HITAKER'S ALMANACK 2002

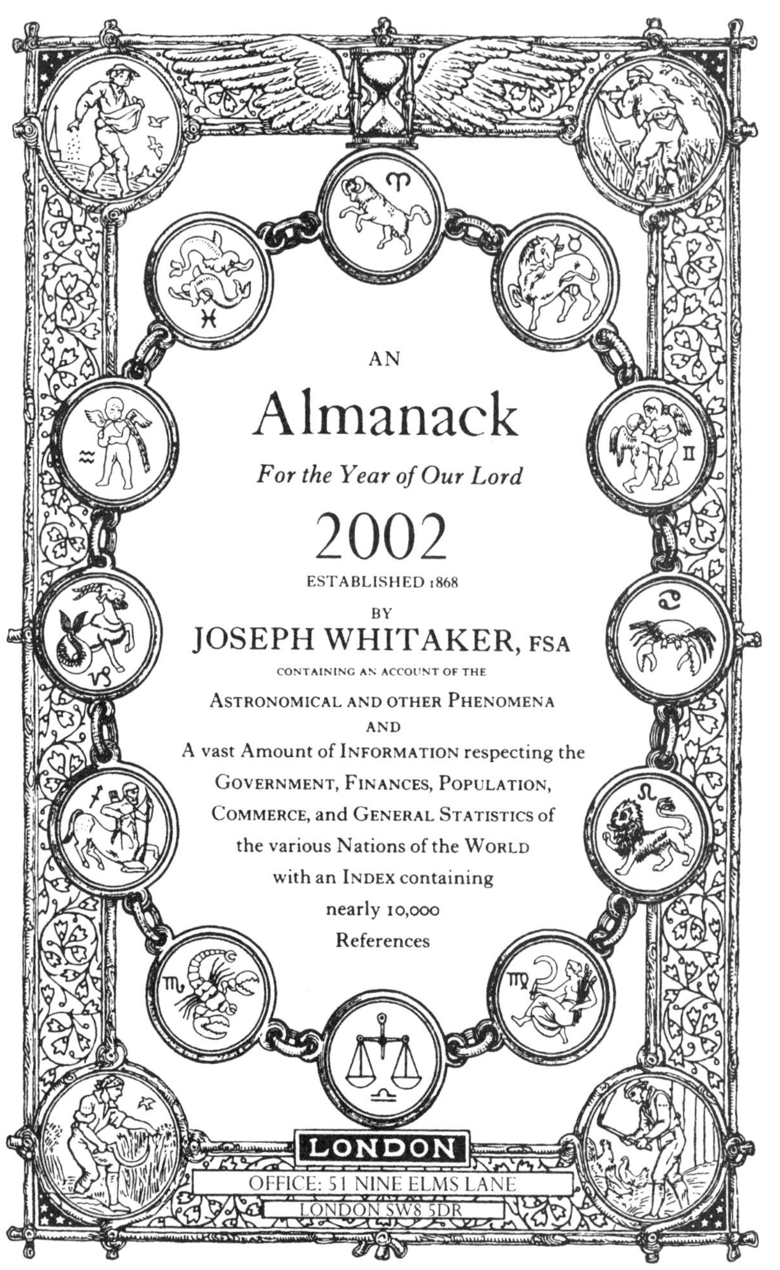


*The traditional design of the title page for Whitaker's Almanack which has appeared in each edition since 18*

# Whitaker's Almanack

# 2002

LONDON
THE STATIONERY OFFICE

THE STATIONERY OFFICE LTD

51 Nine Elms Lane, London SW8 5DR

Whitaker's Almanack published annually since 1868



Standard edition

Cloth covers
0 11 7022 799

Leather binding
0 11 7022 772
Designed by Douglas Martin
Jacket designed by Compendium
Jacket photographs: PA Photos, Ltd
Typeset in Great Britain by Tradespools Ltd, Frome, Somerset
Printed in Great Britian by The Stationery Office Ltd, Parliamentary Press, London.
Bound by William Clowes Ltd, Beccles, Suffolk.

Whitaker's Almanack Countries of the World Section was compiled with the assistance of: Flagmaster, the quarterly publication of the © Flag institute; Military Balance 2000-2001, published by Oxford University Press for © The International Institute for Strategic Studies; OTS1 Overseas Trade Statistics — United Kingdom Trade with Countries outside the European Community - December 2000 © The Stationary Office Ltd 2000; Overseas Trade Statistics of the United Kingdom with Countries within the European Community (Intrastat) December 2000 © The Stationary Office Ltd 2000; People in Power © Cambridge International Reference on Current Affairs (CIRCA) Ltd 2001; The Diplomatic Service List 2000 © Crown Copyright 1999; The London Diplomatic List © Crown Copyright 2000; UN Demographic Yearbook 1998 © United Nations; UN Statistical Year book 1997 data © United Nations; UNESCO Statistical Yearbook 2000 © UNESCO 2000; World Bank Atlas 2001 ©; International Bank for Reconstruction and Development/World Bank; World Mineral Statistics 1995–99 (British Geological Survey 1999) © NERC; Yearbook of Labour Statistics 2000 © International Labour Organization.

Published by The Stationery Office and available from:

**The Publications Centre**
(mail, telephone and fax orders only)
PO Box 276, London SW8 5DT
General enquiries/Telephone orders 0870-600 5522

**The Stationery Office Bookshops**
123 Kingsway, London WC2B 6PQ
020-7242 6393 Fax 020-7242 6394
16 Arthur Street, Belfast BTI 4GD
028-9023 8451 Fax 020-9023 5401
68-69 Bull Street, Birmingham B4 6AD
0121-236 9696 Fax 0121-236-9699
33 Wine Street, Cardiff CF1 2BZ
0117-926 4306 Fax 0117-929 4515
The Stationery Office Oriel Bookshop
18-19 High Street, Cardiff CF1 2BZ
029-2039 5548 Fax 029-2038 4347
71 Lothian Road, Edinburgh EH3 9AZ
0870-606 5566 Fax 0870-606 5588
9-21 Princess Street, Manchester M60 8AS
0161-834 7201 Fax 0161-833 0634

**The Stationery Office's Accredited Agents**
(*see* Yellow Pages)
*and through good booksellers*



EDITORIAL CONTACT DETAILS
Tel: 020-7873 8442
Fax: 020-7873 8723
Email: whitakers.almanack@theso.co.uk
Web: www.whitakers-almanack.co.uk
www.thestationeryoffice.com
www.clicktso.com

# Contents

# ʾreface

) THE 134TH ANNUAL VOLUME

'elcome to the 134th edition of Whitaker's Almanack. I had hoped that this edition would have its primary focus on the ne 2001 general election. An election year is always an important one in the compilation of Whitaker's Almanack as so any of our sections are totally revised to reflect the changes in parliament and government in general. This edition cludes all the information you would expect to find including a fully updated list of MPs, comprehensive election results d details of all the new cabinet and shadow cabinet posts.

However, the terrorist attack on the World Trade Centre twin towers in New York City on the 11 September 2001 has ghlighted a greater need than ever for understanding and information to help us come to terms with such all compassing 'world changing' events. The attack has sent enormous shock waves around the world. The media has quite ghtly flooded us with news, commentary and analysis of this event, examining both its impact on future events and the ctors that may have caused it. However, such media coverage can sometimes leave us wanting to know more of the ckground and to expand our knowledge of certain regions and peoples of the world. We want to read up on the storical and political transitions of certain countries, to appreciate religious motivations and cultural differences and to derstand more clearly the infrastructures and people within our own country involved in responding to this sort of orld crisis. Whitaker's Almanack can help to provide answers to some of the many questions that may arise over the eeks and months to come and tries to live up to its descriptive by-line of offering 'information for a changing world'. (*A ief summary of the media coverage of the attack on the twin towers is given in the Stop Press section at the back of this edition.*)

To those who are familiar with Whitaker's Almanack, the breadth of its coverage is no doubt one of the key motivations r its usage. I have always been in awe of the diversity of its content and would like to take this opportunity to draw rhaps newer readers to sections such the events of the year, a detailed chronological summary of news events both in the K and around the world. The latter sections of Whitaker's Almanack carry many fascinating articles on subjects such as chitecture, literature, the theatre, film, broadcasting and sport, all adding to the distinctive style of the Whitaker's manack appraisal of the year.

This edition of Whitaker's Almanack has also seen a change in editorship. I took over the compilation of the Whitaker's manack series in January of this year and hope to have done it justice in this short time. As always we are grateful to hear aders comments and suggestions. My warmest thanks go to my team and the many contributors who made this edition ossible. Thank you also to the many individuals and organisations who assisted with our research.

VANESSA WHITE
*Editor*

/HITAKER'S ALMANACK
HE STATIONERY OFFICE
l Nine Elms Lane, London SW8 5DR
'EL: 020-7873 8442
AX: 020-7873 8723
-MAIL: whitakers.almanack@theso.co.uk
Veb: www.whitakers-almanack.co.uk
www.thestationeryoffice.com
www.clicktso.com

# [T]he Year 2002

## [C]HRONOLOGICAL CYCLES AND ERAS

| | |
|---|---|
| ominical Letter | F |
| olden Number (Lunar Cycle) | VIII |
| lian Period | 6715 |
| oman Indiction | 10 |
| olar Cycle | 23 |

| | *Beginning* |
|---|---|
| panese year Heisei 14 | 1 January |
| hinese year of the Horse | 12 February |
| egnal year 51 | 6 February |
| indu new year | 13 April |
| dian (Saka) year 1924 | 22 March |
| uslim year AH 1423 | 15 March |
| kh new year | 13 April |
| wish year AM 5763 | 7 September |
| oman year 2755 AUC | |

## ELIGIOUS CALENDARS

### HRISTIAN

| | |
|---|---|
| piphany | 6 January |
| resentation of Christ in the Temple | 2 February |
| sh Wednesday | 13 February |
| he Annunciation | 25 March |
| laundy Thursday | 28 March |
| ood Friday | 29 March |
| aster Day (western churches) | 31 March |
| aster Day (Eastern Orthodox) | 5 May |
| ogation Sunday | 5 May |
| scension Day | 9 May |
| entecost (Whit Sunday) | 19 May |
| rinity Sunday | 26 May |
| orpus Christi | 30 May |
| ll Saints' Day | 1 November |
| dvent Sunday | 1 December |
| hristmas Day | 25 December |

### IINDU

| | |
|---|---|
| Makara Sankranti | 14 January |
| Vasant Panchami (Sarasvati-puja) | 17 February |
| Mahashivaratri | 12 March |
| Ioli | 28 March |
| Chaitra (Hindu new year) | 13 April |
| Ramanavami | 21 April |
| Raksha-bandhan | 22 August |
| anmashtami | 30 August |
| Ganesh Chaturthi, first day | 10 September |
| Ganesh festival, last day | 20 September |
| Durga-puja | 7 October |
| Navaratri festival, first day | 7 October |
| Sarasvati-puja | 12 October |
| Dasara | 15 October |
| Diwali, first day | 2 November |
| Diwali, last day | 6 November |

### JEWISH

| | |
|---|---|
| Purim, | 26 February |
| Passover, first day | 28 March |
| Feast of Weeks, first day | 17 May |
| Jewish new year, first day | 7 September |
| Yom Kippur (Day of Atonement) | 16 September |
| Feast of Tabernacles, first day | 21 September |
| Chanucah, first day | 30 November |

### MUSLIM

| | |
|---|---|
| Muslim new year | 15 March |
| Ramadan, first day | 6 November |

### SIKH

| | |
|---|---|
| Birthday of Guru Gobind Singh Ji | 5 January |
| Baisakhi Mela (Sikh new year) | 13 April |
| Martyrdom of Guru Arjan Dev Ji | 16 June |
| Birthday of Guru Nanak Dev Ji | 11 November |
| Martyrdom of Guru Tegh Bahadur Ji | 24 November |

## CIVIL CALENDAR

| | |
|---|---|
| Accession of Queen Elizabeth II | 6 February |
| Duke of York's birthday | 19 February |
| St David's Day | 1 March |
| Earl of Wessex birthday | 10 March |
| Commonwealth Day | 11 March |
| St Patrick's Day | 17 March |
| Birthday of Queen Elizabeth II | 21 April |
| St George's Day | 23 April |
| Europe Day | 9 May |
| Coronation of Queen Elizabeth II | 2 June |
| Duke of Edinburgh's birthday | 10 June |
| The Queen's Official Birthday | 15 June |
| Queen Elizabeth the Queen Mother's birthday | 4 August |
| Princess Royal's birthday | 15 August |
| Princess Margaret's birthday | 21 August |
| Lord Mayor's Day | 9 November |
| Remembrance Sunday | 10 November |
| Prince of Wales's birthday | 14 November |
| Wedding Day of Queen Elizabeth II | 20 November |
| St Andrew's Day | 30 November |

## LEGAL CALENDAR

### LAW TERMS

| | |
|---|---|
| Hilary Term | 11 January to 27 March |
| Easter Term | 9 April to 31 May |
| Trinity Term | 18 June to 31 July |
| Michaelmas Term | 1 October to 21 December |

### QUARTER DAYS

*England, Wales and Northern Ireland*

| | |
|---|---|
| Lady | 25 March |
| Midsummer | 24 June |
| Michaelmas | 29 September |
| Christmas | 25 December |

### TERM DAYS

*Scotland*

| | |
|---|---|
| Candlemas | 28 February |
| Whitsunday | 28 May |
| Lammas | 28 August |
| Martinmas | 28 November |
| Removal Terms | 28 May, 28 November |

# 2002

## JANUARY

| | | | | | |
|---|---|---|---|---|---|
| *Sunday* | | 6 | 13 | 20 | 27 |
| *Monday* | | 7 | 14 | 21 | 28 |
| *Tuesday* | 1 | 8 | 15 | 22 | 29 |
| *Wednesday* | 2 | 9 | 16 | 23 | 30 |
| *Thursday* | 3 | 10 | 17 | 24 | 31 |
| *Friday* | 4 | 11 | 18 | 25 | |
| *Saturday* | 5 | 12 | 19 | 26 | |

## FEBRUARY

| | | | | | |
|---|---|---|---|---|---|
| *Sunday* | | 3 | 10 | 17 | 24 |
| *Monday* | | 4 | 11 | 18 | 25 |
| *Tuesday* | | 5 | 12 | 19 | 26 |
| *Wednesday* | | 6 | 13 | 20 | 27 |
| *Thursday* | | 7 | 14 | 21 | 28 |
| *Friday* | 1 | 8 | 15 | 22 | |
| *Saturday* | 2 | 9 | 16 | 23 | |

## MARCH

| | | | | | |
|---|---|---|---|---|---|
| *Sunday* | | 3 | 10 | 17 | 24 |
| *Monday* | | 4 | 11 | 18 | 25 |
| *Tuesday* | | 5 | 12 | 19 | 26 |
| *Wednesday* | | 6 | 13 | 20 | 27 |
| *Thursday* | | 7 | 14 | 21 | 28 |
| *Friday* | 1 | 8 | 15 | 22 | 29 |
| *Saturday* | 2 | 9 | 16 | 23 | 30 |

## APRIL

| | | | | | |
|---|---|---|---|---|---|
| *Sunday* | | 7 | 14 | 21 | 28 |
| *Monday* | 1 | 8 | 15 | 22 | 29 |
| *Tuesday* | 2 | 9 | 16 | 23 | 30 |
| *Wednesday* | 3 | 10 | 17 | 24 | |
| *Thursday* | 4 | 11 | 18 | 25 | |
| *Friday* | 5 | 12 | 19 | 26 | |
| *Saturday* | 6 | 13 | 20 | 27 | |

## MAY

| | | | | | |
|---|---|---|---|---|---|
| *Sunday* | | 5 | 12 | 19 | 26 |
| *Monday* | | 6 | 13 | 20 | 27 |
| *Tuesday* | | 7 | 14 | 21 | 28 |
| *Wednesday* | 1 | 8 | 15 | 22 | 29 |
| *Thursday* | 2 | 9 | 16 | 23 | 30 |
| *Friday* | 3 | 10 | 17 | 24 | 31 |
| *Saturday* | 4 | 11 | 18 | 25 | |

## JUNE

| | | | | | |
|---|---|---|---|---|---|
| *Sunday* | | 2 | 9 | 16 | 23 |
| *Monday* | | 3 | 10 | 17 | 24 |
| *Tuesday* | | 4 | 11 | 18 | 25 |
| *Wednesday* | | 5 | 12 | 19 | 26 |
| *Thursday* | | 6 | 13 | 20 | 27 |
| *Friday* | | 7 | 14 | 21 | 28 |
| *Saturday* | 1 | 8 | 15 | 22 | 29 |

## JULY

| | | | | | |
|---|---|---|---|---|---|
| *Sunday* | | 7 | 14 | 21 | 28 |
| *Monday* | 1 | 8 | 15 | 22 | 29 |
| *Tuesday* | 2 | 9 | 16 | 23 | 30 |
| *Wednesday* | 3 | 10 | 17 | 24 | 31 |
| *Thursday* | 4 | 11 | 18 | 25 | |
| *Friday* | 5 | 12 | 19 | 26 | |
| *Saturday* | 6 | 13 | 20 | 27 | |

## AUGUST

| | | | | | |
|---|---|---|---|---|---|
| *Sunday* | | 4 | 11 | 18 | 25 |
| *Monday* | | 5 | 12 | 19 | 26 |
| *Tuesday* | | 6 | 13 | 20 | 27 |
| *Wednesday* | | 7 | 14 | 21 | 28 |
| *Thursday* | 1 | 8 | 15 | 22 | 29 |
| *Friday* | 2 | 9 | 16 | 23 | 30 |
| *Saturday* | 3 | 10 | 17 | 24 | 31 |

## SEPTEMBER

| | | | | | |
|---|---|---|---|---|---|
| *Sunday* | 1 | 8 | 15 | 22 | 29 |
| *Monday* | 2 | 9 | 16 | 23 | 30 |
| *Tuesday* | 3 | 10 | 17 | 24 | |
| *Wednesday* | 4 | 11 | 18 | 25 | |
| *Thursday* | 5 | 12 | 19 | 26 | |
| *Friday* | 6 | 13 | 20 | 27 | |
| *Saturday* | 7 | 14 | 21 | 28 | |

## OCTOBER

| | | | | | |
|---|---|---|---|---|---|
| *Sunday* | | 6 | 13 | 20 | 27 |
| *Monday* | | 7 | 14 | 21 | 28 |
| *Tuesday* | 1 | 8 | 15 | 22 | 29 |
| *Wednesday* | 2 | 9 | 16 | 23 | 30 |
| *Thursday* | 3 | 10 | 17 | 24 | 31 |
| *Friday* | 4 | 11 | 18 | 25 | |
| *Saturday* | 5 | 12 | 19 | 26 | |

## NOVEMBER

| | | | | | |
|---|---|---|---|---|---|
| *Sunday* | | 3 | 10 | 17 | 24 |
| *Monday* | | 4 | 11 | 18 | 25 |
| *Tuesday* | | 5 | 12 | 19 | 26 |
| *Wednesday* | | 6 | 13 | 20 | 27 |
| *Thursday* | | 7 | 14 | 21 | 28 |
| *Friday* | 1 | 8 | 15 | 22 | 29 |
| *Saturday* | 2 | 9 | 16 | 23 | 30 |

## DECEMBER

| | | | | | |
|---|---|---|---|---|---|
| *Sunday* | 1 | 8 | 15 | 22 | 29 |
| *Monday* | 2 | 9 | 16 | 23 | 30 |
| *Tuesday* | 3 | 10 | 17 | 24 | 31 |
| *Wednesday* | 4 | 11 | 18 | 25 | |
| *Thursday* | 5 | 12 | 19 | 26 | |
| *Friday* | 6 | 13 | 20 | 27 | |
| *Saturday* | 7 | 14 | 21 | 28 | |

| PUBLIC HOLIDAYS | *England and Wales* | *Scotland* | *Northern Ireland* |
|---|---|---|---|
| New Year | †1 January | 1, †2 January | †1 January |
| St Patrick's Day | – | – | ‡18 March |
| *Good Friday | 29 March | 29 March | 29 March |
| Easter Monday | 1 April | – | 1 April |
| Early May | †6 May | 6 May | †6 May |
| Golden Jubilee | 3 June | 3 June | 3 June |
| Spring | 4 June | †4 June | 4 June |
| Battle of the Boyne | – | – | ‡12 July |
| Summer | 26 August | 5 August | 26 August |
| *Christmas | 25, 26 December | 25, †26 December | 25, 26 Decembe |

*In England, Wales and Northern Ireland, Christmas Day and Good Friday are common law holidays
In the Channel Islands, Liberation Day is a bank and public holiday
† Subject to royal proclamation
‡ Subject to proclamation by the Secretary of State for Northern Ireland

# 003

### NUARY

| | | | | | |
|---|---|---|---|---|---|
| nday | | 5 | 12 | 19 | 26 |
| onday | | 6 | 13 | 20 | 27 |
| esday | | 7 | 14 | 21 | 28 |
| ednesday | 1 | 8 | 15 | 22 | 29 |
| ursday | 2 | 9 | 16 | 23 | 30 |
| iday | 3 | 10 | 17 | 24 | 31 |
| turday | 4 | 11 | 18 | 25 | |

### FEBRUARY

| | | | | | |
|---|---|---|---|---|---|
| *Sunday* | | 2 | 9 | 16 | 23 |
| *Monday* | | 3 | 10 | 17 | 24 |
| *Tuesday* | | 4 | 11 | 18 | 25 |
| *Wednesday* | | 5 | 12 | 19 | 26 |
| *Thursday* | | 6 | 13 | 20 | 27 |
| *Friday* | | 7 | 14 | 21 | 28 |
| *Saturday* | 1 | 8 | 15 | 22 | |

### MARCH

| | | | | | |
|---|---|---|---|---|---|
| *Sunday* | | 2 | 9 | 16 | 23 | 30 |
| *Monday* | | 3 | 10 | 17 | 24 | 31 |
| *Tuesday* | | 4 | 11 | 18 | 25 | |
| *Wednesday* | | 5 | 12 | 19 | 26 | |
| *Thursday* | | 6 | 13 | 20 | 27 | |
| *Friday* | | 7 | 14 | 21 | 28 | |
| *Saturday* | 1 | 8 | 15 | 22 | 29 | |

### PRIL

| | | | | | |
|---|---|---|---|---|---|
| nday | | 6 | 13 | 20 | 27 |
| onday | | 7 | 14 | 21 | 28 |
| uesday | 1 | 8 | 15 | 22 | 29 |
| ednesday | 2 | 9 | 16 | 23 | 30 |
| hursday | 3 | 10 | 17 | 24 | |
| riday | 4 | 11 | 18 | 25 | |
| aturday | 5 | 12 | 19 | 26 | |

### MAY

| | | | | | |
|---|---|---|---|---|---|
| *Sunday* | | 4 | 11 | 18 | 25 |
| *Monday* | | 5 | 12 | 19 | 26 |
| *Tuesday* | | 6 | 13 | 20 | 27 |
| *Wednesday* | | 7 | 14 | 21 | 28 |
| *Thursday* | 1 | 8 | 15 | 22 | 29 |
| *Friday* | 2 | 9 | 16 | 23 | 30 |
| *Saturday* | 3 | 10 | 17 | 24 | 31 |

### JUNE

| | | | | | |
|---|---|---|---|---|---|
| *Sunday* | 1 | 8 | 15 | 22 | 29 |
| *Monday* | 2 | 9 | 16 | 23 | 30 |
| *Tuesday* | 3 | 10 | 17 | 24 | |
| *Wednesday* | 4 | 11 | 18 | 25 | |
| *Thursday* | 5 | 12 | 19 | 26 | |
| *Friday* | 6 | 13 | 20 | 27 | |
| *Saturday* | 7 | 14 | 21 | 28 | |

### LY

| | | | | | |
|---|---|---|---|---|---|
| unday | | 6 | 13 | 20 | 27 |
| londay | | 7 | 14 | 21 | 28 |
| uesday | 1 | 8 | 15 | 22 | 29 |
| Vednesday | 2 | 9 | 16 | 23 | 30 |
| hursday | 3 | 10 | 17 | 24 | 31 |
| riday | 4 | 11 | 18 | 25 | |
| aturday | 5 | 12 | 19 | 26 | |

### AUGUST

| | | | | | | |
|---|---|---|---|---|---|---|
| *Sunday* | | 3 | 10 | 17 | 24 | 31 |
| *Monday* | | 4 | 11 | 18 | 25 | |
| *Tuesday* | | 5 | 12 | 19 | 26 | |
| *Wednesday* | | 6 | 13 | 20 | 27 | |
| *Thursday* | | 7 | 14 | 21 | 28 | |
| *Friday* | 1 | 8 | 15 | 22 | 29 | |
| *Saturday* | 2 | 9 | 16 | 23 | 30 | |

### SEPTEMBER

| | | | | | |
|---|---|---|---|---|---|
| *Sunday* | | 7 | 14 | 21 | 28 |
| *Monday* | 1 | 8 | 15 | 22 | 29 |
| *Tuesday* | 2 | 9 | 16 | 23 | 30 |
| *Wednesday* | 3 | 10 | 17 | 24 | |
| *Thursday* | 4 | 11 | 18 | 25 | |
| *Friday* | 5 | 12 | 19 | 26 | |
| *Saturday* | 6 | 13 | 20 | 27 | |

### CTOBER

| | | | | | |
|---|---|---|---|---|---|
| unday | | 5 | 12 | 19 | 26 |
| londay | | 6 | 13 | 20 | 27 |
| uesday | | 7 | 14 | 21 | 28 |
| Vednesday | 1 | 8 | 15 | 22 | 29 |
| hursday | 2 | 9 | 16 | 23 | 30 |
| riday | 3 | 10 | 17 | 24 | 31 |
| aturday | 4 | 11 | 18 | 25 | |

### NOVEMBER

| | | | | | | |
|---|---|---|---|---|---|---|
| *Sunday* | | 2 | 9 | 16 | 23 | 30 |
| *Monday* | | 3 | 10 | 17 | 24 | |
| *Tuesday* | | 4 | 11 | 18 | 25 | |
| *Wednesday* | | 5 | 12 | 19 | 26 | |
| *Thursday* | | 6 | 13 | 20 | 27 | |
| *Friday* | | 7 | 14 | 21 | 28 | |
| *Saturday* | 1 | 8 | 15 | 22 | 29 | |

### DECEMBER

| | | | | | |
|---|---|---|---|---|---|
| *Sunday* | | 7 | 14 | 21 | 28 |
| *Monday* | 1 | 8 | 15 | 22 | 29 |
| *Tuesday* | 2 | 9 | 16 | 23 | 30 |
| *Wednesday* | 3 | 10 | 17 | 24 | 31 |
| *Thursday* | 4 | 11 | 18 | 25 | |
| *Friday* | 5 | 12 | 19 | 26 | |
| *Saturday* | 6 | 13 | 20 | 27 | |

| UBLIC HOLIDAYS | *England and Wales* | *Scotland* | *Northern Ireland* |
|---|---|---|---|
| New Year | †1 January | 1, †2 January | †1 January |
| t Patrick's Day | — | — | ‡17 March |
| Good Friday | 18 April | 18 April | 18 April |
| Easter Monday | 21 April | — | 21 April |
| Early May | †5 May | 5 May | †5 May |
| pring | 26 May | †26 May | 26 May |
| Battle of the Boyne | — | — | ‡14 July |
| ummer | 25 August | 4 August | 25 August |
| Christmas | 25, 26 December | 25, †26 December | 25, 26 December |

In England, Wales and Northern Ireland, Christmas Day and Good Friday are common law holidays
n the Channel Islands, Liberation Day is a bank and public holiday
† Subject to royal proclamation
‡ Subject to proclamation by the Secretary of State for Northern Ireland

## FORTHCOMING EVENTS 2002

*Provisional dates

### January

| | |
|---|---|
| 12–27 | London International Mime Festival |
| 16–20 | Art 2002, Business Design Centre, London |

### February

| | |
|---|---|
| 1–3 | Labour Party Conference, Cardiff Indoor Arena |
| 18–19 May | American Sublime, Tate Britain |

### March

| | |
|---|---|
| 2–10 | Bath Literature Festival |
| 6–1 April | Ideal Home Exhibition, Earls Court |
| 7–10 | Crufts Dog Show, NEC Birmingham |
| 8–10 | Liberal-Democrat Party Conference, MICC Manchester |
| 8–17 | National Science Week |
| 17–19 | London Book Fair |

### April

| | |
|---|---|
| 14 | London Marathon |

### May

| | |
|---|---|
| 17–2 June | Bath International Music Festival |
| 18–19 | London Tattoo, Wembley Arena |
| 23–24 | Chelsea Flower Show, Royal Hospital, Chelsea |
| 31–9 June | The Hay Festival, Hay on Wye |

### June

| | |
|---|---|
| 6–15 | Hampton Court Palace Music Festival |
| 7–23 | The Aldeburgh Festival |
| 8 | Trooping the Colour – the Queen's Birthday Parade, Horse Guards Palace |
| 11–9 August | Royal Academy Summer Exhibition |
| 25–27 | Wisley Flower Show, RHS Garden, Woking |
| 25–11 July | City of London Festival |
| 29–14 July | Cheltenham International Festival of Music |
| 29–24 August | Kenwood House – Lakeside Concerts, Hampstead |

### July

| | |
|---|---|
| 1–4 | The Royal Show, National Agricultural Centre, Stoneleigh Park |
| 2–7 | Hampton Court Palace Flower Show |
| *6–15 July | York Early Music Festival |
| 11–21 | Buxton Festival |
| 18–27 | The Welsh Proms, St David's Hall, Cardiff |
| 19–14 September | BBC Promenade Concerts, Royal Albert Hall |

### August

| | |
|---|---|
| 2–24 August | Edinburgh Military Tattoo |
| 13–2 September | Edinburgh International Festival |
| *4–11 | National Eisteddfod of Wales |
| *17–23 | Three Choirs Festival, Hereford |
| 20–22 | Wisley Flower Show, RHS Garden, Woking |
| 25–16 | Notting Hill Carnival, London |
| 30–3 November | Blackpool Illuminations |

### September

| | |
|---|---|
| 7 | Braemar Royal Highland Gathering |
| *14–23 | Southampton International Boat Show |

### October

| | |
|---|---|
| 7–10 | Conservative Party Conference, BIC Bournemouth |
| *8–8 December | Glyndebourne Festival Opera Season |

### November

| | |
|---|---|
| 3 | London to Brighton Veteran Car Run |
| 10 | Lord Mayor's Procession and Show London |
| 20 November–1 December | Huddersfield Contemporary Music Festival |
| *7–22 | London Film Festival, NFT and Odeon West End Cinema |

## SPORTS EVENTS

### Athletics

| | |
|---|---|
| 1–3 March | European Indoor Championships, Vienna |
| 25 July–24 August | Commonwealth Games, Manchester |

### Cricket

*Test Matches*

| | |
|---|---|
| 16–20 May | England v. Sri Lanka, 1st, Lord's |
| 30 May–3 June | England v. Sri Lanka, 2nd, Edgbaston |
| 13–17 June | England v. Sri Lanka, 3rd, Old Trafford |
| 25–29 July | England v. India, 1st, Lord's |
| 8–12 August | England v. India, 2nd, Trent Bridge |
| 22–26 August | England v. India, 3rd, Headingley |
| 5–9 September | England v. India, 4th, Oval |

*NatWest Series*

| | |
|---|---|
| 27 June | England v. Sri Lanka, Headingly |
| 29 June | England v. India, Lord's |
| 30 June | India v. England, Oval |
| 2 July | England v. Sri Lanka, Headingly |
| 4 July | England v. India, Durham |
| 7 July | England v. Sri Lanka, Old Trafford |
| 9 July | England v. India, Oval |
| 13 July | The Final |

### Curling

| | |
|---|---|
| 5–14 April | World Championships, Bismark, ND, USA |

### Equestrian Events

| | |
|---|---|
| 2–5 May | The Mitsubishi Motors Badminton Horse Trials, Badminton |
| 15–19 May | Royal Windsor Horse Show, Home Park, Windsor |
| 29 August–1 September | Burghley Horse Trials, Stamford |
| 5–8 September | Blenheim Horse Trials |
| *26–30 September | Horse of the Year Show, Wembley Arena, London |
| 18–22 December | International Show Jumping Championships, Olympia |

OTBALL

| | |
|---|---|
| February | Worthington Cup Final |
| lay | FA Cup Final, Millennium Stadium, Cardiff |
| lay | Scottish FA Cup Final, Hampden Park, Glasgow |
| lay | Welsh FA Cup Final, Millennium Stadium, Cardiff |
| lay | UEFA Cup Final |
| May | UEFA Champions League Final |
| May–30 June | FIFA World Cup Finals, Japan and South Korea |

LF

| | |
|---|---|
| 8 June | Royal Porthcawl GC/Pyle and Kenfig GC |
| –14 July | Loch Lomond Invitational |
| –21 July | The Open, The Honourable Company of Edinburgh Golfers, Muirfield |
| –30 September | Ryder Cup, The Belfry |

ORSERACING

| | |
|---|---|
| March | Cheltenham Gold Cup |
| -6 April | The Martell Grant National, Aintree |
| April | Stakis Casinos Scottish Grand National, Ayr |
| 7 April | Whitbread Gold Cup, Sandown Park |
| 9 April–12 August | Windsor Evening Race Meeting Season |
| –6 May | 1000 Guineas, Newmarket |
| June | The Vodaphone Derby, Epsom |
| 8–21 June | Royal Ascot |
| –11 July | Newmarket July |
| 7 July | King George VI and Queen Elizabeth Diamond Stakes, Ascot |
| 0 July–3 August | Glorious Goodwood |
| 1–14 September | St Leger, Doncaster |
| November | Hennessy Cognac Gold Cup, Newbury |

IOTOR SPORTS

| | |
|---|---|
| 2–14 July | Formula 1: The British Grand Prix, Silverstone |
| –7 June | Motorcycles: TT Races, Isle of Man |

OLYMPICS

| | |
|---|---|
| 8–24 February | Winter Olympic Games, Salt Lake |
| 7–16 March | Winter Paralympic Games, Salt Lake |

ROWING AND YACHTING

| | |
|---|---|
| 3–13 | 48th London Boat Show |
| 3–7 July | Henley Royal Regatta |
| 24 March | The Oxford and Cambridge Boat Race |

RUGBY LEAGUE

| | |
|---|---|
| 27 April | Challenge Cup Final, Murrayfield, Edinburgh |

RUGBY UNION

| | SIX NATIONS |
|---|---|
| 2 February | Scotland v. England, Murrayfield |
| 3 February | Ireland v. Wales, Lansdowne Road |
| 16 February | Italy v. Scotland, Rome; Wales v. France, Cardiff; England v. Ireland, Twickenham |
| 2 March | Ireland v. Scotland, Lansdowne Road; Wales v. Italy, Cardiff; France v. England, Paris |
| 23 March | Ireland v. Italy, Lansdowne Road; Scotland v. France, Murrayfield; England v. Wales, Twickenham |
| 6 April | Wales v. Scotland, Cardiff; France v. Ireland, Paris |
| 7 April | Italy v. England, Rome |

SHOOTING

| | |
|---|---|
| 29 June–13 July | Imperial Meeting, Bisley |
| 25 July–3 August | Commonwealth Games, Bisley |

SNOOKER

| | |
|---|---|
| 3–10 February | Benson & Hedges Masters, Wembley Conference Centre, London |
| 20 April–6 May | Embassy World Championship, Crucible Theatre, Sheffield |

TENNIS

| | |
|---|---|
| 10–16 June | Stella Artois Tournament, Queens Club |
| 24 June–7 July | The All-England Championships, Wimbledon, London |
| 4–8 December | Honda Challenge, Royal Albert Hall |

## CENTENARIES OF 2002

**1602**
14 February — Francesco Cavalli, Italian composer, born

**1702**
8 March — William III Orange, Dutch King 1689–1702, died

**1802**
26 February — Victor Hugo, French novelist and poet, born
6 March — Sir Edwin Landseer, painter and sculptor, born
18 April — Erasmus Darwin, physician, free-thinker, poet and grandfather of Charles Darwin, died
12 June — Harriet Martineau, essayist and novelist, born
24 July — Alexandre Dumas, French novelist and playwright, born
15 November — George Romney, painter, died

**1902**
5 January — Stella Gibbons, novelist, journalist and poet, born
31 January — Tallulah Bankhead, American actress, born
4 February — Charles Lindbergh, American aviator, born
27 February — John Steinbeck, American novelist, born
16 March — Dame Lucie Rie, Austrian-British potter, born
17 March — Bobby Jones, American golfer, born
26 March — Cecil Rhodes, colonialist, founder of Rhodesia, died
28 March — Dame Flora Robson, actress, born
29 March — Sir William Walton, composer, born
23 April — Halldor Laxness, Icelandic writer and Nobel literature laureate 1995, born
6 June — Lord Kings Norton Cox, aeronautical engineer, industrialist, chancellor of Cranfield University 1969-97, born
18 June — Samuel Butler, novelist, essayist and critic, died
28 June — Richard Rodgers, American composer, born
28 July — Sir Karl Popper, Austrian-British philosopher of natural and social science, born
31 July — Sir George Allen, cricketer, born
16 August — Georgette Heyer, novelist, born
19 August — Ogden Nash, American humorous poet born
20 September — Florence Smith, poet, born
21 September — Sir Allen Lane, pioneer of paperback publishing, born
29 September — Émile Zola, French novelist, died
29 October — Susie Cooper, potter, born
9 December — R. A. Butler, Conservative politician, born
19 December — Sir Ralph Richardson, actor, born

## CENTENARIES OF 2003

**1503**
14 December — Nostradamus, astrologer, physician and seer, born
11 January — Girolamo Mazzola, painter, born

**1603**
24 March — Elizabeth I, Tudor Queen of England 1558-1603, died

**1703**
15/16 May — Charles Perrault, poet, prose writer and storyteller; wrote 'Tales of Mother Goose', died
26 May — Samuel Pepys, diarist, died
17 June — John Wesley, co-founder of the Methodist movement, born
5 October — Jonathan Edwards, theologian and metaphysician, born

**1803**
3 March — Alexandre Gabriel Decamps, painter, of the Romantic school, born
25 May — Edward Bulwer Lytton, novelist, playwright, poet, essayist and politician, born
25 May — Ralph Waldo, Emerson, lecturer, poet and essayist, born
5 July — George Borrow, writer and traveller, born
16 October — Robert Stephenson, engineer, born
29 November — Christian Doppler, physicist, developed 'Doppler's Principle', born
11 December — Hector Berlioz, composer, born
21 December — Sir Joseph Whitworth, engineer, born

**1903**
10 January — Dame Barbara Hepworth, sculptor, born
11 January — Alan Paton, novelist, born
19 January — Sir Alfred Beit, financier and philanthropist, born
13 February — Georges Simenon, novelist, born
22 February — Hugo Wolf, composer, died
24 March — Malcolm Muggeridge, television broadcaster, born
2 May — Dr Benjamin Spock, paediatrician and child psychologist, born
8 May — Paul Gauguin, post-Impressionist painter, died
12 May — Sir Lennox Berkeley, composer, born
29 May — Bob Hope, actor, born
6 June — Aram Ilich Khachaturian, composer, born
19 June — Walter Hammond, cricketer, born
25 June — George Orwell, author, born
1 July — Amy Johnson, aviator, born
2 July — Lord Home of the Hirsel, Alec Douglas-Home, Prime Minister 1963-4, born
17 July — James M. Whistler, painter, died
18 August — Marcel Carne, film director, born
24 August — Graham Sutherland, painter, born
25 September — Mark Rothko, painter, born
28 October — Evelyn Waugh, novelist, born
13 November — Camille Pissarro, painter, died
4 December — Alfred Leslie Rowse, historian, born
13 December — John Piper, painter, born
28 December — George Gissing, novelist, died

# ıstronomy

ıe following pages give astronomical data for each ›nth of the year 2002. There are four pages of data for :h month. All data are given for 0h Greenwich Mean ıme (GMT), i.e. at the midnight at the beginning of the y named. This applies also to data for the months when itish Summer Time is in operation (for dates, *see* below).
The astronomical data are given in a form suitable for servation with the naked eye or with a small telescope. ıese data do not attempt to replace the *Astronomical manac* for professional astronomers.
A fuller explanation of how to use the astronomical data given on pages 71–3.

ıLENDAR FOR EACH MONTH

ıe calendar for each month shows dates of religious, civil d legal significance for the year 2002.
The days in bold type are the principal holy days and the stivals and greater holy days of the Church of England as t out in the calendar authorized for use from 1997. bservance of certain festivals and greater holy days is ınsferred if the day falls on a principal holy day. The lendar shows the date on which holy days and festivals e to be observed in 2002.
The days in small capitals are dates of significance in the lendars of non-Anglican denominations and non-hristian religions.
The days in italic type are dates of civil and legal gnificance. The royal anniversaries shown in italic type e the days on which the Union flag is to be flown.
The rest of the calendar comprises days of general terest and the dates of birth or death of well-known eople.
Fuller explanations of the various calendars can be ›und under Time Measurement and Calendars (pages ı–9).
The zodiacal signs through which the Sun is passing ıring each month are illustrated. The date of transition om one sign to the next, to the nearest hour, is given nder Astronomical Phenomena.

JLIAN DATE

'he Julian date on 2002 January 0.0 is 2452274.5. To find ıe Julian date for any other date in 2002 (at 0h GMT), add ıe day-of-the-year number on the extreme right of the ılendar for each month to the Julian date for January 0.0.

## EASONS

'he seasons are defined astronomically as follows:

| | |
|---|---|
| *pring* | from the vernal equinox to the summer solstice |
| *ummer* | from the summer solstice to the autumnal equinox |
| *ıutumn* | from the autumnal equinox to the winter solstice |
| *Vinter* | from the winter solstice to the vernal equinox |

The seasons in 2002 are:

*Northern hemisphere*

| | |
|---|---|
| Vernal equinox | March 20d 19h GMT |
| Summer solstice | June 21d 13h GMT |
| Autumnal equinox | September 23d 05h GMT |
| Winter solstice | December 22d 01h GMT |

*Southern hemisphere*

| | |
|---|---|
| Autumnal equinox | March 20d 19h GMT |
| Winter solstice | June 21d 13h GMT |
| Vernal equinox | September 23d 05h GMT |
| Summer solstice | December 22d 01h GMT |

The longest day of the year, measured from sunrise to sunset, is at the summer solstice. The longest day in the United Kingdom will fall on 21 June in 2002. *See also* page 81.

The shortest day of the year is at the winter solstice. The shortest day in the United Kingdom will fall on 22 December in 2002. *See also* page 81.

The equinox is the point at which day and night are of equal length all over the world. *See also* page 81.

In popular parlance, the seasons in the northern hemisphere comprise the following months:

| | |
|---|---|
| *Spring* | March, April, May |
| *Summer* | June, July, August |
| *Autumn* | September, October, November |
| *Winter* | December, January, February |

## BRITISH SUMMER TIME

British Summer Time is the legal time for general purposes during the period in which it is in operation (*see also* page 75). During this period, clocks are kept one hour ahead of Greenwich Mean Time. The hour of changeover is 01h Greenwich Mean Time. The duration of Summer Time in 2002 is from March 31 01h GMT to October 27 01h GMT.

# January 2002

FIRST MONTH, 31 DAYS. *Janus*, god of the portal, facing two ways, past and future

| | | | |
|---|---|---|---|
| 1 | *Tuesday* | **Naming and Circumcision of Jesus.** *Bank Holiday in UK.* | 1 |
| 2 | *Wednesday* | *Bank Holiday in Scotland.* Alexander William Kinglake d. 1891 | 2 |
| 3 | *Thursday* | Bill Travers b. 1922. Jeremiah Horrocks d. 1641 | 3 |
| 4 | *Friday* | Augustus John b. 1878. Donald Campbell d. 1967 | 4 |
| 5 | *Saturday* | Stella Gibbons b. 1902. Queen Catherine de Medici d. 1589 | 5 |
| 6 | *Sunday* | **The Epiphany. 2nd S. of Christmas.** | 6 |
| 7 | *Monday* | Hirohito Michinomiya d. 1989. | *week 1 day* 7 |
| 8 | *Tuesday* | Dennis Wheatley b. 1897. En-lai Chou d. 1976 | 8 |
| 9 | *Wednesday* | Richard Nixon b. 1913. Metropolitan Line, Paddington to Holborn Hill, first underground trains in operation (journey took 20 mins) 1863 | 9 |
| 10 | *Thursday* | Lucila Godoy de Alcayaga d. 1957. Penny Post introduced 1840 | 10 |
| 11 | *Friday* | *Hilary Law Sittings begin.* Louis François Roubillacd.1762 | 11 |
| 12 | *Saturday* | Charles Perrault b. 1628. | 12 |
| 13 | *Sunday* | **1st S. of Epiphany.** Independent Labour Party founded 1893 | 13 |
| 14 | *Monday* | Albert Schweitzer b. 1875. Jean Ingres d. 1867 | *week 2 day* 14 |
| 15 | *Tuesday* | Ivor Novello b. 1893. Rosa Luxemburg d. 1919 | 15 |
| 16 | *Wednesday* | Léo Delibes d. 1891. Start of Prohibition in the USA 1920 | 16 |
| 17 | *Thursday* | David Lloyd George b. 1963. George Bancroft d. 1891 | 17 |
| 18 | *Friday* | A. A. Milne b. 1882. Captain Scott reaches the South Pole 1912 | 18 |
| 19 | *Saturday* | Sir Alfred Beit b. 1903. William Congreve d. 1729 | 19 |
| 20 | *Sunday* | **2nd S. of Epiphany**. First assembly of the House of Commons 1265 | 20 |
| 21 | *Monday* | King Louis XVI d. 1793. Concorde entered service 1976 | *week 3 day* 21 |
| 22 | *Tuesday* | Capture of Tobruk 1941 | 22 |
| 23 | *Wednesday* | Sergey Eisenstein b. 1898. Charles Kingsley d. 1875 | 23 |
| 24 | *Thursday* | William Congreve b. 1670. Amedeo Modigliani d. 1920 | 24 |
| 25 | *Friday* | **Conversion of St Paul.** Virginia Woolf b. 1882 | 25 |
| 26 | *Saturday* | Sir Henry Cotton b. 1907. Edward G. Robinson d. 1973 | 26 |
| 27 | *Sunday* | **9th S. before Easter.** Johann Gottlieb Fichte d. 1814 | 27 |
| 28 | *Monday* | Sir Henry Stanley b. 1841. Joseph Alexandrovich Brodsky d. 1996 | *week 4 day* 28 |
| 29 | *Tuesday* | Robert Lee Frost d. 1963. Institution of the V.C. 1856 | 29 |
| 30 | *Wednesday* | Charles Bradlaugh d. 1891. Hitler formed Nazi government in Germany 1933 | 30 |
| 31 | *Thursday* | Jean Simmons b. 1929. Jean Giraudoux d. 1944 | 31 |

## Astronomical Phenomena

| d | h | |
|---|---|---|
| 1 | 06 | Jupiter at opposition |
| 2 | 15 | Earth at perihelion (147 million km) |
| 12 | 00 | Mercury at greatest elongation E.19° |
| 13 | 13 | Venus in conjunction with Moon. Venus 1° N. |
| 14 | 12 | Venus in superior conjunction |
| 15 | 05 | Mercury in conjunction with Moon. Mercury 4° N. |
| 18 | 21 | Mercury at stationary point |
| 19 | 03 | Mars in conjunction with Moon. Mars 5° N. |
| 20 | 06 | Sun's longitude 300°♒ |
| 24 | 16 | Saturn in conjunction with Moon. Saturn 0°.06 S. |
| 26 | 12 | Venus in conjunction with Mercury . Venus 4° S. |
| 26 | 19 | Jupiter in conjunction with Moon. Jupiter 0°.9 S. |
| 27 | 19 | Mercury in inferior conjunction |
| 28 | 14 | Neptune in conjunction |

## Minima of Algol

| d | h | d | h | d | h |
|---|---|---|---|---|---|
| 1 | 23.6 | 13 | 10.9 | 24 | 22.2 |
| 4 | 20.5 | 16 | 07.8 | 27 | 19.0 |
| 7 | 17.3 | 19 | 04.6 | 30 | 15.9 |
| 10 | 14.1 | 22 | 01.4 | | |

## Constellations

The following constellations are near the meridian at

| | d | h | | d | h |
|---|---|---|---|---|---|
| December | 1 | 24 | January | 16 | 21 |
| December | 16 | 23 | February | 1 | 20 |
| January | 1 | 22 | February | 15 | 19 |

Draco (below the Pole), Ursa Minor (below the Pole), Camelopardus, Perseus, Auriga, Taurus, Orion, Eridanus and Lepus

## The Moon

| Phases, Apsides and Node | d | h | m |
|---|---|---|---|
| ☾ Last Quarter | 6 | 03 | 55 |
| ● New Moon | 13 | 13 | 29 |
| ☽ First Quarter | 21 | 17 | 46 |
| ○ Full Moon | 28 | 22 | 50 |
| | | | |
| Perigee (365,384km) | 2 | 07 | 21 |
| Apogee (405,538km) | 18 | 08 | 55 |
| Perigee (359,983km) | 30 | 09 | 06 |

Mean longitude of ascending node on January 1, 86°

THE SUN S.D 16′.1

| Day | Right Ascension | Dec. | Equation of Time | Rise 52° | Rise 56° | Transit | Set 52° | Set 56° | Sidereal time | Transit of First Point of Aries |
|---|---|---|---|---|---|---|---|---|---|---|
| | h m s | ° ′ | m s | h m | h m | h m | h m | h m | h m s | h m s |
| **1** | 18 45 10 | 23 02 | – 3 17 | 8 08 | 8 31 | 12 04 | 15 59 | 15 36 | 6 41 53 | 17 15 17 |
| **2** | 18 49 35 | 22 57 | – 3 46 | 8 08 | 8 31 | 12 04 | 16 00 | 15 37 | 6 45 50 | 17 11 21 |
| **3** | 18 54 00 | 22 52 | – 4 13 | 8 08 | 8 31 | 12 04 | 16 01 | 15 39 | 6 49 46 | 17 07 25 |
| **4** | 18 58 24 | 22 46 | – 4 41 | 8 08 | 8 30 | 12 05 | 16 02 | 15 40 | 6 53 43 | 17 03 29 |
| **5** | 19 02 47 | 22 39 | – 5 08 | 8 07 | 8 30 | 12 05 | 16 04 | 15 41 | 6 57 39 | 16 59 33 |
| **6** | 19 07 11 | 22 32 | – 5 35 | 8 07 | 8 29 | 12 06 | 16 05 | 15 43 | 7 01 36 | 16 55 37 |
| **7** | 19 11 34 | 22 25 | – 6 01 | 8 07 | 8 29 | 12 06 | 16 06 | 15 44 | 7 05 32 | 16 51 41 |
| **8** | 19 15 56 | 22 18 | – 6 27 | 8 06 | 8 28 | 12 07 | 16 08 | 15 46 | 7 09 29 | 16 47 45 |
| **9** | 19 20 18 | 22 09 | – 6 52 | 8 06 | 8 27 | 12 07 | 16 09 | 15 47 | 7 13 26 | 16 43 49 |
| **10** | 19 24 39 | 22 01 | – 7 17 | 8 05 | 8 26 | 12 07 | 16 10 | 15 49 | 7 17 22 | 16 39 54 |
| **11** | 19 29 00 | 21 52 | – 7 41 | 8 04 | 8 26 | 12 08 | 16 12 | 15 51 | 7 21 19 | 16 35 58 |
| **12** | 19 33 20 | 21 42 | – 8 05 | 8 04 | 8 25 | 12 08 | 16 13 | 15 52 | 7 25 15 | 16 32 02 |
| **13** | 19 37 40 | 21 33 | – 8 28 | 8 03 | 8 24 | 12 09 | 16 15 | 15 54 | 7 29 12 | 16 28 06 |
| **14** | 19 41 59 | 21 22 | – 8 51 | 8 02 | 8 23 | 12 09 | 16 16 | 15 56 | 7 33 08 | 16 24 10 |
| **15** | 19 46 18 | 21 12 | – 9 13 | 8 01 | 8 21 | 12 09 | 16 18 | 15 58 | 7 37 05 | 16 20 14 |
| **16** | 19 50 35 | 21 01 | – 9 34 | 8 00 | 8 20 | 12 10 | 16 19 | 16 00 | 7 41 02 | 16 16 18 |
| **17** | 19 54 53 | 20 49 | – 9 54 | 7 59 | 8 19 | 12 10 | 16 21 | 16 02 | 7 44 58 | 16 12 22 |
| **18** | 19 59 09 | 20 37 | –10 14 | 7 59 | 8 18 | 12 10 | 16 23 | 16 03 | 7 48 55 | 16 08 26 |
| **19** | 20 03 24 | 20 25 | –10 33 | 7 57 | 8 17 | 12 11 | 16 24 | 16 05 | 7 52 51 | 16 04 30 |
| **20** | 20 07 39 | 20 12 | –10 52 | 7 56 | 8 15 | 12 11 | 16 26 | 16 07 | 7 56 48 | 16 00 34 |
| **21** | 20 11 53 | 19 59 | –11 09 | 7 55 | 8 14 | 12 11 | 16 28 | 16 09 | 8 00 44 | 15 56 39 |
| **22** | 20 16 07 | 19 46 | –11 26 | 7 54 | 8 12 | 12 12 | 16 30 | 16 11 | 8 04 41 | 15 52 43 |
| **23** | 20 20 19 | 19 32 | –11 42 | 7 53 | 8 11 | 12 12 | 16 31 | 16 14 | 8 08 37 | 15 48 47 |
| **24** | 20 24 31 | 19 18 | –11 57 | 7 52 | 8 09 | 12 12 | 16 33 | 16 16 | 8 12 34 | 15 44 51 |
| **25** | 20 28 42 | 19 03 | –12 12 | 7 50 | 8 08 | 12 12 | 16 35 | 16 18 | 8 16 31 | 15 40 55 |
| **26** | 20 32 52 | 18 49 | –12 25 | 7 49 | 8 06 | 12 13 | 16 37 | 16 20 | 8 20 27 | 15 36 59 |
| **27** | 20 37 02 | 18 33 | –12 38 | 7 48 | 8 04 | 12 13 | 16 38 | 16 22 | 8 24 24 | 15 33 03 |
| **28** | 20 41 10 | 18 18 | –12 50 | 7 46 | 8 03 | 12 13 | 16 40 | 16 24 | 8 28 20 | 15 29 07 |
| **29** | 20 45 18 | 18 02 | –13 01 | 7 45 | 8 01 | 12 13 | 16 42 | 16 26 | 8 32 17 | 15 25 11 |
| **30** | 20 49 25 | 17 46 | –13 11 | 7 43 | 7 59 | 12 13 | 16 44 | 16 28 | 8 36 13 | 15 21 15 |
| **31** | 20 53 31 | 17 29 | –13 21 | 7 42 | 7 57 | 12 13 | 16 46 | 16 30 | 8 40 10 | 15 17 19 |

DURATION OF TWILIGHT (in minutes)

| *Latitude* | 52° | 56° | 52° | 56° | 52° | 56° | 52° | 56° |
|---|---|---|---|---|---|---|---|---|
| | 1 January | | 11 January | | 21 January | | 31 January | |
| *Civil* | 41 | 47 | 40 | 45 | 38 | 43 | 37 | 41 |
| *Nautical* | 84 | 96 | 82 | 93 | 80 | 90 | 78 | 87 |
| *Astronomical* | 125 | 141 | 123 | 138 | 120 | 134 | 117 | 130 |

THE NIGHT SKY

*Mercury* is at greatest eastern elongation on the 11th, and is visible for the first three weeks of the month. During this period it is an evening object, its magnitude fading from -0.7 to + 1.0. Mercury is visible for a short while at the end of evening civil twilight, low in the south-western sky. After becoming lost in the evening twilight it passes through inferior conjunction on the 27th. On the evening of the 15th the thin crescent Moon, 2 days old, is 9 degrees to the left of Mercury, low above the south-western horizon, though this will require very good conditions for successful observation.

*Venus* passes through superior conjunction on the 14th and is therefore unsuitably placed for observation throughout the month.

*Mars*, magnitude +0.9, is visible in the south-western sky in the evenings. During the month the planet will be seen moving eastwards, south of the Square of Pegasus. Unusually, it can be said that for the whole month, for the whole of mainland Britain, it is visible until about 21h 30m L.M.T. (i.e. when it has reached an altitude of 5 degrees in the western sky). The crescent Moon will be seen 7 degrees south of the planet on the evening of the 18th, while it will be about 10 degrees to the left of it on the following evening.

*Jupiter*, magnitude -2.7, is at opposition on the 1st and is therefore visible throughout the hours of darkness. Jupiter is retrograding slowly in the western part of the constellation of Gemini. On the early evening of the 26th Jupiter will be seen only about 0.1 degrees from the lower limb of the gibbous Moon.

*Saturn*, magnitude -0.2, is an evening object and visible in the southern and south-western sky for the greater part of the night. Saturn is moving slowly westwards in the constellation of Taurus, north of the Hyades. The gibbous Moon will be seen near the planet on the evening of the 24th.

## THE MOON

| Day | RA | Dec. | Hor. par. | Semi-diam | Sun's co-long. | PA of Bright Limb | Phase | Age | Rise 52° | Rise 56° | Transit | Set 52° | Set 56° |
|---|---|---|---|---|---|---|---|---|---|---|---|---|---|
| | h m | ° | ′ | ′ | ° | ° | % | d | h m | h m | h m | h m | h m |
| **1** | 8 16 | +22.8 | 59.8 | 16.3 | 113 | 95 | 97 | 17.1 | 18 24 | 18 02 | 1 38 | 10 00 | 10 23 |
| **2** | 9 17 | +19.9 | 60.0 | 16.3 | 125 | 102 | 91 | 18.1 | 19 49 | 19 33 | 2 38 | 10 35 | 10 52 |
| **3** | 10 16 | +15.8 | 60.0 | 16.3 | 138 | 107 | 84 | 19.1 | 21 14 | 21 04 | 3 34 | 11 01 | 11 13 |
| **4** | 11 12 | +10.7 | 59.8 | 16.3 | 150 | 110 | 74 | 20.1 | 22 38 | 22 33 | 4 28 | 11 23 | 11 30 |
| **5** | 12 05 | + 5.2 | 59.4 | 16.2 | 162 | 112 | 63 | 21.1 | 23 59 | — | 5 18 | 11 42 | 11 44 |
| **6** | 12 57 | – 0.6 | 59.0 | 16.1 | 174 | 113 | 52 | 22.1 | — | 0 00 | 6 07 | 12 00 | 11 57 |
| **7** | 13 48 | – 6.3 | 58.5 | 15.9 | 186 | 112 | 41 | 23.1 | 1 20 | 1 26 | 6 56 | 12 19 | 12 11 |
| **8** | 14 39 | –11.5 | 58.0 | 15.8 | 198 | 109 | 30 | 24.1 | 2 39 | 2 51 | 7 45 | 12 39 | 12 27 |
| **9** | 15 31 | –16.1 | 57.5 | 15.7 | 210 | 106 | 21 | 25.1 | 3 58 | 4 15 | 8 36 | 13 04 | 12 46 |
| **10** | 16 25 | –19.9 | 57.0 | 15.5 | 223 | 101 | 13 | 26.1 | 5 14 | 5 36 | 9 28 | 13 34 | 13 12 |
| **11** | 17 20 | –22.5 | 56.5 | 15.4 | 235 | 95 | 7 | 27.1 | 6 25 | 6 51 | 10 21 | 14 13 | 13 46 |
| **12** | 18 16 | –24.0 | 56.1 | 15.3 | 247 | 87 | 2 | 28.1 | 7 28 | 7 56 | 11 15 | 15 01 | 14 33 |
| **13** | 19 11 | –24.2 | 55.6 | 15.1 | 259 | 68 | 0 | 29.1 | 8 19 | 8 46 | 12 08 | 15 59 | 15 32 |
| **14** | 20 05 | –23.1 | 55.2 | 15.0 | 271 | 287 | 0 | 0.4 | 8 59 | 9 23 | 12 59 | 17 04 | 16 40 |
| **15** | 20 58 | –21.0 | 54.8 | 14.9 | 284 | 266 | 2 | 1.4 | 9 30 | 9 50 | 13 47 | 18 12 | 17 53 |
| **16** | 21 47 | –17.9 | 54.4 | 14.8 | 296 | 259 | 6 | 2.4 | 9 54 | 10 09 | 14 33 | 19 21 | 19 07 |
| **17** | 22 35 | –14.2 | 54.2 | 14.8 | 308 | 254 | 11 | 3.4 | 10 13 | 10 24 | 15 16 | 20 29 | 20 20 |
| **18** | 23 20 | – 9.9 | 54.1 | 14.7 | 320 | 251 | 18 | 4.4 | 10 30 | 10 37 | 15 57 | 21 37 | 21 32 |
| **19** | 0 04 | – 5.3 | 54.1 | 14.7 | 332 | 249 | 25 | 5.4 | 10 45 | 10 48 | 16 38 | 22 44 | 22 43 |
| **20** | 0 47 | – 0.5 | 54.3 | 14.8 | 344 | 249 | 34 | 6.4 | 10 59 | 10 58 | 17 19 | 23 51 | 23 55 |
| **21** | 1 30 | + 4.4 | 54.6 | 14.9 | 357 | 249 | 43 | 7.4 | 11 15 | 11 09 | 18 0 | — | — |
| **22** | 2 15 | + 9.2 | 55.1 | 15.0 | 9 | 250 | 53 | 8.4 | 11 31 | 11 22 | 18 44 | 1 01 | 1 09 |
| **23** | 3 02 | +13.7 | 55.8 | 15.2 | 21 | 253 | 62 | 9.4 | 11 52 | 11 37 | 19 31 | 2 12 | 2 25 |
| **24** | 3 52 | +17.8 | 56.6 | 15.4 | 33 | 257 | 72 | 10.4 | 12 17 | 11 58 | 20 22 | 3 26 | 3 44 |
| **25** | 4 46 | +21.1 | 57.5 | 15.7 | 45 | 262 | 81 | 11.4 | 12 52 | 12 28 | 21 17 | 4 41 | 5 04 |
| **26** | 5 44 | +23.4 | 58.5 | 15.9 | 57 | 268 | 89 | 12.4 | 13 38 | 13 11 | 22 17 | 5 53 | 6 20 |
| **27** | 6 46 | +24.3 | 59.3 | 16.2 | 69 | 277 | 95 | 13.4 | 14 40 | 14 12 | 23 19 | 6 58 | 7 25 |
| **28** | 7 49 | +23.6 | 60.1 | 16.4 | 82 | 291 | 99 | 14.4 | 15 55 | 15 31 | — | 7 50 | 8 15 |
| **29** | 8 52 | +21.3 | 60.6 | 16.5 | 94 | 26 | 100 | 15.4 | 17 21 | 17 02 | 0 21 | 8 31 | 8 50 |
| **30** | 9 53 | +17.5 | 60.9 | 16.6 | 106 | 94 | 98 | 16.4 | 18 49 | 18 37 | 1 20 | 9 01 | 9 16 |
| **31** | 10 52 | +12.5 | 60.9 | 16.6 | 118 | 104 | 94 | 17.4 | 20 17 | 20 11 | 2 17 | 9 26 | 9 35 |

## MERCURY

| Day | RA | Dec. | Diam. | Phase | Transit | 5° high 52° | 5° high 56° |
|---|---|---|---|---|---|---|---|
| | h m | ° | ″ | % | h m | h m | h m |
| 1 | 19 52 | -23.0 | 5 | 87 | 13 11 | 16 17 | 15 42 |
| 3 | 20 05 | -22.3 | 6 | 84 | 13 16 | 16 28 | 15 56 |
| 5 | 20 17 | -21.5 | 6 | 79 | 13 21 | 16 39 | 16 09 |
| 7 | 20 29 | -20.6 | 6 | 75 | 13 24 | 16 50 | 16 22 |
| 9 | 20 39 | -19.7 | 6 | 69 | 13 27 | 16 59 | 16 33 |
| 11 | 20 49 | -18.7 | 7 | 62 | 13 28 | 17 07 | 16 43 |
| 13 | 20 57 | -17.7 | 7 | 54 | 13 27 | 17 13 | 16 51 |
| 15 | 21 02 | -16.8 | 7 | 45 | 13 24 | 17 17 | 16 56 |
| 17 | 21 06 | -16.0 | 8 | 35 | 13 19 | 17 16 | 16 57 |
| 19 | 21 06 | -15.4 | 8 | 25 | 13 11 | 17 12 | 16 53 |
| 21 | 21 04 | -14.9 | 9 | 16 | 13 00 | 17 03 | 16 45 |
| 23 | 20 58 | -14.7 | 9 | 9 | 12 46 | 16 49 | 16 31 |
| 25 | 20 50 | -14.7 | 10 | 4 | 12 29 | 16 32 | 16 14 |
| 27 | 20 41 | -14.9 | 10 | 1 | 12 12 | 16 13 | 15 54 |
| 29 | 20 30 | -15.3 | 10 | 1 | 11 54 | 7 55 | 8 14 |
| 31 | 20 21 | -15.8 | 10 | 4 | 11 36 | 7 41 | 8 01 |

## VENUS

| Day | RA | Dec. | Diam. | Phase | Transit | 5° high 52° | 5° high 56° |
|---|---|---|---|---|---|---|---|
| | h m | ° | ″ | % | h m | h m | h m |
| 1 | 18 31 | -23.6 | 10 | 100 | 11 50 | 14 48 | 14 11 |
| 6 | 18 59 | -23.3 | 10 | 100 | 11 58 | 14 59 | 14 22 |
| 11 | 19 26 | -22.7 | 10 | 100 | 12 05 | 15 12 | 14 38 |
| 16 | 19 53 | -21.9 | 10 | 100 | 12 13 | 15 27 | 14 55 |
| 21 | 20 19 | -20.7 | 10 | 100 | 12 19 | 15 43 | 15 15 |
| 26 | 20 45 | -19.3 | 10 | 100 | 12 26 | 16 01 | 15 35 |
| 31 | 21 11 | -17.6 | 10 | 100 | 12 31 | 16 18 | 15 56 |

## MARS

| Day | RA | Dec. | Diam. | Phase | Transit | 5° high 52° | 5° high 56° |
|---|---|---|---|---|---|---|---|
| 1 | 23 13 | - 5.8 | 6 | 89 | 16 30 | 21 28 | 21 20 |
| 6 | 23 26 | - 4.3 | 6 | 89 | 16 24 | 21 30 | 21 23 |
| 11 | 23 39 | - 2.8 | 6 | 90 | 16 17 | 21 31 | 21 26 |
| 16 | 23 53 | - 1.2 | 6 | 90 | 16 11 | 21 33 | 21 29 |
| 21 | 0 06 | + 0.3 | 6 | 90 | 16 04 | 21 34 | 21 32 |
| 26 | 0 19 | + 1.8 | 6 | 91 | 15 58 | 21 36 | 21 34 |
| 31 | 0 32 | + 3.3 | 5 | 91 | 15 51 | 21 37 | 21 37 |

## SUNRISE AND SUNSET

| | London | | Bristol | | Birmingham | | Manchester | | Newcastle | | Glasgow | | Belfast | |
|---|---|---|---|---|---|---|---|---|---|---|---|---|---|---|
| | 0°05′ | 51°30′ | 2°35′ | 51°28′ | 1°55′ | 52°28′ | 2°15′ | 53°28′ | 1°37′ | 54°59′ | 4°14′ | 55°52′ | 5°56′ | 54°35′ |
| | h m | h m | h m | h m | h m | h m | h m | h m | h m | h m | h m | h m | h m | h m |
| **1** | 8 06 | 16 02 | 8 16 | 16 12 | 8 18 | 16 04 | 8 25 | 16 00 | 8 31 | 15 49 | 8 47 | 15 54 | 8 46 | 16 09 |
| **2** | 8 06 | 16 03 | 8 16 | 16 13 | 8 18 | 16 05 | 8 25 | 16 01 | 8 31 | 15 50 | 8 47 | 15 55 | 8 46 | 16 10 |
| **3** | 8 06 | 16 04 | 8 16 | 16 14 | 8 18 | 16 07 | 8 25 | 16 03 | 8 31 | 15 51 | 8 47 | 15 56 | 8 46 | 16 11 |
| **4** | 8 05 | 16 05 | 8 15 | 16 15 | 8 18 | 16 08 | 8 24 | 16 04 | 8 30 | 15 53 | 8 46 | 15 58 | 8 45 | 16 12 |
| **5** | 8 05 | 16 06 | 8 15 | 16 17 | 8 17 | 16 09 | 8 24 | 16 05 | 8 30 | 15 54 | 8 46 | 15 59 | 8 45 | 16 14 |
| **6** | 8 05 | 16 08 | 8 15 | 16 18 | 8 17 | 16 10 | 8 23 | 16 06 | 8 29 | 15 55 | 8 45 | 16 00 | 8 44 | 16 15 |
| **7** | 8 04 | 16 09 | 8 14 | 16 19 | 8 17 | 16 12 | 8 23 | 16 08 | 8 29 | 15 57 | 8 45 | 16 02 | 8 44 | 16 16 |
| **8** | 8 04 | 16 10 | 8 14 | 16 20 | 8 16 | 16 13 | 8 22 | 16 09 | 8 28 | 15 58 | 8 44 | 16 04 | 8 43 | 16 18 |
| **9** | 8 04 | 16 12 | 8 13 | 16 22 | 8 15 | 16 14 | 8 22 | 16 11 | 8 28 | 16 00 | 8 43 | 16 05 | 8 43 | 16 19 |
| **10** | 8 03 | 16 13 | 8 13 | 16 23 | 8 15 | 16 16 | 8 21 | 16 12 | 8 27 | 16 01 | 8 42 | 16 07 | 8 42 | 16 21 |
| **11** | 8 02 | 16 14 | 8 12 | 16 25 | 8 14 | 16 17 | 8 20 | 16 14 | 8 26 | 16 03 | 8 42 | 16 08 | 8 41 | 16 23 |
| **12** | 8 02 | 16 16 | 8 12 | 16 26 | 8 14 | 16 19 | 8 20 | 16 15 | 8 25 | 16 05 | 8 41 | 16 10 | 8 40 | 16 24 |
| **13** | 8 01 | 16 17 | 8 11 | 16 28 | 8 13 | 16 20 | 8 19 | 16 17 | 8 24 | 16 06 | 8 40 | 16 12 | 8 39 | 16 26 |
| **14** | 8 00 | 16 19 | 8 10 | 16 29 | 8 12 | 16 22 | 8 18 | 16 18 | 8 23 | 16 08 | 8 39 | 16 14 | 8 38 | 16 28 |
| **15** | 7 59 | 16 20 | 8 09 | 16 31 | 8 11 | 16 23 | 8 17 | 16 20 | 8 22 | 16 10 | 8 38 | 16 16 | 8 37 | 16 29 |
| **16** | 7 59 | 16 22 | 8 08 | 16 32 | 8 10 | 16 25 | 8 16 | 16 22 | 8 21 | 16 12 | 8 36 | 16 17 | 8 36 | 16 31 |
| **17** | 7 58 | 16 24 | 8 08 | 16 34 | 8 09 | 16 27 | 8 15 | 16 23 | 8 20 | 16 13 | 8 35 | 16 19 | 8 35 | 16 33 |
| **18** | 7 57 | 16 25 | 8 07 | 16 35 | 8 08 | 16 28 | 8 14 | 16 25 | 8 19 | 16 15 | 8 34 | 16 21 | 8 34 | 16 35 |
| **19** | 7 56 | 16 27 | 8 06 | 16 37 | 8 07 | 16 30 | 8 13 | 16 27 | 8 18 | 16 17 | 8 33 | 16 23 | 8 33 | 16 36 |
| **20** | 7 55 | 16 28 | 8 05 | 16 39 | 8 06 | 16 32 | 8 12 | 16 29 | 8 16 | 16 19 | 8 31 | 16 25 | 8 32 | 16 38 |
| **21** | 7 54 | 16 30 | 8 03 | 16 40 | 8 05 | 16 34 | 8 11 | 16 31 | 8 15 | 16 21 | 8 30 | 16 27 | 8 30 | 16 40 |
| **22** | 7 52 | 16 32 | 8 02 | 16 42 | 8 04 | 16 35 | 8 09 | 16 32 | 8 14 | 16 23 | 8 28 | 16 29 | 8 29 | 16 42 |
| **23** | 7 51 | 16 34 | 8 01 | 16 44 | 8 02 | 16 37 | 8 08 | 16 34 | 8 12 | 16 25 | 8 27 | 16 31 | 8 28 | 16 44 |
| **24** | 7 50 | 16 35 | 8 00 | 16 45 | 8 01 | 16 39 | 8 07 | 16 36 | 8 11 | 16 27 | 8 25 | 16 33 | 8 26 | 16 46 |
| **25** | 7 49 | 16 37 | 7 59 | 16 47 | 8 00 | 16 41 | 8 05 | 16 38 | 8 09 | 16 29 | 8 24 | 16 35 | 8 25 | 16 48 |
| **26** | 7 48 | 16 39 | 7 57 | 16 49 | 7 58 | 16 42 | 8 04 | 16 40 | 8 08 | 16 31 | 8 22 | 16 37 | 8 23 | 16 50 |
| **27** | 7 46 | 16 41 | 7 56 | 16 51 | 7 57 | 16 44 | 8 02 | 16 42 | 8 06 | 16 33 | 8 21 | 16 39 | 8 22 | 16 52 |
| **28** | 7 45 | 16 42 | 7 55 | 16 52 | 7 56 | 16 46 | 8 01 | 16 44 | 8 05 | 16 35 | 8 19 | 16 42 | 8 20 | 16 54 |
| **29** | 7 43 | 16 44 | 7 53 | 16 54 | 7 54 | 16 48 | 7 59 | 16 46 | 8 03 | 16 37 | 8 17 | 16 44 | 8 18 | 16 56 |
| **30** | 7 42 | 16 46 | 7 52 | 16 56 | 7 53 | 16 50 | 7 58 | 16 48 | 8 01 | 16 39 | 8 15 | 16 46 | 8 17 | 16 58 |
| **31** | 7 40 | 16 48 | 7 50 | 16 58 | 7 51 | 16 52 | 7 56 | 16 49 | 7 59 | 16 41 | 8 13 | 16 48 | 8 15 | 17 00 |

## JUPITER

| *Day* | *RA* | | *Dec.* | | *Transit* | | *5° high* | | | |
|---|---|---|---|---|---|---|---|---|---|---|
| | | | | | | | 52° | | 56° | |
| | h | m | ° | ′ | h | m | h | m | h | m |
| 1 | 6 | 46.4 | +23 | 01 | 0 | 04 | 7 | 35 | 7 | 53 |
| 11 | 6 | 40.6 | +23 | 08 | 23 | 15 | 6 | 51 | 7 | 09 |
| 21 | 6 | 35.2 | +23 | 14 | 22 | 30 | 6 | 07 | 6 | 25 |
| 31 | 6 | 30.7 | +23 | 19 | 21 | 47 | 5 | 23 | 5 | 42 |

Diameters – equatorial 47″ polar 44″

## SATURN

| *Day* | *RA* | | *Dec.* | | *Transit* | | *5° high* | | | |
|---|---|---|---|---|---|---|---|---|---|---|
| | | | | | | | 52° | | 56° | |
| | h | m | ° | ′ | h | m | h | m | h | m |
| 1 | 4 | 31.7 | +20 | 04 | 21 | 46 | 5 | 03 | 5 | 17 |
| 11 | 4 | 29.3 | +20 | 01 | 21 | 04 | 4 | 21 | 4 | 35 |
| 21 | 4 | 27.5 | +19 | 59 | 20 | 23 | 3 | 40 | 3 | 54 |
| 31 | 4 | 26.5 | +19 | 59 | 19 | 43 | 2 | 59 | 3 | 13 |

Diameters – equatorial 20″ polar 18″
Rings – major axis 45″ minor axis 20″

## URANUS

| *Day* | *RA* | | *Dec.* | | *Transit* | | *10° high* | | | |
|---|---|---|---|---|---|---|---|---|---|---|
| | | | | | | | 52° | | 56° | |
| | h | m | ° | ′ | h | m | h | m | h | m |
| 1 | 21 | 40.2 | -14 | 41 | 14 | 56 | 18 | 20 | 17 | 55 |
| 11 | 21 | 42.1 | -14 | 32 | 14 | 19 | 17 | 44 | 17 | 19 |
| 21 | 21 | 44.2 | -14 | 21 | 13 | 41 | 17 | 08 | 16 | 43 |
| 31 | 21 | 46.3 | -14 | 10 | 13 | 04 | 16 | 32 | 16 | 08 |

Diameter 4″

## NEPTUNE

| *Day* | *RA* | | *Dec.* | | *Transit* | | *10° high* | | | |
|---|---|---|---|---|---|---|---|---|---|---|
| | | | | | | | 52° | | 56° | |
| | h | m | ° | ′ | h | m | h | m | h | m |
| 1 | 20 | 39.3 | -18 | 18 | 13 | 55 | 16 | 50 | 16 | 15 |
| 11 | 20 | 40.7 | -18 | 13 | 13 | 17 | 16 | 13 | 15 | 39 |
| 21 | 20 | 42.3 | -18 | 07 | 12 | 40 | 15 | 36 | 15 | 02 |
| 31 | 20 | 43.8 | -18 | 02 | 12 | 02 | 14 | 59 | 14 | 25 |

Diameter 2″

# February 2002

SECOND MONTH, 28 or 29 DAYS. *Februa*, Roman festival of Purification

| | | | |
|---|---|---|---|
| **1** | *Friday* | Clark Gable b. 1901. Piet Mondrian d. 1944 | 32 |
| **2** | *Saturday* | **The Presentation of Christ in the Temple (Candlemas).** | 33 |
| **3** | *Sunday* | **8th S. before Easter.** Elizabeth Blackwell b. 1821 | 34 |
| **4** | *Monday* | Pierre Marivaux b. 1688. RNLI founded 1824 | *week 5 day* 35 |
| **5** | *Tuesday* | William S. Burroughs b. 1914. Sir Robert Peel b. 1788 | 36 |
| **6** | *Wednesday* | *Queen's Accession 1952.* Christopher Marlowe b. 1564 | 37 |
| **7** | *Thursday* | Sir Thomas More b. 1478. Joseph Sheridan Le Fanu d. 1873 | 38 |
| **8** | *Friday* | Sir Giles Gilbert Scott d. 1960. Rt. Hon. Enoch Powell d. 1998 | 39 |
| **9** | *Saturday* | Edward Carson b. 1854. Yuri Andropov d. 1984 | 40 |
| **10** | *Sunday* | **7th S. before Easter.** PAYE introduced 1944 | 41 |
| **11** | *Monday* | Sir Vivian Fuchs b. 1908. Sergey Eisenstein d. 1948 | *week 6 day* 42 |
| **12** | *Tuesday* | Shrove Tuesday. *Chinese Year of the Horse* | 43 |
| **13** | *Wednesday* | **Ash Wednesday**. Queen Catherine Howard d. 1542 | 44 |
| **14** | *Thursday* | St Valentines Day. William Sherman d. 1891 | 45 |
| **15** | *Friday* | Henry Hunt d. 1835. Introduction of decimal currency in Britain 1971 | 46 |
| **16** | *Saturday* | Angela Carter d. 1992. Giosue Carducci d. 1907 | 47 |
| **17** | *Sunday* | **1st S. in Lent.** Sir John Jones b. 1923 | 48 |
| **18** | *Monday* | Queen Mary I Tudor b. 1516. Fra Angelico d. 1455 | *week 7 day* 49 |
| **19** | *Tuesday* | *Duke of York b. 1960.* Luigi Boccherini b. 1743 | 50 |
| **20** | *Wednesday* | Honoré Daumier b. 1808. Joseph Hume d. 1855 | 51 |
| **21** | *Thursday* | Léo Delibes b. 1836. Battle of Verdun 1915 | 52 |
| **22** | *Friday* | Sir John Mills b. 1908. Oskar Kokoschka d. 1980 | 53 |
| **23** | *Saturday* | George Watts b. 1817. Stefan Zweig d. 1942 | 54 |
| **24** | *Sunday* | **2nd S. in Lent.** Nikolai Bukharin (Bulganin) d. 1975 | 55 |
| **25** | *Monday* | Sir John Tenniel d. 1914. Tennessee Williams d. 1983 | *week 8 day* 56 |
| **26** | *Tuesday* | John Philip Kemble d. 1823. First issue of £1 and £2 notes 1797 | 57 |
| **27** | *Wednesday* | Antoinette Sibley b. 1939. Ivan Pavlov d. 1936 | 58 |
| **28** | *Thursday* | Sir John Tenniel b. 1820. Albert Lippert d. 1998 | 59 |

## Astronomical Phenomena

| d | h | |
|---|---|---|
| 8 | 02 | Saturn at stationary point |
| 8 | 17 | Mercury at stationary point |
| 10 | 07 | Mercury in conjunction with Moon. Mercury 5° N. |
| 12 | 23 | Venus in conjunction with Moon. Venus 3° N. |
| 13 | 17 | Uranus in conjunction |
| 17 | 04 | Mars in conjunction with Moon. Mars 5° N. |
| 18 | 20 | Sun's longitude 330° ♓ |
| 21 | 00 | Saturn in conjunction with Moon. Saturn 0°.2 S. |
| 21 | 16 | Mercury at greatest elongation W.27° |
| 23 | 02 | Jupiter in conjunction with Moon. Jupiter 0°.9 S. |

## Minima of Algol

| d | h | d | h | d | h |
|---|---|---|---|---|---|
| 2 | 12.7 | 14 | 00.0 | 25 | 11.3 |
| 5 | 09.5 | 16 | 20.8 | 28 | 08.1 |
| 8 | 06.3 | 19 | 17.6 | | |
| 11 | 03.1 | 22 | 14.4 | | |

## Constellations

The following constellations are near the meridian at

| | d | h | | d | h |
|---|---|---|---|---|---|
| January | 1 | 24 | February | 15 | 21 |
| January | 16 | 23 | March | 1 | 20 |
| February | 1 | 22 | March | 16 | 19 |

Draco (below the Pole), Camelopardus, Auriga, Taurus, Gemini, Orion, Canis Minor, Monoceros, Lepus, Canis Major and Puppis

## The Moon

| Phases, Apsides and Node | d | h | m |
|---|---|---|---|
| ☾ Last Quarter | 4 | 13 | 33 |
| ● New Moon | 12 | 07 | 41 |
| ☽ First Quarter | 20 | 12 | 02 |
| ○ Full Moon | 27 | 09 | 17 |
| Apogee (406,382km) | 14 | 22 | 32 |
| Perigee (356,893km) | 27 | 19 | 50 |

Mean longitude of ascending node on February 1, 85°

## THE SUN

S.D 16′.1

| Day | Right Ascension | Dec. | Equation of Time | Rise 52° | Rise 56° | Transit | Set 52° | Set 56° | Sidereal time | Transit of First Point of Aries |
|---|---|---|---|---|---|---|---|---|---|---|
| | h m s | ° ′ | m s | h m | h m | h m | h m | h m | h m s | h m s |
| 1 | 20 57 36 | 17 13 | −13 30 | 7 40 | 7 55 | 12 14 | 16 47 | 16 33 | 8 44 06 | 15 13 24 |
| 2 | 21 01 41 | 16 56 | −13 38 | 7 39 | 7 53 | 12 14 | 16 49 | 16 35 | 8 48 03 | 15 09 28 |
| 3 | 21 05 44 | 16 38 | −13 45 | 7 37 | 7 51 | 12 14 | 16 51 | 16 37 | 8 52 00 | 15 05 32 |
| 4 | 21 09 47 | 16 20 | −13 51 | 7 35 | 7 49 | 12 14 | 16 53 | 16 39 | 8 55 56 | 15 01 36 |
| 5 | 21 13 49 | 16 02 | −13 57 | 7 34 | 7 47 | 12 14 | 16 55 | 16 41 | 8 59 53 | 14 57 40 |
| 6 | 21 17 51 | 15 44 | −14 01 | 7 32 | 7 45 | 12 14 | 16 57 | 16 44 | 9 03 49 | 14 53 44 |
| 7 | 21 21 51 | 15 26 | −14 05 | 7 30 | 7 43 | 12 14 | 16 59 | 16 46 | 9 07 46 | 14 49 48 |
| 8 | 21 25 51 | 15 07 | −14 09 | 7 29 | 7 41 | 12 14 | 17 01 | 16 48 | 9 11 42 | 14 45 52 |
| 9 | 21 29 50 | 14 48 | −14 11 | 7 27 | 7 39 | 12 14 | 17 02 | 16 50 | 9 15 39 | 14 41 56 |
| 0 | 21 33 48 | 14 29 | −14 13 | 7 25 | 7 37 | 12 14 | 17 04 | 16 52 | 9 19 35 | 14 38 00 |
| 1 | 21 37 45 | 14 09 | −14 13 | 7 23 | 7 35 | 12 14 | 17 06 | 16 55 | 9 23 32 | 14 34 04 |
| 2 | 21 41 42 | 13 49 | −14 14 | 7 21 | 7 33 | 12 14 | 17 08 | 16 57 | 9 27 29 | 14 30 09 |
| 3 | 21 45 38 | 13 29 | −14 13 | 7 19 | 7 30 | 12 14 | 17 10 | 16 59 | 9 31 25 | 14 26 13 |
| 4 | 21 49 33 | 13 09 | −14 11 | 7 17 | 7 28 | 12 14 | 17 12 | 17 01 | 9 35 22 | 14 22 17 |
| 5 | 21 53 27 | 12 49 | −14 09 | 7 15 | 7 26 | 12 14 | 17 14 | 17 03 | 9 39 18 | 14 18 21 |
| 6 | 21 57 21 | 12 28 | −14 06 | 7 14 | 7 24 | 12 14 | 17 15 | 17 06 | 9 43 15 | 14 14 25 |
| 7 | 22 01 14 | 12 07 | −14 03 | 7 12 | 7 21 | 12 14 | 17 17 | 17 08 | 9 47 11 | 14 10 29 |
| 8 | 22 05 06 | 11 46 | −13 58 | 7 10 | 7 19 | 12 14 | 17 19 | 17 10 | 9 51 08 | 14 06 33 |
| 9 | 22 08 58 | 11 25 | −13 53 | 7 08 | 7 17 | 12 14 | 17 21 | 17 12 | 9 55 04 | 14 02 37 |
| 0 | 22 12 49 | 11 04 | −13 48 | 7 05 | 7 14 | 12 14 | 17 23 | 17 14 | 9 59 01 | 13 58 41 |
| 1 | 22 16 39 | 10 42 | −13 41 | 7 03 | 7 12 | 12 14 | 17 25 | 17 16 | 10 02 58 | 13 54 45 |
| 2 | 22 20 28 | 10 20 | −13 34 | 7 01 | 7 09 | 12 14 | 17 27 | 17 19 | 10 06 54 | 13 50 49 |
| 3 | 22 24 17 | 9 58 | −13 26 | 6 59 | 7 07 | 12 13 | 17 28 | 17 21 | 10 10 51 | 13 46 54 |
| 4 | 22 28 05 | 9 36 | −13 18 | 6 57 | 7 04 | 12 13 | 17 30 | 17 23 | 10 14 47 | 13 42 58 |
| 5 | 22 31 53 | 9 14 | −13 09 | 6 55 | 7 02 | 12 13 | 17 32 | 17 25 | 10 18 44 | 13 39 02 |
| 6 | 22 35 40 | 8 52 | −12 59 | 6 53 | 7 00 | 12 13 | 17 34 | 17 27 | 10 22 40 | 13 35 06 |
| 7 | 22 39 26 | 8 29 | −12 49 | 6 51 | 6 57 | 12 13 | 17 36 | 17 29 | 10 26 37 | 13 31 10 |
| 8 | 22 43 12 | 8 07 | −12 38 | 6 49 | 6 55 | 12 13 | 17 37 | 17 32 | 10 30 33 | 13 27 14 |

## DURATION OF TWILIGHT (in minutes)

| Latitude | 52° | 56° | 52° | 56° | 52° | 56° | 52° | 56° |
|---|---|---|---|---|---|---|---|---|
| | 1 February | | 11 February | | 21 February | | 28 February | |
| Civil | 37 | 41 | 35 | 39 | 34 | 38 | 34 | 37 |
| Nautical | 77 | 86 | 75 | 83 | 74 | 81 | 73 | 80 |
| Astronomical | 117 | 130 | 114 | 126 | 113 | 124 | 112 | 124 |

## THE NIGHT SKY

*Mercury*, although it attains greatest western elongation on the 21st, is unsuitably placed for observation from these latitudes.

*Venus* is too close to the Sun for observation during the first half of the month but then becomes visible as an evening object, magnitude -3.9, low above the west-south-western horizon for a short while after sunset.

*Mars*, magnitude +1.2, continues to be visible as an evening object in the south-western sky. Mars is in the constellation of Pisces but enters Aries at the very end of the month. The crescent Moon will be seen passing about degrees below the planet on the evening of the 16th.

*Jupiter* is a conspicuous evening object in the southern skies, magnitude -2.5. It is almost stationary in the western part of Gemini. On the evenings of the 22nd and 23rd the gibbous Moon is in the vicinity of the planet. The four Galilean satellites are readily observable with a small telescope or even a good pair of binoculars provided that they are held rigidly.

*Saturn*, magnitude 0.0, continues to be visible in the southern and south-western part of the sky in the evenings. It reaches its second stationary point on the 8th, in Taurus, resuming its direct motion. The Moon, near First Quarter, is near the planet on the evenings of the 20th and 21st.

*Zodiacal Light*. The evening cone may be observed stretching up from the western horizon, along the ecliptic, after the end of twilight, from the beginning of the month up to the 13th. This faint phenomenon is only visible under good conditions and in the absence of both moonlight and artificial lighting.

THE MOON

| Day | RA | Dec. | Hor. par. | Semi-diam | Sun's co-long. | PA of Bright Limb | Phase | Age | Rise 52° | Rise 56° | Transit | Set 52° | Set 56° |
|---|---|---|---|---|---|---|---|---|---|---|---|---|---|
| | h m | ° | ′ | ′ | ° | ° | % | d | h m | h m | h m | h m | h m |
| **1** | 11 48 | + 6.9 | 60.6 | 16.5 | 130 | 108 | 87 | 18.4 | 21 43 | 21 42 | 3 11 | 9 46 | 9 50 |
| **2** | 12 42 | + 0.9 | 60.0 | 16.4 | 142 | 110 | 78 | 19.4 | 23 06 | 23 11 | 4 02 | 10 05 | 10 04 |
| **3** | 13 35 | − 5.0 | 59.4 | 16.2 | 154 | 110 | 67 | 20.4 | — | — | 4 52 | 10 24 | 10 18 |
| **4** | 14 27 | −10.5 | 58.6 | 16.0 | 167 | 108 | 56 | 21.4 | 0 28 | 0 38 | 5 42 | 10 44 | 10 33 |
| **5** | 15 19 | −15.3 | 57.9 | 15.8 | 179 | 105 | 45 | 22.4 | 1 48 | 2 03 | 6 33 | 11 07 | 10 51 |
| **6** | 16 13 | −19.3 | 57.2 | 15.6 | 191 | 101 | 35 | 23.4 | 3 05 | 3 26 | 7 24 | 11 36 | 11 15 |
| **7** | 17 07 | −22.1 | 56.5 | 15.4 | 203 | 96 | 25 | 24.4 | 4 18 | 4 42 | 8 17 | 12 11 | 11 46 |
| **8** | 18 02 | −23.8 | 55.9 | 15.2 | 215 | 89 | 17 | 25.4 | 5 22 | 5 50 | 9 10 | 12 56 | 12 28 |
| **9** | 18 57 | −24.3 | 55.4 | 15.1 | 227 | 82 | 10 | 26.4 | 6 16 | 6 44 | 10 02 | 13 50 | 13 23 |
| **10** | 19 51 | −23.5 | 55.0 | 15.0 | 240 | 74 | 5 | 27.4 | 6 59 | 7 24 | 10 54 | 14 53 | 14 28 |
| **11** | 20 43 | −21.7 | 54.7 | 14.9 | 252 | 62 | 2 | 28.4 | 7 32 | 7 53 | 11 43 | 16 00 | 15 39 |
| **12** | 21 33 | −18.8 | 54.4 | 14.8 | 264 | 22 | 0 | 29.4 | 7 58 | 8 15 | 12 29 | 17 09 | 16 53 |
| **13** | 22 21 | −15.2 | 54.1 | 14.8 | 276 | 280 | 1 | 0.7 | 8 19 | 8 31 | 13 13 | 18 17 | 18 06 |
| **14** | 23 07 | −11.1 | 54.0 | 14.7 | 288 | 262 | 3 | 1.7 | 8 36 | 8 44 | 13 55 | 19 25 | 19 19 |
| **15** | 23 51 | − 6.5 | 54.0 | 14.7 | 301 | 255 | 7 | 2.7 | 8 51 | 8 55 | 14 36 | 20 33 | 20 30 |
| **16** | 0 34 | − 1.7 | 54.0 | 14.7 | 313 | 253 | 12 | 3.7 | 9 05 | 9 05 | 15 16 | 21 40 | 21 42 |
| **17** | 1 17 | + 3.2 | 54.2 | 14.8 | 325 | 252 | 19 | 4.7 | 9 20 | 9 16 | 15 57 | 22 48 | 22 54 |
| **18** | 2 01 | + 8.0 | 54.5 | 14.9 | 337 | 252 | 27 | 5.7 | 9 36 | 9 27 | 16 39 | 23 57 | — |
| **19** | 2 47 | +12.6 | 55.0 | 15.0 | 349 | 254 | 35 | 6.7 | 9 54 | 9 41 | 17 23 | — | 0 08 |
| **20** | 3 35 | +16.7 | 55.7 | 15.2 | 1 | 257 | 45 | 7.7 | 10 16 | 9 59 | 18 11 | 1 09 | 1 25 |
| **21** | 4 26 | +20.2 | 56.4 | 15.4 | 14 | 261 | 55 | 8.7 | 10 45 | 10 23 | 19 03 | 2 21 | 2 43 |
| **22** | 5 21 | +22.8 | 57.3 | 15.6 | 26 | 266 | 65 | 9.7 | 11 24 | 10 58 | 19 59 | 3 33 | 3 59 |
| **23** | 6 19 | +24.2 | 58.3 | 15.9 | 38 | 272 | 75 | 10.7 | 12 17 | 11 49 | 20 58 | 4 40 | 5 08 |
| **24** | 7 20 | +24.2 | 59.3 | 16.2 | 50 | 280 | 84 | 11.7 | 13 24 | 12 58 | 21 59 | 5 37 | 6 04 |
| **25** | 8 23 | +22.6 | 60.2 | 16.4 | 62 | 288 | 92 | 12.7 | 14 45 | 14 23 | 23 00 | 6 22 | 6 45 |
| **26** | 9 25 | +19.4 | 60.9 | 16.6 | 74 | 299 | 97 | 13.7 | 16 13 | 15 57 | 23 59 | 6 57 | 7 15 |
| **27** | 10 25 | +14.9 | 61.3 | 16.7 | 87 | 331 | 100 | 14.7 | 17 44 | 17 34 | — | 7 25 | 7 36 |
| **28** | 11 24 | + 9.3 | 61.4 | 16.7 | 99 | 84 | 99 | 15.7 | 19 13 | 19 10 | 0 55 | 7 47 | 7 53 |

MERCURY

| Day | RA | Dec. | Diam. | Phase | Transit | 5° high 52° | 5° high 56° |
|---|---|---|---|---|---|---|---|
| | h m | ° | ″ | % | h m | h m | h m |
| 1 | 20 16 | −16.1 | 10 | 6 | 11 28 | 7 35 | 7 55 |
| 3 | 20 09 | −16.6 | 10 | 12 | 11 14 | 7 23 | 7 44 |
| 5 | 20 04 | −17.1 | 10 | 18 | 11 01 | 7 14 | 7 36 |
| 7 | 20 01 | −17.6 | 9 | 24 | 10 51 | 7 07 | 7 30 |
| 9 | 20 01 | −18.0 | 9 | 30 | 10 44 | 7 02 | 7 25 |
| 11 | 20 02 | −18.3 | 8 | 36 | 10 38 | 6 58 | 7 22 |
| 13 | 20 06 | −18.6 | 8 | 41 | 10 34 | 6 56 | 7 20 |
| 15 | 20 11 | −18.7 | 8 | 46 | 10 31 | 6 54 | 7 18 |
| 17 | 20 17 | −18.8 | 8 | 51 | 10 29 | 6 52 | 7 17 |
| 19 | 20 24 | −18.8 | 7 | 55 | 10 29 | 6 52 | 7 16 |
| 21 | 20 32 | −18.7 | 7 | 58 | 10 29 | 6 51 | 7 16 |
| 23 | 20 40 | −18.5 | 7 | 61 | 10 30 | 6 50 | 7 15 |
| 25 | 20 50 | −18.2 | 7 | 64 | 10 31 | 6 50 | 7 13 |
| 27 | 20 59 | −17.9 | 6 | 67 | 10 33 | 6 49 | 7 12 |
| 29 | 21 10 | −17.4 | 6 | 70 | 10 36 | 6 48 | 7 10 |
| 31 | 21 20 | −16.9 | 6 | 72 | 10 39 | 6 47 | 7 09 |

VENUS

| Day | RA | Dec. | Diam. | Phase | Transit | 5° high 52° | 5° high 56° |
|---|---|---|---|---|---|---|---|
| | h m | ° | ″ | % | h m | h m | h m |
| 1 | 21 16 | −17.3 | 10 | 100 | 12 32 | 16 22 | 16 00 |
| 6 | 21 41 | −15.4 | 10 | 100 | 12 38 | 16 40 | 16 2[illegible] |
| 11 | 22 05 | −13.3 | 10 | 99 | 12 42 | 16 58 | 16 4[illegible] |
| 16 | 22 29 | −11.1 | 10 | 99 | 12 46 | 17 16 | 17 0[illegible] |
| 21 | 22 53 | − 8.7 | 10 | 99 | 12 50 | 17 33 | 17 2[illegible] |
| 26 | 23 16 | − 6.3 | 10 | 99 | 12 54 | 17 50 | 17 4[illegible] |
| 31 | 23 39 | − 3.8 | 10 | 98 | 12 57 | 18 07 | 18 0[illegible] |

MARS

| Day | RA | Dec. | Diam. | Phase | Transit | 5° high 52° | 5° high 56° |
|---|---|---|---|---|---|---|---|
| 1 | 0 35 | + 3.6 | 5 | 91 | 15 50 | 21 37 | 21 3[illegible] |
| 6 | 0 48 | + 5.1 | 5 | 92 | 15 44 | 21 38 | 21 3[illegible] |
| 11 | 1 02 | + 6.6 | 5 | 92 | 15 37 | 21 39 | 21 4[illegible] |
| 16 | 1 15 | + 8.0 | 5 | 92 | 15 31 | 21 40 | 21 4[illegible] |
| 21 | 1 28 | + 9.4 | 5 | 93 | 15 24 | 21 41 | 21 4[illegible] |
| 26 | 1 42 | +10.8 | 5 | 93 | 15 18 | 21 42 | 21 4[illegible] |
| 31 | 1 55 | +12.1 | 5 | 93 | 15 12 | 21 42 | 21 4[illegible] |

## SUNRISE AND SUNSET

| Day | London 0°05′ 51°30′ h m | h m | Bristol 2°35′ 51°28′ h m | h m | Birmingham 1°55′ 52°28′ h m | h m | Manchester 2°15′ 53°28′ h m | h m | Newcastle 1°37′ 54°59′ h m | h m | Glasgow 4°14′ 55°52′ h m | h m | Belfast 5°56′ 54°35′ h m | h m |
|---|---|---|---|---|---|---|---|---|---|---|---|---|---|---|
| 1 | 7 39 | 16 49 | 7 49 | 17 00 | 7 50 | 16 54 | 7 54 | 16 51 | 7 58 | 16 43 | 8 12 | 16 50 | 8 13 | 17 02 |
| 2 | 7 37 | 16 51 | 7 47 | 17 01 | 7 48 | 16 55 | 7 53 | 16 53 | 7 56 | 16 45 | 8 10 | 16 52 | 8 11 | 17 04 |
| 3 | 7 36 | 16 53 | 7 46 | 17 03 | 7 46 | 16 57 | 7 51 | 16 55 | 7 54 | 16 47 | 8 08 | 16 54 | 8 10 | 17 06 |
| 4 | 7 34 | 16 55 | 7 44 | 17 05 | 7 45 | 16 59 | 7 49 | 16 57 | 7 52 | 16 49 | 8 06 | 16 57 | 8 08 | 17 08 |
| 5 | 7 33 | 16 57 | 7 42 | 17 07 | 7 43 | 17 01 | 7 47 | 16 59 | 7 50 | 16 52 | 8 04 | 16 59 | 8 06 | 17 10 |
| 6 | 7 31 | 16 59 | 7 41 | 17 09 | 7 41 | 17 03 | 7 46 | 17 01 | 7 48 | 16 54 | 8 02 | 17 01 | 8 04 | 17 12 |
| 7 | 7 29 | 7 00 | 7 39 | 17 11 | 7 39 | 17 05 | 7 44 | 17 03 | 7 46 | 16 56 | 8 00 | 17 03 | 8 02 | 17 14 |
| 8 | 7 27 | 17 02 | 7 37 | 17 12 | 7 38 | 17 07 | 7 42 | 17 05 | 7 44 | 16 58 | 7 58 | 17 05 | 8 00 | 17 16 |
| 9 | 7 26 | 17 04 | 7 36 | 17 14 | 7 36 | 17 09 | 7 40 | 17 07 | 7 42 | 17 00 | 7 56 | 17 08 | 7 58 | 17 19 |
| 10 | 7 24 | 17 06 | 7 34 | 17 16 | 7 34 | 17 11 | 7 38 | 17 09 | 7 40 | 17 02 | 7 53 | 17 10 | 7 56 | 17 21 |
| 11 | 7 22 | 17 08 | 7 32 | 17 18 | 7 32 | 17 13 | 7 36 | 17 11 | 7 38 | 17 04 | 7 51 | 17 12 | 7 54 | 17 23 |
| 12 | 7 20 | 17 10 | 7 30 | 17 20 | 7 30 | 17 14 | 7 34 | 17 13 | 7 36 | 17 06 | 7 49 | 17 14 | 7 52 | 17 25 |
| 13 | 7 18 | 17 11 | 7 28 | 17 21 | 7 28 | 17 16 | 7 32 | 17 15 | 7 34 | 17 08 | 7 47 | 17 16 | 7 50 | 17 27 |
| 14 | 7 17 | 17 13 | 7 26 | 17 23 | 7 26 | 17 18 | 7 30 | 17 17 | 7 32 | 17 11 | 7 45 | 17 19 | 7 48 | 17 29 |
| 15 | 7 15 | 17 15 | 7 25 | 17 25 | 7 24 | 17 20 | 7 28 | 17 19 | 7 29 | 17 13 | 7 42 | 17 21 | 7 46 | 17 31 |
| 16 | 7 13 | 17 17 | 7 23 | 17 27 | 7 22 | 17 22 | 7 26 | 17 21 | 7 27 | 17 15 | 7 40 | 17 23 | 7 43 | 17 33 |
| 17 | 7 11 | 17 19 | 7 21 | 17 29 | 7 20 | 17 24 | 7 24 | 17 23 | 7 25 | 17 17 | 7 38 | 17 25 | 7 41 | 17 35 |
| 18 | 7 09 | 17 21 | 7 19 | 17 31 | 7 18 | 17 26 | 7 22 | 17 25 | 7 23 | 17 19 | 7 35 | 17 27 | 7 39 | 17 37 |
| 19 | 7 07 | 17 22 | 7 17 | 17 32 | 7 16 | 17 28 | 7 20 | 17 27 | 7 20 | 17 21 | 7 33 | 17 29 | 7 37 | 17 39 |
| 20 | 7 05 | 17 24 | 7 15 | 17 34 | 7 14 | 17 30 | 7 17 | 17 29 | 7 18 | 17 23 | 7 31 | 17 32 | 7 35 | 17 41 |
| 21 | 7 03 | 17 26 | 7 13 | 17 36 | 7 12 | 17 31 | 7 15 | 17 31 | 7 16 | 17 25 | 7 28 | 17 34 | 7 32 | 17 43 |
| 22 | 7 01 | 17 28 | 7 11 | 17 38 | 7 10 | 17 33 | 7 13 | 17 33 | 7 14 | 17 27 | 7 26 | 17 36 | 7 30 | 17 45 |
| 23 | 6 59 | 17 30 | 7 09 | 17 40 | 7 08 | 17 35 | 7 11 | 17 35 | 7 11 | 17 29 | 7 24 | 17 38 | 7 28 | 17 47 |
| 24 | 6 57 | 17 31 | 7 07 | 17 41 | 7 06 | 17 37 | 7 09 | 17 37 | 7 09 | 17 31 | 7 21 | 17 40 | 7 25 | 17 49 |
| 25 | 6 55 | 17 33 | 7 04 | 17 43 | 7 03 | 17 39 | 7 06 | 17 39 | 7 07 | 17 33 | 7 19 | 17 42 | 7 23 | 17 51 |
| 26 | 6 52 | 17 35 | 7 02 | 17 45 | 7 01 | 17 41 | 7 04 | 17 41 | 7 04 | 17 36 | 7 16 | 17 44 | 7 21 | 17 53 |
| 27 | 6 50 | 17 37 | 7 00 | 17 47 | 6 59 | 17 43 | 7 02 | 17 42 | 7 02 | 17 38 | 7 14 | 17 47 | 7 18 | 17 56 |
| 28 | 6 48 | 17 38 | 6 58 | 17 49 | 6 57 | 17 44 | 7 00 | 17 44 | 6 59 | 17 40 | 7 11 | 17 49 | 7 16 | 17 58 |

## JUPITER

| Day | *RA* h | m | *Dec.* ° | ′ | *Transit* h | m | *5° high* 52° h | m | 56° h | m |
|---|---|---|---|---|---|---|---|---|---|---|
| | 6 | 30.3 | +23 | 20 | 21 | 42 | 5 | 19 | 5 | 37 |
| | 6 | 27.0 | +23 | 23 | 21 | 00 | 4 | 37 | 4 | 55 |
| | 6 | 25.1 | +23 | 26 | 20 | 19 | 3 | 56 | 4 | 14 |
| | 6 | 24.5 | +23 | 27 | 19 | 39 | 3 | 16 | 3 | 35 |

Diameters – equatorial 44″ polar 41″

## SATURN

| Day | *RA* h | m | *Dec.* ° | ′ | *Transit* h | m | *5° high* 52° h | m | 56° h | m |
|---|---|---|---|---|---|---|---|---|---|---|
| 1 | 4 | 26.4 | +19 | 59 | 19 | 39 | 2 | 55 | 3 | 09 |
| 11 | 4 | 26.2 | +20 | 02 | 19 | 00 | 2 | 16 | 2 | 30 |
| 21 | 4 | 26.8 | +20 | 06 | 18 | 21 | 1 | 38 | 1 | 52 |
| 31 | 4 | 28.2 | +20 | 11 | 17 | 43 | 1 | 00 | 1 | 15 |

Diameters – equatorial 19″ polar 17″
Rings – major axis 43″ minor axis 19″

## URANUS

| Day | *RA* h | m | *Dec.* ° | ′ | *Transit* h | m | *10° high* 52° h | m | 56° h | m |
|---|---|---|---|---|---|---|---|---|---|---|
| | 21 | 46.5 | –14 | 09 | 13 | 00 | 9 | 32 | 9 | 57 |
| | 21 | 48.8 | –13 | 57 | 12 | 23 | 8 | 54 | 9 | 18 |
| | 21 | 51.0 | –13 | 46 | 11 | 46 | 8 | 15 | 8 | 39 |
| | 21 | 53.2 | –13 | 34 | 11 | 09 | 7 | 37 | 8 | 00 |

Diameter 4″

## NEPTUNE

| Day | *RA* h | m | *Dec.* ° | ′ | *Transit* h | m | *10° high* 52° h | m | 56° h | m |
|---|---|---|---|---|---|---|---|---|---|---|
| 1 | 20 | 44.0 | –18 | 01 | 11 | 58 | 9 | 00 | 9 | 34 |
| 11 | 20 | 45.5 | –17 | 55 | 11 | 20 | 8 | 22 | 8 | 55 |
| 21 | 20 | 47.0 | –17 | 50 | 10 | 42 | 7 | 43 | 8 | 16 |
| 31 | 20 | 48.4 | –17 | 44 | 10 | 04 | 7 | 04 | 7 | 37 |

Diameter 2″

# March 2002

THIRD MONTH, 31 DAYS. *Mars*, Roman god of battle

| | | | |
|---|---|---|---|
| **1** | *Friday* | **St David's Day**. Girolamo Frescobaldi d. 1643 | 60 |
| **2** | *Saturday* | Ivar Kreuger b. 1880. Cardinal Archbishop Hume b. 1923 | 61 |
| **3** | *Sunday* | **3rd S. in Lent.** Abolition of Serfdom in Russia 1861 | 62 |
| **4** | *Monday* | Bernard Haitink b. 1929 | *week* 9 *day* 63 |
| **5** | *Tuesday* | Gerardus Mercator b. 1512. Franz Mesmer d. 1815 | 64 |
| **6** | *Wednesday* | Frankie Howerd b. 1922. Melina Mercouri d. 1994 | 65 |
| **7** | *Thursday* | 1st Earl of Snowdon, Antony Armstrong Jones. b. 1930. Anstide Briand d. 1932 | 66 |
| **8** | *Friday* | Lynn Seymour b. 1939. Count Ferdinand von Zeppelin d. 1917 | 67 |
| **9** | *Saturday* | Comte de Mirabeau Honoré Riqueti b. 1749. Jules Mazarin d. 1661 | 68 |
| **10** | *Sunday* | **4th S. in Lent.** Mothering Sunday. *Earl of Wessex b. 1964.* | 69 |
| **11** | *Monday* | Commonwealth Day. Harold Wilson b. 1916 | *week* 10 *day* 70 |
| **12** | *Tuesday* | Bishop George Berkeley b. 1685. Saint Gregory d. 604 | 71 |
| **13** | *Wednesday* | Odette Hallowes d. 1995. First submarine telephone lines laid 1891 | 72 |
| **14** | *Thursday* | Jim Clark b. 1936. Busby Berkeley d. 1976 | 73 |
| **15** | *Friday* | MUSLIM NEW YEAR. Andrew Jackson b. 1767 | 74 |
| **16** | *Saturday* | George Ohm b. 1787. William Beveridge d. 1963 | 75 |
| **17** | *Sunday* | **5th S. in Lent.** Ronnie Kray d. 1995 | 76 |
| **18** | *Monday* | St Patrick's Day. *Bank Holiday in Northern Ireland.* | *week* 11 *day* 77 |
| **19** | *Tuesday* | **St Joseph of Nazareth.** Sir John Jones d. 1998 | 78 |
| **20** | *Wednesday* | Sir Michael Redgrave b. 1908. Beverley Cross d. 1998 | 79 |
| **21** | *Thursday* | Paul Tortelier b. 1914. Sir Michael Redgrave d. 1985 | 80 |
| **22** | *Friday* | Stephen Sondheim b. 1930. Jonathan Edwards d. 1758 | 81 |
| **23** | *Saturday* | Princess Eugenie of York b. 1990. Sir Roger Bannister b. 1929 | 82 |
| **24** | *Sunday* | **Palm Sunday.** E. H. Shepard d. 1976 | 83 |
| **25** | *Monday* | **The Annunciation.** Achille-Claude Debussy d. 1918 | *week* 12 *day* 84 |
| **26** | *Tuesday* | William Hague b. 1961. Robert Lee Frost b. 1874 | 85 |
| **27** | *Wednesday* | *Hilary Law Sittings end.* Mstislav Rostropovich b. 1927 | 86 |
| **28** | *Thursday* | **Maundy Thursday.** PASSOVER begins. | 87 |
| **29** | *Friday* | **Good Friday.** *Bank Holiday in UK.* | 88 |
| **30** | *Saturday* | Easter Eve. James Cagney d. 1986 | 89 |
| **31** | *Sunday* | **Easter Day.** Robert Bunsen b. 1811 | 90 |

### Astronomical Phenomena

| d | h | |
|---|---|---|
| 1 | 15 | Jupiter at stationary point |
| 12 | 03 | Mercury in conjunction with Moon. Mercury 3° N. |
| 15 | 10 | Venus in conjunction with Moon. Venus 4° N. |
| 18 | 03 | Mars in conjunction with Moon. Mars 4° N. |
| 20 | 10 | Saturn in conjunction with Moon. Saturn 0.4° S |
| 20 | 15 | Pluto at stationary point |
| 20 | 19 | Sun's longitude 0°♈ |
| 22 | 12 | Jupiter in conjunction with Moon. Jupiter 1° S |

### Minima of Algol

| d | h | d | h | d | h |
|---|---|---|---|---|---|
| 3 | 04.9 | 14 | 16.2 | 26 | 03.5 |
| 6 | 01.7 | 17 | 13.0 | 29 | 00.3 |
| 8 | 22.5 | 20 | 09.8 | 31 | 21.1 |
| 11 | 19.4 | 23 | 06.6 | | |

### Constellations

The following constellations are near the meridian at

| | d | h | | d | h |
|---|---|---|---|---|---|
| February | 1 | 24 | March | 16 | 21 |
| February | 15 | 23 | April | 1 | 20 |
| March | 1 | 22 | April | 15 | 19 |

Cepheus (below the Pole), Camelopardus, Lynx, Gemini, Cancer, Leo, Canis Minor, Hydra, Monoceros, Canis Major and Puppis

### The Moon

| Phases, Apsides and Node | d | h | m |
|---|---|---|---|
| ☾ Last Quarter | 6 | 01 | 24 |
| ● New Moon | 14 | 02 | 02 |
| ☽ First Quarter | 22 | 02 | 28 |
| ○ Full Moon | 28 | 18 | 25 |
| | | | |
| Apogee (406,707km) | 14 | 01 | 25 |
| Perigee (357,013km) | 28 | 07 | 48 |

Mean longitude of ascending node on March 1, 83°

## ΓHE SUN

S.D 16′.1

| Day | Right Ascension | Dec. | Equation of Time | Rise 52° | Rise 56° | Transit | Set 52° | Set 56° | Sidereal time | Transit of First Point of Aries |
|---|---|---|---|---|---|---|---|---|---|---|
| | h m s | ° ′ | m s | h m | h m | h m | h m | h m | h m s | h m s |
| 1 | 22 46 57 | −7 44 | −12 27 | 6 46 | 6 52 | 12 12 | 17 39 | 17 34 | 10 34 30 | 13 23 18 |
| 2 | 22 50 42 | −7 21 | −12 15 | 6 44 | 6 50 | 12 12 | 17 41 | 17 36 | 10 38 26 | 13 19 22 |
| 3 | 22 54 26 | −6 58 | 12 03 | 6 42 | 6 47 | 12 12 | 17 43 | 17 38 | 10 42 23 | 13 15 26 |
| 4 | 22 58 10 | −6 35 | −11 50 | 6 40 | 6 45 | 12 12 | 17 45 | 17 40 | 10 46 20 | 13 11 30 |
| 5 | 23 01 53 | −6 12 | −11 37 | 6 38 | 6 42 | 12 12 | 17 46 | 17 42 | 10 50 16 | 13 07 34 |
| 6 | 23 05 36 | −5 49 | −11 24 | 6 35 | 6 39 | 12 11 | 17 48 | 17 44 | 10 54 13 | 13 03 39 |
| 7 | 23 09 19 | −5 26 | −11 10 | 6 33 | 6 37 | 12 11 | 17 50 | 17 46 | 10 58 09 | 12 59 43 |
| 8 | 23 13 01 | −5 03 | −10 55 | 6 31 | 6 34 | 12 11 | 17 52 | 17 48 | 11 02 06 | 12 55 47 |
| 9 | 23 16 43 | −4 39 | −10 41 | 6 29 | 6 32 | 12 11 | 17 54 | 17 51 | 11 06 02 | 12 51 51 |
| 0 | 23 20 25 | −4 16 | −10 26 | 6 26 | 6 29 | 12 10 | 17 55 | 17 53 | 11 09 59 | 12 47 55 |
| 1 | 23 24 06 | −3 52 | −10 10 | 6 24 | 6 26 | 12 10 | 17 57 | 17 55 | 11 13 55 | 12 43 59 |
| 2 | 23 27 47 | −3 29 | − 9 55 | 6 22 | 6 24 | 12 10 | 17 59 | 17 57 | 11 17 52 | 12 40 03 |
| 3 | 23 31 27 | −3 05 | − 9 39 | 6 19 | 6 21 | 12 10 | 18 01 | 17 59 | 11 21 49 | 12 36 07 |
| 4 | 23 35 07 | −2 41 | − 9 22 | 6 17 | 6 19 | 12 09 | 18 02 | 18 01 | 11 25 45 | 12 32 11 |
| 5 | 23 38 47 | −2 18 | − 9 06 | 6 15 | 6 16 | 12 09 | 18 04 | 18 03 | 11 29 42 | 12 28 15 |
| 6 | 23 42 27 | −1 54 | − 8 49 | 6 13 | 6 13 | 12 09 | 18 06 | 18 05 | 11 33 38 | 12 24 19 |
| 7 | 23 46 07 | −1 30 | − 8 32 | 6 10 | 6 11 | 12 08 | 18 08 | 18 07 | 11 37 35 | 12 20 24 |
| 8 | 23 49 46 | −1 07 | − 8 15 | 6 08 | 6 08 | 12 08 | 18 09 | 18 09 | 11 41 31 | 12 16 28 |
| 9 | 23 53 25 | −0 43 | − 7 57 | 6 06 | 6 06 | 12 08 | 18 11 | 18 11 | 11 45 28 | 12 12 32 |
| 0 | 23 57 04 | −0 19 | − 7 40 | 6 03 | 6 03 | 12 08 | 18 13 | 18 13 | 11 49 24 | 12 08 36 |
| 1 | 0 00 43 | +0 05 | − 7 22 | 6 01 | 6 00 | 12 07 | 18 14 | 18 15 | 11 53 21 | 12 04 40 |
| 2 | 0 04 22 | +0 28 | − 7 04 | 5 59 | 5 58 | 12 07 | 18 16 | 18 17 | 11 57 18 | 12 00 44 |
| 3 | 0 08 00 | +0 52 | − 6 46 | 5 56 | 5 55 | 12 07 | 18 18 | 18 19 | 12 01 14 | 11 56 48 |
| 4 | 0 11 39 | +1 16 | − 6 28 | 5 54 | 5 52 | 12 06 | 18 20 | 18 21 | 12 05 11 | 11 52 52 |
| 5 | 0 15 17 | +1 39 | − 6 10 | 5 52 | 5 50 | 12 06 | 18 21 | 18 24 | 12 09 07 | 11 48 56 |
| 6 | 0 18 55 | +2 03 | − 5 52 | 5 49 | 5 47 | 12 06 | 18 23 | 18 26 | 12 13 04 | 11 45 00 |
| 7 | 0 22 34 | +2 26 | − 5 33 | 5 47 | 5 44 | 12 05 | 18 25 | 18 28 | 12 17 00 | 11 41 05 |
| 8 | 0 26 12 | +2 50 | − 5 15 | 5 45 | 5 42 | 12 05 | 18 27 | 18 30 | 12 20 57 | 11 37 09 |
| 9 | 0 29 50 | +3 13 | − 4 57 | 5 42 | 5 39 | 12 05 | 18 28 | 18 32 | 12 24 53 | 11 33 13 |
| 0 | 0 33 29 | +3 37 | − 4 39 | 5 40 | 5 37 | 12 04 | 18 30 | 18 34 | 12 28 50 | 11 29 17 |
| 1 | 0 37 07 | +4 00 | − 4 20 | 5 38 | 5 34 | 12 04 | 18 32 | 18 36 | 12 32 47 | 11 25 21 |

## )URATION OF TWILIGHT (in minutes)

| atitude | 52° | 56° | 52° | 56° | 52° | 56° | 52° | 56° |
|---|---|---|---|---|---|---|---|---|
| | 1 March | | 11 March | | 21 March | | 31 March | |
| 'ivil | 34 | 37 | 34 | 37 | 34 | 37 | 34 | 38 |
| lautical | 73 | 80 | 73 | 80 | 74 | 81 | 75 | 84 |
| stronomical | 112 | 124 | 113 | 125 | 115 | 128 | 120 | 135 |

## 'HE NIGHT SKY

*lercury*, remains too close to the Sun for observation roughout the month.

*Venus*, magnitude -3.9, is visible as an evening object, w in the western sky after sunset. The thin crescent loon, only 1.7 days old, will be seen about 5 degrees to the ft of Venus on the evening of the 15th.

*Mars* continues to be visible in the south-western sky in e early evenings, magnitude +1.4. Its slightly reddish ppearance is an aid to its identification. Mars is in the nstellation of Aries. The crescent Moon will be seen ıssing about 6 degrees below Mars on the evening of the 'th.

*Jupiter*, magnitude -2.3, continues to be visible as a nspicuous evening object in the south-western quadrant the sky from shortly after sunset until well after idnight. Jupiter reaches its second stationary point in e western part of Gemini on the 1st and then resumes its direct motion. On the evenings of the 21st and 22nd the Moon, near First Quarter, is near the planet.

*Saturn* is still an evening object in the western sky but before the end of the month it will be too low in the sky to be visible after midnight. Its magnitude is +0.1. The crescent Moon is in the vicinity of Saturn on the evenings of the 19th and 20th. On the last day of the month Saturn is 4 degrees north of Aldebaran. The rings of Saturn present a beautiful spectacle to the observer with a small telescope. The Earth passed through the ring plane twice in 1995 and since then the rings have been slowly opening up: the diameter of the minor axis is now 20 arcseconds, marginally greater than the polar diameter of the planet itself. The rings will not be at their maximum opening until early next year.

*Zodiacal Light*. The evening cone may be observed, stretching up from the western horizon, along the ecliptic, after the end of twilight, from the beginning of the month up to the 15th.

## THE MOON

| Day | RA | | Dec. | Hor. par. | Semi-diam | Sun's co-long. | PA of Bright Limb | Phase | Age | Rise 52° | | Rise 56° | | Transit | | Set 52° | | Set 56° | |
|---|---|---|---|---|---|---|---|---|---|---|---|---|---|---|---|---|---|---|---|
| | h | m | ° | ′ | ′ | ° | ° | % | d | h | m | h | m | h | m | h | m | h | m |
| **1** | 12 | 20 | + 3.2 | 61.2 | 16.7 | 111 | 102 | 96 | 16.7 | 20 | 41 | 20 | 43 | 1 | 49 | 8 | 07 | 8 | 08 |
| **2** | 13 | 15 | − 3.0 | 60.7 | 16.5 | 123 | 106 | 90 | 17.7 | 22 | 08 | 22 | 15 | 2 | 42 | 8 | 27 | 8 | 22 |
| **3** | 14 | 09 | − 8.9 | 59.9 | 16.3 | 135 | 107 | 82 | 18.7 | 23 | 32 | 23 | 45 | 3 | 34 | 8 | 47 | 8 | 37 |
| **4** | 15 | 03 | −14.2 | 59.1 | 16.1 | 147 | 105 | 72 | 19.7 | — | | — | | 4 | 26 | 9 | 09 | 8 | 54 |
| **5** | 15 | 58 | −18.5 | 58.1 | 15.8 | 159 | 101 | 61 | 20.7 | 0 | 53 | 1 | 12 | 5 | 19 | 9 | 36 | 9 | 16 |
| **6** | 16 | 53 | −21.8 | 57.2 | 15.6 | 172 | 97 | 51 | 21.7 | 2 | 09 | 2 | 33 | 6 | 12 | 10 | 10 | 9 | 45 |
| **7** | 17 | 49 | −23.8 | 56.4 | 15.4 | 184 | 91 | 40 | 22.7 | 3 | 17 | 3 | 45 | 7 | 06 | 10 | 52 | 10 | 24 |
| **8** | 18 | 44 | −24.5 | 55.7 | 15.2 | 196 | 85 | 31 | 23.7 | 4 | 15 | 4 | 43 | 7 | 59 | 11 | 44 | 11 | 16 |
| **9** | 19 | 39 | −24.0 | 55.1 | 15.0 | 208 | 79 | 22 | 24.7 | 5 | 01 | 5 | 27 | 8 | 51 | 12 | 44 | 12 | 18 |
| **10** | 20 | 31 | −22.3 | 54.7 | 14.9 | 220 | 73 | 15 | 25.7 | 5 | 36 | 5 | 59 | 9 | 40 | 13 | 50 | 13 | 28 |
| **11** | 21 | 21 | −19.7 | 54.3 | 14.8 | 233 | 66 | 9 | 26.7 | 6 | 03 | 6 | 22 | 10 | 27 | 14 | 58 | 14 | 41 |
| **12** | 22 | 09 | −16.2 | 54.1 | 14.7 | 245 | 59 | 4 | 27.7 | 6 | 25 | 6 | 39 | 11 | 11 | 16 | 07 | 15 | 55 |
| **13** | 22 | 55 | −12.2 | 54.0 | 14.7 | 257 | 45 | 1 | 28.7 | 6 | 43 | 6 | 52 | 11 | 54 | 17 | 16 | 17 | 08 |
| **14** | 23 | 40 | − 7.6 | 53.9 | 14.7 | 269 | 347 | 0 | 29.7 | 6 | 58 | 7 | 03 | 12 | 35 | 18 | 23 | 18 | 20 |
| **15** | 0 | 23 | − 2.8 | 54.0 | 14.7 | 281 | 272 | 1 | 0.9 | 7 | 13 | 7 | 14 | 13 | 15 | 19 | 31 | 19 | 32 |
| **16** | 1 | 06 | + 2.1 | 54.1 | 14.7 | 294 | 259 | 3 | 1.9 | 7 | 27 | 7 | 24 | 13 | 55 | 20 | 39 | 20 | 44 |
| **17** | 1 | 50 | + 7.0 | 54.3 | 14.8 | 306 | 256 | 8 | 2.9 | 7 | 42 | 7 | 34 | 14 | 37 | 21 | 48 | 21 | 58 |
| **18** | 2 | 35 | +11.7 | 54.6 | 14.9 | 318 | 255 | 13 | 3.9 | 7 | 58 | 7 | 47 | 15 | 20 | 22 | 58 | 23 | 13 |
| **19** | 3 | 22 | +15.9 | 55.1 | 15.0 | 330 | 257 | 21 | 4.9 | 8 | 19 | 8 | 02 | 16 | 06 | — | | — | |
| **20** | 4 | 11 | +19.6 | 55.6 | 15.2 | 342 | 260 | 29 | 5.9 | 8 | 44 | 8 | 23 | 16 | 56 | 0 | 10 | 0 | 30 |
| **21** | 5 | 04 | +22.4 | 56.3 | 15.3 | 355 | 265 | 39 | 6.9 | 9 | 18 | 8 | 53 | 17 | 49 | 1 | 21 | 1 | 45 |
| **22** | 6 | 00 | +24.2 | 57.1 | 15.6 | 7 | 270 | 49 | 7.9 | 10 | 03 | 9 | 35 | 18 | 45 | 2 | 28 | 2 | 56 |
| **23** | 6 | 58 | +24.6 | 58.0 | 15.8 | 19 | 276 | 60 | 8.9 | 11 | 02 | 10 | 34 | 19 | 43 | 3 | 27 | 3 | 56 |
| **24** | 7 | 58 | +23.6 | 58.9 | 16.1 | 31 | 283 | 70 | 9.9 | 12 | 15 | 11 | 50 | 20 | 42 | 4 | 16 | 4 | 41 |
| **25** | 8 | 59 | +21.1 | 59.8 | 16.3 | 43 | 289 | 80 | 10.9 | 13 | 38 | 13 | 19 | 21 | 40 | 4 | 54 | 5 | 14 |
| **26** | 9 | 59 | +17.2 | 60.6 | 16.5 | 55 | 296 | 89 | 11.9 | 15 | 06 | 14 | 53 | 22 | 37 | 5 | 24 | 5 | 38 |
| **27** | 10 | 57 | +12.1 | 61.1 | 16.7 | 68 | 303 | 95 | 12.9 | 16 | 36 | 16 | 29 | 23 | 32 | 5 | 48 | 5 | 57 |
| **28** | 11 | 54 | + 6.1 | 61.4 | 16.7 | 80 | 318 | 99 | 13.9 | 18 | 06 | 18 | 05 | — | | 6 | 08 | 6 | 12 |
| **29** | 12 | 49 | − 0.2 | 61.3 | 16.7 | 92 | 58 | 100 | 14.9 | 19 | 35 | 19 | 40 | 0 | 25 | 6 | 27 | 6 | 2[illegible] |
| **30** | 13 | 45 | − 6.5 | 60.9 | 16.6 | 104 | 98 | 98 | 15.9 | 21 | 03 | 21 | 14 | 1 | 19 | 6 | 47 | 6 | 4[illegible] |
| **31** | 14 | 40 | −12.3 | 60.3 | 16.4 | 116 | 103 | 93 | 16.9 | 22 | 30 | 22 | 46 | 2 | 12 | 7 | 08 | 6 | 5[illegible] |

## MERCURY

| Day | RA | | Dec. | Diam. | Phase | Transit | | 5° high 52° | | 5° high 56° | |
|---|---|---|---|---|---|---|---|---|---|---|---|
| | h | m | ° | ″ | % | h | m | h | m | h | m |
| 1 | 21 | 10 | −17.4 | 6 | 70 | 10 | 36 | 6 | 48 | 7 | 10 |
| 3 | 21 | 20 | −16.9 | 6 | 72 | 10 | 39 | 6 | 47 | 7 | 09 |
| 5 | 21 | 31 | −16.2 | 6 | 74 | 10 | 42 | 6 | 46 | 7 | 06 |
| 7 | 21 | 42 | −15.5 | 6 | 76 | 10 | 45 | 6 | 45 | 7 | 04 |
| 9 | 21 | 54 | −14.7 | 6 | 78 | 10 | 49 | 6 | 43 | 7 | 01 |
| 11 | 22 | 05 | −13.8 | 6 | 80 | 10 | 52 | 6 | 41 | 6 | 58 |
| 13 | 22 | 17 | −12.9 | 6 | 82 | 10 | 56 | 6 | 39 | 6 | 55 |
| 15 | 22 | 29 | −11.8 | 5 | 84 | 11 | 01 | 6 | 37 | 6 | 51 |
| 17 | 22 | 42 | −10.7 | 5 | 85 | 11 | 05 | 6 | 34 | 6 | 47 |
| 19 | 22 | 54 | − 9.5 | 5 | 87 | 11 | 10 | 6 | 32 | 6 | 44 |
| 21 | 23 | 07 | − 8.2 | 5 | 89 | 11 | 14 | 6 | 29 | 6 | 40 |
| 23 | 23 | 19 | − 6.8 | 5 | 90 | 11 | 19 | 6 | 26 | 6 | 36 |
| 25 | 23 | 32 | − 5.4 | 5 | 92 | 11 | 24 | 6 | 24 | 6 | 31 |
| 27 | 23 | 45 | − 3.8 | 5 | 94 | 11 | 30 | 6 | 21 | 6 | 27 |
| 29 | 23 | 59 | − 2.3 | 5 | 95 | 11 | 35 | 6 | 18 | 6 | 23 |
| 31 | 0 | 13 | − 0.6 | 5 | 97 | 11 | 41 | 6 | 15 | 6 | 19 |

## VENUS

| Day | RA | | Dec. | Diam. | Phase | Transit | | 5° high 52° | | 5° high 56° | |
|---|---|---|---|---|---|---|---|---|---|---|---|
| | h | m | ° | ″ | % | h | m | h | m | h | m |
| 1 | 23 | 30 | − 4.8 | 10 | 98 | 12 | 56 | 18 | 00 | 17 | 5[illegible] |
| 6 | 23 | 53 | − 2.2 | 10 | 98 | 12 | 59 | 18 | 17 | 18 | 1[illegible] |
| 11 | 0 | 15 | + 0.3 | 10 | 97 | 13 | 02 | 18 | 33 | 18 | 3[illegible] |
| 16 | 0 | 38 | + 2.9 | 10 | 97 | 13 | 05 | 18 | 49 | 18 | 4[illegible] |
| 21 | 1 | 01 | + 5.5 | 10 | 96 | 13 | 08 | 19 | 05 | 19 | 0[illegible] |
| 26 | 1 | 23 | + 7.9 | 10 | 96 | 13 | 11 | 19 | 21 | 19 | 2[illegible] |
| 31 | 1 | 46 | +10.4 | 10 | 95 | 13 | 14 | 19 | 37 | 19 | 4[illegible] |

## MARS

| Day | RA | | Dec. | Diam. | Phase | Transit | | 5° high 52° | | 5° high 56° | |
|---|---|---|---|---|---|---|---|---|---|---|---|
| 1 | 1 | 50 | +11.6 | 5 | 93 | 15 | 14 | 21 | 42 | 21 | 4[illegible] |
| 6 | 2 | 03 | +12.8 | 5 | 94 | 15 | 08 | 21 | 43 | 21 | 5[illegible] |
| 11 | 2 | 17 | +14.1 | 5 | 94 | 15 | 02 | 21 | 43 | 21 | 5[illegible] |
| 16 | 2 | 30 | +15.3 | 5 | 94 | 14 | 56 | 21 | 43 | 21 | 5[illegible] |
| 21 | 2 | 44 | +16.4 | 5 | 95 | 14 | 50 | 21 | 44 | 21 | 5[illegible] |
| 26 | 2 | 58 | +17.5 | 4 | 95 | 14 | 44 | 21 | 44 | 21 | 5[illegible] |
| 31 | 3 | 12 | +18.4 | 4 | 95 | 14 | 38 | 21 | 44 | 21 | 5[illegible] |

## SUNRISE AND SUNSET

| | London 0°05′ 51°30′ | | Bristol 2°35′ 51°28′ | | Birmingham 1°55′ 52°28′ | | Manchester 2°15′ 53°28′ | | Newcastle 1°37′ 54°59′ | | Glasgow 4°14′ 55°52′ | | Belfast 5°56′ 54°35′ | |
|---|---|---|---|---|---|---|---|---|---|---|---|---|---|---|
| | h m | h m | h m | h m | h m | h m | h m | h m | h m | h m | h m | h m | h m | h m |
| 1 | 6 46 | 17 40 | 6 56 | 17 50 | 6 55 | 17 46 | 6 57 | 17 46 | 6 57 | 17 42 | 7 09 | 17 51 | 7 14 | 18 00 |
| 2 | 6 44 | 17 42 | 6 54 | 17 52 | 6 52 | 17 48 | 6 55 | 17 48 | 6 55 | 17 44 | 7 06 | 17 53 | 7 11 | 18 02 |
| 3 | 6 42 | 17 44 | 6 52 | 17 54 | 6 50 | 17 50 | 6 53 | 17 50 | 6 52 | 17 46 | 7 04 | 17 55 | 7 09 | 18 04 |
| 4 | 6 40 | 17 45 | 6 49 | 17 56 | 6 48 | 17 52 | 6 50 | 17 52 | 6 50 | 17 48 | 7 01 | 17 57 | 7 06 | 18 06 |
| 5 | 6 37 | 17 47 | 6 47 | 17 57 | 6 46 | 17 54 | 6 48 | 17 54 | 6 47 | 17 50 | 6 59 | 17 59 | 7 04 | 18 08 |
| 6 | 6 35 | 17 49 | 6 45 | 17 59 | 6 43 | 17 55 | 6 46 | 17 56 | 6 45 | 17 52 | 6 56 | 18 01 | 7 02 | 18 09 |
| 7 | 6 33 | 17 51 | 6 43 | 18 01 | 6 41 | 17 57 | 6 43 | 17 58 | 6 42 | 17 54 | 6 54 | 18 03 | 6 59 | 18 11 |
| 8 | 6 31 | 17 52 | 6 41 | 18 03 | 6 39 | 17 59 | 6 41 | 18 00 | 6 40 | 17 56 | 6 51 | 18 06 | 6 57 | 18 13 |
| 9 | 6 29 | 17 54 | 6 38 | 18 04 | 6 37 | 18 01 | 6 39 | 18 02 | 6 37 | 17 58 | 6 48 | 18 08 | 6 54 | 18 15 |
| 10 | 6 26 | 17 56 | 6 36 | 18 06 | 6 34 | 18 03 | 6 36 | 18 03 | 6 35 | 18 00 | 6 46 | 18 10 | 6 52 | 18 17 |
| 11 | 6 24 | 17 58 | 6 34 | 18 08 | 6 32 | 18 04 | 6 34 | 18 05 | 6 32 | 18 02 | 6 43 | 18 12 | 6 49 | 18 19 |
| 12 | 6 22 | 17 59 | 6 32 | 18 09 | 6 30 | 18 06 | 6 31 | 18 07 | 6 30 | 18 04 | 6 41 | 18 14 | 6 47 | 18 21 |
| 13 | 6 20 | 18 01 | 6 30 | 18 11 | 6 27 | 18 08 | 6 29 | 18 09 | 6 27 | 18 06 | 6 38 | 18 16 | 6 44 | 18 23 |
| 14 | 6 17 | 18 03 | 6 27 | 18 13 | 6 25 | 18 10 | 6 27 | 18 11 | 6 25 | 18 08 | 6 36 | 18 18 | 6 42 | 18 25 |
| 15 | 6 15 | 18 05 | 6 25 | 18 15 | 6 23 | 18 12 | 6 24 | 18 13 | 6 22 | 18 10 | 6 33 | 18 20 | 6 39 | 18 27 |
| 16 | 6 13 | 18 06 | 6 23 | 18 16 | 6 20 | 18 13 | 6 22 | 18 15 | 6 20 | 18 12 | 6 30 | 18 22 | 6 37 | 18 29 |
| 17 | 6 10 | 18 08 | 6 20 | 18 18 | 6 18 | 18 15 | 6 19 | 18 16 | 6 17 | 18 14 | 6 28 | 18 24 | 6 34 | 18 31 |
| 18 | 6 08 | 18 10 | 6 18 | 18 20 | 6 16 | 18 17 | 6 17 | 18 18 | 6 15 | 18 16 | 6 25 | 18 26 | 6 32 | 18 33 |
| 19 | 6 06 | 18 11 | 6 16 | 18 21 | 6 13 | 18 19 | 6 15 | 18 20 | 6 12 | 18 18 | 6 22 | 18 28 | 6 29 | 18 35 |
| 20 | 6 04 | 18 13 | 6 14 | 18 23 | 6 11 | 18 20 | 6 12 | 18 22 | 6 09 | 18 20 | 6 20 | 18 30 | 6 27 | 18 37 |
| 21 | 6 01 | 18 15 | 6 11 | 18 25 | 6 09 | 18 22 | 6 10 | 18 24 | 6 07 | 18 22 | 6 17 | 18 32 | 6 24 | 18 39 |
| 22 | 5 59 | 18 16 | 6 09 | 18 26 | 6 06 | 18 24 | 6 07 | 18 26 | 6 04 | 18 24 | 6 15 | 18 34 | 6 22 | 18 41 |
| 23 | 5 57 | 18 18 | 6 07 | 18 28 | 6 04 | 18 26 | 6 05 | 18 27 | 6 02 | 18 25 | 6 12 | 18 36 | 6 19 | 18 43 |
| 24 | 5 55 | 18 20 | 6 05 | 18 30 | 6 01 | 18 28 | 6 02 | 18 29 | 5 59 | 18 27 | 6 09 | 18 38 | 6 17 | 18 45 |
| 25 | 5 52 | 18 21 | 6 02 | 18 31 | 5 59 | 18 29 | 6 00 | 18 31 | 5 57 | 18 29 | 6 07 | 18 40 | 6 14 | 18 46 |
| 26 | 5 50 | 18 23 | 6 00 | 18 33 | 5 57 | 18 31 | 5 58 | 18 33 | 5 54 | 18 31 | 6 04 | 18 42 | 6 12 | 18 48 |
| 27 | 5 48 | 18 25 | 5 58 | 18 35 | 5 54 | 18 33 | 5 55 | 18 35 | 5 52 | 18 33 | 6 01 | 18 44 | 6 09 | 18 50 |
| 28 | 5 45 | 18 27 | 5 55 | 18 36 | 5 52 | 18 35 | 5 53 | 18 37 | 5 49 | 18 35 | 5 59 | 18 46 | 6 07 | 18 52 |
| 29 | 5 43 | 18 28 | 5 53 | 18 38 | 5 50 | 18 36 | 5 50 | 18 38 | 5 47 | 18 37 | 5 56 | 18 48 | 6 04 | 18 54 |
| 30 | 5 41 | 18 30 | 5 51 | 18 40 | 5 47 | 18 38 | 5 48 | 18 40 | 5 44 | 18 39 | 5 54 | 18 51 | 6 02 | 18 56 |
| 31 | 5 39 | 18 32 | 5 49 | 18 42 | 5 45 | 18 40 | 5 45 | 18 42 | 5 41 | 18 41 | 5 51 | 18 53 | 5 59 | 18 58 |

## JUPITER

| Day | RA | | Dec. | | Transit | | 5° high 52° | | 56° | |
|---|---|---|---|---|---|---|---|---|---|---|
| | h | m | ° | ′ | h | m | h | m | h | m |
| 1 | 6 | 24.5 | +23 | 27 | 19 | 47 | 3 | 24 | 3 | 42 |
| 11 | 6 | 25.2 | +23 | 27 | 19 | 08 | 2 | 45 | 3 | 04 |
| 21 | 6 | 27.2 | +23 | 27 | 18 | 31 | 2 | 08 | 2 | 26 |
| 31 | 6 | 30.5 | +23 | 26 | 17 | 55 | 1 | 32 | 1 | 50 |

Diameters – equatorial 40″ polar 38″

## SATURN

| Day | RA | | Dec. | | Transit | | 5° high 52° | | 56° | |
|---|---|---|---|---|---|---|---|---|---|---|
| | h | m | ° | ′ | h | m | h | m | h | m |
| 1 | 4 | 27.9 | +20 | 10 | 17 | 51 | 1 | 08 | 1 | 22 |
| 11 | 4 | 29.8 | +20 | 17 | 17 | 13 | 0 | 31 | 0 | 46 |
| 21 | 4 | 32.5 | +20 | 25 | 16 | 37 | 23 | 52 | 0 | 10 |
| 31 | 4 | 35.8 | +20 | 34 | 16 | 01 | 23 | 16 | 23 | 31 |

Diameters – equatorial 18″ polar 16″
Rings – major axis 41″ minor axis 18″

## URANUS

| Day | RA | | Dec. | | Transit | | 10° high 52° | | 56° | |
|---|---|---|---|---|---|---|---|---|---|---|
| | h | m | ° | ′ | h | m | h | m | h | m |
| 1 | 21 | 52.8 | –13 | 37 | 11 | 17 | 7 | 45 | 8 | 08 |
| 11 | 21 | 54.9 | –13 | 25 | 10 | 39 | 7 | 06 | 7 | 29 |
| 21 | 21 | 57.0 | –13 | 15 | 10 | 02 | 6 | 28 | 6 | 50 |
| 31 | 21 | 58.8 | –13 | 05 | 9 | 25 | 5 | 49 | 6 | 11 |

Diameter 4″

## NEPTUNE

| Day | RA | | Dec. | | Transit | | 10° high 52° | | 56° | |
|---|---|---|---|---|---|---|---|---|---|---|
| | h | m | ° | ′ | h | m | h | m | h | m |
| 1 | 20 | 48.1 | –17 | 45 | 10 | 12 | 7 | 12 | 7 | 45 |
| 11 | 20 | 49.4 | –17 | 40 | 9 | 34 | 6 | 33 | 7 | 06 |
| 21 | 20 | 50.6 | –17 | 36 | 8 | 56 | 5 | 55 | 6 | 27 |
| 31 | 20 | 51.6 | –17 | 32 | 8 | 17 | 5 | 16 | 5 | 48 |

Diameter 2″

# April 2002

FOURTH MONTH, 30 DAYS. *Aperire*, to open; Earth opens to receive seed

| | | | |
|---|---|---|---|
| **1** | *Monday* | *Bank Holiday in England, Wales and Northern Ireland.* | *week* 13 *day* 91 |
| **2** | *Tuesday* | Sir Alec Guinness b. 1914. Comte de Mirabeau Honoré Riqueti d. 1791 | 92 |
| **3** | *Wednesday* | Leslie Howard b. 1893. Richard D'Oyly Carte d. 1901 | 93 |
| **4** | *Thursday* | Maurice de Vlaminck b. 1876. Zulfikar Ali Bhutto d. 1979 | 94 |
| **5** | *Friday* | Jean-Honoré Fragonard b. 1732. Chiang Kai-Shek d. 1975 | 95 |
| **6** | *Saturday* | Alexander Herzen b. 1812. Modern Olympic Games revived at Athens 1896 | 96 |
| **7** | *Sunday* | **1st S. after Easter.** Dick Turpin d. 1739 | 97 |
| **8** | *Monday* | General Omar Bradley d. 1981. Entente Cordiale signed 1904 | *week* 14 *day* 98 |
| **9** | *Tuesday* | *Easter Law Sittings begin.* François Rabelais d. 1553 | 99 |
| **10** | *Wednesday* | Antonia White d. 1980. Battle of Toulouse 1814 | 100 |
| **11** | *Thursday* | Masaru Ibuka b. 1908. Francis Durbridge d. 1998 | 101 |
| **12** | *Friday* | Beverley Cross b. 1931. First manned space flight by Yuri Gagarin in Vostok 1 1961 | 102 |
| **13** | *Saturday* | HINDU NEW YEAR. SIKH NEW YEAR | 103 |
| **14** | *Sunday* | **2nd S. after Easter.** Abraham Lincoln shot 1865 | 104 |
| **15** | *Monday* | Il-sung Kim b. 1912. Jean Genet d. 1986 | *week* 15 *day* 105 |
| **16** | *Tuesday* | Francisco de Goya y Lucientes d. 1828. Battle of Culloden 1746 | 106 |
| **17** | *Wednesday* | Thornton Wilder b. 1897. Rhodesia became Zimbabwe 1980 | 107 |
| **18** | *Thursday* | Louis-Adolphe Thiers b. 1797. San Francisco earthquake 1906 | 108 |
| **19** | *Friday* | b. Frankie Howerd d. 1992. Battle of Lexington 1775 | 109 |
| **20** | *Saturday* | Johann Agricola b. 1494. Adolf Hitler b. 1889 | 110 |
| **21** | *Sunday* | **3rd S. after Easter.** *Queen Elizabeth II b. 1926.* | 111 |
| **22** | *Monday* | Madame de Stael Anne Necker b. 1766. Richard Nixon d. 1994 | *week* 16 *day* 112 |
| **23** | *Tuesday* | **St George.** Paulette Goddard d. 1990 | 113 |
| **24** | *Wednesday* | Marshal Philippe Pétain b. 1856. Bill Edrich d. 1986 | 114 |
| **25** | *Thursday* | **St Mark.** Vladimir Nemirovich-Danchenko d. 1943 | 115 |
| **26** | *Friday* | Rudolf Hess b. 1894. Sid James d. 1976 | 116 |
| **27** | *Saturday* | Mary Wollstonecraft Godwin b. 1759. William Macready d. 1873 | 117 |
| **28** | *Sunday* | **4th S. after Easter.** The League of Nations founded 1919 | 118 |
| **29** | *Monday* | Sir Thomas Beecham b. 1870 | *week* 17 *day* 119 |
| **30** | *Tuesday* | Sir Henry Bishop d. 1855. George Washington inaugurated as the first President of the USA 1789 | 120 |

### Astronomical Phenomena

| d | h | |
|---|---|---|
| 7 | 09 | Mercury in superior conjunction |
| 13 | 10 | Mercury in conjunction with Moon. Mercury 4° N. |
| 14 | 19 | Venus in conjunction with Moon. Venus 3° N. |
| 16 | 00 | Mars in conjunction with Moon. Mars 2° N. |
| 16 | 20 | Saturn in conjunction with Moon. Saturn 0°.8 S. |
| 18 | 23 | Jupiter in conjunction with Moon. Jupiter 2° S. |
| 20 | 06 | Sun's longitude 30°♉ |

### Minima of Algol

| d | h | d | h | d | h |
|---|---|---|---|---|---|
| 3 | 17.9 | 15 | 05.2 | 26 | 16.5 |
| 6 | 14.7 | 18 | 02.0 | 29 | 13.3 |
| 9 | 11.6 | 20 | 22.8 | | |
| 12 | 08.4 | 23 | 19.7 | | |

### Constellations

The following constellations are near the meridian at

| | d | h | | d | h |
|---|---|---|---|---|---|
| March | 1 | 24 | April | 15 | 2 |
| March | 16 | 23 | May | 1 | 2 |
| April | 1 | 22 | May | 16 | 1 |

Cepheus (below the Pole), Cassiopeia (below the Pole Ursa Major, Leo Minor, Leo, Sextans, Hydra and Crate

### The Moon

| Phases, Apsides and Node | d | h | m |
|---|---|---|---|
| ☾ Last Quarter | 4 | 15 | 2 |
| ● New Moon | 12 | 19 | 2 |
| ☽ First Quarter | 20 | 12 | 4 |
| ○ Full Moon | 27 | 03 | 0 |
| | | | |
| Apogee (406,390km) | 10 | 05 | 4 |
| Perigee (360,096km) | 25 | 16 | 3 |

Mean longitude of ascending node on April 1, 82°

THE SUN S.D 16′.1

| Day | Right Ascension | Dec. + | Equation of Time | Rise 52° | Rise 56° | Transit | Set 52° | Set 56° | Sidereal time | Transit of First Point of Aries |
|---|---|---|---|---|---|---|---|---|---|---|
| | h m s | ° ′ | m s | h m | h m | h m | h m | h m | h m s | h m s |
| 1 | 0 40 46 | 4 23 | −4 02 | 5 36 | 5 31 | 12 04 | 18 33 | 18 38 | 12 36 43 | 11 21 25 |
| 2 | 0 44 24 | 4 46 | −3 45 | 5 33 | 5 29 | 12 04 | 18 35 | 18 40 | 12 40 40 | 11 17 29 |
| 3 | 0 48 03 | 5 09 | −3 27 | 5 31 | 5 26 | 12 03 | 18 37 | 18 42 | 12 44 36 | 11 13 33 |
| 4 | 0 51 42 | 5 32 | −3 09 | 5 29 | 5 23 | 12 03 | 18 38 | 18 44 | 12 48 33 | 11 09 37 |
| 5 | 0 55 21 | 5 55 | −2 52 | 5 26 | 5 21 | 12 03 | 18 40 | 18 46 | 12 52 29 | 11 05 41 |
| 6 | 0 59 00 | 6 18 | −2 34 | 5 24 | 5 18 | 12 02 | 18 42 | 18 48 | 12 56 26 | 11 01 45 |
| 7 | 1 02 40 | 6 41 | −2 17 | 5 22 | 5 16 | 12 02 | 18 44 | 18 50 | 13 00 22 | 10 57 50 |
| 8 | 1 06 20 | 7 03 | −2 01 | 5 20 | 5 13 | 12 02 | 18 45 | 18 52 | 13 04 19 | 10 53 54 |
| 9 | 1 09 59 | 7 26 | −1 44 | 5 17 | 5 10 | 12 02 | 18 47 | 18 54 | 13 08 16 | 10 49 58 |
| 10 | 1 13 40 | 7 48 | −1 28 | 5 15 | 5 08 | 12 01 | 18 49 | 18 56 | 13 12 12 | 10 46 02 |
| 11 | 1 17 20 | 8 10 | −1 12 | 5 13 | 5 05 | 12 01 | 18 50 | 18 58 | 13 16 09 | 10 42 06 |
| 12 | 1 21 01 | 8 32 | −0 56 | 5 11 | 5 03 | 12 01 | 18 52 | 19 00 | 13 20 05 | 10 38 10 |
| 13 | 1 24 42 | 8 54 | −0 40 | 5 08 | 5 00 | 12 01 | 18 54 | 19 02 | 13 24 02 | 10 34 14 |
| 14 | 1 28 23 | 9 16 | −0 25 | 5 06 | 4 58 | 12 00 | 18 56 | 19 04 | 13 27 58 | 10 30 18 |
| 15 | 1 32 05 | 9 37 | −0 10 | 5 04 | 4 55 | 12 00 | 18 57 | 19 06 | 13 31 55 | 10 26 22 |
| 16 | 1 35 47 | 9 59 | +0 04 | 5 02 | 4 53 | 12 00 | 18 59 | 19 08 | 13 35 51 | 10 22 26 |
| 17 | 1 39 30 | 10 20 | +0 18 | 5 00 | 4 50 | 12 00 | 19 01 | 19 10 | 13 39 48 | 10 18 30 |
| 18 | 1 43 12 | 10 41 | +0 32 | 4 57 | 4 48 | 11 59 | 19 02 | 19 12 | 13 43 44 | 10 14 35 |
| 19 | 1 46 56 | 11 02 | +0 45 | 4 55 | 4 45 | 11 59 | 19 04 | 19 14 | 13 47 41 | 10 10 39 |
| 20 | 1 50 39 | 11 23 | +0 58 | 4 53 | 4 43 | 11 59 | 19 06 | 19 17 | 13 51 38 | 10 06 43 |
| 21 | 1 54 23 | 11 43 | +1 11 | 4 51 | 4 40 | 11 59 | 19 08 | 19 19 | 13 55 34 | 10 02 47 |
| 22 | 1 58 08 | 12 04 | +1 23 | 4 49 | 4 38 | 11 59 | 19 09 | 19 21 | 13 59 31 | 9 58 51 |
| 23 | 2 01 52 | 12 24 | +1 35 | 4 47 | 4 35 | 11 58 | 19 11 | 19 23 | 14 03 27 | 9 54 55 |
| 24 | 2 05 38 | 12 44 | +1 46 | 4 45 | 4 33 | 11 58 | 19 13 | 19 25 | 14 07 24 | 9 50 59 |
| 25 | 2 09 23 | 13 04 | +1 57 | 4 43 | 4 31 | 11 58 | 19 14 | 19 27 | 14 11 20 | 9 47 03 |
| 26 | 2 13 09 | 13 23 | +2 08 | 4 41 | 4 28 | 11 58 | 19 16 | 19 29 | 14 15 17 | 9 43 07 |
| 27 | 2 16 56 | 13 42 | +2 17 | 4 39 | 4 26 | 11 58 | 19 18 | 19 31 | 14 19 13 | 9 39 11 |
| 28 | 2 20 43 | 14 02 | +2 27 | 4 37 | 4 24 | 11 57 | 19 19 | 19 33 | 14 23 10 | 9 35 15 |
| 29 | 2 24 31 | 14 20 | +2 36 | 4 35 | 4 21 | 11 57 | 19 21 | 19 35 | 14 27 07 | 9 31 20 |
| 30 | 2 28 19 | 14 39 | +2 44 | 4 33 | 4 19 | 11 57 | 19 23 | 19 37 | 14 31 03 | 9 27 24 |

DURATION OF TWILIGHT (in minutes)

| *Latitude* | 52° | 56° | 52° | 56° | 52° | 56° | 52° | 56° |
|---|---|---|---|---|---|---|---|---|
| | 1 April | | 11 April | | 21 April | | 30 April | |
| *Civil* | 34 | 38 | 35 | 39 | 37 | 42 | 39 | 44 |
| *Nautical* | 76 | 84 | 79 | 89 | 83 | 96 | 89 | 106 |
| *Astronomical* | 120 | 136 | 127 | 147 | 137 | 165 | 152 | 204 |

THE NIGHT SKY

*Mercury* passes through superior conjunction on the 7th and about ten days later becomes visible as an evening object, low above the west- north-western horizon for a short while, around the end of evening civil twilight. During this period its magnitude fades from -1.2 to 0.0. This is the most favourable evening apparition of the year for observers in the latitudes of the British Isles.

*Venus* continues to be visible for a short time in the evenings, low in the western sky after sunset. Its magnitude is -3.9. The crescent Moon, only 2 days old, will be seen about 3 degrees below and to the left of the planet, on the evening of the 14th.

*Mars*, magnitude +1.6, is visible for a short while low above the western horizon in the evenings. Early in the month Mars moves from Aries eastwards into Taurus, passing between the two open clusters, the Pleiades and the Hyades. Mars passes 6 degrees north of Aldebaran on the 29th. On the evening of the 15th the crescent Moon, three days old, passes 4 degrees below the planet.

*Jupiter* is an evening object, magnitude -2.1, visible in the south-western sky until midnight. The crescent Moon will be seen only 2 degrees to the right of Jupiter on the evening of the 18th.

*Saturn*, magnitude +0.1, is still an evening object in the western sky, though continuing to draw closer to the Sun. By the end of the month it will be too low to be detected two hours after sunset. On the evening of the 16th the crescent Moon will occult Saturn (*see* page 67 for details).

## THE MOON

| Day | RA | Dec. | Hor. par. | Semi-diam | Sun's co-long. | PA of Bright Limb | Phase | Age | Rise 52° | Rise 56° | Transit | Set 52° | Set 56° |
|---|---|---|---|---|---|---|---|---|---|---|---|---|---|
| | h m | ° | ′ | ′ | ° | ° | % | d | h m | h m | h m | h m | h m |
| **1** | 15 37 | −17.2 | 59.4 | 16.2 | 128 | 101 | 85 | 17.9 | 23 52 | — | 3 07 | 7 34 | 7 16 |
| **2** | 16 34 | −21.0 | 58.5 | 15.9 | 141 | 98 | 77 | 18.9 | — | 0 14 | 4 02 | 8 05 | 7 42 |
| **3** | 17 31 | −23.6 | 57.5 | 15.7 | 153 | 93 | 67 | 19.9 | 1 07 | 1 34 | 4 58 | 8 45 | 8 18 |
| **4** | 18 28 | −24.7 | 56.6 | 15.4 | 165 | 87 | 57 | 20.9 | 2 10 | 2 39 | 5 53 | 9 35 | 9 06 |
| **5** | 19 24 | −24.5 | 55.8 | 15.2 | 177 | 82 | 47 | 21.9 | 3 01 | 3 29 | 6 46 | 10 34 | 10 06 |
| **6** | 20 18 | −23.1 | 55.1 | 15.0 | 189 | 76 | 37 | 22.9 | 3 40 | 4 04 | 7 37 | 11 39 | 11 15 |
| **7** | 21 09 | −20.6 | 54.6 | 14.9 | 201 | 71 | 28 | 23.9 | 4 09 | 4 29 | 8 25 | 12 48 | 12 29 |
| **8** | 21 58 | −17.3 | 54.3 | 14.8 | 214 | 66 | 20 | 24.9 | 4 32 | 4 48 | 9 10 | 13 57 | 13 43 |
| **9** | 22 44 | −13.4 | 54.0 | 14.7 | 226 | 62 | 13 | 25.9 | 4 51 | 5 02 | 9 53 | 15 05 | 14 56 |
| **10** | 23 29 | − 8.9 | 54.0 | 14.7 | 238 | 58 | 7 | 26.9 | 5 06 | 5 13 | 10 34 | 16 13 | 16 08 |
| **11** | 0 12 | − 4.1 | 54.0 | 14.7 | 250 | 53 | 3 | 27.9 | 5 21 | 5 23 | 11 14 | 17 21 | 17 21 |
| **12** | 0 55 | + 0.9 | 54.1 | 14.7 | 263 | 40 | 1 | 28.9 | 5 34 | 5 33 | 11 55 | 18 29 | 18 33 |
| **13** | 1 39 | + 5.8 | 54.3 | 14.8 | 275 | 311 | 0 | 0.2 | 5 49 | 5 43 | 12 36 | 19 38 | 19 47 |
| **14** | 2 23 | +10.7 | 54.6 | 14.9 | 287 | 265 | 1 | 1.2 | 6 05 | 5 54 | 13 19 | 20 49 | 21 03 |
| **15** | 3 10 | +15.1 | 55.0 | 15.0 | 299 | 260 | 5 | 2.2 | 6 23 | 6 09 | 14 04 | 22 01 | 22 20 |
| **16** | 3 59 | +19.0 | 55.4 | 15.1 | 311 | 261 | 9 | 3.2 | 6 47 | 6 27 | 14 53 | 23 13 | 23 37 |
| **17** | 4 51 | +22.1 | 55.9 | 15.2 | 324 | 264 | 16 | 4.2 | 7 17 | 6 53 | 15 44 | — | — |
| **18** | 5 46 | +24.1 | 56.5 | 15.4 | 336 | 268 | 24 | 5.2 | 7 58 | 7 30 | 16 39 | 0 22 | 0 49 |
| **19** | 6 43 | +24.9 | 57.1 | 15.6 | 348 | 274 | 34 | 6.2 | 8 51 | 8 22 | 17 35 | 1 23 | 1 52 |
| **20** | 7 42 | +24.3 | 57.8 | 15.8 | 0 | 279 | 44 | 7.2 | 9 58 | 9 31 | 18 32 | 2 14 | 2 41 |
| **21** | 8 40 | +22.3 | 58.6 | 16.0 | 12 | 285 | 55 | 8.2 | 11 15 | 10 53 | 19 29 | 2 54 | 3 17 |
| **22** | 9 38 | +18.9 | 59.3 | 16.2 | 25 | 291 | 66 | 9.2 | 12 38 | 12 22 | 20 24 | 3 25 | 3 43 |
| **23** | 10 35 | +14.3 | 60.0 | 16.3 | 37 | 295 | 77 | 10.2 | 14 05 | 13 55 | 21 18 | 3 50 | 4 02 |
| **24** | 11 31 | + 8.8 | 60.5 | 16.5 | 49 | 299 | 86 | 11.2 | 15 32 | 15 28 | 22 10 | 4 11 | 4 17 |
| **25** | 12 25 | + 2.6 | 60.8 | 16.6 | 61 | 302 | 93 | 12.2 | 17 00 | 17 02 | 23 03 | 4 30 | 4 31 |
| **26** | 13 20 | − 3.7 | 60.9 | 16.6 | 73 | 307 | 98 | 13.2 | 18 29 | 18 36 | 23 56 | 4 48 | 4 44 |
| **27** | 14 15 | − 9.8 | 60.6 | 16.5 | 86 | 353 | 100 | 14.2 | 19 57 | 20 11 | — | 5 08 | 4 58 |
| **28** | 15 11 | −15.2 | 60.1 | 16.4 | 98 | 94 | 99 | 15.2 | 21 24 | 21 44 | 0 50 | 5 31 | 5 16 |
| **29** | 16 09 | −19.7 | 59.4 | 16.2 | 110 | 98 | 95 | 16.2 | 22 45 | 23 11 | 1 46 | 5 59 | 5 38 |
| **30** | 17 08 | −22.9 | 58.5 | 16.0 | 122 | 95 | 89 | 17.2 | 23 57 | — | 2 43 | 6 36 | 6 10 |

## MERCURY

| Day | RA | Dec. | Diam. | Phase | Transit | 5° high 52° | 5° high 56° |
|---|---|---|---|---|---|---|---|
| | h m | ° | ″ | % | h m | h m | h m |
| 1 | 0 19 | + 0.3 | 5 | 98 | 11 44 | 6 14 | 6 17 |
| 3 | 0 34 | + 2.0 | 5 | 99 | 11 51 | 6 11 | 6 12 |
| 5 | 0 48 | + 3.8 | 5 | 100 | 11 57 | 6 08 | 6 08 |
| 7 | 1 03 | + 5.6 | 5 | 100 | 12 04 | 18 05 | 18 07 |
| 9 | 1 18 | + 7.5 | 5 | 100 | 12 11 | 18 22 | 18 25 |
| 11 | 1 33 | + 9.3 | 5 | 99 | 12 19 | 18 39 | 18 44 |
| 13 | 1 48 | +11.2 | 5 | 97 | 12 26 | 18 56 | 19 02 |
| 15 | 2 04 | +13.0 | 5 | 94 | 12 34 | 19 13 | 19 21 |
| 17 | 2 19 | +14.7 | 5 | 90 | 12 41 | 19 30 | 19 39 |
| 19 | 2 34 | +16.3 | 6 | 85 | 12 49 | 19 45 | 19 57 |
| 21 | 2 49 | +17.8 | 6 | 79 | 12 55 | 20 00 | 20 13 |
| 23 | 3 03 | +19.1 | 6 | 73 | 13 02 | 20 14 | 20 28 |
| 25 | 3 17 | +20.3 | 6 | 66 | 13 07 | 20 26 | 20 41 |
| 27 | 3 30 | +21.3 | 7 | 60 | 13 12 | 20 36 | 20 53 |
| 29 | 3 42 | +22.2 | 7 | 53 | 13 16 | 20 45 | 21 02 |
| 31 | 3 53 | +22.9 | 7 | 47 | 13 18 | 20 51 | 21 09 |

## VENUS

| Day | RA | Dec. | Diam. | Phase | Transit | 5° high 52° | 5° high 56° |
|---|---|---|---|---|---|---|---|
| | h m | ° | ″ | % | h m | h m | h m |
| 1 | 1 51 | +10.8 | 10 | 95 | 13 15 | 19 40 | 19 46 |
| 6 | 2 15 | +13.1 | 11 | 94 | 13 18 | 19 56 | 20 04 |
| 11 | 2 38 | +15.3 | 11 | 93 | 13 23 | 20 12 | 20 22 |
| 16 | 3 02 | +17.3 | 11 | 93 | 13 27 | 20 27 | 20 39 |
| 21 | 3 27 | +19.1 | 11 | 92 | 13 32 | 20 42 | 20 56 |
| 26 | 3 52 | +20.7 | 11 | 91 | 13 37 | 20 57 | 21 13 |
| 31 | 4 18 | +22.1 | 11 | 90 | 13 43 | 21 11 | 21 28 |

## MARS

| Day | RA | Dec. | Diam. | Phase | Transit | 5° high 52° | 5° high 56° |
|---|---|---|---|---|---|---|---|
| 1 | 3 15 | +18.6 | 4 | 95 | 14 37 | 21 43 | 21 57 |
| 6 | 3 29 | +19.6 | 4 | 96 | 14 32 | 21 43 | 21 57 |
| 11 | 3 43 | +20.4 | 4 | 96 | 14 26 | 21 42 | 21 57 |
| 16 | 3 57 | +21.2 | 4 | 96 | 14 21 | 21 42 | 21 57 |
| 21 | 4 11 | +21.9 | 4 | 97 | 14 15 | 21 40 | 21 57 |
| 26 | 4 26 | +22.5 | 4 | 97 | 14 10 | 21 39 | 21 56 |
| 31 | 4 40 | +23.0 | 4 | 97 | 14 05 | 21 37 | 21 55 |

## SUNRISE AND SUNSET

| | London | | Bristol | | Birmingham | | Manchester | | Newcastle | | Glasgow | | Belfast | |
|---|---|---|---|---|---|---|---|---|---|---|---|---|---|---|
| | 0°05′ | 51°30′ | 2°35′ | 51°28′ | 1°55′ | 52°28′ | 2°15′ | 53°28′ | 1°37′ | 54°59′ | 4°14′ | 55°52′ | 5°56′ | 54°35′ |
| | h m | h m | h m | h m | h m | h m | h m | h m | h m | h m | h m | h m | h m | h m |
| 1 | 5 36 | 18 33 | 5 46 | 18 43 | 5 43 | 18 42 | 5 43 | 18 44 | 5 39 | 18 43 | 5 48 | 18 55 | 5 57 | 19 00 |
| 2 | 5 34 | 18 35 | 5 44 | 18 45 | 5 40 | 18 43 | 5 41 | 18 46 | 5 36 | 18 45 | 5 46 | 18 57 | 5 54 | 19 02 |
| 3 | 5 32 | 18 37 | 5 42 | 18 47 | 5 38 | 18 45 | 5 38 | 18 48 | 5 34 | 18 47 | 5 43 | 18 59 | 5 52 | 19 04 |
| 4 | 5 30 | 18 38 | 5 40 | 18 48 | 5 36 | 18 47 | 5 36 | 18 49 | 5 31 | 18 49 | 5 41 | 19 01 | 5 49 | 19 06 |
| 5 | 5 27 | 18 40 | 5 37 | 18 50 | 5 33 | 18 48 | 5 33 | 18 51 | 5 29 | 18 51 | 5 38 | 19 03 | 5 47 | 19 08 |
| 6 | 5 25 | 18 42 | 5 35 | 18 52 | 5 31 | 18 50 | 5 31 | 18 53 | 5 26 | 18 53 | 5 35 | 19 05 | 5 44 | 19 09 |
| 7 | 5 23 | 18 43 | 5 33 | 18 53 | 5 29 | 18 52 | 5 29 | 18 55 | 5 24 | 18 55 | 5 33 | 19 07 | 5 42 | 19 11 |
| 8 | 5 21 | 18 45 | 5 31 | 18 55 | 5 26 | 18 54 | 5 26 | 18 57 | 5 21 | 18 57 | 5 30 | 19 09 | 5 39 | 19 13 |
| 9 | 5 18 | 18 47 | 5 28 | 18 57 | 5 24 | 18 55 | 5 24 | 18 58 | 5 19 | 18 59 | 5 28 | 19 11 | 5 37 | 19 15 |
| 10 | 5 16 | 18 48 | 5 26 | 18 58 | 5 22 | 18 57 | 5 22 | 19 00 | 5 16 | 19 01 | 5 25 | 19 13 | 5 34 | 19 17 |
| 11 | 5 14 | 18 50 | 5 24 | 19 00 | 5 20 | 18 59 | 5 19 | 19 02 | 5 14 | 19 03 | 5 23 | 19 15 | 5 32 | 19 19 |
| 12 | 5 12 | 18 52 | 5 22 | 19 02 | 5 17 | 19 01 | 5 17 | 19 04 | 5 11 | 19 04 | 5 20 | 19 17 | 5 29 | 19 21 |
| 13 | 5 10 | 18 53 | 5 20 | 19 03 | 5 15 | 19 02 | 5 15 | 19 06 | 5 09 | 19 06 | 5 17 | 19 19 | 5 27 | 19 23 |
| 14 | 5 07 | 18 55 | 5 17 | 19 05 | 5 13 | 19 04 | 5 12 | 19 08 | 5 06 | 19 08 | 5 15 | 19 21 | 5 25 | 19 25 |
| 15 | 5 05 | 18 57 | 5 15 | 19 07 | 5 11 | 19 06 | 5 10 | 19 09 | 5 04 | 19 10 | 5 12 | 19 23 | 5 22 | 19 27 |
| 16 | 5 03 | 18 58 | 5 13 | 19 08 | 5 08 | 19 08 | 5 08 | 19 11 | 5 02 | 19 12 | 5 10 | 19 25 | 5 20 | 19 29 |
| 17 | 5 01 | 19 00 | 5 11 | 19 10 | 5 06 | 19 09 | 5 05 | 19 13 | 4 59 | 19 14 | 5 07 | 19 27 | 5 17 | 19 30 |
| 18 | 4 59 | 19 02 | 5 09 | 19 12 | 5 04 | 19 11 | 5 03 | 19 15 | 4 57 | 19 16 | 5 05 | 19 29 | 5 15 | 19 32 |
| 19 | 4 57 | 19 03 | 5 07 | 19 13 | 5 02 | 19 13 | 5 01 | 19 17 | 4 54 | 19 18 | 5 02 | 19 31 | 5 13 | 19 34 |
| 20 | 4 55 | 19 05 | 5 05 | 19 15 | 5 00 | 19 15 | 4 59 | 19 19 | 4 52 | 19 20 | 5 00 | 19 33 | 5 10 | 19 36 |
| 21 | 4 53 | 19 07 | 5 03 | 19 17 | 4 58 | 19 16 | 4 56 | 19 20 | 4 50 | 19 22 | 4 58 | 19 35 | 5 08 | 19 38 |
| 22 | 4 50 | 19 08 | 5 01 | 19 18 | 4 55 | 19 18 | 4 54 | 19 22 | 4 47 | 19 24 | 4 55 | 19 37 | 5 06 | 19 40 |
| 23 | 4 48 | 19 10 | 4 59 | 19 20 | 4 53 | 19 20 | 4 52 | 19 24 | 4 45 | 19 26 | 4 53 | 19 39 | 5 03 | 19 42 |
| 24 | 4 46 | 19 12 | 4 56 | 19 22 | 4 51 | 19 22 | 4 50 | 19 26 | 4 43 | 19 28 | 4 50 | 19 41 | 5 01 | 19 44 |
| 25 | 4 44 | 19 13 | 4 54 | 19 23 | 4 49 | 19 23 | 4 48 | 19 28 | 4 40 | 19 30 | 4 48 | 19 43 | 4 59 | 19 46 |
| 26 | 4 42 | 19 15 | 4 52 | 19 25 | 4 47 | 19 25 | 4 45 | 19 29 | 4 38 | 19 32 | 4 46 | 19 45 | 4 57 | 19 48 |
| 27 | 4 40 | 19 17 | 4 50 | 19 27 | 4 45 | 19 27 | 4 43 | 19 31 | 4 36 | 19 34 | 4 43 | 19 47 | 4 54 | 19 50 |
| 28 | 4 38 | 19 18 | 4 49 | 19 28 | 4 43 | 19 28 | 4 41 | 19 33 | 4 34 | 19 36 | 4 41 | 19 49 | 4 52 | 19 51 |
| 29 | 4 37 | 19 20 | 4 47 | 19 30 | 4 41 | 19 30 | 4 39 | 19 35 | 4 31 | 19 38 | 4 39 | 19 51 | 4 50 | 19 53 |
| 30 | 4 35 | 19 22 | 4 45 | 19 31 | 4 39 | 19 32 | 4 37 | 19 37 | 4 29 | 19 39 | 4 36 | 19 53 | 4 48 | 19 55 |

## JUPITER

| *Day* | *RA* | | *Dec.* | | *Transit* | | *5° high* | | | |
|---|---|---|---|---|---|---|---|---|---|---|
| | | | | | | | 52° | | 56° | |
| | h | m | ° | ′ | h | m | h | m | h | m |
| 1 | 6 | 30.9 | +23 | 25 | 17 | 52 | 1 | 28 | 1 | 47 |
| 11 | 6 | 35.5 | +23 | 23 | 17 | 17 | 0 | 53 | 1 | 12 |
| 21 | 6 | 41.1 | +23 | 18 | 16 | 43 | 0 | 19 | 0 | 37 |
| 31 | 6 | 47.6 | +23 | 12 | 16 | 10 | 23 | 42 | 0 | 04 |

Diameters — equatorial 36″ polar 34″

## SATURN

| *Day* | *RA* | | *Dec.* | | *Transit* | | *5° high* | | | |
|---|---|---|---|---|---|---|---|---|---|---|
| | | | | | | | 52° | | 56° | |
| | h | m | ° | ′ | h | m | h | m | h | m |
| 1 | 4 | 36.1 | +20 | 35 | 15 | 57 | 23 | 13 | 23 | 28 |
| 11 | 4 | 40.0 | +20 | 44 | 15 | 22 | 22 | 39 | 22 | 54 |
| 21 | 4 | 44.4 | +20 | 54 | 14 | 47 | 22 | 05 | 22 | 20 |
| 31 | 4 | 49.2 | +21 | 04 | 14 | 12 | 21 | 31 | 21 | 46 |

Diameters — equatorial 17″ polar 15″
Rings — major axis 39″ minor axis 17″

## URANUS

| *Day* | *RA* | | *Dec.* | | *Transit* | | *10° high* | | | |
|---|---|---|---|---|---|---|---|---|---|---|
| | | | | | | | 52° | | 56° | |
| | h | m | ° | ′ | h | m | h | m | h | m |
| 1 | 21 | 59.0 | −13 | 04 | 9 | 21 | 5 | 45 | 6 | 07 |
| 11 | 22 | 00.7 | −12 | 56 | 8 | 43 | 5 | 06 | 5 | 29 |
| 21 | 22 | 02.1 | −12 | 48 | 8 | 05 | 4 | 28 | 4 | 50 |
| 31 | 22 | 03.2 | −12 | 43 | 7 | 27 | 3 | 49 | 4 | 11 |

Diameter 4″

## NEPTUNE

| *Day* | *RA* | | *Dec.* | | *Transit* | | *10° high* | | | |
|---|---|---|---|---|---|---|---|---|---|---|
| | | | | | | | 52° | | 56° | |
| | h | m | ° | ′ | h | m | h | m | h | m |
| 1 | 20 | 51.7 | −17 | 31 | 8 | 14 | 5 | 12 | 5 | 44 |
| 11 | 20 | 52.5 | −17 | 28 | 7 | 35 | 4 | 33 | 5 | 05 |
| 21 | 20 | 53.1 | −17 | 26 | 6 | 56 | 3 | 54 | 4 | 26 |
| 31 | 20 | 53.5 | −17 | 24 | 6 | 17 | 3 | 15 | 3 | 47 |

Diameter 2″

# May 2002

FIFTH MONTH, 31 DAYS, *Maia*, goddess of growth and increase

| | | | |
|---|---|---|---|
| **1** | *Wednesday* | **SS. Philip and James.** Great Exhibition opened 1851 | |
| **2** | *Thursday* | Senator Joseph McCarthy d. 1957. Berlin surrendered to Russian troops 1945 | 122 |
| **3** | *Friday* | Richard D'Oyly Carte b. 1844. Opening of Festival of Britain 1951 | 123 |
| **4** | *Saturday* | Joseph Whitaker b. 1820. Marshal Josip Tito d. 1980 | 124 |
| **5** | *Sunday* | **5th S. after Easter.** EASTER DAY (Eastern Orthodox) | 125 |
| **6** | *Monday* | *Bank Holiday in UK.* Tony Blair b. 1953. | *week* 18 *day* 126 |
| **7** | *Tuesday* | Caspar Friedrich d. 1840. Lusitania torpedoed 1915 | 127 |
| **8** | *Wednesday* | Harry Truman b. 1884. Restoration of the British Monarchy 1660 | 128 |
| **9** | *Thursday* | **Ascension Day.** John Brown b. 1800 | 129 |
| **10** | *Friday* | Owen Brannigan d. 1973. Resignation of Chamberlain 1940 | 130 |
| **11** | *Saturday* | Irving Berlin b. 1888. Prime Minister Spencer Perceval assassinated 1812 | 131 |
| **12** | *Sunday* | **S. after Ascension (6th after Easter).** Coronation of George VI and Queen Elizabeth 1937 | 132 |
| **13** | *Monday* | John Nash d. 1835. Gary Cooper d. 1961 | *week* 19 *day* 133 |
| **14** | *Tuesday* | **St Matthias.** Thomas Gainsborough b. 1727 | 134 |
| **15** | *Wednesday* | Edwin Muir b. 1887. Charles Perrault d. 1703 | 135 |
| **16** | *Thursday* | Sir John Hare b. 1844. Russian spacecraft Venus 5 touched down on Venus 1969 | 136 |
| **17** | *Friday* | FEAST OF WEEKS begins. Summer Time Act came into force 1916 | 137 |
| **18** | *Saturday* | Pope John Paul II b. 1920. Napoleon proclaimed Emperor of the French 1804 | 138 |
| **19** | *Sunday* | **Pentecost (Whit Sunday).** Nathaniel Hawthorne d. 1864 | 139 |
| **20** | *Monday* | Mary Lamb d. 1847. First solo transatlantic flight by a woman completed by Amelia Earhart 1932 | *week* 20 *day* 140 |
| **21** | *Tuesday* | Andrey Sakharov b. 1921. Christopher Columbus d. 1506 | 141 |
| **22** | *Wednesday* | Elizabeth David d. 1992. Blackwall Tunnel opened 1897 | 142 |
| **23** | *Thursday* | Heinrich Himmler d. 1945. Coalition Ministry dissolved 1945 | 143 |
| **24** | *Friday* | Joseph Alexandrovich Brodsky b. 1940. Field Marshall 1st Earl Archibald Percival Wavell d. 1950 | 144 |
| **25** | *Saturday* | Robert Capa d. 1954. Consecration of re-built Coventry Cathedral 1962 | 145 |
| **26** | *Sunday* | **Trinity Sunday.** Saint Augustine d. 604/5 | 146 |
| **27** | *Monday* | Arnold Bennett b. 1867. Habeus Corpus Act passed 1679 | *week* 21 *day* 147 |
| **28** | *Tuesday* | Patrick White b. 1912. Jean Muir d. 1995 | 148 |
| **29** | *Wednesday* | Erich Honecker d. 1994. Oak Apple Day - Restoration of Charles II 1660 | 149 |
| **30** | *Thursday* | **Corpus Christi.** Christopher Marlowe d. 1593 | 150 |
| **31** | *Friday* | **Visit of the Virgin Mary to Elizabeth.** *Easter Law Sittings end.* | 151 |

## ASTRONOMICAL PHENOMENA

| d | h | |
|---|---|---|
| 4 | 04 | Mercury at greatest elongation E.21° |
| 4 | 06 | Saturn in conjunction with Mars. Saturn 2° S. |
| 7 | 12 | Saturn in conjunction with Venus. Saturn 2° S. |
| 10 | 20 | Mars in conjunction with Venus. Mars 0°.3 S. |
| 13 | 12 | Neptune at stationary point |
| 13 | 22 | Mercury in conjunction with Moon. Mercury 2° N. |
| 14 | 08 | Saturn in conjunction with Moon. Saturn 1° S. |
| 14 | 19 | Mars in conjunction with Moon. Mars 0°.6 N. |
| 14 | 23 | Venus in conjunction with Moon. Venus 0°.8 N. |
| 15 | 19 | Mercury at stationary point |
| 16 | 12 | Jupiter in conjunction with Moon. Jupiter 2° S. |
| 21 | 05 | Sun's longitude 60°♊ |
| 27 | 07 | Mercury in inferior conjunction |

## MINIMA OF ALGOL

Algol is inconveniently situated for observation during May

## CONSTELLATIONS

The following constellations are near the meridian at

| | d | h | | d | h |
|---|---|---|---|---|---|
| April | 1 | 24 | May | 16 | 2 |
| April | 15 | 23 | June | 1 | 2 |
| May | 1 | 22 | June | 15 | 1 |

Cepheus (below the Pole), Cassiopeia (below the Pole), Ursa Minor, Ursa Major, Canes Venatici, Coma Berenices, Bootes, Leo, Virgo, Crater, Corvus and Hydra

## THE MOON

| Phases, Apsides and Node | d | h | m |
|---|---|---|---|
| ☾ Last Quarter | 4 | 07 | 1 |
| ● New Moon | 12 | 10 | 4 |
| ☽ First Quarter | 19 | 19 | 4 |
| ○ Full Moon | 26 | 11 | 5 |
| Apogee (405,452km) | 7 | 19 | 2 |
| Perigee (365,006km) | 23 | 15 | 4 |

Mean longitude of ascending node on May 1, 80°

'HE SUN S.D 16′.1

| ay | Right Ascension | Dec. + | Equation of Time | Rise 52° | Rise 56° | Transit | Set 52° | Set 56° | Sidereal time | Transit of First Point of Aries |
|---|---|---|---|---|---|---|---|---|---|---|
| | h m s | ° ′ | m s | h m | h m | h m | h m | h m | h m s | h m s |
| 1 | 2 32 08 | 14 57 | +2 52 | 4 31 | 4 17 | 11 57 | 19 24 | 19 39 | 14 35 00 | 9 23 28 |
| 2 | 2 35 57 | 15 15 | +2 59 | 4 29 | 4 14 | 11 57 | 19 26 | 19 41 | 14 38 56 | 9 19 32 |
| 3 | 2 39 47 | 15 33 | +3 06 | 4 27 | 4 12 | 11 57 | 19 28 | 19 43 | 14 42 53 | 9 15 36 |
| 4 | 2 43 37 | 15 51 | +3 12 | 4 25 | 4 10 | 11 57 | 19 29 | 19 45 | 14 46 49 | 9 11 40 |
| 5 | 2 47 28 | 16 08 | +3 18 | 4 23 | 4 08 | 11 57 | 19 31 | 19 47 | 14 50 46 | 9 07 44 |
| 6 | 2 51 20 | 16 25 | +3 23 | 4 22 | 4 06 | 11 57 | 19 33 | 19 49 | 14 54 42 | 9 03 48 |
| 7 | 2 55 12 | 16 42 | +3 27 | 4 20 | 4 04 | 11 57 | 19 34 | 19 51 | 14 58 39 | 8 59 52 |
| 8 | 2 59 04 | 16 59 | +3 31 | 4 18 | 4 01 | 11 56 | 19 36 | 19 53 | 15 02 36 | 8 55 56 |
| 9 | 3 02 58 | 17 15 | +3 34 | 4 16 | 3 59 | 11 56 | 19 38 | 19 55 | 15 06 32 | 8 52 00 |
| 0 | 3 06 52 | 17 31 | +3 37 | 4 15 | 3 57 | 11 56 | 19 39 | 19 57 | 15 10 29 | 8 48 05 |
| 1 | 3 10 46 | 17 47 | +3 39 | 4 13 | 3 55 | 11 56 | 19 41 | 19 59 | 15 14 25 | 8 44 09 |
| 2 | 3 14 41 | 18 02 | +3 41 | 4 11 | 3 53 | 11 56 | 19 42 | 20 01 | 15 18 22 | 8 40 13 |
| 3 | 3 18 37 | 18 17 | +3 42 | 4 10 | 3 51 | 11 56 | 19 44 | 20 02 | 15 22 18 | 8 36 17 |
| 4 | 3 22 33 | 18 32 | +3 42 | 4 08 | 3 50 | 11 56 | 19 46 | 20 04 | 15 26 15 | 8 32 21 |
| 5 | 3 26 30 | 18 46 | +3 42 | 4 06 | 3 48 | 11 56 | 19 47 | 20 06 | 15 30 11 | 8 28 25 |
| 6 | 3 30 27 | 19 00 | +3 41 | 4 05 | 3 46 | 11 56 | 19 49 | 20 08 | 15 34 08 | 8 24 29 |
| 7 | 3 34 25 | 19 14 | +3 40 | 4 04 | 3 44 | 11 56 | 19 50 | 20 10 | 15 38 05 | 8 20 33 |
| 8 | 3 38 23 | 19 28 | +3 38 | 4 02 | 3 42 | 11 56 | 19 52 | 20 12 | 15 42 01 | 8 16 37 |
| 9 | 3 42 22 | 19 41 | +3 36 | 4 01 | 3 40 | 11 56 | 19 53 | 20 14 | 15 45 58 | 8 12 41 |
| 0 | 3 46 21 | 19 54 | +3 33 | 3 59 | 3 39 | 11 56 | 19 55 | 20 15 | 15 49 54 | 8 08 45 |
| 1 | 3 50 21 | 20 06 | +3 29 | 3 58 | 3 37 | 11 57 | 19 56 | 20 17 | 15 53 51 | 8 04 50 |
| 2 | 3 54 22 | 20 18 | +3 25 | 3 57 | 3 36 | 11 57 | 19 57 | 20 19 | 15 57 47 | 8 00 54 |
| 3 | 3 58 23 | 20 30 | +3 21 | 3 55 | 3 34 | 11 57 | 19 59 | 20 20 | 16 01 44 | 7 56 58 |
| 4 | 4 02 24 | 20 42 | +3 16 | 3 54 | 3 32 | 11 57 | 20 00 | 20 22 | 16 05 40 | 7 53 02 |
| 5 | 4 06 26 | 20 53 | +3 11 | 3 53 | 3 31 | 11 57 | 20 02 | 20 24 | 16 09 37 | 7 49 06 |
| 6 | 4 10 29 | 21 03 | +3 05 | 3 52 | 3 30 | 11 57 | 20 03 | 20 25 | 16 13 34 | 7 45 10 |
| 7 | 4 14 32 | 21 14 | +2 58 | 3 51 | 3 28 | 11 57 | 20 04 | 20 27 | 16 17 30 | 7 41 14 |
| 8 | 4 18 35 | 21 24 | +2 51 | 3 50 | 3 27 | 11 57 | 20 05 | 20 28 | 16 21 27 | 7 37 18 |
| 9 | 4 22 39 | 21 33 | +2 44 | 3 49 | 3 26 | 11 57 | 20 07 | 20 30 | 16 25 23 | 7 33 22 |
| 0 | 4 26 44 | 21 43 | +2 36 | 3 48 | 3 24 | 11 57 | 20 08 | 20 31 | 16 29 20 | 7 29 26 |
| 1 | 4 30 48 | 21 51 | +2 28 | 3 47 | 3 23 | 11 58 | 20 09 | 20 33 | 16 33 16 | 7 25 30 |

'URATION OF TWILIGHT (in minutes)

| atitude | 52° | 56° | 52° | 56° | 52° | 56° | 52° | 56° |
|---|---|---|---|---|---|---|---|---|
| | 1 May | | 11 May | | 21 May | | 31 May | |
| 'ivil | 39 | 44 | 41 | 48 | 44 | 53 | 46 | 57 |
| 'autical | 89 | 106 | 97 | 120 | 106 | 141 | 115 | 187 |
| stronomical | 152 | 204 | 176 | TAN | TAN | TAN | TAN | TAN |

'HE NIGHT SKY

*lercury*, its magnitude fading from 0.0 to +1.0, is visible as 1 evening object for the first week of the month, low bove the west-north-western horizon for a short while round the end of evening civil twilight. Thereafter it is o close to the Sun for observation, passing through ferior conjunction on the 27th.

*'he Moon and the planets on the evening of the 14th.*

On this occasion the Moon and the planets Venus, Mars ipiter and Saturn will all be within 20 degrees of each ther. At the end of evening civil twilight Jupiter should be early visible, almost due west, with Venus about 20 egrees to its right. The crescent Moon, only 2.4 days old, ill be 2 or 3 degrees below Venus. Mars, the faintest of ese planets, will be about 2 degrees below and to the ght of Venus. Saturn will also be difficult to detect since it ill be 7 degrees below and 4 degrees to the right of Venus.

*Venus*, magnitude -3.9, is visible as a brilliant object in e western sky for nearly two hours after sunset. Venus is oving eastwards at a rate of over 1 degree per day, passing both Saturn and Mars. It passes Saturn at midday on the 7th and in the evening will be seen about 2.5 degrees above this planet. On the evening of the 10th Venus passes 0.3 degrees north of Mars and this close conjunction should help observers to locate the fainter planet. Venus is 6 degrees north of Aldebaran on the 4th.

*Mars*, magnitude +1.7, continues to be visible as an evening object low above the west-north-western horizon for a short while after dusk. Early in the month Mars and Saturn are close together and on the 4th Mars passes 2 degrees north of Saturn, the latter being several times brighter and therefore a useful guide to locating Mars. Mars is coming towards the end of its evening apparition and will be lost to view shortly before the end of the month.

*Jupiter*, magnitude -1.9, is still visible as an evening object, in the south-western sky, though by the end of the month it is only visible for about two hours after sunset.

*Saturn*, magnitude +0.1, becomes increasingly difficult to detect low in the western sky in the gathering evening twilight and is unlikely to be seen after the middle of the month.

## THE MOON

| Day | RA | Dec. | Hor. par. | Semi-diam | Sun's co-long. | PA of Bright Limb | Phase | Age | Rise 52° | Rise 56° | Transit | Set 52° | Set 56° |
|---|---|---|---|---|---|---|---|---|---|---|---|---|---|
| | h m | ° | ′ | ′ | ° | ° | % | d | h m | h m | h m | h m | h m |
| **1** | 18 07 | –24.6 | 57.6 | 15.7 | 134 | 90 | 81 | 18.2 | — | 0 26 | 3 41 | 7 22 | 6 53 |
| **2** | 19 05 | –24.9 | 56.7 | 15.5 | 146 | 85 | 73 | 19.2 | 0 55 | 1 25 | 4 37 | 8 19 | 7 50 |
| **3** | 20 01 | –23.9 | 55.9 | 15.2 | 159 | 79 | 63 | 20.2 | 1 40 | 2 06 | 5 30 | 9 24 | 8 58 |
| **4** | 20 54 | –21.7 | 55.2 | 15.0 | 171 | 74 | 53 | 21.2 | 2 13 | 2 35 | 6 20 | 10 34 | 10 12 |
| **5** | 21 44 | –18.5 | 54.7 | 14.9 | 183 | 70 | 43 | 22.2 | 2 38 | 2 56 | 7 07 | 11 44 | 11 27 |
| **6** | 22 31 | –14.7 | 54.3 | 14.8 | 195 | 67 | 34 | 23.2 | 2 58 | 3 11 | 7 50 | 12 53 | 12 42 |
| **7** | 23 17 | –10.3 | 54.1 | 14.7 | 207 | 64 | 25 | 24.2 | 3 14 | 3 23 | 8 32 | 14 01 | 13 55 |
| **8** | 0 00 | – 5.6 | 54.1 | 14.7 | 220 | 62 | 18 | 25.2 | 3 29 | 3 33 | 9 13 | 15 09 | 15 07 |
| **9** | 0 43 | – 0.6 | 54.2 | 14.8 | 232 | 61 | 11 | 26.2 | 3 42 | 3 42 | 9 53 | 16 17 | 16 20 |
| **10** | 1 27 | + 4.4 | 54.4 | 14.8 | 244 | 60 | 6 | 27.2 | 3 56 | 3 52 | 10 34 | 17 26 | 17 33 |
| **11** | 2 11 | + 9.3 | 54.7 | 14.9 | 256 | 58 | 2 | 28.2 | 4 11 | 4 03 | 11 16 | 18 37 | 18 49 |
| **12** | 2 57 | +14.0 | 55.1 | 15.0 | 269 | 45 | 0 | 29.2 | 4 29 | 4 16 | 12 01 | 19 50 | 20 07 |
| **13** | 3 46 | +18.1 | 55.5 | 15.1 | 281 | 273 | 0 | 0.6 | 4 51 | 4 32 | 12 49 | 21 03 | 21 25 |
| **14** | 4 38 | +21.5 | 56.0 | 15.3 | 293 | 264 | 2 | 1.6 | 5 19 | 4 56 | 13 40 | 22 14 | 22 41 |
| **15** | 5 33 | +23.8 | 56.5 | 15.4 | 305 | 266 | 7 | 2.6 | 5 56 | 5 29 | 14 35 | 23 19 | 23 49 |
| **16** | 6 30 | +25.0 | 57.0 | 15.5 | 318 | 271 | 13 | 3.6 | 6 45 | 6 16 | 15 31 | — | — |
| **17** | 7 28 | +24.7 | 57.5 | 15.7 | 330 | 277 | 21 | 4.6 | 7 48 | 7 20 | 16 28 | 0 14 | 0 42 |
| **18** | 8 27 | +23.0 | 58.0 | 15.8 | 342 | 282 | 30 | 5.6 | 9 01 | 8 38 | 17 24 | 0 57 | 1 22 |
| **19** | 9 24 | +20.0 | 58.6 | 16.0 | 354 | 287 | 41 | 6.6 | 10 22 | 10 04 | 18 18 | 1 30 | 1 49 |
| **20** | 10 20 | +15.8 | 59.0 | 16.1 | 7 | 291 | 52 | 7.6 | 11 46 | 11 33 | 19 11 | 1 56 | 2 10 |
| **21** | 11 14 | +10.6 | 59.5 | 16.2 | 19 | 295 | 64 | 8.6 | 13 10 | 13 04 | 20 02 | 2 17 | 2 25 |
| **22** | 12 07 | + 4.8 | 59.8 | 16.3 | 31 | 296 | 74 | 9.6 | 14 35 | 14 34 | 20 52 | 2 35 | 2 38 |
| **23** | 13 00 | – 1.3 | 60.0 | 16.4 | 43 | 297 | 84 | 10.6 | 16 00 | 16 05 | 21 43 | 2 53 | 2 51 |
| **24** | 13 53 | – 7.4 | 60.1 | 16.4 | 55 | 296 | 92 | 11.6 | 17 26 | 17 37 | 22 35 | 3 11 | 3 04 |
| **25** | 14 48 | –13.1 | 59.9 | 16.3 | 68 | 295 | 97 | 12.6 | 18 53 | 19 10 | 23 30 | 3 31 | 3 19 |
| **26** | 15 45 | –18.0 | 59.5 | 16.2 | 80 | 298 | 100 | 13.6 | 20 18 | 20 41 | — | 3 56 | 3 38 |
| **27** | 16 43 | –21.7 | 58.9 | 16.1 | 92 | 93 | 100 | 14.6 | 21 36 | 22 04 | 0 27 | 4 28 | 4 04 |
| **28** | 17 43 | –24.1 | 58.2 | 15.9 | 104 | 94 | 97 | 15.6 | 22 42 | 23 12 | 1 25 | 5 10 | 4 41 |
| **29** | 18 42 | –25.0 | 57.4 | 15.7 | 116 | 89 | 92 | 16.6 | 23 34 | — | 2 22 | 6 03 | 5 33 |
| **30** | 19 40 | –24.5 | 56.7 | 15.4 | 128 | 83 | 86 | 17.6 | — | 0 02 | 3 18 | 7 06 | 6 38 |
| **31** | 20 36 | –22.7 | 55.9 | 15.2 | 141 | 78 | 78 | 18.6 | 0 13 | 0 37 | 4 11 | 8 15 | 7 52 |

## MERCURY

| Day | RA | Dec. | Diam. | Phase | Transit | 5° high 52° | 5° high 56° |
|---|---|---|---|---|---|---|---|
| | h m | ° | ″ | % | h m | h m | h m |
| 1 | 3 53 | +22.9 | 7 | 47 | 13 18 | 20 51 | 21 09 |
| 3 | 4 02 | +23.4 | 8 | 41 | 13 20 | 20 55 | 21 13 |
| 5 | 4 11 | +23.7 | 8 | 35 | 13 20 | 20 57 | 21 16 |
| 7 | 4 18 | +24.0 | 9 | 30 | 13 19 | 20 56 | 21 15 |
| 9 | 4 24 | +24.0 | 9 | 25 | 13 16 | 20 54 | 21 13 |
| 11 | 4 28 | +24.0 | 9 | 20 | 13 12 | 20 49 | 21 08 |
| 13 | 4 31 | +23.8 | 10 | 16 | 13 07 | 20 42 | 21 00 |
| 15 | 4 32 | +23.4 | 10 | 12 | 13 00 | 20 32 | 20 50 |
| 17 | 4 32 | +23.0 | 11 | 9 | 12 52 | 20 21 | 20 38 |
| 19 | 4 31 | +22.5 | 11 | 6 | 12 43 | 20 08 | 20 25 |
| 21 | 4 29 | +21.8 | 12 | 3 | 12 32 | 19 53 | 20 09 |
| 23 | 4 26 | +21.1 | 12 | 2 | 12 21 | 19 38 | 19 53 |
| 25 | 4 22 | +20.4 | 12 | 1 | 12 09 | 19 21 | 19 36 |
| 27 | 4 18 | +19.6 | 12 | 0 | 11 57 | 4 48 | 4 34 |
| 29 | 4 13 | +18.9 | 12 | 0 | 11 45 | 4 40 | 4 27 |
| 31 | 4 09 | +18.2 | 12 | 1 | 11 33 | 4 32 | 4 20 |

## VENUS

| Day | RA | Dec. | Diam. | Phase | Transit | 5° high 52° | 5° high 56° |
|---|---|---|---|---|---|---|---|
| | h m | ° | ″ | % | h m | h m | h m |
| 1 | 4 18 | 22.1 | 11 | 90 | 13 43 | 21 11 | 21 2[illegible] |
| 6 | 4 43 | +23.3 | 12 | 88 | 13 49 | 21 24 | 21 4[illegible] |
| 11 | 5 10 | +24.1 | 12 | 87 | 13 56 | 21 36 | 21 5[illegible] |
| 16 | 5 36 | +24.7 | 12 | 86 | 14 03 | 21 46 | 22 0[illegible] |
| 21 | 6 02 | +25.0 | 12 | 85 | 14 09 | 21 54 | 22 1[illegible] |
| 26 | 6 29 | +25.0 | 12 | 83 | 14 16 | 22 01 | 22 2[illegible] |
| 31 | 6 55 | +24.7 | 13 | 82 | 14 22 | 22 05 | 22 2[illegible] |

## MARS

| Day | RA | Dec. | Diam. | Phase | Transit | 5° high 52° | 5° high 56° |
|---|---|---|---|---|---|---|---|
| 1 | 4 40 | +23.0 | 4 | 97 | 14 05 | 21 37 | 21 55 |
| 6 | 4 55 | +23.5 | 4 | 97 | 13 59 | 21 34 | 21 53 |
| 11 | 5 09 | +23.8 | 4 | 98 | 13 54 | 21 31 | 21 50 |
| 16 | 5 24 | +24.1 | 4 | 98 | 13 49 | 21 28 | 21 47 |
| 21 | 5 38 | +24.3 | 4 | 98 | 13 44 | 21 24 | 21 43 |
| 26 | 5 53 | +24.4 | 4 | 98 | 13 39 | 21 19 | 21 39 |
| 31 | 6 07 | +24.4 | 4 | 99 | 13 33 | 21 14 | 21 33 |

## UNSET AND SUNRISE

| | London | | Bristol | | Birmingham | | Manchester | | Newcastle | | Glasgow | | Belfast | |
|---|---|---|---|---|---|---|---|---|---|---|---|---|---|---|
| | 0°05′ | 51°30′ | 2°35′ | 51°28′ | 1°55′ | 52°28′ | 2°15′ | 53°28′ | 1°37′ | 54°59′ | 4°14′ | 55°52′ | 5°56′ | 54°35′ |
| | h m | h m | h m | h m | h m | h m | h m | h m | h m | h m | h m | h m | h m | h m |
| 1 | 4 33 | 19 23 | 4 43 | 19 33 | 4 37 | 19 34 | 4 35 | 19 38 | 4 27 | 19 41 | 4 34 | 19 55 | 4 46 | 19 57 |
| 2 | 4 31 | 19 25 | 4 41 | 19 35 | 4 35 | 19 35 | 4 33 | 19 40 | 4 25 | 19 43 | 4 32 | 19 57 | 4 44 | 19 59 |
| 3 | 4 29 | 19 26 | 4 39 | 19 36 | 4 33 | 19 37 | 4 31 | 19 42 | 4 23 | 19 45 | 4 30 | 19 59 | 4 42 | 20 01 |
| 4 | 4 27 | 19 28 | 4 37 | 19 38 | 4 31 | 19 39 | 4 29 | 19 44 | 4 21 | 19 47 | 4 27 | 20 01 | 4 39 | 20 03 |
| 5 | 4 25 | 19 30 | 4 35 | 19 40 | 4 29 | 19 40 | 4 27 | 19 45 | 4 19 | 19 49 | 4 25 | 20 03 | 4 37 | 20 05 |
| 6 | 4 24 | 19 31 | 4 34 | 19 41 | 4 27 | 19 42 | 4 25 | 19 47 | 4 16 | 19 51 | 4 23 | 20 05 | 4 35 | 20 06 |
| 7 | 4 22 | 19 33 | 4 32 | 19 43 | 4 26 | 19 44 | 4 23 | 19 49 | 4 14 | 19 53 | 4 21 | 20 07 | 4 33 | 20 08 |
| 8 | 4 20 | 19 34 | 4 30 | 19 44 | 4 24 | 19 45 | 4 21 | 19 51 | 4 12 | 19 55 | 4 19 | 20 09 | 4 31 | 20 10 |
| 9 | 4 18 | 19 36 | 4 29 | 19 46 | 4 22 | 19 47 | 4 19 | 19 52 | 4 10 | 19 56 | 4 17 | 20 11 | 4 29 | 20 12 |
| 10 | 4 17 | 19 38 | 4 27 | 19 48 | 4 20 | 19 49 | 4 18 | 19 54 | 4 09 | 19 58 | 4 15 | 20 13 | 4 28 | 20 14 |
| 11 | 4 15 | 19 39 | 4 25 | 19 49 | 4 19 | 19 50 | 4 16 | 19 56 | 4 07 | 20 00 | 4 13 | 20 15 | 4 26 | 20 16 |
| 12 | 4 14 | 19 41 | 4 24 | 19 51 | 4 17 | 19 52 | 4 14 | 19 58 | 4 05 | 20 02 | 4 11 | 20 17 | 4 24 | 20 17 |
| 13 | 4 12 | 19 42 | 4 22 | 19 52 | 4 15 | 19 54 | 4 12 | 19 59 | 4 03 | 20 04 | 4 09 | 20 19 | 4 22 | 20 19 |
| 14 | 4 10 | 19 44 | 4 21 | 19 54 | 4 14 | 19 55 | 4 11 | 20 01 | 4 01 | 20 06 | 4 07 | 20 21 | 4 20 | 20 21 |
| 15 | 4 09 | 19 45 | 4 19 | 19 55 | 4 12 | 19 57 | 4 09 | 20 03 | 3 59 | 20 07 | 4 05 | 20 22 | 4 19 | 20 23 |
| 16 | 4 07 | 19 47 | 4 18 | 19 57 | 4 11 | 19 58 | 4 07 | 20 04 | 3 58 | 20 09 | 4 03 | 20 24 | 4 17 | 20 24 |
| 17 | 4 06 | 19 48 | 4 16 | 19 58 | 4 09 | 20 00 | 4 06 | 20 06 | 3 56 | 20 11 | 4 02 | 20 26 | 4 15 | 20 26 |
| 18 | 4 05 | 19 50 | 4 15 | 20 00 | 4 08 | 20 01 | 4 04 | 20 07 | 3 54 | 20 13 | 4 00 | 20 28 | 4 14 | 20 28 |
| 19 | 4 03 | 19 51 | 4 13 | 20 01 | 4 06 | 20 03 | 4 03 | 20 09 | 3 53 | 20 14 | 3 58 | 20 30 | 4 12 | 20 29 |
| 20 | 4 02 | 19 53 | 4 12 | 20 03 | 4 05 | 20 04 | 4 01 | 20 11 | 3 51 | 20 16 | 3 56 | 20 32 | 4 10 | 20 31 |
| 21 | 4 01 | 19 54 | 4 11 | 20 04 | 4 03 | 20 06 | 4 00 | 20 12 | 3 49 | 20 18 | 3 55 | 20 33 | 4 09 | 20 33 |
| 22 | 3 59 | 19 55 | 4 09 | 20 05 | 4 02 | 20 07 | 3 59 | 20 14 | 3 48 | 20 19 | 3 53 | 20 35 | 4 07 | 20 34 |
| 23 | 3 58 | 19 57 | 4 08 | 20 07 | 4 01 | 20 09 | 3 57 | 20 15 | 3 46 | 20 21 | 3 52 | 20 37 | 4 06 | 20 36 |
| 24 | 3 57 | 19 58 | 4 07 | 20 08 | 4 00 | 20 10 | 3 56 | 20 17 | 3 45 | 20 22 | 3 50 | 20 38 | 4 05 | 20 37 |
| 25 | 3 56 | 19 59 | 4 06 | 20 09 | 3 58 | 20 12 | 3 55 | 20 18 | 3 44 | 20 24 | 3 49 | 20 40 | 4 03 | 20 39 |
| 26 | 3 55 | 20 01 | 4 05 | 20 11 | 3 57 | 20 13 | 3 53 | 20 19 | 3 42 | 20 26 | 3 47 | 20 41 | 4 02 | 20 40 |
| 27 | 3 54 | 20 02 | 4 04 | 20 12 | 3 56 | 20 14 | 3 52 | 20 21 | 3 41 | 20 27 | 3 46 | 20 43 | 4 01 | 20 42 |
| 28 | 3 53 | 20 03 | 4 03 | 20 13 | 3 55 | 20 15 | 3 51 | 20 22 | 3 40 | 20 28 | 3 45 | 20 45 | 3 59 | 20 43 |
| 29 | 3 52 | 20 04 | 4 02 | 20 14 | 3 54 | 20 17 | 3 50 | 20 23 | 3 39 | 20 30 | 3 43 | 20 46 | 3 58 | 20 45 |
| 30 | 3 51 | 20 06 | 4 01 | 20 15 | 3 53 | 20 18 | 3 49 | 20 25 | 3 38 | 20 31 | 3 42 | 20 47 | 3 57 | 20 46 |
| 31 | 3 50 | 20 07 | 4 00 | 20 17 | 3 52 | 20 19 | 3 48 | 20 26 | 3 36 | 20 33 | 3 41 | 20 49 | 3 56 | 20 47 |

## JPITER

| *ay* | *RA* | | *Dec.* | | *Transit* | | *5° high* | | | |
|---|---|---|---|---|---|---|---|---|---|---|
| | | | | | | | 52° | | 56° | |
| | h | m | ° | ′ | h | m | h | m | h | m |
| | 6 | 47.6 | +23 | 12 | 16 | 10 | 23 | 42 | 0 | 04 |
| | 6 | 54.9 | +23 | 04 | 15 | 38 | 23 | 09 | 23 | 27 |
| | 7 | 02.8 | +22 | 54 | 15 | 07 | 22 | 37 | 22 | 55 |
| | 7 | 11.2 | +22 | 41 | 14 | 36 | 22 | 05 | 22 | 22 |

iameters – equatorial 34″ polar 32″

## SATURN

| *Day* | *RA* | | *Dec.* | | *Transit* | | *5° high* | | | |
|---|---|---|---|---|---|---|---|---|---|---|
| | | | | | | | 52° | | 56° | |
| | h | m | ° | ′ | h | m | h | m | h | m |
| 1 | 4 | 49.2 | +21 | 04 | 14 | 12 | 21 | 31 | 21 | 46 |
| 11 | 4 | 54.2 | +21 | 14 | 13 | 38 | 20 | 58 | 21 | 13 |
| 21 | 4 | 59.5 | +21 | 23 | 13 | 04 | 20 | 25 | 20 | 40 |
| 31 | 5 | 05.0 | +21 | 32 | 12 | 30 | 19 | 52 | 20 | 08 |

Diameters – equatorial 17″ polar 15″
Rings – major axis 38″ minor axis 17″

## RANUS

| *ay* | *RA* | | *Dec.* | | *Transit* | | *10° high* | | | |
|---|---|---|---|---|---|---|---|---|---|---|
| | | | | | | | 52° | | 56° | |
| | h | m | ° | ′ | h | m | h | m | h | m |
| | 22 | 03.2 | –12 | 43 | 7 | 27 | 3 | 49 | 4 | 11 |
| | 22 | 04.1 | –12 | 38 | 6 | 49 | 3 | 10 | 3 | 31 |
| | 22 | 04.7 | –12 | 36 | 6 | 10 | 2 | 31 | 2 | 52 |
| | 22 | 04.9 | –12 | 35 | 5 | 31 | 1 | 52 | 2 | 13 |

iameter 4″

## NEPTUNE

| *Day* | *RA* | | *Dec.* | | *Transit* | | *10° high* | | | |
|---|---|---|---|---|---|---|---|---|---|---|
| | | | | | | | 52° | | 56° | |
| | h | m | ° | ′ | h | m | h | m | h | m |
| 1 | 20 | 53.5 | –17 | 24 | 6 | 17 | 3 | 15 | 3 | 47 |
| 11 | 20 | 53.6 | –17 | 24 | 5 | 38 | 2 | 35 | 3 | 07 |
| 21 | 20 | 53.6 | –17 | 24 | 4 | 59 | 1 | 56 | 2 | 28 |
| 31 | 20 | 53.3 | –17 | 25 | 4 | 19 | 1 | 17 | 1 | 49 |

Diameter 2″

# June 2002

SIXTH MONTH, 30 DAYS. *Junius*, Roman *gens* (family)

| | | | |
|---|---|---|---|
| 1 | *Saturday* | Leslie Howard d. 1943. Battle of Glorious First of June 1794 | 15 |
| 2 | *Sunday* | **1st S. after Trinity.** *Coronation Day 1953.* | 15 |
| 3 | *Monday* | *Golden Jubilee Bank Holiday in UK.* Elisabeth Powell d. 1995 | *week 22 day* 15 |
| 4 | *Tuesday* | *Bank Holiday in UK.* Lord Thorneycroft George Thorneycroft d. 1994 | 15 |
| 5 | *Wednesday* | David Hare b. 1947. William Sidney Porter d. 1910 | 15 |
| 6 | *Thursday* | Dame Ninette de Valois b. 1898. Robert Francis Kennedy d. 1968 | 15 |
| 7 | *Friday* | Beau Brummell b. 1778. Dorothy Parker d. 1967 | 15 |
| 8 | *Saturday* | Frink Lloyd Wright b. 1969. Andrew Jackson d. 1845 | 15 |
| 9 | *Sunday* | **2nd S. after Trinity.** Saint Columba d. 597 | 16 |
| 10 | *Monday* | *Duke of Edinburgh b. 1921.* Sir Henry Coward d. 1944 | *week 23 day* 16 |
| 11 | *Tuesday* | **St. Barnabus.** Dame Millicent Fawcett b. 1847 | 16 |
| 12 | *Wednesday* | Charles Kingsley b. 1819. John Ireland d. 1962 | 16 |
| 13 | *Thursday* | Fanny Burney b. 1752. Boxer Rebellion broke out 1900 | 16 |
| 14 | *Friday* | Sam Wanamaker b. 1919. Battle of Naseby 1645 | 16 |
| 15 | *Saturday* | *Queen's Official Birthday.* First non-stop transatlantic flight 1919 | 16 |
| 16 | *Sunday* | **3rd S. after Trinity.** Imre Nagy d. 1958 | 16 |
| 17 | *Monday* | Beryl Reid b. 1920. Joseph Addison d. 1719 | *week 24 day* 16 |
| 18 | *Tuesday* | *Trinity Law Sittings begin.* Samuel Butler d. 1902 | 16 |
| 19 | *Wednesday* | James I b. 1566. Sir Joseph Banks d. 1820 | 17 |
| 20 | *Thursday* | Jacques Offenbach b. 1819. Willem Barents d. 1597 | 17 |
| 21 | *Friday* | Prince William of Wales b. 1982. King Edward III d. 1377 | 17 |
| 22 | *Saturday* | Darius Milhaud d. 1974. Coronation of George V 1911 | 17 |
| 23 | *Sunday* | **4th S. after Trinity.** Cecil James Sharp d. 1924 | 17 |
| 24 | *Monday* | **John the Baptist.** Marie François Carnot d. 1894 | *week 25 day* 17 |
| 25 | *Tuesday* | Antonio Gaudí b. 1852. Colonel George Custer d. 1876 | 17 |
| 26 | *Wednesday* | Francisco Pizarro d. 1541. UN Charter signed at San Francisco 1945 | 17 |
| 27 | *Thursday* | Charles Stewart Parnell b. 1846. Joseph Smith d. 1844 | 17 |
| 28 | *Friday* | Luigi Pirandello b. 1867. Coronation of Queen Victoria 1838 | 17 |
| 29 | *Saturday* | **SS. Peter and Paul.** Paul Klee d. 1940 | 18 |
| 30 | *Sunday* | **5th S. after Trinity.** Margery Allingham d. 1966 | 18 |

## Astronomical Phenomena

| d | h | |
|---|---|---|
| 3 | 00 | Uranus at stationary point |
| 3 | 23 | Jupiter in conjunction with Venus. Jupiter 2° S. |
| 7 | 05 | Pluto at opposition |
| 8 | 15 | Mercury at stationary point |
| 9 | 11 | Saturn in conjunction |
| 9 | 13 | Mercury in conjunction with Moon. Mercury 3° S. |
| 10 | 21 | Saturn in conjunction with Moon. Saturn 1° S. |
| 11 | 00 | Annular eclipse of Sun (see page 66) |
| 12 | 12 | Mars in conjunction with Moon. Mars 0°.9 S. |
| 13 | 04 | Jupiter in conjunction with Moon. Jupiter 2° S. |
| 13 | 22 | Venus in conjunction with Moon. Venus 1° S. |
| 21 | 13 | Sun's longitude 90°♋ |
| 21 | 14 | Mercury at greatest elongation W.23° |

## Minima of Algol

Algol is inconveniently situated for observation during June

## Constellations

| | d | h | | d | h |
|---|---|---|---|---|---|
| May | 1 | 24 | June | 15 | 2 |
| May | 16 | 23 | July | 1 | 2 |
| June | 1 | 22 | July | 16 | 1 |

Cassiopeia (below the Pole), Ursa Minor, Draco, Urs Major, Canes Venatici, Bootes, Corona, Serpens, Virg and Libra

## The Moon

| Phases, Apsides and Node | d | h | m |
|---|---|---|---|
| ☾ Last Quarter | 3 | 00 | 0 |
| ● New Moon | 10 | 23 | 4 |
| ☽ First Quarter | 18 | 00 | 2 |
| ○ Full Moon | 24 | 21 | 4 |
| | | | |
| Apogee (404,484km) | 4 | 13 | ( |
| Perigee (369,343km) | 19 | 07 | 3 |

Mean longitude of ascending node on June 1, 78

## HE SUN

S.D 16′.1

| Day | Right Ascension | Dec. + | Equation of Time | Rise 52° | Rise 56° | Transit | Set 52° | Set 56° | Sidereal time | Transit of First Point of Aries |
|---|---|---|---|---|---|---|---|---|---|---|
| | h m s | ° ′ | m s | h m | h m | h m | h m | h m | h m s | h m s |
| 1 | 4 34 54 | 22 00 | +2 19 | 3 46 | 3 22 | 11 58 | 20 10 | 20 34 | 16 37 13 | 7 21 35 |
| 2 | 4 38 59 | 22 08 | +2 10 | 3 45 | 3 21 | 11 58 | 20 11 | 20 35 | 16 41 10 | 7 17 39 |
| 3 | 4 43 06 | 22 16 | +2 01 | 3 45 | 3 20 | 11 58 | 20 12 | 20 37 | 16 45 06 | 7 13 43 |
| 4 | 4 47 12 | 22 23 | +1 51 | 3 44 | 3 19 | 11 58 | 20 13 | 20 38 | 16 49 03 | 7 09 47 |
| 5 | 4 51 19 | 22 30 | +1 40 | 3 43 | 3 18 | 11 58 | 20 14 | 20 39 | 16 52 59 | 7 05 51 |
| 6 | 4 55 26 | 22 37 | +1 30 | 3 43 | 3 18 | 11 59 | 20 15 | 20 40 | 16 56 56 | 7 01 55 |
| 7 | 4 59 34 | 22 43 | +1 19 | 3 42 | 3 17 | 11 59 | 20 16 | 20 41 | 17 00 52 | 6 57 59 |
| 8 | 5 03 41 | 22 49 | +1 07 | 3 42 | 3 16 | 11 59 | 20 17 | 20 42 | 17 04 49 | 6 54 03 |
| 9 | 5 07 50 | 22 54 | +0 56 | 3 41 | 3 15 | 11 59 | 20 18 | 20 43 | 17 08 45 | 6 50 07 |
| 10 | 5 11 58 | 22 59 | +0 44 | 3 41 | 3 15 | 11 59 | 20 18 | 20 44 | 17 12 42 | 6 46 11 |
| 11 | 5 16 07 | 23 03 | +0 32 | 3 40 | 3 14 | 12 00 | 20 19 | 20 45 | 17 16 39 | 6 42 15 |
| 12 | 5 20 15 | 23 08 | +0 20 | 3 40 | 3 14 | 12 00 | 20 20 | 20 46 | 17 20 35 | 6 38 19 |
| 13 | 5 24 25 | 23 11 | +0 07 | 3 40 | 3 14 | 12 00 | 20 21 | 20 47 | 17 24 32 | 6 34 24 |
| 14 | 5 28 34 | 23 15 | −0 06 | 3 40 | 3 13 | 12 00 | 20 21 | 20 47 | 17 28 28 | 6 30 28 |
| 15 | 5 32 43 | 23 17 | −0 18 | 3 39 | 3 13 | 12 00 | 20 22 | 20 48 | 17 32 25 | 6 26 32 |
| 16 | 5 36 53 | 23 20 | −0 31 | 3 39 | 3 13 | 12 01 | 20 22 | 20 49 | 17 36 21 | 6 22 36 |
| 17 | 5 41 02 | 23 22 | −0 44 | 3 39 | 3 13 | 12 01 | 20 23 | 20 49 | 17 40 18 | 6 18 40 |
| 18 | 5 45 12 | 23 24 | −0 57 | 3 39 | 3 13 | 12 01 | 20 23 | 20 50 | 17 44 14 | 6 14 44 |
| 19 | 5 49 21 | 23 25 | −1 10 | 3 39 | 3 13 | 12 01 | 20 23 | 20 50 | 17 48 11 | 6 10 48 |
| 20 | 5 53 31 | 23 26 | −1 23 | 3 39 | 3 13 | 12 01 | 20 24 | 20 50 | 17 52 08 | 6 06 52 |
| 21 | 5 57 40 | 23 26 | −1 36 | 3 40 | 3 13 | 12 02 | 20 24 | 20 50 | 17 56 04 | 6 02 56 |
| 22 | 6 01 50 | 23 26 | −1 49 | 3 40 | 3 13 | 12 02 | 20 24 | 20 51 | 18 00 01 | 5 59 00 |
| 23 | 6 05 59 | 23 26 | −2 02 | 3 40 | 3 14 | 12 02 | 20 24 | 20 51 | 18 03 57 | 5 55 04 |
| 24 | 6 10 09 | 23 25 | −2 15 | 3 40 | 3 14 | 12 02 | 20 24 | 20 51 | 18 07 54 | 5 51 09 |
| 25 | 6 14 18 | 23 24 | −2 28 | 3 41 | 3 14 | 12 03 | 20 24 | 20 51 | 18 11 50 | 5 47 13 |
| 26 | 6 18 27 | 23 22 | −2 41 | 3 41 | 3 15 | 12 03 | 20 24 | 20 51 | 18 15 47 | 5 43 17 |
| 27 | 6 22 37 | 23 20 | −2 53 | 3 42 | 3 15 | 12 03 | 20 24 | 20 50 | 18 19 43 | 5 39 21 |
| 28 | 6 26 46 | 23 18 | −3 06 | 3 42 | 3 16 | 12 03 | 20 24 | 20 50 | 18 23 40 | 5 35 25 |
| 29 | 6 30 54 | 23 15 | −3 18 | 3 43 | 3 17 | 12 03 | 20 24 | 20 50 | 18 27 37 | 5 31 29 |
| 30 | 6 35 03 | 23 12 | −3 30 | 3 43 | 3 17 | 12 04 | 20 23 | 20 49 | 18 31 33 | 5 27 33 |

### Duration of Twilight (in minutes)

| *Latitude* | 52° | 56° | 52° | 56° | 52° | 56° | 52° | 56° |
|---|---|---|---|---|---|---|---|---|
| | 1 June | | 11 June | | 21 June | | 31 June | |
| *Civil* | 46 | 58 | 48 | 61 | 49 | 63 | 48 | 61 |
| *Nautical* | 116 | TAN | 124 | TAN | 127 | TAN | 124 | TAN |
| *Astronomical* | TAN | TAN | TAN | TAN | TAN | TAN | TAN | TAN |

### The Night Sky

*Mercury*, is at greatest western elongation on the 21st, but the long duration of twilight renders observation impossible.

*Venus*, magnitude -4.0, is visible as a brilliant object in the western sky in the evenings. Although it is continuing to increase its eastern elongation from the Sun, the period available for observation actually decreases slightly during the month because it is moving southwards in declination and also because the Sun is setting about a quarter of an hour later at the end of the month than it is at the beginning. On the evening of the 3rd Venus passes 1.6 degrees north of Jupiter, while on the 9th it passes 5 degrees south of Pollux.

*Mars* is too close to the Sun for observation.

*Jupiter*, magnitude -1.9, is coming towards the end of its period of visibility and will only be detected during the first half of the month, low in the western sky for a diminishing period after sunset. The waxing crescent Moon is near Jupiter on the evenings of the 12th and 13th.

*Saturn* passes through conjunction on the 9th and thus remains too close to the Sun for observation throughout the month.

## THE MOON

| Day | RA | Dec. | Hor. par. | Semi-diam | Sun's co-long. | PA of Bright Limb | Phase | Age | Rise 52° | Rise 56° | Transit | Set 52° | Set 56° |
|---|---|---|---|---|---|---|---|---|---|---|---|---|---|
| | h m | ° | ′ | ′ | ° | ° | % | d | h m | h m | h m | h m | h m |
| **1** | 21 28 | –19.8 | 55.3 | 15.1 | 153 | 74 | 69 | 19.6 | 0 42 | 1 01 | 5 00 | 9 27 | 9 0 |
| **2** | 22 16 | –16.1 | 54.8 | 14.9 | 165 | 70 | 60 | 20.6 | 1 04 | 1 18 | 5 46 | 10 38 | 10 2 |
| **3** | 23 03 | –11.8 | 54.4 | 14.8 | 177 | 67 | 50 | 21.6 | 1 21 | 1 31 | 6 28 | 11 47 | 11 3 |
| **4** | 23 47 | – 7.1 | 54.2 | 14.8 | 189 | 65 | 41 | 22.6 | 1 36 | 1 42 | 7 10 | 12 55 | 12 5 |
| **5** | 0 30 | – 2.2 | 54.2 | 14.8 | 202 | 65 | 32 | 23.6 | 1 50 | 1 52 | 7 50 | 14 03 | 14 0 |
| **6** | 1 13 | + 2.8 | 54.4 | 14.8 | 214 | 65 | 23 | 24.6 | 2 03 | 2 01 | 8 30 | 15 11 | 15 1 |
| **7** | 1 57 | + 7.8 | 54.7 | 14.9 | 226 | 66 | 16 | 25.6 | 2 18 | 2 11 | 9 12 | 16 21 | 16 3 |
| **8** | 2 43 | +12.5 | 55.1 | 15.0 | 238 | 68 | 9 | 26.6 | 2 34 | 2 23 | 9 56 | 17 34 | 17 4 |
| **9** | 3 31 | +16.9 | 55.6 | 15.1 | 251 | 71 | 4 | 27.6 | 2 54 | 2 38 | 10 43 | 18 48 | 19 0 |
| **10** | 4 22 | +20.5 | 56.1 | 15.3 | 263 | 76 | 1 | 28.6 | 3 19 | 2 58 | 11 33 | 20 01 | 20 2 |
| **11** | 5 16 | +23.3 | 56.7 | 15.5 | 275 | 203 | 0 | 0.0 | 3 53 | 3 28 | 12 27 | 21 10 | 21 3 |
| **12** | 6 14 | +24.8 | 57.3 | 15.6 | 287 | 265 | 1 | 1.0 | 4 39 | 4 10 | 13 24 | 22 10 | 22 3 |
| **13** | 7 13 | +24.9 | 57.8 | 15.7 | 300 | 272 | 5 | 2.0 | 5 38 | 5 10 | 14 22 | 22 57 | 23 2 |
| **14** | 8 13 | +23.6 | 58.2 | 15.9 | 312 | 278 | 10 | 3.0 | 6 50 | 6 25 | 15 19 | 23 34 | 23 5 |
| **15** | 9 11 | +20.8 | 58.6 | 16.0 | 324 | 284 | 18 | 4.0 | 8 10 | 7 50 | 16 15 | — | — |
| **16** | 10 08 | +16.8 | 58.9 | 16.0 | 336 | 288 | 28 | 5.0 | 9 33 | 9 19 | 17 08 | 0 01 | 0 1 |
| **17** | 11 02 | +11.9 | 59.1 | 16.1 | 349 | 291 | 38 | 6.0 | 10 57 | 10 48 | 17 59 | 0 24 | 0 3 |
| **18** | 11 55 | + 6.2 | 59.3 | 16.2 | 1 | 294 | 50 | 7.0 | 12 20 | 12 17 | 18 48 | 0 42 | 0 4 |
| **19** | 12 46 | + 0.3 | 59.4 | 16.2 | 13 | 294 | 61 | 8.0 | 13 43 | 13 45 | 19 37 | 0 59 | 0 5 |
| **20** | 13 38 | – 5.7 | 59.3 | 16.2 | 25 | 293 | 72 | 9.0 | 15 06 | 15 15 | 20 28 | 1 17 | 1 1 |
| **21** | 14 31 | –11.4 | 59.2 | 16.1 | 37 | 291 | 82 | 10.0 | 16 30 | 16 45 | 21 20 | 1 35 | 1 2 |
| **22** | 15 25 | –16.4 | 59.0 | 16.1 | 50 | 287 | 90 | 11.0 | 17 54 | 18 14 | 22 14 | 1 58 | 1 4 |
| **23** | 16 22 | –20.5 | 58.6 | 16.0 | 62 | 282 | 96 | 12.0 | 19 14 | 19 40 | 23 11 | 2 25 | 2 0 |
| **24** | 17 20 | –23.4 | 58.1 | 15.8 | 74 | 273 | 99 | 13.0 | 20 25 | 20 55 | — | 3 02 | 2 3 |
| **25** | 18 20 | –24.9 | 57.6 | 15.7 | 86 | 140 | 100 | 14.0 | 21 24 | 21 53 | 0 08 | 3 49 | 3 2 |
| **26** | 19 18 | –24.9 | 56.9 | 15.5 | 98 | 93 | 99 | 15.0 | 22 09 | 22 35 | 1 05 | 4 48 | 4 1 |
| **27** | 20 15 | –23.5 | 56.3 | 15.3 | 111 | 85 | 95 | 16.0 | 22 42 | 23 04 | 2 00 | 5 56 | 5 3 |
| **28** | 21 09 | –20.9 | 55.7 | 15.2 | 123 | 79 | 90 | 17.0 | 23 07 | 23 23 | 2 51 | 7 08 | 6 4 |
| **29** | 21 59 | –17.5 | 55.1 | 15.0 | 135 | 74 | 83 | 18.0 | 23 26 | 23 38 | 3 39 | 8 20 | 8 0 |
| **30** | 22 47 | –13.3 | 54.7 | 14.9 | 147 | 71 | 75 | 19.0 | 23 42 | 23 50 | 4 23 | 9 31 | 9 2 |

## MERCURY

| Day | RA | Dec. | Diam. | Phase | Transit | 5° high 52° | 5° high 56° |
|---|---|---|---|---|---|---|---|
| | h m | ° | ″ | % | h m | h m | h m |
| 1 | 4 08 | +17.9 | 12 | 2 | 11 28 | 4 28 | 4 16 |
| 3 | 4 04 | +17.3 | 12 | 4 | 11 17 | 4 20 | 4 09 |
| 5 | 4 02 | +16.9 | 12 | 6 | 11 07 | 4 13 | 4 02 |
| 7 | 4 01 | +16.6 | 11 | 9 | 10 58 | 4 05 | 3 54 |
| 9 | 4 00 | +16.4 | 11 | 12 | 10 50 | 3 58 | 3 47 |
| 11 | 4 01 | +16.4 | 10 | 16 | 10 43 | 3 51 | 3 41 |
| 13 | 4 03 | +16.5 | 10 | 19 | 10 38 | 3 45 | 3 34 |
| 15 | 4 07 | +16.7 | 9 | 23 | 10 33 | 3 39 | 3 28 |
| 17 | 4 11 | +17.1 | 9 | 27 | 10 30 | 3 34 | 3 22 |
| 19 | 4 17 | +17.5 | 9 | 31 | 10 28 | 3 29 | 3 17 |
| 21 | 4 23 | +18.0 | 8 | 35 | 10 27 | 3 25 | 3 13 |
| 23 | 4 31 | +18.6 | 8 | 40 | 10 27 | 3 22 | 3 09 |
| 25 | 4 40 | +19.2 | 8 | 45 | 10 28 | 3 19 | 3 05 |
| 27 | 4 50 | +19.9 | 7 | 49 | 10 31 | 3 17 | 3 03 |
| 29 | 5 01 | +20.5 | 7 | 55 | 10 34 | 3 17 | 3 02 |
| 31 | 5 13 | +21.2 | 7 | 60 | 10 39 | 3 17 | 3 01 |

## VENUS

| Day | RA | Dec. | Diam. | Phase | Transit | 5° high 52° | 5° high 56° |
|---|---|---|---|---|---|---|---|
| | h m | ° | ″ | % | h m | h m | h m |
| 1 | 7 00 | +24.6 | 13 | 82 | 14 24 | 22 05 | 22 2 |
| 6 | 7 26 | +23.9 | 13 | 80 | 14 30 | 22 07 | 22 2 |
| 11 | 7 51 | +23.0 | 14 | 79 | 14 35 | 22 06 | 22 2 |
| 16 | 8 16 | +21.8 | 14 | 77 | 14 40 | 22 04 | 22 2 |
| 21 | 8 40 | +20.4 | 14 | 75 | 14 45 | 21 59 | 22 1 |
| 26 | 9 04 | +18.7 | 15 | 74 | 14 49 | 21 53 | 22 0 |
| 31 | 9 27 | +16.9 | 15 | 72 | 14 52 | 21 46 | 21 5 |

## MARS

| Day | RA | Dec. | Diam. | Phase | Transit | 5° high 52° | 5° high 56° |
|---|---|---|---|---|---|---|---|
| 1 | 6 10 | +24.4 | 4 | 99 | 13 32 | 21 13 | 21 3 |
| 6 | 6 25 | +24.3 | 4 | 99 | 13 27 | 21 07 | 21 2 |
| 11 | 6 39 | +24.2 | 4 | 99 | 13 22 | 21 00 | 21 2 |
| 16 | 6 53 | +23.9 | 4 | 99 | 13 16 | 20 53 | 21 1 |
| 21 | 7 07 | +23.6 | 4 | 99 | 13 11 | 20 45 | 21 0 |
| 26 | 7 21 | +23.2 | 4 | 99 | 13 05 | 20 37 | 20 5 |
| 31 | 7 35 | +22.7 | 4 | 100 | 12 59 | 20 28 | 20 4 |

## UNSET AND SUNRISE

| London | | | | Bristol | | | | Birmingham | | | | Manchester | | | | Newcastle | | | | Glasgow | | | | Belfast | | | |
|---|---|---|---|---|---|---|---|---|---|---|---|---|---|---|---|---|---|---|---|---|---|---|---|---|---|---|---|
| 0°05′ | | 51°30′ | | 2°35′ | | 51°28′ | | 1°55′ | | 52°28′ | | 2°15′ | | 53°28′ | | 1°37′ | | 54°59′ | | 4°14′ | | 55°52′ | | 5°56′ | | 54°35′ | |
| h | m | h | m | h | m | h | m | h | m | h | m | h | m | h | m | h | m | h | m | h | m | h | m | h | m | h | m |
| 3 | 49 | 20 | 08 | 3 | 59 | 20 | 18 | 3 | 51 | 20 | 20 | 3 | 47 | 20 | 27 | 3 | 35 | 20 | 34 | 3 | 40 | 20 | 50 | 3 | 55 | 20 | 49 |
| 3 | 48 | 20 | 09 | 3 | 58 | 20 | 19 | 3 | 50 | 20 | 21 | 3 | 46 | 20 | 28 | 3 | 34 | 20 | 35 | 3 | 39 | 20 | 52 | 3 | 54 | 20 | 50 |
| 3 | 47 | 20 | 10 | 3 | 58 | 20 | 20 | 3 | 50 | 20 | 22 | 3 | 45 | 20 | 29 | 3 | 33 | 20 | 36 | 3 | 38 | 20 | 53 | 3 | 53 | 20 | 51 |
| 3 | 47 | 20 | 11 | 3 | 57 | 20 | 21 | 3 | 49 | 20 | 23 | 3 | 45 | 20 | 31 | 3 | 33 | 20 | 38 | 3 | 37 | 20 | 54 | 3 | 52 | 20 | 52 |
| 3 | 46 | 20 | 12 | 3 | 56 | 20 | 22 | 3 | 48 | 20 | 24 | 3 | 44 | 20 | 32 | 3 | 32 | 20 | 39 | 3 | 36 | 20 | 55 | 3 | 52 | 20 | 53 |
| 3 | 46 | 20 | 13 | 3 | 56 | 20 | 23 | 3 | 48 | 20 | 25 | 3 | 43 | 20 | 33 | 3 | 31 | 20 | 40 | 3 | 35 | 20 | 56 | 3 | 51 | 20 | 54 |
| 3 | 45 | 20 | 14 | 3 | 55 | 20 | 23 | 3 | 47 | 20 | 26 | 3 | 43 | 20 | 34 | 3 | 30 | 20 | 41 | 3 | 35 | 20 | 57 | 3 | 50 | 20 | 55 |
| 3 | 45 | 20 | 14 | 3 | 55 | 20 | 24 | 3 | 47 | 20 | 27 | 3 | 42 | 20 | 34 | 3 | 30 | 20 | 42 | 3 | 34 | 20 | 58 | 3 | 50 | 20 | 56 |
| 3 | 44 | 20 | 15 | 3 | 54 | 20 | 25 | 3 | 46 | 20 | 28 | 3 | 41 | 20 | 35 | 3 | 29 | 20 | 43 | 3 | 33 | 20 | 59 | 3 | 49 | 20 | 57 |
| 3 | 44 | 20 | 16 | 3 | 54 | 20 | 26 | 3 | 46 | 20 | 29 | 3 | 41 | 20 | 36 | 3 | 29 | 20 | 43 | 3 | 33 | 21 | 00 | 3 | 49 | 20 | 58 |
| 3 | 43 | 20 | 17 | 3 | 54 | 20 | 27 | 3 | 45 | 20 | 30 | 3 | 41 | 20 | 37 | 3 | 28 | 20 | 44 | 3 | 32 | 21 | 01 | 3 | 48 | 20 | 59 |
| 3 | 43 | 20 | 17 | 3 | 53 | 20 | 27 | 3 | 45 | 20 | 30 | 3 | 40 | 20 | 38 | 3 | 28 | 20 | 45 | 3 | 32 | 21 | 02 | 3 | 48 | 21 | 00 |
| 3 | 43 | 20 | 18 | 3 | 53 | 20 | 28 | 3 | 45 | 20 | 31 | 3 | 40 | 20 | 38 | 3 | 27 | 20 | 46 | 3 | 32 | 21 | 03 | 3 | 47 | 21 | 00 |
| 3 | 43 | 20 | 19 | 3 | 53 | 20 | 28 | 3 | 45 | 20 | 31 | 3 | 40 | 20 | 39 | 3 | 27 | 20 | 46 | 3 | 31 | 21 | 03 | 3 | 47 | 21 | 01 |
| 3 | 43 | 20 | 19 | 3 | 53 | 20 | 29 | 3 | 44 | 20 | 32 | 3 | 40 | 20 | 39 | 3 | 27 | 20 | 47 | 3 | 31 | 21 | 04 | 3 | 47 | 21 | 02 |
| 3 | 42 | 20 | 20 | 3 | 53 | 20 | 29 | 3 | 44 | 20 | 33 | 3 | 40 | 20 | 40 | 3 | 27 | 20 | 48 | 3 | 31 | 21 | 05 | 3 | 47 | 21 | 02 |
| 3 | 42 | 20 | 20 | 3 | 53 | 20 | 30 | 3 | 44 | 20 | 33 | 3 | 39 | 20 | 40 | 3 | 27 | 20 | 48 | 3 | 31 | 21 | 05 | 3 | 47 | 21 | 03 |
| 3 | 42 | 20 | 20 | 3 | 53 | 20 | 30 | 3 | 44 | 20 | 33 | 3 | 39 | 20 | 41 | 3 | 27 | 20 | 48 | 3 | 31 | 21 | 05 | 3 | 47 | 21 | 03 |
| 3 | 43 | 20 | 21 | 3 | 53 | 20 | 31 | 3 | 44 | 20 | 34 | 3 | 39 | 20 | 41 | 3 | 27 | 20 | 49 | 3 | 31 | 21 | 06 | 3 | 47 | 21 | 03 |
| 3 | 43 | 20 | 21 | 3 | 53 | 20 | 31 | 3 | 44 | 20 | 34 | 3 | 40 | 20 | 41 | 3 | 27 | 20 | 49 | 3 | 31 | 21 | 06 | 3 | 47 | 21 | 04 |
| 3 | 43 | 20 | 21 | 3 | 53 | 20 | 31 | 3 | 45 | 20 | 34 | 3 | 40 | 20 | 42 | 3 | 27 | 20 | 49 | 3 | 31 | 21 | 06 | 3 | 47 | 21 | 04 |
| 3 | 43 | 20 | 21 | 3 | 53 | 20 | 31 | 3 | 45 | 20 | 34 | 3 | 40 | 20 | 42 | 3 | 27 | 20 | 50 | 3 | 31 | 21 | 06 | 3 | 47 | 21 | 04 |
| 3 | 43 | 20 | 22 | 3 | 54 | 20 | 31 | 3 | 45 | 20 | 34 | 3 | 40 | 20 | 42 | 3 | 28 | 20 | 50 | 3 | 32 | 21 | 07 | 3 | 48 | 21 | 04 |
| 3 | 44 | 20 | 22 | 3 | 54 | 20 | 31 | 3 | 45 | 20 | 35 | 3 | 41 | 20 | 42 | 3 | 28 | 20 | 50 | 3 | 32 | 21 | 07 | 3 | 48 | 21 | 04 |
| 3 | 44 | 20 | 22 | 3 | 54 | 20 | 31 | 3 | 46 | 20 | 35 | 3 | 41 | 20 | 42 | 3 | 28 | 20 | 50 | 3 | 32 | 21 | 07 | 3 | 48 | 21 | 04 |
| 3 | 44 | 20 | 22 | 3 | 55 | 20 | 31 | 3 | 46 | 20 | 35 | 3 | 41 | 20 | 42 | 3 | 29 | 20 | 50 | 3 | 33 | 21 | 06 | 3 | 49 | 21 | 04 |
| 3 | 45 | 20 | 22 | 3 | 55 | 20 | 31 | 3 | 47 | 20 | 34 | 3 | 42 | 20 | 42 | 3 | 29 | 20 | 49 | 3 | 33 | 21 | 06 | 3 | 49 | 21 | 04 |
| 3 | 45 | 20 | 21 | 3 | 56 | 20 | 31 | 3 | 47 | 20 | 34 | 3 | 42 | 20 | 42 | 3 | 30 | 20 | 49 | 3 | 34 | 21 | 06 | 3 | 50 | 21 | 04 |
| 3 | 46 | 20 | 21 | 3 | 56 | 20 | 31 | 3 | 48 | 20 | 34 | 3 | 43 | 20 | 41 | 3 | 30 | 20 | 49 | 3 | 35 | 21 | 06 | 3 | 51 | 21 | 03 |
| 3 | 47 | 20 | 21 | 3 | 57 | 20 | 31 | 3 | 48 | 20 | 34 | 3 | 44 | 20 | 41 | 3 | 31 | 20 | 49 | 3 | 35 | 21 | 05 | 3 | 51 | 21 | 03 |

## PITER

| y | RA | | Dec. | | Transit | | 5° high | | | |
|---|---|---|---|---|---|---|---|---|---|---|
| | | | | | | | 52° | | 56° | |
| | h | m | ° | ′ | h | m | h | m | h | m |
| | 7 | 12.0 | +22 | 39 | 14 | 33 | 22 | 01 | 22 | 19 |
| | 7 | 20.8 | +22 | 24 | 14 | 02 | 21 | 29 | 21 | 46 |
| | 7 | 30.0 | +22 | 06 | 13 | 32 | 20 | 57 | 21 | 14 |
| | 7 | 39.3 | +21 | 46 | 13 | 02 | 20 | 25 | 20 | 41 |

ameters – equatorial 32 polar 30″

## SATURN

| Day | RA | | Dec. | | Transit | | 5° high | | | |
|---|---|---|---|---|---|---|---|---|---|---|
| | | | | | | | 52° | | 56° | |
| | h | m | ° | ′ | h | m | h | m | h | m |
| 1 | 5 | 05.6 | +21 | 33 | 12 | 27 | 5 | 05 | 4 | 49 |
| 11 | 5 | 11.1 | +21 | 40 | 11 | 53 | 4 | 30 | 4 | 14 |
| 21 | 5 | 16.7 | +21 | 47 | 11 | 19 | 3 | 56 | 3 | 40 |
| 31 | 5 | 22.2 | +21 | 53 | 10 | 45 | 3 | 21 | 3 | 05 |

Diameters – equatorial 16″ polar 15″
Rings – major axis 37″ minor axis 17″

## RANUS

| y | RA | | Dec. | | Transit | | 10° high | | | |
|---|---|---|---|---|---|---|---|---|---|---|
| | | | | | | | 52° | | 56° | |
| | h | m | ° | ′ | h | m | h | m | h | m |
| | 22 | 05.0 | –12 | 35 | 5 | 27 | 1 | 48 | 2 | 09 |
| | 22 | 04.9 | –12 | 35 | 4 | 47 | 1 | 08 | 1 | 30 |
| | 22 | 04.5 | –12 | 38 | 4 | 08 | 0 | 29 | 0 | 51 |
| | 22 | 03.8 | –12 | 42 | 3 | 28 | 23 | 45 | 0 | 11 |

ameter 4″

## NEPTUNE

| Day | RA | | Dec. | | Transit | | 10° high | | | |
|---|---|---|---|---|---|---|---|---|---|---|
| | | | | | | | 52° | | 56° | |
| | h | m | ° | ′ | h | m | h | m | h | m |
| 1 | 20 | 53.3 | –17 | 25 | 4 | 15 | 1 | 13 | 1 | 45 |
| 11 | 20 | 52.8 | –17 | 27 | 3 | 36 | 0 | 33 | 1 | 05 |
| 21 | 20 | 52.1 | –17 | 30 | 2 | 56 | 23 | 50 | 0 | 26 |
| 31 | 20 | 51.3 | –17 | 34 | 2 | 15 | 23 | 10 | 23 | 42 |

Diameter 2″

# July 2002

SEVENTH MONTH, 31 DAYS, *Julius* Caesar, formerly *Quintilis*, fifth month of Roman pre-Julia
calendar

| | | | |
|---|---|---|---|
| **1** | *Monday* | Robert Mitchum d. 1997. Battle of the Boyne 1690 | *week* 26 *day* 18 |
| **2** | *Tuesday* | Sir Robert Peel d. 1850. Battle of Marston Moor 1644 | 18 |
| **3** | *Wednesday* | **St Thomas.** Ken Russell b. 1927 | 18 |
| **4** | *Thursday* | Nathaniel Hawthorne b. 1804. James Monroe d. 1831 | 18 |
| **5** | *Friday* | George Borrow b. 1803. Walter Gropius d. 1969 | 18 |
| **6** | *Saturday* | George W Bush b. 1946. Aneurin Bevan d. 1960 | 18 |
| **7** | *Sunday* | **6th S. after Trinity.** Georg S. Ohm d. 1854 | 18 |
| **8** | *Monday* | Count Ferdinand von Zeppelin b. 1838. Il-sung Kim d. 1994 | *week* 27 *day* 18 |
| **9** | *Tuesday* | David Hockney b. 1937. Jan Van Eyck d. 1441 | 19 |
| **10** | *Wednesday* | Marcel Proust b. 1871. George Stubbs d. 1806 | 19 |
| **11** | *Thursday* | King Robert I b. 1274. Lord Laurence Olivier d. 1989 | 19 |
| **12** | *Friday* | Amedeo Modigliani b. 1884. Kenneth More d. 1982 | 19 |
| **13** | *Saturday* | Sir Reginald Goodall b. 1901. Titus Oates d. 1705 | 19 |
| **14** | *Sunday* | **7th S. after Trinity.** Madame de Stael Anne Necker d. 1817 | 19 |
| **15** | *Monday* | Sir Harrison Birtwistle b. 1934. Royal Society received its charter 1662 | *week* 28 *day* 19 |
| **16** | *Tuesday* | Baroness Llewelyn-Davies of Hastoe b. 1915. Sir Stephen Spender d. 1995 | 19 |
| **17** | *Wednesday* | Jean Muir b. 1928. Adam Smith d. 1790 | 19 |
| **18** | *Thursday* | William Makepeace Thackeray b. 1811. Spanish Civil War began 1936 | 19 |
| **19** | *Friday* | Sir James Goldsmith d. 1997. *Mary Rose* sank 1545 | 20 |
| **20** | *Saturday* | Elisabeth Powell b. 1901. Andrew Lang d. 1912 | 20 |
| **21** | *Sunday* | **8th S. after Trinity.** Salvator Rosa b. 1615 | 20 |
| **22** | *Monday* | **Mary Magdalene.** Michael Denison d. 1998 | *week* 29 *day* 20 |
| **23** | *Tuesday* | Raymond Chandler b. 1888. Marshal Philippe Pétain d. 1951 | 20 |
| **24** | *Wednesday* | E. F. Benson b. 1867. Isaac Bashevis Singer d. 1991 | 20 |
| **25** | *Thursday* | **St James.** First cross-channel flight by Bleriot 1909 | 20 |
| **26** | *Friday* | Lord Thorneycroft b. 1909. George Bernard Shaw b. 1856 | 20 |
| **27** | *Saturday* | James Mason d. 1984. Sealing of charter establishing the Bank of England 1694 | 20 |
| **28** | *Sunday* | **9th S. after Trinity.** Sir Garfield Sobers b. 1936 | 20 |
| **29** | *Monday* | Benito Mussolini b. 1883. Frans Hals d. 1666 | *week* 30 *day* 21 |
| **30** | *Tuesday* | Emily Brontë b. 1818. Claudette Colbert d. 1996 | 21 |
| **31** | *Wednesday* | *Trinity Law Sittings end.* Saint Ignatius Loyola d. 1556 | 21 |

## Astronomical Phenomena

| d | h | |
|---|---|---|
| 2 | 12 | Saturn in conjunction with Mercury. Saturn 0°.2 N. |
| 3 | 13 | Jupiter in conjunction with Mars. Jupiter 0°.8 S. |
| 6 | 04 | Earth at aphelion (152 million km.) |
| 8 | 12 | Saturn in conjunction with Moon. Saturn 2° S. |
| 9 | 09 | Mercury in conjunction with Moon. Mercury 2° S. |
| 10 | 23 | Jupiter in conjunction with Moon. Jupiter 3° S. |
| 11 | 04 | Mars in conjunction with Moon. Mars 2° S. |
| 13 | 15 | Venus in conjunction with Moon. Venus 4° S. |
| 20 | 01 | Jupiter in conjunction |
| 20 | 16 | Jupiter in conjunction with Mercury. Jupiter 1° S. |
| 21 | 02 | Mercury in superior conjunction |
| 23 | 00 | Sun's longitude 120°♌ |
| 25 | 15 | Mars in conjunction with Mercury. Mars 0°.6 S. |

## Minima of Algol

| d | h | d | h | d | h |
|---|---|---|---|---|---|
| 1 | 15.2 | 13 | 02.5 | 24 | 13.7 |
| 4 | 12.0 | 15 | 23.3 | 27 | 10.5 |
| 7 | 08.8 | 18 | 20.1 | 30 | 07.3 |
| 10 | 05.6 | 21 | 16.9 | | |

## Constellations

The following constellations are near the meridian at

| | d | h | | d | h |
|---|---|---|---|---|---|
| June | 1 | 24 | July | 16 | 21 |
| June | 15 | 23 | August | 1 | 20 |
| July | 1 | 22 | August | 16 | 19 |

Ursa Minor, Draco, Corona, Hercules, Lyra, Serper
Ophiuchus, Libra, Scorpius and Sagittarius

## The Moon

| Phases, Apsides and Node | d | h |
|---|---|---|
| ☾ Last Quarter | 2 | 17 |
| ● New Moon | 10 | 10 |
| ☽ First Quarter | 17 | 04 |
| ○ Full Moon | 24 | 09 |
| Apogee (404,171km) | 2 | 07 |
| Perigee (367,876km) | 14 | 13 |
| Apogee (404,707km) | 30 | 01 |

Mean longitude of ascending node on July 1, 77°

## HE SUN

S.D 16′.1

| ry | Right Ascension | Dec. + | Equation of Time | Rise 52° | Rise 56° | Transit | Set 52° | Set 56° | Sidereal time | Transit of First Point of Aries |
|---|---|---|---|---|---|---|---|---|---|---|
| | h m s | ° ′ | m s | h m | h m | h m | h m | h m | h m s | h m s |
| 1 | 6 39 11 | 23 08 | −3 42 | 3 44 | 3 18 | 12 04 | 20 23 | 20 49 | 18 35 30 | 5 23 37 |
| 2 | 6 43 19 | 23 04 | −3 53 | 3 45 | 3 19 | 12 04 | 20 23 | 20 49 | 18 39 26 | 5 19 41 |
| 3 | 6 47 27 | 22 59 | −4 04 | 3 46 | 3 20 | 12 04 | 20 22 | 20 48 | 18 43 23 | 5 15 45 |
| 4 | 6 51 35 | 22 55 | −4 16 | 3 46 | 3 21 | 12 04 | 20 22 | 20 47 | 18 47 19 | 5 11 49 |
| 5 | 6 55 42 | 22 49 | −4 26 | 3 47 | 3 22 | 12 05 | 20 21 | 20 47 | 18 51 16 | 5 07 54 |
| 6 | 6 59 49 | 22 44 | −4 37 | 3 48 | 3 23 | 12 05 | 20 21 | 20 46 | 18 55 12 | 5 03 58 |
| 7 | 7 03 56 | 22 38 | −4 47 | 3 49 | 3 24 | 12 05 | 20 20 | 20 45 | 18 59 09 | 5 00 02 |
| 8 | 7 08 02 | 22 31 | −4 57 | 3 50 | 3 25 | 12 05 | 20 20 | 20 44 | 19 03 06 | 4 56 06 |
| 9 | 7 12 08 | 22 24 | −5 06 | 3 51 | 3 26 | 12 05 | 20 19 | 20 43 | 19 07 02 | 4 52 10 |
| 10 | 7 16 14 | 22 17 | −5 15 | 3 52 | 3 28 | 12 05 | 20 18 | 20 42 | 19 10 59 | 4 48 14 |
| 11 | 7 20 19 | 22 09 | −5 24 | 3 53 | 3 29 | 12 05 | 20 17 | 20 41 | 19 14 55 | 4 44 18 |
| 12 | 7 24 24 | 22 01 | −5 32 | 3 54 | 3 30 | 12 06 | 20 16 | 20 40 | 19 18 52 | 4 40 22 |
| 13 | 7 28 28 | 21 53 | −5 39 | 3 55 | 3 32 | 12 06 | 20 15 | 20 39 | 19 22 48 | 4 36 26 |
| 14 | 7 32 31 | 21 44 | −5 47 | 3 56 | 3 33 | 12 06 | 20 15 | 20 38 | 19 26 45 | 4 32 30 |
| 15 | 7 36 35 | 21 35 | −5 53 | 3 58 | 3 34 | 12 06 | 20 14 | 20 36 | 19 30 41 | 4 28 34 |
| 16 | 7 40 37 | 21 26 | −5 59 | 3 59 | 3 36 | 12 06 | 20 12 | 20 35 | 19 34 38 | 4 24 38 |
| 17 | 7 44 40 | 21 16 | −6 05 | 4 00 | 3 37 | 12 06 | 20 11 | 20 34 | 19 38 35 | 4 20 43 |
| 18 | 7 48 41 | 21 06 | −6 10 | 4 01 | 3 39 | 12 06 | 20 10 | 20 32 | 19 42 31 | 4 16 47 |
| 19 | 7 52 42 | 20 55 | −6 15 | 4 03 | 3 41 | 12 06 | 20 09 | 20 31 | 19 46 28 | 4 12 51 |
| 20 | 7 56 43 | 20 44 | −6 18 | 4 04 | 3 42 | 12 06 | 20 08 | 20 29 | 19 50 24 | 4 08 55 |
| 21 | 8 00 43 | 20 33 | −6 22 | 4 05 | 3 44 | 12 06 | 20 07 | 20 28 | 19 54 21 | 4 04 59 |
| 22 | 8 04 42 | 20 21 | −6 25 | 4 07 | 3 46 | 12 06 | 20 05 | 20 26 | 19 58 17 | 4 01 03 |
| 23 | 8 08 41 | 20 09 | −6 27 | 4 08 | 3 47 | 12 06 | 20 04 | 20 25 | 20 02 14 | 3 57 07 |
| 24 | 8 12 39 | 19 57 | −6 29 | 4 09 | 3 49 | 12 06 | 20 03 | 20 23 | 20 06 11 | 3 53 11 |
| 25 | 8 16 37 | 19 44 | −6 30 | 4 11 | 3 51 | 12 07 | 20 01 | 20 21 | 20 10 07 | 3 49 15 |
| 26 | 8 20 34 | 19 31 | −6 30 | 4 12 | 3 52 | 12 07 | 20 00 | 20 19 | 20 14 04 | 3 45 19 |
| 27 | 8 24 30 | 19 18 | −6 30 | 4 14 | 3 54 | 12 07 | 19 58 | 20 18 | 20 18 00 | 3 41 23 |
| 28 | 8 28 26 | 19 04 | −6 29 | 4 15 | 3 56 | 12 06 | 19 57 | 20 16 | 20 21 57 | 3 37 28 |
| 29 | 8 32 21 | 18 50 | −6 28 | 4 17 | 3 58 | 12 06 | 19 55 | 20 14 | 20 25 53 | 3 33 32 |
| 30 | 8 36 16 | 18 36 | −6 26 | 4 18 | 4 00 | 12 06 | 19 54 | 20 12 | 20 29 50 | 3 29 36 |
| 31 | 8 40 10 | 18 22 | −6 24 | 4 20 | 4 02 | 12 06 | 19 52 | 20 10 | 20 33 46 | 3 25 40 |

## URATION OF TWILIGHT (in minutes)

| *atitude* | 52° | 56° | 52° | 56° | 52° | 56° | 52° | 56° |
|---|---|---|---|---|---|---|---|---|
| | 1 July | | 11 July | | 21 July | | 31 July | |
| *ivil* | 48 | 61 | 47 | 58 | 44 | 53 | 42 | 49 |
| *autical* | 124 | TAN | 117 | TAN | 107 | 146 | 98 | 123 |
| *stronomical* | TAN | TAN | TAN | TAN | TAN | TAN | 182 | TAN |

## HE NIGHT SKY

*lercury* passes through superior conjunction on the 21st nd therefore is unsuitably placed for observation roughout the month.

*Venus* continues to be visible as a brilliant object in the estern sky after sunset. Its magnitude is -4.1. The rescent Moon, 3 days old, passes within 4 degrees of enus on the evening of the 13th. On the 10th Venus asses 1 degree north of Regulus.

*Mars* continues to be unsuitably placed for observation.

*Jupiter* passes through conjunction on the 20th and is erefore too close to the Sun for observation.

*Saturn* is too close to the Sun for observation at first but as it slowly emerges from the morning twilight it may be detected by the middle of the month, low above the eastern horizon, for a short while before the brightening sky inhibits observation. Its magnitude is +0.1.

Twilight. Reference to the section above shows that astronomical twilight lasts all night for a period around the summer solstice (i.e. in June and July), even in southern England. Under these conditions the sky never gets completely dark as the Sun is always less than 18 degrees below the horizon.

## THE MOON

| Day | RA | | Dec. | Hor. par. | Semi-diam | Sun's co-long. | PA of Bright Limb | Phase | Age | Rise 52° | | Rise 56° | | Transit | | Set 52° | | Set 56° | |
|---|---|---|---|---|---|---|---|---|---|---|---|---|---|---|---|---|---|---|---|
| | h | m | ° | ′ | ′ | ° | ° | % | d | h | m | h | m | h | m | h | m | h | m |
| **1** | 23 | 32 | − 8.7 | 54.4 | 14.8 | 159 | 68 | 66 | 20.0 | 23 | 56 | — | | 5 | 05 | 10 | 40 | 10 | 3 |
| **2** | 0 | 16 | − 3.8 | 54.3 | 14.8 | 172 | 67 | 57 | 21.0 | — | | 0 | 00 | 5 | 46 | 11 | 48 | 11 | 4 |
| **3** | 0 | 59 | + 1.2 | 54.3 | 14.8 | 184 | 67 | 47 | 22.0 | 0 | 10 | 0 | 09 | 6 | 26 | 12 | 56 | 12 | 5 |
| **4** | 1 | 42 | + 6.1 | 54.5 | 14.8 | 196 | 68 | 38 | 23.0 | 0 | 24 | 0 | 19 | 7 | 06 | 14 | 04 | 14 | 1 |
| **5** | 2 | 27 | +11.0 | 54.9 | 14.9 | 208 | 70 | 29 | 24.0 | 0 | 39 | 0 | 29 | 7 | 49 | 15 | 15 | 15 | 2 |
| **6** | 3 | 13 | +15.4 | 55.4 | 15.1 | 221 | 73 | 20 | 25.0 | 0 | 57 | 0 | 43 | 8 | 34 | 16 | 28 | 16 | 4 |
| **7** | 4 | 03 | +19.3 | 56.0 | 15.3 | 233 | 77 | 13 | 26.0 | 1 | 20 | 1 | 01 | 9 | 23 | 17 | 42 | 18 | 0 |
| **8** | 4 | 57 | +22.4 | 56.7 | 15.4 | 245 | 83 | 7 | 27.0 | 1 | 50 | 1 | 26 | 10 | 16 | 18 | 54 | 19 | 2 |
| **9** | 5 | 54 | +24.4 | 57.4 | 15.6 | 257 | 92 | 2 | 28.0 | 2 | 30 | 2 | 02 | 11 | 12 | 19 | 58 | 20 | 2 |
| **10** | 6 | 53 | +25.0 | 58.1 | 15.8 | 270 | 116 | 0 | 29.0 | 3 | 25 | 2 | 56 | 12 | 11 | 20 | 52 | 21 | [illegible] |
| **11** | 7 | 54 | +24.1 | 58.6 | 16.0 | 282 | 257 | 0 | 0.6 | 4 | 34 | 4 | 07 | 13 | 10 | 21 | 33 | 21 | 5 |
| **12** | 8 | 54 | +21.7 | 59.1 | 16.1 | 294 | 275 | 3 | 1.6 | 5 | 53 | 5 | 31 | 14 | 08 | 22 | 05 | 22 | 2 |
| **13** | 9 | 53 | +17.9 | 59.4 | 16.2 | 306 | 283 | 9 | 2.6 | 7 | 18 | 7 | 02 | 15 | 03 | 22 | 29 | 22 | 4 |
| **14** | 10 | 49 | +13.1 | 59.6 | 16.2 | 319 | 288 | 16 | 3.6 | 8 | 43 | 8 | 33 | 15 | 55 | 22 | 49 | 22 | 5 |
| **15** | 11 | 43 | + 7.5 | 59.6 | 16.2 | 331 | 291 | 26 | 4.6 | 10 | 07 | 10 | 03 | 16 | 46 | 23 | 06 | 23 | 0 |
| **16** | 12 | 35 | + 1.6 | 59.5 | 16.2 | 343 | 292 | 36 | 5.6 | 11 | 31 | 11 | 32 | 17 | 35 | 23 | 23 | 23 | 2 |
| **17** | 13 | 26 | − 4.4 | 59.3 | 16.1 | 355 | 292 | 48 | 6.6 | 12 | 54 | 13 | 00 | 18 | 25 | 23 | 41 | 23 | 3 |
| **18** | 14 | 18 | −10.2 | 59.0 | 16.1 | 8 | 290 | 59 | 7.6 | 14 | 17 | 14 | 29 | 19 | 15 | — | | 23 | 4 |
| **19** | 15 | 11 | −15.3 | 58.6 | 16.0 | 20 | 287 | 70 | 8.6 | 15 | 39 | 15 | 57 | 20 | 08 | 0 | 02 | — | |
| **20** | 16 | 06 | −19.6 | 58.2 | 15.9 | 32 | 282 | 80 | 9.6 | 16 | 59 | 17 | 23 | 21 | 02 | 0 | 27 | 0 | 0 |
| **21** | 17 | 03 | −22.8 | 57.8 | 15.7 | 44 | 276 | 88 | 10.6 | 18 | 12 | 18 | 41 | 21 | 58 | 0 | 59 | 0 | 3 |
| **22** | 18 | 01 | −24.6 | 57.3 | 15.6 | 56 | 268 | 94 | 11.6 | 19 | 15 | 19 | 45 | 22 | 55 | 1 | 42 | 1 | [illegible] |
| **23** | 19 | 00 | −25.0 | 56.8 | 15.5 | 69 | 256 | 98 | 12.6 | 20 | 04 | 20 | 32 | 23 | 50 | 2 | 36 | 2 | 0 |
| **24** | 19 | 56 | −24.1 | 56.3 | 15.3 | 81 | 223 | 100 | 13.6 | 20 | 41 | 21 | 05 | — | | 3 | 40 | 3 | [illegible] |
| **25** | 20 | 51 | −21.9 | 55.7 | 15.2 | 93 | 103 | 99 | 14.6 | 21 | 09 | 21 | 28 | 0 | 42 | 4 | 50 | 4 | 2 |
| **26** | 21 | 43 | −18.7 | 55.3 | 15.1 | 105 | 84 | 97 | 15.6 | 21 | 30 | 21 | 44 | 1 | 31 | 6 | 03 | 5 | 4 |
| **27** | 22 | 31 | −14.7 | 54.8 | 14.9 | 117 | 77 | 93 | 16.6 | 21 | 47 | 21 | 57 | 2 | 17 | 7 | 15 | 7 | 0 |
| **28** | 23 | 17 | −10.2 | 54.5 | 14.8 | 130 | 73 | 87 | 17.6 | 22 | 02 | 22 | 07 | 3 | 00 | 8 | 25 | 8 | 1 |
| **29** | 0 | 01 | − 5.3 | 54.3 | 14.8 | 142 | 70 | 80 | 18.6 | 22 | 16 | 22 | 16 | 3 | 41 | 9 | 33 | 9 | 3 |
| **30** | 0 | 44 | − 0.3 | 54.2 | 14.8 | 154 | 69 | 72 | 19.6 | 22 | 29 | 22 | 26 | 4 | 2 | 10 | 41 | 10 | 4 |
| **31** | 1 | 27 | + 4.7 | 54.2 | 14.8 | 166 | 69 | 64 | 20.6 | 22 | 44 | 22 | 36 | 5 | 02 | 11 | 49 | 11 | 5 |

## MERCURY

| Day | RA | | Dec. | Diam. | Phase | Transit | | 5° high 52° | | 5° high 56° | |
|---|---|---|---|---|---|---|---|---|---|---|---|
| | h | m | ° | ″ | % | h | m | h | m | h | m |
| 1 | 5 | 13 | +21.2 | 7 | 60 | 10 | 39 | 3 | 17 | 3 | 01 |
| 3 | 5 | 27 | +21.8 | 6 | 66 | 10 | 45 | 3 | 19 | 3 | 02 |
| 5 | 5 | 41 | +22.4 | 6 | 71 | 10 | 51 | 3 | 22 | 3 | 05 |
| 7 | 5 | 56 | +22.9 | 6 | 77 | 10 | 59 | 3 | 27 | 3 | 09 |
| 9 | 6 | 13 | +23.3 | 6 | 83 | 11 | 08 | 3 | 33 | 3 | 15 |
| 11 | 6 | 30 | +23.5 | 5 | 88 | 11 | 17 | 3 | 41 | 3 | 23 |
| 13 | 6 | 48 | +23.6 | 5 | 92 | 11 | 28 | 3 | 51 | 3 | 32 |
| 15 | 7 | 06 | +23.5 | 5 | 96 | 11 | 38 | 4 | 02 | 3 | 43 |
| 17 | 7 | 25 | +23.2 | 5 | 98 | 11 | 49 | 4 | 15 | 3 | 56 |
| 19 | 7 | 43 | +22.7 | 5 | 99 | 12 | 00 | 19 | 30 | 19 | 47 |
| 21 | 8 | 02 | +22.1 | 5 | 100 | 12 | 10 | 19 | 36 | 19 | 52 |
| 23 | 8 | 20 | +21.3 | 5 | 99 | 12 | 20 | 19 | 40 | 19 | 56 |
| 25 | 8 | 37 | +20.4 | 5 | 98 | 12 | 29 | 19 | 44 | 19 | 58 |
| 27 | 8 | 54 | +19.3 | 5 | 97 | 12 | 38 | 19 | 46 | 19 | 59 |
| 29 | 9 | 10 | +18.2 | 5 | 95 | 12 | 46 | 19 | 47 | 19 | 59 |
| 31 | 9 | 25 | +17.0 | 5 | 93 | 12 | 53 | 19 | 47 | 19 | 58 |

## VENUS

| Day | RA | | Dec. | Diam. | Phase | Transit | | 5° high 52° | | 5° high 56° | |
|---|---|---|---|---|---|---|---|---|---|---|---|
| | h | m | ° | ″ | % | h | m | h | m | h | m |
| 1 | 9 | 27 | +16.9 | 15 | 72 | 14 | 52 | 21 | 46 | 21 | 5 |
| 6 | 9 | 49 | +14.9 | 16 | 70 | 14 | 54 | 21 | 37 | 21 | 4 |
| 11 | 10 | 11 | +12.8 | 16 | 68 | 14 | 56 | 21 | 28 | 21 | 3 |
| 16 | 10 | 32 | +10.6 | 17 | 66 | 14 | 58 | 21 | 17 | 21 | 2 |
| 21 | 10 | 52 | + 8.2 | 18 | 64 | 14 | 58 | 21 | 06 | 21 | 0 |
| 26 | 11 | 12 | + 5.8 | 18 | 62 | 14 | 58 | 20 | 53 | 20 | 5 |
| 31 | 11 | 32 | + 3.4 | 19 | 60 | 14 | 58 | 20 | 40 | 20 | 3 |

## MARS

| Day | RA | | Dec. | Diam. | Phase | Transit | | 5° high 52° | | 5° high 56° | |
|---|---|---|---|---|---|---|---|---|---|---|---|
| 1 | 7 | 35 | +22.7 | 4 | 100 | 12 | 59 | 20 | 28 | 20 | 4 |
| 6 | 7 | 49 | +22.2 | 4 | 100 | 12 | 53 | 20 | 19 | 20 | 3 |
| 11 | 8 | 03 | +21.6 | 4 | 100 | 12 | 47 | 20 | 09 | 20 | 2 |
| 16 | 8 | 16 | +20.9 | 4 | 100 | 12 | 41 | 19 | 59 | 20 | 1 |
| 21 | 8 | 29 | +20.2 | 4 | 100 | 12 | 34 | 19 | 48 | 20 | 0 |
| 26 | 8 | 43 | +19.4 | 4 | 100 | 12 | 28 | 19 | 37 | 19 | 5 |
| 31 | 8 | 56 | +18.5 | 4 | 100 | 12 | 21 | 19 | 25 | 19 | 3 |

## SUNRISE AND SUNSET

| Day | London 0°05′ 51°30′ rise h m | set h m | Bristol 2°35′ 51°28′ rise h m | set h m | Birmingham 1°55′ 52°28′ rise h m | set h m | Manchester 2°15′ 53°28′ rise h m | set h m | Newcastle 1°37′ 54°59′ rise h m | set h m | Glasgow 4°14′ 55°52′ rise h m | set h m | Belfast 5°56′ 54°35′ rise h m | set h m |
|---|---|---|---|---|---|---|---|---|---|---|---|---|---|---|
| 1 | 3 47 | 20 21 | 3 57 | 20 30 | 3 49 | 20 33 | 3 44 | 20 41 | 3 32 | 20 48 | 3 36 | 21 05 | 3 52 | 21 03 |
| 2 | 3 48 | 20 20 | 3 58 | 20 30 | 3 50 | 20 33 | 3 45 | 20 40 | 3 33 | 20 48 | 3 37 | 21 04 | 3 53 | 21 02 |
| 3 | 3 49 | 20 20 | 3 59 | 20 30 | 3 51 | 20 33 | 3 46 | 20 40 | 3 34 | 20 47 | 3 38 | 21 04 | 3 54 | 21 02 |
| 4 | 3 49 | 20 20 | 4 00 | 20 29 | 3 51 | 20 32 | 3 47 | 20 39 | 3 34 | 20 47 | 3 39 | 21 03 | 3 54 | 21 01 |
| 5 | 3 50 | 20 19 | 4 00 | 20 29 | 3 52 | 20 32 | 3 48 | 20 39 | 3 35 | 20 46 | 3 40 | 21 03 | 3 55 | 21 01 |
| 6 | 3 51 | 20 18 | 4 01 | 20 28 | 3 53 | 20 31 | 3 49 | 20 38 | 3 36 | 20 45 | 3 41 | 21 02 | 3 56 | 21 00 |
| 7 | 3 52 | 20 18 | 4 02 | 20 28 | 3 54 | 20 30 | 3 50 | 20 38 | 3 37 | 20 45 | 3 42 | 21 01 | 3 57 | 20 59 |
| 8 | 3 53 | 20 17 | 4 03 | 20 27 | 3 55 | 20 30 | 3 51 | 20 37 | 3 39 | 20 44 | 3 43 | 21 00 | 3 58 | 20 58 |
| 9 | 3 54 | 20 17 | 4 04 | 20 26 | 3 56 | 20 29 | 3 52 | 20 36 | 3 40 | 20 43 | 3 44 | 20 59 | 4 00 | 20 58 |
| 10 | 3 55 | 20 16 | 4 05 | 20 26 | 3 57 | 20 28 | 3 53 | 20 35 | 3 41 | 20 42 | 3 45 | 20 58 | 4 01 | 20 57 |
| 11 | 3 56 | 20 15 | 4 06 | 20 25 | 3 58 | 20 27 | 3 54 | 20 34 | 3 42 | 20 41 | 3 47 | 20 57 | 4 02 | 20 56 |
| 12 | 3 57 | 20 14 | 4 07 | 20 24 | 3 59 | 20 27 | 3 55 | 20 33 | 3 43 | 20 40 | 3 48 | 20 56 | 4 03 | 20 55 |
| 13 | 3 58 | 20 13 | 4 08 | 20 23 | 4 00 | 20 26 | 3 56 | 20 32 | 3 45 | 20 39 | 3 49 | 20 55 | 4 04 | 20 54 |
| 14 | 3 59 | 20 12 | 4 09 | 20 22 | 4 02 | 20 25 | 3 58 | 20 31 | 3 46 | 20 38 | 3 51 | 20 54 | 4 06 | 20 52 |
| 15 | 4 00 | 20 11 | 4 11 | 20 21 | 4 03 | 20 24 | 3 59 | 20 30 | 3 47 | 20 36 | 3 52 | 20 53 | 4 07 | 20 51 |
| 16 | 4 02 | 20 10 | 4 12 | 20 20 | 4 04 | 20 23 | 4 00 | 20 29 | 3 49 | 20 35 | 3 54 | 20 51 | 4 08 | 20 50 |
| 17 | 4 03 | 20 09 | 4 13 | 20 19 | 4 05 | 20 21 | 4 01 | 20 28 | 3 50 | 20 34 | 3 55 | 20 50 | 4 10 | 20 49 |
| 18 | 4 04 | 20 08 | 4 14 | 20 18 | 4 07 | 20 20 | 4 03 | 20 27 | 3 52 | 20 33 | 3 57 | 20 48 | 4 11 | 20 48 |
| 19 | 4 05 | 20 07 | 4 16 | 20 17 | 4 08 | 20 19 | 4 04 | 20 25 | 3 53 | 20 31 | 3 58 | 20 47 | 4 13 | 20 46 |
| 20 | 4 07 | 20 06 | 4 17 | 20 16 | 4 09 | 20 18 | 4 06 | 20 24 | 3 55 | 20 30 | 4 00 | 20 45 | 4 14 | 20 45 |
| 21 | 4 08 | 20 05 | 4 18 | 20 14 | 4 11 | 20 16 | 4 07 | 20 23 | 3 56 | 20 28 | 4 02 | 20 44 | 4 16 | 20 43 |
| 22 | 4 09 | 20 03 | 4 19 | 20 13 | 4 12 | 20 15 | 4 09 | 20 21 | 3 58 | 20 27 | 4 03 | 20 42 | 4 17 | 20 42 |
| 23 | 4 11 | 20 02 | 4 21 | 20 12 | 4 14 | 20 14 | 4 10 | 20 20 | 3 59 | 20 25 | 4 05 | 20 41 | 4 19 | 20 40 |
| 24 | 4 12 | 20 01 | 4 22 | 20 11 | 4 15 | 20 12 | 4 12 | 20 18 | 4 01 | 20 24 | 4 07 | 20 39 | 4 21 | 20 39 |
| 25 | 4 13 | 19 59 | 4 24 | 20 09 | 4 16 | 20 11 | 4 13 | 20 17 | 4 03 | 20 22 | 4 08 | 20 37 | 4 22 | 20 37 |
| 26 | 4 15 | 19 58 | 4 25 | 20 08 | 4 18 | 20 09 | 4 15 | 20 15 | 4 04 | 20 20 | 4 10 | 20 36 | 4 24 | 20 36 |
| 27 | 4 16 | 19 56 | 4 26 | 20 06 | 4 19 | 20 08 | 4 16 | 20 14 | 4 06 | 20 19 | 4 12 | 20 34 | 4 25 | 20 34 |
| 28 | 4 18 | 19 55 | 4 28 | 20 05 | 4 21 | 20 06 | 4 18 | 20 12 | 4 08 | 20 17 | 4 14 | 20 32 | 4 27 | 20 32 |
| 29 | 4 19 | 19 53 | 4 29 | 20 03 | 4 22 | 20 05 | 4 19 | 20 10 | 4 10 | 20 15 | 4 16 | 20 30 | 4 29 | 20 30 |
| 30 | 4 21 | 19 52 | 4 31 | 20 02 | 4 24 | 20 03 | 4 21 | 20 09 | 4 11 | 20 13 | 4 17 | 20 28 | 4 31 | 20 29 |
| 31 | 4 22 | 19 50 | 4 32 | 20 00 | 4 26 | 20 01 | 4 23 | 20 07 | 4 13 | 20 11 | 4 19 | 20 26 | 4 32 | 20 27 |

## JUPITER

| *Day* | *RA* h | m | *Dec.* ° | ′ | *Transit* h | m | *5° high* 52° h | m | 56° h | m |
|---|---|---|---|---|---|---|---|---|---|---|
| 1 | 7 | 39.3 | +21 | 46 | 13 | 02 | 20 | 25 | 20 | 41 |
| 11 | 7 | 48.7 | +21 | 24 | 12 | 32 | 19 | 53 | 20 | 09 |
| 21 | 7 | 58.1 | +20 | 59 | 12 | 02 | 19 | 20 | 19 | 36 |
| 31 | 8 | 07.4 | +20 | 33 | 11 | 32 | 18 | 48 | 19 | 03 |

Diameters – equatorial 31 polar 30″

## SATURN

| *Day* | *RA* h | m | *Dec.* ° | ′ | *Transit* h | m | *5° high* 52° h | m | 56° h | m |
|---|---|---|---|---|---|---|---|---|---|---|
| 1 | 5 | 22.2 | +21 | 53 | 10 | 45 | 3 | 21 | 3 | 05 |
| 11 | 5 | 27.5 | +21 | 58 | 10 | 11 | 2 | 47 | 2 | 30 |
| 21 | 5 | 32.6 | +22 | 02 | 9 | 37 | 2 | 12 | 1 | 56 |
| 31 | 5 | 37.4 | +22 | 04 | 9 | 02 | 1 | 37 | 1 | 21 |

Diameters – equatorial 17″ polar 15″
Rings – major axis 38″ minor axis 17″

## URANUS

| *Day* | *RA* h | m | *Dec.* ° | ′ | *Transit* h | m | *10° high* 52° h | m | 56° h | m |
|---|---|---|---|---|---|---|---|---|---|---|
| 1 | 22 | 03.8 | −12 | 42 | 3 | 28 | 23 | 45 | 0 | 11 |
| 11 | 22 | 02.9 | −12 | 47 | 2 | 47 | 23 | 06 | 23 | 28 |
| 21 | 22 | 01.7 | −12 | 54 | 2 | 07 | 22 | 26 | 22 | 48 |
| 31 | 22 | 00.4 | −13 | 01 | 1 | 26 | 21 | 46 | 22 | 09 |

Diameter 4″

## NEPTUNE

| *Day* | *RA* h | m | *Dec.* ° | ′ | *Transit* h | m | *10° high* 52° h | m | 56° h | m |
|---|---|---|---|---|---|---|---|---|---|---|
| 1 | 20 | 51.3 | −17 | 34 | 2 | 15 | 23 | 10 | 23 | 42 |
| 11 | 20 | 50.4 | −17 | 37 | 1 | 35 | 22 | 30 | 23 | 03 |
| 21 | 20 | 49.3 | −17 | 42 | 0 | 55 | 21 | 50 | 22 | 23 |
| 31 | 20 | 48.2 | −17 | 46 | 0 | 14 | 21 | 11 | 21 | 44 |

Diameter 2″

# August 2002

EIGHTH MONTH, 31 DAYS, *Augustus*, formerly *Sextilis*, sixth month of Roman pre-Julian calendar

| | | | | |
|---|---|---|---|---|
| **1** | *Thursday* | Richard Wilson b. 1714. Battle of the Nile (Aboukir Bay) 1798 | | 21 |
| **2** | *Friday* | William II d. 1100. King William II Normandy d. 1100 | | 21 |
| **3** | *Saturday* | 1st Earl Baldwin of Bewdley Stanley Baldwin b. 1867. Ida Lupino d. 1995 | | 21 |
| **4** | *Sunday* | **10th S. after Trinity.** *Queen Elizabeth the Queen Mother b. 1900.* | | 21 |
| **5** | *Monday* | *Bank Holiday in Scotland.* Thomas Newcomen d. 1729 | *week* 31 *day* | 21 |
| **6** | *Tuesday* | **The Transfiguration.** Anne Hathaway d. 1623 | | 21 |
| **7** | *Wednesday* | Oliver Hardy d. 1957. Konstantin Stanislavsky d. 1938 | | 21 |
| **8** | *Thursday* | Princess Beatrice of York b. 1988. Nixon resigned over Watergate scandal 1974 | | 22 |
| **9** | *Friday* | Joe Mercer d. 1990. Second atomic bomb dropped, Nagasaki 1945 | | 22 |
| **10** | *Saturday* | Sir Charles Napier b. 1782 | | 22 |
| **11** | *Sunday* | **11th S. after Trinity.** Edith Wharton d. 1937 | | 22 |
| **12** | *Monday* | William Blake d. 1827. Glorious Twelfth - start of grouse shooting season | *week* 32 *day* | 22 |
| **13** | *Tuesday* | Ben Hogan b. 1912. Sir Basil Spence b. 1907 | | 22 |
| **14** | *Wednesday* | Ira Sankey d. 1908. William Randolph Hearst d. 1951 | | 22 |
| **15** | *Thursday* | **Blessed Virgin Mary.** *Princess Royal b. 1950.* | | 22 |
| **16** | *Friday* | Ted Hughes b. 1930. Stewart Granger d. 1993 | | 22 |
| **17** | *Saturday* | Wilfred Scawen Blunt b. 1840. Ludwig Mies van der Rohe d. 1969 | | 22 |
| **18** | *Sunday* | **12th S. after Trinity.** Guido Reni d. 1642 | | 23 |
| **19** | *Monday* | John Flamsteed b. 1646. Julius Marx d. 1977 | *week* 33 *day* | 23 |
| **20** | *Tuesday* | Gen. William Booth d. 1912. George Adamson d. 1989 | | 23 |
| **21** | *Wednesday* | *Princess Margaret b. 1930.* Leon Trotsky d. 1940 | | 23 |
| **22** | *Thursday* | Achille-Claude Debussy b. 1862. Jean-Honoré Fragonard d. 1806 | | 23 |
| **23** | *Friday* | King Louis XVI b. 1754. 1st Duke of Buckingham George Villiers d. 1628 | | 23 |
| **24** | *Saturday* | **St Bartholomew.** Cardinal Cormac Murphy O'Connor b. 1932. | | 23 |
| **25** | *Sunday* | **13th S. after Trinity.** Erich Honecker b. 1912 | | 23 |
| **26** | *Monday* | *Bank Holiday in England, Wales and Northern Ireland.* Charles Boyer d. 1978 | *week* 34 *day* | 23 |
| **27** | *Tuesday* | Tiziano Vecellio Titian d. 1576. Battle of Dresden 1813 | | 23 |
| **28** | *Wednesday* | 1st Duke of Buckingham. George Villiers b. 1592. John Huston d. 1987 | | 24 |
| **29** | *Thursday* | Jean Ingres b. 1780. Joseph Wright d. 1797 | | 24 |
| **30** | *Friday* | Mary Wollenstonecraft Shelly b. 1797. Denis Healy b. 1917 | | 24 |
| **31** | *Saturday* | Clive Lloyd b. 1944. John Bunyan d. 1688 | | 24 |

## Astronomical Phenomena

| d | h | |
|---|---|---|
| 2 | 01 | Neptune at opposition |
| 5 | 03 | Saturn in conjunction with Moon. Saturn 2° S. |
| 7 | 19 | Jupiter in conjunction with Moon. Jupiter 3° S. |
| 8 | 20 | Mars in conjunction with Moon. Mars 3° S. |
| 10 | 04 | Mercury in conjunction with Moon. Mercury 4° S. |
| 10 | 22 | Mars in conjunction |
| 12 | 03 | Venus in conjunction with Moon. Venus 6° S. |
| 20 | 01 | Uranus at opposition |
| 22 | 13 | Venus at greatest elongation E.46° |
| 23 | 07 | Sun's longitude 150°♍ |
| 26 | 11 | Pluto at stationary point |

## Minima of Algol

| d | h | d | h | d | h |
|---|---|---|---|---|---|
| 2 | 04.1 | 13 | 15.4 | 25 | 02.6 |
| 5 | 00.9 | 16 | 12.2 | 27 | 23.4 |
| 7 | 21.7 | 19 | 09.0 | 30 | 20.2 |
| 10 | 18.6 | 22 | 05.8 | | |

## Constellations

The following constellations are near the meridian at

| | d | h | | d | h |
|---|---|---|---|---|---|
| July | 1 | 24 | August | 16 | 21 |
| July | 16 | 23 | September | 1 | 20 |
| August | 1 | 22 | September | 15 | 19 |

Draco, Hercules, Lyra, Cygnus, Sagitta, Ophiuchus Serpens, Aquila and Sagittarius

## The Moon

| Phases, Apsides and Node | d | h | m |
|---|---|---|---|
| ☾ Last Quarter | 1 | 10 | 2 |
| ● New Moon | 8 | 19 | 1 |
| ☽ First Quarter | 15 | 10 | 1 |
| ○ Full Moon | 22 | 22 | 2 |
| ☾ Last Quarter | 31 | 02 | 3 |
| | | | |
| Perigee (362,945km) | 10 | 23 | 2 |
| Apogee (405,669km) | 26 | 17 | 3 |

Mean longitude of ascending node on August 1, 75°

## THE SUN

S.D 16′.1

| Day | Right Ascension | Dec. + | Equation of Time | Rise 52° | Rise 56° | Transit | Set 52° | Set 56° | Sidereal time | Transit of First Point of Aries |
|---|---|---|---|---|---|---|---|---|---|---|
| | h m s | ° ′ | m s | h m | h m | h m | h m | h m | h m s | h m s |
| 1 | 8 44 03 | 18 07 | −6 20 | 4 21 | 4 03 | 12 06 | 19 50 | 20 08 | 20 37 43 | 3 21 44 |
| 2 | 8 47 56 | 17 52 | −6 17 | 4 23 | 4 05 | 12 06 | 19 49 | 20 06 | 20 41 40 | 3 17 48 |
| 3 | 8 51 49 | 17 36 | −6 13 | 4 24 | 4 07 | 12 06 | 19 47 | 20 04 | 20 45 36 | 3 13 52 |
| 4 | 8 55 40 | 17 21 | −6 08 | 4 26 | 4 09 | 12 06 | 19 45 | 20 02 | 20 49 33 | 3 09 56 |
| 5 | 8 59 31 | 17 05 | −6 02 | 4 28 | 4 11 | 12 06 | 19 43 | 20 00 | 20 53 29 | 3 06 00 |
| 6 | 9 03 22 | 16 48 | −5 56 | 4 29 | 4 13 | 12 06 | 19 42 | 19 58 | 20 57 26 | 3 02 04 |
| 7 | 9 07 12 | 16 32 | −5 50 | 4 31 | 4 15 | 12 06 | 19 40 | 19 55 | 21 01 22 | 2 58 08 |
| 8 | 9 11 01 | 16 15 | −5 43 | 4 32 | 4 17 | 12 06 | 19 38 | 19 53 | 21 05 19 | 2 54 13 |
| 9 | 9 14 50 | 15 58 | −5 35 | 4 34 | 4 19 | 12 06 | 19 36 | 19 51 | 21 09 15 | 2 50 17 |
| 10 | 9 18 38 | 15 41 | −5 26 | 4 35 | 4 21 | 12 05 | 19 34 | 19 49 | 21 13 12 | 2 46 21 |
| 11 | 9 22 26 | 15 23 | −5 17 | 4 37 | 4 23 | 12 05 | 19 32 | 19 47 | 21 17 09 | 2 42 25 |
| 12 | 9 26 13 | 15 05 | −5 08 | 4 39 | 4 24 | 12 05 | 19 30 | 19 44 | 21 21 05 | 2 38 29 |
| 13 | 9 29 59 | 14 47 | −4 58 | 4 40 | 4 26 | 12 05 | 19 28 | 19 42 | 21 25 02 | 2 34 33 |
| 14 | 9 33 45 | 14 29 | −4 47 | 4 42 | 4 28 | 12 05 | 19 26 | 19 40 | 21 28 58 | 2 30 37 |
| 15 | 9 37 31 | 14 10 | −4 36 | 4 44 | 4 30 | 12 05 | 19 24 | 19 37 | 21 32 55 | 2 26 41 |
| 16 | 9 41 15 | 13 52 | −4 24 | 4 45 | 4 32 | 12 04 | 19 22 | 19 35 | 21 36 51 | 2 22 45 |
| 17 | 9 45 00 | 13 33 | −4 12 | 4 47 | 4 34 | 12 04 | 19 20 | 19 33 | 21 40 48 | 2 18 49 |
| 18 | 9 48 43 | 13 13 | −3 59 | 4 48 | 4 36 | 12 04 | 19 18 | 19 30 | 21 44 44 | 2 14 53 |
| 19 | 9 52 27 | 12 54 | −3 46 | 4 50 | 4 38 | 12 04 | 19 16 | 19 28 | 21 48 41 | 2 10 58 |
| 20 | 9 56 09 | 12 34 | −3 32 | 4 52 | 4 40 | 12 03 | 19 14 | 19 25 | 21 52 38 | 2 07 02 |
| 21 | 9 59 51 | 12 15 | −3 17 | 4 53 | 4 42 | 12 03 | 19 12 | 19 23 | 21 56 34 | 2 03 06 |
| 22 | 10 03 33 | 11 55 | −3 02 | 4 55 | 4 44 | 12 03 | 19 10 | 19 20 | 22 00 31 | 1 59 10 |
| 23 | 10 07 14 | 11 34 | −2 47 | 4 57 | 4 46 | 12 03 | 19 08 | 19 18 | 22 04 27 | 1 55 14 |
| 24 | 10 10 55 | 11 14 | −2 31 | 4 58 | 4 48 | 12 02 | 19 05 | 19 15 | 22 08 24 | 1 51 18 |
| 25 | 10 14 35 | 10 54 | −2 15 | 5 00 | 4 50 | 12 02 | 19 03 | 19 13 | 22 12 20 | 1 47 22 |
| 26 | 10 18 15 | 10 33 | −1 59 | 5 01 | 4 52 | 12 02 | 19 01 | 19 10 | 22 16 17 | 1 43 26 |
| 27 | 10 21 55 | 10 12 | −1 42 | 5 03 | 4 54 | 12 02 | 18 59 | 19 08 | 22 20 13 | 1 39 30 |
| 28 | 10 25 34 | 9 51 | −1 24 | 5 05 | 4 56 | 12 01 | 18 57 | 19 05 | 22 24 10 | 1 35 34 |
| 29 | 10 29 13 | 9 30 | −1 06 | 5 06 | 4 58 | 12 01 | 18 54 | 19 03 | 22 28 06 | 1 31 38 |
| 30 | 10 32 51 | 9 08 | −0 48 | 5 08 | 5 00 | 12 01 | 18 52 | 19 00 | 22 32 03 | 1 27 43 |
| 31 | 10 36 30 | 8 47 | −0 30 | 5 10 | 5 02 | 12 00 | 18 50 | 18 58 | 22 36 00 | 1 23 47 |

## DURATION OF TWILIGHT (in minutes)

| Latitude | 52° | 56° | 52° | 56° | 52° | 56° | 52° | 56° |
|---|---|---|---|---|---|---|---|---|
| | 1 August | | 11 August | | 21 August | | 31 August | |
| Civil | 41 | 49 | 39 | 45 | 37 | 42 | 35 | 40 |
| Nautical | 97 | 121 | 90 | 107 | 84 | 97 | 79 | 90 |
| Astronomical | 179 | TAN | 154 | 210 | 139 | 168 | 128 | 148 |

## THE NIGHT SKY

*Mercury* remains too close to the Sun for observation throughout the month.

*Venus*, magnitude -4.3, is visible low in the western sky in the evenings after sunset. Although greatest eastern elongation (46°) occurs on the 22nd, Venus is only visible for a short time after sunset. On the evenings of the 11th and 12th the crescent Moon is near the planet.

*Mars* remains too close to the Sun for observation, as it passes through conjunction on the 10th.

*Jupiter*, after the first week or ten days of the month, becomes visible as a morning object, low above the eastern horizon for a short while before sunrise, magnitude -1.8. Jupiter is in the constellation of Cancer.

*Saturn* continues to be visible as a morning object, magnitude +0.1. By the end of the month it is visible low above the eastern horizon at midnight. During the early hours of the 5th the old crescent Moon will be seen 1 degree above Saturn.

*Uranus* is at opposition on the 20th, on the boundary between Capricornus and Aquarius. Uranus is barely visible to the naked eye as its magnitude is +5.7, but it is readily located with only small optical aid.

*Neptune* is at opposition on the 2nd, in Capricornus. It is not visible to the naked eye since its magnitude is +7.8.

*Meteors*. The maximum of the famous Perseid meteor shower occurs on the night of the 12th-13th. Conditions are favourable since the 4–day old crescent Moon sets in the late evening, before the radiant has reached an altitude of about 30 degrees.

## THE MOON

| Day | RA | Dec. | Hor. par. | Semi-diam | Sun's co-long. | PA of Bright Limb | Phase | Age | Rise 52° | Rise 56° | Transit | Set 52° | Set 56° |
|---|---|---|---|---|---|---|---|---|---|---|---|---|---|
| | h m | ° | ′ | ′ | ° | ° | % | d | h m | h m | h m | h m | h m |
| **1** | 2 11 | + 9.5 | 54.5 | 14.8 | 178 | 71 | 54 | 21.6 | 23 00 | 22 48 | 5 43 | 12 58 | 13 09 |
| **2** | 2 57 | +14.1 | 54.9 | 15.0 | 191 | 73 | 45 | 22.6 | 23 20 | 23 03 | 6 26 | 14 09 | 14 25 |
| **3** | 3 45 | +18.1 | 55.5 | 15.1 | 203 | 77 | 35 | 23.6 | 23 46 | 23 24 | 7 13 | 15 22 | 15 43 |
| **4** | 4 36 | +21.5 | 56.2 | 15.3 | 215 | 82 | 26 | 24.6 | — | 23 55 | 8 03 | 16 34 | 17 00 |
| **5** | 5 31 | +23.9 | 57.0 | 15.5 | 227 | 88 | 17 | 25.6 | 0 21 | — | 8 58 | 17 42 | 18 11 |
| **6** | 6 29 | +25.0 | 57.8 | 15.8 | 240 | 95 | 10 | 26.6 | 1 09 | 0 40 | 9 55 | 18 41 | 19 10 |
| **7** | 7 30 | +24.7 | 58.6 | 16.0 | 252 | 105 | 4 | 27.6 | 2 12 | 1 43 | 10 55 | 19 28 | 19 53 |
| **8** | 8 31 | +22.8 | 59.4 | 16.2 | 264 | 123 | 1 | 28.6 | 3 28 | 3 03 | 11 54 | 20 03 | 20 23 |
| **9** | 9 31 | +19.4 | 59.9 | 16.3 | 276 | 229 | 0 | 0.2 | 4 53 | 4 34 | 12 52 | 20 31 | 20 45 |
| **10** | 10 30 | +14.8 | 60.3 | 16.4 | 288 | 275 | 2 | 1.2 | 6 21 | 6 08 | 13 47 | 20 53 | 21 01 |
| **11** | 11 26 | + 9.2 | 60.4 | 16.5 | 301 | 285 | 7 | 2.2 | 7 49 | 7 42 | 14 3 | 21 11 | 21 15 |
| **12** | 12 20 | + 3.1 | 60.3 | 16.4 | 313 | 288 | 14 | 3.2 | 9 15 | 9 15 | 15 30 | 21 29 | 21 27 |
| **13** | 13 13 | − 3.1 | 60.0 | 16.3 | 325 | 290 | 24 | 4.2 | 10 40 | 10 45 | 16 21 | 21 47 | 21 46 |
| **14** | 14 06 | − 9.0 | 59.5 | 16.2 | 337 | 289 | 34 | 5.2 | 12 05 | 12 16 | 17 12 | 22 07 | 21 54 |
| **15** | 14 59 | −14.4 | 58.9 | 16.1 | 350 | 286 | 45 | 6.2 | 13 28 | 13 45 | 18 04 | 22 30 | 22 12 |
| **16** | 15 54 | −18.9 | 58.3 | 15.9 | 2 | 282 | 57 | 7.2 | 14 49 | 15 12 | 18 58 | 23 00 | 22 36 |
| **17** | 16 50 | −22.3 | 57.7 | 15.7 | 14 | 277 | 67 | 8.2 | 16 04 | 16 32 | 19 53 | 23 39 | 23 11 |
| **18** | 17 47 | −24.4 | 57.1 | 15.6 | 26 | 271 | 77 | 9.2 | 17 09 | 17 39 | 20 49 | — | 23 58 |
| **19** | 18 45 | −25.2 | 56.6 | 15.4 | 39 | 263 | 85 | 10.2 | 18 02 | 18 31 | 21 44 | 0 28 | — |
| **20** | 19 41 | −24.5 | 56.1 | 15.3 | 51 | 256 | 92 | 11.2 | 18 42 | 19 07 | 22 37 | 1 29 | 1 00 |
| **21** | 20 36 | −22.6 | 55.6 | 15.1 | 63 | 246 | 96 | 12.2 | 19 12 | 19 33 | 23 26 | 2 37 | 2 12 |
| **22** | 21 28 | −19.7 | 55.2 | 15.0 | 75 | 229 | 99 | 13.2 | 19 35 | 19 50 | — | 3 49 | 3 29 |
| **23** | 22 17 | −15.9 | 54.8 | 14.9 | 87 | 151 | 100 | 14.2 | 19 53 | 20 04 | 0 13 | 5 01 | 4 47 |
| **24** | 23 04 | −11.5 | 54.5 | 14.8 | 99 | 90 | 99 | 15.2 | 20 08 | 20 15 | 0 57 | 6 12 | 6 02 |
| **25** | 23 48 | − 6.7 | 54.2 | 14.8 | 112 | 78 | 96 | 16.2 | 20 22 | 20 24 | 1 38 | 7 21 | 7 16 |
| **26** | 0 31 | − 1.7 | 54.1 | 14.7 | 124 | 74 | 91 | 17.2 | 20 35 | 20 33 | 2 19 | 8 29 | 8 29 |
| **27** | 1 14 | + 3.4 | 54.1 | 14.7 | 136 | 72 | 85 | 18.2 | 20 49 | 20 43 | 2 59 | 9 37 | 9 41 |
| **28** | 1 57 | + 8.3 | 54.2 | 14.8 | 148 | 72 | 78 | 19.2 | 21 04 | 20 53 | 3 39 | 10 45 | 10 54 |
| **29** | 2 42 | +12.9 | 54.4 | 14.8 | 160 | 74 | 70 | 20.2 | 21 22 | 21 07 | 4 21 | 11 55 | 12 09 |
| **30** | 3 29 | +17.1 | 54.8 | 14.9 | 173 | 76 | 61 | 21.2 | 21 45 | 21 24 | 5 06 | 13 06 | 13 25 |
| **31** | 4 18 | +20.7 | 55.4 | 15.1 | 185 | 80 | 51 | 22.2 | 22 15 | 21 50 | 5 54 | 14 17 | 14 41 |

## MERCURY

| Day | RA | Dec. | Diam. | Phase | Transit | 5° high 52° | 5° high 56° |
|---|---|---|---|---|---|---|---|
| | h m | ° | ″ | % | h m | h m | h m |
| 1 | 9 33 | +16.3 | 5 | 92 | 12 57 | 19 47 | 19 57 |
| 3 | 9 47 | +15.0 | 5 | 90 | 13 03 | 19 46 | 19 55 |
| 5 | 10 01 | +13.6 | 5 | 87 | 13 09 | 19 45 | 19 52 |
| 7 | 10 14 | +12.3 | 5 | 85 | 13 14 | 19 42 | 19 48 |
| 9 | 10 27 | +10.8 | 5 | 83 | 13 19 | 19 39 | 19 44 |
| 11 | 10 39 | + 9.4 | 6 | 81 | 13 23 | 19 36 | 19 40 |
| 13 | 10 50 | + 8.0 | 6 | 79 | 13 26 | 19 32 | 19 35 |
| 15 | 11 01 | + 6.6 | 6 | 76 | 13 29 | 19 28 | 19 29 |
| 17 | 11 12 | + 5.2 | 6 | 74 | 13 32 | 19 23 | 19 24 |
| 19 | 11 22 | + 3.8 | 6 | 72 | 13 34 | 19 18 | 19 18 |
| 21 | 11 32 | + 2.4 | 6 | 70 | 13 36 | 19 13 | 19 11 |
| 23 | 11 41 | + 1.1 | 6 | 67 | 13 37 | 19 07 | 19 05 |
| 25 | 11 50 | − 0.2 | 6 | 65 | 13 38 | 19 02 | 18 58 |
| 27 | 11 58 | − 1.4 | 7 | 62 | 13 38 | 18 55 | 18 51 |
| 29 | 12 06 | − 2.6 | 7 | 60 | 13 38 | 18 49 | 18 43 |
| 31 | 12 13 | − 3.8 | 7 | 57 | 13 37 | 18 42 | 18 35 |

## VENUS

| Day | RA | Dec. | Diam. | Phase | Transit | 5° high 52° | 5° high 56° |
|---|---|---|---|---|---|---|---|
| | h m | ° | ″ | % | h m | h m | h m |
| 1 | 11 36 | + 2.9 | 20 | 59 | 14 58 | 20 38 | 20 36 |
| 6 | 11 54 | + 0.4 | 20 | 57 | 14 57 | 20 24 | 20 21 |
| 11 | 12 13 | − 2.1 | 22 | 55 | 14 55 | 20 10 | 20 04 |
| 16 | 12 31 | − 4.5 | 23 | 52 | 14 54 | 19 55 | 19 47 |
| 21 | 12 48 | − 6.9 | 24 | 50 | 14 51 | 19 39 | 19 30 |
| 26 | 13 05 | − 9.3 | 25 | 47 | 14 48 | 19 23 | 19 11 |
| 31 | 13 21 | −11.5 | 27 | 44 | 14 45 | 19 07 | 18 52 |

## MARS

| Day | RA | Dec. | Diam. | Phase | Transit | 5° high 52° | 5° high 56° |
|---|---|---|---|---|---|---|---|
| 1 | 8 58 | +18.4 | 4 | 100 | 12 20 | 5 16 | 5 04 |
| 6 | 9 11 | +17.4 | 4 | 100 | 12 13 | 5 15 | 5 03 |
| 11 | 9 24 | +16.5 | 4 | 100 | 12 06 | 5 13 | 5 03 |
| 16 | 9 36 | +15.5 | 4 | 100 | 11 59 | 5 12 | 5 02 |
| 21 | 9 49 | +14.4 | 4 | 100 | 11 52 | 5 10 | 5 01 |
| 26 | 10 01 | +13.3 | 4 | 100 | 11 44 | 5 08 | 5 01 |
| 31 | 10 13 | +12.2 | 4 | 100 | 11 37 | 5 07 | 5 00 |

## SUNRISE AND SUNSET

| | London | | Bristol | | Birmingham | | Manchester | | Newcastle | | Glasgow | | Belfast | |
|---|---|---|---|---|---|---|---|---|---|---|---|---|---|---|
| | 0°05′ | 51°30′ | 2°35′ | 51°28′ | 1°55′ | 52°28′ | 2°15′ | 53°28′ | 1°37′ | 54°59′ | 4°14′ | 55°52′ | 5°56′ | 54°35′ |
| | h m | h m | h m | h m | h m | h m | h m | h m | h m | h m | h m | h m | h m | h m |
| **1** | 4 24 | 19 49 | 4 34 | 19 59 | 4 27 | 20 00 | 4 24 | 20 05 | 4 15 | 20 10 | 4 21 | 20 24 | 4 34 | 20 25 |
| **2** | 4 25 | 19 47 | 4 35 | 19 57 | 4 29 | 19 58 | 4 26 | 20 03 | 4 17 | 20 08 | 4 23 | 20 22 | 4 36 | 20 23 |
| **3** | 4 27 | 19 45 | 4 37 | 19 55 | 4 30 | 19 56 | 4 28 | 20 02 | 4 18 | 20 06 | 4 25 | 20 20 | 4 37 | 20 21 |
| **4** | 4 28 | 19 44 | 4 38 | 19 54 | 4 32 | 19 55 | 4 29 | 20 00 | 4 20 | 20 04 | 4 27 | 20 18 | 4 39 | 20 19 |
| **5** | 4 30 | 19 42 | 4 40 | 19 52 | 4 33 | 19 53 | 4 31 | 19 58 | 4 22 | 20 02 | 4 29 | 20 16 | 4 41 | 20 17 |
| **6** | 4 31 | 19 40 | 4 41 | 19 50 | 4 35 | 19 51 | 4 33 | 19 56 | 4 24 | 20 00 | 4 30 | 20 14 | 4 43 | 20 15 |
| **7** | 4 33 | 19 38 | 4 43 | 19 48 | 4 37 | 19 49 | 4 34 | 19 54 | 4 26 | 19 58 | 4 32 | 20 12 | 4 45 | 20 13 |
| **8** | 4 34 | 19 37 | 4 44 | 19 46 | 4 38 | 19 47 | 4 36 | 19 52 | 4 27 | 19 55 | 4 34 | 20 10 | 4 46 | 20 11 |
| **9** | 4 36 | 19 35 | 4 46 | 19 45 | 4 40 | 19 45 | 4 38 | 19 50 | 4 29 | 19 53 | 4 36 | 20 07 | 4 48 | 20 09 |
| **10** | 4 37 | 19 33 | 4 48 | 19 43 | 4 42 | 19 43 | 4 39 | 19 48 | 4 31 | 19 51 | 4 38 | 20 05 | 4 50 | 20 07 |
| **11** | 4 39 | 19 31 | 4 49 | 19 41 | 4 43 | 19 41 | 4 41 | 19 46 | 4 33 | 19 49 | 4 40 | 20 03 | 4 52 | 20 05 |
| **12** | 4 41 | 19 29 | 4 51 | 19 39 | 4 45 | 19 39 | 4 43 | 19 44 | 4 35 | 19 47 | 4 42 | 20 01 | 4 54 | 20 03 |
| **13** | 4 42 | 19 27 | 4 52 | 19 37 | 4 47 | 19 37 | 4 45 | 19 42 | 4 37 | 19 45 | 4 44 | 19 58 | 4 55 | 20 00 |
| **14** | 4 44 | 19 25 | 4 54 | 19 35 | 4 48 | 19 35 | 4 46 | 19 40 | 4 39 | 19 42 | 4 46 | 19 56 | 4 57 | 19 58 |
| **15** | 4 45 | 19 23 | 4 55 | 19 33 | 4 50 | 19 33 | 4 48 | 19 38 | 4 40 | 19 40 | 4 48 | 19 54 | 4 59 | 19 56 |
| **16** | 4 47 | 19 21 | 4 57 | 19 31 | 4 52 | 19 31 | 4 50 | 19 36 | 4 42 | 19 38 | 4 50 | 19 51 | 5 01 | 19 54 |
| **17** | 4 49 | 19 19 | 4 59 | 19 29 | 4 53 | 19 29 | 4 52 | 19 33 | 4 44 | 19 36 | 4 52 | 19 49 | 5 03 | 19 52 |
| **18** | 4 50 | 19 17 | 5 00 | 19 27 | 4 55 | 19 27 | 4 53 | 19 31 | 4 46 | 19 33 | 4 54 | 19 47 | 5 05 | 19 49 |
| **19** | 4 52 | 19 15 | 5 02 | 19 25 | 4 56 | 19 25 | 4 55 | 19 29 | 4 48 | 19 31 | 4 56 | 19 44 | 5 06 | 19 47 |
| **20** | 4 53 | 19 13 | 5 03 | 19 23 | 4 58 | 19 23 | 4 57 | 19 27 | 4 50 | 19 29 | 4 58 | 19 42 | 5 08 | 19 45 |
| **21** | 4 55 | 19 11 | 5 05 | 19 21 | 5 00 | 19 21 | 4 58 | 19 25 | 4 52 | 19 26 | 4 59 | 19 39 | 5 10 | 19 42 |
| **22** | 4 57 | 19 09 | 5 07 | 19 19 | 5 01 | 19 19 | 5 00 | 19 22 | 4 54 | 19 24 | 5 01 | 19 37 | 5 12 | 19 40 |
| **23** | 4 58 | 19 07 | 5 08 | 19 17 | 5 03 | 19 16 | 5 02 | 19 20 | 4 55 | 19 22 | 5 03 | 19 34 | 5 14 | 19 38 |
| **24** | 5 00 | 19 05 | 5 10 | 19 15 | 5 05 | 19 14 | 5 04 | 19 18 | 4 57 | 19 19 | 5 05 | 19 32 | 5 16 | 19 35 |
| **25** | 5 01 | 19 03 | 5 11 | 19 12 | 5 06 | 19 12 | 5 05 | 19 16 | 4 59 | 19 17 | 5 07 | 19 29 | 5 17 | 19 33 |
| **26** | 5 03 | 19 00 | 5 13 | 19 10 | 5 08 | 19 10 | 5 07 | 19 13 | 5 01 | 19 14 | 5 09 | 19 27 | 5 19 | 19 31 |
| **27** | 5 04 | 18 58 | 5 15 | 19 08 | 5 10 | 19 07 | 5 09 | 19 11 | 5 03 | 19 12 | 5 11 | 19 24 | 5 21 | 19 28 |
| **28** | 5 06 | 18 56 | 5 16 | 19 06 | 5 11 | 19 05 | 5 11 | 19 09 | 5 05 | 19 09 | 5 13 | 19 22 | 5 23 | 19 26 |
| **29** | 5 08 | 18 54 | 5 18 | 19 04 | 5 13 | 19 03 | 5 12 | 19 06 | 5 07 | 19 07 | 5 15 | 19 19 | 5 25 | 19 23 |
| **30** | 5 09 | 18 52 | 5 19 | 19 02 | 5 15 | 19 01 | 5 14 | 19 04 | 5 09 | 19 04 | 5 17 | 19 17 | 5 27 | 19 21 |
| **31** | 5 11 | 18 49 | 5 21 | 18 59 | 5 16 | 18 58 | 5 16 | 19 02 | 5 10 | 19 02 | 5 19 | 19 14 | 5 28 | 19 18 |

## JUPITER

| *Day* | *RA* | | *Dec.* | | *Transit* | | *5° high* | | | |
|---|---|---|---|---|---|---|---|---|---|---|
| | | | | | | | 52° | | 56° | |
| | h | m | ° | ′ | h | m | h | m | h | m |
| 1 | 8 | 08.4 | +20 | 31 | 11 | 29 | 4 | 14 | 3 | 59 |
| 11 | 8 | 17.5 | +20 | 03 | 10 | 59 | 3 | 46 | 3 | 32 |
| 21 | 8 | 26.5 | +19 | 34 | 10 | 29 | 3 | 19 | 3 | 05 |
| 31 | 8 | 35.1 | +19 | 04 | 9 | 58 | 2 | 51 | 2 | 37 |

Diameters - equatorial 32″ polar 30″

## SATURN

| *Day* | *RA* | | *Dec.* | | *Transit* | | *5° high* | | | |
|---|---|---|---|---|---|---|---|---|---|---|
| | | | | | | | 52° | | 56° | |
| | h | m | ° | ′ | h | m | h | m | h | m |
| 1 | 5 | 37.8 | +22 | 05 | 8 | 59 | 1 | 34 | 1 | 17 |
| 11 | 5 | 42.2 | +22 | 07 | 8 | 24 | 0 | 59 | 0 | 42 |
| 21 | 5 | 46.1 | +22 | 08 | 7 | 48 | 0 | 23 | 0 | 06 |
| 31 | 5 | 49.4 | +22 | 08 | 7 | 12 | 23 | 44 | 23 | 27 |

Diameters - equatorial 17″ polar 16″
Rings- major axis 39″ minor axis 18″

## URANUS

| *Day* | *RA* | | *Dec.* | | *Transit* | | *10° high* | | | |
|---|---|---|---|---|---|---|---|---|---|---|
| | | | | | | | 52° | | 56° | |
| | h | m | ° | ′ | h | m | h | m | h | m |
| 1 | 22 | 00.2 | −13 | 02 | 1 | 22 | 21 | 42 | 22 | 05 |
| 11 | 21 | 58.8 | −13 | 10 | 0 | 42 | 21 | 02 | 21 | 25 |
| 21 | 21 | 57.2 | −13 | 18 | 0 | 01 | 20 | 23 | 20 | 45 |
| 31 | 21 | 55.7 | −13 | 26 | 23 | 16 | 19 | 43 | 20 | 06 |

Diameter 4″

## NEPTUNE

| *Day* | *RA* | | *Dec.* | | *Transit* | | *10° high* | | | |
|---|---|---|---|---|---|---|---|---|---|---|
| | | | | | | | 52° | | 56° | |
| | h | m | ° | ′ | h | m | h | m | h | m |
| 1 | 20 | 48.1 | −17 | 47 | 0 | 10 | 3 | 10 | 2 | 37 |
| 11 | 20 | 47.0 | −17 | 51 | 23 | 26 | 2 | 29 | 1 | 56 |
| 21 | 20 | 46.0 | −17 | 55 | 22 | 46 | 1 | 48 | 1 | 14 |
| 31 | 20 | 45.0 | −17 | 59 | 22 | 05 | 1 | 07 | 0 | 33 |

Diameter 2″

# September 2002

NINTH MONTH, 30 DAYS, *Septem* (seven), seventh month of Roman pre-Julian calendar

| | | | |
|---|---|---|---|
| 1 | *Sunday* | **14th S. after Trinity.** James Corbett b. 1866 | 244 |
| 2 | *Monday* | John Howard b. 1726. Formal surrender of Japan (aboard USS Missouri) and end of World War II 1945 | *week 35 day* 245 |
| 3 | *Tuesday* | Oliver Cromwell d. 1658. Battle of Dunbar 1650 | 246 |
| 4 | *Wednesday* | Darius Milhaud b. 1892. Forth Road Bridge opened 1964 | 247 |
| 5 | *Thursday* | King Louis XIV b. 1638. Jean Rook d. 1991 | 248 |
| 6 | *Friday* | Austin Reed b. 1873. Gertrude Lawrence d. 1952 | 249 |
| 7 | *Saturday* | JEWISH NEW YEAR. Queen Catherine Parr d. 1548 | 250 |
| 8 | *Sunday* | **15th S. after Trinity.** Peter Sellers b. 1925 | 251 |
| 9 | *Monday* | John Curry b. 1949. Burgess Meredith d. 1997 | *week 36 day* 252 |
| 10 | *Tuesday* | Arnold Palmer b. 1929. Wilfred Scawen Blunt d. 1922 | 253 |
| 11 | *Wednesday* | O. Henry b. 1862. Battle of Malplaquet 1709 | 254 |
| 12 | *Thursday* | Louis MacNeice b. 1907. Jean-Philippe Rameau d. 1764 | 255 |
| 13 | *Friday* | Claudette Colbert b. 1903. Andrea Mantegna d. 1506 | 256 |
| 14 | *Saturday* | **Holy Cross Day.** Augustus Pugin d. 1852 | 257 |
| 15 | *Sunday* | **16th S. after Trinity.** Prince Henry of Wales b. 1984. | 258 |
| 16 | *Monday* | YOM KIPPUR. Marc Bolan d. 1977 | *week 37 day* 259 |
| 17 | *Tuesday* | Hildegard of Bingen d. 1179. Constitution of the USA was signed 1787 | 260 |
| 18 | *Wednesday* | Dr. Samuel Johnson b. 1709. Jimi Hendrix d. 1970 | 261 |
| 19 | *Thursday* | Zandra Rhodes b. 1940. Hermes Pan d. 1990 | 262 |
| 20 | *Friday* | Kenneth More b. 1914. Battle of the Alma 1854 | 263 |
| 21 | *Saturday* | **St Matthew.** FEAST OF TABERNACLES. | 264 |
| 22 | *Sunday* | **17th S. after Trinity.** Queen Anne of Cleves b. 1515 | 265 |
| 23 | *Monday* | Aldo Moro b. 1916. Dorothy Lamour d. 1996 | *week 38 day* 266 |
| 24 | *Tuesday* | Theophrastus von Hohenheim d. 1541. George Cross introduced 1940 | 267 |
| 25 | *Wednesday* | Dmitry Shostakovich b. 1906. Battle of Stamford Bridge 1066 | 268 |
| 26 | *Thursday* | Ivan Pavlov b. 1849. Hugh Lofting d. 1947 | 269 |
| 27 | *Friday* | Professor R. V. Jones b. 1911. Sylvia Pankhurst d. 1960 | 270 |
| 28 | *Saturday* | Georges Clemenceau b. 1841. Leslie Crowther d. 1996 | 271 |
| 29 | *Sunday* | **St Michael and All Angels. 18th S. after Trinity.** | 272 |
| 30 | *Monday* | Truman Capote b. 1924. George Whitefield d. 1770 | *week 39 day* 273 |

## ASTRONOMICAL PHENOMENA

| d | h | |
|---|---|---|
| 1 | 10 | Mercury at greatest elongation E.27° |
| 1 | 17 | Saturn in conjunction with Moon. Saturn 2° S. |
| 4 | 15 | Jupiter in conjunction with Moon. Jupiter 4° S. |
| 6 | 12 | Mars in conjunction with Moon. Mars 4° S. |
| 8 | 22 | Mercury in conjunction with Moon. Mercury 8° S. |
| 10 | 07 | Venus in conjunction with Moon. Venus 7° S. |
| 14 | 20 | Mercury at stationary point |
| 23 | 05 | Sun's longitude 180°♎ |
| 26 | 11 | Venus at greatest brilliancy |
| 27 | 19 | Mercury in inferior conjunction |
| 29 | 03 | Saturn in conjunction with Moon. Saturn 3° S. |

## MINIMA OF ALGOL

| d | h | d | h | d | h |
|---|---|---|---|---|---|
| 2 | 17.0 | 14 | 04.3 | 25 | 15.5 |
| 5 | 13.8 | 17 | 01.1 | 28 | 12.3 |
| 8 | 10.6 | 19 | 21.9 | | |
| 11 | 07.5 | 22 | 18.7 | | |

## CONSTELLATIONS

The following constellations are near the meridian at

| | d | h | | d | h |
|---|---|---|---|---|---|
| August | 1 | 24 | September | 15 | 21 |
| August | 16 | 23 | October | 1 | 20 |
| September | 1 | 22 | October | 16 | 19 |

Draco, Cepheus, Lyra, Cygnus, Vulpecula, Sagitta, Delphinus, Equuleus, Aquila, Aquarius and Capricornus

## THE MOON

| Phases, Apsides and Node | d | h | m |
|---|---|---|---|
| ● New Moon | 7 | 03 | 10 |
| ☽ First Quarter | 13 | 18 | 08 |
| ○ Full Moon | 21 | 13 | 59 |
| ☾ Last Quarter | 29 | 17 | 03 |
| | | | |
| Perigee (358,754km) | 8 | 03 | 11 |
| Apogee (406,341km) | 23 | 03 | 11 |

Mean longitude of ascending node on September 1, 73°

## HE SUN

S.D 16′.1

| ay | Right Ascension | Dec. | Equation of Time | Rise 52° | Rise 56° | Transit | Set 52° | Set 56° | Sidereal time | Transit of First Point of Aries |
|---|---|---|---|---|---|---|---|---|---|---|
| | h m s | ° ′ | m s | h m | h m | h m | h m | h m | h m s | h m s |
| 1 | 10 40 08 | +8 25 | −0 11 | 5 11 | 5 04 | 12 00 | 18 48 | 18 55 | 22 39 56 | 1 19 51 |
| 2 | 10 43 45 | +8 04 | +0 08 | 5 13 | 5 06 | 12 00 | 18 45 | 18 52 | 22 43 53 | 1 15 55 |
| 3 | 10 47 22 | +7 42 | +0 27 | 5 15 | 5 08 | 11 59 | 18 43 | 18 50 | 22 47 49 | 1 11 59 |
| 4 | 10 50 59 | +7 20 | +0 46 | 5 16 | 5 10 | 11 59 | 18 41 | 18 47 | 22 51 46 | 1 08 03 |
| 5 | 10 54 36 | +6 57 | +1 06 | 5 18 | 5 11 | 11 59 | 18 39 | 18 45 | 22 55 42 | 1 04 07 |
| 6 | 10 58 13 | +6 35 | +1 26 | 5 19 | 5 13 | 11 58 | 18 36 | 18 42 | 22 59 39 | 1 00 11 |
| 7 | 11 01 49 | +6 13 | +1 46 | 5 21 | 5 15 | 11 58 | 18 34 | 18 39 | 23 03 35 | 0 56 15 |
| 8 | 11 05 25 | +5 50 | +2 07 | 5 23 | 5 17 | 11 58 | 18 32 | 18 37 | 23 07 32 | 0 52 19 |
| 9 | 11 09 01 | +5 28 | +2 27 | 5 24 | 5 19 | 11 57 | 18 29 | 18 34 | 23 11 29 | 0 48 23 |
| 10 | 11 12 37 | +5 05 | +2 48 | 5 26 | 5 21 | 11 57 | 18 27 | 18 32 | 23 15 25 | 0 44 28 |
| 11 | 11 16 13 | +4 42 | +3 09 | 5 28 | 5 23 | 11 57 | 18 25 | 18 29 | 23 19 22 | 0 40 32 |
| 12 | 11 19 48 | +4 20 | +3 30 | 5 29 | 5 25 | 11 56 | 18 22 | 18 26 | 23 23 18 | 0 36 36 |
| 13 | 11 23 24 | +3 57 | +3 51 | 5 31 | 5 27 | 11 56 | 18 20 | 18 24 | 23 27 15 | 0 32 40 |
| 14 | 11 26 59 | +3 34 | +4 12 | 5 32 | 5 29 | 11 56 | 18 18 | 18 21 | 23 31 11 | 0 28 44 |
| 15 | 11 30 34 | +3 11 | +4 34 | 5 34 | 5 31 | 11 55 | 18 15 | 18 18 | 23 35 08 | 0 24 48 |
| 16 | 11 34 09 | +2 48 | +4 55 | 5 36 | 5 33 | 11 55 | 18 13 | 18 16 | 23 39 04 | 0 20 52 |
| 17 | 11 37 45 | +2 24 | +5 16 | 5 37 | 5 35 | 11 55 | 18 11 | 18 13 | 23 43 01 | 0 16 56 |
| 18 | 11 41 20 | +2 01 | +5 38 | 5 39 | 5 37 | 11 54 | 18 08 | 18 10 | 23 46 58 | 0 13 00 |
| 19 | 11 44 55 | +1 38 | +5 59 | 5 41 | 5 39 | 11 54 | 18 06 | 18 08 | 23 50 54 | 0 09 04 |
| 20 | 11 48 30 | +1 15 | +6 21 | 5 42 | 5 41 | 11 53 | 18 04 | 18 05 | 23 54 51 | 0 05 08 |
| 21 | 11 52 05 | +0 51 | +6 42 | 5 44 | 5 43 | 11 53 | 18 01 | 18 02 | 23 58 47 | { 0 01 13<br>23 57 17 |
| 22 | 11 55 40 | +0 28 | +7 03 | 5 45 | 5 45 | 11 53 | 17 59 | 18 00 | 0 02 44 | 23 53 21 |
| 23 | 11 59 16 | +0 05 | +7 25 | 5 47 | 5 47 | 11 52 | 17 57 | 17 57 | 0 06 40 | 23 49 25 |
| 24 | 12 02 51 | −0 19 | +7 46 | 5 49 | 5 49 | 11 52 | 17 54 | 17 54 | 0 10 37 | 23 45 29 |
| 25 | 12 06 27 | −0 42 | +8 07 | 5 50 | 5 51 | 11 52 | 17 52 | 17 52 | 0 14 33 | 23 41 33 |
| 26 | 12 10 02 | −1 05 | +8 28 | 5 52 | 5 53 | 11 51 | 17 50 | 17 49 | 0 18 30 | 23 37 37 |
| 27 | 12 13 38 | −1 29 | +8 48 | 5 54 | 5 54 | 11 51 | 17 47 | 17 46 | 0 22 27 | 23 33 41 |
| 28 | 12 17 15 | −1 52 | +9 08 | 5 55 | 5 56 | 11 51 | 17 45 | 17 44 | 0 26 23 | 23 29 45 |
| 29 | 12 20 51 | −2 15 | +9 29 | 5 57 | 5 58 | 11 50 | 17 43 | 17 41 | 0 30 20 | 23 25 49 |
| 30 | 12 24 28 | −2 39 | +9 49 | 5 59 | 6 00 | 11 50 | 17 40 | 17 39 | 0 34 16 | 23 21 54 |

## URATION OF TWILIGHT (in minutes)

| atitude | 52° | 56° | 52° | 56° | 52° | 56° | 52° | 56° |
|---|---|---|---|---|---|---|---|---|
| | 1 September | | 11 September | | 21 September | | 30 September | |
| ivil | 35 | 39 | 34 | 38 | 34 | 37 | 34 | 37 |
| autical | 79 | 89 | 76 | 85 | 74 | 82 | 73 | 80 |
| stronomical | 127 | 147 | 120 | 136 | 116 | 129 | 113 | 125 |

## HE NIGHT SKY

*lercury* is at greatest eastern elongation on the 1st and asses through inferior conjunction on the 27th, but ontinues to remain too close to the Sun for observation.

*Venus*, magnitude -4.5, is a magnificent object in the outh-western sky in the early evenings for a very short me after sunset. Venus passes 0.9 degrees south of Spica n the 1st. The planet is gradually drawing closer to the un and being well south of the equator is unlikely to be een from the latitudes of the British Isles after the first ortnight in September. Only observers much farther outh will be able to see the planet at its greatest brilliancy n the 26th.

*Mars* is too close to the Sun for observation at first but uring the last few days of the month it may be glimpsed as difficult morning object, low above the eastern horizon for a short while before twilight inhibits observation. Mars, magnitude +1.8, is in the constellation of Leo.

*Jupiter*, magnitude -1.9, continues to be visible as a conspicuous morning object in the south-eastern quadrant of the sky. Jupiter is moving eastwards in Cancer. On the morning of the 4th the old crescent Moon will be seen approaching the planet.

*Saturn*, magnitude +0.1, is still a morning object, now visible in the eastern sky well before midnight. The old crescent Moon is near the planet on the mornings of the 1st and 2nd, and again on the 29th. Also on the 1st, Venus passes only 0.9 degrees south of Spica.

*Zodiacal Light*. The morning cone may be seen reaching up from the eastern horizon along the ecliptic, before the beginning of morning twilight, from the 6th to the 19th.

## THE MOON

| Day | RA | Dec. | Hor. par. | Semi-diam | Sun's co-long. | PA of Bright Limb | Phase | Age | Rise 52° | Rise 56° | Transit | Set 52° | Set 56° |
|---|---|---|---|---|---|---|---|---|---|---|---|---|---|
| | h m | ° | ′ | ′ | ° | ° | % | d | h m | h m | h m | h m | h m |
| **1** | 5 11 | +23.4 | 56.1 | 15.3 | 197 | 85 | 41 | 23.2 | 22 55 | 22 27 | 6 45 | 15 26 | 15 5 |
| **2** | 6 07 | +25.0 | 57.0 | 15.5 | 209 | 91 | 31 | 24.2 | 23 50 | 23 20 | 7 40 | 16 28 | 16 5 |
| **3** | 7 05 | +25.2 | 57.9 | 15.8 | 221 | 98 | 22 | 25.2 | — | — | 8 38 | 17 19 | 17 4 |
| **4** | 8 05 | +23.9 | 58.8 | 16.0 | 234 | 106 | 13 | 26.2 | 1 00 | 0 32 | 9 36 | 17 59 | 18 2 |
| **5** | 9 06 | +21.1 | 59.7 | 16.3 | 246 | 114 | 7 | 27.2 | 2 21 | 1 59 | 10 35 | 18 30 | 18 4 |
| **6** | 10 05 | +16.9 | 60.4 | 16.5 | 258 | 127 | 2 | 28.2 | 3 48 | 3 33 | 11 31 | 18 54 | 19 0 |
| **7** | 11 03 | +11.6 | 60.9 | 16.6 | 270 | 182 | 0 | 29.2 | 5 18 | 5 09 | 12 26 | 19 14 | 19 2 |
| **8** | 11 59 | + 5.4 | 61.1 | 16.7 | 283 | 272 | 1 | 0.9 | 6 48 | 6 45 | 13 19 | 19 32 | 19 3 |
| **9** | 12 53 | − 1.0 | 61.0 | 16.6 | 295 | 284 | 5 | 1.9 | 8 17 | 8 20 | 14 12 | 19 50 | 19 4 |
| **10** | 13 48 | − 7.3 | 60.6 | 16.5 | 307 | 287 | 12 | 2.9 | 9 45 | 9 54 | 15 04 | 20 10 | 19 5 |
| **11** | 14 43 | −13.1 | 60.0 | 16.3 | 319 | 286 | 21 | 3.9 | 11 12 | 11 27 | 15 58 | 20 32 | 20 [illegible] |
| **12** | 15 39 | −18.0 | 59.2 | 16.1 | 332 | 283 | 31 | 4.9 | 12 37 | 12 58 | 16 53 | 21 00 | 20 3 |
| **13** | 16 36 | −21.8 | 58.4 | 15.9 | 344 | 278 | 42 | 5.9 | 13 56 | 14 23 | 17 49 | 21 36 | 21 0 |
| **14** | 17 34 | −24.3 | 57.6 | 15.7 | 356 | 273 | 53 | 6.9 | 15 05 | 15 36 | 18 45 | 22 23 | 21 5 |
| **15** | 18 32 | −25.3 | 56.9 | 15.5 | 8 | 266 | 63 | 7.9 | 16 02 | 16 32 | 19 40 | 23 21 | 22 5 |
| **16** | 19 29 | −25.0 | 56.2 | 15.3 | 20 | 260 | 73 | 8.9 | 16 45 | 17 12 | 20 33 | — | — |
| **17** | 20 24 | −23.3 | 55.6 | 15.1 | 33 | 253 | 81 | 9.9 | 17 17 | 17 39 | 21 24 | 0 27 | 0 0 |
| **18** | 21 16 | −20.6 | 55.1 | 15.0 | 45 | 247 | 88 | 10.9 | 17 41 | 17 58 | 22 11 | 1 38 | 1 1 |
| **19** | 22 05 | −17.0 | 54.7 | 14.9 | 57 | 241 | 94 | 11.9 | 18 00 | 18 13 | 22 55 | 2 49 | 2 3 |
| **20** | 22 52 | −12.7 | 54.4 | 14.8 | 69 | 232 | 98 | 12.9 | 18 16 | 18 24 | 23 37 | 4 01 | 3 5 |
| **21** | 23 36 | − 7.9 | 54.2 | 14.8 | 81 | 209 | 100 | 13.9 | 18 30 | 18 33 | — | 5 10 | 5 0 |
| **22** | 0 20 | − 2.9 | 54.0 | 14.7 | 93 | 112 | 100 | 14.9 | 18 43 | 18 42 | 0 18 | 6 19 | 6 1 |
| **23** | 1 03 | + 2.2 | 54.0 | 14.7 | 106 | 82 | 98 | 15.9 | 18 56 | 18 51 | 0 57 | 7 26 | 7 3 |
| **24** | 1 46 | + 7.2 | 54.0 | 14.7 | 118 | 76 | 95 | 16.9 | 19 10 | 19 00 | 1 38 | 8 35 | 8 4 |
| **25** | 2 30 | +11.9 | 54.1 | 14.8 | 130 | 75 | 90 | 17.9 | 19 26 | 19 12 | 2 19 | 9 44 | 9 5 |
| **26** | 3 15 | +16.3 | 54.4 | 14.8 | 142 | 76 | 83 | 18.9 | 19 47 | 19 28 | 3 02 | 10 55 | 11 1 |
| **27** | 4 03 | +20.0 | 54.8 | 14.9 | 154 | 79 | 76 | 19.9 | 20 13 | 19 49 | 3 48 | 12 05 | 12 2 |
| **28** | 4 54 | +22.9 | 55.3 | 15.1 | 166 | 83 | 67 | 20.9 | 20 48 | 20 20 | 4 37 | 13 14 | 13 4 |
| **29** | 5 48 | +24.9 | 56.0 | 15.3 | 179 | 89 | 57 | 21.9 | 21 36 | 21 05 | 5 30 | 14 18 | 14 4 |
| **30** | 6 45 | +25.5 | 56.8 | 15.5 | 191 | 95 | 47 | 22.9 | 22 37 | 22 08 | 6 25 | 15 12 | 15 4 |

## MERCURY

| Day | RA | Dec. | Diam. | Phase | Transit | 5° high 52° | 5° high 56° |
|---|---|---|---|---|---|---|---|
| | h m | ° | ″ | % | h m | h m | h m |
| 1 | 12 17 | − 4.3 | 7 | 55 | 13 36 | 18 39 | 18 32 |
| 3 | 12 23 | − 5.3 | 7 | 52 | 13 35 | 18 32 | 18 24 |
| 5 | 12 29 | − 6.2 | 8 | 48 | 13 32 | 18 24 | 18 15 |
| 7 | 12 33 | − 7.1 | 8 | 45 | 13 29 | 18 17 | 18 07 |
| 9 | 12 37 | − 7.8 | 8 | 41 | 13 25 | 18 09 | 17 59 |
| 11 | 12 40 | − 8.3 | 8 | 36 | 13 19 | 18 01 | 17 50 |
| 13 | 12 42 | − 8.7 | 9 | 31 | 13 13 | 17 52 | 17 41 |
| 15 | 12 42 | − 8.9 | 9 | 26 | 13 05 | 17 44 | 17 32 |
| 17 | 12 41 | − 8.9 | 9 | 21 | 12 56 | 17 35 | 17 24 |
| 19 | 12 39 | − 8.6 | 10 | 16 | 12 45 | 17 26 | 17 15 |
| 21 | 12 35 | − 8.0 | 10 | 11 | 12 32 | 17 17 | 17 07 |
| 23 | 12 29 | − 7.1 | 10 | 6 | 12 19 | 17 09 | 17 00 |
| 25 | 12 22 | − 6.0 | 10 | 3 | 12 04 | 17 01 | 16 52 |
| 27 | 12 15 | − 4.7 | 10 | 1 | 11 49 | 6 47 | 6 54 |
| 29 | 12 08 | − 3.3 | 10 | 1 | 11 34 | 6 24 | 6 30 |
| 31 | 12 02 | − 1.9 | 10 | 3 | 11 20 | 6 03 | 6 08 |

## VENUS

| Day | RA | Dec. | Diam. | Phase | Transit | 5° high 52° | 5° high 56° |
|---|---|---|---|---|---|---|---|
| | h m | ° | ″ | % | h m | h m | h m |
| 1 | 13 24 | −12.0 | 27 | 43 | 14 44 | 19 03 | 18 4 |
| 6 | 13 40 | −14.1 | 29 | 40 | 14 40 | 18 46 | 18 2 |
| 11 | 13 54 | −16.1 | 31 | 37 | 14 34 | 18 28 | 18 0 |
| 16 | 14 08 | −17.9 | 34 | 34 | 14 28 | 18 09 | 17 4 |
| 21 | 14 20 | −19.5 | 36 | 30 | 14 20 | 17 49 | 17 2 |
| 26 | 14 30 | −20.9 | 39 | 26 | 14 10 | 17 29 | 16 5 |
| 31 | 14 37 | −22.0 | 43 | 22 | 13 58 | 17 08 | 16 3 |

## MARS

| Day | RA | Dec. | Diam. | Phase | Transit | 5° high 52° | 5° high 56° |
|---|---|---|---|---|---|---|---|
| 1 | 10 16 | +12.0 | 4 | 100 | 11 35 | 5 07 | 5 0 |
| 6 | 10 28 | +10.9 | 4 | 100 | 11 28 | 5 05 | 4 5 |
| 11 | 10 40 | + 9.7 | 4 | 100 | 11 20 | 5 03 | 4 5 |
| 16 | 10 52 | + 8.5 | 4 | 100 | 11 12 | 5 02 | 4 5 |
| 21 | 11 04 | + 7.2 | 4 | 100 | 11 04 | 5 00 | 4 5 |
| 26 | 11 15 | + 6.0 | 4 | 99 | 10 56 | 4 59 | 4 5 |
| 31 | 11 27 | + 4.7 | 4 | 99 | 10 48 | 4 57 | 4 5 |

## SUNRISE AND SUNSET

| Day | London rise | London set | Bristol rise | Bristol set | Birmingham rise | Birmingham set | Manchester rise | Manchester set | Newcastle rise | Newcastle set | Glasgow rise | Glasgow set | Belfast rise | Belfast set |
|---|---|---|---|---|---|---|---|---|---|---|---|---|---|---|
| | 0°05′ | 51°30′ | 2°35′ | 51°28′ | 1°55′ | 52°28′ | 2°15′ | 53°28′ | 1°37′ | 54°59′ | 4°14′ | 55°52′ | 5°56′ | 54°35′ |
| | h m | h m | h m | h m | h m | h m | h m | h m | h m | h m | h m | h m | h m | h m |
| 1 | 5 12 | 18 47 | 5 22 | 18 57 | 5 18 | 18 56 | 5 18 | 18 59 | 5 12 | 18 59 | 5 21 | 19 12 | 5 30 | 19 16 |
| 2 | 5 14 | 18 45 | 5 24 | 18 55 | 5 20 | 18 54 | 5 19 | 18 57 | 5 14 | 18 57 | 5 23 | 19 09 | 5 32 | 19 14 |
| 3 | 5 16 | 18 43 | 5 26 | 18 53 | 5 21 | 18 52 | 5 21 | 18 54 | 5 16 | 18 54 | 5 25 | 19 07 | 5 34 | 19 11 |
| 4 | 5 17 | 18 40 | 5 27 | 18 50 | 5 23 | 18 49 | 5 23 | 18 52 | 5 18 | 18 52 | 5 27 | 19 04 | 5 36 | 19 09 |
| 5 | 5 19 | 18 38 | 5 29 | 18 48 | 5 25 | 18 47 | 5 25 | 18 50 | 5 20 | 18 49 | 5 29 | 19 01 | 5 38 | 19 06 |
| 6 | 5 20 | 18 36 | 5 30 | 18 46 | 5 26 | 18 45 | 5 26 | 18 47 | 5 22 | 18 47 | 5 31 | 18 59 | 5 39 | 19 04 |
| 7 | 5 22 | 18 34 | 5 32 | 18 44 | 5 28 | 18 42 | 5 28 | 18 45 | 5 23 | 18 44 | 5 33 | 18 56 | 5 41 | 19 01 |
| 8 | 5 24 | 18 31 | 5 34 | 18 41 | 5 30 | 18 40 | 5 30 | 18 42 | 5 25 | 18 42 | 5 35 | 18 54 | 5 43 | 18 59 |
| 9 | 5 25 | 18 29 | 5 35 | 18 39 | 5 31 | 18 38 | 5 32 | 18 40 | 5 27 | 18 39 | 5 36 | 18 51 | 5 45 | 18 56 |
| 10 | 5 27 | 18 27 | 5 37 | 18 37 | 5 33 | 18 35 | 5 33 | 18 38 | 5 29 | 18 37 | 5 38 | 18 48 | 5 47 | 18 54 |
| 11 | 5 28 | 18 25 | 5 38 | 18 35 | 5 35 | 18 33 | 5 35 | 18 35 | 5 31 | 18 34 | 5 40 | 18 46 | 5 49 | 18 51 |
| 12 | 5 30 | 18 22 | 5 40 | 18 32 | 5 36 | 18 30 | 5 37 | 18 33 | 5 33 | 18 32 | 5 42 | 18 43 | 5 50 | 18 48 |
| 13 | 5 32 | 18 20 | 5 42 | 18 30 | 5 38 | 18 28 | 5 39 | 18 30 | 5 35 | 18 29 | 5 44 | 18 40 | 5 52 | 18 46 |
| 14 | 5 33 | 18 18 | 5 43 | 18 28 | 5 40 | 18 26 | 5 40 | 18 28 | 5 36 | 18 27 | 5 46 | 18 38 | 5 54 | 18 43 |
| 15 | 5 35 | 18 15 | 5 45 | 18 25 | 5 41 | 18 23 | 5 42 | 18 25 | 5 38 | 18 24 | 5 48 | 18 35 | 5 56 | 18 41 |
| 16 | 5 36 | 18 13 | 5 46 | 18 23 | 5 43 | 18 21 | 5 44 | 18 23 | 5 40 | 18 21 | 5 50 | 18 32 | 5 58 | 18 38 |
| 17 | 5 38 | 18 11 | 5 48 | 18 21 | 5 45 | 18 19 | 5 46 | 18 20 | 5 42 | 18 19 | 5 52 | 18 30 | 6 00 | 18 36 |
| 18 | 5 40 | 18 08 | 5 50 | 18 18 | 5 46 | 18 16 | 5 47 | 18 18 | 5 44 | 18 16 | 5 54 | 18 27 | 6 01 | 18 33 |
| 19 | 5 41 | 18 06 | 5 51 | 18 16 | 5 48 | 18 14 | 5 49 | 18 16 | 5 46 | 18 14 | 5 56 | 18 25 | 6 03 | 18 31 |
| 20 | 5 43 | 18 04 | 5 53 | 18 14 | 5 50 | 18 11 | 5 51 | 18 13 | 5 48 | 18 11 | 5 58 | 18 22 | 6 05 | 18 28 |
| 21 | 5 44 | 18 02 | 5 54 | 18 12 | 5 51 | 18 09 | 5 52 | 18 11 | 5 49 | 18 09 | 6 00 | 18 19 | 6 07 | 18 26 |
| 22 | 5 46 | 17 59 | 5 56 | 18 09 | 5 53 | 18 07 | 5 54 | 18 08 | 5 51 | 18 06 | 6 02 | 18 17 | 6 09 | 18 23 |
| 23 | 5 48 | 17 57 | 5 58 | 18 07 | 5 55 | 18 04 | 5 56 | 18 06 | 5 53 | 18 03 | 6 04 | 18 14 | 6 11 | 18 21 |
| 24 | 5 49 | 17 55 | 5 59 | 18 05 | 5 56 | 18 02 | 5 58 | 18 03 | 5 55 | 18 01 | 6 06 | 18 11 | 6 12 | 18 18 |
| 25 | 5 51 | 17 52 | 6 01 | 18 02 | 5 58 | 18 00 | 5 59 | 18 01 | 5 57 | 17 58 | 6 07 | 18 09 | 6 14 | 18 16 |
| 26 | 5 52 | 17 50 | 6 02 | 18 00 | 6 00 | 17 57 | 6 01 | 17 58 | 5 59 | 17 56 | 6 09 | 18 06 | 6 16 | 18 13 |
| 27 | 5 54 | 17 48 | 6 04 | 17 58 | 6 02 | 17 55 | 6 03 | 17 56 | 6 01 | 17 53 | 6 11 | 18 03 | 6 18 | 18 10 |
| 28 | 5 56 | 17 45 | 6 06 | 17 55 | 6 03 | 17 53 | 6 05 | 17 54 | 6 03 | 17 51 | 6 13 | 18 01 | 6 20 | 18 08 |
| 29 | 5 57 | 17 43 | 6 07 | 17 53 | 6 05 | 17 50 | 6 07 | 17 51 | 6 05 | 17 48 | 6 15 | 17 58 | 6 22 | 18 05 |
| 30 | 5 59 | 17 41 | 6 09 | 17 51 | 6 07 | 17 48 | 6 08 | 17 49 | 6 06 | 17 45 | 6 17 | 17 55 | 6 24 | 18 03 |

## JUPITER

| *Day* | *RA* | | *Dec.* | | *Transit* | | *5° high* 52° | | 56° | |
|---|---|---|---|---|---|---|---|---|---|---|
| | h | m | ° | ′ | h | m | h | m | h | m |
| 1 | 8 | 35.9 | +19 | 01 | 9 | 55 | 2 | 48 | 2 | 35 |
| 11 | 8 | 44.1 | +18 | 32 | 9 | 24 | 2 | 19 | 2 | 07 |
| 21 | 8 | 51.8 | +18 | 03 | 8 | 52 | 1 | 51 | 1 | 38 |
| 31 | 8 | 58.9 | +17 | 36 | 8 | 20 | 1 | 21 | 1 | 09 |

Diameters - equatorial 33″ polar 31″

## SATURN

| *Day* | *RA* | | *Dec.* | | *Transit* | | *5° high* 52° | | 56° | |
|---|---|---|---|---|---|---|---|---|---|---|
| | h | m | ° | ′ | h | m | h | m | h | m |
| 1 | 5 | 49.7 | +22 | 08 | 7 | 09 | 23 | 40 | 23 | 23 |
| 11 | 5 | 52.4 | +22 | 08 | 6 | 32 | 23 | 03 | 22 | 46 |
| 21 | 5 | 54.4 | +22 | 08 | 5 | 55 | 22 | 26 | 22 | 09 |
| 31 | 5 | 55.6 | +22 | 08 | 5 | 17 | 21 | 48 | 21 | 31 |

Diameters - equatorial 18″ polar 17″
Rings- major axis 41″ minor axis 18″

## URANUS

| *Day* | *RA* | | *Dec.* | | *Transit* | | *10° high* 52° | | 56° | |
|---|---|---|---|---|---|---|---|---|---|---|
| | h | m | ° | ′ | h | m | h | m | h | m |
| 1 | 21 | 55.6 | −13 | 27 | 23 | 12 | 2 | 49 | 2 | 26 |
| 11 | 21 | 54.1 | −13 | 35 | 22 | 31 | 2 | 07 | 1 | 44 |
| 21 | 21 | 52.8 | −13 | 42 | 21 | 50 | 1 | 26 | 1 | 02 |
| 31 | 21 | 51.7 | −13 | 47 | 21 | 10 | 0 | 45 | 0 | 21 |

Diameter 4″

## NEPTUNE

| *Day* | *RA* | | *Dec.* | | *Transit* | | *10° high* 52° | | 56° | |
|---|---|---|---|---|---|---|---|---|---|---|
| | h | m | ° | ′ | h | m | h | m | h | m |
| 1 | 20 | 44.9 | −18 | 00 | 22 | 01 | 1 | 03 | 0 | 29 |
| 11 | 20 | 44.0 | −18 | 03 | 21 | 21 | 0 | 22 | 23 | 44 |
| 21 | 20 | 43.3 | −18 | 06 | 20 | 41 | 23 | 38 | 23 | 04 |
| 31 | 20 | 42.8 | −18 | 08 | 20 | 01 | 22 | 58 | 22 | 24 |

Diameter 2″

# October 2002

TENTH MONTH, 31 DAYS. *Octo* (eighth), eighth month of Roman pre-Julian calendar

| | | | | |
|---|---|---|---|---|
| **1** | *Tuesday* | *Michaelmas Law Sittings begin.* People's Republic of China formally proclaimed 1949 | | 274 |
| **2** | *Wednesday* | Julius Marx b. 1890. Dr Marie Stopes d. 1958 | | 275 |
| **3** | *Thursday* | Jean Anouilh d. 1987. 1st British Atomic Bomb tested off north west coast of Australia 1952 | | 276 |
| **4** | *Friday* | Sir Arthur Whitten Brown d. 1948. Printing of first English (Coverdale) Bible 1535 | | 277 |
| **5** | *Saturday* | Jonathan Edwards b. 1703. *R101* disaster 1930 | | 278 |
| **6** | *Sunday* | **19th S. after Trinity.** William Tyndale d. 1536 | | 279 |
| **7** | *Monday* | Archbishop William Laud b. 1573. Cyril Cusack d. 1993 | *week* 40 *day* | 280 |
| **8** | *Tuesday* | Clement Attlee d. 1967. Great Fire of Chicago 1871 | | 281 |
| **9** | *Wednesday* | André Maurois d. 1967. Breathalyser tests came into force 1967 | | 282 |
| **10** | *Thursday* | Fridtjof Nansen b. 1861. Viscount Nuffield b. 1877 | | 283 |
| **11** | *Friday* | Johann Albert Fabricius b. 1668. Andy Stewart d. 1993 | | 284 |
| **12** | *Saturday* | Ramsay Macdonald b. 1866. Anatole France d. 1924 | | 285 |
| **13** | *Sunday* | **20th S. after Trinity.** Prince of Wales Edward b. 1453 | | 286 |
| **14** | *Monday* | Hon. George Grenville b. 1712. Erwin Rommel d. 1944 | *week* 41 *day* | 287 |
| **15** | *Tuesday* | Dr Marie Stopes b. 1880. First manned balloon flight (Jean de Rozier) 1783 | | 288 |
| **16** | *Wednesday* | Günter Grass b. 1927. Nicholas Ridley d. 1555 | | 289 |
| **17** | *Thursday* | Sir Philip Sidney b. 1586. Arthur Miller b. 1915 | | 290 |
| **18** | *Friday* | **St Luke.** Viscount Palmerston d. 1865 | | 291 |
| **19** | *Saturday* | Jonathan Swift d. 1745. Surrender of British Troops, American War of Independence 1781 | | 292 |
| **20** | *Sunday* | **21st S. after Trinity.** Arthur Rimbaud b. 1854 | | 293 |
| **21** | *Monday* | Geoffrey Boycott b. 1940. Arthur Schnitzler d. 1931 | *week* 42 *day* | 294 |
| **22** | *Tuesday* | Joan Fontaine b. 1917. Thomas Sheraton d. 1806 | | 295 |
| **23** | *Wednesday* | Pierre Larousse b. 1817. Zane Grey d. 1939 | | 296 |
| **24** | *Thursday* | 1st Baron Gladwyn Gladwyn Jebb d. 1996. United Nations formally came into existence 1945 | | 297 |
| **25** | *Friday* | Johann Strauss b. 1825. Battle of Agincourt 1415 | | 298 |
| **26** | *Saturday* | Alma Cogan d. 1966. Founding of Royal Marines 1664 | | 299 |
| **27** | *Sunday* | **9th S. before Christmas. Last Sunday after Trinity** | | 300 |
| **28** | *Monday* | **SS Simon and Jude.** John Locke d. 1704 | *week* 43 *day* | 301 |
| **29** | *Tuesday* | Sir Walter Raleigh d. 1618. International Red Cross founded 1863 | | 302 |
| **30** | *Wednesday* | Louis Malle b. 1932. Dame Rose Macaulay d. 1958 | | 303 |
| **31** | *Thursday* | Kai-Shek Chiang b. 1887. Mrs Indira Gandhi d. 1984 | | 304 |

## Astronomical Phenomena

| d | h | |
|---|---|---|
| 2 | 09 | Jupiter in conjunction with Moon. Jupiter 4° S. |
| 5 | 04 | Mars in conjunction with Moon. Mars 4° S. |
| 5 | 12 | Mercury in conjunction with Moon. Mercury 5° S. |
| 6 | 19 | Mercury at stationary point |
| 8 | 15 | Venus in conjunction with Moon. Venus 9° S. |
| 10 | 19 | Venus at stationary point |
| 11 | 13 | Saturn at stationary point |
| 13 | 07 | Mercury at greatest elongation W.18° |
| 20 | 14 | Neptune at stationary point |
| 23 | 14 | Sun's longitude 210°♏ |
| 26 | 09 | Saturn in conjunction with Moon. Saturn 3° S. |
| 30 | 00 | Jupiter in conjunction with Moon. Jupiter 4° S. |
| 31 | 12 | Venus in inferior conjunction |

## Minima of Algol

| d | h | d | h | d | h |
|---|---|---|---|---|---|
| 1 | 09.1 | 12 | 20.4 | 24 | 07.6 |
| 4 | 05.9 | 15 | 17.2 | 27 | 04.4 |
| 7 | 02.8 | 18 | 14.0 | 30 | 01.3 |
| 9 | 23.6 | 21 | 10.8 | | |

## Constellations

The following constellations are near the meridian at

| | d | h | | d | h |
|---|---|---|---|---|---|
| September | 1 | 24 | October | 16 | 21 |
| September | 15 | 23 | November | 1 | 20 |
| October | 1 | 22 | November | 15 | 19 |

Ursa Major (below the Pole), Cepheus, Cassiopeia Cygnus, Lacerta, Andromeda, Pegasus, Capricornus Aquarius and Piscis Austrinus

## The Moon

| Phases, Apsides and Node | d | h | m |
|---|---|---|---|
| ● New Moon | 6 | 11 | 18 |
| ☽ First Quarter | 13 | 05 | 33 |
| ○ Full Moon | 21 | 07 | 20 |
| ☾ Last Quarter | 29 | 05 | 28 |
| | | | |
| Perigee (356,918km) | 6 | 13 | 10 |
| Apogee (406,369km) | 20 | 04 | 24 |

Mean longitude of ascending node on October 1, 72°

HE SUN S.D 16′.1

| ay | Right Ascension | Dec. – | Equation of Time | Rise 52° | Rise 56° | Transit | Set 52° | Set 56° | Sidereal time | Transit of First Point of Aries |
|---|---|---|---|---|---|---|---|---|---|---|
| | h m s | ° ′ | m s | h m | h m | h m | h m | h m | h m s | h m s |
| 1 | 12 28 05 | 3 02 | +10 08 | 6 00 | 6 02 | 11 50 | 17 38 | 17 36 | 0 38 13 | 23 17 58 |
| 2 | 12 31 42 | 3 25 | +10 27 | 6 02 | 6 04 | 11 49 | 17 36 | 17 33 | 0 42 09 | 23 14 02 |
| 3 | 12 35 19 | 3 48 | +10 46 | 6 04 | 6 06 | 11 49 | 17 33 | 17 31 | 0 46 06 | 23 10 06 |
| 4 | 12 38 57 | 4 12 | +11 05 | 6 05 | 6 08 | 11 49 | 17 31 | 17 28 | 0 50 02 | 23 06 10 |
| 5 | 12 42 36 | 4 35 | +11 23 | 6 07 | 6 10 | 11 48 | 17 29 | 17 25 | 0 53 59 | 23 02 14 |
| 6 | 12 46 14 | 4 58 | +11 41 | 6 09 | 6 12 | 11 48 | 17 27 | 17 23 | 0 57 56 | 22 58 18 |
| 7 | 12 49 53 | 5 21 | +11 59 | 6 11 | 6 14 | 11 48 | 17 24 | 17 20 | 1 01 52 | 22 54 22 |
| 8 | 12 53 33 | 5 44 | +12 16 | 6 12 | 6 16 | 11 48 | 17 22 | 17 18 | 1 05 49 | 22 50 26 |
| 9 | 12 57 12 | 6 07 | +12 33 | 6 14 | 6 18 | 11 47 | 17 20 | 17 15 | 1 09 45 | 22 46 30 |
| 0 | 13 00 53 | 6 30 | +12 49 | 6 16 | 6 20 | 11 47 | 17 18 | 17 13 | 1 13 42 | 22 42 34 |
| 1 | 13 04 33 | 6 52 | +13 05 | 6 17 | 6 23 | 11 47 | 17 15 | 17 10 | 1 17 38 | 22 38 39 |
| 2 | 13 08 14 | 7 15 | +13 21 | 6 19 | 6 25 | 11 47 | 17 13 | 17 07 | 1 21 35 | 22 34 43 |
| 3 | 13 11 56 | 7 37 | +13 35 | 6 21 | 6 27 | 11 46 | 17 11 | 17 05 | 1 25 31 | 22 30 47 |
| 4 | 13 15 38 | 8 00 | +13 50 | 6 23 | 6 29 | 11 46 | 17 09 | 17 02 | 1 29 28 | 22 26 51 |
| 5 | 13 19 21 | 8 22 | +14 04 | 6 24 | 6 31 | 11 46 | 17 06 | 17 00 | 1 33 25 | 22 22 55 |
| 6 | 13 23 04 | 8 44 | +14 17 | 6 26 | 6 33 | 11 46 | 17 04 | 16 57 | 1 37 21 | 22 18 59 |
| 7 | 13 26 48 | 9 06 | +14 30 | 6 28 | 6 35 | 11 45 | 17 02 | 16 55 | 1 41 18 | 22 15 03 |
| 8 | 13 30 32 | 9 28 | +14 42 | 6 29 | 6 37 | 11 45 | 17 00 | 16 52 | 1 45 14 | 22 11 07 |
| 9 | 13 34 17 | 9 50 | +14 54 | 6 31 | 6 39 | 11 45 | 16 58 | 16 50 | 1 49 11 | 22 07 11 |
| 0 | 13 38 02 | 10 12 | +15 05 | 6 33 | 6 41 | 11 45 | 16 56 | 16 48 | 1 53 07 | 22 03 15 |
| 1 | 13 41 48 | 10 33 | +15 16 | 6 35 | 6 43 | 11 45 | 16 54 | 16 45 | 1 57 04 | 21 59 19 |
| 2 | 13 45 35 | 10 55 | +15 25 | 6 37 | 6 45 | 11 44 | 16 52 | 16 43 | 2 01 00 | 21 55 24 |
| 3 | 13 49 23 | 11 16 | +15 34 | 6 38 | 6 47 | 11 44 | 16 50 | 16 40 | 2 04 57 | 21 51 28 |
| 4 | 13 53 11 | 11 37 | +15 43 | 6 40 | 6 49 | 11 44 | 16 48 | 16 38 | 2 08 53 | 21 47 32 |
| 5 | 13 56 59 | 11 58 | +15 51 | 6 42 | 6 52 | 11 44 | 16 46 | 16 36 | 2 12 50 | 21 43 36 |
| 6 | 14 00 49 | 12 18 | +15 58 | 6 44 | 6 54 | 11 44 | 16 44 | 16 33 | 2 16 47 | 21 39 40 |
| 7 | 14 04 39 | 12 39 | +16 04 | 6 45 | 6 56 | 11 44 | 16 42 | 16 31 | 2 20 43 | 21 35 44 |
| 8 | 14 08 30 | 12 59 | +16 09 | 6 47 | 6 58 | 11 44 | 16 40 | 16 29 | 2 24 40 | 21 31 48 |
| 9 | 14 12 22 | 13 19 | +16 14 | 6 49 | 7 00 | 11 44 | 16 38 | 16 27 | 2 28 36 | 21 27 52 |
| 0 | 14 16 15 | 13 39 | +16 18 | 6 51 | 7 02 | 11 44 | 16 36 | 16 24 | 2 32 33 | 21 23 56 |
| 1 | 14 20 08 | 13 59 | +16 21 | 6 53 | 7 04 | 11 44 | 16 34 | 16 22 | 2 36 29 | 21 20 00 |

URATION OF TWILIGHT (in minutes)

| atitude | 52° | 56° | 52° | 56° | 52° | 56° | 52° | 56° |
|---|---|---|---|---|---|---|---|---|
| | 1 October | | 11 October | | 21 October | | 31 October | |
| ivil | 34 | 37 | 34 | 37 | 34 | 38 | 35 | 39 |
| Vautical | 73 | 80 | 73 | 80 | 74 | 81 | 75 | 83 |
| Astronomical | 113 | 125 | 112 | 124 | 113 | 124 | 114 | 126 |

HE NIGHT SKY

*Mercury* reaches greatest western elongation (18°) on the 3th and is visible as a morning object after the first week of he month, low above the east-south-eastern horizon round the time of morning civil twilight. During the last veek of the month it is getting too close to the Sun to be letected, even though its magnitude has brightened to 1.0. This is the most favourable morning apparition of the ear for observers in the latitudes of the British Isles. For ome days around the 10th Mercury will only be a few legrees east of Mars.

*Venus* is unsuitably placed for observation throughout )ctober. Although it is still 37 degrees from the Sun at the eginning of the month, its declination of -23 degrees ompletely nullifies this apparently favourable elongation, s seen from the latitudes of the British Isles. Venus passes apidly through inferior conjunction on the last day of the nonth, becoming visible early in November.

*Mars*, magnitude +1.8, continues to be visible in the pre-dawn sky, low above the east-south-eastern horizon. Early in the month Mars moves eastwards from Leo into Virgo. Under good conditions on the morning of the 5th, about 1 hour before sunrise, the old Moon, less than 2 days before New, may be seen about 4 degrees to the left of the planet.

*Jupiter*, is a conspicuous object in the south-eastern quadrant of the sky in the mornings until twilight inhibits observation. By the end of the month the planet is visible low above the eastern horizon by midnight. The Moon is near Jupiter on the mornings of the 2nd and the 30th.

The four Galilean satellites are readily observable with a small telescope or even a good pair of binoculars provided that they are held rigidly.

*Saturn* continues to be visible as a morning object, magnitude -0.1. It reaches its first stationary point on the 11th, in the constellation of Orion, just south of the Taurus-Gemini border, some 15 degrees north of Betelgeuse. On the morning of the 26th the gibbous Moon passes 2 degrees north of Saturn.

## THE MOON

| Day | RA | Dec. | Hor. par. | Semi-diam | Sun's co-long. | PA of Bright Limb | Phase | Age | Rise 52° | Rise 56° | Transit | Set 52° | Set 56° |
|---|---|---|---|---|---|---|---|---|---|---|---|---|---|
| | h m | ° | ′ | ′ | ° | ° | % | d | h m | h m | h m | h m | h m |
| **1** | 7 43 | +24.8 | 57.7 | 15.7 | 203 | 101 | 37 | 23.9 | 23 51 | 23 26 | 7 22 | 15 55 | 16 2 |
| **2** | 8 42 | +22.6 | 58.6 | 16.0 | 215 | 107 | 26 | 24.9 | — | — | 8 18 | 16 29 | 16 4 |
| **3** | 9 40 | +19.0 | 59.6 | 16.2 | 227 | 113 | 17 | 25.9 | 1 15 | 0 56 | 9 15 | 16 55 | 17 0 |
| **4** | 10 37 | +14.2 | 60.4 | 16.5 | 240 | 119 | 9 | 26.9 | 2 43 | 2 30 | 10 09 | 17 16 | 17 2 |
| **5** | 11 33 | + 8.3 | 61.0 | 16.6 | 252 | 126 | 4 | 27.9 | 4 12 | 4 06 | 11 03 | 17 35 | 17 3 |
| **6** | 12 29 | + 1.9 | 61.4 | 16.7 | 264 | 147 | 1 | 28.9 | 5 42 | 5 42 | 11 56 | 17 52 | 17 5 |
| **7** | 13 24 | − 4.7 | 61.4 | 16.7 | 276 | 265 | 1 | 0.5 | 7 13 | 7 19 | 12 50 | 18 11 | 18 0 |
| **8** | 14 20 | −10.9 | 61.1 | 16.6 | 289 | 282 | 4 | 1.5 | 8 44 | 8 56 | 13 44 | 18 32 | 18 1 |
| **9** | 15 17 | −16.5 | 60.5 | 16.5 | 301 | 283 | 9 | 2.5 | 10 13 | 10 32 | 14 41 | 18 58 | 18 3 |
| **10** | 16 16 | −20.9 | 59.7 | 16.3 | 313 | 280 | 17 | 3.5 | 11 39 | 12 04 | 15 38 | 19 31 | 19 0 |
| **11** | 17 16 | −23.9 | 58.7 | 16.0 | 325 | 275 | 27 | 4.5 | 12 56 | 13 25 | 16 37 | 20 15 | 19 4 |
| **12** | 18 15 | −25.4 | 57.8 | 15.7 | 337 | 269 | 37 | 5.5 | 13 59 | 14 30 | 17 34 | 21 11 | 20 3 |
| **13** | 19 14 | −25.4 | 56.9 | 15.5 | 350 | 263 | 48 | 6.5 | 14 47 | 15 16 | 18 29 | 22 16 | 21 4 |
| **14** | 20 10 | −24.1 | 56.1 | 15.3 | 2 | 257 | 58 | 7.5 | 15 22 | 15 46 | 19 21 | 23 26 | 23 0 |
| **15** | 21 04 | −21.5 | 55.4 | 15.1 | 14 | 252 | 68 | 8.5 | 15 48 | 16 07 | 20 09 | — | — |
| **16** | 21 54 | −18.1 | 54.9 | 15.0 | 26 | 247 | 76 | 9.5 | 16 08 | 16 22 | 20 54 | 0 39 | 0 2 |
| **17** | 22 41 | −13.9 | 54.5 | 14.8 | 38 | 243 | 84 | 10.5 | 16 24 | 16 34 | 21 36 | 1 50 | 1 3 |
| **18** | 23 26 | − 9.2 | 54.2 | 14.8 | 51 | 240 | 90 | 11.5 | 16 38 | 16 43 | 22 17 | 3 00 | 2 5 |
| **19** | 0 09 | − 4.3 | 54.0 | 14.7 | 63 | 236 | 95 | 12.5 | 16 51 | 16 52 | 22 57 | 4 09 | 4 0 |
| **20** | 0 52 | + 0.9 | 54.0 | 14.7 | 75 | 231 | 98 | 13.5 | 17 04 | 17 00 | 23 37 | 5 17 | 5 1 |
| **21** | 1 35 | + 5.9 | 54.0 | 14.7 | 87 | 201 | 100 | 14.5 | 17 17 | 17 09 | — | 6 25 | 6 3 |
| **22** | 2 18 | +10.8 | 54.1 | 14.7 | 99 | 91 | 100 | 15.5 | 17 33 | 17 20 | 0 18 | 7 34 | 7 4 |
| **23** | 3 04 | +15.4 | 54.3 | 14.8 | 111 | 80 | 97 | 16.5 | 17 51 | 17 34 | 1 01 | 8 45 | 9 0 |
| **24** | 3 51 | +19.3 | 54.6 | 14.9 | 123 | 79 | 94 | 17.5 | 18 15 | 17 53 | 1 46 | 9 56 | 10 1 |
| **25** | 4 42 | +22.5 | 55.0 | 15.0 | 136 | 82 | 88 | 18.5 | 18 47 | 18 19 | 2 34 | 11 07 | 11 3 |
| **26** | 5 35 | +24.7 | 55.4 | 15.1 | 148 | 86 | 81 | 19.5 | 19 29 | 18 59 | 3 25 | 12 12 | 12 4 |
| **27** | 6 30 | +25.7 | 56.0 | 15.3 | 160 | 92 | 73 | 20.5 | 20 24 | 19 54 | 4 18 | 13 09 | 13 3 |
| **28** | 7 26 | +25.4 | 56.7 | 15.4 | 172 | 98 | 63 | 21.5 | 21 32 | 21 05 | 5 13 | 13 55 | 14 2 |
| **29** | 8 24 | +23.7 | 57.5 | 15.7 | 184 | 103 | 53 | 22.5 | 22 50 | 22 28 | 6 08 | 14 30 | 14 5 |
| **30** | 9 20 | +20.6 | 58.3 | 15.9 | 196 | 109 | 42 | 23.5 | — | 23 58 | 7 03 | 14 57 | 15 1 |
| **31** | 10 16 | +16.3 | 59.1 | 16.1 | 209 | 113 | 31 | 24.5 | 0 13 | — | 7 56 | 15 19 | 15 3 |

## MERCURY

| Day | RA | Dec. | Diam. | Phase | Transit | 5° high 52° | 5° high 56° |
|---|---|---|---|---|---|---|---|
| | h m | ° | ″ | % | h m | h m | h m |
| 1 | 12 02 | −1.9 | 10 | 3 | 11 20 | 6 03 | 6 08 |
| 3 | 11 57 | −0.7 | 9 | 8 | 11 08 | 5 45 | 5 49 |
| 5 | 11 55 | +0.3 | 9 | 15 | 10 59 | 5 30 | 5 33 |
| 7 | 11 54 | +1.0 | 8 | 23 | 10 51 | 5 19 | 5 22 |
| 9 | 11 57 | +1.3 | 8 | 33 | 10 46 | 5 12 | 5 15 |
| 11 | 12 01 | +1.3 | 7 | 42 | 10 43 | 5 10 | 5 12 |
| 13 | 12 08 | +0.9 | 7 | 52 | 10 42 | 5 11 | 5 13 |
| 15 | 12 16 | +0.2 | 7 | 61 | 10 43 | 5 15 | 5 18 |
| 17 | 12 26 | −0.6 | 6 | 69 | 10 45 | 5 21 | 5 25 |
| 19 | 12 36 | −1.7 | 6 | 75 | 10 48 | 5 30 | 5 34 |
| 21 | 12 47 | −2.9 | 6 | 81 | 10 51 | 5 39 | 5 45 |
| 23 | 12 59 | −4.2 | 6 | 85 | 10 55 | 5 50 | 5 57 |
| 25 | 13 11 | −5.5 | 5 | 89 | 10 59 | 6 01 | 6 09 |
| 27 | 13 23 | −6.9 | 5 | 92 | 11 03 | 6 13 | 6 22 |
| 29 | 13 35 | −8.2 | 5 | 94 | 11 08 | 6 25 | 6 36 |
| 31 | 13 48 | −9.6 | 5 | 96 | 11 12 | 6 37 | 6 50 |

## VENUS

| Day | RA | Dec. | Diam. | Phase | Transit | 5° high 52° | 5° high 56° |
|---|---|---|---|---|---|---|---|
| | h m | ° | ″ | % | h m | h m | h m |
| 1 | 14 37 | −22.0 | 43 | 22 | 13 58 | 17 08 | 16 3 |
| 6 | 14 42 | −22.9 | 46 | 17 | 13 42 | 16 46 | 16 1 |
| 11 | 14 44 | −23.3 | 50 | 13 | 13 24 | 16 24 | 15 4 |
| 16 | 14 41 | −23.2 | 54 | 8 | 13 01 | 16 02 | 15 2 |
| 21 | 14 35 | −22.6 | 58 | 5 | 12 35 | 15 42 | 15 0 |
| 26 | 14 26 | −21.4 | 60 | 2 | 12 06 | 15 24 | 14 5 |
| 31 | 14 15 | −19.7 | 62 | 1 | 11 36 | 15 07 | 14 4 |

## MARS

| Day | RA | Dec. | Diam. | Phase | Transit | 5° high 52° | 5° high 56° |
|---|---|---|---|---|---|---|---|
| 1 | 11 27 | + 4.7 | 4 | 99 | 10 48 | 4 57 | 4 5 |
| 6 | 11 39 | + 3.5 | 4 | 99 | 10 40 | 4 56 | 4 5 |
| 11 | 11 51 | + 2.2 | 4 | 99 | 10 32 | 4 54 | 4 5 |
| 16 | 12 02 | + 0.9 | 4 | 99 | 10 24 | 4 53 | 4 5 |
| 21 | 12 14 | − 0.4 | 4 | 99 | 10 16 | 4 51 | 4 5 |
| 26 | 12 26 | − 1.6 | 4 | 98 | 10 08 | 4 50 | 4 5 |
| 31 | 12 37 | − 2.9 | 4 | 98 | 10 00 | 4 49 | 4 5 |

## SUNRISE AND SUNSET

| | London | | Bristol | | Birmingham | | Manchester | | Newcastle | | Glasgow | | Belfast | |
|---|---|---|---|---|---|---|---|---|---|---|---|---|---|---|
| | 0°05′ | 51°30′ | 2°35′ | 51°28′ | 1°55′ | 52°28′ | 2°15′ | 53°28′ | 1°37′ | 54°59′ | 4°14′ | 55°52′ | 5°56′ | 54°35′ |
| | h m | h m | h m | h m | h m | h m | h m | h m | h m | h m | h m | h m | h m | h m |
| **1** | 6 01 | 17 39 | 6 11 | 17 49 | 6 08 | 17 45 | 6 10 | 17 46 | 6 08 | 17 43 | 6 19 | 17 53 | 6 25 | 18 00 |
| **2** | 6 02 | 17 36 | 6 12 | 17 46 | 6 10 | 17 43 | 6 12 | 17 44 | 6 10 | 17 40 | 6 21 | 17 50 | 6 27 | 17 58 |
| **3** | 6 04 | 17 34 | 6 14 | 17 44 | 6 12 | 17 41 | 6 14 | 17 41 | 6 12 | 17 38 | 6 23 | 17 48 | 6 29 | 17 55 |
| **4** | 6 05 | 17 32 | 6 15 | 17 42 | 6 13 | 17 38 | 6 15 | 17 39 | 6 14 | 17 35 | 6 25 | 17 45 | 6 31 | 17 53 |
| **5** | 6 07 | 17 30 | 6 17 | 17 40 | 6 15 | 17 36 | 6 17 | 17 37 | 6 16 | 17 33 | 6 27 | 17 42 | 6 33 | 17 50 |
| **6** | 6 09 | 17 27 | 6 19 | 17 37 | 6 17 | 17 34 | 6 19 | 17 34 | 6 18 | 17 30 | 6 29 | 17 40 | 6 35 | 17 48 |
| **7** | 6 10 | 17 25 | 6 20 | 17 35 | 6 19 | 17 32 | 6 21 | 17 32 | 6 20 | 17 28 | 6 31 | 17 37 | 6 37 | 17 45 |
| **8** | 6 12 | 17 23 | 6 22 | 17 33 | 6 20 | 17 29 | 6 23 | 17 30 | 6 22 | 17 25 | 6 33 | 17 35 | 6 39 | 17 43 |
| **9** | 6 14 | 17 21 | 6 24 | 17 31 | 6 22 | 17 27 | 6 24 | 17 27 | 6 24 | 17 23 | 6 35 | 17 32 | 6 41 | 17 41 |
| **10** | 6 15 | 17 18 | 6 25 | 17 28 | 6 24 | 17 25 | 6 26 | 17 25 | 6 26 | 17 20 | 6 37 | 17 30 | 6 42 | 17 38 |
| **11** | 6 17 | 17 16 | 6 27 | 17 26 | 6 26 | 17 22 | 6 28 | 17 22 | 6 28 | 17 18 | 6 39 | 17 27 | 6 44 | 17 36 |
| **12** | 6 19 | 17 14 | 6 29 | 17 24 | 6 27 | 17 20 | 6 30 | 17 20 | 6 30 | 17 15 | 6 41 | 17 25 | 6 46 | 17 33 |
| **13** | 6 20 | 17 12 | 6 30 | 17 22 | 6 29 | 17 18 | 6 32 | 17 18 | 6 31 | 17 13 | 6 43 | 17 22 | 6 48 | 17 31 |
| **14** | 6 22 | 17 10 | 6 32 | 17 20 | 6 31 | 17 16 | 6 34 | 17 16 | 6 33 | 17 11 | 6 45 | 17 20 | 6 50 | 17 28 |
| **15** | 6 24 | 17 08 | 6 34 | 17 18 | 6 33 | 17 13 | 6 35 | 17 13 | 6 35 | 17 08 | 6 47 | 17 17 | 6 52 | 17 26 |
| **16** | 6 26 | 17 05 | 6 35 | 17 15 | 6 34 | 17 11 | 6 37 | 17 11 | 6 37 | 17 06 | 6 49 | 17 15 | 6 54 | 17 24 |
| **17** | 6 27 | 17 03 | 6 37 | 17 13 | 6 36 | 17 09 | 6 39 | 17 09 | 6 39 | 17 03 | 6 52 | 17 12 | 6 56 | 17 21 |
| **18** | 6 29 | 17 01 | 6 39 | 17 11 | 6 38 | 17 07 | 6 41 | 17 06 | 6 41 | 17 01 | 6 54 | 17 10 | 6 58 | 17 19 |
| **19** | 6 31 | 16 59 | 6 41 | 17 09 | 6 40 | 17 05 | 6 43 | 17 04 | 6 43 | 16 59 | 6 56 | 17 07 | 7 00 | 17 17 |
| **20** | 6 32 | 16 57 | 6 42 | 17 07 | 6 42 | 17 03 | 6 45 | 17 02 | 6 45 | 16 56 | 6 58 | 17 05 | 7 02 | 17 14 |
| **21** | 6 34 | 16 55 | 6 44 | 17 05 | 6 43 | 17 00 | 6 47 | 17 00 | 6 47 | 16 54 | 7 00 | 17 02 | 7 04 | 17 12 |
| **22** | 6 36 | 16 53 | 6 46 | 17 03 | 6 45 | 16 58 | 6 49 | 16 58 | 6 49 | 16 52 | 7 02 | 17 00 | 7 06 | 17 10 |
| **23** | 6 38 | 16 51 | 6 48 | 17 01 | 6 47 | 16 56 | 6 50 | 16 55 | 6 51 | 16 49 | 7 04 | 16 58 | 7 08 | 17 08 |
| **24** | 6 39 | 16 49 | 6 49 | 16 59 | 6 49 | 16 54 | 6 52 | 16 53 | 6 53 | 16 47 | 7 06 | 16 55 | 7 10 | 17 05 |
| **25** | 6 41 | 16 47 | 6 51 | 16 57 | 6 51 | 16 52 | 6 54 | 16 51 | 6 55 | 16 45 | 7 08 | 16 53 | 7 12 | 17 03 |
| **26** | 6 43 | 16 45 | 6 53 | 16 55 | 6 52 | 16 50 | 6 56 | 16 49 | 6 57 | 16 43 | 7 10 | 16 51 | 7 14 | 17 01 |
| **27** | 6 45 | 16 43 | 6 55 | 16 53 | 6 54 | 16 48 | 6 58 | 16 47 | 6 59 | 16 40 | 7 12 | 16 48 | 7 16 | 16 59 |
| **28** | 6 46 | 16 41 | 6 56 | 16 51 | 6 56 | 16 46 | 7 00 | 16 45 | 7 01 | 16 38 | 7 14 | 16 46 | 7 18 | 16 57 |
| **29** | 6 48 | 16 39 | 6 58 | 16 49 | 6 58 | 16 44 | 7 02 | 16 43 | 7 04 | 16 36 | 7 17 | 16 44 | 7 20 | 16 54 |
| **30** | 6 50 | 16 37 | 7 00 | 16 47 | 7 00 | 16 42 | 7 04 | 16 41 | 7 06 | 16 34 | 7 19 | 16 42 | 7 22 | 16 52 |
| **31** | 6 52 | 16 36 | 7 02 | 16 46 | 7 01 | 16 40 | 7 06 | 16 39 | 7 08 | 16 32 | 7 21 | 16 39 | 7 24 | 16 50 |

## JUPITER

| *Day* | *RA* | | *Dec.* | | *Transit* | | *5° high* | | | |
|---|---|---|---|---|---|---|---|---|---|---|
| | | | | | | | 52° | | 56° | |
| | h | m | ° | ′ | h | m | h | m | h | m |
| 1 | 8 | 58.9 | +17 | 36 | 8 | 20 | 1 | 21 | 1 | 09 |
| 11 | 9 | 05.3 | +17 | 11 | 7 | 47 | 0 | 50 | 0 | 39 |
| 21 | 9 | 10.8 | +16 | 48 | 7 | 13 | 0 | 18 | 0 | 08 |
| 31 | 9 | 15.5 | +16 | 29 | 6 | 38 | 23 | 42 | 23 | 32 |

Diameters – equatorial 35″ polar 33″

## SATURN

| *Day* | *RA* | | *Dec.* | | *Transit* | | *5° high* | | | |
|---|---|---|---|---|---|---|---|---|---|---|
| | | | | | | | 52° | | 56° | |
| | h | m | ° | ′ | h | m | h | m | h | m |
| 1 | 5 | 55.6 | +22 | 08 | 5 | 17 | 21 | 48 | 21 | 31 |
| 11 | 5 | 56.1 | +22 | 07 | 4 | 38 | 21 | 09 | 20 | 52 |
| 21 | 5 | 55.7 | +22 | 07 | 3 | 58 | 20 | 29 | 20 | 12 |
| 31 | 5 | 54.6 | +22 | 06 | 3 | 18 | 19 | 49 | 19 | 32 |

Diameters – equatorial 19″ polar 18″
Rings – major axis 44″ minor axis 19″

## URANUS

| *Day* | *RA* | | *Dec.* | | *Transit* | | *10° high* | | | |
|---|---|---|---|---|---|---|---|---|---|---|
| | | | | | | | 52° | | 56° | |
| | h | m | ° | ′ | h | m | h | m | h | m |
| 1 | 21 | 51.7 | −13 | 47 | 21 | 10 | 0 | 45 | 0 | 21 |
| 11 | 21 | 50.8 | −13 | 52 | 20 | 30 | 0 | 04 | 23 | 36 |
| 21 | 21 | 50.1 | −13 | 54 | 19 | 50 | 23 | 20 | 22 | 56 |
| 31 | 21 | 49.8 | −13 | 56 | 19 | 10 | 22 | 40 | 22 | 16 |

Diameter 4″

## NEPTUNE

| *Day* | *RA* | | *Dec.* | | *Transit* | | *10° high* | | | |
|---|---|---|---|---|---|---|---|---|---|---|
| | | | | | | | 52° | | 56° | |
| | h | m | ° | ′ | h | m | h | m | h | m |
| 1 | 20 | 42.8 | −18 | 08 | 20 | 01 | 22 | 58 | 22 | 24 |
| 11 | 20 | 42.5 | −18 | 09 | 19 | 22 | 22 | 18 | 21 | 44 |
| 21 | 20 | 42.4 | −18 | 10 | 18 | 42 | 21 | 39 | 21 | 04 |
| 31 | 20 | 42.5 | −18 | 10 | 18 | 03 | 21 | 00 | 20 | 25 |

Diameter 2″

# November 2002

ELEVENTH MONTH, 30 DAYS, *Novem* (nine), ninth month of Roman pre-Julian calendar

| | | | |
|---|---|---|---|
| 1 | *Friday* | **All Saints' Day.** Michael Denison b. 1915 | 305 |
| 2 | *Saturday* | Queen Marie Antoinette b. 1755. Jenny Lind d. 1887 | 306 |
| 3 | *Sunday* | **4th S. before Advent.** First dog launched into space in Sputnik II 1957 | 307 |
| 4 | *Monday* | Guido Reni b. 1575. Russian troops invaded Budapest 1956 | *week* 44 *day* 308 |
| 5 | *Tuesday* | Jacques Tati d. 1982. Battle of Inkerman 1854 | 309 |
| 6 | *Wednesday* | RAMADAN begins. Abraham Lincoln elected 16th President of the USA 1860 | 310 |
| 7 | *Thursday* | Joan Sutherland b. 1926. Gene Tunney d. 1978 | 311 |
| 8 | *Friday* | Bram Stoker b. 1847. Anya Seton d. 1990 | 312 |
| 9 | *Saturday* | King Edward VII Saxe-Coburg and Gotha b. 1841. Ramsay Macdonald d. 1937 | 313 |
| 10 | *Sunday* | **3rd S. before Advent.** Remembrance Sunday. | 314 |
| 11 | *Monday* | Ned Kelly d. 1880. Armistice Day 1918 | *week* 45 *day* 315 |
| 12 | *Tuesday* | Auguste Rodin b. 1840. Harry R. Haldeman d. 1993 | 316 |
| 13 | *Wednesday* | Dr George Carey b. 1935. King Edward III b. 1312 | 317 |
| 14 | *Thursday* | *Prince of Wales b. 1948.* Gottfried Leibniz d. 1716 | 318 |
| 15 | *Friday* | Daniel Barenboim b. 1942. Aneurin Bevan b. 1897 | 319 |
| 16 | *Saturday* | Burgess Meredith b. 1907. Lucia Popp d. 1993 | 320 |
| 17 | *Sunday* | **2nd S. before Advent.** Auguste Rodin d. 1917 | 321 |
| 18 | *Monday* | Marcel Proust d. 1922. Consecration of St Peter's Church, Rome 1626 | *week* 46 *day* 322 |
| 19 | *Tuesday* | Nicolas Poussin d. 1665. Gettysburg Address by Lincoln 1863 | 323 |
| 20 | *Wednesday* | *Queen's Wedding Day 1947.* Thomas Chatterton b. 1752 | 324 |
| 21 | *Thursday* | Malcolm Williamson b. 1931. Edward Bawden d. 1989 | 325 |
| 22 | *Friday* | Sir Peter Hall b. 1930. Mae West d. 1981 | 326 |
| 23 | *Saturday* | Michael Gough b. 1917. Louis Malle d. 1995 | 327 |
| 24 | *Sunday* | **S. next before Advent.** Georges Clemenceau d. 1929 | 328 |
| 25 | *Monday* | Francis Durbridge b. 1912. Upton Sinclair d. 1968 | *week* 47 *day* 329 |
| 26 | *Tuesday* | Sir Henry Coward b. 1849. John McAdam d. 1836 | 330 |
| 27 | *Wednesday* | Alexander Dubcek b. 1921. Eugene O'Neill d. 1953 | 331 |
| 28 | *Thursday* | Friedrich Engels b. 1820. Kenneth Connor d. 1993 | 332 |
| 29 | *Friday* | Christian Doppler b. 1803. Claudio Monteverdi d. 1643 | 333 |
| 30 | *Saturday* | **St Andrew.** CHANUCAH. | 334 |

### Astronomical Phenomena

| d | h | |
|---|---|---|
| 2 | 20 | Mars in conjunction with Moon. Mars 3° S. |
| 4 | 06 | Uranus at stationary point |
| 4 | 08 | Venus in conjunction with Mercury. Venus 6° S. |
| 4 | 10 | Venus in conjunction with Moon. Venus 8° S. |
| 4 | 10 | Mercury in conjunction with Moon. Mercury 2° S. |
| 14 | 05 | Mercury in superior conjunction |
| 21 | 07 | Venus at stationary point |
| 22 | 12 | Sun's longitude 240° ♐ |
| 22 | 12 | Saturn in conjunction with Moon. Saturn 3° S. |
| 26 | 10 | Jupiter in conjunction with Moon. Jupiter 4° S. |

### Minima of Algol

| d | h | d | h | d | h |
|---|---|---|---|---|---|
| 1 | 22.1 | 13 | 09.3 | 24 | 20.6 |
| 4 | 18.9 | 16 | 06.1 | 27 | 17.4 |
| 7 | 15.7 | 19 | 03.0 | 30 | 14.2 |
| 10 | 12.5 | 21 | 23.8 | | |

### Constellations

The following constellations are near the meridian at

| | d | h | | d | h |
|---|---|---|---|---|---|
| October | 1 | 24 | November | 15 | 21 |
| October | 16 | 23 | December | 1 | 20 |
| November | 1 | 22 | December | 16 | 19 |

Ursa Major (below the Pole), Cepheus, Cassiopeia, Andromeda, Pegasus, Pisces, Aquarius and Cetus

### The Moon

| Phases, Apsides and Node | d | h | m |
|---|---|---|---|
| ● New Moon | 4 | 20 | 34 |
| ☽ First Quarter | 11 | 20 | 52 |
| ○ Full Moon | 20 | 01 | 34 |
| ☾ Last Quarter | 27 | 15 | 46 |
| | | | |
| Perigee (358,146km) | 4 | 00 | 40 |
| Apogee (405,823km) | 16 | 11 | 20 |

Mean longitude of ascending node on November 1, 70°

THE SUN S.D 16′.1

| Day | Right Ascension | Dec. – | Equation of Time | Rise 52° | Rise 56° | Transit | Set 52° | Set 56° | Sidereal time | Transit of First Point of Aries |
|---|---|---|---|---|---|---|---|---|---|---|
| | h m s | ° ′ | m s | h m | h m | h m | h m | h m | h m s | h m s |
| 1 | 14 24 02 | 14 18 | +16 23 | 6 54 | 7 06 | 11 44 | 16 32 | 16 20 | 2 40 26 | 21 16 04 |
| 2 | 14 27 57 | 14 37 | +16 25 | 6 56 | 7 09 | 11 44 | 16 30 | 16 18 | 2 44 22 | 21 12 09 |
| 3 | 14 31 53 | 14 56 | +16 26 | 6 58 | 7 11 | 11 44 | 16 28 | 16 16 | 2 48 19 | 21 08 13 |
| 4 | 14 35 50 | 15 15 | +16 26 | 7 00 | 7 13 | 11 44 | 16 27 | 16 13 | 2 52 16 | 21 04 17 |
| 5 | 14 39 47 | 15 33 | +16 25 | 7 02 | 7 15 | 11 44 | 16 25 | 16 11 | 2 56 12 | 21 00 21 |
| 6 | 14 43 46 | 15 52 | +16 23 | 7 03 | 7 17 | 11 44 | 16 23 | 16 09 | 3 00 09 | 20 56 25 |
| 7 | 14 47 45 | 16 10 | +16 20 | 7 05 | 7 19 | 11 44 | 16 21 | 16 07 | 3 04 05 | 20 52 29 |
| 8 | 14 51 45 | 16 27 | +16 17 | 7 07 | 7 21 | 11 44 | 16 20 | 16 05 | 3 08 02 | 20 48 33 |
| 9 | 14 55 46 | 16 45 | +16 13 | 7 09 | 7 23 | 11 44 | 16 18 | 16 03 | 3 11 58 | 20 44 37 |
| 10 | 14 59 47 | 17 02 | +16 08 | 7 11 | 7 26 | 11 44 | 16 17 | 16 02 | 3 15 55 | 20 40 41 |
| 11 | 15 03 50 | 17 19 | +16 02 | 7 12 | 7 28 | 11 44 | 16 15 | 16 00 | 3 19 51 | 20 36 45 |
| 12 | 15 07 53 | 17 35 | +15 55 | 7 14 | 7 30 | 11 44 | 16 13 | 15 58 | 3 23 48 | 20 32 49 |
| 13 | 15 11 57 | 17 51 | +15 48 | 7 16 | 7 32 | 11 44 | 16 12 | 15 56 | 3 27 45 | 20 28 54 |
| 14 | 15 16 02 | 18 07 | +15 39 | 7 18 | 7 34 | 11 44 | 16 11 | 15 54 | 3 31 41 | 20 24 58 |
| 15 | 15 20 08 | 18 23 | +15 30 | 7 19 | 7 36 | 11 45 | 16 09 | 15 52 | 3 35 38 | 20 21 02 |
| 16 | 15 24 14 | 18 38 | +15 20 | 7 21 | 7 38 | 11 45 | 16 08 | 15 51 | 3 39 34 | 20 17 06 |
| 17 | 15 28 22 | 18 53 | +15 09 | 7 23 | 7 40 | 11 45 | 16 06 | 15 49 | 3 43 31 | 20 13 10 |
| 18 | 15 32 30 | 19 08 | +14 57 | 7 25 | 7 42 | 11 45 | 16 05 | 15 48 | 3 47 27 | 20 09 14 |
| 19 | 15 36 39 | 19 22 | +14 45 | 7 26 | 7 44 | 11 45 | 16 04 | 15 46 | 3 51 24 | 20 05 18 |
| 20 | 15 40 49 | 19 36 | +14 31 | 7 28 | 7 46 | 11 46 | 16 03 | 15 44 | 3 55 20 | 20 01 22 |
| 21 | 15 45 00 | 19 49 | +14 17 | 7 30 | 7 48 | 11 46 | 16 01 | 15 43 | 3 59 17 | 19 57 26 |
| 22 | 15 49 11 | 20 03 | +14 02 | 7 31 | 7 50 | 11 46 | 16 00 | 15 42 | 4 03 14 | 19 53 30 |
| 23 | 15 53 24 | 20 15 | +13 47 | 7 33 | 7 52 | 11 46 | 15 59 | 15 40 | 4 07 10 | 19 49 34 |
| 24 | 15 57 37 | 20 28 | +13 30 | 7 35 | 7 54 | 11 47 | 15 58 | 15 39 | 4 11 07 | 19 45 39 |
| 25 | 16 01 51 | 20 40 | +13 13 | 7 36 | 7 56 | 11 47 | 15 57 | 15 38 | 4 15 03 | 19 41 43 |
| 26 | 16 06 05 | 20 52 | +12 54 | 7 38 | 7 58 | 11 47 | 15 56 | 15 36 | 4 19 00 | 19 37 47 |
| 27 | 16 10 21 | 21 03 | +12 36 | 7 39 | 7 59 | 11 48 | 15 55 | 15 35 | 4 22 56 | 19 33 51 |
| 28 | 16 14 37 | 21 14 | +12 16 | 7 41 | 8 01 | 11 48 | 15 55 | 15 34 | 4 26 53 | 19 29 55 |
| 29 | 16 18 54 | 21 24 | +11 55 | 7 42 | 8 03 | 11 48 | 15 54 | 15 33 | 4 30 50 | 19 25 59 |
| 30 | 16 23 12 | 21 35 | +11 34 | 7 44 | 8 05 | 11 49 | 15 53 | 15 32 | 4 34 46 | 19 22 03 |

DURATION OF TWILIGHT (in minutes)

| Latitude | 52° | 56° | 52° | 56° | 52° | 56° | 52° | 56° |
|---|---|---|---|---|---|---|---|---|
| | 1 November | | 11 November | | 21 November | | 30 November | |
| *Civil* | 36 | 40 | 37 | 41 | 38 | 43 | 40 | 45 |
| *Nautical* | 75 | 84 | 78 | 87 | 80 | 90 | 82 | 93 |
| *Astronomical* | 115 | 127 | 117 | 130 | 120 | 134 | 123 | 138 |

THE NIGHT SKY

*Mercury* passes through superior conjunction on the 14th and thus remains too close to the Sun for observation throughout the month.

*Venus*, magnitude -4.4, becomes visible as a morning object after the first week of the month. It is then visible above the south-eastern horizon before dawn. Venus is now moving rapidly away from the Sun and by the end of the month can be detected low above the horizon nearly three hours before sunrise.

*Mars* is still a morning object, magnitude +1.8, moving steadily eastwards in the constellation of Virgo, passing 3 degrees north of Spica on the 20th. The old crescent Moon will be seen near Mars on the mornings of the 2nd and 3rd.

*Jupiter*, magnitude -2.2, continues to be visible as a conspicuous morning object, though now visible well before midnight. At the very beginning of the month the planet moves eastwards from Cancer into Leo. The gibbous Moon will be near Jupiter on the morning of the 26th.

*Saturn* is now visible for the greater part of the night as it approaches opposition next month, magnitude -0.3. The gibbous Moon is near the planet on the 22nd and 23rd. The rings of Saturn present a beautiful spectacle to the observer with a small telescope. The Earth passed through the ring plane twice in 1995 and since then the rings have been slowly opening up: the diameter of the minor axis is now 20 arcseconds, marginally greater than the polar diameter of the planet itself. The rings will not be at their maximum opening until early next year.

*Meteors*. The Leonid meteor shower, associated with Comet Tempel-Tuttle, does not usually provide a very noticeable display to the casual observer, but on rare occasions spectacular displays of short duration have been observed. There is a possibility of such a display in the early morning hours of the 18th, though the gibbous Moon will create interference.

## THE MOON

| Day | RA | Dec. | Hor. par. | Semi-diam | Sun's co-long. | PA of Bright Limb | Phase | Age | Rise 52° | Rise 56° | Transit | Set 52° | Set 56° |
|---|---|---|---|---|---|---|---|---|---|---|---|---|---|
| | h m | ° | ′ | ′ | ° | ° | % | d | h m | h m | h m | h m | h m |
| **1** | 11 10 | +10.9 | 59.9 | 16.3 | 221 | 117 | 21 | 25.5 | 1 39 | 1 30 | 8 48 | 15 38 | 15 44 |
| **2** | 12 04 | + 4.9 | 60.6 | 16.5 | 233 | 119 | 12 | 26.5 | 3 07 | 3 04 | 9 40 | 15 55 | 15 55 |
| **3** | 12 58 | − 1.6 | 61.1 | 16.6 | 245 | 121 | 5 | 27.5 | 4 36 | 4 38 | 10 32 | 16 12 | 16 07 |
| **4** | 13 54 | − 8.1 | 61.2 | 16.7 | 257 | 126 | 1 | 28.5 | 6 06 | 6 15 | 11 26 | 16 31 | 16 21 |
| **5** | 14 50 | −14.1 | 61.1 | 16.6 | 270 | 240 | 0 | 0.1 | 7 38 | 7 53 | 12 22 | 16 55 | 16 37 |
| **6** | 15 49 | −19.2 | 60.6 | 16.5 | 282 | 279 | 2 | 1.1 | 9 08 | 9 31 | 13 21 | 17 24 | 17 01 |
| **7** | 16 50 | −23.0 | 59.9 | 16.3 | 294 | 278 | 7 | 2.1 | 10 33 | 11 01 | 14 21 | 18 04 | 17 35 |
| **8** | 17 52 | −25.2 | 59.0 | 16.1 | 306 | 273 | 13 | 3.1 | 11 46 | 12 17 | 15 21 | 18 56 | 18 24 |
| **9** | 18 54 | −25.8 | 58.0 | 15.8 | 318 | 267 | 22 | 4.1 | 12 42 | 13 13 | 16 19 | 19 59 | 19 29 |
| **10** | 19 53 | −24.8 | 57.1 | 15.6 | 331 | 261 | 31 | 5.1 | 13 24 | 13 50 | 17 14 | 21 11 | 20 45 |
| **11** | 20 48 | −22.6 | 56.2 | 15.3 | 343 | 255 | 41 | 6.1 | 13 53 | 14 14 | 18 05 | 22 24 | 22 04 |
| **12** | 21 40 | −19.3 | 55.5 | 15.1 | 355 | 251 | 51 | 7.1 | 14 15 | 14 31 | 18 51 | 23 37 | 23 23 |
| **13** | 22 28 | −15.2 | 54.9 | 15.0 | 7 | 247 | 61 | 8.1 | 14 33 | 14 43 | 19 35 | — | — |
| **14** | 23 14 | −10.6 | 54.5 | 14.8 | 19 | 245 | 70 | 9.1 | 14 47 | 14 53 | 20 16 | 0 48 | 0 39 |
| **15** | 23 58 | − 5.7 | 54.2 | 14.8 | 31 | 243 | 78 | 10.1 | 15 00 | 15 02 | 20 56 | 1 57 | 1 53 |
| **16** | 0 40 | − 0.6 | 54.0 | 14.7 | 44 | 242 | 86 | 11.1 | 15 12 | 15 10 | 21 36 | 3 06 | 3 06 |
| **17** | 1 23 | + 4.5 | 54.0 | 14.7 | 56 | 242 | 92 | 12.1 | 15 25 | 15 19 | 22 16 | 4 14 | 4 18 |
| **18** | 2 07 | + 9.5 | 54.2 | 14.8 | 68 | 243 | 96 | 13.1 | 15 40 | 15 29 | 22 58 | 5 23 | 5 32 |
| **19** | 2 52 | +14.2 | 54.4 | 14.8 | 80 | 243 | 99 | 14.1 | 15 57 | 15 41 | 23 43 | 6 34 | 6 48 |
| **20** | 3 39 | +18.4 | 54.7 | 14.9 | 92 | 201 | 100 | 15.1 | 16 19 | 15 58 | — | 7 46 | 8 06 |
| **21** | 4 29 | +21.8 | 55.0 | 15.0 | 104 | 81 | 99 | 16.1 | 16 48 | 16 22 | 0 31 | 8 57 | 9 23 |
| **22** | 5 22 | +24.3 | 55.4 | 15.1 | 116 | 83 | 96 | 17.1 | 17 27 | 16 57 | 1 21 | 10 05 | 10 35 |
| **23** | 6 17 | +25.6 | 55.9 | 15.2 | 129 | 88 | 92 | 18.1 | 18 18 | 17 47 | 2 14 | 1 06 | 1 37 |
| **24** | 7 13 | +25.6 | 56.4 | 15.4 | 141 | 94 | 85 | 19.1 | 19 22 | 18 53 | 3 09 | 11 55 | 12 24 |
| **25** | 8 10 | +24.3 | 56.9 | 15.5 | 153 | 100 | 77 | 20.1 | 20 36 | 20 13 | 4 04 | 12 33 | 12 58 |
| **26** | 9 06 | +21.6 | 57.5 | 15.7 | 165 | 105 | 68 | 21.1 | 21 56 | 21 38 | 4 58 | 13 02 | 13 21 |
| **27** | 10 01 | +17.6 | 58.1 | 15.8 | 177 | 110 | 57 | 22.1 | 23 19 | 23 07 | 5 50 | 13 25 | 13 38 |
| **28** | 10 54 | +12.7 | 58.8 | 16.0 | 189 | 113 | 46 | 23.1 | — | — | 6 41 | 13 44 | 13 52 |
| **29** | 11 46 | + 7.0 | 59.4 | 16.2 | 202 | 115 | 35 | 24.1 | 0 43 | 0 37 | 7 31 | 14 00 | 14 03 |
| **30** | 12 38 | + 0.9 | 59.9 | 16.3 | 214 | 116 | 25 | 25.1 | 2 07 | 2 07 | 8 20 | 14 16 | 14 14 |

## MERCURY

| Day | RA | Dec. | Diam. | Phase | Transit | 5° high 52° | 5° high 56° |
|---|---|---|---|---|---|---|---|
| | h m | ° | ″ | % | h m | h m | h m |
| 1 | 13 54 | −10.3 | 5 | 97 | 11 14 | 6 43 | 6 57 |
| 3 | 14 06 | −11.6 | 5 | 98 | 11 19 | 6 56 | 7 11 |
| 5 | 14 19 | −12.9 | 5 | 99 | 11 24 | 7 08 | 7 25 |
| 7 | 14 31 | −14.2 | 5 | 99 | 11 28 | 7 21 | 7 39 |
| 9 | 14 44 | −15.4 | 5 | 100 | 11 33 | 7 34 | 7 53 |
| 11 | 14 56 | −16.5 | 5 | 100 | 11 38 | 7 46 | 8 07 |
| 13 | 15 09 | −17.7 | 5 | 100 | 11 43 | 7 59 | 8 22 |
| 15 | 15 22 | −18.7 | 5 | 100 | 11 47 | 8 11 | 8 36 |
| 17 | 15 35 | −19.7 | 5 | 100 | 11 52 | 8 23 | 8 50 |
| 19 | 15 48 | −20.6 | 5 | 100 | 11 57 | 8 35 | 9 05 |
| 21 | 16 01 | −21.5 | 5 | 100 | 12 03 | 15 17 | 14 45 |
| 23 | 16 14 | −22.3 | 5 | 99 | 12 08 | 15 16 | 14 42 |
| 25 | 16 27 | −23.0 | 5 | 99 | 12 13 | 15 15 | 14 39 |
| 27 | 16 40 | −23.6 | 5 | 98 | 12 19 | 15 15 | 14 37 |
| 29 | 16 53 | −24.2 | 5 | 98 | 12 24 | 15 15 | 14 35 |
| 31 | 17 07 | −24.6 | 5 | 97 | 12 30 | 15 17 | 14 35 |

## VENUS

| Day | RA | Dec. | Diam. | Phase | Transit | 5° high 52° | 5° high 56° |
|---|---|---|---|---|---|---|---|
| | h m | ° | ″ | % | h m | h m | h m |
| 1 | 14 13 | −19.3 | 62 | 1 | 11 30 | 7 57 | 8 22 |
| 6 | 14 03 | −17.3 | 61 | 1 | 11 00 | 7 13 | 7 35 |
| 11 | 13 56 | −15.3 | 59 | 4 | 10 33 | 6 33 | 6 51 |
| 16 | 13 51 | −13.5 | 55 | 8 | 10 10 | 5 58 | 6 15 |
| 21 | 13 51 | −12.2 | 52 | 12 | 9 50 | 5 30 | 5 45 |
| 26 | 13 54 | −11.4 | 48 | 17 | 9 34 | 5 09 | 5 23 |
| 31 | 14 00 | −11.0 | 44 | 21 | 9 21 | 4 54 | 5 08 |

## MARS

| Day | RA | Dec. | Diam. | Phase | Transit | 5° high 52° | 5° high 56° |
|---|---|---|---|---|---|---|---|
| 1 | 12 40 | − 3.2 | 4 | 98 | 9 59 | 4 48 | 4 54 |
| 6 | 12 52 | − 4.4 | 4 | 98 | 9 51 | 4 47 | 4 54 |
| 11 | 13 03 | − 5.7 | 4 | 98 | 9 43 | 4 46 | 4 54 |
| 16 | 13 15 | − 6.9 | 4 | 97 | 9 35 | 4 45 | 4 55 |
| 21 | 13 27 | − 8.1 | 4 | 97 | 9 27 | 4 44 | 4 55 |
| 26 | 13 39 | − 9.3 | 4 | 97 | 9 20 | 4 43 | 4 55 |
| 31 | 13 51 | −10.5 | 4 | 96 | 9 12 | 4 42 | 4 55 |

## UNRISE AND SUNSET

| | London 0°05′ 51°30′ | | Bristol 2°35′ 51°28′ | | Birmingham 1°55′ 52°28′ | | Manchester 2°15′ 53°28′ | | Newcastle 1°37′ 54°59′ | | Glasgow 4°14′ 55°52′ | | Belfast 5°56′ 54°35′ | |
|---|---|---|---|---|---|---|---|---|---|---|---|---|---|---|
| | h m | h m | h m | h m | h m | h m | h m | h m | h m | h m | h m | h m | h m | h m |
| 1 | 6 53 | 16 34 | 7 03 | 16 44 | 7 03 | 16 38 | 7 08 | 16 37 | 7 10 | 16 30 | 7 23 | 16 37 | 7 26 | 16 48 |
| 2 | 6 55 | 16 32 | 7 05 | 16 42 | 7 05 | 16 37 | 7 09 | 16 35 | 7 12 | 16 28 | 7 25 | 16 35 | 7 28 | 16 46 |
| 3 | 6 57 | 16 30 | 7 07 | 16 40 | 7 07 | 16 35 | 7 11 | 16 33 | 7 14 | 16 26 | 7 27 | 16 33 | 7 30 | 16 44 |
| 4 | 6 59 | 16 28 | 7 09 | 16 38 | 7 09 | 16 33 | 7 13 | 16 31 | 7 16 | 16 24 | 7 29 | 16 31 | 7 32 | 16 42 |
| 5 | 7 00 | 16 27 | 7 10 | 16 37 | 7 11 | 16 31 | 7 15 | 16 29 | 7 18 | 16 22 | 7 31 | 16 29 | 7 34 | 16 40 |
| 6 | 7 02 | 16 25 | 7 12 | 16 35 | 7 13 | 16 29 | 7 17 | 16 27 | 7 20 | 16 20 | 7 34 | 16 27 | 7 36 | 16 38 |
| 7 | 7 04 | 16 23 | 7 14 | 16 33 | 7 14 | 16 28 | 7 19 | 16 26 | 7 22 | 16 18 | 7 36 | 16 25 | 7 38 | 16 36 |
| 8 | 7 06 | 16 22 | 7 16 | 16 32 | 7 16 | 16 26 | 7 21 | 16 24 | 7 24 | 16 16 | 7 38 | 16 23 | 7 40 | 16 35 |
| 9 | 7 08 | 16 20 | 7 17 | 16 30 | 7 18 | 16 24 | 7 23 | 16 22 | 7 26 | 16 14 | 7 40 | 16 21 | 7 42 | 16 33 |
| 0 | 7 09 | 16 19 | 7 19 | 16 29 | 7 20 | 16 23 | 7 25 | 16 20 | 7 28 | 16 12 | 7 42 | 16 19 | 7 44 | 16 31 |
| 1 | 7 11 | 16 17 | 7 21 | 16 27 | 7 22 | 16 21 | 7 27 | 16 19 | 7 30 | 16 10 | 7 44 | 16 17 | 7 46 | 16 29 |
| 2 | 7 13 | 16 16 | 7 23 | 16 26 | 7 23 | 16 19 | 7 29 | 16 17 | 7 32 | 16 09 | 7 46 | 16 15 | 7 48 | 16 27 |
| 3 | 7 14 | 16 14 | 7 24 | 16 24 | 7 25 | 16 18 | 7 30 | 16 16 | 7 34 | 16 07 | 7 48 | 16 13 | 7 50 | 16 26 |
| 4 | 7 16 | 16 13 | 7 26 | 16 23 | 7 27 | 16 16 | 7 32 | 16 14 | 7 36 | 16 05 | 7 50 | 16 12 | 7 52 | 16 24 |
| 5 | 7 18 | 16 11 | 7 28 | 16 21 | 7 29 | 16 15 | 7 34 | 16 12 | 7 38 | 16 04 | 7 52 | 16 10 | 7 53 | 16 23 |
| 6 | 7 20 | 16 10 | 7 30 | 16 20 | 7 31 | 16 14 | 7 36 | 16 11 | 7 40 | 16 02 | 7 54 | 16 08 | 7 55 | 16 21 |
| 7 | 7 21 | 16 09 | 7 31 | 16 19 | 7 32 | 16 12 | 7 38 | 16 09 | 7 42 | 16 00 | 7 56 | 16 07 | 7 57 | 16 19 |
| 8 | 7 23 | 16 07 | 7 33 | 16 18 | 7 34 | 16 11 | 7 40 | 16 08 | 7 44 | 15 59 | 7 58 | 16 05 | 7 59 | 16 18 |
| 9 | 7 25 | 16 06 | 7 35 | 16 16 | 7 36 | 16 10 | 7 41 | 16 07 | 7 46 | 15 57 | 8 00 | 16 04 | 8 01 | 16 16 |
| 0 | 7 26 | 16 05 | 7 36 | 16 15 | 7 38 | 16 08 | 7 43 | 16 05 | 7 48 | 15 56 | 8 02 | 16 02 | 8 03 | 16 15 |
| 1 | 7 28 | 16 04 | 7 38 | 16 14 | 7 39 | 16 07 | 7 45 | 16 04 | 7 50 | 15 55 | 8 04 | 16 01 | 8 05 | 16 14 |
| 2 | 7 30 | 16 03 | 7 39 | 16 13 | 7 41 | 16 06 | 7 47 | 16 03 | 7 51 | 15 53 | 8 06 | 15 59 | 8 07 | 16 12 |
| 3 | 7 31 | 16 02 | 7 41 | 16 12 | 7 43 | 16 05 | 7 48 | 16 02 | 7 53 | 15 52 | 8 08 | 15 58 | 8 09 | 16 11 |
| 4 | 7 33 | 16 01 | 7 43 | 16 11 | 7 44 | 16 04 | 7 50 | 16 01 | 7 55 | 15 51 | 8 10 | 15 56 | 8 10 | 16 10 |
| 5 | 7 34 | 16 00 | 7 44 | 16 10 | 7 46 | 16 03 | 7 52 | 16 00 | 7 57 | 15 49 | 8 12 | 15 55 | 8 12 | 16 09 |
| 6 | 7 36 | 15 59 | 7 46 | 16 09 | 7 48 | 16 02 | 7 54 | 15 59 | 7 59 | 15 48 | 8 14 | 15 54 | 8 14 | 16 08 |
| 7 | 7 37 | 15 58 | 7 47 | 16 08 | 7 49 | 16 01 | 7 55 | 15 58 | 8 00 | 15 47 | 8 16 | 15 53 | 8 16 | 16 07 |
| 8 | 7 39 | 15 57 | 7 49 | 16 07 | 7 51 | 16 00 | 7 57 | 15 57 | 8 02 | 15 46 | 8 17 | 15 52 | 8 17 | 16 06 |
| 9 | 7 40 | 15 56 | 7 50 | 16 07 | 7 52 | 15 59 | 7 58 | 15 56 | 8 04 | 15 45 | 8 19 | 15 51 | 8 19 | 16 05 |
| 0 | 7 42 | 15 56 | 7 52 | 16 06 | 7 54 | 15 58 | 8 00 | 15 55 | 8 05 | 15 44 | 8 21 | 15 50 | 8 21 | 16 04 |

## UPITER

| )ay | *RA* | | *Dec.* | | *Transit* | | *5° high* 52° | | 56° | |
|---|---|---|---|---|---|---|---|---|---|---|
| | h | m | ° | ′ | h | m | h | m | h | m |
| 1 | 9 | 15.9 | +16 | 28 | 6 | 34 | 23 | 39 | 23 | 28 |
| 1 | 9 | 19.4 | +16 | 14 | 5 | 59 | 23 | 04 | 22 | 54 |
| 1 | 9 | 21.8 | +16 | 05 | 5 | 22 | 22 | 28 | 22 | 18 |
| 1 | 9 | 22.9 | +16 | 02 | 4 | 43 | 21 | 50 | 21 | 40 |

)iameters - equatorial 39″ polar 36″

## SATURN

| *Day* | *RA* | | *Dec.* | | *Transit* | | *5° high* 52° | | 56° | |
|---|---|---|---|---|---|---|---|---|---|---|
| | h | m | ° | ′ | h | m | h | m | h | m |
| 1 | 5 | 54.4 | +22 | 06 | 3 | 13 | 19 | 44 | 19 | 28 |
| 11 | 5 | 52.5 | +22 | 05 | 2 | 32 | 19 | 03 | 18 | 47 |
| 21 | 5 | 49.9 | +22 | 05 | 1 | 50 | 18 | 21 | 18 | 05 |
| 31 | 5 | 46.8 | +22 | 04 | 1 | 08 | 17 | 39 | 17 | 22 |

Diameters - equatorial 20″ polar 18″
Rings- major axis 46″ minor axis 20″

## JRANUS

| )ay | *RA* | | *Dec.* | | *Transit* | | *10° high* 52° | | 56° | |
|---|---|---|---|---|---|---|---|---|---|---|
| | h | m | ° | ′ | h | m | h | m | h | m |
| 1 | 21 | 49.8 | −13 | 56 | 19 | 06 | 22 | 36 | 22 | 12 |
| 1 | 21 | 49.9 | −13 | 55 | 18 | 27 | 21 | 57 | 21 | 33 |
| 1 | 21 | 50.3 | −13 | 53 | 17 | 48 | 21 | 18 | 20 | 54 |
| 1 | 21 | 51.0 | −13 | 49 | 17 | 10 | 20 | 40 | 20 | 16 |

)iameter 4″

## NEPTUNE

| *Day* | *RA* | | *Dec.* | | *Transit* | | *10° high* 52° | | 56° | |
|---|---|---|---|---|---|---|---|---|---|---|
| | h | m | ° | ′ | h | m | h | m | h | m |
| 1 | 20 | 42.6 | −18 | 09 | 17 | 59 | 20 | 56 | 20 | 21 |
| 11 | 20 | 42.9 | −18 | 08 | 17 | 20 | 20 | 17 | 19 | 43 |
| 21 | 20 | 43.5 | −18 | 06 | 16 | 42 | 19 | 39 | 19 | 04 |
| 31 | 20 | 44.3 | −18 | 03 | 16 | 03 | 19 | 00 | 18 | 26 |

Diameter 2″

# December 2002

TWELFTH MONTH, 31 DAYS. *Decem* (ten), tenth month of Roman pre-Julian calendar

| | | | | |
|---|---|---|---|---|
| **1** | *Sunday* | **Advent Sunday.** Samuel Courtauld d. 1947 | | 335 |
| **2** | *Monday* | Georges Seurat b. 1859. Hernan Cortés d. 1547 | *week* 48 *day* | 336 |
| **3** | *Tuesday* | Hernando Cortés d. 1894. Battle of Austerlitz 1805 | | 337 |
| **4** | *Wednesday* | Edith Cavell b. 1865. Luigi Galvani d. 1798 | | 338 |
| **5** | *Thursday* | Fritz Lang b. 1890. Sir Henry Wotton d. 1639 | | 339 |
| **6** | *Friday* | George Chisholm d. 1997. Finland declared its independence 1917 | | 340 |
| **7** | *Saturday* | Ferdinand de Lesseps d. 1894. Thornton Wilder d. 1975 | | 341 |
| **8** | *Sunday* | **2nd S. of Advent.** Jean Sibelius b. 1865 | | 342 |
| **9** | *Monday* | Douglas Fairbanks Junior b. 1909. R. A. Butler b. 1902 | *week* 49 *day* | 343 |
| **10** | *Tuesday* | Paolo Uccello d. 1475. Nobel Prizes awarded for the first time 1901 | | 344 |
| **11** | *Wednesday* | Colley Cibber d. 1757. Abdication of Edward VIII and accession of George VI 1936 | | 345 |
| **12** | *Thursday* | Edward G. Robinson b. 1893. Frank Sinatra b. 1915 | | 346 |
| **13** | *Friday* | Glen Byam Shaw b. 1904. L. P. Hartley d. 1972 | | 347 |
| **14** | *Saturday* | Pierre Puvis de Chavannes b. 1824. 1st Earl Baldwin of Bewdley Stanley Baldwin d. 1947 | | 348 |
| **15** | *Sunday* | **3rd S. of Advent.** Sir George Cayley d. 1857 | | 349 |
| **16** | *Monday* | Quentin Bell d. 1996. Cromwell becomes Lord Protector 1653 | *week* 50 *day* | 350 |
| **17** | *Tuesday* | Professor R. V. Jones d. 1997. First flight by Wright Brothers 1903 | | 351 |
| **18** | *Wednesday* | Paul Klee b. 1879. Abolition of Slavery in USA 1865 | | 352 |
| **19** | *Thursday* | Jean Genet b. 1910. Leonid Brezhnev b. 1906 | | 353 |
| **20** | *Friday* | Artur Rubinstein d. 1982 | | 354 |
| **21** | *Saturday* | *Michaelmas Law Sittings end.* Mayflower Pilgrims land at Plymouth Rock 1620 | | 355 |
| **22** | *Sunday* | **4th S. of Advent.** Sir Henry Cotton d. 1987 | | 356 |
| **23** | *Monday* | Richard Arkwright b. 1732. Thomas Malthus d. 1834 | *week* 51 *day* | 357 |
| **24** | *Tuesday* | Saint Ignatius Loyola b. 1491. William Makepeace Thackeray d. 1863 | | 358 |
| **25** | *Wednesday* | **Christmas Day.** *Bank Holiday in UK.* | | 359 |
| **26** | *Thursday* | **St Stephen.** Boxing Day. *Bank Holiday in UK.* | | 360 |
| **27** | *Friday* | **St John.** Sergei Esenin d. 1925 | | 361 |
| **28** | *Saturday* | **Holy Innocents.** Dame Maggie Smith b. 1934 | | 362 |
| **29** | *Sunday* | **1st S. of Christmas.** Rainer Maria Rilke d. 1926 | | 363 |
| **30** | *Monday* | L. P. Hartley b. 1895. Irving Lazar d. 1993 | *week* 52 *day* | 364 |
| **31** | *Tuesday* | John Denver b. 1943. The farthing ceased to be legal tender 1960 | | 365 |

## Astronomical Phenomena

| d | h | |
|---|---|---|
| 1 | 11 | Mars in conjunction with Moon. Mars 2° S. |
| 1 | 15 | Venus in conjunction with Moon. Venus 2° S. |
| 4 | 08 | Total eclipse of Sun (see page 66) |
| 4 | 12 | Jupiter at stationary point |
| 5 | 04 | Mercury in conjunction with Moon. Mercury 0°.6 S. |
| 7 | 01 | Venus at greatest brilliancy |
| 9 | 17 | Pluto in conjunction |
| 17 | 17 | Saturn at opposition |
| 19 | 15 | Saturn in conjunction with Moon. Saturn 3° S. |
| 22 | 01 | Sun's longitude 270° ♑ |
| 23 | 14 | Jupiter in conjunction with Moon. Jupiter 4° S. |
| 26 | 05 | Mercury at greatest elongation E.20° |
| 30 | 01 | Mars in conjunction with Moon. Mars 1° S. |
| 30 | 08 | Venus in conjunction with Moon. Venus 2° N. |

## Minima of Algol

| d | h | d | h | d | h |
|---|---|---|---|---|---|
| 3 | 11.0 | 14 | 22.3 | 26 | 09.6 |
| 6 | 07.9 | 17 | 19.1 | 29 | 06.4 |
| 9 | 04.7 | 20 | 15.9 | | |
| 12 | 01.5 | 23 | 12.8 | | |

## Constellations

The following constellations are near the meridian at

| | d | h | | d | h |
|---|---|---|---|---|---|
| November | 1 | 24 | December | 16 | 21 |
| November | 15 | 23 | January | 1 | 20 |
| December | 1 | 22 | January | 16 | 19 |

Ursa Major (below the Pole), Ursa Minor (below the Pole), Cassiopeia, Andromeda, Perseus, Triangulum, Aries, Taurus, Cetus and Eridanus

## The Moon

| Phases, Apsides and Node | d | h | m |
|---|---|---|---|
| ● New Moon | 4 | 07 | 34 |
| ☽ First Quarter | 11 | 15 | 49 |
| ○ Full Moon | 19 | 19 | 10 |
| ☾ Last Quarter | 27 | 00 | 31 |
| | | | |
| Perigee (362,272km) | 2 | 08 | 43 |
| Apogee (404,950km) | 14 | 03 | 52 |
| Perigee (367,874km) | 30 | 00 | 57 |

Mean longitude of ascending node on December 1, 69°

HE SUN S.D 16′.1

| ay | Right Ascension | Dec. – | Equation of Time | Rise 52° | Rise 56° | Transit | Set 52° | Set 56° | Sidereal time | Transit of First Point of Aries |
|---|---|---|---|---|---|---|---|---|---|---|
| | h m s | ° ′ | m s | h m | h m | h m | h m | h m | h m s | h m s |
| 1 | 16 27 30 | 21 44 | +11 13 | 7 45 | 8 06 | 11 49 | 15 52 | 15 31 | 4 38 43 | 19 18 07 |
| 2 | 16 31 49 | 21 54 | +10 50 | 7 47 | 8 08 | 11 49 | 15 52 | 15 30 | 4 42 39 | 19 14 11 |
| 3 | 16 36 09 | 22 02 | +10 27 | 7 48 | 8 10 | 11 50 | 15 51 | 15 29 | 4 46 36 | 19 10 15 |
| 4 | 16 40 29 | 22 11 | +10 03 | 7 49 | 8 11 | 11 50 | 15 51 | 15 29 | 4 50 32 | 19 06 19 |
| 5 | 16 44 50 | 22 19 | + 9 39 | 7 51 | 8 13 | 11 51 | 15 50 | 15 28 | 4 54 29 | 19 02 23 |
| 6 | 16 49 11 | 22 27 | + 9 14 | 7 52 | 8 14 | 11 51 | 15 50 | 15 27 | 4 58 25 | 18 58 28 |
| 7 | 16 53 33 | 22 34 | + 8 49 | 7 53 | 8 16 | 11 51 | .15 49 | 15 27 | 5 02 22 | 18 54 32 |
| 8 | 16 57 56 | 22 40 | + 8 23 | 7 54 | 8 17 | 11 52 | 15 49 | 15 26 | 5 06 19 | 18 50 36 |
| 9 | 17 02 19 | 22 47 | + 7 56 | 7 56 | 8 18 | 11 52 | 15 49 | 15 26 | 5 10 15 | 18 46 40 |
| 0 | 17 06 42 | 22 52 | + 7 29 | 7 57 | 8 20 | 11 53 | 15 49 | 15 26 | 5 14 12 | 18 42 44 |
| 1 | 17 11 06 | 22 58 | + 7 02 | 7 58 | 8 21 | 11 53 | 15 48 | 15 25 | 5 18 08 | 18 38 48 |
| 2 | 17 15 30 | 23 03 | + 6 35 | 7 59 | 8 22 | 11 54 | 15 48 | 15 25 | 5 22 05 | 18 34 52 |
| 3 | 17 19 55 | 23 07 | + 6 07 | 8 00 | 8 23 | 11 54 | 15 48 | 15 25 | 5 26 01 | 18 30 56 |
| 4 | 17 24 20 | 23 11 | + 5 38 | 8 01 | 8 24 | 11 55 | 15 48 | 15 25 | 5 29 58 | 18 27 00 |
| 5 | 17 28 45 | 23 15 | + 5 10 | 8 02 | 8 25 | 11 55 | 15 48 | 15 25 | 5 33 54 | 18 23 04 |
| 6 | 17 33 10 | 23 18 | + 4 41 | 8 02 | 8 26 | 11 56 | 15 49 | 15 25 | 5 37 51 | 18 19 08 |
| 7 | 17 37 36 | 23 20 | + 4 12 | 8 03 | 8 27 | 11 56 | 15 49 | 15 25 | 5 41 48 | 18 15 13 |
| 8 | 17 42 01 | 23 23 | + 3 43 | 8 04 | 8 28 | 11 57 | 15 49 | 15 25 | 5 45 44 | 18 11 17 |
| 9 | 17 46 27 | 23 24 | + 3 13 | 8 05 | 8 28 | 11 57 | 15 49 | 15 26 | 5 49 41 | 18 07 21 |
| 0 | 17 50 54 | 23 25 | + 2 44 | 8 05 | 8 29 | 11 58 | 15 50 | 15 26 | 5 53 37 | 18 03 25 |
| 1 | 17 55 20 | 23 26 | + 2 14 | 8 06 | 8 30 | 11 58 | 15 50 | 15 26 | 5 57 34 | 17 59 29 |
| 2 | 17 59 46 | 23 26 | + 1 44 | 8 06 | 8 30 | 11 59 | 15 51 | 15 27 | 6 01 30 | 17 55 33 |
| 3 | 18 04 12 | 23 26 | + 1 15 | 8 07 | 8 30 | 11 59 | 15 51 | 15 28 | 6 05 27 | 17 51 37 |
| 4 | 18 08 39 | 23 25 | + 0 45 | 8 07 | 8 31 | 12 00 | 15 52 | 15 28 | 6 09 23 | 17 47 41 |
| 5 | 18 13 05 | 23 24 | + 0 15 | 8 07 | 8 31 | 12 00 | 15 53 | 15 29 | 6 13 20 | 17 43 45 |
| 6 | 18 17 31 | 23 23 | − 0 15 | 8 08 | 8 31 | 12 00 | 15 53 | 15 30 | 6 17 17 | 17 39 49 |
| 7 | 18 21 58 | 23 21 | − 0 44 | 8 08 | 8 32 | 12 01 | 15 54 | 15 30 | 6 21 13 | 17 35 53 |
| 8 | 18 26 24 | 23 18 | − 1 14 | 8 08 | 8 32 | 12 01 | 15 55 | 15 31 | 6 25 10 | 17 31 57 |
| 9 | 18 30 50 | 23 15 | − 1 43 | 8 08 | 8 32 | 12 02 | 15 56 | 15 32 | 6 29 06 | 17 28 02 |
| 0 | 18 35 15 | 23 12 | − 2 13 | 8 08 | 8 32 | 12 02 | 15 57 | 15 33 | 6 33 03 | 17 24 06 |
| 1 | 18 39 41 | 23 08 | − 2 42 | 8 08 | 8 32 | 12 03 | 15 58 | 15 35 | 6 36 59 | 17 20 10 |

URATION OF TWILIGHT (in minutes)

| atitude | 52° | 56° | 52° | 56° | 52° | 56° | 52° | 56° |
|---|---|---|---|---|---|---|---|---|
| | 1 December | | 11 December | | 21 December | | 31 December | |
| ivil | 40 | 45 | 41 | 47 | 41 | 47 | 41 | 47 |
| autical | 82 | 93 | 84 | 96 | 85 | 97 | 84 | 96 |
| stronomical | 123 | 138 | 125 | 141 | 126 | 142 | 125 | 141 |

HE NIGHT SKY

*Iercury* remains too close to the Sun for most of )ecember. However, for the last week of the month it ıay be detected low above the south-western horizon round the end of evening civil twilight. During this eriod its magnitude fades from -0.5 to +0.2.

*Venus* is a magnificent object in the early mornings, ttaining its greatest brilliancy (magnitude -4.7) on the th. It completely dominates the south-eastern sky for everal hours before sunrise. Venus is only a few degrees ast of Mars. The old crescent Moon will be seen pproaching Venus on the morning of the 1st and again n the 30th. These dates are favourable for locating Venus n daylight, if the observer keeps in shadow, say 1 hour fter sunrise. On the first occasion Venus will be found bout 3.6 degrees to the left and below the Moon, while on he second occasion it will be 3 degrees above the Moon.

*Mars*, magnitude +1.6, continues to be visible for several hours in the south-eastern sky in the early mornings. The old crescent Moon is close to Mars on the mornings of the 1st and 30th.

*Jupiter*, magnitude -2.4, is still a prominent morning object in the southern sky, but already visible in the east in the late evening. Jupiter reaches its first stationary point on the 4th, commencing its retrograde motion and returning from Leo back into Cancer. The gibbous Moon is near Jupiter on the morning of the 23rd.

*Saturn*, magnitude -0.5, reaches opposition on the 17th and is therefore visible throughout the hours of darkness. Saturn is moving slowly retrograde in the constellation of Taurus. The Full Moon is near Saturn on the 19th.

*Meteors*. The maximum of the well-known Geminid meteor shower occurs on the night of the 13th-14th. Conditions are not favourable before about 02h since the bright gibbous Moon will be above the horizon until then.

## THE MOON

| *Day* | *RA* | *Dec.* | *Hor. par.* | *Semi-diam* | *Sun's co-long.* | *PA of Bright Limb* | *Phase* | *Age* | *Rise* 52° | *Rise* 56° | *Transit* | *Set* 52° | *Set* 56° |
|---|---|---|---|---|---|---|---|---|---|---|---|---|---|
| | h m | ° | ′ | ′ | ° | ° | % | d | h m | h m | h m | h m | h m |
| **1** | 13 31 | − 5.5 | 60.3 | 16.4 | 226 | 115 | 15 | 26.1 | 3 34 | 3 39 | 9 11 | 14 34 | 14 2 |
| **2** | 14 25 | −11.5 | 60.5 | 16.5 | 238 | 113 | 8 | 27.1 | 5 02 | 5 14 | 10 05 | 14 54 | 14 4 |
| **3** | 15 22 | −17.0 | 60.5 | 16.5 | 250 | 109 | 2 | 28.1 | 6 32 | 6 51 | 11 01 | 15 19 | 14 5 |
| **4** | 16 22 | −21.4 | 60.2 | 16.4 | 262 | 101 | 0 | 29.1 | 8 01 | 8 26 | 12 01 | 15 53 | 15 2 |
| **5** | 17 24 | −24.4 | 59.6 | 16.3 | 275 | 281 | 1 | 0.7 | 9 22 | 9 52 | 13 02 | 16 39 | 16 0 |
| **6** | 18 27 | −25.7 | 58.9 | 16.1 | 287 | 273 | 4 | 1.7 | 10 28 | 11 00 | 14 03 | 17 38 | 17 0 |
| **7** | 19 29 | −25.4 | 58.1 | 15.8 | 299 | 266 | 9 | 2.7 | 11 18 | 11 47 | 15 01 | 18 48 | 18 2 |
| **8** | 20 27 | −23.6 | 57.2 | 15.6 | 311 | 260 | 16 | 3.7 | 11 54 | 12 17 | 15 55 | 20 04 | 19 4 |
| **9** | 21 22 | −20.6 | 56.4 | 15.4 | 323 | 255 | 25 | 4.7 | 12 19 | 12 37 | 16 44 | 21 19 | 21 0 |
| **10** | 22 12 | −16.7 | 55.6 | 15.2 | 336 | 251 | 34 | 5.7 | 12 38 | 12 51 | 17 30 | 22 33 | 22 2 |
| **11** | 23 00 | −12.2 | 55.0 | 15.0 | 348 | 248 | 44 | 6.7 | 12 54 | 13 02 | 18 13 | 23 43 | 23 3 |
| **12** | 23 44 | − 7.3 | 54.5 | 14.9 | 360 | 246 | 53 | 7.7 | 13 07 | 13 11 | 18 53 | — | — |
| **13** | 0 28 | − 2.2 | 54.3 | 14.8 | 12 | 245 | 63 | 8.7 | 13 20 | 13 19 | 19 33 | 0 52 | 0 5 |
| **14** | 1 10 | + 3.0 | 54.1 | 14.8 | 24 | 246 | 72 | 9.7 | 13 33 | 13 28 | 20 13 | 2 00 | 2 0 |
| **15** | 1 53 | + 8.0 | 54.2 | 14.8 | 36 | 247 | 80 | 10.7 | 13 46 | 13 37 | 20 54 | 3 09 | 3 1 |
| **16** | 2 38 | +12.8 | 54.4 | 14.8 | 49 | 249 | 87 | 11.7 | 14 02 | 13 48 | 21 38 | 4 19 | 4 3 |
| **17** | 3 24 | +17.2 | 54.7 | 14.9 | 61 | 253 | 93 | 12.7 | 14 22 | 14 03 | 22 25 | 5 30 | 5 4 |
| **18** | 4 13 | +20.9 | 55.1 | 15.0 | 73 | 259 | 97 | 13.7 | 14 49 | 14 24 | 23 15 | 6 43 | 7 0 |
| **19** | 5 06 | +23.7 | 55.6 | 15.1 | 85 | 270 | 99 | 14.7 | 15 24 | 14 55 | — | 7 54 | 8 2 |
| **20** | 6 01 | +25.4 | 56.1 | 15.3 | 97 | 51 | 100 | 15.7 | 16 12 | 15 41 | 0 08 | 8 58 | 9 2 |
| **21** | 6 58 | +25.8 | 56.6 | 15.4 | 109 | 84 | 98 | 16.7 | 17 13 | 16 43 | 1 03 | 9 52 | 10 2 |
| **22** | 7 56 | +24.7 | 57.1 | 15.5 | 121 | 93 | 95 | 17.7 | 18 25 | 18 00 | 1 59 | 10 35 | 11 0 |
| **23** | 8 53 | +22.3 | 57.5 | 15.7 | 133 | 100 | 89 | 18.7 | 19 45 | 19 25 | 2 54 | 11 07 | 11 2 |
| **24** | 9 49 | +18.6 | 58.0 | 15.8 | 146 | 106 | 81 | 19.7 | 21 07 | 20 53 | 3 47 | 11 31 | 11 4 |
| **25** | 10 42 | +13.9 | 58.4 | 15.9 | 158 | 110 | 72 | 20.7 | 22 29 | 22 22 | 4 38 | 11 51 | 12 0 |
| **26** | 11 34 | + 8.4 | 58.7 | 16.0 | 170 | 112 | 62 | 21.7 | 23 52 | 23 50 | 5 27 | 12 07 | 12 1 |
| **27** | 12 25 | + 2.4 | 59.1 | 16.1 | 182 | 113 | 50 | 22.7 | — | — | 6 16 | 12 23 | 12 2 |
| **28** | 13 16 | − 3.7 | 59.3 | 16.2 | 194 | 113 | 39 | 23.7 | 1 15 | 1 18 | 7 05 | 12 39 | 12 3 |
| **29** | 14 08 | − 9.7 | 59.5 | 16.2 | 206 | 111 | 28 | 24.7 | 2 39 | 2 49 | 7 55 | 12 57 | 12 4 |
| **30** | 15 02 | −15.2 | 59.6 | 16.2 | 219 | 108 | 18 | 25.7 | 4 06 | 4 22 | 8 48 | 13 19 | 13 0 |
| **31** | 15 59 | −19.9 | 59.5 | 16.2 | 231 | 102 | 10 | 26.7 | 5 33 | 5 55 | 9 45 | 13 48 | 13 2 |

## MERCURY

| *Day* | *RA* | *Dec.* | *Diam.* | *Phase* | *Transit* | *5° high* 52° | *5° high* 56° |
|---|---|---|---|---|---|---|---|
| | h m | ° | ″ | % | h m | h m | h m |
| 1 | 17 07 | −24.6 | 5 | 97 | 12 30 | 15 17 | 14 35 |
| 3 | 17 20 | −25.0 | 5 | 96 | 12 35 | 15 19 | 14 35 |
| 5 | 17 34 | −25.3 | 5 | 95 | 12 41 | 15 22 | 14 36 |
| 7 | 17 47 | −25.5 | 5 | 94 | 12 47 | 15 26 | 14 39 |
| 9 | 18 01 | −25.6 | 5 | 92 | 12 52 | 15 31 | 14 43 |
| 11 | 18 15 | −25.7 | 5 | 91 | 12 58 | 15 36 | 14 49 |
| 13 | 18 28 | −25.6 | 5 | 88 | 13 03 | 15 43 | 14 57 |
| 15 | 18 41 | −25.4 | 5 | 86 | 13 09 | 15 50 | 15 05 |
| 17 | 18 54 | −25.1 | 6 | 83 | 13 13 | 15 58 | 15 15 |
| 19 | 19 06 | −24.7 | 6 | 80 | 13 18 | 16 07 | 15 25 |
| 21 | 19 18 | −24.3 | 6 | 76 | 13 22 | 16 15 | 15 36 |
| 23 | 19 29 | −23.7 | 6 | 71 | 13 25 | 16 23 | 15 46 |
| 25 | 19 39 | −23.1 | 7 | 65 | 13 26 | 16 31 | 15 56 |
| 27 | 19 48 | −22.4 | 7 | 58 | 13 27 | 16 37 | 16 04 |
| 29 | 19 55 | −21.7 | 7 | 50 | 13 25 | 16 41 | 16 10 |
| 31 | 20 00 | −21.1 | 8 | 41 | 13 22 | 16 43 | 16 13 |

## VENUS

| *Day* | *RA* | *Dec.* | *Diam.* | *Phase* | *Transit* | *5° high* 52° | *5° high* 56° |
|---|---|---|---|---|---|---|---|
| | h m | ° | ″ | % | h m | h m | h m |
| 1 | 14 00 | −11.0 | 44 | 21 | 9 21 | 4 54 | 5 0 |
| 6 | 14 10 | −11.1 | 41 | 26 | 9 11 | 4 44 | 4 5 |
| 11 | 14 21 | −11.5 | 38 | 30 | 9 03 | 4 38 | 4 5 |
| 16 | 14 35 | −12.1 | 35 | 34 | 8 57 | 4 36 | 4 5 |
| 21 | 14 50 | −13.0 | 32 | 37 | 8 52 | 4 37 | 4 5 |
| 26 | 15 07 | −14.0 | 30 | 41 | 8 50 | 4 41 | 4 5 |
| 31 | 15 25 | −15.0 | 28 | 44 | 8 48 | 4 46 | 5 0 |

## MARS

| *Day* | *RA* | *Dec.* | *Diam.* | *Phase* | *Transit* | *5° high* 52° | *5° high* 56° |
|---|---|---|---|---|---|---|---|
| 1 | 13 51 | −10.5 | 4 | 96 | 9 12 | 4 42 | 4 5 |
| 6 | 14 04 | −11.6 | 4 | 96 | 9 05 | 4 42 | 4 5 |
| 11 | 14 16 | −12.7 | 4 | 96 | 8 57 | 4 41 | 4 5 |
| 16 | 14 29 | −13.8 | 4 | 95 | 8 50 | 4 40 | 4 5 |
| 21 | 14 41 | −14.9 | 4 | 95 | 8 43 | 4 40 | 4 5 |
| 26 | 14 54 | −15.8 | 4 | 95 | 8 36 | 4 39 | 4 5 |
| 31 | 15 07 | −16.8 | 5 | 94 | 8 29 | 4 39 | 5 0 |

## NRISE AND SUNSET

| London | | Bristol | | Birmingham | | Manchester | | Newcastle | | Glasgow | | Belfast | |
|---|---|---|---|---|---|---|---|---|---|---|---|---|---|
| 0°05′ | 51°30′ | 2°35′ | 51°28′ | 1°55′ | 52°28′ | 2°15′ | 53°28′ | 1°37′ | 54°59′ | 4°14′ | 55°52′ | 5°56′ | 54°35′ |
| h m | h m | h m | h m | h m | h m | h m | h m | h m | h m | h m | h m | h m | h m |
| 7 43 | 15 55 | 7 53 | 16 05 | 7 55 | 15 58 | 8 01 | 15 54 | 8 07 | 15 43 | 8 23 | 15 49 | 8 22 | 16 03 |
| 7 45 | 15 54 | 7 55 | 16 05 | 7 57 | 15 57 | 8 03 | 15 53 | 8 09 | 15 43 | 8 24 | 15 48 | 8 24 | 16 02 |
| 7 46 | 15 54 | 7 56 | 16 04 | 7 58 | 15 57 | 8 04 | 15 53 | 8 10 | 15 42 | 8 26 | 15 47 | 8 25 | 16 01 |
| 7 47 | 15 53 | 7 57 | 16 03 | 7 59 | 15 56 | 8 06 | 15 52 | 8 12 | 15 41 | 8 27 | 15 46 | 8 27 | 16 01 |
| 7 49 | 15 53 | 7 58 | 16 03 | 8 01 | 15 55 | 8 07 | 15 52 | 8 13 | 15 41 | 8 29 | 15 46 | 8 28 | 16 00 |
| 7 50 | 15 52 | 8 00 | 16 03 | 8 02 | 15 55 | 8 09 | 15 51 | 8 15 | 15 40 | 8 30 | 15 45 | 8 29 | 16 00 |
| 7 51 | 15 52 | 8 01 | 16 02 | 8 03 | 15 55 | 8 10 | 15 51 | 8 16 | 15 40 | 8 32 | 15 45 | 8 31 | 15 59 |
| 7 52 | 15 52 | 8 02 | 16 02 | 8 04 | 15 54 | 8 11 | 15 50 | 8 17 | 15 39 | 8 33 | 15 44 | 8 32 | 15 59 |
| 7 53 | 15 52 | 8 03 | 16 02 | 8 06 | 15 54 | 8 12 | 15 50 | 8 18 | 15 39 | 8 34 | 15 44 | 8 33 | 15 58 |
| 7 55 | 15 51 | 8 04 | 16 02 | 8 07 | 15 54 | 8 13 | 15 50 | 8 20 | 15 39 | 8 36 | 15 43 | 8 35 | 15 58 |
| 7 56 | 15 51 | 8 05 | 16 01 | 8 08 | 15 54 | 8 15 | 15 50 | 8 21 | 15 38 | 8 37 | 15 43 | 8 36 | 15 58 |
| 7 57 | 15 51 | 8 06 | 16 01 | 8 09 | 15 54 | 8 16 | 15 50 | 8 22 | 15 38 | 8 38 | 15 43 | 8 37 | 15 58 |
| 7 58 | 15 51 | 8 07 | 16 01 | 8 10 | 15 54 | 8 17 | 15 49 | 8 23 | 15 38 | 8 39 | 15 43 | 8 38 | 15 58 |
| 7 58 | 15 51 | 8 08 | 16 01 | 8 11 | 15 54 | 8 18 | 15 49 | 8 24 | 15 38 | 8 40 | 15 43 | 8 39 | 15 58 |
| 7 59 | 15 51 | 8 09 | 16 02 | 8 12 | 15 54 | 8 18 | 15 50 | 8 25 | 15 38 | 8 41 | 15 43 | 8 40 | 15 58 |
| 8 00 | 15 52 | 8 10 | 16 02 | 8 12 | 15 54 | 8 19 | 15 50 | 8 26 | 15 38 | 8 42 | 15 43 | 8 41 | 15 58 |
| 8 01 | 15 52 | 8 11 | 16 02 | 8 13 | 15 54 | 8 20 | 15 50 | 8 27 | 15 38 | 8 43 | 15 43 | 8 41 | 15 58 |
| 8 02 | 15 52 | 8 11 | 16 02 | 8 14 | 15 54 | 8 21 | 15 50 | 8 27 | 15 38 | 8 44 | 15 43 | 8 42 | 15 58 |
| 8 02 | 15 52 | 8 12 | 16 03 | 8 15 | 15 55 | 8 22 | 15 50 | 8 28 | 15 39 | 8 44 | 15 43 | 8 43 | 15 59 |
| 8 03 | 15 53 | 8 13 | 16 03 | 8 15 | 15 55 | 8 22 | 15 51 | 8 29 | 15 39 | 8 45 | 15 44 | 8 44 | 15 59 |
| 8 03 | 15 53 | 8 13 | 16 03 | 8 16 | 15 55 | 8 23 | 15 51 | 8 29 | 15 40 | 8 46 | 15 44 | 8 44 | 15 59 |
| 8 04 | 15 54 | 8 14 | 16 04 | 8 16 | 15 56 | 8 23 | 15 52 | 8 30 | 15 40 | 8 46 | 15 45 | 8 45 | 16 00 |
| 8 04 | 15 54 | 8 14 | 16 04 | 8 17 | 15 57 | 8 24 | 15 52 | 8 30 | 15 41 | 8 47 | 15 45 | 8 45 | 16 00 |
| 8 05 | 15 55 | 8 15 | 16 05 | 8 17 | 15 57 | 8 24 | 15 53 | 8 31 | 15 41 | 8 47 | 15 46 | 8 45 | 16 01 |
| 8 05 | 15 56 | 8 15 | 16 06 | 8 18 | 15 58 | 8 24 | 15 54 | 8 31 | 15 42 | 8 47 | 15 47 | 8 46 | 16 02 |
| 8 05 | 15 56 | 8 15 | 16 06 | 8 18 | 15 59 | 8 25 | 15 54 | 8 31 | 15 43 | 8 47 | 15 47 | 8 46 | 16 03 |
| 8 06 | 15 57 | 8 15 | 16 07 | 8 18 | 15 59 | 8 25 | 15 55 | 8 31 | 15 44 | 8 48 | 15 48 | 8 46 | 16 03 |
| 8 06 | 15 58 | 8 16 | 16 08 | 8 18 | 16 00 | 8 25 | 15 56 | 8 32 | 15 45 | 8 48 | 15 49 | 8 46 | 16 04 |
| 8 06 | 15 59 | 8 16 | 16 09 | 8 18 | 16 01 | 8 25 | 15 57 | 8 32 | 15 45 | 8 48 | 15 50 | 8 46 | 16 05 |
| 8 06 | 16 00 | 8 16 | 16 10 | 8 18 | 16 02 | 8 25 | 15 58 | 8 32 | 15 46 | 8 48 | 15 51 | 8 46 | 16 06 |
| 8 06 | 16 01 | 8 16 | 16 11 | 8 18 | 16 03 | 8 25 | 15 59 | 8 31 | 15 48 | 8 48 | 15 52 | 8 46 | 16 07 |

## PITER

| y | *RA* | | *Dec.* | | *Transit* | | *5° high* | | | |
|---|---|---|---|---|---|---|---|---|---|---|
| | | | | | | | 52° | | 56° | |
| | h | m | ° | ′ | h | m | h | m | h | m |
| | 9 | 22.9 | +16 | 02 | 4 | 43 | 21 | 50 | 21 | 40 |
| | 9 | 22.8 | +16 | 05 | 4 | 04 | 21 | 10 | 21 | 00 |
| | 9 | 21.3 | +16 | 14 | 3 | 23 | 20 | 28 | 20 | 18 |
| | 9 | 18.7 | +16 | 29 | 2 | 41 | 19 | 45 | 19 | 34 |

ameters - equatorial 42″ polar 40″

## SATURN

| *Day* | *RA* | | *Dec.* | | *Transit* | | *5° high* | | | |
|---|---|---|---|---|---|---|---|---|---|---|
| | | | | | | | 52° | | 56° | |
| | h | m | ° | ′ | h | m | h | m | h | m |
| 1 | 5 | 46.8 | +22 | 04 | 1 | 08 | 8 | 33 | 8 | 49 |
| 11 | 5 | 43.4 | +22 | 04 | 0 | 25 | 7 | 50 | 8 | 06 |
| 21 | 5 | 39.8 | +22 | 03 | 23 | 38 | 7 | 07 | 7 | 23 |
| 31 | 5 | 36.4 | +22 | 02 | 22 | 55 | 6 | 24 | 6 | 41 |

Diameters - equatorial 21″ polar 19″
Rings- major axis 47″ minor axis 21″

## RANUS

| y | *RA* | | *Dec.* | | *Transit* | | *10° high* | | | |
|---|---|---|---|---|---|---|---|---|---|---|
| | | | | | | | 52° | | 56° | |
| | h | m | ° | ′ | h | m | h | m | h | m |
| | 21 | 51.0 | −13 | 49 | 17 | 10 | 20 | 40 | 20 | 16 |
| | 21 | 52.0 | −13 | 43 | 16 | 31 | 20 | 02 | 19 | 39 |
| | 21 | 53.3 | −13 | 36 | 15 | 53 | 19 | 25 | 19 | 02 |
| | 21 | 54.8 | −13 | 27 | 15 | 15 | 18 | 49 | 18 | 26 |

ameter 4″

## NEPTUNE

| *Day* | *RA* | | *Dec.* | | *Transit* | | *10° high* | | | |
|---|---|---|---|---|---|---|---|---|---|---|
| | | | | | | | 52° | | 56° | |
| | h | m | ° | ′ | h | m | h | m | h | m |
| 1 | 20 | 44.3 | −18 | 03 | 16 | 03 | 19 | 00 | 18 | 26 |
| 11 | 20 | 45.4 | −17 | 59 | 15 | 25 | 18 | 23 | 17 | 49 |
| 21 | 20 | 46.5 | −17 | 55 | 14 | 47 | 17 | 45 | 17 | 12 |
| 31 | 20 | 47.8 | −17 | 50 | 14 | 09 | 17 | 08 | 16 | 35 |

Diameter 2″

## RISING AND SETTING TIMES

### TABLE 1. SEMI-DIURNAL ARCS (HOUR ANGLES AT RISING/SETTING)

| *Dec.* | *Latitude* 0° | 10° | 20° | 30° | 40° | 45° | 50° | 52° | 54° | 56° | 58° | 60° | De |
|---|---|---|---|---|---|---|---|---|---|---|---|---|---|
| | h m | h m | h m | h m | h m | h m | h m | h m | h m | h m | h m | h m | |
| 0° | 6 00 | 6 00 | 6 00 | 6 00 | 6 00 | 6 00 | 6 00 | 6 00 | 6 00 | 6 00 | 6 00 | 6 00 | |
| 1° | 6 00 | 6 01 | 6 01 | 6 02 | 6 03 | 6 04 | 6 05 | 6 05 | 6 06 | 6 06 | 6 06 | 6 07 | |
| 2° | 6 00 | 6 01 | 6 03 | 6 05 | 6 07 | 6 08 | 6 10 | 6 10 | 6 11 | 6 12 | 6 13 | 6 14 | |
| 3° | 6 00 | 6 02 | 6 04 | 6 07 | 6 10 | 6 12 | 6 14 | 6 15 | 6 17 | 6 18 | 6 19 | 6 21 | |
| 4° | 6 00 | 6 03 | 6 06 | 6 09 | 6 13 | 6 16 | 6 19 | 6 21 | 6 22 | 6 24 | 6 26 | 6 28 | |
| 5° | 6 00 | 6 04 | 6 07 | 6 12 | 6 17 | 6 20 | 6 24 | 6 26 | 6 28 | 6 30 | 6 32 | 6 35 | |
| 6° | 6 00 | 6 04 | 6 09 | 6 14 | 6 20 | 6 24 | 6 29 | 6 31 | 6 33 | 6 36 | 6 39 | 6 42 | |
| 7° | 6 00 | 6 05 | 6 10 | 6 16 | 6 24 | 6 28 | 6 34 | 6 36 | 6 39 | 6 42 | 6 45 | 6 49 | |
| 8° | 6 00 | 6 06 | 6 12 | 6 19 | 6 27 | 6 32 | 6 39 | 6 41 | 6 45 | 6 48 | 6 52 | 6 56 | |
| 9° | 6 00 | 6 06 | 6 13 | 6 21 | 6 31 | 6 36 | 6 44 | 6 47 | 6 50 | 6 54 | 6 59 | 7 04 | |
| 10° | 6 00 | 6 07 | 6 15 | 6 23 | 6 34 | 6 41 | 6 49 | 6 52 | 6 56 | 7 01 | 7 06 | 7 11 | 1 |
| 11° | 6 00 | 6 08 | 6 16 | 6 26 | 6 38 | 6 45 | 6 54 | 6 58 | 7 02 | 7 07 | 7 12 | 7 19 | 1 |
| 12° | 6 00 | 6 09 | 6 18 | 6 28 | 6 41 | 6 49 | 6 59 | 7 03 | 7 08 | 7 13 | 7 20 | 7 26 | 1 |
| 13° | 6 00 | 6 09 | 6 19 | 6 31 | 6 45 | 6 53 | 7 04 | 7 09 | 7 14 | 7 20 | 7 27 | 7 34 | 1 |
| 14° | 6 00 | 6 10 | 6 21 | 6 33 | 6 48 | 6 58 | 7 09 | 7 14 | 7 20 | 7 27 | 7 34 | 7 42 | 1 |
| 15° | 6 00 | 6 11 | 6 22 | 6 36 | 6 52 | 7 02 | 7 14 | 7 20 | 7 27 | 7 34 | 7 42 | 7 51 | 1 |
| 16° | 6 00 | 6 12 | 6 24 | 6 38 | 6 56 | 7 07 | 7 20 | 7 26 | 7 33 | 7 41 | 7 49 | 7 59 | 1 |
| 17° | 6 00 | 6 12 | 6 26 | 6 41 | 6 59 | 7 11 | 7 25 | 7 32 | 7 40 | 7 48 | 7 57 | 8 08 | 1 |
| 18° | 6 00 | 6 13 | 6 27 | 6 43 | 7 03 | 7 16 | 7 31 | 7 38 | 7 46 | 7 55 | 8 05 | 8 17 | 1 |
| 19° | 6 00 | 6 14 | 6 29 | 6 46 | 7 07 | 7 21 | 7 37 | 7 45 | 7 53 | 8 03 | 8 14 | 8 26 | 1 |
| 20° | 6 00 | 6 15 | 6 30 | 6 49 | 7 11 | 7 25 | 7 43 | 7 51 | 8 00 | 8 11 | 8 22 | 8 36 | 2 |
| 21° | 6 00 | 6 16 | 6 32 | 6 51 | 7 15 | 7 30 | 7 49 | 7 58 | 8 08 | 8 19 | 8 32 | 8 47 | 2 |
| 22° | 6 00 | 6 16 | 6 34 | 6 54 | 7 19 | 7 35 | 7 55 | 8 05 | 8 15 | 8 27 | 8 41 | 8 58 | 2 |
| 23° | 6 00 | 6 17 | 6 36 | 6 57 | 7 23 | 7 40 | 8 02 | 8 12 | 8 23 | 8 36 | 8 51 | 9 09 | 2 |
| 24° | 6 00 | 6 18 | 6 37 | 7 00 | 7 28 | 7 46 | 8 08 | 8 19 | 8 31 | 8 45 | 9 02 | 9 22 | 2 |
| 25° | 6 00 | 6 19 | 6 39 | 7 02 | 7 32 | 7 51 | 8 15 | 8 27 | 8 40 | 8 55 | 9 13 | 9 35 | 2 |
| 26° | 6 00 | 6 20 | 6 41 | 7 05 | 7 37 | 7 57 | 8 22 | 8 35 | 8 49 | 9 05 | 9 25 | 9 51 | 2 |
| 27° | 6 00 | 6 21 | 6 43 | 7 08 | 7 41 | 8 03 | 8 30 | 8 43 | 8 58 | 9 16 | 9 39 | 10 08 | 2 |
| 28° | 6 00 | 6 22 | 6 45 | 7 12 | 7 46 | 8 08 | 8 37 | 8 52 | 9 08 | 9 28 | 9 53 | 10 28 | 2 |
| 29° | 6 00 | 6 22 | 6 47 | 7 15 | 7 51 | 8 15 | 8 45 | 9 01 | 9 19 | 9 41 | 10 10 | 10 55 | 2 |
| 30° | 6 00 | 6 23 | 6 49 | 7 18 | 7 56 | 8 21 | 8 54 | 9 11 | 9 30 | 9 55 | 10 30 | 12 00 | 3 |
| 35° | 6 00 | 6 28 | 6 59 | 7 35 | 8 24 | 8 58 | 9 46 | 10 15 | 10 58 | 12 00 | 12 00 | 12 00 | 3 |
| 40° | 6 00 | 6 34 | 7 11 | 7 56 | 8 59 | 9 48 | 12 00 | 12 00 | 12 00 | 12 00 | 12 00 | 12 00 | 4 |
| 45° | 6 00 | 6 41 | 7 25 | 8 21 | 9 48 | 12 00 | 12 00 | 12 00 | 12 00 | 12 00 | 12 00 | 12 00 | 4 |
| 50° | 6 00 | 6 49 | 7 43 | 8 54 | 12 00 | 12 00 | 12 00 | 12 00 | 12 00 | 12 00 | 12 00 | 12 00 | 5 |
| 55° | 6 00 | 6 58 | 8 05 | 9 42 | 12 00 | 12 00 | 12 00 | 12 00 | 12 00 | 12 00 | 12 00 | 12 00 | 5 |
| 60° | 6 00 | 7 11 | 8 36 | 12 00 | 12 00 | 12 00 | 12 00 | 12 00 | 12 00 | 12 00 | 12 00 | 12 00 | 6 |
| 65° | 6 00 | 7 29 | 9 25 | 12 00 | 12 00 | 12 00 | 12 00 | 12 00 | 12 00 | 12 00 | 12 00 | 12 00 | 6 |
| 70° | 6 00 | 7 56 | 12 00 | 12 00 | 12 00 | 12 00 | 12 00 | 12 00 | 12 00 | 12 00 | 12 00 | 12 00 | 7 |
| 75° | 6 00 | 8 45 | 12 00 | 12 00 | 12 00 | 12 00 | 12 00 | 12 00 | 12 00 | 12 00 | 12 00 | 12 00 | 7 |
| 80° | 6 00 | 12 00 | 12 00 | 12 00 | 12 00 | 12 00 | 12 00 | 12 00 | 12 00 | 12 00 | 12 00 | 12 00 | 8 |

### TABLE 2. CORRECTION FOR REFRACTION AND SEMI-DIAMETER

| | m | m | m | m | m | m | m | m | m | m | m | m | |
|---|---|---|---|---|---|---|---|---|---|---|---|---|---|
| 0° | 3 | 3 | 4 | 4 | 4 | 5 | 5 | 5 | 6 | 6 | 6 | 7 | |
| 10° | 3 | 3 | 4 | 4 | 4 | 5 | 5 | 6 | 6 | 6 | 7 | 7 | 1 |
| 20° | 4 | 4 | 4 | 4 | 5 | 5 | 6 | 7 | 7 | 8 | 8 | 9 | 2 |
| 25° | 4 | 4 | 4 | 4 | 5 | 6 | 7 | 8 | 8 | 9 | 11 | 13 | 2 |
| 30° | 4 | 4 | 4 | 5 | 6 | 7 | 8 | 9 | 11 | 14 | 21 | — | 3 |

NB: Regarding Table 1. If latitude and declination are of the same sign, take out the respondent directly. If they are of opposite signs, subtract the respondent from 12h.
*Example:*

| Lat. | Dec. | Semi-diurnal arc |
|---|---|---|
| +52° | +20° | 7h 51m |
| +52° | –20° | 4h 09m |

Table 1 gives the complete range of declinations in ca any user wishes to calculate semi-diurnal arcs for bodi other than the Sun and Moon.

## UNRISE AND SUNSET

he local mean time of sunrise or sunset may be found by taining the hour angle from Table 1 and applying it to e time of transit. The hour angle is negative for sunrise d positive for sunset. A small correction to the hour gle, which always has the effect of increasing it merically, is necessary to allow for the Sun's semi-ameter (16′) and for refraction (34′); it is obtained from able 2. The resulting local mean time may be converted to the standard time of the country by taking the fference between the longitude of the standard meridian the country and that of the place, adding it to the local ean time if the place is west of the standard meridian, and btracting it if the place is east.

*ample* – Required the New Zealand Mean Time (12h st on GMT) of sunset on May 23 at Auckland, latitude ° 50′ S. (or minus), longitude 11h 39m E. Taking the clination as +20°.6 (page 33), we find:

| | | h | m |
|---|---|---|---|
| ew Zealand Standard Time | + | 12 | 00 |
| ongitude | – | 11 | 39 |
| ongitudinal Correction | + | 0 | 21 |
| abular entry for Lat. 30° and Dec. 20°, opposite signs | + | 5 | 11 |
| oportional part for 6° 50′ of Lat. | – | | 15 |
| oportional part for 0°.6 of Dec. | – | | 2 |
| orrection (Table 2) | + | | 5 |
| our angle | | 4 | 58 |
| n transits (page 33) | | 11 | 57 |
| ongitudinal correction | + | | 21 |
| New Zealand Mean Time | | 17 | 16 |

## OONRISE AND MOONSET

is possible to calculate the times of moonrise and moonset ing Table 1, though the method is more complicated cause the apparent motion of the Moon is much more pid and also more variable than that of the Sun.

ABLE 3. LONGITUDE CORRECTION

| 40m | 45m | 50m | 55m | 60m | 65m | 70m |
|---|---|---|---|---|---|---|
| m | m | m | m | m | m | m |
| 2 | 2 | 2 | 2 | 3 | 3 | 3 |
| 3 | 4 | 4 | 5 | 5 | 5 | 6 |
| 5 | 6 | 6 | 7 | 8 | 8 | 9 |
| 7 | 8 | 8 | 9 | 10 | 11 | 12 |
| 8 | 9 | 10 | 11 | 13 | 14 | 15 |
| 10 | 11 | 13 | 14 | 15 | 16 | 18 |
| 12 | 13 | 15 | 16 | 18 | 19 | 20 |
| 13 | 15 | 17 | 18 | 20 | 22 | 23 |
| 15 | 17 | 19 | 21 | 23 | 24 | 26 |
| 17 | 19 | 21 | 23 | 25 | 27 | 29 |
| 18 | 21 | 23 | 25 | 28 | 30 | 32 |
| 20 | 23 | 25 | 28 | 30 | 33 | 35 |
| 22 | 24 | 27 | 30 | 33 | 35 | 38 |
| 23 | 26 | 29 | 32 | 35 | 38 | 41 |
| 25 | 28 | 31 | 34 | 38 | 41 | 44 |
| 27 | 30 | 33 | 37 | 40 | 43 | 47 |
| 28 | 32 | 35 | 39 | 43 | 46 | 50 |
| 30 | 34 | 38 | 41 | 45 | 49 | 53 |
| 32 | 36 | 40 | 44 | 48 | 51 | 55 |
| 33 | 38 | 42 | 46 | 50 | 54 | 58 |
| 35 | 39 | 44 | 48 | 53 | 57 | 61 |
| 37 | 41 | 46 | 50 | 55 | 60 | 64 |
| 38 | 43 | 48 | 53 | 58 | 62 | 67 |
| 40 | 45 | 50 | 55 | 60 | 65 | 70 |

The parallax of the Moon, about 57′, is near to the sum of the semi-diameter and refraction but has the opposite effect on these times. It is thus convenient to neglect all three quantities in the method outlined below.

*Notation*

$\phi$ = latitude of observer
$\lambda$ = longitude of observer (measured positively towards the west)
$T_{-1}$ = time of transit of Moon on previous day
$T_0$ = time of transit of Moon on day in question
$T_1$ = time of transit of Moon on following day
$\delta_0$ = approximate declination of Moon
$\delta_R$ = declination of Moon at moonrise
$\delta_S$ = declination of Moon at moonset
$h_0$ = approximate hour angle of Moon
$h_R$ = hour angle of Moon at moonrise
$h_S$ = hour angle of Moon at moonset
$t_R$ = time of moonrise
$t_S$ = time of moonset

*Method*

1. With arguments $\phi$, $\delta_0$ enter Table 1 on page 64 to determine $h_0$ where $h_0$ is negative for moonrise and positive for moonset.
2. Form approximate times from
   $t_R = T_0 + \lambda + h_0$
   $t_S = T_0 + \lambda + h_0$
3. Determine $\delta_R$, $\delta_S$ for times $t_R$, $t_S$ respectively.
4. Re-enter Table 1 on page 64 with
   (*a*) arguments $\phi$, $\delta_R$ to determine $h_R$
   (*b*) arguments $\phi$, $\delta_S$ to determine $h_S$
5. Form $t_R = T_0 + \lambda + h_R + AX$
   $t_S = T_0 + \lambda + h_S + AX$

where $A = (\lambda + h)$

and $X = (T_0 - T_{-1})$ if $(\lambda + h)$ is negative
$X = (T_1 - T_0)$ if $(\lambda + h)$ is positive

AX is the respondent in Table 3.

*Example* – To find the times of moonrise and moonset at Vancouver ($\phi = +49°$, $\lambda = +8h\ 12m$) on 2002 March 11. The starting data (page 26) are:

$T_{-1}$ = 9h 40m
$T_0$ = 10h 27m
$T_1$ = 11h 11m
$\delta_0$ = –19°

1. $h_0$ = 4h 26m
2. Approximate values
   $t_R$ = 11d 10h 27m + 8h 12m + (-4h 26m)
   = 11d 14h 13m
   $t_S$ = 11d 10h 27m + 8h 12m + (+4h 26m)
   = 11d 23h 05m
3. $\delta_R$ = -17°.6
   $\delta_S$ = -16°.3
4. $h_R$ = -4h 34m
   $h_S$ = +4h 41m
5. $t_R$ = 11d 10h 27m + 8h 12m + (-4h 34m) + 7m
   = 11d 14h 12m
   $t_S$ = 11d 10h 27m + 8h 12m + (+4h 41m) + 23m
   = 11d 23h 43m

To get the LMT of the phenomenon the longitude is subtracted from the GMT thus:

Moonrise = 11d 14h 12m - 8h 12m = 11d 06h 00m
Moonset = 11d 23h 43m - 8h 12m = 11d 15h 31m

## ECLIPSES AND OCCULTATIONS 2002

### Eclipses

During 2002 there will be two eclipses, both of the Sun. (Penumbral eclipses are not mentioned in this section as they are so difficult to observe).

1. An annular eclipse of the sun on June 10-11 is visible as a partial eclipse from western Asia, Indonesia, the Philippine Islands, northern Australia, the Pacific Ocean and most of North America (except the north-east and southern Mexico). The eclipse begins at 20h 52m and ends at 02h 37m. The track of annularity starts in the Celebes Sea, crosses the Pacific Ocean, and then passes just south of Lower California and ends on the west coast of Mexico, south-west of Guadalajara. Annularity begins at 21h 54m and ends at 01h 35m. The maximum duration is 23s.

2. A total eclipse of the Sun on December 4 is visible as a partial eclipse from the south-east Atlantic Ocean, Africa, Madagascar, part of Antarctica, the Indian Ocean, Australia (except the extreme east) and Indonesia. The partial phase begins at 04h 51m and ends at 10h 11m. The track of totality starts in the south-west Atlantic and crosses Angola, Zambia, extreme north-east Namibia, northern Botswana, southern Zimbabwe and extreme north-east of South Africa and Mozambique. It then crosses the southern Indian Ocean before ending in south-eastern Australia. The total phase begins at 05h 50m and ends at 09h 12m. The maximum duration is 2m 04s.

### Lunar Occultations

Observations of the times of occultations are made by both amateur and professional astronomers. Such observations are later analysed to yield accurate positions of the Moon; this is one method of determining the difference between ephemeris time and universal time.

Many of the observations made by amateurs are obtained with the use of a stop-watch which is compared with a time-signal immediately after the observation. Thus an accuracy of about one-fifth of a second is obtainable, though the observer's personal equation may amount to one-third or one-half of a second.

The list on page 67 includes most of the occultations visible under favourable conditions in the British Isles. No occultation is included unless the star is at least 10° above the horizon and the Sun sufficiently far below the horizon to permit the star to be seen with the naked eye or with a small telescope. The altitude limit is reduced from 10° to 2° for stars and planets brighter than magnitude 2.0 and such occultations are also predicted in daylight.

The column Phase shows (i) whether a disappearance (D) or reappearance (R) is to be observed; and (ii) whether it is at the dark limb (D) or bright limb (B). The column headed 'El. of Moon' gives the elongation of the Moon from the Sun, in degrees. The elongation increases from 0° at New Moon to 180° at Full Moon and on to 360° (or 0°) at New Moon again. Times and position angles (*P*), reckoned from the north point in the direction north, east, south, west, are given for Greenwich (lat. 51° 30′, long. 0°) and Edinburgh (lat. 56° 00′, long. 3° 12′ west).

The coefficients *a* and *b* are the variations in the GMT for each degree of longitude (positive to the west) and latitude (positive to the north) respectively; they enable approximate times (to within about 1m generally) to be found for any point in the British Isles. If the point of observation is $\Delta\lambda$ degrees west and $\Delta\phi$ degrees north, the approximate time is found by adding $a.\Delta\lambda + b.\Delta\phi$ to the given GMT.

*Example:* the disappearance of ZC5 on October 18 Coventry, found from both Greenwich and Edinburgh.

| | Greenwich | Edinburg |
|---|---|---|
| | ° | |
| Longitude | 0.0 | +3 |
| Long. of Coventry | +1.5 | +1 |
| $\Delta\lambda$ | +1.5 | –1 |
| Latitude | +51.5 | +56 |
| Lat. of Coventry | +52.4 | +52 |
| $\Delta\phi$ | +0.9 | –3 |
| | h m | h m |
| GMT | 21 06.1 | 21 02 |
| $a.\Delta\lambda$ | – 3.6 | + 2 |
| $b.\Delta\phi$ | + 0.2 | – 2 |
| | 21 02.7 | 21 02 |

If the occultation is given for one station but not t other, the reason for the suppression is given by t following code:

N = star not occulted
A = star's altitude less than 10° (2° for bright stars a planets)
S = Sun not sufficiently below the horizon
G = occultation is of very short duration

In some cases the coefficients *a* and *b* are not given; this because the occultation is so short that prediction for oth places by means of these coefficients would not be reliab

UNAR OCCULTATIONS 2002

| | | ZCNo. | Mag. | Phase | El. of Moon | Greewich UT | | a | b | P | Edinburgh UT | | a | b | P |
|---|---|---|---|---|---|---|---|---|---|---|---|---|---|---|---|
| | | | | | | h | m | m | m | ° | h | m | m | m | ° |
| anuary | 17 | 3396 | 7.9 | D.D. | 46 | 17 | 32.9 | –1.2 | –0.7 | 73 | 17 | 27.2 | –0.9 | –0.3 | 60 |
| | 21 | 303 | 6.6 | D.D. | 90 | 18 | 31.9 | –0.8 | +1.9 | 24 | 18 | 40.5 | –0.2 | +2.9 | 4 |
| | 21 | 322 | 5.7 | D.D. | 92 | 23 | 00.1 | –0.4 | +1.0 | 21 | 23 | 09.3 | G | | 351 |
| | 24 | 691 | 6.6 | D.D. | 125 | 18 | 28.8 | –1.5 | +0.7 | 95 | 18 | 29.4 | –1.1 | +1.2 | 81 |
| | 25 | 828 | 6.5 | D.D. | 137 | 17 | 20.0 | –0.3 | +2.2 | 49 | 17 | 30.2 | –0.1 | +2.5 | 35 |
| | 25 | 861 | 6.5 | D.D. | 140 | 23 | 20.4 | –1.1 | –2.6 | 128 | 23 | 07.4 | –1.2 | –1.6 | 111 |
| | 31 | 1702 | 4.2 | R.D. | 222 | 22 | 23.8 | –0.4 | +1.3 | 276 | 22 | 27.7 | –0.3 | +1.0 | 290 |
| ebruary | 21 | 766 | 6.0 | D.D. | 105 | 17 | 44.5 | –1.6 | +0.2 | 102 | S | | | | |
| | 21 | 784 | 6.2 | D.D. | 107 | 22 | 12.6 | –1.2 | +0.1 | 53 | 22 | 10.7 | –1.2 | +0.9 | 37 |
| | 21 | 792 | 5.1 | D.D. | 108 | 24 | 01.5 | –0.2 | –2.1 | 112 | 23 | 51.6 | –0.4 | –1.9 | 102 |
| | 22 | 923 | 6.9 | D.D. | 117 | 18 | 09.5 | –1.1 | +1.6 | 68 | 18 | 14.6 | –0.8 | +2.1 | 52 |
| | 22 | 956 | 6.3 | D.D. | 120 | 23 | 32.8 | –0.9 | –0.9 | 77 | 23 | 26.1 | –1.0 | –0.6 | 66 |
| arch | 2 | 1921 | 5.9 | R.D. | 220 | 4 | 49.5 | –1.1 | –1.3 | 294 | 4 | 40.6 | –1.0 | –1.2 | 296 |
| | 2 | 1924 | 5.8 | R.D. | 221 | 5 | 34.7 | –1.0 | –1.4 | 282 | 5 | 25.4 | –1.0 | –1.3 | 284 |
| | 17 | 352 | 7.3 | D.D. | 41 | 19 | 15.8 | –0.6 | 0.0 | 43 | 19 | 15.3 | –0.5 | +0.6 | 26 |
| | 19 | 593 | 5.8 | D.D. | 63 | 19 | 56.1 | G | | 160 | 19 | 28.6 | –0.9 | –3.2 | 124 |
| | 21 | 887 | 7.1 | D.D. | 87 | 21 | 08.1 | –0.7 | –2.4 | 121 | 20 | 56.0 | –0.8 | –1.9 | 109 |
| | 22 | 1041 | 8.0 | D.D. | 99 | 20 | 01.8 | –1.6 | +0.7 | 58 | 20 | 02.4 | –1.5 | +1.9 | 41 |
| | 22 | 1052 | 6.8 | D.D. | 101 | 23 | 12.8 | –1.0 | –0.3 | 50 | 23 | 08.9 | –1.3 | +0.3 | 39 |
| pril | 16 | Saturn | 0.2 | D.D. | 46 | 21 | 00.2 | G | | 147 | 20 | 46.6 | +0.2 | –3.0 | 131 |
| | 16 | Saturn | 0.2 | R B. | 46 | 21 | 26.0 | G | | 200 | 21 | 26.0 | –0.4 | –0.1 | 214 |
| | 18 | 1019 | 6.7 | D.D. | 70 | 22 | 59.2 | G | | 25 | N | | | | |
| | 22 | 1535 | 7.1 | D.D. | 121 | 20 | 59.1 | –1.7 | –0.2 | 86 | 20 | 54.3 | –1.6 | +0.3 | 77 |
| | 23 | 1659 | 6.8 | D.D. | 135 | 21 | 46.3 | –1.8 | 0.0 | 83 | 21 | 41.7 | –1.7 | +0.4 | 75 |
| ay | 14 | Saturn | 0.1 | D.D. | 21 | 6 | 44.4 | G | | 161 | 6 | 41.7 | G | | 137 |
| | 14 | Saturn | 0.1 | R.D. | 21 | 6 | 47.1 | G | | 167 | 7 | 06.2 | G | | 191 |
| une | 19 | 1941 | 4.8 | D.D. | 115 | 21 | 56.5 | G | | 196 | 21 | 44.8 | G | | 192 |
| | 22 | 2337 | 6.4 | D.D. | 154 | 21 | 30.5 | –0.9 | –0.5 | 147 | S | | G | | 22 |
| uly | 20 | 2434 | 5.6 | D.D. | 137 | 21 | 07.0 | G | | 31 | 21 | 08.1 | G | | 22 |
| | 28 | 3536 | 4.7 | R.D. | 233 | 23 | 53.5 | –1.0 | +1.4 | 288 | 23 | 57.1 | –0.9 | +1.5 | 294 |
| eptember | 13 | 2500 | 3.4 | D.D. | 91 | 19 | 09.4 | –1.5 | –1.0 | 128 | 19 | 01.2 | –1.3 | –0.7 | 125 |
| | 14 | 2657 | 6.7 | D.D. | 103 | 19 | 21.2 | –1.6 | –0.1 | 69 | A | | | | |
| | 18 | 3227 | 6.4 | D.D. | 150 | 22 | 22.4 | –1.2 | +0.6 | 44 | 22 | 22.0 | –0.9 | +0.7 | 35 |
| | 19 | 3349 | 4.2 | D.D. | 161 | 22 | 28.7 | –1.1 | +1.1 | 39 | 22 | 30.4 | –0.9 | +1.1 | 30 |
| | 23 | 249 | 4.7 | R.D. | 205 | 20 | 25.7 | G | | 169 | 20 | 39.3 | G | | 180 |
| | 24 | 354 | 5.5 | R.D. | 216 | 20 | 47.9 | –0.2 | +1.7 | 268 | 20 | 55.1 | –0.2 | +1.8 | 273 |
| ctober | 12 | 2750 | 2.1 | D.D. | 83 | 15 | 21.5 | –1.9 | +2.0 | 39 | A | | | | |
| | 12 | 2750 | 2.1 | R.B. | 83 | 16 | 06.0 | –1.0 | –0.2 | 327 | A | | | | |
| | 15 | 3178 | 6.2 | D.D. | 119 | 18 | 05.6 | –1.2 | +1.6 | 33 | A | | | | |
| | 18 | 3536 | 4.7 | D.D. | 152 | 18 | 36.9 | –0.8 | +1.9 | 62 | 18 | 43.2 | –0.7 | +1.9 | 58 |
| | 18 | 5 | 4.7 | D.D. | 153 | 21 | 06.1 | –2.4 | +0.2 | 109 | 21 | 02.2 | –1.6 | +0.8 | 97 |
| ovember | 9 | 2862 | 8.0 | D.D. | 65 | 17 | 20.7 | G | | 19 | A | | | | |
| | 11 | 3141 | 6.0 | D.D. | 88 | 17 | 15.9 | –1.8 | +0.4 | 98 | 17 | 13.0 | –1.4 | +0.6 | 92 |
| | 12 | 3276 | 7.4 | D.D. | 101 | 19 | 24.1 | –1.1 | +0.6 | 42 | 19 | 23.7 | –0.8 | +0.6 | 32 |
| | 13 | 3396 | 7.9 | D.D. | 112 | 20 | 52.6 | –0.1 | +1.7 | 6 | DB | | | | |
| | 24 | 1117 | 5.1 | R.D. | 228 | 5 | 25.3 | –1.2 | –1.4 | 280 | 5 | 15.3 | –1.0 | –1.5 | 290 |
| ecember | 8 | 3087 | 7.7 | D.D. | 57 | 17 | 52.0 | –1.4 | –1.0 | 91 | A | | | | |
| | 10 | 3343 | 5.8 | D.D. | 80 | 17 | 33.0 | –1.0 | +0.9 | 36 | 17 | 34.5 | –0.7 | +1.0 | 26 |
| | 11 | 3480 | 7.3 | D.D. | 92 | 19 | 36.2 | –0.8 | +0.7 | 36 | 19 | 37.7 | –0.5 | +0.9 | 21 |
| | 11 | 3484 | 6.8 | D.D. | 92 | 20 | 57.5 | –1.2 | –1.0 | 80 | 20 | 50.6 | –0.9 | –0.6 | 65 |
| | 13 | 150 | 6.2 | D.D. | 114 | 20 | 12.6 | –2.9 | –2.0 | 115 | 20 | 01.2 | –1.8 | –0.3 | 94 |
| | 21 | 1170 | 3.7 | R.D. | 204 | 18 | 36.5 | +0.2 | +1.0 | 285 | 18 | 41.6 | +0.1 | +1.0 | 296 |
| | 26 | 1702 | 4.2 | R.D. | 260 | 5 | 53.3 | –0.5 | –2.1 | 344 | 5 | 42.4 | –0.3 | –2.2 | 351 |

## MEAN PLACES OF STARS 2002.5

| *Name* | *Mag.* | *RA* h | m | *Dec.* ° | ′ | *Spectrum* |
|---|---|---|---|---|---|---|
| $\alpha$ And *Alpheratz* | 2.1 | 0 | 08.5 | +29 | 06 | A0*p* |
| $\beta$ Cassiopeiae *Caph* | 2.3 | 0 | 09.3 | +59 | 10 | F5 |
| $\gamma$ Pegasi *Algenib* | 2.8 | 0 | 13.4 | +15 | 12 | B2 |
| $\beta$ Mensae | 2.9 | 0 | 25.9 | –77 | 14 | G0 |
| $\alpha$ Phoenicis | 2.4 | 0 | 26.4 | –42 | 18 | K0 |
| $\alpha$ Cassiopeiae *Schedar* | 2.2 | 0 | 40.7 | +56 | 33 | K0 |
| $\beta$ Ceti *Diphda* | 2.0 | 0 | 43.7 | –17 | 58 | K0 |
| $\gamma$ Cassiopeiae* | Var. | 0 | 56.9 | +60 | 44 | B0*p* |
| $\beta$ *Andromedae Mirach* | 2.1 | 1 | 09.9 | +35 | 38 | M0 |
| $\delta$ Cassiopeiae | 2.7 | 1 | 26.0 | +60 | 15 | A5 |
| $\alpha$ Eridani *Achernar* | 0.5 | 1 | 37.8 | –57 | 13 | B5 |
| $\beta$ Arietis *Sheratan* | 2.6 | 1 | 54.8 | +20 | 49 | A5 |
| $\gamma$ Andromedae *Almak* | 2.3 | 2 | 04.1 | +42 | 21 | K0 |
| $\alpha$ Arietis *Hamal* | 2.0 | 2 | 07.3 | +23 | 28 | K2 |
| $\alpha$ Ursae Minoris *Polaris* | *2.0* | 2 | 34.7 | +89 | 17 | F8 |
| $\beta$ Persei *Algol** | Var. | 3 | 08.3 | +40 | 58 | B8 |
| $\alpha$ Persei *Mirfak* | 1.8 | 3 | 24.5 | +49 | 52 | F5 |
| $\eta$ Tauri *Alcyone* | 2.9 | 3 | 47.6 | +24 | 07 | B5*p* |
| $\alpha$ Tauri *Aldebaran* | 0.9 | 4 | 36.1 | +16 | 31 | K5 |
| $\beta$ Orionis *Rigel* | 0.1 | 5 | 14.7 | –8 | 12 | B8*p* |
| $\alpha$ Aurigae *Capella* | 0.1 | 5 | 16.9 | +46 | 00 | G0 |
| $\gamma$ Orionis *Bellatrix* | 1.6 | 5 | 25.3 | +6 | 21 | B2 |
| $\beta$ Tauri *Elnath* | 1.7 | 5 | 26.5 | +28 | 37 | B8 |
| $\delta$ Orionis | 2.2 | 5 | 32.1 | –0 | 18 | B0 |
| $\alpha$ Leporis | 2.6 | 5 | 32.8 | –17 | 49 | F0 |
| $\varepsilon$ Orionis | 1.7 | 5 | 36.3 | –1 | 12 | B0 |
| $\zeta$ Orionis | 1.8 | 5 | 40.9 | –1 | 56 | B0 |
| $\kappa$ Orionis | 2.1 | 5 | 47.9 | –9 | 40 | B0 |
| $\alpha$ Orionis *Betelgeuse** | Var. | 5 | 55.3 | +7 | 24 | M0 |
| $\beta$ Aurigae *Menkalinan* | 1.9 | 5 | 59.7 | +44 | 57 | A0*p* |
| $\beta$ CMa *Mirzam* | 2.0 | 6 | 22.8 | –17 | 57 | B1 |
| $\alpha$ Carinae *Canopus* | –0.7 | 6 | 24.0 | –52 | 42 | F0 |
| $\gamma$ Geminorum *Alhena* | 1.9 | 6 | 37.9 | +16 | 24 | A0 |
| $\alpha$ Canis Majoris *Sirius* | –1.5 | 6 | 45.3 | –16 | 43 | A0 |
| $\varepsilon$ Canis Majoris | 1.5 | 6 | 58.7 | –28 | 59 | B1 |
| $\delta$ Canis Majoris | 1.9 | 7 | 08.5 | –26 | 24 | F8*p* |
| $\alpha$ Geminorum *Castor* | 1.6 | 7 | 34.8 | +31 | 53 | A0 |
| $\alpha$ CMi *Procyon* | 0.4 | 7 | 39.4 | +5 | 13 | F5 |
| $\beta$ Geminorum *Pollux* | 1.1 | 7 | 45.5 | +28 | 01 | K0 |
| $\zeta$ Puppis | 2.3 | 8 | 03.7 | –40 | 01 | Od |
| $\gamma$ Velorum | 1.8 | 8 | 09.6 | –47 | 21 | Oa*p* |
| $\varepsilon$ Carinae | 1.9 | 8 | 22.6 | –59 | 31 | K0 |
| $\delta$ Velorum | 2.0 | 8 | 44.8 | –54 | 43 | A0 |
| $\lambda$ Velorum *Suhail* | 2.2 | 9 | 08.1 | –43 | 27 | K5 |
| $\beta$ Carinae | 1.7 | 9 | 13.2 | –69 | 44 | A0 |
| $\iota$ Carinae | 2.2 | 9 | 17.2 | –59 | 17 | F0 |
| $\kappa$ Velorum | 2.6 | 9 | 22.2 | –55 | 01 | B3 |
| $\alpha$ Hydrae *Alphard* | 2.0 | 9 | 27.7 | –8 | 40 | K2 |
| $\alpha$ Leonis *Regulus* | 1.3 | 10 | 08.5 | +11 | 57 | B8 |
| $\gamma$ Leonis *Algeiba* | 1.9 | 10 | 20.1 | +19 | 50 | K0 |
| $\beta$ Ursae Majoris *Merak* | 2.4 | 11 | 02.0 | +56 | 22 | A0 |
| $\alpha$ Ursae Majoris *Dubhe* | 1.8 | 11 | 03.9 | +61 | 44 | K0 |
| $\delta$ Leonis | 2.6 | 11 | 14.2 | +20 | 31 | A3 |
| $\beta$ Leonis *Denebola* | 2.1 | 11 | 49.2 | +14 | 33 | A2 |
| $\gamma$ Ursae Majoris *Phecda* | 2.4 | 11 | 54.0 | +53 | 41 | A0 |

| *Name* | *Mag.* | *RA* h | m | *Dec.* ° | ′ | *Spectrum* |
|---|---|---|---|---|---|---|
| $\gamma$ Corvi | 2.6 | 12 | 15.9 | -17 | 33 | B |
| $\alpha$ Crucis | 1.0 | 12 | 26.7 | -63 | 07 | B |
| $\gamma$ Crucis | 1.6 | 12 | 31.3 | -57 | 08 | M |
| $\gamma$ Centauri | 2.2 | 12 | 41.7 | -48 | 58 | A |
| $\gamma$ Virginis | 2.7 | 12 | 41.8 | -1 | 28 | F |
| $\beta$ Crucis | 1.3 | 12 | 47.9 | -59 | 42 | B |
| $\varepsilon$ Ursae Majoris *Alioth* | 1.8 | 12 | 54.1 | +55 | 57 | A0 |
| $\alpha$ Canum Venaticorum | 2.9 | 12 | 56.1 | +38 | 18 | A0 |
| $\zeta$ Ursae Majoris *Mizar* | 2.1 | 13 | 24.0 | +54 | 55 | A2 |
| $\alpha$ Virginis *Spica* | 1.0 | 13 | 25.3 | -11 | 10 | B |
| $\varepsilon$ Centauri | 2.6 | 13 | 40.0 | -53 | 29 | B |
| $\eta$ Ursae Majoris *Alkaid* | 1.9 | 13 | 47.6 | +49 | 18 | B |
| $\beta$ Centauri *Hadar* | 0.6 | 14 | 04.0 | -60 | 23 | B |
| $\theta$ Centauri | 2.1 | 14 | 06.8 | -36 | 23 | K |
| $\alpha$ Bootis *Arcturus* | 0.0 | 14 | 15.8 | +19 | 10 | K |
| $\alpha$ Centauri *Rigil Kent* | 0.1 | 14 | 39.8 | -60 | 51 | G |
| $\varepsilon$ Bootis | 2.4 | 14 | 45.1 | +27 | 04 | K |
| $\beta$ UMi *Kochab* | 2.1 | 14 | 50.7 | +74 | 09 | K |
| $\gamma$ Ursae Minoris | 3.1 | 15 | 20.7 | +71 | 50 | A |
| $\alpha$ CrB *Alphecca* | 2.2 | 15 | 34.8 | +26 | 42 | A |
| $\beta$ Trianguli Australis | 3.0 | 15 | 55.4 | -63 | 26 | F |
| $\delta$ Scorpii | 2.3 | 16 | 00.5 | -22 | 38 | B |
| $\beta$ Scorpii | 2.6 | 16 | 05.6 | -19 | 49 | B |
| $\alpha$ Scorpii *Antares* | 1.0 | 16 | 29.6 | -26 | 26 | M |
| $\alpha$ Trianguli Australis | 1.9 | 16 | 48.9 | -69 | 02 | K |
| $\varepsilon$ Scorpii | 2.3 | 16 | 50.3 | -34 | 18 | K |
| $\alpha$ Herculis† | Var. | 17 | 14.8 | +14 | 23 | M |
| $\lambda$ Scorpii | 1.6 | 17 | 33.8 | -37 | 06 | B |
| $\alpha$ Ophiuchi *Rasalhague* | 2.1 | 17 | 35.1 | +12 | 34 | A |
| $\theta$ Scorpii | 1.9 | 17 | 37.5 | -43 | 00 | F |
| $\kappa$ Scorpii | 2.4 | 17 | 42.7 | -39 | 02 | B |
| $\gamma$ Draconis | 2.2 | 17 | 56.7 | +51 | 29 | K |
| $\varepsilon$ Sgr Kaus *Australis* | 1.9 | 18 | 24.3 | -34 | 23 | A |
| $\alpha$ Lyrae *Vega* | 0.0 | 18 | 37.0 | +38 | 47 | A |
| $\sigma$ Sagittarii | 2.0 | 18 | 55.4 | -26 | 18 | B |
| $\beta$ Cygni *Albireo* | 3.1 | 19 | 30.8 | +27 | 58 | K |
| $\alpha$ Aquilae *Altair* | 0.8 | 19 | 50.9 | +8 | 52 | A |
| $\alpha$ Capricorni | 3.8 | 20 | 18.2 | -12 | 32 | G |
| $\gamma$ Cygni | 2.2 | 20 | 22.3 | +40 | 16 | F8 |
| $\alpha$ Pavonis | 1.9 | 20 | 25.8 | -56 | 44 | B |
| $\alpha$ Cygni *Deneb* | 1.3 | 20 | 41.5 | +45 | 17 | A2 |
| $\alpha$ Cephei *Alderamin* | 2.4 | 21 | 18.6 | +62 | 36 | A |
| $\varepsilon$ Pegasi | 2.4 | 21 | 44.3 | +9 | 53 | K |
| $\delta$ Capricorni | 2.9 | 21 | 47.2 | -16 | 07 | A |
| $\alpha$ Gruis | 1.7 | 22 | 08.4 | -46 | 57 | B |
| $\delta$ Cephei† | 3.7 | 22 | 29.3 | +58 | 26 |  |
| $\beta$ Gruis | 2.1 | 22 | 42.8 | -46 | 52 | M |
| $\alpha$ PsA *Fomalhaut* | 1.2 | 22 | 57.8 | -29 | 37 | A |
| $\beta$ Pegasi *Scheat* | 2.4 | 23 | 03.9 | +28 | 06 | M |
| $\alpha$ Pegasi *Markab* | 2.5 | 23 | 04.9 | +15 | 13 | A |

*$\gamma$ Cassiopeiae, 2000 mag. 2.2. $\beta$ Persei, mag. 2.1 to 3.4 $\alpha$ Orionis, mag. 0.1 to 1.2.

†$\alpha$ Herculis, mag. 3.1 to 3.9. $\delta$ Cephei, mag. 3.7 to 4.4 spectrum F5 to G0.

The positions of heavenly bodies on the celestial sphere are defined by two co-ordinates, right ascension and declination, which are analogous to longitude and latitude on the surface of the Earth. If we imagine the plane of the terrestrial equator extended indefinitely, it will cut the celestial sphere in a great circle known as the celestial equator. Similarly the plane of the Earth's orbit, when extended, cuts in the great circle called the ecliptic. The two intersections of these circles are known as the First Point of Aries and the First Point of Libra. If from any star a perpendicular be drawn to the celestial equator, the length of this perpendicular is the star's declination. The arc, measured eastwards along the equator from the First Point of Aries to the foot of this perpendicular, is the right ascension. An alternative definition of right ascension is that it is the angle at the celestial pole (where the Earth's axis, if prolonged, would meet the sphere) between the great circles to the First Point of Aries and to the star.

The plane of the Earth's equator has a slow movement, so that our reference system for right ascension and declination is not fixed. The consequent alteration in these quantities from year to year is called precession. In right ascension it is an increase of about 3 seconds a year for equatorial stars, and larger or smaller changes in either direction for stars near the poles, depending on the right ascension of the star. In declination it varies between +20″ and –20″ according to the right ascension of the star.

A star or other body crosses the meridian when the sidereal time is equal to its right ascension. The altitude is then a maximum, and may be deduced by remembering that the altitude of the elevated pole is numerically equal to the latitude, while that of the equator at its intersection with the meridian is equal to the co-latitude, or complement of the latitude.

Thus in London (lat. 51° 30′) the meridian altitude of Sirius is found as follows:

| | ° | ′ |
|---|---|---|
| Altitude of equator | 38 | 30 |
| Declination south | 16 | 43 |
| Difference | 21 | 47 |

The altitude of Capella (Dec. +46° 00′) at lower transit is:

| | | |
|---|---|---|
| Altitude of pole | 51 | 30 |
| Polar distance of star | 44 | 00 |
| Difference | 7 | 30 |

The brightness of a heavenly body is denoted by its magnitude. Omitting the exceptionally bright stars Sirius and Canopus, the twenty brightest stars are of the first magnitude, while the faintest stars visible to the naked eye are of the sixth magnitude. The magnitude scale is a precise one, as a difference of five magnitudes represents a ratio of 100 to 1 in brightness. Typical second magnitude stars are Polaris and the stars in the belt of Orion. The scale is most easily fixed in memory by comparing the stars with Norton's *Star Atlas* (*see* page 71). The stars Sirius and Canopus and the planets Venus and Jupiter are so bright that their magnitudes are expressed by negative numbers. A small telescope will show stars down to the ninth or tenth magnitude, while stars fainter than the twentieth magnitude may be photographed by long exposures with the largest telescopes.

MEAN AND SIDEREAL TIME

Acceleration

| h | m | s | m | s | s |
|---|---|---|---|---|---|
| 1 | 0 | 10 | 0 | 00 | 0 |
| 2 | 0 | 20 | 3 | 02 | 1 |
| 3 | 0 | 30 | 9 | 07 | 2 |
| 4 | 0 | 39 | 15 | 13 | 3 |
| 5 | 0 | 49 | 21 | 18 | 4 |
| 6 | 0 | 59 | 27 | 23 | 5 |
| 7 | 1 | 09 | 33 | 28 | 6 |
| 8 | 1 | 19 | 39 | 34 | 7 |
| 9 | 1 | 29 | 45 | 39 | 8 |
| 10 | 1 | 39 | 51 | 44 | 9 |
| 11 | 1 | 48 | 57 | 49 | 10 |
| 12 | 1 | 58 | 60 | 00 | |
| 13 | 2 | 08 | | | |
| 14 | 2 | 18 | | | |
| 15 | 2 | 28 | | | |
| 16 | 2 | 38 | | | |
| 17 | 2 | 48 | | | |
| 18 | 2 | 57 | | | |
| 19 | 3 | 07 | | | |
| 20 | 3 | 17 | | | |
| 21 | 3 | 27 | | | |
| 22 | 3 | 37 | | | |
| 23 | 3 | 47 | | | |
| 24 | 3 | 57 | | | |

Retardation

| h | m | s | m | s | s |
|---|---|---|---|---|---|
| 1 | 0 | 10 | 0 | 00 | 0 |
| 2 | 0 | 20 | 3 | 03 | 1 |
| 3 | 0 | 29 | 9 | 09 | 2 |
| 4 | 0 | 39 | 15 | 15 | 3 |
| 5 | 0 | 49 | 21 | 21 | 4 |
| 6 | 0 | 59 | 27 | 28 | 5 |
| 7 | 1 | 09 | 33 | 34 | 6 |
| 8 | 1 | 19 | 39 | 40 | 7 |
| 9 | 1 | 28 | 45 | 46 | 8 |
| 10 | 1 | 38 | 51 | 53 | 9 |
| 11 | 1 | 48 | 57 | 59 | 10 |
| 12 | 1 | 58 | 60 | 00 | |
| 13 | 2 | 08 | | | |
| 14 | 2 | 18 | | | |
| 15 | 2 | 27 | | | |
| 16 | 2 | 37 | | | |
| 17 | 2 | 47 | | | |
| 18 | 2 | 57 | | | |
| 19 | 3 | 07 | | | |
| 20 | 3 | 17 | | | |
| 21 | 3 | 26 | | | |
| 22 | 3 | 36 | | | |
| 23 | 3 | 46 | | | |
| 24 | 3 | 56 | | | |

The length of a sidereal day in mean time is 23h 56m 04s.09. Hence 1h MT = 1h+9s.86 ST and 1h ST = 1h–9s.83 MT.

To convert an interval of mean time to the corresponding interval of sidereal time, enter the acceleration table with the given mean time (taking the hours and the minutes and seconds separately) and add the acceleration obtained to the given mean time. To convert an interval of sidereal time to the corresponding interval of mean time, take out the retardation for the given sidereal time and subtract.

The columns for the minutes and seconds of the argument are in the form known as critical tables. To use these tables, find in the appropriate left-hand column the two entries between which the given number of minutes and seconds lies; the quantity in the right-hand column between these two entries is the required acceleration or retardation. Thus the acceleration for 11m 26s (which lies between the entries 9m 07s and 15m 13s) is 2s. If the given number of minutes and seconds is a tabular entry, the required acceleration or retardation is the entry in the right-hand column above the given tabular entry, e.g. the retardation for 45m 46s is 7s.

*Example* – Convert 14h 27m 35s from ST to MT

| | h | m | s |
|---|---|---|---|
| Given ST | 14 | 27 | 35 |
| Retardation for 14h | | 2 | 18 |
| Retardation for 27m 35s | | | 5 |
| Corresponding MT | 14 | 25 | 12 |

For further explanation, *see* pages 73–74.

## ECLIPSES AND SHADOW TRANSITS OF JUPITER'S SATELLITES 2002

| *GMT* *d* | *h* | *m* | *Sat.* | *Phen.* |
|---|---|---|---|---|
| JANUARY | | | | |
| 2 | 19 | 18 | II | Sh.E |
| 4 | 04 | 32 | I | Sh.I |
| 5 | 03 | 23 | III | Ec.R |
| 5 | 04 | 07 | I | Ec.R |
| 5 | 20 | 58 | IV | Ec.R |
| 5 | 23 | 01 | I | Sh.I |
| 6 | 01 | 16 | I | Sh.E |
| 6 | 05 | 48 | II | Sh.I |
| 6 | 22 | 36 | I | Ec.R |
| 7 | 19 | 44 | I | Sh.E |
| 8 | 02 | 49 | II | Ec.R |
| 9 | 19 | 06 | II | Sh.I |
| 9 | 21 | 55 | II | Sh.E |
| 13 | 00 | 55 | I | Sh.I |
| 13 | 03 | 10 | I | Sh.E |
| 14 | 00 | 31 | I | Ec.R |
| 14 | 04 | 59 | IV | Sh.I |
| 14 | 19 | 24 | I | Sh.I |
| 14 | 21 | 39 | I | Sh.E |
| 15 | 18 | 17 | III | Sh.I |
| 15 | 18 | 59 | I | Ec.R |
| 15 | 21 | 21 | III | Sh.E |
| 16 | 21 | 43 | II | Sh.I |
| 17 | 00 | 32 | II | Sh.E |
| 18 | 18 | 43 | II | Ec.R |
| 20 | 02 | 50 | I | Sh.I |
| 21 | 02 | 26 | I | Ec.R |
| 21 | 21 | 18 | I | Sh.I |
| 21 | 23 | 33 | I | Sh.E |
| 22 | 20 | 54 | I | Ec.R |
| 22 | 22 | 16 | III | Sh.I |
| 23 | 01 | 21 | III | Sh.E |
| 24 | 00 | 20 | II | Sh.I |
| 24 | 03 | 08 | II | Sh.E |
| 25 | 21 | 19 | II | Ec.R |
| 28 | 04 | 21 | I | Ec.R |
| 28 | 23 | 13 | I | Sh.I |
| 29 | 01 | 28 | I | Sh.E |
| 29 | 22 | 49 | I | Ec.R |
| 30 | 02 | 15 | III | Sh.I |
| 30 | 19 | 57 | I | Sh.E |
| 30 | 23 | 00 | IV | Sh.I |
| 31 | 02 | 02 | IV | Sh.E |
| 31 | 02 | 57 | II | Sh.I |
| FEBRUARY | | | | |
| 1 | 23 | 55 | II | Ec.R |
| 2 | 19 | 26 | III | Ec.R |
| 3 | 19 | 03 | II | Sh.E |
| 5 | 01 | 08 | I | Sh.I |
| 5 | 03 | 23 | I | Sh.E |
| 6 | 00 | 44 | I | Ec.R |
| 6 | 19 | 37 | I | Sh.I |
| 6 | 21 | 52 | I | Sh.E |
| 7 | 19 | 13 | I | Ec.R |
| 9 | 02 | 31 | II | Ec.R |
| 9 | 20 | 18 | III | Ec.D |
| 9 | 23 | 27 | III | Ec.R |
| 10 | 18 | 52 | II | Sh.I |
| 10 | 21 | 40 | II | Sh.E |
| 12 | 03 | 03 | I | Sh.I |
| 13 | 02 | 39 | I | Ec.R |
| 13 | 21 | 32 | I | Sh.I |
| 13 | 23 | 47 | I | Sh.E |
| 14 | 21 | 08 | I | Ec.R |
| 16 | 20 | 13 | IV | Sh.E |
| 17 | 00 | 18 | III | Ec.D |
| 17 | 21 | 28 | II | Sh.I |
| 18 | 00 | 16 | II | Sh.E |
| 20 | 23 | 27 | I | Sh.I |
| 21 | 01 | 42 | I | Sh.E |
| 21 | 23 | 03 | I | Ec.R |
| 22 | 20 | 10 | I | Sh.E |
| 25 | 00 | 05 | II | Sh.I |
| 25 | 00 | 17 | IV | Ec.D |
| 26 | 21 | 03 | II | Ec.R |
| 27 | 21 | 24 | III | Sh.E |
| 28 | 01 | 22 | I | Sh.I |
| MARCH | | | | |
| 1 | 00 | 59 | I | Ec.R |
| 1 | 19 | 51 | I | Sh.I |
| 1 | 22 | 06 | I | Sh.E |
| 2 | 19 | 27 | I | Ec.R |
| 5 | 23 | 40 | II | Ec.R |
| 6 | 22 | 15 | III | Sh.I |
| 7 | 01 | 25 | III | Sh.E |
| 8 | 21 | 46 | I | Sh.I |
| 9 | 00 | 01 | I | Sh.E |
| 9 | 21 | 23 | I | Ec.R |
| 13 | 21 | 48 | IV | Ec.R |
| 14 | 21 | 23 | II | Sh.E |
| 15 | 23 | 41 | I | Sh.I |
| 16 | 23 | 18 | I | Ec.R |
| 17 | 20 | 25 | I | Sh.E |
| 21 | 21 | 12 | II | Sh.I |
| 21 | 23 | 59 | II | Sh.E |
| 24 | 20 | 06 | I | Sh.I |
| 24 | 20 | 18 | III | Ec.D |
| 24 | 22 | 21 | I | Sh.E |
| 24 | 23 | 33 | III | Ec.R |
| 28 | 23 | 47 | II | Sh.I |
| 30 | 20 | 52 | II | Ec.R |
| 31 | 22 | 01 | I | Sh.I |
| APRIL | | | | |
| 1 | 21 | 37 | I | Ec.R |
| 6 | 23 | 30 | II | Ec.R |
| 7 | 23 | 09 | IV | Sh.I |
| 8 | 23 | 32 | I | Ec.R |
| 9 | 20 | 41 | I | Sh.E |
| 11 | 21 | 29 | III | Sh.E |
| 15 | 21 | 04 | II | Sh.E |
| 16 | 22 | 37 | I | Sh.E |
| 18 | 22 | 16 | III | Sh.I |
| 22 | 20 | 52 | II | Sh.I |
| 23 | 22 | 17 | I | Sh.I |
| 24 | 21 | 51 | I | Ec.R |
| SEPTEMBER | | | | |
| 16 | 03 | 46 | I | Sh.E |
| 23 | 03 | 23 | I | Sh.I |
| 27 | 03 | 56 | III | Ec.D |
| OCTOBER | | | | |
| 5 | 03 | 18 | II | Ec.D |
| 8 | 04 | 16 | I | Ec.D |
| 9 | 03 | 55 | I | Sh.E |
| 14 | 02 | 55 | II | Sh.E |
| 16 | 03 | 32 | I | Sh.I |
| 21 | 02 | 39 | II | Sh.I |
| 23 | 05 | 25 | I | Sh.I |
| 24 | 02 | 32 | I | Ec.D |
| 25 | 02 | 10 | I | Sh.E |
| 26 | 03 | 52 | IV | Sh.E |
| 28 | 05 | 14 | II | Sh.I |
| 31 | 04 | 25 | I | Ec.D |
| NOVEMBER | | | | |
| 1 | 01 | 47 | I | Sh.I |
| 1 | 04 | 03 | I | Sh.E |
| 2 | 03 | 20 | III | Ec.R |
| 6 | 02 | 52 | II | Ec.D |
| 8 | 03 | 40 | I | Sh.I |
| 8 | 05 | 56 | I | Sh.E |
| 9 | 03 | 44 | III | Ec.D |
| 13 | 05 | 25 | II | Ec.D |
| 15 | 02 | 35 | II | Sh.E |
| 15 | 05 | 33 | I | Sh.I |
| 16 | 02 | 41 | I | Ec.D |
| 17 | 02 | 17 | I | Sh.E |
| 20 | 00 | 44 | IV | Ec.D |
| 20 | 01 | 16 | III | Sh.E |
| 20 | 05 | 31 | IV | Ec.R |
| 22 | 02 | 18 | II | Sh.I |
| 22 | 05 | 10 | II | Sh.E |
| 23 | 04 | 34 | I | Ec.D |
| 24 | 01 | 54 | I | Sh.I |
| 24 | 04 | 10 | I | Sh.E |
| 27 | 01 | 41 | III | Sh.I |
| 27 | 05 | 13 | III | Sh.E |
| 29 | 04 | 53 | II | Sh.I |
| 30 | 23 | 49 | II | Ec.D |
| DECEMBER | | | | |
| 1 | 03 | 47 | I | Sh.I |
| 1 | 06 | 03 | I | Sh.E |
| 2 | 00 | 56 | I | Ec.D |
| 3 | 00 | 32 | I | Sh.E |
| 4 | 05 | 38 | III | Sh.I |
| 6 | 23 | 33 | IV | Ec.R |
| 7 | 23 | 14 | III | Ec.R |
| 8 | 02 | 22 | II | Ec.D |
| 8 | 05 | 40 | I | Sh.I |
| 9 | 02 | 50 | I | Ec.D |
| 9 | 23 | 41 | II | Sh.E |
| 10 | 00 | 09 | I | Sh.I |
| 10 | 02 | 25 | I | Sh.E |
| 14 | 23 | 35 | III | Ec.D |
| 15 | 03 | 12 | III | Ec.R |
| 15 | 04 | 55 | II | Ec.D |
| 15 | 05 | 08 | IV | Sh.I |
| 16 | 04 | 44 | I | Ec.D |
| 16 | 23 | 23 | II | Sh.I |
| 17 | 02 | 02 | I | Sh.I |
| 17 | 02 | 17 | II | Sh.E |
| 17 | 04 | 18 | I | Sh.E |
| 17 | 23 | 12 | I | Ec.D |
| 18 | 22 | 46 | I | Sh.E |
| 22 | 03 | 33 | III | Ec.D |
| 23 | 06 | 38 | I | Ec.D |
| 24 | 01 | 59 | II | Sh.I |
| 24 | 03 | 55 | I | Sh.I |
| 24 | 04 | 53 | II | Sh.E |
| 24 | 06 | 11 | I | Sh.E |
| 25 | 01 | 06 | I | Ec.D |
| 25 | 22 | 23 | I | Sh.I |
| 26 | 00 | 40 | I | Sh.E |
| 31 | 04 | 35 | II | Sh.I |
| 31 | 05 | 48 | I | Sh.I |
| 31 | 23 | 06 | IV | Sh.I |

Jupiter's satellites transit across the disk from east to west, and pass behind the disk from west to east. The shadows that they cast also transit across the disk. With the exception at times of Satellite IV, the satellites also pass through the shadow of the planet, i.e. they are eclipsed. Just before opposition the satellite disappears in the shadow to the west of the planet and reappears from occultation on the east limb. Immediately after opposition the satellite is occulted at the west limb and reappears from eclipse to the east of the planet. At times approximately two to four months before and after opposition, both phases of eclipses of Satellite III may be seen. When Satellite IV is eclipsed, both phases may be seen.

The times given refer to the centre of the satellite. As the satellite is of considerable size, the immersion and emersion phases are not instantaneous. Even when the satellite enters or leaves the shadow along a radius of the shadow, the phase can last for several minutes. With Satellite IV, grazing phenomena can occur so that the light from the satellite may fade and brighten again without a complete eclipse taking place.

The list of phenomena gives most of the eclipses and shadow transits visible in the British Isles under favourable conditions.

| | |
|---|---|
| Ec. = Eclipse | R. = Reappearance |
| Sh. = Shadow transit | I. = Ingress |
| D. = Disappearance | E. = Egress |

## EXPLANATION OF ASTRONOMICAL DATA

Positions of the heavenly bodies are given only to the degree of accuracy required by amateur astronomers for setting telescopes, or for plotting on celestial globes or star atlases. Where intermediate positions are required, linear interpolation may be employed.

Definitions of the terms used cannot be given here. They must be sought in astronomical literature and textbooks. Probably the best source for the amateur is Norton's *Star Atlas and Reference Handbook* (Longman, 18th edition, 1989; £26.99), which contains an introduction to observational astronomy, and a series of star maps showing stars visible to the naked eye. Certain more extended ephemerides are available in the British Astronomical Association Handbook, an annual popular among amateur astronomers (Secretary: Burlington House, Piccadilly, London W1J 0DU).

A special feature has been made of the times when the various heavenly bodies are visible in the British Isles. Since two columns, calculated for latitudes 52° and 56°, are devoted to risings and settings, the range 50° to 58° can be covered by interpolation and extrapolation. The times given in these columns are Greenwich Mean Times for the meridian of Greenwich. An observer west of this meridian must add his/her longitude (in time) and vice versa.

In accordance with the usual convention in astronomy, + and – indicate respectively north and south latitudes or declinations.

All data are, unless otherwise stated, for 0h Greenwich Mean Time (GMT), i.e. at the midnight at the beginning of the day named. Allowance must be made for British Summer Time during the period that this is in operation (*see* pages 15 and 75).

### PAGE ONE OF EACH MONTH

The calendar for each month is explained on page 15.

Under the heading Astronomical Phenomena will be found particulars of the more important conjunctions of the Sun, Moon and planets with each other, and also the dates of other astronomical phenomena of special interest.

Times of Minima of Algol are approximate times of the middle of the period of diminished light.

The Constellations listed each month are those that are near the meridian at the beginning of the month at 22h local mean time. Allowance must be made for British Summer Time if necessary. The fact that any star crosses the meridian 4m earlier each night or 2h earlier each month may be used, in conjunction with the lists given each month, to find what constellations are favourably placed at any moment. The table preceding the list of constellations may be extended indefinitely at the rate just quoted.

The principal phases of the Moon are the GMTs when the difference between the longitude of the Moon and that of the Sun is 0°, 90°, 180° or 270°. The times of perigee and apogee are those when the Moon is nearest to, and farthest from, the Earth, respectively. The nodes or points of intersection of the Moon's orbit and the ecliptic make a complete retrograde circuit of the ecliptic in about 19 years. From a knowledge of the longitude of the ascending node and the inclination, whose value does not vary much from 5°, the path of the Moon among the stars may be plotted on a celestial globe or star atlas.

### PAGE TWO OF EACH MONTH

The Sun's semi-diameter, in arc, is given once a month.

The right ascension and declination (Dec.) is that of the true Sun. The right ascension of the mean Sun is obtained by applying the equation of time, with the sign given, to the right ascension of the true Sun, or, more easily, by applying 12h to the Sidereal Time. The direction in which the equation of time has to be applied in different problems is a frequent source of confusion and error. Apparent Solar Time is equal to the Mean Solar Time plus the Equation of Time. For example, at noon on August 8 the Equation of Time is –5m 39s and thus at 12h Mean Time on that day the Apparent Time is 12h –5m 39s = 11h 54m 21s.

The Greenwich Sidereal Time at 0h and the Transit of the First Point of Aries (which is really the mean time when the sidereal time is 0h) are used for converting mean time to sidereal time and vice versa.

The GMT of transit of the Sun at Greenwich may also be taken as the local mean time (LMT) of transit in any longitude. It is independent of latitude. The GMT of transit in any longitude is obtained by adding the longitude to the time given if west, and vice versa.

#### LIGHTING-UP TIME

The legal importance of sunrise and sunset is that the Road Vehicles Lighting Regulations 1989 (SI 1989 No. 1796) make the use of front and rear position lamps on vehicles compulsory during the period between sunset and sunrise. Headlamps on vehicles are required to be used during the hours of darkness on unlit roads or whenever visibility is seriously reduced. The hours of darkness are defined in these regulations as the period between half an hour after sunset and half an hour before sunrise.

In all laws and regulations 'sunset' refers to the local sunset, i.e. the time at which the Sun sets at the place in question. This common-sense interpretation has been upheld by legal tribunals. Thus the necessity for providing for different latitudes and longitudes, as already described, is evident.

#### SUNRISE AND SUNSET

The times of sunrise and sunset are those when the Sun's upper limb, as affected by refraction, is on the true horizon of an observer at sea-level. Assuming the mean refraction to be 34′, and the Sun's semi-diameter to be 16′, the time given is that when the true zenith distance of the Sun's centre is 90°+34′+16′ or 90° 50′, or, in other words, when the depression of the Sun's centre below the true horizon is 50′. The upper limb is then 34′ below the true horizon, but is brought there by refraction. An observer on a ship might see the Sun for a minute or so longer, because of the dip of the horizon, while another viewing the sunset over hills or mountains would record an earlier time. Nevertheless, the moment when the true zenith distance of the Sun's centre is 90° 50′ is a precise time dependent only on the latitude and longitude of the place, and independent of its altitude above sea-level, the contour of its horizon, the vagaries of refraction or the small seasonal change in the Sun's semi-diameter; this moment is suitable in every way as a definition of sunset (or sunrise) for all statutory purposes. (For further information, *see* footnote on page 72.)

#### TWILIGHT

Light reaches us before sunrise and continues to reach us for some time after sunset. The interval between darkness and sunrise or sunset and darkness is called twilight. Astronomically speaking, twilight is considered to begin or end when the Sun's centre is 18° below the horizon, as no light from the Sun can then reach the observer. As thus defined twilight may last several hours; in high latitudes at the summer solstice the depression of 18° is not reached, and twilight lasts from sunset to sunrise.

The need for some sub-division of twilight is met by dividing the gathering darkness into four stages.

(1) *Sunrise or Sunset*, defined as above
(2) *Civil twilight*, which begins or ends when the Sun's centre is 6° below the horizon. This marks the time when operations requiring daylight may commence or must cease. In England it varies from about 30 to 60 minutes after sunset and the same interval before sunrise
(3) *Nautical twilight*, which begins or ends when the Sun's centre is 12° below the horizon. This marks the time when it is, to all intents and purposes, completely dark
(4) *Astronomical twilight*, which begins or ends when the Sun's centre is 18° below the horizon. This marks theoretical perfect darkness. It is of little practical importance, especially if nautical twilight is tabulated

To assist observers the durations of civil, nautical and astronomical twilights are given at intervals of ten days. The beginning of a particular twilight is found by subtracting the duration from the time of sunrise, while the end is found by adding the duration to the time of sunset. Thus the beginning of astronomical twilight in latitude 52°, on the Greenwich meridian, on March 11 is found as 06h 24m–113m = 04h 31m and similarly the end of civil twilight as 17h 57m+34m = 18h 31m. The letters TAN (twilight all night) are printed when twilight lasts all night.

Under the heading The Night Sky will be found notes describing the position and visibility of the planets and other phenomena.

## PAGE THREE OF EACH MONTH

The Moon moves so rapidly among the stars that its position is given only to the degree of accuracy that permits linear interpolation. The right ascension (RA) and declination (Dec.) are geocentric, i.e. for an imaginary observer at the centre of the Earth. To an observer on the surface of the Earth the position is always different, as the altitude is always less on account of parallax, which may reach 1°.

The lunar terminator is the line separating the bright from the dark part of the Moon's disk. Apart from irregularities of the lunar surface, the terminator is elliptical, because it is a circle seen in projection. It becomes the full circle forming the limb, or edge, of the Moon at New and Full Moon. The selenographic longitude of the terminator is measured from the mean centre of the visible disk, which may differ from the visible centre by as much as 8°, because of libration.

Instead of the longitude of the terminator the Sun's selenographic co-longitude (Sun's co-long.) is tabulated. It is numerically equal to the selenographic longitude of the morning terminator, measured eastwards from the mean centre of the disk. Thus its value is approximately 270° at New Moon, 360° at First Quarter, 90° at Full Moon and 180° at Last Quarter.

The Position Angle (PA) of the Bright Limb is the position angle of the midpoint of the illuminated limb, measured eastwards from the north point on the disk. The Phase column shows the percentage of the area of the Moon's disk illuminated; this is also the illuminated percentage of the diameter at right angles to the line of cusps. The terminator is a semi-ellipse whose major axis is the line of cusps, and whose semi-minor axis is determined by the tabulated percentage; from New Moon to Full Moon the east limb is dark, and vice versa.

The times given as moonrise and moonset are those when the upper limb of the Moon is on the horizon of an observer at sea-level. The Sun's horizontal parallax (Hor. par.) is about 9″, and is negligible when considering sunrise and sunset, but that of the Moon averages about 57′. Hence the computed time represents the moment when the true zenith distance of the Moon is 90° 50′ (as for the Sun) minus the horizontal parallax. The time required for the Sun or Moon to rise or set is about four minutes (except in high latitudes). *See also* page 65 and footnote below.

The GMT of transit of the Moon over the meridian of Greenwich is given; these times are independent of latitude but must be corrected for longitude. For places in the British Isles it suffices to add the longitude if west, and vice versa. For other places a further correction is necessary because of the rapid movement of the Moon relative to the stars. The entire correction is conveniently determined by first finding the west longitude $\lambda$ of the place. If the place is in west longitude, $\lambda$ is the ordinary west longitude; if the place is in east longitude $\lambda$ is the complement to 24h (or 360°) of the longitude and will be greater than 12h (or 180°). The correction then consists of two positive portions, namely $\lambda$ and the fraction $\lambda/24$ (or $\lambda°/360$) multiplied by the difference between consecutive transits. Thus for Christchurch, New Zealand, the longitude is 11h 31m east, so $\lambda$=12h 29m and the fraction $\lambda/24$ is 0.52. The transit on the local date 2002 September 1 is found as follows:

| | | d h m |
|---|---|---|
| GMT of transit at Greenwich | August | 31 05 54 |
| $\lambda$ | | 12 29 |
| 0.52×(5h 54m - 5h 06m) | | 25 |
| GMT of transit at Christchurch | | 31 18 48 |
| Corr. to NZ Standard Time | | 12 00 |
| Local standard time of transit | September | 1 06 48 |

As is evident, for any given place the quantities $\lambda$ and the correction to local standard time may be combined permanently, being here 24h 29m.

Positions of Mercury are given for every second day, and those of Venus and Mars for every fifth day; they may be interpolated linearly. The diameter (Diam.) is given in seconds of arc. The phase is the illuminated percentage of the disk. In the case of the inner planets this approaches 100 at superior conjunction and 0 at inferior conjunction. When the phase is less than 50 the planet is crescent-shaped or horned; for greater phases it is gibbous. In the case of the exterior planet Mars, the phase approaches 100 at conjunction and opposition, and is a minimum at the quadratures.

Since the planets cannot be seen when on the horizon, the actual times of rising and setting are not given; instead, the time when the planet has an apparent altitude of 5° has been tabulated. If the time of transit is between 00h and 12h the time refers to an altitude of 5° above the eastern horizon; if between 12h and 24h, to the western horizon. The phenomenon tabulated is the one that occurs between

---

SUNRISE, SUNSET AND MOONRISE, MOONSET

The tables have been constructed for the meridian of Greenwich and for latitudes 52° and 56°. They give Greenwich Mean Time (GMT) throughout the year. To obtain the GMT of the phenomenon as seen from any other latitude and longitude in the British Isles, first interpolate or extrapolate for latitude by the usual rules of proportion. To the time thus found, the longitude (expressed in time) is to be added if west (as it usually is in Great Britain) or subtracted if east. If the longitude is expressed in degrees and minutes of arc, it must be converted to time at the rate of 1°=4m and 15′=1m.

A method of calculating rise and set times for other places in the world is given on pages 64 and 65

sunset and sunrise. The times given may be interpolated for latitude and corrected for longitude, as in the case of the Sun and Moon.

The GMT at which the planet transits the Greenwich meridian is also given. The times of transit are to be corrected to local meridians in the usual way, as already described.

## PAGE FOUR OF EACH MONTH

The GMTs of sunrise and sunset for seven cities, whose adopted positions in longitude (W.) and latitude (N.) are given immediately below the name, may be used not only for these phenomena, but also for lighting-up times (*see* page 71 for a fuller explanation).

The particulars for the four outer planets resemble those for the planets on Page Three of each month, except that, under Uranus and Neptune, times when the planet is 10° high instead of 5° high are given; this is because of the inferior brightness of these planets. The diameters given for the rings of Saturn are those of the major axis (in the plane of the planet's equator) and the minor axis respectively. The former has a small seasonal change due to the slightly varying distance of the Earth from Saturn, but the latter varies from zero when the Earth passes through the ring plane every 15 years to its maximum opening half-way between these periods. The rings were last open at their widest extent (and Saturn at its brightest) in 1988; this will occur again in 2002. The Earth passed through the ring plane in 1995–6 and will do so again in 2009.

## TIME

From the earliest ages, the natural division of time into recurring periods of day and night has provided the practical time-scale for the everyday activities of the human race. Indeed, if any alternative means of time measurement is adopted, it must be capable of adjustment so as to remain in general agreement with the natural time-scale defined by the diurnal rotation of the Earth on its axis. Ideally the rotation should be measured against a fixed frame of reference; in practice it must be measured against the background provided by the celestial bodies. If the Sun is chosen as the reference point, we obtain Apparent Solar Time, which is the time indicated by a sundial. It is not a uniform time but is subject to variations which amount to as much as a quarter of an hour in each direction. Such wide variations cannot be tolerated in a practical time-scale, and this has led to the concept of Mean Solar Time in which all the days are exactly the same length and equal to the average length of the Apparent Solar Day.

The positions of the stars in the sky are specified in relation to a fictitious reference point in the sky known as the First Point of Aries (or the Vernal Equinox). It is therefore convenient to adopt this same reference point when considering the rotation of the Earth against the background of the stars. The time-scale so obtained is known as Apparent Sidereal Time.

### Greenwich Mean Time

The daily rotation of the Earth on its axis causes the Sun and the other heavenly bodies to appear to cross the sky from east to west. It is convenient to represent this relative motion as if the Sun really performed a daily circuit around a fixed Earth. Noon in Apparent Solar Time may then be defined as the time at which the Sun transits across the observer's meridian. In Mean Solar Time, noon is similarly defined by the meridian transit of a fictitious Mean Sun moving uniformly in the sky with the same average speed as the true Sun. Mean Solar Time observed on the meridian of the transit circle telescope of the Old Royal Observatory at Greenwich is called Greenwich Mean Time (GMT). The mean solar day is divided into 24 hours and, for astronomical and other scientific purposes, these are numbered 0 to 23, commencing at midnight. Civil time is usually reckoned in two periods of 12 hours, designated a.m. (*ante meridiem*, i.e. before noon) and p.m. (*post meridiem*, i.e. after noon).

### Universal Time

Before 1925 January 1, GMT was reckoned in 24 hours commencing at noon; since that date it has been reckoned from midnight. To avoid confusion in the use of the designation GMT before and after 1925, since 1928 astronomers have tended to use the term Universal Time (UT) or Weltzeit (WZ) to denote GMT measured from Greenwich Mean Midnight.

In precision work it is necessary to take account of small variations in Universal Time. These arise from small irregularities in the rotation of the Earth. Observed astronomical time is designated UT0. Observed time corrected for the effects of the motion of the poles (giving rise to a 'wandering' in longitude) is designated UT1. There is also a seasonal fluctuation in the rate of rotation of the Earth arising from meteorological causes, often called the annual fluctuation. UT1 corrected for this effect is designated UT2 and provides a time-scale free from short-period fluctuations. It is still subject to small secular and irregular changes.

### Apparent Solar Time

As mentioned above, the time shown by a sundial is called Apparent Solar Time. It differs from Mean Solar Time by an amount known as the Equation of Time, which is the total effect of two causes which make the length of the apparent solar day non-uniform. One cause of variation is that the orbit of the Earth is not a circle but an ellipse, having the Sun at one focus. As a consequence, the angular speed of the Earth in its orbit is not constant; it is greatest at the beginning of January when the Earth is nearest the Sun.

The other cause is due to the obliquity of the ecliptic; the plane of the equator (which is at right angles to the axis of rotation of the Earth) does not coincide with the ecliptic (the plane defined by the apparent annual motion of the Sun around the celestial sphere) but is inclined to it at an angle of 23° 26′. As a result, the apparent solar day is shorter than average at the equinoxes and longer at the solstices. From the combined effects of the components due to obliquity and eccentricity, the equation of time reaches its maximum values in February (–14 minutes) and early November (+16 minutes). It has a zero value on four dates during the year, and it is only on these dates (approximately April 15, June 14, September 1 and December 25) that a sundial shows Mean Solar Time.

### Sidereal Time

A sidereal day is the duration of a complete rotation of the Earth with reference to the First Point of Aries. The term sidereal (or 'star') time is a little misleading since the time-scale so defined is not exactly the same as that which would be defined by successive transits of a selected star, as there is a small progressive motion between the stars and the First Point of Aries due to the precession of the Earth's axis. This makes the length of the sidereal day shorter than the true period of rotation by 0.008 seconds. Superimposed on this steady precessional motion are small oscillations (nutation), giving rise to fluctuations in apparent sidereal time amounting to as much as 1.2 seconds. It is therefore customary to employ Mean Sidereal Time, from which these fluctuations have been removed. The conversion of GMT to Greenwich sidereal time (GST) may be performed by adding the value of the GST at 0h on the day in question (Page Two of each month) to the GMT converted to sidereal time using the table on page 069.

*Example* – To find the GST at August 8d 02h 41m 11s GMT

| | h | m | s |
|---|---|---|---|
| GST at 0h | 21 | 05 | 19 |
| GMT | 2 | 41 | 11 |
| Acceleration for 2h | | | 20 |
| Acceleration for 41m 11s | | | 7 |
| Sum = GST = | 23 | 46 | 57 |

If the observer is not on the Greenwich meridian then his/her longitude, measured positively westwards from Greenwich, must be subtracted from the GST to obtain Local Sidereal Time (LST). Thus, in the above example, an observer 5h east of Greenwich, or 19h west, would find the LST as 4h 46m 57s.

### Ephemeris Time

An analysis of observations of the positions of the Sun, Moon and planets taken over an extended period is used in preparing ephemerides. (An ephemeris is a table giving the apparent position of a heavenly body at regular intervals of time, e.g. one day or ten days, and may be used to compare current observations with tabulated positions.) Discrepancies between the positions of heavenly bodies observed over a 300-year period and their predicted positions arose because the time-scale to which the observations were related was based on the assumption that the rate of rotation of the Earth is uniform. It is now known that this rate of rotation is variable. A revised time-scale, Ephemeris Time (ET), was devised to bring the ephemerides into agreement with the observations.

The second of ET is defined in terms of the annual motion of the Earth in its orbit around the Sun(1/31556925.9747 of the tropical year for 1900 January 0d 12h ET). The precise determination of ET from astronomical observations is a lengthy process as the requisite standard of accuracy can only be achieved by averaging over a number of years.

In 1976 the International Astronomical Union adopted Terrestrial Dynamical Time (TDT), a new dynamical time-scale for general use whose scale unit is the SI second (*see* Atomic Time). TDT was renamed Terrestrial Time (TT) in 1991. ET is now of little more than historical interest.

### Terrestrial Time

The uniform time system used in computing the ephemerides of the solar system is Terrestrial Time (TT), which has replaced ET for this purpose. Except for the most rigorous astronomical calculations, it may be assumed to be the same as ET. During 2002 the estimated difference TT–UT is about 67 seconds.

### Atomic Time

The fundamental standards of time and frequency must be defined in terms of a periodic motion adequately uniform, enduring and measurable. Progress has made it possible to use natural standards, such as atomic or molecular oscillations. Continuous oscillations are generated in an electrical circuit, the frequency of which is then compared or brought into coincidence with the frequency characteristic of the absorption or emission by the atoms or molecules when they change between two selected energy levels. The National Physical Laboratory (NPL) routinely uses clocks of high stability produced by locking a quartz oscillator to the frequencies defined by caesium or hydrogen atoms.

International Atomic Time (TAI), established through international collaboration, is formed by combining the readings of many caesium clocks and was set close to the astronomically-based Universal Time (UT) near the beginning of 1958. It was formally recognized in 1971 and since 1988 January 1 has been maintained by the International Bureau of Weights and Measures (BIPM). The second markers are generated according to the International System (SI) definition adopted in 1967 at the 13th General Conference of Weights and Measures: 'The second is the duration of 9 192 631 770 periods of the radiation corresponding to the transition between the two hyperfine levels of the ground state of the caesium-133 atom.'

Civil time in almost all countries is now based on Co-ordinated Universal Time (UTC), which was adopted for scientific purposes on 1972 January 1. UTC differs from TAI by an integer number of seconds (determined from studies of the rate of rotation of the Earth) and was designed to make both atomic time and UT accessible with accuracies appropriate for most users. The UTC time-scale is adjusted by the insertion (or, in principle, omission) of leap seconds in order to keep it within ±0.9 s of UT. These leap seconds are introduced, when necessary, at the same instant throughout the world, either at the end of December or at the end of June. So, for example, the 22nd leap second occurred at 0h UTC on 1999 January 1. All leap seconds so far have been positive, with 61 seconds in the final minute of the UTC month. The time 23h 59m 60s UTC is followed one second later by 0h 0m 00s of the first day of the following month. Notices concerning the insertion of leap seconds are issued by the International Earth Rotation Service (IERS) at the Observatoire de Paris.

### Radio Time-Signals

UTC is made generally available through time-signals and standard frequency broadcasts such as MSF in the UK, CHU in Canada and WWV and WWVH in the USA. These are based on national time-scales that are maintained in close agreement with UTC and provide traceability to the national time-scale and to UTC. The markers of seconds in the UTC scale coincide with those of TAI.

To disseminate the national time-scale in the UK, special signals are broadcast on behalf of the National Physical Laboratory from the BT radio station at Rugby (call-sign MSF). The signals are controlled from a caesium beam atomic frequency standard and consist of a precise frequency carrier of 60 kHz which is switched off, after being on for at least half a second, to mark every second. The first second of the minute begins with a period of 500 ms with the carrier switched off, to serve as a minute marker. In the other seconds the carrier is always off for at least one tenth of a second at the start and then it carries an on-off code giving the British clock time and date, together with information identifying the start of the next minute. Changes to and from summer time are made following government announcements. Leap seconds are inserted as announced by the IERS and information provided by them on the difference between UTC and UT is also signalled. Other broadcast signals in the UK include the BBC six pips signal, the BT Timeline ('speaking clock'), the NPL

Truetime service for computers, and a coded time-signal on the BBC 198 kHz transmitters which is used for timing in the electricity supply industry. From 1972 January 1 the six pips on the BBC have consisted of five short pips from second 55 to second 59 (six pips in the case of a leap second) followed by one lengthened pip, the start of which indicates the exact minute. From 1990 February 5 these signals have been controlled by the BBC with seconds markers referenced to the satellite-based US navigation system GPS (Global Positioning System) and time and day referenced to the MSF transmitter. Formerly they were generated by the Royal Greenwich Observatory. The BT Timeline is compared daily with the National Physical Laboratory caesium beam atomic frequency standard at the Rugby radio station. The NPL Truetime service is directly connected to the national time scale.

Accurate timing may also be obtained from the signals of international navigation systems such as the ground-based Omega, or the satellite-based American GPS or Russian GLONASS systems.

### Standard Time

Since 1880 the standard time in Britain has been Greenwich Mean Time (GMT); a statute that year enacted that the word 'time' when used in any legal document relating to Britain meant, unless otherwise specifically stated, the mean time of the Greenwich meridian. Greenwich was adopted as the universal meridian on 13 October 1884. A system of standard time by zones is used world-wide, standard time in each zone differing from that of the Greenwich meridian by an integral number of hours, either fast or slow. The large territories of the USA and Canada are divided into zones approximately 7.5° on either side of central meridians. (For time zones of countries of the world, *see* Index.)

Variations from the standard time of some countries occur during part of the year; they are decided annually and are usually referred to as Summer Time or Daylight Saving Time.

At the 180th meridian the time can be either 12 hours fast on Greenwich Mean Time or 12 hours slow, and a change of date occurs. The internationally recognized date or calendar line is a modification of the 180th meridian, drawn so as to include islands of any one group on the same side of the line, or for political reasons. The line is indicated by joining up the following co-ordinates:

| *Lat.* | *Long.* | *Lat.* | *Long.* |
|---|---|---|---|
| 60° S. | 180° | 48° N. | 180° |
| 51° S. | 180° | 53° N. | 170° E. |
| 45° S. | 172.5° W. | 65.5° N. | 169° W. |
| 15° S. | 172.5° W. | 75° N. | 180° |
| 5° S. | 180° | | |

Changes to the date line would require an international conference.

### British Summer Time

In 1916 an Act ordained that during a defined period of that year the legal time for general purposes in Great Britain should be one hour in advance of Greenwich Mean Time. The Summer Time Acts 1922 and 1925 defined the period during which Summer Time was to be in force, stabilizing practice until the Second World War.

During the war the duration of Summer Time was extended and in the years 1941 to 1945 and in 1947 Double Summer Time (two hours in advance of Greenwich Mean Time) was in force. After the war, Summer Time was extended each year in 1948–52 and 1961–4 by Order in Council.

Between 1968 October 27 and 1971 October 31 clocks were kept one hour ahead of Greenwich Mean Time throughout the year. This was known as British Standard Time.

The most recent legislation is the Summer Time Act 1972, which enacted that 'the period of summer time for the purposes of this Act is the period beginning at two o'clock, Greenwich mean time, in the morning of the day after the third Saturday in March or, if that day is Easter Day, the day after the second Saturday in March, and ending at two o'clock, Greenwich mean time, in the morning of the day after the fourth Saturday in October.'

The duration of Summer Time can be varied by Order in Council and in recent years alterations have been made to bring the operation of Summer Time in Britain closer to similar provisions in other countries of the European Union; for instance, since 1981 the hour of changeover has been 01h Greenwich Mean Time.

The duration of Summer Time in 2002 is:

March 31 01h GMT to October 27 01h GMT

## MEAN REFRACTION

| Alt. ° | Alt. ′ | Ref. ′ | Alt. ° | Alt. ′ | Ref. ′ | Alt. ° | Alt. ′ | Ref. ′ |
|---|---|---|---|---|---|---|---|---|
| 1 | 20 | | 3 | 12 | | 7 | 54 | |
| | | 21 | | | 13 | | | 6 |
| 1 | 30 | | 3 | 34 | | 9 | 27 | |
| | | 20 | | | 12 | | | 5 |
| 1 | 41 | | 4 | 00 | | 11 | 39 | |
| | | 19 | | | 11 | | | 4 |
| 1 | 52 | | 4 | 30 | | 15 | 00 | |
| | | 18 | | | 10 | | | 3 |
| 2 | 05 | | 5 | 06 | | 20 | 42 | |
| | | 17 | | | 9 | | | 2 |
| 2 | 19 | | 5 | 50 | | 32 | 20 | |
| | | 16 | | | 8 | | | 1 |
| 2 | 35 | | 6 | 44 | | 62 | 17 | |
| | | 15 | | | 7 | | | 0 |
| 2 | 52 | | 7 | 54 | | 90 | 00 | |
| | | 14 | | | | | | |
| 3 | 12 | | | | | | | |

The refraction table is in the form of a critical table (*see* page 69)

## ASTRONOMICAL CONSTANTS

| | |
|---|---|
| Solar parallax | 8″.794 |
| Astronomical unit | 149597870 km |
| Precession for the year 2002 | 50″.291 |
| Precession in right ascension | 3s.075 |
| Precession in declination | 20″.043 |
| Constant of nutation | 9″.202 |
| Constant of aberration | 20″.496 |
| Mean obliquity of ecliptic (2002) | 23° 26′ 21″ |
| Moon's equatorial hor. parallax | 57′ 02″.70 |
| Velocity of light in vacuo per second | 299792.5 km |
| Solar motion per second | 20.0 km |
| Equatorial radius of the Earth | 6378.140 km |
| Polar radius of the Earth | 6356.755 km |
| North galactic pole (IAU standard) | RA 12h 49m (1950.0). Dec. +27°.4 N. |
| Solar apex | RA 18h 06m Dec.+30° |
| Length of year (in mean solar days) | |
| Tropical | 365.24219 |
| Sidereal | 365.25636 |
| Anomalistic (perihelion to perihelion) | 365.25964 |
| Eclipse | 346.62000 |

| Length of month (mean values) | d | h | m | s |
|---|---|---|---|---|
| New Moon to New | 29 | 12 | 44 | 02.9 |
| Sidereal | 27 | 07 | 43 | 11.5 |
| Anomalistic (perigee to perigee) | 27 | 13 | 18 | 33.2 |

## ELEMENTS OF THE SOLAR SYSTEM

| Orb | Mean distance from Sun (Earth = 1) | Mean distance from Sun km $10^6$ | Sidereal period days | Synodic period days | Incl. of orbit to ecliptic ° ′ | Diameter km | Mass (Earth = 1) | Period of rotation on axis days |
|---|---|---|---|---|---|---|---|---|
| Sun | — | — | — | — | — | 1,392,530 | 332,946 | 25–35* |
| Mercury | 0.39 | 58 | 88.0 | 116 | 7 00 | 4,879 | 0.0553 | 58.646 |
| Venus | 0.72 | 108 | 224.7 | 584 | 3 24 | 12,104 | 0.8150 | 243.019*r* |
| Earth | 1.00 | 150 | 365.3 | — | — | 12,756*e* | 1.0000 | 0.997 |
| Mars | 1.52 | 228 | 687.0 | 780 | 1 51 | 6,794*e* | 0.1074 | 1.026 |
| Jupiter | 5.20 | 778 | 4,332.6 | 399 | 1 18 | 142,984*e*<br>133,708p | 317.89 | 0.410*e* |
| Saturn | 9.54 | 1427 | 10,759.2 | 378 | 2 29 | 120,536*e*<br>108,728p | 95.18 | 0.426*e* |
| Uranus | 19.18 | 2870 | 30,684.6 | 370 | 0 46 | 51,118*e* | 14.54 | 0.718*r* |
| Neptune | 30.06 | 4497 | 60,191.0 | 367 | 1 46 | 49,528*e* | 17.15 | 0.671 |
| Pluto | 39.80 | 5954 | 91,708.2 | 367 | 17 09 | 2,302 | 0.002 | 6.387 |

*e* equatorial, *p* polar, *r* retrograde, * depending on latitude

## THE SATELLITES

| Name | Star mag. | Mean distance from primary | Sidereal period of revolution |
|---|---|---|---|
| | | km | d |
| **EARTH** | | | |
| I Moon | — | 384,400 | 27.322 |
| **MARS** | | | |
| I Phobos | 12 | 9,378 | 0.319 |
| II Deimos | 13 | 23,459 | 1.262 |
| **JUPITER** | | | |
| XVI Metis | 17 | 127,960 | 0.295 |
| XV Adrastea | 19 | 128,980 | 0.298 |
| V Amalthea | 14 | 181,300 | 0.498 |
| XIV Thebe | 16 | 221,900 | 0.675 |
| I Io | 5 | 421,600 | 1.769 |
| II Europa | 5 | 670,900 | 3.552 |
| III Ganymede | 5 | 1,070,000 | 7.155 |
| IV Callisto | 6 | 1,883,000 | 16.689 |
| XIII Leda | 20 | 11,094,000 | 239 |
| VI Himalia | 15 | 11,480,000 | 251 |
| X Lysithea | 18 | 11,720,000 | 259 |
| VII Elara | 17 | 11,737,000 | 260 |
| XII Ananke | 19 | 21,200,000 | 631*r* |
| XI Carme | 18 | 22,600,000 | 692*r* |
| VIII Pasiphae | 17 | 23,500,000 | 735*r* |
| IX Sinope | 18 | 23,700,000 | 758*r* |
| 199JI | - | 23,960,000 | 719 |
| **SATURN** | | | |
| XVIII Pan | — | 133,583 | 0.575 |
| XV Atlas | 18 | 137,640 | 0.602 |
| XVI Prometheus | 16 | 139,353 | 0.613 |
| XVII Pandora | 16 | 141,700 | 0.629 |
| XI Epimetheus | 15 | 151,422 | 0.695 |
| X Janus | 14 | 151,472 | 0.695 |
| I Mimas | 13 | 185,520 | 0.942 |
| II Enceladus | 12 | 238,020 | 1.370 |
| III Tethys | 10 | 294,660 | 1.888 |
| XIII Telesto | 19 | 294,660 | 1.888 |
| XIV Calypso | 19 | 294,660 | 1.888 |
| IV Dione | 10 | 377,400 | 2.737 |
| XII Helene | 18 | 377,400 | 2.737 |
| V Rhea | 10 | 527,040 | 4.518 |
| VI Titan | 8 | 1,221,850 | 15.945 |
| VII Hyperion | 14 | 1,481,100 | 21.277 |
| VIII Iapetus | 11 | 3,561,300 | 79.330 |
| IX Pheobe | 16 | 12,952,000 | 550.48r |
| **URANUS** | | | |
| VI Cordelia | - | 49,750 | 0.335 |
| VII Orphelia | - | 53,760 | 0,376 |
| VIII Bianca | - | 59,170 | 0.435 |
| IX Cressida | - | 61,780 | 0.464 |
| X Desdemona | - | 62,660 | 0.474 |
| XI Juliet | - | 64,360 | 0.493 |
| XII Portia | - | 66,100 | 0.513 |
| XIII Rosalind | - | 69,930 | 0.558 |
| XIV Belinda | - | 75,260 | 0.624 |
| S/1986U10 | - | 76,420 | 0.638 |
| XV Puck | - | 86,000 | 0.762 |
| V Miranda | 17 | 129,800 | 1.413 |
| I Ariel | 14 | 191,200 | 2.520 |
| II Umbriel | 15 | 266,000 | 4.144 |
| III Titania | 14 | 435,800 | 8.706 |
| IV Oberon | 14 | 583,600 | 13.463 |
| XVI Caliban | - | 7,164,600 | 579.4 |
| XX Stephano | - | 9,608,400 | 900 |
| XVII Sycorax | - | 12,174,700 | 1,283.7 |
| XVIII Prospero | - | 16,668,000 | 2056 |
| XIX Setebos | - | 18,288,000 | 2363 |
| **NEPTUNE** | | | |
| III Naiad | 25 | 48,230 | 0.294 |
| IV Thalassa | 24 | 50,070 | 0.311 |
| V Despina | 23 | 52,530 | 0.335 |
| VI Galatea | 22 | 61,950 | 0.429 |
| VII Larissa | 22 | 73,550 | 0.555 |
| VIII Proteus | 20 | 117,650 | 1.122 |
| I Triton | 13 | 354,760 | 5.877 |
| II Nereid | 19 | 5,513,400 | 360.136 |
| **PLUTO** | | | |
| I Charon | 17 | 19,600 | 6.387 |

## THE EARTH

The shape of the Earth is that of an oblate spheroid or solid of revolution whose meridian sections are ellipses not differing much from circles, whilst the sections at right angles are circles. The length of the equatorial axis is about 12,756 km, and that of the polar axis is 12,714 km. The mean density of the Earth is 5.5 times that of water, although that of the surface layer is less. The Earth and Moon revolve about their common centre of gravity in a lunar month; this centre in turn revolves round the Sun in a plane known as the ecliptic, that passes through the Sun's centre. The Earth's equator is inclined to this plane at an angle of 23.4°. This tilt is the cause of the seasons. In mid-latitudes, and when the Sun is high above the Equator, not only does the high noon altitude make the days longer, but the Sun's rays fall more directly on the Earth's surface; these effects combine to produce summer. In equatorial regions the noon altitude is large throughout the year, and there is little variation in the length of the day. In higher latitudes the noon altitude is lower, and the days in summer are appreciably longer than those in winter.

The average velocity of the Earth in its orbit is 30 km a second. It makes a complete rotation on its axis in about 23h 56m of mean time, which is the sidereal day. Because of its annual revolution round the Sun, the rotation with respect to the Sun, or the solar day, is more than this by about four minutes (*see* page 73). The extremity of the axis of rotation, or the North Pole of the Earth, is not rigidly fixed, but wanders over an area roughly 20 metres in diameter.

## TERRESTRIAL MAGNETISM

The Earth's main magnetic field corresponds approximately to that of a very strong small bar magnet near the centre of the Earth, but with appreciable smooth spatial departures. The origin of the main field is not fully understood but is generally ascribed to electric currents associated with fluid motions in the Earth's core. As a result not only does the main field vary in strength and direction from place to place, but also with time. Superimposed on the main field are local and regional anomalies whose magnitudes may in places approach that of the main field; these are due to the influence of mineral deposits in the Earth's crust. A small proportion of the field is of external origin, mostly associated with electric currents in the ionosphere. The configuration of the external field and the ionisation of the atmosphere depend on the incident particle and radiation flux from the Sun. There are, therefore, short-term and non-periodic as well as diurnal, 27-day, seasonal and 11-year periodic changes in the magnetic field, dependent upon the position of the Sun and the degree of solar activity.

A magnetic compass points along the horizontal component of a magnetic line of force. These lines of force converge on the 'magnetic dip-poles', the places where the Earth's magnetic field is vertical. These poles move with time, and their present approximate adopted mean positions are 81°.4 N., 111°.0 W. and 64°.6 S., 138°.2 E.

There is also a 'magnetic equator', at all points of which the vertical component of the Earth's magnetic field is zero and a magnetised needle remains horizontal. This line runs between 2° and 12° north of the geographical equator in Asia and Africa, turns sharply south off the west African coast, and crosses South America through Brazil, Bolivia and Peru; it recrosses the geographical equator in mid-Pacific.

Reference has already been made to secular changes in the Earth's field. The following table indicates the changes in magnetic declination (or variation of the compass). Declination is the angle in the horizontal plane between the direction of true north and that in which a magnetic compass points. Similar, though much smaller, changes have occurred in 'dip' or magnetic inclination. Secular changes differ throughout the world. Although the London observations suggest a cycle with a period of several hundred years, an exact repetition is unlikely.

| *London* | | | | *Greenwich* | | | |
|---|---|---|---|---|---|---|---|
| 1580 | 11° | 15′ | E. | 1900 | 16° | 29′ | W. |
| 1622 | 5° | 56′ | E. | 1925 | 13° | 10′ | W. |
| 1665 | 1° | 22′ | W. | 1950 | 9° | 07′ | W. |
| 1730 | 13° | 00′ | W. | 1975 | 6° | 39′ | W. |
| 1773 | 21° | 09′ | W. | 1998 | 3° | 32′ | W. |
| 1850 | 22° | 24′ | W. | | | | |

In order that up-to-date information on declination may be available, many governments publish magnetic charts on which there are lines (isogonic lines) passing through all places at which specified values of declination will be found at the date of the chart.

In the British Isles, isogonic lines now run approximately north-east to south-west. Though there are considerable local deviations due to geological causes, a rough value of magnetic declination may be obtained by assuming that at 50° N. on the meridian of Greenwich, the value in 2002 is 2°19′ west and allowing an increase of 13′ for each degree of latitude northwards and one of 27′ for each degree of longitude westwards. For example, at 53° N., 5° W., declination will be about 2°19′+39′+135′, i.e. 5°13′ west. The average annual change at the present time is about 12′ decrease.

The number of magnetic observatories is about 180, irregularly distributed over the globe. There are three in Great Britain, run by the British Geological Survey: at Hartland, north Devon; at Eskdalemuir, Dumfries and Galloway; and at Lerwick, Shetland Islands. The following are some recent annual mean values of the magnetic elements for Hartland.

| *Year* | *Declination West* ° | ′ | *Dip or inclination* ° | ′ | *Horizontal force* gauss | *Vertical force* gauss |
|---|---|---|---|---|---|---|
| 1960 | 9 | 59 | 66 | 44 | 0.1871 | 0.4350 |
| 1965 | 9 | 30 | 66 | 34 | 0.1887 | 0.4354 |
| 1970 | 9 | 06 | 66 | 26 | 0.1903 | 0.4364 |
| 1975 | 8 | 32 | 66 | 17 | 0.1921 | 0.4373 |
| 1980 | 7 | 44 | 66 | 10 | 0.1933 | 0.4377 |
| 1985 | 6 | 56 | 66 | 08 | 0.1938 | 0.4380 |
| 1990 | 6 | 15 | 66 | 10 | 0.1939 | 0.4388 |
| 1995 | 5 | 33 | 66 | 07 | 0.1946 | 0.4395 |
| 2000 | 4 | 44 | 66 | 07 | 0.1951 | 0.4405 |

As well as navigation at sea, in the air and on land by compass the oil industry depends on the Earth's magnetic field as a directional reference. They use magnetic survey tools when drilling well-bores and require accurate estimates of the local magnetic field, taking into account the crustal and external fields.

### MAGNETIC STORMS

Occasionally, sometimes with great suddenness, the Earth's magnetic field is subject for several hours to marked disturbance. During a severe storm in 1989 the declination at Lerwick changed by almost 8° in less than an hour. In many instances such disturbances are accompanied by widespread displays of aurorae, marked changes in the incidence of cosmic rays, an increase in the reception of 'noise' from the Sun at radio frequencies, and rapid changes in the ionosphere and induced electric currents within the Earth which adversely affect satellite operations, telecommunications and electric power transmission systems. The disturbances are caused by changes in the stream of ionised particles which emanates from the Sun and through which the Earth is continuously passing. Some of these changes are associated with visible eruptions on the Sun, usually in the region of sun-spots. There is a marked tendency for disturbances to recur after intervals of about 27 days, the apparent period of rotation of the Sun on its axis, which is consistent with the sources being located on particular areas of the Sun.

## ARTIFICIAL SATELLITES

To consider the orbit of an artificial satellite, it is best to imagine that one is looking at the Earth from a distant point in space. The Earth would then be seen to be rotating about its axis inside the orbit described by the rapidly revolving satellite. The inclination of a satellite orbit to the Earth's equator (which generally remains almost constant throughout the satellite's lifetime) gives at once the maximum range of latitudes over which the satellite passes. Thus a satellite whose orbit has an inclination of 53° will pass overhead all latitudes between 53° S. and 53° N., but would never be seen in the zenith of any place nearer the poles than these latitudes. If we consider a particular place on the earth, whose latitude is less than the inclination of the satellite's orbit, then the Earth's rotation carries this place first under the northbound part of the orbit and then under the southbound portion of the orbit, these two occurrences being always less than 12 hours apart for satellites moving in direct orbits (i.e. to the east). (For satellites in retrograde orbits, the words 'northbound' and 'southbound' should be interchanged in the preceding statement.) As the value of the latitude of the observer increases and approaches the value of the inclination of the orbit, so this interval gets shorter until (when the latitude is equal to the inclination) only one overhead passage occurs each day.

### Observation of Satellites

The regression of the orbit around the Earth causes alternate periods of visibility and invisibility, though this is of little concern to the radio or radar observer. To the visual observer the following cycle of events normally occurs (though the cycle may start in any position): invisibility, morning observations before dawn, invisibility, evening observations after dusk, invisibility, morning observations before dawn, and so on. With reasonably high satellites and for observers in high latitudes around the summer solstice, the evening observations follow the morning observations without interruption as sunlight passing over the polar regions can still illuminate satellites which are passing over temperate latitudes at local midnight. At the moment all satellites rely on sunlight to make them visible, though a satellite with a flashing light has been suggested for a future launching. The observer must be in darkness or twilight in order to make any useful observations. (For durations of twilight, and sunrise and sunset times, *see* Page Two of each month.)

Some of the satellites are visible to the naked eye and much interest has been aroused by the spectacle of a bright satellite disappearing into the Earth's shadow. The event is even more interesting telescopically as the disappearance occurs gradually as the satellite traverses the Earth's penumbral shadow, and during the last few seconds before the eclipse is complete the satellite may change colour (in suitable atmospheric conditions) from yellow to red. This is because the last rays of sunlight are refracted through the denser layers of our atmosphere before striking the satellite.

Some satellites rotate about one or more axes so that a periodic variation in brightness is observed. This was particularly noticeable in several of the Soviet satellites.

Satellite research has provided some interesting results, including a revised value of the Earth's oblateness (1/298.2), and the discovery of the Van Allen radiation belts.

### Launchings

Apart from their names, e.g. Cosmos 6 Rocket, the satellites are also classified according to their date of launch. Thus 1961 $\alpha$ refers to the first satellite launching of 1961. A number following the Greek letter indicated the relative brightness of the satellites put in orbit. From the beginning of 1963 the Greek letters were replaced by numbers and the numbers by roman letters e.g. 1963–01A. For all satellites successfully injected into orbit the following table gives the designation and names of the main objects, the launch date and some initial orbital data. These are the inclination to the equator ($i$), the nodal period of revolution ($P$), and the apogee and perigee heights.

Although most of the satellites launched are injected into orbits less than 1,000 km high, there are an increasing number of satellites in geostationary orbits, i.e. where the orbital inclination is zero, the eccentricity close to zero, and the period of revolution is 1436.1 minutes. Thus the satellite is permanently situated over the equator at one selected longitude at a mean height of 35,786 km. This geostationary band is crowded. In one case there are four television satellites (Astra 1A, Astra 1B, Astra 1C and Astra 1D) orbiting within a few tens of kilometres of each other. In the sky they appear to be separated by only a few arc minutes.

In 1997 a number of *Iridium* satellites were launched into high inclination orbits. These are owned by the mobile telephone company Cellnet. For visual observers, these satellites have the interesting characteristic that the large aeriels they carry can, when in exactly the right orientation with respect to the Sun and the observer, give off a 'flare' in brightness which can on occasion attain a magnitude of –6, much brighter than Venus. The flare can be visible to the naked eye for nearly a minute.

The Russian Space Station, Mir, 1986-17A, which was launched in 1986 was successfully de-orbited on March 23 2001. The re-entry was carried out in several stages, the first small burn to lower the orbit occurring at 00h 33m. The main de-orbit burn began at 05h 07m, which lowered the perigee height to 80km. The new International Space Station ISS, 1998-67A, is currently being assembled in an orbit of similar size and inclination to Mir. It will become even brighter as more parts are added to it. When passing over Britain it can appear to be almost as bright as Jupiter on favourable transits, though only visible for four or five minutes on each pass.

## ARTIFICIAL SATELLITE LAUNCHES 2000–2001

| Designation | Satellite | Launch date | P | i | Apogee height | Perigee height |
|---|---|---|---|---|---|---|
| 2000– | | | m | ° | km | km |
| 011 | Garuda 1, rocket | February 12 | 908.0 | 10.2 | 36007 | 13380 |
| 012 | Superbird 4, rocket | February 18 | 1417.9 | 0.2 | 35792 | 35088 |
| 013 | Express 6A, rocket, platform, rocket | March 12 | 1432.5 | 0.3 | 35752 | 35702 |
| 014 | MTI, rocket | March 12 | 96.6 | 97.4 | 614 | 577 |
| 015 | Fregat Rocket /Cluster II | March 20 | 320.4 | 64.7 | 18033 | 256 |
| 016 | Asiastar, Insat 3B, Sylda 5,rocket | March 21 | 636.6 | 7.0 | 35694 | 598 |
| 017 | Image, rocket, rocket | March 25 | 856.3 | 90.0 | 46005 | 1000 |
| 018 | Soyuz TM-30, rocket | April 4 | 91.1 | 51.7 | 340 | 339 |
| 019 | Sesat | April 17 | 1449.8 | 0.1 | 36083 | 36046 |
| 020 | Galaxy IVR | April 19 | 1435.9 | 0.1 | 35803 | 35784 |
| 021 | Progress M-2 | April 25 | 91.2 | 51.7 | 344 | 340 |
| 022 | GOES-L, rocket | May 3 | 999.0 | 5.9 | 42242 | 11219 |
| 023 | Cosmos 2370, Soyuz rocket | May 3 | 90.0 | 64.8 | 316 | 254 |
| 024 | USA 149 DSP, rocket, rocket | May 8 | (No elements available) | | | |
| 025 | USA 150 Navstar 47, rocket, rocket | May 11 | 356.9 | 39.2 | 20410 | 189 |
| 026 | Dummysat-01, Dummysat-02, rocket | May 16 | 95.7 | 86.4 | 571 | 556 |
| 027 | STS-101 Atlantis F21 | May 19 | 91.5 | 51.6 | 365 | 353 |
| 028 | Eutelsat W4, rocket | May 24 | 835.4 | 20.0 | 45789 | 243 |
| 029 | Gorizont 33, rocket, tank | June 6 | 619.0 | 48.8 | 35001 | 382 |
| 030 | TSX-5, rocket | June 7 | 106.3 | 69.0 | 1717 | 416 |
| 031 | Express 3A, rocket, platform, rocket | June 24 | 637.5 | 48.7 | 36076 | 260 |
| 032 | Unknown, rocket | June 25 | 1438.3 | 1.1 | 35871 | 35808 |
| 033 | Nadezhda, Tzinghua 1,Snap 1,rocket | June 28 | 98.7 | 98.2 | 721 | 696 |
| 034 | TDRS-8, rocket | June 30 | 480.9 | 27.1 | 27683 | 249 |
| 035 | Sirius-1, rocket, platform, rocket | June 30 | 995.2 | 63.4 | 47127 | 6177 |
| 036 | Cosmos 2371,rocket, platform, rocket | July 5 | 633.9 | 48.7 | 35890 | 265 |
| 037 | Zvezda, rocket | July 12 | 91.0 | 51.6 | 367 | 299 |
| 038 | Echostar 6, rocket | July 14 | 673.9 | 26.7 | 38027 | 162 |
| 039 | Ruben, Champ/Mita, rocket | July 15 | 93.6 | 87.3 | 489 | 435 |
| 040 | GPS Navstar 48, rocket, rocket | July 16 | 357.9 | 39.0 | 20465 | 197 |
| 041 | Cluster II/FM7 & FM6, rocket | July 16 | 321.4 | 64.7 | 18085 | 263 |
| 042 | Mightysat II.1, rocket | July 19 | 96.0 | 97.9 | 598 | 561 |
| 043 | Pas-9, rocket | July 28 | 1427.4 | 0.1 | 35798 | 35456 |
| 044 | Progress M1–3, rocket | August 6 | 89.2 | 51.4 | 259 | 227 |
| 045 | Cluster II/FM-5 Rumba, FM-4 Tango, rocket | August 9 | 597.3 | 65.0 | 33998 | 254 |
| 046 | Nilesat, rocket | August | 1005.8 | 0.4 | 35744 | 18012 |
| 047 | Lacrosse 4 USA 152 Onyx, rocket | August 17 | 98.4 | 68.1 | 704 | 676 |
| 048 | DM-F3, rocket | August 23 | 361.0 | 27.7 | 20654 | 200 |
| 049 | Raduga 1–5, rocket, platform | August 28 | 1472.5 | 2.3 | 36595 | 36420 |
| 050 | PRC 44 ZY-2, rocket | September 1 | 94.3 | 97.5 | 505 | 487 |
| 051 | Sirius-2, rocket, platform, rocket | September 5 | 994.5 | 63.4 | 47070 | 6205 |
| 052 | Eutelsat W1, rocket | September 6 | 633.0 | 7.0 | 35783 | 324 |
| 053 | STS-106 Atlantis F22 | September 8 | 90.7 | 51.6 | 344 | 292 |
| 054 | Astra 2B, GE-7, rocket, platform | September 14 | 1318.8 | 0.4 | 35774 | 31166 |
| 055 | NOAA 16, rocket | September 21 | 102.1 | 98.8 | 877 | 861 |
| 056 | Cosmos 2372, rocket | September 25 | 90.0 | 64.8 | 344 | 223 |
| 057 | Tiungsat-1, Megsat, Unisat, Saudisat-1A, Saudisat-1B, rocket | September 26 | 97.5 | 64.6 | 656 | 647 |
| 058 | Cosmos 2373, rocket | September 29 | 89.4 | 70.4 | 290 | 223 |
| 059 | GE-1A, rocket, platform, rocket | October 1 | 630.2 | 48.6 | 35733 | 229 |
| 060 | Nsat-110, rocket | October 6 | 1430.6 | 0.0 | 35753 | 35610 |

## ARTIFICIAL SATELLITE LAUNCHES 2000–2001

| Designation | Satellite | Launch date | P | *i* | Apogee height | Perigee height |
|---|---|---|---|---|---|---|
| 2000– | | | m | ° | km | km |
| 061 | Hete-2, rocket | October 9 | 97.1 | 2.0 | 649 | 608 |
| 062 | STS-92 Discovery F-18 | October 11 | 92.2 | 51.6 | 393 | 387 |
| 063 | Cosmos 2374–6, platform, rocket, rocket | October 13 | 675.6 | 64.9 | 19140 | 19136 |
| 064 | Progress M-43, rocket | October 16 | 88.8 | 51.7 | 245 | 201 |
| 065 | DSCS-III B-11 USA-153, rocket, IUS | October 20 | (No elements available) | | | |
| 066 | Thuraya-1, rocket | October 21 | 632.2 | 6.4 | 35821 | 243 |
| 067 | GE-6, rocket, platform, rocket, platform | October 21 | 746.2 | 18.7 | 35785 | 5985 |
| 068 | Europe *star FM-1, rocket | October 29 | 655.7 | 7.0 | 36981 | 288 |
| 069 | Abeidou-1 (Navsat), rocket | October 30 | 753.2 | 25.0 | 41901 | 208 |
| 070 | Soyuz TM-31, rocket | October 31 | 89.7 | 51.6 | 282 | 260 |
| 071 | GPS Navstar 49 USA-154, rocket, PAM-D | November 10 | 724.3 | 55.1 | 20510 | 20191 |
| 072 | PAS-1R. Amsat P3D, Oscar 40, STRV-1C, STRV-1D, rocket, Sylda, ASAP | November 16 | 704.2 | 6.5 | 39077 | 627 |
| 073 | Progress M1–4, rocket | November 16 | 89.9 | 51.6 | 281 | 274 |
| 074 | Quickbird 1 (Cosmos Rocket) | November 20 | 91.5 | 65.8 | 614 | 81 |
| 075 | EO-1, SAC-C, Munin, rocket, DPAF | November 21 | 98.8 | 98.3 | 721 | 704 |
| 076 | Anik F1, rocket | November 21 | 864.8 | 3.0 | 41232 | 6169 |
| 077 | Sirius 3, rocket, platform, rocket | November 30 | 1141.9 | 63.4 | 47085 | 12539 |
| 078 | STS-97 | December 1 | 89.8 | 51.6 | 335 | 218 |
| 079 | Eros A-1, rocket | December 5 | 94.7 | 97.4 | 520 | 504 |
| 080 | USA-155, rocket | December 6 | (No elements available) | | | |
| 081 | Astra 2D, GE-8, LDREX, rocket, Sylda | December 20 | 630.3 | 2.0 | 35746 | 224 |
| 082 | Beidou 1B, rocket | December 20 | 752.7 | 25.0 | 41882 | 203 |
| 2001– | | | | | | |
| 001 | SZ-2, rocket | January 9 | 91.2 | 42.6 | 346 | 341 |
| 002 | Turksat 2A, rocket | January 10 | 1428.4 | 0.2 | 35748 | 35547 |
| 003 | Progress M1–5, rocket | January 24 | 90.5 | 51.7 | 319 | 297 |
| 004 | GPS Navstar 50 = USA-156, rocket, PAM-D | January 30 | 356.6 | 39.2 | 20410 | 173 |
| 005 | Sicral 1, Skynet 4F, rocket, Spelda | February 7 | 840.5 | 2.4 | 35763 | 10508 |
| 006 | STS-98 Atlantis F23 | February 7 | 91.7 | 51.6 | 376 | 363 |
| 007 | Odin, rocket | February 20 | 97.1 | 97.9 | 634 | 624 |
| 008 | Progress M1–44, rocket | February 26 | 90.0 | 51.6 | 295 | 278 |
| 009 | Milstar DFS-4, rocket | February 27 | (No elements available) | | | |
| 010 | STS-102 Discovery F19 | March 8 | 89.6 | 51.6 | 286 | 246 |

# Time Measurement and Calendars

## MEASUREMENTS OF TIME

Measurements of time are based on the time taken by the earth to rotate on its axis (day); by the moon to revolve round the earth (month); and by the earth to revolve round the sun (year). From these, which are not commensurable, certain average or mean intervals have been adopted for ordinary use.

### THE DAY

The day begins at midnight and is divided into 24 hours of 60 minutes, each of 60 seconds. The hours are counted from midnight up to 12 noon (when the sun crosses the meridian), and these hours are designated a.m. (*ante meridiem*); and again from noon up to 12 midnight, which hours are designated p.m. (*post meridiem*), except when the 24-hour reckoning is employed. The 24-hour reckoning ignores a.m. and p.m., numbering the hours 0 to 23 from midnight.

Colloquially the 24 hours are divided into day and night, day being the time while the sun is above the horizon (including the four stages of twilight defined on page 72). Day is subdivided into morning, the early part of daytime, ending at noon; afternoon, from noon to about 6 p.m.; and evening, which may be said to extend from 6 p.m. until midnight. Night, the dark period between day and day, begins at the close of astronomical twilight (*see* page 72) and extends beyond midnight to sunrise the next day.

The names of the days are derived from Old English translations or adaptations of the Roman titles.

| | | |
|---|---|---|
| *Sunday* | Sun | Sol |
| *Monday* | Moon | Luna |
| *Tuesday* | Tiw/Tyr (god of war) | Mars |
| *Wednesday* | Woden/Odin | Mercury |
| *Thursday* | Thor | Jupiter |
| *Friday* | Frigga/Freyja (goddess of love) | Venus |
| *Saturday* | Saeternes | Saturn |

### THE MONTH

The month in the ordinary calendar is approximately the twelfth part of a year, but the lengths of the different months vary from 28 (or 29) days to 31.

### THE YEAR

The equinoctial or tropical year is the time that the earth takes to revolve round the sun from equinox to equinox, i.e. 365.24219 mean solar days, or 365 days 5 hours 48 minutes and 45 seconds.

The calendar year usually consists of 365 days but a year containing 366 days is called bissextile (*see* Roman calendar, page 89) or leap year, one day being added to the month of February so that a date 'leaps over' a day of the week. In the Roman calendar the day that was repeated was the sixth day before the beginning of March, the equivalent of 24 February.

A year is a leap year if the date of the year is divisible by four without remainder, unless it is the last year of the century. The last year of a century is a leap year only if its number is divisible by 400 without remainder, e.g. the years 1800 and 1900 had only 365 days but the year 2000 has 366 days.

### THE SOLSTICE

A solstice is the point in the tropical year at which the sun attains its greatest distance, north or south, from the Equator. In the northern hemisphere the furthest point north of the Equator marks the summer solstice and the furthest point south the winter solstice.

The date of the solstice varies according to locality. For example, if the summer solstice falls on 21 June late in the day by Greenwich time, that day will be the longest of the year at Greenwich though it may be by only a second, but it will fall on 22 June, local date, in Japan, and so 22 June will be the longest day there. The date of the solstice is also affected by the length of the tropical year, which is 365 days 6 hours less about 11 minutes 15 seconds. If a solstice happens late on 21 June in one year, it will be nearly six hours later in the next (unless the next year is a leap year), i.e. early on 22 June, and that will be the longest day.

This delay of the solstice does not continue because the extra day in leap year brings it back a day in the calendar. However, because of the 11 minutes 15 seconds mentioned above, the additional day in leap year brings the solstice back too far by 45 minutes, and the time of the solstice in the calendar is earlier, in a four-year pattern, as the century progresses. The last year of a century is in most cases not a leap year, and the omission of the extra day puts the date of the solstice later by about six hours too much. Compensation for this is made by the fourth centennial year being a leap year. The solstice has become earlier in date throughout this century and, because the year 2000 is a leap year, the solstice will get earlier still throughout the 21st century.

The date of the winter solstice, the shortest day of the year, is affected by the same factors as the longest day.

At Greenwich the sun sets at its earliest by the clock about ten days before the shortest day. The daily change in the time of sunset is due in the first place to the sun's movement southwards at this time of the year, which diminishes the interval between the sun's transit and its setting. However, the daily decrease of the Equation of Time causes the time of apparent noon to be continuously later day by day, which to some extent counteracts the first effect. The rates of the change of these two quantities are not equal or uniform; their combination causes the date of earliest sunset to be 12 or 13 December at Greenwich. In more southerly latitudes the effect of the movement of the sun is less, and the change in the time of sunset depends on that of the Equation of Time to a greater degree, and the date of earliest sunset is earlier than it is at Greenwich, e.g. on the Equator it is about 1 November.

### THE EQUINOX

The equinox is the point at which the sun crosses the Equator and day and night are of equal length all over the world. This occurs in March and September.

### DOG DAYS

The days about the heliacal rising of the Dog Star, noted from ancient times as the hottest period of the year in the northern hemisphere, are called the Dog Days. Their incidence has been variously calculated as depending on the Greater or Lesser Dog Star (Sirius or Procyon) and their duration has been reckoned as from 30 to 54 days. A generally accepted period is from 3 July to 15 August.

## CHRISTIAN CALENDAR

In the Christian chronological system the years are distinguished by cardinal numbers before or after the birth of Christ, the period being denoted by the letters BC (Before Christ) or, more rarely, AC (*Ante Christum*), and AD (*Anno Domini* – In the Year of Our Lord). The correlative dates of the epoch are the fourth year of the 194th Olympiad, the 753rd year from the foundation of Rome, AM 3761 in Jewish chronology, and the 4714th year of the Julian period. The actual date of the birth of Christ is somewhat uncertain.

The system was introduced into Italy in the sixth century. Though first used in France in the seventh century, it was not universally established there until about the eighth century. It has been said that the system was introduced into England by St Augustine (AD 596), but it was probably not generally used until some centuries later. It was ordered to be used by the Bishops at the Council of Chelsea (AD 816).

### THE JULIAN CALENDAR

In the Julian calendar (adopted by the Roman Empire in 45 BC, *see* page 89) all the centennial years were leap years, and for this reason towards the close of the 16th century there was a difference of ten days between the tropical and calendar years; the equinox fell on 11 March of the calendar, whereas at the time of the Council of Nicaea (AD 325), it had fallen on 21 March. In 1582 Pope Gregory ordained that 5 October should be called 15 October and that of the end-century years only the fourth should be a leap year (*see* page 81).

### THE GREGORIAN CALENDAR

The Gregorian calendar was adopted by Italy, France, Spain and Portugal in 1582, by Prussia, the Roman Catholic German states, Switzerland, Holland and Flanders on 1 January 1583, by Poland in 1586, Hungary in 1587, the Protestant German and Netherland states and Denmark in 1700, and by Great Britain and Dominions (including the North American colonies) in 1752, by the omission of eleven days (3 September being reckoned as 14 September). Sweden omitted the leap day in 1700 but observed leap days in 1704 and 1708, and reverted to the Julian calendar by having two leap days in 1712; the Gregorian calendar was adopted in 1753 by the omission of eleven days (18 February being reckoned as 1 March). Japan adopted the calendar in 1872, China in 1912, Bulgaria in 1915, Turkey and Soviet Russia in 1918, Yugoslavia and Romania in 1919, and Greece in 1923.

In the same year that the change was made in England from the Julian to the Gregorian calendar, the beginning of the new year was also changed from 25 March to 1 January (*see* page 86).

### THE ORTHODOX CHURCHES

Some Orthodox Churches still use the Julian reckoning but the majority of Greek Orthodox Churches and the Romanian Orthodox Church have adopted a modified 'New Calendar', observing the Gregorian calendar for fixed feasts and the Julian for movable feasts.

The Orthodox Church year begins on 1 September. There are four fast periods and, in addition to Pascha (Easter), twelve great feasts, as well as numerous commemorations of the saints of the Old and New Testaments throughout the year.

### THE DOMINICAL LETTER

The dominical letter is one of the letters A–G which ar[e] used to denote the Sundays in successive years. If the firs[t] day of the year is a Sunday the letter is A; if the second, B[;] the third, C; and so on. A leap year requires two letters, th[e] first for 1 January to 29 February, the second for 1 Marc[h] to 31 December (*see* page 84).

### EPIPHANY

The feast of the Epiphany, commemorating the manifes[-]tation of Christ, later became associated with the offerin[g] of gifts by the Magi. The day was of great importance fro[m] the time of the Council of Nicaea (AD 325), as the primat[e] of Alexandria was charged at every Epiphany feast with th[e] announcement in a letter to the churches of the date of th[e] forthcoming Easter. The day was also of importance i[n] Britain as it influenced dates, ecclesiastical and lay, e.g[.] Plough Monday, when work was resumed in the fields, fel[l] on the Monday in the first full week after Epiphany.

### LENT

The Teutonic word *Lent*, which denotes the fast precedin[g] Easter, originally meant no more than the spring season[,] but from Anglo-Saxon times at least it has been used as th[e] equivalent of the more significant Latin term Quadrage[-]sima, meaning the 'forty days' or, more literally, th[e] fortieth day. Ash Wednesday is the first day of Lent, whic[h] ends at midnight before Easter Day.

### PALM SUNDAY

Palm Sunday, the Sunday before Easter and the beginnin[g] of Holy Week, commemorates the triumphal entry o[f] Christ into Jerusalem and is celebrated in Britain (wher[e] palm is not available) by branches of willow gathered fo[r] use in the decoration of churches on that day.

### MAUNDY THURSDAY

Maundy Thursday is the day before Good Friday, th[e] name itself being a corruption of *dies mandati* (day of th[e] mandate) when Christ washed the feet of the disciples an[d] gave them the mandate to love one another.

### EASTER DAY

Easter Day is the first Sunday after the full moon which happens on, or next after, the 21st day of March; if the full moon happens on a Sunday, Easter Day is the Sunday after.

This definition is contained in an Act of Parliament (24 Geo. II c. 23) and explanation is given in the preamble to the Act that the day of full moon depends on certain tables that have been prepared. These tables are summarized in the early pages of the Book of Common Prayer. The moon referred to is not the real moon of the heavens, but a hypothetical moon on whose 'full' the date of Easter depends, and the lunations of this 'calendar' moon consist of twenty-nine and thirty days alternately, with certain necessary modifications to make the date of its full agree as nearly as possible with that of the real moon, which is known as the Paschal Full Moon.

### A FIXED EASTER

In 1928 the House of Commons agreed to a motion for the third reading of a bill proposing that Easter Day shall, in the calendar year next but one after the commencement of the Act and in all subsequent years, be the first Sunday after the second Saturday in April. Easter would thus fall on the cond or third Sunday in April, i.e. between 9 and 15 April nclusive). A clause in the Bill provided that before it shall me into operation, regard shall be had to any opinion pressed officially by the various Christian churches. fforts by the World Council of Churches to secure a nanimous choice of date for Easter by its member urches have so far been unsuccessful.

### OGATION DAYS

ogation Days are the Monday, Tuesday and Wednesday receding Ascension Day and from the fifth century were bserved as public fasts with solemn processions and pplications. The processions were discontinued as ligious observances at the Reformation, but survive in e ceremony known as 'beating the parish bounds'. ogation Sunday is the Sunday before Ascension Day.

### EMBER DAYS

The Ember Days at the four seasons are the Wednesday, Friday and Saturday (*a*) before the third Sunday in Advent, (*b*) before the second Sunday in Lent, and (*c*) before the Sundays nearest to the festivals of St Peter and of St Michael and All Angels.

### TRINITY SUNDAY

Trinity Sunday is eight weeks after Easter Day, on the Sunday following Pentecost (Whit Sunday). Subsequent Sundays are reckoned in the Book of Common Prayer calendar of the Church of England as 'after Trinity'. Thomas Becket (1118–70) was consecrated Archbishop of Canterbury on the Sunday after Whit Sunday and his first act was to ordain that the day of his consecration should be held as a new festival in honour of the Holy Trinity. This observance spread from Canterbury throughout the whole of Christendom.

## OVABLE FEASTS TO THE YEAR 2035

| *ear* | *Ash Wednesday* | *Easter* | *Ascension* | *Pentecost (Whit Sunday)* | *Advent Sunday* |
|---|---|---|---|---|---|
| 002 | 13 February | 31 March | 9 May | 19 May | 1 December |
| 003 | 5 March | 20 April | 29 May | 8 June | 30 November |
| 004 | 25 February | 11 April | 20 May | 30 May | 28 November |
| 005 | 9 February | 27 March | 5 May | 15 May | 27 November |
| 006 | 1 March | 16 April | 25 May | 4 June | 3 December |
| 007 | 21 February | 8 April | 17 May | 27 May | 2 December |
| 008 | 6 February | 23 March | 1 May | 11 May | 30 November |
| 009 | 25 February | 12 April | 21 May | 31 May | 29 November |
| 010 | 17 February | 4 April | 13 May | 23 May | 28 November |
| 011 | 9 March | 24 April | 2 June | 12 June | 27 November |
| 012 | 22 February | 8 April | 17 May | 27 May | 2 December |
| 013 | 13 February | 31 March | 9 May | 19 May | 1 December |
| 014 | 5 March | 20 April | 29 May | 8 June | 30 November |
| 015 | 18 February | 5 April | 14 May | 24 May | 29 November |
| 016 | 10 February | 27 March | 5 May | 15 May | 27 November |
| 017 | 1 March | 16 April | 25 May | 4 June | 3 December |
| 018 | 14 February | 1 April | 10 May | 20 May | 2 December |
| 019 | 6 March | 21 April | 30 May | 9 June | 1 December |
| 020 | 26 February | 12 April | 21 May | 31 May | 29 November |
| 021 | 17 February | 4 April | 13 May | 23 May | 28 November |
| 022 | 2 March | 17 April | 26 May | 5 June | 27 November |
| 023 | 22 February | 9 April | 18 May | 28 May | 3 December |
| 024 | 14 February | 31 March | 9 May | 19 May | 1 December |
| 025 | 5 March | 20 April | 29 May | 8 June | 30 November |
| 026 | 18 February | 5 April | 14 May | 24 May | 29 November |
| 027 | 10 February | 28 March | 6 May | 16 May | 28 November |
| 028 | 1 March | 16 April | 25 May | 4 June | 3 December |
| 029 | 14 February | 1 April | 10 May | 20 May | 2 December |
| 030 | 6 March | 21 April | 30 May | 9 June | 1 December |
| 031 | 26 February | 13 April | 22 May | 1 June | 30 November |
| 032 | 11 February | 28 March | 6 May | 16 May | 28 November |
| 033 | 2 March | 17 April | 26 May | 5 June | 27 November |
| 034 | 22 February | 9 April | 18 May | 28 May | 3 December |
| 035 | 7 February | 25 March | 3 May | 13 May | 2 December |

### NOTES

*sh Wednesday* (first day in Lent) can fall at earliest on 4 February and at latest on 10 March

*Iothering Sunday* (fourth Sunday in Lent) can fall at earliest on 1 March and at latest on 4 April

*aster Day* can fall at earliest on 22 March and at latest on 25 April

*scension Day* is forty days after Easter Day and can fall at earliest on 30 April and at latest on 3 June

*Pentecost (Whit Sunday)* is seven weeks after Easter and can fall at earliest on 10 May and at latest on 13 June

*Trinity Sunday* is the Sunday after Whit Sunday

*Corpus Christi* falls on the Thursday after Trinity Sunday

*Sundays after Pentecost* – there are not less than 18 and not more than 23

*Advent Sunday* is the Sunday nearest to 30 November

## EASTER DAYS AND DOMINICAL LETTERS 1500 TO 2035

Dates up to and including 1752 are according to the Julian calendar. For dominical letters in leap years, *see* page 82

| | | 1500–1599 | 1600–1699 | 1700–1799 | 1800–1899 | 1900–1999 | 2000–203 |
|---|---|---|---|---|---|---|---|
| *March* | | | | | | | |
| d | 22 | 1573 | 1668 | 1761 | 1818 | | |
| e | 23 | 1505/16 | 1600 | 1788 | 1845/56 | 1913 | 2008 |
| f | 24 | | 1611/95 | 1706/99 | | 1940 | |
| g | 25 | 1543/54 | 1627/38/49 | 1722/33/44 | 1883/94 | 1951 | 2035 |
| A | 26 | 1559/70/81/92 | 1654/65/76 | 1749/58/69/80 | 1815/26/37 | 1967/78/89 | |
| b | 27 | 1502/13/24/97 | 1608/87/92 | 1785/96 | 1842/53/64 | 1910/21/32 | 2005/16 |
| c | 28 | 1529/35/40 | 1619/24/30 | 1703/14/25 | 1869/75/80 | 1937/48 | 2027/32 |
| d | 29 | 1551/62 | 1635/46/57 | 1719/30/41/52 | 1807/12/91 | 1959/64/70 | |
| e | 30 | 1567/78/89 | 1651/62/73/84 | 1746/55/66/77 | 1823/34 | 1902/75/86/97 | |
| f | 31 | 1510/21/32/83/94 | 1605/16/78/89 | 1700/71/82/93 | 1839/50/61/72 | 1907/18/29/91 | 2002/13/2 |
| *April* | | | | | | | |
| g | 1 | 1526/37/48 | 1621/32 | 1711/16 | 1804/66/77/88 | 1923/34/45/56 | 2018/29 |
| A | 2 | 1553/64 | 1643/48 | 1727/38 | 1809/20/93/99 | 1961/72 | |
| b | 3 | 1575/80/86 | 1659/70/81 | 1743/63/68/74 | 1825/31/36 | 1904/83/88/94 | |
| c | 4 | 1507/18/91 | 1602/13/75/86/97 | 1708/79/90 | 1847/58 | 1915/20/26/99 | 2010/21 |
| d | 5 | 1523/34/45/56 | 1607/18/29/40 | 1702/13/24/95 | 1801/63/74/85/96 | 1931/42/53 | 2015/26 |
| e | 6 | 1539/50/61/72 | 1634/45/56 | 1729/35/40/60 | 1806/17/28/90 | 1947/58/69/80 | |
| f | 7 | 1504/77/88 | 1667/72 | 1751/65/76 | 1822/33/44 | 1901/12/85/96 | |
| g | 8 | 1509/15/20/99 | 1604/10/83/94 | 1705/87/92/98 | 1849/55/60 | 1917/28 | 2007/12 |
| A | 9 | 1531/42 | 1615/26/37/99 | 1710/21/32 | 1871/82 | 1939/44/50 | 2023/34 |
| b | 10 | 1547/58/69 | 1631/42/53/64 | 1726/37/48/57 | 1803/14/87/98 | 1955/66/77 | |
| c | 11 | 1501/12/63/74/85/96 | 1658/69/80 | 1762/73/84 | 1819/30/41/52 | 1909/71/82/93 | 2004 |
| d | 12 | 1506/17/28 | 1601/12/91/96 | 1789 | 1846/57/68 | 1903/14/25/36/98 | 2009/20 |
| e | 13 | 1533/44 | 1623/28 | 1707/18 | 1800/73/79/84 | 1941/52 | 2031 |
| f | 14 | 1555/60/66 | 1639/50/61 | 1723/34/45/54 | 1805/11/16/95 | 1963/68/74 | |
| g | 15 | 1571/82/93 | 1655/66/77/88 | 1750/59/70/81 | 1827/38 | 1900/06/79/90 | 2001 |
| A | 16 | 1503/14/25/36/87/98 | 1609/20/82/93 | 1704/75/86/97 | 1843/54/65/76 | 1911/22/33/95 | 2006/17/2 |
| b | 17 | 1530/41/52 | 1625/36 | 1715/20 | 1808/70/81/92 | 1927/38/49/60 | 2022/33 |
| c | 18 | 1557/68 | 1647/52 | 1731/42/56 | 1802/13/24/97 | 1954/65/76 | |
| d | 19 | 1500/79/84/90 | 1663/74/85 | 1747/67/72/78 | 1829/35/40 | 1908/81/87/92 | |
| e | 20 | 1511/22/95 | 1606/17/79/90 | 1701/12/83/94 | 1851/62 | 1919/24/30 | 2003/14/2 |
| f | 21 | 1527/38/49 | 1622/33/44 | 1717/28 | 1867/78/89 | 1935/46/57 | 2019/30 |
| g | 22 | 1565/76 | 1660 | 1739/53/64 | 1810/21/32 | 1962/73/84 | |
| A | 23 | 1508 | 1671 | | 1848 | 1905/16 | 2000 |
| b | 24 | 1519 | 1603/14/98 | 1709/91 | 1859 | | 2011 |
| c | 25 | 1546 | 1641 | 1736 | 1886 | 1943 | |

## HINDU CALENDAR

The Hindu calendar is a luni-solar calendar of twelve months, each containing 29 days, 12 hours. Each month is divided into a light fortnight (Shukla or Shuddha) and a dark fortnight (Krishna or Vadya) based on the waxing and waning of the moon. In most parts of India the month starts with the light fortnight, i.e. the day after the new moon, although in some regions it begins with the dark fortnight, i.e. the day after the full moon.

The new year begins in the month of Chaitra (March/April) and ends in the month of Phalgun (March). The twelve months, Chaitra, Vaishakh, Jyeshtha, Ashadh, Shravan, Bhadrapad, Ashvin, Kartik, Margashirsh, Paush, Magh and Phalgun, have Sanskrit names derived from twelve asterisms (constellations). There are regional variations to the names of the months but the Sanskrit names are understood throughout India.

Every lunar month must have a solar transit and is termed pure (shuddha). The lunar month without a solar transit is impure (mala) and called an intercalary month. An intercalary month occurs approximately every 32 lunar months, whenever the difference between the Hindu year of 360 lunar days (354 days 8 hours solar time) and the 365 days 6 hours of the solar year reaches the length of on Hindu lunar month (29 days 12 hours).

The leap month may be added at any point in the Hind year. The name given to the month varies according t when it occurs but is taken from the month immediatel following it. There is no leap month in 2002.

The days of the week are called Raviwar (Sunday Somawar (Monday), Mangalwar (Tuesday), Budhawa (Wednesday), Guruwar (Thursday), Shukrawar (Friday and Shaniwar (Saturday). The names are derived from th Sanskrit names of the Sun, the Moon and five planets Mars, Mercury, Jupiter, Venus and Saturn.

Most fasts and festivals are based on the lunar calenda but a few are determined by the apparent movement of th Sun, e.g. Sankranti and Pongal (in southern India), whic are celebrated on 14/15 January to mark the start of th Sun's apparent journey northwards and a change o season.

Festivals celebrated throughout India are Chaitra (th New Year), Raksha-bandhan (the renewal of the kinshi bond between brothers and sisters), Navaratri (a nine night festival dedicated to the goddess Parvati), Dasar ıe victory of Rama over the demon army), Diwali (a stival of lights), Makara Sankranti, Shivaratri (dedicated Shiva), and Holi (a spring festival).

Regional festivals are Durga-puja (dedicated to the ıddess Durga (Parvati)), Sarasvati-puja (dedicated to the ıddess Sarasvati), Ganesh Chaturthi (worship of Ganesh the fourth day (Chaturthi) of the light half of ıadrapad), Ramanavami (the birth festival of the god ama) and Janmashtami (the birth festival of the god rishna).

The main festivals celebrated in Britain are Navaratri, asara, Durga-puja, Diwali, Holi, Sarasvati-puja, Ganesh haturthi, Raksha-bandhan, Ramanavami and Janmash-mi.

For dates of the main festivals in 2002, *see* page 9.

## :WISH CALENDAR

he story of the Flood in the Book of Genesis indicates the ;e of a calendar of some kind and that the writers cognized thirty days as the length of a lunation. .owever, after the diaspora, Jewish communities were ft in considerable doubt as to the times of fasts and stivals. This led to the formation of the Jewish calendar used today. It is said that this was done in AD 358 by abbi Hillel II, though some assert that it did not happen ıtil much later.

The calendar is luni-solar, and is based on the lengths of ıe lunation and of the tropical year as found by ipparchus (*c*.120 BC), which differ little from those lopted at the present day. The year AM 5762 (2000-2001) the 5th year of the 304th Metonic (Minor or Lunar) cycle f 19 years and the 22st year of the 206th Solar (or Major) ʹcle of 28 years since the Era of the Creation. Jews hold ıat the Creation occurred at the time of the autumnal quinox in the year known in the Christian calendar as 760 BC (954 of the Julian period). The epoch or starting oint of Jewish chronology corresponds to 7 October 761 BC. At the beginning of each solar cycle, the Tekufah f Nisan (the vernal equinox) returns to the same day and the same hour.

The hour is divided into 1080 minims, and the month etween one new moon and the next is reckoned as 29 ays, 12 hours, 793 minims. The normal calendar year, ılled a Regular Common year, consists of 12 months of ) days and 29 days alternately. Since 12 months such as ıese comprise only 354 days, in order that each of them ıall not diverge greatly from an average place in the solar ear, a 13th month is occasionally added after the fifth ıonth of the civil year (which commences on the first day f the month Tishri), or as the penultimate month of the cclesiastical year (which commences on the first day of ıe month Nisan). The years when this happens are called mbolismic or leap years.

Of the 19 years that form a Metonic cycle, seven are leap ears; they occur at places in the cycle indicated by the ımbers 3, 6, 8, 11, 14, 17 and 19, these places being hosen so that the accumulated excesses of the solar years ıould be as small as possible.

A Jewish year is of one of the following six types:

| | |
|---|---|
| Iinimal Common | 353 days |
| :egular Common | 354 days |
| 'ull Common | 355 days |
| Iinimal Leap | 383 days |
| :egular Leap | 384 days |
| 'ull Leap | 385 days |

The Regular year has alternate months of 30 and 29 days. In a Full year, whether common or leap, Marcheshvan, the second month of the civil year, has 30 days instead of 29; in Minimal years Kislev, the third month, has 29 instead of 30. The additional month in leap years is called Adar I and precedes the month called Adar in Common years. Adar II is called Adar Sheni in leap years, and the usual Adar festivals are kept in Adar Sheni. Adar I and Adar II always have 30 days, but neither this, nor the other variations mentioned, is allowed to change the number of days in the other months, which still follow the alternation of the normal twelve.

These are the main features of the Jewish calendar, which must be considered permanent because as a Jewish law it cannot be altered except by a great Sanhedrin.

The Jewish day begins between sunset and nightfall. The time used is that of the meridian of Jerusalem, which is 2h 21m in advance of Greenwich Mean Time. Rules for the beginning of sabbaths and festivals were laid down for the latitude of London in the 18th century and hours for nightfall are now fixed annually by the Chief Rabbi.

### JEWISH CALENDAR 5762–3

AM 5762 (762) is a Regular Common year of 12 months, 50 sabbaths and 354 days. AM 5763 (763) is a Full leap year of 13 months, 55 sabbaths and 385 days.

| Month (first day) | AM 5762 | AM 5763 |
|---|---|---|
| *Tishri* 1 | 18 September 2001 | 7 September 2002 |
| *Marcheshvan* 1 | 18 October | 7 October |
| *Kislev* 1 | 16 November | 6 November |
| *Tebet* 1 | 16 December | 6 December |
| *Shebat* 1 | 14 January 2002 | 4 January 2003 |
| **Adar* 1 | 13 February | 3 February |
| †*Adar* II | | 5 March |
| *Nisan* 1 | 14 March | 3 April |
| *Iyar* 1 | 13 April | 3 May |
| *Sivan* 1 | 12 May | 1 June |
| *Tammuz* 1 | 11 June | 1 July |
| *Ab* 1 | 10 July | 30 July |
| *Elul* 1 | 9 August | 29 August |

*Known as Adar Rishon in leap years
†Known as Adar Sheni in leap years

### JEWISH FASTS AND FESTIVALS

For dates of principal festivals in 2002, *see* page 9.

| | |
|---|---|
| *Tishri* 1–2 | Rosh Hashanah (New Year) |
| *Tishri* 3 | *Fast of Gedaliah |
| *Tishri* 10 | Yom Kippur (Day of Atonement) |
| *Tishri* 15–21 | Succoth (Feast of Tabernacles) |
| *Tishri* 21 | Hoshana Rabba |
| *Tishri* 22 | Shemini Atseret (Solemn Assembly) |
| *Tishri* 23 | Simchat Torah (Rejoicing of the Law) |
| *Kislev* 25 | Chanucah (Dedication of the Temple) begins |
| *Tebet* 10 | Fast of Tebet |
| †*Adar* 13 | §Fast of Esther |
| †*Adar* 14 | Purim |
| †*Adar* 15 | Shushan Purim |
| *Nisan* 15–22 | Pesach (Passover) |
| *Sivan* 6–7 | Shavuot (Feast of Weeks) |
| *Tammuz* 17 | *Fast of Tammuz |
| *Ab* 9 | *Fast of Ab |

*If these dates fall on the sabbath the fast is kept on the following day
†Adar Sheni in leap years
§This fast is observed on Adar 11 (or Adar Sheni 11 in leap years) if Adar 13 falls on a sabbath

## THE MUSLIM CALENDAR

The Muslim era is dated from the *Hijrah*, or flight of the Prophet Muhammad from Mecca to Medina, the corresponding date of which in the Julian calendar is 16 July AD 622. The lunar *hijri* calendar is used principally in Iran, Egypt, Malaysia, Pakistan, Mauritania, various Arab states and certain parts of India. Iran uses the solar *hijri* calendar as well as the lunar *hijri* calendar.The dating system was adopted about AD 639, commencing with the first day of the month Muharram.

The lunar calendar consists of twelve months containing an alternate sequence of 30 and 29 days, with the intercalation of one day at the end of the twelfth month at stated intervals in each cycle of 30 years. The object of the intercalation is to reconcile the date of the first day of the month with the date of the actual new moon.

Some adherents still take the date of the evening of the first physical sighting of the crescent of the new moon as that of the first of the month. If cloud obscures the moon the present month may be extended to 30 days, after which the new month will begin automatically regardless of whether the moon has been seen. (Under religious law a month must have less than 31 days.) This means that the beginning of a new month and the date of religious festivals can vary from the published calendars.

In each cycle of 30 years, 19 years are common and contain 354 days, and 11 years are intercalary (leap years) of 355 days, the latter being called *kabisah*. The mean length of the Hijrah years is 354 days 8 hours 48 minutes and the period of mean lunation is 29 days 12 hours 44 minutes.

To ascertain if a year is common or kabisah, divide it by 30: the quotient gives the number of completed cycles and the remainder shows the place of the year in the current cycle. If the remainder is 2, 5, 7, 10, 13, 16, 18, 21, 24, 26 or 29, the year is kabisah and consists of 355 days.

### MUSLIM CALENDAR 1422-23

Hijrah year 1422 AH (remainder 12) is a common year, 1423 AH (remainder 13) is a kabisah year.

| Month (length) | 1423 (1422) AH |
|---|---|
| *Dhû'l-Qa'da* (30) | (15 January) |
| *Dhû'l-Hijjah* (29 or 30) | (15 February) |
| *Muharram* (30) | 15 March |
| *Safar* (29) | 14 April |
| *Rabi' I* (30) | 14 May |
| *Rabi' II* (29) | 12 June |
| *Jumada I* (30) | 12 July |
| *Jumada II* (29) | 10 August |
| *Rajab* (30) | 9 September |
| *Sha'ban* (29) | 8 October |
| *Ramadân* (30) | 6 November |
| *Shawwâl* (29) | 6 December |

### MUSLIM FESTIVALS

Ramadan is a month of fasting for all Muslims because it is the month in which the revelation of the *Qur'an* (Koran) began. During Ramadan Muslims abstain from food, drink and sexual pleasure from dawn until after sunset throughout the month.

The two major festivals are *Id al-Fitr* and *Id al-Adha*. Id al-Fitr marks the end of the Ramadan fast and is celebrated on the day after the sighting of the new moon of the following month. Id al-Adha, the festival of sacrifice (also known as the great festival), celebrates the submission of the Prophet Ibrahim (Abraham) to God. Id al-Adha falls on the tenth day of Dhul-Hijjah, coinciding with the da when those on *hajj* (pilgrimage to Mecca) sacrifice animal

Other days accorded special recognition are:

| | |
|---|---|
| *Muharram* 1 | New Year's Day |
| *Muharram* 10 | Ashura (the day Prophet Noah left the Ark and Prophet Moses was saved from Pharaoh (Sunni the death of the Prophet's grandson Husain (Shi'ite)) |
| *Rabi'u-l-Awwal* (*Rabi' I*) 12 | Mawlid al-Nabi (birthday of th Prophet Muhammad) |
| *Rajab* 27 | Laylat al-Isra' wa'l-Mi'raj (The Night of Journey and Ascensio |
| *Ramadân* One of the odd-numbered nights in the last 10 of the month | Laylat al-Qadr (Night of Powe |
| *Dhû'l-Hijjah* 10 | Id al-Adha (Festival of Sacrifice |

## THE SIKH CALENDAR

The Sikh calendar is a lunar calendar of 365 days divide into 12 months. The length of the months varies betwee 29 and 32 days.

There are no prescribed feast days and no fastin periods. The main celebrations are Baisakhi Mela (the ne year and the anniversary of the founding of the Khalsa Diwali Mela (festival of light), Hola Mohalla Mela ( spring festival held in the Punjab), and the Gurpurb (anniversaries associated with the ten Gurus).

For dates of the major celebrations in 2002, *see* page 9

## CIVIL AND LEGAL CALENDAR

### THE HISTORICAL YEAR

Before 1752, two calendar systems were used in Englanc The civil or legal year began on 25 March and th historical year on 1 January. Thus the civil or legal date 2 March 1658 was the same day as the historical date 2 March 1659; a date in that portion of the year is written a 24 March 165$^{8}/_{9}$, the lower figure showing the historica year.

### THE NEW YEAR

In England in the seventh century, and as late as the 13th the year was reckoned from Christmas Day, but in the 12t century the Church in England began the year with th feast of the Annunciation of the Blessed Virgin ('Lad Day') on 25 March and this practice was adopted generall in the 14th century. The civil or legal year in the Britis Dominions (exclusive of Scotland) began with Lady Da until 1751. But in and since 1752 the civil year has begu with 1 January. New Year's Day in Scotland was change from 25 March to 1 January in 1600.

Elsewhere in Europe, 1 January was adopted as the firs day of the year by Venice in 1522, German states in 1544 Spain, Portugal and the Roman Catholic Netherlands i 1556, Prussia, Denmark and Sweden in 1559, France i 1564, Lorraine in 1579, the Protestant Netherlands i 1583, Russia in 1725, and Tuscany in 1751.

GNAL YEARS

gnal years are the years of a sovereign's reign and each ins on the anniversary of his or her accession, e.g. nal year 51 of the present Queen begins on 6 February 2.

The system was used for dating Acts of Parliament until 2. The Summer Time Act 1925, for example, is quoted 5 and 16 Geo. V c. 64, because it became law in the liamentary session which extended over part of both of se regnal years. Acts of a parliamentary session during ch a sovereign died were usually given two year nbers, the regnal year of the deceased sovereign and regnal year of his or her successor, e.g. those passed 952 were dated 16 Geo. VI and 1 Elizabeth II. Since 2 Acts of Parliament have been dated by the calendar r.

ARTER AND TERM DAYS

ly days and saints days were the usual means in early es for setting the dates of future and recurrent ointments. The quarter days in England and Wales the feast of the Nativity (25 December), the feast of the nunciation (25 March), the feast of St John the Baptist June) and the feast of St Michael and All Angels (29 tember).

The term days in Scotland are Candlemas (the feast of Purification), Whitsunday, Lammas (Loaf Mass), and rtinmas (St Martin's Day). These fell on 2 February, 15 y, 1 August and 11 November respectively. However, the Term and Quarter Days (Scotland) Act 1990, the es of the term days were changed to 28 February ndlemas), 28 May (Whitsunday), 28 August (Lammas) 28 November (Martinmas).

D-LETTER DAYS

l-letter days were originally the holy days and saints s indicated in early ecclesiastical calendars by letters nted in red ink. The days to be distinguished in this way e approved at the Council of Nicaea in AD 325.

These days still have a legal significance, as judges of the een's Bench Division wear scarlet robes on red-letter s falling during the law sittings. The days designated as -letter days for this purpose are:

*y and saints days*

e Conversion of St Paul, the Purification, Ash Wednes-, the Annunciation, the Ascension, the feasts of St rk, SS Philip and James, St Matthias, St Barnabas, St n the Baptist, St Peter, St Thomas, St James, St Luke, Simon and Jude, All Saints, St Andrew

*il calendar* (for dates, *see* page 9)

e anniversaries of The Queen's accession, The Queen's hday and The Queen's coronation, The Queen's cial birthday, the birthday of the Duke of Edinburgh, birthday of Queen Elizabeth the Queen Mother, the hday of the Prince of Wales, St David's Day and Lord yor's Day

BLIC HOLIDAYS

blic holidays are divided into two categories, common and statutory. Common law holidays are holidays 'by it and custom'; in England, Wales and Northern and these are Good Friday and Christmas Day.

Statutory public holidays, known as bank holidays, were t established by the Bank Holidays Act 1871. They e, literally, days on which the banks (and other public itutions) were closed and financial obligations due on t day were payable the following day. The legislation rently governing public holidays in the UK, which is Banking and Financial Dealings Act 1971, stipulates the days that are to be public holidays in England, Wales, Scotland and Northern Ireland.

Certain holidays (indicated by * below) are granted annually by royal proclamation, either throughout the UK or in any place in the UK. The public holidays are:

*England and Wales*

*New Year's Day
Easter Monday
*The first Monday in May
The last Monday in May
The last Monday in August
26 December, if it is not a Sunday
27 December when 25 or 26 December is a Sunday

*Scotland*

New Year's Day, or if it is a Sunday, 2 January
2 January, or if it is a Sunday, 3 January
Good Friday
The first Monday in May
*The last Monday in May
The first Monday in August
Christmas Day, or if it is a Sunday, 26 December
*Boxing Day – if Christmas Day falls on a Sunday, 26 December is given in lieu and an alternative day is given for Boxing Day

*Northern Ireland*

New Year's Day
7 March, or if it is a Sunday, 18 March
Easter Monday
*The first Monday in May
The last Monday in May
*12 July, or if it is a Sunday, 13 July
The last Monday in August
26 December, if it is not a Sunday
27 December if 25 or 26 December is a Sunday

For dates of public holidays in 2002 and 2003, *see* pages 10–11.

---

## CHRONOLOGICAL CYCLES AND ERAS

---

SOLAR (OR MAJOR) CYCLE

The solar cycle is a period of twenty-eight years in any corresponding year of which the days of the week recur on the same day of the month.

METONIC (LUNAR, OR MINOR) CYCLE

In 432 BC, Meton, an Athenian astronomer, found that 235 lunations are very nearly, though not exactly, equal in duration to 19 solar years and so after 19 years the phases of the Moon recur on the same days of the month (nearly). The dates of full moon in a cycle of 19 years were inscribed in figures of gold on public monuments in Athens, and the number showing the position of a year in the cycle is called the golden number of that year.

JULIAN PERIOD

The Julian period was proposed by Joseph Scaliger in 1582. The period is 7980 Julian years, and its first year coincides with the year 4713 BC. The figure of 7980 is the product of the number of years in the solar cycle, the Metonic cycle and the cycle of the Roman indiction (28 × 19 × 15).

## Roman Indiction

The Roman indiction is a period of fifteen years, instituted for fiscal purposes about AD 300.

## Epact

The epact is the age of the calendar Moon, diminished by one day, on 1 January, in the ecclesiastical lunar calendar.

## Chinese Calendar

A lunar calendar was the sole calendar in use in China until 1911, when the government adopted the new (Gregorian) calendar for official and most business activities. The Chinese tend to follow both calendars, the lunar calendar playing an important part in personal life, e.g. birth celebrations, festivals, marriages; and in rural villages the lunar calendar dictates the cycle of activities, denoting the change of weather and farming activities.

The lunar calendar is used in Hong Kong, Singapore, Malaysia, Tibet and elsewhere in south-east Asia. The calendar has a cycle of 60 years. The new year begins at the first new moon after the sun enters the sign of Aquarius, i.e. the new year falls between 21 January and 19 February in the Gregorian calendar.

Each year in the Chinese calendar is associated with one of 12 animals: the rat, the ox, the tiger, the rabbit, the dragon, the snake, the horse, the goat or sheep, the monkey, the chicken or rooster, the dog, and the pig.

The date of the Chinese new year and the astrological sign for the years 2001–2005 are:

| | | |
|---|---|---|
| 2001 | 24 January | Snake |
| 2002 | 12 February | Horse |
| 2003 | 1 February | Goat or Sheep |
| 2004 | 22 January | Monkey |
| 2005 | 9 February | Chicken or Rooster |

## Coptic Calendar

In the Coptic calendar, which is used in parts of Egypt and Ethiopia, the year is made up of 12 months of 30 days each, followed, in general, by five complementary days. Every fourth year is an intercalary or leap year and in these years there are six complementary days. The intercalary year of the Coptic calendar immediately precedes the leap year of the Julian calendar. The era is that of Diocletian or the Martyrs, the origin of which is fixed at 29 August AD 284 (Julian date).

## Indian Eras

In addition to the Muslim reckoning, other eras are used in India. The Saka era of southern India, dating from 3 March AD 78, was declared the national calendar of the Republic of India with effect from 22 March 1957, to be used concurrently with the Gregorian calendar. As revised, the year of the new Saka era begins at the spring equinox, with five successive months of 31 days and seven of 30 days in ordinary years, and six months of each length in leap years. The year AD 2002 is 1924 of the revised Saka era.

The year AD 2002 corresponds to the following years in other eras:

Year 2059 of the Vikram Samvat era
Year 1409 of the Bengali San era
Year 1178 of the Kollam era
Vedanga Jyotisa year 3 of the five-yearly cycle (385th cycle of Paitamah Siddhanta)
Year 6003 of the Kaliyuga era
Year 2546 of the Buddha Nirvana era

## Japanese Calendar

The Japanese calendar is essentially the same as [illegible] Gregorian calendar, the years, months and weeks being the same length and beginning on the same days as those the Gregorian calendar. The numeration of the years different, based on a system of epochs or periods each which begins at the accession of an Emperor or ot[illegible] important occurrence. The method is not unlike t British system of regnal years, except that each year o period closes on 31 December. The Japanese chronolo begins about AD 650 and the three latest epochs are defir by the reigns of Emperors, whose actual names are [illegible] necessarily used:

*Epoch*
Taishō 1 August 1912 to 25 December 1926
Shōwa 26 December 1926 to 7 January 1989
Heisei 8 January 1989

The year Heisei 14 begins on 1 January 2002.

The months are known as First Month, Second Mon etc., First Month being equivalent to January. The days the week are Nichiyōbi (Sun-day), Getsuyōbi (Moc day), Kayōbi (Fire-day), Suiyōbi (Water-day), Mokuy (Wood-day), Kinyōbi (Metal-day), Doyōbi (Earth-day

## The Masonic Year

Two dates are quoted in warrants, dispensations, e[illegible] issued by the United Grand Lodge of England, those [illegible] the current year being expressed as *Anno Domini* 200[illegible] *Anno Lucis* 6000. This *Anno Lucis* (year of light) is based the Book of Genesis 1:3, the 4000-year difference be[illegible] derived, in modified form, from *Ussher's Notation*, pu lished in 1654, which places the Creation of the World 4004 BC.

## Olympiads

Ancient Greek chronology was reckoned in Olympia cycles of four years corresponding with the perio Olympic Games held on the plain of Olympia in Elis or every four years. The intervening years were the fi second, etc., of the Olympiad, which received the name the victor at the Games. The first recorded Olympiad that of Choroebus, 776 BC.

## Zoroastrian Calendar

Zoroastrians, followers of the Iranian prophet Zarathus tra (known to the Greeks as Zoroaster) are mostly to found in Iran and in India, where they are known Parsees.

The Zoroastrian era dates from the coronation of [illegible] last Zoroastrian Sasanian king in AD 631. The Zoroastri calendar is divided into twelve months, each comprisi 30 days, followed by five holy days of the Gathas at the e of each year to make the year consist of 365 days.

In order to synchronize the calendar with the solar y of 365 days, an extra month was intercalated once eve 120 years. However, this intercalation ceased in the 1 century and the New Year, which had fallen in the spri slipped back to August. Because intercalation ceased different times in Iran and India, there was one mont difference between the calendar followed in Iran (Kad calendar) and that followed by the Parsees (Shens calendar). In 1906 a group of Zoroastrians decided bring the calendar back in line with the seasons again a restore the New Year to 21 March each year (Fa calendar).

The Shenshai calendar (New Year in August) is mai used by Parsees. The Fasli calendar (New Year, 21 Mar is mainly used by Zoroastrians living in Iran, in the Indi subcontinent, or away from Iran.

## E ROMAN CALENDAR

nan historians adopted as an epoch the foundation of ne, which is believed to have happened in the year 753 The ordinal number of the years in Roman reckoning llowed by the letters AUC (*ab urbe condita*), so that the 2002 is 2755 AUC (MMDCCLV). The calendar that know has developed from one said to have been blished by Romulus using a year of 304 days divided ten months, beginning with March. To this Numa ed January and February, making the year consist of 12 nths of 30 and 29 days alternately, with an additional so that the total was 355. It is also said that Numa ered an intercalary month of 22 or 23 days in alternate rs, making 90 days in eight years, to be inserted after 23 ruary.

Iowever, there is some doubt as to the origination and details of the intercalation in the Roman calendar. It is ain that some scheme of this kind was inaugurated and fully carried out, for in the year 46 BC Julius Caesar found that the calendar had been allowed to fall into some confusion. He sought the help of the Egyptian astronomer Sosigenes, which led to the construction and adoption (45 BC) of the Julian calendar, and, by a slight alteration, to the Gregorian calendar now in use. The year 46 BC was made to consist of 445 days and is called the Year of Confusion.

In the Roman (Julian) calendar the days of the month were counted backwards from three fixed points, or days, and an intervening day was said to be so many days before the next coming point, the first and last being counted. These three points were the Kalends, the Nones, and the Ides. Their positions in the months and the method of counting from them will be seen in the table below. The year containing 366 days was called *bissextillis annus*, as it had a doubled sixth day (*bissextus dies*) before the March Kalends on 24 February – *ante diem sextum Kalendas Martias*, or a.d. VI Kal. Mart.

| *ent of month* | *March, May, July, October have thirty-one days* | *January, August, December have thirty-one day* | *April, June, September, November have thirty day* | *February has twenty-eight days, and in leap year twenty-nine* |
|---|---|---|---|---|
| | Kalendis | Kalendis | Kalendis | Kalendis |
| | VI | IV ante | IV ante | IV ante |
| | V ante | III Nonas | III Nonas | III Nonas |
| | IV Nonas | pridie Nonas | pridie Nonas | pridie Nonas |
| | III | Nonis | Nonis | Nonis |
| | pridie Nonas | VIII | VIII | VIII |
| | Nonis | VII | VII | VII |
| | VIII | VI ante | VI ante | VI ante |
| | VII | V Idus | V Idus | V Idus |
| | VI ante | IV | IV | IV |
| | V Idus | III | III | III |
| | IV | pridie Idus | pridie Idus | pridie Idus |
| | III | Idibus | Idibus | Idibus |
| | pridie Idus | XIX | XVIII | XVI |
| | Idibus | XVIII | XVII | XV |
| | XVII | XVII | XVI | XIV |
| | XVI | XVI | XV | XIII |
| | XV | XV | XIV | XII |
| | XIV | XIV | XIII | XI |
| | XIII | XIII | XII ante Kalendas | X ante |
| | XII | XII ante Kalendas | XI (of the month | IX Kalendas |
| | XI ante Kalendas | XI (of the month | X following) | VIII Martias |
| | X (of the month | X following) | IX | VII |
| | IX following) | IX | VIII | *VI |
| | VIII | VIII | VII | V |
| | VII | VII | VI | IV |
| | VI | VI | V | III |
| | V | V | IV | pridie Kalendas |
| | IV | IV | III | |
| | III | III | pridie Kalendas (Maias, Quinctilis, Octobris, Decembris) | |
| | pridie Kalendas (Aprilis, Iunias, Sextilis, Novembris) | pridie Kalendas (Februarias, Septembris, Ianuarias) | | |

* (repeated in leap year)

# Calendar for Any Year 1780–2040

To select the correct calendar for any year between 1780 and 2040, consult the index below
* leap year

| Year | | Year | | Year | | Year | | Year | | Year | | Year | | Year |
|---|---|---|---|---|---|---|---|---|---|---|---|---|---|---|
| 1780 | N* | 1813 | K | 1846 | I | 1879 | G | 1912 | D* | 1945 | C | 1978 | A | 2011 |
| 1781 | C | 1814 | M | 1847 | K | 1880 | J* | 1913 | G | 1946 | E | 1979 | C | 2012 |
| 1782 | E | 1815 | A | 1848 | N* | 1881 | M | 1914 | I | 1947 | G | 1980 | F* | 2013 |
| 1783 | G | 1816 | D* | 1849 | C | 1882 | A | 1915 | K | 1948 | J* | 1981 | I | 2014 |
| 1784 | J* | 1817 | G | 1850 | E | 1883 | C | 1916 | N* | 1949 | M | 1982 | K | 2015 |
| 1785 | M | 1818 | I | 1851 | G | 1884 | F* | 1917 | C | 1950 | A | 1983 | M | 2016 |
| 1786 | A | 1819 | K | 1852 | J* | 1885 | I | 1918 | E | 1951 | C | 1984 | B* | 2017 |
| 1787 | C | 1820 | N* | 1853 | M | 1886 | K | 1919 | G | 1952 | F* | 1985 | E | 2018 |
| 1788 | F* | 1821 | C | 1854 | A | 1887 | M | 1920 | J* | 1953 | I | 1986 | G | 2019 |
| 1789 | I | 1822 | E | 1855 | C | 1888 | B* | 1921 | M | 1954 | K | 1987 | I | 2020 |
| 1790 | K | 1823 | G | 1856 | F* | 1889 | E | 1922 | A | 1955 | M | 1988 | L* | 2021 |
| 1791 | M | 1824 | J* | 1857 | I | 1890 | G | 1923 | C | 1956 | B* | 1989 | A | 2022 |
| 1792 | B* | 1825 | M | 1858 | K | 1891 | I | 1924 | F* | 1957 | E | 1990 | C | 2023 |
| 1793 | E | 1826 | A | 1859 | M | 1892 | L* | 1925 | I | 1958 | G | 1991 | E | 2024 |
| 1794 | G | 1827 | C | 1860 | B* | 1893 | A | 1926 | K | 1959 | I | 1992 | H* | 2025 |
| 1795 | I | 1828 | F* | 1861 | E | 1894 | C | 1927 | M | 1960 | L* | 1993 | K | 2026 |
| 1796 | L* | 1829 | I | 1862 | G | 1895 | E | 1928 | B* | 1961 | A | 1994 | M | 2027 |
| 1797 | A | 1830 | K | 1863 | I | 1896 | H* | 1929 | E | 1962 | C | 1995 | A | 2028 |
| 1798 | C | 1831 | M | 1864 | L* | 1897 | K | 1930 | G | 1963 | E | 1996 | D* | 2029 |
| 1799 | E | 1832 | B* | 1865 | A | 1898 | M | 1931 | I | 1964 | H* | 1997 | G | 2030 |
| 1800 | G | 1833 | E | 1866 | C | 1899 | A | 1932 | L* | 1965 | K | 1998 | I | 2031 |
| 1801 | I | 1834 | G | 1867 | E | 1900 | C | 1933 | A | 1966 | M | 1999 | K | 2032 |
| 1802 | K | 1835 | I | 1868 | H* | 1901 | E | 1934 | C | 1967 | A | 2000 | N* | 2033 |
| 1803 | M | 1836 | L* | 1869 | K | 1902 | G | 1935 | E | 1968 | D* | 2001 | C | 2034 |
| 1804 | B* | 1837 | A | 1870 | M | 1903 | I | 1936 | H* | 1969 | G | 2002 | E | 2035 |
| 1805 | E | 1838 | C | 1871 | A | 1904 | L* | 1937 | K | 1970 | I | 2003 | G | 2036 |
| 1806 | G | 1839 | E | 1872 | D* | 1905 | A | 1938 | M | 1971 | K | 2004 | J* | 2037 |
| 1807 | I | 1840 | H* | 1873 | G | 1906 | C | 1939 | A | 1972 | N* | 2005 | M | 2038 |
| 1808 | L* | 1841 | K | 1874 | I | 1907 | E | 1940 | D* | 1973 | C | 2006 | A | 2039 |
| 1809 | A | 1842 | M | 1875 | K | 1908 | H* | 1941 | G | 1974 | E | 2007 | C | 2040 |
| 1810 | C | 1843 | A | 1876 | N* | 1909 | K | 1942 | I | 1975 | G | 2008 | F* | |
| 1811 | E | 1844 | D* | 1877 | C | 1910 | M | 1943 | K | 1976 | J* | 2009 | I | |
| 1812 | H* | 1845 | G | 1878 | E | 1911 | A | 1944 | N* | 1977 | M | 2010 | K | |

## A

| | *January* | *February* | *March* |
|---|---|---|---|
| Sun. | 1 8 15 22 29 | 5 12 19 26 | 5 12 19 26 |
| Mon. | 2 9 16 23 30 | 6 13 20 27 | 6 13 20 27 |
| Tue. | 3 10 17 24 31 | 7 14 21 28 | 7 14 21 28 |
| Wed. | 4 11 18 25 | 1 8 15 22 | 1 8 15 22 29 |
| Thur. | 5 12 19 26 | 2 9 16 23 | 2 9 16 23 30 |
| Fri. | 6 13 20 27 | 3 10 17 24 | 3 10 17 24 31 |
| Sat. | 7 14 21 28 | 4 11 18 25 | 4 11 18 25 |

| | *April* | *May* | *June* |
|---|---|---|---|
| Sun. | 2 9 16 23 30 | 7 14 21 28 | 4 11 18 25 |
| Mon. | 3 10 17 24 | 1 8 15 22 29 | 5 12 19 26 |
| Tue. | 4 11 18 25 | 2 9 16 23 30 | 6 13 20 27 |
| Wed. | 5 12 19 26 | 3 10 17 24 31 | 7 14 21 28 |
| Thur. | 6 13 20 27 | 4 11 18 25 | 1 8 15 22 29 |
| Fri. | 7 14 21 28 | 5 12 19 26 | 2 9 16 23 30 |
| Sat. | 1 8 15 22 29 | 6 13 20 27 | 3 10 17 24 |

| | *July* | *August* | *September* |
|---|---|---|---|
| Sun. | 2 9 16 23 30 | 6 13 20 27 | 3 10 17 24 |
| Mon. | 3 10 17 24 31 | 7 14 21 28 | 4 11 18 25 |
| Tue. | 4 11 18 25 | 1 8 15 22 29 | 5 12 19 26 |
| Wed. | 5 12 19 26 | 2 9 16 23 30 | 6 13 20 27 |
| Thur. | 6 13 20 27 | 3 10 17 24 31 | 7 14 21 28 |
| Fri. | 7 14 21 28 | 4 11 18 25 | 1 8 15 22 29 |
| Sat. | 1 8 15 22 29 | 5 12 19 26 | 2 9 16 23 30 |

| | *October* | *November* | *December* |
|---|---|---|---|
| Sun. | 1 8 15 22 29 | 5 12 19 26 | 3 10 17 24 31 |
| Mon. | 2 9 16 23 30 | 6 13 20 27 | 4 11 18 25 |
| Tue. | 3 10 17 24 31 | 7 14 21 28 | 5 12 19 26 |
| Wed. | 4 11 18 25 | 1 8 15 22 29 | 6 13 20 27 |
| Thur. | 5 12 19 26 | 2 9 16 23 30 | 7 14 21 28 |
| Fri. | 6 13 20 27 | 3 10 17 24 | 1 8 15 22 29 |
| Sat. | 7 14 21 28 | 4 11 18 25 | 2 9 16 23 30 |

Easter Days
March 26 1815, 1826, 1837, 1967, 1978, 1989
April 2 1809, 1893, 1899, 1961
April 9 1871, 1882, 1939, 1950, 2023, 2034
April 16 1786, 1797, 1843, 1854, 1865, 1911
1922, 1933, 1995, 2006, 2017
April 23 1905

## B (leap year)

| | *January* | *February* | *March* |
|---|---|---|---|
| Sun. | 1 8 15 22 29 | 5 12 19 26 | 4 11 18 25 |
| Mon. | 2 9 16 23 30 | 6 13 20 27 | 5 12 19 26 |
| Tue. | 3 10 17 24 31 | 7 14 21 28 | 6 13 20 27 |
| Wed. | 4 11 18 25 | 1 8 15 22 29 | 7 14 21 28 |
| Thur. | 5 12 19 26 | 2 9 16 23 | 1 8 15 22 29 |
| Fri. | 6 13 20 27 | 3 10 17 24 | 2 9 16 23 30 |
| Sat. | 7 14 21 28 | 4 11 18 25 | 3 10 17 24 31 |

| | *April* | *May* | *June* |
|---|---|---|---|
| Sun. | 1 8 15 22 29 | 6 13 20 27 | 3 10 17 24 |
| Mon. | 2 9 16 23 30 | 7 14 21 28 | 4 11 18 25 |
| Tue. | 3 10 17 24 | 1 8 15 22 29 | 5 12 19 26 |
| Wed. | 4 11 18 25 | 2 9 16 23 30 | 6 13 20 27 |
| Thur. | 5 12 19 26 | 3 10 17 24 31 | 7 14 21 28 |
| Fri. | 6 13 20 27 | 4 11 18 25 | 1 8 15 22 29 |
| Sat. | 7 14 21 28 | 5 12 19 26 | 2 9 16 23 30 |

| | *July* | *August* | *September* |
|---|---|---|---|
| Sun. | 1 8 15 22 29 | 5 12 19 26 | 2 9 16 23 |
| Mon. | 2 9 16 23 30 | 6 13 20 27 | 3 10 17 24 |
| Tue. | 3 10 17 24 31 | 7 14 21 28 | 4 11 18 25 |
| Wed. | 4 11 18 25 | 1 8 15 22 29 | 5 12 19 26 |
| Thur. | 5 12 19 26 | 2 9 16 23 30 | 6 13 20 27 |
| Fri. | 6 13 20 27 | 3 10 17 24 31 | 7 14 21 28 |
| Sat. | 7 14 21 28 | 4 11 18 25 | 1 8 15 22 29 |

| | *October* | *November* | *December* |
|---|---|---|---|
| Sun. | 7 14 21 28 | 4 11 18 25 | 2 9 16 23 |
| Mon. | 1 8 15 22 29 | 5 12 19 26 | 3 10 17 24 |
| Tue. | 2 9 16 23 30 | 6 13 20 27 | 4 11 18 25 |
| Wed. | 3 10 17 24 31 | 7 14 21 28 | 5 12 19 26 |
| Thur. | 4 11 18 25 | 1 8 15 22 29 | 6 13 20 27 |
| Fri. | 5 12 19 26 | 2 9 16 23 30 | 7 14 21 28 |
| Sat. | 6 13 20 27 | 3 10 17 24 | 1 8 15 22 29 |

Easter Days
April 1 1804, 1888, 1956, 2040
April 8 1792, 1860, 1928, 2012
April 22 1832, 1984

| | *January* | *February* | *March* |
|---|---|---|---|
| n. | 7 14 21 28 | 4 11 18 25 | 4 11 18 25 |
| n. | 1 8 15 22 29 | 5 12 19 26 | 5 12 19 26 |
| e. | 2 9 16 23 30 | 6 13 20 27 | 6 13 20 27 |
| d. | 3 10 17 24 31 | 7 14 21 28 | 7 14 21 28 |
| ur. | 4 11 18 25 | 1 8 15 22 | 1 8 15 22 29 |
| | 5 12 19 26 | 2 9 16 23 | 2 9 16 23 30 |
| | 6 13 20 27 | 3 10 17 24 | 3 10 17 24 31 |

| | *April* | *May* | *June* |
|---|---|---|---|
| n. | 1 8 15 22 29 | 6 13 20 27 | 3 10 17 24 |
| n. | 2 9 16 23 30 | 7 14 21 28 | 4 11 18 25 |
| e. | 3 10 17 24 | 1 8 15 22 29 | 5 12 19 26 |
| d. | 4 11 18 25 | 2 9 16 23 30 | 6 13 20 27 |
| ur. | 5 12 19 26 | 3 10 17 24 31 | 7 14 21 28 |
| | 6 13 20 27 | 4 11 18 25 | 1 8 15 22 29 |
| | 7 14 21 28 | 5 12 19 26 | 2 9 16 23 30 |

| | *July* | *August* | *September* |
|---|---|---|---|
| n. | 1 8 15 22 29 | 5 12 19 26 | 2 9 16 23 30 |
| n. | 2 9 16 23 30 | 6 13 20 27 | 3 10 17 24 |
| e. | 3 10 17 24 31 | 7 14 21 28 | 4 11 18 25 |
| d. | 4 11 18 25 | 1 8 15 22 29 | 5 12 19 26 |
| ur. | 5 12 19 26 | 2 9 16 23 30 | 6 13 20 27 |
| | 6 13 20 27 | 3 10 17 24 31 | 7 14 21 28 |
| | 7 14 21 28 | 4 11 18 25 | 1 8 15 22 29 |

| | *October* | *November* | *December* |
|---|---|---|---|
| n. | 7 14 21 28 | 4 11 18 25 | 2 9 16 23 30 |
| n. | 1 8 15 22 29 | 5 12 19 26 | 3 10 17 24 31 |
| e. | 2 9 16 23 30 | 6 13 20 27 | 4 11 18 25 |
| d. | 3 10 17 24 31 | 7 14 21 28 | 5 12 19 26 |
| ur. | 4 11 18 25 | 1 8 15 22 29 | 6 13 20 27 |
| | 5 12 19 26 | 2 9 16 23 30 | 7 14 21 28 |
| | 6 13 20 27 | 3 10 17 24 | 1 8 15 22 29 |

STER DAYS
rch 25 1883, 1894, 1951, 2035
il 1 1866, 1877, 1923, 1934, 1945, 2018, 2029
il 8 1787, 1798, 1849, 1855, 1917, 2007
il 15 1781, 1827, 1838, 1900, 1906, 1979, 1990, 2001
il 22 1810, 1821, 1962, 1973

## E

| | *January* | *February* | *March* |
|---|---|---|---|
| Sun. | 6 13 20 27 | 3 10 17 24 | 3 10 17 24 31 |
| Mon. | 7 14 21 28 | 4 11 18 25 | 4 11 18 25 |
| Tue. | 1 8 15 22 29 | 5 12 19 26 | 5 12 19 26 |
| Wed. | 2 9 16 23 30 | 6 13 20 27 | 6 13 20 27 |
| Thur. | 3 10 17 24 31 | 7 14 21 28 | 7 14 21 28 |
| Fri. | 4 11 18 25 | 1 8 15 22 | 1 8 15 22 29 |
| Sat. | 5 12 19 26 | 2 9 16 23 | 2 9 16 23 30 |

| | *April* | *May* | *June* |
|---|---|---|---|
| Sun. | 7 14 21 28 | 5 12 19 26 | 2 9 16 23 30 |
| Mon. | 1 8 15 22 29 | 6 13 20 27 | 3 10 17 24 |
| Tue. | 2 9 16 23 30 | 7 14 21 28 | 4 11 18 25 |
| Wed. | 3 10 17 24 | 1 8 15 22 29 | 5 12 19 26 |
| Thur. | 4 11 18 25 | 2 9 16 23 30 | 6 13 20 27 |
| Fri. | 5 12 19 26 | 3 10 17 24 31 | 7 14 21 28 |
| Sat. | 6 13 20 27 | 4 11 18 25 | 1 8 15 22 29 |

| | *July* | *August* | *September* |
|---|---|---|---|
| Sun. | 7 14 21 28 | 4 11 18 25 | 1 8 15 22 29 |
| Mon. | 1 8 15 22 29 | 5 12 19 26 | 2 9 16 23 30 |
| Tue. | 2 9 16 23 30 | 6 13 20 27 | 3 10 17 24 |
| Wed. | 3 10 17 24 31 | 7 14 21 28 | 4 11 18 25 |
| Thur. | 4 11 18 25 | 1 8 15 22 29 | 5 12 19 26 |
| Fri. | 5 12 19 26 | 2 9 16 23 30 | 6 13 20 27 |
| Sat. | 6 13 20 27 | 3 10 17 24 31 | 7 14 21 28 |

| | *October* | *November* | *December* |
|---|---|---|---|
| Sun. | 6 13 20 27 | 3 10 17 24 | 1 8 15 22 29 |
| Mon. | 7 14 21 28 | 4 11 18 25 | 2 9 16 23 30 |
| Tue. | 1 8 15 22 29 | 5 12 19 26 | 3 10 17 24 31 |
| Wed. | 2 9 16 23 30 | 6 13 20 27 | 4 11 18 25 |
| Thur. | 3 10 17 24 31 | 7 14 21 28 | 5 12 19 26 |
| Fri. | 4 11 18 25 | 1 8 15 22 29 | 6 13 20 27 |
| Sat. | 5 12 19 26 | 2 9 16 23 30 | 7 14 21 28 |

EASTER DAYS
March 24 1799
March 31 1782, 1793, 1839, 1850, 1861, 1907, 1918, 1929, 1991, 2002, 2013
April 7 1822, 1833, 1901, 1985
April 14 1805, 1811, 1895, 1963, 1974
April 21 1867, 1878, 1889, 1935, 1946, 1957, 2019, 2030

## (LEAP YEAR)

| | *January* | *February* | *March* |
|---|---|---|---|
| n. | 7 14 21 28 | 4 11 18 25 | 3 10 17 24 31 |
| n. | 1 8 15 22 29 | 5 12 19 26 | 4 11 18 25 |
| e. | 2 9 16 23 30 | 6 13 20 27 | 5 12 19 26 |
| d. | 3 10 17 24 31 | 7 14 21 28 | 6 13 20 27 |
| ur. | 4 11 18 25 | 1 8 15 22 29 | 7 14 21 28 |
| | 5 12 19 26 | 2 9 16 23 | 1 8 15 22 29 |
| | 6 13 20 27 | 3 10 17 24 | 2 9 16 23 30 |

| | *April* | *May* | *June* |
|---|---|---|---|
| n. | 7 14 21 28 | 5 12 19 26 | 2 9 16 23 30 |
| n. | 1 8 15 22 29 | 6 13 20 27 | 3 10 17 24 |
| e. | 2 9 16 23 30 | 7 14 21 28 | 4 11 18 25 |
| d. | 3 10 17 24 | 1 8 15 22 29 | 5 12 19 26 |
| ur. | 4 11 18 25 | 2 9 16 23 30 | 6 13 20 27 |
| | 5 12 19 26 | 3 10 17 24 31 | 7 14 21 28 |
| | 6 13 20 27 | 4 11 18 25 | 1 8 15 22 29 |

| | *July* | *August* | *September* |
|---|---|---|---|
| n. | 7 14 21 28 | 4 11 18 25 | 1 8 15 22 29 |
| n. | 1 8 15 22 29 | 5 12 19 26 | 2 9 16 23 30 |
| e. | 2 9 16 23 30 | 6 13 20 27 | 3 10 17 24 |
| d. | 3 10 17 24 31 | 7 14 21 28 | 4 11 18 25 |
| ur. | 4 11 18 25 | 1 8 15 22 29 | 5 12 19 26 |
| | 5 12 19 26 | 2 9 16 23 30 | 6 13 20 27 |
| | 6 13 20 27 | 3 10 17 24 31 | 7 14 21 28 |

| | *October* | *November* | *December* |
|---|---|---|---|
| n. | 6 13 20 27 | 3 10 17 24 | 1 8 15 22 29 |
| n. | 7 14 21 28 | 4 11 18 25 | 2 9 16 23 30 |
| e. | 1 8 15 22 29 | 5 12 19 26 | 3 10 17 24 31 |
| d. | 2 9 16 23 30 | 6 13 20 27 | 4 11 18 25 |
| ur. | 3 10 17 24 31 | 7 14 21 28 | 5 12 19 26 |
| | 4 11 18 25 | 1 8 15 22 29 | 6 13 20 27 |
| | 5 12 19 26 | 2 9 16 23 30 | 7 14 21 28 |

STER DAYS
rch 24 1940
rch 31 1872, 2024
ril 7 1844, 1912, 1996
il 14 1816, 1968

## F (LEAP YEAR)

| | *January* | *February* | *March* |
|---|---|---|---|
| Sun. | 6 13 20 27 | 3 10 17 24 | 2 9 16 23 30 |
| Mon. | 7 14 21 28 | 4 11 18 25 | 3 10 17 24 31 |
| Tue. | 1 8 15 22 29 | 5 12 19 26 | 4 11 18 25 |
| Wed. | 2 9 16 23 30 | 6 13 20 27 | 5 12 19 26 |
| Thur. | 3 10 17 24 31 | 7 14 21 28 | 6 13 20 27 |
| Fri. | 4 11 18 25 | 1 8 15 22 29 | 7 14 21 28 |
| Sat. | 5 12 19 26 | 2 9 16 23 | 1 8 15 22 29 |

| | *April* | *May* | *June* |
|---|---|---|---|
| Sun. | 6 13 20 27 | 4 11 18 25 | 1 8 15 22 29 |
| Mon. | 7 14 21 28 | 5 12 19 26 | 2 9 16 23 30 |
| Tue. | 1 8 15 22 29 | 6 13 20 27 | 3 10 17 24 |
| Wed. | 2 9 16 23 30 | 7 14 21 28 | 4 11 18 25 |
| Thur. | 3 10 17 24 | 1 8 15 22 29 | 5 12 19 26 |
| Fri. | 4 11 18 25 | 2 9 16 23 30 | 6 13 20 27 |
| Sat. | 5 12 19 26 | 3 10 17 24 31 | 7 14 21 |

| | *July* | *August* | *September* |
|---|---|---|---|
| Sun. | 6 13 20 27 | 3 10 17 24 31 | 7 14 21 28 |
| Mon. | 7 14 21 28 | 4 11 18 25 | 1 8 15 22 29 |
| Tue. | 1 8 15 22 29 | 5 12 19 26 | 2 9 16 23 30 |
| Wed. | 2 9 16 23 30 | 6 13 20 27 | 3 10 17 24 |
| Thur. | 3 10 17 24 31 | 7 14 21 28 | 4 11 18 25 |
| Fri. | 4 11 18 25 | 1 8 15 22 29 | 5 12 19 26 |
| Sat. | 5 12 19 26 | 2 9 16 23 30 | 6 13 20 27 |

| | *October* | *November* | *December* |
|---|---|---|---|
| Sun. | 5 12 19 26 | 2 9 16 23 30 | 7 14 21 28 |
| Mon. | 6 13 20 27 | 3 10 17 24 | 1 8 15 22 29 |
| Tue. | 7 14 21 28 | 4 11 18 25 | 2 9 16 23 30 |
| Wed. | 1 8 15 22 29 | 5 12 19 26 | 3 10 17 24 31 |
| Thur. | 2 9 16 23 30 | 6 13 20 27 | 4 11 18 25 |
| Fri. | 3 10 17 24 31 | 7 14 21 28 | 5 12 19 26 |
| Sat. | 4 11 18 25 | 1 8 15 22 29 | 6 13 20 27 |

EASTER DAYS
March 23 1788, 1856, 2008
April 6 1828, 1980
April 13 1884, 1952, 2036
April 20 1924

## G

| | January | February | March |
|---|---|---|---|
| Sun. | 5 12 19 26 | 2 9 16 23 | 2 9 16 23 30 |
| Mon. | 6 13 20 27 | 3 10 17 24 | 3 10 17 24 31 |
| Tue. | 7 14 21 28 | 4 11 18 25 | 4 11 18 25 |
| Wed. | 1 8 15 22 29 | 5 12 19 26 | 5 12 19 26 |
| Thur. | 2 9 16 23 30 | 6 13 20 27 | 6 13 20 27 |
| Fri. | 3 10 17 24 31 | 7 14 21 28 | 7 14 21 28 |
| Sat. | 4 11 18 25 | 1 8 15 22 | 1 8 15 22 29 |

| | April | May | June |
|---|---|---|---|
| Sun. | 6 13 20 27 | 4 11 18 25 | 1 8 15 22 29 |
| Mon. | 7 14 21 28 | 5 12 19 26 | 2 9 16 23 30 |
| Tue. | 1 8 15 22 29 | 6 13 20 27 | 3 10 17 24 |
| Wed. | 2 9 16 23 30 | 7 14 21 28 | 4 11 18 25 |
| Thur. | 3 10 17 24 | 1 8 15 22 29 | 5 12 19 26 |
| Fri. | 4 11 18 25 | 2 9 16 23 30 | 6 13 20 27 |
| Sat. | 5 12 19 26 | 3 10 17 24 31 | 7 14 21 28 |

| | July | August | September |
|---|---|---|---|
| Sun. | 6 13 20 27 | 3 10 17 24 31 | 7 14 21 28 |
| Mon. | 7 14 21 28 | 4 11 18 25 | 1 8 15 22 29 |
| Tue. | 1 8 15 22 29 | 5 12 19 26 | 2 9 16 23 30 |
| Wed. | 2 9 16 23 30 | 6 13 20 27 | 3 10 17 24 |
| Thur. | 3 10 17 24 31 | 7 14 21 28 | 4 11 18 25 |
| Fri. | 4 11 18 25 | 1 8 15 22 29 | 5 12 19 26 |
| Sat. | 5 12 19 26 | 2 9 16 23 30 | 6 13 20 27 |

| | October | November | December |
|---|---|---|---|
| Sun. | 5 12 19 26 | 2 9 16 23 30 | 7 14 21 28 |
| Mon. | 6 13 20 27 | 3 10 17 24 | 1 8 15 22 29 |
| Tue. | 7 14 21 28 | 4 11 18 25 | 2 9 16 23 30 |
| Wed. | 1 8 15 22 29 | 5 12 19 26 | 3 10 17 24 31 |
| Thur. | 2 9 16 23 30 | 6 13 20 27 | 4 11 18 25 |
| Fri. | 3 10 17 24 31 | 7 14 21 28 | 5 12 19 26 |
| Sat. | 4 11 18 25 | 1 8 15 22 29 | 6 13 20 27 |

Easter Days

| | |
|---|---|
| March 23 | 1845, 1913 |
| March 30 | 1823, 1834, 1902, 1975, 1986, 1997 |
| April 6 | 1806, 1817, 1890, 1947, 1958, 1969 |
| April 13 | 1800, 1873, 1879, 1941, 2031 |
| April 20 | 1783, 1794, 1851, 1862, 1919, 1930, 2003, 2014, 2025 |

## H (leap year)

| | January | February | March |
|---|---|---|---|
| Sun. | 5 12 19 26 | 2 9 16 23 | 1 8 15 22 29 |
| Mon. | 6 13 20 27 | 3 10 17 24 | 2 9 16 23 30 |
| Tue. | 7 14 21 28 | 4 11 18 25 | 3 10 17 24 31 |
| Wed. | 1 8 15 22 29 | 5 12 19 26 | 4 11 18 25 |
| Thur. | 2 9 16 23 30 | 6 13 20 27 | 5 12 19 26 |
| Fri. | 3 10 17 24 31 | 7 14 21 28 | 6 13 20 27 |
| Sat. | 4 11 18 25 | 1 8 15 22 29 | 7 14 21 28 |

| | April | May | June |
|---|---|---|---|
| Sun. | 5 12 19 26 | 3 10 17 24 31 | 7 14 21 28 |
| Mon. | 6 13 20 27 | 4 11 18 25 | 1 8 15 22 29 |
| Tue. | 7 14 21 28 | 5 12 19 26 | 2 9 16 23 30 |
| Wed. | 1 8 15 22 29 | 6 13 20 27 | 3 10 17 24 |
| Thur. | 2 9 16 23 30 | 7 14 21 28 | 4 11 18 25 |
| Fri. | 3 10 17 24 | 1 8 15 22 29 | 5 12 19 26 |
| Sat. | 4 11 18 25 | 2 9 16 23 30 | 6 13 20 27 |

| | July | August | September |
|---|---|---|---|
| Sun. | 5 12 19 26 | 2 9 16 23 30 | 6 13 20 27 |
| Mon. | 6 13 20 27 | 3 10 17 24 31 | 7 14 21 28 |
| Tue. | 7 14 21 28 | 4 11 18 25 | 1 8 15 22 29 |
| Wed. | 1 8 15 22 29 | 5 12 19 26 | 2 9 16 23 30 |
| Thur. | 2 9 16 23 30 | 6 13 20 27 | 3 10 17 24 |
| Fri. | 3 10 17 24 31 | 7 14 21 28 | 4 11 18 25 |
| Sat. | 4 11 18 25 | 1 8 15 22 29 | 5 12 19 26 |

| | October | November | December |
|---|---|---|---|
| Sun. | 4 11 18 25 | 1 8 15 22 29 | 6 13 20 27 |
| Mon. | 5 12 19 26 | 2 9 16 23 30 | 7 14 21 28 |
| Tue. | 6 13 20 27 | 3 10 17 24 | 1 8 15 22 29 |
| Wed. | 7 14 21 28 | 4 11 18 25 | 2 9 16 23 30 |
| Thur. | 1 8 15 22 29 | 5 12 19 26 | 3 10 17 24 31 |
| Fri. | 2 9 16 23 30 | 6 13 20 27 | 4 11 18 25 |
| Sat. | 3 10 17 24 31 | 7 14 21 28 | 5 12 19 26 |

Easter Days

| | |
|---|---|
| March 29 | 1812, 1964 |
| April 5 | 1896 |
| April 12 | 1868, 1936, 2020 |
| April 19 | 1840, 1908, 1992 |

## I

| | January | February | March |
|---|---|---|---|
| Sun. | 4 11 18 25 | 1 8 15 22 | 1 8 15 22 |
| Mon. | 5 12 19 26 | 2 9 16 23 | 2 9 16 23 |
| Tue. | 6 13 20 27 | 3 10 17 24 | 3 10 17 24 |
| Wed. | 7 14 21 28 | 4 11 18 25 | 4 11 18 25 |
| Thur. | 1 8 15 22 29 | 5 12 19 26 | 5 12 19 26 |
| Fri. | 2 9 16 23 30 | 6 13 20 27 | 6 13 20 27 |
| Sat. | 3 10 17 24 31 | 7 14 21 28 | 7 14 21 28 |

| | April | May | June |
|---|---|---|---|
| Sun. | 5 12 19 26 | 3 10 17 24 31 | 7 14 21 |
| Mon. | 6 13 20 27 | 4 11 18 25 | 1 8 15 22 |
| Tue. | 7 14 21 28 | 5 12 19 26 | 2 9 16 23 |
| Wed. | 1 8 15 22 29 | 6 13 20 27 | 3 10 17 24 |
| Thur. | 2 9 16 23 30 | 7 14 21 28 | 4 11 18 25 |
| Fri. | 3 10 17 24 | 1 8 15 22 29 | 5 12 19 26 |
| Sat. | 4 11 18 25 | 2 9 16 23 30 | 6 13 20 27 |

| | July | August | September |
|---|---|---|---|
| Sun. | 5 12 19 26 | 2 9 16 23 30 | 6 13 20 |
| Mon. | 6 13 20 27 | 3 10 17 24 31 | 7 14 21 |
| Tue. | 7 14 21 28 | 4 11 18 25 | 1 8 15 22 |
| Wed. | 1 8 15 22 29 | 5 12 19 26 | 2 9 16 23 |
| Thur. | 2 9 16 23 30 | 6 13 20 27 | 3 10 17 24 |
| Fri. | 3 10 17 24 31 | 7 14 21 28 | 4 11 18 25 |
| Sat. | 4 11 18 25 | 1 8 15 22 29 | 5 12 19 26 |

| | October | November | December |
|---|---|---|---|
| Sun. | 4 11 18 25 | 1 8 15 22 29 | 6 13 20 |
| Mon. | 5 12 19 26 | 2 9 16 23 30 | 7 14 21 |
| Tue. | 6 13 20 27 | 3 10 17 24 | 1 8 15 22 |
| Wed. | 7 14 21 28 | 4 11 18 25 | 2 9 16 23 |
| Thur. | 1 8 15 22 29 | 5 12 19 26 | 3 10 17 24 |
| Fri. | 2 9 16 23 30 | 6 13 20 27 | 4 11 18 25 |
| Sat. | 3 10 17 24 31 | 7 14 21 28 | 5 12 19 26 |

Easter Days

| | |
|---|---|
| March 22 | 1818 |
| March 29 | 1807, 1891, 1959, 1970 |
| April 5 | 1795, 1801, 1863, 1874, 1885, 1931, 1942, 1953, 2015, 2026, 2037 |
| April 12 | 1789, 1846, 1857, 1903, 1914, 1925, 1998, 2009 |
| April 19 | 1829, 1835, 1981, 1987 |

## J (leap year)

| | January | February | March |
|---|---|---|---|
| Sun. | 4 11 18 25 | 1 8 15 22 29 | 7 14 21 28 |
| Mon. | 5 12 19 26 | 2 9 16 23 | 1 8 15 22 29 |
| Tue. | 6 13 20 27 | 3 10 17 24 | 2 9 16 23 30 |
| Wed. | 7 14 21 28 | 4 11 18 25 | 3 10 17 24 31 |
| Thur. | 1 8 15 22 29 | 5 12 19 26 | 4 11 18 25 |
| Fri. | 2 9 16 23 30 | 6 13 20 27 | 5 12 19 26 |
| Sat. | 3 10 17 24 31 | 7 14 21 28 | 6 13 20 27 |

| | April | May | June |
|---|---|---|---|
| Sun. | 4 11 18 25 | 2 9 16 23 30 | 6 13 20 27 |
| Mon. | 5 12 19 26 | 3 10 17 24 31 | 7 14 21 28 |
| Tue. | 6 13 20 27 | 4 11 18 25 | 1 8 15 22 29 |
| Wed. | 7 14 21 28 | 5 12 19 26 | 2 9 16 23 30 |
| Thur. | 1 8 15 22 29 | 6 13 20 27 | 3 10 17 24 |
| Fri. | 2 9 16 23 30 | 7 14 21 28 | 4 11 18 25 |
| Sat. | 3 10 17 24 | 1 8 15 22 29 | 5 12 19 26 |

| | July | August | September |
|---|---|---|---|
| Sun. | 4 11 18 25 | 1 8 15 22 29 | 5 12 19 26 |
| Mon. | 5 12 19 26 | 2 9 16 23 30 | 6 13 20 27 |
| Tue. | 6 13 20 27 | 3 10 17 24 31 | 7 14 21 28 |
| Wed. | 7 14 21 28 | 4 11 18 25 | 1 8 15 22 29 |
| Thur. | 1 8 15 22 29 | 5 12 19 26 | 2 9 16 23 30 |
| Fri. | 2 9 16 23 30 | 6 13 20 27 | 3 10 17 24 |
| Sat. | 3 10 17 24 31 | 7 14 21 28 | 4 11 18 25 |

| | October | November | December |
|---|---|---|---|
| Sun. | 3 10 17 24 31 | 7 14 21 28 | 5 12 19 26 |
| Mon. | 4 11 18 25 | 1 8 15 22 29 | 6 13 20 27 |
| Tue. | 5 12 19 26 | 2 9 16 23 30 | 7 14 21 28 |
| Wed. | 6 13 20 27 | 3 10 17 24 | 1 8 15 22 29 |
| Thur. | 7 14 21 28 | 4 11 18 25 | 2 9 16 23 30 |
| Fri. | 1 8 15 22 29 | 5 12 19 26 | 3 10 17 24 31 |
| Sat. | 2 9 16 23 30 | 6 13 20 27 | 4 11 18 25 |

Easter Days

| | |
|---|---|
| March 28 | 1880, 1948, 2032 |
| April 4 | 1920 |
| April 11 | 1784, 1852, 2004 |
| April 18 | 1824, 1976 |

| | *January* | *February* | *March* |
|---|---|---|---|
| n. | 3 10 17 24 31 | 7 14 21 28 | 7 14 21 28 |
| on. | 4 11 18 25 | 1 8 15 22 | 1 8 15 22 29 |
| e. | 5 12 19 26 | 2 9 16 23 | 2 9 16 23 30 |
| ed. | 6 13 20 27 | 3 10 17 24 | 3 10 17 24 31 |
| ur. | 7 14 21 28 | 4 11 18 25 | 4 11 18 25 |
| . | 1 8 15 22 29 | 5 12 19 26 | 5 12 19 26 |
| . | 2 9 16 23 30 | 6 13 20 27 | 6 13 20 27 |
| | *April* | *May* | *June* |
| n. | 4 11 18 25 | 2 9 16 23 30 | 6 13 20 27 |
| on. | 5 12 19 26 | 3 10 17 24 31 | 7 14 21 28 |
| e. | 6 13 20 27 | 4 11 18 25 | 1 8 15 22 29 |
| ed. | 7 14 21 28 | 5 12 19 26 | 2 9 16 23 30 |
| ur. | 1 8 15 22 29 | 6 13 20 27 | 3 10 17 24 |
| . | 2 9 16 23 30 | 7 14 21 28 | 4 11 18 25 |
| . | 3 10 17 24 | 1 8 15 22 29 | 5 12 19 26 |
| | *July* | *August* | *September* |
| n. | 4 11 18 25 | 1 8 15 22 29 | 5 12 19 26 |
| on. | 5 12 19 26 | 2 9 16 23 30 | 6 13 20 27 |
| e. | 6 13 20 27 | 3 10 17 24 31 | 7 14 21 28 |
| ed. | 7 14 21 28 | 4 11 18 25 | 1 8 15 22 29 |
| ur. | 1 8 15 22 29 | 5 12 19 26 | 2 9 16 23 30 |
| . | 2 9 16 23 30 | 6 13 20 27 | 3 10 17 24 |
| . | 3 10 17 24 31 | 7 14 21 28 | 4 11 18 25 |
| | *October* | *November* | *December* |
| n. | 3 10 17 24 31 | 7 14 21 28 | 5 12 19 26 |
| on. | 4 11 18 25 | 1 8 15 22 29 | 6 13 20 27 |
| e. | 5 12 19 26 | 2 9 16 23 30 | 7 14 21 28 |
| ed. | 6 13 20 27 | 3 10 17 24 | 1 8 15 22 29 |
| ur. | 7 14 21 28 | 4 11 18 25 | 2 9 16 23 30 |
| . | 1 8 15 22 29 | 5 12 19 26 | 3 10 17 24 31 |
| . | 2 9 16 23 30 | 6 13 20 27 | 4 11 18 25 |

ASTER DAYS
arch 28 1869, 1875, 1937, 2027
ril 4 1790, 1847, 1858, 1915, 1926, 1999, 2010, 2021
ril 11 1819, 1830, 1841, 1909, 1971, 1982, 1993
ril 18 1802, 1813, 1897, 1954, 1965
ril 25 1886, 1943, 2038

## M

| | *January* | *February* | *March* |
|---|---|---|---|
| Sun. | 2 9 16 23 30 | 6 13 20 27 | 6 13 20 27 |
| Mon. | 3 10 17 24 31 | 7 14 21 28 | 7 14 21 28 |
| Tue. | 4 11 18 25 | 1 8 15 22 | 1 8 15 22 29 |
| Wed. | 5 12 19 26 | 2 9 16 23 | 2 9 16 23 30 |
| Thur. | 6 13 20 27 | 3 10 17 24 | 3 10 17 24 31 |
| Fri. | 7 14 21 28 | 4 11 18 25 | 4 11 18 25 |
| Sat. | 1 8 15 22 29 | 5 12 19 26 | 5 12 19 26 |
| | *April* | *May* | *June* |
| Sun. | 3 10 17 24 | 1 8 15 22 29 | 5 12 19 26 |
| Mon. | 4 11 18 25 | 2 9 16 23 30 | 6 13 20 27 |
| Tue. | 5 12 19 26 | 3 10 17 24 31 | 7 14 21 28 |
| Wed. | 6 13 20 27 | 4 11 18 25 | 1 8 15 22 29 |
| Thur. | 7 14 21 28 | 5 12 19 26 | 2 9 16 23 30 |
| Fri. | 1 8 15 22 29 | 6 13 20 27 | 3 10 17 24 |
| Sat. | 2 9 16 23 30 | 7 14 21 28 | 4 11 18 25 |
| | *July* | *August* | *September* |
| Sun. | 3 10 17 24 31 | 7 14 21 28 | 4 11 18 25 |
| Mon. | 4 11 18 25 | 1 8 15 22 29 | 5 12 19 26 |
| Tue. | 5 12 19 26 | 2 9 16 23 30 | 6 13 20 27 |
| Wed. | 6 13 20 27 | 3 10 17 24 31 | 7 14 21 28 |
| Thur. | 7 14 21 28 | 4 11 18 25 | 1 8 15 22 29 |
| Fri. | 1 8 15 22 29 | 5 12 19 26 | 2 9 16 23 30 |
| Sat. | 2 9 16 23 30 | 6 13 20 27 | 3 10 17 24 |
| | *October* | *November* | *December* |
| Sun. | 2 9 16 23 30 | 6 13 20 27 | 4 11 18 25 |
| Mon. | 3 10 17 24 31 | 7 14 21 28 | 5 12 19 26 |
| Tue. | 4 11 18 25 | 1 8 15 22 29 | 6 13 20 27 |
| Wed. | 5 12 19 26 | 2 9 16 23 30 | 7 14 21 28 |
| Thur. | 6 13 20 27 | 3 10 17 24 | 1 8 15 22 29 |
| Fri. | 7 14 21 28 | 4 11 18 25 | 2 9 16 23 30 |
| Sat. | 1 8 15 22 29 | 5 12 19 26 | 3 10 17 24 31 |

EASTER DAYS
March 27 1785, 1842, 1853, 1910, 1921, 2005
April 3 1825, 1831, 1983, 1994
April 10 1803, 1814, 1887, 1898, 1955, 1966, 1977, 2039
April 17 1870, 1881, 1927, 1938, 1949, 2022, 2033
April 24 1791, 1859, 2011

## (LEAP YEAR)

| | *January* | *February* | *March* |
|---|---|---|---|
| n. | 3 10 17 24 31 | 7 14 21 28 | 6 13 20 27 |
| on. | 4 11 18 25 | 1 8 15 22 29 | 7 14 21 28 |
| e. | 5 12 19 26 | 2 9 16 23 | 1 8 15 22 29 |
| ed. | 6 13 20 27 | 3 10 17 24 | 2 9 16 23 30 |
| ur. | 7 14 21 28 | 4 11 18 25 | 3 10 17 24 31 |
| . | 1 8 15 22 29 | 5 12 19 26 | 4 11 18 25 |
| . | 2 9 16 23 30 | 6 13 20 27 | 5 12 19 26 |
| | *April* | *May* | *June* |
| n. | 3 10 17 24 | 1 8 15 22 29 | 5 12 19 26 |
| on. | 4 11 18 25 | 2 9 16 23 30 | 7 14 21 28 |
| e. | 5 12 19 26 | 3 10 17 24 31 | 1 8 15 22 29 |
| ed. | 6 13 20 27 | 4 11 18 25 | 2 9 16 23 30 |
| ur. | 7 14 21 28 | 5 12 19 26 | 3 10 17 24 |
| . | 1 8 15 22 29 | 6 13 20 27 | 4 11 18 25 |
| . | 2 9 16 23 30 | 7 14 21 28 | |
| | *July* | *August* | *September* |
| n. | 3 10 17 24 31 | 7 14 21 28 | 4 11 18 25 |
| on. | 4 11 18 25 | 1 8 15 22 29 | 5 12 19 26 |
| e. | 5 12 19 26 | 2 9 16 23 30 | 6 13 20 27 |
| ed. | 6 13 20 27 | 3 10 17 24 31 | 7 14 21 28 |
| ur. | 7 14 21 28 | 4 11 18 25 | 1 8 15 22 29 |
| i. | 1 8 15 22 29 | 5 12 19 26 | 2 9 16 23 30 |
| t. | 2 9 16 23 30 | 6 13 20 27 | 3 10 17 24 |
| | *October* | *November* | *December* |
| n. | 2 9 16 23 30 | 6 13 20 27 | 4 11 18 25 |
| on. | 3 10 17 24 31 | 7 14 21 28 | 5 12 19 26 |
| e. | 4 11 18 25 | 1 8 15 22 29 | 6 13 20 27 |
| ed. | 5 12 19 26 | 2 9 16 23 30 | 7 14 21 28 |
| ur. | 6 13 20 27 | 3 10 17 24 | 1 8 15 22 29 |
| i. | 7 14 21 28 | 4 11 18 25 | 2 9 16 23 30 |
| t. | 1 8 15 22 29 | 5 12 19 26 | 3 10 17 24 31 |

ASTER DAYS
arch 27 1796, 1864, 1932, 2016
pril 3 1836, 1904, 1988
pril 17 1808, 1892, 1960

## N (LEAP YEAR)

| | *January* | *February* | *March* |
|---|---|---|---|
| Sun. | 2 9 16 23 30 | 6 13 20 27 | 5 12 19 26 |
| Mon. | 3 10 17 24 31 | 7 14 21 28 | 6 13 20 27 |
| Tue. | 4 11 18 25 | 1 8 15 22 29 | 7 14 21 28 |
| Wed. | 5 12 19 26 | 2 9 16 23 | 1 8 15 22 29 |
| Thur. | 6 13 20 27 | 3 10 17 24 | 2 9 16 23 30 |
| Fri. | 7 14 21 28 | 4 11 18 25 | 3 10 17 24 31 |
| Sat. | 1 8 15 22 29 | 5 12 19 26 | 4 11 18 25 |
| | *April* | *May* | *June* |
| Sun. | 2 9 16 23 30 | 7 14 21 28 | 4 11 18 25 |
| Mon. | 3 10 17 24 | 1 8 15 22 29 | 5 12 19 26 |
| Tue. | 4 11 18 25 | 2 9 16 23 30 | 6 13 20 27 |
| Wed. | 5 12 19 26 | 3 10 17 24 31 | 7 14 21 28 |
| Thur. | 6 13 20 27 | 4 11 18 25 | 1 8 15 22 29 |
| Fri. | 7 14 21 28 | 5 12 19 26 | 2 9 16 23 30 |
| Sat. | 1 8 15 22 29 | 6 13 20 27 | 3 10 17 24 |
| | *July* | *August* | *September* |
| Sun. | 2 9 16 23 30 | 6 13 20 27 | 3 10 17 24 |
| Mon. | 3 10 17 24 31 | 7 14 21 28 | 4 11 18 25 |
| Tue. | 4 11 18 25 | 1 8 15 22 29 | 5 12 19 26 |
| Wed. | 5 12 19 26 | 2 9 16 23 30 | 6 13 20 27 |
| Thur. | 6 13 20 27 | 3 10 17 24 31 | 7 14 21 28 |
| Fri. | 7 14 21 28 | 4 11 18 25 | 1 8 15 22 29 |
| Sat. | 1 8 15 22 29 | 5 12 19 26 | 2 9 16 23 30 |
| | *October* | *November* | *December* |
| Sun. | 1 8 15 22 29 | 5 12 19 26 | 3 10 17 24 31 |
| Mon. | 2 9 16 23 30 | 6 13 20 27 | 4 11 18 25 |
| Tue. | 3 10 17 24 31 | 7 14 21 28 | 5 12 19 26 |
| Wed. | 4 11 18 25 | 1 8 15 22 29 | 6 13 20 27 |
| Thur. | 5 12 19 26 | 2 9 16 23 30 | 7 14 21 28 |
| Fri. | 6 13 20 27 | 3 10 17 24 | 1 8 15 22 29 |
| Sat. | 7 14 21 28 | 4 11 18 25 | 2 9 16 23 30 |

EASTER DAYS
March 26 1780
April 2 1820, 1972
April 9 1944
April 16 2028
April 23 1848, 1916, 2000

## GEOLOGICAL TIME

The earth is thought to have come into existence approximately 4,600 million years ago, but for nearly half this time, the Archean era, it was uninhabited. Life is generally believed to have emerged in the succeeding Proterozoic era. The Archean and the Proterozoic eras are often together referred to as the Precambrian.

Although primitive forms of life, e.g. algae and bacteria, existed during the Proterozoic era, it is not until the strata of Palaeozoic rocks is reached that abundant fossilised remains appear.

Since the Precambrian, there have been three great geological eras:

### PALAEOZOIC ('ancient life') *c.*570–*c.*245 million years ago

*Cambrian* – Mainly sandstones, slate and shales; limestones in Scotland. Shelled fossils and invertebrates, e.g. trilobites and brachiopods appear
*Ordovician* – Mainly shales and mudstones, e.g. in north Wales; limestones in Scotland. First fishes
*Silurian* – Shales, mudstones and some limestones, found mostly in Wales and southern Scotland
*Devonian* – Old red sandstone, shale, limestone and slate, e.g. in south Wales and the West Country
*Carboniferous* – Coal-bearing rocks, millstone grit, limestone and shale. First traces of land-living life
*Permian* – Marls, sandstones and clays. First reptile fossils

There were two great phases of mountain building in the Palaeozoic era: the Caledonian, characterised in Britain by NE–SW lines of hills and valleys; and the later Hercyian, widespread in west Germany and adjacent areas, and in Britain exemplified in E.–W. lines of hills and valleys.

The end of the Palaeozoic era was marked by the extensive glaciations of the Permian period in the southern continents and the decline of amphibians. It was succeeded by an era of warm conditions.

### MESOZOIC ('middle forms of life') *c.* 245–*c.*65 million years ago

*Triassic* – Mostly sandstone, e.g. in the West Midlands
*Jurassic* – Mainly limestones and clays, typically displayed in the Jura mountains, and in England in a NE–SW belt from Lincolnshire and the Wash to the Severn and the Dorset coast
*Cretaceous* – Mainly chalk, clay and sands, e.g. in Kent and Sussex

Giant reptiles were dominant during the Mesozoic era, but it was at this time that marsupial mammals first appeared, as well as *Archaeopteryx lithographica*, the earliest known species of bird. Coniferous trees and flowering plants also developed during the era and, with the birds and the mammals, were the main species to survive into the Cenozoic era. The giant reptiles became extinct.

### CENOZOIC ('recent life') from *c.* 65 million years ago

*Palaeocene*, *Eocene* } The emergence of new forms of life, including existing species

*Oligocene* – Fossils of a few still existing species
*Miocene* – Fossil remains show a balance of existing and extinct species
*Pliocene* – Fossil remains show a majority of still existing species
*Pleistocene* – The majority of remains are those of st existing species
*Holocene* – The present, post-glacial period. Existi species only, except for a few exterminated by man

In the last 25 million years, from the Miocene through t Pliocene periods, the Alpine-Himalayan and the circur Pacific phases of mountain building reached their clima During the Pleistocene period ice-sheets repeatec locked up masses of water as land ice; its weight depress the land, but the locking-up of the water lowered the se level by 100–200 metres. The glaciations and interglaci of the Ice Age are difficult to date and classify, but rece scientific opinion considers the Pleistocene period to ha begun approximately 1.64 million years ago. The la glacial retreat, merging into the Holocene period, w 10,000 years ago.

## HUMAN DEVELOPMENT

Any consideration of the history of mankind must sta with the fact that all members of the human race belong one species of animal, i.e. *Homo sapiens*, the definition o species being in biological terms that all its members c interbreed. As a species of mammal it is possible to gro man with other similar types, known as the primate Amongst these is found a sub-group, the apes, whi includes, in addition to man, the chimpanzees, gorilla orang-utans and gibbons. All lack a tail, have should blades at the back, and a Y-shaped chewing pattern on t surface of their molars, as well as showing the more gener primate characteristics of four incisors, a thumb which able to touch the fingers of the same hand, and finger ar toe nails instead of claws. The factors available to scienti study suggest that human beings have chimpanzees ar gorillas as their nearest relatives in the animal worl However, there remains the possibility that there on lived creatures, now extinct, which were closer to mode man than the chimpanzees and gorillas, and which share with modern man the characteristics of having flat fac (i.e. the absence of a pronounced muzzle), being biped and possessing large brains.

There are two broad groups of extinct apes recognise by specialists. The ramapithecines, the remains of whic mainly jaw fragments, have been found in east Africa, Asi and Turkey. They lived about 14 to 8 million years ag and from the evidence of their teeth it seems they chewe more in the manner of modern man than the oth presently living apes. The second group, the austral pithecines, have left more numerous remains among which sub-groups may be detected, although the ge graphic spread is limited to south and east Africa. Livir between 5 and 1.5 million years ago, they were clos relatives of modern man to the extent that they walke upright, did not have an extensive muzzle and had simil types of pre-molars. The first australopithecine remai were recognised at Taung in South Africa in 1924 ar subsequent discoveries include those at the Olduvai Gorg in Tanzania. The most impressive discovery was made Hadar, Ethiopia, in 1974 when about half a skeleto known as 'Lucy', was found.

Also in east Africa, between 2 million and 1.5 millio years ago, lived a hominid group which not only walke upright, had a flat face, and a large brain case, but als made simple pebble and flake stone tools. On prese evidence these habilines seem to have been the first peop to make tools, however crude. This facility is related to th larger brain size and human beings are the only animals

EOLOGICAL TIME

| Era | Period | Epoch | Date began* | Evolutionary stages |
|---|---|---|---|---|
| Cenozoic | Quaternary | Holocene | 0.01 | Man |
| | | Pleistocene | 1.64 | |
| | Tertiary | Pliocene | 5.2 | |
| | | Milocene | 23.3 | |
| | | Oligocene | 35.4 | |
| | | Eocene | 56.5 | |
| | | Palaeocene | 65.0 | |
| Mesozoic | Cretaceous | | 145.6 | |
| | Jurassic | | 208.0 | First birds |
| | Triassic | | 245.0 | First Mammals |
| Palaeozoic | Permian | | 290.0 | First Reptiles |
| | Carboniferous | | 362.5 | First amphibians and insects |
| | Devonian | | 408.5 | |
| | Silurian | | 439.0 | |
| | Ordovician | | 510.0 | First fishes |
| | Cambrian | | 570.0 | First invertebrates |
| Precambrian | | | 4,600.0 | First primitive life forms, e.g. algae and bacteria |

* millions of years ago

make implements to be used in other processes. These early pebble tool users, because of their distinctive characteristics, have been grouped as a separate sub-species, now extinct, of the genus *Homo* and are known as *Homo habilis*.

The use of fire, again a human characteristic, is associated with another group of extinct hominids whose remains, about a million years old, are found in south and east Africa, China, Indonesia, north Africa and Europe. Mastery of the techniques of making fire probably helped the colonisation of the colder northern areas and in this respect the site of Vertesszollos in Hungary is of particular importance. *Homo erectus* is the name given to this group of fossils and it includes a number of famous individual discoveries, e.g. Solo Man, Heidelberg Man, and especially Peking Man who lived at the cave site at Choukoutien which has yielded evidence of fire and burnt bone.

The well-known group Neanderthal Man, or *Homo sapiens neandertalensis*, is an extinct form of modern man who lived between about 100,000 and 40,000 years ago, thus spanning the last Ice Age. Indeed, its ability to adapt to the cold climate on the edge of the ice-sheets is one of its characteristic features, the remains being found only in Europe, Asia and the Middle East. Complete neanderthal skeletons were found during excavations at Tabun in Israel, together with evidence of tool-making and the use of fire. Distinguished by very large brains, it seems that neanderthal man was the first to develop recognisable social customs, especially deliberate burial rites. Why the neanderthalers became extinct is not clear but it may be connected with the climatic changes at the end of the Ice Ages, which would have seriously affected their food supplies; possibly they became too specialised for their own good.

The Swanscombe skull is the only known human fossil remains found in England. Some specialists see Swanscombe Man (or, more probably, woman) as a neanderthaler. Others group these remains together with the Steinheim skull from Germany, seeing both as a separate sub-species. There is too little evidence as yet on which to form a final judgement.

Modern Man, *Homo sapiens sapiens*, the surviving sub-species of *Homo sapiens*, had evolved to our present physical condition and had colonised much of the world by about 30,000 years ago. There are many previously distinguished individual specimens, e.g. Cromagnon Man, which may now be grouped together as *Homo sapiens sapiens*. It was modern man who spread to the American continent by crossing the landbridge between Siberia and Alaska and thence moved south through North America and into South America. Equally it is modern man who over the last 30,000 years has been responsible for the major developments in technology, art and civilisation generally.

One of the problems for those studying fossil man is the lack in many cases of sufficient quantities of fossil bone for analysis. It is important that theories should be tested against evidence, rather than the evidence being made to fit the theory. The Piltdown hoax is a well-known example of 'fossils' being forged to fit what was seen in some quarters as the correct theory of man's evolution.

## CULTURAL DEVELOPMENT

The Eurocentric bias of early archaeologists meant that the search for a starting point for the development and transmission of cultural ideas, especially by migration, trade and warfare, concentrated unduly on Europe and the Near East. The Three Age system, whereby pre-history was divided into a Stone Age, a Bronze Age and an Iron Age, was devised by Christian Thomsen, curator of th National Museum of Denmark in the early 19th centur to facilitate the classification of the museum's collection The descriptive adjectives referred to the materials fro which the implements and weapons were made and cam to be regarded as the dominant features of the societies t which they related. The refinement of the Three Ag system once dominated archaeological thought an remains a generally accepted concept in the popul mind. However, it is now seen by archaeologists as a inadequate model for human development.

Common sense suggests that there were no complet breaks between one so-called Age and another, any mo than contemporaries would have regarded 1485 as complete break between medieval and modern Englis history. Nor can the Three Age system be applie universally. In some areas it is necessary to insert a Copp Age, while in Africa south of the Sahara there would see to be no Bronze Age at all; in Australia, Old Stone Ag societies survived, while in South America, New Ston Age communities existed into modern times. Th civilisations in other parts of the world clearly invalida a Eurocentric theory of human development.

The concept of the 'Neolithic revolution', associate with the domestication of plants and animals, was development of particular importance in the huma cultural pattern. It reflected change from the primitiv hunter/gatherer economies to a more settled agricultur way of life and therefore, so the argument goes, mad possible the development of urban civilisation. Howeve it can no longer be argued that this 'revolution' took plac only in one area from which all development stemme Though it appears that the cultivation of wheat and barle was first undertaken, together with the domestication cattle and goats/sheep in the Fertile Crescent (the are bounded by the rivers Tigris and Euphrates), there evidence that rice was first deliberately planted and pig domesticated in south-east Asia, maize first cultivated i Central America and llamas first domesticated in Sout America. It has been recognised in recent years th cultural changes can take place independently of eac other in different parts of the world at different rates an different times. There is no need for a general diffusioni theory.

Although scholars will continue to study the particul societies which interest them, it may be possible to obtain reliable chronological framework, in absolute terms years, against which the cultural development of an particular area may be set. The development an refinement of radio-carbon dating and other scientifi methods of producing absolute chronologies is enablin the cross-referencing of societies to be undertaken. As th techniques of dating become more rigorous in applicatio and the number of scientifically obtained dates increase the attainment of an absolute chronology for prehistori societies throughout the world comes closer to bein achieved.

# Tidal Tables

## CONSTANTS

The constant tidal difference may be used in conjunction with the time of high water at a standard port shown in the predictions data (pages 98–103) to find the time of high water at any of the ports or places listed below.

These tidal differences are very approximate and should be used only as a guide to the time of high water at the places below. More precise local data should be obtained for navigational and other nautical purposes.

All data allow high water time to be found in Greenwich Mean Time; this applies to data for the months when British Summer Time is in operation and the hour's time difference should be allowed for. Ports marked * are in a different time zone and the standard time zone difference also needs to be added/subtracted to give local time.

EXAMPLE

Required time of high water at Stranraer at 2 January 2002
Appropriate time of high water at Greenock

| | |
|---|---|
| Afternoon tide 2 January | 1423hrs |
| Tidal difference | –0020hrs |
| High water at Stranraer | 1403hrs |

The columns headed 'Springs' and 'Neaps' show the height, in metres, of the tide above datum for mean high water springs and mean high water neaps respectively.

| Port | | Diff. h | m | Springs m | Neaps m |
|---|---|---|---|---|---|
| Aberdeen | *Leith* | –1 | 19 | 4.4 | 3.4 |
| Antwerp (Prosperpolder) | *London* | +0 | 50 | 5.8 | 4.8 |
| Ardrossan | *Greenock* | –0 | 15 | 3.2 | 2.6 |
| Avonmouth | *London* | –6 | 45 | 12.2 | 9.8 |
| Ayr | *Greenock* | –0 | 25 | 3.0 | 2.5 |
| Barrow (Docks) | *Liverpool* | 0 | 00 | 9.3 | 7.1 |
| Belfast | *London* | –2 | 47 | 3.5 | 3.0 |
| Blackpool | *Liverpool* | –0 | 10 | 8.9 | 7.0 |
| Boulogne | *London* | –2 | 44 | 8.9 | 7.2 |
| Calais | *London* | –2 | 04 | 7.2 | 5.9 |
| Cherbourg | *London* | –6 | 00 | 6.4 | 5.0 |
| Cobh | *Liverpool* | –5 | 55 | 4.2 | 3.2 |
| Cowes | *London* | –2 | 38 | 4.2 | 3.5 |
| Dartmouth | *London* | +4 | 25 | 4.9 | 3.8 |
| Dieppe | *London* | –3 | 03 | 9.3 | 7.3 |
| Douglas, IoM | *Liverpool* | –0 | 04 | 6.9 | 5.4 |
| Dover | *London* | –2 | 52 | 6.7 | 5.3 |
| Dublin | *London* | –2 | 05 | 4.1 | 3.4 |
| Dun Loaghaire | *London* | –2 | 10 | 4.1 | 3.4 |
| Dunkirk | *London* | –1 | 54 | 6.0 | 4.9 |
| Fishguard | *Liverpool* | –4 | 01 | 4.8 | 3.4 |
| Fleetwood | *Liverpool* | 0 | 00 | 9.2 | 7.3 |
| Flushing | *London* | –0 | 15 | 4.7 | 3.9 |
| Folkestone | *London* | –3 | 04 | 7.1 | 5.7 |
| Galway | *Liverpool* | –6 | 08 | 5.1 | 3.9 |
| Glasgow | *Greenock* | +0 | 26 | 4.7 | 4.0 |
| Harwich | *London* | –2 | 06 | 4.0 | 3.4 |
| Le Havre | *London* | –3 | 55 | 7.9 | 6.6 |
| Heysham | *Liverpool* | +0 | 05 | 9.4 | 7.4 |
| Holyhead | *Liverpool* | –0 | 50 | 5.6 | 4.4 |
| *Hook of Holland | *London* | –0 | 01 | 2.1 | 1.7 |
| Hull (Albert Dock) | *London* | –7 | 40 | 7.5 | 5.8 |
| Immingham | *London* | –8 | 00 | 7.3 | 5.8 |
| Larne | *London* | –2 | 40 | 2.8 | 2.5 |
| Lerwick | *Leith* | –3 | 48 | 2.2 | 1.6 |
| Londonderry | *London* | –5 | 37 | 2.7 | 2.1 |
| Lowestoft | *London* | –4 | 25 | 2.4 | 2.1 |
| Margate | *London* | –1 | 53 | 4.8 | 3.9 |
| Milford Haven | *Liverpool* | –5 | 08 | 7.0 | 5.2 |
| Morecambe | *Liverpool* | +0 | 07 | 9.5 | 7.4 |
| Newhaven | *London* | –2 | 46 | 6.7 | 5.1 |
| Oban | *Greenock* | +5 | 43 | 4.0 | 2.9 |
| *Ostend | *London* | –1 | 32 | 5.1 | 4.2 |
| Plymouth | *London* | +4 | 05 | 5.5 | 4.4 |
| Portland | *London* | +5 | 09 | 2.1 | 1.4 |
| Portsmouth | *London* | –2 | 38 | 4.7 | 3.8 |
| Ramsgate | *London* | –2 | 32 | 5.2 | 4.1 |
| Richmond Lock | *London* | +1 | 00 | 4.9 | 3.7 |
| Rosslare Harbour | *Liverpool* | –5 | 24 | 1.9 | 1.4 |
| Rosyth | *Leith* | +0 | 09 | 5.8 | 4.7 |
| *Rotterdam | *London* | +1 | 45 | 2.0 | 1.7 |
| St Helier | *London* | +4 | 48 | 11.0 | 8.1 |
| St Malo | *London* | +4 | 27 | 12.2 | 9.2 |
| St Peter Port | *London* | +4 | 54 | 9.3 | 7.0 |
| Scrabster | *Leith* | –6 | 06 | 5.0 | 4.0 |
| Sheerness | *London* | –1 | 19 | 5.8 | 4.7 |
| Shoreham | *London* | –2 | 44 | 6.3 | 4.9 |
| Southampton (1st high water) | *London* | –2 | 54 | 4.5 | 3.7 |
| Spurn Head | *London* | –8 | 25 | 6.9 | 5.5 |
| Stornoway | *Liverpool* | –4 | 16 | 4.8 | 3.7 |
| Stranraer | *Greenock* | –0 | 20 | 3.0 | 2.4 |
| Stromness | *Leith* | –5 | 26 | 3.6 | 2.7 |
| Swansea | *London* | –7 | 35 | 9.5 | 7.2 |
| Tees (River Entrance) | *Leith* | +1 | 09 | 5.5 | 4.3 |
| Tilbury | *London* | –0 | 49 | 6.4 | 5.4 |
| Tobermory | *Liverpool* | –5 | 11 | 4.4 | 3.3 |
| Tyne River (North Shields) | *London* | –10 | 30 | 5.0 | 3.9 |
| Ullapool | *Leith* | –7 | 40 | 5.2 | 3.9 |
| Walton-on-the-Naze | *London* | –2 | 10 | 4.2 | 3.4 |
| Wick | *Leith* | –3 | 26 | 3.5 | 2.8 |
| Zeebrugge | *London* | –0 | 55 | 4.8 | 3.9 |

## PREDICTIONS

The data on pages 98–103 are daily predictions of the time and height of high water at London Bridge, Liverpool, Greenock and Leith. The time of the of the data is Greenwich Mean Time; this applies also to data for the months when British Summer Time is in operation and the hour's time difference should be allowed for. The datum of predictions for each port shows the difference of height, in metres from Ordnance data (Newlyn).

JANUARY 2002 *High Water* GMT

| | | London Bridge | | | | Liverpool | | | | Greenock | | | | Leith | | | |
|---|---|---|---|---|---|---|---|---|---|---|---|---|---|---|---|---|---|
| | | *Datum of Predictions 3.20m below | | | | *Datum of Predictions 4.93m below | | | | *Datum of Predictions 1.62m below | | | | *Datum of Predictions 2.90m below | | | |
| | | hr | ht m | hr | ht m | hr | ht m | hr | ht m | hr | ht m | hr | ht m | hr | ht m | hr | ht m |
| 1 | Tuesday | 02 48 | 6.9 | 15 14 | 7.1 | 00 05 | 9.4 | 12 26 | 9.5 | 01 34 | 3.3 | 13 41 | 3.7 | 03 35 | 5.6 | 15 54 | 5.6 |
| 2 | Wednesday | 03 32 | 6.9 | 16 01 | 7.2 | 00 53 | 9.4 | 13 13 | 9.6 | 02 22 | 3.3 | 14 23 | 3.8 | 04 20 | 5.7 | 16 37 | 5.6 |
| 3 | Thursday | 04 15 | 6.8 | 16 48 | 7.1 | 01 41 | 9.3 | 14 01 | 9.5 | 03 10 | 3.3 | 15 06 | 3.8 | 05 08 | 5.6 | 17 24 | 5.5 |
| 4 | Friday | 04 59 | 6.8 | 17 37 | 7.0 | 02 30 | 9.1 | 14 51 | 9.3 | 03 59 | 3.2 | 15 52 | 3.7 | 05 58 | 5.4 | 18 15 | 5.4 |
| 5 | Saturday | 05 46 | 6.6 | 18 28 | 6.7 | 03 22 | 8.8 | 15 44 | 9.0 | 04 51 | 3.2 | 16 41 | 3.6 | 06 51 | 5.2 | 19 11 | 5.2 |
| 6 | Sunday | 06 37 | 6.4 | 19 25 | 6.4 | 04 18 | 8.4 | 16 42 | 8.6 | 05 47 | 3.1 | 17 35 | 3.5 | 07 52 | 4.9 | 20 18 | 5.1 |
| 7 | Monday | 07 38 | 6.2 | 20 29 | 6.2 | 05 22 | 8.1 | 17 47 | 8.3 | 06 48 | 3.0 | 18 37 | 3.3 | 08 59 | 4.8 | 21 28 | 5.0 |
| 8 | Tuesday | 08 49 | 6.1 | 21 36 | 6.1 | 06 31 | 7.9 | 18 58 | 8.2 | 07 59 | 3.0 | 19 50 | 3.2 | 10 06 | 4.7 | 22 35 | 4.9 |
| 9 | Wednesday | 09 59 | 6.1 | 22 40 | 6.2 | 07 41 | 8.0 | 20 08 | 8.2 | 09 14 | 3.0 | 21 15 | 3.2 | 11 12 | 4.8 | 23 40 | 5.0 |
| 10 | Thursday | 11 04 | 6.3 | 23 38 | 6.4 | 08 43 | 8.3 | 21 09 | 8.4 | 10 15 | 3.2 | 22 23 | 3.2 | 12 13 | 4.9 | — | — |
| 11 | Friday | 12 02 | 6.5 | — | — | 09 36 | 8.6 | 22 02 | 8.7 | 11 06 | 3.3 | 23 19 | 3.2 | 00 40 | 5.1 | 13 07 | 5.0 |
| 12 | Saturday | 00 31 | 6.6 | 12 56 | 6.7 | 10 23 | 8.9 | 22 47 | 8.8 | 11 51 | 3.4 | — | — | 01 34 | 5.2 | 13 54 | 5.2 |
| 13 | Sunday | 01 20 | 6.7 | 13 46 | 6.8 | 11 04 | 9.1 | 23 28 | 8.9 | 00 08 | 3.2 | 12 33 | 3.5 | 02 22 | 5.2 | 14 35 | 5.3 |
| 14 | Monday | 02 04 | 6.7 | 14 31 | 6.8 | 11 43 | 9.2 | — | — | 00 53 | 3.2 | 13 11 | 3.6 | 03 04 | 5.2 | 15 14 | 5.3 |
| 15 | Tuesday | 02 43 | 6.7 | 15 12 | 6.8 | 00 05 | 8.9 | 12 20 | 9.2 | 01 34 | 3.2 | 13 48 | 3.6 | 03 44 | 5.2 | 15 50 | 5.3 |
| 16 | Wednesday | 03 17 | 6.6 | 15 48 | 6.6 | 00 41 | 8.8 | 12 56 | 9.1 | 02 11 | 3.2 | 14 23 | 3.6 | 04 21 | 5.1 | 16 25 | 5.3 |
| 17 | Thursday | 03 48 | 6.5 | 16 21 | 6.5 | 01 15 | 8.7 | 13 31 | 9.0 | 02 47 | 3.2 | 14 57 | 3.6 | 04 57 | 5.0 | 16 59 | 5.2 |
| 18 | Friday | 04 19 | 6.5 | 16 54 | 6.5 | 01 50 | 8.5 | 14 08 | 8.8 | 03 23 | 3.2 | 15 32 | 3.5 | 05 33 | 4.9 | 17 35 | 5.1 |
| 19 | Saturday | 04 53 | 6.4 | 17 30 | 6.4 | 02 26 | 8.3 | 14 45 | 8.6 | 04 00 | 3.2 | 16 07 | 3.4 | 06 11 | 4.8 | 18 15 | 4.9 |
| 20 | Sunday | 05 31 | 6.3 | 18 09 | 6.3 | 03 04 | 8.0 | 15 25 | 8.3 | 04 38 | 3.1 | 16 46 | 3.3 | 06 53 | 4.6 | 18 58 | 4.7 |
| 21 | Monday | 06 14 | 6.2 | 18 54 | 6.1 | 03 47 | 7.7 | 16 11 | 7.9 | 05 20 | 3.0 | 17 28 | 3.1 | 07 39 | 4.5 | 19 46 | 4.6 |
| 22 | Tuesday | 07 02 | 6.0 | 19 44 | 6.0 | 04 39 | 7.4 | 17 07 | 7.6 | 06 06 | 2.9 | 18 18 | 3.0 | 08 31 | 4.4 | 20 42 | 4.4 |
| 23 | Wednesday | 07 59 | 5.8 | 20 42 | 5.9 | 05 42 | 7.2 | 18 12 | 7.5 | 06 58 | 2.9 | 19 16 | 2.9 | 09 31 | 4.3 | 21 48 | 4.4 |
| 24 | Thursday | 09 03 | 5.8 | 21 48 | 5.8 | 06 54 | 7.3 | 19 21 | 7.7 | 08 00 | 2.8 | 20 30 | 2.8 | 10 35 | 4.4 | 22 57 | 4.5 |
| 25 | Friday | 10 13 | 5.9 | 22 58 | 6.0 | 08 02 | 7.7 | 20 27 | 8.0 | 09 15 | 2.9 | 21 49 | 2.9 | 11 39 | 4.6 | — | — |
| 26 | Saturday | 11 23 | 6.1 | — | — | 09 01 | 8.2 | 21 25 | 8.5 | 10 22 | 3.1 | 22 54 | 3.0 | 00 03 | 4.7 | 12 39 | 4.8 |
| 27 | Sunday | 00 01 | 6.3 | 12 26 | 6.5 | 09 52 | 8.8 | 22 17 | 8.9 | 11 14 | 3.3 | 23 47 | 3.1 | 01 02 | 5.0 | 13 30 | 5.1 |
| 28 | Monday | 00 57 | 6.6 | 13 22 | 6.8 | 10 40 | 9.2 | 23 07 | 9.3 | 12 00 | 3.4 | — | — | 01 53 | 5.3 | 14 15 | 5.4 |
| 29 | Tuesday | 01 47 | 6.8 | 14 13 | 7.1 | 11 27 | 9.6 | 23 54 | 9.6 | 00 38 | 3.2 | 12 45 | 3.6 | 02 38 | 5.6 | 14 57 | 5.6 |
| 30 | Wednesday | 02 35 | 7.0 | 15 02 | 7.3 | 12 14 | 9.9 | — | — | 01 28 | 3.3 | 13 30 | 3.7 | 03 22 | 5.8 | 15 39 | 5.7 |
| 31 | Thursday | 03 20 | 7.1 | 15 49 | 7.4 | 00 42 | 9.7 | 13 01 | 10.0 | 02 16 | 3.3 | 14 13 | 3.8 | 04 06 | 5.8 | 16 22 | 5.8 |

FEBRUARY 2002 *High Water* GMT

| | | London Bridge | | | | Liverpool | | | | Greenock | | | | Leith | | | |
|---|---|---|---|---|---|---|---|---|---|---|---|---|---|---|---|---|---|
| 1 | Friday | 04 03 | 7.1 | 16 35 | 7.4 | 01 29 | 9.7 | 13 48 | 10.0 | 03 01 | 3.3 | 14 57 | 3.9 | 04 52 | 5.8 | 17 08 | 5. |
| 2 | Saturday | 04 46 | 7.1 | 17 20 | 7.3 | 02 14 | 9.5 | 14 34 | 9.7 | 03 44 | 3.3 | 15 40 | 3.9 | 05 39 | 5.6 | 17 55 | 5. |
| 3 | Sunday | 05 29 | 7.0 | 18 06 | 7.0 | 03 00 | 9.2 | 15 21 | 9.3 | 04 27 | 3.3 | 16 24 | 3.7 | 06 28 | 5.3 | 18 47 | 5 |
| 4 | Monday | 06 13 | 6.7 | 18 55 | 6.6 | 03 49 | 8.7 | 16 12 | 8.7 | 05 11 | 3.2 | 17 10 | 3.6 | 07 22 | 5.0 | 19 48 | 5. |
| 5 | Tuesday | 07 03 | 6.4 | 19 51 | 6.1 | 04 44 | 8.1 | 17 11 | 8.1 | 05 58 | 3.0 | 18 00 | 3.3 | 08 24 | 4.7 | 20 58 | 4. |
| 6 | Wednesday | 08 08 | 6.1 | 20 58 | 5.8 | 05 51 | 7.7 | 18 25 | 7.7 | 06 54 | 2.9 | 18 59 | 3.1 | 09 32 | 4.5 | 22 10 | 4. |
| 7 | Thursday | 09 28 | 5.9 | 22 09 | 5.8 | 07 10 | 7.5 | 19 48 | 7.6 | 08 23 | 2.9 | 20 35 | 2.9 | 10 43 | 4.5 | 23 24 | 4. |
| 8 | Friday | 10 43 | 5.9 | 23 14 | 5.9 | 08 24 | 7.8 | 20 58 | 7.9 | 09 52 | 3.0 | 22 16 | 2.9 | 11 55 | 4.6 | — | — |
| 9 | Saturday | 11 47 | 6.2 | — | — | 09 22 | 8.2 | 21 52 | 8.2 | 10 49 | 3.1 | 23 16 | 3.0 | 00 34 | 4.7 | 12 58 | 4. |
| 10 | Sunday | 00 11 | 6.2 | 12 43 | 6.5 | 10 10 | 8.6 | 22 37 | 8.5 | 11 36 | 3.3 | — | — | 01 31 | 4.9 | 13 47 | 5. |
| 11 | Monday | 01 03 | 6.5 | 13 33 | 6.7 | 10 52 | 9.0 | 23 17 | 8.7 | 00 04 | 3.0 | 12 19 | 3.4 | 02 16 | 5.0 | 14 27 | 5. |
| 12 | Tuesday | 01 48 | 6.6 | 14 17 | 6.8 | 11 29 | 9.1 | 23 51 | 8.8 | 00 47 | 3.1 | 12 58 | 3.5 | 02 54 | 5.1 | 15 02 | 5. |
| 13 | Wednesday | 02 28 | 6.6 | 14 57 | 6.8 | — | — | 12 04 | 9.2 | 01 24 | 3.1 | 13 34 | 3.5 | 03 28 | 5.2 | 15 34 | 5. |
| 14 | Thursday | 03 02 | 6.6 | 15 30 | 6.6 | 00 23 | 8.8 | 12 38 | 9.2 | 01 57 | 3.1 | 14 07 | 3.5 | 03 59 | 5.1 | 16 04 | 5. |
| 15 | Friday | 03 32 | 6.5 | 15 59 | 6.6 | 00 55 | 8.8 | 13 10 | 9.1 | 02 27 | 3.1 | 14 37 | 3.4 | 04 30 | 5.1 | 16 35 | 5. |
| 16 | Saturday | 04 00 | 6.5 | 16 28 | 6.5 | 01 26 | 8.7 | 13 43 | 9.0 | 02 56 | 3.1 | 15 07 | 3.4 | 05 03 | 5.0 | 17 07 | 5. |
| 17 | Sunday | 04 30 | 6.5 | 17 00 | 6.6 | 01 58 | 8.6 | 14 15 | 8.8 | 03 27 | 3.2 | 15 39 | 3.4 | 05 37 | 4.9 | 17 42 | 5 |
| 18 | Monday | 05 04 | 6.5 | 17 36 | 6.5 | 02 30 | 8.4 | 14 50 | 8.5 | 04 00 | 3.1 | 16 13 | 3.3 | 06 14 | 4.8 | 18 19 | 4. |
| 19 | Tuesday | 05 42 | 6.4 | 18 17 | 6.4 | 03 05 | 8.1 | 15 29 | 8.2 | 04 36 | 3.1 | 16 51 | 3.1 | 06 55 | 4.6 | 19 01 | 4. |
| 20 | Wednesday | 06 26 | 6.3 | 19 03 | 6.1 | 03 49 | 7.7 | 16 19 | 7.7 | 05 17 | 3.0 | 17 34 | 2.9 | 07 41 | 4.4 | 19 50 | 4. |
| 21 | Thursday | 07 18 | 6.0 | 19 57 | 5.9 | 04 47 | 7.3 | 17 24 | 7.4 | 06 04 | 2.8 | 18 29 | 2.8 | 08 38 | 4.3 | 20 56 | 4. |
| 22 | Friday | 08 20 | 5.8 | 21 01 | 5.7 | 06 01 | 7.2 | 18 41 | 7.3 | 07 03 | 2.7 | 19 43 | 2.7 | 09 48 | 4.2 | 22 16 | 4. |
| 23 | Saturday | 09 31 | 5.8 | 22 18 | 5.7 | 07 23 | 7.4 | 20 00 | 7.7 | 08 25 | 2.7 | 21 21 | 2.7 | 11 03 | 4.4 | 23 36 | 4. |
| 24 | Sunday | 10 53 | 6.0 | 23 34 | 6.0 | 08 35 | 7.9 | 21 07 | 8.2 | 09 51 | 2.9 | 22 40 | 2.9 | — | — | 12 12 | 4. |
| 25 | Monday | — | — | 12 06 | 6.4 | 09 34 | 8.6 | 22 03 | 8.9 | 10 52 | 3.1 | 23 37 | 3.1 | 00 42 | 4.9 | 13 09 | 5 |
| 26 | Tuesday | 00 36 | 6.4 | 13 06 | 6.8 | 10 24 | 9.3 | 22 52 | 9.4 | 11 42 | 3.4 | — | — | 01 36 | 5.3 | 13 55 | 5. |
| 27 | Wednesday | 01 29 | 6.8 | 13 58 | 7.2 | 11 12 | 9.8 | 23 39 | 9.8 | 00 27 | 3.2 | 12 29 | 3.6 | 02 21 | 5.6 | 14 38 | 5. |
| 28 | Thursday | 02 17 | 7.1 | 14 46 | 7.4 | 11 58 | 10.1 | — | — | 01 16 | 3.3 | 13 14 | 3.7 | 03 04 | 5.9 | 15 19 | 5. |

## MARCH 2002 *High Water* GMT

| | London Bridge | | | | Liverpool | | | | Greenock | | | | Leith | | | |
|---|---|---|---|---|---|---|---|---|---|---|---|---|---|---|---|---|
| | *Datum of Predictions 3.20m below | | | | *Datum of Predictions 4.93m below | | | | *Datum of Predictions 1.62m below | | | | *Datum of Predictions 2.90m below | | | |
| | hr | ht m | hr | ht m | hr | ht m | hr | ht m | hr | ht m | hr | ht m | hr | ht m | hr | ht m |
| 1 Friday | 03 02 | 7.2 | 15 32 | 7.6 | 00 24 | 10.0 | 12 43 | 10.3 | 02 00 | 3.3 | 13 58 | 3.8 | 03 47 | 5.9 | 1602 | 6.0 |
| 2 Saturday | 03 44 | 7.3 | 16 15 | 7.5 | 01 09 | 9.9 | 13 28 | 10.2 | 02 41 | 3.4 | 14 41 | 3.9 | 04 31 | 5.8 | 1647 | 6.0 |
| 3 Sunday | 04 25 | 7.4 | 16 58 | 7.3 | 01 52 | 9.7 | 14 11 | 9.9 | 03 19 | 3.4 | 15 22 | 3.9 | 05 16 | 5.6 | 1734 | 5.8 |
| 4 Monday | 05 06 | 7.2 | 17 39 | 7.0 | 02 35 | 9.3 | 14 55 | 9.3 | 03 55 | 3.4 | 16 03 | 3.8 | 06 03 | 5.3 | 1825 | 5.4 |
| 5 Tuesday | 05 47 | 6.9 | 18 21 | 6.6 | 03 18 | 8.8 | 15 42 | 8.6 | 04 33 | 3.3 | 16 45 | 3.5 | 06 52 | 4.9 | 1923 | 5.0 |
| 6 Wednesday | 06 32 | 6.5 | 19 07 | 6.1 | 04 08 | 8.1 | 16 38 | 7.8 | 05 15 | 3.1 | 17 30 | 3.2 | 07 50 | 4.6 | 2032 | 4.7 |
| 7 Thursday | 07 29 | 6.0 | 20 08 | 5.6 | 05 12 | 7.5 | 17 55 | 7.2 | 06 05 | 2.9 | 18 24 | 2.9 | 08 59 | 4.4 | 2147 | 4.4 |
| 8 Friday | 08 58 | 5.6 | 21 37 | 5.4 | 06 39 | 7.2 | 19 29 | 7.1 | 07 11 | 2.8 | 19 38 | 2.7 | 10 14 | 4.3 | 2308 | 4.4 |
| 9 Saturday | 10 23 | 5.7 | 22 49 | 5.6 | 08 02 | 7.4 | 20 42 | 7.5 | 09 28 | 2.8 | 22 12 | 2.7 | 11 35 | 4.4 | — | — |
| 10 Sunday | 11 28 | 6.0 | 23 48 | 6.0 | 09 03 | 7.9 | 21 35 | 8.0 | 10 30 | 3.0 | 23 06 | 2.9 | 00 25 | 4.6 | 1243 | 4.6 |
| 11 Monday | 12 24 | 6.4 | — | — | 09 51 | 8.4 | 22 19 | 8.4 | 11 18 | 3.2 | 23 50 | 3.0 | 01 20 | 4.8 | 1332 | 4.9 |
| 12 Tuesday | 00 41 | 6.3 | 13 13 | 6.7 | 10 32 | 8.8 | 22 56 | 8.7 | 12 00 | 3.3 | — | — | 02 02 | 5.0 | 1411 | 5.1 |
| 13 Wednesday | 01 27 | 6.6 | 13 57 | 6.8 | 11 09 | 9.1 | 23 29 | 8.8 | 00 28 | 3.0 | 12 39 | 3.4 | 02 36 | 5.1 | 1443 | 5.2 |
| 14 Thursday | 02 07 | 6.7 | 14 34 | 6.8 | 11 42 | 9.1 | — | — | 01 03 | 3.0 | 13 14 | 3.3 | 03 06 | 5.1 | 1512 | 5.3 |
| 15 Friday | 02 42 | 6.6 | 15 05 | 6.7 | 00 00 | 8.9 | 12 14 | 9.1 | 01 33 | 3.0 | 13 44 | 3.3 | 03 34 | 5.2 | 1540 | 5.3 |
| 16 Saturday | 03 11 | 6.5 | 15 33 | 6.6 | 00 30 | 8.9 | 12 45 | 9.1 | 01 59 | 3.1 | 14 11 | 3.3 | 04 02 | 5.2 | 1609 | 5.3 |
| 17 Sunday | 03 38 | 6.5 | 16 00 | 6.6 | 00 59 | 8.8 | 13 15 | 9.0 | 02 25 | 3.1 | 14 39 | 3.3 | 04 33 | 5.1 | 1640 | 5.2 |
| 18 Monday | 04 06 | 6.6 | 16 31 | 6.6 | 01 28 | 8.8 | 13 46 | 8.8 | 02 53 | 3.2 | 15 11 | 3.3 | 05 06 | 5.0 | 1714 | 5.1 |
| 19 Tuesday | 04 38 | 6.6 | 17 05 | 6.6 | 01 58 | 8.6 | 14 19 | 8.6 | 03 25 | 3.2 | 15 45 | 3.2 | 05 41 | 4.9 | 1750 | 4.9 |
| 20 Wednesday | 05 15 | 6.6 | 17 44 | 6.5 | 02 31 | 8.3 | 14 56 | 8.2 | 03 58 | 3.1 | 16 21 | 3.1 | 06 19 | 4.7 | 1831 | 4.7 |
| 21 Thursday | 05 59 | 6.4 | 18 29 | 6.2 | 03 11 | 7.9 | 15 45 | 7.8 | 04 34 | 3.0 | 17 02 | 2.9 | 07 02 | 4.5 | 1921 | 4.5 |
| 22 Friday | 06 50 | 6.1 | 19 22 | 5.8 | 04 07 | 7.5 | 16 50 | 7.3 | 05 17 | 2.8 | 17 55 | 2.7 | 07 56 | 4.3 | 2025 | 4.3 |
| 23 Saturday | 07 52 | 5.8 | 20 25 | 5.6 | 05 24 | 7.1 | 18 13 | 7.2 | 06 15 | 2.7 | 19 14 | 2.6 | 09 08 | 4.2 | 2148 | 4.3 |
| 24 Sunday | 09 05 | 5.7 | 21 46 | 5.6 | 06 53 | 7.3 | 19 39 | 7.5 | 07 42 | 2.7 | 21 04 | 2.6 | 10 32 | 4.3 | 2312 | 4.6 |
| 25 Monday | 10 32 | 5.9 | 23 10 | 6.0 | 08 12 | 7.9 | 20 49 | 8.2 | 09 22 | 2.8 | 22 27 | 2.8 | 11 46 | 4.6 | — | — |
| 26 Tuesday | 11 48 | 6.4 | — | — | 09 13 | 8.6 | 21 44 | 8.9 | 10 29 | 3.1 | 23 22 | 3.0 | 00 21 | 5.0 | 1244 | 5.1 |
| 27 Wednesday | 00 13 | 6.4 | 12 47 | 6.9 | 10 04 | 9.3 | 22 33 | 9. | 11 20 | 3.4 | — | — | 01 14 | 5.4 | 1331 | 5.5 |
| 28 Thursday | 01 06 | 6.8 | 13 38 | 7.3 | 10 51 | 9.9 | 23 18 | 9.9 | 00 10 | 3.2 | 12 08 | 3.6 | 01 59 | 5.7 | 1414 | 5.8 |
| 29 Friday | 01 54 | 7.2 | 14 25 | 7.5 | 11 37 | 10.2 | — | — | 00 55 | 3.3 | 12 54 | 3.7 | 02 42 | 5.9 | 1457 | 6.0 |
| 30 Saturday | 02 38 | 7.3 | 15 09 | 7.6 | 00 02 | 10.0 | 12 21 | 10.2 | 01 37 | 3.4 | 13 39 | 3.8 | 03 24 | 5.9 | 1541 | 6.1 |
| 31 Sunday | 03 21 | 7.5 | 15 52 | 7.5 | 00 45 | 10.0 | 13 05 | 10.1 | 02 15 | 3.4 | 14 21 | 3.8 | 04 07 | 5.8 | 1626 | 6.0 |

## APRIL 2002 *High Water* GMT

| | London Bridge | | | | Liverpool | | | | Greenock | | | | Leith | | | |
|---|---|---|---|---|---|---|---|---|---|---|---|---|---|---|---|---|
| 1 Monday | 04 03 | 7.4 | 16 32 | 7.3 | 01 27 | 9.7 | 13 47 | 9.7 | 02 50 | 3.5 | 15 02 | 3.8 | 04 51 | 5.6 | 17 14 | 5.7 |
| 2 Tuesday | 04 43 | 7.3 | 17 10 | 7.0 | 02 08 | 9.3 | 14 30 | 9.1 | 03 25 | 3.4 | 15 41 | 3.7 | 05 37 | 5.3 | 18 06 | 5.3 |
| 3 Wednesday | 05 25 | 7.0 | 17 48 | 6.6 | 02 50 | 8.7 | 15 15 | 8.4 | 04 02 | 3.3 | 16 23 | 3.4 | 06 25 | 4.9 | 19 04 | 4.9 |
| 4 Thursday | 06 08 | 6.5 | 18 27 | 6.1 | 03 36 | 8.1 | 16 10 | 7.6 | 04 43 | 3.2 | 17 08 | 3.1 | 07 21 | 4.6 | 20 10 | 4.5 |
| 5 Friday | 07 02 | 6.0 | 19 17 | 5.6 | 04 38 | 7.4 | 17 28 | 7.0 | 05 32 | 3.0 | 18 02 | 2.8 | 08 28 | 4.3 | 21 22 | 4.3 |
| 6 Saturday | 08 32 | 5.6 | 20 59 | 5.3 | 06 07 | 7.1 | 19 01 | 6.9 | 06 35 | 2.8 | 19 15 | 2.6 | 09 43 | 4.2 | 22 42 | 4.3 |
| 7 Sunday | 09 59 | 5.6 | 22 19 | 5.5 | 07 30 | 7.3 | 20 13 | 7.2 | 08 48 | 2.7 | 21 50 | 2.6 | 11 04 | 4.3 | — | — |
| 8 Monday | 11 02 | 6.0 | 23 19 | 5.9 | 08 32 | 7.7 | 21 06 | 7.8 | 10 02 | 2.9 | 22 41 | 2.8 | 00 00 | 4.5 | 12 14 | 4.5 |
| 9 Tuesday | 11 57 | 6.4 | — | — | 09 22 | 8.2 | 21 49 | 8.2 | 10 50 | 3.1 | 23 22 | 2.9 | 00 55 | 4.7 | 13 04 | 4.8 |
| 10 Wednesday | 00 11 | 6.3 | 12 45 | 6.7 | 10 03 | 8.6 | 22 26 | 8.5 | 11 32 | 3.2 | 23 59 | 3.0 | 01 35 | 4.9 | 13 43 | 5.0 |
| 11 Thursday | 00 58 | 6.5 | 13 28 | 6.8 | 10 41 | 8.9 | 22 59 | 8.7 | 12 10 | 3.2 | — | — | 02 08 | 5.0 | 14 15 | 5.1 |
| 12 Friday | 01 39 | 6.6 | 14 04 | 6.8 | 11 15 | 9.0 | 23 30 | 8.8 | 00 32 | 3.0 | 12 45 | 3.2 | 02 37 | 5.1 | 14 44 | 5.2 |
| 13 Saturday | 02 14 | 6.6 | 14 35 | 6.7 | 11 46 | 9.0 | — | — | 01 02 | 3.0 | 13 14 | 3.2 | 03 04 | 5.2 | 15 12 | 5.3 |
| 14 Sunday | 02 45 | 6.5 | 15 04 | 6.6 | 00 00 | 8.9 | 12 17 | 9.0 | 01 27 | 3.1 | 13 41 | 3.2 | 03 33 | 5.2 | 15 43 | 5.3 |
| 15 Monday | 03 13 | 6.5 | 15 32 | 6.6 | 00 29 | 8.8 | 12 47 | 8.9 | 01 53 | 3.2 | 14 12 | 3.2 | 04 04 | 5.2 | 16 15 | 5.2 |
| 16 Tuesday | 03 43 | 6.6 | 16 04 | 6.6 | 00 59 | 8.8 | 13 19 | 8.8 | 02 22 | 3.2 | 14 45 | 3.2 | 04 38 | 5.1 | 16 51 | 5.1 |
| 17 Wednesday | 04 17 | 6.6 | 16 39 | 6.6 | 01 31 | 8.7 | 13 55 | 8.6 | 02 54 | 3.3 | 15 21 | 3.1 | 05 13 | 5.0 | 17 29 | 5.0 |
| 18 Thursday | 04 56 | 6.6 | 17 18 | 6.4 | 02 06 | 8.4 | 14 35 | 8.2 | 03 28 | 3.2 | 15 59 | 3.0 | 05 51 | 4.8 | 18 13 | 4.8 |
| 19 Friday | 05 41 | 6.4 | 18 03 | 6.2 | 02 49 | 8.1 | 15 25 | 7.8 | 04 03 | 3.1 | 16 43 | 2.8 | 06 35 | 4.6 | 19 05 | 4.6 |
| 20 Saturday | 06 33 | 6.1 | 18 56 | 5.8 | 03 46 | 7.6 | 16 31 | 7.4 | 04 46 | 2.9 | 17 42 | 2.6 | 07 29 | 4.4 | 20 08 | 4.5 |
| 21 Sunday | 07 36 | 5.9 | 20 01 | 5.6 | 05 02 | 7.3 | 17 54 | 7.3 | 05 46 | 2.8 | 19 08 | 2.6 | 08 42 | 4.3 | 21 29 | 4.5 |
| 22 Monday | 08 51 | 5.8 | 21 24 | 5.7 | 06 29 | 7.5 | 19 18 | 7.6 | 07 14 | 2.7 | 20 50 | 2.6 | 10 06 | 4.4 | 22 49 | 4.7 |
| 23 Tuesday | 10 17 | 6.1 | 22 44 | 6.0 | 07 47 | 8.0 | 20 26 | 8.3 | 08 54 | 2.9 | 22 06 | 2.8 | 11 18 | 4.7 | 23 55 | 5.0 |
| 24 Wednesday | 11 27 | 6.6 | 23 46 | 6.5 | 08 48 | 8.7 | 21 20 | 8.9 | 10 02 | 3.1 | 23 00 | 3.0 | 12 16 | 5.1 | — | — |
| 25 Thursday | — | — | 12 23 | 7.0 | 09 40 | 9.3 | 22 09 | 9.4 | 10 56 | 3.4 | 23 46 | 3.2 | 00 48 | 5.4 | 13 05 | 5.5 |
| 26 Friday | 00 39 | 6.9 | 13 14 | 7.3 | 10 28 | 9.8 | 22 54 | 9.8 | 11 44 | 3.5 | — | — | 01 34 | 5.6 | 13 50 | 5.8 |
| 27 Saturday | 01 28 | 7.2 | 14 01 | 7.5 | 11 14 | 10.0 | 23 37 | 9.9 | 00 30 | 3.3 | 12 31 | 3.6 | 02 17 | 5.8 | 14 34 | 6.0 |
| 28 Sunday | 02 14 | 7.3 | 14 45 | 7.4 | 11 58 | 10.0 | — | — | 01 11 | 3.4 | 13 17 | 3.7 | 03 00 | 5.8 | 15 20 | 6.0 |
| 29 Monday | 02 59 | 7.4 | 15 27 | 7.3 | 00 19 | 9.8 | 12 42 | 9.7 | 01 48 | 3.4 | 14 00 | 3.7 | 03 44 | 5.7 | 16 08 | 5.8 |
| 30 Tuesday | 03 42 | 7.4 | 16 06 | 7.1 | 01 01 | 9.5 | 13 25 | 9.3 | 02 24 | 3.5 | 14 42 | 3.6 | 04 28 | 5.5 | 16 57 | 5.6 |

MAY 2002 *High Water* GMT

| | | London Bridge | | | | Liverpool | | | | Greenock | | | | Leith | | | |
|---|---|---|---|---|---|---|---|---|---|---|---|---|---|---|---|---|---|
| | | *Datum of Predictions 3.20m below | | | | *Datum of Predictions 4.93m below | | | | *Datum of Predictions 1.62m below | | | | *Datum of Predictions 2.90m below | | | |
| | | hr | ht m | hr | ht m | hr | ht m | hr | ht m | hr | ht m | hr | ht m | hr | ht m | hr | ht m |
| 1 | Wednesday | 04 24 | 7.2 | 16 44 | 6.9 | 01 42 | 9.1 | 14 07 | 8.8 | 03 00 | 3.5 | 15 23 | 3.5 | 05 13 | 5.3 | 17 49 | 5.2 |
| 2 | Thursday | 05 07 | 6.9 | 17 20 | 6.5 | 02 24 | 8.7 | 14 52 | 8.2 | 03 38 | 3.4 | 16 06 | 3.3 | 06 01 | 5.0 | 18 45 | 4.8 |
| 3 | Friday | 05 52 | 6.5 | 17 58 | 6.1 | 03 10 | 8.1 | 15 44 | 7.5 | 04 19 | 3.2 | 16 53 | 3.0 | 06 55 | 4.7 | 19 45 | 4.5 |
| 4 | Saturday | 06 44 | 6.0 | 18 44 | 5.7 | 04 08 | 7.6 | 16 55 | 7.0 | 05 08 | 3.0 | 17 49 | 2.8 | 07 58 | 4.4 | 20 50 | 4.3 |
| 5 | Sunday | 08 02 | 5.6 | 20 05 | 5.4 | 05 29 | 7.2 | 18 19 | 6.9 | 06 08 | 2.8 | 18 57 | 2.6 | 09 07 | 4.3 | 22 00 | 4.2 |
| 6 | Monday | 09 24 | 5.6 | 21 38 | 5.5 | 06 47 | 7.3 | 19 29 | 7.1 | 07 34 | 2.7 | 20 49 | 2.6 | 10 18 | 4.3 | 23 13 | 4.3 |
| 7 | Tuesday | 10 27 | 5.9 | 22 41 | 5.8 | 07 51 | 7.6 | 20 25 | 7.5 | 09 16 | 2.8 | 21 56 | 2.7 | 11 27 | 4.4 | — | — |
| 8 | Wednesday | 11 21 | 6.2 | 23 34 | 6.1 | 08 43 | 8.0 | 21 10 | 8.0 | 10 12 | 3.0 | 22 42 | 2.9 | 00 12 | 4.6 | 12 22 | 4.7 |
| 9 | Thursday | 12 08 | 6.5 | — | — | 09 27 | 8.4 | 21 49 | 8.3 | 10 56 | 3.1 | 23 21 | 2.9 | 00 56 | 4.8 | 13 03 | 4.9 |
| 10 | Friday | 00 21 | 6.4 | 12 51 | 6.7 | 10 06 | 8.6 | 22 25 | 8.6 | 11 34 | 3.1 | 23 56 | 3.0 | 01 30 | 4.9 | 13 39 | 5.0 |
| 11 | Saturday | 01 03 | 6.5 | 13 28 | 6.7 | 10 42 | 8.8 | 22 57 | 8.7 | 12 08 | 3.1 | — | — | 02 02 | 5.1 | 14 11 | 5.1 |
| 12 | Sunday | 01 41 | 6.6 | 14 03 | 6.7 | 11 15 | 8.8 | 23 29 | 8.8 | 00 26 | 3.1 | 12 40 | 3.1 | 02 33 | 5.2 | 14 44 | 5.2 |
| 13 | Monday | 02 16 | 6.6 | 14 35 | 6.7 | 11 48 | 8.8 | — | — | 00 55 | 3.1 | 13 11 | 3.1 | 03 05 | 5.2 | 15 18 | 5.2 |
| 14 | Tuesday | 02 50 | 6.6 | 15 09 | 6.7 | 00 01 | 8.8 | 12 22 | 8.8 | 01 24 | 3.2 | 13 47 | 3.1 | 03 38 | 5.2 | 15 54 | 5.2 |
| 15 | Wednesday | 03 25 | 6.6 | 15 43 | 6.6 | 00 35 | 8.8 | 12 59 | 8.8 | 01 57 | 3.3 | 14 25 | 3.1 | 04 13 | 5.2 | 16 32 | 5.2 |
| 16 | Thursday | 04 03 | 6.7 | 16 20 | 6.6 | 01 12 | 8.7 | 13 39 | 8.6 | 02 32 | 3.3 | 15 05 | 3.0 | 04 50 | 5.1 | 17 14 | 5.1 |
| 17 | Friday | 04 44 | 6.6 | 17 01 | 6.4 | 01 53 | 8.6 | 14 24 | 8.4 | 03 07 | 3.3 | 15 48 | 2.9 | 05 31 | 4.9 | 18 00 | 4.9 |
| 18 | Saturday | 05 32 | 6.5 | 17 47 | 6.2 | 02 40 | 8.3 | 15 16 | 8.0 | 03 46 | 3.2 | 16 39 | 2.8 | 06 18 | 4.8 | 18 53 | 4.8 |
| 19 | Sunday | 06 25 | 6.3 | 18 40 | 6.0 | 03 38 | 8.0 | 16 20 | 7.7 | 04 32 | 3.1 | 17 45 | 2.7 | 07 13 | 4.6 | 19 56 | 4.7 |
| 20 | Monday | 07 28 | 6.1 | 19 46 | 5.8 | 04 48 | 7.8 | 17 36 | 7.6 | 05 34 | 2.9 | 19 04 | 2.6 | 08 23 | 4.6 | 21 09 | 4.7 |
| 21 | Tuesday | 08 42 | 6.1 | 21 05 | 5.9 | 06 05 | 7.9 | 18 51 | 7.8 | 06 56 | 2.9 | 20 25 | 2.7 | 09 40 | 4.7 | 22 22 | 4.8 |
| 22 | Wednesday | 09 57 | 6.3 | 22 16 | 6.2 | 07 17 | 8.2 | 19 57 | 8.3 | 08 24 | 3.0 | 21 36 | 2.9 | 10 49 | 4.9 | 23 27 | 5.0 |
| 23 | Thursday | 11 02 | 6.6 | 23 18 | 6.5 | 08 20 | 8.7 | 20 54 | 8.8 | 09 34 | 3.2 | 22 32 | 3.0 | 11 47 | 5.2 | — | — |
| 24 | Friday | 11 58 | 7.0 | — | — | 09 15 | 9.1 | 21 44 | 9.2 | 10 30 | 3.3 | 23 20 | 3.1 | 00 21 | 5.3 | 12 39 | 5.4 |
| 25 | Saturday | 00 13 | 6.9 | 12 50 | 7.2 | 10 05 | 9.4 | 22 30 | 9.5 | 11 20 | 3.4 | — | — | 01 10 | 5.4 | 13 28 | 5.6 |
| 26 | Sunday | 01 04 | 7.1 | 13 37 | 7.3 | 10 53 | 9.6 | 23 14 | 9.6 | 00 04 | 3.3 | 12 09 | 3.5 | 01 55 | 5.6 | 14 16 | 5.7 |
| 27 | Monday | 01 53 | 7.2 | 14 22 | 7.2 | 11 38 | 9.5 | 23 57 | 9.5 | 00 46 | 3.3 | 12 56 | 3.5 | 02 39 | 5.6 | 15 04 | 5.7 |
| 28 | Tuesday | 02 40 | 7.2 | 15 05 | 7.1 | 12 22 | 9.3 | — | — | 01 25 | 3.4 | 13 41 | 3.4 | 03 23 | 5.6 | 15 53 | 5.6 |
| 29 | Wednesday | 03 25 | 7.2 | 15 45 | 7.0 | 00 39 | 9.3 | 13 06 | 9.0 | 02 03 | 3.5 | 14 25 | 3.4 | 04 08 | 5.4 | 16 42 | 5.4 |
| 30 | Thursday | 04 09 | 7.0 | 16 22 | 6.7 | 01 21 | 9.0 | 13 48 | 8.6 | 02 41 | 3.5 | 15 08 | 3.3 | 04 53 | 5.2 | 17 32 | 5.1 |
| 31 | Friday | 04 52 | 6.8 | 16 58 | 6.5 | 02 03 | 8.7 | 14 31 | 8.2 | 03 20 | 3.4 | 15 53 | 3.1 | 05 39 | 5.0 | 18 22 | 4.8 |

JUNE 2002 *High Water* GMT

| | | London Bridge | | | | Liverpool | | | | Greenock | | | | Leith | | | |
|---|---|---|---|---|---|---|---|---|---|---|---|---|---|---|---|---|---|
| 1 | Saturday | 05 36 | 6.4 | 17 36 | 6.2 | 02 47 | 8.3 | 15 18 | 7.7 | 04 01 | 3.3 | 16 40 | 3.0 | 06 28 | 4.8 | 19 15 | 4 |
| 2 | Sunday | 06 24 | 6.1 | 18 20 | 5.9 | 03 37 | 7.9 | 16 13 | 7.3 | 04 47 | 3.1 | 17 33 | 2.8 | 07 23 | 4.6 | 20 09 | 4. |
| 3 | Monday | 07 21 | 5.8 | 19 18 | 5.7 | 04 39 | 7.5 | 17 22 | 7.0 | 05 41 | 3.0 | 18 29 | 2.7 | 08 22 | 4.4 | 21 06 | 4. |
| 4 | Tuesday | 08 29 | 5.7 | 20 35 | 5.6 | 05 52 | 7.4 | 18 33 | 7.1 | 06 44 | 2.8 | 19 29 | 2.7 | 09 23 | 4.4 | 22 06 | 4. |
| 5 | Wednesday | 09 35 | 5.8 | 21 46 | 5.7 | 06 57 | 7.5 | 19 33 | 7.3 | 07 58 | 2.8 | 20 36 | 2.7 | 10 24 | 4.4 | 23 05 | 4. |
| 6 | Thursday | 10 31 | 6.0 | 22 44 | 5.9 | 07 55 | 7.7 | 20 25 | 7.7 | 09 13 | 2.8 | 21 42 | 2.8 | 11 21 | 4.5 | 23 59 | 4. |
| 7 | Friday | 11 22 | 6.2 | 23 36 | 6.1 | 08 44 | 8.0 | 21 09 | 8.1 | 10 09 | 2.9 | 22 34 | 2.9 | 12 13 | 4.7 | — | — |
| 8 | Saturday | 12 08 | 6.4 | — | — | 09 27 | 8.3 | 21 48 | 8.4 | 10 52 | 2.9 | 23 15 | 3.0 | 00 44 | 4.8 | 12 58 | 4. |
| 9 | Sunday | 00 23 | 6.3 | 12 51 | 6.6 | 10 07 | 8.5 | 22 24 | 8.6 | 11 30 | 3.0 | 23 52 | 3.1 | 01 24 | 5.0 | 13 39 | 5. |
| 10 | Monday | 01 07 | 6.5 | 13 31 | 6.7 | 10 45 | 8.7 | 23 00 | 8.8 | 12 07 | 3.0 | — | — | 02 02 | 5.1 | 14 18 | 5. |
| 11 | Tuesday | 01 49 | 6.6 | 14 11 | 6.7 | 11 23 | 8.8 | 23 37 | 8.9 | 00 26 | 3.2 | 12 46 | 3.0 | 02 39 | 5.2 | 14 57 | 5. |
| 12 | Wednesday | 02 30 | 6.7 | 14 50 | 6.7 | 12 03 | 8.8 | — | — | 01 01 | 3.3 | 13 28 | 3.0 | 03 16 | 5.2 | 15 36 | 5. |
| 13 | Thursday | 03 11 | 6.8 | 15 29 | 6.7 | 00 17 | 9.0 | 12 45 | 8.8 | 01 38 | 3.3 | 14 12 | 3.0 | 03 54 | 5.3 | 16 17 | 5. |
| 14 | Friday | 03 54 | 6.8 | 16 10 | 6.6 | 01 00 | 8.9 | 13 30 | 8.8 | 02 16 | 3.4 | 14 57 | 3.0 | 04 34 | 5.2 | 17 01 | 5. |
| 15 | Saturday | 04 39 | 6.8 | 16 52 | 6.5 | 01 46 | 8.9 | 14 18 | 8.6 | 02 56 | 3.4 | 15 46 | 2.9 | 05 17 | 5.2 | 17 49 | 5. |
| 16 | Sunday | 05 27 | 6.7 | 17 38 | 6.4 | 02 35 | 8.7 | 15 09 | 8.4 | 03 38 | 3.4 | 16 40 | 2.9 | 06 04 | 5.1 | 18 41 | 5. |
| 17 | Monday | 06 19 | 6.5 | 18 29 | 6.3 | 03 30 | 8.5 | 16 07 | 8.2 | 04 26 | 3.3 | 17 41 | 2.8 | 06 58 | 4.9 | 19 39 | 4. |
| 18 | Tuesday | 07 18 | 6.4 | 19 31 | 6.1 | 04 31 | 8.4 | 17 12 | 8.0 | 05 24 | 3.1 | 18 45 | 2.8 | 08 01 | 4.9 | 20 45 | 4. |
| 19 | Wednesday | 08 24 | 6.3 | 20 40 | 6.1 | 05 38 | 8.3 | 18 21 | 8.0 | 06 32 | 3.1 | 19 52 | 2.8 | 09 12 | 4.9 | 21 53 | 4. |
| 20 | Thursday | 09 31 | 6.3 | 21 47 | 6.2 | 06 46 | 8.3 | 19 27 | 8.2 | 07 49 | 3.1 | 21 01 | 2.9 | 10 19 | 5.0 | 22 57 | 4. |
| 21 | Friday | 10 35 | 6.5 | 22 51 | 6.4 | 07 52 | 8.5 | 20 28 | 8.5 | 09 04 | 3.1 | 22 03 | 3.0 | 11 21 | 5.1 | 23 56 | 5. |
| 22 | Saturday | 11 33 | 6.7 | 23 50 | 6.7 | 08 52 | 8.7 | 21 22 | 8.8 | 10 07 | 3.2 | 22 56 | 3.1 | 12 19 | 5.2 | — | — |
| 23 | Sunday | 12 27 | 6.9 | — | — | 09 47 | 8.9 | 22 11 | 9.1 | 11 02 | 3.2 | 23 44 | 3.2 | 00 48 | 5.2 | 13 14 | 5. |
| 24 | Monday | 00 45 | 6.9 | 13 17 | 7.0 | 10 37 | 9.0 | 22 56 | 9.2 | 11 53 | 3.3 | — | — | 01 37 | 5.3 | 14 05 | 5. |
| 25 | Tuesday | 01 37 | 7.0 | 14 04 | 7.0 | 11 24 | 9.0 | 23 40 | 9.2 | 00 27 | 3.3 | 12 42 | 3.2 | 02 23 | 5.4 | 14 54 | 5. |
| 26 | Wednesday | 02 26 | 7.0 | 14 47 | 6.9 | 12 08 | 8.9 | — | — | 01 09 | 3.4 | 13 29 | 3.2 | 03 08 | 5.4 | 15 41 | 5. |
| 27 | Thursday | 03 13 | 7.0 | 15 28 | 6.8 | 00 22 | 9.2 | 12 50 | 8.8 | 01 48 | 3.4 | 14 14 | 3.1 | 03 52 | 5.4 | 16 27 | 5. |
| 28 | Friday | 03 56 | 6.9 | 16 04 | 6.7 | 01 03 | 9.0 | 13 30 | 8.5 | 02 26 | 3.5 | 14 57 | 3.1 | 04 34 | 5.2 | 17 11 | 5. |
| 29 | Saturday | 04 37 | 6.7 | 16 39 | 6.5 | 01 43 | 8.8 | 14 09 | 8.3 | 03 04 | 3.4 | 15 39 | 3.0 | 05 16 | 5.1 | 17 54 | 4. |
| 30 | Sunday | 05 17 | 6.5 | 17 15 | 6.4 | 02 23 | 8.5 | 14 49 | 8.0 | 03 43 | 3.3 | 16 22 | 3.0 | 05 58 | 4.9 | 18 38 | 4. |

ULY 2002 *High Water* GMT

| | London Bridge | | | | Liverpool | | | | Greenock | | | | Leith | | | |
|---|---|---|---|---|---|---|---|---|---|---|---|---|---|---|---|---|
| | *Datum of Predictions 3.20m below | | | | *Datum of Predictions 4.93m below | | | | *Datum of Predictions 1.62m below | | | | *Datum of Predictions 2.90m below | | | |
| | hr | ht m | hr | ht m | hr | ht m | hr | ht m | hr | ht m | hr | ht m | hr | ht m | hr | ht m |
| 1 Monday | 05 56 | 6.3 | 17 55 | 6.2 | 03 05 | 8.2 | 15 31 | 7.7 | 04 24 | 3.2 | 17 06 | 2.9 | 06 43 | 4.8 | 19 23 | 4.5 |
| 2 Tuesday | 06 39 | 6.0 | 18 41 | 6.0 | 03 51 | 7.9 | 16 20 | 7.4 | 05 08 | 3.1 | 17 52 | 2.9 | 07 32 | 4.6 | 20 12 | 4.4 |
| 3 Wednesday | 07 28 | 5.9 | 19 35 | 5.8 | 04 44 | 7.6 | 17 18 | 7.2 | 05 57 | 2.9 | 18 40 | 2.8 | 08 25 | 4.5 | 21 05 | 4.3 |
| 4 Thursday | 08 23 | 5.8 | 20 37 | 5.7 | 05 45 | 7.5 | 18 25 | 7.2 | 06 51 | 2.8 | 19 30 | 2.8 | 09 22 | 4.4 | 22 00 | 4.3 |
| 5 Friday | 09 24 | 5.8 | 21 41 | 5.8 | 06 50 | 7.5 | 19 28 | 7.4 | 07 53 | 2.7 | 20 28 | 2.8 | 10 20 | 4.4 | 22 58 | 4.4 |
| 6 Saturday | 10 25 | 6.0 | 22 44 | 5.9 | 07 51 | 7.7 | 20 23 | 7.8 | 09 03 | 2.8 | 21 35 | 2.8 | 11 20 | 4.5 | 23 56 | 4.6 |
| 7 Sunday | 11 22 | 6.2 | 23 42 | 6.1 | 08 45 | 7.9 | 21 11 | 8.2 | 10 06 | 2.8 | 22 34 | 2.9 | 12 18 | 4.6 | — | — |
| 8 Monday | 12 15 | 6.4 | — | — | 09 33 | 8.3 | 21 55 | 8.5 | 10 57 | 2.9 | 23 20 | 3.0 | 00 49 | 4.8 | 13 10 | 4.8 |
| 9 Tuesday | 00 35 | 6.4 | 13 04 | 6.6 | 10 19 | 8.5 | 22 37 | 8.8 | 11 43 | 3.0 | — | — | 01 36 | 5.0 | 13 56 | 5.0 |
| 0 Wednesday | 01 25 | 6.6 | 13 50 | 6.7 | 11 03 | 8.8 | 23 20 | 9.1 | 00 02 | 3.2 | 12 29 | 3.0 | 02 18 | 5.2 | 14 39 | 5.3 |
| 1 Thursday | 02 13 | 6.8 | 14 35 | 6.8 | 11 49 | 8.9 | — | — | 00 43 | 3.3 | 13 16 | 3.0 | 02 58 | 5.3 | 15 21 | 5.4 |
| 2 Friday | 02 59 | 7.0 | 15 18 | 6.8 | 00 04 | 9.2 | 12 35 | 9.1 | 01 23 | 3.4 | 14 05 | 3.0 | 03 38 | 5.4 | 16 03 | 5.5 |
| 3 Saturday | 03 45 | 7.0 | 16 01 | 6.8 | 00 50 | 9.3 | 13 21 | 9.1 | 02 05 | 3.5 | 14 53 | 3.0 | 04 19 | 5.5 | 16 47 | 5.5 |
| 4 Sunday | 04 31 | 7.1 | 16 43 | 6.8 | 01 37 | 9.3 | 14 08 | 9.1 | 02 47 | 3.5 | 15 41 | 3.0 | 05 02 | 5.5 | 17 34 | 5.4 |
| 5 Monday | 05 17 | 7.0 | 17 27 | 6.7 | 02 25 | 9.3 | 14 56 | 8.9 | 03 30 | 3.5 | 16 30 | 3.0 | 05 49 | 5.4 | 18 23 | 5.3 |
| 6 Tuesday | 06 06 | 6.8 | 18 13 | 6.6 | 03 15 | 9.1 | 15 47 | 8.6 | 04 16 | 3.5 | 17 20 | 3.0 | 06 39 | 5.3 | 19 17 | 5.1 |
| 7 Wednesday | 06 58 | 6.6 | 19 06 | 6.4 | 04 08 | 8.8 | 16 43 | 8.3 | 05 06 | 3.4 | 18 12 | 2.9 | 07 36 | 5.1 | 20 17 | 4.9 |
| 8 Thursday | 07 57 | 6.3 | 20 08 | 6.2 | 05 08 | 8.4 | 17 47 | 8.0 | 06 03 | 3.2 | 19 09 | 2.9 | 08 43 | 5.0 | 21 23 | 4.7 |
| 9 Friday | 09 02 | 6.2 | 21 17 | 6.1 | 06 15 | 8.1 | 18 57 | 7.9 | 07 08 | 3.1 | 20 20 | 2.8 | 09 53 | 4.9 | 22 29 | 4.7 |
| 0 Saturday | 10 08 | 6.2 | 22 27 | 6.2 | 07 28 | 8.1 | 20 06 | 8.1 | 08 31 | 3.0 | 21 37 | 2.9 | 11 01 | 4.9 | 23 34 | 4.8 |
| 1 Sunday | 11 10 | 6.3 | 23 33 | 6.4 | 08 37 | 8.2 | 21 06 | 8.4 | 09 51 | 3.0 | 22 38 | 3.0 | 12 08 | 5.0 | — | — |
| 2 Monday | 12 07 | 6.5 | — | — | 09 37 | 8.4 | 21 59 | 8.7 | 10 54 | 3.0 | 23 29 | 3.2 | 00 35 | 4.9 | 13 08 | 5.1 |
| 3 Tuesday | 00 32 | 6.6 | 13 00 | 6.7 | 10 28 | 8.6 | 22 45 | 9.0 | 11 48 | 3.1 | — | — | 01 29 | 5.1 | 14 01 | 5.2 |
| 4 Wednesday | 01 26 | 6.8 | 13 49 | 6.8 | 11 14 | 8.7 | 23 27 | 9.1 | 00 14 | 3.3 | 12 38 | 3.1 | 02 15 | 5.2 | 14 47 | 5.3 |
| 5 Thursday | 02 15 | 6.9 | 14 33 | 6.8 | 11 56 | 8.8 | — | — | 00 56 | 3.4 | 13 23 | 3.1 | 02 57 | 5.3 | 15 29 | 5.3 |
| 6 Friday | 03 01 | 6.9 | 15 13 | 6.8 | 00 07 | 9.1 | 12 35 | 8.7 | 01 35 | 3.4 | 14 04 | 3.0 | 03 37 | 5.3 | 16 09 | 5.2 |
| 7 Saturday | 03 42 | 6.8 | 15 47 | 6.7 | 00 44 | 9.1 | 13 10 | 8.6 | 02 12 | 3.4 | 14 41 | 3.0 | 04 14 | 5.3 | 16 46 | 5.1 |
| 8 Sunday | 04 18 | 6.7 | 16 19 | 6.6 | 01 20 | 9.0 | 13 44 | 8.5 | 02 47 | 3.4 | 15 17 | 3.0 | 04 50 | 5.2 | 17 22 | 5.0 |
| 9 Monday | 04 51 | 6.5 | 16 50 | 6.5 | 01 56 | 8.8 | 14 18 | 8.3 | 03 21 | 3.4 | 15 53 | 3.0 | 05 26 | 5.1 | 17 59 | 4.8 |
| 0 Tuesday | 05 24 | 6.4 | 17 26 | 6.4 | 02 32 | 8.5 | 14 53 | 8.1 | 03 55 | 3.3 | 16 30 | 3.0 | 06 04 | 5.0 | 18 39 | 4.7 |
| 1 Wednesday | 06 00 | 6.3 | 18 05 | 6.3 | 03 10 | 8.2 | 15 32 | 7.8 | 04 32 | 3.2 | 17 09 | 3.0 | 06 45 | 4.8 | 19 23 | 4.5 |

UGUST 2002 *High Water* GMT

| | London Bridge | | | | Liverpool | | | | Greenock | | | | Leith | | | |
|---|---|---|---|---|---|---|---|---|---|---|---|---|---|---|---|---|
| 1 Thursday | 06 41 | 6.1 | 18 50 | 6.1 | 03 53 | 7.9 | 16 17 | 7.5 | 05 12 | 3.0 | 17 51 | 2.9 | 07 31 | 4.6 | 20 12 | 4.4 |
| 2 Friday | 07 28 | 6.0 | 19 42 | 5.9 | 04 44 | 7.6 | 17 14 | 7.3 | 05 59 | 2.9 | 18 38 | 2.8 | 08 25 | 4.4 | 21 08 | 4.3 |
| 3 Saturday | 08 23 | 5.8 | 20 42 | 5.7 | 05 46 | 7.3 | 18 24 | 7.2 | 06 56 | 2.7 | 19 32 | 2.8 | 09 27 | 4.3 | 22 09 | 4.3 |
| 4 Sunday | 09 28 | 5.8 | 21 51 | 5.7 | 06 56 | 7.3 | 19 36 | 7.5 | 08 07 | 2.7 | 20 40 | 2.8 | 10 34 | 4.3 | 23 14 | 4.4 |
| 5 Monday | 10 38 | 5.9 | 23 03 | 5.9 | 08 06 | 7.6 | 20 39 | 7.9 | 09 27 | 2.7 | 21 54 | 2.9 | 11 43 | 4.5 | — | — |
| 6 Tuesday | 11 43 | 6.2 | — | — | 09 06 | 8.0 | 21 31 | 8.4 | 10 36 | 2.9 | 22 53 | 3.0 | 00 17 | 4.7 | 12 45 | 4.8 |
| 7 Wednesday | 00 08 | 6.3 | 12 41 | 6.5 | 09 59 | 8.5 | 22 19 | 8.9 | 11 30 | 3.0 | 23 41 | 3.2 | 01 12 | 4.9 | 13 37 | 5.1 |
| 8 Thursday | 01 05 | 6.6 | 13 32 | 6.7 | 10 48 | 8.9 | 23 04 | 9.3 | 12 19 | 3.1 | — | — | 01 58 | 5.2 | 14 21 | 5.4 |
| 9 Friday | 01 56 | 7.0 | 14 19 | 6.9 | 11 35 | 9.2 | 23 50 | 9.6 | 00 25 | 3.4 | 13 08 | 3.1 | 02 39 | 5.5 | 15 04 | 5.6 |
| 0 Saturday | 02 44 | 7.2 | 15 03 | 7.0 | 12 21 | 9.4 | — | — | 01 08 | 3.5 | 13 56 | 3.2 | 03 19 | 5.7 | 15 45 | 5.8 |
| 1 Sunday | 03 30 | 7.3 | 15 45 | 7.1 | 00 35 | 9.8 | 13 06 | 9.5 | 01 51 | 3.6 | 14 41 | 3.2 | 04 00 | 5.8 | 16 29 | 5.8 |
| 2 Monday | 04 15 | 7.3 | 16 26 | 7.1 | 01 21 | 9.8 | 13 51 | 9.4 | 02 34 | 3.7 | 15 24 | 3.2 | 04 43 | 5.8 | 17 13 | 5.7 |
| 3 Tuesday | 04 59 | 7.2 | 17 07 | 7.1 | 02 07 | 9.7 | 14 35 | 9.2 | 03 16 | 3.7 | 16 05 | 3.2 | 05 28 | 5.7 | 18 00 | 5.4 |
| 4 Wednesday | 05 44 | 7.0 | 17 50 | 6.9 | 02 53 | 9.4 | 15 21 | 8.9 | 03 58 | 3.7 | 16 46 | 3.2 | 06 17 | 5.5 | 18 51 | 5.2 |
| 5 Thursday | 06 30 | 6.6 | 18 36 | 6.6 | 03 42 | 8.9 | 16 12 | 8.4 | 04 43 | 3.5 | 17 30 | 3.1 | 07 12 | 5.3 | 19 48 | 4.9 |
| 6 Friday | 07 22 | 6.2 | 19 32 | 6.2 | 04 38 | 8.3 | 17 13 | 7.9 | 05 31 | 3.3 | 18 20 | 2.9 | 08 18 | 5.0 | 20 54 | 4.6 |
| 7 Saturday | 08 27 | 5.9 | 20 47 | 5.9 | 05 48 | 7.7 | 18 31 | 7.6 | 06 28 | 3.0 | 19 25 | 2.8 | 09 33 | 4.7 | 22 05 | 4.5 |
| 8 Sunday | 09 41 | 5.7 | 22 10 | 5.8 | 07 12 | 7.5 | 19 51 | 7.7 | 07 52 | 2.8 | 21 15 | 2.8 | 10 49 | 4.7 | 23 19 | 4.6 |
| 9 Monday | 10 49 | 5.9 | 23 20 | 6.1 | 08 30 | 7.7 | 20 56 | 8.1 | 09 52 | 2.8 | 22 24 | 3.0 | 12 04 | 4.8 | — | — |
| 20 Tuesday | 11 50 | 6.2 | — | — | 09 30 | 8.1 | 21 48 | 8.6 | 10 56 | 3.0 | 23 16 | 3.2 | 00 27 | 4.8 | 13 08 | 4.9 |
| 21 Wednesday | 00 20 | 6.5 | 12 44 | 6.5 | 10 19 | 8.4 | 22 33 | 8.9 | 11 47 | 3.0 | — | — | 01 23 | 5.0 | 13 57 | 5.1 |
| 22 Thursday | 01 14 | 6.8 | 13 32 | 6.7 | 11 02 | 8.6 | 23 13 | 9.1 | 00 01 | 3.3 | 12 32 | 3.1 | 02 07 | 5.2 | 14 37 | 5.2 |
| 23 Friday | 02 02 | 7.0 | 14 16 | 6.8 | 11 39 | 8.7 | 23 49 | 9.2 | 00 42 | 3.4 | 13 11 | 3.1 | 02 44 | 5.3 | 15 13 | 5.2 |
| 24 Saturday | 02 44 | 7.0 | 14 54 | 6.8 | 12 13 | 8.8 | — | — | 01 20 | 3.4 | 13 47 | 3.1 | 03 19 | 5.4 | 15 46 | 5.2 |
| 25 Sunday | 03 21 | 6.8 | 15 27 | 6.7 | 00 22 | 9.1 | 12 44 | 8.7 | 01 54 | 3.4 | 14 18 | 3.1 | 03 50 | 5.4 | 16 17 | 5.2 |
| 26 Monday | 03 52 | 6.7 | 15 54 | 6.6 | 00 55 | 9.0 | 13 15 | 8.6 | 02 25 | 3.4 | 14 47 | 3.1 | 04 21 | 5.3 | 16 49 | 5.1 |
| 27 Tuesday | 04 20 | 6.5 | 16 23 | 6.5 | 01 26 | 8.9 | 13 45 | 8.5 | 02 54 | 3.4 | 15 17 | 3.2 | 04 53 | 5.2 | 17 23 | 5.0 |
| 28 Wednesday | 04 48 | 6.5 | 16 54 | 6.5 | 01 58 | 8.7 | 14 16 | 8.3 | 03 25 | 3.3 | 15 49 | 3.2 | 05 28 | 5.1 | 17 59 | 4.8 |
| 29 Thursday | 05 21 | 6.4 | 17 29 | 6.4 | 02 32 | 8.4 | 14 50 | 8.1 | 03 57 | 3.2 | 16 24 | 3.1 | 06 06 | 4.9 | 18 39 | 4.7 |
| 30 Friday | 05 59 | 6.3 | 18 10 | 6.3 | 03 10 | 8.1 | 15 30 | 7.7 | 04 34 | 3.1 | 17 03 | 3.0 | 06 48 | 4.7 | 19 25 | 4.5 |
| 31 Saturday | 06 41 | 6.1 | 18 58 | 6.0 | 03 57 | 7.6 | 16 22 | 7.3 | 05 16 | 2.9 | 17 48 | 2.9 | 07 37 | 4.4 | 20 19 | 4.3 |

## SEPTEMBER 2002 *High Water* GMT

| | | London Bridge | | | | Liverpool | | | | Greenock | | | | Leith | | | |
|---|---|---|---|---|---|---|---|---|---|---|---|---|---|---|---|---|---|
| | | *Datum of Predictions 3.20m below | | | | *Datum of Predictions 4.93m below | | | | *Datum of Predictions 1.62m below | | | | *Datum of Predictions 2.90m below | | | |
| | | hr | ht m | hr | ht m | hr | ht m | hr | ht m | hr | ht m | hr | ht m | hr | ht m | hr | ht m |
| 1 | Sunday | 07 33 | 5.8 | 19 56 | 5.8 | 04 58 | 7.2 | 17 31 | 7.1 | 06 12 | 2.7 | 18 44 | 2.8 | 08 40 | 4.3 | 21 25 | 4. |
| 2 | Monday | 08 35 | 5.6 | 21 05 | 5.7 | 06 13 | 7.1 | 18 54 | 7.2 | 07 26 | 2.6 | 19 55 | 2.8 | 09 55 | 4.3 | 22 38 | 4. |
| 3 | Tuesday | 09 53 | 5.6 | 22 27 | 5.8 | 07 36 | 7.4 | 20 12 | 7.7 | 09 01 | 2.7 | 21 20 | 2.9 | 11 13 | 4.5 | 23 49 | 4. |
| 4 | Wednesday | 11 14 | 5.9 | 23 45 | 6.2 | 08 46 | 7.9 | 21 11 | 8.4 | 10 24 | 2.9 | 22 28 | 3.1 | 12 22 | 4.8 | — | — |
| 5 | Thursday | 12 17 | 6.4 | — | — | 09 42 | 8.5 | 22 00 | 9.1 | 11 19 | 3.1 | 23 19 | 3.3 | 00 47 | 5.0 | 13 16 | 5. |
| 6 | Friday | 00 45 | 6.7 | 13 10 | 6.7 | 10 30 | 9.1 | 22 46 | 9.6 | 12 07 | 3.2 | — | — | 01 34 | 5.3 | 14 00 | 5. |
| 7 | Saturday | 01 37 | 7.1 | 13 57 | 7.0 | 11 16 | 9.5 | 23 31 | 9.9 | 00 05 | 3.5 | 12 53 | 3.3 | 02 16 | 5.7 | 14 42 | 5. |
| 8 | Sunday | 02 24 | 7.4 | 14 40 | 7.2 | 12 00 | 9.7 | — | — | 00 50 | 3.7 | 13 37 | 3.3 | 02 56 | 5.9 | 15 23 | 6. |
| 9 | Monday | 03 09 | 7.5 | 15 22 | 7.3 | 00 15 | 10.1 | 12 44 | 9.8 | 01 33 | 3.8 | 14 18 | 3.4 | 03 37 | 6.1 | 16 05 | 6. |
| 10 | Tuesday | 03 52 | 7.5 | 16 03 | 7.3 | 00 59 | 10.1 | 13 27 | 9.7 | 02 16 | 3.9 | 14 56 | 3.4 | 04 20 | 6.1 | 16 49 | 5. |
| 11 | Wednesday | 04 34 | 7.3 | 16 43 | 7.3 | 01 43 | 9.8 | 14 10 | 9.4 | 02 57 | 3.9 | 15 33 | 3.4 | 05 06 | 5.9 | 17 35 | 5. |
| 12 | Thursday | 05 16 | 7.0 | 17 24 | 7.1 | 02 28 | 9.4 | 14 53 | 8.9 | 03 37 | 3.8 | 16 10 | 3.4 | 05 55 | 5.6 | 18 24 | 5. |
| 13 | Friday | 05 57 | 6.6 | 18 08 | 6.7 | 03 15 | 8.7 | 15 41 | 8.3 | 04 18 | 3.6 | 16 51 | 3.2 | 06 51 | 5.2 | 19 20 | 4. |
| 14 | Saturday | 06 42 | 6.1 | 19 00 | 6.2 | 04 10 | 8.0 | 16 42 | 7.7 | 05 04 | 3.3 | 17 39 | 3.1 | 07 59 | 4.8 | 20 28 | 4. |
| 15 | Sunday | 07 42 | 5.6 | 20 21 | 5.7 | 05 26 | 7.3 | 18 08 | 7.3 | 05 57 | 3.0 | 18 39 | 2.9 | 09 17 | 4.6 | 21 44 | 4. |
| 16 | Monday | 09 13 | 5.4 | 21 55 | 5.7 | 07 03 | 7.2 | 19 35 | 7.5 | 07 19 | 2.7 | 20 53 | 2.9 | 10 38 | 4.5 | 23 03 | 4. |
| 17 | Tuesday | 10 28 | 5.6 | 23 05 | 6.0 | 08 19 | 7.5 | 20 40 | 8.0 | 09 55 | 2.8 | 22 07 | 3.1 | 11 58 | 4.7 | — | — |
| 18 | Wednesday | 11 29 | 6.0 | — | — | 09 15 | 8.0 | 21 31 | 8.5 | 10 50 | 3.0 | 22 57 | 3.3 | 00 15 | 4.8 | 12 58 | 4. |
| 19 | Thursday | 00 03 | 6.5 | 12 23 | 6.4 | 10 01 | 8.4 | 22 13 | 8.9 | 11 34 | 3.1 | 23 40 | 3.4 | 01 08 | 5.0 | 13 43 | 5. |
| 20 | Friday | 00 55 | 6.8 | 13 10 | 6.7 | 10 40 | 8.7 | 22 51 | 9.1 | 12 13 | 3.2 | — | — | 01 50 | 5.2 | 14 19 | 5. |
| 21 | Saturday | 01 40 | 7.0 | 13 53 | 6.9 | 11 15 | 8.8 | 23 25 | 9.2 | 00 20 | 3.5 | 12 48 | 3.2 | 02 24 | 5.4 | 14 50 | 5. |
| 22 | Sunday | 02 20 | 7.0 | 14 30 | 6.8 | 11 46 | 8.8 | 23 56 | 9.1 | 00 57 | 3.5 | 13 19 | 3.2 | 02 54 | 5.4 | 15 18 | 5. |
| 23 | Monday | 02 54 | 6.8 | 15 01 | 6.7 | 12 14 | 8.8 | — | — | 01 29 | 3.4 | 13 47 | 3.2 | 03 23 | 5.4 | 15 47 | 5. |
| 24 | Tuesday | 03 21 | 6.7 | 15 27 | 6.6 | 00 26 | 9.0 | 12 43 | 8.8 | 01 58 | 3.4 | 14 13 | 3.3 | 03 52 | 5.4 | 16 17 | 5. |
| 25 | Wednesday | 03 46 | 6.6 | 15 53 | 6.5 | 00 56 | 8.9 | 13 12 | 8.7 | 02 25 | 3.4 | 14 41 | 3.3 | 04 23 | 5.3 | 16 49 | 5. |
| 26 | Thursday | 04 13 | 6.6 | 16 23 | 6.5 | 01 26 | 8.7 | 13 42 | 8.5 | 02 55 | 3.3 | 15 11 | 3.3 | 04 57 | 5.2 | 17 24 | 5. |
| 27 | Friday | 04 44 | 6.5 | 16 57 | 6.5 | 01 58 | 8.5 | 14 14 | 8.3 | 03 27 | 3.3 | 15 45 | 3.3 | 05 34 | 5.0 | 18 02 | 4. |
| 28 | Saturday | 05 20 | 6.4 | 17 38 | 6.4 | 02 35 | 8.1 | 14 52 | 7.9 | 04 02 | 3.1 | 16 21 | 3.2 | 06 16 | 4.7 | 18 45 | 4. |
| 29 | Sunday | 06 02 | 6.2 | 18 26 | 6.1 | 03 21 | 7.7 | 15 43 | 7.5 | 04 42 | 2.9 | 17 03 | 3.0 | 07 05 | 4.5 | 19 37 | 4. |
| 30 | Monday | 06 52 | 5.8 | 19 24 | 5.8 | 04 23 | 7.2 | 16 53 | 7.1 | 05 36 | 2.7 | 17 58 | 2.9 | 08 06 | 4.3 | 20 46 | 4. |

## OCTOBER 2002 *High Water* GMT

| | | London Bridge | | | | Liverpool | | | | Greenock | | | | Leith | | | |
|---|---|---|---|---|---|---|---|---|---|---|---|---|---|---|---|---|---|
| 1 | Tuesday | 07 54 | 5.6 | 20 33 | 5.7 | 05 43 | 7.0 | 18 21 | 7.2 | 06 59 | 2.6 | 19 16 | 2.8 | 09 25 | 4.3 | 22 06 | 4 |
| 2 | Wednesday | 09 12 | 5.5 | 21 58 | 5.8 | 07 13 | 7.3 | 19 45 | 7.7 | 08 44 | 2.7 | 20 48 | 2.9 | 10 46 | 4.5 | 23 20 | 4 |
| 3 | Thursday | 10 43 | 5.8 | 23 21 | 6.3 | 08 25 | 8.0 | 20 47 | 8.5 | 10 10 | 2.9 | 22 01 | 3.2 | 11 56 | 4.9 | — | - |
| 4 | Friday | 11 49 | 6.3 | — | — | 09 20 | 8.7 | 21 37 | 9.2 | 11 02 | 3.2 | 22 54 | 3.4 | 00 19 | 5.1 | 12 50 | 5 |
| 5 | Saturday | 00 21 | 6.8 | 12 41 | 6.8 | 10 07 | 9.3 | 22 23 | 9.8 | 11 47 | 3.3 | 23 41 | 3.6 | 01 07 | 5.5 | 13 35 | 5 |
| 6 | Sunday | 01 13 | 7.2 | 13 28 | 7.1 | 10 52 | 9.7 | 23 08 | 10.1 | 12 30 | 3.4 | — | — | 01 49 | 5.8 | 14 17 | 6 |
| 7 | Monday | 01 59 | 7.5 | 14 13 | 7.3 | 11 35 | 9.9 | 23 51 | 10.2 | 00 27 | 3.8 | 13 11 | 3.5 | 02 30 | 6.1 | 14 58 | 6 |
| 8 | Tuesday | 02 44 | 7.5 | 14 56 | 7.4 | 12 18 | 9.9 | — | — | 01 12 | 3.9 | 13 50 | 3.6 | 03 13 | 6.2 | 15 40 | 6 |
| 9 | Wednesday | 03 26 | 7.5 | 15 38 | 7.5 | 00 35 | 10.1 | 13 01 | 9.8 | 01 55 | 3.9 | 14 27 | 3.6 | 03 58 | 6.2 | 16 24 | 5 |
| 10 | Thursday | 04 07 | 7.3 | 16 20 | 7.4 | 01 19 | 9.7 | 13 43 | 9.4 | 02 36 | 3.9 | 15 02 | 3.6 | 04 46 | 5.9 | 17 10 | 5 |
| 11 | Friday | 04 47 | 7.0 | 17 02 | 7.1 | 02 04 | 9.2 | 14 26 | 8.9 | 03 16 | 3.8 | 15 40 | 3.6 | 05 37 | 5.6 | 17 59 | 5 |
| 12 | Saturday | 05 26 | 6.6 | 17 47 | 6.7 | 02 51 | 8.5 | 15 14 | 8.3 | 03 57 | 3.6 | 16 21 | 3.4 | 06 35 | 5.1 | 18 55 | 4 |
| 13 | Sunday | 06 05 | 6.1 | 18 39 | 6.1 | 03 46 | 7.7 | 16 15 | 7.6 | 04 43 | 3.3 | 17 09 | 3.2 | 07 44 | 4.8 | 20 04 | 4 |
| 14 | Monday | 06 54 | 5.6 | 20 03 | 5.6 | 05 07 | 7.1 | 17 43 | 7.3 | 05 39 | 2.9 | 18 10 | 3.0 | 08 59 | 4.5 | 21 21 | 4 |
| 15 | Tuesday | 08 42 | 5.3 | 21 34 | 5.6 | 06 42 | 7.0 | 19 08 | 7.4 | 07 08 | 2.7 | 20 08 | 3.0 | 10 18 | 4.5 | 22 38 | 4 |
| 16 | Wednesday | 10 00 | 5.5 | 22 40 | 6.0 | 07 54 | 7.4 | 20 12 | 7.9 | 09 37 | 2.9 | 21 37 | 3.1 | 11 36 | 4.6 | 23 48 | 4 |
| 17 | Thursday | 11 00 | 5.9 | 23 37 | 6.4 | 08 48 | 7.9 | 21 02 | 8.4 | 10 27 | 3.0 | 22 29 | 3.3 | 12 34 | 4.9 | — | - |
| 18 | Friday | 11 53 | 6.4 | — | — | 09 32 | 8.3 | 21 45 | 8.8 | 11 07 | 3.2 | 23 13 | 3.4 | 00 41 | 5.0 | 13 17 | 5 |
| 19 | Saturday | 00 26 | 6.8 | 12 41 | 6.7 | 10 10 | 8.6 | 22 23 | 9.0 | 11 43 | 3.3 | 23 52 | 3.5 | 01 22 | 5.2 | 13 51 | 5 |
| 20 | Sunday | 01 11 | 7.0 | 13 23 | 6.8 | 10 44 | 8.8 | 22 57 | 9.1 | 12 16 | 3.3 | — | — | 01 56 | 5.3 | 14 21 | 5 |
| 21 | Monday | 01 49 | 6.9 | 14 00 | 6.8 | 11 15 | 8.9 | 23 27 | 9.1 | 00 28 | 3.4 | 12 47 | 3.3 | 02 26 | 5.4 | 14 48 | 5 |
| 22 | Tuesday | 02 21 | 6.8 | 14 31 | 6.6 | 11 43 | 8.9 | 23 56 | 9.0 | 01 00 | 3.4 | 13 14 | 3.4 | 02 54 | 5.4 | 15 16 | 5 |
| 23 | Wednesday | 02 48 | 6.7 | 14 59 | 6.6 | 12 12 | 8.9 | — | — | 01 28 | 3.3 | 13 40 | 3.4 | 03 24 | 5.4 | 15 47 | 5 |
| 24 | Thursday | 03 14 | 6.6 | 15 27 | 6.5 | 00 26 | 8.9 | 12 42 | 8.8 | 01 56 | 3.3 | 14 08 | 3.5 | 03 57 | 5.3 | 16 20 | 5 |
| 25 | Friday | 03 42 | 6.6 | 15 58 | 6.6 | 00 58 | 8.7 | 13 13 | 8.6 | 02 28 | 3.3 | 14 40 | 3.5 | 04 33 | 5.2 | 16 54 | 5 |
| 26 | Saturday | 04 14 | 6.6 | 16 34 | 6.6 | 01 32 | 8.5 | 13 47 | 8.4 | 03 03 | 3.3 | 15 14 | 3.5 | 05 11 | 5.0 | 17 32 | 4 |
| 27 | Sunday | 04 50 | 6.5 | 17 16 | 6.4 | 02 11 | 8.2 | 14 28 | 8.1 | 03 40 | 3.1 | 15 49 | 3.4 | 05 54 | 4.8 | 18 14 | 4 |
| 28 | Monday | 05 33 | 6.2 | 18 05 | 6.2 | 02 59 | 7.8 | 15 20 | 7.7 | 04 21 | 3.0 | 16 30 | 3.2 | 06 44 | 4.6 | 19 06 | 4 |
| 29 | Tuesday | 06 23 | 5.9 | 19 04 | 5.9 | 04 01 | 7.3 | 16 29 | 7.4 | 05 17 | 2.8 | 17 24 | 3.1 | 07 44 | 4.5 | 20 14 | 4 |
| 30 | Wednesday | 07 24 | 5.6 | 20 13 | 5.8 | 05 20 | 7.2 | 17 52 | 7.4 | 06 43 | 2.7 | 18 42 | 3.0 | 08 59 | 4.5 | 21 35 | 4 |
| 31 | Thursday | 08 41 | 5.6 | 21 36 | 5.9 | 06 46 | 7.4 | 19 13 | 7.9 | 08 22 | 2.8 | 20 14 | 3.1 | 10 18 | 4.7 | 22 48 | 4 |

## NOVEMBER 2002 *High Water* GMT

| | London Bridge | | | | Liverpool | | | | Greenock | | | | Leith | | | |
|---|---|---|---|---|---|---|---|---|---|---|---|---|---|---|---|---|
| | *Datum of Predictions 3.20m below | | | | *Datum of Predictions 4.93m below | | | | *Datum of Predictions 1.62m below | | | | *Datum of Predictions 2.90m below | | | |
| | hr | ht m | hr | ht m | hr | ht m | hr | ht m | hr | ht m | hr | ht m | hr | ht m | hr | ht m |
| 1 Friday | 10 08 | 5.9 | 22 53 | 6.4 | 07 57 | 8.1 | 20 17 | 8.6 | 09 42 | 3.0 | 21 30 | 3.3 | 11 26 | 5.0 | 23 47 | 5.2 |
| 2 Saturday | 11 15 | 6.4 | 23 53 | 6.8 | 08 53 | 8.8 | 21 10 | 9.3 | 10 35 | 3.2 | 22 27 | 3.5 | 12 21 | 5.4 | — | — |
| 3 Sunday | 12 09 | 6.8 | — | — | 09 41 | 9.4 | 21 58 | 9.8 | 11 21 | 3.4 | 23 16 | 3.7 | 00 37 | 5.6 | 13 08 | 5.7 |
| 4 Monday | 00 45 | 7.2 | 12 59 | 7.1 | 10 26 | 9.8 | 22 44 | 10.1 | 12 03 | 3.5 | — | — | 01 22 | 5.9 | 13 51 | 5.9 |
| 5 Tuesday | 01 33 | 7.4 | 13 46 | 7.3 | 11 10 | 9.9 | 23 29 | 10.1 | 00 03 | 3.8 | 12 44 | 3.6 | 02 06 | 6.1 | 14 33 | 6.0 |
| 6 Wednesday | 02 18 | 7.4 | 14 32 | 7.4 | 11 53 | 9.9 | — | — | 00 50 | 3.9 | 13 23 | 3.7 | 02 52 | 6.1 | 15 17 | 5.9 |
| 7 Thursday | 03 01 | 7.4 | 15 17 | 7.4 | 00 13 | 9.9 | 12 37 | 9.7 | 01 34 | 3.9 | 14 01 | 3.7 | 03 40 | 6.0 | 16 01 | 5.8 |
| 8 Friday | 03 42 | 7.2 | 16 01 | 7.3 | 00 58 | 9.5 | 13 20 | 9.4 | 02 17 | 3.8 | 14 39 | 3.8 | 04 30 | 5.8 | 16 48 | 5.5 |
| 9 Saturday | 04 22 | 6.9 | 16 46 | 7.0 | 01 43 | 9.0 | 14 04 | 8.9 | 02 59 | 3.7 | 15 17 | 3.7 | 05 23 | 5.5 | 17 37 | 5.2 |
| 10 Sunday | 05 00 | 6.6 | 17 32 | 6.6 | 02 30 | 8.4 | 14 51 | 8.4 | 03 43 | 3.5 | 16 00 | 3.6 | 06 20 | 5.1 | 18 32 | 4.9 |
| 11 Monday | 05 38 | 6.2 | 18 25 | 6.1 | 03 24 | 7.7 | 15 49 | 7.8 | 04 31 | 3.2 | 16 48 | 3.4 | 07 24 | 4.7 | 19 38 | 4.7 |
| 12 Tuesday | 06 22 | 5.8 | 19 37 | 5.7 | 04 36 | 7.2 | 17 05 | 7.5 | 05 29 | 3.0 | 17 47 | 3.2 | 08 31 | 4.5 | 20 49 | 4.5 |
| 13 Wednesday | 07 51 | 5.4 | 21 00 | 5.7 | 06 01 | 7.0 | 18 25 | 7.4 | 06 44 | 2.8 | 19 07 | 3.1 | 09 41 | 4.4 | 22 00 | 4.5 |
| 14 Thursday | 09 21 | 5.5 | 22 05 | 5.9 | 07 13 | 7.2 | 19 31 | 7.7 | 08 42 | 2.9 | 20 48 | 3.1 | 10 52 | 4.5 | 23 06 | 4.7 |
| 15 Friday | 10 23 | 5.8 | 23 00 | 6.2 | 08 09 | 7.6 | 20 25 | 8.1 | 09 43 | 3.0 | 21 50 | 3.3 | 11 53 | 4.7 | — | — |
| 16 Saturday | 11 16 | 6.1 | 23 50 | 6.5 | 08 56 | 8.1 | 21 10 | 8.5 | 10 27 | 3.2 | 22 38 | 3.3 | 00 01 | 4.8 | 12 39 | 4.9 |
| 17 Sunday | 12 04 | 6.4 | — | — | 09 35 | 8.4 | 21 50 | 8.7 | 11 05 | 3.3 | 23 19 | 3.4 | 00 46 | 5.0 | 13 16 | 5.0 |
| 18 Monday | 00 34 | 6.7 | 12 47 | 6.6 | 10 11 | 8.7 | 22 25 | 8.9 | 11 41 | 3.3 | 23 56 | 3.3 | 01 23 | 5.1 | 13 48 | 5.2 |
| 19 Tuesday | 01 12 | 6.7 | 13 26 | 6.6 | 10 43 | 8.8 | 22 58 | 8.9 | 12 13 | 3.4 | — | — | 01 56 | 5.2 | 14 18 | 5.3 |
| 20 Wednesday | 01 46 | 6.7 | 14 00 | 6.6 | 11 14 | 8.9 | 23 29 | 8.9 | 00 29 | 3.3 | 12 43 | 3.5 | 02 28 | 5.3 | 14 49 | 5.3 |
| 21 Thursday | 02 17 | 6.7 | 14 33 | 6.6 | 11 45 | 8.9 | — | — | 01 00 | 3.3 | 13 11 | 3.5 | 03 02 | 5.3 | 15 22 | 5.3 |
| 22 Friday | 02 48 | 6.6 | 15 06 | 6.6 | 00 02 | 8.9 | 12 18 | 8.9 | 01 32 | 3.3 | 13 43 | 3.6 | 03 37 | 5.3 | 15 56 | 5.3 |
| 23 Saturday | 03 19 | 6.6 | 15 41 | 6.6 | 00 38 | 8.8 | 12 54 | 8.8 | 02 08 | 3.3 | 14 17 | 3.6 | 04 14 | 5.2 | 16 31 | 5.2 |
| 24 Sunday | 03 53 | 6.6 | 16 20 | 6.6 | 01 16 | 8.6 | 13 33 | 8.6 | 02 46 | 3.2 | 14 52 | 3.6 | 04 54 | 5.1 | 17 10 | 5.0 |
| 25 Monday | 04 31 | 6.5 | 17 04 | 6.5 | 01 59 | 8.4 | 14 17 | 8.4 | 03 27 | 3.1 | 15 30 | 3.5 | 05 38 | 5.0 | 17 53 | 4.9 |
| 26 Tuesday | 05 14 | 6.3 | 17 54 | 6.3 | 02 48 | 8.1 | 15 09 | 8.1 | 04 13 | 3.0 | 16 13 | 3.4 | 06 28 | 4.8 | 18 44 | 4.8 |
| 27 Wednesday | 06 03 | 6.1 | 18 51 | 6.1 | 03 46 | 7.7 | 16 12 | 7.9 | 05 12 | 2.9 | 17 06 | 3.2 | 07 25 | 4.7 | 19 46 | 4.7 |
| 28 Thursday | 07 02 | 5.9 | 19 57 | 6.0 | 04 56 | 7.6 | 17 24 | 7.9 | 06 27 | 2.8 | 18 16 | 3.2 | 08 33 | 4.7 | 21 01 | 4.7 |
| 29 Friday | 08 15 | 5.8 | 21 11 | 6.1 | 06 12 | 7.7 | 18 37 | 8.1 | 07 48 | 2.9 | 19 36 | 3.2 | 09 45 | 4.8 | 22 13 | 4.9 |
| 30 Saturday | 09 34 | 6.0 | 22 22 | 6.4 | 07 23 | 8.1 | 19 43 | 8.6 | 09 04 | 3.0 | 20 54 | 3.3 | 10 52 | 5.0 | 23 14 | 5.2 |

## DECEMBER 2002 *High Water* GMT

| | London Bridge | | | | Liverpool | | | | Greenock | | | | Leith | | | |
|---|---|---|---|---|---|---|---|---|---|---|---|---|---|---|---|---|
| 1 Sunday | 10 41 | 6.4 | 23 24 | 6.7 | 08 23 | 8.7 | 20 42 | 9.1 | 10 03 | 3.2 | 21 58 | 3.5 | 11 50 | 5.2 | — | — |
| 2 Monday | 11 40 | 6.7 | — | — | 09 15 | 9.1 | 21 35 | 9.5 | 10 53 | 3.4 | 22 52 | 3.6 | 00 08 | 5.5 | 12 41 | 5.5 |
| 3 Tuesday | 00 18 | 7.0 | 12 34 | 7.0 | 10 03 | 9.5 | 22 24 | 9.7 | 11 38 | 3.5 | 23 42 | 3.7 | 00 59 | 5.7 | 13 28 | 5.6 |
| 4 Wednesday | 01 08 | 7.2 | 13 25 | 7.2 | 10 49 | 9.7 | 23 11 | 9.7 | 12 21 | 3.6 | — | — | 01 48 | 5.8 | 14 12 | 5.7 |
| 5 Thursday | 01 55 | 7.2 | 14 14 | 7.3 | 11 34 | 9.7 | 23 57 | 9.6 | 00 31 | 3.7 | 13 02 | 3.7 | 02 37 | 5.9 | 14 57 | 5.7 |
| 6 Friday | 02 40 | 7.1 | 15 01 | 7.3 | 12 18 | 9.6 | — | — | 01 18 | 3.7 | 13 42 | 3.8 | 03 27 | 5.8 | 15 43 | 5.6 |
| 7 Saturday | 03 22 | 7.0 | 15 48 | 7.1 | 00 42 | 9.3 | 13 02 | 9.4 | 02 04 | 3.6 | 14 22 | 3.8 | 04 17 | 5.6 | 16 30 | 5.5 |
| 8 Sunday | 04 02 | 6.8 | 16 33 | 6.9 | 01 27 | 8.9 | 13 46 | 9.0 | 02 48 | 3.5 | 15 02 | 3.8 | 05 09 | 5.3 | 17 18 | 5.3 |
| 9 Monday | 04 40 | 6.6 | 17 18 | 6.6 | 02 13 | 8.4 | 14 31 | 8.7 | 03 33 | 3.4 | 15 45 | 3.7 | 06 01 | 5.1 | 18 09 | 5.0 |
| 10 Tuesday | 05 18 | 6.3 | 18 05 | 6.3 | 03 00 | 7.9 | 15 20 | 8.2 | 04 21 | 3.2 | 16 30 | 3.5 | 06 55 | 4.8 | 19 04 | 4.8 |
| 11 Wednesday | 05 59 | 6.0 | 18 58 | 5.9 | 03 53 | 7.5 | 16 17 | 7.8 | 05 13 | 3.1 | 17 22 | 3.3 | 07 51 | 4.5 | 20 05 | 4.6 |
| 12 Thursday | 06 53 | 5.7 | 20 02 | 5.7 | 04 58 | 7.2 | 17 24 | 7.6 | 06 10 | 3.0 | 18 21 | 3.2 | 08 49 | 4.4 | 21 06 | 4.5 |
| 13 Friday | 08 11 | 5.6 | 21 09 | 5.7 | 06 10 | 7.1 | 18 32 | 7.6 | 07 10 | 2.9 | 19 28 | 3.1 | 09 48 | 4.4 | 22 06 | 4.5 |
| 14 Saturday | 09 26 | 5.6 | 22 08 | 5.8 | 07 15 | 7.3 | 19 34 | 7.7 | 08 18 | 2.9 | 20 46 | 3.1 | 10 47 | 4.4 | 23 04 | 4.6 |
| 15 Sunday | 10 26 | 5.8 | 23 01 | 6.0 | 08 10 | 7.7 | 20 27 | 8.0 | 09 27 | 3.0 | 21 52 | 3.1 | 11 43 | 4.6 | 23 57 | 4.7 |
| 16 Monday | 11 19 | 6.0 | 23 49 | 6.2 | 08 56 | 8.0 | 21 13 | 8.3 | 10 20 | 3.1 | 22 42 | 3.1 | 12 31 | 4.8 | — | — |
| 17 Tuesday | 12 07 | 6.3 | — | — | 09 36 | 8.4 | 21 53 | 8.5 | 11 04 | 3.3 | 23 24 | 3.2 | 00 44 | 4.9 | 13 13 | 5.0 |
| 18 Wednesday | 00 32 | 6.4 | 12 51 | 6.4 | 10 13 | 8.7 | 22 30 | 8.7 | 11 41 | 3.4 | — | — | 01 27 | 5.0 | 13 50 | 5.1 |
| 19 Thursday | 01 12 | 6.6 | 13 32 | 6.5 | 10 49 | 8.8 | 23 07 | 8.8 | 00 01 | 3.2 | 12 15 | 3.4 | 02 06 | 5.1 | 14 27 | 5.2 |
| 20 Friday | 01 51 | 6.6 | 14 11 | 6.6 | 11 24 | 9.0 | 23 44 | 8.9 | 00 37 | 3.2 | 12 48 | 3.5 | 02 44 | 5.2 | 15 02 | 5.3 |
| 21 Saturday | 02 28 | 6.7 | 14 51 | 6.7 | 12 02 | 9.0 | — | — | 01 15 | 3.2 | 13 23 | 3.6 | 03 21 | 5.3 | 15 38 | 5.3 |
| 22 Sunday | 03 05 | 6.6 | 15 31 | 6.8 | 00 24 | 8.9 | 12 42 | 9.0 | 01 55 | 3.2 | 14 00 | 3.6 | 04 00 | 5.3 | 16 15 | 5.3 |
| 23 Monday | 03 42 | 6.6 | 16 13 | 6.8 | 01 07 | 8.8 | 13 25 | 9.0 | 02 37 | 3.2 | 14 39 | 3.6 | 04 41 | 5.3 | 16 54 | 5.2 |
| 24 Tuesday | 04 21 | 6.6 | 16 58 | 6.7 | 01 51 | 8.7 | 14 10 | 8.9 | 03 21 | 3.1 | 15 19 | 3.6 | 05 24 | 5.2 | 17 37 | 5.2 |
| 25 Wednesday | 05 03 | 6.5 | 17 45 | 6.6 | 02 38 | 8.5 | 14 59 | 8.7 | 04 08 | 3.1 | 16 03 | 3.5 | 06 12 | 5.1 | 18 25 | 5.1 |
| 26 Thursday | 05 50 | 6.3 | 18 38 | 6.4 | 03 31 | 8.3 | 15 53 | 8.6 | 05 00 | 3.0 | 16 52 | 3.4 | 07 04 | 5.0 | 19 20 | 5.0 |
| 27 Friday | 06 43 | 6.2 | 19 36 | 6.3 | 04 29 | 8.1 | 16 54 | 8.4 | 05 59 | 2.9 | 17 49 | 3.3 | 08 03 | 4.8 | 20 24 | 4.9 |
| 28 Saturday | 07 46 | 6.1 | 20 42 | 6.2 | 05 36 | 7.9 | 18 01 | 8.3 | 07 03 | 2.9 | 18 54 | 3.3 | 09 10 | 4.8 | 21 35 | 4.9 |
| 29 Sunday | 08 58 | 6.1 | 21 51 | 6.2 | 06 45 | 8.0 | 19 10 | 8.4 | 08 16 | 3.0 | 20 11 | 3.2 | 10 17 | 4.8 | 22 43 | 5.0 |
| 30 Monday | 10 09 | 6.2 | 22 56 | 6.4 | 07 53 | 8.3 | 20 17 | 8.6 | 09 28 | 3.1 | 21 28 | 3.3 | 11 20 | 5.0 | 23 46 | 5.2 |
| 31 Tuesday | 11 15 | 6.4 | 23 54 | 6.6 | 08 53 | 8.7 | 21 17 | 8.9 | 10 28 | 3.2 | 22 33 | 3.4 | 12 18 | 5.1 | — | — |

# World Geographical Statistics

## THE EARTH

The shape of the Earth is that of an oblate spheroid or solid of revolution whose meridian sections are ellipses, whilst the sections at right angles are circles.

### Dimensions

Equatorial diameter = 12,756.27 km (7,926.38 miles)
Polar diameter = 12,713.50 km (7,899.80 miles)
Equatorial circumference = 40,075.01 km (24,901.46 miles)
Polar circumference = 40,007.86 km (24,859.73 miles)
Mass = 5,974,000,000,000,000,000,000 tonnes ($5.879 \times 10^{21}$ tons)

The equatorial circumference is divided into 360 degrees of longitude, which is measured in degrees, minutes and seconds east or west of the Greenwich meridian (0°) to 180°, the meridian 180° E. coinciding with 180° W. This dateline was internationally ratified on 13 October 1884.

Distance north and south of the Equator is measured in degrees, minutes and seconds of latitude. The Equator is 0°, the North Pole is 90° N. and the South Pole is 90° S. The Tropics lie at 23° 27′ N. (Tropic of Cancer) and 23° 27′ S. (Tropic of Capricorn). The Arctic Circle lies at 66° 33′ N. and the Antarctic Circle at 66° 33′ S. (NB The Tropics and the Arctic and Antarctic circles are affected by the slow decrease in obliquity of the ecliptic, of about 0.47 arcseconds per year. The effect of this is that the Arctic and Antarctic circles are currently moving towards their respective poles by about 14 metres per annum, while the Tropics move towards the Equator by the same amount.

### Area, etc.

The surface area of the Earth is 510,069,120 $km^2$ (196,938,800 $miles^2$), of which the water area is 70.92 per cent and the land area is 29.08 per cent.

The radial velocity on the Earth's surface at the Equator is 1,669.79 km per hour (1,037.56 m.p.h.). The Earth's mean velocity in its orbit around the Sun is 107,229 km per hour (66,629 m.p.h.). The Earth's mean distance from the Sun is 149,597,870 km (92,955,807 miles).

## OCEANS

### Area

| | $km^2$ | $miles^2$ |
|---|---|---|
| Pacific | 166,240,000 | 64,186,300 |
| Atlantic | 86,550,000 | 33,420,000 |
| Indian | 73,427,000 | 28,350,500 |
| Arctic | 9,485,000 | 5,105,700 |

The division by the Equator of the Pacific into the North and South Pacific and the Atlantic into the North and South Atlantic makes a total of six oceans.

### Greatest Depths

| Greatest depth | location | metres | feet |
|---|---|---|---|
| Mariana Trench | Pacific | 10,924 | 35,840 |
| Puerto Rico Trench | Atlantic | 8,605 | 28,232 |
| Java (Sunda) Trench | Indian | 7,125 | 23,376 |
| Molloy Deep | Arctic | 5,680 | 18,400 |

## SEAS

### Area

| | $km^2$ | $miles^2$ |
|---|---|---|
| South China | 2,974,600 | 1,148,500 |
| Caribbean | 2,515,900 | 971,400 |
| Mediterranean | 2,509,900 | 969,100 |
| Bering | 2,261,000 | 873,000 |
| Gulf of Mexico | 1,507,600 | 582,100 |
| Okhotsk | 1,392,000 | 537,500 |
| Japan | 1,012,900 | 391,100 |
| Hudson Bay | 730,100 | 281,900 |
| East China | 664,600 | 256,600 |
| Andaman | 564,880 | 218,100 |
| Black Sea | 507,900 | 196,100 |
| Red Sea | 453,000 | 174,900 |
| North Sea | 427,100 | 164,900 |
| Baltic Sea | 382,000 | 147,500 |
| Yellow Sea | 294,000 | 113,500 |
| Persian/Arabian Gulf | 230,000 | 88,800 |

### Greatest Depths

| | *Maximum depth* metres | feet |
|---|---|---|
| Caribbean | 8,605 | 28,232 |
| East China (Ryu Kyu Trench) | 7,507 | 24,629 |
| South China | 7,258 | 23,812 |
| Mediterranean (Ionian Basin) | 5,150 | 16,896 |
| Andaman | 4,267 | 14,000 |
| Bering | 3,936 | 12,913 |
| Gulf of Mexico | 3,504 | 11,496 |
| Okhotsk | 3,365 | 11,040 |
| Japan | 3,053 | 10,016 |
| Red Sea | 2,266 | 7,434 |
| Black Sea | 2,212 | 7,257 |
| North Sea | 439 | 1,440 |
| Hudson Bay | 111 | 364 |
| Baltic Sea | 90 | 295 |
| Persian Gulf | 73 | 240 |
| Yellow Sea | 58 | 190 |

## THE CONTINENTS

There are six geographic continents, although America is often divided politically into North and Central America, and South America.

Africa is surrounded by sea except for the narrow isthmus of Suez in the north-east, through which is cut the Suez Canal. Its extreme longitudes are 17° 20′ W. at Cape Verde, Senegal, and 51° 24′ E. at Ras Hafun, Somalia. The extreme latitudes are 37° 20′ N. at Cape Blanc, Tunisia, and 34° 50′ S. at Cape Agulhas, South Africa, about 4,400 miles apart. The Equator passes through the middle of the continent.

North America, including Mexico, is surrounded by ocean except in the south, where the isthmian states of Central America link North America with South America. Its extreme longitudes are 168° 5′ W. at Cape

Prince of Wales, Alaska, and 55° 40′ W. at Cape Charles, Newfoundland. The extreme continental latitudes are the tip of the Boothia peninsula, NW Territories, Canada (71° 51′ N.) and 14° 22′ N. at Ocós in the south of Mexico.

SOUTH AMERICA lies mostly in the southern hemisphere; the Equator passes through the north of the continent. It is surrounded by ocean except where it is joined to Central America in the north by the narrow isthmus through which is cut the Panama Canal. Its extreme longitudes are 34° 47′ W. at Cape Branco in Brazil and 81° 20′ W. at Punta Pariña, Peru. The extreme continental latitudes are 12° 25′ N. at Punta Gallinas, Colombia, and 53° 54′ S. at the southernmost tip of the Brunswick peninsula, Chile. Cape Horn, on Cape Island, Chile, lies at 55° 59′ S.

ANTARCTICA lies almost entirely within the Antarctic Circle (66° 34′ S.) and is the largest of the world's glaciated areas. The continent has an area of 5.1 million square miles, 99 per cent of which is permanently ice-covered. The ice amounts to some 7.2 million cubic miles and represents more than 90 per cent of the world's fresh water. The environment is too hostile for unsupported human habitation. *See also* pages 786–7

ASIA is the largest continent and occupies 29.6 per cent of the world's land surface. The extreme longitudes are 26° 05′ E. at Baba Buran, Turkey and 169° 40′ W. at Mys Dežneva (East Cape), Russia, a distance of about 6,000 miles. Its extreme northern latitude is 77° 45′ N. at Cape Celjuskin, Russia, and it extends over 5,000 miles south to about 1° 15′ N. of the Equator.

AUSTRALIA is the smallest of the continents and lies in the southern hemisphere. It is entirely surrounded by ocean. Its extreme longitudes are 113° 11′ E. at Steep Point and 153° 11′ E. at Cape Byron. The extreme latitudes are 10° 42′ S. at Cape York and 39° S. at South East Point, Tasmania.

EUROPE, including European Russia, is the smallest continent in the northern hemisphere. Its extreme latitudes are 71° 11′ N. at North Cape in Norway, and 36° 23′ N. at Cape Matapan in southern Greece, a distance of about 2,400 miles. Its breadth from Cabo Carvoeiro in Portugal (9° 34′ W.) in the west to the Kara River, north of the Urals (66° 30′ E.) in the east is about 3,300 miles. The division between Europe and Asia is generally regarded as the watershed of the Ural Mountains; down the Ural river to Gur'yev, Kazakhstan; across the Caspian Sea to Apsheronskiy Poluostrov, near Baku; along the watershed of the Caucasus Mountains to Anapa and thence across the Black Sea to the Bosporus in Turkey; across the Sea of Marmara to Çanakkale Boğazi (Dardanelles).

| | *Area* km$^2$ | miles$^2$ |
|---|---|---|
| Asia | 43,998,000 | 16,988,000 |
| *America | 41,918,000 | 16,185,000 |
| Africa | 29,800,000 | 11,506,000 |
| Antarctica | 13,209,000 | 5,100,000 |
| †Europe | 9,699,000 | 3,745,000 |
| Australia | 7,618,493 | 2,941,526 |

*North and Central America has an area of 24,255,000 km{Sup}2 (9,365,000 miles$^2$)
†Includes 5,571,000 km$^2$ (2,151,000 miles$^2$) of former USSR territory, including the Baltic states, Belarus, Moldova, the Ukraine, that part of Russia west of the Ural Mountains and Kazakhstan west of the Ural river. European Turkey (24,378 km$^2$/9,412 miles$^2$) comprises territory to the west and north of the Bosporus and the Dardanelles

## GLACIATED AREAS

It is estimated that 15,915,000 km$^2$ (6,145,000 miles$^2$) or 10.73 per cent of the world's land surface is permanently covered with ice.

| | *Area* km$^2$ | miles$^2$ |
|---|---|---|
| South Polar regions | 13,830,000 | 5,340,000 |
| North Polar regions (incl. Greenland or Kalaallit Nunaat) | 1,965,000 | 758,500 |
| Alaska-Canada | 58,800 | 22,700 |
| Asia | 37,800 | 14,600 |
| South America | 11,900 | 4,600 |
| Europe | 10,700 | 4,128 |
| New Zealand | 1,015 | 391 |
| Africa | 238 | 92 |

The largest glacier is the 515 km/320 mile-long Lambert-Fisher Ice Passage, Antarctica.

## PENINSULAS

| | *Area* km$^2$ | miles$^2$ |
|---|---|---|
| Arabian | 3,250,000 | 1,250,000 |
| Southern Indian | 2,072,000 | 800,000 |
| Alaskan | 1,500,000 | 580,000 |
| Labradorian | 1,300,000 | 500,000 |
| Scandinavian | 800,300 | 309,000 |
| Iberian | 584,000 | 225,500 |

## LARGEST ISLANDS

| *Island, and Ocean* | *Area* km$^2$ | miles$^2$ |
|---|---|---|
| Greenland (Kalaallit Nunaat), Arctic | 2,175,500 | 840,000 |
| New Guinea, Pacific | 792,500 | 306,000 |
| Borneo, Pacific | 725,450 | 280,100 |
| Madagascar, Indian | 587,040 | 226,658 |
| Baffin Island, Arctic | 507,451 | 195,928 |
| Sumatra, Indian | 427,350 | 165,000 |
| Honshu, Pacific | 227,413 | 87,805 |
| *Great Britain, Atlantic | 218,077 | 84,200 |
| Victoria Island, Arctic | 217,292 | 83,897 |
| Ellesmere Island, Arctic | 196,236 | 75,767 |
| Sulawesi (Celebes), Indian | 189,036 | 72,987 |
| South Island, NZ, Pacific | 151,213 | 58,384 |
| Java, Indian | 126,650 | 48,900 |
| North Island, NZ, (Pacific) | 114,487 | 44,204 |
| Cuba, Atlantic | 110,862 | 42,804 |
| Newfoundland, Atlantic | 108,855 | 42,030 |
| Luzon, Pacific | 105,360 | 40,680 |
| Iceland, Atlantic | 102,820 | 39,700 |
| Mindanao, Pacific | 95,247 | 36,775 |
| Ireland, Atlantic | 82,462 | 31,839 |

*Mainland only

## LARGEST DESERTS

| | Area (approx.) km$^2$ | miles$^2$ |
|---|---|---|
| The Sahara, N. Africa | 9,000,000 | 3,500,000 |
| Australian Desert (Great Sandy, Gibson and Great Victoria) | 1,350,000 | 520,000 |
| The Gobi, Mongolia/China | 1,300,000 | 500,000 |
| Arabian Desert | 1,000,000 | 385,000 |
| Kalahari Desert, Botswana/ Namibia/S. Africa | 570,000 | 220,000 |
| Taklimakan Shamo, Mongolia/China | 320,000 | 125,000 |
| *Kara Kum, Turkmenistan | 310,000 | 120,000 |
| Namib Desert, Namibia | 285,000 | 110,000 |
| Thar Desert, India/Pakistan | 260,000 | 100,000 |
| Somali Desert, Somalia | 260,000 | 100,000 |
| Atacama Desert, Chile | 180,000 | 70,000 |
| Sonoran Desert, USA/Mexico | 180,000 | 70,000 |
| Dasht-e Lut, Iran | 52,000 | 20,000 |
| Mojave Desert, USA | 38,850 | 15,000 |

*Together with the Kyzyl Kum known as the Turkestan Desert

## DEEPEST DEPRESSIONS

| | Maximum depth below sea level metres | feet |
|---|---|---|
| Dead Sea, Jordan/Israel | 408 | 1,338 |
| Lake Assal, Djibouti | 156 | 511 |
| Turfan Depression, Sinkiang, China | 153 | 505 |
| Qattara Depression, Egypt | 132 | 436 |
| Mangyshlak peninsula, Kazakhstan | 131 | 433 |
| Danakil Depression, Ethiopia | 116 | 383 |
| Death Valley, California, USA | 86 | 282 |
| Salton Sink, California, USA | 71 | 235 |
| W. of Ustyurt plateau, Kazakhstan | 70 | 230 |
| Prikaspiyskaya Nizmennost', Russia/Kazakhstan | 67 | 220 |
| Lake Sarykamysh, Uzbekistan/ Turkmenistan | 45 | 148 |
| El Faiyûm, Egypt | 44 | 147 |
| Península Valdés, Chubut, Argentina | 40 | 131 |
| Lake Eyre, South Australia | 16 | 52 |

The world's largest exposed depression is the Prikaspiyskaya Nizmennost' covering the hinterland of the northern third of the Caspian Sea, which is itself 28 m (92 ft) below sea level.

Western Antarctica and Central Greenland largely comprise crypto-depressions under ice burdens. The Antarctic Bentley subglacial trench has a bedrock 2,538 m (8,326 ft) below sea-level. In Greenland (lat. 73° N., long. 39° W.) the bedrock is 365 m (1,197 ft) below sea-level.

Nearly one quarter of the area of The Netherlands lies marginally below sea-level, an area of more than 10,000 km$^2$/3,860 miles$^2$.

## LONGEST MOUNTAIN RANGES

| *Range, and location* | *Length* km | miles |
|---|---|---|
| Cordillera de Los Andes, W. South America | 7,200 | 4,500 |
| Rocky Mountains, W. North America | 4,800 | 3,000 |
| Himalaya-Karakoram-Hindu Kush, S. Central Asia | 3,800 | 2,400 |
| Great Dividing Range, E. Australia | 3,600 | 2,250 |
| Trans-Antarctic Mts, Antarctica | 3,500 | 2,200 |
| Atlantic Coast Range, E. Brazil | 3,000 | 1,900 |
| West Sumatran-Javan Range, Indonesia | 2,900 | 1,800 |
| Aleutian Range, Alaska and NW Pacific | 2,650 | 1,650 |
| Tien Shan, S. Central Asia | 2,250 | 1,400 |
| Central New Guinea Range, Irian Jaya/ Papua New Guinea | 2,000 | 1,250 |

## HIGHEST MOUNTAINS

The world's 8,000-metre mountains (with six subsidiary peaks) are all in the Himalaya-Karakoram-Hindu Kush ranges.

| *Mountain* | *Height* metres | feet |
|---|---|---|
| Mt Everest* | 8,850 | 29,035 |
| K2 (Chogori)† | 8,611 | 28,251 |
| Kangchenjunga | 8,586 | 28,169 |
| Lhotse | 8,501 | 27,890 |
| Makalu I | 8,462 | 27,762 |
| Lhotse Shar (II) | 8,383 | 27,504 |
| Cho Oyu | 8,201 | 26,906 |
| Dhaulagiri I | 8,167 | 26,794 |
| Manaslu I (Kutang I) | 8,156 | 26,760 |
| Nanga Parbat (Diamir) | 8,125 | 26,660 |
| Annapurna I | 8,091 | 26,546 |
| Gasherbrum I (Hidden Peak) | 8,068 | 26,470 |
| Broad Peak I | 8,046 | 26,400 |
| Shisham Pangma (Gosainthan) | 8,013 | 26,287 |
| Gasherbrum II | 8,034 | 26,360 |
| Makalu South-East | 8,010 | 26,280 |
| Broad Peak Central | 8,000 | 26,246 |

*Named after Sir George Everest (1790–1866), Surveyor-General of India 1830–43, in 1863. He pronounced his name Eve-rest

†Formerly Col. H. H. Godwin-Austen (1834-1923)

The culminating summits in the other major mountain ranges are:

| *Mountain, by range or country* | *Height* metres | feet |
|---|---|---|
| Pik Pobedy, Tien Shan | 7,439 | 24,406 |
| Cerro Aconcagua, Cordillera de Los Andes | 6,960 | 22,834 |
| Mt McKinley (*S. Peak*), Alaska Range | 6,194 | 20,320 |
| Kilimanjaro (Kibo), Tanzania | 5,894 | 19,340 |
| Hkakabo Razi, Myanmar | 5,881 | 19,296 |
| El'brus, (*W. Peak*), Caucasus | 5,642 | 18,510 |
| Citlaltépetl (Orizaba), Sierra Madre Oriental, Mexico | 5,610 | 18,405 |
| Vinson Massif, E. Antarctica | 4,897 | 16,066 |
| Puncak Jaya, Central New Guinea Range | 4,884 | 16,023 |
| Mt Blanc, Alps | 4,807 | 15,771 |

| *Mountain, by range or country* | *Height* metres | feet |
|---|---|---|
| Klyuchevskaya Sopka, Kamchatka peninsula, Russia | 4,750 | 15,584 |
| Ras Dashan, Ethiopian Highlands | 4,620 | 15,158 |
| Zard Kuh, Zagros Mts, Iran | 4,547 | 14,921 |
| Mt Kirkpatrick, Trans Antarctic | 4,529 | 14,860 |
| Mt Belukha, Altai Mts, Russia/ Kazakhstan | 4,505 | 14,783 |
| Mt Elbert, Rocky Mountains | 4,400 | 14,433 |
| Mt Rainier, Cascade Range, N. America | 4,392 | 14,410 |
| Nevado de Colima, Sierra Madre Occidental, Mexico | 4,268 | 14,003 |
| Jebel Toubkal, Atlas Mts, N. Africa | 4,165 | 13,665 |
| Kinabalu, Crocker Range, Borneo | 4,101 | 13,455 |
| Kerinci, West Sumatran-Javan Range, Indonesia | 3,800 | 12,467 |
| Jabal an NabiShu'ayb, N. Tihamat, Yemen | 3,760 | 12,336 |
| Mt Cook (Aorangi), Southern Alps, New Zealand | 3,754 | 12,315 |
| Teotepec, Sierra Madre del Sur, Mexico | 3,703 | 12,149 |
| Thaban Ntlenyana, Drakensberg, South Africa | 3,482 | 11,425 |
| Pico de Bandeira, Atlantic Coast Range | 2,890 | 9,482 |
| Shishaldin, Aleutian Range | 2,861 | 9,387 |
| Kosciusko, Great Dividing Range | 2,228 | 7,310 |

## HIGHEST VOLCANOES

| *Volcano (last major eruption), and location* | *Height* metres | feet |
|---|---|---|
| Ojos del Salado (1981), Andes, Argentina/Chile | 6,880 | 22,572 |
| Llullaillaco (1877), Andes, Argentina/Chile | 6,723 | 22,057 |
| San Pedro (1960), Andes, Chile | 6,199 | 20,325 |
| Guallatiri (1960, 1993), Andes, Chile | 6,071 | 19,918 |
| Cotopaxi (1940, 1975), Andes, Ecuador | 5,897 | 19,347 |
| Tupungatito (1986), Andes, Chile | 5,640 | 18,504 |
| Láscar (2000), Andes, Chile | 5,591 | 18,346 |
| Popocatépetl (1999-2001), Mexico | 5,465 | 17,930 |
| Nevado del Ruiz (1985, 1991), Colombia | 5,321 | 17,457 |
| Sangay (1998), Andes, Ecuador | 5,188 | 17,021 |
| Irruputancu (1995), Chile | 5,163 | 16,939 |
| Klyuchevskaya Sopka (1999), Kamchatka peninsula, Russia | 4,835 | 15,863 |
| Guagua Pichincha (1999), Andes, Ecuador | 4,784 | 15,696 |
| Purace (1977), Colombia | 4,756 | 15,601 |
| Wrangel (1907), Alaska, USA | 4,316 | 14,028 |
| Shasta (1786), California, USA | 4,316 | 14,162 |
| Galeras (1993), Colombia | 4,275 | 14,028 |
| Mauna Loa (1984, 1987), Hawaii Is. | 4,170 | 13,680 |
| Cameroon (2000), Cameroon | 4,095 | 13,435 |

### Other Notable Volcanoes

| | *Height* metres | feet |
|---|---|---|
| Erebus (1998), Ross Island, Antarctica | 3,794 | 12,450 |
| Fuji (1708), Honshu, Japan | 3,775 | 12,388 |
| Santa Maria (1902, 1998), Guatemala | 3,772 | 12,375 |
| Semeru (since 1967), Java, Indonesia | 3,675 | 12,060 |
| Mt Etna (1169, 1669, 1993, 1996-9, 2000), Sicily, Italy | 3,368 | 11,053 |
| Raung (1993, 1997), Java, Indonesia | 3,322 | 10,932 |
| Sheveluch (1997, 1999, 2000), Kamchatka, Russia | 3,283 | 10,771 |
| Llaima (1995), Chile | 3,125 | 10,253 |
| Mt St Helens (1980, 1986, 1991, 1998), Washington State, USA | 2,549 | 8,363 |
| Beerenberg (1985), Jan Mayen Island | 2,277 | 7,470 |
| Pinatubo (1991, 1995), Luzon, Philippines | 1,598 | 5,249 |
| Hekla (1981, 1991, 2000), Iceland | 1,491 | 4,892 |
| Mt Unzen (1792, 1991, 1996, 2000), Kyushu, Japan | 1,360 | 4,462 |
| Vesuvius (AD 79, 1631, 1944), Italy | 1,281 | 4,203 |
| Kilauea (1996, 1997, 2000), Hawaii, USA | 1,249 | 4,009 |
| Soufrière (1979, 1997), St Vincent | 1,178 | 3,865 |
| Soufrière Hills (1997–2000), Montserrat | 914 | 3,001 |
| Stromboli (1996, 1997-9, 2000), Lipari Is., Italy | 926 | 3,038 |
| Krakatau (1883, 1995, 1999, 2001), Sunda Strait, Indonesia | 813 | 2,667 |
| Santoríni (Thíra) (1628 BC, 1950), Aegean Sea, Greece | 564 | 1,850 |
| Tristan da Cunha (1961), South Atlantic | 243 | 800 |
| Surtsey (1963–7), off Iceland | 173 | 568 |

## LARGEST LAKES

The areas of some of these lakes are subject to seasonal variation.

| | *Area* $km^2$ | $miles^2$ | *Length* km | miles |
|---|---|---|---|---|
| Caspian Sea, Iran/ Azerbaijan/Russia/ Turkmenistan/ Kazakhstan | 371,000 | 143,000 | 1,171 | 728 |
| *Michigan–Huron, USA/Canada | 117,610 | 45,300 | 1,010 | 627 |
| Superior, Canada/ USA | 82,100 | 31,700 | 563 | 350 |
| Victoria, Uganda/ Tanzania/Kenya | 69,500 | 26,828 | 362 | 225 |
| Tanganyika, Dem. Rep. of Congo/ Tanzania/Zambia/ Burundi | 32,900 | 12,665 | 725 | 450 |
| Great Bear, Canada | 31,328 | 12,096 | 309 | 192 |
| ‡Aral Sea, Kazakhstan/ Uzbekistan | 30,700 | 11,850 | 320 | 200 |
| †Baykal (*Baikal*), Russia | 30,500 | 11,776 | 620 | 385 |
| Malawi (Nyasa), Tanzania/Malawi/ Mozambique | 28,900 | 11,150 | 580 | 360 |
| Great Slave, Canada | 28,570 | 11,031 | 480 | 298 |
| Erie, Canada/USA | 25,670 | 9,910 | 388 | 241 |
| Winnipeg, Canada | 24,390 | 9,417 | 428 | 266 |
| Ontario, Canada/USA | 19,010 | 7,340 | 310 | 193 |

| | Area km$^2$ | miles$^2$ | Length km | miles |
|---|---|---|---|---|
| Balkhash, Kazakhstan | 18,427 | 7,115 | 605 | 376 |
| Ladozhskoye (*Ladoga*), Russia | 17,700 | 6,835 | 193 | 120 |

*Lakes Michigan and Huron are regarded as lobes of the same lake. The Michigan lobe has an area of 57,750 km$^2$ (22,300 miles$^2$) and the Huron lobe an area of 59,570 km$^2$ (23,000 miles$^2$)
†World's deepest lake (1,940 m/6,365 ft)
‡ Northern part (Little Aral Sea) dammed off in 1997

UNITED KINGDOM, BY COUNTRY

| | Area km$^2$ | miles$^2$ | Length km | miles |
|---|---|---|---|---|
| Lough Neagh, Northern Ireland | 381.73 | 147.39 | 28.90 | 18.00 |
| Loch Lomond, Scotland | 71.12 | 27.46 | 36.44 | 22.64 |
| Windermere, England | 14.74 | 5.69 | 16.90 | 10.50 |
| Lake Vyrnwy, Wales (artificial) | 4.53 | 1.75 | 7.56 | 4.70 |
| Llyn Tegid (*Bala*), Wales (natural) | 4.38 | 1.69 | 5.80 | 3.65 |

## LONGEST RIVERS

| *River, source and outflow* | Length km | miles |
|---|---|---|
| Nile (*Bahr-el-Nil*), R. Luvironza, Burundi – E. Mediterranean Sea | 6,725 | 4,180 |
| Amazon (*Amazonas*), Lago Villafro, Peru – S. Atlantic Ocean | 6,448 | 4,007 |
| Yangtze-Kiang (*Chang Jiang*), Kunlun Mts, W. China – Yellow Sea | 6,380 | 3,964 |
| Mississippi-Missouri-Red Rock, Montana – Gulf of Mexico | 5,970 | 3,710 |
| Yenisey-Angara, W. Mongolia – Kara Sea | 5,536 | 3,440 |
| Huang He (*Yellow River*), Bayan Har Shan range, central China – Yellow Sea | 5,463 | 3,395 |
| Ob'-Irtysh, W. Mongolia – Kara Sea | 5,410 | 3,362 |
| Lena-Kirenga, R. Kirenga, W. of Lake Baykal – Laptev Sea, Arctic Ocean | 4,400 | 2,734 |
| Amur-Argun, R. Argun, Khingan Mts, N. China – Sea of Okhotsk | 4,416 | 2,744 |
| Zaïre (*Congo*), R. Lualaba, Dem. Rep. of Congo-Zambia – S. Atlantic Ocean | 4,665 | 2,900 |
| Mekong, Lants'ang, Tibet – South China Sea | 4,345 | 2,700 |
| Mackenzie-Peace, Tatlatui Lake, British Columbia – Beaufort Sea | 4,240 | 2,635 |
| Paraná-Río de la Plata, R. Paranáiba, central Brazil – S. Atlantic Ocean | 4,240 | 2,635 |
| Niger, Loma Mts, Guinea – Gulf of Guinea, E. Atlantic Ocean | 4,170 | 2,590 |
| Murray-Darling, SE Queensland – Lake Alexandrina, S. Australia | 3,717 | 2,310 |
| Volga, Valdai plateau – Caspian Sea | 3,685 | 2,290 |

OTHER NOTABLE RIVERS

| | km | miles |
|---|---|---|
| Rio Grande, USA–Mexican border | 3,057 | 1,900 |
| Ganges-Brahmaputra, R. Matsang, SW Tibet – Bay of Bengal | 2,900 | 1,800 |
| Indus, R. Sengge, SW Tibet – N. Arabian Sea | 2,897 | 1,800 |
| Danube (*Donau*), Black Forest, SW Germany – Black Sea | 2,856 | 1,775 |
| Tigris-Euphrates, R. Murat, E. Turkey – Persian Gulf | 2,800 | 1,740 |
| Zambezi, NW Zambia – S. Indian Ocean | 2,735 | 1,700 |
| Irrawaddy, R. Mali Hka, Myanmar – Andaman Sea | 2,151 | 1,337 |
| Don, SE of Novomoskovsk – Sea of Azov | 1,969 | 1,224 |

BRITISH ISLES

| | km | miles |
|---|---|---|
| Shannon, Co. Cavan, Rep. of Ireland – Atlantic Ocean | 386 | 240 |
| Severn, Powys, Wales – Bristol Channel | 354 | 220 |
| Thames, Gloucestershire, England – North Sea | 346 | 215 |
| Tay, Perthshire, Scotland – North Sea | 188 | 117 |
| Clyde, Lanarkshire, Scotland – Firth of Clyde | 158 | 98½ |
| Tweed, Peeblesshire, Scotland – North Sea | 155 | 96½ |
| Bann (Upper and Lower), Co. Down, N. Ireland – Atlantic Ocean | 122 | 76 |

## GREATEST WATERFALLS – BY HEIGHT

| *Waterfall, river and location* | *Total drop* metres | feet | *Greatest single leap* metres | feet |
|---|---|---|---|---|
| Saltó Angel, Carrao Auyán Tepuí, Venezuela | 979 | 3,212 | 807 | 2,648 |
| Utigård, Jostedal Glacier, Norway | 800 | 2,625 | 600 | 1,970 |
| Mongefossen, Monge, Norway | 774 | 2,540 | — | — |
| Yosemite, Yosemite Creek, USA | 739 | 2,425 | 435 | 1,430 |
| *Østre Mardøla Foss, Mardals, Norway | 655 | 2,149 | 296 | 974 |
| *Tyssestrengene, Tysso, Norway | 646 | 2,120 | 289 | 948 |
| Cuquenán, Arabopó, Venezuela | 610 | 2,000 | — | — |
| Tugela, Tugela, Natal, S. Africa | 580 | 1,904 | 410 | 1,350 |
| Sutherland, Arthur, NZ | 580 | 1,904 | 248 | 815 |

*Volume much affected by hydroelectric harnessing

BRITISH ISLES, BY COUNTRY

| | metres | feet | |
|---|---|---|---|
| Eas a' Chuàl Aluinn, Glas Bheinn, Sutherland, Scotland | 200 | 658 | |
| Powerscourt Falls, Dargle, Co. Wicklow, Rep. of Ireland | 106 | 350 | |
| Pistyll-y-Llyn, Powys/ Dyfed border, Wales | *c.*72 | *c.*235 | (cascades) |
| Pistyll Rhyadr, Clwyd/ Powys border, Wales | 71.5 | 235 | (single leap) |
| Caldron Snout, R. Tees, Cumbria/Durham, England | 61 | 200 | (cascades) |

## GREATEST WATERFALLS – BY VOLUME

| *Waterfall, river and location* | *Mean annual flow* m^3/sec | galls/sec |
|---|---|---|
| Inga (Congo dam site), Dem. Rep. of Congo | 43,000 | 9,460,000 |
| Khône, Mekong, Laos | 42,500 | 9,350,000 |
| Boyoma (Stanley), R. Lualaba, Dem. Rep. of Congo | *c.*17,000 | *c.*3,750,000 |
| Guayra (Sete Quedas), Brazil | 13,000 | 2,860,000 |
| Rio Paraná, Argentina/ Paraguay | 11,900 | 2,619,000 |
| Niagara (Horseshoe), R. Niagara/Lake Erie–Lake Ontario | 6,000 | 1,320,000 |
| Paulo Afonso, R. São Francisco, Brazil | 2,830 | 622,500 |
| Urubupunga, Alto Parañá, Brazil | 2,745 | 604,000 |
| Cataratas del Iguazú, R. Iguaçu, Brazil/Argentina | 1,743 | 380,000 |
| Patos-Maribando, Rio Grande, Brazil | 1,500 | 330,000 |
| Churchill, R. Churchill, Canada | 1,132 | 215,000 |
| Victoria (*Mosi-oa-tunya*), R. Zambezi, Zambia/Zimbabwe | 1,087 | 242,000 |

## TALLEST DAMS

| | metres | feet |
|---|---|---|
| *Rogun, R. Vakhsh, Tajikistan | 335 | 1,098 |
| Nurek, R. Vakhsh, Tajikistan | 300 | 984 |
| Grande Dixence, Switzerland | 285 | 935 |
| *Longtan, R. Hangshui, China | 285 | 935 |
| Inguri, Georgia | 272 | 892 |
| Borucu, Costa Rica | 269 | 883 |
| Vaiont, Italy | 262 | 859 |
| Manuel M. Torres, Chicoasén, Mexico | 261 | 856 |
| Tehri, R. Bhagivathi, India | 261 | 856 |

*Under construction

The world's most massive dam is the Syncrude Tailings dam in Alberta, Canada, which will have a volume of 540 million cubic metres/706 million cubic yards.

The Three Gorges Chang Jiang (Yangtze) Dam, China, with a crest length of 1,983 m/6,505 ft, is due for completion in 2009 (stage 3).

The Yacyretá-Apipe dam across the River Paraná, Argentina-Paraguay, is being completed to a length of 69,600 m/43.24 miles.

## TALLEST INHABITED BUILDINGS

| *Building and city* | *Height* metres | feet |
|---|---|---|
| Pearl of the Orient | 468 | 1535 |
| Shanghai World Financial Centre | 460 | 1,509 |
| Chongqing Tower, China | 457 | 1,499 |
| Petronas Towers I and II, Kuala Lumpur, Malaysia (1998) | 451.9 | 1,482 |
| Sears Tower, Chicago[1] (1974) | 443 | 1,454 |
| Jin Mao, Shanghai, China (1999) | 420 | 1,378 |
| Xianmen Fairwell International Centre, China (2002) | 397 | 1,302 |
| Plaza Rakyat, Kuala Lumpur, Malaysia (1999) | 382 | 1,254 |
| Empire State Building, New York[2] (1931) | 381 | 1,250 |
| Central Plaza, Hong Kong (1992) | 373 | 1,227 |
| Bank of China Tower, Hong Kong (1998) | 368 | 1,209 |
| Emirates Tower One (2000) | 350 | 1,148 |
| Amoco Building, Chicago (1973) | 346 | 1,136 |
| Central Station, Hong Kong | 346 | 1,136 |
| John Hancock Center, Chicago (1969 | 343 | 1,127 |
| Shun Hing Square, Shenzhen, China (1996) | 384 | 1,260 |
| CITIC Plaza, Guangzhou, China (1996) | 391 | 1,283 |
| Chicago Beach Tower, Dubai (1999) | 321 | 1,053 |
| Sky Central Plaza, Guangzhou | 322 | 1,056 |
| Baiyoke Tower, Bangkok, Thailand (1998) | 320 | 1,050 |

1. With TV antennae, 520 m/1,707 ft

Note: The two World Trade Center towers, One or North (1972) 110 stories, 415 m 1,368 ft or 521.2 m 1,716 ft with TV antennae; and Two or South (1973) 110 stories, 415 m, 1,362 ft, were destroyed by two terrorist hijacked aircraft on 11 September 2001.

2. With TV tower (added 1950–1), 430.9 m/1,414 ft

## TALLEST STRUCTURES

| *Structure and location* | *Height* metres | feet |
|---|---|---|
| *Warszawa Radio Mast, Konstantynow, Poland (1974) | 646 | 2,120 |
| KVLY (formerly KTHI)-TV Mast, Blanchard, North Dakota (guyed) (1963) | 629 | 2,063 |
| CN Tower, Metro Centre, Toronto, Canada (1975) | 555 | 1,822 |
| Ostankino Tower, Moscow (1967) | 540 | 1,772 |

*Collapsed during renovation, August 1991. New structure planned on a site at Solkajawski

## LONGEST BRIDGES – BY SPAN

| *Bridge and location* | *Length* Metres | feet |
|---|---|---|
| SUSPENSION SPANS | | |
| Akashi-Kaikyo, Shikoku, Japan (1998) | 1,990 | 6,529 |
| Storebaelt East Bridge, Denmark (1998) | 1,624 | 5,328 |
| Humber Estuary, Humberside, England (1981) | 1,410 | 4,626 |
| Jiangyin (Yangtze), China (1999) | 1,385 | 4,544 |
| Tsing Ma, Hong Kong, China (1997) | 1,377 | 4,518 |
| Verrazano Narrows, Brooklyn–Staten I, USA (1964) | 1,298 | 4,260 |
| Golden Gate, San Francisco Bay, USA (1937) | 1,280 | 4,200 |
| Hoga Kusten, Sweden (1997) | 1,210 | 3,970 |
| Mackinac Straits, Michigan, USA (1957) | 1,158 | 3,800 |
| Chesapeake Bay No.2, Viginia, USA (1999) | 1,158 | 3,800 |
| Minami Bisan-Seto, Japan (1988) | 1,100 | 3,609 |
| Bosporus II, Istanbul, Turkey (1988) | 1,089 | 3,576 |
| Bosporus I, Istanbul, Turkey (1973) | 1,074 | 3,524 |
| George Washington, Hudson River, New York City, USA (1931) | 1,067 | 3,500 |
| Kurushima III, Japan (1999) | 1,030 | 3,379 |
| Kurushima II, Japan (1999) | 1,020 | 3,346 |
| Ponte 25 de Abril (Tagus), Lisbon, Portugal (1966) | 1,013 | 3,323 |
| Firth of Forth (road), nr Edinburgh, Scotland | 1,006 | 3,300 |
| Kita Bisan-Seto, Japan | 990 | 3,248 |
| *Severn River, Severn Estuary, England | 988 | 3,240 |

*The main span of the 5.15 km/3.2 mile long Second Severn bridging, opened in 1996, is 456 m/1,496 ft.

| *Bridge and location* | *Length* Metres | feet |
|---|---|---|
| CANTILEVER SPANS | | |
| Pont de Québec (rail-road), St Lawrence, Canada (1997) | 548.6 | 1,800 |
| Ravenswood, W. Virginia, USA | 525.1 | 1,723 |
| Firth of Forth (rail), nr Edinburgh, Scotland (two spans of 1,170ft each) (1890) | 521.2 | 1,710 |
| Nanko, Osaka, Japan (1974) | 510.0 | 1,673 |
| Commodore Barry, Chester, Pennsylvania, USA | 494.3 | 1,622 |
| Greater New Orleans, Louisiana, USA (1988) | 480.0 | 1,575 |
| Howrah (rail-road), Calcutta, India (1936-43) | 457.2 | 1,500 |
| STEEL ARCH SPANS | | |
| New River Gorge, Fayetteville, W. Virginia, USA (1977) | 518.0 | 1,700 |
| Bayonne (Kill van Kull), Bayonne, NJ – Staten I., USA (1931) | 503.5 | 1,652 |
| Sydney Harbour, Sydney, Australia (1932) | 502.9 | 1,650 |

The 'floating' bridging at Evergreen Point, Seattle, Washington State, USA (1963), is 3,839 m/12,596 ft long, of which 2,310 m/7,578 ft floats.

The longest stretch of bridgings of any kind is that carrying the Interstate 55 and Interstate 10 highways at Manchac, Louisiana (1979), on twin concrete trestles over 55.21 km/34.31 miles.

## LONGEST VEHICULAR TUNNELS

| *Tunnel and location* | *Length* km | miles |
|---|---|---|
| *Seikan (rail), Tsugaru Channel, Japan (1988) | 53.90 | 33.49 |
| *Channel Tunnel, (rail) Cheriton, Kent – Sangatte, Calais (1994) | 49.94 | 31.03 |
| Moscow metro, Belyaevo - Bittsevsky, Moscow, Russia (1979) | 37.90 | 23.50 |
| Northern line tube, East Finchley – Morden, London (1939) | 27.84 | 17.30 |
| Laerdal-Aurland Road Link (2000) | 24.51 | 15.22 |
| *Oshimizu (rail), Honshu, Japan (1982) | 22.17 | 13.78 |
| Simplon II (rail), Brigue, Switzerland – Iselle, Italy (1922) | 19.82 | 12.31 |
| Simplon I (rail), Brigue, Switzerland – Iselle, Italy (1906) | 19.80 | 12.30 |
| Vereina, Switzerland (1999) | 19.06 | 11.84 |
| *Shin-Kanmon (rail), Kanmon Strait, Japan (1975) | 18.68 | 11.61 |
| Appennino (rail), Vernio, Italy (1934) | 18.49 | 11.49 |
| St Gotthard (road), Göschenen – Airolo, Switzerland (1981) | 16.91 | 10.51 |

*Sub-aqueous

The longest non-vehicular tunnelling in the world is the Delaware Aqueduct in New York State, USA, constructed in 1937–44 to a length of 168.9 km/105 miles.

St Gotthard (rail) tunnel (2010) will be 56.9 km/33.6 miles.

### BRITAIN – RAIL TUNNELS

| | miles | yards |
|---|---|---|
| Severn, Bristol - Newport (1873-86) | 4 | 484 |
| Totley, Manchester – Sheffield | 3 | 950 |
| Standedge, Manchester - Huddersfield (1811) | 3 | 66 |
| Sodbury, Swindon – Bristol | 2 | 924 |
| Disley, Stockport – Sheffield | 2 | 346 |
| Ffestiniog, Llandudno – Blaenau Ffestiniog | 2 | 338 |
| Bramhope, Leeds – Harrogate | 2 | 241 |
| Cowburn, Manchester – Sheffield | 2 | 182 |

The longest road tunnel in Britain is the Mersey Road Tunnel (1934), 3.42 km/2 miles 228 yards long. The longest canal tunnel, at Standedge, W. Yorks, is 5.13 km/3 miles 330 yards long; it was closed in 1944 but is currently being restored.

## LONGEST SHIP CANALS

| *Canal (opening date)* | *Length* km | miles | *Min. depth* metres | feet |
|---|---|---|---|---|
| White Sea-Baltic (formerly Stalin) (1933), of which Canalised river; 51.5 km/32 miles | 235 | 146.02 | 5.0 | 16.5 |
| *Suez (1869) Links Red and Mediterranean Seas | 162 | 100.60 | 12.9 | 42.3 |
| V. I. Lenin Volga-Don (1952) Links Black and Caspian Seas | 100 | 62.20 | n/a | n/a |
| Kiel (or North Sea) (1895) Links North and Baltic Seas | 98 | 60.90 | 13.7 | 45.0 |
| *Houston (1940) Links inland city with sea | 91 | 56.70 | 10.4 | 34.0 |
| Alphonse XIII (1926) Gives Seville access to sea | 85 | 53.00 | 7.6 | 25.0 |
| Panama (1914) Links Pacific Ocean and Caribbean Sea; lake chain, 78.9 km/49 miles dug | 82 | 50.71 | 12.5 | 41.0 |
| Manchester Ship (1894) Links city with Irish Channel | 64 | 39.70 | 8.5 | 28.0 |
| Welland (1932) Circumvents Niagara Falls and Rapids | 43.5 | 27.00 | 8.8 | 29.0 |
| Brussels (Rupel Sea) (1922) Renders Brussels an inland port | 32 | 19.80 | 6.4 | 21.0 |

*Has no locks

The first section of China's Grand Canal, running 1,782 km/1,107 miles from Beijing to Hangzhou, was opened AD 610 and completed in 1283. Today it is limited to 2,000 tonne vessels.

The St Lawrence Seaway comprises the Beauharnois, Welland and Welland Bypass and Seaway 54–59 canals, and allows access to Duluth, Minnesota, USA via the Great Lakes from the Atlantic end of Canada's Gulf of St Lawrence, a distance of 3,769 km/2,342 miles. The St Lawrence Canal, completed in 1959, is 293 km/182 miles long.

# Distances from London by Air

This list details the distances in miles from London, Heathrow, to various cities (airports) abroad.

| *To* | *Miles* |
|---|---|
| Abidjan | 3,197 |
| Abu Dhabi (International) | 3,425 |
| Addis Ababa | 3,675 |
| Adelaide (International) | 10,111 |
| Aden | 3,670 |
| Algiers | 1,035 |
| 'Ammān (Queen Alia) | 2,287 |
| Amsterdam | 230 |
| Ankara (Esenboga) | 1,770 |
| Athens | 1,500 |
| Atlanta | 4,198 |
| Auckland | 11,404 |
| Baghdād (Saddam) | 2,551 |
| Bahrain | 3,163 |
| Baku | 2,485 |
| Bangkok | 5,928 |
| Barbados | 4,193 |
| Barcelona (Muntadas) | 712 |
| Basel | 447 |
| Beijing (Capital) | 5,063 |
| Beirut | 2,161 |
| Belfast (Aldergrove) | 325 |
| Belgrade | 1,056 |
| Berlin (Tegel) | 588 |
| Bermuda | 3,428 |
| Bern | 476 |
| Bogotá | 5,262 |
| Bombay (Mumbai) | 4,478 |
| Boston | 3,255 |
| Brasília | 5,452 |
| Bratislava | 817 |
| Brisbane (Eagle Farm) | 10,273 |
| Brussels | 217 |
| Bucharest (Otopeni) | 1,307 |
| Budapest | 923 |
| Buenos Aires | 6,915 |
| Cairo (International) | 2,194 |
| Calcutta | 4,958 |
| Calgary | 4,357 |
| Canberra | 10,563 |
| Cape Town | 6,011 |
| Caracas | 4,639 |
| Casablanca (Mohamed V) | 1,300 |
| Chicago (O'Hare) | 3,941 |
| Cologne | 331 |
| Colombo (Katunayake) | 5,411 |
| Copenhagen | 608 |
| Dakar | 2,706 |
| Dallas (Fort Worth) | 4,736 |
| Dallas (Lovefield) | 4,732 |
| Damascus (International) | 2,223 |
| Dar-es-Salaam | 4,662 |
| Darwin | 8,613 |
| Delhi | 4,180 |
| Denver | 4,655 |
| Detroit (Metropolitan) | 3,754 |
| Dhahran | 3,143 |
| Dhaka | 4,976 |
| Doha | 3,253 |
| Dubai | 3,414 |
| Dublin | 279 |
| Durban | 5,937 |
| Düsseldorf | 310 |
| Entebbe | 4,033 |
| Frankfurt (Main) | 406 |
| Freetown | 3,046 |
| Geneva | 468 |
| Gibraltar | 1,084 |
| Gothenburg (Landvetter) | 664 |
| Hamburg | 463 |
| Harare | 5,156 |
| Havana | 4,647 |
| Helsinki (Vantaa) | 1,148 |
| Hobart | 10,826 |
| Ho Chi Minh City | 6,345 |
| Hong Kong | 5,990 |
| Honolulu | 7,220 |
| Houston (Intercontinental) | 4,821 |
| Houston (William P. Hobby) | 4,837 |
| Islamabad | 3,767 |
| Istanbul | 1,560 |
| Jakarta (Halim Perdanakusuma) | 7,295 |
| Jeddah | 2,947 |
| Johannesburg | 5,634 |
| Kabul | 3,558 |
| Karachi | 3,935 |
| Kathmandu | 4,570 |
| Khartoum | 3,071 |
| Kiev (Borispol) | 1,357 |
| Kiev (Julyany) | 1,337 |
| Kingston, Jamaica | 4,668 |
| Kuala Lumpur (Subang) | 6,557 |
| Kuwait | 2,903 |
| Lagos | 3,107 |
| Larnaca | 2,036 |
| Lima | 6,303 |
| Lisbon | 972 |
| Lomé | 3,129 |
| Los Angeles (International) | 5,439 |
| Madras | 5,113 |
| Madrid | 773 |
| Malta | 1,305 |
| Manila | 6,685 |
| Marseille | 614 |
| Mauritius | 6,075 |
| Melbourne (Essendon) | 10,504 |
| Melbourne (Tullamarine) | 10,499 |
| Mexico City | 5,529 |
| Miami | 4,414 |
| Milan (Linate) | 609 |
| Minsk | 1,176 |
| Montego Bay | 4,687 |
| Montevideo | 6,841 |
| Montreal (Mirabel) | 3,241 |
| Moscow (Sheremetievo) | 1,557 |
| Munich (Franz Josef Strauss) | 584 |
| Muscat | 3,621 |
| Nairobi (Jomo Kenyatta) | 4,248 |
| Naples | 1,011 |
| Nassau | 4,333 |
| New York (J. F. Kennedy) | 3,440 |
| Nice | 645 |
| Oporto | 806 |
| Oslo (Fornebu) | 722 |
| Ottawa | 3,321 |
| Palma, Majorca (Son San Juan) | 836 |
| Paris (Charles de Gaulle) | 215 |
| Paris (Le Bourget) | 215 |
| Paris (Orly) | 227 |
| Perth, Australia | 9,008 |
| Port of Spain | 4,404 |
| Prague | 649 |
| Pretoria | 5,602 |
| Reykjavík (Domestic) | 1,167 |
| Reykjavík (Keflavík) | 1,177 |
| Rhodes | 1,743 |
| Rio de Janeiro | 5,745 |
| Riyadh (King Khaled) International | 3,067 |
| Rome (Fiumicino) | 895 |
| St John's, Newfoundland | 2,308 |
| St Petersburg | 1,314 |
| Salzburg | 651 |
| San Francisco | 5,351 |
| São Paulo | 5,892 |
| Sarajevo | 1,017 |
| Seoul (Kimpo) | 5,507 |
| Shanghai | 5,725 |
| Shannon | 369 |
| Singapore (Changi) | 6,756 |
| Sofia | 1,266 |
| Stockholm (Arlanda) | 908 |
| Suva | 10,119 |
| Sydney (Kingsford Smith) | 10,568 |
| Tangier | 1,120 |
| Tehran | 2,741 |
| Tel Aviv | 2,227 |
| Tōkyō (Narita) | 5,956 |
| Toronto | 3,544 |
| Tripoli (International) | 1,468 |
| Tunis | 1,137 |
| Turin (Caselle) | 570 |
| Ulaanbaatar | 4,340 |
| Valencia | 826 |
| Vancouver | 4,707 |
| Venice (Tessera) | 715 |
| Vienna (Schwechat) | 790 |
| Vladivostok | 5,298 |
| Warsaw | 912 |
| Washington (Dulles) | 3,665 |
| Wellington | 11,692 |
| Yangon/Rangoon | 5,582 |
| Yokohama (Aomori) | 5,647 |
| Zagreb | 848 |
| Zürich | 490 |

# The United Kingdom

The United Kingdom comprises Great Britain (England, Wales and Scotland) and Northern Ireland. The Isle of Man and the Channel Islands are Crown dependencies with their own legislative systems, and not a part of the United Kingdom.

## AREA AS AT 31 MARCH 1981

| | Land miles$^2$ | km$^2$ | *Inland water miles$^2$ | km$^2$ | Total miles$^2$ | km$^2$ |
|---|---|---|---|---|---|---|
| United Kingdom | 93,006 | 240,883 | 1,242 | 3,218 | 94,248 | 244,101 |
| England | 50,058 | 129,652 | 293 | 758 | 50,351 | 130,410 |
| Wales | 7,965 | 20,628 | 50 | 130 | 8,015 | 20,758 |
| Scotland | 29,767 | 77,097 | 653 | 1,692 | 30,420 | 78,789 |
| †Northern Ireland | 5,225 | 13,532 | 249 | 628 | 5,467 | 14,160 |
| Isle of Man | 221 | 572 | — | — | 221 | 572 |
| Channel Islands | 75 | 194 | — | — | 75 | 194 |

*Excluding tidal water
†Excluding certain tidal waters that are parts of statutory areas in Northern Ireland

## POPULATION

The first official census of population in England, Wales and Scotland was taken in 1801 and a census has been taken every ten years since, except in 1941 when there was no census because of war. The last official census in the United Kingdom was taken in April 2001.

The first official census of population in Ireland was taken in 1841. However, all figures given below refer only to the area which is now Northern Ireland. Figures for Northern Ireland in 1921 and 1931 are estimates based on the censuses taken in 1926 and 1937 respectively.

Estimates of the population of England before 1801, calculated from the number of baptisms, burials and marriages, are:

| | | | |
|---|---|---|---|
| 1570 | 4,160,221 | 1670 | 5,773,646 |
| 1600 | 4,811,718 | 1700 | 6,045,008 |
| 1630 | 5,600,517 | 1750 | 6,517,035 |

| *Thousands* | United Kingdom Total | Male | Female | England and Wales Total | Male | Female | Scotland Total | Male | Female | Northern Ireland Total | Male | Female |
|---|---|---|---|---|---|---|---|---|---|---|---|---|
| CENSUS RESULTS 1801–1991 | | | | | | | | | | | | |
| 1801 | — | — | — | 8,893 | 4,255 | 4,638 | 1,608 | 739 | 869 | — | — | — |
| 1811 | 13,368 | 6,368 | 7,000 | 10,165 | 4,874 | 5,291 | 1,806 | 826 | 980 | — | — | — |
| 1821 | 15,472 | 7,498 | 7,974 | 12,000 | 5,850 | 6,150 | 2,092 | 983 | 1,109 | — | — | — |
| 1831 | 17,835 | 8,647 | 9,188 | 13,897 | 6,771 | 7,126 | 2,364 | 1,114 | 1,250 | — | — | — |
| 1841 | 20,183 | 9,819 | 10,364 | 15,914 | 7,778 | 8,137 | 2,620 | 1,242 | 1,378 | 1,649 | 800 | 849 |
| 1851 | 22,259 | 10,855 | 11,404 | 17,928 | 8,781 | 9,146 | 2,889 | 1,376 | 1,513 | 1,443 | 698 | 745 |
| 1861 | 24,525 | 11,894 | 12,631 | 20,066 | 9,776 | 10,290 | 3,062 | 1,450 | 1,612 | 1,396 | 668 | 728 |
| 1871 | 27,431 | 13,309 | 14,122 | 22,712 | 11,059 | 11,653 | 3,360 | 1,603 | 1,757 | 1,359 | 647 | 712 |
| 1881 | 31,015 | 15,060 | 15,955 | 25,974 | 12,640 | 13,335 | 3,736 | 1,799 | 1,936 | 1,305 | 621 | 684 |
| 1891 | 34,264 | 16,593 | 17,671 | 29,003 | 14,060 | 14,942 | 4,026 | 1,943 | 2,083 | 1,236 | 590 | 646 |
| 1901 | 38,237 | 18,492 | 19,745 | 32,528 | 15,729 | 16,799 | 4,472 | 2,174 | 2,298 | 1,237 | 590 | 647 |
| 1911 | 42,082 | 20,357 | 21,725 | 36,070 | 17,446 | 18,625 | 4,761 | 2,309 | 2,452 | 1,251 | 603 | 648 |
| 1921 | 44,027 | 21,033 | 22,994 | 37,887 | 18,075 | 19,811 | 4,882 | 2,348 | 2,535 | 1,258 | 610 | 648 |
| 1931 | 46,038 | 22,060 | 23,978 | 39,952 | 19,133 | 20,819 | 4,843 | 2,326 | 2,517 | 1,243 | 601 | 642 |
| 1951 | 50,225 | 24,118 | 26,107 | 43,758 | 21,016 | 22,742 | 5,096 | 2,434 | 2,662 | 1,371 | 668 | 703 |
| 1961 | 52,709 | 25,481 | 27,228 | 46,105 | 22,304 | 23,801 | 5,179 | 2,483 | 2,697 | 1,425 | 694 | 731 |
| 1971 | 55,515 | 26,952 | 28,562 | 48,750 | 23,683 | 25,067 | 5,229 | 2,515 | 2,714 | 1,536 | 755 | 781 |
| 1981 | 55,848 | 27,104 | 28,742 | 49,155 | 23,873 | 25,281 | 5,131 | 2,466 | 2,664 | *1,533 | 750 | 783 |
| 1991 | 56,467 | 27,344 | 29,123 | 49,890 | 24,182 | 25,707 | 4,999 | 2,392 | 2,607 | 1,578 | 769 | 809 |
| †RESIDENT POPULATION: PROJECTIONS (MID-YEAR) | | | | | | | | | | | | |
| 2001 | 59, 954 | 29,581 | 30,372 | 53,137 | 26,258 | 26,879 | 5,109 | 2,485 | 2,624 | 1,708 | 839 | 869 |
| 2011 | 61,773 | 30,696 | 30,077 | 54,915 | 27,328 | 27,587 | 5,087 | 2,492 | 2,595 | 1,771 | 876 | 895 |
| 2021 | 63,642 | 31,717 | 31,925 | 56,763 | 28,325 | 28,437 | 5,058 | 2,487 | 2,570 | 1,821 | 904 | 917 |

*Figures include 44,500 non-enumerated persons
† Projections are 1996 based
*Source:* The Stationery Office – *Annual Abstract 2001*; ONS – Census reports (Crown copyright)

ISLANDS: Census Results 1901–91

| | Isle of Man Total | Male | Female | Jersey Total | Male | Female | *Guernsey Total | Male | Female |
|---|---|---|---|---|---|---|---|---|---|
| 901 | 54,752 | 25,496 | 29,256 | 52,576 | 23,940 | 28,636 | 40,446 | 19,652 | 20,794 |
| 911 | 52,016 | 23,937 | 28,079 | 51,898 | 24,014 | 27,884 | 41,858 | 20,661 | 21,197 |
| 921 | 60,284 | 27,329 | 32,955 | 49,701 | 22,438 | 27,263 | 38,315 | 18,246 | 20,069 |
| 931 | 49,308 | 22,443 | 26,865 | 50,462 | 23,424 | 27,038 | 40,643 | 19,659 | 20,984 |
| 951 | 55,123 | 25,749 | 29,464 | 57,296 | 27,282 | 30,014 | 43,652 | 21,221 | 22,431 |
| 961 | 48,151 | 22,060 | 26,091 | 57,200 | 27,200 | 30,000 | 45,068 | 21,671 | 23,397 |
| 971 | 56,289 | 26,461 | 29,828 | 72,532 | 35,423 | 37,109 | 51,458 | 24,792 | 26,666 |
| 981 | 64,679 | 30,901 | 33,778 | 77,000 | 37,000 | 40,000 | 53,313 | 25,701 | 27,612 |
| 991 | 69,788 | 33,693 | 36,095 | 84,082 | 40,862 | 43,220 | 58,867 | 28,297 | 30,570 |

Population of Guernsey, Herm, Jethou and Lithou. Figures for 1901–71 record all persons present on census night; census figures r 1981 and 1991 record all persons resident in the islands on census night
*urce:* 1991 Census

## ESIDENT POPULATION

### IID-YEAR ESTIMATE

| | 1989 | 1999 |
|---|---|---|
| Jnited Kingdom | 57,365,000 | 59,501,000 |
| ngland | 47,809,000 | 49,753,000 |
| Vales | 2,869,000 | 2,937,000 |
| cotland | 5,097,000 | 5,119,000 |
| Jorthern Ireland | 1,590,000 | 1,692,000 |

*urce:* The Stationery Office – *Annual Abstract of Statistics 2001* Crown copyright)

### Y AGE AND SEX 1999

| *Iales* | *Under 18* | *65 and over* |
|---|---|---|
| Jnited Kingdom | 6,963,000 | 3,845,000 |
| ngland | 5,801,000 | 3,231,000 |
| Vales | 344,000 | 210,000 |
| cotland | 581,000 | 315,000 |
| Jorthern Ireland | 237,000 | 89,000 |
| *'emales* | *Under 18* | *60 and over* |
| Jnited Kingdom | 6,614,000 | 6,908,000 |
| ngland | 5,506,000 | 5,760,000 |
| Vales† | 291,000 | 376,000 |
| cotland | 555,000 | 606,000 |
| Jorthern Ireland | 226,000 | 169,000 |

1998 figures
*ource:* The Stationery Office – *Annual Abstract of Statistics 2001* Crown copyright)

### Y ETHNIC GROUP (1991 CENSUS (GREAT RITAIN))

| *thnic group* | *Estimated population* | *As % of ethnic minority population* |
|---|---|---|
| Caribbean | 500,000 | 16.6 |
| African | 212,000 | 7 |
| Other black | 178,000 | 5.9 |
| ndian | 840,000 | 27.9 |
| Pakistani | 477,000 | 15.8 |
| Bangladeshi | 163,000 | 5.4 |
| Chinese | 157,000 | 5.2 |
| Other Asian | 198,000 | 6.6 |
| Other | 290,000 | 9.6 |
| Total ethnic minority groups | 3,015,000 | 100 |
| White | 51,874,000 | — |
| All ethnic groups | 54,889,000 | — |

*ource:* The Stationery Office – *Population Trends* 72 (Crown opyright)

## AVERAGE DENSITY *Persons per hectare*

| | 1981 | 1991 |
|---|---|---|
| England | 3.55 | 3.61 |
| Wales | 1.34 | 1.36 |
| Scotland | 0.66 | 0.65 |
| Northern Ireland | 1.12 | 1.11 |

*Sources:* ONS – Census reports (Crown copyright)

## IMMIGRATION 1999

*Acceptances for settlement in the UK by nationality*

| *Region* | *Number of persons* |
|---|---|
| Europe: total | 15,990 |
| European Economic Area | 10 |
| Remainder of Europe | 15,980 |
| Americas: total | 8,520 |
| USA | 3,760 |
| Canada | 1,010 |
| Africa: total | 27,020 |
| Asia: total | 40,090 |
| Indian sub-continent | 21,440 |
| Middle East | 5,590 |
| Oceania: total | 4,120 |
| British Overseas Citizens | 560 |
| Stateless | 820 |
| Total | 97,120 |

*Source:* The Stationery Office – *Annual Abstract of Statistics 2001* (Crown copyright)

## LIVE BIRTHS AND BIRTH RATES 1998

| | *Live births* | *Birth rate** |
|---|---|---|
| United Kingdom | 700,000 | 11.8 |
| England and Wales | 622,000 | 11.8 |
| Scotland | 55,000 | 10.8 |
| Northern Ireland | 23,000 | 13.6 |

*Live births per 1,000 population
*Source:* The Stationery Office – *Annual Abstract of Statistics 2001* (Crown copyright)

## LEGAL ABORTIONS 1999

| *Age group* | *England and Wales* | *Scotland*† |
|---|---|---|
| Under 16 | 3,603 | 251 |
| 16-19 | 32,807 | 2,630 |
| 20-34 | 112,635 | 7,704 |
| 35-44 | 24,096 | 1,536 |
| 45 and over | 502 | 23 |
| Total | 173,643 | 12,144 |

† provisional
*Source:* The Stationery Office – *Annual Abstract of Statistics 2001* (Crown copyright)

## BIRTHS OUTSIDE MARRIAGE (UK)

| *Age group* | 1989 | 1999 |
|---|---|---|
| Under 20 | 49,000 | 49,000 |
| 20-24 | 79,000 | 77,000 |
| 25-29 | 46,000 | 68,000 |
| Over 30 | 32,000 | 77,000 |
| Total | 207,000 | 272,000 |

*Source:* The Stationery Office – *Annual Abstract of Statistics 2001* (Crown copyright)

## MARRIAGE AND DIVORCE 1999

| | *Marriages* | *Divorces* |
|---|---|---|
| United Kingdom | 301,083 | 158,746 |
| England and Wales | 263,515 | 144,556 |
| Scotland | 29,940 | 11,864 |
| Northern Ireland | 7,628 | 2,326 |

*Source:* The Stationery Office – *Annual Abstract of Statistics 2001* (Crown copyright)

## DEATHS AND DEATH RATES 1999

| *Males* | *Deaths* | *Death rat* |
|---|---|---|
| United Kingdom | 300,368 | 10. |
| England and Wales | 264,299 | 10. |
| Scotland | 28,605 | 11. |
| Northern Ireland | 7,464 | 8. |
| *Females* | | |
| United Kingdom | 331,694 | 11. |
| England and Wales | 291,819 | 10. |
| Scotland | 31,676 | 11. |
| Northern Ireland | 8,199 | 8. |

* Deaths per 1,000 population
*Sources:* The Stationery Office – *Annual Abstract of Statisti 2001* (Crown copyright); ONS; General Register Office fc Scotland; General Register Office (Northern Ireland)

## INFANT MORTALITY 1999
*deaths of infants under 1 year of age per 1,000 live birth*

| | *Number* |
|---|---|
| United Kingdom | 5.8 |
| England and Wales | 5.8 |
| Scotland | 5.0 |
| Northern Ireland | 6.4 |

*Source:* The Stationery Office – *Annual Abstract of Statistics 200* (Crown copyright)

## LIFE EXPECTANCY LIFE TABLES 1997–99 (INTERIM FIGURES)

| Age | England and Wales Male | England and Wales Female | Scotland Male | Scotland Female | Northern Ireland Male | Northern Ireland Female |
|---|---|---|---|---|---|---|
| 0 | 75.1 | 80.0 | 72.6 | 78.1 | 74.3 | 79.5 |
| 5 | 70.7 | 75.5 | 68.1 | 73.5 | 69.8 | 75.0 |
| 10 | 65.7 | 70.5 | 63.2 | 68.5 | 64.9 | 70.1 |
| 15 | 60.8 | 65.5 | 58.3 | 63.6 | 59.9 | 65.1 |
| 20 | 55.9 | 60.6 | 53.5 | 58.7 | 55.1 | 60.2 |
| 25 | 51.2 | 55.7 | 48.8 | 53.8 | 50.4 | 55.3 |
| 30 | 46.4 | 50.8 | 44.1 | 48.9 | 45.6 | 50.4 |
| 35 | 41.4 | 45.9 | 39.4 | 44.0 | 40.9 | 45.5 |
| 40 | 36.8 | 41.1 | 34.7 | 39.2 | 36.1 | 40.6 |
| 45 | 32.2 | 36.3 | 30.1 | 34.5 | 31.4 | 35.9 |
| 50 | 27.6 | 31.7 | 25.7 | 29.9 | 26.9 | 31.3 |
| 55 | 23.2 | 27.2 | 21.5 | 25.5 | 22.6 | 26.7 |
| 60 | 19.1 | 22.8 | 17.7 | 21.3 | 18.5 | 22.4 |
| 65 | 15.3 | 18.7 | 14.2 | 17.4 | 14.8 | 18.3 |
| 70 | 12.0 | 14.9 | 11.1 | 13.8 | 11.6 | 14.5 |
| 75 | 9.2 | 11.5 | 8.5 | 10.6 | 8.9 | 11.1 |
| 80 | 6.9 | 8.6 | 6.4 | 7.9 | 6.6 | 8.3 |
| 85 | 5.1 | 6.3 | 4.7 | 5.6 | 4.9 | 6.0 |
| 90 | 3.9 | 4.6 | 3.5 | 3.8 | 4.1 | 4.3 |

*Source:* The Stationery Office – *Annual Abstract of Statistics 2001* (Crown copyright)

## EATHS ANALYSED BY CAUSE 1999

| | *England* and *Wales* | *Scotland* | *N. Ireland* |
|---|---|---|---|
| OTAL DEATHS | 556,118 | 60,281 | 15,663 |
| eaths from natural causes | 537,166 | 57,649 | 14,942 |
| fectious and parasitic diseases | 3,613 | 498 | 47 |
| eoplasms | 136,181 | 14,966 | 3,654 |
| Malignant neoplasm of stomach | 6,139 | 650 | 187 |
| Malignant neoplasm of trachea, bronchus and lung | 29,493 | 3,961 | 781 |
| Malignant neoplasm of breast | 11,670 | 1,136 | 289 |
| Malignant neoplasm of uterus | 1,231 | 138 | 26 |
| Malignant neoplasm of cervix | 1,107 | 122 | 36 |
| Benign and unspecified neoplasms | 1,656 | 124 | 67 |
| Leukaemia | 3,680 | 313 | 104 |
| ndocrine, nutritional and metabolic diseases and immunity disorders | 7,560 | 870 | 118 |
| Diabetes mellitus | 5,963 | 670 | 93 |
| Nutritional deficiencies | 59 | 17 | 3 |
| ther metabolic and immunity disorders | 1,150 | 147 | 20 |
| iseases of blood and blood-forming organs | 1,855 | 204 | 24 |
| Anaemias | 584 | 80 | 9 |
| ental disorders | 11,173 | 1,901 | 190 |
| iseases of the nervous system and sense organs | 10,192 | 971 | 284 |
| eningitis | 182 | 19 | 3 |
| iseases of the circulatory system | 219,087 | 24,787 | 6,423 |
| heumatic heart disease | 1,638 | 173 | 35 |
| Hypertensive disease | 3,324 | 353 | 68 |
| Ischaemic heart disease | 115,119 | 13,337 | 3,568 |
| Diseases of pulmonary circulation and other forms of heart disease | 26,462 | 2,638 | 768 |
| Cerebrovascular disease | 56,051 | 6,785 | 1,680 |
| iseases of the respiratory system | 97,755 | 8,870 | 3,161 |
| Influenza | 585 | 62 | 5 |
| Pneumonia | 59,273 | 4,526 | 2,130 |
| Bronchitis, emphysema | 3,452 | 322 | 93 |
| Asthma | 1,364 | 119 | 38 |
| iseases of the digestive system | 21,698 | 2,787 | 507 |
| Ulcer of stomach and duodenum | 4,011 | 337 | 80 |
| Appendicitis | 133 | 9 | 3 |
| Hernia of the abdominal cavity and other intestinal obstruction | 2,126 | 213 | 49 |
| Chronic liver disease and cirrhosis | 4,718 | 896 | 92 |
| iseases of the genitourinary system | 7,299 | 936 | 242 |
| Nephritis, nephrotic syndrome and nephrosis | 2,952 | 540 | 155 |
| Hyperplasia of prostate | 200 | 16 | 4 |
| omplications of pregnancy, childbirth and the puerperium | 30 | 7 | — |
| Abortion | 5 | — | — |
| iseases of the skin and subcutaneous tissue | 1,152 | 90 | 27 |
| iseases of the musculo-skeletal system | 3,554 | 295 | 54 |
| ongenital anomalies | 1,194 | 157 | 93 |
| ertain conditions originating in the perinatal period | 116 | 137 | 69 |
| Birth trauma, hypoxia, birth asphyxia and other respiratory conditions | 72 | 54 | 21 |
| igns, symptoms and ill-defined conditions | 14,707 | 355 | 161 |
| udden infant death syndrome | 222 | 41 | 3 |
| eaths from injury and poisoning | 16,517 | 2,450 | 609 |
| ll accidents | 10,625 | 1,428 | 430 |
| Motor vehicle accidents | 3,003 | 320 | 134 |
| uicide and self-inflicted injury | 3,690 | 637 | 121 |
| ll other external causes | 2,202 | 385 | 58 |

*ource*: The Stationery Office – *Annual Abstract of Statistics 2001* (Crown copyright)

# The National Flag

The national flag of the United Kingdom is the Union Flag, generally known as the Union Jack.

The Union Flag is a combination of the cross of St George, patron saint of England, the cross of St Andrew, patron saint of Scotland, and a cross similar to that of St Patrick, patron saint of Ireland.

*Cross of St George:* cross Gules in a field Argent (red cross on a white ground)

*Cross of St Andrew:* saltire Argent in a field Azure (white diagonal cross on a blue ground)

*Cross of St Patrick:* saltire Gules in a field Argent (red diagonal cross on a white ground)

The Union Flag was first introduced in 1606 after the union of the kingdoms of England and Scotland under one sovereign. The cross of St Patrick was added in 1801 after the union of Great Britain and Ireland.

## Flying the Union Flag

The correct orientation of the Union Flag when flying is with the broader diagonal band of white uppermost in the hoist (i.e. near the pole) and the narrower diagonal band of white uppermost in the fly (i.e. furthest from the pole).

It is the practice to fly the Union Flag daily on some customs houses. In all other cases, flags are flown on government buildings by command of The Queen. It is now customary for the Union Flag to be flown at Buckingham Palace when The Queen is not present.

Days for hoisting the Union Flag are notified to the Department for Culture, Media and Sport by The Queen's command and communicated by the department to the other government departments. On the days appointed, the Union Flag is flown on government buildings in the United Kingdom from 8 a.m. to sunset.

## Days for Flying Flags

| | |
|---|---|
| The Queen's Accession | 6 February |
| Birthday of The Duke of York | 19 February |
| *St David's Day (in Wales only) | 1 March |
| Birthday of The Earl of Wessex | 10 March |
| Commonwealth Day** (2002) | 11 March |
| Birthday of The Queen | 21 April |
| *St George's Day (in England only) | 23 April |
| †Europe Day | 9 May |
| Coronation Day | 2 June |
| Birthday of The Duke of Edinburgh | 10 June |
| The Queen's Official Birthday (2002) | 15 June |
| Birthday of Queen Elizabeth the Queen Mother | 4 August |
| Birthday of The Princess Royal | 15 August |
| Birthday of The Princess Margaret | 21 August |
| Remembrance Sunday (2002) | 10 November |
| Birthday of The Prince of Wales | 14 November |
| The Queen's Wedding Day | 20 November |
| *St Andrew's Day (in Scotland only) | 30 November |

‡The opening of Parliament by The Queen
‡The prorogation of Parliament by The Queen

*Where a building has two or more flagstaffs, the appropriate national flag may be flown in addition to the Union Flag, but not in a superior position

**Commonwealth Day is always the second Monday in March

†The Union Flag should fly alongside the European flag. O[n] government buildings that have only one flagpole, the Union Flag should take precedence

‡Flags are flown whether or not The Queen performs the ceremony in person. Flags are flown only in the Greater London area

## Flags at Half-Mast

Flags are flown at half-mast (i.e. two-thirds up between th[e] top and bottom of the flagstaff) on the following occasion[s]:

(a) From the announcement of the death up to the funer[al] of the Sovereign, except on Proclamation Day, whe[n] flags are hoisted right up from 11 a.m. to sunset
(b) The funerals of members of the royal family, subject [to] special commands from The Queen in each case
(c) The funerals of foreign rulers, subject to speci[al] commands from The Queen in each case
(d) The funerals of prime ministers and ex-prim[e] ministers of the UK, subject to special comman[d] from The Queen in each case
(e) Other occasions by special command of The Queen

On occasions when days for flying flags coincide with day[s] for flying flags at half-mast, the following rules a[re] observed. Flags are flown:

(a) although a member of the royal family, or a nea[r] relative of the royal family, may be lying dead, unles[s] special commands are received from The Queen t[o] the contrary
(b) although it may be the day of the funeral of a foreig[n] ruler

If the body of a very distinguished subject is lying at [a] government office, the flag may fly at half-mast on tha[t] office until the body has left (provided it is a day on whic[h] the flag would fly) and then the flag is to be hoisted righ[t] up. On all other government buildings the flag will fly a[s] usual.

## The Royal Standard

The Royal Standard is hoisted only when The Queen [is] actually present in the building, and never when He[r] Majesty is passing in procession.

# The Royal Family

## 'HE SOVEREIGN

LIZABETH II, by the Grace of God, of the United ;ingdom of Great Britain and Northern Ireland and of er other Realms and Territories Queen, Head of the ;ommonwealth, Defender of the Faith

ler Majesty Elizabeth Alexandra Mary of Windsor, elder aughter of King George VI and of HM Queen Elizabeth ıe Queen Mother
*'orn* 21 April 1926, at 17 Bruton Street, London W1
*scended the throne* 6 February 1952
*'rowned* 2 June 1953, at Westminster Abbey
*Iarried* 20 November 1947, in Westminster Abbey, IRH The Prince Philip, Duke of Edinburgh
*fficial residences:* Buckingham Palace, London SW1A 1AA; Vindsor Castle, Berks; Palace of Holyroodhouse, dinburgh
*rivate residences:* Sandringham, Norfolk; Balmoral Castle, berdeenshire

## IUSBAND OF THE QUEEN

IRH THE PRINCE PHILIP, DUKE OF EDINBURGH, KG, KT, M, GBE, AC, QSO, PC, Ranger of Windsor Park
*'orn* 10 June 1921, son of Prince and Princess Andrew of ;reece and Denmark, naturalised a British subject 1947, reated Duke of Edinburgh, Earl of Merioneth and Baron ;reenwich 1947

## :HILDREN OF THE QUEEN

IRH THE PRINCE OF WALES (Prince Charles Philip rthur George), KG, KT, GCB and Great Master of the )rder of the Bath, AK, QSO, PC, ADC(p)
*'orn* 14 November 1948, created Prince of Wales and Earl f Chester 1958, succeeded as Duke of Cornwall, Duke of :othesay, Earl of Carrick and Baron Renfrew, Lord of the sles and Prince and Great Steward of Scotland 1952
*Iarried* 29 July 1981 Lady Diana Frances Spencer (Diana, 'rincess of Wales (1961–97), youngest daughter of the 8th :arl Spencer and the Hon. Mrs Shand Kydd), marriage lissolved 1996
*ssue:*
1) HRH Prince William of Wales (Prince William Arthur Philip Louis), *born* 21 June 1982
2) HRH Prince Henry of Wales (Prince Henry Charles Albert David), *born* 15 September 1984

*'esidences of the Prince of Wales:* St James's Palace, London W1A 1BS; Highgrove, Doughton, Tetbury, Glos GL8 8TN

IRH THE PRINCESS ROYAL (Princess Anne Elizabeth lice Louise), KG, GCVO
*'orn* 15 August 1950, declared The Princess Royal 1987
*Iarried* (1) 14 November 1973 Captain Mark Anthony 'eter Phillips, CVO (*born* 22 September 1948); marriage lissolved 1992; (2) 12 December 1992 Captain Timothy ames Hamilton Laurence, MVO, RN (*born* 1 March 1955)
*ssue:*
1) Peter Mark Andrew Phillips, *born* 15 November 1977
(2) Zara Anne Elizabeth Phillips, *born* 15 May 1981

*Residence:* Gatcombe Park, Minchinhampton, Glos

HRH THE DUKE OF YORK (Prince Andrew Albert Christian Edward), CVO, ADC(P)
*Born* 19 February 1960, created Duke of York, Earl of Inverness and Baron Killyleagh 1986
*Married* 23 July 1986 Sarah Margaret Ferguson, now Sarah, Duchess of York (*born* 15 October 1959, younger daughter of Major Ronald Ferguson and Mrs Hector Barrantes), marriage dissolved 1996
*Issue:*
(1) HRH Princess Beatrice of York (Princess Beatrice Elizabeth Mary), *born* 8 August 1988
(2) HRH Princess Eugenie of York (Princess Eugenie Victoria Helena), *born* 23 March 1990

*Residences:* Buckingham Palace, London SW1A 1AA; Sunninghill Park, Ascot, Berks

HRH THE EARL OF WESSEX (Prince Edward Antony Richard Louis), CVO
*Born* 10 March 1964, created Earl of Wessex, Viscount Severn 1999
*Married* 19 June 1999 Sophie Helen Rhys-Jones, now HRH The Countess of Wessex (*born* 20 January 1965, daughter of Mr and Mrs Christopher Rhys-Jones)
*Residence:* Bagshot Park, Bagshot, Surrey GU19 5HS

## SISTER OF THE QUEEN

HRH THE PRINCESS MARGARET, COUNTESS OF SNOWDON, CI, GCVO, Royal Victorian Chain, Dame Grand Cross of the Order of St John of Jerusalem
*Born* 21 August 1930, younger daughter of King George VI and HM Queen Elizabeth the Queen Mother
*Married* 6 May 1960 Antony Charles Robert Armstrong-Jones, GCVO (*born* 7 March 1930, created Earl of Snowdon 1961); marriage dissolved 1978
*Issue:*
(1) David Albert Charles, Viscount Linley, *born* 3 November 1961, *married* 8 October 1993 the Hon. Serena Stanhope, and has issue, Hon. Charles Patrick Inigo Armstrong-Jones, *born* 1 July 1999
(2) Lady Sarah Chatto (Sarah Frances Elizabeth), *born* 1 May 1964, *married* 14 July 1994 Daniel Chatto, and has issue, Samuel David Benedict Chatto, *born* 28 July 1996; Arthur Robert Nathaniel Chatto, *born* 5 February 1999

*Residence:* Kensington Palace, London W8 4PU

## MOTHER OF THE QUEEN

HM QUEEN ELIZABETH THE QUEEN MOTHER (Elizabeth Angela Marguerite), Lady of the Garter, Lady of the Thistle, CI, GCVO, GBE, Dame Grand Cross of the Order of St John of Jerusalem, Royal Victorian Chain, Lord Warden and Admiral of the Cinque Ports and Constable of Dover Castle
*Born* 4 August 1900, youngest daughter of the 14th Earl of Strathmore and Kinghorne
*Married* 26 April 1923 (as Lady Elizabeth Bowes-Lyon) Prince Albert, Duke of York, afterwards King George VI (*see* page 126)

*Residences:* Clarence House, St James's Palace, London SW1A 1BA; Royal Lodge, Windsor Great Park, Berks; Castle of Mey, Caithness

## AUNT OF THE QUEEN

HRH PRINCESS ALICE, DUCHESS OF GLOUCESTER (Alice Christabel), GCB, CI, GCVO, GBE, Grand Cordon of Al Kamal
*Born* 25 December 1901, third daughter of the 7th Duke of Buccleuch and Queensberry
*Married* 6 November 1935 (as Lady Alice Montagu-Douglas-Scott) Prince Henry, Duke of Gloucester, third son of King George V (*see* page 126)
*Residence:* Kensington Palace, London W8 4PU

## COUSINS OF THE QUEEN

HRH THE DUKE OF GLOUCESTER (Prince Richard Alexander Walter George), KG, GCVO, Grand Prior of the Order of St John of Jerusalem
*Born* 26 August 1944
*Married* 8 July 1972 Birgitte Eva van Deurs, now HRH The Duchess of Gloucester, GCVO (*born* 20 June 1946, daughter of Asger Henriksen and Vivian van Deurs)
*Issue:*
(1) Earl of Ulster (Alexander Patrick Gregers Richard), *born* 24 October 1974
(2) Lady Davina Windsor (Davina Elizabeth Alice Benedikte), *born* 19 November 1977
(3) Lady Rose Windsor (Rose Victoria Birgitte Louise), *born* 1 March 1980
*Residence:* Kensington Palace, London W8 4PU

HRH THE DUKE OF KENT (Prince Edward George Nicholas Paul Patrick), KG, GCMG, GCVO, ADC(P)
*Born* 9 October 1935
*Married* 8 June 1961 Katharine Lucy Mary Worsley, now HRH The Duchess of Kent, GCVO (*born* 22 February 1933, daughter of Sir William Worsley, Bt.)
*Issue:*
(1) Earl of St Andrews (George Philip Nicholas), *born* 26 June 1962, *married* 9 January 1988 Sylvana Tomaselli, and has issue, Edward Edmund Maximilian George, Baron Downpatrick, *born* 2 December 1988; Lady Marina Charlotte Alexandra Katharine Windsor, *born* 30 September 1992; Lady Amelia Sophia Theodora Mary Margaret Windsor, *born* 24 August 1995
(2) Lady Helen Taylor (Helen Marina Lucy), *born* 28 April 1964, *married* 18 July 1992 Timothy Taylor, and has issue, Columbus George Donald Taylor, *born* 6 August 1994; Cassius Edward Taylor, *born* 26 December 1996
(3) Lord Nicholas Windsor (Nicholas Charles Edward Jonathan), *born* 25 July 1970
*Residence:* Wren House, Palace Green, London W8 4PY

HRH PRINCESS ALEXANDRA, THE HON. LADY OGILVY (Princess Alexandra Helen Elizabeth Olga Christabel), GCVO
*Born* 25 December 1936
*Married* 24 April 1963 The Rt. Hon. Sir Angus Ogilvy, KCVO (*born* 14 September 1928, second son of 12th Earl of Airlie)
*Issue:*
(1) James Robert Bruce Ogilvy, *born* 29 February 1964, *married* 30 July 1988 Julia Rawlinson, and has issue, Flora Alexandra Ogilvy, *born* 15 December 1994; Alexander Charles Ogilvy, *born* 12 November 1996
(2) Marina Victoria Alexandra, Mrs Mowatt, *born* 31 July 1966, *married* 2 February 1990 Paul Mowatt (marriage dissolved 1997), and has issue, Zenouska May Mowatt, *born* 26 May 1990; Christian Alexander Mowatt, *born* 4 June 1993
*Residence:* Thatched House Lodge, Richmond Park, Surrey

HRH PRINCE MICHAEL OF KENT (Prince Michael George Charles Franklin), KCVO
*Born* 4 July 1942
*Married* 30 June 1978 Baroness Marie-Christine Agnes Hedwig Ida von Reibnitz, now HRH Princess Michael of Kent (*born* 15 January 1945, daughter of Baron Gunther von Reibnitz)
*Issue:*
(1) Lord Frederick Windsor (Frederick Michael George David Louis), *born* 6 April 1979
(2) Lady Gabriella Windsor (Gabriella Marina Alexandra Ophelia), *born* 23 April 1981
*Residences:* Kensington Palace, London W8 4PU; Nether Lypiatt Manor, Stroud, Glos GL6 7LS

## ORDER OF SUCCESSION

1 HRH The Prince of Wales
2 HRH Prince William of Wales
3 HRH Prince Henry of Wales
4 HRH The Duke of York
5 HRH Princess Beatrice of York
6 HRH Princess Eugenie of York
7 HRH The Earl of Wessex
8 HRH The Princess Royal
9 Peter Phillips
10 Zara Phillips
11 HRH The Princess Margaret, Countess of Snowdon
12 Viscount Linley
13 Hon. Charles Armstrong-Jones
14 Lady Sarah Chatto
15 Samuel Chatto
16 Arthur Chatto
17 HRH The Duke of Gloucester
18 Earl of Ulster
19 Lady Davina Windsor
20 Lady Rose Windsor
21 HRH The Duke of Kent
22 Baron Downpatrick
23 Lady Marina Charlotte Windsor
24 Lady Amelia Windsor
25 Lord Nicholas Windsor
26 Lady Helen Taylor
27 Columbus Taylor
28 Cassius Taylor
29 Lord Frederick Windsor
30 Lady Gabriella Windsor
31 HRH Princess Alexandra, the Hon. Lady Ogilvy
32 James Ogilvy
33 Alexander Ogilvy
34 Flora Ogilvy
35 Marina, Mrs Paul Mowatt
36 Christian Mowatt
37 Zenouska Mowatt
38 The Earl of Harewood

The Earl of St Andrews and HRH Prince Michael of Kent both lost the right of succession to the throne through marriage to a Roman Catholic. Their children remain in succession provided that they are in communion with the Church of England.

# Private Secretaries to the Royal Family

ote to readers: the complete listings of members of the oyal Households as published in previous editions of *'hitaker's Almanack* are no longer made available for iblication by Buckingham Palace. We apologise for any convenience this may cause.

## HE QUEEN

*fice:* Buckingham Palace, London SW1A 1AA
el: 020-7930 4832
'eb: www.royal.gov.uk
*ivate Secretary to The Queen*, Sir Robin Janvrin, KCVO, CB

## RINCE PHILIP, THE DUKE OF DINBURGH

*fice:* Buckingham Palace, London SW1A 1AA
el: 020-7930 4832
*ivate Secretary*, Brig. M. G. Hunt-Davis, CVO, CBE

## UEEN ELIZABETH THE QUEEN MOTHER

*fice:* Clarence House, St James's Palace, London SW1A A Tel: 020-7930 3141
*ivate Secretary*, Capt. Sir Alastair Aird, GCVO

## HE PRINCE OF WALES

*ffice:* St James's Palace, London SW1A 1BS
el: 020-7930 4832
*rivate Secretary*, S. M. J. Lamport, CVO

## HE DUKE OF YORK

*ffice:* Buckingham Palace, London SW1A 1AA
'el: 020-7930 4832
*rivate Secretary*, Miss C. Manly, OBE

## HE EARL AND COUNTESS OF WESSEX

*ffice:* The Old Stables, Bagshot Park, Surrey GU19 5PJ
'el: 01276-700 843/022
*rivate Secretary*, Lt.-Col. S. G. O'Dwyer, LVO

## HE PRINCESS ROYAL

*ffice:* Buckingham Palace, London SW1A 1AA
'el: 020-7930 4832
*rivate Secretary*, Col. T. Earl, OBE

## THE PRINCESS MARGARET, COUNTESS OF SNOWDON

*Office:* Kensington Palace, London W8 4PU
Tel: 020-7930 3141
*Private Secretary*, The Viscount Ullswater, PC

## PRINCESS ALICE, DUCHESS OF GLOUCESTER AND THE DUKE AND DUCHESS OF GLOUCESTER

*Office:* Kensington Palace, London W8 4PU
Tel: 020-7937 6374
*Private Secretary*, Maj. N. M. L. Barne, LVO

## THE DUKE OF KENT

*Office:* St James's Palace, London, SW1A 1BQ
Tel: 020-7930 4872
*Private Secretary*, N. C. Adamson, OBE

## THE DUCHESS OF KENT

*Office:* Palace Green, London, W8 4PU
Tel: 020-7937 2928
*Personal Secretary*, Miss V. Uttley, OBE

## PRINCE AND PRINCESS MICHAEL OF KENT

*Office:* Kensington Palace, London W8 4PU
Tel: 020-7938 3519
*Private Secretary*, N. Chance

## PRINCESS ALEXANDRA, THE HON. LADY OGILVY

*Office:* Buckingham Palace, London SW1A 1AA
Tel: 020-7930 1860
*Private Secretary*, Lt.-Col. R. Macfarlane

# Offices of the Royal Household

## PRIVATE SECRETARY'S OFFICE

The Private Secretary, assisted by the three Assistant Private Secretaries, is responsible for:

- Informing and advising The Queen on constitutional, governmental and political matters in the UK, her other realms and the wider Commonwealth, including communications with the Prime Minister and Government Departments.

- Organising The Queen's domestic and overseas official programme, including the Presentation of Credentials by incoming foreign ambassadors from overseas countries.
- The Queen's speeches and messages, The Queen's patronage, The Queen's photographs and official presents, portraits of The Queen and dedications and congratulatory messages.
- Communications in connection with the role of the Royal Family and other members of the Royal Family and their households.
- Dealing with correspondence to The Queen from members of the public.
- Organising and co-ordinating Royal travel through the Royal Travel Office.
- Co-ordinating and initiating research to support engagements by members of the Royal Family through the Co-ordination and Research Unit.

The Private Secretary is also responsible for communications and media affairs. The Communications Secretary reports to the Private Secretary and is responsible for:

- Developing communications strategies to enhance the public understanding of the role of the royal family, including an education strategy, encompassing website development and other multi-media initiatives.
- Co-ordinating communications across the Households, including the publication of internal newsletters and related literature.
- The Buckingham Palace Press Office.

Within the Press Office, the Press Secretary, assisted by the Deputy Press Secretary and two Assistant Press Secretaries, is responsible for:

- Briefing the British and international media on the role and duties of The Queen and issues relating to the Royal Family.
- Responding to media enquiries.
- Arranging media facilities in the United Kingdom and overseas to support royal functions and engagements.
- The management of the Royal website.

The Private Secretary is Keeper of the Royal Archives and is responsible for the care of the records of the Sovereign and the Royal Household from previous reigns, which are preserved in the Royal Archives at Windsor, where they are managed by the Assistant Keeper (a post combined with that of the Librarian of the Royal Library, q.v.) and made available for historical research. As keeper, it is the Private Secretary's responsibility to ensure the proper management of the records of the present reign with a view to their transfer to the archives as and when appropriate. The Private Secretary is an *ex officio* trustee of the Royal Collection Trust.

## PRIVY PURSE AND TREASURER'S OFFICE

The Keeper of the Privy Purse and Treasurer to the Queen, assisted by the Deputy Treasurer (who is also Deputy Keeper of the Privy Purse) and the Assistant Keeper of the Privy Purse, is responsible for:

- The Queen's Civil List, which is the money paid from the Government's Consolidated Fund to meet official expenditure relating to the Queen's duties as Head of State and Head of the Commonwealth.
- Through the Director of Personnel, the identification, planning and management of personnel policy across the Household, the administration of all pension schemes provided for the Household and Private Estates employees, and the allocation employee and pensioner housing.
- Information technology systems for the household.
- Internal audit services.
- All insurance matters.
- The Privy Purse, which is mainly financed by the n income of the Duchy of Lancaster, and which mee both official expenditure incurred by The Queen Sovereign and private expenditure.
- Liaison with other members of the Royal Family ar their Households on Financial matters.
- The Queen's private estates at Sandringham ar Balmoral, The Queen's Racing Establishment and t Royal Studs and liaison with the Ascot Authority.
- The Home Park at Windsor and liaison with t Crown Estate Commissioners concerning the Hon Park and the Great Park at Windsor.
- The Royal Philatelic Collection, which is managed l the Keeper of the Royal Philatelic Collection.
- Administrative aspects of the Military Knights Windsor and the Royal Almonry.
- Administration of the Royal Victorian Order, which the Keeper of the Privy Purse is Secretar Long and Faithful Service Medals, and the Queen Cups, Medals and Prizes, and Policy on Commer orative Medals.

The Keeper of the Privy Purse is one of three Roy Trustees (in respect of his responsibilities for the Civ List) and is Receiver General of the Duchy of Lancast and a member of the Duchy's Council.

The Keeper of the Privy Purse is also responsible f property services for the Occupied Royal Palaces England, which comprise Buckingham Palace, St Jame Palace and Clarence House, Marlborough House Mew the residential, office and general areas of Kensingtc Palace, Windsor Castle and related areas and building Frogmore House, and Hampton Court Mews ar Paddocks. The costs of property services for the Occupie Royal Palaces are met from a Grant-in-aid from th Department for Culture, Media and Sport.

The Director of Property Services, assisted by th Director of Finance, Property Services, has day to da responsibility for the Royal Household's Property Sec tion, which is responsible for:

- Fire, health and safety issues.
- Repairs and refurbishment of buildings and ne buildings work.
- Utilities and telephones.
- Putting up stages, flags and tents and other work i connection with ceremonial occasions and garde parties and other official functions.

The Property Section is also responsible, in effect on sub-contract basis from the Department for Cultur Media and Sport, for the maintenance of Marlboroug House (Which is occupied by the Commonwealt Secretariat).

The Keeper of the Privy Purse, assisted by the Director Finance, Property Services, also oversees Royal Commu nications and Information expenditure, which is met fror the Property Services Grant-in-aid.

The Keeper of the Privy Purse is responsible for th financial aspects of royal travel, which are overseen on day to day basis by the Director of Finance, Royal Trave who is also the Director of Finance, Property Service The costs of official royal travel by aeroplane and train a t from a Grant-in-aid provided by the Department of ansport.

e Keeper of the Privy Purse is an *ex officio* trustee of the yal Collection Trust and is also chairman of its trading bsidiary Royal Collection Enterprises Limited (see yal Collection Department). He is also an *ex officio* stee of the Historic Royal Palaces Trust.

e Queen's Civil List and the Grants-in-aid for property vices and royal travel are provided by the Government return for the surrender by the Sovereign of the net plus from the Crown Estate and other hereditary venues.

## ASTER OF THE HOUSEHOLD'S EPARTMENT

e Master of the Household, assisted by the Deputy aster of the Household (who is also Equerry to the ieen, q.v.), is responsible for the staff and domestic angements at Buckingham Palace, Windsor Castle and Palace of Holyroodhouse and at Balmoral Castle and ndringham House when The Queen is in residence. ese arrangements include:

- The provision of meals for The Queen and other members of the Royal Family, their guests and Royal Household employees.
- Service by liveried staff at meals, receptions and other events.
- Travel arrangements for employees and the movement of baggage between the Royal residences.
- Cleaning and laundry
- Furnishings and the internal decorative appearance of the Occupied Royal Palaces in collaboration with the Director of the Royal Collection.
- Liaison with the Royalty and Diplomatic Protection Department of the Metropolitan Police concerning security procedures at the Occupied Royal Palaces.

ie Master of the Household is responsible for The ieen's official entertaining, both at home and overseas, cluding preparation of guest lists, invitations and seating ins, and overseeing aspects of The Queen's private tertaining.

## ORD CHAMBERLAIN'S OFFICE

ie Comptroller, Lord Chamberlain's Office, assisted by Assistant Comptroller, is responsible for:

- The organisation of all ceremonial engagements, including state visits to The Queen in the United Kingdom, royal weddings and royal funerals, the state opening of Parliament, Guards of Honour at Buckingham Palace, Investitures, and the Garter and Thistle ceremonies.
- Garden Parties at Buckingham Palace and Palace at Holyroodhouse (except for catering and tents).
- The Crown Jewels, which are part of the Royal Collection, when they are in use on state occasions.
- Co-ordination of the arrangements for The Queen to be represented at funerals and memorial services and at the arrival and departure of visiting Heads of State.
- Advising on matters of precedence, style and titles, dress, flying of flags, gun salutes, mourning and other ceremonial questions.
- Supervising the applications from tradesmen for Royal Warrants of Appointment.
- Advising on the commercial use of royal emblems and contemporary royal photographs.
- The Ecclesiastical Household, the Medical Household, the Body Guards and certain ceremonial appointments such as Gentlemen Ushers and Pages of Honour.
- The personal Lords in Waiting, who represent The Queen on various occasions and escort the visiting Head of State during incoming state visits.
- The Queen's Bargemaster and Watermen and The Queen's Swans.

The Comptroller, Lord Chamberlain's Office is also responsible for the Royal Mews, assisted by the Crown Equerry, who has day-to-day responsibility for:

- The provision of carriage processions for the State Opening of Parliament, State Visits, Trooping of the Colour, Royal Ascot, the Garter Ceremony, the Thistle Service, the Presentation of credentials to The Queen by incoming foreign Ambassadors and High Commissioners, and other state and ceremonial occasions.
- The provision of chauffeur-driven cars.
- Co-ordinating the travelling and transport arrangements by road in respect of The Queen's official engagements.
- Supervision and administration of the Royal Mews at Buckingham Palace, Windsor Castle, Hampton Court and the Palace of Holyroodhouse.

The Comptroller, Lord Chamberlain's Office also has overall responsibility for the Marshal of the Diplomatic Corps, who is responsible for the relationship between the Royal Household and the Diplomatic Heads of Mission in London; and the Secretary of the central chancery of the orders of Knighthood, who administers the Orders of Chivalry and their records, makes arrangements for the recipients at Investitures and the distribution of insignia, and ensures the proper public notification of awards through the London Gazette. The Secretary of the Central Chancery is also the Assistant Comptroller.

## ROYAL COLLECTION DEPARTMENT

The Royal Collection, which contains a large number of works of art of all kinds, is held by The Queen as Sovereign in trust for her successors and the nation and is not owned by her as an individual. The administration, conservation and presentation of the Royal Collection are funded by the Royal Collection Trust solely from income from visitors to Windsor Castle, Buckingham Palace and the Palace of Holyroodhouse in Edinburgh. The Royal Collection Trust is chaired by the Prince of Wales. The Lord Chamberlain, the Private Secretary and the Keeper of the Privy Purse are *ex officio* trustees and there are three external trustees appointed by The Queen.

The Director of the Royal Collection is responsible for:

- The administration and custodial control of the Royal Collection in all royal residences.
- The care, display, conservation and restoration of items in the Collection.
- Initiating and assisting research into the Collection and publishing catalogues and books on the Collection.
- Making the Collection accessible to the public by display in places open to the public (including the unoccupied palaces), The Queen's Gallery at Buckingham Palace and the Queen's Gallery at the Palace of Holyroodhouse, by travelling exhibitions organised by museums and galleries in the United Kingdom and abroad.
- Educating and informing the public about the Collection.

The Surveyor of the Queen's Pictures is responsible for pictures and miniatures, the Royal Librarian is responsible for all the books, manuscripts, coins and medals, insignia and works of art on paper including the watercolours, prints and drawings in the Print Room at Windsor Castle, and the Surveyor of the Queen's Works of art is responsible for furniture, ceramics and the other decorative arts in the Collection.

The Director of the Royal Collection has overall responsibility for the trading activities that fund the Royal Collection Department. These are administered by Royal Collection Enterprises Limited, the trading subsidiary of The Royal Collection Trust, which is run by the Managing Director, Royal Collection Enterprises. Th company, whose chairman is the Keeper of the Priv Purse, is responsible for:

- Managing access by the public to Windsor Cast (including Frogmore House), Buckingham Palac (including the Royal Mews and The Queen's Gallery and the Palace of Holyroodhouse.
- Running shops at each location.
- Managing the images and intellectual property righ of the Royal Collection.

The Director of the Royal Collection is also an *ex offic* trustee of the Historic Royal Palaces Trust.

# Royal Salutes

### ENGLAND

A salute of 62 guns is fired on the wharf at the Tower of London on the following occasions:

(a) the anniversaries of the birth, accession and coronation of the Sovereign
(b) the anniversary of the birth of HM Queen Elizabeth the Queen Mother
(c) the anniversary of the birth of HRH Prince Philip, Duke of Edinburgh

A salute of 41 guns only is fired on extraordinary and triumphal occasions, e.g. on the occasion of the Sovereign opening, proroguing or dissolving Parliament in person, or when passing through London in procession, except when otherwise ordered.

A salute of 41 guns is fired from the two saluting stations in London (the Tower of London and Hyde Park) on the occasion of the birth of a royal infant.

*Constable of the Royal Palace and Fortress of London*, Gen. Sir Roger Wheeler, GCB, CBE
*Lieutenant of the Tower of London*, Lt.-Gen. Sir Roderick Cordy-Simpson, KBE, CB
*Resident Governor and Keeper of the Jewel House*, Maj.-Gen. Geoffrey Field, CB, OBE
*Master Gunner of St James's Park*, Gen. Sir Alex Harley KBE, CB
*Master Gunner within the Tower*, Col. James Ferguson, T

### SCOTLAND

Royal salutes are authorised at Edinburgh Castle an Stirling Castle, although in practice Edinburgh Castle i the only operating saluting station in Scotland.

A salute of 21 guns is fired on the following occasions

(a) the anniversaries of the birth, accession and corona tion of the Sovereign
(b) the anniversary of the birth of HM Queen Elizabet the Queen Mother
(c) the anniversary of the birth of HRH Prince Philip Duke of Edinburgh

A salute of 21 guns is fired in Edinburgh on the occasio of the opening of the General Assembly of the Church c Scotland.

A salute of 21 guns may also be fired in Edinburgh on th arrival of HM The Queen, HM Queen Elizabeth th Queen Mother, or a member of the royal family who is Royal Highness on an official visit.

# Royal Finances

## FUNDING

### THE CIVIL LIST

The Civil List dates back to the late 17th century. It was originally used by the sovereign to supplement hereditary revenues for paying the salaries of judges, ambassadors and other government officers as well as the expenses of the royal household. In 1760 on the accession of George III it was decided that the Civil List would be provided by Parliament to cover all relevant expenditure in return for the King surrendering the hereditary revenues of the Crown. At that time Parliament undertook to pay the salaries of judges, ambassadors, etc. In 1831 Parliament agreed also to meet the costs of the royal palaces in return for a reduction in the Civil List. Each sovereign has agreed to continue this arrangement.

The Civil List paid to The Queen is charged on the Consolidated Fund. Until 1972, the amount of money allocated annually under the Civil List was set for th duration of a reign. The system was then altered to a fixe annual payment for ten years but from 1975 high inflatio made an annual review necessary. The system of payment reverted to the practice of a fixed annual payment for te years from 1 January 1991.

The Civil List Acts provide for other members of th royal family to receive parliamentary annuities fror government funds to meet the expenses of carrying ou their official duties. Since 1975 The Queen has reim bursed the Treasury for the annuities paid to the Duke o Gloucester, the Duke of Kent and Princess Alexandra Since 1993 The Queen has reimbursed all the annuitie except those paid to herself, Queen Elizabeth the Quee Mother and the Duke of Edinburgh.

The Prince of Wales does not receive a parliamentar annuity. He derives his income from the revenues of th Duchy of Cornwall and these monies meet the official an private expenses of the Prince of Wales and his family.

The annual payments for the years 1991–2001:

| | |
|---|---|
| The Queen | £7,900,000 |
| Queen Elizabeth the Queen Mother | 643,000 |
| The Duke of Edinburgh | 359,000 |
| The Duke of York | 249,000 |
| †The Earl of Wessex | 141,000 |
| The Princess Royal | 228,000 |
| The Princess Margaret, Countess of Snowdon | 219,000 |
| Princess Alice, Duchess of Gloucester | 87,000 |
| The Duke of Gloucester | 175,000 |
| The Duke of Kent | 236,000 |
| Princess Alexandra | 225,000 |
| | 10,462,000 |
| Refunded to the Treasury | 1,560,000 |
| Total | 8,902,000 |

† The Earl of Wessex's annuity was increased from £96,000 upon his marriage in June 1999

GRANTS-IN-AID

The royal household receives grants-in-aid from two government departments to meet various official expenses. The Department for Culture, Media and Sport provides grant-in-aid to pay for the upkeep of English occupied royal palaces, which are used as offices, for official and ceremonial purposes and to which there is public access, and to meet the cost of media and information services. The Royal Travel grant-in-aid is provided by the Department of the Environment, Transport and the Regions to meet the cost of official royal travel by air and rail, using mainly aircraft from 32 (The Royal) Squadron, chartered commercial aircraft for major overseas state visits and the Royal Train.

Grants-in-aid for 2000–2001 were:

| | |
|---|---|
| Property Services and Communications and Information | £15,000,000 |
| Royal Travel | 5,400,000 |

THE PRIVY PURSE

The funds received by the Privy Purse pay for official expenses incurred by The Queen as head of state and for some of The Queen's private expenditure. The revenues of the Duchy of Lancaster are the principal source of income for the Privy Purse. The revenues of the Duchy were retained by George III in 1760 when the hereditary revenues were surrendered in exchange for the Civil List.

PERSONAL INCOME

The Queen's personal income derives mostly from investments, and is used to meet private expenditure.

DEPARTMENTAL VOTES

Items of expenditure connected with the official duties of the royal family which fall directly on votes of government departments include:

Ministry of Defence – equerries
Foreign and Commonwealth Office – Marshal of the Diplomatic Corps; costs (other than travel costs) associated with overseas visits at the request of government departments
HM Treasury – Central Chancery of the Orders of Knighthood
The Post Office – postal services

## TAXATION

The sovereign is not legally liable to pay income tax, capital gains tax or inheritance tax. After income tax was reintroduced in 1842, some income tax was paid voluntarily by the sovereign but over a long period these payments were phased out. In 1992 The Queen offered to pay tax on a voluntary basis from 6 April 1993, and the Prince of Wales offered to pay tax on a voluntary basis on his income from the Duchy of Cornwall. (He was already taxed in all other respects.)

The main provisions for The Queen and the Prince of Wales to pay tax, set out in a Memorandum of Understanding on Royal Taxation presented to Parliament on 11 February 1993, are that The Queen will pay income tax and capital gains tax in respect of her private income and assets, and on the proportion of the income and capital gains of the Privy Purse used for private purposes. Inheritance tax will be paid on The Queen's assets, except for those which pass to the next sovereign, whether automatically or by gift or bequest. The Prince of Wales will pay income tax on income from the Duchy of Cornwall used for private purposes.

The Prince of Wales has confirmed that he intends to pay tax on the same basis following his accession to the throne.

Other members of the royal family are subject to tax as for any taxpayer.

# Military Ranks and Titles

## THE QUEEN

*Lord High Admiral of the United Kingdom*

*Colonel-in-Chief*

The Life Guards; The Blues and Royals (Royal Horse Guards and 1st Dragoons); The Royal Scots Dragoon Guards (Carabiniers and Greys); The Queen's Royal Lancers; Royal Tank Regiment; Corps of Royal Engineers; Grenadier Guards; Coldstream Guards; Scots Guards; Irish Guards; Welsh Guards; The Royal Welsh Fusiliers; The Queen's Lancashire Regiment; The Argyll and Sutherland Highlanders (Princess Louise's); The Royal Green Jackets; Adjutant General's Corps; The Royal Mercian and Lancastrian Yeomanry; The Governor General's Horse Guards (of Canada); The King's Own Calgary Regiment; Canadian Forces Military Engineers Branch; Royal 22e Regiment (of Canada); Governor-General's Foot Guards (of Canada); The Canadian Grenadier Guards; Le Regiment de la Chaudiere (of Canada); 2nd Bn Royal New Brunswick Regiment (North Shore); The 48th Highlanders of Canada; The Argyll and Sutherland Highlanders of Canada (Princess Louise's); The Calgary Highlanders; Royal Australian Engineers; Royal Australian Infantry Corps; Royal Australian Army Ordnance Corps; Royal Australian Army Nursing Corps; The Corps of Royal New Zealand Engineers; Royal New Zealand Infantry Regiment; Royal Malta Artillery; The Malawi Rifles

*Affiliated Colonel-in-Chief*
The Queen's Gurkha Engineers

*Captain-General*
Royal Regiment of Artillery; The Honourable Artillery Company; Combined Cadet Force Association; Royal Regiment of Canadian Artillery; Royal Regiment of Australian Artillery; Royal Regiment of New Zealand Artillery; Royal New Zealand Armoured Corps

*Patron*
Royal Army Chaplains' Department

*Air Commodore-in-Chief*
Royal Auxiliary Air Force; Royal Air Force Regiment; Air Reserve (of Canada); Royal Australian Air Force Reserve; Territorial Air Force (of New Zealand)

*Commandant-in-Chief*
Royal Air Force College, Cranwell

*Hon. Air Commodore*
RAF Marham

## HRH THE PRINCE PHILIP, DUKE OF EDINBURGH

*Admiral of the Fleet*
*Field Marshal*
*Marshal of the Royal Air Force*

*Admiral of the Fleet, Royal Australian Navy*
*Field Marshal, Australian Military Forces*
*Marshal of the Royal Australian Air Force*

*Admiral of the Fleet, Royal New Zealand Navy*
*Field Marshal, New Zealand Army*
*Marshal of the Royal New Zealand Air Force*
*Captain-General, Royal Marines*

*Admiral*
Royal Canadian Sea Cadets

*Colonel-in-Chief*
The Royal Gloucestershire, Berkshire and Wiltshire Regiment; The Highlanders (Seaforth, Gordons and Camerons); Corps of Royal Electrical and Mechanical Engineers; Intelligence Corps; Army Cadet Force Association; The Royal Canadian Regiment; The Royal Hamilton Light Infantry (Wentworth Regiment) (of Canada); The Cameron Highlanders of Ottawa; The Queen's Own Cameron Highlanders of Canada; The Seaforth Highlanders of Canada; The Royal Canadian Army Cadets; The Royal Corps of Australian Electrical and Mechanical Engineers; The Australian Cadet Corps

*Deputy Colonel-in-Chief*
The Queen's Royal Hussars (Queen's Own and Royal Irish)

*Colonel*
Grenadier Guards

*Hon. Colonel*
City of Edinburgh Universities Officers' Training Corps; The Trinidad and Tobago Regiment

*Air Commodore-in-Chief*
Air Training Corps; Royal Canadian Air Cadets

*Hon. Air Commodore*
RAF Kinloss

## HM QUEEN ELIZABETH THE QUEEN MOTHER

*Colonel-in-Chief*
1st The Queen's Dragoon Guards; The Queen's Roya Hussars (Queen's Own and Royal Irish); 9th/12t Royal Lancers (Prince of Wales's); The King's Regi ment; The Royal Anglian Regiment; The Ligh Infantry; The Black Watch (Royal Highland Regi ment); Royal Army Medical Corps; The Black Watc (Royal Highland Regiment) of Canada; The Toront Scottish Regiment; Canadian Forces Medical Services Royal Australian Army Medical Corps; Royal Nev Zealand Army Medical Corps

*Hon. Colonel*
The Royal Yeomanry; The London Scottish; Inns c Court and City Yeomanry

*Commandant-in-Chief*
Women in the Royal Navy; Women, Royal Air Force Royal Air Force Central Flying School

## HRH THE PRINCE OF WALES

*Rear Admiral*, Royal Navy
*Major-General*, Army
*Air Vice-Marshal*, Royal Air Force

*Colonel-in-Chief*
The Royal Dragoon Guards; The 22nd (Cheshire Regiment; The Royal Regiment of Wales (24th/41s Foot); The Parachute Regiment; The Royal Gurkh Rifles; Army Air Corps; The Royal Canadian Dra goons; Lord Strathcona's Horse (Royal Canadians Royal Regiment of Canada; Royal Winnipeg Rifles; Ai Reserve Group of Air Command (of Canada); Roya Australian Armoured Corps; The Royal Pacific Island Regiment; Queen's Own Yeomanry

*Deputy Colonel-in-Chief*
The Highlanders (Seaforth, Gordons and Camerons)

*Colonel*
Welsh Guards

*Air Commodore-in-Chief*
Royal New Zealand Air Force

*Hon. Air Commodore*
RAF Valley

## HRH THE DUKE OF YORK

*Commander*, Royal Navy

*Admiral*
Sea Cadet Corps

*Colonel-in-Chief*
The Staffordshire Regiment (The Prince of Wales's) The Royal Irish Regiment (27th (Inniskilling), 83rd 87th and The Ulster Defence Regiment); Royal New Zealand Army Logistic Regiment; The Queen's York Rangers (First Americans)

*Hon. Air Commodore*
RAF Lossiemouth

ꝛH THE PRINCESS ROYAL

*ɪr Admiral*
Chief Commandant for Women in the Royal Navy

*lonel-in-Chief*
The King's Royal Hussars; Royal Corps of Signals; The Royal Scots (The Royal Regiment); The Worcestershire and Sherwood Foresters Regiment (29th/45th Foot); The Royal Logistic Corps; 8th Canadian Hussars (Princess Louise's); Canadian Forces Communications and Electronics Branch; The Grey and Simcoe Foresters; The Royal Regina Rifle Regiment; Royal Australian Corps of Signals; Royal New Zealand Corps of Signals; Royal New Zealand Nursing Corps

*lonel*
Blues and Royals

*filiated Colonel-in-Chief*
The Queen's Gurkha Signals; The Queen's Own Gurkha Transport Regiment

*ɪn. Colonel*
University of London Officers' Training Corps

*ɔn. Air Commodore*
RAF Lyneham; University of London Air Squadron

RH THE PRINCESS MARGARET, ƆUNTESS OF SNOWDON

*lonel-in-Chief*
The Light Dragoons; The Royal Highland Fusiliers (Princess Margaret's Own Glasgow and Ayrshire Regiment); Queen Alexandra's Royal Army Nursing Corps; The Royal Highland Fusiliers of Canada; The Princess Louise Fusiliers (of Canada); The Bermuda Regiment

*ɛputy Colonel-in-Chief*
The Royal Anglian Regiment

*ɔn. Air Commodore*
RAF Coningsby

RH PRINCESS ALICE, DUCHESS OF LOUCESTER

*r Chief Marshal*

*lonel-in-Chief*
The King's Own Scottish Borderers; Royal Australian Corps of Transport

*ɛputy Colonel-in-Chief*
The King's Royal Hussars; The Royal Anglian Regiment

*r Chief Commandant*
Women, Royal Air Force

RH THE DUKE OF GLOUCESTER

*ɔn. Air Marshal*

*ɛputy Colonel-in-Chief*
The Royal Gloucestershire, Berkshire and Wiltshire Regiment; The Royal Logistic Corps

*ɔn. Colonel*
Royal Monmouthshire Royal Engineers (Militia)

*Hon. Air Commodore*
RAF Odiham

HRH THE DUCHESS OF GLOUCESTER

*Colonel-in-Chief*
Royal Australian Army Educational Corps; Royal New Zealand Army Educational Corps; Royal Army Dental Corps

*Deputy Colonel-in-Chief*
Adjutant-General's Corps

HRH THE DUKE OF KENT

*Field Marshal*
*Hon. Air Chief Marshal*

*Colonel-in-Chief*
The Royal Regiment of Fusiliers; The Devonshire and Dorset Regiment; The Lorne Scots (Peel, Dufferin and Hamilton Regiment)

*Deputy Colonel-in-Chief*
The Royal Scots Dragoon Guards (Carabiniers and Greys)

*Colonel*
Scots Guards

*Hon. Air Commodore*
RAF Leuchars

HRH THE DUCHESS OF KENT

*Hon. Major-General*

*Colonel-in-Chief*
The Prince of Wales's Own Regiment of Yorkshire

*Deputy Colonel-in-Chief*
The Royal Dragoon Guards; Adjutant-General's Corps; The Royal Logistic Corps

HRH PRINCE MICHAEL OF KENT

*Major (retd)*, The Royal Hussars (Prince of Wales's Own)

*Hon. Commodore*
*Royal Naval Reserve*

HRH PRINCESS ALEXANDRA, THE HON. LADY OGILVY

*Patron*
Queen Alexandra's Royal Naval Nursing Service

*Colonel-in-Chief*
The King's Own Royal Border Regiment; The Queen's Own Rifles of Canada; The Canadian Scottish Regiment (Princess Mary's)

*Deputy Colonel-in-Chief*
The Queen's Royal Lancers; The Light Infantry

*Deputy Hon. Colonel*
The Royal Yeomanry

*Patron and Air Chief Commandant*
Princess Mary's Royal Air Force Nursing Service

# The House of Windsor

King George V assumed by royal proclamation (17 July 1917) for his House and family, as well as for all descendants in the male line of Queen Victoria who are subjects of these realms, the name of Windsor.

KING GEORGE V (George Frederick Ernest Albert), second son of King Edward VII, *born* 3 June 1865; *married* 6 July 1893 HSH Princess Victoria Mary Augusta Louise Olga Pauline Claudine Agnes of Teck (Queen Mary, *born* 26 May 1867; *died* 24 March 1953); *succeeded* to the throne 6 May 1910; *died* 20 January 1936. *Issue:*

1. HRH Prince Edward Albert Christian George Andrew Patrick David, *born* 23 June 1894, *succeeded* to the throne as King Edward VIII, 20 January 1936; *abdicated* 11 December 1936; created *Duke of Windsor* 1937; *married* 3 June 1937, Mrs Wallis Simpson (Her Grace The Duchess of Windsor, *born* 19 June 1896; *died* 24 April 1986), *died* 28 May 1972

2. HRH Prince Albert Frederick Arthur George, *born* 14 December 1895, *created* Duke of York 1920; *married* 26 April 1923, Lady Elizabeth Bowes-Lyon, youngest daughter of the 14th Earl of Strathmore and Kinghorne (HM Queen Elizabeth the Queen Mother, *see* page 117), *succeeded* to the throne as King George VI, 11 December 1936; *died* 6 February 1952, having had issue (*see* page 117)

3. HRH Princess (Victoria Alexandra Alice) Mary, *born* 25 April 1897, *created* Princess Royal 1932; *married* 28 February 1922, Viscount Lascelles, later the 6th Earl of Harewood (1882–1947), *died* 28 March 1965. *Issue:*
(1) George Henry Hubert Lascelles, 7th Earl of Harewood, KBE, *born* 7 February 1923; *married* (1) 1949, Maria (Marion) Stein (marriage dissolved 1967); *issue*, (*a*) David Henry George, Viscount Lascelles, *born* 1950; (*b*) James Edward, *born* 1953; (*c*) (Robert) Jeremy Hugh, *born* 1955; (2) 1967, Mrs Patri Tuckwell; *issue*, (*d*) Mark Hubert, *born* 1964
(2) Gerald David Lascelles (1924-98), *married* (1) 1952, M Angela Dowding (marriage dissolved 1978); *issue*, (*a*) He Ulick, *born* 1953; (2) 1978, Mrs Elizabeth Colvin; *issue*, (*b*) Mar David, *born* 1962

4. HRH Prince Henry William Frederick Albert, *born* 31 Ma 1900, *created* Duke of Gloucester, Earl of Ulster and Ba Culloden 1928, *married* 6 November 1935, Lady Alice Christa Montagu-Douglas-Scott, daughter of the 7th Duke of Buccle (HRH Princess Alice, Duchess of Gloucester, *see* page 118); *died* June 1974. *Issue:*
(1) HRH Prince William Henry Andrew Frederick, *born* December 1941; *accidentally killed* 28 August 1972
(2) HRH Prince Richard Alexander Walter George (HRH T Duke of Gloucester), *see* page 118

5. HRH Prince George Edward Alexander Edmund, *born* December 1902, *created* Duke of Kent, Earl of St Andrews a Baron Downpatrick 1934, *married* 29 November 1934, HR Princess Marina of Greece and Denmark (*born* 30 November 1906; *died* 27 August 1968); *killed on active service*, 25 August 19 *Issue:*
(1) HRH Prince Edward George Nicholas Paul Patrick (HR The Duke of Kent), *see* page 118
(2) HRH Princess Alexandra Helen Elizabeth Olga Christa (HRH Princess Alexandra, the Hon. Lady Ogilvy), *see* page 1
(3) HRH Prince Michael George Charles Franklin (HRH Prir Michael of Kent), *see* page 118

6. HRH Prince John Charles Francis, *born* 12 July 19C *died* 18 January 1919

---

# Descendants of Queen Victoria

QUEEN VICTORIA (Alexandrina Victoria), *born* 24 May 1819; *succeeded* to the throne 20 June 1837; *married* 10 February 1840 (Francis) Albert Augustus Charles Emmanuel, Duke of Saxony, Prince of Saxe-Coburg and Gotha (HRH Albert, Prince Consort, *born* 26 August 1819, *died* 14 December 1861); *died* 22 January 1901. *Issue:*

1. HRH Princess Victoria Adelaide Mary Louisa (Princess Royal) (1840–1901), *m.* 1858, Friedrich III (1831–88), German Emperor March–June 1888. *Issue:*
(1) HIM Wilhelm II (1859–1941), German Emperor 1888–1918, *m.* (1) 1881 Princess Augusta Victoria of Schleswig-Holstein-Sonderburg-Augustenburg (1858–1921); (2) 1922 Princess Hermine of Reuss (1887–1947). *Issue:*
(*a*) Prince Wilhelm (1882–1951), *Crown Prince* 1888–1918, *m.* 1905 Duchess Cecilie of Mecklenburg-Schwerin; *issue:* Prince Wilhelm (1906–40); Prince Louis Ferdinand (1907–94), *m.* 1938 Grand Duchess Kira (*see* page 128); Prince Hubertus (1909–50); Prince Friedrich Georg (1911–66); Princess Alexandrine Irene (1915–80); Princess Cecilie (1917–75)
(*b*) Prince Eitel-Friedrich (1883–1942), *m.* 1906 Duchess Sophie of Oldenburg (marriage dissolved 1926)
(*c*) Prince Adalbert (1884–1948), *m.* 1914 Duchess Adelheid of Saxe-Meiningen; *issue:* Princess Victoria Marina (1917–81); Prince Wilhelm Victor (1919–89)
(*d*) Prince August Wilhelm (1887–1949), *m.* 1908 Princess Alexandra of Schleswig-Holstein-Sonderburg-Glücksburg (marriage dissolved 1920); *issue:* Prince Alexander (1912–85)
(*e*) Prince Oskar (1888–1958), *m.* 1914 Countess von Ruppin; *issue:* Prince Oskar (1915–39); Prince Burchard (1917–88); Princess Herzeleide (1918–89); Prince Wilhelm-Karl (*b.* 1922)
(*f*) Prince Joachim (1890–1920), *m.* 1916 Princess Marie of Anhalt; *issue:* Prince (Karl) Franz Joseph (1916–75), and has issue
(*g*) Princess Viktoria Luise (1892–1980), *m.* 1913 Ernst, Du of Brunswick 1913–18 (1887–1953); *issue:* Prince Ernst (191 87); Prince Georg (*b.* 1915), *m.* 1946 Princess Sophie of Gree (*see* page 128) and has issue (two sons, one daughter); Prince Frederika (1917–81), *m.* 1938 Paul I, King of the Hellenes ( page 128); Prince Christian (1919–81); Prince Welf Heinri (*b.* 1923)
(2) Princess Charlotte (1860–1919), *m.* 1878 Bernhard, Duke Saxe-Meiningen 1914 (1851–1914). *Issue:*
Princess Feodora (1879–1945), *m.* 1898 Prince Heinrich XXX Reuss
(3) Prince Heinrich (1862–1929), *m.* 1888 Princess Irene of Hes (*see* page 128). *Issue:*
(*a*) Prince Waldemar (1889–1945), *m.* Princess Calixta Agnes Lippe
(*b*) Prince Sigismund (1896–1978), *m.*1919 Princess Charlo of Saxe-Altenburg; *issue:* Princess Barbara (1920–94); Prin Alfred (*b.* 1924)
(*c*) Prince Heinrich (1900–4)
(4) Prince Sigismund (1864–6)
(5) Princess Victoria (1866–1929), *m.* (1) 1890, Prince Adolf Schaumburg-Lippe (1859–1916); (2) 1927 Alexander Zubkov
(6) Prince Waldemar (1868–79)
(7) Princess Sophie (1870–1932), *m.* 1889 Constantine I (186 1923), King of the Hellenes 1913–17, 1920–3. *Issue:*
(*a*) George II (1890–1947), King of the Hellenes 1923–4 a 1935–47, *m.* 1921 Princess Elisabeth of Roumania (marria dissolved 1935) (*see* page 127)
(*b*) Alexander I (1893–1920), King of the Hellenes 1917–20, 1919 Aspasia Manos; *issue:* Princess Alexandra (1921–93), 1944 King Petar II of Yugoslavia (*see* below)
(*c*) Princess Helena (1896–1982), *m.* 1921 King Carol Roumania (*see* below), (marriage dissolved 1928)

(*d*) Paul I (1901–64), King of the Hellenes 1947–64, *m.* 1938 Princess Frederika of Brunswick (*see* page 126); *issue:* King Constantine II (*b.* 1940), *m.* 1964 Princess Anne-Marie of Denmark (*see* page 128), and has issue (three sons, two daughters); Princess Sophie (*b.* 1938), *m.* 1962 Juan Carlos I of Spain (*see* page 128); Princess Irene (*b.* 1942)
(*e*) Princess Irene (1904–74), *m.* 1939 4th Duke of Aosta; *issue:* Prince Amedeo, 5th Duke of Aosta (*b.* 1943)
(*f*) Princess Katherine (Lady Katherine Brandram) (*b.* 1913), *m.* 1947 Major R. C. A. Brandram, MC, TD; *issue:* R. Paul G. A. Brandram (*b.* 1948)
(8) Princess Margarethe (1872–1954), *m.* 1893 Prince Friedrich Karl of Hesse (1868–1940). *Issue:*
(*a*) Prince Friedrich Wilhelm (1893–1916)
(*b*) Prince Maximilian (1894–1914)
(*c*) Prince Philipp (1896–1980), *m.* 1925 Princess Mafalda of Italy; *issue:* Prince Moritz (*b.* 1926); Prince Heinrich (1927-2000); Prince Otto (*b.* 1937); Princess Elisabeth (*b.* 1940)
(*d*) Prince Wolfgang (1896–1989), *m.* (1) 1924 Princess Marie Alexandra of Baden; (2) 1948 Ottilie Möller
(*e*) Prince Richard (1901–69)
(*f*) Prince Christoph (1901–43), *m.* 1930 Princess Sophie of Greece (*see* below) and has issue (two sons, three daughters)

HRH Prince Albert Edward (HM King Edward VII), *b.* 9 ovember 1841, *m.* 1863 HRH Princess Alexandra of Denmark 344–1925), *succeeded* to the throne 22 January 1901, *d.* 6 May 1910. *ue:*
(1) Albert Victor, Duke of Clarence and Avondale (1864–92)
(2) George (HM King George V) (*see* page 126)
(3) Louise (1867–1931) Princess Royal 1905–31, *m.* 1889 1st Duke of Fife (1849–1912). *Issue:*
(*a*) Princess Alexandra, Duchess of Fife (1891–1959), *m.* 1913 Prince Arthur of Connaught (*see* page 128)
(*b*) Princess Maud (1893–1945), *m.* 1923 11th Earl of Southesk (1893–1992); *issue:* The Duke of Fife (*b.* 1929)
(4) Victoria (1868–1935)
(5) Maud (1869–1938), *m.* 1896 Prince Carl of Denmark (1872–1957), later King Haakon VII of Norway 1905–57. *Issue:*
(*a*) Olav V (1903–91), King of Norway 1957–91, *m.* 1929 Princess Märtha of Sweden (1901–54); *issue:* Princess Ragnhild (*b.* 1930); Princess Astrid (*b.* 1932); Harald V, King of Norway (*b.* 1937)
(6) Alexander (6–7 April 1871)

HRH Princess Alice Maud Mary (1843–78), *m.* 1862 Prince ıdwig (1837–92), Grand Duke of Hesse 1877–92. *Issue:*
(1) Victoria (1863–1950), *m.* 1884 *Admiral of the Fleet* Prince Louis of Battenberg (1854–1921), *cr.* 1st Marquess of Milford Haven 1917. *Issue:*
(*a*) Alice (1885–1969), *m.* 1903 Prince Andrew of Greece (1882–1944); *issue:* Princess Margarita (1905–81), *m.* 1931 Prince Gottfried of Hohenlohe-Langenburg (*see* below); Princess Theodora (1906–69), *m.* Prince Berthold of Baden (1906–63) and has issue (two sons, one daughter); Princess Cecilie (1911–37), *m.* George, Grand Duke of Hesse (*see* below); Princess Sophie (*b.* 1914), *m.* (1) 1930 Prince Christoph of Hesse (*see* above); (2) 1946 Prince Georg of Hanover (*see* page 127); Prince Philip, Duke of Edinburgh (*b.* 1921) (*see* page 117)
(*b*) Louise (1889–1965), *m.* 1923 Gustaf VI Adolf (1882–1973), King of Sweden 1950–73
(*c*) George, 2nd Marquess of Milford Haven (1892–1938), *m.* 1916 Countess Nadejda, daughter of Grand Duke Michael of Russia; *issue:* Lady Tatiana (1917–88); David Michael, 3rd Marquess (1919–70)
(*d*) Louis, 1st Earl Mountbatten of Burma (1900–79), *m.* 1922 Edwina Ashley, daughter of Lord Mount Temple; *issue:* Patricia, Countess Mountbatten of Burma (*b.* 1924), Pamela (*b.* 1929)
(2) Elizabeth (1864–1918), *m.* 1884 Grand Duke Sergius of Russia (1857–1905)
(3) Irene (1866–1953), *m.* 1888 Prince Heinrich of Prussia (*see* page 126)
(4) Ernst Ludwig (1868–1937), Grand Duke of Hesse 1892–1918, *m.* (1) 1894 Princess Victoria Melita of Saxe-Coburg (*see* below) (marriage dissolved 1901); (2) 1905 Princess Eleonore of Solms-Hohensolmslich. *Issue:*
(*a*) Princess Elizabeth (1895–1903)
(*b*) George, Hereditary Grand Duke of Hesse (1906–37), *m.* Princess Cecilie of Greece (*see* above), and had issue, two sons, accidentally killed with parents 1937
(*c*) Ludwig, Prince of Hesse (1908–68), *m.* 1937 Margaret, daughter of 1st Lord Geddes
(5) Frederick William (1870–3)
(6) Alix (Tsaritsa of Russia) (1872–1918), *m.* 1894 Nicholas II (1868–1918) Tsar of All the Russias 1894–1917, assassinated 16 July 1918. *Issue:*
(*a*) Grand Duchess Olga (1895–1918)
(*b*) Grand Duchess Tatiana (1897–1918)
(*c*) Grand Duchess Marie (1899–1918)
(*d*) Grand Duchess Anastasia (1901–18)
(*e*) Alexis, Tsarevich of Russia (1904–18)
(7) Marie (1874–8)

4. HRH Prince Alfred Ernest Albert, Duke of Edinburgh, *Admiral of the Fleet* (1844–1900), *m.* 1874 Grand Duchess Marie Alexandrovna of Russia (1853–1920); succeeded as Duke of Saxe-Coburg and Gotha 22 August 1893. *Issue:*
(1) Alfred, Prince of Saxe-Coburg (1874–99)
(2) Marie (1875–1938), *m.* 1893 Ferdinand (1865–1927), King of Roumania 1914–27. *Issue:*
(*a*) Carol II (1893–1953), King of Roumania 1930–40, *m.* (2) 1921 Princess Helena of Greece (*see* above) (marriage dissolved 1928); *issue:* Michael (*b.* 1921), King of Roumania 1927–30, 1940–7, *m.* 1948 Princess Anne of Bourbon-Parma, and has issue (five daughters)
(*b*) Elisabeth (1894–1956), *m.* 1921 George II, King of the Hellenes (*see* page 126)
(*c*) Marie (1900–61), *m.* 1922 Alexander (1888–1934), King of Yugoslavia 1921–34; *issue:* Petar II (1923–70), King of Yugoslavia 1934–45, *m.* 1944 Princess Alexandra of Greece (*see* above) and has issue (Crown Prince Alexander, *b.* 1945); Prince Tomislav (*b.* 1928), *m.* (1) 1957 Princess Margarita of Baden (daughter of Princess Theodora of Greece and Prince Berthold of Baden, *see* above); (2) 1982 Linda Bonney; and has issue (three sons, one daughter); Prince Andrej (1929–90), *m.* (1) 1956 Princess Christina of Hesse (daughter of Prince Christoph of Hesse and Princess Sophie of Greece, *see* above); (2) 1963 Princess Kira-Melita of Leiningen (*see* below); and has issue (three sons, two daughters)
(*d*) Prince Nicolas (1903–78)
(*e*) Princess Ileana (1909–91), *m.* (1) 1931 Archduke Anton of Austria; (2) 1954 Dr Stefan Issarescu; *issue:* Archduke Stefan (*b.* 1932); Archduchess Maria Ileana (1933–59); Archduchess Alexandra (*b.* 1935); Archduke Dominic (*b.* 1937); Archduchess Maria Magdalena (*b.* 1939); Archduchess Elisabeth (*b.* 1942)
(*f*) Prince Mircea (1913–16)
(3) Victoria Melita (1876–1936), *m.* (1) 1894 Grand Duke Ernst Ludwig of Hesse (*see* above) (marriage dissolved 1901); (2) 1905 the Grand Duke Kirill of Russia (1876–1938). *Issue:*
(*a*) Marie Kirillovna (1907–51), *m.* 1925 Prince Friedrich Karl of Leiningen; *issue:* Prince Emich (1926–91); Prince Karl (1928–90); Princess Kira-Melita (*b.* 1930), *m.* Prince Andrej of Yugoslavia (*see* above); Princess Margarita (*b.* 1932); Princess Mechtilde (*b.* 1936); Prince Friedrich (*b.* 1938)
(*b*) Kira Kirillovna (1909–67), *m.* 1938 Prince Louis Ferdinand of Prussia (*see* page 127); *issue:* Prince Friedrich Wilhelm (*b.* 1939); Prince Michael (*b.* 1940); Princess Marie (*b.* 1942); Princess Kira (*b.* 1943); Prince Louis Ferdinand (1944–77); Prince Christian (*b.* 1946); Princess Xenia (1949–92)
(*c*) Vladimir Kirillovich (1917–92), *m.* 1948 Princess Leonida Bagration-Mukhransky; *issue:* Grand Duchess Maria (*b.* 1953), and has issue
(4) Alexandra (1878–1942), *m.* 1896 Ernst, Prince of Hohenlohe Langenburg. *Issue:*
(*a*) Gottfried (1897–1960), *m.* 1931 Princess Margarita of Greece (*see* above); *issue:* Prince Kraft (*b.* 1935), Princess Beatrice (1936–97), Prince Georg Andreas (*b.* 1938), Prince Ruprecht (1944–76); Prince Albrecht (1944–92)
(*b*) Maria (1899–1967), *m.* 1916 Prince Friedrich of Schleswig-Holstein-Sonderburg-Glücksburg; *issue:* Prince Peter (1922–80); Princess Marie (*b.* 1927)
(*c*) Princess Alexandra (1901–63)
(*d*) Princess Irma (1902–86)

(5) Princess Beatrice (1884–1966), *m.* 1909 Alfonso of Orleans, Infante of Spain. *Issue:*

(*a*) Prince Alvaro (*b.* 1910), *m.* 1937 Carla Parodi-Delfino; *issue:* Doña Gerarda (*b.* 1939); Don Alonso (1941–75); Doña Beatriz (*b.* 1943); Don Alvaro (*b.* 1947)

(*b*) Prince Alonso (1912–36)

(*c*) Prince Ataulfo (1913–74)

5. HRH PRINCESS HELENA Augusta Victoria (1846–1923), *m.* 1866 Prince Christian of Schleswig-Holstein-Sonderburg-Augustenburg (1831–1917). *Issue:*

(1) Prince Christian Victor (1867–1900)

(2) Prince Albert (1869–1931), Duke of Schleswig-Holstein 1921–31

(3) Princess Helena (1870–1948)

(4) Princess Marie Louise (1872–1956), *m.* 1891 Prince Aribert of Anhalt (marriage dissolved 1900)

(5) Prince Harold (12–20 May 1876)

6. HRH PRINCESS LOUISE Caroline Alberta (1848–1939), *m.* 1871 the Marquess of Lorne, afterwards 9th Duke of Argyll (1845–1914); without issue

7. HRH PRINCE ARTHUR William Patrick Albert, Duke of Connaught, *Field Marshal* (1850–1942), *m.* 1879 Princess Louisa of Prussia (1860–1917). *Issue:*

(1) Margaret (1882–1920), *m.* 1905 Crown Prince Gustaf Adolf (1882–1973), afterwards King of Sweden 1950–73. *Issue:*

(*a*) Gustaf Adolf, Duke of Västerbotten (1906–47), *m.* 1932 Princess Sibylla of Saxe-Coburg-Gotha (*see* below); *issue:* Princess Margaretha (*b.* 1934); Princess Birgitta (*b.* 1937); Princess Désirée (*b.* 1938); Princess Christina (*b.* 1943); Carl XVI Gustaf, King of Sweden (*b.* 1946)

(*b*) Count Sigvard Bernadotte (*b.* 1907), *m.*; *issue:* Count Michael (*b.* 1944)

(*c*) Princess Ingrid (Queen Mother of Denmark) (1910–2000), *m.* 1935 Frederick IX (1899–1972), King of Denmark 1947–72; *issue:* Margrethe II, Queen of Denmark (*b.* 1940); Princess Benedikte (*b.* 1944); Princess Anne-Marie (*b.* 1946), *m.* 1964 Constantine II of Greece (*see* page 127)

(*d*) Prince Bertil, Duke of Halland (1912–97), *m.* 1976 Mrs Lilian Craig

(*e*) Count Carl Bernadotte (*b.* 1916), *m.* (1) 1946 Mrs Kerstin Johnson; (2) 1988 Countess Gunnila Bussler

(2) Arthur (1883–1938), *m.* 1913 HH the Duchess of Fife (*see* page 127). *Issue:*

Alastair Arthur, 2nd Duke of Connaught (1914–43)

(3) (Victoria) Patricia (1886–1974), *m.* 1919 Adm. Hon. S Alexander Ramsay. *Issue:*

Alexander Ramsay of Mar (*b.* 1919), *m.* 1956 Hon. Flora Fras (Lady Saltoun)

8. HRH PRINCE LEOPOLD George Duncan Albert, Duke of Albar (1853–84), *m.* 1882 Princess Helena of Waldeck (1861–1922). *Issu*

(1) Alice (1883–1981), *m.* 1904 Prince Alexander of Teck (1874 1957), *cr.* 1st Earl of Athlone 1917. *Issue:*

(*a*) Lady May (1906–94), *m.* 1931 Sir Henry Abel-Smith, KCMC KCVO, DSO; *issue:* Anne (*b.* 1932); Richard (*b.* 1933); Elizabeth (*b.* 1936)

(*b*) Rupert, Viscount Trematon (1907–28)

(*c*) Prince Maurice (March–September 1910)

(2) Charles Edward (1884–1954), Duke of Albany 1884 unt title suspended 1917, Duke of Saxe-Coburg-Gotha 1900–18 *m.* 1905 Princess Victoria Adelheid of Schleswig-Holstein Sonderburg-Glücksburg. *Issue:*

(*a*) Prince Johann Leopold (1906–72), and has issue

(*b*) Princess Sibylla (1908–72), *m.* 1932 Prince Gustav Adolf o Sweden (*see* above)

(*c*) Prince Dietmar Hubertus (1909–43)

(*d*) Princess Caroline (1912–83), and has issue

(*e*) Prince Friedrich Josias (*b.* 1918), and has issue

9. HRH PRINCESS BEATRICE Mary Victoria Feodore (1857–1944) *m.* 1885 Prince Henry of Battenberg (1858–96). *Issue:*

(1) Alexander, 1st Marquess of Carisbrooke (1886–1960), *m.* 1917 Lady Irene Denison. *Issue:*

Lady Iris Mountbatten (1920–82), *m.*; *issue:* Robin A. Bryan (*b.* 1957)

(2) Victoria Eugénie (1887–1969), *m.* 1906 Alfonso XIII (1886–1941) King of Spain 1886–1931. *Issue:*

(*a*) Prince Alfonso (1907–38)

(*b*) Prince Jaime (1908–75), and has issue

(*c*) Princess Beatrice (*b.* 1909), and has issue

(*d*) Princess Maria (1911–96), and has issue

(*e*) Prince Juan (1913–93), Count of Barcelona; *issue:* Princess Maria (*b.* 1936); Juan Carlos I, King of Spain (*b.* 1938), *m.* 1962 Princess Sophie of Greece (*see* page 127) and has issue (one son, two daughters); Princess Margarita (*b.* 1939)

(*f*) Prince Gonzalo (1914–34)

(3) Major Lord Leopold Mountbatten (1889–1922)

(4) Maurice (1891–1914), died of wounds received in action

# Kings and Queens

## ENGLISH KINGS AND QUEENS 927 TO 1603

### HOUSES OF CERDIC AND DENMARK

*Reign*

927–939 ÆTHELSTAN
Son of Edward the Elder, by Ecgwynn, and grandson of Alfred
Acceded to Wessex and Mercia *c.*924, established direct rule over Northumbria 927, effectively creating the Kingdom of England
*Reigned* 15 years

939–946 EDMUND I
*Born* 921, son of Edward the Elder, by Eadgifu
*Married* (1) Ælfgifu (2) Æthelflæd
*Killed* aged 25, *reigned* 6 years

946–955 EADRED
Son of Edward the Elder, by Eadgifu
*Reigned* 9 years

955–959 EADWIG
*Born* before 943, son of Edmund and Ælfgifu
*Married* Ælfgifu
*Reigned* 3 years

959–975 EDGAR I
*Born* 943, son of Edmund and Ælfgifu
*Married* (1) Æthelflæd (2) Wulfthryth (3) Ælfthryth
*Died* aged 32, *reigned* 15 years

975–978 EDWARD I (the Martyr)
*Born c.*962, son of Edgar and Æthelflæd
*Assassinated* aged *c.*16, *reigned* 2 years

978–1016 ÆTHELRED (the Unready)
*Born c.*968/969, son of Edgar and Ælfthryth
*Married* (1) Ælfgifu (2) Emma, daughter of Richard I, count of Normandy
1013–14 dispossessed of kingdom by Swegn Forkbeard (king of Denmark 987–1014)
*Died* aged *c.*47, *reigned* 38 years

1016 EDMUND II (Ironside)
*Born* before 993, son of Æthelred and Ælfgifu
*Married* Ealdgyth
*Died* aged over 23, *reigned* 7 months (April–November)

1016–1035 CNUT (Canute)
*Born c.*995, son of Swegn Forkbeard, king of Denmark, and Gunhild
*Married* (1) Ælfgifu (2) Emma, widow of Æthelred the Unready

Gained submission of West Saxons 1015, Northumbrians 1016, Mercia 1016, king of all England after Edmund's death
King of Denmark 1019–35, king of Norway 1028–35
*Died* aged *c*.40, *reigned* 19 years

035–1040 HAROLD I (Harefoot)
*Born c*.1016/17, son of Cnut and Ælfgifu
*Married* Ælfgifu
1035 recognized as regent for himself and his brother Harthacnut; 1037 recognized as king
*Died* aged *c*.23, *reigned* 4 years

040–1042 HARTHACNUT
*Born c*.1018, son of Cnut and Emma
Titular king of Denmark from 1028
Acknowledged king of England 1035–7 with Harold I as regent; effective king after Harold's death
*Died* aged *c*.24, *reigned* 2 years

042–1066 EDWARD II (the Confessor)
*Born* between 1002 and 1005, son of Æthelred the Unready and Emma
*Married* Eadgyth, daughter of Godwine, earl of Wessex
*Died* aged over 60, *reigned* 23 years

066 HAROLD II (Godwinesson)
*Born c*.1020, son of Godwine, earl of Wessex, and Gytha
*Married* (1) Eadgyth (2) Ealdgyth
*Killed* in battle aged *c*.46, *reigned* 10 months (January–October)

## 'HE HOUSE OF NORMANDY

066–1087 WILLIAM I (the Conqueror)
*Born* 1027/8, son of Robert I, duke of Normandy; obtained the Crown by conquest
*Married* Matilda, daughter of Baldwin, count of Flanders
*Died* aged *c*.60, *reigned* 20 years

087–1100 WILLIAM II (Rufus)
*Born* between 1056 and 1060, third son of William I; succeeded his father in England only
*Killed* aged *c*.40, *reigned* 12 years

100–1135 HENRY I (Beauclerk)
*Born* 1068, fourth son of William I
*Married* (1) Edith or Matilda, daughter of Malcolm III of Scotland (2) Adela, daughter of Godfrey, count of Louvain
*Died* aged 67, *reigned* 35 years

135–1154 STEPHEN
*Born* not later than 1100, third son of Adela, daughter of William I, and Stephen, count of Blois
*Married* Matilda, daughter of Eustace, count of Boulogne
1141 (February–November) held captive by adherents of Matilda, daughter of Henry I, who contested the crown until 1153
*Died* aged over 53, *reigned* 18 years

## THE HOUSE OF ANJOU (PLANTAGENETS)

154–1189 HENRY II (Curtmantle)
*Born* 1133, son of Matilda, daughter of Henry I, and Geoffrey, count of Anjou
*Married* Eleanor, daughter of William, duke of Aquitaine, and divorced queen of Louis VII of France
*Died* aged 56, *reigned* 34 years

189–1199 RICHARD I (Coeur de Lion)
*Born* 1157, third son of Henry II
*Married* Berengaria, daughter of Sancho VI, king of Navarre
*Died* aged 42, *reigned* 9 years

199–1216 JOHN (Lackland)
*Born* 1167, fifth son of Henry II
*Married* (1) Isabella or Avisa, daughter of William, earl of Gloucester (divorced) (2) Isabella, daughter of Aymer, count of Angoulême
*Died* aged 48, *reigned* 17 years

1216–1272 HENRY III
*Born* 1207, son of John and Isabella of Angoulême
*Married* Eleanor, daughter of Raymond, count of Provence
*Died* aged 65, *reigned* 56 years

1272–1307 EDWARD I (Longshanks)
*Born* 1239, eldest son of Henry III
*Married* (1) Eleanor, daughter of Ferdinand III, king of Castile (2) Margaret, daughter of Philip III of France
*Died* aged 68, *reigned* 34 years

1307–1327 EDWARD II
*Born* 1284, eldest surviving son of Edward I and Eleanor
*Married* Isabella, daughter of Philip IV of France
*Deposed* January 1327, *killed* September 1327 aged 43, *reigned* 19 years

1327–1377 EDWARD III
*Born* 1312, eldest son of Edward II
*Married* Philippa, daughter of William, count of Hainault
*Died* aged 64, *reigned* 50 years

1377–1399 RICHARD II
*Born* 1367, son of Edward (the Black Prince), eldest son of Edward III
*Married* (1) Anne, daughter of Emperor Charles IV (2) Isabelle, daughter of Charles VI of France
*Deposed* September 1399, *killed* February 1400 aged 33, *reigned* 22 years

## THE HOUSE OF LANCASTER

1399–1413 HENRY IV
*Born* 1366, son of John of Gaunt, fourth son of Edward III, and Blanche, daughter of Henry, duke of Lancaster
*Married* (1) Mary, daughter of Humphrey, earl of Hereford (2) Joan, daughter of Charles, king of Navarre, and widow of John, duke of Brittany
*Died* aged *c.* 47, *reigned* 13 years

1413–1422 HENRY V
*Born* 1387, eldest surviving son of Henry IV and Mary
*Married* Catherine, daughter of Charles VI of France
*Died* aged 34, *reigned* 9 years

1422–1471 HENRY VI
*Born* 1421, son of Henry V
*Married* Margaret, daughter of René, duke of Anjou and count of Provence
*Deposed* March 1461, *restored* October 1470
*Deposed* April 1471, *killed* May 1471 aged 49, *reigned* 39 years

## THE HOUSE OF YORK

1461–1483 EDWARD IV
*Born* 1442, eldest son of Richard of York (grandson of Edmund, fifth son of Edward III, and son of Anne, great-granddaughter of Lionel, third son of Edward III)
*Married* Elizabeth Woodville, daughter of Richard, Lord Rivers, and widow of Sir John Grey
*Acceded* March 1461, *deposed* October 1470, *restored* April 1471
*Died* aged 40, *reigned* 21 years

1483 EDWARD V
*Born* 1470, eldest son of Edward IV
*Deposed* June 1483, *died* probably July–September 1483, aged 12, *reigned* 2 months (April–June)

1483–1485 RICHARD III
*Born* 1452, fourth son of Richard of York
*Married* Anne Neville, daughter of Richard, earl of Warwick, and widow of Edward, Prince of Wales, son of Henry VI
*Killed* in battle aged 32, *reigned* 2 years

## THE HOUSE OF TUDOR

1485–1509 HENRY VII
*Born* 1457, son of Margaret Beaufort (great-granddaughter of John of Gaunt, fourth son of

| | |
|---|---|
| | Edward III) and Edmund Tudor, earl of Richmond<br>*Married* Elizabeth, daughter of Edward IV<br>*Died* aged 52, *reigned* 23 years |
| 1509–1547 | HENRY VIII<br>*Born* 1491, second son of Henry VII<br>*Married* (1) Catherine, daughter of Ferdinand II, king of Aragon, and widow of his elder brother Arthur (divorced) (2) Anne, daughter of Sir Thomas Boleyn (executed) (3) Jane, daughter of Sir John Seymour (died in childbirth) (4) Anne, daughter of John, duke of Cleves (divorced) (5) Catherine Howard, niece of the Duke of Norfolk (executed) (6) Catherine, daughter of Sir Thomas Parr and widow of Lord Latimer<br>*Died* aged 55, *reigned* 37 years |
| 1547–1553 | EDWARD VI<br>*Born* 1537, son of Henry VIII and Jane Seymour<br>*Died* aged 15, *reigned* 6 years |
| 1553 | JANE<br>*Born* 1537, daughter of Frances (daughter of Mary Tudor, the younger daughter of Henry VII) and Henry Grey, duke of Suffolk<br>*Married* Lord Guildford Dudley, son of the Duke of Northumberland<br>*Deposed* July 1553, *executed* February 1554 aged 16, *reigned* 14 days |
| 1553–1558 | MARY I<br>*Born* 1516, daughter of Henry VIII and Catherine of Aragon<br>*Married* Philip II of Spain<br>*Died* aged 42, *reigned* 5 years |
| 1558–1603 | ELIZABETH I<br>*Born* 1533, daughter of Henry VIII and Anne Boleyn<br>*Died* aged 69, *reigned* 44 years |

## BRITISH KINGS AND QUEENS SINCE 1603

### THE HOUSE OF STUART

| *Reign* | |
|---|---|
| 1603–1625 | JAMES I (VI OF SCOTLAND)<br>*Born* 1566, son of Mary, queen of Scots (granddaughter of Margaret Tudor, elder daughter of Henry VII), and Henry Stewart, Lord Darnley<br>*Married* Anne, daughter of Frederick II of Denmark<br>*Died* aged 58, *reigned* 22 years<br>(*see also* page 133) |
| 1625–1649 | CHARLES I<br>*Born* 1600, second son of James I<br>*Married* Henrietta Maria, daughter of Henry IV of France<br>*Executed* 1649 aged 48, *reigned* 23 years<br>COMMONWEALTH DECLARED 19 May 1649<br>1649–53 Government by a council of state<br>1653–8 Oliver Cromwell, *Lord Protector*<br>1658–9 Richard Cromwell, *Lord Protector* |
| 1660–1685 | CHARLES II<br>*Born* 1630, eldest son of Charles I<br>*Married* Catherine, daughter of John IV of Portugal<br>*Died* aged 54, *reigned* 24 years |
| 1685–1688 | JAMES II (VII of Scotland)<br>*Born* 1633, second son of Charles I<br>*Married* (1) Lady Anne Hyde, daughter of Edward, earl of Clarendon (2) Mary, daughter of Alphonso, duke of Modena<br>Reign ended with flight from kingdom December 1688<br>*Died* 1701 aged 67, *reigned* 3 years<br>INTERREGNUM 11 December 1688 to 12 February 1689 |
| 1689–1702 | WILLIAM III<br>*Born* 1650, son of William II, prince of Orange, and Mary Stuart, daughter of Charles I<br>*Married* Mary, elder daughter of James II<br>*Died* aged 51, *reigned* 13 years |
| *and*<br>1689–1694 | MARY II<br>*Born* 1662, elder daughter of James II and Anne<br>*Died* aged 32, *reigned* 5 years |
| 1702–1714 | ANNE<br>*Born* 1665, younger daughter of James II and Anne<br>*Married* Prince George of Denmark, son of Frederick III of Denmark<br>*Died* aged 49, *reigned* 12 years |

### THE HOUSE OF HANOVER

| | |
|---|---|
| 1714–1727 | GEORGE I (Elector of Hanover)<br>*Born* 1660, son of Sophia (daughter of Frederick, elector palatine, and Elizabeth Stuart, daughter of James I) and Ernest Augustus, elector of Hanover<br>*Married* Sophia Dorothea, daughter of George William, duke of Lüneburg-Celle<br>*Died* aged 67, *reigned* 12 years |
| 1727–1760 | GEORGE II<br>*Born* 1683, son of George I<br>*Married* Caroline, daughter of John Frederick, margrave of Brandenburg-Anspach<br>*Died* aged 76, *reigned* 33 years |
| 1760–1820 | GEORGE III<br>*Born* 1738, son of Frederick, eldest son of George II<br>*Married* Charlotte, daughter of Charles Louis, duke of Mecklenburg-Strelitz<br>*Died* aged 81, *reigned* 59 years<br>REGENCY 1811–20<br>Prince of Wales regent owing to the insanity of George III |
| 1820–1830 | GEORGE IV<br>*Born* 1762, eldest son of George III<br>*Married* Caroline, daughter of Charles, duke of Brunswick-Wolfenbüttel<br>*Died* aged 67, *reigned* 10 years |
| 1830–1837 | WILLIAM IV<br>*Born* 1765, third son of George III<br>*Married* Adelaide, daughter of George, duke of Saxe-Meiningen<br>*Died* aged 71, *reigned* 7 years |
| 1837–1901 | VICTORIA<br>*Born* 1819, daughter of Edward, fourth son of George III<br>*Married* Prince Albert of Saxe-Coburg and Gotha<br>*Died* aged 81, *reigned* 63 years |

### THE HOUSE OF SAXE-COBURG AND GOTHA

| | |
|---|---|
| 1901–1910 | EDWARD VII<br>*Born* 1841, eldest son of Victoria and Albert<br>*Married* Alexandra, daughter of Christian IX of Denmark<br>*Died* aged 68, *reigned* 9 years |

### THE HOUSE OF WINDSOR

| | |
|---|---|
| 1910–1936 | GEORGE V<br>*Born* 1865, second son of Edward VII<br>*Married* Victoria Mary, daughter of Francis, duke of Teck<br>*Died* aged 70, *reigned* 25 years |
| 1936 | EDWARD VIII<br>*Born* 1894, eldest son of George V<br>*Married* (1937) Mrs Wallis Simpson<br>*Abdicated* 1936, *died* 1972 aged 77, *reigned* 10 months (20 January to 11 December) |
| 1936–1952 | GEORGE VI<br>*Born* 1895, second son of George V<br>*Married* Lady Elizabeth Bowes-Lyon, daughter of 14th Earl of Strathmore and Kinghorne (*see also* page 117)<br>*Died* aged 56, *reigned* 15 years |

1952– ELIZABETH II
*Born* 1926, elder daughter of George VI
*Married* Philip, son of Prince Andrew of Greece (*see also* page 117)

## KINGS AND QUEENS OF SCOTS 1016 TO 1603

*Reign*

1016–1034 MALCOLM II
*Born c.*954, son of Kenneth II
Acceded to Alba 1005, secured Lothian *c.*1016, obtained Strathclyde for his grandson Duncan *c.*1016, thus reigning over an area approximately the same as that governed by later rulers of Scotland
*Died* aged *c.*80, *reigned* 18 years

### THE HOUSE OF ATHOLL

1034–1040 DUNCAN I
Son of Bethoc, daughter of Malcolm II, and Crinan, mormaer of Atholl
*Married* a cousin of Siward, earl of Northumbria
*Reigned* 5 years

1040–1057 MACBETH
*Born c.*1005, son of a daughter of Malcolm II and Finlaec, mormaer of Moray
*Married* Gruoch, granddaughter of Kenneth III
*Killed* aged *c.*52, *reigned* 17 years

1057–1058 LULACH
*Born c.*1032, son of Gillacomgan, mormaer of Moray, and Gruoch (and stepson of Macbeth)
*Died* aged *c.*26, *reigned* 7 months (August–March)

1058–1093 MALCOLM III (Canmore)
*Born c.*1031, elder son of Duncan I
*Married* (1) Ingibiorg (2) Margaret (St Margaret), granddaughter of Edmund II of England
*Killed* in battle aged *c.*62, *reigned* 35 years

1093–1097 DONALD III BÁN
*Born c.*1033, second son of Duncan I
*Deposed* May 1094, *restored* November 1094, *deposed* October 1097, *reigned* 3 years

1094 DUNCAN II
*Born c.*1060, elder son of Malcolm III and Ingibiorg
*Married* Octreda of Dunbar
*Killed* aged *c.*34, *reigned* 6 months (May–November)

1097–1107 EDGAR
*Born c.*1074, second son of Malcolm III and Margaret
*Died* aged *c.*32, *reigned* 9 years

1107–1124 ALEXANDER I (The Fierce)
*Born c.*1077, fifth son of Malcolm III and Margaret
*Married* Sybilla, illegitimate daughter of Henry I of England
*Died* aged *c.*47, *reigned* 17 years

1124–1153 DAVID I (The Saint)
*Born c.*1085, sixth son of Malcolm III and Margaret
*Married* Matilda, daughter of Waltheof, earl of Huntingdon
*Died* aged *c.*68, *reigned* 29 years

1153–1165 MALCOLM IV (The Maiden)
*Born c.*1141, son of Henry, earl of Huntingdon, second son of David I
*Died* aged *c.*24, *reigned* 12 years

1165–1214 WILLIAM I (The Lion)
*Born c.*1142, brother of Malcolm IV
*Married* Ermengarde, daughter of Richard, viscount of Beaumont
*Died* aged *c.*72, *reigned* 49 years

1214–1249 ALEXANDER II
*Born* 1198, son of William I
*Married* (1) Joan, daughter of John, king of England (2) Marie, daughter of Ingelram de Coucy *Died* aged 50, *reigned* 34 years

1249–1286 ALEXANDER III
*Born* 1241, son of Alexander II and Marie
*Married* (1) Margaret, daughter of Henry III of England (2) Yolande, daughter of the Count of Dreux
*Killed* accidentally aged 44, *reigned* 36 years

1286–1290 MARGARET (The Maid of Norway)
*Born* 1283, daughter of Margaret (daughter of Alexander III) and Eric II of Norway
*Died* aged 7, *reigned* 4 years
FIRST INTERREGNUM 1290–2
Throne disputed by 13 competitors. Crown awarded to John Balliol by adjudication of Edward I of England

### THE HOUSE OF BALLIOL

1292–1296 JOHN (Balliol)
*Born c.*1250, son of Dervorguilla, great-great-granddaughter of David I, and John de Balliol
*Married* Isabella, daughter of John, earl of Surrey
*Abdicated* 1296, *died* 1313 aged *c.*63, *reigned* 3 years
SECOND INTERREGNUM 1296–1306
Edward I of England declared John Balliol to have forfeited the throne for contumacy in 1296 and took the government of Scotland into his own hands

### THE HOUSE OF BRUCE

1306–1329 ROBERT I (Bruce)
*Born* 1274, son of Robert Bruce and Marjorie, countess of Carrick, and great-grandson of the second daughter of David, earl of Huntingdon, brother of William I
*Married* (1) Isabella, daughter of Donald, earl of Mar (2) Elizabeth, daughter of Richard, earl of Ulster
*Died* aged 54, *reigned* 23 years

1329–1371 DAVID II
*Born* 1324, son of Robert I and Elizabeth
*Married* (1) Joanna, daughter of Edward II of England (2) Margaret Drummond, widow of Sir John Logie (divorced)
*Died* aged 46, *reigned* 41 years
1332 Edward Balliol, son of John Balliol, crowned King of Scots September, expelled December
1333–6 Edward Balliol restored as King of Scots

### THE HOUSE OF STEWART

1371–1390 ROBERT II (Stewart)
*Born* 1316, son of Marjorie (daughter of Robert I) and Walter, High Steward of Scotland
*Married* (1) Elizabeth, daughter of Sir Robert Mure of Rowallan (2) Euphemia, daughter of Hugh, earl of Ross
*Died* aged 74, *reigned* 19 years

1390–1406 ROBERT III
*Born c.*1337, son of Robert II and Elizabeth
*Married* Annabella, daughter of Sir John Drummond of Stobhall
*Died* aged *c.*69, *reigned* 16 years

1406–1437 JAMES I
*Born* 1394, son of Robert III
*Married* Joan Beaufort, daughter of John, earl of Somerset
*Assassinated* aged 42, *reigned* 30 years

1437–1460 JAMES II
*Born* 1430, son of James I
*Married* Mary, daughter of Arnold, duke of Gueldres
*Killed* accidentally aged 29, *reigned* 23 years

1460–1488 JAMES III
*Born* 1452, son of James II
*Married* Margaret, daughter of Christian I of Denmark
*Assassinated* aged 36, *reigned* 27 years

1488–1513 JAMES IV
*Born* 1473, son of James III
*Married* Margaret Tudor, daughter of Henry VII of England
*Killed* in battle aged 40, *reigned* 25 years

| | |
|---|---|
| 1513–1542 | JAMES V<br>*Born* 1512, son of James IV<br>*Married* (1) Madeleine, daughter of Francis I of France (2) Mary of Lorraine, daughter of the Duc de Guise<br>*Died* aged 30, *reigned* 29 years |
| 1542–1567 | MARY<br>*Born* 1542, daughter of James V and Mary<br>*Married* (1) the Dauphin, afterwards Francis II of France (2) Henry Stewart, Lord Darnley (3) James Hepburn, earl of Bothwell<br>*Abdicated* 1567, prisoner in England from 1568, *executed* 1587, *reigned* 24 years |
| 1567–1625 | JAMES VI (and I of England)<br>*Born* 1566, son of Mary, queen of Scots, and Henry, Lord Darnley<br>Acceded 1567 to the Scottish throne, *reigned* 58 years<br>Succeeded 1603 to the English throne, so joining the English and Scottish crowns in one person. The two kingdoms remained distinct until 1707 when the parliaments of the kingdoms became conjoined<br>For British Kings and Queens since 1603, *see* pages 130–1 |

## WELSH SOVEREIGNS AND PRINCES

Wales was ruled by sovereign princes from the earliest times until the death of Llywelyn in 1282. The first English Prince of Wales was the son of Edward I, who was born in Caernarvon town on 25 April 1284. According to a discredited legend, he was presented to the Welsh chieftains as their prince, in fulfilment of a promise that they should have a prince who 'could not speak a word of English' and should be native born. This son, who afterwards became Edward II, was created 'Prince of Wales and Earl of Chester' at the Lincoln Parliament on 7 February 1301.

The title Prince of Wales is borne after individual conferment and is not inherited at birth, though some Princes have been declared and styled Prince of Wales but never formally so created (*s.*). The title was conferred on Prince Charles by The Queen on 26 July 1958. He was invested at Caernarvon on 1 July 1969.

### INDEPENDENT PRINCES AD 844 TO 1282

| | |
|---|---|
| 844–878 | Rhodri the Great |
| 878–916 | Anarawd, son of Rhodri |
| 916–950 | Hywel Dda, the Good |
| 950–979 | Iago ab Idwal (or Ieuaf) |
| 979–985 | Hywel ab Ieuaf, the Bad |
| 985–986 | Cadwallon, his brother |
| 986–999 | Maredudd ab Owain ap Hywel Dda |
| 999–1008 | Cynan ap Hywel ab Ieuaf |
| 1018–1023 | Llywelyn ap Seisyll |
| 1023–1039 | Iago ab Idwal ap Meurig |
| 1039–1063 | Gruffydd ap Llywelyn ap Seisyll |
| 1063–1075 | Bleddyn ap Cynfyn |
| 1075–1081 | Trahaern ap Caradog |
| 1081–1137 | Gruffydd ap Cynan ab Iago |
| 1137–1170 | Owain Gwynedd |
| 1170–1194 | Dafydd ab Owain Gwynedd |
| 1194–1240 | Llywelyn Fawr, the Great |
| 1240–1246 | Dafydd ap Llywelyn |
| 1246–1282 | Llywelyn ap Gruffydd ap Llywelyn |

### ENGLISH PRINCES SINCE 1301

| | |
|---|---|
| 1301 | Edward (Edward II) |
| 1343 | Edward the Black Prince, son of Edward III |
| 1376 | Richard (Richard II), son of the Black Prince |
| 1399 | Henry of Monmouth (Henry V) |
| 1454 | Edward of Westminster, son of Henry VI |
| 1471 | Edward of Westminster (Edward V) |
| 1483 | Edward, son of Richard III (d. 1484) |
| 1489 | Arthur Tudor, son of Henry VII |
| 1504 | Henry Tudor (Henry VIII) |
| 1610 | Henry Stuart, son of James I (d. 1612) |
| 1616 | Charles Stuart (Charles I) |
| *c.*1638 (*s.*) | Charles Stuart (Charles II) |
| 1688 (*s.*) | James Francis Edward Stuart (The Old Pretender), son of James II (d. 1766) |
| 1714 | George Augustus (George II) |
| 1729 | Frederick Lewis, son of George II (d. 1751) |
| 1751 | George William Frederick (George III) |
| 1762 | George Augustus Frederick (George IV) |
| 1841 | Albert Edward (Edward VII) |
| 1901 | George (George V) |
| 1910 | Edward (Edward VIII) |
| 1958 | Charles, son of Elizabeth II |

## PRINCESSES ROYAL

The style Princess Royal is conferred at the Sovereign's discretion on his or her eldest daughter. It is an honorary title, held for life, and cannot be inherited or passed on. It was first conferred on Princess Mary, daughter of Charles I, in approximately 1642.

| | |
|---|---|
| *c.*1642 | Princess Mary (1631–60), daughter of Charles I |
| 1727 | Princess Anne (1709–59), daughter of George II |
| 1766 | Princess Charlotte (1766–1828), daughter of George III |
| 1840 | Princess Victoria (1840–1901), daughter of Victoria |
| 1905 | Princess Louise (1867–1931), daughter of Edward VII |
| 1932 | Princess Mary (1897–1965), daughter of George V |
| 1987 | Princess Anne (b. 1950), daughter of Elizabeth II |

# Precedence

## ENGLAND AND WALES

- The Sovereign
- The Prince Philip, Duke of Edinburgh
- The Prince of Wales
- The Sovereign's younger sons
- The Sovereign's grandsons
- The Sovereign's cousins
- Archbishop of Canterbury
- Lord High Chancellor
- Archbishop of York
- The Prime Minister
- Lord President of the Council
- Speaker of the House of Commons
- Lord Privy Seal
- Ambassadors and High Commissioners
- Lord Great Chamberlain
- Earl Marshal
- Lord Steward of the Household
- Lord Chamberlain of the Household
- Master of the Horse
- Dukes, according to their patent of creation:
  - (1) of England
  - (2) of Scotland
  - (3) of Great Britain
  - (4) of Ireland
  - (5) those created since the Union
- Ministers and Envoys
- Eldest sons of Dukes of Blood Royal
- Marquesses, according to their patent of creation:
  - (1) of England
  - (2) of Scotland
  - (3) of Great Britain
  - (4) of Ireland
  - (5) those created since the Union
- Dukes' eldest sons
- Earls, according to their patent of creation:
  - (1) of England
  - (2) of Scotland
  - (3) of Great Britain
  - (4) of Ireland
  - (5) those created since the Union
- Younger sons of Dukes of Blood Royal
- Marquesses' eldest sons
- Dukes' younger sons
- Viscounts, according to their patent of creation:
  - (1) of England
  - (2) of Scotland
  - (3) of Great Britain
  - (4) of Ireland
  - (5) those created since the Union
- Earls' eldest sons
- Marquesses' younger sons
- Bishops of London, Durham and Winchester
- Other English Diocesan Bishops, according to seniority of consecration
- Suffragan Bishops, according to seniority of consecration
- Secretaries of State, if of the degree of a Baron
- Barons, according to their patent of creation:
  - (1) of England
  - (2) of Scotland
  - (3) of Great Britain
  - (4) of Ireland
  - (5) those created since the Union
- Treasurer of the Household
- Comptroller of the Household
- Vice-Chamberlain of the Household
- Secretaries of State under the degree of Baron
- Viscounts' eldest sons
- Earls' younger sons
- Barons' eldest sons
- Knights of the Garter
- Privy Counsellors
- Chancellor of the Exchequer
- Chancellor of the Duchy of Lancaster
- Lord Chief Justice of England
- Master of the Rolls
- President of the Family Division
- Vice-Chancellor
- Lords Justices of Appeal
- Judges of the High Court
- Viscounts' younger sons
- Barons' younger sons
- Sons of Life Peers
- Baronets, according to date of patent
- Knights of the Thistle
- Knights Grand Cross of the Bath
- Members of the Order of Merit
- Knights Grand Commanders of the Star of India
- Knights Grand Cross of St Michael and St George
- Knights Grand Commanders of the Indian Empire
- Knights Grand Cross of the Royal Victorian Order
- Knights Grand Cross of the British Empire
- Companions of Honour
- Knights Commanders of the Bath
- Knights Commanders of the Star of India
- Knights Commanders of St Michael and St George
- Knights Commanders of the Indian Empire
- Knights Commanders of the Royal Victorian Order
- Knights Commanders of the British Empire
- Knights Bachelor
- Vice-Chancellor of the County Palatine of Lancaster
- Judges of the Technology and Construction Court
- Circuit judges and judges of the Mayor's and City of London Court
- Companions of the Bath
- Companions of the Star of India
- Companions of St Michael and St George
- Companions of the Indian Empire
- Commanders of the Royal Victorian Order
- Commanders of the British Empire
- Companions of the Distinguished Service Order
- Lieutenants of the Royal Victorian Order
- Officers of the British Empire
- Companions of the Imperial Service Order
- Eldest sons of younger sons of Peers
- Baronets' eldest sons
- Eldest sons of Knights, in the same order as their fathers
- Members of the Royal Victorian Order
- Members of the British Empire
- Younger sons of the younger sons of Peers
- Baronets' younger sons
- Younger sons of Knights, in the same order as their fathers
- Naval, Military, Air, and other Esquires by office

## SCOTLAND

- The Sovereign
- The Prince Philip, Duke of Edinburgh
- The Lord High Commissioner to the General Assembly (while that Assembly is sitting)
- The Duke of Rothesay (eldest son of the Sovereign)
- The Sovereign's younger sons
- The Sovereign's cousins
- Lord-Lieutenants
- Lord Provosts of those Cities
- Sheriffs Principal, successively, within their own localities and during holding of office
- Lord Chancellor of Great Britain
- Moderator of the General Assembly of the Church of Scotland
- Keepers of the Great Seal
- The Presiding Officer
- The Secretary of State for Scotland
- Hereditary Lord High Constable of Scotland
- Hereditary Master of the Household
- Dukes, in same order as in England
- Eldest sons of Dukes of the Blood Royal
- Marquesses, as in England
- Dukes' eldest sons
- Earls, as in England
- Younger sons of Dukes of Blood Royal

Marquesses' eldest sons
Dukes' younger sons
Lord Justice General
Lord Clerk Register
Lord Advocate
The Advocate-General
Lord Justice Clerk
Viscounts, as in England
Earls' eldest sons
Marquesses' younger sons
Lord-Barons, as in England
Viscounts' eldest sons
Earls' younger sons
Lord-Barons' eldest sons
Knights of the Garter
Knights of the Thistle
Privy Counsellors
Senators of College of Justice (Lords of Session)
Viscounts' younger sons
Lord-Barons' younger sons
Sons of Life Peers
Baronets
Knights Grand Cross, Grand Commander, and Knight Commanders, as in England
Solicitor-General for Scotland
Lord Lyon King of Arms
Sheriffs Principal, except as shown above
Knights Bachelor
Sheriffs
Commanders of the Royal Victorian Order
Companions of Orders, as in England
Commanders of the British Empire
Lieutenants of the Royal Victorian Order
Companions of the Distinguished Service Order
Eldest sons of younger sons of Peers
Baronets' eldest sons
Knights' eldest sons, as in England
Members of the Royal Victorian Order
Baronets' younger sons
Knights' younger sons
Queen's Counsel
Esquires
Gentlemen

### Women

Women take the same rank as their husbands or as their brothers; but the daughter of a peer marrying a commoner retains her title as Lady or Honourable. Daughters of peers rank next immediately after the wives of their elder brothers, and before their younger brothers' wives. Daughters of peers marrying peers of lower degree take the same order of precedence as that of their husbands; thus the daughter of a Duke marrying a Baron becomes of the rank of Baroness only, while her sisters married to commoners retain their rank and take precedence of the Baroness. Merely official rank on the husband's part does not give any similar precedence to the wife.

Peeresses in their own right take the same precedence as peers of the same rank, i.e. from their date of creation.

### Local Precedence

*England and Wales*

No written code of county or city order of precedence has been promulgated, but in counties the Lord Lieutenant stands first, and secondly (normally) the Sheriff, and therefore in cities and boroughs the Lord Lieutenant has social precedence over the Mayor; but at city or borough functions the Lord Mayor or Mayor will preside. At Oxford and Cambridge the High Sheriff takes precedence of the Vice-Chancellor.

*Scotland*

The Lord Provosts of the city districts of Aberdeen, Dundee, Edinburgh and Glasgow are Lord Lieutenants for those districts *ex officio* and take precedence as such.

# ·orms of address

: is only possible to cover here the forms of address for eers, baronets and knights, their wife and children, and rivy Counsellors. Greater detail should be sought in one f the publications devoted to the subject.

Both formal and social forms of address are given where sage differs; nowadays, the social form is generally referred to the formal, which increasingly is used only or official documents and on very formal occasions.

'_ represents forename
_ represents surname

BARON – *Envelope (formal)*, The Right Hon. Lord _; *(social)*, The Lord_. *Letter (formal)*, My Lord; *(social)*, Dear Lord_. *Spoken*, Lord_.

BARON'S WIFE–*Envelope (formal)*, The Right Hon. Lady_; *(social)*, The Lady_. *Letter (formal)*, My Lady; *(social)*, Dear Lady_. *Spoken*, Lady_.

BARON'S CHILDREN – *Envelope*, The Hon. F_S_. *Letter*, Dear Mr/Miss/Mrs S_. *Spoken*, Mr/Miss/Mrs S_.

BARONESS IN OWN RIGHT – *Envelope*, may be addressed in same way as a Baron's wife or, if she prefers *(formal)*, The Right Hon. the Baroness _; *(social)*, The Baroness_. Otherwise as for a Baron's wife.

BARONET – *Envelope*, Sir F_S_, Bt. *Letter (formal)*, Dear Sir; *(social)*, Dear Sir F_. *Spoken*, Sir F_.

BARONET'S WIFE – *Envelope*, Lady S_. *Letter (formal)*, Dear Madam; *(social)*, Dear Lady S_. *Spoken*, Lady S_.

COUNTESS IN OWN RIGHT – As for an Earl's wife.

COURTESY TITLES–The heir apparent to a Duke, Marquess or Earl uses the highest of his father's other titles as a courtesy title. (For list, *see* pages 165–6.) The holder of a courtesy title is not styled The Most Hon. or The Right Hon., and in correspondence 'The' is omitted before the title. The heir apparent to a Scottish title may use the title 'Master' (*see* below).

DAME – *Envelope*, Dame F_S_, followed by appropriate post-nominal letters. *Letter (formal)*, Dear Madam; *(social)*, Dear Dame F_. *Spoken*, Dame F_.

DUKE–*Envelope (formal)*, His Grace the Duke of_ ; *(social)*, The Duke of_. *Letter (formal)*, My Lord Duke; *(social)*, Dear Duke. *Spoken (formal)*, Your Grace; *(social)*, Duke.

DUKE'S WIFE–*Envelope (formal)*, Her Grace the Duchess of_; *(social)*, The Duchess of_. *Letter (formal)*, Dear Madam; *(social)*, Dear Duchess. *Spoken*, Duchess.

DUKE'S ELDEST SON – *see* Courtesy titles.

DUKE'S YOUNGER SONS – *Envelope*, Lord F_S_. *Letter (formal)*, My Lord; *(social)*, Dear Lord F_. *Spoken (formal)*, My Lord; *(social)*, Lord F_.

DUKE'S DAUGHTER–*Envelope*, Lady F_S_. *Letter (formal)*, Dear Madam; *(social)*, Dear Lady F_. *Spoken*, Lady F_.

EARL –*Envelope (formal)*, The Right Hon. the Earl (of)_; *(social)*, The Earl (of)_. *Letter (formal)*, My Lord; *(social)*, Dear Lord _. *Spoken (formal)*, My Lord; *(social)*, Lord _S WIFE – *Envelope (formal)*, The Right Hon. the Countess (of)_; *(social)*, The Countess (of)_. *Letter (formal)*, Madam; *(social)*, Lady_. *Spoken (formal)*, Madam; *(social)*, Lady_.

EARL'S CHILDREN – *Eldest son, see* Courtesy titles. *Younger sons*, The Hon. F_S_ (for forms of address, *see* Baron's children). *Daughters*, Lady F_S_ (for forms of address, *see* Duke's daughter).

KNIGHT (BACHELOR) – *Envelope*, Sir F_S_. *Letter (formal)*, Dear Sir; *(social)*, Dear Sir F_. *Spoken*, Sir F_.

KNIGHT (ORDERS OF CHIVALRY) – *Envelope*, Sir F_S_ , followed by appropriate post-nominal letters. Otherwise as for Knight Bachelor.

KNIGHT'S WIFE – As for Baronet's wife.

LIFE PEER – As for Baron/Baroness in own right.

LIFE PEER'S WIFE – As for Baron's wife.

LIFE PEER'S CHILDREN – As for Baron's children.

MARQUESS–*Envelope (formal)*, The Most Hon. the Marquess of _; *(social)*, The Marquess of_. *Letter (formal)*, My Lord; *(social)*, Dear Lord_. *Spoken (formal)*, My Lord; *(social)*, Lord_.

MARQUESS'S WIFE – *Envelope (formal)*, The Most Hon. the Marchioness of _; *(social)*, The Marchioness of_. *Letter (formal)*, Madam; *(social)*, Dear Lady_. *Spoken*, Lady_.

MARQUESS'S CHILDREN–*Eldest son, see* Courtesy titles. *Younger sons*, Lord F_S_ (for forms of address, *see* Duke's younger sons). *Daughters*, Lady F_S_ (for forms of address, *see* Duke's daughter).

MASTER–The title is used by the heir apparent to a Scottish peerage, though usually the heir apparent to a Duke, Marquess or Earl uses his courtesy title rather than 'Master'. *Envelope*, The Master of_. *Letter (formal)*, Dear Sir; *(social)*, Dear Master of _. *Spoken (formal)*, Master, or Sir; *(social)*, Master, or Mr S_.

MASTER'S WIFE–Addressed as for the wife of the appropriate peerage style, otherwise as Mrs S_.

PRIVY COUNSELLOR–*Envelope*, The Right (or Rt.) Hon. F_S_. *Letter*, Dear Mr/Miss/Mrs S_. *Spoken*, Mr/Miss/Mrs S_. It is incorrect to use the letters PC after the name in conjunction with the prefix The Right Hon., unless the Privy Counsellor is a peer below the rank of Marquess and so is styled The Right Hon. because of his rank. In this case only, the post-nominal letters may be used in conjunction with the prefix The Right Hon.

VISCOUNT–*Envelope (formal)*, The Right Hon. the Viscount_; *(social)*, The Viscount_. *Letter (formal)*, My Lord; *(social)*, Dear Lord_. *Spoken*, Lord_.

VISCOUNT'S WIFE – *Envelope (formal)*, The Right Hon. the Viscountess_; *(social)*, The Viscountess_. *Letter (formal)*, Madam; *(social)*, Dear Lady _. *Spoken*, Lady _.

VISCOUNT'S CHILDREN – As for Baron's children.

# The Peerage

## and Members of the House of Lords

The rules which govern the creation and succession of peerages are extremely complicated. There are, technically, five separate peerages, the Peerage of England, of Scotland, of Ireland, of Great Britain, and of the United Kingdom. The Peerage of Great Britain dates from 1707 when an Act of Union combined the two kingdoms of England and Scotland and separate peerages were discontinued. The Peerage of the United Kingdom dates from 1801 when Great Britain and Ireland were combined under an Act of Union. Some Scottish peers have received additional peerages of Great Britain or of the United Kingdom since 1707, and some Irish peers additional peerages of the United Kingdom since 1801.

The Peerage of Ireland was not entirely discontinued from 1801 but holders of Irish peerages, whether predating or created subsequent to the Union of 1801, were not entitled to sit in the House of Lords if they had no additional English, Scottish, Great Britain or United Kingdom peerage. However, they are eligible for election to the House of Commons and to vote in parliamentary elections. An Irish peer holding a peerage of a lower grade which enabled him to sit in the House of Lords was introduced there by the title which enabled him to sit, though for all other purposes he was known by his higher title.

In the Peerage of Scotland there is no rank of Baron; the equivalent rank is Lord of Parliament, abbreviated to 'Lord' (the female equivalent is 'Lady'). All peers of England, Scotland, Great Britain or the United Kingdom who are 21 years or over, and of British, Irish or Commonwealth nationality were entitled to sit in the House of Lords until the House of Lords Act 1999, when hereditary peers lost the right to sit. Ninety-two hereditaries are to remain in the House of Lords for a transitional period. In the list below, these peers are indicated by the **. Ten hereditary peers received Life Peerages in 1999 enabling them to remain in the reformed chamber, and two further hereditary peers reverted to sitting by virtue of the Life Peerages they already held.

### Hereditary Women Peers

Most hereditary peerages pass on death to the nearest male heir, but there are exceptions, and several are held by women.

A woman peer in her own right retains her title after marriage, and if her husband's rank is the superior she is designated by the two titles jointly, the inferior one second. Her hereditary claim still holds good in spite of any marriage whether higher or lower. No rank held by a woman can confer any title or even precedence upon her husband but the rank of a hereditary woman peer in her own right is inherited by her eldest son (or in some cases daughter).

After the Peerage Act 1963, hereditary women peers in their own right were entitled to sit in the House of Lords, subject to the same qualifications as men, until the House of Lords Act 1999.

### Life Peers

Since 1876 non-hereditary or life peerages have been conferred on certain eminent judges to enable the judicial functions of the House of Lords to be carried out. These Lords are known as Lords of Appeal or law lords and, to date, such appointments have all been male.

Since 1958 life peerages have been conferred upon distinguished men and women from all walks of life, giving them seats in the House of Lords in the degree of Baron or Baroness. They are addressed in the same way as hereditary Lords and Barons, and their children have similar courtesy titles.

### Peerages Extinct Since the Last Edition

EARLDOMS: Munster (cr. 1831)

VISCOUNTCIES: Lambert (cr. 1945); Leverhulme (cr. 1922)

LIFE PEERAGES: Aldington (cr. 1999); Bellwin (cr. 1979); Brooke of Ystrafellte (cr. 1964); Cledwyn of Penrhos (cr. 1979); Cocks of Hartcliffe (cr. 1987); Cowdry of Tonbridge (cr. 1997); Denton of Wakefield (cr. 1991); Greenhill of Harrow (cr. 1974); Hamlyn (cr. 1998); Harmar-Nicholls (cr. 1974); Harris of Greenwich (cr. 1974); Hartwell (cr. 1968); Kelvedon (cr. 1997); Low (cr. 1999); Lovell-Davis (cr. 1974); McConnell (cr. 1995); MacKay of Ardbrecknish (cr. 1991); Molloy (cr. 1981); Morris of Castle Morris (cr. 1990); Onslow of Woking (cr. 1997); Packenham of Cowely (cr. 1999); Plowden (cr. 1959); Prentice (cr. 1992); Ryder of Warsaw (cr. 1979); Sefton of Garston (cr. 1978); Shepherd of Spalding (cr. 1999); Sieff of Brimpton (cr. 1980); Taylor of Gryfe (cr. 1968).

### Disclaimer of Peerages

The Peerage Act 1963 enables peers to disclaim their peerages for life. Peers alive in 1963 could disclaim within twelve months after the passing of the Act (31 July 1963); a person subsequently succeeding to a peerage may disclaim within 12 months (one month if an MP) after the date of succession, or of reaching 21, if later. The disclaimer is irrevocable but does not affect the descent of the peerage after the disclaimant's death, and children of a disclaimed peer may, if they wish, retain their precedence and any courtesy titles and styles borne as children of a peer. The disclaimer permitted the disclaimant to sit in the House of Commons if elected as an MP. As the House of Lords Act 1999 removed hereditary peers from the House of Lords, they are now entitled to sit in the House of Commons without having to disclaim their titles.

The following peerages are currently disclaimed:

EARLDOMS: Durham (1970); Selkirk (1994)

VISCOUNTCIES: Hailsham (1963); Stansgate (1963)

BARONIES: Altrincham (1963); Merthyr (1977); Reith (1972); Sanderson of Ayot (1971); Silkin (1972)

PEERS WHO ARE MINORS (i.e. under 21 years of age)

EARLS: Craven (*b.* 1989)

### Contractions and Symbols

- S. Scottish title
- I. Irish title
- * The peer holds also an Imperial title, specified after the name by Engl., Brit. or UK
- ** Hereditary peer remaining in the House of Lords for a transitional period
- ° there is no 'of' in the title
- *b.* born
- *s.* succeeded
- *m.* married
- *w.* widower or widow
- *M.* minor
- † heir not ascertained at time of going to press

# Iereditary Peers

## EERS OF THE BLOOD ROYAL

*tyle*, His Royal Highness The Duke of _/His Royal Highness the Earl of_
*tyle of address* (*formal*) May it please your Royal Highness; (*informal*) Sir

| *'reated* | *Title, order of succession, name, etc.* | *Heir* |
|---|---|---|
| | *Dukes* | |
| 337 | *Cornwall*, Charles, Prince of Wales, *s.* 1952 (*see* page 117) | ‡ |
| 398 | *Rothesay*, Charles, Prince of Wales, *s.* 1952 (*see* page 117) | ‡ |
| 986 | *York* (1st), The Prince Andrew, Duke of York (*see* page 117) | None |
| 928 | *Gloucester* (2nd), Prince Richard, Duke of Gloucester, *s.* 1974 (*see* page 118) | Earl of Ulster (*see* page 118) |
| 934 | *Kent* (2nd), Prince Edward, Duke of Kent, *s.* 1942 (*see* page 118) | Earl of St Andrews (*see* page 118) |
| | *Earl* | |
| 999 | *Wessex* (1st), The Prince Edward, Earl of Wessex (*see* page 117) | None |

The title is not hereditary but is held by the Sovereign's eldest son from the moment of his birth or the Sovereign's accession

## )UKES

*'oronet*, Eight strawberry leaves
*tyle*, His Grace the Duke of _
*Vife's style*, Her Grace the Duchess of _
*'ldest son's style*, Takes his father's second title as a courtesy title
*'ounger sons' style*, 'Lord' before forename and family name
*)aughters' style*, 'Lady' before forename and family name
'or forms of address, *see* page 135

| *'reated* | *Title, order of succession, name, etc.* | *Heir* |
|---|---|---|
| 868 I. | *Abercorn (5th)*, James Hamilton, KG, *b.* 1934, *s.* 1979, *m.* | Marquess of Hamilton, *b.* 1969 |
| 701 S.* | *Argyll (13th) and 6th UK Duke Argyll, 1892*, Torquhil Campbell, *b.* 1968, *s.* 2001 | None |
| 703 S. | *Atholl (11th)*, John Murray, *b.* 1929, *s.* 1996, *m.* | Marquess of Tullibardine, *b.* 1960 |
| 682 | *Beaufort (11th)*, David Robert Somerset, *b.* 1928, *s.* 1984, *w.* | Marquess of Worcester, *b.* 1952 |
| 694 | *Bedford (13th)*, John Robert Russell, *b.* 1917, *s.* 1953, *m.* | Marquess of Tavistock, *b.* 1940 |
| 663 S.* | *Buccleuch (9th) and Queensberry (11th) (S. 1684) and 8th Eng. Earl, Doncaster*, 1662, Walter Francis John Montagu Douglas Scott, KT, VRD, *b.* 1923, *s.* 1973, *m.* | Earl of Dalkeith, *b.* 1954 |
| 694 | *Devonshire (11th)*, Andrew Robert Buxton Cavendish, KG, MC, PC, *b.* 1920, *s.* 1950, *m.* | Marquess of Hartington, CBE, *b.* 1944 |
| 947 | *Edinburgh (1st)*, HRH The Prince Philip, Duke of Edinburgh, (*see* page 117) | The Prince of Wales §, (see *page 117)* |
| 900 | *Fife (3rd) and 12th Scott. Earl, Southesk, 1633, (S. 1992)*, James George Alexander Bannerman Carnegie, *b.* 1929, *s.* 1959 (*see* page 128) | Earl of Southesk, *b.* 1961 |
| 675 | *Grafton (11th)*, Hugh Denis Charles FitzRoy, KG, *b.* 1919, *s.* 1970, *m.* | Earl of Euston, *b.* 1947 |
| 643 S.* | *Hamilton (15th) and Brandon (12th) (Brit. 1711)*, Angus Alan Douglas Douglas-Hamilton, *b.* 1938, *s.* 1973, *Premier Peer of Scotland* | Marquess of Douglas and Clydesdale, *b.* 1978 |
| 766 I.* | *Leinster (8th) and 8th Brit. Visct., Leinster, 1747*, Gerald FitzGerald, *b.* 1914, *s.* 1976, *m., Premier Duke and Marquess of Ireland* | Marquess of Kildare, *b.* 1948 |
| 719 | *Manchester (12th)*, Angus Charles Drogo Montagu, *b.* 1938, *s.* 1985, *m.* | Viscount Mandeville, *b.* 1962 |
| 702 | *Marlborough (11th)*, John George Vanderbilt Henry Spencer-Churchill, *b.* 1926, *s.* 1972, *m.* | Marquess of Blandford, *b.* 1955 |
| 707 S.* | ** *Montrose (8th) and 6th Brit. Earl, Graham*, 1722, James Graham, *b.* 1935, *s.* 1992, *m.* | Marquess of Graham, *b.* 1973 |
| 483 | ** *Norfolk (17th) and 12th Eng. Baron, Beaumont, 1309, s. 1971, and 4th UK Baron Howard of Glossop, 1869, S. 1972*, Miles Francis Stapleton Fitzalan-Howard, KG, GCVO, CB, CBE, MC, *b.* 1915, *s.* 1975, *m., Premier Duke and Earl Marshal* | Earl of Arundel and Surrey, *b.* 1956 |

In June 1999 Buckingham Palace revealed that the current Earl of Wessex would be given the Dukedom of Edinburgh when the present title returns to the Crown

| Created | Title, order of succession, name, etc. | Heir |
|---|---|---|
| 1766 | *Northumberland (12th)*, Ralph George Algernon Percy, *b.* 1956, *s.* 1995, *m.* | Earl Percy, *b.* 1984 |
| 1675 | *Richmond (10th) and Gordon (5th) (UK 1876) and Scott. Duke Lennox (10th)*, Charles Henry Gordon Lennox, *b.* 1929, *s.* 1989, *m.* | Earl of March and Kinrara, *b.* 195 |
| 1707 S.* | *Roxburghe (10th) and 5th UK Earl, Innes*, 1837, Guy David Innes-Ker, *b.* 1954, *s.* 1974, *m., Premier Baronet of Scotland* | Marquess of Bowmont and Cessford, *b.* 1981 |
| 1703 | *Rutland (11th)*, David Charles Robert Manners, *b.* 1959, *s.* 1999, *m.* | Marquis of Granby, *b.* 1999 |
| 1684 | *St Albans (14th)*, Murray de Vere Beauclerk, *b.* 1939, *s.* 1988, *m.* | Earl of Burford, *b.* 1965 |
| 1547 | *Somerset (19th)*, John Michael Edward Seymour, *b.* 1952, *s.* 1984, *m.* | Lord Seymour, *b.* 1982 |
| 1833 | *Sutherland (7th) and 6th UK Earl, Ellesmere, 1846*, Francis Ronald Egerton, *b.* 1940, *s.* 2000, *m.* | Marquess of Stafford, *b.* 1975 |
| 1814 | *Wellington (8th) and 9th Irish Earl, Mornington*, 1760, Arthur Valerian Wellesley, KG, LVO, OBE, MC, *b.* 1915, *s.* 1972, *m.* | Marquess of Douro, *b.* 1945 |
| 1874 | *Westminster (6th)*, Gerald Cavendish Grosvenor, OBE, *b.* 1951, *s.* 1979, *m.* | Earl Grosvenor, *b.* 1991 |

## MARQUESSES

*Coronet*, Four strawberry leaves alternating with four silver balls
*Style*, The Most Hon. the Marquess (of) _ . In Scotland the spelling 'Marquis' is preferred for pre-Union creations
*Wife's style*, The Most Hon. the Marchioness (of) _
*Eldest son's style*, Takes his father's second title as a courtesy title
*Younger sons' style*, 'Lord' before forename and family name
*Daughters' style*, 'Lady' before forename and family name
For forms of address, *see* page 135

| Created | Title, order of succession, name, etc. | Heir |
|---|---|---|
| 1916 | *Aberdeen and Temair (6th) and Scott. Earl, Aberdeen*, 1682, Alastair Ninian John Gordon, *b.* 1920, *s.* 1984, *m.* | Earl Haddo, *b.* 1955 |
| 1876 | *Abergavenny (6th)*, Christopher George Charles Nevill, *b.* 1955, *s.* 2000, *m.* | David M. R. N., *b.* 1941 |
| 1821 | *Ailesbury (8th)*, Michael Sidney Cedric Brudenell-Bruce, *b.* 1926, *s.* 1974 | Earl of Cardigan, *b.* 1952 |
| 1831 | *Ailsa (8th) and 20th Scott. Earl, Cassillis*, 1509, Archibald Angus Charles Kennedy, *b.* 1956, *s.* 1994 | Lord David Kennedy, *b.* 1958 |
| 1815 | *Anglesey (7th)*, George Charles Henry Victor Paget, *b.* 1922, *s.* 1947, *m.* | Earl of Uxbridge, *b.* 1950 |
| 1789 | *Bath (7th)*, Alexander George Thynn, *b.* 1932, *s.* 1992, *m.* | Viscount Weymouth, *b.* 1974 |
| 1826 | *Bristol (8th)*, Frederick William Augustus Hervey, *b.* 1979, *s.* 1999 | Timothy H. H., *b.* 1960 |
| 1796 | *Bute (7th) and 12th Scott. Earl, Dumfries*, 1633, John Colum Crichton-Stuart, *b.* 1958, *s.* 1993, *m.* | Earl of Dumfries, *b.* 1989 |
| 1812 | °*Camden (6th)*, David George Edward Henry Pratt, *b.* 1930, *s.* 1983 | Earl of Brecknock, *b.* 1965 |
| 1815 | ** *Cholmondeley (7th) and 11th Irish Visct., Cholmondeley*, 1661, David George Philip Cholmondeley, *b.* 1960, *s.* 1990, *Lord Great Chamberlain* | Charles G. C., *b.* 1959 |
| 1816 | °*Conyngham (7th) and 7th UK Baron, Minster*, 1821, Frederick William Henry Francis Conyngham, *b.* 1924, *s.* 1974, *m.* | Earl of Mount Charles, *b.* 195 |
| 1791 I.* | *Donegall (7th) and 7th Brit. Baron, Fisherwick, 1970 and 6th Brit. Baron Templemore, 1831, S. 1953*, Dermot Richard Claud Chichester, LVO, *b.* 1916, *s.* 1975, *w.* | Earl of Belfast, *b.* 1952 |
| 1789 I.* | *Downshire (8th) and 8th Brit. Earl, Hillsborough*, 1772, (Arthur) Robin Ian Hill, *b.* 1929, *s.* 1989, *m.* | Earl of Hillsborough, *b.* 1959 |
| 1801 I.* | *Ely (8th) and 8th UK Baron, Loftus*, 1801, Charles John Tottenham, *b.* 1913, *s.* 1969, *m.* | Viscount Loftus, *b.* 1943 |
| 1801 | *Exeter (8th)*, (William) Michael Anthony Cecil, *b.* 1935, *s.* 1988, *m.* | Lord Burghley, *b.* 1970 |
| 1800 I.* | *Headfort (6th) and 4th UK Baron, Kenlis*, 1831, Thomas Geoffrey Charles Michael Taylour, *b.* 1932, *s.* 1960, *m.* | Earl of Bective, *b.* 1959 |
| 1793 | *Hertford (9th) and 10th Irish Baron, Conway*, 1712, Henry Jocelyn Seymour, *b.* 1958, *s.* 1997, *m.* | Earl of Yarmouth, *b.* 1958 |
| 1599 S.* | *Huntly (13th) and 5th UK Baron, Meldrum*, 1815, Granville Charles Gomer Gordon, *b.* 1944, *s.* 1987, *m., Premier Marquess of Scotland* | Earl of Aboyne, *b.* 1973 |
| 1784 | *Lansdowne (9th) and 9th Irish Earl, Kerry*, 1723, Charles Maurice Mercer NairnePetty-Fitzmaurice, *b.* 1941, *s.* 1999, *m.* | Earl of Shelbourne, *b.* 1941 |
| 1902 | *Linlithgow (4th) and 10th Scott. Earl, Hopetoun*, 1703, Adrian John Charles Hope, *b.* 1946, *s.* 1987, *m.* | Earl of Hopetown, *b.* 1969 |
| 1816 I.* | *Londonderry (9th) and 6th UK Earl, Vane*, 1823, Alexander Charles Robert Vane-Tempest-Stewart, *b.* 1937, *s.* 1955, *m.* | Viscount Castlereagh, *b.* 1972 |

| Created | Title, order of succession, name, etc. | Heir |
|---|---|---|
| 701 S.* | *Lothian (12th) and 6th UK Baron, Kerr*, 1821, Peter Francis Walter Kerr, KCVO, *b.* 1922, *s.* 1940, *m.* | Earl of Ancram, PC, MP, *b.* 1945 |
| 917 | *Milford Haven (4th)*, George Ivar Louis Mountbatten, *b.* 1961, *s.* 1970, *m.* | Earl of Medina, *b.* 1991 |
| 838 | *Normanby (5th) and 9th Irish Baron, Mulgrave*, 1767, Constantine Edmund Walter Phipps, *b.* 1954, *s.* 1994, *m.* | Earl of Mulgrave, *b.* 1994 |
| 812 | *Northampton (7th)*, Spencer Douglas David Compton, *b.* 1946, *s.* 1978, *m.* | Earl Compton, *b.* 1973 |
| 682 S. | *Queensberry (12th)*, David Harrington Angus Douglas, *b.* 1929, *s.* 1954 | Viscount Drumlanrig, *b.* 1967 |
| 926 | *Reading (4th)*, Simon Charles Henry Rufus Isaacs, *b.* 1942, *s.* 1980, *m.* | Viscount Erleigh, *b.* 1986 |
| 789 | *Salisbury (6th)*, Robert Edward Peter Cecil, *b.* 1916, *s.* 1972, *m.* | Viscount Cranborne, PC, *b.* 1946 (*see also* Baron Cecil) |
| 800 I.* | *Sligo (11th) and 11th UK Baron, Monteagle*, 1806, Jeremy Ulick Browne, *b.* 1939, *s.* 1991, *m.* | Sebastian U. B., *b.* 1964 |
| 787 | ° *Townshend (7th)*, George John Patrick Dominic Townshend, *b.* 1916, *s.* 1921, *w.* | Viscount Raynham, *b.* 1945 |
| 694 | ° *Tweeddale (13th) and 4th UK Baron Tweeddale*, 1881, Edward Douglas John Hay, *b.* 1947, *s.* 1979 | Lord Charles D. M. H., *b.* 1947 |
| 789 I.* | *Waterford (8th) and 8th Brit. Baron Tyrone*, 1786, John Hubert de la Poer Beresford, *b.* 1933, *s.* 1934, *m.* | Earl of Tyrone, *b.* 1958 |
| 551 | *Winchester (18th)*, Nigel George Paulet, *b.* 1941, *s.* 1968, *m.*, *Premier Marquess of England* | Earl of Wiltshire, *b.* 1969 |
| 892 | *Zetland (4th) and 6th UK Earl, Zetland, 1838 and 7th Brit. Baron Dundas*, 1794, Lawrence Mark Dundas, *b.* 1937, *s.* 1989, *m.* | Earl of Ronaldshay, *b.* 1965 |

## EARLS

*Coronet*, Eight silver balls on stalks alternating with eight gold strawberry leaves
*Style*, The Right Hon. the Earl (of) _
*Wife's style*, The Right Hon. the Countess (of) _
*Eldest son's style*, Takes his father's second title as a courtesy title
*Younger sons' style*, 'The Hon.' before forename and family name
*Daughters' style*, 'Lady' before forename and family name
For forms of address, *see* page 135

| Created | Title, order of succession, name, etc. | Heir |
|---|---|---|
| 1639 S. | *Airlie (13th)*, David George Coke Patrick Ogilvy, KT, GCVO, PC, *b.* 1926, *s.* 1968, *m.* | Lord Ogilvy, *b.* 1958 |
| 1696 | *Albemarle (10th)*, Rufus Arnold Alexis Keppel, *b.* 1965, *s.* 1979 | Crispian W. J. K., *b.* 1948 |
| 1952 | ° *Alexander of Tunis (2nd)*, Shane William Desmond Alexander, *b.* 1935, *s.* 1969, *m.* | Hon. Brian J. A., *b.* 1939 |
| 1662 | *Annandale and Hartfell (11th)*, Patrick Andrew Wentworth Hope Johnstone, *b.* 1941, *m.*, claim established 1985 | Lord Johnstone, *b.* 1971 |
| 1789 | ° *Annesley (10th)*, Patrick Annesley, *b.* 1924, *s.* 1979, *m.* | Hon. Philip H. A., *b.* 1927 |
| 1785 | *Antrim (9th)*, Alexander Randal Mark McDonnell, *b.* 1935, *s.* 1977, *m.* | Viscount Dunluce, *b.* 1967 |
| 1762 | ** *Arran (9th) and 5th UK Baron Sudley*, 1884, Arthur Desmond Colquhoun Gore, *b.* 1938, *s.* 1983, *m.* | Paul A. G., CMG, CVO, *b.* 1921 |
| 1955 | °** *Attlee (3rd)*, John Richard Attlee, *b.* 1956, *s.* 1991, *m.* | None |
| 1714 | *Aylesford (11th)*, Charles Ian Finch-Knightley, *b.* 1918, *s.* 1958, *w.* | Lord Guernsey, *b.* 1947 |
| 1937 | °** *Baldwin of Bewdley (4th)*, Edward Alfred Alexander Baldwin, *b.* 1938, *s.* 1976, *m.* | Viscount Corvedale, *b.* 1973 |
| 1922 | *Balfour (4th)*, Gerald Arthur James Balfour, *b.* 1925, *s.* 1968, *m.* | Roderick F. A. G., *b.* 1948 |
| 1772 | ° *Bathurst (8th)*, Henry Allen John Bathurst, *b.* 1927, *s.* 1943, *m.* | Lord Apsley, *b.* 1961 |
| 1919 | ° *Beatty (3rd)*, David Beatty, *b.* 1946, *s.* 1972, *m.* | Viscount Borodale, *b.* 1973 |
| 1797 | *Belmore (8th)*, John Armar Lowry-Corry, *b.* 1951, *s.* 1960, *m.* | Viscount Corry, *b.* 1985 |
| 1739 | *Bessborough (11th) and 8th UK Baron Duncannon*, 1834, Arthur Mountifort Longfield Ponsonby, *b.* 1912, *s.* 1993, *m.* | Viscount Duncannon, *b.* 1941 |
| 1815 | *Bradford (7th)*, Richard Thomas Orlando Bridgeman, *b.* 1947, *s.* 1981, *m.* | Viscount Newport, *b.* 1980 |
| 1469 | *Buchan (17th) and 8th UK Baron Erskine*, 1806, Malcolm Harry Erskine, *b.* 1930, *s.* 1984, *m.* | Lord Cardross, *b.* 1960 |
| 1746 | *Buckinghamshire (10th)*, (George) Miles Hobart-Hampden, *b.* 1944, *s.* 1983, *m.* | Sir John Hobart, Bt., *b.* 1945 |
| 1800 | ° *Cadogan (8th)*, Charles Gerald John Cadogan, *b.* 1937, *s.* 1997, *m.* | Viscount Chelsea, *b.* 1966 |
| 1878 | ° *Cairns (6th)*, Simon Dallas Cairns, CBE, *b.* 1939, *s.* 1989, *m.* | Viscount Garmoyle, *b.* 1965 |
| 1455 | ** *Caithness (20th)*, Malcolm Ian Sinclair, PC, *b.* 1948, *s.* 1965, *w.* | Lord Berriedale, *b.* 1981 |

| *Created* | *Title, order of succession, name, etc.* | *Heir* |
|---|---|---|
| 1800 | *Caledon* (*7th*), Nicholas James Alexander, *b.* 1955, *s.* 1980, *m.* | Viscount Alexander, *b.* 19 |
| 1661 | *Carlisle* (*13th*) *and 13th Scott. Baron Ruthven of Freeland*, 1651, George William Beaumont Howard, *b.* 1949, *s.* 1994 | Hon. Philip C. W. H., *b.* 1963 |
| 1793 | *Carnarvon* (*8th*), George Reginald Oliver Molyneux Herbert, *b.* 1956, *s.* 2001, *m.* | Hon. George K. O. M. H. *b.* 1992 |
| 1748 I.* | *Carrick* (*10th*) *and 4th UK Baron Butler*, 1912, David James Theobald Somerset Butler, *b.* 1953, *s.* 1992, *m.* | Viscount Ikerrin, *b.* 1975 |
| 1800 I.° | *Castle Stewart* (*8th*), Arthur Patrick Avondale Stuart, *b.* 1928, *s.* 1961, *m.* | Viscount Stuart, *b.* 1953 |
| 1814 | ° *Cathcart* (*7th*) *and 16th Scott. Baron Cathcart*, 1447, Charles Alan Andrew Cathcart, *b.* 1952, *s.* 1999, *m.* | Lord Greenock, *b.* 1952 |
| 1647 | *Cavan*. The 12th Earl died in 1988. Heir had not established his claim to the title at the time of going to press | Roger C. Lambart, *b.* 194 |
| 1827 | ° *Cawdor* (*7th*), Colin Robert Vaughan Campbell, *b.* 1962, *s.* 1993, *m.* | Hon. Frederick W. C., *b.* 1965 |
| 1801 | *Chichester* (*9th*), John Nicholas Pelham, *b.* 1944, *s.* 1944, *m.* | Richard A. H. P., *b.* 1952 |
| 1803 I. | *Clancarty* (*9th*) *and 8th UK Visct. Clancarty*, 1823, Nicholas Power Richard Le Poer Trench, *b.* 1952, *s.* 1995 | None |
| 1776 I. | *Clanwilliam* (*7th*) *and 5th UK Baron Clanwilliam*, 1828, John Herbert Meade, *b.* 1919, *s.* 1989, *m.* | Lord Gillford, *b.* 1960 |
| 1776 | *Clarendon* (*7th*), George Frederick Laurence Hyde Villiers, *b.* 1933, *s.* 1955, *m.* | Lord Hyde, *b.* 1976 |
| 1620 I. | *Cork and Orrery* (*14th*) (*I. 1660*) *and 10th Brit. Baron Boyle of Marston*, 1711, John William Boyle, DSC, *b.* 1916, *s.* 1995, *m.* | Viscount Dungarvan, *b.* 1945 |
| 1850 | *Cottenham* (*8th*), Kenelm Charles Everard Digby Pepys, *b.* 1948, *s.* 1968, *m.* | Viscount Crowhurst, *b.* 19 |
| 1762 I. | ** *Courtown* (*9th*) *and 8th Brit. Baron Saltersford*, 1796, James Patrick Montagu Burgoyne Winthrop Stopford, *b.* 1954, *s.* 1975, *m.* | Viscount Stopford, *b.* 198 |
| 1697 | *Coventry* (*11th*), George William Coventry, *b.* 1934, *s.* 1940, *m.* | Francis H. C., *b.* 1912 |
| 1857 | ° *Cowley* (*7th*), Garret Graham Wellesley, *b.* 1934, *s.* 1975, *m.* | Viscount Dangan, *b.* 1965 |
| 1892 | *Cranbrook* (*5th*), Gathorne Gathorne-Hardy, *b.* 1933, *s.* 1978, *m.* | Lord Medway, *b.* 1968 |
| 1801 | *Craven* (*9th*), Benjamin Robert Joseph Craven, *b.* 1989, *s.* 1990 | Rupert J. E. C., *b.* 1926 |
| 1398 S.* | *Crawford* (*29th*) *and Balcarres* (*12th*) (*s. 1651*) *and 5th UK Baron, Wigan, 1826 and Baron Balniel* (*life peerage, 1974*), Robert Alexander Lindsay, KT, PC, *b.* 1927, *s.* 1975, *m., Premier Earl on Union Roll* | Lord Balniel, *b.* 1958 |
| 1861 | *Cromartie* (*5th*), John Ruaridh Blunt Grant Mackenzie, *b.* 1948, *s.* 1989, *m.* | Viscount Tarbat, *b.* 1987 |
| 1901 | *Cromer* (*4th*), Evelyn Rowland Esmond Baring, *b.* 1946, *s.* 1991, *m.* | Viscount Errington, b 199 |
| 1633 S.* | *Dalhousie* (*17th*) *and 5th UK Baron Ramsay*, 1875, James Hubert Ramsay, *b.* 1948, *s.* 1999, *m.* | Lord Ramsay, *b.* 1948 |
| 1725 I. | *Darnley* (*11th*) *and 20th Engl. Baron Clifton of Leighton Bromswold*, 1608, Adam Ivo Stuart Bligh, *b.* 1941, *s.* 1980, *m.* | Lord Clifton, *b.* 1968 |
| 1711 | *Dartmouth* (*10th*), William Legge, *b.* 1949, *s.* 1997 | Hon. Rupert L., *b.* 1951 |
| 1761 | ° *De La Warr* (*11th*), William Herbrand Sackville, *b.* 1948, *s.* 1988, *m.* | Lord Buckhurst, *b.* 1979 |
| 1622 | *Denbigh* (*12th*) *and Desmond* (*11th*) (*I. 1622*), Alexander Stephen Rudolph Feilding, *b.* 1970, *s.* 1995, *m.* | William D. F, *b.* 1939 |
| 1485 | *Derby* (*19th*), Edward Richard William Stanley, *b.* 1962, *s.* 1994, *m.* | Lord Stanley, *b.* 1998 |
| 1553 | *Devon* (*18th*), Hugh Rupert Courtenay, *b.* 1942, *s.* 1998, *m.* | Lord Courtenay, *b.* 1942 |
| 1800 I.* | *Donoughmore* (*8th*) *and 8th UK Visct. Hutchinson*, 1821, Richard Michael John Hely-Hutchinson, *b.* 1927, *s.* 1981, *m.* | Viscount Suirdale, *b.* 1952 |
| 1661 I.* | *Drogheda* (*12th*) *and 3rd UK Baron Moore*, 1954, Henry Dermot Ponsonby Moore, *b.* 1937, *s.* 1989, *m.* | Viscount Moore, *b.* 1983 |
| 1837 | *Ducie* (*7th*), David Leslie Moreton, *b.* 1951, *s.* 1991, *m.* | Lord Moreton, *b.* 1981 |
| 1860 | *Dudley* (*4th*), William Humble David Ward, *b.* 1920, *s.* 1969, *m.* | Viscount Ednam, *b.* 1947 |
| 1660 S.* | ** *Dundee* (*12th*) *and 2nd UK Baron Glassary*, 1954, Alexander Henry Scrymgeour, *b.* 1949, *s.* 1983, *m.* | Lord Scrymgeour, *b.* 1982 |
| 1669 S. | *Dundonald* (*15th*), Iain Alexander Douglas Blair Cochrane, *b.* 1961, *s.* 1986, *m.* | Lord Cochrane, *b.* 1991 |
| 1686 S. | *Dunmore* (*12th*), Malcolm Kenneth Murray, *b.* 1946, *s.* 1995, *m.* | Hon. Geoffrey C. M., *b.*1949 |
| 1822 I. | *Dunraven and Mount-Earl* (*7th*), Thady Windham Thomas Wyndham-Quin, *b.* 1939, *s.* 1965, *m.* | None |
| 1833 | *Durham*, Antony Claud Frederick Lambton, *b.* 1922, *s.* 1970, *m.*, Disclaimed for life 1970 | Hon. Edward R. L. (Baron Durham), *b.* 1961 |
| 1837 | *Effingham* (*7th*) *and 17th Engl. Baron Howard of Effingham*, 1554, David Mowbray Algernon Howard, *b.* 1939, *s.* 1996, *m.* | Lord Howard of Effinghan *b.* 1971 |
| 1507 S.* | *Eglinton* (*18th*) *and Winton* (*9th*) *and 6th UK Earl Winton*, 1859, Archibald George Montgomerie, *b.* 1939, *s.* 1966, *m.* | Lord Montgomerie, *b.* 196 |
| 1733 I.* | *Egmont* (*11th*) *and 9th Brit. Baron Lovel and Holland*, 1762, Frederick George Moore Perceval, *b.* 1914, *s.* 1932, *m.* | Viscount Perceval, *b.* 1934 |
| 1821 | *Eldon* (*5th*), John Joseph Nicholas Scott, *b.* 1937, *s.* 1976, *m.* | Viscount Encombe, *b.* 196 |

| ;reated | *Title, order of succession, name, etc.* | *Heir* |
|---|---|---|
| 633 S.* | *Elgin (11th) and Kincardine (15th) (s. 1647) and 4th UK Baron, Elgin*, 1849, Andrew Douglas Alexander Thomas Bruce, KT, *b.* 1924, *s.* 1968, *m.* | Lord Bruce, *b.* 1961 |
| 789 I.* | *Enniskillen (7th) and 5th UK Baron, Grinstead*, 1815, Andrew John Galbraith Cole, *b.* 1942, *s.* 1989, *m.* | Arthur G. C., *b.* 1920 |
| 876 I.* | *Erne (3rd) and 3rd UK Baron Fermanagh, 1876*, Henry George Victor John Crichton, *b.* 1937, *m.* | Viscount Crichton, *b.* 1971 |
| 452 S. | ** *Erroll (24th)*, Merlin Sereld Victor Gilbert Hay, *b.* 1948, *s.* 1978, *m.*, *Hereditary Lord High Constable and Knight Marischal of Scotland* | Lord Hay, *b.* 1984 |
| 661 | *Essex (10th)*, Robert Edward de Vere Capell, *b.* 1920, *s.* 1981, *m.* | Viscount Malden, *b.* 1944 |
| 711 | °** *Ferrers (13th)*, Robert Washington Shirley, PC, *b.* 1929, *s.* 1954, *m.* | Viscount Tamworth, *b.* 1952 |
| 789 | ° *Fortescue (8th)*, Charles Hugh Richard Fortescue, *b.* 1951, *s.* 1993, *m.* | Hon. Martin D. F., *b.* 1924 |
| 841 | *Gainsborough (5th)*, Anthony Gerard Edward Noel, *b.* 1923, *s.* 1927, *m.* | Viscount Campden, *b.* 1950 |
| 623 S.* | *Galloway (13th) and 6th Brit. Baron of Garlies*, 1796, Randolph Keith Reginald Stewart, *b.* 1928, *s.* 1978, *w.* | Andrew C. S., *b.* 1949 |
| 703 S.* | *Glasgow (10th) and 4th UK Baron, Farlie*, 1897, Patrick Robin Archibald Boyle, *b.* 1939, *s.* 1984, *m.* | Viscount of Kelburn, *b.* 1978 |
| 806 I.* | *Gosford (7th) and 5th UK Baron, Worlingham*, 1835, Charles David Nicholas Alexander John Sparrow Acheson, *b.* 1942, *s.* 1966, *m.* | Hon. Patrick B. V. M. A., *b.* 1915 |
| 945 | *Gowrie (2nd) and 3rd UK Baron Ruthven of Gowrie*, 1919, Alexander Patric Greysteil Hore-Ruthven, PC, *b.* 1939, *s.* 1955, *m.* | Viscount Ruthven of Canberra, *b.* 1964 |
| 684 I.* | *Granard (10th) and 5th UK Baron, Granard*, 1806, Peter Arthur Edward Hastings Forbes, *b.* 1957, *s.* 1992, *m.* | Viscount Forbes, *b.* 1981 |
| 833 | ° *Granville (6th)*, Granville George Fergus Leveson-Gower, *b.* 1959, *s.* 1996, *m.* | Hon. Niall J. L.-G., *b.* 1963 |
| 806 | ° *Grey (6th)*, Richard Fleming George Charles Grey, *b.* 1939, *s.* 1963, *m.* | Philip K. G., *b.* 1940 |
| 752 | *Guilford (10th)*, Piers Edward Brownlow North, *b.* 1971, *s.* 1999, *m.* | Hon. Charles E. N., *b.* 1918 |
| 619 | *Haddington (13th)*, John George Baillie-Hamilton, *b.* 1941, *s.* 1986, *m.* | Lord Binning, *b.* 1985 |
| 919 | ° *Haig (2nd)*, George Alexander Eugene Douglas Haig, OBE, *b.* 1918, *s.* 1928, *m.* | Viscount Dawick, *b.* 1961 |
| 944 | *Halifax (3rd) and 5th UK Visct., Halifax*, 1866, Charles Edward Peter Neil Wood, *b.* 1944, *s.* 1980, *m.* | Lord Irwin, *b.* 1977 |
| 898 | *Halsbury (4th)*, Adam Edward Giffard, *b.* 1934, *s.* 2000, *m.* | † |
| 754 | *Hardwicke (10th)*, Joseph Philip Sebastian Yorke, *b.* 1971, *s.* 1974 | Charles E. Y., *b.* 1951 |
| 812 | *Harewood (7th)*, George Henry Hubert Lascelles, KBE, *b.* 1923, *s.* 1947, *m.* (*see also* page 127) | Viscount Lascelles, *b.* 1950 (*see also* page 126) |
| 742 | *Harrington (11th) and 8th Brit. Visct. Stanhope of Mahon*, 1717, William Henry Leicester Stanhope, *b.* 1922, *s.* 1929, *m.* | Viscount Petersham, *b.* 1945 |
| 809 | *Harrowby (7th)*, Dudley Danvers Granville Coutts Ryder, TD, *b.* 1922, *s.* 1987, *m.* | Viscount Sandon, *b.* 1951 |
| 605 | ** *Home (15th)*, David Alexander Cospatrick Douglas-Home, CVO, *b.* 1943, *s.* 1995, *m.* | Lord Dunglass, *b.* 1987 |
| 821 | ° ** *Howe (7th)*, Frederick Richard Penn Curzon, *b.* 1951, *s.* 1984, *m.* | Viscount Curzon, *b.* 1994 |
| 529 | *Huntingdon (16th)*, William Edward Robin Hood Hastings Bass, LVO, *b.* 1948, *s.* 1990, *m.* | Hon. Simon A. R. H. H. B., *b.* 1950 |
| 885 | *Iddesleigh (4th)*, Stafford Henry Northcote, *b.* 1932, *s.* 1970, *m.* | Viscount St Cyres, *b.* 1957 |
| 756 | *Ilchester (9th)*, Maurice Vivian de Touffreville Fox-Strangways, *b.* 1920, *s.* 1970, *m.* | Hon. Raymond G. F.-S., *b.* 1921 |
| 1929 | *Inchcape (4th)*, (Kenneth) Peter (Lyle) Mackay, *b.* 1943, *s.* 1994, *m.* | Viscount Glenapp, *b.* 1979 |
| 1919 | *Iveagh (4th)*, Arthur Edward Rory Guinness, *b.* 1969, *s.* 1992 | Hon. Rory M. B. G., *b.* 1974 |
| 1925 | ° *Jellicoe (2nd) and Baron Jellicoe of Southampton* (*life peerage, 1999*), George Patrick John Rushworth Jellicoe, KBE, DSO, MC, PC, FRS, *b.* 1918, *s.* 1935, *m.* | Viscount Brocas, *b.* 1950 |
| 1697 | *Jersey (10th) and 13th Visct. Grandison*, 1620, George Francis William Child Villiers, *b.* 1976, *s.* 1998 | Hon. Jamie C. V., *b.* 1994 |
| 1822 I. | *Kilmorey (6th)*, Richard Francis Needham, KT, PC, *b.* 1942, *s.* 1977, *m.* (does not use title) | Viscount Newry and Morne, *b.* 1966 |
| 1866 | *Kimberley (4th)*, John Wodehouse, *b.* 1924, *s.* 1941, *m.* | Lord Wodehouse, *b.* 1951 |
| 1768 I. | *Kingston (11th)*, Barclay Robert Edwin King-Tenison, *b.* 1943, *s.* 1948, *m.* | Viscount Kingsborough, *b.* 1969 |
| 1633 S.* | *Kinnoull (15th) and 9th Brit. Baron Hay of Pedwardine*, 1711, Arthur William George Patrick Hay, *b.* 1935, *s.* 1938, *m.* | Viscount Dupplin, *b.* 1962 |
| 1677 S.* | *Kintore (13th) and 3rd UK Visct. Stonehaven*, 1938, Michael Canning William John Keith, *b.* 1939, *s.* 1989, *m.* | Lord Inverurie, *b.* 1976 |
| 1914 | ° *Kitchener of Khartoum (3rd)*, Henry Herbert Kitchener, TD, *b.* 1919, *s.* 1937 | None |
| 1624 | *Lauderdale (17th)*, Patrick Francis Maitland, *b.* 1911, *s.* 1968, *m.* | Viscount Maitland, *b.* 1937 |
| 1837 | *Leicester (7th)*, Edward Douglas Coke, *b.* 1936, *s.* 1994, *m.* | Viscount Coke, *b.* 1965 |
| 1641 S.* | *Leven (14th) and Melville (13th) (s. 1690)*, Alexander Robert Leslie Melville, *b.* 1924, *s.* 1947, *m.* | Lord Balgonie, *b.* 1954 |
| 1831 | *Lichfield (5th)*, Thomas Patrick John Anson, *b.* 1939, *s.* 1960 | Viscount Anson, *b.* 1978 |

| *Created* | *Title, order of succession, name, etc.* | *Heir* |
|---|---|---|
| 1803 I.* | *Limerick (6th) and 6th UK Baron Foxford*, 1815, Patrick Edmund Pery, KBE, *b.* 1930, *s.* 1967, *m.* | Viscount Glentworth, *b.* 1963 |
| 1572 | *Lincoln (18th)*, Robert Edward Fiennes-Clinton, *s.* 2001 | † |
| 1633 S. | ** *Lindsay (16th)*, James Randolph Lindesay-Bethune, *b.* 1955, *s.* 1989, *m.* | Viscount Garnock, *b.* 1990 |
| 1626 | *Lindsey (14th) and Abingdon (9th) (1682)*, Richard Henry Rupert Bertie, *b.* 1931, *s.* 1963, *m.* | Lord Norreys, *b.* 1958 |
| 1776 I. | *Lisburne (8th)*, John David Malet Vaughan, *b.* 1918, *s.* 1965, *m.* | Viscount Vaughan, *b.* 1945 |
| 1822 I.* | ** *Listowel (6th) and 4th UK Baron Hare*, 1869, Francis Michael Hare, *b.* 1964, *s.* 1997, *m.* | Hon. Timothy P. H., *b.* 1966 |
| 1905 | ** *Liverpool (5th)*, Edward Peter Bertram Savile Foljambe, *b.* 1944, *s.* 1969, *m.* | Viscount Hawkesbury, *b.* 1972 |
| 1945 | ° *Lloyd George of Dwyfor (3rd)*, Owen Lloyd George, *b.* 1924, *s.* 1968, *m.* | Viscount Gwynedd, *b.* 195 |
| 1785 I.* | *Longford (8th) and 2nd UK Baron Pakenham*, 1945, Thomas Frank Dermot Pakenham, *s.* 2001, *m.* | Hon. Edward M. P., *b.* 197 |
| 1807 | *Lonsdale (7th)*, James Hugh William Lowther, *b.* 1922, *s.* 1953, *m.* | Viscount Lowther, *b.* 1949 |
| 1838 | *Lovelace (5th) and 12th Brit. Baron King*, 1725, Peter Axel William Locke King, *b.* 1951, *s.* 1964, *m.* | None |
| 1795 I.* | *Lucan (7th) and 3rd UK Baron Bingham*, 1934, Richard John Bingham, *b.* 1934, *s.* 1964, *m.* | Lord Bingham, *b.* 1967 |
| 1880 | *Lytton (5th) and 18th Engl. Baron, Wentworth*, 1529, John Peter Michael Scawen Lytton, *b.* 1950, *s.* 1985, *m.* | Viscount Knebworth, *b.* 1989 |
| 1721 | *Macclesfield (9th)*, Richard Timothy George Mansfield Parker, *b.* 1943, *s.* 1992, *m.* | Hon. J. David G. P., *b.* 194 |
| 1800 | *Malmesbury (6th)*, William James Harris, TD, *b.* 1907, *s.* 1950, *w.* | Viscount FitzHarris, *b.* 194 |
| 1776 & 1792 | *Mansfield and Mansfield (8th) and 14th Scott. Visct. Stormont*, 1621, William David Mungo James Murray, *b.* 1930, *s.* 1971, *m.* | Viscount Stormont, *b.* 195 |
| 1565 S.* | ***Mar (14th) and Kellie (16th) (S. 1616) and Baron Erkine of Alloa Tower (life peerage, 2000)*, James Thorne Erskine, *b.* 1949, *s.* 1994, *m.* | Hon. Alexander D. E., *b.* 1952 |
| 1785 I. | *Mayo (10th)*, Terence Patrick Bourke, *b.* 1929, *s.* 1962 | Lord Naas, *b.* 1953 |
| 1627 I.* | *Meath (15th) and 6th UK Baron, Chaworth*, 1831, John Anthony Brabazon, *b.* 1941, *s.* 1998, *m.* | Lord Ardee, *b.* 1941 |
| 1766 | *Mexborough (8th)*, John Christopher George Savile, *b.* 1931, *s.* 1980, *m.* | Viscount Pollington, *b.* 195 |
| 1813 | *Minto (6th)*, Gilbert Edward George Lariston Elliot-Murray-Kynynmound, OBE, *b.* 1928, *s.* 1975, *m.* | Viscount Melgund, *b.* 1953 |
| 1562 S.* | *Moray (20th) and 12th Brit. Baron Stuart of Castle Stuart*, 1796, Douglas John Moray Stuart, *b.* 1928, *s.* 1974, *m.* | Lord Doune, *b.* 1966 |
| 1815 | *Morley (6th)*, John St Aubyn Parker, KCVO, *b.* 1923, *s.* 1962, *m.* | Viscount Boringdon, *b.* 195 |
| 1458 | *Morton (22nd)*, John Charles Sholto Douglas, *b.* 1927, *s.* 1976, *m.* | Lord Aberdour, *b.* 1952 |
| 1789 | *Mount Edgcumbe (8th)*, Robert Charles Edgcumbe, *b.* 1939, *s.* 1982 | Piers V. E., *b.* 1946 |
| 1805 | ° *Nelson (9th)*, Peter John Horatio Nelson, *b.* 1941, *s.* 1981, *m.* | Viscount Merton, *b.* 1971 |
| 1660 S. | *Newburgh (12th)*, Don Filippo Giambattista Camillo Francesco Aldo Ma Rospigliosi, *b.* 1942, *s.* 1986, *m.* | Princess Donna Benedetta F. M. R., *b.* 1974 |
| 1827 I. | *Norbury (6th)*, Noel Terence Graham-Toler, *b.* 1939, *s.* 1955, *m.* | Viscount Glandine, *b.* 1967 |
| 1806 I.* | *Normanton (6th) and 9th Brit. Baron Mendip, 1794, and 4th UK Baron, Somerton*, 1873, Shaun James Christian Welbore Ellis Agar, *b.* 1945, *s.* 1967, *m.* | Viscount Somerton, *b.* 198 |
| 1647 S.** | *Northesk (14th)*, David John MacRae Carnegie, *b.* 1954, *s.* 1994, *m.* | Lord Rosehill, *b.* 1980 |
| 1801 | ** *Onslow (7th)*, Michael William Coplestone Dillon Onslow, *b.* 1938, *s.* 1971, *m.* | Viscount Cranley, *b.* 1967 |
| 1696 S. | *Orkney (9th)*, (Oliver) Peter St John, *b.* 1938, *s.* 1998, *m.* | Viscount Kirkwall, *b.* 1969 |
| 1328 | *Ormonde and Ossory*. The 8th Marquess of Ormonde died in 1997, when the marquessate became extinct. The heir to his earldoms had not established his claim at the time of going to press. | Viscount Mountgarret, *b.* 1936 (*see page* 146) |
| 1925 | *Oxford and Asquith (2nd)*, Julian Edward George Asquith, KCMG, *b.* 1916, *s.* 1928, *w.* | Viscount Asquith, OBE, *b.* 1952 |
| 1929 | °** *Peel (3rd) and 4th UK Viscount Peel*, 1895, William James Robert Peel, *b.* 1947, *s.* 1969, *m.* | Viscount Clanfield, *b.* 1976 |
| 1551 | *Pembroke (17th) and Montgomery (14th) (1605)*, Henry George Charles Alexander Herbert, *b.* 1939, *s.* 1969 | Lord Herbert, *b.* 1978 |
| 1605 | *Perth (17th)*, John David Drummond, PC, *b.* 1907, *s.* 1951, *w.* | Viscount Strathallan, *b.* 193 |
| 1905 | *Plymouth (3rd) and 15th Engl. Baron, Windsor*, 1529, Other Robert Ivor Windsor-Clive, *b.* 1923, *s.* 1943, *m.* | Viscount Windsor, *b.* 1951 |
| 1785 | *Portarlington (7th)*, George Lionel Yuill Seymour Dawson-Damer, *b.* 1938, *s.* 1959, *m.* | Viscount Carlow, *b.* 1965 |
| 1689 | *Portland (12th)*, Count Timothy Charles Robert Noel Bentinck, *b.* 1953, *s.* 1997, *m.* | Viscount Woodstock, *b.* 1984 |
| 1743 | *Portsmouth (10th)*, Quentin Gerard Carew Wallop, *b.* 1954, *s.* 1984, *m.* | Viscount Lymington, *b.* 1981 |

| *Created* | *Title, order of succession, name, etc.* | *Heir* |
|---|---|---|
| 1804 | *Powis (8th) and 9th Irish Baron, Clive*, 1762, John George Herbert, *b.* 1952, *s.* 1993, *m.* | Viscount Clive, *b.* 1979 |
| 1765 | *Radnor (8th)*, Jacob Pleydell-Bouverie, BT, *b.* 1927, *s.* 1968, *m.* | Viscount Folkestone, *b.* 1955 |
| 1831 I.* | *Ranfurly (7th) and 8th UK Baron, Ranfurly*, 1826, Gerald Françoys Needham Knox, *b.* 1929, *s.* 1988, *m.* | Edward J. K., *b.* 1957 |
| 1771 | *Roden (10th)*, Robert John Jocelyn, *b.* 1938, *s.* 1993, *m.* | Viscount Jocelyn, *b.* 1989 |
| 1801 | *Romney (7th)*, Michael Henry Marsham, *b.* 1910, *s.* 1975, *m.* | Julian C. M., *b.* 1948 |
| 1703 S.* | *Rosebery (7th) and 3rd UK Earl Midlothian*, 1911, Neil Archibald Primrose, *b.* 1929, *s.* 1974, *m.* | Lord Dalmeny, *b.* 1967 |
| 1806 I. | *Rosse (7th)*, William Brendan Parsons, *b.* 1936, *s.* 1979, *m.* | Lord Oxmantown, *b.* 1969. |
| 1801 | ** *Rosslyn (7th)*, Peter St Clair-Erskine, *b.* 1958, *s.* 1977, *m.* | Lord Loughborough, *b.* 1986 |
| 1457 S. | *Rothes (21st)*, Ian Lionel Malcolm Leslie, *b.* 1932, *s.* 1975, *m.* | Lord Leslie, *b.* 1958 |
| 1861 | °** *Russell (5th)*, Conrad Sebastian Robert Russell, FBA, *b.* 1937, *s.* 1987, *m.* | Viscount Amberley, *b.* 1968 |
| 1915 | ° *St Aldwyn (3rd)*, Michael Henry Hicks Beach, *b.* 1950, *s.* 1992, *m.* | Hon. David S. H. B., *b.* 1955 |
| 1815 | *St Germans (10th)*, Peregrine Nicholas Eliot, *b.* 1941, *s.* 1988 | Lord Eliot, *b.* 1966 |
| 1660 | ** *Sandwich (11th)*, John Edward Hollister Montagu, *b.* 1943, *s.* 1995, *m.* | Viscount Hinchingbrooke, *b.* 1969 |
| 1690 | *Scarbrough (12th) and 13th Irish Visct. Lumley*, 1628, Richard Aldred Lumley, *b.* 1932, *s.* 1969, *m.* | Viscount Lumley, *b.* 1973 |
| 1701 S. | *Seafield (13th)*, Ian Derek Francis Ogilvie-Grant, *b.* 1939, *s.* 1969, *m.* | Viscount Reidhaven, *b.* 1963 |
| 1882 | ** *Selborne (4th)*, John Roundell Palmer, KBE, FRS, *b.* 1940, *s.* 1971, *m.* | Viscount Wolmer, *b.* 1971 |
| 1646 S. | *Selkirk*. Disclaimed for life 1994. (*see* Lord Selkirk of Douglas, page 161) | Hon. John A. D.-H., *b.* 1978 |
| 1672 | *Shaftesbury (10th)*, Anthony Ashley-Cooper, *b.* 1938, *s.* 1961, *m.* | Lord Ashley, *b.* 1977 |
| 1756 I.* | *Shannon (9th) and 8th Brit. Baron Carleton*, 1786, Richard Bentinck Boyle, *b.* 1924, *s.* 1963 | Viscount Boyle, *b.* 1960 |
| 1442 | ** *Shrewsbury and Waterford (22nd) and 7th Engl. Earl Talbot*, 1784, Charles Henry John Benedict Crofton Chetwynd Chetwynd-Talbot, *b.* 1952, *s.* 1980, *m.*, *Premier Earl of England and Ireland* | Viscount Ingestre, *b.* 1978 |
| 1961 | *Snowdon (1st) and Baron Armstrong-Jones (life peerage, 1999)*, Antony Charles Robert Armstrong-Jones, GCVO, *b.* 1930, *m. Constable of Caernarfon Castle* (*see also* page 117) | Viscount Linley, *b.* 1961 |
| 1765 | ° *Spencer (9th)*, Charles Edward Maurice Spencer, *b.* 1964, *s.* 1992 | Viscount Althorp, *b.* 1994 |
| 1703 S.* | *Stair (14th) and 7th UK Baron, Oxenfoord*, 1841, John David James Dalrymple, *b.* 1961, *s.* 1996 | Hon. David H. D., *b.* 1963 |
| 1984 | *Stockton (2nd)*, Alexander Daniel Alan Macmillan, MEP, *b.* 1943, *s.* 1986, *m.* | Viscount Macmillan of Ovenden, *b.* 1974 |
| 1821 | *Stradbroke (6th)*, Robert Keith Rous, *b.* 1937, *s.* 1983, *m.* | Viscount Dunwich, *b.* 1961 |
| 1847 | *Strafford (8th)*, Thomas Edmund Byng, *b.* 1936, *s.* 1984, *m.* | Viscount Enfield, *b.* 1964 |
| 1606 S.* | *Strathmore and Kinghorne (18th) and 16th Scott. Earl, Strathmore, 1677 and 18th Scott. Earl, Kinghorne, 1606 and 5th UK Earl, Strathmore and Kinghorne*, 1937, Michael Fergus Bowes Lyon, *b.* 1957, *s.* 1987, *m.* | Lord Glamis, *b.* 1986 |
| 1603 | *Suffolk (21st) and Berkshire (14th) (1626)*, Michael John James George Robert Howard, *b.* 1935, *s.* 1941, *m.* | Viscount Andover, *b.* 1974 |
| 1955 | *Swinton (2nd)*, David Yarburgh Cunliffe-Lister, *b.* 1937, *s.* 1972, *m.* | Hon. Nicholas J. C.-L., *b.* 1939 |
| 1714 | *Tankerville (10th)*, Peter Grey Bennet, *b.* 1956, *s.* 1980 | Revd the Hon. George A. G. B., *b.* 1925 |
| 1822 | ° *Temple of Stowe (8th)*, (Walter) Grenville Algernon Temple-Gore-Langton, *b.* 1924, *s.* 1988, *m.* | Lord Langton, *b.* 1955 |
| 1815 | *Verulam (7th) and 11th Irish Visct. Grimston, 1719 and 16th Scott. Baron Forrester of Corstorphine*, 1633, John Duncan Grimston, *b.* 1951, *s.* 1973, *m.* | Viscount Grimston, *b.* 1978 |
| 1729 | ° *Waldegrave (13th)*, James Sherbrooke Waldegrave, *b.* 1940, *s.* 1995, *m.* | Viscount Chewton, *b.* 1986 |
| 1759 | *Warwick (9th) and Brooke (9th) (Brit. 1746)*, Guy David Greville, *b.* 1957, *s.* 1996, *m.* | Lord Brooke, *b.* 1982 |
| 1633 S.* | *Wemyss (12th) and March (8th) and 5th UK Baron Wemyss*, 1821, Francis David Charteris, KT, *b.* 1912, *s.* 1937, *m.* | Lord Neidpath, *b.* 1948 |
| 1621 I. | *Westmeath (13th)*, William Anthony Nugent, *b.* 1928, *s.* 1971, *m.* | Hon. Sean C. W. N., *b.* 1965 |
| 1624 | *Westmorland (16th)*, Anthony David Francis Henry Fane, *b.* 1951, *s.* 1993, *m.* | Hon. Harry St C. F., *b.* 1953 |
| 1876 | *Wharncliffe (5th)*, Richard Alan Montagu Stuart Wortley, *b.* 1953, *s.* 1987, *m.* | Viscount Carlton, *b.* 1980 |
| 1801 | *Wilton (8th) and Ebury (1857)*, Francis Egerton Grosvenor, *b.* 1934, *s.* 1999, *m.* | Hon. Julian F. M. G., *b.* 1959 |
| 1628 | *Winchilsea (17th) and Nottingham (12th) (1681)*, Daniel James Hatfield Finch Hatton, *b.* 1967, *s.* 1999, *m.* | Hon. Robin H. F.-H., *b.* 1939 |
| 1766 | ° *Winterton (8th)*, (Donald) David Turnour, *b.* 1943, *s.* 1991, *m.* | Robert C. T., *b.* 1950 |
| 1956 | *Woolton (3rd)*, Simon Frederick Marquis, *b.* 1958, *s.* 1969, *m.* | None |
| 1837 | *Yarborough (8th)*, Charles John Pelham, *b.* 1963, *s.* 1991, *m.* | Lord Worsley, *b.* 1990 |

## COUNTESSES IN THEIR OWN RIGHT

*Style*, The Right Hon. the Countess (of) _
*Husband*, Untitled
*Children's style*, As for children of an Earl
For forms of address, *see* page 135

| *Created* | | *Title, order of succession, name, etc.* | *Heir* |
|---|---|---|---|
| 1643 | S. | *Dysart (11th in line)*, Rosamund Agnes Greaves, *b.* 1914, *s.* 1975 | Lady Katherine Grant of Rothiemurchus, *b.* 1918 |
| 1633 | S. | *Loudoun (13th in line)*, Barbara Huddleston Abney-Hastings, *b.* 1919, *s.* 1960, *m.* | Lord Mauchline, *b.* 1942 |
| c.1115 | S. | ** *Mar (31st in line)*, Margaret of Mar, *b.* 1940, *s.* 1975, *m.*, *Premier Earldom of Scotland* | Mistress of Mar, *b.* 1963 |
| 1947 | | ° *Mountbatten of Burma (2nd in line)*, Patricia Edwina Victoria Knatchbull, CBE, *b.* 1924, *s.* 1979, *m.* | Lord Romsey, *b.* 1947 |
| c.1235 | S. | *Sutherland (24th in line)*, Elizabeth Millicent Sutherland, *b.* 1921, *s.* 1963, *m.* | Lord Strathnaver, *b.* 1947 |

## VISCOUNTS

*Coronet*, Sixteen silver balls
*Style*, The Right Hon. the Viscount _
*Wife's style*, The Right Hon. the Viscountess _
*Children's style*, 'The Hon.' before forename and family name
In Scotland, the heir apparent to a Viscount may be styled 'The Master of _ (title of peer)'
For forms of address, *see* page 135

| *Created* | | *Title, order of succession, name, etc.* | *Heir* |
|---|---|---|---|
| 1945 | | *Addison (4th)*, William Matthew Wand Addison, *b.* 1945, *s.* 1992, *m.* | Hon. Paul W. A., *b.* 1973 |
| 1946 | | *Alanbrooke (3rd)*, Alan Victor Harold Brooke, *b.* 1932, *s.* 1972 | None |
| 1919 | | ** *Allenby (3rd)*, Lt.-Col. Michael Jaffray Hynman Allenby, *b.* 1931, *s.* 1984, *m.* | Hon. Henry J. H. A., *b.* 1968 |
| 1911 | | *Allendale (3rd)*, Wentworth Hubert Charles Beaumont, *b.* 1922, *s.* 1956 | Hon. Wentworth P. I. B., *b.* 1948 |
| 1642 | S. | *Arbuthnott (16th)*, John Campbell Arbuthnott, KT, CBE, DSC, FRSE, *b.* 1924, *s.* 1966, *m.* | Master of Arbuthnott, *b.* 1950 |
| 1751 | I. | *Ashbrook (11th)*, Michael Llowarch Warburton Flower, *b.* 1935, *s.* 1995, *m.* | Hon. Rowland F. W. F., *b.* 1975 |
| 1917 | | ** *Astor (4th)*, William Waldorf Astor, *b.* 1951, *s.* 1966, *m.* | Hon. William W. A., *b.* 1979 |
| 1781 | I. | *Bangor (8th)*, William Maxwell David Ward, *b.* 1948, *s.* 1993, *m.* | Hon. E. Nicholas W., *b.* 1953 |
| 1925 | | *Bearsted (5th)*, Nicholas Alan Samuel, *b.* 1950, *s.* 1996, *m.* | Hon. Harry R. S., *b.* 1988 |
| 1963 | | *Blakenham (2nd)*, Michael John Hare, *b.* 1938, *s.* 1982, *m.* | Hon. Caspar J. H., *b.* 1972 |
| 1935 | | ** *Bledisloe (3rd)*, Christopher Hiley Ludlow Bathurst, QC, *b.* 1934, *s.* 1979 | Hon. Rupert E. L. B., *b.* 1964 |
| 1712 | | *Bolingbroke (7th) and St John (8th) (1716)*, Kenneth Oliver Musgrave St John, *b.* 1927, *s.* 1974 | Hon. Henry F. St J., *b.* 1957 |
| 1960 | | *Boyd of Merton (2nd)*, Simon Donald Rupert Neville Lennox-Boyd, *b.* 1939, *s.* 1983, *m.* | Hon. Benjamin A. L.-B., *b.* 1964 |
| 1717 | I.* | *Boyne (11th) and 5th UK Baron Brancepeth*, 1866, Gustavus Michael Stucley Hamilton-Russell, *b.* 1965, *s.* 1995, *m.* | Brian G. H.-R., *b.* 1940 |
| 1929 | | *Brentford (4th)*, Crispin William Joynson-Hicks, *b.* 1933, *s.* 1983, *m.* | Hon. Paul W. J.-H., *b.* 1971 |
| 1929 | | ** *Bridgeman (3rd)*, Robin John Orlando Bridgeman, *b.* 1930, *s.* 1982, *m.* | Hon. William O. C. B., *b.* 1968 |
| 1868 | | *Bridport (4th) and 7th Duke, Bronte in Sicily, 1799 and 6th Irish Baron Bridport*, 1794, Alexander Nelson Hood, *b.* 1948, *s.* 1969, *m.* | Hon. Peregrine A. N. H., *b.* 1974 |
| 1952 | | ** *Brookeborough (3rd)*, Alan Henry Brooke, *b.* 1952, *s.* 1987, *m.* | Hon. Christopher A. B., *b.* 1954 |
| 1933 | | *Buckmaster (3rd)*, Martin Stanley Buckmaster, OBE, *b.* 1921, *s.* 1974 | Hon. Colin J. B., *b.* 1923 |
| 1939 | | *Caldecote (3rd)*, Piers James Hampden Inskip, *b.* 1947, *s.* 1999, *m.* | Hon. Thomas J. H. I., *b.* 1985 |
| 1941 | | *Camrose (4th)*, Adrian Michael Berry, *s.* 2001, *m.* | Hon. Jonathan W. B., *b.* 1970 |
| 1954 | | *Chandos (3rd) and Baron Lyttelton of Aldershot (life peerage, 2000)* Thomas Orlando Lyttelton, *b.* 1953, *s.* 1980, *m.* | Hon. Oliver A. L., *b.* 1986 |

| *Created* | *Title, order of succession, name, etc.* | *Heir* |
|---|---|---|
| 665 I.* | *Charlemont (14th) and 18th Irish Baron Caulfield of Charlemont*, 1620, John Day Caulfeild, *b.* 1934, *s.* 1985, *m.* | Hon. John D. C., *b.* 1966 |
| 921 | *Chelmsford (4th) and UK Baron Chelmsford*, 1858, Frederic Corin Piers Thesiger, *b.* 1962, *s.* 1999 | To Barony only, Sir Wilfred P. T., KBE, *b.* 1910 |
| 717 I. | *Chetwynd (10th)*, Adam Richard John Casson Chetwynd, *b.* 1935, *s.* 1965, *m.* | Hon. Adam D. C., *b.* 1969 |
| 911 | *Chilston (4th)*, Alastair George Akers-Douglas, *b.* 1946, *s.* 1982, *m.* | Hon. Oliver I. A.-D., *b.* 1973 |
| 902 | *Churchill (3rd) and 5th UK Baron Churchill*, 1815, Victor George Spencer, *b.* 1934, *s.* 1973 | To Barony only, Richard H. R. S., *b.* 1926 |
| 718 | *Cobham (11th) and 8th Irish Baron Westcote*, 1776, John William Leonard Lyttelton, *b.* 1943, *s.* 1977, *m.* | Hon. Christopher C. L., *b.* 1947 |
| 1902 | ** *Colville of Culross (4th) and 13th Scott. Baron Colville of Culcross*, 1604, John Mark Alexander Colville, QC, *b.* 1933, *s.* 1945, *m.* | Master of Colville, *b.* 1959 |
| 1826 | *Combermere (6th)*, Thomas Robert Wellington Stapleton-Cotton, *s.* 2001 | Hon. David P. D., *b.* 1932 |
| 1917 | *Cowdray (4th) and 4th UK Baron Cowdray*, 1910, Michael Orlando Weetman Pearson, *b.* 1944, *s.* 1995, *m.* | Hon. Peregrine J. D. P., *b.* 1994 |
| 1927 | ** *Craigavon (3rd)*, Janric Fraser Craig, *b.* 1944, *s.* 1974 | None |
| 1886 | *Cross (3rd)*, Assheton Henry Cross, *b.* 1920, *s.* 1932 | None |
| 1943 | *Daventry (4th)*, James Edward FitzRoy Newdegate, *b.* 1960, *s.* 2000, *m.* | Hon. Humphrey J. F. N., *b.* 1995 |
| 1937 | *Davidson (2nd)*, John Andrew Davidson, *b.* 1928, *s.* 1970, *m.* | Hon. Malcolm W. M. D., *b.* 1934 |
| 1956 | *De L'Isle (2nd) and 7th UK Baron de L'Isle and Dudley*, 1835, Philip John Algernon Sidney, MBE, *b.* 1945, *s.* 1991, *m.* | Hon. Philip W. E. S., *b.* 1985 |
| 1776 I.* | *De Vesci (7th) and 8th Irish Baron Knapton*, 1750, Thomas Eustace Vesey, *b.* 1955, *s.* 1983, *m.* | Hon. Oliver I. V., *b.* 1991 |
| 1917 | *Devonport (3rd)*, Terence Kearley, *b.* 1944, *s.* 1973 | Chester D. H. K., *b.* 1932 |
| 1964 | *Dilhorne (2nd)*, John Mervyn Manningham-Buller, *b.* 1932, *s.* 1980, *m.* | Hon. James E. M.-B., *b.* 1956 |
| 1622 I. | *Dillon (22nd)*, Henry Benedict Charles Dillon, *b.* 1973, *s.* 1982 | Hon. Richard A. L. D., *b.* 1948 |
| 1785 I. | *Doneraile (10th)*, Richard Allen St Leger, *b.* 1946, *s.* 1983, *m.* | Hon. Nathaniel W. R. St J. St L., *b.* 1971 |
| 1680 I.* | *Downe (11th) and 4th UK Baron Dawnay*, 1897, John Christian George Dawnay, *b.* 1935, *s.* 1965, *m.* | Hon. Richard H. D., *b.* 1967 |
| 1959 | *Dunrossil (3rd)*, Andrew William Reginald Morrison, *b.* 1953, *s.* 2000, *m.* | Hon. Callum A. B. M., *b.* 1994 |
| 1964 | *Eccles (2nd)*, John Dawson Eccles, CBE, *b.* 1931, *s.* 1999, *m.* | Hon. William D. E., *b.* 1960 |
| 1897 | *Esher (4th)*, Lionel Gordon Baliol Brett, CBE, *b.* 1913, *s.* 1963, *m.* | Hon. Christopher L. B. B., *b.* 1936 |
| 1816 | *Exmouth (10th)*, Paul Edward Pellew, *b.* 1940, *s.* 1970, *m.* | Hon. Edward F. P., *b.* 1978 |
| 1620 S. | ** *Falkland (15th)*, Lucius Edward William Plantagenet Cary, *b.* 1935, *s.* 1984, *m.*, *Premier Scottish Viscount on the Roll* | Master of Falkland, *b.* 1963 |
| 1720 | *Falmouth (9th) and 26th Engl. Baron Le Despencer*, 1264, George Hugh Boscawen, *b.* 1919, *s.* 1962, *m.* | Hon. Evelyn A. H. B., *b.* 1955 |
| 1720 I.* | *Gage (8th) and 7th Brit. Baron Gage*, 1790, (Henry) Nicolas Gage, *b.* 1934, *s.* 1993, *m.* | Hon. Henry W. G., *b.* 1975 |
| 1727 I. | *Galway (12th)*, George Rupert Monckton-Arundell, *b.* 1922, *s.* 1980, *m.* | Hon. J. Philip M., *b.* 1952 |
| 1478 I.* | *Gormanston (17th) and 5th UK Baron Gormanston*, 1868, Jenico Nicholas Dudley Preston, *b.* 1939, *s.* 1940, *w.*, *Premier Viscount of Ireland* | Hon. Jenico F. T. P., *b.* 1974 |
| 1816 I. | *Gort (9th)*, Foley Robert Standish Prendergast Vereker, *b.* 1951, *s.* 1995, *m.* | Hon. Robert F. P. V., *b.* 1993 |
| 1900 | ** *Goschen (4th)*, Giles John Harry Goschen, *b.* 1965, *s.* 1977, *m.* | John A. G., *b.* 1992 |
| 1849 | *Gough (5th)*, Shane Hugh Maryon Gough, *b.* 1941, *s.* 1951 | None |
| 1937 | *Greenwood (3rd)*, Michael George Hamar Greenwood, *b.* 1923, *s.* 1998 | None |
| 1929 | *Hailsham*. Disclaimed for life 1963 (*see* Lord Hailsham of St Marylebone, page 159) | Rt. Hon. Douglas M. Hogg, QC, MP, *b.* 1945 |
| 1891 | *Hambleden (4th)*, William Herbert Smith, *b.* 1930, *s.* 1948, *m.* | Hon. William H. B. S., *b.* 1955 |
| 1884 | *Hampden (6th)*, Anthony David Brand, *b.* 1937, *s.* 1975, *m.* | Hon. Francis A. B., *b.* 1970 |
| 1936 | *Hanworth (3rd)*, David Stephen Geoffrey Pollock, *b.* 1946, *s.* 1996, *m.* | Hon. Richard C. S. P., *b.* 1951 |
| 1791 I. | *Harberton (10th)*, Thomas de Vautort Pomeroy, *b.* 1910, *s.* 1980, *w.* | Henry R. P., *b.* 1958 |
| 1846 | *Hardinge (6th)*, Charles Henry Nicholas Hardinge, *b.* 1956, *s.* 1984, *m.* | Hon. Andrew H. H., *b.* 1960 |
| 1791 I. | *Hawarden (9th)*, (Robert) Connan Wyndham Leslie Maude, *b.* 1961, *s.* 1991, *m.* | Hon. Varian J. C. E. M., *b.* 1997 |
| 1960 | *Head (2nd)*, Richard Antony Head, *b.* 1937, *s.* 1983, *m.* | Hon. Henry J. H., *b.* 1980 |
| 1550 | *Hereford (18th)*, Robert Milo Leicester Devereux, *b.* 1932, *s.* 1952, *Premier Viscount of England* | Hon. Charles R. de B. D., *b.* 1975 |
| 1842 | *Hill (8th)*, Antony Rowland Clegg-Hill, *b.* 1931, *s.* 1974, *m.* | Peter D. R. C. C.-H., *b.* 1945 |
| 1796 | *Hood (8th) and 7th Irish Baron, Hood* 1782, Henry Lyttleton Alexander Hood, *b.* 1958, *s.* 1999, *m.* | Hon. Archibald L. S. H., *b.* 1993 |
| 1956 | *Ingleby (2nd)*, Martin Raymond Peake, *b.* 1926, *s.* 1966, *w.* | None |
| 1945 | *Kemsley (3rd)*, Richard Gomer Berry, *b.* 1951, *s.* 1999, *m.* | Hon. Edward A. M., *b.* 1960 |
| 1911 | *Knollys (3rd)*, David Francis Dudley Knollys, *b.* 1931, *s.* 1966, *m.* | Hon. Patrick N. M. K., *b.* 1962 |

| *Created* | *Title, order of succession, name, etc.* | *Heir* |
|---|---|---|
| 1895 | *Knutsford (6th)*, Michael Holland-Hibbert, *b.* 1926, *s.* 1986, *m.* | Hon. Henry T. H.-H., *b.* 1959 |
| 1954 | *Leathers (3rd)*, Christopher Graeme Leathers, *b.* 1941, *s.* 1996, *m.* | Hon. James F. L., *b.* 1969 |
| 1781 I. | *Lifford (9th)*, (Edward) James Wingfield Hewitt, *b.* 1949, *s.* 1987, *m.* | Hon. James T. W. H., *b.* 1979 |
| 1921 | *Long (4th)*, Richard Gerard Long, CBE, *b.* 1929, *s.* 1967, *m.* | Hon. James R. L., *b.* 1960 |
| 1957 | *Mackintosh of Halifax (3rd)*, (John) Clive Mackintosh, *b.* 1958, *s.* 1980, *m.* | Hon. Thomas H. G. M., *b.* 198 |
| 1955 | *Malvern (3rd)*, Ashley Kevin Godfrey Huggins, *b.* 1949, *s.* 1978 | Hon. M. James H., *b.* 1928 |
| 1945 | *Marchwood (3rd)*, David George Staveley Penny, *b.* 1936, *s.* 1979, *w.* | Hon. Peter G. W. P., *b.* 1965 |
| 1942 | *Margesson (2nd)*, Francis Vere Hampden Margesson, *b.* 1922, *s.* 1965, *m.* | Capt. Hon. Richard F. D. M., *b.* 1960 |
| 1660 I.* | *Massereene (14th) and Ferrard (7th) (1797) and 7th UK Baron, Oriel*, 1821, John David Clotworthy Whyte-Melville Foster Skeffington, *b.* 1940, *s.* 1992, *m.* | Hon. Charles J. C. W.-M. F. S *b.* 1973 |
| 1802 | *Melville (9th)*, Robert David Ross Dundas, *b.* 1937, *s.* 1971, *m.* | Hon. Robert H. K. D., *b.* 1984 |
| 1916 | *Mersey (4th) and 13th Scott. Lord Nairne, 1681 s. 1995*, Richard Maurice Clive Bigham, *b.* 1934, *s.* 1979, *m.* | Master of Nairne, *b.* 1966 |
| 1717 I.* | *Midleton (12th) and 9th Brit. Baron Brodrick of Peper Harow*, 1796, Alan Henry Brodrick, *b.* 1949, *s.* 1988, *m.* | Hon. Ashley R. B., *b.* 1980 |
| 1962 | *Mills (3rd)*, Christopher Philip Roger Mills, *b.* 1956, *s.* 1988, *m.* | None |
| 1716 I. | *Molesworth (12th)*, Robert Bysse Kelham Molesworth, *b.* 1959, *s.* 1997 | Hon. William J. C. M., *b.* 1960 |
| 1801 I.* | *Monck (7th) and 4th UK Baron, Monck*, 1866, Charles Stanley Monck, *b.* 1953, *s.* 1982. Does not use title. | Hon. George S. M., *b.* 1957 |
| 1957 | *Monckton of Brenchley (2nd)*, Maj.-Gen. Gilbert Walter Riversdale Monckton, CB, OBE, MC, *b.* 1915, *s.* 1965, *m.* | Hon. Christopher W. M., *b.* 1952 |
| 1946 | *Montgomery of Alamein (2nd)*, David Bernard Montgomery, CBE, *b.* 1928, *s.* 1976, *m.* | Hon. Henry D. M., *b.* 1954 |
| 1550 I.* | *Mountgarret (17th) and 4th UK Baron Mountgarret*, 1911, Richard Henry Piers Butler, *b.* 1936, *s.* 1966, *m.* | Hon. Piers J. R. B., *b.* 1961 |
| 1952 | *Norwich (2nd)*, John Julius Cooper, CVO, *b.* 1929, *s.* 1954, *m.* | Hon. Jason C. D. B. C., *b.* 1959 |
| 1651 S.** | *of Oxfuird (13th)*, George Hubbard Makgill, CBE, *b.* 1934, *s.* 1986, *m.* | Master of Oxfuird, *b.* 1969 |
| 1873 | *Portman (10th)*, Christopher Edward Berkeley Portman, *b.* 1958, *s.* 1999, *m.* | Hon. Luke O. B. P., *b.* 1984 |
| 1743 I.* | *Powerscourt (10th) and 4th UK Baron Powerscourt*, 1885, Mervyn Niall Wingfield, *b.* 1935, *s.* 1973, *m.* | Hon. Mervyn A. W., *b.* 1963 |
| 1900 | *Ridley (4th)*, Matthew White Ridley, KG, GCVO, TD, *b.* 1925, *s.* 1964, *m.*, *Lord Steward* | Hon. Matthew W. R., *b.* 1958 |
| 1960 | *Rochdale (2nd)*, St John Durival Kemp, *b.* 1938, *s.* 1993, *m.* | Hon. Jonathan H. D. K., *b.* 196 |
| 1919 | *Rothermere (4th)*, (Harold) Jonathan Esmond Vere Harmsworth, *b.* 1967, *s.* 1998, *m.* | Hon. Esmond V. H., *b.* 1967 |
| 1937 | *Runciman of Doxford (3rd) and 4th UK Baron, Runciman*, 1933, Walter Garrison Runciman (Garry), CBE, FBA, *b.* 1934, *s.* 1989, *m.* | Hon. David W. R., *b.* 1967 |
| 1918 | ** *St Davids (3rd) and 20th Engl. Baron Strange of Knokin, 1299 and 8th Engl. Baron, Hungerford, 1426 and Baron De Moleyns*, 1445, Colwyn Jestyn John Philipps, *b.* 1939, *s.* 1991, *m.* | Hon. Rhodri C. P., *b.* 1966 |
| 1801 | *St Vincent (7th)*, Ronald George James Jervis, *b.* 1905, *s.* 1940, *m.* | Hon. Edward R. J. J., *b.* 1951 |
| 1937 | *Samuel (3rd)*, David Herbert Samuel, OBE, PH.D., *b.* 1922, *s.* 1978, *m.* | Hon. Dan J. S., *b.* 1925 |
| 1911 | *Scarsdale (3rd) and 7th Brit. Baron Scarsdale*, 1761, Francis John Nathaniel Curzon, *b.* 1924, *s.* 1977, *m.* | Hon. Peter G. N. C., *b.* 1949 |
| 1905 | *Selby (5th)*, Edward Thomas William Gully, *b.* 1967, *s.* 1997, *m.* | Hon. Christopher R. T. G., *b.* 1993 |
| 1805 | *Sidmouth (7th)*, John Tonge Anthony Pellew Addington, *b.* 1914, *s.* 1976, *m.* | Hon. Jeremy F. A., *b.* 1947 |
| 1940 | ** *Simon (3rd)*, Jan David Simon, *b.* 1940, *s.* 1993, *m.* | None |
| 1960 | ** *Slim (2nd)*, John Douglas Slim, OBE, *b.* 1927, *s.* 1970, *m.* | Hon. Mark W. R. S., *b.* 1960 |
| 1954 | *Soulbury (2nd)*, James Herwald Ramsbotham, *b.* 1915, *s.* 1971, *w.* | Hon. Sir Peter E. R., GCMG, GCVO, *b.* 1919 |
| 1776 I. | *Southwell (7th)*, Pyers Anthony Joseph Southwell, *b.* 1930, *s.* 1960, *m.* | Hon. Richard A. P. S., *b.* 1956 |
| 1942 | *Stansgate*, Rt. Hon. Anthony Neil Wedgwood Benn, *b.* 1925, *s.* 1960, *m.* Disclaimed for life 1963. | Stephen M. W. B., *b.* 1951 |
| 1959 | *Stuart of Findhorn (3rd)*, James Dominic Stuart, *b.* 1948, *s.* 1999, *m.* | Hon. Andrew M. S., *b.* 1957 |
| 1957 | ** *Tenby (3rd)*, William Lloyd George, *b.* 1927, *s.* 1983, *m.* | Hon. Timothy H. G. L. G., *b.* 1962 |
| 1952 | *Thurso (3rd)*, John Archibald Sinclair, *b.* 1953, *s.* 1995, *m.* | Hon. James A. R. S., *b.* 1984 |
| 1721 | *Torrington (11th)*, Timothy Howard St George Byng, *b.* 1943, *s.* 1961, *m.* | John L. B., MC, *b.* 1919 |
| 1936 | *Trenchard (3rd)*, Hugh Trenchard, *b.* 1951, *s.* 1987, *m.* | Hon. Alexander T. T., *b.* 1978 |
| 1921 | *Ullswater (2nd)*, Nicholas James Christopher Lowther, PC, *b.* 1942, *s.* 1949, *m.* | Hon. Benjamin J. L., *b.* 1975 |
| 1621 I. | *Valentia (15th)*, Richard John Dighton Annesley, *b.* 1929, *s.* 1983, *m.* | Hon. Francis W. D. A., *b.* 1959 |
| 1952 | ** *Waverley (3rd)*, John Desmond Forbes Anderson, *b.* 1949, *s.* 1990 | Hon. Forbes A. R. A., *b.* 1996 |
| 1938 | *Weir (3rd)*, William Kenneth James Weir, *b.* 1933, *s.* 1975, *m.* | Hon. James W. H. W., *b.* 1965 |

| Created | Title, order of succession, name, etc. | Heir |
|---|---|---|
| 1918 | *Wimborne (4th) and 5th UK Baron Wimborne*, 1880, Ivor Mervyn Vigors Guest, *b.* 1968, *s.* 1993 | Hon. Julien J. G., *b.* 1945 |
| 1923 | *Younger of Leckie (4th) and Baron Younger of Prestwick (life peerage, 1992)*, George Kenneth Hotson Younger, KT, KCVO, TD, PC, *b.* 1931, *s.* 1997, *m.* | Hon. James E. G. Y., *b.* 1955 |

## BARONS/LORDS

*Coronet*, Six silver balls
*Style*, The Right Hon. the Lord _ . In the Peerage of Scotland there is no rank of Baron; the equivalent rank is Lord of Parliament (*see* page 136) and Scottish peers should always be styled 'Lord', never 'Baron'
*Wife's style*, The Right Hon. the Lady _
*Children's style*, 'The Hon.' before forename and family name
In Scotland, the heir apparent to a Lord may be styled 'The Master of _ (title of peer)'
For forms of address, *see* page 135

| Created | Title, order of succession, name, etc. | Heir |
|---|---|---|
| 1911 | *Aberconway (3rd)*, Charles Melville McLaren, *b.* 1913, *s.* 1953, *m.* | Hon. H. Charles M., *b.* 1948 |
| 1873 | ** *Aberdare (4th)*, Morys George Lyndhurst Bruce, KBE, PC, *b.* 1919, *s.* 1957, *m.* | Hon. Alastair J. L. B., *b.* 1947 |
| 1835 | *Abinger (8th)*, James Richard Scarlett, *b.* 1914, *s.* 1943, *m.* | Hon. James H. S., *b.* 1959 |
| 1869 | *Acton (4th) and Baron Acton of Bridgnorth (life peerage, 2000)*, Richard Gerald Lyon-Dalberg-Acton, *b.* 1941, *s.* 1989, *m.* | Hon. John C. F. H. L.-D.-A., *b.* 1966 |
| 1887 | ** *Addington (6th)*, Dominic Bryce Hubbard, *b.* 1963, *s.* 1982 | Hon. Michael W. L. H., *b.* 1965 |
| 1896 | *Aldenham (6th) and Hunsdon of Hunsdon (4th) (1923)*, Vicary Tyser Gibbs, *b.* 1948, *s.* 1986, *m.* | Hon. Humphrey W. F. G., *b.* 1989 |
| 1962 | *Aldington (2nd)*, Charles Harold Stuart Low, *b.* 1948, *s.* 2001, *m.* | Hon. Philip T. A. L., *b.* 1990 |
| 1945 | *Altrincham*. John Edward Poynder Grigg, *b.* 1924, *s.* 1955, *m.* Disclaimed for life 1963. | Hon. Anthony U. D. D. G.., *b.* 1934 |
| 1929 | *Alvingham (2nd)*, Maj.-Gen. Robert Guy Eardley Yerburgh, CBE, *b.* 1926, *s.* 1955, *m.* | Capt. Hon. Robert R. G. Y., *b.* 1956 |
| 1892 | *Amherst of Hackney (4th)*, William Hugh Amherst Cecil, *b.* 1940, *s.* 1980, *m.* | Hon. H. William A. C., *b.* 1968 |
| 1881 | ** *Ampthill (4th)*, Geoffrey Denis Erskine Russell, CBE, PC, *b.* 1921, *s.* 1973 | Hon. David W. E. R., *b.* 1947 |
| 1947 | *Amwell (3rd)*, Keith Norman Montague, *b.* 1943, *s.* 1990, *m.* | Hon. Ian K. M., *b.* 1973 |
| 1863 | *Annaly (6th)*, Luke Richard White, *b.* 1954, *s.* 1990, *m.* | Hon. Luke H. W., *b.* 1990 |
| 1885 | *Ashbourne (4th)*, Edward Barry Greynville Gibson, *b.* 1933, *s.* 1983, *m.* | Hon. Edward C. d'O. G., *b.* 1967 |
| 1835 | *Ashburton (7th)*, John Francis Harcourt Baring, KG, KCVO, *b.* 1928, *s.* 1991, *m.* | Hon. Mark F. R. B., *b.* 1958 |
| 1892 | *Ashcombe (4th)*, Henry Edward Cubitt, *b.* 1924, *s.* 1962, *m.* | Mark E. C., *b.* 1964 |
| 1911 | *Ashton of Hyde (3rd)*, Thomas John Ashton, TD, *b.* 1926, *s.* 1983, *m.* | Hon. Thomas H. A., *b.* 1958 |
| 1800 I. | *Ashtown (7th)*, Nigel Clive Crosby Trench, KCMG, *b.* 1916, *s.* 1990, *m.* | Hon. Roderick N. G. T., *b.* 1944 |
| 1956 | ** *Astor of Hever (3rd)*, John Jacob Astor, *b.* 1946, *s.* 1984, *m.* | Hon. Charles G. J. A., *b.* 1990 |
| 1789 I.* | *Auckland (10th) and 10th Brit. Baron Auckland*, 1793, Robert Ian Burnard Eden, *b.* 1962, *s.* 1997, *m.* | Hon. Ronald J. E., *b.* 1931 |
| 1313 | *Audley*. The 25th Lord Audley died in July 1997, leaving three co-heiresses. | |
| 1900 | ** *Avebury (4th)*, Eric Reginald Lubbock, *b.* 1928, *s.* 1971, *m.* | Hon. Lyulph A. J. L., *b.* 1954 |
| 1718 I. | *Aylmer (13th)*, Michael Anthony Aylmer, *b.* 1923, *s.* 1982, *m.* | Hon. A. Julian A., *b.* 1951 |
| 1929 | *Baden-Powell (3rd)*, Robert Crause Baden-Powell, *b.* 1936, *s.* 1962, *m.* | Hon. David M. B.-P., *b.* 1940 |
| 1780 | *Bagot (9th)*, Heneage Charles Bagot, *b.* 1914, *s.* 1979, *m.* | Hon. C. H. Shaun B., *b.* 1944 |
| 1953 | *Baillieu (3rd)*, James William Latham Baillieu, *b.* 1950, *s.* 1973, *m.* | Hon. Robert L. B., *b.* 1979 |
| 1607 S. | *Balfour of Burleigh (8th)*, Robert Bruce, FRSE, *b.* 1927, *s.* 1967, *m.* | Hon. Victoria B., *b.* 1973 |
| 1945 | *Balfour of Inchrye (2nd)*, Ian Balfour, *b.* 1924, *s.* 1988, *m.* | None |
| 1924 | *Banbury of Southam (3rd)*, Charles William Banbury, *b.* 1953, *s.* 1981, *m.* | None |
| 1698 | *Barnard (11th)*, Harry John Neville Vane, TD, *b.* 1923, *s.* 1964 | Hon. Henry F. C. V., *b.* 1959 |
| 1887 | *Basing (5th)*, Neil Lutley Sclater-Booth, *b.* 1939, *s.* 1983, *m.* | Hon. Stuart W. S.-B., *b.* 1969 |
| 1917 | *Beaverbrook (3rd)*, Maxwell William Humphrey Aitken, *b.* 1951, *s.* 1985, *m.* | Hon. Maxwell F. A., *b.* 1977 |
| 1647 S. | *Belhaven and Stenton (13th)*, Robert Anthony Carmichael Hamilton, *b.* 1927, *s.* 1961, *m.* | Master of Belhaven, *b.* 1953 |
| 1848 I. | *Bellew (7th)*, James Bryan Bellew, *b.* 1920, *s.* 1981, *m.* | Hon. Bryan E. B., *b.* 1943 |

| *Created* | *Title, order of succession, name, etc.* | *Heir* |
|---|---|---|
| 1856 | *Belper* (*5th*), Richard Henry Strutt, *b.* 1941, *s.* 1999, *m.* | Michael H. Richard H. S., *b.* 1969 |
| 1938 | *Belstead* (*2nd*) *and Baron Ganzoni* (*life peerage, 1999*), John Julian Ganzoni, PC, *b.* 1932, *s.* 1958 | None |
| 1421 | *Berkeley* (*18th*) *and Baron Gueterbock* (*life peerage, 2000*), Anthony Fitzhardinge Gueterbock, OBE, *b.* 1939, *s.* 1992, *m.* | Hon. Thomas F. G., *b.* 1969 |
| 1922 | *Bethell* (*4th*), Nicholas William Bethell, MEP, *b.* 1938, *s.* 1967, *m.* | Hon. James N. B., *b.* 1967 |
| 1938 | *Bicester* (*3rd*), Angus Edward Vivian Smith, *b.* 1932, *s.* 1968 | Hugh C. V. S., *b.* 1934 |
| 1903 | *Biddulph* (*5th*), (Anthony) Nicholas Colin Maitland Biddulph, *b.* 1959, *s.* 1988, *m.* | Hon. Robert J. M. B., *b.* 1994 |
| 1938 | *Birdwood* (*3rd*), Mark William Ogilvie Birdwood, *b.* 1938, *s.* 1962, *m.* | None |
| 1958 | *Birkett* (*2nd*), Michael Birkett, *b.* 1929, *s.* 1962, *m.* | Hon. Thomas B., *b.* 1982 |
| 1907 | *Blyth* (*4th*), Anthony Audley Rupert Blyth, *b.* 1931, *s.* 1977, *m.* | Hon. Riley A. J. B., *b.* 1955 |
| 1797 | *Bolton* (*8th*), Harry Algar Nigel Orde-Powlett, *b.* 1954, *s.* 2001, *m.* | Hon. Thomas O.-P., *b.* 1979 |
| 1452 S. | *Borthwick* (*24th*), John Hugh Borthwick, *b.* 1940, *s.* 1997, *m.* | Hon. James H. A. B. of Glengelt, *b.* 1940 |
| 1922 | *Borwick* (*4th*), James Hugh Myles Borwick, MC, *b.* 1917, *s.* 1961, *m.* | Hon. Robin S. B., *b.* 1927 |
| 1761 | *Boston* (*10th*), Timothy George Frank Boteler Irby, *b.* 1939, *s.* 1978, *m.* | Hon. George W. E. B. I., *b.* 1971 |
| 1942 | ** *Brabazon of Tara* (*3rd*), Ivon Anthony Moore-Brabazon, *b.* 1946, *s.* 1974, *m.* | Hon. Benjamin R. M.-B., *b.* 1983 |
| 1880 | *Brabourne* (*7th*), John Ulick Knatchbull, CBE, *b.* 1924, *s.* 1943, *m.* | Lord Romsey, *b.* 1947 |
| 1925 | *Bradbury* (*3rd*), John Bradbury, *b.* 1940, *s.* 1994, *m.* | Hon. John B., *b.* 1973 |
| 1962 | *Brain* (*2nd*), Christopher Langdon Brain, *b.* 1926, *s.* 1966, *m.* | Hon. Michael C. B., *b.* 1928 |
| 1938 | *Brassey of Apethorpe* (*3rd*), David Henry Brassey, OBE, *b.* 1932, *s.* 1967, *m.* | Hon. Edward B., *b.* 1964 |
| 1788 | *Braybrooke* (*10th*), Robin Henry Charles Neville, *b.* 1932, *s.* 1990, *m.* | George N., *b.* 1943 |
| 1957 | ** *Bridges* (*2nd*), Thomas Edward Bridges, GCMG, *b.* 1927, *s.* 1969, *m.* | Hon. Mark T. B., *b.* 1954 |
| 1945 | *Broadbridge* (*4th*), Martin Hugh Broadbridge, *b.* 1929, *s.* 2000, *m.* | Hon. Richard J. M. B., *b.* 1959 |
| 1933 | *Brocket* (*3rd*), Charles Ronald George Nall-Cain, *b.* 1952, *s.* 1967, *m.* | Hon. Alexander C. C. N.-C., *b.* 1984 |
| 1860 | ** *Brougham and Vaux* (*5th*), Michael John Brougham, CBE, *b.* 1938, *s.* 1967 | Hon. Charles W. B., *b.* 1971 |
| 1945 | *Broughshane* (*3rd*), (William) Kensington Davison, DSO, DFC, *b.* 1914, *s.* 1995 | None |
| 1776 | *Brownlow* (*7th*), Edward John Peregrine Cust, *b.* 1936, *s.* 1978, *m.* | Hon. Peregrine E. Q. C., *b.* 197 |
| 1942 | *Bruntisfield* (*2nd*), John Robert Warrender, OBE, MC, TD, *b.* 1921, *s.* 1993, *m.* | Hon. Michael J. V. W., *b.* 1949 |
| 1950 | *Burden* (*3rd*), Andrew Philip Burden, *b.* 1959, *s.* 1995 | Hon. Fraser W. E. B., *b.* 1964 |
| 1529 | *Burgh* (*7th*), Alexander Peter Willoughby Leith, *b.* 1935, *s.* 1959, *m.* | Hon. A. Gregory D. L., *b.* 1958 |
| 1903 | ** *Burnham* (*6th*), Hugh John Frederick Lawson, *b.* 1931, *s.* 1993, *m.* | Hon. Harry F. A. L., *b.* 1968 |
| 1897 | *Burton* (*3rd*), Michael Evan Victor Baillie, *b.* 1924, *s.* 1962, *m.* | Hon. Evan M. R. B., *b.* 1949 |
| 1643 | *Byron* (*13th*), Robert James Byron, *b.* 1950, *s.* 1989, *m.* | Hon. Charles R. G. B., *b.* 1990 |
| 1937 | *Cadman* (*3rd*), John Anthony Cadman, *b.* 1938, *s.* 1966, *m.* | Hon. Nicholas A. J. C., *b.* 1977 |
| 1945 | *Calverley* (*3rd*), Charles Rodney Muff, *b.* 1946, *s.* 1971, *m.* | Hon. Jonathan E. M., *b.* 1975 |
| 1383 | *Camoys* (*7th*), (Ralph) Thomas Campion George Sherman Stonor, GCVO, PC, *b.* 1940, *s.* 1976, *m.*, *Lord Chamberlain* | Hon. R. William R. T. S., *b.* 1974 |
| 1715 I. | *Carbery* (*11th*), Peter Ralfe Harrington Evans-Freke, *b.* 1920, *s.* 1970, *m.* | Hon. Michael P. E.-F., *b.* 1942 |
| 1834 I.* | *Carew* (*7th*) *and 7th UK Baron, Carew*, 1838, Patrick Thomas Conolly-Carew, *b.* 1938, *s.* 1994, *m.* | Hon. William P. C.-C., *b.* 1973 |
| 1916 | *Carnock* (*4th*), David Henry Arthur Nicolson, *b.* 1920, *s.* 1982 | Nigel N., MBE, *b.* 1917 |
| 1796 I.* | *Carrington* (*6th*) *and 6th Brit. Baron Carrington, 1797 and Baron Carington of Upton* (*life peerage, 1999*), Peter Alexander Rupert Carington, KG, GCMG, CH, MC, PC, *b.* 1919, *s.* 1938, *m.* | Hon. Rupert F. J. C., *b.* 1948 |
| 1812 | *Castlemaine* (*8th*), Roland Thomas John Handcock, MBE, *b.* 1943, *s.* 1973, *m.* | Hon. Ronan M. E. H., *b.* 1989 |
| 1936 | *Catto* (*3rd*), Innes Gordon Catto, *b.* 1950, *s.* 2001, *m.* | † |
| 1918 | *Cawley* (*4th*), John Francis Cawley, *b.* 1946, *s.* 2001, *m.* | Hon. William R. H. C., *b.* 1981 |
| 1603 | *Cecil.* A subsidiary title of the Marquess of Salisbury. His heir Viscount Cranborne, was given a Writ in Acceleration in this title to enable him to sit in the House of Lords whilst his father is still alive (*see also* page 139). | |
| 1937 | *Chatfield* (*2nd*), Ernle David Lewis Chatfield, *b.* 1917, *s.* 1967, *m.* | None |
| 1858 | *Chesham* (*6th*), Nicholas Charles Cavendish, *b.* 1941, *s.* 1989, *m.* | Hon. Charles G. C. C., *b.* 1974 |
| 1945 | *Chetwode* (*2nd*), Philip Chetwode, *b.* 1937, *s.* 1950, *m.* | Hon. Roger C., *b.* 1968 |
| 1945 | *Chorley* (*2nd*), Roger Richard Edward Chorley, *b.* 1930, *s.* 1978, *m.* | Hon. Nicholas R. D. C., *b.* 1966 |
| 1858 | *Churston* (*5th*), John Francis Yarde-Buller, *b.* 1934, *s.* 1991, *m.* | Hon. Benjamin F. A. Y.-B., *b.* 1974 |
| 1946 | *Citrine* (*3rd*), Ronald Eric Citrine, *b.* 1919, *s.* 1997, *m.* Does not use title. | None |
| 1800 | *Clanmorris* (*8th*), Simon John Ward Bingham, *b.* 1937, *s.* 1988, *m.* | Robert D. de B. B., *b.* 1942 |

| *reated* | *Title, order of succession, name, etc.* | *Heir* |
|---|---|---|
| 672 | *Clifford of Chudleigh (14th)*, Thomas Hugh Clifford, *b.* 1948, *s.* 1988, *m.* | Hon. Alexander T. H. C., *b.* 1985 |
| 299 | *Clinton (22nd)*, Gerard Nevile Mark Fane Trefusis, *b.* 1934, *m.* Title called out of abeyance 1965. | Hon. Charles P. R. F. T., *b.* 1962 |
| 955 | *Clitheroe (2nd)*, Ralph John Assheton, *b.* 1929, *s.* 1984, *m.* | Hon. Ralph C. A., *b.* 1962 |
| 919 | *Clwyd (3rd)*, (John) Anthony Roberts, *b.* 1935, *s.* 1987, *m.* | Hon. J. Murray R., *b.* 1971 |
| 948 | *Clydesmuir (3rd)*, David Ronald Colville, *b.* 1949, *s.* 1996, *m.* | Hon. Richard C., *b.* 1980 |
| 960 | ** *Cobbold (2nd)*, David Antony Fromanteel Lytton Cobbold, *b.* 1937, *s.* 1987, *m.* | Hon. Henry F. L. C., *b.* 1962 |
| 919 | *Cochrane of Cults (4th)*, (Ralph Henry) Vere Cochrane, *b.* 1926, *s.* 1990, *m.* | Hon. Thomas H. V. C., *b.* 1957 |
| 954 | *Coleraine (2nd)*, (James) Martin (Bonar) Law, *b.* 1931, *s.* 1980, *m.* | Hon. James P. B. L., *b.* 1975 |
| 873 | *Coleridge (5th)*, William Duke Coleridge, *b.* 1937, *s.* 1984, *m.* | Hon. James D. C., *b.* 1967 |
| 946 | *Colgrain (3rd)*, David Colin Campbell, *b.* 1920, *s.* 1973, *m.* | Hon. Alastair C. L. C., *b.* 1951 |
| 917 | ** *Colwyn (3rd)*, (Ian) Anthony Hamilton-Smith, CBE, *b.* 1942, *s.* 1966, *m.* | Hon. Craig P. H.-S., *b.* 1968 |
| 956 | *Colyton (2nd)*, Alisdair John Munro Hopkinson, *b.* 1958, *s.* 1996, *m.* | Hon. James P. M. H., *b.* 1983 |
| 841 | *Congleton (8th)*, Christopher Patrick Parnell, *b.* 1930, *s.* 1967, *m.* | Hon. John P. C. P., *b.* 1959 |
| 927 | *Cornwallis (3rd)*, Fiennes Neil Wykeham Cornwallis, OBE, *b.* 1921, *s.* 1982, *m.* | Hon. F. W. Jeremy C., *b.* 1946 |
| 874 | *Cottesloe (5th)*, Cdr. John Tapling Fremantle, *b.* 1927, *s.* 1994, *m.* | Hon. Thomas F. H. F., *b.* 1966 |
| 929 | *Craigmyle (4th)*, Thomas Columba Shaw, *b.* 1960, *s.* 1998, *m.* | Hon. Alexander F. S., *b.* 1988 |
| 899 | *Cranworth (3rd)*, Philip Bertram Gurdon, *b.* 1940, *s.* 1964, *m.* | Hon. Sacha W. R. G., *b.* 1970 |
| 959 | ** *Crathorne (2nd)*, Charles James Dugdale, *b.* 1939, *s.* 1977, *m.* | Hon. Thomas A. J. D., *b.* 1977 |
| 892 | *Crawshaw (5th)*, David Gerald Brooks, *b.* 1934, *s.* 1997, *m.* | Hon. John P. B., *b.* 1938 |
| 940 | *Croft (3rd)*, Bernard William Henry Page Croft, *b.* 1949, *s.* 1997, *m.* | None |
| 797 I. | *Crofton (7th)*, Guy Patrick Gilbert Crofton, *b.* 1951, *s.* 1989, *m.* | Hon. E. Harry P. C., *b.* 1988 |
| 375 | *Cromwell (7th)*, Godfrey John Bewicke-Copley, *b.* 1960, *s.* 1982, *m.* | Hon. David G. B.-C., *b.* 1997 |
| 947 | *Crook (2nd)*, Douglas Edwin Crook, *b.* 1926, *s.* 1989, *m.* | Hon. Robert D. E. C., *b.* 1955 |
| 914 | *Cunliffe (3rd)*, Roger Cunliffe, *b.* 1932, *s.* 1963, *m.* | Hon. Henry C., *b.* 1962 |
| 927 | *Daresbury (4th)*, Peter Gilbert Greenall, *b.* 1953, *s.* 1996, *m.* | Hon. Thomas E. G., *b.* 1984 |
| 924 | *Darling (2nd)*, Robert Charles Henry Darling, *b.* 1919, *s.* 1936, *m.* | Hon. R. Julian H. D., *b.* 1944 |
| 946 | *Darwen (3rd)*, Roger Michael Davies, *b.* 1938, *s.* 1988, *m.* | Hon. Paul D., *b.* 1962 |
| 932 | *Davies (3rd)*, David Davies, *b.* 1940, *s.* 1944, *m.* | Hon. David D. D., *b.* 1975 |
| 812 I. | *Decies (7th)*, Marcus Hugh Tristram de la Poer Beresford, *b.* 1948, *s.* 1992, *m.* | Hon. Robert M. D. de la P. B., *b.* 1988 |
| 299 | *de Clifford (27th)*, John Edward Southwell Russell, *b.* 1928, *s.* 1982, *m.* | Hon. William S. R., *b.* 1930 |
| 851 | *De Freyne (7th)*, Francis Arthur John French, *b.* 1927, *s.* 1935, *m.* | Hon. Fulke C. A. J. F., *b.* 1957 |
| 821 | *Delamere (5th)*, Hugh George Cholmondeley, *b.* 1934, *s.* 1979, *m.* | Hon. Thomas P. G. C., *b.* 1968 |
| 838 | *de Mauley (6th)*, Gerald John Ponsonby, *b.* 1921, *s.* 1962, *m.* | Hon. Col. Thomas M. P., *b.* 1930 |
| 937 | ** *Denham (2nd)*, Bertram Stanley Mitford Bowyer, KBE, PC, *b.* 1927, *s.* 1948, *m.* | Hon. Richard G. G. B., *b.* 1959 |
| 834 | *Denman (5th)*, Charles Spencer Denman, CBE, MC, TD, *b.* 1916, *s.* 1971, *w.* | Hon. Richard T. S. D., *b.* 1946 |
| 885 | *Deramore (6th)*, Richard Arthur de Yarburgh-Bateson, *b.* 1911, *s.* 1964, *m.* | None |
| 887 | *De Ramsey (4th)*, John Ailwyn Fellowes, *b.* 1942, *s.* 1993, *m.* | Hon. Freddie J. F., *b.* 1978 |
| 264 | *de Ros (28th)*, Peter Trevor Maxwell, *b.* 1958, *s.* 1983, *m.*, *Premier Baron of England* | Hon. Finbar J. M., *b.* 1988 |
| 881 | *Derwent (5th)*, Robin Evelyn Leo Vanden-Bempde-Johnstone, LVO, *b.* 1930, *s.* 1986, *m.* | Hon. Francis P. H. V.-B.-J., *b.* 1965 |
| 831 | *de Saumarez (7th)*, Eric Douglas Saumarez, *b.* 1956, *s.* 1991, *m.* | Hon. Victor T. S., *b.* 1956 |
| 910 | *de Villiers (3rd)*, Arthur Percy de Villiers, *b.* 1911, *s.* 1934 | Hon. Alexander C. de V., *b.* 1940 |
| 1930 | *Dickinson (2nd)*, Richard Clavering Hyett Dickinson, *b.* 1926, *s.* 1943, *m.* | Hon. Martin H. D., *b.* 1961 |
| 1620 I.* | *Digby (12th)*, Edward Henry Kenelm Digby, KCVO, *b.* 1924, *s.* 1964, *m.* | Hon. Henry N. K. D., *b.* 1954 |
| 1765 | *Digby (6th)*, Edward Henry Kenelm Digby, KCVO, *b.* 1924, *m.* | Hon. Henry N. K. D., *b.* 1954 |
| 1615 | *Dormer (17th)*, Geoffrey Henry Dormer, *b.* 1920, *s.* 1995, *m.* | Hon. William R. D., *b.* 1960 |
| 1943 | *Dowding (3rd)*, Piers Hugh Tremenheere Dowding, *b.* 1948, *s.* 1992 | Hon. Mark D. J. D., *b.* 1949 |
| 1800 I. | *Dufferin and Clandeboye*. The 10th Baron died in 1991. Heir had not established his claim to the title at the time of going to press. | Sir John Blackwood, Bt., *b.* 1944 |
| 1929 | *Dulverton (3rd)*, (Gilbert) Michael Hamilton Wills, *b.* 1944, *s.* 1992 | Hon. Robert A. H. W., *b.* 1983 |
| 1800 I. | *Dunalley (7th)*, Henry Francis Cornelius Prittie, *b.* 1948, *s.* 1992, *m.* | Hon. Joel H. P., *b.* 1981 |
| 1324 I. | *Dunboyne (28th)*, Patrick Theobald Tower Butler, VRD, *b.* 1917, *s.* 1945, *m.* | Hon. John F. B., *b.* 1951 |
| 1892 | *Dunleath (6th)*, Brian Henry Mulholland, *b.* 1950, *s.* 1997, *m.* | Hon. Andrew H. M., *b.* 1981 |
| 1439 I. | *Dunsany (20th)*, Edward John Carlos Plunkett, *b.* 1939, *s.* 1999, *m.* | Hon. Randal P., *b.* 1983 |
| 1780 | *Dynevor (9th)*, Richard Charles Uryan Rhys, *b.* 1935, *s.* 1962 | Hon. Hugo G. U. R., *b.* 1966 |
| 1963 | *Egremont (2nd)* and 7th UK Baron Leconfield, 1859, John Max Henry Scawen Wyndham, *b.* 1948, *s.* 1972, *m.* | Hon. George R. V. W., *b.* 1983 |
| 1643 | *Elibank (14th)*, Alan D'Ardis Erskine-Murray, *b.* 1923, *s.* 1973, *w.* | Master of Elibank, *b.* 1964 |

| *Created* | *Title, order of succession, name, etc.* | *Heir* |
|---|---|---|
| 1802 | *Ellenborough (8th)*, Richard Edward Cecil Law, *b.* 1926, *s.* 1945, *m.* | Maj. Hon. Rupert E. H. L., *b.* 1955 |
| 1509 S.* | *Elphinstone (19th)* and 5th UK Baron Elphinstone, 1885, Alexander Mountstuart Elphinstone, *b.* 1980, *s.* 1994 | Hon. Angus J. E., *b.* 1982 |
| 1934 | ** *Elton (2nd)*, Rodney Elton, TD, *b.* 1930, *s.* 1973, *m.* | Hon. Edward P. E., *b.* 1966 |
| 1627 S. | *Fairfax of Cameron (14th)*, Nicholas John Albert Fairfax, *b.* 1956, *s.* 1964, *m.* | Hon. Edward N. T. F., *b.* 1984 |
| 1961 | *Fairhaven (3rd)*, Ailwyn Henry George Broughton, *b.* 1936, *s.* 1973, *m.* | Maj. Hon. James H. A. B., *b.* 1963 |
| 1916 | *Faringdon (3rd)*, Charles Michael Henderson, *b.* 1937, *s.* 1977, *m.* | Hon. James H. H., *b.* 1961 |
| 1756 | *Farnham (12th)*, Barry Owen Somerset Maxwell, *b.* 1931, *s.* 1957, *m.* | Hon. Simon K. M., *b.* 1933 |
| 1856 | *Fermoy (6th)*, Patrick Maurice Burke Roche, *b.* 1967, *s.* 1984, *m.* | Hon. E. Hugh B. R., *b.* 1972 |
| 1826 | *Feversham (6th)*, Charles Antony Peter Duncombe, *b.* 1945, *s.* 1963, *m.* | Hon. Jasper O. S. D., *b.* 1968 |
| 1798 I. | *ffrench (8th)*, Robuck John Peter Charles Mario ffrench, *b.* 1956, *s.* 1986, *m.* | Hon. John C. M. J. F. ff., *b.* 192 |
| 1909 | *Fisher (3rd)*, John Vavasseur Fisher, DSC, *b.* 1921, *s.* 1955, *m.* | Hon. Patrick V. F., *b.* 1953 |
| 1295 | *Fitzwalter (21st)* (Fitzwalter) Brook Plumptre, *b.* 1914, *m.* Title called out of abeyance 1953. | Hon. Julian B. P., *b.* 1952 |
| 1776 | *Foley (8th)*, Adrian Gerald Foley, *b.* 1923, *s.* 1927, *m.* | Hon. Thomas H. F., *b.* 1961 |
| 1445 | *Forbes (22nd)*, Nigel Ivan Forbes, KBE, *b.* 1918, *s.* 1953, *m.*, *Premier Lord of Scotland* | Master of Forbes, *b.* 1946 |
| 1821 | *Forester (8th)* (George Cecil) Brooke Weld-Forester, *b.* 1938, *s.* 1977, *m.* | Hon. C. R. George W.-F., *b.* 1975 |
| 1922 | *Forres (4th)*, Alastair Stephen Grant Williamson, *b.* 1946, *s.* 1978, *m.* | Hon. George A. M. W., *b.* 197 |
| 1917 | *Forteviot (4th)*, John James Evelyn Dewar, *b.* 1938, *s.* 1993, *m.* | Hon. Alexander J. E. D., *b.* 197 |
| 1951 | ** *Freyberg (3rd)*, Valerian Bernard Freyberg, *b.* 1970, *s.* 1993 | None |
| 1917 | *Gainford (3rd)*, Joseph Edward Pease, *b.* 1921, *s.* 1971, *m.* | Hon. George P., *b.* 1926 |
| 1818 | *Garvagh (5th)*, (Alexander Leopold Ivor) George Canning, *b.* 1920, *s.* 1956, *m.* | Hon. Spencer G. S. de R. C., *b.* 1953 |
| 1942 | ** *Geddes (3rd)*, Euan Michael Ross Geddes, *b.* 1937, *s.* 1975, *m.* | Hon. James G. N. G., *b.* 1969 |
| 1876 | *Gerard (5th)*, Anthony Robert Hugo Gerard, *b.* 1949, *s.* 1992, *m.* | Hon. Rupert B. C. G., *b.* 1981 |
| 1824 | *Gifford (6th)*, Anthony Maurice Gifford, QC, *b.* 1940, *s.* 1961, *m.* | Hon. Thomas A. G., *b.* 1967 |
| 1917 | *Gisborough (3rd)*, Thomas Richard John Long Chaloner, *b.* 1927, *s.* 1951, *m.* | Hon. T. Peregrine L. C., *b.* 196 |
| 1960 | *Gladwyn (2nd)*, Miles Alvery Gladwyn Jebb, *b.* 1930, *s.* 1996 | None |
| 1899 | *Glanusk (5th)*, Christopher Russell Bailey, *b.* 1942, *s.* 1997, *m.* | Hon. Charles H. B., *b.* 1976 |
| 1918 | ** *Glenarthur (4th)*, Simon Mark Arthur, *b.* 1944, *s.* 1976, *m.* | Hon. Edward A. A., *b.* 1973 |
| 1911 | *Glenconner (3rd)*, Colin Christopher Paget Tennant, *b.* 1926, *s.* 1983, *m.* | Hon. Cody T., *b.* 1994 |
| 1964 | *Glendevon (2nd)*, Julian John Somerset Hope, *b.* 1950, *s.* 1996 | Hon. Jonathan C. H., *b.* 1952 |
| 1922 | *Glendyne (3rd)*, Robert Nivison, *b.* 1926, *s.* 1967, *m.* | Hon. John N., *b.* 1960 |
| 1939 | ** *Glentoran (3rd)* (Thomas) Robin (Valerian) Dixon, CBE, *b.* 1935, *s.* 1995, *m.* | Hon. Daniel G. D., *b.* 1959 |
| 1909 | *Gorell (4th)*, Timothy John Radcliffe Barnes, *b.* 1927, *s.* 1963, *m.* | Hon. Ronald A. H. B., *b.* 1931 |
| 1953 | *Grantchester (3rd)*, Christopher John Suenson-Taylor, *b.* 1951, *s.* 1995, *m.* | Hon. Jesse D. S.-T., *b.* 1977 |
| 1782 | *Grantley (8th)*, Richard William Brinsley Norton, *b.* 1956, *s.* 1995 | Hon. Francis J. H. N., *b.* 1960 |
| 1794 I. | *Graves (9th)*, Evelyn Paget Graves, *b.* 1926, *s.* 1994, *m.* | Hon. Timothy E. G., *b.* 1960 |
| 1445 S. | *Gray (22nd)*, Angus Diarmid Ian Campbell-Gray, *b.* 1931, *s.* 1946, *m.* | Master of Grey, *b.* 1964 |
| 1950 | *Greenhill (3rd)*, Malcolm Greenhill, *b.* 1924, *s.* 1989 | None |
| 1927 | ** *Greenway (4th)*, Ambrose Charles Drexel Greenway, *b.* 1941, *s.* 1975, *m.* | Hon. Mervyn S. K. G., *b.* 1942 |
| 1902 | *Grenfell (3rd) and Baron Grenfell of Kilvey (life peerage, 2000)*, Julian Pascoe Francis St Leger Grenfell, *b.* 1935, *s.* 1976, *m.* | Francis P. J. G., *b.* 1938 |
| 1944 | *Gretton (4th)*, John Lysander Gretton, *b.* 1975, *s.* 1989 | None |
| 1397 | *Grey of Codnor (6th)*, Richard Henry Cornwall-Legh, *b.* 1936, *s.* 1996, *m.* | Hon. Richard S. C. C.-L., *b.* 1976 |
| 1955 | *Gridley (3rd)*, Richard David Arnold Gridley, *b.* 1956, *s.* 1996, *m.* | Hon. Carl R. G., *b.* 1981 |
| 1964 | *Grimston of Westbury (2nd)*, Robert Walter Sigismund Grimston, *b.* 1925, *s.* 1979, *m.* | Hon. Robert J. S. G., *b.* 1951 |
| 1886 | *Grimthorpe (4th)*, Christopher John Beckett, OBE, *b.* 1915, *s.* 1963, *m.* | Hon. Edward J. B., *b.* 1954 |
| 1945 | *Hacking (3rd)*, Douglas David Hacking, *b.* 1938, *s.* 1971, *m.* | Hon. Douglas F. H., *b.* 1968 |
| 1950 | *Haden-Guest (5th)*, Christopher Haden-Guest, *b.* 1948, *s.* 1996, *m.* | Hon. Nicholas H.-G., *b.* 1951 |
| 1886 | *Hamilton of Dalzell (4th)*, James Leslie Hamilton, *b.* 1938, *s.* 1990, *m.* | Hon. Gavin G. H., *b.* 1968 |
| 1874 | *Hampton (6th)*, Richard Humphrey Russell Pakington, *b.* 1925, *s.* 1974, *m.* | Hon. John H. A. P., *b.* 1964 |
| 1939 | *Hankey (3rd)*, Donald Robin Alers Hankey, *b.* 1938, *s.* 1996, *m.* | Hon. Alexander M. A. H., *b.* 1947 |
| 1958 | *Harding of Petherton (2nd)*, John Charles Harding, *b.* 1928, *s.* 1989, *m.* | Hon. William A. J. H., *b.* 1969 |
| 1910 | *Hardinge of Penshurst (4th)*, Julian Alexander Hardinge, *b.* 1945, *s.* 1997 | Hon. Hugh F. H., *b.* 1948 |
| 1876 | *Harlech (6th)*, Francis David Ormsby-Gore, *b.* 1954, *s.* 1985, *m.* | Hon. Jasset D. C. O.-G., *b.* 198 |

| Created | *Title, order of succession, name, etc.* | *Heir* |
|---|---|---|
| 1939 | *Harmsworth (3rd)*, Thomas Harold Raymond Harmsworth, *b.* 1939, *s.* 1990, *m.* | Hon. Dominic M. E. H., *b.* 1973 |
| 1815 | *Harris (8th)*, Anthony Harris, *b.* 1942, *s.* 1996, *m.* | Anthony J. T. H., *b.* 1915 |
| 1954 | *Harvey of Tasburgh (2nd)*, Peter Charles Oliver Harvey, *b.* 1921, *s.* 1968, *w.* | Charles J. G. H., *b.* 1951 |
| 1295 | *Hastings (22nd)*, Edward Delaval Henry Astley, *b.* 1912, *s.* 1956, *m.* | Hon. Delaval T. H. A., *b.* 1960 |
| 1835 | *Hatherton (8th)*, Edward Charles Littleton, *b.* 1950, *s.* 1985, *m.* | Hon. Thomas E. L., *b.* 1977 |
| 1776 | *Hawke (11th)*, Edward George Hawke, TD, *b.* 1950, *s.* 1992, *m.* | Hon. William M. T. H., *b.* 1995 |
| 1927 | *Hayter (3rd)*, George Charles Hayter Chubb, KCVO, CBE, *b.* 1911, *s.* 1967, *m.* | Hon. G. William M. C., *b.* 1943 |
| 1945 | *Hazlerigg (2nd)*, Arthur Grey Hazlerigg, MC, TD, *b.* 1910, *s.* 1949, *w.* | Hon. Arthur G. H., *b.* 1951 |
| 1943 | *Hemingford (3rd)* (Dennis) Nicholas Herbert, *b.* 1934, *s.* 1982, *m.* | Hon. Christopher D. C. H., *b.* 1973 |
| 1906 | *Hemphill (5th)*, Peter Patrick Fitzroy Martyn Martyn-Hemphill, *b.* 1928, *s.* 1957, *m.* | Hon. Charles A. M. M.-H., *b.* 1954 |
| 1799 I.* | ** *Henley (8th) and 6th UK Baron Northington*, 1885, Oliver Michael Robert Eden, *b.* 1953, *s.* 1977, *m.* | Hon. John W. O. E., *b.* 1988 |
| 1800 I.* | *Henniker (8th)* and 4th UK Baron Hartismere, 1866, John Patrick Edward Chandos Henniker-Major, KCMG, CVO, MC, *b.* 1916, *s.* 1980, *m.* | Hon. Mark I. P. C. H.-M., *b.* 1947 |
| 1886 | *Herschell (3rd)*, Rognvald Richard Farrer Herschell, *b.* 1923, *s.* 1929, *m.* | None |
| 1935 | *Hesketh (3rd)*, Thomas Alexander Fermor-Hesketh, KBE, PC, *b.* 1950, *s.* 1955, *m.* | Hon. Frederick H. F.-H., *b.* 1988 |
| 1828 | *Heytesbury (6th)*, Francis William Holmes à Court, *b.* 1931, *s.* 1971, *m.* | Hon. James W. H. à. C., *b.* 1967 |
| 1886 | *Hindlip (6th)*, Charles Henry Allsopp, *b.* 1940, *s.* 1993, *m.* | Hon. Henry W. A., *b.* 1973 |
| 1950 | *Hives (3rd)*, Matthew Peter Hives, *b.* 1971, *s.* 1997 | Hon. Michael B. H., *b.* 1926 |
| 1912 | *Hollenden (4th)*, Ian Hampden Hope-Morley, *b.* 1946, *s.* 1999, *m.* | Hon. Edward H.-M., *b.* 1981 |
| 1897 | *HolmPatrick (4th)*, Hans James David Hamilton, *b.* 1955, *s.* 1991, *m.* | Hon. Ion H. J. H., *b.* 1956 |
| 1797 I. | *Hotham (8th)*, Henry Durand Hotham, *b.* 1940, *s.* 1967, *m.* | Hon. William B. H., *b.* 1972 |
| 1881 | *Hothfield (6th)*, Anthony Charles Sackville Tufton, *b.* 1939, *s.* 1991, *m.* | Hon. William S. T., *b.* 1977 |
| 1597 | *Howard de Walden (9th)*. The 9th Baron Howard de Walden died in 1999, leaving four co-heiresses. | |
| 1930 | *Howard of Penrith (3rd)*, Philip Esme Howard, *b.* 1945, *s.* 1999, *m.* | Hon. Thomas Philip H., *b.* 1974 |
| 1960 | *Howick of Glendale (2nd)*, Charles Evelyn Baring, *b.* 1937, *s.* 1973, *m.* | Hon. David E. C. B., *b.* 1975 |
| 1796 I. | *Huntingfield (7th)*, Joshua Charles Vanneck, *b.* 1954, *s.* 1994, *m.* | Hon. Gerard C. A. V., *b.* 1985 |
| 1866 | ** *Hylton (5th)*, Raymond Hervey Jolliffe, *b.* 1932, *s.* 1967, *m.* | Hon. William H. M. J., *b.* 1967 |
| 1933 | *Iliffe (3rd)*, Robert Peter Richard Iliffe, *b.* 1944, *s.* 1996, *m.* | Hon. Edward R. I., *b.* 1968 |
| 1543 I. | *Inchiquin (18th)*, Conor Myles John O'Brien, *b.* 1943, *s.* 1982, *m.* | Murrough R. O., *b.* 1910 |
| 1962 | *Inchyra (2nd)*, Robert Charles Reneke Hoyer Millar, *b.* 1935, *s.* 1989, *m.* | Hon. C. James C. H. M., *b.* 1962 |
| 1964 | ** *Inglewood (2nd)* (William) Richard Fletcher-Vane, MEP, *b.* 1951, *s.* 1989, *m.* | Hon. Henry W. F. F.-V., *b.* 1990 |
| 1919 | *Inverforth (4th)*, Andrew Peter Weir, *b.* 1966, *s.* 1982 | Hon. John V. W., *b.* 1935 |
| 1941 | *Ironside (2nd)*, Edmund Oslac Ironside, *b.* 1924, *s.* 1959, *m.* | Hon. Charles E. G. I., *b.* 1956 |
| 1952 | *Jeffreys (3rd)*, Christopher Henry Mark Jeffreys, *b.* 1957, *s.* 1986, *m.* | Hon. Arthur M. H. J., *b.* 1989 |
| 1906 | *Joicey (5th)*, James Michael Joicey, *b.* 1953, *s.* 1993, *m.* | Hon. William J. J., *b.* 1990 |
| 1937 | *Kenilworth (4th)*, (John) Randle Siddeley, *b.* 1954, *s.* 1981, *m.* | Hon. William R. J. S., *b.* 1992 |
| 1935 | *Kennet (2nd)*, Wayland Hilton Young, *b.* 1923, *s.* 1960, *m.* | Hon. W. A. Thoby Y., *b.* 1957 |
| 1776 I.* | *Kensington (8th)*, Hugh Ivor Edwardes, *b.* 1933, *s.* 1981, *m.* | Hon. W. Owen A. E., *b.* 1964 |
| 1886 | *Kensington (5th)*, Hugh Ivor Edwardes, *b.* 1933, *m.* | Hon. W. Owen A. E., *b.* 1964 |
| 1951 | *Kenswood (2nd)*, John Michael Howard Whitfield, *b.* 1930, *s.* 1963, *m.* | Hon. Michael C. W., *b.* 1955 |
| 1788 | *Kenyon (6th)*, Lloyd Tyrell-Kenyon, *b.* 1947, *s.* 1993, *m.* | Hon. Lloyd N. T.-K., *b.* 1972 |
| 1947 | *Kershaw (4th)*, Edward John Kershaw, *b.* 1936, *s.* 1962, *m.* | Hon. John C. E. K., *b.* 1971 |
| 1943 | *Keyes (2nd)*, Roger George Bowlby Keyes, *b.* 1919, *s.* 1945, *m.* | Hon. Charles W. P. K., *b.* 1951 |
| 1909 | *Kilbracken (3rd)*, John Raymond Godley, DSC, *b.* 1920, *s.* 1950 | Hon. Christopher J. G., *b.* 1945 |
| 1900 | *Killanin (4th)* (George) Redmond Fitzpatrick Morris, *b.* 1947, *s.* 1999, *m.* | Luke M. G. M., *b.* 1975 |
| 1943 | *Killearn (3rd)*, Victor Miles George Aldous Lampson, *b.* 1941, *s.* 1996, *m.* | Hon. Miles H. M. L., *b.* 1977 |
| 1789 I. | *Kilmaine (7th)*, John David Henry Browne, *b.* 1948, *s.* 1978, *m.* | Hon. John F. S. B., *b.* 1983 |
| 1831 | *Kilmarnock (7th)*, Alastair Ivor Gilbert Boyd, *b.* 1927, *s.* 1975, *m.* | Hon. Robin J. B., *b.* 1941 |
| 1941 | *Kindersley (3rd)*, Robert Hugh Molesworth Kindersley, *b.* 1929, *s.* 1976, *m.* | Hon. Rupert J. M. K., *b.* 1955 |
| 1223 I. | *Kingsale (35th)*, John de Courcy, *b.* 1941, *s.* 1969, *Premier Baron of Ireland* | Nevinson R. de C., *b.* 1920 |
| 1902 | *Kinross (5th)*, Christopher Patrick Balfour, *b.* 1949, *s.* 1985, *m.* | Hon. Alan I. B., *b.* 1978 |
| 1951 | *Kirkwood (3rd)*, David Harvie Kirkwood, PH.D., *b.* 1931, *s.* 1970, *m.* | Hon. James S. K., *b.* 1937 |
| 1800 I. | *Langford (9th)*, Col. Geoffrey Alexander Rowley-Conwy, OBE, *b.* 1912, *s.* 1953, *m.* | Hon. Owain G. R.-C., *b.* 1958 |
| 1942 | *Latham (2nd)*, Dominic Charles Latham, *b.* 1954, *s.* 1970 | Anthony M. L., *b.* 1954 |
| 1431 | *Latymer (8th)*, Hugo Nevill Money-Coutts, *b.* 1926, *s.* 1987, *m.* | Hon. Crispin J. A. N. M.-C., *b.* 1955 |
| 1869 | *Lawrence (5th)*, David John Downer Lawrence, *b.* 1937, *s.* 1968 | None |
| 1947 | *Layton (3rd)*, Geoffrey Michael Layton, *b.* 1947, *s.* 1989, *m.* | Hon. David L., *b.* 1914 |

| *Created* | | *Title, order of succession, name, etc.* | *Heir* |
|---|---|---|---|
| 1839 | | *Leigh (5th)*, John Piers Leigh, *b.* 1935, *s.* 1979, *m.* | Hon. Christopher D. P. L., *b.* 1960 |
| 1962 | | *Leighton of St Mellons (3rd)*, Robert William Henry Leighton Seager, *b.* 1955, *s.* 1998 | Hon. Simon J. L. S., *b.* 1957 |
| 1797 | | *Lilford (7th)*, George Vernon Powys, *b.* 1931, *s.* 1949, *m.* | Hon. Mark V. P., *b.* 1975 |
| 1945 | | *Lindsay of Birker (3rd)*, James Francis Lindsay, *b.* 1945, *s.* 1994, *m.* | Alexander S. L., *b.* 1940 |
| 1758 I. | | *Lisle (8th)*, Patrick James Lysaght, *b.* 1931, *s.* 1998 | Hon. John N. G. L., *b.* 1960 |
| 1850 | | *Londesborough (9th)*, Richard John Denison, *b.* 1959, *s.* 1968, *m.* | Hon. James F. D., *b.* 1990 |
| 1541 I. | | *Louth (16th)*, Otway Michael James Oliver Plunkett, *b.* 1929, *s.* 1950, *m.* | Hon. Jonathan O. P., *b.* 1952 |
| 1458 S.* | | *Lovat (16th) and 5th UK Baron, Lovat*, 1837, Simon Fraser, *b.* 1977, *s.* 1995 | Hon. Jack F., *b.* 1984 |
| 1946 | | *Lucas of Chilworth (2nd)*, Michael William George Lucas, *b.* 1926, *s.* 1967, *m.* | Hon. Simon W. L., *b.* 1957 |
| 1663 | ** | *Lucas (11th) and Dingwall (14th) (s. 1609)*, Ralph Matthew Palmer, *b.* 1951, *s.* 1991 | Hon. Lewis E. P., *b.* 1987 |
| 1929 | ** | *Luke (3rd)*, Arthur Charles St John Lawson-Johnston, *b.* 1933, *s.* 1996, *m.* | Hon. Ian J. St J. L.-J., *b.* 1963 |
| 1914 | ** | *Lyell (3rd)*, Charles Lyell, *b.* 1939, *s.* 1943 | None |
| 1859 | | *Lyveden (6th)*, Ronald Cecil Vernon, *b.* 1915, *s.* 1973, *m.* | Hon. Jack L. V., *b.* 1938 |
| 1959 | | *MacAndrew (3rd)*, Christopher Anthony Colin MacAndrew, *b.* 1945, *s.* 1989, *m.* | Hon. Oliver C. J. M., *b.* 1983 |
| 1776 I. | | *Macdonald (8th)*, Godfrey James Macdonald of Macdonald, *b.* 1947, *s.* 1970, *m.* | Hon. Godfrey E. H. T. M., *b.* 1982 |
| 1949 | | *Macdonald of Gwaenysgor (2nd)*, Gordon Ramsay Macdonald, *b.* 1915, *s.* 1966, *m.* | None |
| 1937 | | *McGowan (3rd)*, Harry Duncan Cory McGowan, *b.* 1938, *s.* 1966, *m.* | Hon. Harry J. C. M., *b.* 1971 |
| 1922 | | *Maclay (3rd)*, Joseph Paton Maclay, *b.* 1942, *s.* 1969, *m.* | Hon. Joseph P. M., *b.* 1977 |
| 1955 | | *McNair (3rd)*, Duncan James McNair, *b.* 1947, *s.* 1989, *m.* | Hon. William S. A. M., *b.* 1958 |
| 1951 | | *Macpherson of Drumochter (2nd)* (James) Gordon Macpherson, *b.* 1924, *s.* 1965, *m.* | Hon. James A. M., *b.* 1979 |
| 1937 | ** | *Mancroft (3rd)*, Benjamin Lloyd Stormont Mancroft, *b.* 1957, *s.* 1987, *m.* | Hon. Arthur L. S. M., *b.* 1995 |
| 1807 | | *Manners (5th)*, John Robert Cecil Manners, *b.* 1923, *s.* 1972, *m.* | Hon. John H. R. M., *b.* 1956 |
| 1922 | | *Manton (3rd)*, Joseph Rupert Eric Robert Watson, *b.* 1924, *s.* 1968, *m.* | Maj. Hon. Miles R. M. W., *b.* 1958 |
| 1908 | | *Marchamley (4th)*, William Francis Whiteley, *b.* 1968, *s.* 1994 | None |
| 1964 | | *Margadale (2nd)*, James Ian Morrison, TD, *b.* 1930, *s.* 1996, *m.* | Hon. Alastair J. M., *b.* 1958 |
| 1961 | | *Marks of Broughton (3rd)*, Simon Richard Marks, *b.* 1950, *s.* 1998, *m.* | Hon. Michael M., *b.* 1989 |
| 1964 | | *Martonmere (2nd)*, John Stephen Robinson, *b.* 1963, *s.* 1989 | David A. R., *b.* 1965 |
| 1776 I. | | *Massy (9th)*, Hugh Hamon John Somerset Massy, *b.* 1921, *s.* 1958, *m.* | Hon. David H. S. M., *b.* 1947 |
| 1935 | | *May (3rd)*, Michael St John May, *b.* 1931, *s.* 1950, *m.* | Hon. Jasper B. St J. M., *b.* 1965 |
| 1928 | | *Melchett (4th)*, Peter Robert Henry Mond, *b.* 1948, *s.* 1973 | None |
| 1925 | | *Merrivale (3rd)*, Jack Henry Edmond Duke, *b.* 1917, *s.* 1951, *m.* | Hon. Derek J. P. D., *b.* 1948 |
| 1911 | | *Merthyr.* Trevor Oswin Lewis, Bt, CBE, *b.* 1935, *s.* 1977, *m.* Disclaimed for life 1977. | David T. L., *b.* 1977 |
| 1919 | | *Meston (3rd)*, James Meston, *b.* 1950, *s.* 1984, *m.* | Hon. Thomas J. D. M., *b.* 1977 |
| 1838 | ** | *Methuen (7th)*, Robert Alexander Holt Methuen, *b.* 1931, *s.* 1994, *m.* | James P. A. M.-C., *b.* 1952 |
| 1711 | | *Middleton (12th)* (Digby) Michael Godfrey John Willoughby, MC, *b.* 1921, *s.* 1970, *m.* | Hon. Michael C. J. W., *b.* 1948 |
| 1939 | | *Milford (4th)*, Guy Wogan Philipps, *b.* 1961, *s.* 1999, *m.* | Hon. Roland A. P., *b.* 1962 |
| 1933 | | *Milne (2nd)*, George Douglass Milne, TD, *b.* 1909, *s.* 1948, *m.* | Hon. George A. M., *b.* 1941 |
| 1951 | ** | *Milner of Leeds (2nd)*, Arthur James Michael Milner, AE, *b.* 1923, *s.* 1967, *m.* | Hon. Richard J. M., *b.* 1959 |
| 1947 | | *Milverton (2nd)*, Revd Fraser Arthur Richard Richards, *b.* 1930, *s.* 1978, *m.* | Hon. Michael H. R., *b.* 1936 |
| 1873 | | *Moncreiff (5th)*, Harry Robert Wellwood Moncreiff, *b.* 1915, *s.* 1942, *w.* | Hon. Rhoderick H. W. M., *b.* 1954 |
| 1884 | | *Monk Bretton (3rd)*, John Charles Dodson, *b.* 1924, *s.* 1933, *m.* | Hon. Christopher M. D., *b.* 1958 |
| 1885 | | *Monkswell (5th)*, Gerard Collier, *b.* 1947, *s.* 1984, *m.* | Hon. James A. C., *b.* 1977 |
| 1728 | ** | *Monson (11th)*, John Monson, *b.* 1932, *s.* 1958, *m.* | Hon. Nicholas J. M., *b.* 1955 |
| 1885 | ** | *Montagu of Beaulieu (3rd)*, Edward John Barrington Douglas-Scott-Montagu, *b.* 1926, *s.* 1929, *m.* | Hon. Ralph D.-S.-M., *b.* 1961 |
| 1839 | | *Monteagle of Brandon (6th)*, Gerald Spring Rice, *b.* 1926, *s.* 1946, *m.* | Hon. Charles J. S. R., *b.* 1953 |
| 1943 | ** | *Moran (2nd)* (Richard) John (McMoran) Wilson, KCMG, *b.* 1924, *s.* 1977, *m.* | Hon. James M. W., *b.* 1952 |
| 1918 | | *Morris (3rd)*, Michael David Morris, *b.* 1937, *s.* 1975, *m.* | Hon. Thomas A. S. M., *b.* 1982 |
| 1950 | | *Morris of Kenwood (2nd)*, Philip Geoffrey Morris, *b.* 1928, *s.* 1954, *m.* | Hon. Jonathan D. M., *b.* 1968 |
| 1831 | | *Mostyn (5th)*, Roger Edward Lloyd Lloyd-Mostyn, MC, *b.* 1920, *s.* 1965, *m.* | Hon. Llewellyn R. L. L.-M., *b.* 1948 |
| 1933 | | *Mottistone (4th)*, David Peter Seely, CBE, *b.* 1920, *s.* 1966, *m.* | Hon. Peter J. P. S., *b.* 1949 |
| 1945 | | *Mountevans (3rd)*, Edward Patrick Broke Evans, *b.* 1943, *s.* 1974, *m.* | Hon. Jeffrey de C. R. E., *b.* 1948 |

| *Created* | *Title, order of succession, name, etc.* | *Heir* |
|---|---|---|
| 1283 | ** *Mowbray (26th), Segrave (27th) and Stourton (23rd) (1448)*, Charles Edward Stourton, CBE, *b.* 1923, *s.* 1965, *m.* | Hon. Edward W. S. S., *b.* 1953 |
| 1932 | *Moyne (3rd)*, Jonathan Bryan Guinness, *b.* 1930, *s.* 1992, *m.* | Hon. Jasper J. R. G., *b.* 1954 |
| 1929 | ** *Moynihan (4th)* Colin Berkeley Moynihan, *b.* 1955, *s.* 1997, *m.* | Hon. Nicholas E. B. M., *b.* 1994 |
| 1781 I. | *Muskerry (9th)* Robert Fitzmaurice Deane, *b.* 1948, *s.* 1988, *m.* | Hon. Jonathan F. D., *b.* 1986 |
| 1627 S.* | *Napier (14th) and Ettrick (5th) (UK 1872)*, Francis Nigel Napier, KCVO, *b.* 1930, *s.* 1954, *m.* | Master of Napier, *b.* 1962 |
| 1868 | *Napier of Magdala (6th)*, Robert Alan Napier, *b.* 1940, *s.* 1987, *m.* | Hon. James R. N., *b.* 1966 |
| 1940 | *Nathan (2nd)*, Roger Carol Michael Nathan, *b.* 1922, *s.* 1963, *m.* | Hon. Rupert H. B. N., *b.* 1957 |
| 1960 | *Nelson of Stafford (3rd)*, Henry Roy George Nelson, *b.* 1943, *s.* 1995, *m.* | Hon. Alistair W. H. N., *b.* 1973 |
| 1959 | *Netherthorpe (3rd)*, James Frederick Turner, *b.* 1964, *s.* 1982, *m.* | Hon. Andrew J. E. T., *b.* 1993 |
| 1946 | *Newall (2nd)*, Francis Storer Eaton Newall, *b.* 1930, *s.* 1963, *m.* | Hon. Richard H. E. N., *b.* 1961 |
| 1776 I. | *Newborough (8th)*, Robert Vaughan Wynn, *b.* 1949, *s.* 1998, *m.* | Hon. Charles H. R. W., *b.* 1923 |
| 1892 | *Newton (5th)*, Richard Thomas Legh, *b.* 1950, *s.* 1992, *m.* | Hon. Piers R. L., *b.* 1979 |
| 1930 | *Noel-Buxton (3rd)*, Martin Connal Noel-Buxton, *b.* 1940, *s.* 1980, *m.* | Hon. Charles C. N.-B., *b.* 1975 |
| 1957 | *Norrie (2nd)* (George) Willoughby Moke Norrie, *b.* 1936, *s.* 1977, *m.* | Hon. Mark W. J. N., *b.* 1972 |
| 1884 | ** *Northbourne (5th)*, Christopher George Walter James, *b.* 1926, *s.* 1982, *m.* | Hon. Charles W. H. J., *b.* 1960 |
| 1866 | ** *Northbrook (6th)*, Francis Thomas Baring, *b.* 1954, *s.* 1990, *m.* | Peter B., *b.* 1939 |
| 1878 | *Norton (8th)*, James Nigel Arden Adderley, *b.* 1947, *s.* 1993, *m.* | Hon. Edward J. A. A., *b.* 1982 |
| 1950 | *Ogmore (2nd)*, Gwilym Rees Rees-Williams, *b.* 1931, *s.* 1976, *m.* | Hon. Morgan R.-W., *b.* 1937 |
| 1870 | *O'Hagan (4th)*, Charles Towneley Strachey, *b.* 1945, *s.* 1961 | Hon. Richard T. S., *b.* 1950 |
| 1868 | *O'Neill (4th)*, Raymond Arthur Clanaboy O'Neill, TD, *b.* 1933, *s.* 1944, *m.* | Hon. Shane S. C. O'N., *b.* 1965 |
| 1836 I.* | *Oranmore and Browne (4th) and 2nd UK Baron, Mereworth*, 1926, Dominick Geoffrey Edward Browne, *b.* 1901, *s.* 1927, *m.* | Hon. Dominick G. T. B., *b.* 1929 |
| 1933 | ** *Palmer (4th)*, Adrian Bailie Nottage Palmer, *b.* 1951, *s.* 1990, *m.* | Hon. Hugo B. R. P., *b.* 1980 |
| 1914 | *Parmoor (4th)*, (Frederick Alfred) Milo Cripps, *b.* 1929, *s.* 1977 | Michael L. S. C., *b.* 1942 |
| 1937 | *Pender (3rd)*, John Willoughby Denison-Pender, *b.* 1933, *s.* 1965, *m.* | Hon. Henry J. R. D.-P., *b.* 1968 |
| 1866 | *Penrhyn (6th)*, Malcolm Frank Douglas-Pennant, DSO, MBE, *b.* 1908, *s.* 1967, *m.* | Hon. Nigel D.-P., *b.* 1909 |
| 1603 | *Petre (18th)*, John Patrick Lionel Petre, *b.* 1942, *s.* 1989, *m.* | Hon. Dominic W. P., *b.* 1966 |
| 1918 | *Phillimore (5th)*, Francis Stephen Phillimore, *b.* 1944, *s.* 1994, *m.* | Hon. Tristan A. S. P., *b.* 1977 |
| 1945 | *Piercy (3rd)*, James William Piercy, *b.* 1946, *s.* 1981 | Hon. Mark E. P. P., *b.* 1953 |
| 1827 | *Plunket (8th)*, Robin Rathmore Plunket, *b.* 1925, *s.* 1975, *m.* | Hon. Shaun A. F. S. P., *b.* 1931 |
| 1831 | *Poltimore (7th)*, Mark Coplestone Bampfylde, *b.* 1957, *s.* 1978, *m.* | Hon. Henry A. W. B., *b.* 1985 |
| 1690 S. | *Polwarth (10th)*, Henry Alexander Hepburne-Scott, TD, *b.* 1916, *s.* 1944, *m.* | Master of Polwarth, *b.* 1947 |
| 1930 | *Ponsonby of Shulbrede (4th) and Baron Ponsonby of Roehampton (life peerage, 2000)*, Frederick Matthew Thomas Ponsonby, *b.* 1958, *s.* 1990 | None |
| 1958 | *Poole (2nd)*, David Charles Poole, *b.* 1945, *s.* 1993, *m.* | Hon. Oliver J. P., *b.* 1972 |
| 1852 | *Raglan (5th)*, FitzRoy John Somerset, *b.* 1927, *s.* 1964 | Hon. Geoffrey S., *b.* 1932 |
| 1932 | *Rankeillour (4th)*, Peter St Thomas More Henry Hope, *b.* 1935, *s.* 1967 | Michael R. H., *b.* 1940 |
| 1953 | *Rathcavan (3rd)*, Hugh Detmar Torrens O'Neill, *b.* 1939, *s.* 1994, *m.* | Hon. François H. N. O'N., *b.* 1984 |
| 1916 | *Rathcreedan (3rd)*, Christopher John Norton, *b.* 1949, *s.* 1990, *m.* | Hon. Adam G. N., *b.* 1952 |
| 1868 | *Rathdonnell (5th)*, Thomas Benjamin McClintock-Bunbury, *b.* 1938, *s.* 1959, *m.* | Hon. William L. M.-B., *b.* 1966 |
| 1911 | *Ravensdale (3rd)*, Nicholas Mosley, MC, *b.* 1923, *s.* 1966, *m.* | Hon. Shaun N. M., *b.* 1949 |
| 1821 | *Ravensworth (8th)*, Arthur Waller Liddell, *b.* 1924, *s.* 1950, *m.* | Hon. Thomas A. H. L., *b.* 1954 |
| 1821 | *Rayleigh (6th)*, John Gerald Strutt, *b.* 1960, *s.* 1988, *m.* | Hon. John F. S., *b.* 1993 |
| 1937 | ** *Rea (3rd)*, John Nicolas Rea, MD, *b.* 1928, *s.* 1981, *m.* | Hon. Matthew J. R., *b.* 1956 |
| 1628 S. | ** *Reay (14th)*, Hugh William Mackay, *b.* 1937, *s.* 1963, *m.* | Master of Reay, *b.* 1965 |
| 1902 | *Redesdale (6th) and Baron Mitford (life peerage 2000)*, Rupert Bertram Mitford, *b.* 1967, *s.* 1991, *m.* | Hon. Bertram D. M., *b.* 2000 |
| 1940 | *Reith*. Christopher John Reith, *b.* 1928, *s.* 1971, *m.* Disclaimed for life 1972. | Hon. James H. J. R., *b.* 1971 |
| 1928 | *Remnant (3rd)*, James Wogan Remnant, CVO, *b.* 1930, *s.* 1967, *m.* | Hon. Philip J. R., *b.* 1954 |
| 1806 | *Rendlesham (8th)*, Charles Anthony Hugh Thellusson, *b.* 1915, *s.* 1943, *w.* | Hon. Charles W. B. T., *b.* 1954 |
| 1933 | *Rennell (3rd)* (John Adrian) Tremayne Rodd, *b.* 1935, *s.* 1978, *m.* | Hon. James R. D. T. R., *b.* 1978 |
| 1964 | *Renwick (2nd)*, Harry Andrew Renwick, *b.* 1935, *s.* 1973, *m.* | Hon. Robert J. R., *b.* 1966 |
| 1885 | *Revelstoke (5th)*, John Baring, *b.* 1934, *s.* 1994 | Hon. James C. B., *b.* 1938 |
| 1905 | *Ritchie of Dundee (5th)* (Harold) Malcolm Ritchie, *b.* 1919, *s.* 1978, *m.* | Hon. C. Rupert R. R., *b.* 1958 |
| 1935 | *Riverdale (3rd)*, Anthony Robert Balfour, *b.* 1960, *s.* 1998 | Hon. David R. B., *b.* 1938 |
| 1961 | *Robertson of Oakridge (2nd)*, William Ronald Robertson, *b.* 1930, *s.* 1974, *m.* | Hon. William B. E. R., *b.* 1975 |
| 1938 | *Roborough (3rd)*, Henry Massey Lopes, *b.* 1940, *s.* 1992, *m.* | Hon. Massey J. H. L., *b.* 1969 |
| 1931 | *Rochester (2nd)*, Foster Charles Lowry Lamb, *b.* 1916, *s.* 1955, *w.* | Hon. David C. L., *b.* 1944 |
| 1934 | *Rockley (3rd)*, James Hugh Cecil, *b.* 1934, *s.* 1976, *m.* | Hon. Anthony R. C., *b.* 1961 |
| 1782 | *Rodney (10th)*, George Brydges Rodney, *b.* 1953, *s.* 1992, *m.* | Nicholas S. H. R., *b.* 1947 |

| *Created* | *Title, order of succession, name, etc.* | *Heir* |
|---|---|---|
| 1651 S.* | *Rollo (14th) and 5th UK Baron Dunning*, 1869, David Eric Howard Rollo, *b.* 1943, *s.* 1997, *m.* | Master , *b.* 1972 |
| 1959 | *Rootes (3rd)*, Nicholas Geoffrey Rootes, *b.* 1951, *s.* 1992, *m.* | William B. R., *b.* 1944 |
| 1796 I.* | *Rossmore (7th) and 6th UK Baron, Rossmore*, 1838, William Warner Westenra, *b.* 1931, *s.* 1958, *m.* | Hon. Benedict W. W., *b.* 1983 |
| 1939 | ** *Rotherwick (3rd)* (Herbert) Robin Cayzer, *b.* 1954, *s.* 1996, *m.* | Hon. H. Robin C., *b.* 1989 |
| 1885 | *Rothschild (4th)* (Nathaniel Charles) Jacob Rothschild, GBE, *b.* 1936, *s.* 1990, *m.* | Hon. Nathaniel P. V. J. R., *b.* 1971 |
| 1911 | *Rowallan (4th)*, John Polson Cameron Corbett, *b.* 1947, *s.* 1993 | Hon. Jason W. P. C. C., *b.* 197 |
| 1947 | *Rugby (3rd)*, Robert Charles Maffey, *b.* 1951, *s.* 1990, *m.* | Hon. Timothy J. H. M., *b.* 197 |
| 1919 | *Russell of Liverpool (3rd)*, Simon Gordon Jared Russell, *b.* 1952, *s.* 1981, *m.* | Hon. Edward C. S. R., *b.* 1985 |
| 1876 | *Sackville (6th)*, Lionel Bertrand Sackville-West, *b.* 1913, *s.* 1965, *m.* | Hugh R. I. S.-W., *b.* 1919 |
| 1964 | *St Helens (2nd)*, Richard Francis Hughes-Young, *b.* 1945, *s.* 1980, *m.* | Hon. Henry T. H.-Y., *b.* 1986 |
| 1559 | ** *St John of Bletso (21st)*, Anthony Tudor St John, *b.* 1957, *s.* 1978, *m.* | Hon. Oliver B. St J., *b.* 1995 |
| 1887 | *St Levan (4th)*, John Francis Arthur St Aubyn, DSC, *b.* 1919, *s.* 1978, *m.* | Hon. O. Piers St. A., *b.* 1920 |
| 1885 | *St Oswald (6th)*, Charles Rowland Andrew Winn, *b.* 1959, *s.* 1999, *m.* | Hon. Rowland C. S. H. W., *b.* 1986 |
| 1960 | *Sanderson of Ayot*. Alan Lindsay Sanderson, *b.* 1931, *s.* 1971, *m.* Disclaimed for life 1971. | Hon. Michael S., *b.* 1959 |
| 1945 | *Sandford (2nd)*, Revd John Cyril Edmondson, DSC, *b.* 1920, *s.* 1959, *m.* | Hon. James J. M. E., *b.* 1949 |
| 1871 | *Sandhurst (5th)* (John Edward) Terence Mansfield, DFC, *b.* 1920, *s.* 1964, *m.* | Hon. Guy R. J. M., *b.* 1949 |
| 1802 | *Sandys (7th)*, Richard Michael Oliver Hill, *b.* 1931, *s.* 1961, *m.* | The Marquess of Downshire, (*see* page 138) |
| 1888 | *Savile (3rd)*, George Halifax Lumley-Savile, *b.* 1919, *s.* 1931 | Hon. Henry L. T. L.-S., *b.* 192 |
| 1447 | *Saye and Sele (21st)*, Nathaniel Thomas Allen Fiennes, *b.* 1920, *s.* 1968, *m.* | Hon. Richard I. F., *b.* 1959 |
| 1826 | *Seaford (6th)*, Colin Humphrey Felton Ellis, *b.* 1946, *s.* 1999, *m.* | Benjamin F. T. E., *b.* 1976 |
| 1932 | ** *Selsdon (3rd)*, Malcolm McEacharn Mitchell-Thomson, *b.* 1937, *s.* 1963, *m.* | Hon. Callum M. M. M.-T., *b.* 1969 |
| 1489 S. | *Sempill (21st)*, James William Stuart Whitemore Sempill, *b.* 1949, *s.* 1995, *m.* | Master of Semphill, *b.* 1979 |
| 1916 | *Shaughnessy (3rd)*, William Graham Shaughnessy, *b.* 1922, *s.* 1938, *w.* | Hon. Michael J. S., *b.* 1946 |
| 1946 | *Shepherd (2nd)*, Malcolm Newton Shepherd, PC, *b.* 1918, *s.* 1954, *w.* | Hon. Graeme G. S., *b.* 1949 |
| 1964 | *Sherfield (2nd)*, Christopher James Makins, *b.* 1942, *s.* 1996, *m.* | Hon. Dwight W. M., *b.* 1951 |
| 1902 | *Shuttleworth (5th)*, Charles Geoffrey Nicholas Kay-Shuttleworth, *b.* 1948, *s.* 1975, *m.* | Hon. Thomas E. K.-S., *b.* 1976 |
| 1950 | *Silkin*. Arthur Silkin, *b.* 1916, *s.* 1972, *m.* Disclaimed for life 1972. | Hon. Christopher L. S., *b.* 1947 |
| 1963 | *Silsoe (2nd)*, David Malcolm Trustram Eve, QC, *b.* 1930, *s.* 1976, *m.* | Hon. Simon R. T. E., *b.* 1966 |
| 1947 | *Simon of Wythenshawe (2nd)*, Roger Simon, *b.* 1913, *s.* 1960, *m.* | Hon. Matthew S., *b.* 1955 |
| 1449 S. | *Sinclair (17th)*, Charles Murray Kennedy St Clair, CVO, *b.* 1914, *s.* 1957, *m.* | Master of Sinclair, *b.* 1968 |
| 1957 | *Sinclair of Cleeve (3rd)*, John Lawrence Robert Sinclair, *b.* 1953, *s.* 1985 | None |
| 1919 | *Sinha (6th)*, Arup Kumar Sinha, *b.* 1966, *s.* 1999 | Hon. Dilip K. S., *b.* 1967 |
| 1828 | ** *Skelmersdale (7th)*, Roger Bootle-Wilbraham, *b.* 1945, *s.* 1973, *m.* | Hon. Andrew B.-W., *b.* 1977 |
| 1916 | *Somerleyton (3rd)*, Savile William Francis Crossley, GCVO, *b.* 1928, *s.* 1959, *m.* | Hon. Hugh F. S. C., *b.* 1971 |
| 1784 | *Somers (9th)*, Philip Sebastian Somers Cocks, *b.* 1948, *s.* 1995 | Alan B. C., *b.* 1930 |
| 1780 | *Southampton (6th)*, Charles James FitzRoy, *b.* 1928, *s.* 1989, *m.* | Hon. Edward C. F., *b.* 1955 |
| 1640 | *Stafford (15th)*, Francis Melfort William Fitzherbert, *b.* 1954, *s.* 1986, *m.* | Hon. Benjamin J. B. F., *b.* 1983 |
| 1938 | *Stamp (4th)*, Trevor Charles Bosworth Stamp, MD, FRCP, *b.* 1935, *s.* 1987, *m.* | Hon. Nicholas C. T. S., *b.* 1978 |
| 1839 | *Stanley of Alderley (8th) and Sheffield (8th) (I. 1738) and 7th UK Baron, Eddisbury*, 1848, Thomas Henry Oliver Stanley, *b.* 1927, *s.* 1971, *m.* | Hon. Richard O. S., *b.* 1956 |
| 1318 | ** *Strabolgi (11th)*, David Montague de Burgh Kenworthy, *b.* 1914, *s.* 1953, *m.* | Andrew D. W. K., *b.* 1967 |
| 1954 | *Strang (2nd)*, Colin Strang, *b.* 1922, *s.* 1978, *m.* | None |
| 1955 | *Strathalmond (3rd)*, William Roberton Fraser, *b.* 1947, *s.* 1976, *m.* | Hon. William G. F., *b.* 1976 |
| 1936 | *Strathcarron (2nd)*, David William Anthony Blyth Macpherson, *b.* 1924, *s.* 1937, *m.* | Hon. Ian D. P. M., *b.* 1949 |
| 1955 | ** *Strathclyde (2nd)*, Thomas Galloway Dunlop du Roy de Blicquy Galbraith, PC, *b.* 1960, *s.* 1985, *m.* | Hon. Charles W. du R. de B. G., *b.* 1962 |
| 1900 | *Strathcona and Mount Royal (4th)*, Donald Euan Palmer Howard, *b.* 1923, *s.* 1959, *m.* | Hon. D. Alexander S. H., *b.* 1961 |
| 1836 | *Stratheden (6th) and Campbell (6th) (1841)* Donald Campbell, *b.* 1934, *s.* 1987, *m.* | Hon. David A. C., *b.* 1963 |
| 1884 | *Strathspey (6th)*, James Patrick Trevor Grant of Grant, *b.* 1943, *s.* 1992, *m.* | Hon. Michael P. F. G., *b.* 1953 |
| 1838 | *Sudeley (7th)*, Merlin Charles Sainthill Hanbury-Tracy, *b.* 1939, *s.* 1941 | D. Andrew J. H.-T., *b.* 1928 |

| Created | Title, order of succession, name, etc. | Heir |
|---|---|---|
| 1786 | *Suffield (11th)*, Anthony Philip Harbord-Hamond, MC, *b.* 1922, *s.* 1951, *w.* | Hon. Charles A. A. H.-H., *b.* 1953 |
| 1893 | *Swansea (4th)*, John Hussey Hamilton Vivian, *b.* 1925, *s.* 1934, *m.* | Hon. Richard A. H. V., *b.* 1957 |
| 1907 | *Swaythling (5th)*, Charles Edgar Samuel Montagu, *b.* 1954, *s.* 1998, *m.* | Hon. Anthony T. S. M., *b.* 1931 |
| 1919 | ** *Swinfen (3rd)*, Roger Mynors Swinfen Eady, *b.* 1938, *s.* 1977, *m.* | Hon. Charles R. P. S. E., *b.* 1971 |
| 1935 | *Sysonby (3rd)*, John Frederick Ponsonby, *b.* 1945, *s.* 1956 | None |
| 1831 I. | *Talbot of Malahide (10th)*, Reginald John Richard Arundell, *b.* 1931, *s.* 1987, *m.* | Hon. Richard J. T. A., *b.* 1957 |
| 1946 | *Tedder (3rd)*, Robin John Tedder, *b.* 1955, *s.* 1994, *m.* | Hon. Benjamin J. T., *b.* 1985 |
| 1884 | *Tennyson (5th)*, Cdr. Mark Aubrey Tennyson, DSC, *b.* 1920, *s.* 1991, *m.* | Lt.-Cdr. James A. T., *b.* 1913 |
| 1940 | *Teviot (2nd)*, Charles John Kerr, *b.* 1934, *s.* 1968, *m.* | Hon. Charles R. K., *b.* 1971 |
| 1616 | *Teynham (20th)*, John Christopher Ingham Roper-Curzon, *b.* 1928, *s.* 1972, *m.* | Hon. David J. H. I. R.-C., *b.* 1965 |
| 1964 | *Thomson of Fleet (2nd)*, Kenneth Roy Thomson, *b.* 1923, *s.* 1976, *m.* | Hon. David K. R. T., *b.* 1957 |
| 1792 | *Thurlow (8th)*, Francis Edward Hovell-Thurlow-Cumming-Bruce, KCMG, *b.* 1912, *s.* 1971, *w.* | Hon. Roualeyn R. H.-T.-C.-B., *b.* 1952 |
| 1876 | *Tollemache (5th)*, Timothy John Edward Tollemache, *b.* 1939, *s.* 1975, *m.* | Hon. Edward J. H. T., *b.* 1976 |
| 1564 S. | *Torphichen (15th)*, James Andrew Douglas Sandilands, *b.* 1946, *s.* 1975, *m.* | Douglas R. A. S., *b.* 1926 |
| 1947 | ** *Trefgarne (2nd)*, David Garro Trefgarne, PC, *b.* 1941, *s.* 1960, *m.* | Hon. George G. T., *b.* 1970 |
| 1921 | *Trevethin (4th) and Oaksey (2nd) (1947)*, John Geoffrey Tristram Lawrence, OBE, *b.* 1929, *s.* 1971, *m.* | Hon. Patrick J. T. L., *b.* 1960 |
| 1880 | *Trevor (5th)*, Marke Charles Hill-Trevor, *b.* 1970, *s.* 1997, *m.* | Hon. Iain R. H.-T., *b.* 1971 |
| 1461 I. | *Trimlestown (21st)*, Raymond Charles Barnewall, *b.* 1930, *s.* 1997 | None |
| 1940 | *Tryon (3rd)*, Anthony George Merrik Tryon, *b.* 1940, *s.* 1976 | Hon. Charles G. B. T., *b.* 1976 |
| 1935 | *Tweedsmuir (3rd)*, William de l'Aigle Buchan, *b.* 1916, *s.* 1996, *m.* | Hon. John W. H. de l'A. B., *b.* 1950 |
| 1523 | *Vaux of Harrowden (10th)*, John Hugh Philip Gilbey, *b.* 1915, *s.* 1977, *m.* | Hon. Anthony W. G., *b.* 1940 |
| 1800 I. | *Ventry (8th)*, Andrew Wesley Daubeny de Moleyns, *b.* 1943, *s.* 1987, *m.* | Hon. Francis W. D. de M., *b.* 1965 |
| 1762 | *Vernon (10th)*, John Lawrance Vernon, *b.* 1923, *s.* 1963, *m.* | Anthony W. Vernon-Harcourt , *b.* 1939 |
| 1922 | *Vestey (3rd)*, Samuel George Armstrong Vestey, *b.* 1941, *s.* 1954, *m.* | Hon. William G. V., *b.* 1983 |
| 1841 | ** *Vivian (6th)*, Nicholas Crespigny Laurence Vivian, *b.* 1935, *s.* 1991, *m.* | Hon. Charles H. C. V., *b.* 1966 |
| 1934 | *Wakehurst (3rd)* (John) Christopher Loder, *b.* 1925, *s.* 1970, *m.* | Hon. Timothy W. L., *b.* 1958 |
| 1723 | ** *Walpole (10th) and 8th Brit. Baron Walpole of Wolterton*, 1756, Robert Horatio Walpole, *b.* 1938, *s.* 1989, *m.* | Hon. Jonathan R. H. W., *b.* 1967 |
| 1780 | *Walsingham (9th)*, John de Grey, MC, *b.* 1925, *s.* 1965, *m.* | Hon. Robert de. G., *b.* 1969 |
| 1936 | *Wardington (2nd)*, Christopher Henry Beaumont Pease, *b.* 1924, *s.* 1950, *m.* | Hon. William S. P., *b.* 1925 |
| 1792 I. | *Waterpark (7th)*, Frederick Caryll Philip Cavendish, *b.* 1926, *s.* 1948, *m.* | Hon. Roderick A. C., *b.* 1959 |
| 1942 | *Wedgwood (4th)*, Piers Anthony Weymouth Wedgwood, *b.* 1954, *s.* 1970, *m.* | John W., *b.* 1919 |
| 1861 | *Westbury (5th)*, David Alan Bethell, CBE, MC, *b.* 1922, *s.* 1961, *m.* | Hon. Richard N. B., *b.* 1950 |
| 1944 | *Westwood (3rd)*, (William) Gavin Westwood, *b.* 1944, *s.* 1991, *m.* | Hon. W. Fergus W., *b.* 1972 |
| 1544/5 | *Wharton (12th)*, Myles Christopher David Robertson, *b.* 1964, *s.* 2000, *m.* | Hon. Christopher J. R., *b.* 1969 |
| 1935 | *Wigram (2nd)* (George) Neville (Clive) Wigram, MC, *b.* 1915, *s.* 1960, *w.* | Maj. Hon. Andrew F. C. W., *b.* 1949 |
| 1491 | ** *Willoughby de Broke (21st)*, Leopold David Verney, *b.* 1938, *s.* 1986, *m.* | Hon. Rupert G. V., *b.* 1966 |
| 1946 | *Wilson (2nd)*, Patrick Maitland Wilson, *b.* 1915, *s.* 1964, *w.* | None |
| 1937 | *Windlesham (3rd) and Baron Hennesy (life peerage, 1999)*, David James George Hennessy, CVO, PC, *b.* 1932, *s.* 1962, *w.* | Hon. James R. H., *b.* 1968 |
| 1951 | *Wise (2nd)*, John Clayton Wise, *b.* 1923, *s.* 1968, *m.* | Hon. Christopher J. C. W., *b.* 1949 |
| 1869 | *Wolverton (7th)*, Christopher Richard Glyn, *b.* 1938, *s.* 1988 | Hon. Andrew J. G., *b.* 1943 |
| 1928 | *Wraxall (2nd)*, George Richard Lawley Gibbs, *b.* 1928, *s.* 1931 | Hon. Sir Eustace H. B. G., *b.* 1929 |
| 1915 | *Wrenbury (3rd)*, Revd John Burton Buckley, *b.* 1927, *s.* 1940, *m.* | Hon. William E. B., *b.* 1966 |
| 1838 | *Wrottesley (6th)*, Clifton Hugh Lancelot de Verdon Wrottesley, *b.* 1968, *s.* 1977 | Hon. Stephen J. W., *b.* 1955 |
| 1829 | *Wynford (8th)*, Robert Samuel Best, MBE, *b.* 1917, *s.* 1943, *m.* | Hon. John P. R. B., *b.* 1950 |
| 1308 | *Zouche (18th)*, James Assheton Frankland, *b.* 1943, *s.* 1965, *m.* | Hon. William T. A. F., *b.* 1984 |

## BARONESSES/LADIES IN THEIR OWN RIGHT

*Style*, The Right Hon. the Lady _ , *or* The Right Hon. the Baroness _ , according to her preference. Either style may be used, except in the case of Scottish titles (indicated by S.), which are not baronies (*see* page 136) and whose holders are always addressed as Lady
*Husband*, Untitled
*Children's style*, As for children of a Baron
For forms of address, *see* page 135

| *Created* | | *Title, order of succession, name, etc.* | *Heir* |
|---|---|---|---|
| 1664 | | *Arlington*, Jennifer Jane Forwood, *b.* 1939, *m.* title called out of abeyance 1999 | Patrick John Dudley Forwood, *b.* 1967 |
| 1455 | | *Berners (16th)*, Pamela Vivien Kirkham, *b.* 1929, *m.* | Hon. Rupert W. T. K., *b.* 1953 |
| 1529 | | *Braye (8th)*, Mary Penelope Aubrey-Fletcher, *b.* 1941, *s.* 1985, *m.* | |
| 1321 | | *Dacre (27th)*, Rachel Leila Douglas-Home, *b.* 1929, *w.* | Hon. James T. A. D.-H., *b.* 195 |
| 1332 | | ** *Darcy de Knayth (18th)*, Davina Marcia Ingrams, DBE, *b.* 1938, *s.* 1943, *w.* | Hon. Caspar D. I., *b.* 1962 |
| 1439 | | *Dudley (14th)*, Barbara Amy Felicity Hamilton, *b.* 1907, *s.* 1972, *m.* | Hon. Jim A. H. Wallace, *b.* 193 |
| 1490 | S. | *Herries of Terregles (14th)*, Anne Elizabeth Fitzalan-Howard, *b.* 1938, *s.* 1975, *w.* | Lady Mary Mumford, *b.* 1940 |
| 1602 | S. | *Kinloss (12th)*, Beatrice Mary Grenville Freeman-Grenville, *b.* 1922, *s.* 1944, *m.* | Master, *b.* 1953 |
| 1445 | S. | ** *Saltoun (20th)*, Flora Marjory Fraser, *b.* 1930, *s.* 1979, *m.* | Hon. Katharine I. M. I. F., *b.* 1957 |
| 1628 | | ** *Strange (16th)* (Jean) Cherry Drummond of Megginch, *b.* 1928, *m.* | Hon. Adam H. D. of M., *b.* 195 |
| 1313 | | *Willoughby de Eresby (27th)*, (Nancy) Jane Marie Heathcote-Drummond-Willoughby, *b.* 1934, *s.* 1983 | |

# Life Peers

New Life Peerages *1 September 2000 to 31 August 2001:*
Victor Abedowale, CBE; Sir Jeremy (Paddy) Ashdown, KBE; Richard Best, OBE; Peter Brooke, CH; Edmund Browne; Dale Campbell-Savours; David Clarke; Paul Condon, QPM; Robin Corbett; Ronald Fearn, OBE; *Prof.* Ilora Finlay; Peter Fowler; Bruce Grocott; *Gen.* Sir Charles Guthrie, GCB, LVO, OBE; Michael Heseltine CH; Valerie Howarth, OBE; Elspeth Howe, CBE; Stephen Jones; Thomas King, CH, PC; Richard Livsey, CBE; John MacGregor, CBE; Robert MacLennon, PC; Ken Maginnis, Sir Robert May, Kt., Janet Michie; John Morris, QC; Sir Claus Moser, KCB, CBE; Sir Herman Ouseley, Kt.; Thomas Pendry, Giles Radice; Robert Sheldon; Sir Stewart Sutherland, Kt.; John Taylor; Peter Temple-Morris;

## CREATED UNDER THE APPELLATE JURISDICTION ACT 1876 (AS AMENDED)

### BARONS

*Created*
1986 *Ackner*, Desmond James Conrad, Ackner, PC, *b.* 1920, *m.*
1980 *Bridge of Harwich*, Nigel Cyprian, Bridge, PC, *b.* 1917, *m.*
1982 *Brightman*, John Anson, Brightman, PC, *b.* 1911, *m.*
1991 *Browne-Wilkinson*, Nicolas Christopher Henry, Browne-Wilkinson, PC, *b.* 1930, *m.*
1996 *Clyde*, James John, Clyde, *b.* 1932, *m. Lord of Appeal in Ordinary*
1986 *Goff of Chieveley*, Robert Lionel Archibald, Goff, PC, *b.* 1926, *m.*
1985 *Griffiths*, (William) Hugh, Griffiths, MC, PC, *b.* 1923, *m.*
1998 *Hobhouse of Woodborough*, John Stewart, Hobhouse, PC, *b.* 1932, *Lord of Appeal in Ordinary*
1995 *Hoffmann*, Leonard Hubert, Hoffmann, PC, *b.* 1934, *m. Lord of Appeal in Ordinary*
1997 *Hutton*, (James) Brian (Edward), Hutton, PC, *b.* 1931, *m. Lord of Appeal in Ordinary*
1988 *Jauncey of Tullichettle*, Charles Eliot, Jauncey, PC, *b.* 1925, *m.*
1977 *Keith of Kinkel*, Henry Shanks, Keith, GBE, PC, *b.* 1922, *m.*
1979 *Lane*, Geoffrey Dawson, Lane, AFC, PC, *b.* 1918, *m.*
1993 *Lloyd of Berwick*, Anthony John Leslie, Lloyd, PC, *b.* 1929, *m.*
1998 *Millett*, Peter Julian, Millett, PC, *b.* 1932, *m. Lord of Appeal in Ordinary*
1992 *Mustill*, Michael John, Mustill, PC, *b.* 1931, *m.*
1994 *Nicholls of Birkenhead*, Donald James, Nicholls, PC, *b.* 1933, *m. Lord of Appeal in Ordinary*
1994 *Nolan*, Michael Patrick, Nolan, PC, *b.* 1928, *m.*
1986 *Oliver of Aylmerton*, Peter Raymond, Oliver, PC, *b.* 1921, *m.*
1999 *Phillips of Worth Matravers*, Nicholas Addison, Phillips, *b.* 1938, *m. Master of the Rolls*
1997 *Saville of Newdigate*, Mark Oliver, Saville, PC, *b.* 1936, *m. Lord of Appeal in Ordinary*
1977 *Scarman*, Leslie George, Scarman, OBE, PC, *b.* 1911, *m.*
1992 *Slynn of Hadley*, Gordon, Slynn, PC, *b.* 1930, *m. Lord of Appeal in Ordinary*
1995 *Steyn*, Johan van Zyl, Steyn, PC, *b.* 1932, *m. Lord of Appeal in Ordinary*
1982 *Templeman*, Sydney William, Templeman, MBE, PC, *b.* 1920, *m.*
1964 *Wilberforce*, Richard Orme, Wilberforce, CMG, OBE, PC, *b.* 1907, *m.*
1992 *Woolf*, Harry Kenneth, Woolf, PC, *b.* 1933, *m. Lord Chief Justice of England and Wales*

## CREATED UNDER THE LIFE PEERAGES ACT 1958

*Hereditary Peer who has been granted a life peerage

### BARONS

2000 **Acton of Bridgnorth*, Lord Acton, *m.* (*see page 147*)
2001 *Adebowale of Thornes*, Victor Olufemi, Adebowale, CBE,
1998 *Ahmed*, Nazir, Ahmed, *b.* 1957, *m.*
1996 *Alderdice*, John Thomas, Alderdice, *b.* 1955, *m.*
1988 *Alexander of Weedon*, Robert Scott, Alexander, QC, *b.* 1936, *m.*
1976 *Allen of Abbeydale*, Philip, Allen, GCB, *b.* 1912, *m.*
1998 *Alli*, Waheed, Alli,
1997 *Alton of Liverpool*, David Patrick Paul, Alton, *b.* 1951, *m.*
1992 *Archer of Sandwell*, Peter Kingsley, Archer, PC, QC, *b.* 1926, *m.*
1992 *Archer of Weston-super-Mare*, Jeffrey Howard, Archer, *b.* 1940, *m.*
1988 *Armstrong of Ilminster*, Robert Temple, Armstrong, GCB, CVO, *b.* 1927, *m.*
1999 **Armstrong-Jones*, Earl of Snowdon, GCVO, *m.* (*see page 143*)
2000 *Ashcroft*, Michael Anthony, Ashcroft, KCMG,
2001 *Ashdown of Norton-sub-Hamdon*, Jeremy John Durham (Paddy), Ashdown, KBE, *m.*
1992 *Ashley of Stoke*, Jack, Ashley, CH, PC, *b.* 1922, *m.*
1993 *Attenborough*, Richard Samuel, Attenborough, CBE, *b.* 1923, *m.*
1998 *Bach*, William Stephen Goulden, Bach, *b.* 1946, *m. Minister of State for Defence Procurement*
1997 *Bagri*, Raj Kumar, Bagri, CBE, *b.* 1930, *m.*
1997 *Baker of Dorking*, Kenneth Wilfred, Baker, CH, PC, *b.* 1934, *m.*
1974 **Balniel*, The Earl of Crawford and Balcarres, *m.* (*see page 140*)
1974 *Barber*, Anthony Perrinott Lysberg, Barber, TD, PC, *b.* 1920, *m.*
1992 *Barber of Tewkesbury*, Derek Coates, Barber, *b.* 1918, *m.*
1983 *Barnett*, Joel, Barnett, PC, *b.* 1923, *m.*
1997 *Bassam of Brighton*, (John) Steven, Bassam, *b.* 1953, *Lord-in-Waiting*
1982 *Bauer*, Prof. Peter Thomas, Bauer, D.SC., FBA, *b.* 1915
1967 *Beaumont of Whitley*, Revd Timothy Wentworth, Beaumont, *b.* 1928, *m.*
1998 *Bell*, Timothy John Leigh, Bell, *b.* 1941, *m.*
2000 *Bernstein of Craigweil*, Alexander, Bernstein, *b.* 1936, *m.*
2001 *Best*, Richard Stuart, Best, OBE, *b.* 1945, *m.*
1997 *Biffen*, (William) John, Biffen, PC, *b.* 1930, *m.*
1996 *Bingham of Cornhill*, Thomas Henry, Bingham, PC, *b.* 1933, *m. Lord of Appeal in Ordinary*

2000 *Birt*, John Francis Hodgess, Birt, *b.* 1944, *m.*
1997 *Blackwell*, Norman Roy, Blackwell, *b.* 1952, *m.*
1971 *Blake*, Robert Norman William, Blake, FBA, *b.* 1916, *w.*
1994 *Blaker*, Peter Allan Renshaw, Blaker, KCMG, PC, *b.* 1922, *m.*
1978 *Blease*, William John, Blease, *b.* 1914, *m.*
1995 *Blyth of Rowington*, James, Blyth, *b.* 1940, *m.*
1980 *Boardman*, Thomas Gray, Boardman, MC, TD, *b.* 1919, *m.*
1996 *Borrie*, Gordon Johnson, Borrie, QC, *b.* 1931, *m.*
1976 *Boston of Faversham*, Terence George, Boston, QC, *b.* 1930, *m.*
1996 *Bowness*, Peter Spencer, Bowness, CBE, *b.* 1943, *m.*
1999 *Bradshaw*, William Peter, Bradshaw, *b.* 1936, *m.*
1998 *Bragg*, Melvyn, Bragg, *b.* 1939, *m.*
1987 *Bramall*, Edwin Noel Westby, Bramall, KG, GCB, OBE, MC, *b.* 1923, *m.*
2000 *Brennan*, Daniel Joseph, Brennan, QC, *b.* 1942, *m.*
1999 *Brett*, William Henry, Brett, *b.* 1942, *m.*
1976 *Briggs*, Asa, Briggs, FBA, *b.* 1921, *m.*
2000 *Brittan of Spennithorne*, Leon, Brittan, PC, QC, *b.* 1939, *m.*
1997 *Brooke of Alverthorpe*, Clive, Brooke, *b.* 1942, *m.*
2001 *Brooke of Sutton Mandeville*, Peter Leonard, Brooke, CH, *b.* 1934, *m.*
1975 *Brookes*, Raymond Percival, Brookes, *b.* 1909, *m.*
1998 *Brookman*, David Keith, Brookman, *b.* 1937, *m.*
1979 *Brooks of Tremorfa*, John Edward, Brooks, *b.* 1927, *m.*
2001 *Browne of Madingley*, Edmund John Phillip, Browne, *b.* 1948
1974 *Bruce of Donington*, Donald William Trevor, Bruce, *b.* 1912, *m.*
1976 *Bullock*, Alan Louis Charles, Bullock, FBA, *b.* 1914, *m.*
1997 *Burlison*, Thomas Henry, Burlison, *b.* 1936, *m.*
1998 *Burns*, Terence, Burns, GCB, *b.* 1944, *m.*
1998 *Butler of Brockwell*, (Frederick Edward) Robin, Butler, GCB, CVO, *b.* 1938, *m.*
1985 *Butterworth*, John Blackstock, Butterworth, CBE, *b.* 1918, *m.*
1978 *Buxton of Alsa*, Aubrey Leland Oakes, Buxton, KCVO, MC, *b.* 1918, *m.*
1987 *Callaghan of Cardiff*, (Leonard) James, Callaghan, KG, PC, *b.* 1912, *m.*
1984 *Cameron of Lochbroom*, Kenneth John, Cameron, PC, *b.* 1931, *m.*
1981 *Campbell of Alloway*, Alan Robertson, Campbell, QC, *b.* 1917, *m.*
1974 *Campbell of Croy*, Gordon Thomas Calthrop, Campbell, MC, PC, *b.* 1921, *m.*
2001 *Campbell-Savours of Allerdale*, Dale Norman, Cambell-Savours, *b.* 1943, *m.*
1999 **Carington of Upton*, Lord Carrington, GCMG, *b.* 1919, *m.* (*see page 148*)
1999 *Carlile of Berriew*, Alexander Charles, Carlile, QC, *b.* 1948, *m.*
1987 *Carlisle of Bucklow*, Mark, Carlisle, QC, PC, *b.* 1929, *m.*
1983 *Carmichael of Kelvingrove*, Neil George, Carmichael, *b.* 1921
1975 *Carr of Hadley*, (Leonard) Robert, Carr, PC, *b.* 1916, *m.*
1987 *Carter*, Denis Victor, Carter, PC, *b.* 1932, *m.* *Chief Whip*
1977 *Carver*, (Richard) Michael (Power), Carver, GCB, CBE, DSO, MC, *b.* 1915, *m.*
1990 *Cavendish of Furness*, (Richard) Hugh, Cavendish, *b.* 1941, *m.*
1996 *Chadlington*, Peter Selwyn, Gummer, *b.* 1942, *m.*
1964 *Chalfont*, (Alun) Arthur, Gwynne Jones, OBE, MC, PC, *b.* 1919, *m.*
1985 *Chapple*, Francis (Frank) Joseph, Chapple, *b.* 1921 *w.*
1987 *Chilver*, (Amos) Henry, Chilver, FRS, FENG., *b.* 1926, *m.*
1977 *Chitnis*, Pratap Chidamber, Chitnis, *b.* 1936, *m.*
1998 *Christopher*, Anthony Martin Grosvenor, Christopher, CBE, *b.* 1925, *m.*
1992 *Clark of Kempston*, William Gibson Haig, Clark, PC, *b.* 1917, *m.*
*Clarke*, David George, Clarke, *m.*
1998 *Clarke of Hampstead*, Anthony James, Clarke, CBE *b.* 1932, *m.*
1998 *Clement-Jones*, Timothy Francis, Clement-Jones CBE, *b.* 1949, *m.*
1990 *Clinton-Davis*, Stanley Clinton, Clinton-Davis, PC, *b.* 1928, *m.*
1978 *Cockfield*, (Francis) Arthur, Cockfield, PC, *b.* 1916 *w.*
2000 *Coe*, Sebastian Newbold, Coe, OBE, *b.* 1956, *m.*
2001 *Condon of Langdon Green*, Paul Leslie, Condon, QPM, *m.*
1981 *Constantine of Stanmore*, Theodore, Constantine, CBE, AE, *b.* 1910, *w.*
1992 *Cooke of Islandreagh*, Victor Alexander, Cooke, OBE, *b.* 1920, *m.*
1996 *Cooke of Thorndon*, Robin Brunskill, Cooke, KBE, PC, PH.D., *b.* 1926, *m.*
1997 *Cope of Berkeley*, John Ambrose, Cope, PC, *b.* 1937 *m.*
2001 *Corbett of Castle Vale*, Robin, Corbett, *b.* 1933, *m.*
1991 *Craig of Radley*, David Brownrigg, Craig, GCB, OBE *b.* 1929, *m.*
1987 *Crickhowell*, (Roger) Nicholas, Edwards, PC, *b.* 1934, *m.*
1978 *Croham*, Douglas Albert Vivian, Allen, GCB, *b.* 1917, *w.*
1995 *Cuckney*, John Graham, Cuckney, *b.* 1925, *m.*
1996 *Currie of Marylebone*, David Anthony, Currie, *b.* 1946, *m.*
1979 *Dacre of Glanton*, Hugh Redwald, Trevor-Roper, *b.* 1914, *w.*
1993 *Dahrendorf*, Ralf, Dahrendorf, KBE, PH.D., D.PHIL., FBA, *b.* 1929, *m.*
1997 *Davies of Coity*, (David) Garfield, Davies, CBE, *b.* 1935, *m.*
1997 *Davies of Oldham*, Bryan, Davies, *b.* 1939, *m.* *Lord-in-Waiting*
1993 *Dean of Harptree*, (Arthur) Paul, Dean, PC, *b.* 1924 *m.*
1998 *Dearing*, Ronald Ernest, Dearing, CB, *b.* 1930, *m.*
1986 *Deedes*, William Francis, Deedes, KBE MC, PC, *b.* 1913, *m.*
1991 *Desai*, Prof. Meghnad Jagdishchandra, Desai, PH.D., *b.* 1940, *m.*
1997 *Dholakia*, Navnit, Dholakia, OBE, *b.* 1937, *m.*
1970 *Diamond*, John, Diamond, PC, *b.* 1907, *m.*
1997 *Dixon*, Donald, Dixon, PC, *b.* 1929, *m.*
1993 *Dixon-Smith*, Robert William, Dixon-Smith, *b.* 1934, *m.*
1988 *Donaldson of Lymington*, John Francis, Donaldson, PC, *b.* 1920, *m.*
1985 *Donoughue*, Bernard, Donoughue, D.PHIL., *b.* 1934
1987 *Dormand of Easington*, John Donkin, Dormand, *b.* 1919, *m.*
1994 *Dubs*, Alfred, Dubs, *b.* 1932, *m.*
1995 *Eames*, Robert Henry Alexander, Eames, PH.D., *b.* 1937, *m.*
1992 *Eatwell*, John Leonard, Eatwell, PH.D., *b.* 1945, *m.*
1983 *Eden of Winton*, John Benedict, Eden, PC, *b.* 1925, *m.*
1999 *Elder*, Thomas Murray, Elder,
1992 *Elis-Thomas*, Dafydd Elis, Elis-Thomas, *b.* 1946, *m.*

985 *Elliott of Morpeth*, Robert William, Elliott, *b.* 1920, *m.*
981 *Elystan-Morgan*, Dafydd Elystan, Elystan-Morgan, *b.* 1932, *m.*
980 *Emslie*, George Carlyle, Emslie, MBE, PC, FRSE, *b.* 1919, *m.*
000 **Erskine of Alloa Tower*, Earl of Mar and Kellie, *m.* *(see page 142)*
997 *Evans of Parkside*, John, Evans, *b.* 1930, *m.*
000 *Evans of Temple Guiting*, Matthew, Evans, CBE, *b.* 1941, *m.*
998 *Evans of Watford*, David Charles, Evans, *b.* 1942, *m.*
992 *Ewing of Kirkford*, Harry, Ewing, *b.* 1931, *m.*
983 *Ezra*, Derek, Ezra, MBE, *b.* 1919, *m.*
997 *Falconer of Thornton*, Charles Leslie, Falconer, QC, *b.* 1951, *m. Minister of State for Housing and Planning*
983 *Fanshawe of Richmond*, Anthony Henry Fanshawe, Royle, KCMG, *b.* 1927, *m.*
999 *Faulkner of Worcester*, Richard Oliver, Faulkner, *b.* 1946, *m.*
001 *Fearn of Southport*, Ronald Cyril, Fearn, OBE, *b.* 1931, *m.*
996 *Feldman*, Basil, Feldman, *b.* 1926, *m.*
999 *Fellowes*, Robert, Fellowes, PC, GCB, GCVO, *b.* 1941, *m.*
999 *Filkin*, David Geoffrey Nigel, Filkin, CBE, *b.* 1944, *Lord-in-Waiting*
983 *Fitt*, Gerard, Fitt, *b.* 1926, *w.*
979 *Flowers*, Brian Hilton, Flowers, FRS, *b.* 1924, *m.*
967 *Foot*, John Mackintosh, Foot, *b.* 1909, *m.*
999 *Forsyth of Drumlean*, Michael Bruce, Forsyth, *b.* 1954, *m.*
982 *Forte*, Charles, Forte, *b.* 1908, *m.*
999 *Foster of Thames Bank*, Norman Robert, Foster, OM, *b.* 1935, *m.*
001 *Fowler of Sutton Coldfield*, (Peter) Norman, Fowler, *b.* 1938, *m.*
989 *Fraser of Carmyllie*, Peter Lovat, Fraser, PC, QC, *b.* 1945, *m.*
997 *Freeman*, Roger Norman, Freeman, PC, *b.* 1942, *m.*
000 *Fyfe of Fairfield*, George Lennox, Fyfe, *b.* 1941, *m.*
982 *Gallacher*, John, Gallacher, *b.* 1920, *m.*
999 **Ganzoni*, Lord Belstead, PC, *(see page 148)*
997 *Garel-Jones*, (William Armand) Thomas Tristan, Garel-Jones, PC, *b.* 1941, *m.*
999 **Gascoyne-Cecil*, The Viscount Cranborne, PC, *m.* *(see Baron Cecil page 148)*
999 *Gavron*, Robert, Gavron, CBE, *b.* 1930, *m.*
992 *Geraint*, Geraint Wyn, Howells, *b.* 1925, *m.*
975 *Gibson*, (Richard) Patrick (Tallentyre), Gibson, *b.* 1916, *m.*
979 *Gibson-Watt*, (James) David, Gibson-Watt, MC, PC, *b.* 1918, *m.*
997 *Gilbert*, John William, Gilbert, PC, PH.D., *b.* 1927, *m.*
992 *Gilmour of Craigmillar*, Ian Hedworth John Little, Gilmour, PC, *b.* 1926, *m.*
994 *Gladwin of Clee*, Derek Oliver, Gladwin, CBE, *b.* 1930, *m.*
977 *Glenamara*, Edward Watson, Short, CH, PC, *b.* 1912, *m.*
001 *Golding of Newcastle-under-Lyme*, Llinos , Golding, *b.* 1933, *m.*
999 *Goldsmith*, Peter Henry, Goldsmith, QC, *b.* 1950, *m. Attorney-General*
997 *Goodhart*, William Howard, Goodhart, QC, *b.* 1933, *m.*
997 *Gordon of Strathblane*, James Stuart, Gordon, CBE, *b.* 1936, *m.*
1999 *Grabiner*, Anthony Stephen, Grabiner, QC, *b.* 1945, *m.*
1983 *Graham of Edmonton*, (Thomas) Edward, Graham, *b.* 1925, *m.*
1983 *Gray of Contin*, James (Hamish) Hector Northey, Gray, PC, *b.* 1927, *m.*
1974 *Greene of Harrow Weald*, Sidney Francis, Greene, CBE, *b.* 1910, *m.*
1975 *Gregson*, John, Gregson, *b.* 1924
2000 **Grenfell of Kilvey*, Lord Grenfell, *(see page 150)*
1991 *Griffiths of Fforestfach*, Brian, Griffiths, *b.* 1941, *m.*
2001 *Grocott*, Bruce Joseph, Grocott, *b.* 1940, *m. Lord-in-Waiting*
2000 **Gueterbock*, Lord Berkeley, OBE, *(see page 148)*
2001 *Guthrie of Craigiebank*, Charles Ronald Llewelyn, Guthrie, GCB, LVO, OBE, *b.* 1938, *m.*
1995 *Habgood*, Rt. Revd John Stapylton, Habgood, PC, PH.D., *b.* 1927, *m.*
1970 *Hailsham of St Marylebone*, Quintin McGarel, Hogg, KG, CH, PC, FRS, *b.* 1907, *w.*
1994 *Hambro*, Charles Eric Alexander, Hambro, *b.* 1930, *m.*
1998 *Hanningfield*, Paul Edward Winston, White, *b.* 1940
1983 *Hanson*, James Edward, Hanson, *b.* 1922, *m.*
1997 *Hardie*, Andrew Rutherford, Hardie, QC, PC, *b.* 1946, *m.*
1997 *Hardy of Wath*, Peter, Hardy, *b.* 1931, *m.*
1998 *Harris of Haringey*, (Jonathan) Toby, Harris, *b.* 1953, *m.*
1979 *Harris of High Cross*, Ralph, Harris, *b.* 1924, *m.*
1996 *Harris of Peckham*, Philip Charles, Harris, *b.* 1942, *m.*
1999 *Harrison*, Lyndon Henry Arthur, Harrison, *b.* 1947, *m.*
1993 *Haskel*, Simon, Haskel, *b.* 1934, *m.*
1998 *Haskins*, Christopher Robin, Haskins, *b.* 1937, *m.*
1990 *Haslam*, Robert, Haslam, *b.* 1923, *m.*
1997 *Hattersley*, Roy Sidney George, Hattersley, PC, *b.* 1932, *m.*
1992 *Hayhoe*, Bernard John (Barney), Hayhoe, PC, *b.* 1925, *m.*
1992 *Healey*, Denis Winston, Healey, CH, MBE, PC, *b.* 1917, *m.*
1999 **Hennessey*, Lord Windlesham, CVO, *w.* *(see page 155)*
2001 *Heseltine of Thenford*, Michael Ray Dibdin, Heseltine, CH, *b.* 1933, *m.*
1997 *Higgins*, Terence Langley, Higgins, KBE, PC, *b.* 1928, *m.*
1979 *Hill-Norton*, Peter John, Hill-Norton, GCB, *b.* 1915, *m.*
2000 *Hodgson of Astley Abbotts*, Robin Granville, Hodgson, CBE, *b.* 1937, *m.*
1997 *Hogg of Cumbernauld*, Norman, Hogg, *b.* 1938, *m.*
1979 *Holderness*, Richard Frederick, Wood, PC, *b.* 1920, *m.*
1991 *Hollick*, Clive Richard, Hollick, *b.* 1945, *m.*
1990 *Holme of Cheltenham*, Richard Gordon, Holme, CBE, *b.* 1936, *m.*
1979 *Hooson*, (Hugh) Emlyn, Hooson, QC, *b.* 1925, *m.*
1995 *Hope of Craighead*, (James Arthur) David, Hope, PC, *b.* 1938, *m. Lord of Appeal in Ordinary*
1992 *Howe of Aberavon*, (Richard Edward) Geoffrey, Howe, CH, PC, QC, *b.* 1926, *m.*
1997 *Howell of Guildford*, David Arthur Russell, Howell, PC, *b.* 1936, *m.*
1978 *Howie of Troon*, William, Howie, *b.* 1924, *m.*
1997 *Hoyle*, (Eric) Douglas Harvey, Hoyle, *b.* 1930, *w.*
1997 *Hughes of Woodside*, Robert, Hughes, *b.* 1932, *m.*
2001 *Hunt of Chesterton*, Julian Charles Roland, Hunt, CBE, *b.* 1941, *m.*

1997 *Hunt of Kings Heath*, Philip Alexander, Hunt, OBE, *b.* 1949, *m.*
1980 *Hunt of Tanworth*, John Joseph Benedict, Hunt, GCB, *b.* 1919, *m.*
1997 *Hunt of Wirral*, David James Fletcher, Hunt, MBE, PC, *b.* 1942, *m.*
1997 *Hurd of Westwell*, Douglas Richard, Hurd, CH, CBE, PC, *b.* 1930, *m.*
1996 *Hussey of North Bradley*, Marmaduke James, Hussey, *b.* 1923, *m.*
1978 *Hutchinson of Lullington*, Jeremy Nicolas, Hutchinson, QC, *b.* 1915, *m.*
1999 *Imbert*, Peter Michael, Imbert, QPM, *b.* 1933, *m.*
1997 *Inge*, Peter Anthony, Inge, GCB, *b.* 1935, *m.*
1982 *Ingrow*, John Aked, Taylor, OBE, TD, *b.* 1917, *m.*
1987 *Irvine of Lairg*, Alexander Andrew Mackay, Irvine, PC, QC, *b.* 1940, *m. Lord Chancellor*
1997 *Islwyn*, Royston John (Roy), Hughes, *b.* 1925, *m.*
1997 *Jacobs*, (David) Anthony, Jacobs, *b.* 1931, *m.*
1997 *Janner of Braunstone*, Greville Ewan, Janner, QC, *b.* 1928, *w.*
1999 **Jellicoe of Southampton*, Earl Jellicoe, KBE, *w.* *(see page 141)*
1987 *Jenkin of Roding*, (Charles) Patrick (Fleeming), Jenkin, PC, *b.* 1926, *m.*
1987 *Jenkins of Hillhead*, Roy Harris, Jenkins, OM, PC, *b.* 1920, *m.*
1981 *Jenkins of Putney*, Hugh Gater, Jenkins, *b.* 1908, *w.*
2000 *Joffe*, Joel Goodman, Joffe, CBE, *b.* 1932, *m.*
1987 *Johnston of Rockport*, Charles Collier, Johnston, TD, *b.* 1915, *m.*
2001 *Jones of Deeside*, Stephen Barry, Jones, *b.* 1937, *m.*
1997 *Jopling*, (Thomas) Michael, Jopling, PC, *b.* 1930, *m.*
2000 *Jordan*, William Brian, Jordan, CBE, *b.* 1936, *m.*
1991 *Judd*, Frank Ashcroft, Judd, *b.* 1935, *m.*
1980 *Keith of Castleacre*, Kenneth Alexander, Keith, *b.* 1916, *m.*
1996 *Kilpatrick of Kincraig*, Robert, Kilpatrick, CBE, *b.* 1926, *m.*
1985 *Kimball*, Marcus Richard, Kimball, *b.* 1928, *m.*
2001 *King*, Thomas Jeremy, King, CH, PC, *b.* 1933, *m.*
1983 *King of Wartnaby*, John Leonard, King, *b.* 1918, *m.*
1999 *King of West Bromwich*, Tarsem, King
1993 *Kingsdown*, Robert (Robin), Leigh-Pemberton, KG, PC, *b.* 1927, *m.*
1994 *Kingsland*, Christopher James, Prout, TD, PC, QC, *b.* 1942
1999 *Kirkham*, Graham, Kirkham, *b.* 1944, *m.*
1975 *Kirkhill*, John Farquharson, Smith, *b.* 1930, *m.*
1987 *Knights*, Philip Douglas, Knights, CBE, QPM, *b.* 1920, *m.*
1991 *Laing of Dunphail*, Hector, Laing, *b.* 1923, *m.*
1999 *Laird*, John Dunn, Laird, *b.* 1944, *m.*
1998 *Laming*, (William) Herbert, Laming, CBE, *b.* 1936, *m.*
1998 *Lamont of Lerwick*, Norman Stewart Hughson, Lamont, PC, *b.* 1942, *m.*
1990 *Lane of Horsell*, Peter Stewart, Lane, *b.* 1925, *w.*
1997 *Lang of Monkton*, Ian Bruce, Lang, PC, *b.* 1940, *m.*
1992 *Lawson of Blaby*, Nigel, Lawson, PC, *b.* 1932, *m.*
2000 *Layard*, Peter Richard Grenville, Layard, *b.* 1934, *m.*
1999 *Lea of Crondall*, David Edward, Lea, OBE, *b.* 1937
1993 *Lester of Herne Hill*, Anthony Paul, Lester, QC, *b.* 1936, *m.*
1997 *Levene of Portsoken*, Peter Keith, Levene, KBE, *b.* 1941, *m.*
1997 *Levy*, Michael Abraham, Levy, *b.* 1944, *m.*
1989 *Lewis of Newnham*, Jack, Lewis, FRS, *b.* 1928, *m.*
1999 *Lipsey*, David Lawrence, Lipsey, *b.* 1948, *m.*
1999 *Livsey*, Richard, Livsey, CBE, *b.* 1948, *m.*
1997 *Lloyd-Webber*, Andrew Lloyd, Webber, *b.* 1948, *m.*
1997 *Lofthouse of Pontefract*, Geoffrey, Lofthouse, *b.* 1925, *w.*
2000 **Lyttelton of Aldershot*, The Viscount Chandos, *m.* *(see page 144)*
1988 *Macaulay of Bragar*, Donald, Macaulay, QC, *b.* 1933, *m.*
1998 *Macdonald of Tradeston*, Angus John, Macdonald, CBE, *b.* 1940, *m. Minister for the Cabinet Office and Chancellor of the Duchy of Lancaster*
1991 *Macfarlane of Bearsden*, Norman Somerville, Macfarlane, KT, FRSE, *b.* 1926, *m.*
2001 *MacGregor of Pulham Market*, John Roddick Russell, MacGregor, CBE, *b.* 1937, *m.*
1979 *Mackay of Clashfern*, James Peter Hymers, Mackay, KT, PC, FRSE, *b.* 1927, *m.*
1995 *Mackay of Drumadoon*, Donald Sage, Mackay, PC, *b.* 1946, *m.*
1999 *Mackenzie of Culkein*, Hector Uisdean, MacKenzie, *b.* 1940
1998 *Mackenzie of Framwellgate*, Brian, Mackenzie, OBE, *b.* 1943, *m.*
1974 *Mackie of Benshie*, George Yull, Mackie, CBE, DSC, DFC, *b.* 1919, *m.*
1996 *MacLaurin of Knebworth*, Ian Charter, MacLaurin, *b.* 1937, *w.*
2001 *Maclennon of Rogart*, Robert Adam Ross, Maclennan, PC, *b.* 1936, *m.*
2001 *Maginnis of Drumglass*, Kenneth Wiggins, Maginnis, *b.* 1938, *m.*
1991 *Marlesford*, Mark Shuldham, Schreiber, *b.* 1931, *m.*
1981 *Marsh*, Richard William, Marsh, PC, *b.* 1928, *m.*
1998 *Marshall of Knightsbridge*, Colin Marsh, Marshall, *b.* 1933, *m.*
1987 *Mason of Barnsley*, Roy, Mason, PC, *b.* 1924, *m.*
2001 *May of Oxford*, Robert McCredie, May, *b.* 1936, *m.*
1997 *Mayhew of Twysden*, Patrick Barnabas Burke, Mayhew, QC, PC, *b.* 1929, *m.*
1984 *McAlpine of West Green*, (Robert) Alistair, McAlpine, *b.* 1942, *m.*
1975 *McCarthy*, William Edward John, McCarthy, D.PHIL., *b.* 1925, *m.*
1976 *McCluskey*, John Herbert, McCluskey, *b.* 1929, *m.*
1989 *McColl of Dulwich*, Ian, McColl, CBE, FRCS, FRCSE, *b.* 1933, *m.*
1982 *McIntosh of Haringey*, Andrew Robert, McIntosh, *b.* 1933, *m. Deputy Chief Whip*
1995 *McNally*, Tom, McNally, *b.* 1943, *m.*
1992 *Merlyn-Rees*, Merlyn, Merlyn-Rees, PC, *b.* 1920, *m.*
1978 *Mishcon*, Victor, Mishcon, QC, *b.* 1915, *m.*
2001 *Mitchell*, Parry Andrew, Mitchell
2000 **Mitford*, Lord Redesdale, *m.* *(see page 153)*
1997 *Molyneaux of Killead*, James Henry, Molyneaux, KBE, PC, *b.* 1920
1997 *Monro of Langholm*, Hector Seymour Peter, Monro, AE, PC, *b.* 1922, *m.*
1992 *Moore of Lower Marsh*, John Edward Michael, Moore, PC, *b.* 1937, *m.*
1986 *Moore of Wolvercote*, Philip Brian Cecil, Moore, GCB, GCVO, CMG, PC, *b.* 1921, *m.*
2000 *Morgan*, Kenneth Owen, Morgan, *b.* 1934, *m.*
2001 *Morris of Aberavon*, John, Morris, QC, *b.* 1931, *m.*
1997 *Morris of Manchester*, Alfred, Morris, PC, *b.* 1928, *m.*
2001 *Moser of Regents Park*, Claus Adolf, Moser, KCB, CBE, *b.* 1922, *m.*
1971 *Moyola*, James Dawson, Chichester-Clark, PC (NI), *b.* 1923, *m.*
1985 *Murray of Epping Forest*, Lionel, Murray, OBE, PC, *b.* 1922, *m.*

979 *Murton of Lindisfarne*, (Henry) Oscar, Murton, OBE, TD, PC, *b.* 1914, *m.*

997 *Naseby*, Michael Wolfgang Laurence, Morris, PC, *b.* 1936, *m.*

997 *Neill of Bladen*, (Francis) Patrick, Neill, QC, *b.* 1926, *m.*

997 *Newby*, Richard Mark, Newby, OBE, *b.* 1953, *m.*

997 *Newton of Braintree*, Antony Harold, Newton, OBE, PC, *b.* 1937, *m.*

994 *Nickson*, David Wigley, Nickson, KBE, FRSE, *b.* 1929, *m.*

975 *Northfield*, (William) Donald, Chapman, *b.* 1923

998 *Norton of Louth*, Philip, Norton, *b.* 1951

997 *Orme*, Stanley, Orme, PC, *b.* 1923, *m.*

001 *Ouseley of Peckham Rye*, Herman George, Ouseley, *m.*

992 *Owen*, David Anthony Llewellyn, Owen, CH, PC, *b.* 1938, *m.*

999 *Oxburgh*, Ernest Ronald, Oxburgh, KBE, FRS, PH.D., *b.* 1934, *m.*

991 *Palumbo*, Peter Garth, Palumbo, *b.* 1935, *m.*

000 *Parekh*, Bhikhu Chhotalal, Parekh, *b.* 1935, *m.*

992 *Parkinson*, Cecil Edward, Parkinson, PC, *b.* 1931, *m.*

975 *Parry*, Gordon Samuel David, Parry, *b.* 1925, *m.*

999 *Patel*, Narendra Babubhai, Patel, *b.* 1938

000 *Patel of Blackburn*, Adam Hafejee, Patel

997 *Patten*, John Haggitt Charles, Patten, PC, *b.* 1945, *m.*

996 *Paul*, Swraj, Paul, *b.* 1931, *m.*

990 *Pearson of Rannoch*, Malcolm Everard MacLaren, Pearson, *b.* 1942, *m.*

2001 *Pendry of Stalybridge*, Thomas, Pendry, *b.* 1934, *m.*

979 *Perry of Walton*, Walter Laing Macdonald, Perry, OBE, FRS, FRSE, *b.* 1921, *m.*

987 *Peston*, Maurice Harry, Peston, *b.* 1931, *m.*

983 *Peyton of Yeovil*, John Wynne William, Peyton, PC, *b.* 1919, *m.*

998 *Phillips of Sudbury*, Andrew Wyndham, Phillips, OBE, *b.* 1939, *m.*

996 *Pilkington of Oxenford*, Revd Canon Peter, Pilkington, *b.* 1933, *w.*

992 *Plant of Highfield*, Prof. Raymond, Plant, PH.D., *b.* 1945, *m.*

1987 *Plumb*, (Charles) Henry, Plumb, *b.* 1925, *m.*

1981 *Plummer of St Marylebone*, (Arthur) Desmond (Herne), Plummer, TD, *b.* 1914, *w.*

2000 **Ponsonby of Roehampton*, Lord Ponsonby of Shulbrede, (*see page 153*)

1990 *Porter of Luddenham*, George, Porter, OM, FRS, *b.* 1920, *m.*

2000 *Powell of Bayswater*, Charles David, Powell, KCMG, *b.* 1941

1987 *Prior*, James Michael Leathes, Prior, PC, *b.* 1927, *m.*

1982 *Prys-Davies*, Gwilym Prys, Prys-Davies, *b.* 1923, *m.*

1997 *Puttnam*, David Terence, Puttnam, CBE, *b.* 1941, *m.*

1987 *Pym*, Francis Leslie, Pym, MC, PC, *b.* 1922, *m.*

1982 *Quinton*, Anthony Meredith, Quinton, FBA, *b.* 1925, *m.*

1994 *Quirk*, Prof. (Charles) Randolph, Quirk, CBE, FBA, *b.* 1920, *m.*

2001 *Radice*, Giles Heneage, Radice, *b.* 1936

1997 *Randall of St Budeaux*, Stuart Jeffrey, Randall, *b.* 1938, *m.*

1978 *Rawlinson of Ewell*, Peter Anthony Grayson, Rawlinson, PC, QC, *b.* 1919, *m.*

1976 *Rayne*, Max, Rayne, *b.* 1918, *m.*

1997 *Razzall*, (Edward) Timothy, Razzall, CBE, *b.* 1943, *m.*

1987 *Rees*, Peter Wynford Innes, Rees, PC, QC, *b.* 1926, *m.*

1988 *Rees-Mogg*, William, Rees-Mogg, *b.* 1928, *m.*

1991 *Renfrew of Kaimsthorn*, (Andrew) Colin, Renfrew, FBA, *b.* 1937, *m.*

1999 *Rennard*, Christopher John, Rennard, MBE, *b.* 1960

1979 *Renton*, David Lockhart-Mure, Renton, KBE, TD, PC, QC, *b.* 1908, *w.*

1997 *Renton of Mount Harry*, (Ronald) Timothy, Renton, PC, *b.* 1932, *m.*

1997 *Renwick of Clifton*, Robin William, Renwick, KCMG, *b.* 1937, *m.*

1990 *Richard*, Ivor Seward, Richard, PC, QC, *b.* 1932, *m.*

1979 *Richardson*, John Samuel, Richardson, LVO, MD, FRCP, *b.* 1910, *w.*

1983 *Richardson of Duntisbourne*, Gordon William Humphreys, Richardson, KG, MBE, TD, PC, *b.* 1915, *m.*

1992 *Rix*, Brian Norman Roger, Rix, CBE, *b.* 1924, *m.*

1997 *Roberts of Conwy*, (Ieuan) Wyn (Pritchard), Roberts, PC, *b.* 1930, *m.*

1999 *Robertson of Port Ellen*, George Islay MacNeill, Robertson, PC, *b.* 1946, *m.*

1992 *Rodger of Earlsferry*, Alan Ferguson, Rodger, PC, QC, FBA, *b.* 1944

1992 *Rodgers of Quarry Bank*, William Thomas, Rodgers, PC, *b.* 1928, *m.*

1999 *Rogan*, Dennis Robert David, Rogan, *b.* 1942, *m.*

1996 *Rogers of Riverside*, Richard George, Rogers, RA, RIBA, *b.* 1933, *m.*

1977 *Roll of Ipsden*, Eric, Roll, KCMG, CB, *b.* 1907, *w.*

2001 *Rooker*, Jeffrey William, Rooker, PC, *b.* 1941, *m.*

2000 *Roper*, John Francis Hodgess, Roper, *b.* 1935, *m.*

1997 *Russell-Johnston*, (David) Russell, Russell-Johnston, *b.* 1932, *m.*

1975 *Ryder of Eaton Hastings*, Sydney Thomas Franklin (Don), Ryder, *b.* 1916, *m.*

1997 *Ryder of Wensum*, Richard Andrew, Ryder, OBE, PC, *b.* 1949, *m.*

1996 *Saatchi*, Maurice, Saatchi, *b.* 1946, *m.*

1989 *Sainsbury of Preston Candover*, John Davan, Sainsbury, KG, *b.* 1927, *m.*

1997 *Sainsbury of Turville*, David John, Sainsbury, *b.* 1940, *m.*

1997 *Sandberg*, Michael Graham Ruddock, Sandberg, CBE, *b.* 1927, *m.*

1985 *Sanderson of Bowden*, Charles Russell, Sanderson, *b.* 1933, *m.*

1998 *Sawyer*, Lawrence (Tom), Sawyer,

2000 *Scott of Foscote*, Richard Rashleigh Folliott, Scott, PC, *b.* 1934, *m. Lord of Appeal in Ordinary*

1997 *Selkirk of Douglas*, James Alexander, Douglas-Hamilton, MSP, PC, QC, *b.* 1942, *m.*

1996 *Sewel*, John Buttifant, Sewel, CBE, *b.* 1946

1999 *Sharman*, Colin Morven, Sharman, OBE, *b.* 1943, *m.*

1994 *Shaw of Northstead*, Michael Norman, Shaw, *b.* 1920, *m.*

1959 *Shawcross*, Hartley William, Shawcross, GBE, PC, QC, *b.* 1923, *m.*

2001 *Sheldon of Ashton-under-Lyne*, Robert Edward, Sheldon, *b.* 1923, *m.*

1994 *Sheppard of Didgemere*, Allan John George, Sheppard, KCVO, *b.* 1932, *m.*

1998 *Sheppard of Liverpool*, David Stuart, Sheppard, *b.* 1929, *m.*

1997 *Shore of Stepney*, Peter David, Shore, PC, *b.* 1924, *m.*

2000 *Shutt of Greetland*, David Trevor , Shutt, OBE

1971 *Simon of Glaisdale*, Jocelyn Edward Salis, Simon, PC, *b.* 1911, *m.*

1997 *Simon of Highbury*, David Alec Gwyn, Simon, CBE, *b.* 1939, *m.*

1997 *Simpson of Dunkeld*, George, Simpson, *b.* 1942, *m.*
1991 *Skidelsky*, Robert Jacob Alexander, Skidelsky, D.PHIL., *b.* 1939, *m.*
1997 *Smith of Clifton*, Trevor Arthur, Smith, *b.* 1937, *m.*
1999 *Smith of Leigh*, Peter Richard Charles, Smith, *b.* 1945, *m.*
1990 *Soulsby of Swaffham Prior*, Ernest Jackson Lawson, Soulsby, PH.D., *b.* 1926, *m.*
1987 *St John of Fawsley*, Norman Antony Francis, St John-Stevas, PC, *b.* 1929
1983 *Stallard*, Albert William, Stallard, *b.* 1921, *m.*
1997 *Steel of Aikwood*, David Martin Scott, Steel, PC, KBE, MSP, *b.* 1938, *m.*
1991 *Sterling of Plaistow*, Jeffrey Maurice, Sterling, CBE, *b.* 1934, *m.*
1987 *Stevens of Ludgate*, David Robert, Stevens, *b.* 1936, *m.*
1999 *Stevenson of Coddenham*, Henry Dennistoun, Stevenson, CBE, *b.* 1945, *m.*
1992 *Stewartby*, (Bernard Harold) Ian (Halley), Stewart, RD, PC, FBA, FRSE, *b.* 1935, *m.*
1981 *Stodart of Leaston*, James Anthony, Stodart, PC, *b.* 1916, *w.*
1983 *Stoddart of Swindon*, David Leonard, Stoddart, *b.* 1926, *m.*
1969 *Stokes*, Donald Gresham, Stokes, TD, FENG., *b.* 1914, *w.*
1997 *Stone of Blackheath*, Andrew Zelig, Stone, *b.* 1942, *m.*
2001 *Sutherland of Houndwood*, Stewart Ross, Sutherland, *b.* 1941, *m.*
1971 *Tanlaw*, Simon Brooke, Mackay, *b.* 1934, *m.*
1996 *Taverne*, Dick, Taverne, QC, *b.* 1928, *m.*
2001 *Taylor*, John David, Taylor, *b.* 1937, *m.*
1978 *Taylor of Blackburn*, Thomas, Taylor, CBE, *b.* 1929, *m.*
1996 *Taylor of Warwick*, John David Beckett, Taylor, *b.* 1952, *m.*
1992 *Tebbit*, Norman Beresford, Tebbit, CH, PC, *b.* 1931, *m.*
2001 *Temple-Morris of Llandaff*, Peter , Temple-Morris, *b.* 1938, *m.*
1996 *Thomas of Gresford*, Donald Martin, Thomas, OBE, QC, *b.* 1937, *m.*
1987 *Thomas of Gwydir*, Peter John Mitchell, Thomas, PC, QC, *b.* 1920, *w.*
1997 *Thomas of Macclesfield*, Terence James, Thomas, CBE, *b.* 1937, *m.*
1981 *Thomas of Swynnerton*, Hugh Swynnerton, Thomas, *b.* 1931, *m.*
1977 *Thomson of Monifieth*, George Morgan, Thomson, KT, PC, *b.* 1921, *m.*
1990 *Tombs*, Francis Leonard, Tombs, FENG., *b.* 1924, *m.*
1998 *Tomlinson*, John Edward, Tomlinson, MEP, *b.* 1939
1994 *Tope*, Graham Norman, Tope, CBE, *b.* 1943, *m.*
1981 *Tordoff*, Geoffrey Johnson, Tordoff, *b.* 1928, *m.*
1999 *Trotman*, Alexander, Trotman, *b.* 1933
1993 *Tugendhat*, Christopher Samuel, Tugendhat, *b.* 1937, *m.*
1990 *Varley*, Eric Graham, Varley, PC, *b.* 1932, *m.*
1996 *Vincent of Coleshill*, Richard Frederick, Vincent, GBE, KCB, DSO, *b.* 1931, *m.*
1985 *Vinson*, Nigel, Vinson, LVO, *b.* 1931, *m.*
1990 *Waddington*, David Charles, Waddington, GCVO, PC, QC, *b.* 1929, *m.*
1990 *Wade of Chorlton*, (William) Oulton, Wade, *b.* 1932, *m.*
1992 *Wakeham*, John, Wakeham, PC, *b.* 1932, *m.*
1999 *Waldegrave of North Hill*, William Arthur, Waldegrave, PC, *b.* 1946, *m.*
1997 *Walker of Doncaster*, Harold, Walker, PC, *b.* 1927, *m.*
1992 *Walker of Worcester*, Peter Edward, Walker, MB PC, *b.* 1932, *m.*
1974 *Wallace of Coslany*, George Douglas, Wallace, *b.* 1906, *m.*
1995 *Wallace of Saltaire*, William John Lawrence, Wallace, PH.D., *b.* 1941, *m.*
1989 *Walton of Detchant*, John Nicholas, Walton, TD, FRCP, *b.* 1922, *m.*
1998 *Warner*, Norman Reginald, Warner, *b.* 1940, *m*
1997 *Watson of Invergowrie*, Michael Goodall, Watso MSP, *b.* 1949, *m.*
1999 *Watson of Richmond*, Alan John, Watson, CBE, *b.* 1941, *m.*
1992 *Weatherill*, (Bruce) Bernard, Weatherill, PC, *b.* 1920, *m.*
1977 *Wedderburn of Charlton*, (Kenneth) William, Wedderburn, FBA, QC, *b.* 1927, *m.*
1976 *Weidenfeld*, (Arthur) George, Weidenfeld, *b.* 1919, *m.*
1980 *Weinstock*, Arnold, Weinstock, *b.* 1924, *m.*
1978 *Whaddon*, (John) Derek, Page, *b.* 1927, *m.*
1996 *Whitty*, John Lawrence (Larry), Whitty, *b.* 194 *m.*
1974 *Wigoder*, Basil Thomas, Wigoder, QC, *b.* 1921, *m*
1985 *Williams of Elvel*, Charles Cuthbert Powell, Williams, CBE, *b.* 1933, *m.*
1992 *Williams of Mostyn*, Gareth Wyn, Williams, QC, *b.* 1941, *m. Lord Privy Seal, Leader of the House o Lords*
1999 *Williamson of Horton*, David (Francis), Williamson, GCMG, CB, *b.* 1934, *m.*
1992 *Wilson of Tillyorn*, David Clive, Wilson, GCMG, PH.D., KT, *b.* 1935, *m.*
1995 *Winston*, Robert Maurice Lipson, Winston, FRCOG, *b.* 1940, *m.*
1985 *Wolfson*, Leonard Gordon, Wolfson, *b.* 1927, *m.*
1991 *Wolfson of Sunningdale*, David, Wolfson, *b.* 1935 *m.*
1999 *Woolmer of Leeds*, Kenneth John, Woolmer, *b.* 1940, *m.*
1994 *Wright of Richmond*, Patrick Richard Henry, Wright, GCMG, *b.* 1931, *m.*
1978 *Young of Dartington*, Michael, Young, PH.D., *b.* 1915, *m.*
1984 *Young of Graffham*, David Ivor, Young, PC, *b.* 1932 *m.*
1992 **Younger of Prestwick*, The Viscount Younger of, Leckie, *m.* (*see page 146*)

## BARONESSES

*Created*

1997 *Amos*, Valerie Ann, Amos, *b.* 1954
2000 *Andrews*, Elizabeth Kay, Andrews, OBE
1996 *Anelay of St Johns*, Joyce Anne, Anelay, DBE, *b.* 1947, *m.*
1999 *Ashton of Upholland*, Catherine Margaret, Ashton, *m.*
1999 *Barker*, Elizabeth Jean, Barker, *b.* 1961
1987 *Blackstone*, Tessa Ann Vosper, Blackstone, PH.D., *b.* 1942, *Minister of State for the Arts*
1987 *Blatch*, Emily May, Blatch, CBE, PC, *b.* 1937, *m.*
1999 *Blood*, May, Blood, MBE, *b.* 1938
1990 *Brigstocke*, Heather Renwick, Brigstocke, *b.* 1929 *m.*
1998 *Buscombe*, Peta Jane, Buscombe, *b.* 1954, *m.*
1996 *Byford*, Hazel, Byford, DBE, *b.* 1941, *m.*
1982 *Carnegy of Lour*, Elizabeth Patricia Carnegy of, Lour, *b.* 1925
1990 *Castle of Blackburn*, Barbara Anne, Castle, PC, *b.* 1910, *w.*
1992 *Chalker of Wallasey*, Lynda, Chalker, PC, *b.* 1942, *m.*
2000 *Cohen of Pimlico*, Janet, Cohen, *b.* 1940, *m.*

982 *Cox*, Caroline Anne, Cox, *b.* 1937, *m.*
998 *Crawley*, Christine Mary, Crawley, MEP, *b.* 1950, *m.*
990 *Cumberlege*, Julia Frances, Cumberlege, CBE, *b.* 1943, *m.*
978 *David*, Nora Ratcliff, David, *b.* 1913, *w.*
993 *Dean of Thornton-le-Fylde*, Brenda, Dean, PC, *b.* 1943, *m.*
974 *Delacourt-Smith of Alteryn*, Margaret Rosalind, Delacourt-Smith, *b.* 1916, *m.*
990 *Dunn*, Lydia Selina, Dunn, DBE, *b.* 1940, *m.*
990 *Eccles of Moulton*, Diana Catherine, Eccles, *b.* 1933, *m.*
972 *Elles*, Diana Louie, Elles, *b.* 1921, *m.*
997 *Emerton*, Audrey Caroline, Emerton, DBE, *b.* 1935
974 *Falkender*, Marcia Matilda, Falkender, CBE, *b.* 1932
994 *Farrington of Ribbleton*, Josephine, Farrington, *b.* 1940, *m. Baroness-in-Waiting*
001 *Finlay of Llandaff*, Ilora Gillian, Finlay, *m.*
974 *Fisher of Rednal*, Doris Mary Gertrude, Fisher, *b.* 1919, *w.*
990 *Flather*, Shreela, Flather, *m.*
997 *Fookes*, Janet Evelyn, Fookes, DBE, *b.* 1936
999 *Gale*, Anita, Gale, *b.* 1940
981 *Gardner of Parkes*, (Rachel) Trixie (Anne), Gardner, *b.* 1927, *m.*
000 *Gibson of Market Rasen*, Anne, Gibson, OBE, *b.* 1940, *m.*
998 *Goudie*, Mary Teresa, Goudie, *b.* 1946, *m.*
993 *Gould of Potternewton*, Joyce Brenda, Gould, *b.* 1932, *m.*
000 *Greengross*, Sally Ralea, Greengross, OBE, *b.* 1935, *m.*
991 *Hamwee*, Sally Rachel, Hamwee, *b.* 1947
999 *Hanham*, Joan Brownlow, Hanham, CBE, *b.* 1939, *m.*
999 *Harris of Richmond*, Angela Felicity, Harris, *b.* 1944
996 *Hayman*, Helene Valerie, Hayman, *b.* 1949, *m.*
991 *Hilton of Eggardon*, Jennifer, Hilton, QPM, *b.* 1936
995 *Hogg*, Sarah Elizabeth Mary, Hogg, *b.* 1946, *m.*
990 *Hollis of Heigham*, Patricia Lesley, Hollis, D.PHIL., *b.* 1941, *m.*
985 *Hooper*, Gloria Dorothy, Hooper, *b.* 1939
001 *Howarth of Breckland*, Valerie Georgina, Howarth, OBE,*m.*
001 *Howe of Idlicote*, Elspeth Rosamond Morton, Howe, CBE, *b.* 1932, *m.*
999 *Howells of St Davids*, Rosalind Patricia-Anne, Howells
1965 *Hylton-Foster*, Audrey Pellew, Hylton-Foster, DBE, *b.* 1908, *w.*
1991 *James of Holland Park*, Phyllis Dorothy White (P. D., James), OBE, *b.* 1920, *w.*
1992 *Jay of Paddington*, Margaret Ann, Jay, PC, *b.* 1939, *m.*
1979 *Jeger*, Lena May, Jeger, *b.* 1915, *w.*
1997 *Kennedy of the Shaws*, Helena Ann, Kennedy, QC, *b.* 1950, *m.*
1997 *Knight of Collingtree*, (Joan Christabel) Jill, Knight, DBE, *b.* 1923, *w.*
1997 *Linklater of Butterstone*, Veronica, Linklater, *b.* 1943, *m.*
1996 *Lloyd of Highbury*, Prof. June Kathleen, Lloyd, DBE, FRCP, FRCPE, FRCGP, *b.* 1928
1978 *Lockwood*, Betty, Lockwood, *b.* 1924, *w.*
1997 *Ludford*, Sarah Ann, Ludford, MEP, *b.* 1951
1997 *Maddock*, Diana Margaret, Maddock, *b.* 1945, *m.*
1991 *Mallalieu*, Ann, Mallalieu, QC, *b.* 1945, *m.*
1970 *Masham of Ilton*, Susan Lilian Primrose, Cunliffe-Lister, *b.* 1935, *m.*
1999 *Massey of Darwen*, Doreen Elizabeth, Massey, *b.* 1938, *m.*
1979 *McFarlane of Llandaff*, Jean Kennedy, McFarlane, *b.* 1926
1999 *McIntosh of Hudnall*, Genista Mary, McIntosh, *b.* 1946
2001 *Michie*, Janet Ray, Michie, *b.* 1934, *m.*
1998 *Miller of Chilthorne Domer*, Susan Elizabeth, Miller, *b.* 1954
1993 *Miller of Hendon*, Doreen, Miller, MBE, *b.* 1933, *m.*
2001 *Morgan of Huyton*, Sally, Morgan, *b.* 1959, *m.*
1997 *Nicholson of Winterbourne*, Emma Harriet, Nicholson, MEP, *b.* 1941, *m.*
1982 *Nicol*, Olive Mary Wendy, Nicol, *b.* 1923, *m.*
2000 *Noakes*, Shiela Valerie, Masters, DBE,*m.*
2000 *Northover*, Lindsay Patricia, Granshaw
1991 *O'Cathain*, Detta, O'Cathain, OBE, *b.* 1938, *m.*
1999 *O'Neill of Bengarve*, Onora Sylvia, O'Neill, CBE, PH.D., *b.* 1941
1989 *Oppenheim-Barnes*, Sally, Oppenheim-Barnes, PC, *b.* 1930, *m.*
1990 *Park of Monmouth*, Daphne Margaret Sybil Désirée, Park, CMG, OBE, *b.* 1921
1991 *Perry of Southwark*, Pauline, Perry, *b.* 1931, *m.*
1974 *Pike*, (Irene) Mervyn (Parnicott), Pike, DBE, *b.* 1918
1997 *Pitkeathley*, Jill Elizabeth, Pitkeathley, OBE, *b.* 1940
1981 *Platt of Writtle*, Beryl Catherine, Platt, CBE, FENG., *b.* 1923, *m.*
1999 *Prashar*, Usha Kumari, Prashar, CBE, *b.* 1948, *m.*
1996 *Ramsay of Cartvale*, Margaret Mildred (Meta), Ramsay, *b.* 1936
1994 *Rawlings*, Patricia Elizabeth, Rawlings, *b.* 1939
1997 *Rendell of Babergh*, Ruth Barbara, Rendell, CBE, *b.* 1930, *m.*
1998 *Richardson of Calow*, Kathleen Margaret, Richardson, OBE, *b.* 1938, *m.*
1997 *Scotland of Asthal*, Patricia Janet, Scotland, QC, *m.*
2000 *Scott of Needham Market*, Rosalind Carol, Scott
1991 *Seccombe*, Joan Anna Dalziel, Seccombe, DBE, *b.* 1930, *m.*
1967 *Serota*, Beatrice, Serota, DBE, *b.* 1919, *m.*
1998 *Sharp of Guildford*, Margaret Lucy, Sharp, *m.*
1973 *Sharples*, Pamela, Sharples, *b.* 1923, *m.*
1995 *Smith of Gilmorehill*, Elizabeth Margaret, Smith, *b.* 1940, *w.*
1999 *Stern*, Vivien Helen, Stern, CBE, *b.* 1941
1996 *Symons of Vernham Dean*, Elizabeth Conway, Symons, *b.* 1951, *Minister of State for Trade and the Foreign and Commonwealth Office*
1992 *Thatcher*, Margaret Hilda, Thatcher, KG, OM, PC, FRS, *b.* 1925, *m.*
1994 *Thomas of Walliswood*, Susan Petronella, Thomas, OBE, *b.* 1935, *m.*
1998 *Thornton*, (Dorothea) Glenys, Thornton, *b.* 1952, *m.*
1980 *Trumpington*, Jean Alys, Barker, PC, *b.* 1922, *w.*
1985 *Turner of Camden*, Muriel Winifred, Turner, *b.* 1927, *m.*
1998 *Uddin*, Manzila Pola, Uddin, *b.* 1959, *m.*
2000 *Walmsley*, Joan Margaret, Walmsley
1985 *Warnock*, Helen Mary, Warnock, DBE, *b.* 1924, *w.*
1999 *Warwick of Undercliffe*, Diana Mary, Warwick, *b.* 1945, *m.*
1999 *Whitaker*, Janet Alison, Whitaker
1996 *Wilcox*, Judith Ann, Wilcox, *w.*
1999 *Wilkins*, Rosalie Catherine, Wilkins, *b.* 1946
1993 *Williams of Crosby*, Shirley Vivien Teresa Brittain, Williams, PC, *b.* 1930, *m.*
1971 *Young*, Janet Mary, Young, PC, *b.* 1926, *m.*
1997 *Young of Old Scone*, Barbara Scott, Young, *b.* 1948

# Lords Spiritual

The Lords Spiritual are the Archbishops of Canterbury and York and 24 diocesan bishops of the Church of England. The Bishops of London, Durham and Winchester always have seats in the House of Lords; the other 21 seats are filled by the remaining diocesan bishops in order of seniority. The Bishop of Sodor and Man and the Bishop of Gibraltar are not eligible to sit in the House of Lords.

## ARCHBISHOPS

*Style*, The Most Revd and Right Hon. the Lord Archbishop of _
*Addressed as* Archbishop, *or* Your Grace

*Introduced to House of Lords*

1991 *Canterbury* (103rd), George Leonard Carey, PC, Ph.D., *b.* 1935, *m.*, *cons.* 1987, *trans.* 1991

1990 *York* (96th), David Michael Hope, KCVO, PC, D.Phil., *b.* 1940, *cons.* 1985, *elected* 1985, *trans.* 1991, 1995

## BISHOPS

*Style*, The Right Revd the Lord Bishop of _
*Addressed as* My Lord
*elected* date of election as diocesan bishop

*Introduced to House of Lords* (as at mid-2001)

1989 *Lichfield* (97th), Keith Norman Sutton, *b.* 1934, *m.*, *cons.* 1978, *elected* 1984

1990 *Bristol* (54th), Barry Rogerson, *b.* 1936, *m.*, *cons.* 1979, *elected* 1985

1993 *Lincoln* (70th), Robert Maynard Hardy, *b.* 1936, *m.*, *cons.* 1980, *elected* 1986

1993 *Oxford* (41st), Richard Douglas Harries, *b.* 1936, *m.*, *cons.* 1987, *elected* 1987

1994 *Birmingham* (7th), Mark Santer, *b.* 1936, *m.*, *cons.* 1981, *elected* 1987

1994 *Durham* (93rd), (Anthony) Michael (Arnold) Turnbull, *b.* 1935, *m.*, *cons.* 1988, *elected* 1988, *trans.* 1994

1995 *Blackburn* (7th), Alan David Chesters, *b.* 1937, *m.*, *cons.* 1989, *elected* 1989

1996 *London* (132nd), Richard John Carew Chartres, *b.* 1947, *m.*, *cons.* 1992

1996 *Winchester* (96th), Michael Charles Scott-Joynt, *b.* 1943, *m.*, *cons.* 1987

1997 *Hereford* (103rd), John Keith Oliver, *b.* 1935, *m.*, *cons.* 1990, *elected* 1990

1997 *Southwark* (9th), Thomas Frederick Butler, *b.* 1940, *m.*, *cons.* 1985, *elected* 1991

1997 *Bath and Wells* (77th), James Lawton Thompson, *b.* 1936, *m.*, *cons.* 1978, *elected* 1991

1997 *Wakefield* (11th), Nigel Simeon McCulloch, *b.* 1942, *m.*, *cons.* 1986, *elected* 1992

1997 *Bradford* (8th), David James Smith, *b.* 1935, *m.*, *cons.* 1987, *elected* 1992

1998 *Manchester* (10th), Christopher John Mayfield, *b.* 1935, *m.*, *cons.* 1985, *elected* 1993

1998 *Salisbury* (77th), David Staffurth Stancliffe, *b.* 1942, *m.*, *cons.* 1993, *elected* 1993

1998 *Gloucester* (39th), David Edward Bentley, *b.* 1935, *m.*, *cons.* 1986, *elected* 1993

1999 *Rochester* (106th), Michael James Nazir-Ali, Ph.D., *b.* 1949, *m.*, *cons.* 1984, *elected* 1995

1999 *Guildford* (8th), John Warren Gladwin, *b.* 1942, *m.*, *cons.* 1994, *elected* 1994

1999 *Portsmouth* (8th), Kenneth William Stevenson, *b.* 1949, *m.*, *cons.* 1995, *elected* 1995

1999 *Derby* (6th), Jonathan Sansbury Bailey, *b.* 1940, *m.*, *cons.* 1992, *elected* 1995

1999 *St Albans* (9th), Christopher William Herbert, *b.* 1944, *m.*, *cons.* 1995, *elected* 1995

2000 *Chelmsford* (8th), John Freeman Perry, *b.* 1935, *m.*, *cons.* 1989, *elected* 1996

2001 *Peterborough* (37th), Ian Cundy, *b.* 1945, *m.*, *cons.* 1992, *elected* 1996

*Bishops awaiting seats, in order of seniority* (as at mid-2001)

*Chester* (40th), Peter Robert Forster, Ph.D., *b.* 1950, *cons.* 1996, *elected* 1996

*St Edmundsbury and Ipswich* (9th), (John Hubert) Richard Lewis, *b.* 1943, *m.*, *cons.* 1992, *elected* 1997

*Truro* (14th), William Ind, *b.* 1942, *m.*, *cons.* 1987, *elected* 1997

*Worcester* (112th), Peter Stephen Maurice Selby, *b.* 1941, *cons.* 1984, *elected* 1997

*Newcastle* (11th), (John) Martin Wharton, *b.* 1944, *m.*, *cons.* 1992, *elected* 1997

*Sheffield* (6th), John Nicholls, *b.* 1943, *m.*, *cons.* 1990, *elected* 1997

*Coventry* (8th), Colin J. Bennetts, *b.* 1940, *m.*, *cons.* 1994, *elected* 1997

*Liverpool* (7th), James Jones, *b.* 1948, *m.*, *cons.* 1994, *elected* 1998

*Leicester* (6th), Timothy John Stevens, *b.* 1946, *m.*, cons. 1999, *elected* 1999

*Southwell* (10th), George Henry Cassidy, *b.* 1942, *m.*, *cons.* 1999, *elected* 1999

*Norwich* (71st), Graham R. James, *b.* 1951, *m.*, *cons.* 1993, *elected* 1999

*Exeter* (70th), Michael L. Langrish, *b.* 1946, *m.*, *cons.* 1993, *elected* 2000

*Ripon and Leeds* (12th), John R. Packer, *b.* 1946, *m.*, *cons.*1996, *elected* 2000

*Ely* (68th) Dr. Anthony Russell, *b.* 1943, *m.*, *cons.* 1988, *elected* 2000

*Carlisle* (65th) Graham Dow, *b.* 1942, *m.*, *cons.* 1985, *elected* 2000

## COURTESY TITLES

From this list it will be seen that, for example, the Marquess of Blandford is heir to the Dukedom of Marlborough, and Viscount Amberley to the Earldom of Russell. Titles of second heirs are also given, and the courtesy title of the father of a second heir is indicated by *; e.g. Earl of Burlington, eldest son of *Marquess of Hartington
For forms of address, *see* page 135

### MARQUESSES

Blandford – *Marlborough, D.*
Bowmont and Cessford – *Roxburghe, D.*
Douglas and Clydesdale – *Hamilton, D.*
Douro – *Wellington, D.*
Graham – *Montrose, D.*
Granby – *Rutland, D.*
Hamilton – *Abercorn, D.*
Hartington – *Devonshire, D.*
Kildare – *Leinster, D.*
Lorne – *Argyll, D.*
Tavistock – *Bedford, D.*
Tullibardine – *Atholl, D.*
Worcester – *Beaufort, D.*

### EARLS

Aboyne – *Huntly, M.*
Ancram – *Lothian, M.*
Arundel and Surrey – *Norfolk, D.*
Bective – *Headfort, M.*
Belfast – *Donegall, M.*
Brecknock – *Camden, M.*
Burford – *St Albans, D.*
Burlington – **Hartington, M.*
Cardigan – *Ailesbury, M.*
Compton – *Northampton, M.*
Dalkeith – *Buccleuch, D.*
Dumfries – *Bute, M.*
Euston – *Grafton, D.*
Glamorgan – **Worcester, M.*
Grosvenor – *Westminster, D.*
Haddo – *Aberdeen and Temair, M.*
Hillsborough – *Downshire, M.*
Hopetoun – *Linlithgow, M.*
March and Kinrara – *Richmond, D.*
Medina – *Milford Haven, M.*
*Mount Charles – *Conyngham, M.*
Mornington – **Douro, M.*
Mulgrave – *Normanby, M.*
Percy – *Northumberland, D.*
Ronaldshay – *Zetland, M.*
*St Andrews – *Kent, D.*
*Shelburne – *Lansdowne, M.*
*Southesk – *Fife, D.*
Sunderland – **Blandford, M.*
*Tyrone – *Waterford, M.*
Ulster – *Gloucester, D.*
*Uxbridge – *Anglesey, M.*
Wiltshire – *Winchester, M.*
Yarmouth – *Hertford, M.*

### VISCOUNTS

Althorp – *Spencer, E.*
Amberley – *Russell, E.*
Andover – *Suffolk and Berkshire, E.*
Anson – *Lichfield, E.*
Asquith – *Oxford and Asquith, E.*
Boringdon – *Morley, E.*
Borodale – *Beatty, E.*
Boyle – *Shannon, E.*
Brocas – *Jellicoe, E.*
Campden – *Gainsborough, E.*
Carlow – *Portarlington, E.*
Carlton – *Wharncliffe, E.*
Castlereagh – *Londonderry, M.*
Chelsea – *Cadogan, E.*
Chewton – *Waldegrave, E.*
Chichester – **Belfast, E.*
Clanfield – *Peel, E.*
Clive – *Powis, E.*
Coke – *Leicester, E.*
Corry – *Belmore, E.*
Corvedale – *Baldwin of Bewdley, E.*
Cranborne – *Salisbury, M.*
Cranley – *Onslow, E.*
Crichton – *Erne, E.*
Crowhurst – *Cottenham, E.*
Curzon – *Howe, E.*
Dangan – *Cowley, E.*
Dawick – *Haig, E.*
Drumlanrig – *Queensberry, M.*
Duncannon – *Bessborough, E.*
Dungarvan – *Cork and Orrery, E.*
Dunluce – *Antrim, E.*
Dunwich – *Stradbroke, E.*
Dupplin – *Kinnoull, E.*
Ebrington – *Fortescue, E.*
Ednam – *Dudley, E.*
Encombe – *Eldon, E.*
Enfield – *Strafford, E.*
Erleigh – *Reading, M.*
Errington – *Cromer, E.*
FitzHarris – *Malmesbury, E.*
Folkestone – *Radnor, E.*
Forbes – *Granard, E.*
Garmoyle – *Cairns, E.*
Garnock – *Lindsay, E.*
Glandine – *Norbury, E.*
Glenapp – *Inchcape, E.*
Glentworth – *Limerick, E.*
Grimstone – *Verulam, E.*
Gwynedd – *Lloyd George of Dwyfor, E.*
Hawkesbury – *Liverpool, E.*
Hinchingbrooke – *Sandwich, E.*
Ikerrin – *Carrick, E.*
Ingestre – *Shrewsbury, E.*
Ipswich – **Euston, E.*
Jocelyn – *Roden, E.*
Kelburn – *Glasgow, E.*
Kilwarlin – *Hillsborough, E.*
Kingsborough – *Kingston, E.*
Kirkwall – *Orkney, E.*
Knebworth – *Lytton, E.*
Lascelles – *Harewood, E.*
Linley – *Snowdon, E.*
Loftus – *Ely, M.*
Lowther – *Lonsdale, E.*
Lumley – *Scarbrough, E.*
Lymington – *Portsmouth, E.*
Macmillan of Ovenden – *Stockton, E.*
Maitland – *Lauderdale, E.*
Malden – *Essex, E.*
Mandeville – *Manchester, D.*
Melgund – *Minto, E.*
Merton – *Nelson, E.*
Moore – *Drogheda, E.*
Newport – *Bradford, E.*
Newry and Mourne – *Kilmorey, E.*
Parker – *Macclesfield, E.*
Perceval – *Egmont, E.*
Petersham – *Harrington, E.*
Pollington – *Mexborough, E.*
Raynham – *Townshend, M.*
Reidhaven – *Seafield, E.*
Ruthven of Canberra – *Gowrie, E.*
St Cyres – *Iddesleigh, E.*
Sandon – *Harrowby, E.*
Savernake – **Cardigan, E.*
Slane – **Mount Charles, E.*
Somerton – *Normanton, E.*
Stopford – *Courtown, E.*
Stormont – *Mansfield, E.*
Strathallan – *Perth, E.*
Stuart – *Castle Stewart, E.*
Suirdale – *Donoughmore, E.*
Tamworth – *Ferrers, E.*
Tarbat – *Cromartie, E.*
Vaughan – *Lisburne, E.*
Weymouth – *Bath, M.*
Windsor – *Plymouth, E.*
Wolmer – *Selborne, E.*
Woodstock – *Portland, E.*

### BARONS (LORD)

Aberdour – *Morton, E.*
Apsley – *Bathurst, E.*
Ardee – *Meath, E.*
Ashley – *Shaftesbury, E.*
Balgonie – *Leven and Melville, E.*
Balniel – *Crawford and Balcarres, E.*
Berriedale – *Caithness, E.*
Bingham – *Lucan, E.*
Binning – *Haddington, E.*
Brooke – *Warwick, E.*
Bruce – *Elgin, E.*
Buckhurst – *De La Warr, E.*
Burghley – *Exeter, M.*
Cardross – *Buchan, E.*
Carnegie – **Southesk, E.*
Clifton – *Darnley, E.*
Cochrane – *Dundonald, E.*
Courtenay – *Devon, E.*
Dalmeny – *Rosebery, E.*
Doune – *Moray, E.*
Downpatrick – **St Andrews, E.*
Dunglass – *Home, E.*
Eliot – *St Germans, E.*
Eskdail – **Dalkeith, E.*
Formartine – **Haddo, E.*
Gillford – *Clanwilliam, E.*
Glamis – *Strathmore, E.*
Greenock – *Cathcart, E.*
Guernsey – *Aylesford, E.*
Hay – *Erroll, E.*
Herbert – *Pembroke, E.*
Howard of Effingham – *Effingham, E.*
Howland – **Tavistock, M.*
Hyde – *Clarendon, E.*
Inverurie – *Kintore, E.*
Irwin – *Halifax, E.*
Johnstone – *Annandale and Hartfell, E.*
Kenlis – **Bective, E.*
Langton – *Temple of Stowe, E.*
La Poer – **Tyrone, E.*
Leslie – *Rothes, E.*
Loughborough – *Rosslyn, E.*
Maltravers – **Arundel and Surrey, E.*
Mauchline – *Loudoun, C.*
Medway – *Cranbrook, E.*
Montgomerie – *Eglinton and Winton, E.*
Moreton – *Ducie, E.*
Naas – *Mayo, E.*
Neidpath – *Wemyss and March, E.*

Norreys – Lindsey and Abingdon, E.
Ogilvy – Airlie, E.
Oxmantown – Rosse, E.
Paget de Beaudesert – *Uxbridge, E.
Porchester – Carnarvon, E.
Ramsay – Dalhousie, E.
Romsey – Mountbatten of Burma, C.
Rosehill – Northesk, E.
Scrymgeour – Dundee, E.
Seymour – Somerset, D.
Stanley – Derby, E.
Strathnaver – Sutherland, C.
Wodehouse – Kimberley, E
Worsley – Yarborough, E.

## PEERS' SURNAMES WHICH DIFFER FROM THEIR TITLES

The following symbols indicate the rank of the peer holding each title:

| | |
|---|---|
| C. | Countess |
| D. | Duke |
| E. | Earl |
| M. | Marquess |
| V. | Viscount |
| * | Life Peer |

Where no designation is given, the title is that of an hereditary Baron or Baroness

Abney-Hastings – Loudoun, C.
Acheson – Gosford, E.
Adderley – Norton
Addington – Sidmouth, V.
Adebowale – A. of Thornes*
Agar – Normanton, E.
Aitken – Beaverbrook
Akers-Douglas – Chilston, V.
Alexander – A. of Tunis, E.
Alexander – A. of Weedon*
Alexander – Caledon, E.
Allen – A. of Abbeydale*
Allen – Croham*
Allsopp – Hindlip
Alton – A. of Liverpool*
Anderson – Waverley, V.
Anelay – A. of St Johns*
Annesley – Valentia, V.
Anson – Lichfield, E.
Archer – A. of Sandwell*
Archer – A. of Weston-super-Mare*
Armstrong – A. of Ilminster*
Armstrong-Jones – Snowdon, E.
Arthur – Glenarthur
Arundell – Talbot of Malahide
Ashdown – A. of Norton-sub-Hamdon*
Ashley – A. of Stoke*
Ashley-Cooper – Shaftesbury, E.
Ashton – A. of Hyde
Ashton – A. of Upholland*
Asquith – Oxford and Asquith, E.
Assheton – Clitheroe
Astley – Hastings
Astor – A. of Hever
Aubrey-Fletcher – Braye
Bailey – Glanusk
Baillie – Burton
Baillie Hamilton – Haddington, E.
Baker – B. of Dorking*
Baldwin – B. of Bewdley, E.
Balfour – B. of Inchrye
Balfour – Kinross
Balfour – Riverdale
Bampfylde – Poltimore
Banbury – B. of Southam
Barber – B. of Tewkesbury*
Baring – Ashburton
Baring – Cromer, E.
Baring – Howick of Glendale
Baring – Northbrook
Baring – Revelstoke
Barker – Trumpington*
Barnes – Gorell
Barnewall – Trimlestown
Bassam – B. of Brighton*
Bathurst – Bledisloe, V.
Beauclerk – St Albans, D.
Beaumont – Allendale, V.
Beaumont – B. of Whitley*
Beckett – Grimthorpe
Benn – Stansgate, V.
Bennet – Tankerville, E.
Bentinck – Portland, E.-
Beresford – Decies
Beresford – Waterford, M.
Bernstein – B. of Craigweil*
Berry – Camrose, V.
Berry – Kemsley, V.
Bertie – Lindsey, E.
Best – Wynford
Bethell – Westbury
Bewicke-Copley – Cromwell
Bigham – Mersey, V.
Bingham – B. of Cornhill*
Bingham – Clanmorris
Bingham – Lucan, E.
Bligh – Darnley, E.
Blyth – B. of Rowington*
Bootle-Wilbraham – Skelmersdale
Boscawen – Falmouth, V.
Boston – B. of Faversham*
Bourke – Mayo, E.
Bowes Lyon – Strathmore,E.
Bowyer – Denham
Boyd – Kilmarnock
Boyle – Cork and Orrery, E.
Boyle – Glasgow, E.
Boyle – Shannon, E.
Brabazon – Meath, E.
Brand – Hampden, V.
Brassey – B. of Apethorpe
Brett – Esher, V.
Bridge – B. of Harwich*
Bridgeman – Bradford, E.
Brittan – B. of Spennithorne*
Brodrick – Midleton, V.
Brooke – Alanbrooke, V.
Brooke – B. of Alverthorpe*
Brooke – Brookeborough, V.
Brooke – B. of Sutton Mandeville*
Brooks – B. of Tremorfa*
Brooks – Crawshaw
Brougham – Brougham and Vaux
Broughton – Fairhaven
Browne – Kilmaine
Browne – B. of Madingley*
Browne – Oranmore and Browne
Browne – Sligo, M.
Bruce – Aberdare
Bruce – Balfour of Burleigh
Bruce – B. of Donington*
Bruce – Elgin and Kincardine, E.
Brudenell-Bruce – Ailesbury, M.
Buchan – Tweedsmuir
Buckley – Wrenbury
Butler – B. of Brockwell*
Butler – Carrick, E.
Butler – Dunboyne
Butler – Mountgarret, V.
Buxton – B. of Alsa*
Byng – Strafford, E.
Byng – Torrington, V.
Callaghan – C. of Cardiff*
Cambell-Savours – C.-S. of Allerdale*
Cameron – C. of Lochbroom*
Campbell – Argyll, D.
Campbell – C. of Alloway*
Campbell – C. of Croy*
Campbell – Cawdor, E.
Campbell – Colgrain
Campbell – Stratheden and Campbell
Campbell-Gray – Gray
Canning – Garvagh
Capell – Essex, E.
Carington – Carrington
Carlisle – C. of Berriew*
Carlisle – C. of Bucklow*
Carmichael – C. of Kelvingrove*
Carnegie – Fife, D.
Carnegie – Northesk, E.
Carr – C. of Hadley*
Cary – Falkland, V.
Castle – C. of Blackburn*
Caulfeild – Charlemont, V.
Cavendish – C. of Furness*
Cavendish – Chesham
Cavendish – Devonshire, D.
Cavendish – Waterpark
Cayzer – Rotherwick
Cecil – Amherst of Hackney
Cecil – Exeter, M.
Cecil – Rockley
Cecil – Salisbury, M.
Chalker – C. of Wallasey*
Chaloner – Gisborough
Charteris – Wemyss and March, E.
Chetwynd-Talbot – Shrewsbury, E.
Chichester – Donegall, M.
Chichester-Clark – Moyola*
Child Villiers – Jersey, E.
Cholmondeley – Delamere
Chubb – Hayter
Clark – C. of Kempston*
Clarke – C. of Hampstead*
Clegg-Hill – Hill, V.
Clifford – C. of Chudleigh
Cochrane – C. of Cults
Cochrane – Dundonald, E.
Cocks – Somers
Cohen – C. of Pimlico*
Coke – Leicester, E.
Cole – Enniskillen, E.
Collier – Monkswell
Colville – Clydesmuir
Colville – C. of Culross, V.
Compton – Northampton,M.
Condon – C. of Langdon Green*
Conolly-Carew – Carew
Constantine – C. of Stanmore*
Cooke – C. of Islandreagh*
Cooke – C. of Thorndon*
Cooper – Norwich, V
Cope – C. of Berkeley*
Corbett – C. of Castle Vale*.
Corbett – Rowallan
Cornwall-Leigh – Grey of Condor
Courtenay – Devon, E.
Craig – C. of Radley*
Craig – Craigavon, V.
Crichton – Erne, E.
Crichton-Stuart – Bute, M.
Cripps – Parmoor
Crossley – Somerleyton
Cubitt – Ashcombe
Cunliffe-Lister – Masham of Ilton*
Cunliffe-Lister – Swinton, E.

Currie – *C. of Marylebone**
Curzon – *Howe, E.*
Curzon – *Scarsdale, V.*
Cust – *Brownlow*
Dalrymple – *Stair, E.*
Daubeny de Moleyns – *Ventry*
Davies – *D. of Coity**
Davies – *Darwen*
Davies – *D. of Oldham**
Davison – *Broughshane*
Dawnay – *Downe, V.*
Dawson-Damer – *Portarlington, E.*
Dean – *D. of Harptree**
Dean – *D. of Thornton-le-Fylde**
Deane – *Muskerry*
de Courcy – *Kingsale*
de Grey – *Walsingham*
Delacourt-Smith – *Delacourt Smith of Alteryn**
Denison – *Londesborough*
Denison-Pender – *Pender*
Devereux – *Hereford, V.*
Dewar – *Forteviot*
De Yarburgh-Bateson – *Deramore*
Dixon – *Glentoran*
Dodson – *Monk Bretton*
Donaldson – *D. of Lymington**
Dormand – *D. of Easington**
Douglas – *Morton, E.*
Douglas – *Queensberry, M.*
Douglas-Hamilton – *Hamilton, D.*
Douglas-Hamilton – *Selkirk, E.*
Douglas-Hamilton – *Selkirk of Douglas**
Douglas-Home – *Dacre*
Douglas-Home – *Home, E.*
Douglas-Pennant–*Penrhyn*
Douglas-Scott-Montagu – *Montagu of Beaulieu*
Drummond – *Perth, E.*
Drummond of Megginch – *Strange*
Dugdale – *Crathorne*
Duke – *Merrivale*
Duncombe – *Feversham*
Dundas – *Melville, V.*
Dundas – *Zetland, M.*
Eady – *Swinfen*
Eccles – *E. of Moulton**
Eden – *Auckland*
Eden – *E. of Winton**
Eden – *Henley*
Edgcumbe – *Mount Edgcumbe, E.*
Edmondson – *Sandford*
Edwardes – *Kensington*
Edwards – *Crickhowell**
Egerton – *Sutherland, D.*
Eliot – *St Germans, E.*
Elliot-Murray-Kynynmound – *Minto, E.*
Ellis – *Seaford*
Erskine – *Buchan, E.*
Erskine – *Mar and Kellie, E.*
Erskine-Murray – *Elibank*
Evans – *E. of Parkside**
Evans – *E. of Temple Guiting**
Evans – *E. of Watford**
Evans – *Mountevans*
Evans-Freke – *Carbery*
Eve – *Silsoe*
Ewing – *E. of Kirkford**
Fairfax – *F. of Cameron*
Falconer – *F. of Thoroton**
Fane – *Westmorland, E.*
Farrington – *F. of Ribbleton**
Faulkner – *F. of Worcester**
Fearn – *F. of Southport**
Feilding – *Denbigh, E.*
Felton – *Seaford*
Fellowes – *De Ramsey*
Fermor-Hesketh – *Hesketh*
Fiennes – *Saye and Sele*
Fiennes-Clinton – *Lincoln, E.*
Finch Hatton – *Winchilsea, E.*
Finch-Knightley – *Aylesford, E.*
Finlay – *F. of Llandaff**
Fisher – *F. of Rednal**
Fitzalan-Howard – *Herries of Terregles*
Fitzalan-Howard – *Norfolk, D.*
FitzGerald – *Leinster, D.*
Fitzherbert – *Stafford*
FitzRoy – *Grafton, D.*
FitzRoy – *Southampton*
FitzRoy Newdegate – *Daventry, V.*
Fletcher-Vane – *Inglewood*
Flower – *Ashbrook, V.*
Foljambe – *Liverpool, E.*
Forbes – *Granard, E.*
Forsyth – *F. of Drumlean**
Forwood – *Arlington*
Foster – *F. of Thames Bank**
Fowler - *F. of Sutton Caulfield**
Fox-Strangways – *Ilchester, E.*
Frankland – *Zouche*
Fraser – *F. of Carmyllie**
Fraser – *F. of Kilmorack**
Fraser – *Lovat*
Fraser – *Saltoun*
Fraser – *Strathalmond*
Freeman-Grenville – *Kinloss*
Fremantle – *Cottesloe*
French – *De Freyne*
Fyfe – *F. of Fairfield**
Galbraith – *Strathclyde*
Ganzoni – *Belstead*
Gardner – *G. of Parkes**
Gathorne-Hardy – *Cranbrook, E.*
Gibbs – *Aldenham*
Gibbs – *Wraxall*
Gibson – *Ashbourne*
Gibson – *G. of Market Rasen**
Giffard – *Halsbury, E.*
Gilbey – *Vaux of Harrowden*
Gilmour – *G. of Craigmillar**
Gladwin – *G. of Clee**
Glyn – *Wolverton*
Godley – *Kilbracken*
Goff – *G. of Chieveley**
Golding – *G. of Newcastle-under-Lyme**
Gordon – *Aberdeen, M.*
Gordon – *G. of Strathblane**
Gordon – *Huntly, M.*
Gordon Lennox – *Richmond, D.*
Gore – *Arran, E.*
Gould – *G. of Potternewton**
Graham – *G. of Edmonton**
Graham – *Montrose, D.*
Graham-Toler – *Norbury, E.*
Granshaw – *Northover**
Grant of Grant – *Strathspey*
Granville – *G. of Eye**
Gray – *G. of Contin**
Greaves – *Dysart, C.*
Greenall – *Daresbury*
Greene – *G. of Harrow Weald**
Greville – *Warwick, E.*
Griffiths – *G. of Fforestfach**
Grigg – *Altrincham*
Grimston – *G. of Westbury*
Grimston – *Verulam, E.*
Grosvenor – *Westminster, D.*
Grosvenor – *Wilton and Ebury, E*
Guest – *Wimborne, V*
Gueterbock – *Berkeley*
Guinness – *Iveagh, E.*
Guinness – *Moyne*
Gully – *Selby, V.*
Gummer – *Chadlington**
Gurdon – *Cranworth*
Guthrie – *G. of Craigiebank**
Gwynne Jones – *Chalfont**
Hamilton – *Abercorn, D.*
Hamilton – *Belhaven and Stenton*
Hamilton – *Dudley*
Hamilton – *H. of Dalzell*
Hamilton – *Holm Patrick*
Hamilton-Russell – *Boyne, V.*
Hamilton-Smith – *Colwyn*
Hanbury-Tracy – *Sudeley*
Handcock – *Castlemaine*
Harbord-Hamond – *Suffield*
Harding – *H. of Petherton*
Hardinge – *H. of Penshurst*
Hardy – *H. of Wath**
Hare – *Blakenham, V.*
Hare – *Listowel, E.*
Harmsworth – *Rothermere, V.*
Harris – *H. of Haringey**
Harris – *H. of High Cross**
Harris – *H. of Peckham**
Harris – *H. of Richmond**
Harris – *Malmesbury, E.*
Harvey – *H. of Tasburgh*
Hastings Bass – *Huntingdon, E.*
Hay – *Erroll, E.*
Hay – *Kinnoull, E.*
Hay – *Tweeddale, M.*
Heathcote-Drummond-Willoughby – *Willoughby de Eresby*
Hely-Hutchinson – *Donoughmore, E.*
Henderson – *Faringdon*
Hennessy – *Windlesham*
Henniker-Major – *Henniker*
Hepburne-Scott – *Polwarth*
Herbert – *Carnarvon, E.*
Herbert – *Hemingford*
Herbert – *Pembroke, E.*
Herbert – *Powis, E.*
Hervey – *Bristol, M.*
Heseltine – *H. of Thenford**
Hewitt – *Lifford, V.*
Hicks Beach – *St Aldwyn, E.*
Hill – *Downshire, M.*
Hill – *Sandys*
Hill-Trevor – *Trevor*
Hilton – *H. of Eggardon**
Hobart-Hampden – *Buckinghamshire, E.*
Hobhouse – *H. of Woodborough**
Hodgson – *H. of Astley Abbotts**
Hogg – *Hailsham of St Marylebone**
Hogg – *H. of Cumbernauld**
Holland-Hibbert – *Knutsford, V.*
Hollis – *H. of Heigham**
Holme – *H. of Cheltenham**
Holmes à Court – *Heytesbury*
Hood – *Bridport, V.*
Hope – *Glendevon*
Hope – *H. of Craighead**
Hope – *Linlithgow, M.*
Hope – *Rankeillour*
Hope Johnstone – *Annandale and Hartfell, E.*
Hope-Morley – *Hollenden*
Hopkinson – *Colyton*
Hore Ruthven – *Gowrie, E.*
Hovell-Thurlow-Cumming-Bruce – *Thurlow*
Howard – *Carlisle, E.*
Howard – *Effingham, E.*
Howard – *H. of Penrith*
Howard – *Strathcona*
Howard – *Suffolk and Berkshire, E.*

Howarth – *H. of Breckland**
Howe – *H. of Aberavon**
Howe – *H. of Idlicote**
Howell – *H. of Guildford**
Howells – *Geraint**
Howells – *H. of St. Davids**
Howie – *H. of Troon**
Hubbard – *Addington*
Huggins – *Malvern, V.*
Hughes – *H. of Woodside**
Hughes – *Islwyn**
Hughes-Young – *St Helens*
Hunt – *H. of Chesterton**
Hunt – *H. of Kings Heath**
Hunt – *H. of Tanworth**
Hunt – *H. of Wirral**
Hurd – *H. of Westwell**
Hussey – *H. of North Bradley**
Hutchinson – *H. of Lullington**
Ingrams – *Darcy de Knayth*
Innes-Ker – *Roxburghe, D.*
Inskip – *Caldecote, V.*
Irby – *Boston*
Irvine – *I. of Lairg**
Isaacs – *Reading, M.*
James – *J. of Holland Park**
James – *Northbourne*
Janner – *J. of Braunstone**
Jauncey – *J. of Tullichettle**
Jay – *J. of Paddington**
Jebb – *Gladwyn*
Jenkin – *J. of Roding**
Jenkins – *J. of Hillhead**
Jenkins – *J. of Putney**
Jervis – *St Vincent, V.*
Jocelyn – *Roden, E.*
Johnston – *J. of Rockport**
Jolliffe – *Hylton*
Jones – *J. of Deeside**
Joynson-Hicks – *Brentford, V.*
Kay-Shuttleworth – *Shuttleworth*
Kearley – *Devonport, V.*
Keith – *K. of Castleacre**
Keith – *K. of Kinkel**
Keith – *Kintore, E.*
Kemp – *Rochdale, V.*
Kennedy – *Ailsa, M*
Kennedy – *K. of the Shaws**.
Kenworthy – *Strabolgi*
Keppel – *Albemarle, E.*
Kerr – *Lothian, M.*
Kerr – *Teviot*
Kilpatrick – *K. of Kincraig**
King – *Lovelace, E.*
King – *K. of Wartnaby**
King – *K. of West Bromwich**
King-Tenison – *Kingston, E.*
Kirkham – *Berners*
Kitchener – *K. of Khartoum, E.*
Knatchbull – *Brabourne*
Knatchbull – *Mountbatten of Burma, C.*
Knight – *K. of Collingtree**
Knox – *Ranfurly, E.*
Laing – *L. of Dunphail**
Lamb – *Rochester*
Lambton – *Durham, E.*
Lamont – *L. of Lerwick**
Lampson – *Killearn*
Lane – *L. of Horsell**
Lang – *L. of Monkton**
Lascelles – *Harewood, E.*
Law – *Coleraine*
Law – *Ellenborough*
Lawrence – *Trevethin and Oaksey*
Lawson – *Burnham*
Lawson – *L. of Blaby**
Lawson-Johnston – *Luke*
Lea – *L. of Crondall**
Leckie – *Younger of Prestwick**
Legge – *Dartmouth, E.*
Legh – *Grey of Codnor*
Legh – *Newton*
Leigh-Pemberton – *Kingsdown**
Leith – *Burgh*
Lennox-Boyd – *Boyd of Merton, V.*
Le Poer Trench – *Clancarty, E.*
Leslie – *Rothes, E.*
Leslie Melville – *Leven and Melville, E.*
Lester – *L. of Herne Hill**
Levene – *L. of Portsoken**
Leveson-Gower – *Granville, E.*
Lewis – *L. of Newnham**
Lewis – *Merthyr*
Liddell – *Ravensworth*
Lindesay-Bethune – *Lindsay, E.*
Lindsay – *Crawford, E.*
Lindsay – *L. of Birker*
Linklater – *L. of Butterstone**
Littleton – *Hatherton*
Llewelyn-Davies – *Llewelyn-Davies of Hastoe**
Lloyd – *L. of Berwick**
Lloyd – *L. of Highbury**
Lloyd George – *Lloyd George of Dwyfor, E.*
Lloyd George – *Tenby, V.*
Lloyd-Mostyn – *Mostyn*
Loder – *Wakehurst*
Lofthouse – *L. of Pontefract**
Lopes – *Roborough*
Lour – *Carneggy of Lour**
Low – *Aldington*
Lowry-Corry – *Belmore, E.*
Lowther – *Lonsdale, E.*
Lowther – *Ullswater, V.*
Lubbock – *Avebury*
Lucas – *L. of Chilworth*
Lumley – *Scarbrough, E.*
Lumley-Savile – *Savile*
Lyon-Dalberg-Acton – *Acton*
Lysaght – *Lisle*
Lyttelton – *Chandos, V.*
Lyttelton – *Cobham, V.*
Lytton Cobbold – *Cobbold*
McAlpine – *M. of West Green**
Macaulay – *M. of Bragar**
McClintock-Bunbury – *Rathdonnell*
McColl – *M. of Dulwich**
Macdonald – *M. of Gwaenysgor*
Macdonald – *M. of Tradeston**
McDonnell – *Antrim, E.*
Macfarlane – *M. of Bearsden**
McFarlane – *M. of Llandaff**
MacGregor – *M. of Pulham Market**
McIntosh – *M. of Haringey**
McIntosh – *M. of Hudnall**
Mackay – *Inchcape, E.*
Mackay – *M. of Clashfern**
Mackay – *M. of Drumadoon**
Mackay – *Reay*
Mackay – *Tanlaw**
MacKenzie – *M. of Culkein**
MacKenzie – *M. of Framwellgate**
Mackenzie – *Cromartie, E.*
Mackie – *M. of Benshie**
Mackintosh – *M. of Halifax, V.*
McLaren – *Aberconway*
MacLaurin – *M. of Knebworth**
MacLennan – *M. of Rogart**
Macmillan – *Stockton, E.*
Macpherson – *M. of Drumochter*
Macpherson – *Strathcarron*
Maffey – *Rugby*
Maginnis – *M. of Drumglass**
Maitland – *Lauderdale, E.*
Makgill – *Oxfuird, V.*
Makins – *Sherfield*
Manners – *Rutland, D.*
Manningham-Buller – *Dilhorne, V.*
Mansfield – *Sandhurst*
Marks – *M. of Broughton*
Marquis – *Woolton, E.*
Marshall – *M. of Knightsbridge**
Marsham – *Romney, E.*
Martyn-Hemphill – *Hemphill*
Mason – *M. of Barnsley**
Massey – *M. of Darwen**
Masters – *Noakes**
Maude – *Hawarden, V.*
Maxwell – *de Ros*
Maxwell – *Farnham*
May – *M. of Oxford**
Mayhew – *M. of Twysden**
Meade – *Clanwilliam, E.*
Mercer Nairne Petty-Fitzmaurice – *Lansdowne, M.*
Millar – *Inchyra*
Miller – *M. of Chiltorne Domer**
Miller – *M. of Hendon**
Milner – *M. of Leeds*
Mitchell-Thomson – *Selsdon*
Mitford – *Redesdale*
Molyneaux – *M. of Killead*
Monckton – *M. of Brenchley, V.*
Monckton-Arundell – *Galway, V.*
Mond – *Melchett*
Money-Coutts – *Latymer*
Monro – *M. of Langholm**
Montagu – *Manchester, D.*
Montagu – *Sandwich, E.*
Montagu – *Swaythling*
Montagu Douglas Scott – *Buccleuch, D.*
Montagu Stuart Wortley – *Wharncliffe, E.*
Montague – *Amwell*
Montgomerie – *Eglinton, E*
Montgomery – *M. of Alamein, V.*
Moore – *Drogheda, E.*
Moore – *M. of Lower Marsh**
Moore – *M. of Wolvercote**
Moore-Brabazon – *Brabazon of Tara*
Moreton – *Ducie, E*
Morgan – *M. of Huyton**.
Morris – *Killanin*
Morris – *M. of Aberavon**
Morris – *M. of Manchester**
Morris – *M. of Naseby**
Morris – *M. of Kenwood*
Morrison – *Dunrossil, V.*
Morrison – *Margadale*
Moser – *M. of Regents Park**
Mosley – *Ravensdale*
Mountbatten – *Milford Haven, M.*
Muff – *Calverley*
Mulholland – *Dunleath*
Murray – *Atholl, D.*
Murray – *Dunmore, E.*
Murray – *Mansfield and Mansfield, E.*
Murray – *M. of Epping Forest**
Murton – *M. of Lindisfarne**
Nall-Cain – *Brocket*
Napier – *Napier and Ettrick*
Napier – *N. of Magdala*
Needham – *Kilmorey, E.*
Neill – *N. of Bladen**
Nelson – *N. of Stafford*
Nevill – *Abergavenny, M.*
Neville – *Braybrooke*
Newton – *N. of Braintree**
Nicholls – *N. of Birkenhead**
Nicolson – *Carnock*
Nicholson – *N. of Winterboune**
Nivison – *Glendyne*
Noel – *Gainsborough, E.*
North – *Guilford, E.*

Northcote – *Iddesleigh, E.*
Norton – *Grantley*
Norton – *N. of Louth**
Norton – *Rathcreedan*
Nugent – *Westmeath, E.*
O'Brien – *Inchiquin*
Ogilvie-Grant – *Seafield, E.*
Ogilvy – *Airlie, E.*
Oliver – *O. of Aylmerton**
O'Neill – *O'N of Bengarve**
O'Neill – *Rathcavan*
Orde-Powlett – *Bolton*
Ormsby-Gore – *Harlech*
Ouseley – *O. of Peckham Rye**
Page – *Whaddon**
Paget – *Anglesey, M.*
Pakenham – *Longford, E.*
Pakington – *Hampton*
Palmer – *Lucas and Dingwall*
Palmer – *Selborne, E.*
Park – *P. of Monmouth**
Parker – *Macclesfield, E.*
Parker – *Morley, E.*
Parnell – *Congleton*
Parsons – *Rosse, E.*
Patel – *P. of Blackburn**
Paulet – *Winchester, M.*
Peake – *Ingleby, V.*
Pearson – *Cowdray, V.*
Pearson – *P. of Rannoch**
Pease – *Gainford*
Pease – *Wardington*
Pelham – *Chichester, E.*
Pelham – *Yarborough, E.*
Pellew – *Exmouth, V*
Pendry – *P. of Stalybridge**.
Penny – *Marchwood, V.*
Pepys – *Cottenham, E.*
Perceval – *Egmont, E.*
Percy – *Northumberland, D.*
Perry – *P. of Southwark**
Perry – *P. of Walton**
Pery – *Limerick, E.*
Peyton – *P. of Yeovil**
Philipps – *Milford*
Philipps – *St Davids, V.*
Phillips – *P. of Sudbury**
Phillips – *P. of Worth Matravers**
Phipps – *Normanby, M.*
Pilkington – *P. of Oxenford**
Plant – *P. of Highfield**
Platt – *P. of Writtle**
Pleydell-Bouverie – *Radnor, E.*
Plummer – *P. of St Marylebone**
Plumptre – *Fitzwalter*
Plunkett – *Dunsany*
Plunkett – *Louth*
Pollock – *Hanworth, V.*
Pomeroy – *Harberton, V.*
Ponsonby – *Bessborough, E.*
Ponsonby – *de Mauley*
Ponsonby – *P. of Shulbrede*
Ponsonby – *Sysonby*
Porter – *P. of Luddenham**
Powell – *P. of Bayswater**
Powys – *Lilford*
Pratt – *Camden, M.*
Preston – *Gormanston, V.*
Primrose – *Rosebery, E.*
Prittie – *Dunalley*
Prout – *Kingsland**
Ramsay – *Dalhousie, E.*
Ramsay – *R. of Cartvale**
Ramsbotham – *Soulbury, V.*
Randall – *R. of St. Budeaux**
Rawlinson – *R. of Ewell**
Rees-Williams – *Ogmore*
Rendell – *R. of Babergh**
Renfrew – *R. of Kaimsthorn**
Renton – *R. of Mount Harry**
Renwick – *R. of Clifton**
Rhys – *Dynevor*
Richards – *Milverton*
Richardson – *R. of Calow**
Richardson – *R. of Duntisbourne**
Ritchie – *R. of Dundee*
Roberts – *Clwyd*
Roberts – *R. of Conway**
Robertson – *R. of Oakridge*
Robertson – *R. of Port Ellen**
Robertson – *Wharton*
Robinson – *Martonmere*
Roche – *Fermoy*
Rodd – *Rennell*
Rodger – *R. of Earlsferry**
Rodgers – *R. of Quarry Bank**
Rogers – *R. of Riverside**
Roll – *R. of Ipsden**
Roper-Curzon – *Teynham*
Rospigliosi – *Newburgh, E.*
Rous – *Stradbroke, E.*
Rowley-Conwy – *Langford*
Royle – *Fanshawe of Richmond**
Runciman – *R. of Doxford, V.*
Russell – *Ampthill*
Russell – *Bedford, D.*
Russell – *de Clifford*
Russell – *R. of Liverpool*
Ryder – *Harrowby, E.*
Ryder – *R. of Eaton Hastings**
Ryder – *R. of Wensum**
Sackville – *De La Warr, E.*
Sackville-West – *Sackville*
Sainsbury – *S. of Preston Candover**
Sainsbury – *S. of Turville**
St Aubyn – *St Levan*
St Clair – *Sinclair*
St Clair-Erskine – *Rosslyn, E.*
St John – *Bolingbroke and St John, V.*
St John – *St John of Blesto*
St John-Stevas – *St John of Fawsley**
St Leger – *Doneraile, V.*
Samuel – *Bearsted, V.*
Sanderson – *S. of Ayot*
Sanderson – *S. of Bowden**
Sandilands – *Torphichen*
Saumarez – *De Saumarez*
Savile – *Mexborough, E.*
Saville – *S. of Newdigate**
Scarlett – *Abinger*
Schreiber – *Marlesford**
Sclater-Booth – *Basing*
Scotland – *S. of Asthal**
Scott – *Eldon, E*
Scott – *S. of Foscotte**
Scott – *S. of Needham Market**.
Scrymgeour – *Dundee, E.*
Seager – *Leighton of St Mellons*
Seely – *Mottistone*
Seymour – *Hertford, M.*
Seymour – *Somerset, D.*
Sharp – *S. of Guildford**
Shaw – *Craigmyle*
Shaw – *S. of Northstead**
Sheldon – *S. of Ashdon-under-Lyne**
Sheppard – *S. of Didgemere**
Sheppard – *S. of Liverpool**
Shirley – *Ferrers, E.*
Shore – *S. of Stepney**
Short – *Glenamara**
Shutt – *S. of Greetland**
Siddeley – *Kenilworth*
Sidney – *De L'Isle, V.*
Simon – *S. of Glaisdale**
Simon – *S. of Highbury**
Simon – *S. of Wythenshawe*
Simpson – *S. of Dunkeld**
Sinclair – *Caithness, E.*
Sinclair – *S. of Cleeve*
Sinclair – *Thurso, V.*
Skeffington – *Massereene, V.*
Slynn – *S. of Hadley**
Smith – *Bicester*
Smith – *Hambleden, V.*
Smith – *Kirkhill**
Smith – *S. of Clifton**
Smith – *S. of Gilmorehill**
Smith – *S. of Leigh**
Somerset – *Beaufort, D.*
Somerset – *Raglan*
Soulsby – *S. of Swaffham Prior**
Spencer – *Churchill, V.*
Spencer-Churchill – *Marlborough, D.*
Spring Rice – *Monteagle of Brandon*
Stanhope – *Harrington, E.*
Stanley – *Derby, E.*
Stanley – *Stanley of Alderley and Sheffield*
Stapleton-Cotton – *Combermere, V.*
Steel – *S. of Aikwood**
Sterling – *S. of Plaistow**
Stevens – *S. of Ludgate**
Stevenson – *S. of Coddenham**
Stewart – *Galloway, E.*
Stewart – *Stewartby**
Stodart – *S. of Leaston**
Stoddart – *S. of Swindon**
Stone – *S. of Blackheath**
Stonor – *Camoys*
Stopford – *Courtown, E.*
Stourton – *Mowbray*
Strachey – *O'Hagan*
Strutt – *Belper*
Strutt – *Rayleigh*
Stuart – *Castle Stewart, E.*
Stuart – *Moray, E.*
Stuart – *S. of Findhorn, V.*
Suenson-Taylor – *Grantchester*
Sutherland – *S. of Houndwood**
Symons – *S. of Vernham Dean**
Taylor – *Ingrow**
Taylor – *T. of Blackburn**
Taylor – *T. of Warwick**
Taylour – *Headfort, M.*
Temple-Gore-Langton – *Temple of Stowe, E*
Temple-Morris – *Temple-Morris of Llandaff**
Tennant – *Glenconner*
Thellusson – *Rendlesham*
Thesiger – *Chelmsford, V.*
Thomas – *T. of Gresford**
Thomas – *T. of Gwydir**
Thomas – *T. of Macclesfield**
Thomas – *T. of Swynnerton**
Thomas – *T. of Walliswood**
Thomson – *T. of Fleet*
Thomson – *T. of Monifieth**
Thynn – *Bath, M.*
Tottenham – *Ely, M.*
Trefusis – *Clinton*
Trench – *Ashtown*
Trevor-Roper – *Dacre of Glanton**
Tufton – *Hothfield*
Turner – *Netherthorpe*
Turner – *T. of Camden**
Turnour – *Winterton, E.*
Tyrell-Kenyon – *Kenyon*
Vanden-Bempde-Johnstone – *Derwent*
Vane – *Barnard*
Vane-Tempest-Stewart – *Londonderry, M.*
Vanneck – *Huntingfield*
Vaughan – *Lisburne, E.*
Vereker – *Gort, V.*
Verney – *Willoughby de Broke*
Vernon – *Lyveden*
Vesey – *De Vesci, V.*
Villiers – *Clarendon, E.*
Vincent – *V. of Coleshill**
Vivian – *Swansea*
Wade – *W. of Chorlton**
Waldegrave – *W. of North Hill**
Walker – *W. of Doncaster**
Walker – *W. of Worcester**
Wallace – *W. of Coslany**
Wallace – *W. of Saltaire**
Wallop – *Portsmouth, E.*
Walton – *W. of Detchant**
Ward – *Bangor, V.*

Ward – *Dudley, E.*
Warrender – *Bruntisfield*
Warwick – *W. of Undercliffe**
Watson – *W. of Invergowrie**
Watson – *Manton*
Watson – *W. of Richmond**
Webber – *Lloyd-Webber**
Wedderburn – *W. of Charlton**
Weir – *Inverforth*
Weld-Forester – *Forester*
Wellesley – *Cowley, E.*
Wellesley – *Wellington, D.*
Westenra – *Rossmore*
White – *Annaly*
White – *Haningfield**
Whiteley – *Marchamley*
Whitfield – *Kenswood*
Williams – *W. of Crosby**
Williams – *W. of Elve**
Williams – *W. of Mostyn**
Williamson – *Forres*
Williamson – *W. of Horton**
Willoughby – *Middleton*
Wills – *Dulverton*
Wilson – *Moran*
Wilson – *W. of Tillyorn**
Windsor – *Gloucester, D.*
Windsor – *Kent, D.*
Windsor-Clive – *Plymouth, E.*
Wingfield – *Powerscourt, V.*
Winn – *St Oswald*
Wodehouse – *Kimberley, E.*
Wolfson – *W. of Sunningdale**
Wood – *Halifax, E.*
Wood – *Holderness**
Woolmer – *W. of Leeds**
Wright – *W. of Richmond**
Wyndham – *Egremont and Leconfield*
Wyndham-Quin – *Dunraven, E.*
Wynn – *Newborough*
Yarde-Buller – *Churston*
Yerburgh – *Alvingham*
Yorke – *Hardwicke, E.*
Young – *Kennet*
Young – *Y. of Dartington**
Young – *Y. of Graffham**
Young – *Y. of Old Scone**
Younger – *Y. of Leckie, V.*

# Orders of Chivalry

## THE MOST NOBLE ORDER OF THE GARTER (1348)

KG
*Ribbon*, Blue
*Motto*, Honi soit qui mal y pense (*Shame on him who thinks evil of it*)

The number of Knights Companions is limited to 24

SOVEREIGN OF THE ORDER
The Queen

LADIES OF THE ORDER
HM Queen Elizabeth the Queen Mother, 1936
HRH The Princess Royal, 1994

ROYAL KNIGHTS
HRH The Prince Philip, Duke of Edinburgh, 1947
HRH The Prince of Wales, 1958
HRH The Duke of Kent, 1985
HRH The Duke of Gloucester, 1997

EXTRA KNIGHTS COMPANIONS AND LADIES
HRH Princess Juliana of the Netherlands, 1958
HRH The Grand Duke of Luxembourg, 1972
HM The Queen of Denmark, 1979
HM The King of Sweden, 1983
HM The King of Spain, 1988
HM The Queen of the Netherlands, 1989
HIM The Emperor of Japan, 1998

KNIGHTS AND LADY COMPANIONS
The Earl of Longford, 1971
The Duke of Grafton, 1976
The Duke of Norfolk, 1983
The Lord Richardson of Duntisbourne, 1983
The Lord Carrington, 1985
The Lord Callaghan of Cardiff, 1987
The Lord Hailsham of St Marylebone, 1988
The Duke of Wellington, 1990
Field Marshal the Lord Bramall, 1990
Sir Edward Heath, 1992
The Viscount Ridley, 1992
The Lord Sainsbury of Preston Candover, 1992
The Lord Ashburton, 1994
The Lord Kingsdown, 1994
Sir Ninian Stephen, 1994
The Baroness Thatcher, 1995
Sir Edmund Hillary, 1995
The Duke of Devonshire, 1996
Sir Timothy Colman, 1996
The Duke of Abercorn, 1999
Sir William Gladstone, 1999
Field Marshal The Lord Inge, 2001
Sir Anthony Acland, 2001

*Prelate*, The Bishop of Winchester
*Chancellor*, The Lord Carrington, KG, GCMG, CH, MC
*Register*, The Dean of Windsor
*Garter King of Arms*, P. Gwynn-Jones, CVO
*Gentleman Usher of the Black Rod*, Lt. Gen. Sir Michael Willcocks, KCB
*Secretary*, D. H. B. Chesshyre, LVO

## THE MOST ANCIENT AND MOST NOBLE ORDER OF THE THISTLE (REVIVED 1687)

KT
*Ribbon*, Green
*Motto*, Nemo me impune lacessit (*No one provokes me with impunity*)

The number of Knights is limited to 16

SOVEREIGN OF THE ORDER
The Queen

LADIES OF THE THISTLE
HM Queen Elizabeth the Queen Mother, 1937
HRH The Princess Royal, 2000

ROYAL KNIGHTS
HRH The Prince Philip, Duke of Edinburgh, 1952
HRH The Prince of Wales, Duke of Rothesay, 1977

KNIGHTS AND LADIES
The Earl of Wemyss and March, 1966
Sir Donald Cameron of Lochiel, 1973
The Duke of Buccleuch and Queensberry, 1978
The Earl of Elgin and Kincardine, 1981
The Lord Thomson of Monifieth, 1981
The Earl of Airlie, 1985
Capt. Sir Iain Tennant, 1986
The Viscount Younger of Leckie, 1995
The Viscount of Arbuthnott, 1996
The Earl of Crawford and Balcarres, 1996
Lady Marion Fraser, 1996
The Lord Macfarlane of Bearsden, 1996
The Lord Mackay of Clashfern, 1997
The Lord Wilson of Tillyorn, 2000

*Chancellor*, The Duke of Buccleuch and Queensberry, KT, VRD
*Dean*, The Very Revd G. I. Macmillan, CVO
*Secretary and Lord Lyon King of Arms*, R. O. Blair, LVO, WS
*Usher of the Green Rod*, Rear-Adm. C. H. Layman, CB, DSO, LVO

## THE MOST HONOURABLE ORDER OF THE BATH (1725)

GCB *Military* GCB *Civil*

GCB Knight (or Dame) Grand Cross
KCB Knight Commander
DCB Dame Commander
CB Companion

*Ribbon*, Crimson
*Motto*, Tria juncta in uno (*Three joined in one*)

Remodelled 1815, and enlarged many times since. The Order is divided into civil and military divisions. Women became eligible for the Order from 1 January 1971

THE SOVEREIGN

GREAT MASTER AND FIRST OR PRINCIPAL KNIGHT GRAND CROSS
HRH The Prince of Wales, KG, KT, GCB

*Dean of the Order*, The Dean of Westminster
*Bath King of Arms*, Gen. Sir Brian Kenny, GCB, CBE
*Registrar and Secretary*, Rear-Adm. D. E. Macey, CB
*Genealogist*, P. Gwynn-Jones, CVO
*Gentleman Usher of the Scarlet Rod*, Air Vice-Marshal Sir Richard Peirse, KCVO, CB
*Deputy Secretary*, The Secretary of the Central Chancery of the Orders of Knighthood

*Chancery*, Central Chancery of the Orders of Knighthood, St James's Palace, London SW1A 1BH

## THE ORDER OF MERIT (1902)

OM *Military*

OM *Civil*

OM

*Ribbon*, Blue and crimson

This Order is designed as a special distinction for eminent men and women without conferring a knighthood upon them. The Order is limited in numbers to 24, with the addition of foreign honorary members. Membership is of two kinds, military and civil, the badge of the former having crossed swords, and the latter oak leaves

THE SOVEREIGN

HRH The Prince Philip, Duke of Edinburgh, 1968
Sir George Edwards, 1971
Revd Prof. Owen Chadwick, KBE, 1983
Sir Andrew Huxley, 1983
Dr Frederick Sanger, 1986
Prof. Sir Ernst Gombrich, 1988
Dr Max Perutz, 1988
Dame Cicely Saunders, 1989
Prof. The Lord Porter of Luddenham, 1989
The Baroness Thatcher, 1990
Dame Joan Sutherland, 1991
Prof. Francis Crick, 1991
Dame Ninette de Valois, 1992
Sir Michael Atiyah, 1992
Lucian Freud, 1993
The Lord Jenkins of Hillhead, 1993
Sir Aaron Klug, 1995
The Lord Foster of Thames Bank, 1997
Sir Denis Rooke, 1997
Sir James Black, 2000
Sir Anthony Caro, 2000
Prof. Sir Roger Penrose, 2000
Sir Tom Stoppard, 2000
*Honorary Member*, Nelson Mandela, 1995

*Secretary and Registrar*, Sir Edward Ford, GCVO, KCB, ERD
*Chancery*, Central Chancery of the Orders of Knighthood, St James's Palace, London SW1A 1BH

## THE MOST DISTINGUISHED ORDER OF ST MICHAEL AND ST GEORGE (1818)

GCMG

KCMG

| | |
|---|---|
| GCMG | Knight (or Dame) Grand Cross |
| KCMG | Knight Commander |
| DCMG | Dame Commander |
| CMG | Companion |

*Ribbon*, Saxon blue, with scarlet centre
*Motto*, Auspicium melioris aevi (*Token of a better age*)

THE SOVEREIGN

GRAND MASTER

HRH The Duke of Kent, KG, GCMG, GCVO, ADC

*Prelate*, The Rt. Revd Simon Barrington-Ward, KCMG
*Chancellor*, Sir Antony Acland, KG, GCMG, GCVO
*Secretary*, The Permanent Under-Secretary of State at the Foreign and Commonwealth Office and Head of the Diplomatic Service
*Registrar*, Sir John Graham, Bt., GCMG
*King of Arms*, Sir Ewen Fergusson, GCMG, GCVO
*Gentleman Usher of the Blue Rod*, Sir John Margetson, KCMG
*Dean*, The Dean of St Paul's
*Deputy Secretary*, The Secretary of the Central Chancery of the Orders of Knighthood
*Chancery*, Central Chancery of the Orders of Knighthood, St James's Palace, London SW1A 1BH

## THE MOST EMINENT ORDER OF THE INDIAN EMPIRE (1868)

| | |
|---|---|
| GCIE | Knight Grand Commander |
| KCIE | Knight Commander |
| CIE | Companion |

*Ribbon*, Imperial purple
*Motto*, Imperatricis auspiciis (*Under the auspices of the Empress*)

THE SOVEREIGN

*Registrar*, The Secretary of the Central Chancery of the Orders of Knighthood
No conferments have been made since 1947

## THE IMPERIAL ORDER OF THE CROWN OF INDIA (1877) FOR LADIES

CI

*Badge*, the royal cipher in jewels within an oval, surmounted by an heraldic crown and attached to a bow of light blue watered ribbon, edged white
The honour does not confer any rank or title upon the recipient
No conferments have been made since 1947

HM The Queen, 1947
HM Queen Elizabeth the Queen Mother, 1931
HRH The Princess Margaret, Countess of Snowdon, 1947
HRH Princess Alice, Duchess of Gloucester, 1937

## THE ROYAL VICTORIAN ORDER (1896)

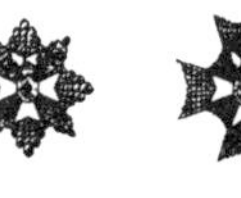

GCVO KCVO

| | |
|---|---|
| GCVO | Knight or Dame Grand Cross |
| KCVO | Knight Commander |
| DCVO | Dame Commander |
| CVO | Commander |
| LVO | Lieutenant |
| MVO | Member |

*Ribbon*, Blue, with red and white edges
*Motto*, Victoria

THE SOVEREIGN

GRAND MASTER
HM Queen Elizabeth the Queen Mother

*Chancellor*, The Lord Chamberlain
*Secretary*, The Keeper of the Privy Purse
*Registrar*, The Secretary of the Central Chancery of the Orders of Knighthood
*Chaplain*, The Chaplain of the Queen's Chapel of the Savoy
*Hon. Genealogist*, D. H. B. Chesshyre, LVO

## [T]HE MOST EXCELLENT [O]RDER OF THE BRITISH [E]MPIRE (1917)

GBE

KBE

[T]he Order was divided into military [a]nd civil divisions in December 1918

[G]BE Knight or Dame Grand Cross
[K]BE Knight Commander
DBE Dame Commander
[C]BE Commander
[O]BE Officer
[M]BE Member

*[R]ibbon*, Rose pink edged with pearl grey with vertical pearl stripe in centre (military division); without vertical pearl stripe (civil division)
*Motto*, For God and the Empire

THE SOVEREIGN

GRAND MASTER
HRH The Prince Philip, Duke of Edinburgh, KG, KT, OM, GBE, PC

*Prelate*, The Bishop of London
*King of Arms*, Air Chief Marshal Sir Patrick Hine, GCB, GBE
*Registrar*, The Secretary of the Central Chancery of the Orders of Knighthood
*Secretary*, The Secretary of the Cabinet and Head of the Home Civil Service
*Dean*, The Dean of St Paul's
*Gentleman Usher of the Purple Rod*, Sir Alexander Michael Graham, GBE, DCL*Chancery*, Central Chancery of the Orders of Knighthood, St James's Palace, London SW1A 1BH

## ORDER OF THE COMPANIONS OF HONOUR (1917)

CH

*Ribbon*, Carmine, with gold edges

This Order consists of one class only and carries with it no title. The number of awards is limited to 65 (excluding honorary members)

Anthony, Rt. Hon. John, 1981
Ashley of Stoke, The Lord, 1975
Astor, Hon. David, 1993
Attenborough, Sir David, 1995
Baker, Dame Janet, 1993
Baker of Dorking, The Lord, 1992
Birtwistle, Sir Harrison, 2001
Brenner, Sydney, 1986
Brook, Peter, 1998
Brooke, Rt. Hon. Peter, 1992
Carrington, The Lord, 1983
De Chastelain, Gen. John, 1999
Doll, Prof. Sir Richard, 1995
Fraser, Rt. Hon. Malcolm, 1977
Freud, Lucian, 1983
Glenamara, The Lord, 1976
Gorton, Rt. Hon. Sir John, 1971
Hailsham of St Marylebone, The Lord, 1974
Hamilton, Richard, 1999
Hawking, Prof. Stephen, 1989
Healey, The Lord, 1979
Heseltine, Rt. Hon. Michael, 1997
Hobsbawm, Prof. Eric, 1998
Hockney, David, 1997
Howe of Aberavon, The Lord, 1996
Hurd of Westwell, The Lord, 1995
Jones, James, 1977
King, Rt. Hon. Tom, 1992
Lange, Rt. Hon. David, 1989
Lessing, Doris, 1999
Major, Rt. Hon. John, 1999
Milstein, César, 1994
Owen, The Lord, 1994
Patten, Rt. Hon. Christopher, 1998
Perutz, Dr Max, 1975
Powell, Sir Philip, 1984
Riley, Bridget, 1999
Sanger, Frederick, 1981
Scofield, Paul, 2000
Sisson, Charles, 1993
Smith, Sir John, 1993
Somare, Rt. Hon. Sir Michael, 1978
Talboys, Rt. Hon. Sir Brian, 1981
Tebbit, The Lord, 1987
Varah, Rev. Dr. Chad, 1999
*Honorary Members*, Lee Kuan Yew, 1970; Dr Joseph Luns, 1971

*Secretary and Registrar*, The Secretary of the Central Chancery of the Orders of Knighthood

## THE DISTINGUISHED SERVICE ORDER (1886)

DSO

*Ribbon*, Red, with blue edges

Bestowed in recognition of especial services in action of commissioned officers in the Navy, Army and Royal Air Force and (since 1942) Mercantile Marine. The members are Companions only. A Bar may be awarded for any additional act of service

## THE IMPERIAL SERVICE ORDER (1902)

ISO

*Ribbon*, Crimson, with blue centre

Appointment as Companion of this Order is open to members of the Civil Services whose eligibility is determined by the grade they hold. The Order consists of The Sovereign and Companions to a number not exceeding 1,900, of whom 1,300 may belong to the Home Civil Services and 600 to Overseas Civil Services. The then Prime Minister announced in March 1993 that he would make no further recommendations for appointments to the Order.

*Secretary*, The Secretary of the Cabinet and Head of the Home Civil Service
*Registrar*, The Secretary of the Central Chancery of the Orders of Knighthood, St James's Palace, London SW1A 1BH

## THE ROYAL VICTORIAN CHAIN (1902)

It confers no precedence on its holders

HM THE QUEEN

HM Queen Elizabeth the Queen Mother, 1937

HRH Princess Juliana of the Netherlands, 1950
HM The King of Thailand, 1960
HM King Zahir Shah of Afghanistan, 1971
HM The Queen of Denmark, 1974
HM The King of Nepal, 1975
HM The King of Sweden, 1975
HM The Queen of the Netherlands, 1982
Gen. Antonio Eanes, 1985
HM The King of Spain, 1986
HM The King of Saudi Arabia, 1987
HRH The Princess Margaret, Countess of Snowdon, 1990
HE Richard von Weizsäcker, 1992
HM The King of Norway, 1994
The Earl of Airlie, 1997
The Duke of Norfolk, 2000

# Baronetage and Knightage

## BARONETS

*Style*, 'Sir' before forename and surname, followed by 'Bt.'
*Wife's style*, 'Lady' followed by surname
For forms of address, *see* page 135

There are five different creations of baronetcies: Baronets of England (creations dating from 1611); Baronets of Ireland (creations dating from 1619); Baronets of Scotland or Nova Scotia (creations dating from 1625); Baronets of Great Britain (creations after the Act of Union 1707 which combined the kingdoms of England and Scotland); and Baronets of the United Kingdom (creations after the union of Great Britain and Ireland in 1801).

*Badge of Baronets of the United Kingdom*

*Badge of Baronets of Nova Scotia*

*Badge of Ulster*

The patent of creation limits the destination of a baronetcy, usually to male descendants of the first baronet, although special remainders allow the baronetcy to pass, if the male issue of sons fail, to the male issue of daughters of the first baronet. In the case of baronetcies of Scotland or Nova Scotia, a special remainder of 'heirs male and of tailzie' allows the baronetcy to descend to heirs general, including women. There are four existing Scottish baronets with such a remainder.

The Official Roll of Baronets is kept at the Home Office by the Registrar of the Baronetage. Anyone who considers that he is entitled to be entered on the Roll may petition the Crown through the Home Secretary. Every person succeeding to a baronetcy must exhibit proofs of succession to the Home Secretary. A person whose name is not entered on the Official Roll will not be addressed or mentioned by the title of baronet in any official document, nor will he be accorded precedence as a baronet.

BARONETCIES EXTINCT SINCE THE LAST EDITION
Corbet (*cr.* 1808); Cradock (*cr.* 1796); Nicholls (now Harmar-Nicholls) (*cr*, 1960); Readhead (*cr.* 1922); Richmond (*cr.*1920)

*Registrar of the Baronetage*, Miss C. E. C. Sinclair
*Assistant Registrar*, Mrs F. G. Bright
*Office*, Home Office, 50 Queen Anne's Gate, London SW1H 9AT. Tel: 020 7273 3498

## KNIGHTS

*Style*, 'Sir' before forename and surname, followed by appropriate post-nominal initials if a Knight Grand Cross, Knight Grand Commander or Knight Commander
*Wife's style*, 'Lady' followed by surname
For forms of address, *see* page 135

The prefix 'Sir' is not used by knights who are clerics of the Church of England, who do not receive the accolade. Their wives are entitled to precedence as the wife of a knight but not to the style of 'Lady'.

### ORDERS OF KNIGHTHOOD

Knight Grand Cross, Knight Grand Commander, and Knight Commander are the higher classes of the Orders of Chivalry (*see* pages 171–3). Honorary knighthoods of these Orders may be conferred on men who are citizens of countries of which The Queen is not head of state. As a rule, the prefix 'Sir' is not used by honorary knights.

### KNIGHTS BACHELOR

The Knights Bachelor do not constitute a Royal Order, but comprise the surviving representation of the ancient State Orders of Knighthood. The Register of Knights Bachelor, instituted by James I in the 17th century, lapsed, and in 1908 a voluntary association under the title of The Society of Knights (now The Imperial Society of Knights Bachelor by Royal Command) was formed with the primary objects of continuing the various registers dating from 1257 and obtaining the uniform registration of every created Knight Bachelor. In 1926 a design for a badge to be worn by Knights Bachelor was approved and adopted; in 1974 a neck badge and miniature were added.

*Knight Principal*, Sir Richard Gaskell
*Prelate*, Rt. Revd and Rt. Hon. The Bishop of London
*Registrar*, Sir Robert Balchin, DL
*Hon. Treasurer*, Sir Paul Judge.
*Clerk to the Council*, R. L. Jenkins, LVO, TD.
*Office*, 21 Old Buildings, Lincoln's Inn, London WC2A 3UJ

## LIST OF BARONETS AND KNIGHTS

*Revised to 31 August 2001*
Peers are not included in this list

| | |
|---|---|
| † | Not registered on the Official Roll of the Baronetage at the time of going to press |
| ( ) | The date of creation of the baronetcy is given in parenthesis |
| I | Baronet of Ireland |
| NS | Baronet of Nova Scotia |
| S | Baronet of Scotland |

If a baronet or knight has a double-barrelled or hyphenated surname, he is listed under the final element of the name

*A full entry in italic type* indicates that the recipient of a knighthood died during the year in which the honour was conferred. The name is included for purposes of record

bal, Sir Tei, Kt., CBE
bbott, Sir Albert Francis, Kt., CBE
bbott, *Adm.* Sir Peter Charles, GBE, KCB
bdy, Sir Valentine Robert Duff, Bt. (1850)
bel, Sir Seselo (Cecil) Charles Geoffrey, Kt., OBE
bercromby, Sir Ian George, Bt. (S. 1636)
cheson, *Prof.* Sir (Ernest) Donald, KBE
ckers, Sir James George, Kt.
ckroyd, Sir Timothy Robert Whyte, Bt. (1956)
cland, Sir Antony Arthur, GCMG, GCVO
cland, *Lt.-Col.* Sir (Christopher) Guy (Dyke), Bt., MVO (1890)
cland, Sir John Dyke, Bt. (1644)
cland, *Maj.-Gen.* Sir John Hugh Bevil, KCB, CBE
dam, Sir Christopher Eric Forbes, Bt. (1917)
dams, Sir Philip George Doyne, KCMG
dams, Sir William James, KCMG
drien, *Hon.* Sir Maurice Latour-, Kt.
dsetts, Sir William Norman, Kt., OBE
dye, Sir John Anthony, KCMG
gnew, Sir Crispin Hamlyn, Bt. (S. 1629)
gnew, Sir John Keith, Bt. (1895)
iken, *Air Chief Marshal* Sir John Alexander Carlisle, KCB
ikens, Sir Richard John Pearson, Kt., QC
†Ainsworth, Sir Anthony Thomas Hugh, Bt. (1916)
ird, *Capt.* Sir Alastair Sturgis, GCVO
ird, Sir (George) John, Bt. (1901)
iry, *Maj.-Gen.* Sir Christopher John, KCVO, CBE
Aitchison, Sir Charles Walter de Lancey, Bt. (1938)
Akehurst, *Gen.* Sir John Bryan, KCB, CBE
Alberti, *Prof.* Kurt George Matthew Mayer, Kt.
Albu, Sir George, Bt. (1912)
Alcock, *Air Chief Marshal* Sir (Robert James) Michael, GCB, KBE
Aldous, *Rt. Hon.* Sir William, Kt.
Alexander, Sir Charles Gundry, Bt. (1945)
Alexander, Sir Claud Hagart-, Bt. (1886)
Alexander, Sir Douglas, Bt. (1921)
Alexander, Sir Michael O'Donal Bjarne, GCMG
†Alexander, Sir Patrick Desmond William Cable-, Bt. (1809)
Allan, Sir Anthony James Allan Havelock-, Bt. (1858)
Allen, *Prof.* Sir Geoffrey, Kt., Ph.D., FRS
Allen, Sir John Derek, Kt., CBE
Allen, *Hon.* Sir Peter Austin Philip Jermyn, Kt.
Allen, Sir Thomas Boaz, Kt., CBE
Allen, *Hon.* Sir William Clifford, KCMG, MP
Allen, Sir William Guilford, Kt.
Alleyne, Sir George Allanmoore Ogarren, Kt.
Alleyne, *Revd* Sir John Olpherts Campbell, Bt. (1769)
Alliance, Sir David, Kt., CBE
Allinson, Sir (Walter) Leonard, KCVO, CMG
Alliott, *Hon.* Sir John Downes, Kt.
Allison, *Air Chief Marshal* Sir John Shakespeare, KCB, CBE
Alment, Sir (Edward) Anthony John, Kt.
Althaus, Sir Nigel Frederick, Kt.
Ambo, *Rt. Revd* George, KBE
Amet, *Hon.* Sir Arnold Karibone, Kt.
Amies, Sir (Edwin) Hardy, KCVO
Amory, Sir Ian Heathcoat, Bt. (1874)
Anderson, Sir John Anthony, KBE
Anderson, *Maj.-Gen.* Sir John Evelyn, KBE
Anderson, Sir John Muir, Kt., CMG
Anderson, *Hon.* Sir Kevin Victor, Kt.
Anderson, Sir Leith Reinsford Steven, Kt., CBE
Anderson, *Vice-Adm.* Sir Neil Dudley, KBE, CB
Anderson, *Prof.* Sir (William) Ferguson, Kt., OBE
Anderton, Sir (Cyril) James, Kt., CBE, QPM
Andrew, Sir Robert John, KCB
Andrews, Sir Derek Henry, KCB, CBE
Andrews, *Hon.* Sir Dormer George, Kt.
Angus, Sir Michael Richardson, Kt.
Annesley, Sir Hugh Norman, Kt., QPM
Anson, *Vice-Adm.* Sir Edward Rosebery, KCB
Anson, Sir John, KCB
Anson, *Rear-Adm.* Sir Peter, Bt., CB (1831)
Anstruther, *Maj.* Sir Ralph Hugo, Bt., GCVO, MC (S. 1694)
Antico, Sir Tristan Venus, Kt.
Antrobus, Sir Charles James, GCMG, OBE
Antrobus, Sir Edward Philip, Bt. (1815)
Appleyard, Sir Leonard Vincent, KCMG
Appleyard, Sir Raymond Kenelm, KBE
Arbuthnot, Sir Keith Robert Charles, Bt. (1823)
Arbuthnot, Sir William Reierson, Bt. (1964)
Arbuthnott, *Prof.* Sir John Peebles, Kt., Ph.D., FRSE
Archdale, *Capt.* Sir Edward Folmer, Bt., DSC, RN (1928)
Arculus, Sir Ronald, KCMG, KCVO
Armitage, *Air Chief Marshal* Sir Michael John, KCB, CBE
Armour, *Prof.* Sir James, Kt., CBE
†Armstrong, Sir Christopher John Edmund Stuart, Bt., MBE (1841)
Armytage, Sir John Martin, Bt. (1738)
Arnold, *Rt. Hon.* Sir John Lewis, Kt.
Arnold, Sir Malcolm Henry, Kt., CBE
Arnold, Sir Thomas Richard, Kt.
Arnott, Sir Alexander John Maxwell, Bt. (1896)
Arrindell, Sir Clement Athelston, GCMG, GCVO, QC
Arthur, *Lt.-Gen.* Sir (John) Norman Stewart, KCB
Arthur, Sir Stephen John, Bt. (1841)
Ash, *Prof.* Sir Eric Albert, Kt., CBE, FRS, FREng.
Ashburnham, Sir James Fleetwood, Bt. (1661)
Ashcroft, Sir Michael, KCMG
Ashdown, *Rt. Hon.* Sir Jeremy John Durham (Paddy), KBE
Ashley, Sir Bernard Albert, Kt.
Ashmore, *Admiral of the Fleet* Sir Edward Beckwith, GCB, DSC
Ashmore, *Vice-Adm.* Sir Peter William Beckwith, KCB, KCVO, DSC
Aske, *Revd* Sir Conan, Bt. (1922)
Askew, Sir Bryan, Kt.
Asscher, Prof. Sir (Adolf) William, Kt., MD, FRCP
Astill, *Hon.* Sir Michael John, Kt.
Aston, Sir Harold George, Kt., CBE
Astwood, *Hon.* Sir James Rufus, KBE
Atcherley, Sir Harold Winter, Kt.
Atiyah, Sir Michael Francis, Kt., OM, Ph.D., FRS
Atkins, *Rt. Hon.* Sir Robert James, Kt.
Atkinson, *Prof.* Sir Anthony Barnes, Kt.
Atkinson, *Air Marshal* Sir David William, KBE
Atkinson, Sir Frederick John, KCB
Atkinson, Sir John Alexander, KCB, DFC
Atkinson, Sir Robert, Kt., DSC, FREng.
Atopare, Sir Sailas, GCMG
Attenborough, Sir David Frederick, Kt., CH, CVO, CBE, FRS
Atwill, Sir (Milton) John (Napier), Kt.
Audland, Sir Christopher John, KCMG
Audley, Sir George Bernard, Kt.
Augier, *Prof.* Sir Fitz-Roy Richard, Kt.
Auld, *Rt. Hon.* Sir Robin Ernest, Kt.
Austin, Sir Anthony Leonard, Bt. (1894)
Austin, *Vice-Adm.* Sir Peter Murray, KCB
Austin, *Air Marshal* Sir Roger Mark, KCB, AFC
Axford, Sir William Ian, Kt.
Ayckbourn, Sir Alan, Kt., CBE
Aykroyd, Sir James Alexander Frederic, Bt. (1929)
Aykroyd, Sir William Miles, Bt., MC (1920)
Aylmer, Sir Richard John, Bt. (I. 1622)
Ayre, Sir Douglas, Kt., JP
Bacha, Sir Bhinod, Kt., CMG
Backhouse, Sir Jonathan Roger, Bt. (1901)
Bacon, Sir Nicholas Hickman Ponsonby, Bt. *Premier Baronet of England* (1611 and 1627)

Bacon, Sir Sidney Charles, Kt., CB, FREng.
Baddeley, Sir John Wolsey Beresford, Bt. (1922)
Baddiley, *Prof.* Sir James, Kt., Ph.D., D.Sc., FRS, FRSE
Badge, Sir Peter Gilmour Noto, Kt.
Badger, Sir Geoffrey Malcolm, Kt.
Baer, Sir Jack Mervyn Frank, Kt.
Bagge, Sir (John) Jeremy Picton, Bt. (1867)
Bagnall, *Air Marshal* Sir Anthony John Crowther, KCB, OBE
Bagnall, *Field Marshal* Sir Nigel Thomas, GCB, CVO, MC
Bailey, Sir Alan Marshall, KCB
Bailey, Sir Brian Harry, Kt., OBE
Bailey, Sir Derrick Thomas Louis, Bt., DFC (1919)
Bailey, Sir John Bilsland, KCB
Bailey, Sir Richard John, Kt., CBE
Bailey, Sir Stanley Ernest, Kt., CBE, QPM
Bailhache, Sir Philip Martin, Kt.
Baillie, Sir Gawaine George Hope, Bt. (1823)
Bain, *Prof.* Sir George Sayers, Kt.
Baines, *Prof.* Sir George Grenfell-, Kt., OBE
†Baird, Sir Charles William Stuart, Bt. (1809)
†Baird, Sir James Andrew Gardiner, Bt. (S. 1695)
Baird, *Lt.-Gen.* Sir James Parlane, KBE, MD
Baird, *Air Marshal* Sir John Alexander, KBE
Baird, *Vice-Adm.* Sir Thomas Henry Eustace, KCB
Bairsto, *Air Marshal* Sir Peter Edward, KBE, CB
Baker, Sir Bryan William, Kt.
Baker, Sir Robert George Humphrey Sherston-, Bt. (1796)
Baker, *Hon.* Sir (Thomas) Scott (Gillespie), Kt.
Balchin, Sir Robert George Alexander, Kt.
Balderstone, Sir James Schofield, Kt.
Baldwin, *Prof.* Sir Jack Edward, Kt., FRS
Baldwin, Sir Peter Robert, KCB
Ball, *Air Marshal* Sir Alfred Henry Wynne, KCB, DSO, DFC
Ball, Sir Charles Irwin, Bt. (1911)
Ball, Sir Christopher John Elinger, Kt.
Ball, *Prof.* Sir Robert James, Kt., Ph.D.
Bamford, Sir Anthony Paul, Kt.
Banham, Sir John Michael Middlecott, Kt.
Bannerman, Sir David Gordon, Bt., OBE (S. 1682)
Bannister, Sir Roger Gilbert, Kt., CBE, DM, FRCP
Barber, Sir (Thomas) David, Bt. (1960)
Barbour, *Very Revd* Sir Robert Alexander Stewart, KCVO, MC
Barclay, Sir Colville Herbert Sanford, Bt. (S. 1668)
Barclay, Sir David Rowat, Kt.
Barclay, Sir Frederick Hugh, Kt.
Barclay, Sir Peter Maurice, Kt., CBE
Barder, Sir Brian Leon, KCMG
Baring, Sir John Francis, Bt. (1911)
Barker, Sir Alwyn Bowman, Kt., CMG
Barker, Sir Colin, Kt.
Barker, *Hon.* Sir (Richard) Ian, Kt.
Barlow, Sir Christopher Hilaro, Bt. (1803)
Barlow, Sir Frank, Kt., CBE
Barlow, Sir (George) William, Kt., FREng.
Barlow, Sir John Kemp, Bt. (1907)
Barlow, Sir Thomas Erasmus, Bt., DSC (1902)
Barnard, Sir Joseph Brian, Kt.
Barnes, Sir (James) David (Francis), Kt., CBE
Barnes, Sir Kenneth, KCB
Barnewall, Sir Reginald Robert, Bt. (I. 1623)
Baron, Sir Thomas, Kt., CBE
Barraclough, *Air Chief Marshal* Sir John, KCB, CBE, DFC, AFC
Barran, Sir David Haven, Kt.
Barran, Sir John Napoleon Ruthven, Bt. (1895)
Barratt, Sir Lawrence Arthur, Kt.
Barratt, Sir Richard Stanley, Kt., CBE, QPM
Barrett, *Lt.-Gen.* Sir David William Scott-, KBE, MC
Barrett, Sir Stephen Jeremy, KCMG
Barrington, Sir Alexander (Fitzwilliam Croker), Bt. (1831)
Barrington, Sir Nicholas John, KCMG, CVO
Barron, Sir Donald James, Kt.
Barrow, *Capt.* Sir Richard John Uniacke, Bt. (1835)
Barrowclough, Sir Anthony Richard, Kt., QC
Barry, Sir (Lawrence) Edward (Anthony Tress), Bt. (1899)
Barter, Sir Peter Leslie Charles, Kt., OBE
†Bartlett, Sir Andrew Alan, Bt. (1913)
Barttelot, *Col.* Sir Brian Walter de Stopham, Bt., OBE (1875)
Batchelor, Sir Ivor Ralph Campbell, Kt., CBE
Bate, Sir David Lindsay, KBE
Bate, Sir (Walter) Edwin, Kt., OBE
Bates, Sir Geoffrey Voltelin, Bt., MC (1880)
Bates, Sir Malcolm Rowland, Kt.
Bates, Sir Richard Dawson Hoult, Bt. (1937)
Batho, Sir Peter Ghislain, Bt. (1928)
Bathurst, *Admiral of the Fleet* Sir (David) Benjamin, GCB
Bathurst, Sir Frederick John Charles Gordon Hervey-, Bt. (1818)
Bathurst, Sir Maurice Edward, Kt., CMG, CBE, QC
Batten, Sir John Charles, KCVO
Battersby, Prof. Sir Alan Rushton, Kt., FRS
Battishill, Sir Anthony Michael William, GCB
Batty, Sir William Bradshaw, Kt., TD
Baxendell, Sir Peter Brian, Kt., CBE, FREng.
Bayliss, Sir Richard Ian Samuel, KCVO, MD, FRCP
Bayne, Sir Nicholas Peter, KCMG
Baynes, Sir John Christopher Malcolm, Bt. (1801)
Bazley, Sir Thomas John Sebastian, Bt. (1869)
Beach, *Gen.* Sir (William Gerald) Hugh, GBE, KCB, MC
Beale, *Lt.-Gen.* Sir Peter John, KBE, FRCP
Beament, Sir James William Longman, Kt., Sc.D., FRS
Beamish, Sir Adrian John, KCMG
Beattie, *Hon.* Sir Alexander Craig, Kt.
Beattie, *Hon.* Sir David Stuart, GCMG, GCVO
Beauchamp, Sir Christopher Radstock Proctor-, Bt. (1745)
Beaumont, *Capt.* the Hon. Sir (Edward) Nicholas (Canning), KCVO
Beaumont, Sir George (Howland Francis), Bt. (1661)
Beaumont, Sir Richard Ashton, KCMG, OBE
Beavis, *Air Chief Marshal* Sir Michael Gordon, KCB, CBE, AFC
Becher, Sir John William Michael Wrixon-, Bt. (1831)
Beck, Sir Edgar Philip, Kt.
†Beckett, Sir Richard Gervase, Bt., QC (1921)
Beckett, Sir Terence Norman, KBE, FREng.
Bedingfeld, *Capt.* Sir Edmund George Felix Paston-, Bt. (1661)
Beddoe, Sir David Sydney Rowe-, Kt.
Bedser, Sir Alec Victor, Kt., CBE
Beecham, Sir Jeremy Hugh, Kt.
Beecham, Sir John Stratford Roland, Bt. (1914)
Beetham, *Marshal of the Royal Air Force* Sir Michael James, GCB, CBE, DFC, AFC
Beevor, Sir Thomas Agnew, Bt. (1784)
Beldam, *Rt. Hon.* Sir (Alexander) Roy (Asplan), Kt.
Belich, Sir James, Kt.
Bell, Sir Brian Ernest, KBE
Bell, Sir (George) Raymond, KCMG, CB
Bell, Sir John Lowthian, Bt. (1885)
Bell, *Hon.* Sir Rodger, Kt.
Bell, Sir (William) Ewart, KCB
Bell, Sir William Hollin Dayrell Morrison-, Bt. (1905)
Bellamy, *Hon.* Sir Christopher William, Kt.
Bellew, Sir Henry Charles Gratton-, Bt. (1838)
Bellinger, Sir Robert Ian, GBE

Bellingham, Sir Anthony Edward Norman, Bt. (1796)
Bengough, *Col.* Sir Piers, KCVO, OBE
Benn, Sir (James) Jonathan, Bt. (1914)
Bennett, *Air Vice-Marshal* Sir Erik Peter, KBE, CB
Bennett, *Rt. Hon.* Sir Frederic Mackarness, Kt.
Bennett, *Hon.* Sir Hugh Peter Derwyn, Kt.
Bennett, Sir John Mokonuiarangi, Kt.
Bennett, *Gen.* Sir Phillip Harvey, KBE, DSO
Bennett, Sir Richard Rodney, Kt., CBE
Bennett, Sir Ronald Wilfrid Murdoch, Bt. (1929)
Benson, Sir Christopher John, Kt.
Benyon, Sir William Richard, Kt.
Beresford, Sir (Alexander) Paul, Kt., MP
Berger, *Vice-Adm.* Sir Peter Egerton Capel, KCB, LVO, DSC
Berghuser, *Hon.* Sir Eric, Kt., MBE
Beringer, *Prof.* Sir John Evelyn, Kt., CBE
Berman, Sir Franklin Delow, KCMG
Bernard, Sir Dallas Edmund, Bt. (1954)
Berney, Sir Julian Reedham Stuart, Bt. (1620)
Berridge, *Prof.* Sir Michael John, Kt., FRS
Berrill, Sir Kenneth Ernest, GBE, KCB
Berriman, Sir David, Kt.
Berry, *Prof.* Sir Colin Leonard, Kt., FRCPath.
Berry, *Prof.* Sir Michael Victor, Kt., FRS
Berthon, *Vice-Adm.* Sir Stephen Ferrier, KCB
Berthoud, Sir Martin Seymour, KCVO, CMG
Best, Sir Richard Radford, KCVO, CBE
Bethune, *Hon.* Sir (Walter) Angus, Kt.
Bett, Sir Michael, Kt., CBE
Bevan, Sir Martyn Evan Evans, Bt. (1958)
Bevan, Sir Nicolas, Kt., CB
Bevan, Sir Timothy Hugh, Kt.
Beverley, *Lt.-Gen.* Sir Henry York La Roche, KCB, OBE, RM
Bibby, Sir Derek James, Bt., MC (1959)
Bichard, Sir Michael George, KCB
Bick, *Hon.* Sir Martin James Moore-, Kt.
Bickersteth, *Rt. Revd* Sir John Monier, KCVO
Biddulph, Sir Ian D'Olier, Bt. (1664)
Bide, Sir Austin Ernest, Kt.
Bidwell, Sir Hugh Charles Philip, GBE
Biggam, Sir Robin Adair, Kt.
Biggs, *Vice-Adm.* Sir Geoffrey William Roger, KCB
Biggs, Sir Norman Paris, Kt.
Bilas, Sir Angmai Simon, Kt., OBE
Billière, *Gen.* Sir Peter Edgar de la Cour de la, KCB, KBE, DSO, MC
Bingham, *Hon.* Sir Eardley Max, Kt., QC
Birch, Sir John Allan, KCVO, CMG
Birch, Sir Roger, Kt., CBE, QPM
Bird, Sir Richard Geoffrey Chapman, Bt. (1922)
Birkin, Sir John Christian William, Bt. (1905)
Birkin, Sir (John) Derek, Kt., TD
Birkmyre, Sir James, Bt. (1921)
Birley, Sir Derek Sydney, Kt.
Birrell, Sir James Drake, Kt.
Birtwistle, Sir Harrison, Kt.
Bischoff, Winfried Franz Wilhelm, Kt.
Bishop, Sir Frederick Arthur, Kt., CB, CVO
Bishop, Sir Michael David, Kt., CBE
Bisson, *Rt. Hon.* Sir Gordon Ellis, Kt.
Black, *Prof.* Sir Douglas Andrew Kilgour, Kt., MD, FRCP
Black, Sir James Whyte, Kt., FRCP, FRS, OM
Black, *Adm.* Sir (John) Jeremy, GBE, KCB, DSO
Black, Sir Robert David, Bt. (1922)
Blackburne, *Hon.* Sir William Anthony, Kt.
Blacker, *Gen.* Sir (Anthony Stephen) Jeremy, KCB, CBE
Blacker, *Gen.* Sir Cecil Hugh, GCB, OBE, MC
Blackett, Sir Hugh Francis, Bt. (1673)
Blackham, *Vice-Adm.* Sir Jeremy Joe, KCB
Blacklock, *Surgeon Capt. Prof.* Sir Norman James, KCVO, OBE
Blackman, Sir Frank Milton, KCVO, OBE
Blackwell, Sir Basil Davenport, Kt., FREng.
Blackwood, Sir John Francis, Bt. (1814) (see also page 149)
Blair, *Lt.-Gen.* Sir Chandos, KCVO, OBE, MC
Blair, Sir Edward Thomas Hunter, Bt. (1786)
Blake, Sir Alfred Lapthorn, KCVO, MC
Blake, Sir Francis Michael, Bt. (1907)
Blake, Sir Peter James, KBE
Blake, Sir (Thomas) Richard (Valentine), Bt. (I. 1622)
Blaker, Sir John, Bt. (1919)
Blakiston, Sir Ferguson Arthur James, Bt. (1763)
Blanch, Sir Malcolm, KCVO
Bland, Sir (Francis) Christopher (Buchan), Kt.
Bland, *Lt.-Col.* Sir Simon Claud Michael, KCVO
Blank, Sir Maurice Victor, Kt.
Blatherwick, Sir David Elliott Spiby, KCMG, OBE
Blelloch, Sir John Nial Henderson, KCB
Blennerhassett, Sir (Marmaduke) Adrian Francis William, Bt. (1809)
Blewitt, *Maj.* Sir Shane Gabriel Basil, GCVO
Blofeld, *Hon.* Sir John Christopher Calthorpe, Kt.
Blois, Sir Charles Nicholas Gervase, Bt. (1686)
Blomefield, Sir Thomas Charles Peregrine, Bt. (1807)
Bloomfield, Sir Kenneth Percy, KCB
Blosse, *Capt.* Sir Richard Hely Lynch-, Bt. (1622)
Blount, Sir Walter Edward Alpin, Bt., DSC (1642)
Blundell, Sir Thomas Leon, Kt., FRS
Blunden, Sir George, Kt.
†Blunden, Sir Philip Overington, Bt. (I. 1766)
Blunt, Sir David Richard Reginald Harvey, Bt. (1720)
Blyth, Sir Charles (Chay), Kt., CBE, BEM
Boardman, *Prof.* Sir John, Kt., FSA, FBA
Bodey, *Hon.* Sir David Roderick Lessiter, Kt., QC
Bodmer, Sir Walter Fred, Kt., Ph.D., FRS
Body, Sir Richard Bernard Frank Stewart, Kt., MP
Boevey, Sir Thomas Michael Blake Crawley-, Bt. (1784)
Bogan, Sir Nagora, KBE
Boileau, Sir Guy (Francis), Bt. (1838)
Boles, Sir Jeremy John Fortescue, Bt. (1922)
Boles, Sir John Dennis, Kt., MBE
Bolland, Sir Edwin, KCMG
Bollers, *Hon.* Sir Harold Brodie Smith, Kt.
Bolt, *Air Marshal* Sir Richard Bruce, KBE, CB, DFC, AFC
Bolton, Sir Frederic Bernard, Kt., MC
Bona, Sir Kina, KBE
Bonallack, Sir Michael Francis, Kt., OBE
Bond, Sir John Reginald Hartnell, Kt.
Bond, Sir Kenneth Raymond Boyden, Kt.
Bond, *Prof.* Sir Michael Richard, Kt., FRCPsych., FRCPGlas., FRCSE
Bondi, *Prof.* Sir Hermann, KCB, FRS
Bonfield, Sir Peter Leahy, Kt., CBE, FREng.
Bonham, *Maj.* Sir Antony Lionel Thomas, Bt. (1852)
Bonington, Sir Christian John Storey, Kt., CBE
Bonsall, Sir Arthur Wilfred, KCMG, CBE
Bonsor, Sir Nicholas Cosmo, Bt. (1925)
Boolell, Sir Satcam, Kt.
Boord, Sir Nicolas John Charles, Bt. (1896)
Boorman, *Lt.-Gen.* Sir Derek, KCB
Booth, Sir Christopher Charles, Kt., MD, FRCP
Booth, Hon. Sir David Alwyn Gore-, KCMG, KCVO
Booth, Sir Douglas Allen, Bt. (1916)
Booth, Sir Gordon, KCMG, CVO
Booth, Sir Josslyn Henry Robert Gore-, Bt. (I. 1760)
Booth, Sir Michael Addison John Wheeler-, KCB

Boothby, Sir Brooke Charles, Bt. (1660)
Boreel, Sir Francis David, Bt. (1645)
Boreham, *Hon.* Sir Leslie Kenneth Edward, Kt.
Bornu, The Waziri of, KCMG, CBE
Borthwick, Sir John Thomas, Bt., MBE (1908)
Borysiewicz, *Prof.* Sir Leszek Krzysztof, Kt.
Bossom, *Hon.* Sir Clive, Bt. (1953)
Boswall, Sir (Thomas) Alford Houstoun-, Bt. (1836)
Boswell, *Lt.-Gen.* Sir Alexander Crawford Simpson, KCB, CBE
Bosworth, Sir Neville Bruce Alfred, Kt., CBE
Bottoms, *Prof.* Sir Anthony Edward, Kt.
Bottomley, Sir James Reginald Alfred, KCMG
Boughey, Sir John George Fletcher, Bt. (1798)
Boulton, Sir Clifford John, GCB
Boulton, Sir (Harold Hugh) Christian, Bt. (1905)
Boulton, Sir William Whytehead, Bt., CBE, TD (1944)
Bourn, Sir John Bryant, KCB
Bovell, *Hon.* Sir (William) Stewart, Kt.
Bowater, Sir Euan David Vansittart, Bt. (1939)
Bowater, Sir (John) Vansittart, Bt. (1914)
Bowden, Sir Andrew, Kt., MBE
Bowden, Sir Frank, Bt. (1915)
Bowen, Sir Geoffrey Fraser, Kt.
Bowen, Sir Mark Edward Mortimer, Bt. (1921)
Bowett, *Prof.* Sir Derek William, Kt., CBE, QC, FBA
†Bowlby, Sir Richard Peregrine Longstaff, Bt. (1923)
Bowman, Sir Jeffery Haverstock, Kt.
Bowman, Sir Paul Humphrey Armytage, Bt. (1884)
Bowness, Sir Alan, Kt., CBE
Boyce, Sir Graham Hugh, KCMG
Boyce, *Adm.* Sir Michael Cecil, GCB, OBE
Boyce, Sir Robert Charles Leslie, Bt. (1952)
Boyd, Sir Alexander Walter, Bt. (1916)
Boyd, Sir John Dixon Iklé, KCMG
Boyd, The Hon. Sir Mark Alexander Lennox-, Kt.
Boyd, *Prof.* Sir Robert Lewis Fullarton, Kt., CBE, D.Sc., FRS
Boyes, Sir Brian Gerald Barratt-, KBE
Boyle, Sir Stephen Gurney, Bt. (1904)
Boynton, Sir John Keyworth, Kt., MC
Boys, *Rt. Hon.* Sir Michael Hardie, GCMG
Boyson, *Rt. Hon.* Sir Rhodes, Kt.
Brabham, Sir John Arthur, Kt., OBE
Bradbeer, Sir John Derek Richardson, Kt., OBE, TD
Bradbury, *Surgeon Vice-Adm.* Sir Eric Blackburn, KBE, CB
Bradford, Sir Edward Alexander Slade, Bt. (1902)
Bradshaw, Sir Kenneth Anthony, KCB
Bradshaw, *Lt.-Gen.* Sir Richard Phillip, KBE
Brain, Sir (Henry) Norman, KBE, CMG
Braithwaite, Sir (Joseph) Franklin Madders, Kt.
Braithwaite, *Rt. Hon.* Sir Nicholas Alexander, Kt., OBE
Braithwaite, Sir Rodric Quentin, GCMG
Bramley, *Prof.* Sir Paul Anthony, Kt.
Branson, Sir Richard Charles Nicholas, Kt.
Bratza, Sir Nicolas Dušan, Kt., QC
Bray, Sir Theodor Charles, Kt., CBE
Brennan, *Hon.* Sir (Francis) Gerard, KBE
Brett, Sir Charles Edward Bainbridge, Kt., CBE
Brickwood, Sir Basil Greame, Bt. (1927)
Bridges, *Hon.* Sir Phillip Rodney, Kt., CMG
Brierley, Sir Ronald Alfred, Kt.
Bright, Sir Graham Frank James, Kt.
Bright, Sir Keith, Kt.
Brigstocke, *Adm.* Sir John Richard, KCB
Brinckman, Sir Theodore George Roderick, Bt. (1831)
†Brisco, Sir Campbell Howard, Bt. (1782)
Briscoe, Sir John Geoffrey James, Bt. (1910)
Brise, Sir John Archibald Ruggles-, Bt., CB, OBE, TD (1935)
Bristow, *Hon.* Sir Peter Henry Rowley, Kt.
Brittan, Sir Samuel, Kt.
Britton, Sir Edward Louis, Kt., CBE
†Broadbent, Sir Andrew George, Bt. (1893)
Brocklebank, Sir Aubrey Thomas, Bt. (1885)
Brodie, Sir Benjamin David Ross, Bt. (1834)
Broers, *Prof.* Sir Alec Nigel, Kt., Ph.D., FRS
Bromhead, Sir John Desmond Gonville, Bt. (1806)
Bromley, Sir Michael Roger, KBE
Bromley, Sir Rupert Charles, Bt. (1757)
†Brooke, Sir Alistair Weston, Bt. (1919)
Brooke, Sir Francis George Windham, Bt. (1903)
Brooke, *Rt. Hon.* Sir Henry, Kt.
Brooke, Sir (Richard) David Christopher, Bt. (1662)
Brooksbank, Sir (Edward) Nicholas, Bt. (1919)
Broom, *Air Marshal* Sir Ivor Gordon, KCB, CBE, DSO, DFC, AFC
Broomfield, Sir Nigel Hugh Robert Allen, KCMG
†Broughton, Sir David Delves, Bt. (1661)
Broun, Sir William Windsor, Bt. (S. 1686)
Brown, Sir Allen Stanley, Kt., CBE
Brown, Sir (Austen) Patrick, KCB
Brown, *Adm.* Sir Brian Thomas, KCB, CBE
Brown, Sir (Cyril) Maxwell Palmer, KCB, CMG
Brown, Sir David, Kt.
Brown, *Vice-Adm.* Sir David Worthington, KCB
Brown, Sir Derrick Holden-, Kt.
Brown, Sir Douglas Denison, Kt.
Brown, *Hon.* Sir Douglas Dunlop, Kt.
Brown, Sir George Francis Richmond, Bt. (1863)
Brown, Sir George Noel, Kt.
Brown, Sir John, Kt.
Brown, Sir John Gilbert Newton, Kt., CBE
Brown, Sir Martin, Kt.
Brown, Sir Mervyn, KCMG, OBE
Brown, Sir Peter Randolph, Kt.
Brown, *Hon.* Sir Ralph Kilner, Kt., OBE, TD
Brown, Sir Robert Crichton-, KCMG, CBE, TD
Brown, *Rt. Hon.* Sir Simon Denis, Kt.
Brown, *Rt. Hon.* Sir Stephen, GBE
Brown, Sir Stephen David Reid, KCVO
Brown, Sir Thomas, Kt.
Brown, Sir William Brian Piggott-, Bt. (1903)
Browne, Sir Anthony Arthur Duncan Montague-, KCMG, CBE, DFC
Browne, Sir (Edmund) John (Phillip), Kt., FREng.
Brownrigg, Sir Nicholas (Gawen), Bt. (1816)
Browse, *Prof.* Sir Norman Leslie, Kt., MD, FRCS
Bruce, Sir (Francis) Michael Ian, Bt. (S. 1628)
Bruce, Sir Hervey James Hugh, Bt. (1804)
Bruce, *Rt. Hon.* Sir (James) Roualeyn Hovell-Thurlow-Cumming-, Kt.
Brunner, Sir John Henry Kilian, Bt. (1895)
Brunton, Sir (Edward Francis) Lauder, Bt. (1908)
Brunton, Sir Gordon Charles, Kt.
Bryan, Sir Arthur, Kt.
Bryan, Sir Paul Elmore Oliver, Kt., DSO, MC
Bryce, *Hon.* Sir (William) Gordon, Kt., CBE
Bryson, *Adm.* Sir Lindsay Sutherland, KCB, FREng.
Buchan, Sir John, Kt., CMG
Buchanan, Sir Andrew George, Bt. (1878)
Buchanan, Sir Charles Alexander James Leith-, Bt. (1775)
Buchanan, *Prof.* Sir Colin Douglas, Kt., CBE
Buchanan, *Vice-Adm.* Sir Peter William, KBE

Cave, Sir Robert Cave-Browne-, Bt. (1641)
Cayley, Sir Digby William David, Bt. (1661)
Cayzer, Sir James Arthur, Bt. (1904)
Cazalet, *Hon.* Sir Edward Stephen, Kt.
Cazalet, Sir Peter Grenville, Kt.
Cecil, *Rear-Adm.* Sir (Oswald) Nigel Amherst, KBE, CB
Chadwick, *Revd Prof.* Sir Henry, KBE
Chadwick, *Rt. Hon.* Sir John Murray, Kt., ED
Chadwick, Sir Joshua Kenneth Burton, Bt. (1935)
Chadwick, *Revd Prof.* Sir (William) Owen, OM, KBE, FBA
Chalmers, Sir Iain Geoffrey, Kt.
Chalmers, Sir Neil Robert, Kt.
Chalstrey, Sir (Leonard) John, Kt., MD, FRCS
Chan, *Rt. Hon.* Sir Julius, GCMG, KBE
Chance, Sir (George) Jeremy ffolliott, Bt. (1900)
Chandler, Sir Colin Michael, Kt.
Chandler, Sir Geoffrey, Kt., CBE
Chaney, *Hon.* Sir Frederick Charles, KBE, AFC
Chantler, *Prof.* Sir Cyril, Kt., MD, FRCP
Chaplin, Sir Malcolm Hilbery, Kt., CBE
Chapman, Sir David Robert Macgowan, Bt. (1958)
Chapman, Sir George Alan, Kt.
Chapman, Sir Sidney Brookes, Kt., MP
Chapman, *Lt-Gen.* Sir Timothy John Granville-, KCB, CBE
Chapple, *Field Marshal* Sir John Lyon, GCB, CBE
Charles, *Hon.* Sir Arthur William Hessin, Kt
Charles, Sir George Frederick Lawrence, KCMG, CBE
Charlton, Sir Robert (Bobby), Kt., CBE
Charnley, Sir (William) John, Kt., CB, FREng.
Chataway, *Rt. Hon.* Sir Christopher, Kt.
Chatfield, Sir John Freeman, Kt., CBE
Chaytor, Sir George Reginald, Bt. (1831)
Checketts, *Sqn. Ldr.* Sir David John, KCVO
Checkland, Sir Michael, Kt.
Cheetham, Sir Nicolas John Alexander, KCMG
Cheshire, *Air Chief Marshal* Sir John Anthony, KBE, CB
Chessells, Sir Arthur David (Tim), Kt.
Chesterton, Sir Oliver Sidney, Kt., MC
Chetwood, Sir Clifford Jack, Kt.
Chetwynd, Sir Arthur Ralph Talbot, Bt. (1795)
Cheung, Sir Oswald Victor, Kt., CBE
Cheyne, Sir Joseph Lister Watson, Bt., OBE (1908)
Chichester, Sir (Edward) John, Bt. (1641)
Chilcot, Sir John Anthony, GCB
Child, Sir (Coles John) Jeremy, Bt. (1919)
Chilton, *Brig.* Sir Frederick Oliver, Kt., CBE, DSO
Chilwell, *Hon.* Sir Muir Fitzherbert, Kt.
Chinn, Sir Trevor Edwin, Kt., CVO
Chipperfield, Sir Geoffrey Howes, KCB
Chisholm, Sir John Alexander Raymond, Kt., FREng.
Chitty, Sir Thomas Willes, Bt. (1924)
Cholmeley, Sir Hugh John Frederick Sebastian, Bt. (1806)
Chow, Sir Chung Kong, Kt.
Chow, Sir Henry Francis, Kt., OBE
Christie, Sir George William Langham, Kt.
Christie, Sir William, Kt., MBE
Chung, Sir Sze-yuen, GBE, FREng.
Clapham, Sir Michael John Sinclair, KBE
Clark, Sir Francis Drake, Bt. (1886)
Clark, Sir John Allen, Kt.
Clark, Sir John Stewart-, Bt., MEP (1918)
Clark, Sir Jonathan George, Bt. (1917)
Clark, Sir Robert Anthony, Kt., DSC
Clark, Sir Robin Chichester-, Kt.
Clark, Sir Terence Joseph, KBE, CMG, CVO
Clark, Sir Thomas Edwin, Kt.
Clarke, *Hon.* Sir Anthony Petr, Kt.
Clarke, Sir Arthur Charles, Kt., CBE
Clarke, Sir (Charles Mansfield) Tobias, Bt. (1831)
Clarke, Sir Ellis Emmanuel Innocent, GCMG
Clarke, Sir Jonathan Dennis, Kt.
Clarke, *Maj.* Sir Peter Cecil, KCVO
Clarke, Sir Robert Cyril, Kt.
Clarke, Sir Rupert William John, Bt., MBE (1882)
Clarke, Sir Stanley William, Kt., CBE
Clay, Sir Richard Henry, Bt. (1841)
Clayton, Sir David Robert, Bt. (1732)
Cleaver, Sir Anthony Brian, Kt.
Cleminson, Sir James Arnold Stacey, KBE, MC
Clerk, Sir John Dutton, Bt., CBE, VRD (S. 1679)
Clerke, Sir John Edward Longueville, Bt. (1660)
Clifford, Sir Roger Joseph, Bt. (1887)
Clothier, Sir Cecil Montacute, KCB, QC
Clucas, Sir Kenneth Henry, KCB
Clutterbuck, *Vice-Adm.* Sir David Granville, KBE, CB
Coates, Sir Anthony Robert Milnes, Bt. (1911)
Coates, Sir David Frederick Charlton, Bt. (1921)
Coats, Sir Alastair Francis Stuart, Bt. (1905)
Coats, Sir William David, Kt.
Cobham, Sir Michael John, Kt., CBE
Cochrane, Sir (Henry) Marc (Sursock), Bt. (1903)
Cockburn, Sir John Elliot, Bt. (S. 1671)
Cockshaw, Sir Alan, Kt., FREng.
Codrington, Sir Simon Francis Bethell, Bt. (1876)
Codrington, Sir William Alexander, Bt. (1721)
†Coghill, Sir Patrick Kendal Farley, Bt. (1778)
Coghlin, *Hon.* Sir Patrick, Kt.
Cohen, Sir Edward, Kt.
Cohen, Sir Ivor Harold, Kt., CBE, TD
Cohen, *Prof.* Sir Philip, Kt., Ph.D, FRS
Cohen, Sir Ronald, Kt.
Cohen, Sir Stephen Harry Waley-, Bt. (1961)
Coldstream, Sir George Phillips, KCB, KCVO, QC
Cole, Sir (Alexander) Colin, KCB, KCVO, TD
Cole, Sir (Robert) William, Kt.
Coleridge, *Hon.* Sir Justice Paul James Duke, Kt.
Coles, Sir (Arthur) John, GCMG
Colfox, Sir (William) John, Bt. (1939)
Collett, Sir Christopher, GBE
Collett, Sir Ian Seymour, Bt. (1934)
Collins, *Hon.* Sir Andrew David, Kt.
Collins, Sir Bryan Thomas Alfred, Kt., OBE, QFSM
Collins, Sir John Alexander, Kt.
Collins, *Hon.* Sir Lawrence Antony, Kt.
Collyear, Sir John Gowen, Kt., FREng.
Colman, *Hon.* Sir Anthony David, Kt.
Colman, Sir Michael Jeremiah, Bt. (1907)
Colman, Sir Timothy, KG
Colquhoun of Luss, Sir Ivar Iain, Bt. (1786)
Colt, Sir Edward William Dutton, Bt. (1694)
Colthurst, Sir Richard La Touche, Bt. (1744)
Coltman, Sir (Arthur) Leycester Scott, KBE, CMG
Colvin, Sir Howard Montagu, Kt., CVO, CBE, FBA
Compton, *Rt. Hon.* Sir John George Melvin, KCMG
Conant, Sir John Ernest Michael, Bt. (1954)
Condon, Sir Paul Leslie, Kt., QPM
Connell, *Hon.* Sir Michael Bryan, Kt.
Connery, Sir Sean, Kt.
Conran, Sir Terence Orby, Kt.
Cons, *Hon.* Sir Derek, Kt.
Constable, Sir Frederic Strickland-, Bt. (1641)
Constantinou, Sir Georkios, Kt., OBE
Cook, *Prof.* Sir Alan Hugh, Kt.
Cook, Sir Christopher Wymondham Rayner Herbert, Bt. (1886)
Cooke, Sir Charles Fletcher-, Kt., QC
Cooke, *Col.* Sir David William Perceval, Bt. (1661)
Cooke, Sir Howard Felix Hanlan, GCMG, GCVO

Cooksey, Sir David James Scott, Kt.
Cooper, *Rt. Hon.* Sir Frank, GCB, CMG
Cooper, Sir (Frederick Howard) Michael Craig-, Kt., CBE, TD
Cooper, *Gen.* Sir George Leslie Conroy, GCB, MC
Cooper, Sir Henry, Kt.
Cooper, Sir Louis Jacques Blom-, Kt., QC
Cooper, Sir Patrick Graham Astley, Bt. (1821)
Cooper, Sir Richard Powell, Bt. (1905)
Cooper, Sir Robert George, Kt., CBE
Cooper, *Maj.-Gen.* Sir Simon Christie, GCVO
Cooper, Sir William Daniel Charles, Bt. (1863)
Coote, Sir Christopher John, Bt., *Premier Baronet of Ireland* (I. 1621)
Copas, *Most Revd* Sir Virgil, KBE, DD
Copisarow, Sir Alcon Charles, Kt.
Corbett, *Maj.-Gen.* Sir Robert John Swan, KCVO, CB
Corby, Sir (Frederick) Brian, Kt.
Corfield, *Rt. Hon.* Sir Frederick Vernon, Kt., QC
Corfield, Sir Kenneth George, Kt., FREng.
Cork, Sir Roger William, Kt.
Corley, Sir Kenneth Sholl Ferrand, Kt.
Cormack, Sir Patrick Thomas, Kt., MP
Corness, Sir Colin Ross, Kt.
Cornforth, Sir John Warcup, Kt., CBE, D.Phil., FRS
Cortazzi, Sir (Henry Arthur) Hugh, GCMG
Cory, Sir (Clinton Charles) Donald, Bt. (1919)
Cossons, Sir Neil, Kt., OBE
Cotter, *Lt.-Col.* Sir Delaval James Alfred, Bt., DSO (I. 1763)
Cotterell, Sir John Henry Geers, Bt. (1805)
Cotton, Sir John Richard, KCMG, OBE
Cotton, *Hon.* Sir Robert Carrington, KCMG
Cotton, Sir William Frederick, Kt., CBE
Cottrell, Sir Alan Howard, Kt., Ph.D., FRS, FREng.
†Cotts, Sir Richard Crichton Mitchell, Bt. (1921)
Couper, Sir (Robert) Nicholas (Oliver), Bt. (1841)
Court, *Hon.* Sir Charles Walter Michael, KCMG, OBE
Courtenay, Sir Thomas Daniel, Kt.
Cousins, *Air Chief Marshal* Sir David, KCB, AFC
Coutts, Sir David Burdett Money-, KCVO
Couzens, Sir Kenneth Edward, KCB
Covacevich, Sir (Anthony) Thomas, Kt., DFC
Coville, *Air Marshal* Sir Christopher Charles Cotton, KCB
Cowan, *Gen.* Sir Samuel, KCB, CBE
Coward, *Vice-Adm.* Sir John Francis, KCB, DSO
Cowen, *Rt. Hon. Prof.* Sir Zelman, GCMG, GCVO, QC
Cowie, Sir Thomas (Tom), Kt., OBE
Cowperthwaite, Sir John James, KBE, CMG
Cox, Sir Alan George, Kt., CBE
Cox, *Prof.* Sir David Roxbee, Kt., FRS
Cox, Sir Geoffrey Sandford, Kt., CBE
Cox, *Vice-Adm.* Sir John Michael Holland, KCB
Cradock, *Rt. Hon.* Sir Percy, GCMG
Craig, Sir (Albert) James (Macqueen), GCMG
Crane, *Hon.* Sir Peter Francis, Kt.
Craufurd, Sir Robert James, Bt. (1781)
Craven, Sir John Anthony, Kt.
Craven, *Air Marshal* Sir Robert Edward, KBE, CB, DFC
Crawford, *Prof.* Sir Frederick William, Kt., FREng.
Crawford, Sir (Robert) Stewart, GCMG, CVO
Crawford, *Vice-Adm.* Sir William Godfrey, KBE, CB, DSC
Creagh, *Maj.-Gen.* Sir (Kilner) Rupert Brazier-, KBE, CB, DSO
Crew, Sir (Michael) Edward, Kt., QPM
Cresswell, *Hon.* Sir Peter John, Kt.
Crill, Sir Peter Leslie, KBE
Cripps, Sir Cyril Humphrey, Kt.
Crisp, Sir (John) Peter, Bt. (1913)
Critchett, Sir Ian (George Lorraine), Bt. (1908)
Crocker, Sir Walter Russell, KBE
Croft, Sir Owen Glendower, Bt. (1671)
Croft, Sir Thomas Stephen Hutton, Bt. (1818)
†Crofton, Sir Hugh Denis, Bt. (1801)
Crofton, *Prof.* Sir John Wenman, Kt.
Crofton, Sir Malby Sturges, Bt. (1838)
Crookenden, *Lt.-Gen.* Sir Napier, KCB, DSO, OBE
Cross, *Air Chief Marshal* Sir Kenneth Brian Boyd, KCB, CBE, DSO, DFC
Crossland, *Prof.* Sir Bernard, Kt., CBE, FREng.
Crossley, Sir Julian Charles, Bt. (1909)
Cruthers, Sir James Winter, Kt.
Cubbon, Sir Brian Crossland, GCB
Cubitt, Sir Hugh Guy, Kt., CBE
Cullen, Sir (Edward) John, Kt., FREng.
Culpin, Sir Robert Paul, Kt.
Cumming, Sir William Gordon Gordon-, Bt. (1804)
Cuninghame, Sir John Christopher Foggo Montgomery-, Bt. (NS 1672)
Cuninghame, Sir Robert Henry Fairlie-, Bt. (S. 1630)
Cunliffe, Sir David Ellis, Bt. (1759)
Cunningham, *Lt.-Gen.* Sir Hugh Patrick, KBE
Cunynghame, Sir Andrew David Francis, Bt. (S. 1702)
†Currie, Sir Donald Scott, Bt. (1847)
Currie, Sir Neil Smith, Kt., CBE
Curry, Sir Donald Thomas Younger, Kt., CBE
Curtis, Sir Barry John, Kt.
Curtis, Sir (Edward) Leo, Kt.
Curtis, *Hon.* Sir Richard Herbert, Kt.
Curtis, Sir William Peter, Bt. (1802)
Curtiss, *Air Marshal* Sir John Bagot, KCB, KBE
Curwen, Sir Christopher Keith, KCMG
Cuschieri, *Prof.* Sir Alfred, Kt.
Cutler, Sir (Arthur) Roden, VC, KCMG, KCVO, CBE
Cutler, Sir Charles Benjamin, KBE, ED
Dacie, *Prof.* Sir John Vivian, Kt., MD, FRS
Dain, Sir David John Michael, KCVO
Dalrymple, *Maj.* Sir Hew Fleetwood Hamilton-, Bt., GCVO, KCVO (S. 1697)
Dalton, Sir Alan Nugent Goring, Kt., CBE
Dalton, *Vice-Adm.* Sir Geoffrey Thomas James Oliver, KCB
Daly, *Lt.-Gen.* Sir Thomas Joseph, KBE, CB, DSO
Dalyell, Sir Tam (Thomas), Bt., MP (NS 1685)
Daniel, Sir Goronwy Hopkin, KCVO, CB, D.Phil.
Daniel, Sir John Sagar, Kt., D.Sc.
Daniel, Sir Wilred St Clair-, Kt., CBE, JP
Daniell, Sir Peter Averell, Kt., TD
Darby, Sir Peter Howard, Kt., CBE, QFSM
Darell, Sir Jeffrey Lionel, Bt., MC (1795)
Dargie, Sir William Alexander, Kt., CBE
Dark, Sir Anthony Michael Beaumont-, Kt.
Darling, Sir Clifford, GCVO
Darvall, Sir (Charles) Roger, Kt., CBE
†Dashwood, Sir Edward John Francis, Bt., *Premier Baronet of Great Britain* (1707)
Dashwood, Sir Richard James, Bt. (1684)
Daunt, Sir Timothy Lewis Achilles, KCMG
Davey, *Hon.* Sir David Herbert Penry-, Kt.
David, Sir Jean Marc, Kt., CBE, QC
David, *His Hon.* Sir Robin (Robert) Daniel George, Kt., QC
Davidge, Sir Leonard Edward, Kt.
Davidson, Sir Robert James, Kt., FREng.
†Davie, Sir Michael Ferguson-, Bt. (1847)
Davies, Sir Alan Seymour, Kt.
Davies, *Hon.* Sir (Alfred William) Michael, Kt.
Davies, Sir (Charles) Noel, Kt.
Davies, *Prof.* Sir David Evan Naughton, Kt., CBE, FRS, FREng.
Davies, *Hon.* Sir (David Herbert) Mervyn, Kt., MC, TD

Davies, Sir David John, Kt.
Davies, Sir Frank John, Kt., CBE
Davies, *Prof.* Sir Graeme John, Kt., FREng.
Davies, Sir John Howard, Kt.
Davies, *Vice-Adm.* Sir Lancelot Richard Bell, KBE
Davies, Sir Peter Maxwell, Kt., CBE
Davies, Sir Rhys Everson, Kt., QC
Davis, Sir Andrew Frank, Kt., CBE
Davis, Sir Colin Rex, Kt., CBE, CH
Davis, Sir (Ernest) Howard, Kt., CMG, OBE
Davis, Sir John Gilbert, Bt. (1946)
Davis, Sir Peter John, Kt.
Davis, *Hon.* Sir Thomas Robert Alexander Harries, KBE
Davison, *Rt. Hon.* Sir Ronald Keith, GBE, CMG
Davson, Sir Christopher Michael Edward, Bt. (1927)
Dawanincura, Sir John Norbert, Kt., OBE
Dawbarn, Sir Simon Yelverton, KCVO, CMG
Dawson, *Hon.* Sir Daryl Michael, KBE, CB
Dawson, Sir Hugh Michael Trevor, Bt. (1920)
Dawtry, Sir Alan (Graham), Kt., CBE, TD
Day, Sir Derek Malcolm, KCMG
Day, *Air Marshal* Sir John Romney, KCB, OBE
Day, Sir (Judson) Graham, Kt.
Day, Sir Michael John, Kt., OBE
Day, Sir Simon James, Kt.
Deakin, Sir (Frederick) William (Dampier), Kt., DSO
Deane, *Hon.* Sir William Patrick, KBE
Dear, Sir Geoffrey James, Kt., QPM
Dearlove, Sir Richard Billing, KCMG, OBE
de Bellaigue, Sir Geoffrey, GCVO
Debenham, Sir Gilbert Ridley, Bt. (1931)
de Deney, Sir Geoffrey Ivor, KCVO
de Hoghton, Sir (Richard) Bernard (Cuthbert), Bt. (1611)
De la Bère, Sir Cameron, Bt. (1953)
de la Rue, Sir Andrew George Ilay, Bt. (1898)
Dellow, Sir John Albert, Kt., CBE
de Montmorency, Sir Arnold Geoffroy, Bt. (I. 1631)
Denholm, Sir John Ferguson (Ian), Kt., CBE
Denman, Sir (George) Roy, KCB, CMG
Denny, Sir Anthony Coningham de Waltham, Bt. (I. 1782)
Denny, Sir Charles Alistair Maurice, Bt. (1913)
Dent, Sir John, Kt., CBE, FREng.
Denton, *Prof.* Sir Eric James, Kt., CBE, FRS
Derbyshire, Sir Andrew George, Kt.
Derham, Sir Peter John, Kt.
de Trafford, Sir Dermot Humphrey, Bt. (1841)
Deverell, *Lt.-Gen.* Sir John Freegard, KCB, OBE
Devesi, Sir Baddeley, GCMG, GCVO
De Ville, Sir Harold Godfrey Oscar, Kt., CBE
Devitt, Sir James Hugh Thomas, Bt. (1916)
de Waal, Sir (Constant Henrik) Henry, KCB, QC
Dewar, Sir John James Evelyn, Bt. (1907)
Dewey, Sir Anthony Hugh, Bt. (1917)
Dewhurst, *Prof.* Sir (Christopher) John, Kt.
d'Eyncourt, Sir Mark Gervais Tennyson-, Bt. (1930)
Dhenin, *Air Marshal* Sir Geoffrey Howard, KBE, AFC, GM, MD
Dhrangadhra, HH the Maharaja Raj Saheb of, KCIE
Dibela, *Hon.* Sir Kingsford, GCMG
Dick, *Maj.-Gen.* Sir Iain Charles Mackay-, KCVO, MBE
Dickenson, Sir Aubrey Fiennes Trotman-, Kt.
Dickinson, Sir Harold Herbert, Kt.
Dickinson, Sir Samuel Benson, Kt.
Dilke, Sir Charles John Wentworth, Bt. (1862)
Dillon, *Rt. Hon.* Sir (George) Brian (Hugh), Kt.
Dixon, Sir Jeremy, Kt.
Dixon, Sir Jonathan Mark, Bt. (1919)
Djanogly, Sir Harry Ari Simon, Kt., CBE
Dobbs, *Capt.* Sir Richard Arthur Frederick, KCVO
Dobson, *Vice-Adm.* Sir David Stuart, KBE
Dobson, *Gen.* Sir Patrick John Howard-, GCB
Dodds, Sir Ralph Jordan, Bt. (1964)
Dodson, Sir Derek Sherborne Lindsell, KCMG, MC
Dodsworth, Sir John Christopher Smith-, Bt. (1784)
Doll, *Prof.* Sir (William) Richard (Shaboe), Kt., CH, OBE, FRS, DM, MD, D.Sc.
Dollery, Sir Colin Terence, Kt.
Donald, Sir Alan Ewen, KCMG
Donald, *Air Marshal* Sir John George, KBE
Donne, *Hon.* Sir Gaven John, KBE
Donne, Sir John Christopher, Kt.
Dookun, Sir Dewoonarain, Kt.
Dorey, Sir Graham Martyn, Kt.
Dorman, Sir Philip Henry Keppel, Bt. (1923)
Dougherty, *Maj.-Gen.* Sir Ivan Noel, Kt., CBE, DSO, ED
Doughty, Sir Graham Martin, Kt.
Doughty, Sir William Roland, Kt.
Douglas, Sir (Edward) Sholto, Kt.
Douglas, *Hon.* Sir Roger Owen, Kt.
Douglas, *Rt. Hon.* Sir William Randolph, KCMG
Dover, *Prof.* Sir Kenneth James, Kt., D.Litt., FBA, FRSE
Dowell, Sir Anthony James, Kt., CBE
Down, Sir Alastair Frederick, Kt., OBE, MC, TD
Downes, Sir Edward Thomas, Kt., CBE
Downey, Sir Gordon Stanley, KCB
Downs, Sir Diarmuid, Kt., CBE, FREng.
Downward, *Maj.-Gen.* Sir Peter Aldcroft, KCVO, CB, DSO, DFC
Downward, Sir William Atkinson, Kt.
Dowson, Sir Philip Manning, Kt., CBE, PRA
Doyle, Sir Reginald Derek Henry, Kt., CBE
D'Oyly, Sir Nigel Hadley Miller, Bt. (1663)
Drake, *Hon.* Sir (Frederick) Maurice, Kt., DFC
Drewry, *Lt-Gen.* Sir Christopher Francis, KCB, CBE
Dreyer, *Adm.* Sir Desmond Parry, GCB, CBE, DSC
Drinkwater, Sir John Muir, Kt., QC
Driver, Sir Antony Victor, Kt.
Driver, Sir Eric William, Kt.
*Drummond, Sir John Richard Gray, Kt., CBE*
Drury, Sir (Victor William) Michael, Kt., OBE
Dryden, Sir John Stephen Gyles, Bt. (1733 and 1795)
du Cann, *Rt. Hon.* Sir Edward Dillon Lott, KBE
†Duckworth, Sir Edward Richard Dyce, Bt. (1909)
du Cros, Sir Claude Philip Arthur Mallet, Bt. (1916)
Duffell, *Lt.-Gen.* Sir Peter Royson, KCB, CBE, MC
Duffus, *Hon.* Sir Herbert George Holwell, Kt.
Duffy, Sir (Albert) (Edward) Patrick, Kt., Ph.D.
Dugdale, Sir William Stratford, Bt., MC (1936)
Dummett, *Prof.* Sir Michael Anthony Eardley, Kt., FBA
Dunbar, Sir Archibald Ranulph, Bt. (S. 1700)
Dunbar, Sir David Hope-, Bt. (S. 1664)
Dunbar, Sir Robert Drummond Cospatrick, Bt. (S. 1698)
Dunbar, Sir James Michael, Bt. (S. 1694)
†Dunbar of Hempriggs, Sir Richard Francis, Bt. (S. 1706)
Duncan, Sir James Blair, Kt.
Duncombe, Sir Philip Digby Pauncefort-, Bt. (1859)
Dunham, Sir Kingsley Charles, Kt., Ph.D., FRS, FRSE, FREng.
Dunlop, Sir Thomas, Bt. (1916)
Dunn, *Air Marshal* Sir Eric Clive, KBE, CB, BEM
Dunn, *Air Marshal* Sir Patrick Hunter, KBE, CB, DFC
Dunn, *Rt. Hon.* Sir Robin Horace Walford, Kt., MC
Dunne, Sir Thomas Raymond, KCVO

Dunning, Sir Simon William Patrick, Bt. (1930)
Dunstan, *Lt.-Gen.* Sir Donald Beaumont, KBE, CB
Dunt, *Vice-Adm.* Sir John Hugh, KCB
†Duntze, Sir Daniel Evans, Bt. (1774)
Dupre, Sir Tumun, Kt., MBE
Dupree, Sir Peter, Bt. (1921)
Durand, Sir Edward Alan Christopher David Percy, Bt. (1892)
Durant, Sir (Robert) Anthony (Bevis), Kt.
Durham, Sir Kenneth, Kt.
Durkin, *Air Marshal* Sir Herbert, KBE, CB
Durrant, Sir William Alexander Estridge, Bt. (1784)
Duthie, *Prof.* Sir Herbert Livingston, Kt.
Duthie, Sir Robert Grieve (Robin), Kt., CBE
Dwyer, Sir Joseph Anthony, Kt.
Dyer, *Prof.* Sir (Henry) Peter (Francis) Swinnerton-, Bt., KBE, FRS (1678)
Dyke, Sir David William Hart, Bt. (1677)
Dyson, *Hon.* Sir John Anthony, Kt.
Eady, *Hon.* Sir David, Kt.
Earle, Sir (Hardman) George (Algernon), Bt. (1869)
Easton, Sir Robert William Simpson, Kt., CBE
Eaton, *Adm.* Sir Kenneth John, GBE, KCB
Eberle, *Adm.* Sir James Henry Fuller, GCB
Ebrahim, Sir (Mahomed) Currimbhoy, Bt. (1910)
Echlin, Sir Norman David Fenton, Bt. (I. 1721)
Eckersley, Sir Donald Payze, Kt., OBE
Edge, *Capt.* Sir (Philip) Malcolm, KCVO
Edge, Sir William, Bt. (1937)
Edmonstone, Sir Archibald Bruce Charles, Bt. (1774)
Edwardes, Sir Michael Owen, Kt.
Edwards, Sir Christopher John Churchill, Bt. (1866)
Edwards, Sir George Robert, Kt., OM, CBE, FRS, FREng.
Edwards, Sir Llewellyn Roy, Kt.
Edwards, *Prof.* Sir Samuel Frederick, Kt., FRS
Egan, Sir John Leopold, Kt.
Egerton, Sir John Alfred Roy, Kt.
Egerton, Sir (Philip) John (Caledon) Grey-, Bt. (1617)
Egerton, Sir Stephen Loftus, KCMG
Eichelbaum, *Rt. Hon.* Sir Thomas, GBE
Elias, Sir Patrick, Kt., QC
Eliott of Stobs, Sir Charles Joseph Alexander, Bt. (S. 1666)
Ellerton, Sir Geoffrey James, Kt., CMG, MBE
Elliot, Sir Gerald Henry, Kt.
Elliott, Sir Clive Christopher Hugh, Bt. (1917)
Elliott, Sir David Murray, KCMG, CB
Elliott, *Prof.* Sir John Huxtable, Kt., FBA
Elliott, Sir Randal Forbes, KBE
Elliott, *Prof.* Sir Roger James, Kt., FRS
Elliott, Sir Ronald Stuart, Kt.
Ellis, Sir Ronald, Kt., FREng.
Ellison, *Col.* Sir Ralph Harry Carr-, KCVO, TD
Elphinstone, Sir John, Bt. (S. 1701)
Elphinstone, Sir John Howard Main, Bt. (1816)
Elton, Sir Arnold, Kt., CBE
Elton, Sir Charles Abraham Grierson, Bt. (1717)
Elwes, Sir Jeremy Vernon, Kt., CBE
Elwood, Sir Brian George Conway, Kt., CBE
Elworthy, Sir Peter Herbert, Kt.
Elyan, Sir (Isadore) Victor, Kt.
Emery, *Rt. Hon.* Sir Peter Frank Hannibal, Kt., MP
Empey, Sir Reginald Norman Morgan, Kt., OBE
Engle, Sir George Lawrence Jose, KCB, QC
English, Sir Terence Alexander Hawthorne, KBE, FRCS
Epstein, *Prof.* Sir (Michael) Anthony, Kt., CBE, FRS
Errington, *Col.* Sir Geoffrey Frederick, Bt., OBE (1963)
Errington, Sir Lancelot, KCB
Erskine, Sir (Thomas) David, Bt. (1821)
Esmonde, Sir Thomas Francis Grattan, Bt. (I. 1629)
Espie, Sir Frank Fletcher, Kt., OBE
Esplen, Sir John Graham, Bt. (1921)
Essenhigh, *Adm.* Sir Nigel Richard, Kt.
Etherton, *Hon.* Sir Terence Michael Elkan Barnet, KT.
Evans, Sir Anthony Adney, Bt. (1920)
Evans, *Rt. Hon.* Sir Anthony Howell Meurig, Kt., RD
Evans, *Prof.* Sir Christopher Thomas, Kt., OBE
Evans, *Air Chief Marshal* Sir David George, GCB, CBE
Evans, *Air Chief Marshal* Sir David Parry-, GCB, CBE
Evans, *Hon.* Sir David Roderick, Kt.
Evans, *Hon.* Sir Haydn Tudor, Kt.
Evans, *Prof.* Sir John Grimley, Kt., FRCP
Evans, Sir John Stanley, Kt., QPM
Evans, Sir Richard Harry, Kt., CBE
Evans, Sir Richard Mark, KCMG, KCVO
Evans, Sir Robert, Kt., CBE, FREng.
Evans, Sir (William) Vincent (John), GCMG, MBE, QC
Eveleigh, *Rt. Hon.* Sir Edward Walter, Kt., ERD
Everard, Sir Robin Charles, Bt. (1911)
Every, Sir Henry John Michael, Bt. (1641)
Ewans, Sir Martin Kenneth, KCMG
†Ewart, Sir William Michael, Bt. (1887)
Ewbank, *Hon.* Sir Anthony Bruce, Kt.
Ewin, Sir (David) Ernest Thomas Floyd, Kt., OBE, LVO
Ewing, Sir (Alistair) Simon Orr-, Bt. (1963)
Ewing, Sir Ronald Archibald Orr-, Bt. (1886)
Eyre, *Maj.-Gen.* Sir James Ainsworth Campden Gabriel, KCVO, CBE
Eyre, Sir Reginald Edwin, Kt.
Eyre, Sir Richard Charles Hastings, Kt., CBE
Faber, Sir Richard Stanley, KCVO, CMG
Fagge, Sir John William Frederick, Bt. (1660)
Fairbairn, Sir (James) Brooke, Bt. (1869)
Fairclough, Sir John Whitaker, Kt., FREng.
Fairhall, *Hon.* Sir Allen, KBE
Fairweather, Sir Patrick Stanislaus, KCMG
Falconer, *Hon.* Sir Douglas William, Kt., MBE
†Falkiner, Sir Benjamin Simon Patrick, Bt. (I. 1778)
Fall, Sir Brian James Proetel, GCVO, KCMG
Falle, Sir Samuel, KCMG, KCVO, DSC
Fang, *Prof.* Sir Harry, Kt., CBE
Fareed, Sir Djamil Sheik, Kt.
Farmer, Sir Thomas, Kt., CBE
Farquhar, Sir Michael Fitzroy Henry, Bt. (1796)
Farquharson, *Rt. Hon.* Sir Donald Henry, Kt.
Farquharson, Sir James Robbie, KBE
Farrell, Sir Terence, Kt., CBE
Farrer, Sir (Charles) Matthew, GCVO
Farrington, Sir Henry Francis Colden, Bt. (1818)
Fat, Sir (Maxime) Edouard (Lim Man) Lim, Kt.
Faulkner, Sir (James) Dennis (Compton), Kt., CBE, VRD
Fawcus, Sir (Robert) Peter, KBE, CMG
Fawkes, Sir Randol Francis, Kt.
Fay, Sir (Humphrey) Michael Gerard, Kt.
Fayrer, Sir John Lang Macpherson, Bt. (1896)
Fearn, Sir (Patrick) Robin, KCMG
Feilden, Sir Bernard Melchior, Kt., CBE
Feilden, Sir Henry Wemyss, Bt., (1846)
Fell, Sir David, KCB
Fender, Sir Brian Edward Frederick, Kt., CMG, Ph.D.
Fenn, Sir Nicholas Maxted, GCMG
Fennell, *Hon.* Sir (John) Desmond Augustine, Kt., OBE
Fennessy, Sir Edward, Kt., CBE
Fergus, Sir Howard Archibald, KBE, CBE
Ferguson, Sir Alexander Chapman, Kt., CBE

Ferguson, Sir Ian Edward Johnson-, Bt. (1906)
Fergusson of Kilkerran, Sir Charles, Bt. (S. 1703)
Fergusson, Sir Ewan Alastair John, GCMG, GCVO
Fergusson, Sir James Herbert Hamilton Colyer-, Bt. (1866)
Feroze, Sir Rustam Moolan, Kt., FRCS
Ferris, *Hon.* Sir Francis Mursell, Kt., TD
ffolkes, Sir Robert Francis Alexander, Bt, OBE (1774)
Field, Sir Malcolm David, Kt.
Fielding, Sir Colin Cunningham, Kt., CB
Fielding, Sir Leslie, KCMG
Fieldsend, *Hon.* Sir John Charles Rowell, KBE
Fiennes, Sir Ranulph Twisleton-Wykeham-, Bt., OBE (1916)
Figg, Sir Leonard Clifford William, KCMG
Figgis, Sir Anthony St John Howard, KCVO, CMG
Figures, Sir Colin Frederick, KCMG, OBE
Fingland, Sir Stanley James Gunn, KCMG
Finlay, Sir David Ronald James Bell, Bt. (1964)
Finney, Sir Thomas, Kt., OBE
Firth, *Prof.* Sir Raymond William, Kt., Ph.D., FBA
Fisher, Sir George Read, Kt., CMG
Fisher, *Hon.* Sir Henry Arthur Pears, Kt.
Fison, Sir (Richard) Guy, Bt., DSC (1905)
†Fitzgerald, *Revd* (Sir) Daniel Patrick, Bt. (1903)
†FitzGerald, Sir Adrian James Andrew, Bt. (1880)
FitzHerbert, Sir Richard Ranulph, Bt. (1784)
Fitzpatrick, *Gen.* Sir (Geoffrey Richard) Desmond, GCB, GCVO, DSO, MBE, MC
Fitzpatrick, *Air Marshal* Sir John Bernard, KBE, CB
Flanagan, Sir Ronald, Kt., OBE
Fletcher, Sir Henry Egerton Aubrey-, Bt. (1782)
Fletcher, Sir James Muir Cameron, Kt.
Fletcher, Sir Leslie, Kt., DSC
Floissac, *Hon.* Sir Vincent Frederick, Kt., CMG, OBE, QC
Floyd, Sir Giles Henry Charles, Bt. (1816)
Foley, *Lt.-Gen.* Sir John Paul, KCB, OBE, MC
Foley, Sir (Thomas John) Noel, Kt., CBE
Follett, *Prof.* Sir Brian Keith, Kt., FRS
Foot, Sir Geoffrey James, Kt.
Foots, Sir James William, Kt.
Forbes, *Maj.* Sir Hamish Stewart, Bt., MBE, MC (1823)
Forbes of Craigievar, Sir John Alexander Cumnock, Bt. (S. 1630)
Forbes, *Vice-Adm.* Sir John Morrison, KCB
Forbes, *Hon.* Sir Thayne John, Kt.
†Forbes, Sir William Daniel Stuart-, Bt. (S. 1626)
Ford, Sir Andrew Russell, Bt. (1929)
Ford, Sir David Robert, KBE, LVO, OBE
Ford, *Maj.* Sir Edward William Spencer, GCVO, KCB, ERD
Ford, *Air Marshal* Sir Geoffrey Harold, KBE, CB, FREng.
Ford, *Prof.* Sir Hugh, Kt., FRS, FREng.
Ford, Sir James Anson St Clair-, Bt. (1793)
Ford, Sir John Archibald, KCMG, MC
Ford, *Gen.* Sir Robert Cyril, GCB, CBE
Foreman, Sir Philip Frank, Kt., CBE, FREng.
Forman, Sir John Denis, Kt., OBE
Forrest, *Prof.* Sir (Andrew) Patrick (McEwen), Kt.
Forrest, *Rear-Adm.* Sir Ronald Stephen, KCVO
Forster, Sir Archibald William, Kt., FREng.
Forte, Hon. Sir Rocco John Vincent, Kt.
Forwood, Sir Dudley Richard, Bt. (1895)
Foster, Sir Andrew William, Kt.
Foster, *Prof.* Sir Christopher David, Kt.
Foster, Sir John Gregory, Bt. (1930)
Foster, Sir Robert Sidney, GCMG, KCVO
Foulis, Sir Ian Primrose Liston-, Bt. (S. 1634)
Foulkes, Sir Arther Alexander, KCMG
Foulkes, Sir Nigel Gordon, Kt.
Fountain, *Hon.* Sir Cyril Stanley Smith, Kt.
Fowden, Sir Leslie, Kt., FRS
Fowke, Sir David Frederick Gustavus, Bt. (1814)
Fowler, Sir (Edward) Michael Coulson, Kt.
Fowler, *Rt. Hon.* Sir (Peter) Norman, Kt., MP
Fox, *Rt. Hon.* Sir (John) Marcus, Kt., MBE
Fox, *Rt. Hon.* Sir Michael John, Kt.
Fox, Sir Paul Leonard, Kt., CBE
France, Sir Christopher Walter, GCB
Francis, Sir Horace William Alexander, Kt., CBE, FREng.
Frank, Sir Douglas George Horace, Kt., QC
Frank, Sir Robert Andrew, Bt. (1920)
Franklin, Sir Michael David Milroy, KCB, CMG
Franklin, Sir Michael George Charles, Kt
Franks, Sir Arthur Temple, KCMG
Fraser, Sir Alasdair MacLeod, Kt.
Fraser, Sir Charles Annand, KCVO
Fraser, *Gen.* Sir David William, GCB, OBE
Fraser, Sir Iain Michael Duncan, Bt. (1943)
Fraser, Sir Ian James, Kt., CBE, MC
Fraser, Sir (James) Campbell, Kt.
Fraser, Sir James Murdo, KBE
Fraser, Sir William Kerr, GCB
Frayling, *Prof.* Sir Christopher John, Kt.
Frederick, Sir Christopher St John, Bt. (1723)
Freeland, Sir John Redvers, KCMG
Freeman, Sir James Robin, Bt. (1945)
Freer, *Air Chief Marshal* Sir Robert William George, GBE, KCB
Freeth, *Hon.* Sir Gordon, KBE
French, *Hon.* Sir Christopher James Saunders, Kt.
Frere, *Vice-Adm.* Sir Richard Tobias, KCB
Fretwell, Sir (Major) John (Emsley), GCMG
Freud, Sir Clement Raphael, Kt.
Froggatt, Sir Leslie Trevor, Kt.
Froggatt, Sir Peter, Kt.
Frossard, Sir Charles Keith, KBE
Frost, Sir David Paradine, Kt., OBE
Frost, Sir Terence Ernest Manitou, Kt., RA
Fry, Sir Peter Derek, Kt.
Fry, *Hon.* Sir William Gordon, Kt.
Fuller, Sir James Henry Fleetwood, Bt. (1910)
Fuller, *Hon.* Sir John Bryan Munro, Kt.
Fung, *Hon.* Sir Kenneth Ping-Fan, Kt., CBE
Furness, Sir Stephen Roberts, Bt. (1913)
Gadsden, Sir Peter Drury Haggerston, GBE, FREng.
Gage, *Hon.* Sir William Marcus, Kt.
Gainsford, Sir Ian Derek, Kt., DDS
Gaius, *Rt. Revd* Saimon, KBE
Gallwey, Sir Philip Frankland Payne-, Bt. (1812)
Galsworthy, Sir Anthony Charles, KCMG
Galway, Sir James, Kt., OBE
Gam, *Rt. Revd* Sir Getake, KBE
Gamble, Sir David Hugh Norman, Bt. (1897)
Gambon, Sir Michael John, Kt., CBE
Garden, *Air Marshal* Sir Timothy, KCB
Gardiner, Sir George Arthur, Kt.
Gardiner, Sir John Eliot, Kt., CBE
Gardner, Sir Robert Henry Bruce-, Bt. (1945)
Garland, *Hon.* Sir Patrick Neville, Kt.
Garland, *Hon.* Sir Ransley Victor, KBE
Garlick, Sir John, KCB
Garner, Sir Anthony Stuart, Kt.
Garnett, *Vice-Adm.* Sir Ian David Graham, KCB
Garnier, *Rear-Adm.* Sir John, KCVO, CBE
Garrett, Sir Anthony Peter, Kt., CBE
Garrick, Sir Ronald, Kt., CBE, FREng.
Garrioch, Sir (William) Henry, Kt.

Garrod, *Lt.-Gen.* Sir (John) Martin Carruthers, KCB, OBE
Garthwaite, Sir (William) Mark (Charles), Bt. (1919)
Gaskell, Sir Richard Kennedy Harvey, Kt.
Gatehouse, *Hon.* Sir Robert Alexander, Kt.
Geno, Sir Makena Viora, KBE
Gent, Sir Christopher Charles, Kt.
George, Sir Arthur Thomas, Kt.
George, *Prof.* Sir Charles Frederick, MD, FRCP
George, Sir Edward, Kt.
George, *Rt. Hon.* Sir Edward Alan John, GBE
George, Sir Richard William, Kt., CVO
Gerken, *Vice-Adm.* Sir Robert William Frank, KCB, CBE
Gery, Sir Robert Lucian Wade-, KCMG, KCVO
Gethin, Sir Richard Joseph St Lawrence, Bt. (I. 1665)
Getty, Sir (John) Paul, KBE
Ghurburrun, Sir Rabindrah, Kt.
Gibb, Sir Francis Ross (Frank), Kt., CBE, FREng.
Gibbings, Sir Peter Walter, Kt.
Gibbons, Sir (John) David, KBE
Gibbons, Sir William Edward Doran, Bt. (1752)
Gibbs, *Hon.* Sir Eustace Hubert Beilby, KCVO, CMG
Gibbs, *Rt. Hon.* Sir Harry Talbot, GCMG, KBE
Gibbs, *Hon.* Sir Richard John Hedley, Kt.
Gibbs, Sir Roger Geoffrey, Kt.
Gibbs, *Field Marshal* Sir Roland Christopher, GCB, CBE, DSO, MC
†Gibson, *Revd* Sir Christopher Herbert, Bt. (1931)
Gibson, Sir Ian, Kt., CBE
Gibson, *Rt. Hon.* Sir Peter Leslie, Kt.
Gibson, *Rt. Hon.* Sir Ralph Brian, Kt.
Giddings, *Air Marshal* Sir (Kenneth Charles) Michael, KCB, OBE, DFC, AFC
Gielgud, Sir (Arthur) John, Kt., OM, CH
Giffard, Sir (Charles) Sydney (Rycroft), KCMG
Gilbert, *Air Chief Marshal* Sir Joseph Alfred, KCB, CBE
Gilbert, Sir Martin John, Kt., CBE
†Gilbey, Sir Walter Gavin, Bt. (1893)
Giles, *Rear-Adm.* Sir Morgan Charles Morgan-, Kt., DSO, OBE, GM
Gill, Sir Anthony Keith, Kt., FREng.
Gillam, Sir Patrick John, Kt.
Gillen, *Hon.* Sir John de Winter, Kt.
Gillett, Sir Robin Danvers Penrose, Bt., GBE, RD (1959)
Gilmour, *Col.* Sir Allan Macdonald, KCVO, OBE, MC
Gilmour, Sir John Edward, Bt., DSO, TD (1897)
Gina, Sir Lloyd Maepeza, KBE
Gingell, *Air Chief Marshal* Sir John, GBE, KCB, KCVO
Girolami, Sir Paul, Kt.
Girvan, *Hon.* Sir (Frederick) Paul, Kt.
Gladstone, Sir (Erskine) William, KG, Bt. (1846)
Glen, Sir Alexander Richard, KBE, DSC
Glenn, Sir (Joseph Robert) Archibald, Kt., OBE
Glidewell, *Rt. Hon.* Sir Iain Derek Laing, Kt.
Glover, *Gen.* Sir James Malcolm, KCB, MBE
Glover, Sir Victor Joseph Patrick, Kt.
Glyn, Sir Richard Lindsay, Bt. (1759 and 1800)
Goavea, Sir Sinaka Vakai, KBE
Gobbo, Sir James Augustine, Kt., AC
Godber, Sir George Edward, GCB, DM
Goff, Sir Robert (William) Davis-, Bt. (1905)
Gold, Sir Arthur Abraham, Kt., CBE
Gold, Sir Joseph, Kt.
Goldberg, *Prof.* Sir Abraham, Kt., MD, D.Sc., FRCP
Goldberg, *Prof.* Sir David Paul Brandes, Kt.
Goldman, Sir Samuel, KCB
Goldring, Sir John Bernard, Kt.
Gombrich, *Prof.* Sir Ernst Hans Josef, Kt., OM, CBE, Ph.D., FBA, FSA
Gomersall, Sir Stephen John, KCMG
Gooch, Sir Timothy Robert, Bt., MBE (1746)
Gooch, Sir Trevor Sherlock (Sir Peter), Bt. (1866)
Good, Sir John Kennedy-, KBE
Goodall, Sir (Arthur) David Saunders, GCMG
Goodall, *Air Marshal* Sir Roderick Harvey, KBE, CB, CBE, AFC RAF
Goode, Prof. Sir Royston Miles, Kt., CBE, QC
Goodenough, Sir Anthony Michael, KCMG
Goodenough, Sir William McLernon, Bt. (1943)
Goodhart, Sir Philip Carter, Kt.
Goodhart, Sir Robert Anthony Gordon, Bt. (1911)
Goodhew, Sir Victor Henry, Kt.
Gooding, Sir Alan, Kt.
Goodison, Sir Alan Clowes, KCMG
Goodison, Sir Nicholas Proctor, Kt.
Goodlad, *Rt. Hon.* Sir Alastair Robertson, KCMG
Goodman, Sir Patrick Ledger, Kt., CBE
Goodson, Sir Mark Weston Lassam, Bt. (1922)
Goodwin, Sir Matthew Dean, Kt., CBE
†Goold, Sir George William, Bt. (1801)
Gordon, Sir Andrew Cosmo Lewis Duff-, Bt. (1813)
Gordon, Sir Charles Addison Somerville Snowden, KCB
Gordon, Sir Gerald Henry, Kt., CBE, QC
Gordon, Sir Keith Lyndell, Kt., CMG
Gordon, Sir (Lionel) Eldred (Peter) Smith-, Bt. (1838)
Gordon, Sir Robert James, Bt. (S. 1706)
Gordon, Sir Sidney Samuel, Kt., CBE
Gordon Lennox, Lord Nicholas Charles, KCMG, KCVO
†Gore, Sir Nigel Hugh St George, Bt. (I. 1622)
Gorham, Sir Richard Masters, Kt., CBE, DFC
Goring, Sir William Burton Nigel, Bt. (1627)
Gorman, Sir John Reginald, Kt., CVO, CBE, MC
Gorst, Sir John Michael, Kt.
Gorton, *Rt. Hon.* Sir John Grey, GCMG, CH
Goschen, Sir Edward Christian, Bt., DSO (1916)
Gosling, Sir (Frederick) Donald, Kt.
Goswell, Sir Brian Lawrence, Kt.
Goulden, Sir (Peter) John, KCMG, GCMG
Goulding, Sir Marrack Irvine, KCMG
Goulding, Sir (William) Lingard Walter, Bt. (1904)
Gourlay, *Gen.* Sir (Basil) Ian (Spencer), KCB, OBE, MC, RM
Gourlay, Sir Simon Alexander, Kt.
Govan, Sir Lawrence Herbert, Kt.
Gow, *Gen.* Sir (James) Michael, GCB
Gowans, Sir James Learmonth, Kt., CBE, FRCP, FRS
†Graaff, Sir David de Villiers, Bt., MBE (1911)
Grabham, Sir Anthony Henry, Kt.
Graham, Sir Alexander Michael, GBE
Graham, Sir James Bellingham, Bt. (1662)
Graham, Sir James Fergus Surtees, Bt. (1783)
Graham, Sir James Thompson, Kt., CMG
Graham, Sir John Alexander Noble, Bt., GCMG (1906)
Graham, Sir John Alistair, Kt.
Graham, Sir John Moodie, Bt. (1964)
Graham, Sir Norman William, Kt., CB
Graham, Sir Peter, KCB, QC
Graham, Sir Peter Alfred, Kt., OBE
Graham, *Lt.-Gen.* Sir Peter Walter, KCB, CBE
†Graham, Sir Ralph Stuart, Bt. (1629)
Graham, *Hon.* Sir Samuel Horatio, Kt., CMG, OBE
Grandy, *Marshal of the Royal Air Force* Sir John, GCB, GCVO, KBE, DSO
Grant, Sir Archibald, Bt. (S. 1705)
Grant, Sir Clifford, Kt.
Grant, Sir (John) Anthony, Kt.
Grant, Sir Patrick Alexander Benedict, Bt. (S. 1688)
Grant, *Lt.-Gen.* Sir Scott Carnegie, KCB

Gray, *Hon.* Sir Charles Anthony St John, Kt., QC
Gray, *Prof.* Sir Denis John Pereira, Kt., OBE, FRCGP
Gray, Sir John Archibald Browne, Kt., Sc.D., FRS
Gray, Sir John Walton David, KBE, CMG
Gray, *Lt.-Gen.* Sir Michael Stuart, KCB, OBE
Gray, Sir Robert McDowall (Robin), Kt.
Gray, Sir William Hume, Bt. (1917)
Graydon, *Air Chief Marshal* Sir Michael James, GCB, CBE
Grayson, Sir Jeremy Brian Vincent Harrington, Bt. (1922)
Green, Sir Allan David, KCB, QC
Green, Sir Andrew Fleming, KCMG
Green, *Hon.* Sir Guy Stephen Montague, KBE
Green, Sir Kenneth, Kt.
Green, Sir Owen Whitley, Kt.
†Green, Sir Simon Lycett, Bt., TD (1886)
Greenaway, Sir John Michael Burdick, Bt. (1933)
Greenbury, Sir Richard, Kt.
Greene, Sir (John) Brian Massy-, Kt.
Greener, Sir Anthony Armitage, Kt.
Greengross, Sir Alan David, Kt.
Greening, *Rear-Adm.* Sir Paul Woollven, GCVO
Greenstock, Sir Jeremy Quentin, KCMG
Greenwell, Sir Edward Bernard, Bt. (1906)
Gregson, Sir Peter Lewis, GCB
Greig, Sir (Henry Louis) Carron, KCVO, CBE
Grenside, Sir John Peter, Kt., CBE
Grey, Sir Anthony Dysart, Bt. (1814)
Grierson, Sir Michael John Bewes, Bt. (S. 1685)
Grierson, Sir Ronald Hugh, Kt.
Griffin, *Maj.* Sir (Arthur) John (Stewart), KCVO
Griffin, Sir (Charles) David, Kt., CBE
Griffiths, Sir Eldon Wylie, Kt.
Griffiths, Sir John Norton-, Bt. (1922)
Grigson, *Hon.* Sir Geoffrey Douglas, Kt.
Grimwade, Sir Andrew Sheppard, Kt., CBE
Grindrod, *Most Revd* Sir John Basil Rowland, KBE
Grinstead, Sir Stanley Gordon, Kt.
Grose, *Vice-Adm.* Sir Alan, KBE
Grossart, Sir Angus McFarlane McLeod, Kt., CBE
Grotrian, Sir Philip Christian Brent, Bt. (1934)
Grove, Sir Charles Gerald, Bt. (1874)
Grove, Sir Edmund Frank, KCVO
Grugeon, Sir John Drury, Kt.
Guinness, Sir Howard Christian Sheldon, Kt., VRD
Guinness, Sir John Ralph Sidney, Kt., CB
Guinness, Sir Kenelm Ernest Lee, Bt. (1867)
Guise, Sir John Grant, Bt. (1783)
Gull, Sir Rupert William Cameron, Bt. (1872)
Gumbs, Sir Emile Rudolph, Kt.
Gunn, *Prof.* Sir John Currie, Kt., CBE
Gunn, Sir Robert Norman, Kt.
Gunn, Sir William Archer, KBE, CMG
†Gunning, Sir Charles Theodore, Bt. (1778)
Gunston, Sir John Wellesley, Bt. (1938)
Gurdon, *Prof.* Sir John Bertrand, Kt., D.Phil., FRS
Guthrie, *Gen.* Sir Charles Ronald Llewelyn, GCB, LVO, OBE
Guthrie, Sir Malcolm Connop, Bt., (1936)
Guy, *Gen.* Sir Roland Kelvin, GCB, CBE, DSO
Habakkuk, Sir John Hrothgar, Kt., FBA
Haddacks, *Vice-Adm.* Sir Paul Kenneth, KCB
Hadfield, Sir Ronald, Kt., QPM
Hadlee, Sir Richard John, Kt., MBE
Hague, *Prof.* Sir Douglas Chalmers, Kt., CBE
Halberg, Sir Murray Gordon, Kt., MBE
Hall, Sir Basil Brodribb, KCB, MC, TD
Hall, Sir Douglas Basil, Bt., KCMG (S. 1687)
Hall, Sir Ernest, Kt., OBE
Hall, Sir (Frederick) John (Frank), Bt. (1923)
Hall, Sir John, Kt.
Hall, Sir John Bernard, Bt. (1919)
Hall, Sir Laurence Charles Brodie-, Kt., AO, CMG
Hall, Sir Percival Burton Curtis, Kt.
Hall, Sir Peter Edward, KBE, CMG
Hall, *Prof.* Sir Peter Geoffrey, Kt., FBA
Hall, Sir Peter Reginald Frederick, Kt., CBE
Hall, Sir Robert de Zouche, KCMG
Hall, *Brig.* Sir William Henry, KBE, DSO, ED
Halliday, *Vice-Adm.* Sir Roy William, KBE, DSC
Halpern, Sir Ralph Mark, Kt.
Halsey, *Revd* Sir John Walter Brooke, Bt. (1920)
Halstead, Sir Ronald, Kt., CBE
Ham, Sir David Kenneth Rowe-, GBE
Hambling, Sir (Herbert) Hugh, Bt. (1924)
Hamburger, Sir Sidney Cyril, Kt., CBE
Hamer, *Hon.* Sir Rupert James, KCMG, ED
Hamilton, *Rt. Hon.* Sir Archibald Gavin, Kt., MP
Hamilton, Sir Edward Sydney, Bt. (1776 and 1819)
Hamilton, Sir James Arnot, KCB, MBE, FREng.
Hamilton, Sir Malcolm William Bruce Stirling-, Bt. (S. 1673)
Hamilton, Sir (Robert Charles) Richard Caradoc, Bt. (S. 1646)
Hammick, Sir Stephen George, Bt. (1834)
Hammond, Sir Anthony Hilgrove, KCB, QC
Hampel, Sir Ronald Claus, Kt.
Hampshire, Sir Stuart Newton, Kt., FBA
Hampson, Sir Stuart, Kt.
Hampton, Sir (Leslie) Geoffrey, Kt.
Hancock, Sir David John Stowell, KCB
Hancock, *Air Marshal* Sir Valston Eldridge, KBE, CB, DFC
Hand, *Most Revd* Geoffrey David, KBE
Handley, Sir David John Davenport-, Kt., OBE
Hanham, Sir Michael William, Bt., DFC (1667)
Hanley, *Rt. Hon.* Sir Jeremy James, KCMG
Hanmer, Sir John Wyndham Edward, Bt. (1774)
Hann, Sir James, Kt., CBE
Hannam, Sir John Gordon, Kt.
Hannay, Sir David Hugh Alexander, GCMG
Hanson, Sir (Charles) Rupert (Patrick), Bt. (1918)
Hanson, Sir John Gilbert, KCMG, CBE
Hardcastle, Sir Alan John, Kt.
Hardie, Sir Douglas Fleming, Kt., CBE
Harding, Sir George William, KCMG, CVO
Harding, *Marshal of the Royal Air Force* Sir Peter Robin, GCB
Harding, Sir Roy Pollard, Kt., CBE
Hardy, Sir David William, Kt.
Hardy, Sir James Gilbert, Kt., OBE
Hardy, Sir Richard Charles Chandos, Bt. (1876)
Hare, Sir David, Kt., FRSL
Hare, Sir Nicholas Patrick, Bt. (1818)
Harford, Sir (John) Timothy, Bt. (1934)
Hargroves, *Brig.* Sir Robert Louis, Kt., CBE
Harington, *Gen.* Sir Charles Henry Pepys, GCB, CBE, DSO, MC
Harington, Sir Nicholas John, Bt. (1611)
Harland, *Air Marshal* Sir Reginald Edward Wynyard, KBE, CB
Harley, *Gen.* Sir Alexander George Hamilton, KBE, CB
Harman, *Gen.* Sir Jack Wentworth, GCB, OBE, MC
Harman, *Hon.* Sir Jeremiah LeRoy, Kt.
Harman, Sir John Andrew, Kt.
Harmsworth, Sir Hildebrand Harold, Bt. (1922)
Harris, *Prof.* Sir Henry, Kt., FRCP, FRCPath., FRS
Harris, Sir Jack Wolfred Ashford, Bt. (1932)
Harris, *Air Marshal* Sir John Hulme, KCB, CBE
Harris, *Prof.* Sir Martin Best, Kt., CBE

Harris, Sir William Gordon, KBE, CB, FREng.
Harrison, Sir David, Kt., CBE, FREng.
Harrison, *Prof.* Sir Donald Frederick Norris, Kt., FRCS
Harrison, Sir Ernest Thomas, Kt., OBE
Harrison, Sir Francis Alexander Lyle, Kt., MBE, QC
Harrison, *Surgeon Vice-Adm.* Sir John Albert Bews, KBE
Harrison, *Hon.* Sir (John) Richard, Kt., ED
Harrison, *Hon.* Sir Michael Guy Vicat, Kt.
Harrison, Sir Michael James Harwood, Bt. (1961)
Harrison, *Prof.* Sir Richard John, Kt., FRS
Harrison, Sir (Robert) Colin, Bt. (1922)
Harrison, Sir Terence, Kt., FREng
Harrop, Sir Peter John, KCB
Hart, Sir Graham Allan, KCB
Hart, *Hon.* Sir Michael Christopher Campbell, Kt.
Hartwell, Sir (Francis) Anthony Charles Peter, Bt. (1805)
Harvey, Sir Charles Richard Musgrave, Bt. (1933)
Harvie, Sir John Smith, Kt., CBE
Haselhurst, *Rt. Hon.* Sir Alan Gordon Barraclough, Kt., MP
Haskard, Sir Cosmo Dugal Patrick Thomas, KCMG, MBE
Haslam, *Rear-Adm.* Sir David William, KBE, CB
Hassett, *Gen.* Sir Francis George, KBE, CB, DSO, LVO
Hastings, Sir Stephen Lewis Edmonstone, Kt., MC
Hatter, Sir Maurice, Kt.
Havelock, Sir Wilfrid Bowen, Kt.
Hawkins, Sir Paul Lancelot, Kt., TD
Hawkins, Sir Richard Caesar, Bt. (1778)
Hawley, Sir Donald Frederick, KCMG, MBE
Hawley, Sir Henry Nicholas, Bt. (1795)
Haworth, Sir Philip, Bt. (1911)
Hawthorne, Sir Nigel Barnard, Kt., CBE
Hawthorne, *Prof.* Sir William Rede, Kt., CBE, Sc.D., FRS, FREng.
Hay, Sir David Osborne, Kt., CBE, DSO
Hay, Sir David Russell, Kt., CBE, FRCP, MD
Hay, Sir Hamish Grenfell, Kt.
Hay, Sir James Brian Dalrymple-, Bt. (1798)
Hay, Sir John Erroll Audley, Bt. (S. 1663)
Hay, Sir Ronald Frederick Hamilton, Bt. (S. 1703)
Hayes, Sir Brian, Kt., CBE, QPM
Hayes, Sir Brian David, GCB
Hayward, Sir Anthony William Byrd, Kt.
Hayward, Sir Jack Arnold, Kt., OBE
Haywood, Sir Harold, KCVO, OBE
Head, Sir Francis David Somerville, Bt. (1838)
Healey, Sir Charles Edward Chadwyck-, Bt. (1919)
Heap, Sir Peter William, KCMG
Heap, *Prof.* Sir Robert Brian, Kt., CBE, FRS
Hearne, Sir Graham James, Kt., CBE
Heath, *Rt. Hon.* Sir Edward Richard George, KG, MBE, MP
Heath, Sir Mark Evelyn, KCVO, CMG
Heathcote, *Brig.* Sir Gilbert Simon, Bt., CBE (1733)
Heathcote, Sir Michael Perryman, Bt. (1733)
Heatley, Sir Peter, Kt., CBE
Heaton, Sir Yvo Robert Henniker-, Bt. (1912)
Heiser, Sir Terence Michael, GCB
Hellaby, Sir (Frederick Reed) Alan, Kt.
Henao, Revd Sir Ravu, Kt., OBE
Henderson, Sir Denys Hartley, Kt.
Henderson, Sir (John) Nicholas, GCMG, KCVO
Henley, Sir Douglas Owen, KCB
Hennessy, Sir James Patrick Ivan, KBE, CMG
†Henniker, Sir Adrian Chandos, Bt. (1813)
Henriques, *Hon.* Sir Richard Henry Quixano, Kt.
Henry, *Rt. Hon.* Sir Denis Robert Maurice, Kt.
Henry, *Hon.* Sir Geoffrey Arama, KBE
†Henry, Sir Patrick Denis, Bt. (1923)
Henry, *Hon.* Sir Trevor Ernest, Kt.
Hepburn, Sir John Alastair Trant Kidd Buchan-, Bt. (1815)
Herbecq, Sir John Edward, KCB
Herbert, *Adm.* Sir Peter Geoffrey Marshall, KCB, OBE
Herbert, Sir Walter William, Kt.
Hermon, Sir John Charles, Kt., OBE, QPM
Heron, Sir Conrad Frederick, KCB, OBE
Heron, Sir Michael Gilbert, Kt.
Hervey, Sir Roger Blaise Ramsay, KCVO, CMG
Heseltine, *Rt. Hon.* Sir William Frederick Payne, GCB, GCVO
Hetherington, Sir Arthur Ford, Kt., DSC, FREng.
Hetherington, Sir Thomas Chalmers, KCB, CBE, TD, QC
Hewetson, Sir Christopher Raynor, Kt., TD
Hewitt, Sir (Cyrus) Lenox (Simson), Kt., OBE
Hewitt, Sir Nicholas Charles Joseph, Bt. (1921)
Heygate, Sir Richard John Gage, Bt. (1831)
Heywood, Sir Peter, Bt. (1838)
Hezlet, *Vice-Adm.* Sir Arthur Richard, KBE, CB, DSO, DSC
Hibbert, Sir Jack, KCB
Hibbert, Sir Reginald Alfred, GCMG
Hickey, Sir Justin, Kt.
Hickman, Sir (Richard) Glenn, Bt. (1903)
Hicks, Sir Robert, Kt.
Hidden, *Hon.* Sir Anthony Brian, Kt.
Hielscher, Sir Leo Arthur, Kt.
Higgins, *Hon.* Sir Malachy Joseph, Kt.
Higginson, Sir Gordon Robert, Kt., Ph.D., FREng.
Hill, Sir Alexander Rodger Erskine-, Bt. (1945)
Hill, Sir Arthur Alfred, Kt., CBE
Hill, Sir Brian John, Kt.
Hill, Sir James Frederick, Bt. (1917)
Hill, Sir John McGregor, Kt., Ph.D., FREng.
Hill, Sir John Maxwell, Kt., CBE, DFC
†Hill, Sir John Rowley, Bt. (I. 1779)
Hill, *Vice-Adm.* Sir Robert Charles Finch, KBE, FREng.
Hillary, Sir Edmund, KG, KBE
Hillhouse, Sir (Robert) Russell, KCB
Hills, Sir Graham John, Kt.
Hine, *Air Chief Marshal* Sir Patrick Bardon, GCB, GBE
Hinston, Sir Harry Lee, Kt.
Hirsch, *Prof.* Sir Peter Bernhard, Kt., Ph.D., FRS
Hirst, *Rt. Hon.* Sir David Cozens-Hardy, Kt.
Hirst, Sir Michael William, Kt.
Hoare, *Prof.* Sir Charles Anthony Richard, Kt., FRS
Hoare, Sir Peter Richard David, Bt. (1786)
Hoare, Sir Timothy Edward Charles, Bt., OBE (I. 1784)
Hobart, Sir John Vere, Bt. (1914)
Hobbs, *Maj.-Gen.* Sir Michael Frederick, KCVO, CBE
Hobday, Sir Gordon Ivan, Kt.
Hobhouse, Sir Charles John Spinney, Bt. (1812)
Hockaday, Sir Arthur Patrick, KCB, CMG
Hockley, *Gen.* Sir Anthony Heritage Farrar-, GBE, KCB, DSO, MC
†Hodge, Sir Andrew Rowland, Bt. (1921)
Hodge, Sir James William, KCVO, CMG
Hodge, Sir Julian Stephen Alfred, Kt.
Hodges, *Air Chief Marshal* Sir Lewis MacDonald, KCB, CBE, DSO, DFC
Hodgkin, Sir Gordon Howard Eliot, Kt., CBE
Hodgkinson, *Air Chief Marshal* Sir (William) Derek, KCB, CBE, DFC, AFC
Hodgson, Sir Maurice Arthur Eric, Kt., FREng.
Hodgson, *Hon.* Sir (Walter) Derek (Thornley), Kt.
Hodson, Sir Michael Robin Adderley, Bt. (I. 1789)
Hoffenberg, *Prof.* Sir Raymond, KBE
Hogg, Sir Christopher Anthony, Kt.
Hogg, *Vice-Adm.* Sir Ian Leslie Trower, KCB, DSC

†Hogg, Sir Piers Michael James, Bt. (1846)
†Hogg, Sir Michael Edward Lindsay-, Bt. (1905)
Holcroft, Sir Peter George Culcheth, Bt. (1921)
Holderness, Sir Martin William, Bt. (1920)
Holden, Sir Edward, Bt. (1893)
Holden, Sir John David, Bt. (1919)
Holder, Sir John Henry, Bt. (1898)
Holdgate, Sir Martin Wyatt, Kt., CB, Ph.D.
Holdsworth, Sir (George) Trevor, Kt., CVO
Holland, *Hon.* Sir Alan Douglas, Kt.
Holland, *Hon.* Sir Christopher John, Kt.
Holland, Sir Clifton Vaughan, Kt.
Holland, Sir Geoffrey, KCB
Holland, Sir Kenneth Lawrence, Kt., CBE, QFSM
Holland, Sir Philip Welsby, Kt.
Holliday, *Prof.* Sir Frederick George Thomas, Kt., CBE, FRSE
Hollings, *Hon.* Sir (Alfred) Kenneth, Kt., MC
Hollis, *Hon.* Sir Anthony Barnard, Kt.
Hollom, Sir Jasper Quintus, KBE
Holloway, *Hon.* Sir Barry Blyth, KBE
Holm, Sir Carl Henry, Kt., OBE
Holm, Sir Ian (Ian Holm Cuthbert), Kt., CBE
Holman, *Hon.* Sir (Edward) James, Kt.
Holmes, *Prof.* Sir Frank Wakefield, Kt.
Holmes, Sir John Eaton, KBE, CMG, CVO
Holmes, Sir Peter Fenwick, Kt., MC
Holroyd, *Air Marshal* Sir Frank Martyn, KBE, CB, FREng.
Holt, *Prof.* Sir James Clarke, Kt.
Holt, Sir Michael, Kt., CBE
Home, Sir William Dundas, Bt. (S. 1671)
Hone, Sir Michael, Kt.
Honeycombe, *Prof.* Sir Robert William Kerr, Kt., FRS, FREng.
Honywood, Sir Filmer Courtenay William, Bt. (1660)
Hood, Sir Harold Joseph, Bt., TD (1922)
Hookway, Sir Harry Thurston, Kt.
Hooper, *Hon.* Sir Anthony, Kt.
Hope, Sir Colin Frederick Newton, Kt.
Hope, *Rt. Revd and Rt. Hon.* Sir David Michael, KCVO
Hope, Sir John Carl Alexander, Bt. (S. 1628)
Hopkin, Sir (William Aylsham) Bryan, Kt., CBE
Hopkins, Sir Anthony Philip, Kt., CBE
Hopkins, Sir Michael John, Kt., CBE, RA, RIBA
Hopwood, *Prof.* Sir David Alan, Kt., FRS
Hordern, *Rt. Hon.* Sir Peter Maudslay, Kt.
Horlick, *Vice-Adm.* Sir Edwin John, KBE, FREng.
Horlick, Sir James Cunliffe William, Bt. (1914)
Horlock, *Prof.* Sir John Harold, Kt., FRS, FREng.
Hornby, Sir Derek Peter, Kt.
Hornby, Sir Simon Michael, Kt.
Horne, Sir Alan Gray Antony, Bt. (1929)
Horsfall, Sir John Musgrave, Bt., MC, TD (1909)
Horsley, *Air Marshal* Sir (Beresford) Peter (Torrington), KCB, CBE, LVO, AFC
†Hort, Sir Andrew Edwin Fenton, Bt. (1767)
*Horton, Sir Robert Baynes, Kt.*
Hosker, Sir Gerald Albery, KCB, QC
Hoskyns, Sir Benedict Leigh, Bt. (1676)
Hoskyns, Sir John Austin Hungerford Leigh, Kt.
Hotung, Sir Joseph Edward, Kt.
Houghton, Sir John Theodore, Kt., CBE, FRS
Houldsworth, Sir Richard Thomas Reginald, Bt. (1887)
Hounsfield, Sir Godfrey Newbold, Kt., CBE
Hourston, Sir Gordon Minto, Kt.
House, *Lt.-Gen.* Sir David George, GCB, KCVO, CBE, MC
Houssemayne du Boulay, Sir Roger William, KCVO, CMG
Howard, Sir David Howarth Seymour, Bt. (1955)
Howard, Sir George Marshall, Kt.
Howard, *Prof.* Sir Michael Eliot, Kt., CBE, MC
Howard, *Maj.-Gen.* Lord Michael Fitzalan-, GCVO, CB, CBE, MC
Howell, Sir Ralph Frederic, Kt.
Howells, Sir Eric Waldo Benjamin, Kt., CBE
Howes, Sir Christopher Kingston, KCVO, CB
Howlett, *Gen.* Sir Geoffrey Hugh Whitby, KBE, MC
Hoyos, *Hon.* Sir Fabriciano Alexander, Kt.
Huggins, *Hon.* Sir Alan Armstrong, Kt.
Hughes, *Hon.* Sir Anthony Philip Gilson, Kt.
Hughes, Sir David Collingwood, Bt. (1773)
Hughes, Hon. Sir Davis, Kt.
Hughes, Sir Jack William, Kt.
Hughes, Sir Trevor Denby Lloyd-, Kt.
Hughes, Sir Trevor Poulton, KCB
Hull, *Prof.* Sir David, Kt.
Hulse, Sir Edward Jeremy Westrow, Bt. (1739)
Hume, Sir Alan Blyth, Kt., CB
Humphreys, Sir (Raymond Evelyn) Myles, Kt.
Hunt, Sir John Leonard, Kt.
Hunt, *Adm.* Sir Nicholas John Streynsham, GCB, LVO
Hunt, *Hon.* Sir Patrick James, Kt.
Hunt, Sir Rex Masterman, Kt., CMG
Hunt, Sir Robert Frederick, Kt., CBE, FREng.
Hunt, Sir Julian Charles Roland, CB, Bt.
Hunter, Sir Alistair John, KCMG
Hunter, Sir Ian Bruce Hope, Kt., MBE
Hunter, *Prof.* Sir Laurence Colvin, Kt., CBE, FRSE
Hurn, Sir (Francis) Roger, Kt.
Hurrell, Sir Anthony Gerald, KCVO, CMG
Hurst, Sir Geoffrey Charles, Kt., MBE
Husbands, Sir Clifford Straugh, GCMG
Hutchinson, *Hon.* Sir Ross, Kt., DFC
Hutchison, *Lt.-Cdr.* Sir (George) Ian Clark, Kt., RN
Hutchison, Sir James Colville, Bt. (1956)
Hutchison, *Rt. Hon.* Sir Michael, Kt.
Hutchison, Sir Robert, Bt. (1939)
Huxley, *Prof.* Sir Andrew Fielding, Kt., OM, FRS
Huxtable, *Gen.* Sir Charles Richard, KCB, CBE
Hyatali, *Hon.* Sir Isaac Emanuel, Kt.
Hyslop, Sir Robert John (Robin) Maxwell-, Kt.
Ibbs, Sir (John) Robin, KBE
Imray, Sir Colin Henry, KBE, CMG
Ingham, Sir Bernard, Kt.
Ingilby, Sir Thomas Colvin William, Bt. (1866)
Inglis, Sir Brian Scott, Kt.
Inglis of Glencorse, Sir Roderick John, Bt. (S. 1703)
Ingram, Sir James Herbert Charles, Bt. (1893)
Ingram, Sir John Henderson, Kt., CBE
Inkin, Sir Geoffrey David, Kt., OBE
†Innes, Sir David Charles Kenneth Gordon, Bt. (NS 1686)
Innes of Edingight, Sir Malcolm Rognvald, KCVO
Innes, Sir Peter Alexander Berowald, Bt. (S. 1628)
Irvine, Sir Donald Hamilton, Kt., CBE, MD, FRCGP
Irving, *Prof.* Sir Miles Horsfall, Kt., MD, FRCS, FRCSE
Isaacs, Sir Jeremy Israel, Kt.
Isham, Sir Ian Vere Gyles, Bt. (1627)
Jack, *Hon.* Sir Alieu Sulayman, Kt.
Jack, Sir David, Kt., CBE, FRS, FRSE
Jack, Sir David Emmanuel, GCMG, MBE
Jack, *Hon.* Sir Raymond Evan, Kt.
Jackling, Sir Roger Tustin, KCB. CBE
Jackson, Sir Barry Trevor, Kt.
Jackson, Sir (John) Edward, KCMG
Jackson, Sir Kenneth Joseph, Kt.
Jackson, *Lt.-Gen.* Sir Michael David, KCB, CBE
Jackson, Sir Michael Roland, Bt. (1902)

Jackson, Sir Nicholas Fane St George, Bt. (1913)
Jackson, Sir Robert, Bt. (1815)
Jackson, *Hon.* Sir Rupert Matthew, Kt., QC
Jackson, Sir William Thomas, Bt. (1869)
Jacob, Sir Isaac Hai, Kt., QC
Jacob, *Hon.* Sir Robert Raphael Hayim (Robin), Kt.
Jacobi, Sir Derek George, Kt., CBE
Jacobi, *Dr* Sir James Edward, Kt., OBE
Jacobs, *Hon.* Sir Kenneth Sydney, KBE
Jacobs, Sir Wilfred Ebenezer, GCMG, GCVO, OBE, QC
Jacomb, Sir Martin Wakefield, Kt.
Jaffray, Sir William Otho, Bt. (1892)
James, Sir Cynlais Morgan, KCMG
James, Sir Jeffrey Russell, KBE, CBE
James, Sir John Nigel Courtenay, KCVO, CBE
James, Sir Stanislaus Anthony, GCMG, OBE
Jamieson, *Air Marshal* Sir David Ewan, KBE, CB
Jansen, Sir Ross Malcolm, KBE
Jansen van Rensburg, *Lt.-Gen.* Sir Jurinus Lindo, Kt.
Janvrin, Sir Robin Berry, KCVO, CB
Jardine of Applegirth, Sir Alexander Maule, Bt. (S. 1672)
Jardine, Sir Andrew Colin Douglas, Bt. (1916)
Jardine, *Maj.* Sir (Andrew) Rupert (John) Buchanan-, Bt., MC (1885)
Jarman, *Prof.* Sir Brian, Kt., OBE
Jarratt, Sir Alexander Anthony, Kt., CB
Jarvis, Sir Gordon Ronald, Kt.
Jawara, *Hon.* Sir Dawda Kairaba, Kt.
Jay, Sir Antony Rupert, Kt., CVO
Jay, Sir Michael Hastings, KCMG
Jeewoolall, Sir Ramesh, Kt.
Jefferson, Sir George Rowland, Kt., CBE, FREng.
Jefferson, Sir Mervyn Stewart Dunnington-, Bt. (1958)
Jeffreys, *Prof.* Sir Alec John, Kt., FRS
Jeffries, *Hon.* Sir John Francis, Kt.
Jehangir, Sir Cowasji, Bt. (1908)
Jejeebhoy, Sir Jamsetjee, Bt. (1857)
Jenkins, Sir Brian Garton, GBE
Jenkins, Sir Elgar Spencer, Kt., OBE
Jenkins, Sir James Christopher, KCB, QC
Jenkins, Sir Michael Nicholas Howard, Kt., OBE
Jenkins, Sir Michael Romilly Heald, KCMG
Jenkinson, Sir John Banks, Bt. (1661)
Jenks, Sir Maurice Arthur Brian, Bt. (1932)
Jenner, *Air Marshall* Sir Timothy Ivo, KCB
Jennings, Sir John Southwood, Kt., CBE, FRSE
Jennings, Sir Peter Neville Wake, Kt., CVO
Jennings, *Prof.* Sir Robert Yewdall, Kt., QC
Jephcott, Sir (John) Anthony, Bt. (1962)
Jessel, Sir Charles John, Bt. (1883)
Jewkes, Sir Gordon Wesley, KCMG
Job, Sir Peter James Denton, Kt.
John, Sir David Glyndwr, KCMG
John, Sir Elton Hercules (Reginald Kenneth Dwight), Kt., CBE
Johns, *Air Chief Marshal* Sir Richard Edward, GCB, CBE, LVO
Johnson, *Gen.* Sir Garry Dene, KCB, OBE, MC
Johnson, Sir John Rodney, KCMG
†Johnson, Sir Patrick Eliot, Bt. (1818)
Johnson, Sir Peter Colpoys Paley, Bt. (1755)
Johnson, *Hon.* Sir Robert Lionel, Kt.
Johnson, Sir Vassel Godfrey, Kt., CBE
Johnston, Sir John Baines, GCMG, KCVO
Johnston, *Lt.-Col.* Sir John Frederick Dame, GCVO, MC
Johnston, *Lt.-Gen.* Sir Maurice Robert, KCB, OBE
Johnston, Sir Thomas Alexander, Bt. (S. 1626)
Johnston, Sir William Robert Patrick Knox- (Sir Robin), Kt., CBE, RD
Johnstone, Sir (George) Richard Douglas, Bt. (S. 1700)
Johnstone, Sir (John) Raymond, Kt., CBE
Jolliffe, Sir Anthony Stuart, GBE
Jolly, Sir Aurthur Richard, KCMG
Jonas, Sir John Peter Jens, Kt., CBE
Jones, *Gen.* Sir (Charles) Edward Webb, KCB, CBE
Jones, Sir Christopher Lawrence-, Bt. (1831)
Jones, Sir David Akers-, KBE, CMG
Jones, *Air Marshal* Sir Edward Gordon, KCB, CBE, DSO, DFC
Jones, Sir Ewart Ray Herbert, Kt., D.Sc., Ph.D., FRS
Jones, Sir Harry George, Kt., CBE
Jones, Sir (John) Derek Alun-, Kt.
Jones, Sir John Henry Harvey-, Kt., MBE
Jones, Sir John Prichard-, Bt. (1910)
Jones, Sir Keith Stephen, Kt.
Jones, *Hon.* Sir Kenneth George Illtyd, Kt.
Jones, Sir Lyndon, Kt.
Jones, Sir (Owen) Trevor, Kt.
Jones, Sir (Peter) Hugh (Jefferd) Lloyd-, Kt.
Jones, Sir Richard Anthony Lloyd, KCB
Jones, Sir Robert Edward, Kt.
Jones, Sir Simon Warley Frederick Benton, Bt. (1919)
Jones, Sir William Gwynoro, Kt.
Jones, Sir Wynn Normington Hugh-, Kt., LVO
†Joseph, *Hon.* Sir James Samuel, Bt. (1943)
Jowitt, *Hon.* Sir Edwin Frank, Kt.
Joyce, *Lt.-Gen.* Sir Robert John Hayman-, KCB, CBE
Judge, *Rt. Hon.* Sir Igor, Kt.
Judge, Sir Paul Rupert, Kt.
Jugnauth, *Rt. Hon.* Sir Anerood, KCMG, QC
Jungius, *Vice-Adm.* Sir James George, KBE
Jupp, *Hon.* Sir Kenneth Graham, Kt., MC
Kaberry, *Hon.* Sir Christopher Donald, Bt. (1960)
Kalms, Sir (Harold) Stanley, Kt.
Kalo, Sir Kwamala, Kt., MBE
Kan Yuet-Keung, Sir, GBE
Kapi, *Hon.* Sir Mari, Kt., CBE
Kaputin, Sir John Rumet, KBE, CMG
Katz, Sir Bernard, Kt., FRS
Kausimae, Sir David Nanau, KBE
Kavali, Sir Thomas, Kt., OBE
Kawashima, Sir Maurice Masaaki, Kt.
Kawharu, *Prof.* Sir Ian Hugh, Kt.
Kay, *Prof.* Sir Andrew Watt, Kt.
Kay, *Hon.* Sir John William, Kt.
Kay, *Hon.* Sir Maurice Ralph, Kt.
Kaye, Sir John Phillip Lister Lister-, Bt. (1812)
Kaye, Sir Paul Henry Gordon, Bt. (1923)
Keane, Sir Richard Michael, Bt. (1801)
Kearney, *Hon.* Sir William John Francis, Kt., CBE
Keeble, Sir (Herbert Ben) Curtis, GCMKeegan, Sir John Desmond Patrick, Kt., OBE
Keene, *Hon.* Sir David Wolfe, Kt.
Keirlie, Sir Dennis Robert, Kt
Keith, *Prof.* Sir James, KBE
Kellett, Sir Stanley Charles, Bt. (1801)
Kelly, Sir Christopher William, KCB
Kelly, Sir David Robert Corbett, Kt., CBE
Kelly, *Rt. Hon.* Sir (John William) Basil, Kt.
Kemakeza, Sir Allan, Kt.
Kemball, *Air Marshal* Sir (Richard) John, KCB, CBE
Kemp, Sir (Edward) Peter, KCB
Kenilorea, *Rt. Hon.* Sir Peter, KBE
Kennaway, Sir John Lawrence, Bt. (1791)
Kennedy, Sir Francis, KCMG, CBE
Kennedy, *Hon.* Sir Ian Alexander, Kt.
Kennedy, Sir Ludovic Henry Coverley, Kt.
†Kennedy, Sir Michael Edward, Bt., (1836)
Kennedy, *Rt. Hon.* Sir Paul Joseph Morrow, Kt.
Kennedy, *Air Chief Marshal* Sir Thomas Lawrie, GCB, AFC
Kenny, Sir Anthony John Patrick, Kt., D.Phil., D.Litt., FBA
Kenny, *Gen.* Sir Brian Leslie Graham, GCB, CBE
Kentridge, Sir Sydney Woolf, KCMG, QC
Kenyon, Sir George Henry, Kt.
Kermode, Sir (John) Frank, Kt., FBA
Kermode, Sir Ronald Graham Quale, KBE
Kerr, *Hon.* Sir Brian Francis, Kt.

Kerr, *Adm.* Sir John Beverley, GCB
Kerr, Sir John (Olav), GCMG, KCMG
Kerr, *Rt. Hon.* Sir Michael Robert Emanuel, Kt.
Kerruish, Sir (Henry) Charles, Kt., OBE
Kerry, Sir Michael James, KCB, QC
Kershaw, Sir (John) Anthony, Kt., MC
Keswick, Sir John Chippendale Lindley, Kt.
Keys, Sir (Alexander George) William, Kt., OBE, MC
Kidd, Sir Robert Hill, KBE, CB
Kikau, *Ratu* Sir Jone Latianara, KBE
Killen, *Hon.* Sir Denis James, KCMG
Killick, Sir John Edward, GCMG
Kimber, Sir Charles Dixon, Bt. (1904)
King, Sir John Christopher, Bt. (1888)
King, *Vice-Adm.* Sir Norman Ross Dutton, KBE
King, Sir Wayne Alexander, Bt. (1815)
Kingman, *Prof.* Sir John Frank Charles, Kt., FRS
Kingsland, Sir Richard, Kt., CBE, DFC
Kinloch, Sir David, Bt. (S. 1686)
Kinloch, Sir David Oliphant, Bt. (1873)
Kipalan, Sir Albert, Kt.
Kirby, *Hon.* Sir Richard Clarence, Kt.
Kirkpatrick, Sir Ivone Elliott, Bt. (S. 1685)
Kirkwood, *Hon.* Sir Andrew Tristram Hammett, Kt.
Kitcatt, Sir Peter Julian, Kt., CB
Kitson, *Gen.* Sir Frank Edward, GBE, KCB, MC
Kitson, Sir Timothy Peter Geoffrey, Kt.
Kleinwort, Sir Richard Drake, Bt. (1909)
Klevan, *Hon.* Sir Rodney (Conrad), Kt., QC
Klug, Sir Aaron, Kt., OM
Kneller, Sir Alister Arthur, Kt.
Knight, Sir Arthur William, Kt.
Knight, Sir Harold Murray, KBE, DSC
Knight, *Air Chief Marshal* Sir Michael William Patrick, KCB, AFC
Knill, *Prof.* Sir John Lawrence, Kt., FREng.
†Knill, Sir Thomas John Pugin Bartholomew, Bt. (1893)
Knowles, Sir Charles Francis, Bt. (1765)
Knowles, Sir Durward Randolph, Kt., OBE
Knowles, Sir Leonard Joseph, Kt., CBE
Knowles, Sir Richard Marchant, Kt.
Knox, Sir Bryce Muir, KCVO, MC, TD
Knox, Sir David Laidlaw, Kt.
Knox, *Hon.* Sir John Leonard, Kt.
Knox, *Hon.* Sir William Edward, Kt.
Koraea, Sir Thomas, Kt.
Kornberg, *Prof.* Sir Hans Leo, Kt., D.Sc., Sc.D., Ph.D., FRS
Korowi, Sir Wiwa, GCMG
Krebs, *Prof.* Sir John Richard, Kt., D.Phil., FRS
Kroto, *Prof.* Sir Harold Walter, Kt., FRS
Kulukundis, Sir Elias George (Eddie), Kt., OBE
Kurongku, *Most Revd* Peter, KBE
Lacon, Sir Edmund Vere, Bt. (1818)
Lacy, Sir Patrick Brian Finucane, Bt. (1921)
Lacy, Sir John Trend, Kt., CBE
Laddie, *Hon.* Sir Hugh Ian Lang, Kt.
Laidlaw, Sir Christophor Charles Fraser, Kt.
Laing, Sir (John) Martin (Kirby), Kt., CBE
Laing, Sir (John) Maurice, Kt.
Laing, Sir (William) Kirby, Kt., FREng.
Laird, Sir Gavin Harry, Kt., CBE
Lake, Sir (Atwell) Graham, Bt. (1711)
Laker, Sir Frederick Alfred, Kt.
Lakin, Sir Michael, Bt. (1909)
Laking, Sir George Robert, KCMG
Lamb, Sir Albert Thomas, KBE, CMG, DFC
Lambert, Sir Anthony Edward, KCMG
Lambert, Sir John Henry, KCVO, CMG
†Lambert, Sir Peter John Biddulph, Bt. (1711)
Lampl, Sir Frank William, Kt.
Landale, Sir David William Neil, KCVO
Landau, Sir Dennis Marcus, Kt.
Lander, Sir Stephen James, KCB
Lane, Prof. Sir David Philip, Kt., FRS, FRSE
Langham, Sir James Michael, Bt. (1660)
Langlands, Sir Robert Alan, Kt.
Langley, *Hon.* Sir Gordon Julian Hugh, Kt.
Langley, *Maj.-Gen.* Sir Henry Desmond Allen, KCVO, MBE
Langrishe, Sir James Hercules, Bt. (I. 1777)
Lankester, Sir Timothy Patrick, KCB
Lapun, *Hon.* Sir Paul, Kt.
Larcom, Sir (Charles) Christopher Royde, Bt. (1868)
Large, Sir Andrew McLeod Brooks, Kt.
Large, Sir Peter, Kt., CBE
Latham, *Hon.* Sir David Nicholas Ramsey, Kt.
Latham, Sir Martin Stuart, Kt., OBE
Latham, Sir Michael Anthony, Kt.
Latham, Sir Richard Thomas Paul, Bt. (1919)
Latimer, Sir (Courtenay) Robert, Kt., CBE
Latimer, Sir Graham Stanley, KBE
Lauder, Sir Piers Robert Dick-, Bt. (S. 1690)
Laughton, Sir Anthony Seymour, Kt.
Laurantus, Sir Nicholas, Kt., MBE
Laurence, Sir Peter Harold, KCMG, MC
Laurie, Sir Robert Bayley Emilius, Bt. (1834)
Lauterpacht, Sir Elihu, Kt., CBE, QC
Lauti, *Rt. Hon.* Sir Toaripi, GCMG
Lavan, *Hon.* Sir John Martin, Kt.
Law, *Adm.* Sir Horace Rochfort, GCB, OBE, DSC
Lawes, Sir (John) Michael Bennet, Bt. (1882)
Lawler, Sir Peter James, Kt., OBE
Lawrence, Sir David Roland Walter, Bt. (1906)
Lawrence, Sir George Alexander Waldemar, Bt. (1858)
Lawrence, Sir Ivan John, Kt., QC
Lawrence, Sir John Patrick Grosvenor, Kt., CBE
Lawrence, Sir William Fettiplace, Bt. (1867)
Laws, *Rt. Hon.* Sir John Grant McKenzie, Kt.
Lawson, Sir Christopher Donald, Kt.
Lawson, *Col.* Sir John Charles Arthur Digby, Bt., DSO, MC (1900)
Lawson, Sir John Philip Howard-, Bt. (1841)
Lawson, *Gen.* Sir Richard George, KCB, DSO, OBE
Layard, *Adm.* Sir Michael Henry Gordon, KCB, CBE
Lea, *Vice-Adm.* Sir John Stuart Crosbie, KBE
Lea, Sir Thomas William, Bt. (1892)
Leach, *Admiral of the Fleet* Sir Henry Conyers, GCB
Leahy, Sir Daniel Joseph, Kt.
Leahy, Sir John Henry Gladstone, KCMG
Learmont, *Gen.* Sir John Hartley, KCB, CBE
Leask, *Lt.-Gen.* Sir Henry Lowther Ewart Clark, KCB, DSO, OBE
Leather, Sir Edwin Hartley Cameron, KCMG, KCVO
Leaver, Sir Christopher, GBE
Le Bailly, *Vice-Adm.* Sir Louis Edward Stewart Holland, KBE, CB
Le Cheminant, *Air Chief Marshal* Sir Peter de Lacey, GBE, KCB, DFC
†Lechmere, Sir Reginald Anthony Hungerford, Bt. (1818)
Ledger, Sir Philip Stevens, Kt., CBE, FRSE
Lee, Sir Arthur James, KBE, MC
Lee, *Air Chief Marshal* Sir David John Pryer, GBE, CB
Lee, *Brig.* Sir Leonard Henry, Kt., CBE
Lee, Sir Quo-wei, Kt., CBE
Leeds, Sir Christopher Anthony, Bt. (1812)
Lees, Sir David Bryan, Kt.
Lees, Sir Thomas Edward, Bt. (1897)
Lees, Sir Thomas Harcourt Ivor, Bt. (1804)
Lees, Sir (William) Antony Clare, Bt. (1937)
Leese, Sir John Henry Vernon, Bt. (1908)
Le Fanu, *Maj.* Sir (George) Victor (Sheridan), KCVO
le Fleming, Sir David Kelland, Bt. (1705)

McCowan, *Rt. Hon.* Sir Anthony James Denys, Kt.
†McCowan, Sir David William, Bt. (1934)
McCullough, *Hon.* Sir (Iain) Charles (Robert), Kt.
MacDermott, *Rt. Hon.* Sir John Clarke, Kt.
McDermott, Sir (Lawrence) Emmet, KBE
Macdonald of Sleat, Sir Ian Godfrey Bosville, Bt. (S. 1625)
Macdonald, Sir Kenneth Carmichael, KCB
McDonald, Sir Tom, Kt., OBE
McDonald, Sir Trevor, Kt., OBE
MacDougall, Sir (George) Donald (Alastair), Kt., CBE, FBA
McDowell, Sir Eric Wallace, Kt., CBE
McDowell, Sir Henry McLorinan, KBE
Mace, *Lt.-Gen.* Sir John Airth, KBE, CB
McEwen, Sir John Roderick Hugh, Bt. (1953)
McFarland, Sir John Talbot, Bt. (1914)
Macfarlane, Sir (David) Neil, Kt.
Macfarlane, Sir George Gray, Kt., CB, FREng.
McFarlane, Sir Ian, Kt.
McGeoch, *Vice-Adm.* Sir Ian Lachlan Mackay, KCB, DSO, DSC
McGrath, Sir Brian Henry, GCVO
Macgregor, Sir Edwin Robert, Bt. (1828)
MacGregor of MacGregor, Sir Gregor, Bt. (1795)
McGregor, Sir Ian Alexander, Kt., CBE, FRS
McGrigor, *Capt.* Sir Charles Edward, Bt. (1831)
McIntosh, *Vice-Adm.* Sir Ian Stewart, KBE, CB, DSO, DSC
McIntosh, Sir Neil William David, Kt., CBE
McIntosh, Sir Ronald Robert Duncan, KCB
McIntyre, Sir Donald Conroy, Kt., CBE
McIntyre, Sir Meredith Alister, Kt.
Mackay, *Hon.* Sir Colin Crichton, Kt.
MacKay, *Prof.* Sir Donald Iain, Kt., FRSE
McKay, Sir John Andrew, Kt., CBE
McKay, Sir William Robert, KCB, CB
Mackechnie, Sir Alistair John, Kt.
McKee, *Maj.* Sir (William) Cecil, Kt., ERD
McKellen, Sir Ian Murray, Kt., CBE
Mackenzie, Sir Alexander Alwyne Henry Charles Brinton Muir-, Bt. (1805)
†Mackenzie, Sir (James William) Guy, Bt. (1890)
Mackenzie, *Gen.* Sir Jeremy John George, GCB, OBE
†Mackenzie, Sir Peter Douglas, Bt. (S. 1673)
†Mackenzie, Sir Roderick McQuhae, Bt. (S. 1703)
McKenzie, Sir Roy Allan, KBE
Mackerras, Sir (Alan) Charles (MacLaurin), Kt., CBE
Mackeson, Sir Rupert Henry, Bt. (1954)
MacKinlay, Sir Bruce, Kt., CBE
McKinnon, Sir James, Kt.
McKinnon, *Hon.* Sir Stuart Neil, Kt.
Mackintosh, Sir Cameron Anthony, Kt.
Macklin, Sir Bruce Roy, Kt., OBE
Mackworth, Sir Digby (John), Bt. (1776)
McLaren, Sir Robin John Taylor, KCMG
McLaughlin, Sir Justice, Kt.
Maclean of Dunconnell, Sir Charles Edward, Bt. (1957)
Maclean, Sir Donald Og Grant, Kt.
MacLean, *Vice-Adm.* Sir Hector Charles Donald, KBE, CB, DSC
Maclean, Sir Lachlan Hector Charles, Bt. (NS 1631)
McLeod, Sir Charles Henry, Bt. (1925)
McLeod, Sir Ian George, Kt.
MacLeod, Sir (John) Maxwell Norman, Bt. (1924)
Macleod, Sir (Nathaniel William) Hamish, KBE
McLintock, Sir (Charles) Alan, Kt.
McLintock, Sir Michael William, Bt. (1934)
Maclure, Sir John Robert Spencer, Bt. (1898)
McMahon, Sir Brian Patrick, Bt. (1817)
McMahon, Sir Christopher William, Kt.
Macmillan, Sir (Alexander McGregor) Graham, Kt.
MacMillan, *Lt.-Gen.* Sir John Richard Alexander, KCB, CBE
McMullin, *Rt. Hon.* Sir Duncan Wallace, Kt.
McMurtry, Sir David, Kt., CBE
Macnaghten, Sir Patrick Alexander, Bt. (1836)
McNamara, *Air Chief Marshal* Sir Neville Patrick, KBE
Macnaughton, *Prof.* Sir Malcolm Campbell, Kt.
McNee, Sir David Blackstock, Kt., QPM
McNulty, Sir (Robert William) Roy, Kt., CBE
MacPhail, Sir Bruce Dugald, Kt.
Macpherson, Sir Ronald Thomas Steward (Tommy), CBE, MC, TD
Macpherson of Cluny, *Hon.* Sir William Alan, Kt., TD
McQuarrie, Sir Albert, Kt.
MacRae, Sir (Alastair) Christopher (Donald Summerhayes), KCMG
Macready, Sir Nevil John Wilfrid, Bt. (1923)
Mactaggart, Sir John Auld, Bt. (1938)
Macwhinnie, Sir Gordon Menzies, Kt., CBE
McWilliam, Sir Michael Douglas, KCMG
McWilliams, Sir Francis, GBE, FREng.
Madden, Sir Peter John, Bt. (1919)
Maddox, Sir John Royden, Kt.
Madel, Sir (William) David, Kt., MP
Madigan, Sir Russel Tullie, Kt., OBE
Magnus, Sir Laurence Henry Philip, Bt. (1917)
Mahon, Sir (John) Denis, Kt., CBE
Mahon, Sir William Walter, Bt. (1819)
Maiden, Sir Colin James, Kt., D.Phil.
Main, Sir Peter Tester, Kt., ERD
Maingard de la Ville ès Offrans, Sir Louis Pierre René, Kt., CBE
Maino, Sir Charles, KBE
†Maitland, Sir Charles Alexander, Bt. (1818)
Maitland, Sir Donald James Dundas, GCMG, OBE
Malbon, *Vice-Adm.* Sir Fabian Michael, KBE
Malcolm, Sir James William Thomas Alexander, Bt. (S. 1665)
Malet, Sir Harry Douglas St Lo, Bt. (1791)
Mallaby, Sir Christopher Leslie George, GCMG, GCVO
Mallick, *Prof.* Sir Netar Prakash, Kt., FRCP, FRCPEd.
Mallinson, Sir William James, Bt. (1935)
Malone, *Hon.* Sir Denis Eustace Gilbert, Kt.
Malpas, Sir Robert, Kt., CBE, FREng
Mamo, Sir Anthony Joseph, Kt., OBE
Mance, *Hon.* Sir Jonathan Hugh, Kt.
Manchester, Sir William Maxwell, KBE
Mander, Sir Charles Marcus, Bt. (1911)
Manduell, Sir John, Kt., CBE
Mann, *Rt. Revd* Sir Michael Ashley, KCVO
Mann, Sir Rupert Edward, Bt. (1905)
Manning, Sir David Geoffrey, KCMG, CMG
Mansel, Sir Philip, Bt. (1622)
Mansfield, *Vice-Adm.* Sir (Edward) Gerard (Napier), KBE, CVO
Mansfield, *Prof.* Sir Peter, Kt., FRS
Mansfield, Sir Philip (Robert Aked), KCMG
Mantell, *Rt. Hon.* Sir Charles Barrie Knight, Kt.
Manton, Sir Edwin Alfred Grenville, Kt.
Manuella, Sir Tulaga, GCMG, MBE
Manzie, Sir (Andrew) Gordon, KCB
Mara, *Rt. Hon. Ratu* Sir Kamisese Kapaiwai Tuimacilai, GCMG, KBE
Margetson, Sir John William Denys, KCMG
Marjoribanks, Sir James Alexander Milne, KCMG
Mark, Sir Robert, GBE
Markham, Sir Charles John, Bt. (1911)
Marking, Sir Henry Ernest, KCVO, CBE, MC

Marling, Sir Charles William Somerset, Bt. (1882)
Marmot, Prof. Sir Michael Gideon, Kt.
Marr, Sir Leslie Lynn, Bt. (1919)
Marriner, Sir Neville, Kt., CBE
Marriott, Sir Hugh Cavendish Smith-, Bt. (1774)
Marsden, Sir Simon Neville Llewelyn, Bt. (1924)
Marsh, *Prof.* Sir John Stanley, Kt., CBE
Marshall, Sir Arthur Gregory George, Kt., OBE
Marshall, Sir Denis Alfred, Kt.
Marshall, *Prof.* Sir (Oshley) Roy, Kt., CBE
Marshall, Sir Peter Harold Reginald, KCMG
Marshall, Sir Robert Braithwaite, KCB, MBE
Marshall, Sir (Robert) Michael, Kt.
Martin, Sir Clive Haydon, Kt., OBE
Martin, Sir George Henry, Kt., CBE
Martin, *Vice-Adm.* Sir John Edward Ludgate, KCB, DSC
Martin, *Prof.* Sir Laurence Woodward, Kt.
Martin, Sir (Robert) Bruce, Kt., QC
Marychurch, Sir Peter Harvey, KCMG
Masefield, Sir Charles Beech Gordon, Kt.
Masefield, Sir Peter Gordon, Kt.
Masire, Sir Ketumile, GCMG
Mason, *Hon.* Sir Anthony Frank, KBE
Mason, Sir (Basil) John, Kt., CB, D.Sc., FRS
Mason, *Prof.* Sir David Kean, Kt., CBE
Mason, Sir Frederick Cecil, KCVO, CMG
Mason, Sir Gordon Charles, Kt., OBE
Mason, Sir John Charles Moir, KCMG
Mason, Sir John Peter, Kt., CBE
Mason, *Prof.* Sir Ronald, KCB, FRS
Matane, Sir Paulias Nguna, Kt., CMG, OBE
Mather, Sir (David) Carol (Macdonell), Kt., MC
Mathers, Sir Robert William, Kt.
Matheson of Matheson, Sir Fergus John, Bt. (1882)
Matheson, Sir (James Adam) Louis, KBE, CMG, FREng.
Mathewson, Sir George Ross, Kt., CBE, Ph.D., FRSE
Matthews, Sir Peter Alec, Kt.
Matthews, Sir Peter Jack, Kt., CVO, OBE, QPM
Matthews, Sir Terence Hedley, Kt., OBE
Maud, The Hon. Sir Humphrey John Hamilton, KCMG
Mawhinney, *Rt. Hon.* Sir Brian Stanley, Kt., MP
Maxwell, Sir Michael Eustace George, Bt. (S. 1681)
Maxwell, Sir Nigel Mellor Heron-, Bt. (S. 1683)
May, *Rt. Hon.* Sir Anthony Tristram Kenneth, Kt.
May, Sir Kenneth Spencer, Kt., CBE
May, *Prof.* Sir Robert McCredie, Kt., FRS
Maynard, *Hon.* Sir Clement Travelyan, Kt.
Mayne, *Very Revd* Sir Michael Clement Otway, KCVO
Meadow, *Prof.* Sir (Samuel) Roy, Kt., FRCP, FRCPE
Medlycott, Sir Mervyn Tregonwell, Bt. (1808)
Megarry, *Rt. Hon.* Sir Robert Edgar, Kt., FBA
Meldrum, Sir George William, LVO
Melhuish, Sir Michael Ramsay, KBE, CMG
Mellon, Sir James, KCMG
Melville, Sir Leslie Galfreid, KBE
Melville, Sir Ronald Henry, KCB
Menter, Sir James Woodham, Kt., Ph.D., Sc.D., FRS
Menteth, Sir James Wallace Stuart-, Bt. (1838)
Merifield, Sir Anthony James, KCVO, CB
Meyer, Sir Anthony John Charles, Bt. (1910)
Meyer, Sir Christopher John Rome, KCMG
Meyjes, Sir Richard Anthony, Kt.
Meyrick, Sir David John Charlton, Bt. (1880)
Meyrick, Sir George Christopher Cadafael Tapps-Gervis-, Bt. (1791)
Miakwe, *Hon.* Sir Akepa, KBE
Michael, Sir Duncan, Kt.
Michael, Sir Peter Colin, Kt., CBE
Middleton, Sir Peter Edward, GCB
Miers, Sir (Henry) David Alastair Capel, KBE, CMG
Milbank, Sir Anthony Frederick, Bt. (1882)
Milburn, Sir Anthony Rupert, Bt. (1905)
Mildmay, Sir Walter John Hugh St John-, Bt. (1772)
Miles, Sir Peter Tremayne, KCVO
Miles, Sir William Napier Maurice, Bt. (1859)
Millais, Sir Geoffrey Richard Everett, Bt. (1885)
Millar, Sir Oliver Nicholas, GCVO, FBA
Millard, Sir Guy Elwin, KCMG, CVO
Miller, Sir Donald John, Kt., FRSE, FREng.
Miller, Sir Harry Holmes, Bt. (1705)
Miller, Sir Hilary Duppa (Hal), Kt.
Miller, *Lt.-Col.* Sir John Mansel, GCVO, DSO, MC
Miller, Sir (Oswald) Bernard, Kt.
Miller, Sir Peter North, Kt.
Miller, Sir Ronald Andrew Baird, Kt., CBE
Miller of Glenlee, Sir Stephen William Macdonald, Bt. (1788)
Miller, Sir William R., Kt.
Millichip, Sir Frederick Albert (Bert), Kt.
Mills, *Vice-Adm.* Sir Charles Piercy, KCB, CBE, DSC
Mills, Sir Ian, Kt.
Mills, Sir Frank, KCVO, CMG
Mills, Sir John Lewis Ernest Watts, Kt., CBE
Mills, Sir Peter Frederick Leighton, Bt. (1921)
Milman, Sir David Patrick, Bt. (1800)
Milne, Sir John Drummond, Kt.
Milner, Sir Timothy William Lycett, Bt. (1717)
Mirrlees, *Prof.* Sir James Alexander, Kt., FBA
Mitchell, *Air Cdre* Sir (Arthur) Dennis, KBE, CVO, DFC, AFC
Mitchell, Sir David Bower, Kt.
Mitchell, Sir Derek Jack, KCB, CVO
Mitchell, *Prof.* Sir (Edgar) William John, Kt., CBE, FRS
Mitchell, *Rt. Hon.* Sir James FitzAllen, KCMG
Mitchell, *Very Revd* Sir Patrick Reynolds, KCVO
Mitchell, *Hon.* Sir Stephen George, Kt.
Mitting, *Hon.* Sir John Edward, Kt.
Moate, Sir Roger Denis, Kt.
Mobbs, Sir (Gerald) Nigel, Kt.
Moberly, Sir John Campbell, KBE, CMG
Moberly, Sir Patrick Hamilton, KCMG
Moffat, Sir Brian Scott, Kt., OBE
Moffat, *Lt.-Gen.* Sir (William) Cameron, KBE
Mogg, *Gen.* Sir (Herbert) John, GCB, CBE, DSO
†Moir, Sir Christopher Ernest, Bt. (1916)
†Molony, Sir Thomas Desmond, Bt. (1925)
Monck, Sir Nicholas Jeremy, KCB
Montagu, Sir Nicholas Lionel John, KCB, CB
Montgomery, Sir (Basil Henry) David, Bt. (1801)
Montgomery, Sir (William) Fergus, Kt.
Mookerjee, Sir Birendra Nath, Kt.
Moollan, Sir Abdool Hamid Adam, Kt.
Moollan, *Hon.* Sir Cassam (Ismael), Kt.
Moon, Sir Peter Wilfred Giles Graham-, Bt. (1855)
†Moon, Sir Roger, Bt. (1887)
Moore, *Most Revd* Sir Desmond Charles, KBE
Moore, Sir Francis Thomas, Kt.
Moore, Sir Henry Roderick, Kt., CBE
Moore, *Maj.-Gen.* Sir (John) Jeremy, KCB, OBE, MC
Moore, Sir John Michael, KCVO, CB, DSC
Moore, Sir Lee Llewellyn, KCMG, QC
Moore, *Vice Adm.* Sir Michael Antony Claës, KBE, LVO
Moore, *Prof.* Sir Norman Winfrid, Bt. (1919)
Moore, Sir Patrick Alfred Caldwell, Kt., CBE

Moore, Sir Patrick William Eisdell, Kt., OBE
Moore, Sir William Roger Clotworthy, Bt., TD (1932)
Morauta, Sir Mekere, Kt.
Mordaunt, Sir Richard Nigel Charles, Bt. (1611)
Moreton, Sir John Oscar, KCMG, KCVO, MC
Morgan, *Vice-Adm.* Sir Charles Christopher, KBE
Morgan, *His Hon. Maj.-Gen.* Sir David John Hughes-, Bt., CB, CBE (1925)
Morgan, Sir Graham, Kt.
Morgan, Sir John Albert Leigh, KCMG
Morison, *Hon.* Sir Thomas Richard Atkin, Kt.
Morland, *Hon.* Sir Michael, Kt.
Morland, Sir Robert Kenelm, Kt.
Morpeth, Sir Douglas Spottiswoode, Kt., TD
†Morris, Sir Allan Lindsay, Bt. (1806)
Morris, *Air Marshal* Sir Arnold Alec, KBE, CB, FREng.
Morris, Sir (James) Richard (Samuel), Kt., CBE, FREng.
Morris, *Rt. Hon.* Sir John, Kt., QC
Morris, Sir Keith Elliot Hedley, KBE, CMG
Morris, *Prof.* Sir Peter John, Kt., FRS
Morris, Sir Trefor Alfred, Kt., CBE, QPM
Morris, *Very Revd* Sir William James, KCVO, Ph.D.
Morrison, Sir (Alexander) Fraser, Kt., CBE
Morrison, *Hon.* Sir Charles Andrew, Kt.
Morrison, Sir Howard Leslie, Kt., OBE
Morrison, Sir Kenneth Duncan, Kt., CBE
Morritt, *Hon.* Sir (Robert) Andrew, Kt., CVO
Morrow, Sir Ian Thomas, Kt.
Morse, Sir Christopher Jeremy, KCMG
Mortimer, Sir Laird, Kt.
Mortimer, Sir John Clifford, Kt., CBE, QC
Morton, *Adm.* Sir Anthony Storrs, GBE, KCB
Morton, Sir (Robert) Alastair (Newton), Kt.
Moseley, Sir George Walker, KCB
Moser, *Prof.* Sir Claus Adolf, KCB, CBE, FBA
Moses, *Hon.* Sir Alan George, Kt.
†Moss, Sir David John Edwards-, Bt. (1868)
Moss, Sir David Joseph, KCVO, CMG
Moss, Sir Stirling Craufurd, Kt., OBE
Mostyn, *Gen.* Sir (Joseph) David Frederick, KCB, CBE
†Mostyn, Sir William Basil John, Bt. (1670)
Mott, Sir John Harmer, Bt. (1930)
Mottram, Sir Richard Clive, KCB
†Mount, Sir (William Robert) Ferdinand, Bt. (1921)
Mountain, Sir Denis Mortimer, Bt. (1922)
Mountfield, Sir Robin, KCB
Mowbray, Sir John, Kt.
Mowbray, Sir John Robert, Bt. (1880)
Muir, Sir Laurence Macdonald, Kt.
†Muir, Sir Richard James Kay, Bt. (1892)
Mulcahy, Sir Geoffrey John, Kt.
Mullens, *Lt.-Gen.* Sir Anthony Richard Guy, KCB, OBE
Mummery, *Hon.* Sir John Frank, Kt.
Munby, *Hon.* Sir James Lawrence, Kt.
Munn, Sir James, Kt., OBE
Munro, Sir Alan Gordon, KCMG
†Munro, Sir Kenneth Arnold William, Bt. (S. 1634)
†Munro, Sir Keith Gordon, Bt. (1825)
Munro, Sir Sydney Douglas Gun-, GCMG, MBE
Muria, *Hon.* Sir Gilbert John Baptist, Kt.
Murphy, Sir Leslie Frederick, Kt.
Murray, *Rt. Hon.* Sir Donald Bruce, Kt.
Murray, Sir James, KCMG
Murray, Sir John Antony Jerningham, Kt., CBE
Murray, *Prof.* Sir Kenneth, Kt., FRCPath., FRS, FRSE
Murray, Sir Nigel Andrew Digby, Bt. (S. 1628)
Murray, Sir Patrick Ian Keith, Bt. (S. 1673)
†Murray, Sir Rowland William, Bt. (S. 1630)
Mursell, Sir Peter, Kt., MBE
Musgrave, Sir Christopher Patrick Charles, Bt. (1611)
Musson, *Gen.* Sir Geoffrey Randolph Dixon, GCB, CBE, DSO
Myers, Sir Philip Alan, Kt., OBE, QPM
Myers, *Prof.* Sir Rupert Horace, KBE
Mynors, Sir Richard Baskerville, Bt. (1964)
Naipaul, Sir Vidiadhar Surajprasad, Kt.
Nairn, Sir Michael, Bt. (1904)
Nairn, Sir Robert Arnold Spencer-, Bt. (1933)
Nairne, *Rt. Hon.* Sir Patrick Dalmahoy, GCB, MC
Naish, Sir (Charles) David, Kt.
Nall, Sir Michael Joseph, Bt., RN (1954)
Namaliu, *Rt. Hon.* Sir Rabbie Langanai, KCMG
†Napier, Sir Charles Joseph, Bt. (1867)
Napier, Sir John Archibald Lennox, Bt. (S. 1627)
Napier, Sir Oliver John, Kt.
Napier, *Rt. Hon.* Sir Richard, GCVO
Nasmith, *Prof.* Sir James Duncan Dunbar-, Kt., CBE, RIBA, FRSE
Neal, Sir Eric James, Kt., CVO
Neal, Sir Leonard Francis, Kt., CBE
Neale, Sir Gerrard Anthony, Kt.
Neave, Sir Paul Arundell, Bt. (1795)
Needham, *Rt. Hon.* Sir Richard (Th Earl of Kilmorey, *see* page 141)
Neill, *Rt. Hon.* Sir Brian Thomas, K
Neill, *Rt. Hon.* Sir Ivan, Kt., PC (NI)
Neill, Sir (James) Hugh, KCVO, CBE, TD
†Nelson, Sir Jamie Charles Vernon Hope, Bt. (1912)
Nelson, *Hon.* Sir Robert Franklyn, K
Nelson, *Air Marshal* Sir (Sidney) Richard (Carlyle), KCB, OBE, MD
Nepean, *Lt.-Col.* Sir Evan Yorke, Bt. (1802)
Neuberger, *Hon.* Sir David Edmond Kt.
Neubert, Sir Michael John, Kt.
Neville, Sir Roger Albert Gartside, Kt., VRD
New, *Maj.-Gen.* Sir Laurence Anthony Wallis, Kt., CB, CBE
Newall, Sir Paul Henry, Kt., TD
Newby, *Prof.* Sir Howard Joseph, Kt CBE
Newington, Sir Michael John, KCMG
Newman, Sir Francis Hugh Cecil, Bt (1912)
Newman, Sir Geoffrey Robert, Bt. (1836)
Newman, *Hon.* Sir George Michael, Kt.
Newman, Sir Kenneth Leslie, GBE, QPM
Newman, *Vice-Adm.* Sir Roy Thomas KCB
Newman, *Col.* Sir Stuart Richard, Kt. CBE, TD
Newsam, Sir Peter Anthony, Kt.
Newton, Sir (Charles) Wilfred, Kt., CBE
Newton, Sir (Harry) Michael (Rex), Bt. (1900)
Newton, Sir Kenneth Garnar, Bt., OBE, TD (1924)
Ngata, Sir Henare Kohere, KBE
Nichol, Sir Duncan Kirkbride, Kt., CBE
Nicholas, Sir David, Kt., CBE
Nicholas, Sir John William, KCVO, CMG
Nicholls, *Air Marshal* Sir John Moreton, KCB, CBE, DFC, AFC
Nicholls, Sir Nigel Hamilton, KCVO, CBE
Nicholls, Sir Charles Harmar-, Bt. (1960)
Nichols, Sir Richard Everard, Kt.
Nicholson, Sir Bryan Hubert, Kt.
†Nicholson, Sir Charles Christian, Bt. (1912)
Nicholson, *Rt. Hon.* Sir Michael, Kt.
Nicholson, Sir Paul Douglas, Kt.
Nicholson, Sir Robin Buchanan, Kt., Ph.D., FRS, FREng.
Nicoll, Sir William, KCMG
Nightingale, Sir Charles Manners Gamaliel, Bt. (1628)
Nightingale, Sir John Cyprian, Kt., CBE, BEM, QPM
Nixon, Sir Simon Michael Christopher, Bt. (1906)

Nixon, Sir Edwin Ronald, Kt., CBE
Noble, Sir David Brunel, Bt. (1902)
Noble, Sir Iain Andrew, Bt., OBE (1923)
Noble, Sir (Thomas Alexander) Fraser, Kt., MBE
Nombri, Sir Joseph Karl, Kt., ISO, BEM
Norman, Sir Arthur Gordon, KBE, DFC
Norman, Sir Mark Annesley, Bt. (1915)
Norman, Sir Robert Henry, Kt., OBE
Norman, Sir Ronald, Kt., OBE
Norrington, Sir Roger Arthur Carver, Kt., CBE
Norris, *Air Chief Marshal* Sir Christopher Neil Foxley-, GCB, DSO, OBE
Norris, Sir Eric George, KCMG
Norriss, Air Marshal Sir Peter Coulson, KBE, CB, AFC
North, Sir Peter Machin, Kt., CBE, QC, DCL, FBA
North, Sir Thomas Lindsay, Kt.
North, Sir (William) Jonathan (Frederick), Bt. (1920)
Norton, *Vice-Adm. Hon.* Sir Nicholas John Hill-, KCB
Norwood, Sir Walter Neville, Kt.
Nossal, Sir Gustav Joseph Victor, Kt., CBE
Nott, *Rt. Hon.* Sir John William Frederic, KCB
Nourse, *Rt. Hon.* Sir Martin Charles, Kt.
Nugent, Sir John Edwin Lavallin, Bt. (I. 1795)
Nugent, *Maj.* Sir Peter Walter James, Bt. (1831)
Nugent, Sir Robin George Colborne, Bt. (1806)
Nursaw, Sir James, KCB, QC
Nurse, Sir Paul Maxime, Kt., Ph.D.
Nuttall, Sir Nicholas Keith Lillington, Bt. (1922)
Nutting, Sir John Grenfell, Bt., QC (1903)
Oakeley, Sir John Digby Atholl, Bt. (1790)
Oakes, Sir Christopher, Bt. (1939)
Oakshott, Hon. Sir Anthony Hendrie, Bt. (1959)
Oates, Sir Thomas, Kt., CMG, OBE
Obolensky, *Prof.* Sir Dimitri, Kt.
O'Brien, Sir Frederick William Fitzgerald, Kt.
O'Brien, Sir Richard, Kt., DSO, MC
O'Brien, Sir Timothy John, Bt. (1849)
O'Brien, *Adm.* Sir William Donough, KCB, DSC
O'Connell, Sir Maurice James Donagh MacCarthy, Bt. (1869)
O'Dea, Sir Patrick Jerad, KCVO
Odell, Sir Stanley John, Kt.
Odgers, Sir Graeme David William, Kt.
O'Dowd, Sir David Joseph, Kt., CBE, QPM
Ogden, Sir (Edward) Michael, Kt., QC
Ogden, Sir Robert, Kt., CBE
Ogilvy, *Rt. Hon.* Sir Angus James Bruce, KCVO
Ogilvy, Sir Francis Gilbert Arthur, Bt. (S. 1626)
Ognall, *Hon.* Sir Harry Henry, Kt.
Ohlson, Sir Brian Eric Christopher, Bt. (1920)
Okeover, *Capt.* Sir Peter Ralph Leopold Walker-, Bt. (1886)
Olewale, *Hon.* Sir Niwia Ebia, Kt.
Oliphant, Sir Mark (Marcus Laurence Elwin), KBE, FRS
O'Loghlen, Sir Colman Michael, Bt. (1838)
Olson, Sir Ralph, Kt.
Olver, Sir Stephen John Linley, KBE, CMG
Omand, Sir David Bruce, KCB
O'Neil, *Hon.* Sir Desmond Henry, Kt.
Ongley, *Hon.* Sir Joseph Augustine, Kt.
O'Nions, Prof. Sir Robert Keith, Kt., FRS, Ph.D.
Onslow, Sir John Roger Wilmot, Bt. (1797)
Oppenheim, Sir Duncan Morris, Kt.
Oppenheimer, Sir Michael Bernard Grenville, Bt. (1921)
Orde, Sir John Alexander Campbell-, Bt. (1790)
O'Regan, *Dr* Sir Stephen Gerard (Tipene), Kt.
O'Reilly, Anthony John Francis, Kt.
Orr, Sir David Alexander, Kt., MC
Orr, Sir John, Kt., OBE
Osborn, Sir John Holbrook, Kt.
Osborn, Sir Richard Henry Danvers, Bt. (1662)
Osborne, Sir Peter George, Bt. (I. 1629)
Osifelo, Sir Frederick Aubarua, Kt., MBE
Osmond, Sir Douglas, Kt., CBE
O'Sullevan, Sir Peter John, Kt., CBE
Oswald, *Admiral of the Fleet* Sir (John) Julian Robertson, GCB
Oswald, Sir (William Richard) Michael, KCVO
Otton, Sir Geoffrey John, KCB
Otton, *Rt. Hon.* Sir Philip Howard, Kt.
Oulton, Sir Antony Derek Maxwell, GCB, QC
Ouseley, *Hon.* Sir Brian Walter, Kt.
Ouseley, Sir Herman George, Kt.
Outram, Sir Alan James, Bt. (1858)
Overall, Sir John Wallace, Kt., CBE, MC
Owen, Sir Geoffrey, Kt.
Owen, Sir Hugh Bernard Pilkington, Bt. (1813)
Owen, Sir Hugo Dudley Cunliffe-, Bt. (1920)
Owen, *Hon.* Sir John Arthur Dalziel, Kt.
Owen, *Hon.* Sir Robert Michael, Kt.
Packer, Sir Richard John, KCB
Page, Sir (Arthur) John, Kt.
Page, Sir Frederick William, Kt., CBE, FREng.
Page, Sir John Joseph Joffre, Kt., OBE
Paget, Sir Julian Tolver, Bt., CVO (1871)
Paget, Sir Richard Herbert, Bt. (1886)
Pain, *Lt.-Gen.* Sir (Horace) Rollo (Squarey), KCB, MC
Pain, *Hon.* Sir Peter Richard, Kt.
Paine, Sir Christopher Hammon, Kt., FRCP, FRCR
Palin, *Air Chief Marshal* Sir Roger Hewlett, KCB, OBE
Palliser, *Rt. Hon.* Sir (Arthur) Michael, GCMG
Palmar, Sir Derek James, Kt.
Palmer, Sir (Charles) Mark, Bt. (1886)
Palmer, Sir Geoffrey Christopher John, Bt. (1660)
Palmer, *Rt. Hon.* Sir Geoffrey Winston Russell, KCMG
Palmer, Sir John Chance, Kt.
Palmer, Sir John Edward Somerset, Bt. (1791)
Palmer, *Maj.-Gen.* Sir (Joseph) Michael, KCVO
Palmer, Sir Reginald Oswald, GCMG, MBE
Pantlin, Sir Dick Hurst, Kt., CBE
Paolozzi, Sir Eduardo Luigi, Kt., CBE, RA
Parbo, Sir Arvi Hillar, Kt.
Park, *Hon.* Sir Andrew Edward Wilson, Kt.
Parker, Sir (Arthur) Douglas Dodds-, Kt.
Parker, Sir Eric Wilson, Kt.
Parker, Sir John, Kt.
Parker, *Hon.* Sir Jonathan Frederic, Kt.
Parker, *Maj.* Sir Michael John, KCVO, CBE
Parker, Sir Peter, KBE, LVO
Parker, Sir Richard (William) Hyde, Bt. (1681)
Parker, *Rt. Hon.* Sir Roger Jocelyn, Kt.
Parker, Sir Thomas John, Kt.
Parker, *Vice-Adm.* Sir (Wilfred) John, KBE, CB, DSC
Parker, Sir William Peter Brian, Bt. (1844)
Parkes, Sir Edward Walter, Kt., FREng.
Parkinson, Sir Nicholas Fancourt, Kt.
Parsons, Sir (John) Michael, Kt.
Parsons, Sir Richard Edmund (Clement Fownes), KCMG
Partridge, Sir Michael John Anthony, KCB
Pascoe, *Gen.* Sir Robert Alan, KCB, MBE
Pasley, Sir John Malcolm Sabine, Bt. (1794)
Paterson, Sir Dennis Craig, Kt.
Patnick, Sir (Cyril) Irvine, Kt., OBE
Patten, *Hon.* Sir Justice Nicholas John, Kt.
Pattie, *Rt. Hon.* Sir Geoffrey Edwin, Kt.
Pattinson, Sir (William) Derek, Kt.

Price, Sir Frank Leslie, Kt.
Price, Sir Norman Charles, KCB
Price, Sir Robert John Green-, Bt. (1874)
Prickett, *Air Chief Marshal* Sir Thomas Other, KCB, DSO, DFC
Prideaux, Sir Humphrey Povah Treverbian, Kt., OBE
Primrose, Sir John Ure, Bt. (1903)
Pringle, *Air Marshal* Sir Charles Norman Seton, KBE, FREng.
Pringle, *Hon.* Sir John Kenneth, Kt.
Pringle, *Lt.-Gen.* Sir Steuart (Robert), Bt., KCB, RM (S. 1683)
Pritchard, Sir Neil, KCMG
Proby, Sir Peter, Bt. (1952)
Prosser, Sir Ian Maurice Gray, Kt.
Pryke, Sir Christopher Dudley, Bt. (1926)
Puapua, *Rt. Hon.* Sir Tomasi, KBE
Pugh, Sir Idwal Vaughan, KCB
Pullinger, Sir (Francis) Alan, Kt., CBE
Pumfrey, *Hon.* Sir Nicholas Richard, Kt.
Pumphrey, Sir (John) Laurence, KCMG
Purchas, *Rt. Hon.* Sir Francis Brooks, Kt.
Purves, Sir William, Kt., CBE, DSO
Purvis, *Vice-Adm.* Sir Neville, KCB
Quicke, Sir John Godolphin, Kt., CBE
Quigley, Sir (William) George (Henry), Kt., CB, Ph.D.
Quilliam, *Hon.* Sir (James) Peter, Kt.
Quilter, Sir Anthony Raymond Leopold Cuthbert, Bt. (1897)
Quinlan, Sir Michael Edward, GCB
Quinton, Sir James Grand, Kt.
Radcliffe, Sir Sebastian Everard, Bt. (1813)
Radda, *Prof.* Sir George Karoly, Kt., CBE, FRS
Rae, *Hon.* Sir Wallace Alexander Ramsay, Kt.
Raeburn, Sir Michael Edward Norman, Bt. (1923)
Raeburn, *Maj.-Gen.* Sir (William) Digby (Manifold), KCVO, CB, DSO, MBE
Raikes, *Vice-Adm.* Sir Iwan Geoffrey, KCB, CBE, DSC
Raison, *Rt. Hon.* Sir Timothy Hugh Francis, Kt.
Ralli, Sir Godfrey Victor, Bt., TD (1912)
Ramdanee, Sir Mookteswar Baboolall Kailash, Kt.
Ramphal, Sir Shridath Surendranath, GCMG
Ramphul, Sir Baalkhristna, Kt.
Ramphul, Sir Indurduth, Kt.
Ramsay, Sir Alexander William Burnett, Bt. (1806)
Ramsay, Sir Allan John (Hepple), KBE, CMG
Ramsbotham, *Gen.* Sir David John, GCB, CBE
Ramsbotham, *Hon.* Sir Peter Edward, GCMG, GCVO
Ramsden, Sir John Charles Josslyn, Bt. (1689)
Randle, *Prof.* Sir Philip John, Kt.
Rank, Sir Benjamin Keith, Kt., CMG
Rankin, Sir Ian Niall, Bt. (1898)
Rasch, Sir Simon Anthony Carne, Bt. (1903)
Rashleigh, Sir Richard Harry, Bt. (1831)
Ratford, Sir David John Edward, KCMG, CVO
Rattee, *Hon.* Sir Donald Keith, Kt.
Rattle, Sir Simon Dennis, Kt., CBE
Rault, Sir Louis Joseph Maurice, Kt.
Rawlins, *Surgeon Vice-Adm.* Sir John Stuart Pepys, KBE
Rawlins, *Prof.* Sir Michael David, Kt., FRCP, FRCPED.
Rawlinson, Sir Anthony Henry John, Bt. (1891)
Read, *Air Marshal* Sir Charles Frederick, KBE, CB, DFC, AFC
Read, Sir John Emms, Kt.
†Reade, Sir Kenneth Ray, Bt. (1661)
Reay, *Lt.-Gen.* Sir (Hubert) Alan John, KBE
Redgrave, *Maj.-Gen.* Sir Roy Michael Frederick, KBE, MC
Redgrave, Sir Steven Geoffrey, Kt., CBE
Redmayne, Sir Nicholas, Bt. (1964)
Redwood, Sir Peter Boverton, Bt. (1911)
Reece, Sir Charles Hugh, Kt.
Reece, Sir James Gordon, Kt.
Rees, Sir David Allan, Kt., Ph.D., D.Sc., FRS
Rees, *Prof.* Sir Martin John, Kt., FRS
Reeve, Sir Anthony, KCMG, KCVO
Reeves, *Most Revd* Paul Alfred, GCMG, GCVO
Reffell, *Adm.* Sir Derek Roy, KCB
Refshauge, *Maj-Gen.* Sir William Dudley, Kt., CBE
Reid, Sir Alexander James, Bt. (1897)
Reid, Sir (Harold) Martin (Smith), KBE, CMG
Reid, Sir Hugh, Bt. (1922)
Reid, Sir Norman Robert, Kt.
Reid, Sir Robert Paul, Kt.
Reid, Sir William Kennedy, KCB
Reiher, Sir Frederick Bernard Carl, KBE, CMG
Reilly, *Lt.-Gen.* Sir Jeremy Calcott, KCB, DSO
Renals, Sir Stanley, Bt. (1895)
Rennie, Sir John Shaw, GCMG, OBE
Renouf, Sir Clement William Bailey, Kt.
Renshaw, Sir (Charles) Maurice Bine, Bt. (1903)
Renwick, Sir Richard Eustace, Bt. (1921)
Reporter, Sir Shapoor Ardeshirji, KBE
Reynolds, Sir David James, Bt. (1923)
Reynolds, Sir Peter William John, Kt., CBE
Rhodes, Sir Basil Edward, Kt., CBE, TD
Rhodes, Sir John Christopher Douglas, Bt. (1919)
Rhodes, Sir Peregrine Alexander, KCMG
Rice, *Maj.-Gen.* Sir Desmond Hind Garrett, KCVO, CBE
Rice, Sir Timothy Miles Bindon, Kt.
Richard, Sir Cliff, Kt., OBE
Richards, Sir Brian Mansel, Kt., CBE, Ph.D.
Richards, Sir (Francis) Brooks, KCMG, DSC
Richards, *Lt.-Gen.* Sir John Charles Chisholm, KCB, KCVO, RM
Richards, Sir Rex Edward, Kt., D.Sc., FRS
Richards, *Hon.* Sir Stephen Price, Kt.
Richardson, Sir Anthony Lewis, Bt. (1924)
Richardson, *Rt. Hon.* Sir Ivor Lloyd Morgan, Kt.
Richardson, Sir (John) Eric, Kt., CBE
Richardson, Sir Michael John de Rougemont, Kt.
Richardson, *Lt.-Gen.* Sir Robert Francis, KCB, CVO, CBE
Richardson, Sir Simon Alaisdair Stewart-, Bt. (S. 1630)
Richardson, Sir Thomas Legh, KCMG
Richmond, *Prof.* Sir Mark Henry, Kt., FRS
Ricketts, Sir Robert Cornwallis Gerald St Leger, Bt. (1828)
Riddell, Sir John Charles Buchanan, Bt., CVO (S. 1628)
Ridley, Sir Adam (Nicholas), Kt.
Ridley, Sir Michael Kershaw, KCVO
Ridsdale, Sir Julian Errington, Kt., CBE
Rifkind, *Rt. Hon.* Sir Malcolm Leslie, KCMG, QC
Rigby, Sir Anthony John, Bt. (1929)
Rimer, *Hon.* Sir Colin Percy Farquharson, Kt.
Ringadoo, *Hon.* Sir Veerasamy, GCMG
Ripley, Sir Hugh, Bt. (1880)
Risk, Sir Thomas Neilson, Kt.
Ritako, Sir Thomas Baha, Kt., MBE
Rix, *Hon.* Sir Bernard Anthony, Kt.
Rix, Sir John, Kt., MBE, FREng.
Robati, Sir Pupuke, KBE, OBE
Robb, Sir John Weddell, Kt.
Roberts, *Hon.* Sir Denys Tudor Emil, KBE, QC
Roberts, Sir Derek Harry, Kt., CBE, FRS, FREng.
Roberts, Sir (Edward Fergus) Sidney, Kt., CBE
Roberts, *Prof.* Sir Gareth Gwyn, Kt., FRS
Roberts, Sir Gilbert Howland Rookehurst, Bt. (1809)
Roberts, Sir Gordon James, Kt., CBE
Roberts, Sir Hugh Ashley, KCVO, CVO
Roberts, Sir Ivor Anthony, KCMG
Roberts, Sir Samuel, Bt. (1919)
Roberts, Sir Stephen James Leake, Kt.
Roberts, Sir William James Denby, Bt. (1909)

Robertson, Sir John Fraser, KCMG, CBE
Robertson, Sir Lewis, Kt., CBE, FRSE
Robertson, *Prof.* Sir Rutherford Ness, Kt., CMG
Robins, Sir Ralph Harry, Kt., FREng.
Robinson, Sir Albert Edward Phineas, Kt.
†Robinson, Sir Christopher Philipse, Bt. (1854)
Robinson, Sir Dominick Christopher Lynch-, Bt. (1920)
Robinson, Sir Ian, Kt.
Robinson, Sir John James Michael Laud, Bt. (1660)
Robinson, Sir Wilfred Henry Frederick, Bt. (1908)
Robson, *Prof.* Sir James Gordon, Kt., CBE
Robson, Sir John Adam, KCMG
Robson, Sir Stephen Arthur, Kt., CB
Roch, *Rt. Hon.* Sir John Ormond, Kt.
Roche, Sir David O'Grady, Bt. (1838)
Roche, Sir Henry John, Kt.
Rodgers, Sir (Andrew) Piers (Wingate Aikin-Sneath), Bt. (1964)
Rodley, *Prof.* Sir Nigel, KBE
Rodrigues, Sir Alberto Maria, Kt., CBE, ED
Roe, *Air Chief Marshal* Sir Rex David, GCB, AFC
Rogers, Sir Frank Jarvis, Kt.
Rogers, *Air Chief Marshal* Sir John Robson, KCB, CBE
Rooke, Sir Denis Eric, Kt., OM, CBE, FRS, FREng.
Ropner, Sir John Bruce Woollacott, Bt. (1952)
Ropner, Sir Robert Douglas, Bt. (1904)
Roscoe, Sir Robert Bell, KBE
Rose, *Rt. Hon.* Sir Christopher Dudley Roger, Kt.
Rose, Sir Clive Martin, GCMG
Rose, Sir David Lancaster, Bt. (1874)
Rose, *Gen.* Sir (Hugh) Michael, KCB, CBE, DSO, QGM
Rose, Sir Julian Day, Bt. (1872 and 1909)
Ross, Sir (James) Keith, Bt., RD, FRCS (1960)
Ross, *Lt.-Gen.* Sir Robert Jeremy, KCB, OBE
Ross, *Lt.-Col.* Sir Walter Hugh Malcolm, KCVO, OBE
Rosser, Sir Melvyn Wynne, Kt.
Rossi, Sir Hugh Alexis Louis, Kt.
Rotblat, *Prof.* Sir Joseph, KCMG, CBE, FRS
Roth, *Prof.* Sir Martin, Kt., MD, FRCP
Rothschild, Sir Evelyn Robert Adrian de, Kt.
Rougier, *Hon.* Sir Richard George, Kt.
Rowell, Sir John Joseph, Kt., CBE
Rowland, *Air Marshal* Sir James Anthony, KBE, DFC, AFC
Rowland, Sir (John) David, Kt.
Rowlands, *Air Marshal* Sir John Samuel, GC, KBE
Rowley, Sir Charles Robert, Bt. (1836) †(1786)
Rowlinson, *Prof.* Sir John Shipley, Kt., FRS
Roxburgh, *Vice-Adm.* Sir John Charles Young, KCB, CBE, DSO, DSC
Royden, Sir Christopher John, Bt. (1905)
Rudd, Sir (Anthony) Nigel (Russell), Kt.
Rudge, Sir Alan Walter, Kt., CBE, FRS
Rumbold, Sir Henry John Sebastian, Bt. (1779)
Rumbold, Sir Jack Seddon, Kt.
Runchorelal, Sir (Udayan) Chinubhai Madhowlal, Bt. (1913)
Rusby, *Vice-Adm.* Sir Cameron, KCB, LVO
†Russell, Sir (Arthur) Mervyn, Bt. (1812)
Russell, Sir Charles Dominic, Bt. (1916)
Russell, *Hon.* Sir David Sturrock West-, Kt.
Russell, Sir George, Kt., CBE
Russell, Sir Muir, KCB
Russell, *Prof.* Sir Peter Edward Lionel, Kt., D.Litt., FBA
Russell, Sir (Robert) Mark, KCMG
Russell, *Rt. Hon.* Sir (Thomas) Patrick, Kt.
Rutter, Sir Frank William Eden, KBE
Rutter, *Prof.* Sir Michael Llewellyn, Kt., CBE, MD, FRS
Ryan, Sir Derek Gerald, Bt. (1919)
Rycroft, Sir Richard John, Bt. (1784)
Ryrie, Sir William Sinclair, KCB
Sabola, *Hon.* Sir Joaquim Claudino Gonsalves-, Kt.
Sachs, *Hon.* Sir Michael Alexander Geddes, Kt.
Sainsbury, *Rt. Hon.* Sir Timothy Alan Davan, Kt.
†St Aubyn, Sir William Molesworth-, Bt. (1689)
†St George, Sir John Avenel Bligh, Bt. (I. 1766)
St Johnston, Sir Kerry, Kt.
Sainty, Sir John Christopher, KCB
Salisbury, Sir Robert William, Kt.
Salt, Sir Patrick MacDonnell, Bt. (1869)
Salt, Sir (Thomas) Michael John, Bt. (1899)
Sampson, Sir Colin, Kt., CBE, QPM
Samuel, Sir John Michael Glen, Bt. (1898)
Samuelson, Sir (Bernard) Michael (Francis), Bt. (1884)
Samuelson, Sir Sydney Wylie, Kt., CBE
Sanders, Sir John Reynolds Mayhew-, Kt.
Sanders, Sir Robert Tait, KBE, CMG
Sanderson, Sir Frank Linton, Bt. (1920)
Sarei, Sir Alexis Holyweek, Kt., CBE
Satchwell, Sir Kevin Joseph, Kt.
Saunders, *Hon.* Sir John Anthony Holt, Kt., CBE, DSO, MC
Saunders, Sir Peter, Kt.
Savage, Sir Ernest Walter, Kt.
Savile, Sir James Wilson Vincent, Kt OBE
Say, *Rt. Revd* Richard David, KCVO
Scheele, Sir Nicholas Vernon, KCMG
Schiemann, *Rt. Hon.* Sir Konrad Hermann Theodor, Kt.
Scholar, Sir Michael Charles, KCB
Scholey, Sir David Gerald, Kt., CBE
Scholey, Sir Robert, Kt., CBE, FREng
Scholtens, Sir James Henry, KCVO
Schreier, Sir Bernard, Kt.
Schubert, Sir Sydney, Kt.
Scipio, Sir Hudson Rupert, Kt.
Scoon, Sir Paul, GCMG, GCVO, OBE
Scott, Sir Anthony Percy, Bt. (1913)
Scott, Sir (Charles) Peter, KBE, CMG
Scott, Sir David Aubrey, GCMG
Scott, Sir Dominic James Maxwell-, Bt. (1642)
Scott, Sir Ian Dixon, KCMG, KCVO, CI
Scott, Sir James Jervoise, Bt. (1962)
Scott, Sir Kenneth Bertram Adam, KCVO, CMG
Scott, Sir Michael, KCVO, CMG
Scott, *Rt. Hon.* Sir Nicholas Paul, KB
Scott, Sir Oliver Christopher Anderson, Bt. (1909)
Scott, *Prof.* Sir Philip John, KBE
Scott, *Rt. Hon.* Sir Richard Rashleigh Folliott, Kt.
Scott, Sir Robert David Hillyer, Kt.
Scott, Sir Walter John, Bt. (1907)
Scott, *Rear-Adm.* Sir (William) Davi (Stewart), KBE, CB
Scowen, Sir Eric Frank, Kt., MD, D.Sc. LL D, FRCP, FRCS
Seale, Sir Clarence David, Kt.
Seale, Sir John Henry, Bt. (1838)
Seaman, Sir Keith Douglas, KCVO, OBE
Sebastian, Sir Cuthbert Montraville, GCMG, OBE
†Sebright, Sir Peter Giles Vivian, Bt. (1626)
Seccombe, Sir (William) Vernon Stephen, Kt.
Seconde, Sir Reginald Louis, KCMG, CVO
Sedley, *Rt. Hon.* Sir Stephen John, Kt
Seely, Sir Nigel Edward, Bt. (1896)
Seeto, Sir Ling James, Kt., MBE
Seeyave, Sir Rene Sow Choung, Kt., CBE
Seligman, Sir Peter Wendel, Kt., CBE
Sellors, Sir Patrick John Holmes-, KCVO, FRCS
Semple, Sir John Laughlin, KCB
Sergeant, Sir Patrick, Kt.
Series, Sir (Joseph Michel) Emile, Kt., CBE
Serota, Sir Nicholas Andrew, Kt.
Serpell, Sir David Radford, KCB, CMG, OBE
†Seton, Sir Charles Wallace, Bt. (S. 1683)
Seton, Sir Iain Bruce, Bt. (S. 1663)
Severne, *Air Vice-Marshal* Sir John de Milt, KCVO, OBE, AFC

Soakimori, Sir Frederick Pa-Nukuanca, KBE, CPM
Soame, Sir Charles John Buckworth-Herne-, Bt. (1697)
Sobers, Sir Garfield St Auburn, Kt.
Solomon, Sir Harry, Kt.
Somare, *Rt. Hon.* Sir Michael Thomas, GCMG, CH
Somers, *Rt. Hon.* Sir Edward Jonathan, Kt.
Somerville, *Brig.* Sir John Nicholas, Kt., CBE
Somerville, Sir Quentin Charles Somerville Agnew-, Bt. (1957)
Sorrell, Sir Martin Stuart, Kt.
Soulsby, Sir Peter Alfred, Kt.
Soutar, *Air Marshal* Sir Charles John Williamson, KBE
South, Sir Arthur, Kt.
Southby, Sir John Richard Bilbe, Bt. (1937)
Southgate, Sir Colin Grieve, Kt.
Southgate, Sir William David, Kt.
Southward, Sir Leonard Bingley, Kt., OBE
Southwood, *Prof.* Sir (Thomas) Richard (Edmund), Kt., FRS
Souyave, *Hon.* Sir (Louis) Georges, Kt.
Sowrey, *Air Marshal* Sir Frederick Beresford, KCB, CBE, AFC
Sparkes, Sir Robert Lyndley, Kt.
Sparrow, Sir John, Kt.
Spearman, Sir Alexander Young Richard Mainwaring, Bt. (1840)
Spedding, *Prof.* Sir Colin Raymond William, Kt., CBE
Speed, Sir (Herbert) Keith, Kt., RD
Speelman, Sir Cornelis Jacob, Bt. (1686)
Speight, *Hon.* Sir Graham Davies, Kt.
Spencer, Sir Derek Harold, Kt., QC
Spencer, *Vice-Adml.* Sir Peter, KCB
Spicer, Sir James Wilton, Kt.
Spicer, Sir Nicholas Adrian Albert, Bt., MB (1906)
Spicer, Sir (William) Michael Hardy, Kt., MP
Spiers, Sir Donald Maurice, Kt., CB, TD
Spooner, Sir James Douglas, Kt.
Spotswood, *Marshal of the Royal Air Force* Sir Denis Frank, GCB, CBE, DSO, DFC
Spratt, *Col.* Sir Greville Douglas, GBE, TD
Spring, Sir Dryden Thomas, Kt.
Squire, *Air Chief Marshal* Sir Peter Ted, KCB, DFC, AFC, GCB
Stabb, *Hon.* Sir William Walter, Kt., QC
Stainton, Sir (John) Ross, Kt., CBE
Stamer, Sir (Lovelace) Anthony, Bt. (1809)
Stanbridge, *Air Vice-Marshal* Sir Brian Gerald Tivy, KCVO, CBE, AFC
Standard, Sir Kenneth Livingstone, Kt., MD
Stanier, Sir Beville Douglas, Bt. (1917)
Stanier, *Field Marshal* Sir John Wilfred, GCB, MBE
Stanley, *Rt. Hon.* Sir John Paul, Kt., MP
Staples, Sir Richard Molesworth, Bt. (I. 1628)
Stark, Sir Andrew Alexander Steel, KCMG, CVO
Starkey, Sir John Philip, Bt. (1935)
Starrit, Sir James, KCVO
Statham, Sir Norman, KCMG, CVO
Staughton, *Rt. Hon.* Sir Christopher Stephen Thomas Jonathan Thayer, Kt.
Staveley, Sir John Malfroy, KBE, MC
Stear, *Air Chief Marshal* Sir Michael James Douglas, KCB, CBE
Steel, Sir David Edward Charles, Kt., DSO, MC, TD
Steel, *Hon.* Sir David William, Kt.
Steele, Sir (Philip John) Rupert, Kt.
Steere, Sir Ernest Henry Lee-, KBE
Stephen, *Rt. Hon.* Sir Ninian Martin, KG, GCMG, GCVO, KBE
Stephens, Sir (Edwin) Barrie, Kt.
Stephenson, Sir Henry Upton, Bt. (1936)
Sternberg, Sir Sigmund, Kt.
Stevens, Sir Jocelyn Edward Greville, Kt., CVO
Stevens, Sir John, Kt.
Stevens, Sir Laurence Houghton, Kt., CBE
Stevenson, *Vice-Adm.* Sir (Hugh) David, KBE
Stevenson, Sir Simpson, Kt.
Stewart, Sir Alan, KBE
Stewart, Sir Alan d'Arcy, Bt. (I. 1623)
Stewart, Sir David James Henderson-, Bt. (1957)
Stewart, Sir David John Christopher, Bt. (1803)
Stewart, Sir Edward Jackson, Kt.
Stewart, *Prof.* Sir Frederick Henry, Kt., Ph.D., FRS, FRSE
Stewart, Sir Houston Mark Shaw-, Bt., MC, TD (S. 1667)
Stewart, Sir James Douglas, Kt.
Stewart, Sir James Moray, KCB
Stewart, Sir (John) Simon (Watson), Bt. (1920)
Stewart, Sir John Young, Kt., OBE
Stewart, Sir Robertson Huntly, Kt., CBE
Stewart, Sir Robin Alastair, Bt. (1960)
Stewart, *Prof.* Sir William Duncan Paterson, Kt., FRS, FRSE
Stibbon, *Gen.* Sir John James, KCB, OBE
Stirling, Sir Alexander John Dickson, KBE, CMG
Stirling, Sir Angus Duncan Aeneas, Kt.
Stockdale, Sir Arthur Noel, Kt.
Stockdale, Sir Thomas Minshull, Bt. (1960)
Stoddart, *Wg Cdr.* Sir Kenneth Maxwell, KCVO, AE
Stoker, *Prof.* Sir Michael George Parke, Kt., CBE, FRCP, FRS, FRSE
Stokes, Sir John Heydon Romaine, Kt.
Stones, Sir William Frederick, Kt., OBE
Stonhouse, *Revd* Sir Michael Philip, Bt. (1628)
Stonor, *Air Marshal* Sir Thomas Henry, KCB
Stoppard, Sir Thomas, Kt., CBE, OB
Storey, *Hon.* Sir Richard, Bt., CBE (1960)
Stott, Sir Adrian George Ellingham, Bt. (1920)
Stoute, Sir Michael Ronald, Kt.
Stow, Sir Christopher Philipson-, Bt., DFC (1907)
Stowe, Sir Kenneth Ronald, GCB, CVO
Stracey, Sir John Simon, Bt. (1818)
Strachan, Sir Curtis Victor, Kt., CVO
Strachey, Sir Charles, Bt. (1801)
Strang Steel, Sir (Fiennes) Michael, Bt. (1938)
Strawson, *Prof.* Sir Peter Frederick, Kt., FBA
Street, *Hon.* Sir Laurence Whistler, KCMG
Streeton, Sir Terence George, KBE, CMG
Stringer, Sir Donald Edgar, Kt., CBE
Stringer, Sir Howard, Kt.
Strong, Sir Roy Colin, Kt., Ph.D., FSA
Stronge, Sir James Anselan Maxwell, Bt. (1803)
Stroud, *Prof.* Sir (Charles) Eric, Kt., FRCP
Strutt, Sir Nigel Edward, Kt., TD
Stuart, Sir James Keith, Kt.
Stuart, Sir Kenneth Lamonte, Kt.
Stuart, Sir Mark Moody-, KCMG
†Stuart, Sir Phillip Luttrell, Bt. (1660)
Stubbs, Sir William Hamilton, Kt., Ph.D.
Stucley, *Lt.* Sir Hugh George Coplestone Bampfylde, Bt. (1859)
Studd, Sir Edward Fairfax, Bt. (1929)
Studd, Sir Peter Malden, GBE, KCVO
Studholme, Sir Henry William, Bt. (1956)
†Style, Sir William Frederick, Bt. (1627)
Sugar, Sir Alan Michael, Kt.
Sugden, Sir Arthur, Kt.
Sullivan, *Hon.* Sir Jeremy Mirth, Kt.
Sullivan, Sir Richard Arthur, Bt. (1804)
Sulston, Sir John Edward, Kt.
Sumner, *Hon.* Sir Christopher John, Kt.
Sutherland, Sir John Brewer, Bt. (1921)
Sutherland, Sir Maurice, Kt.
Sutherland, *Prof.* Sir Stewart Ross, Kt., FBA
Sutherland, Sir William George MacKenzie, Kt.
Suttie, Sir James Edward Grant-, Bt. (S. 1702)
Sutton, Sir Frederick Walter, Kt., OBE
Sutton, *Air Marshal* Sir John Matthias Dobson, KCB

utton, Sir Richard Lexington, Bt. (1772)
waffield, Sir James Chesebrough, Kt., CBE, RD
waine, Sir John Joseph, Kt., CBE
wan, Sir Conrad Marshall John Fisher, KCVO, Ph.D.
wan, Sir John William David, KBE
wann, Sir Michael Christopher, Bt., TD (1906)
wanwick, Sir Graham Russell, Kt., MBE
wartz, *Hon.* Sir Reginald William Colin, KBE, ED
weeney, Sir George, Kt.
weetnam, Sir (David) Rodney, KCVO, CBE, FRCS
winburn, *Lt.-Gen.* Sir Richard Hull, KCB
winson, Sir John Henry Alan, Kt., OBE
Swinton, *Maj.-Gen.* Sir John, KCVO, OBE
Swire, Sir Adrian Christopher, Kt.
Swire, Sir John Anthony, Kt., CBE
Swynnerton, Sir Roger John Massy, Kt., CMG, OBE, MC
Sykes, Sir Francis John Badcock, Bt. (1781)
Sykes, Sir Hugh Ridley, Kt.
Sykes, Sir John Charles Anthony le Gallais, Bt. (1921)
Sykes, *Prof.* Sir (Malcolm) Keith, Kt.
Sykes, Sir Richard, Kt.
Sykes, Sir Tatton Christopher Mark, Bt. (1783)
Symington, *Prof.* Sir Thomas, Kt., MD, FRSE
Symons, *Vice-Adm.* Sir Patrick Jeremy, KBE
Synge, Sir Robert Carson, Bt. (1801)
Tait, *Adm.* Sir (Allan) Gordon, KCB, DSC
Talbot, *Hon.* Sir Hilary Gwynne, Kt.
Talboys, *Rt. Hon.* Sir Brian Edward, CH, KCB
Tancred, Sir Henry Lawson-, Bt. (1662)
Tangaroa, *Hon.* Sir Tangoroa, Kt., MBE
Tange, Sir Arthur Harold, Kt., CBE
Tapsell, Sir Peter Hannay Bailey, Kt., MP
Tate, Sir (Henry) Saxon, Bt. (1898)
Tavaiqia, *Ratu* Sir Josaia, KBE
Tavare, Sir John, Kt., CBE
Tavener, *Prof.* Sir John Kenneth, Kt.
Taylor, *Lt.-Gen.* Sir Allan Macnab, KBE, MC
Taylor, Sir (Arthur) Godfrey, Kt.
Taylor, Sir Cyril Julian Hebden, Kt.
Taylor, Sir Edward Macmillan (Teddy), Kt., MP
Taylor, *Rt. Revd* John Bernard, KCVO
Taylor, Sir John Lang, KCMG
Taylor, Sir Nicholas Richard Stuart, Bt. (1917)
Taylor, *Prof.* Sir William, Kt., CBE
Teagle, *Vice-Adm.* Sir Somerford Francis, KBE
Tebbit, Sir Donald Claude, GCMG
Telford, Sir Robert, Kt., CBE, FREng.
Temple, Sir Rawden John Afamado, Kt., CBE, QC
Temple, *Maj.* Sir Richard Anthony Purbeck, Bt., MC (1876)
Templeton, Sir John Marks, Kt.
Tenison, Sir Richard Hanbury-, KCVO
Tennant, Sir Anthony John, Kt.
Tennant, *Capt.* Sir Iain Mark, KT
Teo, Sir Fiatau Penitala, GCMG, GCVO, ISO, MBE
Terry, *Air Marshal* Sir Colin George, KBE, CB
Terry, Sir Michael Edward Stanley Imbert-, Bt. (1917)
Terry, *Air Chief Marshal* Sir Peter David George, GCB, AFC
Thatcher, Sir Denis, Bt., MBE, TD (1990)
Thesiger, Sir Wilfred Patrick, KBE, DSO
Thomas, Sir Derek Morison David, KCMG
Thomas, Sir (Godfrey) Michael (David), Bt. (1694)
Thomas, Sir Jeremy Cashel, KCMG
Thomas, Sir (John) Alan, Kt.
Thomas, Sir John Maldwyn, Kt.
Thomas, *Prof.* Sir John Meurig, Kt., FRS
Thomas, Sir Keith Vivian, Kt.
Thomas, Sir Quentin Jeremy, Kt., CB
Thomas, Sir Robert Evan, Kt.
Thomas, *Hon.* Sir Roger John Laugharne, Kt.
Thomas, *Hon.* Sir Swinton Barclay, Kt.
Thomas, Sir William James Cooper, Bt., TD (1919)
Thomas, Sir (William) Michael (Marsh), Bt. (1918)
Thompson, Sir Christopher Peile, Bt. (1890)
Thompson, Sir Clive Malcolm, Kt.
Thompson, Sir Donald, Kt.
Thompson, Sir Gilbert Williamson, Kt., OBE
Thompson, *Surgeon Vice-Adm.* Sir Godfrey James Milton-, KBE
Thompson, Sir (Humphrey) Simon Meysey-, Bt. (1874)
Thompson, *Prof.* Sir Michael Warwick, Kt., D.Sc
Thompson, Sir Nicholas Annesley, Bt. (1963)
Thompson, Sir Paul Anthony, Bt. (1963)
Thompson, Sir Peter Anthony, Kt.
Thompson, Sir Thomas d'Eyncourt John, Bt. (1806)
Thomson, Sir (Frederick Douglas) David, Bt. (1929)
Thomson, Sir John Adam, GCMG
Thomson, Sir John (Ian) Sutherland, KBE, CMG
Thomson, Sir Mark Wilfrid Home, Bt. (1925)
Thomson, Sir Thomas James, Kt., CBE, FRCP
Thorn, Sir John Samuel, Kt., OBE
Thorne, Sir Neil Gordon, Kt., OBE, TD
Thorne, Sir Peter Francis, KCVO, CBE
Thornton, Sir (George) Malcolm, Kt.
Thornton, Sir Peter Eustace, KCB
Thornton, Sir Richard Eustace, KCVO, OBE
†Thorold, Sir (Anthony) Oliver, Bt. (1642)
Thorpe, *Hon.* Sir Mathew Alexander, Kt.
Thouron, Sir John Rupert Hunt, KBE
Thwaites, Sir Bryan, Kt., Ph.D.
Tibbits, *Capt.* Sir David Stanley, Kt., DSC
Tickell, Sir Crispin Charles Cervantes, GCMG, KCVO
Tidbury, Sir Charles Henderson, Kt.
Tikaram, Sir Moti, KBE
Tilt, Sir Robin Richard, Kt.
Tims, Sir Michael David, KCVO
Tindle, Sir Ray Stanley, Kt., CBE
Tippet, *Vice-Adm.* Sir Anthony Sanders, KCB
†Tipping, Sir David Gwynne Evans-, Bt. (1913)
Tirvengadum, Sir Harry Krishnan, Kt.
Titman, Sir John Edward Powis, KCVO
Tod, *Air Marshal* Sir John Hunter Hunter-, KBE, CB
Tod, *Vice-Adm.* Sir Jonathan James Richard, KCB, CBE
Todd, *Prof.* Sir David, Kt., CBE
Todd, Sir Ian Pelham, KBE, FRCS
Todd, *Hon.* Sir (Reginald Stephen) Garfield, Kt.
Tollemache, Sir Lyonel Humphry John, Bt. (1793)
Tololo, Sir Alkan, KBE
Tomkins, Sir Edward Emile, GCMG, CVO
Tomkys, Sir (William) Roger, KCMG
Tomlinson, *Prof.* Sir Bernard Evans, Kt., CBE
Tomlinson, *Hon.* Sir Stephen Miles, Kt.
Tooley, Sir John, Kt.
Tooth, Sir (Hugh) John Lucas-, Bt. (1920)
ToRobert, Sir Henry Thomas, KBE
Tory, Sir Geofroy William, KCMG
Touche, Sir Anthony George, Bt. (1920)
Touche, Sir Rodney Gordon, Bt. (1962)
Toulson, *Hon.* Sir Roger Grenfell, Kt.
Tovey, Sir Brian John Maynard, KCMG
ToVue, Sir Ronald, Kt., OBE
Towneley, Sir Simon Peter Edmund Cosmo William, KCVO
Townsend, Sir Cyril David, Kt.
Traill, Sir Alan Towers, GBE
Trant, *Gen.* Sir Richard Brooking, KCB

Treacher, *Adm.* Sir John Devereux, KCB
Trehane, Sir (Walter) Richard, Kt.
Treitel, *Prof.* Sir Guenter Heinz, Kt., FBA, QC
Trelawny, Sir John Barry Salusbury-, Bt. (1628)
Trench, Sir Peter Edward, Kt., CBE, TD
Trescowthick, Sir Donald Henry, KBE
†Trevelyan, Sir Edward (Norman), Bt. (1662)
Trevelyan, Sir Geoffrey Washington, Bt. (1874)
Trezise, Sir Kenneth Bruce, Kt., OBE
Trippier, Sir David Austin, Kt., RD
Tritton, Sir Anthony John Ernest, Bt. (1905)
Trollope, Sir Anthony Simon, Bt. (1642)
Trotter, Sir Neville Guthrie, Kt.
Trotter, Sir Ronald Ramsay, Kt.
Troubridge, Sir Thomas Richard, Bt. (1799)
Troup, *Vice-Adm.* Sir (John) Anthony (Rose), KCB, DSC
Trowbridge, *Rear-Adm.* Sir Richard John, KCVO
Truscott, Sir George James Irving, Bt. (1909)
Tsang, Sir Donald Yam-keun, KBE
Tuck, Sir Bruce Adolph Reginald, Bt. (1910)
Tucker, *Hon.* Sir Richard Howard, Kt.
Tuckey, *Hon.* Sir Simon Lane, Kt.
Tuita, Sir Mariano Kelesimalefo, Kt., OBE
Tuite, Sir Christopher Hugh, Bt., Ph.D. (1622)
Tuivaga, Sir Timoci Uluiburotu, Kt.
Tumim, *His Hon.* Sir Stephen, Kt.
Tupper, Sir Charles Hibbert, Bt. (1888)
Turbott, Sir Ian Graham, Kt., CMG, CVO
Turing, Sir John Dermot, Bt. (S. 1638)
Turnbull, Sir Andrew, KCB, CVO
Turner, Sir Colin William Carstairs, Kt., CBE, DFC
Turner, *Hon.* Sir Michael John, Kt.
Turnquest, Sir Orville Alton, GCMG, QC
Tuti, *Revd* Dudley, KBE
Tweedie, *Prof.* Sir David Philip, Kt.
Tyree, Sir (Alfred) William, Kt., OBE
Tyrwhitt, Sir Reginald Thomas Newman, Bt. (1919)
Unsworth, *Hon.* Sir Edgar Ignatius Godfrey, Kt., CMG
Unwin, Sir (James) Brian, KCB
Ure, Sir John Burns, KCMG, LVO
Urquhart, Sir Brian Edward, KCMG, MBE
Urwick, Sir Alan Bedford, KCVO, CMG
*Usher, Sir Andrew John, Bt. (1899)*
Usher, Sir Leonard Gray, KBE
Ustinov, Sir Peter Alexander, Kt., CBE
Utting, Sir William Benjamin, Kt., CB
Vai, Sir Mea, Kt., CBE, ISO
Vallance, Sir Iain David Thomas, Kt.
Vallat, Sir Francis Aimé, GBE, KCMG, QC
Vallings, *Vice-Adm.* Sir George Montague Francis, KCB
Vanderfelt, Sir Robin Victor, KBE
Vane, Sir John Robert, Kt., D.Phil., D.Sc., FRS
Vardy, Sir Peter, Kt.
Vasquez, Sir Alfred Joseph, Kt., CBE, QC
Vaughan, Sir Gerard Folliott, Kt., FRCP
Vavasour, Sir Eric Michael Joseph Marmaduke, Bt. (1828)
Veale, Sir Alan John Ralph, Kt., FREng.
Venner, Sir Kenneth Dwight Vincent, KBE
Vereker, Sir John Michael Medlicott, KCB
†Verney, Sir John Sebastian, Bt. (1946)
Verney, *Hon.* Sir Lawrence John, Kt., TD
Verney, Sir Ralph Bruce, Bt., KBE (1818)
Vernon, Sir James, Kt., CBE
Vernon, Sir Nigel John Douglas, Bt. (1914)
Vernon, Sir (William) Michael, Kt.
Vestey, Sir (John) Derek, Bt. (1921)
Vial, Sir Kenneth Harold, Kt., CBE
Vickers, *Lt.-Gen.* Sir Richard Maurice Hilton, KCB, CVO, OBE
Vincent, Sir William Percy Maxwell, Bt. (1936)
Vinelott, *Hon.* Sir John Evelyn, Kt.
Vines, Sir William Joshua, Kt., CMG
von Schramek, Sir Eric Emil, Kt.
†Vyvyan, Sir Ralph Ferrers Alexander, Bt. (1645)
Waddell, Sir James Henderson, Kt., CB
Wade, *Prof.* Sir Henry William Rawson, Kt., QC, FBA
Wade, *Air Chief Marshal* Sir Ruthven Lowry, KCB, DFC
Waine, *Rt. Revd* John, KCVO
Waite, *Rt. Hon.* Sir John Douglas, Kt.
Wake, Sir Hereward, Bt., MC (1621)
Wakefield, Sir (Edward) Humphry (Tyrell), Bt. (1962)
Wakefield, Sir Norman Edward, Kt.
Wakefield, Sir Peter George Arthur, KBE, CMG
Wakeford, *Air Marshal* Sir Richard Gordon, KCB, OBE, LVO, AFC
Wakeley, Sir John Cecil Nicholson, Bt., FRCS (1952)
†Wakeman, Sir Edward Offley Bertram, Bt. (1828)
Wales, Sir Robert Andrew, Kt.
Walford, Sir Christopher Rupert, Kt.
Walker, *Revd* Alan Edgar, Kt., OBE
Walker, *Gen.* Sir Antony Kenneth Frederick, KCB
Walker, Sir Baldwin Patrick, Bt. (1856)
Walker, Sir (Charles) Michael, GCMG
Walker, Sir David Alan, Kt.
Walker, Sir Harold Berners, KCMG
Walker, *Maj.* Sir Hugh Ronald, Bt. (1906)
Walker, Sir James Graham, Kt., MBE
Walker, Sir James Heron, Bt. (1868)
Walker, Sir John Ernest, Kt., D.Phil., FRS
Walker, *Air Marshal* Sir John Robert, KCB, CBE, AFC
Walker, *Gen.* Sir Michael John Dawson, GCB, CMG, CBE
Walker, Sir Michael Leolin Forestier-, Bt. (1835)
Walker, Sir Miles Rawstron, Kt., CBE
Walker, Sir Patrick Jeremy, KCB
Walker, *Rt. Hon.* Sir Robert, Kt.
Walker, Sir Rodney Myerscough, Kt.
Walker, *Hon.* Sir Timothy Edward, Kt.
Wall, Sir John Anthony, Kt., CBE
Wall, Sir (John) Stephen, KCMG, LVO
Wall, *Hon.* Sir Nicholas Peter Rathbone, Kt.
Wall, Sir Robert William, Kt., OBE
Wallace, *Lt.-Gen.* Sir Christopher Brooke Quentin, KBE
Wallace, Sir Ian James, Kt., CBE
Waller, *Hon.* Sir (George) Mark, Kt.
Waller, Sir Robert William, Bt. (I. 1780)
Walley, Sir John, KBE, CB
Wallis, Sir Peter Gordon, KCVO
Wallis, Sir Timothy William, Kt.
Walmsley, *Vice-Adm.* Sir Robert, KCB
Walsh, *Prof.* Sir John Patrick, KBE
†Walsham, Sir Timothy John, Bt. (1831)
Walters, *Prof.* Sir Alan Arthur, Kt.
Walters, Sir Dennis Murray, Kt., MBE
Walters, Sir Frederick Donald, Kt.
Walters, Sir Peter Ingram, Kt.
Walters, Sir Roger Talbot, KBE, FRIBA
Wamiri, Sir Akapite, KBE
Wan, Sir Wamp, Kt., MBE
Wanstall, *Hon.* Sir Charles Gray, Kt.
Ward, *Rt. Hon.* Sir Alan Hylton, Kt.
Ward, Sir John Devereux, Kt., CBE
Ward, Sir Joseph James Laffey, Bt. (1911)
Ward, *Maj.-Gen.* Sir Philip John Newling, KCVO, CBE
Ward, *Rt. Rev.* Simon Barrington-, KCMG
Ward, Sir Timothy James, Kt.
Wardale, Sir Geoffrey Charles, KCB
Wardlaw, Sir Henry (John), Bt. (S. 1631)
Waring, Sir (Alfred) Holburt, Bt. (1935)
Warmington, Sir David Marshall, Bt. (1908)
Warner, Sir (Edward Courtenay) Henry, Bt. (1910)
Warner, Sir Edward Redston, KCMG, OBE
Warner, *Prof.* Sir Frederick Edward, Kt., FRS, FREng.
Warner, Sir Gerald Chierici, KCMG

Warner, *Hon.* Sir Jean-Pierre Frank Eugene, Kt.
Warren, Sir (Frederick) Miles, KBE
Warren, Sir Kenneth Robin, Kt.
Warren, Sir Michael Blackley, Bt. (1784)
Wass, Sir Douglas William Gretton, GCB
Waterhouse, *Hon.* Sir Ronald Gough, Kt.
Waterlow, Sir Christopher Rupert, Bt. (1873)
Waterlow, Sir (James) Gerard, Bt. (1930)
Waters, *Gen.* Sir (Charles) John, GCB, CBE
Waters, Sir (Thomas) Neil (Morris), Kt.
Wates, Sir Christopher Stephen, Kt.
Watkins, *Rt. Hon.* Sir Tasker, VC, GBE
Watson, Sir Andrew Michael Milne-, Bt. (1937)
Watson, Sir Bruce Dunstan, Kt.
Watson, *Prof.* Sir David John, Kt., Ph.D.
Watson, Sir (James) Andrew, Bt. (1866)
Watson, Sir John Forbes Inglefield-, Bt. (1895)
Watson, *Vice-Adm.* Sir Philip Alexander, KBE, LVO
Watson, Sir Ronald Matthew, Kt., CBE
Watt, *Surgeon Vice-Adm.* Sir James, KBE, FRCS
Watt, Sir James Harvie-, Bt. (1945)
Watts, Sir John Augustus Fitzroy, KCMG, CBE
Watts, Sir Arthur Desmond, KCMG
Watts, *Lt.-Gen.* Sir John Peter Barry Condliffe, KBE, CB, MC
Wauchope, Sir Roger (Hamilton) Don-, Bt. (S. 1667)
Weatherall, *Prof.* Sir David John, Kt., FRS
Weatherall, *Vice-Adm.* Sir James Lamb, KCVO, KBE
Weatherstone, Sir Dennis, KBE
Webb, *Prof.* Sir Adrian Leonard, Kt.
Webb, Sir Thomas Langley, Kt.
Webster, *Very Revd* Alan Brunskill, KCVO
Webster, *Vice-Adm.* Sir John Morrison, KCB
Webster, *Hon.* Sir Peter Edlin, Kt.
Wedderburn, Sir Andrew John Alexander Ogilvy-, Bt. (1803)
Wedgwood, Sir (Hugo) Martin, Bt. (1942)
Weekes, Sir Everton DeCourcey, KCMG, OBE
Weinberg, Sir Mark Aubrey, Kt.
Weir, Sir Michael Scott, KCMG
Weir, Sir Roderick Bignell, Kt.
Welby, Sir (Richard) Bruno Gregory, Bt. (1801)
Welch, Sir John Kemp-, Kt.
Welch, Sir John Reader, Bt. (1957)
Weldon, Sir Anthony William, Bt. (I. 1723)
Weller, Sir Arthur Burton, Kt., CBE
Wellings, Sir Jack Alfred, Kt., CBE
†Wells, Sir Christopher Charles, Bt. (1944)
Wells, Sir John Julius, Kt.
Wells, Sir William Henry Weston, Kt., FRICS
West, *Vice-Adm.* Sir Alan William John, KCB
Westbrook, Sir Neil Gowanloch, Kt., CBE
Westerman, Sir (Wilfred) Alan, Kt., CBE
Weston, Sir Michael Charles Swift, KCMG, CVO
Weston, Sir (Philip) John, KCMG
Whalen, Sir Geoffrey Henry, Kt., CBE
Wheeler, Sir Harry Anthony, Kt., OBE
Wheeler, *Air Chief Marshal* Sir (Henry) Neil (George), GCB, CBE, DSO, DFC, AFC
Wheeler, *Rt. Hon.* Sir John Daniel, Kt.
Wheeler, Sir John Hieron, Bt. (1920)
Wheeler, *Gen.* Sir Roger Neil, GCB, CBE
Wheler, Sir Edward Woodford, Bt. (1660)
Whent, Sir Gerald Arthur, Kt., CBE
Whishaw, Sir Charles Percival Law, Kt.
Whitaker, Sir John James Ingham (Jack), Bt. (1936)
White, *Prof.* Sir Christopher John, Kt., CVO
White, Sir Christopher Robert Meadows, Bt. (1937)
White, *Hon.* Sir Christopher Stuart Stuart-, Kt.
White, Sir David Harry, Kt.
White, Sir Frank John, Kt.
White, Sir George Stanley James, Bt. (1904)
White, *Wg Cdr.* Sir Henry Arthur Dalrymple-, Bt., DFC (1926)
White, *Adm.* Sir Hugo Moresby, GCB, CBE
White, *Hon.* Sir John Charles, Kt., MBE
White, Sir John Albert
White, Sir John Woolmer, Bt. (1922)
White, Sir Lynton Stuart, Kt., MBE, TD
White, Sir Nicholas Peter Archibald, Bt. (1802)
White, *Adm.* Sir Peter, GBE
Whitehead, Sir John Stainton, GCMG, CVO
Whitehead, Sir Rowland John Rathbone, Bt. (1889)
Whiteley, Sir Hugo Baldwin Huntington-, Bt. (1918)
Whiteley, *Gen.* Sir Peter John Frederick, GCB, OBE, RM
Whitfield, Sir William, Kt., CBE
Whitford, *Hon.* Sir John Norman Keates, Kt.
Whitmore, Sir Clive Anthony, GCB, CVO
Whitmore, Sir John Henry Douglas, Bt. (1954)
Whitney, Sir Raymond William, Kt., OBE, MP
Wickerson, Sir John Michael, Kt.
Wicks, Sir Nigel Leonard, GCB, CVO, CBE
†Wigan, Sir Michael Iain, Bt. (1898)
Wiggin, Sir Alfred William (Jerry), Kt., TD
†Wiggin, Sir Charles Rupert John, Bt. (1892)
Wigram, *Maj.* Sir Edward Robert Woolmore, Bt. (1805)
Wignall, Sir Trevor Charles, Kt.
Wilbraham, Sir Richard Baker, Bt. (1776)
Wilford, Sir (Kenneth) Michael, GCMG
Wilkes, *Prof.* Sir Maurice Vincent, Kt.
Wilkes, *Gen.* Sir Michael John, KCB, CBE
Wilkins, Sir Graham John, Kt.
Wilkinson, Sir (David) Graham (Brook) Bt. (1941)
Wilkinson, *Prof.* Sir Denys Haigh, Kt., FRS
Wilkinson, Sir Philip William, Kt.
Willcocks, Sir David Valentine, Kt., CBE, MC
Willcocks, *Lt.-Gen.* Sir Michael Alan, Kt., CB
Williams, Sir Alastair Edgcumbe James Dudley-, Bt. (1964)
Williams, Sir Alwyn, Kt., Ph.D., FRS, FRSE
Williams, Sir Arthur Dennis Pitt, Kt.
Williams, Sir (Arthur) Gareth Ludovic Emrys Rhys, Bt. (1918)
Williams, *Prof.* Sir Bernard Arthur Owen, Kt., FBA
Williams, *Prof.* Sir Bruce Rodda, KBE
Williams, Sir Charles Othniel, Kt.
Williams, Sir Daniel Charles, GCMG, QC
Williams, *Adm.* Sir David, GCB
Williams, *Prof.* Sir David Glyndwr Tudor, Kt.
Williams, Sir David Innes, Kt.
Williams, Sir David Reeve, Kt., CBE
Williams, *Hon.* Sir Denys Ambrose, KCMG
Williams, Sir Donald Mark, Bt. (1866)
Williams, *Prof.* Sir (Edward) Dillwyn, Kt., FRCP
Williams, *Hon.* Sir Edward Stratten, KCMG, KBE
Williams, Sir Francis Owen Garbett, Kt., CBE
Williams, *Prof.* Sir Glanmor, Kt., CBE, FBA
Williams, Sir Henry Sydney, Kt., OBE
Williams, Sir (John) Kyffin, Kt., OBE, DL, RA
Williams, Sir (Lawrence) Hugh, Bt. (1798)
Williams, Sir Leonard, KBE, CB
Williams, Sir Osmond, Bt., MC (1909)
Williams, Sir Peter Michael, Kt.
Williams, *Prof.* Sir Robert Evan Owen, Kt., MD, FRCP

Williams, Sir (Robert) Philip Nathaniel, Bt. (1915)
Williams, Sir Robin Philip, Bt. (1953)
Williams, Sir (William) Maxwell (Harries), Kt.
Williamson, *Marshal of the Royal Air Force* Sir Keith Alec, GCB, AFC
Williamson, Sir Robert Brian, Kt., CBE
Willink, Sir Charles William, Bt. (1957)
Willis, *Vice-Adm.* Sir (Guido) James, KBE
Willis, *Air Chief Marshal* Sir John Frederick, GBE, KCB
Willison, *Lt.-Gen.* Sir David John, KCB, OBE, MC
Willison, Sir John Alexander, Kt., OBE
Wills, Sir David James Vernon, Bt. (1923)
Wills, Sir David Seton, Bt. (1904)
Wilmot, Sir Henry Robert, Bt. (1759)
Wilmot, Sir Michael John Assheton Eardley-, Bt. (1821)
Wilsey, *Gen.* Sir John Finlay Willasey, GCB, CBE
Wilshaw, Sir Michael, Kt.
Wilson, *Prof.* Sir Alan Geoffrey, Kt.
Wilson, *Lt.-Gen.* Sir (Alexander) James, KBE, MC
Wilson, Sir Anthony, Kt.
Wilson, *Vice-Adm.* Sir Barry Nigel, KCB
Wilson, *Lt.-Col.* Sir Blair Aubyn Stewart-, KCVO
Wilson, Sir Charles Haynes, Kt.
Wilson, *Prof.* Sir Colin Alexander St John, Kt., RA, FRIBA
Wilson, Sir David, Bt. (1920)
Wilson, Sir David Mackenzie, Kt.
Wilson, Sir Geoffrey Masterman, KCB, CMG
Wilson, Sir James William Douglas, Bt. (1906)
Wilson, *Brig.* Sir Mathew John Anthony, Bt., OBE, MC (1874)
Wilson, *Hon.* Sir Nicholas Allan Roy, Kt.
Wilson, Sir Patrick Michael Ernest David McNair-, Kt.
Wilson, Sir Richard Thomas James, KCB, GCB
Wilson, Sir Robert, Kt., CBE
Wilson, *Rt. Revd* Roger Plumpton, KCVO, DD
Wilson, Sir Robert Peter, KCMG
Wilson, *Air Chief Marshal* Sir (Ronald) Andrew (Fellowes), KCB, AFC
Wilson, *Hon.* Sir Ronald Darling, KBE, CMG
Wilton, Sir (Arthur) John, KCMG, KCVO, MC
Wingate, *Capt.* Sir Miles Buckley, KCVO
Winkley, Sir David Ross, Kt.
Winnington, Sir Francis Salwey William, Bt. (1755)
Winskill, *Air Cdre* Sir Archibald Little, KCVO, CBE, DFC
Winterbottom, Sir Walter, Kt., CBE
Wisdom, Sir Norman, Kt., OBE
Wiseman, Sir John William, Bt. (1628)
Wolfendale, *Prof.* Sir Arnold Whittaker, Kt., FRS
Wolfson, Sir Brian Gordon, Kt.
Wolseley, Sir Charles Garnet Richard Mark, Bt. (1628)
†Wolseley, Sir James Douglas, Bt. (I. 1745)
Wolstenholme, Sir Gordon Ethelbert Ward, Kt., OBE
Wombwell, Sir George Philip Frederick, Bt. (1778)
Womersley, Sir Peter John Walter, Bt. (1945)
Woo, Sir Leo Joseph, Kt.
Woo, Sir Po-Shing, Kt.
Wood, Sir Alan Marshall Muir, Kt., FRS, FREng.
Wood, Sir Andrew Marley, GCMG
Wood, Sir Anthony John Page, Bt. (1837)
Wood, Sir David Basil Hill-, Bt. (1921)
Wood, Sir Frederick Ambrose Stuart, Kt.
Wood, Sir Ian Clark, Kt., CBE
Wood, *Prof.* Sir John Crossley, Kt., CBE
Wood, *Hon.* Sir John Kember, Kt., MC
Wood, Sir Martin Francis, Kt., OBE
Wood, Sir Russell Dillon, KCVO, VRD
Wood, Sir William Alan, KCVO, CB
Woodard, *Rear Adm.* Sir Robert Nathaniel, KCVO
Woodcock, Sir John, Kt., CBE, QPM
Woodhead, *Vice-Adm.* Sir (Anthony) Peter, KCB
Woodhouse, *Rt. Hon.* Sir (Arthur) Owen, KBE, DSC
Wooding, Sir Norman Samuel, Kt., CBE
Woodroffe, *Most Revd* George Cuthbert Manning, KBE
Woodroofe, Sir Ernest George, Kt., Ph.D.
Woods, Sir Colin Philip Joseph, KCVO, CBE
Woods, Sir Robert Kynnersley, Kt., CBE
Woodward, *Hon.* Sir (Albert) Edward, Kt., OBE
Woodward, *Adm.* Sir John Forster, GBE, KCB
Worsley, *Gen.* Sir Richard Edward, GCB, OBE
Worsley, Sir (William) Marcus (John), Bt. (1838)
Worsthorne, Sir Peregrine Gerard, Kt.
Wratten, *Air Chief Marshal* Sir William John, GBE, CB, AFC
Wraxall, Sir Charles Frederick Lascelles, Bt. (1813)
Wrey, Sir George Richard Bourchier Bt. (1628)
Wrigglesworth, Sir Ian William, Kt.
Wright, Sir Allan Frederick, KBE
Wright, Sir David John, KCMG, LVO
Wright, Sir Denis Arthur Hepworth GCMG
Wright, Sir Edward Maitland, Kt., D.Phil., LL D, D.Sc., FRSE
Wright, *Hon.* Sir (John) Michael, Kt.
Wright, Sir (John) Oliver, GCMG, GCVO, DSC
Wright, Sir Paul Hervé Giraud, KCMG, OBE
Wright, Sir Peter Robert, Kt., CBE
Wright, Sir Richard Michael Cory-, Bt. (1903)
Wrightson, Sir Charles Mark Garmondsway, Bt. (1900)
Wrigley, *Prof.* Sir Edward Anthony (Sir Tony), Kt., Ph.D., PBA
Wu, Sir Gordon Ying Sheung, KCMG
Wynn, Sir David Watkin Williams-, Bt. (1688)
Yacoub, *Prof.* Sir Magdi Habib, Kt., FRCS
Yaki, Sir Roy, KBE
Yang, *Hon.* Sir Ti Liang, Kt.
Yapp, Sir Stanley Graham, Kt.
Yardley, Sir David Charles Miller, Kt., LL D
Yarranton, Sir Peter George, Kt.
Yarrow, Sir Eric Grant, Bt., MBE (1916)
Yellowlees, Sir Henry, KCB
Yocklunn, Sir John (Soong Chung), KCVO
Yoo Foo, Sir (François) Henri, Kt.
Young, Sir Brian Walter Mark, Kt.
Young, Sir Colville Norbert, GCMG, MBE
Young, Sir Dennis Charles, KCMG
Young, *Rt. Hon.* Sir George Samuel Knatchbull, Bt., MP (1813)
Young, *Hon.* Sir Harold William, KCMG
Young, Sir John Kenyon Roe, Bt. (1821)
Young, *Hon.* Sir John McIntosh, KCMG
Young, Sir John Robertson, KCMG
Young, Sir Leslie Clarence, Kt., CBE
Young, Sir Nicholas Charles, Kt.
Young, Sir Richard Dilworth, Kt.
Young, Sir Roger William, Kt.
Young, Sir Stephen Stewart Templeton, Bt. (1945)
Young, Sir William Neil, Bt. (1769)
Younger, *Maj.-Gen.* Sir John William, Bt., CBE (1911)
Yuwi, Sir Matiabe, KBE
Zeeman, *Prof.* Sir (Erik) Christopher, Kt., FRS
Zissman, Sir Bernard Philip, Kt.
Zochonis, Sir John Basil, Kt.
Zoleveke, Sir Gideon Pitabose, KBE
Zunz, Sir Gerhard Jacob (Jack), Kt., FREng.
Zurenuoc, Sir Zibang, KBE

# Dames Grand Cross and Dames Commanders

*tyle*, 'Dame' before forename and surname, followed by ppropriate post-nominal initials. Where such an award is nade to a lady already in enjoyment of a higher title, the ppropriate initials follow her name
*Iusband*, Untitled
or forms of address, *see* page 135

Dame Grand Cross and Dame Commander are the higher lasses for women of the Order of the Bath, the Order of St Michael and St George, the Royal Victorian Order, and the Order of the British Empire. Dames Grand Cross rank after the wives of Baronets and before the wives of Knights Grand Cross. Dames Commanders rank after the wives of Knights Grand Cross and before the wives of Knights Commanders.

Honorary Dames Commanders may be conferred on women who are citizens of countries of which The Queen is not head of state.

---

LIST OF DAMES
*evised to 31 August 2001*

---

Vomen peers in their own right and fe peers are not included in this list. emale members of the royal family re not included in this list; details of ne orders they hold are given on ages 117–8

If a dame has a double barrelled or yphenated surname, she is listed nder the final element of the name

*I full entry in italic type* indicates that he recipient of an honour died during he year in which the honour was onferred. The name is included for he purposes of record

Abaijah, Dame Josephine, DBE
Abel Smith, Lady, DCVO
Abergavenny, The Marchioness of, DCVO
Airlie, The Countess of, DCVO
Albemarle, The Countess of, DBE
Albon, Dame Yvonne Jeanne, DBE
Allen, *Prof.* Dame Ingrid Victoria, DBE, CBE, DL
Anderson, *Brig. Hon.* Dame Mary Mackenzie (Mrs Pihl), DBE
Andrews, Dame Julie, DBE
Anglesey, The Marchioness of, DBE
Anson, Lady (Elizabeth Audrey), DBE
Anstee, Dame Margaret Joan, DCMG
Arden, *Hon.* Dame Mary Howarth (Mrs Mance), DBE
Bainbridge, Dame Beryl, DBE
Baker, Dame Janet Abbott (Mrs Shelley), CH, DBE
Ballin, Dame Reubina Ann, DBE
Barletta, Dame Nelia, DBE
Barrow, Dame Jocelyn Anita (Mrs Downer), DBE
Barstow, Dame Josephine Clare (Mrs Anderson), DBE
Basset, Lady Elizabeth, DCVO
Bassey, Dame Shirley, DBE
Bean, Dame Majorie Louise, DBE
Beaurepaire, Dame Beryl Edith, DBE
Beer, *Prof.* Dame Gillian Patricia Kempster, DBE, FBA
Bergquist, *Prof.* Dame Patricia Rose, DBE
Berry, Dame Alice Miriam, DBE
Bewley, Dame Beulah Rosemary, DBE
Black, *Hon.* Dame Jill Margaret, DBE
Blaize, Dame Venetia Ursula, DBE
Blaxland, Dame Helen Frances, DBE
Booth, *Hon.* Dame Margaret Myfanwy Wood, DBE
Bowman, Dame (Mary) Elaine Kellett-, DBE
Bowtell, Dame Ann Elizabeth, DCB
Boyd, Dame Vivienne Myra, DBE
Bracewell, *Hon.* Dame Joyanne Winifred (Mrs Copeland), DBE
Brain, Dame Margaret Anne (Mrs Wheeler), DBE
Brazill, Dame Josephine (Sister Mary Philippa), DBE
Bridges, Dame Mary Patricia, DBE
Browne, Lady Moyra Blanche Madeleine, DBE
Bryans, Dame Anne Margaret, DBE
Buttfield, Dame Nancy Eileen, DBE
Byatt, Dame Antonia Susan, DBE, FRSL
Bynoe, Dame Hilda Louisa, DBE
Caldicott, Dame Fiona, DBE, FRCP, FRCPsych.
Cartwright, Dame Silvia Rose, DBE
Casey, Dame Stella Katherine, DBE
Charles, Dame (Mary) Eugenia, DBE
Chesterton, Dame Elizabeth Ursula, DBE
Clark, *Prof.* Dame Jill MacLeod, DBE
Clark, *Prof.* Dame (Margaret) June, DBE, Ph.D.
Collins, Dame Diana Clavering, DBE
Clay, Dame Marie Mildred, DBE
Clayton, Dame Barbara Evelyn (Mrs Klyne), DBE
Cleland, Dame Rachel, DBE
Coll, Dame Elizabeth Anne Loosemore Esteve-, DBE
Collarbone, Dame Patricia, DBE
Corsar, The Hon. Dame Mary Drummond, DBE
Davies, Dame Audrey Joan, DBE
Davies, Dame Wendy Patricia, DBE
Davis, Dame Karlene Cecile, DBE
Daws, Dame Joyce Margaretta, DBE
Cates, Dame Emma De-, DBE
Dell, Dame Miriam Patricia, DBE
Dench, Dame Judith Olivia (Mrs Williams), DBE
Descartes, Dame Marie Selipha Sesenne, BEM
Devonshire, The Duchess of, DCVO
Digby, Lady, DBE
Donaldson, Dame (Dorothy) Mary (Lady Donaldson of Lymington), GBE
Duffield, Dame Vivien Louise, DBE, CBE
Dugdale, Kathryn, Lady, DCVO
Dumont, Dame Ivy Leona, DCMG
Dyche, Dame Rachael Mary, DBE
Ebsworth, *Hon.* Dame Ann Marian, DBE
Ellison, Dame Jill, DBE
Else, Dame Jean, DBE
Engel, Dame Pauline Frances (Sister Pauline Engel), DBE
Evans, Dame Anne Elizabeth Jane, DBE
Evans, Dame Lois Marie Browne-, DBE
Evans, Dame Hilda Mary, DBE, BEM
Evison, Dame Helen June Patricia, DBE
Fenner, Dame Peggy Edith, DBE
Fielding, Dame Pauline, DBE
Fitton, Dame Doris Alice (Mrs Mason), DBE
Fort, Dame Maeve Geraldine, DCMG, DCVO
Fraser, Dame Dorothy Rita, DBE
Friend, Dame Phyllis Muriel, DBE
Fritchie, Dame Irene Tordoff (Dame Rennie Fritchie), DBE
Frost, Dame Phyllis Irene, DBE
Fry, Dame Margaret Louise, DBE
Gallagher, Dame Monica Josephine, DBE
Gardiner, Dame Helen Louisa, DBE, MVO
Giles, *Air Comdt.* Dame Pauline (Mrs Parsons), DBE, RRC
Goltra, Dame Seipp, DBE
Goodman, Dame Barbara, DBE
Gordon, Dame Minita Elmira, GCMG, GCVO
Gow, Dame Jane Elizabeth (Mrs Whiteley), DBE
Grafton, The Duchess of, GCVO
Grant, Dame Mavis, DBE
Green, Dame Mary Georgina, DBE
Grey, Dame Beryl Elizabeth (Mrs Svenson), DBE
Grimthorpe, The Lady, DCVO
Guilfoyle, Dame Margaret Georgina Constance, DBE
Guthardt, *Revd Dr* Dame Phyllis Myra, DBE
Haig, Dame Mary Alison Glen-, DBE
Hale, *Hon.* Dame Brenda Marjorie (Mrs Farrand), DBE
Hallett, Dame Heather Carol, DBE, QC
Harper, Dame Elizabeth Margaret Way, DBE
Dames Grand Cross and Dame Commanders
Heilbron, *Hon.* Dame Rose, DBE
Herbison, Dame Jean Marjory, DBE, CMG
Hercus, *Hon.* Dame (Margaret) Ann, DCMG

Higgins, *Prof.* Dame Julia Stretton, DBE, CBE, FRS
Higgins, *Prof.* Dame Rosalyn, DBE, QC
Hill, *Air Cdre* Dame Felicity Barbara, DBE
Hiller, Dame Wendy (Mrs Gow), DBE
Hine, Dame Deirdre Joan, DBE, FRCP
Hird, Dame Thora (Mrs Scott), DBE
Hogg, *Hon.* Dame Mary Claire (Mrs Koops), DBE
Hollows, Dame Sharon, DBE
Hurley, *Prof.* Dame Rosalinde (Mrs Gortvai), DBE
Hussey, Lady Susan Katharine (Lady Hussey of North Bradley), DCVO
Imison, Dame Tamsyn, DBE
Isaacs, Dame Albertha Madeline, DBE
James, Dame Naomi Christine (Mrs Haythorne), DBE
Jenkins, Dame (Mary) Jennifer (Lady Jenkins of Hillhead), DBE
Jones, Dame Gwyneth (Mrs Haberfeld-Jones), DBE
Jones, Dame (Lilian) Pauline Neville-, DCMG
Keegan, Dame Geraldine Mary Marcella, DBE, OBE
Kekedo, Dame Rosalina Violet, DBE
Kelleher, Dame Joan, DBE
Kelly, Dame Lorna May Boreland, DBE
Kershaw, Dame Janet Elizabeth Murray (Dame Betty), DBE
Kettlewell, *Comdt.* Dame Marion Mildred, DBE
Kilpatrick, Dame Judith Ann Gladys, DBE
King, Dame Thea, DBE, OBE
Kirby, Dame Georgina Kamiria, DBE
Kirk, Dame (Lucy) Ruth, DBE
Kramer, *Prof.* Dame Leonie Judith, DBE
Laine, Dame Cleo (Clementine) Dinah (Mrs Dankworth), DBE
Lamb, Dame Dawn Ruth, DBE
Lewis, Dame Edna Leofrida (Lady Lewis), DBE
Litchfield, Dame Ruby Beatrice, DBE
Lott, Dame Felicity Ann Emwhyla (Mrs Woolf), DBE
Louisy, Dame (Calliopa) Pearlette, DBE, GCSL, GCMG
Lowrey, *Air Comdt.* Dame Alice, DBE, RRC
Lympany, Dame Moura, DBE
Lynn, Dame Vera (Mrs Lewis), DBE
Mackinnon, Dame (Una) Patricia, DBE
McKechnie, Dame Sheila Marshall, DBE, OBE
McLaren, Dame Anne Laura, DBE, FRCOG, FRS
Macmillan of Ovenden, Katharine, Viscountess, DBE
Major, Dame Malvina Lorraine (Mrs Fleming), DBE
Major, Dame Norma Christina Elizabeth, DBE
Markova, Dame Alicia, DBE
Metcalf, Dame Helen, DBE
Metge, *Dr* Dame (Alice) Joan, DBE
Middleton, Dame Elaine Madoline, DCMG, MBE
Miller, Dame Mary Elizabeth Hedley-, DCVO, CB
Mills, Dame Barbara Jean Lyon, DBE, QC
Mitchell, Dame Mona, DCVO
Moores, Dame Yvonne, DBE
Morrison, *Hon.* Dame Mary Anne, DCVO
Mueller, Dame Anne Elisabeth, DCB
Muirhead, Dame Lorna Elizabeth Fox, DBE
Muldoon, Thea Dale, Lady, DBE, QSO
Mumford, Lady Mary Katharine, DCVO
Munro, Dame Alison, DBE
Murdoch, Dame Elisabeth Joy, DBE
Murray, Dame (Alice) Rosemary, DBE, D.Phil.
Ogilvie, Dame Bridget Margaret, DBE, Ph.D., D.Sc.
Oliver, Dame Gillian Frances, DBE
Ollerenshaw, Dame Kathleen Mary, DBE, D.Phil.
Oxenbury, Dame Shirley Anne, DBE
Park, Dame Merle Florence (Mrs Bloch), DBE
Paterson, Dame Betty Fraser Ross, DBE
Peake, *Air Cdre* Dame Felicity Hyde, DBE, AE
Penhaligon, Dame Annette (Mrs Egerton), DBE
Peters, Dame Mary Elizabeth, DBE, CBE
Poole, Dame Avril Anne Barker, DBE
Porter, Dame Shirley (Lady Porter), DBE
Powell, Dame Sally Ann Vickers, DBE
Prendergast, Dame Simone Ruth, DBE
Prentice, Dame Winifred Eva, DBE
Preston, Dame Frances Olivia Campbell-, DCVO
Price, Dame Margaret Berenice, DBE
Purves, Dame Daphne Helen, DBE
Pyke, Lady, DBE
Quinn, Dame Sheila Margaret Imelda, DBE
Rafferty, *Hon.* Anne Judith, DBE
Rankin, Lady Jean Margaret Florence, DCVO
Rees, *Prof.* Dame Lesley Howard, DBE
Reeves, Dame Helen May, DBE
Richardson, Dame Mary, DBE
Riddelsdell, Dame Mildred, DCB, CBE
Ridley, Dame (Mildred) Betty, DBE
Ridsdale, Dame Victoire Evelyn Patricia (Lady Ridsdale), DBE
Rigg, Dame Diana, DBE
Rimington, Dame Stella, DCB
Robertson, *Cmdt.* Dame Nancy Margaret, DBE
Robottom, Dame Marlene, DBE
Roe, Dame Raigh Edith, DBE
Rothschild, Hon. Dame Miriam Louisa, DBE, FRS
Rue, Dame (Elsie) Rosemary, DBE
Rumbold, *Rt. Hon.* Dame Angela Claire Rosemary, DBE
Runciman of Doxford, The Viscountess, DBE
Salas, Dame Margaret Laurence, DBE
Salmond, *Prof.* Dame Mary Anne, DBE
Saunders, Dame Cicely Mary Strode, OM, DBE, FRCP
Sawyer, *Hon.* Dame Joan Augusta, DBE
Schwarzkopf, Dame Elisabeth Friederike Marie Olga Legge-, DBE
Scott, Barbara, DBE
Scott, Dame Jean Mary Monica Maxwell-, DCVO
Seward, Dame Margaret Helen Elizabeth, DBE
Shenfield, Dame Barbara Estelle, DBE
Sherlock, *Prof.* Dame Sheila Patricia Violet, DBE, MD, FRCP
Shirley, Dame Stephanie, DBE
Shovelton, Dame Helena, DBE
Sibley, Dame Antoinette (Mrs Corbett), DBE
Sloss, *Rt. Hon.* Dame (Ann) Elizabeth (Oldfield) Butler-, DBE
Smieton, Dame Mary Guillan, DBE
Smith, Dame Dela, DBE
Smith, *Hon.* Dame Janet Hilary (Mrs Mathieson), DBE
Smith, Dame Margaret Natalie (Maggie) (Mrs Cross), DBE
Smith, Dame Margot, DBE
Smyth, Dame Frances Mary, DBE
Soames, Mary, Lady, DBE
Southgate, Prof. Dame Lesley Jill, DBE
Spark, Dame Muriel Sarah, DBE
Spencer, Dame Rosemary Jane, DCMG
Steel, *Hon.* Dame (Anne) Heather (Mrs Beattie), DBE
Stephens, *Air Cmdt.* Dame Anne, DBE
Stewart, Dame Muriel Acadia, DBE
Strachan, Dame Valerie Patricia Marie, DCB
Strathern, *Prof.* Dame Anne Marilyn, DBE
Sutherland, Dame Joan (Mrs Bonynge), OM, DBE
Sutherland, Dame Veronica Evelyn, DBE, CMG
Szaszy, Dame Miraka Petricevich, DBE
Taylor, Dame Elizabeth, DBE
Taylor, Dame Jean Elizabeth, DCVO
Te Atairangikaahu, Te Arikinui, Dame, DBE
Te Kanawa, Dame Kiri Janette, DBE
Thomas, Dame Maureen Elizabeth (Lady Thomas), DBE
Thorneycroft, Carla, Lady, DBE
Tinson, Dame Sue, DBE
Tizard, Dame Catherine Anne, GCMG, GCVO, DBE
Tokiel, Dame Rosa, DBE
Trotter, Dame Janet Olive, DBE
Uprichard, Dame Mary Elizabeth, DBE
Varley, Dame Joan Fleetwood, DBE
Wagner, Dame Gillian Mary Millicent (Lady Wagner), DBE
Wall, (Alice) Anne, (Mrs Michael Wall), DCVO
Warburton, Dame Anne Marion, DCVO, CMG
Warwick, Dame Margaret Elizabeth Harvey Turner-, DBE, FRCP, FRCPEd.
Waterhouse, Dame Rachel Elizabeth, DBE, Ph.D.
Webb, Prof. Dame Patricia, DBE
Weir, Dame Gillian Constance (Mrs Phelps), DBE
Weston, Dame Margaret Kate, DBE
Williamson, Dame (Elsie) Marjorie, DBE, Ph.D.
Winstone, Dame Dorothy Gertrude, DBE, CMG
Wong Yick-ming, Dame Rosanna, DBE
Wright, Dame Clarice Betty, DBE
Wright, Dame Gail, DBE

# Decorations and Medals

## PRINCIPAL DECORATIONS AND MEDALS
*In order of precedence*

VICTORIA CROSS (VC), 1856 (*see* page 208)
GEORGE CROSS (GC), 1940 (*see* pages 208–9)

BRITISH ORDERS OF KNIGHTHOOD AND DISTINGUISHED SERVICE ORDER.

*Baronet's Badge*
*Knight Bachelor's Badge*

DECORATIONS

*Conspicuous Gallantry Cross* (CGC), 1995
*Royal Red Cross* Class I (RRC), 1883
*Distinguished Service Cross* (DSC), 1914. For all ranks for actions at sea
*Military Cross* (MC), December 1914. For all ranks for actions on land
*Distinguished Flying Cross* (DFC), 1918. For all ranks for acts of gallantry when flying in active operations against the enemy
*Air Force Cross* (AFC), 1918. For all ranks for acts of courage when flying, although not in active operations against the enemy
*Royal Red Cross* Class II (ARRC)
*Order of British India*
*Kaisar-i-Hind Medal*
*Order of St John*

MEDALS FOR GALLANTRY AND DISTINGUISHED CONDUCT

*Union of South Africa Queen's Medal for Bravery*, in Gold
*Distinguished Conduct Medal* (DCM), 1854
*Conspicuous Gallantry Medal* (CGM), 1874
*Conspicuous Gallantry Medal (Flying)*
*George Medal* (GM), 1940
*Queen's Police Medal for Gallantry*
*Queen's Fire Service Medal for Gallantry*
*Royal West African Frontier Force Distinguished Conduct Medal*
*King's African Rifles Distinguished Conduct Medal*
*Indian Distinguished Service Medal*
*Union of South Africa Queen's Medal for Bravery*, in Silver
*Distinguished Service Medal* (DSM), 1914
*Military Medal* (MM), 1916
*Distinguished Flying Medal* (DFM), 1918
*Air Force Medal* (AFM)
*Constabulary Medal (Ireland)*
*Medal for Saving Life at Sea*
*Sea Gallantry Medal*
*Indian Order of Merit* (Civil)
*Indian Police Medal for Gallantry*
*Ceylon Police Medal for Gallantry*
*Sierra Leone Police Medal for Gallantry*
*Sierra Leone Fire Brigades Medal for Gallantry*
*Colonial Police Medal for Gallantry* (CPM)
*Queen's Gallantry Medal* (QGM), 1974
*Royal Victorian Medal* (RVM), Gold, Silver and Bronze
*British Empire Medal* (BEM), (formerly the Medal of the Order of the British Empire, for Meritorious Service; also includes the Medal of the Order awarded before 29 December 1922)
*Canada Medal*
*Queen's Police* (QPM) *and Queen's Fire Service Medals* (QFSM) *for Distinguished Service*
*Queen's Volunteer Reserves Medal*
*Queen's Medal for Chiefs*

WAR MEDALS AND STARS (in order of date)

Polar Medals (in order of date)

POLICE MEDALS FOR VALUABLE SERVICE

JUBILEE, CORONATION AND DURBAR MEDALS

*King George V, King George VI and Queen Elizabeth II Long and Faithful Service Medals*

EFFICIENCY AND LONG SERVICE DECORATIONS AND MEDALS

*Medal for Meritorious Service*
*Accumulated Campaign Service Medal*
*The Medal for Long Service and Good Conduct* (Military)
*Naval Long Service and Good Conduct Medal*
*Royal Marines Meritorious Service Medal*
*Royal Air Force Meritorious Service Medal*
*Royal Air Force Long Service and Good Conduct Medal*
*Medal for Long Service and Good Conduct (Ulster Defence Regiment)*
*Police Long Service and Good Conduct Medal*
*Fire Brigade Long Service and Good Conduct Medal*
*Colonial Police and Fire Brigades Long Service Medals*
*Colonial Prison Service Medal*
*Hong Kong Disciplined Services Medal*
*Army Emergency Reserve Decoration* (ERD), 1952
*Volunteer Officers' Decoration* (VD)
*Volunteer Long Service Medal*
*Volunteer Officers' Decoration* for India and the Colonies
*Volunteer Long Service Medal* for India and the Colonies
*Colonial Auxiliary Forces Officers' Decoration*
*Colonial Auxiliary Forces Long Service Medal*
*Medal for Good Shooting* (Naval)
*Militia Long Service Medal*
*Imperial Yeomanry Long Service Medal*
*Territorial Decoration* (TD), 1908
*Efficiency Decoration* (ED)
*Territorial Efficiency Medal*
*Efficiency Medal*
*Special Reserve Long Service and Good Conduct Medal*
*Decoration for Officers, Royal Navy Reserve* (RD), 1910
*Decoration for Officers*, RNVR (VRD)
*Royal Naval Reserve Long Service and Good Conduct Medal*
*RNVR Long Service and Good Conduct Medal*
*Royal Naval Auxiliary Sick Berth Reserve Long Service and Good Conduct Medal*
*Royal Fleet Reserve Long Service and Good Conduct Medal*
*Royal Naval Wireless Auxiliary Reserve Long Service and Good Conduct Medal*
*Air Efficiency Award* (AE), 1942
*Volunteer Reserves Service Medal*
*Ulster Defence Regiment Medal*
*Northern Ireland Home Service Medal*
*The Queen's Medal*. For champion shots in the RN, RM, RNZN, Army, RAF
*Cadet Forces Medal*, 1950
*Coastguard Auxiliary Service Long Service Medal* (formerly Coast Life Saving Corps Long Service Medal)
*Special Constabulary Long Service Medal*
*Royal Observer Corps Medal*
*Civil Defence Long Service Medal*

*Ambulance Service (Emergency Duties) Long Service and Good Conduct Medal*
*Royal Fleet Auxiliary Service Medal*
*Rhodesia Medal*
*Royal Ulster Constabulary Service Medal*
*Northern Ireland Prison Service Medal*
*Service Medal of the Order of St John*
*Badge of the Order of the League of Mercy*
*Voluntary Medical Service Medal*, 1932
*Women's Voluntary Service Medal*
*Colonial Special Constabulary Medal*

FOREIGN ORDERS, DECORATIONS AND MEDALS (IN ORDER OF DATE)

## THE VICTORIA CROSS (1856)

FOR CONSPICUOUS BRAVERY

VC

*Ribbon*, Crimson, for all Services (until 1918 it was blue for the Royal Navy)

Instituted on 29 January 1856, the Victoria Cross was awarded retrospectively to 1854, the first being held by Lt. C. D. Lucas, RN, for bravery in the Baltic Sea on 21 June 1854 (gazetted 24 February 1857). The first 62 Crosses were presented by Queen Victoria in Hyde Park, London, on 26 June 1857.

The Victoria Cross is worn before all other decorations, on the left breast, and consists of a cross-pattée of bronze, one and a half inches in diameter, with the Royal Crown surmounted by a lion in the centre, and beneath there is the inscription *For Valour*. Holders of the VC receive a tax-free annuity of £1,300, irrespective of need or other conditions. In 1911, the right to receive the Cross was extended to Indian soldiers, and in 1920 to matrons, sisters and nurses, and the staff of the Nursing Services and other services pertaining to hospitals and nursing, and to civilians of either sex regularly or temporarily under the orders, direction or supervision of the naval, military, or air forces of the Crown.

SURVIVING RECIPIENTS OF THE VICTORIA CROSS

*as at 31 August 2001*

Annand, *Capt.* R. W. (Durham Light Infantry)
1940 *World War*
Bhan Bhagta Gurung, *Havildar* (2nd Gurkha Rifles)
1945 *World War*
Bhandari Ram, *Capt.* (10th Baluch Regiment)
1944 *World War*
Chapman, *Sgt.* E. T., BEM (Monmouthshire Regiment)
1945 *World War*
Cruickshank, *Flt. Lt.* J. A. (RAFVR)
1944 *World War*
Cutler, *Capt.* Sir Roden, AK, KCMG, KCVO, CBE (Australian Military Forces, 2/5th Field Artillery)
1941 *World War*
Fraser, *Lt.-Cdr.* I. E., DSC (RNR)
1945 *World War*
Gardner, *Capt.* P. J., MC (Royal Tank Regiment)
1941 *World War*
Gould, *Lt.* T. W. (RN)
1942 *World War*
Kenna, *Pte.* E. (Australian Military Forces, 2/4th (NSW))
1945 *World War*
Lachhiman Gurung, *Havildar* (8th Gurkha Rifles)
1945 *World War*
Norton, *Capt.* G. R., MM (South African Forces, Kaffrarian Rifles)
1944 *World War*
Payne, *WO* K., DSC (USA) (Australian Army Training Team)
1969 *Vietnam*
Rambahadur Limbu, *Capt.*, MVO (10th Princess Mary's Gurkha Rifles)
1965 *Sarawak*
Reid, *Flt. Lt.* W. (RAFVR)
1943 *World War*
Smith, *Sgt.* E. A., CD (Seaforth Highlanders of Canada)
1944 *World War*
Speakman-Pitts, *Sgt.* W. (Black Watch, attached KOSB)
1951 *Korea*
Tulbahadur Pun, *Lt.* (6th Gurkha Rifles)
1944 *World War*
Umrao Singh, *Sub Major* (Royal Indian Artillery)
1944 *World War*
Watkins, *Maj. Rt. Hon.* Sir Tasker, GBE (Welch Regiment)
1944 *World War*
Wilson, *Lt.-Col.* E. C. T. (East Surrey Regiment)
1940 *World War*

## THE GEORGE CROSS (1940)

FOR GALLANTRY

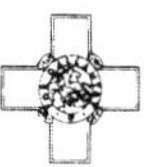

GC

*Ribbon*, Dark blue, threaded through a bar adorned with laurel leaves

Instituted 24 September 1940 (with amendments, 3 November 1942)

The George Cross is worn before all other decorations (except the VC) on the left breast (when worn by a woman it may be worn on the left shoulder from a ribbon of the same width and colour fashioned into a bow). It consists of a plain silver cross with four equal limbs, the cross having in the centre a circular medallion bearing a design showing St George and the Dragon. The inscription *For Gallantry* appears round the medallion and in the angle of each limb of the cross is the Royal cypher 'G VI' forming a circle concentric with the medallion. The reverse is plain and bears the name of the recipient and the date of the award. The cross is suspended by a ring from a bar adorned with laurel leaves on dark blue ribbon one and a half inches wide.

The cross is intended primarily for civilians; awards to the fighting services are confined to actions for which purely military honours are not normally granted. It is awarded only for acts of the greatest heroism or of the most conspicuous courage in circumstances of extreme danger. From 1 April 1965, holders of the Cross have received a tax-free annuity, which is now £1,300. The cross has twice been awarded collectively rather than to an individual: to Malta (1942) and the Royal Ulster Constabulary (1999).

The royal warrant which ordained that the grant of the Empire Gallantry Medal should cease authorised holders of that medal to return it to the Central Chancery of the Orders of Knighthood and to receive in exchange the George Cross. A similar provision applied to posthumous awards of the Empire Gallantry Medal made after the outbreak of war in 1939. In October 1971 all surviving holders of the Albert Medal and the Edward Medal exchanged those decorations for the George Cross.

### Surviving Recipients of the George Cross

*as at 31 August 2001*

If the recipient originally received the Empire Gallantry Medal (EGM), the Albert Medal (AM) or the Edward Medal (EM), this is indicated by the initials in parenthesis.

Archer, *Col.* B. S. T., GC, OBE, ERD, 1941
Bamford, J., GC, 1952
Beaton, J., GC, CVO, 1974
Bridge, *Lt.-Cdr.* J., GC, GM and Bar, 1944
Butson, *Lt.-Col.* A. R. C., GC, CD, MD (AM), 1948
Bywater, R. A. S., GC, GM, 1944
Errington, H., GC, 1941
Farrow, K., GC (AM), 1948
Flintoff, H. H., GC (EM), 1944
Gledhill, A. J., GC, 1967
Gregson, J. S., GC (AM), 1943
Hawkins, E., GC (AM), 1943
Johnson, *WO1 (SSM)* B., GC, 1990
Kinne, D. G., GC, 1954
Lowe, A. R., GC (AM), 1949
Lynch, J., GC, BEM (AM), 1948
Moore, R. V., GC, CBE, 1940
Naughton, F., GC (EGM), 1937
Pratt, M. K., GC, 1978
Purves, Mrs M., GC (AM), 1949
Raweng, Awang anak, GC, 1951
Riley, G., GC (AM), 1944
Rowlands, *Air Marshal* Sir John, GC, KBE, 1943
Sinclair, *Air Vice-Marshal* Sir Laurence, GC, KCB, CBE, DSO, 1941
Stevens, H. W., GC, 1958
Styles, *Lt.-Col.* S. G., GC, 1972
Walker, C., GC, 1972
Walker, C. H., GC (AM), 1942
Walton, E. W. K., GC (AM), DSO, 1948
Wilcox, C., GC (EM), 1949
Wiltshire, S. N., GC (EGM), 1930
Wooding, E. A., GC (AM), 1945

# Chiefs of Clans and Names in Scotland

Only chiefs of whole Names or Clans are included, except certain special instances (marked *) who, though not chiefs of a whole name, were or are for some reason (e.g. the Macdonald forfeiture) independent. Under decision (*Campbell-Gray*, 1950) that a bearer of a 'double or triple-barrelled' surname cannot be held chief of a part of such, several others cannot be included in the list at present.

THE ROYAL HOUSE: HM The Queen

AGNEW: Sir Crispin Agnew of Lochnaw, Bt., QC, 6 Palmerston Road, Edinburgh EH9 1TN

ANSTRUTHER: Sir Ralph Anstruther of that Ilk, Bt., GCVO, MC, Balcaskie, Pittenweem, Fife KY10 2RD

ARBUTHNOTT: The Viscount of Arbuthnott, KT, CBE, DSC, Arbuthnott House, Laurencekirk, Kincardineshire AB30 1PA

BARCLAY: Peter C. Barclay of Towie Barclay and of that Ilk, 69 Oakwood Court, W14 8JF

BORTHWICK: The Lord Borthwick, Crookston, Heriot, Midlothian EH38 5YS

BOYD: The Lord Kilmarnock, 194 Regent's Park Road, London NW1 8XP

BOYLE: The Earl of Glasgow, Kelburn, Fairlie, Ayrshire KA29 0BE

BRODIE: Ninian Brodie of Brodie, Brodie Castle, Forres, Morayshire IV36 0TE

BRUCE: The Earl of Elgin and Kincardine, KT, Broomhall, Dunfermline, Fife KY11 3DU

BUCHAN: David S. Buchan of Auchmacoy, Auchmacoy House, Ellon, Aberdeenshire

BURNETT: J. C. A. Burnett of Leys, Crathes Castle, Banchory, Kincardineshire

CAMERON: Sir Donald Cameron of Lochiel, KT, CVO, TD, Achnacarry, Spean Bridge, Inverness-shire

CAMPBELL: The Duke of Argyll, Inveraray, Argyll PA32 8XF

CARMICHAEL: Richard J. Carmichael of Carmichael, Carmichael, Thankerton, Biggar, Lanarkshire

CARNEGIE: The Duke of Fife, Elsick House, Stonehaven, Kincardineshire AB3 2NT

CATHCART: The Earl Cathcart, 14 Smith Terrace, SW3 4DL

CHARTERIS: The Earl of Wemyss and March, KT, Gosford House, Longniddry, East Lothian EH32 0PX

CLAN CHATTAN: M. K. Mackintosh of Clan Chattan, Maxwell Park, Gwelo, Zimbabwe

CHISHOLM: Hamish Chisholm of Chisholm (*The Chisholm*), Elmpine, Beck Row, Bury St Edmunds, Suffolk

COCHRANE: The Earl of Dundonald, Lochnell Castle, Ledaig, Argyllshire

COLQUHOUN: Sir Ivar Colquhoun of Luss, Bt., Camstraddan, Luss, Dunbartonshire G83 8NX

CRANSTOUN: David A. S. Cranstoun of that Ilk, Corehouse, Lanark

CRICHTON: vacant

CUMMING: Sir William Cumming of Altyre, Bt., Altyre, Forres, Moray

DARROCH: Capt. Duncan Darroch of Gourock, The Red House, Branksome Park Road, Camberley, Surrey

DAVIDSON: Alister G. Davidson of Davidston, 21 Winscombe Street, Takapuna, Auckland, New Zealand

DEWAR: Michael Dewar of that Ilk and Vogrie, Rectory Farm House, Charleton Musgrove, Wincanton, Somerset BA9 8ET

DRUMMOND: The Earl of Perth, PC, Stobhall, Perth PH2 6DR

DUNBAR: Sir James Dunbar of Mochrum, Bt., 211 Gardenville Drive, Yorktown, Va 23693, USA

DUNDAS: David D. Dundas of Dundas, 8 Derna Road, Kenwyn 7700, South Africa

DURIE: Andrew Durie of Durie, CBE, Finnich Malise, Croftamie, Stirlingshire G63 0HA

ELIOTT: Mrs Margaret Eliott of Redheugh, Redheugh, Newcastleton, Roxburghshire

ERSKINE: The Earl of Mar and Kellie, Erskine House, Kirk Wynd, Alloa, Clackmannan FK10 4JF

FARQUHARSON: Capt. A. Farquharson of Invercauld, MC, Invercauld, Braemar, Aberdeenshire AB35 5TT

FERGUSSON: Sir Charles Fergusson of Kilkerran, Bt., Kilkerran, Maybole, Ayrshire

FORBES: The Lord Forbes, KBE, Balforbes, Alford, Aberdeenshire AB33 8DR

FORSYTH: Alistair Forsyth of that Ilk, Ethie Castle, by Arbroath, Angus DD11 5SP

FRASER: The Lady Saltoun, Inverey House, Braemar, Aberdeenshire AB35 5YB

* FRASER (OF LOVAT): The Lord Lovat, Beaufort Lodge, Beauly, Inverness-shire IV4 7AZ

GAYRE: R. Gayre of Gayre and Nigg, Minard Castle, Minard, Inverary, Argyll PA32 8YB

GORDON: The Marquess of Huntly, Aboyne Castle, Aberdeenshire AB34 5JP

GRAHAM: The Duke of Montrose, Buchanan Auld House, Drymen, Stirlingshire

GRANT: The Lord Strathspey, The School House, Lochbuie, Mull, Argyllshire PA62 6AA

GRIERSON: Sir Michael Grierson of Lag, Bt., 40C Palace Road, London SW2 3NJ

HAIG: The Earl Haig, OBE, Bemersyde, Melrose, Roxburghshire TD6 9DP

HALDANE: Martin Haldane of Gleneagles, Gleneagles, Auchterarder, Perthshire

HANNAY: Ramsey Hannay of Kirkdale and of that Ilk, Cardoness House, Gatehouse-of-Fleet, Kirkcudbrightshire

HAY: The Earl of Erroll, Woodbury Hall, Sandy, Beds

HENDERSON: John Henderson of Fordell, 7 Owen Street, Toowoomba, Queensland, Australia

HUNTER: Pauline Hunter of Hunterston, Plovers Ridge, Lon Cecrist, Treaddur Bay, Holyhead, Gwynedd

IRVINE OF DRUM: David C. Irvine of Drum, Holly Leaf Cottage, Inchmarlo, Banchory, Aberdeenshire AB31 4BR

JARDINE: Sir Alexander Jardine of Applegirth, Bt., Ash House, Thwaites, Millom, Cumbria LA18 5HY

JOHNSTONE: The Earl of Annandale and Hartfell, Raehills, Lockerbie, Dumfriesshire

KEITH: The Earl of Kintore, The Stables, Keith Hall, Inverurie, Aberdeenshire AB51 0LD

KENNEDY: The Marquess of Ailsa, Cassillis House, Maybole, Ayrshire

KERR: The Marquess of Lothian, KCVO, Ferniehurst Castle, Jedburgh, Roxburghshire TN8 6NX

KINCAID: Arabella Kincaid of Stoneyeld, Downton Kincaid, Ludlow, Shropshire

LAMONT: Peter N. Lamont of that Ilk, 209 Bungarribee Road, Blacktown, Australia

LEASK: Madam Leask of Leask, 1 Vincent Road, Sheringham, Norfolk

LENNOX: Edward J. H. Lennox of that Ilk, Tods Top Farm, Downton on the Rock, Ludlow, Shropshire

LESLIE: The Earl of Rothes, Tanglewood, West Tytherley, Salisbury, Wilts SP5 1LX

LINDSAY: The Earl of Crawford and Balcarres, KT, PC, Balcarres, Colinsburgh, Fife

LOCKHART: Angus H. Lockhart of the Lee, Newholme, Dunsyre, Lanark

LUMSDEN: Gillem Lumsden of that Ilk and Blanerne, Stapely Howe, Hoe Benham, Newbury, Berks
MACALESTER: William St J. S. McAlester of Loup and Kennox, Dun Skeig, 27 Durnham Road, Burton, Christchurch, Dorset BH23 7ND
MCBAIN: J. H. McBain of McBain, 7025 North Finger Rock Place, Tucson, Arizona, USA
MACDONALD: The Lord Macdonald (*The Macdonald of Macdonald*), Kinloch Lodge, Sleat, Isle of Skye
*MACDONALD OF CLANRANALD: Ranald A. Macdonald of Clanranald, Mornish House, Killin, Perthshire FK21 8TX
*MACDONALD OF SLEAT (CLAN HUSTEAIN): Sir Ian Macdonald of Sleat, Bt., Thorpe Hall, Rudston, Driffield, N. Humberside YO25 0JE
*MACDONELL OF GLENGARRY: Ranald MacDonell of Glengarry, Elonbank, Castle Street, Fortrose, Ross-shire IV10 8TH
MACDOUGALL: vacant
MACDOWALL: Fergus D. H. Macdowall of Garthland, 16 Rowe Road, Ottawa, Ontario K29 2ZS
MACGREGOR: Brig. Sir Gregor MacGregor of MacGregor, Bt., Bannatyne, Newtyle, Blairgowrie, Perthshire PH12 8TR
MACINTYRE: James W. MacIntyre of Glenoe, 15301 Pine Orchard Drive, Apartment 3H, Silver Spring, Maryland, USA
MACKAY: The Lord Reay, 98 Oakley Street, London SW3
MACKENZIE: The Earl of Cromartie, Castle Leod, Strathpeffer, Ross-shire IV14 9AA
MACKINNON: Madam Anne Mackinnon of Mackinnon, 16 Purleigh Road, Bridgwater, Somerset
MACKINTOSH: *The Mackintosh of Mackintosh*, Moy Hall, Inverness IV13 7YQ
MACLAREN: Donald MacLaren of MacLaren and Achleskine, Achleskine, Kirkton, Balquhidder, Lochearnhead
MACLEAN: The Hon. Sir Lachlan Maclean of Duart, Bt., CVO, Arngask House, Glenfarg, Perthshire PH2 9QA
MACLENNAN: Ruaraidh MacLennan of MacLennan, Oldmill, Dores, Inverness-shire IV2 6R
MACLEOD: John MacLeod of MacLeod, Dunvegan Castle, Isle of Skye
MACMILLAN: George MacMillan of MacMillan, Finlaystone, Langbank, Renfrewshire
MACNAB: J. C. Macnab of Macnab (*The Macnab*), Leuchars Castle Farmhouse, Leuchars, Fife KY16 0EY
MACNAGHTEN: Sir Patrick Macnaghten of Macnaghten and Dundarave, Bt., Dundarave, Bushmills, Co. Antrim
MACNEACAIL: Iain Macneacail of Macneacail and Scorrybreac, 12 Fox Street, Ballina, NSW, Australia
MACNEIL OF BARRA: Ian R. Macneil of Barra (*The Macneil of Barra*), 95/6 Grange Loan, Edinburgh
MACPHERSON: The Hon. Sir William Macpherson of Cluny, TD, Newtown Castle, Blairgowrie, Perthshire
MACTAVISH: E. S. Dugald MacTavish of Dunardry, 2519 Vivaldi Lane, Four Seasons Estates, Gambrills, MD21 054, USA
MACTHOMAS: Andrew P. C. MacThomas of Finegand, c/o Roslin Cottage, Pitmedden, Aberdeenshire AB41 7NY
MAITLAND: The Earl of Lauderdale, 12 St Vincent Street, Edinburgh
MAKGILL: The Viscount of Oxfuird, Kenback, Stoke, Nr Andover, Hampshire SP11 0NP
MALCOLM (MACCALLUM): Robin N. L. Malcolm of Poltalloch, Duntrune Castle, Lochgilphead, Argyll
MAR: The Countess of Mar, St Michael's Farm, Great Witley, Worcs WR6 6JB
MARJORIBANKS: Andrew Marjoribanks of that Ilk, 10 Newark Street, Greenock
MATHESON: Maj. Sir Fergus Matheson of Matheson, Bt., Old Rectory, Hedenham, Bungay, Suffolk NR35 2LD
MENZIES: David R. Menzies of Menzies, Wester Auchnagallin Farmhouse, Braes of Castle Grant, Grantown on Spey PH26 3PL
MOFFAT: Madam Moffat of that Ilk, St Jasual, Bullocks Farm Lane, Wheeler End Common, High Wycombe
MONCREIFFE: Peregrine Moncreiffe of Moncreiffe, Easter Moncreiffe, Bride of Earn, Perthshire
MONTGOMERIE: The Earl of Eglinton and Winton, Balhomie, Cargill, Perth PH2 6DS
MORRISON: Dr Iain M. Morrison of Ruchdi, Magnolia Cottage, The Street, Walberton, Sussex
MUNRO: Hector W. Munro of Foulis, Foulis Castle, Evanton, Ross-shire IV16 9UX
MURRAY: The Duke of Atholl, Blair Castle, Blair Atholl, Perthshire
NESBITT (or NISBET): Mark Nesbitt of that Ilk, 1 Pier Head, Wapping High Street, London E12 1PN
NICOLSON: The Lord Carnock, 90 Whitehall Court, London SW1A 2EL
OGILVY: The Earl of Airlie, KT, GCVO, PC, Cortachy Castle, Kirriemuir, Angus
RAMSAY: The Earl of Dalhousie, Brechin Castle, Brechin, Angus DD7 6SH
RATTRAY: James S. Rattray of Rattray, Craighall, Rattray, Perthshire
RIDDELL; Sir John Riddell of Riddell, CB. CVO, Hepple, Morpeth, Northumberland
ROBERTSON: Alexander G. H. Robertson of Struan (*Struan-Robertson*), The Breach Farm, Goudhurst Road, Cranbrook, Kent
ROLLO: The Lord Rollo, Pitcairns, Dunning, Perthshire
ROSE: Miss Elizabeth Rose of Kilravock, Kilravock Castle, Croy, Inverness
ROSS: David C. Ross of that Ilk and Balnagowan, Shandwick, Perth Road, Stanley, Perthshire
RUTHVEN: The Earl of Gowrie, PC, 34 King Street, Covent Garden, London WC2
SCOTT: The Duke of Buccleuch and Queensberry, KT, VRD, Bowhill, Selkirk
SCRYMGEOUR: The Earl of Dundee, Birkhill, Cupar, Fife
SEMPILL: The Lord Sempill, 3 Vanburgh Place, Edinburgh, EH6 8AE
SHAW: John Shaw of Tordarroch, East Craig an Ron, 22 Academy Mead, Fortrose IV10 8TW
SINCLAIR: The Earl of Caithness, 137 Claxton Grove, London W6 8HB
SKENE: Danus Skene of Skene, Nether Pitlour, Strathmiglo, Fife
STIRLING: Fraser J. Stirling of Cader, 44A Oakley Street, London SW3 5HA
STRANGE: Maj. Timothy Strange of Balcaskie, Little Holme, Porton Road, Amesbury, Wilts
SUTHERLAND: The Countess of Sutherland, House of Tongue, Brora, Sutherland
SWINTON: John Swinton of that Ilk, 123 Superior Avenue SW, Calgary, Alberta, Canada
TROTTER: Alexander Trotter of Mortonhall, Charterhall, Duns, Berwickshire
URQUHART: Kenneth T. Urquhart of Urquhart, 507 Jefferson Park Avenue, Jefferson, New Orleans, La. 70121, USA
WALLACE: Ian F. Wallace of that Ilk, 5 Lennox Street, Edinburgh EH4 1QB
WEDDERBURN OF THAT ILK: The Master of Dundee, Birkhill, Cupar, Fife
WEMYSS: David Wemyss of that Ilk, Invermay, Forteviot, Perthshire

# The Privy Council

The Sovereign in Council, or Privy Council, was the chief source of executive power until the system of Cabinet government developed in the 18th century. Now the Privy Council's main functions are to advise the Sovereign and to exercise its own statutory responsibilities independent of the Sovereign in Council (*see also* page 215).

Membership of the Privy Council is automatic upon appointment to certain government and judicial positions in the United Kingdom, e.g. Cabinet ministers must be Privy Counsellors and are sworn in on first assuming office. Membership is also accorded by The Queen to eminent people in the UK and independent countries of the Commonwealth of which Her Majesty is Queen, on the recommendation of the British Prime Minister. Membership of the Council is retained for life, except for very occasional removals.

The administrative functions of the Privy Council are carried out by the Privy Council Office (*see* page 354) under the direction of the President of the Council, who is always a member of the Cabinet.

*President of the Council*, The Rt. Hon. Robin Cook, MP
*Clerk of the Council*, A. Galloway

MEMBERS *as at 31 August 2001*

HRH The Duke of Edinburgh, 1951
HRH The Prince of Wales, 1977

Aberdare, Lord, 1974
Ackner, Lord, 1980
Airlie, Earl of, 1984
Aldington, Lord, 1954
Aldous, Sir William, 1995
Alebua, Ezekiel, 1988
Alison, Michael, 1981
Ampthill, Lord, 1995
Ancram, Michael, 1996
Anderson, Donald, 2000
Anthony, Douglas, 1971
Arbuthnot, James, 1998
Archer of Sandwell, Lord, 1977
Arden, Dame Mary, 2000
Armstrong, Hilary, 1999
Arnold, Sir John, 1979
Arthur, Hon. Owen, 1995
Ashdown of Norton-sub-Hamdon, Lord, 1989
Ashley of Stoke, Lord, 1979
Atkins, Sir Robert, 1995
Auld, Sir Robin, 1995
Baker of Dorking, Lord, 1984
Barber, Lord, 1963
Barnett, Lord, 1975
Beckett, Margaret, 1993
Beith, Alan, 1992
Beldam, Sir Roy, 1989
Belstead, Lord, 1983
Benn, Anthony, 1964
Bennett, Sir Frederic, 1985
Biffen, Lord, 1979
Bingham of Cornhill, Lord, 1986
Birch, William, 1992
Bisson, Sir Gordon, 1987
Blackstone, Baroness, 2001
Blair, Tony, 1994
Blaker, Lord, 1983
Blanchard, Peter, 1998
Blatch, Baroness, 1993
Blunkett, David, 1997
Boateng, Paul, 1999
Bolger, James, 1991
Booth, Albert, 1976
Boothroyd, Baroness, 1992
Boscawen, Hon. Robert, 1992
Bottomley, Virginia, 1992
Boyd, Colin, 2000
Boyson, Sir Rhodes, 1987
Bradley, Keith, 2001
Brathwaite, Sir Nicholas, 1991
Bridge of Harwich, Lord, 1975
Brightman, Lord, 1979
Brittan of Spennithorne, Lord, 1981
Brook, Sir Henry, 1996
Brooke of Sutton Mandeville, Lord, 1988
Brown, Gordon, 1996
Brown, Nicholas, 1997
Brown, Sir Simon, 1992
Brown, Sir Stephen, 1983
Browne-Wilkinson, Lord, 1983
Butler, Sir Adam, 1984
Butler-Sloss, Dame Elizabeth, 1988
Buxton, Sir Richard, 1997
Byers, Stephen, 1998
Caborn, Richard, 1999
Caithness, Earl of, 1990
Callaghan of Cardiff, Lord, 1964
Cameron of Lochbroom, Lord, 1984
Camoys, Lord, 1997
Campbell of Croy, Lord, 1970
Campbell, Walter Menzies, 1999
Campbell, Sir William, 1999
Canterbury, The Archbishop of, 1991
Carlisle of Bucklow, Lord, 1979
Carr of Hadley, Lord, 1963
Carrington of Upton, Lord, 1959
Carswell, Sir Robert, 1993
Carter, Lord, 1997
Casey, Sir Maurice, 1986
Castle of Blackburn, Baroness, 1964
Chadwick, Sir John, 1997
Chalfont, Lord, 1964
Chalker of Wallasey, Baroness, 1987
Chan, Sir Julius, 1981
Chataway, Sir Christopher, 1970
Clark of Windermere, Lord, 1997
Clark, Helen, 1990
Clark of Kempston, Lord, 1990
Clarke, Sir Anthony, 1998
Clarke, Charles, 2001
Clarke, Kenneth, 1984
Clarke, Thomas, 1997
Clinton-Davis, Lord, 1998
Clyde, Lord, 1996
Cockfield, Lord, 1982
Colman, Fraser, 1986
Compton, Sir John, 1983
Concannon, John, 1978
Cook, Robin, 1996
Cooke of Thorndon, Lord, 1977
Cooper, Sir Frank, 1983
Cope of Berkeley, Lord, 1988
Corfield, Sir Frederick, 1970
Coulsfield, Lord, 2000
Cowen, Sir Zelman, 1981
Cradock, Sir Percy, 1993
Cranborne, Viscount, 1994
Crawford and Balcarres, Earl of, 1972
Creech, *Hon.* Wyatt, 1999
Crickhowell, Lord, 1979
Croom-Johnson, Sir David, 1984
Cullen, *Hon.* Lord, 1997
Cunningham, Jack, 1993
Curry, David, 1996
Darling, Alistair, 1997
Davies, Denzil, 1978
Davies, Ronald, 1997
Davis, David, 1997
Davis, Terence, 1999
Davison, Sir Ronald, 1978
Dean of Harptree, Lord, 1991
Dean of Thornton-le-Fylde, Baroness, 1998
Deedes, Lord, 1962
Denham, John, 2000
Denham, Lord, 1981
Devonshire, Duke of, 1964
Diamond, Lord, 1965
Dillon, Sir Brian, 1982
Dixon, Lord, 1996
Dobson, Frank, 1997
Donaldson of Lymington, Lord, 1979
Dorrell, Stephen, 1994
Douglas, Sir William, 1977
du Cann, Sir Edward, 1964
Dunn, Sir Robin, 1980
Dyson, Sir John, 2001
East, Paul, 1998
Eden of Winton, Lord, 1972
Eggar, Timothy, 1995
Eichelaum, Sir Thomas, 1989
Elias, *Hon.* Dame, Sian, 1999
Emery, Sir Peter, 1993
Emslie, Lord, 1972
Erroll of Hale, Lord, 1960
Esquivel, Manuel, 1986
Evans, Sir Anthony, 1992
Eveleigh, Sir Edward, 1977
Farquharson, Sir Donald, 1989
Fellowes, Lord, 1990
Ferrers, Earl, 1982
Field, Frank, 1997
Floissac, Sir Vincent, 1992
Foot, Michael, 1974
Forsyth of Drumlean, The Lord, 1995
Forth, Eric, 1997

Foster, Derek, 1993
Fowler, Lord, 1979
Fox, Sir Marcus, 1995
Fox, Sir Michael, 1981
Fraser, Malcolm, 1976
Fraser of Carmyllie, Lord, 1989
Freeman, John, 1966
Freeman, Lord, 1993
Freeson, Reginald, 1976
Garel-Jones, Lord, 1992
Gault, Thomas, 1992
George, Bruce, 2000
George, Sir Edward, 1999
Georges, Telford, 1986
Gibbs, Sir Harry, 1972
Gibson, Sir Peter, 1993
Gibson, Sir Ralph, 1985
Gibson-Watt, Lord, 1974
Gilbert, Lord, 1978
Gilmour of Craigmillar, Lord, 1973
Glenamara, Lord, 1964
Glidewell, Sir Iain, 1985
Goff of Chieveley, Lord, 1982
Goodlad, Sir Alastair, 1992
Gorton, Sir John, 1968
Gowrie, Earl of, 1984
Graham, Sir Douglas, 1998
Graham of Edmonton, Lord, 1998
Gray of Contin, Lord, 1982
Griffiths, Lord, 1980
Gummer, John, 1985
Habgood, Rt. Revd Lord, 1983
Hague, William, 1995
Hailsham of St Marylebone, Lord, 1956
Hain, Peter, 2001
Hale, Dame Brenda, 1999
Hamilton, Sir Archie, 1991
Hanley, Sir Jeremy, 1994
Hardie, Lord, 1997
Hardie Boys, Sir Michael, 1989
Harman, Harriet, 1997
Harrison, Walter, 1977
Haselhurst, Sir Alan, 1999
Hattersley, Lord, 1975
Hayhoe, Lord, 1985
Hayman, Baroness, 2000
Healey, Lord, 1964
Heath, Sir Edward, 1955
Heathcoat-Amory, David, 1996
Henry, Sir Denis, 1993
Henry, John, 1996
Heseltine, Lord, 1979
Heseltine, Sir William, 1986
Hesketh, Lord, 1991
Hewitt, Patricia, 2001
Higgins, Lord, 1979
Hirst, Sir David, 1992
Hobhouse, Sir John, 1993
Hoffmann, Lord, 1992
Hogg, Hon. Douglas, 1992
Holderness, Lord, 1959
Hollis of Heigham, Baroness, 1999
Holme of Cheltenham, Lord, 2000
Hoon, Geoffrey, 1999
Hope of Craighead, Lord, 1989
Hordern, Sir Peter, 1993
Howard, Michael, 1990
Howe of Aberavon, Lord, 1972
Howell of Guildford, Lord, 1979
Hunt, Jonathan, 1989
Hunt of Wirral, Lord, 1990
Hurd of Westwell, Lord, 1982
Hutchison, Sir Michael, 1995
Hutton, Lord, 1988
Hutton, John, 2001
Ingraham, Hubert, 1993
Ingram, Adam, 1998
Irvine of Lairg, Lord, 1997
Jack, Michael, 1997
Janvrin, Sir Robin, 1998
Jauncey of Tullichettle, Lord, 1988
Jay of Paddington, Baroness, 1998
Jellicoe, Earl, 1963
Jenkin of Roding, Lord, 1973
Jenkins of Hillhead, Lord, 1964
Jones, Aubrey, 1955
Jones, Lord, 1999
Jopling, Lord, 1979
Jowell, Tessa, 1998
Judge, Sir Igor, 1996
Jugnauth, Sir Anerood, 1987
Kaufman, Gerald, 1978
Kay, Sir John, 2000
Keene, Sir David, 2000
Keith, Sir Kenneth, 1998
Keith of Kinkel, Lord, 1976
Kelly, Sir Basil, 1984
Kelvedon, Lord, 1980
Kenilorea, Sir Peter, 1979
Kennedy, Charles, 1999
Kennedy, Sir Paul, 1992
Kerr, Sir Michael, 1981
King of Bridgwater, Lord, 1979
Kingsdown, Lord, 1987
Kingsland, Lord, 1994
Kinnock, Neil, 1983
Kirkwood, Lord, 2000
Knight, Gregory, 1995
Lamont of Lerwick, Lord, 1986
Lane, Lord, 1975
Lang of Monkton, Lord, 1990
Lange, David, 1984
Latasi, Kamuta, 1996
Latham, Sir David, 2000
Lauti, Sir Toaripi, 1979
Laws, Sir John, 1999
Lawson of Blaby, Lord, 1981
Lawton, Sir Frederick, 1972
Leggatt, Sir Andrew, 1990
Leonard, Rt. Revd Graham, 1981
Liddell, Mrs Helen, 1998
Lilley, Peter, 1990
Lloyd of Berwick, Lord, 1984
Lloyd, Sir Peter, 1994
London, The Bishop of, 1995
Longmore, Sir Andrew, 2001
Louisy, Allan, 1981
Luce of Adur, Lord, 1986
Lyell, Sir Nicholas, 1990
Mabon, Dickson, 1977
McCartney, Ian, 1999
McCollum, Sir Liam, 1997
McCowan, Sir Anthony, 1989
MacDermott, Sir John, 1987
Macdonald of Tradeston, Lord, 1999
MacGregor of Pulham Market, Lord, 1985
MacIntyre, Duncan, 1980
Mackay, Andrew, 1998
McKay, Ian, 1992
Mackay of Clashfern, Lord, 1979
Mackay of Drumadoon, Lord, 1996
McKinnon, Donald, 1992
Maclean, David, 1995
Maclean, Lord, 2001
McLeish, Henry, 2000
Maclennan of Rogart, Lord, 1997
McMullin, Sir Duncan, 1980
Major, John, 1987
Mance, Sir Jonathan, 1999
Mandelson, Peter, 1998
Mantell, Sir Charles, 1997
Mara, Ratu Sir Kamisese, 1973
Marnoch, Lord, 2001
Marsh, Lord, 1966
Martin, Michael, 2000
Mason of Barnsley, Lord, 1968
Maude, Hon. Francis, 1992
Mawhinney, Sir Brian, 1994
May, Sir Anthony, 1998
Mayhew of Twysden, Lord, 1986
Meacher, Michael, 1997
Megarry, Sir Robert, 1978
Mellor, David, 1990
Merlyn-Rees, Lord, 1974
Michael, Alun, 1998
Milburn, Alan, 1998
Millan, Bruce, 1975
Millett, Lord, 1994
Milligan, Lord, 2000
Mitchell, Sir James, 1985
Molyneaux of Killead, Lord, 1983
Monro of Langholm, Lord, 1995
Moore, Michael, 1990
Moore of Lower Marsh, Lord, 1986
Moore of Wolvercote, Lord, 1977
Morgan, Rhodri, 2000
Morris, Charles, 1978
Morris, Estelle, 1999
Morris of Aberavon, Lord, 1970
Morris of Manchester, Lord, 1979
Morritt, Sir Robert, 1994
Mowlam, Marjorie, 1997
Moyle, Roland, 1978
Mummery, Sir John, 1996
Murphy, Paul, 1998
Murray, *Hon.* Lord, 1974
Murray, Sir Donald, 1989
Murray of Epping Forest, Lord, 1976
Murton of Lindisfarne, Lord, 1976
Mustill, Lord, 1985
Nairne, Sir Patrick, 1982
Namaliu, Sir Rabbie, 1989
Naseby, Lord, 1994
Needham, Sir Richard, 1994
Neill, Sir Brian, 1985
Newton of Braintree, Lord, 1988
Nicholls of Birkenhead, Lord, 1995
Nicholson, Sir Michael, 1995
Nolan, Lord, 1991
Nott, Sir John, 1979
Nourse, Sir Martin, 1985
Oakes, Gordon, 1979
O'Connor, Sir Patrick, 1980
O'Donnell, Turlough, 1979
O'Flynn, Francis, 1987
Ogilvy, Sir Angus, 1997
Oliver of Aylmerton, Lord, 1980
Onslow of Woking, Lord, 1988
Oppenheim-Barnes, Baroness, 1979
Orme, Lord, 1974
Osbourne, Lord, 2001
Otton, Sir Philip, 1995
Owen, Lord, 1976
Paeniu, Bikenibeu, 1991
Palliser, Sir Michael, 1983
Palmer, Sir Geoffrey, 1986
Parker, Sir Jonathan, 2000
Parker, Sir Roger, 1983
Parkinson, Lord, 1981
Patten, Christopher, 1989
Patten, Lord, 1990

Patterson, Percival, 1993
Pattie, Sir Geoffrey, 1987
Pendry, Lord, 2000
Penrose, Lord, 2000
Perth, Earl of, 1957
Peters, Winston, 1998
Peyton of Yeovil, Lord, 1970
Phillips of Worth Matravers, Lord, 1995
Pill, Sir Malcolm, 1995
Pindling, Sir Lynden, 1976
Portillo, Michael, 1992
Potter, Sir Mark, 1996
Prentice, Lord, 1966
Prescott, John, 1994
Price, George, 1982
Prior, Lord, 1970
Prosser, Lord, 2000
Puapua, Sir Tomasi, 1982
Purchas, Sir Francis, 1982
Pym, Lord, 1970
Quin, Ms Joyce, 1998
Radice, Lord, 1999
Raison, Sir Timothy, 1982
Ramsden, James, 1963
Rawlinson of Ewell, Lord, 1964
Raynsford, Nick, 2001
Redwood, John, 1993
Rees, Lord, 1983
Reid, John, 1998
Renton, Lord, 1962
Renton of Mount Harry, Lord, 1989
Richard, Lord, 1993
Richardson, Sir Ivor, 1978
Richardson of Duntisbourne, Lord, 1976
Rifkind, Sir Malcolm, 1986
Roberts of Conwy, Lord, 1991
Robertson of Port Ellen, Lord, 1997
Roch, Sir John, 1993
Rodger of Earlsferry, Lord, 1992
Rodgers of Quarry Bank, Lord, 1975
Rooker of Perry Barr, Lord, 1999
Rose, Sir Christopher, 1992
Ross, *Hon.* Lord, 1985
Rumbold, Dame Angela, 1991
Russell, Sir Patrick, 1987
Ryder of Wensum, Lord, 1990
Sainsbury, Sir Timothy, 1992
St John of Fawsley, Lord, 1979
Sandiford, Erskine, 1989
Saville of Newdigate, Lord, 1994
Scarman, Lord, 1973
Schiemann, Sir Konrad, 1995
Scott, Sir Nicholas, 1989
Scott, Sir Richard, 1991
Seaga, Edward, 1981
Sedley, Sir Stephen, 1999
Selkirk of Douglas, Lord, 1996
Shawcross, Lord, 1946
Shearer, Hugh, 1969
Sheldon, Lord, 1977
Shephard, Gillian, 1992
Shipley, Jennifer, 1998
Shore of Stepney, Lord, 1967
Short, Clare, 1997
Simmonds, Kennedy, 1984
Simon of Glaisdale, Lord, 1961
Sinclair, Ian, 1977
Slade, Sir Christopher, 1982
Slynn of Hadley, Lord, 1992
Smith, Andrew, 1997
Smith, Christopher, 1997
Smith, Sir Geoffrey Johnson, 1996
Somare, Sir Michael, 1977
Somers, Sir Edward, 1981
Spellar, John, 2001
Stanley, Sir John, 1984
Staughton, Sir Christopher, 1988
Steel of Aikwood, Lord, 1977
Stephen, Sir Ninian, 1979
Stewartby, Lord, 1989
Steyn, Lord, 1992
Stodart of Leaston, Lord, 1974
Strang, Gavin, 1997
Strathclyde, Lord, 1995
Straw, Jack, 1997
Stuart-Smith, Sir Murray, 1988
Sutherland, Lord, 2000
Symons of Vernham Dean, Baroness, 2001
Talboys, Sir Brian, 1977
Taylor, Ann, 1997
Tebbit, Lord, 1981
Templeman, Lord, 1978
Thatcher, Baroness, 1970
Thomas, Edmund, 1996
Thomas of Gwydir, Lord, 1964
Thomas, Sir Swinton, 1994
Thomson of Monifieth, Lord, 1966
Thorpe, Jeremy, 1967
Thorpe, Sir Matthew, 1995
Tipping, Andrew, 1998
Tizard, Robert, 1986
Trefgarne, Lord, 1989
Trimble, David, 1997
Trumpington, Baroness, 1992
Tuckey, Sir Simon, 1998
Ullswater, Viscount, 1994
Upton, Simon, 1999
Varley, Lord, 1974
Waddington, Lord, 1987
Waite, Sir John, 1993
Wakeham, Lord, 1983
Waldegrave of North Hill, Lord, 1990
Walker of Doncaster, Lord, 1979
Walker of Worcester, Lord, 1970
Walker, Sir Robert, 1997
Wallace, James, 2000
Waller, Sir Mark, 1996
Ward, Sir Alan, 1995
Watkins, Sir Tasker, 1980
Weatherill, Lord, 1980
Wheeler, Sir John, 1993
Widdecombe, Ann, 1997
Wigley, Dafydd, 1997
Wilberforce, Lord, 1964
Williams, Alan, 1977
Williams of Crosby, Baroness, 1974
Williams of Mostyn, Lord
Windlesham, Lord, 1973
Winti, Paias, 1987
Withers, Reginald, 1977
Woolfe, Sir David, 2000
Woodhouse, Sir Owen, 1974
Woolf, Lord, 1986
Wylie, *Hon.* Lord, 1970
York, The Archbishop of, 1991
Young, Baroness, 1981
Young, Sir George, 1993
Young of Graffham, Lord, 1984
Younger of Leckie, Viscount, 1979
Zacca, Edward, 1992

# The Privy Council of Northern Ireland

The Privy Council of Northern Ireland had responsibilities in Northern Ireland similar to those of the Privy Council in Great Britain until the Northern Ireland Act 1974 instituted direct rule and a UK Cabinet minister became responsible for the functions previously exercised by the Northern Ireland government.

Membership of the Privy Council of Northern Ireland is retained for life. Since the Northern Ireland Constitution Act 1973 no further appointments have been made. The postnominal initials PC (NI) are used to differentiate its members from those of the Privy Council.

## MEMBERS *as at 31 August 2001*

Bailie, Robin, 1971
Bleakley, David, 1971
Craig, William, 1963
Dobson, John, 1969
Kelly, Sir Basil, 1969
Kirk, Herbert, 1962
Long, William, 1966
McConnell, The Lord, 1964
McIvor, Basil, 1971
Moyola, Lord, 1966
Neill, Sir Ivan, 1950
Porter, Sir Robert, 1969
Taylor, John, MP, 1970
West, Henry, 1960

# Parliament

The United Kingdom constitution is not contained in any single document but has evolved in the course of time, formed partly by statute, partly by common law and partly by convention. A constitutional monarchy, the United Kingdom is governed by Ministers of the Crown in the name of the Sovereign, who is head both of the state and of the government.

The organs of government are the legislature (Parliament), the executive and the judiciary. The executive consists of HM Government (Cabinet and other Ministers), government departments, local authorities (*see* Local Government and Government Departments and Public Offices). The judiciary (*see* Law Courts and Offices) pronounces on the law, both written and unwritten, interprets statutes and is responsible for the enforcement of the law; the judiciary is independent of both the legislature and the executive.

## THE MONARCHY

The Sovereign personifies the state and is, in law, an integral part of the legislature, head of the executive, head of the judiciary, commander-in-chief of all armed forces of the Crown and 'Supreme Governor' of the Church of England. The seat of the monarchy is in the United Kingdom. In the Channel Islands and the Isle of Man, which are Crown dependencies, the Sovereign is represented by a Lieutenant-Governor. In the member states of the Commonwealth of which the Sovereign is head of state, her representative is a Governor-General; in UK dependencies the Sovereign is usually represented by a Governor, who is responsible to the British Government.

Although in practice the powers of the monarchy are now very limited, restricted mainly to the advisory and ceremonial, there are important acts of government which require the participation of the Sovereign. These include summoning, proroguing and dissolving Parliament, giving royal assent to bills passed by Parliament, appointing important office-holders, e.g. government ministers, judges, bishops and governors, conferring peerages, knighthoods and other honours, and granting pardon to a person wrongly convicted of a crime. The Sovereign appoints the Prime Minister; by convention this office is held by the leader of the political party which enjoys, or can secure, a majority of votes in the House of Commons. In international affairs the Sovereign as head of state has the power to declare war and make peace, to recognise foreign states and governments, to conclude treaties and to annex or cede territory. However, as the Sovereign entrusts executive power to Ministers of the Crown and acts on the advice of her Ministers, which she cannot ignore, royal prerogative powers are in practice exercised by Ministers, who are responsible to Parliament.

Ministerial responsibility does not diminish the Sovereign's importance to the smooth working of government. She holds meetings of the Privy Council (*see* below), gives audiences to her Ministers and other officials at home and overseas, receives accounts of Cabinet decisions, reads dispatches and signs state papers; she must be informed and consulted on every aspect of national life; and she must show complete impartiality.

### COUNSELLORS OF STATE

In the event of the Sovereign's absence abroad, it is necessary to appoint Counsellors of State under letters patent to carry out the chief functions of the Monarch, including the holding of Privy Councils and giving royal assent to acts passed by Parliament. The normal procedure is to appoint as Counsellors three or four members of the royal family among those remaining in the UK.

In the event of the Sovereign on accession being under the age of 18 years, or at any time unavailable or incapacitated by infirmity of mind or body for the performance of the royal functions, provision is made for a regency.

## THE PRIVY COUNCIL

The Sovereign in Council, or Privy Council, was the chief source of executive power until the system of Cabinet government developed. Nowadays its main function is to advise the Sovereign to approve Orders in Council and to advise on the issue of royal proclamations. The Council's own statutory responsibilities (independent of the powers of the Sovereign in Council) include powers of supervision over the registering bodies for the medical and allied professions. A full Council is summoned only on the death of the Sovereign or when the Sovereign announces his or her intention to marry. (For full list of Counsellors, *see* The Privy Council section.)

There are a number of advisory Privy Council committees, whose meetings the Sovereign does not attend. Some are prerogative committees, such as those dealing with legislative matters submitted by the legislatures of the Channel Islands and the Isle of Man or with applications for charters of incorporation; and some are provided for by statute, e.g. those for the universities of Oxford and Cambridge and the Scottish universities.

The Judicial Committee of the Privy Council is the final court of appeal from courts of the UK dependencies, courts of independent Commonwealth countries which have retained the right of appeal, courts of the Channel Islands and the Isle of Man, some professional and disciplinary committees, and church sources. The Committee is composed of Privy Counsellors who hold, or have held, high judicial office, although usually only three or five hear each case.

Administrative work is carried out by the Privy Council Office under the direction of the President of the Council, a Cabinet Minister.

## PARLIAMENT

Parliament is the supreme law-making authority and can legislate for the UK as a whole or for any parts of it separately (the Channel Islands and the Isle of Man are Crown dependencies and not part of the UK). The main functions of Parliament are to pass laws, to provide (by voting taxation) the means of carrying on the work of government and to scrutinise government policy and administration, particularly proposals for expenditure.

International treaties and agreements are by custom presented to Parliament before ratification.

Parliament emerged during the late 13th and early 14th centuries. The officers of the King's household and the King's judges were the nucleus of early Parliaments, joined by such ecclesiastical and lay magnates as the King might summon to form a prototype 'House of Lords', and occasionally by the knights of the shires, burgesses and proctors of the lower clergy. By the end of Edward III's reign a 'House of Commons' was beginning to appear; the first known Speaker was elected in 1377.

Parliamentary procedure is based on custom and precedent, partly formulated in the Standing Orders of both Houses of Parliament, and each House has the right to control its own internal proceedings and to commit for contempt. The system of debate in the two Houses is similar; when a motion has been moved, the Speaker proposes the question as the subject of a debate. Members speak from wherever they have been sitting. Questions are decided by a vote on a simple majority. Draft legislation is introduced, in either House, as a bill. Bills can be introduced by a Government Minister or a private Member, but in practice the majority of bills which become law are introduced by the Government. To become law, a bill must be passed by each House (for parliamentary stages, *see* Bill, page 220) and then sent to the Sovereign for the royal assent, after which it becomes an Act of Parliament.

Proceedings of both Houses are public, except on extremely rare occasions. The minutes (called Votes and Proceedings in the Commons, and Minutes of Proceedings in the Lords) and the speeches (*The Official Report of Parliamentary Debates*, Hansard) are published daily. Proceedings are also recorded for transmission on radio and television and stored in the Parliamentary Recording Unit before transfer to the National Sound Archive. Television cameras have been allowed into the House of Lords since 1985 and into the House of Commons since 1989; committee meetings may also be televised.

By the Parliament Act of 1911, the maximum duration of a Parliament is five years (if not previously dissolved), the term being reckoned from the date given on the writs for the new Parliament. The maximum life has been prolonged by legislation in such rare circumstances as the two world wars (31 January 1911 to 25 November 1918; 26 November 1935 to 15 June 1945). Dissolution and writs for a general election are ordered by the Sovereign on the advice of the Prime Minister. The life of a Parliament is divided into sessions, usually of one year in length, beginning and ending most often in October or November.

### Devolution

The Scottish Parliament elected in 1999 has legislative power over all devolved matters, i.e. matters not reserved to Westminster or otherwise outside its powers. The National Assembly for Wales elected in May 1999 has power to make secondary legislation in the areas where executive functions have been transferred to it. The New Northern Ireland Assembly elected in June 1998 was due to be formally established by legislation in 1999. The Assembly started sitting in July 1998. Following suspension in February 2000, it resumed sitting on 5 June 2000. It will have legislative authority in the fields currently administered by the Northern Ireland departments.

## THE HOUSE OF LORDS

London SW1A 0PW
Tel: 020-7219 3000
Information Office: 020-7219 3107
E-mail: hlinfo@parliament.uk
Web: www.parliament.uk

The members of the House of Lords consist of the Lords Spiritual and Temporal. The Lords Spiritual are the Archbishops of Canterbury and York, the Bishops of London, Durham and Winchester, and the 21 senior diocesan bishops of the Church of England. The Lords Temporal currently consist of, life peers created under the Life Peerages Act 1958, 92 hereditary peers elected under the House of Lords Act 1999, and those Lords of Appeal in Ordinary created life peers under the Appellate Jurisdiction Act 1876, as amended (i.e. Law Lords). The House of Lords Act provides for 92 hereditary peers (42 Conservative, 28 cross-bench, three Liberal Democrat, two Labour, the Earl Marshal, the Lord Great Chamberlain and 15 others) to remain in the House of Lords until longer-term reform of the House has been carried out; elections to select those who remain were held in October and November 1999.

Peers are disqualified from sitting in the House if they are:

- aliens, i.e. any peer who is not a British citizen, a Commonwealth citizen (under the British Nationality Act 1981) or a citizen of the Republic of Ireland
- under the age of 21
- undischarged bankrupts or, in Scotland, those whose estate is sequestered
- convicted of treason

Bishops retire from their sees on reaching the age of 70 and cease to be members of the house at that time.

Peers who do not wish to attend sittings of the House of Lords may apply for leave of absence for the duration of a Parliament.

Until the beginning of this century the House of Lords had considerable power, being able to veto any bill submitted to it by the House of Commons, but those powers were greatly reduced by the Parliament Acts of 1911 and 1949 (*see* page 221).

Combined with its legislative role, the House of Lords has judicial powers as the ultimate Court of Appeal for courts in Great Britain and Northern Ireland, except for criminal cases in Scotland. These powers are exercised by the Lord Chancellor and the Lords of Appeal in Ordinary (the Law Lords) (*see* Law Courts and Officers).

Members of the House of Lords are unpaid. However, they are entitled to reimbursement of travelling expenses on parliamentary business within the UK and certain other expenses incurred for the purpose of attendance at sittings of the House, within a maximum for each day of £84.00 for overnight subsistence, £37.00 for day subsistence and incidental travel, and £36.00 for secretarial costs, postage and certain additional expenses.

### Composition *as at 25 July 2001*

Archbishops and Bishops, 26
Life peers under the Appellate Jurisdiction Act 1876, 28
Life peers under the Life Peerages Act 1958, 569 (113 women)
Peers under the House of Lords Act 1999, 92 (4 women)
Total 715
Of whom:
Peers on leave of absence from the House, 6

STATE OF PARTIES *as at 25 July 2001**
Conservative, 223
Labour, 195
Liberal Democrats, 61
Cross-bench, 173
Archbishops and Bishops, 26
Other, 31
Total: 709
* Excluding peers on leave of absence from the House

## OFFICERS

The House is presided over by the Lord Chancellor, who is *ex officio* Speaker of the House. A panel of deputy Speakers is appointed by Royal Commission. The first deputy Speaker is the Chairman of Committees, appointed at the beginning of each session, a salaried officer of the House who takes the chair in committee of the whole House and in some select committees. He is assisted by a panel of deputy chairmen, headed by the salaried Principal Deputy Chairman of Committees, who is also chairman of the European Communities Committee of the House.

The permanent officers include the Clerk of the Parliaments, who is in charge of the administrative and procedural staff collectively known as the Parliament Office; the Gentleman Usher of the Black Rod, who is also Serjeant-at-Arms in attendance upon the Lord Chancellor and is responsible for security and for accommodation and services in the House of Lords; and the Yeoman Usher who is Deputy Serjeant-at-Arms and assists Black Rod in his duties.

*Speaker* (£173,875), The Lord Irvine of Lairg, PC, QC
*Private Secretary*, Ms E. Hutchinson
*Chairman of Committees* (£68,283), The Lord Tordoff
*Principal Deputy Chairman of Committees* (£63,626), The Lord Brabazon of Tara

DEPARTMENT OF THE CLERK OF THE PARLIAMENTS
*Clerk of the Parliaments* (£132,603), J. M. Davies
*Clerk Assistant* (£64,768– £100,292), P. D. G. Hayter
*Reading Clerk and Principal Finance Officer* (£64,768–£101,292), M. G. Pownall
*Counsel to Chairman of Committees* (£64,768–£104,292), Sir James Nursaw, KCB, QC: Dr C. S. Kerse; D. W. Saunders
*Principal Clerks* (£48,552–£77,869), J. A. Vallance White, CB (*Judicial Office and Fourth Clerk at the Table*); B. P. Keith (*Journals*); D. R. Beamish (*Committees and Overseas Office*); R. H. Walters, D.Phil. (*Clerk of Public Bills*)
*Chief Clerks* (£48,552–£77,869), E. C. Ollard, D.Phil. (*Establishment Officer*); T. V. Mohan (*Private Bills*); S. P. Burton (*Public Bills*); A. Makower; T. V. Mohan (*Select Committees*)
*Senior Clerks* (£32,931–£49,896), Miss M. B. Robertson (*seconded as Secretary to the Leader of the House and Chief Whip*); T. E. Radice; D. J. Batt; E. R. Morgan; J. A. Vaughan; Miss C. Salmon; Mr A. Rawsthorne; A. J. Mackersie; Miss K. Ball; P. F. Wogan
*Clerks* (£20,000–£27,500), R. A. McLean; C. S. Johnson; Miss C. K. S. K. Mawson; Mr T. Elias; Miss A. Murphy; R. R. Neal
*Clerk of the Records* (£48,552–£77,869), S. K. Ellison
*Assistant Clerks of the Records* (£32,931–£49,896), D. L. Prior; Dr C. Shenton; P. F. Grey
*Librarian* (£53,534–£87,598), D. L. Jones
*Deputy Librarian* (£37,293–£60,509), P. G. Davis, PH.D.
*Senior Library Clerks* (£32,931–£49,896), Miss I. L. Victory, Ph.D.; S. Kennedy; H. C. Deadman
*Library Clerk* (£20,000–£27,500), I. S. Cruse; A. J. C. Brocklehurst
*Examiners of Petitions for Private Bills* (£48,552–£77,869), T. V. Morgan; F. A. Cramer
*Editor, Official Report (Hansard)*, (£48,552–£77,869), Mrs C. J. Bowden
*Deputy Editor, Official Report* (£37, 293–£60,509), Miss J. A. Bradshaw

DEPARTMENT OF THE GENTLEMAN USHER OF THE BLACK ROD
*Gentleman Usher of the Black Rod and Serjeant-at-Arms* (£64,768–£104, 292), Lt.-Gen. Sir Michael Willcocks
*Yeoman Usher of the Black Rod and Deputy Serjeant-at-Arms* (£32,931–£49,896), Brig. H. D. C. Duncan, MBE

## SELECT COMMITTEES

The main House of Lords select committees, as at June 2001, are as follows:
*European Union – Chair*, The Lord Brabazon of Tara; *Clerk*, T.V. Mohan
*European Union – Sub-committees:*
*A (Economic and Financial Affairs, Trade and External Relations) – Chair*, The Lord Grenfell; *Clerk*, Miss A. E. Murphy
*B (Energy, Industry and Transport) – Chair*, The Lord Brook of Alverthorpe; *Clerk*, P. F. M. Wogan
*C (Common Foreign and Security Policy) – Chair*, The Lord Jopling; *Clerk*, D. Batt
*D (Environment, Agriculture, Public Health and Consumer Protection) – Chair*, The Earl of Selborne; *Clerk*, T. E. Radice
*E (Law and Institutions) – Chair*, The Lord Scott of Foscote; *Clerk*, S. P. Burton
*F (Social Affairs, Education and Home Affairs) – Chair*, The Lord Harris of Richmond; *Clerk*, Dr C. S. Johnson
*Science and Technology – Chair*, Lord Oxburgh, FRCOG; *Clerk*, A. Makower
*Delegated Powers and Deregulation – Chair*, The Lord Alexander of Weedon, QC; *Clerk*, Dr F. P. Tudor
*Constitution Committee – Chair*, The Lord Norton of Louth; *Clerk*, S. P. Burton
*Economic Affairs – Chair*, The Lord Preston; *Clerk*, Ms C. Salmon
*Animals in Scientific Procedures – Chair*, The Lord Smith of Clifton; *Clerk*, Anon
*Stem Cell Research – Chair*, The Bishop of Oxford; *Clerk*, A. R. Rawsthorne

## THE HOUSE OF COMMONS

London SW1A 0AA
Tel 020-7219 3000
Information Office: 020-7219 4272
Forthcoming business: 020-7219 5532
E-mail: hcinfo@parliament.uk
Web: www.parliament.uk

The members of the House of Commons are elected by universal adult suffrage. For electoral purposes, the United Kingdom is divided into constituencies, each of which returns one member to the House of Commons, the member being the candidate who obtains the largest number of votes cast in the constituency. To ensure equitable representation, the four Boundary Commissions keep constituency boundaries under review and recommend any redistribution of seats which may seem necessary because of population movements, etc. The number of seats was raised to 640 in 1945, reduced to 625 in 1948, and subsequently rose to 630 in 1955, 635 in 1970, 650 in 1983, 651 in 1992 and 659 in 1997. Of the present 659 seats, there are 529 for England, 40 for Wales, 72 for Scotland and 18 for Northern Ireland. The number of

Scottish MPs at Westminster is likely to be cut by about 12 by 2007.

An electoral reform commission headed by Lord Jenkins of Hillhead proposed in October 1998 that the 'first-past-the-post' system of electing members of the House of Commons should be replaced by an alternative vote top-up system, under which 80–85 per cent of MPs would be elected by an alternative vote method and the remaining 15–20 per cent by an open-list system of proportional representation. A referendum will be held on the proposals at an unspecified future date.

## ELECTIONS

Elections are by secret ballot, each elector casting one vote; voting is not compulsory. For entitlement to vote in parliamentary elections, *see* Legal Notes section. When a seat becomes vacant between general elections, a by-election is held.

British subjects and citizens of the Irish Republic can stand for election as Members of Parliament (MPs) provided they are 21 or over and not subject to disqualification. Those disqualified from sitting in the House include:

- undischarged bankrupts
- people sentenced to more than one year's imprisonment
- members of the House of Lords (but hereditary peers not sitting in the Lords are eligible)
- holders of certain offices listed in the House of Commons Disqualification Act 1975, e.g. members of the judiciary, Civil Service, regular armed forces, police forces, some local government officers and some members of public corporations and government commissions

A candidate does not require any party backing but his or her nomination for election must be supported by the signatures of ten people registered in the constituency. A candidate must also deposit with the returning officer £500, which is forfeit if the candidate does not receive more than 5 per cent of the votes cast. All election expenses at a general election, except the candidate's personal expenses, are subject to a statutory limit of £5,483, plus 4.6 pence for each elector in a borough constituency or 6.2 pence for each elector in a county constituency.

*See* pages for an alphabetical list of MPs, pages for the results of the last general election, and page for the results of by-elections since the general election.

## STATE OF PARTIES *as at 18 July 2001*

Conservative, 164 (14 women)
Labour, 411 (94 women)
Liberal Democrats, 52 (5 women)
Plaid Cymru, 4
Scottish Nationalist, 5 (1 woman)
Sinn Fein, 4 (1 woman)
Social Democratic Labour, 3
Ulster Democratic Unionist, 5 (1 woman)
Ulster Unionist, 6 (1 woman)
Independent (Dr Richard Taylor-Wyre Forest), 1
The Speaker and three Deputy Speakers, 4
Total, 659 (118 women)
Government majority, 167

## BUSINESS

The week's business of the House is outlined each Thursday by the Leader of the House, after consultation between the Chief Government Whip and the Chief Opposition Whip. A quarter to a third of the time will be taken up by the Government's legislative programme and the rest by other business. As a rule, bills likely to raise political controversy are introduced in the Commons before going on to the Lords, and the Commons claims exclusive control in respect of national taxation and expenditure. Bills such as the Finance Bill, which imposes taxation, and the Consolidated Fund Bills, which authorise expenditure, must begin in the Commons. A bill of which the financial provisions are subsidiary may begin in the Lords; and the Commons may waive its rights in regard to Lords' amendments affecting finance.

The Commons has a public register of MPs' financial and certain other interests; this is published annually as a House of Commons paper. Members must also disclose any relevant financial interest or benefit in a matter before the House when taking part in a debate, in certain other proceedings of the House, or in consultations with other MPs, with Ministers or with civil servants.

## MEMBERS' PAY AND ALLOWANCES

Since 1911 members of the House of Commons have received salary payments; facilities for free travel were introduced in 1924. Salary rates since 1911 are as follows:

| | | | |
|---|---|---|---|
| 1911 | £400 p.a. | 1984 Jan | £16,106 p.a. |
| 1931 | 360 | 1985 Jan | 16,904 |
| 1934 | 380 | 1986 Jan | 17,702 |
| 1935 | 400 | 1987 Jan | 18,500 |
| 1937 | 600 | 1988 Jan | 22,548 |
| 1946 | 1,000 | 1989 Jan | 24,107 |
| 1954 | 1,250 | 1990 Jan | 26,701 |
| 1957 | 1,750 | 1991 Jan | 28,970 |
| 1964 | 3,250 | 1992 Jan | 30,854 |
| 1972 Jan | 4,500 | 1994 Jan | 31,687 |
| 1975 June | 5,750 | 1995 Jan | 33,189 |
| 1976 June | 6,062 | 1996 Jan | 34,085 |
| 1977 July | 6,270 | 1996 July | 43,000 |
| 1978 June | 6,897 | 1997 April | 43,860 |
| 1979 June | 9,450 | 1998 April | 45,066 |
| 1980 June | 11,750 | 1999 April | 47,008 |
| 1981 June | 13,950 | 2000 April | 48,371 |
| 1982 June | 14,510 | 2001 April | 49,822 |
| 1983 June | 15,308 | | |

In 1969 MPs were granted an allowance for secretarial and research expenses, now known as the Office Costs Allowance. From April 2001 the allowance is £52,760 a year.

Since 1972 MPs have been able to claim reimbursement for the additional cost of staying overnight away from their main residence while on parliamentary business; this is known as the Additional Costs Allowance and from April 2001 is £13,622 a year.

Since 1980 each MP in receipt of the Office Costs Allowance has been able to contribute sums to an approved pension scheme for the provision of a pension, or other benefits, for or in respect of persons whose salary is met by him/her from the Office Costs Allowance.

## MEMBERS' PENSIONS

Pension arrangements for MPs were first introduced in 1964. The arrangements currently provide a pension of one-fiftieth of salary for each year of pensionable service with a maximum of two-thirds of salary at age 65. Pension is payable normally at age 65, for men and women, or on later retirement. Pensions may be paid earlier, e.g. on retirement due to ill health or at age 60 after 20 years' service. The widow/widower of a former MP receives a pension of five-eighths of the late MP's pension. Pensions are index-linked. Members currently contribute six per cent of salary to the pension fund; there is an Exchequer contribution, currently slightly more than the amount contributed by MPs.

The House of Commons Members' Fund provides for annual or lump sum grants to ex-MPs, their widows or widowers, and children whose incomes are below certain limits or who are experiencing severe hardship. Members contribute £24 a year and the Exchequer £215,000 a year to the fund.

## OFFICERS AND OFFICIALS

The House of Commons is presided over by the Speaker, who has considerable powers to maintain order in the House. A deputy Speaker, called the Chairman of Ways and Means, and two Deputy Chairmen may preside over sittings of the House of Commons; they are elected by the House, and, like the Speaker, neither speak nor vote other than in their official capacity.

The staff of the House are employed by a Commission chaired by the Speaker. The heads of the six House of Commons departments are permanent officers of the House, not MPs. The Clerk of the House is the principal adviser to the Speaker on the privileges and procedures of the House, the conduct of the business of the House, and committees. The Serjeant-at-Arms is responsible for security, ceremonial, and for accommodation in the Commons part of the Palace of Westminster.

*Speaker* (£114,543), The Rt. Hon. Michael J. Martin, MP (Glasgow Springburn)
*Chairman of Ways and Means* (£82,697), Sir Alan Haselhurst, MP (Saffron Walden)
*First Deputy Chairman of Ways and Means* (£78,539), Sylvia Heal, MP
*Second Deputy Chairman of Ways and Means* (£78,539), Sir Michael Lord, MP (Suffolk Central and Ipswich North)

### OFFICES OF THE SPEAKER AND CHAIRMAN OF WAYS AND MEANS

*Speaker's Secretary* (£45,810–£73,470), N. Bevan, CB
*Chaplain to the Speaker*, Revd Canon R. Wright
*Secretary to the Chairman of Ways and Means* (£30,967–£46,848 –£45,795), M. Hennessy

### DEPARTMENT OF THE CLERK OF THE HOUSE

*Clerk of the House of Commons* (£123,787), W. R. McKay, CB
*Clerk Assistant* (£70,905–£110,428), R. B. Sands
*Clerk of Committees* (£70,905–£11,428), G. Cubie
*Clerk of Legislation* (£70,905–£110,428), D. G. Millar
*Principal Clerks* (£64,768–£104,292)
*Journals*, A. J. Hastings, CB
*Table Office*, Ms H. E. Irwin
*Principal Clerks* (£53,534–£87,598)
*Overseas Office*, R. W. G. Wilson
*Bills*, Ms H. E. Irwin
*Select Committees*, Mrs J. Sharpe; D. L. Natzler; R. J. Rogers
*Delegated Legislation*, W. A. Proctor
*Deputy Principal Clerks* (£48,552–£77,869), Ms A. Barry; C. R. M. Ward, Ph.D.; D. W. N. Doig; A. Sandall; A. R. Kennon; L. C. Laurence Smyth; S. J. Patrick; D. J. Gerhold; C. J. Poyser; D. F. Harrison; S. J. Priestley; A. H. Doherty; P. A. Evans; R. I. S. Phillips; R. G. James, Ph.D.; Ms P. A. Helme; D. R. Lloyd; J. S. Benger, D.Phil.; N. P. Walker; M. D. Hamlyn; Mrs E. J. Flood; A. Y. A. Azad; C. G. Lee; C.D. Stanton
*Senior Clerks* (£31,710–£47,972), K. J. Brown, OBE, M. Clark; T. Goldsmith; D. H. Griffths (*acting*) M. Hennessy; Mrs J. N. St J. Mulley; T. W. P. Healey; J. D. Whatley; Mrs C. Oxborough; S. T. Fiander (*acting*); Ms R. Melling, CBE (*acting*)
*Examiners of Petitions for Private Bills*, F. A. Cranmer; Dr F. P. Tudor
*Registrar of Members' Interests* (£53,534–£87,598), Ms A. Barry
*Taxing Officer*, F. A. Cranmer

### VOTE OFFICE

*Deliverer of the Vote* (£48,552–£77,869), J. F. Collins
*Deputy Deliverers of the Vote* (£31,710–£58,164), O. B. T. Sweeney (*Parliamentary*); F. W. Hallett (*Production*); A. Powell (*Development*)

### SPEAKER'S COUNSEL

*Speaker's Counsel and Head of Legal Services Office* (£64,768–£104,292), J. E. G. Vaux
*Speaker's Counsel* (*European legislation*) (£64,768–£104,292), M. Carpenter
*Assistant Counsel* (£48,552–£77,869), A. Akbar; P. Brooksbank

### DEPARTMENT OF THE SERJEANT-AT-ARMS

*Serjeant-at-Arms* (£64,768–£104,292), M. J. A. Cummins
*Deputy Serjeant-at-Arms* (£48,552–£77,869), R. M. Morton
*Assistant Serjeants-at-Arms* (£35,914–£58,164), P. A. J. Wright; J. M. Robertson; M. Harvey

### DEPARTMENT OF THE LIBRARY

*Librarian* (£64,768–£104,292), Miss P. Baines
*Directors* (£48,552–£77,869), K. G. Cuninghame; Mrs J. Wainwright; R. Clements; Mrs C. Gillie; R; Miss E. M. McInnes.
*Heads of Sections* (£35,914–£58,164), C. Pond, Ph.D.; Mrs C. Andrews; Mrs J. Lourie; C. Barclay; Mrs C. Gillie; RG. Allen; R. Cracknell; E. Wood; P. Richards, Ph.D.
*Senior Library Clerks* (£31,710–£47,972), Ms F. Poole; T. Edmonds; Ms O. Gay; Dr D. Gore; B. Winetrobe; Miss M. Baber; Ms A. Walker; Mrs H. Holden; Mrs P. Carling; S. Wise; Mrs J. Hough; Mrs K. Greener; Ms P. Strickland; Miss V. Miller; M. P. Hillyard; Ms J. Roll; Ms W. Wilson; S. Wise; E. Wood; P. Bowers, Ph.D.; A. Seely; G. Danby, Ph.D.; B. C. Morgan; Miss L. Conway; C. Blair, Ph.D.; G. Vidler; C. Sear; Ms F. Whittle; M. Oakes (*period*); Ms G. Garton Grimwood; Ms S. Broadbridge (*period* )

### DEPARTMENT OF FINANCE AND ADMINISTRATION

*Director of Finance and Administration* (£64,768–£104,292), A. J. Walker
*Director of Operations* (£48,552–£77,869), A. A. Cameron
*Director of Personnel Policy* (£48,552–£77,869) Ms S. Craig
*Director of Finance Policy* (£48,552–£77,869), M. Barram
*Director of Internal Review Services* (£35,914–£58,164), R. Russell

### DEPARTMENT OF THE OFFICIAL REPORT

*Editor* (£53,534–£87,598), I. Church
*Deputy Editors* (£44,038–£69,178), W. G. Garland; Miss L. Sutherland; Ms C. Fogarty

### REFRESHMENT DEPARTMENT

*Director of Catering Services* (£53,534–£87,598), Mrs S. Harrison
*Catering Operations Manager (Outbuildings* (£31,710–£47,972), Ms Della Herd
*Executive Chef* (£31,710–£47,972), D. Dorricott
*Financial Controller* (£31,710–£47,972), Mr Robert Gibbs

## SELECT COMMITTEES

The more important committees, as at July 2001, are:

DEPARTMENTAL COMMITTEES

*Accomodation and Works Chair*, Derek Conway, MP
*Administration Chair*, Mrs Marion Roe
*Culture, Media and Sport Chair*, Rt. Hon. Gerald Kaufman, MP; *Clerks*, C. G. Lee; R. Cooke
*Defence Chair*, Rt. Hon. Bruce George, MP; *Clerks*, P. A. Evans; Mrs C. Oxborough
*Education and Skills Chair*, Barry Sheerman,MP; *Clerks*, L. C. Laurence-Smyth; T. P.W. Healey
*Environment, Food and Rural Affairs Chair*, Rt. Hon. David Curry, MP; *Clerks*, Dr. D. F. Harrison; H. Yardley; G. Devine
*Foreign Affairs Chair*, Rt. Hon. Donald Anderson, MP; *Clerks*, E. P. Silk; Ms T. Brufal
*Health Chair*, David Hinchliffe, MP; *Clerks*, J. S. Benger, D.Phil.; T. Goldsmith
*Home Affairs Chair*, Chris Mullin, MP; *Clerks*, A. R. Kennon; M. P. Atkins
*International Development Chair*, Tony Baldry, MP; *Clerks*, A. Y. A. Azad; Ms J. Hughes
*Northern Ireland – Chair*, Michael Mates, MP; *Clerk*, C. R. M. Ward
*Scottish Affairs – Chair*, to be announced; *Clerk*, J. D. Whatley
*Trade and Industry – Chair*, Martin O'Neill, MP; *Clerks*, D. L. Natzler; Ms C. Littleboy
*Transport, Local Government and the Regions Chair*, Hon. Mrs Gwyneth Dunwoody, MP
*Treasury – Chair*, Rt. Hon. John McFall, MP; *Clerks*, S. J. Patrick; M. Egan
*Treasury sub-committee: Chair*, Michael Fallon, MP; *Clerk*, M. Egan
*Urban Affairs sub committee: Chair*, Andrew Bennett, MP
*Welsh Affairs – Chair*, Martyn Jones, MP; *Clerk*, Ms P. A. Helme
*Work and Pensions – Chair*, Archy Kirkwood, MP

NON-DEPARTMENTAL COMMITTEES

*Selection – Chair*, John McWilliam, MP
*Statutory Instruments – Chair*, David Tredinnick, MP
*Deregulation and Regulatory Reform – Chair*, Peter Pike, MP; *Clerk*, Mrs S. Craig
*Environmental Audit – Chair*, John Horam, MP; *Clerk*, F. J. Reid
*European Scrutiny – Chair*, James Hood, MP; *Clerks*, Mrs E. J. Flood; Mrs S. Craig
*Human Rights (Joint Committee) – Chair*, Jean Carston
*Modernisation of the House of Commons – Chair*, Rt. Hon. Robin Cook, MP; *Clerks*, C. B. Winnifrith, CB; A. Sandall
*Procedure – Chair*, Nicholas Winterton, MP; *Clerks*, Dr R. G. James; Ms S. McGlashan
*Public Accounts – Chair*, Rt. Hon. David Davis, MP; *Clerk*, K. J. Brown, OBE
*Public Administration – Chair*, Tony Wright, MP; *Clerk*, Ms A. Barry

## PARLIAMENTARY INFORMATION

The following is a short glossary of aspects of the work of Parliament. Unless otherwise stated, references are to House of Commons procedures.

BILL – Proposed legislation is termed a bill. The stages of a public bill (for private bills, *see* page 221) in the House of Commons are as follows:
*First Reading:* This stage nowadays merely constitutes an order to have the bill printed
*Second Reading:* The debate on the principles of the bill
*Committee Stage:* The detailed examination of a bill, clause by clause. In most cases this takes place in a standing committee, or the whole House may act as a committee. A special standing committee may take evidence before embarking on detailed scrutiny of the bill. Very rarely, a bill may be examined by a select committee (*see* page)
*Report Stage:* Detailed review of a bill as amended in committee
*Third Reading:* Final debate on a bill
Public bills go through the same stages in the House of Lords, except that in almost all cases the committee stage is taken in committee of the whole House.

A bill may start in either House, and has to pass through both Houses to become law. Both Houses have to agree the same text of a bill, so that the amendments made by the second House are then considered in the originating House, and if not agreed, sent back or themselves amended, until agreement is reached.

CHILTERN HUNDREDS – A nominal office of profit under the Crown, the acceptance of which requires an MP to vacate his/her seat. The Manor of Northstead is similar. These are the only means by which an MP may resign.

CONSOLIDATED FUND BILL – A bill to authorise issue of money to maintain Government services. The bill is dealt with without debate.

EARLY DAY MOTION – A motion put on the notice paper by an MP without in general the real prospect of its being debated. Such motions are expressions of back-bench opinion.

FATHER OF THE HOUSE – The Member whose continuous service in the House of Commons is the longest. The present Father of the House is the Rt. Hon. Tam Dalyell.

HOURS OF MEETING – The House of Commons normally meets Monday, Tuesday and Wednesday at 2.30 p.m., Thursdays at 11.30 a.m. and some Fridays at 9.30 a.m. There are ten Fridays without sittings in each session. (*See also* Westminster Hall Sittings, below.) The House of Lords normally meets at 2.30 p.m. Monday to Wednesday and at 3 p.m. on Thursday. In the latter part of the session, the House of Lords sometimes sits on Fridays at 11 a.m.

LEADER OF THE OPPOSITION – In 1937 the office of Leader of the Opposition was recognised and a salary was assigned to the post. Since April 2001 this has been £110,481 (including parliamentary salary of £49,822). The present Leader of the Opposition is Iain Duncan Smith.

THE LORD CHANCELLOR – The Lord High Chancellor of Great Britain is (*ex officio*) the Speaker of the House of Lords. Unlike the Speaker of the House of Commons, he is a member of the Government, takes part in debates and votes in divisions. He has none of the powers to maintain order that the Speaker in the Commons has, these powers being exercised in the Lords by the House as a whole. The Lord Chancellor sits in the Lords on one of the Woolsacks, couches covered with red cloth and stuffed with wool. If he wishes to address the House in any way except formally as Speaker, he leaves the Woolsack.

NORTHERN IRELAND GRAND COMMITTEE – The Northern Ireland Grand Committee consists of all MPs representing constituencies in Northern Ireland, together with not more than 25 other MPs nominated by the Committee of Selection. The business of the committee includes questions, short debates, ministerial statements, bills, legislative proposals and other matters relating exclusively to Northern Ireland, and delegated legislation.

The Northern Ireland Affairs Committee is one of the departmental select committees, empowered to examine the expenditure, administration and policy of the Northern Ireland Office and the administration and expenditure of the Crown Solicitor's Office.

OPPOSITION DAY – A day on which the topic for debate is chosen by the Opposition. There are 20 such days in a normal session. On 17 days, subjects are chosen by the Leader of the Opposition; on the remaining three days by the leader of the next largest opposition party.

PARLIAMENT ACTS 1911 AND 1949 – Under these Acts, bills may become law without the consent of the Lords, though the House of Lords has the power to delay a public bill for 13 months from its first second reading in the House of Commons.

PRIME MINISTER'S QUESTIONS – The Prime Minister answers questions from 3.00 to 3.30 p.m. on Wednesdays.

PRIVATE BILL – A bill promoted by a body or an individual to give powers additional to, or in conflict with, the general law, and to which a special procedure applies to enable people affected to object.

PRIVATE MEMBER'S BILL – A public bill promoted by a Member who is not a member of the Government.

PRIVATE NOTICE QUESTION – A question adjudged of urgent importance on submission to the Speaker (in the Lords, the Leader of the House), answered at the end of oral questions, usually at 3.30 p.m.

PRIVILEGE – The following are covered by the privilege of Parliament:

(i) freedom from interference in going to, attending at, and going from, Parliament
(ii) freedom of speech in parliamentary proceedings
(iii) the printing and publishing of anything relating to the proceedings of the two Houses is subject to privilege
(iv) each House is the guardian of its dignity and may punish any insult to the House as a whole

QUESTION TIME – Oral questions are answered by Ministers in the Commons from 2.30 to 3.30 p.m. Monday to Wednesday and 11.30 a.m. to 12.30 p.m. on Thursdays. Questions are also taken at the start of the Lords sittings, with a daily limit of four oral questions.

ROYAL ASSENT – The royal assent is signified by letters patent to such bills and measures as have passed both Houses of Parliament (or bills which have been passed under the Parliament Acts 1911 and 1949). The Sovereign has not given royal assent in person since 1854. On occasion, for instance in the prorogation of Parliament, royal assent may be pronounced to the two Houses by Lords Commissioners. More usually royal assent is notified to each House sitting separately in accordance with the Royal Assent Act 1967. The old French formulae for royal assent are then endorsed on the acts by the Clerk of the Parliaments.

The power to withhold assent resides with the Sovereign but has not been exercised in the UK since 1707.

SELECT COMMITTEES – Consisting usually of ten to fifteen members of all parties, select committees are a means used by both Houses in order to investigate certain matters.

Most select committees in the House of Commons are tied to departments: each committee investigates subjects within a government department's remit. There are other select committees dealing with public accounts (i.e. the spending by the Government of money voted by Parliament) and European legislation, and also domestic committees dealing, for example, with privilege and procedure. Major select committees usually take evidence in public; their evidence and reports are published by The Stationery Office. House of Commons select committees are reconstituted after a general election. For main committees, *see* page 220.

The principal select committee in the House of Lords is that on the European Communities, which has, at present, six sub-committees dealing with all areas of Community policy. The House of Lords also has a select committee on science and technology, which appoints sub-committees to deal with specific subjects, and a select committee on delegated powers and deregulation. For committees, *see* page 217. In addition, *ad hoc* select committees have been set up from time to time to investigate specific subjects. There are also some joint committees of the two Houses, e.g. the committees on statutory instruments and on parliamentary privilege.

THE SPEAKER – The Speaker of the House of Commons is the spokesman and chairman of the Chamber. He or she is elected by the House at the beginning of each Parliament or when the previous Speaker retires or dies. The Speaker neither speaks in debates nor votes in divisions except when the voting is equal.

VACANT SEATS – When a vacancy occurs in the House of Commons during a session of Parliament, the writ for the by-election is moved by a Whip of the party to which the member whose seat has been vacated belonged. If the House is in recess, the Speaker can issue a warrant for a writ, should two members certify to him that a seat is vacant.

The Welsh Affairs Committee, one of the departmental select committees, was empowered to examine the expenditure, administration and policy of the Welsh Office. Following devolution, the role of the select committee has been questioned. If it continues, it will be concerned with the role and responsibilities of the relevant Secretary of State and on occasion the policy of the UK departments as it affects Wales.

WESTMINSTER HALL SITTINGS – Following a report by the Modernisation of the House of Commons Select Committee, the Commons decided in May 1999 to set up a second debating forum. It is known as 'Westminster Hall' and sittings are in the Grand Committee Room on Tuesdays and Wednesdays from 9.30 a.m. to 2 p.m. and Thursdays from 2.30 p.m. for up to three hours. Sittings will be open to the public at the times indicated.

WHIPS – In order to secure the attendance of Members of a particular party in Parliament, particularly on the occasion of an important vote, Whips (originally known as 'Whippers-in') are appointed. The written appeal or circular letter issued by them is also known as a 'whip', its urgency being denoted by the number of times it is underlined. Failure to respond to a three-line whip is tantamount in the Commons to secession (at any rate temporarily) from the party. Whips are provided with office accommodation in both Houses, and Government and some Opposition Whips receive salaries from public funds.

PARLIAMENTARY EDUCATION UNIT – Norman Shaw Building (North), London SW1A 2TT.
Tel: 020-7219 2105
E-mail: edunit@parliament.uk
Web: www.explore-parliament.uk

## GOVERNMENT OFFICE

The Government is the body of Ministers responsible for the administration of national affairs, determining policy and introducing into Parliament any legislation necessary to give effect to government policy. The majority of Ministers are members of the House of Commons but members of the House of Lords or of neither House may also hold ministerial responsibility. The Lord Chancellor is always a member of the House of Lords. The Prime Minister is, by current convention, always a member of the House of Commons.

### THE PRIME MINISTER

The office of Prime Minister, which had been in existence for nearly 200 years, was officially recognised in 1905 and its holder was granted a place in the table of precedence. The Prime Minister, by tradition also First Lord of the Treasury and Minister for the Civil Service, is appointed by the Sovereign and is usually the leader of the party which enjoys, or can secure, a majority in the House of Commons. Other Ministers are appointed by the Sovereign on the recommendation of the Prime Minister, who also allocates functions amongst Ministers and has the power to obtain their resignation or dismissal individually.

The Prime Minister informs the Sovereign of state and political matters, advises on the dissolution of Parliament, and makes recommendations for important Crown appointments, the award of honours, etc.

As the chairman of Cabinet meetings and leader of a political party, the Prime Minister is responsible for translating party policy into government activity. As leader of the Government, the Prime Minister is responsible to Parliament and to the electorate for the policies and their implementation.

The Prime Minister also represents the nation in international affairs, e.g. summit conferences.

### THE CABINET

The Cabinet developed during the 18th century as an inner committee of the Privy Council, which was the chief source of executive power until that time. The Cabinet is composed of about 20 Ministers chosen by the Prime Minister, usually the heads of government departments (generally known as Secretaries of State unless they have a special title, e.g. Chancellor of the Exchequer), the leaders of the two Houses of Parliament, and the holders of various traditional offices.

The Cabinet's functions are the final determination of policy, control of government and co-ordination of government departments. The exercise of its functions is dependent upon enjoying majority support in the House of Commons. Cabinet meetings are held in private, taking place once or twice a week during parliamentary sittings and less often during a recess. Proceedings are confidential, the members being bound by their oath as Privy Counsellors not to disclose information about the proceedings.

The convention of collective responsibility means that the Cabinet acts unanimously even when Cabinet Ministers do not all agree on a subject. The policies of departmental Ministers must be consistent with the policies of the Government as a whole, and once the Government's policy has been decided, each Minister is expected to support it or resign.

The convention of ministerial responsibility holds a Minister, as the political head of his or her department, accountable to Parliament for the department's work. Departmental Ministers usually decide all matters within their responsibility, although on matters of political importance they normally consult their colleagues collectively. A decision by a departmental Minister is binding on the Government as a whole.

## POLITICAL PARTIES

Before the reign of William and Mary the principal officers of state were chosen by and were responsible to the Sovereign alone and not to Parliament or the nation at large. Such officers acted sometimes in concert with one another but more often independently, and the fall of one did not, of necessity, involve that of others, although all were liable to be dismissed at any moment.

In 1693 the Earl of Sunderland recommended to William III the advisability of selecting a ministry from the political party which enjoyed a majority in the House of Commons and the first united ministry was drawn in 1696 from the Whigs, to which party the King owed his throne. This group became known as the Junto and was regarded with suspicion as a novelty in the political life of the nation, being a small section meeting in secret apart from the main body of Ministers. It may be regarded as the forerunner of the Cabinet and in course of time it led to the establishment of the principle of joint responsibility of Ministers, so that internal disagreement caused a change of personnel or resignation of the whole body of Ministers.

The accession of George I, who was unfamiliar with the English language, led to a disinclination on the part of the Sovereign to preside at meetings of his Ministers and caused the appearance of a Prime Minister, a position first acquired by Robert Walpole in 1721 and retained by him without interruption for 20 years and 326 days.

### DEVELOPMENT OF PARTIES

In 1828 the Whigs became known as Liberals, a name originally given to it by its opponents to imply laxity of principles, but gradually accepted by the party to indicate its claim to be pioneers and champions of political reform and progressive legislation. In 1861 a Liberal Registration Association was founded and Liberal Associations became widespread. In 1877 a National Liberal Federation was formed, with headquarters in London. The Liberal Party was in power for long periods during the second half of the 19th-century and for several years during the first quarter of the 20th-century, but after a split in the party the numbers elected were small from 1931. In 1988, a majority of the Liberals agreed on a merger with the Social Democratic Party under the title Social and Liberal Democrats; since 1989 they have been known as the Liberal Democrats. A minority continue separately as the Liberal Party.

Soon after the change from Whig to Liberal the Tory Party became known as Conservative, a name believed to have been invented by John Wilson Croker in 1830 and to have been generally adopted about the time of the passing of the Reform Act of 1832 to indicate that the preservation of national institutions was the leading principle of the party. After the Home Rule crisis of 1886 the dissentient Liberals entered into a compact with the Conservatives, under which the latter undertook not to contest their seats, but a separate Liberal Unionist organisation was maintained until 1912, when it was united with the Conservatives.

Labour candidates for Parliament made their first appearance at the general election of 1892, when there were 27 standing as Labour or Liberal-Labour. In 1900 the Labour Representation Committee was set up in order to establish a distinct Labour group in Parliament, with its own whips, its own policy, and a readiness to co-operate with any party which might be engaged in promoting legislation in the direct interest of labour. In 1906 the LRC became known as the Labour Party.

The Council for Social Democracy was announced by four former Labour Cabinet Ministers in January 1981 and in March 1981 the Social Democratic Party was launched. Later that year the SDP and the Liberal Party formed an electoral alliance. In 1988 a majority of the SDP agreed on a merger with the Liberal Party but a minority continued as a separate party under the SDP title. In 1990 it was decided to wind up the party organisation and its three sitting MPs were known as independent social democrats. None were returned at the 1992 general election.

Plaid Cymru was founded in 1926 to provide an independent political voice for Wales and to campaign for self-government in Wales.

The Scottish National Party was founded in 1934 to campaign for independence for Scotland.

The Social Democratic and Labour Party was founded in 1970, emerging from the civil rights movement of the 1960s, with the aim of promoting reform, reconciliation and partnership across the sectarian divide in Northern Ireland and of opposing violence from any quarter.

The Ulster Democratic Unionist Party was founded in 1971 to resist moves by the Ulster Unionist Party which were considered a threat to the Union. Its aim is to maintain Northern Ireland as an integral part of the UK.

The Ulster Unionist Council first met formally in 1905. Its objectives are to maintain Northern Ireland as an integral part of the UK and to promote the aims of the Ulster Unionist Party.

### Government and Opposition

The government of the day is formed by the party which wins the largest number of seats in the House of Commons at a general election, or which has the support of a majority of members in the House of Commons. By tradition, the leader of the majority party is asked by the Sovereign to form a government, while the largest minority party becomes the official Opposition with its own leader and a 'Shadow Cabinet'. Leaders of the Government and Opposition sit on the front benches of the Commons with their supporters (the back-benchers) sitting behind them.

### Financial Support

Financial support to Opposition parties in the House of Commons was introduced in 1975 and is commonly known as Short Money, after Edward Short, the Leader of the House at that time, who introduced the scheme. At 1 April 2001 the financial support was:

| | |
|---|---|
| Conservative | £3,545,032 |
| Liberal Democrats | 1,138,615 |
| Plaid Cymru | 64,918 |
| SNP | 141,296 |
| SDLP | 56,787 |
| Democratic Unionists | 35,546 |
| Ulster Unionists | 145,612 |

A specific allocation for the Leader of the Opposition's office was introduced in April 1999 and has been set at £500,000 a year.

Financial support to the Opposition parties in the House of Lords was introduced in 1996 and is commonly known as Cranborne Money.

The parties included here are those with MPs sitting in the House of Commons in the present Parliament. Addresses of other political parties may be found in the Societies and Institutions section.

### COMMONWEALTH PARLIAMENTARY ASSOCIATION (1911)

Suite 700, Westminster House, 7 Millbank, London SW1P 3JA.
Tel: 020-7799 1460; Fax: 020-7222 6073;
Email: hq.sec@cpahq.org; Web:www.cpahq.org;

The Commonwealth Parliamentary Association consists of 170 branches in the national, state, provincial or territorial parliaments in the countries of the Commonwealth. Conferences and general assemblies are held every year in different countries of the Commonwealth.

*President (2001–2002)*, Rt. Hon. Kandi Nehova, MP

### COMMONWEALTH PARLIAMENTARY ASSOCIATION (UK BRANCH)

Westminster Hall, Houses of Parliament, London SW1A 0AA. Tel: 020-7219 5373; Fax: 020-7233 1202;
Email: cpa@parliament.uk
*Hon. President, The Lord Chancellor*, The Lord Irvine of Laird
*Chairman of Branch*, Rt. Hon. Tony Blair, MP
*Chairman of the Executive Committee*, Tom Cox, MP
*Secretary*, A. Pearson

### CONSERVATIVE PARTY

Conservative Central Office, 32 Smith Square, London SW1P 3HH
Tel: 020-7222 9000; Fax: 020-7222 1135
E-mail: ccoffice@conservative-party.org.uk
Web: www.conservatives.com
*See* Stop Press for details of the Opposition leader and Shadow Cabinet.

### SCOTTISH CONSERVATIVE AND UNIONIST CENTRAL OFFICE

83 Princes Street, Edinburgh EH2 2ER
Tel: 0131-247 6890; Fax: 0131-247 6891
Email: central.office@scottishtories.org.uk;
Web: www.scottishtories.org.uk
*Chairman*, D. Mitchell
*Deputy Chairman*, B. Walker
*Hon. Treasurer*, to be announced
*Acting Director*, M. McDonald

### LABOUR PARTY

Millbank Tower, Millbank, London SW1P 4GT
Tel: 08705-900 200; Fax: 020-7802 1234
E-mail: join@labour.org.uk
Web: www.labour.org.uk
*Parliamentary Party Leader*, Rt. Hon. Tony Blair, MP
*Deputy Party Leader*, Rt. Hon. John Prescott, MP
*Leader in the Lords*, Lord Williams of Mostyn, QC
*Chair*, Clive Soley, MP
*Vice-Chair*, Tony Lloyd, MP
*Treasurer*, Ms M. Prosser
*General Secretary*, Ms M. McDonagh
*General Secretary, Scottish Labour Party*, L. Quinn

### LIBERAL DEMOCRATS

4 Cowley Street, London SW1P 3NB
Tel: 020-7222 7999; Fax: 020-7799 2170
E-mail: libdems@cix.co.uk
Web: www.libdems.org.uk
*President*, Lord Dholakia
*Hon. Treasurer*, Reg Clark

*Chief Executive*, Hugh Rickard
*Parliamentary Party Leader*, Rt. Hon. Charles Kennedy, MP
*Shadow Leader in the House of Commons*, Paul Tyler, MP
*Leader in the Lords*, The Lord Rodgers of Quarry Bank, PC

LIBERAL DEMOCRAT SPOKESMEN *as at August 2001*

*Deputy Leader*, Rt. Hon. Alan Beith, MP
*Culture, Media and Sport, Constitution*, Rt. Hon. Nick Harvey, MP
*Defence*, Paul Keetch, MP
*Education and Skills*, Phil Willis, MP
*Environment,Food and Rural Affairs*, Malcolm Bruce, MP
*Foreign Affairs, Defence and Europe*, Rt. Hon. Menzies Campbell, MP
*Home Affairs*, Simon Hughes, MP
*Health*, Dr Evans Harry, MP
*International Development*, Dr Jenny Tonge, MP
*Social Security and Welfare*, Prof. Steve Webb, MP
*Trade and Industry*, Dr Vincent Cable, MP
*Transport, Local Government and the Regions*, Don Foster, MP
*Treasury*, Matthew Taylor, MP
*Scotland*, Rt. Hon. Michael Moore, MP
*Wales and Northern Ireland*, Lempit Opik, MP
*Chair of the Parliamentary Party*, Mark Oaten, MP

LIBERAL DEMOCRAT WHIPS

*House of Lords*, The Lord Roper of Thorney Island
*House of Commons*, Andrew Stunell, MP (*Chief Whip*)

## WELSH LIBERAL DEMOCRATS

Bay View House, 102 Bute Street, Cardiff CF10 5AD
Tel: 029-2031 3400; Fax: 029-2031 3401
E-mail: ldwales@cix.co.uk

*Party President*, Clive Lindley
*Party Leader*, L. Opik, MP
*Chairman*, P. Lloyd
*Treasurer*, N. Burree
*Secretary*, J. Burree
*Administrative Officer*, Ms J. Batchelor
*Chief Executive*, C. Lines

## SCOTTISH LIBERAL DEMOCRATS

4 Clifton Terrace, Edinburgh EH12 5DR
Tel: 0131-337 2314; Fax: 0131-337 3566
E-mail: scotlibdem@cix.co.uk
Web: www.scotlibdems.org.uk

*Party President*, Malcolm Bruce, MP
*Party Leader*, Jim Wallace, MSP
*Convener*, Cllr I. Yuill
*Vice Convener*, Neil Wallace; Moira Craig
*Treasurer*, D. R. Sullivan
*Chief Executive*, K. Croft

## PLAID CYMRU – THE PARTY OF WALES

18 Park Grove, Cardiff CF10 3BN
Tel: 029-2064 6000; Fax: 029-2064 6001
E-mail: post@plaidcymru.org
Web: www.plaidcymru.org

*Party President*, Ieuan Wyn Jones, AM
*Chairman*, E. Jones, AM
*Hon. Treasurer*, Jeff Canning
*Chief Executive/General Secretary*, K. Davies

## SCOTTISH NATIONAL PARTY

6 North Charlotte Street, Edinburgh EH2 4JH
Tel: 0131-226 3661; Fax: 0131-225 9597
Web: www.snp.org.uk

*Parliamentary Party Leader*, John Swinney, MSP
*Chief Whip*, K. Ullrich, MSP
*National Convener*, Alex Salmond, MP
*Senior Vice-Convener*, John Swinney, MSP
*National Treasurer*, Jim Mather
*National Secretary*, Stewart Hosie

## NORTHERN IRELAND

## SINN FEIN

147 Andersonstown Road, Belfast BT11 9BW
Tel: 028- 9030 1719; Web: www.sinnfein.ie
*Party President*, Gerry Adams, MP
*Vice President*, Pat Doherty, MP
*Chief Negotiator*, Martin McGuinnes, MP

## SOCIAL DEMOCRATIC AND LABOUR PARTY

Cranmore House, 121 Ormeau Road, Belfast BT7 1SH
Tel: 028-9024 7700; Fax: 028-9023 6699
E-mail: sdlp@indigo.ie
Web: www.sdlp.ie

*Parliamentary Party Leader*, vacant
*Deputy Leader*, Seamus Mallon, MP
*Chief Whip*, Eddie McGrady, MP
*Chairman*, A. Attwood, MLA
*Hon. Treasurer*, J. Stephenson
*General Secretary*, Mrs G. Cosgrove

## ULSTER DEMOCRATIC UNIONIST PARTY

91 Dundela Avenue, Belfast BT4 3BU
Tel: 028-9047 1155; Fax: 028-9047 1797
E-mail: info@dup.org.uk
Web: www.dup.org.uk

*Parliamentary Party Leader*, Ian Paisley, MP, MEP, MLA
*Deputy Leader*, Peter Robinson, MP, MLA
*Chairman*, M. Morrow, MLA
*Chief Executive*, A. Ewart
*Hon. Treasurer*, G. Campbell, MP, MLA
*Party Secretary*, N. Dodds, MP, MLA

## ULSTER UNIONIST PARTY

3 Glengall Street, Belfast BT12 5AE
Tel: 028-9032 4601; Fax: 028-9024 6738
E-mail: uup@uup.org
Web: www.uup.org

*Party Leader*, Rt. Hon. David Trimble, MP
*Chief Whip*, Cllr. Roy Beggs, MP

ULSTER UNIONIST COUNCIL

*President*, Revd Martin Smyth, MP
*Leader*, Rt. Hon. David Trimble, MP, MLA
*Chairman of the Executive Committee*, James Cooper
*Hon. Treasurer*, J. Allen, OBE
*Vice Chairman*, D. McConnell, OBE
*Vice President*, Jeffrey Donaldson, MP; Sir Reg Empey, OBE, MLA; Cllr K. Maginnis; Jim Nicholson, MEP

## MEMBERS OF PARLIAMENT

*Abbott, Ms Diane (*b.* 1953) *Lab.*, *Hackney North and Stoke Newington*, Maj. 13,651
*Adams, Gerard (Gerry) (*b.* 1948) *SF*, *Belfast West*, Maj. 19,342
*Adams, Mrs K. Irene JP (*b.* 1948) *Lab.*, *Paisley North*, Maj. 9,321
*Ainger, Nicholas R. (*b.* 1949) *Lab.*, *Carmarthen West and Pembrokeshire South*, Maj. 4,538
*Ainsworth, Peter M. (*b.* 1956) *C.*, *Surrey East*, Maj. 13,203
*Ainsworth, Robert W. (*b.* 1952) *Lab.*, *Coventry North East*, Maj. 15,751
*Alexander, Douglas G. (*b.* 1967) *Lab.*, *Paisley South*, Maj. 11,910
Allan, Richard B. (*b.* 1966) *LD*, *Sheffield Hallam*, Maj. 9,347
*Allen, Graham W. (*b.* 1953) *Lab.*, *Nottingham North*, Maj. 12,240
*Amess, David A. A. (*b.* 1952) *C.*, *Southend West*, Maj. 7,941
*Ancram, Rt. Hon. Michael A.F.J.K. (Earl of Ancram) (*b.* 1945) *C.*, *Devizes*, Maj. 11,896
*Anderson, Rt. Hon. Donald (*b.* 1939) *Lab.*, *Swansea East*, Maj. 16,148
*Anderson, Mrs Janet (*b.* 1949) *Lab.*, *Rossendale and Darwen*, Maj. 5,223
*Arbuthnot, Rt. Hon. James N. (*b.* 1952) *C.*, *Hampshire North East*, Maj. 13,257
*Armstrong, Rt. Hon. Hilary J. (*b.* 1945) *Lab.*, *Durham North West*, Maj. 16,333
Atherton, Ms Candy K. (*b.* 1955) *Lab.*, *Falmouth and Camborne*, Maj. 4,527
Atkins, Ms Charlotte (*b.* 1950) *Lab.*, *Staffordshire Moorlands*, Maj. 5,838
*Atkinson, David A. (*b.* 1940) *C.*, *Bournemouth East*, Maj. 3,434
*Atkinson, Peter L. (*b.* 1943) *C.*, *Hexham*, Maj. 2,529
*Austin, John E. (*b.* 1944) *Lab.*, *Erith and Thamesmead*, Maj. 11,167
Bacon, Richard (*b.* 1962) *C.*, *Norfolk South*, Maj. 6,893
*Bailey, Adrian (*b.* 1945) *Lab. Co-op*, *West Bromwich West*, Maj. 11,355
Baird, Vera (*b.* 1950) *Lab.*, *Redcar*, Maj. 13,443
*Baker, Norman (*b.* 1957) *LD*, *Lewes*, Maj. 9,710
*Baldry, Anthony B. (*b.* 1950) *C.*, *Banbury*, Maj. 5,219
*Banks, Anthony L. (*b.* 1943) *Lab.*, *West Ham*, Maj. 15,645
Barker, Gregory (*b.* 1966) *C.*, *Bexhill and Battle*, Maj. 10,503
*Barnes, Harold (*b.* 1936) *Lab.*, *Derbyshire North East*, Maj. 12,258
Baron, John (*b.* 1959) *C.*, *Billericay*, Maj. 5,013
Barrett, John (*b.* 1954) *LD*, *Edinburgh West*, Maj. 7,589
*Barron, Rt. Hon. Kevin J. (*b.* 1946) *Lab.*, *Rother Valley*, Maj. 14,882
*Battle, John D. (*b.* 1951) *Lab.*, *Leeds West*, Maj. 14,935
*Bayley, Hugh (*b.* 1952) *Lab.*, *City of York*, Maj. 13,779
Beard, Nigel C. (*b.* 1936) *Lab.*, *Bexleyheath and Crayford*, Maj. 1,472
*Beckett, Rt. Hon. Margaret (*b.* 1943) *Lab.*, *Derby South*, Maj. 13,855
Begg, Ms Anne (*b.* 1955) *Lab.*, *Aberdeen South*, Maj. 4,388
*Beggs, Roy (*b.* 1936) *UUP*, *Antrim East*, Maj. 128
*Beith, Rt. Hon. Alan J. (*b.* 1943) *LD*, *Berwick upon Tweed*, Maj. 8,458
*Bell, Stuart (*b.* 1938) *Lab.*, *Middlesbrough*, Maj. 16,330
Bellingham, Henry (*b.* 1955) *Lab.*, *Norfolk North West*, Maj. 3,485
*Benn, Hilary J. (*b.* 1953) *Lab.*, *Leeds Central*, Maj. 14,381
*Bennett, Andrew F. (*b.* 1939) *Lab.*, *Denton and Reddish*, Maj. 15,330
*Benton, Joseph E. (*b.* 1933) *Lab.*, *Bootle*, Maj. 19,043
Bercow, John S. (*b.* 1963) *C.*, *Buckingham*, Maj. 13,325
*Beresford, Sir Paul (*b.* 1946) *C.*, *Mole Valley*, Maj. 10,153
*Berry, Dr Roger D.PHIL. (*b.* 1948) *Lab.*, *Kingswood*, Maj. 13,962
*Best, Harold (*b.* 1939) *Lab.*, *Leeds North West*, Maj. 5,236
*Betts, Clive J. C. (*b.* 1950) *Lab.*, *Sheffield Attercliffe*, Maj. 18,844
Blackman, Ms Elizabeth M. (*b.* 1949) *Lab.*, *Erewash*, Maj. 6,932
*Blair, Rt. Hon. Anthony C. L. (*b.* 1953) *Lab.*, *Sedgefield*, Maj. 17,713
Blears, Hazel A. (*b.* 1956) *Lab.*, *Salford*, Maj. 11,012
Blizzard, Robert J. (*b.* 1950) *Lab.*, *Waveney*, Maj. 8,553
*Blunkett, Rt. Hon. David (*b.* 1947) *Lab.*, *Sheffield Brightside*, Maj. 17,049
*Blunt, Crispin J. R. (*b.* 1960) *C.*, *Reigate*, Maj. 8,025
*Boateng, Rt. Hon. Paul Y. (*b.* 1951) *Lab.*, *Brent South*, Maj. 17,380
Borrow, David S. (*b.* 1952) *Lab.*, *Ribble South*, Maj. 3,792
*Boswell, Timothy E. (*b.* 1942) *C.*, *Daventry*, Maj. 9,649
*Bottomley, Peter J. (*b.* 1944) *C.*, *Worthing West*, Maj. 9,037
*Bottomley, Rt. Hon. Virginia H. B. M. (*b.* 1948) *C.*, *Surrey South West*, Maj. 861
*Bradley, Rt. Hon. Keith J. C. (*b.* 1950) *Lab.*, *Manchester Withington*, Maj. 11,524
Bradley, Peter C. S. (*b.* 1953) *Lab.*, *Wrekin, The*, Maj. 3,587
Bradshaw, Benjamin P. J. (*b.* 1960) *Lab.*, *Exeter*, Maj. 11,759
*Brady, Graham (*b.* 1967) *C.*, *Altrincham and Sale West*, Maj. 2,941
Brake, Thomas A. (*b.* 1962) *LD*, *Carshalton and Wallington*, Maj. 4,547
*Brazier, Julian W. H. TD (*b.* 1953) *C.*, *Canterbury*, Maj. 2,069
Breed, Colin E. (*b.* 1947) *LD*, *Cornwall South East*, Maj. 5,375
Brennan, Kevin (*b.* 1959) *Lab.*, *Cardiff West*, Maj. 11,321
Brooke, Annette (*b.* 1947) *LD*, *Dorset Mid and Poole North*, Maj. 384
*Brown, Rt. Hon. J. Gordon PH.D. (*b.* 1951) *Lab.*, *Dunfermline East*, Maj. 15,063
*Brown, Rt. Hon. Nicholas H. (*b.* 1950) *Lab.*, *Newcastle upon Tyne East and Wallsend*, Maj. 14,223
Brown, Russell L. (*b.* 1951) *Lab.*, *Dumfries*, Maj. 8,834
Browne, Desmond (*b.* 1952) *Lab.*, *Kilmarnock and Loudoun*, Maj. 10,334
*Browning, Mrs Angela F. (*b.* 1946) *C.*, *Tiverton and Honiton*, Maj. 6,284
*Bruce, Malcolm G. (*b.* 1944) *LD*, *Gordon*, Maj. 7,879
Bryant, Chris (*b.* 1962) *Lab.*, *Rhondda*, Maj. 16,047
Buck, Ms Karen P. (*b.* 1958) *Lab.*, *Regent's Park and Kensington North*, Maj. 10,266
*Burden, Richard H. (*b.* 1954) *Lab.*, *Birmingham Northfield*, Maj. 7,798
Burgon, Colin (*b.* 1948) *Lab.*, *Elmet*, Maj. 4,171
Burnett, John P. A. (*b.* 1945) *LD*, *Devon West and Torridge*, Maj. 1,194
*Burnham, Andy (*b.* 1970) *Lab.*, *Leigh*, Maj. 16,362
*Burns, Simon H. M. (*b.* 1952) *C.*, *Chelmsford West*, Maj. 6,261
Burnside, David (*b.* 1952) *UUP*, *Antrim South*, Maj. 1,011

Burstow, Paul K. (*b.* 1962) *LD*, *Sutton and Cheam*, Maj. 4,304
Burt, Alastair (*b.* 1955) *C.*, *Bedfordshire North East*, Maj. 8,577
*Butterfill, John V. (*b.* 1941) *C.*, *Bournemouth West*, Maj. 4,718
*Byers, Rt. Hon. Stephen J. (*b.* 1953) *Lab.*, *Tyneside North*, Maj. 20,668
Cable, Dr J. Vincent (*b.* 1943) *LD*, *Twickenham*, Maj. 7,655
*Caborn, Rt. Hon. Richard G. (*b.* 1943) *Lab.*, *Sheffield Central*, Maj. 12,544
Cairns, David (*b.* 1966) *Lab.*, *Greenock and Inverclyde*, Maj. 9,890
Calton, Patsy (*b.* 1948) *LD*, *Cheadle*, Maj. 33
Cameron, David (*b.* 1966) *C.*, *Witney*, Maj. 7,973
Campbell, Alan (*b.* 1957) *Lab.*, *Tynemouth*, Maj. 8,678
*Campbell, Mrs Anne (*b.* 1940) *Lab.*, *Cambridge*, Maj. 8,579
Campbell, Gregory (*b.* 1953) *DUP*, *Londonderry East*, Maj. 1,901
*Campbell, Ronald (*b.* 1943) *Lab.*, *Blyth Valley*, Maj. 12,188
*Campbell, Rt. Hon. W. Menzies CBE, QC (*b.* 1941) *LD*, *Fife North East*, Maj. 9,736
*Cann, James C. (*b.* 1946) *Lab.*, *Ipswich*, Maj. 8,081
*Caplin, Ivor K. (*b.* 1958) *Lab.*, *Hove*, Maj. 3,171
Carmichael, Alistair (*b.* 1965) *LD*, *Orkney and Shetland*, Maj. 3,475
Casale, Roger M. (*b.* 1960) *Lab.*, *Wimbledon*, Maj. 3,744
*Cash, William N. P. (*b.* 1940) *C.*, *Stone*, Maj. 6,036
Caton, Martin P. (*b.* 1951) *Lab.*, *Gower*, Maj. 7,395
*Cawsey, Ian A. (*b.* 1960) *Lab.*, *Brigg and Goole*, Maj. 3,961
Challen, Colin (*b.* 1953) *Lab.*, *Morley and Rothwell*, Maj. 12,090
*Chapman, J. K. (Ben) (*b.* 1940) *Lab.*, *Wirral South*, Maj. 5,049
*Chapman, Sir Sydney (*b.* 1935) *C.*, *Chipping Barnet*, Maj. 2,701
*Chaytor, David M. (*b.* 1949) *Lab.*, *Bury North*, Maj. 6,532
*Chidgey, David W. G. (*b.* 1942) *LD*, *Eastleigh*, Maj. 3,058
*Chope, Christopher R. OBE (*b.* 1947) *C.*, *Christchurch*, Maj. 13,544
*Clapham, Michael (*b.* 1943) *Lab.*, *Barnsley West and Penistone*, Maj. 12,352
*Clappison, W. James (*b.* 1956) *C.*, *Hertsmere*, Maj. 4,902
Clark, Ms Helen R. (*b.* 1954) *Lab.*, *Peterborough*, Maj. 384
Clark, Dr Lynda M. QC (*b.* 1949) *Lab.*, *Edinburgh Pentlands*, Maj. 1,742
Clark, Paul G. (*b.* 1957) *Lab.*, *Gillingham*, Maj. 2,272
Clarke, Anthony R. (*b.* 1963) *Lab.*, *Northampton South*, Maj. 885
*Clarke, Rt. Hon. Charles R. (*b.* 1950) *Lab.*, *Norwich South*, Maj. 8,816
*Clarke, Rt. Hon. Kenneth H. QC (*b.* 1940) *C.*, *Rushcliffe*, Maj. 7,357
*Clarke, Rt. Hon. Thomas CBE (*b.* 1941) *Lab.*, *Coatbridge and Chryston*, Maj. 15,314
*Clelland, David G. (*b.* 1943) *Lab.*, *Tyne Bridge*, Maj. 14,889
*Clifton-Brown, Geoffrey R. (*b.* 1953) *C.*, *Cotswold*, Maj. 11,983
*Clwyd, Anne (*b.* 1937) *Lab.*, *Cynon Valley*, Maj. 12,998
*Coaker, Vernon R. (*b.* 1953) *Lab.*, *Gedling*, Maj. 5,598
*Coffey, Ms M. Ann (*b.* 1946) *Lab.*, *Stockport*, Maj. 11,569
*Cohen, Harry M. (*b.* 1949) *Lab.*, *Leyton and Wanstead*, Maj. 12,904
Coleman, Iain (*b.* 1958) *Lab.*, *Hammersmith and Fulham*, Maj. 2,015
Collins, Timothy W. G. CBE (*b.* 1964) *C.*, *Westmorland and Lonsdale*, Maj. 3,147
Colman, Anthony (*b.* 1943) *Lab.*, *Putney*, Maj. 2,771
*Connarty, Michael (*b.* 1947) *Lab.*, *Falkirk East*, Maj. 10,712
Conway, Derek (*b.* 1953) *C.*, *Old Bexley and Sidcup*, Maj. 3,345
*Cook, Frank (*b.* 1935) *Lab.*, *Stockton North*, Maj. 14,647
*Cook, Rt. Hon. R. F. (Robin) (*b.* 1946) *Lab.*, *Livingston*, Maj. 10,616
Cooper, Ms Yvette (*b.* 1969) *Lab.*, *Pontefract and Castleford*, Maj. 16,378
*Corbyn, Jeremy B. (*b.* 1949) *Lab.*, *Islington North*, Maj. 12,958
*Cormack, Sir Patrick FSA (*b.* 1939) *C.*, *Staffordshire South*, Maj. 6,881
*Corston, Ms Jean A. (*b.* 1942) *Lab.*, *Bristol East*, Maj. 13,392
Cotter, Brian J. (*b.* 1938) *LD*, *Weston-super-Mare*, Maj. 338
*Cousins, James M. (*b.* 1944) *Lab.*, *Newcastle upon Tyne Central*, Maj. 11,605
*Cox, Thomas M. (*b.* 1930) *Lab.*, *Tooting*, Maj. 10,400
*Cran, James D. (*b.* 1944) *C.*, *Beverley and Holderness*, Maj. 781
Cranston, Ross F. QC (*b.* 1948) *Lab.*, *Dudley North*, Maj. 6,800
*Crausby, David A. (*b.* 1946) *Lab.*, *Bolton North East*, Maj. 8,422
Cruddas, Jon (*b.* 1965) *Lab.*, *Dagenham*, Maj. 8,693
Cryer, Mrs C. Ann (*b.* 1939) *Lab.*, *Keighley*, Maj. 4,005
Cryer, John R. (*b.* 1964) *Lab.*, *Hornchurch*, Maj. 1,482
*Cummings, John S. (*b.* 1943) *Lab.*, *Easington*, Maj. 21,949
*Cunningham, Rt. Hon. Dr J. A. (Jack) PH.D. (*b.* 1939) *Lab.*, *Copeland*, Maj. 4,964
*Cunningham, James D. (*b.* 1941) *Lab.*, *Coventry South*, Maj. 8,279
Cunningham, Tony (*b.* 1952) *Lab.*, *Workington*, Maj. 10,850
*Curry, Rt. Hon. David M. (*b.* 1944) *C.*, *Skipton and Ripon*, Maj. 12,930
Curtis-Thomas, Ms Claire (*b.* 1958) *Lab.*, *Crosby*, Maj. 8,353
Daisley, Paul (*b.* 1957) *Lab.*, *Brent East*, Maj. 13,047
*Dalyell, Tam (*b.* 1932) *Lab.*, *Linlithgow*, Maj. 9,129
*Darling, Rt. Hon. Alistair M. (*b.* 1953) *Lab.*, *Edinburgh Central*, Maj. 8,142
Davey, Edward J. (*b.* 1965) *LD*, *Kingston and Surbiton*, Maj. 15,676
Davey, Ms Valerie (*b.* 1940) *Lab.*, *Bristol West*, Maj. 4,426
David, Wayne (*b.* 1957) *Lab.*, *Caerphilly*, Maj. 14,425
*Davidson, Ian G. (*b.* 1950) *Lab. Co-op.*, *Glasgow Pollok*, Maj. 11,268
*Davies, Rt. Hon. D. J. Denzil (*b.* 1938) *Lab.*, *Llanelli*, Maj. 6,403
Davies, Geraint R. (*b.* 1960) *Lab.*, *Croydon Central*, Maj. 3,984
*Davies, J. Quentin (*b.* 1944) *C.*, *Grantham and Stamford*, Maj. 4,518
*Davis, Rt. Hon. David M. (*b.* 1948) *C.*, *Haltemprice and Howden*, Maj. 1,903
*Davis, Rt. Hon. Terence A. G. (*b.* 1938) *Lab.*, *Birmingham Hodge Hill*, Maj. 11,618
Dawson, T. Hilton (*b.* 1953) *Lab.*, *Lancaster and Wyre*, Maj. 481
Dean, Ms Janet E. A. (*b.* 1949) *Lab.*, *Burton*, Maj. 4,849
*Denham, Rt. Hon. John Y. (*b.* 1953) *Lab.*, *Southampton Itchen*, Maj. 11,223
*Dhanda, Parmjit (*b.* 1971) *Lab.*, *Gloucester*, Maj. 3,880
*Dismore, Andrew H. (*b.* 1954) *Lab.*, *Hendon*, Maj. 7,417
Djanogly, Jonathan (*b.* 1965) *C.*, *Huntingdon*, Maj. 12,792

Dobbin, James (*b.* 1941) *Lab. Co-op.*, *Heywood and Middleton*, Maj. 11,670
*Dobson, Rt. Hon. Frank G. (*b.* 1940) *Lab.*, *Holborn and St Pancras*, Maj. 11,175
Dodds, Nigel MLA (*b.* 1958) *DUP*, *Belfast North*, Maj. 6,387
Doherty, Pat (*b.* 1945) *SF*, *Tyrone West*, Maj. 5,040
Donaldson, Jeffrey M. (*b.* 1962) *UUP*, *Lagan Valley*, Maj. 18,342
*Donohoe, Brian H. (*b.* 1948) *Lab.*, *Cunninghame South*, Maj. 11,230
Doran, Frank (*b.* 1949) *Lab.*, *Aberdeen Central*, Maj. 6,646
*Dorrell, Rt. Hon. Stephen J. (*b.* 1952) *C.*, *Charnwood*, Maj. 7,739
Doughty, Sue (*b.* 1955) *LD*, *Guildford*, Maj. 538
*Dowd, James P. (*b.* 1951) *Lab.*, *Lewisham West*, Maj. 11,920
Drew, David E. (*b.* 1952) *Lab. Co-op.*, *Stroud*, Maj. 5,039
Drown, Ms Julia K. (*b.* 1962) *Lab.*, *Swindon South*, Maj. 7,341
*Duncan, Alan J. C. (*b.* 1957) *C.*, *Rutland and Melton*, Maj. 8,612
Duncan, Peter (*b.* 1965) *C.*, *Galloway and Upper Nithsdale*, Maj. 74
*Duncan Smith, G. Iain (*b.* 1954) *C.*, *Chingford and Woodford Green*, Maj. 5,487
*Dunwoody, Hon. Mrs Gwyneth P. (*b.* 1930) *Lab.*, *Crewe and Nantwich*, Maj. 9,906
*Eagle, Ms Angela (*b.* 1961) *Lab.*, *Wallasey*, Maj. 12,276
Eagle, Ms Maria (*b.* 1961) *Lab.*, *Liverpool Garston*, Maj. 12,494
Edwards, Huw W. E. (*b.* 1953) *Lab.*, *Monmouth*, Maj. 384
Efford, Clive S. (*b.* 1958) *Lab.*, *Eltham*, Maj. 6,996
*Ellman, Ms Louise J. (*b.* 1945) *Lab. Co-op.*, *Liverpool Riverside*, Maj. 13,950
*Ennis, Jeffrey (*b.* 1952) *Lab.*, *Barnsley East and Mexborough*, Maj. 16,789
*Etherington, William (*b.* 1941) *Lab.*, *Sunderland North*, Maj. 13,354
*Evans, Nigel M. (*b.* 1957) *C.*, *Ribble Valley*, Maj. 11,238
Ewing, Annabelle (*b.* 1960) *SNP*, *Perth*, Maj. 48
*Fabricant, Michael (*b.* 1950) *C.*, *Lichfield*, Maj. 4,426
*Fallon, Michael C. (*b.* 1952) *C.*, *Sevenoaks*, Maj. 10,154
Farrelly, Paul (*b.* 1962) *Lab.*, *Newcastle under Lyme*, Maj. 9,986
*Field, Rt. Hon. Frank (*b.* 1942) *Lab.*, *Birkenhead*, Maj. 15,591
*Field, Mark (*b.* 1934) *C.*, *Cities of London and Westminster*, Maj. 4,499
*Fisher, Mark (*b.* 1944) *Lab.*, *Stoke-on-Trent Central*, Maj. 11,845
*Fitzpatrick, James (*b.* 1952) *Lab.*, *Poplar and Canning Town*, Maj. 14,104
*Fitzsimons, Ms Lorna (*b.* 1967) *Lab.*, *Rochdale*, Maj. 5,655
*Flight, Howard E. (*b.* 1948) *C.*, *Arundel and South Downs*, Maj. 13,704
*Flint, Ms Caroline L. (*b.* 1961) *Lab.*, *Don Valley*, Maj. 9,520
Flook, Adrian (*b.* 1963) *C.*, *Taunton*, Maj. 235
*Flynn, Paul P. (*b.* 1935) *Lab.*, *Newport West*, Maj. 9,304
Follett, Ms D. Barbara (*b.* 1942) *Lab.*, *Stevenage*, Maj. 8,566
*Forth, Rt. Hon. Eric (*b.* 1944) *C.*, *Bromley and Chislehurst*, Maj. 9,037
*Foster, Rt. Hon. Derek (*b.* 1937) *Lab.*, *Bishop Auckland*, Maj. 13,926
*Foster, Donald M. E. (*b.* 1947) *LD*, *Bath*, Maj. 9,894
*Foster, Michael J. (*b.* 1946) *Lab.*, *Hastings and Rye*, Maj. 4,308
Foster, Michael (*b.* 1963) *Lab.*, *Worcester*, Maj. 5,766
*Foulkes, George (*b.* 1942) *Lab. Co-op.*, *Carrick, Cumnock and Doon Valley*, Maj. 14,856
*Fox, Dr Liam (*b.* 1961) *C.*, *Woodspring*, Maj. 8,798
Francis, David Hywel (*b.* 1946) *Lab.*, *Aberavon*, Maj. 16,108
Francois, Mark PH.D. (*b.* 1965) *C.*, *Rayleigh*, Maj. 8,290
*Gale, Roger J. (*b.* 1943) *C.*, *Thanet North*, Maj. 6,650
*Galloway, George (*b.* 1954) *Lab.*, *Glasgow Kelvin*, Maj. 7,260
*Gapes, Michael J. (*b.* 1952) *Lab. Co-op.*, *Ilford South*, Maj. 13,997
Gardiner, Barry S. (*b.* 1957) *Lab.*, *Brent North*, Maj. 10,205
*Garnier, Edward H. QC (*b.* 1952) *C.*, *Harborough*, Maj. 5,252
George, Andrew H. (*b.* 1958) *LD*, *St Ives*, Maj. 10,053
*George, Rt. Hon. Bruce T. (*b.* 1942) *Lab.*, *Walsall South*, Maj. 9,931
*Gerrard, Neil F. (*b.* 1942) *Lab.*, *Walthamstow*, Maj. 15,181
*Gibb, Nicholas J. (*b.* 1960) *C.*, *Bognor Regis and Littlehampton*, Maj. 5,643
*Gibson, Dr Ian (*b.* 1938) *Lab.*, *Norwich North*, Maj. 5,863
*Gidley, Sandra (*b.* 1957) *LD*, *Romsey*, Maj. 2,370
Gildernew, Michelle (*b.* 1970) *SF*, *Fermanagh and South Tyrone*, Maj. 53
*Gillan, Mrs Cheryl E. K. (*b.* 1952) *C.*, *Chesham and Amersham*, Maj. 11,882
Gilroy, Mrs Linda (*b.* 1949) *Lab. Co-op.*, *Plymouth Sutton*, Maj. 7,517
*Godsiff, Roger D. (*b.* 1946) *Lab.*, *Birmingham Sparkbrook and Small Heath*, Maj. 16,246
Goggins, Paul G. (*b.* 1953) *Lab.*, *Wythenshawe and Sale East*, Maj. 12,608
Goodman, Paul (*b.* 1960) *C.*, *Wycombe*, Maj. 3,168
Gray, James W. (*b.* 1954) *C.*, *Wiltshire North*, Maj. 3,878
Grayling, Chris (*b.* 1962) *C.*, *Epsom and Ewell*, Maj. 10,080
Green, Damian H. (*b.* 1956) *C.*, *Ashford*, Maj. 7,359
Green, Mathew (*b.* 1970) *LD*, *Ludlow*, Maj. 1,630
*Greenway, John R. (*b.* 1946) *C.*, *Ryedale*, Maj. 4,875
*Grieve, Dominic C. R. (*b.* 1956) *C.*, *Beaconsfield*, Maj. 11,065
*Griffiths, Ms Jane P. (*b.* 1954) *Lab.*, *Reading East*, Maj. 5,588
*Griffiths, Nigel (*b.* 1955) *Lab.*, *Edinburgh South*, Maj. 5,499
*Griffiths, Winston J. (*b.* 1943) *Lab.*, *Bridgend*, Maj. 10,045
Grogan, John T. (*b.* 1961) *Lab.*, *Selby*, Maj. 2,138
*Gummer, Rt. Hon. John S. (*b.* 1939) *C.*, *Suffolk Coastal*, Maj. 4,326
*Hague, Rt. Hon. William J. (*b.* 1961) *C.*, *Richmond*, Maj. 16,319
*Hain, Rt. Hon. Peter G. (*b.* 1950) *Lab.*, *Neath*, Maj. 14,816
*Hall, Michael T. (*b.* 1952) *Lab.*, *Weaver Vale*, Maj. 9,637
Hall, Patrick (*b.* 1951) *Lab.*, *Bedford*, Maj. 6,157
*Hamilton, Fabian (*b.* 1955) *Lab.*, *Leeds North East*, Maj. 7,089
Hamilton, David (*b.* 1950) *Lab.*, *Midlothian*, Maj. 9,014
Hammond, Philip (*b.* 1955) *C.*, *Runnymede and Weybridge*, Maj. 8,360
*Hancock, Michael T. CBE (*b.* 1946) *LD*, *Portsmouth South*, Maj. 6,094
*Hanson, David G. (*b.* 0) *Lab.*, *Delyn*, Maj. 8,065
*Harman, Rt. Hon. Harriet QC (*b.* 1950) *Lab.*, *Camberwell and Peckham*, Maj. 14,123
*Harris, Dr Evan (*b.* 1965) *LD*, *Oxford West and Abingdon*, Maj. 9,185
Harris, Tom (*b.* 1964) *Lab.*, *Glasgow Cathcart*, Maj. 10,816
*Harvey, Nicholas B. (*b.* 1961) *LD*, *Devon North*, Maj. 2,984
*Haselhurst, Rt. Hon. Sir Alan (*b.* 1937) *C.*, *Saffron Walden*, Maj. 12,004

Havard, Dai (*b.* 1949) *Lab.*, *Merthyr Tydfil and Rhymney*, Maj. 14,923
Hawkins, Nick (*b.* 0) *C.*, *Surrey Heath*, Maj. 10,819
Hayes, John H. (*b.* 1958) *C.*, *South Holland and the Deepings*, Maj. 11,099
*Heal, Mrs Sylvia L (*b.* 1942) *Lab.*, *Halesowen and Rowley Regis*, Maj. 7,359
*Heald, Oliver (*b.* 1954) *C.*, *Hertfordshire North East*, Maj. 3,444
Healey, John (*b.* 1960) *Lab.*, *Wentworth*, Maj. 16,449
Heath, David W. CBE (*b.* 1954) *LD*, *Somerton and Frome*, Maj. 668
*Heathcoat-Amory, Rt. Hon. David P. (*b.* 1949) *C.*, *Wells*, Maj. 2,796
*Henderson, Douglas J. (*b.* 1949) *Lab.*, *Newcastle upon Tyne North*, Maj. 14,450
Henderson, Ivan J. (*b.* 1958) *Lab.*, *Harwich*, Maj. 2,596
*Hendrick, Mark (*b.* 1958) *Lab.Co-op*, *Preston*, Maj. 12,268
Hendry, Charles (*b.* 1959) *C.*, *Wealden*, Maj. 13,772
Hepburn, Stephen (*b.* 1959) *Lab.*, *Jarrow*, Maj. 17,595
*Heppell, John (*b.* 1948) *Lab.*, *Nottingham East*, Maj. 10,320
Hermon, Lady Sylvia (*b.* 1956) *UUP*, *Down North*, Maj. 7,324
Hesford, Stephen (*b.* 1957) *Lab.*, *Wirral West*, Maj. 4,035
Hewitt, Rt. Hon. Patricia H. (*b.* 1948) *Lab.*, *Leicester West*, Maj. 9,639
Heyes, David (*b.* 1946) *Lab.*, *Ashton under Lyne*, Maj. 15,518
*Hill, T. Keith (*b.* 1943) *Lab.*, *Streatham*, Maj. 14,270
*Hinchliffe, David M. (*b.* 1948) *Lab.*, *Wakefield*, Maj. 7,954
Hoban, Mark (*b.* 1964) *C.*, *Fareham*, Maj. 7,009
*Hodge, Mrs Margaret E. MBE (*b.* 1944) *Lab.*, *Barking*, Maj. 9,534
*Hoey, Ms Catharine (Kate) L. (*b.* 1946) *Lab.*, *Vauxhall*, Maj. 13,018
*Hogg, Rt. Hon. Douglas M. QC (*b.* 1945) *C.*, *Sleaford and North Hykeham*, Maj. 8,622
Holmes, Paul (*b.* 1957) *LD*, *Chesterfield*, Maj. 2,586
*Hood, James (*b.* 1948) *Lab.*, *Clydesdale*, Maj. 7,794
*Hoon, Rt. Hon. Geoffrey W. (*b.* 1953) *Lab.*, *Ashfield*, Maj. 13,268
Hope, Philip I. (*b.* 1955) *Lab. Co-op.*, *Corby*, Maj. 5,700
Hopkins, Kelvin P. (*b.* 1941) *Lab.*, *Luton North*, Maj. 9,977
*Horam, John R. (*b.* 1939) *C.*, *Orpington*, Maj. 269
*Howard, Rt. Hon. Michael QC (*b.* 1941) *C.*, *Folkestone and Hythe*, Maj. 5,907
*Howarth, Rt. Hon. Alan CBE (*b.* 1967) *Lab.*, *Newport East*, Maj. 9,874
*Howarth, George E. (*b.* 1949) *Lab.*, *Knowsley North and Sefton East*, Maj. 18,927
Howarth, J. Gerald D. (*b.* 1947) *C.*, *Aldershot*, Maj. 6,564
*Howells, Dr Kim S. PH.D. (*b.* 1946) *Lab.*, *Pontypridd*, Maj. 17,684
Hoyle, Lindsay H. (*b.* 1957) *Lab.*, *Chorley*, Maj. 8,444
*Hughes, Ms Beverley J. (*b.* 1950) *Lab.*, *Stretford and Urmston*, Maj. 13,239
*Hughes, Kevin M. (*b.* 1952) *Lab.*, *Doncaster North*, Maj. 15,187
*Hughes, Simon H. W. (*b.* 1951) *LD*, *Southwark North and Bermondsey*, Maj. 9,632
Humble, Mrs Jovanka (Joan) (*b.* 1951) *Lab.*, *Blackpool North and Fleetwood*, Maj. 5,721
*Hume, John MEP (*b.* 1937) *SDLP*, *Foyle*, Maj. 11,550
*Hunter, Andrew R. F. (*b.* 1943) *C.*, *Basingstoke*, Maj. 880
Hurst, Alan A. (*b.* 1945) *Lab.*, *Braintree*, Maj. 358
*Hutton, Rt. Hon. John M. P. (*b.* 1955) *Lab.*, *Barrow and Furness*, Maj. 9,889
Iddon, Brian (*b.* 1940) *Lab.*, *Bolton South East*, Maj. 12,871
*Illsley, Eric E. (*b.* 1955) *Lab.*, *Barnsley Central*, Maj. 15,130
*Ingram, Rt. Hon. Adam P. (*b.* 1947) *Lab.*, *East Kilbride*, Maj. 12,755
*Jack, Rt. Hon. J. Michael (*b.* 1946) *C.*, *Fylde*, Maj. 9,610
*Jackson, Ms Glenda M. CBE (*b.* 1936) *Lab.*, *Hampstead and Highgate*, Maj. 7,876
*Jackson, Mrs Helen M. (*b.* 1939) *Lab.*, *Sheffield Hillsborough*, Maj. 14,569
*Jackson, Robert V. (*b.* 1946) *C.*, *Wantage*, Maj. 5,600
*Jamieson, David C. (*b.* 1947) *Lab.*, *Plymouth Devonport*, Maj. 13,033
*Jenkin, Hon. Bernard C. (*b.* 1959) *C.*, *Essex North*, Maj. 7,186
*Jenkins, Brian D. (*b.* 1942) *Lab.*, *Tamworth*, Maj. 4,598
*Johnson, Alan A. (*b.* 1950) *Lab.*, *Hull West and Hessle*, Maj. 10,951
Johnson, Boris (*b.* 1964) *C.*, *Henley*, Maj. 8,458
Johnson, Ms Melanie J. (*b.* 1955) *Lab.*, *Welwyn Hatfield*, Maj. 1,196
Jones, Ms Helen M. (*b.* 1954) *Lab.*, *Warrington North*, Maj. 15,156
*Jones, Jonathan O. (*b.* 1954) *Lab. Co-op.*, *Cardiff Central*, Maj. 659
Jones, Kevan (*b.* 1964) *Lab.*, *Durham North*, Maj. 18,683
*Jones, Ms Lynne M. PH.D. (*b.* 1951) *Lab.*, *Birmingham Selly Oak*, Maj. 10,339
*Jones, Martyn D. (*b.* 1947) *Lab.*, *Clwyd South*, Maj. 8,898
*Jones, Nigel D. (*b.* 1948) *LD*, *Cheltenham*, Maj. 5,255
*Jowell, Rt. Hon. Tessa J. H. D. (*b.* 1947) *Lab.*, *Dulwich and West Norwood*, Maj. 12,310
*Joyce, Eric (*b.* 1960) *Lab.*, *Falkirk West*, Maj. 8,532
*Kaufman, Rt. Hon. Gerald B. (*b.* 1930) *Lab.*, *Manchester Gorton*, Maj. 11,304
Keeble, Ms Sally C. (*b.* 1951) *Lab.*, *Northampton North*, Maj. 7,893
Keen, Mrs Ann L. (*b.* 1948) *Lab.Co-op*, *Brentford and Isleworth*, Maj. 10,318
*Keen, D. Alan (*b.* 1937) *Labour Co-op*, *Feltham and Heston*, Maj. 12,657
*Keetch, Paul S. (*b.* 1961) *LD*, *Hereford*, Maj. 968
*Kelly, Ms Ruth M. (*b.* 1968) *Lab.*, *Bolton West*, Maj. 5,518
*Kemp, Fraser (*b.* 1958) *Lab.*, *Houghton and Washington East*, Maj. 19,818
*Kennedy, Rt. Hon. Charles P. (*b.* 1959) *LD*, *Ross, Skye and Inverness West*, Maj. 12,952
*Kennedy, Mrs Jane E. (*b.* 1958) *Lab.*, *Liverpool Wavertree*, Maj. 12,319
*Key, S. Robert (*b.* 1945) *C.*, *Salisbury*, Maj. 8,703
*Khabra, Piara S. (*b.* 1922) *Lab.*, *Ealing Southall*, Maj. 13,683
*Kidney, David N. (*b.* 1955) *Lab.*, *Stafford*, Maj. 5,032
*Kilfoyle, Peter (*b.* 1946) *Lab.*, *Liverpool Walton*, Maj. 17,996
King, Andrew (*b.* 1948) *Lab.*, *Rugby and Kenilworth*, Maj. 2,877
*King, Ms Oona T. (*b.* 1967) *Lab.*, *Bethnal Green and Bow*, Maj. 10,057
*Kirkbride, Miss Julie (*b.* 1960) *C.*, *Bromsgrove*, Maj. 8,138
*Kirkwood, Archibald J. (*b.* 1946) *LD*, *Roxburgh and Berwickshire*, Maj. 7,511
Knight, Rt. Hon. Greg (*b.* 1949) *C.*, *Yorkshire East*, Maj. 4,682
Knight, Jim (*b.* 1965) *Lab.*, *Dorset South*, Maj. 153
*Kumar, Dr Ashok (*b.* 1956) *Lab.*, *Middlesbrough South and Cleveland East*, Maj. 9,351
*Ladyman, Dr Stephen J. (*b.* 1952) *Lab.*, *Thanet South*, Maj. 1,792
Laing, Mrs Eleanor F. (*b.* 1958) *C.*, *Epping Forest*, Maj. 8,426
*Lait, Ms Jacqueline A. H. (*b.* 1947) *C.*, *Beckenham*, Maj. 4,959

Lamb, Norman (*b.* 1957) *LD*, *Norfolk North*, Maj. 483
*Lammy, David (*b.* 1972) *Lab.*, *Tottenham*, Maj. 16,916
*Lansley, Andrew D. CBE (*b.* 1956) *C.*, *Cambridgeshire South*, Maj. 8,403
*Lawrence, Mrs Jacqueline R. (*b.* 1948) *Lab.*, *Preseli Pembrokeshire*, Maj. 2,946
Laws, David (*b.* 1965) *LD*, *Yeovil*, Maj. 3,928
*Laxton, Robert (*b.* 1944) *Lab.*, *Derby North*, Maj. 6,982
Lazarowicz, Mark (*b.* 1953) *Lab. Co-op.*, *Edinburgh North and Leith*, Maj. 8,817
*Leigh, Edward J. E. (*b.* 1950) *C.*, *Gainsborough*, Maj. 8,071
*Lepper, David (*b.* 1945) *Lab. Co-op.*, *Brighton Pavilion*, Maj. 9,643
Leslie, Christopher M. (*b.* 1972) *Lab.*, *Shipley*, Maj. 1,428
Letwin, Oliver (*b.* 1956) *C.*, *Dorset West*, Maj. 1,414
*Levitt, Tom (*b.* 1954) *Lab.*, *High Peak*, Maj. 4,489
*Lewis, Ivan (*b.* 1967) *Lab.*, *Bury South*, Maj. 12,772
*Lewis, Dr Julian M. (*b.* 1951) *C.*, *New Forest East*, Maj. 3,829
*Lewis, Terence (*b.* 1935) *Lab.*, *Worsley*, Maj. 11,787
*Liddell, Rt. Hon. Helen (*b.* 1950) *Lab.*, *Airdrie and Shotts*, Maj. 12,340
Liddell-Grainger, Ian (*b.* 1959) *C.*, *Bridgwater*, Maj. 4,987
*Lidington, David R. PH.D. (*b.* 1956) *C.*, *Aylesbury*, Maj. 10,009
*Lilley, Rt. Hon. Peter B. (*b.* 1943) *C.*, *Hitchin and Harpenden*, Maj. 6,663
Linton, J. Martin (*b.* 1944) *Lab.*, *Battersea*, Maj. 5,053
*Lloyd, Anthony J. (*b.* 1950) *Lab.*, *Manchester Central*, Maj. 13,742
*Llwyd, Elfyn (*b.* 1951) *PC*, *Meirionnydd nant Conwy*, Maj. 5,684
*Lord, Sir Michael N. (*b.* 1938) *C.*, *Suffolk Central and Ipswich North*, Maj. 3,469
*Loughton, Timothy P. (*b.* 1962) *C.*, *Worthing East and Shoreham*, Maj. 6,139
*Love, Andrew (*b.* 1949) *Lab. Co-op.*, *Edmonton*, Maj. 9,772
Lucas, Ian (*b.* 1960) *Lab.*, *Wrexham*, Maj. 9,188
*Luff, Peter J. (*b.* 1955) *C.*, *Worcestershire Mid*, Maj. 10,627
Luke, Ian (*b.* 1951) *Lab.*, *Dundee East*, Maj. 4,475
Lyons, John (*b.* 1950) *Lab.*, *Strathkelvin and Bearsden*, Maj. 11,717
*MacDonald, Calum A. PH.D. (*b.* 1956) *Lab.*, *Western Isles*, Maj. 1,074
*MacDougall, John (*b.* 1947) *Lab.*, *Fife Central*, Maj. 10,075
*Mackay, Rt. Hon. Andrew J. (*b.* 1949) *C.*, *Bracknell*, Maj. 6,713
*Mackinlay, Andrew S. (*b.* 1949) *Lab.*, *Thurrock*, Maj. 9,997
*Maclean, Rt. Hon. David J. (*b.* 1953) *C.*, *Penrith and the Border*, Maj. 14,677
*MacShane, Denis PH.D. (*b.* 1948) *Lab.*, *Rotherham*, Maj. 13,077
Mactaggart, Ms Fiona M. (*b.* 1953) *Lab.*, *Slough*, Maj. 12,508
*McAvoy, Thomas M. (*b.* 1943) *Lab. Co-op.*, *Glasgow Rutherglen*, Maj. 12,625
*McCabe, Stephen J. (*b.* 1955) *Lab.*, *Birmingham Hall Green*, Maj. 6,648
*McCafferty, Ms Christine (*b.* 1945) *Lab.*, *Calder Valley*, Maj. 3,094
*McCartney, Rt. Hon. Ian (*b.* 1951) *Lab.*, *Makerfield*, Maj. 17,750
McDonagh, Ms Siobhain A. (*b.* 1960) *Lab.*, *Mitcham and Morden*, Maj. 13,785
McDonnell, John M. (*b.* 1951) *Lab.*, *Hayes and Harlington*, Maj. 13,466
*McFall, John (*b.* 1944) *Lab. Co-op.*, *Dumbarton*, Maj. 9,575
*McGrady, Edward K. (*b.* 1935) *SDLP*, *Down South*, Maj. 13,858
McGuinness, Martin (*b.* 1950) *SF*, *Ulster Mid*, Maj. 9,953
McGuire, Anne (*b.* 1949) *Lab.*, *Stirling*, Maj. 6,274
*McIntosh, Miss Anne C. B. (*b.* 1954) *C.*, *Vale of York*, Maj. 12,517
McIsaac, Ms Shona (*b.* 1960) *Lab.*, *Cleethorpes*, Maj. 5,620
McKechin, Anne (*b.* 1961) *Lab.*, *Glasgow Maryhill*, Maj. 9,888
McKenna, Ms Rosemary CBE (*b.* 1941) *Lab.*, *Cumbernauld and Kilsyth*, Maj. 7,520
*McLoughlin, Patrick A. (*b.* 1957) *C.*, *Derbyshire West*, Maj. 7,370
*McNamara, J. Kevin (*b.* 1934) *Lab.*, *Hull North*, Maj. 10,721
*McNulty, Anthony J. (*b.* 1958) *Lab.*, *Harrow East*, Maj. 11,124
*McWalter, Tony (*b.* 1945) *Lab. Co-op.*, *Hemel Hempstead*, Maj. 3,742
*McWilliam, John D. (*b.* 1941) *Lab.*, *Blaydon*, Maj. 7,809
Mahmood, Khalid (*b.* 1961) *Lab.*, *Birmingham Perry Barr*, Maj. 8,753
*Mahon, Mrs Alice (*b.* 1937) *Lab.*, *Halifax*, Maj. 6,129
Malins, Humfrey J. CBE (*b.* 1945) *C.*, *Woking*, Maj. 6,759
*Mallaber, Ms C. Judith (*b.* 1951) *Lab.*, *Amber Valley*, Maj. 7,227
*Mallon, Seamus (*b.* 1936) *SDLP*, *Newry and Armagh*, Maj. 3,575
*Mandelson, Rt. Hon. Peter B. (*b.* 1953) *Lab.*, *Hartlepool*, Maj. 14,571
Mann, John (*b.* 1960) *Lab.*, *Bassetlaw*, Maj. 9,748
*Maples, John C. (*b.* 1943) *C.*, *Stratford-upon-Avon*, Maj. 11,802
Marris, Robert (*b.* 1955) *Lab.*, *Wolverhampton South West*, Maj. 3,487
*Marsden, Gordon (*b.* 1953) *Lab.*, *Blackpool South*, Maj. 8,262
*Marsden, Paul W. B. (*b.* 1968) *Lab.*, *Shrewsbury and Atcham*, Maj. 3,579
*Marshall, David PH.D (*b.* 1941) *Lab.*, *Glasgow Shettleston*, Maj. 9,818
*Marshall, James PH.D. (*b.* 1941) *Lab.*, *Leicester South*, Maj. 13,243
*Marshall-Andrews, Robert G. QC (*b.* 1944) *Lab.*, *Medway*, Maj. 3,780
*Martin, Rt. Hon. Michael J. (*b.* 1945) *The Speaker Lab.*, *Glasgow Springburn*, Maj. 11,378
*Martlew, Eric A. (*b.* 1949) *Lab.*, *Carlisle*, Maj. 5,702
*Mates, Michael J. (*b.* 1934) *C.*, *Hampshire East*, Maj. 8,890
*Maude, Rt. Hon. Francis A. A. (*b.* 1953) *C.*, *Horsham*, Maj. 13,666
*Mawhinney, Rt. Hon. Sir Brian PH.D. (*b.* 1940) *C.*, *Cambridgeshire North West*, Maj. 8,101
*May, Mrs Theresa M. (*b.* 1956) *C.*, *Maidenhead*, Maj. 3,284
*Meacher, Rt. Hon. Michael H. (*b.* 1939) *Lab.*, *Oldham West and Royton*, Maj. 13,365
*Meale, J. Alan (*b.* 1949) *Lab.*, *Mansfield*, Maj. 11,038
Mercer, Patrick OBE (*b.* 1956) *C.*, *Newark*, Maj. 4,073
*Merron, Ms Gillian J. (*b.* 1959) *Lab.*, *Lincoln*, Maj. 8,420
*Michael, Rt. Hon. Alun E. (*b.* 1943) *Lab. Co-op.*, *Cardiff South and Penarth*, Maj. 12,287
*Milburn, Rt. Hon. Alan (*b.* 1958) *Lab.*, *Darlington*, Maj. 9,529
Miliband, David (*b.* 1966) *Lab.*, *South Shields*, Maj. 14,090
*Miller, Andrew P. (*b.* 1949) *Lab.*, *Ellesmere Port and Neston*, Maj. 10,861
*Mitchell, Austin V. D.PHIL. (*b.* 1934) *Lab.*, *Great Grimsby*, Maj. 11,484
Mitchell, Andrew (*b.* 1956) *C.*, *Sutton Coldfield*, Maj. 10,104
*Moffatt, Mrs Laura J. (*b.* 1954) *Lab.*, *Crawley*, Maj. 6,770

*Moonie, Dr Lewis G. (*b.* 1947) *Lab. Co-op.*, *Kirkcaldy*, Maj. 8,963
*Moore, Michael (*b.* 1965) *LD*, *Tweeddale, Ettrick and Lauderdale*, Maj. 5,157
*Moran, Ms Margaret (*b.* 1955) *Lab.*, *Luton South*, Maj. 10,133
Morgan, Ms Julie (*b.* 1944) *Lab.*, *Cardiff North*, Maj. 6,165
*Morley, Elliot A. (*b.* 1952) *Lab.*, *Scunthorpe*, Maj. 10,372
*Morris, Rt. Hon. Estelle (*b.* 1952) *Lab.*, *Birmingham Yardley*, Maj. 2,578
*Moss, Malcolm D. (*b.* 1943) *C.*, *Cambridgeshire North East*, Maj. 6,373
Mountford, Ms Kali C. J. (*b.* 1954) *Lab.*, *Colne Valley*, Maj. 4,639
*Mudie, George E. (*b.* 1945) *Lab.*, *Leeds East*, Maj. 12,643
*Mullin, Christopher J. (*b.* 1947) *Lab.*, *Sunderland South*, Maj. 13,667
Munn, Meg (*b.* 1959) *Lab.Co-op*, *Sheffield Heeley*, Maj. 11,704
Murphy, Denis (*b.* 1948) *Lab.*, *Wansbeck*, Maj. 13,101
Murphy, Jim (*b.* 1967) *Lab.*, *Eastwood*, Maj. 9,141
*Murphy, Rt. Hon. Paul P. (*b.* 1948) *Lab.*, *Torfaen*, Maj. 16,280
Murrison, Andrew (*b.* 1961) *C.*, *Westbury*, Maj. 5,294
Naysmith, J. Douglas (*b.* 1941) *Lab. Co-op.*, *Bristol North West*, Maj. 11,087
Norman, Archibald J. (*b.* 1954) *C.*, *Tunbridge Wells*, Maj. 9,730
Norris, Dan (*b.* 1960) *Lab.*, *Wansdyke*, Maj. 5,113
*Oaten, Mark (*b.* 1964) *LD*, *Winchester*, Maj. 9,634
*O'Brien, Michael (*b.* 1954) *Lab.*, *Warwickshire North*, Maj. 9,639
*O'Brien, Stephen (*b.* 1957) *C.*, *Eddisbury*, Maj. 4,568
*O'Brien, William (*b.* 1929) *Lab.*, *Normanton*, Maj. 9,937
*O'Hara, Edward (*b.* 1937) *Lab.*, *Knowsley South*, Maj. 21,316
*Olner, William J. (*b.* 1942) *Lab.*, *Nuneaton*, Maj. 7,535
*O'Neill, Martin J. (*b.* 1945) *Lab.*, *Ochil*, Maj. 5,349
Öpik, Lembit (*b.* 1965) *LD*, *Montgomeryshire*, Maj. 6,234
*Organ, Ms Diana M. (*b.* 1952) *Lab.*, *Forest of Dean*, Maj. 2,049
Osborne, Mrs Sandra C. (*b.* 1956) *Lab.*, *Ayr*, Maj. 2,545
Osborne, George (*b.* 1971) *C.*, *Tatton*, Maj. 8,611
*Ottaway, Richard G. J. (*b.* 1945) *C.*, *Croydon South*, Maj. 8,697
*Owen, Albert (*b.* 1960) *Lab.*, *Ynys Môn*, Maj. 800
*Page, Richard L. (*b.* 1941) *C.*, *Hertfordshire South West*, Maj. 8,181
*Paice, James E. T. (*b.* 1949) *C.*, *Cambridgeshire South East*, Maj. 8,990
*Paisley, Revd Ian R. K. MEP (*b.* 1926) *DUP*, *Antrim North*, Maj. 14,224
Palmer, Nicholas D. (*b.* 1950) *Lab.*, *Broxtowe*, Maj. 5,873
*Paterson, Owen W. (*b.* 1956) *C.*, *Shropshire North*, Maj. 6,241
*Pearson, Ian P. PH.D. (*b.* 1959) *Lab.*, *Dudley South*, Maj. 6,817
*Perham, Ms Linda (*b.* 1947) *Lab.*, *Ilford North*, Maj. 2,115
Picking, Anne (*b.* 1958) *Lab.*, *East Lothian*, Maj. 10,830
*Pickles, Eric J. (*b.* 1952) *C.*, *Brentwood and Ongar*, Maj. 2,821
*Pickthall, Colin (*b.* 1944) *Lab.*, *Lancashire West*, Maj. 9,643
*Pike, Peter L. (*b.* 1937) *Lab.*, *Burnley*, Maj. 10,498
*Plaskitt, James A. (*b.* 1954) *Lab.*, *Warwick and Leamington*, Maj. 5,953
Pollard, Kerry P. (*b.* 1944) *Lab.*, *St Albans*, Maj. 4,466
*Pond, Christopher R. (*b.* 1952) *Lab.*, *Gravesham*, Maj. 4,862
*Pope, Gregory J. (*b.* 1960) *Lab.*, *Hyndburn*, Maj. 8,219
*Portillo, Rt. Hon. Michael (*b.* 1953) *C.*, *Kensington and Chelsea*, Maj. 8,771
Pound, Stephen P. (*b.* 1948) *Lab.*, *Ealing North*, Maj. 11,837
*Powell, Sir Raymond (*b.* 1928) *Lab.*, *Ogmore*, Maj. 14,574
*Prentice, Ms Bridget T. (*b.* 1952) *Lab.*, *Lewisham East*, Maj. 8,959
*Prentice, Gordon (*b.* 1951) *Lab.*, *Pendle*, Maj. 4,275
*Prescott, Rt. Hon. John L. (*b.* 1938) *Lab.*, *Hull East*, Maj. 15,325
Price, Adam (*b.* 1968) *PC*, *Carmarthen East and Dinefwr*, Maj. 2,590
*Primarolo, Ms Dawn (*b.* 1954) *Lab.*, *Bristol South*, Maj. 14,181
*Prisk, Mark (*b.* 1962) *C.*, *Hertford and Stortford*, Maj. 5,603
*Prosser, Gwynfor M. (*b.* 1943) *Lab.*, *Dover*, Maj. 5,199
Pugh, John (*b.* 1949) *LD*, *Southport*, Maj. 3,007
*Purchase, Kenneth (*b.* 1939) *Lab. Co-op.*, *Wolverhampton North East*, Maj. 9,965
Purnell, James (*b.* 1970) *Lab.*, *Stalybridge and Hyde*, Maj. 8,859
*Quin, Rt. Hon. Joyce G. (*b.* 1944) *Lab.*, *Gateshead East and Washington West*, Maj. 17,904
*Quinn, Lawrence W. (*b.* 1956) *Lab.*, *Scarborough and Whitby*, Maj. 3,585
*Rammell, William E. (*b.* 1959) *Lab.*, *Harlow*, Maj. 5,228
*Randall, A. John (*b.* 1955) *C.*, *Uxbridge*, Maj. 2,098
Rapson, Sydney N. J. (*b.* 1942) *Lab.*, *Portsmouth North*, Maj. 5,134
*Raynsford, Rt. Hon. W. R. N. (Nick) (*b.* 1945) *Lab.*, *Greenwich and Woolwich*, Maj. 13,433
*Redwood, Rt. Hon. John A. D.PHIL. (*b.* 1951) *C.*, *Wokingham*, Maj. 5,994
Reed, Andrew J. (*b.* 1964) *Lab.*, *Loughborough*, Maj. 6,378
Reid, Alan (*b.* 1954) *LD*, *Argyll and Bute*, Maj. 1,653
*Reid, Rt. Hon. John PH.D. (*b.* 1947) *Lab.*, *Hamilton North and Bellshill*, Maj. 13,561
*Rendel, David D. (*b.* 1949) *LD*, *Newbury*, Maj. 2,415
*Robathan, Andrew R. G. (*b.* 1951) *C.*, *Blaby*, Maj. 6,209
*Robertson, John (*b.* 1952) *Lab.*, *Glasgow Anniesland*, Maj. 11,054
Robertson, Angus (*b.* 1945) *SNP*, *Moray*, Maj. 11,054
Robertson, Hugh (*b.* 1962) *C.*, *Faversham and Mid Kent*, Maj. 4,183
Robertson, Laurence A. (*b.* 1958) *C.*, *Tewkesbury*, Maj. 8,663
*Robinson, Geoffrey (*b.* 1938) *Lab.*, *Coventry North West*, Maj. 10,874
Robinson, Iris MLA (*b.* 1949) *DUP*, *Strangford*, Maj. 1,110
*Robinson, Peter D. (*b.* 1948) *DUP*, *Belfast East*, Maj. 7,117
*Roche, Mrs Barbara M. R. (*b.* 1954) *Lab.*, *Hornsey and Wood Green*, Maj. 10,614
*Roe, Mrs Marion A. (*b.* 1936) *C.*, *Broxbourne*, Maj. 8,993
*Rooney, Terence H. (*b.* 1950) *Lab.*, *Bradford North*, Maj. 8,969
Rosindell, Andrew (*b.* 1966) *C.*, *Romford*, Maj. 5,977
*Ross, Ernest (*b.* 1942) *Lab.*, *Dundee West*, Maj. 6,800
*Roy, Frank (*b.* 1958) *Lab.*, *Motherwell and Wishaw*, Maj. 10,956
*Ruane, Christopher S. (*b.* 1958) *Lab.*, *Vale of Clwyd*, Maj. 5,761
*Ruddock, Mrs Joan M. (*b.* 1943) *Lab.*, *Lewisham Deptford*, Maj. 15,293
Ruffley, David L. (*b.* 1962) *C.*, *Bury St Edmunds*, Maj. 2,503
Russell, Ms Christine M. (*b.* 1945) *Lab.*, *City of Chester*, Maj. 6,894
*Russell, Robert E. (*b.* 1946) *LD*, *Colchester*, Maj. 5,553
*Ryan, Ms Joan M. (*b.* 1955) *Lab.*, *Enfield North*, Maj. 2,291

*Salmond, Alexander E. A. (*b.* 1954) *SNP, Banff and Buchan*, Maj. 10,503
Salter, Martin J. (*b.* 1954) *Lab., Reading West*, Maj. 8,849
*Sanders, Adrian M. (*b.* 1959) *LD, Torbay*, Maj. 6,708
*Sarwar, Mohammad (*b.* 1952) *Lab., Glasgow Govan*, Maj. 6,400
*Savidge, Malcolm K. (*b.* 1946) *Lab., Aberdeen North*, Maj. 4,449
*Sawford, Philip A. (*b.* 1950) *Lab., Kettering*, Maj. 665
*Sayeed, Jonathan (*b.* 1948) *C., Bedfordshire Mid*, Maj. 8,066
*Sedgemore, Brian C. J. (*b.* 1937) *Lab., Hackney South and Shoreditch*, Maj. 15,049
Selous, Andres (*b.* 1962) *C., Bedfordshire South West*, Maj. 776
*Shaw, Jonathan R. (*b.* 1966) *Lab., Chatham and Aylesford*, Maj. 4,340
*Sheerman, Barry J. (*b.* 1940) *Lab. Co-op., Huddersfield*, Maj. 10,046
*Shephard, Rt. Hon. Gillian P. (*b.* 1940) *C., Norfolk South West*, Maj. 9,366
*Shepherd, Richard C. S. (*b.* 1942) *C., Aldridge-Brownhills*, Maj. 3,768
Sheridan, Jim (*b.* 1952) *Lab., Renfrewshire West*, Maj. 8,575
*Shipley, Ms Debra A. (*b.* 1957) *Lab., Stourbridge*, Maj. 3,812
*Short, Rt. Hon. Clare (*b.* 1946) *Lab., Birmingham Ladywood*, Maj. 18,143
Simmonds, Mark (*b.* 1964) *C., Boston and Skegness*, Maj. 515
Simon, Sion (*b.* 1969) *Lab., Birmingham Erdington*, Maj. 9,962
*Simpson, Alan J. (*b.* 1948) *Lab., Nottingham South*, Maj. 9,989
*Simpson, Keith (*b.* 1949) *C., Norfolk Mid*, Maj. 4,562
Singh, Marsha (*b.* 1954) *Lab., Bradford West*, Maj. 4,165
*Skinner, Dennis E. (*b.* 1932) *Lab., Bolsover*, Maj. 18,777
*Smith, Rt. Hon. Andrew D. (*b.* 1951) *Lab., Oxford East*, Maj. 10,344
*Smith, Ms Angela E. (*b.* 1959) *Lab. Co-op., Basildon*, Maj. 7,738
*Smith, Rt. Hon. Christopher R. PH.D. (*b.* 1951) *Lab., Islington South and Finsbury*, Maj. 7,280
*Smith, Ms Geraldine (*b.* 1961) *Lab., Morecambe and Lunesdale*, Maj. 5,092
*Smith, Ms Jacqui (*b.* 1962) *Lab., Redditch*, Maj. 2,484
*Smith, John W. P. (*b.* 1951) *Lab., Vale of Glamorgan*, Maj. 4,700
*Smith, Llewellyn T. (*b.* 1944) *Lab., Blaenau Gwent*, Maj. 19,313
*Smith, Sir Robert BT. (*b.* 1958) *LD, Aberdeenshire West and Kincardine*, Maj. 4,821
*Smyth, Revd W. Martin (*b.* 1931) *UUP, Belfast South*, Maj. 5,399
*Soames, Hon. A. Nicholas W. (*b.* 1948) *C., Sussex Mid*, Maj. 6,898
*Soley, Clive S. (*b.* 1939) *Lab., Ealing Acton and Shepherd's Bush*, Maj. 10,789
Southworth, Ms Helen M. (*b.* 1956) *Lab., Warrington South*, Maj. 7,387
*Spellar, Rt. Hon. John F. (*b.* 1947) *Lab., Warley*, Maj. 11,850
Spelman, Mrs Caroline A. (*b.* 1958) *C., Meriden*, Maj. 3,784
*Spicer, Sir Michael (*b.* 1943) *C., Worcestershire West*, Maj. 5,374
Spink, Dr Robert (*b.* 1948) *C., Castle Point*, Maj. 985
*Spring, Richard J. G. (*b.* 1946) *C., Suffolk West*, Maj. 4,295
*Squire, Ms Rachel A. (*b.* 1954) *Lab., Dunfermline West*, Maj. 10,980
*Stanley, Rt. Hon. Sir John (*b.* 1942) *C., Tonbridge and Malling*, Maj. 8,250
Starkey, Dr Phyllis M. (*b.* 1947) *Lab., Milton Keynes South West*, Maj. 6,978
*Steen, Anthony (*b.* 1939) *C., Totnes*, Maj. 3,597
*Steinberg, Gerald N. (*b.* 1945) *Lab., City of Durham*, Maj. 13,441
*Stevenson, George W. (*b.* 1938) *Lab., Stoke-on-Trent South*, Maj. 10,489
*Stewart, David J. (*b.* 1956) *Lab., Inverness East, Nairn and Lochaber*, Maj. 4,716
*Stewart, Ian (*b.* 1950) *Lab., Eccles*, Maj. 14,528
*Stinchcombe, Paul D. (*b.* 1962) *Lab., Wellingborough*, Maj. 2,355
*Stoate, Dr Howard G. A. (*b.* 1954) *Lab., Dartford*, Maj. 3,306
*Strang, Rt. Hon Dr Gavin (*b.* 1943) *Lab., Edinburgh East and Musselburgh*, Maj. 12,168
*Straw, Rt. Hon. J. W. (Jack) (*b.* 1946) *Lab., Blackburn*, Maj. 9,249
*Streeter, Gary N. (*b.* 1955) *C., Devon South West*, Maj. 7,144
*Stringer, Graham E. (*b.* 1950) *Lab., Manchester Blackley*, Maj. 14,464
*Stuart, Mrs Gisela G. (*b.* 1955) *Lab., Birmingham Edgbaston*, Maj. 4,698
*Stunell, Andrew (*b.* 1942) *LD, Hazel Grove*, Maj. 8,435
*Sutcliffe, Gerard (*b.* 1953) *Lab., Bradford South*, Maj. 9,662
Swayne, Desmond A. (*b.* 1956) *C., New Forest West*, Maj. 13,191
Swire, Hugo (*b.* 1959) *C., Devon East*, Maj. 8,195
*Syms, Robert A. R. (*b.* 1956) *C., Poole*, Maj. 7,166
Tami, Mark (*b.* 1963) *Lab., Alyn and Deeside*, Maj. 9,222
*Tapsell, Sir Peter (*b.* 1930) *C., Louth and Horncastle*, Maj. 7,554
*Taylor, Rt. Hon. Ann (*b.* 1947) *Lab., Dewsbury*, Maj. 7,449
*Taylor, Ms Dari J. (*b.* 1944) *Lab., Stockton South*, Maj. 9,086
Taylor, David L. (*b.* 1946) *Lab., Leicestershire North West*, Maj. 8,157
*Taylor, Sir Edward (Teddy) (*b.* 1937) *C., Rochford and Southend East*, Maj. 7,034
*Taylor, Ian C. MBE (*b.* 1945) *C., Esher and Walton*, Maj. 11,538
*Taylor, John M. (*b.* 1941) *C., Solihull*, Maj. 9,407
*Taylor, Matthew O. J. (*b.* 1963) *LD, Truro and St Austell*, Maj. 8,065
Taylor, Dr Richard (*b.* 1935) *KHHC, Wyre Forest*, Maj. 17,630
Thomas, Gareth (*b.* 1954) *Lab., Clwyd West*, Maj. 1,115
*Thomas, Gareth R. (*b.* 1967) *Lab., Harrow West*, Maj. 6,156
*Thomas, Simon (*b.* 1963) *PC, Ceredigion*, Maj. 3,944
*Thurso, John (*b.* 1953) *LD, Caithness, Sutherland and Easter Ross*, Maj. 2,744
*Timms, Stephen C. (*b.* 1955) *Lab., East Ham*, Maj. 21,032
*Tipping, S. P. (Paddy) (*b.* 1949) *Lab., Sherwood*, Maj. 9,373
Todd, Mark W. (*b.* 1954) *Lab., Derbyshire South*, Maj. 7,851
Tonge, Dr Jennifer L. (*b.* 1941) *LD, Richmond Park*, Maj. 4,964
*Touhig, J. Donnelly (Don) (*b.* 1947) *Lab. Co-op., Islwyn*, Maj. 15,309
*Tredinnick, David A. S. (*b.* 1950) *C., Bosworth*, Maj. 2,280
*Trend, Hon. Michael St J. CBE (*b.* 1952) *C., Windsor*, Maj. 8,889
*Trickett, Jon H. (*b.* 1950) *Lab., Hemsworth*, Maj. 15,636
*Trimble, Rt. Hon. W. David (*b.* 1944) *UUP, Upper Bann*, Maj. 2,058
Truswell, Paul A. (*b.* 1955) *Lab., Pudsey*, Maj. 5,626

Turner, Andrew (*b.* 1953) *C.*, *Isle of Wight*, Maj. 2,826
*Turner, Dennis (*b.* 1942) *Lab. Co-op.*, *Wolverhampton South East*, Maj. 12,464
Turner, Desmond S. (*b.* 1939) *Lab.*, *Brighton Kemptown*, Maj. 4,922
*Turner, Neil (*b.* 1945) *Lab.*, *Wigan*, Maj. 13,743
*Twigg, J. Derek (*b.* 1959) *Lab.*, *Halton*, Maj. 17,428
*Twigg, Stephen (*b.* 1966) *Lab.*, *Enfield Southgate*, Maj. 5,546
*Tyler, Paul A. CBE (*b.* 1941) *LD*, *Cornwall North*, Maj. 9,832
*Tynan, Bill (*b.* 1940) *Lab.*, *Hamilton South*, Maj. 10,775
*Tyrie, Andrew G. (*b.* 1957) *C.*, *Chichester*, Maj. 11,355
*Vaz, N. Keith A. S. (*b.* 1956) *Lab.*, *Leicester East*, Maj. 13,422
*Viggers, Peter J. (*b.* 1938) *C.*, *Gosport*, Maj. 2,621
*Vis, R. J. (Rudi) (*b.* 1941) *Lab.*, *Finchley and Golders Green*, Maj. 3,716
*Walley, Ms Joan L. (*b.* 1949) *Lab.*, *Stoke-on-Trent North*, Maj. 11,784
*Walter, Robert J. (*b.* 1948) *C.*, *Dorset North*, Maj. 3,797
*Ward, Ms Claire M. (*b.* 1972) *Lab.*, *Watford*, Maj. 5,555
*Wareing, Robert N. (*b.* 1930) *Lab.*, *Liverpool West Derby*, Maj. 15,853
*Waterson, Nigel C. (*b.* 1950) *C.*, *Eastbourne*, Maj. 2,154
Watkinson, Angela (*b.* 1941) *C.*, *Upminster*, Maj. 1,241
*Watson, Tom (*b.* 1967) *Lab.*, *West Bromwich East*, Maj. 9,763
Watts, David L. (*b.* 1951) *Lab.*, *St Helens North*, Maj. 15,901
Webb, Prof. Steven J. (*b.* 1965) *LD*, *Northavon*, Maj. 9,877
Weir, Michael (*b.* 1957) *SNP*, *Angus*, Maj. 3,611
White, Brian A. R. (*b.* 1957) *Lab.*, *Milton Keynes North East*, Maj. 1,829
*Whitehead, Alan P. V. (*b.* 1950) *Lab.*, *Southampton Test*, Maj. 11,207
*Whittingdale, John F. L. OBE (*b.* 1959) *C.*, *Maldon and Chelmsford East*, Maj. 8,462
*Wicks, Malcolm H. (*b.* 1947) *Lab.*, *Croydon North*, Maj. 16,858
*Widdecombe, Rt. Hon. Ann N. (*b.* 1947) *C.*, *Maidstone and the Weald*, Maj. 10,318
Wiggin, Bill (*b.* 1966) *C.*, *Leominster*, Maj. 10,367
*Wilkinson, John A. D. (*b.* 1940) *C.*, *Ruislip-Northwood*, Maj. 7,537
*Willetts, David L. (*b.* 1956) *C.*, *Havant*, Maj. 4,207
*Williams, Rt. Hon. Alan J. (*b.* 1930) *Lab.*, *Swansea West*, Maj. 9,550
*Williams, Betty (*b.* 1944) *Lab.*, *Conwy*, Maj. 6,219
Williams, Hywel (*b.* 1953) *PC*, *Caernarfon*, Maj. 3,511
Williams, Roger (*b.* 1948) *LD*, *Brecon and Radnorshire*, Maj. 751
*Willis, G. Philip (*b.* 1941) *LD*, *Harrogate and Knaresborough*, Maj. 8,845
Wills, Michael D. (*b.* 1952) *Lab.*, *Swindon North*, Maj. 8,105
*Wilshire, David (*b.* 1943) *C.*, *Spelthorne*, Maj. 3,262
*Wilson, Brian D. H. (*b.* 1948) *Lab.*, *Cunninghame North*, Maj. 8,398
*Winnick, David J. (*b.* 1933) *Lab.*, *Walsall North*, Maj. 9,391
*Winterton, Mrs J. Ann (*b.* 1941) *C.*, *Congleton*, Maj. 7,134
*Winterton, Nicholas R. (*b.* 1938) *C.*, *Macclesfield*, Maj. 7,200
Winterton, Ms Rosalie (*b.* 1958) *Lab.*, *Doncaster Central*, Maj. 11,999
Wishart, Peter (*b.* 1962) *SNP*, *Tayside North*, Maj. 3,283
*Wood, Michael R. (*b.* 1946) *Lab.*, *Batley and Spen*, Maj. 5,064
Woodward, Shaun (*b.* 1958) *Lab.*, *St Helens South*, Maj. 8,985
*Woolas, Philip J. (*b.* 1959) *Lab.*, *Oldham East and Saddleworth*, Maj. 2,726
*Worthington, Anthony (*b.* 1941) *Lab.*, *Clydebank and Milngavie*, Maj. 10,724
*Wray, James (*b.* 1938) *Lab.*, *Glasgow Baillieston*, Maj. 9,839
Wright, Anthony D. (*b.* 1954) *Lab.*, *Great Yarmouth*, Maj. 4,564
*Wright, Anthony W. D.PHIL. (*b.* 1948) *Lab.*, *Cannock Chase*, Maj. 10,704
Wright, David (*b.* 1967) *Lab.*, *Telford*, Maj. 8,383
*Wyatt, Derek M. (*b.* 1949) *Lab.*, *Sittingbourne and Sheppey*, Maj. 3,509
*Yeo, Timothy S. K. (*b.* 1945) *C.*, *Suffolk South*, Maj. 5,081
*Young, Rt. Hon. Sir George BT. (*b.* 1941) *C.*, *Hampshire North West*, Maj. 12,009
Younger-Ross, Richard (*b.* 1953) *LD*, *Teignbridge*, Maj. 3,011

*Sitting MPs
For By-elections since 1997 *see* page 268
For MPs who stood down and defeated MPs *see* page 269.

# GENERAL ELECTION STATISTICS

## MAJORITIES IN THE COMMONS SINCE 1970

| *Year* | *Party* | *Maj.* |
|---|---|---|
| 1970 | Conservative | 31 |
| 1974 Feb. | No majority | |
| 1974 Oct. | Labour | 5 |
| 1979 | Conservative | 43 |
| 1983 | Conservative | 144 |
| 1987 | Conservative | 102 |
| 1992 | Conservative | 21 |
| 1997 | Labour | 178 |
| 2001 | Labour | 165 |

## DISTRIBUTION OF SEATS BY COUNTRY 2001

| | England | Wales | Scotland | N. Ireland |
|---|---|---|---|---|
| Conservative | 165 | — | 1 | — |
| Labour | 323 | 34 | 55 | — |
| Lib. Dem. | 40 | 2 | 10 | — |
| SNP | — | — | 5 | — |
| Plaid Cymru | — | 4 | — | — |
| Other | 1 | — | 1* | 18 |

* The Speaker

## VOTES CAST 1997 AND 2001

| | 1997 | 2001 |
|---|---|---|
| Conservative | 9,600,940 | 8,357,622 |
| Labour | 13,517,911 | 10,724,895 |
| Liberal Democrats | 5,243,440 | 4,812,833 |
| Scottish Nationalist | 622,260 | 464,305 |
| Plaid Cymru | 161,030 | 195,892 |
| N. Ireland parties | 780,920 | 635,735 |
| Others | 1,361,701 | 1,177,516 |
| Total | 31,287,702 | 26,368,798 |

## SIZE OF ELECTORATE 2001

| | |
|---|---|
| England | 37,101,328 |
| Wales | 2,238,211 |
| Scotland | 4,001,018 |
| Northern Ireland | 1,205,097 |
| Total | 44,545,654 |

# PARLIAMENTARY CONSTITUENCIES AS AT 7 JUNE 2001

The results of voting in each parliamentary division at the general election of 7 June 2001 are given below. The majority in the 1997 general election, and any by-election between 1997 and 2001, is given below the 2001 result.

*Symbols*

| | |
|---|---|
| * | Sitting MP |
| † | Previously MP in another seat |

*Abbreviations*

| | |
|---|---|
| *AL* | Asian League |
| *Alliance* | Alliance |
| *Anti-Corrupt* | Anti-Corruption Forum |
| *BNP* | British National Party |
| *Bean* | New Millennium Bean |
| *CPA* | Christian Peoples Alliance |
| *Ch. D.* | Christian Democrat |
| *Choice* | People's Choice |
| *Comm.* | Communist Party |
| *Community* | Independent Community Candidate Empowering Change |
| *C.* | Conservative |
| *Country* | Countryside Party |
| *Customer* | Direct Customer Service Party |
| *DUP* | Democratic Unionist Party |
| *Def Welfare* | Defend The Welfare State Against Blairism |
| *Elvis* | Church of the Militant Elvis Party |
| *Ext. Club* | Club Extinction Club |
| *FDP* | Fancy Dress Party |
| *FP* | Freedom Party |
| *Green* | Green Party |
| *Grey* | Grey Party |
| *IOW* | Isle of Wight Party |
| *Ind.* | Independent |
| *Ind. UU* | Independent United Unionist |
| *Ind. Vote* | Independent - Vote for Yourself Party |
| *JLDP* | John Lillburne Democratic Party |
| *JP* | Justice Party |
| *KHHC* | Kidderminster Hospital and Health Concern |
| *LCA* | Legalise Cannabis Alliance |
| *LD* | Liberal Democrat |
| *LP* | Liberated Party |
| *Lab.* | Labour |
| *Lab. Co-op.* | Labour and Co-operative |
| *Left* | All Left Alliance |
| *Lib.* | Liberal |
| *Loony* | Monster Raving Loony Party |
| *Low Excise* | Lower Excise Duty Party |
| *Marxist* | Marxist Party |
| *Meb. Ker.* | Mebyon Kernow |
| *Muslim* | Muslim Party |
| *NBP* | New Britain Party |
| *NF* | National Front |
| *NI Unionist* | Northern Ireland Unionist |
| *PC* | Plaid Cymru |
| *PF* | Pathfinders |
| *PJP* | People's Justice Party |
| *PUP* | Progressive Unionist Party |
| *Pacifist* | Pacifist for Peace, Justice, Cooperation, Environment |
| *Pensioner* | Pensioner Coalition |
| *Pro Euro C* | Pro Euro Conservative Party |
| *ProLife* | ProLife Alliance |
| *Prog Dem* | Progress Democratic Party Members Decide Policy |
| *Qari* | Qari |
| *R & R Loony* | Rock & Roll Loony Party |
| *RP* | Rate Payer |
| *Ref. UK* | Reform UK |
| *Reform* | Reform 2000 |
| *Res.* | Motor Residents and Motorists of Great Britain |
| *SDLP* | Social Democratic and Labour Party |
| *SF* | Sinn Fein |
| *SNP* | Scottish National Party |
| *SSP* | Scottish Socialist Party |
| *Scot. Ref.* | Scottish Freedom Referendum Party |
| *Scot. U.* | Scottish Unionist |
| *Soc.* | Socialist Party |
| *Soc. Alt.* | Socialist Alternative Party |
| *Soc. Lab.* | Socialist Labour Party |
| *Socialist* | Socialist |
| *Speaker* | The Speaker |
| *Stuck* | Stuckist |
| *Sunrise* | Chairman of Sunrise Radio |
| *Tatton* | Tatton Group Independent |
| *Third* | Third Way |
| *Truth* | Truth Party |
| *UK Ind.* | UK Independence Party |
| *UKU* | United Kingdom Unionist |
| *UUP* | Ulster Unionist Party |
| *Unrep.* | Unrepresented People's Party |
| *WFLOE* | Women for Life on Earth |
| *WP* | Workers' Party |
| *WRP* | Workers' Revolutionary Party |
| *Wessex Reg.* | Wessex Regionalist |
| *Women's Co.* | Women's Coalition |
| *Wrestling* | Jam Wrestling Party |

## ENGLAND

### Aldershot
*E.*78,262 *T.* 45,315 (57.90%) C. hold
*Gerald Howarth, *C.* 19,106
Adrian Collett, *LD* 12,542
Luke Akehurst, *Lab.* 11,391
Derek Rumsey, *UK Ind.* 797
Adam Stacey, *Green* 630
Arthur Pendragon, *Ind.* 459
Alan Hope, *Loony* 390
*C. majority* 6,564 (14.49%)
1.13% swing LD to C.
(1997, C. maj. 6,621 (12.22%))

### Aldridge-Brownhills
*E.*62,388 *T.* 37,810 (60.60%) C. hold
*Richard Shepherd, *C.* 18,974
Ian Geary, *Lab.* 15,206
Mrs Monica Howes, *LD* 3,251
John Rothery, *Soc. All.* 379
*C. majority* 3,768 (9.97%)
2.26% swing Lab. to C.
(1997, C. maj. 2,526 (5.44%))

### Altrincham & Sale West
*E.*71,820 *T.* 43,568 (60.66%) C. hold
*Graham Brady, *C.* 20,113
Ms Janet Baugh, *Lab.* 17,172
Christopher Gaskell, *LD* 6,283
*C. majority* 2,941 (6.75%)
1.92% swing Lab. to C.
(1997, C. maj. 1,505 (2.91%))

### Amber Valley
*E.*73,798 *T.* 44,513 (60.32%) Lab. hold
*Ms Judy Mallaber, *Lab.* 23,101
Ms Gillian Shaw, *C.* 15,874
Ms Kate Smith, *LD* 5,538
*Lab. majority* 7,227 (16.24%)
2.49% swing Lab. to C.
(1997, Lab. maj. 11,613 (21.21%))

### Arundel & South Downs
*E.*70,956 *T.* 45,889 (64.67%) C. hold
*Howard Flight, *C.* 23,969
Derek Deedman, *LD* 10,265
Charles Taylor, *Lab.* 9,488
Robert Perrin, *UK Ind.* 2,167
*C. majority* 13,704 (29.86%)
1.26% swing LD to C.
(1997, C. maj. 14,035 (27.34%))

### Ashfield
*E.*73,428 *T.* 39,350 (53.59%) Lab. hold
*Rt. Hon. G. Hoon, *Lab.* 22,875
Julian Leigh, *C.* 9,607
Bill Smith, *LD* 4,428
Melvin Harby, *Ind.* 1,471
George Watson, *Soc. All.* 589
Ms Katrina Howse, *Soc. Lab.* 380
*Lab. majority* 13,268 (33.72%)
5.60% swing Lab. to C.
(1997, Lab. maj. 22,728 (44.91%))

### Ashford
*E.*76,699 *T.* 47,937 (62.50%) C. hold
*Damien Green, *C.* 22,739
John Adams, *Lab.* 15,380
Keith Fitchett, *LD* 7,236
Richard Boden, *Green* 1,353
David Waller, *UK Ind.* 1,229
*C. majority* 7,359 (15.35%)
2.84% swing Lab. to C.
(1997, C. maj. 5,355 (9.68%))

### Ashton under Lyne
*E.*72,820 *T.* 35,764 (49.11%) Lab. hold
David Heyes, *Lab.* 22,340
Tim Charlesworth, *C.* 6,822
Mrs Kate Fletcher, *LD* 4,237
Roger Woods, *BNP* 1,617
Nigel Rolland, *Green* 748
*Lab. majority* 15,518 (43.39%)
2.59% swing Lab. to C.
(1997, Lab. maj. 22,965 (48.57%))

### Aylesbury
*E.*80,002 *T.* 49,087 (61.36%) C. hold
*David Lidington, *C.* 23,230
Peter Jones, *LD* 13,221
Keith White, *Lab.* 11,388
Justin Harper, *UK Ind.* 1,248
*C. majority* 10,009 (20.39%)
2.88% swing LD to C.
(1997, C. maj. 8,419 (14.63%))

### Banbury
*E.*83,392 *T.* 51,515 (61.77%) C. hold
*Tony Baldry, *C.* 23,271
Leslie Sibley, *Lab.* 18,052
Tony Worgan, *LD* 8,216
Bev Cotton, *Green* 1,281
Stephen Harris, *UK Ind.* 695
*C. majority* 5,219 (10.13%)
1.02% swing Lab. to C.
(1997, C. maj. 4,737 (8.10%))

### Barking
*E.*55,229 *T.* 25,126 (45.49%) Lab. hold
*Mrs Margaret Hodge, *Lab.* 15,302
Mike Weatherley, *C.* 5,768
Anura Keppetipola, *LD* 2,450
Mark Toleman, *BNP* 1,606
*Lab. majority* 9,534 (37.94%)
5.14% swing Lab. to C.
(1997, Lab. maj. 15,896 (48.22%))

### Barnsley Central
*E.*60,086 *T.* 27,543 (45.84%) Lab. hold
*Eric Illsley, *Lab.* 19,181
Alan Hartley, *LD* 4,051
Ian McCord, *C.* 3,608
Henry Rajch, *Soc. All.* 703
*Lab. majority* 15,130 (54.93%)
6.26% swing Lab. to LD
(1997, Lab. maj. 24,501 (67.15%))

### Barnsley East & Mexborough
*E.*65,655 *T.* 32,509 (49.51%) Lab. hold
*Jeff Ennis, *Lab.* 21,945
Mrs Sharron Brook, *LD* 5,156
Matthew Offord, *C.* 4,024
Terry Robinson, *Soc. Lab.* 722
George Savage, *UK Ind.* 662
*Lab. majority* 16,789 (51.64%)
5.57% swing Lab. to LD
(1997, Lab. maj. 26,763 (61.76%))

### Barnsley West & Penistone
*E.*65,291 *T.* 34,564 (52.94%) Lab. hold
*Michael Clapham, *Lab.* 20,244
William Rowe, *C.* 7,892
Miles Crompton, *LD* 6,428
*Lab. majority* 12,352 (35.74%)
2.59% swing Lab. to C.
(1997, Lab. maj. 17,267 (40.91%))

### Barrow & Furness
*E.*64,746 *T.* 39,020 (60.27%) Lab. hold
*Rt. Hon. J. Hutton, *Lab.* 21,724
James Airey, *C.* 11,835
Barry Rabone, *LD* 4,750
John Smith, *UK Ind.* 711
*Lab. majority* 9,889 (25.34%)
2.36% swing Lab. to C.
(1997, Lab. maj. 14,497 (30.06%))

### Basildon
*E.*74,121 *T.* 40,875 (55.15%) Lab. Co-op hold
*Ms Angela Smith, *Lab. Co-op* 21,551
Dominic Schofield, *C.* 13,813
Ms Jane Smithard, *LD* 3,691
Frank Mallon, *UK Ind.* 1,397
Dick Duane, *Soc. All.* 423
*Lab. Co-op majority* 7,738 (18.93%)
3.04% swing Lab. Co-op to C.
(1997, Lab. maj. 13,280 (25.02%))

### Basingstoke
*E.*79,110 *T.* 47,995 (60.67%) C. hold
*Andrew Hunter, *C.* 20,490
Jon Hartley, *Lab.* 19,610
Steve Sollitt, *LD* 6,693
Mrs Kim-Elisbeth Graham, *UK Ind.* 1,202
*C. majority* 880 (1.83%)
1.18% swing C. to Lab.
(1997, C. maj. 2,397 (4.19%))

### Bassetlaw
*E.*68,302 *T.* 38,895 (56.95%) Lab. hold
John Mann, *Lab.* 21,506
Mrs Alison Holley, *C.* 11,758
Neil Taylor, *LD* 4,942
Kevin Meloy, *Soc. Lab.* 689
*Lab. majority* 9,748 (25.06%)
5.68% swing Lab. to C.
(1997, Lab. maj. 17,460 (36.43%))

### Bath
*E.*71,372 *T.* 46,296 (64.87%) LD hold
*Don Foster, *LD* 23,372
Ashley Fox, *C.* 13,478
Ms Marilyn Hawkings, *Lab.* 7,269
Mike Boulton, *Green* 1,469
Andrew Tettenborn, *UK Ind.* 708
*LD majority* 9,894 (21.37%)
2.06% swing C. to LD
(1997, LD maj. 9,319 (17.26%))

### Batley & Spen
*E.*63,665 *T.* 38,542 (60.54%) Lab. hold
*Mike Wood, *Lab.* 19,224
Mrs Elizabeth Peacock, *C.* 14,160
Ms Kath Pinnock, *LD* 3,989
Clive Lord, *Green* 595
Allen Burton, *UK Ind.* 574
*Lab. majority* 5,064 (13.14%)
0.03% swing C. to Lab.
(1997, Lab. maj. 6,141 (13.08%))

### Battersea
*E.*67,495 *T.* 36,804 (54.53%) Lab. hold

*Martin Linton, *Lab.* 18,498
Mrs Lucy Shersby, *C.* 13,445
Ms Siobhan Vitelli, *LD* 4,450
Thomas Barber, *Ind.* 411
*Lab. majority* 5,053 (13.73%)
1.21% swing C. to Lab.
(1997, Lab. maj. 5,360 (11.31%))

BEACONSFIELD
*E.*68,378 *T.* 42,044 (61.49%) C. hold
*Dominic Grieve, *C.* 22,233
Stephen Lathrope, *Lab.* 9,168
Stephen Lloyd, *LD* 9,017
Andrew Moffatt, *UK Ind.* 1,626
*C. majority* 13,065 (31.07%)
0.95% swing Lab. to C.
(1997, C. maj. 13,987 (27.86%))

BECKENHAM
*E.*72,241 *T.* 45,562 (63.07%) C. hold
*Mrs Jacqui Lait, *C.* 20,618
Richard Watts, *Lab.* 15,659
Alex Feakes, *LD* 7,308
Ms Karen Moran, *Green* 961
Christopher Pratt, *UK Ind.* 782
Rif Winfield, *Lib.* 234
*C. majority* 4,959 (10.88%)
0.89% swing Lab. to C.
(1997 Nov by-election, C. maj. 1,227 (3.85%); (1997, C. maj. 4,953 (9.11%))

BEDFORD
*E.*67,763 *T.* 40,579 (59.88%) Lab. hold
*Patrick Hall, *Lab.* 19,454
Mrs Nicky Attenborough, *C.* 13,297
Michael Headley, *LD* 6,425
Dr Richard Rawlins, *Ind.* 973
Mrs Jennifer Lo Bianco, *UK Ind.* 430
*Lab. majority* 6,157 (15.17%)
0.89% swing Lab. to C.
(1997, Lab. maj. 8,300 (16.96%))

BEDFORDSHIRE MID
*E.*70,594 *T.* 46,638 (66.07%) C. hold
*Jonathan Sayeed, *C.* 22,109
James Valentine, *Lab.* 14,043
Graham Mabbutt, *LD* 9,205
Christopher Laurence, *UK Ind.* 1,281
*C. majority* 8,066 (17.29%)
1.89% swing Lab. to C.
(1997, C. maj. 7,090 (13.51%))

BEDFORDSHIRE NORTH EAST
*E.*69,451 *T.* 45,246 (65.15%) C. hold
Alastair Burt, *C.* 22,586
Philip Ross, *Lab.* 14,009
Dan Rogerson, *LD* 7,409
Ms Ros Hill, *UK Ind.* 1,242
*C. majority* 8,577 (18.96%)
3.64% swing Lab. to C.
(1997, C. maj. 5,883 (11.68%))

BEDFORDSHIRE SOUTH WEST
*E.*72,126 *T.* 43,854 (60.80%) C. hold
Andrew Selous, *C.* 18,477
Andrew Date, *Lab.* 17,701
Martin Pantling, *LD* 6,473
Tom Wise, *UK Ind.* 1,203
*C. majority* 776 (1.77%)
0.76% swing Lab. to C.
(1997, C. maj. 132 (0.24%))

BERWICK-UPON-TWEED
*E.*56,918 *T.* 36,308 (63.79%) LD hold
*Rt. Hon. A. Beith, *LD* 18,651
Glen Sanderson, *C.* 10,193
Martin Walker, *Lab.* 6,435
John Pearson, *UK Ind.* 1,029
*LD majority* 8,458 (23.30%)
0.94% swing C. to LD
(1997, LD maj. 8,042 (19.24%))

BETHNAL GREEN & BOW
*E.*79,192 *T.* 38,470 (48.58%) Lab. hold
*Ms Oona King, *Lab.* 19,380
Shahagir Faruk, *C.* 9,323
Ms Janet Ludlow, *LD* 5,946
Ms Anna Bragga, *Green* 1,666
Michael Davidson, *BNP* 1,267
Dennis Delderfield, *NBP* 888
*Lab. majority* 10,057 (26.14%)
0.44% swing C. to Lab.
(1997, Lab. maj. 11,285 (25.26%))

BEVERLEY & HOLDERNESS
*E.*75,146 *T.* 46,375 (61.71%) C. hold
*James Cran, *C.* 19,168
Ms Pippa Langford, *Lab.* 18,387
Stewart Willie, *LD* 7,356
Stephen Wallis, *UK Ind.* 1,464
*C. majority* 781 (1.68%)
0.08% swing Lab. to C.
(1997, C. maj. 811 (1.53%))

BEXHILL & BATTLE
*E.*69,010 *T.* 44,783 (64.89%) C. hold
Greg Barker, *C.* 21,555
Stephen Hardy, *LD* 11,052
Ms Anne Moore-Williams, *Lab.* 8,702
Nigel Farage, *UK Ind.* 3,474
*C. majority* 10,503 (23.45%)
0.40% swing LD to C.
(1997, C. maj. 11,100 (22.66%))

BEXLEYHEATH & CRAYFORD
*E.*63,580 *T.* 40,378 (63.51%) Lab. hold
*Nigel Beard, *Lab.* 17,593
David Evennett, *C.* 16,121
Nickolas O'Hare, *LD* 4,476
Colin Smith, *BNP* 1,408
John Dunford, *UK Ind.* 780
*Lab. majority* 1,472 (3.65%)
1.72% swing Lab. to C.
(1997, Lab. maj. 3,415 (7.08%))

BILLERICAY
*E.*78,528 *T.* 45,598 (58.07%) C. hold
John Baron, *C.* 21,608
Ms Amanda Campbell, *Lab.* 16,595
Frank Bellard, *LD* 6,323
Nick Yeomans, *UK Ind.* 1,072
*C. majority* 5,013 (10.99%)
4.27% swing Lab. to C.
(1997, C. maj. 1,356 (2.45%))

BIRKENHEAD
*E.*60,726 *T.* 28,967 (47.70%) Lab. hold
*Rt. Hon. F. Field, *Lab.* 20,418
Brian Stewart, *C.* 4,827
Roy Wood, *LD* 3,722
*Lab. majority* 15,591 (53.82%)
0.86% swing Lab. to C.
(1997, Lab. maj. 21,843 (55.55%))

BIRMINGHAM EDGBASTON
*E.*67,405 *T.* 37,749 (56.00%) Lab. hold
*Ms Gisela Stuart, *Lab.* 18,517
Nigel Hastilow, *C.* 13,819
Ms Nicola Davies, *LD* 4,528
John Gretton, *Pro Euro C* 454
Sam Brackenbury, *Soc. Lab.* 431
*Lab. majority* 4,698 (12.45%)
1.23% swing C. to Lab.
(1997, Lab. maj. 4,842 (9.99%))

BIRMINGHAM ERDINGTON
*E.*65,668 *T.* 30,604 (46.60%) Lab. hold
Sion Llewelyn Simon, *Lab.* 17,375
Oliver Lodge, *C.* 7,413
Ms Sandra Johnson, *LD* 3,602
Michael Shore, *NF* 681
Steve Goddard, *Soc. All.* 669
Mark Nattrass, *UK Ind.* 521
Ms Judith Sambrook-Marshall, *Soc. Lab.* 343
*Lab. majority* 9,962 (32.55%)
0.62% swing C. to Lab.
(1997, Lab. maj. 12,657 (31.32%))

BIRMINGHAM HALL GREEN
*E.*57,563 *T.* 33,084 (57.47%) Lab. hold
*Stephen McCabe, *Lab.* 18,049
Chris White, *C.* 11,401
Punjab Singh, *LD* 2,926
Peter Johnson, *UK Ind.* 708
*Lab. majority* 6,648 (20.09%)
0.02% swing Lab. to C.
(1997, Lab. maj. 8,420 (20.14%))

BIRMINGHAM HODGE HILL
*E.*55,254 *T.* 26,465 (47.90%) Lab. hold
*Rt. Hon. T. Davis, *Lab.* 16,901
Mrs Debbie Lewis, *C.* 5,283
Alistair Dow, *LD* 2,147
Lee Windridge, *BNP* 889
Parwez Hussain, *PJP* 561
Dennis Cridge, *Soc. Lab.* 284
Harvey Vivian, *UK Ind.* 275
Ayub Khan, *Muslim* 125
*Lab. majority* 11,618 (43.90%)
1.16% swing C. to Lab.
(1997, Lab. maj. 14,200 (41.58%))

BIRMINGHAM LADYWOOD
*E.*71,113 *T.* 31,493 (44.29%) Lab. hold
*Rt. Hon. Ms C. Short, *Lab.* 21,694
Benjamin Prentice, *C.* 3,551
Mahmood Chaudhry, *LD* 2,586
Allah Ditta, *PJP* 2,112
Surinder Virdee, *Soc. Lab.* 443
Mahmood Hussain, *Muslim* 432
James Caffery, *ProLife* 392
Dr Anneliese Nattrass, *UK Ind.* 283
*Lab. majority* 18,143 (57.61%)
1.59% swing Lab. to C.
(1997, Lab. maj. 23,082 (60.78%))

BIRMINGHAM NORTHFIELD
*E.*55,922 *T.* 29,534 (52.81%) Lab. hold
*Richard Burden, *Lab.* 16,528
Nils Purser, *C.* 8,730
Trevor Sword, *LD* 3,322
Stephen Rogers, *UK Ind.* 550
Clive Walder, *Soc. All.* 193
Zane Carpenter, *Soc. Lab.* 151
Andrew Chaffer, *Comm.* 60

*Lab. majority* 7,798 (26.40%)
1.53% swing Lab. to C.
(1997, Lab. maj. 11,443 (29.46%))

BIRMINGHAM PERRY BARR
*E*.71,121 *T*. 37,417 (52.61%) Lab. hold
Khalid Mahmood, *Lab.* 17,415
David Binns, *C.* 8,662
Jon Hunt, *LD* 8,566
Avtar Singh Jouhl, *Soc. Lab.* 1,544
Ms Caroline Johnson, *Soc. All.* 465
Ms Natalya Nattrass, *UK Ind.* 352
Michael Roche, *Marxist* 221
Robert Davidson, *Muslim* 192
*Lab. majority* 8,753 (23.39%)
8.96% swing Lab. to C.
(1997, Lab. maj. 18,957 (41.32%))

BIRMINGHAM SELLY OAK
*E*.71,237 *T*. 40,100 (56.29%) Lab. hold
*Dr Lynne Jones, *Lab.* 21,015
Ken Hardeman, *C.* 10,676
David Osborne, *LD* 6,532
Barney Smith, *Green* 1,309
Mrs Beryl Williams, *UK Ind.* 568
*Lab. majority* 10,339 (25.78%)
1.04% swing Lab. to C.
(1997, Lab. maj. 14,088 (27.87%))

BIRMINGHAM SPARKBROOK & SMALL HEATH
*E*.74,358 *T*. 36,647 (49.28%) Lab. hold
*Roger Godsiff, *Lab.* 21,087
Qassim Afzal, *LD* 4,841
Shafaq Hussain, *PJP* 4,770
Iftkhar Hussain, *C.* 3,948
Gul Mohammed, *Ind.* 662
Wayne Vincent, *UK Ind.* 634
Abdul Aziz, *Muslim* 401
Salman Mirza, *Soc. All.* 304
*Lab. majority* 16,246 (44.33%)
5.31% swing Lab. to LD
(1997, Lab. maj. 19,526 (46.76%))

BIRMINGHAM YARDLEY
*E*.52,444 *T*. 30,013 (57.23%) Lab. hold
*Rt. Hon. Ms E. Morris, *Lab.* 14,085
John Hemming, *LD* 11,507
Barrie Roberts, *C.* 3,941
Alan Ware, *UK Ind.* 329
Colin Wren, *Soc. Lab.* 151
*Lab. majority* 2,578 (8.59%)
2.74% swing Lab. to LD
(1997, Lab. maj. 5,315 (14.07%))

BISHOP AUCKLAND
*E*.67,377 *T*. 38,559 (57.23%) Lab. hold
*Rt. Hon. D. Foster, *Lab.* 22,680
Mrs Fiona McNish, *C.* 8,754
Chris Foote-Wood, *LD* 6,073
Carl Bennett, *Green* 1,052
*Lab. majority* 13,926 (36.12%)
4.85% swing Lab. to C.
(1997, Lab. maj. 21,064 (45.82%))

BLABY
*E*.73,907 *T*. 47,642 (64.46%) C. hold
*Andrew Robathan, *C.* 22,104
David Morgan, *Lab.* 15,895
Geoff Welsh, *LD* 8,286
Edward Scott, *BNP* 1,357
*C. majority* 6,209 (13.03%)
0.48% swing Lab. to C.
(1997, C. maj. 6,474 (12.08%))

BLACKBURN
*E*.72,621 *T*. 40,484 (55.75%) Lab. hold
*Rt. Hon. J. Straw, *Lab.* 21,808
John Cotton, *C.* 12,559
Imtiaz Patel, *LD* 3,264
Mrs Dorothy Baxter, *UK Ind.* 1,185
Paul Morris, *Ind.* 577
Terence Cullen, *Soc. Lab.* 559
Frederick Nichol, *Socialist* 532
*Lab. majority* 9,249 (22.85%)
3.79% swing Lab. to C.
(1997, Lab. maj. 14,451 (30.43%))

BLACKPOOL NORTH & FLEETWOOD
*E*.74,456 *T*. 42,581 (57.19%) Lab. hold
*Ms Joan Humble, *Lab.* 21,610
Alan Vincent, *C.* 15,889
Steven Bate, *LD* 4,132
Colin Porter, *UK Ind.* 950
*Lab. majority* 5,721 (13.44%)
1.60% swing Lab. to C.
(1997, Lab. maj. 8,946 (16.64%))

BLACKPOOL SOUTH
*E*.74,311 *T*. 38,792 (52.20%) Lab. hold
*Gordon Marsden, *Lab.* 21,060
David Morris, *C.* 12,798
Ms Doreen Holt, *LD* 4,115
Mrs Val Cowell, *UK Ind.* 819
*Lab. majority* 8,262 (21.30%)
0.67% swing Lab. to C.
(1997, Lab. maj. 11,616 (22.63%))

BLAYDON
*E*.64,574 *T*. 37,086 (57.43%) Lab. hold
*John McWilliam, *Lab.* 20,340
Peter Maughan, *LD* 12,531
Mark Watson, *C.* 4,215
*Lab. majority* 7,809 (21.06%)
7.55% swing Lab. to LD
(1997, Lab. maj. 16,605 (36.16%))

BLYTH VALLEY
*E*.63,274 *T*. 34,550 (54.60%) Lab. hold
*Ronnie Campbell, *Lab.* 20,627
Jeff Reid, *LD* 8,439
Wayne Daley, *C.* 5,484
*Lab. majority* 12,188 (35.28%)
3.24% swing Lab. to LD
(1997, Lab. maj. 17,736 (41.75%))

BOGNOR REGIS & LITTLEHAMPTON
*E*.66,903 *T*. 38,968 (58.25%) C. hold
*Nick Gibb, *C.* 17,602
George O'Neill, *Lab.* 11,959
Ms Pamela Peskett, *LD* 6,846
George Stride, *UK Ind.* 1,779
Ms Lilias Rider Haggard Cheyne, *Green* 782
*C. majority* 5,643 (14.48%)
0.64% swing C. to Lab.
(1997, C. maj. 7,321 (15.76%))

BOLSOVER
*E*.67,537 *T*. 38,271 (56.67%) Lab. hold
*Dennis Skinner, *Lab.* 26,249
Simon Massey, *C.* 7,472
Ms Marie Bradley, *LD* 4,550
*Lab. majority* 18,777 (49.06%)
4.10% swing Lab. to C.
(1997, Lab. maj. 27,149 (57.26%))

BOLTON NORTH EAST
*E*.69,514 *T*. 38,950 (56.03%) Lab. hold
*David Crausby, *Lab.* 21,166
Michael Winstanley, *C.* 12,744
Tim Perkins, *LD* 4,004
Kenneth McIvor, *Green* 629
Ms Lynne Lowe, *Soc. Lab.* 407
*Lab. majority* 8,422 (21.62%)
2.06% swing Lab. to C.
(1997, Lab. maj. 12,669 (25.74%))

BOLTON SOUTH EAST
*E*.68,140 *T*. 34,154 (50.12%) Lab. hold
*Dr Brian Iddon, *Lab.* 21,129
Haroon Rashid, *C.* 8,258
Frank Harasiwka, *LD* 3,941
Dr William John Kelly, *Soc. Lab.* 826
*Lab. majority* 12,871 (37.69%)
5.74% swing Lab. to C.
(1997, Lab. maj. 21,311 (49.16%))

BOLTON WEST
*E*.66,033 *T*. 41,214 (62.41%) Lab. hold
*Ms Ruth Kelly, *Lab.* 19,381
James Stevens, *C.* 13,863
Ms Barbara Ronson, *LD* 7,573
David Toomer, *Soc. All.* 397
*Lab. majority* 5,518 (13.39%)
0.50% swing Lab. to C.
(1997, Lab. maj. 7,072 (14.39%))

BOOTLE
*E*.56,320 *T*. 27,594 (49.00%) Lab. hold
*Joe Benton, *Lab.* 21,400
Jim Murray, *LD* 2,357
Miss Judith Symes, *C.* 2,194
Dave Flynn, *Soc. Lab.* 971
Peter Glover, *Soc. All.* 672
*Lab. majority* 19,043 (69.01%)
4.05% swing Lab. to LD
(1997, Lab. maj. 28,421 (74.36%))

BOSTON & SKEGNESS
*E*.69,010 *T*. 40,313 (58.42%) C. hold
Mark Simmonds, *C.* 17,298
Ms Elaine Bird, *Lab.* 16,783
Duncan Moffatt, *LD* 4,994
Cyril Wakefield, *UK Ind.* 717
Martin Harrison, *Green* 521
*C. majority* 515 (1.28%)
0.06% swing C. to Lab.
(1997, C. maj. 647 (1.39%))

BOSWORTH
*E*.69,992 *T*. 45,106 (64.44%) C. hold
*David Tredinnick, *C.* 20,030
Andrew Furlong, *Lab.* 17,750
Jon Ellis, *LD* 7,326
*C. majority* 2,280 (5.05%)
1.54% swing Lab. to C.
(1997, C. maj. 1,027 (1.97%))

BOURNEMOUTH EAST
*E*.60,454 *T*. 35,799 (59.22%) C. hold
*David Atkinson, *C.* 15,501
Andrew Garratt, *LD* 12,067
Paul Nicholson, *Lab.* 7,107
George Chamberlaine, *UK Ind.* 1,124
*C. majority* 3,434 (9.59%)
0.21% swing C. to LD

(1997, C. maj. 4,346 (10.01%))

BOURNEMOUTH WEST
*E.*62,038 *T.* 33,648 (54.24%) C. hold
*John Butterfill, *C.* 14,417
David Stokes, *Lab.* 9,699
Ms Fiona Hornby, *LD* 8,468
Mrs Cynthia Blake, *UK Ind.* 1,064
*C. majority* 4,718 (14.02%)
1.54% swing C. to Lab.
(1997, C. maj. 5,710 (13.90%))

BRACKNELL
*E.*81,118 *T.* 49,225 (60.68%) C. hold
*Rt. Hon. A. Mackay, *C.* 22,962
Ms Janet Keene, *Lab.* 16,249
Ray Earwicker, *LD* 8,424
Lawrence Boxall, *UK Ind.* 1,266
Ms Dominica Roberts, *ProLife* 324
*C. majority* 6,713 (13.64%)
1.97% swing C. to Lab.
(1997, C. maj. 10,387 (17.58%))

BRADFORD NORTH
*E.*66,454 *T.* 35,017 (52.69%) Lab. hold
*Terry Rooney, *Lab.* 17,419
Zahid Iqbal, *C.* 8,450
David Ward, *LD* 6,924
John Brayshaw, *BNP* 1,613
Steven Schofield, *Green* 611
*Lab. majority* 8,969 (25.61%)
2.44% swing Lab. to C.
(1997, Lab. maj. 12,770 (30.49%))

BRADFORD SOUTH
*E.*68,450 *T.* 35,137 (51.33%) Lab. hold
*Gerry Sutcliffe, *Lab.* 19,603
Graham Tennyson, *C.* 9,941
Alexander Wilson-Fletcher, *LD* 3,717
Peter North, *UK Ind.* 783
Tony Kelly, *Soc. Lab.* 571
Ateeq Siddique, *Soc. All.* 302
George Riseborough, *Def Welfare* 220
*Lab. majority* 9,662 (27.50%)
0.61% swing Lab. to C.
(1997, Lab. maj. 12,936 (28.71%))

BRADFORD WEST
*E.*71,620 *T.* 38,370 (53.57%) Lab. hold
*Marsha Singh, *Lab.* 18,401
Mohammed Riaz, *C.* 14,236
John Robinson, *Green* 2,672
Abdul Rauf Khan, *LD* 2,437
Imran Hussain, *UK Ind.* 427
Farhan Khokhar, *AL* 197
*Lab. majority* 4,165 (10.85%)
1.17% swing C. to Lab.
(1997, Lab. maj. 3,877 (8.51%))

BRAINTREE
*E.*79,157 *T.* 50,315 (63.56%) Lab. hold
*Alan Hurst, *Lab.* 21,123
Brooks Newmark, *C.* 20,765
Peter Turner, *LD* 5,664
James Abbott, *Green* 1,241
Michael Nolan, *LCA* 774
Charles Cole, *UK Ind.* 748
*Lab. majority* 358 (0.71%)
0.95% swing Lab. to C.
(1997, Lab. maj. 1,451 (2.61%))

BRENT EAST
*E.*58,095 *T.* 28,992 (49.90%) Lab. gain
Paul Daisley, *Lab.* 18,325
David Gauke, *C.* 5,278
Ms Nowsheen Bhatti, *LD* 3,065
Ms Simone Aspis, *Green* 1,361
Ms Sarah Macken, *ProLife* 392
Ms Iris Cremer, *Soc. Lab.* 383
Ashwin Tanna, *UK Ind.* 188
*Lab. majority* 13,047 (45.00%)
0.01% swing Lab. to C.
(1997, Lab. maj. 15,882 (45.03%))

BRENT NORTH
*E.*58,789 *T.* 33,939 (57.73%) Lab. hold
*Barry Gardiner, *Lab.* 20,149
Philip Allott, *C.* 9,944
Paul Lorber, *LD* 3,846
*Lab. majority* 10,205 (30.07%)
9.77% swing C. to Lab.
(1997, Lab. maj. 4,019 (10.53%))

BRENT SOUTH
*E.*55,891 *T.* 28,637 (51.24%) Lab. hold
*Rt. Hon. P. Boateng, *Lab.* 20,984
Carupiah Selvarajah, *C.* 3,604
Havard Hughes, *LD* 3,098
Mick McDonnell, *Soc. All.* 491
Thomas Mac Stiofain (Res. Motor) 460
*Lab. majority* 17,380 (60.69%)
1.81% swing C. to Lab.
(1997, Lab. maj. 19,691 (57.08%))

BRENTFORD & ISLEWORTH
*E.*84,049 *T.* 44,514 (52.96%) Lab. hold
*Ms Ann Keen, *Lab.* 23,275
Tim Mack, *C.* 12,957
Gareth Hartwell, *LD* 5,994
Nic Ferriday, *Green* 1,324
Gerald Ingram, *UK Ind.* 412
Danny Faith, *Soc. All.* 408
Asa Khaira, *Ind.* 144
*Lab. majority* 10,318 (23.18%)
1.26% swing Lab. to C.
(1997, Lab. maj. 14,424 (25.70%))

BRENTWOOD & ONGAR
*E.*64,695 *T.* 43,542 (67.30%) C. hold
*Eric Pickles, *C.* 16,558
†Martin Bell (Ind Bell) 13,737
David Kendall, *LD* 6,772
Ms Diana Johnson, *Lab.* 5,505
Ken Gulleford, *UK Ind.* 611
Peter Pryke, *Ind.* 239
David Bishop, *Elvis* 68
Tony Appleton, *Ind.* 52
*C. majority* 2,821 (6.48%)
(1997, C. maj. 9,690 (19.10%))

BRIDGWATER
*E.*74,079 *T.* 47,847 (64.59%) C. hold
Ian Liddell-Grainger, *C.* 19,354
Ian Thorn, *LD* 14,367
William Monteith, *Lab.* 12,803
Ms Vicky Gardner, *UK Ind.* 1,323
*C. majority* 4,987 (10.42%)
3.57% swing LD to C.
(1997, C. maj. 1,796 (3.28%))

BRIGG & GOOLE
*E.*63,536 *T.* 41,054 (64.62%) Lab. hold
*Ian Cawsey, *Lab.* 20,066
Don Stewart, *C.* 16,105
David Nolan, *LD* 3,796
Godfrey Bloom, *UK Ind.* 688
Michael Kenny, *Soc. Lab.* 399
*Lab. majority* 3,961 (9.65%)
2.00% swing Lab. to C.
(1997, Lab. maj. 6,389 (13.65%))

BRIGHTON KEMPTOWN
*E.*67,621 *T.* 39,203 (57.97%) Lab. hold
*Dr Desmond Turner, *Lab.* 18,745
Geoffrey Theobald, *C.* 13,823
Ms Jan Marshall, *LD* 4,064
Hugh Miller, *Green* 1,290
Dr James Chamberlain-Webber, *UK Ind.* 543
John McLeod, *Soc. Lab.* 364
Dave Dobbs, *Free* 227
Ms Elaine Cook, *ProLife* 147
*Lab. majority* 4,922 (12.56%)
2.45% swing C. to Lab.
(1997, Lab. maj. 3,534 (7.66%))

BRIGHTON PAVILION
*E.*69,200 *T.* 40,723 (58.85%) Lab. Co-op hold
*David Lepper, *Lab. Co-op* 19,846
David Gold, *C.* 10,203
Ms Ruth Berry, *LD* 5,348
Keith Taylor, *Green* 3,806
Ian Fyvie, *Soc. Lab.* 573
Bob Dobbs, *Free* 409
Stuart Hutchin, *UK Ind.* 361
Ms Marie Paragallo, *ProLife* 177
*Lab. Co-op majority* 9,643 (23.68%)
1.63% swing Lab. Co-op to C.
(1997, Lab. maj. 13,181 (26.93%))

BRISTOL EAST
*E.*70,279 *T.* 40,334 (57.39%) Lab. hold
*Ms Jean Corston, *Lab.* 22,180
Jack Lo-Presti, *C.* 8,788
Brian Niblett, *LD* 6,915
Geoff Collard, *Green* 1,110
Roger Marsh, *UK Ind.* 572
Mike Langley, *Soc. Lab.* 438
Andy Pryor, *Soc. All.* 331
*Lab. majority* 13,392 (33.20%)
0.16% swing Lab. to C.
(1997, Lab. maj. 16,159 (33.52%))

BRISTOL NORTH WEST
*E.*76,756 *T.* 46,692 (60.83%) Lab. Co-op hold
*Doug Naysmith, *Lab. Co-op* 24,436
Charles Hansard, *C.* 13,349
Peter Tyzack, *LD* 7,387
Miss Diane Carr, *UK Ind.* 1,149
Vince Horrigan, *Soc. Lab.* 371
*Lab. Co-op majority* 11,087 (23.74%)
1.57% swing C. to Lab. Co-op
(1997, Lab. maj. 11,382 (20.60%))

BRISTOL SOUTH
*E.*72,490 *T.* 40,970 (56.52%) Lab. hold
*Ms Dawn Primarolo, *Lab.* 23,299
Richard Eddy, *C.* 9,118
James Main, *LD* 6,078
Glenn Vowles, *Green* 1,233
Brian Drummond, *Soc. All.* 496
Chris Prasad, *UK Ind.* 496
Giles Shorter, *Soc. Lab.* 250
*Lab. majority* 14,181 (34.61%)
2.08% swing Lab. to C.
(1997, Lab. maj. 19,328 (38.77%))

BRISTOL WEST
*E.*84,821 *T.* 55,665 (65.63%) Lab. hold
*Ms Valerie Davey, *Lab.* 20,505
Stephen Williams, *LD* 16,079
Mrs Pamela Chesters, *C.* 16,040
John Devaney, *Green* 1,961
Bernard Kennedy, *Soc. Lab.* 590
Simon Muir, *UK Ind.* 490
*Lab. majority* 4,426 (7.95%)
0.37% swing LD to Lab.
(1997, Lab. maj. 1,493 (2.38%))

BROMLEY & CHISLEHURST
*E.*68,763 *T.* 43,231 (62.87%) C. hold
*Rt. Hon. E. Forth, *C.* 21,412
Ms Sue Polydorou, *Lab.* 12,375
Geoff Payne, *LD* 8,180
Rob Bryant, *UK Ind.* 1,264
*C. majority* 9,037 (20.90%)
0.09% swing C. to Lab.
(1997, C. maj. 11,118 (21.08%))

BROMSGROVE
*E.*68,115 *T.* 45,684 (67.07%) C. hold
*Miss Julie Kirkbride, *C.* 23,640
Peter McDonald, *Lab.* 15,502
Mrs Margaret Rowley, *LD* 5,430
Ian Gregory, *UK Ind.* 1,112
*C. majority* 8,138 (17.81%)
4.22% swing Lab. to C.
(1997, C. maj. 4,895 (9.38%))

BROXBOURNE
*E.*68,982 *T.* 37,845 (54.86%) C. hold
*Mrs Marion Roe, *C.* 20,487
David Prendergast, *Lab.* 11,494
Ms Julia Davies, *LD* 4,158
Martin Harvey, *UK Ind.* 858
John Cope, *BNP* 848
*C. majority* 8,993 (23.76%)
4.80% swing Lab. to C.
(1997, C. maj. 6,653 (14.16%))

BROXTOWE
*E.*73,675 *T.* 49,004 (66.51%) Lab. hold
*Nick Palmer, *Lab.* 23,836
Mrs Pauline Latham, *C.* 17,963
David Watts, *LD* 7,205
*Lab. majority* 5,873 (11.98%)
1.20% swing C. to Lab.
(1997, Lab. maj. 5,575 (9.59%))

BUCKINGHAM
*E.*65,270 *T.* 45,272 (69.36%) C. hold
*John Bercow, *C.* 24,296
Mark Seddon, *Lab.* 10,971
Ms Isobel Wilson, *LD* 9,037
Christopher Silcock, *UK Ind.* 968
*C. majority* 13,325 (29.43%)
2.18% swing Lab. to C.
(1997, C. maj. 12,386 (25.08%))

BURNLEY
*E.*66,393 *T.* 36,884 (55.55%) Lab. hold
*Peter Pike, *Lab.* 18,195
Robert Frost, *C.* 7,697
Paul Wright, *LD* 5,975
Steven Smith, *BNP* 4,151
Richard Buttrey, *UK Ind.* 866
*Lab. majority* 10,498 (28.46%)
4.62% swing Lab. to C.
(1997, Lab. maj. 17,062 (37.71%))

BURTON
*E.*75,194 *T.* 46,457 (61.78%) Lab. hold
*Ms Janet Dean, *Lab.* 22,783
Mrs Maggie Punyer, *C.* 17,934
David Fletcher, *LD* 4,468
Ian Crompton, *UK Ind.* 984
John Taylor, *ProLife* 288
*Lab. majority* 4,849 (10.44%)
0.59% swing Lab. to C.
(1997, Lab. maj. 6,330 (11.62%))

BURY NORTH
*E.*71,108 *T.* 44,788 (62.99%) Lab. hold
*David Chaytor, *Lab.* 22,945
John Walsh, *C.* 16,413
Bryn Hackley, *LD* 5,430
*Lab. majority* 6,532 (14.58%)
0.15% swing C. to Lab.
(1997, Lab. maj. 7,866 (14.29%))

BURY SOUTH
*E.*67,276 *T.* 39,539 (58.77%) Lab. hold
*Ivan Lewis, *Lab.* 23,406
Mrs Nicola Le Page, *C.* 10,634
Tim Pickstone, *LD* 5,499
*Lab. majority* 12,772 (32.30%)
3.80% swing C. to Lab.
(1997, Lab. maj. 12,433 (24.70%))

BURY ST EDMUNDS
*E.*76,146 *T.* 50,257 (66.00%) C. hold
*David Ruffley, *C.* 21,850
Mark Ereira, *Lab.* 19,347
Richard Williams, *LD* 6,998
John Howlett, *UK Ind.* 831
Mike Brundle, *Ind.* 651
Michael Benwell, *Soc. Lab.* 580
*C. majority* 2,503 (4.98%)
2.16% swing Lab. to C.
(1997, C. maj. 368 (0.66%))

CALDER VALLEY
*E.*75,298 *T.* 47,425 (62.98%) Lab. hold
*Mrs Christine McCafferty, *Lab.* 20,244
Mrs Sue Robson-Catling, *C.* 17,150
Michael Taylor, *LD* 7,596
Steve Hutton, *Green* 1,034
John Nunn, *UK Ind.* 729
Philip Lockwood, *LCA* 672
*Lab. majority* 3,094 (6.52%)
2.27% swing Lab. to C.
(1997, Lab. maj. 6,255 (11.07%))

CAMBERWELL & PECKHAM
*E.*53,694 *T.* 25,104 (46.75%) Lab. hold
*Rt. Hon. Ms H. Harman, *Lab.* 17,473
Donnachadh McCarthy, *LD* 3,350
Jonathan Morgan, *C.* 2,740
Storm Poorun, *Green* 805
John Mulrenan, *Soc. All.* 478
Robert Adams, *Soc. Lab.* 188
Frank Sweeney, *WRP* 70
*Lab. majority* 14,123 (56.26%)
0.91% swing Lab. to LD
(1997, Lab. maj. 16,351 (57.43%))

CAMBRIDGE
*E.*70,663 *T.* 42,836 (60.62%) Lab. hold
*Ms Anne Campbell, *Lab.* 19,316
David Howarth, *LD* 10,737
Graham Stuart, *C.* 9,829
Stephen Lawrence, *Green* 1,413
Howard Senter, *Soc. All.* 716
Len Baynes, *UK Ind.* 532
Ms Clare Underwood, *ProLife* 232
Ms Margaret Courtney, *WRP* 61
*Lab. majority* 8,579 (20.03%)
8.64% swing Lab. to LD
(1997, Lab. maj. 14,137 (27.54%))

CAMBRIDGESHIRE NORTH EAST
*E.*79,891 *T.* 48,051 (60.15%) C. hold
*Malcolm Moss, *C.* 23,132
Dil Owen, *Lab.* 16,759
Richard Renaut, *LD* 6,733
John Stevens, *UK Ind.* 1,189
Tony Hoey, *ProLife* 238
*C. majority* 6,373 (13.26%)
2.03% swing Lab. to C.
(1997, C. maj. 5,101 (9.20%))

CAMBRIDGESHIRE NORTH WEST
*E.*70,569 *T.* 43,956 (62.29%) C. hold
*Rt. Hon. Sir B. Mawhinney, *C.* 21,895
Ms Anthea Cox, *Lab.* 13,794
Alastair Taylor, *LD* 6,957
Barry Hudson, *UK Ind.* 881
David Hall, *Ind.* 429
*C. majority* 8,101 (18.43%)
1.27% swing Lab. to C.
(1997, C. maj. 7,754 (15.88%))

CAMBRIDGESHIRE SOUTH
*E.*72,095 *T.* 48,341 (67.05%) C. hold
*Andrew Lansley, *C.* 21,387
Ms Amanda Taylor, *LD* 12,984
Dr Joan Herbert, *Lab.* 11,737
Simon Saggers, *Green* 1,182
Mrs Helene Davies, *UK Ind.* 875
Ms Beata Klepacka, *ProLife* 176
*C. majority* 8,403 (17.38%)
0.58% swing LD to C.
(1997, C. maj. 8,712 (16.23%))

CAMBRIDGESHIRE SOUTH EAST
*E.*81,663 *T.* 51,886 (63.54%) C. hold
*James Paice, *C.* 22,927
Ms Sal Brinton, *LD* 13,937
Andrew Inchley, *Lab.* 13,714
Neil Scarr, *UK Ind.* 1,308
*C. majority* 8,990 (17.33%)
0.27% swing C. to LD
(1997, C. maj. 9,349 (16.46%))

CANNOCK CHASE
*E.*73,423 *T.* 41,064 (55.93%) Lab. hold
*Dr Tony Wright, *Lab.* 23,049
Gavin Smithers, *C.* 12,345
Stewart Reynolds, *LD* 5,670
*Lab. majority* 10,704 (26.07%)
0.79% swing Lab. to C.
(1997, Lab. maj. 14,478 (27.65%))

CANTERBURY
*E.*74,159 *T.* 45,132 (60.86%) C. hold
*Julian Brazier, *C.* 18,711
Ms Emily Thornberry, *Lab.* 16,642
Peter Wales, *LD* 8,056
Ms Hazel Dawe, *Green* 920
Ms Lisa Moore, *UK Ind.* 803
*C. majority* 2,069 (4.58%)
1.37% swing C. to Lab.
(1997, C. maj. 3,964 (7.33%))

CARLISLE
*E.*58,811 *T.* 34,909 (59.36%) Lab. hold
*Eric Martlew, *Lab.* 17,856
Mike Mitchelson, *C.* 12,154
John Guest, *LD* 4,076
Colin Paisley, *LCA* 554
Paul Wilcox, *Soc. All.* 269
*Lab. majority* 5,702 (16.33%)
6.04% swing Lab. to C.
(1997, Lab. maj. 12,390 (28.41%))

CARSHALTON & WALLINGTON
*E.*67,337 *T.* 40,612 (60.31%) LD hold
*Tom Brake, *LD* 18,289
Ken Andrew, *C.* 13,742
Ms Margaret Cooper, *Lab.* 7,466
Simon Dixon, *Green* 614
Martin Haley, *UK Ind.* 501
*LD majority* 4,547 (11.20%)
3.26% swing C. to LD
(1997, LD maj. 2,267 (4.68%))

CASTLE POINT
*E.*68,108 *T.* 39,763 (58.38%) Con gain
Dr Robert Spink, *C.* 17,738
*Ms Christine Butler, *Lab.* 16,753
Billy Boulton, *LD* 3,116
Ron Hurrell, *UK Ind.* 1,273
Douglas Roberts, *Ind.* 663
Nik Searle, *Truth* 220
*C. majority* 985 (2.48%)
2.39% swing Lab. to C.
(1997, Lab. maj. 1,116 (2.30%))

CHARNWOOD
*E.*74,836 *T.* 48,265 (64.49%) C. hold
*Rt. Hon. S. Dorrell, *C.* 23,283
Sean Sheahan, *Lab.* 15,544
Ms Susan King, *LD* 7,835
Jamie Bye, *UK Ind.* 1,603
*C. majority* 7,739 (16.03%)
2.77% swing Lab. to C.
(1997, C. maj. 5,900 (10.50%))

CHATHAM & AYLESFORD
*E.*69,759 *T.* 39,735 (56.96%) Lab. hold
*Jonathan Shaw, *Lab.* 19,180
Sean Holden, *C.* 14,840
David Lettington, *LD* 4,705
Gregory Knopp, *UK Ind.* 1,010
*Lab. majority* 4,340 (10.92%)
2.62% swing C. to Lab.
(1997, Lab. maj. 2,790 (5.68%))

CHEADLE
*E.*69,002 *T.* 43,606 (63.20%) LD gain
Ms Patsy Calton, *LD* 18,477
*Stephen Day, *C.* 18,444
Howard Dawber, *Lab.* 6,086
Vincent Cavanagh, *UK Ind.* 599
*LD majority* 33 (0.08%)
3.07% swing C. to LD
(1997, C. maj. 3,189 (6.07%))

CHELMSFORD WEST
*E.*78,291 *T.* 48,143 (61.49%) C. hold
*Simon Burns, *C.* 20,446
Adrian Longden, *Lab.* 14,185
Stephen Robinson, *LD* 11,197
Mrs Eleanor Burgess, *Green* 837
Ken Wedon, *UK Ind.* 785
Christopher Philbin, *LCA* 693
*C. majority* 6,261 (13.01%)
0.62% swing C. to Lab.
(1997, C. maj. 6,691 (11.42%))

CHELTENHAM
*E.*67,563 *T.* 41,835 (61.92%) LD hold
*Nigel Jones, *LD* 19,970
Rob Garnham, *C.* 14,715
Andy Erlam, *Lab.* 5,041
Keith Bessant, *Green* 735
Dancing Ken Hanks, *Loony* 513
Jim Carver, *UK Ind.* 482
Anthony Gates, *ProLife* 272
Roger Everest, *Ind.* 107
*LD majority* 5,255 (12.56%)
0.32% swing LD to C.
(1997, LD maj. 6,645 (13.21%))

CHESHAM & AMERSHAM
*E.*70,021 *T.* 45,283 (64.67%) C. hold
*Mrs Cheryl Gillan, *C.* 22,867
John Ford, *LD* 10,985
Ken Hulme, *Lab.* 8,497
Ian Harvey, *UK Ind.* 1,367
Nick Wilkins, *Green* 1,114
Ms Gillian Duval, *ProLife* 453
*C. majority* 11,882 (26.24%)
0.16% swing C. to LD
(1997, C. maj. 13,859 (26.55%))

CHESTER, CITY OF
*E.*70,382 *T.* 44,877 (63.76%) Lab. hold
*Ms Christine Russell, *Lab.* 21,760
David Jones, *C.* 14,866
Tony Dawson, *LD* 6,589
Allan Weddell, *UK Ind.* 899
George Rogers, *Ind.* 763
*Lab. majority* 6,894 (15.36%)
1.70% swing Lab. to C.
(1997, Lab. maj. 10,553 (18.76%))

CHESTERFIELD
*E.*73,252 *T.* 44,441 (60.67%) LD gain
Paul Holmes, *LD* 21,249
Reg Race, *Lab.* 18,663
Simon Hitchcock, *C.* 3,613
Ms Jeannie Robinson, *Soc. All.* 437
Bill Harrison, *Soc. Lab.* 295
Christopher Rawson, *Ind.* 184
*LD majority* 2,586 (5.82%)
8.53% swing Lab. to LD
(1997, Lab. maj. 5,775 (11.24%))

CHICHESTER
*E.*77,703 *T.* 49,512 (63.72%) C. hold
*Andrew Tyrie, *C.* 23,320
Ms Lynne Ravenscroft, *LD* 11,965
Ms Celia Barlow, *Lab.* 10,627
Douglas Denny, *UK Ind.* 2,308
Gavin Graham, *Green* 1,292
*C. majority* 11,355 (22.93%)
2.74% swing LD to C.
(1997, C. maj. 9,734 (17.45%))

CHINGFORD & WOODFORD GREEN
*E.*63,252 *T.* 36,982 (58.47%) C. hold
*Iain Duncan Smith, *C.* 17,834
Ms Jessica Webb, *Lab.* 12,347
John Beanse, *LD* 5,739
Ms Jean Griffin, *BNP* 1,062
*C. majority* 5,487 (14.84%)
0.99% swing Lab. to C.
(1997, C. maj. 5,714 (12.85%))

CHIPPING BARNET
*E.*70,217 *T.* 42,456 (60.46%) C. hold
*Sir Sydney Chapman, *C.* 19,702
Damien Welfare, *Lab.* 17,001
Sean Hooker, *LD* 5,753
*C. majority* 2,701 (6.36%)
2.14% swing Lab. to C.
(1997, C. maj. 1,035 (2.09%))

CHORLEY
*E.*77,036 *T.* 47,952 (62.25%) Lab. hold
*Lindsay Hoyle, *Lab.* 25,088
Peter Booth, *C.* 16,644
Stephen Fenn, *LD* 5,372
Graham Frost, *UK Ind.* 848
*Lab. majority* 8,444 (17.61%)
0.25% swing C. to Lab.
(1997, Lab. maj. 9,870 (17.10%))

CHRISTCHURCH
*E.*73,503 *T.* 49,567 (67.44%) C. hold
*Christopher Chope, *C.* 27,306
Ms Dorothy Webb, *LD* 13,762
Ms Judith Begg, *Lab.* 7,506
Ms Margaret Strange, *UK Ind.* 993
*C. majority* 13,544 (27.32%)
11.74% swing LD to C.
(1997, C. maj. 2,165 (3.85%))

CITIES OF LONDON & WESTMINSTER
*E.*71,935 *T.* 33,975 (47.23%) C. hold
Mark Field, *C.* 15,737
Michael Katz, *Lab.* 11,238
Martin Horwood, *LD* 5,218
Hugo Charlton, *Green* 1,318
Colin Merton, *UK Ind.* 464
*C. majority* 4,499 (13.24%)
0.54% swing Lab. to C.
(1997, C. maj. 4,881 (12.16%))

CLEETHORPES
*E.*68,392 *T.* 42,418 (62.02%) Lab. hold
*Ms Shona McIsaac, *Lab.* 21,032
Stephen Howd, *C.* 15,412
Gordon Smith, *LD* 5,080
Ms Janet Hatton, *UK Ind.* 894
*Lab. majority* 5,620 (13.25%)
2.47% swing Lab. to C.
(1997, Lab. maj. 9,176 (18.18%))

COLCHESTER
*E.*78,955 *T.* 43,736 (55.39%) LD hold
*Bob Russell, *LD* 18,627
Kevin Bentley, *C.* 13,074
Chris Fegan, *Lab.* 10,925
Roger Lord, *UK Ind.* 631
Leonard Overy-Owen, *Grey* 479
*LD majority* 5,553 (12.70%)
4.83% swing C. to LD
(1997, LD maj. 1,581 (3.04%))

COLNE VALLEY
*E.*74,192 *T.* 46,987 (63.33%) Lab. hold
*Ms Kali Mountford, *Lab.* 18,967
Philip Davies, *C.* 14,328
Gordon Beever, *LD* 11,694
Richard Plunkett, *Green* 1,081
Dr Arthur Quarmby, *UK Ind.* 917
*Lab. majority* 4,639 (9.87%)
0.65% swing C. to Lab.
(1997, Lab. maj. 4,840 (8.58%))

CONGLETON
*E.*71,941 *T.* 45,083 (62.67%) C. hold
*Mrs Ann Winterton, *C.* 20,872
John Flanagan, *Lab.* 13,738
David Lloyd-Griffiths, *LD* 9,719
Bill Young, *UK Ind.* 754
*C. majority* 7,134 (15.82%)
1.08% swing Lab. to C.
(1997, C. maj. 6,130 (11.48%))

COPELAND
*E.*53,526 *T.* 34,750 (64.92%) Lab. hold
*Rt. Hon. Dr J. Cunningham, *Lab.* 17,991
Mike Graham, *C.* 13,027
Mark Gayler, *LD* 3,732
*Lab. majority* 4,964 (14.28%)
7.30% swing Lab. to C.
(1997, Lab. maj. 11,944 (28.89%))

CORBY
*E.*72,304 *T.* 47,222 (65.31%) Lab. Co-op hold
*Phil Hope, *Lab. Co-op* 23,283
Andrew Griffith, *C.* 17,583
Kevin Scudder, *LD* 4,751
Ian Gillman, *UK Ind.* 855
Andrew Dickson, *Soc. Lab.* 750
*Lab. Co-op majority* 5,700 (12.07%)
4.95% swing Lab. Co-op to C.
(1997, Lab. maj. 11,860 (21.98%))

CORNWALL NORTH
*E.*84,662 *T.* 53,983 (63.76%) LD hold
*Paul Tyler, *LD* 28,082
John Weller, *C.* 18,250
Mike Goodman, *Lab.* 5,257
Steve Protz, *UK Ind.* 2,394
*LD majority* 9,832 (18.21%)
2.79% swing LD to C.
(1997, LD maj. 13,933 (23.79%))

CORNWALL SOUTH EAST
*E.*79,090 *T.* 51,753 (65.44%) LD hold
*Colin Breed, *LD* 23,756
Ashley Gray, *C.* 18,381
Bill Stevens, *Lab.* 6,429
Graham Palmer, *UK Ind.* 1,978
Dr Ken George, *Meb. Ker.* 1,209
*LD majority* 5,375 (10.39%)
0.45% swing LD to C.
(1997, LD maj. 6,480 (11.28%))

COTSWOLD
*E.*68,154 *T.* 45,981 (67.47%) C. hold
*Geoffrey Clifton-Brown, *C.* 23,133
Ms Angela Lawrence, *LD* 11,150
Richard Wilkins, *Lab.* 10,383
Mrs Jill Stopps, *UK Ind.* 1,315
*C. majority* 11,983 (26.06%)
1.33% swing LD to C.
(1997, C. maj. 11,965 (23.41%))

COVENTRY NORTH EAST
*E.*73,998 *T.* 37,265 (50.36%) Lab. hold
*Bob Ainsworth, *Lab.* 22,739
Gordon Bell, *C.* 6,988
Geoffrey Sewards, *LD* 4,163
Dave Nellist, *Soc. All.* 2,638
Edward Sheppard, *BNP* 737
*Lab. majority* 15,751 (42.27%)
2.34% swing Lab. to C.
(1997, Lab. maj. 22,569 (46.94%))

COVENTRY NORTH WEST
*E.*76,652 *T.* 42,551 (55.51%) Lab. hold
*Geoffrey Robinson, *Lab.* 21,892
Andrew Fairburn, *C.* 11,018
Napier Penlington, *LD* 5,832
Ms Christine Oddy, *Ind.* 3,159
Mark Benson, *UK Ind.* 650
*Lab. majority* 10,874 (25.56%)
2.50% swing Lab. to C.
(1997, Lab. maj. 16,601 (30.56%))

COVENTRY SOUTH
*E.*72,527 *T.* 40,096 (55.28%) Lab. hold
*Jim Cunningham, *Lab.* 20,125
Ms Heather Wheeler, *C.* 11,846
Vincent McKee, *LD* 5,672
Rob Windsor, *Soc. All.* 1,475
Ms Irene Rogers, *Ind.* 564
Timothy Logan, *Soc. Lab.* 414
*Lab. majority* 8,279 (20.65%)
0.61% swing Lab. to C.
(1997, Lab. maj. 10,953 (21.86%))

CRAWLEY
*E.*71,626 *T.* 39,522 (55.18%) Lab. hold
*Ms Laura Moffatt, *Lab.* 19,488
Henry Smith, *C.* 12,718
Ms Linda Seekings, *LD* 5,009
Brian Galloway, *UK Ind.* 1,137
Ms Claire Staniford, *Loony* 388
Arshad Khan, *JP* 271
Karl Stewart, *Soc. Lab.* 260
Ms Muriel Hirsch, *Soc. All.* 251
*Lab. majority* 6,770 (17.13%)
3.05% swing Lab. to C.
(1997, Lab. maj. 11,707 (23.22%))

CREWE & NANTWICH
*E.*69,040 *T.* 41,547 (60.18%) Lab. hold
*Mrs Gwyneth Dunwoody, *Lab.* 22,556
Donald Potter, *C.* 12,650
David Cannon, *LD* 5,595
Roger Croston, *UK Ind.* 746
*Lab. majority* 9,906 (23.84%)
3.69% swing Lab. to C.
(1997, Lab. maj. 15,798 (31.22%))

CROSBY
*E.*57,375 *T.* 36,866 (64.25%) Lab. hold
*Ms Claire Curtis-Thomas, *Lab.* 20,327
Robert Collinson, *C.* 11,974
Tim Drake, *LD* 4,084
Mark Holt, *Soc. Lab.* 481
*Lab. majority* 8,353 (22.66%)
3.19% swing C. to Lab.
(1997, Lab. maj. 7,182 (16.27%))

CROYDON CENTRAL
*E.*77,567 *T.* 45,860 (59.12%) Lab. hold
*Geraint Davies, *Lab.* 21,643
David Congdon, *C.* 17,659
Paul Booth, *LD* 5,156
James Feisenberger, *UK Ind.* 545
Ms Lynda Miller, *BNP* 449
John Cartwright, *Loony* 408
*Lab. majority* 3,984 (8.69%)
0.85% swing C. to Lab.
(1997, Lab. maj. 3,897 (6.99%))

CROYDON NORTH
*E.*76,600 *T.* 41,882 (54.68%) Lab. hold
*Malcolm Wicks, *Lab.* 26,610
Simon Allison, *C.* 9,752
Ms Sandra Lawman, *LD* 4,375
Alan Smith, *UK Ind.* 606
Don Madgwick, *Soc. All.* 539
*Lab. majority* 16,858 (40.25%)
2.63% swing C. to Lab.
(1997, Lab. maj. 18,398 (35.00%))

CROYDON SOUTH
*E.*73,402 *T.* 45,060 (61.39%) C. hold
*Richard Ottaway, *C.* 22,169
Gerry Ryan, *Lab.* 13,472
Ms Anne Gallop, *LD* 8,226
Mrs Kathleen Garner, *UK Ind.* 998
Mark Samuel, *Choice* 195
*C. majority* 8,697 (19.30%)
1.35% swing C. to Lab.
(1997, C. maj. 11,930 (22.01%))

DAGENHAM
*E.*59,340 *T.* 27,580 (46.48%) Lab. hold
Jon Cruddas, *Lab.* 15,784
Michael White, *C.* 7,091
Adrian Gee-Turner, *LD* 2,820
David Hill, *BNP* 1,378
Berlyne Hamilton, *Soc. All.* 262
Robert Siggins, *Soc. Lab.* 245
*Lab. majority* 8,693 (31.52%)
7.82% swing Lab. to C.
(1997, Lab. maj. 17,054 (47.16%))

DARLINGTON
*E.*64,328 *T.* 40,754 (63.35%) Lab. hold
*Rt. Hon. A. Milburn, *Lab.* 22,479
Tony Richmond, *C.* 12,950
Robert Adamson, *LD* 4,358
Alan Docherty, *Soc. All.* 469
Craig Platt, *Ind.* 269
Ms Amanda Rose, *Soc. Lab.* 229
*Lab. majority* 9,529 (23.38%)
4.94% swing Lab. to C.
(1997, Lab. maj. 16,025 (33.27%))

DARTFORD
*E.*72,258 *T.* 44,740 (61.92%) Lab. hold
*Howard Stoate, *Lab.* 21,466
Bob Dunn, *C.* 18,160
Graham Morgan, *LD* 3,781
Mark Croucher, *UK Ind.* 989
Keith Davenport, *FDP* 344
*Lab. majority* 3,306 (7.39%)
0.47% swing Lab. to C.
(1997, Lab. maj. 4,328 (8.32%))

DAVENTRY
*E.*86,537 *T.* 56,684 (65.50%) C. hold
*Tim Boswell, *C.* 27,911
Kevin Quigley, *Lab.* 18,262
Jamie Calder, *LD* 9,130
Peter Baden, *UK Ind.* 1,381
*C. majority* 9,649 (17.02%)
2.54% swing Lab. to C.
(1997, C. maj. 7,378 (11.95%))

DENTON & REDDISH
*E.*69,236 *T.* 33,593 (48.52%) Lab. hold
*Andrew Bennett, *Lab.* 21,913
Paul Newman, *C.* 6,583
Roger Fletcher, *LD* 4,152
Alan Cadwallender, *UK Ind.* 945
*Lab. majority* 15,330 (45.63%)
0.78% swing C. to Lab.
(1997, Lab. maj. 20,311 (44.08%))

### Derby North
*E.*76,489 *T.* 44,054 (57.60%) Lab. hold
*Bob Laxton, *Lab.* 22,415
Barrie Holden, *C.* 15,433
Robert Charlesworth, *LD* 6,206
*Lab. majority* 6,982 (15.85%)
1.53% swing Lab. to C.
(1997, Lab. maj. 10,615 (18.91%))

### Derby South
*E.*77,366 *T.* 43,075 (55.68%) Lab. hold
*Rt. Hon. Mrs M. Beckett, *Lab.* 24,310
Simon Spencer, *C.* 10,455
Anders Hanson, *LD* 8,310
*Lab. majority* 13,855 (32.16%)
0.54% swing C. to Lab.
(1997, Lab. maj. 16,106 (31.08%))

### Derbyshire North East
*E.*71,527 *T.* 42,124 (58.89%) Lab. hold
*Harry Barnes, *Lab.* 23,437
James Hollingsworth, *C.* 11,179
Mark Higginbottom, *LD* 7,508
*Lab. majority* 12,258 (29.10%)
3.08% swing Lab. to C.
(1997, Lab. maj. 18,321 (35.25%))

### Derbyshire South
*E.*81,010 *T.* 51,945 (64.12%) Lab. hold
*Mark Todd, *Lab.* 26,338
James Hakewill, *C.* 18,487
Russell Eagling, *LD* 5,233
John Blunt, *UK Ind.* 1,074
Paul Liversuch, *Soc. Lab.* 564
James Taylor, *Ind.* 249
*Lab. majority* 7,851 (15.11%)
4.09% swing Lab. to C.
(1997, Lab. maj. 13,967 (23.29%))

### Derbyshire West
*E.*75,067 *T.* 50,589 (67.39%) C. hold
*Patrick McLoughlin, *C.* 24,280
Stephen Clamp, *Lab.* 16,910
Jeremy Beckett, *LD* 7,922
Stuart Bavester, *UK Ind.* 672
Nick Delves, *Loony* 472
Robert Goodall, *Ind.* 333
*C. majority* 7,370 (14.57%)
2.99% swing Lab. to C.
(1997, C. maj. 4,885 (8.59%))

### Devizes
*E.*83,655 *T.* 53,249 (63.65%) C. hold
*Rt. Hon. M. Ancram, *C.* 25,159
Jim Thorpe, *Lab.* 13,263
Ms Helen Frances, *LD* 11,756
Alan Wood, *UK Ind.* 1,521
Ludovic Kennedy, *Ind.* 1,078
Ms Vanessa Potter, *Loony* 472
*C. majority* 11,896 (22.34%)
1.88% swing Lab. to C.
(1997, C. maj. 9,782 (16.29%))

### Devon East
*E.*70,278 *T.* 47,837 (68.07%) C. hold
Hugo Swire, *C.* 22,681
Tim Dumper, *LD* 14,486
Phil Starr, *Lab.* 7,974
David Wilson, *UK Ind.* 2,696
*C. majority* 8,195 (17.13%)
1.44% swing LD to C.
(1997, C. maj. 7,489 (14.25%))

### Devon North
*E.*72,100 *T.* 49,254 (68.31%) LD hold
*Nick Harvey, *LD* 21,784
Clive Allen, *C.* 18,800
Ms Viv Gale, *Lab.* 4,995
Roger Knapman, *UK Ind.* 2,484
Tony Bown, *Green* 1,191
*LD majority* 2,984 (6.06%)
2.61% swing LD to C.
(1997, LD maj. 6,181 (11.27%))

### Devon South West
*E.*70,922 *T.* 46,904 (66.13%) C. hold
*Gary Streeter, *C.* 21,970
Christopher Mavin, *Lab.* 14,826
Phil Hutty, *LD* 8,616
Roger Bullock, *UK Ind.* 1,492
*C. majority* 7,144 (15.23%)
0.58% swing Lab. to C.
(1997, C. maj. 7,433 (14.07%))

### Devon West & Torridge
*E.*78,976 *T.* 55,684 (70.51%) LD hold
*John Burnett, *LD* 23,474
Geoffrey Cox, *C.* 22,280
David Brenton, *Lab.* 5,959
Bob Edwards, *UK Ind.* 2,674
Martin Quinn, *Green* 1,297
*LD majority* 1,194 (2.14%)
0.58% swing LD to C.
(1997, LD maj. 1,957 (3.31%))

### Dewsbury
*E.*62,344 *T.* 36,651 (58.79%) Lab. hold
*Rt. Hon. Mrs A. Taylor, *Lab.* 18,524
Robert Cole, *C.* 11,075
Ian Cuthbertson, *LD* 4,382
Russell Smith, *BNP* 1,632
Ms Brenda Smithson, *Green* 560
David Peace, *UK Ind.* 478
*Lab. majority* 7,449 (20.32%)
0.50% swing C. to Lab.
(1997, Lab. maj. 8,323 (19.33%))

### Don Valley
*E.*66,244 *T.* 36,630 (55.30%) Lab. hold
*Ms Caroline Flint, *Lab.* 20,009
James Browne, *C.* 10,489
Phillip Smith, *LD* 4,089
Tony Wilde, *Ind.* 800
David Cooper, *UK Ind.* 777
Nigel Ball, *Soc. Lab.* 466
*Lab. majority* 9,520 (25.99%)
3.84% swing Lab. to C.
(1997, Lab. maj. 14,659 (33.66%))

### Doncaster Central
*E.*65,087 *T.* 33,902 (52.09%) Lab. hold
*Ms Rosie Winterton, *Lab.* 20,034
Gary Meggitt, *C.* 8,035
Michael Southcombe, *LD* 4,390
David Gordon, *UK Ind.* 926
Ms Janet Terry, *Soc. All.* 517
*Lab. majority* 11,999 (35.39%)
2.85% swing Lab. to C.
(1997, Lab. maj. 17,856 (41.10%))

### Doncaster North
*E.*62,124 *T.* 31,363 (50.48%) Lab. hold
*Kevin Hughes, *Lab.* 19,788
Mrs Anita Kapoor, *C.* 4,601
Colin Ross, *LD* 3,323
Martin Williams, *Ind.* 2,926
John Wallis, *UK Ind.* 725
*Lab. majority* 15,187 (48.42%)
3.28% swing Lab. to C.
(1997, Lab. maj. 21,937 (54.99%))

### Dorset Mid & Poole North
*E.*66,675 *T.* 43,718 (65.57%) LD gain
Ms Annette Brooke, *LD* 18,358
*Christopher Fraser, *C.* 17,974
James Selby-Bennett, *Lab.* 6,765
Jeff Mager, *UK Ind.* 621
*LD majority* 384 (0.88%)
1.11% swing C. to LD
(1997, C. maj. 681 (1.34%))

### Dorset North
*E.*72,140 *T.* 47,821 (66.29%) C. hold
*Robert Walter, *C.* 22,314
Miss Emily Gasson, *LD* 18,517
Mark Wareham, *Lab.* 5,334
Peter Jenkins, *UK Ind.* 1,019
Joseph Duthie, *Low Excise* 391
Mrs Cora Bone, *Ind.* 246
*C. majority* 3,797 (7.94%)
1.36% swing LD to C.
(1997, C. maj. 2,746 (5.23%))

### Dorset South
*E.*69,233 *T.* 45,345 (65.50%) Lab. gain
Jim Knight, *Lab.* 19,027
*Ian Cameron Bruce, *C.* 18,874
Andrew Canning, *LD* 6,531
Laurence Moss, *UK Ind.* 913
*Lab. majority* 153 (0.34%)
0.25% swing C. to Lab.
(1997, C. maj. 77 (0.16%))

### Dorset West
*E.*74,016 *T.* 49,571 (66.97%) C. hold
*Oliver Letwin, *C.* 22,126
Simon Green, *LD* 20,712
Richard Hyde, *Lab.* 6,733
*C. majority* 1,414 (2.85%)
0.29% swing C. to LD
(1997, C. maj. 1,840 (3.44%))

### Dover
*E.*69,025 *T.* 44,960 (65.14%) Lab. hold
*Gwyn Prosser, *Lab.* 21,943
Paul Watkins, *C.* 16,744
Antony Hook, *LD* 5,131
Lee Speakman, *UK Ind.* 1,142
*Lab. majority* 5,199 (11.56%)
5.05% swing Lab. to C.
(1997, Lab. maj. 11,739 (21.66%))

### Dudley North
*E.*68,964 *T.* 38,564 (55.92%) Lab. hold
*Ross Cranston, *Lab.* 20,095
Andrew Griffiths, *C.* 13,295
Richard Burt, *LD* 3,352
Simon Darby, *BNP* 1,822
*Lab. majority* 6,800 (17.63%)
1.08% swing Lab. to C.
(1997, Lab. maj. 9,457 (19.79%))

### Dudley South
*E.*65,578 *T.* 36,344 (55.42%) Lab. hold
*Ian Pearson, *Lab.* 18,109
Jason Sugarman, *C.* 11,292
Ms Lorely Burt, *LD* 5,421
John Westwood, *UK Ind.* 859
Ms Angela Thompson, *Soc. All.* 663

*Lab. majority* 6,817 (18.76%)
4.22% swing Lab. to C.
(1997, Lab. maj. 13,027 (27.19%))

DULWICH & WEST NORWOOD
*E.*70,497 *T.* 38,247 (54.25%) Lab. hold
*Rt. Hon. Ms T. Jowell, *Lab.* 20,999
Nick Vineall, *C.* 8,689
Ms Caroline Pidgeon, *LD* 5,806
Ms Jenny Jones, *Green* 1,914
Brian Kelly, *Soc. All.* 839
*Lab. majority* 12,310 (32.19%)
2.29% swing Lab. to C.
(1997, Lab. maj. 16,769 (36.76%))

DURHAM NORTH
*E.*67,610 *T.* 38,568 (57.04%) Lab. hold
Kevan Jones, *Lab.* 25,920
Matthew Palmer, *C.* 7,237
Ms Carole Field, *LD* 5,411
*Lab. majority* 18,683 (48.44%)
3.65% swing Lab. to C.
(1997, Lab. maj. 26,299 (55.75%))

DURHAM NORTH WEST
*E.*67,062 *T.* 39,226 (58.49%) Lab. hold
*Rt. Hon. Ms H. Armstrong, *Lab.* 24,526
William Clouston, *C.* 8,193
Alan Ord, *LD* 5,846
Ms Joan Hartnell, *Soc. Lab.* 661
*Lab. majority* 16,333 (41.64%)
5.90% swing Lab. to C.
(1997, Lab. maj. 24,754 (53.44%))

DURHAM, CITY OF
*E.*69,633 *T.* 41,486 (59.58%) Lab. hold
*Gerry Steinberg, *Lab.* 23,254
Ms Carol Woods, *LD* 9,813
Nick Cartmell, *C.* 7,167
Mrs Chris Williamson, *UK Ind.* 1,252
*Lab. majority* 13,441 (32.40%)
7.82% swing Lab. to LD
(1997, Lab. maj. 22,504 (45.80%))

EALING ACTON & SHEPHERD'S BUSH
*E.*70,697 *T.* 37,201 (52.62%) Lab. hold
*Clive Soley, *Lab.* 20,144
Miss Justine Greening, *C.* 9,355
Martin Tod, *LD* 6,171
Nick Grant, *Soc. All.* 529
Andrew Lawrie, *UK Ind.* 476
Carlos Rule, *Soc. Lab.* 301
Ms Rebecca Ng, *ProLife* 225
*Lab. majority* 10,789 (29.00%)
1.77% swing Lab. to C.
(1997, Lab. maj. 15,647 (32.55%))

EALING NORTH
*E.*77,524 *T.* 44,957 (57.99%) Lab. hold
*Stephen Pound, *Lab.* 25,022
Charles Walker, *C.* 13,185
Francesco Fruzza, *LD* 5,043
Ms Astra Seibe, *Green* 1,039
Daniel Moss, *UK Ind.* 668
*Lab. majority* 11,837 (26.33%)
4.94% swing C. to Lab.
(1997, Lab. maj. 9,160 (16.44%))

EALING SOUTHALL
*E.*82,373 *T.* 46,828 (56.85%) Lab. hold
*Piara Khabra, *Lab.* 22,239
Daniel Kawczynski, *C.* 8,556
Avtar Lit, *Sunrise* 5,764
Baldev Sharma, *LD* 4,680
Ms Jane Cook, *Green* 2,119
Salvinder Dhillon, *Community* 1,214
Mushtaq Choudhry, *Ind.* 1,166
Harpal Brar, *Soc. Lab.* 921
Mohammed Bhutta, *Qari* 169
*Lab. majority* 13,683 (29.22%)
5.00% swing Lab. to C.
(1997, Lab. maj. 21,423 (39.21%))

EASINGTON
*E.*61,532 *T.* 33,010 (53.65%) Lab. hold
*John Cummings, *Lab.* 25,360
Philip Lovel, *C.* 3,411
Christopher Ord, *LD* 3,408
Dave Robinson, *Soc. Lab.* 831
*Lab. majority* 21,949 (66.49%)
2.57% swing Lab. to C.
(1997, Lab. maj. 30,012 (71.64%))

EAST HAM
*E.*71,255 *T.* 37,277 (52.31%) Lab. hold
*Stephen Timms, *Lab.* 27,241
Peter Campbell, *C.* 6,209
Ms Bridget Fox, *LD* 2,600
Rod Finlayson, *Soc. Lab.* 783
Ms Johinda Pandhal, *UK Ind.* 444
*Lab. majority* 21,032 (56.42%)
3.95% swing C. to Lab.
(1997, Lab. maj. 19,358 (48.53%))

EASTBOURNE
*E.*73,784 *T.* 44,770 (60.68%) C. hold
*Nigel Waterson, *C.* 19,738
Chris Berry, *LD* 17,584
Ms Gillian Roles, *Lab.* 5,967
Barry Jones, *UK Ind.* 907
Ms Theresia Williamson, *Lib.* 574
*C. majority* 2,154 (4.81%)
0.51% swing LD to C.
(1997, C. maj. 1,994 (3.79%))

EASTLEIGH
*E.*74,603 *T.* 47,573 (63.77%) LD hold
*David Chidgey, *LD* 19,360
Conor Burns, *C.* 16,302
Sam Jaffa, *Lab.* 10,426
Stephen Challis, *UK Ind.* 849
Ms Martha Lyn, *Green* 636
*LD majority* 3,058 (6.43%)
2.54% swing C. to LD
(1997, LD maj. 754 (1.35%))

ECCLES
*E.*68,764 *T.* 33,182 (48.25%) Lab. hold
*Ian Stewart, *Lab.* 21,395
Peter Caillard, *C.* 6,867
Bob Boyd, *LD* 4,920
*Lab. majority* 14,528 (43.78%)
2.09% swing Lab. to C.
(1997, Lab. maj. 21,916 (47.96%))

EDDISBURY
*E.*69,181 *T.* 44,387 (64.16%) C. hold
*Stephen O'Brien, *C.* 20,556
Bill Eyres, *Lab.* 15,988
Paul Roberts, *LD* 6,975
David Carson, *UK Ind.* 868
*C. majority* 4,568 (10.29%)
3.95% swing Lab. to C.
(1999 Jul by-election, C. maj. 1,606)
(1997, C. maj. 1,185 (2.39%))

EDMONTON
*E.*62,294 *T.* 34,774 (55.82%) Lab. Co-op hold
*Andy Love, *Lab. Co-op* 20,481
David Burrowes, *C.* 10,709
Douglas Taylor, *LD* 2,438
Miss Gwyneth Rolph, *UK Ind.* 406
Erol Basarik, *Reform* 344
Howard Medwell, *Soc. All.* 296
Dr Ram Saxena, *Ind.* 100
*Lab. Co-op majority* 9,772 (28.10%)
0.97% swing Lab. Co-op to C.
(1997, Lab. maj. 13,472 (30.04%))

ELLESMERE PORT & NESTON
*E.*68,147 *T.* 41,528 (60.94%) Lab. hold
*Andrew Miller, *Lab.* 22,964
Gareth Williams, *C.* 12,103
Stuart Kelly, *LD* 4,828
Henry Crocker, *UK Ind.* 824
Geoff Nicholls, *Green* 809
*Lab. majority* 10,861 (26.15%)
2.18% swing Lab. to C.
(1997, Lab. maj. 16,036 (30.51%))

ELMET
*E.*70,041 *T.* 45,937 (65.59%) Lab. hold
*Colin Burgon, *Lab.* 22,038
Andrew Millard, *C.* 17,867
Ms Madeleine Kirk, *LD* 5,001
Andrew Spence, *UK Ind.* 1,031
*Lab. majority* 4,171 (9.08%)
3.57% swing Lab. to C.
(1997, Lab. maj. 8,779 (16.22%))

ELTHAM
*E.*57,519 *T.* 33,792 (58.75%) Lab. hold
*Clive Efford, *Lab.* 17,855
Mrs Sharon Massey, *C.* 10,859
Martin Morris, *LD* 4,121
Terry Jones, *UK Ind.* 706
Andrew Graham, *Ind.* 251
*Lab. majority* 6,996 (20.70%)
1.37% swing Lab. to C.
(1997, Lab. maj. 10,182 (23.45%))

ENFIELD NORTH
*E.*67,756 *T.* 38,143 (56.29%) Lab. hold
*Ms Joan Ryan, *Lab.* 17,888
Nick De Bois, *C.* 15,597
Ms Hilary Leighter, *LD* 3,355
Ramon Johns, *BNP* 605
Brian Hall, *UK Ind.* 247
Michael Akerman, *ProLife* 241
Richard Course, *Ind.* 210
*Lab. majority* 2,291 (6.01%)
4.15% swing Lab. to C.
(1997, Lab. maj. 6,822 (14.31%))

ENFIELD SOUTHGATE
*E.*66,418 *T.* 41,908 (63.10%) Lab. hold
*Stephen Twigg, *Lab.* 21,727
John Flack, *C.* 16,181
Wayne Hoban, *LD* 2,935
Ms Elaine Graham-Leigh, *Green* 662
Roy Freshwater, *UK Ind.* 298
Andrew Malakouna, *Ind.* 105
*Lab. majority* 5,546 (13.23%)
5.08% swing C. to Lab.
(1997, Lab. maj. 1,433 (3.08%))

EPPING FOREST
*E.*72,645 *T.* 42,414 (58.39%) C. hold

*Mrs Eleanor Laing, *C.* 20,833
Christopher Naylor, *Lab.* 12,407
Michael Heavens, *LD* 7,884
Andrew Smith, *UK Ind.* 1,290
*C. majority* 8,426 (19.87%)
4.98% swing Lab. to C.
(1997, C. maj. 5,252 (9.91%))

EPSOM & EWELL
*E.*74,266 *T.* 46,643 (62.81%) C. hold
Chris Grayling, *C.* 22,430
Charles Mansell, *Lab.* 12,350
John Vincent, *LD* 10,316
G. Webster-Gardiner, *UK Ind.* 1,547
*C. majority* 10,080 (21.61%)
0.17% swing Lab. to C.
(1997, C. maj. 11,525 (21.27%))

EREWASH
*E.*78,484 *T.* 48,596 (61.92%) Lab. hold
*Ms Liz Blackman, *Lab.* 23,915
Gregor MacGregor, *C.* 16,983
Martin Garnett, *LD* 5,586
Ms Louise Smith, *UK Ind.* 692
Steven Belshaw, *BNP* 591
R U Seerius, *Loony* 428
Peter Waldock, *Soc. Lab.* 401
*Lab. majority* 6,932 (14.26%)
0.44% swing Lab. to C.
(1997, Lab. maj. 9,135 (15.14%))

ERITH & THAMESMEAD
*E.*66,371 *T.* 33,351 (50.25%) Lab. hold
*John Austin, *Lab.* 19,769
Mark Brooks, *C.* 8,602
James Kempton, *LD* 3,800
Hardev Dhillon, *Soc. Lab.* 1,180
*Lab. majority* 11,167 (33.48%)
4.21% swing Lab. to C.
(1997, Lab. maj. 17,424 (41.90%))

ESHER & WALTON
*E.*73,541 *T.* 45,531 (61.91%) C. hold
*Ian Taylor, *C.* 22,296
Joe McGowan, *Lab.* 10,758
Mark Marsh, *LD* 10,241
Bernard Collignon, *UK Ind.* 2,236
*C. majority* 11,538 (25.34%)
0.86% swing C. to Lab.
(1997, C. maj. 14,528 (27.07%))

ESSEX NORTH
*E.*71,680 *T.* 44,944 (62.70%) C. hold
*Bernard Jenkin, *C.* 21,325
Philip Hawkins, *Lab.* 14,139
Trevor Ellis, *LD* 7,867
George Curtis, *UK Ind.* 1,613
*C. majority* 7,186 (15.99%)
2.65% swing Lab. to C.
(1997, C. maj. 5,476 (10.69%))

EXETER
*E.*81,942 *T.* 52,616 (64.21%) Lab. hold
*Ben Bradshaw, *Lab.* 26,194
Mrs Anne Jobson, *C.* 14,435
Richard Copus, *LD* 6,512
David Morrish, *Lib.* 2,596
Paul Edwards, *Green* 1,240
John Stuart, *UK Ind.* 1,109
Francis Choules, *Soc. All.* 530
*Lab. majority* 11,759 (22.35%)
1.71% swing C. to Lab.
(1997, Lab. maj. 11,705 (18.92%))

FALMOUTH & CAMBORNE
*E.*72,833 *T.* 46,820 (64.28%) Lab. hold
*Ms Candy Atherton, *Lab.* 18,532
Nick Serpell, *C.* 14,005
Julian Brazil, *LD* 11,453
John Browne, *UK Ind.* 1,328
Ms Hilda Wasley, *Meb. Ker.* 853
Paul Holmes, *Lib.* 649
*Lab. majority* 4,527 (9.67%)
2.33% swing C. to Lab.
(1997, Lab. maj. 2,688 (5.01%))

FAREHAM
*E.*72,678 *T.* 45,447 (62.53%) C. hold
Mark Hoban, *C.* 21,389
James Carr, *Lab.* 14,380
Hugh Pritchard, *LD* 8,503
William O'Brien, *UK Ind.* 1,175
*C. majority* 7,009 (15.42%)
2.21% swing C. to Lab.
(1997, C. maj. 10,358 (19.85%))

FAVERSHAM & KENT MID
*E.*67,995 *T.* 41,051 (60.37%) C. hold
Hugh Robertson, *C.* 18,739
Grahame Birchall, *Lab.* 14,556
Mike Sole, *LD* 5,529
Jim Gascoyne, *UK Ind.* 828
Ms Penny Kemp, *Green* 799
Norman Davidson, *R & R Loony* 600
*C. majority* 4,183 (10.19%)
0.89% swing Lab. to C.
(1997, C. maj. 4,173 (8.41%))

FELTHAM & HESTON
*E.*73,229 *T.* 36,177 (49.40%) Lab. Co-op hold
*Alan Keen, *Lab. Co-op* 21,406
Mrs Liz Mammatt, *C.* 8,749
Andy Darley, *LD* 4,998
Surinder Cheema, *Soc. Lab.* 651
Warwick Prachar, *Ind.* 204
Asa Khaira, *Ind.* 169
*Lab. Co-op majority* 12,657 (34.99%)
1.11% swing C. to Lab. Co-op
(1997, Lab. maj. 15,273 (32.76%))

FINCHLEY & GOLDERS GREEN
*E.*76,175 *T.* 43,675 (57.34%) Lab. hold
*Rudi Vis, *Lab.* 20,205
John Marshall, *C.* 16,489
Ms Sarah Teather, *LD* 5,266
Ms Miranda Dunn, *Green* 1,385
John de Roeck, *UK Ind.* 330
*Lab. majority* 3,716 (8.51%)
1.08% swing C. to Lab.
(1997, Lab. maj. 3,189 (6.34%))

FOLKESTONE & HYTHE
*E.*71,503 *T.* 45,855 (64.13%) C. hold
*Rt. Hon. M. Howard, *C.* 20,645
Peter Carroll, *LD* 14,738
Albert Catterall, *Lab.* 9,260
John Baker, *UK Ind.* 1,212
*C. majority* 5,907 (12.88%)
0.36% swing LD to C.
(1997, C. maj. 6,332 (12.17%))

FOREST OF DEAN
*E.*66,240 *T.* 44,607 (67.34%) Lab. hold
*Ms Diana Organ, *Lab.* 19,350
Mark Harper, *C.* 17,301
David Gayler, *LD* 5,762
Simon Pickering, *Green* 1,254
Allen Prout, *UK Ind.* 661
Gerald Morgan, *Ind.* 279
*Lab. majority* 2,049 (4.59%)
4.02% swing Lab. to C.
(1997, Lab. maj. 6,343 (12.64%))

FYLDE
*E.*72,207 *T.* 44,737 (61.96%) C. hold
*Rt. Hon. M. Jack, *C.* 23,383
John Stockton, *Lab.* 13,773
John Begg, *LD* 6,599
Mrs Lesley Brown, *UK Ind.* 982
*C. majority* 9,610 (21.48%)
2.13% swing Lab. to C.
(1997, C. maj. 8,963 (17.22%))

GAINSBOROUGH
*E.*65,871 *T.* 42,319 (64.25%) C. hold
*Edward Leigh, *C.* 19,555
Alan Rhodes, *Lab.* 11,484
Steve Taylor, *LD* 11,280
*C. majority* 8,071 (19.07%)
2.39% swing Lab. to C.
(1997, C. maj. 6,826 (14.29%))

GATESHEAD EAST & WASHINGTON WEST
*E.*64,041 *T.* 33,615 (52.49%) Lab. hold
*Rt. Hon. Ms J. Quin, *Lab.* 22,903
Ron Beadle, *LD* 4,999
Ms Elizabeth Campbell, *C.* 4,970
Martin Rouse, *UK Ind.* 743
*Lab. majority* 17,904 (53.26%)
4.04% swing Lab. to LD
(1997, Lab. maj. 24,950 (57.92%))

GEDLING
*E.*68,540 *T.* 43,816 (63.93%) Lab. hold
*Vernon Coaker, *Lab.* 22,383
Jonathan Bullock, *C.* 16,785
Tony Gillam, *LD* 4,648
*Lab. majority* 5,598 (12.78%)
2.74% swing C. to Lab.
(1997, Lab. maj. 3,802 (7.29%))

GILLINGHAM
*E.*70,898 *T.* 42,212 (59.54%) Lab. hold
*Paul Clark, *Lab.* 18,782
Tim Butcher, *C.* 16,510
Jonathan Hunt, *LD* 5,755
Tony Scholefield, *UK Ind.* 933
Wynford Vaughan, *Soc. All.* 232
*Lab. majority* 2,272 (5.38%)
0.74% swing C. to Lab.
(1997, Lab. maj. 1,980 (3.91%))

GLOUCESTER
*E.*81,144 *T.* 48,223 (59.43%) Lab. hold
Parmjit Dhanda, *Lab.* 22,067
Paul James, *C.* 18,187
Tim Bullamore, *LD* 6,875
Terry Lines, *UK Ind.* 822
Stewart Smyth, *Soc. All.* 272
*Lab. majority* 3,880 (8.05%)
3.11% swing Lab. to C.
(1997, Lab. maj. 8,259 (14.26%))

GOSPORT
*E.*69,626 *T.* 39,789 (57.15%) C. hold
*Peter Viggers, *C.* 17,364
Richard Williams, *Lab.* 14,743
Roger Roberts, *LD* 6,011

John Bowles, *UK Ind.* 1,162
Kevin Chetwynd, *Soc. Lab.* 509
*C. majority* 2,621 (6.59%)
3.18% swing C. to Lab.
(1997, C. maj. 6,258 (12.94%))

GRANTHAM & STAMFORD
*E.*74,459 *T.* 46,289 (62.17%) C. hold
*Quentin Davies, *C.* 21,329
John Robinson, *Lab.* 16,811
Ms Jane Carr, *LD* 6,665
Miss Marilyn Swain, *UK Ind.* 1,484
*C. majority* 4,518 (9.76%)
2.34% swing Lab. to C.
(1997, C. maj. 2,692 (5.08%))

GRAVESHAM
*E.*69,590 *T.* 43,639 (62.71%) Lab. hold
*Chris Pond, *Lab.* 21,773
Jacques Arnold, *C.* 16,911
Bruce Parmenter, *LD* 4,031
William Jenner, *UK Ind.* 924
*Lab. majority* 4,862 (11.14%)
0.15% swing C. to Lab.
(1997, Lab. maj. 5,779 (10.85%))

GREAT GRIMSBY
*E.*63,157 *T.* 33,017 (52.28%) Lab. hold
*Austin Mitchell, *Lab.* 19,118
James Cousins, *C.* 7,634
Andrew de Freitas, *LD* 6,265
*Lab. majority* 11,484 (34.78%)
1.46% swing Lab. to C.
(1997, Lab. maj. 16,244 (37.70%))

GREAT YARMOUTH
*E.*69,131 *T.* 40,366 (58.39%) Lab. hold
*Tony Wright, *Lab.* 20,344
Charles Reynolds, *C.* 15,780
Maurice Leeke, *LD* 3,392
Bertie Poole, *UK Ind.* 850
*Lab. majority* 4,564 (11.31%)
3.21% swing Lab. to C.
(1997, Lab. maj. 8,668 (17.73%))

GREENWICH & WOOLWICH
*E.*62,530 *T.* 32,536 (52.03%) Lab. hold
*Rt. Hon. N. Raynsford, *Lab.* 19,691
Richard Forsdyke, *C.* 6,258
Russell Pyne, *LD* 5,082
Stan Gain, *UK Ind.* 672
Miss Kirstie Paton, *Soc. All.* 481
Ms Margaret Sharkey, *Soc. Lab.* 352
*Lab. majority* 13,433 (41.29%)
1.79% swing Lab. to C.
(1997, Lab. maj. 18,128 (44.87%))

GUILDFORD
*E.*76,046 *T.* 47,842 (62.91%) LD gain
Ms Sue Doughty, *LD* 20,358
*Nick St Aubyn, *C.* 19,820
Ms Joyce Still, *Lab.* 6,558
Ms Sonya Porter, *UK Ind.* 736
John Morris, *Pacifist* 370
*LD majority* 538 (1.12%)
4.77% swing C. to LD
(1997, C. maj. 4,791 (8.41%))

HACKNEY NORTH & STOKE NEWINGTON
*E.*60,444 *T.* 29,621 (49.01%) Lab. hold
*Ms Diane Abbott, *Lab.* 18,081
Mrs Pauline Dye, *C.* 4,430
Ms Meral Ece, *LD* 4,170
Chit Yen Chong, *Green* 2,184
Sukant Chandan, *Soc. Lab.* 756
*Lab. majority* 13,651 (46.09%)
0.74% swing Lab. to C.
(1997, Lab. maj. 15,627 (47.57%))

HACKNEY SOUTH & SHOREDITCH
*E.*63,990 *T.* 30,347 (47.42%) Lab. hold
*Brian Sedgemore, *Lab.* 19,471
Tony Vickers, *LD* 4,422
Paul White, *C.* 4,180
Ms Cecilia Prosper, *Soc. All.* 1,401
Saim Kokshal, *Reform* 471
Ivan Beavis, *Comm.* 259
William Rogers, *WRP* 143
*Lab. majority* 15,049 (49.59%)
2.60% swing LD to Lab.
(1997, Lab. maj. 14,980 (44.39%))

HALESOWEN & ROWLEY REGIS
*E.*65,683 *T.* 39,274 (59.79%) Lab. hold
*Ms Sylvia Heal, *Lab.* 20,804
Les Jones, *C.* 13,445
Patrick Harley, *LD* 4,089
Alan Sheath, *UK Ind.* 936
*Lab. majority* 7,359 (18.74%)
1.23% swing Lab. to C.
(1997, Lab. maj. 10,337 (21.20%))

HALIFAX
*E.*69,870 *T.* 40,390 (57.81%) Lab. hold
*Ms Alice Mahon, *Lab.* 19,800
James Walsh, *C.* 13,671
John Durkin, *LD* 5,878
Mrs Helen Martinek, *UK Ind.* 1,041
*Lab. majority* 6,129 (15.17%)
3.50% swing Lab. to C.
(1997, Lab. maj. 11,212 (22.18%))

HALTEMPRICE & HOWDEN
*E.*67,055 *T.* 43,928 (65.51%) C. hold
*Rt. Hon. D. Davis, *C.* 18,994
John Neal, *LD* 17,091
Leslie Howell, *Lab.* 6,898
Ms Joanne Robinson, *UK Ind.* 945
*C. majority* 1,903 (4.33%)
5.41% swing C. to LD
(1997, C. maj. 7,514 (15.16%))

HALTON
*E.*63,673 *T.* 34,470 (54.14%) Lab. hold
*Derek Twigg, *Lab.* 23,841
Chris Davenport, *C.* 6,413
Peter Walker, *LD* 4,216
*Lab. majority* 17,428 (50.56%)
1.33% swing Lab. to C.
(1997, Lab. maj. 23,650 (53.22%))

HAMMERSMITH & FULHAM
*E.*79,302 *T.* 44,700 (56.37%) Lab. hold
*Iain Coleman, *Lab.* 19,801
Matthew Carrington, *C.* 17,786
Jon Burden, *LD* 5,294
Daniel Lopez Dias, *Green* 1,444
Gerald Roberts, *UK Ind.* 375
*Lab. majority* 2,015 (4.51%)
1.30% swing Lab. to C.
(1997, Lab. maj. 3,842 (7.11%))

HAMPSHIRE EAST
*E.*78,802 *T.* 50,289 (63.82%) C. hold
*Michael Mates, *C.* 23,950
Robert Booker, *LD* 15,060
Ms Barbara Burfoot, *Lab.* 9,866
Stephen Coles, *UK Ind.* 1,413
*C. majority* 8,890 (17.68%)
1.13% swing C. to LD
(1997, C. maj. 11,590 (19.93%))

HAMPSHIRE NORTH EAST
*E.*71,323 *T.* 43,947 (61.62%) C. hold
*Rt. Hon. J. Arbuthnot, *C.* 23,379
Mike Plummer, *LD* 10,122
Barry Jones, *Lab.* 8,744
Graham Mellstrom, *UK Ind.* 1,702
*C. majority* 13,257 (30.17%)
1.00% swing LD to C.
(1997, C. maj. 14,398 (28.17%))

HAMPSHIRE NORTH WEST
*E.*76,359 *T.* 48,631 (63.69%) C. hold
*Rt. Hon. Sir G. Young, *C.* 24,374
Mick Mumford, *Lab.* 12,365
Alex Bentley, *LD* 10,329
Stanley Oram, *UK Ind.* 1,563
*C. majority* 12,009 (24.69%)
1.53% swing Lab. to C.
(1997, C. maj. 11,551 (21.13%))

HAMPSTEAD & HIGHGATE
*E.*65,309 *T.* 35,407 (54.21%) Lab. hold
*Ms Glenda Jackson, *Lab.* 16,601
Andrew Mennear, *C.* 8,725
Jonathan Simpson, *LD* 7,273
Andrew Cornwell, *Green* 1,654
Ms Helen Cooper, *Soc. All.* 559
Thomas McDermott, *UK Ind.* 316
Ms Sister XNunoftheabove, *Ind.* 144
Ms Mary Teale, *ProLife* 92
Amos Klein, *Ind.* 43
*Lab. majority* 7,876 (22.24%)
3.96% swing Lab. to C.
(1997, Lab. maj. 13,284 (30.17%))

HARBOROUGH
*E.*73,300 *T.* 46,427 (63.34%) C. hold
*Edward Garnier, *C.* 20,748
Ms Jill Hope, *LD* 15,496
Raj Jethwa, *Lab.* 9,271
David Knight, *UK Ind.* 912
*C. majority* 5,252 (11.31%)
0.49% swing C. to LD
(1997, C. maj. 6,524 (12.30%))

HARLOW
*E.*67,074 *T.* 40,115 (59.81%) Lab. hold
*Bill Rammell, *Lab.* 19,169
Robert Halfon, *C.* 13,941
Ms Lorna Spenceley, *LD* 5,381
Tony Bennett, *UK Ind.* 1,223
John Hobbs, *Soc. All.* 401
*Lab. majority* 5,228 (13.03%)
4.48% swing Lab. to C.
(1997, Lab. maj. 10,514 (21.99%))

HARROGATE & KNARESBOROUGH
*E.*65,185 *T.* 42,179 (64.71%) LD hold
*Phil Willis, *LD* 23,445
Andrew Jones, *C.* 14,600
Alastair MacDonald, *Lab.* 3,101
Bill Brown, *UK Ind.* 761
John Cornforth, *ProLife* 272
*LD majority* 8,845 (20.97%)

3.94% swing C. to LD
(1997, LD maj. 6,236 (13.09%))

HARROW EAST
*E.*81,575 *T.* 48,077 (58.94%) Lab. hold
*Tony McNulty, *Lab.* 26,590
Peter Wilding, *C.* 15,466
George Kershaw, *LD* 6,021
*Lab. majority* 11,124 (23.14%)
3.02% swing C. to Lab.
(1997, Lab. maj. 9,738 (17.09%))

HARROW WEST
*E.*73,505 *T.* 46,648 (63.46%) Lab. hold
*Gareth Thomas, *Lab.* 23,142
Danny Finkelstein, *C.* 16,986
Christopher Noyce, *LD* 5,995
Peter Kefford, *UK Ind.* 525
*Lab. majority* 6,156 (13.20%)
5.42% swing C. to Lab.
(1997, Lab. maj. 1,240 (2.36%))

HARTLEPOOL
*E.*67,652 *T.* 38,051 (56.25%) Lab. hold
*Rt. Hon. P. Mandelson, *Lab.* 22,506
Gus Robinson, *C.* 7,935
Nigel Boddy, *LD* 5,717
Arthur Scargill, *Soc. Lab.* 912
Ian Cameron, *Ind.* 557
John Booth, *Ind.* 424
*Lab. majority* 14,571 (38.29%)
0.54% swing Lab. to C.
(1997, Lab. maj. 17,508 (39.38%))

HARWICH
*E.*77,539 *T.* 48,115 (62.05%) Lab. hold
*Ivan Henderson, *Lab.* 21,951
Ian Sproat, *C.* 19,355
Peter Wilcock, *LD* 4,099
Tony Finnegan-Butler, *UK Ind.* 2,463
Clive Lawrance, *Ind.* 247
*Lab. majority* 2,596 (5.40%)
1.56% swing C. to Lab.
(1997, Lab. maj. 1,216 (2.28%))

HASTINGS & RYE
*E.*70,632 *T.* 41,218 (58.36%) Lab. hold
*Michael Foster, *Lab.* 19,402
Mark Coote, *C.* 15,094
Graem Peters, *LD* 4,266
Alan Coomber, *UK Ind.* 911
Ms Sally Phillips, *Green* 721
Mrs Gillian Bargery, *Ind.* 486
John Ord-Clarke, *Loony* 198
Brett McLean, *R & R Loony* 140
*Lab. majority* 4,308 (10.45%)
2.62% swing C. to Lab.
(1997, Lab. maj. 2,560 (5.21%))

HAVANT
*E.*70,246 *T.* 40,437 (57.56%) C. hold
*David Willetts, *C.* 17,769
Peter Guthrie, *Lab.* 13,562
Ms Helena Cole, *LD* 7,508
Kevin Jacks, *Green* 793
Tim Cuell, *UK Ind.* 561
Roy Stanley, *Ind.* 244
*C. majority* 4,207 (10.40%)
1.34% swing Lab. to C.
(1997, C. maj. 3,729 (7.72%))

HAYES & HARLINGTON
*E.*57,561 *T.* 32,403 (56.29%) Lab. hold
*John McDonnell, *Lab.* 21,279
Robert McLean, *C.* 7,813
Ms Nahid Boethe, *LD* 1,958
Gary Burch, *BNP* 705
Wally Kennedy, *Soc. Alt.* 648
*Lab. majority* 13,466 (41.56%)
3.39% swing C. to Lab.
(1997, Lab. maj. 14,291 (34.78%))

HAZEL GROVE
*E.*65,107 *T.* 38,478 (59.10%) LD hold
*Andrew Stunell, *LD* 20,020
Ms Nadine Bargery, *C.* 11,585
Martin Miller, *Lab.* 6,230
Gerald Price, *UK Ind.* 643
*LD majority* 8,435 (21.92%)
1.01% swing LD to C.
(1997, LD maj. 11,814 (23.95%))

HEMEL HEMPSTEAD
*E.*72,086 *T.* 45,833 (63.58%) Lab. Co-op hold
*Tony McWalter, *Lab. Co-op* 21,389
Paul Ivey, *C.* 17,647
Neil Stuart, *LD* 5,877
Barry Newton, *UK Ind.* 920
*Lab. Co-op majority* 3,742 (8.16%)
0.78% swing C. to Lab. Co-op
(1997, Lab. maj. 3,636 (6.60%))

HEMSWORTH
*E.*67,948 *T.* 35,227 (51.84%) Lab. hold
*Jon Trickett, *Lab.* 23,036
Mrs Elizabeth Truss, *C.* 7,400
Ed Waller, *LD* 3,990
Paul Turek, *Soc. Lab.* 801
*Lab. majority* 15,636 (44.39%)
4.19% swing Lab. to C.
(1997, Lab. maj. 23,992 (52.76%))

HENDON
*E.*78,212 *T.* 40,851 (52.23%) Lab. hold
*Andrew Dismore, *Lab.* 21,432
Richard Evans, *C.* 14,015
Wayne Casey, *LD* 4,724
Craig Crosbie, *UK Ind.* 409
Ms Stella Taylor, *WRP* 164
Michael Stewart, *Prog Dem* 107
*Lab. majority* 7,417 (18.16%)
2.93% swing C. to Lab.
(1997, Lab. maj. 6,155 (12.30%))

HENLEY
*E.*69,081 *T.* 44,401 (64.27%) C. hold
Boris Johnson, *C.* 20,466
Ms Catherine Bearder, *LD* 12,008
Ms Janet Mathews, *Lab.* 9,367
Philip Collings, *UK Ind.* 1,413
Oliver Tickell, *Green* 1,147
*C. majority* 8,458 (19.05%)
1.31% swing C. to LD
(1997, C. maj. 11,167 (21.66%))

HEREFORD
*E.*70,305 *T.* 44,624 (63.47%) LD hold
*Paul Keetch, *LD* 18,244
Mrs Virginia Taylor, *C.* 17,276
David Hallam, *Lab.* 6,739
Clive Easton, *UK Ind.* 1,184
David Gillett, *Green* 1,181
*LD majority* 968 (2.17%)
5.24% swing LD to C.
(1997, LD maj. 6,648 (12.65%))

HERTFORD & STORTFORD
*E.*75,141 *T.* 47,176 (62.78%) C. hold
Mark Prisk, *C.* 21,074
Simon Speller, *Lab.* 15,471
Ms Mione Goldspink, *LD* 9,388
Stuart Rising, *UK Ind.* 1,243
*C. majority* 5,603 (11.88%)
0.37% swing C. to Lab.
(1997, C. maj. 6,885 (12.62%))

HERTFORDSHIRE NORTH EAST
*E.*68,790 *T.* 44,645 (64.90%) C. hold
*Oliver Heald, *C.* 19,695
Ivan Gibbons, *Lab.* 16,251
Ms Alison Kingman, *LD* 7,686
Michael Virgo, *UK Ind.* 1,013
*C. majority* 3,444 (7.71%)
0.89% swing Lab. to C.
(1997, C. maj. 3,088 (5.94%))

HERTFORDSHIRE SOUTH WEST
*E.*73,367 *T.* 47,269 (64.43%) C. hold
*Richard Page, *C.* 20,933
Graham Dale, *Lab.* 12,752
Ed Featherstone, *LD* 12,431
Colin Dale-Mills, *UK Ind.* 847
Ms Julia Goffin, *ProLife* 306
*C. majority* 8,181 (17.31%)
0.39% swing C. to Lab.
(1997, C. maj. 10,021 (18.08%))

HERTSMERE
*E.*68,780 *T.* 41,505 (60.34%) C. hold
*James Clappison, *C.* 19,855
Ms Hilary Broderick, *Lab.* 14,953
Paul Thompson, *LD* 6,300
James Dry, *Soc. Lab.* 397
*C. majority* 4,902 (11.81%)
2.85% swing Lab. to C.
(1997, C. maj. 3,075 (6.11%))

HEXHAM
*E.*59,807 *T.* 42,413 (70.92%) C. hold
*Peter Atkinson, *C.* 18,917
Paul Brannen, *Lab.* 16,388
Philip Latham, *LD* 6,380
Alan Patterson, *UK Ind.* 728
*C. majority* 2,529 (5.96%)
2.74% swing Lab. to C.
(1997, C. maj. 222 (0.49%))

HEYWOOD & MIDDLETON
*E.*73,005 *T.* 38,779 (53.12%) Lab. Co-op hold
*Jim Dobbin, *Lab. Co-op* 22,377
Mrs Marilyn Hopkins, *C.* 10,707
Ian Greenhalgh, *LD* 4,329
Philip Burke, *Lib.* 1,021
Ms Christine West, *Ch. D.* 345
*Lab. Co-op majority* 11,670 (30.09%)
2.30% swing Lab. Co-op to C.
(1997, Lab. maj. 17,542 (34.70%))

HIGH PEAK
*E.*73,774 *T.* 48,114 (65.22%) Lab. hold
*Tom Levitt, *Lab.* 22,430
Simon Chapman, *C.* 17,941
Peter Ashenden, *LD* 7,743
*Lab. majority* 4,489 (9.33%)
3.03% swing Lab. to C.
(1997, Lab. maj. 8,791 (15.38%))

HITCHIN & HARPENDEN
*E.*67,196 *T.* 44,924 (66.86%) C. hold
*Rt. Hon. P. Lilley, *C.* 21,271
Alan Amos, *Lab.* 14,608
John Murphy, *LD* 8,076
John Saunders, *UK Ind.* 606
Peter Rigby, *Ind.* 363
*C. majority* 6,663 (14.83%)
1.06% swing Lab. to C.
(1997, C. maj. 6,671 (12.72%))

HOLBORN & ST PANCRAS
*E.*62,813 *T.* 31,129 (49.56%) Lab. hold
*Rt. Hon. F. Dobson, *Lab.* 16,770
Nathaniel Green, *LD* 5,595
Mrs Roseanne Serelli, *C.* 5,258
Rob Whitley, *Green* 1,875
Ms Candy Udwin, *Soc. All.* 971
Joti Brar, *Soc. Lab.* 359
Magnus Nielsen, *UK Ind.* 301
*Lab. majority* 11,175 (35.90%)
8.31% swing Lab. to LD
(1997, Lab. maj. 17,903 (47.11%))

HORNCHURCH
*E.*61,008 *T.* 35,557 (58.28%) Lab. hold
*John Cryer, *Lab.* 16,514
Robin Squire, *C.* 15,032
Ms Sarah Lea, *LD* 2,928
Lawrence Webb, *UK Ind.* 893
Mr David Durant, *Third* 190
*Lab. majority* 1,482 (4.17%)
4.38% swing Lab. to C.
(1997, Lab. maj. 5,680 (12.93%))

HORNSEY & WOOD GREEN
*E.*75,967 *T.* 44,063 (58.00%) Lab. hold
*Ms Barbara Roche, *Lab.* 21,967
Ms Lynne Featherstone, *LD* 11,353
Jason Hollands, *C.* 6,921
Ms Jayne Forbes, *Green* 2,228
Ms Louise Christian, *Soc. All.* 1,106
Ms Ella Rule, *Soc. Lab.* 294
Erdil Ataman, *Reform* 194
*Lab. majority* 10,614 (24.09%)
13.21% swing Lab. to LD
(1997, Lab. maj. 20,499 (39.82%))

HORSHAM
*E.*79,604 *T.* 50,770 (63.78%) C. hold
*Rt. Hon. F. Maude, *C.* 26,134
Hubert Carr, *LD* 12,468
Ms Janet Sully, *Lab.* 10,267
Hugo Miller, *UK Ind.* 1,472
Jim Duggan, *Ind.* 429
*C. majority* 13,666 (26.92%)
0.46% swing LD to C.
(1997, C. maj. 14,862 (26.00%))

HOUGHTON & WASHINGTON EAST
*E.*67,946 *T.* 33,641 (49.51%) Lab. hold
*Fraser Kemp, *Lab.* 24,628
Tony Devenish, *C.* 4,810
Richard Ormerod, *LD* 4,203
*Lab. majority* 19,818 (58.91%)
2.29% swing Lab. to C.
(1997, Lab. maj. 26,555 (63.49%))

HOVE
*E.*70,889 *T.* 41,988 (59.23%) Lab. hold
*Ivor Caplin, *Lab.* 19,253
Mrs Jenny Langston, *C.* 16,082
Harold de Souza, *LD* 3,823
Ms Anthea Ballam, *Green* 1,369
Andy Richards, *Soc. All.* 531
Richard Franklin, *UK Ind.* 358
Nigel Donovan, *Lib.* 316
Simon Dobbshead, *Free* 196
Thomas Major, *Ind.* 60
*Lab. majority* 3,171 (7.55%)
0.34% swing Lab. to C.
(1997, Lab. maj. 3,959 (8.23%))

HUDDERSFIELD
*E.*64,349 *T.* 35,383 (54.99%) Lab. Co-op hold
*Barry Sheerman, *Lab. Co-op* 18,840
Paul Baverstock, *C.* 8,794
Neil Bentley, *LD* 5,300
John Phillips, *Green* 1,254
Mrs Judith Longman, *UK Ind.* 613
Graham Hellawell, *Soc. All.* 374
George Randall, *Soc. Lab.* 208
*Lab. Co-op majority* 10,046 (28.39%)
3.59% swing Lab. Co-op to C.
(1997, Lab. maj. 15,848 (35.57%))

HULL EAST
*E.*66,473 *T.* 30,875 (46.45%) Lab. hold
*Rt. Hon. J. Prescott, *Lab.* 19,938
Ms Jo Swinson, *LD* 4,613
Ms Sandip Verma, *C.* 4,276
Ms Jeanette Jenkinson, *UK Ind.* 1,218
Ms Linda Muir, *Soc. Lab.* 830
*Lab. majority* 15,325 (49.64%)
5.94% swing Lab. to LD
(1997, Lab. maj. 23,318 (57.60%))

HULL NORTH
*E.*63,022 *T.* 28,633 (45.43%) Lab. hold
*Kevin McNamara, *Lab.* 16,364
Ms Simone Butterworth, *LD* 5,643
Paul Charlson, *C.* 4,902
Ms Tineka Robinson, *UK Ind.* 655
Roger Smith, *Soc. All.* 490
Carl Wagner, *LCA* 478
Christopher Veasey, *Ind.* 101
*Lab. majority* 10,721 (37.44%)
6.89% swing Lab. to LD
(1997, Lab. maj. 19,705 (50.79%))

HULL WEST & HESSLE
*E.*63,077 *T.* 28,916 (45.84%) Lab. hold
*Alan Johnson, *Lab.* 16,880
John Sharp, *C.* 5,929
Ms Angela Wastling, *LD* 4,364
John Cornforth, *UK Ind.* 878
David Harris, *Ind.* 512
David Skinner, *Soc. Lab.* 353
*Lab. majority* 10,951 (37.87%)
1.38% swing Lab. to C.
(1997, Lab. maj. 15,525 (40.48%))

HUNTINGDON
*E.*78,604 *T.* 49,089 (62.45%) C. hold
Jonathan Djanogly, *C.* 24,507
Michael Pope, *LD* 11,715
Takki Sulaiman, *Lab.* 11,211
Derek Norman, *UK Ind.* 1,656
*C. majority* 12,792 (26.06%)
7.26% swing C. to LD
(1997, C. maj. 18,140 (31.84%))

HYNDBURN
*E.*66,445 *T.* 38,243 (57.56%) Lab. hold
*Greg Pope, *Lab.* 20,900
Peter Britcliffe, *C.* 12,681
Bill Greene, *LD* 3,680
John Tomlin, *UK Ind.* 982
*Lab. majority* 8,219 (21.49%)
1.11% swing Lab. to C.
(1997, Lab. maj. 11,448 (23.71%))

ILFORD NORTH
*E.*68,893 *T.* 40,234 (58.40%) Lab. hold
*Ms Linda Perham, *Lab.* 18,428
Vivian Bendall, *C.* 16,313
Gavin Stollar, *LD* 4,717
Martin Levin, *UK Ind.* 776
*Lab. majority* 2,115 (5.26%)
0.67% swing Lab. to C.
(1997, Lab. maj. 3,224 (6.60%))

ILFORD SOUTH
*E.*76,025 *T.* 41,295 (54.32%) Lab. Co-op hold
*Mike Gapes, *Lab. Co-op* 24,619
Suresh Kuma, *C.* 10,622
Ralph Scott, *LD* 4,647
Harun Khan, *UK Ind.* 1,407
*Lab. Co-op majority* 13,997 (33.90%)
2.75% swing C. to Lab. Co-op
(1997, Lab. maj. 14,200 (28.39%))

IPSWICH
*E.*68,198 *T.* 38,873 (57.00%) Lab. hold
*Jamie Cann, *Lab.* 19,952
Edward Wild, *C.* 11,871
Terry Gilbert, *LD* 5,904
William Vinyard, *UK Ind.* 624
Peter Leach, *Soc. All.* 305
Shaun Gratton, *Soc. Lab.* 217
*Lab. majority* 8,081 (20.79%)
0.40% swing Lab. to C.
(1997, Lab. maj. 10,439 (21.58%))

ISLE OF WIGHT
*E.*106,305 *T.* 63,482 (59.72%) Con gain
Andrew Turner, *C.* 25,223
*Dr Peter Brand, *LD* 22,397
Ms Deborah Gardiner, *Lab.* 9,676
David Lott, *UK Ind.* 2,106
David Holmes, *Ind.* 1,423
Paul Scivier, *Green* 1,279
Philip Murray, *IOW* 1,164
James Spensley, *Soc. Lab.* 214
*C. majority* 2,826 (4.45%)
6.61% swing LD to C.
(1997, LD maj. 6,406 (8.76%))

ISLINGTON NORTH
*E.*61,970 *T.* 30,216 (48.76%) Lab. hold
*Jeremy Corbyn, *Lab.* 18,699
Ms Laura Willoughby, *LD* 5,741
Neil Rands, *C.* 3,249
Chris Ashby, *Green* 1,876
Steve Cook, *Soc. Lab.* 512
Emine Hassan, *Reform* 139
*Lab. majority* 12,958 (42.88%)
6.38% swing Lab. to LD
(1997, Lab. maj. 19,955 (55.64%))

ISLINGTON SOUTH & FINSBURY
*E.*59,515 *T.* 28,206 (47.39%) Lab. hold
*Rt. Hon. C. Smith, *Lab.* 15,217
Keith Sharp, *LD* 7,937

Mrs Nicky Morgan, *C.* 3,860
Ms Janine Booth, *Soc. All.* 817
Thomas McCarthy, *Ind.* 267
Charles Thomson, *Stuck* 108
*Lab. majority* 7,280 (25.81%)
7.71% swing Lab. to LD
(1997, Lab. maj. 14,563 (41.24%))

JARROW
*E.*63,172 *T.* 34,479 (54.58%) Lab. hold
*Stephen Hepburn, *Lab.* 22,777
James Selby, *LD* 5,182
Donald Wood, *C.* 5,056
Alan Badger, *UK Ind.* 716
Alan Le Blond, *Ind.* 391
John Bissett, *Soc.* 357
*Lab. majority* 17,595 (51.03%)
1.37% swing Lab. to LD
(1997, Lab. maj. 21,933 (49.91%))

KEIGHLEY
*E.*68,349 *T.* 43,333 (63.40%) Lab. hold
*Ms Ann Cryer, *Lab.* 20,888
Simon Cooke, *C.* 16,883
Mike Doyle, *LD* 4,722
Michael Cassidy, *UK Ind.* 840
*Lab. majority* 4,005 (9.24%)
2.30% swing Lab. to C.
(1997, Lab. maj. 7,132 (13.85%))

KENSINGTON & CHELSEA
*E.*62,007 *T.* 28,038 (45.22%) C. hold
*Rt. Hon. M. Portillo, *C.* 15,270
Simon Stanley, *Lab.* 6,499
Ms Kishwer Falkner, *LD* 4,416
Ms Julia Stephenson, *Green* 1,158
Nicholas Hockney, *UK Ind.* 416
Ms Josephine Quintavalle, *ProLife* 179
Ginger Crab, *Wrestling* 100
*C. majority* 8,771 (31.28%)
2.81% swing Lab. to C.
(1999 Nov by-election, C. maj. 6,706 (34.37%); 1997, C. maj. 9,519 (25.66%))

KETTERING
*E.*79,697 *T.* 53,752 (67.45%) Lab. hold
*Philip Sawford, *Lab.* 24,034
Philip Hollobone, *C.* 23,369
Roger Aron, *LD* 5,469
Barry Mahoney, *UK Ind.* 880
*Lab. majority* 665 (1.24%)
0.45% swing C. to Lab.
(1997, Lab. maj. 189 (0.33%))

KINGSTON & SURBITON
*E.*72,687 *T.* 49,093 (67.54%) LD hold
*Edward Davey, *LD* 29,542
David Shaw, *C.* 13,866
Phil Woodford, *Lab.* 4,302
Chris Spruce, *Green* 572
Miss Amy Burns, *UK Ind.* 438
John Hayball, *Soc. Lab.* 319
Jeremy Middleton, *Unrep.* 54
*LD majority* 15,676 (31.93%)
15.92% swing C. to LD
(1997, LD maj. 56 (0.10%))

KINGSWOOD
*E.*80,531 *T.* 52,676 (65.41%) Lab. hold
*Dr Roger Berry, *Lab.* 28,903
Robert Marven, *C.* 14,941
Christopher Greenfield, *LD* 7,747
David Smith, *UK Ind.* 1,085
*Lab. majority* 13,962 (26.51%)
1.35% swing C. to Lab.
(1997, Lab. maj. 14,253 (23.80%))

KNOWSLEY NORTH & SEFTON EAST
*E.*70,781 *T.* 37,517 (53.00%) Lab. hold
*George Howarth, *Lab.* 25,035
Keith Chapman, *C.* 6,108
Richard Roberts, *LD* 5,173
Ron Waugh, *Soc. Lab.* 574
Thomas Rossiter, *Ind.* 356
David Jones, *Ind.* 271
*Lab. majority* 18,927 (50.45%)
1.08% swing Lab. to C.
(1997, Lab. maj. 26,147 (52.61%))

KNOWSLEY SOUTH
*E.*70,681 *T.* 36,590 (51.77%) Lab. hold
*Eddie O'Hara, *Lab.* 26,071
David Smithson, *LD* 4,755
Paul Jemetta, *C.* 4,250
Alan Fogg, *Soc. Lab.* 1,068
Ms Mona McNee, *Ind.* 446
*Lab. majority* 21,316 (58.26%)
5.27% swing Lab. to LD
(1997, Lab. maj. 30,708 (64.53%))

LANCASHIRE WEST
*E.*72,858 *T.* 42,971 (58.98%) Lab. hold
*Colin Pickthall, *Lab.* 23,404
Jeremy Myers, *C.* 13,761
John Thornton, *LD* 4,966
David Hill, *Ind.* 523
David Braid (Indep Braid) 317
*Lab. majority* 9,643 (22.44%)
4.42% swing Lab. to C.
(1997, Lab. maj. 17,119 (31.28%))

LANCASTER & WYRE
*E.*78,964 *T.* 52,350 (66.30%) Lab. hold
*Hilton Dawson, *Lab.* 22,556
Steve Barclay, *C.* 22,075
Ms Liz Scott, *LD* 5,383
Prof John Whitelegg, *Green* 1,595
Dr John Whittaker, *UK Ind.* 741
*Lab. majority* 481 (0.92%)
0.64% swing Lab. to C.
(1997, Lab. maj. 1,295 (2.20%))

LEEDS CENTRAL
*E.*65,497 *T.* 27,306 (41.69%) Lab. hold
*Hilary Benn, *Lab.* 18,277
Miss Victoria Richmond, *C.* 3,896
Stewart Arnold, *LD* 3,607
David Burgess, *UK Ind.* 775
Steve Johnson, *Soc. All.* 751
*Lab. majority* 14,381 (52.67%)
1.62% swing Lab. to C.
(1999 Jun by-election, Lab. maj. 2,293 (17.39%); 1997, Lab. maj. 20,689 (55.90%))

LEEDS EAST
*E.*56,400 *T.* 29,055 (51.52%) Lab. hold
*George Mudie, *Lab.* 18,290
Barry Anderson, *C.* 5,647
Brian Jennings, *LD* 3,923
Raymond Northgreaves, *UK Ind.* 634
Mark King, *Soc. Lab.* 419
Peter Socrates, *Ind.* 142
*Lab. majority* 12,643 (43.51%)
2.64% swing Lab. to C.
(1997, Lab. maj. 17,466 (48.80%))

LEEDS NORTH EAST
*E.*64,123 *T.* 39,773 (62.03%) Lab. hold
*Fabian Hamilton, *Lab.* 19,540
Owain Rhys, *C.* 12,451
Jonathan Brown, *LD* 6,325
Ms Celia Foote (Left All) 770
Jeffrey Miles, *UK Ind.* 382
Colin Muir, *Soc. Lab.* 173
Mohammed Zaman, *Ind.* 132
*Lab. majority* 7,089 (17.82%)
1.27% swing C. to Lab.
(1997, Lab. maj. 6,959 (15.29%))

LEEDS NORTH WEST
*E.*72,945 *T.* 42,451 (58.20%) Lab. hold
*Harold Best, *Lab.* 17,794
Adam Pritchard, *C.* 12,558
David Hall-Matthews, *LD* 11,431
Simon Jones, *UK Ind.* 668
*Lab. majority* 5,236 (12.33%)
2.27% swing C. to Lab.
(1997, Lab. maj. 3,844 (7.79%))

LEEDS WEST
*E.*64,218 *T.* 32,094 (49.98%) Lab. hold
*John Battle, *Lab.* 19,943
Kris Hopkins, *C.* 5,008
Darren Finlay, *LD* 3,350
David Blackburn, *Green* 2,573
William Finley, *UK Ind.* 758
Noel Nowosielski, *Lib.* 462
*Lab. majority* 14,935 (46.54%)
1.31% swing Lab. to C.
(1997, Lab. maj. 19,771 (49.16%))

LEICESTER EAST
*E.*65,527 *T.* 40,661 (62.05%) Lab. hold
*Keith Vaz, *Lab.* 23,402
John Mugglestone, *C.* 9,960
Ms Harpinder Athwal, *LD* 4,989
Dave Roberts, *Soc. Lab.* 837
Clive Potter, *BNP* 772
Shirley Bennett, *Ind.* 701
*Lab. majority* 13,442 (33.06%)
4.22% swing Lab. to C.
(1997, Lab. maj. 18,422 (41.49%))

LEICESTER SOUTH
*E.*72,671 *T.* 42,142 (57.99%) Lab. hold
*Jim Marshall, *Lab.* 22,958
Richard Hoile, *C.* 9,715
Parmjit Singh Gill, *LD* 7,243
Ms Margaret Layton, *Green* 1,217
Arnold Gardner, *Soc. Lab.* 676
Kirti Ladwa, *UK Ind.* 333
*Lab. majority* 13,243 (31.42%)
1.43% swing Lab. to C.
(1997, Lab. maj. 16,493 (34.28%))

LEICESTER WEST
*E.*65,267 *T.* 33,219 (50.90%) Lab. hold
*Rt. Hon. Ms P. Hewitt, *Lab.* 18,014
Chris Shaw, *C.* 8,375
Andrew Vincent, *LD* 5,085
Matthew Gough, *Green* 1,074
Sean Kirkpatrick, *Soc. Lab.* 350
Steve Score, *Soc. All.* 321
*Lab. majority* 9,639 (29.02%)
1.21% swing Lab. to C.
(1997, Lab. maj. 12,864 (31.44%))

LEICESTERSHIRE NORTH WEST
*E.*68,414 *T.* 45,009 (65.79%) Lab. Co-op hold
*David Taylor, *Lab. Co-op* 23,431
Nick Weston, *C.* 15,274
Charlie Fraser-Fleming, *LD* 4,651
William Nattrass, *UK Ind.* 1,021
Robert Nettleton, *Ind.* 632
*Lab. Co-op majority* 8,157 (18.12%)
3.64% swing Lab. Co-op to C.
(1997, Lab. maj. 13,219 (25.41%))

LEIGH
*E.*71,054 *T.* 35,298 (49.68%) Lab. hold
Andrew Burnham, *Lab.* 22,783
Andrew Oxley, *C.* 6,421
Ray Atkins, *LD* 4,524
William Kelly, *Soc. Lab.* 820
Chris Best, *UK Ind.* 750
*Lab. majority* 16,362 (46.35%)
3.50% swing Lab. to C.
(1997, Lab. maj. 24,496 (53.35%))

LEOMINSTER
*E.*68,695 *T.* 46,729 (68.02%) Con gain
Bill Wiggin, *C.* 22,879
Ms Celia Downie, *LD* 12,512
Stephen Hart, *Lab.* 7,872
Ms Pippa Bennett, *Green* 1,690
Christopher Kingsley, *UK Ind.* 1,590
John Haycock, *Ind.* 186
*C. majority* 10,367 (22.19%)
2.35% swing LD to C.
(1997, C. maj. 8,835 (17.48%))

LEWES
*E.*66,332 *T.* 45,433 (68.49%) LD hold
*Norman Baker, *LD* 25,588
Simon Sinnatt, *C.* 15,878
Paul Richards, *Lab.* 3,317
John Harvey, *UK Ind.* 650
*LD majority* 9,710 (21.37%)
9.36% swing C. to LD
(1997, LD maj. 1,300 (2.65%))

LEWISHAM DEPTFORD
*E.*62,869 *T.* 29,107 (46.30%) Lab. hold
*Joan Ruddock, *Lab.* 18,915
Ms Cordelia McCartney, *C.* 3,622
Andrew Wiseman, *LD* 3,409
Darren Johnson, *Green* 1,901
Ian Page, *Soc. All.* 1,260
*Lab. majority* 15,293 (52.54%)
1.78% swing Lab. to C.
(1997, Lab. maj. 18,878 (56.11%))

LEWISHAM EAST
*E.*58,302 *T.* 30,040 (51.52%) Lab. hold
*Ms Bridget Prentice, *Lab.* 16,116
David McInnes, *C.* 7,157
David Buxton, *LD* 4,937
Barry Roberts, *BNP* 1,005
Ms Jean Kysow, *Soc. All.* 464
Maurice Link, *UK Ind.* 361
*Lab. majority* 8,959 (29.82%)
1.30% swing Lab. to C.
(1997, Lab. maj. 12,127 (32.42%))

LEWISHAM WEST
*E.*60,947 *T.* 30,815 (50.56%) Lab. hold
*Jim Dowd, *Lab.* 18,816
Gary Johnson, *C.* 6,896
Richard Thomas, *LD* 4,146
Frederick Pearson, *UK Ind.* 485
Nick Long, *Ind.* 472
*Lab. majority* 11,920 (38.68%)
0.25% swing C. to Lab.
(1997, Lab. maj. 14,337 (38.19%))

LEYTON & WANSTEAD
*E.*61,549 *T.* 33,718 (54.78%) Lab. hold
*Harry Cohen, *Lab.* 19,558
Edward Heckels, *C.* 6,654
Alex Wilcock, *LD* 5,389
Ashley Gunstock, *Green* 1,030
Ms Sally Labern, *Soc. All.* 709
M. Skaife D'Ingerthorp, *UK Ind.* 378
*Lab. majority* 12,904 (38.27%)
0.17% swing Lab. to C.
(1997, Lab. maj. 15,186 (38.62%))

LICHFIELD
*E.*63,794 *T.* 41,680 (65.34%) C. hold
*Michael Fabricant, *C.* 20,480
Martin Machray, *Lab.* 16,054
Phillip Bennion, *LD* 4,462
John Phazey, *UK Ind.* 684
*C. majority* 4,426 (10.62%)
5.06% swing Lab. to C.
(1997, C. maj. 238 (0.49%))

LINCOLN
*E.*66,299 *T.* 37,125 (56.00%) Lab. hold
*Ms Gillian Merron, *Lab.* 20,003
Mrs Christine Talbot, *C.* 11,583
Ms Lisa Gabriel, *LD* 4,703
Roger Doughty, *UK Ind.* 836
*Lab. majority* 8,420 (22.68%)
0.61% swing Lab. to C.
(1997, Lab. maj. 11,130 (23.91%))

LIVERPOOL GARSTON
*E.*65,094 *T.* 32,651 (50.16%) Lab. hold
*Ms Maria Eagle, *Lab.* 20,043
Ms Paula Keaveney, *LD* 7,549
Miss Helen Sutton, *C.* 5,059
*Lab. majority* 12,494 (38.27%)
2.05% swing Lab. to LD
(1997, Lab. maj. 18,417 (42.36%))

LIVERPOOL RIVERSIDE
*E.*74,827 *T.* 25,503 (34.08%) Lab. Co-op hold
*Ms Louise Ellman, *Lab. Co-op* 18,201
Richard Marbrow, *LD* 4,251
Miss Judith Edwards, *C.* 2,142
Ms Cathy Wilson, *Soc. All.* 909
*Lab. Co-op majority* 13,950 (54.70%)
1.23% swing Lab. Co-op to LD
(1997, Lab. maj. 21,799 (57.16%))

LIVERPOOL WALTON
*E.*66,237 *T.* 28,458 (42.96%) Lab. hold
*Peter Kilfoyle, *Lab.* 22,143
Kiron Reid, *LD* 4,147
Stephen Horgan, *C.* 1,726
Paul Forrest, *UK Ind.* 442
*Lab. majority* 17,996 (63.24%)
2.00% swing Lab. to LD
(1997, Lab. maj. 27,038 (67.24%))

LIVERPOOL WAVERTREE
*E.*72,555 *T.* 32,138 (44.29%) Lab. hold
*Ms Jane Kennedy, *Lab.* 20,155
Christopher Newby, *LD* 7,836
Geoffrey Allen, *C.* 3,091
Michael Lane, *Soc. Lab.* 359
Mark O'Brien, *Soc. All.* 349
Neil Miney, *UK Ind.* 348
*Lab. majority* 12,319 (38.33%)
2.29% swing Lab. to LD
(1997, Lab. maj. 19,701 (42.91%))

LIVERPOOL WEST DERBY
*E.*67,921 *T.* 30,907 (45.50%) Lab. hold
*Robert Wareing, *Lab.* 20,454
Steve Radford, *Lib.* 4,601
Patrick Moloney, *LD* 3,366
Bill Clare, *C.* 2,486
*Lab. majority* 15,853 (51.29%)
5.15% swing Lab. to Lib.
(1997, Lab. maj. 25,965 (61.59%))

LOUGHBOROUGH
*E.*70,077 *T.* 44,254 (63.15%) Lab. Co-op hold
*Andy Reed, *Lab. Co-op* 22,016
Neil Lyon, *C.* 15,638
Ms Julie Simons, *LD* 5,667
John Bigger, *UK Ind.* 933
*Lab. Co-op majority* 6,378 (14.41%)
1.75% swing C. to Lab. Co-op
(1997, Lab. maj. 5,712 (10.91%))

LOUTH & HORNCASTLE
*E.*71,556 *T.* 44,460 (62.13%) C. hold
*Sir Peter Tapsell, *C.* 21,543
David Bolland, *Lab.* 13,989
Ms Fiona Martin, *LD* 8,928
*C. majority* 7,554 (16.99%)
1.59% swing Lab. to C.
(1997, C. maj. 6,900 (13.81%))

LUDLOW
*E.*63,053 *T.* 43,124 (68.39%) LD gain
Matthew Green, *LD* 18,620
Martin Taylor-Smith, *C.* 16,990
Nigel Knowles, *Lab.* 5,785
Jim Gaffney, *Green* 871
Phil Gutteridge, *UK Ind.* 858
*LD majority* 1,630 (3.78%)
8.27% swing C. to LD
(1997, C. maj. 5,909 (12.77%))

LUTON NORTH
*E.*65,998 *T.* 39,126 (59.28%) Lab. hold
*Kelvin Hopkins, *Lab.* 22,187
Mrs Amanda Sater, *C.* 12,210
Dr Bob Hoyle, *LD* 3,795
Colin Brown, *UK Ind.* 934
*Lab. majority* 9,977 (25.50%)
2.58% swing C. to Lab.
(1997, Lab. maj. 9,626 (20.34%))

LUTON SOUTH
*E.*68,985 *T.* 39,351 (57.04%) Lab. hold
*Ms Margaret Moran, *Lab.* 21,719
Gordon Henderson, *C.* 11,586
Rabi Martins, *LD* 4,292
Marc Scheimann, *Green* 798
Charles Lawman, *UK Ind.* 578
Joe Hearne, *Soc. All.* 271
Robert Bolton, *WRP* 107
*Lab. majority* 10,133 (25.75%)
1.13% swing C. to Lab.
(1997, Lab. maj. 11,319 (23.49%))

MACCLESFIELD
E.73,123 T. 45,585 (62.34%) C. hold
*Nicholas Winterton, *C.* 22,284
Stephen Carter, *Lab.* 15,084
Mike Flynn, *LD* 8,217
*C. majority* 7,200 (15.79%)
0.09% swing C. to Lab.
(1997, C. maj. 8,654 (15.97%))

MAIDENHEAD
E.68,130 T. 43,318 (63.58%) C. hold
*Mrs Theresa May, *C.* 19,506
Ms Kathryn Newbound, *LD* 16,222
John O'Farrell, *Lab.* 6,577
Dr Denis Cooper, *UK Ind.* 741
Lloyd Clarke, *Loony* 272
*C. majority* 3,284 (7.58%)
7.98% swing C. to LD
(1997, C. maj. 11,981 (23.54%))

MAIDSTONE & THE WEALD
E.74,002 T. 45,577 (61.59%) C. hold
*Rt. Hon. Miss A. Widdecombe, *C.* 22,621
Mark Davis, *Lab.* 12,303
Ms Allison Wainman, *LD* 9,064
John Botting, *UK Ind.* 978
Neil Hunt, *Ind.* 611
*C. majority* 10,318 (22.64%)
2.36% swing Lab. to C.
(1997, C. maj. 9,603 (17.91%))

MAKERFIELD
E.68,457 T. 34,856 (50.92%) Lab. hold
*Rt. Hon. I. McCartney, *Lab.* 23,879
Mrs Jane Brooks, *C.* 6,129
David Crowther, *LD* 3,990
Malcolm Jones, *Soc. All.* 858
*Lab. majority* 17,750 (50.92%)
3.61% swing Lab. to C.
(1997, Lab. maj. 26,177 (58.15%))

MALDON & CHELMSFORD EAST
E.69,201 T. 44,100 (63.73%) C. hold
*John Whittingdale, *C.* 21,719
Russell Kennedy, *Lab.* 13,257
Ms Jane Jackson, *LD* 7,002
Geoffrey Harris, *UK Ind.* 1,135
Walter Schwarz, *Green* 987
*C. majority* 8,462 (19.19%)
0.37% swing C. to Lab.
(1997, C. maj. 10,039 (19.92%))

MANCHESTER BLACKLEY
E.59,111 T. 26,523 (44.87%) Lab. hold
*Graham Stringer, *Lab.* 18,285
Lance Stanbury, *C.* 3,821
Gary Riding, *LD* 3,015
Kevin Barr, *Soc. Lab.* 485
Ms Karen Reissmann, *Soc. All.* 461
Aziz Bhatti, *Anti-Corrupt* 456
*Lab. majority* 14,464 (54.53%
0.13% swing Lab. to C.
(1997, Lab. maj. 19,588 (54.79%))

MANCHESTER CENTRAL
E.66,268 T. 25,928 (39.13%) Lab. hold
*Tony Lloyd, *Lab.* 17,812
Philip Hobson, *LD* 4,070
Aaron Powell, *C.* 2,328
Ms Vanessa Hall, *Green* 1,018
Ron Sinclair, *Soc. Lab.* 484
Ms Terrenia Brosnan, *ProLife* 216
*Lab. majority* 13,742 (53.00%)
2.84% swing Lab. to LD
(1997, Lab. maj. 19,682 (58.69%))

MANCHESTER GORTON
E.63,834 T. 27,229 (42.66%) Lab. hold
*Rt. Hon. G. Kaufman, *Lab.* 17,099
Ms Jackie Pearcey, *LD* 5,795
Christopher Causer, *C.* 2,705
Bruce Bingham, *Green* 835
Rashid Bhatti, *UK Ind.* 462
Ms Kirsty Muir, *Soc. Lab.* 333
*Lab. majority* 11,304 (41.51%)
3.12% swing Lab. to LD
(1997, Lab. maj. 17,342 (47.76%))

MANCHESTER WITHINGTON
E.67,480 T. 35,050 (51.94%) Lab. hold
*Rt. Hon. K. Bradley, *Lab.* 19,239
Ms Yasmin Zalzala, *LD* 7,715
Julian Samways, *C.* 5,349
Ms Michelle Valentine, *Green* 1,539
John Clegg, *Soc. All.* 1,208
*Lab. majority* 11,524 (32.88%)
7.53% swing Lab. to LD
(1997, Lab. maj. 18,581 (42.20%))

MANSFIELD
E.66,748 T. 36,852 (55.21%) Lab. hold
*Alan Meale, *Lab.* 21,050
William Wellesley, *C.* 10,012
Tim Hill, *LD* 5,790
*Lab. majority* 11,038 (29.95%)
6.65% swing Lab. to C.
(1997, Lab. maj. 20,518 (43.26%))

MEDWAY
E.64,930 T. 38,610 (59.46%) Lab. hold
*Robert Marshall-Andrews, *Lab.* 18,914
Mark Reckless, *C.* 15,134
Geoffrey Juby, *LD* 3,604
Ms Nikki Sinclaire, *UK Ind.* 958
*Lab. majority* 3,780 (9.79%)
1.08% swing Lab. to C.
(1997, Lab. maj. 5,354 (11.96%))

MERIDEN
E.74,439 T. 44,559 (59.86%) C. hold
*Mrs Caroline Spelman, *C.* 21,246
Ms Christine Shawcroft, *Lab.* 17,462
Nigel Hicks, *LD* 4,941
Richard Adams, *UK Ind.* 910
*C. majority* 3,784 (8.49%)
3.71% swing Lab. to C.
(1997, C. maj. 582 (1.07%))

MIDDLESBROUGH
E.67,659 T. 33,717 (49.83%) Lab. hold
*Stuart Bell, *Lab.* 22,783
Alex Finn, *C.* 6,453
Keith Miller, *LD* 3,512
Geoff Kerr-Morgan, *Soc. All.* 577
Kai Andersen, *Soc. Lab.* 392
*Lab. majority* 16,330 (48.43%)
2.92% swing Lab. to C.
(1997, Lab. maj. 25,018 (54.28%))

MIDDLESBROUGH SOUTH & CLEVELAND EAST
E.71,485 T. 43,991 (61.54%) Lab. hold
*Dr Ashok Kumar, *Lab.* 24,321
Mrs Barbara Harpham, *C.* 14,970
Ms Linda Parrish, *LD* 4,700
*Lab. majority* 9,351 (21.26%)
0.73% swing C. to Lab.
(1997, Lab. maj. 10,607 (19.79%))

MILTON KEYNES NORTH EAST
E.75,526 T. 47,094 (62.35%) Lab. hold
*Brian White, *Lab.* 19,761
Mrs Marion Rix, *C.* 17,932
David Yeoward, *LD* 8,375
Michael Phillips, *UK Ind.* 1,026
*Lab. majority* 1,829 (3.88%)
1.71% swing C. to Lab.
(1997, Lab. maj. 240 (0.47%))

MILTON KEYNES SOUTH WEST
E.76,607 T. 45,384 (59.24%) Lab. hold
*Dr Phyllis Starkey, *Lab.* 22,484
Iain Stewart, *C.* 15,506
Nazar Mohammad, *LD* 4,828
Alan Francis, *Green* 957
Clive Davies, *UK Ind.* 848
Patrick Denning, *LCA* 500
Dave Bradbury, *Soc. All.* 261
*Lab. majority* 6,978 (15.38%)
2.45% swing Lab. to C.
(1997, Lab. maj. 10,292 (20.28%))

MITCHAM & MORDEN
E.65,671 T. 37,961 (57.80%) Lab. hold
*Ms Siobhain McDonagh, *Lab.* 22,936
Harry Stokes, *C.* 9,151
Nicholas Harris, *LD* 3,820
Tom Walsh, *Green* 926
John Tyndall, *BNP* 642
Adrian Roberts, *UK Ind.* 486
*Lab. majority* 13,785 (36.31%)
3.83% swing C. to Lab.
(1997, Lab. maj. 13,741 (28.66%))

MOLE VALLEY
E.67,770 T. 47,072 (69.46%) C. hold
*Sir Paul Beresford, *C.* 23,790
Ms Celia Savage, *LD* 13,637
Dan Redford, *Lab.* 7,837
Ron Walters, *UK Ind.* 1,333
William Newton, *ProLife* 475
*C. majority* 10,153 (21.57%)
1.41% swing LD to C.
(1997, C. maj. 10,221 (18.74%))

MORECAMBE & LUNESDALE
E.68,607 T. 41,655 (60.72%) Lab. hold
*Ms Geraldine Smith, *Lab.* 20,646
David Nuttall, *C.* 15,554
Chris Cotton, *LD* 3,817
Gregg Beaman, *UK Ind.* 935
Ms Cherith Adams, *Green* 703
*Lab. majority* 5,092 (12.22%)
0.05% swing C. to Lab.
(1997, Lab. maj. 5,965 (12.12%))

MORLEY & ROTHWELL
E.71,815 T. 38,442 (53.53%) Lab. hold
Colin Challen, *Lab.* 21,919
David Schofield, *C.* 9,829
Stewart Golton, *LD* 5,446
John Bardsley, *UK Ind.* 1,248
*Lab. majority* 12,090 (31.45%)
0.35% swing Lab. to C.
(1997, Lab. maj. 14,750 (32.14%))

NEW FOREST EAST
*E.*66,767 *T.* 42,178 (63.17%) C. hold
*Dr Julian Lewis, *C.* 17,902
Brian Dash, *LD* 14,073
Alan Goodfellow, *Lab.* 9,141
William Howe, *UK Ind.* 1,062
*C. majority* 3,829 (9.08%)
0.78% swing C. to LD
(1997, C. maj. 5,215 (10.63%))

NEW FOREST WEST
*E.*67,806 *T.* 44,087 (65.02%) C. hold
*Desmond Swayne, *C.* 24,575
Mike Bignell, *LD* 11,384
Ms Crada Onuegbu, *Lab.* 6,481
Michael Clark, *UK Ind.* 1,647
*C. majority* 13,191 (29.92%)
3.57% swing LD to C.
(1997, C. maj. 11,332 (22.78%))

NEWARK
*E.*71,089 *T.* 45,147 (63.51%) Con gain
Patrick Mercer, *C.* 20,983
*Ms Fiona Jones, *Lab.* 16,910
David Harding-Price, *LD* 5,970
Donald Haxby, *Ind.* 822
Ian Thomson, *Soc. All.* 462
*C. majority* 4,073 (9.02%)
7.41% swing Lab. to C.
(1997, Lab. maj. 3,016 (5.80%))

NEWBURY
*E.*75,490 *T.* 50,807 (67.30%) LD hold
*David Rendel, *LD* 24,507
Richard Benyon, *C.* 22,092
Steve Billcliffe, *Lab.* 3,523
Ms Delphine Gray-Fisk, *UK Ind.* 685
*LD majority* 2,415 (4.75%)
5.16% swing LD to C.
(1997, LD maj. 8,517 (15.08%))

NEWCASTLE UPON TYNE CENTRAL
*E.*67,970 *T.* 34,870 (51.30%) Lab. hold
*Jim Cousins, *Lab.* 19,169
Stephen Psallidas, *LD* 7,564
Aidan Ruff, *C.* 7,414
Gordon Potts, *Soc. Lab.* 723
*Lab. majority* 11,605 (33.28%)
5.44% swing Lab. to LD
(1997, Lab. maj. 16,480 (35.75%))

NEWCASTLE UPON TYNE EAST & WALLSEND
*E.*61,494 *T.* 32,694 (53.17%) Lab. hold
*Rt. Hon. N. Brown, *Lab.* 20,642
David Ord, *LD* 6,419
Tim Troman, *C.* 3,873
Andrew Gray, *Green* 651
Dr Harash Narang, *Ind.* 563
Ms Blanch Carpenter, *Soc. Lab.* 420
Martin Levy, *Comm.* 126
*Lab. majority* 14,223 (43.50%)
8.53% swing Lab. to LD
(1997, Lab. maj. 23,811 (57.25%))

NEWCASTLE UPON TYNE NORTH
*E.*63,208 *T.* 36,368 (57.54%) Lab. hold
*Doug Henderson, *Lab.* 21,874
Phillip Smith, *C.* 7,424
Graham Soult, *LD* 7,070
*Lab. majority* 14,450 (39.73%)
1.50% swing Lab. to C.
(1997, Lab. maj. 19,332 (42.74%))

NEWCASTLE-UNDER-LYME
*E.*65,739 *T.* 38,674 (58.83%) Lab. hold
Paul Farrelly, *Lab.* 20,650
Mike Flynn, *C.* 10,664
Jerry Roodhouse, *LD* 5,993
Robert Fyson, *Ind.* 773
Paul Godfrey, *UK Ind.* 594
*Lab. majority* 9,986 (25.82%)
4.60% swing Lab. to C.
(1997, Lab. maj. 17,206 (35.02%))

NORFOLK MID
*E.*74,911 *T.* 52,548 (70.15%) C. hold
*Keith Simpson, *C.* 23,519
Daniel Zeichner, *Lab.* 18,957
Ms V. Clifford-Jackson, *LD* 7,621
John Agnew, *UK Ind.* 1,333
Peter Reeve, *Green* 1,118
*C. majority* 4,562 (8.68%)
3.18% swing Lab. to C.
(1997, C. maj. 1,336 (2.33%))

NORFOLK NORTH
*E.*80,061 *T.* 56,220 (70.22%) LD gain
Norman Lamb, *LD* 23,978
*David Prior, *C.* 23,495
Michael Gates, *Lab.* 7,490
Mike Sheridan, *Green* 649
Paul Simison, *UK Ind.* 608
*LD majority* 483 (0.86%)
1.53% swing C. to LD
(1997, C. maj. 1,293 (2.20%))

NORFOLK NORTH WEST
*E.*77,387 *T.* 51,203 (66.16%) Con gain
Henry Bellingham, *C.* 24,846
*Dr George Turner, *Lab.* 21,361
Dr Ian Mack, *LD* 4,292
Ian Durrant, *UK Ind.* 704
*C. majority* 3,485 (6.81%)
4.57% swing Lab. to C.
(1997, Lab. maj. 1,339 (2.33%))

NORFOLK SOUTH
*E.*82,710 *T.* 55,929 (67.62%) C. hold
Richard Bacon, *C.* 23,589
Dr Anne Lee, *LD* 16,696
Mark Wells, *Lab.* 13,719
Ms Stephanie Ross-Wagenknecht, *Green* 1,069
Joseph Neal, *UK Ind.* 856
*C. majority* 6,893 (12.32%)
0.22% swing LD to C.
(1997, C. maj. 7,378 (11.88%))

NORFOLK SOUTH WEST
*E.*83,903 *T.* 52,949 (63.11%) C. hold
*Rt. Hon. Mrs G. Shephard, *C.* 27,633
Ms Anne Hanson, *Lab.* 18,267
Gordon Dean, *LD* 5,681
Ian Smith, *UK Ind.* 1,368
*C. majority* 9,366 (17.69%)
6.75% swing Lab. to C.
(1997, C. maj. 2,464 (4.19%))

NORMANTON
*E.*65,392 *T.* 34,155 (52.23%) Lab. hold
*William O'Brien, *Lab.* 19,152
Graham Smith, *C.* 9,215
Stephen Pearson, *LD* 4,990
Mick Appleyard, *Soc. Lab.* 798
*Lab. majority* 9,937 (29.09%)
3.93% swing Lab. to C.
(1997, Lab. maj. 15,893 (36.96%))

NORTHAMPTON NORTH
*E.*74,124 *T.* 41,494 (55.98%) Lab. hold
*Ms Sally Keeble, *Lab.* 20,507
John Whelan, *C.* 12,614
Richard Church, *LD* 7,363
Dusan Torbica, *UK Ind.* 596
Gordon White, *Soc. All.* 414
*Lab. majority* 7,893 (19.02%)
0.16% swing Lab. to C.
(1997, Lab. maj. 10,000 (19.34%))

NORTHAMPTON SOUTH
*E.*85,271 *T.* 51,029 (59.84%) Lab. hold
*Tony Clarke, *Lab.* 21,882
Shailesh Vara, *C.* 20,997
Andrew Simpson, *LD* 6,355
Derek Clark, *UK Ind.* 1,237
Miss Tina Harvey, *LP* 362
Ms Clare Johnson, *ProLife* 196
*Lab. majority* 885 (1.73%)
0.22% swing C. to Lab.
(1997, Lab. maj. 744 (1.30%))

NORTHAVON
*E.*78,841 *T.* 55,758 (70.72%) LD hold
*Steve Webb, *LD* 29,217
Dr Carrie Ruxton, *C.* 19,340
Robert Hall, *Lab.* 6,450
Mrs Carmen Carver, *UK Ind.* 751
*LD majority* 9,877 (17.71%)
7.15% swing C. to LD
(1997, LD maj. 2,137 (3.42%))

NORWICH NORTH
*E.*74,911 *T.* 45,614 (60.89%) Lab. hold
*Dr Ian Gibson, *Lab.* 21,624
Ms Kay Mason, *C.* 15,761
Ms Moira Toye, *LD* 6,750
Robert Tinch, *Green* 797
Guy Cheyney, *UK Ind.* 471
Michael Betts, *Ind.* 211
*Lab. majority* 5,863 (12.85%)
2.17% swing Lab. to C.
(1997, Lab. maj. 9,470 (17.20%))

NORWICH SOUTH
*E.*65,792 *T.* 42,592 (64.74%) Lab. hold
*Rt. Hon. C. Clarke, *Lab.* 19,367
Andrew French, *C.* 10,551
Andrew Aalders-Dunthorne, *LD* 9,640
Adrian Holmes, *Green* 1,434
Alun Buffrey, *LCA* 620
Edward Manningham, *Soc. All.* 507
Tarquin Mills, *UK Ind.* 473
*Lab. majority* 8,816 (20.70%)
3.67% swing Lab. to C.
(1997, Lab. maj. 14,239 (28.03%))

NOTTINGHAM EAST
*E.*65,339 *T.* 29,731 (45.50%) Lab. hold
*John Heppell, *Lab.* 17,530
Richard Allan, *C.* 7,210
Tim Ball, *LD* 3,874
Pete Radcliff, *Soc. All.* 1,117
*Lab. majority* 10,320 (34.71%)
2.04% swing Lab. to C.
(1997, Lab. maj. 15,419 (38.80%))

### NOTTINGHAM NORTH
*E.*64,281 *T.* 30,042 (46.74%) Lab. hold
*Graham Allen, *Lab.* 19,392
Martin Wright, *C.* 7,152
Rob Lee, *LD* 3,177
Andrew Botham, *Soc. Lab.* 321
*Lab. majority* 12,240 (40.74%)
2.34% swing Lab. to C.
(1997, Lab. maj. 18,801 (45.42%))

### NOTTINGHAM SOUTH
*E.*73,049 *T.* 36,605 (50.11%) Lab. hold
*Alan Simpson, *Lab.* 19,949
Mrs Wendy Manning, *C.* 9,960
Kevin Mulloy, *LD* 6,064
David Bartrop, *UK Ind.* 632
*Lab. majority* 9,989 (27.29%)
0.13% swing Lab. to C.
(1997, Lab. maj. 13,364 (27.55%))

### NUNEATON
*E.*72,101 *T.* 43,312 (60.07%) Lab. hold
*Bill Olner, *Lab.* 22,577
Mark Lancaster, *C.* 15,042
Tony Ferguson, *LD* 4,820
Brian James, *UK Ind.* 873
*Lab. majority* 7,535 (17.40%)
3.95% swing Lab. to C.
(1997, Lab. maj. 13,540 (25.30%))

### OLD BEXLEY & SIDCUP
*E.*67,841 *T.* 42,133 (62.11%) C. hold
Derek Conway, *C.* 19,130
Jim Dickson, *Lab.* 15,785
Ms Belinda Ford, *LD* 5,792
Mrs Janice Cronin, *UK Ind.* 1,426
*C. majority* 3,345 (7.94%)
0.49% swing Lab. to C.
(1997, C. maj. 3,569 (6.95%))

### OLDHAM EAST & SADDLEWORTH
*E.*74,511 *T.* 45,420 (60.96%) Lab. hold
*Phil Woolas, *Lab.* 17,537
Howard Sykes, *LD* 14,811
Craig Heeley, *C.* 7,304
Michael Treacy, *BNP* 5,091
Ms Barbara Little, *UK Ind.* 677
*Lab. majority* 2,726 (6.00%)
0.13% swing Lab. to LD
(1997, Lab. maj. 3,389 (6.26%))

### OLDHAM WEST & ROYTON
*E.*69,409 *T.* 39,962 (57.57%) Lab. hold
*Rt. Hon. M. Meacher, *Lab.* 20,441
Duncan Reed, *C.* 7,076
Nick Griffin, *BNP* 6,552
Marc Ramsbottom, *LD* 4,975
David Roney, *Green* 918
*Lab. majority* 13,365 (33.44%)
0.99% swing Lab. to C.
(1997, Lab. maj. 16,201 (35.42%))

### ORPINGTON
*E.*74,423 *T.* 50,912 (68.41%) C. hold
*John Horam, *C.* 22,334
Chris Maines, *LD* 22,065
Chris Purnell, *Lab.* 5,517
John Youles, *UK Ind.* 996
*C. majority* 269 (0.53%)
2.19% swing C. to LD
(1997, C. maj. 2,952 (4.91%))

### OXFORD EAST
*E.*74,421 *T.* 39,848 (53.54%) Lab. hold
*Rt. Hon. A. Smith, *Lab.* 19,681
Steve Goddard, *LD* 9,337
Ms Cheryl Potter, *C.* 7,446
Pritam Singh, *Green* 1,501
John Lister, *Soc. All.* 708
Peter Gardner, *UK Ind.* 570
Fahim Ahmed, *Soc. Lab.* 274
Ms Linda Hodge, *ProLife* 254
Pathmanathan Mylvaganan, *Ind.* 77
*Lab. majority* 10,344 (25.96%)
8.08% swing Lab. to LD
(1997, Lab. maj. 16,665 (34.81%))

### OXFORD WEST & ABINGDON
*E.*79,915 *T.* 51,568 (64.53%) LD hold
*Dr Evan Harris, *LD* 24,670
Ed Matts, *C.* 15,485
Ms Gillian Kirk, *Lab.* 9,114
Mike Woodin, *Green* 1,423
Marcus Watney, *UK Ind.* 451
Ms Sigrid Shreeve, *Ind.* 332
Robert Twigger, *Ext. Club* 93
*LD majority* 9,185 (17.81%)
3.77% swing C. to LD
(1997, LD maj. 6,285 (10.27%))

### PENDLE
*E.*62,870 *T.* 39,732 (63.20%) Lab. hold
*Gordon Prentice, *Lab.* 17,729
Rasjid Skinner, *C.* 13,454
David Whipp, *LD* 5,479
Christian Jackson, *BNP* 1,976
Graham Cannon, *UK Ind.* 1,094
*Lab. majority* 4,275 (10.76%)
6.13% swing Lab. to C.
(1997, Lab. maj. 10,824 (23.02%))

### PENRITH & THE BORDER
*E.*67,776 *T.* 44,249 (65.29%) C. hold
*Rt. Hon. D. Maclean, *C.* 24,302
Kenneth Geyve Walker, *LD* 9,625
Michael Boaden, *Lab.* 8,177
Thomas Lowther, *UK Ind.* 938
Mark Gibson, *LCA* 870
John Moffat, *Ind.* 337
*C. majority* 14,677 (33.17%)
6.13% swing LD to C.
(1997, C. maj. 10,233 (20.90%))

### PETERBOROUGH
*E.*64,918 *T.* 39,812 (61.33%) Lab. hold
*Mrs Helen Brinton, *Lab.* 17,975
Stewart Jackson, *C.* 15,121
Nick Sandford, *LD* 5,761
Julian Fairweather, *UK Ind.* 955
*Lab. majority* 2,854 (7.17%)
3.98% swing Lab. to C.
(1997, Lab. maj. 7,323 (15.12%))

### PLYMOUTH DEVONPORT
*E.*73,666 *T.* 41,719 (56.63%) Lab. hold
*David Jamieson, *Lab.* 24,322
John Glen, *C.* 11,289
Keith Baldry, *LD* 4,513
Michael Parker, *UK Ind.* 958
Tony Staunton, *Soc. All.* 334
Rob Hawkins, *Soc. Lab.* 303
*Lab. majority* 13,033 (31.24%)
2.73% swing Lab. to C.
(1997, Lab. maj. 19,067 (36.70%))

### PLYMOUTH SUTTON
*E.*68,438 *T.* 39,073 (57.09%) Lab. Co-op hold
*Mrs Linda Gilroy, *Lab. Co-op* 19,827
Oliver Colvile, *C.* 12,310
Alan Connett, *LD* 5,605
Alan Whitton, *UK Ind.* 970
Henry Leary, *Soc. Lab.* 361
*Lab. Co-op majority* 7,517 (19.24%)
0.29% swing Lab. Co-op to C.
(1997, Lab. maj. 9,440 (19.81%))

### PONTEFRACT & CASTLEFORD
*E.*63,181 *T.* 31,391 (49.68%) Lab. hold
*Ms Yvette Cooper, *Lab.* 21,890
Ms Pamela Singleton, *C.* 5,512
Wesley Paxton, *LD* 2,315
John Burdon, *UK Ind.* 739
Trevor Bolderson, *Soc. Lab.* 605
John Gill, *Soc. All.* 330
*Lab. majority* 16,378 (52.17%)
4.99% swing Lab. to C.
(1997, Lab. maj. 25,725 (62.15%))

### POOLE
*E.*64,644 *T.* 39,233 (60.69%) C. hold
*Robert Syms, *C.* 17,710
David Watt, *Lab.* 10,544
Nick Westbrook, *LD* 10,011
John Bass, *UK Ind.* 968
*C. majority* 7,166 (18.27%)
1.15% swing C. to Lab.
(1997, C. maj. 5,298 (11.32%))

### POPLAR & CANNING TOWN
*E.*75,173 *T.* 34,108 (45.37%) Lab. hold
*Jim Fitzpatrick, *Lab.* 20,862
Robert Marr, *C.* 6,758
Ms Alexi Sugden, *LD* 3,795
Paul Borg, *BNP* 1,743
Dr Kambiz Boomla, *Soc. All.* 950
*Lab. majority* 14,104 (41.35%)
3.41% swing Lab. to C.
(1997, Lab. maj. 18,915 (48.17%))

### PORTSMOUTH NORTH
*E.*64,256 *T.* 36,866 (57.37%) Lab. hold
*Syd Rapson, *Lab.* 18,676
Chris Day, *C.* 13,542
Darren Sanders, *LD* 3,795
William McCabe, *UK Ind.* 559
Brian Bundy, *Ind.* 294
*Lab. majority* 5,134 (13.93%)
2.19% swing C. to Lab.
(1997, Lab. maj. 4,323 (9.55%))

### PORTSMOUTH SOUTH
*E.*77,095 *T.* 39,215 (50.87%) LD hold
*Mike Hancock, *LD* 17,490
Philip Warr, *C.* 11,396
Graham Heaney, *Lab.* 9,361
John Molyneux, *Soc. All.* 647
Michael Tarrant, *UK Ind.* 321
*LD majority* 6,094 (15.54%)
3.58% swing C. to LD
(1997, LD maj. 4,327 (8.37%))

### PRESTON
*E.*72,077 *T.* 36,041 (50.00%) Lab. Co-op hold
*Mark Hendrick, *Lab. Co-op* 20,540
Graham O'Hare, *C.* 8,272
Bill Chadwick, *LD* 4,746

Bilal Patel, *Ind.* 1,241
Richard Merrick, *Green* 1,019
The Rev David Braid, *Ind.* 223
*Lab. Co-op majority* 12,268 (34.04%)
2.41% swing Lab. Co-op to C.
(2000 Nov by-election, Lab. maj. 4,426)
(1997, Lab. maj. 18,680 (38.86%))

PUDSEY
*E.*71,405 *T.* 45,175 (63.27%) Lab. hold
*Paul Truswell, *Lab.* 21,717
John Procter, *C.* 16,091
Stephen Boddy, *LD* 6,423
David Sewards, *UK Ind.* 944
*Lab. majority* 5,626 (12.45%)
0.34% swing C. to Lab.
(1997, Lab. maj. 6,207 (11.77%))

PUTNEY
*E.*60,643 *T.* 34,254 (56.48%) Lab. hold
*Tony Colman, *Lab.* 15,911
Michael Simpson, *C.* 13,140
Tony Burrett, *LD* 4,671
Ms Pat Wild, *UK Ind.* 347
Ms Yvonne Windsor, *ProLife* 185
*Lab. majority* 2,771 (8.09%)
0.66% swing C. to Lab.
(1997, Lab. maj. 2,976 (6.76%))

RAYLEIGH
*E.*70,073 *T.* 42,773 (61.04%) C. hold
Mark Francois, *C.* 21,434
Paul Clark, *Lab.* 13,144
Geoff Williams, *LD* 6,614
Colin Morgan, *UK Ind.* 1,581
*C. majority* 8,290 (19.38%)
0.72% swing C. to Lab.
(1997, C. maj. 10,684 (20.83%))

READING EAST
*E.*74,637 *T.* 43,618 (58.44%) Lab. hold
*Ms Jane Griffiths, *Lab.* 19,531
Barry Tanswell, *C.* 13,943
Tom Dobrashian, *LD* 8,078
Ms Miriam Kennett, *Green* 1,053
Miss Amy Thornton, *UK Ind.* 525
Darren Williams, *Soc. All.* 394
Peter Hammerson, *Ind.* 94
*Lab. majority* 5,588 (12.81%)
2.63% swing C. to Lab.
(1997, Lab. maj. 3,795 (7.55%))

READING WEST
*E.*71,688 *T.* 41,986 (58.57%) Lab. hold
*Martin Salter, *Lab.* 22,300
Stephen Reid, *C.* 13,451
Ms Polly Martin, *LD* 5,387
David Black, *UK Ind.* 848
*Lab. majority* 8,849 (21.08%)
7.44% swing C. to Lab.
(1997, Lab. maj. 2,997 (6.20%))

REDCAR
*E.*66,179 *T.* 38,198 (57.72%) Lab. hold
Ms Vera Baird, *Lab.* 23,026
Chris Main, *C.* 9,583
Stan Wilson, *LD* 4,817
John Taylor, *Soc. Lab.* 772
*Lab. majority* 13,443 (35.19%)
4.53% swing Lab. to C.
(1997, Lab. maj. 21,664 (44.25%))

REDDITCH
*E.*62,543 *T.* 37,032 (59.21%) Lab. hold
*Ms Jacqui Smith, *Lab.* 16,899
Mrs Karen Lumley, *C.* 14,415
Michael Ashall, *LD* 3,808
George Flynn, *UK Ind.* 1,259
Richard Armstrong, *Green* 651
*Lab. majority* 2,484 (6.71%)
3.49% swing Lab. to C.
(1997, Lab. maj. 6,125 (13.69%))

REGENT'S PARK & KENSINGTON NORTH
*E.*75,886 *T.* 37,052 (48.83%) Lab. hold
*Ms Karen Buck, *Lab.* 20,247
Peter Wilson, *C.* 9,981
David Boyle, *LD* 4,669
Dr Paul Miller, *Green* 1,268
China Mieville, *Soc. All.* 459
Alan Crisp, *UK Ind.* 354
Ms Charlotte Regan, *Ind.* 74
*Lab. majority* 10,266 (27.71%)
1.63% swing Lab. to C.
(1997, Lab. maj. 14,657 (30.96%))

REIGATE
*E.*65,023 *T.* 39,474 (60.71%) C. hold
*Crispin Blunt, *C.* 18,875
Simon Charleton, *Lab.* 10,850
Ms Jane Kulka, *LD* 8,330
Stephen Smith, *UK Ind.* 1,062
Harold Green, *Ref. UK* 357
*C. majority* 8,025 (20.33%)
2.13% swing Lab. to C.
(1997, C. maj. 7,741 (16.07%))

RIBBLE SOUTH (SOUTH RIBBLE)
*E.*73,794 *T.* 46,130 (62.51%) Lab. hold
*David Borrow, *Lab.* 21,386
Adrian Owens, *C.* 17,594
Mark Alcock, *LD* 7,150
*Lab. majority* 3,792 (8.22%)
0.49% swing Lab. to C.
(1997, Lab. maj. 5,084 (9.20%))

RIBBLE VALLEY
*E.*74,319 *T.* 49,171 (66.16%) C. hold
*Nigel Evans, *C.* 25,308
Mike Carr, *LD* 14,070
Marcus Johnstone, *Lab.* 9,793
*C. majority* 11,238 (22.85%)
5.63% swing LD to C.
(1997, C. maj. 6,640 (11.60%))

RICHMOND (YORKS)
*E.*65,360 *T.* 44,034 (67.37%) C. hold
*Rt. Hon. W. Hague, *C.* 25,951
Ms Fay Tinnion, *Lab.* 9,632
Edward Forth, *LD* 7,890
Mrs Melodie Staniforth, *Loony* 561
*C. majority* 16,319 (37.06%)
8.00% swing Lab. to C.
(1997, C. maj. 10,051 (21.05%))

RICHMOND PARK
*E.*72,663 *T.* 49,151 (67.64%) LD hold
*Dr Jenny Tonge, *LD* 23,444
Tom Harris, *C.* 18,480
Barry Langford, *Lab.* 5,541
James Page, *Green* 1,223
Peter St John Howe, *UK Ind.* 348
Raymond Perrin, *Ind.* 115
*LD majority* 4,964 (10.10%)
2.45% swing C. to LD
(1997, LD maj. 2,951 (5.19%))

ROCHDALE
*E.*69,506 *T.* 39,412 (56.70%) Lab. hold
*Ms Lorna Fitzsimons, *Lab.* 19,406
Paul Rowen, *LD* 13,751
Ms Elaina Cohen, *C.* 5,274
Nick Harvey, *Green* 728
Mohammed Salim, *Ind.* 253
*Lab. majority* 5,655 (14.35%)
2.45% swing LD to Lab.
(1997, Lab. maj. 4,545 (9.45%))

ROCHFORD & SOUTHEND EAST
*E.*69,991 *T.* 37,452 (53.51%) C. hold
*Sir Teddy Taylor, *C.* 20,058
Chris Dandridge, *Lab.* 13,024
Stephen Newton, *LD* 2,780
Adrian Hedges, *Green* 990
Brian Lynch, *Lib.* 600
*C. majority* 7,034 (18.78%)
4.86% swing Lab. to C.
(1997, C. maj. 4,225 (9.07%))

ROMFORD
*E.*59,893 *T.* 35,701 (59.61%) Con gain
Andrew Rosindell, *C.* 18,931
*Ms Eileen Gordon, *Lab.* 12,954
Nigel Meyer, *LD* 2,869
Stephen Ward, *UK Ind.* 533
Frank McAllister, *BNP* 414
*C. majority* 5,977 (16.74%)
9.14% swing Lab. to C.
(1997, Lab. maj. 649 (1.54%))

ROMSEY
*E.*70,584 *T.* 48,459 (68.65%) LD hold
*Mrs Sandra Gidley, *LD* 22,756
Paul Raynes, *C.* 20,386
Stephen Roberts, *Lab.* 3,986
Anthony McCabe, *UK Ind.* 730
Derrick Large, *LCA* 601
*LD majority* 2,370 (4.89%)
10.73% swing C. to LD
(2000 May by-election, LD maj. 3,311 (8.55%); 1997, C. maj. 8,585 (16.56%))

ROSSENDALE & DARWEN
*E.*70,280 *T.* 41,358 (58.85%) Lab. hold
*Ms Janet Anderson, *Lab.* 20,251
George Lee, *C.* 15,028
Brian Dunning, *LD* 6,079
*Lab. majority* 5,223 (12.63%)
4.38% swing Lab. to C.
(1997, Lab. maj. 10,949 (21.38%))

ROTHER VALLEY
*E.*69,174 *T.* 36,803 (53.20%) Lab. hold
*Rt. Hon. K. Barron, *Lab.* 22,851
James Duddridge, *C.* 7,969
Ms Win Knight, *LD* 4,603
David Cutts, *UK Ind.* 1,380
*Lab. majority* 14,882 (40.44%)
5.22% swing Lab. to C.
(1997, Lab. maj. 23,485 (50.88%))

ROTHERHAM
*E.*57,931 *T.* 29,354 (50.67%) Lab. hold
*Denis MacShane, *Lab.* 18,759
Richard Powell, *C.* 5,682

Charles Hall, *LD* 3,117
Peter Griffith, *UK Ind.* 730
Dick Penycate, *Green* 577
Ms Freda Smith, *Soc. All.* 352
Geoffrey Bartholomew, *JLDP* 137
*Lab. majority* 13,077 (44.55%)
6.24% swing Lab. to C.
(1997, Lab. maj. 21,469 (57.02%))

RUGBY & KENILWORTH
*E.*79,764 *T.* 53,796 (67.44%) Lab. hold
*Andy King, *Lab.* 24,221
David Martin, *C.* 21,344
Ms Gwen Fairweather, *LD* 7,444
Paul Garratt, *UK Ind.* 787
*Lab. majority* 2,877 (5.35%)
2.27% swing C. to Lab.
(1997, Lab. maj. 495 (0.81%))

RUISLIP-NORTHWOOD
*E.*60,788 *T.* 37,141 (61.10%) C. hold
*John Wilkinson, *C.* 18,115
Ms Gillian Travis, *Lab.* 10,578
Mike Cox, *LD* 7,177
Graham Lee, *Green* 724
Ian Edward, *BNP* 547
*C. majority* 7,537 (20.29%)
1.46% swing Lab. to C.
(1997, C. maj. 7,794 (17.38%))

RUNNYMEDE & WEYBRIDGE
*E.*75,569 *T.* 42,426 (56.14%) C. hold
*Philip Hammond, *C.* 20,646
Ms Jane Briginshaw, *Lab.* 12,286
Chris Bushill, *LD* 6,924
Christopher Browne, *UK Ind.* 1,332
Charles Gilman, *Green* 1,238
*C. majority* 8,360 (19.70%)
0.27% swing Lab. to C.
(1997, C. maj. 9,875 (19.16%))

RUSHCLIFFE
*E.*81,839 *T.* 54,446 (66.53%) C. hold
*Rt. Hon. K. Clarke, *C.* 25,869
Paul Fallon, *Lab.* 18,512
Jeremy Hargreaves, *LD* 7,395
Ken Browne, *UK Ind.* 1,434
Ashley Baxter, *Green* 1,236
*C. majority* 7,357 (13.51%)
2.69% swing Lab. to C.
(1997, C. maj. 5,055 (8.14%))

RUTLAND & MELTON
*E.*72,448 *T.* 47,056 (64.95%) C. hold
*Alan Duncan, *C.* 22,621
Matthew O'Callaghan, *Lab.* 14,009
Kim Lee, *LD* 8,386
Peter Baker, *UK Ind.* 1,223
Christopher Davies, *Green* 817
*C. majority* 8,612 (18.30%)
0.76% swing Lab. to C.
(1997, C. maj. 8,836 (16.78%))

RYEDALE
*E.*66,543 *T.* 43,899 (65.97%) C. hold
*John Greenway, *C.* 20,711
Keith Orrell, *LD* 15,836
David Ellis, *Lab.* 6,470
Stephen Feaster, *UK Ind.* 882
*C. majority* 4,875 (11.11%)
0.37% swing LD to C.
(1997, C. maj. 5,058 (10.37%))

SAFFRON WALDEN
*E.*76,724 *T.* 50,040 (65.22%) C. hold
*Rt. Hon. Sir A. Haselhurst, *C.* 24,485
Mrs E. Tealby-Watson, *LD* 12,481
Ms Tania Rogers, *Lab.* 11,305
Richard Glover, *UK Ind.* 1,769
*C. majority* 12,004 (23.99%)
2.73% swing LD to C.
(1997, C. maj. 10,573 (18.53%))

SALFORD
*E.*54,152 *T.* 22,514 (41.58%) Lab. hold
*Ms Hazel Blears, *Lab.* 14,649
Norman Owen, *LD* 3,637
Chris King, *C.* 3,446
Peter Grant, *Soc. All.* 414
Ms Hazel Wallace, *Ind.* 216
Roy Masterson, *Ind.* 152
*Lab. majority* 11,012 (48.91%)
4.89% swing Lab. to LD
(1997, Lab. maj. 17,069 (51.53%))

SALISBURY
*E.*80,538 *T.* 52,603 (65.31%) C. hold
*Robert Key, *C.* 24,527
Ms Y. Emmerson-Peirce, *LD* 15,824
Ms Sue Mallory, *Lab.* 9,199
Malcolm Wood, *UK Ind.* 1,958
Hamish Soutar, *Green* 1,095
*C. majority* 8,703 (16.54%)
2.88% swing LD to C.
(1997, C. maj. 6,276 (10.78%))

SCARBOROUGH & WHITBY
*E.*75,213 *T.* 47,523 (63.18%) Lab. hold
*Lawrie Quinn, *Lab.* 22,426
John Sykes, *C.* 18,841
Tom Pearce, *LD* 3,977
Jonathan Dixon, *Green* 1,049
John Jacob, *UK Ind.* 970
Ms Theresa Murray, *ProLife* 260
*Lab. majority* 3,585 (7.54%)
0.94% swing Lab. to C.
(1997, Lab. maj. 5,124 (9.43%))

SCUNTHORPE
*E.*59,689 *T.* 33,625 (56.33%) Lab. hold
*Elliot Morley, *Lab.* 20,096
Bernard Theobald, *C.* 9,724
Bob Tress, *LD* 3,156
John Cliff, *UK Ind.* 347
David Patterson, *Ind.* 302
*Lab. majority* 10,372 (30.85%)
1.62% swing Lab. to C.
(1997, Lab. maj. 14,173 (34.09%))

SEDGEFIELD
*E.*64,925 *T.* 40,258 (62.01%) Lab. hold
*Rt. Hon. A. Blair, *Lab.* 26,110
Douglas Carswell, *C.* 8,397
Andrew Duffield, *LD* 3,624
Andrew Spence, *UK Ind.* 974
Brian Gibson, *Soc. Lab.* 518
Christopher Driver, *R & R Loony* 375
Ms Helen John, *WFLOE* 260
*Lab. majority* 17,713 (44.00%)
4.69% swing Lab. to C.
(1997, Lab. maj. 25,143 (53.37%))

SELBY
*E.*77,924 *T.* 50,272 (64.51%) Lab. hold
*John Grogan, *Lab.* 22,652
Michael Mitchell, *C.* 20,514
Jeremy Wilcock, *LD* 5,569
Ms Helen Kenwright, *Green* 902
Bob Lewis, *UK Ind.* 635
*Lab. majority* 2,138 (4.25%)
1.28% swing Lab. to C.
(1997, Lab. maj. 3,836 (6.81%))

SEVENOAKS
*E.*66,648 *T.* 42,614 (63.94%) C. hold
*Michael Fallon, *C.* 21,052
Ms Caroline Humphreys, *Lab.* 10,898
Clive Gray, *LD* 9,214
Mrs Lisa Hawkins, *UK Ind.* 1,155
Mark Ellis, *PF* 295
*C. majority* 10,154 (23.83%)
1.48% swing Lab. to C.
(1997, C. maj. 10,461 (20.86%))

SHEFFIELD ATTERCLIFFE
*E.*68,386 *T.* 35,824 (52.38%) Lab. hold
*Clive Betts, *Lab.* 24,287
John Perry, *C.* 5,443
Ms Gail Smith, *LD* 5,092
Ms Pauline Arnott, *UK Ind.* 1,002
*Lab. majority* 18,844 (52.60%)
1.69% swing C. to Lab.
(1997, Lab. maj. 21,818 (49.23%))

SHEFFIELD BRIGHTSIDE
*E.*54,711 *T.* 25,552 (46.70%) Lab. hold
*Rt. Hon. D. Blunkett, *Lab.* 19,650
Matthew Wilson, *C.* 2,601
Ms Alison Firth, *LD* 2,238
Brian Wilson, *Soc. All.* 361
Robert Morris, *Soc. Lab.* 354
Mark Suter, *UK Ind.* 348
*Lab. majority* 17,049 (66.72%)
0.81% swing C. to Lab.
(1997, Lab. maj. 19,954 (58.92%))

SHEFFIELD CENTRAL
*E.*62,018 *T.* 30,069 (48.48%) Lab. hold
*Rt. Hon. R. Caborn, *Lab.* 18,477
Ali Qadar, *LD* 5,933
Miss Noelle Brelsford, *C.* 3,289
Bernard Little, *Green* 1,008
Nick Riley, *Soc. All.* 754
David Hadfield, *Soc. Lab.* 289
Ms Charlotte Schofield, *UK Ind.* 257
Michael Driver, *WRP* 62
*Lab. majority* 12,544 (41.72%)
2.36% swing Lab. to LD
(1997, Lab. maj. 16,906 (46.43%))

SHEFFIELD HALLAM
*E.*60,288 *T.* 38,246 (63.44%) LD hold
*Richard Allan, *LD* 21,203
John Harthman, *C.* 11,856
Ms Gillian Furniss, *Lab.* 4,758
Leslie Arnott, *UK Ind.* 429
*LD majority* 9,347 (24.44%)
3.12% swing C. to LD
(1997, LD maj. 8,271 (18.19%))

SHEFFIELD HEELEY
*E.*62,758 *T.* 34,139 (54.40%) Lab. hold
Ms Meg Munn, *Lab.* 19,452
David Willis, *LD* 7,748
Ms Carolyn Abbott, *C.* 4,864
Rob Unwin, *Green* 774
Brian Fischer, *Soc. Lab.* 667
David Dunn, *UK Ind.* 634
*Lab. majority* 11,704 (34.28%)

2.60% swing Lab. to LD
(1997, Lab. maj. 17,078 (39.48%))

SHEFFIELD HILLSBOROUGH
*E.*75,097 *T.* 42,536 (56.64%) Lab. hold
*Ms Helen Jackson, *Lab.* 24,170
John Commons, *LD* 9,601
Graham King, *C.* 7,801
Peter Webb, *UK Ind.* 964
*Lab. majority* 14,569 (34.25%)
1.62% swing LD to Lab.
(1997, Lab. maj. 16,451 (31.02%))

SHERWOOD
*E.*75,670 *T.* 45,900 (60.66%) Lab. hold
*Paddy Tipping, *Lab.* 24,900
Brandon Lewis, *C.* 15,527
Peter Harris, *LD* 5,473
*Lab. majority* 9,373 (20.42%)
4.66% swing Lab. to C.
(1997, Lab. maj. 16,812 (29.74%))

SHIPLEY
*E.*69,577 *T.* 46,020 (66.14%) Lab. hold
*Christopher Leslie, *Lab.* 20,243
David Senior, *C.* 18,815
Ms Helen Wright, *LD* 4,996
Martin Love, *Green* 1,386
Walter Whitacker, *UK Ind.* 580
*Lab. majority* 1,428 (3.10%)
1.28% swing Lab. to C.
(1997, Lab. maj. 2,996 (5.67%))

SHREWSBURY & ATCHAM
*E.*74,964 *T.* 49,909 (66.58%) Lab. hold
*Paul Marsden, *Lab.* 22,253
Miss Anthea McIntyre, *C.* 18,674
Jonathan Rule, *LD* 6,173
Henry Curteis, *UK Ind.* 1,620
Ms Emma Bullard, *Green* 931
James Gollins, *Ind.* 258
*Lab. majority* 3,579 (7.17%)
2.08% swing C. to Lab.
(1997, Lab. maj. 1,670 (3.02%))

SHROPSHIRE NORTH
*E.*73,716 *T.* 46,520 (63.11%) C. hold
*Owen Paterson, *C.* 22,631
Michael Ion, *Lab.* 16,390
Ben Jephcott, *LD* 5,945
David Trevanion, *UK Ind.* 1,165
Russell Maxfield, *Ind.* 389
*C. majority* 6,241 (13.42%)
4.58% swing Lab. to C.
(1997, C. maj. 2,195 (4.26%))

SITTINGBOURNE & SHEPPEY
*E.*65,825 *T.* 37,858 (57.51%) Lab. hold
*Derek Wyatt, *Lab.* 17,340
Adrian Lee, *C.* 13,831
Ms Elvie Lowe, *LD* 5,353
Michael Young, *R & R Loony* 673
Robert Oakley, *UK Ind.* 661
*Lab. majority* 3,509 (9.27%)
2.54% swing C. to Lab.
(1997, Lab. maj. 1,929 (4.18%))

SKIPTON & RIPON
*E.*75,201 *T.* 49,126 (65.33%) C. hold
*Rt. Hon. D. Curry, *C.* 25,736
Bernard Bateman, *LD* 12,806
Michael Dugher, *Lab.* 8,543
Mrs Nancy Holdsworth, *UK Ind.* 2,041
*C. majority* 12,930 (26.32%)
2.47% swing LD to C.
(1997, C. maj. 11,620 (21.38%))

SLEAFORD & NORTH HYKEHAM
*E.*74,561 *T.* 48,719 (65.34%) C. hold
*Rt. Hon. D. Hogg, *C.* 24,190
Ms Elizabeth Donnelly, *Lab.* 15,568
Robert Arbon, *LD* 7,894
Michael Ward-Barrow, *UK Ind.* 1,067
*C. majority* 8,622 (17.70%)
4.03% swing Lab. to C.
(1997, C. maj. 5,123 (9.64%))

SLOUGH
*E.*72,429 *T.* 38,998 (53.84%) Lab. hold
*Ms Fiona MacTaggart, *Lab.* 22,718
Mrs Diana Coad, *C.* 10,210
Keith Kerr, *LD* 4,109
Michael Haines, *Ind.* 859
John Lane, *UK Ind.* 738
Choudry Nazir, *Ind.* 364
*Lab. majority* 12,508 (32.07%)
2.34% swing C. to Lab.
(1997, Lab. maj. 13,071 (27.39%))

SOLIHULL
*E.*77,094 *T.* 48,271 (62.61%) C. hold
*John Taylor, *C.* 21,935
Ms Jo Byron, *LD* 12,528
Brendan O'Brien, *Lab.* 12,373
Andy Moore, *UK Ind.* 1,061
Ms Stephanie Pyne, *ProLife* 374
*C. majority* 9,407 (19.49%)
0.07% swing LD to C.
(1997, C. maj. 11,397 (19.35%))

SOMERTON & FROME
*E.*74,991 *T.* 52,684 (70.25%) LD hold
*David Heath, *LD* 22,983
Jonathan Marland, *C.* 22,315
Andrew Perkins, *Lab.* 6,113
Peter Bridgwood, *UK Ind.* 919
Ms Jean Pollock, *Lib.* 354
*LD majority* 668 (1.27%)
0.52% swing C. to LD
(1997, LD maj. 130 (0.23%))

SOUTH HOLLAND & THE DEEPINGS
*E.*73,880 *T.* 46,202 (62.54%) C. hold
*John Hayes, *C.* 25,611
Graham Walker, *Lab.* 14,512
Ms Grace Hill, *LD* 4,761
Malcolm Charlesworth, *UK Ind.* 1,318
*C. majority* 11,099 (24.02%)
4.04% swing Lab. to C.
(1997, C. maj. 7,991 (15.94%))

SOUTH SHIELDS
*E.*61,802 *T.* 30,448 (49.27%) Lab. hold
David Miliband, *Lab.* 19,230
Miss Joanna Gardner, *C.* 5,140
Marshall Grainger, *LD* 5,127
Alan Hardy, *UK Ind.* 689
Roger Nettleship, *Ind.* 262
*Lab. majority* 14,090 (46.28%)
5.28% swing Lab. to C.
(1997, Lab. maj. 22,153 (56.84%))

SOUTHAMPTON ITCHEN
*E.*76,603 *T.* 41,373 (54.01%) Lab. hold
*Rt. Hon. J. Denham, *Lab.* 22,553
Mrs Caroline Nokes, *C.* 11,330
Mark Cooper, *LD* 6,195
Kim Rose, *UK Ind.* 829
Gavin Marsh, *Soc. All.* 241
Michael Holmes, *Soc. Lab.* 225
*Lab. majority* 11,223 (27.13%)
0.37% swing C. to Lab.
(1997, Lab. maj. 14,209 (26.38%))

SOUTHAMPTON TEST
*E.*73,893 *T.* 41,575 (56.26%) Lab. hold
*Alan Whitehead, *Lab.* 21,824
Richard Gueterbock, *C.* 10,617
John Shaw, *LD* 7,522
Garry Rankin-Moore, *UK Ind.* 792
Mark Abel, *Soc. All.* 442
Paramjit Bahia, *Soc. Lab.* 378
*Lab. majority* 11,207 (26.96%)
0.43% swing C. to Lab.
(1997, Lab. maj. 13,684 (26.10%))

SOUTHEND WEST
*E.*64,116 *T.* 37,375 (58.29%) C. hold
*David Amess, *C.* 17,313
Paul Fisher, *Lab.* 9,372
Richard de Ste Croix, *LD* 9,319
Brian Lee, *UK Ind.* 1,371
*C. majority* 7,941 (21.25%)
2.64% swing Lab. to C.
(1997, C. maj. 2,615 (5.62%))

SOUTHPORT
*E.*70,785 *T.* 41,153 (58.14%) LD hold
John Pugh, *LD* 18,011
Laurence Jones, *C.* 15,004
Paul Brant, *Lab.* 6,816
David Green, *Lib.* 767
Gerry Kelley, *UK Ind.* 555
*LD majority* 3,007 (7.31%)
2.44% swing LD to C.
(1997, LD maj. 6,160 (12.18%))

SOUTHWARK NORTH & BERMONDSEY
*E.*73,527 *T.* 36,862 (50.13%) LD hold
*Simon Hughes, *LD* 20,991
Kingsley Abrams, *Lab.* 11,359
Ewan Wallace, *C.* 2,800
Ms Ruth Jenkins, *Green* 752
Ms Lianne Shore, *NF* 612
Rob McWhirter, *UK Ind.* 271
John Davies, *Ind.* 77
*LD majority* 9,632 (26.13%)
8.91% swing Lab. to LD
(1997, LD maj. 3,387 (8.30%))

SPELTHORNE
*E.*68,731 *T.* 41,794 (60.81%) C. hold
*David Wilshire, *C.* 18,851
Andrew Shaw, *Lab.* 15,589
Martin Rimmer, *LD* 6,156
Richard Squire, *UK Ind.* 1,198
*C. majority* 3,262 (7.80%)
0.56% swing Lab. to C.
(1997, C. maj. 3,473 (6.69%))

ST ALBANS
*E.*66,040 *T.* 43,761 (66.26%) Lab. hold
*Kerry Pollard, *Lab.* 19,889
Charles Elphicke, *C.* 15,423
Nick Rijke, *LD* 7,847
Christopher Sherwin, *UK Ind.* 602

*Lab. majority* 4,466 (10.21%)
0.71% swing C. to Lab.
(1997, Lab. maj. 4,459 (8.78%))

### St Helens North
*E.*70,545 *T.* 37,601 (53.30%) Lab. hold
*Dave Watts, *Lab.* 22,977
Simon Pearce, *C.* 7,076
John Beirne, *LD* 6,609
Stephen Whatham, *Soc. Lab.* 939
*Lab. majority* 15,901 (42.29%)
2.64% swing Lab. to C.
(1997, Lab. maj. 23,417 (47.57%))

### St Helens South
*E.*65,122 *T.* 33,804 (51.91%) Lab. hold
†Shaun Woodward, *Lab.* 16,799
Brian Spencer, *LD* 7,814
Dr Lee Rotherham, *C.* 4,675
Neil Thompson, *Soc. All.* 2,325
Mike Perry, *Soc. Lab.* 1,504
Bryan Slater, *UK Ind.* 336
Michael Murphy, *Ind.* 271
David Braid, *Ind.* 80
*Lab. majority* 8,985 (26.58%)
14.33% swing Lab. to LD
(1997, Lab. maj. 23,739 (53.63%))

### St Ives
*E.*74,256 *T.* 49,266 (66.35%) LD hold
*Andrew George, *LD* 25,413
Miss Joanna Richardson, *C.* 15,360
William Morris, *Lab.* 6,567
Mick Faulkner, *UK Ind.* 1,926
*LD majority* 10,053 (20.41%)
3.55% swing C. to LD
(1997, LD maj. 7,170 (13.30%))

### Stafford
*E.*67,934 *T.* 44,366 (65.31%) Lab. hold
*David Kidney, *Lab.* 21,285
Philip Cochrane, *C.* 16,253
Ms Jeanne Pinkerton, *LD* 4,205
Earl of Bradford, *UK Ind.* 2,315
Michael Hames, *R & R Loony* 308
*Lab. majority* 5,032 (11.34%)
1.50% swing C. to Lab.
(1997, Lab. maj. 4,314 (8.34%))

### Staffordshire Moorlands
*E.*66,760 *T.* 42,658 (63.90%) Lab. hold
*Ms Charlotte Atkins, *Lab.* 20,904
Marcus Hayes, *C.* 15,066
John Redfern, *LD* 5,928
Paul Gilbert, *UK Ind.* 760
*Lab. majority* 5,838 (13.69%)
2.99% swing Lab. to C.
(1997, Lab. maj. 10,049 (19.66%))

### Staffordshire South
*E.*69,925 *T.* 42,180 (60.32%) C. hold
*Sir Patrick Cormack, *C.* 21,295
Paul Kalinauckas, *Lab.* 14,414
Ms Jo Harrison, *LD* 4,891
Mike Lynch, *UK Ind.* 1,580
*C. majority* 6,881 (16.31%)
0.51% swing Lab. to C.
(1997, C. maj. 7,821 (15.30%))

### Stalybridge & Hyde
*E.*66,265 *T.* 32,046 (48.36%) Lab. hold
James Purnell, *Lab.* 17,781
Andrew Reid, *C.* 8,922
Brendon Jones, *LD* 4,327
Frank Bennett, *UK Ind.* 1,016
*Lab. majority* 8,859 (27.64%)
3.36% swing Lab. to C.
(1997, Lab. maj. 14,806 (34.36%))

### Stevenage
*E.*69,203 *T.* 42,453 (61.35%) Lab. hold
*Ms Barbara Follett, *Lab.* 22,025
Graeme Quar, *C.* 13,459
Harry Davies, *LD* 6,027
Steve Glennon, *Soc. All.* 449
Antal Losonczi, *Ind.* 320
Ms Sarah Bell, *ProLife* 173
*Lab. majority* 8,566 (20.18%)
1.18% swing Lab. to C.
(1997, Lab. maj. 11,582 (22.54%))

### Stockport
*E.*66,397 *T.* 35,383 (53.29%) Lab. hold
*Ms Ann Coffey, *Lab.* 20,731
John Allen, *C.* 9,162
Mark Hunter, *LD* 5,490
*Lab. majority* 11,569 (32.70%)
3.91% swing Lab. to C.
(1997, Lab. maj. 18,912 (40.52%))

### Stockton North
*E.*65,192 *T.* 35,427 (54.34%) Lab. hold
*Frank Cook, *Lab.* 22,470
Ms Amanda Vigar, *C.* 7,823
Ms Mary Wallace, *LD* 4,208
Bill Wennington, *Green* 926
*Lab. majority* 14,647 (41.34%)
3.34% swing Lab. to C.
(1997, Lab. maj. 21,357 (48.02%))

### Stockton South
*E.*71,026 *T.* 44,209 (62.24%) Lab. hold
*Ms Dari Taylor, *Lab.* 23,414
Tim Devlin, *C.* 14,328
Mrs Suzanne Fletcher, *LD* 6,012
Lawrie Coombes, *Soc. All.* 455
*Lab. majority* 9,086 (20.55%)
0.84% swing Lab. to C.
(1997, Lab. maj. 11,585 (22.23%))

### Stoke-on-Trent Central
*E.*59,750 *T.* 28,300 (47.36%) Lab. hold
*Mark Fisher, *Lab.* 17,170
Ms Jill Clark, *C.* 5,325
Gavin Webb, *LD* 4,148
Richard Wise, *Ind.* 1,657
*Lab. majority* 11,845 (41.86%)
3.83% swing Lab. to C.
(1997, Lab. maj. 19,924 (49.51%))

### Stoke-on-Trent North
*E.*57,998 *T.* 30,115 (51.92%) Lab. hold
*Ms Joan Walley, *Lab.* 17,460
Benjamin Browning, *C.* 5,676
Henry Jebb, *LD* 3,580
Lee Wanger, *Ind.* 3,399
*Lab. majority* 11,784 (39.13%)
2.92% swing Lab. to C.
(1997, Lab. maj. 17,392 (44.98%))

### Stoke-on-Trent South
*E.*70,032 *T.* 36,028 (51.45%) Lab. hold
*George Stevenson, *Lab.* 19,366
Philip Bastiman, *C.* 8,877
Christopher Coleman, *LD* 4,724
Adrian Knapper, *Ind.* 1,703
Steven Batkin, *BNP* 1,358
*Lab. majority* 10,489 (29.11%)
5.23% swing Lab. to C.
(1997, Lab. maj. 18,303 (39.58%))

### Stone
*E.*68,847 *T.* 45,642 (66.29%) C. hold
*William Cash, *C.* 22,395
John Palfreyman, *Lab.* 16,359
Brendan McKeown, *LD* 6,888
*C. majority* 6,036 (13.22%)
3.01% swing Lab. to C.
(1997, C. maj. 3,818 (7.20%))

### Stourbridge
*E.*64,610 *T.* 39,924 (61.79%) Lab. hold
*Ms Debra Shipley, *Lab.* 18,823
Stephen Eyre, *C.* 15,011
Chris Bramall, *LD* 4,833
John Knotts, *UK Ind.* 763
Mick Atherton, *Soc. Lab.* 494
*Lab. majority* 3,812 (9.55%)
0.91% swing Lab. to C.
(1997, Lab. maj. 5,645 (11.36%))

### Stratford-on-Avon
*E.*85,241 *T.* 54,914 (64.42%) C. hold
*John Maples, *C.* 27,606
Dr Susan Juned, *LD* 15,804
Mushtaq Hussain, *Lab.* 9,164
Ronald Mole, *UK Ind.* 1,184
Mick Davies, *Green* 1,156
*C. majority* 11,802 (21.49%)
0.61% swing C. to LD
(1997, C. maj. 14,106 (22.72%))

### Streatham
*E.*76,021 *T.* 36,998 (48.67%) Lab. hold
*Keith Hill, *Lab.* 21,041
Roger O'Brien, *LD* 6,771
Stephen Hocking, *C.* 6,639
Mohammed Sajid, *Green* 1,641
Greg Tucker, *Soc. All.* 906
*Lab. majority* 14,270 (38.57%)
5.33% swing Lab. to LD
(1997, Lab. maj. 18,423 (41.04%))

### Stretford & Urmston
*E.*70,924 *T.* 38,973 (54.95%) Lab. hold
*Ms Beverley Hughes, *Lab.* 23,804
Jonathan Mackie, *C.* 10,565
John Bridges, *LD* 3,891
Ms Katie Price, *Ind.* 713
*Lab. majority* 13,239 (33.97%)
2.98% swing C. to Lab.
(1997, Lab. maj. 13,640 (28.01%))

### Stroud
*E.*78,878 *T.* 55,175 (69.95%) Lab. Co-op hold
*David Drew, *Lab. Co-op* 25,685
Neil Carmichael, *C.* 20,646
Ms Janice Beasley, *LD* 6,036
Kevin Cranston, *Green* 1,913
Adrian Blake, *UK Ind.* 895
*Lab. Co-op majority* 5,039 (9.13%)
2.24% swing C. to Lab. Co-op
(1997, Lab. maj. 2,910 (4.66%))

### Suffolk Central & Ipswich North
*E.*74,200 *T.* 47,104 (63.48%) C. hold
*Michael Lord, *C.* 20,924

Ms Carole Jones, *Lab.* 17,455
Mrs Ann Elvin, *LD* 7,593
Jonathan Wright, *UK Ind.* 1,132
*C. majority* 3,469 (7.36%)
0.33% swing Lab. to C.
(1997, C. maj. 3,538 (6.70%))

### Suffolk Coastal
*E.*75,963 *T.* 50,407 (66.36%) C. hold
*Rt. Hon. J. Gummer, *C.* 21,847
Nigel Gardner, *Lab.* 17,521
Tony Schur, *LD* 9,192
Michael Burn, *UK Ind.* 1,847
*C. majority* 4,326 (8.58%)
1.40% swing Lab. to C.
(1997, C. maj. 3,254 (5.79%))

### Suffolk South
*E.*68,408 *T.* 45,293 (66.21%) C. hold
*Tim Yeo, *C.* 18,748
Marc Young, *Lab.* 13,667
Mrs Tessa Munt, *LD* 11,296
Derek Allen, *UK Ind.* 1,582
*C. majority* 5,081 (11.22%)
1.59% swing Lab. to C.
(1997, C. maj. 4,175 (8.03%))

### Suffolk West
*E.*71,220 *T.* 42,445 (59.60%) C. hold
*Richard Spring, *C.* 20,201
Michael Jeffreys, *Lab.* 15,906
Robin Martlew, *LD* 5,017
Will Burrows, *UK Ind.* 1,321
*C. majority* 4,295 (10.12%)
3.16% swing Lab. to C.
(1997, C. maj. 1,867 (3.80%))

### Sunderland North
*E.*60,846 *T.* 29,820 (49.01%) Lab. hold
*Bill Etherington, *Lab.* 18,685
Michael Harris, *C.* 5,331
John Lennox, *LD* 3,599
Neil Herron, *Ind.* 1,518
David Guynan, *BNP* 687
*Lab. majority* 13,354 (44.78%)
3.38% swing Lab. to C.
(1997, Lab. maj. 19,697 (51.55%))

### Sunderland South
*E.*64,577 *T.* 31,187 (48.29%) Lab. hold
*Chris Mullin, *Lab.* 19,921
Jim Boyd, *C.* 6,254
Mark Greenfield, *LD* 3,675
Joseph Dobbie, *BNP* 576
Joseph Moore, *UK Ind.* 470
Ms Rosalyn Warner, *Loony* 291
*Lab. majority* 13,667 (43.82%)
2.68% swing Lab. to C.
(1997, Lab. maj. 19,638 (49.18%))

### Surrey East
*E.*75,049 *T.* 47,049 (62.69%) C. hold
*Peter Ainsworth, *C.* 24,706
Jeremy Pursehouse, *LD* 11,503
Ms Jo Tanner, *Lab.* 8,994
Anthony Stone, *UK Ind.* 1,846
*C. majority* 13,203 (28.06%)
0.23% swing LD to C.
(1997, C. maj. 15,093 (27.61%))

### Surrey Heath
*E.*75,858 *T.* 45,102 (59.46%) C. hold
*Nicholas Hawkins, *C.* 22,401
Mark Lelliott, *LD* 11,582
James Norman, *Lab.* 9,640
Nigel Hunt, *UK Ind.* 1,479
*C. majority* 10,819 (23.99%)
2.89% swing C. to LD
(1997, C. maj. 16,287 (29.76%))

### Surrey South West
*E.*74,127 *T.* 49,592 (66.90%) C. hold
*Rt. Hon. Mrs V. Bottomley, *C.* 22,462
Simon Cordon, *LD* 21,601
Martin Whelton, *Lab.* 4,321
Timothy Clark, *UK Ind.* 1,208
*C. majority* 861 (1.74%)
1.52% swing C. to LD
(1997, C. maj. 2,694 (4.77%))

### Sussex Mid
*E.*70,632 *T.* 45,822 (64.87%) C. hold
*Nicholas Soames, *C.* 21,150
Ms Lesley Wilkins, *LD* 14,252
Paul Mitchell, *Lab.* 8,693
Petrina Holdsworth, *UK Ind.* 1,126
Peter Berry, *Loony* 601
*C. majority* 6,898 (15.05%)
1.12% swing LD to C.
(1997, C. maj. 6,854 (12.82%))

### Sutton & Cheam
*E.*63,648 *T.* 39,723 (62.41%) LD hold
*Paul Burstow, *LD* 19,382
Lady Olga Maitland, *C.* 15,078
Ms Lisa Homan, *Lab.* 5,263
*LD majority* 4,304 (10.84%)
3.19% swing C. to LD
(1997, LD maj. 2,097 (4.45%))

### Sutton Coldfield
*E.*71,856 *T.* 43,452 (60.47%) C. hold
Andrew Mitchell, *C.* 21,909
Robert Pocock, *Lab.* 11,805
Martin Turner, *LD* 8,268
Mike Nattrass, *UK Ind.* 1,186
Ian Robinson, *Ind.* 284
*C. majority* 10,104 (23.25%)
2.58% swing C. to Lab.
(1997, C. maj. 14,885 (28.41%))

### Swindon North
*E.*69,335 *T.* 42,328 (61.05%) Lab. hold
*Michael Wills, *Lab.* 22,371
Nick Martin, *C.* 14,266
David Nation, *LD* 4,891
Brian Lloyd, *UK Ind.* 800
*Lab. majority* 8,105 (19.15%)
1.61% swing C. to Lab.
(1997, Lab. maj. 7,688 (15.93%))

### Swindon South
*E.*71,080 *T.* 43,384 (61.04%) Lab. hold
*Ms Julia Drown, *Lab.* 22,260
Simon Coombs, *C.* 14,919
Geoff Brewer, *LD* 5,165
Mrs Vicki Sharp, *UK Ind.* 713
Roly Gillard, *R & R Loony* 327
*Lab. majority* 7,341 (16.92%)
2.94% swing C. to Lab.
(1997, Lab. maj. 5,645 (11.04%))

### Tamworth
*E.*69,596 *T.* 40,250 (57.83%) Lab. hold
*Brian Jenkins, *Lab.* 19,722
Ms Luise Gunter, *C.* 15,124
Ms Jennifer Pinkett, *LD* 4,721
Paul Southeran, *UK Ind.* 683
*Lab. majority* 4,598 (11.42%)
1.81% swing Lab. to C.
(1997, Lab. maj. 7,496 (15.04%))

### Tatton
*E.*64,954 *T.* 41,278 (63.55%) Con gain
George Osborne, *C.* 19,860
Steve Conquest, *Lab.* 11,249
Mike Ash, *LD* 7,685
Mark Sheppard, *UK Ind.* 769
Peter Sharratt, *Ind.* 734
Mrs Viviane Allinson, *Tatton* 505
John Batchelor, *Ind.* 322
Jonathan Boyd Hunt, *Ind.* 154
*C. majority* 8,611 (20.86%)
(1997: Ind. maj 11,077 (22.70%))

### Taunton
*E.*81,651 *T.* 55,225 (67.64%) Con gain
Adrian Flook, *C.* 23,033
*Mrs Jackie Ballard, *LD* 22,798
Andrew Govier, *Lab.* 8,254
Michael Canton, *UK Ind.* 1,140
*C. majority* 235 (0.43%)
2.21% swing LD to C.
(1997, LD maj. 2,443 (4.00%))

### Teignbridge
*E.*85,533 *T.* 59,310 (69.34%) LD gain
Richard Younger-Ross, *LD* 26,343
*Patrick Nicholls, *C.* 23,332
Christopher Bain, *Lab.* 7,366
Paul Viscount Exmouth, *UK Ind.* 2,269
*LD majority* 3,011 (5.08%)
2.76% swing C. to LD
(1997, C. maj. 281 (0.45%))

### Telford
*E.*59,486 *T.* 30,875 (51.90%) Lab. hold
David Wright, *Lab.* 16,854
Andrew Henderson, *C.* 8,471
Ms Sally Wiggin, *LD* 3,983
Ms Nicola Brookes, *UK Ind.* 1,098
Mike Jeffries, *Soc. All.* 469
*Lab. majority* 8,383 (27.15%)
1.63% swing Lab. to C.
(1997, Lab. maj. 11,290 (30.42%))

### Tewkesbury
*E.*70,276 *T.* 45,195 (64.31%) C. hold
*Laurence Robertson, *C.* 20,830
Keir Dhillon, *Lab.* 12,167
Stephen Martin, *LD* 11,863
Charles Vernall, *Ind.* 335
*C. majority* 8,663 (19.17%)
0.19% swing C. to Lab.
(1997, C. maj. 9,234 (17.71%))

### Thanet North
*E.*70,581 *T.* 41,868 (59.32%) C. hold
*Roger Gale, *C.* 21,050
James Stewart Laing, *Lab.* 14,400
Seth Proctor, *LD* 4,603
John Moore, *UK Ind.* 980
David Shortt, *Ind.* 440
Thomas Holmes, *NF* 395
*C. majority* 6,650 (15.88%)
5.12% swing Lab. to C.
(1997, C. maj. 2,766 (5.65%))

THANET SOUTH
E.61,462 T. 39,431 (64.16%) Lab. hold
*Dr Stephen Ladyman, *Lab.* 18,002
Mark Macgregor, *C.* 16,210
Guy Voizey, *LD* 3,706
William Baldwin, *Ind.* 770
Terry Eccott, *UK Ind.* 501
Bernard Franklin, *NF* 242
*Lab. majority* 1,792 (4.54%)
0.92% swing Lab. to C.
(1997, Lab. maj. 2,878 (6.39%))

THURROCK
E.76,524 T. 37,362 (48.82%) Lab. hold
*Andrew Mackinlay, *Lab.* 21,121
Mike Penning, *C.* 11,124
John Lathan, *LD* 3,846
Christopher Sheppard, *UK Ind.* 1,271
*Lab. majority* 9,997 (26.76%)
4.90% swing Lab. to C.
(1997, Lab. maj. 17,256 (36.55%))

TIVERTON & HONITON
E.80,646 T. 55,784 (69.17%) C. hold
*Mrs Angela Browning, *C.* 26,258
Jim Barnard, *LD* 19,974
Ms Isabel Owen, *Lab.* 6,647
Alan Langmaid, *UK Ind.* 1,281
Matthew Burgess, *Green* 1,030
Mrs Jennifer Roach, *Lib.* 594
*C. majority* 6,284 (11.26%)
4.23% swing LD to C.
(1997, C. maj. 1,653 (2.80%))

TONBRIDGE & MALLING
E.65,939 T. 42,436 (64.36%) C. hold
*Rt. Hon. Sir J. Stanley, *C.* 20,956
Ms Victoria Hayman, *Lab.* 12,706
Ms Merilyn Canet, *LD* 7,605
Ms Lynn Croucher, *UK Ind.* 1,169
*C. majority* 8,250 (19.44%)
0.67% swing C. to Lab.
(1997, C. maj. 10,230 (20.78%))

TOOTING
E.68,447 T. 37,591 (54.92%) Lab. hold
*Tom Cox, *Lab.* 20,332
Alexander Nicoll, *C.* 9,932
Simon James, *LD* 5,583
Matthew Ledbury, *Green* 1,744
*Lab. majority* 10,400 (27.67%)
2.45% swing Lab. to C.
(1997, Lab. maj. 15,011 (32.56%))

TORBAY
E.72,409 T. 47,569 (65.69%) LD hold
*Adrian Sanders, *LD* 24,015
Christian Sweeting, *C.* 17,307
John McKay, *Lab.* 4,484
Graham Booth, *UK Ind.* 1,512
Ms Pam Neale, *Ind.* 251
*LD majority* 6,708 (14.10%)
7.04% swing C. to LD
(1997, LD maj. 12 (0.02%))

TOTNES
E.72,548 T. 49,246 (67.88%) C. hold
*Anthony Steen, *C.* 21,914
Ms Rachel Oliver, *LD* 18,317
Thomas Wildy, *Lab.* 6,005
Craig Mackinlay, *UK Ind.* 3,010
*C. majority* 3,597 (7.30%)
2.84% swing LD to C.
(1997, C. maj. 877 (1.63%))

TOTTENHAM
E.65,567 T. 31,601 (48.20%) Lab. hold
*David Lammy, *Lab.* 21,317
Ms Uma Fernandes, *C.* 4,401
Ms Meher Khan, *LD* 3,008
Peter Budge, *Green* 1,443
Weyman Bennett, *Soc. All.* 1,162
Unver Shefki, *Reform* 270
*Lab. majority* 16,916 (53.53%)
0.03% swing Lab. to C.
(2000 Jun by-election, Lab. maj. 5,646 (34.39%); 1997, Lab. maj. 20,200 (53.58%))

TRURO & ST AUSTELL
E.79,219 T. 50,295 (63.49%) LD hold
*Matthew Taylor, *LD* 24,296
Tim Bonner, *C.* 16,231
David Phillips, *Lab.* 6,889
James Wonnacott, *UK Ind.* 1,664
Conan Jenkin, *Meb. Ker.* 1,137
John Lee, *Ind.* 78
*LD majority* 8,065 (16.04%)
3.00% swing LD to C.
(1997, LD maj. 12,501 (22.03%))

TUNBRIDGE WELLS
E.64,534 T. 40,201 (62.29%) C. hold
*Archie Norman, *C.* 19,643
Keith Brown, *LD* 9,913
Ian Carvell, *Lab.* 9,332
Victor Webb, *UK Ind.* 1,313
*C. majority* 9,730 (24.20%)
4.34% swing LD to C.
(1997, C. maj. 7,506 (15.52%))

TWICKENHAM
E.74,135 T. 49,938 (67.36%) LD hold
*Dr Vincent Cable, *LD* 24,344
Nick Longworth, *C.* 16,689
Dean Rogers, *Lab.* 6,903
Ms Judy Maciejowska, *Green* 1,423
Ray Hollebone, *UK Ind.* 579
*LD majority* 7,655 (15.33%)
3.98% swing C. to LD
(1997, LD maj. 4,281 (7.36%))

TYNE BRIDGE
E.58,900 T. 26,032 (44.20%) Lab. hold
*David Clelland, *Lab.* 18,345
James Cook, *C.* 3,456
Jonathan Wallace, *LD* 3,213
James Fitzpatrick, *Soc. Lab.* 533
Samuel Robson, *Soc. All.* 485
*Lab. majority* 14,889 (57.19%)
4.27% swing Lab. to C.
(1997, Lab. maj. 22,906 (65.73%))

TYNEMOUTH
E.65,184 T. 43,903 (67.35%) Lab. hold
*Alan Campbell, *Lab.* 23,364
Karl Poulsen, *C.* 14,686
Ms Penny Reid, *LD* 5,108
Michael Rollings, *UK Ind.* 745
*Lab. majority* 8,678 (19.77%)
1.14% swing Lab. to C.
(1997, Lab. maj. 11,273 (22.04%))

TYNESIDE NORTH
E.64,914 T. 37,569 (57.88%) Lab. hold
*Rt. Hon. S. Byers, *Lab.* 26,127
Mark Ruffell, *C.* 5,459
Simon Reed, *LD* 4,649
Alan Taylor, *UK Ind.* 770
Pete Burnett, *Soc. All.* 324
Ken Capstick, *Soc. Lab.* 240
*Lab. majority* 20,668 (55.01%)
2.02% swing Lab. to C.
(1997, Lab. maj. 26,643 (59.05%))

UPMINSTER
E.56,829 T. 33,851 (59.57%) C. gain
Mrs Angela Watkinson, *C.* 15,410
*Keith Darvill, *Lab.* 14,169
Peter Truesdale, *LD* 3,183
Terry Murray, *UK Ind.* 1,089
*C. majority* 1,241 (3.67%)
5.18% swing Lab. to C.
(1997, Lab. maj. 2,770 (6.70%))

UXBRIDGE
E.58,066 T. 33,418 (57.55%) C. hold
*John Randall, *C.* 15,751
David Salisbury-Jones, *Lab.* 13,653
Ms Catherine Royce, *LD* 3,426
Paul Cannons, *UK Ind.* 588
*C. majority* 2,098 (6.28%)
2.26% swing Lab. to C.
(1997 Jul by-election, C. maj. 3,766 (11.82%); 1997, C. maj. 724 (1.75%))

VALE OF YORK
E.73,335 T. 48,490 (66.12%) C. hold
*Miss Anne McIntosh, *C.* 25,033
Christopher Jukes, *Lab.* 12,516
Greg Stone, *LD* 9,799
Peter Thornber, *UK Ind.* 1,142
*C. majority* 12,517 (25.81%)
3.78% swing Lab. to C.
(1997, C. maj. 9,721 (18.25%))

VAUXHALL
E.74,474 T. 33,392 (44.84%) Lab. hold
*Ms Kate Hoey, *Lab.* 19,738
Anthony Bottrall, *LD* 6,720
Gareth Compton, *C.* 4,489
Shane Collins, *Green* 1,485
Ms Theresa Bennett, *Soc. All.* 853
Martin Boyd, *Ind.* 107
*Lab. majority* 13,018 (38.99%)
4.39% swing Lab. to LD
(1997, Lab. maj. 18,660 (47.77%))

WAKEFIELD
E.75,750 T. 41,254 (54.46%) Lab. hold
*David Hinchcliffe, *Lab.* 20,592
Mrs Thelma Karran, *C.* 12,638
Douglas Dale, *LD* 5,097
Ms Sarah Greenwood, *Green* 1,075
Ms Janice Cannon, *UK Ind.* 677
Abdul Aziz, *Soc. Lab.* 634
Mick Griffiths, *Soc. All.* 541
*Lab. majority* 7,954 (19.28%)
4.82% swing Lab. to C.
(1997, Lab. maj. 14,604 (28.93%))

WALLASEY
E.64,889 T. 37,346 (57.55%) Lab. hold
*Ms Angela Eagle, *Lab.* 22,718
Mrs Lesley Rennie, *C.* 10,442
Peter Reisdorf, *LD* 4,186
*Lab. majority* 12,276 (32.87%)
3.92% swing Lab. to C.
(1997, Lab. maj. 19,074 (40.72%))

WALSALL NORTH
*E.*66,020 *T.* 32,312 (48.94%) Lab. hold
*David Winnick, *Lab.* 18,779
Melvin Pitt, *C.* 9,388
Michael Heap, *LD* 2,923
Mrs Jenny Mayo, *UK Ind.* 812
Dave Church, *Soc. All.* 410
*Lab. majority* 9,391 (29.06%)
(1997, Lab. maj. 12,588 (29.07%))

WALSALL SOUTH
*E.*62,657 *T.* 34,899 (55.70%) Lab. hold
*Rt. Hon. B. George, *Lab.* 20,574
Mike Bird, *C.* 10,643
Bill Tomlinson, *LD* 2,365
Derek Bennett, *UK Ind.* 974
Peter Smith, *Soc. All.* 343
*Lab. majority* 9,931 (28.46%)
1.15% swing C. to Lab.
(1997, Lab. maj. 11,312 (26.16%))

WALTHAMSTOW
*E.*64,403 *T.* 34,429 (53.46%) Lab. hold
*Neil Gerrard, *Lab.* 21,402
Nick Boys Smith, *C.* 6,221
Peter Dunphy, *LD* 5,024
Simon Donovan, *Soc. Alt.* 806
William Phillips, *BNP* 389
Ms Gerda Mayer, *UK Ind.* 298
Ms Barbara Duffy, *ProLife* 289
*Lab. majority* 15,181 (44.09%)
0.64% swing C. to Lab.
(1997, Lab. maj. 17,149 (42.81%))

WANSBECK
*E.*62,989 *T.* 37,419 (59.41%) Lab. hold
*Denis Murphy, *Lab.* 21,617
Alan Thompson, *LD* 8,516
Mrs Rachael Lake, *C.* 4,774
Michael Kirkup, *Ind.* 1,076
Dr Nic Best, *Green* 954
Gavin Attwell, *UK Ind.* 482
*Lab. majority* 13,101 (35.01%)
7.25% swing Lab. to LD
(1997, Lab. maj. 22,367 (49.52%))

WANSDYKE
*E.*70,728 *T.* 49,047 (69.35%) Lab. hold
*Dan Norris, *Lab.* 22,706
Chris Watt, *C.* 17,593
Ms Gail Coleshill, *LD* 7,135
Francis Hayden, *Green* 958
Peter Sandell, *UK Ind.* 655
*Lab. majority* 5,113 (10.42%)
0.83% swing C. to Lab.
(1997, Lab. maj. 4,799 (8.77%))

WANTAGE
*E.*76,129 *T.* 49,129 (64.53%) C. hold
*Robert Jackson, *C.* 19,475
Stephen Beer, *Lab.* 13,875
Neil Fawcett, *LD* 13,776
David Brooks-Saxl, *Green* 1,062
Count Nicholas Tolstoy, *UK Ind.* 941
*C. majority* 5,600 (11.40%)
0.31% swing Lab. to C.
(1997, C. maj. 6,039 (10.77%))

WARLEY
*E.*58,071 *T.* 31,415 (54.10%) Lab. hold
*Rt. Hon. J. Spellar, *Lab.* 19,007
Mark Pritchard, *C.* 7,157
Ron Cockings, *LD* 3,315
Harbhajan Dardi, *Soc. Lab.* 1,936
*Lab. majority* 11,850 (37.72%)
1.00% swing Lab. to C.
(1997, Lab. maj. 15,451 (39.73%))

WARRINGTON NORTH
*E.*72,445 *T.* 38,910 (53.71%) Lab. hold
*Ms Helen Jones, *Lab.* 24,026
James Usher, *C.* 8,870
Roy Smith, *LD* 5,232
Jack Kirkham, *UK Ind.* 782
*Lab. majority* 15,156 (38.95%)
0.43% swing C. to Lab.
(1997, Lab. maj. 19,527 (38.10%))

WARRINGTON SOUTH
*E.*74,283 *T.* 45,487 (61.23%) Lab. hold
*Ms Helen Southworth, *Lab.* 22,409
Ms Caroline Mosley, *C.* 15,022
Roger Barlow, *LD* 7,419
Mrs Joan Kelley, *UK Ind.* 637
*Lab. majority* 7,387 (16.24%)
1.69% swing Lab. to C.
(1997, Lab. maj. 10,807 (19.62%))

WARWICK & LEAMINGTON
*E.*81,405 *T.* 53,539 (65.77%) Lab. hold
*James Plaskitt, *Lab.* 26,108
David Campbell Bannerman, *C.* 20,155
Ms Linda Forbes, *LD* 5,964
Ms Clare Kime, *Soc. All.* 664
Greville Warwick, *UK Ind.* 648
*Lab. majority* 5,953 (11.12%)
2.73% swing C. to Lab.
(1997, Lab. maj. 3,398 (5.65%))

WARWICKSHIRE NORTH
*E.*73,828 *T.* 44,409 (60.15%) Lab. hold
*Mike O'Brien, *Lab.* 24,023
Geoff Parsons, *C.* 14,384
William Powell, *LD* 5,052
John Flynn, *UK Ind.* 950
*Lab. majority* 9,639 (21.71%)
2.76% swing Lab. to C.
(1997, Lab. maj. 14,767 (27.23%))

WATFORD
*E.*75,724 *T.* 46,372 (61.24%) Lab. hold
*Ms Claire Ward, *Lab.* 20,992
Michael McManus, *C.* 15,437
Duncan Hames, *LD* 8,088
Ms Denise Kingsley, *Green* 900
Edmund Stewart-Mole, *UK Ind.* 535
Jon Berry, *Soc. All.* 420
*Lab. majority* 5,555 (11.98%)
0.75% swing C. to Lab.
(1997, Lab. maj. 5,792 (10.48%))

WAVENEY
*E.*76,585 *T.* 47,167 (61.59%) Lab. hold
*Bob Blizzard, *Lab.* 23,914
Lee Scott, *C.* 15,361
David Young, *LD* 5,370
Brian Aylett, *UK Ind.* 1,097
Graham Elliot, *Green* 983
Rupert Mallin, *Soc. All.* 442
*Lab. majority* 8,553 (18.13%)
1.93% swing Lab. to C.
(1997, Lab. maj. 12,453 (21.99%))

WEALDEN
*E.*83,066 *T.* 52,756 (63.51%) C. hold
Charles Hendry, *C.* 26,279
Steve Murphy, *LD* 12,507
Ms Kathy Fordham, *Lab.* 10,705
Keith Riddle, *UK Ind.* 1,539
Julian Salmon, *Green* 1,273
Cyril Thornton, *Pensioner* 453
*C. majority* 13,772 (26.11%) 1.03% swing LD to C.
(1997, C. maj. 14,204 (24.04%))

WEAVER VALE
*E.*68,236 *T.* 39,271 (57.55%) Lab. hold
*Mike Hall, *Lab.* 20,611
Carl Cross, *C.* 10,974
Nigel Griffiths, *LD* 5,643
Michael Cooksley, *Ind.* 1,484
Jim Bradshaw, *UK Ind.* 559
*Lab. majority* 9,637 (24.54%)
1.65% swing Lab. to C.
(1997, Lab. maj. 13,448 (27.84%))

WELLINGBOROUGH
*E.*77,389 *T.* 51,006 (65.91%) Lab. hold
*Paul Stinchcombe, *Lab.* 23,867
Peter Bone, *C.* 21,512
Peter Gaskell, *LD* 4,763
Anthony Ellwood, *UK Ind.* 864
*Lab. majority* 2,355 (4.62%)
2.14% swing C. to Lab.
(1997, Lab. maj. 187 (0.33%))

WELLS
*E.*74,189 *T.* 51,314 (69.17%) C. hold
*Rt. Hon. D. Heathcoat-Amory, *C.* 22,462
Graham Oakes, *LD* 19,666
Andy Merryfield, *Lab.* 7,915
Steve Reed, *UK Ind.* 1,104
Colin Bex, *Wessex Reg.* 167
*C. majority* 2,796 (5.45%)
2.25% swing LD to C.
(1997, C. maj. 528 (0.94%))

WELWYN HATFIELD
*E.*67,004 *T.* 42,821 (63.91%) Lab. hold
*Ms Melanie Johnson, *Lab.* 18,484
Grant Shapps, *C.* 17,288
Daniel Cooke, *LD* 6,021
Malcolm Biggs, *UK Ind.* 798
Ms Fiona Pinto, *ProLife* 230
*Lab. majority* 1,196 (2.79%)
3.89% swing Lab. to C.
(1997, Lab. maj. 5,595 (10.57%))

WENTWORTH
*E.*64,033 *T.* 33,778 (52.75%) Lab. hold
*John Healey, *Lab.* 22,798
Mike Roberts, *C.* 6,349
David Wildgoose, *LD* 3,652
John Wilkinson, *UK Ind.* 979
*Lab. majority* 16,449 (48.70%)
4.32% swing Lab. to C.
(1997, Lab. maj. 23,959 (57.34%))

WEST BROMWICH EAST
*E.*61,198 *T.* 32,664 (53.37%) Lab. hold
Tom Watson, *Lab.* 18,250
David MacFarlane, *C.* 8,487
Ian Garrett, *LD* 4,507
Steven Grey, *UK Ind.* 835
Sheera Johal, *Soc. Lab.* 585
*Lab. majority* 9,763 (29.89%)
1.43% swing Lab. to C.
(1997, Lab. maj. 13,584 (32.74%))

WEST BROMWICH WEST
E.66,777 T. 31,840 (47.68%) Lab. Co-op hold
*Adrian Bailey, *Lab. Co-op* 19,352
Mrs Karen Bissell, *C.* 7,997
Mrs Sadie Smith, *LD* 2,168
John Salvage, *BNP* 1,428
Kevin Walker, *UK Ind.* 499
Baghwant Singh, *Soc. Lab.* 396
*Lab. Co-op majority* 11,355 (35.66%)
(2000 Nov by-election, Lab. maj. 3,232 (17.12%); 1997: Speaker maj 15,423 (42.03%))

WEST HAM
E.59,828 T. 29,273 (48.93%) Lab. hold
*Tony Banks, *Lab.* 20,449
Syed Kamall, *C.* 4,804
Paul Fox, *LD* 2,166
Ms Jackie Chandler Oatts, *Green* 1,197
Gerard Batten, *UK Ind.* 657
*Lab. majority* 15,645 (53.45%)
2.24% swing Lab. to C.
(1997, Lab. maj. 19,494 (57.92%))

WESTBURY
E.75,911 T. 50,628 (66.69%) C. hold
Dr Andrew Murrison, *C.* 21,299
David Vigar, *LD* 16,005
Ms Sarah Cardy, *Lab.* 10,847
Charles Booth-Jones, *UK Ind.* 1,261
Bob Gledhill, *Green* 1,216
*C. majority* 5,294 (10.46%)
0.12% swing C. to LD
(1997, C. maj. 6,068 (10.69%))

WESTMORLAND & LONSDALE
E.70,637 T. 47,903 (67.82%) C. hold
*Tim Collins, *C.* 22,486
Tim Farron, *LD* 19,339
John Bateson, *Lab.* 5,234
Robert Gibson, *UK Ind.* 552
Tim Bell, *Ind.* 292
*C. majority* 3,147 (6.57%)
1.17% swing C. to LD
(1997, C. maj. 4,521 (8.90%))

WESTON-SUPER-MARE
E.74,343 T. 46,680 (62.79%) LD hold
*Brian Cotter, *LD* 18,424
John Penrose, *C.* 18,086
Derek Kraft, *Lab.* 9,235
Bill Lukins, *UK Ind.* 650
John Peverelle, *Ind.* 206
Richard Sibley, *Ind.* 79
*LD majority* 338 (0.72%)
0.83% swing LD to C.
(1997, LD maj. 1,274 (2.39%))

WIGAN
E.64,040 T. 33,591 (52.45%) Lab. hold
*Neil Turner, *Lab.* 20,739
Mark Page, *C.* 6,996
Trevor Beswick, *LD* 4,970
Dave Lowe, *Soc. All.* 886
*Lab. majority* 13,743 (40.91%)
5.38% swing Lab. to C.
(1999 Sept by-election, Lab. maj. 6,729)
(1997, Lab. maj. 22,643 (51.67%))

WILTSHIRE NORTH
E.79,524 T. 52,948 (66.58%) C. hold
*James Gray, *C.* 24,090
Hugh Pym, *LD* 20,212
Ms Jo Garton, *Lab.* 7,556
Neil Dowdney, *UK Ind.* 1,090
*C. majority* 3,878 (7.32%)
0.67% swing LD to C.
(1997, C. maj. 3,475 (5.99%))

WIMBLEDON
E.63,930 T. 41,109 (64.30%) Lab. hold
*Roger Casale, *Lab.* 18,806
Stephen Hammond, *C.* 15,062
Martin Pierce, *LD* 5,341
Rajeev Thacker, *Green* 1,007
Roger Glencross, *Bean* 479
Ms Mariana Bell, *UK Ind.* 414
*Lab. majority* 3,744 (9.11%)
1.47% swing C. to Lab.
(1997, Lab. maj. 2,980 (6.17%))

WINCHESTER
E.81,852 T. 59,158 (72.27%) LD hold
*Mark Oaten, *LD* 32,282
Andrew Hayes, *C.* 22,648
Stephen Wyeth, *Lab.* 3,498
Ms Joan Martin, *UK Ind.* 664
Ms Henrietta Rouse, *Wessex Reg.* 66
*LD majority* 9,634 (16.29%)
8.14% swing C. to LD
(1997 Nov by-election, LD maj. 21,556 (39.64%)
(1997, LD maj. 2 (0.00%))

WINDSOR
E.69,136 T. 42,110 (60.91%) C. hold
*Michael Trend, *C.* 19,900
Nick Pinfield, *LD* 11,011
Mark Muller, *Lab.* 10,137
John Fagan, *UK Ind.* 1,062
*C. majority* 8,889 (21.11%)
0.79% swing LD to C.
(1997, C. maj. 9,917 (19.53%))

WIRRAL SOUTH
E.60,653 T. 39,818 (65.65%) Lab. hold
*Ben Chapman, *Lab.* 18,890
Anthony Millard, *C.* 13,841
Phillip Gilchrist, *LD* 7,087
*Lab. majority* 5,049 (12.68%)
0.94% swing Lab. to C.
(1997, Lab. maj. 7,004 (14.56%))

WIRRAL WEST
E.62,294 T. 40,475 (64.97%) Lab. hold
*Stephen Hesford, *Lab.* 19,105
Chris Lynch, *C.* 15,070
Simon Holbrook, *LD* 6,300
*Lab. majority* 4,035 (9.97%)
2.06% swing C. to Lab.
(1997, Lab. maj. 2,738 (5.84%))

WITNEY
E.74,624 T. 49,203 (65.93%) C. gain
David Cameron, *C.* 22,153
Michael Bartlet, *Lab.* 14,180
Gareth Epps, *LD* 10,000
Mark Stevenson, *Green* 1,100
Barry Beadle, *Ind.* 1,003
Kenneth Dukes, *UK Ind.* 767
*C. majority* 7,973 (16.20%)
1.87% swing Lab. to C.
(1997, C. maj. 7,028 (12.46%))

WOKING
E.71,163 T. 42,910 (60.30%) C. hold
*Humfrey Malins, *C.* 19,747
Alan Hilliar, *LD* 12,988
Sabir Hussain, *Lab.* 8,714
Michael Harvey, *UK Ind.* 1,461
*C. majority* 6,759 (15.75%)
2.30% swing LD to C.
(1997, C. maj. 5,678 (11.15%))

WOKINGHAM
E.68,430 T. 43,848 (64.08%) C. hold
*Rt. Hon. J. Redwood, *C.* 20,216
Dr Royce Longton, *LD* 14,222
Matthew Syed, *Lab.* 7,633
Franklin Carstairs, *UK Ind.* 897
Peter "Top Cat" Owen, *Loony* 880
*C. majority* 5,994 (13.67%)
2.51% swing C. to LD
(1997, C. maj. 9,365 (18.69%))

WOLVERHAMPTON NORTH EAST
E.60,486 T. 31,494 (52.07%) Lab. Co-op hold
*Ken Purchase, *Lab. Co-op* 18,984
Ms Maria Miller, *C.* 9,019
Steven Bourne, *LD* 2,494
Thomas McCartney, *UK Ind.* 997
*Lab. Co-op majority* 9,965 (31.64%)
0.14% swing C. to Lab. Co-op
(1997, Lab. maj. 12,987 (31.37%))

WOLVERHAMPTON SOUTH EAST
E.53,931 T. 27,297 (50.61%) Lab. Co-op hold
*Dennis Turner (Lab. Co-op.) 18,409
Adrian Pepper, *C.* 5,945
Peter Wild, *LD* 2,389
James Barry, *NF* 554
*Lab. Co-op majority* 12,464 (45.66%)
1.04% swing C. to Lab. Co-op
(1997, Lab. maj. 15,182 (43.58%))

WOLVERHAMPTON SOUTH WEST
E.67,171 T. 40,897 (60.88%) Lab. hold
Robert Marris, *Lab.* 19,735
David Chambers, *C.* 16,248
Mike Dixon, *LD* 3,425
Ms Wendy Walker, *Green* 805
Doug Hope, *UK Ind.* 684
*Lab. majority* 3,487 (8.53%)
0.97% swing Lab. to C.
(1997, Lab. maj. 5,118 (10.46%))

WOODSPRING
E.71,023 T. 48,758 (68.65%) C. hold
*Dr Liam Fox, *C.* 21,297
Chanel Stevens, *Lab.* 12,499
Colin Eldridge, *LD* 11,816
David Shopland, *Ind.* 1,412
Dr Richard Lawson, *Green* 1,282
Fraser Crean, *UK Ind.* 452
*C. majority* 8,798 (18.04%)
2.86% swing C. to Lab.
(1997, C. maj. 7,734 (14.08%))

WORCESTER
E.71,255 T. 44,210 (62.04%) Lab. hold
*Michael Foster, *Lab.* 21,478
Richard Adams, *C.* 15,712

Paul Chandler, *LD* 5,578
Richard Chamings, *UK Ind.* 1,442
*Lab. majority* 5,766 (13.04%)
0.67% swing Lab. to C.
(1997, Lab. maj. 7,425 (14.38%))

WORCESTERSHIRE MID
*E.*71,985 *T.* 44,897 (62.37%) C. hold
*Peter Luff, *C.* 22,937
David Bannister, *Lab.* 12,310
R. Woodthorpe-Browne, *LD* 8,420
Tony Eaves, *UK Ind.* 1,230
*C. majority* 10,627 (23.67%)
2.57% swing Lab. to C.
(1997, C. maj. 9,412 (18.52%))

WORCESTERSHIRE WEST
*E.*66,769 *T.* 44,807 (67.11%) C. hold
*Sir Michael Spicer, *C.* 20,597
Mike Hadley, *LD* 15,223
Waquar Azmi, *Lab.* 6,275
Ian Morris, *UK Ind.* 1,574
Malcolm Victory, *Green* 1,138
*C. majority* 5,374 (11.99%)
2.10% swing LD to C.
(1997, C. maj. 3,846 (7.80%))

WORKINGTON
*E.*65,965 *T.* 41,822 (63.40%) Lab. hold
Tony Cunningham, *Lab.* 23,209
Tim Stoddart, *C.* 12,359
Ian Francis, *LD* 5,214
John Peacock, *LCA* 1,040
*Lab. majority* 10,850 (25.94%)
6.93% swing Lab. to C.
(1997, Lab. maj. 19,656 (39.81%))

WORSLEY
*E.*69,300 *T.* 35,363 (51.03%) Lab. hold
*Terry Lewis, *Lab.* 20,193
Tobias Ellwood, *C.* 8,406
Robert Bleakley, *LD* 6,188
Ms Dorothy Entwistle, *Soc. Lab.* 576
*Lab. majority* 11,787 (33.33%)
2.30% swing Lab. to C.
(1997, Lab. maj. 17,741 (37.93%))

WORTHING EAST & SHOREHAM
*E.*71,890 *T.* 43,068 (59.91%) C. hold
*Tim Loughton, *C.* 18,608
Daniel Yates, *Lab.* 12,469
Paul Elgood, *LD* 9,876
Jim McCulloch, *UK Ind.* 1,195
Christopher Baldwin, *LCA* 920
*C. majority* 6,139 (14.25%)
1.14% swing C. to Lab.
(1997, C. maj. 5,098 (9.89%))

WORTHING WEST
*E.*72,419 *T.* 43,209 (59.67%) C. hold
*Peter Bottomley, *C.* 20,508
James Walsh, *LD* 11,471
Alan Butcher, *Lab.* 9,270
Tim Cross, *UK Ind.* 1,960
*C. majority* 9,037 (20.91%)
2.96% swing LD to C.
(1997, C. maj. 7,713 (15.00%))

WREKIN, THE
*E.*65,837 *T.* 41,490 (63.02%) Lab. hold
*Peter Bradley, *Lab.* 19,532
Jacob Rees-Mogg, *C.* 15,945
Ian Jenkins, *LD* 4,738
Denis Brookes, *UK Ind.* 1,275
*Lab. majority* 3,587 (8.65%)
0.98% swing C. to Lab.
(1997, Lab. maj. 3,025 (6.69%))

WYCOMBE
*E.*74,647 *T.* 44,974 (60.25%) C. hold
Paul Goodman, *C.* 19,064
Chauhdry Shafique, *Lab.* 15,896
Ms Dee Tomlin, *LD* 7,658
Christopher Cooke, *UK Ind.* 1,059
John Laker, *Green* 1,057
David Fitton, *Ind.* 240
*C. majority* 3,168 (7.04%)
1.26% swing Lab. to C.
(1997, C. maj. 2,370 (4.53%))

WYRE FOREST
*E.*72,152 *T.* 49,062 (68.00%) KHHC gain
Dr Richard Taylor, *KHHC* 28,487
*David Lock, *Lab.* 10,857
Mark Simpson, *C.* 9,350
James Millington, *UK Ind.* 368
*KHHC majority* 17,630 (35.93%)
(1997, Lab. maj. 6,946 (12.62%))

WYTHENSHAWE & SALE EAST
*E.*72,127 *T.* 35,055 (48.60%) Lab. hold
*Paul Goggins, *Lab.* 21,032
Mrs Susan Fildes, *C.* 8,424
Ms Vanessa Tucker, *LD* 4,320
Lance Crookes, *Green* 869
Fred Shaw, *Soc. Lab.* 410
*Lab. majority* 12,608 (35.97%)
1.49% swing C. to Lab.
(1997, Lab. maj. 15,019 (32.99%))

YEOVIL
*E.*75,977 *T.* 48,132 (63.35%) LD hold
David Laws, *LD* 21,266
Marco Forgione, *C.* 17,338
Joe Conway, *Lab.* 7,077
Neil Boxall, *UK Ind.* 1,131
Alex Begg, *Green* 786
Tony Prior, *Lib.* 534
*LD majority* 3,928 (8.16%)
6.47% swing LD to C.
(1997, LD maj. 11,403 (21.10%))

YORK, CITY OF
*E.*80,431 *T.* 47,980 (59.65%) Lab. hold
*Hugh Bayley, *Lab.* 25,072
Michael McIntyre, *C.* 11,293
Andrew Waller, *LD* 8,519
Bill Shaw, *Green* 1,465
Frank Ormston, *Soc. All.* 674
Richard Bate, *UK Ind.* 576
Graham Cambridge, *Loony* 381
*Lab. majority* 13,779 (28.72%)
3.23% swing Lab. to C.
(1997, Lab. maj. 20,523 (35.17%))

YORKSHIRE EAST
*E.*72,342 *T.* 43,314 (59.87%) C. hold
Rt. Hon. G. Knight, *C.* 19,861
Ms Tracey Simpson-Laing, *Lab.* 15,179
Ms Mary-Rose Hardy, *LD* 6,300
Trevor Pearson, *UK Ind.* 1,661
Paul Dessoy, *Ind.* 313
*C. majority* 4,682 (10.81%)
1.99% swing Lab. to C.
(1997, C. maj. 3,337 (6.82%))

## WALES

ABERAVON
*E.*49,660 *T.* 30,190 (60.79%) Lab. hold
Hywel Francis, *Lab.* 19,063
Ms Lisa Turnbull, *PC* 2,955
Chris Davies, *LD* 2,933
Ali Miraj, *C.* 2,296
Andrew Tutton, *RP* 1,960
Captain Beany, *Bean* 727
Mr Martin Chapman, *Soc. All.* 256
*Lab. majority* 16,108 (53.36%)
6.08% swing Lab. to PC
(1997, Lab. maj. 21,571 (59.98%))

ALYN & DEESIDE
*E.*60,478 *T.* 35,421 (58.57%) Lab. hold
Mark Tami, *Lab.* 18,525
Mark Isherwood, *C.* 9,303
Derek Burnham, *LD* 4,585
Richard Coombs, *PC* 1,182
Klaus Armstrong-Braun, *Green* 881
William Crawford, *UK Ind.* 481
Max Cooksey, *Ind.* 253
Glyn Davies, *Comm.* 211
*Lab. majority* 9,222 (26.04%)
6.53% swing Lab. to C.
(1997, Lab. maj. 16,403 (39.10%))

BLAENAU GWENT
*E.*53,353 *T.* 31,725 (59.46%) Lab. hold
*Llew Smith, *Lab.* 22,855
Adam Rykala, *PC* 3,542
Edward Townsend, *LD* 2,945
Huw Williams, *C.* 2,383
*Lab. majority* 19,313 (60.88%)
6.68% swing Lab. to PC
(1997, Lab. maj. 28,035 (70.74%))

BRECON & RADNORSHIRE
*E.*52,247 *T.* 37,516 (71.81%) LD hold
Roger Williams, *LD* 13,824
Dr Felix Aubel, *C.* 13,073
Huw Irranca-Davis, *Lab.* 8,024
Brynach Parri, *PC* 1,301
Ian Mitchell, *Ind.* 762
Mrs Elizabeth Phillips, *UK Ind.* 452
Robert Nicholson, *Ind.* 80
*LD majority* 751 (2.00%)
4.94% swing LD to C.
(1997, LD maj. 5,097 (11.89%))

BRIDGEND
*E.*61,496 *T.* 37,004 (60.17%) Lab. hold
*Win Griffiths, *Lab.* 19,422
Ms Tania Brisby, *C.* 9,377
Ms Jean Barraclough, *LD* 5,330
Ms Monica Mahoney, *PC* 2,652

Ms Sara Jeremy, *ProLife* 223
*Lab. majority* 10,045 (27.15%)
4.05% swing Lab. to C.
(1997, Lab. maj. 15,248 (35.24%))

CAERNARFON
*E.*47,354 *T.* 29,053 (61.35%) PC hold
Hywel Williams, *PC* 12,894
Martin Eaglestone, *Lab.* 9,383
Ms Bronwen Naish, *C.* 4,403
Mel ab Owain, *LD* 1,823
Ifor Lloyd, *UK Ind.* 550
*PC majority* 3,511 (12.08%)
4.75% swing PC to Lab
(1997, PC maj. 7,449 (21.59%))

CAERPHILLY
*E.*67,593 *T.* 38,831 (57.45%) Lab. hold
Wayne David, *Lab.* 22,597
Lindsay Whittle, *PC* 8,172
David Simmonds, *C.* 4,413
Rob Roffe, *LD* 3,649
*Lab. majority* 14,425 (37.15%)
10.49% swing Lab. to PC
(1997, Lab. maj. 25,839 (57.08%))

CARDIFF CENTRAL
*E.*59,785 *T.* 34,842 (58.28%) Lab. Co-op. hold
*Jon Owen Jones, *Lab. Co-op* 13,451
Ms Jenny Willott, *LD* 12,792
Gregory Walker, *C.* 5,537
Richard Grigg, *PC* 1,680
Stephen Bartley, *Green* 661
Julian Goss, *Soc. All.* 283
Frank Hughes, *UK Ind.* 221
Ms Madeleine Jeremy, *ProLife* 217
Lab. Co-op. maj 659 (1.89%) 8.43% swing Lab. Co-op. to LD
(1997, Lab. maj. 7,923 (18.75%))

CARDIFF NORTH
*E.*62,634 *T.* 43,240 (69.04%) Lab. hold
*Ms Julie Morgan, *Lab.* 19,845
Alastair Watson, *C.* 13,680
John Dixon, *LD* 6,631
Sion Jobbins, *PC* 2,471
Don Hulston, *UK Ind.* 613
*Lab. majority* 6,165 (14.26%)
1.25% swing Lab. to C.
(1997, Lab. maj. 8,126 (16.76%))

CARDIFF SOUTH & PENARTH
*E.*62,125 *T.* 35,751 (57.55%) Lab. Co-op. hold
*Rt. Hon. A. Michael, *Lab. Co-op* 20,094
Ms Maureen Kelly Owen, *C.* 7,807
Dr Rodney Berman, *LD* 4,572
Ms Lila Haines, *PC* 1,983
Justin Callan, *UK Ind.* 501
Dave Bartlett, *Soc. All.* 427
Ms Anne Savoury, *ProLife* 367
Lab. Co-op. maj 12,287 (34.37%)
0.81% swing Con to Lab. Co-op.
(1997, Lab. maj. 13,881 (32.74%))

CARDIFF WEST
*E.*58,348 *T.* 34,083 (58.41%) Lab. hold
Kevin Brennan, *Lab.* 18,594
Andrew Davies, *C.* 7,273
Ms Jacqui Gasson, *LD* 4,458
Delme Bowen, *PC* 3,296
Ms Joyce Jenking, *UK Ind.* 462
*Lab. majority* 11,321 (33.22%)
2.79% swing Lab. to C.
(1997, Lab. maj. 15,628 (38.80%))

CARMARTHEN EAST & DINEFWR
*E.*54,035 *T.* 38,053 (70.42%) PC gain
Adam Price, *PC* 16,130
*Alan Williams, *Lab.* 13,540
David N Thomas, *C.* 4,912
Doiran Evans, *LD* 2,815
Mike Squires, *UK Ind.* 656
*PC majority* 2,590 (6.81%)
7.54% swing Lab. to PC
(1997, Lab. maj. 3,450 (8.27%))

CARMARTHEN WEST & PEMBROKESHIRE SOUTH
*E.*56,518 *T.* 36,916 (65.32%) Lab. hold
*Nick Ainger, *Lab.* 15,349
Robert Wilson, *C.* 10,811
Llyr Hughes Griffiths, *PC* 6,893
William Jeremy, *LD* 3,248
Ian Phillips, *UK Ind.* 537
Nick Turner, *Customer* 78
*Lab. majority* 4,538 (12.29%)
5.14% swing Lab. to C.
(1997, Lab. maj. 9,621 (22.57%))

CEREDIGION
*E.*56,118 *T.* 34,606 (61.67%) PC hold
*Simon Thomas, *PC* 13,241
Mark Williams, *LD* 9,297
Paul Davies, *C.* 6,730
David Grace, *Lab.* 5,338
*PC majority* 3,944 (11.40%)
6.89% swing PC to LD
(2000 Feb by-election: PC maj 4,948 (19.74%); 1997, PC maj. 6,961 (17.33%))

CLWYD SOUTH
*E.*53,680 *T.* 33,496 (62.40%) Lab. hold
*Martyn Jones, *Lab.* 17,217
Tom Biggins, *C.* 8,319
Dyfed Edwards, *PC* 3,982
David Griffiths, *LD* 3,426
Mrs Edwina Theunissen, *UK Ind.* 552
*Lab. majority* 8,898 (26.56%)
4.25% swing Lab. to C.
(1997, Lab. maj. 13,810 (35.07%))

CLWYD WEST
*E.*53,960 *T.* 34,600 (64.12%) Lab. hold
*Gareth Thomas, *Lab.* 13,426
Jimmy James, *C.* 12,311
Elfed Williams, *PC* 4,453
Ms Bobbie Feeley, *LD* 3,934
Matthew Guest, *UK Ind.* 476
*Lab. majority* 1,115 (3.22%)
0.68% swing Lab. to C.
(1997, Lab. maj. 1,848 (4.59%))

CONWY
*E.*54,751 *T.* 34,366 (62.77%) Lab. hold
*Mrs Betty Williams, *Lab.* 14,366
David Logan, *C.* 8,147
Ms Vicky Macdonald, *LD* 5,800
Ms Ann Owen, *PC* 5,665
Alan Barham, *UK Ind.* 388
*Lab. majority* 6,219 (18.10%)
3.66% swing Con to Lab
(1997, Lab. maj. 1,596 (3.84%))

CYNON VALLEY
*E.*48,591 *T.* 26,958 (55.48%) Lab. hold
*Ms Ann Clwyd, *Lab.* 17,685
Steven Cornelius, *PC* 4,687
Ian Parry, *LD* 2,541
Julian Waters, *C.* 2,045
*Lab. majority* 12,998 (48.22%)
5.44% swing Lab. to PC
(1997, Lab. maj. 19,755 (59.10%))

DELYN
*E.*54,732 *T.* 34,636 (63.28%) Lab. hold
*David Hanson, *Lab.* 17,825
Paul Brierley, *C.* 9,220
Tudor Jones, *LD* 5,329
Paul Rowlinson, *PC* 2,262
*Lab. majority* 8,605 (24.84%)
2.29% swing Lab. to C.
(1997, Lab. maj. 11,693 (29.42%))

GOWER
*E.*58,943 *T.* 37,353 (63.37%) Lab. hold
*Martin Caton, *Lab.* 17,676
John Bushell, *C.* 10,281
Ms Sheila Waye, *LD* 4,507
Ms Sian Caiach, *PC* 3,865
Ms Tina Shrewsbury, *Green* 607
Darran Hickery, *Soc. Lab.* 417
*Lab. majority* 7,395 (19.80%)
5.11% swing Lab. to C.
(1997, Lab. maj. 13,007 (30.02%))

ISLWYN
*E.*51,230 *T.* 31,691 (61.86%) Lab. Co-op. hold
*Don Touhig, *Lab. Co-op* 19,505
Kevin Etheridge, *LD* 4,196
Leigh Thomas, *PC* 3,767
Philip Howells, *C.* 2,543
Paul Taylor, *Ind.* 1,263
Ms Mary Millington, *Soc. Lab.* 417
Lab. Co-op. maj 15,309 (48.31%)
8.71% swing Lab. Co-op. to LD
(1997, Lab. maj. 23,931 (65.73%))

LLANELLI
*E.*58,148 *T.* 36,198 (62.25%) Lab. hold
*Rt. Hon. D. Davies, *Lab.* 17,586
Dyfan Jones, *PC* 11,183
Simon Hayes, *C.* 3,442
Ken Rees, *LD* 3,065
Ms Jan Cliff, *Green* 515
John Willock, *Soc. Lab.* 407
*Lab. majority* 6,403 (17.69%)
10.62% swing Lab. to PC
(1997, Lab. maj. 16,039 (38.92%))

MEIRIONNYDD NANT CONWY
*E.*33,175 *T.* 21,068 (63.51%) PC hold
*Elfyn Llwyd, *PC* 10,459
Ms Denise Idris Jones, *Lab.* 4,775
Ms Lisa Francis, *C.* 3,962
Dafydd Raw-Rees, *LD* 1,872
*PC majority* 5,684 (26.98%)
0.36% swing PC to Lab
(1997, PC maj. 6,805 (27.69%))

MERTHYR TYDFIL & RHYMNEY
*E.*55,368 *T.* 31,684 (57.22%) Lab. hold
Dai Havard, *Lab.* 19,574
Robert Hughes, *PC* 4,651
Keith Rogers, *LD* 2,385
Richard Cuming, *C.* 2,272

Jeff Edwards, *Ind.* 1,936
Ken Evans, *Soc. Lab.* 692
Anthony Lewis, *ProLife* 174
*Lab. majority* 14,923 (47.10%)
11.80% swing Lab. to PC
(1997, Lab. maj. 27,086 (69.20%))

MONMOUTH
*E.*62,202 *T.* 44,462 (71.48%) Lab. hold
*Huw Edwards, *Lab.* 19,021
Roger Evans, *C.* 18,637
Neil Parker, *LD* 5,080
Marc Hubbard, *PC* 1,068
David Rowlands, *UK Ind.* 656
*Lab. majority* 384 (0.86%)
3.83% swing Lab. to C.
(1997, Lab. maj. 4,178 (8.52%))

MONTGOMERYSHIRE
*E.*44,243 *T.* 28,983 (65.51%) LD hold
*Lembit Opik, *LD* 14,319
David Jones, *C.* 8,085
Paul Davies, *Lab.* 3,443
David Senior, *PC* 1,969
David William Rowlands, *UK Ind.* 786
Miss Ruth Davies, *ProLife* 210
Reg Taylor, *Ind.* 171
*LD majority* 6,234 (21.51%)
0.88% swing Con to LD
(1997, LD maj. 6,303 (19.74%))

NEATH
*E.*56,107 *T.* 35,020 (62.42%) Lab. hold
*Rt. Hon. P. Hain, *Lab.* 21,253
Alun Llywelyn, *PC* 6,437
David Davies, *LD* 3,335
David Devine, *C.* 3,310
Huw Pudner, *Soc. All.* 483
Gerardo Brienza, *ProLife* 202
*Lab. majority* 14,816 (42.31%)
11.56% swing Lab. to PC
(1997, Lab. maj. 26,741 (64.84%))

NEWPORT EAST
*E.*56,118 *T.* 31,282 (55.74%) Lab. hold
*Rt. Hon. A. Howarth, *Lab.* 17,120
Ian Oakley, *C.* 7,246
Alistair Cameron, *LD* 4,394
Madoc Batcup, *PC* 1,519
Ms Liz Screen, *Soc. Lab.* 420
Neal Reynolds, *UK Ind.* 410
Robert Griffiths, *Comm.* 173
*Lab. majority* 9,874 (31.56%)
2.36% swing Lab. to C.
(1997, Lab. maj. 13,523 (36.29%))

NEWPORT WEST
*E.*59,742 *T.* 35,063 (58.69%) Lab. hold
*Paul Flynn, *Lab.* 18,489
Dr William Morgan, *C.* 9,185
Ms Veronica Watkins, *LD* 4,095
Anthony Salkeld, *PC* 2,510
Hugh Moelwyn-Hughes, *UK Ind.* 506
Terry Cavill, *BNP* 278
*Lab. majority* 9,304 (26.54%)
4.81% swing Lab. to C.
(1997, Lab. maj. 14,537 (36.16%))

OGMORE
*E.*52,185 *T.* 30,353 (58.16%) Lab. hold
*Sir Ray Powell, *Lab.* 18,833
Ms Angela Pulman, *PC* 4,259
Ian Lewis, *LD* 3,878
Richard Hill, *C.* 3,383
*Lab. majority* 14,574 (48.02%)
9.46% swing Lab. to PC
(1997, Lab. maj. 24,447 (64.22%))

PONTYPRIDD
*E.*66,105 *T.* 38,309 (57.95%) Lab. hold
*Dr Kim Howells, *Lab.* 22,963
Bleddyn Hancock, *PC* 5,279
Ms Prudence Dailey, *C.* 5,096
Eric Brooke, *LD* 4,152
Ms Sue Warry, *UK Ind.* 603
Joseph Biddulph, *ProLife* 216
*Lab. majority* 17,684 (46.16%)
5.61% swing Lab. to PC
(1997, Lab. maj. 23,129 (50.44%))

PRESELI PEMBROKESHIRE
*E.*54,283 *T.* 36,777 (67.75%) Lab. hold
*Ms Jackie Lawrence, *Lab.* 15,206
Stephen Crabb, *C.* 12,260
Rhys Sinnet, *PC* 4,658
Alexander Dauncey, *LD* 3,882
Ms Trish Bowen, *Soc. Lab.* 452
Hugh Jones, *UK Ind.* 319
*Lab. majority* 2,946 (8.01%)
6.29% swing Lab. to C.
(1997, Lab. maj. 8,736 (20.60%))

RHONDDA
*E.*56,059 *T.* 34,002 (60.65%) Lab. hold
Chris Bryant, *Lab.* 23,230
Ms Leanne Wood, *PC* 7,183
Peter Hobbins, *C.* 1,557
Gavin Cox, *LD* 1,525
Glyndwr Summers, *Ind.* 507
*Lab. majority* 16,047 (47.19%)
6.95% swing Lab. to PC
(1997, Lab. maj. 24,931 (61.09%))

SWANSEA EAST
*E.*57,273 *T.* 30,072 (52.51%) Lab. hold
*Rt. Hon. D. Anderson, *Lab.* 19,612
John Ball, *PC* 3,464
Robert Speht, *LD* 3,064
Paul Morris, *C.* 3,026
Tony Young, *Green* 463
Tim Jenkins, *UK Ind.* 443
*Lab. majority* 16,148 (53.70%)
9.15% swing Lab. to PC
(1997, Lab. maj. 25,569 (66.12%))

SWANSEA WEST
*E.*57,074 *T.* 32,100 (56.24%) Lab. hold
*Rt. Hon. A. Williams, *Lab.* 15,644
Ms Margaret Harper, *C.* 6,094
Mike Day, *LD* 5,313
Ian Titherington, *PC* 3,404
Richard Lewis, *UK Ind.* 653
Martyn Shrewsbury, *Green* 626
Alec Thraves, *Soc. All.* 366
*Lab. majority* 9,550 (29.75%)
2.99% swing Lab. to C.
(1997, Lab. maj. 14,459 (35.73%))

TORFAEN
*E.*61,110 *T.* 35,242 (57.67%) Lab. hold
*Rt. Hon. P. Murphy, *Lab.* 21,883
Jason Evans, *C.* 5,603
Alan Masters, *LD* 3,936
Stephen Smith, *PC* 2,720
Mrs Brenda Vipass, *UK Ind.* 657
Steve Bell, *Soc. All.* 443
*Lab. majority* 16,280 (46.19%)
5.27% swing Lab. to C.
(1997, Lab. maj. 24,536 (56.74%))

VALE OF CLWYD
*E.*51,247 *T.* 32,346 (63.12%) Lab. hold
*Chris Ruane, *Lab.* 16,179
Brendan Murphy, *C.* 10,418
Graham Rees, *LD* 3,058
John Penri Williams, *PC* 2,300
William Campbell, *UK Ind.* 391
*Lab. majority* 5,761 (17.81%)
2.54% swing Lab. to C.
(1997, Lab. maj. 8,955 (22.89%))

VALE OF GLAMORGAN
*E.*67,071 *T.* 45,184 (67.37%) Lab. hold
*John Smith, *Lab.* 20,524
Lady Susan Inkin, *C.* 15,824
Dewi Smith, *LD* 5,521
Chris Franks, *PC* 2,867
Niall Warry, *UK Ind.* 448
*Lab. majority* 4,700 (10.40%)
4.57% swing Lab. to C.
(1997, Lab. maj. 10,532 (19.54%))

WREXHAM
*E.*50,465 *T.* 30,048 (59.54%) Lab. hold
Ian Lucas, *Lab.* 15,934
Ms Felicity Elphick, *C.* 6,746
Ron Davies, *LD* 5,153
Malcolm Evans, *PC* 1,783
Mrs Jane Brookes, *UK Ind.* 432
*Lab. majority* 9,188 (30.58%)
0.86% swing Lab. to C.
(1997, Lab. maj. 11,762 (32.30%))

YNYS MON
*E.*53,117 *T.* 34,018 (64.04%) Lab. gain
Albert Owen, *Lab.* 11,906
Eilian Williams, *PC* 11,106
Albie Fox, *C.* 7,653
Nick Bennett, *LD* 2,772
Francis Wykes, *UK Ind.* 359
Ms Nona Donald, *Ind.* 222
*Lab. majority* 800 (2.35%)
4.28% swing PC to Lab
(1997, PC maj. 2,481 (6.21%))

## SCOTLAND

### Aberdeen Central
*E.*50,098 *T.* 26,429 (52.75%) Lab. hold
*Frank Doran, *Lab.* 12,025
Wayne Gault, *SNP* 5,379
Ms Eleanor Anderson, *LD* 4,547
Stewart Whyte, *C.* 3,761
Andy Cumbers, *SSP* 717
*Lab. majority* 6,646 (25.15%)
4.24% swing Lab. to SNP
(1997, Lab. maj. 10,801 (30.32%))

### Aberdeen North
*E.*52,746 *T.* 30,357 (57.55%) Lab. hold
*Malcolm Savidge, *Lab.* 13,157
Dr Alasdair Allan, *SNP* 8,708
Jim Donaldson, *LD* 4,991
Richard Cowling, *C.* 3,047
Ms Shona Forman, *SSP* 454
*Lab. majority* 4,449 (14.66%)
5.70% swing Lab. to SNP
(1997, Lab. maj. 10,010 (26.06%))

### Aberdeen South
*E.*58,907 *T.* 36,890 (62.62%) Lab. hold
*Ms Anne Begg, *Lab.* 14,696
Ian Yuill, *LD* 10,308
Moray Macdonald, *C.* 7,098
Ian Angus, *SNP* 4,293
David Watt, *SSP* 495
*Lab. majority* 4,388 (11.89%)
2.13% swing LD to Lab.
(1997, Lab. maj. 3,365 (7.64%))

### Aberdeenshire West & Kincardine
*E.*61,180 *T.* 37,914 (61.97%) LD hold
*Sir Robert Smith, *LD* 16,507
Tom Kerr, *C.* 11,686
Kevin Hutchens, *Lab.* 4,669
John Green, *SNP* 4,634
Alan Manley, *SSP* 418
*LD majority* 4,821 (12.72%)
3.28% swing C. to LD
(1997, LD maj. 2,662 (6.16%))

### Airdrie & Shotts
*E.*58,349 *T.* 31,736 (54.39%) Lab. hold
*Rt. Hon. Ms H. Liddell, *Lab.* 18,478
Ms Alison Lindsay, *SNP* 6,138
John Love, *LD* 2,376
Gordon McIntosh, *C.* 1,960
Ms Mary Dempsey, *Scot. U.* 1,439
Kenny McGuigan, *SSP* 1,171
Chris Herriot, *Soc. Lab.* 174
*Lab. majority* 12,340 (38.88%)
0.73% swing SNP to Lab.
(1997, Lab. maj. 15,412 (37.42%))

### Angus
*E.*59,004 *T.* 35,013 (59.34%) SNP hold
Michael Weir, *SNP* 12,347
Marcus Booth, *C.* 8,736
Ian McFatridge, *Lab.* 8,183
Peter Nield, *LD* 5,015
Bruce Wallace, *SSP* 732
*SNP majority* 3,611 (10.31%)
6.67% swing SNP to C.
(1997, SNP maj. 10,189 (23.66%))

### Argyll & Bute
*E.*49,175 *T.* 30,957 (62.95%) LD hold
Alan Reid, *LD* 9,245
Hugh Raven, *Lab.* 7,592
David Petrie, *C.* 6,436
Ms Agnes Samuel, *SNP* 6,433
Des Divers, *SSP* 1,251
*LD majority* 1,653 (5.34%)
9.60% swing LD to Lab.
(1997, LD maj. 6,081 (17.03%))

### Ayr
*E.*55,630 *T.* 38,560 (69.32%) Lab. hold
*Ms Sandra Osborne, *Lab.* 16,801
Phil Gallie, *C.* 14,256
Jim Mather, *SNP* 4,621
Stuart Ritchie, *LD* 2,089
James Stewart, *SSP* 692
Joseph Smith, *UK Ind.* 101
*Lab. majority* 2,545 (6.60%)
4.01% swing Lab. to C.
(1997, Lab. maj. 6,543 (14.62%))

### Banff & Buchan
*E.*56,496 *T.* 30,806 (54.53%) SNP hold
*Alex Salmond, *SNP* 16,710
Alexander Wallace, *C.* 6,207
Edward Harris, *Lab.* 4,363
Douglas Herbison, *LD* 2,769
Ms Alice Rowan, *SSP* 447
Eric Davidson, *UK Ind.* 310
*SNP majority* 10,503 (34.09%)
1.06% swing C. to SNP
(1997, SNP maj. 12,845 (31.97%))

### Caithness, Sutherland & Easter Ross
*E.*41,225 *T.* 24,867 (60.32%) LD hold
Viscount John Thurso, *LD* 9,041
Michael Meighan, *Lab.* 6,297
John Macadam, *SNP* 5,273
Robert Rowantree, *C.* 3,513
Ms Karn Mabon, *SSP* 544
Gordon Campbell, *Ind.* 199
*LD majority* 2,744 (11.03%)
1.64% swing Lab. to LD
(1997, LD maj. 2,259 (7.75%))

### Carrick, Cumnock & Doon Valley
*E.*64,919 *T.* 40,107 (61.78%) Lab. Co-op hold
*George Foulkes, *Lab. Co-op* 22,174
Gordon Miller, *C.* 7,318
Tom Wilson, *SNP* 6,258
Ms Amy Rogers, *LD* 2,932
Ms Amanda McFarlane, *SSP* 1,058
James McDaid, *Soc. Lab.* 367
*Lab. Co-op majority* 14,856 (37.04%)
2.90% swing Lab. Co-op to C.
(1997, Lab. maj. 21,062 (42.84%))

### Clydebank & Milngavie
*E.*52,534 *T.* 32,491 (61.85%) Lab. hold
*Tony Worthington, *Lab.* 17,249
Jim Yuill, *SNP* 6,525
Rod Ackland, *LD* 3,909
Dr Catherine Pickering, *C.* 3,514
Ms Dawn Brennan, *SSP* 1,294
*Lab. majority* 10,724 (33.01%)
0.54% swing Lab. to SNP
(1997, Lab. maj. 13,320 (34.08%))

### Clydesdale
*E.*64,423 *T.* 38,222 (59.33%) Lab. hold
*Jimmy Hood, *Lab.* 17,822
Jim Wright, *SNP* 10,028
Kevin Newton, *C.* 5,034
Ms Moira Craig, *LD* 4,111
Paul Cockshott, *SSP* 974
Donald MacKay, *UK Ind.* 253
*Lab. majority* 7,794 (20.39%)
5.01% swing Lab. to SNP
(1997, Lab. maj. 13,809 (30.41%))

### Coatbridge & Chryston
*E.*52,178 *T.* 30,311 (58.09%) Lab. hold
*Rt. Hon. T. Clarke, *Lab.* 19,807
Peter Kearney, *SNP* 4,493
Alistair Tough, *LD* 2,293
Patrick Ross-Taylor, *C.* 2,171
Ms Lynne Sheridan, *SSP* 1,547
*Lab. majority* 15,314 (50.52%)
0.39% swing Lab. to SNP
(1997, Lab. maj. 19,295 (51.30%))

### Cumbernauld & Kilsyth
*E.*49,739 *T.* 29,699 (59.71%) Lab. hold
*Ms Rosemary McKenna, *Lab.* 16,144
David McGlashan, *SNP* 8,624
John O'Donnell, *LD* 1,934
Ms Alison Ross, *C.* 1,460
Kenny McEwan, *SSP* 1,287
Thomas Taylor, *Scot. Ref.* 250
*Lab. majority* 7,520 (25.32%)
2.78% swing Lab. to SNP
(1997, Lab. maj. 11,128 (30.89%))

### Cunninghame North
*E.*54,993 *T.* 33,816 (61.49%) Lab. hold
*Brian Wilson, *Lab.* 15,571
Campbell Martin, *SNP* 7,173
Richard Wilkinson, *C.* 6,666
Ross Chmiel, *LD* 3,060
Sean Scott, *SSP* 964
Ms Louise McDaid, *Soc. Lab.* 382
*Lab. majority* 8,398 (24.83%)
3.51% swing Lab. to SNP
(1997, Lab. maj. 11,039 (26.84%))

### Cunninghame South
*E.*49,982 *T.* 28,009 (56.04%) Lab. hold
*Brian Donohoe, *Lab.* 16,424
Bill Kidd, *SNP* 5,194
Mrs Pam Paterson, *C.* 2,682
John Boyd, *LD* 2,094
Ms Rosemary Byrne, *SSP* 1,233
Bobby Cochrane, *Soc. Lab.* 382
*Lab. majority* 11,230 (40.09%)
0.93% swing Lab. to SNP
(1997, Lab. maj. 14,869 (41.95%))

### Dumbarton
*E.*56,267 *T.* 33,994 (60.42%) Lab. Co-op hold
*John McFall, *Lab. Co-op* 16,151
Iain Robertson, *SNP* 6,576
Eric Thompson, *LD* 5,265
Peter Ramsay, *C.* 4,648
Les Robertson, *SSP* 1,354
*Lab. Co-op majority* 9,575 (28.17%)
0.89% swing SNP to Lab. Co-op
(1997, Lab. maj. 10,883 (26.38%))

DUMFRIES
*E.*62,931 *T.* 42,586 (67.67%) Lab. hold
*Russell Brown, *Lab.* 20,830
John Charteris, *C.* 11,996
John Ross Scott, *LD* 4,955
Gerry Fisher, *SNP* 4,103
John Dennis, *SSP* 702
*Lab. majority* 8,834 (20.74%)
0.64% swing C. to Lab.
(1997, Lab. maj. 9,643 (19.47%))

DUNDEE EAST
*E.*56,535 *T.* 32,358 (57.24%) Lab. hold
Iain Luke, *Lab.* 14,635
Stewart Hosie, *SNP* 10,160
Alan Donnelly, *C.* 3,900
Raymond Lawrie, *LD* 2,784
Harvey Duke, *SSP* 879
*Lab. majority* 4,475 (13.83%)
5.38% swing Lab. to SNP
(1997, Lab. maj. 9,961 (24.58%))

DUNDEE WEST
*E.*53,760 *T.* 29,242 (54.39%) Lab. hold
*Ernie Ross, *Lab.* 14,787
Gordon Archer, *SNP* 7,987
Ian Hail, *C.* 2,656
Ms Elizabeth Dick, *LD* 2,620
Jim McFarlane, *SSP* 1,192
*Lab. majority* 6,800 (23.25%)
3.65% swing Lab. to SNP
(1997, Lab. maj. 11,859 (30.56%))

DUNFERMLINE EAST
*E.*52,811 *T.* 30,086 (56.97%) Lab. hold
*Rt. Hon. G. Brown, *Lab.* 19,487
John Mellon, *SNP* 4,424
Stuart Randall, *C.* 2,838
John Mainland, *LD* 2,281
Andy Jackson, *SSP* 770
Tom Dunsmore, *UK Ind.* 286
*Lab. majority* 15,063 (50.07%)
0.60% swing Lab. to SNP
(1997, Lab. maj. 18,751 (51.26%))

DUNFERMLINE WEST
*E.*54,293 *T.* 30,975 (57.05%) Lab. hold
*Ms Rachel Squire, *Lab.* 16,370
Brian Goodall, *SNP* 5,390
Russell McPhate, *LD* 4,832
James Mackie, *C.* 3,166
Ms Kate Stewart, *SSP* 746
Alastair Harper, *UK Ind.* 471
*Lab. majority* 10,980 (35.45%)
0.77% swing SNP to Lab.
(1997, Lab. maj. 12,354 (33.91%))

EAST KILBRIDE
*E.*66,572 *T.* 41,690 (62.62%) Lab. hold
*Rt. Hon. A. Ingram, *Lab.* 22,205
Archie Buchanan, *SNP* 9,450
Ewan Hawthorn, *LD* 4,278
Mrs Margaret McCulloch, *C.* 4,238
David Stevenson, *SSP* 1,519
*Lab. majority* 12,755 (30.59%)
2.52% swing Lab. to SNP
(1997, Lab. maj. 17,384 (35.63%))

EAST LOTHIAN
*E.*58,987 *T.* 36,871 (62.51%) Lab. hold
Mrs Anne Picking, *Lab.* 17,407
Hamish Mair, *C.* 6,577
Ms Judy Hayman, *LD* 6,506
Ms Hilary Brown, *SNP* 5,381
Derrick White, *SSP* 624
Jake Herriot, *Soc. Lab.* 376
*Lab. majority* 10,830 (29.37%)
1.68% swing Lab. to C.
(1997, Lab. maj. 14,221 (32.74%))

EASTWOOD
*E.*68,378 *T.* 48,368 (70.74%) Lab. hold
*Jim Murphy, *Lab.* 23,036
Raymond Robertson, *C.* 13,895
Allan Steele, *LD* 6,239
Stewart Maxwell, *SNP* 4,137
Peter Murray, *SSP* 814
Dr Manar Tayan, *Ind.* 247
*Lab. majority* 9,141 (18.90%)
6.35% swing C. to Lab.
(1997, Lab. maj. 3,236 (6.19%))

EDINBURGH CENTRAL
*E.*66,089 *T.* 34,390 (52.04%) Lab. hold
*Rt. Hon. A. Darling, *Lab.* 14,495
Andrew Myles, *LD* 6,353
Alastair Orr, *C.* 5,643
Dr Ian McKee, *SNP* 4,832
Graeme Farmer, *Green* 1,809
Kevin Williamson, *SSP* 1,258
*Lab. majority* 8,142 (23.68%)
5.15% swing Lab. to LD
(1997, Lab. maj. 11,070 (25.90%))

EDINBURGH EAST & MUSSELBURGH
*E.*59,241 *T.* 34,454 (58.16%) Lab. hold
*Rt. Hon. Dr G. Strang, *Lab.* 18,124
Rob Munn, *SNP* 5,956
Gary Peacock, *LD* 4,981
Peter Finnie, *C.* 3,906
Derek Durkin, *SSP* 1,487
*Lab. majority* 12,168 (35.32%)
0.41% swing SNP to Lab.
(1997, Lab. maj. 14,530 (34.50%))

EDINBURGH NORTH & LEITH
*E.*62,475 *T.* 33,234 (53.20%) Lab. hold
Mark Lazarowicz, *Lab.* 15,271
Sebastian Tombs, *LD* 6,454
Ms Kaukab Stewart, *SNP* 5,290
Iain Mitchell, *C.* 4,626
Ms Catriona Grant, *SSP* 1,334
Don Jacobsen, *Soc. Lab.* 259
*Lab. majority* 8,817 (26.53%)
3.67% swing Lab. to LD
(1997, Lab. maj. 10,978 (26.81%))

EDINBURGH PENTLANDS
*E.*59,841 *T.* 38,932 (65.06%) Lab. hold
*Dr Lynda Clark, *Lab.* 15,797
Sir Malcolm Rifkind, *C.* 14,055
David Walker, *LD* 4,210
Stewart Gibb, *SNP* 4,210
James Mearns, *SSP* 555
William McMurdo, *UK Ind.* 105
*Lab. majority* 1,742 (4.47%)
3.08% swing Lab. to C.
(1997, Lab. maj. 4,862 (10.63%))

EDINBURGH SOUTH
*E.*64,012 *T.* 37,166 (58.06%) Lab. hold
*Nigel Griffiths, *Lab.* 15,671
Ms Marilyne MacLaren, *LD* 10,172
Geoffrey Buchan, *C.* 6,172
Ms Heather Williams, *SNP* 3,683
Colin Fox, *SSP* 933
Ms Linda Hendry, *LCA* 535
*Lab. majority* 5,499 (14.80%)
7.19% swing Lab. to LD
(1997, Lab. maj. 11,452 (25.54%))

EDINBURGH WEST
*E.*61,895 *T.* 39,478 (63.78%) LD hold
John Barrett, *LD* 16,719
Ms Elspeth Alexandra, *Lab.* 9,130
Iain Whyte, *C.* 8,894
Alyn Smith, *SNP* 4,047
Bill Scott, *SSP* 688
*LD majority* 7,589 (19.22%)
2.59% swing LD to Lab.
(1997, LD maj. 7,253 (15.22%))

FALKIRK EAST
*E.*57,633 *T.* 33,702 (58.48%) Lab. hold
*Michael Connarty, *Lab.* 18,536
Ms Isabel Hutton, *SNP* 7,824
Bill Stevenson, *C.* 3,252
Ms Karen Utting, *LD* 2,992
Tony Weir, *SSP* 725
Raymond Stead, *Soc. Lab.* 373
*Lab. majority* 10,712 (31.78%)
0.20% swing Lab. to SNP
(1997, Lab. maj. 13,385 (32.18%))

FALKIRK WEST
*E.*53,583 *T.* 30,891 (57.65%) Lab. hold
*Eric Joyce, *Lab.* 16,022
David Kerr, *SNP* 7,490
Simon Murray, *C.* 2,321
Hugh O'Donnell, *LD* 2,203
William Buchanan, *Ind.* 1,464
Ms Mhairi McAlpine, *SSP* 707
Hugh Lynch, *Ind.* 490
Ronnie Forbes, *Soc. Lab.* 194
*Lab. majority* 8,532 (27.62%)
4.15% swing Lab. to SNP
2000 Dec by-election, Lab. maj. 705 (3.61%) (1997, Lab. maj. 13,783 (35.92%))

FIFE CENTRAL
*E.*59,597 *T.* 32,512 (54.55%) Lab. hold
John MacDougall, *Lab.* 18,310
David Alexander, *SNP* 8,235
Ms Elizabeth Riches, *LD* 2,775
Jeremy Balfour, *C.* 2,351
Ms Morag Balfour, *SSP* 841
*Lab. majority* 10,075 (30.99%)
1.33% swing Lab. to SNP
(1997, Lab. maj. 13,713 (33.64%))

FIFE NORTH EAST
*E.*61,900 *T.* 34,692 (56.05%) LD hold
*Rt. Hon. M. Campbell, *LD* 17,926
Mike Scott-Hayward, *C.* 8,190
Ms Claire Brennan, *Lab.* 3,950
Ms Kris Murray-Browne, *SNP* 3,596
Keith White, *SSP* 610
Mrs Leslie Von Goetz, *LCA* 420
*LD majority* 9,736 (28.06%)
1.66% swing C. to LD
(1997, LD maj. 10,356 (24.75%))

GALLOWAY & UPPER NITHSDALE
*E.*52,756 *T.* 35,914 (68.08%) C. gain
Peter Duncan, *C.* 12,222
Malcolm Fleming, *SNP* 12,148

Thomas Sloan, *Lab.* 7,258
Neil Wallace, *LD* 3,698
Andy Harvey, *SSP* 588
*C. majority* 74 (0.21%)
6.80% swing SNP to C.
(1997, SNP maj. 5,624 (13.39%))

GLASGOW ANNIESLAND
*E.*53,290 *T.* 26,722 (50.14%) Lab. hold
*John Robertson, *Lab.* 15,102
Grant Thoms, *SNP* 4,048
Christopher McGinty, *LD* 3,244
Stewart Connell, *C.* 2,651
Charlie McCarthy, *SSP* 1,486
Ms Katherine McGavigan, *Soc. Lab.* 191
*Lab. majority* 11,054 (41.37%)
1.68% swing Lab. to SNP
2000 Nov by-election, Lab. maj. 6,337 (31.35%) (1997, Lab. maj. 15,154 (44.73%))

GLASGOW BAILLIESTON
*E.*49,268 *T.* 23,261 (47.21%) Lab. hold
*Jimmy Wray, *Lab.* 14,200
Lachlan McNeill, *SNP* 4,361
David Comrie, *C.* 1,580
Jim McVicar, *SSP* 1,569
Charles Dundas, *LD* 1,551
*Lab. majority* 9,839 (42.30%)
2.15% swing Lab. to SNP
(1997, Lab. maj. 14,840 (46.59%))

GLASGOW CATHCART
*E.*52,094 *T.* 27,386 (52.57%) Lab. hold
Tom Harris, *Lab.* 14,902
Mrs Josephine Docherty, *SNP* 4,086
Richard Cook, *C.* 3,662
Tom Henery, *LD* 3,006
Ronnie Stevenson, *SSP* 1,730
*Lab. majority* 10,816 (39.49%)
1.80% swing SNP to Lab.
(1997, Lab. maj. 12,245 (35.90%))

GLASGOW GOVAN
*E.*54,068 *T.* 25,284 (46.76%) Lab. hold
*Mohammad Sarwar, *Lab.* 12,464
Ms Karen Neary, *SNP* 6,064
Bob Stewart, *LD* 2,815
Mark Menzies, *C.* 2,167
Willie McGartland, *SSP* 1,531
John Foster, *Comm.* 174
Badar Mirza, *Ind.* 69
*Lab. majority* 6,400 (25.31%)
8.14% swing SNP to Lab.
(1997, Lab. maj. 2,914 (9.04%))

GLASGOW KELVIN
*E.*61,534 *T.* 26,802 (43.56%) Lab. hold
*George Galloway, *Lab.* 12,014
Ms Tamsin Mayberry, *LD* 4,754
Frank Rankin, *SNP* 4,513
Miss Davina Rankin, *C.* 2,388
Ms Heather Ritchie, *SSP* 1,847
Tim Shand, *Green* 1,286
*Lab. majority* 7,260 (27.09%)
4.85% swing Lab. to LD
(1997, Lab. maj. 9,665 (29.60%))

GLASGOW MARYHILL
*E.*55,431 *T.* 22,231 (40.11%) Lab. hold
Ms Ann McKechin, *Lab.* 13,420
Alex Dingwall, *SNP* 3,532
Stuart Callison, *LD* 2,372
Gordon Scott, *SSP* 1,745
Gawain Towler, *C.* 1,162
*Lab. majority* 9,888 (44.48%)
1.76% swing Lab. to SNP
(1997, Lab. maj. 14,264 (47.99%))

GLASGOW POLLOK
*E.*49,201 *T.* 25,277 (51.37%) Lab. Co-op hold
*Ian Davidson, *Lab. Co-op* 15,497
David Ritchie, *SNP* 4,229
Keith Baldassara, *SSP* 2,522
Ms Isabel Nelson, *LD* 1,612
Rory O'Brien, *C.* 1,417
*Lab. Co-op majority* 11,268 (44.58%)
1.27% swing SNP to Lab. Co-op
(1997, Lab. maj. 13,791 (42.04%))

GLASGOW RUTHERGLEN
*E.*51,855 *T.* 29,213 (56.34%) Lab. Co-op hold
*Tommy McAvoy, *Lab. Co-op* 16,760
Ms Anne McLaughlin, *SNP* 4,135
David Jackson, *LD* 3,689
Malcolm Macaskill, *C.* 3,301
Bill Bonnar, *SSP* 1,328
*Lab. Co-op majority* 12,625 (43.22%)
0.48% swing SNP to Lab. Co-op
(1997, Lab. maj. 15,007 (42.25%))

GLASGOW SHETTLESTON
*E.*51,557 *T.* 20,465 (39.69%) Lab. hold
*David Marshall, *Lab.* 13,235
Jim Byrne, *SNP* 3,417
Ms Rosie Kane, *SSP* 1,396
Lewis Hutton, *LD* 1,105
Campbell Murdoch, *C.* 1,082
Murdo Ritchie, *Soc. Lab.* 230
*Lab. majority* 9,818 (47.97%)
5.60% swing Lab. to SNP
(1997, Lab. maj. 15,868 (59.18%))

GLASGOW SPRINGBURN
*E.*55,192 *T.* 24,104 (43.67%) Speaker hold
*Rt. Hon. M. Martin, *Speaker* 16,053
Sandy Bain, *SNP* 4,675
Ms Carolyn Leckie, *SSP* 1,879
Daniel Houston, *Scot. U.* 1,289
Richard Silvester, *Ind.* 208
Speaker maj 11,378 (47.20%)
(1997, Lab. maj. 17,326 (54.87%))

GORDON
*E.*59,996 *T.* 35,001 (58.34%) LD hold
*Malcolm Bruce, *LD* 15,928
Mrs Nanette Milne, *C.* 8,049
Mrs Rhona Kemp, *SNP* 5,760
Ellis Thorpe, *Lab.* 4,730
John Sangster, *SSP* 534
*LD majority* 7,879 (22.51%)
2.97% swing C. to LD
(1997, LD maj. 6,997 (16.57%))

GREENOCK & INVERCLYDE
*E.*47,884 *T.* 28,419 (59.35%) Lab. hold
David Cairns, *Lab.* 14,929
Chic Brodie, *LD* 5,039
Andrew Murie, *SNP* 4,248
Alistair Haw, *C.* 3,000
Davey Landels, *SSP* 1,203
*Lab. majority* 9,890 (34.80%)
3.77% swing Lab. to LD
(1997, Lab. maj. 13,040 (37.59%))

HAMILTON NORTH & BELLSHILL
*E.*53,539 *T.* 30,404 (56.79%) Lab. hold
*Rt. Hon. Dr J. Reid, *Lab.* 18,786
Chris Stephens, *SNP* 5,225
Bill Frain Bell, *C.* 2,649
Keith Legg, *LD* 2,360
Ms Shareen Blackall, *SSP* 1,189
Steve Mayes, *Soc. Lab.* 195
*Lab. majority* 13,561 (44.60%)
0.16% swing Lab. to SNP
(1997, Lab. maj. 17,067 (44.92%))

HAMILTON SOUTH
*E.*46,665 *T.* 26,750 (57.32%) Lab. hold
*Bill Tynan, *Lab.* 15,965
John Wilson, *SNP* 5,190
John Oswald, *LD* 2,381
Neil Richardson, *C.* 1,876
Ms Gena Mitchell, *SSP* 1,187
Ms Janice Murdoch, *UK Ind.* 151
*Lab. majority* 10,775 (40.28%)
3.85% swing Lab. to SNP
1999 Sep by-election, Lab. maj. 556 (2.86%) (1997, Lab. maj. 15,878 (47.98%))

INVERNESS EAST, NAIRN & LOCHABER
*E.*67,139 *T.* 42,461 (63.24%) Lab. hold
*David Stewart, *Lab.* 15,605
Angus MacNeil, *SNP* 10,889
Ms Patsy Kenton, *LD* 9,420
Richard Jenkins, *C.* 5,653
Steve Arnott, *SSP* 894
*Lab. majority* 4,716 (11.11%)
3.10% swing SNP to Lab.
(1997, Lab. maj. 2,339 (4.90%))

KILMARNOCK & LOUDOUN
*E.*61,049 *T.* 37,665 (61.70%) Lab. hold
*Des Browne, *Lab.* 19,926
John Brady, *SNP* 9,592
Donald Reece, *C.* 3,943
John Stewart, *LD* 3,177
Jason Muir, *SSP* 1,027
*Lab. majority* 10,334 (27.44%)
6.07% swing SNP to Lab.
(1997, Lab. maj. 7,256 (15.30%))

KIRKCALDY
*E.*51,559 *T.* 28,157 (54.61%) Lab. Co-op hold
*Dr Lewis Moonie, *Lab. Co-op* 15,227
Ms Shirley-Anne Somerville, *SNP* 6,264
Scott Campbell, *C.* 3,013
Andrew Weston, *LD* 2,849
Dougie Kinnear, *SSP* 804
*Lab. Co-op majority* 8,963 (31.83%)
0.60% swing SNP to Lab. Co-op
(1997, Lab. maj. 10,710 (30.63%))

LINLITHGOW
*E.*54,599 *T.* 31,655 (57.98%) Lab. hold
*Tam Dalyell, *Lab.* 17,207
Jim Sibbald, *SNP* 8,078
Gordon Lindhurst, *C.* 2,836
Martin Oliver, *LD* 2,628
Eddie Cornoch, *SSP* 695
Ms Helen Cronin, *R & R Loony* 211

*Lab. majority* 9,129 (28.84%)
0.75% swing SNP to Lab.
(1997, Lab. maj. 10,838 (27.33%))

LIVINGSTON
*E.*64,850 *T.* 36,033 (55.56%) Lab. hold
*Rt. Hon. R. Cook, *Lab.* 19,108
Graham Sutherland, *SNP* 8,492
Gordon Mackenzie, *LD* 3,969
Ian Mowat, *C.* 2,995
Ms Wendy Milne, *SSP* 1,110
Robert Kingdon, *UK Ind.* 359
*Lab. majority* 10,616 (29.46%)
1.02% swing SNP to Lab.
(1997, Lab. maj. 11,747 (27.43%))

MIDLOTHIAN
*E.*48,625 *T.* 28,724 (59.07%) Lab. hold
David Hamilton, *Lab.* 15,145
Ian Goldie, *SNP* 6,131
Ms Jacqueline Bell, *LD* 3,686
Robin Traquair, *C.* 2,748
Bob Goupillot, *SSP* 837
Terence Holden, *ProLife* 177
*Lab. majority* 9,014 (31.38%)
1.69% swing SNP to Lab.
(1997, Lab. maj. 9,870 (28.00%))

MORAY
*E.*58,008 *T.* 33,223 (57.27%) SNP hold
Angus Robertson, *SNP* 10,076
Mrs Catriona Munro, *Lab.* 8,332
Frank Spencer-Nairn, *C.* 7,677
Ms Linda Gorn, *LD* 5,224
Ms Norma Anderson, *SSP* 821
Bill Jappy, *Ind.* 802
Nigel Kenyon, *UK Ind.* 291
*SNP majority* 1,744 (5.25%)
8.25% swing SNP to Lab.
(1997, SNP maj. 5,566 (14.00%))

MOTHERWELL & WISHAW
*E.*52,418 *T.* 29,673 (56.61%) Lab. hold
*Frank Roy, *Lab.* 16,681
Jim McGuigan, *SNP* 5,725
Mark Nolan, *C.* 3,155
Iain Brown, *LD* 2,791
Stephen Smellie, *SSP* 1,260
Ms Claire Watt, *Soc. Lab.* 61
*Lab. majority* 10,956 (36.92%)
1.00% swing SNP to Lab.
(1997, Lab. maj. 12,791 (34.93%))

OCHIL
*E.*57,554 *T.* 35,303 (61.34%) Lab. hold
*Martin O'Neill, *Lab.* 16,004
Keith Brown, *SNP* 10,655
Alasdair Campbell, *C.* 4,235
Paul Edie, *LD* 3,253
Ms Pauline Thompson, *SSP* 751
Flash Gordon Approaching, *Loony* 405
*Lab. majority* 5,349 (15.15%)
2.26% swing SNP to Lab.
(1997, Lab. maj. 4,652 (10.63%))

ORKNEY & SHETLAND
*E.*31,909 *T.* 16,733 (52.44%) LD hold
Alistair Carmichael, *LD* 6,919
Robert Mochrie, *Lab.* 3,444
John Firth, *C.* 3,121
John Mowat, *SNP* 2,473
Peter Andrews, *SSP* 776
*LD majority* 3,475 (20.77%)
6.48% swing LD to Lab.
(1997, LD maj. 6,968 (33.72%))

PAISLEY NORTH
*E.*47,994 *T.* 27,153 (56.58%) Lab. hold
*Ms Irene Adams, *Lab.* 15,058
George Adam, *SNP* 5,737
Ms Jane Hook, *LD* 2,709
Craig Stevenson, *C.* 2,404
Jim Halfpenny, *SSP* 982
Robert Graham, *ProLife* 263
*Lab. majority* 9,321 (34.33%)
1.61% swing Lab. to SNP
(1997, Lab. maj. 12,814 (37.54%))

PAISLEY SOUTH
*E.*53,351 *T.* 30,536 (57.24%) Lab. hold
*Douglas Alexander, *Lab.* 17,830
Brian Lawson, *SNP* 5,920
Brian O'Malley, *LD* 3,178
Andrew Cossar, *C.* 2,301
Ms Frances Curran, *SSP* 835
Ms Patricia Graham, *ProLife* 346
Terence O'Donnell, *Ind.* 126
*Lab. majority* 11,910 (39.00%)
2.44% swing SNP to Lab.
(1997 Nov by-election, Lab. maj. 2,731)
(1997, Lab. maj. 12,750 (34.13%))

PERTH
*E.*61,497 *T.* 37,816 (61.49%) SNP hold
Ms Annabelle Ewing, *SNP* 11,237
Miss Elizabeth Smith, *C.* 11,189
Ms Marion Dingwall, *Lab.* 9,638
Ms Vicki Harris, *LD* 4,853
Frank Byrne, *SSP* 899
*SNP majority* 48 (0.13%)
3.46% swing SNP to C.
(1997, SNP maj. 3,141 (7.05%))

RENFREWSHIRE WEST
*E.*52,889 *T.* 33,497 (63.33%) Lab. gain
James Sheridan, *Lab.* 15,720
Ms Carol Puthucheary, *SNP* 7,145
David Sharpe, *C.* 5,522
Ms Clare Hamblen, *LD* 4,185
Ms Arlene Nunnery, *SSP* 925
*Lab. majority* 8,575 (25.60%)
2.77% swing SNP to Lab.
(1997, Lab. maj. 7,979 (20.05%))

ROSS, SKYE & INVERNESS WEST
*E.*56,522 *T.* 34,812 (61.59%) LD hold
*Rt. Hon. C. Kennedy, *LD* 18,832
Donald Crichton, *Lab.* 5,880
Ms Jean Urquhart, *SNP* 4,901
Angus Laing, *C.* 3,096
Dr Eleanor Scott, *Green* 699
Stuart Topp, *SSP* 683
Philip Anderson, *UK Ind.* 456
James Crawford, *Country* 265
*LD majority* 12,952 (37.21%)
13.57% swing Lab. to LD
(1997, LD maj. 4,019 (10.06%))

ROXBURGH & BERWICKSHIRE
*E.*47,059 *T.* 28,797 (61.19%) LD hold
*Archy Kirkwood, *LD* 14,044
George Turnbull, *C.* 6,533
Ms C. Maxwell-Stuart, *Lab.* 4,498
Roderick Campbell, *SNP* 2,806
Ms Amanda Millar, *SSP* 463
Peter Neilson, *UK Ind.* 453
*LD majority* 7,511 (26.08%)
1.73% swing C. to LD
(1997, LD maj. 7,906 (22.63%))

STIRLING
*E.*53,097 *T.* 35,930 (67.67%) Lab. hold
*Ms Anne McGuire, *Lab.* 15,175
Geoff Mawdsley, *C.* 8,901
Ms Fiona Macaulay, *SNP* 5,877
Clive Freeman, *LD* 4,208
Dr Clarke Mullen, *SSP* 1,012
Mark Ruskell, *Green* 757
*Lab. majority* 6,274 (17.46%)
1.27% swing C. to Lab.
(1997, Lab. maj. 6,411 (14.93%))

STRATHKELVIN & BEARSDEN
*E.*62,729 *T.* 41,486 (66.14%) Lab. hold
John Lyons, *Lab.* 19,250
Gordon Macdonald, *LD* 7,533
Calum Smith, *SNP* 6,675
Murray Roxburgh, *C.* 6,635
Willie Telfer, *SSP* 1,393
*Lab. majority* 11,717 (28.24%)
7.44% swing Lab. to LD
(1997, Lab. maj. 16,292 (32.77%))

TAYSIDE NORTH
*E.*61,645 *T.* 38,517 (62.48%) SNP hold
Peter Wishart, *SNP* 15,441
Murdo Fraser, *C.* 12,158
Thomas Docherty, *Lab.* 5,715
Ms Julia Robertson, *LD* 4,363
Ms Rosie Adams, *SSP* 620
Ms Tina MacDonald, *Ind.* 220
*SNP majority* 3,283 (8.52%)
0.30% swing SNP to C.
(1997, SNP maj. 4,160 (9.13%))

TWEEDDALE, ETTRICK & LAUDERDALE
*E.*51,966 *T.* 33,217 (63.92%) LD hold
*Michael Moore, *LD* 14,035
Keith Geddes, *Lab.* 8,878
Andrew Brocklehurst, *C.* 5,118
Richard Thomson, *SNP* 4,108
Norman Lockhart, *SSP* 695
John Hein, *Lib.* 383
*LD majority* 5,157 (15.53%)
5.86% swing Lab. to LD
(1997, LD maj. 1,489 (3.81%))

WESTERN ISLES
*E.*21,807 *T.* 13,159 (60.34%) Lab. hold
*Calum MacDonald, *Lab.* 5,924
Alasdair Nicholson, *SNP* 4,850
Douglas Taylor, *C.* 1,250
John Horne, *LD* 849
Ms Joanne Telfer, *SSP* 286
*Lab. majority* 1,074 (8.16%)
7.02% swing Lab. to SNP
(1997, Lab. maj. 3,576 (22.20%)

## NORTHERN IRELAND

### ANTRIM EAST
*E.*60,897 *T.*36,000 (59.12%) UUP hold
*Roy Beggs, *UUP* 13,101
Sammy Wilson, *DUP* 12,973
John Mathews, *Alliance* 4,483
Danny O'Connor, *SDLP* 2,641
Robert Mason, *Ind* 1,092
Ms Jeanette Graffin, *SF* 903
Alan Greer, *C.* 807
*UUP majority* 128 (0.36%)
9.48% swing UUP to DUP
(1997, UUP maj. 6,389 (18.60%))

### ANTRIM NORTH
*E.*74,451 *T.*49,217 (66.11%) DUP hold
*Revd Ian Paisley, *DUP* 24,539
Lexie Scott, *UUP* 10,315
Sean Farren, *SDLP* 8,283
John Kelly, *SF* 4,822
Miss Jayne Dunlop, *Alliance* 1,258
*DUP majority* 14,224 (28.90%)
3.01% swing UUP to DUP
(1997, DUP maj. 10,574 (22.89%))

### ANTRIM SOUTH
*E.*70,651 *T.*44,158 (62.50%) UUP gain
David Burnside, *UUP* 16,366
*Revd Robert McCrea, *DUP* 15,355
Sean McKee, *SDLP* 5,336
Martin Meehan, *SF* 4,160
David Ford, *Alliance* 1,969
Norman Boyd, *NI Unionist* 972
*UUP majority* 1,011 (2.29%)
10.21% swing UUP to DUP
(2000 Sep by-election, DUP maj. 822)
(1997, UUP maj. 16,611 (41.33%))

### BELFAST EAST
*E.*58,455 *T.*36,829 (63.00%) DUP hold
*Peter Robinson, *DUP* 15,667
Tim Lemon, *UUP* 8,550
Dr David Alderdice, *Alliance* 5,832
David Ervine, *PUP* 3,669
Joe O'Donnell, *SF* 1,237
Ms Ciara Farren, *SDLP* 880
Terry Dick, *C.* 800
Joe Bell, *WP* 123
Rainbow George Weiss, *Ind. Vote* 71
*DUP majority* 7,117 (19.32%)
1.01% swing UUP to DUP
(1997, DUP maj. 6,754 (17.30%))

### BELFAST NORTH
*E.*60,941 *T.*40,932 (67.17%) DUP gain
Nigel Dodds, *DUP* 16,718
Gerry Kelly, *SF* 10,331
Alban Maginness, *SDLP* 8,592
*Cecil Walker, *UUP* 4,904
Ms Marcella Delaney, *WP* 253
Rainbow George Weiss, *Ind. Vote* 134
*DUP majority* 6,387 (15.60%)
(1997, UUP maj. 13,024 (31.42%))

### BELFAST SOUTH
*E.*59,436 *T.*37,952 (63.85%) UUP hold
*Revd Martin Smyth, *UUP* 17,008
Dr Alasdair McDonnell, *SDLP* 11,609
Prof Monica McWilliams (Women's Co.) 2,968
Alex Maskey, *SF* 2,894
Ms Geraldine Rice, *Alliance* 2,042
Ms Dawn Purvis, *PUP* 1,112
Paddy Lynn, *WP* 204
Rainbow George Weiss, *Ind. Vote* 115
*UUP majority* 5,399 (14.23%)
1.29% swing SDLP to UUP
(1997, UUP maj. 4,600 (11.65%))

### BELFAST WEST
*E.*59,617 *T.* 40,982 (68.74%) SF hold
*Gerry Adams, *SF* 27,096
Alex Attwood, *SDLP* 7,754
The Rev Eric Smyth, *DUP* 2,641
Chris McGimpsey, *UUP* 2,541
John Lowry, *WP* 736
Mr David Kerr, *Third* 116
Rainbow George Weiss, *Ind. Vote* 98
*SF majority* 19,342 (47.20%)
14.98% swing SDLP to SF
(1997, SF maj. 7,909 (17.24%))

### DOWN NORTH
*E.*63,212 *T.*37,189 (58.83%) UUP gain
Lady Sylvia Hermon, *UUP* 20,833
*Robert McCartney, *UKU* 13,509
Ms Marietta Farrell, *SDLP* 1,275
Julian Robertson, *C.* 815
Chris Carter, *Ind* 444
Eamon McConvey, *SF* 313
*UUP majority* 7,324 (19.69%)
11.83% swing UKU to UUP
(1997, UKU maj. 1,449 (3.96%))

### DOWN SOUTH
*E.*73,519 *T.* 52,074 (70.83%) SDLP hold
*Eddie McGrady, *SDLP* 24,136
Mick Murphy, *SF* 10,278
Dermot Nesbitt, *UUP* 9,173
Jim Wells, *DUP* 7,802
Ms Betty Campbell, *Alliance* 685
*SDLP majority* 13,858 (26.61%)
7.97% swing SDLP to SF
(1997, SDLP maj. 9,933 (20.08%))

### FERMANAGH & SOUTH TYRONE
*E.*66,640 *T.* 51,974 (77.99%) SF gain
Ms Michelle Gildernew, *SF* 17,739
James Cooper, *UUP* 17,686
Tommy Gallagher, *SDLP* 9,706
Jim Dixon, *Ind. UU* 6,843
*SF majority* 53 (0.10%)
14.22% swing UUP to SF
(1997, UUP maj. 13,688 (28.34%))

### FOYLE
*E.*70,943 *T.* 48,879 (68.90%) SDLP hold
*John Hume, *SDLP* 24,538
Mitchel McLaughlin, *SF* 12,988
William Hay, *DUP* 7,414
Andrew Davidson, *UUP* 3,360
Colm Cavanagh, *Alliance* 579
*SDLP majority* 11,550 (23.63%)
2.47% swing SDLP to SF
(1997, SDLP maj. 13,664 (28.57%))

### LAGAN VALLEY
*E.*72,671 *T.*45,941 (63.22%) UUP hold
*Jeffrey Donaldson, *UUP* 25,966
Seamus Close, *Alliance* 7,624
Edwin Poots, *DUP* 6,164
Ms Patricia Lewsley, *SDLP* 3,462
Paul Butler, *SF* 2,725
*UUP majority* 18,342 (39.93%)
0.86% swing Alliance to UUP
(1997, UUP maj. 16,925 (38.20%))

### LONDONDERRY EAST
*E.*60,276 *T.*39,869 (66.14%) DUP gain
Gregory Campbell, *DUP* 12,813
*William Ross, *UUP* 10,912
John Dallat, *SDLP* 8,298
Francie Brolly, *SF* 6,221
Mrs Yvonne Boyle, *Alliance* 1,625
*DUP majority* 1,901 (4.77%)
7.36% swing UUP to DUP
(1997, UUP maj. 3,794 (9.95%))

### NEWRY & ARMAGH
*E.*72,466 *T.* 55,621 (76.75%) SDLP hold
*Seamus Mallon, *SDLP* 20,784
Conor Murphy, *SF* 17,209
Paul Berry, *DUP* 10,795
Mrs Sylvia McRoberts, *UUP* 6,833
*SDLP majority* 3,575 (6.43%)
7.75% swing SDLP to SF
(1997, SDLP maj. 4,889 (9.17%))

### STRANGFORD
*E.*72,192 *T.*43,254 (59.92%) DUP gain
Mrs Iris Robinson, *DUP* 18,532
*David McNarry, *UUP* 17,422
Kieran McCarthy, *Alliance* 2,902
Danny McCarthy, *SDLP* 2,646
Liam Johnstone, *SF* 930
Cedric Wilson, *NI Unionist* 822
*DUP majority* 1,110 (2.57%)
8.32% swing UUP to DUP
(1997, UUP maj. 5,852 (14.07%))

### TYRONE WEST
*E.*60,739 *T.* 48,530 (79.90%) SF gain
Pat Doherty, *SF* 19,814
*William Thompson, *UUP* 14,774
Ms Brid Rodgers, *SDLP* 13,942
*SF majority* 5,040 (10.39%)
7.05% swing UUP to SF
(1997, UUP maj. 1,161 (2.51%))

### ULSTER MID
*E.*61,390 *T.*49,936 (81.34%) SF hold
*Martin McGuinness, *SF* 25,502
Ian McCrea, *DUP* 15,549
Ms Eilis Haughey, *SDLP* 8,376
Francie Donnelly, *WP* 509
*SF majority* 9,953 (19.93%)
8.11% swing DUP to SF
(1997, SF maj. 1,883 (3.71%))

### UPPER BANN
*E.*72,574 *T.*51,036 (70.32%) UUP hold
*Rt. Hon. D. Trimble, *UUP* 17,095
David Simpson, *DUP* 15,037
Dr Dara O'Hagan, *SF* 10,770
Ms Dolores Kelly, *SDLP* 7,607
Tom French, *WP* 527
*UUP majority* 2,058 (4.03%)
14.05% swing UUP to DUP
(1997, UUP maj. 9,252 (19.36%))

## BY-ELECTIONS SINCE THE 1997 GENERAL ELECTION

**UXBRIDGE**
(31 July 1997)
*E.*57,446 *T.*55.5%

| | |
|---|---|
| J. Randall, *C.* | 16, 288 |
| A. Slaughter, *Lab.* | 12,522 |
| K. Kerr, *LD* | 1,792 |
| 'Lord Sutch', *Loony* | 396 |
| Ms J. Leonard, *Soc.* | 259 |
| Ms F. Taylor, *BNP* | 205 |
| I. Anderson, *Nat. Dem.* | 157 |
| J. McCauley, *NF* | 110 |
| H. Middleton, *Original Lib. Party* | 69 |
| J. Feisenberger, *UK Ind.* | 39 |
| R. Carroll, *Emerald Rainbow Islands Dream Ticket* | 30 |
| *C. majority* | 3,766 |

**PAISLEY SOUTH**
(6 November 1997)
*E.*54,386 *T.*43.1%

| | |
|---|---|
| D. Alexander, *Lab.* | 10,346 |
| I. Blackford, *SNP* | 7,615 |
| Ms E. McCartin, *LD* | 2,582 |
| Ms S. Laidlaw, *C.* | 1,643 |
| J. Deighan, *ProLife* | 578 |
| F. Curran, *Soc. All. Fighting Corruption* | 306 |
| C. McLauchlan, *Scottish Ind. Lab.* | 155 |
| C. Herriot, *Soc. Lab.* | 153 |
| K. Blair, *NLP* | 57 |
| *Lab. majority* | 2,731 |

**BECKENHAM**
(20 November 1997)
*E.*73,232 *T.*43.6%

| | |
|---|---|
| Ms J. Lait, *C.* | 13,162 |
| R. Hughes, *Lab.* | 11,935 |
| Ms R. Vetterlein, *LD* | 5,864 |
| P. Rimmer, *Lib.* | 330 |
| J. McAuley, *NF* | 267 |
| L. Mead, *New Britain Ref.* | 237 |
| T. Campion, *Social Foundation* | 69 |
| J. Small, *NLP* | 44 |
| *C. majority* | 1, 227 |

**WINCHESTER**
(20 November 1997)
*E.*79,116 *T.*68.7%

| | |
|---|---|
| M. Oaten, *LD* | 37,006 |
| G. Malone, *C.* | 15,450 |
| P. Davies, *Lab.* | 944 |
| R. Page, *Ref./UK Ind.* | 521 |
| Lord' Sutch, *Loony* | 316 |
| R. Huggett, *Literal Dem.* | 59 |
| Ms R. Barry, *NLP* | 48 |
| R. Everest, *European C.* | 40 |
| *LD majority* | 21,556 |

**LEEDS CENTRAL**
(10 June 1999)
*E.*67,280 *T.*19.6%

| | |
|---|---|
| H. Benn, *Lab.* | 6,361 |
| P. Wild, *LD* | 4,068 |
| E. Wild, *C.* | 1,618 |
| D. Blackburn, *Green* | 478 |
| R. Northgreaves, *UK Ind.* | 353 |
| C. Hill, *C.* | 258 |
| J. Fitzgerald, *Equal Parenting Campaign* | 51 |
| *Lab. majority* | 2, 293 |

**EDDISBURY**
(22 July 1999)
*E.*67,086 *T.*51.4 %

| | |
|---|---|
| S. O'Brien, *C.* | 15,465 |
| Ms M. Hanson, *Lab.* | 13,859 |
| P. Roberts, *LD* | 4,757 |
| A. Hope, *Loony* | 238 |
| R. Everest, *Ind. Euro C.* | 98 |
| Ms D. Grice, *NLP* | 80 |
| *C. majority* | 1,606 |

**WIGAN**
(23 September 1999)
*E.*64,775 *T.*25.0%

| | |
|---|---|
| N. Turner, *Lab.* | 9,641 |
| T. Peet, *C.* | 2,912 |
| J. Rule, *LD* | 2,148 |
| J. Whittaker, *UK Ind.* | 834 |
| W. Kelly, *Soc. Lab.* | 240 |
| C. Maile, *Green* | 190 |
| S. Ebbs, *Nat. Dem. Res.* | 100 |
| P. Davis, *NLP* | 64 |
| D. Braid, *Rev.* | 58 |
| *C. majority* | 6,729 |

**HAMILTON SOUTH**
(23 September 1999)
*E.*47,081 *T.*41.3%

| | |
|---|---|
| B. Tynan, *Lab.* | 7,172 |
| A. Ewing, *SNP* | 6,616 |
| S. Blackall, *SSP* | 1,847 |
| C. Ferguson, *C.* | 1,406 |
| S. Mungall, *Watson* | 1,075 |
| M. MacLaren, *LD* | 634 |
| M. Burns, *ProLife.* | 257 |
| T. Dewar, *Soc. Lab.* | 238 |
| J. Reid, *SU* | 113 |
| A. McConnachie, *UK Ind.* | 61 |
| G. Stidolph, *NLP* | 18 |
| J. Moray, *SQ* | 17 |
| *Lab. majority* | 556 |

**KENSINGTON AND CHELSEA**
(25 November 1999)
*E.*65,806 *T.*29.7%

| | |
|---|---|
| Rt. Hon. M. Portillo, *C.* | 11,004 |
| R. Atkinson, *Lab.* | 4, 298 |
| R. Woodthorpe Browne, *LD* | 1,831 |
| J. Stevens, *ProECP* | 740 |
| D. Hockney, *UK Ind.* | 450 |
| H. Charlton, *Green* | 446 |
| C. de Vere Beauclerk, *Dem.* | 182 |
| C. Paisley, *LCA* | 141 |
| M. Irwin, *LWLC* | 97 |
| G. Oliver, *UKPP* | 75 |
| S. Scott-Fawcett, *Ref.* | 57 |
| L. Hodges, *DSSP* | 48 |
| G. Valente, *NLP* | 35 |
| L. Lovebucket, *PNDTP* | 26 |
| J. Davies, Ind. *ESCC* | 24 |
| P. May, *EPP* | 24 |
| A. Hope, *Loony* | 20 |
| T. Samuelson, *Stop* | 15 |
| *C. majority* | 6,706 |

**CEREDIGION**
(3 February 2000)
*E.*55,025 *T.* 45.6%

| | |
|---|---|
| S. Thomas, *PC* | 10,716 |
| M. Williams, *LD* | 5,768 |
| P. Davies, *C.* | 4,138 |
| M. Battle, *Lab.* | 3,612 |
| J. Bufton, *UK Ind.* | 487 |
| J. Berkeley Davies, *Ind. Green* | 289 |
| M. Shipton, *Match.* | 55 |
| *PC majority* | 4,948 |

**ROMSEY**
(4 May 2000)
*E.*69,701 *T.* 55.5%

| | |
|---|---|
| S. Gidley, *LD* | 19,571 |
| T. Palmer, *C* | 16,260 |
| A. Howard, *Lab* | 1,451 |
| G. Rankin-Moore, *UK Ind* | 901 |
| D. Large, *LCA* | 417 |
| T. Lamont, *Ind* | 109 |
| *LD majority* | 3,311 |

**TOTTENHAM**
(22 June 2000)
*E.*64,554 *T.*25.4%

| | |
|---|---|
| D. Lammy, *Lab.* | 8,785 |
| D. Hames, *LD* | 3,139 |
| J. Ellison, *C* | 2,634 |
| W. Bennett, *London Soc. All.* | 885 |
| P. Budge, *Green* | 606 |
| E. Basarik, *Reform 2000* | 177 |
| A. Tanna, *UK Ind* | 136 |
| D. de Braam, *Ind. C.* | 55 |
| *Lab. majority* | 5,646 |

**SOUTH ANTRIM**
(21 September 2000)
*E.*71,047 *T.*43.0%

| | |
|---|---|
| W. McCrea, *DUP* | 11,601 |
| D. Burnside, *UUP* | 10,779 |
| D. McClelland, *SDLP* | 3,496 |
| M. Meehan, *SF* | 2,611 |
| D. Ford, *Alliance* | 2,031 |
| D. Collins, *NLP* | 49 |
| *DUP majority* | 822 |

**PRESTON**
(23 November 2000)
*E.*72,229 *T.*29.6%

| | |
|---|---|
| M. Hendrick, *Lab* | 9,765 |
| G. O'Hare, *C.* | 5,339 |
| W. Chadwick, *LD* | 3,454 |
| T. Cartwright, *Lancashire Social Alliance* | 1,210 |
| G. Beaman, *UK Ind* | 458 |
| R. Merrick, *Green* | 441 |
| P Garrett, *Preston Alliance, Christian People's Alliance* | 416 |
| C. Jackson, *BNP* | 229 |
| D. Franklin-Braid, *Battle of Britain Christian Alliance* | 51 |
| *Lab. majority* | 4,426 |

**WEST BROMWICH WEST**
(23 November 2000)
*E.*68,408 *T.*27.6%

| | |
|---|---|
| A. Bailey, *Lab* | 9,640 |
| K. Bissell, *C.* | 6,408 |
| S. Smith, *LD* | 1,791 |
| N. Griffin, *BNP* | 794 |
| J. Oakton, *UK Ind* | 246 |
| *Lab. majority* | 3,232 |

**GLASGOW, ANNIESLAND**
(23 November 2000)
*E.*52,609 *T.*38.4%

| | |
|---|---|
| J. Robertson, *Lab* | 10,539 |
| G. Thomas, *SNP* | 4,202 |
| D. Luckhurst, C. | 2,188 |
| C. McGinty, *LD* | 1,630 |
| C. McCarthy, *Scottish Socialist* | 1,441 |
| W. Lyden, *Family* | 212 |
| *Lab. majority* | 6,337 |

**FALKIRK WEST**
(21 December 2000)
*E.*53,851 *T.*36.2%

| | |
|---|---|
| E. Joyce, *Lab* | 8,492 |
| D. Kerr, *SNP* | 7,787 |
| C. Stevenson C. | 1,621 |
| I. Hunter, *Scottish Socialist* | 989 |
| H O'Donnell, *LD* | 615 |
| *Lab. majority* | 705 |

## RETIRING MPS

Ashdown, Rt. Hon. Sir Paddy; KBE, *LD*, *Yeovil*; Ashton, Joe, *Lab.*, *Bassetlaw*; Benn, Rt. Hon. Tony, *Lab.*, *Chesterfield*; Bermingham, Gerry, *Lab.*, *St Helens South*; Body, Sir Richard, *C.*, *Boston & Skegness*; Brooke, Rt. Hon. Peter; CH, *C.*, *Cities of London & Westminster*; Campbell-Savours, Dale, *Lab.*, *Workington*; Chisholm, Malcolm; MSP, *Lab.*, *Edinburgh North & Leith*; Church, Judith, *Lab.*, *Dagenham;* Clark, Rt. Hon. Dr David, *Lab.*, *South Shields*; Clark, Dr Michael, *C.*, *Rayleigh*; Clarke, Eric, *Lab.*, *Midlothian*; Corbett, Robin, *Lab.*, *Birmingham Erdington*; Cunliffe, Lawrence, *Lab.*, *Leigh*; Cunningham, Roseanna; MSP, *SNP*, *Perth*; Davies, Rt. Hon. Ron; AM, *Lab.*, *Caerphilly*; Emery, Rt. Hon. Sir Peter, *C.*, *Devon East*; Ewing, Margaret; MSP, *SNP*, *Moray*; Faber, David, *C.*, *Westbury*; Fearn, Ronnie; OBE, *LD*, *Southport*; Fowler, Rt. Hon. Sir Norman, *C.*, *Sutton Coldfield*; Fyfe, Maria, *Lab.*, *Glasgow Maryhill*; Galbraith, Sam; MSP, *Lab.*, *Strathkelvin & Bearsden*; Gill, Christopher; RD, *C.*, *Ludlow*; Godman, Dr Norman A, *Lab.*, *Greenock & Inverclyde*; Golding, Llin, *Lab.*, *Newcastle-under-Lyme*; Gorman, Teresa, *C.*, *Billericay*; Gorrie, Donald; MSP, *LD*, *Edinburgh West*; Graham, Thomas, *Scot Lab.*, *Renfrewshire West*; Grocott, Bruce, *Lab.*, *Telford*; Gunnell, John, *Lab.*, *Morley & Rothwell*; Hamilton, Rt. Hon. Sir Archibald, *C.*, *Epsom & Ewell*; Heath, Rt. Hon. Sir Edward; KG MBE, *C.*, *Old Bexley & Sidcup*; Heseltine, Rt. Hon. Michael; CH, *C.*, *Henley*; Home Robertson, John; MSP, *Lab.*, *East Lothian*; Johnson Smith, Rt. Hon. Sir Geoffrey, *C.*, *Wealden*; Jones, Ieuan Wyn; AM, *PC*, *Ynys Mon*; Jones, Jenny, *Lab.*, *Wolverhampton South West*; Jones, Rt. Hon. Barry, *Lab.*, *Alyn & Deeside*; King, Rt. Hon. Tom; CH, *C.*, *Bridgwater*; Kingham, Tess, *Lab.*, *Gloucester*; Livingstone, Ken, *Ind.*, *Brent East*; Livsey, Richard, *LD*, *Brecon & Radnorshire*; Lloyd, Rt. Hon. Sir Peter, *C.*, *Fareham*; Lyell, Rt. Hon. Sir; Nicholas; QC, *C.*, *Bedfordshire North East*; MacGregor, Rt. Hon. John; OBE, *C.*, *Norfolk South*; Maclennan, Rt. Hon. Robert, *LD*, *Caithness, Sutherland & Easter Ross*; Madel, Sir David, *C.*, *Bedfordshire South West*; Maginnis, Ken, UU, *Fermanagh & South Tyrone*; Major, Rt. Hon. John; CH, *C.*, *Huntingdon*; Marek, Dr John; MP, *Lab.*, *Wrexham*; Maxton, John, *Lab.*, *Glasgow Cathcart*; McAllion, John; MSP, *Lab.*, *Dundee East*; McLeish, Rt. Hon. Henry; MSP, *Lab.*, *Fife Central*; Michie, Bill, *Lab.*, *Sheffield Heeley*; Michie, Hon Janet Ray, *LD*, *Argyll & Bute*; Morgan, Alasdair; MSP, *SNP*, *Galloway & Upper Nithsdale*; Morgan, Rt. Hon. Rhodri; AM, *Lab.*, *Cardiff West*; Morris, Rt. Hon. Sir John; QC, *Lab.*, *Aberavon*; Mowlam, Rt. Hon. Mo, *Lab.*, *Redcar*; Pendry, Rt. Hon. Tom, *Lab.*, *Stalybridge & Hyde*; Radice, Rt. Hon. Giles, *Lab.*, *Durham North*; Rogers, Allan R, *Lab.*, *Rhondda*; Rooker, Rt. Hon. Jeff, *Lab.*, *Birmingham Perry Barr*; Rowe, Andrew, *C.*, *Faversham & Mid Kent*; Rowlands, Ted, *Lab.*, *Merthyr Tydfil & Rhymney*; Sheldon, Rt. Hon. Robert, *Lab.*, *Ashton-under-Lyne*; Snape, Peter, *Lab.*, *West Bromwich East*; Swinney, John; MSP, *SNP*, *Tayside North*; Taylor, Rt. Hon. Dr John D, UU, *Strangford*; Temple-Morris, Peter, *Lab.*, *Leominster*; Townend, John, *C.*, *Yorkshire East*; Wallace, Rt. Hon. Jim; QC, MSP, *LD*, *Orkney & Shetland*; Wardle, Charles, *Ind.*, *Bexhill & Battle*; Wells, Bowen, *C.*, *Hertford & Stortford*; Welsh, Andrew; MSP. MP, *SNP*, *Angus*; Whitney, Sir Raymond; OBE, *C.*, *Wycombe*; Wigley, Rt. Hon. Dafydd; AM, *PC*, *Caernarfon*

## DEFEATED MPS

Balard, Jackie, *LD*, *Taunton*; Bell, Martin, *Ind.*, *Tatton (contesting Brentwood and Ongar)*; Brand, Dr Peter, *LD*, *Isle of Wight*; Bruce, Ian, *C.*, *Dorset South*; Butler, Christine, *Lab.*, *Castle Point*; Darvill, Keith, *Lab.*, *Upminster*; Day, Stephen, *C.*, *Cheadle*; Fraser, Christopher, *C.*, *Dorset Mid and Poole North*; Gordon, Eileen, *Lab.*, *Romford*; Jones, Fiona, *Lab.*, *Newark*; Lock, David, *Lab.*, *Wyre Forest*; McCartney, Robert, *UK Unionist*, *Down North*; McCrea, Rev. Dr William, *DUP*, *Antrim South*; Nicholls, Patrick, *C.*, *Teignbridge*; Prior, David, *C.*, *Norfolk North*; Ross, William, *UU*, *Londonderry East*; St Aubyn, Nick, *C.*, *Guildford*; Thompson, William, *UU*, *Tyrone West*; Turner, Dr. George, *Lab.*, *Norfolk North West*; Walker, Cecil, *UU*, *Belfast North*; Wynne Williams, Alan, *Lab.*, *Carmarthen East and Dinefwr*

### DEFEATED MPs BY PARTY

| | |
|---|---|
| Labour, | 7 |
| Conservative, | 6 |
| Ulster Unionist, | 3 |
| Liberal Democrat, | 2 |
| Democratic Unionist Party, | 1 |
| Independent, | 1 |
| United Kingdom Unionist, | 1 |
| TOTAL | 21 |

# Regional Government

## GREATER LONDON AUTHORITY (GLA)

Romney House, 43 Marsham Street, London SW21P 3PY
Tel: 020-7983 4000; Press Office: 020-7983 4071/4072/4090/4067/4228; Email: mayor@london.gov.uk;
Web: www.london.gov.uk

On the 7 May 1998 London voted in favour of the formation of the Greater London Authority. The first elections to the GLA were on Thursday, 4 May 2000 and the new Authority took over its responsibilities on 3 July 2000.

The structure and objectives of the GLA stem from its eight main areas of responsibility. These are transport, planning, economic development and regeneration, the environment, police, fire and emergency planning, culture and health. The bodies that co-ordinate these functions and report to the GLA are: Transport for London (TfL), London Development Agency (LDA), Metropolitan Police Authority (MPA), London Fire and Emergency Planning Authority (LFEPA). The GLA also absorbs a number of other London bodies, such as the London Planning Advisory Committee, the London Ecology Unit and the London Research Centre.

The GLA consists of a directly elected Mayor, The Mayor of London and a separately elected assembly, The London Assembly. The Mayor has the key role of decision making with the Assembly performing the tasks of regulating and scrutinising these decisions. In addition, the GLA has around 400 permanent staff to support the activities of the Mayor and the Assembly, which are overseen by a Head of Paid Service. The Mayor may appoint two political advisors but he/she may not appoint the Chief Executive the Monitoring Officer or the Chief Finance Officer. These must be appointed by the Assembly.

The Mayor is also responsible for appointing a Cabinet. The Cabinet functions as part of the Mayor's objective of eliminating barriers to effective decision making and enabling the GLA to speak with one voice on behalf of London. The function of the Mayor's Cabinet is to provide the Mayor with the most sound advice on policy and strategy. Meetings of the Cabinet are designed to be a powerful forum for discussing the issues affecting Londoners. The Cabinet is not intended to fit the Whitehall Cabinet model in that GLA members will not be bound by the convention of collective responsibility, the absence of which does not mean that the Mayor will devolve or federalise his powers. All decisions are made by the Mayor acting on the honest advice of his Cabinet. Cabinet members can be broadly categorised into (a) those with specific policy brief (e.g. in the areas of planning, policing or fire and civil defence) and (b) those who have been chosen to give advice and/or reflect political breadth.

The role of the Mayor can be broken down into a number of key areas: to represent and promote London at home and abroad and speak up for Londoners; to devise strategies and plans to tackle London-wide issues, such as transport, economic development and regeneration, air quality, noise, waste, bio-diversity, planning and culture; to set budgets for the Transport for London, the London Development Agency, the Metropolitan Police Authority and the London Fire and Emergency Planning Authority; to control new transport and economic development bodies and appoint their members; to make appointments to the new police and fire authorities; to publish regular reports on the state of the environment in London.

The role of the Assembly can be broken down into a number of key areas:

- to provide a check and balance on the Mayor
- to scrutinise the Mayor
- to have the power to amend the Mayor's budget by a majority of 2/3
- to investigate issues of London wide significance and make proposals to the Mayor
- to provide the Deputy Mayor and the members serving on the police, fire and emergency planning authorities.

### ELECTIONS AND THE VOTING SYSTEMS

The Assembly will be elected every four years at the same time as the Mayor and consists of 25 members. There is one member from each of the 14 GLA Constituencies topped up with 11 London members who are representatives of political parties or individuals standing as independent candidates.

The GLA constituencies are: Barnet and Camden; Bexley and Bromley; Brent and Harrow; City and London East, covering Barking and Dagenham and the City of London; Newham and Tower Hamlets; Croydon and Sutton; Ealing and Hillingdon; Enfield and Haringey; Greenwich and Lewisham; Havering and Redbridge; North East, covering Hackney, Islington and Waltham Forest; Lambeth and Southwark; West Central, covering Hammersmith and Fulham, Kensington and Chelsea and Westminster; South West, covering Hounslow, Kingston upon Thames and Richmond upon Thames; Merton and Wandsworth.

### FUNCTIONS AND STRUCTURE

Every aspect of the Assembly and its activities must be open to the view of the public and therefore accountable. Assembly meetings are open to the public and the reports it produces are available to the public. Other measures such as a twice yearly 'people's question time' also take place. The meetings where the Assembly questions the Mayor are also open to the public.

### FUNDING

The GLA is responsible for funding Transport for London, the London Development Agency, the Metropolitan Police Authority and the London Fire and Emergency Planning Authority. Budgets are set by the Mayor, and scrutinised by the Assembly. Funds are allocated subject to safeguards on service standards

### TRANSPORT FOR LONDON (TfL)

The TfL is run by a board of 8-15 members appointed by the Mayor. Its role is:

- to manage the buses, Croydon Tramlink and the Docklands Light Railway (DLR).
- to manage the underground once Public Private partnership contracts are in place
- to manage an important network of roads to be known as the GLA Road Network
- to regulate taxis and minicabs
- to run the London River services and promote the river for passenger and freight movement
- to help to co-ordinate the Dial-a-Ride and Taxicard schemes for door-to-door services for transport users with mobility problems
- to take responsibility for traffic lights

London Borough Councils maintain the role of highway and traffic authorities for 95 per cent of London's roads.

*Transport Commissioner for London*, Robert Kiley

### Spatial Development Strategy (SDS)

The Mayor of London is responsible for strategic planning in London in the form of a Spatial Planning Strategy. This sets priorities and provides direction for the future development of London. It replaces regional planning guidance provided by the Secretary of State. The SDS incorporates the key aspects of the many other areas of the Mayor's responsibility including sustainable development, transport, economic development, housing, the built environment, the natural and open environment, waste, town centres, cultural and community facilities, London's Capital and World City roles and the River Thames.

London Borough Councils continue to deal with all planning applications and produce development plans.

### London Development Agency (LDA)

The LDA promotes economic development and regeneration. It is one of the eight regional development agencies set up around the country to perform this task. The key aspects of the LDA's role are:

- to promote business efficiency, investment and competitiveness
- to promote employment
- to enhance the skills of local people
- to create sustainable development

The London Boroughs retain powers to promote economic development in their local areas.

### The Environment

The Mayor is required to formulate strategies to tackle London's environmental issues including the quality of water, air and land; the use of energy and London's contribution to climate change targets; ground water levels and traffic emissions; municipal waste management.

### Metropolitan Police Authority (MPA)

This body, which oversees the policing of London consists of 12 members of the assembly, including the deputy Mayor, 4 magistrates and 7 independents. One of the independents was appointed by the Home Secretary. The role of the MPA is:

- to maintain an efficient and effective police force
- to publish and annual policing plan
- to set police targets and monitor performance
- to be part of the appointment, discipline and removal of senior officers
- to be responsible for the performance budget

The boundaries of the metropolitan police districts have been changed to be in line with the 32 London boroughs. Areas beyond the GLA remit have been incorporated into the Surrey, Hertfordshire and Essex police areas. The City of London has its own police force.

### London Fire and Emergency Planning Authority (LFEPA)

On 3 July 2000 the existing London Fire and Civil defence authority became the London Fire and Emergency Planning Authority. It consists of 17 members, 9 drawn from the assembly and 8 nominated by the London Boroughs. The role of LFEPA is:

- to set the strategy for the provision of fire services
- to ensure that the fire brigade can meet all the normal requirements efficiently
- to ensure that effective arrangements are made for the fire brigade to receive emergency calls and deal with them promptly
- to ensure that information useful to the development of the fire brigades is gathered
- to assist the boroughs with their emergency planning training and exercises.

### Health

Healthcare in London continues to be the remit of the NHS and the London Ambulance Service. The NHS London Regional Office are fully supported by the GLA in its development of strategies to improve the health of Londoners.

### The Cultural Strategy Group for London (CSGL)

The GLA aims to provide a wide ranging culture strategy, encompassing the arts, sport and tourism. The CSGL provides advice and guidance to the GLA on this matter. Its role is:

- to produce a strategy for the cultural development of London
- to endorse and bid for major sporting events which London may host
- to develop the creative industries' contribution to the London economy
- to take over management of Trafalgar Square and Parliament Square
- to develop a policy for the development of tourism in London

The GLA will be housed at the temporary address shown above until its new premises are complete. The new GLA building is being built on a brown field site on the south bank of the river Thames, adjacent to Tower Bridge. The building is a distinctive glass globe with a purpose built assembly chamber and offices for 400 people. It will stand fifty metres high, with 21,700 square metres of floor space.

### Salaries *as at March 2001*

| | |
|---|---|
| *Mayor*, | £86,832 |
| *Deputy Mayor*, | £53,243 |
| *Assembly Member*, | £35,436 |

### Mayor's Advisory Cabinet

*Deputy Mayor and Spatial development and strategic planning*, Nicky Gavron
*Police*, Toby Harris
*Human rights and equalities*, Graham Tope
*Chair, London Fire and Emergency Planning Authority*, Val Shawcross
*Environment*, Darren Johnson
*City and business*, Judith Mayhew
*Homelessness*, Glenda Jackson
*Consultation and local government*, John McDonnell
*Chair of the London Development Agency*, George Barlow
*Regeneration*, Kumar Murshid
*Race relations*, Lee Jasper
*Women and equality*, Diane Abbott
*Community relations*, Richard Stone
*London Voluntary Services Council*, Sean Baine
*Disability rights*, Caroline Gooding

## GREATER LONDON ASSEMBLY MEMBERS
*as at 31 July 2001*

*The Mayor*, Ken Livingstone (*Ind.*)
Anderson, Victor (*Green*), *London List*
Arnold, Jeanette Arnold (*Lab.*) *London List*
Arbour, Anthony (*C.*), *South West*, maj. 7,059
Barnes, Richard (*C.*), *Ealing and Hillingdon*, maj. 6,812
Briggs, John (*Lab.*), *City and East*, maj. 26,121
Bloom, Louise (*LD*), *London List*
Bray, Angie (*C.*), *West Central*, maj. 18,279
Coleman, Brian (*C.*), *Barnet and Camden*, maj. 551
Duvall, Len (*Lab.*), *Greenwich and Lewisham*, maj. 17,985
Evans, Jeremy Roger (*C.*), *Havering and Redbridge*, maj. 8,269
Featherstone, Lynne (*LD*), *London List*
Gavron, Nicky (*Lab.*), *Enfield and Haringey*, maj. 3,302
Hamwee, Baroness (Sally) (*LD*), *London List*
Harris, Lord Toby (*Lab.*), *Brent and Harrow*, maj. 4,380
Heath, Samantha (*Lab.*), *London List*
Hillier, Meg (*Lab.*), *North East*, maj. 17,603
Howlett, Elizabeth (*C.*), *Merton and Wandsworth*, maj. 12,870
Johnson, Darren (*Green*), *London List*
Jones, Jennifer (*Green*), *London List*
Neill, Bob (*C.*), *Bexley and Bromley*, maj. 34,559
Ollerenshaw, Eric (*C.*), *London List*
Pelling, Andrew John (*C.*), *Croydon and Sutton*, maj. 17,087
Phillips, Trevor (*Lab.*), *London List*
Shawcross, Valerie (*Lab.*), *Lambeth and Southwark*, maj. 15,493
Tope, Graham (*LD*), *London List*

## OVERALL RESULTS IN MAYORAL ELECTION AS AT MAY 2000

| *First Pref* | *Party* | *Votes* | % |
|---|---|---|---|
| Ken Livingstone | Ind. | 667,877 | 39.0 |
| Steven Norris | C. | 464,434 | 27.1 |
| Frank Dobson | Lab. | 223,884 | 13.1 |
| Susan Kramer | LD | 203,452 | 11.9 |
| Ram Gidoomal | CPA | 42,060 | 2.4 |
| Darren Johnson | Green | 38,121 | 2.2 |
| Michael Newland | BNP | 33,569 | 2.0 |
| Damian Hockney | UK Ind | 16,234 | 1.0 |
| Geoffrey Ben-Nathan | PMSS | 9,956 | 0.6 |
| Ashwin Kumar Tanna | Ind. | 9,015 | 0.5 |
| Geoffrey Clements | Natural Law Party | 5,470 | 0.3 |
| *Second Pref* | *Party* | *Votes* | % |
| Susan Kramer | LD | 404,815 | 28.5 |
| Frank Dobson | Lab. | 228,095 | 16.0 |
| Darren Johnson | Green | 192,764 | 13.6 |
| Steven Norris | C. | 188,041 | 13.2 |
| Ken Livingstone | Ind. | 178,809 | 12.6 |
| Ram Gidoomal | CPA | 56,489 | 4.0 |
| Michael Newland | BNP | 45,337 | 3.2 |
| Damian Hockney | UK Ind. | 43,672 | 3.1 |
| Ashwin Kumar Tanna | Ind. | 41,766 | 2.9 |
| Geoffrey Ben-Nathan | PMSS | 23,021 | 1.6 |
| Geoffrey Clements | Natural Law Party | 18,185 | 1.3 |

## THE NATIONAL ASSEMBLY FOR WALES

Cathays Park, Cardiff CF1 3NQ
Tel: 029-2082 5111
National Assembly Information Line: 029-2089 8200
E-mail: webmaster@wales.gov.uk
Web: www.wales.gov.uk

In July 1997 the Government announced plans to establish a National Assembly for Wales. In a referendum on 18 September 1997 about 50 per cent of the electorate voted, of whom 50.3 per cent voted in favour of the Assembly. Elections are to be held every four years. The First elections were held on 6 May 1999 when about 46 per cent of the electorate voted. The first session was held on 10 May 1999 and the Assembly was officially opened on 26 May at Crickhowell House, Cardiff; a new building to house the Assembly is under construction in Cardiff.

The Assembly has 60 members (including the Presiding Officer), comprising 40 constituency members and 20 additional regional members from party lists. It can introduce only secondary legislation and has no power to raise or lower income tax.

The National Assembly for Wales has responsibility in Wales for ministerial functions relating to health and personal social services; education, except for terms and conditions of service and student awards; training; the Welsh language, arts and culture; the implementation of the Citizen's Charter in Wales; local government; housing; water and sewerage; environmental protection; sport; agriculture and fisheries; forestry; land use, including town and country planning and countryside and nature conservation; new towns; non-departmental public bodies and appointments in Wales; ancient monuments and historic buildings and the Welsh Arts Council; roads; tourism; financial assistance to industry; the Strategic Development Scheme in Wales and the Programme for the Valleys; and the operation of the European Regional Development Fund in Wales and other European Union matters.

SALARIES FROM 1 APRIL 2001:

| | |
|---|---|
| First Secretary | £68,158 |
| Assembly Secretary/Presiding Officer | £35,357 |
| Assembly Members | £38,000* |

*Reduced by two-thirds if the member is already an MP or an MEP

First Secretary, Assembly Member and Presiding Officer also receive the Assembly Member salary

THE WELSH CABINET
*First Secretary of the Assembly and Acting Minister for Economic Development*, Rhodri Morgan, AM
*Principal Private Secretary*, L. Conway
*Special Advisers*, P. Griffiths; M. Drakeford; Dr R. Jones; L. Punter; N. Bennett; M. Hines
*Deputy First Minister (acting)*, Jenny Randerson, AM
*Minister for Education and Lifelong Learning*, Jane Davidson, AM
*Minister for Health and Social Services*, Jane Hutt, AM
*Minister for Finance and Communities*, Edwina Hunt, AM
*Minister for Rural Affairs*, Carwyn Jones, AM
*Minister for Environment, Planning and Transport*, Sue Essex, AM
*Minister for Sport, Culture and the Welsh Language*, Jenny Randerson, AM
*Minister for Assembly Business*, Andrew Davies, AM
*Permanent Secretary (G1)*, J. D. Shortridge
*Clerk to the Assembly*, P. Silk , CB

OFFICE OF THE PRESIDING OFFICER
*Deputy Clerk (G3)*, vacant

COMMITTEE SECRETARIAT
*Grade 5*, Ms M. Knox

CABINET EXECUTIVE
*Head*, B. Mitchell

CABINET SECRETARIAT
*Grade 5*, L. Conway

OFFICE OF THE COUNSEL GENERAL
*Counsel General*, W. Roddick, QC

COMMUNICATIONS DIRECTORATE
*Head*, M. Brooke

FINANCE GROUP
*Principal Finance Officer (G3)*, D. T. Richards

## ECONOMIC AFFAIRS, TRANSPORT, PLANNING AND ENVIRONMENT

*Senior Director (G2)*, D. W. Jones

AGRICULTURE DEPARTMENT
*Head of Department (G3)*, H. D. Brodie

ECONOMIC DEVELOPMENT DEPARTMENT
*Head of Department (G3)*, D. Pritchard

## SOCIAL POLICY AND LOCAL GOVERNMENT

*Senior Director (G2)*, G. C. G. Craig

TRAINING AND EDUCATION DEPARTMENT
*Head of Department (G3)*, R. J. Davies

OFFICE OF HM CHIEF INSPECTOR FOR SCHOOLS IN WALES – ESTYN
†*Chief Inspector (G4)*, Miss S. Lewis

SOCIAL SERVICES AND COMMUNITIES GROUP
*Director*, Ms H. Thomas

LOCAL GOVERNMENT GROUP
*Head of Group (G3)*, A. Peat

NHS DIRECTORATE
*Director (G3)*, vacant

HEALTH PROTECTION AND IMPROVEMENT DIRECTORATE
*Chief Medical Officer (G3)*, Dr R. Hall
*Chief Dental Officer (G5)*, P. Langmaid
*Chief Scientific Adviser (G5)*, Dr J. A. V. Pritchard
*Chief Pharmaceutical Adviser (G5)*, Miss C. W. Howells
*Chief Environmental Health Adviser (G5)*, R. Alexander

NURSING DIVISION
*Chief Nursing Officer*, Miss R. Kennedy

TRANSPORT, PLANNING AND ENVIRONMENT GROUP
*Head of Group (G3)*, M. L. Evans
*Director of Transport (G4)*, R. Shaw

## EXECUTIVE AGENCIES

CADW: WELSH HISTORIC MONUMENTS
Crown Building, Cathays Park, Cardiff CF1 3NQ
Tel: 029-2050 0200; Fax: 029-2082 6375

Cadw supports the preservation, conservation, appreciation and enjoyment of the built heritage in Wales.
*Chief Executive*, T. Cassidy

PLANNING INSPECTORATE
Crown Buildings, Cathays Park, Cardiff CF1 3NQ
Tel: 029-2082 5150 ; Fax: 029-2082 5111
*Chief Executive and Chief Planning Inspector (G3)*, K. Powell

---

MEMBERS OF THE WELSH ASSEMBLY
AS AT MAY 2001

---

Barrett, Ms Lorraine, *Lab. Co-op., Cardiff South and Penarth*, maj. 6,803
Bates, Mick, *LD, Montgomeryshire*, maj. 5,504
Black, Peter, *LD, South Wales West region*
Bourne, Prof. Nicholas, *C., Wales Mid and West region*
Burham, Elenor, *LD, Wales North region*
Butler, Ms Rosemary, *Lab., Newport West*, maj. 4,710
Cairns, Alun, *C., South Wales West region*
Chapman, Ms Christine, *Lab. Co-op., Cynon Valley*, maj. 677
Dafis, Cynog G., *PC, Wales Mid and West region*
Davidson, Ms Jane, *Lab., Pontypridd*, maj. 1,575
Davies, Andrew, *Lab., Swansea West*, maj. 1,926
Davies, David, *C., Monmouth*, maj. 2,712
Davies, Geraint, *PC, Rhondda*, maj. 2,285
Davies, Glyn, *C., Wales Mid and West region*
Davies, Ms Janet, *PC, South Wales West region*
Davies, Ms Jocelyn, *PC, South Wales East region*
Davies, Rt. Hon. Ronald, *Lab., Caerphilly*, maj. 2,861
Edwards, Richard, *Lab., Preseli Pembrokeshire*, maj. 2,738
Elis Thomas, Dafydd, *PC, Meirionnydd Nant Conwy*, maj. 8,742
Essex, Ms Sue, *Lab., Cardiff North*, maj. 2,304
Evans, Delyth, *Lab., Wales Mid and West region*
Feld, Ms Val, *Lab., Swansea East*, maj. 3,781
German, Michael, *LD, South Wales East region*
Gibbons, Brian, *Lab., Aberavon*, maj. 6,743
Graham, William, *C., South Wales East region*
Gregory, Ms Janice, *Lab., Ogmore*, maj. 4,565
Griffiths, John, *Lab. Co-op., Newport East*, maj. 5,111

Gwyther, Ms Christine, *Lab.*, *Carmarthen West and Pembrokeshire South*, maj. 1,492
Halford, Ms Alison, *Lab.*, *Delyn*, maj. 5,417
Hancock, Brian, *PC*, *Islwyn*, maj. 604
Hart, Ms Edwina, *Lab.*, *Gower*, maj. 3,160
Hutt, Ms Jane, *Lab.*, *Vale of Glamorgan*, maj. 926
Jarman, Ms Pauline, *PC*, *South Wales Central region*
Jones, Ms Ann, *Lab.*, *Vale of Clwyd*, maj. 3,341
Jones, Carwyn, *Lab.*, *Bridgend*, maj. 4,258
Jones, Elin, *PC*, *Ceredigion*, maj. 10,249
Jones, Gareth, *PC*, *Conwy*, maj. 114
Jones, Ms Helen Mary, *PC*, *Llanelli*, maj. 688
Jones, Ieuan W., *PC*, *Ynys Môn*, maj. 9,288
Law, Peter, *Lab. Co-op.*, *Blaenau Gwent*, maj. 10,568
Lewis, Huw, *Lab. Co-op.*, *Merthyr Tydfil and Rhymney*, maj. 4,214
Lloyd, Dr David, *PC*, *South Wales West region*
Marek, John, Ph.D., *Lab.*, *Wrexham*, maj. 6,472
Melding, David, *C.*, *South Wales Central region*
Middlehurst, Tom, *Lab.*, *Alyn and Deeside*, maj. 6,359
Morgan, H. Rhodri, *Lab.*, *Cardiff West*, maj. 10,859
Morgan, Jonathan, *C.*, *South Wales Central region*
Neagle, Ms Lynne, *Lab.*, *Torfaen*, maj. 5,285
Pugh, Alun, *Lab.*, *Clwyd West*, maj. 760
Randerson, Ms Jenny, *LD*, *Cardiff Central*, maj. 3,168
Richards, Rod, *C.*, *Wales North region*
Rogers, Peter, *C.*, *Wales North region*
Ryder, Ms Janet, *PC*, *Wales North region*
Sinclair, Ms Karen, *Lab.*, *Clwyd South*, maj. 3,685
Thomas, Ms Gwenda, *Lab.*, *Neath*, maj. 2,618
Thomas, Owen John, *PC*, *South Wales Central region*
Thomas, Rhodri, *PC*, *Carmarthen East and Dinefwr*, maj. 6,980
Wigley, Rt. Hon. Dafydd, *PC*, *Caernarfon*, maj. 12,273
Williams, Ms Kirsty, *LD*, *Brecon and Radnorshire*, maj. 5,852
Williams, Dr Phil, *PC*, *South Wales East region*

STATE OF THE PARTIES *as at May 2001*

| | Constituency AMs | Regional AMs | Total |
|---|---|---|---|
| Labour | 27 | 1 | 28 |
| Plaid Cymru | 8† | 8 | 16† |
| Conservative | 1 | 8 | 9 |
| Liberal Democrats | 3 | 3 | 6 |
| The Presiding Officer (The Lord Elis-Thomas) | 1 | 0 | 1 |

† Excludes the Presiding Officer, who has no party allegiance while in post

# Welsh Assembly AS AT JULY 2001

## CONSTITUENCIES

ABERAVON (S. WALES WEST)
*E.* 49,786 *T.* 46.79%

| | |
|---|---|
| B. Gibbons, *Lab.* | 11,941 |
| Ms J. Davies, *PC* | 5,198 |
| K. Davies, *LD* | 3,165 |
| Ms M. E. Davies, *C.* | 1,624 |
| Beany, *Bean* | 849 |
| D. Pudner, *United Soc.* | 517 |

*Lab. majority* 6,743

ALYN AND DEESIDE (WALES N.)
*E.* 59,386 *T.* 32.04%

| | |
|---|---|
| T. Middlehurst, *Lab.* | 9,772 |
| N. Formstone, *C.* | 3,413 |
| Ms A. Owen, *PC* | 2,304 |
| J. Clarke, *LD* | 1,879 |
| J. Cooksey, *Ind.* | 1,333 |
| G. Davies, *Comm.* | 329 |

*Lab. majority* 6,359

BLAENAU GWENT (S. WALES EAST)
*E.* 53,919 *T.* 48.21%

| | |
|---|---|
| P. Law, *Lab. Co-op.* | 16,069 |
| P. Williams, *PC* | 5,501 |
| K. Rogers, *LD* | 2,980 |
| D. Thomas, *C.* | 1,444 |

*Lab. Co-op. majority* 10,568

BRECON AND RADNORSHIRE (WALES MID AND W.)
*E.* 51,166 *T.* 57.10%

| | |
|---|---|
| Ms K. Williams, *LD* | 13,022 |
| N. Bourne, *C.* | 7,170 |
| I. Janes, *Lab. Co-op.* | 5,165 |
| D. Patterson, *PC* | 2,356 |
| M. Shaw, *Ind.* | 1,502 |

*LD majority* 5,852

BRIDGEND (S. WALES WEST)
*E.* 60,234 *T.* 41.56%

| | |
|---|---|
| C. Jones, *Lab.* | 9,321 |
| A. Cairns, *C.* | 5,063 |
| J. Canning, *PC* | 4,919 |
| R. Humphreys, *LD* | 3,910 |
| A. Jones, *Ind.* | 1,819 |

*Lab. majority* 4,258

CAERNARFON (WALES N.)
*E.* 47,213 *T.* 60.32%

| | |
|---|---|
| D. Wigley, *PC* | 18,748 |
| T. Jones, *Lab.* | 6,475 |
| Ms B. Naish, *C.* | 2,464 |
| D. Shankland, *LD* | 791 |

*PC majority* 12,273

CAERPHILLY (S. WALES EAST)
*E.* 65,997 *T.* 43.20%

| | |
|---|---|
| R. Davies, *Lab.* | 12,602 |
| R. Gough, *PC* | 9,741 |
| M. German, *LD* | 3,543 |
| Ms M. Taylor, *C.* | 2,213 |
| T. Richards, *United Soc.* | 412 |

*Lab. majority* 2,861

CARDIFF CENTRAL (S. WALES CENTRAL)
*E.* 57,815 *T.* 44.75%

| | |
|---|---|
| Ms J. Randerson, *LD* | 10,937 |
| M. Drakeford, *Lab.* | 7,769 |
| O. J. Thomas, *PC* | 3,795 |
| S. Jones, *C.* | 3,034 |
| J. Goss, *United Soc.* | 338 |

*LD majority* 3,168

CARDIFF NORTH (S. WALES CENTRAL)
*E.* 61,398 *T.* 51.33%

| | |
|---|---|
| Ms S. Essex, *Lab.* | 12,198 |
| J. Morgan, *C.* | 9,894 |
| A. Meikle, *LD* | 5,088 |
| C. Mann, *PC* | 4,337 |

*Lab. majority* 2,304

CARDIFF SOUTH AND PENARTH (S. WALES CENTRAL)
*E.* 61,149 *T.* 37.67%

| | |
|---|---|
| Ms L. Barrett, *Lab. Co-op.* | 11,057 |
| Ms M. Davies, *C.* | 4,254 |
| J. Rowlands, *PC* | 3,931 |
| Ms J. Maw-Cornish, *LD* | 2,890 |
| D. Bartlett, *United Soc.* | 355 |
| J. Foreman, *Ind. Lab.* | 339 |
| T. Davies, *Celtic All.* | 210 |

*Lab. Co-op. majority* 6,803

CARDIFF WEST (S. WALES CENTRAL)
*E.* 57,717 *T.* 40.22%

| | |
|---|---|
| R. Morgan, *Lab.* | 14,305 |
| Ms M. Boult, *C.* | 3,446 |
| Ms E. Bush, *PC* | 3,402 |
| D. Garrow-Smith, *LD* | 2,063 |

*Lab. majority* 10,859

CARMARTHEN EAST AND DINEFWR (WALES MID AND W.)
*E.* 53,634 *T.* 60.88%

| | |
|---|---|
| R. Thomas, *PC* | 17,328 |
| C. Llewellyn, *Lab.* | 10,348 |
| Ms H. Stoddart, *C.* | 2,776 |
| Ms J. Hughes, *LD* | 2,202 |

*PC majority* 6,980

CARMARTHEN WEST AND PEMBROKESHIRE SOUTH (WALES MID AND W.)
*E.* 55,655 *T.* 50.58%

| | |
|---|---|
| Ms C. Gwyther, *Lab.* | 9,891 |

R. Llewellyn, *PC* 8,399
D. Edwards, *C.* 5,079
E. Davies, *Ind.* 2,090
R. Williams, *LD* 1,875
G. Fry, *TFPW* 815
*Lab. majority* 1,492

CEREDIGION (WALES MID AND W.)
*E.* 55,311 *T.* 57.67%
E. Jones, *PC* 15,258
Ms M. Battle, *Lab.* 5,009
D. Lloyd Evans, *Ind.* 4,114
D. Evans, *LD* 3,571
H. Lloyd Davies, *C.* 2,944
D. Bradney, *Green* 1,002
*PC majority* 10,249

CLWYD SOUTH (WALES N.)
*E.* 53,843 *T.* 40.51%
Ms K. Sinclair, *Lab.* 9,196
H. Williams, *PC* 5,511
D. R. Jones, *C.* 4,167
D. Burnham, *LD* 2,432
M. Jones, *United Soc.* 508
*Lab. majority* 3,685

CLWYD WEST (WALES N.)
*E.* 53,952 *T.* 46.77%
A. Pugh, *Lab.* 7,824
R. Richards, *C.* 7,064
Ms E. Williams, *PC* 6,886
Ms R. Feeley, *LD* 3,462
*Lab. majority* 760

CONWY (WALES N.)
*E.* 55,189 *T.* 49.11%
G. Jones, *PC* 8,285
Ms C. Sherrington, *Lab.* 8,171
D. I. Jones, *C.* 5,006
*Ms C. Humphreys, *LD* 4,480
G. Edwards, *Ind.* 1,160
*PC majority* 114
**C. Humphreys resigned in April 2001. Replaced by Ms E. Burham.*

CYNON VALLEY (S. WALES CENTRAL)
*E.* 47,619 *T.* 45.50%
Ms C. Chapman, *Lab. Co-op.* 9,883
P. Richards, *PC* 9,206
Ms A. Willott, *LD* 1,531
E. Hayward, *C.* 1,046
*Lab. Co-op. majority* 677

DELYN (WALES N.)
*E.* 54,047 *T.* 44.13%
Ms A. Halford, *Lab.* 10,672
Ms K. Lumley, *C.* 5,255
Ms M. Ellis, *PC* 4,837
Ms E. Burnham, *LD* 3,089
*Lab. majority* 5,417

GOWER (S. WALES WEST)
*E.* 58,523 *T.* 47.33%
Ms E. Hart, *Lab.* 9,813
D. Jones, *PC* 6,653
A. Jones, *C.* 3,912
H. Evans, *LD* 3,260
R. Lewis, *Ind.* 2,307
I. Richard, *PRP* 1,755
*Lab. majority* 3,160

ISLWYN (S. WALES EAST)
*E.* 50,600 *T.* 47.29%
B. Hancock, *PC* 10,042
S. Williams, *Lab.* 9,438
Ms C. Bennett, *LD* 2,351
C. Stevens, *C.* 1,621
I. Thomas, *United Soc.* 475
*PC majority* 604

LLANELLI (WALES MID AND W.)
*E.* 58,371 *T.* 48.63%
Ms H. M. Jones, *PC* 11,973
Ms A. Garrard, *Lab. Co-op.* 11,285
T. Dumper, *LD* 2,920
B. Harding, *C.* 1,864
A. Popham, *Ind.* 345
*PC majority* 688

MEIRIONNYDD NANT CONWY (WALES MID AND W.)
*E.* 32,922 *T.* 57.33%
D. Elis Thomas, *PC* 12,034
Ms D. Jones, *Lab.* 3,292
O. J. Williams, *C.* 2,170
G. Worley, *LD* 1,378
*PC majority* 8,742

MERTHYR TYDFIL AND RHYMNEY (S. WALES EAST)
*E.* 55,858 *T.* 44.91%
H. Lewis, *Lab. Co-op.* 11,024
A. Cox, *PC* 6,810
A. Rogers, *Ind.* 3,746
E. Jones, *LD* 1,682
Ms C. Hyde, *C.* 1,246
M. Jenkins, *United Soc.* 580
*Lab. Co-op. majority* 4,214

MONMOUTH (S. WALES EAST)
*E.* 61,999 *T.* 51.13%
D. Davies, *C.* 12,950
Ms C. Short, *Lab.* 10,238
C. Lines, *LD* 4,639
M. Hubbard, *PC* 1,964
A. Carrington, *TFPW* 1,911
*C. majority* 2,712

MONTGOMERYSHIRE (WALES MID AND W.)
*E.* 43,386 *T.* 49.41%
M. Bates, *LD* 10,374
G. Davies, *C.* 4,870
D. Senior, *PC* 3,554
C. Hewitt, *Lab.* 2,638
*LD majority* 5,504

NEATH (S. WALES WEST)
*E.* 56,085 *T.* 47.95%
Ms G. Thomas, *Lab.* 12,234
T. Jones, *PC* 9,616
D. Davies, *LD* 2,631
Ms J. Chambers, *C.* 1,895
N. Duncan, *United Soc.* 519
*Lab. majority* 2,618

NEWPORT EAST (S. WALES EAST)
*E.* 54,196 *T.* 35.45%
J. Griffiths, *Lab. Co-op.* 9,497
M. Major, *C.* 4,386
A. Cameron, *LD* 2,684
C. Holland, *PC* 2,647
*Lab. Co-op. majority* 5,111

NEWPORT WEST (S. WALES EAST)
*E.* 57,243 *T.* 42.34%
Ms R. Butler, *Lab.* 11,538
W. Graham, *C.* 6,828
R. Vickery, *PC* 3,053
Ms V. Watkins, *LD* 2,820
*Lab. majority* 4,710

OGMORE (S. WALES WEST)
*E.* 51,998 *T.* 41.54%
Ms J. Gregory, *Lab.* 10,407
J. Rogers, *PC* 5,842
R. Hughes, *Ind.* 2,439
Ms S. Waye, *LD* 1,496
C. Smart, *C.* 1,415
*Lab. majority* 4,565

PONTYPRIDD (S. WALES CENTRAL)
*E.* 64,597 *T.* 45.71%
Ms J. Davidson, *Lab.* 11,330
B. Hancock, *PC* 9,755
G. Orsi, *LD* 5,240
Ms S. Ingerfield, *C.* 2,485
P. Phillips, *Ind.* 436
R. Griffiths, *Comm.* 280
*Lab. majority* 1,575

PRESELI PEMBROKESHIRE (WALES MID AND W.)
*E.* 54,225 *T.* 53.63%
R. Edwards, *Lab.* 9,977
C. Bryant, *PC* 7,239
F. Aubel, *C.* 6,585
D. Lloyd, *LD* 3,338
A. Luke, *Ind.* 1,944
*Lab. majority* 2,738

RHONDDA (S. WALES CENTRAL)
*E.* 55,398 *T.* 50.22%
G. Davies, *PC* 13,558
W. David, *Lab.* 11,273
M. Williams, *LD* 1,303
G. Summers, *Ind.* 913
P. Hobbins, *C.* 774
*PC majority* 2,285

SWANSEA EAST (S. WALES WEST)
*E.* 57,766 *T.* 36.07%
*Ms V. Feld, *Lab.* 9,495
J. Ball, *PC* 5,714
P. Black, *LD* 3,963
W.Hughes, *C.* 1,663
*Lab. majority* 3,781
**Awaiting by-election results following the death of Ms Feld, See Stop Press*

SWANSEA WEST (S. WALES WEST)
*E.* 59,369 *T.* 39.97%
A. Davies, *Lab.* 8,217
D. Lloyd, *PC* 6,291
P. Valerio, *C.* 3,643
J. Newbury, *LD* 3,543
D. Evans, *Ind.* 996
J. Harris, *PRP* 774
A. Thraves, *United Soc.* 263
*Lab. majority* 1,926

TORFAEN (S. WALES EAST)
*E.* 61,037 *T.* 39.19%

| | |
|---|---|
| Ms L. Neagle, *Lab.* | 9,080 |
| M. Gough, *Ind. Lab.* | 3,795 |
| Ms I. Nutt, *Ind.* | 2,828 |
| N. Turner, *PC* | 2,614 |
| Ms J. Gray, *LD* | 2,614 |
| Ms K. Thomas, *C.* | 2,152 |
| S. Smith, *Local Soc.* 839 | |

*Lab. majority* 5,285

VALE OF CLWYD (WALES N.)
*E.* 51,124 *T.* 43.43%

| | |
|---|---|
| Ms A. Jones, *Lab.* | 8,359 |
| R. Salisbury, *C.* | 5,018 |
| Ms S. Brynach, *PC* | 4,295 |
| G. Clague, *Dem. All.* | 1,908 |
| P. Lloyd, *LD* | 1,376 |
| D. Roberts, *Ind.* | 661 |
| D. Pennant, *Ind.* | 586 |

*Lab. majority* 3,341

VALE OF GLAMORGAN (S. WALES CENTRAL)
*E.* 67,804 *T.* 48.31%

| | |
|---|---|
| Ms J. Hutt, *Lab.* | 11,448 |
| D. Melding, *C.* | 10,522 |
| C. Franks, *PC* | 7,848 |
| F. Little, *LD* | 2,938 |

*Lab. majority* 926

WREXHAM (WALES N.)
*E.* 50,932 *T.* 34.19%

| | |
|---|---|
| J. Marek, *Lab.* | 9,239 |
| Ms C. O'Toole, *LD* | 2,767 |
| Ms F. Elphick, *C.* | 2,747 |
| Ms J. Ryder, *PC* | 2,659 |

*Lab. majority* 6,472

YNYS MON (WALES N.)
*E.* 52,571 *T.* 59.56%

| | |
|---|---|
| I. W. Jones, *PC* | 16,469 |
| A. Owen, *Lab.* | 7,181 |
| P. Rogers, *C.* | 6,031 |
| J. Clarke, *LD* | 1,630 |

*PC majority* 9,288

## REGIONS

SOUTH WALES CENTRAL
*E.* 473,494 *T.* 45.51%

| | |
|---|---|
| *Lab.* | 79,564 (36.92%) |
| *PC* | 58,080 (26.95%) |
| *C.* | 34,944 (16.22%) |
| *LD* | 30,911 (14.35%) |
| *Green* | 5,336 (2.48%) |
| *Soc. Lab.* | 2,822 (1.31%) |
| *Ind. Matt.* | 1,524 (0.71%) |
| *NLP* | 665 (0.31%) |
| *Comm.* | 652 (0.30%) |
| *United Soc.* | 602 (0.28%) |
| *Ind. Phill.* | 378 (0.18%) |

*Lab. majority* 21,484
(May 1997, Lab. maj. 131,398)
Additional Members elected: J. Morgan, *C.*; D. Melding, *C.*; Ms P. Jarman, *PC*; O. J. Thomas, *PC*

SOUTH WALES EAST
*E.* 460,846 *T.* 43.95%

| | |
|---|---|
| *Lab.* | 83,953 (41.45%) |
| *PC* | 49,139 (24.26%) |
| *C.* | 33,947 (16.76%) |
| *LD* | 24,757 (12.22%) |
| *Soc. Lab.* | 4,879 (2.41%) |
| *Green* | 4,055 (2.00%) |
| *United Soc.* | 903 (0.45%) |
| *NLP* | 898 (0.44%) |

*Lab. majority* 34,814
(May 1997, Lab. maj. 163,134)
Additional Members elected: W. Graham, *C.*; M. German, *LD*; Ms J. Davies, *PC*; Dr P. Williams, *PC*

SOUTH WALES WEST
*E.* 393,758 *T.* 42.44%

| | |
|---|---|
| *Lab.* | 70,625 (42.26%) |
| *PC* | 50,757 (30.37%) |
| *C.* | 20,993 (12.56%) |
| *LD* | 18,527 (11.09%) |
| *Green* | 4,082 (2.44%) |
| *United Soc.* | 1,257 (0.75%) |
| *NLP* | 676 (0.40%) |
| *PRP* | 204 (0.12%) |

*Lab. majority* 19,868
(May 1997, Lab. maj. 142,286)
Additional Members elected: A. Cairns, *C.*; P. Black, *LD*; Dr D. Lloyd, *PC*; Ms J. Davies, *PC*

WALES MID AND WEST
*E.* 404,667 *T.* 54.21%

| | |
|---|---|
| *PC* | 84,554 (38.55%) |
| *Lab.* | 53,842 (24.55%) |
| *C.* | 36,622 (16.70%) |
| *LD* | 31,683 (14.44%) |
| *Green* | 7,718 (3.52%) |
| *Soc. Lab.* | 3,019 (1.38%) |
| *Ind. Turner* | 1,214 (0.55%) |
| *NLP* | 705 (0.32%) |

*PC majority* 30,712
(May 1997, Lab. maj. 52,382)
Additional Members elected: G. Davies, *C.*; Prof. N. Bourne, *C.*; *A. Michael, *Lab.*; C. Dafis, *PC*
**A. Michael resigned in March 2000. Replaced by D. Evans.*

WALES NORTH
*E.* 478,252 *T.* 45.06%

| | |
|---|---|
| *Lab.* | 73,673 (34.19%) |
| *PC* | 69,518 (32.26%) |
| *C.* | 41,700 (19.35%) |
| *LD* | 22,130 (10.27%) |
| *Green* | 4,667 (2.17%) |
| *Rhuddlan* | 1,353 (0.63%) |
| *NLP* | 917 (0.43%) |
| *United Soc.* | 828 (0.38%) |
| *Comm.* | 714 (0.33%) |

*Lab. majority* 4,155
(May 1997, Lab. maj. 80,590)
Additional Members elected: P. Rogers, *C.*; R. Richards, *C.*; Ms C. Humphreys, *LD*; Ms J. Ryder, *PC*
**C. Humpreys resigned in April 2001. Replaced by Ms E. Burham.*

## THE SCOTTISH PARLIAMENT

Edinburgh EH99 1SP. Tel: 0131-348 5000;
Web www.scotland.gov.uk

In July 1997 the Government announced plans to establish a Scottish Parliament. In a referendum on 11 September 1997 about 62 per cent of the electorate voted, of whom 74.3 per cent voted in favour of the Parliament and 63.5 in favour of its having tax-raising powers. Elections are to be held every four years. The first elections were held on 6 May 1999 when about 59 per cent of the electorate voted. The first session was held on 12 May 1999 and the Scottish Parliament was officially opened on 1 July 1999 at the Edinburgh Assembly Hall; a new building to house the Parliament is under construction in Edinburgh.

The Scottish Parliament has 129 members (including the Presiding Officer), comprising 73 constituency members and 56 additional regional members from party lists. It can introduce primary legislation and has the power to raise or lower the basic rate of income tax by up to three pence in the pound.

The Scottish Parliament is responsible for: education, health, law, environment, economic development, local government, housing, police, fire services, planning, financial assistance to industry, tourism, some transport, heritage and the arts, agriculture, forestry, food standards.

SALARIES FROM 1 APRIL 2001:

| | |
|---|---|
| First Minister | £68,159* |
| Ministers | £35,358* |
| Lord Advocate | £86,103 |
| Solicitor-General for Scotland | £73,684 |
| Junior Ministers | £18,342* |
| MSPs | £42,493† |
| Presiding Officer | £35,358 |
| Deputy Presiding Officers | £18,342 |

*In addition to the MSP salary
†Reduced by two-thirds if the member is already an MP or an MEP

## THE SCOTTISH EXECUTIVE

St Andrew's House, Regent Road, Edinburgh EH1 3DG
Tel: 0131-556 8400; E-mail: ceu@scotland.gov.uk
Web: www.scotland.gov.uk

The Scottish Executive is responsible in Scotland for all matters not reserved to Westminster under devolution, including education, health, social work, law and order, agriculture and the environment. In addition there are a number of Scottish departments for which the Executive has some degree of responsibility; these include the Scottish Courts Administration, the General Register Office, the National Archives of Scotland (formerly the Scottish Record Office) and the Department of the Registers of Scotland.

*First Minister*, The Rt. Hon. Henry McLeish, MSP (*Lab.*)
*Deputy First Minister and Minister for Justice*, Jim Wallace, QC, MSP (*LD*)
*Finance Minister*, Jack McConnell, MSP (*Lab.*)
*Minister for Health and Community Care*, Susan Deacon, MSP (*Lab.*)
*Minister for Transport and Planning*, Sarah Boyack, MSP (*Lab.*)
*Minister for Enterprise and Lifelong Learning*, Wendy Alexander, MSP (*Lab.*)
*Minister for Finance and Local Government*, Angus MacKay, MSP (*Lab.*)
*Minister for Environment and Rural Development*, Ross Finnie, MSP (*LD*)
*Minister for Education, Europe and External and External Affairs*, Jack McConnell MSP (*Lab.*)
*Minister for Parliament and Chief Whip*, Tom McCabe, MSP (*Lab.*)
*Lord Advocate*, Colin Boyd, QC
*Solicitor General*, Neil Davidson, QC

### JUNIOR MINISTERS (NOT MEMBERS OF THE SCOTTISH EXECUTIVE)

*Deputy Minister for Social Justice*, Margaret Curran, MSP (*Lab.*)
*Deputy Minister for Community Care*, Iain Gray, MSP
*Deputy Minister for Finance and Local Government*, Peter Peacock, MSP (*Lab.*)
*Deputy Minister Health and Community Care*, Malcolm Chisholm, MSP (*Lab.*)
*Deputy Minister for Enterprise and Lifelong Learning*, Alasdair Morrison, MSP
*Deputy Minister for Education, Europe and External Affairs*, Nicol Stephen, MSP (*Lab.*)
*Deputy Minister for Sport*, The Arts and Culture, Allan Wilson, MSP (*Lab.*)
*Deputy Minister for Environment and Rural Development*, Rhonda Brankin, MSP (*Lab.*)
*Deputy Minister for Parliament and Whip*, Euan Robertson, MSP (*LD*)

## SCOTTISH EXECUTIVE CORPORATE SERVICES

16 Waterloo Place, Edinburgh EH1 3DN
Tel: 0131-556 8400

*Principal Establishment Officer (SCS)*, Mrs A. Robson
*Head of Personnel (SCS)*, Dr Ingrid Clayden

### DIRECTORATE OF ADMINISTRATIVE SERVICES

Saughton House, Broomhouse Drive, Edinburgh EH11 3DX
Tel: 0131-556 8400

*Director of Administrative Services (SCS)*, J. Meldrum
*Director of Information Technology (SCS)*, P. Gray
*Director of Procurement and Commercial Services*, N. Bowd
*Director of Corporate Development*, I. Walford
*Director of Accommodation*, P. A. Rhodes
*Chief Quantity Surveyor (SCS)*, A. J. Wyllie
*Head of Procurement (SCS)*, N. Bowd

## SCOTTISH EXECUTIVE FINANCE

Victoria Quay, Edinburgh EH6 6QQ
Tel: 0131-556 8400

*Principal Finance Officer (SCS)*, Dr P. S. Collings
*Head of Accountancy Services Unit*, I. M. Smith

## SCOTTISH EXECUTIVE SECRETARIAT

St Andrew's House, Regent Road, Edinburgh EH1 3DG
Tel: 0131-556 8400

*Head of Secretariat*, R. S. B. Gordon, CB
*Constitutional Policy and Parliamentary Secretariat*, C. M. A. Lugton
*Head, Cabinet Secretariat*, B. Campbell
*Head, Audit Unit*, W.T. Tait
*Head of Accountancy Services Unit*, I. M. Smith
*Head, External Relations*, B. Doig
*Head, Brussels Office*, G. Calder
*Chief Economic Adviser*, A. W. Goudie
*Legal Secretary to the Lord Advocate*, P. J. Layden
*Head, Equality and Voluntary Issues*, V. M. Macniven

### SCOTTISH EXECUTIVE POLICY UNIT

*Head of Unit (SCS)*, P. J. Rycroft

### SCOTTISH EXECUTIVE INFORMATION DIRECTORATE

For the Scottish Executive and certain UK services in Scotland

*Head of New Media Presentation (SCS)*, R. Williams
*Head of News*, O. D. Kelly

### SOLICITOR'S OFFICE

*Solicitor (SCS)*, R. M. Henderson
*Deputy Solicitor (SCS)*, J. S. G. Maclean

## SCOTTISH EXECUTIVE RURAL AFFAIRS DEPARTMENT

Pentland House, 47 Robb's Loan, Edinburgh EH14 1TY
Tel: 0131-556 8400

*Head of Department (SCS)*, J. S. Graham
*Group Heads (SCS)*, D. J. Crawley (*Food and Agriculture*); S. F. Hampson (*Environment*); A. J. Rushworth (*Agriculture and Biological Research*); A. J. Robertson (*Chief Agriculture Officer*)
*Chief Agricultural Economist*, A. Moxey
*Chief Food and Dairy Officer*, S. D. Rooke
*Senior Principal Scientific Officers*, Dr Linda Saunderson; Dr Maureen Bruce

### EXECUTIVE AGENCIES

#### FISHERIES RESEARCH SERVICES

Marine Laboratory, PO Box 101, Victoria Road, Aberdeen AB11 9DB
Tel: 01224-876544; Fax: 01224-295511

*Chief Executive*, Dr A. D. Hawkins
*Deputy Director*, Dr R. Stagg

#### SCOTTISH AGRICULTURAL SCIENCE AGENCY

82 Craigs Road, East Craig, Edinburgh EH12 8NJ
Tel: 0131-244 8890; Fax: 0131-244 8988

*Director*, Dr R. K. M. Hay

#### SCOTTISH FISHERIES PROTECTION AGENCY

Pentland House, 47 Robb's Loan, Edinburgh EH14 1TY
Tel: 0131-556 8400; Fax: 0131-244 6086

*Chief Executive*, Capt. P. Du Vivier, RN

## SCOTTISH EXECUTIVE DEVELOPMENT DEPARTMENT

Victoria Quay, Edinburgh EH6 6QQ
Tel: 0131-556 8400

*Head of Department (SCS)*, K. MacKenzie, CB
*Heads of Groups (SCS)*, D. J. Belfall; J. S. B. Martin
*Senior Economic Adviser (SCS)*, N. Jackson

PROFESSIONAL STAFF
*Chief Planner (SCS)*, J. MacKinnon

INQUIRY REPORTERS
2 Greenside Lane, Edinburgh EH1 3AG
Tel: 0131-244 5649; Fax: 0131-244 5680

*Chief Reporter (SCS)*, R. M. Hickman

TRUNK ROADS DESIGN AND CONSTRUCTION DIVISION
Victoria Quay, Edinburgh EH6 6QQ
Tel: 0131-556 8400

*Chief Engineers (SCS)*, J. A. Howison (*Roads*); N. B. MacKenzie (*Bridges*)

## SCOTTISH EXECUTIVE EDUCATION DEPARTMENT

Victoria Quay, Edinburgh EH6 6QQ
Tel: 0131-556 8400

*Secretary (SCS)*, J. Elvidge
*Under-Secretaries (SCS)*, Mrs G. Stewart; Dr M. Ewart; Ms I. Low
*Chief Statistician (SCS)*, R. C. Wishart
*Chief Architect (SCS)*, J. E. Gibbons, Ph.D., FSA Scot.
*Chief Inspector of Social Work Services*, A. Skinner
*Assistant Chief Inspectors*, V. A. Cox ; D. Perrott; I. C. Robertson

HM INSPECTORS OF SCHOOLS
*Senior Chief Inspector (SCS)*, D. A. Osler
*Depute Senior Chief Inspectors (SCS)*, G. H. C. Donaldson
*Chief Inspectors (SCS)*, P. Banks; J. Boyes; W. C. Calder; F. Crawford; Miss K. M. Fairweather; A. S. McGlynn; H. M. Stalker

EXECUTIVE AGENCIES

HISTORIC SCOTLAND
Longmore House, Salisbury Place, Edinburgh EH9 1SH
Tel: 0131-668 8600; Fax: 0131-668 8699

*Chief Executive (G3)*, G. N. Munro

SCOTTISH PUBLIC PENSIONS AGENCY
St Margaret's House, 151 London Road, Edinburgh EH8 7TG
Tel: 0131-556 8400; Fax: 0131-244 3334

*Chief Executive*, R. Garden

## SCOTTISH EXECUTIVE ENTERPRISE AND LIFELONG LEARNING DEPARTMENT

Meridian Court, 5 Cadogan Street, Glasgow G2 6AT
Tel 0141-248 2855

*Secretary (SCS)*, E. Frizzell
*Under Secretary (SCS)*, vacant
*Industrial Adviser*, D. B. Blair
*Scientific Adviser*, Prof. D. J. Tedford

ECONOMIC DEVELOPMENT, ADVICE AND EMPLOYMENT ISSUES
*Under-Secretaries (SCS)*, M. B. Foulis

ENTERPRISE AND INDUSTRIAL EXPANSION
Meridian Court, 5 Cadogan Street, Glasgow G2 6AT
Tel: 0141-248 2855

*Under-Secretary (SCS)*, S. Hampson
*Industrial Adviser*, D. Blair

LIFELONG LEARNING GROUP
Europa House, 450 Argyle Street G2 8LG
Tel: 0141-248 2855
*Under Secretary (SCS)*, E. J. Weeple

LOCATE IN SCOTLAND
120 Bothwell Street, Glasgow G2 7JP
Tel: 0141-248 2700

*Director (SCS)*, M. Togneri

SCOTTISH TRADE INTERNATIONAL
120 Bothwell Street, Glasgow G2 7JP
Tel: 0141-248 2700

*Director*, D. Taylor

EXECUTIVE AGENCY

STUDENT AWARDS AGENCY FOR SCOTLAND
Gyleview House, 3 Redheughs Rigg, Edinburgh EH12 9HH
Tel: 0131-476 8212; Fax: 0131-244 5887

*Chief Executive*, K. MacRae

## SCOTTISH EXECUTIVE HEALTH DEPARTMENT

St Andrew's House, Edinburgh EH1 3DG
Tel: 0131-244 2410

NATIONAL HEALTH SERVICE IN SCOTLAND MANAGEMENT EXECUTIVE
*Chief Executive (SCS)*, T. Jones
*Director of Nursing*, Miss A. Jarvie
*Chief Medical Officer*, Dr M. Armstrong
*Head of Community Care*, T. Teale
*Chief Pharmacist (SCS)*, W. Scott
*Chief Scientist*, Prof. Roland Young
*Chief Dental Officer*, T. R. Watkins

PUBLIC HEALTH POLICY UNIT
*Director*, Geofrey Robinson
*Head of Policy and Chief Medical Officer (SCS)*, Dr Armstrong Keel

STATE HOSPITAL
Carstairs Junction, Lanark ML11 8RP
Tel: 01555-840293

*Chairman*, D. N. James
*General Manager*, R. Manson

COMMON SERVICES AGENCY
Trinity Park House, South Trinity Road, Edinburgh EH5 3SE
Tel: 0131-552 6255

*Chairman*, G. R. Scaife, CB
*General Manager*, Dr F. Gibb

## SCOTTISH EXECUTIVE JUSTICE DEPARTMENT

Saughton House, Broomhouse Drive, Edinburgh EH11 3XD
Tel: 0131-556 8400

*Secretary (SCS)*, J. Gallagher
*Under-Secretaries (SCS)*, C. Baxter; N. G. Campbell; V. Macniven

SOCIAL WORK AND SERVICES GROUP AND INSPECTORATE
James Craig Walk, Edinburgh EH1 3BA
Tel: 0131-556 8400

*Under Secretary (SCS)*, Mrs G. M. Stewart
*Chief Inspector of Social Work and Services for Scotland*, A. Skinner

OTHER APPOINTMENTS
*HM Chief Inspector of Constabulary*, W. Taylor, QPM
*HM Chief Inspector of Prisons*, C. Fairweather, OBE
*Commandant, Scottish Police College*, H. I. Watson, OBE, QPM
*HM Chief Inspector of Fire Services*, D. Davis, CBE, QFSM
*Head of Training, Scottish Fire Service Training School*, J. Robson

## OFFICE OF THE SCOTTISH PARLIAMENTARY COUNSEL

Victoria Quay, Edinburgh EH6 6QQ
Tel: 0131-556 8400

*First Scottish Parliamentary Counsel*, J. C. McCluskie, CB, QC
*Scottish Parliamentary Counsel*, G. M. Clark; C. A. M. Wilson

## PRIVATE LEGISLATION OFFICE UNDER THE PRIVATE LEGISLATION PROCEDURE (SCOTLAND) ACT 1936

50 Frederick Street, Edinburgh EH2 1EN
Tel: 0131-226 6499

*Senior Counsel*, G. S. Douglas, QC
*Junior Counsel*, N. M. P. Morrison

EXECUTIVE AGENCIES

NATIONAL ARCHIVES OF SCOTLAND

REGISTERS OF SCOTLAND

SCOTTISH PRISON SERVICE

GENERAL REGISTER OFFICE FOR SCOTLAND
New Register House, Edinburgh EH1 3YT
Tel: 0131-334 0380; Fax: 0131-314 4400;
Web www.gro-scotland.gov.uk

*Registrar-General (SCS)*, J. N. Randall

MENTAL WELFARE COMMISSION FOR SCOTLAND
K Floor, Argyle House, 3 Lady Lawson Street, Edinburgh EH3 9SH
Tel: 0131-222 6111

*Chairman*, I. J. Miller, OBE
*Vice-Chairman*, Mrs N. Bennie

## MEMBERS OF THE SCOTTISH PARLIAMENT

Adam, Brian, *SNP, Scotland North East region*
Aitken, William, *C., Glasgow region*
Alexander, Ms Wendy, *Lab., Paisley North*, maj. 4,616
Baillie, Ms Jackie, *Lab., Dumbarton*, maj. 4,758
Barrie, Scott, *Lab., Dunfermline West*, maj. 5,021
Boyack, Ms Sarah, *Lab., Edinburgh Central*, maj. 4,626
Brankin, Ms Rhona, *Lab. Co-op., Midlothian*, maj. 5,525
Brown, Robert, *LD, Glasgow region*
Butler, Bill, *Lab., Glasgow Anniesland*, maj. 5,376
Campbell, Colin, *SNP, Scotland West region*
Canavan, Dennis A., MP, *Lab., Falkirk West*, maj. 12,192
Chisholm, Malcolm G. R., MP, *Lab., Edinburgh North and Leith*, maj. 7,736
Craigie, Ms Cathy, *Lab., Cumbernauld and Kilsyth*, maj. 4,259
Crawford, Bruce, *SNP, Scotland Mid and Fife region*
Cunningham, Ms Roseanna, MP, *SNP, Perth*, maj. 2,027
Curran, Ms Margaret, *Lab., Glasgow Baillieston*, maj. 3,072
Davidson, David, *C., Scotland North East region*
Deacon, Ms Susan, *Lab., Edinburgh East and Musselburgh*, maj. 6,714
Selkirk of Douglas, The Lord, PC, QC, *C., Lothians region*
Eadie, Ms Helen, *Lab. Co-op., Dunfermline East*, maj. 8,699
Elder, Ms Dorothy, *SNP, Glasgow region*
Ewing, Fergus, *SNP, Inverness East, Nairn and Lochaber*, maj. 441
Ewing, Mrs Margaret A., MP, *SNP, Moray*, maj. 4,129
Ewing, Dr Winnifred, *SNP, Highlands and Islands region*
Fabiani, Ms Linda, *SNP, Scotland Central region*
Farquhar-Munro, John, *LD, Ross, Skye and Inverness West*, maj. 1,539
Ferguson, Ms Patricia, *Lab., Glasgow Maryhill*, maj. 4,326
Fergusson, Alex, *C., Scotland South region*
Finnie, Ross, *LD, Scotland West region*
Fitzpatrick, Brian, *Lab., Strathkelvin and Bearsden*, maj. 7,829
Fraser, Murdo, *C., Scotland Mid and Fife region*
Gallie, Phil, *C., Scotland South region*
Gibson, Kenneth, *SNP, Glasgow region*
Gillon, Ms Karen, *Lab., Clydesdale*, maj. 3,880 *(elected as Karen Turnbull)*
Godman, Ms Patricia, *Lab., Renfrewshire West*, maj. 2,893
Goldie, Miss Annabel, *C., Scotland West region*
Gorrie, Donald C. E., MP, OBE, *LD, Scotland Central region*
Grahame, Ms Christine, *SNP, Scotland South region (elected as Christine Creech)*
Grant, Ms Rhoda, *Lab., Highlands and Islands region*
Gray, Iain, *Lab., Edinburgh Pentlands*, maj. 2,885
Hamilton, Duncan, *SNP, Highlands and Islands region*
Harding, Keith, *C., Scotland Mid and Fife region*
Harper, Robin, *Green, Lothians region*
Henry, Hugh, *Lab., Paisley South*, maj. 4,495
Home Robertson, John D., MP, *Lab., East Lothian*, maj. 10,946
Hughes, Ms Janice, *Lab., Glasgow Rutherglen*, maj. 7,287
Hyslop, Ms Fiona, *SNP, Lothians region*
Ingram, Adam, *SNP, Scotland South region*
Jackson, Gordon, QC, *Lab., Glasgow Govan*, maj. 1,756
Jackson, Dr Sylvia, *Lab., Stirling*, maj. 3,981
Jamieson, Ms Cathy, *Lab. Co-op., Carrick, Cumnock and Doon Valley*, maj. 8,803
Jamieson, Ms Margaret, *Lab., Kilmarnock and Loudoun*, maj. 2,760
Jenkins, Ian, *LD, Tweeddale, Ettrick and Lauderdale*, maj. 4,478
Johnstone, Alex, *C., Scotland North East region*
Kerr, Andy, *Lab., East Kilbride*, maj. 6,499
Lamont, Johann, *Lab. Co-op., Glasgow Pollock*, maj. 4,642
Livingstone, Ms Marilyn, *Lab. Co-op., Kirkcaldy*, maj. 4,475
Lochhead, Richard, *SNP, Scotland North East region*
Lyon, George, *LD, Argyll and Bute*, maj. 2,057
McAllion, John, MP, *Lab., Dundee East*, maj. 2,854
MacAskill, Kenny, *SNP, Lothians region*
McAveety, Frank, *Lab. Co-op., Glasgow Shettleston*, maj. 5,467
McCabe, Tom, *Lab., Hamilton South*, maj. 7,176
McConnell, Jack, *Lab., Motherwell and Wishaw*, maj. 5,076
Macdonald, Lewis, *Lab., Aberdeen Central*, maj. 2,696
MacDonald, Ms Margo, *SNP, Lothians region*

MacGrigor, Jamie, *C., Highlands and Islands region*
McGugan, Ms Irene, *SNP, Scotland North East region*
Macintosh, Ken, *Lab., Eastwood*, maj. 2,125
McIntosh, Mrs Lindsay, *C., Scotland Central region*
MacKay, Angus, *Lab., Edinburgh South*, maj. 5,424
MacLean, Ms Kate, *Lab., Dundee West*, maj. 121
McLeish, Henry B., MP, *Lab., Fife Central*, maj. 8,675
McLeod, Ms Fiona, *SNP, Scotland West region*
McLetchie, David, *C., Lothians region*
McMahon, Michael, *Lab., Hamilton North and Bellshill*, maj. 5,606
Macmillan, Ms Maureen, *Lab., Highlands and Islands region*
McNeil, Duncan, *Lab., Greenock and Inverclyde*, maj. 4,313
McNeill, Ms Pauline, *Lab., Glasgow Kelvin*, maj. 4,408
McNulty, Des, *Lab., Clydebank and Milngavie*, maj. 4,710
Martin, Paul, *Lab., Glasgow Springburn*, maj. 7,893
Marwick, Ms Tricia, *SNP, Scotland Mid and Fife region*
Matheson, Michael, *SNP, Scotland Central region*
Monteith, Brian, *C., Scotland Mid and Fife region*
Morgan, Alasdair N., MP, *SNP, Galloway and Upper Nithsdale*, maj. 3,201
Morrison, Alasdair, *Lab., Western Isles*, maj. 2,093
Muldoon, Bristow, *Lab., Livingston*, maj. 3,904
Mulligan, Ms Mary, *Lab., Linlithgow*, maj. 2,928
Mundell, David, *C., Scotland South region*
Murray, Dr Elaine, *Lab., Dumfries*, maj. 3,654
Neil, Alex, *SNP, Scotland Central region*
Oldfather, Ms Irene, *Lab., Cunninghame South*, maj. 6,541
Paterson, Gil, *SNP, Scotland Central region*
Peacock, Peter, *Lab., Highlands and Islands region*
Peattie, Ms Cathy, *Lab., Falkirk East*, maj. 4,139
Quinan, Lloyd, *SNP, Scotland West region*
Radcliffe, Ms Nora, *LD, Gordon*, maj. 4,195
Raffan, Keith, *LD, Scotland Mid and Fife region*
Reid, George, *SNP, Scotland Mid and Fife region*
Robison, Ms Shona, *SNP, Scotland North East region*
Robson, Euan, *LD, Roxburgh and Berwickshire*, maj. 3,585
Rumbles, Mike, *LD, Aberdeenshire West and Kincardine*, maj. 2,289
Russell, Michael, *SNP, Scotland South region*
Scanlon, Mrs Mary, *C., Highlands and Islands region*
Scott, John, *C., Ayr*, maj. 3,344
Scott, Tavish, *LD, Shetland*, maj. 3,194
Sheridan, Tommy, *SSP, Glasgow region*
Simpson, Richard, *Lab., Ochil*, maj. 1,303
Smith, Ms Elaine, *Lab., Coatbridge and Chryston*, maj. 10,404
Smith, Iain, *LD, Fife North East*, maj. 5,064
Smith, Ms Margaret, *LD, Edinburgh West*, maj. 4,583
Steel, Rt. Hon. Sir David (The Lord Steel of Aikwood), KBE, PC, *LD, Lothians region*
Stephen, Nicol, *LD, Aberdeen South*, maj. 1,760
Stone, Jamie, *LD, Caithness, Sutherland and Easter Ross*, maj. 4,391
Sturgeon, Ms Nicola, *SNP, Glasgow region*
Swinney, John R., MP, *SNP, Tayside North*, maj. 4,192
Thomson, Ms Elaine, *Lab., Aberdeen North*, maj. 398
Tosh, Murray, *C., Scotland South region*
Ullrich, Ms Kay, *SNP, Scotland West region*
Wallace, Ben, *C., Scotland North East region*
Wallace, James R., MP, QC, *LD, Orkney*, maj. 4,619
Watson, Mike (The Lord Watson of Invergowrie), *Lab., Glasgow Cathcart*, maj. 5,374
Welsh, Andrew P., MP, *SNP, Angus*, maj. 8,901
White, Ms Sandra, *SNP, Glasgow region*
Whitefield, Ms Karen, *Lab., Airdrie and Shotts*, maj. 8,985
Wilson, Allan, *Lab., Cunninghame North*, maj. 4,796
Wilson, Andrew, *SNP, Scotland Central region*
Young, John, OBE, *C., Scotland West region*

STATE OF THE PARTIES *as at July 2001*

| | Constituency MSPs | Regional MSPs | Total |
|---|---|---|---|
| Scottish Labour Party | 52 | 3 | 55 |
| Scottish National Party | 7 | 28 | 35 |
| Scottish Conservative and Unionist Party | 1 | 18 | 19 |
| Scottish Liberal Democrats | 12 | 4† | 16† |
| Scottish Green Party | 0 | 1 | 1 |
| Scottish Socialist Party | 0 | 1 | 1 |
| Independent (Dennis Canavan) | 1 | 0 | 1 |
| The Presiding Officer (Rt. Hon. Sir David Steel, KBE, MSP) | 0 | 1 | 1 |

† *Excludes the Presiding Officer, who has no party allegiance while in post*

*Deputy Presiding Officers*, Patricia Ferguson, MSP (*Lab.*); George Reid, MSP (*SNP*)

# Scottish Parliament

## CONSTITUENCIES

ABERDEEN CENTRAL
*(Scotland North East region)*
*E.* 52,715 *T.* 50.26%

| | |
|---|---|
| L. Macdonald, *Lab.* | 10,305 |
| R. Lochhead, *SNP* | 7,609 |
| Ms E. Anderson, *LD* | 4,403 |
| T. Mason, *C.* | 3,655 |
| A. Cumbers, *SSP* | 523 |

*Lab. majority* 2,696

ABERDEEN NORTH
*(Scotland North East region)*
*E.* 54,553 *T.* 51.00%

| | |
|---|---|
| Ms E. Thomson, *Lab.* | 10,340 |
| B. Adam, *SNP* | 9,942 |
| J. Donaldson, *LD* | 4,767 |
| I. Haughie, *C.* | 2,772 |

*Lab. majority* 398

ABERDEEN SOUTH
*(Scotland North East region)*
*E.* 60,579 *T.* 57.26%

| | |
|---|---|
| N. Stephen, *LD* | 11,300 |
| M. Elrick, *Lab.* | 9,540 |
| Ms N. Milne, *C.* | 6,993 |
| Ms I. McGugan, *SNP* | 6,651 |
| S. Sutherland, *SWP* | 206 |

*LD majority* 1,760

ABERDEENSHIRE WEST AND KINCARDINE
*(Scotland North East region)*
*E.* 60,702 *T.* 58.87%

| | |
|---|---|
| M. Rumbles, *LD* | 12,838 |
| B. Wallace, *C.* | 10,549 |
| Ms M. Watt, *SNP* | 7,699 |
| G. Guthrie, *Lab.* | 4,650 |

*LD majority* 2,289

AIRDRIE AND SHOTTS
*(Scotland Central region)*
*E.* 58,481 *T.* 56.79%

| | |
|---|---|
| Ms K. Whitefield, *Lab.* | 18,338 |
| G. Paterson, *SNP* | 9,353 |
| P. Ross-Taylor, *C.* | 3,177 |
| D. Miller, *LD* | 2,345 |

*Lab. majority* 8,985

ANGUS
*(Scotland North East region)*
*E.* 59,891 *T.* 57.66%

| | |
|---|---|
| A. Welsh, *SNP* | 16,055 |
| R. Harris, *C.* | 7,154 |
| I. McFatridge, *Lab.* | 6,914 |
| R. Speirs, *LD* | 4,413 |

*SNP majority* 8,901

ARGYLL AND BUTE
*(Highlands and Islands region)*
*E.* 49,609 *T.* 64.86%

| | |
|---|---|
| G. Lyon, *LD* | 11,226 |
| D. Hamilton, *SNP* | 9,169 |
| H. Raven, *Lab.* | 6,470 |

D. Petrie, *C.* 5,312
*LD majority* 2,057

AYR
*(Scotland South region)*
*E.* 56,338 *T.* 66.48%
I. Welsh, *Lab.* 14,263
P. Gallie, *C.* 14,238
R. Mullin, *SNP* 7,291
Ms E. Morris, *LD* 1,662
*Lab. majority* 25
By-election held on 16 March 2000 *see* p 284

BANFF AND BUCHAN
*(Scotland North East region)*
*E.* 57,639 *T.* 55.06%
A. Salmond, *SNP* 16,695
D. Davidson, *C.* 5,403
M. Mackie, *LD* 5,315
Ms M. Harris, *Lab.* 4,321
*SNP majority* 11,292
By-election held on 7 June 2001 *see* p 284

CAITHNESS, SUTHERLAND AND EASTER ROSS
*(Highlands and Islands region)*
*E.* 41,581 *T.* 62.60%
J. Stone, *LD* 10,691
J. Hendry, *Lab.* 6,300
Ms J. Urquhart, *SNP* 6,035
R. Jenkins, *C.* 2,167
J. Campbell, *Ind.* 554
E. Stewart, *Ind.* 282
*LD majority* 4,391

CARRICK, CUMNOCK AND DOON VALLEY
*(Scotland South region)*
*E.* 65,580 *T.* 62.66%
Ms C. Jamieson, *Lab. Co-op.* 19,667
A. Ingram, *SNP* 10,864
J. Scott, *C.* 8,123
D, Hannay, *LD* 2,441
*Lab. Co-op. majority* 8,803

CLYDEBANK AND MILNGAVIE
*(Scotland West region)*
*E.* 52,461 *T.* 63.55%
D. McNulty, *Lab.* 15,105
J. Yuill, *SNP* 10,395
R. Ackland, *LD* 4,149
Ms D. Luckhurst, *C.* 3,688
*Lab. majority* 4,710

CLYDESDALE
*(Scotland South region)*
*E.* 64,262 *T.* 60.61%
Ms K. Turnbull, *Lab.* 16,755
Ms A. Winning, *SNP* 12,875
C. Cormack, *C.* 5,814
Ms S. Grieve, *LD* 3,503
*Lab. majority* 3,880

COATBRIDGE AND CHRYSTON
*(Scotland Central region)*
*E.* 52,178 *T.* 57.87%
Ms E. Smith, *Lab.* 17,923
P. Kearney, *SNP* 7,519
G. Lind, *C.* 2,867
Ms J. Hook, *LD* 1,889
*Lab. majority* 10,404

CUMBERNAULD AND KILSYTH
*(Scotland Central region)*
*E.* 49,395 *T.* 61.97%
Ms C. Craigie, *Lab.* 15,182
A. Wilson, *SNP* 10,923
H. O'Donnell, *LD* 2,029
R. Slack, *C.* 1,362
K. McEwan, *SSP* 1,116
*Lab. majority* 4,259

CUNNINGHAME NORTH
*(Scotland West region)*
*E.* 55,867 *T.* 59.95%
A. Wilson, *Lab.* 14,369
Ms K. Ullrich, *SNP* 9,573
M. Johnston, *C.* 6,649
C. Irving, *LD* 2,900
*Lab. majority* 4,796

CUNNINGHAME SOUTH
*(Scotland South region)*
*E.* 50,443 *T.* 56.06%
Ms I. Oldfather, *Lab.* 14,936
M. Russell, *SNP* 8,395
M. Tosh, *C.* 3,229
S. Ritchie, *LD* 1,717
*Lab. majority* 6,541

DUMBARTON
*(Scotland West region)*
*E.* 56,090 *T.* 61.86%
Ms J. Baillie, *Lab.* 15,181
L. Quinan, *SNP* 10,423
D. Reece, *C.* 5,060
P. Coleshill, *LD* 4,035
*Lab. majority* 4,758

DUMFRIES
*(Scotland South region)*
*E.* 63,162 *T.* 60.93%
Ms E. Murray, *Lab.* 14,101
D. Mundell, *C.* 10,447
S.Norris, *SNP* 7,625
N. Wallace, *LD* 6,309
*Lab. majority* 3,654

DUNDEE EAST
*(Scotland North East region)*
*E.* 57,222 *T.* 55.33%
J. McAllion, *Lab.* 13,703
Ms S. Robison, *SNP* 10,849
I. Mitchell, *C.* 4,428
R. Lawrie, *LD* 2,153
H. Duke, *SSP* 530
*Lab. majority* 2,854

DUNDEE WEST
*(Scotland North East region)*
*E.* 55,725 *T.* 52.19%
Ms K. MacLean, *Lab.* 10,925
C. Cashley, *SNP* 10,804
G. Buchan, *C.* 3,345
Ms E. Dick, *LD* 2,998
J. McFarlane, *SSP* 1,010
*Lab. majority* 121

DUNFERMLINE EAST
*(Scotland Mid and Fife region)*
*E.* 52,087 *T.* 56.94%
Ms H. Eadie, *Lab. Co-op.* 16,576
D. McCarthy, *SNP* 7,877
Ms C. Ruxton, *C.* 2,931
F. Lawson, *LD* 2,275
*Lab. Co-op. majority* 8,699

DUNFERMLINE WEST
*(Scotland Mid and Fife region)*
*E.* 53,112 *T.* 57.75%
S. Barrie, *Lab.* 13,560
D. Chapman, *SNP* 8,539
Ms E. Harris, *LD* 5,591
J. Mackie, *C.* 2,981
*Lab. majority* 5,021

EAST KILBRIDE
*(Scotland Central region)*
*E.* 66,111 *T.* 62.49%
A. Kerr, *Lab.* 19,987
Ms L. Fabiani, *SNP* 13,488
C. Stevenson, *C.* 4,465
E. Hawthorn, *LD* 3,373
*Lab. majority* 6,499

EAST LOTHIAN
*(Scotland South region)*
*E.* 58,579 *T.* 64.16%
J. Home Robertson, *Lab.* 19,220
C. Miller, *SNP* 8,274
Ms C. Richard, *C.* 5,941
Ms J. Hayman, *LD* 4,147
*Lab. majority* 10,946

EASTWOOD
*(Scotland West region)*
*E.* 67,248 *T.* 67.51%
K. Macintosh, *Lab.* 16,970
J. Young, *C.* 14,845
Ms R. Findlay, *SNP* 8,760
Ms A. McCurley, *LD* 4,472
M. Tayan, *Ind.* 349
*Lab. majority* 2,125

EDINBURGH CENTRAL
*(Lothians region)*
*E.* 65,945 *T.* 56.73%
Ms S. Boyack, *Lab.* 14,224
I. McKee, *SNP* 9,598
A. Myles, *LD* 6,187
Ms J. Low, *C.* 6,018
K. Williamson, *SSP* 830
B. Allingham, *Ind. Dem.* 364
W. Wallace, *Braveheart* 191
*Lab. majority* 4,626

EDINBURGH EAST AND MUSSELBURGH
*(Lothians region)*
*E.* 60,167 *T.* 61.48%
Ms S. Deacon, *Lab.* 17,086
K. MacAskill, *SNP* 10,372
J. Balfour, *C.* 4,600
Ms M. Thomas, *LD* 4,100
D. White, *SSP* 697
M. Heavey, *Ind. You* 134
*Lab. majority* 6,714

EDINBURGH NORTH AND LEITH
*(Lothians region)*
*E.* 62,976 *T.* 58.19%
M. Chisholm, *Lab.* 17,203
Ms A. Dana, *SNP* 9,467
J. Sempill, *C.* 5,030
S. Tombs, *LD* 4,039
R. Brown, *SSP* 907
*Lab. majority* 7,736

EDINBURGH PENTLANDS
(*Lothians region*)
*E.* 60,029 *T.* 65.97%

| | |
|---|---|
| I. Gray, *Lab.* | 14,343 |
| D. McLetchie, *C.* | 11,458 |
| S. Gibb, *SNP* | 8,770 |
| I. Gibson, *LD* | 5,029 |

*Lab. majority* 2,885

EDINBURGH SOUTH
(*Lothians region*)
*E.* 64,100 *T.* 62.61%

| | |
|---|---|
| A. MacKay, *Lab.* | 14,869 |
| Ms M. MacDonald, *SNP* | 9,445 |
| M. Pringle, *LD* | 8,961 |
| I. Whyte, *C.* | 6,378 |
| W. Black, *SWP* | 482 |

*Lab. majority* 5,424

EDINBURGH WEST
(*Lothians region*)
*E.* 61,747 *T.* 67.34%

| | |
|---|---|
| Ms M. Smith, *LD* | 15,161 |
| Lord J. Douglas-Hamilton, *C.* | 10,578 |
| Ms C. Fox, *Lab.* | 8,860 |
| G. Sutherland, *SNP* | 6,984 |

*LD majority* 4,583

FALKIRK EAST
(*Scotland Central region*)
*E.* 57,345 *T.* 61.40%

| | |
|---|---|
| Ms C. Peattie, *Lab.* | 15,721 |
| K. Brown, *SNP* | 11,582 |
| A. Orr, *C.* | 3,399 |
| G. McDonald, *LD* | 2,509 |

R. Stead, *Soc. Lab.* 1,643
V. MacGrain, *SFPP* 358
*Lab. majority* 4,139

FALKIRK WEST
(*Scotland Central region*)
*E.* 53,404 *T.* 63.04%
D. Canavan, *Falkirk W.* 18,511

| | |
|---|---|
| R. Martin, *Lab.* | 6,319 |
| M. Matheson, *SNP* | 5,986 |
| G. Miller, *C.* | 1,897 |
| A. Smith, *LD* | 954 |

*Falkirk W. majority* 12,192

FIFE CENTRAL
(*Scotland Mid and Fife region*)
*E.* 58,850 *T.* 55.82%

| | |
|---|---|
| H. McLeish, *Lab.* | 18,828 |
| Ms P. Marwick, *SNP* | 10,153 |
| Ms J. A. Liston, *LD* | 1,953 |
| K. Harding, *C.* | 1,918 |

*Lab. majority* 8,675

FIFE NORTH EAST
(*Scotland Mid and Fife region*)
*E.* 60,886 *T.* 59.03%

| | |
|---|---|
| I. Smith, *LD* | 13,590 |
| E. Brocklebank, *C.* | 8,526 |
| C. Welsh, *SNP* | 6,373 |
| C. Milne, *Lab.* | 5,175 |
| D. Macgregor, *Ind.* | 1,540 |
| R. Beveridge, *Ind.* | 737 |

*LD majority* 5,064

GALLOWAY AND UPPER NITHSDALE
(*Scotland South region*)
*E.* 53,057 *T.* 66.56%

| | |
|---|---|
| A. Morgan, *SNP* | 13,873 |
| A. Fergusson, *C.* | 10,672 |
| J. Stevens, *Lab.* | 7,209 |
| Ms J. Mitchell, *LD* | 3,562 |

*SNP majority* 3,201

GLASGOW ANNIESLAND
(*Glasgow region*)
*E.* 54,378 *T.* 52.37%

| | |
|---|---|
| D. Dewar, *Lab.* | 16,749 |
| K. Stewart, *SNP* | 5,756 |
| W. Aitken, *C.* | 3,032 |
| I. Brown, *LD* | 1,804 |
| Ms A. Lynch, *SSP* | 1,000 |
| E. Boyd, *Soc. Lab.* | 139 |

*Lab. majority* 10,993
By-election held on 23 November 2000 *see* p 284

GLASGOW BAILLIESTON
(*Glasgow region*)
*E.* 49,068 *T.* 48.32%

| | |
|---|---|
| Ms M. Curran, *Lab.* | 11,289 |
| Ms D. Elder, *SNP* | 8,217 |
| J. McVicar, *SSP* | 1,864 |
| Ms K. Pickering, *C.* | 1,526 |
| Ms J. Fryer, *LD* | 813 |

*Lab. majority* 3,072

GLASGOW CATHCART
(*Glasgow region*)
*E.* 51,338 *T.* 52.55%

| | |
|---|---|
| M. Watson, *Lab.* | 12,966 |
| Ms M. Whitehead, *SNP* | 7,592 |
| Ms M. Leishman, *C.* | 3,311 |
| C. Dick, *LD* | 2,187 |
| R. Slorach, *SWP* | 920 |

*Lab. majority* 5,374

GLASGOW GOVAN
(*Glasgow region*)
*E.* 53,257 *T.* 49.52%

| | |
|---|---|
| G. Jackson, *Lab.* | 11,421 |
| Ms N. Sturgeon, *SNP* | 9,665 |
| Ms T. Ahmed-Sheikh, *C.* | 2,343 |
| M. Aslam Khan, *LD* | 1,479 |
| C. McCarthy, *SSP* | 1,275 |

J. Foster, *Comm. Brit.* 190
*Lab. majority* 1,756

GLASGOW KELVIN
(*Glasgow region*)
*E.* 61,207 *T.* 46.34%

| | |
|---|---|
| Ms P. McNeill, *Lab.* | 12,711 |
| Ms S. White, *SNP* | 8,303 |
| Ms M. Craig, *LD* | 3,720 |
| A. Rasul, *C.* | 2,253 |
| Ms H. Ritchie, *SSP* | 1,375 |

*Lab. majority* 4,408

GLASGOW MARYHILL
(*Glasgow region*)
*E.* 56,469 *T.* 40.75%

| | |
|---|---|
| Ms P. Ferguson, *Lab.* | 11,455 |
| W. Wilson, *SNP* | 7,129 |
| Ms C. Hamblen, *LD* | 1,793 |
| G. Scott, *SSP* | 1,439 |
| M. Fry, *C.* | 1,194 |

*Lab. majority* 4,326

GLASGOW POLLOCK
(*Glasgow region*)
*E.* 47,970 *T.* 54.37%

| | |
|---|---|
| J. Lamont, *Lab. Co-op.* | 11,405 |
| K. Gibson, *SNP* | 6,763 |
| T. Sheridan, *SSP* | 5,611 |
| R. O'Brien, *C.* | 1,370 |
| J. King, *LD* | 931 |

*Lab. Co-op. majority* 4,642

GLASGOW RUTHERGLEN
(*Glasgow region*)
*E.* 51,012 *T.* 56.89%

| | |
|---|---|
| Ms J. Hughes, *Lab.* | 13,442 |
| T. Chalmers, *SNP* | 6,155 |
| R. Brown, *LD* | 5,798 |
| I. Stewart, *C.* | 2,315 |
| W. Bonnar, *SSP* | 832 |

J. Nisbet, *Soc. Lab.* 481
*Lab. majority* 7,287

GLASGOW SHETTLESTON
(*Glasgow region*)
*E.* 50,592 *T.* 40.58%

| | |
|---|---|
| F. McAveety, *Lab. Co-op.* | 11,078 |
| J. Byrne, *SNP* | 5,611 |
| Ms R. Kane, *SSP* | 1,640 |
| C. Bain, *C.* | 1,260 |
| L. Clarke, *LD* | 943 |

*Lab. Co-op. majority* 5,467

GLASGOW SPRINGBURN
(*Glasgow region*)
*E.* 55,670 *T.* 43.77%

| | |
|---|---|
| P. Martin, *Lab.* | 14,268 |
| J. Brady, *SNP* | 6,375 |
| M. Roxburgh, *C.* | 1,293 |
| M. Dunnigan, *LD* | 1,288 |
| J. Friel, *SSP* | 1,141 |

*Lab. majority* 7,893

GORDON
(*Scotland North East region*)
*E.* 59,497 *T.* 56.51%

| | |
|---|---|
| Ms N. Radcliffe, *LD* | 12,353 |
| A. Stronach, *SNP* | 8,158 |
| A. Johnstone, *C.* | 6,602 |
| Ms G. Carlin-Kulwicki, *Lab.* | 3,950 |
| H. Watt, *Ind.* | 2,559 |

*LD majority* 4,195

GREENOCK AND INVERCLYDE
(*Scotland West region*)
*E.* 48,584 *T.* 58.95%

| | |
|---|---|
| D. McNeil, *Lab.* | 11,817 |
| R. Finnie, *LD* | 7,504 |
| I. Hamilton, *SNP* | 6,762 |
| R. Wilkinson, *C.* | 1,699 |
| D. Landels, *SSP* | 857 |

*Lab. majority* 4,313

HAMILTON NORTH AND BELLSHILL
(*Scotland Central region*)
*E.* 53,992 *T.* 57.82%

| | |
|---|---|
| M. McMahon, *Lab.* | 15,227 |
| Ms K. McAlorum, *SNP* | 9,621 |
| S. Thomson, *C.* | 3,199 |
| Ms J. Struthers, *LD* | 2,105 |
| Ms K. McGavigan, *Soc. Lab.* | 1,064 |

*Lab. majority* 5,606

HAMILTON SOUTH
(*Scotland Central region*)
*E.* 46,765 *T.* 55.43%

T. McCabe, *Lab.* 14,098
A. Ardrey, *SNP* 6,922
Ms M. Mitchell, *C.* 2,918
J. Oswald, *LD* 1,982
*Lab. majority* 7,176

INVERNESS EAST, NAIRN AND LOCHABER
*(Highlands and Islands region)*
*E.* 66,285 *T.* 63.10%
F. Ewing, *SNP* 13,825
Ms J. Aitken, *Lab.* 13,384
D. Fraser, *LD* 8,508
Ms M. Scanlon, *C.* 6,107
*SNP majority* 441

KILMARNOCK AND LOUDOUN
*(Scotland Central region)*
*E.* 61,454 *T.* 64.03%
Ms M. Jamieson, *Lab.* 17,345
A. Neil, *SNP* 14,585
L. McIntosh, *C.* 4,589
J. Stewart, *LD* 2,830
*Lab. majority* 2,760

KIRKCALDY
*(Scotland Mid and Fife region)*
*E.* 51,640 *T.* 54.88%
M. Livingstone, *Lab. Co-op.* 13,645
S. Hosie, *SNP* 9,170
M. Scott-Hayward, *C.* 2,907
J. Mainland, *LD* 2,620
*Lab. Co-op. majority* 4,475

LINLITHGOW
*(Lothians region)*
*E.* 54,262 *T.* 62.26%
Ms M. Mulligan, *Lab.* 15,247
S. Stevenson, *SNP* 12,319
G. Lindhurst, *C.* 3,158
J. Barrett, *LD* 2,643
Ms I. Ovenstone, *Ind.* 415
*Lab. majority* 2,928

LIVINGSTON
*(Lothians region)*
*E.* 62,060 *T.* 58.93%
B. Muldoon, *Lab.* 17,313
G. McCarra, *SNP* 13,409
D. Younger, *C.* 3,014
M. Oliver, *LD* 2,834
*Lab. majority* 3,904

MIDLOTHIAN
*(Lothians region)*
*E.* 48,374 *T.* 61.51%
Ms R. Brankin, *Lab. Co-op.* 14,467
A. Robertson, *SNP* 8,942
J. Elder, *LD* 3,184
G. Turnbull, *C.* 2,544
D. Pryde, *Ind.* 618
*Lab. Co-op. majority* 5,525

MORAY
*(Highlands and Islands region)*
*E.* 58,388 *T.* 57.50%
Mrs M. Ewing, *SNP* 13,027
A. Farquharson, *Lab.* 8,898
A. Findlay, *C.* 8,595
Ms P. Kenton, *LD* 3,056
*SNP majority* 4,129

MOTHERWELL AND WISHAW
*(Scotland Central region)*
*E.* 52,613 *T.* 57.71%
J. McConnell, *Lab.* 13,955
J. McGuigan, *SNP* 8,879
W. Gibson, *C.* 3,694
J. Milligan, *Soc. Lab.* 1,941
R. Spillane, *LD* 1,895
*Lab. majority* 5,076

OCHIL
*(Scotland Mid and Fife region)*
*E.* 57,083 *T.* 64.58%
R. Simpson, *Lab.* 15,385
G. Reid, *SNP* 14,082
*N. Johnston, *C.* 4,151
Earl of Mar and Kellie, *LD* 3,249
*Lab. majority* 1,303
*N. Johnston resigned on 10 August 2001. He was replaced by Murdo Fraser

ORKNEY
*(Highlands and Islands region)*
*E.* 15,658 *T.* 56.95%
J. Wallace, *LD* 6,010
C. Zawadzki, *C.* 1,391
J. Mowat, *SNP* 917
A. Macleod, *Lab.* 600
*LD majority* 4,619

PAISLEY NORTH
*(Scotland West region)*
*E.* 49,020 *T.* 56.61%
Ms W. Alexander, *Lab.* 13,492
I. Mackay, *SNP* 8,876
P. Ramsay, *C.* 2,242
Ms T. Mayberry, *LD* 2,133
Ms F. Macdonald, *SSP* 1,007
*Lab. majority* 4,616

PAISLEY SOUTH
*(Scotland West region)*
*E.* 53,637 *T.* 57.15%
H. Henry, *Lab.* 13,899
W. Martin, *SNP* 9,404
S. Callison, *LD* 2,974
Ms S. Laidlaw, *C.* 2,433
P. Mack, *Ind.* 1,273
Ms J. Forrest, *SWP* 673
*Lab. majority* 4,495

PERTH
*(Scotland Mid and Fife region)*
*E.* 61,034 *T.* 61.27%
Ms R. Cunningham, *SNP* 13,570
I. Stevenson, *C.* 11,543
Ms J. Richards, *Lab.* 8,725
C. Brodie, *LD* 3,558
*SNP majority* 2,027

RENFREWSHIRE WEST
*(Scotland West region)*
*E.* 52,452 *T.* 64.89%
Ms P. Godman, *Lab.* 12,708
C. Campbell, *SNP* 9,815
Ms A. Goldie, *C.* 7,243
N. Ascherson, *LD* 2,659
A. McGraw, *Ind.* 1,136
P. Clark, *SWP* 476
*Lab. majority* 2,893

ROSS, SKYE AND INVERNESS WEST
*(Highlands and Islands region)*
*E.* 55,845 *T.* 63.42%
J. Farquhar-Munro, *LD* 11,652
D. Munro, *Lab.* 10,113
J. Mather, *SNP* 7,997
J. Scott, *C.* 3,351
D. Briggs, *Ind.* 2,302
*LD majority* 1,539

ROXBURGH AND BERWICKSHIRE
*(Scotland South region)*
*E.* 47,639 *T.* 58.52%
E. Robson, *LD* 11,320
A. Hutton, *C.* 7,735
S. Crawford, *SNP* 4,719
Ms S. McLeod, *Lab.* 4,102
*LD majority* 3,585

SHETLAND
*(Highlands and Islands region)*
*E.* 16,978 *T.* 58.77%
T. Scott, *LD* 5,435
J. Wills, *Lab.* 2,241
W. Ross, *SNP* 1,430
G. Robinson, *C.* 872
*LD majority* 3,194

STIRLING
*(Scotland Mid and Fife region)*
*E.* 52,904 *T.* 67.68%
Ms S. Jackson, *Lab.* 13,533
Ms A. Ewing, *SNP* 9,552
B. Monteith, *C.* 9,158
I. Macfarlane, *LD* 3,407
S. Kilgour, *Ind.* 155
*Lab. majority* 3,981

STRATHKELVIN AND BEARSDEN
*(Scotland West region)*
*E.* 63,111 *T.* 67.17%
S. Galbraith, *Lab.* 21,505
Ms F. McLeod, *SNP* 9,384
C. Ferguson, *C.* 6,934
Ms A. Howarth, *LD* 4,144
Ms M. Richards, *Anti-Drug* 423
*Lab. majority* 12,121
By-election held on 7 June 2001 *see below*

TAYSIDE NORTH
*(Scotland Mid and Fife region)*
*E.* 61,795 *T.* 61.58%
J. Swinney, *SNP* 16,786
M. Fraser, *C.* 12,594
Ms M. Dingwall, *Lab.* 5,727
P. Regent, *LD* 2,948
*SNP majority* 4,192

TWEEDDALE, ETTRICK AND LAUDERDALE
*(Scotland South region)*
*E.* 51,577 *T.* 65.37%
I. Jenkins, *LD* 12,078
Ms C. Creech, *SNP* 7,600
G. McGregor, *Lab.* 7,546
J. Campbell, *C.* 6,491
*LD majority* 4,478

WESTERN ISLES
*(Highlands and Islands region)*
*E.* 22,412 *T.* 62.26%

| | |
|---|---|
| A. Morrison, *Lab.* | 7,248 |
| A. Nicholson, *SNP* | 5,155 |
| J. MacGrigor, *C.* | 1,095 |
| J. Horne, *LD* | 456 |

*Lab. majority* 2,093

## BY-ELECTIONS

AYR (16 March 2000)
*T.* 57%

| | |
|---|---|
| J. Scott, *C.* | 12,580 |
| J. Mather, *SNP* | 9,236 |
| R. Millar, *Lab.* | 7,054 |
| J. Stewart, *SSP* | 1,345 |
| S. Ritchie, *LD* | 800 |
| G. Corbett, *Green* | 460 |
| W. Botcherby, *Ind.* | 186 |
| A. McConnachie, *UK Ind* | 113 |
| R. Graham, *ProLife* | 111 |
| K. Dhillon, *Ind* | 15 |

*C. majority* 3,344

GLASGOW ANNIESLAND
(23 November 2000)
*T.* 20,221

| | |
|---|---|
| Bill Butler, *Lab.* | 9,838 |
| Tom Chalmers, *SNP* | 4,462 |
| Kate Pickering, *C.* | 2,148 |
| R. Kane, *SSP* | 1,429 |
| Judith Fryer, *LD* | 1,384 |
| Alasdair Whitelaw, *Green* | 662 |
| Murdo Ritchie, *Lab.* | 298 |

*Lab. majority* 5,376

BANFF AND BUCHAN (7 June 2001)
*T.* 30,838

| | |
|---|---|
| Stewart Stevenson, *SNP* | 15,386 |
| Ted Brocklebank, *C.* | 6,819 |
| Megan Harris, *Lab.* | 4,597 |
| Canon Kenyon Wright, *LD* | 3,231 |
| Peter Anderson, *SSP* | 682 |

*SNP majority* 8,567

STRATHKELVIN AND BEARSDEN
(7 June 2001)
*T.* 41,734

| | |
|---|---|
| Brian Fitzpatrick, *Lab.* | 15,401 |
| Jean M. Turner, *Ind.* | 7,275 |
| John Morrison, *LD* | 7,147 |
| Janet E. Law, *SNP* | 6,457 |
| Charles Ferguson, *C.* | 5,037 |

*Lab. majority*, 8,126

## REGIONS

GLASGOW
*E.* 531,956 *T.* 48.19%

| | |
|---|---|
| *Lab.* | 112,588 (43.92%) |
| *SNP* | 65,360 (25.50%) |
| *C.* | 20,239 (7.90%) |
| *SSP* | 18,581 (7.25%) |
| *LD* | 18,473 (7.21%) |
| *Green* | 10,159 (3.96%) |
| *Soc. Lab.* | 4,391 (1.71%) |
| *ProLife* | 2,357 (0.92%) |
| *SUP* | 2,283 (0.89%) |
| *Comm. Brit.* | 521 (0.20%) |
| *Humanist* | 447 (0.17%) |
| *NLP* | 419 (0.16%) |
| *SPGB* | 309 (0.12%) |
| *Choice* | 221 (0.09%) |

*Lab. majority* 47,228
(May 1997, Lab. maj. 166,061)
Additional Members elected: W. Aitken, *C.*; R. Brown, *LD*; Ms D. Elder, *SNP*; Ms S. White, *SNP*; Ms N. Sturgeon, *SNP*; K. Gibson, *SNP*; T. Sheridan, *SSP*

HIGHLANDS AND ISLANDS
*E.* 326,553 *T.* 61.76%

| | |
|---|---|
| *SNP* | 55,933 (27.73%) |
| *Lab.* | 51,371 (25.47%) |
| *LD* | 43,226 (21.43%) |
| *C.* | 30,122 (14.94%) |
| *Green* | 7,560 (3.75%) |
| *Ind. Noble* | 3,522 (1.75%) |
| *Soc. Lab.* | 2,808 (1.39%) |
| *Highlands* | 2,607 (1.29%) |
| *SSP* | 1,770 (0.88%) |
| *Mission* | 1,151 (0.57%) |
| *Int. Ind.* | 712 (0.35%) |
| *NLP* | 536 (0.27%) |
| *Ind. R.* | 354 (0.18%) |

*SNP majority* 4,562
(May 1997, LD maj. 1,388)

Additional Members
J. MacGrigor, *C.*; Mrs M. Scanlon, *C.*; Ms M. MacMillan, *Lab.*; P. Peacock, *Lab.*; Ms R. Grant, *Lab.*; Mrs W. Ewing, *SNP*; D. Hamilton, *SNP*

LOTHIANS
*E.* 539,656 *T.* 61.25%

| | |
|---|---|
| *Lab.* | 99,908 (30.23%) |
| *SNP* | 85,085 (25.74%) |
| *C.* | 52,067 (15.75%) |
| *LD* | 47,565 (14.39%) |
| *Green* | 22,848 (6.91%) |
| *Soc. Lab.* | 10,895 (3.30%) |
| *SSP* | 5,237 (1.58%) |
| *Lib.* | 2,056 (0.62%) |
| *Witchery* | 1,184 (0.36%) |
| *ProLife* | 898 (0.27%) |
| *Rights* | 806 (0.24%) |
| *NLP* | 564 (0.17%) |
| *Braveheart* | 557 (0.17%) |
| *SPGB* | 388 (0.12%) |
| *Ind. Voice* | 256 (0.08%) |
| *Ind. Ind.* | 145 (0.04%) |
| *Anti-Corr.* | 54 (0.02%) |

*Lab. majority* 14,823
(May 1997, Lab. maj. 101,991)

Additional Members
Lord James Douglas Hamilton, *C.*; D. McLetchie, *C.*; Rt. Hon. Sir David Steel, *LD*; K. MacAskill, *SNP*; Ms M. MacDonald, *SNP*; Ms F. Hyslop, *SNP*; R. Harper, *Green*

SCOTLAND CENTRAL
*E.* 551,733 *T.* 59.90%

| | |
|---|---|
| *Lab.* | 129,822 (39.28%) |
| *SNP* | 91,802 (27.78%) |
| *C.* | 30,243 (9.15%) |
| *Falkirk W.* | 27,700 (8.38%) |
| *LD* | 20,505 (6.20%) |
| *Soc. Lab.* | 10,956 (3.32%) |
| *Green* | 5,926 (1.79%) |
| *SSP* | 5,739 (1.74%) |
| *SUP* | 2,886 (0.87%) |
| *ProLife* | 2,567 (0.78%) |
| *SFPP* | 1,373 (0.42%) |
| *NLP* | 719 (0.22%) |
| *Ind. Prog.* | 248 (0.08%) |

*Lab. majority* 38,020
(May 1997, Lab. maj. 143,376)

Additional Members
Mrs L. McIntosh, *C.*; D. Gorrie, *LD*; A. Neil, *SNP*; M. Matheson, *SNP*; Ms L. Fabiani, *SNP*; A. Wilson, *SNP*; G. Paterson, *SNP*

SCOTLAND MID AND FIFE
*E.* 509,387 *T.* 60.01%

| | |
|---|---|
| *Lab.* | 101,964 (33.36%) |
| *SNP* | 87,659 (28.68%) |
| *C.* | 56,719 (18.56%) |
| *LD* | 38,896 (12.73%) |
| *Green* | 11,821 (3.87%) |
| *Soc. Lab.* | 4,266 (1.40%) |
| *SSP* | 3,044 (1.00%) |
| *ProLife* | 735 (0.24%) |
| *NLP* | 558 (0.18%) |

*Lab. majority* 14,305
(May 1997, Lab. maj. 54,087)

Additional Members
*N. Johnston, *C.*; B. Monteith, *C.*; K. Harding, *C.*; K. Raffan, *LD*; B. Crawford, *SNP*; G. Reid, *SNP*; Ms P. Marwick, *SNP*; *N. Johnston *resigned on 10 August 2001. He was replaced by Murdo Fraser*

SCOTLAND NORTH EAST
*E.* 518,521 *T.* 55.05%

| | |
|---|---|
| *SNP* | 92,329 (32.35%) |
| *Lab.* | 72,666 (25.46%) |
| *C.* | 52,149 (18.27%) |
| *LD* | 49,843 (17.46%) |
| *Green* | 8,067 (2.83%) |
| *Soc. Lab.* | 3,557 (1.25%) |
| *SSP* | 3,016 (1.06%) |
| *Ind. Watt.* | 2,303 (0.81%) |
| *Ind. SB* | 770 (0.27%) |
| *NLP* | 746 (0.26%) |

*SNP majority* 19,663
(May 1997, Lab. maj. 17,518)

Additional Members
D. Davidson, *C.*; A. Johnstone, *C.*; B. Wallace, *C.*; R. Lochhead, *SNP*; Ms S. Robison, *SNP*; B. Adam, *SNP*; Ms I. McGugan, *SNP*

SCOTLAND SOUTH
*E.* 510,634 *T.* 62.35%

| | |
|---|---|
| *Lab.* | 98,836 (31.04%) |
| *SNP* | 80,059 (25.15%) |
| *C.* | 68,904 (21.64%) |
| *LD* | 38,157 (11.99%) |
| *Soc. Lab.* | 13,887 (4.36%) |
| *Green* | 9,468 (2.97%) |

| | |
|---|---|
| *Lib.* | 3,478 (1.09%) |
| *SSP* | 3,304 (1.04%) |
| *UK Ind.* | 1,502 (0.47%) |
| *NLP* | 775 (0.24%) |

*Lab. majority* 18,777
(May 1997, Lab. maj. 79,585)

Additional Members
P. Gallie, *C.*; D. Mundell, *C.*; M. Tosh, *C.*; A. Fergusson, *C.*; M. Russell, *SNP*; A. Ingram, *SNP*; Ms C. Creech, *SNP*

SCOTLAND WEST
*E.* 498,466 *T.* 62.27%

| | |
|---|---|
| *Lab.* | 119,663 (38.55%) |
| *SNP* | 80,417 (25.91%) |
| *C.* | 48,666 (15.68%) |
| *LD* | 34,095 (10.98%) |
| *Green* | 8,175 (2.63%) |
| *SSP* | 5,944 (1.91%) |
| *Soc. Lab.* | 4,472 (1.44%) |
| *ProLife* | 3,227 (1.04%) |
| *Individual* | 2,761 (0.89%) |
| *SUP* | 1,840 (0.59%) |
| *NLP* | 589 (0.19%) |
| *Ind. Water* | 565 (0.18%) |

*Lab. majority* 39,246
(May 1997, Lab. maj. 115,995)

Additional Members
Miss A. Goldie, *C.*; J. Young, *C.*; R. Finnie, *LD*; L. Quinan, *SNP*; Ms F. McLeod, *SNP*; Ms K. Ullrich, *SNP*; C. Campbell, *SNP*

## NORTHERN IRELAND ASSEMBLY

Parliament Buildings, Stormont, Belfast BT4 3XX
Tel: 028-9052 1333; Fax: 028-9052 1961
Web: www.ni-assembly.gov.uk

The Assembly has 108 members elected by single transferable vote (six from each of the 18 Westminster constituencies). The first elections took place on 25 June 1998 and members met for the first time on 1 July. Safeguards ensure that key decisions have cross-community support. The executive powers of the Assembly are discharged by an Executive Committee comprising a First Minister and Deputy First Minister (jointly elected by the Assembly on a cross-community basis) and up to ten ministers with departmental responsibilities. Ministerial posts are allocated on the basis of the number of seats each party holds.

The Assembly met in shadow form, pending the establishment of an Executive and the transfer of powers from Parliament. Following devolution it has executive and legislative authority over those areas formerly the responsibility of the Northern Ireland government departments. Its powers might be extended further in future.

Power was initially due to be transferred to the new Executive on 10 March 1999, but disagreements emerged over whether Sinn Fein should be allowed to enter the Executive before IRA weapons had been decommissioned. Further deadlines of 2 April and 30 June were also missed. On 15 July the Assembly met to nominate ministers, with the transfer of power to follow on 18 July. However, as the decommissioning issue had still not been resolved, Unionists failed to nominate ministers (the UUP boycotting the meeting itself) and the process collapsed. On 20 July the two prime ministers announced a review of the implementation of the Agreement to be facilitated by Senator George Mitchell. The scope of the review was tightly drawn, focusing only on the practical implementation of the three principles set out above, effectively decommissioning the Executive. The timing of the review dove-tailed with the inevitably sensitive publication of the Patten Commission's report on policing.

Following a series of meetings involving the parties in London, Mitchell's interim report of 15 November stated that he was increasingly more confident that the parties could find a way through the impasse.

On 18 November, following statements from the UUP, Sinn Fein and one from the IRA, Senator Mitchell concluded the review indicating that he now believed there was a basis for devolution to occur, for the institutions to be established and for decommissioning to take place as soon as possible. He concluded that devolution should take effect, the Executive Committee should meet and paramilitary organisations should appoint their authorised representatives to the IICD in that order and all in the same day. On 20 November the Secretary of State announced support for the Mitchell proposals and stated that the assembly should meet on 29 November for the purpose of running d'Hondt procedure for appointing shadow ministers and devolution should take effect after the necessary Parliamentary procedures had been completed on 2 December 1999.

Powers were devolved to Assembly and other institutions established on 2 December on a basis agreed by the parties during the Mitchell review. The Mitchell review created the expectation that the establishment of the institutions and the appointment of authorised representatives produced conditions in which Sinn Fein could influence bringing about the start of decommissioning. But it was a matter of political reality that if decommissioning did not occur by the end of January 2000 it would be very difficult for David Trimble to continue as leader of the Ulster Unionist Party beyond this. In Late November the Council of the UUP had endorsed the Mitchell outcome but, reflecting the political reality, also recommend that progress on the timing and modalities of decommissioning be reviewed at the end of January 2000 through reports presented to the two governments by the IICD.

Devolution and the institutions were able to flourish on the basis of sufficient cross community support. Unfortunately that support began to ebb when the anticipated progress on decommissioning failed to materialise at the end of January. The two Governments took receipt of General de Chastelain's 31 January report but held back publication in order to explore any hope of credible progress on decommissioning. Both governments tried further efforts to gain clarity on the decommissioning issue.

The Secretary of State announced the suspension legislation on 3 February and warned publicly that it would come into effect on Friday 11 February . On the morning of 11 February , there was some sign that a new IRA proposal was emerging. The Irish Government presented a new position from its leadership. There were still only words and no timescale, but it did include clearer and less equivocal words than before. Unfortunately this was not enough to avert the collapse of the institutions.

Suspension meant that the Assembly could not meet or conduct any business. Parliament Buildings remained open for use by Assembly Members for the purpose of carrying out constituency work and they continued to be paid salaries and allowances - set at the lower pre-devolution shadow rate to reflect the suspension of Assembly business.

Following a period of intensive discussions with pro-Agreement parties during 4 and 5 May at Hillsborough, the Prime Minister and Taoiseach issued a joint statement committing both Government's proposals. On May 6, the

IRA responded with a significant and forthcoming statement in which they recognised that:

- the implementation of what the Governments had agreed would provide a new context in which Republicans could pursue their political objectives peacefully.
- in that new context the IRA leadership would initiate a process that would completely and verifiably put arms beyond use.
- the IRA would renew contact with the Decommissioning Commission.
- agreed, as a confidence building measure, to open a number of arms dumps to independent inspectors reporting to the Decommissioning Commission on a regular basis to verify that arms remain secure.

The pro-Agreement parties welcomed these developments. The UUP leader, David Trimble said that the IRA statement 'appeared to break new ground'. The Prime Minister and the Taoiseach announced on 8 May that they were asking the former Finnish President Martti Ahtisaari and Cyril Ramaphosa, the ANC negotiator, to become the independent inspectors. On 9 May, the Chief Constable of the RUC recognised that the IRA statement marked a significant reduction in the overall threat and announced a number of measures, spread across Northern Ireland, designed as a return to more normal policing.

The Government published the Police Bill on 16 May and gave assurances to Unionists that the legal description of the new police service would incorporate the RUC, while the operational and working name would change to Police Service of Northern Ireland. The Government also took an enabling power to resolve the flying of flags over Government buildings if the devolved Executive could not.

A week later than originally envisaged the Ulster Unionist Council endorsed the Government's proposals on 27 May and devolved government was restored to Northern Ireland with effect from midnight on 29 May 2000.

Following considerable political unrest, David Trimble resigned as Northern Ireland First Minister on 30 June 2001. His resignation was an ultimatum to encourage the IRA to start decommissioning their weapons. The administrative elements of his post have been passed to Sir Reg Empey. The future of the Assembly remains uncertain at the time of going to press.

SALARIES *as at April 2001*

| | |
|---|---|
| First Minister | £108,471* |
| Deputy First Minister | £108,471* |
| Assembly Member | £40,315 |

*Also receive the Assembly Member salary

## NORTHERN IRELAND EXECUTIVE

CASTLE BUILDINGS, STORMONT, BELFAST BT4 3SG
Tel: 028-9052 0700; Fax: 028-9052 8195
Web: www.northernireland.gov.uk

*First Minister*, vacant
*Deputy First Minister*, Seamus Mallon, MLA
*Minister of Agriculture and Rural Development*, Brid Rogers, MLA
*Minster of Culture and Arts and Leisure*, Michael McGimpsey, MLA
*Minister of Education*, Martin McGuiness, MLA
*Minister for Enterprise, Trade and Investment*, Sir Reg Empey, MLA
*Minister for Environment*, Sam Foster, MLA
*Minister for Finance and Personnel*, Mark Durkan, MLA
*Minister of Health, Social Services and Public Safety*, Bairbre de Brún, MLA
*Minister of Higher and Further Education, Training and Employment*, Sean Farren, MLA
*Minister for Regional Development*, Gregory Campbell, MLA
*Minister for Social Development*, Morris Morrow, MLA

## OFFICE OF THE FIRST MINISTER AND DEPUTY MINISTER

Castle Buildings, Stormont Estate, Belfast BT4 3SR
Tel: 028-9052 8400
*First Minister*, vacant
*Deputy First Minister*, Seamus Mallon, MLA

## DEPARTMENT OF AGRICULTURE AND RURAL DEVELOPMENT

Dundonald House, Upper Newtownards Road, Belfast BT4 3SB
Tel: 028-9052 0100; Fax: 028-9052 5015

*Minister for Agriculture and Rural Development*, Brid Rodgers, MLA
*Permanent Secretary (SCS)*, Peter Small
*Under-Secretaries (SCS)*, (Central Services and Rural Development); (Food, Farming and Environmental Policy); (Veterinary); (Science); (Agri-Food Development)

EXECUTIVE AGENCIES

RIVERS AGENCY, 4 Hospital Road, Belfast BT8 8JP. Tel: 028-9025 3355
FOREST SERVICE, Dundonald House, Upper Newtownards Road, Belfast BT4 3SB. Tel: 028-9052 4480

## DEPARTMENT OF CULTURE, ARTS AND LEISURE

20-24 York Street, Belfast BT15 1AQ
Tel: 028-9025 8825

*Minister for Culture, Arts and Leisure*, Michael McGimpsey, MLA
*Permanent Secretary (SCS)*, Dr Aideen Meginley

## DEPARTMENT OF EDUCATION

Rathgael House, 43 Balloo Road, Bangor, Co. Down BT19 7PR
Tel: 028-9127 9279; Fax: 028-9127 9100

*Minister of Education*, Martin McGuinness, MLA
*Permanent Secretary (SCS)*, Jerry McGinn

## DEPARTMENT OF ENTERPRISE, TRADE AND INVESTMENT

Netherleigh, Massey Avenue, Belfast BT4 2JP
Tel: 028-9052 9900; Fax: 028 9052 9550

*Minister for Enterprise, Trade and Investment*, Sir Reg Empey, MLA
*Permanent Secretary (SCS)*, Bruce Robinson
*Under-Secretaries (SCS)*, Greg McConnell (Policy Group); R. Hamilton (Management Services Group)
INDUSTRIAL DEVELOPMENT BOARD, IDB House, 64 Chichester Street, Belfast BT1 4JX. Tel: 028-9023 3233

EXECUTIVE AGENCIES

INDUSTRIAL RESEARCH AND TECHNOLOGY UNIT, 17 Antrim Road, Lisburn BT28 3AL. Tel: 028-9262 3000

## DEPARTMENT OF THE ENVIRONMENT FOR NORTHERN IRELAND

Clarence Court, 10–18 Adelaide Street, Belfast BT2 8GB
Tel: 028-90 540540

*Minister for the Environment*, Sam Foster, MLA
*Permanent Secretary (SCS)*, Stephen Quinn
*Under-Secretaries (SCS)*, C. Smith (Local Government and Planning); F. Dillon (Environment and Heritage, Road Safety, DVT (NI), DVL (NI) and Environmental Policy)

EXECUTIVE AGENCIES

DRIVER AND VEHICLE LICENSING AGENCY (NORTHERN IRELAND), County Hall, Castlerock Road, Coleraine, Co. Londonderry BT51 3HS. Tel: 028-703 41469

DRIVER AND VEHICLE TESTING AGENCY (NORTHERN IRELAND), Balmoral Road, Belfast BT12 6QL. Tel: 028-90681 831

ENVIRONMENT AND HERITAGE SERVICE, Commonwealth House, Castle Street, Belfast BT1 1GU. Tel: 028-90251477

PLANNING SERVICE, Clarence Court, 10–18 Adelaide Street, Belfast BT2 8GB. Tel: 028-9054 0540

ADVISORY BODIES

HISTORIC BUILDINGS COUNCIL FOR NORTHERN IRELAND, c/o Environment and Heritage Service, Historic Monuments and Buildings, Commonwealth House, Castle Street, Belfast BT1 1GU. Tel: 028-9025 1477

COUNCIL FOR NATURE CONSERVATION AND THE COUNTRYSIDE, c/o Environment and Heritage Service, Commonwealth House, Castle Street, Belfast BT1 1GU. Tel: 028-9025 1477

## DEPARTMENT OF FINANCE AND PERSONNEL

Rathgael House, Balloo Road, Bangor BT19 7NA
Tel: 028-9127 9279
*Minister of Finance and Personnel*, Mark Durkan, MLA
*Permanent Secretary (SCS)*, P. Carvill
*Under-Secretaries (SCS)*, Dr A. MacCormick (Central Finances Group); Carol Muir (Central Personnel Group) J. Goldring (Law Reform)

GENERAL REGISTER OFFICE (NORTHERN IRELAND), Oxford House, 49–55 Chichester Street, Belfast BT1 4HH. Tel: 028-9025 2000. *Registrar-General (G5)*

EXECUTIVE AGENCIES

BUSINESS DEVELOPMENT SERVICE, Craigantlet Buildings, Stoney Road, Belfast BT4 3SX. Tel: 028-9052 0400

CONSTRUCTION SERVICE, Churchill House, Victoria Square, Belfast BT1 4QW. Tel: 028-9052 0250

GOVERNMENT PURCHASING AGENCY, Rosepark House, Upper Newtownards Road, Belfast BT4 3NR. Tel: 028-9052 0400

LAND REGISTERS OF NORTHERN IRELAND, Lincoln Building, 27-45 Great Victoria Street, Belfast BT2 7SL. Tel: 028-9025 1555

NORTHERN IRELAND STATISTICS AND RESEARCH AGENCY, McAuley House, 2-14 Castle Street, Belfast BT1 1SA. Tel: 028-9034 8100

RATE COLLECTION AGENCY, Oxford House, 49–55 Chichester Street, Belfast BT1 4HH Tel: 028-9025 2252

VALUATION AND LANDS AGENCY, Queen's Court, 56–66 Upper Queen Street, Belfast BT1 6FD. Tel: 028-9025 0700

## DEPARTMENT OF HEALTH SOCIAL SERVICES AND PUBLIC SAFETY NORTHERN IRELAND

Castle Buildings, Stormont, Belfast BT4 3SJ
Tel: 028-9052 0000; Fax: 028-9052 0572
*Minister for Health, Social Services and Public Safety*: Bairbre de Brún, MLA
*Permanent Secretary (SCS)*, Clive Gowdy
*Chief Medical Officer (SCS)*, Dr H. Campbell
*Under-Secretaries (SCS)*, D. Hill (Planning and Resources Group); P. Simpson (HPSS Management Group)

EXECUTIVE AGENCIES

NORTHERN IRELAND HEALTH AND SOCIAL SERVICES ESTATES AGENCY, Stoney Road, Dundonald, Belfast BT16 1US. Tel: 028-9052 0025

## DEPARTMENT FOR EMPLOYMENT AND LEARNING

Adelaide House, Adelaide Street, Belfast BT2 8FD
Tel: 028-9025 7777; Fax: 028-9025 7783
*Minister for Higher and Further Education, Training and Employment*, Sean Farren, MLA
*Permanent Secretary (SCS)*, Allan Shannon
*Private Secretary (SCS)*, (Training and Employment Agency) Bernie Rooney

## DEPARTMENT FOR REGIONAL DEVELOPMENT

Clarence Court, 10-18 Adelaide Street, Belfast BT2 8GB
Tel: 028-9054 0540; Fax: 028-9054 0064
*Minister for Regional Development*, Gregory Cambell, MLA
*Permanent Secretary (SCS)*, N. Hamilton
*Deputy Secretaries (SCS)*, Paul Swinney (Strategic Planning, Transport and Finance); Linda Brown (Roads, Water, Personnel and Management Services)

## DEPARTMENT FOR SOCIAL DEVELOPMENT

Churchill House, Victoria Square, Belfast BT2 4BA
Tel: 028-9056 9100
*Minister for Social Development*, Morris Morrow
*Permanent Secretary (SCS)*, John Hunter
*Deputy Secretaries (SCS)*, Cliff Radcliffe (Urban Regeneration and Community Development); vacant (Resources, Housing and Social Group)

## OTHER BODIES

BRITISH-IRISH COUNCIL
NORTH/SOUTH MINISTERIAL COUNCIL
CIVIC FORUM
BRITISH-IRISH INTERGOVERNMENTAL CONFERENCE

## NORTHERN IRELAND ASSEMBLY MEMBERS AS AT 31 JULY 2001

Adams, Gerry, *(SF)*, *West Belfast*
Adamson, Dr Ian, *(UUP)*, *East Belfast*
*Agnew, Fraser, *(UUAP)*, *North Belfast*
Alderdice, Lord, *(Speaker)*, *East Belfast*
Armitage, Ms Pauline, *(UUP)*, *East Londonderry*
Armstrong, Billy, *(UUP)*, *Mid Ulster*
Attwood, Alex, *(SDLP)*, *West Belfast*
Beggs, Roy, *(UUP)*, *East Antrim*
Bell, Billy, *(UUP) Lagan Valley*
Bell, Eileen, *(All.)*, *North Down*
Berry, Paul, *(DUP)*, *Newry and Armagh*
Birnie, Esmond, *(UUP)*, *South Belfast*
†Boyd, Norman, *(NIUP)*, *South Antrim*
Bradley, P. J. *(SDLP)*, *South Down*
Brun, Ms Bairbre de, *(SF)*, *West Belfast*
Byrne, Joe, *(SDLP)*, *West Tyrone*
Campbell, Gregory, *(DUP)*, *East Londonderry*
Carrick, Mervyn, *(DUP)*, *Upper Bann*
Carson, Ms Joan, *(UUP)*, *Ferm and South Tyrone*
Close, Seamus, *(All.)*, *Lagan Valley*

Clyde, Wilson, (*DUP*), *South Antrim*
Cobain, Fred, (*UUP*), *North Belfast*
Coulter, Robert, (*UUP*), *North Antrim*
**Courtney, Anne, (*SDLP*), *Foyle*
Dallat, John, (*SDLP*), *East Londonderry*
Davis, Ivan, (*UUP*), *Lagan Valley*
Dodds, Nigel, (*DUP*), *North Belfast*
Doherty, Arthur, (*SDLP*), *East Londonderry*
Doherty, Pat, (*SF*), *West Tyrone*
*Douglas, Boyd, (*UUAP*), *East Londonderry*
Durkan, Mark, (*SDLP*), *Foyle*
Empey, Reg, (*UUP*), *East Belfast*
Ervine, David, (*PUP*), *East Belfast*
Farren, Sean, (*SDLP*), *North Antrim*
Fee, John, (*SDLP*), *Newry and Armagh*
Ford, David, (*All.*), *South Antrim*
Foster, Sam, (*UUP*), *Ferm and South Tyrone*
Gallagher, Tommy, (*SDLP*), *Ferm and South Tyrone*
Gibson, Oliver, (*DUP*), *West Tyrone*
Gildernew, Michelle, (*SF*), *Ferm and South Tyrone*
‡Gorman, John, (*UUP*), *North Down*
***Hamilton, Tom, (*UUP*), *Strangford*
Hanna, Carmel, (*SDLP*), *South Belfast*
Haughey, Denis, (*SDLP*), *Mid Ulster*
Hay, William, (*DUP*), *Foyle*
Hendron, Joe, (*SDLP*), *West Belfast*
Hilditch, David, (*DUP*), *East Antrim*
Hussey, Derek, (*UUP*), *West Tyrone*
Hutchinson, Bill, (*PUP*), *North Belfast*
§Hutchinson, Roger, (*Ind Unionist*), *East Antrim*
Kane, Gardiner, (*DUP*), *North Antrim*
Kelly, Gerry (*SF*), *North Belfast*
Kelly, John, (*SF*), *Mid Ulster*
Kennedy, Danny, (*UUP*), *Newry and Armagh*
Leslie, James, (*UUP*), *North Antrim*
Lewsley, Patricia, (*SDLP*), *Lagan Valley*
Maginness, Alban, (*SDLP*), *North Belfast*
Mallon, Seamus, (*SDLP*), *Newry and Armagh*
Maskey, Alex, (*SF*), *West Belfast*
McCarthy, Keiran, (*All.*), *Strangford*
McCartney, Robert, (*UKUP*), *North Down*
McClarty, David, (*UUP*), *East Londonderry*
McCrea, William, (*DUP*), *Mid Ulster*
‡McClelland, Donovan, (*SDLP*), *South Antrim*
McDonnell, Alasdair, (*SDLP*), *South Belfast*
McElduff, Barry, (*SF*), *West Tyrone*
McFarland, Alan, (*UUP*), *North Down*
McGimpsey, Michael, (*UUP*), *South Belfast*
McGrady, Eddie, (*SDLP*), *South Down*
McGuiness, Martin, (*SF*), *Mid Ulster*
McHugh, Gerry, (*SF*), *Ferm and South Tyrone*
McLaughlin, Mitchel, (*SF*), *Foyle*
McMenamin, Eugene, (*SDLP*), *West Tyrone*
McNamee, Pat, (*SF*), *Newry and Armagh*
McWilliams, Prof. Monica, (*NIWC*), *South Belfast*
Molloy, Francie, (*SF*), *Mid Ulster*
Murphy, Connor, (*SF*), *Newry and Armagh*
Murphy, Mick, (*SF*), *South Down*
‡Morrice, Ms Jane, (*NIWC*), *North Down*
Morrow, Maurice, (*DUP*), *Ferm and South Tyrone*
Neeson, Sean, (*All.*), *East Antrim*
Nelis, Ms Mary, (*SF*), *Foyle*
Nesbitt, Dermot, (*UUP*), *South Down*
O'Connor, Danny, (*SDLP*), *East Antrim*
O'Hagan, Dara, (*SF*), *Upper Bann*
O'Neill, Eamon, (*SDLP*), *South Down*
Paisley, Rev Dr Ian, (*DUP*), *North Antrim*
Poots, Edwin, (*DUP*), *Lagan Valley*
Ramsey, Sue, (*SF*), *West Belfast*
Robinson, Iris, (*DUP*), *Strangford*
Robinson, Ken, (*UUP*), East Anrtim
Robinson, Mark, (*DUP*), *South Belfast*
Robinson, Peter, (*DUP*), *East Belfast*
†Roche, Patrick, (*NIUP*), *Lagan Valley*
Rodgers, Brid, (*SDLP*), *Upper Bann*
Savage, George, (*UUP*), *Upper Bann*
Shannon, Jim, (*DUP*), *Strangford*
Shipley-Dalton, Duncan, (*UUP*), *South Antrim*
Taylor, The Rt. Hon. John, (*UUP*), *Strangford*
Tierney, John, (*SDLP*), *Foyle*
Trimble, The Rt. Hon. David, (*UUP*), *Upper Bann*
Watson, Denis, (*UUAP*), *Upper Bann*
Weir, Peter, (*UUP*), *North Down*
Wells, Jim, (*DUP*), *South Down*
†Wilson, Cedric, (*NIUP*), *Strangford*
Wilson, Jim, (*UUP*) *South Antrim*
Wilson, Sammy, (*DUP*), *East Belfast*

* Elected as independent candidates, formed the United Unionist Assembly Party (UUAP) with effect from 21 September 1998
† Elected as UK Unionist Candidates, formed Northern Ireland Unionist Party (NIUP) with effect from 15 January 1999
‡ Elected as Deputy Speakers of the Northern Ireland Assembly 31 January 2000
§ Mr Hutchinson was expelled from the Northern Ireland Unionist Party (NIUP) with effect from 2 December 1999
** John Hume, MP, MEP, resigned from the Northern Ireland Assembly with effect from 1 December 2000. He was replaced by Anne Courtney
*** Tom Benson died on 24 December 2000. He was replaced by Tom Hamilton

## POLITICAL COMPOSITION

| | | |
|---|---|---|
| UUP | Ulster Unionist Party | 28 |
| SDLP | Social Democratic and Labour Party | 24 |
| DUP | Democratic Unionist Party | 20 |
| SF | Sinn Fein | 18 |
| All. | All. | 6 |
| *NIUP | Northern Ireland Unionist Party | 3 |
| †UUAP | United Unionist Assembly Party | 3 |
| NIWC | Northern Ireland Women's Coalition | 2 |
| PUP | Progressive Unionist Party | 2 |
| UKUP | UK Unionist Party | 1 |
| ‡Ind Unionist | Independent Unionist | 1 |

# The Government

## THE CABINET AS AT 8 JUNE 2001

*Prime Minister, First Lord of the Treasury and Minister for the Civil Service*
The Rt. Hon. Anthony (Tony) Blair, MP, since May 1997
*Deputy Prime Minister and First Secretary of State*
The Rt. Hon. John Prescott, MP, since May 1997
*Chancellor of the Exchequer*
The Rt. Hon. Gordon Brown, MP, since May 1997
*Secretary of State for Foreign and Commonwealth Affairs*
The Rt. Hon Jack Straw, MP, since June 2001
*Lord Chancellor*
The Lord Irvine of Lairg, PC, QC, since May 1997
*Secretary of State for the Home Department*
The Rt. Hon. David Blunkett, MP, since June 2001
*Secretary of State for Education and Skills*
The Rt. Hon. Estelle Morris, MP, since June 2001
*President of the Council and Leader of the House of Commons*
The Rt. Hon. Robin Cook, MP, since June 2001
*Minister for the Cabinet Office and Chancellor of the Duchy of Lancaster*
The Rt. Hon. Lord MacDonald of Tradeston, CBE
*Secretary of State for Scotland*
The Rt. Hon. Helen Liddell, MP, since June 2001
*Secretary of State for Defence*
The Rt. Hon. Geoff Hoon, MP, since October 1999
*Secretary of State for Health*
The Rt. Hon. Alan Milburn, MP, since October 1999
*Parliamentary Secretary to the Treasury (Chief Whip)*
The Rt. Hon. Hilary Armstrong, MP, since June 2001
*Secretary of State for Culture, Media and Sport*
The Rt. Hon. Tessa Jowell, MP, since June 2001
*Secretary of State for Northern Ireland*
The Rt. Hon. Dr John Reid, MP, since June 2001
*Secretary of State for Wales*
The Rt. Hon. Paul Murphy, MP, since July 1999
*Secretary of State for International Development*
The Rt. Hon. Clare Short, MP, since May 1997
*Secretary of State for Work and Pensions*
The Rt. Hon. Alistair Darling, MP, since July 1998
*Secretary of State for Environment, Food and Rural Affairs*
The Rt. Hon. Margaret Beckett, MP, since June 2001
*Secretary of State for Transport, Local Government and The Regions*
The Rt. Hon. Stephen Byers, MP, since June 2001
*Lord Privy Seal, Leader of the House of Lords, The Lord* Williams of Mostyn, QC, since June 2001
*Secretary of State for Trade and Industry and Minister for Women*
The Rt. Hon. Patricia Hewitt, MP, since June 2001
*Chief Secretary to the Treasury*
The Rt. Hon. Andrew Smith, MP, since October 1999
*Minister without Portfolio and Party Chair*
Charles Clarke, MP

The Government Chief Whip in the House of Lords will attend Cabinet meetings although they are not members of the Cabinet.
* Appointed as Lord Privy Seal

## LAW OFFICERS

*Attorney-General*
Lord Goldsmith, QC, since June 2001
*Lord Advocate*
Colin Boyd, QC, since February 2000
*Solicitor-General*
The Rt. Hon. Harriet Harman, QC, MP, since June 2001
*Solicitor-General for Scotland*
Neil Davidson, QC, since February 2001
*Advocate-General for Scotland*
Dr Lynda Clark, QC, MP, since May 1999

## MINISTERS OF STATE

*Cabinet Office*
Ms Barbara Roche, MP
Baroness Morgan of Huyton
*Culture and Media*
The Rt. Hon. Richard Caborn, MP (*Sport*)
The Rt. Hon. Baroness Blackstone (*Arts*)
*Defence*
The Rt. Hon. Adam Ingram, MP (*Armed Forces*)
Lord Bach (*Defence Procurement*)
*Education and Skills*
Stephen Timms, MP (*Schools*)
Mrs Margaret Hodge, MP, MBE (*Universities*)
*Environment, Food and Rural Affairs*
The Rt. Hon. Michael Meacher, MP (*Environment*)
The Rt. Hon. Alun Michael, MP (*Rural Affairs*)
*Foreign and Commonwealth Office*
Peter Hain, MP (*Minister for Europe*)
The Rt. Hon. Baroness Symons of Vernham Dean (*Trade and FCO*)
*Health*
John Hutton, MP (*NHS Structure and Resources*)
Ms Jacqui Smith, MP (*Social Care and Mental Health*)
*Home Office*
The Rt. Hon. John Denham, MP (*Crime Reduction Policing and Community Safety*)
The Rt. Hon. Keith Bradley, MP (*Criminal Justice Sentencing and Law Reform*)
The Lord Rooker of Perry Barr (*Citizenship and Immigration*)
*Northern Ireland Office*
Ms Jane Kennedy, MP
*Scotland Office*
George Foulkes, MP
*Trade and Industry*
Douglas Alexander, MP (*E-Commerce and Competitiveness*)
The Rt. Hon. Baroness Symons of Vernham Dean (*Trade and Investment*)
Brian Wilson, MP (*Industry and Energy*)
Alan Johnson, MP (*Employment Relations and the Regions*)
*Transport, Local Government and the Regions*
The Rt. Hon. John Spellar, MP (*Transport*)
The Rt. Hon. Nick Raynsford, MP (*Local Government and the Regions*)
Lord Falconer of Thoroton, QC (*Housing, Planning and Regeneration*)

*Treasury*
Dawn Primarolo, MP (*Paymaster-General*)
The Rt. Hon. Paul Boateng, MP (*Financial Secretary*)
Ms Ruth Kelly, MP (*Economic Secretary*)
*Work and Pensions*
The Rt. Hon. Nick Brown, MP (*Work*)
The Rt. Hon. Ian McCartney, MP (*Pensions*)

## UNDER-SECRETARIES OF STATE

*Cabinet*
Christopher Leslie§, MP
*Culture, Media and Sport*
Dr Kim Howells, MP
*Defence*
Dr Lewis Moonie, MP (*Veterans*)
Lord Bach of Lutterworth (*Defence Procurement*)
*Education and Skills*
Baroness Ashton of Upholland (*Early Years and Skill Standards*)
Ivan Lewis, MP (*Young People and Learning*)
John Healey, MP (*Adult Skills*)
*Environment, Food and Rural Affairs*
Elliot Morley, MP (*Animal Health and Welfare and Fisheries*)
The Lord Whitty (*Food and Farming*)
*Foreign and Commonwealth Office*
Ben Bradshaw, MP
Baroness Amos
Dr Denis MacShane, MP
*Health*
Ms Hazel Blears, MP
The Lord Hunt of King's Heath, OBE
Yvette Cooper, MP
*Home Office*
Ms Beverley Hughes, MP (*Community and Custodial Sentences*)
Robert Ainsworth, MP (*Anti-Drugs Co-ordination and Organised Crime*)
Ms Angela Eagle, MP (*Europe, Community and Race*)
*International Development*
Hilary Benn, MP
*Lord Chancellor's Department*
Baroness Scotland of Asthal, QC
Michael Wills, MP
Ms Rosie Winterton, MP
*Northern Ireland Office*
Des Browne, MP
*Trade and Industry*
Lord Sainsbury of Turville (*Science and Innovation*)
Ms Melanie Johnson§, MP (*Competition, Consumers and Markets*)
Nigel Griffiths§, MP (*Small Business*)
*Transport, Local Government and the Regions*
David Jamieson, MP (*Transport*)
Ms Sally Keeble, MP (*Housing, Planning and Regeneration*)
Dr Alan Whitehead, MP (*Local Government and the Regions*)
*Wales Office*
Don Touhig, MP
*Work and Pensions*
The Rt. Hon. Baroness Hollis of Heigham
Malcolm Wicks, MP
Marcia Eagle, MP

§ Unpaid

## GOVERNMENT WHIPS

### HOUSE OF LORDS

*Captain of the Honourable Corps of Gentlemen-at-Arms (Chief Whip)*
The Rt. Hon.The Lord Carter, PC
*Captain of The Queen's Bodyguard of the Yeoman of the Guard (Deputy Chief Whip)*
The Lord McIntosh of Haringey
*Lords-in-Waiting*
The Lord Davies of Oldham
The Lord Grocott
The Lord Filkin, CBE
The Lord Bassam of Brighton
*Baronesses-in-Waiting*
The Baroness Farrington of Ribbleton

### HOUSE OF COMMONS

*Parliamentary Secretary to the Treasury (Chief Whip)*
The Rt. Hon. Hilary Armstrong, MP
*Treasurer of HM Household (Deputy Chief Whip)*
Keith Hill, MP
*Comptroller of HM Household*
Thomas McAvoy, MP
*Vice-Chamberlain of HM Household*
Gerry Sutcliffe, MP
*Lords Commissioners*
Mrs Anne McGuire, MP; John Heppell, MP; Tony McNulty, MP; Nick Ainger, MP; Graham Stringer, MP
*Assistant Whips*
Ian Pearson, MP; Ms Angela Smith, MP; Ivor Caplin, MP; Jim Fitzpatrick, MP; Fraser Kemp, MP; Philip Woolas, MP; Dan Norris, MP

# Government Departments and Public Offices

This section covers central Government departments, executive agencies, regulatory bodies, other statutory independent organisations, and bodies which are government-financed or whose head is appointed by a Government Minister.

THE CIVIL SERVICE

Under the Next Steps programme, launched in 1988, many semi-autonomous executive agencies have been established to carry out much of the work of the Civil Service. Executive agencies operate within a framework set by the responsible minister which specifies policies, objectives and available resources. All executive agencies are set annual performance targets by their Minister. Each agency has a chief executive, who is responsible for the day-to-day operations of the agency and who is accountable to the minister for the use of resources and for meeting the agency's targets. The minister accounts to Parliament for the work of the agency. Nearly 80 per cent of civil servants now work in executive agencies. In October 1999 there were about 466,500 permanent civil servants.

The Senior Civil Service was created in 1996 and on 1 April 2000 comprised 3,180 staff from Permanent Secretary to the former Grade 5 level, including all agency chief executives. All Government departments and executive agencies are now responsible for their own pay and grading systems for civil servants outside the Senior Civil Service. In practice the grades of the former Open structure are still in use in some organisations. The Open structure represented the following:

| *Grade* | *Title* |
|---|---|
| 1 | Permanent Secretary |
| 1A | Second Permanent Secretary |
| 2 | Deputy Secretary |
| 3 | Under-Secretary |
| 4 | Chief Scientific Officer B, Professional and Technology Directing A |
| 5 | Assistant Secretary, Deputy Chief Scientific Officer, Professional and Technology Directing B |
| 6 | Senior Principal, Senior Principal Scientific Officer, Professional and Technology Superintending Grade |
| 7 | Principal, Principal Scientific Officer, Principal Professional and Technology Officer |

## SALARIES 2001–2

MINISTERIAL SALARIES *from 1 April 2001*

Ministers who are Members of the House of Commons receive a parliamentary salary (£49,822) in addition to their ministerial salary.

| | |
|---|---|
| *Prime Minister | £113,596 |
| *Cabinet minister (Commons) | £68,157 |
| *†Cabinet minister (Lords) | £88,562 |
| Minister of State (Commons) | £35,356 |
| Minister of State (Lords) | £68,283 |
| Parliamentary Under-Secretary (Commons) | £26,835 |
| Parliamentary Under-Secretary (Lords) | £58,941 |

† Except the Lord Chancellor, who receives a salary of £173,875

SPECIAL ADVISERS' SALARIES *from 1 April 2001*

Special advisers to Government Ministers are paid out of public funds; their salaries are negotiated individually, but are usually in the range £28,328 to £82,867.

CIVIL SERVICE SALARIES *from 1 April 2001*

*Senior Civil Service (SCS)*

| | |
|---|---|
| Secretary of the Cabinet and Head of the Home Civil Service | £98,400–£168,910 |
| Permanent Secretary | £104,292 –£179,022 |
| Band 9 | £92,696 –£131,276 |
| Band 8 | £84,811 –£123,856 |
| Band 7 | £77,635 –£116,904 |
| Band 6 | £70,905 –£110,428 |
| Band 5 | £64,768 –£104,292 |
| Band 4 | £59,088 –£98,494 |
| Band 3 | £53,534 –£87,598 |
| Band 2 | £48,552 –£77,869 |
| Band 1 | £44,038 –£69,178 |

Staff are placed in pay bands according to their level of responsibility and taking account of other factors such as experience and marketability. Movement within and between bands is based on performance.

*Other Civil Servants*

Following the delegation of responsibility for pay and grading to Government departments and agencies from 1 April 1996, it is no longer possible to show service-wide pay rates for staff outside the Senior Civil Service. The following table will however give an indication of the percentage of civil servants at a given salary level.

Non-Industrial Staff by Gross Salary Band
*as at 1 April 2000*

| *Salary Band* | *Per Cent* |
|---|---|
| £5,001–£10,000 | 6.1 |
| £10,001–£15,000 | 36.8 |
| £15,001–£20,000 | 23.2 |
| £20,001–£25,000 | 16.8 |
| £25,001–£30,000 | 6.9 |
| £30,001–£35,000 | 3.4 |
| £35,001–£40,000 | 1.9 |
| £40,001–£45,000 | 1.4 |
| £45,001–£50,000 | 0.8 |
| £50,001–£55,000 | 0.4 |
| £55,001–£60,000 | 0.3 |
| £60,001–£65,000 | 0.2 |
| £65,001–£70,000 | 0.1 |
| £70,001–£75,000 | 0.1 |
| £75,001 + | 0.1 |

*Source:* Government Statistical Service – *Civil Service Statistics 2000*

## GOVERNMENT DEPARTMENTS

### THE CABINET OFFICE

70 Whitehall, London SW1A 2AS
Tel: 020-7270 3000
Web: www.cabinet-office.gov.uk

The Cabinet Office has responsibility for a wide range of work. This includes a secretariat role for the Cabinet and Civil Contingencies work, devolution and regional work, a central role for civil service strategy and management, public service reform, government policy delivery, social exclusion and work for women and equality. The department also takes the lead on issues such as e-government and regulatory impact.

*Prime Minister and Minister for the Civil Service*, The Rt. Hon. Antony (Tony) Blair, MP
*Deputy Prime Minister and First Secretary of State*, The Rt. Hon. John Prescott, MP
*Minister for the Cabinet Office and Chancellor of the Duchy of Lancaster*, The Rt. Hon. The Lord MacDonald of Tradeston, CBE
*Principal Private Secretary (SCS)*, Dr J. Fuller
*Parliamentary Private Secretary*, Alan Campbell, MP
*Private Secretary*, Fiona Butler
*Minister of State*, Barbara Roche, MP
*Private Secretary*, Mark Langdale
*Parliamentary Secretary*, Tom Levitt, MP
*Minister of State*, Baroness Morgan of Huyton
*Private Secretary*, N. Pitts
*Parliamentary Private Secretary*, Magaret Moran, MP
*Parliamentary Under-Secretary of State*, Christopher Leslie, MP
*Secretary of the Cabinet and Head of the Home Civil Service*, Sir Richard Wilson, KCB
*Private Secretary (SCS)*, A. Allbellry
*Permanent Secretary*, Ms M. MacDonald
*Private Secretary*, Julie Eason

### PRIME MINISTER'S OFFICE

10 Downing Street, London SW1A 2AA
Tel: 020-7270 3000; Fax: 020-7925 0918
Web: www.number-10.gov.uk

*Prime Minister*, The Rt. Hon. Antony (Tony) Blair, MP
*Principal Private Secretary*, Jeremy Heywood
*Chief of Staff*, Jonathan Powell
*Deputy Chief of Staff*, P. McFadden
*Private Secretaries*, Claire Sumner (*Parliamentary Affairs*); David North (*Home Affairs*); Simon Virley (*Economic Affairs*); Anna Wechsberg, Michael Tatham (*Assistants on Foreign Affairs*)
*Personal Assistant to PM (Diary)*, Katie Kay
*Political Secretary*, Robert Hill
*Head of Policy Unit*, Andrew Adonis
*Policy Directorate*: Carey Oppenheim; Ed Richards, Brian Hackland; Simon Virley; Geoffrey Norris; Mike Emmerich; Sarah Hunter; Simon Stevens; Justin Russell; David North; Clare Sumner; Alasdair McGowan
*Parliamentary Private Secretary*, David Hanson, MP
*Research and Information Unit*, Phil Bassett
*Corporate Communications*, James Humphreys
*Director of Communications and Strategy*, Alastair Campbell
*Strategic Communications Unit*, Peter Hyman
*Executive Secretary*, Pat Dixon
*Director of Events and Visits*, Fiona Millar
*Director of Government Relations*, Anji Hunter
*Secretary for Appointments, and Ecclesiastical Secretary to the Lord Chancellor*, William Chapman
*Head of Secretariat and Advisor on Foreign Policy and Head of Overseas Defence Secretariat*, Sir David Manning
*Parliamentary Clerk*, Clive Barbour

### SECRETARIATS

#### ECONOMIC AND DOMESTIC SECRETARIAT

*Head (SCS)*, S. Chakrabarti
*Deputy Heads (SCS)*, Ms. L. Bell; P. Britton

#### DEFENCE AND OVERSEAS AFFAIRS SECRETARIAT

*Foreign Policy*, M. Tatham; A. Wechberg; I. Lloyd; R. Liddle
*Delivery Unit Head*, M. Barber
*Office of Public Service Reform Head*; W. Thomson
*Forward Strategy Unit Head*; G. Mulgan

#### EUROPEAN AFFAIRS SECRETARIAT

*Head (SCS)*, S. Wall
*Deputy Heads (SCS)*, M. Donnelly

#### CONSTITUTION SECRETARIAT

*Director (SCS)*, J. Tross
*Head of Other Constitutional Reform Team (SCS)*, Ms J. Simpson
*Head of Legal Advisers*, Ms R. Jeffreys

#### CENTRAL SECRETARIAT

*Director (SCS)*, Ms S. Phippard
*Deputy Director (SCS)*, P. Calcutt, OBE

#### CEREMONIAL BRANCH

Ashley House, 2 Monck Street, London SW1P 2BQ
Tel: 020-7270 1234
*Honours Nomination Unit:* Tel: 020-7276 2775
*Ceremonial Officer (SCS)*, Mrs G. Catto

### PUBLIC SERVICE DELIVERY

#### MODERNISING PUBLIC SERVICES GROUP

*Director (SCS)*, J. Stephens
*Deputy Directors (SCS)*, S. O'Leary, OBE; M. Sweetman; A. Whysall; J. Cowper

#### CENTRAL IT UNIT

Tel: 020-7270 1234
*Director (SCS)*, D. Cooke
*Deputy Directors (SCS)*, J. Crump; M. Gladwyn; Mrs A. Steward; I. White; P. Waller

#### REGULATORY IMPACT UNIT

*Director (SCS)*, P. Wynn Owen
*Deputy Directors (SCS)*, D. Hayler; C. Hayes; Ms A. French
*Legal Adviser*, P. Bovey

#### MODERNISING GOVERNMENT

*Director*, A. Wells
*Deputy Director (SCS)*, J. Cowper

### CIVIL SERVICE MANAGEMENT

#### CENTRAL GOVERNMENT NATIONAL TRAINING ORGANISATION (CGNTO)

Room 69/1 GOOGS, Horse Guards Road, London SW1P 3AL Tel: 020-7270 1597; Fax: 020-7270 6640; Email: secretariat@cgnto.org.uk

*Council Members*, B. Fox; J. Barker; R. Green; Ms A. Perkins; R. Dudding; C. MacDonald; B. Mitchell; B. Richardson; M. Grannatt; P. Joyce; J. Sheldon; Cllr J. Stocks; N. Starritt; D. Laughrin; I. Magee
*Head of Secretariat*, John Barker

CENTRE FOR MANAGEMENT AND POLICY STUDIES (CMPS)

*Director-General*, Prof. R. Amman
*Directors (SCS)*, R. Green; S. Duncan

CIVIL SERVICE COLLEGE DIRECTORATE

Sunningdale Park, Larch Avenue, Ascot, Berks SL5 0QE
Tel: 01344-634000; Fax: 01344-634233
11 Belgrave Road, London SW1 4RB
Tel: 020-7834 6644; Fax: 01344-634451
1 St Colme Street, Edinburgh EH3 6AA
Tel: 0131-220 8267; Fax: 0131-220 8367

The Civil Service College Directorate of CMPS which is part of the Cabinet Office provides training in management and professional skills for the public and private sectors.
*Director*, E. Wooldridge
*Deputy Directors* M. Barnes; R. Behrens; E. Goodison; G. Llewellyn; M. Timmis

CIVIL SERVICE CORPORATE MANAGEMENT COMMAND

*Senior Director (SCS)*, B. M. Fox, CB
*Directors (SCS)*, J. Barker; Ms S. Hinkley, CBE
*Deputy Directors (SCS)*, Ms A. Schofield; Ms J. Lemprière; C. J. Parry; Ms E. Goodison; D. G. Pain; S. Mitha

GOVERNMENT INFORMATION AND COMMUNICATION SERVICES

*Head of Government Information and Communication Services (SCS)*, M. Granatt
*Director, Development Centre (SCS)*, C. Skinner
*Deputy Director*, Ms S. Jenkins

OFFICE OF THE COMMISSIONER FOR PUBLIC APPOINTMENTS (OCPA)

Tel: 020-7270 6472

The role of the Commissioner for Public Appointments is to monitor, regulate, report and advise on 12,500 ministerial public appointments to executive non-departmental public bodies, public corporations, nationalised industries, utility regulators and NHS bodies. The Commissioner is appointed by an Order-in-Council.
*Commissioner*, Dame Rennie Fritchie
*Head of Office (SCS)*, J. Barron

OFFICE OF THE CIVIL SERVICE COMMISSIONERS (OCSC)

3rd Floor, 35 Great Smith Street, London, SW1P 3BQ
Tel: 020-7276 2615; Fax: 020-7276 2606

The Civil Service Commissioners are responsible for upholding the principle of selection on merit on the basis of fair and open competition in recruitment to the Civil Service. They also hear and determine appeals in cases of concerns about propriety and conscience raised by civil servants under the Civil Service Code which cannot be resolved through internal procedures. The Commissioners are appointed by Order-in-Council.
*First Commissioner*, The Baroness Usha Prashar, CBE
*Commissioners (part-time)*, D. Bell; P. Bounds; J.Boyle; Ms B. Curtis; Ms S. Forbes; Dame Rennie Fritchie; Prof. E. Gallagher, CBE; J. Hamill, CB; G. Lemos; A. Macdonald, CB; G. Maddrell; Rabbi Julia Neuberger; G. Peacock, CBE; Dr M. Semple, OBE; J. Shrigley; C. Stevens, CB
*Secretary to the Commissioners and Head of the Office (SCS)*, J. K. Barron

## CROSS-CUTTING ISSUES

SOCIAL EXCLUSION UNIT

Tel: 020-7270 5211

*Director of Unit (SCS)*, Ms M. Wallace, OBE
*Deputy Directors*, Ms Z. Peatfield; A. Patel

UK ANTI DRUGS CO-ORDINATION UNIT

Tel: 020-7270 5399

*UK Anti-Drugs Co-ordinator* (£106,057), K. Hellawell
*Deputy Co-ordinator*, M. Trace
*Private Secretary*, V. Baggarley
*Director*, J. Critchley

WOMEN'S UNIT

10 Great George Street, London SW1P 3AE
Tel: 020-7273 8808
*Head of Unit (SCS)*, Ms F. Reynolds, CBE
*Deputy Director*, G. Kidd

PERFORMANCE AND INNOVATION UNIT

Tel: 020-7270 1512

*Director (SCS)*, vacant
*Deputy Director (SCS)*, J. Rentoul

## INFORMATION, ESTABLISHMENT AND ORGANISATION

Queen Anne's Chambers, 28 Broadway, London SW1H 9JS

*Director of Information (SCS)*, P. Martin
*Principal Establishment and Finance Officer (SCS)*, P. Wardle
*Deputy Directors (SCS)*, Miss E. Chennells; D. Brennan; R. Harris; K. Tolladay
*Ministers' Adviser on Agencies*, C. Brendish, CBE

HER MAJESTY'S STATIONERY OFFICE

St Clements House, 2–16 Colegate, Norwich NR3 1BQ
Tel: 01603-621000

*Controller (SCS)*, Mrs C. Tullo

## EXECUTIVE AGENCY

GOVERNMENT CAR AND DESPATCH AGENCY

46 Ponton Road, London SW8 5AX
Tel: 020-7217 3839; Fax: 020-7217 3840;
Email: info@gcda.gsi.gov.uk The Agency provides secure transport and document transfers between Government departments.
*Chief Executive*, N. Matheson

---

# CENTRAL OFFICE OF INFORMATION

Hercules Road, London SE1 7DU
Tel: 020-7928 2345; Fax: 020-7928 5037

---

The Central Office of Information (COI) is a Government department which offers consultancy, procurement and project management services to central Government for publicity. Administrative responsibility for the COI rests with the Minister for the Cabinet Office.
*Chief Executive (G3)*, Miss Carol Fisher
*Senior Personal Secretary*, Mrs Ira MacMull

MANAGEMENT BOARD

*Members*, K. Williamson; P. Buchanan; I. Hamilton; R. Haslam; Mrs S. Whetton; M. Reid
*Secretary*, Mrs I. MacMull

DIRECTORS

*Director, Client Services*, I. Hamilton
*Director, Marketing Communications*, P. Buchanan
*Director, Films, Radio and Events*, S. Whetton
*Director, Publications*, M. Reid
*Director, Central Services*, K. Williamson
*Director, Regional Network*, R. Haslam

NETWORK OFFICES

EASTERN, 2nd Floor, Block A1, Westbrook Centre, Milton Road, Cambridge CB4 1YG. *Network Director*, Ms. M. Basham
MIDLANDS EAST, Belgrave Centre, Talbot Street, Nottingham NG1 5GG. *Network Director*, P. Smith
MIDLANDS WEST, Five Ways House, Islington Row, Middleway, Edgbaston, Birmingham B15 1SH. *Network Director* , B. Garner
NORTH-EAST, Wellbar House, Gallowgate, Newcastle upon Tyne NE1 4TB. *Network Director*, Ms L. Taylor
NORTH-WEST, Sunley Tower, Piccadilly Plaza, Manchester M1 4BD. *Network Director*, Mrs E. Jones
SOUTH-EAST, Hercules Road, London SE1 7DU. *Network Director*, Ms V. Burdon
SOUTH-WEST, The Pithay, Bristol BS1 2NF. *Network Director*, P. Whitbread
YORKSHIRE AND HUMBERSIDE, City House, New Station Street, Leeds LS1 4JG. *Network Director*, Ms W. Miller

## DEPARTMENT FOR CULTURE, MEDIA AND SPORT

2–4 Cockspur Street, London SW1Y 5DH
Tel: 020-7211 6200; Fax: 020-7211 6032
Email: enquiries@culture.gov.uk
Web: www.culture.gov.uk

The Department for Culture, Media and Sport was established in July 1997 and is responsible for Government policy relating to the arts, broadcasting, the press, museums and galleries, libraries, sport and recreation, historic buildings and ancient monuments, tourism, and the music industry.

*Secretary of State for Culture, Media and Sport*, The Rt. Hon. Tessa Jowell, MP
*Principal Private Secretary*, Simon Cooper
*Special Advisers*, Bill Bush; Ms Ruth Mackenzie, OBE
*Parliamentary Private Secretary*, Bill Rammell, MP;
*Minister of State*, Baroness Tessa Blackstone (*Arts, Museums and Galleries*)
*Private Secretary*, David McLaren
*Minister of State*, Richard Caborn, MP (*Sport*)
*Parliamentary Private Secretary*, Ben Chapman, MP
*Private Secretary*, Graeme Cornell
*Parliamentary Under-Secretary*, Kim Howells, MP
*Private Secretary*, Tim Owen Edmunds
*Permanent Secretary* (*SCS*), Nicholas Kroll

MUSEUMS, GALLERIES, LIBRARIES AND HERITAGE GROUP

*Head of Group* (*SCS*), Ms A. Stewart
*Head, Museums, Libraries and Archives* (*SCS*), J. Evans
*Head, Architecture and Historic Environment* (*SCS*), C. Pullman
*Head, Museums, and Libraries Sponsorship Unit* (*AU*), H. Bauer
*Director, Government Art Collection* (*SCS*), P. Johnson

STRATEGY AND COMMUNICATION GROUP

*Head of Group* (*SCS*), vacant
*Head of News*, P. Fearney
*Head of Communications*, G. Newsom
*Head of Strategy*, vacant

CORPORATE SERVICES GROUP

*Head of Group* (*SCS*), vacant
*Head, Finance and Planning Division* (*SCS*), A. McLellan
*Head, National Lottery Division* (*SCS*), J. Zest
*Head, Personnel and Central Services Division* (*SCS*), P. Heron
*Head, Public Appointments and Honours Unit*, S. Roberts
*Head, Internal Audit*, D. Rix

CREATIVE INDUSTRIES AND BROADCASTING GROUP

*Head of Group* (*SCS*), A. Ramsay
*Head, Broadcasting Division* (*SCS*), D. Kahn
*Head, Creative Industries Division* (*SCS*), M. Seeney

REGIONS, TOURISM, MILLENNIUM AND INTERNATIONAL GROUP

*Head of Group*, B. Leonard
*Head, Tourism Division* (*SCS*), S. Broadley
*Head, Millennium Unit*, H. Ind
*Head, Local, Regional and International Division* (*SCS*), P. Douglas

EDUCATION, TRAINING, ARTS AND SPORT

*Head of Group*, Ms P. Drew
*Head, Arts Division* (*SCS*), A. Davey
*Head, Sports Division* (*SCS*), H. Reeves
*Head, Education* (*SCS*), vacant
*QUEST Chief Executive, (SCS)*, T. Suter

### EXECUTIVE AGENCY

ROYAL PARKS AGENCY

The Old Police House, Hyde Park, London W2 2UH
Tel: 020-7298 2000; Fax: 020-7298 2005

The Agency is responsible for maintaining and developing the royal parks.
*Chief Executive* (*G5*), W. Weston

## DEPARTMENT FOR EDUCATION AND SKILLS

Sanctuary Buildings, Great Smith Street, London SW1P 3BT Tel: 0870-001 2345; Fax: 020-7925 6000
Email: info@dfes.gov.uk Web: www.dfes.gov.uk
Caxton House, Tothill Street, London SW1H 9NF
Tel: 020-7273 3000; Fax: 020-7273 5124
Castle View House, East Lane, Runcorn,WA7 2GJ.
Tel: 0114-275 3275; Fax: 0114-259 4724
Mowden Hall, Staindrop Road, Darlington DL3 9BG.
Tel: 01325-460155

The Department for Education and Employment was formed in July 1995, bringing together the functions of the former Department for Education with the training and labour market functions of the former Employment Department. It includes an executive agency, the Employment Service. The Department aims to support economic growth and improve the nation's competitiveness and quality of life by raising standards of education and training and by promoting an efficient and flexible labour market. The department was renamed following the 2001 general election.

*Secretary of State for Education and Skills*, The Rt. Hon. Estelle Morris, MP
*Principal Private Secretary*, Mike Wardle
*Special Advisers*, vacant
*Parliamentary Private Secretary*, David Lammy, MP
*Private Secretary*, D. Jefferson
*Minister of State (Schools)*, Stephen Timms, MP
*Parliamentary Private Secretary*, Vernon Coaker, MP
*Private Secretary*, Nick Carson
*Minister in the Lords*, Baroness Catherine Blackstone
*Private Secretary*, M. Hopkinson
*Minister of State (Universities)*, Margaret Hodge, MBE, MP
*Parliamentary Under-Secretaries of State*, John Healey, MP (*Adult Skills*); Ivan Lewis, MP (*Young People and Learning*); Baroness Catherine Ashton of Upholland, (*Early Years and School Standards*)
*Parliamentary Private Secretary*, Mike Foster, MP
*Private Secretaries*, Margaret Doherty; Steve Bartlett; J. Grundy; Karen Lumley
*Permanent Secretary*, David Normington, CB

## EMPLOYMENT, EQUALITY AND INTERNATIONAL RELATIONS DIRECTORATE

*Director-General*, P. Shaw

### INTERNATIONAL

*Director*, C. Tucker, CB
*Heads of Divisions*, Ms W. Harris (*European Union*); J. Evans (*European Social Fund*); M. Evans (*International Relations*)

### EMPLOYMENT POLICY

*Director*, M. J. Richardson
*Heads of Divisions*, J. Moore (*Structural Unemployment Policy*); J. Fuller (*Adults Disadvantage Policy Division*); C. Hunter (*Welfare to Work*); B. Wells (*Economy and Labour Market*); N. Atkinson (*Learning and Workbank Project*); M. Daly (*DfEE/ES New Agency Division*)

### OPPORTUNITY AND DIVERSITY GROUP

*Director*, Ms S. Trundle, OBE
*Heads of Divisions*, Ms J. Eastabrook, (*Equality and Diversity Division*); Ms E. Tillett (*Disability Policy Division*); M. Craske (*Work Permits UK*)

### EARLY YEARS AND CHILDCARE UNIT

*Heads of Divisions*, A. Cranston (*Quality Standards*); C. Slowcock (*Affordability and Accessibility Division*)

## FINANCE AND ANALYTICAL SERVICES DIRECTORATE

*Director-General*, P. Makeham

### FINANCE

*Director*, Ms R. Thompson
*Heads of Divisions*, Mrs S. Todd (*Expenditure*); vacant (*Capital Investment*); Dr J. Pugh (*Programmes*); R. Wye (*Efficiency*); M. Maddox; P. Connor (*Financial Accounting*); N. Thirtle (*Internal Audit*)

### ANALYTICAL SERVICES

*Director General*, P. Makeham
*Director*, P. Johnson
*Heads of Divisions*, M. Britton (*Qualifications, Pupil Assessment and IT*); J. Elliott (*Youth and Further Education*); A. Ray (*Higher Education, Evaluation Strategy and International*); Dr B. Butcher (*Employability and Adult Learning*); R. Bartholomew (*Equal Opportunities and Research Programmes*); Ms A. Brown (*Schools, Teachers and Resources*)

## LIFELONG LEARNING DIRECTORATE

*Director-General*, N. Stuart
*Heads of Division below the Director General*, A. Clarke; (*Prisoners Learning and Skills Unit*); J. Temple (*Strategy and Funding*); M. Boo (*Adult Basic Skills*)

## DIRECTORATES UNDER THE DIRECTOR GENERAL

### ADULT BASIC SKILLS STRATEGY UNIT

*Director*, S. Pember

### ADULT LEARNING GROUP

*Director*, D. Grover
*Heads of Divisions*, T. Down (*Access to Learning for Adults Division*); O. Crouch (*Lifelong Learning and Technologies Division*); E. Galvin (*Skills for Employment*); H. Tollyfield (*Workplace Learning Division*); P. Thorpe (*Review of Basic Skills Agency*)

### CONNEXIONS SERVICE UNIT

*Director*, A. Weinstock
*Heads of Divisions*, J. Haywood (*Activities for Young People and Volunteering Division*); P. Bailey (*Communications Division*); S. Geary (*Partnership Formation & Delivery Division*); C. Tyler (*Policy and Strategy Division*); J. Mackey (*Quality Unit*); Jane Benham (*Standards and Effectiveness Unit*)

### HIGHER EDUCATION GROUP

*Director*, N. Sanders
*Heads of Division*, M. Hipkins (*Higher Education Funding and Organisation Division*); N. Flint (*Student Support Division 1*); N. Graham (*Student Support Division 2*); P. Cohen (*Quality and Employability Division*)

### LEARNING DELIVERY AND STANDARDS GROUP

*Director*, P. Lauener
*Heads of Divisions*, S. Hillier (*FE Funding Division*); P. Mucklow (*Learning and Skills Council and Partnership Division*); S. Orr (*Raising Standards Division*); J. Reid (*Learning Skills Council*); R. Hinchcliffe and M. Stock (*LSC/ALI Information and Business Systems Division*); P. Houten (*Transition Division*); M. Stark (*LSC Corporate Planning Division*)

### QUALIFICATIONS AND YOUNG PEOPLE GROUP

*Director*, R. Hull
*Heads of Divisions*, S. Marshall (*Qualifications for Work Division*); C. Johnson (*School and College Qualifications Division*); T. Fellowes (*Young People Learner Support Division*); A. Davies (*Young People's Policy Division*)

## LEGAL ADVISER'S OFFICE

*Director*, D. Macrae
*Heads of Divisions*, S. Harker (*Legal Advisers Division 1, School*); F. Clarke (*Legal Advisers Division 2, Post 16*); D. Aries (*Legal Advisers Division 3, HE and Teachers and Support Directorates*); D. Collins (*Legal Advisers Division 4, Equality and External*); P. Kilgarriff (*Legal Advisers Division 5, Standards*)

## CORPORATE SERVICES AND DEVELOPMENT DIRECTORATE

*Director-General*, S. Thomas
*Heads of Divisions*, T. Eves (*Personnel Division*); J. McIntyre (*Learning Academy*) C. Moore (*Information Service Division*); P. Neill; G. Archer (*Leadership and Change Division*); D. Jarvis (*Equal Opportunities Unit*)

## SCHOOLS DIRECTORATE

*Director-General*, H. Williams

### CURRICULUM AND COMMUNICATIONS GROUP

*Director*, I. Wilde
*Heads of Divisions*, G. McKenzie (*Curriculum Division*); S. Edwards (*School Communications Division*); D. Brown (*NGFL-National Grid for Learning Division*); N. Baxter (*Parents and Performance Division*); D. Palmer (*ICT Strategy Unit*); vacant (*Future Development of the NGFL*)

### PUPIL SUPPORT AND INCLUSION GROUP

*Director*, T. Jeffrey
*Heads of Divisions*, B. Shaw (*School Inclusion Division*); Ms S. Johnson and Ms. R. Pratt (*Schools Plus*); M. Phipps; (*Pupil Support and Independent Schools Division*); C. Wells

### SURE START UNIT

*Director*, N. Eisenstadt
*Head of Division*, A. Esunshile
*Divisional Managers*, J. Doughty; T. A. McCully (*Children and Young People's Unit*); T. Finkelstein (*Policy*)

### TEACHERS GROUP

*Director*, S. Kershaw
*Heads of Divisions*, G. Holley (*Teachers' Supply and Training Division*); A. Jackson (*Teacher's Pay and Policy Division*); P. Swift (*School Leadership Division*); P. Jones (*Teacher's Standards and Pensions Division*); R. Harrison (*Teacher's Professional Development Division*); M. Williams (*Teacher Rapid Response Unit*)

### SCHOOL ORGANISATION AND FUNDING GROUP

*Director*, H. Williams
*Heads of Divisions*, K. Beeton (*Schools Capital and Buildings Division*); M. Patel (*Architects and Building*); A. Wye (*School and LEA Funding Division*); C. Macready (*School Admissions Organisation and Governance Division*)

### STANDARDS AND EFFECTIVENESS UNIT

*Acting Director*, S. Crowne
*Heads of Divisions*, R. Wood (*Diversity and Best Practice Division*); vacant (*LEA Improvement Division*); S. Adamson (*Pupil Standards Division*); C. Wormald (*School Improvements and Excellence*); S. Imbriano (*Local Implementation Unit*)
*Divisional Managers*, C. Bienkowska (*Diversity in Secondary Education*); J. Benham (*14 to 19 year-olds*); S. Crowne (City Academies Unit)
*Heads of Division*, R. Graham (*Schools Communications Unit*); J. Coles (*Green Paper Implementation Division*)

### STRATEGY AND COMMUNICATIONS DIRECTORATE

*Director*, P. Wanless
*Heads of Divisions*, J. Simpson (*Media Relations Division*); T. Cook (*Deputy Head of Media Relations*); C. Bicknell (*Communications and Knowledge Management Division*); M. Lord (*Strategy Division*); N. Houston (*Team Leader*) (*Speeches, Presentations and General Briefing Unit*); Y. Diamond (*Welfare to Work Communication Division*); J. Ross (*Publicity Division*); G. McKenzies (*Regional Policy Division*); B. Glickman (*Employer Relations*)
*Private Office Head of Division*, N. Roache

## EXECUTIVE AGENCY

### THE EMPLOYMENT SERVICE

Caxton House, Tothill Street, London SW1H 9NA
Tel: 020-7273 6060; Fax: 020-7273 6099

The aims of the Employment Service are to contribute to high levels of employment and growth by helping all people without a job to find work and by helping employers to fill their vacancies, and to help individuals lead rewarding working lives.

From 1 October 2001 The Employment Service, and some parts of the Benefits Agency will merge into a new organisation called 'Jobcentre Plus.'

*Chief Executive*, L. Lewis, CB
*Director of Jobcentre Services*, Ms C. Dodgson,
*Director of Human Resources*, K. White
*Director of Welfare to Work Delivery*, R. Foster
*Director for Finance, Commercial and Corporate Services*, M. Neale
*Non-Executive Directors*, R. Dykes; Ms L. de Groot; C. Cox
*Regional Directors*, M. Groves (*East Midlands and Eastern*); S. Holt, OBE (*London and South-East*); V. Robinson; OBE (*Northern*); L. Brown; (*North-West*); Ms D. Ross; (*South-West*); Ms R. Thew (*West Midlands*); R. Lasko (*Yorkshire and Humberside*)
*Director for Scotland*, A. R. Brown
*Director for Wales*, Mrs S. Keyse

---

## DEPARTMENT FOR ENVIRONMENT, FOOD AND RURAL AFFAIRS

Nobel House, 17 Smith Square, London SW1P 3JR
Tel: 020-7238 3000; Fax: 020-7238 6591
Email: helpline@infdefra.gov.uk
Web: www.defra.gov.uk

---

The Department for Environment, Food, and Rural Affairs is responsible for Government policies on agriculture, horticulture and fisheries in England and for policies relating to the safety and quality of food in the UK as a whole, including composition, labelling, additives, contaminants and new production processes. In association with the agriculture departments of the Scottish Executive, the National Assembly for Wales and the Northern Ireland Office and with the Intervention Board, the Ministry is responsible for negotiations in the EU on the common agricultural and fisheries policies, and for single European market questions relating to its responsibilities. Its remit also includes international agricultural and food trade policy.

The department exercises responsibilities for the protection and enhancement of the countryside and the marine environment, for flood defence and for other rural issues. It is the licensing authority for veterinary medicines and the registration authority for pesticides. It administers policies relating to the control of animal, plant and fish diseases. It provides scientific, technical and professional services and advice to farmers, growers and ancillary industries, and it commissions research to assist in the formulation and assessment of policy and to underpin applied research and development work done by industry. Responsibility for food safety and standards was transferred to the new Food Standards Agency in April 2000.

*Ssecretary of State for Environment, Food and Rural Affairs*, The Rt. Hon. Margaret Beckett, MP
*Principal Private Secretary (G7)*, Andrew Slade
*Private Secretary*, Alexia Flowerday
*Parliamentary Private Secretary*, Andrew Reed, MP
*Special Advisers*, Sheila Watson; Nicci Collins
*Minister of State (Environment)*, The Rt. Hon. Michael Meacher, MP
*Parliamentary Private Secretary*, Terry Rooney, MP
*Private Secretary*, Gabriel Edwards
*Minister of State (Rural Affairs)*, The Rt. Hon. A. Michael, MP
*Parliamentary Private Secretary*, Peter Bradley, MP
*Private Secretary*, Becky Taylor
*Parliamentary Under-Secretary*, Elliot Morley, MP
*Private Secretary*, Robert Hitchen
*Parliamentary Under Secretary*, The Lord Whitty
*Permanent Secretary (SCS)*, Brian Bender, CB

## ESTABLISHMENTS GROUP

*Director of Establishments (SCS)*, R. A. Saunderson

## CORPORATE SERVICES DIVISION

*Head of Division (SCS)*, B. Jones

### Personnel Division

*Head of Division (SCS)*, Ms T. Newell

### Building and Estate Management

Eastbury House, 30–34 Albert Embankment, London SE1 7TL
Tel: 020-7238 6000

*Head of Division (SCS)*, J. A. S. Nickson

## INFORMATION TECHNOLOGY DIRECTORATE

Government Buildings, Epsom Road, Guildford, Surrey GU1 2LD Tel: 01483-403757

## E-BUSINESS

*E-Business Director*, D. Rossington
*IT Director*, S. Soper
*Assistant Director (Applications)*, P. Barber
*Assistant Director (Infrastructure)*, D. Brown
*Assistant Director (E-Business)*, A. Hill

## COMMUNICATIONS DIRECTORATE

Nobel House, 17 Smith Square, London SW1P 3JR
Tel: 020-7238 6000; Helpline 0645-335577

*Director of Communications (SCS)*, R. Lowson
*Head of News*, M. Smith
*Chief Publicity Officer (G7)*, N. Wagstaffe
*Principal Librarian (G7)*, P. McShane

## AGENCY OWNERSHIP UNIT

3-8 Whitehall House (West Block), London SW1A 2HH
*Head of Unit (SCS)*, Dr M. Tas

## FINANCE DEPARTMENT

3–8 Whitehall Place (West Block), London SW1A 2HH
Tel: 020-7238 6000

*Finance Director, (SCS)*, P. Elliott

### Financial Policy Division

*Head of Division (SCS)*, F. Marlow

### Procurement and Contracts Division

19–29 Woburn Place, London WC1H 0LU
Tel: 020-7273 3000

*Head of Division (SCS)*, D. Rabey

### Audit, Consultancy and Management Services

19–29 Woburn Place, London WC1H 0LU
Tel: 020-7273 3000

*Director of Audit (SCS)*, D. V. Fisher

### Resource Management Strategy Unit

19–29 Woburn Place, London WC1H 0LU
Tel: 020-7273 3000

*Head of Unit (SCS)*, D. V. Fisher

### Resource Management Division

Foss House, Kings Pool, 1–2 Peasholme Green, York YO1 7PX Tel: 01904-455328

*Head of Division (G6)*, R. Atkinson

### Business Improvement Division

*Head of Unit (G7)*, Ms. J. Flint and G. Holt

## LEGAL DEPARTMENT

55 Whitehall, London SW1A 2EY
Tel: 020-7238 6000

*Legal Adviser and Solicitor (SCS)*, Miss K. M. S. Morton
*Principal Assistant Solicitors (SCS)*, S. Parker; Ms C. A. Crisham

### Legal Divisions

*Assistant Solicitor, Division A1*, P. Davis
*Assistant Solicitor, Division A2*, Ms A. Werbicki
*Assistant Solicitor, Division A3*, C. Gregory
*Assistant Solicitor, Division A4* , C. Allen
*Assistant Solicitor, Division A5* , N. Lambert
*Assistant Solicitor, Division A6*, B. Dickinson
*Assistant Solicitor, Division B1*, Ms S. Spence
*Assistant Solicitor, Division B2*, M. Patel
*Assistant Solicitor, Division B3*, I. Corbett

### Investigation Unit

*Chief Investigation Officer (G7)*, Miss J. Panting

## ECONOMICS AND STATISTICS

3–8 Whitehall Place (West Block), London SW1A 2HH
Tel: 020-7238 6000
*Director of Economics and Statistics Group (SCS)*, D. Thompson

### Divisions

*Senior Economic Adviser, Economics and Statistics (Farm Business) (G6)*, J. Watson
*Senior Economic Adviser, Economics (International) (SCS)*, N. Atkinson
*Senior Economic Adviser, Economics (Resource Use) (SCS)*, J. P. Muriel

### Statistics Division

Foss House, Kings Pool, 1–2 Peasholme Green, York YO1 7PX Tel: 01904-455332

*Chief Statistician (Commodities and Food) (SCS)*, S. Platt
*Chief Statistician (Census and Surveys) (SCS)*, P. F. Helm

## CHIEF SCIENTIST'S GROUP

Cromwell House, Dean Stanley Street, Westminster, London, SW1P 3JH.
Tel: 020-7238 6000

*Chief Scientist* (*SCS*), Dr D. W. F. Shannon

DIVISIONS

*Head, Agriculture, Environment and Food Technology* (*SCS*), Dr J. C. Sherlock
*Head, Veterinary, Food and Aquatic Science* (*SCS*), vacant
*Head, Research Policy and International* (*SCS*), A. R. Burne

## FISHERIES DEPARTMENT

Nobel House, 17 Smith Square, London SW1P 3JR
*Fisheries Director* (*SCS*), S. Wentworth

DIVISIONS

*Head, Fisheries I* (*SCS*), P. M. Boyling
*Head, Fisheries II* (*SCS*), R. Cowan
*Head, Fisheries III* (*SCS*), C. Ryder
*Head, Fisheries IV* (*SCS*), B. S. Edwards
*Chief Inspector, Sea Fisheries Inspectorate* (*G6*), S. G. Ellson

## AGRICULTURAL CROPS AND COMMODITIES DIRECTORATE

3–8 Whitehall Place (West Block), London SW1A 2HH
Tel: 020-7238 6000

*Director General* (*SCS*), vacant

## EUROPEAN UNION AND INTERNATIONAL POLICY

*Director* (*SCS*), A. J. Lebrecht

DIVISIONS

*Head, European Union and Agriculture Strategy* (*SCS*), T. Eddy
*Head, European Union and International Division* (*SCS*), D. Dawson
*Head, Cap Schemes Policy*, Ms J. Purnell

## AGRICULTURE GROUP

*Head of Group* (*SCS*), D. Hunter

DIVISIONS

*Head, Horticulture, Potatoes and HMI* (*SCS*), D. Jones
*Head Genetic Modification and Industrial Crops*, Ms S. Henry
*Head, Arable Crops* (*SCS*), A. Kuyk
*Head, Beef and Sheep* (*SCS*), I. Llewelyn
*Head, Livestock Schemes* (*SCS*), A. Taylor
*Head, Milk, Pigs, Eggs and Poultry* (*SCS*), G. Ross
*Head Plant Health and PHSI*, S. Hunter

## FOOD INDUSTRY, COMPETITIVENESS AND CONSUMERS

*Director*, (*SCS*), J. Robbs

DIVISIONS

*Head, Food and Drinks Industry* (*SCS*), C. Young
*Head, International Relations and Export Promotion* (*SCS*), N. Denton
*Head, Agricultural Resources and Better Regulations* (*SCS*), L. Harris
*Head, Marketing, Competition and Consumers* (*SCS*), Ms J. Allfrey
*Head, Flood and Coastal Defence* (*SCS*), J. Park

PLANT VARIETY RIGHTS OFFICE AND SEED DIVISION

White House Lane, Huntingdon road, Cambridge CB3 0LF
*Head of Office* (*SCS*), H. Hamilton

## POLICY AND CORPORATE STRATEGY

3–8 Whitehall Place (West Block), London SW1A 2HH
Tel: 020-7238 6000

*Director*, B. Harding
EAST OF ENGLAND, Building A, Westbrook Centre, Milton Road, Cambridge, CB4 1YG. Tel: 01223-346700. *Rural Director*, J. Rabagliati
EAST MIDLANDS, The Belgrave Centre, The Stanley Place, Talbot Street, Nottingham, NG1 5GG. *Rural Director*, Graham Norbury
NORTH-EAST, Welbar House, Gallowgate, Newcastle-upon-Tyne, NE1 4TD. Tel: 0191-201 3300. *Rural Director*, John Bainton
NORTH WEST, Sunley Tower, Picadilly Plaza, Manchester, M1 4BE. Tel: 0161-952 4000. *Regional Director*, Neil Cumberlidge
SOUTH-EAST, Bridge House, 1 Walnut Tree Close, Guildford, Surrey, GU1 4GA. Tel: 01483-882255. *Regional Director*, Alison Parker
SOUTH-WEST, 4th and 5th Floors, The Pithay, Bristol, BS1 2PB. Tel: 0117-900 1700. *Regional Director*, Tim Render
WEST MIDLANDS, 77 Paradise Circus, Queensway, Birmingham, B1 2DT. Tel: 0121-212 5000. *Regional Director*, Brin Davies
YORKSHIRE AND THE HUMBERSIDE, PO Box 213, City House, New Station Street, Leeds, LS1 4US. Tel: 0113-280 0600. *Regional Director*, (*Acting*), Ms C. Deakins

## ANIMAL HEALTH AND ENVIRONMENT GROUP

*Deputy Secretary* (*SCS*), Ms J. Bacon

## ENVIRONMENT AND RURAL DEVELOPMENT GROUP

*Head of Group*, Mrs K. A. J. Brown

DIVISIONS

*Head, Conservation Management*, J. Osmond
*Head, Rural Division*, Ms. L. Cornish
*Head, Land Use*, A. Perrins
*Head, Rural Marine and Environment*, P. Cleasby
*Head, Corporate Strategy Unit*, Ms A. Tarran

## RURAL DEVELOPMENT SERVICE

*Head of Group*, S. Nason
*Technical Advice*, A. Hooper
*Business Process Director*, J. Robinson

## RURAL DEVELOPMENT CENTRES

EAST, Government Buildings, Brooklands Avenue Cambridge, CB2 2DR , Tel: 01223-462727. *Regional Manager*, M. Edwards
EAST-MIDLANDS , Block 7, Government Buildings, Chalfont Drive, Nottingham, NG8 3SN. Tel: 0115-929 1191. *Regional Manager*, S. Buckenham
NORTH-EAST , Government Buildings Kenton Bar, Newcastle-upon-Tyne, NE5 3EW. Tel: 0191-286 3377. *Regional Manager*, F. Gough
NORTH-WEST , Electra Way, Crewe Business Park, Crewe, Cheshire, CW1 6GJ. Tel: 01270-754000. *Regional Manager*, Tony Percival

SOUTH-EAST , Government Buildings, Coley Park, Reading, Berkshire, RG1 6DT. Tel: 01189-581 222, *Regional Manager*, Nick Beard

SOUTH-WEST , Block 3, Government Buildings, Burghill Road, Westbury-on-Trym, Bristol, BS10 6NJ. Tel: 0117-959 1000. *Regional Manager*, David Sisson

WEST MIDLANDS , Block C, Government Buildings, Whittington Road, Worcester, WR5 2LQ. Tel: 01905-763355. *Regional Manager*, C. Deakin

YORKSHIRE AND THE HUMBERSIDE , Government Buildings, Otley Road, Lawnswood, Leeds, LS16 5QT. Tel: 0113 261 3333. *Regional Manager*, M. Silverwood

## ANIMAL HEALTH GROUP

1A Page Street, London SW1P 4PQ. Tel: 020-7904 6000

*Head of Group (SCS)*, N. Thornton

### DIVISIONS

*Head of Animal Indentification and Animal International Trade*, Mrs V. Smith
*Animal Disease Control*, R. Hathaway
*Head Animal Health Services*, Ms C. Harold
*Animal Welfare*, G. Noble
*TSE Group Director*, P. Nash
*Head, BSE and Scrapie*, J. A. Bailey
*Head Sheep TSE*, N. Cleary

## ANIMAL HEALTH AND ENVIRONMENT DIRECTORATE

Nobel House, 17 Smith Square, London, SW1P 3JR
*Director General*, Ms J. Bacon

## WILDLIFE AND COUNTRYSIDE GROUP

Eland House, Bressenden Place, London, SW1E 5DU Tel: 020-7944 3000.
*Director*, Ms S. Lamberet

### DIVISIONS

*Countryside*, S. Carter
*European Wildlife*, H. Neal
*Global Wildlife*, M. Brasher
*Rural Development*, H. Cleary
*Rural Task Force Secretariat*, C. Dunabin

## CHIEF VETERINARY OFFICER'S GROUP

1A Page Street, London SW1P 4PQ. Tel: 020-7904 6000

*Chief Veterinary Officer (SCS)*, J. M. Scudamore
*Deputy Chief Veterinary Officer (Services) (SCS)*, M. Atkinson

### DIVISIONS

*Head of Veterinary Services East (SCS)*, G. Jones
*Head of Veterinary Services West (SCS)*, J. Cross
*Head of Veterinary Services North (SCS)*, R. Drummond
*Head of Veterinary Services Resources (SCS)*, Ms B. Phillip
*Assistant Chief Veterinary Officer* (Scotland), L. Gardner
*Head of Veterinary Services (Scotland) (SCS)*, D. McIntosh
*Assistant Chief Veterinary Officer (Wales)*, A. Edwards
*Deputy Chief Veterinary Officer (Policy) (SCS)*, R. Cawthorne
*Head, Veterinary International Trade Team (SCS)*, R. A. Bell
*Head, Veterinary Notifiable Disease Team (Exotic Diseases) (SCS)*, Dr D. Matthews
*Head, Veterinary Notifiable Disease Team (Endemic Animal Diseases and Zoonosis) (SCS)*, vacant
*Head, Welfare Team (SCS)*, D. Pritchard

## EXECUTIVE AGENCIES

### CENTRAL SCIENCE LABORATORY

Sand Hutton, York YO41 1LZ
Tel: 01904-462000; Fax: 01904-462111

The agency provides advice, technical and enforcement support, underpinned by appropriate research, to meet both the statutory and policy objectives of DEFRA; and it provides research and development and advice on a commercial basis to other government departments and to public and private sector organisations both overseas and UK-based.

The main areas are: safeguarding food supplies through the identification and control of invertebrate pests, plant pests and diseases; the management of vertebrate wildlife; food and consumer safety with the emphasis on the microbiological and chemical safety, and the quality and nutritional value of food. The agency is also concerned with environmental protection through the investigation of the impact of agriculture on the environment, and the promotion of biodiversity in agricultural habitats.

*Chief Executive (G3)*, Prof. M. Roberts
*Research Directors (G5)*, Prof. Tony Hardy (*Agriculture and Environment*); Prof. John Gilbert (*Food*)
*Commercial Director*, Dr Robert Bolton
*Corporate Services Director*, Dr Helen Crews
*Finance and Procurement Director*, Richard Shaw

### CENTRE FOR ENVIRONMENT, FISHERIES AND AQUACULTURE SCIENCE

Pakefield Road, Lowestoft, Suffolk NR33 0HT
Tel: 01502-562244; Fax: 01502-513865

The Agency, established in April 1997, provides research and consultancy services in fisheries science and management, aquaculture, fish health and hygiene, environmental impact assessment, and environmental quality assessment.
*Chief Executive*, Dr P. Greig-Smith

### PESTICIDES SAFETY DIRECTORATE

Mallard House, Kings Pool, 3 Peasholme Green, York YO1 7PX. Tel: 01904-640500; Fax: 01904-455733

The Pesticides Safety Directorate is responsible for the evaluation and approval of agricultural pesticides and the development of policies relating to them, in order to protect consumers, users and the environment.
*Chief Executive (G4)*, Dr H. K. Wilson
*Director (Policy) (G5)*, Dr S. Popple
*Director (Approvals) (G5)*, R. Davis

### VETERINARY LABORATORIES AGENCY

Woodham Lane, New Haw, Addlestone, Surrey KT15 3NB
Tel: 01932-341111; Fax: 01932-347046

The Veterinary Laboratories Agency provides scientific and technical expertise in animal and public health.
*Chief Executive*, Dr S. Edwards
*Director of Research*, Dr J. A. Morris
*Director of Surveillance and Laboratory Services*, R. Hancock
*Director of Finance*, C. Morrey
*Laboratory Secretary*, C. Edwards

### VETERINARY MEDICINES DIRECTORATE

Woodham Lane, New Haw, Addlestone, Surrey KT15 3LS
Tel: 01932-336911; Fax: 01932-336618

The Veterinary Medicines Directorate is responsible for all aspects of the authorisation and control of veterinary medicines, including post-authorisation surveillance of residues in animals and animal products, and the provision of policy advice to Ministers.

*Chief Executive* (*G4*), Dr J. M. Rutter
*Director* (*Policy*) (*G5*), R. Anderson
*Director* (*Licensing*) (*G5*), S. Dean
*Secretary and Head of Business Unit* (*G6*), J. FitzGerald
*Licensing Manager, Pharmaceuticals and Feed Additives* (*G6*), J. P. O'Brien
*Licensing Manager, Immunologicals* (*G6*), Dr D. J. K. Mackay

---

FOREIGN AND COMMONWEALTH OFFICE
King Charles Street, London SW1A 2AH
Tel: 020-7270 1500
Web: www.fco.gov.uk

---

The Foreign and Commonwealth Office provides, through its staff in the UK and through its diplomatic missions abroad, the means of communication between the British Government and other governments and international governmental organisations on all matters falling within the field of international relations. It is responsible for alerting the British Government to the implications of developments overseas; for promoting British interests overseas; for protecting British citizens abroad; for explaining British policies to, and cultivating relationships with, governments overseas; for the discharge of British responsibilities to the overseas territories; for entry clearance (through the Joint Entry Clearance Unit, with the Home Office) and for promoting British business overseas (jointly with the Department of Trade and Industry through British Trade International).

*Secretary of State for Foreign and Commonwealth Affairs*, The Rt. Hon. Jack Straw, MP
*Principal Private Secretary*, Simon McDonald
*Special Advisers*, Michael Williams; Ed Owen
*Parliamentary Private Secretary*, Colin Pickthall, MP
*Minister for Europe*, The Rt. Hon. Peter Hain, MP
*Private Secretary*, James Morrison
*Minister of State for Trade*, The Rt. Hon. Baroness Symons of Vernham Dean,
*Private Secretary*, Robin Gwynn
*Parliamentary Under-Secretary of State*, Ben Bradshaw, MP
*Private Secretary*, Hugo Shorter
*Parliamentary Under-Secretary of State*, Dr. Denis MacShane, MP
*Private Secretary*, Fiona Gibb
*Parliamentary Under-Secretary of State*, Baroness Amos
*Private Secretary*, David Cairns
*Parliamentary Private Secretaries*, Charlotte Atkins, MP; Caroline Flint, MP
*Permanent Under-Secretary of State and Head of HM Diplomatic Service*, Sir John Kerr, KCMG
*Private Secretary*, Susan Hyland
*Chief Executive*, †*British Trade International*, Sir David Wright, KCMG, LVO
*Deputy Under-Secretaries*, Peter Collecott (*Chief Clerk*); Michael. Arthur, CMG (*Economic Director*); M. Wood, CMG (*Legal Adviser*); Peter Westmacott, CMG, LVO; Emyr Jones Parry, CMG (*Political Director*); Stephen Wright, CMG

DIRECTORS

*Africa*, M. Lyall Grant
*Americas/Overseas Territories*, R. Wilkinson, CVO
*International Security*, W. Ehrman
*Wider Europe*, J. Macgregor, CVO
*European Union*, K. Darroch, CMG
*Chief Executive FCO Services*, S. Sage
*Global Issues*, N. Brewer
*South East Europe*, A. Charlton CMG
*Middle East and North Africa*, A. Goulty CMG
*Asia Pacific*, R. Marsden
*British Trade International*, D. Hall CMG
*Personnel*, D. Holt
*Public Services*, D. Reddaway
*Resources*, S. Gass

HEADS OF DEPARTMENTS

*African Department (Equatorial)*, F. Baker
*African Department* (*Southern*), A. Pocock
*Aviation and Maritime Department*, C. Segar
*Central and North-West European Department*, Sir John Ramsden, Bt.
*Change Management Unit*, Ms S. Matthews
*China/Hong Kong Department*, A. Seaton
*Common Foreign and Security Policy Department*, T. Barrow
*Commonwealth Co-ordination*, C. Bright
*Consular Division*, J. Watt
*Counter-Terrorism Policy Department*, K. Bloomfield
*Cultural Relations Department*, Dr M. Reilly
*Diplomatic Service Families Association;* E. Salvesen
*Diplomatic Service Trade Union Side* (*DSTUS*), S. Watson
*Drugs and International Crime Department*, M. Ryder
*Eastern Department*, S. Butt
*Eastern Adriatic Department*, S. Wordsworth
*Economic Policy*, C. Butler
*Environment Policy*, J. Ashton
*Estate Strategy*, J. Metcalfe
*European Unit* (*Bi-lateral*), K. Pierce
*European Union Department* (*External*), S. Featherstone
*European Union Department* (*Internal*), J. Bevan
*Financial Compliance Unit*, D. Major
*FCO Association*, D. Burns *(Chairman)*
*FCO Services*, J. Clark (*Head, Conference and Visits Group*); J. Elgie (*Head, Estates Group*); J. Thompson, MBE (*Head, Information Management Group*); V. Life (*Head Management Consultancy Services*); V. Davies (*Head Language Group*); Ms J. Link (*Head, Resource Management Group*); M. Carr (*Head, Support Group*); N. Stickells (*Head, Technical Group*)
*Human Rights Policy*; Dr C. Browne
*Internal Audit* (*FCO/DFID*), R. Elias
*IT Strategy Unit*, M. Kirk
*Joint Entry Clearance* Unit (*Joint FCO/Home Office Unit*), R. Brinkley
*Latin America and Caribbean Department*, J. Dew
*Legal Advisers*, M. Wood, CMG
*Middle East Department*, W. Patey
*National Audit Office*, J. Pearce
*Near East and North Africa Department*, C. Prentice
*News*, J. Williams
*Non-Proliferation Department*, T. Dowse
*North America Department*, N. Armour
*North-East Asia and Pacific Department*, N. Archer
*Organisation for Security Co-operation in Europe*, P. January
*Overseas Territories Department*, A. Huckle
*Parliamentary Relations and Devolution*, M. Hutton
*Personnel Command*, T. Simmons (*Performance and Development*); Ms E. Kennedy (*Asst. Director, *Medical and Welfare*); P. Jones (*Personnel Management* ); S.

Wightman (*Personnel Policy*); R. White (*Personnel Services*); C. Edgerton and T. Malcomson (*Prosper*); A. Cookson-Hall (*Recruitment*); G. Deacon (*Interchange*); C. Dharwarker (*Training*); R. Clarke (*Policy Planning Staff*)
*Protocol Department*, Mrs K. F. Colvin
*Public Diplomacy*, J. Buck
*Purchasing Directorate*, M. Gower
*Quality and Efficiency*, K. Jackson
*Records and Historical*, H. Yasamee
*Research Analysis*, R. D. Lavers
*Resource Accounting*, M. Brown
*Resource Budgeting*, M. Williamson
*Science and Technology*, R. Barnett
*Security Strategy Unit*, J. Macgregor
*Security Policy*, A. M. Thomson
*South Asia*, S. N. Evans, OBE
*South-East Asian Department*, R. Gordon
*Southern European*, G. Gillham
*United Nations*, S. Pattison
*Whitehall Liaison Department*, M. Kidd

BRITISH TRADE INTERNATIONAL

*Central Services Group*
*Group Director*, D. Hall

REGIONAL GROUP

*Group Director*, I. Jones

INTERNATIONAL GROUP

*Group Director*, Q. Quayle

BUSINESS GROUP

*Group Director*, D. Warren
*Strategy and Communications Group*
*Group Director*, S. Lyle Smythe

INVEST UK

*Chief Executive*, W. Pedder

*Joint Foreign and Commonwealth Office/Department for International Development department
† Joint Foreign and Commonwealth Office/Department of Trade and Industry directorate

## EXECUTIVE AGENCY

WILTON PARK CONFERENCE CENTRE

Wiston House, Steyning, W. Sussex BN44 3DZ
Tel: 01903-815020; Fax: 01903-879647

Wilton Park organises international affairs conferences and is hired out to Government departments and commercial users.
*Chief Executive*, C. B. Jennings

## CORPS OF QUEEN'S MESSENGERS

Support Group, Foreign and Commonwealth Office, London SW1A 2AH Tel: 020-7270 2779

*Superintendent of the Corps of Queen's Messengers*, A. C. Brown
*Queen's Messengers*, P. Allen; R. Allen; Maj. A. N. D. Bols; Maj. P. C. H. Dening-Smitherman; Sqn. Ldr. J. S. Frizzell; Capt. N. C. E. Gardner; Maj. D. A. Griffiths; A. Hill; R. Long; Maj. K. J. Rowbottom; Maj. M. R. Senior; Maj. J. E. A. Andre; W. Lisle; Maj. J. H. Steele; J. A. Hatfield; P. J. Hearn; D. J. Bufton

## DEPARTMENT OF HEALTH

Richmond House, 79 Whitehall, London SW1A 2NL
Tel: 020-7210 3000
Web: www.open.gov.uk/doh/dhhome.htm

The Department of Health is responsible for the provision of the National Health Service in England and for social care, including oversight of personal social services run by local authorities in England for children (except day care, which is now the responsibility of the DfES), the elderly, the infirm, the handicapped and other persons in need. It is responsible for health promotion and has functions relating to public and environmental health, food safety and nutrition. The Department is also responsible for the ambulance and emergency first aid services, under the Civil Defence Act 1948. The Department represents the UK at the European Union and other international organisations including the World Health Organisation. It also supports UK-based healthcare and pharmaceutical industries. Responsibility for food safety was transferred to the Food Standards Agency in April 2000.
*Secretary of State for Health*, The Rt. Hon. Alan Milburn, MP
*Principal Private Secretary*, H. Rodgers
*Private Secretaries*, S. Sinclair; S. Waring
*Special Advisers*, P. Corrigan; D. Murphy
*Parliamentary Private Secretary*, M. Hall , MP
*Minister of State*, The Rt. Hon. John Hutton, MP (*Structure and Resources*)
*Private Secretary*, T. Fretten
*Parliamentary Private Secretary*, Claire Ward, MP
*Minister of State*, Jacqui Smith, MP (*Social Care and Mental Health*)
*Private Secretary*, J. Adedeji
*Parliamentary Under-Secretaries of State*, Yvette Cooper, MP; The Lord Hunt of Kings Heath, OBE; Hazel Blears, MP
*Parliamentary Private Secretary*, Andy Love, MP
*Private Secretaries*, P. Mcnaught; Ms H. McLain; K. Holton
*Parliamentary Clerk*, J. Mean
*Permanent Secretary* (*SCS*), N. Crisp
*Private Secretary*, R. Wetterstand
*Chief Medical Officer* (*SCS*), Prof. L. Donaldson, FRCSEd, FRCP
*Chief Executive, Operations Officer* (*SCS*), Neil McKay

STATISTICS DIVISION

*Director of Statistics* (*SCS*), J. Fox
*Chief Statisticians* (*SCS*), R. K. Willmer; A. Roberts; J. Stokoe; A. Sutherland

INTERNATIONAL AND CONSTITUTIONAL BRANCH (ICB)
*Branch Head* (*SCS*), N. Boyd

PERSONNEL SERVICES

*Director of Personnel* (*SCS*), F. Goldhill
*Heads of Branches* (*SCS*), C. Muir; Mrs W. Honeyghan-Williams; J. Sinclair

INFORMATION SERVICES DIVISION

*Head of Division* (*SCS*), Dr A. A. Holt
*Heads of Branches*, Mrs L. Wishart; C. Horsey; M. Rainsford; Mrs J. Dainty; R. Long; P. G. Cobb; Mrs D. McDonagh
*Joint Service Managers*, P. Dowler and T. Shaw

### Resource Management

*Head of Division (SCS)*, D. Clark
*Head of Branch*, S. Mitchell,

### Finance Directorate

*Director of Finance*, (SCS), R. Douglas
*Deputy Directors of Finance*, C. Daws; vacant
*Head of Branches*, L. Eccles; I. Ellul; M. Sturges, J. Stopes-Roe; J. Tomlinson; P. Coates; P. Taylor; A. MacLellan; P. Kendall

### Medicines, Pharmacy and Industry Division (MPI)

*Head of Division*, A. McKeon
*Heads of Branches*, M. Brownlee; K. Guiness; J. Middleton; Dr J. Smith

### Economics and Operational Research Division (Health)

*Chief Economic Adviser (SCS)*, C. H. Smee, CBE
*Heads of Branches*, Dr S. Harding; Dr G. Royston; A. Hare; N. York;

### Communications Directorate

*Director of Communications (SCS)*, vacant
*Deputy Directors*, S. Jarvis (*Media*); W. Roberts (*Campaigns*); P. Addison-Child (*Corporate Communications*)

## SOLICITOR'S OFFICE

*Solicitor (SCS)*, M. Morgan, CB
*Director of Legal Services (SCS)*, Mrs G. S. Kerrigan

## PUBLIC HEALTH POLICY GROUP

### Public Health Division

*Head of Division*, Prof. D. Nutbeam
*Heads of Branches*, M. Fry; Ms I. Sharp; M. Haroon; R. Carter; D. Harper; Ms C. Hamlyn; E. Waterhouse, Dr Pui-Ling; Dr D. Macpherson; Mrs E. Johnson; Dr M. O'Mahony

### Winter and Emergency Services Capacity Planning Team (West)

*Division Head*, Ms A. Sergeant
*Head of Branch*, C. Hetherington

## SOCIAL CARE GROUP

*Chief Social Services Inspector*, Ms D. Platt, CBE
*Head of Social Care Policy*, D. Walden
*Deputy Chief Inspectors*, D. Gilroy; Ms A. Nottage
*Heads of Branches (SCS)*, Miss A. Stephenson; R. Wilson (*Section Head*); Ms. C. Brock; B. Clark; Ms A. Gross; R. Campbell; C. Hume
*Assistant Chief Inspector (HQ)*, J. Cleary
*Assistant Chief Inspectors (Regions)*, J. Cypher; B. Riddell; A. Jones; C. P. Brearley; J. Fraser; Mrs L. Hoare; Ms J. Owen; Miss F. McCabe; R. Balfe; J. Bolton

## NURSING GROUP

*Chief Nursing Officer/Director of Nursing (SCS)*, Ms S. Mullally
*Assistant Chief Nursing Officers (SCS)*, Mrs G. Stephens; D. Moore; K. Billingham

### Quality Management Branch

*Branch Head*, Julian Brookes

## RESEARCH AND DEVELOPMENT DIVISION

*Director of Research and Development*, Prof. Sir John Pattison
*Heads of Branches (SCS)*, Dr P. Greenaway; Mrs J. Griffin; Ms A. Kauder; M. Taylor

## NHS EXECUTIVE

Quarry House, Quarry Hill, Leeds LS2 7UE
Tel: 0113-254 5000

*Chief Executive*, N. Crisp
*Director of Human Resources*, A. Foster
*Director of Finance*, R. Douglas
*Health Services Director*, Dr S. Adam
*Director of Research and Development*, Prof. Sir John Pattison
*Head of Planning*, M. P. Dash
*Director of National Cancer Services*, Prof. M. Richards, CBE
*Director of Counter Fraud Services*, J. Gee
*Director of Operation*, R. Kerr, CBE

### Human Resources

*Director of Human Resources*, A. Foster
*Deputy Director of Human Resources (SCS)*, S. Barnett
*Heads of Branches*, B. Dyson; R. Mailly; Ms J. Hargadon; S. Barnett; R. Cairncross; T. Sands; H. Fields; D. Amos; Dr R. J. Moore

### Information Policy Unit

*Head of Unit (SCS)*, Dr P. Drury

### Planning Division

*Director (SCS)*, vacant
*Chief Economic Adviser*, C. Smee, CBE
*Head of Planning*, Ms P. Dash
*Head of Information Policy Unit*, P. Drury
*Director of Statistics*, J. Fox

### Health Services Directorate

*Director (SCS)*, Dr Sheila Adam
*Heads of Branches*, Ms J. McKessack; L. Percival; Ms K. Tyson; H. Shirely-Quirk; A. Sheehan; J. Mahoney; A. Humphrey; A. Mithani; Dr G. Chapman; Dr J. Carpenter; J. Boyington; Dr F. Harvey; Ms H. Robinson; A. Berland; Ms K. Tyson; A. Sheehan; Ms S. White; Ms K. Doran; R. Webster; L. Smith, R. Armstrong; Prof. Ian Phillip; Ms H. Gwynn

### Primary Care Division

*Head of Division*, Ms K. Dovan
*Chief Dental Officer*, Dame Margaret Seward
*Chief Pharmaceutical Officer*, Dr J. Smith
*Heads of Branches*, Miss H. Robinson (*Dental and Optical Services*); K. Guinness (*Pharmacy and Prescribing*); vacant (*White Paper Implementation Team*); R. Webster (*General Medical Services*); H. Gwynn (*Cardiac Services*)

### Finance Directorate

*Director (SCS)*, R. Douglas
*Deputy Directors*, Ms C. Daws; vacant
*Heads of Branches*, M. Sturges; P. Coates; P. Taylor; A. MacLellan; I. Ellul; J. Stopes-Roe; L. Eccles; J. Tomlinson

### Performance Directorate

*Heads of Branches*, S. Peck; Dr J. Bibby, Ms J. Copeland

DIRECTORATE OF COUNTER FRAUD SERVICES

*Director*, J. Gee

## REGIONAL OFFICES

– *see* Social Welfare section

## ADVISORY COMMITTEES

ADVISORY COMMITTEE ON THE MICROBIOLOGICAL SAFETY OF FOOD Room 808C, Aviation House, 125 Kingsway, London, WC2B 6NH. Tel: 020-7276 8946.
*Chairman*, Prof. D. Georgarla, CBE, Ph.D.

COMMITTEE ON THE SAFETY OF MEDICINES, Market Towers, 1 Nine Elms Lane, London SW8 5NQ. Tel: 020-7273 0000. *Director*, I. Hudson Breckenridge, CBE, FRCP, FRCPEd., FRSE

MEDICINES COMMISSION, Market Towers, 1 Nine Elms Lane, London SW8 5NQ. Tel: 020-7273 0652. *Chairman*, Prof. D. H. Lawson, CBE, FRCPEd, FRCP(Glas)

## SPECIAL HEALTH AUTHORITIES

DENTAL VOCATIONAL TRAINING AUTHORITY, Master's House, Temple Grove, Compton Place Road, Eastbourne, E. Sussex BN20 8AD. Tel: 01323-431189. *Chairman*, R. Davies; *Secretary*, Ms J. Verity

FAMILY HEALTH SERVICES APPEAL AUTHORITY, 30 Victoria Avenue, Harrogate HG1 5PR. Tel: 01423-535415. *Chief Executive*, D. J. Laverick

HEALTH DEVELOPMENT AGENCY, Trevelyan House, 30 Great Peter Street, London SW1P 2HW. Tel: 0171-222 5300. *Chair*, Ms Y. Buckland; *Chief Executive*, Prof R. Parish

MENTAL HEALTH ACT COMMISSION – *see* page 343

MICROBIOLOGICAL RESEARCH AUTHORITY, Porton Down, Salisbury, Wilts SP4 0JG. Tel: 01980-612100. *Chairman*, Sir William Stewart, FRS; *Director*, Dr R. H. Gilmour

NATIONAL BLOOD SERVICE , Oak House, Reeds Crescent, Watford, Herts WD24 4QN. Tel: 01923-486800. *Chairman*, M. Fogden, CB; *Chief Executive*, M. Gorham

NATIONAL INSTITUTE OF CLINICAL EXCELLENCE, 90 Long Acre, London WC2E 9RZ. Tel: 020-7849 3444. *Chairman*, Sir Michael Rawlins; *Chief Executive*, A. Dillon

NHS INFORMATION AUTHORITY, 15 Frederick Road, Edgbaston, Birmingham B15 1JD. Tel: 0121-625 1992. *Chairman*, Prof. A. Bellingham, CBE; *Chief Executive*, N. Bell

NHS LITIGATION AUTHORITY, Mapier Health, 24-28 High Holburn, London WC13 6AZ. Tel: 020-7430 8700. *Chief Executive*, S. Walker

NHS PURCHASING AND SUPPLY AGENCY, Premier House, 60 Caversham Road, Reading, Berks RG1 7EB. Tel 0118-980 8600. *Chairman*, D. Hall, CBE, TD; *Chief Executive*, D. Eaton

PRESCRIPTION PRICING AUTHORITY, Bridge House, 152 Pilgrim Street, Newcastle upon Tyne NE1 6SN. Tel: 0191-232 5371. *Chairman*, Prof. D. J. Johns; *Chief Executive*, N. Scholte

UK TRANSPLANT SUPPORT SERVICE AUTHORITY, Fox Den Road, Stoke Gifford, Bristol BS34 8RR. Tel: 0117-975 7575. *Chairman*, J. F. Shaw; *Chief Executive*, Mrs R. Balderson

## SPECIAL HOSPITALS

ASHWORTH HOSPITAL, Parkbourn, Maghull, Merseyside L31 1HW. Tel: 0151-473 0303. *Chief Executive*, L. Boswell

BROADMOOR HOSPITAL, Crowthorne, Berks RG45 7EG. Tel: 01344-773111. *Chief Executive*, Dr J. Hollyman

RAMPTON HOSPITAL, Retford, Notts DN22 0PD. Tel: 01777-248321. *Chief Executive*, J. Taylor

## EXECUTIVE AGENCIES

### MEDICINES CONTROL AGENCY (MCA)

Market Towers, 1 Nine Elms Lane, London SW8 5NQ
Tel: 020-7273 0000; Fax: 020-7273 0353

The MCA is responsible for safeguarding public health by ensuring all medicines on the UK market meet appropriate standards of safety, quality and efficacy. This is achieved by a system of licensing, inspection, enforcement and monitoring of medicines after they have been licensed.
*Chief Executive*, Dr K. H. Jones, CB

### MEDICAL DEVICES AGENCY

Hannibal House, Elephant and Castle, London SE1 6TQ
Tel: 020-7972 8000; Fax: 020-7972 8108;
Email mail@medical-devices.gov.uk;
Web www.medical-devices.gov.uk

The Agency safeguards the performance, quality and safety of medical devices and ensures that they comply with relevant EU directives.
*Chief Executive*, Dr D. Jefferys

### NHS ESTATES

1 Trevelyan Square, Boar Lane, Leeds LS1 6AE
Tel: 0113-254 7000; Fax: 0113-254 7299;
Email: nhs.estates@doh.gov.uk

NHS Estates provides advice and guidance in the area of healthcare estate and facilities management to the NHS and the healthcare industry.
*Acting Chief Executive*, Peter Wearmouth

### NHS PENSIONS

Hesketh House, 200–220 Broadway, Fleetwood, Lancs FY7 8LG. Tel: 01253-774774; Fax: 01253-774860

NHS Pensions administers the NHS occupational pension scheme.
*Chief Executive*, A. F. Cowan

---

# HOME OFFICE

Home Office, Room 1024, 50 Queen Anne's Gate, London SW1H 9AT
Tel: 020-7273 4000; Fax: 020-7273 2190
Email: gen.ho@gtnet.gov.uk
Web: www.homeoffice.gov.uk

---

The Home Office deals with those internal affairs in England and Wales which have not been assigned to other Government departments. The Home Secretary personally is the link between The Queen and the public, and exercises certain powers on her behalf, including that of the royal pardon.

The Home Office's statement of purpose is to build a safe, just and tolerant society, enhancing opportunities for all and in which rights and responsibilities go hand in hand, and the protection and security of the public are maintained and enhanced; to support and mobilise communities so that, through active citizenship, they are able to shape policy and improvement for their locality, overcome nuisance, anti-social behaviour, maintain and enhance social cohesion and enjoy their homes and public spaces peacefully; to deliver the Departments policies and responsibilities fairly, effectively and efficiently, through the most up to date project and day to day management; and to make the best use of resources and the development of partnership working. These are also supported by the Department's aims, which reflect the priorities of the Government and the Home Secretary in areas of crime, citizenship and communities. They are to reduce crime and the fear of crime; to reduce organised and international crime; to combat terrorism and other threats to national security; to ensure the effective delivery of justice; to deliver effective custodial and community sentences; to reduce re-offending and protect the public; to reduce the availability and abuse of dangerous drugs; to regulate entry to and settlement in the United Kingdom effectively in the interests of sustainable growth and social inclusion; and to support strong active communities in which people of all races and backgrounds are valued and participate on equal terms.

The Home Office delivers these aims by working through the prison, probation and immigration services; its agencies and non-departmental public bodies, including Forensic Science Service, Police Information Technology Organisation, UK Passport Agency; and by working with partners in private, public and voluntary sectors, individuals and communities.

The Home Secretary is also the link between the UK Government and the governments of the Channel Islands and the Isle of Man.

*Secretary of State for the Home Department*, The Rt. Hon. David Blunkett, MP
*Principal Private Secretary* (*SCS*), Ms H. Jackson
*Private Secretaries*, G. Hills; S. Harrison; Ms M. Goldstein, Judith Simpson
*Special Advisers*, Nick Pearce; Katherine Raymond; Sophie Linden; Huw Evans
*Minister of State*, The Rt. Hon. John Denham, MP
*Private Secretary*, Richard Riley
*Minister of State*, The Rt. Hon. Keith Bradley, MP
*Private Secretary*, J. Laurie
*Minister of State*, Lord Rooker of Perry Barr
*Private Secretary*, C. Cumming
*Parliamentary Under-Secretaries of State*, Bob Ainsworth, MP; Beverley Hughes, MP
*Private Secretaries*, Peter Grime
*Parliamentary Clerk*, Ms D. Caddle
*Permanent Under-Secretary of State* (*SCS*), J. Grieve
*Private Secretary*, Phillip. Colligan
*Chief Medical Officer* (*at Department of Health*), Prof. L. Donaldson, QHP, FRCSEd, FRCP

## COMMUNICATION DIRECTORATE

*Director* (*SCS*), B. Butler
*Deputy Director of Communication* (*Head of News*), Julia Simpson, *Deputy Director of Communication* (*Head of Corporate Communication Strategy*) (*SCS*), A. Nash; (*Head of Strategic Communications*) (*SCS*), P. Teare; *Head of Internal Communications*) (*SCS*), P. Samuels
*Assistant Director and Head of Information Services Group* (*G6*), P. Griffiths
*Head of Business Support Group* (*G6*), *G. Samples*

## CONSTITUTIONAL AND COMMUNITY POLICY DIRECTORATE

*Director* (*SCS*), Miss C. Sinclair
*Heads of Units* (*SCS*), E. L. Avery; Dr R. Richmond; T. Cobley; J. Lane; M. Boyle

### Animals (Scientific Procedures) Inspectorate

*Chief Inspector* (*SCS*), Dr J. Richmond
*Superintendent Inspector* (*SCS*), Dr J. Anderson
*Inspectors* (*G6*), Dr R. Curtis; Dr V. Navaratnam; Dr C. Wilkins; P. Buckley; Dr M. Hinton; Dr A. M. Farmer; Mrs S. Houlton; D. Buist

### Gaming Board for Great Britain

— *see* page 334

## CORPORATE DEVELOPMENT AND SERVICES GROUP

Grenadier House, 99–105 Horseferry Road, London SW1P 2DD
Tel: 020-7273 4000
Queen Anne's Gate, London SW1H 9AT
Tel: 020-7273 4000

*Director* (*SCS*), Ms L. Lockyer
*Heads of Units* (*SCS*), Ms D. Loudon; Ms E. Moody; B. Gudgin; J. Potts; N. Benger; G. Jones; T. Edwards; D. McDonaugh; F. Spencer; S. Whaston
*Senior Principals* (*G6*), P. Roascorla, P. Vagg, J. Lawler; M. Fitzpatrick; V. Clayton; C. McCombie; D. G. Jones

## CRIMINAL POLICY GROUP

*Directors* (*SCS*), Mrs S. Street; D. Cooke; Dr E. Wallis
*Heads of Units* (*SCS*), S. Atkins; Bob Eagle; M. Lewer; Dr D. Jones; I. Chisholm; S. Hickson; A. M. Field; T. Williams; M. Gladwyn; J. Sedgwick; Lord Warner; Miss C. Stewart; H. Webber; T. Woolfenden
*Senior Principals* (*G6*), S. Bryans; D. Grice; J. Furniss; Mrs A. Johnstone; S. Limpkin (*G5*); R. Ritchie; S. Trimmins; D. Perry; M. Wilkinson; S. Hart; D. Rigby

### Home Office Crime Prevention College

The Hawkhills, Easingwold, York YO6 3EG
Tel: 01347-825060
*Director*, S. Trimmins

### HM Inspectorate of Probation

*Chief Inspector* (*SCS*), Sir. G. Smith, CBE
*Deputy Chief Inspector* (*G5*), J. Furnis
*Assistant Chief Inspector* (*G6*), J. Kuipers

## IMMIGRATION AND NATIONALITY DIRECTORATE, AND EUROPEAN AND INTERNATIONAL UNIT

Advance House, 15 Wellesley Road, Croydon, Surrey CR9 3LY Tel: 020-8760 3023
Apollo House, 36 Wellesley Road, Croydon, Surrey CR9 3RR Tel: 020-8760 0333
50 Queen Anne's Gate, London SW1H 9AT
Tel: 020-7273 4000
India Buildings, 3rd Floor, Water Street, Liverpool L2 0QN
Tel: 0151-237 5200

*Director-General* (*SCS*), S. Boys Smith
*Deputy Directors-General* (*SCS*), P. Welch, (*Policy*); Dr C. Mace (Operations)
*Heads of Directorates* (*SCS*), J. Actan; U. Wiffen; M. Craske; R. Reynolds

## WORK PERMITS UK

Moorfort, Sheffield, S1 4PQ.
*Director*, M. Caske

IMMIGRATION SERVICE

*Director (Ports) (SCS)*, P. Higgins
*Deputy Director (G6)*, D. Roberts; D. Ingham
*Director (Enforcement) (SCS)*, I. Boon
*Deputy Director (G6)*, C. Harbin, A. Ramlagan-Singh

EUROPEAN INTERNATIONAL UNIT

*Head of Unit (SCS)*, L. Pallett

## LEGAL ADVISERS' BRANCH

*Legal Adviser (SCS)*, D. Seymour
*Deputy Legal Advisers (SCS)*, D. Noble; T. Middleton
*Assistant Legal Advisers (SCS)*, R. J. Clayton; J. R. O'Meara; S. Bramley; C. Price; H. Carter; S. Weston; R. Collins-Rice; R. Davies; C. Osborn

## ORGANISED AND INTERNATIONAL CRIME DIRECTORATE

*Director (SCS)*, J. Warne
*Deputy Director*, Dr K. Collins

## PLANNING, FINANCE AND PERFOMANCE GROUP

50 Queen Anne's Gate, London SW1H 9AT
Tel: 020-7273 4000
Horseferry House, Dean Ryle Street, London SW1P 2AW
Tel: 020-7273 4000

*Directors (SCS)*, R. Fulton; L. Haugh
*Heads of Units* (G7), A. Potter; A. Corry; *Senior Principals (G6)*, K. Venosi; B. Sanders; C. Jones

## POLICING AND CRIME REDUCTION GROUP

*Director (SCS)*, J. Lyon
*Director of Police Services and Volume Crime (SCS)*, J. Daniell
*Senior Principals (G6)*, S. Pike; C. Lee; B. Lane; A. McFarlane; R. Henderson; S. King; S. Trimmins; Dr S. Martin; P. McFarlane; D. Buge; J. Cooke; P. Duffin; C. Passey; T. Hepple
*Heads of Units (SCS)*, J. Duke-Evans; V. Hogg; J. Nicholson; B. Moxam; P. Pugh; C. Byrne; M. Du Pulford; R. Karnicki; C. Everett

NATIONAL POLICE TRAINING

*National Director of Police Training*, C. Mould
*Corporate Services; Senior Principal (G6)*, S. Wells

NATIONAL POLICE TRAINING

Bramshill House, Bramshill, Hook, Hants RG27 0JW
Tel: 01256-602100
*Head of Higher Training*, I. McDonald

HENDON DATA CENTRE

Aerodrome Road, Colindale, London NW9 5LN
Tel: 020-8200 2424

*Head of Unit (G6)*, J. Ladley

POLICE SCIENTIFIC DEVELOPMENT BRANCH

Sandridge, St Albans, Herts AL4 9HQ
Tel: 01727-865051

*Director (SCS)*, B. R. Coleman, OBE
*Chief Scientist/Deputy Director (G6)*, Dr P. Young

Langhurst House, Langhurstwood Road, Nr Horsham, W. Sussex RH12 4WX
Tel: 01403-255451
*Head of Langhurst Facility (G6)*, M. Thompson

## UK ANTI DRUGS CO-ORDINATION UNIT

4 Central Buildings, Matthew Parker Street, London, SW1H 9NL. Tel: 020 -7270 1234
*Director*, S. Killen
*Deputy Director (SCS)*, J. Lempriese
*Senior Principals (G6)*, T. Campbell; K. Lidbetter

## HM INSPECTORATE OF CONSTABULARY

*HM Chief Inspector of Constabulary (SCS)*, Sir David O'Dowd, CBE, QPM
*HM Inspectors (SCS)*, D. Crompton, CBE, QPM; K. Povey, QPM; C. Smith, CBE, CVO, QPM; P. J. Winship, CBE, QPM; D. Blakey, CBE, QPM
*Senior Principal (G6)*, L. Robinson

METROPOLITAN POLICE COMMITTEE AND SECRETARIAT

Clive House, Petty France, London SW1H 9HD
Tel: 020-7273 4000

*Head of Secretariat (SCS)*, P. Honour

## RESEARCH, DEVELOPMENT AND STATISTICS DIRECTORATE

*Director (SCS)*, Dr P. Wiles
*Heads of Units (SCS)*, Prof. D. Pyle; Mrs C. Lehman; D. Moxam; Dr J. Yovell; C. Lewis; P. Ward C. Willis; *Senior Principals (G6)*, P. Ibrahim M. Koudra; L. Singer; Mrs P. Mayhew, OBE; B. Webb; J. Simmons; P. Dowdeswell; P. Collier; M. Collidge

## HM INSPECTORATE OF PRISONS

*HM Chief Inspector*, Sir David Ramsbotham, GCB, CBE
*HM Deputy Chief Inspector*, C. Allen
*HM Inspectors (Governor 1)*, R. Jacques; G. Hughes; J. Podmore

## PRISONS OMBUDSMAN

— *see* page 354

## PAROLE BOARD FOR ENGLAND AND WALES

— *see* page 353

## HM PRISON SERVICE

— *see* Prison Service Section pages 391–5

## UK PASSPORT SERVICE

Globe House, 89 Ecclestone Square, London SW1V 1PN
Tel: 020-7901 2000

*Chief Executive (SCS)*, B. L. Herdan
*Deputy Chief Executive and Director of Operations (G6)*, K. J. Sheehan
*Director of Systems (G6)*, J. Davies
*Director Finance*; A. Cook
*Director of Human Resources*, R. Mycroft

CRIMINAL RECORDS BUREAU, Horton House, Exchange Flags, Liverpool L2 3YL. Tel: 0151-236 8068.
*Director of Operation* , K. Broadbent
*Programme Manager (G7)*, G. Ryan

DEPARTMENT FOR INTERNATIONAL DEVELOPMENT
94 Victoria Street, London SW1E 5JL
Tel: 020-7917 7000; Fax: 020-7917 0019
Web: www.dfid.gov.uk
Abercrombie House, Eaglesham Road, East Kilbride, Glasgow G75 8EA
Tel: 01355-844000; Fax: 01355-844099

The Department for International Development (DFID) is the UK Government department responsible for promoting development and the reduction of poverty.

The governments aim is to strengthening the department and increase its budget. The central focus of the Government's policy, set out in the 1997 White Paper on International Development, is a commitment to the internationally agreed target to halve the proportion of people living in extreme poverty by 2015, together with associated targets, including basic health care provision and universal access to primary education, by the same date. A second White Paper on International Development, published in December 2000, reaffirmed this commitment, while focusing specifically on how to manage the process of globalisation to benefit poor people. DFID seeks to work in partnership with governments committed to these targets, and with business, civil society and the research community.

DFID also works with multilateral institutions including the World Bank, United Nations agencies and the European Community. The bulk of assistance is concentrated on the poorest countries in Asia and sub-Saharan Africa. DFID also contributes to poverty elimination and sustainable development in middle-income countries in Latin America, the Caribbean and elsewhere. In the transition countries of central and Eastern Europe, DFID is working to ensure the process of change brings benefits to all people, and particularly to the poorest.

*Secretary of State for International Development*, The Rt. Hon. Clare Short, MP
*Private Secretary*, Anna Bewes
*Special Advisers*, Susan Cox; David Mepham
*Parliamentary Private Secretary*, Dennis Turner, MP
*Parliamentary Under-Secretary*, Hilary Benn, MP
*Private Secretary*, James Price
*Permanent Secretary* (*SCS*), Sir John Vereker, KCB
*Private Secretary*, Joanne Graham

## PROGRAMMES

*Director-General* (*SCS*), B. R. Ireton

### AFRICA DIVISION

*Head* (*SCS*), G. Stegmann
*Heads of Departments*, T. Craddock (*SCS, Africa Great Lakes and Horn*); O. Barder (*Africa Policy and Economics*); B. Thomson (*SCS, West and North Africa*); J. Winter (*DFID Central Africa*); M. Wood (*SCS, DFIDCA Malawi*); E. Cassidy (*DFIDCA Mozambique*); Ms H. Mealins (*DFIDCA Zambia*); M. Wyatt (*DFID Eastern Africa*); D. Bell (*DFID Eastern Africa Kenya*); Ms C. Sergeant (*DFID Eastern Africa Tanzania*); M. Hammond (*DFID Eastern Africa Uganda*); P. Spray (*DFID Nigeria*); S. Sharpe (*SCS, DFID Southern Africa*)

### ASIA AND PACIFIC

*Head* (*SCS*), M. Dinham
*Heads of Departments* (*SCS*), P. Grant (*Asia Regional Economics and Policy*); Ms M. H. Vowles (*SCS, Eastern Asia and Pacific*); C. Austin (*Western Asia*); P. Ackroyd (*SCS, DFID Bangladesh*); R. Graham-Harrison (*SCS, DFID India*); D. Wod (*DFID Nepal*); J. Medhurst (*DFID Pacific*); M. Mallalieu (*SCS, DFID South East Asia*)

### EASTERN EUROPE AND WESTERN HEMISPHERE DIVISION

*Head* (*SCS*), Ms C. Miller
*Heads of Departments* (*SCS*), Ms B. Killen (*Americas and Transition Economies Policy*); S. Ray (SCS, Central and South Eastern Europe); D. Batt (*SCS, Eastern Europe and Central Asia*); vacant (*Latin America*); Ms R. Eyben (*SCS, DFID Bolivia*); D. Curran (*DFID Caribbean*); Ms G. Taylor (*DFID Central America*); C. Warren (*Overseas Territories Unit*); J. Kerby (*SCS UK Delegation to the EBRD*)

### INTERNATIONAL DIVISION

*Director* (*SCS*), J. A. L. Faint
*Heads of Departments* (SCS), Dr M. Kapila (*Conflict and Humanitarian Affairs*) A. Smith (*European Affairs*); Ms C. Cund (*International Financial Institutions*); M. Mosselmans (*United Nations Commonwealth*); A. Beattie (*UK Permanent Representation to the UN Food and Agriculture Agencies*); D. L. Stanton (*UK Permanent Delegation to UNESCO*)

### CIVIL SOCIETY DEPARTMENT

*Head*, R. Calvert

### RURAL LIVELIHOODS AND ENVIRONMENT

*Chief Natural Resources Adviser* (*SCS*), A. J. Bennett, CMG
*Head, Environment Policy Department* (*SCS*), A. Davis
*Head, Rural Livelihoods*, J. M. Scott

## RESOURCES

*Director-General* (*SCS*), R. G. Manning, CB

### ECONOMICS, BUSINESS AND STATISTICS DIVISION

*Chief Economist* (*SCS*) A. Wood
*Heads of Departments* (*SCS*) P. Landymore (*Economic Policy and Research*); D. L. Stanton (*Chief Enterprise Development Adviser*); Ms C. Seymour-Smith (*International Trade*); Ms V. Harris (*Private Sector Policy*); A. Williams (*Chief Statistician*)

### FINANCE AND DEVELOPMENT POLICY DIVISION

*Principal Finance Officer (SCS)*, M. Lowcock
*Heads of Department*, R. Teuten (*Acting, Development Policy*); C. Kirk; (*SCS, Evaluation*); K. Sparkhall (*SCS, Finance*); M. Smithson (*Accounts*); R. A. Elias (*SCS, Internal Audit*); S. Chard (*SCS, Procurement*)

### HUMAN RESOURCES DIVISION

*Head* (SCS), D. Fish
*Heads of Departments*, J. Anning (*Human Resources Operations*); D. Richards; (*Human Resources Policy*); P. Brough (*Overseas Pensions*)

### ADVISORY GROUPS

*Heads of Departments* (*SCS*), Prof. Stephen Matlin (*Chief Education Adviser*); R. Wilson (*Chief Governance Adviser*); Dr J. Lob-Levyt (*Chief Health and Population Adviser*); J.W. Hodges (*Chief Engineering Adviser*); Dr M. Schultz (*Chief Social Development Adviser*); Prof. Stephen Matlin (*Chief Education Adviser*); R. Wilson (*Chief Governance Adviser*); Dr J. Lob-Levyt (*Chief Health and Population Adviser*); J.W. Hodges (*Chief Engineering Adviser*); Dr M. Schultz (*Chief Social Development Adviser*)

INFORMATION SYSTEMS AND SERVICES DEPARTMENT
*Head (SCS)*, D. Gillett

INFORMATION DEPARTMENT
*Head (SCS)*, R. Calvert

## OTHER RELATED ORGANISATIONS

CDC CAPITAL PARTNERS
One Bessborough Gardens, London SW1V 2JQ
Tel: 020-7828 4488; Fax: 020-7282 6505
The Commonwealth Development Corporation has now become CDC Capital Partners, a public limited company with the Department of International Development as its 100% shareholder. At a later date CDC plans to become a public-private partnership with the Government maintaining the majority of the shareholding.
*Chairman*, The Lord Cairns, CBE
*Deputy Chairman*, Ms J. Almond
*Chief Executive*, Dr A. Gillespie

---

## LORD CHANCELLOR'S DEPARTMENT
Selborne House, 54–60 Victoria Street, London SW1E 6QW
Tel: 020-7210 8500
Email: enquiries.lcdhq@gtnet.gov.uk
Web: www.open.gov.uk/lcd

---

The Lord Chancellor appoints Justices of the Peace (except in the Duchy of Lancaster) and advises the Crown on the appointment of most members of the higher judiciary. He is responsible for promoting general reforms in the civil law, for the procedure of the civil courts and for the Community Legal Service. He is a member of the Cabinet. He also has ministerial responsibility for magistrates' courts, which are administered locally. Administration of the Supreme Court and county courts in England and Wales was taken over by the Court Service, an executive agency of the department, in 1995.

The Lord Chancellor is also responsible for ensuring that letters patent and other formal documents are passed in the proper form under the Great Seal of the Realm, of which he is the custodian. The work in connection with this is carried out under his direction in the Office of the Clerk of the Crown in Chancery.

The Lord Chancellor is also the senior Lord of Appeal in Ordinary and speaker of the House of Lords.

*Lord Chancellor* (£173,875), The Lord Irvine of Lairg, PC, QC
*Principal Private Secretary*, Ms Debra Matthews
*Special Adviser*, Gary Hart
*Parliamentary Under-Secretary*, Baroness Scotland of Asthal, QC; Michael Wills, MP; Rosie Winterton, MP
*Private Secretaries*, David Liddemore; Mel Charles
*Parliamentary Private Secretaries*, Laura Moffatt, MP; Gordon Marsden, MP
*Permanent Secretary*, Sir Hayden Phillips, KCB
*Private Secretary*, Bridgete Lee

CROWN OFFICE
House of Lords, London SW1A 0PW
Tel: 020-7219 4713
*Clerk of the Crown in Chancery*, Sir Hayden Phillips, KCB
*Deputy Clerk of the Crown in Chancery*, M. Huebner, CB
*Clerk of the Chamber*, C. I. P. Denyer

JUDICIAL GROUP
Tel: 020-7210 8500
*Director General*, Mrs J. Williams
*Director (SCS)*, Mrs E. J. Grimsey
*Heads of Divisions (SCS)*, D. E. Staff (*Policy and Conditions of Service*); D. Gladwell (*Senior Appointment and Silk*); Mrs C. Pulford (*District Bench and Tribunals*); S. Humphries (*Magistrates' Appointments*)

JUDICIAL STUDIES BOARD
9th Floor, Millbank Tower, London SW1P 4QW
Tel: 020-7925 4762
*Secretary* (SCS), E. S. Adams

POLICY GROUP
Tel: 020-7210 8719
*Director-General (SCS)*, Ms J. MacNaughton
*Heads of Divisions (SCS)*, A. Cogbill (*Civil Justice and Legal Services Directorate*); J. Tanner (*Civil Justice*); H. Burns (*Civil Law Development*); D. A. Hill (*Public Legal Services)*; C. Myerscough (*Community Legal Services*); P. Harris (*Legal Services*); Ms A. Finlay (*Public and Private Rights Directorate*); Ms M. Pigott, Ms J. Killick (*Family Policy*); B. Wells (*Administrative Justice*); D. Lye (Children and Advisory Service); Ms C. Colins, Ms K. Di Lorenzo (*Human Rights and Constitution Division*); Mrs K. Allen (*Policy Group Secretariat*); M. Ormerod (*Criminal Justice Group*); M. Kron (*Criminal Courts Review*); P. Stockton (*Criminal Justice*); Ms. S. Field (*Magistrates' Court*); P. White (*Magistrates' Courts IT*)

LEGAL ADVISER'S GROUP
Tel: 020-7210 0711
*Modernising Government*, D. Nooney
*Legal Adviser (SCS)*, P. Jenkins
*Heads of Divisions (SCS)*, P. Fish (*Legal Advice and Litigation*); A. Wallace (*International and Common Law Services*); M. Collon (*Drafting Services*)

COMMUNICATIONS GROUP
Tel: 020-7210 8672
*Director of Communications (SCS)*, A. Percival, LVO

CORPORATE SERVICES GROUP
Tel: 020-7210 8503
*Director of Corporate Services (SCS)*, Ms. J. Rowe
*Heads of Divisions (SCS)*, R. Sams (*Personnel*); S. Smith (*Finance*) A. Pay (*Accountancy*); A. Rummins (*Internal Assurance*); A. Maultby (*Information Management Unit*); R. Atkinson (*Facilities and Support Services*); K. Garrett (*Statutory Publications*); vacant (*Information Technology*); B. Eadie (*Corporate Services Secretariat*)

ECCLESIASTICAL PATRONAGE
10 Downing Street, London SW1A 2AA
Tel: 020-7930 4433
*Secretary for Ecclesiastical Patronage*, J. H. Holroyd, CB
*Assistant Secretary for Ecclesiastical Patronage*, N. C. Wheeler

HM MAGISTRATES' COURTS' SERVICE INSPECTORATE
Southside, 105 Victoria Street, London SW1E 6QJ
Tel: 020-7210 1655
*Chief Inspector (SCS)*, C. J. A. Chivers

*Senior Inspectors (SCS)*, D. Gear; C. Monson; Ms S. Steel; Dr S. Dixon

LORD CHANCELLOR'S ADVISORY COMMITTEE ON STATUTE LAW

Room 6.06, Selborne House, 54–60 Victoria Street, London SW1E 6QW
Tel: 020-7210 2615; Fax: 020-7210 2678

The Advisory Committee advises the Lord Chancellor on all matters relating to the revision, modernisation and publication of the statute book.
*Chairman*, The Lord Chancellor, The Rt. Hon. the Lord Irvine of Lairg
*Deputy Chairman*, Sir Hayden Phillips, KCB
*Members*, The Hon. Mr Justice Carnwath, CVO; The Hon. Lord Gill; J. M. Davies; J. C. McCluskie, CB, QC; R. Henderson; P. Jenkins; Mrs C. Tullo; W. R. McKay, CB; K. Garrett; E. G. Cauldwell, CB; P. J. Layden, TD; G. Gray; Miss J. Wheldon, CB, QC; Ms J. Rowe; A. Pawsey
*Secretary*, N. Hodgett

## EXECUTIVE AGENCY

THE COURT SERVICE

Southside, 105 Victoria Street, London SW1E 6QT
Tel: 020-7210 1646; Fax: 020-7210 2059;
E mail cust.ser.cs@gtnet.gov.uk;
Web www.courtservice.gov.uk

The Court Service provides administrative support to the Supreme Court, the Crown Court, county courts and a number of tribunals in England and Wales.
*Chief Executive (SCS)*, I. Magee
*Director of Field Services*, P. Handcock
*Director of Operational Policy (SCS)*, Miss B. Kenny
*Director of Finance (SCS)*, P. Commins
*Change Director (SCS)*, vacant
*Director of Purchasing and Contract Management (SCS)*, C. Lyne
*Director of Information Services Division (SCS)*, Ms A. Vernon
*Director of Personnel and Training (SCS)*, Ms H. Dudley
*Director of Civil and Family Business (SCS)*, J. Sills; *Director of Crown Court Operations (SCS)*, M. Camley; *Director of Tribunals (SCS)*, S. Smith

SUPREME COURT GROUP

Strand, London WC2A 2LL
Tel: 020-7936 6000
*Director (SCS)*, I. Hyams

---

## NORTHERN IRELAND OFFICE

11 Millbank, London SW1P 4PN
Tel: 020-7210 3000
Castle Buildings, Stormont, Belfast BT4 3SG
Tel: 01232-520700; Fax: 01232-528195
Web: www.nio.gov.uk

---

The Northern Ireland Office was established in 1972, when the Northern Ireland (Temporary Provisions) Act transferred the legislative and executive powers of the Northern Ireland Parliament and Government to the UK Parliament and a Secretary of State.

The Northern Ireland Office is responsible primarily for security issues, law and order and prisons, and for matters relating to the political and constitutional future of the province. It also deals with international issues as they affect Northern Ireland. Following an earlier suspension of the Assembly, devolution took place on 29 May 2000.

Under the terms of the 1998 Belfast Agreement, power was due to be devolved to the New Northern Ireland Assembly in 1999; the Assembly would then have taken on responsibility for the relevant areas of work currently undertaken by the departments of the Northern Ireland Office. In December 1998 the creation of ten new departments was agreed: agriculture and rural development; the environment; regional development; social development; education; higher education, training and employment; enterprise, trade and investment, culture, arts and leisure; health, social services and public safety; and finance and personnel. Each department is headed by a member of the power-sharing executive which is headed by the First Minister and Deputy First Minister. Six cross-border implementation bodies have also been established, dealing with inland waterways, food safety, trade and business development, EU programmes, language, and aquaculture.
*Secretary of State for Northern Ireland*, The Rt. Hon. Dr John Reid, MP
*Parliamentary Private Secretary*, Gillian Merron, MP
*Minister of State*, Jane Kennedy, MP
*Parliamentary Private Secretary*, Shona McIsaac, MP
*Parliamentary Under-Secretary of State*, Des Browne, MP
*Permanent Under-Secretary of State (SCS)*, Sir Joseph Pilling, CB
*Second Permanent Under-Secretary of State, Head of the Northern Ireland Civil Service*, Gerry Loughran

NORTHERN IRELAND INFORMATION SERVICE

Castle Buildings, Stormont, Belfast BT4 3SG
Tel: 01232-520700

EXECUTIVE AGENCIES

COMPENSATION AGENCY, Royston House, Upper Queen Street, Belfast BT1 6FD. Tel: 01232-2499444
FORENSIC SCIENCE AGENCY, Seapark, 151 Belfast Road, Carrickfergus, Co. Antrim BT38 8PL. Tel: 01232-365744
NORTHERN IRELAND PRISON SERVICE, *see* Prison Service section

---

## SCOTLAND OFFICE

Dover House, Whitehall, London SW1A 2AU
Tel: 020-7270 6754; Fax: 020-7270 6812;
Web: www.scottishsecretary.gov.uk

---

The Scotland Office is the department of the Secretary of State for Scotland, who represents Scottish interests in the Cabinet on matters reserved to the UK Parliament, i.e. constitutional matters, financial and economic matters, defence and international relations, immigration, social security, various matters relating to the single market with the UK (energy, transport, consumer protection) and employment. It also supports the Advocate General, the legal adviser to the UK Government on Scottish law. *See also* Scottish Executive, Regional Government section
*Secretary of State for Scotland*, The Rt. Hon. Helen Liddell, MP
*Private Secretary*, Ms J. Colquhoun
*Minister of State*, George Foulkes, MP
*Private Secretary*, Greig Chalmers
*Parliamentary Private Secretary*, Jim Murphy, MP; Sandra Osborne, MP
*Advocate-General for Scotland*, Dr Lynda Clark, QC, MP
*Private Secretary*, Gary Whyte

## DEPARTMENT OF TRADE AND INDUSTRY

1 Victoria Street, London SW1H 0ET
Tel: 020-7215 5000; Fax: 020-7222 2629
Web: www.dti.gov.uk

The Department is responsible for international trade policy, including the development of UK trade interests in the European Union, GATT, OECD, UNCTAD and other international organisations; policy in relation to industry and commerce, including industrial relations policy; policy towards small firms; regional industrial assistance; legislation and policy in relation to the Post Office; competition policy and consumer protection; the development of national policies in relation to all forms of energy and the development of new sources of energy, including international aspects of energy policy; policy on science and technology research and development; space policy; standards, quality and design; and company legislation.

*Secretary of State for Trade and Industry, Minister for Women, and E-Minister in Cabinet*, The Rt. Hon. Patricia Hewitt, MP
*Principal Private Secretary*, Ms Bernadette Kelly
*Private Secretaries*, Elleanor Brooks; Damien Nussbourn
*Minister of State*, Douglas Alexander, MP (*E-Commerce and Competitiveness*)
*Minister of State*, The Rt. Hon. Baroness Symons of Vernham Dean (*Trade and Investment and Deputy Leader of the House of Lords*)
*Minister of State for Industry and Energy*, Brian Wilson, MP
*Minister of State, for the Regions and Employment Relations*, Alan Johnson, MP
*Parliamentary Under-Secretaries of State*, Melanie Johnson, MP (*Competition, Consumers and Markets*); The Lord Sainsbury of Turville, MP (*Science and Innovation*); Nigel Griffiths, MP (*Small Business*)
*Private Secretaries*, Gareth Maybury; Ms Gaynor-. Jeffrey; Ms Becky Eggleton
*Parliamentary Clerk*, Tim Williams
*Permanent Secretary*, Robin Young, CB
*Private Secretary*, Fergus Harradence
*Chief Scientific Adviser and Head of Office of Science and Technology*, Prof. David King
*Private Secretary*, Anne Harris
*British Trade International Chief Executive*, Sir David Wright, KCMG, LVO
*Directors-General*, Dr J. Taylor, OBE, FEng, FRS (*Director-General of the Research Councils*); R. Carden (*Trade Policy*); M. Gibson (*Enterprise and Innovation*); Dr C. Bell (*Competition and Markets Group*); D. Nissen, CB (*The Solicitor*); Ms A. Walker (*Energy*); J. Phillips (*Resources and Services*); J. Spencer (*Business Competitiveness*)

### DIVISIONAL ORGANISATION

#### †British National Space Centre

*Director-General* (*SCS*), Dr C. Hicks
*Deputy Director-General* (*SCS*), D. Leadbeater
*Directors* (*SCS*), A. Cooper; Dr P. Murdin; Miss P. Freedman

#### BPT Directorate - BNFL Public Private Partnership

*Directors*, J. Rhodes; Dr. D. Walker
*Deputy Directors*, Ms R. Loebl; Ms P. Ciniewicz; N. Woodage

#### Central Directorate

*Director of Competitiveness Unit* (*SCS*), S. Lyle Smythe
*Directors* (*SCS*), S. Chambers; E. Zimmon

#### †Chemicals and Biotechnology Directorate

*Director of Chemicals and Biotechnology* (*SCS*), D. Davis
*Directors* (*SCS*), Ms M. Darnbrough; Dr D. Jennings
Directorate/Newsroom
*Deputy Director of News* (*SCS*), I. Heppleshile
*Director of Public Information* (*SCS*), P. Burke

#### †Communications and Information Industries Directorate

*Director of Communications and Information Industries* (*SCS*), W. MacIntyre
*Directors* (*SCS*), N. Worman; D. Lumley; D. Love; C. Holmes; Mrs G. Alliston

#### Coal Directorate

*Director of Coal Directorate* (*SCS*) R. Wright
*Directors* (*SCS*) G. Rigs; A. Taylor; S. Pride

#### Company Law and Investigations Directorate

*Director of Company Law and Investigations* (*SCS*), R. Rogers
*Directors* (*SCS*), J. Grewe; G. Harp; J. Gardner; J. Sibley; R. Burns; Ms B. Chase; A. Robertshaw; K. Harre; P. Masson

#### Competition Policy and Utilities Review Directorate

*Director of Team* (*SCS*), Ms R. Anderson
*Directors* (*SCS*), P. Sellers; J. Swift; D. Miner; J. May; R. Bent

#### Consumer Affairs Directorate

*Director of Consumer Affairs* (*SCS*), J. Rees
*Directors* (*SCS*), P. Wilson; C. Durkin; B. Habbajam; A. Willcocks

#### Consumer Goods, Business and Postal Services Directorate

*Director of Consumer Goods, Business and Postal Services* (*SCS*), D. Davis
*Directors* (*SCS*), B. Hopson; Ms J. Britton; M. Higsen

#### Economics and Statistics Directorate

*Chief Economic Adviser* (*SCS*), D. R. Coates
*Directors* (*SCS*), K. Warwick; G. Everitt; A. Rees

#### Employment Relations Directorate

*Director of Industrial Relations* (*SCS*), M. Beatson; J. Munday; S. Rhodes: J. Startup

#### Energy Policy, Analysis, Technology Council

*Director of Energy Policy, Analysis, Technology and Coal* (*SCS*), N. Hirst
*Directors* (*SCS*), G. C. White; N. Peace; J. Doddrell; Dr A. Heyes; G. White

#### Energy Utilities Directorate (ENU)

*Deputy Director General*, N. Hirst
*Director*, I. Fletcher
*Deputy Director*, Dr G. Bryce

#### †Engineering Industries Directorate

*Director of Engineering Industries* (*SCS*), M. O'Shea
*Directors* (*SCS*), J. Hunt; N. Carter ; R. Kingcombe; H. Brown; I. Cameron; J. Dennis; S. Bishop

ENGINEERING INSPECTORATE

*Director of Engineering Inspectorate* (*SCS*), Dr P. Fenwick

ENVIRONMENT DIRECTORATE

*Director of Environment* (*SCS*), Dr J. Dennis
*Director* (*SCS*), D. Prior

ESTATES AND FACILITIES MANAGEMENT DIRECTORATE

*Director* (*SCS*), M. Coolican

EUROPEAN POLICY DIRECTORATE

Kingsgate House, 66–74 Victoria Street, London SW1E 6SW

*Directors* (*SCS*), J. Alty; H. Savill

EXPORT CONTROL AND NON-PROLIFERATION DIRECTORATE
Kingsgate House, 66–74 Victoria Street, London SW1E 6SW

*Director of Export Control and Non-Proliferation* (*SCS*), Ms S. Haird
*Director* (*SCS*), J. Neve

FINANCE AND RESOURCE MANAGEMENT DIRECTORATE

*Director of Finance and Resource Management* (*SCS*), E. Hosker
*Directors* (*SCS*), P. Lloyd; R. Niblett

‡INDUSTRY ECONOMICS AND STATISTICS DIRECTORATE

*Director* (*SCS*), Dr N. Owen

†INFORMATION MANAGEMENT AND PROCESS ENGINEERING DIRECTORATE

*Director* (*SCS*), R. Wheeler

INNOVATION SERVICES

*Director of Innovation Policy and Standards* (*SCS*), Dr A. Kaddie
*Directors* (*SCS*), J. Barber; D. Reed; S. I. Chanik

†INTERNAL AUDIT DIRECTORATE

*Director of Internal Audit* (*SCS*), C. Juman

INTERNATIONAL ECONOMICS DIRECTORATE

Kingsgate House, 66–74 Victoria Street, London SW1E 6SW

*Director* (*SCS*), C. Moir

INVEST UK

*Chief Executive* (*SCS*), W. Pedder
*Director, Operations*, A. Morgan
*Director, International*, D. Cockerham

LEGAL RESOURCE MANAGEMENT AND BUSINESS LAW UNIT

10 Victoria Street, London SW1H 0NN

*The Solicitor and Director-General* (*SCS*), D. Nissen, CB
*Director* (*SCS*), C. Warren

LEGAL SERVICES DIRECTORATE A

10 Victoria Street, London SW1H 0NN

*Director of Legal A* (*SCS*), J. Stanley
*Legal Directors* (*SCS*), J. Roberts; S. Hyett; Miss G. Richmond

LEGAL SERVICES DIRECTORATE B

10 Victoria Street, London SW1H 0NN

*Director of Legal B* (*SCS*), A. Brett-Holt
*Legal Directors* (*SCS*), R. Baker; B. Welch; R. Perkins; Ms S. Hardy; C. Raikes; Ms N. Arora

LEGAL SERVICES DIRECTORATE C

10 Victoria Street, London SW1H 0NN

*Director of Legal C* (*SCS*), P. Beug
*Legal Directors* (*SCS*), M. Bucknill; A. Woods; M. Smith; T. Susman; B. Welch

LEGAL SERVICES DIRECTORATE D

10 Victoria Street, London SW1H 0NN

*Director of Legal D* (*SCS*), S. Milligan; L. Nawbatt

TRADE POLICY

Kingsgate House, 66–74 Victoria Street, London SW1E 6SW

*Director* (*SCS*), Dr E. Draige

NUCLEAR INDUSTRIES DIRECTORATE

*Director of Nuclear Industries* (*SCS*), H. Leiser
*Directors* (*SCS*), I. Downing; S. Bowen; P. Robinson; Dr P. Heyes

OFFICE OF SCIENCE AND TECHNOLOGY: SCIENCE AND ENGINEERING BASE DIRECTORATE

Albany House, 84–86 Petty France, London SW1H 9ST

*Director, Science and Engineering Base* (*SCS*), C. Henshall
*Directors* (*SCS*), Dr F. Saunders; R. King; Dr K. Root

OFFICE OF SCIENCE AND TECHNOLOGY: TRANSDEPARTMENTAL SCIENCE AND TECHNOLOGY DIRECTORATE

Albany House, 84–86 Petty France, London SW1H 9ST

*Director, Transdepartmental Science and Technology* (*SCS*), Ms J. Durning
*Directors* (*SCS*), S. Spivey; M. Parker; Ms J. Darrell

OIL AND GAS DIRECTORATE

1 Victoria Street, London SW1H 0ET

*Director of Oil and Gas* (*SCS*), G. Dart
*Directors* (*SCS*), J. R. V. Brooks, CBE; Dr A. Eggington; S. Toole; M. Graham

Atholl House, 86–88 Guild Street, Aberdeen AB11 6AR
Tel: 01224-254059

*Director of Reform and Energy Regulation*, K. Long
*Directors of Oil and Gas* (*SCS*), S. Toole; J. Campbell

REGIONAL ASSISTANCE DIRECTORATE

*Director of Regional Assistance* (*SCS*), A. Steele

REGIONAL EUROPEAN FUNDS DIRECTORATE

*Director* (*SCS*), J. Neve

REGIONAL POLICY DIRECTORATE

*Director* (*SCS*), P. Bunn

SENIOR STAFF MANAGEMENT DIRECTORATE
*Director* (*SCS*), Ms K. Elliott

SMALL BUSINESS SERVICE
*Chief Executive*, D. Irwin
*Deputy Chief Executive*, Dr D. Evans
*Directors*, H. Merrifield; P. Jackson; J. Hobday; M. Cocks; R. Allpress

STAFF PERSONNEL OPERATIONS DIRECTORATE

*Director (SCS)*, R. Heyhoe

STAFF POLICY AND PAY DIRECTORATE

*Director (SCS)*, F. Sonne

TRADE POLICY DIRECTORATE

Kingsgate House, 66–74 Victoria Street, London SW1E 6SW

*Director (SCS)*, C. Bridge

TRADE FACILITATION AND IMPORT POLICY DIRECTORATE

Kingsgate House, 66–74 Victoria Street, London SW1E 6SW

*Director (SCS)*, A. Berry

## BRITISH TRADE INTERNATIONAL

Kingsgate House, 66–74 Victoria Street, London SW1E 6SW
Tel: 020-7215 5000

British Trade International brings together the Department of Trade and Industry and the Foreign and Commonwealth Office export and investment operations.
*Chairmen*, The Rt. Hon. Baroness Symons of Vernham Dean (*Minister for Trade, DTI*)
*Vice-Chairmen*, HRH The Duke of York GCMG, GCVO; Sir David John, KCMG
*Chief Executive*, Sir David Wright, KCMG, LVO
*Group Members*, R. Turner, OBE; V. Brown; A. Summers; Ms G. Goucher, MBE; R. Orgill; K. Pathak; P. Westmacott; W. Thomson; G. Robson; D. Jones; J. Spencer; P. Mason; A. Hingston

TRADE PARTNERS UK

The Trade Partners UK network provides services to British exporters and investors at home and overseas.
*Deputy Chief Executive and Group Director, Central Services Group (SCS)*, D. Hall
*Group Director, Regional Group*, I. Jones
*Group Director, International Group (SCS)*, Q. Quayle
*Group Director, Business Group (SCS)*, D. Warren
*Group Director, Strategy and Communications Group (SCS)*, J. Reynolds

## EXECUTIVE AGENCIES

COMPANIES HOUSE

Companies House, Crown Way, Cardiff CF14 3UZ
Tel: 0870-333 3636; Fax: 029-2038 0900
*London Information Centre*, 21 Bloomsbury Street, London WC1B 3XD
*Edinburgh*, 37 Castle Terrace, Edinburgh EH1 2EB
Tel: 0131-535 5800; Fax: 0131-535 5820;
Web: www.companies.gov.uk
*Birmingham*, Central Library, Chamberlain Square,
*Leeds*, 25 Queen Street, Leeds, LS1 2TW; 9am to 4pm
*Manchester*, 75 Mosley Street, Manchester, M2 2HR; 9am to 4pm
*Glasgow*, Small Business Gateway, 7 West George Street, Glasgow, G2 1BQ; 9am to 5pm

Companies House incorporates companies, registers company documents and provides company information.
*Registrar of Companies for England and Wales*, J. Holden
*Registrar for Scotland*, J. Henderson

EMPLOYMENT TRIBUNALS SERVICE

19–29 Woburn Place, London WC1H 0LU
Tel: 020-7273 8666; Fax: 020-7273 8670

The Service became an executive agency in 1997 and brought together the administrative support for the employment tribunals and the Employment Appeal Tribunal.
*Chief Executive*, R. Heathcote

THE INSOLVENCY SERVICE

PO Box 203, 21 Bloomsbury Street, London WC1B 3QW
Tel: 020-7637 1110; Fax: 020-7636 4709

The Service administers and investigates the affairs of bankrupts and companies in compulsory liquidation; deals with the disqualification of directors in all corporate failures; regulates insolvency practitioners and their professional bodies; provides banking and investment services for bankruptcy and liquidation estates; and advises Ministers on insolvency policy issues.
*Inspector-General and Chief Executive*, D. J. Flynn
*Deputy Inspectors-Generals*, D. J. Flynn; L. T. Cramp

NATIONAL WEIGHTS AND MEASURES LABORATORY (NWML)

Stanton Avenue, Teddington, Middx TW11 0JZ
Tel: 020-8943 7272; Fax: 020-8943 7270;
Web: www.nwml.gov.uk

The Laboratory administers weights and measures legislation, carries out type examination, calibration and testing, and runs courses on legal meteorological topics.
*Chief Executive*, Dr S. Bennett

PATENT OFFICE

— *see* page 353

RADIOCOMMUNICATIONS AGENCY

Wyndham House, 189 Marsh Wall, London E14 9SX
Tel: 020-7211 0211; Fax: 020-7211 0507;
Email: library@ra.gsi.gov.uk; Web www.radio.gov.uk

The Agency is responsible for the management of the radio spectrum used for civilian purposes within the UK. It also represents UK radio interests internationally.
*Chief Executive*, D. Hendon

---

## DEPARTMENT OF TRANSPORT, LOCAL GOVERNMENT AND THE REGIONS

Eland House, Bressenden Place, London SW1E 5DU
Great Minster House, 76 Marsham Street, London SW1P 4DR
Ashdown House, 123 Victoria Street, London SW1E 6DE Tel: 020-7944 3000 Web: www.dtlr.gov.uk

---

Due to major changes at Whitehall following the 2001 General Election, the DETR has been re-organised to create the Department for Transport, Local Government and the Regions (DTLR).

Environment Protection and Wildlife & Countryside policy have moved to the former MAFF to create the Department for Environment, Food and Rural Affairs (DEFRA).

Construction has moved to the DTI although DTLR retain Building Regulations, which have been merged with Fire Policy from the Home Office to create a new Directorate.

Responsibility for Local and Parliamentary bylaws has also moved from the Home Office to DTLR.

Sponsorship of the RDAs has moved to the DTI and the Regional Co-ordination Unit and Government Offices now report to the Cabinet Office.

The Department's Ministers are based at Eland House.

*Secretary of State for Transport, Local Government and the Regions*, The Rt. Hon. Stephen Byers, MP
*Private Secretary*, Peter Unwin
*Special Advisers*, Jo Moore; Dan Corrie
*Parliamentary Private Secretary*, David Watts, MP
*Minister of State for Transport*, The Rt. Hon. John Spellar, MP
Private Secretary, *Phil West*
*Special Adviser*, A. Long
*Parliamentary Private Secretary*, D. Watts, MP
*Minister of State, Local Government and The Regions*, The Rt. Hon. Nick Raynsford, MP
*Private Secretary*, Matt Leach
*Parliamentary Private Secretary*, Linda Gilray, MP
*Minister of State for Housing, Planning and Regeneration*, The Rt. Hon. Lord Falconer of Thoroton, QC, MP
*Parliamentary Private Secretary*, Paul Clark, MP
*Parliamentary Under-Secretaries of State*, David Jamieson, MP (*Transport*); Sally Keeble, MP (*Housing, Planning and Regeneration*); Dr Alan Whitehead, MP (*Local Government and the Regions*)
*Private Secretaries*, Rory O'Donnell; Kirsty Gibson; Shane Snow; Tom Wechsler; P. West

* Based at Eland House
† Based at Ashdown House
‡ Based at Great Minster House

## *DIRECTORATE OF COMMUNICATION

*Director of Communication (SCS)*, A. Evans

## DIRECTORATE OF FINANCE

*Director of Finance*, P. Ward

## DIRECTORATE OF LAW

*Legal Director*, D. Hogg

## *HOUSING, URBAN POLICY AND PLANNING (HUPP)

*Director-General (SCS)*, G. Turton, CB

### Housing

*Director (SCS)*, M. Gahagan, CB
*Heads of Divisons (SCS)*, B. Provan (*Housing Care and Support*); B. Oelman (*Housing Data and Statistics*) A.Waquar (*Research, Analysis and Evaluation*); P. Cox (*Housing and Urban Economics*); M. Jones (*Housing Policy, Renewal and Ownership*); M. Faulkner (*Housing Private Rented Sector*); N. McDonald (*Local Authority Housing*); R. Horsman (*Housing Associations and Private Finance*); B. Hill (*Homelessness and Housing Management*)

### Urban Policy Unit

*Director*, Dr P. Evans
*Heads of Divisions*, S. Bonfanti (*Urban White Paper*); J. Bridges (*Strategic Development*); J. Sienkiewicz (*Thames Gateway*); M. Leigh-Pollitt (*LPD-Land and Property*); P. Houston (*Physical Regeneration and English Partnerships*); vacant (*Regional Funding*)

### Planning

*Director*, P. Britton
*Divisional Managers*, J. Channing (*Planning Policies*); L. Hicks (*Minerals and Waste Policy*); C. Bowden (*Development Control Policy*); M. Ash (*Plans, Compensation and International*); A. Gray (*Environmental Assessment, Transport and Works, Management and Finance*); P. Capell (*Planning and Land Use Statistics*)

### Rough Sleepers Unit

*Divisional Director*, L. Casey

### Integrated Transport Taskforce Team

*Director-General (SCS)*, W. Rickett
*Deputy Director (SCS)*, Ms M. Phillips, CB
*Heads of Divisons (SCS)*, Ms L. Robinson (*Transport, Delivery and Presentation*); I. Todd (*Transport, Environment and Taxation*); D. Hulls (*Transport Finance*); Ms B. Hills (*Transport Strategy*)

### Commercial, Housing and Local Government

*Director (SCS)*, C. Muttukamaru
*Heads of Divisions (SCS)*, J. Comber (*Environment (National)*; D. Jordan (*Local Government (Finance)*; Ms P. Conlon (*Local Government (General)*; J. Wright (*Housing and Land*); N. Thomas (*Greater London Authority Implementation*); D. Aries (*Commercial and Establishments*); Ms D. Phillips (*Devolution and Regional Government*)

## *LOCAL AND REGIONAL GOVERNMENT GROUP

*Director-General (SCS)*, P. Wood

### Local Government Directorate

*Director (SCS)*, A. Whetnall
*Heads of Divisions (SCS)*, P. Rowsell (*Local Government Sponsorship*); J. R. Footitt (*Local Government Competition and Quality*); T. Redpath (*Local Government Legislation*); T. Crossley (*Local Government Pensions*); vacant (*Electoral Reform*); J. Haunton (*G7*) (*Local Government Modernisation*); V. Sherwood (*SEO*) (*Honours Secretariat*)

### Local Government Finance Policy Directorate

*Director (SCS)*, M. Lambirth
*Heads of Divisions (SCS)*, R. Davies (*Modernisation and Grant Distribution*); S. Claughton (*Taxation, Valuation and General Policy*); M. Green (*Statistics, Payments and IT Division*); P. Williams (*Capital Finance and Accountancy Advice*)

### Regional Policy Unit

*Director (SCS)*, R. Allan
*Heads of Divisions (SCS)*, A. Murray (*Devolution and Regional Governance*)

### Fire and Building Regulations

*Director*, vacant
*Divisional Managers*, P. Everall (*Building Regulations*); E. Guy (*Fire Policy Unit*); D. Peace (*Fire Research and Development*); G. Meldrum (*HM Fire Service Inspectorate*)

## ‡ TRANSPORT STRATEGY, ROADS AND LOCAL TRANSPORT (TSRLT)

*Director-General (SCS)*, W. Pickett
*Director DVO Group*, J. Plowman

### INTEGRATED AND LOCAL TRANSPORT

*Director*, A. Davis
*Divisional Managers*, R. Verge (*DVO Secretariat*); M. Walsh (*Economics, Local Transport and General*); K. Lloyd (*Local Transport Policy*); M. Talbot (*Traffic Management*); H. Hillier (*Transport Statistics: Personal Travel*); J. Rogers and A. Rutherford (*Buses and Taxis*)

### MOBILITY UNIT

*Head of Unit*, A. Frye, OBE,
*Director Roads and Traffic*, D. Roberts
*Divisional Managers*, A. Oliver (*Transport Statistics: Roads*); R. Jones (*Licensing, Road Worthiness and Insurance*); R. Peel (*Road Safety*); T. Carter (*Road Safety: Chief Medical Advisor*); H. Chipping (*Roads Policy*); M. Fendick (*Vehicle Standards and Engineering*)

### TRANSPORT STRATEGY

*Director*, D. Phillips, CB
*Divisional Managers*, T. Worsley (*Integrated Transport Economics and Appraisal*); P. Collins (*Multi-Modal Studies Division*); G. Smith (*Transport Research Unit*); L. Robinson (*Transport Strategy and Finance*) E. Sampson (*Transport Technology and Telematics*); L. Packer (*Transport, Environment and Taxation*)

## ‡RAILWAYS, AVIATION LOGISTICS AND MARITIME (RALM)

*Director-General (SCS)*, D. Rowlands

### RAILWAYS

*Director (SCS)*, R. Linnard
*Heads of Divisions (SCS)*, Ms A. Munro (*Railways Major Project*); S. Connolly (*Railways Economics and Finance*); P. Thomas (*Railways International and General*); M. Coulshed (*Railways Sponsorship*)

### AVIATION

*Director (SCS)*, R. Griffins
*Heads of Divisions (SCS)*, M. Fawcett (*Airports Policy*); M. Mann (*Economics, Aviation, Maritime and International*); Ms E. Duthie (*Aviation Environmental*); M. Smethers (*Multilateral*); A. T. Baker (*International Aviation Negotiation*); D. McMillan (*Air Traffic*); I. McBrayne (*Civil Aviation*)

### TRANSPORT SECURITY

*Director (SCS)*, I. Devlin
*Deputy Director of Transport Security*, W. Gillan

### LONDON UNDERGROUND TASK GROUP

*Director (SCS)*, M. Fuhr
*Heads of Divisions (SCS)*, I. Jordan (*London Underground Task Group 1*); R. Bennett (*London Underground Task Group 2*); E. West (*London Underground Task Group 3*) P. Sanders (*London Underground Task Group 4*)

### LOGISTICS AND MARITIME TRANSPORT

*Director (SCS)*, B. Wadsworth
*Divisional Managers*, J. Lang (*Marine Accident Investigation Branch*); S. Reeves (*Ports Policy*); Ms B. A. Bostock (*Road Haulage Regulation*); T. Wellburn (*Road Haulage Sponsorship and Logistics*); T. Allan (*Logistics and Maritime Transport*); M. Hughes (*Transport Statistics Freight*); D. Liston-Jones (*Traffic Area Network Unit*); D. Cooke (*Shipping Policy 1*); G. D. Rowe (*Shipping Policy 2*); J. F. Wall, CMG (*Shipping Policy 3*)

## *STRATEGY AND CORPORATE SERVICES GROUP

*Director (SCS)*, R. S. Dudding

## EXECUTIVE AGENCIES

### DRIVER AND VEHICLE LICENSING AGENCY

Longview Road, Morriston, Swansea SA6 7JL
Tel: 01792-782 341; Fax: 01792-782 793
Web www.dvla.gov.uk

The Agency is responsible for registering and licensing drivers and vehicles, and the collection and enforcement of vehicle exercise duty.
*Chief Executive*, C. Bennett

### DRIVING STANDARDS AGENCY

Stanley House, Talbot Street, Nottingham NG1 5GU
Tel: 0115-901 2500; Fax: 0115-901 2940
Web www.dsa.gov.uk

The Agency is responsible for carrying out theory and practical driving tests for car drivers, motorcyclists, bus and lorry drivers and for maintaining the registers of Approved Driving Instructors and Large Goods Vehicle Instructors, as well as supervising Compulsory Basic Training (CBT) for learner motorcyclists. There are five area offices, which manage over 430 practical test centres across Britain.
*Chief Executive*, G. Austin

### FIRE SERVICE COLLEGE

Moreton-in-Marsh, Gloucestershire, GL56 0RH
Tel: 01608-650 831; Fax: 01608-651 788;
Web: www.fireservicecollege.ac.uk

The Fire Service College provides unique facilities for both practical and theoretical fire fighting, fire safety and accident and emergency training.
*Chief Executive*, T. Glossop

### HIGHWAYS AGENCY

St Christopher House, Southwark Street, London SE1 0TE
Tel: 020-7921 4574; Fax:020-7921 4592
Web: www.highways.gov.uk

The Agency is responsible for delivering the DTLR's road programme and for maintaining the national road network in England.
*Chief Executive*, T. Matthews

### MARITIME AND COASTGUARD AGENCY

Spring Place, 105 Commercial Road, Southampton SO15 1EG
Tel: 023-8032 9100; Fax: 023-8032 9477
Web: www.mcga.gov.uk

The Agency aims to develop, promote and enforce high standards of marine safety and pollution prevention; to minimise the loss of life among seafarers and coastal users; and to minimise pollution from ships to sea and coastline.
*Chief Executive*, M. Storey
*Chief Coastguard*, J. Astbury

### ORDNANCE SURVEY

Romsey Road, Maybush, Southampton, SO16 4GU.
Tel: 023-8079 2000; Fax: 023-8079 2660;
Web: www.ordsvy.gov.uk

The Ordnance Survey department carries out official surveying and definitive mapping of Great Britain.
*Chief Executive*, V. Lawrence

PLANNING INSPECTORATE

Crown Buildings, Cathays Park, Cardiff CF10 3NQ.
Tel: 029-2082 3866; Fax; 029- 2082 5150;
Web: www.planning-inspectorate.gov.uk

The Inspectorate appeals against the decisions of local authorities on planning applications and appeals against local authority enforcement notices. Also provides inspectors to hold enquiries into objections to local authority planning.
*Chief Executive and Chief Planning Inspector*, C. Shepley

QUEEN ELIZABETH II CONFERENCE CENTRE

Broad Sanctuary, London SW1P 3EE
Tel: 020-7222 5000; Fax: 020-7798 4200
Web: www.qeiicc.co.uk

The Centre provides secure conference facilities for national and international government and private sector use.
*Chief Executive*, M. C. Buck, CBE

THE RENT SERVICE

Clifton House, 1st Floor, 87-113 Euston Road, London NW1 2RA Tel: 020-7554 2450 Fax: 020-7554 2490
Web: www.vca.gov.uk

The Agency combines 77 independent units previously administered by local authorities.
*Chief Executive*, D. Harvey

VEHICLE CERTIFICATION AGENCY

1 Eastgate Office Centre, Eastgate Road, Bristol BS5 6XX
Tel: 0117-951 5151; Fax: 0117-952 4103;
Web: www.vca.gov.uk

The Agency brings together 77 independent units previously administered by local authorities. It tests and certificates vehicles to UK and international Standards.
*Chief Executive*, D. W. Harvey

VEHICLE INSPECTORATE (VI)

Berkeley House, Croydon Street, Bristol BS5 0DA
Tel: 0117-954 3200; Fax: 0117-954 3212
Web www.via.gov.uk

The Agency tests and certifies the roadworthiness of heavy goods and public service vehicles and supervises MOT testing.
*Chief Executive*, M. Newey

## TRAFFIC AREA OFFICES AND COMMISSIONERS

*Senior Traffic Commissioner*, M. W. Betts, CBE

*Eastern*, G. Simms
*North-Eastern*, T. Macartney
*North-Western*, B. Bell
*Scottish*, M. W. Betts, CBE
*South-Eastern and Metropolitan*, C. Heaps
*Western*, P. Brown
*Wales and West Midlands*, D. Dixon

## HM TREASURY

Parliament Street, London SW1P 3AG
Tel: 020-7270 5000
Email: public.enquiries@hm-treasury.gov.uk
Web: www.hm-treasury.gov.uk

The Office of the Lord High Treasurer has been continuously in commission for well over 200 years. The Lord High Commissioners of HM Treasury are the First Lord of the Treasury (who is also the Prime Minister), the Chancellor of the Exchequer and five junior Lords. This Board of Commissioners is assisted at present by the Chief Secretary, the Parliamentary Secretary (who is also the Government Chief Whip in the House of Commons), the Paymaster-General, the Financial Secretary, and the Economic Secretary. The Prime Minister as First Lord is not primarily concerned in the day-to-day aspects of Treasury business; neither are the Parliamentary Secretary and the Junior Lords as Government Whips. Treasury business is managed by the Chancellor of the Exchequer and the other Treasury Ministers, assisted by the Permanent Secretary.

The Chief Secretary is responsible for public expenditure planning and control; public sector pay; value for money in the public services; public service agreements public/private partnerships and procurement policy; strategic oversight of banking, financial services and insurance; departmental investment strategies; including the Capital, Modernisation Fund and Invest to Save Budget; welfare reform; devolution; and resource accounting and budgeting.

The Paymaster-General is responsible for the Inland Revenue and the Valuation Office, with overall responsibility for the Finance Bill. She leads on personal taxation, business taxation, European and international tax issues.

The Financial Secretary is responsible for Customs and Excise; growth and productivity; science, research and development; competition and deregulation policy; export credit; VAT and road and fuel duties; and parliamentary financial business (Public Accounts Committee, National Audit Office).

The Economic Secretary is responsible for National Savings, the Debt Management Office, the National Investment and Loans Office, the Office of National Statistics, the Royal Mint, and the Government Actuary's Department; banking, financial services and insurance; foreign exchange reserves; debt management policy; financial services tax issues and charity taxation. She provides support to the Chancellor on EU issues.

*Prime Minister and First Lord of the Treasury*, The Rt. Hon. Anthony (Tony) Blair, MP
*Chancellor of the Exchequer*, The Rt. Hon. Gordon Brown, MP
*Principal Private Secretary*, Tom Scholar
*Private Secretaries*, Beth Russell ; Mark Bowman
*Special Advisers*, Ed Miliband; Ian Austin; Paul Andrew; Spencer Livermore
*Council of Economic Advisers*, Chris Wales; Paul Gregg; Ms Shriti Vadera; Paul Gregg; Maeve Sherlock, Stewart Wood
*Parliamentary Private Secretaries*, Mrs Ann Keen, MP, Joan Ryan, MP; Chris Pond, MP; Helen Southworth, MP
*Chief Secretary to the Treasury*, The Rt. Hon. Andrew Smith, MP
*Chief Economic Adviser to the Treasury*, Ed Balls
*Private Secretary*, Lucy Makinson
*Paymaster-General*, Dawn Primarolo, MP

*Private Secretary*, Heidi Popperwell
*Financial Secretary to the Treasury*, The Rt. Hon. Paul Boateng , MP
*Private Secretary*, Helen Watson
*Economic Secretary to the Treasury*, Ruth Kelly, MP
*Private Secretary*, Niki Cleal
*Parliamentary Clerk, David Martin*
*Parliamentary Secretary to the Treasury and Government Chief Whip*, The Rt. Hon. Hilary Armstrong, MP
*Private Secretary*, Roy Stone
*Treasurer of HM Household and Deputy Chief Whip*, Keith Hill , MP
*Comptroller of HM Household*, Thomas McAvoy, MP
*Vice-Chamberlain of HM Household*, Gerry Sutcliffe, MP
*Lord Commissioners of the Treasury (Whips)*, Anne McGuire, MP; John Heppel, MP; Nick Ainger, MP; Tony McNulty, MP; Graham Stringer, MP; *Assistant Whips*, Ian Pearson, MP; Fraser Kemp, MP; Angela Smith , MP; Ivor Caplin, MP; Phil Woolas, MP; Dan Norris, MP; Jim Fitzpatrick, MP
*Permanent Secretary to the Treasury*, Sir Andrew Turnbull, KCB

## DIRECTORATES

*Head of Ministerial Support Team (SCS)*, T. Scholar
*Head of Communications and Strategy Team (SCS)*, M. Elham
*Head of Strategy Finance and Purchasing Team (SCS)*, R. Brightwell

### Macroeconomic Policy and International finance

*Managing Director*, G. O'Donnell
*Directors (SCS)*, S. Brooks; S. Pickford; J. Cunliffe; J. Taylor; I. Rogers
*Heads of Teams (SCS)*, C. M. Kelly; A. Kilpatrick; D. Ramsden; M. Glycopantis; P. Mills; J. de Berkker; G. Lloyd; R. Lawrence K. Peters; A. Lewis; M. Richardson; D. Lawton; M. Manuel

### Budget and Public Finances

*Managing Director (SCS)*, R. Culpin
*Directors (SCS)*, N. Holgate ; C. J. Mowl
*Heads of Teams (SCS)*, P. Curwen; P. Betts; S. Pickford; I. Taylor; M. P. Williams; G. Parker; A. Gibbs; D. Deaton; C. Maxwell; P. Rankin; M. Swan; M. Dawes; A. Sharples; A. Ritche; P. Williams; W. Nye

### Public Services

*Managing Director*, N. Macpherson
*Directors*, M. Aldred; L. de Groot; A. Sharples; J. Grice
*Heads of Teams*, R. Brown; A. Bridges; R. Dunn; H. John; J. Richardson; P. Kane; M. Wheatley; D. Franklin; P. Brook; A. Charlesworth

### Corporate Services And Development (CSD)

*Managing Director (SCS)*, H. Douglas
*Heads of Teams (SCS)*, C. Pearson; J. Dodds; P. Pelger; R. Brightwell

### Financial Management, Reporting and Audit

*Managing Director (SCS)*, A. Likierman
*Director and Head of Treasury Office of Accounts Team (SCS)*, B. Glicksman
*Heads of Teams (SCS)*, D. Loweth; K. Ross; I. Carruthers; R. Brightwell
*Heads of Teams*, K. Ross; C. Butler; Miss A. M. Jones; I. Carruthers; D. Loweth

### Finance, Regulation and Industry

*Managing Director (SCS)*, J. Cunliffe
*Directors (SCS)*, H. J. Bush, CB; R. Fellgett
*Heads of Teams (SCS)*, S. Mullen; S. Meek; D. Griffiths; J. Halligan; P. Rutnan; P. Schofield; J. Kingman; R. Bent; S. Beckett; D. Storey

## EXECUTIVE AGENCIES

### National Savings

— *see* pages 625–6

### Office for National Statistics

— *see* page 349

### Royal Mint

— *see* page 357

### United Kingdom Debt Management Office

Eastcheap Court, 11 Philpot Lane, London, EC3M 8UD
Tel: 020-7862 6500; Fax: 020- 7862 6509

The UK Debt Management Office was launched as an executive agency of the Treasury in April 1998 after the transfer from the Bank of England to the Treasury of responsibility for debt management, the sale of gilts and oversight of the gilts market. It took over responsibility for the management of the Exchequer's daily cash flows in April 2000.
*Chief Executive*, M. L. Williams

## OTHER BODIES

### Office of Government Commerce (OGC)

Fleetbank House, 2-6 Salisbury Square, London EC4Y 8JX
Tel: 020-7211 1300; Web: www.ogc.gov.uk
The Office of Government Commerce was set up on the 1 April 2000. It is a unique body within government, overseen by a supervisory board of Ministers and officials from across the departments of government. Its aim is to achieve the best value for money for the Government's commercial relationships and coherence of purchasing activity across 200 Government departments, non-governmental bodies and agencies. The OGC is an office of HM Treasury.
*Chief Executive*, P. Gershon
*Deputy Chief Executive*, B. Rigby

### OGC.Buying.Solutions

Royal Liver Building, Pier Head, Liverpool L3 1PE
Tel: 0151-227 4262; Fax: 0151-258 1249
Web: www. ogcbuyingsolutions.gov.uk

The Agency provides a professional purchasing service to Government departments and other public bodies. From April 2000 it became part of the Office of Government Commerce reporting to the Chief Secretary to the Treasury.
*Chief Executive (SCS)*, D. J. Court

---

## THE TREASURY SOLICITOR

### Department of HM Procurator-General and Treasury Solicitor

Queen Anne's Chambers, 28 Broadway, London SW1H 9JS Tel: 020-7210 3000; Fax: 020-7210 3004

---

The Treasury Solicitor's Department provides legal services for many Government departments. Those without their own lawyers are provided with legal advice, and both they and other departments are provided with litigation services. The Treasury Solicitor is also the Queen's Proctor, and is responsible for collecting Bona Vacantia on behalf of the Crown. The Department became an executive agency in 1996.

*HM Procurator-General and Treasury Solicitor (SCS)*, Juliet Wheldon
*Deputy Treasury Solicitor (SCS)*, Anthony M. Inglese

LITIGATION DIVISION

*SCS*, R. Aitken; Mrs D. Babar; Peter Bennett; David Brummell; Lee John-Charles; Anthony D. Lawton; A. Leithead; B. McHenry; Barrie McKay; Peter R. Messer; Ms Lyndsey Nicoll; Mrs J. B. C. Oliver; David Palmer; Stephen Parkinson; Roland Phillips; A. J. Sandal

QUEEN'S PROCTOR DIVISION

*Queen's Proctor (SCS)*, Juliet Wheldon
*Assistant Queen's Proctor (SCS)*, Sue Cochrane

RESOURCES AND SERVICES DIVISION

*Principal Establishment and Finance Officer and Security Officer (SCS)*, J. P. Burnett
*Assistant Director Establishments (G7)*, Ms H. Donnelly
*Assistant Director Finance (G7)*, C. A. Woolley
*Assistant Director Information Systems (G7)*, M. Gabbidon
*Business Support Manager (SEO)*, E. Blishen
*Assistant Director Personnel and Training*, Ms M Esplin

BONA VACANTIA DIVISION

*SCS*, Ms L. Addison

EUROPEAN DIVISION

*SCS*, J. E. Collins; A. Ridout; M. C. P. Thomas

CULTURE, MEDIA AND SPORT DIVISION

*SCS*, Ms I. Letwin

CABINET OFFICE AND CENTRAL ADVISORY DIVISION

*SCS*, M. C. L. Carpenter; C. House

MINISTRY OF DEFENCE ADVISORY DIVISION

Metropole Building, Northumberland Avenue, London WC2N 5BL Tel: 020-7218 4691

*SCS*, N. Beach; Mrs V. Collett; M. Hemming; Ms F. Nash

DEPARTMENT FOR EDUCATION AND EMPLOYMENT ADVISORY DIVISION

Caxton House, Tothill Street, London SW1H 9NF
Tel: 020-7273 3000

*SCS*, F. D. W. Clarke; Ms D. Collins; S. T. Harker; P. Kilgarriff; N. A. D. Lambert; D. Macrae; A. Preston

HM TREASURY ADVISORY DIVISION

Allington Towers, 19 Allington Street, London SW1E 5EB
Tel: 020-7270 3000

*SCS*, M. A. Blythe; J. R. J. Braggins; Ms R. Ford; J. Jones; R. Ricks; Miss J. V. Stokes

CONSTITUTIONAL REFORM DIVISION

70 Whitehall, London SW1A 2AS
Tel: 020-7270 6093

*SCS*, Miss R. A. Jeffreys

## WALES OFFICE

Gwydyr House, Whitehall, London SW1A 2ER
Tel: 020-7270 0549;
Email: wales@planning-inspectorate.gov.uk

The Wales Office is the Office of the Secretary of State for Wales, who represents Welsh interests in the Cabinet.

*Secretary of State for Wales*, The Rt. Hon. Paul Murphy, MP
*Parliamentary Under-Secretary*, Don Touhig, MP
*Head of Department*, Ms Alison. Jackson

## DEPARTMENT FOR WORK AND PENSIONS

Richmond House, 79 Whitehall, London SW1A 2NS
Tel: 020-7238 0800; Web: dwp.gov.uk

The Department for Work and Pensions was formed on 8 June 2001 from parts of the former Department of Social Security and Department for Education and Employment and the Employment Service. The Department provides people of working age, pensioners and children with the advice and help they need to achieve financial independence and to make the most of life. Its stated aims are to create a single point of delivery for jobs, benefits advice and support through a modern nationwide service called Jobcentre Plus; to provide employers with a professional service for filling job vacancies; to provide a new Pension Service; to provide information and support to today's and tomorrow's pensioners; to ensure delivery of a simplified and efficient Child Support system and quality of opportunity and social inclusion for all.

*Secretary of State for Work and Pensions*, The Rt. Hon. Alistair Darling, MP
*Principal Private Secretary*, Neil Couling
*Special Advisers*, Andrew Maugham
*Ministers of State*, The Rt. Hon. Nick Brown, MP(*Work*); The Rt. Hon. Ian McCartney, MP (*Pensions*)
*Privaties Secretary for Work* , D. Jefferson; A. Holt; S. Jones
*Private Secretary for Pensions*, D. Whitehead
*Private Secretary for Work*, D. Jefferson; A. Holt; S. Jones
*Private Secretary for Disabled People*, E. Davies
*Parliamentary Under-Secretaries of State*, The Baroness Hollis of Heigham, D.Phil. (*Children and the Family*); Malcolm Wicks, MP (*Work*); Marion Eagle, MP (*Pensions*)
*Private Secretaries*, C. Jennings; Ms M. Curran
*Parliamentary Private Secretaries*, Anne Coffey, MP; Bob Blizzard, MP
*Permanent Secretary (SCS)*, Ms R. Lomax
*Private Secretary*, J. Tunstall

### CORPORATE SERVICES DEPARTMENT

*Director (SCS)*, S. Hickey

HUMAN RESOURCES DIRECTORATE

*Director*, K. White

ANALYTICAL SERVICES DIVISION

The Adelphi, 1–11 John Adam Street, London WC2N 6HT
Tel: 020-7962 8000

*Director (SCS)*, D. Stanton
*Chief Statistician (SCS)*, F. Johnson
*Director Information Centre (SCS)*, N. Dyson
*Senior Economic Advisers (SCS)*, J. Ball; G. Harris; R. Enden; T. Huddleston

*Operational Research Service (SCS)*, D. Barnbrook
*Chief Research Officers (SCS)*, G. Clark; S. Rice

FINANCE DIRECTORATE

*Director*, J. Codling

## COMMUNICATIONS DIRECTORATE

*Director (SCS)*, S. MacDowall
*Deputy Directors* (SCS), J. Bretherton; A. Hall
*Head of Media Relations*, (SCS), K. Young
*Head of Marketing* (SCS), S. O'Neil

## PENSIONS, CHILDREN AND DISABLED CLIENT GROUPS DIRECTORATE

*Director (SCS)*, P. R. C. Gray
*Director, Children (SCS)*, H. Ghosh
*Director, Disability and Carer Benefits (SCS)*, D. Burton
*Director, Pensions Credit Programme (SCS)*, G. McCorkell
*Director, Pensions Change and Specification*, H. Reynolds

## WORKING AGE GROUP

*Director (SCS)*, U. Brennan
*Director, Change*, S. Hewitt
Director, Strategy, *R. Devereux*
*Director, Employment*, M. Richardson

## SOLICITOR'S OFFICE

*Solicitor and Head of Law and Special Policy Group (SCS)*, Mrs M. A. Morgan, CB

SOLICITOR'S DIVISION A

New Court, 48 Carey Street, London WC2A 2LS
Tel: 020-7412 1326
*Legal Director (SCS)*, J. A. Catlin
*Assistant Legal Director (SCS)*, Ms F. A. Logan; S. Cooper; Ms C. Cooper; P. Milledge; Ms A. McGaughrin

SOLICITOR'S DIVISION B

New Court, 48 Carey Street, London WC2A 2LS
Tel: 020-7412 1528
*Solicitor and Head of Law and Special Policy Group (SCS)*, Mrs M. A. Morgan, CB
*Assistant Solicitors (SCS)*, Ms S. Edwards; R. S. Powell; Mrs A. James

SOLICITOR'S DIVISION C

New Court, 48 Carey Street, London WC2A 2LS
Tel: 020-7412 1342

*Legal Director (SCS)*, Mrs G. S. Kerrigan
*Assistant Solicitors (SCS)*, Miss M. E. Trefgarne; Mrs S. Walker; K. Baulblys; D. Dunleavy; Ms R. Sandby-Thomas

## BENEFIT FRAUD INSPECTORATE

Berkeley House, 12A North Park Road, Harrogate HG1 5QA Tel: 01423-832922

*Director-General (SCS)*, C. Bull

## EXECUTIVE AGENCIES

APPEALS SERVICE AGENCY

— *see* Tribunals Section

DWP BENEFITS AGENCY

Quarry House, Quarry Hill, Leeds LS2 7UA
Tel: 0113-232 4000

The Agency administers claims for and payments of social security benefits.
*Chief Executive*, A. Cleveland
*Private Secretary*, R. Baldwin
*Directors*, J. Codling (*Finance*); M. Fisher (*Personnel and Communications*); S. Heminsley (*Strategic and Planning*); A. Cleveland (*Operations Support*); N. Haighton (*Projects*)
*Medical Policy*
*Principal Medical Officers*, Dr M. Aylward; Dr P. Dewis; Dr P. Sawney; Dr A. Braidwood; Dr P. Stidolph

CHILD SUPPORT AGENCY

DSS and Inland Revenue, CSA, Long Benton, Benton Park Road, Newcastle upon Tyne NE98 1YX
Tel: 0191-213 5000

The Agency was set up in April 1993. It is responsible for the administration of the Child Support Act and for the assessment, collection and enforcement of maintenance payments for all new cases.
*Chief Executive*, Ms F. Boardman
*Directors*, M. Davison; C. Peters; M. Isaacs; T. Read

WAR PENSIONS AGENCY

Norcross, Blackpool, Lancs FY5 3WP
Tel: 01253-338816
Email: warpensions@gtnet.gov.uk

The Agency administers the payment of war disablement and war widows' pensions and provides welfare services and support to war disablement pensioners, war widows and their dependants and carers.
*Acting Chief Executive*, A. Burnham
*Secretary*, C. Pike

## ADVISORY BODIES

SOCIAL SECURITY ADVISORY COMMITTEE
New Court, 48 Carey Street, London WC2A 2LS.
Tel: 020-7412 1508; Fax: 020-7412 1570;
Email: ssac@ms42.dwp.gov.uk; Web www.ssac.org.uk
*Chairman*, Sir Thomas Boyd-Carpenter, KBE; *Secretary*, Ms G. Saunders

## PUBLIC OFFICES

### ADJUDICATOR'S OFFICE

Haymarket House, 28 Haymarket, London SW1Y 4SP
Tel: 020-7930 2292; Fax: 020-7930 2298;
Web: www.adjucatorsoffice.gov.uk

The Adjudicator's Office opened in 1993 and investigates complaints about the way the Inland Revenue (including the Valuation Office Agency) and Customs and Excise have handled a person's affairs.

*The Adjudicator*, Dame Barbara Mills, DBE, QC
*Head of Office*, C. Gordon

### ADVISORY, CONCILIATION AND ARBITRATION SERVICE

Brandon House, 180 Borough High Street, London SE1 1LW Tel: 020-7210 3613; Fax: 020-7210 3708

The Advisory, Conciliation and Arbitration Service (ACAS) was set up under the Employment Protection Act 1975 (the provisions now being found in the Trade Union and Labour Relations (Consolidation) Act 1992). ACAS is directed by a Council consisting of a full-time chairman and part-time employer, trade union and independent members, all appointed by the Secretary of State for Trade and Industry. The functions of the Service are to promote the improvement of industrial relations in general, to provide facilities for conciliation, mediation and arbitration as means of avoiding and resolving industrial disputes, and to provide advisory and information services on industrial relations matters to employers, employees and their representatives.

ACAS has regional offices in Birmingham, Bristol, Cardiff, Fleet, Glasgow, Leeds, Liverpool, London, Manchester, Newcastle upon Tyne and Nottingham.

*Chairman*, R. Donaghy, OBE
*Chief Conciliator* (*G4*), D. Evans

### ANCIENT MONUMENTS BOARD FOR SCOTLAND

Longmore House, Salisbury Place, Edinburgh EH9 1SH Tel: 0131-668 8764; Fax: 0131-668 8765;
Email: ancient.monuments@scotland.gov.uk

The Ancient Monuments Board for Scotland advises the Scottish Ministers on the exercise of their functions, under the Ancient Monuments and Archaeological Areas Act 1979, of providing protection for monuments of national importance.

*Chairman*, Prof. Michael Lynch, Ph.D., FRSE, FSA Scot.
*Members*, AR. J. Mercer, FRSE, FSA, FSA Scot.; Miss Lisbeth. M. Thoms, FSA Scot.; J. Higgitt, FSA, FSA Scot.; Dr C. Swanson, Ph.D., FSA Scot.; M. Baughan; Dr J. Cannizzo, Ph.D., FSA Scot.; Dr S. Peake, Ph.D.; M. J. Taylor; Ms Jill. Harden, FSA Scot.; A. Saville, FSA Scot; Cllr J. A. McFadden, CBE; Cllr E. F. Scott, FSA Scot; Prof C. D. Morris, FRSE, FSA, FSA Scot; A.P.K. Wright, OBE
*Secretary*, R. A. J. Dalziel
*Assessor*, Dr D. J. Breeze, Ph.D., FRSE, FSA, FSA Scot.

### ANCIENT MONUMENTS BOARD FOR WALES

Crown Buildings, Cathays Park, Cardiff CF10 3NQ
Tel: 029-2050 0200; Fax: 029-2082 6375;
Email: cadw@wales.gsi.gov.uk;
Web: www.cadw.wales.gov.uk

The Ancient Monuments Board for Wales advises the National Assembly for Wales on its statutory functions in respect of ancient monuments.

*Chairman*, Prof. R. R. Davies, CBE, D.Phil. FBA
*Members*, R. G. Keen; Prof. W. Davies, Ph.D. FBA, FSA; M. J. Garner; Prof. R. A. Griffiths, Ph.D., D.Litt.; R. Brewer, FSA; Prof. A. Whittle, D.Phil, FBA; C. Musson, MBE, FSA; Prof. M. Adhoose-Green, Ph.D., FSA
*Secretary*, Mrs J. Booker

### ARTS COUNCILS

The Arts Council of Great Britain was established as an independent body in 1946 to be the principal channel for the Government's support of the arts. In 1994 the Scottish and Welsh Arts Councils became autonomous and the Arts Council of Great Britain became the Arts Council of England.

The Arts Councils are responsible for the distribution of the proceeds of the National Lottery allocated to the arts. (*see* Lotteries and Gaming Section).

### ARTS COUNCIL OF ENGLAND

14 Great Peter Street, London SW1P 3NQ
Tel: 020-7333 0100; Fax: 020-7973 6590;
Web: www.artscouncil.org.uk

The Arts Council is the national, strategic policy body for the arts. It works in partnership with the Regional Arts Boards, which are responsible for funding and development of the arts in their areas. The Arts Council and the Regional Arts Boards commission new work, conduct research, provide advice and information, promote the case for publicly funded arts and work together to create partnerships and access new money for artistic activity. It receives funding from Government, but is an independent non-political body working at arm's length from the Government.

There are currently proposals to combine the Arts Council and the 10 Regional Arts Boards to create a new national arts funding and development organisation.

The Government grant for 2001–2002 is £252 million.

*Chairman*, G. Robinson
*Members*, D. Brierley, CBE, D. Bull , CBE; E. Cooper; A. Kapoor; Prof. J. MacGregor; B. McMaster, CBE; Dr J. Ritterman; W. Sieghart H. Strong
*Chief Executive*, P. Hewitt

#### REGIONAL ARTS BOARDS

Web: www.arts.org.uk

EAST ENGLAND ARTS, Cherry Hinton Hall, Cherry Hinton Road, Cambridge CB1 8DW. Tel: 01223-215355. *Chair*, Prof. S. Timperley
EAST MIDLANDS ARTS BOARD, Mountfields House, Epinal Way, Loughborough, Leics LE11 0QE. Tel: 01509-218292. *Acting Chair*, S. Lowe
LONDON ARTS , 2 Pear Tree Court, London, ECIR ODS Tel: 020-7608 6100. *Chair*, Lady Hollick

NORTHERN ARTS BOARD, Central Square, Forth Street, Newcastle upon Tyne NE7 3PJ. Tel: 0191-255 8500.
*Chair*, G. Loggie

NORTH-WEST ARTS BOARD, Manchester House, 22 Bridge Street, Manchester M3 3AB. Tel: 0161-834 6644.
*Chair*, T. Bloxham, MBE

SOUTH-EAST ARTS BOARD, Union House, Eridge Road, Tunbridge Wells, Kent TN4 8HF. Tel: 01892-507200.
*Joint Chair*, J. White; N. Chapman

SOUTHERN ARTS , 13 St Clement Street, Winchester SO23 9DQ. Tel: 01962-855099. *Chair*, D. Astor

SOUTH WEST ARTS, Bradninch Place, Gandy Street, Exeter EX4 3LS. Tel: 01392-218188.
*Chair*, Prof. A. Livingston

WEST MIDLANDS ARTS BOARD, 82 Granville Street, Birmingham B1 2LH. Tel: 0121-631 3121.
*Chair*, R. Natkiel

YORKSHIRE ARTS BOARD, 21 Bond Street, Dewsbury, W. Yorks WF13 1AX. Tel: 01924-455555. *Chair*, R. Guthrie

## SCOTTISH ARTS COUNCIL

12 Manor Place, Edinburgh EH3 7DD
Tel: 0131-226 6051; Fax: 0131-225 9833;
Email: administrator@scottisharts.org.uk;
Web: www.sac.org.uk

The Scottish Arts Council funds arts organisations in Scotland with the concept of providing leadership and developing new ideas and initiatives. It has two main sources of funding: the Scottish Executive (2001–2002: £34.9m) and Lottery funding through the Department of Culture, Media and Sport (2001–2002: £207m).

*Chairman*, J. Boyle
*Members*, Ms S. Ainsley; Cllr E. Cameron; R. Chester; W. English; J. Faulds; Ms D. Idiens; Ms M. Marshall; Dr Ann Matheson, OBE; J. Scott Moncrieff; R. Presswood; W. Speirs; J. Baker; L. Mitchell
*Director*, Ms T. Jackson

## ARTS COUNCIL OF WALES

9 Museum Place, Cardiff CF10 3NX
Tel: 029-2037 6500; Fax: 029-2022 1447

The Arts Council of Wales funds arts organisations in Wales and is funded by the National Assembly for Wales. The grant for 2000–2001 was £15.4 million.

*Chairman*, Ms S. Crouch
*Members*, D. Davies; Dr H. Walford Davies; E. Fivet; S. Garrett; E. ap Gwyn; H. James; D. Jones; P. Ryan, OBE; R. Davies; G. Lewis; A. Lloyd; C. Thomas
*Acting Chief Executive*, F. Medley

## ARTS COUNCIL OF NORTHERN IRELAND

MacNeice House, 77 Malone Road, Belfast BT9 6AQ
Tel: 028-90-38 5210; Fax: 028-9066 1715;
Email; publicaffairs@artscouncil-ni.org;
Web: www.artscouncil-ni.org

The Arts Council of Northern Ireland is the prime distributor of Government funds in support of the arts in Northern Ireland. It is funded by the Department of Culture, Arts and Leisure, and the grant for 2001–2002 is £7.881 million including £250,000 for 'cultural traditional funding.'

*Chairman*, Prof. B. Walker
*Vice-Chairman*, Ms E. O'Baoill
*Members*, Ms M. Armstrong; D. Boyd; Dr M. Crozier; R. Dunn; Dr T. Maginess; D. Hyndman; Ms J. Jordan; J. Kerr; Prof. B. McClelland; Ms G. Moriarty; A. Shortt; Mrs. M. Yeomans
*Chief Executive*, Ms R. McDonough

# ART GALLERIES AND ASSOCIATED BODIES

## NATIONAL GALLERIES OF SCOTLAND

The Mound, Edinburgh EH2 2EL
Tel: 0131-624 6200; Fax: 0131-343 3250

The National Galleries of Scotland comprise the National Gallery of Scotland, the Scottish National Portrait Gallery, the Scottish National Gallery of Modern Art and the Dean Gallery. There are also outstations at Paxton House, Berwickshire, and Duff House, Banffshire. Total Government grant-in-aid for 2001–2002 is £7.7 million.

### TRUSTEES

*Chairman of the Trustees*, Mr B.Ivory, CBE
*Trustees*, Ms V. Atkinson; J. Hunter Blair; DL; G. J. N. Gemmell, CBE; Lord Gordon of Strathblane, CBE; A. P. Leitch; Prof. Christina Lodder; Dr I. McKenzie Smith, OBE; G. Weaver; Prof. I. Whyte

### OFFICERS

*Director-General* (*G4*), T. Clifford
*Keeper of Conservation* (*G6*), M. Gallagher
*Head of Press and Information* (*G7*), C. Black
*Head of Education* (*G7*), M. Finn *Registrar* (*G7*), Miss A. Buddle
*Buildings* (*G7*), R. Galbraith
*Director, National Gallery of Scotland* (*G6*), M. Clarke
*Director, Scottish National Portrait Gallery* (*G6*), J. Holloway
*Curator of Photography*, Miss S. F. Stevenson
*Director, Scottish National Gallery of Modern Art and Dean Gallery* (*G6*), R. Calvocoressi

## NATIONAL GALLERY

Trafalgar Square, London WC2N 5DN
Tel: 020-7839 3321; Fax: 020-7747 2403

The National Gallery, which houses a permanent collection of western painting from the 13th to the 20th century, was founded in 1824, following a parliamentary grant of £60,000 for the purchase and exhibition of the Angerstein collection of pictures. The present site was first occupied in 1838; an extension to the north of the building with a public entrance in Orange Street was opened in 1975, and the Sainsbury wing was opened in 1991. Total Government grant-in-aid for 2000–2001 was £19.215 million.

### BOARD OF TRUSTEES

*Chairman*, P. Scott, QC
*Trustees*, Sir Mark Richmond, SC.D., FRS; Sir Ewen Fergusson, GCMG, CGVO; Lord R. Gavron, CBE; P. Hughes, CBE C.Le Brun; Dr D. Landau; Sir Colin Southgate; J. Snow; Prof. Dawn Ades; Lady Hopkins; M. Getty; R. Sondhi; Prof. J. Higgins

### OFFICERS

*Director*, R. N. MacGregor
*Keeper*, Dr N. Penny
*Head of Curational Department*, Dr S. Foister
*Senior Curator*, D. Jaffé
*Chief Restorer*, M. H. Wyld, CBE
*Head of Exhibitions*, M. J. Wilson
*Scientific Adviser*, Dr A. Roy
*Director of Administration*, J. MacAuslan
*Director of Communications*, D. Savelkoul
*Head of Education*, K. Adler

## NATIONAL PORTRAIT GALLERY

St Martin's Place, London WC2H 0HE
Tel: 020-7306 0055; Fax: 020-7306 0056

A grant was made in 1856 to form a gallery of the portraits of the most eminent persons in British history. The present building was opened in 1896 and the Ondaatje wing; including a new Balcony Gallery, Tudor Gallery, IT Gallery, State-of-the-art Lecture Theatre, and roof-top restaurant opened in May 2001. There are four regional partnerships displaying portraits in appropriate settings: Montacute House, Beningbrough Hall and Bodelwyddan Castle. Total Government grant-in-aid for 2001–2002 is £5.460 million.

BOARD OF TRUSTEES

*Chairman*, Sir D. Scholey, CBE
*Trustees*, The Rt. Hon. Margaret Beckett, MP; Prof. Phillip King; Ms F. Fraser; Ms T. Green; M. Hastings; T. Phillips, RA; Prof. The Earl Russell, FBA; Ms C. Tomalin; D. Scholey, CBE; Ms A. Shulman; Sir John Weston; Baroness Willoughby de Eresby; Prof. D. Cannadine; Prof. L. Jordanova
*Director (G3)*, C. Saumarez Smith, Ph.D.

## ROYAL FINE ART COMMISSION FOR SCOTLAND

Bakehouse Close, 146 Canongate, Edinburgh EH8 8DD
Tel: 0131-556 6699; Fax: 0131-556 6633;
Web: www.royfinartcomforsco.gov.uk

The Commission was established in 1927 and advises Ministers and local authorities on the visual impact and quality of design of construction projects. It is an independent body and gives its opinions impartially.

*Chairman*, The Rt. Hon. The Lord Cameron of Lochbroom, PC, FRSE
*Commissioners*, Ms J. Malvenan; R. G. Maund; M. Murray; D. Page; B. Rae; Prof. R. Russell; M. Turnbull; A. Wright
*Secretary*, C. Prosser

## TATE BRITAIN

Millbank, London SW1P 4RG
Tel: 020-7887 8000; Fax: 020-7887 8007
Web: www.tate.org.uk

Tate Britain displays the national collection of British art. The gallery opened in 1897, the cost of erection (£80,000) being defrayed by Sir Henry Tate, who also contributed the nucleus of the present collection. The Turner wing was opened in 1910, and further galleries and a new sculpture hall followed in 1937. In 1979 a further extension was built, and the Clore Gallery, for the Turner collection, was opened in 1987. Tate consists of four galleries: Tate Britain and Tate Modern in London, Tate Liverpool and Tate St Ives.

BOARD OF TRUSTEES

*Chairman*, D. Verey
*Trustees*, Prof. Dawn Ades; Ms V. Barnsley; The Hon. P. Doig; Prof. J. Latto; Sir Christopher Mallaby, GCMG, GCVO; J. Snow; J. Studzinski; Ms G. Wearing; C. Ofili

OFFICERS

*Director*, Sir Nicholas Serota
*Director of National Programmes*, S. Nairne
*Director of Collections*, J. Lewison
*Director, Tate Modern*, vacant
*Director, Tate Britain*, S. Deuchar
*Curator, Tate Liverpool*, C. Gruneberg
*Curator, Tate St Ives*, S. Daniel-McElvoy

## TATE MODERN

Bankside, London SE1 9TG
Tel: 020-7887 8000

Opened on 11 May 2000, Tate Modern displays the Tate collection of international modern art dating from 1900 to the present day. It includes works by Dalí, Picasso, Matisse, and Warhol as well as many contemporary works. It is housed in the former Bankside Power Station in London, redesigned by the Swiss architects Herzog & de Meuron.

## WALLACE COLLECTION

Hertford House, Manchester Square, London W1M 6BN
Tel: 020-7563 9516; Fax: 020-7224 2155

The Wallace Collection was bequeathed to the nation by the widow of Sir Richard Wallace, Bt. in 1897, and Hertford House was subsequently acquired by the Government. Total Government grant-in-aid for 1999–2000 was £2.453 million.

*Director*, vacant
*Head of Administration*, N. Paladina

---

## ASSEMBLY OMBUDSMAN FOR NORTHERN IRELAND AND NORTHERN IRELAND COMMISSIONER FOR COMPLAINTS

Progressive House, 33 Wellington Place, Belfast BT1 6HN Tel: 028-9023 3821; Fax: 028-9023 4912;
Email: ombudsman@ni-ombudsman.org.uk;
Web: www.ni-ombudsman.org.uk

---

The Ombudsman is appointed under legislation with powers to investigate complaints by people claiming to have sustained injustice in consequence of maladministration arising from action taken by a Northern Ireland Government department, or any other public body within his remit. Staff are presently seconded from the Northern Ireland Civil Service.

*Ombudsman*, T. Frawley
*Deputy Ombudsman*, J. MacQuarrie
*Directors*, C. O'Hare; R. Doherty; H. Mallon

---

## AUDIT COMMISSIONS

---

## ACCOUNTS COMMISSION FOR SCOTLAND

*see* Audit Scotland

## AUDIT COMMISSION FOR LOCAL AUTHORITIES AND THE NATIONAL HEALTH SERVICE IN ENGLAND AND WALES

1 Vincent Square, London SW1P 2PN
Tel: 020-7828 1212; Fax: 020-7976 6187

The Audit Commission was set up in 1983 and is responsible for appointing external auditors to local authorities, including the Greater London Authority, and local National Health Service bodies in England and Wales. It is also responsible for promoting the proper stewardship of public finances and value for money in the services provided by local authorities and health bodies.

The Commission has a chairman, a deputy chairman and up to 18 members who are appointed by the Secretary of State for the Transport, Local Government and the Regions in consultation with the Secretary of State for Wales and the Health Secretaries in England and Wales.
*Chair*, Dame Helena Shovelton, DBE
*Deputy Chairman*, A. Fresko
*Members*, J. R. Foster; Sir Ronald Watson, CBE; Dr P. Lane; G. Lemos; N. Skellett; C. Swinson; D. Moss; Ms R. Lowe; Cllr R. Arthur; Sir David Williams; Prof. S. Richards; Dr J. Curson; Sir G. Hart; Ms E. Filkin; B. Wolfe; Ms J. Baddeley
*Controller of Audit*, A. Foster
*Commission Secretary*, C. Morales-Oyarce
*Chief Executive of District Audit Service*, A. Meekings

## AUDIT SCOTLAND

110 George Street, Edinburgh EH2 4LH
Tel: 0131-477 1234; Fax: 0131-477 4567;
Web: www.audit-scotland.gov.uk

Audit Scotland was set up on 1 April 2000 to provide services to the Accounts Commission and the Auditor General for Scotland. Together they help to ensure that the Scottish Executive and public sector bodies in Scotland are held accountable for the proper, efficient and effective use of around £17 billion of public funds.

Audit Scotland's work covers around 250 bodies including local authorities, police and fire boards; NHS boards and trusts; further education colleges; water authorities; departments of the Scottish Executive; executive agencies such as the Prison Service and non-departmental public bodies such as Scottish Enterprise.

Audit Scotland carries out financial and regularity audits to ensure that the public sector bodies adhere to the highest standards of financial management and governance. It also performs audits to ensure that these bodies achieve the best value for money. All of Audit Scotland's work in connection with local authorities, fire and police boards is carries out for the Accounts Commission while its other work is undertaken for the Auditor General.
*Auditor General*, R. W. Black
*Controller of Audit*, R. Hinds
*Secretary*, W. F. Magee

## BANK OF ENGLAND

Threadneedle Street, London EC2R 8AH
Tel: 020-7601 4444; Fax: 020-7601 4771;
Email: enquiries@bankofengland.co.uk;
Web: www.bankofengland

The Bank of England was incorporated in 1694 under royal charter. It is the banker of the Government and manages the note issue. Since May 1997 it has been operationally independent and its Monetary Policy Committee has had responsibility for setting short-term interest rates to meet the Government's inflation target. As the central reserve bank of the country, the Bank keeps the accounts of British banks, who maintain with it a proportion of their cash resources, and of most overseas central banks. The Bank has three main areas of activity: Monetary Stability, Market Operations and Financial Stability. Its responsibility for banking supervision has been transferred to the Financial Services Authority. (*See also* Financial Services Regulation section).
*Governor*, The Rt. Hon. E. A. J. George
*Deputy Governors*, D. Clementi; M. A. King
*Non-Executive Directors*, R. Bailie, OBE; Sir David Cooksey; H. J. Davies; Sir Ian Gibson; Ms S. McKechnie, OBE; W. Morris; J. Neill, CBE, Ph.D.; N. I. Simms; J. Stretton; Ms K. A. O'Donovan; G. Hall; Dr D. Julius; Sir J. Bond; Ms M Francis; Ms B Blow; Sir B. S. Moffat
*Monetary Policy Committee*, The Governor; the Deputy Governors; I. Plenderleith; J. Vickers; Dr S. Wadhwani; Prof. S. Nickell, C. J. Allsopp; C, Bean; Ms K. Barker
*Advisers to the Governor*, Sir Peter Petrie; M. Glover
*Chief Cashier and Deputy Director, Banking and Market Services*, Ms M. V. Lowther
*Chief Registrar*, G. P. Sparkes
*General Manager, Printing Works*, M. Thompson
*Secretary*, P. D. Rodgers
*The Auditor*, K. Butler

## BOARD OF CUSTOMS AND EXCISE

*New King's Beam House, 22 Upper Ground, London SE1 9PJ; Tel: 020-7620 1313;
National Advice Line: 0845 010 900;
Web: www.open.gov.uk/customs/c&ehome.htm

Commissioners of Customs were first appointed in 1671 and housed by the King in London. The Excise Department was formerly under the Inland Revenue Department and was amalgamated with the Customs Department in 1909.

HM Customs and Excise is responsible for collecting and administering customs and excise duties and VAT, and advises the Chancellor of the Exchequer on any matters connected with them. The Department is also responsible for preventing and detecting the evasion of revenue laws and for enforcing a range of prohibitions and restrictions on the importation of certain classes of goods. In addition, the Department undertakes certain agency work on behalf of other departments, including the compilation of UK overseas trade statistics from customs import and export documents.

### THE BOARD

*Chairman (G1)*, R. Broadbent
*Private Secretaries*, Ms D. Morris, Ms A. Lakemen
*Commissioners (G3)*, P. R. H. Allen; M. R. Brown; R. N. McAfee; M. W. Norgrove; T. Byrne; M. Eland; M. Hansons (*Non Executive*) Ms R. Pickauence; D. Spencer
*Solicitor*, D. Pickup

* Unless otherwise stated, this is the address and telephone number of directorates of the Board

### COMMUNICATIONS DIVISION

Tel: 020-7865 5335
*Head of Communications Division*, P. Rose

### LOGISTICS GROUP

Alexander House, 21 Victoria Avenue, Southend-on-Sea SS99 1AA Tel: 01702-348944
*Director*, A. Fazer

### ENFORCEMENT GROUP

*Director*, T. Byrne

### POLICY GROUP

*Director*, M. Eland

### HUMAN RESOURCE GROUP

*Director*, M. Rickwood

TARIFF AND STATISTICAL OFFICE

Portcullis House, 27 Victoria Avenue, Southend-on-Sea SS2 6AL Tel: 01702-348944
*Controller*, M. McDowall

ACCOUNTING SERVICES DIVISION

Alexander House, 21 Victoria Avenue, Southend-on-Sea SS99 1AA Tel: 01702-348944
*Accountant and Comptroller-General*, D. Robinson

NATIONAL INVESTIGATION SERVICE

Custom House, Lower Thames Street, London EC3R 6EE Tel: 020-7283 5353
*Chief Investigation Officer*, P. Evans

SOLICITOR'S OFFICE
*Solicitor*, D. Pickup
*Deputy Solicitor*, G. Fotherby

## BOARD OF INLAND REVENUE

Somerset House, Strand, London WC2R 1LB
Tel: 020-7438 6622

The Board of Inland Revenue was constituted under the Inland Revenue Board Act 1849. The Board administers and collects direct taxes – income tax, corporation tax, capital gains tax, inheritance tax, stamp duty, and petroleum revenue tax – and advises the Chancellor of the Exchequer on policy questions involving them. The Department's Valuation Office is an executive agency responsible for valuing property for tax purposes. The Contributions Agency of the Department for Work and Pensions which is responsible for the collection of contributions under the National Insurance scheme, became part of the Inland Revenue in April 1999 and is now an executive office called the National Insurance Contributions Office. The Contributions Unit of the Social Security Agency in Northern Ireland also transferred to the Inland Revenue in April 1999.

THE BOARD

*Chairman* (*G1*), N. Montagu, CB
*Private Secretary*, S. Hardy
*Deputy Chairmen* (*G2*), T. J. Flesher; A. Chaut

DIVISIONS

*Director, Human Resources Division* (*G3*), A. Walker
*Director of Business* (*G3*), J. Yard
*Head, Strategy and Planning*, S. Norris
*Principal of Financial Institutions* (*G3*), R. R. Martin
*Director, Business Operations* (*G3*), S. Banyard
*Director of Analysis Research* (*G3*), R. G. Ward
*Director Business Tax* (*G3*), Mary Hay
*Director International* (*G3*), G. Makhlouf
*Director of Special Compliance*, J. Middleton
*Director, Personal Tax* (*G3*), T. Orhinal
*Director, Capital and Savings* (*G3*), M. Williams
*Head, Revenue Policy* (*G3*), D. Hartnett

### EXECUTIVE OFFICES

ACCOUNTS OFFICE (CUMBERNAULD), St Mungo's Road, Cumbernauld, Glasgow G70 5TR. *Director*, A. Geddes, OBE
ACCOUNTS OFFICE (SHIPLEY), Shipley, Bradford, W. Yorks BD98 8AA. *Director*, vacant
INLAND REVENUE CAPITAL TAXES, Ferrers House, PO Box 38, Castle Meadow Road, Nottingham NG2 1BB. *Director*, J. Lee Pemberton
CAPITAL TAXES OFFICE (SCOTLAND), Meldrum House, 15 Drumshugh Gardens, Edinburgh, EH3 7UG. *Registrar*, Mrs J. Templeton
MARKETING AND COMMUNICATIONS, Ground Floor, New Wing Somerset House, Strand, London WC2R 1LB. *Director of Communications*, Ms N. Walters
ENFORCEMENT OFFICE, Durrington Bridge House, Barrington Road, Worthing, W. Sussex BN12 4SE. *Director*, D. Ellis
FINANCIAL ACCOUNTING OFFICE, South Block, Barrington Road, Worthing, W. Sussex BN12 4XH. *Director*, Ms M. McLeish
CENTRE FOR NON-RESIDENTS , St John's House, Merton Road, Bootle L269BB; Fitz Roy House, PO Box 46, Castle Meadow, Nottingham NG2 1BD. *Director*, J. Johnson
INTERNAL AUDIT OFFICE, 2nd Floor (North), 22 Kingsway, London WC2B 6NR. *Director*, N. R. Buckley
NATIONAL INSURANCE CONTRIBUTIONS OFFICE, DSS Longbenton, Benton Park Road, Newcastle upon Tyne NE98 1ZZ. *Chief Executive* (*G3*), B. Woodley
OIL TAXATION OFFICE, Melbourne House, Aldwych, London WC2B 4LL. *Director*, R. Dyall
SAVINGS PENSIONS AND SHARES, Yorke House, PO Box 62, Castle Meadow Road, Nottingham NG2 1BG. *Director*, R. Hurcombe
SOLICITOR'S OFFICE, East Wing, Somerset House, London WC2R 1LB. *Solicitor* (*G2*), P. Ridd
SOLICITOR'S OFFICE (SCOTLAND), Clarendon House, 114–116 George Street, Edinburgh EH2 4LH. *Solicitor*, I. K. Laing
SPECIAL COMPLIANCE OFFICE, Angel Court, 199 Borough High Street, London SE1 1HZ. *Director*, J. Middleton
STAMP OFFICE, Ground Floor, PO Box 38, Ferrers House, Castle Meadow, Nottingham NG2 1BB. *Director*, vacant
TRAINING OFFICE, Lawress Hall, Riseholme Park, Lincoln LN2 2BJ. *Director*, Ms L. Hinnigan

### REGIONAL EXECUTIVE OFFICES

INLAND REVENUE CENTRAL ENGLAND, Churchgate, New Road, Peterborough PE1 1TD. *Director*, E. McKeegan
INLAND REVENUE LARGE BUSINESS OFFICE, 1st Floor North, 22 Kingsway, London WC2B 6NR. *Director*, S. Jones
INLAND REVENUE LONDON, New Court, Carey Street, London WC2A 2JE. *Director*, C. R. Massingale
INLAND REVENUE NORTHERN ENGLAND, The Triad, Stanley Road, Bootle, Merseyside L75 2DD. *Director*, G. W. Lunn
INLAND REVENUE SOUTHERN ENGLAND 4th Floor, Dukes Court, Dukes Street, Woking GU21 5XR. *Director*, T. Sleeman
INLAND REVENUE WALES, 1st Floor, Phase II Building, Ty Glas Avenue, Llanishen, Cardiff CF14 5TS. *Director*, J. Harra
INLAND REVENUE SCOTLAND, Clarendon House, 114–116 George Street, Edinburgh EH2 4LH. *Director*, I. S. Gerrie
INLAND REVENUE NORTHERN IRELAND, Dorchester House, 52–58 Great Victoria Street, Belfast BT2 7QE. *Director*, D. Hinstridge

### VALUATION OFFICE AGENCY

New Court, 48 Carey Street, London WC2A 2JE
Tel: 020-7506 1700; Fax: 020-7506 1998;
Web: www.voa.gov.uk
50 Frederick Street, Edinburgh EH2 1NG

Tel: 0131-465 0701; Fax 0131-465 0799
*Chief Executive*, M. A. Johns
*Chief Valuer, Scotland*, A. Ainslie
*Chief Valuer, Wales*, P. Clement

## ADJUDICATOR'S OFFICE

— *see* page 318

## BOUNDARY COMMISSIONS

The Commissions are constituted under the Parliamentary Constituencies Act 1986. The Speaker of the House of Commons is *ex officio* chairman of all four commissions in the UK. Each of the four commissions is required by law to keep the parliamentary constituencies in their part of the UK under review. The latest Boundary Commission report for England was completed in April 1995, and its proposals took effect at the 1997 general election. The next report must be submitted before April 2006. The latest Scottish report was completed in December 1994, with the European constituencies completed in April 1996.

### ENGLAND

1 Drummond Gate, London SW1V 2QQ
Tel: 020-7533 5177; Fax: 020-7533 5176
*Deputy Chairman*, The Hon. Mr Justice Harrison
*Joint Secretaries*, R. Farrance; M. Rawlings

### WALES

1 Drummond Gate, London SW1V 2QQ
Tel: 020-7533 5172; Fax: 020-7533 5176
*Deputy Chairman*, The Hon. Mr Justice Kay
*Joint Secretaries*, R. Farrance; M. Rawlings

### SCOTLAND

3 Drumsheugh Gardens, Edinburgh EH3 7QJ
Tel: 0131-538 7510; Fax: 0131-538 7240
*Deputy Chairman*, The Hon. Lady Cosgrove
*Secretary*, R. Smith

### NORTHERN IRELAND

REL Division, 11 Millbank, London SW1P 4QE
Tel: 020-7210 6569
*Deputy Chairman*, The Hon. Mr Justice Coghlin
*Secretary*, Mrs L. Rogers

## BRITISH BROADCASTING CORPORATION

Broadcasting House, Portland Place, London W1A 1AA Tel: 020-7580 4468;
BBC Information Line: 0870 010 0222;
Web: www.bbc.co.uk
Television Centre, Wood Lane, London W12 7RJ

The BBC was incorporated under royal charter in 1926 as successor to the British Broadcasting Company Ltd. The BBC's current charter came into force on 1 May 1996 and extends to 31 December 2006. The chairman, vice-chairman and other governors are appointed by The Queen-in-Council. The BBC is financed by revenue from receiving licences for the home services and by grant-in-aid from Parliament for the World Service (radio).
For services, *see* Broadcasting section.

### BOARD OF GOVERNORS

*Chairman*, Sir Christopher Bland
*Vice-Chairman*, G. Davies
*National Governors*, Prof. F. Monds (*N. Ireland*); R. S. Jones, OBE (*Wales*); Sir Robert Smith (*Scotland*)
*Governors*, Sir Richard Eyre, CBE; D. Gleeson; Dame Pauline Neville-Jones, DCMG; A. Young; Ms H. Rabbatts; Baroness Hogg; R. Sondhi

### BOARD OF MANAGEMENT

#### EXECUTIVE COMMITTEE

*Director-General and Editor-in-Chief* G. Dyke (from April 2000)
*Directors*, M.Thompson (*Television*); Ms J. Abramsky (*Radio*); M. Byford (*BBC World Service*); R. Sambrook (*News*); G. Benson (*Joint Director, Factual and Learning*) A. Yentob (*Drama, Entertainment and Children*); R. Flynn (*Business Commercial*); P. Loughrey (*National and Regions*); J. Smith (*Finance, and Business Affairs*); G. Jones (*Human Resources and Internal Communcations*); A. Duncan (*Marketing and Communications*); M. Stevenson (*Joint Director, Factual and Learning*); P. Salmon (*Sport*); Ms C. Thomson (*Public Policy*); Ms C. Fairbairn (*Strategy and Distribution*); A. Highfield (*New Media and Distribution*);
*Chief Executives*, D. Green (*Acting*), *BBC Resources and Technology Ltd*); P. Langsdale (*BBC Technology*); R. Gavin (*BBC Worldwide*)

#### OTHER SENIOR STAFF

*Controller, BBC1*, L. Heggessey
*Controller, BBC2*, Ms J. Root
*Controller, Radio 1*, A. Parfitt
*Controller, Radio 2*, J. Moir
*Controller, Radio 3*, R. Wright
*Controller, Radio 4*, H. Boaden
*Controller, Radio 5 Live*, B. Shennan
*Controller, BBC Scotland*, J. McCormick
*Controller, BBC Wales*, M. Richards
*Controller, BBC N. Ireland*, A. Carragher
*Controller, English Regions*, A. Griffee
*Secretary*, G. Milner

## THE BRITISH COUNCIL

10 Spring Gardens, London SW1A 2BN
Tel: 020-7930 8466; Fax: 020-7839 6347
Bridgewater House, 58 Whitworth Street, Manchester M1 6BB Tel: 0161-957 7000; Fax: 0161-957 7111; 11 Portland Place, London W1B 1EJ Tel: 020-7930 3194; Fax: 020-7389 3199

The British Council was established in 1934, incorporated by Royal Charter in 1940 and granted a supplemental charter in 1993. It is an independent, non-political organisationwhich promotes Britain abroad. It is the UK's international organisation for educational and cultural relations. The British Council is represented in 229 towns and cities in 111 countries. Total income in 2000–2001, including Foreign and Commonwealth Office grants and contracted money, was £451.560 million.
*Chairman*, The Baroness Kennedy of The Shaws, QC
*Deputy Chairman*, Sir Tim Lankester, KCB
*Director-General*, D. Green, CMG

BRITISH FILM COMMISSION
10 Little Portland Street, London W1N 5DF
Tel: 020-7224 5000; Fax: 020-7224 1013

The British Film Commission was set up in 1991 and is funded by the Department for Culture, Media and Sport. The Commission promotes the UK as an international production centre, encourages the use of locations, facilities, services and personnel, and provides, at no charge to the film makers, comprehensive advice and information relating to the practical aspects of filming in the UK.

In April 2000, the Government. launched the Film Council to take a leading role in the development of the British film industry.

*Commissioner and Chief Executive*, S. Norris

BRITISH FILM INSTITUTE
21 Stephen Street, London W1T 1LN
Tel: 020-7255 1444; Fax: 020-7436 0439;
Web: www.bfi.org.uk

The British Film Institute was established in in 1933. It consists of three main departments: bfi Education, which comprises the bfi National Library, bfi publishing and bfi education projects, which encourages life-long learning about the moving image; bfi Exhibition, which runs the National Film Theatre, the London Film Festival and supports local cinemas and festivals UK wide; and bfi Collections, which preserves and promotes the UK's moving image heritage. The bfi also runs the London Imax Cinema, featuring the UK's largest screen. In April 2000, the Government launched the Film Council to take a leading role in the development of the British film industry.

*Chairman*, Ms J. Bakewell, CBE
*Deputy Chairman*, E. Senat
*Director*, J. Teckman
*Deputy Director*, R. Collins

BRITISH PHARMACOPOEIA COMMISSION
Market Towers, 1 Nine Elms Lane, London SW8 5NQ Tel: 020-7273 0561; Fax: 020-7273 0566

The British Pharmacopoeia Commission sets standards for medicinal products used in human and veterinary medicines and is responsible for publication of the British Pharmacopoeia (a publicly available statement of the standard that a product must meet throughout its shelf-life), the British Pharmacopoeia (Veterinary) and the selection of British Approved Names. It has 13 members who are appointed by the Secretary of State for Health, the Minister for Environment, Food and Rural Affairs, the Scottish Ministers, the National Assembly for Wales, and the relevant Northern Ireland departments.

*Chairman*, Prof. D. Calam, OBE, D.Phil.
*Vice-Chairman*, Prof. J. A. Goldsmith
*Secretary and Scientific Director*, Dr R. C. Hutton

BRITISH STANDARDS INSTITUTION (BSI)
389 Chiswick High Road, London W4 4AL
Tel: 020-8996 9000; Fax: 020-8996 7344

The British Standards Institution is the recognised authority in the UK for the preparation and publication of national standards for industrial and consumer products. About 90 per cent of its standards work is now internationally linked. British Standards are issued for voluntary adoption, though in a number of cases compliance with a British Standard is required by legislation. Industrial and consumer products certified as complying with the relevant British Standard may carry the Institution's certification trade mark, known as the 'Kitemark'.

*Chairman*, V. E. Thomas, CBE

BRITISH TOURIST AUTHORITY
Thames Tower, Black's Road, London W6 9EL
Tel: 020-8846 9000; Fax: 020-8563 0302

Established under the Development of Tourism Act 1969, the British Tourist Authority is responsible for promoting tourism to Britain from overseas. It also has a general responsibility for the promotion and development of tourism and tourist facilities within Britain as a whole, and for advising the Secretary of State for Culture, Media and Sport on tourism matters.

*Chairman*, D. Quarmby
*Chief Executive*, J. Hamblin

BRITISH WATERWAYS
Willow Grange, Church Road, Watford, Herts WD17 4QA Tel: 01923-226422; Fax: 01923-201400;
Email: enquirieshq@britishwaterways.co.uk
Web: www.britishwaterways.co.uk

British Waterways conserves and manages over 2,000 miles of canals and rivers in England, Scotland and Transport, Local Government and the Regions. Its responsibilities include maintaining the waterways and structures on and around them; looking after wildlife and the waterway environment; and ensuring that canals and rivers are safe and enjoyable places to visit.

*Chairman (part-time)*, Dr G. Greener
*Members (part-time)*, D. Langslow; I. Darling; H. Gorden; Ms C. Dobson; P. King; P. Soulsby; C. Christie
*Chief Executive*, D. Fletcher

BROADCASTING STANDARDS COMMISSION
7 The Sanctuary, London SW1P 3JS
Tel: 020-7808 1000; Fax: 020-7233 0397

The Commission was established in April 1997 under the Broadcasting Act 1996. It is an independent organisation representing the interests of the consumer, and its remit covers all television and radio broadcasting. The Commission considers the portrayal of violence and sexual conduct and matters of taste and decency. It also provides redress for people who believe they have been unfairly treated or subjected to unwarranted infringement of privacy. The Commission conducts research into stan-

dards and fairness in broadcasting and produces codes of practice, and it considers and adjudicates on complaints. Members of the Commission are appointed by the Secretary of State for Culture, Media and Sport. The appointments are part-time.
*Chair*, Lord Dobs of Battersea
*Deputy Chairmen* (£34,000–£36,000), Ms J. Leighton; Lady S. Warner
*Commissioners*, D. Boulton; U. Dholakia; G. Elliott; S. Heppel, CB; Revd Rose Hudson Wilkin; The Rt. Revd R. Holloway; Ms M. Redfern; Ms S. O'Sullivan;
*Director*, P. Bolt

---

THE BROADS AUTHORITY
Thomas Harvey House, 18 Colegate, Norwich NR3 1BQ Tel: 01603-610734; Fax: 01603-765710; Web: www.broads-authority.gov.uk

---

The Broads Authority is a special statutory authority set up under the Norfolk and Suffolk Broads Act 1988. The functions of the Authority are to conserve and enhance the natural beauty of the Broads; to provide integrated management of the land and water space of the area; to promote the enjoyment of the Broads by the public; and to protect the interests of navigation. The Authority comprises 35 members, appointed by the local authorities in the area covered, environmental conservation bodies, the Environment Agency, and the Great Yarmouth Port Authority.
*Chairman*, The Viscountess Knollys
*Chief Executive*, Dr J. Packman

---

CENTRAL ARBITRATION COMMITTEE
Third Floor, Discovery House, 28–42 Banner Street, London EC1Y 8QE Tel: 020-7251 9747; Fax: 020 7251 3114; Web: www.cac.gov.uk

---

The Central Arbitration Committee determines claims for statutory recognition and de-recognition of trade unions under the Employment Relations Act 1999, it also adjudicates on disclosure of information cases, issues relating to the European Works Council Directive and arbitrates on trade disputes.
*Chairman*, Sir Michael Burton
*Secretary*, C. Johnston

---

CERTIFICATION OFFICE FOR TRADE UNIONS AND EMPLOYERS' ASSOCIATIONS
180 Borough High Street, London SE1 1LW
Tel: 020-7210 3734/5; Fax: 020-7210 3612

---

The Certification Office is an independent statutory authority. The Certification Officer is appointed by the Secretary of State for Trade and Industry and is responsible for receiving and scrutinising annual returns from trade unions and employers' associations; for determining complaints concerning trade union elections, certain ballots and certain breaches of trade union rules; for ensuring observance of statutory requirements governing mergers between trade unions and employers' associations; for overseeing the political funds and finances of trade unions and employers' associations; and for certifying the independence of trade unions.
*Certification Officer*, Mr Cockburn
*Assistant Certification Officer*, G. S. Osborne

SCOTLAND

58 Frederick Street, Edinburgh EH2 1NB
Tel: 0131-226 3224; Fax: 0131-200 1300
*Assistant Certification Officer for Scotland*, J. L. J. Craig

---

CHARITY COMMISSION
Harmsworth House, 13–15 Bouverie Street, London EC4Y 8DP Tel: 0870 333 0123; Fax: 020-7674 2310
Web: www.charity-commission.gov.uk
2nd Floor, 20 King's Parade, Queen's Dock, Liverpool L3 4DQ Tel: 0870 333 0123; Fax: 0151-703 1555
Woodfield House, Tangier, Taunton, Somerset TA1 4BL Tel: 0870 333 0123; Fax: 01823-345003

---

The Charity Commission for England and Wales is the Government Department whose aim is to give the public confidence in the integrity of charity. It also carries out the functions of the registration, monitoring and support of charities and the investigation of alleged wrong-doing. The Commission maintains a computerised register of some 187,000 charities. It is accountable to the courts and for its efficiency to the Home Secretary. There are five Commissioners appointed by the Home Office for a fixed term and the Commission has Offices in London, Liverpool and Taunton.
*Chief Commissioner* (*G3*), J. Stoker
*Legal Commissioner* (*G3*), M. Carpenter
*Commissioners* (*part-time*) (*G4*), D. Taylor; Ms J. Warburton; Ms J. Unwin
*Heads of Legal Sections* (*G5*), J. A. Dutton; G. S. Goodchild; K. M. Dibble; S. Slack
*Director of Operations* (*G4*), S. Gillespie
*Head of Policy Division* (*G5*), Ms R. Chapman
*Establishment Officer* (*G5*), Ms C. Stewart
*Information Systems Controller* (*G5*), K. Chaun

The offices responsible for charities in Scotland and Northern Ireland are:
SCOTLAND – Scottish Charities Office, Crown Office, 25 Chambers Street, Edinburgh EH1 1LA. Tel: 0131-226 2626
NORTHERN IRELAND – Department for Social Development, Charities Branch, 5th Floor, Churchill House, Victoria Square, Belfast BT1 4SD

---

CHURCH COMMISSIONERS
1 Millbank, London SW1P 3JZ
Tel: 020-7898 1000; Fax: 020-7898 1131
Email: commissioners.enquiry@c-of-e.org
Web: www.churchcommissioners

---

The Church Commissioners were established in 1948 by the amalgamation of Queen Anne's Bounty (established 1704) and the Ecclesiastical Commissioners (established 1836). They are responsible for the management of most of the Church of England's assets, the income from which is predominantly used to pay, house and pension the clergy. The Commissioners own 128,000 acres of agricultural land, a number of residential estates in central London, and commercial property in Great Britain. They also carry out administrative duties in connection with pastoral reorganisation and redundant churches.

The Commissioners are: the Archbishops of Canterbury and of York; four bishops, three clergy and four lay persons elected by the respective houses of the General Synod; two deans or provosts elected by all the deans and provosts; three persons nominated by The Queen; three persons nominated by the Archbishops of Canterbury and York; three persons nominated by the Archbishops after consultation with others including the lord mayors of London and York and the vice-chancellors of the universities of Oxford and Cambridge; the First Lord of the Treasury; the Lord President of the Council; the Home Secretary; the Lord Chancellor; the Secretary of State for Culture, Media and Sport; and the Speaker of the House of Commons.

INCOME AND EXPENDITURE

| *for year ended 31 December 2000* | |
|---|---|
| £160m | *£ million* |
| Net income | 125.3 |
| Investments | 76.8 |
| Property | 41.4 |
| Interest from loans, etc. | 16.1 |
| Total expenditure | 160.0 |
| Parish ministry support | 22.4 |
| Bishop and cathedral clergy stipends | 6.7 |
| Bishops' housing | 3.0 |
| Grants to cathedrals | 2.5 |
| Financial provision for resigning clergy | 1.2 |
| Clergy pensions and CHARM subsidy | 92.4 |
| Transitional support for pension contributions | 11.3 |
| Church buildings | 1.2 |
| Bishops' working cost | 9.3 |
| Commissioners' administration of national church functions | 5.0 |
| Administration costs of other church bodies | 2.0 |

CHURCH ESTATES COMMISSIONERS

*First*, vacant
*Second*, S. Bell, MP
*Third*, The Viscountess Brentford

OFFICERS

*Secretary*, H. H. Hughes
*Deputy Secretary (Finance and Investment)*, C. W. Daws
*Official Solicitor*, S. Jones
*Assistant Secretaries*:
*The Accountant*, M. Adams
*Management Accountant*, B. J. Hardy
*Chief Surveyor and Deputy Secretary*, A. C. Brown
*Computer Manager*, J. W. Ferguson
*Bishoprics Secretary*, R. Badger
*Investments Manager*, M. Chaloner
*Pastoral, Houses and Redundant Churches*, M. D. Elengorn
*Senior Architect*, J. A. Taylor

## CIVIL AVIATION AUTHORITY

CAA House, 45–59 Kingsway, London WC2B 6TE
Tel: 020-7379 7311; Fax: 020-7240 1153;
Web: www.caa.co.uk

The CAA is responsible for the economic regulation of UK airlines and for the safety regulation of UK civil aviation by the certification of airlines and aircraft and by licensing aerodromes, flight crew and aircraft engineers.

The CAA advises the Government on aviation issues, represents consumer interests, conducts economic and scientific research, produces statistical data, and provides specialist services and other training and consultancy services to clients world-wide. It also regulates UK airspace and runs the ATOL flight and air holiday protection scheme.

*Chairman*, Sir Malcolm Field
*Secretary*, R. J. Britton

## THE COAL AUTHORITY

200 Lichfield Lane, Mansfield, Notts NG18 4RG
Tel: 01623-427162; Fax: 01623-622072;
Email: coalauthority@coal.gov.uk;
Web: www.coal.gov.uk

The Coal Authority was established under the Coal Industry Act 1994 to manage certain functions previously undertaken by British Coal, including ownership of unworked coal. It is responsible for licensing coal mining operations and for providing information on coal reserves and past and future coal mining. It settles subsidence claims not falling on coal mining operators. It deals with the management and disposal of property, and with surface hazards such as abandoned coal mine shafts.

*Chairman*, J. Harris, DL
*Chief Executive*, Dr I. Roxburgh

## COLLEGE OF ARMS (OR HERALDS COLLEGE)

Queen Victoria Street, London EC4V 4BT
Tel: 020-7248 2762; Fax: 020-7248 6448
Email: enquiries@college-of-arms.gov.uk;
Web: www.college-of-arms.gov.uk

The Sovereign's Officers of Arms (Kings, Heralds and Pursuivants of Arms) were first incorporated by Richard III. The powers vested by the Crown in the Earl Marshal (the Duke of Norfolk) with regard to state ceremonial are largely exercised through the College. The College is also the official repository of the arms and pedigrees of English, Welsh, Northern Irish and Commonwealth (except Canadian) families and their descendants, and its records include official copies of the records of Ulster King of Arms, the originals of which remain in Dublin. The 13 officers of the College specialise in genealogical and heraldic work for their respective clients.

Arms have been and still are granted by letters patent from the Kings of Arms. A right to arms can only be established by the registration in the official records of the College of Arms of a pedigree showing direct male line descent from an ancestor already appearing therein as being entitled to arms, or by making application through the College of Arms for a grant of arms. Grants are made to corporations as well as to individuals.

The College of Arms is open Monday–Friday 10–4.

*Earl Marshal*, The Duke of Norfolk, KG, GCVO, CB, CBE, MC

KINGS OF ARMS

*Garter*, P. L. Gwynn-Jones, CVO, FSA
*Clarenceux*, D. H. B. Chesshyre, LVO, FSA
*Norroy and Ulster*, T. Woodcock, LVO, FSA

HERALDS

*Richmond (and Earl Marshal's Secretary)*, P. L. Dickinson
*York*, H. E. Paston-Bedingfeld
*Chester (and Registrar)*, T. H. S. Duke

*Lancaster*, R. J. B. Noel
*Windsor*, W. G. Hunt, TD

PURSUIVANTS

*Rouge Croix*, D. V. White
*Rouge Dragon*, C. E. A. Cheesman

## COMMISSION FOR ARCHITECTURE AND THE BUILT ENVIRONMENT

The Tower Building, 11 York Road, London SE1 7NX Tel: 020-7960 2400; Fax: 020-7960 2444; Email: enquiries@cabe.org.uk; Web: www.cabe.org.uk

The Commission for Architecture and the Built Environment (CABE) is responsible for promoting the importance of high quality architecture and urban design and encouraging the understanding of architecture through educational and regional initiatives CABE offers free advice to Local Authorities, public sector clients and others embarking on building projects of any size or purpose.
*Chairman*, Sir Stuart Lipton
*Chief Executive*, J. Rouse

## COMMISSION FOR INTEGRATED TRANSPORT

Romney House, 5th Floor, Tufton Street, London SW1P 3RA Tel: 020-7944 4101; Fax: 020-7944 2919; Email: cfit@dtlr.gsi.gov.uk; Web: www.cfit.gov.uk

The Commission for Integrated Transport was proposed in the 1998 Transport White Paper and was set up in June 1999. Its role is to provide independent expert advice to the Government in order to achieve a transport system that supports sustainable development. Members of the Commission are appointed by the Secretary of State for Transport, Local Government and the Regions.
*Chairman* (£25,000), Prof. D. Begg
*Vice-Chairman* (£17,500), Sir Trevor Chinn
*Members* (£5,000 each), Lord Bradshaw; L. Christensen, CBE; N. Gavron; S. Joseph; D. Leeder; Ms L. Matson; W. Morris; J. O'Brien; Ms V. Palmer; M. Parker; N. Reilly
*Ex-Officio Members*, Sir Malcolm Field (*Chairman, Civil Aviation Authority*); T. Matthews (*Chief Executive, Highways Agency*); Sir Alastair Morton (*Chairman, British Railways Board and Head, Strategic Rail Authority*); Ms J. Wilmot (*Chair, Disabled Persons Transport Advisory Committee*)
*Secretary* (*G7*), A. Braithwaite

## COMMISSION FOR RACIAL EQUALITY

Elliot House, 10–12 Allington Street, London SW1E 5EH Tel: 020-7828 7022; Fax: 020-7630 7605

The Commission was established in 1977 under the Race Relations Act 1976. Its duties are to work towards the elimination of discrimination and promote equality of opportunity, to encourage good relations between different racial groups and to monitor the working of the Race Relations Act. It is funded by the Home Office.
*Chairman*, Gurbux Singh (£81,000)
*Deputy Chairmen*, Ms B. Bernard; Dr M. Jogee
*Commissioners*, M. Amran; Dr R. Chandran; M. Hastings; S. Malik; Ms J. Mellor; P. Passley; Ms S. Patel; B. Purkiss; Ms C. Short; Dr J. Singh; R. Singh; Ms G. Sootarsing; K. Jandu
*Acting Chief Executive*, A. Housley

## COMMITTEE ON STANDARDS IN PUBLIC LIFE

35 Great Smith Street, London SW1P 3BQ Tel: 020-7276 2595; Fax: 020-7276 2585; Email: nigel.wicks@gtnet.gov.uk; Web: www.public-standards.gov.uk

The Committee on Standards in Public Life was set up in October 1994. It is a standing body whose chairman and members are appointed by the Prime Minister; three members are nominated by the leaders of the three main political parties. The committee's remit is to examine concerns about standards of conduct of all holders of public office, including arrangements relating to financial and commercial activities, and to make recommendations as to any changes in present arrangements which might be required to ensure the highest standards of propriety in public life. It is also charged with reviewing issues in relation to the funding of political parties. The committee does not investigate individual allegations of misconduct.
*Chair*, Sir Nigel Wicks
*Members*, Ms A.Abraham; Prof. Alice Brown; Sir Anthony Cleaver; The Lord Goodhart, QC; F. Heaton The Rt. Hon. J. MacGregor, OBE, R. Donaghy, OBE; Rabbi Julia Neuberger; The Lord Shore of Stepney,
*Secretary (SCS)*, Mrs S. Tyerman

## COMMONWEALTH INSTITUTE

230 Kensington High Street, London W8 6NQ Tel: 020-7603 4535; Fax: 020-7602 7374; Email: info@commonwealth.org.uk; Web: www.commonwealth.org.uk

The Commonwealth Institute is an independent agency working with young people across the Commonwealth. Central to the Institute's mission is running schools education programmes, supplying learning resources and support to schools, teachers and young people, on citizenship, development and issues dealing with managing and celebrating cultural diversity.

The Institute was established in 1958 as an independent statutory body funded by the British Government. In January 2000, the Institute became an Independent Commonwealth agency after forty years as an agency of the Foreign and Commonwealth Office. It is a registered charity and a company limited by guarantee. It is controlled by a Board of Trustees elected by a Board of Governors. All the Commonwealth High Commissioners in London are *ex-officio* governors of the Institute in addition to other governors appointed by the Board of Trustees.
*Chairman*, D. A. Thompson
*Vice-Chairman*, Lord Fellowes
*Chief Executive*, D. French
*Commercial Director*, P. Kennedy
*Director of Education*, S. Brace
*Finance Director*, Ms J. Curry
*Director of Public Affairs*, G. Carter

COMMUNITIES FUND
St Vincent House, 16 Suffolk Street, London SW1Y 4NL Tel: 020-7747 5299; Fax: 020-7747 5220; Web: www.nlcb.org.uk

The Fund was set up under the National Lottery Act 1993 to distribute funds from the Lottery to support charitable, benevolent and philanthropic organisations. The chair and members are appointed by the Secretary of State for Culture, Media and Sport. The Fund's main aim is to help meet the needs of those at greatest disadvantage in society and to improve the quality of life in the community through grants programmes in the UK and an international grants programme for UK-based agencies working abroad.
*Chair*, Lady Brittan, CBE
*Deputy Chairman*, Dame Valerie Stracham
*Members*, T. Baring, CBE; R. Bevan; S. Burkeman; J. Carroll; A. Clark; D. Graham; K. Hampton; Prof. J. Kearney; M. Lee; B. Lowndes, MBE; S. Malley; R. Martineau; Dr N. Stewart, OBE; E. Watkins; B. Whitaker, CBE *Chief Executive*, N. Pittman

COMMONWEALTH WAR GRAVES COMMISSION
2 Marlow Road, Maidenhead, Berks SL6 7DX
Tel: 01628-634221; Fax: 01628-771208;
Email: generalenq@cwgc.org; Web: www.cwgc.org

The Commonwealth War Graves Commission (formerly Imperial War Graves Commission) was founded by royal charter in 1917. It is responsible for the commemoration of 1,693,786 members of the forces of the Commonwealth who fell in the two world wars. More than one million graves are maintained in 23,247 burial grounds throughout the world. Over three-quarters of a million men and women who have no known grave or who were cremated are commemorated by name on memorials built by the Commission.

The funds of the Commission are derived from the six participating governments, i.e. the UK, Canada, Australia, India, New Zealand and South Africa.
*President*, HRH The Duke of Kent, KG, GCMG, GCVO, ADC
*Chairman*, The Secretary of State for Defence in the UK
*Vice-Chairman*, Gen. Sir John Wilsey, GCB, CBE, DC
*Members*, The High Commissioners in London for New Zealand, South Africa, India, Australian and Canada; Mrs L. Golding, MP; J. Wilkinson, MP; Sir John Gray, KBE, CMG; P. D. Orchard-Lisle, CBE, TD; Air Chief Marshal Sir Michael Stear, KCB, CBE, DL,; Dame Susan Tinson, DBE; Gen. Sir John Keegan, OBE; Adm. Sir Peter Abbott, GBE
*Director-General and Secretary to the Commission*, R. E. Kellaway
*Deputy Director-General*, R. J. Dalley
*Legal Adviser and Solicitor*, G. C. Reddie
*Directors*, D. R. Parker (*Information and Secretariat*); A. Coombe (*Works*); R. D. Wilson (*Administration*); D. C. Parker (*Horticulture*); D. G. Stacey (*Personnel*)

IMPERIAL WAR GRAVES ENDOWMENT FUND

*Trustees*, A. C. Barker (*Chairman*); C. G. Clarke; Gen. Sir John Wilsey, DC, CBE
*Secretary to the Trustees*, R. D. Wilson

COMMUNITIES FUND
St Vincent House, 16 Suffolk Street, London SW1Y 4NL Tel: 020-7747 5299; Fax: 020-7747 5220; Web: www.nlcb.org.uk

The Fund was set up under the National Lottery Act 1993 to distribute funds from the Lottery to support charitable, benevolent and philanthropic organisations. The chair and members are appointed by the Secretary of State for Culture, Media and Sport. The Fund's main aim is to help meet the needs of those at greatest disadvantage in society and to improve the quality of life in the community through grants programmes in the UK and an international grants programme for UK-based agencies working abroad.
*Chair*, Lady Brittan, CBE
*Deputy Chairman*, Dame Valerie Stracham
*Members*, T. Baring, CBE; R. Bevan; S. Burkeman; J. Carroll; A. Clark; D. Graham; K. Hampton; Prof. J. Kearney; M. Lee; B. Lowndes, MBE; S. Malley; R. Martineau; Dr N. Stewart, OBE; E. Watkins; B. Whitaker, CBE
*Chief Executive*, N. Pittman

COMPETITION COMMISSION
New Court, 48 Carey Street, London WC2A 2JT
Tel: 020-7271 0100; Fax: 020-7271 0367

The Commission was established in 1948 as the Monopolies and Restrictive Practices Commission (later the Monopolies and Mergers Commission); it became the Competition Commission in April 1999 under the Competition Act 1998. Its role is to investigate and report on matters which are referred to it by the Secretary of State for Trade and Industry or the Director-General of Fair Trading or, in the case of regulated utilities, by the appropriate regulator. It has no power to initiate its own investigations.

The Appeals Tribunal of the Competition Commission hears appeals against decisions by the Director-General of Fair Trading and the utility regulators in respect of the prohibitions on anti-competitive agreements and abuse of a dominant position.

The Commission has a full-time chairman, two part-time deputy chairmen and about 36 reporting panel members and 25 specialist panel members to carry out investigations. All are appointed by the Secretary of State for Trade and Industry.
*Chairman*, Dr D. Morris, Ph.D.
*Deputy Chairmen*, Prof. P. Geroski; Mrs D. P. B. Kingsmill, CBE
*President, Appeal Tribunals*, His Hon. Sir Chrisopher Bellamy, QC
*Members* Prof. J. Beatson, QC; R. Bertram; Mrs S. Brown; Prof. M. Cave; A. T. Clothier; R. H. F. Croft, CB; C. Darke; N. Garthwaite; Prof. C. Graham; G. H. Hadley; D. B. Hammond; Ms J. C. Hanratty; C. Henderson, CB; D. J. Jenkins, MBE; P. MacKay, CB; Dr E. M. Monck; Ms K. M. H. Mortimer; R. J. Munson; Prof. D. M. G. Newbery, FBA; Dr Gill Owen; Prof. D. Parker; A. Pryor, CB; R. A. Rawlinson; Prof. Judith Rees; T. S. Richmond, MBE; J. Rickford; E. J. Seddon; Dame Helena Shovelton, DBE; G. H. Stacy, CBE; J. D. Stark; Prof. A. Steele; M. R. Webster; A. M. Young
*Appeal Panel Members*, Prof. A. Bain, OBE, M. Blair, QC; Sir Christopher Bellamy, QC; P. Clayton; B. D. Colgate; M.

Davey; P. Grant-Hutchinson; Prof. P. Grinyer; Mrs S. Hewitt; Ms A. M. Kelly; The Rt. Hon. A. Lewis; G. Mather; P. Quigley; Prof. J. Pickering; M. R. Prosser, OBE; Dr A. J. Pryor, CB; A. Scott, TD; Mrs V. Smith-Hillman; Prof P. Stoneman; D. L. Summers; Prof. G. Zellick

*Appeal Panel Registrar*, C. Dhanowa

*Secretary*, R. Foster

## COUNCIL ON TRIBUNALS

7th Floor, 22 Kingsway, London WC2B 6LE
Tel: 020-7947 7045; Fax: 020-7947 7044;
Web: www.council-on-tribunals.gov.uk

The Council on Tribunals is an independent body that operates under the Tribunals and Inquiries Act 1992. It consists of 16 members appointed by the Lord Chancellor and the Scottish Ministers; one member is appointed to represent the interests of people in Wales. The Scottish Committee of the Council generally considers Scottish tribunals and matters relating only to Scotland.

The Council advises on and keeps under review the constitution and working of administrative tribunals, and considers and reports on administrative procedures relating to statutory inquiries. Some 80 tribunals are currently under the Council's supervision. It is consulted by and advises Government departments on a wide range of subjects relating to adjudicative procedures.

*Chairman*, The Rt. Hon. The Lord Newton of Braintree

*Members*, The Parliamentary Commissioner for Administration (*ex officio*); R. J. Elliot, WS (*Chairman of the Scottish Committee*); Mrs C. Berkeley; S. M. D. Brown; S. R. Davie, CB; J. H. Eames; Mrs A. Galbraith; Mrs S. R. Howdle; I. J. Irvine; S. Jones, CBE; Prof.G. Richardson; I. D. Penman, CB; D. G. Readings; E. P. Roberts; P. A. A. Waring

*Secretary*, Mrs P. J. Fairbairn

### SCOTTISH COMMITTEE OF THE COUNCIL ON TRIBUNALS

44 Palmerston Place, Edinburgh EH12 5BJ
Tel: 0131-220 1236; Fax: 0131-225 4271;
Email: sccot@gtnet.gov.uk

*Chairman*, R. J. Elliot

*Members*, The Parliamentary Commissioner for Administration (*ex officio*); Mrs M. Wood

*Secretary*, Mrs E. M. MacRae

## CONSIGNIA

148 Old Street, London EC1V 9HQ
Tel: 020-7250 2888

Crown services for the carriage of Government dispatches were set up in about 1516. The conveyance of public correspondence began in 1635 and the mail service was made a parliamentary responsibility with the setting up of a Post Office in 1657. Telegraphs came under Post Office control in 1870 and the Post Office Telephone Service began in 1880. The National Girobank service of the Post Office began in 1968. The Post Office ceased to be a Government department in 1969 when responsibility for the running of the postal, telecommunications, giro and remittance services was transferred to a public authority called The Post Office. The 1981 British Telecommunications Act separated the functions of the Post Office, making it solely responsible for postal services and Girobank. Girobank was privatised in 1990. The Postal Services Act 2000 turned The Post Office into a wholly owned public limited company establishing a regulatory regime under the Postal Service Commission. The Post Office Group changed its name to Consignia plc on 26 March 2001 when its new corporate structure took effect.

The chairman, chief executive and members of the Consignia Board are appointed by the Secretary of State for Trade and Industry but responsibility for the running of Consignia as a whole rests with the Board in its corporate capacity.

### CONSIGNIA BOARD

*Chairman*, Dr N. Bain

*Chief Executive*, J. Roberts, CBE

*Members*, M. Cassoni (*Managing Director, Finance*); J. Cope (*Managing Director, Strategy and Personnel*)

*Secretary*, J. Evans

## COUNTRYSIDE AGENCY

John Dower House, Crescent Place, Cheltenham, Glos GL50 3RA Tel: 01242-521381;
Fax: 01242-584270

The Countryside Agency was set up in April 1999 by the merger of the Countryside Commission with parts of the Rural Development Commission. It is a Government agency which promotes the conservation and enhancement of the countryside in England and undertakes activities aimed at stimulating job creation and the provision of essential services in the countryside. The Agency is funded by an annual grant from the Department Transport, Local Government and the Regions, and board members are appointed by the Secretary of State.

*Chairman*, E. Cameron

*Deputy Chair*, Ms P. Warhurst

*Members*, Ms K. Ashbrook; Ms J. Bradbury; the Rt. Revd Bishop of Norwich; M. Doughty; Dr Victoria Edwards, FRICS; P. Fane; A. Hams, OBE; Prof. P. Lowe; Ms C. Mack; FCA; L. Frank-Riley; Ms F. Rowe; Ms S. Stapley

*Chief Executive*, R. G. Wakeford

*Directors*, Miss M. A. Clark, OBE; D. Coleman; J. Tomlinson; S. Sleet

## COUNTRYSIDE COUNCIL FOR WALES/ CYNGOR CEFN GWLAD CYMRU

Plas Penrhos, Ffordd Penrhos, Bangor LL57 2LQ
Tel: 01248-385500; Fax: 01248-385505

The Countryside Council for Wales is the Government's statutory adviser on sustaining natural beauty, wildlife and the opportunity for outdoor enjoyment in Wales and its inshore waters. It is funded by the National Assembly for Wales and accountable to the First Secretary, who appoints its members.

*Chairman*, J. Lloyd Jones, OBE

*Chief Executive*, P. E. Loveluck, CBE

*Senior Director and Chief Scientist*, Dr M. E. Smith

*Director, Countryside Policy*, Dr J. Taylor

*Director, Conservation*, Dr D. Parker

## COURT OF THE LORD LYON

HM New Register House, Edinburgh EH1 3YT
Tel: 0131-556 7255; Fax: 0131-557 2148

The Court of the Lord Lyon is the Scottish Court of Chivalry (including the genealogical jurisdiction of the *Ri-Sennachie* of Scotland's Celtic Kings). The Lord Lyon King of Arms has jurisdiction, subject to appeal to the Court of Session and the House of Lords, in questions of heraldry and the right to bear arms. The Court also administers the Scottish Public Register of All Arms and Bearings and the Public Register of All Genealogies. Pedigrees are established by decrees of Lyon Court and by letters patent. As Royal Commissioner in Armory, the Lord Lyon grants patents of arms (which constitute the grantee and heirs noble in the Noblesse of Scotland) to 'virtuous and well-deserving' Scotsmen and to petitioners (personal or corporate) in The Queen's overseas realms of Scottish connection, and issues birthbrieves.
*Lord Lyon King of Arms*, R. O. Blair, LVO, WS

### HERALDS

*Albany*, J. A. Spens, MVO, RD, WS
*Rothesay*, Sir Crispin Agnew of Lochnaw, Bt., QC
*Ross*, C. J. Burnett, FSA Scot.

### PURSUIVANTS

*Unicorn*, Alastair Campbell of Airds, FSA Scot.
*Carrick*, Mrs C. G. W. Roads, MVO, FSA Scot.

### EXTRAORDINARY OFFICERS

*Orknell Herald Extrordinary*, Sir Malcolm Innes of Edingight, KCVO, WS
*Linlithgow Pursuant Extraordinary*, J. C. G. George
*Lyon Clerk and Keeper of Records*, Mrs C. G. W. Roads, MVO, FSA Scot.
*Procurator-Fiscal*, D. I. K. MacLeod, WS
*Herald Painter*, Mrs J. Phillips
*Macer*, A. M. Clark

## COVENT GARDEN MARKET AUTHORITY

Covent House, New Covent Garden Market, London SW8 5NX
Tel: 020-7720 2211; Fax: 020-7622 5307;
Email: info@cgma.gov.uk; Web: www.cgma.gov.uk

The Covent Garden Market Authority is constituted under the Covent Garden Market Acts 1961 to 1977, the members being appointed by the Minister of Environment, Food and Rural Affairs. The Authority owns and operates the 56-acre New Covent Garden Markets (fruit, vegetables, flowers) which have been trading since 1974.
*Chairman (part-time)*, L. Mills, CBE
*General Manager*, Dr P. M. Liggins
*Secretary*, C. Farey

## CRIMINAL CASES REVIEW COMMISSION

Alpha Tower, Suffolk Street Queensway, Birmingham B1 1TT
Tel: 0121-633 1800; Fax: 0121-633 1823/1804

The Criminal Cases Review Commission is an independent body set up under the Criminal Appeal Act 1995. It is a non-departmental public body reporting to Parliament via the Home Secretary. It is responsible for investigating suspected miscarriages of justice in England, Wales and Northern Ireland, and deciding whether or not to refer cases back to an appeal court. Membership of the Commission is by royal appointment; the senior executive staff are appointed by the Commission.
*Chairman*, Sir Frederick Crawford, FREng.
*Members*, B. Capon; L. Elks; A. Foster; Ms F. King; J. Knox; D. Kyle; Prof. L. Leigh; J. MacKeith; K. Singh; B. Skitt; E. Weiss
*Chief Executive*, vacant
*Director of Finance and Personnel*, D. Robson
*Legal Advisers*, J. Wagstaff; M. Aspinall
*Police Adviser*, R. Barrington

## CRIMINAL INJURIES COMPENSATION AUTHORITY (CICA)

Morley House, Holborn Viaduct, London EC1A 2JQ
Tel: 020-7842 6800; Fax: 020-7436 0804;
Web: www.cica.gov.uk
Tay House, 300 Bath Street, Glasgow G2 4JR
Tel: 0141-331 2726; Fax: 0141-331 2287

All applications for compensation for personal injury arising from crimes of violence in England, Scotland and Wales are dealt with at the above locations. (Separate arrangements apply in Northern Ireland.) Applications received up to 31 March 1996 are assessed on the basis of common law damages under the 1990 compensation scheme. Applications received later than 1 April 1996 are assessed under a tariff-based scheme, made under the Criminal Injuries Compensation Act 1995, by the Criminal Injuries Compensation Authority (CICA). There is a separate avenue of appeal to the Criminal Injuries Compensation Appeals Panel (CICAP). In 1999-2000 total compensation paid was £194.34 million.
*Chief Executive*, Howard Webber
*Deputy Chief Executive*, E. McKeown
*Head of Legal Services*, Ms A. M. Johnstone
*Press enquiries*, Ms J Hay

## CRIMINAL INJURIES COMPENSATION APPEALS PANEL (CICAP)

11th Floor, Cardinal Tower, 12 Farringdon Road, London EC1M 3HS
Tel: 020-7549 4600; Fax: 020-7549 4643;
Email: info@cicap.gov.uk; Web: www.cicap.gov.uk
*Chairman*, Michael Lewer, QC
*Secretary*, Ms V. Jenson

## CROFTERS COMMISSION

4–6 Castle Wynd, Inverness IV2 3EQ
Tel: 01463-663450; Fax: 01463-711820

The Crofters Commission was established in 1955 under the Crofters (Scotland) Act. It advises the Scottish Ministers on all matters relating to crofting. It seeks to develop and promote thriving crofting communities and to simplify relevant legislation. It administers the Crofting Counties Agricultural Grants Scheme, Livestock Improvement Schemes and the Croft Entrant Scheme. It also provides a free enquiry service.
*Chairman*, I. MacAskill
*Chief Executive*, S. Rankin

## CROWN ESTATE

16 Carlton House Terrace, London SW1Y 5AH
Tel: 020-7210 4377; Fax: 020-7930 8187

The Crown Estate includes substantial blocks of urban property, primarily in London, almost 120,000 hectares of agricultural land and extensive marine holdings throughout the United Kingdom. Its origins go back to the reign of King Edward the Confessor and, until the accession of King George III, the Sovereign received its rents and profits. However, since 1760 the annual surplus, after deducting management expenses, has been surrendered by the Sovereign to Parliament to help meet the cost of civil government. In return, the Sovereign receives the Civil List and the Government meets other official expenditure incurred in support of the Sovereign.

In the year ended 31 March 2001, the gross revenue from the Crown Estate totalled £204.9 million and £147.7 million was paid to the Exchequer as surplus revenue.

*First Commissioner and Chairman (part-time)*, Sir Denys Henderson
*Second Commissioner and Chief Executive*, R, Bright
*Commissioners (part-time)*, The Lord De Ramsey; I. D. Grant, CBE; Mrs H. M. R. Chapman, CBE, FRICS; R. R. Spinney, FRICS; D. T. Y. Curry, CBE
*Director of Urban Estates*, D. A. Bickmore
*Rural Estate*, C. Bourchier
*Urban, Central London Estate*, Ms E. Miller
*Urban, Regent Street Estate*, M. W. Dillon
*Urban, Regional Estate*, A. Meakin
*Urban, Residential Estate*, R, Wyatt
*Urban, Special Projects*, L. Colgan
*Marine Estate*, F. G. Parrish
*Finance and Information Systems*, J. G. Lelliott
*Internal Audit*, J. Ford
*Corporate Policy and Personnel*, M. J. Gravestock
*Commuinications Manager*, I. Belcher

### SCOTLAND

10 Charlotte Square, Edinburgh EH2 4BR
Tel: 0131-226 7241; Fax: 0131-220 1366
*Head of Scottish Estate*, M. Cunliffe

### WINDSOR ESTATE

The Great Park, Windsor, Berks SL4 2HT
Tel: 01753-860222; Fax: 01753-859617
*Deputy Ranger*, P. Everrett

## DEER COMMISSION FOR SCOTLAND

Knowsley, 82 Fairfield Road, Inverness IV3 5LH
Tel: 01463-231751; Fax: 01463-712931;
Email: deercom@aol.com; Web: www.dcs.gov.uk

The Deer Commission for Scotland has the general functions of furthering the conservation and control of deer in Scotland. It has the statutory duty, with powers, to prevent damage to agriculture, forestry and the habitat by deer. It is funded by the Scottish Executive.

*Chairman (part-time)*, A. Raven
*Director*, N. Reiter
*Technical Director*, D. Balharry

## DESIGN COUNCIL

34 Bow Street, London WC2E 7DL
Tel: 020-7420 5200; Fax: 020-7420 5300

The Design Council is a campaigning and lobbying organisation which works with partners in business, education and Government to promote the effective use of good design. It is a registered charity with a Royal Charter and is funded by grant-in-aid from the Department of Trade and Industry.

*Chairman*, C. Frayling
*Chief Executive*, A. Summers

## DISABILITY RIGHTS COMMISSION (DRC)

DRC, Stratford upon Avon CV37 9BR
Helpline: 08457-622633; Web: www.drc-gb.org

The Commission is an executive non-departmental public body established in April 2000. Its role is to advise Government on issues of discrimination against disabled people and the operation of the Disability Discrimination Act 1995. It promotes good practice to employers and service providers and provides advice, information and sometimes legal support to disabled people.

*Chair*, B. Massie
*Chief Executive*, R. Niven
*Commissioners*, Saghir Alam; Ms K. Allen; Ms J. Campbell; M. Deveney; R. Exell; Dr K. Fitzpatrick; J. Hougham; P. Humphrey; C. Low; Mrs E. Noad; Ms E. Rank-Petruzzietto; Ms P. Russell; J. Strachan; Ms J. White

## THE DUCHY OF CORNWALL

10 Buckingham Gate, London SW1E 6LA
Tel: 020-7834 7346; Fax: 020-7931 9541

The Duchy of Cornwall was created by Edward III in 1337 for the support of his eldest son Edward, later known as the Black Prince. It is the oldest of the English duchies. The duchy is acquired by inheritance by the sovereign's eldest son either at birth or on the accession of his parent to the throne, whichever is the later. The primary purpose of the estate remains to provide an income for the Prince of Wales. The estate is mainly agricultural and based in the south-west of England. A recent purchase has increased the landholding to approximately 150,000 acres in 26 counties. The duchy also has some residential property, a number of shops and offices, and a Stock Exchange portfolio. Prince Charles is the 24th Duke of Cornwall.

### THE PRINCE'S COUNCIL

*Chairman*, HRH The Prince of Wales, KG, KT, GCB
*Lord Warden of the Stannaries*, The Earl Peel
*Receiver-General*, The Rt. Hon. J. H. Leigh-Pemberton
*Attorney-General to the Prince of Wales*, N. Underhill, QC
*Secretary and Keeper of the Records*, W. R. A. Ross
*Other members*, R. Broadhurst; A. M. J. Galsworthy; W. N. Hood, CBE; Sir Christopher Howes, CB; S. Lamport; The Marquess of Lansdowne; J. E. Pugsley

### OTHER OFFICERS

*Auditors*, I. Brindle; R. Hughes
*Sheriff* (2001–2002), J. M. Williams

## THE DUCHY OF LANCASTER

Lancaster Place, Strand, London WC2E 7ED
Tel: 020-7836 8277; Fax: 020-7836 3098

The estates and jurisdiction known as the Duchy of Lancaster have belonged to the reigning monarch since 1399 when John of Gaunt's son came to the throne as Henry IV. As the Lancaster Inheritance it goes back as far as 1265 when Henry III granted his youngest son Edmund lands and possessions following the Baron's war. In 1267 Henry gave Edmund the County, Honor and Castle of Lancaster and created him the first Earl of Lancaster. In 1351 Edward III created Lancaster a County Palatine.

The Chancellor of the Duchy of Lancaster is responsible for the administration of the Duchy, the appointment of justices of the peace in Lancashire, Greater Manchester and Merseyside and ecclesiastical patronage in the Duchy gift.

*Chancellor of the Duchy of Lancaster (and Minister for the Cabinet Office)*, The Rt. Hon.The Lord Macdonald of Tradeston, CBE
*Chairman of the Duchy Council*, Sir Michael Bunbury, Bt
*Attorney-General*, M. T. F. Briggs, QC
*Receiver-General*, Sir Michael Peat, KCVO
*Clerk of the Council and Chief Executive*, P. R. Clarke
*Secretary for Appointments*, Col. F. N. J. Davies

## ECGD (EXPORT CREDITS GUARANTEE DEPARTMENT)

PO Box 2200, 2 Exchange Tower, Harbour Exchange Square, London E14 9GS
Tel: 020-7512 7000; Fax: 020-7512 7649

ECGD (Export Credits Guarantee Department), the UK's official export credit insurer, is a Government department responsible to the Secretary of State for Trade and Industry and functions under the Export and Investment Guarantees Act 1991. This enables ECGD to facilitate UK exports by making available export credit insurance to firms engaged in selling overseas and to guarantee repayment to banks providing finance for capital goods. The Act also empowers ECGD to insure UK companies investing overseas against political risks such as war, expropriation and restrictions on remittances.

*Chief Executive*, H. V. B. Brown
*Group Directors (G3)*, V. P. Lunn-Rockliffe (*Portfolio Asset Management*); J. R. Weiss (*Business*); T. M. Jaffray (*Risk Management*)

### DIVISIONS

*Director, Finance (G5)*, R. J. Healey
*Director, Central Services (G5)*, S. R. Dodgson
*Directors, Business Divisions (G5)*, G. G. Welsh *(Division A)*; R. Gotts *(Division B)*; M. D. Pentecost *(Division C)*; J.C.W. Croall *(Capital Management)*
*Director, Office of the General Counsel (G5)*, N. Ridley
*Director, International Debt (G5)*, Ms L. Woods
*Director, Claims (G5)*, R. F. Lethbridge
*Director, Active Portfolio Management* ), J. S. Snowdon
*Director, Strategy and Communications*, J. Ormerod
*Director, Risk Management*, P. J. Radford
*Director, IT Services (G6)*, E. J. Walsby
*Director, Internal Audit (G6)*, G. Cassell
*Director, Operational Research (G6)*, Ms R. Kaufman

### EXPORT GUARANTEES ADVISORY COUNCIL

*Chairman*, D. H. A. Harrison, CBE
*Other Members*, E. L. Airey; J. Armitt; A. Brown, J. Elkington; Prof. J. Kydd; D. MacLachlan; Prof. K. Phylaktis; A. Shepherd; Dr R. Thamotheram; Sir David Wright

## ENGLISH HERITAGE (HISTORIC BUILDINGS AND MONUMENTS COMMISSION FOR ENGLAND)

23 Savile Row, London W1S 2ET Tel: 020-7973 3000; Fax: 020-7973 3001

English Heritage was established under the National Heritage Act 1983. On 1 April 1999 it merged with the Royal Commission on the Historical Monuments of England to become the new lead body for England's historic environment. Its duties are to carry out and sponsor archaeological, architectural and scientific survey and research designed to increase the understanding of England's past and its changing condition; to offer expert advice and skills and give grants to secure the preservation of listed buildings, cathedrals, churches, archaeological sites, ancient monuments and historic houses of England; to encourage the imaginative re-use of historic buildings to aid regeneration of the centres of cities, towns and villages; to manage the historic monuments and historic buildings in England; and to curate and make publicly accessible the National Monuments Record, whose records of over one million historic sites and buildings, and collections of more that 12 million photographs, maps, drawings and reports constitute the central database and archive to England's historic environment.

*Chairman*, Sir Neil Cossons
*Commissioners*, Miss A. Arrowsmith; M. Cairns; Ms B. Cherry; HRH The Duke of Gloucester, KG, GCVO; P. Gough, CBE; J. Grenville; L. Grossman; Ms K. McLeod; Prof. R. Morris, FSA; L. Sparks; Miss S. Underwood
*Chief Executive*, Ms P. Alexander

NATIONAL MONUMENTS RECORD, National Monuments Record Centre, Kemble Drive, Swindon SN2 2GZ. Tel: 01793-414600; Fax: 01793-414606. *London Search Room:* 55 Blandford Street, London SW1H 3AF. Tel: 020-7208 8200; Fax: 020-7224 5333

## ENGLISH NATURE

Northminster House, Peterborough PE1 1UA
Tel: 01733-455000; Fax: 01733-568834

English Nature (the Nature Conservancy Council for England) was established in 1991 and is responsible for advising the Secretary of State for the Transport, Local Government and the Regions on nature conservation in England. It promotes, directly and through others, the conservation of England's wildlife and natural features. It selects, establishes and manages National Nature Reserves and identifies and notifies Sites of Special Scientific Interest. It provides advice and information about nature conservation, and supports and conducts research relevant to these functions. Through the Joint Nature Conservation Committee, it works with its sister organisations in Scotland and Wales on UK and international nature conservation issues.

*Chairman*, M. Doughty
*Chief Executive*, D. Arnold-Forster
*Directors*, Dr K. L. Duff; Miss C. E. M. Wood; Ms S. Collins; A. E. Brown

---

THE ENVIRONMENT AGENCY
Rio House, Waterside Drive, Aztec West, Almondsbury, Bristol BS32 4UD
Tel: 01454-624400; Fax: 01454-624409;
Email: enquiries@environment-agency.gov.uk

---

The Environment Agency was established in 1996 under the Environment Act 1995 and is a non-departmental public body sponsored by the Department of the Environment, Food and Rural Affairs and the National Assembly for Wales. The Agency is responsible for pollution prevention and control in England and Wales, and for the management and use of water resources, including flood defences, fisheries and navigation. It has head offices in London and Bristol and eight regional offices.

THE BOARD

*Chairman*, Sir John Harman
*Members*, C. Beardwood; A. J. P. Dalton; A. Dare, CBE; E. Gallagher; N. Haigh, OBE; C. Hampson, CBE; Prof. R. Macrory; Prof. Jacqueline McGlade; G. Manning, OBE; Dr A. Powell; Prof. D. Ritchie; A. Rogers; G. Wardell

THE EXECUTIVE

*Chief Executive*, B. Young
*Director of Finance*, N. Reader
*Director of Personnel*, G. Duncan
*Director of Environmental Protection*, Dr P. Leinster
*Director of Water Management*, G. Mance
*Director of Operations*, A. Robertson
*Director of Corporate Affairs*, H. McCallum
*Director of Legal Services*, R. Navarro
*Chief Scientist*, Dr John Murlis

---

EQUAL OPPORTUNITIES COMMISSION
Arndale House, Arndale Centre, Manchester M4 3EQ
Tel: 0161-833 9244; Fax: 0161-838 8312

---

*Press Office*, 36 Broadway, London SW1H 0XH. Tel: 020-7222 1110
*Other Offices*, St Stephens House, 279 Bath Street, Glasgow G2 4JL Tel: 0141-248 5833; Windsor House, Windsor Place, Cardiff CF10 3GE Tel: 029-2034 3552

The Commission was set up in 1975 as a result of the passing of the Sex Discrimination Act. It works towards the elimination of discrimination on the grounds of sex or marital status and to promote equality of opportunity between men and women generally. It is responsible to The Cabinet Office.
*Chair*, Ms J. Mellor
*Deputy Chair*, Ms J. Watson
*Members*, T. Akpeki; S. Ashtiany; R. Arashad, OBE; K. Carberry; Ms F. Cannon; J. Drake;. Hodder; S. Pearce; R. Penn; S. Pierce; Prof. T. Rees; S. Sharma; Dr J. Stringer; T. Woodcraft
*Chief Executive*, L. Berry
*Acting Chief Executive*, G. Ashmore

---

EQUALITY COMMISSION FOR NORTHERN IRELAND
Equality House, 7–9 Shaftesbury Square, Belfast, BT2 7DP Tel: 028-9050 0600; Fax: 028-9033 1544;
Email: information@equalityni.org;
Web: www.equallityni.org

---

The Equality Commission was set up in 1999 and is responsible for promoting equality and eliminating discrimination on the grounds of race, disability, gender, religion and political opinion.
*Chief Commissioner*, Ms J. Harbison
*Chief Executive*, E. Collins

---

FILM COUNCIL
10 Little Portland Street, London W1W 7JG
Tel: 020-7861 7861; Fax: 020-7861 7862

---

The Council was created in April 2000 by the Department for Culture, Media and Sport to develop a coherent strategy for the development and leadership of film culture and the film industry. It is responsible for the majority of the Department for Culture, Media and Sport funding for film as well as lottery and grant-in-aid (with the exception of the National Film and Television School).
*Chairman*, A. Parker
*Deputy Chairman*, S. Till
*Chief Executive*, J. Woodward

---

FOOD STANDARDS AGENCY (UK)
Aviation House, 125 Kingsway, London, WC2 BNH
Tel: 020-7276 8100; Fax: 020-7276 84104;
Web: www.foodstandards.gov.uk

---

The Food Standards Agency was established by Act of Parliament (the Food Standards Act 1999) in April 2000 to protect public health from risks arising in connection with the consumption of food, and otherwise to protect the interests of consumers in relation to food. The Agency has the general function of developing policy in these areas and provides information and advice to the Government, other public bodies and consumers. It also sets standards for and monitors food law enforcement by local authorities. The Agency is a UK body and has executive offices in Scotland, Wales and Northern Ireland. It is advised by advisory committees on food safety matters of special interest to each of these areas.
*Chairman*, Prof. Sir John Krebs
*Deputy Chairman*, Ms S. Leather
*Chief Executive*, G. J. F. Podger

EXECUTIVE AGENCY

MEAT HYGIENE SERVICE

Foss House, Kings Pool, 1–2 Peasholme Green, York YO1 7PX Tel: 01904-455501; Fax: 01904-455502

The Agency was launched in April 1995 and from the 1 April became an executive agency of the Food Standards Agency. It protects public health and promotes animal welfare through veterinary supervision and meat inspection in licensed fresh meat establishments.
*Chief Executive* (*G4*), C. S. Lawson

## FOOD STANDARDS AGENCY SCOTLAND

St Magnus House, 25 Guild Street, Aberdeen, AB11 6NJ
Tel: 01224 285100; Fax: 01224 285167;
Email: scotland@foodstandards.gsi.gov.uk;
Web: www foodstandards.gov.uk

## FOOD STANDARDS AGENCY WALES

1st Floor, Southgate House, Wood Street, Cardiff CF10 1EW Tel: 029-2067 8999;
Email: foodstandards@Wales.gsi.gov.uk
Web: www.foodstandards.gov.uk/wales

*Advisory Committee for Wales*
*Chair*, Ms A. Hemingway

## FOOD STANDARDS AGENCY NORTHERN IRELAND

10b and 10c Clarendon Road, Belfast, BT1 3BG
Tel: 028-9041 7700; Fax: 028-9041 7726;
Email: gerry.rickard@dhsspsni.gov.uk;
Web: www.foodstandards.gov.uk/n_ireland

*Advisory Committee for Northern Ireland*
*Chairman*, M. Walker

## FOREIGN COMPENSATION COMMISSION

Room SG/III, Old Admiralty Building, Whitehall, London SW1A 2PA
Tel: 020-7008 1321; Fax: 020-7008 0160

The Commission was set up by the Foreign Compensation Act 1950 primarily to distribute, under Orders in Council, funds received from other governments in accordance with agreements to pay compensation for expropriated British property and other losses sustained by British nationals.

*Chairman*, A. W. E. Wheeler, CBE
*Secretary*, A. N. Grant

## FORESTRY COMMISSION

231 Corstorphine Road, Edinburgh EH12 7AT
Tel: 0131-334 0303; Fax: 0131-334 3047

The Forestry Commission is the Government department responsible for forestry policy in Great Britain. It reports directly to forestry Ministers (i.e. the Minister of Environment, Food and Rural Affairs., the Scottish Ministers and the National Assembly for Wales), to whom it is responsible for advice on forestry policy and for the implementation of that policy.

The Commission's principal objectives are to protect Britain's forests and woodlands; expand Britain's forest area; enhance the economic value of the forest resources; conserve and improve the biodiversity, landscape and cultural heritage of forests and woodlands; develop opportunities for woodland recreation; and increase public understanding of and community participation in forestry. Forest Enterprise, a trading body operating as an executive agency of the Commission, manages its forestry estate on a multi-use basis.

*Chairman (part-time)*, Sir Peter Hutchison, Bt., CBE
*Director-General and Deputy Chairman (G2)*, D. J. Bills
*Secretary to the Commissioners (G5)*, F. Strang

FOREST ENTERPRISE HEADQUARTERS, 231 Corstorphine Road, Edinburgh EH12 7AT. Tel: 0131-334 0303. *Chief Executive*, Dr B. McIntosh

FOREST RESEARCH, Alice Holt Lodge, Wrecclesham, Farnham, Surrey GU10 4LU. Tel: 01420-222555; Northern Research Station, Roslin, Midlothian EH25 9SY. Tel: 0131-445 2176. *Chief Executive*, J. Dewar

## FRIENDLY SOCIETIES COMMISSION

15th Floor, 25 The North Colonnade, Canary Wharf, London E14 5HS
Tel: 020-7676 1000; Fax: 020-7676 9700;
Web: www.fsa.gov.uk

The Friendly Societies Commission was established by the Friendly Societies Act 1992. It is responsible for the supervision of friendly societies and administers the system of prudential regulation. It also advises the Treasury and other Government departments on matters relating to friendly societies.

The Government has decided that the functions of the Commission should pass to the Financial Services Authority on implementation of the Financial Services and Markets Act.

FRIENDLY SOCIETIES COMMISSION

*Chairman*, M. Roberts
*Commissioners*, F. da Rocha; *B. Richardson; *J. A. Geddes; *Ms S. Brown; *Ms P. Triggs

* non executive

SECRETARIAT

Miss J. Erskine; Miss L. Gammans

## GAMING BOARD FOR GREAT BRITAIN

Berkshire House, 168–173 High Holborn, London WC1V 7AA Tel: 020-7306 6200; Fax: 020-7306 6266;
Web: www.gbgb.org.uk

The Board was established in 1968 and is responsible to the Home Secretary. It is the regulatory body for casinos, bingo clubs, gaming machines and the larger society and all local authority lotteries in Great Britain. Its functions are to ensure that those involved in organising gaming and lotteries are fit and proper to do so and to keep gaming free from criminal infiltration; to ensure that gaming and lotteries are run fairly and in accordance with the law; and to advise the Home Secretary on developments in gaming and lotteries.

*Chairman (part-time)* (£39,826 ), P. Dean, CBE
*Secretary*, T. Kavanagh

## GOVERNMENT ACTUARY'S DEPARTMENT

New King's Beam House, 22 Upper Ground, London SE1 9RJ
Tel: 020-7211 2601; Fax: 020-7211 2640/2650;
Email: enquiries@gad.gov.uk; Web: www.gad.gov.uk

The Government Actuary provides a consulting service to Government departments, the public sector, and overseas governments. The actuaries advise on social security schemes and superannuation arrangements in the public sector at home and abroad, on population and other statistical studies, and on supervision of insurance companies and pension funds.

*Government Actuary*, C. D. Daykin, CB

*Directing Actuaries*, D. G. Ballantine; A. G. Young
*Chief Actuaries*, E. I. Battersby; I. A. Boonin; A. I. Johnston; D. Lewis; G. T. Russell

## GOVERNMENT HOSPITALITY

Lancaster House, Stable Yard, St James's, London SW1A 1BB Tel: 020-7008 8196; Fax: 020-7210 4301

The Government Hospitality Fund was instituted in 1908 for the purpose of organising official hospitality on a regular basis with a view to the promotion of international goodwill. It is responsible to the Foreign and Commonwealth Office.

Government Hospitality is now incorporated as part of the Foreign and Commonwealth Office's Conference and Visitors Group.

*Minister in Charge*, Dr Dennis MacShane
*Head of Government Hospitality*, R. Alexander

## GOVERNMENT OFFICES FOR THE REGIONS

The Government Offices for the Regions manage expenditure programmes amounting to over £7 billion per year for various Government Departments. The programmes cover areas such as sustainable development, Neighbourhood Renewal, Social Inclusion, regeneration, competitiveness and rural affairs.

Government Offices handle land use planning, housing and countryside work, road schemes decisions, local transport priorities, transport interaction with land uses planning and statutory casework. Government Offices have a sponsorship role for the eight Regional Development Agencies and the London Development Agency and are also involved in training and education and business support issues.

REGIONAL CO-ORDINATION UNIT, Riverwalk House, 157–161 Millbank, London SW1P 4RR Tel: 020-7217 3595; Fax: 020-7217 3590
Email: username.rcu@go-regions.gsi.gov.uk

*Director General*, R. Smith
*Director (G3)*, A. Wells
*Directors*, A. Modu *(Corporate Relations)*; A. Sargeant *(Strategy)*; T. Vokes *(Business Development)*

### EAST MIDLANDS

*Secretariat:* The Belgrave Centre, Stanley Place, Talbot Street, Nottingham NG1 5GG
Tel: 0115-971 9971; Fax: 0115-971 2404;
Email: enquiries.goem@go-regions.gsi.gov.uk;
Web: www.go-em.gov.uk

*Regional Director (G3)*, D. Morrison
*Directors (G5)*, Dr S. Kennett (*Infrastructure and Community Affairs*); S. Brookes (*Regional Crime Reduction*); G. Norbury (*European and Rural Affairs Policy)*, R. Poole (*Industry, Education and Skills , Leicestershire and Derby*); R. Smith (*Corporate Affairs*)

### EAST OF ENGLAND

*Secretariat:* Building A, Westbrook Centre, Milton Road, Cambridge CB4 1YG
Tel: 01223 346719; Fax: 01223-346705
Email: username.go-east@go-regions.gsi.gov.uk

*Regional Director (G3)*, A. Riddell
*Directors (G5)*, Ms C. Bowdler (*Planning and Transport*); M. Oldham (*Business and Europe*); J. Street (*Learning and Local Government*); (*G6*), J. Rabagliati (*DEFRA, Agriculture, Countryside and Sustainability*); H. Cooper (*Temporary Strategy and Services*); H. Tam (*HO Community Safety and Regeneration)*

### GOVERNMENT OFFICE LONDON

*Secretariat:* Riverwalk House, 157–161 Millbank, London SW1P 4RR
Tel: 020-7217 3456; Fax: 020-7217 3450
Email: username.gol@go-regions.gsi.gov.uk

*Regional Director (G3)*, L. Meek
*Directors (G3)*, J. Anderson and S. Webber (*Job Share Government/FGLA Liaison Unit*); S. Ebanja (*Local Government and Europe*); C. Lyons (*Corporate and Change Management*); A. Melville (*London Co-Ordination and Environment Division*); E. Roy (*Crime Reduction*); K. Timmins (*Trade and Industry*); R. Wragg (*Skills and Education*)

### NORTH-EAST

*Secretariat:* Wellbar House, Gallow Gate, Newcastle upon Tyne NE1 4TD Tel: 0191-201 3300; Fax: 0191-201 3300;
Web: www.go-ne.gov.uk
Email: general.enquiries.gone@go-regions.gsi.gov.uk

*Regional Director (G3)*, Dr R. Dobbie, CB
*Directors (G5)*, J. Darlington (*Planning, Environment and Transport*); D. Caudle (*Education, Skills, Enterprise and Regeneration*); J. Bainton (*DEFRA*); A. Brown (*Crime Reduction*); D. Pearce (*Strategy and Resources*); D. Slater (*Competitiveness in Europe*)

### NORTH-WEST

*Secretariat:* 12th Floor, Sunley Tower, Piccadilly Plaza, Manchester M1 4BE
Tel: 0161-952 4000; Fax: 0161-952 4099

*Regional Director (G3)*, K. Barnes
*Directors (G5)*, P. Styche (*Communities*); Dr D. Highham (*Business and Europe*); (*G6*), I. Jamieson (*Business and Europe*); Ms S. Yates (*Europe, Liverpool*); E. Hughes (*Planning and Environment/Regional Policy and Co-ordination*); D. Duff, OBE (*Tec Transition*); D. Hopewell (*Corporate Services*); N. Burke (*Education and Social Exclusion*); M. Hill (*Commonwealth Games*); J. Flannon (*Objective 1*); Dr D. Higham (*Business Connexions*); T. Walker (*Small Business Team*)

### SOUTH-EAST

*Secretariat:* 2nd Floor, Bridge House, 1 Walnut Tree Close, Guildford, Surrey GU1 4GA
Tel: 01483-882481; Fax: 01483-882250

*Regional Director (G3)*, D. Saunders
*Directors (G5)*, C. Byrne (*Hants/IOW*); S. Burt (*Skills and Enterprise Berks/Oxon/Bucks*); A. Campbell (A. Campbell (*Regeneration, Housing and Environment, Kent*); A. Parker (*DEFRA and Europe, Surrey and Sussex*); C. Dixon (*Transport and Strategy*); P. Craggs (*Finance and Corporate Management*); H. Marriage (*Crime Reduction*)

### SOUTH-WEST

*Secretariat:* 4th and 5th Floor, The Pithay, Bristol BS1 2PB
Tel: 0117-900 1700; Fax: 0117-900 1900;
Email: receptionist.gosw@go-regions.gsi.gov.uk;
Web: www.gosw.gov.uk

*Regional Director (G3)*, Ms J. Henderson

*Directors* (*G5*), R. Bayly (*Transport, Devon and Cornwall*); C. Carrington (*Local Government and Neighbourhood Renewal-Former West/West of England*); T. Shearer (*Enterprise Intelligence and Young People-Gloucestershire/Wiltshire*); (*G6*) M. Davey (*Corporate Services*); P. Rowlandson (*Crime Reduction*); T. Render (*Food Farming and Rural Development, Somerset and Dorset*)

WEST MIDLANDS

*Secretariat:* 6th Floor, 77 Paradise Circus, Queensway, Birmingham B1 2DT
Tel: 0121-212 5050; Fax: 0121-212 1010;
Email: enquiries.gowm@go-regions.gsi.gov.uk

*Regional Director* (*G3*), G. Garbutt
*Directors* (*G5*), C. Marsh (*Corporate Affairs and Europe*); P. Holland (*Local Government*); (*G6*) C. Beesley (*Business and Learning Division*); B. Davies (*DEFRA*); M. Greary (*Crime Reduction*)

YORKSHIRE AND THE HUMBER

*Secretariat:* PO Box 213, City House, New Station Street, Leeds LS1 4US
Tel: 0113-280 0600; Fax: 0113-283 6394
Email: enquiries.goyh@go-regions.gsi.gov.uk

*Regional Director* (*G3*), F. Everiss
*Directors* (*G5*), G. Dyche (*HO Crime Reduction and Voluntary Sector*); S. Perryman (*People and Communities*); (*G6*), J. Jarvis (*Regional Affairs*); N. Best (*Corporate Services*); G. Kingston (*DEFRA-Rural*); I. Mills (*Europe*); S. Yates (*Objective 1*); M. Jackson (*Competitiveness and Sensibilities*)

---

## HEALTH AND SAFETY COMMISSION

Rose Court, 2 Southwark Bridge, London SE1 9HS
Tel: 020-7717 6000; Fax: 020-7717 6644

---

The Health and Safety Commission was created under the Health and Safety at Work etc. Act 1974, with duties to reform health and safety law, to propose new regulations, and generally to promote the protection of people at work and of the public from hazards arising from industrial and commercial activity, including major industrial accidents and the transportation of hazardous materials.

*Chairman*, W. Callaghan
*Members*, J. Donovan; M. Rooney; Ms J. Edmond-Smith; G. Brumwell; Ms M. Burns; S. Hamid; A. Chowdry; O. Tudor; R. Symons, CBE
*Secretary*, A. Adams

---

## HEALTH AND SAFETY EXECUTIVE

Rose Court, 2 Southwark Bridge, London SE1 9HS
Tel: 020-7717 6000; Fax: 020-7717 6717

---

The Health and Safety Executive is the Health and Safety Commission's major instrument. Through its inspectorates it enforces health and safety law in the majority of industrial premises. The Executive advises the Commission in its major task of laying down safety standards through regulations and practical guidance for many industrial processes. The Executive is also the licensing authority for nuclear installations and the reporting officer on the severity of nuclear incidents in Britain, and it is responsible for the Channel Tunnel Safety Authority.

*Director-General*, T. Walker
*Deputy Director-General*, D. C. T. Eves, CB
*Director, Field Operations Unit*, Dr A. Ellis
*Director, Safety Policy*, N. Starling
*Director, Health Directorate*, S. Caldwell
*Director/Chief Inspector of the Nuclear Safety Directorate*, L. Williams
*Director, Strategy and Analytical Support Directorate*, Dr P. Graham
*Director, Hazardous Installations Directorate and Chief Scientist*, Dr P. Davies
*Director, Resource and Planning Directorate*, R. Hiller
*Director Railways Directorate*, C. Norris

---

## HIGHLANDS AND ISLANDS ENTERPRISE

Bridge House, 20 Bridge Street, Inverness IV1 1QR
Tel: 01463-234171; Fax: 01463-244469
Email: hie.general@hient.co.uk;
Web: www.hie.co.uk

---

Highlands and Islands Enterprise (HIE) was set up under the Enterprise and New Towns (Scotland) Act 1991. Its role is to design, direct and deliver enterprise development, training, environmental and social projects and services. HIE is made up of a strategic core body and ten Local Enterprise Companies (LECs) to which many of its individual functions are delegated.

*Chairman*, Dr J. Hunter
*Chief Executive*, J. R. S Cumming

---

## HISTORIC BUILDINGS COUNCIL FOR SCOTLAND

Longmore House, Salisbury Place, Edinburgh EH9 1SH Tel: 0131-668 8799; Fax: 0131-668 8788

---

The Historic Buildings Council for Scotland is the advisory body to the Scottish Ministers on matters related to buildings of special architectural or historical interest and in particular to proposals for awards by them of grants for the repair of buildings of outstanding architectural or historical interest or lying within outstanding conservation areas.

*Chairman*, Sir Raymond Johnstone, CBE
*Members*, R. Cairns; Mrs P. Chalmers; Bishop M. Conti; Ms L. Davidson; Mrs A. Dundas-Bekker; Revd G. Forbes; Dr J. Frew; D. Gauci; M. Hopton; E. Jamieson; Mrs P. Robertson; Ms F. Sinclair
*Secretary*, Mrs S. Williamson

---

## HISTORIC BUILDINGS COUNCIL FOR WALES

Cathays Park, Cardiff CF1 3NQ
Tel: 029-2050 0200; Fax: 029-20-82 6375

---

The Council's function is to advise the National Assembly for Wales on the historic buildings through Cadw: Welsh Historic Monuments, which is an executive agency of the Assembly.

*Chairman*, T. Lloyd, FSA
*Members*, Dr P. Morgan; Mrs S. Furse; Dr S. Unwin; Dr E. William; Miss E. Evans; Dr R. Wools
*Secretary*, Mrs J. Booker

## HISTORIC ROYAL PALACES

Hampton Court Palace, East Molesey, Surrey KT8 9AU Tel: 020-8781 9500; Fax: 020-8781 9754

Historic Royal Palaces is a non-departmental public body with charitable status. The Secretary of State for Culture, Media and Sport is still accountable to Parliament for the care, conservation and presentation of the palaces, which are owned by the Sovereign in right of the Crown. The chairman of the trustees is appointed by The Queen on the advice of the Secretary of State.

Historic Royal Palaces is responsible for the Tower of London, Hampton Court Palace, Kensington Palace State Apartments and the Royal Ceremonial Dress Collection, Kew Palace with Queen Charlotte's Cottage, and the Banqueting House, Whitehall.

TRUSTEES

*Chairman*, The Earl of Airlie, KT, GCVO, PC
*Appointed by The Queen*, The Lord Luce, GCVO, DL; Sir Michael Peat, KCVO; H. Roberts, CVO, FSA
*Appointed by the Secretary of State*, M. Herbert, CBE; Ms A. Heylin, OBE; S. Jones, LVO; Ms J. Sharman, CBE
*Ex officio*, Field Marshal the Lord Inge, GCB (*Constable of the Tower of London*)

OFFICERS

*Chief Executive*, A. Coppin
*Director of Finance*, Ms A. McLeish
*Director of Human Resources*, G. Josephs
*Director, Palaces Group*, H. Player
*Resident Governor, HM Tower of London*, Maj.-Gen. G. Field, CB, OBE
*Retail Director*, Ms A. Boyes
*Marketing Director*, D. Homan
*Director of Conservation*, Vacant

## HOME-GROWN CEREALS AUTHORITY

Caledonia House, 223 Pentonville Road, London N1 9HY Tel: 020-7520 3926; Fax: 020-7520 3954

Set up under the Cereals Marketing Act 1965, the HGCA Board consists of seven members representing UK cereal growers, seven representing dealers in, or processors of, grain and two independent members. HGCA's functions are to improve the production and marketing of UK-grown cereals and oilseeds through a research and development programme, to provide a market information service, and to promote UK cereals in export markets.

*Chairman (part-time)* (£23,576), A. Pike
*Chief Executive*, P. V. Biscoe

## HONOURS SCRUTINY COMMITTEE

Ashley House, 2 Monck Street, London SW1P 2BQ
Tel: 020-7276 2770; Fax: 020-7276 2766

The functions of the Honours Scrutiny Committee (a committee of Privy Councillors) are set out in full in an Order of Council. The Prime Minister submits certain particulars to the Committee about persons proposed to be recommended for honour at any level other than a peerage for their political services, or for an honour at the level of Knight or Dame for non-political services. The Committee, after such enquiry as it thinks fit, reports to the Prime Minister whether, so far as it believes, the political candidates are fit and proper persons to be recommended and for any non-political candidate, who may have made a political donation, whether this was a factor in the recommendation for an honour.

*Chairman*, The Lord Thomson of Monifieth, KT, PC
*Members*, The Baroness Dean of Thornton-le-Fylde, PC; The Lord Hurd of Westwell, CH, CBE
*Secretary*, Mrs P. G. W. Catto

## HORSERACE TOTALISATOR BOARD

Tote House, 74 Upper Richmond Road, London SW15 2SU Tel: 020-8874 6411; Fax: 020-8874 6107; Web: www.tote.co.uk

The Horserace Totalisator Board (the Tote) was established by the Betting, Gaming and Lotteries Act 1963. Its function is to operate totalisators on approved racecourses in Great Britain, and it also provides on- and off-course cash and credit offices. Under the Horserace Totalisator and Betting Levy Board Act 1972, it is further empowered to offer bets at starting price (or other bets at fixed odds) on any sporting event, and under the Horserace Totalisator Board Act 1997 to take bets on any event, except the National Lottery. The chairman and members of the Board are appointed by the Secretary of State, Department of Culture, Media and Sport.

The Government announced in March 2000 that the Tote would be sold to a racing trust, subject to the necessary legislation going through Parliament.

*Chairman*, P. I. Jones
*Chief Executive*, W. J. Heaton

## HOUSING CORPORATION

149 Tottenham Court Road, London W1T 7BN
Tel: 020-7393 2000; Fax: 020-7393 2111;
Email: enquiries@housingcorp.gsx.gov.uk;
Web: www.housingcorp.gov.uk

Established by Parliament in 1964, the Housing Corporation regulates, funds and promotes the proper performance of registered social landlords, which are non-profit making bodies run by voluntary committees. There are over 2,200 registered social landlords, most of which are housing associations, and they now provide homes for more than 1.5 million people. Under the Housing Act 1996, the Corporation's regulatory role was widened to embrace new types of landlords, in particular local housing companies. The Corporation is funded by the Department of Transport, Local Government and the Regions.

*Chairman*, The Rt. Hon. the Baroness Dean of Thornton-le-Fylde, PC
*Deputy Chairman*, E. Armitage
*Chief Executive*, Dr N. Perry

## HUMAN FERTILISATION AND EMBRYOLOGY AUTHORITY

Paxton House, 30 Artillery Lane, London E1 7LS
Tel: 020-7377 5077; Fax: 020-7377 1871

The Human Fertilization and Embryology Authority (HFEA) was established under the Human Fertilisation and Embryology Act 1990. Its function is to license the following activities: the creation or use of embryos outside

the body in the provision of infertility treatment services; the use of donated gametes in infertility treatment; the storage of gametes or embryos; and research on human embryos. It maintains a confidential database of all such treatments and of egg and sperm donors, and provides information to patients, clinics and the public. The HFEA also keeps under review information about embryos and, when requested to do so, gives advice to the Secretary of State for Health.
*Chairman*, Lady Julia Tugendhat
*Deputy Chairman*, Mrs J. Denton
*Members*, Prof. Brenda Almond; Dr S. Avery; Prof T. Baldwin; Prof. D. Barlow; Prof. P. Brande; Prof. I. Cameron; J. Denton; Prof. Christine Gosden; Prof. A. Grubb; Prof. H. Leese; Prof. S. Lewis; Dr Anne McLaren; Dr S. Muhammed; Ms S. Nathan; Ms S. Nebhrajani; The Rt. Revd the Lord Bishop of Rochester; Dr F. Shenfield; Mrs L. Woods
*Chief Executive*, Dr M. Dalziel

---

HUMAN GENETICS COMMISSION
Area 652C, Skipton House, 80 London Road, London, SE1 6LH
Tel: 020-7972 1578; Fax: 020-7972 1717;
Email: hgc@doh.gov.uk; Web: www.hgc.gov.uk

---

The Human Genetics Commission was established in 1999, subsuming three previous advisory committees. Its remit is to give Ministers strategic advice on how developments in human genetics will impact on people and on health care, focusing in particular on the special and ethical implications.
*Chairman*, Baroness H. Kennedy of the Shaws, QC
*Vice Chair*, Prof. A. McCall Smith
*Members* Dr W. Albert, Prof. E. Anionwu; Prof. J. Burn; Ms R. Evans; Prof. P. Goodfellow; Dr H. Harris; Prof. J. Harris; Ms H. Newiss; Revd Dr J. Polkinghorne; Prof. M. Richards; Dr G. Samuels; Mr G. Watts; Mr P. Webb; Prof. V. von Heyningen; Ms R. Deech; Mrs J. Axelby; Dr Patrick Morrison; Dr R. Skinner
*Head of Secretariat*, Mark Bale

---

INDEPENDENT HOUSING OMBUDSMAN
Norman House, 105–109 Strand, London WC2R 0AA
Tel: 020-7836 3630; 0345-125973; Fax: 020-7836 3900; Email: ombudsman@ihos.org.uk;
Web: www.ihos.org.uk

---

The Independent Housing Ombudsman (IHO) was established in 1997 under the Housing Act 1996. The Ombudsman deals with complaints against registered social landlords (not including local authorities) and some private landlords. IHO is also managing the pilot Tenancy Deposit Scheme aimed at protecting the deposits of private tenants and resolving any disputes over their return quickly, cheaply and fairly.
*Ombudsman*, M. Biles
*Chair of Board*, K. Lampard
*General Manager*, L. Greenberg

---

INDEPENDENT INTERNATIONAL COMMISSION ON DECOMMISSIONING
Dublin Castle, Block M, Ship Street, Dublin 2
Tel: 00 353 1-478 0111; Fax: 00 353 1-478 0600
Rosepark House, Upper Newtownards Road, Belfast BT4 3NX
Tel: 028-90-48 8600; Fax: 028-9048 8601

---

The Commission was established by agreement between the British and Irish Governments in August 1997. Its objective is to facilitate the decommissioning of illegally-held firearms and explosives in accordance with the relevant legislation in both jurisdictions. Its members are appointed jointly by the two Governments; staff are appointed by the Commission. All are drawn from countries other than the UK and the Republic of Ireland.
*Chairman*, Gen. J. de Chastelain (Canada)
*Commissioners*, Brig. T. Nieminen (Finland); A. Sens (USA)
*Chief of Staff*, C. E. Garrard (Canada)

---

INDEPENDENT REVIEW SERVICE FOR THE SOCIAL FUND
4th Floor, Centre City Podium, 5 Hill Street, Birmingham B5 4UB
Tel: 0121-606 2100; Fax: 0121-606 2180

---

The Social Fund Commissioner is appointed by the Secretary of State for Work and Pensions. The Commissioner appoints Social Fund Inspectors, who provide an independent review of decisions made by Social Fund Officers in the Benefits Agency of the Department of Work and Pensions.
*Social Fund Commissioner*, Sir R. Tilt

---

INDEPENDENT TELEVISION COMMISSION
33 Foley Street, London W1P 7LB
Tel: 0845-601 3608; Fax: 020-7306 7800

---

The Independent Television Commission replaced the Independent Broadcasting Authority in 1991. The Commission is responsible for licensing and regulating all commercially funded television services broadcast from the UK. Members are appointed by the Secretary of State for Culture, Media and Sport.
*Chairman*, Sir Robin Biggam
*Members*, A. Balls, CB; C. Brendish; Ms B. Donoghue; Sir Michael Checkland; Ms J. Goffe; J. Kelly; C. Bharucha (*Member for Northern Ireland*); Prof. D. L. Morgan, D.Phil. (*Member for Wales*); Dr M. Shea, CVO (*Member for Scotland*)
*Chief Executive*, P. Hodgson
*Secretary and Director of Administration*, M. Redley

---

INDUSTRIAL INJURIES ADVISORY COUNCIL
6th Floor, The Adelphi, 1–11 John Adam Street, London WC2N 6HT
Tel: 020-7962 8066; Fax: 020-7712 2255;
Email: iiac@dial.pipex.com; Web: www.iiac.org.uk

---

The Industrial Injuries Advisory Council is a statutory body under the Social Security Administration Act 1992 which considers and advises the Secretary of State for

Social Security on regulations and other questions relating to industrial injuries benefits or their administration.
*Chairman*, Prof. A. J. Newman Taylor, OBE, FRCP
*Secretary*, H. Leigh

---

## INFORMATION COMMISSIONER'S OFFICE

Wycliffe House, Water Lane, Wilmslow, Cheshire SK9 5AF Tel: 01625-545745; Fax: 01625-524510;
Email: data@dataprotection.gov.uk;
Web: www.dataprotection.gov.uk

---

The Data Protection Act 1998 sets rules for processing personal information and applies to some paper records as well as those held on computers.

The Data Protection Act works in two ways. It says those who record and use personal information (data controllers) must be open about how the information is used and must follow the eight principles of 'good information handling'. It also gives data subjects (individuals who are the subject of personal data) certain rights.

The Commissioner has a number of specific duties under the Act. She is given discretion in the manner in which she fulfils those duties and much of her work, and that of her staff involves informal advice and consultation with data controllers, and data subjects and the various bodies that represent them.

It is the Commissioner's duty to compile and maintain the register of data controllers, and provide facilities for members of the public to examine the register; promote observance of the data protection principles; and disseminate information to the public about the Act and her function under the Act. The Commissioner also has the power to produce codes of practice.

The Commissioner reports annually to parliament on the performance of her functions under the Act and has obligations to assess breaches of the Act.

The Information Commissioner is also responsible for Freedom of Information.
*Commissioner*, Mrs E. France

---

## JOINT NATURE CONSERVATION COMMITTEE

Monkstone House, City Road, Peterborough PE1 1JY
Tel: 01733-562626; Fax: 01733-555948

---

The Committee was established under the Environmental Protection Act 1990. It advises the Government and others on UK and international nature conservation issues and disseminates knowledge on these subjects. It establishes common standards for the monitoring of nature conservation and research, and provides guidance to English Nature, Scottish Natural Heritage, the Countryside Council for Wales and the Department of the Environment for Northern Ireland.
*Chairman*, Sir Angus Stirling
*Managing Director*, D. Steer
*Director*, Dr M. A. Vincent

---

# LAND REGISTRIES

---

## HM LAND REGISTRY

Lincoln's Inn Fields, London WC2A 3PH
Tel: 020-7917 8888; Fax: 020-7955 0110

The registration of title to land was first introduced in England and Wales by the Land Registry Act 1862; HM Land Registry operates today under the Land Registration Acts 1925 to 1997. The object of registering title to land is to create and maintain a register of landowners whose title is guaranteed by the state and so to simplify the transfer, mortgage and other dealings with real property. Registration on sale is now compulsory throughout England and Wales. The register has been open to inspection by the public since 1990.

HM Land Registry is an executive agency and Trading Fund administered under the Lord Chancellor by the Chief Land Registrar.

### HEADQUARTERS OFFICE

*Chief Land Registrar and Chief Executive*, P. Collis
*Solicitor to Land Registry*, C. J. West
*Director of Corporate Services*, E. G. Beardsall
*Director of Operations*, A. Howarth
*Director of Practice and Legal Services*, J. V. Timothy
*Director of Information Systems*, P. J. Smith, OBE
*Director of Facilities*, P. R. Laker
*Director of Personnel*, J. Hodder
*Director of Finance*, Ms H. Jackson
*Director of Communication*, A. Pemberton
*Director of Service Development*, P. Norman

### COMPUTER SERVICES DIVISION

Burrington Way, Plymouth PL5 3LP
Tel: 01752-635600
*Head of IT Services Division*, P. A. Maycock
*Head of IT Development Division*, J. Formby
*Head of IT Management Services*, K. Deards

### LAND CHARGES AND AGRICULTURAL CREDITS DEPARTMENT

Burrington Way, Plymouth PL5 3LP
Tel: 01752-635600
*Superintendent of Land Charges*, J. Hughes

### DISTRICT LAND REGISTRIES

BIRKENHEAD (OLD MARKET) – Old Market House, Hamilton Street, Birkenhead CH41 5FL. Tel: 0151-473 1110. *District Land Registrar*, P. J. Brough

BIRKENHEAD (ROSEBRAE ) – Rosebrae Court, Woodside Ferry Approach, Birkenhead CH41 6DU. Tel: 0151-472 6666. *District Land Registrar*, M. G. Garwood

COVENTRY – Leigh Court, Torrington Avenue, Newline Coventry CV4 9XZ. Tel: 024-7686 0860. *District Land Registrar*, T. H. O. Lewis

CROYDON – Sunley House, Bedford Park, Croydon CR9 3LE. Tel: 020-8781 9100. *District Land Registrar*, F. M. Twambley

DURHAM (BOLDON HOUSE) – Boldon House, Wheatlands Way, Pity Me, Durham DH1 5GJ. Tel: 0191-301 2345. *District Land Registrar*, R. B. Fearnley

DURHAM (SOUTHFIELD HOUSE) – Southfield House, Southfield Way, Durham DH1 5TR. Tel: 0191-301 3500. *District Land Registrar*, P. J. Timothy

GLOUCESTER – Twyver House, Bruton Way, Gloucester GL1 1DQ. Tel: 01452-511111. *District Land Registrar*, W. W. Budden

HARROW – Lyon House, Lyon Road, Harrow, Middx HA1 2EU. Tel: 020-8235 1181. *District Land Registrar*, C. Tate

KINGSTON UPON HULL – Earle House, Portland Street, Hull HU2 8JN. Tel: 01482-223244. *District Land Registrar*, S. R. Coveney

LANCASHIRE – Wrea Brook Court, Lytham Road, Warton, Preston PR4 1TE. Tel: 01772 836 700 *District Land Registrar*, Mrs L. Wallwork
LEICESTER – Westbridge Place, Leicester LE3 5DR. Tel: 0116-265 4000. *District Land Registrar*, Mrs J. A. Goodfellow
LYTHAM – Birkenhead House, East Beach, Lytham, Lancs FY8 5AB. Tel: 01253-849849. *District Land Registrar*, J. G. Cooper
NOTTINGHAM (EAST) – Robins Wood Road, Nottingham NG8 3RQ. Tel: 0115-906 5353. *District Land Registrar*, P. A. Brown
NOTTINGHAM (WEST) – Chalfont Drive, Nottingham NG8 3RN. Tel: 0115-935 1166. *District Land Registrar*, Ms A. M. Goss
PETERBOROUGH – Touthill Close, City Road, Peterborough PE1 1XN. Tel: 01733-288288. *District Land Registrar*, C. W. Martin
PLYMOUTH – Plumer House, Tailyour Road, Crownhill, Plymouth PL6 5HY. Tel: 01752-636000. *District Land Registrar*, A. J. Pain
PORTSMOUTH – St Andrew's Court, St Michael's Road, Portsmouth PO1 2JH. Tel: 023-9276 8888. *District Land Registrar*, S. R. Sehrawat
STEVENAGE – Brickdale House, Swingate, Stevenage, Herts SG1 1XG. Tel: 01438-788888. *District Land Registrar*, M. Croker
SWANSEA – Ty Bryn Glas, High Street, Swansea SA1 1PW. Tel: 01792-458877. *District Land Registrar*, G. A. Hughes
TELFORD – Parkside Court, Hall Park Way, Telford TF3 4LR. Tel: 01952-290355. *District Land Registrar*, A. M. Lewis
TUNBRIDGE WELLS – Forest Court, Forest Road, Tunbridge Wells, Kent TN2 5AQ. Tel: 01892-510015. *District Land Registrar*, G. R. Tooke
WALES – Ty Cwm Tawe, Phoenix Way, Llansamlet, Swansea SA7 9FQ. Tel: 01792-355000. *District Land Registrar*, T. M. Lewis
WEYMOUTH – Melcombe Court, 1 Cumberland Drive, Weymouth, Dorset DT4 9TT. Tel: 01305-363636. *District Land Registrar*, Mrs P. M. Reeson
YORK – James House, James Street, York YO10 3YZ. Tel: 01904-450000. *District Land Registrar*, Mrs R. F. Lovel

## REGISTERS OF SCOTLAND

Meadowbank House, 153 London Road, Edinburgh EH8 7AU
Tel: 0131-659 6111; Fax: 0131-479 3688
Customer Service Centre: 0845-6070161

Registers of Scotland is the executive agency responsible for framing and maintaining records relating to property and other legal documents in Scotland. The agency holds 15 registers: two property registers (General Register of Sasines and Land Register of Scotland) and 13 chancery and judicial registers (Register of Deeds in the Books of Council and Session; Register of Protests; Register of Judgments; Register of Service of Heirs; Register of the Great Seal; Register of the Quarter Seal; Register of the Prince's Seal; Register of Crown Grants; Register of Sheriffs' Commissions; Register of the Cachet Seal; Register of Inhibitions and Adjudications; Register of Entails; and Register of Hornings).

*Chief Executive and Keeper of the Registers of Scotland*, A. W. Ramage
*Deputy Keeper*, A. G. Rennie
*Managing Director*, F. Manson

## LAW COMMISSION

Conquest House, 37–38 John Street, London WC1N 2BQ Tel: 020-7453 1220; Fax: 020-7453 1297; Web: www.lawcom.gov.uk

The Law Commission was set up in 1965, under the Law Commissions Act 1965, to make proposals to the Government for the examination of the law in England and Wales and for its revision where it is unsuited for modern requirements, obscure, or otherwise unsatisfactory. It recommends to the Lord Chancellor programmes for the examination of different branches of the law and suggests whether the examination should be carried out by the Commission itself or by some other body. The Commission is also responsible for the preparation of Consolidation and Statute Law (Repeals) Bills.

*Chairman*, The Hon. Mr Justice Carnwath, CVO
*Commissioners*, C. Harpum; Miss D. Faber; Judge A. Wilkie, QC; Prof H. Beale
*Secretary*, M. W. Sayers

## LAW OFFICERS' DEPARTMENTS

Legal Secretariat to the Law Officers, Attorney-General's Chambers, 9 Buckingham Gate, London SW1E 6JP Tel: 020-7271 2400; Fax: 020-7271 2430; Email: lslo@gtnet.gov.uk; Web: www.lslo.gov.uk
Attorney-General's Chambers, Royal Courts of Justice, Belfast BT1 3JY
Tel: 02890 546082; Fax: 02890-546049

The Law Officers of the Crown for England and Wales are the Attorney-General and the Solicitor-General. The Attorney-General, assisted by the Solicitor-General, is the chief legal adviser to the Government and is also ultimately responsible for all Crown litigation. He has overall responsibility for the work of the Law Officers' Departments (the Treasury Solicitor's Department, the Crown Prosecution Service, the Serious Fraud Office and the Legal Secretariat to the Law Officers). He has a specific statutory duty to superintend the discharge of their duties by the Director of Public Prosecutions (who heads the Crown Prosecution Service) and the Director of the Serious Fraud Office. The Director of Public Prosecutions for Northern Ireland is also responsible to the Attorney-General for the performance of his functions. The Attorney-General has additional responsibilities in relation to aspects of the civil and criminal law.

*Attorney-General* (*£90,125), The Lord Goldsmith, QC
*Private Secretary*, R. Cazalet
*Parliamentary Private Secretary*, M. Foster, DL, MP
*Solicitor-General*, Rt. Hon. Harriet Harman, QC
*Legal Secretary* (*G2*), D. Brammell
**Deputy Legal Secretary* (*G3*), S. Parkinson
In addition to a parliamentary salary of £48,371

## LEARNING AND SKILLS COUNCIL

Cheylesmore House, Quinton Road, Coventry, West Midlands, CV1 2WT

The Learning and Skills Council was established in April 2001 to replace the Further Education Funding and the Training and Enterprise Councils. It is a non-departmental public body that advises the government on future National Learning Targets and is responsible for the

allocation of £6 billion of public money. Its objective is to ensure that high quality post-16 provision is available to meet the needs of employers, individuals and communities. The LSC operates through 47 local departments, which work to promote the equality of opportunity in the workplace, aiming to ensure that the needs of the most disadvantaged in the labour market are met. These local departments in most cases have coterminous boundaries with Small business service franchises.
*Chairman*, B. Sanderson
*Chief Executive*, J. Harwood

## LEGAL SERVICES COMMISSION

85 Gray's Inn Road, London WC1X 8TX
Tel: 020-7759 0000; Web: www.legalservices.gov.uk

On 1 April 2000, the Legal Aid Board was replaced by the Legal Services Commission (LSC), which runs two schemes - the civil scheme for funding civil cases as part of the Community Legal Service, and the Criminal Defence Service. The LSC has an important role in co-ordinating and working in a partnership with other funders of legal services, such as local authorities. The LSC also directly funds legal services for eligible clients.

The Criminal Defence Services provides access to advice, assistance and representation to people accused of a crime, as the interests of justice require.
*Chairman*, P. G. Birch, CBE
*Members*, S. Orchard, CBE (*Chief Executive*); M. Barnes, CBE; R. Buxton (*Director of Operations*); A. Edwards; P. Ely; B. Harvey (*Director of Resources and Supplier Development*); Ms J. Herzog; Mrs S. Hewitt; Ms Y. Mosquito; R. Penn; J. Shearer

# LIBRARIES

## THE BRITISH LIBRARY

96 Euston Road, London NW1 2DB
Tel: 020-7412 7000

The British Library was established in 1973. It is the UK's national library and occupies a key position in the library and information network. The Library aims to serve scholarship, research, industry, commerce and all other major users of information. Its services are based on collections which include over 18 million volumes, 1 million discs, and 55,000 hours of tape recordings. The Library is now based at two sites: London (St Pancras and Colindale) and Boston Spa, W. Yorks. Government grant-in-aid to the British Library in 2001-2002 is £86.2 million. The Library's sponsoring department is the Department for Culture, Media and Sport.

Access to the reading rooms at St Pancras is limited to holders of a British Library Reader's Pass; information about eligibility is available from the Reader Admissions Office. The exhibition galleries and public areas are open to all, free of charge.

Opening hours of services vary; some services may close for one week each year. Specific information should be checked by telephone.

### British Library Board

*Chairman*, Dr J. M. Ashworth
*Chief Executive and Deputy Chairman*, L. Brindley
*Part-time Members*, H. Boyd-Carpenter, CVO; Prof. M. Anderson, OBE, FBA, FRSE; C. G. R. Leach, Ph.D.; B. Naylor; Prof. Jessica Rawson, CBE, FBA; J. Ritblat, FRICS; The Viscount Runciman of Doxford, CBE, FBA; P. Scherer; Prof. L. Colley, FRHist; S. Olswang

### British Library, Boston Spa

Boston Spa, Wetherby, W. Yorks LS23 7BQ
Tel: 01937-546000

### British Library, St Pancras

96 Euston Road, London NW1 2DB
Tel: 020-7412 7000

Press and Public Relations. Tel: 020-7412 7111

Exhibitions Service and Visitor Services. Tel: 020-7412 7332

Education Service. Tel: 020-7412 7797

Reader Services and Collection Development.
*Reader Admissions*. Tel: 020-7412 7677
*Reader Services*. Tel: 020-7412 7676
*West European Collections, Slavonic and East European Collections, English Language Collections*. Tel: 020-7412 7676
*Newspaper Library*, Colindale Avenue, London NW9 5HE. Tel: 020-7412 7353

National Preservation Office. Tel: 020-7412 7612

Special Collections. Tel: 020-7412 7513
*Oriental and India Office Collections*. Tel: 020-7412 7873
*Western Manuscripts*. Tel: 020-7412 7513
*Map Library*. Tel: 020-7412 7700
*Music Library*. Tel: 020-7412 7772
*Philatelic Collections*. Tel: 020-7412 7635
*National Sound Archive*. Tel: 020-7412 7440

Science, Technology and Business
*Science and Technology*. Tel: 020-7412 7494/7496
*British and EPO Patents*. Tel: 020-7412 7919
*Foreign Patents*. Tel: 020-7412 7902
*Business*. Tel: 020-7412 7454
*Social Policy Information Service*. Tel: 020-7412 7536

Libraries and Information Commission (former) – *see* Resource: The Council for Museums, Libraries and Archives

## NATIONAL LIBRARY OF SCOTLAND

George IV Bridge, Edinburgh EH1 1EW
Tel: 0131-226 4531; Fax: 0131-622 4803

The Library, which was founded as the Advocates' Library in 1682, became the National Library of Scotland in 1925. It is funded by the Scottish Executive. It contains about seven million books and pamphlets, 20,000 current periodicals, 350 newspaper titles and 120,000 manuscripts. It has an unrivalled Scottish collection.

The Reading Room is for reference and research which cannot conveniently be pursued elsewhere. Admission is by ticket issued to an approved applicant. Opening hours: Reading Room, weekdays, 9.30–8.30 (Wednesday, 10–8.30); Saturday 9.30–1. Map Library, weekdays, 9.30–5 (Wednesday, 10–5); Saturday 9.30–1. Exhibition, weekdays, 10–5; Saturday 10–5; Sunday 2–5. Scottish Science Library, weekdays, 9.30–5 (Wednesday, 10–8.30).
*Chairman of the Trustees*, Prof. Michael Anderson, OBE, Ph.D., FBA, FRSE
*Librarian and Secretary to the Trustees* (*G4*), I. D. McGowan
*Secretary of the Library* (*G6*), M. C. Graham
*Director of General Collections*, C. Newton
*Director of Special Collections*, M. C. T. Simpson
*Director of Public Services*, A. M. Marchbank

## NATIONAL LIBRARY OF WALES/ LLYFRGELL GENEDLAETHOL CYMRU

Aberystwyth SY23 3BU
Tel: 01970-632800; Fax: 01970-615709

The National Library of Wales was founded by royal charter in 1907, and is funded by the National Assembly for Wales. It contains about four million printed books, 40,000 manuscripts, four million deeds and documents, numerous maps, prints and drawings, and a sound and moving image collection. It specialises in manuscripts and books relating to Wales and the Celtic peoples. It is the repository for pre-1858 Welsh probate records, manorial records and tithe documents, and certain legal records. Readers' room open weekdays, 9.30–6 (Saturday 9.30–5); closed first week of October. Admission by reader's ticket to the Reading Rooms but free entry to the exhibition programme.

*President*, Dr R. Brinley Jones
*Librarian (G4)*, A. M. W. Green
*Heads of Departments (G6)*, M. W. Mainwaring (*Corporate Services*); G. Jenkins (*Collection Services*); Dr W. R. M. Griffiths (*Public Services*)

## LIGHTHOUSE AUTHORITIES

## CORPORATION OF TRINITY HOUSE

Trinity House, Tower Hill, London EC3N 4DH
Tel: 020-7481 6900; Fax: 020-7480 7662

Trinity House, the first general lighthouse and pilotage authority in the kingdom, was granted its first charter by Henry VIII in 1514. The Corporation is the general lighthouse authority for England, Wales and the Channel Islands and maintains 72 lighthouses, 13 major floating aids to navigation (e.g. light vessels) and more than 420 buoys. The Corporation also has certain statutory jurisdiction over aids to navigation maintained by local harbour authorities and is responsible for dealing with wrecks dangerous to navigation, except those occurring within port limits or wrecks of HM ships.

The Trinity House Lighthouse Service is maintained out of the General Lighthouse Fund which is provided from light dues levied on ships calling at ports of the UK and the Republic of Ireland. The Corporation is also a deep-sea pilotage authority and a charitable organisation.

The affairs of the Corporation are controlled by a board of Elder Brethren and the Secretary. A separate board, which comprises Elder Brethren, senior staff and outside representatives, currently controls the Lighthouse Service. The Elder Brethren also act as nautical assessors in marine cases in the Admiralty Division of the High Court of Justice.

### ELDER BRETHREN

*Master*, HRH The Prince Philip, Duke of Edinburgh, KG KT
*Deputy Master*, Rear-Adm. P. B. Rowe, CBE, LVO
*Wardens*, Capt. C. M. C. Stewart; Sir Brian Shaw
*Elder Brethren*, HRH The Prince of Wales, KG, KT; HRH The Duke of York, CVO, ADC; Capt. Sir David Tibbits, DSC, RN; Capt. D. A. G. Dickins; Capt. J. E. Bury; Capt. J. A. N. Bezant, DSC, RD, RNR (retd.); Capt. D. J. Cloke; Capt. Sir Miles Wingate, KCVO; The Rt. Hon. Sir Edward Heath, KG, MBE, Capt. I. R. C. Saunders; Capt. P. F. Mason, CBE; Capt.T. Woodfield, OBE; The Lord Simon of Glaisdale; Capt. D. T. Smith, RN; Cdr. Sir Robin Gillett, Bt., GBE, RD, RNR; Capt. Sir Malcolm Edge, KCVO; The Lord Cuckney; Capt. D. J. Orr; The Lord Carrington, KG, GCMG, CH, MC, PC; The Lord Mackay of Clashfern, KT, PC; Sir Adrian Swire; The Lord Sterling of Plaistow, CBE, RNR; Cdr. M. J. Rivett-Carnac, RN; Adm. Sir Jock Slater, GCB, LVO, ADC; Capt. J. R. Burton-Hall, RD; Capt. I. Gibb, FRSA; Cdre P. J. Melson, CBE, RN; Capt. D. C. Glass

### OFFICERS

*Secretary*, R. F. Dobb
*Director of Finance*, K. W. Clark
*Director of Engineering*, D. Golden
*Director of Administration*, D. I. Brewer
*Head of Human Resources*, P. F. Morgan
*Legal and Insurance Manager*, J. D. Price
*Navigation Manager*, Mrs K. Hossain
*Head of Management Services*, S. J. W. Dunning
*Deputy Director of Engineering*, P. N. Hyde
*Senior Inspector of Shipping*, J. R. Dunnett
*Media and Communication Officer*, H. L. Cooper

## NORTHERN LIGHTHOUSE BOARD

84 George Street, Edinburgh EH2 3DA
Tel: 0131-473 3100; Fax: 0131-220 2093;
Email: enquiries@nlb.org.uk; Web: www.nlb.org.uk

The Lighthouse Board is the general lighthouse authority for Scotland and the Isle of Man. The board owes its origin to an Act of Parliament passed in 1786. At present the Commissioners operate under the Merchant Shipping Act 1995 and are 19 in number.

The Commissioners control 83 major automatic lighthouses, 117 minor lights and many lighted and unlighted buoys. They have a fleet of two motor vessels.

### COMMISSIONERS

The Lord Advocate; the Solicitor-General for Scotland; the Lord Provosts of Edinburgh, Glasgow and Aberdeen; the Provost of Inverness; the Convener of Argyll and Bute Council; the Sheriffs-Principal of North Strathclyde, Tayside, Central and Fife, Grampian, Highlands and Islands, South Strathclyde, Dumfries and Galloway, Lothians and Borders, and Glasgow and Strathkelvin; Capt. D. M. Cowell; Adm. Sir Michael Livesay, KCB; The Lord Maclay; P. MacKay, CB; Capt. K. MacLeod

### OFFICERS

*Chief Executive*, Capt. J. B. Taylor, RN
*Director of Finance*, D. Gorman
*Director of Engineering*, M. Waddell
*Director of Operations and Navigational Requirements*, P. J. Christmas

## LOCAL COMMISSIONERS

## COMMISSION FOR LOCAL ADMINISTRATION IN ENGLAND

21 Queen Anne's Gate, London SW1H 9BU
Tel: 020-7915 3210; Fax: 020-7233 0396

Local Commissioners (local government ombudsmen) are responsible for investigating complaints from members of the public against local authorities (but not town and parish councils); English Partnerships (planning matters only); Housing Action Trusts; education appeal committees; police authorities and certain other authorities.The Commissioners are appointed by the Crown on the recommendation of the Secretary of State for Transport, Local Government, and the Regions.

Certain types of action are excluded from investigation, including personnel matters and commercial transactions unless they relate to the purchase or sale of land. Complaints can be sent direct to the Local Government Ombudsman or through a councillor, although the Local Government Ombudsman will not consider a complaint unless the council has had an opportunity to investigate and reply to a complainant.

A free leaflet 'Complaint about the council? How to complain to the Local Government Ombudsman' is available from the Commission's office.

*Chairman and Chief Executive of the Commission and Local Commissioner* (£132,603), E. B. C. Osmotherly, CB
*Vice-Chairman and Local Commissioner* (£100,420), Mrs P. A. Thomas
*Local Commissioner* (£99,420), J. R. White
*Member (ex officio)*, The Parliamentary Commissioner for Administration
*Deputy Chief Executive and Secretary* (£62,658), N. J. Karney

## COMMISSION FOR LOCAL ADMINISTRATION IN WALES

Derwen House, Court Road, Bridgend CF31 1BN
Tel: 01656-661325; Fax: 01656-658317;
Email: enquiries@ombudsman-wales.org;
Web: www.ombudsman-wales.org

The Local Commissioner for Wales has similar powers to the Local Commissioners in England, but by the end of 2001 he will also have additional powers (similar to the Standards Board for England) to investigate allegations made against local authority members of misconduct. The Commissioner is appointed by the Crown on the recommendation of the Secretary of State for Wales. A free leaflet 'Your Local Government Ombudsman in Wales' is available from the Commissioners office.

*Local Commissioner*, E. R. Moseley
*Secretary*, D. Bowen
*Member (ex officio)*, The Parliamentary Commissioner for Administration

## COMMISSIONER FOR LOCAL ADMINISTRATION IN SCOTLAND

23 Walker Street, Edinburgh EH3 7HX
Tel: 0131-225 5300; Fax: 0131-225 9495;
Email: commissioner@ombudslgscot.org.uk;
Web: www.ombudslgscot.org.uk

The Local Commissioner for Scotland has similar powers to the Local Commissioners in England, and is appointed by the Crown on the recommendation of the First Minister.

*Local Commissioner*, I. F. Smith
*Deputy Commissioner and Secretary*, Ms J. H. Renton

---

## LONDON REGIONAL TRANSPORT

55 Broadway, London SW1H 0BD
Tel: 020-7222 5600

---

Subject to the financial objectives and principles approved by the Secretary of State for Transport, Local Government and the Regions, London Regional Transport has a general duty to provide or secure the provision of public transport services for Greater London.

*Chairman (non-executive)*, B. Kiley
*Member, and Managing Director of London Underground Ltd*, D. Smith

---

## LORD GREAT CHAMBERLAIN'S OFFICE

House of Lords, London SW1A 0PW
Tel: 020-7219 3100; Fax: 020-7219 2500

---

The Lord Great Chamberlain is a Great Officer of State, the office being hereditary since the grant of Henry I to the family of De Vere, Earls of Oxford. It is now a joint hereditary office between the Cholmondeley and Carington families. The Lord Great Chamberlain is responsible for the royal apartments of the Palace of Westminster, i.e. The Queen's Robing Room, the Royal Gallery and, in conjunction with the Lord Chancellor and the Speaker, Westminster Hall. The Lord Great Chamberlain has particular responsibility for the internal administrative arrangements within the House of Lords for State Openings of Parliament.

*Lord Great Chamberlain*, The Marquess of Cholmondeley
*Secretary to the Lord Great Chamberlain*, Lt.-Gen. Sir Michael Willcocks, KCB
*Clerks to the Lord Great Chamberlain*, Ms J. Perodeau; Ms A. Feuz

---

## LORD PRIVY SEAL'S OFFICE

Privy Council Office, 68 Whitehall, London SW1A 2AT Tel: 020-7270 3000;
Web: www.cabinetoffice.gov.uk

---

The Lord Privy Seal is a member of the Cabinet and Leader of the House of Lords. He has no departmental portfolio, but is a member of a number of Cabinet committees. He is responsible to the Prime Minister for the organisation of Government business in the House and has a responsibility to the House itself to advise it on procedural matters and other difficulties which arise.

*Lord Privy Seal, Leader of the House of Lords*, The Lord Williams of Mostyn, QC, PC
*Principal Private Secretary*, P. Richardson
*Private Secretary (House of Lords)*, Miss M. Robertson

---

## MENTAL HEALTH ACT COMMISSION

Maid Marian House, 56 Hounds Gate, Nottingham NG1 6BG Tel: 0115-943 7100; Fax: 0115-943 7101

---

The Mental Health Act Commission was established in 1983. Its functions are to keep under review the operation of the Mental Health Act 1983; to visit and meet patients detained under the Act; to investigate complaints falling within the Commission's remit; to operate the consent to treatment safeguards in the Mental Health Act; to publish a biennial report on its activities; to monitor the implementation of the Code of Practice; and to advise Ministers. Commissioners are appointed by the Secretary of State for Health.

*Chairman*, Miss M. Clayton
*Vice-Chairman*, Prof. R. Williams
*Chief Executives*, P. Hampshire

## MILLENNIUM COMMISSION

Portland House, Stag Place, London SW1E 5EZ
Tel: 020-7880 2001; Fax: 020-7880 2000;
Email: info@millennium.gov.uk

The Millennium Commission was established in February 1994 and is accountable to the Department for Culture, Media and Sport. It is an independent body which distributes money from National Lottery proceeds to projects to mark the millennium.

*Chairman*, The Rt. Hon. T. Jowell, MP
*Members*, Dr H. Couper; The Earl of Dalkeith; Ms F. Benjamin; The Rt. Hon. M. Heseltine, MP; Ms J. Donovan, CBE; M. D' Ancona. Lord Gletoran
*Director*, M. O'Connor

## MUSEUMS

### THE BRITISH MUSEUM

Great Russell Street, London WC1B 3DG
Tel: 020-7323 8000; Fax: 020-7323 8616

The British Museum houses the national collection of antiquities, ethnography, coins and paper money, medals, and prints and drawings. The British Museum may be said to date from 1753, when Parliament approved the holding of a public lottery to raise funds for the purchase of the collections of Sir Hans Sloane and the Harleian manuscripts, and for their proper housing and maintenance. The building (Montagu House) was opened in 1759. The present buildings were erected between 1823 and the present day, and the original collection has increased to its present dimensions by gifts and purchases. Total government grant-in-aid for 2000–2001 was £34.8 million.

BOARD OF TRUSTEES

*Appointed by the Sovereign*, HRH The Duke of Gloucester, KG, GCVO
*Appointed by the Prime Minister*, C. Allen-Jones; H. Askari; N. Barber; Dame Gillian Beer, FBA; Sir John Boyd, KCMG; Sir John Browne, FREng.; The Rt. Hon. Countess of Dalkeith; Sir Michael Hopkins, CBE, RA, RIBA; Dr J. Montagu, FBA; Sir Claus Moser, KCB, CBE, FBA; Sir Joseph Hotung; Prof. M. Kemp, FBA; Prof. Barry Cunliffe, CBE; D. Lindsell; C. McCall, QC; Sir Martin Rees, FRS, Dr Anna Ritchie; E. Salama
*Nominated by the Learned Societies*, Prof. Jean Thomas, CBE (*Royal Society*); T. Phillips, RA (*Royal Academy*); Sir Keith Thomas, FBA (*British Academy*)
*Appointed by the Trustees of the British Museum*, G. C. Greene, CBE (*Chairman*); Sir David Attenborough, CH, CVO, CBE, FRS; Dr Jennifer Montagu, FBA; Sir Claus Moser, KCB, CBE, FBA; J. Tusa

OFFICERS

*Director*, Dr R. G. W. Anderson, FRSC, FSA
*Managing Director*, Ms S. Taverne
*Director of Marketing and Public Affairs*, Dr C. Homden
*Director of Finance and Resources*, C. Herring
*Secretary*, T. Doubleday
*Head of Exhibitions*, G. A. L. House
*Head of Media Relations*, A. E. Hamilton
*Head of Design*, Miss M. Hall, OBE
*Head of Education*, J. F. Reeve
*Director of Operations*, C. E. I. Jones
*Head of Building Development and Planning*, K. T. Stannard
*Head of Building Management*, T. R. A. Giles
*Head of Finance*, D. Allcorn
*Director of Human Resources*, I. Black ,
*Head of Visitor Services*, Ms L. Lee
*Head of Membership Development*, Ms S. Carthew
*Head of Marketing Communications*, M. Ladds

KEEPERS

*Senior Keeper*, Dr B. J. Mack
*Keeper of Prints and Drawings*, A. V. Griffiths
*Keeper of Coins and Medals*, Dr A. M. Burnett
*Keeper of Egyptian Antiquities*, W. V. Davies
*Keeper of Ancient Near East Antiquities*, Dr J. E. Curtis
*Keeper of Greek and Roman Antiquities*, Dr D. J. R. Williams
*Keeper of Medieval and Modern Europe*, J. Cherry
*Keeper of Prehistory and Early Europe*, Dr C. Malone
*Keeper of Japanese Antiquities*, V. T. Harris
*Keeper of Oriental Antiquities*, R. J. Knox
*Keeper of Ethnography*, Dr B. Durrans
*Keeper of Scientific Research*, Dr S. G. E. Bowman
*Keeper of Conservation*, W. A. Oddy

### IMPERIAL WAR MUSEUM

Lambeth Road, London SE1 6HZ
Tel: 020-7416 5320; Fax: 020-7416 5374

The Museum, founded in 1917, illustrates and records all aspects of the two world wars and other military operations involving Britain and the Commonwealth since 1914. It was opened in its present home, formerly Bethlem Hospital or Bedlam, in 1936. The Museum also administers *HMS Belfast* in the Pool of London, Duxford Airfield near Cambridge and the Cabinet War Rooms in Westminster.

Government grant-in-aid for 2001-2002 is £11.347 million.

OFFICERS

*Director-General*, R. W. K. Crawford
*Secretary and Director of Finance*, J. Card
*Assistant Directors*, D. A. Needham (*Administration*); Miss K. J. Carmichael (*Collections*); G. Marsh (*Planning and Development*)
*Director of Duxford Airfield*, E. O. Inman, OBE
*Director of HMS Belfast*, E. J. Wenzel

KEEPERS

*Public Services Division*, C. Dowling, D.Phil.
*Department of Documents*, R. W. A. Suddaby
*Department of Exhibits and Firearms*, D. J. Penn
*Department of Printed Books*, R. Golland
*Department of Art*, Miss A. H. Weight
*Department of Film*, R. B. N. Smither
*Department of Sound Records*, Mrs M. A. Brooks
*Department of Marketing and Trading*, Miss A. Godwin
*Curator of the Cabinet War Rooms*, P. Reed

### MUSEUM OF LONDON

London Wall, London EC2Y 5HN
Tel: 020-7600 3699; Fax: 020-7600 1058;
Email: info@museumoflondon.org.uk;
Web: www.museumoflondon.org.uk

The Museum of London illustrates the history of London from prehistoric times to the present day. It opened in 1976 and is based on the amalgamation of the former Guildhall Museum and London Museum. The Museum is controlled by a Board of Governors, appointed (nine each) by the Government and the Corporation of London. The

Museum is currently funded jointly by the Department for Culture, Media and Sport and the Corporation of London, each contributing £4.519 million in 2000–2001.
*Chairman of Board of Governors*, R. Hambro
*Director*, Dr S. Thurley

## NATIONAL ARMY MUSEUM

Royal Hospital Road, London SW3 4HT
Tel: 020-7730 0717; Fax: 020-7823 6573;
Web: www.national-army-museum.ac.uk;
Email: info@national-army-museum.ac.uk

The National Army Museum covers the history of five centuries of the British Army. It was established by royal charter in 1960. Total Government grant-in-aid for 1999–2000 was £4.5 million.
*Director*, I. G. Robertson
*Assistant Directors*, D. K. Smurthwaite; A. J. Guy; P. B. Boyden

## NATURAL HISTORY MUSEUM

Cromwell Road, London SW7 5BD
Tel: 020-7942 5000

The Natural History Museum originates from the natural history departments of the British Museum, which grew extensively during the 19th century; in 1860 the natural history collection was moved from Bloomsbury to a new location. Part of the site of the 1862 International Exhibition in South Kensington was acquired for the new museum, and the Museum opened to the public in 1881. In 1963 the Natural History Museum became completely independent with its own board of trustees. The Walter Rothschild Zoological Museum, Tring, bequeathed by the second Lord Rothschild, has formed part of the Museum since 1938. The Geological Museum merged with the Natural History Museum in 1985. Total Government grant-in-aid for 2001-2002 is £32.377 million.

### BOARD OF TRUSTEES

*Appointed by the Prime Minister*, The Lord Oxburgh, KBE, Ph.D., FRS (*Chairman*); Sir Crispin Tickell, GCMG, KCVO; Dame Anne McLaren, DBE, FRS, FRCOG; Sir Richard Sykes, FRS; Miss J. Mayhew; Ms J. Bennett; Prof. M. Hassell, FRS; O. Stocken
*Appointed by the Secretary of State for Culture, Media and Sport*, Prof. C. Leaver, CBE, FRS,
*Appointed by the Trustees of the Natural History Museum*, The Lord Palumbo; Prof. Sir K. O'Nions, FRS; Prof. Linda Partridge, FRS, FRSE

### SENIOR STAFF

*Director*, Dr N. R. Chalmers
*Director of Science*, Prof. P. Henderson, D.Phil
*Head of Audit and Review*, D. Thorpe
*Keeper of Botany*, Dr R. Bateman
*Director of Development and Marketing*, Ms S. Ament
*Keeper of Entomology*, Dr R. Vane-Wright
*Director of Estates*, K. Rellis
*Head of Education and Exhibitions*, Dr G. Clarke
*Director of Finance*, N. Greenwood
*Head of Library and Information Services*, Dr R. G. Lester
*Keeper of Mineralogy*, Prof. A. Fleet
*Keeper of Palaeontology*, Prof. S. K. Donovan
*Director of Human Resources*, D. Hill
*Head of Visitor Services*, D. Candlin
*Keeper of Zoology*, Prof. P. Rainbow
*Policy and Planning Co-ordinator*, vacant
*Director, Tring Zoological Museum*, Mrs T. Wild

## NATIONAL MARITIME MUSEUM

Greenwich, London SE10 9NF
Tel: 020-8858 4422; Fax: 020-8312 6632

Established by Act of Parliament in 1934, the National Maritime Museum illustrates the maritime history of Great Britain in the widest sense, underlining the importance of the sea and its influence on the nation's power, wealth, culture, technology and institutions. The Museum is in three groups of buildings in Greenwich Park – the main building, the Queen's House (built by Inigo Jones, 1616–35) and the Royal Observatory (including Wren's Flamsteed House). In May 1999, a £20 million Heritage Lottery supported project opened 16 new galleries in a glazed courtyard in the Museum's west wing. Total Government grant-in-aid for 1999–2000 was £10.425 million.
*Director*, R. Clare

## NATIONAL MUSEUMS AND GALLERIES ON MERSEYSIDE

PO Box 33, 127 Dale Street, Liverpool L69 3LA
Tel: 0151-207 0001; Fax: 0151-478 4790

The Board of Trustees of the National Museums and Galleries on Merseyside is responsible for the Liverpool Museum, the Merseyside Maritime Museum (incorporating HM Customs and Excise National Museum), the Museum of Liverpool Life, the Lady Lever Art Gallery, the Walker Art Gallery and Sudley House, and the Conservation Centre. Total Government grant-in-aid for 2001–2002 is £13.6 million.
*Chairman of the Board of Trustees*, D. McDonnell
*Director*, Dr David Fleming
*Keeper of Art Galleries*, J. Treuherz
*Keeper of Conservation*, A. Durham
*Keeper, Liverpool Museum*, Ms L. Knowles
*Keeper, Merseyside Maritime Museum and Museum of Liverpool Life*, M. Stammers

## NATIONAL MUSEUMS AND GALLERIES OF WALES/AMGUEDDFEYDD AC ORIELAU CENEDLAETHOL CYMRU

Cathays Park, Cardiff CF10 3NP
Tel: 029-2039 7951; Fax: 029-2037 3219;
Email: post@nmgw.ac.uk; Web: www/nmgw.ac.uk

The National Museums and Galleries of Wales comprise the National Museum and Gallery Cardiff, the Museum of Welsh Life St Fagans, Big Pit National Museum of Wales, Blaenafon, the Roman Legionary Museum Caerleon, Turner House Gallery Penarth, the Welsh Slate Museum Llanberis, the Segontium Roman Museum Caernarfon and the Museum of the Welsh Woollen Industry Dre-fach, Felindre. Total funding from the National Assembly for Wales for 2000–2001 is £16 million.
*President*, M. C. T. Prichard, CBE
*Vice-President*, R. G. Thomas, OBE

### OFFICERS

*Director*, A. Southall
*Directors*, Dr E. William (*Collections and Education and Deputy Director*); J. Williams-Davies (*Museum of Welsh Life*); M. Tooby (*National Museum and Gallery*); R. Gwyn (*Strategic Communications*); M. Richards (*Resource Planning*)
*Keeper of Geology*, M. G. Bassett, Ph.D.
*Keeper of Bio-diversity and Systematic Biology*, Dr P. G. Oliver
*Keeper of Art*, O. Fairclough
*Keeper of Archaeology*, R. Brewer

*Manager, Roman Legionary Museum*, B. Lewis
*Keeper in Charge, Turner House Gallery*, O. Fairclough
*Keeper, Welsh Slate Museum and Segontium Roman Museum*, D. Roberts, Ph.D.
*Manager, Museum of the Welsh Woollen Industry*, S. Moss
*Manager, Big Pit National Museum of Wales*, P. Walker

## NATIONAL MUSEUMS OF SCOTLAND

Chambers Street, Edinburgh EH1 1JF
Tel: 0131-225 7534; Fax: 0131-220 4819

The National Museums of Scotland comprise the Royal Museum of Scotland, the Scottish United Services Museum, the Museum of Scottish County Life, the Museum of Flight, Shambellie House Museum of Costume and the Museum of Scotland. Total funding from the Scottish Executive for 2001–2002 is £17.0 million.

### BOARD OF TRUSTEES

*Chairman*, Sir Robert Smith, FSA Scot.
*Members*, Prof. T. Devine; Dr L. Glasser, MBE, FRSE; G. Johnston, OBE, TD; Ms C. Macaulay; N. McIntosh, CBE; Mrs N. Mahal; Prof. A. Manning, OBE; Prof. J. Murray; Sir William Purves, CBE, DSO; Dr A. Ritchie, OBE; I. Smith; The Lord Wilson of Tillyorn, GCMG

### OFFICERS

*Director*, vacant
*Acting Director*, Miss D. Idiens, FRSA, FSA Scot.
*Development Director*, C. McCallum
*Keeper of Archaeology*, D. V. Clarke, Ph.D., FSA, FSA Scot.
*Keeper of Geology and Zoology*, M. Shaw, D.Phil.
*Keeper of Social and Technological History*, G. Sprott
*Head of Public Affairs*, Ms M. Bryden
*Head of Museum Services*, S. R. Elson, FSA Scot.
*Acting Keeper of History and Applied Art*, Dr D. Caldwell, FSA

## RESOURCE: THE COUNCIL FOR MUSEUMS, ARCHIVES AND LIBRARIES

16 Queen Anne's Gate, London SW1H 9AA
Tel: 020-72733 1444; Fax: 020-72733 1404;
Web: www.resource.gov.uk

On 1 April 2000, the Museums and Galleries Commission and the Library and Information Commission merged to form Resource: The Council for Museums, Archives and Libraries. This new strategic agency will work with museums, libraries and archives across the UK.
*Chairman*, Lord Evans
*Chief Executive*, N. Mackay
*Board Members*, L. Grossman; V. Gray; M. Wood; A. Chowdhury; Dr M. Crozier; V. Griffiths; N. Hodgson; M. Jones; N. MacGregor; E. J. Ryder; M. Stevenson; Prof. L. Young; A. Watkin; D. Barrie

## ROYAL AIR FORCE MUSEUM

Grahame Park Way, London NW9 5LL
Tel: 020-8205 2266; Fax: 020-8200 1751

Situated on the former airfield at RAF Hendon, the Museum illustrates the development of aviation from before the Wright brothers to the present-day RAF. Total Government grant-in-aid for 2001–2002, including funding for the aerospace museum at Cosford, is £5.245 million.
*Director*, Dr M. A. Fopp
*Assistant Directors*, H. Hall; A. Wright
*Senior Keeper*, P. Elliott

## THE SCIENCE MUSEUM

Exhibition Road, London SW7 2DD
Tel: 0870 870 4868; Fax: 020-7942 4447

The Science Museum, part of the National Museum of Science and Industry, houses the national collections of science, technology, industry and medicine. The Museum began as the science collection of the South Kensington Museum and first opened in 1857. In 1883 it acquired the collections of the Patent Museum and in 1909 the science collections were transferred to the new Science Museum, leaving the art collections with the Victoria and Albert Museum. The Wellcome Wing was opened in July 2000.

Some of the Museum's commercial aircraft, agricultural machinery, and road and rail transport collections are at Wroughton, Wilts. The National Museum of Science and Industry also incorporates the National Railway Museum, York and the National Museum of Photography, Film and Television, Bradford.

Total Government grant-in-aid for 2000–1 was £24,329 million.

### BOARD OF TRUSTEES

*Chairman*, Sir Peter Williams, CBE, Ph.D., FREng.
*Members*, HRH The Duke of Kent, KG, GCMG, GCVO, ADC; Dr M. Archer; Prof. Anne Dowling; G. Dyke; Prof. Susan Greenfield; Dr Ann Grocock; Mrs A. Higham, OBE; Mrs J. Kennedy, OBE; Dr N. Myhrvold; Dame Bridget Ogilvie, DBE; The Lord Puttnam, CBE; Sir Michael Quinlan, GCB; D. E. Rayner, CBE; Prof. M. Richards; M. G. Smith; Sir Christopher Wates

### OFFICERS

*Director*, Dr. L. Sharp
*Head of Personnel and Legal Services*, A. Mather
*Head of Finance*, Ms A. Caine
*Head of Information Systems*, S. Gordon
*Head of Estates*, J. Bevin
*Assistant Director and Head of Collections Division*, D. Swade
*Head of Physical Sciences and Engineering Group (acting)*, Dr A. Q. Morton
*Head of Life and Communications Technologies Group*, Dr R. F. Bud
*Head of Collections Management Group*, Dr S. Keene
*Assistant Director and Head of Public Affairs Division*, C. M. Pemberton
*Head of Corporate Relations*, F. Kirk
*Head of Commercial Development*, M. Sullivan
*Head of Marketing and Communications*, R. Hopson
*Head of Wellcome Wing Commercial and Access*, B. Jones
*Assistant Director, Wellcome Wing Project Director and Head of Science Communication Division*, Prof. J. R. Durant
*Head of Education and Programmes*, Dr R. Jackson
*Head of Exhibition and Wellcome Wing Content*, Dr G. Farmelo
*Head of Design*, T. Molloy
*Head of National Railway Museum*, A. Scott
*Head of National Museum of Photography, Film and Television*, Ms A. Nevill

## VICTORIA AND ALBERT MUSEUM

Cromwell Road, London SW7 2RL
Tel: 020-7942 2000

The Victoria and Albert Museum is the national museum of fine and applied art and design. It descends directly from the Museum of Manufactures, which opened in Marlborough House in 1852 after the Great Exhibition of 1851. The Museum was moved in 1857 to become part of the South Kensington Museum. It was renamed the Victoria and Albert Museum in 1899. It also houses the National Art Library and Print Room.

The Museum administers three branch museums: the National Museum of Childhood in Bethnal Green, the Theatre Museum in Covent Garden, and the Wellington Museum at Apsley House. The museum in Bethnal Green was opened in 1872 and the building is the most important surviving example of the type of glass and iron construction used by Paxton for the Great Exhibition. Total Government grant-in-aid for 2001–2002 is £32.387 million.

BOARD OF TRUSTEES

*Chairman*, Paula Ridley
*Deputy Chairman*, J. Scott, CBE, FSA
*Members*, Prof M. Buck; Penelope, Viscountess Cobham; R. Dickins CBE; Sir Christopher Frayling, Ph.D.; Sir Terence Heiser, GCB; Mrs J. Gordon Clark; Mrs A. Heseltine; R. Mather; P. Rogers; A. Snow; Sir Christopher White, CVO, FBA
*Acting Secretary to the Board of Trustees*, J.F.Rider

OFFICERS

*Director*, M. Jones, MA
*Assistant Director*, J. W. Close
*Senior Chief Curator*, Dr D. Swallow
*Chief Curator, Ceramics and Glass*, Dr O. Watson
*Director of Collections*, vacant
*Director of Collections Services*, vacant
*Head of Conservation*, Dr J. Ashley-Smith
*Director of Corporate Communications*, vacant
*Director of Development*, Mrs L. Blythe
*Director of Facilities Management*, vacant
*Chief Curator, Far Eastern*, Miss R. Kerr
*Director of Finance and Central Services*, Miss R. M. Sykes
*Chief Curator, Furniture and Woodwork*, C. Wilk
*Chief Curator, Indian and South-East Asian*, R. Crill
*Head of Information Systems Services*, I. Croxford
*Director of Learning and Visitor Services*, D. Anderson, OBE
*Director of Major Projects*, Mrs G. F. Miles
*Chief Curator, Metalwork, Silver and Jewellery*, vacant
*Chief Librarian, National Art Library*, vacant
*Director of Personnel*, Mrs G. Henchley
*Chief Curator, Prints, Drawings and Paintings*, Miss S. B. Lambert
*Head of Records and Collections Services*, A. Seal
*Acting Head of Research*, C. Sargentson
*Chief Curator, Sculpture*, Dr P. E. D. Williamson
*Acting Chief Curator, Textiles and Dress*, L. Parry
*Managing Director, V. and A. Enterprises Ltd*, M. Cass
*Director of the National Museum of Childhood*, Ms D. Lees
*Director of the Theatre Museum*, Miss M. Benton
*Director of the Wellington Museum*, Miss A. Robinson

---

## NATIONAL AUDIT OFFICE

157–197 Buckingham Palace Road, London SW1W 9SP
Tel: 020-7798 7000; Fax: 020-7828 3774
Audit House, 23–24 Park Place, Cardiff CF1 3BA
Tel: 02920-378661; Fax: 02920 678501;
Email: enqiries@nao.gsi.gov.uk
Web: www.nao.gov.uk

---

The National Audit Office came into existence under the National Audit Act 1983 to replace and continue the work of the former Exchequer and Audit Department. The Act reinforced the Office's total financial and operational independence from the Government and brought its head, the Comptroller and Auditor-General, into a closer relationship with Parliament as an officer of the House of Commons.

The National Audit Office provides independent information, advice and assurance to Parliament and the public about all aspects of the financial operations of Government departments and many other bodies receiving public funds. It does this by examining and certifying the accounts of these organisations and by regularly publishing reports to Parliament on the results of its value for money investigations of the economy, efficiency and effectiveness with which public resources have been used. The National Audit Office is also the auditor by agreement of the accounts of certain international and other organisations. In addition, the Office authorises the issue of public funds to Government departments.

*Comptroller and Auditor-General*, Sir John Bourn, KCB
*Private Secretary*, M. Davies
*Deputy Comptroller and Auditor-General*, T. Burr
*Deputy Auditor-General*, M. C. Pfleger
*Assistant Auditors-General*, J. Colman; J. Marshall; Miss C. Mawhood; M. Sinclair; Ms W. Kenway-Smith

---

## NATIONAL CONSUMER COUNCIL

20 Grosvenor Gardens, London SW1W 0DH
Tel: 020-7730 3469; Fax: 020-7730 0191;
Web: www.ncc.org.uk

---

The National Consumer Council (NCC) was set up by the Government in 1975 to give an independent voice to consumers in the UK. Its role is to advocate the consumer interest to decision-makers in national and local government, industry and regulatory bodies, business and the professions. It does this through a combination of research and campaigning. NCC is a non-profit making company limited by guarantee and is largely funded by grant-in-aid from the Department of Trade and Industry.

*Chairman*, D. Hutton, CBE
*Director*, Ms A. Bradley

---

## NATIONAL ENDOWMENT FOR SCIENCE, TECHNOLOGY AND THE ARTS (NESTA)

Fishmongers' Chambers, 110 Upper Thames Street, London EC4R 3TW Tel: 020-7645 9500;
Fax: 020-7645 9501

---

The National Endowment for Science, Technology and the Arts (NESTA) was established under the National Lottery Act 1998 with a £200 million endowment from the proceeds of the National Lottery. Its aims are to help talented individuals; to enable innovative ideas to be successfully commercially exploited; and to promote public knowledge of science, technology and the arts.

*Chairman*, The Lord Puttnam, CBE
*Trustees*, Dame Bridget Ogilvie, DBE; Prof. Sir Martin Rees, FRS; Dr C. Evans, OBE; Ms C. Vorderman; D. Wardell; F. Matarasso; The Baroness McIntosh of Hudnall; Ms C. McKeever; Ms J. Kirkpatrick; Ms S. Hunter; D. Alexander; D. Wanless
*Chief Executive*, J. Newton

## NATIONAL HERITAGE MEMORIAL FUND

7 Holbein Place, London SW1W 8NR
Tel: 020-7591 6000; Fax: 020-7591 6001

The National Heritage Memorial Fund is an independent body established in 1980 as a memorial to those who have died for the UK. The Fund is empowered by the National Heritage Act 1980 to give financial assistance towards the cost of acquiring, maintaining or preserving land, buildings, works of art and other objects of outstanding interest which are also of importance to the national heritage. The Fund is administered by 13 trustees who are appointed by the Prime Minister.

The National Lottery Act 1993 designated the Fund as distributor of the heritage share of proceeds from the National Lottery. As a result, the Fund now operates two funds: the Heritage Memorial Fund and the Heritage Lottery Fund. The Heritage Memorial Fund receives an annual grant from the Department for Culture, Media and Sport; the grant for 2000 - 2001 is £5 million.

*Chairman*, L. Forgan
*Trustees*, Prof. C. Baines; R. Boas; N. Dodd; Sir Angus Grossart; G. Waterfield; Mrs P. Lankester; P. Wilson; S. Palmer; Earl of Dalkeith; Prof. T. Pritchard; Ms M. A. Sieghart; J. Wright
*Director*, Ms A. Case

## NATIONAL INVESTMENT AND LOANS OFFICE

1 King Charles Street, London SW1A 2AP
Tel: 020-7270 3861; Fax: 020-7270 3860

The National Investment and Loans Office is a non-ministerial Government department which was set up in 1980 by the merger of the National Debt Office and the Public Works Loan Board. The Office provides the staff and administrative support for the National Debt Commissioners, the Public Works Loan Commissioners and the Office of HM Paymaster-General. The National Debt Office is responsible for managing the investment portfolios of certain public funds and the management of some residual operations relating to the national debt. The function of the Public Works Loan Board is to make loans from the National Loans Fund to local authorities and certain other statutory bodies, primarily for capital purposes.

The Office of HM Paymaster-General has continuously existed in its present form since 1836; the Paymaster-General has responsibilities assigned from time to time by the Prime Minister and is currently a Treasury minister. The Assistant Paymaster-General is responsible for the banking and financial information services provided to the Government and public sector bodies by the Office of HM Paymaster-General.

*Director*, I. Peattie
*Establishment Officer*, D. Hockey

### NATIONAL DEBT OFFICE

020-7270 3868

*Comptroller-General*, Ian Peattie

### PUBLIC WORKS LOAN BOARD

020-7270 3874

*Chairman*, A. D. Loehnis, CMG
*Deputy Chairman*, Miss V. J. Di Palma, OBE
*Other Commissioners*, Mrs R. V. Hale; J. A. Parkes, CBE; B. Tanner, CBE; Mrs R. Terry; D. W. Midgley; L. M. Nippers; Mrs S. Wood
*Secretary*, Ian Peattie
*Assistant Secretary*, M. Frankel

### OFFICE OF HM PAYMASTER-GENERAL

020-7270 6074

*Paymaster-General*, Dawn Primarolo, MP
*Assistant Paymaster-General*, I. Peattie
*Head of Banking*, L. Palmer
*Banking Manager*, P. Harris

## NATIONAL LOTTERY COMMISSION

2 Monck Street, London SW1P 2BQ
Tel: 020-7227 2000; Fax: 020-7227 2005;
Web: www.natlotcomm.gov.uk

The National Lottery Commission replaced the Office of the National Lottery (OFLOT) in April 1999 under the National Lottery Act 1998. The Commission is responsible for the granting, varying and enforcing of licences to run the National Lottery. Its duties are to ensure that the National Lottery is run with all due propriety, that the interests of players are protected, and, subject to these two objectives, that returns to the 'good causes' are maximised.

*Chairman*, Lord Terry Burns
*Commissioners*, Ms H. Spicer; B. Pomeroy; R. Gilmore; T. Horwsby
*Chief Executive*, M. Harris
*Director of Licensing*, K. Jones
*Director of Compliance and Resources*, Ms M. Phillips

*See also* Lotteries and Gaming section

## NATIONAL PHYSICAL LABORATORY

Queens Road, Teddington, Middx TW11 0LW
Tel: 020-8977 3222; Fax: 020-8943 6458

The Laboratory is the UK's national standards laboratory. It develops, maintains and disseminates national measurement standards for physical quantities such as mass, length, time, temperature, voltage, force and pressure. It also conducts underpinning research on engineering materials and information technology and disseminates good measurement practice. It is Government-owned but contractor-operated.

*Managing Director*, Dr R. McGuiness
*Director of Marketing and Knowledge Transfer*, D. C. Richardson

## NATIONAL RADIOLOGICAL PROTECTION BOARD

Chilton, Didcot, Oxon OX11 0RQ
Tel: 01235-831600; Fax: 01235-833891;
Web: www.nrpb.org.uk

The National Radiological Protection Board is an independent statutory body created by the Radiological Protection Act 1970. It is the national point of authoritative reference on radiological protection for both ionising and non-ionising radiations, and has issued recommendations on limiting human exposure to electromagnetic fields and radiation from a range of sources,

including X-rays, the Sun, base stations and mobile phones. Its sponsoring department is the Department of Health.
*Chairman*, Sir Walter Bodmer, Ph.D., FRCPath., FRS
*Director*, Prof. R. H. Clarke

---

NATIONAL SAVINGS
375 Kensington High Street, London W14 8SD
Tel: 020-7348 9200; Fax: 020-7048 9755;
Web: www.nationalsavings.co.uk

---

National Savings was established as a Government department in 1969. It became an executive agency of the Treasury in 1996 and is responsible for the design, marketing and administration of savings and investment products for personal savers and investors. In April 1999 Siemens Business Services took over all the back office functions at National Savings.
*Chief Executive*, P. Bareau
*Personnel Director*, D. S. Speedie
*Finance Director*, T. Bayley
*Commercial Director*, W. Cattanach
*Sourcing Director*, Ms J. Bevan

For details of schemes, *see* National Savings section

---

NEW OPPORTUNITIES FUND
Heron House, 322 High Holborn, London WC1V 7PW Tel: 020-7211 1800; Fax: 020-7211 1750;
Email: enquiries@nof.org.uk; Web: www.nof.org.uk

---

The New Opportunities Fund is a Lottery Distributor created to distribute grants to health, education and environment projects across the UK. The New Opportunities Fund intends to fund projects that will improve people's quality of life, address the needs of those people who are most disadvantaged in society, encourage community participation and complement relevent local and national strategies and programmes.
*Chair of the Board*, The Baroness Pitkeathley
*Members of the Board*, Ms J. Barrow; Prof. E. Bolton, CB; Ms N. Clarke; Prof. A. Patmore, CBE; D. Mackie; D. Campbell; Prof. S. Griffiths; Prof. B. Gaad
*Chief Executive*, S. Dunmore

---

NORTHERN IRELAND AUDIT OFFICE
106 University Street, Belfast BT7 1EU
Tel: 02890-251000; Fax: 02890-251106

---

The primary aim of the Northern Ireland Audit Office is to provide independent assurance, information and advice to the Northern Ireland Assembly on the proper accounting for Northern Ireland departmental and certain other public expenditure, revenue, assets and liabilities; on regularity and propriety; and on the economy, efficiency and effectiveness of the use of resources.
*Comptroller and Auditor-General for Northern Ireland*, J. M. Dowdall

---

NORTHERN IRELAND HUMAN RIGHTS COMMISSION
Temple Court, 39–41 North Street, Belfast BT1 1NA
Tel: 028-9024 3987; Fax: 028-9024 7844;
Email: nihrc@belfast.org.uk; Web: www.nihrc.org

---

The Northern Ireland Human Rights Commission was set up in March 1999. Its main functions are to keep under review the law and practice relating to human rights in Northern Ireland, to advise the Government and to promote an awareness of human rights in Northern Ireland. It can also take cases to court.The Commission currently consists of one full-time commissioner and eight part-time commissioners, all appointed by the Secretary of State for Northern Ireland.
*Chief Commissioner* (£57,500), Prof. B. Dickson
*Commissioners* (£8,000 each), Prof. C. Bell; Ms M-A. Dinsmore, QC; T. Donnelly, MBE; The Revd H. Good, OBE; Prof. T. Hadden; Ms P. Kelly; Ms I. McCormack; F. McGuinness

---

OCCUPATIONAL PENSIONS REGULATORY AUTHORITY
Invicta House, Trafalgar Place, Brighton BN1 4DW
Tel: 01273-627600; Fax: 01273-627760;
Email: helpdesk@opra.gov.uk

---

The Occupational Pensions Regulatory Authority (OPRA) was set up under the Pensions Act 1995 and became fully operational on 6 April 1997. It is the independent, statutory regulator of occupational and stakeholder pension schemes in the UK.
*Chairman*, H. Maunsell, OBE
*Chief Executive*, Mrs C. Instance

---

OFFICE FOR NATIONAL STATISTICS
1 Drummond Gate, London SW1V 2QQ
Tel: 020-7533 5888; Email: info@statistics.gov.uk;
Web: www.statistics.gov.uk

---

The Office for National Statistics was created in 1996 by the merger of the Central Statistical Office and the Office of PopulationCensuses and Surveys. It is both a government department and an executive agency of the Treasury and is responsible for preparing and interpreting key economic statistics for Government policy; collecting and publishing business statistics; publishing annual and monthly statistical digests; providing researchers, analysts and other customers with a statistical service; administration of the marriage laws and local registration of births, marriages and deaths in England and Wales; provision of population estimates and projections and statistics on health and other demographic matters in England and Wales; population censuses in England and Wales; surveys for Government departments and public bodies; and promoting these functions within the UK, the European Union and internationally to provide a statistical service to meet European Union and international requirements.

Following the publication of the White Paper, 'Building Trust in Statistics', National Statistics was launched in June 2000. Headed by the National Statistician, with an independent Statistics Commission, providing assurance to Parliament about the integrity of official statistics and statistical practice. The National Statistics brand encompasses the output of the ONS, plus many of the key public interest statistics produced by other Government departments.

*National Statistician, Registrar General for England and Wales and the Head of the Government Statistical Service*, L. Cook
*Directors*, Ms S. Linacre (*Method and Quality*); J. Kidgell (*Economic Statistics*); K. Drunnell (*Social Statistics*); J. Pullinger (*Information Age Access Project*); P. Walton (*Business Change*)
*Principal Establishment Officer*, E. Williams
*Head of Communication*, Ms H. Rafalowska
*Parliamentary Clerk*, J. Bailey

FAMILY RECORDS CENTRE, 1 Myddelton Street, London EC1R 1UW. Tel: 020-8392 5300

## OFFICE FOR STANDARDS IN EDUCATION (OFSTED)

Alexandra House, 33 Kingsway, London WC2B 6SE
Tel: 020-7421 6800; Fax: 020-7421 6707

OFSTED is a non-ministerial Government department established under the Education (Schools Act) 1992 to keep the Secretary of State and the public informed about the standards and management of schools in England, and to establish and monitor an independent inspection system for maintained schools in England. Its inspection role also includes the inspection of local education authorities, teacher training institutions, youth work and funded education. Its staff include HMI, who draw on inspection evidence to report on good practice in schools and on a wide range of educational issues.

*See also* Education section.

*HM Chief Inspector*, M. J.Tomlinson, CBE
*Directors of Inspection*, D. Taylor; E. Passmore
*Director of Policy, Planning and Resources*, J. M. Phillips, CBE
*Director of Early Years*, M. Smith
*Director of Finance*, P. Jolly
*Director of Corporate Services*, R. Knight

DIVISION MANAGERS

*Personnel Management*, A. White
*Contracts*, C. Bramley
*Communications, Media and Public Relations*, J. Lawson
*Information Systems*, M. Worthy
*Administrative Support and Estate Management*, K. Francis
*Early Years Inspection Quality*, D. Bradley
*Inspection Quality*, P. Matthews
*LEA Inspections*, D. Singleton
*School Improvement*, K. Cross
*Primary*, K. Lloyd
*Secondary*, M. Raleigh
*Curriculum Advice and Inspection*, B. McCafferty
*Post-Compulsory*, S. Grix
*Special Educational Needs*, C. Marshall
*Research, Analysis and International*, G. Goodwin
*Teacher Education*, C. Gould
*Nursery Education Scheme*, D. Bradley
There are about 200 HM Inspectors

## OFFICE FOR THE REGULATION OF ELECTRICITY AND GAS

Brookmount Buildings, 42 Fountain Street, Belfast BT1 5EE Tel: 028-9031 1575 (*Electricity*); 028-9031 4212 (*Gas*); Fax: 028-9031 1740;
Email: ofreg@nics.gov.uk;
Web: www.ofreg.nics.gov.uk

The Office for the Regulation of Electricity and Gas (OFREG) is the combined regulatory body for the electricity and gas supply industries in Northern Ireland.
*Director-General of Electricity Supply and Director-General of Gas for Northern Ireland*, D. B. McIldoon

## OFFICE OF GAS AND ELECTRICITY MARKETS

9 Millbank, London, SW1P 3GE.
Tel: 020-7901 7000; Fax: 020-7901 7066
SCOTLAND: Regent Court, 70 West Regent Street, Glasgow G2 2QZ
Tel: 0141-331 2678; Fax: 0141-331 2777

The Office of Gas and Electricity Markets (Ofgem) regulates the gas and electricity industries in England, Scotland and Wales. Ofgem's aim is to bring choice and value to all gas and electricity customers by prompting competition and regulating monopolies. Ofgem is governed by an authority and its powers are provided for under the Gas Act 1986, the Electricity Act 1989 and the Utilities Act 2000.
*Chief Executive*, C. McCarthy
*Managing Directors*, J. Neilson (*Customers and Supply*); Dr Marshall, CBE (*Competition and Trading Arrangements*); R. Ramsay (*Regulation and Financial Affairs*); C. Coulthard (*Scotland*)
*Chief Operating Officer*, Ms G. Whittington

## OFFICE OF FAIR TRADING

Fleetbank House, 2–6 Salisbury Square, London EC4Y 8JX Tel: 020-7211 8000; Fax: 020-7211 8800

The Office of Fair Trading is a non-ministerial Government department headed by the Director-General of Fair Trading. It keeps commercial activities in the UK under review and seeks to protect consumers against unfair trading practices. The Director-General's consumer protection duties under the Fair Trading Act 1973, together with his responsibilities under the Consumer Credit Act 1974, the Estate Agents Act 1979, the Control of Misleading Advertisements Regulations 1988, and the Unfair Terms in Consumer Contracts Regulations 1999, are administered by the Office's Consumer Affairs Division. The Competition Policy Division is concerned with monopolies and mergers (under the Fair Trading Act 1973) and the Director-General's other responsibilities for competition matters, including those under the Competition Act 1998, the Financial Services Act 1986 and the Broadcasting Act 1990. The Office is the UK competent authority on the application of the European Commission's competition rules, and also liaises with the Commission on consumer protection initiatives.
*Director-General*, J. Vickers

CONSUMER AFFAIRS DIVISION
*Director* (*G3*), Miss C. Banks
*Branch Directors* (*G5*), R. Watson; M. Graham; D. Wray

COMPETITION POLICY DIVISION
*Divisional Director (G3)*, Mrs M. J. Bloom
*Branch Directors (G5)*, A. J. White; A. Walker-Smith; E. L. Whitehorn; S. Wood; Dr D. Mason; Dr G. Davis; A. Williams
*Chief Economist*, vacant

LEGAL DIVISION
*Divisional Director (G3)*, Miss P. Edwards
*Branch Directors (G5)*, M. A. Khan; S. Brindley
*Establishment and Finance Officer (G5)*, Mrs R. Heyhoe
*Chief Information Officer (G6)*, M. Ricketts

COMMUNICATIONS DIVISION
*Director of Communications (Chief Information Officer) (G5)*, M. Ricketts

RESOURCES AND SERVICES
*Director of Resources and Services (Chief Establishment and Finance Officer) (G5)*, D. Fisher

---

## OFFICE OF MANPOWER ECONOMICS
Oxford House, 76 Oxford Street, London W1N 9FD
Tel: 020-7467 7244; Fax: 020-7467 7248

---

The Office of Manpower Economics was set up in 1971. It is an independent non-statutory organisation which is responsible for servicing independent review bodies which advise on the pay of various public service groups, the Pharmacists Review Panel and the Police Negotiating Board. The Office is also responsible for servicing *ad hoc* bodies of inquiry and for undertaking research into pay and associated matters as requested by the Government.
*OME Director*, M. J. Horsman
*Director, Health Secretariat, and OME Deputy Director*, G. S. Charles
*Director, Armed Forces' Secretariat*, C. Haworth
*Director, Senior Salaries and Police Negotiating Board Secretariat*, Ms R. McCarthy-Ward
*Director, School Teachers' Secretariat*, Mrs E. M. Melling
*Director, Prison Service Secretariat*, M. C. Cahill
*Press Liaison Officer*, C. P. Jordan

---

## OFFICE OF TELECOMMUNICATIONS (OFTEL)
50 Ludgate Hill, London EC4M 7JJ
Tel: 020-7634 8700; Fax: 020-7 634 8943;
Web: www.oftel.gov.uk

---

The Office of Telecommunications (Oftel) is the regulator, or 'watchdog', for the UK telecommunications industry. Oftel is a Government department but is independent of ministerial control. Oftel's aim is for customers to get the best deal in terms of quality, choice and value for money. Its strategy to achieve this goal is through four objectives: effective competition benefiting consumers; well informed consumers; adequately protected consumers; and prevention of significant anti-competitive practice. Oftel is responsible for ensuring that holders of telecommunications licences comply with their licence conditions, and has powers under the Competition Act 1999 to deal with anti-competitive practices and cartels. The Director-General has a duty to consider all reasonable complaints about telecommunications services.

Oftel, is one of the first regulators, along with the Independent Television Commission, the Broadcast Standards Council, the Radio Authority and the Radio Communications Agency that under Government plans will merge to become the Office of Communication, the new regulator for the communications sector.
*Director-General*, D. Edmonds
*Director of Operations*, Miss A. Lambert
*Director of Regulatory Policy*, C. Kenny
*Director of Compliance*, K. Long
*Director of Technology*, P. Walker
*Director of Strategy and Forecasting*, A. Bell
*Director of Business Support*, D. Smith
*Director of Communications*, D. Stroud

---

## OFFICE OF THE LEGAL SERVICES OMBUDSMAN
22 Oxford Court, Oxford Street, Manchester M2 3WQ Tel: 0845 601 0794; Fax: 0161-236 2651;
Email: enquiries.olso@gtnet.gov.uk

---

The Legal Services Ombudsman is appointed by the Lord Chancellor under the Courts and Legal Services Act 1990 to oversee the handling of complaints against solicitors, barristers, licensed conveyancers, legal executives and patent agents by their professional bodies. A complainant must first complain to the relevant professional body before raising the matter with the Ombudsman. The Ombudsman is independent of the legal profession and her services are free of charge.
*Legal Services Ombudsman*, Ms A. Abraham
*Secretary Manager*, S. D. Entwistle

### OFFICE OF THE SCOTTISH LEGAL SERVICES OMBUDSMAN
17 Waterloo Place, Edinburgh, EH1 3DL
Tel: 0131-244 3055; Fax: 0131-244 3065;
Email: Ombudsman@slso.org.uk; Web: www.slso.org.uk

The Ombudsman is appointed by Scottish Ministers, and cannot be a lawyer.
*Scottish Legal Services Ombudsman*, Ms L. Costelloe Baker

---

## OFFICE OF THE LORD ADVOCATE
Crown Office, 25 Chambers Street, Edinburgh EH1 1LA Tel: 0131-226 2626; Fax: 0131-226 6910

---

The Law Officers for Scotland are the Lord Advocate and the Solicitor-General for Scotland.
*Lord Advocate*, The Rt. Hon. Colin Boyd, QC
*Solicitor-General for Scotland*, Neil F. Davidson, QC
*Private Secretary to the Law Officers*, J. Gibbons

---

## OFFICE OF THE PARLIAMENTARY COMMISSIONER FOR ADMINISTRATION AND HEALTH SERVICE COMMISSIONER
Millbank Tower, Millbank, London SW1P 4QP
Tel: 0845-015 4033; Fax: 020-7217 4000
Web: www.ombudsman.org.uk

---

The Parliamentary Commissioner for Administration (the Parliamentary Ombudsman) is independent of Government and is an officer of Parliament. He is responsible for investigating complaints referred to him by MPs from members of the public who claim to have sustained injustice in consequence of maladministration by or on behalf of Government departments and certain non-departmental public bodies. In March 1999 an additional 158 public bodies were brought within the jurisdiction of the Parliamentary Commissioner. Certain types of action by Government departments or bodies are excluded from investigation. The Parliamentary Commissioner is also responsible for investigating complaints, referred by MPs, alleging that access to official information has been wrongly refused under the Code of Practice on Access to Government Information 1994.

The Health Service Commissioners (the Health Service Ombudsmen) for England, for Scotland and for Wales are responsible for investigating complaints against National Health Service authorities and trusts that are not dealt with by those authorities to the satisfaction of the complainant. Complaints can be referred direct by the member of the public who claims to have sustained injustice or hardship in consequence of the failure in a service provided by a relevant body, failure of that body to provide a service or in consequence of any other action by that body. The Ombudsmens' jurisdiction now covers complaints about family doctors, dentists, pharmacists and opticians, and complaints about actions resulting from clinical judgement.

The Health Service Ombudsmen are also responsible for investigating complaints that information has been wrongly refused under the Code of Practice on Openness in the National Health Service 1995. The three offices are presently held by the Parliamentary Commissioner.

*Parliamentary Commissioner and Health Service Commissioner* (*G1*), M. S. Buckley
*Deputy Parliamentary Commissioner* (*G3*), A. Watson
*Deputy Health Service Commissioner* (*G3*), Ms H. Scott
*Directors, Parliamentary Commissioner* (*G5*), G. Monk; D. Reynolds; Ms C. Corrigan;
*Directors, Health Service Commissioners* (*G5*), Ms H. Bainbridge; N. J. Jordan; D. R. G. Pinchin; L. Charlton
*Finance and Establishment Officer* (*G5*), J. Stevens

For Scotland, *see* Scottish Parliamentary Commissioner for Administration

For Wales, *see* Welsh Administration Ombudsman

## OFFICE OF THE PENSIONS OMBUDSMAN

6th Floor, 11 Belgrave Road, London SW1V 1RB
Tel: 020-7834 9144; Fax: 020-7821 0065

The Pensions Ombudsman is appointed under the Pension Schemes Act 1993 as amended by the Pensions Act 1995. He investigates and decides complaints and disputes concerning occupational pension schemes. Complaints concerning personal pensions would normally be dealt with only if outside the jurisdiction of the Personal Investment Authority. The Ombudsman is completely independent and there is no charge for bringing a complaint or dispute to him.

*Pensions Ombudsman*, Dr J. T. Farrand, QC

## OFFICE OF THE RAIL REGULATOR

1 Waterhouse Square, 138–142 Holborn, London EC1N 2TQ Tel: 020-7282 2000; Fax: 020-7282 2047;
Email: orr@dial.pipex.com;
Web: www.rail-reg.gov.uk

The Office of the Rail Regulator was set up under the Railways Act 1993. The Regulator's main functions are the licensing of operators of railway assets; the approval of agreements for access by those operators to track, stations and light maintenance depots; the enforcement of domestic competition law; and consumer protection. The Rail Regulator will become subject to strategic guidance from the Secretary of State.

*Rail Regulator*, T. Winsor
*Director of Strategy Planning and Communications*, K. Webb
*Director of Network Regulation*, M. Beswick
*Director of Access, Competition and Licensing*, S. Gooding
*Chief Economist and Director of Economics and Finance*, T. Martin
*Chief Legal Adviser and Director of Legal Services*, S. Barrett-Williams

## OFFICE OF WATER SERVICES

Centre City Tower, 7 Hill Street, Birmingham B5 4UA Tel: 0121-625 1300; Fax: 0121-625 1400;
Email: enquiries@ofwat.gsi.gov.uk;
Web: www.ofwat.gov.uk

The Office of Water Services (Ofwat) was set up under the Water Act 1989 and is a non-ministerial Government department headed by the Director-General of Water Services. It is the independent economic regulator of the water and sewerage companies in England and Wales. Ofwat's main duties are to ensure that the companies can finance and carry out the functions specified in the Water Industry Act 1991 and to protect the interests of water customers. There are ten regional customer service committees which are concerned solely with the interests of water customers. Representation of customer interests at national level is the responsibility of the Ofwat National Customer Council (ONCC).

*Director-General of Water Services*, P. Fletcher
*Chairman, Ofwat National Customer Council*, M. Terry

## OMBUDSMEN

— *see* Local Commissioners *and* Parliamentary Commissioner. For non-statutory Ombudsmen, *see* Index

## ORDNANCE SURVEY

Romsey Road, Maybush, Southampton SO16 4GU
Tel: 023-8079 2000; Fax: 023-8079 2615

Ordnance Survey is the national mapping agency for Britain. It is a Government department and executive agency operating as a Trading Fund and reporting to the Secretary of State for Transport, Local Government and the Regions.

*Director-General and Chief Executive*, Ms V. Lawrence

## PARADES COMMISSION

12th Floor, Windsor House, 6–12 Bedford Street, Belfast BT2 7EL
Tel: 029-9054 8900; Fax: 029-9032 2988

The Parades Commission was set up under the Public Processions (Northern Ireland) Act 1998. Its function is to encourage and facilitate local accommodation on contentious parades; where this is not possible, the Commission is empowered to make legal determinations about such parades, which may include imposing conditions on aspects of the notified parade.

The chairman and members are appointed by the Secretary of State for Northern Ireland; the membership must, as far as is practicable, be representative of the community in Northern Ireland.
*Chairman*, A. J. Holland
*Members*, J. Cousins; Revd R. Magee; W. Martin; P. Osborne; Sir J. Pringle; P. Quinn
*Secretary (G5)*, A. Elliott

## PARLIAMENTARY COMMISSIONER FOR STANDARDS

House of Commons, London SW1A 0AA
Tel: 020-7219 0320

Following recommendations of the Committee on Standards in Public Life, the House of Commons agreed to the appointment of an independent Parliamentary Commissioner for Standards with effect from November 1995. The Commissioner has responsibility for maintaining and monitoring the operation of the Register of Members' Interests; advising Members of Parliament and the Select Committee on Sandards and Privileges, on the interpretation of the rules on disclosure and advocacy, and on other questions of propriety; and receiving and, if she thinks fit, investigating complaints about the conduct of MPs.
*Parliamentary Commissioner for Standards*, Ms E. Filkin

## PARLIAMENTARY COUNSEL

36 Whitehall, London SW1A 2AY
Tel: 020-7210 6611; Fax: 020-7210 6632

Parliamentary Counsel draft all Government bills (i.e. primary legislation) except those relating exclusively to Scotland. They also advise on all aspects of parliamentary procedure in connection with such bills and draft Government amendments to them as well as any motions (including financial resolutions) necessary to secure their introduction into, and passage through, Parliament.
*First Counsel (SCS)*, E. G. Caldwell, CB
*Counsel (SCS)*, E. G. Bowman, CB; G. B. Sellers, CB; E. R. Sutherland, CB; P. F. A. Knowles, CB; S. C. Laws, CB; R. S. Parker, CB; Miss C. E. Johnston, CB; P. J. Davies, CB; J. M. Sellers

## PAROLE BOARD FOR ENGLAND AND WALES

Abell House, John Islip Street, London SW1P 4LH
Tel: 020-7217 5314; Fax: 020-7217 5793;
Email: info@paroleboard.gov.uk
Web: www.paroleboard.gov.uk

The Board was constituted under the Criminal Justice Act 1967 and continued under the Criminal Justice Act 1991. It is an executive non-departmental public body and its duty is to advise the Home Secretary with respect to matters referred to it by him which are connected with the early release or recall of prisoners. Its functions include giving directions concerning the release on licence of prisoners serving discretionary life sentences and of certain prisoners serving long-term determinate sentences.
*Chairman*, D. Hatch, CBE
*Vice-Chairman*, The Hon. Mr Justice Scott Baker
*Chief Executive*, J. Casey

## PAROLE BOARD FOR SCOTLAND

Saughton House, Broomhouse Drive, Edinburgh EH11 3XD Tel: 0131-244 8755; Fax: 0131-244 69740

The Board directs and advises the Scottish Minister on the release of prisoners on licence, and related matters.
*Chairman*, Dr J. J. McManus
*Vice-Chairman*, H. Hyslop
*Secretary*, H. P. Boyle

## PATENT OFFICE

Concept House, Cardiff Road, Newport NP10 8QQ
Tel: 0845-9500505; Fax: 01633-814444;
Email: enquiries@patent.gov.uk
Web: www.patent.gov.uk

The Patent Office is an executive agency of the Department of Trade and Industry. The duties of the Patent Office are to administer the Patent Acts, the Registered Designs Act and the Trade Marks Act, and to deal with questions relating to the Copyright, Designs and Patents Act 1988. The Search and Advisory Service carries out commercial searches through patent information.
*Comptroller-General*, Ms A. Brimelow
*Director, Intellectual Property Policy Directorate*, G. Jenkins
*Director, Patents and Designs*, R. J. Marchant
*Director and Assistant Registrar of Trade Marks*, P. Lawrence
*Director, Administration and Resources and Secretary to the Patent Office*, C. Clancy
*Director, Copyright*, A. Murphy
*Director, Finance*, J. Thompson

## HM PAYMASTER-GENERAL, OFFICE

— *see* National Investment and Loans Office

## PENSIONS COMPENSATION BOARD

11 Belgrave Road, London SW1V 1RB
Tel: 020-7828 9794; Fax: 020-7931 7239

The Pensions Compensation Board was established under the Pensions Act 1995 and is funded by a levy paid by all eligible occupational pension schemes. Its function is to compensate occupational pension schemes for losses due to dishonesty where the employer is insolvent.
*Chairman*, Dr J. T. Farrand, QC
*Secretary*, M. Lydon

## POLICE COMPLAINTS AUTHORITY

10 Great George Street, London SW1P 3AE
Tel: 020-7273 6450; Fax: 020-7273 6401;
Web: www.pca.gov.uk

The Police Complaints Authority was established under the Police and Criminal Evidence Act 1984 to provide an independent system for dealing with complaints by members of the public against police officers in England and Wales. It is funded by the Home Office. The authority has powers to supervise the investigation of certain categories of serious complaints and examines all completed investigations to decide whether officers should face misconduct proceedings. It does not deal with police operational matters; these are usually dealt with by the Chief Constable of the relevant force.

*Chairman*, Sir Alistair Graham
*Deputy Chair*, M. Meacher
*2nd Deputy Chair*, I. Bynoe
*Members*, Mrs A. Boustred; Ms J. Dobry; J. Elliott; D. Gear; Miss M. Mian; Mrs C. Mitchell; D. Petch; Mrs W. Towers; S. Swindell; D. Hughes; D. Glass; L. Pilkington; A. Macdougall

---

POLICE OMBUDSMAN FOR NORTHERN IRELAND
New Cathedral Buildings, St Anne's Square, 11 Church Street, Belfast BT 1PG
Tel: 028-9082 8600; Fax: 028-9082 8659;
Web: www.policeombudsman.org;
Email: info@policeombudsman.org

Founded in November 2000 under the Police (Northern Ireland) Act 1998, the function of the Police Ombudsman for Northern Ireland is to investigate complaints against the police in an impartial, efficient, effective and (as far as possible) transparent way, to win the confidence of the public and the police. It must report on trends in complaints and react to incidents involving the police, where it is in the public interest, even if no individual complaint has been made.
*Ombudsman*, N. O'Loan

---

PORT OF LONDON AUTHORITY
Bakers' Hall, 7 Harp Lane, London EC3R 6LB
Tel: 020-7743 7900; Fax: 020-7743 7999;
Web: www.portoflondon.co.uk

The Port of London Authority is a public trust constituted under the Port of London Act 1908 and subsequent legislation. It is the governing body for the Port of London, covering the tidal portion of the River Thames from Teddington to the seaward limit. The Board comprises a chairman and up to seven but not less than four non-executive members appointed by the Secretary of State for Transport, Local Government and the Regions, and up to four but not less than one executive members appointed by the Board.
*Chairman*, S. Sherrard
*Vice-Chairman*, The Baroness Wilcox
*Chief Executive*, S. Cuthbert
*Secretary*, G. E. Ennals

PRIME MINISTER'S OFFICE
— *see* page 292

---

PRISONS OMBUDSMAN FOR ENGLAND AND WALES
Ashley House, 2 Monck Street, London SW1P 2BQ
Tel: 020-7276 2876; Fax: 020-7276 2860
Email: prisonsombudsman@homeoffice.gsi.gov.uk

The post of Prisons Ombudsman was instituted in 1994. The Ombudsman is appointed by the Home Secretary and is an independent point of appeal for prisoners' grievances about their lives in prison, including disciplinary issues. The Ombudsman can investigate complaints about almost any aspect of prison life, assuming prisoners have completed the Prison Service's internal complaints procedure.
*Prisons Ombudsman*, S. Shaw

For Scotland, *see* Scottish Prisons Complaints Commission

---

PRIVY COUNCIL OFFICE
2 Carlton Gardens, London SW1Y 5AA
Tel: 020-7210 1033; Fax: 020-7210 1071

The Office is responsible for the arrangements leading to the making of all royal proclamations and Orders in Council; for certain formalities connected with ministerial changes; for considering applications for the granting (or amendment) of royal charters; for the scrutiny and approval of by-laws and statutes of chartered bodies; and for the appointment of high sheriffs and many Crown and Privy Council appointments to governing bodies.
*President of the Council (and Leader of the House of Commons)*, The Rt. Hon. Margaret Beckett, MP
  *Private Secretary*, R. Holderness
*Parliamentary Secretary*, Paddy Tipping, MP
*Clerk of the Council*, A. Galloway
*Deputy Clerk of the Council*, G. Donald
*Senior Clerk*, M. McCullagh
*Registrar*, J. Watherston

---

PUBLIC HEALTH LABORATORY SERVICE
61 Colindale Avenue, London NW9 5DF
Tel: 020-8200 1295; Fax: 020-8358 3130/3131;
Email: phls@phls.nhs.uk

The Public Health Laboratory Service comprises eight groups of laboratories, the Central Public Health Laboratory, the Communicable Disease Surveillance Centre, a Regional Epidemiology service and the Headquarters. The PHLS seeks to protect the population from infection through detection, diagnosis, surveillance, prevention and control of infections and communicable diseases. It keeps track of what infections are appearing where, advises on remedial or preventive action and provides clinical diagnostic services.
*Chairman*, Lord Leslie Turnberg, MD
*Deputy Chairman*, R. Tabor
*Director*, Dr D. Walford, FRCP, FRCPath.
*Deputy Directors*, Prof. B. I. Duerden, MD, FRCPath. (*Medical Director*); K. M. Saunders (*Corporate Planning and Resources*)

CENTRAL PUBLIC HEALTH LABORATORY

Colindale Avenue, London NW9 5HT
*Director*, Prof. S. P. Borriello

COMMUNICABLE DISEASES SURVEILLANCE CENTRE

Colindale Avenue NW9 5EQ
*Director*, Dr A. Nicoll

PHLS GROUPS OF LABORATORIES AND GROUP DIRECTORS

*East*, Dr P. M. B. White
*Midlands*, Dr R. E. Warren
*North*, Dr N. F. Lightfoot
*North-West*, Dr I. Farrell
*South-West*, Prof. K. A. V. Cartwright
*London and South-East*, Dr R. Gross
*Trent*, Dr P. J. Wilkinson
*Wales*, Dr A. J. Howard

OTHER SPECIAL LABORATORIES AND UNITS

ANAEROBE REFERENCE UNIT, Public Health Laboratory, Cardiff. *Head*, Prof. B. I. Duerden
ANTIVIRAL SUSCEPTIBILITY REFERENCE UNIT, Public Health Laboratory, Birmingham. *Head*, Dr D. P. Pillay
CRYPTOSPRORIDIUM REFERENCE UNIT, Public Health Laboratory, Rhyl. *Head*, Dr Rachel Chalmers
FOOD MICROBIOLOGY RESEARCH UNIT, Public Health Laboratory, Exeter. *Head*, Prof. T. J. Humphrey
GENITO-URINARY INFECTIONS REFERENCE LABORATORY, Public Health Laboratory, Bristol. *Head*, Dr A. J. Herring
LEPTOSPIRA REFERENCE LABORATORY, Public Health Laboratory, Hereford. *Director*, Dr T. J. Coleman
LYME DISEASE REFERENCE UNIT, Public Health Laboratory, Southampton. *Head*, Dr S. O'Connell
MALARIA REFERENCE LABORATORY, London School of Hygiene and Tropical Medicine, London WC1E 7HT. *Directors*, Prof. D. J. Bradley; Dr D. C. Warhurst
MENINGOCOCCAL REFERENCE LABORATORY, Public Health Laboratory, Manchester. *Director*, Dr E. Kaczmarski
MYCOBACTERIUM REFERENCE UNIT, Public Health Laboratory, Dulwich, London. *Director*, Dr F. Drobniewski
MYCOLOGY REFERENCE LABORATORY, Public Health Laboratory, Bristol. *Head*, University of Leeds. *Head*, Prof. E. G. V. Evans
PARASITOLOGY REFERENCE LABORATORY, Hospital for Tropical Diseases, London. *Director*, Dr P. L. Chiodini
TOXOPLASMA REFERENCE LABORATORY, Public Health Laboratory, Swansea. *Head*, D. H. M. Joynson
WATER AND ENVIRONMENTAL MICROBIOLOGY RESEARCH UNIT, Public Health Laboratory, Nottingham. *Head*, Dr J. V. Lee

## PUBLIC GUARDIANSHIP OFFICE

Stewart House, 24 Kingsway, London WC2B 6JX
Tel 020-7664 7000; Fax 020-7664 7702
COURT FUNDS OFFICE, 22 Kingsway, London WC2B 6LE Tel 020-7936 6000; Fax 020-7936 6882;
Email: custerv@guardianship.gov.uk
Web: www.gurdianship.gov.uk

The Public Guardianship Office (PGO) is the administrative office of the Court of Protection, based within the Lord Chancellor's Department.

Established on the 1st of April 2001, it has taken over the mental health functions previously undertaken by the Public Trust Office (PTO), which also provides services that promote the financial and social well being of people with mental incapacity.

*Chief Executive (Accountant-General)*, D. Lye
*Director of Finance*, I. Rees
*Director of Client Services*, K. Launchbury
*Director of Mental Health*, F. Eddy
*Interim Director of Human Resource*, H. Daley
*Director of Communication*, L. Joy

## PUBLIC WORKS LOAN BOARD

— *see* National Investment and Loans Office TY

## QUEST (THE QUALITY, EFFICIENCY AND STANDARDS TEAM)

c/o Department for Culture, Media and Sport,
2–4 Cockspur Street, London SW1Y 5DH
Tel: 020-7211 2206; Fax: 020-7211 2220

Quest was established in 1999. Its role is to monitor the quality of performance in organisations sponsored by the Department for Culture, Media and Sport and to provide independent advice to the Secretary of State.

*Chief Executive*, T. Suter

## THE RADIO AUTHORITY

Holbrook House, 14 Great Queen Street, London WC2B 5DG Tel: 020-7430 2724; Fax: 020-7405 7062;
Web: www.radioauthority.org.uk

The Radio Authority was established in 1991 under the Broadcasting Act 1990. It is the regulator and licensing authority for all independent radio services. Members of the Authority are appointed by the Secretary of State for Culture, Media and Sport; senior executive staff are appointed by the Authority.

*Chairman*, Richard Hooper
*Deputy Chairman*, David Witherow
*Members*, M. Adair; T. Prag; G. Talfan Davies; F. Sharkey; Ms S. Hewitt; Ms S. Nathan; Ms K. O'Rourke
*Chief Executive*, T. Stoller
*Deputy Chief Executive*, D. Vick
*Secretary to the Authority and Director of Legal Affairs*, Ms E. Salomon

# RECORD OFFICES

## ADVISORY COUNCIL ON PUBLIC RECORDS

*Secretariat:* Public Record Office, Kew, Richmond, Surrey TW9 4DU
Tel: 020-8876 3444 ext. 2351; Fax: 020-8392 5295
Web: www.pro.gov.uk/advisorycouncil/default.htm

Council members are appointed by the Lord Chancellor, under the Public Records Act 1958, to advise him on matters concerning public records in general and, in particular, on those aspects of the work of the Public Record Office which affect members of the public who make use of it.

*Chairman*, The Master of the Rolls
*Secretary*, T. R. Padfield

## CORPORATION OF LONDON RECORDS OFFICE

Guildhall, London EC2P 2EJ
Tel: 020-7332 1251; Fax: 020-7710 8682
Email: clro@corpoflondon.gov.uk
Web: www.cityoflondon.gov.uk/archives/clro

The Corporation of London Records Office contains the municipal archives of the City of London which are regarded as the most complete collection of ancient municipal records in existence. The collection includes charters of William the Conqueror, Henry II, and later kings and queens to 1957; ancient custumals: Liber Horn, Dunthorne, Custumarum, Ordinacionum, Memorandorum and Albus, Liber de Antiquis Legibus, and collections

of statutes; continuous series of judicial rolls and books from 1252 and Council minutes from 1275; records of the Old Bailey and Guildhall sessions from 1603; financial records from the 16th century; the records of London Bridge from the 12th century; and numerous subsidiary series and miscellanea of historical interest.
*Keeper of the City Records*, The Town Clerk
*City Archivist*, J. R. Sewell, OBE
*Deputy City Archivist*, J. M. Bankes

## HISTORICAL MANUSCRIPTS COMMISSION

Quality House, Quality Court, Chancery Lane, London WC2A 1HP Tel: 020-7242 1198; Fax: 020-7831 3550; Email: nra@hmc.gov.uk; Web: www.hmc.gov.uk

The Commission was set up by royal warrant in 1869 to enquire and report on collections of papers of value for the study of history which were in private hands. In 1959 a new warrant enlarged these terms of reference to include all historical records, wherever situated, outside the Public Records and gave it added responsibilities as a central co-ordinating body to promote, assist and advise on their proper preservation and storage. The Commission is sponsored by the Department for Culture, Media and Sport.

The Commission also maintains the National Register of Archives (NRA), which contains over 43,000 unpublished lists and catalogues of manuscript collections describing the holdings of local record offices, national and university libraries, specialist repositories and others in the UK and overseas. The NRA can be searched using computerised indices which are available in the Commission's search room.

The Commission also administers the Manorial and Tithe Documents Rules on behalf of the Master of the Rolls.
*Chairman*, The Lord Bingham of Cornhill, PC
*Commissioners*, Sir Patrick Cormack, FSA, MP; The Lord Egremont and Leconfield; Sir Matthew Farrer, GCVO; Sir John Sainty, KCB, FSA; Very Revd H. E. C. Stapleton, FSA; Sir Keith Thomas, FBA; The Earl of Scarbrough; A. Dundas-Bekker; Mrs S. J. Davies, Ph.D.; Prof. Peter Clarke; Mr Victor Gray; A. Prochaska, Ph.D.; Miss R. Dunhill, FSA; Dr Caroline Barron, FSA; Prof. T. C. Smout, CBE, Ph.D., FBA, FRSE, FSAScot.; Prof. Lola Young
*Secretary*, C. J. Kitching, Ph.D., FSA

## HOUSE OF LORDS RECORD OFFICE (THE PARLIAMENTARY ARCHIVES)

House of Lords, London SW1A 0PW
Tel: 020-7219 3074; Fax: 020-7219 2570
Web: www.parliament.uk; Email: hlro@parliament.uk

Since 1497, the records of Parliament have been kept within the Palace of Westminster. They are in the custody of the Clerk of the Parliaments. In 1946 a record department was established to supervise their preservation and their availability to the public. The search room of the office is open to the public by appointment.

Some three million documents are preserved, including Acts of Parliament from 1497, journals of the House of Lords from 1510, minutes and committee proceedings from 1610, and papers laid before Parliament from 1531. Amongst the records are the Petition of Right, the Death Warrant of Charles I, the Declaration of Breda, and the Bill of Rights. The House of Lords Record Office also has charge of the journals of the House of Commons (from 1547), and other surviving records of the Commons (from 1572), including documents relating to private bill legislation from 1818. Among other documents are the records of the Lord Great Chamberlain, the political papers of certain members of the two Houses, and documents relating to Parliament acquired on behalf of the nation. A permanent exhibition was established in the Royal Gallery in 1979.
*Clerk of the Records*, S. K. Ellison
*Assistant Clerks of the Records*, D. L. Prior; Dr C. Shenton

## NATIONAL ARCHIVES OF SCOTLAND

HM General Register House, Edinburgh EH1 3YY
Tel: 0131-535 1314; Fax: 0131-535 1360
Web: www.nas.gov.uk; Email: enquiries@nas.gov.uk

The history of the national archives of Scotland can be traced back to the 13th century. The National Archives of Scotland (formerly the Scottish Record Office) is an executive agency of the Scottish Executive and keeps the administrative records of pre-Union Scotland, the registers of central and local courts of law, the public registers of property rights and legal documents, and many collections of local and church records and private archives. Certain groups of records, mainly the modern records of Government departments in Scotland, the Scottish railway records, the plans collection, and private archives of an industrial or commercial nature, are preserved in the branch repository at the West Register House in Charlotte Square. The National Register of Archives (Scotland) is based in the West Register House.
*Keeper of the Records of Scotland*, G. P. MacKenzie
*Deputy Keeper*, Dr P. D. Anderson

## THE PUBLIC RECORD OFFICE

Kew, Richmond, Surrey TW9 4DU
Tel: 020-8876 3444; Fax: 020-8878 8905

The Public Record Office, originally established in 1838 under the Master of the Rolls, was placed under the direction of the Lord Chancellor in 1958; it became an executive agency in 1992. The Lord Chancellor appoints a Keeper of Public Records, whose duties are to co-ordinate and supervise the selection of records of Government departments and the law courts for permanent preservation, to safeguard the records and to make them available to the public. There is a separate record office for Scotland, now called the National Archives of Scotland.

The Office holds records of central Government dating from the Domesday Book (1086) to the present. Under the Public Records Act 1967 they are normally open to inspection when 30 years old, and are then available, without charge, in the reading rooms.
*Keeper of Public Records (G3)*, Mrs S. Tyacke, CB
*Director, Public Services Division (G5)*, Dr E. Hallam Smith
*Director, Government, Corporate and Information Services Division (G5)*, Dr D. Simpson

## PUBLIC RECORD OFFICE OF NORTHERN IRELAND

66 Balmoral Avenue, Belfast BT9 6NY
Tel: 02890-251318; Fax: 02890-255999

The Public Record Office of Northern Ireland is responsible for identifying and preserving Northern Ireland's archival heritage and making it available to the public. It is an executive agency of the Department of Culture, Arts and Leisure.
*Chief Executive*, Dr G. Slater

## SCOTTISH RECORDS ADVISORY COUNCIL

HM General Register House, Edinburgh EH1 3YY
Tel: 0131-535 1314; Fax: 0131-535 1360;
Web: www.nas.gov.uk

The Council was established under the Public Records (Scotland) Act 1937. Its members are appointed by the First Minister and it may submit proposals or make representations to the First Minister, the Lord Justice General or the Lord President of the Court of Session on questions relating to the public records of Scotland.
*Chairman*, Prof. H. MacQueen
*Secretary*, Dr A. Rosie

## REGISTRAR OF PUBLIC LENDING RIGHT

Richard House, Sorbonne Close, Stockton on Tees TS17 6DA Tel: 01642-604699; Fax: 01642-615641

Under the Public Lending Right system, in operation since 1983, payment is made from public funds to authors whose books are lent out from public libraries. Payment is made once a year and the amount each author receives is proportionate to the number of times (established from a sample) that each registered book has been lent out during the previous year. The Registrar of PLR, who is appointed by the Secretary of State for Culture, Media and Sport, compiles the register of authors and books. From 1 July 2000 authors resident in all EC countries are eligible to apply. (The term 'author' covers writers, illustrators, translators, and some editors/compilers.)

A payment of 2.49 pence was made in 2000–2001 for each estimated loan of a registered book, up to a top limit of £6,000 for the books of any one registered author; the money for loans above this level is used to augment the remaining PLR payments. In February 2001, the sum of £4,477 million was made available for distribution to 30,127 registered authors and assignees as the annual payment of PLR.
*Registrar*, Dr J. G. Parker
*Chairman of Advisory Committee*, C. Francis

## REVIEW BODIES

The secretariat for these bodies is provided by the Office of Manpower Economics (*see* page 351)

### ARMED FORCES PAY

The Review Body on Armed Forces Pay was appointed in 1971. It advises the Prime Minister and Government on the pay and allowances of members of naval, military and air forces of the Crown.
*Chairman*, The Baroness Dean of Thornton-le-Fylde, PC
*Members*, Mrs K. Coleman, OBE; J. Davies; Vice-Adm. Sir Toby Frere, KCB; The Lord Gladwin of Clee, CBE; Prof. D. Greenaway; Prof. The Lord Patel of Dunkeld; M. Ward

### DOCTORS' AND DENTISTS'

The Review Body on Doctors' and Dentists' Remuneration was set up in 1971. It advises the Prime Minister and Government on the remuneration of doctors and dentists taking any part in the National Health Service.
*Chairman*, M. Blair, QC
*Members*, Prof. F. Burchill; Prof. A. Dow; A. Hawksworth; Miss C. Hui; Dr G. Jones; R. Malone

### NURSING STAFF, MIDWIVES, HEALTH VISITORS AND PROFESSIONS ALLIED TO MEDICINE

The Review Body for nursing staff, midwives, health visitors and professions allied to medicine was set up in 1983. It advises the Prime Minister and Government on the remuneration of nursing staff, midwives and health visitors employed in the National Health Service; and also of physiotherapists, radiographers, occupational therapists, orthoptists, chiropodists, dietitians and related grades employed in the National Health Service.
*Chairman*, Prof. C. Booth
*Members*, M. Banerjee; J. Bartlett; Mrs M. Davies; C. Monks, OBE; Prof P. Weetman; D. Evans; Sir Patrick Symons

### SCHOOL TEACHERS

The School Teachers' Review Body (STRB) was set up under the School Teachers' Pay and Conditions Act 1991. It is required to examine and report on such matters relating to the statutory conditions of employment of school teachers in England and Wales as may be referred to it by the Secretary of State for Education and Skills.
*Chairman*, A. Vineall
*Members*, C. Ferguson; R. Gardner; P. Gedling; Miss J. Langdon; R. Pearson; J. Singh; Mrs P. Sloane

### SENIOR SALARIES

The Senior Salaries Review Body (formerly the Top Salaries Review Body) was set up in 1971 to advise the Prime Minister on the remuneration of the judiciary, senior civil servants and senior officers of the armed forces. In 1993 its remit was extended to cover the pay, pensions and allowances of MPs, Ministers and others whose pay is determined by a Ministerial and Other Salaries Order, and the allowances of peers. It also advises on the pay of officers and members of the devolved Parliament and Assemblies.
*Chairman*, Sir Michael Perry, CBE

## PRISON SERVICE

The Prison Service Pay Review Body (PSPRB) was set up in 2001. It makes independent recommendations on the pay of prison governors, prison officers and related grades for the Prison Service in England and Wales and for the Northern Ireland Prison.
*Chairman*, Sir Toby Frere, KCB
*Members*, D. Bourn; B. Brewer; A. Faulder; A. Gallico; P. Heard; F. Horisk; Prof. A. Smith

## ROYAL BOTANIC GARDEN EDINBURGH

20A Inverleith Row, Edinburgh EH3 5LR
Tel: 0131-552 7171; Fax: 0131-248 2901;
Email: press@rbge.org.uk; Web: www.rbge.org.uk

The Royal Botanic Garden Edinburgh (RBGE) originated as the Physic Garden, established in 1670 beside the Palace of Holyroodhouse. The Garden moved to its present 28-hectare site at Inverleith, Edinburgh, in 1821. There are also three Regional Gardens: Benmore Botanic Garden, near Dunoon, Argyll; Logan Botanic Garden, near Stranraer, Wigtownshire; and Dawyck Botanic Garden, near Stobo, Peeblesshire. Since 1986 RBGE has been administered by a board of trustees established under the National Heritage (Scotland) Act 1985. It receives an annual grant from the Rural Affairs Department of the Scottish Executive.

RBGE is an international centre for scientific research on plant diversity and for horticulture education and conservation. It has an extensive library, a herbarium with over two million preserved plant specimens, and over 20,00 species in the living collections. Public opening hours: Edinburgh site, daily (except Christmas Day and New Year's Day) November–January 9.30–4; February and October 9.30–5; March and September 9.30–6; April–August 9.30–7; Regional Gardens, 1 March–31 October 9.30–6. Admission free to Edinburgh site; admission charge to Regional Gardens.

*Chairman of the Board of Trustees*, Dr P. Nicholson
*Regius Keeper*, Prof. S. Blackmore, FRSE

## ROYAL BOTANIC GARDENS KEW

Richmond, Surrey TW9 3AB
Tel: 020-8332 5000; Fax: 020-8332 5197
Wakehurst Place, Ardingly, nr Haywards Heath, W. Sussex RH17 6TN
Tel: 01444-894066; Fax: 01444-894069

The Royal Botanic Gardens (RBG) Kew were originally laid out as a private garden for Kew House for George III's mother, Princess Augusta, in 1759. They were much enlarged in the 19th century, notably by the inclusion of the grounds of the former Richmond Lodge. In 1965 the garden at Wakehurst Place was acquired; it is owned by the National Trust and managed by RBG Kew. Under the National Heritage Act 1983 a board of trustees was set up to administer the gardens, which in 1984 became an independent body supported by grant-in-aid from the Department of Environment, Food and Rural Affairs.

The functions of RBG Kew are to carry out research into plant sciences, to disseminate knowledge about plants and to provide the public with the opportunity to gain knowledge and enjoyment from the gardens' collections. There are extensive national reference collections of living and preserved plants and a comprehensive library and archive. The main emphasis is on plant conservation and bio-diversity.

The gardens are open daily (except Christmas Day and New Year's Day) from 9.30 a.m. (Wakehurst, 10 a.m.). The closing hour varies from 4 p.m. in mid-winter to 6 p.m. on weekdays and 7.30 p.m. on Sundays and Bank Holidays in mid-summer. Admission, 2001, £6.50 (free for children under 16); concessionary schemes available. Glasshouses (Kew only), 9.30–4.30 (winter); 9.30–5.30 (summer). No dogs except guide-dogs for the blind.

BOARD OF TRUSTEES

*Chairman*, The Viscount Blakenham
*Members*, Sir Jeffery Bowman (*Queen's Trustee*); Miss M. Black, CBE; Prof. M. Crawley; Prof. H. Dickinson; Miss A. Ford; Mrs R. Franklin; S. de Grey, CBE; R. Lapthorne, CBE; I. Oag; Prof. J. S. Parker; Prof. C. Payne, OBE
*Director*, Prof. P. Crane, FRS

## ROYAL COMMISSION FOR THE EXHIBITION OF 1851

Sherfield Building, Imperial College of Science, Technology and Medicine, London SW7 2AZ
Tel: 020-7594 8790; Fax: 020-7594 8794;
Email: royalcom1851@ic.ac.uk;
Web: www.royalcommission1851.org.uk

The Royal Commission was incorporated by supplemental charter as a permanent commission after winding up the affairs of the Great Exhibition of 1851. Its object is to promote scientific and artistic education by means of funds derived from its Kensington estate, purchased with the surplus left over from the Great Exhibition. Annual charitable expenditure on educational grants is about £1 million.

*President*, HRH The Prince Philip, Duke of Edinburgh, KG, KT, PC
*Chairman, Board of Management*, Sir Alan Rudge, CBE, FRS, FREng.
*Secretary to Commissioners*, J. P. W. Middleton, CB

## ROYAL COMMISSION ON ENVIRONMENTAL POLLUTION

1st Floor, Steel House, 11 Tothill Street, London SW1H 9RE Tel: 020-7273 6635;
Email: enquiries@rcep.org.uk;
Web: www.rcep.org.uk

The Commission was set up in 1970 to advise on national and international matters concerning the pollution of the environment.

*Chairman*, Prof. Sir Thomas Blundell
*Members*, Revd Prof. M. C. Banner; Dr I. Graham-Bryce; CBE; Prof. R. Clift, OBE, FREng.; J. Flemming; Sir Brian Folett, FRS; Sir Martin Holdgate, CB; Prof. B. Hoskins, CBE, FRS; Prof. R. Macrory; Sir Michael Marmot, Ph.D.; Mrs C. Miller, FRSA; Dr Susan Owens, OBE; Prof. Jane Plant, CBE, FRSA; J. Roberts
*Secretary*, D. R. Lewis

## ROYAL COMMISSION ON THE ANCIENT AND HISTORICAL MONUMENTS OF SCOTLAND

John Sinclair House, 16 Bernard Terrace, Edinburgh EH8 9NX
Tel: 0131-662 1456; Fax: 0131-662 1477

The Royal Commission was established in 1908 and is appointed to provide for the survey and recording of ancient and historical monuments connected with the culture, civilisation and conditions of life of the people in Scotland from the earliest times. It is funded by the Scottish Executive.The Commission compiles and maintains the National Monuments Record of Scotland as the national record of the archaeological and historical environment. The National Monuments Record is open for reference Monday–Friday 9.30–4.30.

*Chairman*, Mrs Kathleen Dalyell,
*Commissioners*, Prof. J. M. Coles, Ph.D., FBA, FSA; Prof. R. A. Paxton, MBE, FRSE; Dr Barbara E. Crawford, FSA, FSAScot.; Miss A. C. Riches, OBE, FSA; J. W. T. Simpson, FSAScot.; Dr M. A. Mackay, Ph.D.; Dr J. Murray, Ph.D.;

Dr A. Macdonald Ph.D., FSAScot; Prof. C. D. Morris, FSA, FRSE, FSAScot; Dr Stana Nenadic, Ph.D.
*Secretary*, R. J. Mercer, FSA, FRSE

ROYAL COMMISSION ON THE ANCIENT AND HISTORICAL MONUMENTS OF WALES
Crown Building, Plas Crug, Aberystwyth SY23 1NJ
Tel: 01970-621200; Fax: 01970-627701

The Royal Commission was established in 1908 and is currently empowered by a Royal Warrant of 2001 to survey, record, publish and maintain a database of ancient and historical and maritime sites and structures, and landscapes in Wales. The Commission is funded by the National Assembly for Wales and is also responsible for the National Monuments Record of Wales, which is open daily for public reference, for the supply of archaeological information to the Ordnance Survey, for the co-ordination of archaeological aerial photography in Wales, and for sponsorship of the regional Sites and Monuments Records.
*Chairman*, Prof. R. A. Griffiths, Ph.D., D.Litt.
*Commissioners*, D. W. Crossley, FSA; J. Newman, FSA; U. B. Smith, Ph.D.; Prof. P. Sims-Williams, FBA; Prof. G. J. Wainwright, MBE, Ph.D., FSA; E. Wiliam, Ph.D., FSA
*Secretary*, P. R. White, FSA

THE ROYAL MINT
Llantrisant, Pontyclun CF72 8YT
Tel: 01443-623060; Fax: 01443-623185;
Web: www.royalmint.com

The prime responsibility of the Royal Mint is the provision of United Kingdom coinage, but it actively competes in world markets for a share of the available circulating coin business and about half of the 25,000 tonnes of coins and blanks it produces annually are exported. The Mint also manufactures special proof and uncirculated quality coins in gold, silver and other metals; military and civil decorations and medals; commemorative and prize medals; and royal and official seals.

The Royal Mint became an executive agency of the Treasury in 1990. The Government announced in July 1999 that the Royal Mint would be given greater commercial freedom to expand its business into new areas and develop partnerships with the private sector.
*Master of the Mint*, The Chancellor of the Exchequer (*ex officio*)
*Deputy Master and Comptroller*, R. de L. Holmes

THE ROYAL NATIONAL THEATRE
South Bank, London, SE1 9PX
Tel: 020-7452 3333; Fax: 020-7452 3344;
Email: secretariat@royalmint.gov.uk

*Chairman*, Sir Christopher Hogg
*Members*, Ms J. Bakewell, CBE; The Hon. P. Benson; Sir David Hancock, KCB; G. Hutchings; Ms K. Jones; Ms S. MacGregor, OBE; B. Okri; M. Oliver; Sir Tom Stoppard, OM, CBE; E. Walker-Arnott; P. Wiegand; Prof. Lola Young; A. Ptaszynski
*Company Secretary*, Mrs M. McGregor
*Director*, T. Nunn, CBE
*Executive Director*, The Baroness McIntosh of Hudnall

RURAL PAYMENTS AGENCY
PO Box 69, Reading RG1 3YD
Tel: 0118-958 3626; Fax: 0118-953 1370

The Rural Payments Agency (previously the Intervention Board) was established as a Government department in 1972 and became an executive agency in 1990. It is responsible for the implementation of European Union regulations covering the market support arrangements of the Common Agricultural Policy. Members are appointed by and are responsible to the agriculture Ministers in the UK.
*Chief Executive* (*G3*), J. McNeill
*Directors* (*G5*), H. MacKinnon (*Operations*); A. Kerr, (*Finance*); vacant (*Corporate Services*); P. Kent (*Legal*); R. Gregg (*Acting Human Resources Director*); J. Welch (*Acting I.S.S*)

SCOTTISH CRIMINAL CASES REVIEW COMMISSION
5th Floor, Portland House, 17 Renfield Street, Glasgow G2 5AH
Tel: 0141-270 7030; Fax: 0141-270 7040

The Commission is a non-departmental public body which started operating on 1 April 1999. It took over from the Secretary of State for Scotland powers to consider alleged miscarriages of justice in Scotland and refer cases meeting the relevant criteria to the High Court for review. Members are appointed by Her Majesty The Queen on the recommendation of the First Minister; senior executive staff are appointed by the Commission.
*Chairperson* (£372 per day), Prof. Sheila McLean
*Members* (£217 per day), A. Bonnington; Prof. P. Duff; The Very Revd G. Forbes; A. Gallen; Sir G. Gordon, CBE, QC; W. Taylor, QC
*Chief Executive*, Ms C. A. Kelly

SCOTTISH ENTERPRISE
120 Bothwell Street, Glasgow G2 7JP
Tel: 0141-248 2700; Fax: 0141-221 3217

Scottish Enterprise was established in 1991 and its purpose is to create jobs and prosperity for the people of Scotland. It is funded largely by the Scottish Executive and is responsible to the Scottish Ministers. Working in partnership with the private and public sectors, Scottish Enterprise aims to further the development of Scotland's economy, to enhance the skills of the Scottish workforce and to promote Scotland's international competitiveness. Scottish Enterprise has a network of 12 Local Enterprise Companies that deliver economic development services at local level.
*Chairman* (£33,883), Sir Ian Robinson, CBE
*Chief Executive*, Dr R. Crawford

SCOTTISH ENVIRONMENT PROTECTION AGENCY
Erskine Court, The Castle Business Park, Stirling FK9 4TR Tel: 01786-457700; Hotline: 0800-60 70 60
Fax: 01786-446885

The Scottish Environment Protection Agency (SEPA) is the public body responsible for environmental protection in Scotland. It regulates potential pollution to land, air and water, the storage, transport and disposal of controlled waste and the safe keeping and disposal of radioactive materials. It does this witin a complex legislative framework of Acts of Parliament, EC Directives and Regulations, granting licenses to operations of industrial processes and waste disposal.
*Chairman*, K. Collins
*Chief Executive*, M. P. Henton

SCOTTISH EXECUTIVE
— *see* Regional Government Section

SCOTTISH HOMES
Thistle House, 91 Haymarket Terrace, Edinburgh EH12 5HE Tel: 0131-313 0044; Fax: 0131-313 2680

Scottish Homes, aims to improve the quality and variety of housing available in Scotland by working in partnership with the public and private sectors. The agency is a major funder of new and improved housing provided by housing associations and private developers. It is also involved in housing research. Board members are appointed by the First Minister.

On 1 November 2001 Scottish Homes became a new executive agency directly accountable to ministers and the Scottish Parliament.
*Chairman*, J. Ward, CBE
*Chief Executive*, B. Millar

SCOTTISH LAW COMMISSION
140 Causewayside, Edinburgh EH9 1PR
Tel: 0131-668 2131; Fax: 0131-662 4900

The Commission keeps the law in Scotland under review and makes proposals for its development and reform. It is responsible to the Scottish Ministers through the Scottish Executive Justice Department.
*Chairman (part-time)*, The Hon. Lord Gill
*Commissioners (full-time)*, Prof. G. Maher; Prof. K. G. C. Reid; Prof. J. M. Thomson; *(part-time)* P. S. Hodge, QC

SCOTTISH LEGAL AID BOARD
44 Drumsheugh Gardens, Edinburgh EH3 7SW
Tel: 0131-226 7061; Fax: 0131-220 4878

The Scottish Legal Aid Board was set up under the Legal Aid (Scotland) Act 1986. It is responsible for ensuring that advice, assistance and representation are available in accordance with the Act. Members are appointed by Scottish Ministers.
*Chairman*, Mrs J. Couper

SCOTTISH NATURAL HERITAGE
12 Hope Terrace, Edinburgh EH9 2AS
Tel: 0131-447 4784; Fax: 0131-446 2277;
Web: www.snh.org.uk

Scottish Natural Heritage was established in 1992 under the Natural Heritage (Scotland) Act 1991. It provides advice on nature conservation to all those whose activities affect wildlife, landforms and features of geological interest in Scotland, and seeks to develop and improve facilities for the enjoyment and understanding of the Scottish countryside. It is funded by the Scottish Executive.
*Chairman*, Dr J. Markland, CBE
*Chief Executive*, R. Crofts, CBE

SCOTTISH PARLIAMENTARY COMMISSIONER FOR ADMINISTRATION
28 Thistle Street, Edinburgh EH2 1EN
Tel: 0845-601 0456; Fax: 0131-226 4447
Web: www.ombudsman.org.uk

The Scottish Parliamentary Commissioner for Administration was appointed in July 1999 to investigate complaints made to him by Members of the Scottish Parliament on behalf of members of the public who have suffered an injustice through maladministration by the Scottish Executive and a wide range of public bodies involved in devolved Scottish affairs.
*Scottish Parliamentary Commissioner for Administration*, M. S. Buckley

SCOTTISH PRISONS COMPLAINTS COMMISSION
Government Buildings, Broomhouse Drive, Edinburgh EH11 3XD
Tel: 0131-244 8423; Fax: 0131-244 8430;
Email: joan.aitken@scotland.gsi.gov.uk

The Commission was established in 1994. It is an independent body to which prisoners in Scottish prisons can make application in relation to any matter where they have failed to obtain satisfaction from the Scottish Prison Service's internal grievance procedures. Clinical judgments made by medical officers, matters which are the subject of legal proceedings and matters relating to sentence, conviction and parole decision-making are excluded from the Commission's jurisdiction. The Commissioner is appointed by the First Minister.
*Commissioner*, Miss J. N. Aitken

SEA FISH INDUSTRY AUTHORITY
18 Logie Mill, Logie Green Road, Edinburgh EH7 4HG
Tel: 0131-558 3331; Fax: 0131-558 1442

Established under the Fisheries Act 1981, the Authority is required to promote the efficiency of the sea fish industry. It carries out research relating to the industry and gives advice on related matters. It provides training, promotes the marketing, consumption and export of sea fish and sea fish products, and may provide financial assistance for the

improvement of fishing vessels in respect of essential safety equipment. It is responsible to the Department of the Environment, Food and Rural Affairs.
*Chairman*, E. Davey
*Chief Executive*, A. C. Fairbairn

## THE SECURITY AND INTELLIGENCE SERVICES

Under the Intelligence Services Act 1994, the Intelligence and Security Committee of Parliamentarians was established to oversee the work of GCHQ, MI5 and MI6; in 1999 an Investigator was appointed to the committee in order to reinforce the authority of its findings and establish public confidence in the oversight system. The Act also established the Intelligence Services Tribunal, which hears complaints made against GCHQ and MI6. The Security Service Tribunal and Commissioner (*see* below) investigate complaints about MI5.

### DEFENCE INTELLIGENCE STAFF

— *see* Defence section

### GOVERNMENT COMMUNICATIONS HEADQUARTERS (GCHQ)

Priors Road, Cheltenham, Glos GL52 5AJ
Tel: 01242-221491; Fax: 01242-574349

GCHQ produces signals intelligence in support of national security and the UK's economic wellbeing, and in the prevention or detection of serious crime. Additionally, GCHQ Communications-Electronics Security Group (CESG) provides advice and assistance to Government departments, the armed forces and other national infrastructure bodies on the security of their communications and information systems. GCHQ was placed on a statutory footing by the Intelligence Services Act 1994 and is headed by a director who is directly accountable to the Foreign Secretary. A new building to house GCHQ is being constructed in Cheltenham, with the anticipated completion date of early 2003.
*Director*, F. N. Richards, CVO, CMG

### INVESTIGATORY POWERS TRIBUNAL

PO Box 33220, London, SW1H 9ZQ Tel: 020-7273 4095

The Investigatory Powers Tribunal replaces the Interception of Communications Tribunal, the Intelligence Services Tribunal, the Security Services Tribunal and the complaints function of the Commissioner appointed under the Police Act 1997.

The Regulation of Investigatory Powers Act 2000 provides for a Tribunal made up of senior members of the legal profession, independent of the Government and appointed by The Queen, to investigate complaints from any person about anything which they believe the Intelligence Services or various public authorities has carried out in relation to them, their property or their communications.
*President*, The Rt. Hon. Lord Justice John Mummery

### NATIONAL CRIMINAL INTELLIGENCE SERVICE

PO Box 8000, London SE11 5EN
Tel: 020-7238 8000; Web: www.ncis.gov.uk

The National Criminal Intelligence Service (NCIS) provides intelligence about serious and organised crime to law enforcement, government and other relevant national and international agencies. On 1 April 1998 NCIS was placed on a statutory footing. It is accountable to the NCIS Service Authority.
*Director-General*, J. Abbott, QPM, CBE

#### SERVICE AUTHORITY

PO Box 2600, London SW1V 2WG
Tel: 020-7238 2600

The Service Authority for NCIS is responsible for ensuring its effective operation. It operates with the Service Authority for the National Crime Squad. There are 26 members of the authorities, of whom the chairman and nine others serve as 'core members' on both authorities.
*Chairman*, Rt. Hon. Sir John Wheeler

### THE SECRET INTELLIGENCE SERVICE (MI6)

PO Box 1300, London SE1 1BD

The Secret Intelligence Service produces secret intelligence in support of the Government's security, defence, foreign and economic policies. It was placed on a statutory footing by the Intelligence Services Act 1994 and is headed by a chief, known as 'C', who is directly accountable to the Foreign Secretary.
*Chief*, Sir R. B. Dearlove, OBE, KCMG

### THE SECURITY SERVICE (MI5)

PO Box 3255, London SW1P 1AE
Tel: 020-7930 9000

The function of the Security Service is the protection of national security, in particular against threats from espionage, terrorism, sabotage and the proliferation of weapons of mass destruction, from the activities of agents of foreign powers, and from actions intended to overthrow or undermine parliamentary democracy by political, industrial or violent means. It is also the Service's function to safeguard the economic well-being of the UK against threats posed by the actions or intentions of persons outside the British Islands. Under the Security Service Act 1996, the Service's role was extended to support the police and customs in the prevention and detection of serious crime.
*Director-General*, Sir Stephen Lander, KCB

## INTELLIGENCE COMMISSIONER

c/o PO Box 33220, London SW1H 1ZQ
Tel: 020-7273 4514

The Commissioner is appointed by the Prime Minister. He keeps under review the issue of warrants by the Home Secretary under the Regulation of Investigatory Powers Act (RIPA) 2000. The Commisioner is also required to submit an annual report on the discharge of his functions to the Prime Minister.
*Commissioner*, The Rt. Hon. Lord Justice Simon Brown

## SENTENCE REVIEW COMMISSIONERS

PO Box 1011, Belfast BT2 7SR
Tel: 01232-549412; Fax: 01232-549427;
Email: sentrev@belfast.org.uk;
Web: www.sentencereview.org.uk

The Sentence Review Commissioners are appointed by the Secretary of State for Northern Ireland to consider

applications from prisoners serving sentences in Northern Ireland for declarations that they are entitled to early release in accordance with the provisions of the Northern Ireland (Sentences) Act 1998. The commissioners have been appointed until 31 July 2005 and are served by staff seconded from the Northern Ireland Office.
*Joint Chairmen*, Sir John Belloch, KCB; B. Currin

## SERIOUS FRAUD OFFICE

Elm House, 10–16 Elm Street, London WC1X 0BJ
Tel: 020-7239 7272; Fax: 020-7837 1689;
Email: public.enquiries@sfo.gsigov.uk

The Serious Fraud Office works under the superintendence of the Attorney-General. Its remit is to investigate and prosecute serious and complex fraud. (Other fraud cases are handled by the fraud divisions of the Crown Prosecution Service.) The scope of its powers covers England, Wales and Northern Ireland. The staff includes lawyers, accountants and other support staff, investigating teams work closely with the police.
*Director*, Mrs R. Wright

## SMALL BUSINESS COUNCIL

1 Victoria Street, London SW1H 0ET Tel: 020-7215 5399; Email: sbcsecretariat@sbs.gsi.gov.uk;
Web: www.businessadviceonline.org

The Small Business Council was set up in March 2000. It is a Non-Departmental Public Body independent of Government acting in an advisory capacity to the Small Business Service. The Council also reports to the Secretary for Trade and Industry on the needs of small businesses.
*Chairman*, W. Sargent

## SMALL BUSINESS SERVICE

1 Victoria Street, London SW1H 0ET
Tel: 020-7215 5365;
Email: enquiries@sbs.gsi.gov.uk;
Web: www.businessadviceonline.org

The Small Business Service was set up by the government in April 2000. The role of the Service will be to provide a voice for small businesses in Government, to improve the coherence and quality of Government support for the small business, and to help small businesses on issues of regulation. There are 45 local Business Link franchises throughout England largely coterminous in their boundaries with the new Learning and Skills Councils.
*Chief Executive*, D. Irwin

## STATISTICS COMMISSION

10 Great George Street, London SW1P 3AE
Tel: 020-7273 8000;
Email: statscom@statscom.org.uk
Web: www.statscom.org.uk

The statistics Commission has been set up to advise on the quality, quality assurance and priority-setting for National Statistics, and on the procedures designed to deliver statistical integrity, to help ensure National Statistics are trustworthy and responsive to public needs. It is independent of both Ministers and the procedures of National Statistics. It operates in a transparent way with the minutes of its meetings, correspondence and evidence it receives, and advice it gives, all normally publicly available for scrutiny.
*Chairman*, Sir John Kingman, FRS

## STRATEGIC RAIL AUTHORITY

55 Victoria Street, London SW1H 0EU
Tel: 020-7654 6000; Fax: 020-7654 6010

The Strategic Rail Authority formally came into being on 1 February 2001 following the passage of the Transport Act 2000.

The SRA's key role is to promote and develop the rail network and encourage integration. As well as providing overall strategic direction for Britain's railways, SRA has responsibility for consumer protection, administering freight grants and steering forward the investment projects. It is responsible for letting and managing passenger rail franchises. The SRA operates under Directions and Guidance Issued by the Secretary of State for Transport, Local Government and the Regions. Where Scotland is concerned it is also subject to Directions from the Scottish Minister for Transport. The SRA has subsumed the powers of the Office of Passenger Rail Franchising (OPRAF) and the British Railways Board (BRB).
*Chairman*, Sir Alastair Morton
*Chief Executive*, Mike Grant

## TOURISM BODIES

The English Tourism Council, the Scottish Tourist Board, the Wales Tourist Board and the Northern Ireland Tourist Board are responsible for developing and marketing the tourist industry in their respective countries.

ENGLISH TOURISM COUNCIL, Thames Tower, Black's Road, London W6 9EL. Tel: 020-8563 3000; Web: www.englishtourism.org.uk.

VISIT SCOTLAND, 23 Ravelston Terrace, Edinburgh EH4 3TP. Tel: 0131-332 2433; Thistle House, Beechwood Park North, Inverness IV2 3ED. Tel: 01463-716996. Web: www.visitscotland.com.

WALES TOURIST BOARD, Brunel House, 2 Fitzalan Road, Cardiff CF24 0UY. Tel: 02920-499909 Fax: 02920-485031 Web: www.visitwales.com

NORTHERN IRELAND TOURIST BOARD, St Anne's Court, 59 North Street, Belfast BT1 1NB. Tel: 028- 9023 1221

## UNITED KINGDOM SPORTS COUNCIL (UK SPORT)

40 Bernard Street, London WC1N 1ST
Tel: 020-7841 9500; Fax: 020-7841 8850;
Web: www.uksport.gov.uk

The UK Sports Council (UK Sport) was established by Royal Charter in January 1997. Its role is to focus on high performance sport at UK level, with the aim of achieving sporting excellence in world competition. It works to combat drug misuse, deals with international relations and supports major events. It also distributes the funds

allocated to sport from the proceeds of the National Lottery.
*Chairman*, Sir Rodney Walker
*Chief Executive*, R. Callicott

UNRELATED LIVE TRANSPLANT REGULATORY AUTHORITY
Department of Health, c/o Room 420, Wellington House, 133–155 Waterloo Road, London SE1 8UG
Tel: 020-7972 4812; Fax: 020-7972 4852

The Unrelated Live Transplant Regulatory Authority (ULTRA) is a statutory body established in 1990. In every case where the transplant of an organ within the definition of the Human Organ Transplants Act 1989 is proposed between a living donor and a recipient who are not genetically related, the proposal must be referred to ULTRA. Applications must be made by registered medical practitioners.

The Authority comprises a chairman and ten members appointed by the Secretary of State for Health. The secretariat is provided by Department of Health officials.
*Chairman*, Prof. Sir Roddy MacSween

UK ATOMIC ENERGY AUTHORITY
Harwell, Didcot, Oxon OX11 0RA
Tel: 01235-820220; Fax: 01235-436401

The UKAEA was established by the Atomic Energy Authority Act 1954 and took over responsibility for the research and development of the civil nuclear power programme. The Authority's commercial arm, AEA Technology PLC, was privatised in 1996. UKAEA is now responsible for the safe management and decommissioning of its radioactive plant and for maximising the income from the buildings and land on its sites. UKAEA also undertakes special nuclear tasks for the Government, including the UK's contribution to the international fusion programme.
*Chairman*, Adm. Sir Kenneth Eaton
*Chief Executive*, Dr J. McKeown

WALES YOUTH AGENCY
Leslie Court, Lon-y-Llyn, Caerphilly CF83 1BQ
Tel: 029-2085 5700; Fax: 029-2085 5701;
Email: wya@wya.org.uk; Web: www.wya.org.uk

The Wales Youth Agency is an independent organisation funded by the National Assembly for Wales to support the youth service in Wales. Its functions include the encouragement and development of the partnership between statutory and voluntary agencies relating to young people; the promotion of staff development and training; and the extension of marketing and information services in the relevant fields. The board of directors do not receive a salary.
*Chairman of the Board of Directors*, R. Noble
*Vice-Chairman of the Board of Directors*, Dr H. Williamson
*Chief Executive*, B. Williams

WELSH ADMINISTRATION OMBUDSMAN
5th Floor, Capital Tower, Greyfriars Road, Cardiff CF10 3AG Tel: 0845-601 0987; Fax: 029-2022 6909;
Email: wao.enquiries@ombudsman.gsi.gov.uk
Web: www.ombudsman.org.uk

The Welsh Administration Ombudsman was appointed in July 1999 to investigate complaints by members of the public who have suffered an injustice through maladministration by the National Assembly for Wales and certain public bodies involved in devolved Welsh affairs.
*Welsh Administration Ombudsman*, M. S. Buckley

WELSH DEVELOPMENT AGENCY
Principality House, The Friary, Cardiff CF10 3FE
Tel: 0845-777 5577; Fax: 01443-845589

The Agency was established under the Welsh Development Agency Act 1975. Its remit is to help further the regeneration of the economy and improve the environment in Wales. Under the Government of Wales Act 1998, the Land Authority for Wales and the Development Board for Rural Wales merged with the Welsh Development Agency. The Agency is sponsored by the National Assembly for Wales.

The Agency's priorities are to create new businesses and to encourage existing small firms to grow. Its main activities include promoting Wales as a location for inward investment, helping to boost the growth, profitability and competitiveness of indigenous Welsh companies, providing investment capital for industry, encouraging investment by the private sector in property development, grant-aiding land reclamation, and stimulating quality urban and rural development.
*Chairman*, Sir David Rowe-Beddoe
*Deputy Chairman*, T. G. Jones, CBE
*Chief Executive*, G. Hawker, CBE

WOMEN'S NATIONAL COMMISSION
Room 56/4, Cabinet Office, Horse Guards Road, London SW1P 3AL
Tel: 020-7238 0386; Fax: 020-7238 0387

The Women's National Commission is an independent advisory committee to the Government. Its remit is to ensure that the informed opinions of women are given their due weight in the deliberations of the Government and in public debate on matters of public interest including those of special interest to women. The Commission's sponsoring department is the Cabinet Office.
*Chair*, Baroness Christine Crawley of Edgbaston
*Director*, Ms J. Veitch

# European Parliament

European Parliament elections take place at five-yearly intervals; the first direct elections to the Parliament were held in 1979. In mainland Britain MEPs were elected in all constituencies on a first-past-the-post basis until the elections of June 1999; in Northern Ireland three MEPs have been elected by the single transferable vote system of proportional representation since 1979. From 1979 to 1994 the number of seats held by the UK in the European Parliament was 81. At the June 1994 election the number of seats increased to 87 (England 71, Wales 5, Scotland 8, Northern Ireland 3).

At the European Parliament elections held on 10 June 1999, all British MEPs were elected under a 'closed-list' regional system of proportional representation, with England being divided into nine regions and Scotland and Wales each constituting a region. Parties submitted a list of candidates for each region in their own order of preference. Voters voted for a party or an independent candidate, and the first seat in each region was allocated to the party or candidate with the highest number of votes. The rest of the seats in each region were then allocated broadly in proportion to each party's share of the vote. Each region returned the following number of members: East Midlands, 6; Eastern, 8; London, 10; North East, 4; North West, 10; South East, 11; South West, 7; West Midlands, 8; Yorkshire and the Humber, 7; Wales, 5; Scotland, 8.

If a vacancy occurs due to the resignation or death of an MEP, the vacancy is filled by the next available person on that party's list. If an independent MEP resigns or dies, a by-election is held. Where an MEP leaves the party on whose list he/she was elected, there is no requirement to resign and he/she can remain in office until the next election.

British subjects and citizens of the Irish Republic are eligible for election to the European Parliament provided they are 21 or over and not subject to disqualification. Since 1994, nationals of member states of the European Union have had the right to vote in elections to the European Parliament in the UK as long as they are entered on the electoral register.

MEPs currently receive a salary from the parliaments or governments of their respective member states, set at the level of the national parliamentary salary and subject to national taxation rules (for salary of British MPs, *see* Parliament section). A proposal that all MEPs should be paid the same rate of salary out of the EU budget, and subject to the EC tax rate, was under negotiation between the European Parliament and the Council of Ministers at the time of going to press.

## UK MEMBERS AS AT 28 JULY 2001

*Denotes membership of the last European Parliament
†*See* Replacements since the last election
‡Subsequently left UK Independence Party and now sits as an independent
**Subsequently left the Conservative Party and sits with the Liberal Democrats

Atkins, Rt. Hon. Sir Robert (*b.* 1946), *C., North West*
Attwooll, Ms Elspeth M.-A. (*b.* 1943), *LD, Scotland*
*Balfe, Richard A. (*b.* 1944), *Lab., London*
Beazley, Christopher J. P. (*b.* 1952), *C., Eastern*
Bethell, The Lord (*b.* 1938), *C., London*
*Bowe, David R. (*b.* 1955), *Lab., Yorkshire and the Humber*
Bowis, John C., OBE (*b.* 1945), *C., London*
Bradbourn, Philip, OBE (*b.* 1951), *C., West Midlands*
Bushill-Matthews, Philip (*b.* 1943), *C., West Midlands*
Callanan, Martin (*b.* 1961), *C., North East*
Cashman, Michael (*b.* 1950), *Lab., West Midlands*
*Chichester, Giles B. (*b.* 1946), *C., South West*
Clegg, Nicholas W. P. (*b.* 1967), *LD, East Midlands*
*Corbett, Richard (*b.* 1955), *Lab., Yorkshire and the Humber*
*Corrie, John A. (*b.* 1935), *C., West Midlands*
Davies, Christopher G. (*b.* 1954), *LD, North West*
Deva, Niranjan J. A. (Nirj), FRSA (*b.* 1948), *C., South East*
†*Donnelly, Alan J. (*b.* 1957), *Lab., North East*
Dover, Den (*b.* 1938), *C., North West*
Duff, Andrew N. (*b.* 1950), *LD, Eastern*
*Elles, James E. M. (*b.* 1949), *C., South East*
Evans, Ms Jillian R. (*b.* 1959), *PC, Wales*
Evans, Jonathan P., FRSA (*b.* 1950), *C., Wales*
*Evans, Robert J. E. (*b.* 1956), *Lab., London*
Farage, Nigel (*b. 1964* ), *UK Ind., South East*
*Ford, J. Glyn (*b.* 1950), *Lab., South West*
Foster, Mrs Jacqui (*b.* 1947), *C., North West*
Gill, Ms Neena (*b.* 1956), *Lab., West Midlands*
Goodwill, Robert (*b.* 1956), *C., Yorkshire and the Humber*
†*Green, Mrs Pauline (*b.* 1948), *Lab., London*
Hannan, Daniel (*b.* 1971), *C., South East*
Harbour, Malcolm (*b.* 1947), *C., West Midlands*
Heaton-Harris, Christopher (*b.* 1967), *C., East Midlands*
Helmer, Roger (*b.* 1944), *C., East Midlands*
‡Holmes, Michael (*b. 1938* ), *UK Ind., South West*
*Howitt, Richard (*b.* 1961), *Lab., Eastern*
Hudghton, Ian (*b.* 1951), *SNP, Scotland*
*Hughes, Stephen S. (*b.* 1952), *Lab., North East*
Huhne, Christopher M. P., OBE (*b.* 1954), *LD, South East*
*Hume, John, MP (*b.* 1937), *SDLP, Northern Ireland*
Inglewood, The Lord (*b.* 1951), *C., North West*
*Jackson, Mrs Caroline F., D.Phil. (*b.* 1946), *C., South West*
Khanbhai, Bashir (*b.* 1945), *C., Eastern*
*Kinnock, Mrs Glenys E. (*b.* 1944), *Lab., Wales*
Kirkhope, Timothy J. R. (*b.* 1945), *C., Yorkshire and the Humber*
Lambert, Ms Jean D. (*b.* 1950), *Green, London*
Lucas, Ms Caroline, Ph.D. (*b.* 1960), *Green, South East*
Ludford, The Baroness (*b.* 1951), *LD, London*
Lynne, Ms Elizabeth (*b.* 1948), *LD, West Midlands*
*McAvan, Ms Linda (*b.* 1962), *Lab., Yorkshire and the Humber*
*McCarthy, Ms Arlene (*b.* 1960), *Lab., North West*
MacCormick, Prof. D. Neil, FBA (*b.* 1941), *SNP, Scotland*
*McMillan-Scott, Edward H. C. (*b.* 1949), *C., Yorkshire and the Humber*
*McNally, Mrs Eryl M. (*b.* 1942), *Lab., Eastern*
*Martin, David W. (*b.* 1954), *Lab., Scotland*
*Miller, William (*b.* 1954), *Lab., Scotland*
Moraes, Claude (*b. 1965*), *Lab., London*
*Morgan, Ms Eluned (*b.* 1967), *Lab., Wales*
*Murphy, Simon F., Ph.D. (*b.* 1962), *Lab., West Midlands*
**Newton Dunn, William F. (Bill) (*b.* 1941), LD, *East Midlands*
Nicholson of Winterbourne, The Baroness (*b.* 1941), *LD, South East*
*Nicholson, James F. (*b.* 1945), *UUP, Northern Ireland*
O'Toole, Ms Barbara M. (Mo) (*b.* 1960), *Lab., North East*

*Paisley, Revd Ian R. K., MP (*b.* 1926), *DUP, Northern Ireland*
Parish, Neil (*b.* 1956), *C., South West*
*Perry, Roy J. (*b.* 1943), *C., South East*
*Provan, James L. C. (*b.* 1936), *C., South East*
Purvis, John R., CBE (*b.* 1938), *C., Scotland*
*Read, Ms I. M. (Mel) (*b.* 1939), *Lab., East Midlands*
*Simpson, Brian (*b.* 1953), *Lab., North West*
*Skinner, Peter W. (*b.* 1959), *Lab., South East*
Stevenson, Struan (*b.* 1948), *C., Scotland*
Stihler, Catherine D. (*elected Catherine Taylor*) (*b.* 1973), *Lab., Scotland*
Stockton, The Earl of (*b.* 1943), *C., South West*
*Sturdy, Robert W. (*b.* 1944), *C., Eastern*
Sumberg, David A. G. (*b.* 1941), *C., North West*
Tannock, Dr Charles (*b.* 1957), *C., London*
Titford, Jeffrey (*b.* 1933 ), *UK Ind., Eastern*
*Titley, Gary (*b.* 1950), *Lab., North West*
Van Orden, Geoffrey (*b.* 1945), *C., Eastern*
Villiers, Ms Theresa (*b.* 1968), *C., London*
Wallis, Ms Diana P. (*b.* 1954), *LD, Yorkshire and the Humber*
*Watson, Graham R. (*b.* 1956), *LD, South West*
*Watts, Mark F. (*b.* 1964), *Lab., South East*
*Whitehead, Philip (*b.* 1937), *Lab., East Midlands*
Wyn, Eurig (*b.* 1944), *PC, Wales*
*Wynn, Terence (*b.* 1946), *Lab., North West*

## UK REGIONS AS AT 10 JUNE 1999

*Abbreviations*

| | |
|---|---|
| *ACPFCA* | Anti-Corruption Pro Family Christian Alliance |
| *AHRPE* | Architect Human Rights Peace in Europe |
| *Anti VAT* | Independent Anti Value Added Tax |
| *EFP* | English Freedom Party |
| *Ind. Profit* | Independent Making a Profit in Europe |
| *Ind. Stable* | Independent Open Democracy for Stability |
| *Lower Tax* | Account for Lower Scottish Taxes |
| *MEP Ind.* | MEP Independent Labour |
| *Soc. All.* | Socialist Alliance |
| *SSP* | Scottish Socialist Party |
| *WW* | Weekly Worker |

For other abbreviations, 233

### EASTERN

(Bedfordshire; Cambridgeshire; Essex; Hertfordshire; Luton; Norfolk; Peterborough; Southend-on-Sea; Suffolk; Thurrock)

| | |
|---|---|
| *E.*4,019,916 | *T.*24.74% |
| *C.* | 425,091 (42.75%) |
| *Lab.* | 250,132 (25.15%) |
| *LD* | 118,822 (11.95%) |
| *UK Ind.* | 88,452 (8.89%) |
| *Green* | 61,334 (6.17%) |
| *Lib.* | 16,861 (1.70%) |
| *Pro Euro C.* | 16,340 (1.64%) |
| *BNP* | 9,356 (0.94%) |
| *Soc. Lab.* | 6,143 (0.62%) |
| *NLP* | 1,907 (0.19%) |
| *C. majority* | 174,959 |

(June 1994, Lab. maj. 90,087)

MEMBERS ELECTED
*R. Sturdy, *C.*
C. Beazley, *C.*
B. Khanbhai, *C.*
G. Van Orden, *C.*
*Ms E. McNally, *Lab.*
*R. Howitt, *Lab.*
A. Duff, *LD*
J. Titford, *UK Ind.*

### EAST MIDLANDS

(Derby; Derbyshire; Leicester; Leicestershire; Lincolnshire; Northamptonshire; Nottingham; Nottinghamshire; Rutland)

| | |
|---|---|
| *E.*3,170,517 | *T.*22.83% |
| *C.* | 285,662 (39.47%) |
| *Lab.* | 206,756 (28.57%) |
| *LD* | 92,398 (12.77%) |
| *UK Ind.* | 54,800 (7.57%) |
| *Green* | 38,954 (5.38%) |
| *Alt. Lab.* | 17,409 (2.41%) |
| *Pro Euro C.* | 11,359 (1.57%) |
| *BNP* | 9,342 (1.29%) |
| *Soc. Lab.* | 5,528 (0.76%) |
| *NLP* | 1,525 (0.21%) |
| *C. majority* | 78,906 |

(June 1994, Lab. maj. 229,680)

MEMBERS ELECTED
R. Helmer, *C.*
**W. Newton Dunn, LD.
C. Heaton-Harris, *C.*
*Ms M. Read, *Lab.*
*P. Whitehead, *Lab.*
N. Clegg, *LD*

### LONDON

| | |
|---|---|
| *E.*4,940,493 | *T.*23.10% |
| *Lab.* | 399,466 (35.00%) |
| *C.* | 372,989 (32.68%) |
| *LD* | 133,058 (11.66%) |
| *Green* | 87,545 (7.67%) |
| *UK Ind.* | 61,741 (5.41%) |
| *Soc. Lab.* | 19,632 (1.72%) |
| *BNP* | 17,960 (1.57%) |
| *Lib.* | 16,951 (1.49%) |
| *Pro Euro C.* | 16,383 (1.44%) |
| *AHRPE* | 4,851 (0.43%) |
| *Anti VAT* | 2,596 (0.23%) |
| *Hum.* | 2,586 (0.23%) |
| *Hemp* | 2,358 (0.21%) |
| *NLP* | 2,263 (0.20%) |
| *WW* | 846 (0.07%) |
| *Lab. majority* | 26,477 |

(June 1994, Lab. maj. 346,850)

MEMBERS ELECTED
Miss T. Villiers, *C.*
Dr C. Tannock, *C.*
The Lord Bethell, *C.*
J. Bowis, *C.*
*Ms P. Green, *Lab.*
C. Moraes, *Lab.*
*R. Evans, *Lab.*
*R. Balfe, *Lab.*
Ms S. Ludford, *LD*
Ms J. Lambert, *Green*

### NORTH EAST

(Co. Durham; Darlington; Hartlepool; Middlesbrough; Northumberland; Redcar and Cleveland; Stockton-on-Tees; Tyne and Wear)

| | |
|---|---|
| *E.*1,954,076 | *T.*19.74% |
| *Lab.* | 162,573 (42.15%) |
| *C.* | 105,573 (27.37%) |
| *LD* | 52,070 (13.50%) |
| *UK Ind.* | 34,063 (8.83%) |
| *Green* | 18,184 (4.71%) |
| *Soc. Lab.* | 4,511 (1.17%) |
| *BNP* | 3,505 (0.91%) |
| *Pro Euro C.* | 2,926 (0.76%) |
| *SPGB* | 1,510 (0.39%) |
| *NLP* | 826 (0.21%) |
| *Lab. majority* | 57,000 |

(June 1994, Lab. maj. 330,689)

MEMBERS ELECTED
M. Callanan, *C.*
*A. Donnelly, *Lab.*
*S. Hughes, *Lab.*
Ms M. O'Toole, *Lab.*

### NORTHERN IRELAND

Northern Ireland forms a three-member seat with a single transferable vote system

| | |
|---|---|
| *E.*1,190,160 | *T.*57.77% |
| *First Count* | |
| *Revd I. Paisley, *DUP* | 192,762 |
| *J. Hume, *SDLP* | 190,731 |
| *J. Nicholson, *UUP* | 119,507 |
| M. McLaughlin, *SF* | 117,643 |
| D. Ervine, *PUP* | 22,494 |
| R. McCartney, *UKU* | 20,283 |
| S. Neeson, *All.* | 14,391 |
| J. Anderson, *NLP* | 998 |

MEMBERS ELECTED
*Revd I. Paisley, *DUP*
*J. Hume, *SDLP*
*J. Nicholson, *UUP* (elected on third count)

### NORTH WEST

(Blackburn-with-Darwen; Blackpool; Cheshire; Cumbria; Greater Manchester; Halton; Lancashire; Merseyside; Warrington)

| | |
|---|---|
| *E.*5,170,524 | *T.*19.67% |
| *C.* | 360,027 (35.39%) |
| *Lab.* | 350,511 (34.46%) |
| *LD* | 119,376 (11.74%) |

| | |
|---|---|
| *UK Ind.* | 66,779 (6.57%) |
| *Green* | 56,828 (5.59%) |
| *Lib.* | 22,640 (2.23%) |
| *BNP* | 13,587 (1.34%) |
| *Soc. Lab.* | 11,338 (1.11%) |
| *Pro Euro C.* | 9,816 (0.97%) |
| *ACPFCA* | 2,251 (0.22%) |
| *NLP* | 2,114 (0.21%) |
| *Ind. Hum.* | 1,049 (0.10%) |
| *WW* | 878 (0.09%) |
| *C. majority* | 9,516 |

(June 1994, Lab. maj. 444,569)

MEMBERS ELECTED

The Lord Inglewood, *C.*
Sir Robert Atkins, *C.*
D. Sumberg, *C.*
D. Dover, *C.*
Mrs J. Foster, *C.*
*Ms A. McCarthy, *Lab.*
*G. Titley, *Lab.*
*T. Wynn, *Lab.*
*B. Simpson, *Lab.*
C. Davies, *LD*

## SCOTLAND

| *E.*3,979,845 | *T.*24.83% |
|---|---|
| *Lab.* | 283,490 (28.68%) |
| *SNP* | 268,528 (27.17%) |
| *C.* | 195,296 (19.76%) |
| *LD* | 96,971 (9.81%) |
| *Green* | 57,142 (5.78%) |
| *SSP* | 39,720 (4.02%) |
| *Pro Euro C.* | 17,781 (1.80%) |
| *UK Ind.* | 12,549 (1.27%) |
| *Soc. Lab.* | 9,385 (0.95%) |
| *BNP* | 3,729 (0.38%) |
| *NLP* | 2,087 (0.21%) |
| *Lower Tax* | 1,632 (0.17%) |
| *Lab. majority* | 14,962 |

(June 1994, Lab. maj. 148,718)

MEMBERS ELECTED

S. Stevenson, *C.*
J. Purvis, *C.*
*D. Martin, *Lab.*
*W. Miller, *Lab.*
Ms C. Taylor, *Lab.*
Ms E. Attwooll, *LD*
*I. Hudghton, *SNP*
Prof. N. MacCormick, *SNP*

## SOUTH EAST

(Bracknell Forest; Brighton and Hove; Buckinghamshire; East Sussex; Hampshire; Isle of Wight; Kent; Medway; Milton Keynes; Oxfordshire; Portsmouth; Reading; Slough; Southampton; Surrey; West Berkshire; West Sussex; Windsor and Maidenhead; Wokingham)

| *E.*5,972,945 | *T.*24.95% |
|---|---|
| *C.* | 661,931 (44.42%) |
| *Lab.* | 292,146 (19.61%) |
| *LD* | 228,136 (15.31%) |
| *UK Ind.* | 144,514 (9.70%) |
| *Green* | 110,571 (7.42%) |
| *Pro Euro C.* | 27,305 (1.83%) |
| *BNP* | 12,161 (0.82%) |
| *Soc. Lab.* | 7,281 (0.49%) |
| *NLP* | 2,767 (0.19%) |
| *Ind. Stable* | 1,857 (0.12%) |
| *Ind. Profit* | 1,400 (0.09%) |
| *C. majority* | 369,785 |

(June 1994, C. maj. 230,122)

MEMBERS ELECTED

*J. Provan, *C.*
*R. Perry, *C.*
D. Hannan, *C.*
*J. Elles, *C.*
N. Deva, *C.*
*P. Skinner, *Lab.*
*M. Watts, *Lab.*
The Baroness Nicholson of Winterbourne, *LD*
C. Huhne, *LD*
Dr Caroline Lucas, *Green*
N. Farage, *UK Ind.*

## SOUTH WEST

(Bath and North-East Somerset; Bournemouth; Bristol; Cornwall; Devon; Dorset; Gloucestershire; North Somerset; Plymouth; Poole; Scilly Isles; Somerset; South Gloucestershire; Swindon; Torbay; Wiltshire)

| *E.*3,747,620 | *T.*27.81% |
|---|---|
| *C.* | 434,645 (41.70%) |
| *Lab.* | 188,362 (18.07%) |
| *LD* | 171,498 (16.45%) |
| *UK Ind.* | 111,012 (10.65%) |
| *Green* | 86,630 (8.31%) |
| *Lib.* | 21,645 (2.08%) |
| *Pro Euro C.* | 11,134 (1.07%) |
| *BNP* | 9,752 (0.94%) |
| *Soc. Lab.* | 5,741 (0.55%) |
| *NLP* | 1,968 (0.19%) |
| *C. majority* | 246,283 |

(June 1994, LD maj. 3,796)

MEMBERS ELECTED

*Dr Caroline Jackson, *C.*
*G. Chichester, *C.*
The Earl of Stockton, *C.*
N. Parish, *C.*
*G. Ford, *Lab.*
*G. Watson, *LD*
M. Holmes, *UK Ind.*

## WALES

| *E.*2,211,162 | *T.*28.33% |
|---|---|
| *Lab.* | 199,690 (31.88%) |
| *PC* | 185,235 (29.57%) |
| *C.* | 142,631 (22.77%) |
| *LD* | 51,283 (8.19%) |
| *UK Ind.* | 19,702 (3.15%) |
| *Green* | 16,146 (2.58%) |
| *Pro Euro C.* | 5,834 (0.93%) |
| *Soc. Lab.* | 4,283 (0.68%) |
| *NLP* | 1,621 (0.26%) |
| *Lab. majority* | 14,455 |

(June 1994, Lab. maj. 368,271)

MEMBERS ELECTED

J. Evans, *C.*
*Ms G. Kinnock, *Lab.*
*Ms E. Morgan, *Lab.*
Ms J. Evans, *PC*
E. Wyn, *PC*

## WEST MIDLANDS

(Herefordshire; Shropshire; Staffordshire; Stoke-on-Trent; Telford and Wrekin; Warwickshire; West Midlands Metropolitan County; Worcestershire)

| *E.*4,001,942 | *T.*21.21% |
|---|---|
| *C.* | 321,719 (37.91%) |
| *Lab.* | 237,671 (28.00%) |
| *LD* | 95,769 (11.28%) |
| *UK Ind.* | 49,621 (5.85%) |
| *Green* | 49,440 (5.83%) |
| *MEP Ind.* | 36,849 (4.34%) |
| *Lib.* | 14,954 (1.76%) |
| *BNP* | 14,344 (1.69%) |
| *Pro Euro C.* | 11,144 (1.31%) |
| *Soc. All.* | 7,203 (0.85%) |
| *Soc. Lab.* | 5,257 (0.62%) |
| *EFP* | 3,066 (0.36%) |
| *NLP* | 1,647 (0.19%) |
| *C. majority* | 84,048 |

(June 1994, Lab. maj. 268,888)

MEMBERS ELECTED

*J. Corrie, *C.*
P. Bushill-Matthews, *C.*
M. Harbour, *C.*
P. Bradbourn, *C.*
*S. Murphy, *Lab.*
M. Cashman, *Lab.*
Ms N. Gill, *Lab.*
Ms E. Lynne, *LD*

## YORKSHIRE AND THE HUMBER

(East Riding of Yorkshire; Kingston-upon-Hull; North East Lincolnshire; North Lincolnshire; North Yorkshire; South Yorkshire; West Yorkshire; York)

| *E.*3,767,227 | *T.*19.75% |
|---|---|
| *C.* | 272,653 (36.64%) |
| *Lab.* | 233,024 (31.32%) |
| *LD* | 107,168 (14.40%) |
| *UK Ind.* | 52,824 (7.10%) |
| *Green* | 42,604 (5.73%) |
| *Alt. Lab.* | 9,554 (1.28%) |
| *BNP* | 8,911 (1.20%) |
| *Pro Euro C.* | 8,075 (1.09%) |
| *Soc. Lab.* | 7,650 (1.03%) |
| *NLP* | 1,604 (0.22%) |
| *C. majority* | 39,629 |

(June 1994, Lab. maj. 344,310)

MEMBERS ELECTED

*E. McMillan-Scott, *C.*
T. Kirkhope, *C.*
R. Goodwill, *C.*
*Ms L. McAvan, *Lab.*
*D. Bowe, *Lab.*
*R. Corbett, *Lab.*
Ms D. Wallis, *LD*

## REPLACEMENTS SINCE THE LAST ELECTION

London 2000; Pauline Green replaced by Mary Honeyball, *Lab*
North East 2000; Alan Donnelly replaced by Gordon Adam, *Lab*

# Law Courts and Offices

## THE JUDICIAL COMMITTEE OF THE PRIVY COUNCIL

The Judicial Committee of the Privy Council is primarily the final court of appeal for the United Kingdom overseas and those independent Commonwealth countries which have retained this avenue of appeal (Antigua and Barbuda, The Bahamas, Barbados, Belize, Brunei, Dominica, Grenada, Jamaica, Kiribati, Mauritius, New Zealand, St Christopher and Nevis, St Lucia, St Vincent and the Grenadines, Trinidad and Tobago, and Tuvalu). The Committee also hears appeals from the Channel Islands and the Isle of Man and the disciplinary and health committees of the medical and allied professions. It has a limited jurisdiction to hear appeals under the Pastoral Measure 1983. In 2000 the Judicial Committee heard 76 appeals and 64 petitions for special leave to appeal.

Under the devolution legislation enacted in 1998, the Judicial Committee of the Privy Council is the final arbiter in disputes as to the legal competence of things done or proposed by the devolved legislative and Executive authorities in Scotland, Wales and Northern Ireland.

The members of the Judicial Committee include the Lord Chancellor, the Lords of Appeal in Ordinary (*see* page 368), other Privy Counsellors who hold or have held high judicial office and certain judges from the Commonwealth countries.

PRIVY COUNCIL OFFICE (JUDICIAL COMMITTEE), Downing Street, London SW1A 2AJ. Tel: 020-7270 0483.
*Registrar of the Privy Council*, J. A. C. Watherston; *Chief Clerk*, F. G. Hart

# The Judicature of England and Wales

The legal system of England and Wales is separate from those of Scotland and Northern Ireland and differs from them in law, judicial procedure and court structure, although there is a common distinction between civil law (disputes between individuals) and criminal law (acts harmful to the community).

The supreme judicial authority for England and Wales is the House of Lords, which is the ultimate Court of Appeal from all courts in Great Britain and Northern Ireland (except criminal courts in Scotland) for all cases except those concerning the interpretation and application of European Community law, including preliminary rulings requested by British courts and tribunals, which are decided by the European Court of Justice (*see* pages 773–81). Under the Human Rights Act 1998, which came into force on 2 October 2000, the European Convention on Human Rights is incorporated into British law; unresolved cases are still referred to the European Court of Human Rights. As a Court of Appeal the House of Lords consists of the Lord Chancellor and the Lords of Appeal in Ordinary (law lords).

### SUPREME COURT OF JUDICATURE

The Supreme Court of Judicature comprises the Court of Appeal, the High Court of Justice and the Crown Court. The High Court of Justice is the superior civil court and is divided into three divisions. The Chancery Division is concerned mainly with equity, bankruptcy and contentious probate business. The Queen's Bench Division deals with commercial and maritime law, serious personal injury and medical negligence cases, cases involving a breach of contract and professional negligence actions. The Family Division deals with matters relating to family law. Sittings are held at the Royal Courts of Justice in London or at 126 District Registries outside the capital. High Court judges sit alone to hear cases at first instance. The Restrictive Practices Court, set up under the Restrictive Trade Practices Act 1956, and the Technology and Construction Court, which deals with cases which require expert evidence on technical and other issues concerning mainly the construction industry, defective products, property valuations, and landlord and tenant disputes, are also currently part of the High Court, although the Restrictive Practices Court is due to be abolished following the establishment of the Competition Commission. Appeals from the High Court are heard in the Court of Appeal (Civil Division), presided over by the Master of the Rolls, and may go on to the House of Lords.

In December 1999 the Lord Chancellor began a wide ranging, independent review of the criminal courts in England and Wales. Lord Justice Auld lead the review into how the criminal courts work at every level.

### CRIMINAL CASES

In criminal matters the decision to prosecute in the majority of cases rests with the Crown Prosecution Service, the independent prosecuting body in England and Wales (*see* page 376). The Service is headed by the Director of Public Prosecutions, who works under the superintendence of the Attorney-General. Certain categories of offence continue to require the Attorney-General's consent for prosecution.

The Crown Court sits in about 90 centres, divided into six circuits, and is presided over by High Court judges, full-time circuit judges, and (part-time recorders and assistant recorders), sitting with a jury in all trials which are contested. Since the 12 April 2000, the Lord Chancellor changed the distinction between assistant recorders and recorders. Consequently, there are now only full recorders. The post of Assistant Recorder remains on the statute book but the Lord Chancellor no longer appoints any. There were 1400 full recorders at 30 June 2000. The Crown Court deals with trials of the more serious criminal offences, the sentencing of offenders committed for sentence by magistrates' courts (when the magistrates consider their own power of sentence inadequate), and appeals from magistrates' courts. Magistrates usually sit with a circuit judge or recorder to deal with appeals and committals for sentence. Appeals from the Crown Court, either against sentence or conviction, are made to the Court of Appeal (Criminal Division), presided over by the Lord Chief Justice. A further appeal from the Court of Appeal to the House of Lords can be brought if a point of law of general public importance is considered to be involved.

Minor criminal offences (summary offences) are dealt with in magistrates' courts, which usually consist of three unpaid lay magistrates (justices of the peace) sitting without a jury, who are advised on points of law and procedure by a legally-qualified clerk to the justices. There were 28,735 justices of the peace at 1 April 2001. In busier courts a full-time, salaried and legally-qualified stipendiary magistrate presides alone. Cases involving people under 18 are heard in youth courts, specially constituted magistrates' courts which sit apart from other courts. Preliminary proceedings in a serious case to decide whether there is evidence to justify committal for trial in the Crown Court are also dealt with in the magistrates' courts. Appeals from magistrates' courts against sentence or conviction are made to the Crown Court. Appeals upon a point of law are made to the High Court, and may go on to the House of Lords.

### Civil Cases

Most minor civil cases are dealt with by the county courts, of which there are about 222 (details may be found in the local telephone directory). Cases are heard by circuit judges, courts or district judges (magistrates courts). There were 399 district judges, and 97 District Judges (magistrates courts), formerly stipendiary magistrates at 1 May 2001. For cases involving small claims there are special simplified procedures. Where there are financial limits on county court jurisdiction, claims which exceed those limits may be tried in the county courts with the consent of the parties, subject to the Court's agreement, or in certain circumstances on transfer from the High Court. Outside London, bankruptcy proceedings can be heard in designated county courts. Magistrates' courts can deal with certain classes of civil case and committees of magistrates license public houses, clubs and betting shops. For the implementation of the Children Act 1989, a new structure of hearing centres was set up in 1991 for family proceedings cases, involving magistrates' courts (family proceedings courts), divorce county courts, family hearing centres and care centres. Appeals in family matters heard in the family proceedings courts go to the Family Division of the High Court; affiliation appeals and appeals from decisions of the licensing committees of magistrates go to the Crown Court. Appeals from county courts may be heard in the High Court of Appeal (civil division) and may go on to the House of Lords.

### Coroners' Courts

Coroners' courts investigate violent and unnatural deaths or sudden deaths where the cause is unknown. Cases may be brought before a local coroner (a senior lawyer or doctor) by doctors, the police, various public authorities or members of the public. Where a death is sudden and the cause is unknown, the coroner may order a post-mortem examination to determine the cause of death rather than hold an inquest in court.

Judicial appointments are made by The Queen; the most senior appointments are made on the advice of the Prime Minister and other appointments on the advice of the Lord Chancellor.

Under the provisions of the Criminal Appeal Act 1995, a Commission was set up to direct and supervise investigations into possible miscarriages of justice and to refer cases to the courts on the grounds of conviction and sentence these functions were formerly the responsibility of the Home Secretary.

## THE HOUSE OF LORDS
AS FINAL COURT OF APPEAL

*The Lord High Chancellor* (£167,760)
The Rt. Hon. the Lord Irvine of Lairg, *born* 1940, *apptd* 1997

Lords of Appeal in Ordinary (each £152,072)
*Style*, The Rt. Hon. Lord—
Rt. Hon. Lord Bingham of Cornhill, *born* 1933, *apptd* 2000
Rt. Hon. Lord Slynn of Hadley, *born* 1930, *apptd* 1992
Rt. Hon. Lord Nicholls of Birkenhead, *born* 1933, *apptd* 1994
Rt. Hon. Lord Steyn, *born* 1932, *apptd* 1995
Rt. Hon. Lord Hoffman, *born* 1934, *apptd* 1995
Rt. Hon. Lord Hope of Craighead, *born* 1938, *apptd* 1996
Rt. Hon. Lord Clyde, *born* 1932, *apptd* 1996
Rt. Hon. Lord Hutton, *born* 1931, *apptd* 1997
Rt. Hon. Lord Saville of Newdigate, *born* 1936, *apptd* 1997
Rt. Hon. Lord Hobhouse of Woodborough, *born* 1932, *apptd* 1998
Rt. Hon. Lord Millett, *born* 1932, *apptd* 1998
Rt. Hon. Lord Scott Foscote , *born* 1934, *apptd* 2000

*Judicial Office of the House of Lords*, House of Lords, London SW1A 0PW. Tel: 020-7219 3111
*Registrar*, The Clerk of the Parliaments (*see* page 217)

## SUPREME COURT OF JUDICATURE

## COURT OF APPEAL

*The Master of the Rolls* (£163,213), The Rt. Hon. Lord Phillips of Worth Matravers, *born* 1938, *apptd* 2000,
*Secretary*, Mrs L. Grace
*Clerk*, Ms J. Jones

Lords Justices of Appeal (each £149,897)
*Style*, The Rt. Hon. Lord/Lady Justice [surname]

Rt. Hon. Sir Paul Kennedy, *born* 1935, *apptd* 1992
Rt. Hon. Sir Simon Brown, *born* 1937, *apptd* 1992
Rt. Hon. Sir Christopher Rose, *born* 1937, *apptd* 1992
Rt. Hon. Sir John Roch, *born* 1934, *apptd* 1993
Rt. Hon. Sir Peter Gibson, *born* 1934, *apptd* 1993
Rt. Hon. Sir Denis Henry, *born* 1931, *apptd* 1993
Rt. Hon. Sir Swinton Thomas, *born* 1931, *apptd* 1994
Rt. Hon. Sir Philip Otton, *born* 1933, *apptd* 1995
Rt. Hon. Sir Robin Auld, *born* 1937, *apptd* 1995
Rt. Hon. Sir Malcolm Pill, *born* 1938, *apptd* 1995
Rt. Hon. Sir William Aldous, *born* 1936, *apptd* 1995
Rt. Hon. Sir Alan Ward, *born* 1938, *apptd* 1995
Rt. Hon. Sir Konrad Schiemann, *born* 1937, *apptd* 1995
Rt. Hon. Sir Mathew Thorpe, *born* 1938, *apptd* 1995
Rt. Hon. Sir Mark Potter, *born* 1937, *apptd* 1996
Rt. Hon. Sir Henry Brooke, *born* 1936, *apptd* 1996
Rt. Hon. Sir Igor Judge, *born* 1941, *apptd* 1996
Rt. Hon. Sir Mark Waller, *born* 1940, *apptd* 1996
Rt. Hon. Sir John Mummery, *born* 1938, *apptd* 1996
Rt. Hon. Sir Charles Mantell, *born* 1937, *apptd* 1997
Rt. Hon. Sir John Chadwick, ED, *born* 1941, *apptd* 1997
Rt. Hon. Sir Robert Walker, *born* 1938, *apptd* 1997
Rt. Hon. Sir Richard Buxton, *born* 1938, *apptd* 1997
Rt. Hon. Sir Anthony May, *born* 1940, *apptd* 1997
Rt. Hon. Sir Simon Tuckey, *born* 1941, *apptd* 1998
Rt. Hon. Sir Anthony Clarke, *born* 1943, *apptd* 1998
Rt. Hon. Sir John Laws, *born* 1945, *apptd* 1999
Rt. Hon. Sir Stephen Sedley, *born* 1939, *apptd* 1999
Rt. Hon. Sir Jonathan Mance, *born* 1943, *apptd* 1999
Rt. Hon. Dame Brenda Hale, *born* 1945, *apptd* 1999
Rt Hon. Sir David Latham, *born* 1942, *apptd* 2000
Rt. Hon Sir John William Kay, *born* 1943, *apptd.* 2000
Rt. Hon. Sir Bernard Anthony Rix, *born* 1944, *apptd.*
Rt. Hon. Sir Jonathan Parker, *born* 1937, *apptd* 2000
Rt. Hon. Dame Mary Howarth Alden, DBE, *born* 1947, *apptd* 2000
Rt. Hon. Sir David Wolfe Keene, *born* 1941, *apptd* 2000

Rt. Hon. Sir John Anthony Dyson, *born* 1943, *apptd* 2001
Rt. Hon. Sir Andrew Centlivres Longmore, *born* 1944, *apptd* 2001

*Ex officio Judges*, The Lord High Chancellor; the Lord Chief Justice of England; the Master of the Rolls; the President of the Family Division; and the Vice-Chancellor

### Court of Appeal (Civil Division)

*Vice-President*, The Rt. Hon. Lord Justice Nourse

### Court of Appeal (Criminal Division)

*Vice-President*, The Rt. Hon. Lord Justice Rose
*Judges*, The Lord Chief Justice of England; the Master of the Rolls; Lords Justices of Appeal; and Judges of the High Court of Justice

### Courts-Martial Appeal Court

*Judges*, The Lord Chief Justice of England; the Master of the Rolls; Lords Justices of Appeal; and Judges of the High Court of Justice

## HIGH COURT OF JUSTICE

## CHANCERY DIVISION

*President*, The Lord High Chancellor
*The Vice-Chancellor* (£157,699), The Rt. Hon. Sir Andrew Moritt, CVO, *born*, 1938 *apptd* 1994
*Clerk*, W. Northfield, BEM

### Judges (each £132,603)

*Style*, The Hon. Mr/Mrs Justice [surname]

Hon. Sir Francis Ferris, TD, *born* 1932, *apptd* 1990
Hon. Sir John Lindsay, *born* 1935, *apptd* 1992
Hon. Sir Edward Evans-Lombe, *born* 1937, *apptd* 1993
Hon. Sir Robin Jacob, *born* 1941, *apptd* 1993
Hon. Sir William Blackburne, *born* 1944, *apptd* 1993
Hon. Sir Gavin Lightman, *born* 1939, *apptd* 1994
Hon. Sir Robert Carnwath, *born* 1945, *apptd* 1994
Hon. Sir Colin Rimer, *born* 1944, *apptd* 1994
Hon. Sir Hugh Laddie, *born* 1946, *apptd* 1995
Hon. Sir Timothy Lloyd, *born* 1946, *apptd* 1996
Hon. Sir David Neuberger, *born* 1948, *apptd* 1996
Hon. Sir Andrew Park, *born* 1939, *apptd* 1997
Hon. Sir Nicholas Pumfrey, *born* 1951, *apptd* 1997
Hon. Sir Michael Hart, *born* 1948, *apptd* 1998
Hon. Sir Lawrence Collins, *born* 1941, *apptd* 2000
Hon. Sir Nicholas John Pattern, *born* 1950, apptd 2000
Hon Sir Terence Michael Barnet Etherton, *born* 1951, *apptd* 2001
Rt. Hon. Sir Andrew Morritt, CVO, *born* 1938, *apptd* 2000

### High Court of Justice in Bankruptcy

*Judges*, The Vice-Chancellor and judges of the Chancery Division of the High Court

### Companies Court

*Judges*, The Vice Chancellor and judges of the Chancery Division of the High Court

### Patent Court (Appellate Section)

*Judge*, The Hon. Mr Justice Jacob

## QUEEN'S BENCH DIVISION

*The Lord Chief Justice of England and Wales* (£171,375) The Rt. Hon. the Lord Woolf, *born* 1933, *apptd* 2000
*Private Secretary*, E. Adams
*Clerk*, J. Bond

*Vice-President*, The Rt. Hon. Lord Justice Kennedy until 1 February 2002 when The Rt. Hon. Lord Justice May will take office.

### Judges (each £132,603)

*Style*, The Hon. Mr/Mrs Justice [surname]

Hon. Sir Patrick Garland, *born* 1929, *apptd* 1985
Hon. Sir Michael Turner, *born* 1931, *apptd* 1985
Hon. Sir Humphrey Potts, *born* 1931, *apptd* 1986
Hon. Sir Richard Rougier, *born* 1932, *apptd* 1986
Hon. Sir Stuart McKinnon, *born* 1938, *apptd* 1988
Hon. Sir Scott Baker, *born* 1937, *apptd* 1988
Hon. Sir Michael Morland, *born* 1929, *apptd* 1989
Hon. Sir Roger Buckley, *born* 1939, *apptd* 1989
Hon. Sir Anthony Hidden, *born* 1936, *apptd* 1989
Hon. Sir Michael Wright, *born* 1932, *apptd* 1990
Hon. Sir John Blofeld, *born* 1932, *apptd* 1990
Hon. Sir Peter Cresswell, *born* 1944, *apptd* 1991
Hon. Dame Ann Ebsworth, DBE, *born* 1937, *apptd* 1992
Hon. Sir Christopher Holland, *born* 1937, *apptd* 1992
Hon. Sir Richard Curtis, *born* 1933, *apptd* 1992
Hon. Dame Janet Smith, DBE, *born* 1940, *apptd* 1992
Hon. Sir Anthony Colman, *born* 1938, *apptd* 1992
Hon. Sir Thayne Forbes, *born* 1938, *apptd* 1993
Hon. Sir Michael Sachs, *born* 1932, *apptd* 1993
Hon. Sir Stephen Mitchell, *born* 1941, *apptd* 1993
Hon. Sir Rodger Bell, *born* 1939, *apptd* 1993
Hon. Sir Michael Harrison, *born* 1939, *apptd* 1993
Hon. Dame Heather Steel, DBE, *born* 1940, *apptd* 1993
Hon. Sir William Gage, *born* 1938, *apptd* 1993
Hon. Sir Thomas Morison, *born* 1939, *apptd* 1993
Hon. Sir Andrew Collins, *born* 1942, *apptd* 1994
Hon. Sir Maurice Kay, *born* 1942, *apptd* 1995
Hon. Sir Anthony Hooper, *born* 1937, *apptd* 1995
Hon. Sir Alexander Butterfield, *born* 1942, *apptd* 1995
Hon. Sir George Newman, *born* 1941, *apptd* 1995
Hon. Sir David Poole, *born* 1938, *apptd* 1995
Hon. Sir Martin Moore-Bick, *born* 1946, *apptd* 1995
Hon. Sir Gordon Langley, *born* 1943, *apptd* 1995
Hon. Sir Roger Thomas, *born* 1947, *apptd* 1996
Hon. Sir Robert Nelson, *born* 1942, *apptd* 1996
Hon. Sir Roger Toulson, *born* 1946, *apptd* 1996
Hon. Sir Michael Astill, *born* 1938, *apptd* 1996
Hon. Sir Alan Moses, *born* 1945, *apptd* 1996
Hon. Sir Timothy Walker, *born* 1946, *apptd* 1996
Hon. Sir David Eady, *born* 1943, *apptd* 1997
Hon. Sir Jeremy Sullivan, *born* 1945, *apptd* 1997
Hon. Sir David Penry-Davey, *born* 1942, *apptd* 1997
Hon. Sir Stephen Richards, *born* 1950, *apptd* 1997
Hon. Sir David Steel, *born* 1943, *apptd* 1998
Hon. Sir Rodney Klevan, *born* 1940, *apptd* 1998
Hon. Sir Charles Gray, *born* 1942, *apptd* 1998
Hon. Sir Nicolas Bratza, *born* 1945, *apptd* 1998
Hon. Sir Michael Burton, *born* 1946, *apptd* 1998
Hon. Sir Rupert Jackson, *born* 1948, *apptd* 1998
Hon. Dame Heather Hallett, *born* 1949, *apptd* 1999
Hon. Sir Patrick Elias, *born* 1947, *apptd* 1999
Hon. Sir Richard Aikens, *born* 1948, *apptd* 1999
Hon. Sir Stephen Silber, *born* 1944, apptd 1999
Hon. Sir Peter Crane, *born* 1940, *apptd* 2000
Hon. Dame Anne Rafferty, *born* 1951, *apptd* 2000
Hon. Sir Geoffrey Grigson, *born* 1944, *apptd* 2000
Hon. Sir Richard Gibbs, *born* 1941, *apptd* 2000
Hon. Sir Richard Henriques, *born* 1943, *apptd* 2000
Hon. Sir Stephen Tomlinson, *born* 1952, *apptd* 2000
Hon. Sir Andrew Smith, *born* 1947, *apptd* 2000
Hon. Sir Stanley Burnton, *born* 1942, *apptd* 2000
Hon. Sir Patrick Hunt, *born* 1943, *apptd* 2000
Hon. Sir Brian Leveson, *born* 1949, *apptd* 2000

Hon. Sir Raymond Jack, *born* 1942, *apptd* 2000
Hon. Sir Duncan Ouseley, *born* 1950, *apptd* 2000
Hon. Sir Colin Mackay, *born* 1943, *apptd* 2001
Hon. Sir John Edward Mitting, *born* 1947, *apptd* 2001
Hon. Sir David Roderick Evans, *born* 1946, *apptd* 2001
Hon. Sir Brian Richard Keith, *born* 1944, *apptd* 2001
Hon. Sir Richard George Bramwell McCombe, *born* 1952 *appt* 2001
Hon. Sir Raymond Evan Jack, *born* 1942, *apptd* 2001
Hon. Sir Robert Michael Owen, *born* 1944, *apptd* 2001

## FAMILY DIVISION

*President* (£157,699), The Rt. Hon. Dame Elizabeth Butler-Sloss, DBE, *born* 1933, *apptd* 1999
*Secretary*, Mrs S. Leung
*Clerk*, Mrs S. Bell

### JUDGES (each £132,603)

Hon. Sir Robert Johnson, *born* 1933, *apptd* 1989
Hon. Dame Joyanne Bracewell, DBE, *born* 1934, *apptd* 1990
Hon. Sir Michael Connell, *born* 1939, *apptd* 1991
Hon. Sir Peter Singer, *born* 1944, *apptd* 1993
Hon. Sir Nicholas Wilson, *born* 1945, *apptd* 1993
Hon. Sir Nicholas Wall, *born* 1945, *apptd* 1993
Hon. Sir Andrew Kirkwood, *born* 1944, *apptd* 1993
Hon. Sir Hugh Bennett, *born* 1943, *apptd* 1995
Hon. Sir Edward Holman, *born* 1947, *apptd* 1995
Hon. Dame Mary Hogg, DBE, *born* 1947, *apptd* 1995
Hon. Sir Christopher Sumner, *born* 1939, *apptd* 1996
Hon. Sir Anthony Hughes, *born* 1948, *apptd* 1997
Hon. Sir Arthur Charles, *born* 1948, *apptd* 1998
Hon. Sir David Bodey, *born* 1947, *apptd* 1998
Hon. Dame Jill Black, *born* 1954, *apptd* 1999
Hon. Sir James Munby, *born* 1949, *apptd* 2000
Hon. Sir Paul Coleridge, *born* 1949, *apptd* 2000

## RESTRICTIVE PRACTICES COURT

Room 410, Thomas More Building, Royal Courts of Justice, Strand, London WC2A 2LL
Tel: 020-7947 6727

*President*, The Hon. Mr Justice Buckley
*Judges*, The Hon. Mr Justice Ferris; The Hon. Mr Justice Lightman
*Lay Members*, B. M. Currie; Sir Lewis Robertson, CBE; R. Garrick, CBE; S. J. Ahearne; J. A. Graham; Mrs D. H. Hatfield; J. A. Scott; B. D. Colgate; J. A. C. King
*Clerk of the Court*, M. Buckley

## TECHNOLOGY AND CONSTRUCTION COURT

St Dunstan's House, 133–137 Fetter Lane, London EC4A 1HD. Tel: 020-7947 7427

### JUDGES (each £107,346)

The Hon. Mr Justice Forbes (*Presiding Judge*)
His Hon. Judge Bowsher, QC
His Hon. Judge Havery, QC
His Hon. Judge Seymour, QC
His Hon. Judge Thornton, QC
His Hon. Judge Wilcox
His Hon. Judge Toulmin, CMG, QC
Her Hon. Judge Kirkham

*Court Manager*, Mrs S. Morson

## LORD CHANCELLOR'S DEPARTMENT

— *see* Government Departments and Public Offices

## SUPREME COURT DEPARTMENTS AND OFFICES

Royal Courts of Justice, London WC2A 2LL
Tel: 020-7947 6000

### DIRECTOR'S OFFICE

*Director*, I. Hyams
*Group Manager and Deputy Director*, J. Selch
*Group Manager, Family Proceedings and Probate Service*, R. P. Knight
*Finance and Performance Officer*, vacant

### ADMIRALTY AND COMMERCIAL REGISTRY AND MARSHAL'S OFFICE

*Registrar* (£79,767), P. Miller
*Admiralty Marshal and Court Manager*, K. Houghton

### BANKRUPTCY DEPARTMENT

*Chief Registrar* (£99,420), M. C. B. Buckley
*Bankruptcy Registrars* (£79,767), W. S. James; J. A. Simmonds; P. J. S. Rawson; S. Baister; G. W. Jaques
*Court Manager*, Mrs J. O'Connor

### CENTRAL OFFICE OF THE SUPREME COURT

*Senior Master of the Supreme Court (QBD), and Queen's Remembrancer* (£99,420), R. L. Turner
*Masters of the Supreme Court (QBD)* (£79,767), D. L. Prebble; G. H. Hodgson; J. Trench; M. Tennant; P. Miller; N. O. G. Murray; I. H. Foster; G. H. Rose; P. G. A. Eyre; H. J. Leslie; J. G. G. Ungley
*Court Manager*, M. A. Brown

### CHANCERY CHAMBERS

*Chief Master of the Supreme Court* (£99,420), J. I. Winegarten
*Masters of the Supreme Court* (£79,767), J. A. Moncaster; R. A. Bowman; N. W. Bragge; T. J. Bowles
*Court Manager*, G. Robinson
*Conveyancing Counsel of the Supreme Court*, W. D. Ainger; H. M. Harrod; A. C. Taussig

### COMPANIES COURT

*Registrar* (£79,767), M. Buckley
*Court Manager*, Mrs O'Connel

### COURT OF APPEAL CIVIL DIVISION

*Head of the Civil Appeals Office* R. A. Venne
*Court Manager*, Miss H. M. Goddard

### COURT OF APPEAL CRIMINAL DIVISION

*Registrar* (£99,420), M. McKenzie, CB, QC
*Deputy Registrar*, Mrs L. G. Knapman
*Chief Clerk*, M. Bishop

### COURTS-MARTIAL APPEALS OFFICE

*Registrar* (£99,420), M. McKenzie, CB, QC
*Chief Clerk*, M. Bishop

### CROWN OFFICE OF THE SUPREME COURT

*Master of the Crown Office, and Queen's Coroner and Attorney* (£99,420), M. McKenzie, CB, QC
*Head of Crown Office*, Mrs L. G. Knapman
*Chief Clerk*, M. Bishop

### EXAMINERS OF THE COURT

Empowered to take examination of witnesses in all Divisions of the High Court

A. G. Dyer; A. W. Hughes; Mrs G. M. Kenne; R. M. Planterose; Miss V. E. I. Selvaratnam

### Supreme Court Costs Office

*Senior Cost Judge* (£99,420), P. T. Hurst
*Masters of the Supreme Court* (£79,767), M. Ellis; T. H. Seager Berry; C. C. Wright; P. R. Rogers; G. N. Pollard; J. E. O'Hare; C. D. N. Campbell
*Court Manager*, D. O'Riordan

### Court of Protection

Stewart House, 24 Kingsway, London WC2B 6HD
Tel: 020-7664 7000

*Master* (£99,420), D. A. Lush

### Election Petitions Office

Room E218, Royal Courts of Justice, Strand, London WC2A 2LL. Tel: 020-7947 6131

The office accepts petitions and deals with all matters relating to the questioning of parliamentary, European Parliament and local government elections, and with applications for relief under the Representation of the People legislation.
*Prescribed Officer*, R. L. Turner
*Chief Clerk*, Miss J. L. Waine

### Office of the Lord Chancellor's Visitors

Stewart House, 24 Kingsway, London WC2B 6HD
Tel: 020-7664 7317

*Legal Visitor*, A. R. Tyrrell
*Medical Visitors*, K. Khan; W. B. Sprey; E. Mateu; S. E. Mahapatra; A. Bailey; A. Kaeser

### Official Receivers' Department

21 Bloomsbury Street, London WC1B 3SS
Tel: 020-7323 3090

*Senior Official Receiver*, M. C. A. Osborne
*Official Receivers*, M. J. Pugh; L. T. Cramp; J. Norris

### Official Solicitor's Department

81 Chancery Lane, London WC2B 6HD
Tel: 020-7911 7105

*Official Solicitor to the Supreme Court*, P. M. Harris
*Deputy Official Solicitor*, H. J. Baker
*Chief Clerk*, R. Lancaster

### Principal Registry (Family Division)

First Avenue House, 42–49 High Holborn, London WC1V 6NP. Tel: 020-7947 6000

*Senior District Judge* (£99,420), G. B. N. A. Angel
*District Judges* (£80,921), B. P. F. Kenworthy-Browne; Mrs K. T. Moorhouse; M. J. Segal; R. Conn; Miss I. M. Plumstead; G. J. Maple; Miss H. C. Bradley; K. J. White; A. R. S. Bassett-Cross; N. A. Grove; M. C. Berry; Miss S. M. Bowman; C. Million; P. Waller; Miss P. Cushing; R. Harper; G. C. Brasse; Miss D. C. Redgrave
*Family and Probate Service Group Manager*, R. P. Knight

*District Probate Registrars*
*Birmingham and Stoke-on-Trent*, C. Marsh
*Brighton and Maidstone*, P. Ellwood
*Bristol, Exeter and Bodmin*, R. H. P. Joyce
*Cardiff, Bangor and Carmarthen*, R. F. Yeldam
*Ipswich, Norwich and Peterborough*, D. N. Mee
*Leeds, Lincoln and Sheffield*, A. P. Dawson
*Liverpool, Lancaster and Chester*, C. Fox
*Manchester and Nottingham*, M. A. Moran
*Newcastle, Carlisle, York and Middlesbrough*, P. Sanderson
*Oxford, Gloucester and Leicester*, R. R. Da Costa
*Winchester*, A. K. Biggs

## JUDGE ADVOCATES

## OFFICE OF THE JUDGE ADVOCATE OF THE FLEET

c/o The Crown Court at Chichester, Southgate, Chichester PO19 1SX. Tel: 01243 520741

*Judge Advocate of the Fleet* (£99,420), His Hon. Judge Sessions

## OFFICE OF THE JUDGE ADVOCATE-GENERAL OF THE FORCES

(*Joint Service for the Army and the Royal Air Force*)
22 Kingsway, London WC2B 6LE. Tel: 020-7218 8089

*Judge Advocate-General* (£99,420), His Hon. Judge J. W. Rant, CB, QC
*Vice-Judge Advocate-General* (£95,666), E. G. Moelwyn-Hughes
*Judge Advocates* (£79,767), M. A. Hunter; J. P. Camp; C. R. Burn; R. C. C. Seymour; I. H. Pearson; R. G. Chapple; J. F. T. Bayliss
*Style for Judge Advocates*, Judge Advocate [surname]

## HIGH COURT AND CROWN COURT CENTRES

First-tier centres deal with both civil and criminal cases and are served by High Court and circuit judges. Second-tier centres deal with criminal cases only and are served by High Court and circuit judges. Third-tier centres deal with criminal cases only and are served only by circuit judges.

### Midland Circuit

*First-tier* – Birmingham, Lincoln, Nottingham, Oxford, Stafford, Warwick
*Second-tier* – Leicester, Northampton, Shrewsbury, Worcester
*Third-tier* – Coventry, Derby, Hereford, Stoke-on-Trent, Wolverhampton
*Circuit Administrator*, P. Risk , The Priory Courts, 6th Floor, 33 Bull Street, Birmingham B4 6DS. Tel: 0121-681 3201
*Group Managers: Birmingham Group*, Mrs D. Ponsonby; *West Midlands/Warwickshire Group*; D. Bennett, *Staffordshire/West Mercia*; A. Phillips, *East Midlands*

### North-Eastern Circuit

*First-tier* – Leeds, Newcastle upon Tyne, Sheffield, Teesside
*Second-tier* – Bradford, York
*Third-tier* – Doncaster, Durham, Kingston-upon-Hull
*Circuit Administrator*, P. J. Farmer, 18th Floor, West Riding House, Albion Street, Leeds LS1 5AA. Tel: 0113-251 1200
*Group Managers:* P. M. Norris *North and West Yorkshire Group, Newcastle upon Tyne Group*, Miss S. Proudlock; *Sheffield Group* D.Keane; *Teesside Group*, Miss E. Yates

### Northern Circuit

*First-tier* – Carlisle, Liverpool, Manchester (Crown Square), Preston

*Third-tier* – Barrow-in-Furness, Bolton, Burnley, Lancaster; Manchester (Minshull Street)
*Circuit Administrator*, R. A. Vincent, 15 Quay Street, Manchester M60 9FD. Tel: 0161-833 1005
*Group Managers:Greater Manchester Group*, Miss G. Hague; *Merseyside Group*, R. Knott; *Lancashire and Cumbria Group*; S. McNally

### South-Eastern Circuit

*First-tier* – Chelmsford, Lewes, Norwich
*Second-tier* – Ipswich, London (Central Criminal Court), Luton, Maidstone, Reading, St Albans
*Third-tier* – Aylesbury, Basildon, Bury St Edmunds, Cambridge, Canterbury, Chichester, Croydon, Guildford, King's Lynn, London (Blackfriars, Harrow, Inner London Sessions House, Isleworth, Kingston, Middlesex Guildhall, Snaresbrook, Southwark, Wood Green, Woolwich), Southend
*Circuit Administrator*, K. Pogson, New Cavendish House, 18 Maltravers Street, London WC2R 3EU. Tel: 020-7947 7235
*Group Managers:* K. Budgen (*London Crime*); D. Thompson (*London City*); L. Lennon (*Kent and Sussex*); M. Littlewood (*East Anglia, Bedfordshire and Hertfordshire*), S. Townley (*Thames Valley, Surrey and Oxford*).

The High Court in Greater London sits at the Royal Courts of Justice.

### Wales and Chester Circuit

*First-tier* – Caernarfon, Cardiff, Chester, Mold, Swansea
*Second-tier* – Carmarthen, Merthyr Tydfil, Newport, Welshpool
*Third-tier* – Dolgellau, Haverfordwest, Knutsford, Warrington
*Circuit Administrator*, N. Chipnall, Churchill House, Churchill Way, Cardiff CF10 4HH. Tel: 029-2041 5500
*Group Managers:South Wales Group*, G. Pickett; *North Wales and Cheshire Group*, G. Kenney; *Swansea Group*, Mrs D. Thomas

### Western Circuit

*First-tier* – Bristol, Exeter, Truro, Winchester
*Second-tier* – Dorchester, Gloucester, Plymouth, Weymouth
*Third-tier* – Barnstaple, Bournemouth, Newport (IOW), Portsmouth, Salisbury, Southampton, Swindon, Taunton
*Circuit Administrator*, D. Ryan, Bridge House, Sion Place, Clifton, Bristol BS8 4BN. Tel: 0117-974 3763
*Group Managers: East Group*, N. Jeffery; *Exeter Group*, D. Gentry; *West Group*, D. Gentry

## CIRCUIT JUDGES

**Senior Circuit Judges*, each £107,346
*Circuit Judges at the Central Criminal Court, London* (*Old Bailey Judges*), each £107,346
*Circuit Judges*, each £99,420
*Style*, His/Her Hon. Judge [surname]
*Senior Presiding Judge*, The Rt. Hon. Lord Justice Judge

### Midland Circuit

*Presiding Judges*, The Hon. Mr Justice Astill (until 1 January 2002 when The Hon. Mr Justice Goldring will take office).

Miss C. Alton; B. J. Appleby, QC; D. P. Bennett; R. S. A. Benson; R. W. A. Bray; D. W. Brunning; N. B. Cameron Coles, QC; J. R. Case; J. J. Cavell; F. A. Chapman; P. N. R. Clark (Shared with South-East Circuit); M. F. Coates; R. R. B. Cole; I. Collis; T. G. E. Corrie; *Mrs P. A. Deeley; P. N. de Mille (Shared with South-East Circuit); C. H. Durman; R. M. Eades; H. W. P. Eccles, QC; T. M. Faber; Miss E. N. Fisher; J. E. Fletcher; A. C. Geddes; R.H. Griffith-Jones; J. Hall; V. E. Hall; A. N. Hamilton; D. R. D. Hamilton; S. T. Hammond; G. C. W. Harris, QC; M. J. Heath; Miss E. J. Hindley, QC; C. R. Hodson; J. R. Hopkin; Mrs H. M. Hughes; R. A. G. Inglis; A. W. P. King; Ms F. M. Kirkham; P. G. McCahill, QC; D. L. McCarthy; A. W. McCreath; M. N. McKenna; A. G. MacDuff, QC; D. D. McEvoy, QC; J. V. Machin; M. H. Mander; L. Marshall; W. D. Matthews; H. R. Mayor, QC; C. Metcalf; A. P. Mitchell; P. R. Morrell; J. I. Morris; M. D. Mott; A. J. D. Nicholl; S. Oliver-Jones, QC; R. Onions; R. T. N. Orme; R. C. C. O'Rorke; J. F. F. Orrell; D. S. Perrett, QC; C. J. Pitchers; D. P. Pugsley; J. R. Pyke; R. J. Rubery; R. Rundell; J. A. O. Shand; D. P. Stanley; M. G. T. Stokes, QC; P. J. Stretton; G. C. Styler; A. B. Taylor; J. J. Teare; R. S. W. F. Tonking; S. Waine; *R.M.Wakerley, QC (Recorder of Birmingham) J. J. Wait; J. C. Warner; C.T. Wide QC

*Following a boundary review in April 2001 the Oxford Circuit has now become part of the South-East Circuit.*

### North-Eastern Circuit

*Presiding Judges*, The Hon. Mr Justice Henriques; The Hon. Mr Justice Bennett

### North and West Yorkshire Group

R. Adams; G. N. Barr Young; J. E. Barry; C. O. J. Behrens; C. Benson; B. Bush; P. J. Charlesworth; G. Cliffe; P. J. Cockroft; G. J. K. Coles; J. Dobkin; J. Dowse; A. C. Finnerty; M. S. Garner; R. A. Grant; S. P. Grenfell; S. J. Gullick; T. S. A. Hawkesworth, QC; P. M. L. Hoffman; R. Ibbotson; N. H. Jones, QC; G. H. Kamil; R. Keen, QC; T. D. Kent-Jones, TD; P. Langan, QC; K. M. P. Macgill; A. G. McCallum; C. I. McGonigal; J. Prophet; R. M. Scott; J. Spencer, QC; T. Walsh; J. S. Wolstenholme

### Newcastle Group

P. J. B. Armstrong; B. Bolton; P. H. Bowers; A. N. J. Briggs; D. M. A. Bryant; M. C. Carr; M. L. Cartlidge; W. H. R. Crawford, QC; E. J. Faulks; P. J. Fox, QC; G. F. R. Harkins; T. D. T. Hodson; A. T. Lancaster; P. Lowden; J. P. Moir; M.G.C. Moorhouse; D. A. Orde; L. Spittle; M. Taylor; C. T. Walton; G. Walford; G. Whitburn, QC; D. R. Wood

### Sheffield Group

T. W. Barber; R. Bartfield; D. R. Bentley, QC; J. W. Bullimore; A. C. Carr; J. Crabtree; J. Cracknell; J. Davies; A. R. Goldsack, QC; P. J. M. Heppel, QC; T. Hewitt; L. Hull; P. Jones; M. K. Mettyear; R. J. Moore; M. J. A. Murphy, QC; J. H. Reddihough; P. E. Robertshaw; J. Shipley; L. Sutcliffe; J. A. Swanson; M. Walker

### Northern Circuit

*Presiding Judge*, The Hon. Mr Justice Perry-Davey; The Hon. Mr Justice Douglas Brown (until 1 January 2001 when The Hon. Mr Justice Leveson will take office).

M. P. Allweis; J. F. Appleton; E. K. Armitage, QC; R. K. Atherton; Miss P. H. Badley; S. W. Baker; R. C. W. Bennett;A. N. H. Blake; C. Bloom, QC; D. J. Boulton; L. F. M. Brown; R. Brown; J. K. Burke, QC; I. B. Campbell; B. I. Caulfield; D. Clark; *D. C. Clarke, QC (*Recorder of Liverpool*); G. M. Clifton; I. W. Crompton; Miss J. M. P. Daley;*R. E. Davies, QC (*Recorder of Manchester*); Miss A. E. Downey; B. R. Duckworth; S. B. Duncan; Miss D. B. Eaglestone;T. K. Earnshaw; G. A. Ensor; D. M. Evans,

QC; S. J. D. Fawcus; P. S. Fish; J. R. B. Geake; D. S. Gee; W. George; J. A. D. Gilliland, QC; N.B.D. Gilmour, QC; I. M. Hamilton; J. A. Hammond; D. Harris, QC; M. Hedley; T. B. Hegarty, QC; M. J. Henshell; F. R. B. Holloway; R. C. Holman; N. J. G. Howarth; G. W. Humphries; C. E. F. James; P. M. Kershaw, QC (*Commercial Circuit Judge*); Miss L. J. Kushner, QC; P. M. Lakin; B. L. Lever; B. W. Lewis; R. J. D. Livesey, QC; A. C. Lowcock; A. P. Lyon; D. Lynch; D. I. Mackay; J. B. Macmillan; D. G. Maddison; B. C. Maddocks; C. J. Mahon; J. A. Morgan; W. P. Morris; T. J. Mort; L. Newton; *C. P. L. Openshaw, QC; F. D. Owen, TD; J. A. Phillips; J. C. Phipps; P. R. Raynor, QC; J. H. Roberts; Miss M. Roddy; Miss G. D. Ruaux; H. S. Singer; E. Slinger; A. C. Smith; W. P. Smith; Miss E. M. Steel; M. Steiger, QC; D. R. Swift; P. Sycamore; C. B. Tetlow; I. J. C. Trigger; Miss B. J. Watson; K. H. P. Wilkinson; B. Woodward

### South-Eastern Circuit

*Presiding Judges*, The Hon. Mr Justice Aikens; The Hon. Mr Justice Moses

J. D. R. Adams; M. F. Addison; P. C. Ader; J. Altman; Mrs S. C. Andrew; A. R. L. Ansell; M. G. Anthony; S. A. Anwyl, QC; E. H. Bailey; M. F. Baker, QC; C. G. Ball, QC; A. F. Balston; G. S. Barham; B. J. Barker, QC; C. J. A. Barnett, QC; W. E. Barnett, QC; R. A. Barratt, QC; K. Bassingthwaighte; *G. A. Bathurst Norman; P. J. L. Beaumont, QC (*Common Serjeant*); N. E. Beddard; R. V. M. E. Behar; Mrs C. V. Bevington; N.C. van der Bijl; I. G. Bing; M. G. Binning; J. E. Bishop; B. M. B. Black; H. O. Blacksell, QC; J. G. Boal, QC; A. V. Bradbury; P. N. Brandt; G. B. Breen; R. G. Brown; J. M. Bull, QC; The Hon. C. W. Byers; H. J. Byrt, QC; J. Q. Campbell; M. J. Carroll; M.T. Caterson; B. E. F. Catlin; *B. L. Charles, QC; P. C. L. Clark; P. C. Clegg; Miss S. Coates; N. J. Coleman; S. H. Colgan; *P. H. Collins, CBE; C. C. Colston, QC; S. S. Coltart; ; C. D. Compston; T. A. C. Coningsby, QC; J. G. Connor; R. D. Connor; M. J. Cook; R. A. Cooke; M. R. Coombe; P. E. Copley; T. G. E. Corrie; P. Crawford, QC; Dr E. Cotran; P. R. Cowell; R. C. Cox; M. L. S. Cripps; C. A. Critchlow; J. F. Crocker; D. L. Croft, QC; D. M. Cryan; P. Curl; Mrs P. M. T. Dangor; A. M. Darroch; M. Dean, QC; P. G. Dedman; J. E. Devaux; M. N. Devonshire, TD; P. Dodgson; P. H. Downes; W. H. Dunn, QC; C. M. Edwards; D. R. Ellis; R. C. Elly; C. Elwen; F. P. L. Evans; Miss D. Faber; J. D. Farnworth; P. Fingret; P. E. J. Focke, QC; P. Ford; G. C. F. Forrester; Ms D. A. Freedman; L. Gerber; C. A. H. Gibson; Miss A. F. Goddard, QC; S. A. Goldstein; C. G. M. Gordon; J. B. Gosschalk; A. A. Goymer; B. S. Green, QC; A. E. Greenwood; P.Grobel; TD, VRD D. A. B. R. Hallgarten, QC; Miss G. Hallon; J. Hamilton; Miss S. Hamilton, QC; C. R. H. Hardy; B. Hargrove, OBE, QC; C. Harris, QC; M. F. Harris; A. M. Harvey; W. G. Hawkesworth; R. G. Hawkins, QC; J. M. Haworth; R. J. Haworth; R. M. Hayward; A. N. Hitching; H. E. G. Hodge, OBE; K. M. J. Hollis; J. F. Holt; A. C. W. Hordern, QC; K. A. D. Hornby; M. Hucker; J.C.A. Hughes; M. J. Hyam (*Recorder of London*); D. A. Inman; A. B. Issard-Davies; D. G. A. Jackson; Dr P. J. E. Jackson; T. J. C. Joseph; I. G. F. Karsten, QC; S. S. Katkhuda; C. J. B. Kemp; M. Kennedy, QC; W. A. Kennedy; A. M. Kenny; A.W.P. King; T. R. King; B. J. Knight, QC; P.E. Knowles; L. G. Krikler; L. H. C. Lait; P. QC; Capt. J. B. R. Langdon, RN; P. H. Latham; R. Laurie; T. Lawrence; D. M. Levy, QC; C. C. D. Lindsay, QC; S. H. Lloyd; F. R. Lockhart; J. A. M. Lowen; Mrs C. M. Ludlow; Capt. S. Lyons; A. G. McDowall; R. J. McGregor-Johnson; B. M. McIntyre; K. A. Machin, QC; R. G. McKinnon; W. N. McKinnon; N. A. McKittrick; K. C. Macrae; T. Maher; F. J. M. Marr-Johnson; D. N. N. Martineau; D. Matheson, QC; N. A. Medawar, QC; D. B. Meier; D. J. Mellor; G. D. Mercer; P.N. De Mille; D. Q. Miller; Miss A. E. Mitchell; D.C. Mitchell; F. I. Mitchell; H. M. Morgan; D. Morton Jack; R. T. Moss; Miss M. J. S. Mowat; T. M. E. Nash; M. H. D. Neligan; Mrs M. F. Norrie; Brig. A. P. Norris, OBE; P. W. O'Brien; M. A. Oppenheimer; D. C. J. Paget, QC; D. J. Parry; A. Patience, QC; Mrs N. Pearce; Prof. D. S. Pearl; Miss V. A. Pearlman; B. P. Pearson; N. A. J. Philpot; T. D. Pillay; D. C. Pitman; J. R. Platt; J. R. Playford, QC; Miss I. M. Plumstead; P. B. Pollock; T. G. Pontius; W. D. C. Poulton; S. Pratt; R. J. C. V. Prendergast; B. H. Pryor, QC; D. W. Radford; J. W. Rant, CB, QC; E. V. P. Reece; D. J. Rennie; J. R. Reid, QC; M. P. Reynolds; M. S. Rich, QC; D. J. Richardson; N. P. Riddell; G. Rivlin, QC; S. D. Robbins; J. M. Roberts; D. A. H. Rodwell, QC; G. H. Rooke, TD, QC; W. M. Rose; T. R. G. Ryland; J. E. A. Samuels, QC; R. B. Sanders; A. R. G. Scott-Gall; J. S. Sennitt; D. Serota, QC; J. L. Sessions; D. R. A. Sich; A. G. Simmons; K. T. Simpson; P. R. Simpson; M. Singh, QC; S. P. Sleeman; C. M. Smith, QC; S. A. R. Smith; Miss Z. P. Smith; E. Southwell; S. B. Spence; S. M. Stephens, QC; N. A. Stewart; D. M. A. Stokes, QC; G. Stone, QC; T. M. F. Stow, QC; J. B. C. Tanzer, QC; A. M. Tapping; C. Thomas; P. J. Thompson; A. G. Y. Thorpe; C. H. Tilling; C. J. M. Tyrer; Mrs A. P. Uziell-Hamilton; J. E. van der Werff; T. L. Viljoen; J. P. Wadsworth, QC; Miss A. P. Wakefield; R. Wakefield; R. Walker; S. P. Waller; A. R. Webb; C. S. Welchman; A. F. Wilkie, QC; S. R. Wilkinson; Miss J. A. Williams; R. J. Winstanley; S.E. Woollam; D. Worsley; M. P. Yelton; M. K. Zeidman, QC; K. H. Zucker, QC

### Wales and Chester Circuit

*Presiding Judges*, The Hon. Mr Justice Richard; The Hon. Mr Justice Connell; The Hon. Mr Justice Thomas (until 1 January 2001 when The Hon. Mr Justice Pitchford will take office).

K. E. Barnett; M. R. Burr; G. H. F. Carson; J. R. Case; N. M. Chambers, QC; S. P. Clarke; J. T. Curran; Miss J. M. P. Daley; G. H. M. Daniel; D. T. A. Davies; J. B. S. Diehl, QC; R. T. Dutton; D. E. H. Edwards; G. O. Edwards, QC; The Lord Elystan-Morgan; P. M. Farmer; M. R. Furness; J. W. Gaskell; D. R. Halbert; D. J. Hale; Miss J. E. Hayward; G. R. Hickinbottom; R. P. Hughes; T. M. Hughes, QC; P. J. Jacobs; G. J. Jones; H. D. H. Jones; G. E. Kilfoil; C. G. Masterman; D. G. Morris; D. C. Morton; T. H. Moseley, QC; G. A. L. Price, QC; P. J. Price, QC; D. W. Richards; P. B. Richards; J. M. T. Rogers, QC; A. A. Wallace; *J. G. Williams, QC; N. F. Woodward

### Western Circuit

*Presiding Judges*, The Hon. Mrs Justice Hallett, DBE; The Hon. Mr Justice Toulson

P. R. Barclay; J. F. Beashel; R. H. Bond; Miss J. A. M. Bonvin; C. L. Boothman; M. J. L. Brodrick; J. M. J. Burford, QC; R. D. H. Bursell, QC; M. G. Cotterill; *T. Crowther, QC;G. W. A. Cottle; K. C. Cutler; P. M. Darlow; S. C. Darwall Smith; Mrs L. H. Davies; J. D. Foley; F. H. S. Gilbert, QC; D. L. Griffiths; J. D. Griggs; Mrs C. M. A. Hagen; J. A. Havelock-Allan, QC; P. J. C. R. Hooton; M. K. Harington; G. B. Hutton; J. R. Jarvis; A. G. H. Jones; C. H. de V. Leigh, QC; T. Longbotham; T. N. Mackean; Miss S. M. D. McKinney; I. S. McKintosh; J. G. McNaught; The Lord Meston, QC; T. J. Milligan; J. O. Neligan; S. K. O'Malley; S. K. Overend; R. Price; R. C. Pryor, QC; M. W. Roach; R. Rucker; J. N. P. Rudd; A. Rutherford; Miss A. O. H. Sander; D. H. D. Selwood; R. M. Shawcross; D. A. Smith, QC; W. E. M. Taylor; P. M. Thomas; A. A. R. Thompson, QC; D. K. Ticehurst, QC; D.

I. H. Tyzack, QC; R. C. B. Wade; D. MacLaren Webster, QC; J. H. Weeks, QC; J. S. Wiggs;

RECORDERS (each £422 per day)

F. A. Abbott; R. D. I. Adam; J. F. Akast; D. J. Ake; R. Akenhead, QC; I. D. G. Alexander, QC; C. D. Allan, QC; C. J. Alldis; J. H. Allen, QC; D. M. Altaras; A. J. Anderson, QC; W. P. Andreae-Jones, QC; Mrs E. H. Andrew; P. J. Andrews, QC; R. A. Anelay, QC; J. M. Appleby; Miss L. E. Appleby, QC; B. J. Argyle; G. K. Arran; S. J. Ashurst; E. G. Aspley; P. Atherton; N. J. Atkinson, QC; D. J. M. Aubrey, QC; D. S. Aubrey; M. G. Austin-Smith, QC; M. J. S. Axtell; W. S. Aylen, QC; P. D. Babb; J. F. Badenoch, QC; P. G. N. Badge; A. B. Baillie; N. R. J. Baker, QC; Miss A. Ball, QC; A. Barker, QC; G. E. Barling, QC; D. N. Barnard; H. J. Barnes; T. P. Barnes, QC; A. J. Barnett; Miss F. J. Baron, QC; D. A. Bartlett; G. R. Bartlett, QC; J. C. T. Barton, QC; D. C. Bate, QC; S. D. Batten, QC; P. D. Batty, QC; J. J. Baughan, QC; J. F. T. Bayliss; R. A. Bayliss; D. M. Bean; C. M. Beale; J. Beatson; S. J. Bedford; R. W. Belben; J. K. Benson; P. C. Benson; R. A. Benson, QC; H. L. Bentham, QC; D. M. Berkson; C. R. Berry; M. Bethel, QC; J. P. V. Bevan; Mrs M. O. Bickford-Smith; N. Bidder; P. V. Birkett, QC; M. I. Birnbaum; W. J. Birtles; P. W. Birts, QC; M. J. Black, QC; B. G. D. Blair, QC; W. J. L. Blair, QC; P. E. Bleasdale; R. H. L. Blomfield, TD; D. J. Blunt, QC; O. S. P. Blunt, QC; G. T. K. Boney, QC; Ms C. Booth, QC; J. J. Boothby; S. N. Bourne-Arton, QC; M. J. Bowerman; Ms M. R. Bowron; W. Boyce; S. C. Boyd, QC; J. J. Boyle; D. L. Bradshaw; W. T. S. Braithwaite, QC; D. J. Brennan, QC; M. L. Brent, QC; G. J. B. G. Brice, QC; A. J. Brigden; D. R. Bright; R. P. Brittain; R. A. Britton; J. Bromley-Davenport; S. C. Brown, QC; D. J. M. Browne, QC; J. N. Browne; A. J. N. Brunner, QC; R. V. Bryan; Miss B. M. Bucknall, QC; J. E. Bullen; J. P. Burke, QC; L. S. Burn; H. W. Burnett, QC; R. H. Burns; F. G. Burrell, QC; K. Bush; A. J. Butcher, QC; C. M. Butler; Miss J. Butler; M. D. Byrne; D. W. Caddick; D. Calvert-Smith, QC; R. Camden Pratt, QC; Miss S. M. C. Cameron, QC; A. N. Campbell, QC; Ms A. R. Campbell; J. M. Caplan, QC; G. M. C. Carey, QC; A. C. Carlile, QC, MP; H. B. H. Carlisle, QC; J. J. Carter-Manning, QC; R. Carus, QC; Mrs J. R. Case; P. D. Cattan; R. M. Challinor; Miss D. C. Champion; C. B. Chandler; V. R. Chapman; J. M. Cherry, QC; A. C. Chippindall; C. F. Chruszcz, QC; C. H. Clark, QC; C. S. C. S. Clarke, QC; T. N. Clark; P. W. Clarke; P. R. J. Clarkson, QC; T. Clayson; A. S. L. Cleary; W. Clegg, QC; P. Clements; T. A. Clover; W. P. Coates; D. J. Cocks, QC; J. J. Coffey, QC; T. A. Coghlan, QC; J. L. Cohen; L. F. R. Cohen, QC; W. J. Coker, QC; A. J. S. Coleman; A. R. Collender, QC; P. N. Collier, QC; M. G. Collins, QC; Mrs J. R. Comyns; D. G. Conlin; A. D. Conrad; C. S. Cook; J. L. Cooke, QC; N. O. Cooke; K. B. Coonan, QC; A. E. M. Cooper; P. J. Cooper, QC; C. J. Cornwall; P. J. Cosgrove, QC; Miss D. R. Cotton, QC; J. S. Coward, QC; T. G. Cowling; Mrs L. M. Cox, QC; P. Crampin, QC; L. S. Crawford; N. Crichton; D. I. Crigman, QC; D. R. Crome; S. R. Crookenden, QC; Mrs J. E. Crowley; J. D. Crowley, QC; T. S. Culver; Miss E. A. M. Curnow, QC; P. D. Curran; J. W. O. Curtis, QC; M. J. Curwen; A. J. G. Dalziel; C. P. M. Davidson; A. M. Davies; A. R. M. Davies; H. Davies; J. T. L. Davies; Miss N. V. Davies, QC; R. L. Davies, QC; N. A. L. Davis, QC; W. E. Davis; A. W. Dawson; D. H. Day, QC; Ms M. R. de Haas, QC; P. A. de la Piquerie; M. A. de Navarro, QC; R. L. Denyer, QC; H. A. D. de Silva; P. N. Digney; C. E. Dines; A. D. Dinkin, QC; D. R. Dobbin; R. S. Dodds; R. A. M. Doggett; Ms B. Dohmann, QC; D. T. Donaldson, QC; A. M. Donne, QC; A. F. S. Donovan; A. K. Dooley; Ms J. M. R. Dowell; M. J. Dudley; J. R. Duggan; P. R. Dunkels, QC; J. D. Durham Hall, QC; R. M. C. N. Edelman, QC; A. J. C. Edis, QC; A. H. Edwards; Miss S. M. Edwards, QC; A. J. C. Edwards-Stuart, QC; A. J. Elleray, QC; G. Elias, QC; E. A. Elliott; J. A. Elvidge; R. M. Englehart, QC; D. A. Evans, QC; D. H. Evans, QC; F. W. H. Evans, QC; G. J. Evans; G. W. R. Evans, QC; I. Evans; M. Evans, QC; M. J. Evans; M. A. Everall, QC; R. B. Farley, QC; D. J. Farrer, QC; P. E. Feinberg, QC; J. F. Q. Fenwick, QC; R. Fernyhough, QC; M. C. Field; R. A. Field, QC; J. E. Finestein; D. T. Fish; D. P. Fisher, QC; G. D. Flather, CBE, QC; R. A. Flowerdew; N. M. Ford, QC; R. A. Fordham, QC; B. C. Forster; M. D. P. Fortune; D. R. Foskett, QC; I. H. Foster; J. R. Foster, QC; D. P. Friedman, QC; S. A. Furst, QC; C. J. E. Gardner, QC; P. R. Garlick, QC; C. R. Garside, QC; R. C. Gaskell; J. B. Gateshill; S. A. G. L. Gault; A. H. Gee, QC; I. W. Geering, QC; D. S. Geey; C. R. George, QC; S. M. Gerlis; D. C. Gerrey; J. S. Gibbons, QC; A. J. Gilbart, QC; N. J. Gilchrist; K. Gillance; N. B. D. Gilmour, QC; L. Giovenne; R. P. Glancy, QC; A. T. Glass, QC; M. G. J. Gledhill; H. B. Globe, QC; Miss E. Gloster, QC; H. K. Goddard, QC; H. A. Godfrey, QC; Ms L. S. Godfrey, QC; J. J. Goldberg, QC; I. S. Goldrein, QC; P. H. Goldsmith, QC; A. J. Goldstaub, QC; L. C. Goldstone, QC; A. J. J. Gompertz, QC; Miss R. M. Goode; J. R. W. Goss; T. J. C. Goudie, QC; G. Gozem; The Lord Grabiner, QC; H. Green, QC; Miss J. E. G. Greenberg, QC; J. C. Greenwood; J. G. Grenfell, QC; D. E. Griffith-Jones; J. P. G. Griffiths, QC; M. G. Grills; M. S. E. Grime, QC; P. H. Gross, QC; B. P. Gulbenkian; J. D. Guthrie, QC; A. S. Hacking, QC; J. W. Haines; N. J. Hall; S. J. Hall; J. P. N. Hallam; G. M. Hamilton, TD, QC; P. L. Hamlin; J. L. Hand, QC; G. T. Harrap; P. J. Harrington, QC; R. D. Harrison; R. M. Harrison, QC; H. M. Harrod; J. M. Harrow; C. A. Hart-Leverton, QC; B. Harvey; J. G. Harvey; M. L. T. Harvey, QC; D. W. Hatton, QC; A. M. D. Havelock-Allan, QC; The Hon. P. N. Havers, QC; R. W. P. H. Hay; Prof. D. J. Hayton; R. Hayward-Smith, QC; R. Hedgeland; A. T. Hedworth, QC; R. A. Henderson, QC; R. C. Herman; M. S. Heslop QC; J. W. Hillyer; A. J. H. Hilton, QC; J. W. Hirst, QC; W. T. J. Hirst; J. D. Hitchen; S. A. Hockman, QC; A. J. C. Hoggett, QC; T. V. Holroyde, QC; R. M. Hone; G. A. J. Hooper; A. D. Hope; S. J. Hopkins; M. A. P. Hopmeier; M. Horowitz, QC; Miss R. Horwood-Smart; C. P. Hotten, QC; B. F. Houlder, QC; M. N. Howard, QC; C. I. Howells; M. J. Hubbard, QC; D. L. Hughes; Miss K. L. Hughes; P. T. Hughes, QC; L. D. Hull; Capt. D. R. Humphrey, RN; W. G. B. Hungerford; D. R. N. Hunt, QC; I. G. A. Hunter, QC; M. A. Hunter; G. N. N. Huskinson; M. Hussain, QC; J. G. K. Hyland; M. D. Inman, QC; P. R. Isaacs; S. L. Isaacs, QC; S. M. Jack; M. R. Jackson; I. E. Jacob; N. F. B. Jarman, QC; J. M. Jarvis, QC; A. H. Jeffreys; D. A. Jeffreys, QC; J. D. Jenkins, QC; J. J. Jenkins; Miss A. M. Jolles; D. A. F. Jones; D. L. Jones; S. E. Jones, QC; W. J. Jones; R. C. Jose; Ms W. R. Joseph, QC; H. M. Joy; P. S. L. Joyce, QC; R. W. S. Juckes; M. L. Kallipetis, QC; Miss L. N. R. Kamill; R. G. Kaye, QC; C. B. Kealy; K. R. Keen, QC; Mrs S. M. Keen; D. Kennett Brown; D. M. Kerr; L. D. Kershen, QC; M. I. Khan; G. M. P. F. Khayat, QC; C. A. Kinch; T. R. A. King, QC; M. S. Knott; C. J. Knox; Miss J. C. M. Korner, QC; S. E. Kramer, QC; P. E. Kyte, QC; N. R. W. Lambert; D. C. Lamdin; D. A. Landau; D. G. Lane, QC; B. F. J. Langstaff, QC; R. B. Latham, QC; S. W. Lawler, QC; Sir Ivan Lawrence, QC; Miss E. A. Lawson, QC; M. H. Lawson, QC; G. S. Lawson-Rogers, QC; P. L. O. Leaver, QC; D. Lederman, QC; B. W. T. Leech; I. Leeming, QC; H. B. G. Lett; A. E. Levy, QC; M. E. Lewer, QC; J. A. Lewis; K. M. J. Lewison, QC; S. J. Linehan, QC; R. A. Lissack, QC; G. W. Little; B. J. E. Livesey, QC; C. G. Llewellyn-Jones, QC; L. J. R. Lobo; C. J. Lockhart-Mummery, QC; A. J. C. Lodge, QC; D. C. Lovell-Pank, QC; G. W. Lowe; Rt. Hon. Sir Nicholas Lyell, QC, MP; R. G. B. McCombe, QC; G. F. McDermott; A. E. McFarlane, QC;

R. D. Machell, QC; D. L. Mackie; I. A. B. McLaren, QC; I. McLeod; N. R. B. Macleod, QC; Ms J. Macur, QC; A. G. Mainds; A. H. R. Maitland; A. R. Malcolm; H. J. Malins; M. E. Mann, QC; The Hon. G. R. J. Mansfield; R. L. Marks; J. W. Marrin, QC; A. L. Marriott, QC; G. M. Marriott; A. S. Marron, QC; P. Marsh; R. G. Marshall-Andrews, QC; G. C. Marson; H. R. A. Martineau; S. A. Maskrey, QC; C. P. Mather; P. R. Matthews; Mrs S. P. Matthews, QC; P. B. Mauleverer, QC; R. B. Mawrey, QC; J. F. M. Maxwell; R. Maxwell, QC; Mrs P. R. May; R. M. J. Meeke; G. M. Mercer; N. F. Merriman, QC; C. S. J. Metcalf; J. T. Milford, QC; K. S. H. Miller; P. W. Miller; R. A. Miller; S. M. Miller, QC; C. J. Millington; C. E. Million; J. B. M. Milmo, QC; D. C. Milne, QC; C. J. M. Miskin, QC; Miss C. M. Miskin; A. R. Mitchell, QC; C. R. Mitchell; D. C. Mitchell; J. R. Mitchell; F. R. Moat; E. G. Moelwyn-Hughes; C. R. D. Moger, QC; D. R. P. Mole, QC; M. G. C. Moorhouse; A. G. Moran, QC; P. B. Morgan; A. P. Morris, QC; C. Morris-Coole; H. A. C. Morrison, OBE; R. F. Morrison; G. E. Morrow, QC; M. G. M. Morse; C. J. Moss, QC; P. C. Mott, QC; R. W. Moxon-Brown, QC; J. H. Muir; F. J. Muller, QC; A. H. Munday, QC; G. S. Murdoch, QC; I. P. Murphy, QC; A. C. Murray; C. M. Murray; N. O. G. Murray; N. J. Mylne, QC; H. G. Narayan; A. R. H. Newman, QC; A. I. Niblett; G. Nice, QC; A. E. R. Noble; B. Nolan, QC; M. C. Norman; J. M. Norris; P. H. Norris; G. Nuttall; J. G. Nutting, QC; D. P. O'Brien, QC; Mrs F. M. T. Oldham, QC; M. D. Oldham; R. W. Onions; M. N. O'Sullivan; N. D. Padfield, QC; Miss A. M. Page, QC; S. R. Page; A. O. Palmer, QC; A. W. Palmer, QC; D. P. Pannick, QC; A. D. W. Pardoe, QC; S. A. B. Parish; P. L. Parker; G. C. Parkins, QC; G. E. Parkinson; M. P. Parroy, QC; D. J. T. Parry; E. O. Parry; N. S. K. Pascoe, QC; Miss A. E. H. Pauffley, QC; J. G. Paulusz; W. E. Pawlak; F. M. Pearce; D. J. Pearce-Higgins, QC; R. J. Pearse Wheatley; The Hon. I. J. C. Peddie, QC; J. V. Pegden; J. Perry, QC; M. Pert, QC; N. M. Peters, QC; J. R. D. Philips; D. J. Phillips, QC; W. B. Phillips; M. A. Pickering, QC; J. K. Pickup; The Hon. B. M. D. Pitt; Miss E. F. Platt, QC; R. Platts; R. O. Plender, QC; Miss J. C. Plumptre; S. D. Popat; A. R. Porten, QC; L. R. Portnoy; J. R. L. Posnansky, QC; Mrs R. M. Poulet, QC; S. R. Powles, QC; D. Price; J. A. Price, QC; J. C. Price; N. P. L. Price, QC; R. Price Lewis; R. B. L. Prior; F. S. K. Privett; H. W. Prosser; A. C. Pugh, QC; G. V. Pugh, QC; G. F. Pulman, QC; C. P. B. Purchas, QC; R. M. Purchas, QC; N. R. Purnell, QC; P. O. Purnell, QC; Q. C. W. Querelle; N. P. Quinn; D. A. Radcliffe; Mrs N. P. Radford, QC; T. W. H. Raggatt, QC; Miss E. A. Ralphs; J. Y. Randall, QC; A. D. Rawley, QC; J. E. Rayner James, QC; J. H. Reddihough; M. H. Redfern, QC; A. R. F. Redgrave, QC; D. W. Rees; G. W. Rees; P. Rees; C. E. Reese, QC; P. C. Reid; R. E. Rhodes, QC; T. Rigby; S. V. Riordan, QC; G. Risius; Miss J. H. Ritchie, QC; T. D. Roberts; A. J. Robertson; G. R. Robertson, QC; V. Robinson, QC; D. E. H. Robson, QC; G. W. Roddick, QC; Miss D. J. Rodgers; P. F. G. Rook, QC; J. G. Ross; J. G. Ross Martyn; P. C. Rouch; J. J. Rowe, QC; R. J. Royce, QC; M. W. Rudland; P. E. B. M. Rueff; A. A. Rumbelow, QC; N. J. Rumfitt, QC; R. J. Rundell; J. R. T. Rylance; C. R. A. Sallon, QC; C. N. Salmon; D. A. Salter; G. R. Sankey, QC; N. L. Sarony; J. H. B. Saunders, QC; M. P. Sayers, QC; R. J. Scholes, QC; T. J. W. Scott; Miss P. Scriven, QC; R. J. Seabrook, QC; C. Seagroatt, QC; W. P. L. Sellick; O. M. Sells, QC; A. J. Seys-Llewellyn; A. R. F. Sharp; P. P. Shears; S. J. Sher, QC; Miss D. A. Sherwin; P. C. H. Simon, QC; Miss E. A. Slade, QC; A. T. Smith, QC; D. Smith; P. W. Smith, QC; R. D. H. Smith, QC; C. J. Smyth; R. C. Southwell, QC, M. H. Spence, QC; Sir Derek Spencer, QC; J. Spencer, QC; M. G. Spencer, QC; R. G. Spencer; S. M. Spencer, QC; R. V. Spencer Bernard; D. P. Spens, QC; R. W. Spon-Smith; D. Steer, QC; Mrs L. J. Stern, QC; A. W. Stevenson, TD; J. S. H. Stewart, QC; S. P. Stewart, QC; W. R. Stewart Smith; A. C. Steynor; G. J. C. Still; D. A. Stockdale, QC; Mrs D. M. Stocken; J. B. Storey, QC; D. M. A. Strachan, QC; M. Stuart-Moore, QC; J. H. Stuart-Smith, QC; F. R. C. Such; A. B. Suckling, QC; Ms L. E. Sullivan, QC; D. M. Sumner; J. P. C. Sumption, QC; M. A. Supperstone, QC; P. J. Susman; R. P. Sutton, QC; N. H. Sweeney; Miss C. J. Swift, QC; M. R. Swift, QC; Miss H. H. Swindells, QC; C. J. M. Symons, QC; J. P. Tabor, QC; J. A. Tackaberry, QC; P. J. Talbot, QC; R. K. K. Talbot; R. B. Tansey, QC; G. F. Tattersall, QC; E. T. H. Teague; N. J. M. Teare, QC; R. H. Tedd, QC; A. D. Temple, QC; V. B. A. Temple, QC; M. H. Tennant; The Lord Thomas of Gresford, OBE, QC; P. A. Thomas; R. L. Thomas, QC; R. M. Thomas; R. U. Thomas, QC; Miss S. M. Thomas; C. F. J. Thompson; R. E. T. Thorn, QC; A. R. Thornhill, QC; P. R. Thornton, QC; A. C. Tickle; M. B. Tillett, QC; J. W. Tinnion; R. N. Titheridge, QC; P. J. H. Towler; J. B. S. Townend, QC; C. M. Treacy, QC; H. B. Trethowan; A. D. H. Trollope, QC; D. W. Tucker; M. G. Tugendhat, QC; H. W. Turcan; D. A. Turner, QC; J. Turner; P. A. Twigg, QC; J. F. Uff, QC; R. P. A. Ullstein, QC; N. E. Underhill, QC; J. G. G. Ungley; P. C. Upward, QC; H. V. C. Vagg; N. P. Valios, QC; D. A. J. Vaughan, QC; M. J. D. Vere-Hodge, QC; C. J. Vosper; S. P. Waine; R. A. Walker, QC; R. J. Walker, QC; Sir Jonah Walker-Smith, Bt.; J. J. Wardlow; B. B. Warner; J. Warren, QC; N. J. Warren; N. R. Warren, QC; D. E. B. Waters; Miss B. J. Watson; Sir James Watson, Bt.; B. J. Waylen; A. S. Webster, QC; M. R. West; L. J. West-Knights; G. B. N. White; W. J. M. White; D. R. B. Whitehouse, QC; R. P. Whitehurst; P. G. Whiteman, QC; P. J. M. Whiteman, TD; A. Whitfield, QC; S. J. P. Widdup; R. Wigglesworth; Mrs M. Wilby; N. V. M. Wilkinson, QC; Miss E. Willers; G. H. G. Williams, QC; J. L. Williams, QC; M. J. Williams; W. L. Williams, QC; Miss H. E. Williamson, QC; S. W. Williamson, QC; A. J. D. Wilson, QC; A. M. Wilson, QC; I. K. R. Wilson; C. Wilson-Smith, QC; G. W. Wingate-Saul, QC; Miss S. E. Wollam; H. Wolton, QC; M. M. Wood, QC; N. A. Wood; R. L. J. Wood, QC; W. R. Wood; Miss S. Woodley, QC; J. T. Woods; W. C. Woodward, QC; A. P. L. Woolman; T. H. Workman; Miss A. M. Worrall, QC; P. F. Worsley, QC; J. J. Wright; N. A. Wright; D. E. M. Young, QC

## DISTRICT JUDGES (MAGISTRATES' COURTS)

The Provincial and Metropolitan Divisions have now been changed, all former Provincial and Metropolitan Stipendiary Magistrates can serve nationally within any district and are now called District Judges (Magistrates' Courts).

*District Judges* (each £80,921)
*Former Provincial Magistrates* (each £79,767 and £4,000 additional London allowance)

M. A. Abelson, *apptd* 1998; Mrs J. H. Alderson, *apptd* 1997; R. W. Anderson, *apptd* 1999; Mrs A. M. Arnold, *apptd* 1999; J. A. Browne, *apptd* 1992; P. H. R. Browning, *apptd* 1994; N. R. Cadbury, *apptd* 1997; G. E. Cawdron, *apptd* 1993; D. J. Chinery, *apptd* 1998; T. G. Cowling, *apptd* 1989; C. R. Darnton, *apptd* 1994; S. N. Day, *apptd* 1991; Mrs S. E. Driver, *apptd* 1995; P. K. Dodd, OBE, *apptd* 1991; P. R. Farmer, *apptd* 1998; J. Finestein, *apptd* 1992; P. J. Firth, *apptd* 1994; M. J. Friel, *apptd* 1997; I. Gillespie, *apptd* 1991; K. A.Gray, *apptd* 1995; M. L. R. Harris, *apptd* 1991; N. P. Heley, *apptd* 1994; Mrs P. A. Hewitt, *apptd* 1990; G.

A. K. Hodgson, *apptd* 1993; R. Holland, *apptd* 1999; M. F. James, *apptd* 1991; J. A. Jellema, *apptd* 1998; P. H. F. Jones, *apptd* 1995; C. M. McColl, *apptd* 1994; D. V. Manning-Davies, *apptd* 1996; D. M. Meredith, *apptd* 1995; B. Morgan, *apptd* 1989; P. F. Nuttall, *apptd* 1991; W. M. Probert, *apptd* 1983; M. A. Rosenberg, *apptd* 1993; Mrs M. Shelvey, *apptd* 1999; P. C. Tain, *apptd* 1992; D. R. G. Tapp, *apptd* 1992; D. L. Thomas, *apptd* 1999; W. D. Thomas, *apptd* 1989; P. S. Ward, *apptd* 1994; P. H. Wassall, *apptd* 1994; G. R. Watkins, *apptd* 1993; Miss P. J. Watkins, *apptd* 1995; N. H. White, *apptd* 1985; C. S. Wiles, *apptd* 1996; J. I. Woollard, *apptd* 1998

### Metropolitan Districts

*Bow Street*, The Chief Magistrate; H. N. Evans, *apptd* 1994; C. L. Pratt, *apptd* 1990; T. Workman, *apptd* 1986
*Camberwell Green*, C. P. M. Davidson, *apptd* 1984; K. Grant, *appt* 1999; R. House, *apptd* 1995; Mrs L. Morgan, *appt* 1995; Miss C. S. R. Tubbs, *apptd* 1996
*Greenwich*, D. A. Cooper, *apptd* 1991; M. Kelly, *apptd* 1992; H. C. F. Riddle, *apptd* 1995; P. S. Wallis, *apptd* 1993
*Highbury Corner*, I. M. Baker, *apptd* 1990; P. A. M. Clark, *apptd* 1996; A. T. Evans, *apptd* 1990; M. A. Johnstone, *apptd* 1980; Mrs L. Morgan, *apptd* 1995; J. Perkins, *apptd* 1999; Miss D. Quick, *apptd* 1986
*Horseferry Road*, G. Breen, *apptd* 1986; A. R. Davies, *apptd* 1985; Mrs K. R. Keating, *apptd* 1987; Mrs E. Rees, *apptd* 1994; G. Wicks, *apptd* 1987
*Inner London and City Family Proceedings Court*, N. Crichton, *apptd* 1987
*Marylebone*, Ms G. Babington-Browne, *apptd* 1991; D. Kennett Brown, *apptd* 1982; Miss E. Roscoe, *apptd* 1994
*South-Western*, A. W. Ormerod, *apptd* 1988; C. D. Voelcker, *apptd* 1982; Miss D. Wickham, *apptd* 1989
*Thames*, A. Baldwin, *apptd* 1990; I. G. Bing, *apptd* 1989; Mrs J. Comyns, *apptd* 1982; S. E. Dawson, *apptd* 1984
*Tower Bridge*, C. S. F. Black, *apptd* 1993; M. Read, *apptd* 1993; S. Somjee, *apptd* 1995
*West London Magistrates' Court*, J. Coleman, *apptd* 1995; T. English, *apptd* 1986; Miss D. Lachhar, apptd 1996; B. Loosley, *apptd* 1989; K. L. Maitland-Davies, *apptd* 1984; J. Philips, *apptd* 1989; D. Simpson, *apptd* 1993; D. L. Thomas, *apptd* 1990

### Greater London Magistrates' Courts

185 Marylebone Road, London, NW1 5QL. Tel: 0845 601-3600

*Justices' Chief Executive and Clerk to the Committee* (£93,203), Maj.-Gen. A. Truluck
*Training Manager* (£27,600–£37,500), Miss J. Whitby

## CROWN PROSECUTION SERVICE

50 Ludgate Hill, London EC4M 7EX
Tel: 020-7796 8000
E-mail enquiries@cps.gov.uk
Web www.cps.gov.uk

The Crown Prosecution Service (CPS) is responsible for the independent review and conduct of criminal proceedings instituted by police forces in England and Wales, with the exception of cases conducted by the Serious Fraud Office and certain minor offences.

The Service is headed by the Director of Public Prosecutions (DPP), who works under the superintendence of the Attorney-General, and a chief executive. The Service comprises a headquarters and 42 Areas, each Area corresponding to a police area in England and Wales. Each Area is headed by a Chief Crown Prosecutor, supported by an Area Business Manager.

*Director of Public Prosecutions (SCS)*, D. Calvert-Smith, QC
*Chief Executive (SCS)*, M. E. Addison
*Directors (SCS)*, C. Newell (*Casework*); G. Patten (*Policy*); J. Graham (*Finance*); L. Carey (*Business Information Systems*); I. Seehra (Human Resources
*Head of Communications (SCS)*, Mrs L. Salisbury
*Head of Management Audit Services (SCS), Ms. R. Read*

## CPS AREAS

### England

CPS Avon and Somerset, 2nd Floor, Froomsgate House, Rupert Street, Bristol BS1 2QJ. Tel: 0117-930 2800. *Chief Crown Prosecutor (SCS)*, D. Archer; *Area Business Manager*, Mrs L. Burton
CPS Bedfordshire, Sceptre House, 7–9 Castle Street, Luton LU1 3AJ. Tel: 01582-816600. *Acting Chief Crown Prosecutor (SCS)*, Mrs S. Brown; *Area Business Manager*, Ms J. Altham
CPS Cambridgeshire, Justinian House, Spitfire Close, Ermine Business Park, Huntingdon, Cambs PE28 6XY. Tel: 01480-825200. *Chief Crown Prosecutor (SCS)*, R. Crowley; *Area Business Manager*, A. Mardell
CPS Cheshire, 2nd Floor, Windsor House, Pepper Street, Chester CH1 1TD. Tel: 01244-408600. *Chief Crown Prosecutor (SCS)*, B. Hughes; *Area Business Manager*, Mrs E. Sherwood
CPS Cleveland,5 Linthorpe Road, Middlesbrough, Cleveland TS1 1TX. Tel: 01642-204500. *Chief Crown Prosecutor (SCS)*, D. Magson; *Area Business Manager*, Mrs M. Phillips
CPS Cumbria, 1st Floor, Stocklund House, Castle Street, Carlisle CA3 8SY. Tel: 01228-882900. *Chief Crown Prosecutor (SCS)*, D. Farmer; *Area Business Manager*, J. Pears
CPS Derbyshire, 7th Floor, St Peter's House, Gower Street, Derby DE1 1SB. Tel: 01332-614000. *Chief Crown Prosecutor (SCS)*, D. Adams; *Area Business Manager*, Mrs A. Clarke
CPS Devon and Cornwall, Hawkins House, Pynes Hill, Rydon Lane, Exeter EX2 5SS. Tel: 01392-288000. *Chief Crown Prosecutor (SCS)*, A. Cresswell; *Area Business Manager*, J. Nettleton
CPS Dorset, 1st Floor, Oxford House, Oxford Road, Bournemouth BH8 8HA. Tel: 01202-498700. *Chief Crown Prosecutor (SCS)*, J. Revell; *Area Business Manager*, J. Putman
CPS Durham, Elvet House, Hallgarth Street, Durham DH1 3AT. Tel: 0191-383 5800. *Chief Crown Prosecutor (SCS)*, J. Corringhan; *Area Business Manager*, to be announced
CPS Essex County House, 100 New London Road, Chelmsford CM2 0RG. Tel: 01245-455800. *Chief Crown Prosecutor (SCS)*, J. Bell; *Area Business Manager*, P. Overett
CPS Gloucestershire, 2 Kimbrose Way, Gloucester GL1 2DB. Tel: 01452-872400. *Chief Crown Prosecutor (SCS)*, W. Cole; *Area Business Manager*, W. Hollins
CPS Greater Manchester, PO Box 237, 8th Floor, Sunlight House, Quay Street, Manchester M60 3PS. Tel: 0161-827 4700. *Chief Crown Prosecutor (SCS)*, T. Taylor; *Area Business Manager*, K. Fox
CPS Hampshire, 3rd Floor, Black Horse House, 810 Leigh Road, Eastleigh, Hants SO50 9FH. Tel: 02380-673800. *Chief Crown Prosecutor (SCS)*, R. Daw; *Area Business Manager*, M. Sunderland

CPS HERTFORDSHIRE, Queen's House, 58 Victoria Street, St Albans, Herts AL1 3HZ. Tel: 01727-798700. *Chief Crown Prosecutor* (*SCS*), C. Ingham; *Area Business Manager*, L. Carroll

CPS HUMBERSIDE, 2nd Floor, King William House, Lowgate, Hull HU1 1RS. Tel: 01482-621000. *Chief Crown Prosecutor* (*SCS*), B. Marshall; *Area Business Manager*, Ms C. Skidmore

CPS KENT, Priory Gate, 29 Union Street, Maidstone, Kent ME14 1PT. Tel: 01622-356300. *Chief Crown Prosecutor* (*SCS*), Ms E. Howe; *Area Business Manager*, K. Mitchell

CPS LANCASHIRE, 3rd Floor, Unicentre, Lord's Walk, Preston PR1 1DH. Tel: 01772-208100. *Chief Crown Prosecutor* (*SCS*), D. Dickenson; *Area Business Manager*, G. Rankin

CPS LEICESTERSHIRE, Princes Court, 34 York Road, Leicester LE1 5TU. Tel: 0116-204 6700. *Chief Crown Prosecutor* (*SCS*), M. Howard; *Area Business Manager*, Ms L. Jones

CPS LINCOLNSHIRE, Crosstrend House, 10A Newport, Lincoln LN1 3DF. Tel: 01522-585900. *Chief Crown Prosecutor* (*SCS*), Ms A. Kerr; *Area Business Manager*, Ms A. Garbett

CPS LONDON (METROPOLITAN), 4th Floor, 50 Ludgate Hill, London EC4M 7EX. Tel: 020-7796 8000. *Chief Crown Prosecutor* (*SCS*), P. Boeuf; *Assistant Chief Crown Prosecutors* (*SCS*): R. Barcaly; Ms M. Werrett; H. Cohen; M. Townsend; *Area Business Manager*, A. Machray

CPS MERSEYSIDE, 7th Floor (South), Royal Liver Building, Pier Head, Liverpool L3 1HN. Tel: 0151-239 6400. *Chief Crown Prosecutor* (*SCS*), J. Holt; *Area Business Manager*, Ms D. King

CPS NORFOLK, Haldin House, Old Bank of England Court, Queen Street, Norwich NR2 4SX. Tel: 01603-693000. *Chief Crown Prosecutor* (*SCS*), P. Tidey; *Area Business Manager*, Ms F. CampbellCPS NORTH YORKSHIRE 6th Floor, Ryedale Building, 60 Piccadilly, York YO1 1NS. Tel: 01904-731700. *Chief Crown Prosecutor* (*SCS*), R. Turnbull; *Area Business Manager*, R. Cragg

CPS NORTHAMPTONSHIRE Beaumont House, Cliftonville, Northampton NN1 5BE. Tel: 01604-823600. *Chief Crown Prosecutor* (*SCS*), C. Chapman; *Area Business Manager*, J. Stephenson

CPS NORTHUMBRIA 1st Floor, Benton House, 136 Sandyford Road, Newcastle upon Tyne NE2 1QE. Tel: 0191-260 4200. *Chief Crown Prosecutor* (*SCS*), Ms N. Reasbeck; *Area Business Manager*, I. Groundwell

CPS NOTTINGHAMSHIRE, 2 King Edward Court, King Edward Street, Nottingham NG1 1EL. Tel: 0115-852 3300. *Chief Crown Prosecutor* (*SCS*), P. Lewis; *Area Business Manager*, Mrs G. Pessol

CPS SOUTH YORKSHIRE, Greenfield House, 32 Scotland Street, Sheffield S3 7DQ. Tel: 0114-229 8600. *Chief Crown Prosecutor* (*SCS*), Mrs J. Walker; *Area Business Manager*, C. Day

CPS STAFFORDSHIRE, 11A Princes Street, Stafford ST16 2EU. Tel: 01785-272200. *Chief Crown Prosecutor* (*SCS*), H. Ireland; *Area Business Manager*, B. Laybourne

CPS SUFFOLK, Saxon House, 1 Cromwell Square, Ipswich IP1 1TS. Tel: 01473-282100. *Chief Crown Prosecutor* (*SCS*), C. Yule; *Area Business Manager*, Mrs A. Saunders

CPS SURREY, One Onslow Street, Guildford, Surrey GU1 4YA. Tel: 01483-468200. *Chief Crown Prosecutor* (*SCS*), Ms S. Hebblethwaite; *Area Business Manager*, M. Wray

CPS SUSSEX Unit 3, Clifton Mews, Clifton Hill, Brighton BN1 3HR. Tel: 01273-765600. *Chief Crown Prosecutor* (*SCS*), Mrs A. Saunders; *Area Business Manager*, B. Shepherd

CPS THAMES VALLEY, The Courtyard, Lombard Street, Abingdon, Oxon OX14 5SE. Tel: 01235-551900. *Chief Crown Prosecutor* (*SCS*), S. Clements; *Area Business Manager*, G. Choldcroft

CPS WARWICKSHIRE, Rossmore House, 10 Newbold Terrace, Leamington Spa, Warks CV32 4EA. Tel: 01926-455000. *Chief Crown Prosecutor* (*SCS*), M. Lynn; *Area Business Manager*, Mrs S. Petyt

CPS WEST MERCIA, Artillery House, Heritage Way, Droitwich, Worcester WR9 8YB. Tel: 01905-825000. *Chief Crown Prosecutor* (*SCS*), J. England; *Area Business Manager*, L. Sutton

CPS WEST MIDLANDS, 14th Floor, Colmore Gate, 2 Colmore Row, Birmingham B3 2QA. Tel: 0121-262 1300. *Chief Crown Prosecutor* (*SCS*), D. Blundell; *Area Business Manager*, M. Grist

CPS WEST YORKSHIRE, Oxford House, Oxford Row, Leeds LS1 3BE Tel: 0113-290 2700. *Chief Crown Prosecutor* (*SCS*), N. Franklin; *Area Business Manager*, R. Stevenson

CPS WILTSHIRE 2nd Floor, Fox Talbot House, Bellinger Close, Malmesbury Road, Chippenham, Wilts SN15 1BN. Tel: 01249-766100. *Chief Crown Prosecutor* (*SCS*), N. Hawkins; *Area Business Manager*, N. Nabi

WALES

CPS DYFED-POWYS, Heol Penlanffos, Tanerdy, Carmarthen, Dyfed SA31 2EZ. Tel: 01267-242100. *Chief Crown Prosecutor* (*SCS*), S. Rowlands; *Area Business Manager*, Mrs C. Jones

CPS GWENT 6th Floor, Chartist Tower, Upper Dock Street, Newport, Gwent NP9 1DW. Tel: 01633-261100. *Chief Crown Prosecutor* (*SCS*), C. Woolley; *Area Business Manager*, Ms H. Phillips

CPS NORTH WALES Bromfield House, Ellice Way, Wrexham LL13 7YW. Tel: 01978 346000. *Chief Crown Prosecutor* (*SCS*), P. Whittaker; *Area Business Manager*, Mrs A. Walsh

CPS SOUTH WALES 20th Floor, Capital Tower, Greyfriars Road, Cardiff CF1 3PL. Tel: 029-2080 3900. *Chief Crown Prosecutor* (*SCS*), H. Heycock; *Area Business Manager*, I. Edmondson

# The Scottish Judicature

Scotland has a legal system separate from and differing greatly from the English legal system in enacted law, judicial procedure and the structure of courts.

In Scotland the system of public prosecution is headed by the Lord Advocate and is independent of the police, who have no say in the decision to prosecute. The Lord Advocate, discharging his functions through the Crown Office in Edinburgh, is responsible for prosecutions in the High Court, sheriff courts and district courts. Prosecutions in the High Court are prepared by the Crown Office and conducted in court by one of the law officers, by an advocate-depute, or by a solicitor advocate. In the inferior courts the decision to prosecute is made and prosecution is preferred by procurators fiscal, who are lawyers and full-time civil servants subject to the directions of the Crown Office. A permanent legally-qualified civil servant known as the Crown Agent is responsible for the running of the Crown Office and the organisation of the Procurator Fiscal Service, of which he is the head.

Scotland is divided into six sheriffdoms, each with a full-time sheriff principal. The sheriffdoms are further divided into sheriff court districts, each of which has a legally-qualified resident sheriff or sheriffs, who are the judges of the court.

In criminal cases sheriffs principal and sheriffs have the same powers; sitting with a jury of 15 members, they may try more serious cases on indictment, or, sitting alone, may try lesser cases under summary procedure. Minor summary offences are dealt with in district courts which are administered by the district and the islands local government authorities and presided over by lay justices of the peace (of whom there are about 4,000) and, in Glasgow only, by district judges (magistrates courts). Juvenile offenders (children under 16) may be brought before an informal children's hearing comprising three local lay people. The superior criminal court is the High Court of Justiciary which is both a trial and an appeal court. Cases on indictment are tried by a High Court judge, sitting with a jury of 15, in Edinburgh and on circuit in other towns. Appeals from the lower courts against conviction or sentence are heard also by the High Court, which sits as an appeal court only in Edinburgh. There is no further appeal to the House of Lords in criminal cases.

In civil cases the jurisdiction of the sheriff court extends to most kinds of action. Appeal against decisions of the sheriff may be made to the sheriff principal and thence to the Court of Session, or direct to the Court of Session, which sits only in Edinburgh. The Court of Session is divided into the Inner and the Outer House. The Outer House is a court of first instance in which cases are heard by judges sitting singly, sometimes with a jury of 12. The Inner House, itself subdivided into two divisions of equal status, is mainly an appeal court. Appeals may be made to the Inner House from the Outer House as well as from the sheriff court. An appeal may be made from the Inner House to the House of Lords.

The judges of the Court of Session are the same as those of the High Court of Justiciary, the Lord President of the Court of Session also holding the office of Lord Justice General in the High Court. Senators of the College of Justice are Lords Commissioners of Justiciary as well as judges of the Court of Session. On appointment, a Senator takes a judicial title, which is retained for life. Although styled 'The Hon./Rt. Hon. Lord —', the Senator is not a peer.

The office of coroner does not exist in Scotland. The local procurator fiscal inquires privately into sudden or suspicious deaths and may report findings to the Crown Agent. In some cases a fatal accident inquiry may be held before the sheriff.

## COURT OF SESSION AND HIGH COURT OF JUSTICIARY

*The Lord President and Lord Justice General* (£163,213)
The Rt. Hon. the Lord Rodger of Earlsferry, *born* 1944, *apptd* 1996
*Secretary*, A. Maxwell

### INNER HOUSE

*Lords of Session* (each £149,897)

#### FIRST DIVISION

The Lord President
Rt. Hon. Lord Prosser (William Prosser), *born* 1934, *apptd* 1986
Rt. Hon. Lord Cameron of Lochbroom, *born* 1931, *apptd* 1989
Hon. Lord Marnoch (Michael Bruce), *born* 1938, *apptd* 1990

#### SECOND DIVISION

*Lord Justice Clerk* (£157,699), The Rt. Hon. Lord Cullen (William Cullen), *born* 1935, *apptd* 1997
Rt. Hon. Lord Kirkwood (Ian Kirkwood), *born* 1932, *apptd* 1987
Rt. Hon. Lord Coulsfield (John Cameron), *born* 1934, *apptd* 1987
Hon. Lord MacLean (Ranald MacLean), *born* 1938, *apptd* 1990.
Hon. Lord Osborne (Kenneth Osborne), *born* 1937, *apptd* 1990
Lord Penrose (George Penrose), *born* 1938, *apptd* 1990

### OUTER HOUSE

*Lords of Session* (each £132,603)

Hon. Lord Abernethy (Alistair Cameron), *born* 1938, *apptd* 1992
Hon. Lord Johnston (Alan Johnston), *born* 1942, *apptd* 1994
Hon. Lord Gill (Brian Gill), *born* 1942, *apptd* 1994
Hon. Lord Hamilton (Arthur Hamilton), *born* 1942, *apptd* 1995
Hon. Lord Dawson (Thomas Dawson), *born* 1948, *apptd* 1995
Hon. Lord Macfadyen (Donald Macfadyen), *born* 1945, *apptd* 1995
Hon. Lady Cosgrove (Hazel Aronson), *born* 1946, ;*apptd* 1996
Hon. Lord Nimmo Smith (William Nimmo Smith), *born* 1942, *apptd* 1996
Hon. Lord Philip (Alexander Philip), *born* 1942, *apptd* 1996
Hon. Lord Kingarth (Derek Emslie), *born* 1949, *apptd* 1997
Hon. Lord Bonomy (Iain Bonomy), *born* 1946, *apptd* 1997
Hon. Lord Eassie (Ronald Mackay), *born* 1945, *apptd* 1997
Hon. Lord Reed (Robert Reed), *born* 1956, *apptd* 1998
Hon. Lord Wheatley (John Wheatley), *born* 1941, *apptd* 2000
Hon. Lady Paton (Ann Paton), *born* 1952, *apptd* 2000
Hon. Lord Carloway (Colin Sutherland), *born* 1954, *apptd* 2000
Hon. Lord Clarke (Matthew Clarke), *born* 1947, *apptd* 2000
Rt. Hon. Lord Hardie (Andrew Hardie), *born* 1946, *apptd* 2000
Rt. Hon. Lord Mackay of Drumadoon (Donald Mackay), *born* 1946, *apptd* 2000
Hon. Lord McEwan (Robin McEwan), *born* 1943, *apptd* 2000
Hon. Lord Menzies (Duncan Menzies), *born* 1953, *apptd* 2001
Hon. Lord Drummond Young (James Drummond Young), *born 1950*, *apptd* 2001

## COURT OF SESSION AND HIGH COURT OF JUSTICIARY

Parliament House, Parliament Square, Edinburgh EH1 1HQ Tel: 0131-225 2595

*Principal Clerk of Session and Justiciary* (£33,391–£55,711), J. L. Anderson
*Deputy Principal Clerk of Justiciary* (£29,277–£45,365), T. Higgins

*Deputy Principal Clerk of Session and Principal Extractor* (£29,277–£45,365), D. Shand
*Deputy in Charge of Offices of Court*, Mrs P. McFarlane
*Deputy Principal Clerk (Keeper of the Rolls)* (£29,277–£5,365), D. Shand
*Depute Clerks of Session and Justiciary* (£22,348–£29,381), N. J. Dowie; I. F. Smith; T. Higgins; T. B. Cruickshank; Q. A. Oliver; F. Shannly; A. S. Moffat; G. G. Ellis; W. Dunn; A. M. Finlayson; C. C. Armstrong; R. Jenkins; J. O. McLean; M. Weir; R. M. Sinclair; E. G. Appelbe; B. Watson; D. W. Cullen; I. D. Martin; N. McGinley; J. Lynn; E. Dickson; K. D. Carter; F. Petrie; D. Fraser; S. M. Fowler; W. G. Combe; R. T. MacPherson; P. A. Johnston; D. Bruton

## SCOTTISH EXECUTIVE JUSTICE DEPARTMENT
Hayweight House, 23 Lauriston Street, Edinburgh EH3 9DQ
Tel: 0131-229 9200

Courts Group is responsible for the provision of sufficient Judges and Sheriffs for the needs of the programme of the supreme and Sheriffs Court in Scotland. It is also responsible for the promotion, through the reform of law of Scotland, of the independence, integrity and quality of the judicial process in civil proceedings (and in relation to evidence, in criminal proceedings). It also has a role in the development of the private international law of Scotland and the relationship between the Scottish Legal System and other legal systems including those in Europe and the United Kingdom; and provides resources for the efficient administration of a number of tribunals and small departments.
*Head of Judicial Appointments and Finance Division* (*SCS*), D. Stewart
*Head of Civil Law and International Division* (*SCS*), P. M. Beaton

### SCOTTISH COURT SERVICE

Hayweight House, 23 Lauriston Street, Edinburgh EH3 9DQ Tel: 0131-229 9200

The Scottish Court Service is an executive agency within the Scottish Executive Justice Department. It is responsible to the Scottish Ministers for the provision of staff, court houses and associated services for the Supreme and Sheriff Courts.
*Chief Executive*, J. Ewing

## SHERIFF COURT OF CHANCERY
27 Chambers Street, Edinburgh EH1 1LB
Tel: 0131-225 2525

The Court deals with service of heirs and completion of title in relation to heritable property.
*Sheriff of Chancery*, C. G. B. Nicholson, QC

## HM COMMISSARY OFFICE
27 Chambers Street, Edinburgh EH1 1LB
Tel: 0131-225 2525

The Office is responsible for issuing confirmation, a legal document entitling a person to execute a deceased person's will, and other related matters.
*Commissary Clerk*, J. M. Ross

## SCOTTISH LAND COURT
1 Grosvenor Crescent, Edinburgh EH12 5ER
Tel: 0131-225 3595

The court deals with disputes relating to agricultural and crofting land in Scotland.
*Chairman* (£107,346), The Hon. Lord McGhie (James McGhie), QC
*Members*, D. J. Houston; D. M. Macdonald; J. Kinloch (*part-time*)
*Principal Clerk*, K. H. R. Graham, WS

## SHERIFFDOMS

### SALARIES

| | |
|---|---|
| Sheriff Principal | £107,346 |
| Sheriff | £99,420 |
| Area Director | £32,293–£63,490 |
| Sheriff Clerk | £12,719–£43,873 |

*Floating Sheriff

## GRAMPIAN, HIGHLANDS AND ISLANDS
*Sheriff Principal*, Sir Stephen John, Bt
*Area Director North*, J. Robertson

### SHERIFFS AND SHERIFF CLERKS
*Aberdeen and Stonehaven*, L. A. S. Jessop; A. Pollock; Mrs A. M. Cowan; C. J. Harris, QC; P. M. Bowman; *G. K. Buchanan; *Sheriff Clerks*, Mrs E. Laing (*Aberdeen*); A. Hempseed (*Stonehaven*)
*Peterhead and Banff*, K. A. McLernan; *D. J. Cusine; *Sheriff Clerk*, (*Peterhead*); *Sheriff Clerk Depute*, Mrs F. L. MacPherson (*Banff*)
*Elgin*, I. A. Cameron; *Sheriff Clerk*, M. McBey
*Inverness, Lochmaddy, Portree, Stornoway, Dingwall, Tain, Wick and Dornoch*, W. J. Fulton; D. Booker-Milburn; J. O. A. Fraser;D. O. Sutherland; *Sheriff Clerks*, A. Bayliss (*Inverness*); M. McBey(*Dingwall*); *Sheriff Clerks Depute*, Miss M. Campbell (*Lochmaddy and Portree*); Miss A. B. Armstrong (*Stornoway*); L. MacLachlan (*Tain*); Mrs J. McEwan (*Wick*); K. Kerr (*Dornoch*)
*Kirkwall and Lerwick*, C. S. Mackenzie; *Sheriff Clerks Depute*, A. Moore (*Kirkwall*); M. Flanagan (*Lerwick*)
*Fort William*, W. D. Small (also *Oban*); *Sheriff Clerk Depute*, S. McKenna

## TAYSIDE, CENTRAL AND FIFE
*Sheriff Principal*, R. A. Dunlop, QC
*Area Director East*, M. Bonar

### SHERIFFS AND SHERIFF CLERKS
*Arbroath and Forfar*, K. A. Veal; *C. N. R. Stein; *Sheriff Clerks*, M. Herbertson (*Arbroath*); S. Munro (*Forfar*)
*Dundee*, R. A. Davidson; A. L. Stewart, QC; J. P. Scott; G. J. Evans (also *Cupar*); P. P. Davies; F. R. Crowe; *Sheriff Clerk*, D. Nicoll
*Perth*, M. J. Fletcher; J. K, Tierney; D. Pyle; *L. D. R. Foulis *Sheriff Clerk*, J. Murphy
*Falkirk*, A. V. Sheehan; A. J. Murphy; *C. Caldwell; *Sheriff Clerk*, R. McMillan
*Stirling*, The Hon. R. E. G. Younger; W. Robertson; W. M. Reid; *Sheriff Clerk*, R. G. McKeand
*Cupar*, G. J. Evans (also *Dundee*); *Sheriff Clerk*, A. Nicol
*Dunfermline*, J. S. Forbes; *G. W. M. Liddle; Mrs I. G. McColl; *R. J. Macleod; N. C. Stewart; *Sheriff Clerk*, W. McCulloch
*Kirkcaldy*, F. J. Keane; Mrs L. G. Patrick; *B. G. Donald; *Sheriff Clerk*, W. Jones

## LOTHIAN AND BORDERS

*Sheriff Principal*, C. G. B. Nicholson, QC
*Area Director East*, M. Bonar

### SHERIFFS AND SHERIFF CLERKS

*Edinburgh*, R. G. Craik, QC (also *Peebles*); R. J. D. Scott (also *Peebles*); Miss I. A. Poole; A. M. Bell; J. M. S. Horsburgh, QC; G. W. S. Presslie (also *Haddington*); J. A. Farrell; A. Lothian; I. D. Macphail, QC; C. N. Stoddart; M. McPartlin; J.D.Allan; N. M. P. Morrison, QC; Miss M. M. Stephen; Mrs M. L. E. Jarvie, QC; *Mrs K. E. C. Mackie; *N. J. MacKinnon; D.W.M. McIntyre; *Sheriff Clerk*, J. Ross
*Peebles*, R. G. Craik, QC (also *Edinburgh*); R. J. D. Scott (also *Edinburgh*); *Sheriff Clerk Depute*, M. L. Kubeczka
*Linlithgow*, H. R. MacLean; G. R. Fleming; *P. Gillam; W. D. Muirhead; *Sheriff Clerk*, R. D. Sinclair
*Haddington*, G. W. S. Presslie (also *Edinburgh*); *Sheriff Clerk*, J. O'Donnell
*Jedburgh and Duns*, T. A. K. Drummond, QC; *Sheriff Clerk*, I. W. Williamson
*Selkirk*, T. A. K. Drummond, QC; *Sheriff Clerk Depute*, L. McFarlane

## NORTH STRATHCLYDE

*Sheriff Principal*, B. A. Kerr, QC
*Area Director West*, I. Scott

### SHERIFFS AND SHERIFF CLERKS

*Oban*, W. D. Small (also *Fort William*); *Sheriff Clerk Depute*, D. Irwin
*Dumbarton*, J. T. Fitzsimons; T. Scott; S. W. H. Fraser; *Sheriff Clerk*, S. Bain
*Paisley*, J. Spy; C. K. Higgins; N. Douglas; D. J. Pender; *W. Dunlop; G. C. Kavanagh (also *Campbeltown*); Mrs I. S. McDonald; *Sheriff Clerk*, Miss S. Hindes
*Greenock*, J. Herald (also *Rothesay*); Sir Stephen Young; *Mrs R. Swanney; *Sheriff Clerk*, J. Tannahill
*Kilmarnock*, T. M. Croan; D. B. Smith; T. F. Russell; *Mrs I. S. Donald; *Sheriff Clerk*, G. Waddell
*Dunoon*, Mrs C. M. A. F. Gimblett; *Sheriff Clerk Depute*, J. McGraw
*Campbeltown*, *W. Dunlop (also *Paisley*); *Sheriff Clerk Depute*, Miss E. Napier
*Rothesay*, J. Herald (also *Greenock*); *Sheriff Clerk Depute*, Mrs C. K. McCormick

## GLASGOW AND STRATHKELVIN

*Sheriff Principal*, E. F. Bowen, QC
*Area Director West*, I. Scott

### SHERIFFS AND SHERIFF CLERKS

*Glasgow*, B. Kearney; B. A. Lockhart; Mrs A. L. A. Duncan; A. C. Henry; J. K. Mitchell; A. G. Johnston; Miss S. A. O. Raeburn, QC; D. Convery; I. A. S. Peebles, QC; C. W. McFarlane, QC; K. M. Maciver; H. Matthews, QC; J. A. Baird; Miss R. E. A. Rae, QC; A. W. Noble; J. D. Friel; Mrs D. M. MacNeill, QC; J. A. Taylor; C. A. L. Scott; * S. Cathcart; *Ms L. M. Ruxton; I. H. L. Miller; Mrs F. L. Reith; W. J. Totten; M. G. O'Grady; *Sheriff Clerk*, C. Binning

## SOUTH STRATHCLYDE, DUMFRIES AND GALLOWAY

*Sheriff Principal*, J. C. McInnes, QC
*Area Director West*, I. Scott

### SHERIFFS AND SHERIFF CLERKS

*Hamilton*, L. Cameron; D. C. Russell; V. J. Canavan (also *Airdrie*); W. E. Gibson; J. H. Stewart; Miss J. Powie H. S. Neilson; S. C. Pender; *Sheriff Clerk*, P. Feeney; T. Welsh, QC; D.M.Bicker; *Mrs M. Smart; *H. K. Small
*Lanark*, Ms N.C. Stewart; *A. D. Vannett; *Sheriff Clerk*, Mrs M. McLean, N. Gow, QC; C. B. Miller; J. McGowan; *Sheriff Clerk*, Miss C. D. Cockburn
*Stranraer and Kirkcudbright*, J. R. Smith (also *Dumfries*); *Sheriff Clerks*, W. McIntosh (*Stranraer*); B. Lindsay (*Kirkcudbright*)
*Dumfries*, K. G. Barr; J. R. Smith (also *Stranraer and Kirkcudbright*); K. A. Ross; *Sheriff Clerk*, P. McGonigle
*Airdrie*, V. J. Canavan (also *Hamilton*); R. H. Dickson; I. C. Simpson; J. C. Morris, QC; A. D. Vannet (also *Lanark*) *Sheriff Clerk*, D. Forrester

## STIPENDIARY MAGISTRATES

### GLASGOW

R. Hamilton, *apptd* 1984; J. B. C. Nisbet, *apptd* 1984; R. B. Christie, *apptd* 1985; Mrs J. A. M. MacLean, *apptd* 1990

## CROWN OFFICE AND PROCURATOR FISCAL SERVICE

### CROWN OFFICE

25 Chambers Street, Edinburgh EH1 1LA
Tel: 0131-226 2626; Web www.crownoffice.gov.uk

*Crown Agent* (£80,020–£116,860), A. C. Normand
*Deputy Crown Agent* (£57,367–£95,625), W. A. Gilchrist

### PROCURATORS FISCAL

#### SALARIES

| | |
|---|---|
| Regional Procurator Fiscal - (*SCS Band 5*) | £62,882–£101,254 |
| Regional Procurator Fiscal - (*SCS Band 4*) | £57,367–£95,6256 |
| | £55,750–£92,930 |
| Procurator Fiscal – upper level | £42,755–£67,163 |
| Procurator Fiscal – lower level | £38,00–£46,200 |

#### GRAMPIAN, HIGHLAND AND ISLANDS REGION

*Regional Procurator Fiscal*, Mrs E. Angiolini (*Aberdeen*)
*Procurators Fiscal*, E. K. Barbour (*Stonehaven*); A. J. M. Colley (*Banff*); A. B. Hutchinson (*Peterhead*); D. J. Dickson (*Elgin*); G. Aitken (*Wick*); J. F. Bamber (*Portree, Lochmaddy*); D. S. Teale (*Stornoway*); G. Napier (*Inverness*); Miss Susenn (*Kirkwall, Lerwick*); A. Wylie (*Fort William*); R. Urquhart (*Dingwall, Dornoch, Tain*)

#### TAYSIDE, CENTRAL AND FIFE REGION

*Regional Procurator Fiscal*, B. K. Heywood (*Dundee*)
*Procurators Fiscal*, J. I. Craigen (*Forfar*); I. A. McLeod (*Perth*); W. J. Gallacher (*Falkirk*); C. Ritchie (*Stirling and Alloa*); E. B. Russell (*Cupar*); R. G. Stott (*Dunfermline*); Miss H. M. Clark (*Kirkcaldy*); A. J. Wheelan (*Arbroath*)

#### LOTHIAN AND BORDERS REGION

*Regional Procurator Fiscal*, N. McFadyen (*Edinburgh*)
*Procurators Fiscal*, Mrs C. P. Dyer (*Linlithgow*); A. J. P. Reith (*Haddington*); A. R. G. Fraser (*Duns, Jedburgh*); Mrs L. E. Thomson (*Selkirk, Peebles*)

North Strathclyde Region

*Regional Procurator Fiscal*, W. A. Gilchrist (*Paisley*)
*Procurators Fiscal*, F. Redman (*Campbeltown*); C. C. Donnelly (*Dumbarton*); W. S. Carnegie (*Greenock, Rothesay*); D. L. Webster (*Dunoon*); J. Watt (*Kilmarnock*); B. R. Maguire (*Oban*)

Glasgow and Strathkelvin Region

*Regional Procurator Fiscal*, L. A. Higson (*Glasgow*)

South Strathclyde, Dumfries and Galloway Region

*Regional Procurator Fiscal*, D. A. Brown (*Hamilton*)
*Procurators Fiscal*, S. R. Houston (*Lanark*); J. T. O'Donnell (*Ayr*); A. S. Kennedy (*Stranraer*); D. J. Howdle (*Dumfries, Kirkudbright*); D. Spiers (*Airdrie*)

# Northern Ireland Judicature

In Northern Ireland the legal system and the structure of courts closely resemble those of England and Wales; there are, however, often differences in enacted law.

The Supreme Court of Judicature of Northern Ireland comprises the Court of Appeal, the High Court of Justice and the Crown Court. The practice and procedure of these courts is similar to that in England. The superior civil court is the High Court of Justice, from which an appeal lies to the Northern Ireland Court of Appeal; the House of Lords is the final civil appeal court.

The Crown Court, served by High Court and county court judges, deals with criminal trials on indictment. Cases are heard before a judge and, except those involving offences specified under emergency legislation, a jury. Appeals from the Crown Court against conviction or sentence are heard by the Northern Ireland Court of Appeal; the House of Lords is the final court of appeal.

The decision to prosecute in cases tried on indictment and in summary cases of a serious nature rests in Northern Ireland with the Director of Public Prosecutions, who is responsible to the Attorney-General. Minor summary offences are prosecuted by the police.

Minor criminal offences are dealt with in magistrates' courts by a legally qualified resident magistrate and, where an offender is under 17, by juvenile courts each consisting of a resident magistrate and two lay members specially qualified to deal with juveniles (at least one of whom must be a woman). On 26 July 2001 there were 901 justices of the peace in Northern Ireland. Appeals from magistrates' courts are heard by the county court, or by the Court of Appeal on a point of law or an issue as to jurisdiction.

Magistrates' courts in Northern Ireland can deal with certain classes of civil case but most minor civil cases are dealt with in county courts. Judgments of all civil courts are enforceable through a centralised procedure administered by the Enforcement of Judgments Office.

## SUPREME COURT OF JUDICATURE

The Royal Courts of Justice, Belfast BT1 3JF
Tel: 028-9023 5111
*Lord Chief Justice of Northern Ireland* (£163,213)
The Rt. Hon. Sir Robert Carswell, *born* 1934, *apptd* 1997
*Principal Secretary*, G. W. Johnston

Lords Justices of Appeal (each £149,897)

*Style*, The Rt. Hon. Lord Justice [surname]

Rt. Hon. Sir Michael Nicholson, *born* 1933, *apptd* 1995
Rt. Hon. Sir William McCollum, *born* 1933, *apptd* 1997
Rt. Hon. Sir Anthony Campbell, *born* 1936, *apptd* 1998

Puisne Judges (each £132,603)

*Style*, The Hon. Mr Justice [surname]

Hon. Sir John Sheil, *born* 1938, *apptd* 1989
Hon. Sir Brian Kerr, *born* 1948, *apptd* 1993
Hon. Sir Malachy Higgins, *born* 1944, *apptd* 1993
Hon. Sir Paul Girvan, *born* 1948, *apptd* 1995
Hon. Sir Patrick Coghlin, *born* 1945, *apptd* 1997
Hon. Sir John Gillen, *born* 1947, *apptd* 1998
Hon. Sir Richard McLaughlin, *born* 1947, *apptd* 1999

Masters of the Supreme Court (each £79,767)

*Master, Queen's Bench and Appeals and Clerk of the Crown*, J. W. Wilson, QC
*Master, High Court*, C.J. McCorry
*Master, Office of Care and Protection*, F. B. Hall
*Master, Chancery Office*, R. A. Ellison
*Master, Bankruptcy and Companies Office*, C. W. G. Redpath
*Master, Probate and Matrimonial Office*, Miss M. McReynolds
*Master, Taxing Office*, J. C. Napier

Official Solicitor

*Official Solicitor to the Supreme Court of Northern Ireland*, Miss B. M. Donnelly

## COUNTY COURTS

Judges (each £107,346)

*Style*, His/Her Hon. Judge [surname]

Judge Curran, QC; Judge Gibson, QC; Judge Markey, QC; Judge McKay, QC; Judge Smyth, QC; Judge Martin (*Chief Social Security and Child Support Commissioner*); Judge Brady, QC; Judge Foote, QC; Her Hon. Judge Philpott, QC; Judge McFarland; Judge Lockie; Her Hon. Judge Kennedy; Judge Finnegan

Recorders (each £107,346)

*Belfast*, Judge Hart, QC
*Londonderry*, Judge Burgess

## MAGISTRATES' COURTS

Resident Magistrates (EACH £79,767)

There are 19 resident magistrates in Northern Ireland.

## CROWN SOLICITOR'S OFFICE

PO Box 410, Royal Courts of Justice, Belfast BT1 3JY
Tel: 028-9054 2555

*Crown Solicitor*, W. A. Palmer

## DEPARTMENT OF THE DIRECTOR OF PUBLIC PROSECUTIONS

Royal Courts of Justice, Belfast BT1 3NX
Tel: 028-9054 2444

*Director of Public Prosecutions*, A. Fraser, CB, QC
*Deputy Director of Public Prosecutions*, W. R. Junkin

## NORTHERN IRELAND COURT SERVICE

Windsor House, Bedford Street, Belfast BT2 7LT
Tel: 028-9032 8594

*Director* (*G3*)

# Tribunals

## AGRICULTURAL LAND TRIBUNALS

c/o Rural and Marine Environment Division, Ministry of Agriculture, Fisheries and Food, Nobel House, 17 Smith Square, London SW1P 3JR
Tel: 020-7238 6991

Agricultural Land Tribunals settle disputes and other issues between agricultural landlords and tenants, and drainage disputes between neighbours.

There are seven tribunals covering England and one covering Wales. For each tribunal the Lord Chancellor appoints a chairman and one or more deputies (barristers or solicitors of at least seven years standing). The Lord Chancellor also appoints lay members to three statutory panels: the 'landowners' panel, the 'farmers' panel and the 'drainage' panel.

Each tribunal is an independent statutory body with jurisdiction only within its own area. A separate tribunal is constituted for each case, and consists of a chairman (who may be the chairman or one of the deputy chairmen) and two lay members nominated by the chairman.

*Chairmen (England)* (£280 a day), W. D. M. Wood; P. A. de la Piquerie; A. G. Donn; His Hon. Judge J. V. Machin; N. Thomas G. L. Newsom; His Hon. Judge Robert Taylor
*Chairman (Wales)* (£280 a day), W. J. Owen

## THE APPEALS SERVICE

Whittington House, 19–30 Alfred Place, London WC1E 7LW
Tel: 020-7712 2600

The Service (formerly the Independent Tribunal Service) is responsible for the functioning of tribunals hearing appeals concerning child support assessments, social security benefits and vaccine damage payments. Judicial authority for the Service rests with the President, while administrative responsibility is exercised by the Appeals Service Agency, which is an executive agency of the Department of Work and Pensions.

*President*, His Hon. Judge Michael Harris
*Chief Executive, Appeals Service Agency*, N. Ward

## COMMONS COMMISSIONERS

Room Zone 1/05b, Temple Quay House, 2 The Square, Temple Quay, Bristol BS1 6EB
Tel: 0117-372 8928

The Commons Commissioners are responsible for deciding disputes arising under the Commons Registration Act 1965. They also enquire into the ownership of unclaimed common land and village greens. Commissioners are appointed by the Lord Chancellor.

*Chief Commons Commissioner (part-time)*, I. L. R. Romer
*Clerk*, P. Lawrence

## COPYRIGHT TRIBUNAL

Harmsworth House, 13–15 Bouverie Street, London EC4Y 8DP
Tel: 020-7596 6510; Fax; Minicom: 0845-9222250 020-7596-6526;
Email: copyright.tribunal@patent.gov.uk;
Web: www.patent.gov.uk

The Copyright Tribunal resolves disputes over copyright licences, principally where there is collective licensing.

The chairman and two deputy chairmen are appointed by the Lord Chancellor. Up to eight ordinary members are appointed by the Secretary of State for Trade and Industry.

*Chairman* (£316 a day), C. P. Tootal
*Secretary*, Miss J. E. M. Durdin

## GENERAL COMMISSIONERS OF INCOME TAX

Lord Chancellor's Department, Selborne House, 54–60 Victoria Street, London SW1E 6QW
Tel: 020-7210 0680

General Commissioners of Income Tax operate under the Taxes Management Act 1970. They are unpaid judicial officers who sit in some 460 Divisions throughout the United Kingdom to hear appeals against decisions by the Inland Revenue on a variety of taxation matters. The Commissioners' jurisdiction was extended in 1999 to hear National Insurance appeals. The Lord Chancellor appoints General Commissioners (except in Scotland, where they are appointed by the Scottish Executive). There are approximately 3,000 General Commissioners appointed throughout the United Kingdom. In each Division, Commissioners appoint a Clerk, who is normally legally qualified, who makes the administrative arrangements for appeal hearings and advises the Commissioners on points of law and procedure. The Lord Chancellor's Department pays the Clerks' remuneration.

Appeals from the General Commissioners are by way of case stated, on a point of law, to the High Court (the Court of Session in Scotland or the Court of Appeal in Northern Ireland).

In 2000, approximately 80,000 cases were listed before the General Commissioners.

## INFORMATION TRIBUNAL

c/o The Home Office, Queen Anne's Gate, London SW1H 9AT
Tel 020-7273 3755

The Information Tribunal determines appeals against decisions of the Information Commissioner. The chairman and deputy chairman are appointed by the Lord Chancellor and must be legally qualified. Lay members are appointed by the Lord Chancellor to represent the interests of data users or data subjects. A tribunal consists of a legally-qualified chairman sitting with equal numbers

of the lay members appointed to represent the interests of data users and data subjects. There is a separate panel of the tribunal which hears national security appeals, the president of this panel is the Rt. Hon. Sir Anthony Evans, RD.
*Chairman*, J. A. C. Spokes, QC
*Secretary*, R. Hartley
*Information Commissoner*, Elizabeth France

## EMPLOYMENT TRIBUNALS

CENTRAL OFFICE (ENGLAND AND WALES)
19–29 Woburn Place, London WC1H 0LU
Tel: 020-7273 8666

Employment Tribunals for England and Wales sit in 12 regions. The tribunals deal with matters of employment law, redundancy, dismissal, contract disputes, sexual, racial and disability discrimination, and related areas of dispute which may arise in the workplace. A central registration unit records all applications and maintains a public register at Southgate Street, Bury St Edmunds, Suffolk IP33 2AQ. The tribunals are funded by the Department of Trade and Industry; administrative support is provided by the Employment Tribunals Service.

Chairmen, who may be full-time or part-time, are legally qualified. They are appointed by the Lord Chancellor. Tribunal members are appointed by the Secretary of State for Trade and Industry.
*President* (£103,516), His Hon. Judge Prophet

CENTRAL OFFICE (SCOTLAND)
Eagle Building, 215 Bothwell Street, Glasgow G2 7TS
Tel: 0141-204 0730

Tribunals in Scotland have the same remit as those in England and Wales. Chairmen are appointed by the Lord President of the Court of Session and lay members by the Secretary of State for Trade and Industry.
*President* (£99,420), C. M. Milne

## EMPLOYMENT APPEAL TRIBUNAL

*Central Office:* Audit House, 58 Victoria Embankment, London EC4Y 0DS
Tel: 020-7273 1041; Fax: 020-7273 1045
*Divisional Office:* 52 Melville Street, Edinburgh EH3 7HF
Tel: 0131-225 3963;
Web: www.employmentappeals.gov.uk

The Employment Appeal Tribunal hears appeals on a question of law arising from any decision of an employment tribunal. A tribunal consists of a high court judge and two lay members, one from each side of industry. They are appointed by The Queen on the recommendation of the Lord Chancellor and the Secretary of State for Trade and Industry. Administrative support is provided by the Employment Tribunals Service.
*President*, The Hon. Mr Justice Lindsay
*Scottish Chairman*, The Hon. Lord Johnston
*Registrar*, P. Donleavy
*Deputy Registrar*, Ms J. Johnson

## IMMIGRATION APPELLATE AUTHORITIES

Taylor House, 88 Rosebery Avenue, London EC1R 4QU
Tel: 020-7862 4200

The Immigration Appellate Authorities' powers are now derived from the immigration and Assylum Act 1999. Immigration Adjudicators hear appeals from immigration decisions concerning the need for, and the refusal of, leave to enter or remain in the UK, refusals to grant asylum, decisions to make deportation orders and directions to remove persons subject to immigration control from the UK.

The Immigration Appeal Tribunal provides a second appellate level for those dissatisfied with an Adjudicator's decision. Leave to appeal needs to be obtained. From the Tribunal there is an appeal to the Court of Appeal on a point of law only.

An adjudicator sits alone. The Tribunal sits in divisions of three, normally a legally qualified member and two lay members.

IMMIGRATION APPEAL TRIBUNAL
Field House, 15–25 Bream's Buildings, Chancery Lane, London, EC4A 1DZ
Tel: 020-7073 4200

*President*, The Hon. Mr Justice Collins
*Deputy President*, C. M. G. Ockelton
*Vice-Presidents*, J. Barnes; K. Eshun; J. R. A. Fox; M. W. Rapinet; G. Warr; M. Rapinet; A. O'Brien-Quinn; Dr H. H. W. Storey; J. G. Freeman; D. K. Allen; K. Drabu; J. Fox; P. Moulden; C. Ockelton; A. Mackey; H. J. E. Latter

IMMIGRATION APPEAL ADJUDICATORS

*Chief Adjudicator*, His Hon. Judge Dunn, QC
*Deputy Chief Adjudicator*, E. Arfon-Jones

## IMMIGRATION SERVICES TRIBUNAL

48/49 Chancery Lane, London WC2A 1JR
Tel: 020-7947 7200; Fax; 020-7947 7215

The Immigration Services Tribunal is an independent Judicial body set up to provide a forum in which appeals against decisions of the Immigration Services Commissioner and complaints made by the Immigration Services Commissioner can be heard and determined. The cases exclusively concern people providing advice and representation services in connection with immigration matters.

The Tribunal forms part of the Court Service. It is the responsibility of the Lord Chancellor. There is a President, who is the judicial head; other judicial members, who must be legally qualified; lay members who must have substantial experience in immigration services or in the law and procedure relating to immigration; and a secretary who is responsible for administration. The tribunal can sit anywhere in the UK.
*President*, Hon. Judge Seddon Crisp
*Members*, D. Bean, QC; G. Marriott; P. Barnett; O. Conway; M. Hoare; S. Maguire; A. Montgomery; I. Newton; M. Quayum; S. Rowland; P. Fisher
*Immigration Services Tribunal Staff*, D. Duncan

## INDUSTRIAL TRIBUNALS AND THE FAIR EMPLOYMENT TRIBUNAL (NORTHERN IRELAND)

Long Bridge House, 20–24 Waring Street, Belfast BT1 2EB
Tel: 028-9032 7666

The industrial tribunal system in Northern Ireland was set up in 1965 and has a similar remit to the employment tribunals in the rest of the UK. There is also in Northern Ireland a Fair Employment Tribunal, which hears and determines individual cases of alleged religious or political discrimination in employment. Employers can appeal to the Fair Employment Tribunal if they consider the directions of the Equality Commission to be unreasonable, inappropriate or unnecessary, and the Equality Commission can make application to the Tribunal for the enforcement of undertakings or directions with which an employer has not complied.

The president, vice-president and part-time chairmen of the Fair Employment Tribunal are appointed by the Lord Chancellor. The full-time chairman and the part-time chairmen of the industrial tribunals and the panel members to both the industrial tribunals and the Fair Employment Tribunal are appointed by the Department of Higher and Further Education Training and Employment.

*President of the Industrial Tribunals and the Fair Employment Tribunal* (£103,516), J. Maguire, CBE
*Vice-President of the Industrial Tribunals and the Fair Employment Tribunal*, Mrs M. P. Price
*Secretary*, Mrs P. McVeigh

## LANDS TRIBUNAL

48–49 Chancery Lane, London WC2A 1JR
Tel: 020-7947 7200

The Lands Tribunal is an independent judicial body which determines questions relating to the valuation of land, rating appeals from valuation tribunals, the discharge or modification of restrictive covenants, and compulsory purchase compensation. The tribunal may also arbitrate under references by consent. The president and members are appointed by the Lord Chancellor.

*President* (£103,516), G. R. Bartlett, QC
*Members* (£95,873), P. H. Clarke, FRICS; N. J. Rose, FRICS; P. R. Francis
*Member (part-time)*, His Hon. Judge Rich, QC
*Registrar*, D. Scannell

## LANDS TRIBUNAL FOR SCOTLAND

1 Grosvenor Crescent, Edinburgh EH12 5ER
Tel: 0131-225 7996

The Lands Tribunal for Scotland has the same remit as the tribunal for England and Wales but also covers questions relating to tenants' rights to buy their homes under the Housing (Scotland) Act 1987. The president is appointed by the Lord President of the Court of Session.

*President* (£103,516), The Hon. Lord McGhie, QC
*Members* (£95,873), J. Devine, FRICS; A. R. MacLeary, FRICS
*Member (part-time)* (£33,409), J. N. Wright, QC
*Clerk*, N. M. Tainsh

## MENTAL HEALTH REVIEW TRIBUNALS

*Secretariat:* Health Service Directorate, Room 326 Wellington House, 133–155 Waterloo Road, London SE1 8UG
Tel: 020-7972 4503/4577; Fax: 020-7972 4884

The Mental Health Review Tribunals are independent judicial bodies which review the cases of patients compulsorily detained under the provisions of the Mental Health Act 1983. They have the power to discharge the patient, to recommend leave of absence, delayed discharge, transfer to another hospital or that a guardianship order be made, to reclassify both restricted and unrestricted patients, and to recommend consideration of a supervision application. There are four tribunals in England, each headed by a regional chairman who is appointed by the Lord Chancellor on a part-time basis. Each tribunal is made up of at least three members, and must include a lawyer, who acts as president, a medical member and a lay member.

There are five regional offices:

LIVERPOOL, 3rd Floor, Cressington House, 249 St Mary's Road, Garston, Liverpool L19 0NF. Tel: 0151-728 5400
LONDON (NORTH), Spur 3, Block 1, Government Buildings, Honeypot Lane, Stanmore, Middx HA7 1AY. Tel: 020-7972 3754
LONDON (SOUTH), Block 3, Crown Offices, Kingston Bypass Road, Surbiton, Surrey KT6 5QN. Tel: 020-8268 4549
NOTTINGHAM, Spur A, Block 5, Government Buildings, Chalfont Drive, Western Boulevard, Nottingham NG8 3RZ. Tel: 0115-942 8308
WALES, 4th Floor, Crown Buildings, Cathays Park, Cardiff CF1 3NQ. Tel: 029-2082 5328

## NATIONAL HEALTH SERVICE TRIBUNAL

380 Rayleigh Rod, Thundersley, Essex, SS7 3TA
Tel: 01268-774481; Fax: 01268-71565

The NHS Tribunal considers representations that the continued inclusion of a doctor, dentist, optician or pharmacist on a health authority's list would be prejudicial to the efficiency of the service concerned. The tribunal sits when required, usually in London. The chairman is appointed by the Lord Chancellor and members by the Secretary of State for Health.

*Chairman*, A. Whitfield, QC
*Deputy Chairmen*, Miss E. Platt, QC; Dr R. N. Ough; S. Rodway; W. Edis; T. Thorne
*Clerk*, T. L. Rayson, OBE, 380 Rayleigh Road, Thundersley, Essex SS7 3TA. Tel 01268 774481

## NATIONAL HEALTH SERVICE TRIBUNAL (SCOTLAND)

*Clerk:* 40 Craiglockhart Road, North, Edinburgh EH14 1BT
Tel: 0131-443 2575

The tribunal considers representations that the continued inclusion of a doctor, dentist, optometrist or pharmacist on a health board's list would be prejudicial to the efficiency of the service concerned. The tribunal sits when required and is composed of a chairman, one lay member, and one practitioner member drawn from a representative

professional panel. The chairman is appointed by the Lord President of the Court of Session, and the lay member and the members of the professional panel are appointed by the First Minister.
*Chairman*, M. G. Thomson, QC
*Lay member*, J. D. M. Robertson
*Clerk to the Tribunal*, W. Bryden

## PENSIONS APPEAL TRIBUNALS

CENTRAL OFFICE (ENGLAND AND WALES)
48–49 Chancery Lane, London WC2A 1JF
Tel: 020-7947 7034; Fax: 020-7947 7492

The Pensions Appeal Tribunals are responsible for hearing appeals from ex-servicemen or women and widows who have had their claims for a war pension rejected by the Secretary of State for Social Security. The Entitlement Appeal Tribunals hear appeals in cases where the Secretary of State has refused to grant a war pension. The Assessment Appeal Tribunals hear appeals against the Secretary of State's assessment of the degree of disablement caused by an accepted condition. The tribunal members are appointed by the Lord Chancellor.
*President* (£76,921), Dr H. M. G. Concannon
*Tribunal Manager*, Miss L. Nay

PENSIONS APPEAL TRIBUNALS FOR SCOTLAND
20 Walker Street, Edinburgh EH3 7HS
Tel: 0131-220 1404
*President* (£307 a day), C. N. McEachran, QC

## OFFICE OF THE SOCIAL SECURITY AND CHILD SUPPORT COMMISSIONERS

5th Floor, Newspaper House, 8–16 Great New Street, London EC4A 3BN
Tel: 020-7353 5145
23 Melville Street, Edinburgh EH3 7PW
Tel: 0131-225 2201

The Social Security Commissioners are the final statutory authority to decide appeals relating to entitlement to social security benefits. The Child Support Commissioners are the final statutory authority to decide appeals relating to child support. Appeals may be made in relation to both matters only on a point of law. The Commissioners' jurisdiction covers England, Wales and Scotland. There are 17 commissioners; they are all qualified lawyers.
*Chief Social Security Commissioner and Chief Child Support Commissioner* (£103,516), His Hon. Judge Machin, QC
*Secretary*, L. Salder (*London*); S. Niven (*Edinburgh*)

## OFFICE OF THE SOCIAL SECURITY COMMISSIONERS AND CHILD SUPPORT COMMISSIONERS FOR NORTHERN IRELAND

Lancashire House, 5 Linenhall Street, Belfast BT2 8AA
Tel: 028-9033 2344; Fax: 028-9031 3510
Email: socialsecuritycommissioners@courtsni.gov.uk

The role of Northern Ireland Social Security Commissioners and Child Support Commissioners is similar to that of the Commissioners in Great Britain. There are two commissioners for Northern Ireland.
*Chief Commissioner* (£103,516), His Hon. Judge Martin, QC
*Deputy Commissioner*, Mrs M. S. Brown
*Registrar of Appeals*, W. R. Brown

## THE SOLICITORS' DISCIPLINARY TRIBUNAL

3rd Floor, Gate House, 1 Farringdon Street, London EC4M 7NS
Tel: 020-7329 4808; Fax: 020-7329 4833

The Solicitors' Disciplinary Tribunal is an independent statutory body whose members are appointed by the Master of the Rolls. The tribunal considers applications made to it alleging either professional misconduct and/or a breach of the statutory rules by which solicitors are bound against an individually named solicitor, former solicitor, registered foreign lawyer, or solicitor's clerk. The president and solicitor members do not receive remuneration.
*President*, A. Issacs
*Clerk*, Mrs S. C. Elson

## THE SCOTTISH SOLICITORS' DISCIPLINE TRIBUNAL

22 Rutland Square, Edinburgh EH1 2BB
Tel: 0131-229 5860

The Scottish Solicitors' Discipline Tribunal is an independent statutory body with a panel of 18 members, ten of whom are solicitors; members are appointed by the Lord President of the Court of Session. Its principal function is to consider complaints of misconduct against solicitors in Scotland.
*Chairman*, J. W. Laughland
*Clerk*, J. M. Barton, WS

## SPECIAL COMMISSIONERS OF INCOME TAX

15–19 Bedford Avenue, London WC1B 3AS
Tel: 020-7631 4242

The Special Commissioners are an independent body appointed by the Lord Chancellor to hear complex appeals against decisions of the Board of Inland Revenue and its officials.
*Presiding Special Commissioner*, His Hon. Stephen Oliver, QC
*Clerk*, R. P. Lester

## SPECIAL IMMIGRATION APPEALS COMMISSION

Taylor House, 88 Rosebery Avenue, London EC1R 4QU
Tel: 020-7862 4200

The Commission was set up under the Special Immigration Appeals Commission Act 1998. Its main function is to consider appeals against orders for deportations in cases which involve, in the main, considerations of national security. Members are appointed by the Lord Chancellor.
*Chairman*, The Hon. Mr Justice Potts
*Secretary*, S. Hill

## TRAFFIC COMMISSIONERS

c/o Scottish Traffic Area, Argyle House, 3 Lady Lawson Street, Edinburgh EH3 9SE
Tel: 0131-529 8500

The Traffic Commissioners are responsible for licensing operators of heavy goods and public service vehicles. They also have responsibility for licensing operators of heavy goods and public service vehicles. They also have responsibility for disciplinary cases involving the conduct of drivers of these vehicles. There are Seven Commissioners in the eight traffic areas covering Britain. Each Traffic Commissioner constitutes a tribunal for the purposes of the Tribunals and Inquiries Act 1992.

*Senior Traffic Commissioner* M. W. Betts, CBE

## TRANSPORT TRIBUNAL

48–49 Chancery Lane, London WC2A 1JR
Tel: 020-7947 7493

The Transport Tribunal hears appeals against decisions made by Traffic Commissioners at public inquiries. The tribunal consists of a legally-qualified president, two legal members who may sit as chairmen, and five lay members. The president and legal members are appointed by the Lord Chancellor and the lay members by the Secretary of State for Transport, Local Government and the Regions.

*President (part-time)*, H. B. H. Carlisle, QC
*Legal member (part-time)* (£258 a day), His Hon. Judge Brodrick; J. Beech
*Lay members* (£258 a day), D. Yeomans; J. W. Whitworth; P. Steel; P. Rogers; L. Milliken
*Secretary*, E. Miles

## VALUATION TRIBUNALS

Valuation Tribunal Management Board 2nd Floor, Walton House, 11 Parade, Leamington Spa, Warks CV32 4DG
Tel: 01926-421875

The Valuation Tribunals hear appeals concerning the council tax, non-domestic rating and land drainage rates in England and Wales. There are 56 tribunals in England and four in Wales; those in England are funded by the Department of Transport Local G'ment and the Regions (DTLR) and those in Wales by the National Assembly for Wales. A separate tribunal is constituted for each hearing, and normally consists of a chairman and two other members. Members are appointed by the local authorities and serve on a voluntary basis. The Valuation Tribunal Management Board considers all matters affecting valuation tribunals in England, and the Council of Wales Valuation Tribunals performs the same function in Wales.

*Chairman, Valuation Tribunal Management Board*, P. Wood, OBE
*Valuation Tribunals National Officer*, B. P. Massen, MBE
*President, Council of Wales Valuation Tribunals*, J. H. Owens

## VAT AND DUTIES TRIBUNALS

15–19 Bedford Avenue, London WC1B 3AS
Tel: 020-7631 4242

VAT and Duties Tribunals are administered by the Lord Chancellor in England and Wales, and by the First Minister in Scotland. They are independent, and decide disputes between taxpayers and Customs and Excise. In England and Wales, the president and chairmen are appointed by the Lord Chancellor and members by the Treasury. Chairmen in Scotland are appointed by the Lord President of the Court of Session.

*President*, His Hon. Stephen Oliver, QC
*Vice-President, England and Wales*, J. D. Demack
*Vice-President, Scotland*, T. G. Coutts, QC
*Vice-President, Northern Ireland*, His Hon. J. McKee, QC
*Registrar*, R. P. Lester

### TRIBUNAL CENTRES

EDINBURGH, 44 Palmerston Place, Edinburgh EH12 5BJ. Tel: 0131-226 3551

LONDON (including Belfast), 15–19 Bedford Avenue, London WC1B 3AS. Tel: 020-7631 4242

MANCHESTER, 9th Floor, Westpoint, 501 Chester Road, Manchester M16 5HU. Tel: 0161-868 6600

# The Police Service

There are 52 police forces in the United Kingdom, each responsible for policing in its area. Most forces' area is coterminous with one or more local authority areas. Policing in London is carried out by the Metropolitan Police and the City of London Police; in Northern Ireland by the Royal Ulster Constabulary (RUC); and by the Isle of Man, States of Jersey, and Guernsey forces in their respective islands and bailiwicks. National services include the National Missing Persons Bureau and the National Crime Squad.

The police authorities of English and Welsh forces comprise local councillors, magistrates and independent members. In Scotland, there are six joint police boards made up of local councillors; the other two police authorities are councils. In London the newly established Metropolitan Police Authority oversees police operations; for the City of London Police, a committee of the Corporation of London exists including councillors and magistrates. In Northern Ireland the Secretary of State appoints the police authority.

Police authorities are financed by central and local government grants and a precept on the council tax. Subject to the approval of the Home Secretary (in England and Wales) and to regulations, they appoint the chief constable. In England and Wales they are responsible for publishing annual policing plans and annual reports, setting local objectives and a budget, and levying the precept. The police authorities in Scotland are responsible for setting a budget, providing the resources necessary to police the area adequately, appointing officers of the rank of Assistant Chief Constable and above, and determining the number of officers and civilian staff in the force. The structure and responsibilities of the police authority in Northern Ireland are under review.

The Home Secretary, the Secretary of State for Northern Ireland and the Scottish Executive are responsible for the organisation, administration and operation of the police service. They make regulations covering matters such as police ranks, discipline, hours of duty, and pay and allowances. All police forces are subject to inspection by HM Inspectors of Constabulary, who report to the Home Secretary, Scottish Executive or Secretary of State for Northern Ireland. In Northern Ireland a commission on policing was established by the Belfast Agreement in April 1998. The Police Act, based on the commission's report and passed in November 2000, provided for the creation of a Policing Board to oversee the RUC.

In April 1999 the Home Secretary set targets for recruitment of officers from ethnic minorities for each force in England and Wales to achieve within ten years. In July 1999 targets for promotion and retention of these officers were also set.

## Complaints

The investigation and resolution of a serious complaint against a police officer in England and Wales is subject to the scrutiny of the Police Complaints Authority. An officer who is dismissed, required to resign or reduced in rank, whether as a result of a complaint or not, may appeal to a police appeals tribunal established by the relevant police authority. In Scotland, chief constables are obliged to investigate a complaint against one of their officers; if there is a suggestion of criminal activity, the complaint is investigated by an independent public prosecutor. In Northern Ireland complaints are investigated by the Police Ombudsman.

## Basic Rates of Pay

*since 1 September 2000*

| | |
|---|---|
| Chief Constable | |
| No fixed term | £75,825–£112,353 |
| Fixed term appointment | £79,620–£117,837 |
| Assistant Chief Constable – designated Deputy | |
| No fixed term | 80% of their Chief Constable's pay or £72,630, whichever is higher |
| Fixed term appointment | 80% of their Chief Constable's pay or £76,260, whichever is higher |
| Assistant Chief Constable | |
| No fixed term | £63,270–£72,630 |
| Fixed term appointment | £66,435–£76,260 |
| Superintendent | £46,038–£57,150 |
| Chief Inspector | £37,830–£42,426 |
| Inspector | £33,849–£38,385 |
| Sergeant | £26,169–£30,522 |
| Constable | £17,133–£27,114 |
| *Metropolitan Police* | |
| Metropolitan Commissioner | £130,469-£143,527 |
| Deputy Commissioner | £106,251–£120,057 |
| Assistant Commissioner | £96,075–£105,780 |
| Commander | £63,270–£76,260 |

The rank of Chief Superintendent was abolished in April 1995. Existing appointments continue and receive the higher ranges of the pay scale for Superintendents

## The Special Constabulary

Each police force has its own special constabulary, made up of volunteers who work in their spare time. Special Constables have full police powers within their force and adjoining force areas, and assist regular officers.

## National Crime Squad

The National Crime Squad (NCS) was established on 1 April 1998, replacing the six regional crime squads in England and Wales. It investigates national and international organised and serious crime. It also supports police forces investigating serious crime. The squad is accountable to the National Crime Squad Service Authority.

*Headquarters:* PO Box 2500, London SW1V 2WF.
Tel: 020-7238 2500

*Director General*, W. Hughes, QPM

## NCS Service Authority

The Service Authority is responsible for ensuring the effective operation of the National Crime Squad. It fulfils a similar role to a police authority. It works alongside the National Criminal Intelligence Service Service Authority. There are 17 members, of whom the chairman and nine others serve as 'core members' on both authorities.

*Headquarters*: PO Box 2600, London SW1V 2WG. Tel: 020-7238 2600
*Chairman*, Rt. Hon. Sir John Wheeler, JP, DL
*Clerk*, T. Simmons
*Treasurer*, S. Atkins

POLICE NATIONAL MISSING PERSONS BUREAU

The Police National Missing Persons Bureau (PNMPB) acts as a central clearing house of information, receiving reports about vulnerable missing persons that are still outstanding after 14 days and details of unidentified persons or remains within 48 hours of being found from all forces in England and Wales. Reports are also received from Scottish police forces, the RUC, and foreign police forces via Interpol.
*Headquarters:* New Scotland Yard, Broadway, London SW1H 0BG. Tel: 020-7230 1212
*Director*, C. J. Coombes

POLICE INFORMATION TECHNOLOGY ORGANISATION

The Police Information Technology Organisation (PITO) develops and manages the delivery of national police information technology services, such as the Police National Computer, co-ordinates the development of local information technology systems where common standards and systems are needed, and provides a procurement service.
*Headquarters:* New Kings Beam House, 22 Upper Ground, London SE1 9QY. Tel: 020-8358 5678
*Chairman*, Sir Edmund Burton
*Chief Executive*, V. Dews

FORENSIC SCIENCE SERVICE

The Forensic Science Service (FSS) provides forensic science support to the police forces in England and Wales for the investigation of scenes of crime, scientific analysis of material, and interpretation of scientific results. The FSS is organised into serious crime, volume crime, drugs and specialist services, supported by intelligence and consultancy services.
*Headquarters:* Priory House, Gooch Street North, Birmingham B5 6QQ. Tel: 0121-607 6800
*Chief Executive*, Dr J. Thompson

## POLICE FORCES AND AUTHORITIES

*Strength:* actual strength of force as at mid 2000
*Chair:* chairman/convener of the police authority/police committee/joint police board

## ENGLAND

AVON AND SOMERSET CONSTABULARY, PO Box 37, Valley Road, Portishead, North Somerset BS20 8QJ. Tel: 01275-818181; Fax: 01275-816112; *Strength*, 2,978; *Chief Constable*, S. Pilkington, QPM

BEDFORDSHIRE POLICE, Police Headquarters, Woburn Road, Kempston, Bedford MK43 9AX. Tel: 01234-841212; Fax: 01234-842006; *Strength*, 1,065; *Chief Constable*, P. Hancock, QPM

CAMBRIDGESHIRE CONSTABULARY, Hinchingbrooke Park, Huntingdon, Cambs PE29 6NP. Tel: 01480-456111; Fax: 01480-422447; *Strength*, 1,288; *Chief Constable*, D. G. Gunn

CHESHIRE CONSTABULARY, Police Headquarters, Nuns Road, Chester CH1 2PP. Tel: 01244-350000; Fax: 01244-612269; *Strength*, 2,029; *Chief Constable*, N. K. Burgess, QPM

CLEVELAND POLICE, PO Box 70, Ladgate Lane, Middlesbrough TS8 9EH. Tel: 01642-326326; Fax: 01642-301200; *Strength*, 1,426; *Chief Constable*, B. Shaw

CUMBRIA CONSTABULARY, Carleton Hall, Penrith, Cumbria CA10 2AU. Tel: 01768-891999; Fax: 01768-217099; *Strength*, 1,029; *Chief Constable*, C. Phillips

DERBYSHIRE CONSTABULARY, Butterley Hall, Ripley, Derbys DE5 3RS. Tel: 01773-570100; Fax: 01773-572225; *Strength*, 1,836; *Chief Constable*, D. F. Coleman

DEVON AND CORNWALL CONSTABULARY, Middlemoor, Exeter EX2 7HQ. Tel: 08705-777444; Fax: 08705-452346; *Strength*, 3,058; *Chief Constable*, Sir John Evans, QPM

DORSET POLICE HEADQUARTERS, Winfrith, Dorchester, Dorset DT2 8DZ. Tel: 01929-462727; Fax: 01202-223987; *Strength*, 1,355; *Chief Constable*, Mrs J. Stichbury

DURHAM CONSTABULARY HEADQUARTERS, Aykley Heads, Durham City DH1 5TT. Tel: 0191-386 4929; Fax: 0191-375 2160; *Strength*, 1,602; *Chief Constable*, G. Hedges, QPM

ESSEX POLICE, PO Box 2, Springfield, Chelmsford, Essex CM2 6DA. Tel: 01245-491491; Fax: 01245-452259; *Strength*, 2,906; *Chief Constable*, D. F. Stevens, QPM, LLB

GLOUCESTERSHIRE CONSTABULARY, Holland House, Lansdown Road, Cheltenham, Glos GL51 6QH. Tel: 01242-521321; Fax: 01242-221362; *Strength*, 1,179; *Chief Constable*, T. Brain

GREATER MANCHESTER POLICE, PO Box 22, Chester House, Boyer Street, Manchester M16 0RE. Tel: 0161-872 5050; Fax: 0161-856 2666; *Strength*, 7,000; *Chief Constable*, D. Wilmot

HAMPSHIRE CONSTABULARY, Police Headquarters, West Hill, Winchester, Hampshire SO22 5DB. Tel: 0845-045 4545; Fax: 01962-871204; *Strength*, 3,465; *Chief Constable*, P. R. Kernaghan, QPM, LLB

HERTFORDSHIRE CONSTABULARY, Stanborough Road, Welwyn Garden City, Herts AL8 6XF. Tel: 01707-354200; Fax: 01707-354409; *Strength*, 1,886; *Chief Constable*, P. Acres

HUMBERSIDE POLICE, Queens Gardens, Kingston upon Hull HU1 3DJ. Tel: 01482-326111; Fax: 01482-220037; *Strength*, 2,000; *Chief Constable*, D. Westwood, QPM

KENT CONSTABULARY, Sutton Road, Maidstone, Kent ME15 9BZ. Tel: 01622-690690; Fax: 01622-690511; *Strength*, 3,325; *Chief Constable*, Sir David Phillips, QPM

LANCASHIRE CONSTABULARY, PO Box 77, Hutton, Preston, Lancashire PR4 5SB. Tel: 01772-614444; Fax: 01772-618843; *Strength*, 3,313; *Chief Contstable*, Ms P. Clare

LEICESTERSHIRE CONSTABULARY, St John's, Narborough, Leicester LE9 5BX. Tel: 0116-222 2222; Fax: 0116-248 2227; *Strength*, 2,017; *Chief Constable*, D. J. Wyrko, QPM

LINCOLNSHIRE POLICE, PO Box 999, Lincoln LN5 7PH. Tel: 01522-532222; Fax: 01522-558229; *Strength*, 1,231; *Chief Constable*, R. J. N. Childs

MERSEYSIDE POLICE, PO Box 59, Canning Place, Liverpool L69 1JD. Tel: 0151-709 6010; Fax: 0151-777 8999; *Strength*, 4,190; *Chief Constable*, N. Bettison, QPM

NORFOLK CONSTABULARY, Police Headquarters, Martineau Lane, Norwich NR1 2DJ. Tel: 01603-768769; Fax: 01603-276215; *Strength*, 1,390; *Chief Constable*, K. Williams

NORTHAMPTONSHIRE POLICE, Wootton Hall, Northampton NN4 0JQ. Tel: 01604-700700; Fax: 01604-703028; *Strength*, 1,171; *Chief Executive*, C. Fox

NORTHUMBRIA POLICE, Force Headquarters, North Road, Ponteland, Newcastle upon Tyne NE20 0BL. Tel: 01661-872555; Fax: 01661-868928; *Strength*, 3,294; *Chief Constable*, C. Strachan

NORTH YORKSHIRE POLICE, Newby Wiske Hall, Newby Wiske, Northallerton, N. Yorks DL7 9HA. Tel: 01609-783131; Fax: 01609-789213; *Strength*, 1,337; *Chief Constable*, D. R. Kenworthy

NOTTINGHAMSHIRE POLICE, Sherwood Lodge, Arnold, Nottingham NG5 8PP. Tel: 0115-967 0999; Fax: 0115-967 0900; *Strength*, 2,258; *Chief Constable*, S. M. Green

SOUTH YORKSHIRE POLICE, Snig Hill, Sheffield S3 8LY. Tel: 0114-220 2020; Fax: 0114-252 3154; *Strength*, 3,202; *Chief Constable*, M. Hedges

STAFFORDSHIRE POLICE, Cannock Road, Stafford ST17 0QG. Tel: 01785-257717; Fax: 01785-232313; *Strength*, 2,211; *Chief Constable*, J. Giffard

SUFFOLK CONSTABULARY HEADQUARTERS, Force Headquarters, Portal Avenue, Martlesham Heath, Ipswich IP5 3QS. Tel: 01473-613500; Fax: 01473-610876; *Strength*, 1,136; *Chief Constable*, P. J. Scott-Lee, QPM

SURREY POLICE, Mount Browne, Sandy Lane, Guildford, Surrey GU3 1HG. Tel: 01483-571212; Fax: 01483-300279; *Strength*, 2,088; *Chief Constable*, D. O'Connor

SUSSEX POLICE, Malling House, Church Lane, Lewes, E. Sussex BN7 2DZ. Tel: 0845-6070 999; Fax: 01273-404274; *Strength*, 2,812; *Chief Constable*, P. C. Whitehouse, QPM

THAMES VALLEY POLICE, Oxford Road, Kidlington, Oxon OX5 2NX. Tel: 01865-846000; Fax: 01865-846160; *Strength*, 3,971; *Chief Constable*, C. Pollard, QPM

WARWICKSHIRE CONSTABULARY, PO Box 4, Leek Wootton, Warwick CV35 7QB. Tel: 01926-415000; Fax: 01926-850362; *Strength*, 920; *Chief Constable*, A. C. Timpson

WEST MERCIA CONSTABULARY, Hindlip Hall, PO Box 55, Worcester WR3 8SP. Tel: 01905-723000; Fax: 01905-454226; *Strength*, 1,936; *Chief Constable*, P. Hampson, QPM

WEST MIDLANDS POLICE, PO Box 52, Lloyd House, Colmore Circus, Queensway, Birmingham B4 6NQ. Tel: 0121-626 5000; Fax: 0121-626 5695; *Strength*, 7,322; *Chief Constable*, Sir Edward Crew, QPM

WEST YORKSHIRE POLICE, PO Box 9, Laburnum Road, Wakefield, W. Yorks WF1 3QP. Tel: 01924-375222; Fax: 01924-292182; *Strength*, 4,839; *Chief Constable*, G. Moore

WILTSHIRE CONSTABULARY, Police Headquarters, London Road, Devizes, Wilts SN10 2DN. Tel: 01380-722341; Fax: 01380-734176; *Strength*, 1,074; *Chief Constable*, Miss E. Neville

## WALES

DYFED-POWYS POLICE, PO Box 99, Llangunnor, Carmarthen, Carmarthenshire SA31 2PF. Tel: 01267-222020; Fax: 01267-222185; *Strength*, 1,064; *Chief Constable*, T. Grange

GWENT POLICE, Police Headquarters, Turnpike Road, Croesyceiliog, Cwmbran, Gwent NP44 2XJ. Tel: 01633-838111; Fax: 01633-865211; *Strength*, 1,260; *Chief Constable*, K. Turner

NORTH WALES POLICE, Glan-y-don, Colwyn Bay, Conwy LL29 8AW. Tel: 01492-517171; Fax: 01492-511232; *Strength*, 1,426; *Chief Constable*, R. Brunstrom

SOUTH WALES POLICE, Police Headquarters, Cowbridge Road, Bridgend CF31 3SU. Tel: 01656-655555; Fax: 01656-869399; *Strength*, 3,105; *Chief Constable*, A. T. Burden

## SCOTLAND

CENTRAL SCOTLAND POLICE, Randolphfield, Stirling FK8 2HD. Tel: 01786-456000; Fax: 01786-451177; *Strength*, 733; *Chief Constable*, A. Cameron *Convenor, Joint Police Board*, I. Miller

DUMFRIES AND GALLOWAY CONSTABULARY, Police Headquarters, Cornwall Mount, Dumfries DG1 1PZ. Tel: 01387-252112; Fax: 01387-260501; *Strength*, 483; *Chief Constable*, D. Strang

FIFE CONSTABULARY, Police Headquarters, Detroit Road, Glenrothes, Fife KY6 2RJ. Tel: 01592-418888; Fax: 01592-418444; *Strength*, 855; *Chief Constable*, P. M. Wilson, QPM, LLB

GRAMPIAN POLICE, Force Headquarters, Queen Street, Aberdeen AB10 1ZA. Tel: 01224-386000; Fax: 01224-643366; *Strength*, 1,221; *Chief Constable*, A. G. Brown *Convenor of Police Authority Committee*, Ms M. Stewart

LOTHIAN AND BORDERS POLICE, Fettes Avenue, Edinburgh EH4 1RB. Tel: 0131-311 3131; Fax: 0131-311 3580; *Strength*, 2,602; *Chief Constable*, Sir Roy Cameron, Kt., QPM *Convenor of Police Authority*, Ms L. Hinds

NORTHERN CONSTABULARY, Police Headquarters, Old Perth Road, Inverness IV2 3SY. Tel: 01463-715555; Fax: 01463-720373; *Strength*, 667; *Chief Constable*, W. Robertson

STRATHCLYDE POLICE, HQ, 173 Pitt Street, Glasgow G2 4JS. Tel: 0141-532 2000; Fax: 0141-532 2475; *Strength*, 7,078; *Chief Constable*, W. Rae, QPM *Convenor of Strathclyde Joint Police Board*, B. A. Mann, CBE, JP

TAYSIDE POLICE, PO Box 59, 4 West Bell Street, Dundee DD1 9JU. Tel: 01382-223200; Fax: 01382-200449; *Strength*, 1,160; *Chief Constable*, J. Vine

## NORTHERN IRELAND

ROYAL ULSTER CONSTABULARY, G. C.

Royal Ulster Constabulary, G. C., RUC Headquarters, Brooklyn, 65 Knock Road, Belfast BT5 6LD. Tel: 028-9065 0222; Fax: 028-9070 0124; *Strength*, 7935; *Chief Constable*, Sir Ronnie Flanagan, KT., OBE

## ISLANDS

ISLAND POLICE FORCE

Island Police Force, Hospital Lane, St Peter Port, Guernsey GY1 2QN. Tel: 01481-725111; Fax: 01481-45136; *Strength*, 137; *Chief Constable*, M. H. Wyeth *President, Committee of Home Affairs*, M. Torode

STATES OF JERSEY POLICE

States of Jersey Police, Rouge Bouillon, PO Box 789, St Helier, Jersey JE2 3ZA. Tel: 01534-612612; Fax: 01534-612116; *Strength*, 240; *Chief Officer*, G. Power *Committee President*, A. Layzell

ISLE OF MAN CONSTABULARY

Isle of Man Constabulary, Police Headquarters, Glencrutchery Road, Douglas, Isle of Man IM2 4RG. Tel: 01624-631212; Fax: 01624-628113; *Strength*, 240; *Chief Constable*, M. Culverhouse *Chairman, Minister for Home Affairs*, A. Bell

---

## METROPOLITAN POLICE SERVICE

New Scotland Yard, Broadway, London SW1H 0BG
Tel 020-7230 1212

---

Strength (July 2001), 25,485

*Commissioner*, Sir John Stevens, QPM

*Deputy Commissioner*, Ian Blair, QPM

OPERATIONAL AREAS

*Assistant Commissioners*, T. Ghaffur *(Policy, Review and Standards)*; M. Todd *(Territorial Policing)*

SPECIALIST OPERATIONS DEPARTMENT

*Assistant Commissioner*, A. C. Veness, QPM

COMPLAINTS INVESTIGATION BUREAU

*Deputy Assistant Commissioner*, A. C. Hayman

PAN LONDON UNITS

*Assistant Commissioner*, B. Hogan-Howe

OTHER DEPARTMENTS

*Director, Public Affairs*, R. Fedorcio
*Solicitor*, D. Hamilton
*Director, Information*, Miss A. Beaton
*Director, Property Services*, T. G. Lawrence

## CITY OF LONDON POLICE

26 Old Jewry, London EC2R 8DJ
Tel: 020-7601 2222

*Strength (July 2001)*, 707

The City of London Police is responsible for policing the City of London. Though small, the area includes one of the most important financial centres in the world and the force has particular expertise in areas such as fraud investigation as well as the areas required of any police force.

The force has a wholly elected police authority, the police committee of the Corporation of London, which appoints the Commissioner.

*Commissioner*, P. Nove, QPM
*Assistant Commissioner*, J. Hart, QPM

## BRITISH TRANSPORT POLICE

15 Tavistock Place, London WC1H 9SJ
Tel: 020-7388 7541

*Strength (March 2001)*, 2,109

British Transport Police is the national police force for the railways in England, Wales and Scotland, including the London Underground system, the Docklands Light Railway, the Midland Metro Tram system and Croydon Tramlink. The Chief Constable reports to the British Transport Police Committee.

*Chief Constable*, I. Johnston, QPM

## MINISTRY OF DEFENCE POLICE

MDP Wethersfield, Braintree, Essex CM7 4AZ
Tel: 01371-854000

*Strength (March 2001)*, 3,526 operational staff and 266 civilian support staff

The Ministry of Defence Police is a civilian police force geared to meeting the requirements of the MOD and other customers including visiting forces, the Royal Mint and the Royal Ordnance. The Policing Team initiative has recently been expanded to meet policing demands across a wider area than previously. Other specialist services include marine policing, dogs, firearms and Police Search Teams.

*Chief Constable*, L. Clarke, OBE

## ROYAL PARKS CONSTABULARY

The Old Police House, Hyde Park, London W2 2UH
Tel: 020-7298 2000

*Strength (August 2001)*, 140

The Royal Parks Constabulary is maintained by the Royal Parks Agency, an executive agency of the Department for Culture, Media and Sport, and is responsible for the policing of eight royal parks in and around London.

*Chief Officer (Acting)*, D. Pollack

## UK ATOMIC ENERGY AUTHORITY CONSTABULARY

Building E6, Culham Science Centre, Abingdon, Oxon OX14 3DB
Tel: 01235-463760

*Strength (June 2001)*, 539

The Constabulary is responsible for policing UK Atomic Energy Authority and British Nuclear Fuels PLC establishments and for escorting nuclear material between establishments.

*Chief Constable*, W. F. Pryke

## STAFF ASSOCIATIONS

Police officers are not permitted to join a trade union or to take strike action. All ranks have their own staff associations.

ASSOCIATION OF CHIEF POLICE OFFICERS OF ENGLAND, WALES AND NORTHERN IRELAND, 7th Floor, 25 Victoria Street, London SW1H 0EX. Tel: 020-7227 3434. Represents Chief Constables, Deputy and Assistant Chief Constables in England, Wales and Northern Ireland; officers of the rank of Commander and above in the Metropolitan and City of London Police and senior civilian members of these forces.

THE POLICE SUPERINTENDENTS' ASSOCIATION OF ENGLAND AND WALES, 67A Reading Road, Pangbourne, Reading RG8 7JD. Tel: 0118-984 4005. Represents officers of the rank of Superintendent.

THE POLICE FEDERATION OF ENGLAND AND WALES, 15–17 Langley Road, Surbiton, Surrey KT6 6LP. Tel: 020-8399 2224. Represents officers up to and including the rank of Chief Inspector.

ASSOCIATION OF CHIEF POLICE OFFICERS IN SCOTLAND, Police Headquarters, Fettes Avenue, Edinburgh EH4 1RB. Tel: 0131-311 3051. Represents the Chief Constables, Deputy and Assistant Chief Constables of the Scottish police forces.

THE ASSOCIATION OF SCOTTISH POLICE SUPERINTENDENTS, Secretariat, 173 Pitt Street, Glasgow G2 4JS. Tel: 0141-221 5796. Represents officers of the rank of Superintendent.

THE SCOTTISH POLICE FEDERATION, 5 Woodside Place, Glasgow G3 7QF. Tel: 0141-332 5234. Represents officers up to and including the rank of Chief Inspector.

THE SUPERINTENDENTS' ASSOCIATION OF NORTHERN IRELAND, RUC Training Centre, Garnerville Road, Belfast BT4 2NX. Tel: 028-9070 0660. Represents Superintendents and Chief Superintendents in the RUC.

THE POLICE FEDERATION FOR NORTHERN IRELAND, Royal Ulster Constabulary, Garnerville, Garnerville Road, Belfast BT4 2NX. Tel: 028-9076 0831. Represents officers up to and including the rank of Chief Inspector.

# The Prison Service

The prison services in the United Kingdom are the responsibility of the Home Secretary, the Scottish Executive Justice Department and the Secretary of State for Northern Ireland. The chief director generals (Chief Executive in Scotland) officers of the Prison Service, the Scottish Prison Service and the Northern Ireland Prison Service are responsible for the day-to-day running of the system.

There are 137 prison establishments in England and Wales, 20 in Scotland and four in Northern Ireland. Convicted prisoners are classified according to their assessed security risk and are housed in establishments appropriate to that level of security. There are no open prisons in Northern Ireland. Female prisoners are housed in women's establishments or in separate wings of mixed prisons. Remand prisoners are, where possible, housed separately from convicted prisoners. Offenders under the age of 21 are usually detained in a young offenders' institution, which may be a separate establishment or part of a prison.

Nine prisons are now run by the private sector, and in England and Wales all escort services have been contracted out to private companies. Two prisons are being built and financed under the Private Finance Initiative and will also be run by private contractors. In Scotland, one prison (Kilmarnock) was built and financed by the private sector and is being operated by private contractors.

There are independent prison inspectorates in England and Wales and Scotland which report annually on conditions and the treatment of prisoners. HM Chief Inspector of Prisons for England and Wales also performs an inspectorate role for prisons in Northern Ireland. Every prison establishment also has an independent board of visitors or visiting committee made up of local volunteers. Any prisoner whose complaint is not satisfied by the internal complaints procedures may complain to the Prisons Ombudsman for England and Wales or the Scottish Prisons Complaints Commission. There is no Prisons Ombudsman for Northern Ireland, but complaints by prisoners regarding maladministration may be made to the Parliamentary Commissioner for Administration.

AVERAGE PRISON POPULATION 2000–2001 (UK)

| | *Remand* | *Sentenced* | *Other* |
|---|---|---|---|
| ENGLAND AND WALES | | | |
| Male | 10,296 | 50,480 | 641 |
| Female | 700 | 2,684 | 22 |
| Total | 10,996 | 53,164 | 663 |
| SCOTLAND | | | |
| Male | n/a | n/a | — |
| Female | n/a | n/a | — |
| Total | 975 | 4,999 | — |
| N. IRELAND | | | |
| Male | 284 | 699 | 5 |
| Female | 9 | 13 | 0 |
| Total | 293 | 712 | 5 |
| UK TOTAL | 12,264 | 58,875 | 673 |

The projected prison population for 2007 in England and Wales is 69,500 if custody rates and sentence lengths remain at 2000 levels

*Sources*: Home Office – *Research Development Statistics;* Scottish Prison Service – *Annual Report and Accounts 1999–2000* Northern Ireland Prison Service – *Annual Report 2000–2001*

SENTENCED PRISON POPULATION BY SEX AND OFFENCE (ENGLAND AND WALES) *as at 30 June 2000.*

| | *Male* | *Female* |
|---|---|---|
| Violence against the person | 10,807 | 410 |
| Sexual offences | 5,070 | 20 |
| Burglary | 8,824 | 158 |
| Robbery | 6,158 | 195 |
| Theft, handling | 4,537 | 507 |
| Fraud and forgery | 885 | 131 |
| Drugs offences | 7,526 | 947 |
| Other offences | 5,829 | 222 |
| Offence not known | 797 | 69 |
| In default of payment of a fine | 80 | 7 |
| Total | 50,514 | 2,666 |

*Source:* Home Office – *Research Development Statistics*

AVERAGE SENTENCED POPULATION BY LENGTH OF SENTENCE 2000 (ENGLAND AND WALES)

| | *Adults* | *Young Offenders* |
|---|---|---|
| Less than 12 months | 6,053 | 2,414 |
| 12 months to less than 4 years | 15,161 | 4,517 |
| 4 years to less than 10 years | 16,181 | 1,338 |
| 10 years less than life | 2,384 | 19 |
| Life | 4,406 | 147 |
| Total | 44,185 | 8,435 |

*Source:* Home Office – *Research Development Statistics*

AVERAGE DAILY SENTENCED POPULATION BY LENGTH OF SENTENCE 1999–2000 (SCOTLAND)

| | *Adults* | *Young Offenders* |
|---|---|---|
| Less than 4 years | 1,987 | 502 |
| 4 years or over (including life) | 2,333 | 176 |
| Total | 4,320 | 678 |

*Source:* Scottish Prison Service – *Annual Report and Accounts 1999–2000*

PRISON SUICIDES 2001 (ENGLAND AND WALES)

| | |
|---|---|
| Males | 73 |
| Females | 8 |
| Total | 81 |
| Rate per 1,000 prisoners in custody | 1.25 |

*Source:* Home Office – *Research Development Statistics*

AVERAGE NUMBER OF PRISON SERVICE STAFF 2000–2001 (GREAT BRITAIN)

| | *England and Wales* | *Scotland* |
|---|---|---|
| No. of prison service staff | 43,845 | 4,870 |

*Sources:* HM Prison Service – *Annual Report and Accounts 2000–2001*; Scottish Prison Service – *Annual Report and Accounts 1999–2000*

OPERATING COSTS OF PRISON SERVICE IN ENGLAND AND WALES 2000–2001

| | £ million |
|---|---|
| Staff costs | 1,094.5 |
| Other operating costs | 925.1 |
| Operating income | (144.8) |
| *Net operating costs before notional charge on capital employed* | 1,874.8 |
| Charge on capital employed | 259.9 |
| *Net operating costs* | 2,134.7 |
| Average cost per prisoner place (reflecting establishment costs only) | £22,890 |

*Source:* HM Prison Service – *Annual Report and Accounts 2000–2001*

OPERATING COSTS OF SCOTTISH PRISON SERVICE 1999–2000

| | £ |
|---|---|
| Total income | 1,734,000 |
| Total expenditure | 219,975,000 |
| Staff costs | 127,724,000 |
| Running costs | 73,489,000 |
| Other current expenditure | 18,762,000 |
| Operating cost | (218,241,000) |
| Cost of capital charges | (23,349,000) |
| Interest payable and similar charges | (15,000) |
| Interest receivable | 93,000 |
| Lockerbie Trial Costs | 3,387 |
| Deficit for financial year | (244,899,000) |
| Average annual cost per prisoner per place | £28,375 |

*Source:* Scottish Prison Service – *Annual Report and Accounts 1999–2000*

OPERATING COSTS OF NORTHERN IRELAND PRISON SERVICE 2000–2001

| | £'000 |
|---|---|
| Income | 105 |
| Expenditure | |
| Staff Costs | 82,256 |
| Depreciation and other charges, | 5,417 |
| Other Operating Costs, | 21,719 |
| Total, | 109,392 |
| Net cost of Operations, | 107,657 |
| Average annual cost per prisoner place | 74,580 |

*Source:* Northern Ireland Prison Service – *Annual Report and Accounts 2000–2001*

## THE PRISON SERVICES

### HM PRISON SERVICE

Cleland House, Page Street, London SW1P 4LN
Tel: 020-7217 6000; Fax: 020-7217 6403

SALARIES 2000–2001

| | |
|---|---|
| Grade1A1 | £42,500–£61,376 |
| Grade 1B | £41,000–£58,573 |
| Grade 1C | £36,500–£52,738 |
| Grade 1D/2A | £32,500–£48,293 |
| Grade 2B/3A | £23,000–£36,346 |
| Grade 2C/3B | £19,000–£37,090 |
| Grade 3C | £18,000–£25,233 |

THE PRISON SERVICE MANAGEMENT BOARD

*Director-General (SCS)*, M. Narey
*Private Secretary*, Ms R. Goodwin
*Staff Officer*, C. Stuart
*Prisons and Probation Minister, Chairman of the Strategy Board for Correctional Services*, Beverley J. Huges, MP
*Director, Criminal Policy Group, Home Office*, Ms S. Street
*Deputy Director-General (SCS)*, P. Wheatley
*Director of High Security Prisons (SCS)*, P. Atherton
*Director of Security (SCS)*, B. Clark
*Director of Personnel (SCS)*, G. Hadley
*Director of Finance Procurement (SCS)*, J. Le Vay
*Director of Corporate Affairs (SCS)*, Ms C. Pelham
*Director of Resettlement (SCS)*, K. D. Sutton
*Head of the Prison Health Policy Unit (SCS)*, Dr F. Harvey
*Non-Executive Members*, Sir Duncan Nichol, CBE; Mrs R. Thomson, CBE; P. Carter; R. Rosser; Lord Laming
*Board Secretary and Head of Secretariat*, Ms C. Checksfield
*Chaplain-General and Archdeacon of the Prison Service*, W. Noblett
*Muslim Advisor*, M. Ahmed
*Race Equality Advisor*, Ms J. Clements
*Legal Adviser*, S. Bramley

AREA MANAGERS (*SCS*)

*Eastern*, M. Spurr; *East Midlands (North)*, D. Shaw; *East Midlands (South)*, M. Egan; *London*, A. Smith; *North East*, R. Mitchell; *North West (Lancashire and Cumbria)*, T. Fitzpatrick; *North West (Manchester, Mersey and Cheshire)*, I. Lockwood; *South East (Thames Valley and Hampshire)*, Mrs S. Payne; *South East (Kent Surrey and Sussex)*, T. Murtagh; *South West*, J. Petherick; *Wales*, J. May; *West Midlands*, B. Payling; *Yorkshire and Humberside*, P. Earnshaw
*Operational Manager for Women's Prisons*, N. Clifford
*Operational Manager for Juvenile Estate*, D. Walplington
*Operational Manager for High Security Prisons*, P. Atherton

PRISON ESTABLISHMENTS – ENGLAND AND WALES

*CNA* – Average number of in use certified normal accommodation places without overcrowding 2000-2001 *Prisoners*, 63,462
*Prisoners/Young Offenders* Average number of prisoners/ young offenders 2000-2001, *Prisoners*, 64,520, *Young Offenders 10,980*

ACKLINGTON, Morpeth, Northumberland NE65 9XH. *CNA*, 782. *Prisoners*, 727. *Governor*, P. Atkinson
ALBANY, Newport, Isle of Wight PO30 5RS. *CNA*, 446. *Prisoners*, 438. *Governor*, K. Munns
ALTCOURSE (private prison), Higher Lane, Fazakerley, Liverpool L9 7AG. *CNA*, 614. *Prisoners*,768. *Director*, W. MacGowan
†‡ASHFIELD (from December 1999), Shortwood Road, Pucklechurch, Bristol BS16 9QT. *CNA*, 407. *Prisoners*, 356. *Director*, D. Bramley
ASHWELL, Oakham, Leics LE15 7LF. *CNA*, 407. *Prisoners*, 384. *Governor*, D. Walmsley
*‡ASKHAM GRANGE, Askham Richard, York YO2 3PT. *CNA*, 132. *Prisoners and Young Offenders*, 120. *Governor*, I. Simmonds
‡AYLESBURY, Bierton Road, Aylesbury, Bucks HP20 1EH. *CNA*, 418. *Young Offenders*, 355. *Governor*, S. Bryans
BEDFORD, St Loyes Street, Bedford MK40 1HG. *CNA*, 352. *Prisoners*, 413. *Governor*, A. Cross
†BELMARSH, Western Way, Thamesmead, London SE28 0EB. *CNA*, 843. *Prisoners*, 817. *Governor*, H. Banks
BIRMINGHAM, Winson Green Road, Birmingham B18 4AS. *CNA*, 722. *Prisoners*, 817. *Governor*, M. Shann

BLAKENHURST (private prison), Hewell Lane, Redditch, Worcs B97 6QS. *CNA*, 647. *Prisoners*, 833. *Director*, P. Siddons

BLANTYRE HOUSE, Goudhurst, Cranbrook, Kent TN17 2NH. *CNA*, 120. *Prisoners*, 109. *Governor*, C. Bartlett

BLUNDESTON, Lowestoft, Suffolk NR32 5BG. *CNA*, 424. *Prisoners*, 412. *Governor*, J. Knight

†‡BRINSFORD, New Road, Featherstone, Wolverhampton WV10 7PY. *CNA*, 477. *Young Offenders*, 473. *Governor*, D. McAllister

BRISTOL, Cambridge Road, Bristol BS7 8PS. *CNA*, 489. *Prisoners*, 537. *Governor*, N. Wall

BRIXTON, PO Box 369, Jebb Avenue, London SW2 5XF. *CNA*, 651. *Prisoners*, 766. *Governor*, S. Twinn

*†‡BROCKHILL, Redditch, Worcs B97 6RD. *CNA*, 166. *Prisoners and Young Offenders*, 151. *Governor*, M. Sheppard

BUCKLEY HALL (private prison), Buckley Farm Lane, Rochdale, Lancs OL12 9DP. *CNA*, 350. *Prisoners*, 367. *Director*, P. Norbury

BULLINGDON, PO Box 50, Bicester, Oxon OX6 0PR. *CNA*, 773. *Prisoners*, 864. *Acting Governor*, L. Serjeant

*‡BULLWOOD HALL, High Road, Hockley, Essex SS5 4TE. *CNA*, 180. *Prisoners and Young Offenders*, 167. *Governor*, Mrs V. Hart

CAMP HILL, Newport, Isle of Wight PO30 5PB. *CNA*, 481 *Prisoners*, 525. *Governor*, S. Metcalf

CANTERBURY, 46 Longport, Canterbury CT1 1PJ. *CNA*, 198. *Prisoners*, 273. *Governor*, Ms J. Galbally

†‡CARDIFF, Knox Road, Cardiff CF2 1UG. *CNA*, 525. *Prisoners and Young Offenders*, 619. *Governor*, J. Thomas-Ferrand

‡CASTINGTON, Morpeth, Northumberland NE65 9XG. *CNA*, 460. *Young Offenders*, 271. *Governor*, M. Lees

CHANNINGS WOOD, Denbury, Newton Abbott, Devon TQ12 6DW. *CNA*, 594. *Prisoners*, 587. *Governor*, N. Evans

†‡CHELMSFORD, 200 Springfield Road, Chelmsford, Essex CM2 6LQ. *CNA*, 50. *Prisoners and Young Offenders*, 459. *Governor*, P. Haley

COLDINGLEY, Bisley, Woking, Surrey GU24 9EX. *CNA*, 370. *Prisoners*, 356 *Governor*, J. Dixon

*COOKHAM WOOD, Rochester, Kent ME1 3LU. *CNA*, 120. *Prisoners*, 146. *Governor*, S. West

DARTMOOR, Princetown, Yelverton, Devon PL20 6RR. *CNA*, 691. *Prisoners*, 636. *Governor*, J. Lawrence

‡DEERBOLT, Bowes Road, Barnard Castle, Co. Durham DL12 9BG. *CNA*, 474. *Young Offenders*, 389. *Governor*, P. Copple

†‡DONCASTER (private prison), Off North Bridge, Marshgate, Doncaster DN5 8UX. *CNA*, 771. *Prisoners and Young Offenders*, 1,048. *Director*, K. Rogers

†‡DORCHESTER, North Square, Dorchester DT1 1JD. *CNA*, 172. *Prisoners and Young Offenders*, 225. *Governor*, R. Bateman

‡DOVER, The Citadel, Western Heights, Dover CT17 9DR. *CNA*, 316. *Young Offenders*, 288. *Governor*, C. Kershaw

DOWNVIEW, Sutton Lane, Sutton, Surrey SM2 5PD. *CNA*, 327. *Prisoners*, 328. *Governor*, B. Chapman

*‡DRAKE HALL, Eccleshall, Staffs ST21 6LQ. *CNA*, 311. *Prisoners and Young Offenders*, 199. *Governor*, P. Tidball

DOVEGATE (Private prison), UTTOXETER, ST14 8XR. *CNA*, 200, *Prisoners and Young Offendlers*, 199. *Director*, P. Wright.

*†DURHAM, Old Elvet, Durham DH1 3HU. *CNA*, 670. *Prisoners*, 696. *Governor*, M. Newell

*‡EAST SUTTON PARK, Sutton Valence, Maidstone, Kent ME17 3DF. *CNA*, 94. *Prisoners and Young Offenders*, 85. *Governor*, Revd R. Carter

*†‡EASTWOOD PARK, Falfield, Wotton-under-Edge, Glos GL12 8DB. *CNA*, 295. *Prisoners and Young Offenders*, 303. *Governor*, P. Winkley.

ELMLEY, Church Road, Eastchurch, Sheerness, Kent ME12 4AY. *CNA*, 763. *Prisoners*, 894. *Governor*, B. Pollett

ERLESTOKE HOUSE, Devizes, Wilts SN10 5TU. *CNA*, 326. *Prisoners*, 315. *Governor*, *Mrs J. Blake*

EVERTHORPE, Brough, E. Yorks HU15 1RB. *CNA*, 438. *Prisoners*, 460. *Governor*, P. Midgley

†‡EXETER, New North Road, Exeter EX4 4EX. *CNA*, 321. *Prisoners and Young Offenders*, 469. *Governor*, G. Deighton

FEATHERSTONE, New Road, Wolverhampton WV10 7PU. *CNA*, 599. *Prisoners*, 592. *Governor*, M. Pascoe

†‡FELTHAM, Bedfont Road, Feltham, Middx TW13 4ND. *CNA*, 860. *Prisoners and Young Offenders*, 660. *Governor*, N. Pascoe

FORD, Arundel, W. Sussex BN18 0BX. *CNA*, 501. *Prisoners*, 319. *Governor*, K. Kan

FOREST BANK, Agecroft Road, Pendlebury, Manchester M27 8UE. *CNA*, 800. *Prisoners*, 726. *Director*, M. Goodwin

*‡FOSTON HALL, Foston, Derbys DE65 5DN. *CNA*, 174. *Prisoners and Young Offenders*, 154. *Governor*, Ms P. Scriven

FRANKLAND, Brasside, Durham DH1 5YD. *CNA*, 653. *Prisoners*, 622. *Governor*, I. Woods

FULL SUTTON, Full Sutton, York YO41 1PS. *CNA*, 603. *Prisoners*, 584. *Governor*, D. Roberts

GARTH, Ulnes Walton Lane, Leyland, Preston PR5 3NE. *CNA*, 633. *Prisoners*, 618. *Governor*, J. Illingsworth

GARTREE, Gallow Field Road, Market Harborough, Leics LE16 7RP. *CNA*, 366. *Prisoners*, 286. *Governor*, S. McAllister

†‡GLEN PARVA, Tigers Road, Wigston, Leicester LE8 4TN. *CNA*, 684. *Young Offenders*,763. *Governor*, C. Bushell

†‡GLOUCESTER, Barrack Square, Gloucester GL1 2JN. *CNA*, 236. *Prisoners and Young Offenders*, 260. *Governor*, R. Booty

GRENDON/SPRING HILL, Grendon Underwood, Aylesbury, Bucks HP18 0TL. *CNA*, 509. *Prisoners*, 434. *Governor*, T. C. Newell

‡GUYS MARSH, Shaftesbury, Dorset SP7 0AH. *CNA*, 487. *Prisoners and Young Offenders*, 507. *Governor*, Mrs D. Calvert

§HASLAR, 2 Dolphin Way, Gosport, Hants PO12 2AW. *CNA*, 160. *Prisoners*, 147. *Governor*, B. Bennett

‡HATFIELD, Thorne Road, Hatfield, Doncaster DN7 6EL. *CNA*, 180. *Young Offenders*, 169. *Governor*, T. Watson

HAVERIGG, Millom, Cumbria LA18 4NA. *CNA*, 554. *Prisoners*, 518. *Governor*, G. Brunskill

HEWELL GRANGE, Redditch, Worcs B97 6QQ. *CNA*, 193. *Prisoners*, 142. *Governor*, N. Croft

HIGH DOWN, Sutton Lane, Sutton, Surrey SM2 5PJ. *CNA*, 649. *Prisoners*, 700. *Governor*, T. Butt

*HIGHPOINT, Stradishall, Newmarket, Suffolk CB8 9YG. *CNA*, 850. *Prisoners*, 794. *Governor*, R. Haley

†‡HINDLEY, Gibson Street, Bickershaw, Wigan, Lancs WN2 5TH. *CNA*, 538. *Prisoners and Young Offenders*, 510. *Governor*, J. Heavens

‡HOLLESLEY BAY COLONY, Woodbridge, Suffolk IP12 3JW. *CNA*, 463. *Prisoners and Young Offenders*, 311. *Governor*, S. Robinson

*†‡HOLLOWAY, Parkhurst Road, London N7 0NU. *CNA*, 517. *Prisoners and Young Offenders*, 470. *Governor*, D. Lancaster

HOLME HOUSE, Holme House Road, Stockton-on-Tees TS18 2QU. *CNA*, 971. *Prisoners*, 918. *Governor*, R. Crouch

†‡HULL, Hedon Road, Hull HU9 5LS. *CNA*, 615. *Prisoners and Young Offenders*, 554. *Governor*, S. Wagstaffe

‡HUNTERCOMBE, Huntercombe Place, Nuffield, Henley-on-Thames RG9 5SB. *CNA*, 360. *Young Offenders*, 325. *Governor*, P. Manwaring

KINGSTON, 122 Milton Road, Portsmouth PO3 6AS. *CNA*, 193. *Prisoners*, 181. *Governor*, A. Munro

KIRKHAM, Freckleton Road, Preston PR4 2RN. *CNA*, 577. *Prisoners*, 479. *Governor*, A. F. Jennings, OBE

KIRKLEVINGTON GRANGE, Yarm, Cleveland TS15 9PA. *CNA*, 183. *Prisoners*, 179. *Governor*, Ms S. Anthony

LANCASTER, The Castle, Lancaster LA1 1YL. *CNA*, 240. *Prisoners*, 229. *Governor*, T. Williams

†‡LANCASTER FARMS, Far Moor Lane, Stone Row Head, off Quernmore Road, Lancaster LA1 3QZ. *CNA*, 496. *Prisoners and Young Offenders*, 457. *Governor*, D. Thomas

LATCHMERE HOUSE, Church Road, Ham Common, Richmond, Surrey TW10 5HH. *CNA*, 193. *Prisoners*, 169. *Governor*, T. Hinchliffe

LEEDS, Armley, Leeds LS12 2TJ. *CNA*, 770. *Prisoners*, 1,256. *Governor*, S. Tasker

LEICESTER, Welford Road, Leicester LE2 7AJ. *CNA*, 219. *Prisoners*, 334. *Governor*, D. Bamber

†‡LEWES, Brighton Road, Lewes, E. Sussex BN7 1EA. *CNA*, 485. *Prisoners and Young Offenders*, 445. *Governor*, P. Carroll

LEYHILL, Wotton-under-Edge, Glos GL12 8BT. *CNA*, 410. *Prisoners*, 319. *Governor*, R. Booty

LINCOLN, Greetwell Road, Lincoln LN2 4BD. *CNA*, 436. *Prisoners*, 486. *Governor*, R. Peacock

§LINDHOLME, Bawtry Road, Hatfield Woodhouse, Doncaster DN7 6EE. *CNA*, 641 *Prisoners*,590. *Governor*, M. Read

LITTLEHEY, Perry, Huntingdon, Cambs PE18 0SR. *CNA*, 624. *Prisoners*, 627. *Governor*, J. Morgan

LIVERPOOL, 68 Hornby Road, Liverpool L9 3DF. *CNA*, 1,216. *Prisoners*, 1,257. *Governor*, C. Sheffield

LONG LARTIN, South Littleton, Evesham, Worcs WR11 5TZ. *CNA*, 599. *Prisoners*, 448. *Governor*, J. Mullen

LOWDHAM GRANGE (private prison), Lowdham, Notts NG14 7TA. *CNA*, 504. *Prisoners*, 489. *Director*, A. Bramley

*†‡LOW NEWTON, Brasside, Durham DH1 5SD. *CNA*, 215. *Prisoners and Young Offenders*, 237. *Governor*, M. Kirby

MAIDSTONE, 36 County Road, Maidstone ME14 1UZ. *CNA*, 549. *Prisoners*, 371. *Governor*, M. Conway

MANCHESTER, Southall Street, Manchester M60 9AH. *CNA*, 953. *Prisoners*, 1,105. *Acting Governor*, J. Smith

‡MOORLAND, Bawtry Road, Hatfield Woodhouse, Doncaster DN7 6BW. *CNA*, 753. *Prisoners and Young Offenders*, 760. *Governor*, B. McCourt

MORTON HALL, Swinderby, Lincoln LN6 9PS. *CNA*, 192. *Prisoners*, 119. *Governor*, M. Murphy

THE MOUNT, Molyneaux Avenue, Bovingdon, Hemel Hempstead HP3 0NZ. *CNA*, 705. *Prisoners*, 717. *Governor*, P. Wailen

*†‡NEW HALL, Dial Wood, Flockton, Wakefield WF4 4AX. *CNA*, 327. *Prisoners and Young Offenders*, 334. *Governor*, V. Bird

†‡NORTHALLERTON, 15A East Road, Northallerton, N. Yorks DL6 1NW. *CNA*, 152. *Prisoners and Young Offenders*, 198. *Governor*, D. P. G. Appleton

NORTH SEA CAMP, Freiston, Boston, Lincs PE22 0QX. *CNA*, 226. *Prisoners*, 182. *Governor*, M. A. Lewis

†‡NORWICH, Mousehold, Norwich NR1 4LU. *CNA*, 561. *Prisoners and Young Offenders*, 652. *Governor*, M. Knight

NOTTINGHAM, Perry Road, Sherwood, Nottingham NG5 3AG. *CNA*, 519. *Prisoners*, 484. *Governor*, K. Beaumont

‡ONLEY, Willoughby, Rugby, Warks CV23 8AP. *CNA*, 640. *Young Offenders*, 576. *Governor*, R. Fielder

†‡PARC (private prison), Heol Hopcyn John, Bridgend CF35 6AR. *CNA*, 844. *Prisoners and Young Offenders*, 869. *Director*, R. Woolford

PARKHURST, Newport, Isle of Wight PO30 5NX. *CNA*, 482. *Prisoners*, 427. *Governor*, D. Kennedy

PENTONVILLE, Caledonian Road, London N7 8TT. *CNA*, 897. *Prisoners*, 1,122. *Governor*, G. Davies

‡PORTLAND, Easton, Portland, Dorset DT5 1DL. *CNA*, 512. *Young Offenders*, 480. *Governor*, K. Lockyer

‡PRESCOED, 47 Maryport Street, Usk, Gwent NP5 1XP. *CNA*, 120. *Prisoners and Young Offenders*, 111. *Governor*, R. J. Comber

PRESTON, 2 Ribbleton Lane, Preston PR1 5AB. *CNA*, 425. *Prisoners*, 542. *Governor*, A. Scott

RANBY, Ranby, Retford, Notts DN22 8EV. *CNA*, 725. *Prisoners*, 738. *Governor*, J. Slater

†‡READING, Forbury Road, Reading RG1 3HY. *CNA*, 204. *Prisoners and Young Offenders*, 229. *Governor*, C. Norman

*RISLEY, Risley, Warrington WA3 6BP. *CNA*, 818. *Prisoners*,790. *Governor*, C. McConnell

†‡ROCHESTER, 1 Fort Road, Rochester, Kent ME1 3QS. *CNA*, 433. *Prisoners and Young Offenders*, 367. *Governor*, T. Robson

RYE HILL (Private Prison), ONLEY, RUGBY CV23 8A9. *CNA*, 600. *Prisoners and Young Offenders*, 458, *Director*, A. Rose-Quirie

*SEND, Ripley Road, Send, Woking, Surrey GU23 7LJ. *CNA*, 220. *Prisoners*, 216. *Governor*, T. Beeston

SHEPTON MALLET, Cornhill, Shepton Mallet, Somerset BA4 5LU. *CNA*, 195. *Prisoners*, 150. *Governor*, B. McAlley

SHREWSBURY, The Dana, Shrewsbury SY1 2HR. *CNA*, 185. *Prisoners*, 325. *Governor*, A. Bramley

STAFFORD, 54 Gaol Road, Stafford ST16 3AW. *CNA*, 627. *Prisoners*, 619. *Governor*, L. Taylor

STANDFORD HILL, Church Road, Eastchurch, Isle of Sheppey, Kent ME12 4AA. *CNA*, 384. *Prisoners*, 332. *Governor*, J. Robinson

STOCKEN, Stocken Hall Road, Stretton, nr Oakham, Leics LE15 7RD. *CNA*, 556. *Prisoners*, 578. *Governor*, R. Curtis

‡STOKE HEATH, Stoke Heath, Market Drayton, Shropshire TF9 2JL. *CNA*, 634. *Young Offenders*, 509. *Governor*, C. James

*‡STYAL, Wilmslow, Cheshire SK9 4HR. *CNA*, 412. *Prisoners and Young Offenders*, 421. *Governor*, Ms M. Moulden

SUDBURY, Ashbourne, Derbys DE6 5HW. *CNA*, 519. *Prisoners*, 498. *Governor*, P. Salter

SWALESIDE, Brabazon Road, Eastchurch, Isle of Sheppey, Kent ME12 4AX. *CNA*, 752. *Prisoners*, 746. *Governor*, E. Willett

†SWANSEA, 200 Oystermouth Road, Swansea SA1 3SR. *CNA*, 249. *Prisoners*, 346. *Governor*, Miss V. O'Dea

‡SWINFEN HALL, Lichfield, Staffs WS14 9QS. *CNA*, 320. *Young Offenders*, 308 *Governor*, Ms J. Mosley

‡THORN CROSS, Arley Road, Appleton Thorn, Warrington WA4 4RL. *CNA*, 316. *Young Offenders*, 212. *Governor*, C. Davies

USK, 47 Maryport Street, Usk, Gwent NP5 1XP. *CNA*, 131. *Prisoners*, 216. *Governor*, R. J. Comber

THE VERNE, Portland, Dorset DT5 1EQ. *CNA*, 552. *Prisoners*, 562. *Governor*, M. Cook

WAKEFIELD, 5 Love Lane, Wakefield WF2 9AG. *CNA*, 746. *Prisoners*, 558. *Governor*, D. Shaw

WANDSWORTH, Heathfield Road, London SW18 3HS. *CNA*, 1,162. *Prisoners*, 1,301. *Governor*, S. Rimmer

WAYLAND, Griston, Thetford, Norfolk IP25 6RL. *CNA*, 620. *Prisoners*, 623. *Governor*, Mrs K. Crawley

WEALSTUN, Wetherby, W. Yorks LS23 7AZ. *CNA*, 616. *Prisoners*, 603. *Governor*, S. Tilley
WEARE, Portland Dock, Castletown, Portland, Dorset DT5 1PZ. *CNA*, 400. *Prisoners*, 374. *Governor*, Ms S. F. McCormick
WELLINGBOROUGH, Millers Park, Doddington Road, Wellingborough, Northants NN8 2NH. *CNA*, 518. *Prisoners*, 449. *Governor*, Dr P. Bennett
‡WERRINGTON, Werrington, Stoke-on-Trent ST9 0DX. *CNA*, 106. *Young Offenders*, 105. *Governor*, S. Habgood
‡WETHERBY, York Road, Wetherby, W. Yorks LS22 5ED. *CNA*, 309. *Young Offenders*, 347. *Governor*, S. McEwan
WHATTON, 14 Cromwell Road, Nottingham NG13 9FQ. *CNA*, 275. *Prisoners*, 272. *Governor*, B. Greenberry
WHITEMOOR, Longhill Road, March, Cambs PE15 0PR. *CNA*, 532. *Prisoners*, 381. *Governor*, B. Perry
*WINCHESTER, Romsey Road, Winchester SO22 5DF. *CNA*,439. *Prisoners*, 590. *Governor*, J. Gomersall
THE WOLDS (private prison), Everthorpe, Brough, E. Yorks HU15 2JZ. *CNA*, 360. *Prisoners*, 397. *Director*, D. McDonnell
†‡§WOODHILL, Tattenhoe Street, Milton Keynes MK4 4DA. *CNA*, 677. *Prisoners and Young Offenders*, 660. *Governor*, B. Mullen
WORMWOOD SCRUBS, PO Box 757, Du Cane Road, London W12 0AE. *CNA*, 1,212. *Prisoners*, 947. *Governor*, K. Munns
WYMOTT, Ulnes Walton Lane, Leyland, Preston PR5 3LW. *CNA*, 809. *Prisoners*, 793. *Governor*, R. Doughty

## SCOTTISH PRISON SERVICE

Calton House, 5 Redheughs Rigg, Edinburgh EH12 9HW
Tel: 0131-556 8400

### SALARIES 2000–2001

Senior managers in the Scottish Prison Service, including governors and deputy governors of prisons, are paid across three pay bands:

| | |
|---|---|
| Band I | £37,375–£37,700 |
| Band H | £31,150 –£48,100 |
| Band G | £26,050–£39,600 |

*Chief Executive of Scottish Prison Service*, A. Cameron
*Director, Human Resources*, P. Russell
*Director, Finance and Information Systems*, W. Pretswell
*Director, Strategy and Business Performance*, B. Allison
*Deputy Director, Rehabilitation and Care*, A. Spencer
*Deputy Director, Estates and Buildings*, D. Bentley
*Operations Director, South and West*, M. Duffy
*Operations Director, North and East*, P. Withers
*Head of Training, Scottish Prison Service College*, J. Matthews
*Head of Communications*, T. Fox

### PRISON ESTABLISHMENTS

*Prisoners/Young Offenders* Average number of prisoners/young offenders 2000–2001
*ABERDEEN, Craiginches, Aberdeen AB9 2HN. *Prisoners*, 181. *Governor*, I. Gunn
BARLINNIE, Barlinnie, Glasgow G33 2QX. *Prisoners*, 1,124. *Governor*, R. L. Houchin
CASTLE HUNTLY, Castle Huntly, Longforgan, nr Dundee DD2 5HL. *Prisoners*, 106. *Governor*, M. McAlpine
*‡CORNTON VALE, Cornton Road, Stirling FK9 5NY. *Prisoners and Young Offenders*, 180. *Governor*, S. Swan
*‡DUMFRIES, Terregles Street, Dumfries DG2 9AX. *Young Offenders*, 137. *Governor*, C. McGeever
EDINBURGH, 33 Stenhouse Road, Edinburgh EH1 3LN. *Prisoners*, 731. *Governor*, R. MacCowan
‡GLENOCHIL, King O'Muir Road, Tullibody, Clackmannanshire FK10 3AD. *Prisoners and Young Offenders*, 573. *Governor*, K. Donegan
GREENOCK, Gateside, Greenock PA16 9AH. *Prisoners*, 236. *Governor*, A. Park
*INVERNESS, Porterfield, Inverness IV2 3HH. *Prisoners*, 122. *Governor*, A. MacDonald
KILMARNOCK (private prison), Bowhouse, Mauchline Road, Kilmarnock KA1 5JH. *Prisoners*, 500. *Director*, J. Bywalec
LOW MOSS, Low Moss, Bishopbriggs, Glasgow G64 2QB. *Prisoners*, 362. *Governor*, E. Murch
NORANSIDE, Noranside, Fern, by Forfar, Angus DD8 3QY. *Prisoners*, 102. *Governor*, K. Rennie
PERTH, 3 Edinburgh Road, Perth PH2 8AT. *Prisoners*, 477. *Governor*, W. Millar
PETERHEAD, Salthouse Head, Peterhead, Aberdeenshire AB4 6YY. *Prisoners*, 297. *Governor*, W. Rattray
‡POLMONT, Brightons, Falkirk, Stirlingshire FK2 0AB. *Young Offenders*, 443. *Governor*, D. Gunn
SHOTTS, Shotts ML7 4LF. *Prisoners*, 467. *Governor*, W. McKinlay

## NORTHERN IRELAND PRISON SERVICE

Dundonald House, Upper Newtownards Road, Belfast BT4 3SU. Tel: 028-9052 2922; Fax 028-9052 5100;
Web: www.niprisonservice.gov.uk

| Salaries 1999–2000 | |
|---|---|
| Governor 1 | £55,536–£57,453 |
| Governor 2 | £50,148–£51,687 |
| Governor 3 | £43,309–£44,532 |
| Governor 4 | £36,317–£38,249 |
| Governor 5 | £25,461–£34,261 |

A Northern Ireland allowance is also payable

### PRISON ESTABLISHMENTS

*Prisoners/Young Offenders* Average number of prisoners/young offenders 2000–2001
†HYDEBANK WOOD, Hospital Road, Belfast BT8 8NA. *Young Offenders*, 136
*‡MAGHABERRY, Old Road, Ballinderry Upper, Lisburn, Co. Antrim BT28 2PT. *Prisoners and Young Offenders*, 481
§MAGILLIGAN, Point Road, Magilligan, Co. Londonderry BT49 0LR. *Prisoners*, 364

*Women's establishment or establishment with units for women
†Remand Centre or establishment with units for remand prisoners
‡Young Offender Institution or establishment with units for young offenders
§Immigration Holding Centre

# Defence

The armed forces of the United Kingdom comprise the Royal Navy, the Army and the Royal Air Force. The Queen is commander-in-chief of all the armed forces. The Ministry of Defence, headed by a Secretary of State, provides the support structure for the armed forces. Within the Ministry of Defence, the Defence Council has overall responsibility for running the armed forces. The Chief of Staff of each service reports through the Chief of the Defence Staff to the Secretary of State on matters relating to the running of his service. The Chief of Staff also chairs the executive committee of the appropriate service board, which manages the service in accordance with centrally determined objectives and budgets. The military-civilian Central Staffs, headed by the Vice-Chief of the Defence Staff and the Second Permanent Under-Secretary of State, are responsible for policy, operational requirements, commitments, financial management, resource planning and civilian personnel management. The Defence Procurement Agency is responsible for purchasing equipment. The Defence Scientific Staff and the Defence Intelligence Staff also form part of the Ministry of Defence.

A permanent Joint Headquarters for the conduct of joint operations was set up at Northwood in 1996. The Joint Headquarters connects the policy and strategic functions of the MoD Head Office with the conduct of operations and is intended to strengthen the policy/executive division. A Joint Rapid Deployment Force was established in August 1996 and a Joint Rapid Reaction Force was set up in April 1999.

Britain pursues its defence and security policies through its membership of NATO (to which most of its armed forces are committed), the Western European Union, the European Union, the Organisation for Security and Co-operation in Europe and the UN (*see* International Organisations section).

## Armed Forces Strengths *as at 1 July 2001*

| | |
|---|---|
| All Services | 203,730 |
| Men | 187,054 |
| Women | 16,676 |
| Royal Naval Services | 41,864 |
| Army | 108,475 |
| Royal Air Force | 53,391 |

*Source:* Ministry of Defence: Defence Analytical Service Agency

## Service Personnel

*1 August 2001*

| | *Royal Navy* | *Army* | *RAF* | *All Services* |
|---|---|---|---|---|
| 1975 strength | 76,200 | 167,100 | 95,000 | 338,300 |
| 1990 strength | 63,200 | 152,800 | 89,700 | 305,700 |
| 1999 strength | 43,700 | 113,500 | 55,200 | 212,400 |
| 2001 strength | 41,864 | 108,475 | 53,391 | 203,730 |

*Source:* Ministry of Defence: *The Military Balance 2000–2001 (OUP)*

## Civilian Personnel

| | |
|---|---|
| 1975 level | 316,700 |
| 1990 level | 172,300 |
| 1999 level | 117,700 |
| 2000 level | 99,142 |
| 2001 level | 98,384 |

*Source:* The Ministry of Defence: *The Military Balance 1999–2000 (OUP) and UK Defence Statistics 2001*

## Deployment of UK Personnel

### Service Personnel In UK *as at July 2000*

| | England | Wales | Scotland | N. Ireland | Unknown | Total |
|---|---|---|---|---|---|---|
| All Services | 143,039 | 3,223 | 15,080 | 8,387 | 566 | 170,295 |
| Officers | 25,039 | 402 | 1,759 | 889 | 147 | 28,236 |
| Other Ranks | 118,000 | 2,821 | 13,321 | 7,498 | 419 | 142,059 |
| Army [2] | 68,040 | 864 | 4,165 | 7,110 | 343 | 80,522 |
| Officers | 9,745 | 106 | 422 | 729 | 36 | 11,038 |
| Ranks | 58,295 | 758 | 3,743 | 6,381 | 307 | 69,484 |
| Navy [1, 2] | 34,858 | 29 | 4,962 | 189 | 13 | 40,051 |
| Officers | 6,496 | 12 | 590 | 15 | 5 | 7,118 |
| Ranks | 28,362 | 17 | 4,372 | 174 | 8 | 32,933 |
| RAF [2] | 40,141 | 2,330 | 5,953 | 1,088 | 210 | 49,722 |
| Officers | 8,798 | 284 | 747 | 145 | 106 | 10,080 |
| Ranks | 31,343 | 2,046 | 5,206 | 943 | 104 | 39,642 |

1. Naval Service personnel on sea service in home waters are included against the local authority containing the home port of their ship.
2. The titles Naval Service, Army and Royal Air Force include Nursing services.
3. The Home battalions of the Royal Irish Regiment are excluded from the UK Northern Ireland figures.

*Source:* Ministry of Defence: Defence Analytical Service Agency

### Service Personnel Overseas

*as at 1 January 2001*

| | |
|---|---|
| All Services | 37,657 |
| Officers | 5,480 |
| Other Ranks | 32,177 |
| Army | 29,372 |
| Officers | 3,668 |
| Ranks | 25,704 |
| Navy | 1,924 |
| Officers | 559 |
| Ranks | 1,365 |
| RAF | 6,361 |
| Officers | 1,253 |
| Ranks | 5,108 |

*Source:* Ministry of Defence: Defence Analytical Service Agency

## Nuclear Forces

Britain's nuclear forces comprise four ballistic missile submarines carrying Trident missiles and equipped with nuclear warheads. All nuclear free-fall bombs have been taken out of service.

## Arms Control

The 1990 Conventional Armed Forces in Europe Treaty (the CFE Treaty), which is currently being revised, commits all NATO and former Warsaw Pact members to limiting five major classes of conventional weapons. In 1968 Britain signed the Nuclear Non-Proliferation Treaty, which was indefinitely and unconditionally extended in 1995 and in 1996 signed a Comprehensive Nuclear Test Ban Treaty. Britain was a party to the 1972 Biological and Toxin Weapons Convention, which provides for a world-wide ban on biological weapons, and the 1993 Chemical Weapons Convention, which came into force in 1997 and provides for a world-wide ban on chemical weapons. In 1997 Britain signed the Ottawa

Convention, which provides for an immediate ban on the use, production and transfer of anti-personnel land-mines; Britain ratified the Convention on 31 July 1998 and it came into force on 1 March 1999.

### Defence Budget

| Estimated Outturn | *£ billion* |
|---|---|
| 2000–2001 | 22.820 |
| 2001–2002 | 23.408 |
| 2002–2003 | 24.036 |
| 2003–2004 | 24.816 |

*Source:* Ministry of Defence: Defence Analytical Service Agency

The defence settlement under the 2000 Comprehensive Spending Review estimates that defence expenditure will rise from approximately £23 billion this year to almost £25 billion by 2004–05.

Over the period of the Spending Review, defence as a percentage of GDP will fall from 2.4 per cent this year to 2.3 per cent by 2003–04, reflecting the fact that GDP is forecast to grow strongly. As a share of total Government expenditure, defence spending will remain at around 6 per cent.

---

## MINISTRY OF DEFENCE

Main Building, Whitehall, London SW1A 2HB
Tel 020-7218 9000
Public Enquiry Office: Tel 020-7218 6645
Web: www.mod.uk

---

For ministerial and civil service salaries, *see* page 291
For Services salaries, *see* pages 406–8
Officers promoted in an acting capacity to a more senior rank are listed under the more senior rank. Promotion to five-star rank is no longer usual in peacetime.

*Secretary of State for Defence*, Rt. Hon. Geoffrey Hoon, MP
  *Private Secretary* (*SCS*), P. Watkins
  *Special Adviser*, R. Taylor
  *Parliamentary Private Secretary*, Mrs L. Blackman
*Minister of State for the Armed Forces*, Adam Ingram, MP
  *Private Secretary* (*SCS*), D. Applegate
*Parliamentary Under Secretary and Minister of State for Defence Procurement*, Lord Bach
  *Private Secretary* (*SCS*), D. E. A. Hatcher
  *Parliamentary Private Secretary*, Gillian Merron, MP
*Parliamentary Under-Secretary of State* (*Veterans*), Dr Lewis Moonie, MP
  *Private Secretary* (*SCS*), K. Alford
*Permanent Under-Secretary of State* (*SCS*), K. R. Tebbit, CMG
*Chief of the Defence Staff*, Admiral Sir Michael Boyce GCB, OBE

### The Defence Council

The Defence Council is responsible for running the Armed Forces. The Crown Office announced that as of the 5th November 1999, the constitution of the defence council would be arranged in the following way. It is chaired by the Principal Secretary of State for Defence and consists of: the Ministers of State for the Armed Forces; the Minister of State for Defence Procurement; the Parliamentary Under-Secretary of State for Defence; the Chief of the Defence Staff; the Permanent Under-Secretary of State of the Ministry of Defence; the Chief of the Naval Staff and First Sea Lord; the Chief of the General Staff; the Chief of the Air Staff; the Vice-Chief of the Defence Staff; the Chief of Defence Procurement for the Ministry of Defence; the Chief Scientific Adviser of the Ministry of Defence; the Chief of Defence Logistics and the Second Permanent Under-Secretary of State of the Ministry of Defence.

## CHIEFS OF STAFF

### Chief of the Naval Staff

*Chief of the Naval Staff and First Sea Lord*, Adm. Sir Nigel Essenhigh, KCB
*Asst Chief of the Naval Staff*, Rear-Adm. T. P. McClement OBE
*Secretariat* (*Naval Staff*) (*SCS*), C. Verey

### Chief of the General Staff

*Chief of the General Staff*, Gen. Sir Michael Walker, GCB, CMG, CBE, ADC
*Asst Chief of the General Staff*, Maj.-Gen. F. R. Dannatt CBE MC; Lt-Gen. K. O'Donoghue, CBE MCBE, MC
*Director-General, Development and Doctrine*, Maj.-Gen. C. L. Elliott, CB, MBE

### Chief of the Air Staff

*Chief of the Air Staff*, Air Chief Marshal Sir Peter Squire AFC, ADC, KCB, DFC, GCB
*Asst Chief of the Air Staff*, Air Vice-Marshal P. O. Sturley
*British-American Community Relations Co-ordinator*, Air Marshal Sir John Kemball, KCB, CBE, RAF (retd)
*Chief Executive, National Air Traffic Services* (*SCS*), D. J. McLauchlan
*Director, Airspace Policy*, Air Vice-Marshal J. R. D. Arscott

## CENTRAL STAFFS

*Vice-Chief of the Defence Staff*, Adm. Sir Anthony Bagnall, KCB, OBE
*Second Permanent Under-Secretary of State* (*SCS*), R. T. Jackling, CB, CBE
*Deputy CDS* (*Equipment Capability*), Vice-Adm. Sir Jeremy Blackham, KCB
*Asst CDS, Operational Requirements* (*Sea Systems*), Rear-Adm. R. J. G. Ward
*Asst CDS, Operational Requirements* (*Land Systems*), to be announced
*Asst CDS, Operational Requirements* (*Air Systems*), Air Vice-Marshal S. M. Nicholl, CBE, AFC
*Deputy CDS* (*Personnel*), Air Marshal M. D. Pledger, KCB, OBE, AFC
*Asst CDS* (*Programmes*), Maj.-Gen. J. P. Kiszely, MC
*Asst Under-Secretary of State* (*Service Personnel Policy*) (*SCS*), D. Bowen
*Defence Housing Executive* (*SCS*), C. J. I. James
*Surgeon-General*, Lt.-Gen. R. C. Menzies, OBE, QHS
*Chief Executive, Defence Medical Training Organisation*, Brig. J. R. Brown
*Chief Executive, Defence Secondary Care Organisation*, C. Callow
*Deputy Under-Secretary of State* (*Resources, Programmes and Finance*) (*SCS*), C. V. Balmer
*Asst Under-Secretary of State* (*Programmes*) (*SCS*), T. A. Woolley
*Asst Under-Secretary of State* (*Systems*) (*SCS*), N. K. J. Witney
*Asst Under-Secretary of State* (*Financial Management*) (*SCS*), D. G. Jones
*Asst Under-Secretary of State* (*General Finance*) (*SCS*), C. Sanders
*Defence Services Secretary*, Maj.-Gen. C. H. Elliott
*Deputy CDS* (*Commitments*), Lt.-Gen. A. D. Pigott, CBE

*Asst CDS (Operations) and Air Officer Commanding No 1 Group*, Air Vice-Marshal G. L. Torpy, CBE, DSO
*Chief of Defence Logistics*, Gen. Sir Samuel Cowan, KCB, CBE
*Chief of Staff to the Chief of Defence Logistics, (Operations and Business Development) and Chief Naval Engineer Officer* Rear-Adm. M. G. Wood, CBE
*Deputy to the Chief of Defence Logistics*, J. R. C. Oughton
*Asst CDS (Logistics)*, Air Vice-Marshal D. C. Couzens
*Director of Policy (SCS)*, R. P. Hatfield, CBE
*Asst CDS (Policy)*, Lt. Gen. J. G. Reith, CBE
*Deputy Under-Secretary of State (Civilian Management) (SCS)*, J. Howe
*Asst Under-Secretary of State, Civilian Management (Personnel) (SCS)*, B. A. E. Taylor
*Chief Constable, MOD Police*, W. E. E. Boreham, OBE
*Asst Under-Secretary of State (Security and Support) (SCS)*, A. G. Rucker
*Legal Adviser (SCS)*, M. J. Hemming
*Director-General, Information and Communications Services (SCS)*, A. C. Sleigh
*Defence Estates (SCS)*, B. L. Hirst
*Commandant, Joint Services Command and Staff College*, Air Vice-Marshal B. K. Burridge, CBE

### Defence Information Staff

*Director-General of Corporate Communications (SCS)*, J. Pitt-Brooke
*Director, News*, M. Howard
*Director, Internal Communications and Media Training (SCS)*, A. Boardman
*Director, Corporate Communications (Navy)*, Cdre H. Edelston
*Director, Corporate Communications (Army)*, Brig. S. Roberts
*Director, Corporate Communications (RAF)*, Air Cdre D. Walker

## DEFENCE INTELLIGENCE STAFF

Old War Office Building, Whitehall, London SW1A 2EU
Tel 020-7218 6645; fax 020-7218 1562

*Chief of Defence Intelligence*, Air Marshall Joseph French, CBE
*Deputy Chief of Defence Intelligence and Head of Defence Intelligence Analysis Staff (SCS)*, Anthony Cragg, CMG
*Director, Intelligence Programmes and Resources (SCS)*, P. I. Bailey
*Director, Defence Intelligence Secretariat and Communications Information Systems (SCS)*, C. A. Younger
*Director, Regional Assessments*, Brig. N. J. Cottam
*Director, Intelligence Global Issues (SCS)*, J. M. Cunningham
*Director-General, Intelligence and Geographic Resources*, Maj.-Gen. M. Laurie

## DEFENCE SCIENTIFIC STAFF

*Chief Scientific Adviser (SCS)*, Prof. Sir Keith O'Nions, FRS
*Chief Scientist*, H. B. Jordan
*Director General (Scrutiny and Analysis) (SCS)*, M. J. Earwicker; P. M. Sutcliffe
*Asst Chief Scientific Adviser (Nuclear) (SCS)*, P. W. Roper
*Nuclear Weapon Safety Adviser (SCS)*, Rear-Adm. Fred Scourse

## SECOND SEA LORD/COMMANDER-IN-CHIEF NAVAL HOME COMMAND

*Second Sea Lord and C.-in-C. Naval Home Command*, Vice-Adm. Sir P. Spencer, ADC
*Director-General, Naval Personnel (Strategy and Plans) and Chief of Staff to Second Sea Lord and C.-in-C. Naval Home Command*, Rear-Adm. R. G. Lockwood
*Asst Under-Secretary of State (Naval Personnel) (SCS)*, E. Cassidy
*Flag Officer Training and Recruiting and Chief Executive, Naval Recruiting and Training Agency*, Rear-Adm. J. Chadwick
*Naval Secretary and Chief Executive, Naval Manning Agency*, Rear-Adm. J. M. de Halpert
*Medical Director, General Navy Surgeon*, Rear-Adm. I. L. Jenkins *Director-General, Naval Chaplaincy Services*, Revd Dr C. Stewart

## NAVAL SUPPORT COMMAND

*Chief of Fleet Support*, Rear-Adm. B. B. Perowne
*Asst Under-Secretary of State (Fleet Support) (SCS)*, D. J. Gould
*Chief Executive, Warships Support Agency (SCS)*, J. Coles
*Chief Naval Engineer Officer*, Rear-Adm. M. G. Wood, CBE
*Flag Officer Scotland, N. England and N. Ireland, and Naval Base Commander Clyde*, Rear-Adm. D. J. Anthony, CBE

## COMMANDER-IN-CHIEF FLEET

*C.-in-C. Fleet*, Adm. Sir Alan West KCB, DSC
*Deputy Commander Fleet*, Vice-Adm. J. Band
*Chief of Staff (Operations) and Flag Officer Submarines*, Rear-Adm. R. P. Stevens, OBE
*Chief of Staff (Corporate Development)*, Rear- Adm. P. D. Greenish
*Flag Officer Surface Flotilla*, Rear-Adm. A. K. Backus, OBE, *Flag Officer Sea Training and Flag Officer Surface Flotilla*, Rear-Adm A. K. Backus, OBE.
*Commander, UK Task Group/Commander, Anti-Submarine Warfare Strike Force*, Rear-Adm. J. M. Burnell-Nugent
*Flag Officer Maritime Aviation*, Rear-Adm. I. R. Henderson, CBE
*Commandant-General, Royal Marines*, Maj.-Gen. R. A. Fry, MBE

## ADJUTANT-GENERAL'S DEPARTMENT

*Adjutant-General*, Lt.-Gen. T. J. Granville-Chapman, KCB, CBE
*Chief of Staff*, Brig. K. H. Cima
*Head, Command Secretariat (SCS)*, M. E. McLoughlin
*Director-General, Army Training and Recruiting and Chief Executive, Army Training and Recruiting Agency*, Maj.-Gen. A. M. D. Palmer, CBE
*Chaplain-General*, Revd Ven. J Blackburn
*Director-General, Army Medical Services*, Maj.-Gen. D. S. Jolliffe, QHP
*Director, Army Legal Services*, Maj.-Gen. G. Risius
*Military Secretary and Chief Executive, Army Personnel Centre*, Maj.-Gen. A. P. Grant Peterkin
*Commandant, Royal Military Academy, Sandhurst*, Maj.-Gen. P. C. C. Trousdell, CB

## COMMANDER-IN-CHIEF LAND COMMAND

*C.-in-C., Land Command*, Gen. Sir Michael Jackson, KCB, CBE, DSO (*Commander-in-Chief Headquarters Land Command*)
*Deputy C.-in-C., Land Command, and Inspector-General, Territorial Army and C-in-C Allied Forces Northern Europe*, Lt.-Gen. C. N. G. Delves, CBE, DSO
*Chief of Staff, HQ Land Command*, Maj.-Gen. F. R. Viggers, MBE
*Deputy Chief of Staff, HQ Land Command*, Maj.-Gen. P. A. Chambers, MBE

## HQ STRIKE COMMAND

*Air Officer Commanding-in-Chief*, Air Chief Marshal Sir John Day, KCB, ADC,

*Chief of Air Staff*, Air Chief marshallSir Peter Squire .
*Deputy Chief of Staff Operations*, Air Vice-Marshal N. J. Sudborough OBE
*Air Officer Logistics and Communications Information Systems*, Air Vice-Marshal P. J. Scott
*Air Officer Administration*, Air Vice-Marshal A. J. Burton
*Head, Command Secretariat (SCS)*, C. J. Wright
*Air Officer Commanding, No. 1 Group*, Air Vice-Marshal G. L. Torpy
*Air Officer Commanding No 3 Group*, Rear Adm. S. Lidbetter
*Air Officer Commanding, No. 38 Group*, Air Vice-Marshal K. D. Filbey, CBE
*Deputy Commander-in-Chief Strike Command*, Air Marshal G. E. Stirrup, KCB

## HQ LOGISTICS COMMAND

*Air Officer Commanding-in-Chief*, Air Vice-Marshal G. Skinner, CBE
*Command Secretary (SCS)*, H. Griffiths
*Air Officer Communications Information Systems and Support Services*, Air Vice-Marshal P. Liddell
*Director-General, Support Management (RAF )*, Air Vice-Marshal P. W. Henderson, CB, MBE

## HQ PERSONNEL AND TRAINING COMMAND

*Air Member for Personnel and Commander-in-Chief Personnel and Training Command and Commander-in-Chief Strike Command*, Air Chief Marshal Sir John Day
*Chief of Staff*, Air Vice-Marshal R. A. Wright, AFC
*Chief Executive, Training Group Defence Agency*, Air Vice-Marshal I. S. Corbitt
*Air Officer Administration and Air Officer Commanding Directly Administered Units*, Air Vice-Marshal C. Davison, MBE
*Commandant, RAF College, Cranwell*, Air Vice-Marshall H. G. Mackay, OBE, AFC
*Air Secretary and Chief Executive, RAF Personnel Management Agency*, Air Vice-Marshal I. M. Stewart, AFC
*Director-General, Medical Services (RAF)*, Air Vice-Marshal C. J. Sharples, QHP
*Director, Legal Services (RAF)*, Air Vice-Marshal J. Weeden
*Chaplain-in-Chief (RAF)*, Revd A. P. Bishop, QHC
*Command Secretary (SCS)*, R. Rooks

## DEFENCE PROCUREMENT AGENCY (DPA)

215 MOD Abbey Wood, Bristol BS34 8JH
Tel: 0117-913 0249; Fax: 0117-913 0902

*Chief of Defence Procurement and Chief Executive, Defence Procurement Agency*, Sir Robert Walmsley, KCB
*Deputy Chief Executive (SCS)*, David Gould
*Executive Director 1 (SCS)*, I. Fauset
*Executive Director 2*, Maj.-Gen P. Gilchrist
*Executive Director 3 (SCS)*, B. M. Thornton
*Executive Director 4, and Controller of the Navy*, Rear-Adm. N. C. F. Guild
*Executive Director 5 (SCS)*, S. Porter
*Executive Director 6 (SCS)*, N. Evans

## OTHER DEFENCE AGENCIES

ARMED FORCES PERSONNEL ADMINSTRATION AGENCY, Building 182, RAF Innsworth, Gloucester GL3 1HW. Tel: 01452-712612 ext. 6250. *Chief Executive*, T. S. Lord

ABRO, Building 200, Monxton Road, Andover, Hants SP11 8HT. Tel: 01264-383295. Acting *Chief Executive*, Dr L. Sammon

ARMY PERSONNEL CENTRE, Kentigern House, 65 Brown Street, Glasgow G2 8EX. Tel: 0141-224 3010. *Chief Executive*, Lt-Gen. A. S. H. Irwin, CBE

ARMY TRAINING AND RECRUITING AGENCY, Trenchard Lines, Upavon, Pewsey, Wilts SN9 6BE. Tel: 01980-615033. *Chief Executive*, Maj.-Gen. A. M. D. Palmer, CBE

BRITISH FORCES POST OFFICE, Inglis Barracks, Mill Hill, London NW7 1PX. Tel: 020-8818 6310.
Email: bfpo@compuserve.com; Web: bfpo.org.uk
*Director and Chief Executive*, Brig. B. J. Cash

CHILDREN'S EDUCATION, HQ SCE, Building 5, Wegberg Military Complex, BFPO 40. Tel: 00-49 2161-908 2372. *Chief Executive*, D. G. Wadsworth

DEFENCE ANALYTICAL SERVICES AGENCY, St. Giles Court, 1–13 St Giles High Street, London WC2H 8LD. Tel: 020-7218 0729; Fax; 020-7218 5203.
*Chief Executive*, C. Youngson

DEFENCE AVIATION REPAIR AGENCY, DARA Head Office, Building 145, St Athan, Barry, Vale of Glamorgan CF62 4WA. Tel: 01446-798893. *Chief Executive*, S. R. Hill, OBE

DEFENCE BILLS AGENCY, Room 410, Mersey House, Drury Lane, Liverpool L2 7PX. Tel: 0151-242 2234.
*Chief Executive*, I. S. Elrick

DEFENCE COMMUNICATION SERVICES AGENCY (DCSA), Building 111 Basil Hill Site, Park Lane, Wilts SN13 9NR. Tel: 01225-814785 *Chief Executive*, Maj.-Gen. A. J. Raper, CBE

DEFENCE COMMUNICATION SERVICES AGENCY/ DIRECTORATE ENGINEERING AND INTEROPERABILITY (DSCA/DEI), RAF Henlow, Beds, SG16 6DN.
Tel: 01462-8515 ext 7625/7250
*Chief Executive*, Brig. J. E.Thomas

DEFENCE DENTAL AGENCY, RAF Halton, Aylesbury, Bucks HP22 5PG. Tel: 01296-623535, ext. 6851. *Chief Executive*, Maj.-Gen. J. A. Gamon , QHDS

DEFENCE ESTATES, St George's House, Blakemore Drive, Sutton Coldfield, W. Midlands B75 7RL. Tel: 0121-311 2140. *Chief Executive*, I. Andrews, CBE

DEFENCE GEOGRAPHIC AND IMAGERY INTELLIGENCE AGENCY (DGIA), Watson Building, Elmwood Avenue, Feltham, Middx TW13 7AH. Tel: 020-8818 2133; Fax: 020-8818 2426 *Chief Executive*, Brig. A. P. Walker, OBE The former Military Survey and the Joint Air Reconnaissance Intelligence Centre (JARIC) converged in April 2000 to form one agency, the DGIA.

DEFENCE HOUSING EXECUTIVE, 8th Floor, St Christopher House, Southwark Street, London SE1 0TD. Tel: 020-7305-2035 *Chief Executive*, J. Wilson

DEFENCE INTELLIGENCE AND SECURITY CENTRE, Chicksands, Shefford, Beds SG17 5PR. Tel: 01462-752125. *Chief Executive*, Brig. C. G. Holtom

DEFENCE MEDICAL TRAINING ORGANISATION, Building 87, Fort Blockhouse, Gosport, Hants PO12 2AB.
Tel: 023-9276 5284/5438
*Chief Executive*, Brig. J. R. Brown

DEFENCE SECONDARY CARE AGENCY, Room 4/168, St Christopher House, Southwark Street, London, SE1 0TD. Tel: 020-7305 6190 . *Chief Executive*, Mr J. Tuckett

DEFENCE STORAGE AND DISTRIBUTION AGENCY, Ploughley Road, Lower Arncott, Bicester, Oxon OX25 2LD. Tel: 01869-256840. *Chief Executive*, Brig. P. D. Foxton, CBE,

DEFENCE TRANSPORT AND MOVEMENTS AGENCY, Monxton Road, Andover, Hants SP11 8HT. Tel: 01264-382537. *Chief Executive*, Air Cdre Whalley

DEFENCE VETTING AGENCY, Room Building 107 , Imphal Barracks, Fulford Road, York YO10 4AS . Tel: 01904 662444 . *Chief Executive*, M. P. B. G. Wilson

DISPOSAL SERVICES AGENCY, 7th Floor, 6 Hercules Road, London SE1 7DJ. Tel: 020-7261 8879; Fax: 020-7261 8696; Email: disposalservices.agency.mod.uk
*Chief Executive*, S. Taylor, CBE

LOGISTIC APPLICATIONS IPT, Monxton Road, Andover, Hants SP11 8HT. Tel: 01264-382025; Email: hq.laipt@gtnet.gov.uk
*Team Leader*, Brig. P. A. Flenagan

MEDICAL SUPPLIES AGENCY, Drummond Barracks, Ludgershall, Andover, Hants SP11 9RU. Tel: 01264-798622. *Acting Chief Executive*, J. Baines

MET OFFICE, London Road, Bracknell, Berks RG12 2SZ. Tel: 01344-420242; Email:enquiries@metoffice.com; Web:www.metoffice.com *Chief Executive*, P. D. Ewins

MINSTRY OF DEFENCE POLICE, Wethersfield, Braintree, Essex CM7 4AZ. Tel: 01371-854000. *Chief Executive*, Chief Constable D. L. Clarke

NAVAL MANNING AGENCY, Victory Building, HM Naval Base, Portsmouth PO1 3LS. Tel: 023-9272 7408. *Chief Executive*, Rear-Adm. J. M. de Halpert

NAVAL RECRUITING AND TRAINING AGENCY, Victory Building, HM Naval Base, Portsmouth PO1 3LS. Tel: 023-9272 7600; Fax: 023-9272 7613 *Chief Executive*, Rear-Adm. P.R. Davies, CBE

PAY AND PERSONNEL AGENCY, Warminster Road, Bath BA1 5AA. Tel: 01225-828533. *Chief Executive*, D.C.J. Ball

QINETIQ PLC, Ively Road, Farnborough, Hants GU14 0LX. Tel: 01252-394500; Web: www.qiuetiq.com. *Chief Executive*, Sir John Chisholm

RAF PERSONNEL MANAGEMENT AGENCY, RAF Innsworth, Gloucester GL3 1EZ. Tel: 01452-712612, ext. 7849. *Chief Executive*, Air Vice-Marshal I. M. Stewart, AFC

RAF SIGNALS ENGINEERING ESTABLISHMENT RAF Henlow, Beds SG16 6DN. Tel: 01452-712612 ext. 7849. *Chief Executive*, Air Vice-Marshal I. M. Stewart, AFC

WARSHIP SUPPORT AGENCY, B Block, Management Suite , Foxhill, Bath BA1 5AB. Tel: 01225-882348; Fax: 01225-884313; Email: cessa@navynet.gtnet.gov.uk
*Chief Executive*, J. D. Coles

TRAINING GROUP DEFENCE AGENCY, RAF Innsworth, Gloucester GL3 1EZ. Tel: 01452-712612, ext. 5344. *Chief Executive*, Air Vice-Marshal I. S. Corbitt

UNITED KINGDOM HYDROGRAPHIC OFFICE, Admiralty Way, Taunton, Somerset TA1 2DN. Tel: 01823-337900.
E-mail: name.surname@ukho.gov.uk
Web: www.ukho.gov.uk *Chief Executive, and National Hydrographer*, Dr David Winford Williams

# The Royal Navy

LORD HIGH ADMIRAL OF THE UNITED KINGDOM
HM The Queen

ADMIRALS OF THE FLEET

HRH The Prince Philip, Duke of Edinburgh, KG, KT, OM, GBE, AC, QSO, PC, *apptd* 1953
The Lord Hill-Norton, GCB, *apptd* 1971
Sir Michael Pollock, GCB, LVO, DSC, *apptd* 1974
Sir Edward Ashmore, GCB, DSC, *apptd* 1977
Sir Henry Leach, GCB, *apptd* 1982
Sir Julian Oswald, GCB, *apptd* 1993
Sir Benjamin Bathurst, GCB, *apptd* 1995

ADMIRALS

Boyce, Sir Michael, GCB, OBE, ADC (*Chief of Defence Staff and Aide-de-Camp to Her Majesty The Queen*)
Abbott, Sir Peter, GBE, KCB (*Vice Chief of the Defence Staff*)
Essenhigh, Sir Nigel, KCB (*Chief of Naval Staff and First Sea Lord*)
Perowne, Sir James, KBE (*Deputy Saclant*)
West, Sir Alan, KCB (*Commander-in-Chief Fleet, Cinceastlant and Commander Allied Naval Forces North Europe*)
Forbes, I. A., CBE (*Deputy Supreme Allied Commander Atlantic*)
Garnett, Sir Ian, KCB (*Chief of Joint Operations Chief of Staff Supreme Headquarters Allied Powers Europe*)

VICE-ADMIRALS

Haddacks, Sir Paul, KCB (*Director of International Military Staff*)
Blackham, Sir Jeremy, KCB (*Deputy CDS (Equipment Capability)*)
Malbon, F. M. (*Director TOPMAST*)
Band, J. (*Deputy Commander-in-Chief Fleet*)
Spencer, Sir P., KCB, ADC (*C.-in-C. Naval Home Command and Second Sea Lord*)

REAR-ADMIRALS

Lippiett, R. J., MBE (*Chief of Staff to Commander, Allied Naval Forces Southern Europe*)
Dunt, P. A. (*Senior Directing Staff (Navy)*)
Stevens, R. P., OBE (*Chief of Staff (Operations), Flag Officer Submarines, COMSUBEASTLANT and COMSUBNORTHWEST*)
Chadwick, J. (*Flag Officer Training and Recruiting and Chief Executive, Naval Recruiting and Training Agency*)
de Halpert, J. M. (*Naval Secretary/Chief Executive, Naval Manning Agency*)
Wood, M. G., CBE (*Director General Defence Logistics (Operations and Business Development)*)
Stanford, C. D. (*Chief of Staff to the Surgeon-General*)
Burnell-Nugent, J. M., CBE (*Commander UK Maritime Forces and Commander Anti Submarine Warfare Striking Force*)
Meyer, S. R. (*Chief of Staff, Permanent Joint Headquarters*)
Backus, A. K., OBE (*Flag officer Sea Training and Flag Officer Surface Flotilla*)
Guild, N. C. F. (*Executive Director 4, Defence Procurement Agency, Controller of the Navy*)
Ward, R. J. G. (*Capability Manager (Strategic Deployment)*)
Dymock, A. K. (*Deputy COMSTRIKFORTHS*)
Anthony, D. J., MBE (*Flag Officer Scotland, N. England and N. Ireland, and Naval Base Commander Clyde*)
Reeve, J. ( *Deputy Chief Executive of the Warship Support Agency*)
Lockwood, R. G. (*Director-General, Naval Personnel (Strategy and Plans) and Chief of Staff to Second Sea Lord and C.-in-C. Naval Home Command*)
Greenish, P. D. (*Chief of Staff (Corporate Development)*)
Stanhope, M., OBE (*Director of Operational Management, NATO Regional Command North*)
McLean, R. A. I., OBE (*Asst Chief of Defence Staff (Resource and Planning)*)
McClement, T. P., OBE (*Asst Chief of Naval Staff*)
S. Lidbetter (*Air Officer Commanding 3 Group/Flag Officer Maritime Aviation, Commander Air East Atlantic and Commander Maritime Air North*)

## HM FLEET *as at autumn 2001*

| | |
|---|---|
| SUBMARINES | |
| Trident | Vanguard, Vengeance, Victorious, Vigilant |
| Fleet | Sceptre, Sovereign, Spartan, Splendid, Superb, Talent, Tireless, Torbay, Trafalgar, Trenchant, Triumph, Turbulent |
| ANTI-SUBMARINE WARFARE CARRIERS | Ark Royal, Illustrious, Invincible |
| ASSAULT SHIPS | Fearless, Intrepid |
| LANDING PLATFORM HELICOPTER | Ocean |
| DESTROYERS | |
| Type 42 | Cardiff, Edinburgh, Exeter, Glasgow, Gloucester, Liverpool, Manchester, Newcastle, Nottingham, Southampton, York |
| FRIGATES | |
| Type 23 | Argyll, Grafton, Iron Duke, Kent, Lancaster, Marlborough, Monmouth, Montrose, Norfolk, Northumberland, Portland, Richmond, Somerset, St Albans, Sutherland, Westminster |
| Type 22 | Campbeltown, Chatham, Cornwall, Coventry, Cumberland, Sheffield |
| OFFSHORE PATROL | |
| Castle Class | Dumbarton Castle, Leeds Castle |
| Island Class | Alderney, Anglesey, Guernsey, Lindisfarne, Shetland |
| MINEHUNTERS | |
| Hunt Class | Atherstone, Brecon, Brocklesby, Cattistock, Chiddingfold, Cottesmore, Dulverton, Hurworth, Ledbury, Middleton, Quorn |
| Sandown Class | Bangor, Blyth, Bridport, Cromer, Grimsby, Inverness, Pembroke, Penzance, Ramsay, Sandown, Shoreham, Walney |
| PATROL CRAFT | |
| River Class | Orwell |
| Coastal Training Craft | Archer, Biter, Blazer, Charger, Dasher, Example, Exploit, Explorer, Express, Puncher, Pursuer, Raider, Smiter, Tracker |
| Gibraltar Search and Rescue Craft | Ranger, Trumpeter |
| ICE PATROL SHIP | Endurance |
| SURVEY SHIPS | Beagle, Gleaner, Roebuck, Scott |

## OTHER PARTS OF THE NAVAL SERVICE

### ROYAL MARINES

The Royal Marines were formed in 1664 and are part of the Naval Service. Their primary purpose is to conduct amphibious and land warfare. The principal operational units are 3 Commando Brigade Royal Marines, an amphibious all-arms brigade trained to operate in arduous environments, which is a core element of the UK's Joint Rapid Reaction Force; Comacchio Group Royal Marines, which is responsible for the security of nuclear weapon facilities; and Special Boat Service Royal Marines, the maritime special forces. The Royal Marines also provide detachments for warships and land-based naval parties as required. The Royal Marines Band Service provides military musical support for the Naval Service. The headquarters of the Royal Marines is at Portsmouth, along with the Royal Marines School of Music, and principal bases are at Plymouth, Arbroath, Poole, Taunton and Chivenor. The Corps of Royal Marines is about 6,500 strong.

*Capability Manager (Information Superiority)*, Maj.-Gen. R. H. G. Fulton
*Chief of Staff, NATO Joint Headquarters North*, Maj.-Gen. D. Wilson, OBE
*Director-General, Joint Doctrine and Concepts Centre*, Maj.-Gen. A. A. Milton, OBE, ADC

### ROYAL MARINES RESERVE (RMR)

The Royal Marines Reserve is a commando-trained volunteer force with the principal role, when mobilised, of supporting the Royal Marines. There are RMR centres in London, Glasgow, Bristol, Liverpool and Newcastle. The current strength of the RMR is about 1,000.
*Director, RMR*, Col. A. W. MacCormick

### ROYAL FLEET AUXILIARY service (RFA)

The Royal Fleet Auxiliary Service is a civilian-manned flotilla of 22 ships. Its primary role is to supply the Royal Navy at sea with food, fuel, ammunition and spares, enabling it to maintain operations away from its home ports. In addition the RFA provides the Royal Navy with sea-borne aviation training facilities as well as secure logistic support and amphibious operations capability for the Army and Royal Marines.

### FLEET AIR ARM

The Fleet Air Arm was founded in 1914 as the Royal Naval Air Service and operates some 240 fixed wing aircraft and helicopters for the Royal Navy. Sea Harrier fighters provide air defence/strike capability for the fleet, and Sea King, Merlin and Lynx helicopters provide commando support, anti-submarine, anti-surface, airborne early warning and search and rescue capability. In 2001 the strength of the FAA was 5,500.

### ROYAL NAVAL RESERVE (RNR)

The Royal Naval Reserve is an integral part of the Naval Service. It comprises up to 3,850 men and women nationwide who volunteer to train in their spare time to enable the Royal Navy to meet its operational commitments, at sea and ashore, in crisis or war.

The standard annual training commitment is 24 days, including 12 days' continuous training. Daily pay scales range from £47 to £154 for officers and from £27 to £67 for ratings. A tax-free bounty is also payable, the amount depending on the length of service.
*Director, Naval Reserves*, Capt C. G. Massie-Taylor, OBE, RN

### QUEEN ALEXANDRA'S ROYAL NAVAL NURSING SERVICE

The first nursing sisters were appointed to naval hospitals in 1884 and the Queen Alexandra's Royal Naval Nursing Service (QARNNS) gained its current title in 1902.

Nursing ratings were introduced in 1960 and men were integrated into the Service in 1982; QARNNS recruits qualified nurses as both officers and ratings and student nurse training can be undertaken in the Service. Female medical assistants were introduced between 1987-1998, although no longer recruited some continue to serve in QARNNS.

*Patron*, HRH Princess Alexandra, the Hon. Lady Ogilvy, GCVO

*Matron-in-Chief and Director of Naval Nursing Services*, Capt. M. Bowen

# The Army

THE QUEEN

FIELD MARSHALS

HRH The Prince Philip, Duke of Edinburgh, KG, KT, OM, GBE, AC, QSO, PC, *apptd* 1953
The Lord Carver, GCB, CBE, DSO, MC, *apptd* 1973
Sir Roland Gibbs, GCB, CBE, DSO, MC, *apptd* 1979
The Lord Bramall, KG, GCB, OBE, MC, *apptd* 1982
The Lord Vincent GBE, KCB, DSO
Sir John Stanier, GCB, MBE, *apptd* 1985
Sir Nigel Bagnall, GCB, CVO, MC, *apptd* 1988
Sir John Chapple, GCB, CBE, *apptd* 1992
HRH The Duke of Kent, KG, GCMG, GCVO, ADC, *apptd* 1993
The Lord Inge, GCB (Col. Green Howards, Col. Cmdt. APTC), *apptd* 1994

GENERALS

Sir Michael Boyce, GCB, OBE, ADC (*Chief of the Defence Staff*)
Walker, Sir Michael, GCB, CMG, CBE, ADC (*Chief of the General Staff*)
Harley, Sir Alexander, KBE, CB, ADC (*Gen.*), Col. Cmdt. RHA
Cowan, Sir Samuel, KCB, CBE, Col. Cmdt. Bde of Gurkhas (*Chief of Defence Logistics*)
Smith, Sir Rupert, KCB, DSO, OBE, QGM, Col. Cmdt. REME (*D.SACEUR*)
Jackson, Sir Michael, KCB, CBE, DSO, Col. Cmdt. Parachute Regiment, Col. Cmdt. AG Corps, Hon. Col. The Rifle Volunteers (*C.-in-C., Land*)
Deverell, Sir John, KCB, OBE, Col. Cmdt. LI, Col. Cmdt. SASC (*Deputy C.-in-C., Land Command, and Inspector-General, Territorial Army and C-in-C Allied Forces Northern Europe*)

LIEUTENANT-GENERALS

Willcocks, Sir Michael, KCB, Col. Cmdt. RA (*UK Military Rep. at NATO HQ*)
Drewry, C. F., CBE (*Commander, ACE Rapid Reaction Corps*)
Pigott, A. D., CBE, Col. The Queen's Gurkha Engineers, Col. Cmdt. RE (*Deputy CDS (Commitments)*)
Menzies, R. C., OBE, QHS (*Surgeon-General*)
Irwin, A. S. H., CBE, General Officer Commanding Northern Ireland; Col. Cmdt. The Scottish Division (*Military Secretary and Chief Executive, Army Personnel Centre*)
Delves, C. N. G. (*Chief of Joint Forces Operational Readiness and Training*)
O'Donoghue, K., CBE (*Asst Chief of the General Staff*)
Reith, J. G., CB, CBE (*Asst CDS (Policy)*)

MAJOR-GENERALS

Sullivan, T. J. CBE (*GOC HQ 4 Div*)
Elliott, C. L., CB, MBE (*Director-General, Development and Doctrine*)
Kiszely, J. P., MC (*Asst CDS (Programmes)*)
Moore-Bick, J. D., CBE, (*Military Assistant to the High Representative in Bosnia-Hercegovina*)
Trousdell, P. C. C., Col. The Queen's Own Gurkha Transport Regiment (*Deputy Commander (Operations) Stabilisation Force Bosnia Hercegovina*)
Chambers, P. A., MBE (*Deputy Chief of Staff, HQ Land Command*)
Besgrove, P. V. R., CBE, Col. Cmdt. REME (*Asst. Chief of Staff (Resources) HQ Allied Forces Southern Europe*)
Searby, R. V. (*Senior British Loan Service Officer, Oman*)
Risius, G. (*Director, Army Legal Services*)
Ramsay, A. I., CBE, DSO, Col. Cmdt. (*Commander British Forces Cyprus*)
Elliott, C. H., CBE (*Defence Services Secretary*)
Pringle, A. R. D., CB, CBE, Col. Cmdt. RGJ (*Chief of Staff to Chief of Joint Operations*)
Raper, A. J., CBE (*Chief Executive, Defence Communications Services Agency*)
Ridgway, A. P., CBE (*Chief of Staff HQ ACE Rapid Reaction Corps*)
Currie, A. P. N. (*Chief of Staff to Adjutant-General*)
Watt, C. R., CBE, (*GOG 1 (UK) Armed Division*)
HRH The Prince of Wales, KG, KT, GCB and Great Master of the Order of the Bath, AK, QSO, PC, ADC(P)
Dannatt, F. R., CBE, MC (*GOC 3 (UK) Divn, Asst Chief of the General Staff*)
Grant Peterkin, A. P., OBE (*General Officer, Commanding 5th Division*)
Palmer, A. M. D., CBE (*Director-General, Army Training and Recruiting and Chief Executive, Army Training and Recruiting Agency*)
Sutherell, J. C. B., CBE, Col. Cmdt. The Queens Division (*Commandant, RMCS*)
Viggers, F. R., MBE (*Chief of Staff, HQ Land Command*)
Gordon, R. D. S., CBE (*GOC HQ 2 Divn*)
Plummer, B. P.
Judd, D. L. (*Quartermaster General*)
Brims, R. V., CBE (*Commander Multinational Divn. (South West) Bosnia Hercegovina*)
Gilchrist, P. (*Master General of the Ordnance, Col. Cmdt. RAC Executive Director 2, Defence Procurement Agency*)
Jolliffe, D. S., QHP (*Director-General, Army Medical Services*)
Cross, T. CBE
Messervy-Whiting, G. G. (*Head Interim Military Staff EU Brussels*)
Figgures, A. C., CBE (*Asst CDS, Operational Requirements (Land Systems)*)
Laurie, M. I., CBE,
McColl, J. C., CBE (*Director-General Intelligence and Geographic Resources*)
Charlton-Weedy, M. A. CBE,
Gamon, J. A. (*Chief Executive of the Defence Dental Agency*)
Holmes, J. T., OBE,
Denaro, A. G. (*Commandant of Sandurst and Middle Eastern Adviser to the Secretary of State for Defence, General Officer Commanding 5th Division*)

## CONSTITUTION OF THE ARMY

The regular forces include the following arms, branches and corps. They are listed in accordance with the order of precedence within the British Army. All enquiries with regard to records of serving personnel (Regular and Territorial Army) should be directed to Relations with the Public, Army Personnel Office, Kentigern House, 65 Brown Street, Glasgow G2 8EX. Tel: 0141-224 2023/3303. DASD, Rm 643, Metroploe Building, Northumberland Avenue, London WC2N 5BP. Contact , RO2 Pubs IM, Tel: 020-7218 2922 or Chief Clerk, Tel: 020-7218 2619

### The Arms

Household Cavalry – The Household Cavalry Regiment (The Life Guards and The Blues and Royals)
Royal Armoured Corps – Cavalry Regiments: 1st The Queen's Dragoon Guards; The Royal Scots Dragoon Guards (Carabiniers and Greys); The Royal Dragoon Guards; The Queen's Royal Hussars (The Queen's Own and Royal Irish); 9th/12th Royal Lancers (Prince of Wales's); The King's Royal Hussars; The Light Dragoons; The Queen's Royal Lancers; Royal Tank Regiment, comprising two regular regiments
Artillery – Royal Regiment of Artillery
Engineers – Corps of Royal Engineers
Signals – Royal Corps of Signals

### The Infantry

The Foot Guards and regiments of Infantry of the Line are grouped in divisions as follows:
Guards Division – Grenadier, Coldstream, Scots, Irish and Welsh Guards. *Divisional Office*, HQ Infantry, Warminster Training Centre, Warminster, Wilts. *Training Centre*, Infantry Training Centre, Vimy Barracks, Catterick, N. Yorks
Scottish Division – The Royal Scots (The Royal Regiment); The Royal Highland Fusiliers (Princess Margaret's Own Glasgow and Ayrshire Regiment); The King's Own Scottish Borderers; The Black Watch (Royal Highland Regiment); The Highlanders (Seaforth, Gordons and Camerons); The Argyll and Sutherland Highlanders (Princess Louise's). *Divisional Office*, HQ Infantry, Warminster Training Centre, Warminster, Wilts. *Training Centre*, Infantry Training Centre, Vimy Barracks, Catterick, N. Yorks
Queen's Division – The Princess of Wales's Royal Regiment (Queen's and Royal Hampshire's); The Royal Regiment of Fusiliers; The Royal Anglian Regiment. *Divisional Office*, HQ Infantry, Warminster Training Centre, Warminster, Wilts. *Training Centre*, Infantry Training Centre, Vimy Barracks, Catterick, N. Yorks
King's Division – The King's Own Royal Border Regiment; The King's Regiment; The Prince of Wales's Own Regiment of Yorkshire; The Green Howards (Alexandra, Princess of Wales's Own Yorkshire Regiment); The Queen's Lancashire Regiment; The Duke of Wellington's Regiment (West Riding). *Divisional Office*, HQ Infantry, Warminster Training Centre, Warminster, Wilts. *Training Centre*, Infantry Training Centre, Vimy Barracks, Catterick, N. Yorks
Prince of Wales's Division – The Devonshire and Dorset Regiment; The Cheshire Regiment; The Royal Welch Fusiliers; The Royal Regiment of Wales (24th/41st Foot); The Royal Gloucestershire, Berkshire and Wiltshire Regiment; The Worcestershire and Sherwood Foresters Regiment (29th/45th Foot); The Staffordshire Regiment (The Prince of Wales's). *Divisional Office*, HQ Infantry, Warminster Training Centre, Warminster, Wilts. *Training Centre*, Infantry Training Centre, Vimy Barracks, Catterick, N. Yorks
Light Division – The Light Infantry; The Royal Green Jackets. *Divisional Office*, HQ Infantry, Warminster Training Centre, Warminster, Wilts. *Training Centre*, Infantry Training Centre, Vimy Barracks, Catterick, N. Yorks
The Royal Irish Regiment (one general service and six home service battalions) – 27th (Inniskilling), 83rd, 87th and the Ulster Defence Regiment. *Regimental HQ* and *Training Centre*, St Patrick's Barracks, BFPO 808
Brigade of Gurkhas – The Royal Gurkha Rifles; The Queen's Gurkha Engineers; Queen's Gurkha Signals; The Queen's Own Gurkha Transport Regiment. *Regimental HQ*, Airfield Camp, Netheravon, Wilts. *Gurkha Company*, Infantry Training Centre, Vimy Barracks, Catterick, N. Yorks
The Parachute Regiment (three regular battalions) – *Regimental HQ*, Browning Barracks, Aldershot, Hants. *Training Centre*, Infantry Training Centre, Vimy Barracks, Catterick, N. Yorks
Special Air Service Regiment – *Regimental HQ* and *Training Centre*, Stirling Lines, Hereford
Army Air Corps – *Regimental HQ* and *Training Centre*, Middle Wallop, Stockbridge, Hants

### Services/Arms*

Royal Army Chaplains' Department – *Regimental HQ*, HQ AG, Upavon, Pewsey, Wilts. *Training Centre*, Armed Forces Chaplaincy Centre, Amport House, Amport, Andover, Hants
The Royal Logistic Corps – *Regimental HQ*, Blackdown Barracks, Deepcut, Camberley, Surrey. *Training Centre*, Princess Royal Barracks, Deepcut, Camberley, Surrey
Royal Army Medical Corps – *Regimental HQ*, *Training Centre*, Defence Medical Services Training Centre, former Army Staff Collge, Slim Road, Cambereley, Surrey.
Corps of Royal Electrical and Mechanical Engineers – *Regimental HQ* and *Training Centre*, Hazebrouck Barracks, Isaac Newton Road, Arborfield, Reading, Berks
Adjutant-General's Corps – *Directorate HQ* and *Training Centre*, Worthy Down, Winchester, Hants
Royal Army Veterinary Corps – *Regimental HQ*, Small Arms School Corps - *Regimental HQ*, Warminster Training Centre, Warminster, Wilts
Royal Army Dental Corps – *Regimental HQ*, Keogh Barracks, Ash Vale, Aldershot, Hants. *Training Centre*, Defence Dental Agency Trainingformer Army Staff Collge, Slim Road, Cambereley, Surrey *Intelligence Corps – *Directorate HQ* and *Training Centre*, Chicksands, Shefford, Beds
Army Physical Training Corps – *Regimental HQ*, Army School of Physical Training, Fox Lines, Queen's Avenue, Aldershot, Hants General Service Corps
Queen Alexandra's Royal Army Nursing Corps – *Regimental HQ*, Former Army Staff Collge, Slim Road, Cambereley, Surrey Corps of Army Music - *Directorate HQ* and *Training Centre*, Army School of Music, Kneller Hall, Kneller Road, Twickenham, Middx

### ARMY EQUIPMENT HOLDINGS *as at August 2000*

| | |
|---|---|
| Tanks | 373 |
| Armoured combat vehicles | 2,920 |
| Artillery pieces | 406 |
| Large landing craft | 2 |
| Helicopters | 232 |

## THE TERRITORIAL ARMY (TA)

The Territorial Army provides formed units and individuals as an essential part of the Army's order of battle for operations across all military tasks in order to ensure that the Army is capable of mounting and sustaining operations at nominated states of readiness. It also provides a basis for regeneration, while at the same time maintaining links with the local community and society at large. From 1 July 1999 its established strength is 41,204.

Members of the TA receive pay at the rate appropriate to their rank. From 1 April 2000, the minimum daily pay for an officer is £47.85 and for a soldier is £27.29. Pay rises with rank and length of service. Members who complete their annual training requirements (27 and 19 days respectively for members of the Independent and Specialist TA) and are certified as efficient receive a single bounty ranging from £110 to £1,290.

*Inspector-General*, Lt.-Gen. C.N.G. Delves, CBE, DSO

### QUEEN ALEXANDRA'S ROYAL ARMY NURSING CORPS

The Queen Alexandra's Royal Army Nursing Corps (QARANC) was founded in 1902 as Queen Alexandra's Imperial Military Nursing Service (QAIMNS) and gained its present title in 1949. The QARANC has trained nurses for the register since 1950 and also trains and employs Health Care Assistants to Level 3 NVQ. The Corps also recruits qualified nurses as Officers and other ranks and in 1992 male nurses already serving in the Army were transferred to the QARANC. QARANC personnel serve in all four corners of the world in both peacetime and operational environments.

*Colonel-in-Chief*, HRH The Princess Margaret, Countess of Snowdon, CI, GCVO

*Director of Army Nursing Services (DANS) and Matron in Chief Army*, Col. B. C. McEvilly

---

# The Royal Air Force

### THE QUEEN

### MARSHALS OF THE ROYAL AIR FORCE

HRH The Prince Philip, Duke of Edinburgh, KG, KT, OM, GBE, AC, QSO, PC, *apptd* 1953
Sir John Grandy, GCB, GCVO, KBE, DSO, *apptd* 1971
Sir Denis Spotswood, GCB, CBE, DSO, DFC, *apptd* 1974
Sir Michael Beetham, GCB, CBE, DFC, AFC, *apptd* 1982
Sir Keith Williamson, GCB, AFC, *apptd* 1985
The Lord Craig of Radley, GCB, OBE, *apptd* 1988

### AIR CHIEF MARSHALS

Johns, Sir Richard, GCB, CBE, LVO, ADC (*Chief of the Air Staff*)
Cheshire, Sir John, KBE, CB Squire, Sir Peter, KCB, DFC, AFC, ADC, GCB (*Chief of the Air Staff*) *Air Officer Commanding-in-Chief, HQ Strike Command, and Commander Allied Air Forces NW Europe*)
Bagnall, Sir Anthony, KCB, OBE (*Vice Chief of Defence Staff and Commander-in-Chief Strike Command*)
Day, Sir John, KCB, OBE (*Air Member for Personnel/C-in-C Personnel and Training Command and Commander-in-Chief Strike Command*)

### AIR MARSHALS

Coville, Sir Christopher, KCB (*Deputy C.-in-C. Allied Forces Central Europe*)
Jenner, T. I., CB (*Chief of Staff*)
Norriss, Sir Peter, KBE, CB, AFC (*Deputy Chief of Defence Procurement (Operations) and Controller of the Navy*)
Pledger, M. D., KCB, OBE, AFC (*Deputy CDS (Personnel)*)
Goodall, R. H., CB, CBE, AFC (*Chief of Staff, Component Command Air North*)
Spink, C. R., CBE (*Director General, Saudi Arabia Armed Forces Project*)

### AIR VICE-MARSHALS

French, J. C., CBE (*Director-General, Intelligence and Geographic Resources*)
Thompson, J. H., CB (*Defence Attache and Head of British Defence Staff Washington*)
Stewart, I. M., AFC (*Air Secretary and Chief Executive, RAF Personnel Management Agency*)
Weeden, J. (*Director, Legal Services (RAF)*)
Wright, R. A., AFC (*Chief of Staff, HQ Personnel and Training Command and Asst Chief of Staff Policy and Requirements SHAPE)*
McIntyre, I. G., QHDS (*Chief Executive, Defence Dental Agency*)
Sharples, C. J., QHP (*Director-General, Medical Services (RAF)*)
Burridge, B. K., CBE (*Commandant, Joint Services Command and Staff College*)
Filbey, K. D., CBE (*AOC No. 38 Group*)
Sturley, P. O., CB, MBE (*Asst. Chief of the Air Staff*))
Henderson, P. W., CB, MBE (*Director-General, Support Management, HQ Logistics Command*)
DAY, N. J., CBE (*Capability Manager (Strike) (Air Systems)*)
Niven, D. M., CBE (*Commander, Joint Helicopter Command*)
Scott, P. J. (*Air Officer Logistics and Communications Information Systems, HQ Strike Command*)
Burton, A. J., OBE (*Air Officer Administration, HQ Strike Command*)
Rimmer, T. W., OBE (*Commander British Forces Cyprus and Administrator of the Sovereign Base Areas of Akrotiri and Dhekelia*)
Nicholson, A. A., CBE, LVO (*Integration and Aerospace Adviser, Defence Procurement Agency*)
HRH The Prince of Wales, KG, KT, GCB and Great Master of the Order of the Bath, AK, QSO, PC, ADC(P)
Gardiner, M. J., OBE (*Deputy Commander, Interim Combined Air Operations Centre No. 4* and *Military Assistant to the High Representative Sarajevo*)
Couzens, D. C. (*Asst CDS (Logistics)*)
Liddell, P. (*Air Officer Communications Information Systems and Support Services*)
Arscott, J. R. D. (*Director, Airspace Policy*)
Skinner, G., CBE (*Air Officer C.-in-C., HQ Logistics Command*)
Corbitt, I. S. (*Air Officer Training and Chief Executive, Training Group Defence Agency)*
Roser, P. W., MBE (*Senior Directing Staff (Air), Royal College of Defence Studies)*
Davison, C., MBE (*Air Officer Administration and Air Officer Commanding Directly Administered Units, HQ Personnel and Training Command*)
Sudborough, N.J, OBE (*Deputy Chief of Staff Operations Strike Command*)
Torpy, G. L., CBE, DSO (*Asst CDS (Operations) and Air Officer Commanding No 1 Group)*
Mackay, H. G, OBE, AFC (*Commandant, RAF College, Cranwell*)
Davidson, C. M. (*Air Officer Administration and Air Officer Commanding Directly Administered Units Headquarters Personnel and Training Command*)
Stirrup, G. E., CB (*Deputy C-in-C)*
Walker P. B. (*Asst Chief of Defence Staff (Operations))*
Hobart D. A. (*Asst Chief of Defence Staff (Policy and Nuclear)*)

## CONSTITUTION OF THE ROYAL AIR FORCE

The RAF consists of three commands: Strike Command, Personnel and Training Command and Logistics Command. Strike Command is responsible for all the RAF's front-line forces.The restructured Strike Command, implemented on 1 April 2000, was split into three organisational groups, each responsible for specific operational duties. No 1 Group now contains the tactical fast jet forces, with No 2 Group providing the overarching enabling forces - Air Transport, Air Refuelling and Strategic Reconnaissance. No 3 Group is comprised of the Nimrod MPA force, Search and Rescue helicopters and the newly created Joint Force 2000 - a combination of the RAF Harrier GR7 and RN Harrier FA2 squadrons. Personnel and Training Command is responsible for personnel administration and training in the RAF. Logistics Command is responsible for all logistics, engineering and material support.

Enquiries regarding records of serving officers should be directed to the RAF Personnel Management Agency (*see* Defence Agencies, above).

## RAF EQUIPMENT *as at 1 July 2001*

| | |
|---|---|
| AIRCRAFT | |
| Tornado | 195 |
| Harrier | 48 |
| Jaguar | 43 |
| Canberra | 4 |
| Nimrod | 24 |
| VC10 | 10 |
| Tristar | 8 |
| Hercules | 50 |
| BAe 125 | 5 |
| BAe 146 | 2 |
| Sentry | 6 |
| Hawk | 98 |
| Domenie | 8 |
| Islander | 1 |
| Jetstream | 10 |
| Tucano | 74 |
| HELICOPTERS | |
| Chinook | 31 |
| Puma | 28 |
| Sea King | 19 |
| Wessex | 11 |
| Gazelle | 1 |

## ROYAL AUXILIARY AIR FORCE (RAUXAF)

Formed in 1924, the Auxiliary Air Force received the prefix 'Royal' in 1947 in recognition of its war record. The RAuxAF amalgamated with the Royal Air Force Volunteer Reserve in 1997. The RAuxAF supports the RAF in many roles, including maritime air operations, air and ground defence of airfields, air movements, aero-medical evacuation, intelligence and public relations. The minimum annual commitment for reservists is 27 days, including 15 days' continuous training. Pay scales are equivalent to regular rates less a percentage, made on a pro-rata daily basis. An annual bounty is also payable, the amount depending on the length of service.

*Air Commodore-in-Chief*, HM The Queen
*Inspector Royal Auxiliary Air Force*, Gp. Capt. R. G. Kemp

## PRINCESS MARY'S ROYAL AIR FORCE NURSING SERVICE

The Princess Mary's Royal Air Force Nursing Service (PMRAFNS) was formed on 1 June 1918 as the Royal Air Force Nursing Service. In June 1923, His Majesty King George V gave his Royal Assent for the Royal Air Force Nursing Service to be known as the Princess Mary's Royal Air Force Nursing Service. Men were integrated into the PMRAFNS in 1980 and now serve as officers and other ranks. Student nurse training is undertaken and qualified RN's, RM's and RMN's are recruited to the commissioned branches of the PMRAFNS.

*Patron and Air Chief Commandant*, HRH Princess Alexandra, the Hon. Lady Ogilvy, GCVO
*Matron-in-Chief and Director RAF Nursing Service*, Air Cdre R. H. Williams

## SERVICE SALARIES

The following rates of pay apply from 1 April 2001. Annual salaries are derived from daily rates in whole pence and rounded to the nearest £.

The pay rates shown are for Army personnel. The rates apply also to personnel of equivalent rank and pay band in the other services (*see* page 407 for table of relative ranks).

| *Rank* | *Daily* | *Annual* |
|---|---|---|
| Second Lieutenant | £51.50 | £18,797.50 |
| Lieutenant | | |
| On appointment | £61.91 | £22,597.15 |
| After 1 year in rank | £63.54 | £23,192.10 |
| After 2 years in rank | £65.17 | £23,787.05 |
| After 3 years in rank | £66.79 | £24,378.35 |
| After 4 years in rank | £68.42 | £24,973.30 |
| Captain | | |
| On appointment | £78.94 | £28,813.10 |
| After 1 year in rank | £81.07 | £29,590.55 |
| After 2 years in rank | £83.21 | £30,371.65 |
| After 3 years in rank | £85.35 | £31,152.75 |
| After 4 years in rank | £87.48 | £31,930.20 |
| After 5 years in rank | £89.62 | £32,711.30 |
| After 6 years in rank | £91.75 | £33,488.75 |
| After 7 years in rank | £92.82 | £33,879.30 |
| After 8 years in rank | £93.89 | £34,269.85 |
| Major | | |
| On appointment | £99.44 | £36,295.60 |
| After 1 year in rank | £101.90 | £37,193.50 |
| After 2 years in rank | £104.35 | £38,087.75 |
| After 3 years in rank | £106.81 | £38,985.65 |
| After 4 years in rank | £109.27 | £39,883.55 |
| After 5 years in rank | £111.73 | £40,781.45 |
| After 6 years in rank | £114.18 | £41,675.70 |
| After 7 years in rank | £116.64 | £42,573.60 |
| After 8 years in rank | £119.10 | £43,471.50 |

| *Rank* | *Daily* | *Annual* |
|---|---|---|
| Lieutenant Colonel | | |
| On appointment | £140.25 | £51,191.25 |
| After 1 year in rank | £142.10 | £51.866.50 |
| After 2 years in rank | £143.95 | £52.541.75 |
| After 3 years in rank | £145.79 | £53,213.35 |
| After 4 years in rank | £147.64 | £53,888.60 |
| After 5 years in rank | £149.48 | £54,560.20 |
| After 6 years in rank | £151.33 | £55,235.45 |
| After 7 years in rank | £153.17 | £55,907.05 |
| After 8 years in rank | £155.03 | £56,585.95 |
| On appointment | £162.41 | £59,279.65 |
| After 1 year in the rank | £164.55 | £60,060.75 |
| After 2 years in the rank | £166.69 | £60.841.85 |
| After 3 years in the rank | £168.82 | £61,619.30 |
| After 4 years in the rank | £170.96 | £62,400.40 |
| After 5 years in the rank | £173.10 | £63,181.50 |
| After 6 years in the rank | £175.23 | £63,958.95 |
| After 7 years in the rank | £177.37 | £64,740.05 |
| After 8 years in the rank | £179.51 | £65,521.15 |
| Brigadier | | |
| On appointment | £194.81 | £71,107.65 |
| After 1 year in the rank | £169.89 | £71,864.85 |
| After 2 years in the rank | £198.96 | £72,620.40 |
| After 3 years in the rank | £201.03 | £73,375.95 |
| After 4 years in the rank | £203.11 | £74,135.15 |

Field Marshal – appointments to this rank will not usually be made in peacetime. The salary for existing holders of the rank is equivalent to the salary of a range 8 General

## SALARIES OF OFFICERS COMMISSIONED FROM THE RANKS (LIEUTENANTS AND CAPTAINS ONLY)

| YEARS OF COMMISSIONED SERVICE | YEARS OF NON-COMMISSIONED SERVICE FROM AGE 18 | | | | | |
|---|---|---|---|---|---|---|
| | *Less than 12 years* | | *12 years but less than 15 years* | | *15 years or more* | |
| | *Daily* | *Annual* | *Daily* | *Annual* | *Daily* | *Annual* |
| On commissioning | £87.19 | £31,824.35 | £91.25 | £33,306.25 | £95.32 | £34,791.80 |
| After 1 year's service | £89.22 | £32,565.30 | £93.29 | £34,050.85 | £97.39 | £35,547.80 |
| After 2 years' service | £91.25 | £33,306.25 | £95.32 | £34,791.80 | £98.75 | £36,043.75 |
| After 3 years' service | £93.29 | £34,050.85 | £97.39 | £35,547.35 | £100.10 | £36,536.50 |
| After 4 years' service | £95.32 | £34,791.80 | £98.75 | £36,043.75 | £101.46 | £37,032.90 |
| After 5 years' service | £97.39 | £35,547.35 | £100.10 | £36,536.50 | £102.81 | £37,525.65 |
| After 6 years' service | £98.75 | £36,043.75 | £101.46 | £37,032.90 | £104.17 | £38,022.05 |
| After 8 years' service | £100.10 | £36,536.50 | £102.81 | £37,525.65 | £105.53 | £38,518.45 |
| After 10 years' service | £101.46 | £37,032.90 | £104.17 | £38,022.05 | £105.53 | £38,518.45 |
| After 12 years' service | £102.81 | £37,525.65 | £105.53 | £38,518.45 | £105.53 | £38,518.45 |
| After 14 years' service | £104.17 | £38,022.05 | £105.53 | £38,518.45 | £105.53 | £38,518.45 |
| After 16 years' service | £105.53 | £38,518.45 | £105.53 | £38,518.45 | £105.53 | £38,518.45 |

## SOLDIERS' SALARIES

The pay structure below officer level is divided into pay bands. Jobs at each rank are allocated to bands according to their score in the job evaluation system. Length of service is from age 18.

Scale A: committed to serve for less than 6 years, or those with less than 9 years' service who are serving on Open Engagement

Scale B: committed to serve for 6 years but less than 9 years

Scale C: committed to serve for 9 years or more, or those with more than 9 years' service who are serving on Open Engagement

Daily rates of pay effective from 1 April 2001 are:

| Rank | Scale A | | | |
|---|---|---|---|---|
| | Lower Band | | Higher Band | |
| | Daily | Annual | Daily | Annual |
| Private | | | | |
| Level 1 | £33.07 | £12,070.55 | £33.07 | £12,070.55 |
| Level 2 | £35.02 | £12,782.30 | £38.38 | £14,008.70 |
| Level 3 | £36.96 | £13.490.40 | £42.36 | £15,461.40 |
| Level 4 | £40.20 | £14,673.00 | £45.55 | £16,625.75 |
| Lance Corporal | | | | |
| Level 5 | £42.36 | £15,461.40 | £50.38 | £18,388.70 |
| Level 6 | £44.13 | £16,107.45 | £52.83 | £19,282.95 |
| Level 7 | £46.03 | £16,800.95 | £55.25 | £20,166.25 |
| Level 8 | £48.13 | £17,567.45 | £57.75 | £21,067.80 |
| Level 9 | £49.88 | £18,206.20 | £60.55 | £22,100.75 |

| | Scale B | | | |
|---|---|---|---|---|
| | Lower Band | | Higher Band | |
| | Daily | Annual | Daily | Annual |
| Corporal | | | | |
| Level 1 | £54.28 | £19,812.20 | £56.37 | £20,575.05 |
| Level 2 | £56.81 | £20,735.65 | £59.95 | £21,881.75 |
| Level 3 | £57.80 | £21,097.00 | £63.51 | £23,181.15 |
| Level 4 | £59.56 | £21,739.40 | £64.99 | £23,721.35 |
| Level 5 | £60.46 | £22,067.90 | £66.57 | £24,298.05 |
| Level 6 | £61.19 | £22,067.90 | £67.95 | £24,801.75 |
| Level 7 | £62.02 | £22,637.30 | £69.43 | £25,341.95 |

| | Scale C | | | |
|---|---|---|---|---|
| | Lower Band | | Higher Band | |
| | Daily | Annual | Daily | Annual |
| Sergeant | | | | |
| Level 1 | £62.81 | £22,925.65 | £68.54 | £25,017.10 |
| Level 2 | £64.44 | £23,520.60 | £70.31 | £25,663.15 |
| Level 3 | £66.06 | £24,111.90 | £72.09 | £26,312.85 |
| Level 4 | £66.73 | £24,356.45 | £73.00 | £26,645.00 |
| Level 5 | £67.93 | £24,794.45 | £74.42 | £27,163.30 |
| Level 6 | £69.31 | £25,298.15 | £75.84 | £27,681.60 |
| Level 7 | £70.93 | £25,889.45 | £77.26 | £28,199.90 |

| | Lower Band | | Higher Band | |
|---|---|---|---|---|
| | Daily | Annual | Daily | Annual |
| Staff Sergeant | | | | |
| Level 1 | £69.31 | £25,298.15 | £77.31 | £28,218.15 |
| Level 2 | £70.42 | £25,703.15 | £79.19 | £28,904.35 |
| Level 3 | £72.71 | £26,539.15 | £81.07 | £29,590.55 |
| Level 4 | £74.41 | £27,159.65 | £82.95 | £30,276.75 |
| Warrant Officer II | | | | |
| Level 5 | £75.43 | £27,531.95 | £84.84 | £30,966.60 |
| Level 6 | £77.31 | £28,218.15 | £86.71 | £31,649.15 |
| Level 7 | £79.19 | £28,904.35 | £87.97 | £32,109.05 |
| Level 8 | £81.07 | £29,590.55 | £89.23 | £32,568.95 |
| Level 9 | £82.91 | £30,262.15 | £90.49 | £33,028.85 |

| | Lower Band | | Higher Band | |
|---|---|---|---|---|
| | Daily | Annual | Daily | Annual |
| Warrant Officer I | | | | |
| Level 1 | £79.95 | £29,181.75 | £87.69 | £32,006.85 |
| Level 2 | £81.51 | £29,751.15 | £89.33 | £32,605.45 |
| Level 3 | £83.07 | £30,320.55 | £90.78 | £33,134.70 |
| Level 4 | £84.64 | £30,893.60 | £92.35 | £33,707.75 |
| Level 5 | £86.20 | £31,463.00 | £93.91 | £34,277.15 |
| Level 6 | £87.69 | £32,006.85 | £95.48 | £34,850.20 |
| Level 7 | £89.33 | £32,605.45 | £97.04 | £35,419.60 |

## RELATIVE RANK – ARMED FORCES

| | *Royal Navy* | *Army* | *Royal Air Force* |
|---|---|---|---|
| 1 | Admiral of the Fleet | Field Marshal | Marshal of the RAF |
| 2 | Admiral (Adm.) | General (Gen.) | Air Chief Marshal |
| 3 | Vice-Admiral (Vice-Adm.) | Lieutenant-General (Lt.-Gen.) | Air Marshal |
| 4 | Rear-Admiral (Rear-Adm.) | Major-General (Maj.-Gen.) | Air Vice-Marshal |
| 5 | Commodore (Cdre) | Brigadier (Brig.) | Air Commodore (Air Cdre) |
| 6 | Captain (Capt.) | Colonel (Col.) | Group Captain (Gp Capt.) |
| 7 | Commander (Cdr.) | Lieutenant-Colonel (Lt.-Col.) | Wing Commander (Wg Cdr.) |
| 8 | Lieutenant-Commander (Lt.-Cdr.) | Major (Maj.) | Squadron Leader (Sqn Ldr) |
| 9 | Lieutenant (Lt.) | Captain (Capt.) | Flight Lieutenant (Flt. Lt.) |
| 10 | Sub-Lieutenant (Sub-Lt.) | Lieutenant (Lt.) | Flying Officer (FO) |
| 11 | Acting Sub-Lieutenant (Acting Sub-Lt.) | Second Lieutenant (2nd Lt.) | Pilot Officer (PO) |

## SERVICE RETIRED PAY ON COMPULSORY RETIREMENT

Those who leave the services having served at least five years, but not long enough to qualify for the appropriate immediate pension, now qualify for a preserved pension and terminal grant, both of which are payable at age 60. The tax-free resettlement grants shown below are payable on release to those who qualify for a preserved pension and who have completed nine years service from age 21 (officers) or 12 years from age 18 (other ranks).

The annual rates for army personnel are given. The rates apply also to personnel of equivalent rank in the other services, including the nursing services.

### OFFICERS

Applicable to officers who give full pay service on the active list on or after 31 March 2001. Senior officers (*) can elect to receive a pension calculated as a percentage of their pensionable earnings.

| *No. of years reckonable service over age 21* | *Capt. and below* | *Major* | *Lt.-Col.* | *Colonel* | *Brigadier* | *Major-General** | *Lieutenant-General** | *General** |
|---|---|---|---|---|---|---|---|---|
| 16 | £9,544 | £11,367 | £14,974 | — | — | — | — | — |
| 17 | £9,984 | £11,907 | £15,667 | — | — | — | — | — |
| 18 | £10,424 | £12,447 | £16,360 | £18,944 | — | — | — | — |
| 19 | £10,864 | £12, 986 | £17,052 | £19,746 | — | — | — | — |
| 20 | £ 11,304 | £13,526 | £17,745 | £20,548 | — | — | — | — |
| 21 | £11,743 | £14,066 | £18,438 | £21,351 | — | — | — | — |
| 22 | £12,183 | £14,606 | £19,131 | £22,153 | £26,345 | — | — | — |
| 23 | £12,623 | £15,146 | £19,823 | £22,955 | £26,345 | — | — | — |
| 24 | £13,063 | £15,686 | £20,516 | £23,757 | £27,152 | £29,496 | — | — |
| 25 | £13,503 | £16,225 | £21,209 | £24,559 | £27,959 | £30,372 | — | — |
| 26 | £13,943 | £16,765 | £21,902 | £25,361 | £28,766 | £31,249 | — | — |
| 27 | £14,383 | £17,305 | £22,595 | £26,163 | £29,573 | £32,125 | £37,176 | — |
| 28 | £14,823 | £17,845 | £23,287 | £26,965 | £30,380 | £33,002 | £38,190 | — |
| 29 | £15,263 | £18,385 | £23,980 | £27, 767 | £31,187 | £33,878 | £39,204 | — |
| 30 | £15,702 | £18,925 | £24,673 | £28,570 | £31,993 | £34,755 | £40,219 | £52, 809 |
| 31 | £16,142 | £19,464 | £25,366 | £29,372 | £32,800 | £35,632 | £41,233 | £54,141 |
| 32 | £16,582 | £20,004 | £26,058 | £30,174 | £32,800 | £36,508 | £42,247 | £55,472 |
| 33 | £17,022 | £20,544 | £26,751 | £30,976 | £34,414 | £37,385 | £43,262 | £56,804 |
| 34 | £17,462 | £21,084 | £27,444 | £31,778 | £35,221 | £38,261 | £44,276 | £58,136 |

### WARRANT OFFICERS, NCOS AND PRIVATES

Applicable to soldiers who give full pay service on or after 31 March 2001.

| *No. of years reckonable service* | *Below Corporal* | *Corporal* | *Sergeant* | *Staff Sergeant* | *Warrant Officer Level II* | *Warrant Officer Level I* |
|---|---|---|---|---|---|---|
| 22 | £5,633 | £7,236 | £8,026 | £9,142 | £9,312 | £10,283 |
| 23 | £5,830 | £7,489 | £8,306 | £9,461 | £9,637 | £10,642 |
| 24 | £6,026 | £7,741 | £8,586 | £9,780 | £9,962 | £11,001 |
| 25 | £6,223 | £7,994 | £8,867 | £10,099 | £10,287 | £11,360 |
| 26 | £6,419 | £8,246 | £9,147 | £10,418 | £10,612 | £11,719 |
| 27 | £6,616 | £8,499 | £9,427 | £10,737 | £10,937 | £12,078 |
| 28 | £6,813 | £8,752 | £9,707 | £11,056 | £11,262 | £12,437 |
| 29 | £7,009 | £9,004 | £9,987 | £11,375 | £11,587 | £12,796 |
| 30 | £7,206 | £9,257 | £10,268 | £11,695 | £11,912 | £13,154 |
| 31 | £7,402 | £9,509 | £10,548 | £12,014 | £12,237 | £13,513 |
| 32 | £7,599 | £9,762 | £10,828 | £12,333 | £12,562 | £13,872 |
| 33 | £7,796 | £10,015 | £11,108 | £12,652 | £12,887 | £14,231 |
| 34 | £7,992 | £10,267 | £11,388 | £12,971 | £13,212 | £14,590 |
| 35 | £8,189 | £10,520 | £11,669 | £13,290 | £13,537 | £14,949 |
| 36 | £8,385 | £10,772 | £11,949 | £13,609 | £13,862 | £15,308 |
| 37 | £8,582 | £11,025 | £12,229 | £13,928 | £14,187 | £15,667 |

### RESETTLEMENT GRANTS

Terminal grants are in each case three times the rate of retired pay or pension. There are special rates of retired pay for certain other ranks not shown above. Lower rates are payable in cases of voluntary retirement.

A gratuity of £3,130 is payable for officers with short service commissions for each year completed. Resettlement grants are: officers £10,765; non-commissioned ranks £7,034.

# Religion in the UK

There are two established, i.e. state, churches in the United Kingdom: the Church of England and the Church of Scotland. There are no established churches in Wales or Northern Ireland, though the Church in Wales, the Scottish Episcopal Church and the Church of Ireland are members of the Anglican Communion.

About 65 per cent of the population of the UK (38.1 million people) would call itself broadly Christian (in the Trinitarian sense), with 45 per cent (26.1 million) identifying with Anglican churches, 10 per cent (5.7 million) with the Roman Catholic Church, 4 per cent (2.6 million) with Presbyterian Churches, 2 per cent (1.3 million) with the Methodist Churches and 4 per cent (2.6 million) with other Christian churches; but only about 8.7 per cent of the population of Great Britain (3.98 million people) regularly attends a Christian church. Church attendance in Northern Ireland is estimated at 30–35 per cent of the population.

About 2 per cent of the population (1.3 million people) is affiliated to non-Trinitarian churches, e.g. Jehovah's Witnesses, the Church of Jesus Christ of Latter-Day Saints (Mormons), the Church of Christ, Scientist and the Unitarian churches.

A further 5 per cent of the population (3.25 million people) are adherents of other faiths, including Hinduism, Islam, Judaism and Sikhism.

About 28 per cent of the population is non-religious.

ADHERENTS TO RELIGIONS IN UK *(millions)*

| | 1975 | 1985 | 1995 |
|---|---|---|---|
| Christian (Trinitarian) | 40.2 | 39.1 | 38.1 |
| Non-Trinitarian | 0.7 | 1.0 | 1.3 |
| Hindu | 0.3 | 0.4 | 0.4 |
| Jew | 0.4 | 0.3 | 0.3 |
| Muslim | 0.4 | 0.9 | 1.2 |
| Sikh | 0.2 | 0.3 | 0.6 |
| Other | 0.1 | 0.3 | 0.3 |
| Total | 42.3 | 42.3 | 42.2 |

PERCENTAGE OF UK POPULATION ADHERING TO RELIGIONS

| | 1975 | 1985 | 1995 |
|---|---|---|---|
| Christian (Trinitarian) | 72 | 69 | 65 |
| Non-Trinitarian | 1 | 2 | 2 |
| Non-Christian religions | 3 | 3 | 5 |
| All religions | 76 | 74 | 72 |

*Source:* Christian Research/Paternoster Publishing – *UK Christian Handbook Religious Trends No. 1 1998–9;* figures in text are for 1995

INTER-CHURCH AND INTER-FAITH CO-OPERATION

The main umbrella body for the Christian churches in the UK is the Churches Together in Britain and Ireland (formerly the Council of Churches for Britain and Ireland). There are also ecumenical bodies in each of the constituent countries of the UK: Churches Together in England, Action of Churches Together in Scotland, CYTUN (Churches Together in Wales), and the Irish Council of Churches. The Free Churches' Council comprises most of the Free Churches in England and Wales, and the Evangelical Alliance represents evangelical Christians.

The Inter Faith Network for the United Kingdom promotes co-operation between faiths, and the Council of Christians and Jews works to improve relations between the two religions. Churches Together in Britain and Ireland also has a Commission on Inter-Faith Relations.

ACTION OF CHURCHES TOGETHER IN SCOTLAND, Scottish Churches House, Kirk Street, Dunblane, Perthshire FK15 0AJ. Tel: 01786-823588; Fax: 01786-825844; E-mail: acts.ecum@dial.pipex.com; Web: www.acts-scotland.org. *General Secretary*, Revd Dr K. Franz

CHURCHES TOGETHER IN BRITAIN AND IRELAND, Inter-Church House, 35–41 Lower Marsh, London SE1 7SA. Tel: 020-7523 2121; Fax: 020-7928 0010; Email: gensec@ctbi.org.uk; Web: www.ctbi.org.uk. *General Secretary*, Dr D. Goodbourn

CHURCHES TOGETHER IN ENGLAND, 27 Tavistock Square, London WC1H 9HH. Tel: 020-7529 8141; Fax: 020-7529 8134; Web: www.churches-together.org.uk. *General Secretary*: The Revd Bill Snelson

COUNCIL OF CHRISTIANS AND JEWS, Camelford House, 87-89 Albert Embankment, London, SE1 7TP. Tel: 020-7820 0090; Fax: 020-7820 0504; Email: cjrelalations@ccj.org.uk; Web: www.ccj.org.uk. *Director*, Sr M. Shepherd, NDS

CYTUN (CHURCHES TOGETHER IN WALES) - Ty John Penri, 11 St Helen's Road, Swansea SA1 4AL. Tel: 01792-460876. *General Secretary*, Revd G. Abraham-Williams

EVANGELICAL ALLIANCE, Whitefield House, 186 Kennington Park Road, London SE11 4BT. Tel: 020-7207 2100; Fax: 020-7207 2150; Email: london@eauk.org; Web: www.eauk.org. *General Director*, Revd J. Edwards

INTER FAITH NETWORK FOR THE UNITED KINGDOM, 5–7 Tavistock Place, London WC1H 9SN. Tel: 020-7388 0008; Fax: 020-7387 7968; Email: ifnet.uk@interfaith.org.uk; Web: www.interfaith.org.uk. *Director*, B. Pearce, OBE

IRISH COUNCIL OF CHURCHES, Inter-Church Centre, 48 Elmwood Avenue, Belfast BT9 6AZ. Tel: 028-9066 3145. *General Secretary*, Dr R. D. Stevens

## Christianity

Christianity is a monotheistic faith based on the person and teachings of Jesus Christ and all Christian denominations claim his authority. Central to its teaching is the concept of God and his son Jesus Christ, who was crucified and resurrected in order to enable mankind to attain salvation.

The Jewish scriptures predicted the coming of a *Messiah*, an 'anointed one', who would bring salvation. To Christians, Jesus of Nazareth, a Jewish rabbi (teacher), who was born in Palestine, was the promised Messiah. Jesus' birth, teachings, crucifixion and subsequent resurrection are recorded in the *Gospels*, which, together with other scriptures that summarise Christian belief, form the *New Testament*. This, together with the Hebrew scriptures, entitled the *Old Testament* by Christians, makes up the *Bible*, the sacred texts of Christianity.

### Beliefs

Christians believe that sin distanced mankind from God, and that Jesus was the Son of God, sent to redeem mankind from that sin by his death. In addition, many believe that Jesus will return again at some future date, triumph over evil and establish a kingdom on earth, thus inaugurating a new age. The Gospel assures Christians that those who believe in Jesus and obey his teachings will be forgiven their sins and will be resurrected from the dead.

### Practices

Christian practices vary widely between different Christian churches, but prayer is universal to all, as is charity, giving for the maintenance of the church buildings, for the work of the church, and to the poor and needy. In addition, certain days of observance, i.e. the *Sabbath*, *Easter*, and *Christmas* are celebrated by most Christians. The Orthodox, Roman Catholic and Anglican churches celebrate many more days of observance, based on saints and significant events in the life of Jesus. The belief in sacraments, physical signs believed to have been ordained by Jesus Christ to symbolise and convey spiritual gifts, varies greatly between Christian denominations; *Baptism* and the *Eucharist* are practised by most Christians. Baptism, symbolising repentance and faith in Jesus is an act marking entry into the Christian community; the Eucharist, the ritual re-enactment of the Last Supper, Jesus' final meal with his disciples, is also practised by most denominations. Other sacraments, such as anointing the sick, the laying on of hands to symbolise the passing on of the office of priesthood or to heal the sick and speaking in tongues, where it is believed that the person is possessed by the Holy Spirit, the Spirit of God, are less common. In denominations where infant baptism is practised, confirmation is common, where the person now repeats the commitments made for him or her at infancy. Matrimony and the ordination of priests are also widely believed to be sacraments. Many Protestants only view baptism and the Eucharist as sacraments; the Quakers and the Salvation Army reject the use of sacraments.

Most Christians believe that God actively guides the Church.

### The Early Church

The apostles were Jesus' first converts and are recognised by Christians as the founders of the Christian community. The new faith spread rapidly throughout the eastern provinces of the Roman Empire. Early Christianity was subject to great persecution until 313 AD, when Emperor Constantine's Edict of Toleration confirmed its right to exist and it became established as the religion of the Roman Empire in 381AD.

The Christian faith was slowly formulated in the first millennium of the Christian era. Between AD 325 and 787 there were seven Oecumenical Councils at which bishops from the entire Christian world assembled to resolve various doctrinal disputes. The estrangement between East and West began after Constantine moved the centre of the Roman Empire from Rome to Constantinople, and it grew after the division of the Roman Empire into eastern and western halves. Linguistic and cultural differences between Greek East and Latin West served to encourage separate ecclesiastical developments which became pronounced in the tenth and early 11th centuries.

Administration of the church was divided between five ancient patriarchates: Rome and all the West, Constantinople (the imperial city – the 'New Rome'), Jerusalem and all Palestine, Antioch and all the East, and Alexandria and all Africa. Of these, only Rome was in the Latin West and after the schism in 1054, Rome developed a structure of authority centralised on the Papacy, while the Orthodox East maintained the style of localised administration.

Papal authority over the doctrine and jurisdiction of the Church in western Europe was unrivalled after the split with the Eastern Orthodox Church until the Protestant Reformation in the 16th century.

### Christianity in Britain

An English Church already existed when Pope Gregory sent Augustine to evangelise the English in AD 596. Conflicts between Church and State during the Middle Ages culminated in the Act of Supremacy in 1534, which repudiated papal supremacy and declared King Henry VIII to be the supreme head of the Church in England. Since 1559 the English monarch has been termed the Supreme Governor of the Church of England.

In 1560 the jurisdiction of the Roman Catholic Church in Scotland was abolished and the first assembly of the Church of Scotland ratified the Confession of Faith, drawn up by a committee including John Knox. In 1592 Parliament passed an Act guaranteeing the liberties of the Church and its presbyterian government. King James VI (James I of England) and later Stuart monarchs attempted to reintroduce episcopacy, but a presbyterian church was finally restored in 1690 and secured by the Act of Settlement (1690) and the Act of Union (1707).

### Porvoo Declaration

The Porvoo Declaration was drawn up by representatives of the British and Irish Anglican churches and the Nordic and Baltic Lutheran churches and was approved by the General Synod of the Church of England in July 1995. Churches that approve the Declaration regard baptised members of each other's churches as members of their own, and allow free interchange of episcopally ordained ministers within the rules of each church.

# Non-Christian Religions

## BAHÁ'Í FAITH

Mirza Husayn-'Ali, known as *Bahá'u'lláh* (Glory of God) was born in Iran in 1817 and became a follower of the *Báb*, a religious reformer and prophet who was imprisoned for his beliefs and executed on the grounds of heresy in 1850. *Bahá'u'lláh* was himself imprisoned in 1852, and in 1853 he had a vision that he was the Promised One foretold by the *Báb*. He was exiled after his release from prison and eventually was exiled to Acre, now in Israel, where he continued to compose the Bahá'í sacred scriptures. He died in 1892 and was succeeded by his son, Abdu'l-Bahá, as spiritual leader, under whose guidance the faith spread to Europe and North America. He was followed by Shoghi Effendi, his grandson, who translated many of *Bahá'u'lláh*'s works into English. Upon his death in 1957, a democratic system of leadership was brought into operation.

The Bahá'í faith recognises the unity and relativity of religious truth and teaches that there is only one God, whose will has been revealed to mankind by a series of messengers, such as Zoroaster, Abraham, Moses, Buddha, Krishna, Christ, Muhammad, the Báb and Bahá'u'lláh, who were seen as the founders of separate religions, but whose common purpose was to bring God's message to mankind. It teaches that all races and both sexes are equal and deserving of equal opportunities and treatment, that education is a fundamental right and encourages a fair distribution of wealth. In addition, mankind is exhorted to establish a world federal system to promote peace, tolerance and the free movement of people, goods and ideas.

A Feast is held every 19 days, which consists of prayer and readings of Bahá'í scriptures, consultation on community business, and social activities. Music, food and beverages usually accompany the proceedings. There is no clergy; each local community elects a local assembly, which co-ordinates community activities, enrols new members, counsels and assists members in need, and conducts Bahá'í marriages and funerals. A national assembly is elected annually by locally elected delegates, and every five years the national spiritual assemblies meet together to elect the Universal House of Justice, the supreme international governing body of the Bahá'í Faith. World-wide there are about 12,535 local spiritual assemblies; there are around five million members residing in about 235 countries, of which 181 have national organisations.

THE BAHÁ'Í INFORMATION OFFICE, 27 Rutland Gate, London SW7 1PD. Tel: 020-7584 2566; Fax: 020-7584 9402; Email: nsa@bahai.org.uk; Web: www.bahai.org.uk; *Secretary General*: The Hon. Barnabas Leith

## BUDDHISM

Buddhism originated in northern India, in the teachings of Siddharta Gautama, who was born near Kapilavastu about 560 BC and became the *Buddha* (Enlightened One).

Fundamental to Buddhism is the concept of rebirth. Each life carries with it the consequences of the conduct of earlier lives (known as the law of *karma*). This cycle of death and rebirth is broken only when the state of *nirvana* has been reached. Buddhism steers a middle path between belief in personal immortality and belief in death as the final end.

The Four Noble Truths of Buddhism (*dukkha*, suffering; *tanha*, a thirst or desire for continued existence which causes dukkha; *nirvana*, the final liberation from desire and ignorance; and *ariya*, the path to nirvana) are all held to be universal and to sum up the *dhamma* or true nature of life. Necessary qualities to promote spiritual development are *sila* (morality), *samadhi* (meditation) and *panna* (wisdom).

There are two main schools of Buddhism: *Theravada* Buddhism, the earliest extant school, which is more traditional, and *Mahayana* Buddhism, which began to develop about 100 years after the Buddha's death and is more liberal; it teaches that all people may attain Buddhahood. Important schools that have developed within Mahayana Buddhism are *Zen* Buddhism, *Nichiren* Buddhism and Pure Land Buddhism or *Amidism*. There are also distinctive Tibetan forms of Buddhism. Buddhism began to establish itself in the West in the early 20th century.

The scripture of Theravada Buddhism is the *Pali Canon*, which dates from the first century BC. Mahayana Buddhism uses a Sanskrit version of the Pali Canon but also has many other works of scripture.

There is no set time for Buddhist worship, which may take place in a temple or in the home. Worship centres around meditation, acts of devotion centring on the image of the Buddha, and, where possible, offerings to a relic of the Buddha. Buddhist festivals vary according to local traditions and within Theravada and Mahayana Buddhism. For religious purposes Buddhists use solar and lunar calendars, the New Year being celebrated in April. Other festivals mark events in the life of the Buddha.

There is no supreme governing authority in Buddhism. In the United Kingdom communities representing all schools of Buddhism have developed and operate independently. The Buddhist Society was established in 1924; it runs courses and lectures, and publishes books about Buddhism. It represents no one school of Buddhism.

There are estimated to be at least 300 million Buddhists world-wide, and more than 500 groups and centres, an estimated 25,000 adherents and up to 20 temples or monasteries in the UK.

THE BUDDHIST SOCIETY, 58 Eccleston Square, London SW1V 1PH. Tel: 020-7834 5858; Fax: 020-7976 5238; Email: info@thebuddhistsociety.org.uk; Web: www.thebuddhistsociety.org.uk. *General Secretary*, R. C. Maddox

FRIENDS OF THE WESTERN BUDDHIST ORDER, London Buddhist Centre, 51 Roman Road, E2 0HU. Tel: 020-8901 1225

THE NETWORK OF BUDDHIST ORGANISATIONS, The Old Courthouse, 43 Renfrew Road, London SE11 4NB. Tel: 020-8682 3442; fax: 020-8767 3210; Email: secretary@nbo.org.uk; Web: www.nbo.org.uk

OFFICE OF TIBET (The Official UK Agency for HH the Dalai Lama) Tibet House, 1 Culworth Street, London NW8 7AF. TEL: 020-7722 5378

SOKA GAKKAI UK, Taplow Court, Taplow, Maidenhead, Berkshire SL6 0ER. Tel: 01628-773 163

## HINDUISM

Hinduism has no historical founder but had become highly developed in India by about 1200 BC. Its adherents originally called themselves Aryans; Muslim invaders first called the Aryans 'Hindus' (derived from 'Sindhu', the name of the river Indus) in the eighth century.

Most Hindus hold that *satya* (truthfulness), *ahimsa* (non-violence), honesty, sincerity and devotion to God are essential for good living. They believe in one supreme spirit (*Brahman*), and in the transmigration of *atman* (the soul). Most Hindus accept the doctrine of *karma* (consequences of actions), the concept of *samsara* (successive lives) and the possibility of all atmans achieving *moksha* (liberation from samsara) through *jnana* (knowledge), *yoga* (meditation), *karma* (work or action) and *bhakti* (devotion).

Most Hindus offer worship to *murtis* (images of deities) representing different incarnations or aspects of Brahman, and follow their *dharma* (religious and social duty) according to the traditions of their *varna* (social class), *ashrama* (stage in life), *jati* (caste) and *kula* (family).

Hinduism's sacred texts are divided into *shruti* ('that which is heard'), including the *Vedas*; or *smriti* ('that which is remembered' ), including the *Ramayana*, the *Mahabharata*, the *Puranas* (ancient myths), and the sacred law books. Most Hindus recognise the authority of the *Vedas*, the oldest holy books, and accept the philosophical teachings of the *Upanishads*, the *Vedanta Sutras* and the *Bhagavad-Gita*.

Brahman is omniscient, omnipotent, limitless and all-pervading, and is usually worshipped in His deity form. Brahma, Vishnu and Shiva are the most important gods worshipped by Hindus; their respective consorts are Saraswati, Lakshmi and Durga or Parvati, also known as Shakti. There are believed to have been ten *avatars* (incarnations) of Vishnu, of whom the most important are Rama and Krishna. Other popular gods are Ganesha,

Hanuman and Subrahmanyam. All gods are seen as aspects of the supreme God, not as competing deities.

Orthodox Hindus revere all gods and goddesses equally, but there are many denominations, including the Hare-Krishna movement (ISKCon), the Arya Samaj, the Swami Narayan Hindu mission and the Satya Sai-Baba movement, in which worship is concentrated on one deity. The *guru* (spiritual teacher) is seen as the source of spiritual guidance.

Hinduism does not have a centrally-trained and ordained priesthood. The pronouncements of the *shankaracharyas* (heads of monasteries) of Shringeri, Puri, Dwarka and Badrinath are heeded by the orthodox but may be ignored by the various sects.

The commonest form of worship is a *puja*, in which offerings of water, flowers, food, fruit, incense and light are made to a deity. Puja may be done either in a home shrine or a *mandir* (temple). Many British Hindus celebrate *samskars* (purification rights) to name a baby, the sacred thread (an initiation ceremony), marriage and cremation.

The largest communities of Hindus in Britain are in Leicester, London, Birmingham and Bradford, and developed as a result of immigration from India, eastern Africa and Sri Lanka.

There are an estimated 800 million Hindus world-wide; there are about 380,000 adherents and over 150 temples in the UK.

ARYA PRATINIDHI SABHA (UK) AND ARYA SAMAJ LONDON, 69A Argyle Road, London W13 0LY. Tel: 020-8991 1732. *President*, Prof. S. N. Bharadwaj

BHARATIYA VIDYA BHAVAN, Institute of Indian Art and Culture, 4A Castletown Road, London W14 9HQ. Tel: 020-7381 4608. *Executive Director*, Dr M. N. Nandakumara

INTERNATIONAL SOCIETY FOR KRISHNA CONSCIOUSNESS (ISKCon), Bhaktivedanta Manor, Dharam Marg, Hilfield Lane, Aldenham, Watford, Herts WD2 8EZ. Tel: 01923-857244; Email: bhaktivedanta.manor@pamho.net; Web: www.iskcon.org. *Governing Body Commissioner*, H. H. Sivarama Swami

NATIONAL COUNCIL OF HINDU TEMPLES (UK), Bhakrivedanta Manor, Dharam Marg, Hilfield Lane, Aldenham, Watford WD2 8EZ. Tel: 01923-856269/ 857244; Email: bimal.krsna.bcs@pamho.net. *Secretary*, V. A. Aery

SWAMINARAYAN HINDU MISSION (SHREE SWAMINARAYAN MANDIR), 105–119 Brentfield Road, London NW10 8JP. Tel: 020-8965 2651; Fax: 020-8965 6313; Email: shm@swaminarayan-baps.org.uk; Web: www.swaminarayan-baps.org.uk. *Secretary*, A. Patel

VISHWA HINDU PARISHAD (UK), 48 Wharfedale Gardens, Thornton Heath, Surrey CR7 6LB. Tel: 020-8684 9716. *General Secretary*, K. Ruparelia

## ISLAM

Islam (which means 'peace arising from submission to the will of Allah' in Arabic) is a monotheistic religion which was taught in Arabia by the Prophet Muhammad, who was born in Mecca (Al-Makkah) in 570 CE. Islam spread to Egypt, North Africa, Spain and the borders of China in the century following the Prophet's death, and is now the predominant religion in Indonesia, the Near and Middle East, northern and parts of western Africa, Pakistan, Bangladesh, Malaysia and some of the former Soviet republics. There are also large Muslim communities in other countries.

For Muslims (adherents of Islam), there is one God (*Allah*), who holds absolute power. His commands were revealed to mankind through the prophets, who include Abraham, Moses and Jesus, but His message was gradually corrupted until revealed finally and in perfect form to Muhammad through the angel *Jibril* (Gabriel) over a period of 23 years. This last, incorruptible message has been recorded in the *Qur'an* (Koran), which contains 114 divisions called *surahs*, each made up of *ayahs*, and is held to be the essence of all previous scriptures. The *Ahadith* are the records of the Prophet Muhammad's deeds and sayings (the *Sunnah*) as recounted by his immediate followers. A culture and a system of law and theology gradually developed to form a distinctive Islamic civilisation. Islam makes no distinction between sacred and worldly affairs and provides rules for every aspect of human life. The *Shari'ah* is the sacred law of Islam based upon prescriptions derived from the Qur'an and the *Sunnah* of the Prophet.

The 'five pillars of Islam' are *shahadah* (a declaration of faith in the oneness and supremacy of Allah and the messengership of Muhammad); *salat* (formal prayer, to be performed five times a day facing the *Ka'bah* (sacred house in the holy city of Makkah); *zakat* (welfare due); *sawm* (fasting during the month of Ramadan); and *hajj* (pilgrimage to Makkah); some Muslims would add *jihad* (striving for the cause of good and resistance to evil).

Two main groups developed among Muslims. *Sunni* Muslims accept the legitimacy of Muhammad's first four *caliphs* (successors as head of the Muslim community) and of the authority of the Muslim community as a whole. About 90 per cent of Muslims are Sunni Muslims. *Shi'ites* recognise only Muhammad's son-in-law Ali as his rightful successor and the *Imams* (descendants of Ali, not to be confused with *imams* (prayer leaders or religious teachers)) as the principal legitimate religious authority. The largest group within Shi'ism is *Twelver Shi'ism*, which has been the official school of law and theology in Iran since the 16th century; other subsects include the *Ismailis* and the *Druze*, the latter being an offshoot of the Ismailis and differing considerably from the main body of Muslims.

There is no organised priesthood, but learned men such as *ulama*, *imams* and *ayatollahs* are accorded great respect. The *Sufis* are the mystics of Islam. Mosques are centres for worship and teaching and also for social and welfare activities.

Islam was first known in western Europe in the eighth century AD when 800 years of Muslim rule began in Spain. Later, Islam spread to eastern Europe. More recently, Muslims came to Europe from Africa, the Middle East and Asia in the late 19th century. Both the Sunni and Shi'ah traditions are represented in Britain, but the majority of Muslims in Britain adhere to Sunni Islam.

Efforts to establish a representative central organisation recognised by all Muslims in Britain are beginning to yield good results. Meanwhile, the Islamic Cultural Centre, which is the London Central Mosque, and the Imams and Mosques Council are influential bodies; there are many other Muslim organisations in Britain.

There are about 1,000 million Muslims world-wide, with nearly two million adherents and about 1,200 mosques in Britain.

IMAMS AND MOSQUES COUNCIL, 20–22 Creffield Road, London W5 3RP. Tel: 020-8992 6636. *Director of the Council and Principal of the Muslim College*, Dr M. A. Z. Badawi

ISLAMIC CULTURAL CENTRE, 146 Park Road, London NW8 7RG. Tel: 020-7724 3363. *Director*, Dr A. Al-Dubayan

MUSLIM COUNCIL OF BRITAIN, P.O. Box 52, Wembley, Middx HA9 0XW. Tel: 020-8903 9024; Fax: 020-8903 9026; Email: admin@mcb.org.uk; Web: www.mcb.org.uk. *Secretary-General*, Yousuf Bhailok

MUSLIM WORLD LEAGUE, 46 Goodge Street, London W1P 1FJ. Tel: 020-7636 7568. *Deputy Director*, G. Rahman

UNION OF MUSLIM ORGANISATIONS OF THE UK AND ÉIRE, 109 Campden Hill Road, London W8 7TL. Tel: 020-7229 0538/7221 6608. *General Secretary*, Dr S. A. Pasha

## JAINISM

Jainism traces its history to Vardhamana Jnatiputra, known as *Tirthankara Mahavira* (The Great Hero) whose traditional dates were 599-527 BC. He was the last of a series of 24 *Jinas* (those who overcome all passions and desires) or *Tirthankaras* (those who show a way across the ocean of life) stretching back to remote antiquity. Born to a noble family in north-eastern Indian, he renounced the world for the life of a wandering ascetic and after 12 years of austerity and meditation he attained enlightenment. He then preached his message until, at the age of 72, he passed away and reached *moksha*, total liberation from the cycle of death and rebirth.

Jains deny the authority of the *Vedas*, the Hindu sacred scriptures. They recognise some of the minor deities of the Hindu pantheon, but the supreme objects of worship are the *Tirthankaras*. The pious Jain does not ask favours from the *Tirthankaras*, but seeks to emulate their example in his or her own life.

Jains believe that the universe is eternal and self-subsisting: there is no omnipotent creator God ruling it and the destiny of the individual is in his or her own hands. *Karma*, the fruit of past actions, determines the place of every living being and rebirth may be in the heavens, on earth as a human, an animal or other lower being, or in the hells. The ultimate goal of existence is *moksha* or *nirvana*, a state of perfect knowledge and tranquility for each individual soul, which can be achieved only by gaining enlightenment.

The path to liberation is defined by the Three Jewels, *samyak darsana* (right thought), *samyak jnana* (right knowledge) and *samyak charitra* (right conduct).

There are about 25,000 Jains in Britain, sizeable communities in North America and East Africa and smaller groups in many other countries.

INSTITUTE OF JAINOLOGY, Unit 18, Silicon Business Centre, 26/28 Wadsworth Road, Greenford, Middx, UB6 7JZ Tel: 020-8997 2300; Fax: 020-8997 4964

JAIN CENTRE, Oxford Street, Leicester, LE1 5XU Tel: 0116-254 3091

## JUDAISM

Judaism is the oldest monotheistic faith. The primary authority of Judaism is the Hebrew Bible or *Tanakh*, which records how the descendants of Abraham were led by Moses out of their slavery in Egypt to Mount Sinai where God's law (*Torah*) was revealed to them as the chosen people. The *Talmud*, which consists of commentaries on the *Mishnah* (the first text of rabbinical Judaism), is also held to be authoritative, and may be divided into two main categories: the *halakah* (dealing with legal and ritual matters) and the *Aggadah* (dealing with theological and ethical matters not directly concerned with the regulation of conduct). The *Midrash* comprises rabbinic writings containing biblical interpretations in the spirit of the Aggadah. The *halakah* has become a source of division; Orthodox Jews regard Jewish law as derived from God and therefore unalterable; Reform and Liberal Jews seek to interpret it in the light of contemporary considerations; and Conservative Jews aim to maintain most of the traditional rituals but to allow changes in accordance with tradition. Reconstructionist Judaism, a 20th-century movement, regards Judaism as a culture rather than a theological system and accepts all forms of Jewish practice.

The family is the basic unit of Jewish ritual, with the synagogue playing an important role as the centre for public worship and religious study. A synagogue is led by a group of laymen who are elected to office. The Rabbi is primarily a teacher and spiritual guide. The Sabbath is the central religious observance. Most British Jews are descendants of either the *Ashkenazim* of central and eastern Europe or the *Sephardim* of Spain, Portugal and the Middle East.

The Chief Rabbi of the United Hebrew Congregations of the Commonwealth is appointed by a Chief Rabbinate Conference, and is the rabbinical authority of the mainstream Orthodox sector of the Ashkenazi Jewish community, the largest body of which is the United Synagogue. His authority is not recognised by the Reform Synagogues of Great Britain (the largest progressive group), the Union of Liberal and Progressive Synagogues, the Union of Orthodox Hebrew Congregations, the Federation of Synagogues, the Sephardi community, or the Assembly of Masorti Synagogues. He is, however, generally recognised both outside the Jewish community and within it as the public religious representative of the totality of British Jewry. The Chief Rabbi is President of the *Beth Din* of the United Synagogue.

A *Beth Din* (Court of Judgement) is a rabbinic court. The *Dayanim* (Assessors) adjudicate in disputes or on matters of Jewish law and tradition; they also oversee dietary law administration.

The Board of Deputies of British Jews, established in 1760, is the representative body of British Jewry. The basis of representation is mainly synagogal, but communal organisations are also represented. It watches over the interests of British Jewry, acts as the central voice of the community and seeks to counter anti-Jewish discrimination and antisemitic activities.

In November 1998 a Consultative Committee was established comprising representatives of the Assembly of Masorti Synagogues, Reform Synagogues of Great Britain, Union of Liberal and Progressive Synagogues and the United Synagogue. The Committee holds discussions to further communal harmony and development.

There are over 12.5 million Jews world-wide; in Great Britain and Ireland there are an estimated 285,000 adherents and about 365 synagogues. Of these, 191 congregations and about 150 rabbis and ministers are under the jurisdiction of the Chief Rabbi; 99 orthodox congregations have a more independent status; and 79 congregations are outside the jurisdiction of the Chief Rabbi.

CHIEF RABBINATE, Adler House, 735 High Road, London N12 0US. Tel: 020-8343 6301. *Chief Rabbi*, Prof. Jonathan Sacks; *Executive Director*, Mrs S. Weinberg

BETH DIN (COURT OF THE CHIEF RABBI), 735 High Road, London N12 0US. Tel: 020-8343 6280; Fax: 020-8343 6257; Email: info@londonbethdin.fsnet.co.uk. *Registrar*, D. Frei; *Dayanim*, Dayan C. Ehrentreu; Dayan I. Binstock; Rabbi C. D. Kaplin; Dayan M. Gelley

BOARD OF DEPUTIES OF BRITISH JEWS, Commonwealth House, 1–19 New Oxford Street, London WC1A 1NU. Tel: 020-7543 5400; Email: info@bod.org.uk; Web: www.bod.org.uk. *President*, Jo Wagerman, OBE; *Director-General*, N. A. Nagler

ASSEMBLY OF MASORTI SYNAGOGUES, 1097 Finchley Road, London NW11 0PU. Tel: 020-8201 8772; Fax: 020-8201 8917; Email: office@masorti.org.uk; Web: www.masorti.org.uk. *Director*, M. Gluckman

FEDERATION OF SYNAGOGUES, 65 Watford Way, London NW4 3AQ. Tel: 020-8202 2263. *Chief Executive*, G. D. Coleman

BETH DIN OF THE FEDERATION OF SYNAGOGUES, 65 Watford Way, London NW4 3AQ. Tel: 020-8202 2263. *Registrar*, Rabbi S. Zaiden; *Dayanim*, Dayan Y. Y. Lichtenstein, Dayan B. Berkovits, Dayan M. D. Elzas

REFORM SYNAGOGUES OF GREAT BRITAIN, The Sternberg Centre for Judaism, 80 East End Road, London N3 2SY. Tel: 020-8349 5640; Fax: 020-8349 5699; Email: admin@reformjudaism.org.uk; Web: www.reformjudaism.org.uk. *Chief Executive*, Rabbi T. Bayfield

SPANISH AND PORTUGUESE JEWS' CONGREGATION, 2 Ashworth Road, London W9 1JY. Tel: 020-7289 2573. *Chief Executive*, H. Miller

UNION OF LIBERAL AND PROGRESSIVE SYNAGOGUES, The Montagu Centre, 21 Maple Street, London W1T 4BE. Tel: 020-7580 1663; Fax: 020-7436 4184; Email: montagu@ulps.org; Web: www.ulps.org. *Executive Director*, Rabbi Dr C. H. Middleburgh

UNION OF ORTHODOX HEBREW CONGREGATIONS, 140 Stamford Hill, London N16 6QT. Tel: 020-8802 6226. *Principal Rabbinical Authority*, M. C. E. Padwa

UNITED SYNAGOGUE HEAD OFFICE, Adler House, 735 High Road, London N12 0US. Tel: 020-8343 8989. *Chief Executive*, J. Wayne

## SIKHISM

The Sikh religion dates from the birth of Guru Nanak in the Punjab in 1469. 'Guru' means teacher but in Sikh tradition has come to represent the divine presence of God giving inner spiritual guidance. Nanak's role as the human vessel of the divine guru was passed on to nine successors, the last of whom (Guru Gobind Singh) died in 1708. The immortal guru is now held to reside in the sacred scripture, *Guru Granth Sahib*, and so to be present in all Sikh gatherings.

Guru Nanak taught that there is one God and that different religions are like different roads leading to the same destination. He condemned religious conflict, ritualism and caste prejudices. The fifth Guru, Guru Arjan Dev, largely compiled the Sikh Holy Book, a collection of hymns (*gurbani*) known as the *Adi Granth*. It includes the writings of the first five Gurus and the ninth Guru, and selected writings of Hindu and Muslim saints whose views are in accord with the Gurus' teachings. Guru Arjan Dev also built the Golden Temple at Amritsar, the centre of Sikhism. The tenth Guru, Guru Gobind Singh, passed on the guruship to the sacred scripture, Guru Granth Sahib. He also founded the *Khalsa*, an order intended to fight against tyranny and injustice. Male initiates to the order added 'Singh' to their given names and women added 'Kaur'. Guru Gobind Singh also made five symbols obligatory: *kaccha* (a special undergarment), *kara* (a steel bangle), *kirpan* (a small sword), *kesh* (long unshorn hair, and consequently the wearing of a turban), and *kangha* (a comb). These practices are still compulsory for those Sikhs who are initiated into the Khalsa (the *Amritdharis*). Those who do not seek initiation are known as *Sehajdharis*.

There are no professional priests in Sikhism; anyone with a reasonable proficiency in the Punjabi language can conduct a service. Worship can be offered individually or communally, and in a private house or a *gurdwara* (temple). Sikhs are forbidden to eat meat prepared by ritual slaughter; they are also asked to abstain from smoking, alcohol and other intoxicants. Such abstention is compulsory for the *Amritdharis*.

There are about 20 million Sikhs world-wide and about 500,000 adherents and 250 gurdwaras in Great Britain. Every gurdwara manages its own affairs and there is no central body in the UK. The Sikh Missionary Society provides an information service.

SIKH MISSIONARY SOCIETY UK, 10 Featherstone Road, Southall, Middx UB2 5AA. Tel: 020-8574 1902. *Hon. General Secretary*, K. S. Rai

WORLD SIKH FOUNDATION (THE SIKH COURIER INTERNATIONAL), 33 Wargrave Road, South Harrow, Middx HA2 8LL. Tel: 020-8864 9228. *Secretary*, Mrs H. B. Bharara

## ZOROASTRIANISM

Zoroastrianism was founded by Zarathushtra (or Zoroaster in its hellenised form) in Persia. Linguistic analysis of the earliest extant Zoroastrian texts suggests that he lived around 1500 BC. Zarathushtra's words are recorded in five poems called the *Gathas*, which, together with other scriptures, forms the *Avestan*.

Zoroastrianism teaches that there is one God, *Ahura Mazda* (the Wise Lord), and that all creation stems ultimately from God; the Gathas teach that human beings have free will, are responsible for their own actions and can choose between good and evil: Choosing *Asha* (truth or righteousness) leads to happiness for the individual and society, whereas choosing evil leads to unhappiness and conflict. The *Gathas* also encourage hard work, good deeds and charitable acts. Zoroastrians believe that after death, the immortal soul is judged by God, and is then sent to paradise or hell.

In Zoroastrian places of worship, an urn containing fire is the central feature; the fire symbolises purity, light, and truth and is a visible symbol of the *Fravashi* or *Farohar*, the presence of *Ahura Mazda* in every human being.

Zoroastrians respect nature and much importance is attached to cultivating land and protecting the air, the earth and water. The practice of leaving corpses on mountain tops or towers developed to avoid pollution.

Zoroastrians were persecuted in Iran following the Arab invasion of Persia in the seventh century AD, which also brought Islam and a group migrated to India in the tenth century AD to avoid harassment and persecution; there are fewer than 150,000 Zoroastrians worldwide.

ZOROASTRIAN ASSOCIATION OF EUROPE, 88 Compayne Gardens, London NW6. Tel: 020-7328 6018

# The Churches

For changes notified after 31 August, *see* Stop-press

## The Church of England

The Church of England is the established (i.e. national) church in England and seeks to serve the nation through its dioceses and parishes. It traces its life back to the first coming of Christianity to England. Its position is defined by the ancient creeds of the Church and by the Thirty-nine articles of Religion (1571), the Book of Common Prayer (1662) and the Ordinal. The Church of England is thus both catholic and reformed. It is the mother church of the Anglican Communion.

### THE ANGLICAN COMMUNION

The Anglican Communion consists of 40 independent provincial or national Christian churches throughout the world, many of which are in Commonwealth countries and originated from missionary activity by the Church of England. Every ten years all the bishops in the Communion meet at the Lambeth Conference, convened by the Archbishop of Canterbury. The Conference has no policy-making authority but is an important forum for discussing and forming consensus around issues common concern. The Anglican Consultative Council was set up in 1968 to liaise between the member churches and provinces of the Anglican Communion. It meets every three years. Meetings of the Anglican primates have taken place every two years since 1979.

There are about 70 million Anglicans and 800 archbishops and bishops world-wide.

### STRUCTURE

The Church of England is divided into the two provinces of Canterbury and York, each under an archbishop. The two provinces are subdivided into 44 dioceses.

Decisions on matters concerning the Church of England are made by the General Synod, established in 1970. It also discusses and expresses opinion on any other matter of religious or public interest. The General Synod has 580 members in total, divided between three houses: the House of Bishops, the House of Clergy and the House of Laity. It is presided over jointly by the Archbishops of Canterbury and York and normally meets twice a year. The Synod has the power, delegated by Parliament, to frame statute law (known as a Measure) on any matter concerning the Church of England. A Measure must be laid before both Houses of Parliament, who may accept or reject it but cannot amend it. Once accepted the Measure is submitted for royal assent and then has the full force of law. In addition to the General Synod, there are Synods at diocesan level

The Archbishops' Council was established in January 1999. Its creation was the result of changes to the Church of England's national structure proposed in 1995 and subsequently approved by the Synod and Parliament. The Council's purpose, set out in the National Institutions Measure 1998, is 'to co-ordinate, promote and further the work and mission of the Church of England. It reports frequently to the General Synod. The Archbishops' Council comprises three *ex-officio* members: the Archbishops of Canterbury and York (joint presidents) and a Church Estates Commissioners, ten elected members: the two persons elected by the Convocations of Prolocutors; the Chairman and Vice-Chairman of the House of Laity, elected by that House; two bishops, two clergy and two lay members each elected by their respective Houses of the General Synod; and up to six members appointed by the two archbishops with the approval of the General Synod.

There are also a number of national Boards, Councils and other bodies working on matters such as social responsibility, mission, Christian unity and education which report to the General Synod through the Archbishops' Council.

GENERAL SYNOD OF THE CHURCH OF ENGLAND, Church House, Great Smith Street, London SW1P 3NZ. Tel: 020-7898 1000. *Joint Presidents*, The Archbishops of Canterbury and York. *Secretary-General*, P. Mawer

HOUSE OF BISHOPS: *Chairman*, The Archbishop of Canterbury; *Vice-Chairman*, The Archbishop of York

HOUSE OF CLERGY: *Chairmen (alternating)*, Canon Bob Baker; Canon Glyn Webster

HOUSE OF LAITY: *Chairman*, Dr Christina Baxter; *Vice-Chairman*, Brian McHenry

ARCHBISHOPS' COUNCIL, Church House, Great Smith Street, London SW1P 3NZ. Tel: 020-7898 1000. *Joint Presidents*, The Archbishops of Canterbury and York. *Secretary-General*, P. Mawer.

### THE ORDINATION OF WOMEN

The canon making it possible for women to be ordained to the priesthood was promulgated in the General Synod in February 1994 and the first 32 women priests were ordained on 12 March 1994.

### MEMBERSHIP

In 1999, 179,000 people were baptised. In 1998 the Church of England had an electoral roll membership of 1.4 million, and each week about 1 million people attended Sunday services. At December 2000 there were two archbishops and 108 diocesan, suffragan and (stipendiary) assistant bishops. In 2000 there were 8,398 other male and 1,140 female full-time stipendiary clergy, and over 16,000 churches and places of worship.

### FULL-TIME DIOCESAN CLERGY 1999 AND CHURCH ELECTORAL ROLLS 1997

| | *Clergy* | | *Membership* |
|---|---|---|---|
| | *Male* | *Female* | |
| Bath and Wells | 210 | 29 | 43,000 |
| Birmingham | 177 | 26 | 19,300 |
| Blackburn | 226 | 13 | 38,600 |
| Bradford | 106 | 10 | 13,100 |
| Bristol | 122 | 20 | 20,400 |
| Canterbury | 159 | 19 | 22,300 |
| Carlisle | 139 | 14 | 25,000 |
| Chelmsford | 367 | 48 | 54,200 |
| Chester | 250 | 25 | 52,100 |
| Chichester | 329 | 9 | 61,300 |
| Coventry | 130 | 17 | 18,200 |
| Derby | 168 | 17 | 21,900 |
| Durham | 211 | 28 | 27,700 |
| | *Clergy* | | *Membership* |
| | *Male* | *Female* | |
| Ely | 130 | 24 | 21,500 |
| Europe | 113 | 13 | 9,100 |
| Exeter | 232 | 19 | 34,600 |
| Gloucester | 141 | 18 | 26,900 |
| Guildford | 170 | 31 | 31,900 |
| Hereford | 96 | 19 | 20,100 |

| | | | |
|---|---|---|---|
| Leicester | 143 | 23 | 16,700 |
| Lichfield | 304 | 46 | 54,800 |
| Lincoln | 187 | 39 | 30,700 |
| Liverpool | 215 | 37 | 33,300 |
| London | 497 | 60 | 59,900 |
| Manchester | 256 | 40 | 39,800 |
| Newcastle | 130 | 16 | 18,300 |
| Norwich | 183 | 18 | 26,800 |
| Oxford | 369 | 71 | 63,200 |
| Peterborough | 151 | 17 | 19,600 |
| Portsmouth | 107 | 10 | 19,300 |
| Ripon and Leeds | 123 | 22 | 20,000 |
| Rochester | 194 | 25 | 32,800 |
| St Albans | 228 | 48 | 46,100 |
| St Edmundsbury and Ipswich | 139 | 15 | 26,500 |
| Salisbury | 199 | 30 | 47,500 |
| Sheffield | 156 | 31 | 21,800 |
| Sodor and Man | 20 | 0 | 2,900 |
| Southwark | 304 | 66 | 47,200 |
| Southwell | 144 | 26 | 18,600 |
| Truro | 124 | 6 | 18,100 |
| Wakefield | 155 | 24 | 24,700 |
| Winchester | 220 | 19 | 43,500 |
| Worcester | 129 | 22 | 23,400 |
| York | 245 | 30 | 39,800 |
| TOTAL | 8,398 | 1,140 | 1,347,400 |

STIPENDS 2001–2002

| | |
|---|---|
| Archbishop of Canterbury | £57,320 |
| Archbishop of York | £50,220 |
| Bishop of London | £46,840 |
| Other diocesan bishops | £31,110 |
| Suffragan bishops | £25,530 |
| Assistant Bishops (full-time) | £25,520 |
| Deans and provosts | £25,530 |
| Residentiary canons | £20,800 |
| Incumbents and clergy of similar status | £16,910* |

*National Stipends Benchmark

## CANTERBURY

103RD ARCHBISHOP AND PRIMATE OF ALL ENGLAND
Most Revd and Rt. Hon. George L. Carey, Ph.D., *cons.* 1987, *trans.* 1991, *apptd* 1991; Lambeth Palace, London SE1 7JU. *Signs* George Cantuar

BISHOPS SUFFRAGAN

*Dover*, Rt. Revd Stephen S. Venner, *cons 1994*, *apptd* 1999; Upway, St Martin's Hill, Canterbury, Kent CT1 1PR
*Maidstone*, Rt. Revd Graham Cray Bishop's House, Pett Lane, Charing, Ashford, Kent TN27 0DL
*Ebbsfleet*, Rt. Revd Andrew Burnham, *cons.* 2001, *apptd* 2001 (provincial episcopal visitor); Bishop's House, Dry Sandsford, Oxon OX13 6JP
*Richborough*, Rt. Revd Edwin Barnes, *cons.* 1995, *apptd* 1995 (provincial episcopal visitor); 14 Hall Place Gardens, St Albans, Herts AL1 3SP

DEAN

Very Revd Robert Andrew Willis, *apptd* 2001

CANONS RESIDENTIARY

P. Brett, *apptd* 1983; R. H. C. Symon, *apptd* 1994; Dr M. Chandler, *apptd* 1995; Ven. J. Pritchard, *apptd* 1996
*Organist*, D. Flood, FRCO, *apptd* 1988

ARCHDEACONS

*Canterbury*, Ven. J. Pritchard, *apptd* 1996
*Maidstone*, Ven. P. Evans, *apptd* 1989

*Vicar-General of Province and Diocese*, Chancellor S. Cameron, QC
*Commissary-General*, His Hon. Judge Richard Walker
*Joint Registrars of the Province*, F. E. Robson, OBE; B. J. T. Hanson, CBE
*Diocesan Registrar and Legal Adviser*, R. H. B. Sturt
*Diocesan Secretary*, D. Kemp, Diocesan House, Lady Wootton's Green, Canterbury CT1 1NQ. Tel: 01227-459401

## YORK

96TH ARCHBISHOP AND PRIMATE OF ENGLAND
Most Revd and Rt. Hon. David M. Hope, KCVO, D.Phil., LL D, *cons.* 1985, *trans.* 1995, *apptd* 1995; Bishopthorpe, York YO23 2GE. *Signs* David Ebor

BISHOPS SUFFRAGAN

*Hull*, Rt. Revd Richard M. C. Frith, *cons.* 1998, *apptd* 1998; Hullen House, Woodfield Lane, Hessle, Hull HU13 0ES
*Selby*, Rt. Revd Humphrey V. Taylor, *cons.* 1991, *apptd* 1991; 10 Precentor's Court, York YO1 2EJ
*Whitby*, Rt. Revd Robert S. Ladds, *cons.* 1999, *apptd* 1999; 60 West Green, Stokesley, Middlesbrough TS9 5BD
*Beverley*, Rt. Revd M. Jarrett, *apptd* 2000 (provincial episcopal visitor); 3 North Lane, Roundhay, Leeds LS8 2QJ

DEAN

Very Revd Raymond Furnell, *apptd* 1994

CANONS RESIDENTIARY

G. Webster, *apptd* 1999; E. R. Norman, Ph.D., DD, *apptd* 1999; J. L. Draper, *apptd* 2000

CANONS LAY

J. L. Mackinlay, *apptd* 2000; Mrs E. C. Rymer, *apptd* 2000; Dr A. J. Warren, *apptd* 2000; Brig. P. J. Lyddon (as Chapter Steward), *apptd* 2000
*Organist*, P. Moore, FRCO, *apptd* 1983

ARCHDEACONS

*Cleveland*, Ven. P. J. Ferguson, *apptd* 2001
*East Riding*, Ven. P. R. W. Harrison, *apptd* 1998
*York*, Ven. R. Seed, *apptd* 1999

*Official Principal and Auditor of the Chancery Court*, Sir John Owen, QC
*Chancellor of the Diocese*, His Hon. Judge Coningsby, QC, *apptd* 1977
*Vicar-General of the Province and Official Principal of the Consistory Court*, His Hon. Judge Coningsby, QC
*Registrar and Legal Secretary*, L. P. M. Lennox
*Diocesan Secretary*, C. Sheppard, Diocesan House, Aviator Court, Clifton Moor, York YO30 4WJ. Tel: 01904-699500

## LONDON (Province of Canterbury)

132ND BISHOP
Rt. Revd and Rt. Hon Richard J. C. Chartres, *cons. 1992*, *apptd. 1995*; The Old Deanery, Dean's Court, London EC4V 5AA. *Signs* Richard Londin

AREA BISHOPS

*Edmonton*, Rt. Revd Peter W. Wheatley, *cons.* 1999, *apptd* 1999; 27 Thurlow Road, London NW3 5PP

*Kensington*, Rt. Revd Michael Colclough, *cons.* 1996, *apptd* 1996; 19 Campden Hill Square, London W8 7JY
*Stepney*, Rt. Revd Dr John M. Sentamu, *cons.* 1996, *apptd* 1996; 63 Coborn Road, London E3 2DB
*Willesden*, Rt. Revd Peter Broadbent, *cons.*, *apptd* 2000; 173 Willesden Lane, London NW6 7YN

BISHOP SUFFRAGAN

*Fulham*, Rt. Revd John Broadhurst, *cons.* 1996, *apptd* 1996; 26 Canonbury Park South, London N1 2FN

DEAN OF ST PAUL'S

Very Revd John H. Moses, Ph.D., *apptd* 1996

CANONS RESIDENTIARY

R. J. Halliburton, *apptd* 1990; S. J. Oliver, *apptd* 1997; P. Buckler, *apptd* 1999; Edmund Newall, *apptd* 2001

*Registrar and Receiver of St Paul's*, vacant

*Organist*, J. Scott, FRCO, *apptd* 1990

ARCHDEACONS

*Charing Cross*, Ven. Dr W. Jacob, *apptd* 1996
*Hackney*, Ven. L. Dennen, *apptd* 1999
*Hampstead*, Ven. M. Lawson, *apptd* 1999
*London*, Ven. P. Delaney, *apptd* 1999
*Middlesex*, Ven. M. Colmer, *apptd* 1996
*Northolt*, Ven. Christopher Chessum, *apptd* 2001

*Chancellor*, Nigel Seed, QC, *apptd* 2001
*Registrar and Legal Secretary*, P. C. E. Morris
*Diocesan Secretary*, K. Robinson, London Diocesan House, 36 Causton Street, London SW1P 4AU. Tel: 020-7932 1100

## DURHAM (Province of York)

70TH BISHOP

Rt. Revd A. Michael A. Turnbull, *cons.* 1988, *apptd* 1994; Auckland Castle, Bishop Auckland DL14 7NR. *Signs* Michael Dunelm

BISHOP SUFFRAGAN

*Jarrow*, Rt. Revd Alan Smithson, *cons.* 1990, *apptd* 1990; The Old Vicarage, Hallgarth, Pittington, Durham DH6 1AB

DEAN

Very Revd John R. Arnold, *apptd* 1989

CANONS RESIDENTIARY

D. W. Brown, *apptd* 1990; T. Willmott, *apptd* 1997; M. Kitchen, *apptd* 1997; D. J. Whittington, *apptd* 1998; D. J. Kennedy, *apptd* 2001

*Organist*, J. B. Lancelot, FRCO, *apptd* 1985

ARCHDEACONS

*Auckland*, Ven. I. Jagger, *apptd* 2001
*Durham*, Ven. T. Willmott, *apptd* 1997
*Sunderland*, Ven. F. White, *apptd* 1997

*Chancellor*, His Hon. Judge Bursell, QC, *apptd* 1989
*Registrar and Legal Secretary*, A. N. Fairclough
*Diocesan Secretary*, J. P. Cryer, Auckland Castle, Bishop Auckland, Co. Durham DL14 7QJ. Tel: 01388-604515

## WINCHESTER (Canterbury)

96TH BISHOP

Rt. Revd Michael C. Scott-Joynt, *cons.* 1987, *trans.* 1995, *apptd* 1995; Wolvesey, Winchester SO23 9ND. *Signs* Michael Winton

BISHOPS SUFFRAGAN

*Basingstoke*, vacant
*Southampton*, Rt. Revd Jonathan M. Gledhill, *cons.* 1996, *apptd* 1996; Ham House, The Crescent, Romsey SO51 7NG

DEAN

Very Revd Michael Till, *apptd* 1996

*Dean of Jersey (A Peculiar)*, Very Revd John Seaford, *apptd* 1993
*Dean of Guernsey (A Peculiar)*, Very Revd Marc Trickey, *apptd* 1995

CANONS RESIDENTIARY

A. K. Walker, *apptd* 1987; C. Stewart, *apptd* 1997; Ven. J. A. Guille, *apptd* 1998

*Organist*, D. Hill, FRCO, *apptd* 1988

ARCHDEACONS

*Bournemouth*, Ven. A. G. Harbidge, *apptd* 1998
*Winchester*, Ven. J. A. Guille, *apptd* 1998

*Chancellor*, C. Clark, *apptd* 1993
*Registrar and Legal Secretary*, P. M. White
*Diocesan Secretary*, R. Anderton, Church House, 9 The Close, Winchester, Hants SO23 9LS. Tel: 01962-844644

## BATH AND WELLS (Canterbury)

76TH BISHOP

Rt. Revd James L. Thompson, *cons.* 1978, *apptd* 1991; The Palace, Wells BA5 2PD. *Signs* James Bath & Wells

BISHOP SUFFRAGAN

*Taunton*, Rt. Revd Andrew John Radford, *cons.* Dec. 1998, *apptd* 1998; The Bishop's Lodge, Monkton Heights, West Monkton, Taunton, Somerset TA2 8LU

DEAN

Very Revd Richard Lewis, *apptd* 1990

CANONS RESIDENTIARY

R. Acworth, *apptd* 1993; P. G. Walker, *apptd* 1994; M. W. Matthews, *apptd* 1997; P. H. F. Woodhouse, *apptd* 2000

*Organist*, M. Archer, *apptd* 1996

ARCHDEACONS

*Bath*, Ven. R. J. S. Evens, *apptd* 1996
*Taunton*, Ven. J. P. C. Reed, *apptd* 1999
*Wells*, Ven. R. Acworth, *apptd* 1993

*Chancellor*, T. Briden, *apptd* 1993
*Registrar and Legal Secretary*, T. Berry
*Diocesan Secretary*, N. Denison, The Old Deanery, Wells, Somerset BA5 2UG. Tel: 01749-670777

## BIRMINGHAM (Canterbury)

7TH BISHOP
Rt. Revd Mark Santer, *cons.* 1981, *apptd* 1987; Bishop's Croft, Harborne, Birmingham B17 0BG. *Signs* Mark Birmingham

BISHOP SUFFRAGAN
*Aston*, Rt. Revd John Austin, *cons.* 1992, *apptd* 1992; Strensham House, 8 Strensham Hill, Moseley, Birmingham B13 8AG

PROVOST
The Very Revd Gordon Mursell, *apptd* 2000

CANONS RESIDENTIARY
Ven. C. J. G. Barton, *apptd* 1990; Revd D. Lee, *apptd* 1996; Revd G. O'Neill, *apptd* 1997

*Organist*, M. Huxley, FRCO, *apptd* 1986

ARCHDEACONS
*Aston*, Ven. C. J. G. Barton, *apptd* 1990
*Birmingham*, Ven. H. J. Osborne, *apptd* 2001

*Chancellor*, His Hon. Judge Aglionby, *apptd* 1970
*Registrar and Legal Secretary*, H. Carslake
*Diocesan Secretary*, J. Drennan, 175 Harborne Park Road, Harborne, Birmingham B17 0BH. Tel: 0121-426 0400

## BLACKBURN (York)

7TH BISHOP
Rt. Revd Alan D. Chesters, *cons.* 1989, *apptd* 1989; Bishop's House, Ribchester Road, Blackburn BB1 9EF. *Signs* Alan Blackburn

BISHOPS SUFFRAGAN
*Burnley*, Rt. Revd John W. Goddard, *cons.* 2000, *apptd* 2000; Dean House, 449 Padiham Road, Burnley BB12 6TE
*Lancaster*, Rt. Revd Stephen Pedley, *cons.* 1998, *apptd* 1997; The Vicarage, Shireshead, Forton, Preston PR3 0AE

PROVOST
Very Revd David Frayne, *apptd* 1992

CANONS RESIDENTIARY
D. M. Galilee, *apptd* 1995; A. D. Hindley, *apptd* 1996; P. J. Ballard, *apptd* 1998; A. Clitherow, *apptd* 2000

*Organist*, R. Tanner, *apptd* 1998

ARCHDEACONS
*Blackburn*, Ven. F. J. Marsh, *apptd* 1996
*Lancaster*, Ven. C. H. Williams, *apptd* 1999

*Chancellor*, J. W. M. Bullimore, *apptd* 1990
*Registrar and Legal Secretary*, T. A. Hoyle
*Diocesan Secretary*, Revd M. J. Wedgeworth, Diocesan Office, Cathedral Close, Blackburn BB1 5AA. Tel: 01254-54421

## BRADFORD (York)

8TH BISHOP
Rt. Revd David J. Smith, *cons.* 1987, *apptd* 1992; Bishopscroft, Ashwell Road, Heaton, Bradford BD9 4AU. *Signs* David Bradford

DEAN
Very Revd John S. Richardson, *apptd* 1990

CANONS RESIDENTIARY
C. G. Lewis, *apptd* 1993; D. Jackson, *apptd* 2000

*Organist*, A. Horsey, FRCO, *apptd* 1986

ARCHDEACONS
*Bradford*, Ven. G. A. Wilkinson, *apptd* 1999
*Craven*, Ven. M. L. Grundy, *apptd* 1994

*Chancellor*, J. de G. Walford, *apptd* 1999
*Registrar and Legal Secretary*, J. G. H. Mackrell
*Diocesan Secretary*, M. Halliday, Cathedral Hall, Stott Hill, Bradford BD1 4ET. Tel: 01274-725958

## BRISTOL (Canterbury)

54TH BISHOP
Rt. Revd Barry Rogerson, *cons.* 1979, *apptd* 1985; Bishop's House, Clifton Hill, Bristol BS8 1BW. *Signs* Barry Bristol:

BISHOP SUFFRAGAN
*Swindon*, Rt. Revd Michael Doe, *cons.* 1994, *apptd* 1994; Mark House, Field Rise, Old Town, Swindon SN1 4HP

DEAN
Very Revd Robert W. Grimley, *apptd* 1997

CANONS RESIDENTIARY
P. F. Johnson, *apptd* 1990; D. R. Holt, *apptd* 1998; B. D. Clover, *apptd* 1999

*Organist*, M. Lee, *apptd* 1998

ARCHDEACONS
*Bristol*, Ven. T. E. McClure, apptd 1999
*Swindon*, Ven. A. F. Hawker, *apptd* 1998

*Chancellor*, Sir David Calcutt, QC, *apptd* 1971
*Registrar and Legal Secretary*, T. Berry
*Diocesan Secretary*, Mrs L. Farrall, Diocesan Church House, 23 Great George Street, Bristol, Avon BS1 5QZ. Tel: 0117-921 4411

## CARLISLE (York)

65TH BISHOP
Rt. Revd Graham Dow, *cons.* 1985, *apptd* 2000; Rose Castle, Dalston, Carlisle CA5 7BZ. *Signs* Graham Carlisle

BISHOP SUFFRAGAN
*Penrith*, Rt. Revd Richard Garrard, *cons.* 1994, *apptd* 1994; Holm Croft, Castle Road, Kendal, Cumbria LA9 7AU

DEAN
Very Revd Graeme P. Knowles, *apptd* 1998

CANONS RESIDENTIARY
R. A. Chapman, *apptd* 1978; D. W. V. Weston, *apptd* 1994; C. Hill, *apptd* 1996

*Organist*, J. Suter, FRCO, *apptd* 1991

ARCHDEACONS
*Carlisle*, vacant
*West Cumberland*, Ven. A. N. Davis, *apptd* 1996
*Westmorland and Furness*, Ven. G. A. Howe, *apptd* 2000

*Chancellor*, His Hon. Judge Aglionby, *apptd* 1991
*Registrar and Legal Secretary*, Mrs S. Holmes

*Diocesan Secretary*, Canon C. Hill, Church House, West Walls, Carlisle CA3 8UE. Tel: 01228-522573

## CHELMSFORD (Canterbury)

8TH BISHOP

Rt. Revd John F. Perry, *cons.* 1989, *apptd* 1996; Bishopscourt, Margaretting, Ingatestone CM4 0HD. *Signs* John Chelmsford

BISHOPS SUFFRAGAN

*Barking*, Rt. Revd Roger F. Sainsbury, *cons.* 1991, *apptd* 1991; 110 Capel Road, Forest Gate, London E7 0JS
*Bradwell*, Rt. Revd Laurence Green, *cons.* 1993, *apptd* 1993; The Vicarage, Orsett Road, Horndon-on-the-Hill, Stanford-le-Hope, Essex SS17 8NS
*Colchester*, vacant

PROVOST

Very Revd Peter S. M. Judd, *apptd* 1997

CANONS RESIDENTIARY

A. Knowles, *apptd* 1998; W. King, *apptd* 2001

*Master of Music*, P. Nardone, *apptd* 2000

ARCHDEACONS

*Colchester*, Ven. M. W. Wallace, *apptd* 1997
*Harlow*, Ven. P. F. Taylor, *apptd* 1996
*Southend*, Ven. David Lowman, *apptd* 2001
*West Ham*, Ven. M. J. Fox, *apptd* 1996

*Chancellor*, George Pulman, *apptd* 2001
*Registrar and Legal Secretary*, B. Hood
*Diocesan Secretary*, D. Phillips, 53 New Street, Chelmsford, Essex CM1 1AT. Tel: 01245-294400

## CHESTER (York)

40TH BISHOP

Rt. Revd Peter R. Forster, Ph.D., *cons.* 1996, *apptd* 1996; Bishop's House, Chester CH1 2JD. *Signs* Peter Cestr

BISHOPS SUFFRAGAN

*Birkenhead*, Rt. Revd David A. Urquhart, *cons.* 2000, *apptd* 2000; Bishop's Lodge, 67 Bidston Road, Oxton, Birkenhead CH43 6TR
*Stockport*, Rt. Revd Nigel Stock, *cons.* 2000, *apptd* 2000; Bishop's Lodge, Back Lane, Dunham Town, Altrincham, Cheshire WA14 4SG

DEAN

vacant

CANONS RESIDENTIARY

J. M. Roff, *apptd* 2000; Dr T. J. Dennis, *apptd* 1994; J. W. S. Newcome, *apptd* 1994; C. P. Burkett, *apptd* 2000

*Organist and Director of Music*, D. G. Poulter, FRCO, *apptd* 1997

ARCHDEACONS

*Chester*, Ven. C. Hewetson, *apptd* 1994
*Macclesfield*, Ven. R. J. Gillings, *apptd* 1994

*Chancellor*, D. G. P. Turner, QC, *apptd* 1998
*Registrar and Legal Secretary*, A. K. McAllester
*Diocesan Secretary*, S. P. A. Marriott, Church House, Lower Lane, Aldford, Chester CH3 6HP. Tel: 01244-620444

## CHICHESTER (Canterbury)

102ND BISHOP

Rt. Revd John Hind, *cons.* 1991, *apptd* 2001; The Palace, Chichester PO19 1PY. *Signs* John Cicestr

BISHOPS SUFFRAGAN

*Horsham*, Rt. Revd Lindsay G. Urwin, *cons.* 1993, *apptd* 1993; Bishop's House, 21 Guildford Road, Horsham, W. Sussex RH12 1LU
*Lewes*, Rt. Revd Wallace P. Benn, *cons.* 1997, *apptd* 1997; 16A Prideaux Road, Eastbourne, E. Sussex BN21 2NB

DEAN

Very Revd John D. Treadgold, LVO, *apptd* 1989

CANONS RESIDENTIARY

J. M. Brotherton, *apptd* 1991; P. G. Atkinson, *apptd* 1997; M. R. J. Manktelow, *apptd* 1997; P. C. Kefford, *apptd* 2001

*Organist*, A. J. Thurlow, FRCO, *apptd* 1980

ARCHDEACONS

*Chichester*, Ven. M. Brotherton, *apptd* 1991
*Horsham*, Ven. W. C. L. Filby, *apptd* 1983
*Lewes and Hastings*, Ven. N. S. Reade, *apptd* 1997

*Chancellor*, M. Hill
*Registrar and Legal Secretary*, C. Butcher
*Diocesan Secretary*, J. Prichard, Diocesan Church House, 211 New Church Road, Hove, E. Sussex BN3 4ED. Tel: 01273-421021

## COVENTRY (Canterbury)

8TH BISHOP

Rt. Revd Colin J. Bennetts; *cons.* 1994, *apptd* 1997; The Bishop's House, 23 Davenport Road, Coventry CV5 6PW. *Signs* Colin Coventry

BISHOP SUFFRAGAN

*Warwick*, Rt. Revd Anthony M. Priddis, *cons.* 1996, *apptd* 1996; 139 Kenilworth Road, Coventry CV4 7AF

DEAN

Very Revd John Irvine, *apptd* 2001

CANONS RESIDENTIARY

J. C. Burch, *apptd* 1995; A. White, *apptd* 1998; S. A. Beake, *apptd* 2000

*Director of Music*, R. Jeffcoat, *apptd* 1997

ARCHDEACONS

*Coventry*, Ven. M. W. Bryant, *apptd* 2001
*Warwick*, Ven. M. J. J. Paget-Wilkes, *apptd* 1990

*Chancellor*, Sir William Gage, *apptd* 1980
*Registrar and Legal Secretary*, D. J. Dumbleton
*Diocesan Secretary*, Mrs I. Chapman, Church House, Palmerston Road, Coventry CV5 6FJ. Tel: 024-7667 4328

## DERBY (Canterbury)

6TH BISHOP

Rt. Revd Jonathan S. Bailey, *cons.* 1992, *apptd* 1995; Derby Church House, Full Street, Derby DE1 3DR. *Signs* Jonathan Derby

BISHOP SUFFRAGAN

*Repton*, Rt. Revd David C. Hawtin, *cons.* 1999, *apptd* 1999; Repton House, Lea, Matlock, Derbys DE4 5JP

PROVOST

Very Revd Michael F. Perham, *apptd* 1998

CANONS RESIDENTIARY

G. A. Chesterman, *apptd* 1989; B. V. Gauge, *apptd* 1999; G. O. Marshall, *apptd* 1992; D. C. Truby, *apptd* 1998

*Organist*, P. Gould, *apptd* 1982

ARCHDEACONS

*Chesterfield*, Ven. D. C. Garnett, *apptd* 1996
*Derby*, Ven. I. Gatford, *apptd* 1992

*Chancellor*, J. W. M. Bullimore, *apptd* 1981
*Registrar and Legal Secretary*, J. S. Battie
*Diocesan Secretary*, R. J. Carey, Derby Church House, Full Street, Derby DE1 3DR. Tel: 01332-382233

## ELY (Canterbury)

BISHOP

Rt. Revd Dr Anthony Russell, *cons.* 1988, *apptd* 2000; The Bishop's House, Ely, Cambs CB7 4DW *Signs* Anthony Ely

BISHOP SUFFRAGAN

*Huntingdon*, Rt. Revd John R. Flack, *cons.* 1997, *apptd* 1996; 14 Lynn Road, Ely, Cambs CB6 1DA

DEAN

Very Revd Michael Higgins, *apptd* 1991

CANONS RESIDENTIARY

J. Inge, *apptd* 1996; P. M. Sills, *apptd* 2000

*Organist*, P. Trepte, FRCO, *apptd* 1991

ARCHDEACONS

*Ely*, Ven. J. Watson, *apptd* 1993
*Huntingdon*, Ven. J. Beer, *apptd* 1997
*Wisbech*, Ven. J. Rone, *apptd* 1995

*Chancellor*, W. Gage, QC
*Joint Registrars*, W. H. Godfrey; P. F. B. Beesley (*Legal Secretary*)
*Diocesan Secretary*, Dr M. Lavis, Bishop Woodford House, Barton Road, Ely, Cambs CB7 4DX. Tel: 01353-652701

## EXETER (CANTERBURY)

70TH BISHOP

Rt. Revd Michael L. Langrish, *cons.* 1993, *apptd* 2000; The Palace, Exeter, EX1 1HY. *Signs* Michael Exon

BISHOPS SUFFRAGAN

*Crediton*, Rt. Revd Richard S. Hawkins, *cons.* 1988, *apptd* 1996; 10 The Close, Exeter EX1 1EZ
*Plymouth*, Rt. Revd John H. Garton, *cons.* 1996, *apptd* 1996; 31 Riverside Walk, Tamerton Foliot, Plymouth PL5 4AQ

DEAN

Very Revd Keith B. Jones, *apptd* 1996

CANONS RESIDENTIARY

N. Collings, *apptd* 1999; D. J. Ison, *apptd* 1997; C. Turner, *apptd* 2001

*Director of Music*, A. T. S. Millington, *apptd* 1999

ARCHDEACONS

*Barnstaple*, Ven. T. Lloyd, *apptd* 1989
*Exeter*, Ven. A. F. Tremlett, *apptd* 1994
*Plymouth*, Ven. T. Wilds, *apptd* 2001
*Totnes*, Preb. R. T. Gilpin, *apptd* 1996

*Chancellor*, Sir David Calcutt, QC, *apptd* 1971
*Registrar and Legal Secretary*, R. K. Wheeler
*Diocesan Secretary*, M. Beedell, Diocesan House, Palace Gate, Exeter, Devon EX1 1HX. Tel: 01392-272686

## GIBRALTAR IN EUROPE (Canterbury)

BISHOP

Rt. Revd Geoffrey Rowell, *cons.* 1994, *apptd* 2001; 14 Tufton Street, London SW1P 3QZ

BISHOP SUFFRAGAN

*In Europe* Rt. Revd Henry Scriven, *cons.* 1995, *apptd* 1994; 14 Tufton Street, London SW1P 3QZ

*Dean, Cathedral Church of the Holy Trinity, Gibraltar*, Very Revd J. K. Robinson
*Chancellor, Pro-Cathedral of St Paul, Valletta, Malta*, Canon A. Woods
*Chancellor, Pro-Cathedral of the Holy Trinity, Brussels, Belgium*, Canon N. Walker

ARCHDEACONS

*Eastern*, Rt. Revd H. Scriven (acting)
*North-West Europe*, Ven. G. G. Allen
*France*, Ven. M. Draper, OBE
*Gibraltar*, Very Revd K. Robinson
*Italy*, Ven. W. G. Reid
*Scandinavia and Germany*, Ven. D. Ratcliff
*Switzerland*, Ven. P. J. Hawker, OBE

*Chancellor*, Sir David Calcutt, QC
*Registrar and Legal Secretary*, J. G. Underwood
*Diocesan Secretary*, A. C. Mumford, 14 Tufton Street, London SW1P 3QZ. Tel: 020-7898 1155

## GLOUCESTER (Canterbury)

39TH BISHOP

Rt. Revd David Bentley, *cons.* 1986, *apptd* 1993; Bishopscourt, Pitt Street, Gloucester GL1 2BQ. *Signs* David Gloucestr

BISHOP SUFFRAGAN

*Tewkesbury*, Rt. Revd John S. Went, *cons.* 1995, *apptd* 1995; Green Acre, 166 Hempsted Lane, Hempsted, Gloucester GL2 5LG

DEAN

Very Revd Nicholas A. S. Bury, *apptd* 1997

CANONS RESIDENTIARY

R. D. M. Grey, *apptd* 1982; N. Chatfield, *apptd* 1992; N. Heavisides, *apptd* 1993; C. H. Morgan, *apptd* 1996

*Organist*, D. Briggs, FRCO, *apptd* 1994

ARCHDEACONS

*Cheltenham*, Ven. H. S. Ringrose, *apptd* 1998
*Gloucester*, Ven. G. H. Sidaway, *apptd* 2000

*Chancellor and Vicar-General*, Ms D. J. Rodgers, *apptd* 1990
*Registrar and Legal Secretary*, C. G. Peak

*Diocesan Secretary*, M. Williams, Church House, College Green, Gloucester GL1 2LY. Tel: 01452-410022

## GUILDFORD (Canterbury)

8TH BISHOP
Rt. Revd John W. Gladwin, *cons.* 1994, *apptd* 1994; Willow Grange, Woking Road, Guildford GU4 7QS. Tel: 01483-590500; Fax: 01483-590501 *Signs* John Guildford

BISHOP SUFFRAGAN

*Dorking*, Rt. Revd Ian Brackley, *cons.* 1996, *apptd* 1995; Dayspring, 13 Pilgrims Way, Guildford GU4 8AD

DEAN

vacant

CANONS RESIDENTIARY

Dr Maureen Palmer, *apptd* 1996; Dr Nicholas Thistlethwaite, *apptd* 1999; Julian Hubbard, *apptd* 1999

*Organist*, S. Farr, FRCO, *apptd* 1999

ARCHDEACONS

*Dorking*, Ven. M. Wilson, *apptd* 1996
*Surrey*, Ven. R. Reiss, *apptd* 1996

*Chancellor*, His Hon. Judge Goodman
*Registrar and Legal Secretary*, P. Beesley
*Diocesan Secretary*, S. Marriott

## HEREFORD (Canterbury)

103RD BISHOP
Rt. Revd John Oliver, *cons.* 1990, *apptd* 1990; The Palace, Hereford HR4 9BN. *Signs* John Hereford

BISHOP SUFFRAGAN

*Ludlow*, Rt. Revd Dr John Saxbee, *cons.* 1994, *apptd* 1994; Bishop's House, Halford, Craven Arms, Shropshire SY7 9BT

DEAN

vacant

CANONS RESIDENTIARY

P. Iles, *apptd* 1983; J. Tiller, *apptd* 1984; M. W. Hooper, *apptd* 1997

*Organist*, Geraint Bowen, FRCO, *apptd* 2001

ARCHDEACONS

*Hereford*, Ven. M. W. Hooper, *apptd* 1997
*Ludlow*, Rt. Revd J. C. Saxbee, *apptd* 1992

*Chancellor*, Roger Kaye QC
*Joint Registrars and Legal Secretaries*, V. T. Jordan; P. F. B. Beesley
*Diocesan Secretary*, Miss S. Green, The Palace, Hereford HR4 9BL. Tel: 01432-353863

## LEICESTER (CANTERBURY)

6TH BISHOP
Rt. Revd Timothy J. Stevens, *cons.* 1995, *apptd* 1999; Bishop's Lodge, 10 Springfield Road, Leicester LE2 3BD. *Signs* Timothy Leicester

STIPENDIARY ASSISTANT BISHOP

vacant

PROVOST

Very Revd Vivienne F. Faull, *apptd* 2000

CANONS RESIDENTIARY

M. T. H. Banks, *apptd* 1988; M. Wilson, *apptd* 1988

*Organist*, J. T. Gregory, *apptd* 1994

ARCHDEACONS

*Leicester*, Ven. M. Edson, *apptd* 1994
*Loughborough*, Ven. I. Stanes, *apptd* 1992

*Chancellor*, vacant
*Registrars and Legal Secretaries*, P. C. E. Morris; R. H. Bloor
*Diocesan Secretary*, A. Howard; Church House, 3–5 St Martin's East, Leicester LE1 5FX. Tel: 0116-262 7445

## LICHFIELD (Canterbury)

97TH BISHOP
Rt. Revd Keith N. Sutton, *cons.* 1978, *apptd* 1984; Bishop's House, The Close, Lichfield WS13 7LG. *Signs* Keith Lichfield

BISHOPS SUFFRAGAN

*Shrewsbury*, vacant
*Stafford*, Rt. Revd Christopher J. Hill, *cons.* 1996, *apptd* 1996; Ash Garth, Broughton Crescent, Barlaston, Staffs ST12 9DD
*Wolverhampton*, Rt. Revd Michael G. Bourke, *cons.* 1993, *apptd* 1993; 61 Richmond Road, Wolverhampton WV3 9JH

DEAN

Very Revd Michael Yorke, *apptd* 1999

CANONS RESIDENTIARY

A. N. Barnard, *apptd* 1977; C. W. Taylor, *apptd* 1995; Ven. C. F. Liley, *apptd* 2001

*Organist*, A. Lumsden, *apptd* 1992

ARCHDEACONS

*Lichfield*, Ven. C. F. Liley, *apptd* 2001
*Salop*, Ven . J. B. Hall, *apptd* 1998
*Stoke-on-Trent*, Ven. A. G. C. Smith, *apptd* 1997
*Walsall*, Ven. A. G. Sadler, *apptd* 1997

*Chancellor*, His Hon. Judge Shand
*Registrar and Legal Secretary*, J. P. Thorneycroft
*Diocesan Secretary*, D. R. Taylor, St Mary's House, The Close, Lichfield, Staffs WS13 7LD. Tel: 01543-306030

## LINCOLN (Canterbury)

70TH BISHOP
Rt. Revd Robert M. Hardy, *cons.* 1980, *apptd* 1987; Bishop's House, Eastgate, Lincoln LN2 1QQ. *Signs* Robert Lincoln

BISHOPS SUFFRAGAN

*Grantham*, Rt. Revd Alastair L. J. Redfern, *cons.* 1997, *apptd* 1997; Fairacre, 234 Barrowby Road, Grantham, Lincs NG31 8NP
*Grimsby*, Rt. Revd David D. J. Rossdale, *cons.* 2000, *apptd* 2000; Bishop's House, Church Lane, Irby-upon-Humber, Grimsby DN37 7JR

DEAN

Very Revd Alexander F. Knight, *apptd* 1998

CANONS RESIDENTIARY

B. R. Davis, *apptd* 1977; A. J. Stokes, *apptd* 1992; V. White, *apptd* 1994

*Organist*, C. S. Walsh, FRCO, *apptd* 1988

ARCHDEACONS

*Lincoln*, Ven. A. Hawes, *apptd* 1995
*Lindsey*, Ven. Dr T. W. Ellis, *apptd* 2001
*Stow*, Ven. Dr T. W. Ellis, *apptd* 2001

*Chancellor*, Peter N. Collier, QC, *apptd* 1999
*Registrar and Legal Secretary*, D. M. Wellman
*Diocesan Secretary*, P. Hamlyn Williams, The Old Palace, Lincoln LN2 1PU. Tel: 01522-529241

## LIVERPOOL (York)

7TH BISHOP
Rt. Revd James Jones, *cons.* 1994, *apptd* 1998; Bishop's Lodge, Woolton Park, Liverpool L25 6DT. *Signs* James Liverpool

BISHOP SUFFRAGAN

*Warrington*, Rt. Revd David Jennings; 34 Central Avenue, Eccleston Park, Prescot, Merseyside L34 2QP

DEAN

Rt. Revd Dean Dr Rupert W. N. Hoare

CANONS RESIDENTIARY

D. J. Hutton, *apptd* 1983; M. C. Boyling, *apptd* 1994; N. T. Vincent, *apptd* 1995

*Organist*, Prof. I. Tracey, *apptd* 1980

ARCHDEACONS

*Liverpool*, Ven. R. L. Metcalf, *apptd* 1994
*Warrington*, Ven. C. D. S. Woodhouse, *apptd* 1981

*Chancellor*, R. G. Hamilton
*Registrar and Legal Secretary*, R. H. Arden
*Diocesan Secretary*, Mike Eastwood, Church House, 1 Hanover Street, Liverpool L1 3DW. Tel: 0151-709 9722

## MANCHESTER (York)

10TH BISHOP
Rt. Revd Christopher J. Mayfield, *cons.* 1985, *apptd* 1993; Bishopscourt, Bury New Road, Manchester M7 4LE. *Signs* Christopher Manchester

BISHOPS SUFFRAGAN

*Bolton*, Rt. Revd David K. Gillett, *cons.* 1999, *apptd* 1999; 4 Bishop's Lodge, Bolton Road, Hawkshaw, Bury BL8 4JN
*Hulme*, Rt. Revd Stephen R. Lowe, *cons.* 1999, *apptd.* 1999; 14 Moorgate Avenue, Withington, Manchester M20 1HE
*Middleton*, Rt. Revd Michael A. O. Lewis, *cons.* 1999, *apptd* 1999; The Hollies, Manchester Road, Rochdale OL11 3QY

DEAN

Very Revd Kenneth Riley, *apptd* 1993

CANONS RESIDENTIARY

J. R. Atherton, Ph.D., *apptd* 1984; P. Denby, *apptd* 1995

*Organist*, C. Stokes, *apptd* 1992

ARCHDEACONS

*Bolton*, Ven. L. M. Davies, *apptd* 1992
*Manchester*, Ven A. Wolstencroft, *apptd* 1998
*Rochdale*, Ven. A. Ballard, *apptd* 2000

## NEWCASTLE (York)

11TH BISHOP
Rt. Revd J. Martin Wharton, *cons.* 1992, *apptd* 1997; Bishop's House, 29 Moor Road South, Gosforth, Newcastle upon Tyne NE3 1PA. *Signs* Martin Newcastle

STIPENDIARY ASSISTANT BISHOP

Rt. Revd Paul Richardson, *cons.* 1987, *apptd* 1999

HON. ASSISTANT BISHOP

Rt. Revd K. E. Gill, *cons.* 1972, *apptd* 1998

PROVOST

Very Revd Nicholas G. Coulton, *apptd* 1990

CANONS RESIDENTIARY

P. R. Strange, *apptd* 1986; Ven. P. Elliott, *apptd* 1993; G. V. Miller, *apptd* 1999

*Organist*, T. G. Hone, FRCO, *apptd* 1987

ARCHDEACONS

*Lindisfarne*, Ven. R. Langley, *apptd* 2001
*Northumberland*, Ven. P. Elliott, *apptd* 1993

*Chancellor*, Prof. D. McClean, *apptd* 1998
*Registrar and Legal Secretary*, Mrs B. J. Lowdon
*Diocesan Secretary*, P. Davies, Church House, Grainger Park Road, Newcastle upon Tyne NE4 8SX. Tel: 0191-273 0120

## NORWICH (Canterbury)

71ST BISHOP
Rt. Revd Graham R. James, *cons.* 1993, *apptd* 2000; Bishop's House, Norwich NR3 1SB. *Signs* Graham Norvic

BISHOPS SUFFRAGAN

*Lynn*, Rt. Revd A. C. Foottit, *cons.* 1999, *apptd* 1999; The Old Vicarage, Castle Acre, King's Lynn, Norfolk PE32 2AA.
*Thetford*, Rt. Revd David J. Atkinson, *cons.* 2001, *apptd* 2001; Rectory Meadow, Bramerton, Norwich NR14 7DW

DEAN

Very Revd Stephen Platten, *apptd* 1995

CANONS RESIDENTIARY

J. M. Haselock, *apptd* 1998; Ven. C. J. Offer, *apptd* 1994; R. J. Hanmer, *apptd* 1994; M. Kitchener, *apptd* 1999

*Organist*, D. Dunnett, *apptd* 1996

ARCHDEACONS

*Lynn*, Ven. M. C. Gray, *apptd* 1999
*Norfolk*, Ven. A. M. Handley, *apptd* 1993
*Norwich*, Ven. C. J. Offer, *apptd* 1994

*Chancellor*, The Hon. Mr Justice Blofeld, *apptd* 1998
*Registrar and Legal Secretary*, J. W. F. Herring
*Diocesan Secretary*, D. Adeney, Diocesan House, 109 Dereham Road, Easton, Norwich, Norfolk NR9 5ES. Tel: 01603-880853

## OXFORD (Canterbury)

41ST BISHOP
Rt. Revd Richard D. Harries, *cons.* 1987, *apptd* 1987; Diocesan Church House, North Hinksey, Oxford OX2 0NB. *Signs* Richard Oxon

AREA BISHOPS
*Buckingham*, Rt. Revd Michael A. Hill *cons.* 1998, *apptd* 1998; 28 Church Street, Great Missenden, Bucks HP16 0AZ
*Dorchester*, Rt. Revd Colin Fletcher, *cons.* 2000, *apptd* 2000; 12 Sandy Lane, Yarnton, Oxon OX5 1PB
*Reading*, Rt. Revd Dominic Walker, *cons.* 1997, *apptd* 1997; Bishop's House, Tidmarsh Lane, Tidmarsh, Reading RG8 8HA

DEAN OF CHRIST CHURCH
Very Revd John H. Drury, *apptd* 1991

CANONS RESIDENTIARY
O. M. T. O'Donovan, D.Phil., *apptd* 1982; M. Parry, *apptd* 2001; J. S. K. Ward, *apptd* 1991; R. Jeffery, *apptd* 1996; Prof. J. Webster, *apptd* 1996; Prof. H. M. R. E. Mayr-Harting, *apptd* 1997; Ven. J. A. Morrison, *apptd* 1998; M. Parry, *apptd* 2001
*Organist*, S. Darlington, FRCO, *apptd* 1985

ARCHDEACONS
*Berkshire*, Ven. N. A. Russell, *apptd* 1998
*Buckingham*, Ven. D. Goldie, *apptd* 1998
*Oxford*, Ven. J. A. Morrison, *apptd* 1998

*Acting Chancellor*, Dr Frank Robson, *apptd* 2001
*Joint Registrars and Legal Secretaries*, Dr F. E. Robson and Revd. J. Rees
*Diocesan Secretary*, R. Pearce, Diocesan Church House, North Hinksey, Oxford OX2 0NB. Tel: 01865-208202

## PETERBOROUGH (Canterbury)

37TH BISHOP
Rt. Revd Ian P. M. Cundy, *cons.* 1992, *apptd* 1996; The Palace, Peterborough PE1 1YA. *Signs* Ian Petriburg

BISHOP SUFFRAGAN
*Brixworth*, Rt. Revd Paul E. Barber, *cons.* 1989, *apptd* 1989; 4 The Avenue, Dallington, Northampton NN1 4RZ

DEAN
Very Revd Michael Bunker, *apptd* 1992

CANONS RESIDENTIARY
T. R. Christie, *apptd* 1980; J. Higham, *apptd* 1983; D. Painter, *apptd* 2000; W. S. Croft, *apptd* 2001
*Organist*, C. S. Gower, FRCO, *apptd* 1977

ARCHDEACONS
*Northampton*, Ven. M. R. Chapman, *apptd* 1991
*Oakham*, Ven. D. Painter, *apptd* 2000

*Chancellor*, T. A. C. Coningsby, QC, *apptd* 1989
*Registrar and Legal Secretary*, R. Hemingray
*Diocesan Secretary*, R. L. Pestell, The Palace, Peterborough, Cambs PE1 1YB. Tel: 01733-887000

## PORTSMOUTH (Canterbury)

8TH BISHOP
Rt. Revd Dr Kenneth W. Stevenson, *cons.* 1995, *apptd* 1995; Bishopsgrove, 26 Osborn Road, Fareham, Hants PO16 7DQ. *Signs* Kenneth Portsmouth

DEAN
The Very Revd Dr William H. Taylor, *apptd* 2000; The Deanery, 13 Pembroke Road, Portsmouth PO1 2NS.

CANONS RESIDENTIARY
D. T. Isaac, *apptd* 1990; G. Kirk, *apptd* 1998
*Organist*, D. J. C. Price, *apptd* 1996

ARCHDEACONS
*Isle of Wight*, Ven. K. M. L. H. Banting, *apptd* 1996
*Portsdown*, Ven. C. Lowson, *apptd* 1999
*The Meon*, Ven. P. Hancock, *apptd* 1999

*Chancellor*, His Hon. Judge Aglionby, *apptd* 1978
*Registrar and Legal Secretary*, Miss H. A. G. Tyler
*Diocesan Secretary*, M. F. Jordan, Cathedral House, St Thomas's Street, Portsmouth, Hants PO1 2HA. Tel: 023-9282 5731

## RIPON AND LEEDS (York)

12TH BISHOP
Rt. Revd John R. Packer, *apptd* 2000; Bishop Mount, Ripon HG4 5DP. *Signs* John Ripon and Leeds

BISHOP SUFFRAGAN
*Knaresborough*, Rt. Revd Frank V. Weston, *cons.* 1997, *apptd* 1997; 16 Shaftesbury Avenue, Roundhay, Leeds LS8 1DT

DEAN
Very Revd John Methuen, *apptd* 1995

CANONS RESIDENTIARY
M. R. Glanville-Smith, *apptd* 1990; K. Punshon, *apptd* 1996
*Organist*, K. Beaumont, FRCO, *apptd* 1994

ARCHDEACONS
*Leeds*, Ven. J. M. Oliver, *apptd* 1992
*Richmond*, Ven. K. Good, *apptd* 1993
*Chancellor*, His Hon. Judge Grenfell, *apptd* 1992
*Registrars and Legal Secretaries*, C. T. Tunnard, Mrs N. Harding
*Diocesan Secretary*, P. M. Arundel, Diocesan Office, St Mary's Street, Leeds LS9 7DP. Tel: 0113-248 7487

## ROCHESTER (Canterbury)

106TH BISHOP
Rt. Revd Dr Michael Nazir-Ali, *cons.* 1984, *apptd* 1994; Bishopscourt, Rochester ME1 1TS. *Signs* Michael Roffen

BISHOP SUFFRAGAN
*Tonbridge*, Rt. Revd Brian A. Smith, *cons.* 1993, *apptd* 1993; Bishop's Lodge, 48 St Botolph's Road, Sevenoaks TN13 3AG

DEAN
Very Revd Edward F. Shotter, *apptd* 1990

CANONS RESIDENTIARY

C. J. Meyrick, *apptd* 1998; Ven. P. Lock, *apptd* 2000

*Organist*, R. Sayer, FRCO, *apptd* 1995

ARCHDEACONS

*Bromley*, Ven. G. Norman, *apptd* 1994
*Rochester*, Ven. P. Lock, *apptd* 2000
*Tonbridge*, Ven. Judith Rose, *apptd* 1996

*Chancellor*, His Hon. Judge Goodman, *apptd* 1971
*Registrar and Legal Secretary*, M. Thatcher
*Diocesan Secretary*, Mrs L. Gilbert, St Nicholas Church, Boley Hill, Rochester ME1 1SL. Tel: 01634-830333

## ST ALBANS (Canterbury)

9TH BISHOP
Rt. Revd Christopher W. Herbert, *cons.* 1995, *apptd* 1995; Abbey Gate House, St Albans AL3 4HD. *Signs* Christopher St Albans

BISHOPS SUFFRAGAN

*Bedford*, Rt. Revd John H. Richardson, *cons.* 1994, *apptd* 1994; 168 Kimbolton Road, Bedford MK41 8DN
*Hertford*, Rt. Revd Christopher R. J. Foster, *cons.* 2001, *apptd* 2001; Hertford House, Abbey Mill Lane, St Albans AL3 4HE

DEAN

Very Revd Christopher Lewis, *apptd* 1993

CANONS RESIDENTIARY

M. Sansom, *apptd* 1988; A. K. Bergquist, *apptd* 1997; I. R. Lane, *apptd* 2000

*Organist*, A. Lucas, *apptd* 1998

ARCHDEACONS

*Bedford*, Ven. M. L. Lesiter, *apptd* 1993
*Hertford*, Ven. T. P. Jones, *apptd* 1997
*St Albans*, Ven. R. I. Cheetham, *apptd* 1999

*Chancellor*, His Hon. Judge Bursell, QC, *apptd* 1992
*Registrar and Legal Secretary*, D. N. Cheetham
*Diocesan Secretary*, S. Pope, Holywell Lodge, 41 Holywell Hill, St Albans AL1 1HE. Tel: 01727-854532

## ST EDMUNDSBURY AND IPSWICH (Canterbury)

9TH BISHOP
Rt. Revd J. H. Richard Lewis, *cons.* 1992, *apptd* 1997; Bishop's House, 4 Park Road, Ipswich IP1 3ST. *Signs* Richard St Edmundsbury and Ipswich

BISHOP SUFFRAGAN

*Dunwich*, Rt. Revd Clive Young, *cons.* 1999, *apptd* 1999; 28 Westerfield Road, Ipswich IP4 2UJ

DEAN

Very Revd J. Atwell, *apptd* 1995

CANONS RESIDENTIARY

A. M. Shaw, *apptd* 1989; M. E. Mingins, *apptd* 1993

*Organist*, J. Thomas, *apptd* 1997

ARCHDEACONS

*Ipswich*, Ven. T. A. Gibson, *apptd* 1987
*Sudbury*, Ven. J. Cox, *apptd* 1995
*Suffolk*, Ven. G. Arrand, *apptd* 1994

*Chancellor*, The Hon. Mr Justice Blofeld, *apptd* 1974
*Registrar and Legal Secretary*, J. Hall
*Diocesan Secretary*, N. Edgell, Churchgates House, Cutler Street, Ipswich IP1 1QU. Tel: 01473-298500

## SALISBURY (Canterbury)

77TH BISHOP
Rt. Revd David S. Stancliffe, *cons.* 1993, *apptd* 1993; South Canonry, The Close, Salisbury SP1 2ER. *Signs* David Sarum

BISHOPS SUFFRAGAN

*Ramsbury*, Rt. Revd Peter F. Hullah, *cons.* 1999, *apptd* 1999
*Sherborne*, vacant

DEAN

Very Revd Derek Watson, *apptd* 1996

CANONS RESIDENTIARY

D. J. C. Davies, *apptd* 1985; D. M. K. Durston, *apptd* 1992; June Osborne, *apptd* 1995

*Organist*, S. R. A. Lole, *apptd* 1997

ARCHDEACONS

*Dorset*, Ven. A. J. Magowan, *apptd* 2000
*Sherborne*, Ven. P. C. Wheatley, *apptd* 1991
*Wilts*, Ven. B. J. Hopkinson, *apptd* 1986 (Sarum), 1998 (Wilts)

*Chancellor*, His Hon. Judge Wiggs, *apptd* 1997
*Registrar and Legal Secretary*, A. Johnson
*Diocesan Secretary*, Revd Karen Curnock, Church House, Crane Street, Salisbury SP1 2QB. Tel: 01722-411922

## SHEFFIELD (York)

6TH BISHOP
Rt. Revd John (Jack) Nicholls, *cons.* 1990, *apptd* 1997; Bishopscroft, Snaithing Lane, Sheffield S10 3LG. *Signs* Jack Sheffield

BISHOP SUFFRAGAN

*Doncaster*, Rt. Revd Cyril Guy Ashton, *cons.* 2000, *apptd* 2000; Bishop's House, 3 Farrington Court, Wickersley, Rotherham S66 1JQ

DEAN

Very Revd Michael Sadgrove, *apptd* 1995

CANONS RESIDENTIARY

C. M. Smith, *apptd* 1991; Jane E. M. Sinclair, *apptd* 1993; Ven. R. F. Blackburn, *apptd* 1999

*Master of Music*, N. Taylor, *apptd* 1997

ARCHDEACONS

*Doncaster*, Ven. R. A. Fitzharris, *apptd* 2001
*Sheffield*, Ven. R. F. Blackburn, *apptd* 1999

*Chancellor*, Prof. J. D. McClean, *apptd* 1992
*Registrar and Legal Secretary*, Mrs M. Myers
*Diocesan Secretary*, C. A. Beck, FCIS, Diocesan Church House, 95–99 Effingham Street, Rotherham S65 1BL. Tel: 01709-511116

## SODOR AND MAN (York)

79TH BISHOP
Rt. Revd Noel D. Jones, CB, *cons.* 1989, *apptd* 1989; The Bishop's House, Quarterbridge Road, Douglas, Isle of Man IM2 3RF. *Signs* Noel Sodor and Man

CANONS
B. H. Kelly, *apptd* 1980; F. H. Bird, *apptd* 1993; D. Whitworth, *apptd* 1996; M. Convery, *apptd* 1999

ARCHDEACON
*Isle of Man*, Ven. B. H. Partington, *apptd* 1996

*Vicar-General and Chancellor*, Ms C. Faulds
*Registrar and Legal Secretary*, C. J. Callow
*Diocesan Secretary*, Mrs C. Roberts, Holly Cottage, Ballaughton Meadows, Douglas, Isle of Man IM2 1JG. Tel: 01624-626994

## SOUTHWARK (Canterbury)

9TH BISHOP
Rt. Revd Thomas F. Butler, *cons.* 1985, *apptd* 1998; Bishop's House, 38 Tooting Bec Gardens, London SW16 1QZ. *Signs* Thomas Southwark

AREA BISHOPS
*Croydon*, Rt. Revd Dr Wilfred D. Wood, DD, *cons.* 1985, *apptd* 1985; St Matthew's House, George Street, Croydon CR0 1PE
*Kingston upon Thames*, Rt. Revd Peter B. Price, *cons.* 1997, *apptd* 1998; *Kingston Episcopal Area Office*, Whitelands College, West Hill, London SW15 3SN
*Woolwich*, Rt. Revd Colin O. Buchanan, *cons.* 1985, *apptd* 1996; 37 South Road, Forest Hill, London SE23 2UJ

DEAN
Very Revd Colin B. Slee, *apptd* 1994

CANONS RESIDENTIARY
Helen Cunliffe, *apptd* 1995; J. John, *apptd* 1997; B. Saunders, *apptd* 1997; A. P. Nunn, *apptd* 1999; S. Roberts, *apptd* 2000

*Organist*, P. Wright, FRCO, *apptd* 1989

ARCHDEACONS
*Croydon*, Ven. V. A. Davies, *apptd* 1994
*Lambeth*, Ven. N. Baines, *apptd* 2000
*Lewisham*, Ven. Christine H. Ardman, *apptd* 2001
*Reigate*, Ven. Daniel Kajumba, *apptd* 2001
*Southwark*, Ven. D. L. Bartles-Smith, *apptd* 1985
*Wandsworth*, Ven. D. Gerrard, *apptd* 1989

*Chancellor*, C. George, QC
*Registrar and Legal Secretary*, P. Morris
*Diocesan Secretary*, S. Parton, Trinity House, 4 Chapel Court, Borough High Street, London SE1 1HW. Tel: 020-7403 8686

## SOUTHWELL (York)

10TH BISHOP
Rt. Revd George H. Cassidy, *cons.* 1999, *apptd* 1999; Bishop's Manor, Southwell NG25 0JR. *Signs* George Southwell

BISHOP SUFFRAGAN
*Sherwood*, Rt. Revd Alan W. Morgan, *cons.* 1989, *apptd* 1989; Dunham House, Westgate, Southwell, Notts NG25 0JL

DEAN
Very Revd David Leaning, *apptd* 1991

CANONS RESIDENTIARY
I. G. Collins, *apptd* 1985; G. A. Hendy *apptd* 1997; R. H. Davey, *apptd* 1999

*Organist*, P. Hale, *apptd* 1989

ARCHDEACONS
*Newark*, Ven. N. Peyton, *apptd* 1999
*Nottingham*, Ven. G. Ogilvie, *apptd* 1996

*Chancellor*, J. Shand, *apptd* 1981
*Registrar and Legal Secretary*, C. C. Hodson
*Diocesan Secretary*, P. Prentis, Dunham House, Westgate, Southwell, Notts NG25 0JL. Tel: 01636-814331

## TRURO (Canterbury)

14TH BISHOP
Rt. Revd William Ind, *cons.* 1987, *apptd* 1997; Lis Escop, Truro TR3 6QQ. *Signs* William Truro

BISHOP SUFFRAGAN
*St Germans*, Revd Royden Screech, *cons.* 2000, *apptd* 2000

DEAN
Very Revd Michael A. Moxon, LVO, *apptd* 1998

CANONS RESIDENTIARY
P. R. Gay, *apptd* 1994; K. P. Mellor, *apptd* 1994; P. A. A. Walker, *apptd* 2001

*Organist*, A. Nethsingha, FRCO, *apptd* 1994

ARCHDEACONS
*Cornwall*, Ven. R. D. C. Whiteman, *apptd* 2000
*Bodmin*, Ven. C. Cohen, *apptd* 2000

*Chancellor*, T. Briden, *apptd* 1998
*Registrar and Legal Secretary*, M. J. Follett
*Diocesan Secretary*, B. C. Laite, Diocesan House, Kenwyn, Truro TR1 1UQ. Tel: 01872-274351

## WAKEFIELD (York)

11TH BISHOP
Rt. Revd Nigel S. McCulloch, *cons.* 1986, *apptd* 1992; Bishop's Lodge, Woodthorpe Lane, Wakefield WF2 6JL. *Signs* Nigel Wakefield

BISHOP SUFFRAGAN
*Pontefract*, Rt. Revd David C. James, *cons.* 1998, *apptd* 1998; Pontefract House, 181A Manygates Lane, Wakefield WF2 7DR

DEAN
Very Revd George P. Nairn-Briggs, *apptd* 1997

CANONS RESIDENTIARY
R. Capper, *apptd* 1997; R. Gage, *apptd* 1997; I. Gaskell, *apptd* 1998; J. Holmes, *apptd* 1998

*Organist*, J. Bielby, FRCO, *apptd* 1972

ARCHDEACONS

*Halifax*, Ven. R. Inwood, *apptd* 1995
*Pontefract*, Ven. A. Robinson, *apptd* 1997

*Chancellor*, P. Collier, QC, *apptd* 1992
*Registrar and Legal Secretary*, L. Box
*Diocesan Secretary*, A. W. Ellis, Church House, 1 South Parade, Wakefield WF1 1LP. Tel: 01924-371802

## WORCESTER (Canterbury)

112TH BISHOP

Rt. Revd Dr Peter S. M. Selby, *cons.* 1984, *apptd* 1997; The Bishop's House, Hartlebury Castle, Kidderminster DY11 7XX. *Signs* Peter Wigorn

AREA BISHOP

*Dudley*, Rt. Revd David S. Waker, *cons.* 2000, *apptd* 2000; The Bishop's House, Bishop's Walk, Cradley Heath B64 7JF

DEAN

Very Revd Peter J. Marshall, *apptd* 1997

CANONS RESIDENTIARY

B. B. Ruddock, *apptd.* 1999; J. D. Tetley, *apptd* 1999
*Organist*, A. Lucas, *apptd* 1996

ARCHDEACONS

*Dudley*, Ven. F. M. Trethewey, *apptd* 2001
*Worcester*, Ven. Dr J. D. Tetley

*Chancellor*, C. Mynors, *apptd* 1999
*Registrar and Legal Secretary*, M. Huskinson
*Diocesan Secretary*, R. Higham, The Old Palace, Deansway, Worcester WR1 2JE. Tel: 01905-20537

## ROYAL PECULIARS

### WESTMINSTER

*The Collegiate Church of St Peter*

*Dean*, Very Revd Dr A. W. Carr, *apptd* 1997
*Sub Dean and Archdeacon*, D. H. Hutt, *apptd* 1995
*Canons of Westminster*, D. H. Hutt, *apptd* 1995; M. J. Middleton, *apptd* 1997; R. Wright, *apptd* 1998; Dr N. T. Wright, *apptd* 1999
*Chapter Clerk and Receiver-General*, Maj.-Gen. D. Burden, CB, CBE, *apptd* 199, Chapter Office, 20 Dean's Yard, London SW1P 3PA
*Organist*, J. O'Donnell, *apptd* 1999
*Registrar*, S. J. Holmes, MVO
*Legal Secretary*, C. Vyse, *apptd* 2000

### WINDSOR

*The Queen's Free Chapel of St George within Her Castle of Windsor*

*Dean*, Rt. Revd D. J. Conner, *apptd* 1998
*Canons Residentiary*, J. A. White, *apptd* 1982; L. F. P. Gunner, *apptd* 1996; B. P. Thompson, Ph.D., *apptd* 1998; J. A. Ovenden, *apptd* 1998
*Chapter Clerk*, Lt.-Col. N. J. Newman, *apptd* 1990, Chapter Office, The Cloisters, Windsor Castle, Windsor, Berks SL4 1NJ
*Organist*, J. Rees-Williams, FRCO, *apptd* 1991

# Other Anglican Churches

## THE CHURCH IN WALES

The Anglican Church was the established church in Wales from the 16th century until 1920, when the estrangement of the majority of Welsh people from Anglicanism resulted in disestablishment. Since then the Church in Wales has been an autonomous province consisting of six sees. The bishops are elected by an electoral college comprising elected lay and clerical members, who also elect one of the diocesan bishops as Archbishop of Wales.

The legislative body of the Church in Wales is the Governing Body, which has 365 members divided between the three orders of bishops, clergy and laity. Its President is the Archbishop of Wales and it meets twice annually. Its decisions are binding upon all members of the Church. The Church's property and finances are the responsibility of the Representative Body. There are about 96,000 members of the Church in Wales, with about 700 stipendiary clergy and 1,142 parishes.

THE GOVERNING BODY OF THE CHURCH IN WALES, 39 Cathedral Road, Cardiff CF1 9XF. Tel: 029-2023 1638. *Secretary-General*, J. W. D. McIntyre

10TH ARCHBISHOP OF WALES, Most Revd Dr Rowan D. Williams, *elected* 1999, installed 2000

BISHOPS

*Bangor* (79*th*), Rt. Revd F. J. Saunders Davies, *b.* 1937, *cons.* 2000, *elected* 1999; Ty'r Esgob, Bangor, Gwynedd LL57 2SS. *Signs* Saunders Bangor, *Stipendiary clergy*, 60
*Llandaff* (102nd), Rt. Revd Dr Barry C. Morgan, *b.* 1947, *cons.* 1993, *translated* 1999; Llys Esgob, The Cathedral Green, Llandaff, Cardiff CF5 2YE. *Signs* Barry Landav. *Stipendiary clergy*, 164
*Monmouth* (8*th*), Most Revd Dr Rowan D. Williams, *b.* 1950, *cons.* 1992, *elected* 1992; Bishopstow, Stow Hill, Newport NP20 4EA. *Signs* Rowan Cambrensis. *Stipendiary clergy*, 106
*St Asaph* (74*th*), Rt. Revd John S. Davies, *b.* 1943, *cons.* 1999, *elected* 1999; Esgobty, St Asaph, Denbighshire LL17 0TW. *Signs* John St Asaph. *Stipendiary clergy*, 112
*St David's* (126*th*), Rt. Revd D. Huw Jones, *b.* 1934, *cons.* 1993, *elected* 1995; Llys Esgob, Abergwili, Carmarthen SA31 2JG. *Signs* Huw St Davids. *Stipendiary clergy*, 124
*Swansea and Brecon* (8*th*), Rt. Revd Anthony E. Pierce, *b.* 1941, *cons.* 1999, *elected* 1999; Ely Tower, Brecon, Powys LD3 9DE. *Signs* Anthony Swansea *Stipendiary clergy*, 86

The stipend of a diocesan bishop of the Church in Wales is £26,674 a year from 1998

## THE SCOTTISH EPISCOPAL CHURCH

The Scottish Episcopal Church was founded after the Act of Settlement (1690) established the presbyterian nature of the Church of Scotland. The Scottish Episcopal Church is in full communion with the Church of England but is autonomous. The governing authority is the General Synod, an elected body of approximately 170 members which meets once a year. The diocesan bishop who convenes and presides at meetings of the General Synod is called the Primus and is elected by his fellow bishops.

There are 48,385 members of the Scottish Episcopal

Church, of whom 30,988 are communicants. There are seven bishops, 457 serving clergy, and 327 churches and places of worship.

THE GENERAL SYNOD OF THE SCOTTISH EPISCOPAL CHURCH, 21 Grosvenor Crescent, Edinburgh EH12 5EE. Tel: 0131-225 6357. *Secretary-General*, J. F. Stuart

PRIMUS OF THE SCOTTISH EPISCOPAL CHURCH, Most Revd A. Bruce Cameron (Bishop of Aberdeen and Orkney), *elected* 2000

BISHOPS

*Aberdeen and Orkney*, A. Bruce Cameron, *b.* 1941, *cons.* 1992, *elected* 1992. *Clergy*, 53
*Argyll and the Isles*, Douglas M. Cameron, *b.* 1935, *cons.* 1993, *elected* 1992. *Clergy*, 24
*Brechin*, Neville Chamberlain, *b.* 1939, *cons.* 1997, *elected* 1997. *Clergy*, 30
*Edinburgh*, Brian Smith, *b.* 1943, *cons.* 1993, *elected* 2001. *Clergy*, 143
*Glasgow and Galloway*, Idris Jones, *b.* 1943, *cons.* 1998, *elected* 1998. *Clergy*, 105
*Moray, Ross and Caithness*, John Crook, *b.* 1940, *cons.* 1999, *elected* 1999. *Clergy*, 32
*St Andrews, Dunkeld and Dunblane*, Michael H. G. Henley, *b.* 1938, *cons.* 1995, *elected* 1995. *Clergy*, 70

The minimum stipend of a diocesan bishop of the Scottish Episcopal Church was £24,354 in 2001 (i.e. 1.5 × the minimum clergy stipend of £16,236)

## THE CHURCH OF IRELAND

The Anglican Church was the established church in Ireland from the 16th century but never secured the allegiance of a majority of the Irish and was disestablished in 1871. The Church of Ireland is divided into the provinces of Armagh and Dublin, each under an archbishop. The provinces are subdivided into 12 dioceses.

The legislative body is the General Synod, which has 660 members in total, divided between the House of Bishops and the House of Representatives. The Archbishop of Armagh is elected by the House of Bishops; other episcopal elections are made by an electoral college.

There are about 375,000 members of the Church of Ireland, with two archbishops, ten bishops, about 550 clergy and about 1,000 churches and places of worship.

CENTRAL OFFICE, Church of Ireland House, Church Avenue, Rathmines, Dublin 6. Tel: 00-353-1-4978422. *Chief Officer and Secretary of the Representative Church Body*, R. H. Sherwood; *Assistant Secretary of the General Synod*, V. F. Beatty

### PROVINCE OF ARMAGH

ARCHBISHOP OF ARMAGH AND PRIMATE OF ALL IRELAND, Most Revd Robert H. A. Eames, PH.D., *b.* 1937, *cons.* 1975, *trans.* 1986. *Clergy*, 51

BISHOPS

*Clogher*, Brian D. A. Hannon, *b.* 1936, *cons.* 1986, *apptd* 1986. *Clergy*, 32
*Connor*, James E. Moore, *b.* 1933, *cons.* 1995, *apptd* 1995. *Clergy*, 106
*Derry and Raphoe*, James Mehaffey, PH.D., *b.* 1931, *cons.* 1980, *apptd* 1980. *Clergy*, 50
*Down and Dromore*, Harold C. Miller, *b.* 1950, *cons.* 1997, *apptd* 1997. *Clergy*, 109
*Kilmore, Elphin and Ardagh*, Kenneth H. Clarke, *b.* 1949, *cons* 2001, *apptd* 2001. *Clergy*, 24
*Tuam, Killala and Achonry*, Richard C. A. Henderson, *b.* 1957, *cons.* 1998, *apptd* 1998. *Clergy*, 12

### PROVINCE OF DUBLIN

ARCHBISHOP OF DUBLIN, BISHOP OF GLENDALOUGH, AND PRIMATE OF IRELAND, Most Revd Walton N. F. Empey, *b.* 1934, *cons.* 1981, *trans.* 1985, 1996. *Clergy*, 90

BISHOPS

*Cashel and Ossory*, John R. W. Neill, *b.* 1945, *cons.* 1986, *trans.* 1997. *Clergy*, 37
*Cork, Cloyne and Ross*, W. Paul Colton, *b.* 1960, *cons.* 1999, *apptd* 1999. *Clergy*, 28
*Limerick and Killaloe*, Michael H. G. Mayes, *b.* 1941, *cons.* 1993, *apptd* 2000
*Meath and Kildare*, (Most Revd) Richard L. Clarke, PH.D., *b.* 1949, *cons.* 1996, *apptd* 1996. *Clergy*, 23

## OVERSEAS

### PRIMATES

PRIMATE AND PRESIDING BISHOP OF AOTEAROA, NEW ZEALAND AND POLYNESIA, Rt. Revd John Paterson (Bishop of Auckland), *cons.* 1995, *apptd* 1998
PRIMATE OF AUSTRALIA, Most Revd Peter Carnley (Archbishop of Perth), *cons.* 1981, *apptd* 2000
PRIMATE OF BRAZIL, Most Revd Glauco Soares de Lima (Bishop of São Paulo), *cons.* 1989, *apptd* 1994
ARCHBISHOP OF THE PROVINCE OF BURUNDI, Most Revd Samuel Ndayisenga (Bishop of Buye), *apptd* 1998
ARCHBISHOP AND PRIMATE OF CANADA, Most Revd Michael G. Peers, *cons.* 1977, *elected* 1986
ARCHBISHOP OF THE PROVINCE OF CENTRAL AFRICA, Most Revd Bernard A. Malango, *elected* 2000
PRIMATE OF THE CENTRAL REGION OF AMERICA, Most Revd Cornelius J. Wilson (Bishop of Costa Rica), *cons.* 1978, *apptd* 1998
ARCHBISHOP OF THE PROVINCE OF CONGO, Most Revd Patrice Byankya Njojo (Bishop of Boga), *cons.* 1980, *apptd* 1992
PRIMATE OF THE PROVINCE OF HONG KONG SHENG KUNG HUI, Most Revd Peter Kwong (Bishop of Hong Kong Island), *cons.*1981, *apptd* 1998
ARCHBISHOP OF THE PROVINCE OF THE INDIAN OCEAN, Most Revd Remi Rabenirina (Bishop of Antananarivo), *cons.* 1984, *apptd* 1995
PRESIDENT-BISHOP OF JERUSALEM AND THE MIDDLE EAST, Most Revd Iraj Mottahedeh, *apptd* 2000A
ARCHBISHOP OF THE PROVINCE OF KENYA, Most Revd Dr David M. Gitari (Bishop of Nairobi), *cons.* 1975, *apptd* 1996
ARCHBISHOP OF THE PROVINCE OF KOREA, Most Revd Paul Hwan Yoon (Bishop of Taejon), *cons.* 1987, *apptd* 2000
ARCHBISHOP OF THE PROVINCE OF MELANESIA, Most Revd Ellison L. Pogo (Bishop of Central Melanesia), *cons.* 1981, *apptd* 1994
ARCHBISHOP OF MEXICO, Most Revd Samuel Espinoza (Bishop of Western Mexico), *cons.* 1981, *elected* 1995
ARCHBISHOP OF THE PROVINCE OF MYANMAR, Most Revd Samuel San Si Htay (Bishop of Yangon), *cons. apptd* 2001
ARCHBISHOP OF THE PROVINCE OF NIGERIA, Most Revd Peter Akinola (Bishop of Abuja), *cons.* 1989, *apptd* 2000
PRIMATE OF NIPPON SEI KO KAI, Rt. Revd John Jun'Ichiro Furumoto (Bishop of Kobe), *elected* 2000
ARCHBISHOP OF PAPUA NEW GUINEA, Most Revd James Ayong (Bishop of Aipo Rongo), *cons.* 1995, *elected* 1996

PRIME BISHOP OF THE PHILIPPINES, Most Revd Ignacio C. Soliba, *cons.* 1991, *apptd* 1997
ARCHBISHOP OF THE PROVINCE OF RWANDA, Most Revd Emmanuel Kolini Mboni (Bishop of Kigali), *cons.* 1980, *apptd* 1997
PRIMATE OF THE PROVINCE OF SOUTH EAST ASIA, Most Revd Ping Chung Yong (Bishop of Sabah), *cons.* 1990 *apptd* 1999
METROPOLITAN OF THE PROVINCE OF SOUTHERN AFRICA, Most Revd Winston H. N. Ndungane (Archbishop of Cape Town), *cons.* 1991, *trans.* 1996
PRESIDING BISHOP OF THE SOUTHERN CONE OF AMERICA, Rt. Revd Maurice Sinclair (Bishop of Northern Argentina), *cons.* 1990
ARCHBISHOP OF THE PROVINCE OF THE SUDAN, Most Revd Joseph Marona (Bishop of Juba) *cons.* 1984, *apptd* 2000
ARCHBISHOP OF THE PROVINCE OF TANZANIA, Most Revd Donald L. Mtetemela (Bishop of Ruaha), *cons.* 1982, *apptd* 1998
ARCHBISHOP OF THE PROVINCE OF UGANDA, Most Revd Livingstone Mpalanyi-Nkoyoyo. *cons.* 1980
PRESIDING BISHOP AND PRIMATE OF THE USA, Most Revd Frank T. Griswold III, *cons.* 1985, *apptd* 1997
ARCHBISHOP OF THE PROVINCE OF WEST AFRICA, Most Revd Robert Okine (Bishop of Koforidua), *cons.* 1981, *apptd* 1993
ARCHBISHOP OF THE PROVINCE OF THE WEST INDIES, Most Revd Drexel Gomez (Bishop of Nassau and the Bahamas), *cons.* 1972, *apptd* 1998

## OTHER CHURCHES AND EXTRA-PROVINCIAL DIOCESES

ANGLICAN CHURCH OF BERMUDA, Rt. Revd Ewen Ratteray, *apptd* 1996
CHURCH OF CEYLON: This Church comes under the Metropolitical authority of the Archbishop of Canterbury.
Bishop of Colombo, Rt. Revd. Kenneth Michael James Fernando, *cons.* 1992
Bishop of Kurunagala, Rt. Revd Andrew O. Kumarage, *cons.* 1984
EPISCOPAL CHURCH OF CUBA, Rt. Revd Jorge Perera Hurtado, *apptd* 1995
LUSITANIAN CHURCH (*Portuguese Episcopal Church*), Rt. Revd Fernando da Luz Soares, *apptd* 1971
SPANISH REFORMED EPISCOPAL CHURCH, Rt. Revd Carlos Lozano Lopez, *apptd* 1995
EXTRA-PROVINCIAL TO PROVINCE IX OF THE EPISCOPAL CHURCH IN THE USA:
PUERTO RICO, Rt. Revd David Andres Alvarez-Velazquez, *cons.* 1987
VENEZUELA, Rt. Revd Orlando Guerrero, *cons.* 1995

## MODERATORS OF CHURCHES IN FULL COMMUNION WITH THE ANGLICAN COMMUNION

CHURCH OF NORTH INDIA, Most Revd Zechariah J. Terom (Bishop of Chotanagpur), *apptd*
CHURCH OF SOUTH INDIA, Most Revd Joseph Samuel (Bishop of East Kerala), *cons.* 1990, *apptd* 2000
CHURCH OF PAKISTAN, Rt. Revd Samuel Azariah, Bishop of Raiwind
CHURCH OF BANGLADESH, Rt. Revd Barnabas Mondal, *cons.* 1975, *apptd* 1975

# The Church of Scotland

The Church of Scotland is the established (i.e. national) church of Scotland. The Church is Reformed and evangelical in doctrine, and presbyterian in constitution, i.e. based on a hierarchy of councils of ministers and elders and, since 1990, of members of a diaconate. At local level the kirk session consists of the parish minister and ruling elders. At district level the presbyteries, of which there are 47, consist of all the ministers in the district, one ruling elder from each congregation, and those members of the diaconate who qualify for membership. The General Assembly is the supreme authority, and is presided over by a Moderator chosen annually by the Assembly. The Sovereign, if not present in person, is represented by a Lord High Commissioner who is appointed each year by the Crown.

The Church of Scotland has about 600,000 members, 1,200 ministers and 1,600 churches. There are about 100 ministers and other personnel working overseas.

*Lord High Commissioner* (2000), HRH The Prince of Wales
*Moderator of the General Assembly* (2001), The Rt. Revd John Miller
*Principal Clerk*, Revd F. A. J. Macdonald
*Depute Clerk*, Revd M. A. MacLean
*Procurator*, P. S. Hodge
*Law Agent and Solicitor of the Church*, Mrs J. S. Wilson
*Parliamentary Agent*, I. McCulloch (*London*)
*General Treasurer*, D. F. Ross
*Secretary, Church and Nation Committee*, Revd Dr D. Sinclair
CHURCH OFFICE, 121 George Street, Edinburgh EH2 4YN. Tel: 0131-225 5722

PRESBYTERIES AND CLERKS

*Edinburgh*, Revd W. P. Graham
*West Lothian*, Revd D. Shaw
*Lothian*, J. D. McCulloch
*Melrose and Peebles*, Revd J. H. Brown
*Duns*, Revd J. S. H. Cutler
*Jedburgh*, Revd A. D. Reid
*Annandale and Eskdale*, Revd C. B. Haston
*Dumfries and Kirkcudbright*, Revd G. M. A. Savage
*Wigtown and Stranraer*, Revd D. W. Dutton
*Ayr*, Revd J. Crichton
*Irvine and Kilmarnock*, Revd R. Travers (acting)
*Ardrossan*, Revd D. Broster
*Lanark*, Revd G. J. Elliott
*Paisley*, Revd D. Kay
*Greenock*, Revd D. Mill
*Glasgow*, Revd A. Cunningham
*Hamilton*, Revd J. H. Wilson
*Dumbarton*, Revd D. P. Munro
*South Argyll*, Revd M. A. J. Gossip
*Dunoon*, Revd R. Samuel
*Lorn and Mull*, Revd J. A. McCormick
*Falkirk*, Revd I. W. Black
*Stirling*, Revd G. G. Gringles
*Dunfermline*, Revd W. E. Farquhar
*Kirkcaldy*, Revd B. L. Tomlinson
*St Andrews*, Revd P. Meager
*Dunkeld and Meigle*, Revd B. Dempsey
*Perth*, Revd D. G. Lawson
*Dundee*, Revd J. A. Roy
*Angus*, Revd M. I. G. Rooney
*Aberdeen*, Revd A. M. Douglas

*Kincardine and Deeside*, Revd J. W. S. Brown
*Gordon*, Revd E. Glen
*Buchan*, Revd R. Neilson
*Moray*, Revd G. Melvyn Wood
*Abernethy*, Revd J. A. I. MacEwan
*Inverness*, Revd A. S. Younger
*Lochaber*, Revd A. Ramsay
*Ross*, Revd T. M. McWilliam
*Sutherland*, Revd J. L. Goskirk
*Caithness*, Mrs M. Gillies, MBE
*Lochcarron/Skye*, Revd A. I. Macarthur
*Uist*, Revd M. Smith
*Lewis*, Revd T. S. Sinclair
*Orkney (Finstown)*, Revd T. Hunt
*Shetland (Lerwick)*, Revd C. H. M.Greig
*England (London)*, Revd W. A. Cairns
*Europe (Geneva)*, Revd J. A. Cowie

The minimum stipend of a minister in the Church of Scotland in 2001 was £18,016

# The Roman Catholic Church

The Roman Catholic Church is one world-wide Christian Church acknowledging as its head the Bishop of Rome, known as the Pope (Father). The Pope is held to be the successor of St Peter and thus invested with the power which was entrusted to St Peter by Jesus Christ. A direct line of succession is therefore claimed from the earliest Christian communities. With the fall of the Roman Empire the Pope also became an important political leader. His temporal power is now limited to the 107 acres of the Vatican City State.

The Pope exercises spiritual authority over the Church with the advice and assistance of the Sacred College of Cardinals, the supreme council of the Church. He is also advised about the concerns of the Church locally by his ambassadors, who liaise with the Bishops' Conference in each country.

In addition to advising the Pope, those members of the Sacred College of Cardinals who are under the age of 80 also elect a successor following the death of a Pope. The assembly of the Cardinals at the Vatican for the election of a new Pope is known as the Conclave in which, in complete seclusion, the Cardinals elect by a secret ballot; a two-thirds majority is necessary before the vote can be accepted as final. When a Cardinal receives the necessary votes, the Dean of the Sacred College formally asks him if he will accept election and the name by which he wishes to be known. On his acceptance of the office the Conclave is dissolved and the First Cardinal Deacon announces the election to the assembled crowd in St Peter's Square. On the first Sunday or Holyday following the election, the new Pope assumes the pontificate at High Mass in St Peter's Square. A new pontificate is dated from the assumption of the pontificate.

The number of cardinals was fixed at 70 by Pope Sixtus V in 1586, but has been steadily increased since the pontificate of John XXIII and at the end of July 2001 stood at 189, plus two cardinals created 'in pectore' (their names being kept secret by the Pope for fear of persecution; they are thought to be Chinese).

The Roman Catholic Church universally and the Vatican City State are run by the Curia, which is made up of the Secretariat of State, the Sacred Council for the Public Affairs of the Church, and various congregations, secretariats and tribunals assisted by commissions and offices. The congregations are permanent commissions for conducting the affairs of the Church and are made up of cardinals, one of whom occupies the office of prefect. Below the Secretariat of State and the congregations are the secretariats and tribunals, all of which are headed by cardinals. (The Curial cardinals are analagous to ministers in charge of government departments.)

The Vatican State has its own diplomatic service, with representatives known as nuncios. Papal nuncios with full diplomatic recognition are given precedence over all other ambassadors to the country to which they are appointed; where precedence is not recognised the Papal representative is known as a pro-nuncio. Where the representation is only to the local churches and not to the government of a country, the Papal representative is known as an apostolic delegate. The Roman Catholic Church has an estimated 890.9 million adherents world-wide.

### Sovereign Pontiff

His Holiness Pope John Paul II (Karol Wojtyla), *born* Wadowice, Poland, 18 May 1920; *ordained priest* 1946; *appointed Archbishop* of Kraków 1964; *created Cardinal* 1967; *assumed pontificate* 16 October 1978

### Secretariat of State

*Secretary of State*, HE Cardinal Angelo Sodano
*First Section (General Affairs)*, HE Cardinal G. Re (Archbishop of Vescovio)
*Second Section (Relations with other states)*, Mgr J. L. Tauran (Archbishop of Telepte)

### Bishops' Conference

The Roman Catholic Church in England and Wales is governed by the Bishops' Conference, membership of which includes the Diocesan Bishops, the Apostolic Exarch of the Ukrainians, the Bishop of the Forces and the Auxiliary Bishops. The Conference is headed by the President (*HE Cardinal Cormac M. O'Connor*) and Vice-President (*Archbishop Kelly*). There are five departments, each with an episcopal chairman: the Department for Christian Life and Worship (the Bishop of Menevia), the Department for Mission and Unity (the Bishop of Portsmouth), the Department for Catholic Education and Formation (the Bishop of Leeds), the Department for Christian Responsibility and Citizenship (the Bishop of East Anglia), and the Department for International Affairs (the Bishop of Leeds).

The Bishops' Standing Committee, made up of all the Archbishops and the chairman of each of the above departments, has general responsibility for continuity and policy between the plenary sessions of the Conference. It prepares the Conference agenda and implements its decisions. It is serviced by a General Secretariat. There are also agencies and consultative bodies affiliated to the Conference.

The Bishops' Conference of Scotland had until recently as its president the late Cardinal Winning of Glasgow and is the permanently constituted assembly of the Bishops of Scotland. To promote its work, the Conference establishes various agencies which have an advisory function in relation to the Conference. The more important of these agencies are called Commissions and each one has a Bishop President who, with the other members of the Commissions, are appointed by the Conference.

The Irish Episcopal Conference has as its president Archbishop Brady of Armagh. Its membership comprises all the Archbishops and Bishops of Ireland and it appoints various Commissions to assist it in its work. There are three types of Commissions: (a) those made up of lay and clerical members chosen for their skills and experience, and staffed by full-time expert secretariats; (b) Commissions whose members are selected from existing institutions and whose services are supplied on a part-time basis; and (c) Commissions of Bishops only.

The Roman Catholic Church in Britain and Ireland has an estimated 8,992,000 members, 11 archbishops, 67 bishops, 11,260 priests, and 8,588 churches and chapels open to the public.

Bishops' Conferences secretariats:

ENGLAND AND WALES, 39 Eccleston Square, London SW1V 1PD. Tel: 020-7630 8220; Fax: 020-7630 5166; Email: secretariat@cbcew.org.uk; Web: www.catholic-ew.org.uk. *General Secretary*, The Revd Andrew Summersgill

SCOTLAND, 64 Aitken Street, Airdrie, Lanarkshire ML6 6LT. *General Secretary*, Mgr Henry Docherty

IRELAND, Iona, 65 Newry Road, Dundalk, Co. Louth. *Executive Secretaries*, Revd Aidan O'Boyle; The Rt. Revd William Lee (Bishop of Waterford and Lismore)

## GREAT BRITAIN

APOSTOLIC NUNCIO TO GREAT BRITAIN
The Most Revd Pablo Puente, 54 Parkside, London SW19 5NE. Tel: 020-8946 1410

## ENGLAND AND WALES

THE MOST REVD ARCHBISHOPS

*Westminster*, H. E. Cardinal Cormac Murphy-O'Connor, *cons.* 1977, *apptd* 2000
*Auxiliaries*, James J. O'Brien, *cons.* 1977; Patrick O'Donoghue, *cons.* 1993; Arthur Roche, *cons* 2001; George Stack, *cons* 2001
*Clergy*, 762
*Archbishop's Residence*, Archbishop's House, Ambrosden Avenue, London SW1P 1QJ. Tel: 020-7798 9033

*Birmingham*, Vincent Nichols, *cons.* 1992, *apptd* 2000
*Auxiliaries*, Philip Pargeter, *cons.* 1990
*Clergy*, 511
*Diocesan Curia*, Cathedral House, St Chad's Queensway, Birmingham B4 6EX. Tel: 0121-236 5535

*Cardiff*, John A. Ward, *cons.* 1980, *apptd* 1983 (*The Rt Revd Edwin Regan has been appointed at present as apostolic administrator whilst the Archbishop recovers from illness*)
*Clergy*, 126
*Diocesan Curia*, Archbishop's House, 41–43 Cathedral Road, Cardiff CF1 9HD. Tel: 029-2022 0411

*Liverpool*, Patrick Kelly, *cons.* 1984, *apptd* 1996
*Auxiliary*, Vincent Malone, *cons.* 1989
*Clergy*, 522
*Diocesan Curia*, Archdiocese of Liverpool, Centre for Evengelisation, Croxteth Drive, Sefton Park, Liverpool L17 1AA. Tel: 0151-522 1000

*Southwark*, Michael Bowen, *cons.* 1970, *apptd* 1977
*Auxiliaries*, John Hine, *cons.* 2001; Howard Tripp, *cons.* 1980; John Jukes, *cons.* 1980
*Clergy*, 518
*Diocesan Curia*, Archbishop's House, 150 St George's Road, London SE1 6HX. Tel: 020-7928 5592

THE RT. REVD BISHOPS

*Arundel and Brighton*, Kieran Conry, *cons.* 2001
*Clergy*, 274. *Diocesan Curia*, Bishop's House, The Upper Drive, Hove, E. Sussex BN3 6NE. Tel: 01273-506387

*Brentwood*, Thomas McMahon, *cons.* 1980, *apptd* 1980. *Clergy*, 175. *Bishop's Office*, Cathedral House, Ingrave Road, Brentwood, Essex CM15 8AT. Tel: 01277-232266

*Clifton*, Declan Lang, *cons.* 2001. *Clergy*, 254. *Diocesan Curia*, Egerton Road, Bishopston, Bristol BS7 8HU. Tel: 0117-983 3907

*East Anglia*, Peter Smith, *cons.* 1995, *apptd* 1995. *Clergy*, 164. *Diocesan Curia*, The White House, 21 Upgate, Poringland, Norwich NR14 7SH. Tel: 01508-492202

*Hallam*, John Rawsthorne, *cons.* 1981, *apptd* 1997. *Clergy*, 91. *Bishop's Residence*, 'Quarters', Carsick Hill Way, Sheffield S10 3LY. Tel: 0114-230 9101

*Hexham and Newcastle*, Michael Ambrose Griffiths, *cons.* 1992. *Clergy*, 261. *Diocesan Curia*, Bishop's House, East Denton Hall, 800 West Road, Newcastle upon Tyne NE5 2BJ. Tel: 0191-228 0003

*Lancaster*, Patrick O'Donoghue, *cons.* 2001
*Clergy*, 248. *Bishop's Residence*, Bishop's House, Cannon Hill, Lancaster LA1 5NG. Tel: 01524-32231

*Leeds*, David Konstant, *cons.* 1977, *apptd* 1985. *Clergy*, 254. *Diocesan Curia*, Hinsley Hall, 62 Headingley Lane, Leeds LS6 2BU. Tel: 0113-261 8000

*Menevia* (*Wales*), Mark Jabalé, *cons.* 2001. *Clergy*, 60. *Diocesan Curia*, 27 Convent Street, Greenhill, Swansea SA1 2BX. Tel: 01792-644017

*Middlesbrough*, John Crowley, *cons.* 1986, *apptd* 1992. *Clergy*, 182. *Diocesan Curia*, 50A The Avenue, Linthorpe, Middlesbrough, Cleveland TS5 6QT. Tel: 01642-850505

*Northampton*, Kevin McDonald, *cons.* 2001. *Clergy*, 159. *Diocesan Curia*, Bishop's House, Marriott Street, Northampton NN2 6AW. Tel: 01604-715635

*Nottingham*, Malcolm McMahon, *cons.* 2000. *Clergy*, 214. *Diocesan Curia*, Willson House, Derby Road, Nottingham NG1 5AW. Tel: 0115-953 9800

*Plymouth*, Christopher Budd, *cons.* 1986. *Clergy*, 170. *Diocesan Curia*, Bishop's House, 31 Wyndham Street West, Plymouth PL1 5RZ. Tel: 01752-224414

*Portsmouth*, F. Crispian Hollis, *cons.* 1987, *apptd* 1989. *Clergy*, 282. *Bishop's Residence*, Bishop's House, Edinburgh Road, Portsmouth, Hants PO1 3HG. Tel: 023-9282 0894

*Salford*, Terence J. Brain, *cons.* 1991, *apptd* 1997. *Clergy*, 380. *Diocesan Curia*, Cathedral House, 250 Chapel Street, Salford M3 5LL. Tel: 0161-834 9052

*Shrewsbury*, Brian Noble, *cons.* 1995, *apptd* 1995. *Clergy* 202. *Diocesan Curia*, 2 Park Road South, Prenton, Wirral CH43 4UX. Tel: 0151-652 9855

*Wrexham* (*Wales*), Edwin Regan, *apptd* 1994. *Clergy*, 83. *Diocesan Curia*, Bishop's House, Sontley Road, Wrexham, Clwyd LL13 7EW. Tel: 01978-262726

## SCOTLAND

THE MOST REVD ARCHBISHOPS

*St Andrews and Edinburgh*, Keith Patrick O'Brien, *cons.* 1985
*Clergy*, 188
*Diocesan Curia*, 113 Whitehouse Loan, Edinburgh EH9 1BD. Tel: 0131-452 8244

*Glasgow*, awaiting appointment
*Clergy*, 257
*Diocesan Curia*, 196 Clyde Street, Glasgow G1 4JY. Tel: 0141-226 5898

THE RT. REVD BISHOPS

*Aberdeen*, Mario Conti, *cons.* 1977. *Clergy*, 54. *Bishop's Residence*, 3 Queen's Cross, Aberdeen AB2 6BR. Tel: 01224-319154

*Argyll and the Isles*, Ian Murray, *cons.* 1999. *Clergy*, 33. *Diocesan Curia*, St Columba's Cathedral, Esplanade, Oban, Argyll PA34 5AB. Tel: 01631-571003

*Dunkeld*, Vincent Logan, *cons.* 1981. *Clergy*, 52. *Diocesan Curia*, 29 Roseangle, Dundee DD1 4LR. Tel: 01382-25453

*Galloway*, Maurice Taylor, *cons.* 1981. *Clergy*, 59. *Diocesan Curia*, 8 Corsehill Road, Ayr KA7 2ST. Tel: 01292-266750

*Motherwell*, Joseph Devine, *cons.* 1977, *apptd* 1983. *Clergy*, 163. *Diocesan Curia*, Coursington Road, Motherwell ML1 1PW. Tel: 01698-269114

*Paisley*, John A. Mone, *cons.* 1984, *apptd* 1988. *Clergy*, 87. *Diocesan Curia*, Cathedral House, 8 East Buchanan Street, Paisley, Renfrewshire PA1 1HS. Tel: 0141-889 3601

## BISHOPRIC OF THE FORCES

Francis Walmsley, *cons.* 1979. Administration: AGPDO, Middle Hill, Aldershot, Hants GU11 1PP. Tel: 01252-349004

## IRELAND

There is one hierarchy for the whole of Ireland. Several of the dioceses have territory partly in the Republic of Ireland and partly in Northern Ireland.

### Apostolic Nuncio to Ireland

Most Revd Giovanni Ceirano (titular Archbishop of Tigimma), 183 Navan Road, Dublin 7. Tel: (00 353) (1) 380577

### The Most Revd Archbishops

*Armagh*, Sean Brady, *cons.* 1995, *apptd* 1996
*Auxiliary*, Gerard Clifford, *cons.* 1991
*Clergy*, 183
*Diocesan Curia*, Ara Coeli, Armagh BT61 7QY. Tel: 028-3752 2045

*Cashel*, Dermot Clifford, *cons.* 1986, *apptd* 1988
*Clergy*, 136
*Archbishop's Residence*, Archbishop's House, Thurles, Co. Tipperary. Tel: (00 353) (504) 21512

*Dublin*, H. E. Cardinal Desmond Connell, *cons.* 1988, *apptd* 1988
*Auxiliaries*, James Moriarty, *cons.* 1991; Eamonn Walsh, *cons.* 1990; Fiachra O'Ceallaigh, *cons* 1994; Martin Drennan, *cons.* 1997; Raymond Field, *cons.* 1997
*Clergy*, 994
*Archbishop's Residence*, Archbishop's House, Drumcondra, Dublin 9. Tel: (00 353) (1) 8373732

*Tuam*, Michael Neary, *cons.* 1992, *apptd* 1995
*Clergy*, 180
*Archbishop's Residence*, Archbishop's House, Tuam, Co. Galway. Tel: (00 353) (93) 24166

### The Most Revd Bishops

*Achonry*, Thomas Flynn, *cons.* 1975. *Clergy*, 62. *Bishop's Residence*, Bishop's House, Ballaghadaderreen, Co. Roscommon. Tel: (00 353) (907) 60021

*Ardagh and Clonmacnois*, Colm O'Reilly, *cons.* 1983. *Clergy*, 100. *Diocesan Office*, Bishop's House, St Michael's, Longford, Co. Longford. Tel: (00 353) (43) 46432

*Clogher*, Joseph Duffy, *cons.* 1979. *Clergy*, 108. *Bishop's Residence*, Bishop's House, Monaghan. Tel: (00 353) (47) 81019

*Clonfert*, John Kirby, *cons.* 1988. *Clergy*, 71. *Bishop's Residence*, St Brendan's, Coorheen, Loughrea, Co. Galway. Tel: (00 353) (91) 41560

*Cloyne*, John Magee, *cons.* 1987. *Clergy*, 158. *Diocesan Centre*, Cobh, Co. Cork. Tel: (00 353) (21) 811430

*Cork and Ross*, John Buckley, *cons.* 1984, *apptd* 1998. *Clergy*, 338. *Diocesan Office*, Bishop's House, Redemption Road, Cork. Tel: (00 353) (21) 301717

*Derry*, Seamus Hegarty, *cons.* 1984, *apptd* 1994. *Clergy*, 157. *Bishop's Residence*, Bishop's House, St Eugene's Cathedral, Derry BT48 9AP. Tel: 028-7126 2302
*Auxiliary*, Francis Lagan, *cons.* 1988

*Down and Connor*, Patrick J. Walsh, *cons.* 1983, *apptd* 1991. *Clergy*, 248. *Bishop's Residence*, Lisbreen, 73 Somerton Road, Belfast, Co. Antrim BT15 4DE. Tel: 028-9077 6185
Auxiliaries, *Anthony Farquhar*, cons. *1983; Michael Dallat*, cons. *1994*

*Dromore*, John McAreavey, *cons.* 1999. *Clergy*, 78. *Bishop's Residence*, Bishop's House, Violet Hill, Newry, Co. Down BT35 6PN. Tel: 028-3026 2444

*Elphin*, Christopher Jones, *cons.* 1994. *Clergy*, 101. *Bishop's Residence*, St Mary's, Sligo. Tel: (00 353) (71) 62670

*Ferns*, Brendon Comiskey, *cons.* 1980. *Clergy*, 161. *Bishop's Office*, Bishop's House, Summerhill, Wexford. Tel: (00 353) (53) 22177

*Galway and Kilmacduagh*, James McLoughlin, *cons.* 1993. *Clergy*, 90. *Diocesan Office*, The Cathedral, Galway. Tel: (00 353) (91) 63566

*Kerry*, William Murphy, *cons.* 1995. *Clergy*, 149. *Bishop's Residence*, Bishop's House, Killarney, Co. Kerry. Tel: (00 353) (64) 31168

*Kildare and Leighlin*, Laurence Ryan, *cons.* 1984. *Clergy*, 136. *Bishop's Residence*, Bishop's House, Carlow. Tel: (00 353) (503) 31102

*Killala*, Thomas Finnegan, *cons.* 1970. *Clergy*, 62. *Bishop's Residence*, Bishop's House, Ballina, Co. Mayo. Tel: (00 353) (96) 21518

*Killaloe*, William Walsh, *cons.* 1994. *Clergy*, 149. *Bishop's Residence*, Westbourne, Ennis, Co. Clare. Tel: (00 353) (65) 28638

*Kilmore*, Leo O'Reilly, *cons.* 1972, *apptd* 2000. *Clergy*, 115. *Bishop's Residence*, Bishop's House, Cullies, Co. Cavan. Tel: (00 353) (49) 31496

*Limerick*, Donal Murray, *cons.* 1996. *Clergy*, 152. *Diocesan Offices*, 66 O'Connell Street, Limerick. Tel: (00 353) (61) 315856

*Meath*, Michael Smith, *cons.* 1984, *apptd* 1990. *Clergy*, 141. *Bishop's Residence*, Bishop's House, Dublin Road, Mullingar, Co. Westmeath. Tel: (00 353) (44) 48841

*Ossory*, Laurence Forristal, *cons.* 1980. *Clergy*, 111. *Bishop's Residence*, Sion House, Kilkenny. Tel: (00 353) (56) 62448

*Raphoe*, Philip Boyce, *cons.* 1995. *Clergy*, 96. *Bishop's Residence*, Ard Adhamhnáin, Letterkenny, Co. Donegal. Tel: (00 353) (74) 21208

*Waterford and Lismore*, William Lee, *cons.* 1993. *Clergy*, 130. *Bishop's Residence*, Woodleigh, Summerville Avenue, Waterford. Tel: (00 353) (51) 71432

## PATRIARCHS IN COMMUNION WITH THE ROMAN CATHOLIC CHURCH

*Alexandria*, HB Cardinal Stephanos II Ghattas (Patriarch for Catholic Copts)

*Antioch*, HB Ignace Antoine II Hayek (Patriarch for Syrian rite Catholics); HB Maximos V. Hakim (Patriarch for Greek Melekite rite Catholics); HE Cardinal Nasrallah Pierre Sfeir (Patriarch for Maronite rite Catholics)

*Jerusalem*, HB Michel Sabbah (Patriarch for Latin rite Catholics); HB Maximos V. Hakim (Patriarch for Greek Melekite rite Catholics)

*Babilonia of the Chaldeans*, HB Raphael I Bidawid

*Cilicia of the Armenians*, HB Jean Pierre XVIII Kasparian (Patriarch for Armenian rite Catholics)

*Oriental India*, Archbishop Raul Nicolau Gonsalves

*Lisbon*, vacant

*Venice*, HE Cardinal Marco Ce

# Other Churches in the UK

## AFRICAN AND AFRO-CARIBBEAN CHURCHES

There are more than 160 Christian churches or groups of African or Afro-Caribbean origin in the UK. These include the Apostolic Faith Church, the Cherubim and Seraphim Church, the New Testament Church Assembly, the New Testament Church of God, the Wesleyan Holiness Church and the Aladura Churches.

The Afro-West Indian United Council of Churches and the Council of African and Afro-Caribbean Churches UK (which was initiated as the Council of African and Allied Churches in 1979 to give one voice to the various Christian churches of African origin in the UK) are the media through which the member churches can work jointly to provide services they cannot easily provide individually.

There are about 70,000 adherents of African and Afro-Caribbean churches in the UK, and over 1,000 congregations. The Afro-West Indian United Council of Churches has about 30,000 individual members, 135 ministers and own over 100 places of worship. The Council of African and Afro-Caribbean Churches UK has about 17,000 members, 250 ministers and 125 congregations.

AFRO-WEST INDIAN UNITED COUNCIL OF CHURCHES, c/o New Testament Church of God, Arcadian Gardens, High Road, London N22 5AA. Tel: 020-8888 9427. *Secretary*, Bishop E. Brown

COUNCIL OF AFRICAN AND AFRO-CARIBBEAN CHURCHES UK, 31 Norton House, Sidney Road, London SW9 0UJ. Tel: 020-7274 5589; Fax: 020-7274 4726. *Chairman*, His Grace The Most Revd Father Olu A. Abiola

## ASSOCIATED PRESBYTERIAN CHURCHES OF SCOTLAND

The Associated Presbyterian Churches came into being in 1989 as a result of a division within the Free Presbyterian Church of Scotland. Following two controversial disciplinary cases, the culmination of deepening differences within the Church, a presbytery was formed calling itself the Associated Presbyterian Churches (APC). The Associated Presbyterian Churches has about 1,000 members, 15 ministers and 20 churches.

*Clerk of the Scottish Presbytery*, Revd A. N. McPhail, Fernhill, Polvinster Road, Oban PA34 5TN. Tel: 01631-567076

## THE BAPTIST CHURCH

Baptists trace their origins to John Smyth, who in 1609 in Amsterdam reinstituted the baptism of conscious believers as the basis of the fellowship of a gathered church. Members of Smyth's church established the first Baptist church in England in 1612. They came to be known as 'General' Baptists and their theology was Arminian, whereas a later group of Calvinists who adopted the baptism of believers came to be known as 'Particular' Baptists. The two sections of the Baptists were united into one body, the Baptist Union of Great Britain and Ireland, in 1891. In 1988 the title was changed to the Baptist Union of Great Britain.

Baptists emphasise the complete autonomy of the local church, although individual churches are linked in various kinds of associations. There are international bodies (such as the Baptist World Alliance) and national bodies, but some Baptist churches belong to neither. However, in Great Britain the majority of churches and associations belong to the Baptist Union of Great Britain. There are also Baptist Unions in Wales, Scotland and Ireland which are much smaller than the Baptist Union of Great Britain, and there is some overlap of membership.

There are over 40 million Baptist church members world-wide; in the Baptist Union of Great Britain there are 144,056 members, 1,756 pastors and 2,125 churches. In the Baptist Union of Scotland there are 14,463 members, 156 pastors and 171 churches. In the Baptist Union of Wales (Undeb Bedyddwyr Cymru) there are 19,850 members, 106 pastors and 498 churches. In the Association of Baptist Churches (formerly the Baptist Union of Ireland) there are 8,436 members, 94 pastors and 111 churches.

*President of the Baptist Union of Great Britain* (2001–2), Revd Peter Worley

*General Secretary*, Revd D. R. Coffey, Baptist House, PO Box 44, 129 Broadway, Didcot, Oxon OX11 8RT. Tel: 01235-517700; Email: baptistuniongb@baptist.org.uk; Web: www.baptist.org.uk

*President of the Baptist Union of Scotland* (2001-2) Revd John Greenshields

*General Secretary*, Revd William Slack, 14 Aytoun Road, Glasgow G41 5RT. Tel: 0141-423 6169; fax: 0141-424 1422; Email; admin@scottishbaptist.org.uk

*General Secretary of the Baptist Union of Wales*, Revd P. D. Richards, 94 Stryd Mansel, Swansea SA1 5TZ. Tel: 01792-655468

*General Secretary of the Association of Baptist Churches in Ireland*, Revd W. Colville, 117 Lisburn Road, Belfast BT9 7AF. Tel: 028-9066 3108

## THE CONGREGATIONAL FEDERATION

The Congregational Federation was founded by members of Congregational churches in England and Wales who did not join the United Reformed Church in 1972. There are also churches in Scotland, France and Australia affiliated to the Federation. The Federation exists to encourage congregations of believers to worship in free assembly, but it has no authority over them and emphasises their right to independence and self-government.

The Federation has 11,104 members, 71 recognised ministers and 313 churches in England, Wales and Scotland.

*President of the Federation* (2001–2), Revd Barry Osborne

*General Secretary*, Revd. M. Heaney, The Congregational Centre, 4–8 Castle Gate, Nottingham NG1 7AS. Tel: 0115-911 1460

## THE FREE CHURCH OF ENGLAND

The Free Church of England is a union of two bodies in the Anglican tradition, the Free Church of England, founded in 1844 as a protest against the Oxford Movement in the established Church, and the Reformed Episcopal Church, founded in America in 1873 but which also had congregations in England. As both Churches sought to maintain the historic faith, tradition and practice of the Anglican Church since the Reformation, they decided to unite as one body in England in 1927. The historic episcopate was conferred on the English Church in 1876 through the line of the American bishops, who had pioneered an open table Communion policy towards members of other denominations.

The Free Church of England has 1,400 members, 41 ministers and 25 churches in England. It also has three house churches and three ministers in New Zealand and one church and one minister in St Petersburg, Russia.

*General Secretary*, Revd R. E. Talbot, 32 Bonnywood Road, Hassocks, W. Sussex BN6 8HR. Tel: 01273-845092

## THE FREE CHURCH OF SCOTLAND

The Free Church of Scotland was formed in 1843 when over 400 ministers withdrew from the Church of Scotland as a result of interference in the internal affairs of the church by the civil authorities. In 1900, all but 26 ministers joined with others to form the United Free Church (most of which rejoined the Church of Scotland in 1929). In 1904 the remaining 26 ministers were recognised by the House of Lords as continuing the Free Church of Scotland.

The Church maintains strict adherence to the Westminster Confession of Faith (1648) and accepts the Bible as the sole rule of faith and conduct. Its General Assembly meets annually. It also has links with Reformed Churches overseas. The Free Church of Scotland has 4,600 communicating members, 90 ministers and 110 churches.

*General Treasurer*, I. D. Gill, The Mound, Edinburgh EH1 2LS. Tel: 0131-226 5286

## THE FREE PRESBYTERIAN CHURCH OF SCOTLAND

The Free Presbyterian Church of Scotland was formed in 1893 by two ministers of the Free Church of Scotland who refused to accept a Declaratory Act passed by the Free Church General Assembly in 1892. The Free Presbyterian Church of Scotland is Calvinistic in doctrine and emphasises observance of the Sabbath. It adheres strictly to the Westminster Confession of Faith of 1648.

The Church has about 3,000 members in Scotland and about 4,000 in overseas congregations. It has 19 ministers and 50 churches in the UK.

*Moderator*, Revd D. J. MacDonald, Free Presbyterian Manse, Evelix, Dornoch, Sutherland IV25 3RD. Tel: 01862-811 138

*Clerk of Synod*, Revd J. MacLeod, 16 Matheson Road, Stornoway, Isle of Lewis HS1 2LA. Tel: 01851-702755

## THE HOLY APOSTOLIC CATHOLIC ASSYRIAN CHURCH OF THE EAST

The Holy Apostolic Catholic Assyrian Church of the East traces its beginnings to the middle of the first century. It spread from Upper Mesopotamia throughout the territories of the Persian Empire. The Church is headed by the Catholicos Patriarch and is episcopal in government. The liturgical language is Syriac (Aramaic).

The Church numbers about 400,000 members in the Middle East, India, Europe, North America and Australasia. There are around 1,000 members in the UK

The Church in Great Britain forms part of the diocese of Europe under Mar Odisho Oraham.

*Representative in Great Britain*, Very Revd Younan Y. Younan, 66 Montague Road, London W7 3PQ. Tel: 020-8579 7259.

## THE INDEPENDENT METHODIST CHURCHES

The Independent Methodist Churches seceded from the Wesleyan Methodist Church in 1805 and remained independent when the Methodist Church in Great Britain was formed in 1932. They are mainly concentrated in the industrial areas of the north of England.

The churches are Methodist in doctrine but their organisation is congregational. All the churches are members of the Independent Methodist Connexion of Churches. The controlling body of the Connexion is the Annual Meeting, to which churches send delegates. The Connexional President is elected annually. Between annual meetings the affairs of the Connexion are handled by departmental committees. Ministers are appointed by the churches and trained through the Connexion. The ministry is open to both men and women and is unpaid.

There are 2,552 members, 108 ministers and 96 churches in Great Britain.

*Connexional President* (2001–2), C. Scholes

*General Secretary*, W. C. Gabb, 66 Kirkstone Drive, Loughborough LE11 3RW. Tel: 01942-223526

## THE LUTHERAN CHURCH

Lutheranism is based on the teachings of Martin Luther, the German leader of the Protestant Reformation. The authority of the scriptures is held to be supreme over Church tradition and creeds, and the key doctrine is that of justification by faith alone.

Lutheranism is one of the largest Protestant denominations and it is particularly strong in northern Europe and the USA. Some Lutheran churches are episcopal, while others have a synodal form of organisation; unity is based on doctrine rather than structure. Most Lutheran churches are members of the Lutheran World Federation, based in Geneva.

Lutheran services in Great Britain are held in seventeen languages to serve members of different nationalities. Services usually follow ancient liturgies. English-language congregations are members either of the Lutheran Church in Great Britain, or of the Evangelical Lutheran Church of England. The Lutheran Church in Great Britain and other Lutheran churches in Britain are members of the Lutheran Council of Great Britain, which represents them and co-ordinates their common work.

There are over 70 million Lutherans world-wide; in Great Britain there are about 100,000 members, 50 clergy and 100 congregations.

*General Secretary of the Lutheran Council of Great Britain*, Revd T. Bruch, 30 Thanet Street, London WC1H 9QH. Tel: 020-7554 2900; Fax 020-7383 3081; Email: enquiries@lutheran.org.uk Web: www.lutheran.org.uk

## THE METHODIST CHURCH

The Methodist movement started in England in 1729 when the Revd John Wesley, an Anglican priest, and his brother Charles met with others in Oxford and resolved to conduct their lives and study by 'rule and method'. In 1739 the Wesleys began evangelistic preaching and the first Methodist chapel was founded in Bristol in the same year. In 1744 the first annual conference was held, at which the Articles of Religion were drawn up. Doctrinal emphases included repentance, faith, the assurance of salvation, social concern and the priesthood of all believers. After John Wesley's death in 1791 the Methodists withdrew from the established Church to form the Methodist Church. Methodists gradually drifted into many groups, but in 1932 the Wesleyan Methodist Church, the United Methodist Church and the Primitive Methodist Church united to form the Methodist Church in Great Britain as it now exists.

The governing body and supreme authority of the Methodist Church is the Conference, but there are also 33 district synods, consisting of all the ministers and selected lay people in each district, and circuit meetings of the ministers and lay people of each circuit.

There are over 60 million Methodists world-wide; in Great Britain (1998 figures) there are 353,330 members, 3,727 ministers, 10,746 lay preachers and 6,452 churches.

*President of the Conference in Great Britain* (2001–2), Revd C. Le Moignan
*Vice-President of the Conference* (2001–2), A. Leck
*Secretary of the Conference*, Revd Dr N. T. Collinson, Methodist Church, Conference Office, 25 Marylebone Road, London NW1 5JR. Tel: 020-7486 5502; Fax: 020-7467 5226;
Email: conferenceoffice@methodistchurch.org.uk;
Web: www.methodist.org.uk

## THE METHODIST CHURCH IN IRELAND

The Methodist Church in Ireland is closely linked to British Methodism but is autonomous. It has a community roll of 55,701, 16,191 members, 200 ministers, 293 lay preachers and 222 churches.

*President of the Methodist Church in Ireland* (2001–2), Revd G. Harold Good, OBE, 49 Old Forge Manor, Belfast BT10 0HY. Tel: 028-9060 4200
*Secretary of the Methodist Church in Ireland*, Revd E. T. I. Mawhinney, 1 Fountainville Avenue, Belfast BT9 6AN. Tel: 028-9032 4554

# THE (EASTERN) ORTHODOX CHURCH

The Eastern (or Byzantine) Orthodox Church is a communion of self-governing Christian churches recognising the honorary primacy of the Oecumenical Patriarch of Constantinople.

The position of Orthodox Christians is that the faith was fully defined during the period of the Oecumenical Councils. In doctrine it is strongly trinitarian, and stresses the mystery and importance of the sacraments. It is episcopal in government. The structure of the Orthodox Christian year differs from that of western Churches.

Orthodox Christians throughout the world are estimated to number about 300 million.

### PATRIARCHS OF THE EASTERN ORTHODOX CHURCH

*Archbishop of Constantinople, New Rome and Oecumenical Patriarch*, Vartholomaeos, *elected* 1991
*Pope and Patriarch of Alexandria and All Africa*, Petros VII, *elected* 1997
*Patriarch of Antioch and All the East*, Ignatios IV, *elected* 1979
*Patriarch of Jerusalem and All Palestine*, vacant
*Patriarch of Moscow and All Russia*, Alexei II, *elected* 1990
*Archbishop of Pec, Metropolitan of Belgrade and Karlovci, Patriarch of Serbia*, Pavle, *elected* 1990
*Archbishop of Bucharest and Patriarch of Romania*, Teoctist, *elected* 1986
*Metropolitan of Sofia and Patriarch of Bulgaria*, Maxim, *elected* 1971
*Archbishop of Tbilisi and Mtskheta, Catholicos-Patriarch of All Georgia*, Ilia II, *elected* 1977

## HEADS OF AUTOCEPHALOUS ORTHODOX CHURCHES

*Archbishop of Cyprus*, Chrysostomos, *elected* 1977
*Archbishop of Athens and All Greece*, Christodoulos, *elected* 1998
*Metropolitan of Warsaw and All Poland*, Sawa, *elected* 1998
*Archbishop of Tirana and All Albania*, Anastas, *elected* 1992
*Archbishop of Prague and All the Czech Lands and Slovakia*, Nikolaj, *elected* 2000

## EASTERN ORTHODOX CHURCHES IN THE UK

### THE PATRIARCHATE OF ANTIOCH

There are ten parishes served by 14 clergy. In Great Britain the Patriarchate is represented by the Revd Fr Samir Gholam, St George's Cathedral, 1A Redhill Street, London NW1 4BG. Tel: 020-7383 0403.

### THE GREEK ORTHODOX CHURCH (PATRIARCHATE OF CONSTANTINOPLE)

The presence of Greek Orthodox Christians in Britain dates back at least to 1677 when Archbishop Joseph Geogirenes of Samos fled from Turkish persecution and came to London. The present Greek cathedral in Moscow Road, Bayswater, was opened for public worship in 1879 and the Diocese of Thyateira and Great Britain was established in 1922. There are now 120 parishes and other communities (including monasteries) in the UK, served by seven bishops, 106 clergy, nine cathedrals and about 93 churches.

In Great Britain the Patriarchate of Constantinople is represented by Archbishop Gregorios of Thyateira and Great Britain, Thyateira House, 5 Craven Hill, London W2 3EN. Tel: 020-7723 4787; fax: 020-7224 9301.

### THE RUSSIAN ORTHODOX CHURCH (PATRIARCHATE OF MOSCOW) AND THE RUSSIAN ORTHODOX CHURCH OUTSIDE RUSSIA

The records of Russian Orthodox Church activities in Britain date from the visit to England of Tsar Peter I in the early 18th century. Clergy were sent from Russia to serve the chapel established to minister to the staff of the Imperial Russian Embassy in London.

In Great Britain the Patriarchate of Moscow is represented by Metropolitan Anthony of Sourozh, 67 Ennismore Gardens, London SW7 1NH. Fax only: 020-7584 9864. He is assisted by one archbishop, one vicar bishop and 28 clergy. There are 27 parishes and smaller communities.

The Russian Orthodox Church Outside Russia is represented by Archbishop Mark of Berlin, Germany and Great Britain, c/o 57 Harvard Road, London W4 4ED. Tel: 020-8742 3493. There are eight communities, including two monasteries, served by nine clergy.

### THE SERBIAN ORTHODOX CHURCH (PATRIARCHATE OF SERBIA)

There are 33 parishes and smaller communities in Great Britain served by 11 clergy. The Patriarchate of Serbia is represented by the Episcopal Vicar, the Very Revd Milenko Zebic, 131 Cob Lane, Bournville, Birmingham B30 1QE. Tel: 0121-486 1220.

OTHER NATIONALITIES

Most of the Ukrainian parishes in Britain have joined the Patriarchate of Constantinople, leaving a small number of Ukrainian parishes in Britain under the care of other patriarchates (not all of which are recognised by the other Orthodox Churches). The Latvian, Polish and some Belorussian parishes are also under the care of the Patriarchate of Constantinople. The Patriarchate of Romania has one parish served by two clergy. The Patriarchate of Bulgaria has one parish served by one priest. The Belorussian Autocephalous Orthodox Church has five parishes served by two priests.

## THE ORIENTAL ORTHODOX CHURCHES

The term 'Oriental Orthodox Churches' is now generally used to describe a group of six ancient eastern churches which reject the Christological definition of the Council of Chalcedon (AD 451) and use Christological terms in different ways from the Eastern Orthodox Church. There are about 34 million members of the Oriental Orthodox Churches.

PATRIARCHS OF THE ORIENTAL ORTHODOX CHURCHES

ARMENIAN ORTHODOX CHURCH – *Supreme Patriarch Catholicos of All Armenians (Etchmiadzin)*, Karekin II, *elected* 1999; *Catholicos of Cilicia*, Aram I, *elected* 1995; *Patriarch of Jerusalem*, Torkom II, *elected* 1994; *Patriarch of Constantinople*, Mesrob II, *elected* 1998

COPTIC ORTHODOX CHURCH – *Pope of Alexandria and Patriarch of the See of St Mark*, Shenouda III, *elected* 1971

ERITREAN ORTHODOX CHURCH – *Patriarch of Eritrea*, Philipos I, *elected* 1998

ETHIOPIAN ORTHODOX CHURCH – *Patriarch of Ethiopia*, Paulos, *elected* 1992

MALANKARA ORTHODOX SYRIAN CHURCH – *Catholicos of the East*, Basilios Mar Thoma Mathews II, *elected* 1991

SYRIAN ORTHODOX CHURCH – *Patriarch of Antioch and All the East*, Ignatius Zakka I, *elected* 1980

## ORIENTAL ORTHODOX CHURCHES IN THE UK

THE ARMENIAN ORTHODOX CHURCH (PATRIARCHATE OF ETCHMIADZIN)

The Armenian Orthodox Church is the longest-established Oriental Orthodox community in Great Britain. It is represented by the Rt. Revd Bishop Nathan Hovhannisian, Armenian Primate of Great Britain, Armenian Vicarage, Iverna Gardens, London W8 6TP. Tel: 020-7937 0152.

THE COPTIC ORTHODOX CHURCH

The Coptic Orthodox Church is the largest Oriental Orthodox community in Great Britain. It has five dioceses (London; Birmingham; Scotland, Ireland and North-East England; the British Orthodox Church; and churches directly under Pope Shenouda III). The senior bishop in Great Britain is Metropolitan Seraphim, 10 Heathwood Gardens, London SE7 8EP. Tel: 020-8854 3090.

THE ERITREAN ORTHODOX CHURCH

In Great Britain the Eritrean Orthodox Church is represented by Bishop Markos, 11 Anfield Close, Weir Road, London SW12 0NT. Tel: 020-8675 5115.

THE ETHIOPIAN ORTHODOX CHURCH

The Ethiopian Orthodox Church in Great Britain is represented by Like Teguhan Tekle Mariam Edwards, PO Box 14738, London N15 3NJ. Tel: 020-8889 9355.

THE MALANKARA ORTHODOX SYRIAN CHURCH

The Malankara Orthodox Syrian Church is part of the Diocese of Europe under Metropolitan Thomas Mar Makarios. His representative in Great Britain is Fr M. S. Skariah, Paramula House, 44 Newbury Road, Newbury Park, Ilford, Essex IG2 7HD. Tel: 020-8599 3836.

THE SYRIAN ORTHODOX CHURCH

The Syrian Orthodox Church in Great Britain comes under the Patriarchal Vicar, whose representative is Fr Touma Hazim Dakkama, Antiochian, 5 Canning Road, Croydon CR0 6QA. Tel: 020-8654 7531. The Indian congregation under the Syrian Patriarch of Antioch is represented by Fr Eldhose Koungampillil, 1 Roslyn Court, Roslyn Avenue, East Barnet, Herts EN4 8DJ. Tel: 020-8368 2794.

THE COUNCIL OF ORIENTAL ORTHODOX CHURCHES, 34 Chertsey Road, Church Square, Shepperton, Middx TW17 9LF. Tel: 020-8368 8447; *Secretary*, Deacon Aziz M. A. Nour

## PENTECOSTAL CHURCHES

Pentecostalism is inspired by the descent of the Holy Spirit upon the apostles at Pentecost. The movement began in Los Angeles, USA, in 1906 and is characterised by baptism with the Holy Spirit, divine healing, speaking in tongues (glossolalia), and a literal interpretation of the scriptures. The Pentecostal movement in Britain dates from 1907. Initially, groups of Pentecostalists were led by laymen and did not organise formally. However, in 1915 the Elim Foursquare Gospel Alliance (more usually called the Elim Pentecostal Church) was founded in Ireland by George Jeffreys and in 1924 about 70 independent assemblies formed a fellowship, the Assemblies of God in Great Britain and Ireland. The Apostolic Church grew out of the 1904–5 revivals in South Wales and was established in 1916, and the New Testament Church of God was established in England in 1953. In recent years many aspects of Pentecostalism have been adopted by the growing charismatic movement within the Roman Catholic, Protestant and Eastern Orthodox churches.

There are about 105 million Pentecostalists worldwide, with about 200,000 adult adherents in Great Britain and Ireland.

THE APOSTOLIC CHURCH, International Administration Offices, PO Box 389, 24–27 St Helens Road, Swansea SA1 1ZH. Tel: 01792-473992. *President*, Pastor R. W. Jones; *Administrator*, Pastor A. Saunders. The Apostolic Church has about 110 churches, 5,500 adherents and 91 ministers

THE ASSEMBLIES OF GOD IN GREAT BRITAIN AND IRELAND, General Offices, 16 Bridgford Road, West Bridgford, Nottingham NG2 6AF. Tel: 0115-981 1188. *General Superintendent*, P.C. Weaver; *General Administrator*, D. H. Gill. The Assemblies of God has 630 churches, about 75,000 adherents (including children) and 890 accredited ministers

THE ELIM PENTECOSTAL CHURCH, PO Box 38, Cheltenham, Glos GL50 3HN. Tel: 01242-519904. *General Superintendent*, Revd J. J. Glass; *Administrator*, Pastor B. Hunter. The Elim Pentecostal Church has 600 churches, 68,500 adherents and 650 accredited ministers

THE NEW TESTAMENT CHURCH OF GOD, Main House, Overstone Park, Overstone, Northampton NN6 0AD. Tel: 01604-643311. *National Overseer*, Revd Dr R. O. Brown. The New Testament Church of God has 104 organised congregations, about 8,500 baptised members, about 10,000 adherents and 256 accredited ministers

## THE PRESBYTERIAN CHURCH IN IRELAND

The Presbyterian Church in Ireland is Calvinistic in doctrine and presbyterian in constitution. Presbyterianism was established in Ireland as a result of the Ulster plantation in the early 17th century, when English and Scottish Protestants settled in the north of Ireland.

There are 21 presbyteries and five regional synods under the chief court known as the General Assembly. The General Assembly meets annually and is presided over by a Moderator who is elected for one year. The ongoing work of the Church is undertaken by 18 boards under which there are a number of specialist committees.

There are about 285,000 Presbyterians in Ireland, mainly in the north, in 557 congregations and with 400 ministers.

*Moderator* (2001–2), Rt. Revd Dr H. A Dunlop

*Clerk of Assembly and General Secretary*, Very Revd Dr S. Hutchinson, Church House, Belfast BT1 6DW. Tel: 028-9032 2284

## THE PRESBYTERIAN CHURCH OF WALES

The Presbyterian Church of Wales or Calvinistic Methodist Church of Wales is Calvinistic in doctrine and presbyterian in constitution. It was formed in 1811 when Welsh Calvinists severed the relationship with the established church by ordaining their own ministers. It secured its own confession of faith in 1823 and a Constitutional Deed in 1826, and since 1864 the General Assembly has met annually, presided over by a Moderator elected for a year. The doctrine and constitutional structure of the Presbyterian Church of Wales was confirmed by Act of Parliament in 1931–2.

The Church has 43,606 members, 119 ministers and 869 churches.

*Moderator* (2001–2), Dr B. F. Roberts

*General Secretary*, Revd W. G. Edwards, 53 Richmond Road, Cardiff CF24 3WJ. Tel: 029-2049 4913

## THE RELIGIOUS SOCIETY OF FRIENDS (QUAKERS)

Quakerism is a movement, not a church, which was founded in the 17th century by George Fox and others in an attempt to revive what they saw as 'primitive Christianity'. The movement was based originally in the Midlands, Yorkshire and north-west England, but there are now Quakers in 36 countries around the world. The colony of Pennsylvania, founded by William Penn, was originally Quaker.

Emphasis is placed on the experience of God in daily life rather than on sacraments or religious occasions. There is no church calendar. Worship is largely silent and there are no appointed ministers; the responsibility for conducting a meeting is shared equally among those present. Social reform and religious tolerance have always been important to Quakers, together with a commitment to non-violence in resolving disputes.

There are 213,800 Quakers world-wide, with over 19,000 in Great Britain and Ireland. There are about 490 meeting houses in Great Britain.

CENTRAL OFFICES: (GREAT BRITAIN) Friends House, 173 Euston Road, London NW1 2BJ. Tel: 020-7663 1000; Fax: 020-7663 1001; Email: qhs@quaker.org.uk; Web: www.quaker.org.uk;(IRELAND) Swanbrook House, Morehampton Road, Dublin 4. Tel: (00 353) (1) 668 3684

## THE SALVATION ARMY

The Salvation Army was founded by a Methodist minister, William Booth, in the east end of London in 1865, and has since become established in 108 countries world-wide. In 1878 it adopted a quasi-military command structure intended to inspire and regulate its endeavours and to reflect its view that the Church was engaged in spiritual warfare. Salvationists emphasise evangelism and the provision of social welfare.

There are over 1.5 million members worldwide, 17,201 active officers (full-time ordained ministers) and 15,670 worship centres and outposts world-wide. In Great Britain and Ireland there are 62,836 members, 1,638 active officers and 810 worship centres.

*International Leader*, Gen. John Gowans

*UK Leader*, Commissioner Alex Hughes

TERRITORIAL HEADQUARTERS, 101 Newington Causeway, London SE1 6BN. Tel: 020-7367 4500

## THE SEVENTH-DAY ADVENTIST CHURCH

The Seventh-day Adventist Church was founded in 1863 in the USA. Its members look forward to the second coming of Christ and observe the Sabbath (the seventh day) as a day of rest, worship and ministry. The Church bases its faith and practice wholly on the Bible and has developed 27 fundamental beliefs.

The World Church is divided into 13 divisions, each made up of unions of churches. The Seventh-day Adventist Church in the British Isles is known as the British Union Conference of Seventh-day Adventists and is a member of the Trans-European Division. In the British Isles the administrative organisation of the church is arranged in three tiers: the local churches; the regional conferences for south England, north England, Wales, Scotland and Ireland; and the national headquarters.

There are over 11 Adventists and 45,715 churches in 205 countries world-wide. In the UK and Ireland there are 20,637 members, 153 ministers and 243 churches.

*President of the British Union Conference*, Pastor C. R. Perry

BRITISH ISLES HEADQUARTERS, Stanborough Park, Watford WD25 6JZ. Tel: 01923-672251

## THE (SWEDENBORGIAN) NEW CHURCH

The New Church is based on the teachings of the 18th century Swedish scientist and theologian Emanuel Swedenborg (1688-1772), who believed that Jesus Christ appeared to him and instructed him to reveal the spiritual meaning of the Bible. He claimed to have visions of the spiritual world, including heaven and hell, and conversations with angels and spirits. He published several theological works, including descriptions of the spiritual world and a Bible commentary.

The Second Coming of Jesus Christ is believed to have already taken place and is still taking place, being not an actual physical reappearance of Christ, but rather His return in spirit. It is also believed that concurrent with our life on earth is life in a parallel spiritual world, of which we are usually unconscious until death, when our final judgement is our realisation of our individual essential nature.

There are around 30,000 Swedenborgians world-wide, with about 1,300 members, 30 Churches and 11 ministers in the UK.

THE GENERAL CONFERENCE OF THE NEW CHURCH, Swedenborg House, 20 Bloomsbury Way, London WC1A 2TH. Tel: 020-7229 9340

THE SWEDENBORG MOVEMENT, 98 Abbotts Drive, Wembley, Middx, HA0 3SQ. Tel: 020-8904 3433

## UNDEB YR ANNIBYNWYR CYMRAEG
*The Union of Welsh Independents*

The Union of Welsh Independents was formed in 1872 and is a voluntary association of Welsh Congregational Churches and personal members. It is mainly Welsh-speaking. Congregationalism in Wales dates back to 1639 when the first Welsh Congregational Church was opened in Gwent. Member churches are Calvinistic in doctrine, although a wide range of interpretations is permitted, and congregationalist in organisation. Each church has complete independence in the government and administration of its affairs.

The Union has 34,885 members, 204 ministers and 514 member churches.

*President of the Union* (2001–2002), Revd I. W. Gryffydd
*General Secretary*, Revd D. Myrddin Hughes, Tyy John Penry, 11 Heol Sant Helen, Swansea SA1 4AL. Tel: 01792-652542

## THE UNITED REFORMED CHURCH

The United Reformed Church was first formed by the union of most of the Congregational churches in England and Wales with the Presbyterian Church of England in 1972.

Congregationalism dates from the mid 16th century. It is Calvinistic in doctrine, and its followers form independent self-governing congregations bound under God by covenant, a principle laid down in the writings of Robert Browne (1550–1633). From the late 16th century the movement was driven underground by persecution, but the cause was defended at the Westminster Assembly in 1643 and the Savoy Declaration of 1658 laid down its principles. Congregational churches formed county associations for mutual support and in 1832 these associations merged to form the Congregational Union of England and Wales.

Presbyterianism in England also dates from the mid 16th century, and was Calvinistic and evangelical in its doctrine. It was governed by a hierarchy of courts.

In the 1960s there was close co-operation locally and nationally between Congregational and Presbyterian Churches. This led to union negotiations and a Scheme of Union, supported by Act of Parliament in 1972. In 1981 a further unification took place, with the Reformed Association of Churches of Christ becoming part of the URC. In 2000 a third union took place, with the Congregational Union of Scotland. In its basis the United Reformed Church reflects local church initiative and responsibility with a conciliar pattern of oversight. The General Assembly is the central body, and is made up of equal numbers of ministers and lay members.

The United Reformed Church is divided into 13 Synods, each with a Synod Moderator, and 78 Districts. There are 96,500 members, 657 full-time stipendiary ministers, 77 part-time stipendiary ministers, 190 non-stipendiary ministers, 10 active church related community workers, and 1,765 local churches.

*General Secretary*, Revd Dr David C. Cornick, 86 Tavistock Place, London WC1H 9RT. Tel: 020-7916 2020; Fax: 7916 2021; Email: david.cornick@urc.org.uk

## THE WESLEYAN REFORM UNION

The Wesleyan Reform Union was founded by Methodists who left or were expelled from Wesleyan Methodism in 1849 following a period of internal conflict. Its doctrine is conservative evangelical and its organisation is congregational, each church having complete independence in the government and administration of its affairs. The main concentration of churches is in Yorkshire.

The Union has 2,072 members, 17 ministers, 127 lay preachers and 110 churches.

*President* (2001–2), B. J. Armitt
*General Secretary*, Revd A. J. Williams, Wesleyan Reform Church House, 123 Queen Street, Sheffield S1 2DU. Tel: 0114-272 1938

# Non-Trinitarian Churches

## CHRISTADELPHIANISM

Christadelphians believe in the Bible as the literal truth and that the Second Coming of Jesus Christ to establish God's kingdom is imminent. Mankind is mortal by nature and only those who have been baptised and saved by their faith in Jesus will be resurrected to eternal life on earth.

Christadelphianism was founded by Dr John Thomas, an Englishman who emigrated to the USA, where he joined a religious group which he left after disagreements on doctrine, taking many of the group with him, who were later to be called Christadelphians. He founded several magazines and returned to England several times, where several congregations had formed on the basis of his teachings.

There are around 18,700 Christadelphians in the UK and some 282 ecclesias (churches).

THE CHRISTADELPHIAN MAGAZINE AND PUBLISHING ASSOCIATION, 404 Shaftmoor Lane, Birmingham B28 8SZ. Tel: 0121-777 6324; fax: 0121-778 5024

## THE CHURCH OF CHRIST, SCIENTIST

The Church of Christ, Scientist was founded by Mary Baker Eddy in the USA in 1879 to 'reinstate primitive Christianity and its lost element of healing'. Christian Science teaches the need for spiritual regeneration and salvation from sin, but is best known for its reliance on prayer alone in the healing of sickness. Adherents believe that such healing is a law, or Science, and is in direct line with that practised by Jesus Christ (revered, not as God, but as the Son of God) and by the early Christian Church.

The denomination consists of The First Church of Christ, Scientist, in Boston, Massachusetts, USA (the Mother Church) and its branch churches in over 60 countries world-wide. Branch churches are democratically governed by their members, while a five-member Board of Directors, based in Boston, is authorised to transact the business of the Mother Church. The Bible and Mary Baker Eddy's book, *Science and Health with Key to the Scriptures*, are used at services; there are no clergy. Those engaged in full-time healing are called practitioners, of whom there are 3,500 world-wide.

No membership figures are available, since Mary Baker Eddy felt that numbers are no measure of spiritual vitality and ruled that such statistics should not be published. There are over 2,400 branch churches world-wide, including nearly 200 in the UK.

CHRISTIAN SCIENCE COMMITTEE ON PUBLICATION, 9 Elysium Gate, 126 New Kings Road, London SW6 4LZ. Tel: 020-7384 8600; Fax: 020-7371 9204; Email: joynesh@compub.org; *District Manager for Great Britain and Ireland*, H. Joynes

## THE CHURCH OF JESUS CHRIST OF LATTER-DAY SAINTS

The Church (often referred to as 'the Mormons') was founded in New York State, USA, in 1830, and came to Britain in 1837. The oldest continuous branch in the world is to be found in Preston, Lancs. Mormons are Christians who claim to belong to the 'Restored Church' of Jesus Christ. They believe that true Christianity died when the last original apostle died, but that it was given back to the world by God and Christ through Joseph Smith, the Church's founder and first president. They accept and use the Bible as scripture, but believe in continuing revelation from God and use additional scriptures, including *The Book of Mormon: Another Testament of Jesus Christ*. The importance of the family is central to the Church's beliefs and practices. Church members set aside Monday evenings as Family Home Evenings when Christian family values are taught. Polygamy was formally discontinued in 1890.

The Church has no paid ministry; local congregations are headed by a leader chosen from amongst their number. The world governing body, based in Utah, USA, is the three-man First Presidency, assisted by the Quorum of the Twelve Apostles.

There are more than 11 million members world-wide, with about 180,000 adherents in Britain in over 350 congregations.

*President of the Europe North Area (including Britain)*, Elder W. Rolfe Kerr

BRITISH HEADQUARTERS, Church Offices, 751 Warwick Road, Solihull, W. Midlands B91 3DQ. Tel: 0121-712 1202

## JEHOVAH'S WITNESSES

The movement now known as Jehovah's Witnesses grew from a Bible study group formed by Charles Taze Russell in 1872 in Pennsylvania, USA. In 1896 it adopted the name of the Watch Tower Bible and Tract Society, and in 1931 its members became known as Jehovah's Witnesses. Jehovah's (God's) Witnesses believe in the Bible as the word of God, and consider it to be inspired and historically accurate. They take the scriptures literally, except where there are obvious indications that they are figurative or symbolic, and reject the doctrine of the Trinity. Witnesses also believe that the earth will remain for ever and that all those approved of by Jehovah will have eternal life on a cleansed and beautified earth; only 144,000 will go to heaven to rule with Christ. They believe that the second coming of Christ began in 1914 and his thousand-year reign on earth is imminent, and that Armageddon (a final battle in which evil will be defeated) will precede Christ's rule of peace. They refuse to take part in military service, and do not accept blood transfusions. They publish two magazines, *The Watchtower* and *Awake!*

The 11-member world governing body is based in New York, USA. Witnesses world-wide are divided into branches, countries or areas, districts, circuits and congregations. There are overseers at each level, and two assemblies are held annually for each circuit. There is no paid ministry, but each congregation has elders assigned to look after various duties and every Witness is assigned homes to visit in their congregation.

There are over 6 million Jehovah's Witnesses world-wide, with 130,000 Witnesses in the UK organised into over 1,400 congregations.

BRITISH ISLES HEADQUARTERS, Watch Tower House, The Ridgeway, London NW7 1RN. Tel: 020-8906 2211 Fax: 020-8371 0051; Email: pr@wtbts.org.uk; Web: www.watchtower.org

## UNITARIAN AND FREE CHRISTIAN CHURCHES

Unitarianism has its historical roots in the Judaeo-Christian tradition but rejects the deity of Christ and the doctrine of the trinity. It allows the individual to embrace insights from all the world's faiths and philosophies, as there is no fixed creed. It is accepted that beliefs may evolve in the light of personal experience.

Unitarian communities first became established in Poland and Transylvania in the 16th century. The first avowedly Unitarian place of worship in the British Isles opened in London in 1774. The General Assembly of Unitarian and Free Christian Churches came into existence in 1928 as the result of the amalgamation of two earlier organisations. There are about 7,000 Unitarians in Great Britain and Ireland, and 150 Unitarian ministers. Nearly 200 self-governing congregations and fellowship groups, including a small number overseas, are members of the General Assembly.

GENERAL ASSEMBLY OF UNITARIAN AND FREE CHRISTIAN CHURCHES, Essex Hall, 1–6 Essex Street, London WC2R 3HY. Tel: 020-7240 2384; Fax: 020-7240 3089; Email: ga@unitarian.org.uk; Web: www.unitarian.org.uk. *General Secretary*, Jeffrey J. Teagl

# Education

Responsibility for education in England lies with the Secretary of State for Education and Skills (formerly of Education and Employment); in Wales, with the First Secretary of the National Assembly for Wales; in Scotland, with Scottish Ministers; and with Education Ministers in Northern Ireland.

The main concerns of the education departments (the Department for Education and Skills (DfES) in England; the National Assembly for Wales Education Department; the Scottish Executive Department of Education and Department of Enterprise and Lifelong Learning; the Department of Education (DED) and Department for Employment and Learning (DEL) (formerly Department of Higher and Further Education, Training and Employment) in the Northern Ireland Executive) are the formulation of national policies for education and the maintenance of consistency in educational standards. They are responsible for the broad allocation of resources for education, for the rate and distribution of educational building and for the supply, training and superannuation of teachers (in England through the Teacher Training Agency).

## Expenditure

In the UK in 1998–9, expenditure on education was (£ million):

| | |
|---|---|
| Schools | 22,482.5 |
| Further and higher education | 12,284.3 |
| Other education and related expenditure | 1,886.3 |

Most of this expenditure, except that for higher and further education, is incurred by local authorities, which make their own expenditure decisions according to their local situations and needs. Expenditure on education by central government departments, in real terms, was (£ million):

| | 2000–1 *estimated outturn* | 2001–2 *planned* |
|---|---|---|
| DfES | 18,549 | 21,583 |
| National Assembly for Wales | 877.4 | 932.4 |
| Scottish Executive | 1,469.6 | 1,672.0 |
| Northern Ireland Assembly | 1,645.0 | 1,660.0 |

The bulk of direct expenditure by the DfES, the National Assembly for Wales and the Scottish Executive is directed towards supporting higher education in universities and colleges through the Higher Education Funding Councils (HEFCs) and further education and, in England and Wales, sixth form colleges, through the funding councils for the sector. In addition, the DfES funds student support in England and Wales, the City Technology Colleges, the City College for the Technology of the Arts, and pays grants under the specialist schools programme.

In Wales the National Assembly also funds curriculum development, educational services and research and supports bilingual education. In Scotland the main elements of central government expenditure, in addition to those outlined above, are grant-aided special schools, student awards and bursaries (through the Student Awards Agency for Scotland), teachers, curriculum development, special educational needs, community education and further and higher education through the Funding Councils. In Northern Ireland the DED also administers the teachers' superannuation scheme, pays teachers' salaries and funds grant-maintained integrated schools, and voluntary grammar schools. The DEL directly funds higher education, student awards and further education.

Current net expenditure on education by local education authorities in England, Wales, and Scotland, and education and library boards in Northern Ireland is (£ million):

| | 2000–1 *estimated outturn* | 2001–2 *planned* |
|---|---|---|
| England | 20,577 | 22,573 |
| Wales | 1,476 | 1,586 |
| Scotland | 2,752.4 | 2,952.8 |
| Northern Ireland | 940* | 912 |

*provisional

## Local Education Administration

In England and Wales the education service is administered by local education authorities (LEAs), which carry the day-to-day responsibility for providing most state primary and secondary education in their areas. They share with the funding bodies the duty to provide adult education to meet local needs.

The LEAs own and maintain most schools and some colleges, build new ones and provide equipment. LEAs are financed largely from the council tax and aggregate external finance from the Department for Transport, Local Government and the Regions in England and the National Assembly for Wales.

All LEA-maintained schools manage their own budgets. The LEA allocates funds to the school, largely on the basis of pupil numbers, and the school governing body is responsible for overseeing spending and for most aspects of staffing, including appointments and dismissals. LEAs have powers to monitor, maintain and improve standards. An Education Association can be set up to take over the management of failing schools where both the LEA and the governing body have not brought about improvements identified as necessary by inspection.

The duty of providing education locally in Scotland rests with the education authorities. They are responsible for the construction of buildings, the employment of teachers and other staff and the provision of equipment and materials. Devolved School Management is in place for all primary, secondary and special schools. Education authorities are required to establish school boards consisting of parents and teachers as well as co-opted members, responsible, among other things, for the appointment of staff.

Education is administered locally in Northern Ireland by five education and library boards, whose costs are met in full by central government. All grant-aided schools include elected parents and teachers on their boards of governors. Provision has been made for schools wishing to provide integrated education to have grant-maintained integrated status from the outset. All schools and colleges of further education have full responsibility for their own budgets, including staffing costs. The Council for Catholic Maintained Schools forms an upper tier of management for Catholic schools and provides advice on matters relating to management and administration.

### The Inspectorate

The Office for Standards in Education (OFSTED) is a non-ministerial government department in England headed by HM Chief Inspector of Schools (HMCI). OFSTED's remit is regularly to inspect and report on all maintained schools in England; local education authorities (supported by the Audit Commission); initial teacher training; youth work; all 16–19 education including sixth form and further education colleges; and funded education for three- and four-year-olds. OFSTED also has responsibility for the regulation of day care services for all children under eight.

Teams of OFSTED-trained accredited inspectors, including educationalists and lay people, carry out inspections in schools according to the Framework for Inspection of Schools to ensure consistency in the process of inspection and the criteria used. HM Inspectors (HMI) within OFSTED report on good practice in schools and on other educational issues based on inspection evidence. From 1997 for secondary and from 1998 for primary, schools are inspected once every six years or more frequently if there is cause. A summary of the inspection report must be sent to the parents of each pupil by the school, followed by a copy of the governors' action plan thereon.

There are about 200 HMIs on OFSTED's permanent staff, about 1,500 registered inspectors, about 7,500 team inspectors, and about 700 lay inspectors, who work on contract to OFSTED.

Estyn: Arolygiaeth Ei Mawrhydi dros Addysg a Hyfforddiant yng Nghymru (Her Majesty's Inspectorate for Education and Training in Wales) inspects funded nursery provision, maintained schools, local education authorities, teacher education and training, work-based training, careers companies, adult and youth education, and colleges of further education in Wales. Its remit also includes advice to the National Assembly for Wales on a wide range of education and training matters.

There are 54 HMIs, 149 registered inspectors and 562 team members in Wales.

HM Inspectorate of Education (HMIE) is an executive agency of the Scottish Executive. HM Inspectors (HMI) inspect or review and report on education in pre-school centres, nursery, primary and special schools, further education institutions (under contract to the Scottish Further Education Funding Council), initial teacher education, community learning; care and welfare of pupils; the education functions of local authorities; and in other contexts as necessary. HMIs work in teams alongside lay members and associate assessors, who are practising teachers seconded for the inspection. The inspection of higher education is the responsibility of inspectors appointed to the Higher Education Funding Council for Scotland.

In 2000–1 there were 87 HMIs and five Chief Inspectors in Scotland.

Inspection is carried out in Northern Ireland by the Education and Training Inspectorate which provides services for the Department of Education and the Department for Employment and Learning, among others. Schools are inspected once every five to seven years. In further education and training, extended inspections are carried out once every four years and focused inspections at least every eight years. In addition to its monitoring and evaluating activity, the Inspectorate also provides advice to Ministers and Departments.

The Inspectorate comprises a Chief Inspector, four assistant inspectors and 56 inspectors. Inspectorate teams also include on occasion lay persons and associate assessors.

## SCHOOLS AND PUPILS

Schooling is compulsory in Great Britain for all children between five and 16 years and between four and 16 years in Northern Ireland. Provision is being increased for pre-school children and many pupils remain at school after the minimum leaving age. No fees are charged in any publicly maintained school in England, Wales and Scotland. In Northern Ireland, fees may be charged in voluntary schools and are paid by pupils in preparatory departments of grammar schools, but pupils admitted to the secondary departments of grammar schools, unless they come from outside the province, do not pay fees.

The 'Parents' Charter', available free from education departments, is a booklet telling parents about the education system. Schools are now required to make available information about themselves, their truancy rates, destinations of leavers, public examination and national test results. Parents in England and Wales must receive a written yearly progress report on all aspects of their child's achievements. There is a similar commitment for Northern Ireland. In Scotland the school report card gives parents information on their child's progress.

### Fall and Rise in Numbers

In primary education, and increasingly in secondary education, pupil numbers in the UK increased through the 1990s. In maintained primary schools they stood at 4.9 million in 1991, had risen to 5.5 million by 2000 but are expected to decline to 4.9 million by 2006. In secondary schools pupil numbers stood at 3.4 million in 1991 and had risen to 3.9 million by 2000, where they are projected to remain until 2010.

### England and Wales

There are two main types of school in England and Wales: publicly maintained schools, which charge no fees; and independent schools, which charge fees. Publicly maintained schools, with the exception in England of City Technology Colleges, are maintained by local education authorities (LEAs).

Publicly funded schools are classified as community, voluntary or foundation schools. Community (formerly county) schools are owned by LEAs and wholly funded by them. They are non-denominational and provide primary and secondary education. Schools in the voluntary category provide primary and secondary education and many have a particular religious ethos. Although the buildings are in many cases provided by the voluntary bodies, they are financially maintained by an LEA. The category comprises two subdivisions, voluntary controlled and voluntary aided. In the case of voluntary controlled schools the LEA bears all costs. In voluntary aided schools, although the managers or governors are responsible for repairs, improvements and alterations to the building, central government may reimburse up to 85 per cent of approved capital expenditure, while the LEA pays for internal maintenance and other running costs. That subdivision also includes schools formerly classed as special agreement and those former grant-maintained schools which were originally voluntary aided or special agreement schools or were founded by promoters. In the case of former special agreement schools, the LEA may, by special agreement, pay between one-half and three-quarters of the cost of building a new or extending an existing school, usually a secondary school. Foundation schools are former grant-maintained schools which were originally county or voluntary controlled schools or were established by the Funding Agency for Schools. Under the previous administration all secondary and primary schools, whether maintained or independent, were eligible to apply for grant-maintained status subject to a ballot of parents. Grant-maintained schools were maintained directly by the Secretary of State (through the Funding Agency for Schools) and the former Welsh Office, not the LEA; those arrangements no longer apply and they are now included in LEA funding arrangements. They are wholly run by their own governing body. About 60 per cent of schools established were secondary schools.

The number of schools by category in 2000 was:

| | *England* | *Wales* |
|---|---|---|
| Maintained schools | 24,288 | 1,872 |
| Community | 16,094 | 1,584 |
| Voluntary | 7,314 | 276 |
| controlled | 2,889 | 116 |
| aided | 4,425 | 160 |
| Foundation | 880 | 12 |
| CTCs and CCTAs* | 15 | – |
| Independent schools | 3,050 | 55 |
| TOTAL | 27,353 | 1,927 |

* In England only

Under the Local Management of Schools initiative, LEAs are required to delegate the entire school budget, including staffing costs, directly to those schools that wish it. LEAs continue to retain responsibility for various common services, including transport and special educational needs units. The LEA acts as admission authority for most community and some voluntary schools.

*Governing bodies* – All publicly maintained schools have a governing body, usually made up of a number of parent and local community representatives, governors appointed by the LEA if the school is LEA maintained, the headteacher (unless he or she chooses otherwise), and serving teachers. Schools can appoint up to four sponsor governors from business who will be expected to provide financial and managerial assistance. Governing bodies are responsible for the overall policies of schools and their academic aims and objectives. They also control matters of school discipline, the appointment and dismissal of staff and act as the admission authority for voluntary aided and all foundation schools.

*City Technology Colleges (CTCs) and City Colleges for the Technology of the Arts (CCTAs)* are state-aided but independent of LEAs. Their aim is to widen the choice of secondary education in disadvantaged urban areas and to teach a broad curriculum with an emphasis on science, technology, business understanding and arts technologies. Capital costs are shared by government and business sponsors, and running costs are covered by a per capita grant from the DfES in line with comparable costs in an LEA maintained school. The first city technology college opened in 1988 in Solihull. The first CCTA, known as Britschool, opened in Croydon in 1991.

*The Specialist Schools Programme* – The programme is open to all state secondary schools in England, which wish to specialise in the teaching of a particular subject area (technology, mathematics and science, modern foreign languages, sports and the arts). The schools must raise £50,000 sponsorship, prepare four-year development plans with measurable targets in the specialist subject area and make provision to involve other schools and the wider community. In return, in addition to the normal funding arrangements, the schools receive business sponsorship (up to four sponsor governors may sit on governing bodies) and a capital grant of up to £100,000 from central government, together with extra annual funding of £123 per pupil (for four years initially) to assist the delivery of an enhanced curriculum. By September 2001, there were 367 technology colleges, 126 language colleges, 101 sports colleges and 91 arts colleges.

*City Academies* – The first City Academies, publicly funded independent secondary schools involving sponsors from the private and voluntary sectors, opened in September 2001. They are usually in deprived communities and replace either seriously failing schools with poor examination results or are established to meet a demand for places.

## SCOTLAND

Education authority schools (known as public schools) are financed by local government, partly through revenue support grants from central government, and partly from local taxation. Devolved management from the local authority to the school is in place for more than 88 per cent of all school level expenditure. A small number of grant-aided schools, mainly in the special sector, are conducted by boards of managers and receive grants direct from the Scottish Executive Education Department. Under the previous administration a category of self-governing schools was created. Such schools opted to be managed entirely by a board of management but remained in the public sector and were funded by direct government grant. Two were established but one has since been returned to the education authority framework.

Independent schools charge fees and receive no direct grant, but are subject to inspection and registration.

The number of schools by category in 2000 was:

| | |
|---|---|
| Publicly maintained schools: | |
| Education authority | 4,850 |
| Self-governing | 1 |
| Independent schools | 209 |
| TOTAL | 5,060 |

## NORTHERN IRELAND

Controlled schools are maintained by the education and library boards with all costs paid from public funds. Voluntary maintained schools, mainly under Roman Catholic management, receive grants towards capital costs and running costs in whole or in part. Voluntary grammar schools may be under denominational or non-denominational management and receive grants from the Department for Education (DED). Voluntary maintained and voluntary grammar schools can apply for designation as a new category of voluntary school, which is eligible for a 100 per cent as opposed to 85 per cent grant. Such schools are managed by a board of governors on which no single interest group has a majority of nominees. All grant-aided schools include elected parents and teachers on their boards of governors, whose responsibilities also include financial management under the Local Management of Schools initiative. All schools now have fully delegated budgets. The majority of children in Northern Ireland are educated in schools which have a religious affiliation. Integrated schools exist to educate Protestant and Roman Catholic children together. There are two types: grant-maintained integrated schools which are funded by DED; and controlled integrated schools funded by the education and library boards. Procedures are in place for balloting parents in existing religiously affiliated schools to determine whether they want their school to become integrated, subject to the satisfaction of certain criteria. By September 2001, 45 integrated schools had been established, 17 of them secondary.

The number of schools by category in 2000–2001 was:

| | |
|---|---|
| Grant-aided schools: | |
| Controlled | 646 |
| Maintained | 542 |
| Voluntary grammar | 54 |
| Integrated schools | 45 |
| Independent schools | 27 |
| TOTAL | 1,314 |

## THE STATE SYSTEM

PRE-SCHOOL EDUCATION – Pre-school education is for children from two to five years and is not compulsory, although a free place is available for each four-year-old who requires it and provision for three-year-olds in the public sector is being increased. Northern Ireland has a compulsory school starting age of four as of September each year but there too pre-school provision is being increased. Pre-school education takes place variously in nursery schools (2,826 in the public sector in 2000), nursery classes in primary schools, or pre-school education centres. The number of children receiving pre-school education in the UK in 1999–2000 was (thousands):

| | |
|---|---|
| In maintained nursery schools | 143.8 |
| In primary schools | 963.0 |
| In non-maintained nursery schools | 71.0 |
| In special schools | 7.0 |
| TOTAL | 1,184.8 |

Education authorities are responsible for planning, co-ordinating and delivering nursery education in their areas using a range of providers on the basis of an Early Years Development Plan, in partnership with parents and the private and voluntary sectors. All providers of pre-school education are subject to inspection.

PRIMARY EDUCATION – Primary education begins at five years in Great Britain and four years in Northern Ireland. In England, Wales and Northern Ireland the transfer to secondary school is generally made at 11 years. In Scotland, the primary school course lasts for seven years and pupils transfer to secondary courses at about the age of 12.

Primary schools consist mainly of infant schools for children aged five to seven, junior schools for those aged seven to 11, and combined junior and infant schools for both age groups. First schools in some parts of England cater for ages five to ten as the first stage of a three-tier system: first, middle and secondary.

Primary schools (UK) 1999–2000

| | |
|---|---|
| No. of primary schools | 23,052 |
| No. of pupils (thousands) | 5,338.3 |
| Pupils aged 2–4 years (thousands) | 992.3 |

Pupil–teacher ratios in maintained primary schools were:

| | 1998–9 | 1999–2000 |
|---|---|---|
| England | 23.5 | 23.3 |
| Wales | 23.0 | 22.3 |
| Scotland | 19.4 | 19.1 |
| Northern Ireland | 19.9 | 20.2 |
| UK | 23.0 | 22.7 |

The average size of classes 'as taught' was 25.3 in 1999–2000.

MIDDLE SCHOOLS – Middle schools (which take children from first schools), mostly in England, cover varying age ranges between eight and 14 and usually lead on to comprehensive upper schools.

SECONDARY EDUCATION – Secondary schools are for children aged 11 to 16 and for those who choose to stay on to 18. At 16, many students prefer to move on to tertiary or sixth form colleges. Most secondary schools in England, Wales and Scotland are co-educational. The largest secondary schools have over 1,500 pupils; thirty-five per cent of schools take over 1,000 pupils.

Secondary schools 1999–2000

| | England | Wales | Scotland | Northern Ireland |
|---|---|---|---|---|
| No. of pupils (000s) | 3,181.8 | 204.2 | 316.6 | 155.0 |
| % 16 to 17 years old | 31.2 | 34.1 | 29.2 | 43.1 |
| Average class size | 22.2 | 20.6 | 19.2 | n/a |
| Pupil–teacher ratio | 17.2 | 16.5 | 13.0 | 14.7 |

In England and Wales the main types of maintained secondary schools (January 2000) were: comprehensive schools (86.2 per cent of pupils in England, 100 per cent in Wales), whose admission arrangements are without reference to ability or aptitude; deemed middle schools for children aged between eight and 14 years who then move on to senior comprehensive schools at 12, 13 or 14 (4.8 per cent of pupils in England); secondary modern schools (3.4 per cent of pupils in England) providing a general education with a practical bias; secondary grammar schools (4.4 per cent of pupils in England) with selective intake providing an academic course from 11 to 16–18 years; and technical schools (0.009 per cent of pupils in England), providing an integrated academic and technical education.

In Scotland all pupils in education authority secondary schools attend schools with a comprehensive intake. Most of these schools provide a full range of courses appropriate to all levels of ability from first to sixth year.

In most areas of Northern Ireland there is a selective system of secondary education with pupils transferring either to grammar schools (34.8 per cent of pupils in 2000) or secondary schools (65.2 per cent of pupils in 2000) at 10–11 years of age. Parents can choose the school they would like their children to attend and all those who apply must be admitted if they meet the criteria. If a school is over-subscribed beyond its statutory admissions number, selection is on the basis of published criteria, which, for most grammar schools, place emphasis on performance in the transfer procedure tests which are set and administered by the Northern Ireland Council for the Curriculum, Examinations and Assessment. When parents consider that a school has not applied its criteria fairly they have access to independent appeals tribunals. Grammar schools provide an academic type of secondary education with A-levels at the end of the seventh year, while secondary non-grammar schools follow a curriculum suited to a wider range of aptitudes and abilities.

SPECIAL EDUCATION – Wherever possible, taking the parents' wishes into account, children with special needs are educated in ordinary schools, which are required to publish their policy for pupils with special educational needs. Local education authorities in England and Wales and education and library boards in Northern Ireland are required to identify and secure provision for the needs of children with learning difficulties, to involve the parents in any decision and draw up a formal statement of the child's special educational needs and how they intend to meet them, all within statutory time limits.

In Scotland, school placing is a matter of agreement between education authorities and parents. Parents have the right to say which school they want their child to attend, and a right of appeal where their wishes are not being met. Whenever possible, children with special needs are integrated into ordinary schools.

Maintained special schools are run by education

authorities which pay all the costs of maintenance, but under the terms of Local Management of Schools, those able and wishing to manage their own budgets may choose to do so. Non-maintained special schools are run by voluntary bodies; they may receive some grant from central government for capital expenditure and for equipment but their current expenditure is met primarily from the fees charged to education authorities for pupils placed in the schools. Some independent schools provide education wholly or mainly for children with special educational needs and are required to meet similar standards to those for maintained and non-maintained special schools.

The number of pupils with statements of special needs in January 2000 was (thousands):

| | |
|---|---|
| In special schools: | |
| Total | 101.0 |
| England | 86.9 |
| Wales | 3.7 |
| Scotland | 6.5 |
| N. Ireland | 3.9 |
| In public sector primary and secondary schools: | |
| Total | 93.7 |
| England | 79.8 |
| Wales | 6.8 |
| Scotland | 4.8 |
| N. Ireland | 2.3 |

### Alternative Provision

There is no legal obligation on parents in the UK to educate their children at school provided that the local education authority is satisfied that the child is receiving full-time education suited to its age, abilities and aptitudes. The education authority need not be informed that a child is being educated at home unless the child is already registered at a state school. In that case the parents must arrange for the child's name to be removed from the school's register (by writing to the headteacher) before education at home can begin. Failure to do so leaves the parents liable to prosecution for condoning non-attendance.

## INDEPENDENT SCHOOLS

Independent schools charge fees and are owned and managed under special trusts, with profits being used for the benefit of the schools concerned. There is a wide variety of provision, from kindergartens to large day and boarding schools, and from experimental schools to traditional institutions. A number of independent schools have been instituted by religious and ethnic minorities.

The term public schools is applied to those independent schools in membership of the Headmasters' and Headmistresses' Conference, the Governing Bodies Association or the Governing Bodies of Girls' Schools Association.

Most independent schools in Scotland follow the same examination system as England, Wales and Northern Ireland, i.e. GCSE followed by A-levels.

Preparatory schools are so-called because they prepare pupils for the common entrance examination to senior independent schools. Most cater for pupils from about seven to 13 years. The common entrance examination is set by the Common Entrance Examination Board, but marked by the independent school to which the pupil intends to go. It is taken at 13 by boys, and between 11 and 13 by girls.

The Assisted Places Scheme was funded by central government in England, Wales and Scotland and enabled children to attend independent secondary schools which their parents could not otherwise afford. It ceased to operate after the September 1997 intake but pupils holding their places at the beginning of the 1997–8 school year will keep them until they have completed their education at their current school.

The number of schools and pupils in 1999–2000 was:

| | No. of Schools | No. of pupils (000s) | % of school population | Pupil-teacher ratio |
|---|---|---|---|---|
| England | 2,204 | 577.3 | 7.4 | 9.9 |
| Wales | 54 | 9.7 | 1.9 | 9.8 |
| Scotland | 176 | 30.2 | 3.6 | 10.3 |
| N. Ireland | 22 | 1.2 | 0.3 | 8.8 |

## THE CURRICULUM

### England

The national curriculum was introduced in primary and secondary schools between autumn 1989 and autumn 1996, for the period of compulsory schooling from five to 16. It is mandatory in all maintained schools. As originally proposed, it was widely criticised for being too prescriptive and time-consuming. Following revision in 1994 its requirements were substantially reduced; the revisions were implemented from September 1995 for key stages one to three and from September 1996 for key stage four. A second review was completed in August 1999 and a revised curriculum was introduced in schools from September 2000.

The statutory subjects at key stages one and two (five–11-year olds) are:

| *Core subjects* | *Foundation subjects* |
|---|---|
| English | Design and technology |
| Mathematics | Information and communication technology |
| Science | History |
| | Geography |
| | Music |
| | Art and design |
| | Physical education |

At key stage three (11- to 14-year-olds) a modern foreign language is introduced. At key stage four (14- to 16-year-olds) pupils are required to continue to study the core subjects, physical education, design and technology and information and communication technology. Citizenship will become a compulsory subject for secondary pupils from September 2002. Other foundation subjects are optional and others, such as drama, dance and classical languages are taught when the resources of individual schools permit. Religious education must be taught across all key stages, following a locally agreed syllabus; parents have the right to remove their children if they wish.

Statutory assessment takes place on entry to primary school and national tests and tasks in English and mathematics at key stage one, with the addition of science at key stages two and three, are in place. Teachers make their own assessments of their pupils' progress to set alongside the test results. At key stage four the GCSE and vocational equivalents are the main form of assessment.

The DfES publishes tables showing pupils' performance in A-level, AS-level, GCSE, GNVQ and Vocational A-level examinations school by school. Local education authorities are required to publish similar information in November each year showing the results of national curriculum tests and teacher assessments for seven, 11- and 14-year-olds. Approximately 600,000 pupils in each of the age groups take the tests each year.

NATIONAL TESTING (TEACHERS' ASSESSMENT RESULTS IN PARENTHESIS) IN CORE SUBJECTS 2000

*Percentage of pupils reaching or exceeding the expected level of performance at that age:*

| | *Key stage 1 7-year olds (level 2)* | *Key stage 2 11-year-olds (level 4)* | *Key stage 3 14-year-olds (level 5)* |
|---|---|---|---|
| English | 84 (83) | 74.5 (70.5) | 63.5 (64.5) |
| Mathematics | 90 (88) | 71.5 (72.5) | 64.5 (66.5) |
| Science | – (88) | 84.5 (79) | 59.5 (61.5) |

National targets for 2004 proposed for 11-year-olds are: 85 per cent to reach level four in English and mathematics and 35 per cent to reach level five. Targets for 14-year-olds are: 75 per cent to reach level five in English, mathematics and information and communication technology and 70 per cent in science by 2004; by 2007, 85 and 80 per cent respectively.

The Qualifications and Curriculum Authority (QCA) is an independent government agency funded by the DfES. It is responsible for ensuring that the curriculum and qualifications available to young people and adults are of high quality, coherent and flexible and its remit ranges from the under-fives to higher level vocational qualifications.

WALES

The national curriculum was introduced simultaneously in Wales and, although it is broadly similar, has separate and distinctive characteristics which are reflected, where appropriate, in the programmes of study. A review of the curriculum in Wales has been completed and changes were introduced from September 2000. Welsh is compulsory for pupils at all key stages, either as a teaching medium or as a second language. In 1999–2000 some 27 per cent of primary schools used Welsh as the sole or main medium of instruction and over five per cent used it for part of the curriculum. More than 23.7 per cent of secondary schools taught Welsh both as a first and second language, while 67.5 per cent taught it as a second language only. Schools perform tests and tasks in Welsh in addition to those in the other subjects of the national curriculum. Approximately 38,000 pupils in each of the age groups take the tests each year.

Information about pupils' performance in examinations and national curriculum tests is made available by schools to parents but will no longer be published.

NATIONAL TESTING (TEACHERS' ASSESSMENT RESULTS IN PARENTHESIS) IN CORE SUBJECTS 2000

*Percentage of pupils reaching or exceeding the expected level of performance at that age:*

| | Key stage 1 7-year-olds (level 2) | Key stage 2 11-year-olds (level 4) | Key stage 3 14-year-olds (level 5) |
|---|---|---|---|
| English | 82.5 (81.5) | 73.5 (69) | 59.5 (62.5) |
| Welsh (first language) | 83.0 (82.7) | 73.0 (70) | 62.0 (65) |
| Mathematics | 90.0 (87.5) | 69.0 (70) | 60.5 (64.5) |
| Science | – (88) | 80.5 (78) | 59.0 (60.5) |

National targets have been set as follows: by 2004 80-85 per cent of 11-year-olds to reach level four or better and 80-85 per cent of 14-year-olds to reach level five or better in English, Welsh (first language), mathematics and science.

Awdurdod Cymwysterau, Cwricwlwm ac Asesu Cymru (ACCAC)/the Qualifications, Curriculum and Assessment Authority for Wales advises government on the matters within its remit. ACCAC is funded by the National Assembly for Wales.

SCOTLAND

The content and management of the curriculum in Scotland are not prescribed by statute but are the responsibility of education authorities and individual headteachers. Advice and guidance are provided by the Scottish Executive Education Department and Learning and Teaching Scotland, which also has a developmental role. Those bodies have produced guidelines on the structure and balance of the curriculum as well as for each of the curriculum areas for the five to 14 age group. There are also guidelines on assessment across the whole curriculum, on reporting to parents, and on standardised national tests for English language and mathematics at five levels. Testing is carried out on a voluntary basis when the teacher deems it appropriate; most pupils are expected to move from one level to the next at roughly two-year intervals. National testing is largely in place in most primary schools but secondary school participation rates are lower.

The curriculum for 14- to 16-year-olds includes study within each of eight modes: language and communication; mathematical studies; science; technology; social studies; creative activities; physical education; and religious and moral education. There is a recommended percentage of time to be devoted to each area over the two years. Provision is made for teaching in Gaelic in Gaelic-speaking areas.

For 16- to 18-year-olds National Qualifications, a unified framework of courses and awards, which brings together both academic and vocational courses, was introduced in 1999. The Scottish Qualifications Authority awards the certificates.

NORTHERN IRELAND

A curriculum common to all grant-aided schools exists. Pupils are required to study religious education and, depending on which key stage they have reached, certain subjects from six broad areas of study: English, mathematics, science and technology; the environment and society; creative and expressive studies and, in key stages three and four, language studies. The statutory curriculum requirements at key stages one to three have been revised and new programmes of study were introduced in September 1996. Six cross-curricular educational themes, which include information technology and education for mutual understanding, are woven through the main subjects of the curriculum. Irish is a foundation subject in schools that use it as a medium of instruction.

The assessment of pupils is broadly in line with practice in England and Wales and takes place at the ages of eight, 11 and 14. The GCSE is used to assess 16-year-olds. From 2001 the Department of Education ceased to publish the national testing results, as a consultation exercise showed that parents and others preferred the option of individual schools providing information to parents.

National targets have been set as follows for achievement by 2002: for key stage 2 (11-year-olds), 77 per cent to reach level four in English and mathematics; and for key stage 3 (14-year-olds), 75 per cent in English and mathematics and 70 per cent in science to reach level five and above.

The Northern Ireland Council for the Curriculum, Examinations and Assessment (NICCEA) monitors and advises the Department of Education and teachers on all matters relating to the curriculum, assessment arrangements and examinations in grant-aided schools. It conducts GCSE, A- and AS-level examinations, pupil assessment at key stages one, two and three and administers the transfer procedure tests.

## PUBLIC EXAMINATIONS AND QUALIFICATIONS

### ENGLAND, WALES AND NORTHERN IRELAND

Until the end of 1987, secondary school pupils at the end of compulsory schooling around the age of 16, and others, took the General Certificate of Education (GCE) Ordinary-level or the Certificate of Secondary Education (CSE). From 1988 these were replaced by a single system of examinations, the General Certificate of Secondary Education (GCSE), which is usually taken after five years of secondary education. The GCSE is the main method of assessing the performance of pupils at age 16 in all national curriculum subjects required to be assessed at the end of compulsory schooling. The structure of the examination is being adapted in accordance with national curriculum requirements; new subject criteria were published in 1995 to govern GCSE syllabuses introduced in 1996 for first examination in 1998. GCSE short-course qualifications are available in some subjects. As a rule the syllabus takes half the time of a full GCSE course.

The GCSE differs from its predecessors in that there are syllabuses based on national criteria covering course objectives, content and assessment methods; differentiated assessment (i.e. different papers or questions for different ranges of ability) and grade-related criteria (i.e. grades awarded on absolute rather than relative performance). The GCSE certificates are awarded on an eight-point scale, A* to G. Grades A to C are the equivalent of the corresponding O-level grades A to C or CSE grade 1. Grades D, E, F and G record achievement at least as high as that represented by CSE grades 2 to 5. All GCSE syllabuses, assessments and grading procedures are monitored by the Qualifications and Curriculum Authority to ensure that they conform to the national criteria

In the UK in 1998–9, 73.9 per cent of all 15 to 16-year-old entrants achieved one or more graded GCSE, SCE Standard Grade, or equivalent result, while 49.1 per cent achieved five or more results at grade C or better.

Students are increasingly encouraged to continue their education post-16. For those who do so, in addition to the vocational qualifications outlined below, there are General Certificate of Education (GCE) Advanced (A-level) examinations. A-level courses usually last two years and have traditionally provided the foundation for entry to higher education. A-level reforms have introduced revised syllabuses from Summer 2000 for examination in summer 2002. Advanced Subsidiary (AS) level examinations replaced Advanced Supplementary level examinations (introduced in 1987 and requiring not less than half the teaching time and content of the corresponding A-level course) for examination in summer 2001. The government is considering changes in response to the criticism that the introduction of AS-level examinations has imposed too heavy a burden in the first year of the A-level course on students and teachers. The new A-level qualification is normally composed of six units (three A2 units and three AS units), the latter being less demanding and constituting the new AS-level qualification, which represents the first half of a full A-level. Students who go on to complete the full A-level will be assessed on their attainment in all six units, which may be taken either in stages or all at the end of the course. Candidates have the choice between end-of-course or staged assessment, with limits on coursework. A-levels and AS-levels are marked on a six-point scale: from A to E (pass) and U (unclassified), which is not certificated.

Many maintained schools offer BTEC Firsts and an increasing number offer BTEC Nationals. National Vocational Qualifications (NVQs) in the form of General NVQs (GNVQs) are also available to students in schools. The Vocational Certificates of Education (VCE) exist at Advanced and AS levels.

In the UK in 1998–9, 33.7 per cent of young students in schools and colleges achieved two or more passes at A-level or SCE H-grade (an increase of 0.2 per cent on the previous year). Of those in Great Britain who entered for A-level or SCE H-grade examinations, the greatest number of entries were in the following subjects: English (13 per cent of students, 9 per cent boys, 16.3 per cent girls); general studies (9.7 per cent of students, 10.0 boys, 9.5 girls); mathematics (9.6 per cent of students, 12.8 per cent boys, 7.0 per cent of girls); and biological sciences (6.9 per cent of students, 5.7 per cent boys, 8.0 per cent girls).

There is also the opportunity for A-level candidates to take additional papers of greater difficulty, known as Advanced Extension Awards (formerly Special-level or Scholarship-level). Papers are available in most of the traditional academic subjects and are marked on a two-point scale (Merit and Distinction).

The City & Guilds Diploma of Vocational Education is intended for a wide ability range. Within guidelines and to meet specified criteria, schools and colleges design their own courses, which stress activity-based learning, core skills which include application of number, communication and information technology, and work experience. The Diploma is of value to those who want to find out what aptitudes they may have and to prepare themselves for work, but who may not yet be committed to a particular occupation. It can be taken alongside GCSEs and can provide a context for the introduction of GNVQ units into the key stage four curriculum.

The various examining boards in England have combined into three Unitary Awarding Bodies (UABs), which offer both academic and vocational qualifications: GNVQs, GCSEs, AS and A-levels. The new bodies are the Assessment and Qualifications Alliance (AQA), Edexcel and Oxford, Cambridge and RSA Examinations (OCR). The UABs are separate bodies, although they work together in many ways to meet the needs of schools and colleges. The Joint Council for General Qualifications (JCGQ) comprises the three English UABs, the Welsh Joint Education Committee and the Northern Ireland Council for the Curriculum, Examinations and Assessment.

### SCOTLAND

Scotland has its own system of public examinations. At the end of the fourth year of secondary education, at about the age of 16, pupils take the Standard Grade of the Scottish Certificate of Education. Standard Grade courses and examinations have been designed to suit every level of ability, with assessment against nationally determined standards of performance.

For most courses there are three separate examination papers at the end of the two-year Standard Grade course. They are set at three levels: Credit (leading to awards at grade 1 or 2); General (leading to awards at grade 3 or 4); and Foundation (leading to awards at grade 5 or 6). Grade 7 is available to those who, although they have completed the course, have not attained any of these levels. Normally pupils will take examinations covering two pairs of grades, either grades 1–4 or grades 3–6. Most candidates take seven or eight Standard Grade examinations.

Post-16 a new system of courses and qualifications is being phased in under the 'Higher Still' reforms, bringing together academic and vocational qualifications. National Qualifications will replace the Certificate of Sixth Year Studies (from 2001–2) and Highers, National Certificate modules, and General Scottish Vocational Qualifications (from 2004) for everyone studying beyond Standard Grade in Scottish schools and further education colleges. Standard Grade and Scottish Vocational Qualifications will remain. National Qualifications are available at five levels: Access, Intermediate 1, Intermediate 2, Higher and Advanced Higher. Courses are made up of internally assessed units with external assessment of the full course determining the grade (A to C). The core skills of communication, numeracy, problem-solving, information technology and working with others are embedded in the Higher Still qualifications, although the skills and levels covered vary between subjects; there are also separate core skills units.

All these qualifications are awarded by the Scottish Qualifications Authority (SQA).

### The International Baccalaureate

The International Baccalaureate is an internationally recognised two-year pre-university course and examination designed to facilitate the mobility of students and to promote international understanding. There are 43 schools and colleges in the UK which offer the International Baccalaureate diploma.

### Records of Achievement

The National Record of Achievement is under review. Subject to evaluation, it will be replaced in England, Wales and Northern Ireland by the 'Progress file' after a three year trial period from July 1999. In Scotland the Scottish Qualifications Authority issues a Scottish Qualifications Certificate recording all qualifications achieved at all levels which it has either awarded or accredited.

## TEACHERS

### England and Wales

New entrants to the teaching profession in state primary and secondary schools are required to be graduates and to have Qualified Teacher Status (QTS). QTS is achieved by successfully completing a course of initial teacher training, traditionally either a Bachelor of Education (B Ed) degree or the Postgraduate Certificate of Education (PGCE) at an accredited institution. New entrants are statutorily required to serve a one-year induction period during which they will have a structured programme of support. In recent years various employment-based routes to QTS have been developed. The Graduate Teacher Programme allows graduates of at least 24 years of age with teaching experience to undergo between one term's and one year's school-based training. The schools involved receive up to £13,000 to cover the trainee's salary in addition to a grant of up to £4,000 for undertaking training. The Registered Teacher Scheme is designed to attract into the teaching profession entrants over 24 years of age without a degree or formal teaching qualification but with at least two years higher education and with relevant experience; entrants are paid a salary and complete a degree while undergoing training. Teachers in further education are not required to have QTS, though roughly half have a teaching qualification and most have industrial, commercial or professional experience. A qualification for aspiring head-teachers, the National Professional Qualification for Headship, was introduced in September 1997 and will be mandatory by 2002. The National College for School Leadership administers this qualification and others and acts as a focus for development and support.

Teacher training is now largely school-based, with student teachers on secondary PGCE courses spending two-thirds of their training in the classroom. Changes have also been made to primary phase teacher training to make it more school-based and to give schools a role in course design and delivery. Individual schools or consortia of schools and CTCs can bid for funds from the DfES to carry out their own teacher training, including recruitment of students, subject to approval of their proposed training programme by the Teacher Training Agency (TTA) and monitoring and evaluation by OFSTED and Estyn. Funds are given to schools to meet the costs of designing and delivering the courses.

The TTA funds all types of teacher training in England, whether run by universities, colleges or schools, and some educational research. In Wales funding is undertaken by the Higher Education Funding Council for Wales (HEFCW). On an integrated England and Wales basis the TTA also acts as a central source of information and advice about entry to teaching, and has responsibilities relating to the continuing professional development of teachers. An independent professional council, the General Teaching Council, has been established to advise the Secretary of State and the TTA, with a separate council for Wales.

The Specialist Teacher Assistant (STA) scheme provides trained support to qualified teachers in the teaching of reading, writing and arithmetic to young pupils.

### Shortage Subjects

The government has introduced various schemes in an attempt to address the shortage of teachers in England and Wales. Graduates training for a PGCE in certain secondary subjects (English, modern foreign languages, mathematics, science, technology, and Welsh (in Wales)), who then take up a teaching post, receive a training salary of £6,000 (£150 per week) and a further £4,000 lump sum after completing their first year of work. In Wales the scheme applies to all postgraduate trainee teachers, although only those teaching shortage subjects receive the lump sum. The latter will moreover be assisted to pay off their student loans over 10 years. Furthermore, providers of initial teacher training in England and Wales may receive funds from the TTA to help promote courses in certain subjects and to offer students on courses in those subjects financial support. The subjects are: design and technology; geography; information technology; mathematics; modern languages; music; religious education; science; and Welsh in Wales. A training salary for postgraduates training as primary teachers was trialled during 2000–1 and for trainee teachers in post-16 non-degree craft subjects from September 2001.

The TTA administers a returners' programme for qualified teachers who wish to refresh their skills before returning to the profession. They benefit from the waiving of course fees, a grant of up to £150 per week while studying and supplementary grants for childcare.

### Scotland

The General Teaching Council (GTC) for Scotland advises central government on matters relating to teacher supply and the professional suitability of all teacher training courses. The GTC is also the body responsible for disciplinary procedures in cases of professional misconduct. All teachers in maintained schools must be registered with the GTC, initially for a two-year probationary period which can be extended if necessary. Only graduates are accepted as entrants to the profession; primary school teachers undertake either a four-year vocational degree course or a one-year postgraduate course, while teachers of academic subjects in secondary schools undertake the latter. Most initial teacher training is classroom-based. The Scottish Qualification for Headship has been introduced for aspiring head teachers. The colleges of education provide both in-service and pre-service training for teachers which is subject to inspection by HM Inspectorate of Education. The colleges are funded by the Scottish Higher Education Funding Council, which also sets intake levels for teacher education courses.

### Northern Ireland

All new entrants to teaching in grant-aided schools are graduates and hold an approved teaching qualification. Initial teacher training is provided by the two universities and two colleges of education, but is integrated with induction and early in-service training, the latter over a period of three years. The colleges are concerned with teacher education mainly for the primary school sector. They also provide B Ed courses for intending secondary school teachers of religious education, commercial studies, and craft, design and technology. With these exceptions, the professional training of teachers for secondary schools is provided in the education departments of the universities. A review of primary and secondary teacher training has taken place as a result of which all student teachers spend more time in the classroom. The General Teaching Council for Northern Ireland is to be established in 2002 to advise government on professional issues, to maintain a register of teachers and to act as a disciplinary body.

### Accreditation of Training Institutions

Advice to central government on the accreditation, content and quality of initial teacher training courses is given in England by the TTA, in Wales by the HEFCW and in Northern Ireland by validating bodies (by the General Teaching Council for Northern Ireland when established). These bodies also monitor and disseminate good practice, assisted in Northern Ireland by the Teacher Education Committee. The GTC performs those functions in Scotland.

### Serving Teachers 1998–9 (*full-time and part-time*)(thousands):

| | |
|---|---|
| Public sector schools | |
| Nursery and primary | 230.2 |
| Secondary | 239.8 |
| Special (public sector and non-maintained) | 18.2 |
| Independent schools | 60.4 |
| Total | 548.6 |

### Salaries

Qualified teachers in England, Wales and Northern Ireland, other than heads and deputy heads, are paid on an 18-point scale. Entry points and placement depend on qualifications and experience. There are additional cash allowances for management responsibilities, special needs work and recruitment and retention factors as calculated by the relevant body, i.e. the governing body or the LEA. The grade of 'Advanced Skills Teacher' was introduced to enhance prospects in the classroom for the most able teachers. High-performing teachers as assessed against national standards receive a performance-related pay increase of an extra £3,000 a year. There is a statutory superannuation scheme in maintained schools.

*Salary scales for teachers in England Wales and Northern Ireland from 1 April 2001 are as follows:*

| | |
|---|---|
| Head | £33,375–£78,783 |
| Deputy head | from £29,499 |
| Advanced skills teacher | £27,973–£44,571 |
| Teacher | £16,038–£31,128 |

Teachers in Scotland are paid on a nine-point scale. The entry point depends on type of qualification and additional allowances are payable under a range of circumstances.

*Salary scales for teachers in Scotland are:*

| | from 1 April 2001 | from 1 April 2002 |
|---|---|---|
| Head | £32,526–£60,252 | £33,826–£62,661 |
| Depute Head | £32,526–£45,084 | £33,826–£46,887 |
| Principal teacher | £28,932–£33,750 | £30,090–£35,100 |
| Senior teacher | £26,424–£27,954 | £27,480–£29,073 |
| Teacher | £16,005–£25,644 | £16,644–£25,670 |

## FURTHER EDUCATION

Further education is defined as provision outside schools to people aged over 16 of education up to and including A-level and its equivalent.

### England and Wales

Further education and sixth form colleges are funded directly by central government through the Learning and Skills Council in England (which assumed the role of the former Further Education Funding Council for England and the Training and Enterprise Councils and operates through 47 regional centres) and the National Council for Education and Training in Wales (formerly the Further Education Funding Council for Wales). The Councils have a duty to secure provision of adequate facilities in their areas and are also responsible for the assessment of quality, in which their inspectors play a key role. The colleges are controlled by autonomous further education corporations, which include substantial representation from industry and commerce, and which own their own assets and employ their own staff. Their funding is determined in part by the number of students enrolled and their level of achievement.

Teaching staff in further education establishments are not necessarily required to have teaching qualifications although many do so, but they are subject to regular appraisal of teaching performance. It is planned to introduce a mandatory professional qualification for college principals.

Much further education tends to be broadly vocational in purpose and employers are often involved in designing courses. It ranges from lower-level technical and commercial courses and government-sponsored training, through courses for those aiming at higher-level posts in industry, commerce and administration, to professional courses. Facilities exist for GCE A- and AS-levels, GCSEs, GNVQs and a full range of vocational qualifications. These courses can form the foundation for progress to higher education qualifications. Many students attend part-time, either through day or block release from employment, or in the evenings.

The main courses and examinations in the vocational field, all of which link in with the National Vocational

Qualification (NVQ) framework, are offered by the following bodies, but there are also many others.

The Edexcel Foundation was formed by the merger of the Business and Technology Education Council (BTEC) and London Examinations. It provides programmes of study across a wide range of subject areas. Qualifications offered include GNVQs, NVQs, GCSEs, AS and A-levels, National and Higher National diplomas and certificates and other BTEC qualifications.

City & Guilds specialise in developing qualifications and assessments for work-related and leisure qualifications. They offer nationally and internationally recognised certificates in over 500 vocational qualifications. The progressive structure of awards spans seven levels, from foundation to the highest level of professional competence.

Oxford, Cambridge and RSA Examinations cover the full range of academic and vocational qualifications. The latter include accounting, business administration, customer service, management, language schemes, information technology and teaching qualifications. A wide range of NVQs and GNVQs are offered and a policy operates of credit accumulation, so that candidates can take a single unit or complete qualifications.

There are 428 further education establishments (of which 105 are sixth form colleges) in England and 24 in Wales. In England (1998–9) there were 963.5 thousand full-time and sandwich-course students and 2,506.1 thousand part-time students. In Wales (1998–9) there were 43.9 thousand full-time and sandwich students and 162.4 thousand part-time students.

### SCOTLAND

Responsibility for further education lies with the Scottish Executive under the Minister for Enterprise and Lifelong Learning. The Executive liaises with the Scottish Further Education Funding Council to administer further education funding. There are 47 further education colleges of which 43 are self-governing incorporated colleges run by their own boards of management. The boards include the principal, staff and student representatives among their ten to 16 members; at least half of whom must have experience of commerce, industry or professional practice. Two colleges, on Orkney and Shetland, are under Islands Council control and two others, Sabhal Mor Ostaig (the Gaelic college on Skye) and Newbattle Abbey are run by trustees.

The Scottish Qualifications Authority (SQA) is the statutory awarding body for qualifications in the national education and training system in Scotland. It is both the main awarding body for qualifications for work including Scottish Vocational Qualifications (SVQs) and is also their accrediting body. The SQA is by statute required clearly to separate its awarding and accrediting functions.

There are three main qualification families in Scottish further education: National Qualifications; Higher National Qualifications (HNC and HND); and SVQs. In addition to Standard Grade qualifications, National Qualifications are available at five levels: Access, Intermediate 1, Intermediate 2, Higher and Advanced Higher. Another feature of the qualifications system is the Scottish Group Award (SGA). SGAs are built up unit by unit and allow opportunity for credit transfer from other qualifications (such as Standard Grade or SVQ) providing a further option for learners, especially adult returners.

Advanced-level HNC/HND qualifications are available in further education colleges and higher education institutions. SQA accredits and awards SVQs which have mutual recognition with the NVQs available in the rest of the UK. SVQs are competence-based qualifications suitable for work-place delivery but they can also be taken in further education colleges and other centres where work-place conditions can be simulated.

In the academic year 1999–2000 there were 38,176 full-time and sandwich-course students and 273,360 part-time students on non-advanced vocational courses of further education in further education colleges (excluding Newbattle Abbey College).

### NORTHERN IRELAND

All further education colleges are free-standing corporate bodies like their counterparts in the rest of the UK. Planning is the responsibility of the Department for Employment and Learning, which funds the colleges directly. The colleges own their own property, are responsible for their own services and employ their own staff.

The governing bodies of the colleges must include at least 50 per cent membership from the professions, local business or industry, or other fields of employment relevant to the activities of the college.

In 2000–1 Northern Ireland had 17 institutions of further education, and there were 20,966 full-time and 58,323 part-time enrolments on vocational further education courses.

### STUDENT SUPPORT

At present 16- to 19-year-olds may receive means-tested discretionary payments from LEAs, while adults may apply for funds including financial help with childcare allocated by central government through the funding bodies. The means-tested Education Maintenance Allowance (EMA) for 16- to 19-year-old students continuing their education beyond school leaving age in both schools and colleges is a weekly allowance worth up to £30 which is being piloted in certain areas in England and Scotland where there are problems of poverty and low staying-on rates. EMAs are payable subject to conditions laid out under a learning agreement. The access fund scheme is also being extended. Various similar options are under consideration in Northern Ireland.

### NATIONAL VOCATIONAL QUALIFICATIONS

National Vocational Qualifications (NVQs) are work-place based occupational qualifications. General National Vocational Qualifications (GNVQs) provide a vocational alternative to academic qualifications in colleges and schools. GNVQs cover six broad categories in the NVQ framework and are aimed at those wishing to familiarise themselves with a range of opportunities. The Vocational A-level, introduced in September 2000, operates at three levels: the three unit vocational A-level (known as Vocational AS), equivalent to one GCE AS-level; the 6 unit Vocational A-level, equivalent to one GCE A-level; and the 12 unit Vocational A-level (double award) equivalent to two A-levels (formerly Advanced GNVQ). Part one GNVQ comprises Intermediate GNVQ, equivalent to two GCSEs at A* to C grade and Foundation GNVQ, equivalent to two GCSEs at D to G grade. The full GNVQ , also at Intermediate and Foundation level, is similarly equivalent to four GCSEs.

## HIGHER EDUCATION

The term higher education is used to describe education above A-level, Higher and Advanced Higher Grade and their equivalent, which is provided in universities, colleges of higher education and in some further education colleges.

The Further and Higher Education Act 1992 and parallel legislation in Scotland removed the distinction between higher education provided by the universities and that provided in England and Wales by the former polytechnics and colleges of higher education and in Scotland by the former central institutions and others. It allowed all polytechnics, and other higher education institutions which satisfy the necessary criteria, to award their own taught course and research degrees and to adopt the title of university. All the polytechnics, art colleges and some colleges of higher education have since done so. The change of name does not affect the legal constitution of the institutions. Funding is by the Higher Education Funding Councils for England, Wales and Scotland and directly by the Department for Employment and Learning in Northern Ireland.

The number of students in higher education in the UK in 1999–2000 was (thousands):

| | |
|---|---|
| Full-time, sandwich | 1,259.7 |
| % female | 53.0% |
| Part-time | 764.4 |
| % female | 55.4% |
| TOTAL | 2,024.1 |
| of which overseas | 11.0% |

The proportion of the 18- to 21-year-old population undertaking full-time and part-time courses in higher education was about 33 per cent in England and Wales, about 40 per cent in Scotland and about 45 per cent in Northern Ireland in 1999–2000. In the same year about twenty-five per cent of undergraduates in the first year of a first degree course were aged 21 years or over, while over 70 per cent of first year postgraduate students were aged 25 years or over. During that period 54.6 per cent of the student population were female (56.5 per cent of UK domiciled undergraduates). Women formed the majority of students in subjects allied to medicine (82.9 per cent), education (72 per cent), languages (69.3 per cent), veterinary science (68.1 per cent), information science (62.3 per cent), biological sciences (60.8 per cent) and social, economic and political studies (60.6 per cent). Men formed the majority of those studying engineering and technology (85.2 per cent), computer science (76.9 per cent), architecture, building and planning (72.2 per cent), physical sciences (62.8 per cent) and mathematics (63.1 per cent).

Responsibility for universities rests in England with the Secretary of State for Education and Skills and with Education Ministers in Scotland, Northern Ireland and Wales. Advice to government on matters relating to the universities is provided by the Higher Education Funding Councils for England, Wales and Scotland, and by the Higher Education Council in Northern Ireland. The Councils receive a block grant from central government which they allocate to the universities and colleges. The grant is allocated directly to institutions by the Department for Employment and Learning in Northern Ireland on the advice of the Northern Ireland Higher Education Council.

There are now 88 universities in the UK, where only 47 existed prior to the Further and Higher Education Acts 1992. Of the 88, 71 are in England (including one federal university), two (one a federal institution) in Wales, 13 in Scotland and two in Northern Ireland.

The pre-1992 universities each have their own system of internal government but broad similarities exist. Most are run by two main bodies: the senate, which deals primarily with academic issues and consists of members elected from within the university; and the council, which is the supreme body and is responsible for all appointments and promotions, and bidding for and allocation of financial resources. At least half the members of the council are drawn from outside the university. Joint committees of senate and council are common.

Those universities which were formerly polytechnics (38) or other higher education institutions (three) and the colleges of higher education (61) are run by higher education corporations, which are controlled by boards of governors. At least half the members of each board must be drawn from industry, business, commerce and the professions.

The non-residential Open University provides courses nationally leading to degrees. Teaching is through a combination of television and radio programmes, correspondence, tutorials, short residential courses and local audio-visual centres. No qualifications are needed for entry. The Open University offers a modular programme of undergraduate courses by credit accumulation and post-experience and postgraduate courses, including a programme of higher degrees which comprises BPhil, MPhil and PhD through research, and MA, MBA and MSc through taught courses. The Open University in England, Wales and Northern Ireland is funded by the Higher Education Funding Council for England (HEFCE) and in Scotland by the Scottish Higher Education Funding Council (SHEFC). The Open University's recurrent grant for 1999–2000 was £133.0 million from the HEFCE and £2.3 million from the Teacher Training Agency. In 2001 about 134,000 undergraduates were registered of whom about 54 per cent were women. Estimated cost (2001) of a six-credit degree was around £4,500 including course fees of about £3,300.

The University for Industry (UfI) was launched in autumn 2000 to promote learning ranging from basic skills to specialised technological and management skills. UfI operates through learning centres. The Scottish UfI operates within the distinctive Scottish system.

The independent University of Buckingham receives no public funding and provides a two-year course (four terms per year) leading to a bachelor's degree. Its tuition fees from October 2001 are £2,625 per term.

## ENGLAND AND WALES

In 1999–2000 full-time and part-time student enrolments were (thousands):

| | |
|---|---|
| *England* | |
| Undergraduates | 1,091.1 |
| % overseas | 9.8% |
| Postgraduates | 262.4 |
| % overseas | 30.4% |
| *Wales* | |
| Undergraduates | 74.3 |
| % overseas | 8.6% |
| Postgraduates | 14.1 |
| % overseas | 30.0% |

Higher education courses funded by the funding bodies are also taught in some further education colleges. In England in 1999–2000 there were about 73.1 thousand full-time and part-time students (4.7 per cent of total higher education student numbers) on such courses and 716 enrolments (0.8 per cent of higher education student numbers) in Wales.

## SCOTLAND

SHEFC funds 22 institutions of higher education, including 13 universities. The universities are broadly managed as described above and the remaining colleges are managed by independent governing bodies which include representatives of industrial, commercial, professional and educational interests. Most of the courses outside the universities have a vocational orientation and a substantial number are sandwich courses.

Student enrolments in 1999–2000 in universities and other higher education institutions were (thousands):

| | |
|---|---|
| Undergraduates | 133.7 |
| % overseas | 7.4% |
| Postgraduates | 48.6 |
| % overseas | 27.3% |

There were about 72 thousand students on higher education courses in further education colleges, amounting to about 27.8 per cent of the total number.

## Northern Ireland

In Northern Ireland higher education is provided in the 17 colleges of further education, the two universities and the two university colleges. These institutions offer a range of courses, which may include first and postgraduate degrees, PGCEs, undergraduate diplomas and certificates, and professional qualifications. Enrolments in higher education institutions in 2000–1 were:

| | |
|---|---|
| Undergraduates | 33,879 |
| % overseas* students | 2.4% |
| Postgraduates | 8,113 |
| % overseas* students | 8.1% |

*classified as non-UK or Republic of Ireland domiciled

In addition to the above, in 2000–1 there were 12,021 enrolments on higher education courses in Northern Ireland institutions of further education, which equates to 22.3 per cent of all higher education enrolments in Northern Ireland.

## Academic Staff

Each university and college appoints its own academic staff on its own conditions. However, there is a common salary structure and, except for Oxford and Cambridge, a common career structure in the pre-1992 universities and a common salary structure for the post-1992 universities. The Universities and Colleges Employers Association acts as a pay agency for universities and colleges.

Teaching staff in higher education require no formal teaching qualification, but the Institute of Teaching and Learning in Higher Education, funded by the funding Councils, has been established to set up an accreditation scheme for higher education teachers and to encourage innovation in teaching and learning. Teacher trainers are required to spend a certain amount of time in schools to ensure that they have sufficient recent practical experience.

In 1999–2000, there were 106,410 full-time and part-time teaching and research staff (UK nationals) in institutions of higher education in the UK.

Salary scales for staff in the pre-1992 universities differ from those in the former polytechnics and colleges; it is planned eventually to amalgamate them. The salary scales for non-clinical academic staff in the pre-1992 universities are (2000–1):

| | |
|---|---|
| Professor | from £37,493 |
| Senior lecturer | £32,510–£39,718 |
| Lecturer grade B | £25,213–£30,967 |
| Lecturer grade A | £18,731–£24,227 |

The salaries of clinical academic staff are kept broadly comparable to those of doctors and dentists in the National Health Service.

Salary scales for lecturers in the former polytechnics, now universities, and colleges of higher education in England, Wales and Northern Ireland are:

| | 1 September 2001 | 1 February 2002 |
|---|---|---|
| Head of Department | from £26,304 | from £26,304 |
| Principal lecturer | £30,519–£38,373 | £31,129–£39,141 |
| Senior lecturer | £24,417–£32,265 | £24,906–£32,910 |
| Lecturer | £19,191–£26,163 | £19,575–£26,686 |

and in Scotland:

| | 1 September 2001 | 1 March 2002 |
|---|---|---|
| Head of Department | £45,697–£51,578 | £46,154–£52,094 |
| Senior Lecturer | £28,999–£42,143 | £29,289–£42,605 |
| Lecturer | £17,616–£35,109 | £17,792–35,460 |

## Finance

Although universities and colleges are expected to look to a wider range of funding sources than before, and to generate additional revenue in collaboration with industry, they are still largely financed, directly or indirectly, from government resources.

In 1999–2000 the total income of institutions of higher education in the UK was £12,779.7 million (£12,087.4 million in 1998–9) comprising (*percentage of income in parenthesis*):

| | 1999–2000 £ million | 1998–9 £ million |
|---|---|---|
| Funding Council grants | £5,147.1 (40.3%) | £4,992.1 (40.7%) |
| Tuition fees and education contracts | £2,872.4 (22.5%) | £2,722.6 (22.5%) |
| Research grants and contracts | £1,973.4 (15.4%) | £1,831.4 (15.2%) |
| Other income* | £2,786.9 (21.8%) | £2,611.2 (21.6%) |

*includes fees, services, endowments and investments

In the academic year 1999–2000 the HEFCE's and HEFCW's recurrent grant to institutions outside their sector for the provision of higher education courses was £143.5 million.

## Courses

In the UK all universities and some colleges award their own degrees and other qualifications and may act as awarding and validating bodies for neighbouring colleges which are not yet accredited. The Quality Assurance Agency for Higher Education, funded by institutional contributions, advises government on applications for degree-awarding powers.

Higher education courses last full-time for at least four weeks or, if part-time, involve more than 60 hours of instruction. Facilities exist for full-time and part-time study, day release, sandwich or block release. Credit accumulation and transfer (CATS) is a system of study which allows a student to achieve a final qualification by accumulating credits for courses of study successfully achieved, or even professional experience, over a period. Credit transfer information and values are carried on an electronic database called ECCTIS 2000, which is available in most careers offices and many schools and colleges.

Higher education courses comprise: first degree and postgraduate (including research); Diploma in Higher Education (DipHE); Higher National Diploma (HND) and Higher National Certificate (HNC); and preparation for professional examinations. The in-service training of teachers is also included, but is funded in England by the Teacher Training Agency, not the HEFCE.

The Diploma of Higher Education (DipHE) is a two-year diploma usually intended to serve as a stepping-stone to a degree course or other further study. The DipHE is awarded by the institution itself if it is accredited; by an accredited institution of its choice if not. The BTEC Higher National Certificate (HNC) is awarded after two years part-time study. The BTEC Higher National Diploma (HND) is awarded after two years full-time, or three years sandwich-course or part-time study.

With the exception of certain Scottish universities where master is sometimes used for a first degree in arts subjects, undergraduate courses lead to the title of Bachelor, Bachelor of Arts (BA) and Bachelor of Science (BSc) being the most common. For a higher degree the titles are: Master of Arts (MA), Master of Science (MSc) and the research degrees of Master of Philosophy (MPhil) and Doctor of Philosophy (PhD or, at a few universities, DPhil).

Most undergraduate courses at universities and colleges of higher education run for three years, but some take up to four years. They include modern language courses and honours courses at Scottish universities and the University of Keele. Professional courses in subjects such as medicine, veterinary science and architecture take longer.

Postgraduate studies vary in length. Certificates, diplomas or masters degrees usually take one year full-time or two years part-time. Research degrees take from two to three years full-time.

Post-experience short courses are forming an increasing part of higher education provision, reflecting the need to update professional and technical training. Most of these courses fund themselves.

### ADMISSIONS

The target proportion of the 18- to 19-year-old age group entering full-time higher education for 2001–2 was set at 33 to 35 per cent. Institutions suffer financial penalties if the number of students laid down for them by the funding Councils is exceeded, but the individual university or college decides which students to accept. The formal entry requirements to most degree courses are two A-levels at grade E or above (or equivalent), and to HND courses one A-level (or equivalent). In practice, most offers of places require qualifications in excess of this, higher requirements usually reflecting the popularity of a course or institution. These requirements do not, however, exclude applications from students with a variety of non-GCSE qualifications or unquantified experience and skills.

For admission to a degree, DipHE or HND, potential students apply through a central clearing house, the Universities and Colleges Admission Service (UCAS). Applicants are supplied with an application form and the UCAS Handbook, available from schools, colleges and careers offices or direct from UCAS, and may apply to a maximum of six institutions/courses. The only exception among universities is the Open University, which conducts its own admissions.

Applications for undergraduate teacher training courses are made through UCAS. Details of initial teacher training courses in Scotland can be obtained from colleges of education and those universities offering such courses, and from the Committee of Scottish Higher Education Principals (COSHEP).

For admission as a postgraduate student, universities and colleges normally require a good first degree in a subject related to the proposed course of study or research, but other experience and qualifications will be considered on merit. Most applications are made to individual institutions but there are two clearing houses of relevance. All postgraduate teacher training courses in England and Wales and most of those in Scotland utilise the Graduate Teacher Training Registry. Applications for post graduate certificate of education (PGCE) courses at institutions in Northern Ireland are made directly to the institutions. For social work the Social Work Admissions System operates.

### FEES

From September 1998 entrants to undergraduate courses have paid, directly to the institution, an annual contribution to their fees (up to £1,075 in 2001–2) depending on their own level of income and that of their spouse or parents. The average cost of a higher education course in the UK is £4,000 and the balance is paid by the education authority or, in Northern Ireland, by the Education and Libraries Board. Students from EU member countries pay fees at home student rates and, if studying at institutions in England, Wales and Northern Ireland, are liable to make an annual contribution to fees assessed against family income. Among the classes of students exempt from payment are: Scottish domiciled and EU students at Scottish institutions; students from England, Wales and Northern Ireland in the fourth year of a four-year degree course at a Scottish institution; existing students with mandatory awards (see below), for whom the grant-awarding body pays; PGCE students; medical students in the fifth year of their course; health professionals on National Health Service bursaries; and full-time or part-time students on benefit or low incomes.

Universities and colleges are free to set their own charges for students from non-EU countries, whose fees are meant to cover the cost of their education. Financial help is available under a number of schemes.

For postgraduate students, the maximum tuition fee that will be reimbursed through the awards system is £2,805 (full-time) or £1,402.50 (part-time) in 2001–2.

## STUDENT SUPPORT

### LOANS

The means-tested interest-free loan is the main form of support for most undergraduate students in the UK who started full-time or sandwich undergraduate courses of higher education from the academic year commencing in September 1998. Students apply through LEAs in England and Wales, education and library boards in Northern Ireland and the Students Awards Agency in Scotland. The maximum loan available to full-time students in 2001–2 is £4,700, of which £3,525 (75%) is not subject to means testing.

Loan rates for 2001–2 (final year rates in parenthesis):

| | |
|---|---|
| Living in college/ lodgings in London area | £4,700 (£4,075) |
| Living in college/ lodgings elsewhere | £3,815 (£3,310) |
| Living in parental home | £2,635 (£1,975) |

Extra income assessed loans are available to students whose courses last over 30 term-time weeks or who need to study abroad in certain high-cost countries. Loans of up to £500 are available to part-time students on low incomes or with dependent children.

Loans are available to students on designated courses, which comprise those full-time or sandwich courses leading to: a degree; the Diploma of Higher Education;

the Higher National Diploma; initial teacher-training courses (not in Scotland), including those for the PGCE and the art teachers' certificate or diploma; a university certificate or diploma course lasting at least three years; and other qualifications which are specifically designated as being comparable to first degree courses. Certain residency conditions also apply. In 1999–2000, 723.6 thousand loans were taken up, to the value of £1,823.0 million.

Repayment arrangements differ for students who embarked upon higher education courses before the 1998–9 academic year and those starting thereafter. The former normally repay on a mortgage-style basis over five to seven years, although repayment can be deferred if annual income is at or below 85 per cent of national average earnings. The latter are not required to make repayments until their annual income is above £10,000 when nine per cent of the income above that amount is taken to repay the loan. Interest on the loan is linked to inflation in line with the Retail Prices Index. Providing repayments have been kept up, the loan is automatically cancelled on death; if the recipient becomes permanently disabled; or at age 65.

### Non-repayable Grants and Allowances

Eligible students, such as single parents and others with dependants, are entitled to apply for various additional means-tested supplementary grants for help in meeting certain living costs, for childcare and for each child at school. Disabled students are eligible for non means-tested Disabled Students Allowances.

### Mandatory grants

Students who started their courses before September 1998 and certain others continue, for the duration of their course, to be eligible for means-tested maintenance grants from which a parental contribution is deductible on a sliding scale dependent on income or, for married students, from their spouse's income. However, a parental contribution is not deducted from the grant to students over 25 years of age who have been self-supporting for any three years before the beginning of their course.

Grants are paid by the local education authority for the area in which the student lives in England, Wales and Northern Ireland. The cost is reimbursed by central government. For students resident in Scotland grants are made by central government through the Student Awards Agency.

The means-tested maintenance grant, usually paid once a term, covers periods of attendance during term as well as the Christmas and Easter vacations, but not the summer vacation.

The basic grant rates for 2000–1 (rates for Scottish students in parenthesis) are:

| | |
|---|---|
| Living in College/lodgings in London area | £2,335 (£2,255) |
| College/lodgings outside London area | £1,900 (£1,825) |
| Parental home | £1,555 (£1,345) |

Additional allowances are available if, for example, the course requires a period of study abroad. Expenditure on mandatory awards in 1999–2000 was £470.9 million.

### Access Funds

Access funds are allocated by central government to the appropriate funding Councils in England and Wales and to the Student Awards Agency in Scotland and administered by further and higher education institutions. In Northern Ireland they are allocated by central government directly to the institution. All students, whether full- or part-time, undergraduate or postgraduate, may apply but those whose courses attract a student loan must already have applied for their full entitlement before applying to the access funds. Access funds may be paid as a short-term loan but are usually paid as a grant. The amount payable depends on individual circumstances and on the amount the institution has available. Some colleges offer non-repayable bursaries from access funds, i.e. a payment for each year of the course, to students who might be prevented from completing their studies due to financial problems.

### Postgraduate Awards

Grants for postgraduate study are discretionary and competition for them is fierce. They comprise: maintenance grants for studentships, which cover students undertaking research degrees or taught masters degrees, are not means-tested and are dependent on the class of first degree (especially for research degrees); and flat-rate maintenance grants which replaced the former 30-week bursaries for new entrants from the academic year 2000–1. There are additional allowances for disabled students, those with dependants and for fieldwork expenses. Postgraduate students, with the exception of students in England, Wales and Northern Ireland on loan-bearing diploma courses such as teacher training, are not eligible to apply for student loans.

Awards are funded by The British Academy, the Higher Education Funding Councils for England and Wales, the Department for Employment and Learning (DEL) for Northern Ireland, and the Scottish Higher Education Funding Council.

Prospective students should apply for awards (depending on the subject domain) to the following bodies: the Arts and Humanities Research Board or to one of the six Research Council in England, Wales and Northern Ireland (where application may also be made to DEL) and to the Student Awards Agency in Scotland.

*The rates of awards in 2001–2 are:*

| | London | Elsewhere |
|---|---|---|
| Studentships | £9,250 | £7,500 |
| Professional and vocational | £5,100 | £4,300 |

## ADULT AND CONTINUING EDUCATION

In the UK, the duty of securing adult and continuing education leading to academic or vocational qualifications is statutory. The Learning and Skills Council in England, the National Council for Education and Training in Wales and the Further Education Funding Council in Scotland are responsible for and fund those courses which take place in their sector and lead to academic and vocational qualifications, prepare students to undertake further or higher education courses, or confer basic skills; the Higher Education Funding Councils fund advanced courses of continuing education. The LEAs have the power, although not the duty, to provide those courses which do not fall within the remit of the funding bodies. Funding in Northern Ireland is through the education and library boards.

Adult education is provided in adult education centres and colleges run by LEAs (England and Wales), further education colleges and evening centres (Scotland), community schools (Northern Ireland), and the adult studies departments of higher education institutions.

The involvement of universities in adult education and continuing education has diversified considerably. Birkbeck College in the University of London caters solely for part-time students. The post-1992 universities and the colleges of higher education, because of their range of courses and flexible patterns of student attendance, provide opportunities in the field of adult and continuing education. The Forum for the Advancement of Continuing Education promotes collaboration between institutions of higher education active in this area. The Open University, in partnership with the BBC, provides distance teaching leading to first degrees, and also offers post-experience and higher degree courses.

Of the voluntary bodies, the biggest is the Workers' Educational Association (WEA) which operates throughout the UK, reaching about 150,000 adult students annually. The further education funding bodies and LEAs make grants towards provision.

NIACE, the National Organisation for Adult Learning, has a broad remit to promote lifelong learning opportunities for adults. NIACE works to develop increased participation in education and training. It does this through research and project work, conferences, publications and the provision of an information service to educational providers. NIACE Cymru, the Welsh committee, receives financial support from the National Assembly for Wales, support in kind from local authorities, and advises government, voluntary bodies and education providers on adult continuing education and training matters in Wales. In Scotland advice on adult and community education, and promotion thereof, is provided by Community Learning Scotland. In Northern Ireland those functions are undertaken by the Department for Employment and Learning.

The Universities' Association for Continuing Education (UACE) represents the continuing education community within higher education and is open to universities and higher education institutions in the UK with additional provision for international, associate and individual members.

### Grants

Adult education bursaries for students at the long-term residential colleges of adult education are the responsibility of the colleges themselves. The awards are administered for the colleges by the Awards Officer of the Residential Colleges Committee for students resident in England. They are funded for colleges in England and Wales by the respective Councils; for colleges in Scotland by the Department for Lifelong Learning and administered by the Scottish Further Education Funding Council; and for colleges in Northern Ireland by the Department for Employment and Learning and administered by the education and library boards.

# Education Directory

## LOCAL EDUCATION AUTHORITY

### ENGLAND

#### County Councils

BEDFORDSHIRE, County Hall, Cauldwell Street, Bedford MK42 9AP. Tel: 01234-363222. *Director*, David Doran

BUCKINGHAMSHIRE, County Hall, Walton Street, Aylesbury HP20 1UA. Tel: 01296-382603. *Chief Education Officer*, P. J. Mooney

CAMBRIDGESHIRE, Education Information Office, Box ELH 1500, Shire Hall, Castle Hill, Cambridge CB3 0AP. Tel: 01223-717667. *Director*, A. Baxter

CHESHIRE, County Hall, Chester CH1 1SQ. Tel: 01244-602424. *Director of Education*, D. Cracknell

CORNWALL, County Hall, Truro TR1 3AY. Tel: 01872-322000. *Director of Education, Arts and Libraries*, J. Harris

CUMBRIA, 5 Portland Square, Carlisle CA1 1PU. Tel: 01228-606877. *Director of Education*, J. Nellist

DERBYSHIRE, County Hall, Matlock DE4 3AG. Tel: 01629-585641. *Chief Education Officer*, R. V. Taylor

DEVON, County Hall, Topsham Road, Exeter EX2 4QG. Tel: 01392-382059. *Director of Education, Arts and Libraries*, A. G. Smith

DORSET, County Hall, Colliton Park, Dorchester DT1 1XJ. Tel: 01305-224164. *Director*, D. Goddard

DURHAM, County Hall, Durham DH1 5UJ. Tel: 0191-383 3319. *Director*, K. Mitchell

EAST SUSSEX, County Hall, St Anne's Crescent, Lewes BN7 1SG. Tel: 01273-481000. *Director of Education*, Ms D. Stokoe

ESSEX, PO Box 47, Chelmsford CM2 6WN. Tel: 01245-492211. *Director of Learning Services*, P. A. Lincoln

GLOUCESTERSHIRE, Shire Hall, Westgate Street, Gloucester GL1 2TG. Tel: 01452-425300. *Acting Director*, S. King

HAMPSHIRE, The Castle, Winchester SO23 8UG. Tel: 01962-841841. *County Education Officer*, A. J. Seber

HERTFORDSHIRE, County Hall, Pegs Lane, Hertford SG13 8DE. Tel: 01992-555555. *Director*, R. Shostak

ISLE OF WIGHT, County Hall, High Street, Newport PO30 1UD. Tel: 01983-823400. *Director*, A. Kaye

KENT, Sessions House, County Hall, Maidstone ME14 1XQ. Tel: 01622-671411. *Strategic Director Education and Libraries*, N. Henwood

LANCASHIRE, PO Box 61, County Hall, Preston PR1 8RJ. Tel: 01772-254868. *Director of Education and Cultural Services*, C. J. Trinick

LEICESTERSHIRE, County Hall, Glenfield, Leicester LE3 8RF. Tel: 0116-265 6301. *Director*, Mrs J. A. M. Strong

LINCOLNSHIRE, County Offices, Newland, Lincoln LN1 1YQ. Tel: 01522-552222. *Director*, Dr C. Berry

NORFOLK, County Hall, Martineau Lane, Norwich NR1 2DH. Tel: 01603-222146. *Director*, Dr B. C. Slater

NORTHAMPTONSHIRE, Education and Community Learning, PO Box 233, County Hall, Northampton NN1 1AZ. Tel: 01604-236252. *Corporate Director*, Mrs B. Bignold

NORTHUMBERLAND, County Hall, Morpeth NE61 2EF. Tel: 01670-533601. *Director*, Dr L. Davis

NORTH YORKSHIRE, County Hall, Northallerton, N. Yorks DL7 8AE. Tel: 01609-780780. *Director*, Miss C. Welbourn

NOTTINGHAMSHIRE, County Hall, West Bridgford, Nottingham NG2 7QP. Tel: 0115-982 3823. *Director*, P. Tulley

OXFORDSHIRE, Education Department, Macclesfield House, New Road, Oxford OX1 1NA. Tel: 01865-815449. *Chief Education Officer*, G. Badman

SHROPSHIRE, The Shirehall, Abbey Foregate, Shrewsbury SY2 6ND. Tel: 01743-254307. *Corporate Director - Education Services*, Mrs E. Nicholson

SOMERSET, County Hall, Taunton TA1 4DY. Tel: 01823-355790. *Corporate Director – Education*, M. Jennings

STAFFORDSHIRE, Education Offices, Tipping Street, Stafford ST16 2DH. Tel: 01785-223121. *Director*, Mrs J. S. Hawkins

SUFFOLK, St Andrew House, County Hall, Ipswich IP4 1LJ. Tel: 01473-584631. *Director*, D. J. Peachey

SURREY, County Hall, Penrhyn Road, Kingston upon Thames KT1 2DJ. Tel: 0845-600 9009. *Director*, Dr P. Gray

WARWICKSHIRE, PO Box 24, 22 Northgate Street, Warwick CV34 4SP. Tel: 01926-410410. *County Education Officer*, E. Wood

WEST SUSSEX, County Hall, Chichester PO19 1RF. Tel: 01243-777129. *Director of Education and the Arts*, R. D. C. Bunker

WILTSHIRE, County Hall, Bythesea Road, Trowbridge BA14 8JB. Tel: 01225-713000. *Chief Education Officer*, R. W. Wolfson

WORCESTERSHIRE, County Hall, Spetchley Road, Worcester WR5 2NP. Tel: 01905-766895. *Director of Educational Services*, J. Kramer

#### Unitary Councils

BARNSLEY, Berneslai Close, Barnsley S70 2HS. Tel: 01226-773500. *Executive Director, Education*, Ms J. Potter

BATH AND NORTH-EAST SOMERSET, PO Box 25, Riverside, Temple Street, Keynsham, Bristol BS31 1DN. Tel: 01225-394200. *Director*, D. Williams

BIRMINGHAM, Education Offices, Margaret Street, Birmingham B3 3BU. Tel: 0121-303 2590. *Chief Education Officer*, Prof. T. Brighouse

BLACKBURN WITH DARWEN, Town Hall, Blackburn BB1 7DY. Tel: 01254-585541. *Director of Education and Training*, M. Pattison

BLACKPOOL, Progress House, Clifton Road, Blackpool FY4 4US. Tel: 01253-476555. *Director of Education and Cultural Services*, Dr D. Sanders

BOLTON, Paderborn House, Civic Centre, Bolton BL1 1JW. Tel: 01204-333333. *Director*, Mrs M. Blenkinsop

BOURNEMOUTH, Dorset House, 20–22 Christchurch Road, Bournemouth BH1 3NL. Tel: 01202-456219. *Director*, K. Shaikh

BRACKNELL FOREST, Edward Elgar House, Skimped Hill Lane, Bracknell, Berks RG12 1LY. Tel: 01344-424642. *Director of Education*, T. Eccleston

EDUCATION BRADFORD, Support Office, Flockton Road, Bradford BD4 7RY. Tel: 01274-751840. *Director of Educational Services*, Mr Paul Brett

BRIGHTON AND HOVE, PO Box 2503, Kings House, Grand Avenue, Hove BN3 2SU. Tel: 01273-290000. *Strategic Director of Education and Lifelong Learning*, D. Hawker

BRISTOL, The Council House, College Green, Bristol BS99 7EB. Tel: 0117-903 7961. *Director of Education and Lifelong Learning*, R. Riddell

BURY, Athenaeum House, Market Street, Bury BL9 0SW. Tel: 0161-253 5652. *Chief Education Officer*, H. Williams

CALDERDALE, Northgate House, Northgate, Halifax HX1 1UN. Tel: 01422-357257. *Director*, Ms C. White

COVENTRY, Council Offices, Earl Street, Coventry CV1 5RS. Tel: 024-7683 1511. *Director*, Ms C. Goodwin

DARLINGTON, Town Hall, Darlington DL1 5QT. Tel: 01325-380651. *Director*, G. Pennington

DERBY, Middleton House, 27 St Mary's Gate, Derby DE1 3NN. Tel: 01332-716924. *Director*, A. Flack

DONCASTER, Directorate of Education and Culture, The Council House, College Road, Doncaster DN1 3AD. Tel: 01302-737103. *Executive Director*, M. Simpson

DUDLEY, Westox House, 1 Trinity Road, Dudley DY1 1JQ. Tel: 01384-814225. *Interim Director of Education*, J. Freeman

EAST RIDING OF YORKSHIRE, County Hall, Beverley HU17 9BA. Tel: 01482-392000. *Director of Education, Leisure and Libraries*, J. Ginnever

GATESHEAD, Civic Centre, Regent Street, Gateshead NE8 1HH. Tel: 0191-433 3000. *Director*, B. H. Edwards

HALTON, Halton Borough Council, Grosvenor House, Halton Lea, Runcorn WA7 2WD. Tel: 0151-424 2061. *Director*, G. Talbot

HARTLEPOOL, Civic Centre, Victoria Road, Hartlepool TS24 8AY. Tel: 01429-266522. *Director*, J. J. Fitt

HEREFORDSHIRE, Education and Conference Centre, 4 Blackfriars Street, Hereford HR4 9ZR. Tel: 01432-260000. *Director*, Dr E. Oram

KINGSTON UPON HULL, Essex House, Manor Street, Kingston upon Hull HU1 1YD. Tel: 01482-613161. *Acting Group Director Learning Services*, Mr S. Jenkins

KIRKLEES, Oldgate House, 2 Oldgate, Huddersfield HD1 6QW. Tel: 01484-225242. *Director of Lifelong Learning*, G. Tonkin

KNOWSLEY, Education Offices, Huyton Hey Road, Huyton, Knowsley L36 9YH. Tel: 0151-443 3220. *Director of Education and Lifelong Learning*, S. Munby

EDUCATION LEEDS, Merrion House, Merrion Way, 110 Merrion Centre, Leeds LS2 8DT. Tel: 0113-247 5590. *Chief Executive*, C. Edwards

LEICESTER, Marlborough House, 38 Welford Road, Leicester LE2 7AA. Tel: 0116-252 7807. *Director*, S. Andrews

LIVERPOOL, 4th Floor, Lewis Buildings, 4 Renshaw Street, Liverpool L1 4AD. Tel: 0151-233 3000. *Executive Director*, C. Hilton

LUTON, Unity House, 111 Stuart Street, Luton LU1 5NP. Tel: 01582-546000. *Corporate Director, Lifelong Learning*, T. Dessent

MANCHESTER, Overseas House, Quay Street, Manchester M3 3BB. Tel: 0161-234 7125. *Chief Education Officer*, D. Johnston

MEDWAY, Compass Centre, Chatham Maritime, Chatham, Kent ME4 4YN. Tel: 01634-331011. *Director*, R. Bolsin

MIDDLESBROUGH, PO Box 69, Vancouver House, Gurney Street, Middlesbrough TS1 1EL. Tel: 01642-262001. *Corporate Director of Education*, Dr B. Comiskey

MILTON KEYNES, Learning and Development Directory, Saxon Court, 502 Avebury Boulevard, Milton Keynes MK9 3HS. Tel: 01908-253325. *Head of School Effectiveness and Early Years Services*, J. McElligott

NEWCASTLE UPON TYNE, Civic Centre, Newcastle upon Tyne NE1 8PU. Tel: 0191-232 8520 ext. 5301. *Director of Education and Libraries*, P. Turner

NORTH EAST LINCOLNSHIRE, Education Department, 7 Eleanor Street, Grimsby DN32 9DU. Tel: 01472-323025. *Director of Learning and Child Care*, G. Hill

NORTH LINCOLNSHIRE, PO Box 35, Hewson House, Station Road, Brigg DN20 8XJ. Tel: 01724-297240. *Director of Education and Personal Development*, Dr T. W. Thomas

NORTH SOMERSET, PO Box 51, Town Hall, Weston-super-Mare BS23 1ZZ. Tel: 01934-888888. *Director*, J. Simpson

NORTH TYNESIDE, Town Hall, High Street East, Wallsend, Tyne & Wear NE28 7RR. Tel: 0191-200 6565. *Chief Education Officer*, Anne Marie Carrie

NOTTINGHAM CITY, Sandfield Centre, Sandfield Road, Lenton, Nottingham NG7 1QH. Tel: 0115-915 0706. *Director*, Heather Tomlinson

OLDHAM, PO Box 40, Civic Centre, West Street, Oldham OL1 1XJ. Tel: 0161-911 4200. *Executive Director*, Ms C. Berry

PETERBOROUGH, Bayard Place, Broadway, Peterborough PE1 1FB. Tel: 01733-748000. *Director*, R. Clayton

DEPARTMENT FOR LIFELONG LEARNING, PLYMOUTH, Plymouth PL1 2AA. Tel: 01752-307400. *Director for Lifelong Learning*, S. Faruqi

POOLE, Civic Centre, Poole, Dorset BH15 2RU. Tel: 01202-633202. *Policy Director – Education*, Dr S. Goodwin

PORTSMOUTH, Civic Offices, Guildhall Square, Portsmouth PO1 2AL. Tel: 023-9284 1209. *City Education Officer*, J. Gaskin

READING, Civic Centre, PO Box 2623, Reading RG1 7WA. Tel: 0118-939 0900. *Director*, A. J. Daykin

REDCAR AND CLEVELAND, Council Offices, Kirkleatham Street, Redcar TS10 1YA. Tel: 01642-444342. *Director*, P. Scott

ROCHDALE, PO Box 70, Municipal Offices, Smith Street, Rochdale OL16 1YD. Tel: 01706-647474. *Director of Education*, T. Piggott

ROTHERHAM, Education Office, Norfolk House, Walker Place, Rotherham S65 1AS. Tel: 01709-382121. *Acting Executive Director for Education, Culture and Leisure Services*, Ms D. Billups

RUTLAND, Catmose, Oakham, Rutland LE15 6HP. Tel: 01572-722577. *Director of Education and Youth*, Ms C. Chambers

ST HELENS, Rivington Centre, Rivington Road, St Helens WA10 4ND. Tel: 01744-455321. *Director of Community Education and Leisure Services*, Ms S. Richardson

SALFORD, Pendlebury Road, Swinton, Manchester. *Director of Education and Leisure*, M. Carriline

SANDWELL, PO Box 41, Shaftesbury House, 402 High Street, West Bromwich B70 9LT. Tel: 0121-525 7366. *Executive Director, Education and Lifelong Learning*, E. Griffiths

SEFTON, Town Hall, Trinity Road, Bootle, Merseyside L20 7AE. Tel: 0151-922 4040. *Director*, Ms E. Simpson

SHEFFIELD, Education Directorate, Leopold Street, Sheffield S1 2HH. Tel: 0114-273 5722. *Executive Director of Education*, J. Crossley-Holland

SLOUGH, Town Hall, Bath Road, Slough SL1 3UQ. Tel: 01753-875712. *Chief Education Officer*, J. Christie

SOLIHULL, PO Box 20, Council House, Solihull B91 3QU. Tel: 0121-704 6656. *Director of Education, Libraries and Arts*, D. Nixon

SOUTHAMPTON, Education Services, Southampton City Council, 5th Floor, Frobisher House, Nelson Gate, Southampton SO15 1S2. Tel: 023-8083 2771. *Director*, R. Hogg

SOUTH GLOUCESTERSHIRE EDUCATION, Bowling Hill, Chipping Sodbury, S. Glos BS37 6JX. Tel: 01454-868686. *Director of Education*, Ms T. Gillespie

SOUTHEND, Civic Centre, Victoria Avenue, Southend-on-Sea SS2 6ER. Tel: 01702-215890. *Education and Library Services Director*, S. Hay

SOUTH TYNESIDE, Town Hall and Civic Offices, Westoe Road, South Shields NE33 2RL. Tel: 0191-427 1717. *Director*, Ms B. Hughes

STOCKPORT, Town Hall, Stockport SK1 3XE. Tel: 0161-474 3808. *Chief Education Officer*, M. K. J. Hunt

STOCKTON-ON-TEES, Municipal Buildings, PO Box 228, Church Road, Stockton-on-Tees TS18 1XE. Tel: 01642-393441. *Director*, S. T. Bradford

STOKE-ON-TRENT, Floor 2, Civic Centre, Glebe Street, Stoke-on-Trent ST4 1HH. Tel: 01782-232014. *Director*, N. Rigby

SUNDERLAND, PO Box 101, Civic Centre, Sunderland SR2 7DN. Tel: 0191-553 1000. *Director of Education and Community Services*, Dr J. A. Williams

SWINDON, Sandord House, Sanford Street, Swindon SN1 1QN. Tel: 01793-463069. *Director, Education and Community*, M. Lusty

TAMESIDE, Council Offices, Wellington Road, Ashton under Lyne, Lancs OL6 6DL. Tel: 0161-342 2201. *Director of Education and Cultural Services*, P. Lawday

TELFORD AND WREKIN, Civic Offices, Telford, Shropshire TF3 4WF. Tel: 01952-202402. *Corporate Director: Education*, Mrs C. Davies

THURROCK, PO Box 118, Grays, Essex RM17 6GF. Tel: 01375-652652. *Interim Director of Education*, Jenny Cairns

TORBAY, Oldway Mansion, Paignton, Devon TQ3 2TE. Tel: 01803-208208. *Director*, G. Cane

TRAFFORD, PO Box 40, Trafford Town Hall, Talbot Road, Stretford, Trafford, Greater Manchester M32 0EL. Tel: 0161-912 1212. *Executive Director, Lifelong Learning*, C. Pratt

WAKEFIELD, County Hall, Bond Street, Wakefield WF1 2QW. Tel: 01924-305500. *Chief Education Officer*, J. McLeod

WALSALL, Civic Centre, Darwall Street, Walsall WS1 1TP. Tel: 01922-652301. *Director*, C. Green

WARRINGTON, New Town House, Buttermarket Street, Warrington, Cheshire WA1 2NJ. Tel: 01925-442901. *Director*, M. L. Roxburgh

WEST BERKSHIRE, Avonbank House, West Street, Newbury, Berks RG14 1BZ. Tel: 01635-519722. *Corporate Director for Children and Young People*, R. Hubbard

WIGAN, Gateway House, Standishgate, Wigan, Lancs WN1 1AE. Tel: 01942-828891. *Director*, R. J. Clark

WINDSOR AND MAIDENHEAD, Town Hall, St Ives Road, Maidenhead, Berks SL6 1RF. Tel: 01628-796367. *Director*, M. Peckham

WIRRAL, Hamilton Building, Conway Street, Birkenhead CH41 4FD. Tel: 0151-666 2121. *Director*, C. Rice

WOKINGHAM, Education and Cultural Services, Shute End, Wokingham, Berks RG40 1WN. Tel: 0118-974 6100. *Director*, A. Roberts

WOLVERHAMPTON, Civic Centre, St Peter's Square, Wolverhampton WV1 1RR. Tel: 01902-554100. *Co-ordinating Director for Lifelong Learning*, R. Lockwood

YORK, 10–12 George Hudson Street, York YO1 6ZG. Tel: 01904-613161. *Director of Education and Leisure*, Patrick Scott

LONDON

*Inner London borough

BARKING AND DAGENHAM, Town Hall, Barking, Essex IG11 7LU. Tel: 020-8227 3181/3662. *Director of Education, Arts and Libraries*, A. Larbalestier

BARNET, The Old Town Hall, Friern Barnet Lane, London N11 3DL. Tel: 020-8359 3048. *Chief Education Officer*, Ms L. Stone

BEXLEY, Hill View, Hill View Drive, Welling, Kent DA16 3RY. Tel: 020-8303 7777. *Director*, P. McGee

BRENT, Chesterfield House, 9 Park Lane, Wembley, Middx HA9 7RW. Tel: 020-8937 3190. *Director of Education, Arts and Libraries*, Ms Jackie Griffin

BROMLEY, Civic Centre, Stockwell Close, Bromley BR1 3UH. Tel: 020-8313 4066. *Director*, K. Davis

*CAMDEN, Crowndale Centre, 218–220 Eversholt Street, London NW1 1BD. Tel: 020-7974 1505. *Director*, R. Litchfield

*CITY OF WESTMINSTER, City Hall, 64 Victoria Street, London SW1E 6QP. Tel: 020-7641 1947. *Director*, J. Harris

*CORPORATION OF LONDON, Education Service, Corporation of London, PO Box 270, Guildhall, London EC2P 2EJ. Tel: 020-7332 1750. *City Education Officer*, D. Smith

CROYDON, Taberner House, Park Lane, Croydon CR9 3JS. Tel: 020-8760 5452. *Director*, D. Sands

EALING, Perceval House, 14–16 Uxbridge Road, London W5 2HL. Tel: 020-8758 5410. *Director*, A. Parker

ENFIELD, PO Box 56, Civic Centre, Silver Street, Enfield, Middx EN1 3XQ. Tel: 020-8379 3201. *Director*, Ms E. Graham

*GREENWICH, Riverside House, Woolwich High Street, London SE18 6DN. Tel: 020-8921 8238. *Director*, G. Gyte

*HACKNEY, Edith Cavell Building, Enfield Road, London N1 5BA. Tel: 020-8356 8436. *Director*, Mr A. Wood

*HAMMERSMITH AND FULHAM, Cambridge House, Cambridge Grove, London W6 0LE. Tel: 020-8748 3020. *Director*, Ms C. Whatford

HARINGEY, 48 Station Road, Wood Green, London N22 7TY. Tel: 020-8489 0000. *Director*, S. Jenkin

HARROW, PO Box 22, Civic Centre, Station Road, Harrow HA1 2UW. Tel: 020-8863 5611. *Director*, P. A. Osburn

HAVERING, The Broxhill Centre, Broxhill Road, Harold Hill, Romford RM4 1XN. Tel: 01708-432488. *Executive Director*, S. Evans

HILLINGDON, Civic Centre, High Street, Uxbridge UB8 1UW. Tel: 01895-250528. *Corporate Director*, P. O'Hear

HOUNSLOW, Civic Centre, Lampton Road, Hounslow, Middx TW3 4DN. Tel: 020-8583 2000. *Director*, J. D. Tricket

*ISLINGTON EDUCATION DEPARTMENT, Laycock Street, Islington, London N1 1TH. Tel: 020-7527 5566. *Director of Education*, J. Slater

*KENSINGTON AND CHELSEA, Town Hall, Hornton Street, London W8 7NX. Tel: 020-7361 3303. *Executive Director*, R. Wood

KINGSTON UPON THAMES, Guildhall 2, Kingston upon Thames KT1 1EU. Tel: 020-8547 5220. *Director*, Mr J. Braithwaite

*LAMBETH LOCAL EDUCATION SERVICES, International House, Canterbury Crescent, London SW9 7QE. Tel: 020-7926 1000. *Acting Director*, A. Wood

*LEWISHAM, 3rd Floor, Laurence House, 1 Catford Road, London SE6 4RU. Tel: 020-8314 8527. *Executive Director – Education and Culture*, Ms F. Sulke

MERTON, Civic Centre, London Road, Morden, Surrey SM4 5DX. Tel: 020-8545 3251. *Acting Director of Education, Leisure and Libraries*, Mr Tony Lenney

NEWHAM, Broadway House, 322 High Street, Stratford, London E15 1AJ. Tel: 020-8430 2000. *Director*, Ms P. Maddison

REDBRIDGE, Lynton House, 255–259 High Road, Ilford, Essex IG1 1NN. Tel: 020-8478 3020. *Director*, E. Grant

RICHMOND UPON THAMES, 1st Floor, Regal House, London Road, Twickenham TW1 3QS. Tel: 020-8891 7500. *Chief Education Officer*, Anji Phillips

*SOUTHWARK, John Smith House, 144–152 Walworth Road, London SE17 1JL. Tel: 020-7525 5050/5001. *Strategic Director of Education and Lifelong Learning*, Dr Roger Smith

SUTTON, The Grove, Carshalton, Surrey SM5 3AL. Tel: 020-8770 5000. *Strategic Director of Learning for Life*, Dr I. Birnbaum

*TOWER HAMLETS, Town Hall, Mulberry Place, 5 Clove Crescent, London E14 2BG. Tel: 020-7364 5000. *Corporate Director – Education*, Ms C. Gilbert

WALTHAM FOREST, Leyton Municipal Offices, High Road, Leyton, London E10 5QJ. Tel: 020-8527 5544 ext. 5015

*WANDSWORTH, Town Hall, Wandsworth High Street, London SW18 2PU. Tel: 020-8871 8013. *Director*, P. Robinson

## WALES

ANGLESEY, Swyddfa'r Sir, Llangefni, Anglesey LL77 7EY. Tel: 01248-752921. *Director of Lifelong Learning and Leisure*, R. P. Jones

BLAENAU GWENT, Victoria House, Victoria Business Park, Ebbw Vale, Blaenau Gwent NP23 8ER. Tel: 01495-355434. *Director*, B. Mawby

BRIDGEND, Sunnyside, Bridgend CF31 4AR. Tel: 01656-642600. *Director of Education, Leisure and Community Services*, D. Matthews

CAERPHILLY, Council Offices, Caerphilly Road, Ystrad Mynach, Hengoed CF82 7EP. Tel: 01443-815588. *Director*, D. Hopkins

CARDIFF, County Hall, Atlantic Wharf, Cardiff CF10 4UW. Tel: 029-2087 2700. *Head of Service – Schools Services*, H. Knight

CARMARTHENSHIRE, Pibwrlwyd, Carmarthen SA31 2NH. Tel: 01267-224501. *Director of Education and Community Services*, A. Davies

CEREDIGION, Swyddfa'r Sir, Marine Terrace, Aberystwyth SY23 2DE. Tel: 01970-633600. *Director*, R. J. Williams

CONWY, Government Buildings, Dinerth Road, Colwyn Bay LL28 4UL. Tel: 01492-575031/032. *Director*, R. E. Williams

DENBIGHSHIRE, Caledfryn, Smithfireld Road, Dengbigh, Denbighshire LL16 3RJ. Tel: 01824-706777. *Director*, S. Bowen

FLINTSHIRE, County Hall, Mold CH7 6ND. Tel: 01352-704010. *Director*, K. McDonogh

GWYNEDD, Shirehall Street, Caernarfon LL55 1SH. Tel: 01286-679162. *Director, Education, Culture and Leisure*, D. Whittall

MERTHYR TYDFIL EDUCATION DEPARTMENT, Ty Keir Hardie, Riverside Court, Avenue De Clichy, Merthyr Tydfil CF47 8XD. Tel: 01685-724600. *Corporate Chief Officer (Education)*, Mr W. V. Morgan

MONMOUTHSHIRE, County Hall, Cwmbran NP44 2XH. Tel: 01633-644487. *Director of Lifelong Learning and Leisure*, P. Cooke

NEATH PORT TALBOT, Civic Centre, Port Talbot SA13 1PJ. Tel: 01639-763298. *Director*, K. Napieralla

NEWPORT, Civic Centre, Newport NP20 4UR. Tel: 01633-232257. *Chief Education Officer*, D. Griffiths

PEMBROKESHIRE, County Hall, Haverfordwest SA61 1TP. Tel: 01437-764551. *Director of Education and Community Services*, G. Davies

POWYS, County Hall, Llandrindod Wells LD1 5LG. Tel: 01597-826000. *Director*, M. Barker

RHONDDA, CYNO, TAFF, Education Centre, Grawen Street, Porth CF39 0BU. Tel: 01443-687666. *Group Director, Education and Children's Services*, D. Jones

SWANSEA, County Hall, Oystermouth Road, Swansea SA1 3SN. Tel: 01792-636351. *Director*, R. Parry

TORFAEN, County Hall, Croesyceiliog, Cwmbran, Torfaen NP44 2WN. Tel: 01633-648610. *Director*, M. de Val

VALE OF GLAMORGAN, Civic Offices, Holton Road, Barry CF63 4RU. Tel: 01446-709138. *Director of Learning and Development*, B. Jeffreys

WREXHAM, Ty Henblas, Queen's Square, Wrexham LL13 8AZ. Tel: 01978-297421. *Director*, T. Garner

## SCOTLAND

ABERDEEN CITY, Summerhill Education Centre, Stronsay Drive, Aberdeen AB15 6JA. Tel: 01224-346060. *Director*, J. Stodter

ABERDEENSHIRE, Woodhill House, Westburn Road, Aberdeen AB16 5GJ. Tel: 01224-665420. *Director*, H. Vernal

ANGUS COUNCIL EDUCATION AUTHORITY, County Buildings, Market Street, Forfar DD8 3WE. Tel: 01307-461460. *Director of Education*, J. Anderson

ARGYLL AND BUTE COUNCIL, EDUCATION, Argyll House, Alexandra Parade, Dunoon PA23 8AJ. Tel: 01369-704000. *Director of Education*, A. C. Morton

CITY OF EDINBURGH, Wellington Court, 10 Waterloo Place, Edinburgh EH1 3EG. Tel: 0131-469 3000. *Director, Education*, Mr R. Jobson

CLACKMANNANSHIRE, Lime Tree House, Alloa FK10 1EX. Tel: 01259-452431. *Acting Executive Director Education and Community Services*, Mr J. Goodall

DUMFRIES AND GALLOWAY, Education Department, 30 Edinburgh Road, Dumfries DG1 1JG. Tel: 01387-260419. *Director for Education*, F. Sanderson

DUNDEE CITY COUNCIL EDUCATION DEPARTMENT, Floor 8, Tayside House, Crichton Street, Dundee DD1 3RJ. Tel: 01382-433088. *Director of Education*, Mrs A. Wilson

EAST AYRSHIRE, Council Headquarters, London Road, Kilmarnock KA3 7BU. Tel: 01563-576017. *Director*, J. Mulgrew

EAST DUNBARTONSHIRE, Boclair House, 100 Milngavie Road, Bearsden, Glasgow G61 2TQ. Tel: 0141-578 8000. *Strategic Director – Community*, Ms S. Bruce

EAST LOTHIAN, John Muir House, Haddington EH41 3HA. Tel: 01620-827562. *Director of Education and Community Services*, A. Blackie

EAST RENFREWSHIRE, Council Offices, Eastwood Park, Rouken Glen Road, Giffnock G46 6UG. Tel: 0141-577 3431. *Director*, Mrs E. J. Currie

FALKIRK, McLaren House, Marchmont Avenue, Polmont, Falkirk FK2 0NZ. Tel: 01324-506600. *Director*, Dr G. Young

FIFE, Fife House, North Street, Glenrothes KY7 5PN. Tel: 01592-413667. *Head of Education*, A. McKay

GLASGOW CITY, Nye Bevan House, 20 India Street, Glasgow G2 4PF. Tel: 0141-287 6898. *Director*, K. Corsar

HIGHLAND, Council Buildings, Glenurquhart Road, Inverness IV3 5NX. Tel: 01463-702802. *Director*, B. Robertson

INVERCLYDE, 105 Dalrymple Street, Greenock PA15 1HT. Tel: 01475-712824. *Director*, B. McLeary

MIDLOTHIAN, Fairfield House, 8 Lothian Road, Dalkeith EH22 3ZG. Tel: 0131-270 7500. *Director*, D. MacKay

MORAY, Council Offices, High Street, Elgin IV30 1BX. Tel: 01343-563171. *Director of Educational Services*, D. M. Duncan

NORTH AYRSHIRE, Cunninghame House, Irvine KA12 8EE. Tel: 01294-324400. *Corporate Director – Educational Services*, J. Travers

NORTH LANARKSHIRE, Municipal Buildings, Kildonan Street, Coatbridge ML5 3BT. Tel: 01236-812222. *Director*, M. O'Neill

ORKNEY ISLANDS, Council Offices, School Place, Kirkwall, Orkney KW15 1NY. Tel: 01856-873535. *Director of Education and Recreation*, L. Manson

PERTH AND KINROSS EDUCATION AND CHILDREN'S SERVICES, Pullar House, 35 Kinnoull Street, Perth PH1 5GD. Tel: 01738-476200. *Education Director and Children's Services*, W. Frew

RENFREWSHIRE COUNCIL EDUCATION AND LEISURE DEPT, Council Headquarters, South Building, Cotton Street, Paisley PA1 1LE. Tel: 0141-842 5601. *Director of Education and Leisure*, Ms S. Rae

SCOTTISH BORDERS, Council Headquarters, Newtown St Boswells, Melrose, Roxburghshire TD6 0SA. Tel: 01835-824000. *Director*, J. Christie

SHETLAND ISLANDS, Hayfield House, Hayfield Lane, Lerwick, Shetland ZE1 0QD. Tel: 01595-744000. *Head of Education Service*, M. Payton

SOUTH AYRSHIRE, County Buildings, Wellington Square, Ayr KA7 1DR. Tel: 01292-612201. *Director of Education, Culture and Lifelong Learning*, M. McCabe

SOUTH LANARKSHIRE, Council Headquarters, Almada Street, Hamilton ML3 0AE. Tel: 01698-454545. *Executive Director*, Ms M. Allan

STIRLING, Viewforth, Stirling FK8 2ET. Tel: 01786-442678. *Director of Children's Services*, G. Jeyes

WEST DUNBARTONSHIRE, Garshake Road, Dumbarton G82 3PU. Tel: 01389-737301. *Director of Education and Cultural Services*, I. McMurdo

EILEAN SIAR/WESTERN ISLES, Council Offices, Sandwick Road, Stornoway, Isle of Lewis HS1 2BW. Tel: 01851-703773. *Director of Education*, M. Macleod

WEST LOTHIAN COUNCIL EDUCATION SERVICES, Lindsay House, South Bridge Street, Bathgate EH48 1TS. Tel: 01506-776000. *Corporate Manager*, R. Stewart

### NORTHERN IRELAND

BELFAST EDUCATION AND LIBRARY BOARD, 40 Academy Street, Belfast BT1 2NQ. Tel: 028-9056 4000. *Chief Executive*, D. Cargo

NORTH EASTERN EDUCATION AND LIBRARY BOARD, County Hall, 182 Galgorm Road, Ballymena, Co. Antrim BT42 1HN. Tel: 028-2565 3333. *Chief Executive*, G. Topping

SOUTH EASTERN EDUCATION AND LIBRARY BOARD, Grahamsbridge Road, Dundonald BT16 2HS. Tel: 028-9056 6200. *Chief Executive*, J. B. Fitzsimons

SOUTHERN EDUCATION AND LIBRARY BOARD, 3 Charlemont Place, The Mall, Armagh BT61 9AX. Tel: 028-3751 2200. *Chief Executive*, Mrs H. McClenagahan

WESTERN EDUCATION AND LIBRARY BOARD, 1 Hospital Road, Omagh, Co. Tyrone BT79 0AW. Tel: 028-8241 1411. *Chief Executive*, P. J. Martin

### ISLANDS

GUERNSEY, The Grange, St Peter Port, Guernsey GY1 1RQ. Tel: 01481-710821. *Director*, D. T. Neale

JERSEY, PO Box 142, Jersey JE4 8QJ. Tel: 01534-509500. *Director*, T. W. McKeon

ISLE OF MAN, Murray House, 5–11 Mount Havelock, Douglas, Isle of Man IM1 2SG. Tel: 01624-685820. *Director*, R. B. Cowin

ISLES OF SCILLY, Town Hall, St Mary's, Isles of Scilly TR21 0LW. Tel: 01720-422537 ext. 145. *Secretary for Education*, P. S. Hygate

## ADVISORY BODIES

### SCHOOLS

BRITISH EDUCATIONAL COMMUNICATIONS AND TECHNOLOGY AGENCY, Milburn Hill Road, Science Park, Coventry CV4 7JJ. Tel: 024-7641 6994; Fax: 024-7641 1418. *Chief Executive*, O. Lynch

EDUCATION OTHERWISE, PO Box 7420, London N9 9SG. Tel: Helpline: 0870-730 0074

INTERNATIONAL BACCALAUREATE ORGANIZATION, Peterson House, Malthouse Avenue, Cardiff Gate, Cardiff CF23 8GL. Tel: 029-2054 7777; Fax: 029-2054 7778. *Director of Academic Affairs*, Dr H. Drennen

LEARNING AND SKILLS COUNCIL, 101 Lockhurst Lane, Coventry CV6 5SF. Tel: 024-7670 3241; Fax: 024-7670 3334

LEARNING AND SKILLS COUNCIL, Cheylesmore House, Quinton Road, Coventry CV1 2WT. Tel: 0845-019 4170; Fax: 024-7686 3100

SPECIAL EDUCATIONAL NEEDS TRIBUNAL, 7th Floor, Windsor House, 50 Victoria Street, London SW1H 0NW. Tel: 020-7925 6925; Fax: 020-7925 6926. *President*, T. Aldridge

### INDEPENDANT SCHOOLS

GOVERNING BODIES ASSOCIATION, The Ancient Foresters, Bush End, Takeley, Bishop's Stortford, Herts CM22 6NN. Tel: 01279-871865; Fax: 01279-871865. *Secretary*, F. V. Morgan

GOVERNING BODIES OF GIRLS' SCHOOLS ASSOCIATION, The Ancient Foresters, Bush End, Takeley, Bishop's Stortford, Herts CM22 6NN. Tel: 01279-871865; Fax: 01279-871865. *Secretary*, F. V. Morgan

INDEPENDENT SCHOOLS COUNCIL, Grosvenor Gardens House, 35–37 Grosvenor Gardens, London SW1W 0BS. Tel: 020-7 798 1590; Fax: 020-7 798 1591. *General Secretary*, Dr A. B. Cooke

INDEPENDENT SCHOOLS EXAMINATIONS BOARD, Jordan House, Christchurch Road, New Milton, Hants BH25 6QJ. Tel: 01425-621111; Fax: 01425-620044. *Administrator*, Mrs J. Williams

### FURTHER EDUCATION

AOSEC, Building 33, The University of Reading, London Road, Reading RG1 5AQ. Tel: 0118-931 6320; Fax: 0118-931 6324. *Chief Executive*, B. J. Knowles

*Regional Advisory Councils*

ASSOCIATION OF COLLEGES IN THE EASTERN REGION, Suite 1, Lancaster House, Meadow Lane, St Ives, Huntingdon, Cambs PE27 4LG. Tel: 01480-468198; Fax: 01480-468601. *Chief Executive*, N. Brenton

CENTRA (EDUCATION AND TRAINING SERVICES) LTD, Duxbury Park, Duxbury Hall Road, Chorley, Lancs PR7 4AT. Tel: 01257-241428; Fax: 01257-260357. *Chief Executive*, P. Wren

EMFEC (East Midland Further Education Council), Robins Wood House, Robins Wood Road, Aspley, Nottingham NG8 3NH. Tel: 0115-854 1616; Fax: 0115-854 1617. *Chief Executive*, Ms J. Gardiner
Learning and Skills Development Agency, Citadel Place, Tinworth Street, London SE11 5EH. Tel: 020-7 840 5400; Fax: 020-7 840 5401. *Chief Executive*, C. Hughes
NCFE, Portland House, New Bridge Street, Newcastle upon Tyne NE1 8AN. Tel: 0191-201 3100; Fax: 0191-2013101. *Chief Executive*, I. M. Sutcliffe
South West Association for Education and Training, Bishops Hull House, Bishops Hull, Taunton, Somerset TA1 5EP. Tel: 01823-335491; Fax: 01823-323388. *Chief Executive*, Ms L. McGrath
Welsh Joint Education Committee, 245 Western Avenue, Cardiff CF5 2YX. Tel: 029-2026 5000; Fax: 029-2057 5894

### Higher Education

Association of Commonwealth Universities, John Foster House, 36 Gordon Square, London WC1H 0PF. Tel: 020-7380 6700; Fax: 020-7387 2655.. *Secretary-General*, Prof. M. G. Gibbons
Northern Ireland Higher Education Council, 4th Floor, Room 407, Adelaide House, 39–49 Adelaide Street, Belfast BT2 8FD. Tel: 028-9025 7722; Fax: 028-9025 7701. *Chairman*, Sir Kenneth Bloomfield
Quality Assurance Agency for Higher Education, Southgate House, Southgate Street, Gloucester GL1 1UB. Tel: 01452-557000; Fax: 01452-557070. *Chief Executive*, J. Randall
Universities Scotland, 53 Hanover Street, Edinburgh EH2 2PJ. Tel: 0131-226 1111; Fax: 0131-226 1100. *Director*, D. Caldwell
Universities UK, Woburn House, 20 Tavistock Square, London WC1H 9HQ. Tel: 020-7 419 4111; Fax: 020-7388 8649. *President*, Prof. R. Floud

## CURRICULUM COUNCILS

Awdurdod Cymwysterau, Cwricwlwm Ac Asesu Cymru/Qualifications, Curriculum and Assessment Authority for Wales, Castle Buildings, Womanby Street, Cardiff CF10 1SX. Tel: 029-20 375400; Fax: 029-20 343612. *Chief Executive*, J. V. Williams
Learning and Teaching Scotland, Gardyne Road, Dundee DD5 1NY. Tel: 01382-443600; Fax: 01382-443645. *Chief Executive*, M. Baughan
Northern Ireland Council for the Curriculum, Examinations and Assessment, Clarendon Dock, 29 Clarendon Road, Belfast BT1 3BG. Tel: 028-9026 1200; Fax: 028-9026 1234. *Chief Executive*, G. Boyd
Qualifications and Curriculum Authority, 83 Piccadilly, London W1Y 8QA. Tel: 020-7509 5555; Fax: 020-7 509 6666. *Chairman*, Sir William Stubbs, PH.D.

## EXAMINING BODIES

Assessment and Qualifications Alliance (AQA), Devas Street, Manchester M15 6EX. Tel: 0161-953 1180; Fax: 0161-273 7572. *Director General*, Ms K. Tattersall
Assessment and Qualifications Alliance (AQA), Stag Hill House, Guildford, Surrey GU2 7XJ. Tel: 01483-506506; Fax: 01483-300152. *Director General*, Ms K. Tattersall
Edexcel, Stewart House, 32 Russell Square, London WC1B 5DN. Tel: 0870-240 9800; Fax: 020-7758 6960. *Chief Executive*, Dr C. Townsend
OCR (Oxford Cambridge and RSA Examinations), Head Office, 1 Regent Street, Cambridge CB2 1GG. Tel: 01223-552552; Fax: 01223-552553. *Chief Executive*, Dr R. McLone
Northern Ireland Council for the Curriculum, Examinations and Assessment, 29 Clarendon Road, Belfast, County Antrim BT1 3BG. Tel: 01232-261200; Fax: 01232-261234. *Chief Executive*, G. Boyd
Welsh Joint Education Committee, 245 Western Avenue, Cardiff CF5 2YX. Tel: 029-2026 5000; Fax: 029-2057 5894. *Chief Executive*, W. G. Roberts

### GCSE – *see* above

Edexcel
Northern Ireland Council for the Curriculum, Examinations and Assessment
Welsh Joint Education Committee

### A-Level – *see* above

Assessment and Qualifications Alliance (AQA)
Edexcel
Northern Ireland Council for the Curriculum, Examinations and Assessment Examinations and Assessment
OCR (Oxford, Cambridge and RSA Examinations)

### Scotland

Scottish Qualifications Authority, Hanover House, 24 Douglas Street, Glasgow G2 7NQ. Tel: 0141-248 7900; Fax: 0141-242 2244. *Chief Executive*, B. Morton

### Further Education – *see* above

City Guilds, 1 Giltspur Street, London EC1A 9DD. Tel: 020-7 294 2468; Fax: 020-7294 2400. *Director-General*, C. Humphries, CBE
Edexcel
OCR (Oxford, Cambridge and RSA Examinations)

## FUNDING COUNCILS

### Further Education

Learning and Skills Council, Cheylesmore House, Quinton Road, Coventry CV1 2WT. Tel: 0845-019 4170; Fax: 024-7686 3100. *Chief Executive*, J. Harwood
National Council – ELWA, Linden Court, The Orchards, Ilex Close, Cardiff CF14 5DZ. Tel: 029-2076 1861; Fax: 029-2076 3163. *Director of Operations*, L. Bloomfield
Scottish Further Education Funding Council, Donaldson House, 97 Haymarket Terrace, Edinburgh EH12 5HD. Tel: 0131-313 6500; Fax: 0131-313 6501. *Chief Executive*, Prof. J. Sizer, CBE

### Higher Education

Higher Education Council–ELWA, Linden Court, The Orchards, Ilex Close, Cardiff CF14 5DZ. Tel: 029-2076 1861; Fax: 029-2076 3163. *Chief Executive*, S. Martin

HIGHER EDUCATION FUNDING COUNCIL FOR ENGLAND, Northavon House, Coldharbour Lane, Bristol BS16 1QD. Tel: 0117-931 7317; Fax: 0117-931 7203. *Chief Executive*, Sir Brian Fender, KT.

SCOTTISH HIGHER EDUCATION FUNDING COUNCIL, Donaldson House, 97 Haymarket Terrace, Edinburgh EH12 5HD. Tel: 0131-313 6500; Fax: 0131-313 6501. *Chief Executive*, Prof. J. Sizer, CBE

STUDENT AWARDS AGENCY FOR SCOTLAND, Gyleview House, 3 Redheughs Rigg, Edinburgh EH12 9HH. Tel: 0131-476 8212; Fax: 0131-244 5717. *Chief Executive*, D. Stephen

STUDENT LOANS COMPANY LTD, 100 Bothwell Street, Glasgow G2 7JD. Tel: 0141-306 2000. *Chief Executive*, C. Ward

TEACHER TRAINING AGENCY, Portland House, Stag Place, London SW1E 5TT. Tel: 020-7925 3700; Fax: 020-7925 3790. *Chairman*, Prof. C. Booth

## ADMISSIONS AND COURSE INFORMATION

CAREERS RESEARCH AND ADVISORY CENTRE, Sheraton House, Castle Park, Cambridge CB3 0AX. Tel: 01223-460277; Fax: 01223-311708. *Chief Executive*, D. Thomas

GRADUATE TEACHER TRAINING REGISTRY, Rosehill, New Barn Lane, Cheltenham, Glos GL52 3LZ. Tel: 01242-544600; Fax: 01242-544962. *Small Systems Unit Manager*, Mrs J. Pearce

SOCIAL WORK ADMISSIONS SYSTEM, Rosehill, New Barn Lane, Cheltenham, Glos GL52 3LZ. Tel: 01242-544600; Fax: 01242-544962. *Small Systems Unit Manager*, Mrs J. Pearce

UNIVERSITIES AND COLLEGES ADMISSIONS SERVICE, Rosehill, New Barn Lane, Cheltenham, Glos GL52 3LZ. Tel: 01242-222444; Fax: 01242-544963. *Chief Executive*, M. A. Higgins

UNIVERSITIES SCOTLAND, 53 Hanover Street, Edingburgh EH2 2PJ. Tel: 0141-353 1880; Fax: 0141-353 1881. *Director*, D. Caldwell

## UNIVERSITIES

UNIVERSITY OF ABERDEEN (1495)
Aberdeen AB24 3FX. Scotland
Tel: 01224-272000
*Chancellor*, The Lord Wilson of Tillyorn, GCMG (1997)
*Rector*, Miss C. Dickson Wright
*Vice-Chancellor and Principal*, Prof. C. D. Rice

UNIVERSITY OF ABERTAY DUNDEE (1994)
Bell Street, Dundee DD1 1HG. Scotland
Tel: 01382-308000
*Chancellor*, The Rt. Hon. Earl of Airlie, KT, GCVO, PC (1994)
*Registrar*, Dr D. Button
*Vice-Chancellor*, Prof. B. King

ANGLIA POLYTECHNIC UNIVERSITY (1992)
Bishop Hall Lane, Chelmsford, Essex CM1 1SQ.
Tel: 01245-493131
*Chancellor*, vacant
*Vice-Chancellor*, M. Malone-Lee, CB

ANGLIA POLYTECHNIC UNIVERSITY (1992)
East Road, Cambridge CB1 1PT.
Tel: 01223-363271
*Chancellor*, vacant
*Vice-Chancellor*, M. Malone-Lee, CB

ASTON UNIVERSITY (1895)
Aston Triangle, Birmingham B4 7ET.
Tel: 0121-359 3611
*Chancellor*, Sir Adrian Cadbury, (1979)
*Registrar and Secretary*, R. D. A. Packham
*Vice-Chancellor*, Prof. M. Wright

UNIVERSITY OF BATH (1966)
Claverton Down, Bath BA2 7AY.
Tel: 01225-826826
*Chancellor*, The Lord Tugendhat, (1998)
*Registrar*, J. A. Bursey
*Vice-Chancellor*, Prof. G. Breakwell

UNIVERSITY OF BIRMINGHAM (1900)
Edgbaston, Birmingham BH15 2TT.
Tel: 0121-414 3344
*Chancellor*, Sir Alexander Jarratt, CB (1983)
*Registrar and Secretary*, D. E. Hall
*Vice-Chancellor*, Prof. M. Sterling, DENG, FRENG

BOURNEMOUTH UNIVERSITY (1992)
Christchurch Road, Bournemouth BH1 3LT.
Tel: 01202-524111
*Chancellor*, The Baroness Cox of Queensbury, (1992)
*Registrar*, N. O. G. Richardson
*Vice-Chancellor*, Prof. G. Slater

BOURNEMOUTH UNIVERSITY (1992)
Fern Barrow, Poole, Dorset BH12 5BB.
Tel: 01202-524111
*Chancellor*, The Baroness Cox of Queensbury, (1992)
*Registrar*, N. O. G. Richardson
*Vice-Chancellor*, Prof. G. Slater

UNIVERSITY OF BRADFORD (1966)
Richmond Road, Bradford, W. Yorks BD7 1DP.
Tel: 01274-232323
*Chancellor*, The Baroness Lockwood of Dewsbury, (1997)
*Registrar and Secretary*, N. J. Andrew
*Vice-Chancellor*, Prof. C. Bell

UNIVERSITY OF BRIGHTON (1992)
Lewes Road, Brighton BN2 4AT.
Tel: 01273-600900
*Chairman of the Board*, C. Hume
*Director*, Prof. Sir David Watson
*Deputy Director*, D. E. House
*Secretary*, Ms C. E. Moon

UNIVERSITY OF BRISTOL (1909)
Tyndall Avenue, Bristol BS8 1TH.
Tel: 0117-928 9000
*Chancellor*, Sir Jeremy Morse, KCMG (1989)
*Registrar*, D. Pretty
*Vice-Chancellor*, Prof. Eric Thomas

BRUNEL UNIVERSITY (1966)
Uxbridge, Middx UB8 3PH.
Tel: 01895-274000
*Academic and Principal Registrar*, J. B. Alexander
*Chancellor*, The Rt. Hon Lord Wakeham, PC, JP, DL, FCA, HON AND UNIV, HON PHD (1998)
*Vice-Chancellor and Principal*, Prof. M. J. H. Sterling, PH.D, FRENG.

UNIVERSITY OF BUCKINGHAM (1983)
Buckingham MK18 1EG.
Tel: 01280-814080

*Chancellor*, Sir Martin Jacomb, (1998)
*Registrar and Secretary*, S. Cooksey
*Vice-Chancellor*, Dr Terence Kealey

UNIVERSITY OF CAMBRIDGE
Trinity Lane, Cambridge CB2 1TN.
Tel: 01223-337733

UNIVERSITY OFFICERS, ETC.

*Chancellor*, HRH The Prince Philip, Duke of Edinburgh, KG, KT, OM, GBE, PC (1977)
*Commissary*, The Lord Oliver of Aylmerton (*Trinity Hall*), PC (1989)
*Deputy High Steward*, The Lord Richardson of Duntisbourne, MBE, TD, PC (1983)
*Director of the Fitzwilliam Museum*, D. D. Robinson (*Clare*), (1995)
*Librarian*, P. K. Fox (*Selwyn*), (1994)
*Orator*, A. J. Bowen (*Jesus*), (1993)
*Proctors*, Dr D. J. Chivers (Selwyn); V. E. Izzet (Christ's), (2001)
*Registrary*, T. J. Mead (*Wolfson*), PH.D. (1997)
*Secretary-General of the Faculties*, D. A. Livesey (*Emmanuel*), PH.D. (1992)
*Treasurer*, Mrs J. Womack (*Trinity Hall*), (1993)
*Vice-Chancellor*, Prof. Sir Alec Broers, FRS (1996)

COLLEGES AND HALLS *with dates of foundation*

CHRIST'S, (1505), *Master*, A. J. Munro, PH.D. (1995)
CHURCHILL, (1960), *Master*, Sir John Boyd, KCMG (1996)
CLARE, (1326), *Master*, Prof. B. A. Hepple, LLD (1993)
CLARE HALL, (1966), *President*, Prof. Dame Gillian Beer, DBE, LITTD., FBA (1994)
CORPUS CHRISTI, (1352), *Master*, Prof. H. Ahmed, PH.D. (2000)
DARWIN, (1964), *Master*, Prof. W. Brown (2000)
DOWNING, (1800), *Master*, Dr S. G. Fleet, PHD (2001)
EMMANUEL, (1584), *Master*, Prof. J. E. Ffowcs-Williams, SC.D. (1996)
FITZWILLIAM, (1966), *Master*, Prof. B. F. G. Johnson (1999)
GIRTON, (1869), *Mistress*, Prof. A. M. Strathern, PH.D. (1998)
GONVILLE AND CAIUS, (1348), *Master*, N. McKendrick (1996)
HOMERTON, (1824) (for B.Ed. Students), *Principal*, Dr K. B. Pretty (1991)
HUGHES HALL, (1885) (for post-graduate students), *President*, Prof. P. Richards, PHD (1998)
JESUS, (1496), *Master*, Prof. R. Mair, SRENG
KING'S, (1441), *Provost*, Prof. P. P. G. B. Bateson, SC.D., FRS (1987)
*LUCY CAVENDISH COLLEGE, (1965) (for women research students and mature and affiliated undergraduates), *President*, Dame Veronica Sutherland (2001)
MAGDALENE, (1542), *Master*, Prof. Sir John Gurdon, D.PHIL., FRS (1995)
*NEW HALL, (1954), *President*, Mrs A. Lonsdale (1996)
*NEWNHAM, (1871), *Principal*, Baroness O'Neill, CBE (1992)
PEMBROKE, (1347), *Master*, Sir Roger Tomkys, KCMG (1992)
PETERHOUSE, (1284), *Master*, Prof. Sir John Meurig Thomas, FRS (1993)
QUEENS', (1448), *President*, The Lord Eatwell (1997)
ROBINSON, (1977), *Warden*, Prof. the Lord Lewis of Newnham, SC.D., FRS (1977)
SELWYN, (1882), *Master*, Prof. R. J. Bowring, LITT.D. (2000)
SIDNEY SUSSEX, (1596), *Master*, Prof. S. J. N. Dawson (1999)
ST CATHARINE'S, (1473), *Master*, Prof. D. S. Ingram, SC.D. (2000)
ST EDMUND'S, (1896), *Master*, Prof. R. B. Heap, SC.D. (1996)
ST JOHN'S, (1511), *Master*, Prof. P. Goddard, PH.D., FRS (1994)
TRINITY, (1546), *Master*, Prof. A. K. Sen , PHD (1998)
TRINITY HALL, (1350), *Master*, Prof. P. Clarke (1984)
WOLFSON, (1965), *President*, G. Johnson, PH.D. (1994)
*College for women only

UNIVERSITY OF CENTRAL ENGLAND IN BIRMINGHAM (1992)
Perry Barr, Birmingham B42 2SU.
Tel: 0121-331 5000
*Chancellor*, I. McArdle
*Registrar and Secretary*, Ms M. Penlington
*Vice-Chancellor*, Dr P. C. Knight, CBE

UNIVERSITY OF CENTRAL LANCASHIRE (1992)
Preston PR1 2HE.
Tel: 01772-201201
*Chancellor*, Richard Evans, (1995)
*Registrar*, Ms L. Munro
*Vice-Chancellor*, Dr M. McVicar

CITY UNIVERSITY (1966)
Northampton Square, London EC1V 0HB.
Tel: 020-7040 5060
*Academic Registrar*, A. H. Sevilleb (until Dec 2001), PH.D.
*Chancellor*, The Rt. Hon. the Lord Mayor of London
*Vice-Chancellor*, Prof. D. W. Rhind

COVENTRY UNIVERSITY (1992)
Priory Street, Coventry CV1 5FB.
Tel: 024-7688 7688
*Academic Registrar*, Dr J. Gledhill, PH.D.
*Chancellor*, The Lord Plumb, DL (1995)
*Secretary*, Mrs L. Arlidge
*Vice-Chancellor*, Dr M. Goldstein, CBE, PH.D.

CRANFIELD UNIVERSITY (1969)
Cranfield, Beds MK43 0AL.
Tel: 01234-750111
*Academic Registrar and Secretary*, D. J. Buck
*Chancellor*, The Lord Vincent of Coleshill, GBE, KCB, DSO (1998)
*Vice-Chancellor*, Prof. F. R. Hartley, D.SC.

DE MONTFORT UNIVERSITY (1992)
The Gateway, Leicester LE1 9BH.
Tel: 0116-255 1551
*Academic Registrar*, V. E. Critchlow
*Chancellor*, Baroness Prashar of Runnymede, CBE (1998)
*Vice-Chancellor*, Prof. P. Tasker

UNIVERSITY OF DERBY (1992)
Kedleston Road, Derby DE22 1GB.
Tel: 01332-590500
*Chancellor*, Sir Christopher Ball, FRSA
*Registrar*, Mrs J. M. Fry, BSC
*Vice-Chancellor*, Prof. R. Waterhouse

UNIVERSITY OF DUNDEE (1967)
Dundee DD1 4HN. Scotland
Tel: 01382-344000
*Academic Secretary*, Dr I. K. Francis
*Chancellor*, Sir James Black, FRCP, FRS (1992)
*Rector*, F. MacAualy, 1998–2001
*Vice-Chancellor*, Sir Alan Langlands

UNIVERSITY OF DURHAM Durham DH1 3HP.
Tel: 0191-374 2000
*Chancellor*, Sir Peter Ustinov, CBE, FRSL, KT, HON DLITT, FRSA, FRSL
*Registrar and Secretary*, J. V. Hogan, PH.D.
*Vice-Chancellor*, Prof. Sir Kenneth Calman, KCB, MD, FRCP, FRCGP, FRCR, FRSE, PH.D.

COLLEGES

COLLINGWOOD, *Principal*, Prof. G. H. Blake, PH.D. (1987)
GRADUATE SOCIETY, *Principal*, M. J. Rowell, PH.D. (2000)
GREY, *Master*, V. E. Watts (1989)
HATFIELD, *Master*, Prof. T. P. Burt, PH.D. (1996)
ST AIDAN'S, *Principal*, J. S. Ashworth (1998)
ST CHAD'S, *Principal*, Revd J. P. M. Cassidy, PH.D. (1997)
ST CUTHBERT'S SOCIETY, *Principal*, B. Robertson (1999)
ST HILD AND ST BEDE, *Principal*, J. A. Pearson, PH.D. (2000)
ST JOHN'S, *Principal*, Rt. Revd. Prof. S. W. Sykes (1999)
ST MARY'S, *Principal*, Miss J. L. Hobbs (1999)
STOCKTON CAMPUS, *Provost*, Prof. Sir Kenneth Calman
TREVELYAN, *Principal*, N. Martin, PHD (2000)
UNIVERSITY, *Master*, Prof. M. E. Tucker, PH.D. (1998)
USHAW, *President*, Revd J. O'Keefe (1996)
VAN MILDERT, *Principal*, G. Patterson (2000)

UNIVERSITY OF EAST ANGLIA (1963)
Norwich NR4 7TJ.
Tel: 01603-456161
*Chancellor*, Sir Geoffrey Allen, FRS, FRENG. (1994)
*Registrar and Secretary*, B. Summers
*Vice-Chancellor*, V. Watts

UNIVERSITY OF EAST LONDON (1898)
Longbridge Road, Dagenham, Essex RM8 2AS.
Tel: 020-8223 3000
*Chancellor*, The Lord Rix, CBE, DL, KT. (1997)
*Registrar and Secretary*, A. Ingle
*Vice-Chancellor*, Prof. F. W. Gould

UNIVERSITY OF EDINBURGH (1583)
South Bridge, Edinburgh EH8 9YL. Scotland
Tel: 0131-650 1000
*Chancellor*, HRH The Prince Philip, Duke of Edinburgh, KG, KT, OM, GBE, PC, FRS (1952)
*Rector*, R. Harper, MSP
*Vice-Chancellor*, Prof. Sir Stewart Sutherland, FBA, FRSE

UNIVERSITY OF ESSEX (1964)
Wivenhoe Park, Colchester CO4 3SQ.
Tel: 01206-873333
*Chancellor*, The Lord Nolan, PC (1997)
*Registrar and Secretary*, T. Rich, PH.D.
*Vice-Chancellor*, Prof. I. Crewe

UNIVERSITY OF EXETER (1955)
The Queen's Drive, Exeter EX4 4QJ.
Tel: 01392-263263
*Chancellor*, The Lord Alexander of Weedon (1998), QC
*Registrar and Secretary*, I. H. C. Powell
*Vice-Chancellor*, Sir Geoffrey Holland, KCB

UNIVERSITY OF GLAMORGAN (1992)
Pontypridd CF37 1DL. Wales
Tel: 01443-480480; Freephone: 0800-716925
*Chancellor*, The Rt. Hon. Lord Merlyn-Rees, PC, QC (1994)
*Registrar*, J. O'Shea
*Secretary*, J. L. Bracegirdle,
*Vice-Chancellor*, Prof. Sir Adrian Webb

UNIVERSITY OF GLASGOW (1451)
University Avenue, Glasgow G12 8QQ. Scotland
Tel: 0141-339 8855
*Chancellor*, Sir William Kerr Fraser, GCB, FRSE
*Vice-Chancellor*, Prof. Sir Graeme Davies, FRENG, FRSE

GLASGOW CALEDONIAN UNIVERSITY (1993)
Cowcaddens Road, Glasgow G4 0BA. Scotland
Tel: 0141-331 3000
*Principal and Vice-Chancellor*, Dr I. A. Johnston, PH.D., CB, FIPO, FRSA
*Pro Vice Chancellor Learning*, Prof. P. Abbott, KBE (1993)
*Secretary to University Court*, B. M. Murphy

UNIVERSITY OF GREENWICH (1992)
Park Row, Greenwich, London SE10 9LS.
Tel: 020-8331 8000
*Academic Registrar*, Miss C. Rose
*Chancellor*, Lord Holme of Cheltenham, CBE
*Vice-Chancellor*, Prof. R. Trainor

HERIOT-WATT UNIVERSITY (1966)
Edinburgh EH14 4AS. Scotland
Tel: 0131-449 5111
*Chancellor*, The Lord Mackay of Clashfern, KT, PC (1979)
*Vice-Chancellor*, Prof. J. S. Archer, FRENG.

UNIVERSITY OF HERTFORDSHIRE (1992)
College Lane, Hatfield, Herts AL10 9AB.
Tel: 01707-284000
*Chancellor*, The Lord MacLaurin of Knebworth, (1996)
*Registrar and Secretary*, P. G. Jeffreys,
*Vice-Chancellor*, Prof. N. K. Buxton,

UNIVERSITY OF HUDDERSFIELD (1992)
Queensgate, Huddersfield HD1 3DH.
Tel: 01484-422288
*Chancellor*, Sir Ernest Hall, OBE (1996)
*Vice-Chancellor*, Prof. J. R. Tarrant

UNIVERSITY OF HULL (1954)
Cottingham Road, Hull HU6 7RX.
Tel: 01482-346311
*Chancellor*, The Lord Armstrong of Ilminster, GCB, CVO (1994)
*Registrar*, D. J. Lock
*Vice-Chancellor*, Dr D. J. Drewry

KEELE UNIVERSITY (1962)
Keele, Staffs ST5 5BG.
Tel: 01782-621111
*Chancellor*, Sir Claus Moser, KCB, CBE, FBA (1986)
*Registrar and Secretary*, S. J. Morris
*Vice-Chancellor*, Prof. J. V. Finch, CBE, DL, PH.D.

UNIVERSITY OF KENT AT CANTERBURY (1965)
Canterbury, Kent CT2 7NZ.
Tel: 01227-764000
*Chancellor*, Sir Crispin Tickell, GCMG, KCVO
*Registrar and Secretary*, N. A. McHard,
*Vice-Chancellor*, Prof. D. Melville, PH.D.

KINGSTON UNIVERSITY (1992)
Kingston upon Thames, Surrey KT1 1LQ.
Tel: 020-8547 2000
*Academic Registrar*, Mrs A. Stokes
*Chancellor*, Sir Peter Hall
*Secretary*, R. S. Abdula, MBE
*Vice-Chancellor*, Prof. P. Scott

UNIVERSITY OF LANCASTER (1964)
Bailrigg, Lancaster LA1 4YW.
Tel: 01524-65201
*Chancellor*, HRH Princess Alexandra, the Hon. Lady Ogilvy, GCVO (1964)
*Secretary*, Miss F. Aiken
*Vice-Chancellor*, Prof. W. Ritchie, OBE

UNIVERSITY OF LEEDS (1904)
Leeds LS2 9JT.
Tel: 0113-243 1751
*Academic Registrar*, A. Parkinson
*Chancellor*, Lord Bragg of Wigton
*Vice-Chancellor*, Prof. A. G. Wilson

LEEDS METROPOLITAN UNIVERSITY (1992)
Calverley Street, Leeds LS1 3HE.
Tel: 0113-283 2600
*Chancellor*, L. Silver, OBE (1989)
*Vice-Chancellor*, Prof. L. Wagner, CBE

UNIVERSITY OF LEICESTER (1957)
University Road, Leicester LE1 7RH.
Tel: 0116-252 2522
*Chancellor*, Sir Michael Atiyah, OM, FRS, PH.D., D.SC. (1995)
*Registrar and Secretary*, K. J. Julian,
*Vice-Chancellor*, Prof. R. Burgess, PH.D.

UNIVERSITY OF LINCOLN (1992)
Brayford Pool, Lincoln, LN7 6TS.
Tel: 01522-882000
*Chancellor*, Dame Elizabeth Esteve
*Registrar*, Dr Kevin Pardoe
*Vice-Chancellor*, Prof. David Chiddick

UNIVERSITY OF LIVERPOOL (1903)
Abercromby Square, Liverpool L69 3BX.
Tel: 0151-794 2000
*Chancellor*, The Lord Owen, CH, PC (1996)
*Registrar and Secretary*, M. D. Carr
*Vice-Chancellor*, Prof. P. N. Love, CBE

LIVERPOOL JOHN MOORES UNIVERSITY (1992)
2 Rodaney Street, Liverpool L3 5UX.
Tel: 0151-231 2121
*Chancellor*, Ms C. Booth, QC
*Registrar and Secretary*, Ms A. Wild
*Vice-Chancellor*, Prof. M. Brown

UNIVERSITY OF LONDON (1836)
Malet Street, London WC1E 7HU.
Tel: 020-7862 8000
*Visitor*, HM The Queen in Council
*Academic Registrar*, Mrs G. F. Roberts
*Chairman of Convocation*, D. D. A. Leslie
*Chairman of the Council*, The Lord Woolf, PC
*Chancellor*, HRH The Princess Royal, KG, GCVO, FRS (1981)
*Director of Administration*, J. R. Davidson
*Vice-Chancellor*, Prof. G. Zellick, PH.D.

COLLEGES

BIRKBECK, Malet Street, London WC1E7HX. *Master*, Prof. T. O'Shea, PH.D. (1998)

GOLDSMITHS COLLEGE, Lewisham Way, New Cross, London SE146NW *Warden*, Prof. B. Pimlott, FBA (1998)

HEYTHROP COLLEGE, Kensington Square, London W85HQ. *Principal*, Revd Dr J. McDade, SJ, BD (1999)

IMPERIAL COLLEGE OF SCIENCE, TECHNOLOGY AND MEDICINE (includes Imperial College Schools of Medicine at Charing Cross, Hammersmith and St Mary's hospitals and at the National Heart and Lung Institute), South Kensington, London SW72AZ. *Rector*, Sir Richard Sykes, FRS (2001)

INSTITUTE OF EDUCATION, 20 Bedford Way, London WC1H0AL. *Director*, Prof. G. Whitty (2000)

KING'S COLLEGE LONDON, (includes King's College School of Medicine and Dentistry, United Medical and Dental Schools of Guy's and St Thomas' Hospitals), Strand, London WC2R2LS. *Principal*, Prof. A. Lucas, PH.D. (1993)

LONDON BUSINESS SCHOOL, Sussex Place, Regent's Park, London NW14SA. *Dean*, Prof. L. D'Andrea Tyson (2002)

LONDON SCHOOL OF ECONOMICS AND POLITICAL SCIENCE, Houghton Street, London WC2A2AE. *Director*, Prof. A. Giddens (1997)

LONDON SCHOOL OF HYGIENE AND TROPICAL MEDICINE, Keppel Street, London WC1E7HT. *Dean*, Prof. A. Hairies (2001)

QUEEN MARY (incorporating St Bartholomew's and the Royal London School of Medicine and Dentistry and the London Hospital Medical College), Mile End Road, London E14NS. *Principal*, Prof. A. Smith, FRS, PH. D. (1998)

ROYAL ACADEMY OF MUSIC, Marylebone Road, London NW12BS. *Principal*, Prof. Curtis Price, PH.D., HON. RAM, FKC (1995)

ROYAL HOLLOWAY, Egham Hill, Egham, Surrey TW20 0EX. *Principal*, Prof. D. Bone, FRSA (2000)

ROYAL VETERINARY COLLEGE, Royal College Street, London NW10TU. *Principal and Dean*, Prof. L. E. Lanyon, CBE (1989)

SCHOOL OF ORIENTAL AND AFRICAN STUDIES, Thornhaugh Street, Russell Square, London WC1H0XG. *Director*, Prof. C. Bundy (2001)

SCHOOL OF PHARMACY, 29–39 Brunswick Square, London WC1N1AX. *Dean*, Prof. A. T. Florence, CBE, PH.D. (1989)

ST GEORGE'S HOSPITAL MEDICAL SCHOOL, Cranmer Terrace, London SW170RE. *Principal*, Prof. R. Boyd (1996)

UNIVERSITY COLLEGE LONDON (including UCL Medical School), Gower Street, London WC1E6BT. *Provost and President*, Prof. Sir C. Llewellyn-Smith, FRS (1998)

INSTITUTES

BRITISH INSTITUTE IN PARIS, 9–11 rue de Constantine, 75340 Paris, Cedex 07, France. *Director*, Prof. C. L. Campos, *London office:* Senate House, Malet Street, London WC1E7HU, OBE, PH.D.

CENTRE FOR DEFENCE STUDIES, King's College London, Strand, London WC2R2LS. *Honorary Director*, Prof. L. Freedman, CBE, FBA

COURTAULD INSTITUTE OF ART, North Block, Somerset House, Strand, London WC2R0RN. *Director*, Prof. E. C. Fernie, CBE, FSA, FRSE

ASSOCIATE INSTITUTES

INSTITUTE OF CANCER RESEARCH, Royal Cancer Hospital, Chester Beatty Laboratories, 17A Onslow Gardens, London SW73AL. *Chief Executive*, Dr P. Rigby

LONDON GUILDHALL UNIVERSITY (1992)
31 Jewry Street, London EC3N 2EY.
Tel: 020-7 320 1000
*Chancellor*, Lord Limerick,
*Patron*, HRH The Prince Philip, Duke of Edinburgh, KG, KT, OM, GBE, PC (1952)
*Secretary and Registrar*, Ms J. Grinstead,
*Vice Chancellor*, Prof. R. Floud, D.PHIL.

SCHOOL OF ADVANCED STUDIES

INSTITUTE OF ADVANCED LEGAL STUDIES, Charles Clore House, 17 Russell Square, London WC1B5DR. *Director*, Prof. B. A. K. Rider

INSTITUTE OF CLASSICAL STUDIES, Senate House, Malet Street, London WC1E 7HU. *Director*, Prof. G. B. Waywell, FSA

INSTITUTE OF COMMONWEALTH STUDIES, 27–28 Russell Square, London WC1B5DS. *Director*, Prof. T. Shaw

INSTITUTE OF ENGLISH STUDIES, Senate House, Malet Street, London WC1E 7HU *Director*, Prof. W. Gould

INSTITUTE OF GERMANIC STUDIES, 29 Russell Square, London WC1B5DP. *Director*, Prof. R. Görner, PH. D.
INSTITUTE OF HISTORICAL RESEARCH, Senate House, Malet Street, London WC1E7HU. *Director*, Prof. D. Cannadine
INSTITUTE OF LATIN AMERICAN STUDIES, 31 Tavistock Square, London WC1H9HA. *Director*, Prof. J. Dunkerley
INSTITUTE OF ROMANCE STUDIES, Senate House, Malet Street, London WC1E7HU. *Director*, Prof. J. Labanyi
INSTITUTE OF UNITED STATES STUDIES, Senate House, Malet Street, London WC1E7HU *Director*, Prof. G. L. McDowell, PH.D.
WARBURG INSTITUTE, Woburn Square, London WC1H0AB. *Director*, Prof. C. N. J. Mann, PH.D., CBE

LOUGHBOROUGH UNIVERSITY (1966)
Loughborough, Leics LE11 3TU.
Tel: 01509-263171
*Chancellor*, Sir Denis Rooke, CBE, FRS, FRENG. (1989)
*Registrar and Secretary*, J. Town
*Vice-Chancellor*, Prof. D.Wallace, FRS, FRSE

UNIVERSITY OF LUTON (1993)
Park Square, Luton LU1 3JU.
Tel: 01582-734111
*Chancellor*, Sir Robin Biggam
*Vice-Chancellor*, Dr D. John

UNIVERSITY OF MANCHESTER (1851)
Oxford Road, Manchester M13 9PL.
Tel: 0161-275 2000
*Chancellor*, The Lord Flowers, FRS (1994)
*Registrar and Secretary*, E. Newcomb, FRSA
*Vice-Chancellor*, Prof. M. B. Harris, CBE, DL, PH.D.

UNIVERSITY OF MANCHESTER INSTITUTE OF SCIENCE AND TECHNOLOGY (UMIST) (1824)
Manchester M60 1QD.
Tel: 0161-236 3311
*Chancellor*, Prof. Sir Roland Smith, PH.D. (1995)
*Registrar and Secretary*, J. Baldwin
*Vice-Chancellor*, Prof. J. Garside, PH.D.

MANCHESTER METROPOLITAN UNIVERSITY (1992)
All Saints, Manchester M15 6BH.
Tel: 0161-247 2000
*Academic Registrar*, J. D. M. Karczewski-Slowikowski
*Chancellor*, The Duke of Westminster, OBE, TD (1993)
*Vice-Chancellor*, Mrs A. V. Burslem, OBE

MIDDLESEX UNIVERSITY (1992)
White Hart Lane, London N17 8HR.
Tel: 020-8 411 5000
*Chancellor*, The Rt. Hon. Lord Sheppard of Didgemere, KT., KGVC
*Registrar*, G. Jones
*Vice-Chancellor*, Prof. M. Driscoll, FRSA

NAPIER UNIVERSITY (1992)
219 Colinton Road, Edinburgh EH14 1DJ. Scotland
Tel: 0131-444 2266
*Academic Registrar*, Mrs L. Fraser
*Chancellor*, The Viscount Younger of Leckie, KT, KCVO, TD, PC, FRSE (1993)
*Vice-Chancellor*, Prof. J. Mavor

UNIVERSITY OF NEWCASTLE UPON TYNE (1834)
6 Kensington Terrace, Newcastle upon Tyne NE1 7RU.
Tel: 0191-222 6000
*Chancellor*, Rt. Hon. C. Patten, CH
*Registrar*, D. E. T. Nicholson
*Vice-Chancellor*, Prof. C. R. W. Edwards

UNIVERSITY OF NORTH LONDON (1992)
166–220 Holloway Road, London N7 8DB.
Tel: 020-7 607 2789
*Secretary*, J. McParland
*Vice-Chancellor*, B. A. Roper

UNIVERSITY OF NORTHUMBRIA AT NEWCASTLE (1992)
Ellison Place, Newcastle upon Tyne NE1 8ST.
Tel: 0191-232 6002
*Chancellor*, The Lord Glenamara, CH, PC (1984)
*Registrar*, Mrs C. Penna
*Vice-Chancellor*, Kel Fidler

UNIVERSITY OF NOTTINGHAM (1948)
University Park, Nottingham NG7 2RD.
Tel: 0115-951 5151
*Chancellor*, Prof. F. Yang (1993)
*Registrar*, K. H. Jones
*Vice-Chancellor*, Prof. Sir Colin Campbell, DL, LLB, FRSA

NOTTINGHAM TRENT UNIVERSITY (1992)
Burton Street, Nottingham NG1 4BU.
Tel: 0115-941 8418
*Chairman of the Board of Governors*, John Peace
*Registrar*, D. W. Samson
*Vice-Chancellor*, Prof. R. Cowell, PH.D.

OPEN UNIVERSITY (1969)
Milton Keynes MK7 6AA.
Tel: 01908-274066
*Chancellor*, Baroness Betty Boothroyd
*Head of Student Services Registry*, Ms H. Niven
*Vice-Chancellor*, Prof. Brenda Gourley

UNIVERSITY OF OXFORD
Wellington Square, Oxford OX1 2JD.
Tel: 01865-270000
*Assessor*, Dr B Ward-Perkins (*Trinity*), *elected* 2001
*Bodley's Librarian*, R. P. Carr (*Balliol*), *elected* 1997
*Chancellor*, The Lord Jenkins of Hillhead (*Balliol*), *elected* 1987, OM, PC
*Director of the Ashmolean Museum*, Dr C. Brown (*Worcester*), *elected* 1998
*High Steward*, The Lord Goff of Chieveley (*Lincoln* and *New College*), *elected* 1990, PC
*Keeper of Archives*, S. Bayiley, elected 2000
*Proctors*, Dr D Womersley (*Jesus*); Prof. G, Walford (*Green*), elected 2001
*Public Orator*, Prof. J. Griffin (*Balliol*), elected 1992
*Registrar of the University*, D. R. Holmes (*St John's*), elected 1998
*Secretary of Faculties*, A. P. Weale (*Worcester*), elected 1984
*Secretary of the Chest*, J. R. Clements (*Merton*), elected 1995
*Surveyor to the University*, P. M. R. Hill (*St Cross*),elected 1993
*Vice-Chancellor*, Dr C. R. Lucas (*Balliol*), elected 1997

OXFORD COLLEGES AND HALLS
with dates of foundation

ALL SOULS (1438), *Warden*, Prof. J. Davis, FBA, PH.D. (1995)
BALLIOL (1263), *Master*, A. Graham (1998)
BLACKFRIARS (1221), *Regent*, Revd F. G. Kerr (1998)
BRASENOSE (1509), *Principal*, The Lord Windlesham, BT, CVO, PC, D.LITT (1989)
CAMPION HALL (1896), *Master*, Revd Dr G. J. Hughes (1998)
CHRIST CHURCH (1546), *Dean*, Very Revd J. H. Drury (1991)
CORPUS CHRISTI (1517), *President*, Sir Timothy Lankester, KCB (1986)

EXETER (1314), *Rector*, Dr M. Butler (1993)
GREEN (1979), *Warden*, Sir John Hanson, KCMG, CBE (1997)
GREYFRIARS (1910), *Warden*, Revd Dr T. G. Weinandy (1996)
HARRIS MANCHESTER (1786), *Principal*, Revd R. Waller, PH.D. (1988)
HERTFORD (1874), *Principal*, Sir Walter Bodmer, FRS, FRCPATH. (1996)
JESUS (1571), *Principal*, Sir Peter North, CBE, QC, FBA (1984)
KEBLE (1868), *Warden*, Dr A. Cameron, CBE, PHD, FBA, FSA (1994)
KELLOGG (1990), *President*, Dr G. P. Thomas (1990)
LADY MARGARET HALL (1878), *Principal*, Sir Brian Fall, GVCO, KCMG (1995)
LINACRE (1962), *Principal*, Dr P. A. Slack, FBA (1996)
LINCOLN (1427), *Rector*, Prof. P. Langford (2000)
MAGDALEN (1458), *President*, A. D. Smith, CBE (1988)
MANSFIELD (1886), *Principal*, Prof. D. I. Marquand, FRSA, FBA, FRHISTS (1996)
MERTON (1264), *Warden*, Dr J. Rawson, CBE, FBA (1994)
NEW COLLEGE (1379), *Warden*, Dr. A. J. Ryan, FBA (1996)
NUFFIELD (1958), *Warden*, Sir Tony Atkinson, FBA (1994)
ORIEL (1326), *Provost*, Dr E. W. Nicholson, DD, FBA (1990)
PEMBROKE (1624), *Master*, Giles Henderson, CBE (2001)
QUEEN'S (1340), *Provost*, Sir Alan Budd, D.PHIL. (1999)
REGENT'S PARK (1810), *Principal*, Revd Dr P. S. Fiddes (1989)
SOMERVILLE (1879), *Principal*, Dame Fiona Caldicott, DBE, FRCP, FRCPSYCH., FRCPI (1996)
ST ANNE'S (1952 (Society of Oxford Home-Students (1879)), *Principal*, Mrs R. L. Deech (1991)
ST ANTONY'S (1953), *Warden*, Sir Marrack Goulding, KCMG (1997)
ST BENET'S HALL (1897), *Master*, Revd H. Wansbrough, OSB (1991)
ST CATHERINE'S (1963), *Master*, Sir Peter Williams, CBE, FRENG., FRS (2000)
ST CROSS (1965), *Master*, Dr R. C. Repp (1987)
ST EDMUND HALL (*c*.1278), *Principal*, Prof. D. M. P. Mingos, FRS, FRSC (1999)
*ST HILDA'S (1893), *Principal*, Judith Milne (2001)
ST HUGH'S (1886), *Principal*, D. Wood, CBE, QC (1991)
ST JOHN'S (1555), *President*, Sir Michael Scholar, KCB (2001)
ST PETER'S (1929), *Master*, Dr J. P. Barron, FSA (1991)
TEMPLETON (1965), *President*, Sir David Rowland (1998)
TRINITY (1554), *President*, The Hon. Michael J. Beloff, QC, FRSA (1996)
UNIVERSITY (1249), *Master*, Baron Butler of Brockwell, GCB, CVO (1998)
WADHAM (1610), *Warden*, J. S. Flemming, FBA (1993)
WOLFSON (1966), *President*, Prof. Sir Gareth Roberts, FRS, PHD (2000)
WORCESTER (1714), *Provost*, R. G. Smethurst (1991)
*WYCLIFFE HALL (1877), *Principal*, Revd Dr A. E. McGrath (1995)

OXFORD BROOKES UNIVERSITY (1992)
Gipsy Lane, Oxford OX3 0BP.
Tel: 01865-484848
*Chancellor*, John Snow
*Deputy Vice-Chancellor (Academic Affairs)*, Linda Challis
*Vice-Chancellor*, Prof. G. Upton

UNIVERSITY OF PAISLEY (1992)
Paisley PA1 2BE. Scotland
Tel: 0141-848 3000
*Chancellor*, Sir Robert Easton, CBE (1993)
*Registrar*, D. Rigg
*Vice-Chancellor and Principal*, Prof. R. W. Shaw, CBE

UNIVERSITY OF PLYMOUTH (1992)
Drake Circus, Plymouth PL4 8AA.
Tel: 01752-600600
*Academic Registrar and University Secretary*, Miss J. Hopkinson
*Vice-Chancellor*, Prof. J. Bull

UNIVERSITY OF PORTSMOUTH (1992)
Winston Churchill Avenue, Portsmouth PO1 2UP.
Tel: 023-9284 8484
*Chancellor*, The Lord Palumbo (1992)
*Pro Vice-Chancellor (Academic)*, A. Glasner
*Pro Vice-Chancellor (Resources)*, Dr M. Bateman
*Vice-Chancellor*, Prof. J. Craven

QUEEN'S UNIVERSITY OF BELFAST (1908)
Belfast BT7 1NN. Northern Ireland
Tel: 028-9024 5133
*Chancellor*, Sen. G. Mitchell
*Registrar*, J. O'Kane
*Vice-Chancellor*, Prof. G. Bain

UNIVERSITY OF READING (1926)
PO Box 217, Reading RG6 6AH.
Tel: 0118-987 5123
*Chancellor*, The Rt. Hon. The Lord Carrington, KG, GCMG, CH, MC, PC (1992)
*Registrar*, D. C. R. Frampton
*Vice-Chancellor*, Prof. R. Williams

ROBERT GORDON UNIVERSITY (1992)
Schoolhill, Aberdeen AB10 1FR. Scotland
Tel: 01224-262000
*Chancellor*, Sir Bob Reid (1993)
*Vice-Chancellor and Principal*, Prof. W. Stevely, B.SC., D.PHIL.

ROYAL COLLEGE OF ART (1837)
Kensington Gore, London SW7 2EU.
Tel: 020-7590 4444
*Provost*, The Earl of Snowdon, GCVO (1995)
*Rector*, Prof. C. Frayling, PH.D.
*Registrar*, A. Selby, B.SC.

ROYAL COLLEGE OF MUSIC
Prince Consort Road, London SW7 2BS.
Tel: 020-7 589 3643
*Dean and Deputy Director*, Dr J. Cox
*Director*, Dr J. Ritterman
*Registrar and Secretary*, K. A. Porter

UNIVERSITY OF SURREY ROEHAMPTON
Roehampton Lane, London SW15 5PU.
Tel: 020-8392 3000/3232
*Chancellor*, HRH The Duke of Kent, KG
*Rector & Chief Executive*, Dr Bernadette Porter
*Secretary*, A. Skinner

UNIVERSITY OF ST ANDREWS (1411)
College Gate, St Andrews, Fife KY16 9AJ. Scotland
Tel: 01334-476161
*Chancellor*, Sir Kenneth Dover, DLITT., FRSE, FBA (1981)
*Rector*, A. Neil (2000–2003)
*Secretary and Registrar*, D. J. Corner
*Vice-Chancellor*, Dr B. Lang

UNIVERSITY OF SALFORD (1967)
Salford, Greater Manchester M5 4WT.
Tel: 0161-295 5000

*Chancellor*, Sir Walter Bodmer, PH.D., FRS
*Registrar*, Dr M. D. Winton, PH.D.
*Vice-Chancellor*, Prof. M. Harloe

UNIVERSITY OF SHEFFIELD (1905)
Western Bank, Sheffield S10 2TN.
Tel: 0114-222 2000
*Chancellor*, Sir Peter Middleton, GCB
*Registrar and Secretary*, Dr D. E. Fletcher, PH.D.
*Vice-Chancellor*, Prof. R. F. Boucher, CBE, PH.D.

SHEFFIELD HALLAM UNIVERSITY (1992)
Howard Street, Sheffield S1 1WB.
Tel: 0114-225 5555
*Chancellor*, Sir Bryan Nicholson (1992)
*Registrar*, Ms J. Tory
*Vice-Chancellor*, Prof. D. Green

UNIVERSITY OF SOUTHAMPTON (1952)
Highfield, Southampton SO17 1BJ.
Tel: 023-8059 5000
*Chancellor*, The Rt Hon. The Earl of Selbourne, KBE, FRS (1996)
*Registrar and Secretary*, J. F. D. Lauwerys
*Vice-Chancellor*, Prof. Sir H. Newby, CBE, PH.D.

SOUTH BANK UNIVERSITY (1992)
103 Borough Road, London SE1 0AA.
Tel: 020-7928 8989
*Chancellor*, Sir Trevor McDonald
*Registrar*, R. Phillips
*Vice-Chancellor*, Prof. D. Hopkin

STAFFORDSHIRE UNIVERSITY (1992)
College Road, Stoke-on-Trent ST4 2DE.
Tel: 01782-294000
*Chancellor*, The Lord Ashley of Stoke, CH, PC (1993)
*Dean of Students and Academic Registrar*, Ms F. Francis
*Vice-Chancellor*, Prof. C. E. King, PH.D., DL, D.LITT, FRSA

UNIVERSITY OF STIRLING (1967)
Stirling FK9 4LA. Scotland
Tel: 01786-473171
*Chancellor*, Dame Diana Rigg, DBE
*Principal and Academic Registrar*, D. G. Wood
*Vice-Chancellor*, Prof.Colin Bell, FRSE

UNIVERSITY OF STRATHCLYDE (1796)
John Anderson Campus, Glasgow G1 1XQ. Scotland
Tel: 0141-552 4400
*Chairman of Court*, Dr R. A. Johnson
*Chancellor*, The Rt. Hon. Lord Hope of Craighead, PC (1998)
*Vice-Chancellor*, Prof. A. Hamnett

UNIVERSITY OF SUNDERLAND (1992)
Ryhope Road, Sunderland SR2 7EE.
Tel: 0191-515 2000
*Chancellor*, The Lord Puttnam of Queensgate, CBE (1998)
*Rector*, Revd P. Hutchinson
*Registrar*, S. Porteous
*Vice-Chancellor*, Prof. P. Fidler, MBE

UNIVERSITY OF SURREY (1966)
Guildford, Surrey GU2 7XH.
Tel: 01483-300800
*Chancellor*, HRH The Duke of Kent, KG, GCMG, GCVO (1977)
*Secretary and Registrar*, H. W. B. Davies
*Vice-Chancellor*, Prof. P. J. Dowling, CBE, FRS, FRENG.

UNIVERSITY OF SUSSEX (1961)
Falmer, Brighton BN1 9RH.
Tel: 01273-606755
*Chancellor*, The Lord Attenborough, KT, CBE (1998)
*Registrar*, N. Gershon
*Vice-Chancellor*, Prof. M. A. M. Smith

UNIVERSITY OF TEESSIDE (1992)
Middlesbrough TS1 3BA.
Tel: 01642-218121
*Chancellor*, The Rt. Hon. Sir Leon Brittan, QC (1993)
*Registrar*, Ms J. Walters
*Vice-Chancellor*, Prof. D. Fraser

THAMES VALLEY UNIVERSITY (1992)
St Mary's Road, Ealing, London W5 5RF.
Tel: 020-8579 5000
*Pro-Chanceller*, The Lord Paul of Marylebone, CBE
*Vice-Chancellor*, Prof. K. Barker, CBE

UNIVERSITY OF ULSTER (1984)
Cromore Road, Coleraine, Co. Londonderry BT52 1SA. Northern Ireland
Tel: 028-7034 4141
*Chancellor*, vacant
*Registrar*, Dr A. Scott
*Vice-Chancellor*, Prof. P. G. McKenna, PH.D.

UNIVERSITY OF WALES (1893)
King Edward VII Avenue, Cathays Park, Cardiff CF10 3NS. Wales
Tel: 029-2038 2656
*Chancellor*, HRH The Prince of Wales, KG, KT, GCB, PC (1976)
*Secretary to the Council*, L. E. Williams, PH.D.
*Secretary-General*, Lynne E. Williams, PH. D.
*Senior Vice-Chancellor*, Prof. D. Llwyd Morgan, D.PHIL., DLITT.

UNIVERSITY OF WALES, ABERYSTWYTH, Old College, King Street, Aberystwyth sy232ax. Tel: 01970-623111. *Vice-Chancellor*, Prof. D. Llwyd Morgan, D.PHIL, D.LITT

UNIVERSITY OF WALES BANGOR, Bangor, ll572dg. Tel: 01248-351151 *Vice-Chancellor*, Prof. H. R. Evans, PH.D., FRENG

MEMBER INSTITUTES

UNIVERSITY OF WALES, CARDIFF, PO Box 920, Cardiff CF103XP. Tel: 01222-874000. *Vice-Chancellor*, Dr D. Grant, CBE, FENG

UNIVERSITY OF WALES, INSTITUTE, CARDIFF, Llandaff Centre, Western Avenue, Cardiff CF5 2SG. Tel: 01222-506070. *Principal*, A. J. Chapman, PH.D.

UNIVERSITY OF WALES, LAMPETER, Lampeter SA487ED. Tel: 01570-422351. *Vice-Chancellor*, Prof. K. G. Robbins, D.LITT, D.PHIL., FRSED

UNIVERSITY OF WALES COLLEGE OF MEDICINE, Heath Park, Cardiff CF144XN. Tel: 01222-747747. *Vice-Chancellor*, Prof. S. Tomlinson, MD, FRCP

UNIVERSITY OF WALES COLLEGE, NEWPORT, Caerleon Campus, PO Box 179, Newport NP6 1YG. Tel: 01633-430088. *Principal*, Prof. K. J. Overshott, PH.D.

UNIVERSITY OF WALES, SWANSEA, Singleton Park, Swansea SA28PP. Tel: 01792-205678. *Vice-Chancellor*, Prof. R. H. Williams, PH.D., D.SC., FRS

UNIVERSITY OF WARWICK (1965)
Coventry CV4 7AL.
Tel: 024-7652 3523
*Chancellor*, Sir Shridath Surendranath Ramphal, GCMG, QC (1989)
*Registrar*, Dr J. W. Nicholls
*Vice-Chancellor*, Prof. V. D. Vondelinde, FRS

UNIVERSITY OF WESTMINSTER (1992)
309 Regent Street, London W1B 2UW.

Tel: 020-7911 5000
*Academic Registrar*, Ms E. Green
*Vice-Chancellor and Rector*, Dr G. M. Copland (1996)

UNIVERSITY OF THE WEST OF ENGLAND (1992)
Coldharbour Lane, Bristol BS16 1QY.
Tel: 0117-965 6261
*Chancellor*, The Rt. Hon. Dame Elizabeth Butler-Sloss, DBE (1993)
*Vice-Chancellor*, A. C. Morris
*Academic Secretary*, Ms C. Webb

UNIVERSITY OF WOLVERHAMPTON (1992)
Wulfruna Street, Wolverhampton WV1 1SB.
Tel: 01902-321000
*Chancellor*, Lord Paul of Marylebone
*Clerk to the Board of Governors*, A. W. Lee
*Vice-Chancellor*, Prof. J. S. Brooks, PH.D.

UNIVERSITY OF YORK (1963)
Heslington, York YO10 5DD.
Tel: 01904-430000
*Chancellor*, Dame Janet Baker, CH, DBE (1991)
*Registrar and Secretary*, D. J. Foster
*Vice-Chancellor*, Prof. R. U. Cooke, PH.D.

## COLLEGES

It is not possible to name here all the colleges offering courses of higher or further education. The list does not include colleges forming part of a polytechnic or a university. The English colleges that follow are confined to those in the Higher Education Funding Council for England sector; there are many more colleges in England providing higher education courses, some with HEFCFE funding.

The list of colleges in Wales, Scotland and Northern Ireland include institutions providing at least one full-time course leading to a first degree granted by an accredited validating body.

### ENGLAND

BATH SPA UNIVERSITY COLLEGE, Newton Park, Newton St Loe, Bath BA2 9BN. Tel: 01225-875875. *Director*, F. Morgan

BISHOP GROSSETESTE COLLEGE, Lincoln LN1 3DY. Tel: 01522-527347. *Principal*, Prof. E. Baker

BOLTON INSTITUTE OF HIGHER EDUCATION, Deane Road, Bolton BL3 5AB. Tel: 01204-528851. *Principal*, Ms M. Temple

BUCKINGHAMSHIRE CHILTERNS UNIVERSITY COLLEGE, Queen Alexandra Road, High Wycombe, Bucks HP11 2JZ. Tel: 01494-603015. *Director*, Prof. P. B. Mogford

CANTERBURY CHRIST CHURCH UNIVERSITY COLLEGE, North Holmes Road, Canterbury, Kent CT1 1QU. Tel: 01227-767700. *Principal*, Prof. M. Wright

THE CENTRAL SCHOOL OF SPEECH AND DRAMA SPEECH AND DRAMA, Embassy Theatre, 64 Eton Avenue, London NW3 3HY. Tel: 020-7 722 8183. *Principal*, Prof. G. Crossley

CHELTENHAM AND GLOUCESTER COLLEGE OF HIGHER EDUCATION COLLEGE OF HIGHER EDUCATION, PO Box 220, The Park, Cheltenham, Glos GL50 2QF. Tel: 01242-532700. *Director*, Miss J. O. Trotter, OBE

CHESTER COLLEGE OF HIGHER EDUCATION, Parkgate Road, Chester CH1 4BJ. Tel: 01244-375444. *Principal*, Prof. T. J. Wheeler

DARTINGTON COLLEGE OF ARTS, Totnes, Devon TQ9 6EJ. Tel: 01803-862224. *Principal*, Prof. K. Thompson

EDGE HILL COLLEGE OF HIGHER EDUCATION, St Helens Road, Ormskirk, Lancs L39 4QP. Tel: 01695-575171. *Chief Executive*, Dr J. Cater

FALMOUTH COLLEGE OF ARTS, Woodlane, Falmouth, Cornwall TR11 4RH. Tel: 01326-211077. *Principal*, Prof. A. G. Livingston

HARPER ADAMS UNIVERSITY COLLEGE, Newport, Shropshire TF10 8NB. Tel: 01952-815000. *Principal*, Prof. E. W. Jones

HOMERTON COLLEGE, Cambridge CB2 2PH. Tel: 01223-507111. *Principal*, Dr K. Pretty, Ph.D.

KENT INSTITUTE OF ART AND DESIGN, Oakwood Park, Maidstone, Kent ME16 8AG. Tel: 01622-757286. *Director*, Prof. V. Grylls

KING ALFRED'S COLLEGE, Sparkford Road, Winchester, Hants SO22 4NR. Tel: 01962-841515. *Principal*, Prof. P. Light

LIVERPOOL HOPE, Hope Park, Liverpool L16 9JD. Tel: 0151-291 3000. *Rector and Chief Executive*, Prof. S. Lee

THE LONDON INSTITUTE, 65 Davies Street, London W1Y 2AA. Tel: 020-7 514 6000. *Rector*, Sir William Stubbs

NEWMAN COLLEGE OF HIGHER EDUCATION, Genners Lane, Bartley Green, Birmingham B32 3NT. Tel: 0121-476 1181. *Principal and Chief Executive*, Mrs P. Taylor

THE COLLEGE OF RIPON AND YORK ST JOHN, Lord Mayor's Walk, York YO31 7EX. Tel: 01904-656771. *Principal*, Prof. D. Willcocks

RCN INSTITUTE, The Royal College of Nursing, 20 Cavendish Square, London W1G 0RN. Tel: 020-7647 3700. *Director*, Prof. A. L. Kitson

ROSE BRUFORD COLLEGE, Lamorbey Park, Sidcup, Kent DA15 9DF. Tel: 020-8 300 3024. *Principal*, Prof. A. Pearce

ROYAL AGRICULTURAL COLLEGE, Cirencester, Glos GL7 6JS. Tel: 01285-652531. *Principal*, Prof. J. B. Dent

ROYAL NORTHERN COLLEGE OF MUSIC, 124 Oxford Road, Manchester M13 9RD. Tel: 0161-907 5200. *Principal*, Prof. E. Gregson

ST MARTIN'S COLLEGE, Lancaster LA1 3JD. Tel: 01524-384384. *Principal and Chief Executive*, Prof. C. J. Carr

SOUTHAMPTON INSTITUTE, East Park Terrace, Southampton SO14 0YN. Tel: 023-80 319000. *Principal*, Dr R. Brown

SURREY INSTITUTE OF ART AND DESIGN, UNIVERSITY COLLEGE, Falkner Road, Farnham, Surrey GU9 7DS. Tel: 01252-722441. *Director*, Prof. E. Thomas

TRINITY AND ALL SAINTS' COLLEGE, Brownberrie Lane, Horsforth, Leeds LS18 5HD. Tel: 0113-283 7100. *Principal*, Dr M. J. Coughlan

UNIVERSITY COLLEGE CHICHESTER, College Lane, Chichester, W. Sussex PO19 4PE. Tel: 01243-816000. *Director*, P. E. D. Robinson

UNIVERSITY COLLEGE NORTHAMPTON, Park Campus, Boughton Green Road, Northampton NN2 7AL. Tel: 01604-735500. *Rector*, Dr S. M. Gaskell

THE COLLEGE OF ST MARK AND ST JOHN, Derriford Road, Plymouth PL6 8BH. Tel: 01752-636700. *Principal*, Dr W. J. Rea

WINCHESTER SCHOOL OF ART, Park Avenue, Winchester, Hants SO23 8DL. Tel: 023-8059 6900. *Principal*, Prof. P. Pilgrim

UNIVERSITY COLLEGE WORCESTER, Henwick Grove, Worcester WR2 6AJ. Tel: 01905-855000. *Principal*, Ms D. Urwin

## WALES

CARMARTHENSHIRE COLLEGE, Graig Campus, Sandy Road, Llanelli SA15 4DN. Tel: 01554-748000. *Principal*, B. Robinson

COLEG LLANDRILLO, Llandudno Road, Rhos-on-Sea, Colwyn Bay, Conwy LL28 4HZ. Tel: 01492-546666. *Principal*, W. S. H. Evans

NORTH EAST WALES INSTITUTE OF HIGHER EDUCATION, Plas Coch, Mold Road, Wrexham LL11 2AW. Tel: 01978-290666. *Principal and Chief Executive*, Prof. M. Scott

SWANSEA INSTITUTE OF HIGHER EDUCATION, Mount Pleasant, Swansea SA1 6ED. Tel: 01792-481000. *Principal*, Prof. D. Warner

TRINITY COLLEGE, College Road, Carmarthen SA31 3EP. Tel: 01267-676767. *Principal*, Dr M. Hughes

UNIVERSITY OF WALES INSTITUTE CARDIFF, Llandaff Campus, Western Avenue, Cardiff CF5 2YB. Tel: 029-20 416070. *Principal*, Prof A. J. Chapman

WELSH COLLEGE OF MUSIC AND DRAMA, Castle Grounds, Cathays Park, Cardiff CF10 3ER. Tel: 029-2034 2854. *Principal*, E. Fivet

## SCOTLAND

BELL COLLEGE OF TECHNOLOGY, Almada Street, Hamilton, Lanarkshire ML3 0JB. Tel: 01698-283100. *Principal*, Dr K. J. MacCallum

DUMFRIES AND GALLOWAY COLLEGE, Heathhall, Dumfries DG1 3QZ. Tel: 01387-261261. *Principal*, T. Jakimciw

FIFE COLLEGE OF FURTHER AND HIGHER EDUCATION, St Brycedale Avenue, Kirkcaldy, Fife KY1 1EX. Tel: 01592-268591. *Principal*, Mrs J. S. R. Johnston

GLASGOW SCHOOL OF ART, 167 Renfrew Street, Glasgow G3 6RQ. Tel: 0141-353 4500. *Director*, Ms S. Reid

INVERNESS COLLEGE, 3 Longman Road, Inverness IV1 1SA. Tel: 01463-273000. *Principal*, Dr G. Clark

LEWS CASTLE COLLEGE, Stornoway, Isle of Lewis HS2 0XR. Tel: 01851-770000. *Principal*, D. Green

MORAY COLLEGE, Moray Street, Elgin, Moray IV30 1JJ. Tel: 01343-576000. *Acting Principal*, Dr Logan

NORTHERN COLLEGE, Hilton Place, Aberdeen AB24 4FA. Tel: 01224-283500. *Principal*, D. Adams

NORTH ISLAND COLLEGE, Ormlie Road, Thurso, Caithness KW14 7EE. Tel: 01847-896161. *Principal*, H. Logan

ORKNEY COLLEGE, Kirkwall, Orkney KW15 1LX. Tel: 01856-569000. *Principal*, P. Scott

QUEEN MARGARET UNIVERSITY COLLEGE, Clerwood Terrace, Edinburgh EH12 8TS. Tel: 0131-317 3000. *Principal*, Prof. J. Stringer

ROYAL SCOTTISH ACADEMY OF MUSIC AND DRAMA, 100 Renfrew Street, Glasgow G2 3DB. Tel: 0141-332 4101. *Principal*, Sir Philip Ledger, Kt., CBE, FRSE

SÀBHAL MOR OSTAIG, Sleat, Isle of Skye IV44 8RQ. Tel: 01471-888000

SAC (SCOTTISH AGRICULTURAL COLLEGE), Central Office, West Mains Road, Edinburgh EH9 3JG. Tel: 0131-535 4000. *Principal*, K. A. Linklater

## NORTHERN IRELAND

ST MARY'S UNIVERSITY COLLEGE, 191 Falls Road, Belfast BT12 6FE. Tel: 028-9032 7678. *Principal*, Very Revd Prof. M. O'Callaghan

## ADULT CONTINUING EDUCATION

COMMUNITY LEARNING SCOTLAND, Rosebery House, 9 Haymarket Terrace, Edinburgh EH12 5EZ. Tel: 0131-313 2488. *Chief Executive*, C. McConnell

NATIONAL INSTITUTE OF ADULT CONTINUING EDUCATION, 21 De Montfort Street, Leicester LE1 7GE. Tel: 0116-204 4200. *Director*, A. Tuckett

NIACE DYSGU CYMRU, Ground Floor, 35 Cathedral Road, Cardiff CF11 9HB. Tel: 029-2037 0900. *Acting Director*, R. Griffiths

THE RESIDENTIAL COLLEGES COMMITTEE, c/o Ruskin College, Oxford OX1 2HE. Tel: 01865-556360. *Awards Officer*, Mrs C. Gregory

THE UNIVERSITIES ASSOCIATION FOR CONTINUING EDUCATION, University of Cambridge Board of Continuing Education, Madingley Hall, Madingley, Cambridge CB3 8AQ. Tel: 01954-280280. *Administrator*, Ms S. Irwin

THE WIDENING PARTICIPATION UNIT, Regional Office, Widening Participation Unit, University of East London, Romford Road, London E15 4LZ. Tel: 020-8223 4936

WORKERS' EDUCATIONAL ASSOCIATION, Temple House, 17 Victoria Park Square, London E2 9PB. Tel: 020-8983 1515. *General Secretary*, R. Lochrie

### LONG-TERM RESIDENTIAL COLLEGES FOR ADULT EDUCATION

COLEG HARLECH/WEA(N), Harlech, Gwynedd LL46 2PU. Tel: 01766-780363. *Principal*, A. Williams

CO-OPERATIVE COLLEGE, Holyoake House, Hanover Street, Manchester M60 0AS. Tel: 0161-246 2909. *Chief Executive and Principal*, M. Wilson

FIRCROFT COLLEGE, 1018 Bristol Road, Selly Oak, Birmingham B29 6LH. Tel: 0121-472 0116. *Principal*, Ms F. Larden

HILLCROFT COLLEGE, South Bank, Surbiton, Surrey KT6 6DF. Tel: 020-8 399 2688. *Principal*, Mrs J. Ireton

NEWBATTLE ABBEY COLLEGE, Newbattle Road, Dalkeith, Midlothian EH22 3LL. Tel: 0131-663 1921. *Principal*, Ms A. Southwood

NORTHERN COLLEGE, Wentworth Castle, Stainborough, Barnsley, S. Yorks S75 3ET. Tel: 01226-776000. *Principal and Chief Executive*, Prof. J. A. Jowitt

PLATER COLLEGE, Pullens Lane, Oxford OX3 0DT. Tel: 01865-740500. *Principal*, M. Blades

RUSKIN COLLEGE, Walton Street, Oxford OX1 2HE. Tel: 01865-554331. *Principal*, J. Durcan

## PROFESSIONAL EDUCATION

*Excluding postgraduate study*

The organisations listed below are those which, by providing specialist training or conducting examinations, control entry into a profession, or are responsible for maintaining a register of those with professional qualifications in their sector.

### EU RECOGNITION

It is now possible for those with professional qualifications obtained in the UK to have these recognised in other European Union countries. A booklet, *Europe Open for Professions*, and further information can be obtained from:

DEPARTMENT OF TRADE AND INDUSTRY, Bay 212, Kingsgate House, 66–74 Victoria Street, London SW1E 6SW. Tel: 020-7215 4648. *Contact*, Mrs P. Campbell

### ACCOUNTANCY

The main bodies granting membership on examination after a period of practical work are:

ASSOCIATION OF CHARTERED CERTIFIED ACCOUNTANTS (ACCA), 29 Lincoln's Inn Fields, London WC2A 3EE. Tel: 020-7396 7000; Email: info@accaglobal.com; Web: www.accaglobal.com. *Chief Executive*, Ms A. Rose

CIMA (THE CHARTERED INSTITUTE OF MANAGEMENT ACCOUNTANTS), 26 Chapter Street, London SW1P 4NP. Web: www.cimaglobal.com. *Chief Executive*, C. Tilley

INSTITUTE OF CHARTERED ACCOUNTANTS IN ENGLAND AND WALES, Chartered Accountants' Hall, PO Box 433, Moorgate Place, London EC2P 2BJ. Tel: 020-7920 8100; Email: comms@icaew.co.uk; Web: www.icaew.co.uk. *Secretary General*, J. Collier

INSTITUTE OF CHARTERED ACCOUNTANTS OF SCOTLAND, CA House, 21 Haymarket Yards, Edinburgh EH12 5BG. Tel: 0131-347 0100; Email: enquiries@icas.org.uk; Web: www.icas.org.uk. *Chief Executive*, D. A. Brew

### ACTUARIAL SCIENCE

Two professional organisations grant qualifications after examination:

THE FACULTY OF ACTUARIES IN SCOTLAND, Maclaurin House, 18 Dublin Street, Edinburgh EH2 3PP. Tel: 0131-240 1300; Email: faculty@actuaries.org.uk; Web: www.actuaries.org.uk.

INSTITUTE OF ACTUARIES, Staple Inn Hall, High Holborn, London WC1V 7QJ. Tel: 020-7632 2100; Email: institute@actuaries.org.uk; Web: www.actuaries.org.uk.

### ARCHITECTURE

The Education Committee of the Royal Institute of British Architects sets standards and guides the whole system of architectural education throughout the UK. RIBA recognises courses at 36 schools of architecture in the UK for exemption from their own examinations as well as 57 courses overseas.

ARCHITECTS REGISTRATION BOARD, 8 Weymouth Street, London W1W 5BU. Tel: 020-7580 5861; Email: info@arb.org.uk; Web: www.arb.org.uk. *Chief Executive and Registrar*, R. Vaughan

ROYAL INSTITUTE OF BRITISH ARCHITECTS, 66 Portland Place, London W1N 4AD. Tel: 020-7580 5533; Email: admin@inst.riba.org; Web: www.architecture.com.

THE ARCHITECTURAL ASSOCIATION (INC.), 34–36 Bedford Square, London WC1B 3ES. Tel: 020-7887 4018; Email: arch-assoc@arch-assoc.org.uk; Web: www.aaschool.ac.uk.

THE PRINCE'S FOUNDATION, 19–22 Charlotte Road, London EC2A 3SG. Tel: 020-7613 8500; Email: info@princes-foundation.org; Web: www.princes-foundation.org/school.

### BANKING

Professional organisations granting qualifications after examination are:

THE CHARTERED INSTITUTE OF BANKERS, 90 Bishopsgate, London EC2N 4DQ. Tel: 020-7444 7111; Email: institute@ifslearning.com; Web: www.ifslearning.com. *Chief Executive Officer*, G. Shreeve

THE CHARTERED INSTITUTE OF BANKERS IN SCOTLAND, Drumsheugh House, 38b Drumsheugh Gardens, Edinburgh EH3 7SW. Tel: 0131-473 7777; Email: info@ciobs.org.uk; Web: www.ciobs.org.uk. *Chief Executive*, C. W. Munn

### BUILDING

Examinations are conducted by:

THE CHARTERED INSTITUTE OF BUILDING, Englemere, King's Ride, Ascot, Berks SL5 7TB. Tel: 01344-630700; Email: reception@ciob.org.uk; Web: www.ciob.org.uk. *Chief Executive*, C. Blythe

RICS (ROYAL INSTITUTE OF CHARTERED SURVEYORS), 12 Great George Street, Parliament Square, London SW1P 3AD. Tel: 020-7222 7000; Web: www.rics.org.uk. *Chief Executive*, J. Parrott

THE INSTITUTE OF CLERKS OF WORKS OF GREAT BRITAIN, 41 The Mall, London W5 3TJ. Tel: 020-8579 2917/8. *General Secretary*, D. McGeorge

### BUSINESS, MANAGEMENT AND ADMINISTRATION

Professional bodies conducting training and/or examinations include:

THE ASSOCIATION OF MBAS, 15 Duncan Terrace, London N1 8BZ. Tel: 020-7837 3375; Email: info@mba.org.uk; Web: www.mba.org.uk. *Director General*, M. A. Jones

THE CAM FOUNDATION, Moore Hall, Cookham, Maidenhead, Berks SL6 9QH. Tel: 01628-427180; Web: www.camfoundation.com. *Chief Executive*, D. Royston-Lee

THE CHARTERED INSTITUTE OF HOUSING, Octavia House, Westwood Business Park, Westwood Way, Coventry CV4 8JP. Tel: 024-7685 1700; Email: customer.services@cih.org; Web: www.cih.org. *Chief Executive*, D. Butler

THE CHARTERED INSTITUTE OF PURCHASING AND SUPPLY, Easton House, Easton on the Hill, Stamford, Lincs PE9 3NZ. Tel: 01780-756777; Email: info@cips.org; Web: www.cips.org. *Chief Executive*, K. James

HENLEY MANAGEMENT COLLEGE, Greenlands, Henley on Thames, Oxon RG9 3AU. Tel: 01491-571454; Web: www.henleymc.ac.uk. *Principal*, S. Watson

THE INSTITUTE OF ADMINISTRATIVE MANAGEMENT, 40 Chatsworth Parade, Petts Wood, Orpington, Kent BR5 1RW. Tel: 01689-875555; Email: enquiries@instam.org; Web: www.instam.org.

INSTITUTE OF CHARTERED SECRETARIES AND ADMINISTRATORS, 16 Park Crescent, London W1B 1AH. Tel: 020-7580 4741; Email: icsa@dial.pipex.com; Web: www.icsa.org.uk. *Chief Executive*, M. J. Ainsworth

INSTITUTE OF CHARTERED SHIPBROKERS, 3 St Helen's Place, London EC3A 6EJ. Tel: 020-7628 5559; Email: info@ics.org.uk; Web: www.ics.org.uk. *Director*, Mrs B. Fletcher

THE INSTITUTE OF EXPORT, Export House, Minerva Business Park, Lynch Wood, Peterborough PE2 6FT. Tel: 01733-404400; Email: institute@export.org.uk; Web: www.export.org.uk. *Director-General*, I. J. Campbell

THE INSTITUTE OF HEALTHCARE MANAGEMENT, 46–48 Grosvenor Gardens, London SW1W 0WN. Tel: 020-7881 9235; Email: enquiries@ihm.org.uk; Web: www.ihm.org.uk. *Chief Executive*, S. Marples

INSTITUTE OF MANAGEMENT, 3rd Floor, 2 Savoy Court, The Strand, London WC2R 0EZ. Tel: 01536-204222; Email: marketing@imgt.org.uk; Web: www.inst-mgt.org.uk. *Director-General*, Ms M. Chapman

CHARTERED INSTITUTE OF PERSONNEL AND DEVELOPMENT, CIPD House, Camp Road, London SW19 4UX. Tel: 020-8971 9000; Email: cipd@cipd.co.uk; Web: www.cipd.co.uk. *Director General*, G. Armstrong

INSTITUTE OF QUALITY ASSURANCE, 12 Grosvenor Crescent, London SW1X 7EE. Tel: 020-7245 6722; Email: iqa@iqa.org; Web: www.iqa.org. *Chief Executive*, Frank Steer

## CHIROPRACTIC

The General Chiropractic Council (GCC) is the statutory regulatory body for chiropractors and its role and remit is defined in the Chiropractors Act 1994. The GCC's register of chiropractors opened in June 1999; nearly 1800 chiropractors are expected to be registered with the GCC by the end of 2001.

BRITISH CHIROPRACTIC ASSOCIATION, Blagrave House, Blagrave Street, Reading, Berks RG1 1QB. Tel: 0118-950 5950; Email: enquiries@chiropractic-uk.co.uk; Web: www.chiropractic-uk.co.uk.

COLLEGE OF CHIROPRACTORS, PO Box 2739, 106 London Street, Reading RG1 4BF. Tel: 0118-950 2070.

GENERAL CHIROPRACTIC COUNCIL, 344-354 Gray's Inn Road, London WC1X 8BP. Tel: 020-7713 5155; Email: enquiries@gcc-uk.org; Web: www.gcc-uk.org.

MCTIMONEY CHIROPRACTIC ASSOCIATION, 21 High Street, Eynsham, OX8 1HE. Tel: 01865-880974; Web: www.mctimoney-chiropractic.org.uk.

SCOTTISH CHIROPRACTIC ASSOCIATION, St Boswells Chiropractic Clinic, 16 Jenny Moores Road, St Boswells, Roxburghshire TD6 0AL. Tel: 01835-824026; Email: sca@scottishborders.co.uk; Web: www.sca-chiropractic.org.uk.

UNITED CHIROPRACTIC ASSOCIATION, 145A London Road, Kingston upon Thames, Surrey KT2 6SR. Tel: 020-8549 0020.

## DANCE

The Council for Dance Education and Training (CDET) has accredited courses at the following: Arts Education Schools, Tring Park and London; Central School of Ballet; Doreen Bird College of Performing Arts; Elmhurst–The School for Dance and Performing Arts; English National Ballet School; The Hammond School; The Italia Conti Academy of Theatre Arts Ltd; Laban Centre, London; Laine Theatre Arts Ltd; London Contemporary Dance School; London Studio Centre; Midlands Academy of Dance and Drama; Merseyside Dance and Drama Centre; Northern Ballet School; Performers College; Stella Mann College; Studios La Pointe; Royal Academy of Dancing; The Urdang Academy.

The accreditation of a course in a school does not necessarily imply that other courses of a different type or duration in the same school are also accredited.

CDET has approved the teacher registration systems of the following: Association of American Dancing; British Ballet Organisation; British Theatre Dance Association; Cecchetti Society; Imperial Society of Teachers of Dancing; Royal Academy of Dancing.

IMPERIAL SOCIETY OF TEACHERS OF DANCING, Imperial House, 22-26 Paul Street, London EC2A 4QE. Tel: 020-7377 1577; Email: admin@istd.org; Web: www.istd.org. *Chief Executive*, M. J. Browne

INTERNATIONAL DANCE TEACHERS' ASSOCIATION, International House, 76 Bennett Road, Brighton BN2 5JL. Tel: 01273-685652; Email: info@idta.co.uk; Web: www.idta.co.uk.

ROYAL ACADEMY OF DANCE, 36 Battersea Square, London SW11 3RA. Tel: 020-7326 8000; Email: info@rad.org.uk. *Chief Executive*, L. Rittner

ROYAL BALLET SCHOOL, 155 Talgarth Road, London W14 9DE. Tel: 020-8748 6335; Web: www.royalballetschool.co.uk. *Director*, Ms G. Stock

## DEFENCE

ROYAL COLLEGE OF DEFENCE STUDIES, Seaford House, 37 Belgrave Square, London SW1X 8NS. Tel: 020-7915 4800; Email: des@rcds.ac.uk; Web: www.rcds.ac.uk. *Commandant*, Lt Gen (Retd) Sir Christopher Wallace

JOINT SERVICES COMMAND AND STAFF COLLEGE, Faringdon Road, Watchfield, Swindon, Wilts SN6 8TS. Tel: 01793-788555; Email: registry@jscsc.org.uk; Web: www.jscsc.org.uk. *Commandant*, Air Vice-Marshal B. K. Burridge

### ROYAL NAVAL COLLEGE

BRITANNIA ROYAL NAVAL COLLEGE, Dartmouth, Devon TQ6 0HJ. Tel: 01803-677108. *Commodore*, Cdre M. W. G. Kerr

### MILITARY COLLEGES

DIRECTORATE OF EDUCATIONAL AND TRAINING SERVICES (ARMY), Trenchard Lines, Upavon, Pewsey, Wilts SN9 6BE. Tel: 01980-618719/618701; Email: dets_a@gtnet.gov.uk. *Director*, Brig. P. S. Purves

ROYAL MILITARY ACADEMY SANDHURST, Camberley, Surrey GU15 4PQ. Tel: 01276-63344. *Commandant*, Maj. Gen. PCC Trousdell

ROYAL MILITARY COLLEGE OF SCIENCE, Cranfield University, RMCS Shrivenham, Swindon SN6 8LA. Tel: 01793-785435; Web: www.rmcs.cranfield.ac.uk.

### ROYAL AIR FORCE COLLEGES

ROYAL AIR FORCE COLLEGE, Cranwell, Sleaford, Lincs NG34 8HB. Tel: 01400-261201; Web: www.cranwell.raf.mod.uk.

ROYAL AIR FORCE TRAINING, DEVELOPMENT AND SUPPORT UNIT, RAF Halton, Aylesbury, Bucks HP22 5PG. Tel: 01296-623535 ext. 6210; Email: octdsu@raf-tdsu.demon.co.uk. *Commanding Officer*, PO J. Turner

ROYAL AIR FORCE COLLEGE, Provides initial training for all officer entrants to the RAF. Also provides initial specialist and postgraduate training for engineering and supply officers. The RAF College is the site of the Joint Elementary Flying School for pilots of all three services, Number 3 Flying Training School and the RAF Central Flying School. It is also the headquarters for the RAF University Air Squadrons, and is responsible for supervision of the Air Cadet Organisation.

*Air Officer Commanding and Commandant*, Air Vice-Marshal H. G. Mackay, OBE, AFC, BSC, FRAES, RAF

## DENTISTRY

In order to practise in the UK, a dentist must be registered with the General Dental Council. To be registered a person must be qualified in one of the following ways: hold the degree or diploma in dental surgery of a university in the UK or hold the licentiate in dental surgery awarded by one of the Royal Surgical Colleges in the UK; completed the Council's statutory examination (soon to be replaced by the International Qualifying Examination (IQE)); be an European Community or European Economic Area national holding an appropriate European diploma; hold a registered overseas diploma or be an EEA national holding a primary dental qualification from outside the EEA but has acquired a right to practise in the EEA. The holder of a dental degree or diploma other than those referred to above may be eligible for temporary registration to enable him or her to practise dentistry in the United Kingdom for a limited period and in specified posts without the need to take further examinations. The Dentists Register and Rolls of Dental Auxiliaries are maintained by:

GENERAL DENTAL COUNCIL, 37 Wimpole Street, London W1G 8DQ. Tel: 020-7887 3800; Email: information@gdc-uk.org Web: www.gdc-uk.org.

## DIETETICS

*See also* FOOD AND NUTRITION SCIENCE

The professional association is the British Dietetic Association. Full membership is open to dieticians holding a recognised qualification, who may also become State Registered Dieticians through the Council for Professions Supplementary to Medicine (*see* Medicine).

THE BRITISH DIETETIC ASSOCIATION, 5th Floor, Charles House, 148-149 Craig Charles Street Queensway, Birmingham B3 3HT. Tel: 0121-200 8080.

## DRAMA

The national validating body for courses providing training in drama for the professional theatre is the National Council for Drama Training. It currently has accredited courses at the following: Academy of Live and Recorded Arts; Arts Educational Schools; Birmingham School of Speech Training and Dramatic Art; Bristol Old Vic Theatre School; Central School of Speech and Drama; Drama Centre, London; Drama Studio, London; Guildford School of Acting; Guildhall School of Music and Drama, London; London Academy of Music and Dramatic Art; Manchester Metropolitan University School of Theatre; Mountview Theatre School; Oxford School of Drama, Woodstock; Queen Margaret University College, Edinburgh; Rose Bruford College, Sidcup; Royal Academy of Dramatic Art, London; Royal Scottish Academy of Music and Drama; Webber Douglas Academy of Dramatic Art, London; Welsh College of Music and Drama.

The accreditation of a course in a school does not necessarily imply that other courses of a different type or duration in the same school are also accredited.

NATIONAL COUNCIL FOR DRAMA TRAINING, 5 Tavistock Place, London WC1H 9SS. Tel: 020-7387 3650; Email: ncdt@lineone.net; Web: www.ncdt.co.uk.

## ENGINEERING

The Engineering Council provides a central resource for supporting and promoting the engineering profession through the nominated engineering institutions represented on its Board for Engineers' Regulation. The Council's register of over 250,000 professionals, qualified to internationally recognised standards, reflects engineers and technicians across the broad spectrum of the industry. Working with and through the institutions, the Council sets the standards for the registration of individuals, and also the accreditation for academic courses in universities and colleges and the practical training in industry.

The principal qualifying bodies are:

THE ENGINEERING COUNCIL, 10 Maltravers Street, London WC2R 3ER. Tel: 020-7240 7891; Email: publicaffairs@engc.org.uk; Web: www.engc.org.uk.

BRITISH COMPUTER SOCIETY, 1 Sanford Street, Swindon SN1 1HJ. Tel: 01793-417417; Email: bcshq@hq.bcs.org.uk; Web: www.bcs.org. *Chief Executive*, Ms J. Scott

CHARTERED INSTITUTE OF BUILDING SERVICES ENGINEERS, 222 Balham High Road, London SW12 9BS. Tel: 020-8675 5211; Email: enquiries@cibse.org.uk; Web: www.cibse.org.uk. *Deputy Secretary*, S. Brown

INSTITUTION OF CHEMICAL ENGINEERS, Davis Building, 165–189 Railway Terrace, Rugby, Warks CV21 3HQ. Tel: 01788-578214; Web: www.icheme.org.

INSTITUTION OF CIVIL ENGINEERS, 1 Great George Street, London SW1P 3AA. Tel: 020-7222 7722; Email: library@ice.org.uk; Web: www.ice.org.uk. *Chief Executive and Secretary*, M. Casebourne

INSTITUTION OF ELECTRICAL ENGINEERS, Savoy Place, London WC2R 0BL. Tel: 020-7344 5445; Email: postmaster@iee.org.uk; Web: www.iee.org.uk. *Chief Executive*, Dr A. Roberts

INSTITUTION OF GAS ENGINEERS, 21 Portland Place, London W1B 1PY. Tel: 020-7636 6603; Email: general@igaseng.demon.co.uk; Web: www.igaseng.com.

THE INSTITUTE OF MARINE ENGINEERS, 80 Coleman Street, London EC2R 5BJ. Tel: 020-7382 2600; Email: imare@imare.org.uk; Web: www.imare.org.uk. *Director-General*, K. F. Read

THE INSTITUTE OF MATERIALS, 1 Carlton House Terrace, London SW1Y 5DB. Tel: 020-7451 7300; Email: admin@materials.org.uk; Web: www.materials.org.uk. *Chief Executive*, Dr B. Rickinson

THE INSTITUTE OF MEASUREMENT AND CONTROL, 87 Gower Street, London WC1E 6AF. Tel: 020-7387 4949; Email: education@instmc.org.uk; Web: www.instmc.org.uk. *Secretary*, M. Yates

INSTITUTION OF MECHANICAL ENGINEERS, 1 Birdcage Walk, London SW1H 9JJ. Tel: 020-7222 7899; Email: enquiries@imeche.org.uk; Web: www.imeche.org.uk. *Director-General*, Sir Michael Moore

INSTITUTION OF MINING AND METALLURGY, Danum House, South Parade, Doncaster, S. Yorks DN1 2DY. Tel: 01302-320486; Email: hq@imm.org.uk; Web: www.imm.org.uk. *Secretary*, Dr G. J. M. Woodrow

THE INSTITUTE OF PHYSICS, 76 Portland Place, London W1B 1NT. Tel: 020-7470 4800; Email: physics@iop.org; Web: www.iop.org. *Chief Executive*, Dr A. Jones

INSTITUTION OF STRUCTURAL ENGINEERS, 11 Upper Belgrave Street, London SW1X 8BH. Tel: 020-7235 4535; Email: mail@istructe.org.uk; Web: www.istructe.org.uk. *Chief Executive and Secretary*, Dr K. J. Eaton

INSTITUTION OF STRUCTURAL ENGINEERS, (Scottish Branch), 15 Beresford Place, East Trinity Road, Edinburgh EH5 3SL. Tel: 0131-552 8852.

ROYAL AERONAUTICAL SOCIETY, 4 Hamilton Place, London W1J 7BQ. Tel: 020-7670 4300; Email: raes@raes.org.uk; Web: www.raes.org.uk.

ROYAL INSTITUTION OF NAVAL ARCHITECTS, 10 Upper Belgrave Street, London SW1X 8BQ. Tel: 020-7235 4622; Email: hq@rina.org.uk; Web: www.rina.org.uk. *Chief Executive*, T. Blakeley

## FILM AND TELEVISION

Postgraduate training for those intending to make a career in film, television and media production is provided by the National Film and Television School, which provides courses in animation direction, documentary direction, fiction direction, producing, screenwriting, screen design, editing, cinematography, screen sound, screen music and television producing/direction. Short courses, enabling professionals to update or expand their skills are run by the National Short Course Training Programme. There is also the Finishing School, a new industry-accredited, Digital Post-Production training workshop and creative laboratory.

NATIONAL FILM AND TELEVISION SCHOOL, Station Road, Beaconsfield, Bucks HP9 1LJ. Tel: 01494-671234; Email: admin@nftsfilm-tv.ac.uk Web: www.nftsfilm-tv.ac.uk. *Director*, S. Bayly

## FOOD AND NUTRITION SCIENCE

*See also* DIETETICS

Scientific and professional bodies include:

THE BRITISH DIETETIC ASSOCIATION, 5th Floor, Charles House, 148-149 Craig Charles Street Queensway, Birmingham B3 3HT. Tel: 0121-200 8080.

## FORESTRY AND TIMBER STUDIES

Professional organisations include:

COMMONWEALTH FORESTRY ASSOCIATION, c/o Oxford Forestry Institute, South Parks Road, Oxford OX1 3RB. Tel: 01865-271037; Email: cfa_oxford@hotmail.com. *Chairman*, Dr J. S. Maini

INSTITUTE OF CHARTERED FORESTERS, 7a St Colme Street, Edinburgh EH3 6AA. Tel: 0131-225 2705; Email: icf@charteredforesters.org; Web: www.charteredforesters.org.

ROYAL FORESTRY SOCIETY OF ENGLAND, WALES AND NORTHERN IRELAND, 102 High Street, Tring, Herts HP23 4AF. Tel: 01442-822028; Email: rfshq@rfs.org.uk; Web: www.rfs.org.uk. *Director*, Dr J. E. Jackson

ROYAL SCOTTISH FORESTRY SOCIETY, Hagg-on-Esk, Canonbie, Dumfriesshire DG14 0BE. Tel: 01387-371518. *President*, P. J. Fothergill

## FUEL AND ENERGY SCIENCE

The principal professional bodies are:

THE INSTITUTE OF PETROLEUM, 61 New Cavendish Street, London W1G 7AR. Tel: 020-7467 7100; Email: ip@petroleum.co.uk; Web: www.petroleum.co.uk. *Director-General*, J. Pym

## HOTELKEEPING, CATERING AND INSTITUTIONAL MANAGEMENT

*See also* DIETETICS, AND FOOD AND NUTRITION SCIENCE

The qualifying professional body in these areas is:

HOTEL AND CATERING INTERNATIONAL MANAGEMENT ASSOCIATION, 191 Trinity Road, London SW17 7HN. Tel: 020-8772 7400; Email: general@hcima.co.uk; Web: www.hcima.org.uk. *Chief Executive*, D. Wood

## INDUSTRIAL AND VOCATIONAL TRAINING

The NTO National Council represents the network of employer-led national training organisations (NTOs). NTOs represent the education and training interests of their respective sectors to government and ensure the development and adoption of occupational standards, particularly through National and Scottish Vocational Qualifications and learning initiatives including Modern Apprenticeship and National Traineeship.

NTO NATIONAL COUNCIL, 10 Meadowcourt, Amos Road, Sheffield S9 1BX. Tel: 0114-261 9926; Email: info@nto-nc.org; Web: www.nto-nc.org.

## INSURANCE

Organisations conducting examinations and awarding diplomas are:

ASSOCIATION OF AVERAGE ADJUSTERS, The Baltic Exchange, St Mary Axe, London EC3A 8BH. Tel: 020-7623 5501; Email: aaa@balticexchange.com; Web: www.average-adjusters.co.uk. *Chairman*, M. Duncan

THE CHARTERED INSTITUTE OF LOSS ADJUSTERS, Peninsular House, 36 Monument Street, London EC3R 8LJ. Tel: 020-7337 9960; Email: info@cila.co.uk; Web: www.cila.co.uk. *Executive Director*, G. L. Cave

THE CHARTERED INSURANCE INSTITUTE, 20 Aldermanbury, London EC2V 7HY. Tel: 020-8989 8464; Email: customer.serv@cii.co.uk; Web: www.cii.co.uk. *Director-General*, A. W. M. Scott

## JOURNALISM

Courses for trainee newspaper journalists are available at 30 centres. One-year full-time courses are available for selected students and 18-week courses for graduates. Particulars of all these courses are available from the National Council for the Training of Journalists. Short courses for mid-career development can be arranged, as can various distance learning courses. The NCTJ also offers Assessor, Internal Verifier (IV) and Accreditation of Prior Achievement (APA) training, and NVQs.

For periodical journalists, there are nine centres running courses approved by the Periodicals Training Council (PTC). The PTC also provides career information for people wishing to join the industry.

NATIONAL COUNCIL FOR THE TRAINING OF JOURNALISTS, Latton Bush Centre, Southern Way, Harlow, Essex CM18 7BL. Tel: 01279-430009; Email: info@nctj.com; Web: www.nctj.com.

THE PERIODICALS TRAINING COUNCIL, Queens House, 55–56 Lincoln Inn Field, London WC2A 3LJ. Tel: 020-7404 4168; Email: training@ppa.co.uk; Web: www.ppa.co.uk/ptc.

## LAW

### THE BAR

Admission to the Bar of England and Wales is controlled by the Inns of Court, admission to the Bar of Northern Ireland by the Honorable Society of the Inn of Court of Northern Ireland and admission as an Advocate of the Scottish Bar is controlled by the Faculty of Advocates. The governing body of the barristers' branch of the legal profession in England and Wales is the General Council of the Bar (the Bar Council). The governing body in Northern Ireland is the Honorable Society of the Inn of Court of Northern Ireland, and the Faculty of Advocates is the governing body of the Scottish Bar. The education and examination of students training for the Bar of England and Wales is regulated by the General Council of the Bar. Those who intend to practise at the Bar of England and Wales must pass the Bar's vocational course. The Inns of Court School of Law is the largest provider of initial training (both full and part time) for those wishing to practise at the Bar, but seven other institutions have been validated to provide the course. Applications are handled by the Bar Council's Centralised Applications Clearing House (CACH).

CACH, The General Council of the Bar, 2–3 Curistor Street, London EC4A 1NE. Tel: 020-7440 4000; Email: CACH@barcouncil.org.uk; Web: www.barcouncil.org.uk. *Chief Executive*, N. Morison

FACULTY OF ADVOCATES, Advocates Library, Parliament House, Edinburgh EH1 1RF. Tel: 0131-226 5071. *Dean*, G. N. H. Emslie

THE GENERAL COUNCIL OF THE BAR, 3 Bedford Row, London WC1R 4DB. Tel: 020-7242 0082; Email: chiefexec@barcouncil.org.uk; Web: www.barcouncil.org.uk.

THE HONORABLE SOCIETY OF THE INN OF COURT OF NORTHERN IRELAND, Royal Courts of Justice, Belfast BT1 3JF. Tel: 028-9056 2349.

INNS OF COURT SCHOOL OF LAW, 4 Gray's Inn Place, Gray's Inn, London WC1R 5DX. Tel: 020-7404 5787; Email: icslcourses@icsl.ac.uk; Web: www.icsl.ac.uk.

#### *The Inns of Court*

GRAY'S INN, 8 South Square, London WC1R 5ET. Tel: 020-7458 7800; Web: www.graysinn.org.uk. *Treasurer*, The Rt. Hon. Sir Paul Kennedy

INNER TEMPLE, London EC4Y 7HL. Tel: 020-7797 8250; Web: www.innertemple.org.uk. *Treasurer*, The Rt. Hon. Sir Swinton Thomas

MIDDLE TEMPLE, London EC4Y 9AT. Tel: 020-7427 4800; Email: studentenquiries@middletemple.org.uk. *Treasurer*, Rt Hon. Lord Alexander of Weedon

HONORABLE SOCIETY OF LINCOLN'S INN, Treasury Office, Lincoln's Inn, London WC2A 3TL. Tel: 020-7405

1393; Email: mail@lincolnsinn.org.uk;
Web: www.lincolnsinn.org.uk.
*Under-Treasurer*, Col. D. Hills

### SOLICITORS

Qualifications for solicitors are obtainable only from one of the Law Societies, which control the education and examination of trainee solicitors and the admission of solicitors.

THE COLLEGE OF LAW, Braboeuf Manor, Portsmouth Road, St Catherine's, Guildford, Surrey GU3 1HA. Tel: 01483-460200; Web: www.lawcol.org.uk.

THE LAW SOCIETY OF ENGLAND AND WALES, 113 Chancery Lane, London WC2A 1PL. Tel: 020-7320 5902; Web: www.lawsociety.org.uk.

LAW SOCIETY OF NORTHERN IRELAND, Law Society House, 98 Victoria Street, Belfast BT1 3JZ. Tel: 028-9023 1614; Email: info@lawsoc-ni.org; Web: www.lawsoc-ni.org.

LAW SOCIETY OF SCOTLAND, 26 Drumsheugh Gardens, Edinburgh EH3 7YR. Tel: 0131-226 7411; Email: lawscot@lawscot.org.uk; Web: www.lawscot.org.uk.

OFFICE FOR THE SUPERVISION OF SOLICITORS, Victoria Court, 8 Dormer Place, Leamington Spa, Warks CV32 5AE. Tel: 01926-820082; Email: enquiries@lawsociety.org.uk; Web: www.oss.lawsociety.org.uk. *Director*, J. Plane

## LIBRARIANSHIP AND INFORMATION SCIENCE/MANAGEMENT

The Library Association accredits degree and postgraduate courses in library and information science which are offered by 17 universities in the UK. A full list of accredited degree and postgraduate courses is available from its International Relations and Information Services Department and on its web site (*see* below) The Association also maintains a professional register of Chartered Members.

THE LIBRARY ASSOCIATION, 7 Ridgmount Street, London WC1E 7AE. Tel: 020-7636 7543 Web: www.la-hq.uk.

## MEDICINE

All doctors must be registered with the General Medical Council (GMC), which is responsible for protecting the public by setting standards for professional practice, overseeing medical education, keeping a register of qualified doctors and taking action where a doctor's fitness to practise is in doubt. A doctor not registered with the GMC is not a "legally qualified" medical practitioner for the purposes of the Medical Act 1983. In order to be eligible for registration, doctors must obtain a primary medical qualification recognised by the GMC and have satisfactorily completed a year of general clinical training. Special arrangements apply to doctors qualified outside the UK. Once registered, doctors undertake general professional and basic specialist training as senior house officers. Further specialist training is provided by the royal colleges, faculties and societies listed below.

The United Examining Board holds qualifying examinations for candidates who have trained overseas. These candidates must also have spent a period at a UK medical school.

GENERAL MEDICAL COUNCIL, 178 Great Portland Street, London W1N 6JE. Tel: 020-7580 7642; Web: www.gmc-uk.org.

UNITED EXAMINING BOARD, Apothecaries Hall, Black Friars Lane, London EC4V 6EJ. Tel: 020-7236 1180; Email: examoffice@apothecaries.org.

### COLLEGES/SOCIETIES HOLDING POSTGRADUATE MEMBERSHIP AND DIPLOMA EXAMINATIONS

FACULTY OF ACCIDENT AND EMERGENCY MEDICINE, 35–43 Lincoln's Inn Fields, London WC2A 3PE. Tel: 020-7405 7071; Email: faem@compuserve.com; Web: www.faem.org.uk. *President*, I. W. R. Anderson

FACULTY OF PUBLIC HEALTH MEDICINE, 4 St Andrews Place, London NW1 4LB. Tel: 020-7935 0243; Email: enquiries@fphm.org.uk; Web: www.fphm.org.uk.

ROYAL COLLEGE OF ANAESTHETISTS, 48–49 Russell Square, London WC1B 4JY. Tel: 020-7813 1900; Email: info@rcoa.ac.uk; Web: www.rcoa.ac.uk. *President*, Prof. P. Hatton

ROYAL COLLEGE OF OBSTETRICIANS AND GYNAECOLOGISTS, 27 Sussex Place, Regent's Park, London NW1 4RG. Tel: 020-7772 6200; Email: coll.sec@rcog.org.uk; Web: www.rcog.org.uk. *College Secretary*, P. A. Barnett

ROYAL COLLEGE OF PAEDIATRICS AND CHILD HEALTH, 50 Hallam Street, London W1W 6DE. Tel: 020-7307 5600; Email: enquiries@rcpch.ac.uk. *Secretary*, L. Tyler

ROYAL COLLEGE OF PATHOLOGISTS, 2 Carlton House Terrace, London SW1Y 5AF. Tel: 020-7451 6700; Email: info@rcpath.org; Web: www.rcpath.org. *Chief Executive*, D. Ross

ROYAL COLLEGE OF PHYSICIANS, 11 St Andrews Place, Regent's Park, London NW1 4LE. Tel: 020-7935 1174; Web: www.rcplondon.ac.uk. *President*, Prof. Sir George Alberti

ROYAL COLLEGE OF PHYSICIANS AND SURGEONS OF GLASGOW, 232–242 St Vincent Street, Glasgow G2 5RJ. Tel: 0141-221 6072; Email: registrar@rcpsglasg.ac.uk; Web: www.rcpsglasg.ac.uk. *President*, Prof. A. R. Lorimer

ROYAL COLLEGE OF PHYSICIANS OF EDINBURGH, 9 Queen Street, Edinburgh EH2 1JQ. Tel: 0131-225 7324; Web: www.rcpe.ac.uk. *President*, Dr N. D. C. Finlayson

ROYAL COLLEGE OF PSYCHIATRISTS, 17 Belgrave Square, London SW1X 8PG. Tel: 020-7235 2351; Email: rcpsych@rcpsych.ac.uk; Web: www.rcpsych.ac.uk. *President*, Prof J. L. Cox

ROYAL COLLEGE OF RADIOLOGISTS, 38 Portland Place, London W1N 4JQ. Tel: 020-7636 4432; Email: enquiries@rcr.ac.uk; Web: www.rcr.ac.uk. *President*, Dr D. V. Ash

ROYAL COLLEGE OF SURGEONS OF EDINBURGH, Nicolson Street, Edinburgh EH8 9DW. Tel: 0131-527 1600; Email: information@rcsed.ac.uk; Web: www.rcsed.ac.uk. *President*, Prof. J. G. Temple

THE ROYAL COLLEGE OF SURGEONS OF ENGLAND, 35–43 Lincoln's Inn Fields, London WC2A 3PE. Tel: 020-7405 3474; Web: www.rcseng.ac.uk. *President*, Prof. Sir Peter Morris

SOCIETY OF APOTHECARIES OF LONDON, 14 Black Friars Lane, London EC4V 6EJ. Tel: 020-7236 1189; Email: clerk@apothecaries.org; Web: www.apothecaries.org. *The Clerk*, R. J. Stringer

## PROFESSIONS SUPPLEMENTARY TO MEDICINE

The standard of professional education in art, drama and music therapies, biomedical sciences, chiropody, dietetics, occupational therapy, orthoptics, prosthetics and orthotics, physiotherapy and radiography is the responsibility of nine professional boards, which also publish an annual register of qualified practitioners. The work of the boards is co-ordinated by the Council for Professions Supplementary to Medicine.

In January 2000 three new boards were established, covering speech and language therapists, clinical scientists and paramedics.

COUNCIL FOR PROFESSIONS SUPPLEMENTARY TO MEDICINE, Park House, 184 Kennington Park Road, London SE11 4BU. Tel: 020-7582 0866; Web: www.cpsm.org.uk.

### ART, DRAMA AND MUSIC THERAPIES

A postgraduate qualification in the relevant therapy is required. There are five institutions in the UK offering courses in art therapy and six offering courses in music therapy.

ASSOCIATION OF PROFESSIONAL MUSIC THERAPISTS, 26 Hamlyn Road, Glastonbury, Somerset BA6 8HT. Tel: 01458-834919; Email: apmtoffice@aol.com; Web: www.apmt.org.uk.

BRITISH ASSOCIATION OF ART THERAPISTS, Mary Ward House, 5 Tavistock Place, London WC1H 9SN. Tel: 020-7383 3774; Web: www.baat.co.uk.

BRITISH ASSOCIATION OF DRAMA THERAPISTS, 41 Broomhouse Lane, London SW6 3DP. Tel: 020-7731 0160; Email: gillian@badth.demon.co.uk.

### BIOMEDICAL SCIENCES

Qualifications from higher education establishments and training in medical laboratories are required for membership of the Institute of Biomedical Science.

INSTITUTE OF BIOMEDICAL SCIENCES, 12 Coldbath Square, London EC1R 5HL. Tel: 020-7713 0214; Email: mail@ibms.org; Web: www.ibms.org.

### CHIROPODY

Professional recognition is granted by the Society of Chiropodists and Podiatrists to students who are awarded BSc. degrees in Podiatry or Podiatric Medicine after attending a course of full-time training for three or four years at one of the 13 recognised schools in the UK (ten in England and Wales, two in Scotland and one in Northern Ireland). Qualifications granted and degrees recognised by the Society are approved for the purpose of State Registration, which is a condition of employment within the National Health Service.

SOCIETY OF CHIROPODISTS AND PODIATRISTS, 1 Fellmongers Path, Tower Bridge Road, London SE1 3LY. Tel: 020-7234 8620; Email: eng@scpod.org; Web: www.feetforlife.org.

### OCCUPATIONAL THERAPY

The professional qualification may be obtained upon successful completion of a validated course in any of the 28 institutions approved by the College of Occupational Therapists. The courses are normally degree-level courses based in higher education institutions.

COLLEGE OF OCCUPATIONAL THERAPISTS, 106–114 Borough High Street, London SE1 1LB. Tel: 020-7357 6480; Email: cot@cot.co.uk; Web: www.cot.co.uk.

FACULTY OF OCCUPATIONAL MEDICINE, 6 St Andrew's Place, London NW1 4LB. Tel: 020-7317 5890; Email: fom@facoccmed.ac.uk; Web: www.facoccmed.ac.uk. *Secretary*, Ms F. Quinn

### ORTHOPTICS

Orthoptists undertake the diagnosis and treatment of all types of squint and other anomalies of binocular vision, working in close collaboration with ophthalmologists. The training and maintenance of professional standards are the responsibility of the Orthoptists Board of the Council for the Professions Supplementary to Medicine. The professional body is the British Orthoptic Society. Training is at degree level.

THE BRITISH ORTHOPTIC SOCIETY, Tavistock House North, Tavistock Square, London WC1H 9HX. Tel: 020-7387 7992; Email: bos@orthoptics.org.uk.

### PHYSIOTHERAPY

Full-time three- or four-year degree courses are available at 30 higher education institutions in the UK. Information about courses leading to eligibility for Membership of the Chartered Society of Physiotherapy and to State Registration is available from the Chartered Society of Physiotherapy.

THE CHARTERED SOCIETY OF PHYSIOTHERAPY, 14 Bedford Row, London WC1R 4ED. Tel: 020-7306 6666; Email: careersadviser@csphysio.org.uk; Web: www.csphysio.org.uk.

### PROSTHETICS AND ORTHOTICS

Prosthetists provide artificial limbs, while orthotists provide devices to support or control a part of the body. It is necessary to obtain an honours degree to become a prosthetist/orthotist. Courses are available at two institutions in the UK.

BRITISH ASSOCIATION OF PROSTHETISTS AND ORTHOTISTS, Sir James Clark Building, Abbey Mill Business Centre, Paisley PA1 1TJ. Tel: 0141-561 7217; Email: admin@bapo.com; Web: www.bapo.com.

### RADIOGRAPHY AND RADIOTHERAPY

In order to practise both diagnostic and therapeutic radiography in the UK, it is necessary to have successfully completed a course of education and training recognised by the Privy Council. Such courses are offered by universities throughout the UK and lead to the award of a degree in radiography. Further information is available from the college.

COLLEGE OF RADIOGRAPHERS, 27 Providence Square, Mill Street, London SE1 2EW. Tel: 020-7740 7200; Email: info@sor.org; Web: www.sor.org.

## COMPLEMENTARY MEDICINE

Professional courses are validated by:

INSTITUTE FOR COMPLEMENTARY MEDICINE, PO Box 194, London SE16 7QZ. Tel: 020-7237 5165; Email: icm@icmedicine.co.uk; Web: www.icmedicine.co.uk. *Director*, A. Baird

## MERCHANT NAVY TRAINING SCHOOLS

### OFFICERS

WARSASH MARITIME CENTRE, Southampton Institute, Newtown Road, Warsash, Southampton SO31 9ZL. Tel: 01489-576161; Email: wmc@solent.ac.uk; Web: www.solent.ac.uk/wmc/. *Head*, J. Milligan

### SEAFARERS

NATIONAL SEA TRAINING CENTRE, North West Kent College, Dering Way, Gravesend, Kent DA12 2JJ. Tel: 01322-629600; Email: rodgermacdonald@nwkent.ac.uk; Web: www.nwkent.ac.uk/nstc. *Director of Faculty – NSTC*, R. MacDonald

## MUSIC

Associated Board of the Royal Schools of Music, conducts graded music examinations in over 80 countries and provides other services to music education through its professional development department and publishing company.

ASSOCIATED BOARD OF THE ROYAL SCHOOLS OF MUSIC, 24 Portland Place, London W1B 1LU. Tel: 020-7636 5400; Email: abrsm@abrsm.ac.uk; Web: www.abrsm.ac.uk.

GUILDHALL SCHOOL OF MUSIC DRAMA, Silk Street, Barbican, London EC2Y 8DT. Tel: 020-7628 2571; Web: www.gsmd.ac.uk. *Principal*, Dr I. Horsbrugh

LONDON COLLEGE OF MUSIC AND MEDIA, Thames Valley University, St Mary's Road, London W5 5RF. Tel: 020-8231 2304; Web: www.elgar.tvu.ac.uk. *Acting Dean*, H. Swain

ROYAL ACADEMY OF MUSIC, Marylebone Road, London NW1 5HT. Tel: 020-7873 7373; Email: registry@ram.ac.uk; Web: www.ram.ac.uk. *Principal*, C. Price

ROYAL COLLEGE OF ORGANISTS, 7 St Andrew Street, London EC4A 3LQ. Tel: 020-7936 3606; Email: admin@rco.org.uk; Web: www.rco.org.uk. *Senior Executive*, A. Dear

ROYAL NORTHERN COLLEGE OF MUSIC, 124 Oxford Road, Manchester M13 9RD. Tel: 0161-907 5200; Email: info@rncm.ac.uk; Web: www.rncm.ac.uk. *Principal*, Prof. E. Gregson

ROYAL SCOTTISH ACADEMY OF MUSIC AND DRAMA, 100 Renfrew Street, Glasgow G2 3DB. Tel: 0141-332 4101; Email: registry@rsamd.ac.uk; Web: www.rsamd.ac.uk. *Principal*, Sir Philip Ledger

TRINITY COLLEGE OF MUSIC, 11–13 Mandeville Place, London W1M 6AQ. Tel: 020-7487 9647; Web: www.tcm.ac.uk. *Principal*, G. Henderson

## NURSING

All nurses must be registered with the UK Central Council for Nursing, Midwifery and Health Visiting. Please note that it will cease to exist in March 2002 and a new regulating body – the Nursing and Midwifery Council – will be set up; its functions were not yet known at the time of going to press. Courses leading to registration as a nurse are at least three years in length. There are also some programmes which are combined with degrees. Students study in colleges of nursing or in institutions of higher education. Courses offer a combination of theoretical and practical experience in a variety of settings. Different courses lead to different types of registration, including Registered Nurse (RN), Registered Mental Nurse (RMN), Registered Mental Handicap Nurse (RMHN), Registered Sick Children's Nurse (RSCN), Registered Midwife (RM) and Registered Health Visitor (RHV). The various national boards, listed below, are responsible for validating courses in nursing. In February 1999 the Government announced plans to replace these boards and the UK Central Council with a single UK-wide body. Health visitors will continue to have separate registration and representation on the new body.

The Royal College of Nursing is the largest professional union representing nurses and provides higher education through its Institute.

ENGLISH NATIONAL BOARD FOR NURSING, MIDWIFERY AND HEALTH VISITING, Victory House, 170 Tottenham Court Road, London W1T 7HA. Tel: 020-7391 6229; Email: ceo@enb.org.uk; Web: www.enb.org.uk.

NATIONAL BOARD FOR NURSING, MIDWIFERY AND HEALTH VISITING FOR NORTHERN IRELAND, Centre House, 79 Chichester Street, Belfast BT1 4JE. Tel: 028-9023 8152; Email: enquiries@nbni.n-i.nhs.uk; Web: www.n-i.nhs.uk/NBNI/index.htm.

NATIONAL BOARD FOR NURSING, MIDWIFERY AND HEALTH VISITING FOR SCOTLAND, 22 Queen Street, Edinburgh EH2 1NT. Tel: 0131-226 7371; Email: david.ferguson@nbs.org.uk; Web: www.nbs.org.uk.

UK CENTRAL COUNCIL FOR NURSING, MIDWIFERY AND HEALTH VISITING, 23 Portland Place, London W1N 4JT. Tel: 020-7637 7181; Email: communication@ukcc.org.uk; Web: www.ukcc.org.uk.

WELSH NATIONAL BOARD FOR NURSING, MIDWIFERY AND HEALTH VISITING, 2nd Floor, Golate House, 101 St Mary Street, Cardiff CF10 1DX. Tel: 029-2026 1400; Email: info@wnb.org.uk; Web: www.wnb.org.uk.

## OPHTHALMIC AND DISPENSING OPTICS

Professional bodies are:

THE ASSOCIATION OF BRITISH DISPENSING OPTICIANS, 6 Hurlingham Business Park, Sulivan Road, London SW6 3DU. Tel: 020-7736 0088; Email: general@abdo.org.uk. *General-Secretary*, Sir Anthony Garrett

THE COLLEGE OF OPTOMETRISTS, 42 Craven Street, London WC2N 5NG. Tel: 020-7839 6000; Email: optometry@college-optometrists.org; Web: www.optometrists.org. *Secretary*, P. D. Leigh

## OSTEOPATHY

Osteopathy is the first of the professions previously outside conventional medical services to achieve statutory recognition under a new body the General Osteopathic Council. Since May 2000 all practising osteopaths have had to be registered with the General Osteopathic Council and the title 'osteopath' is protected by law. To gain entry to the register all newly qualified osteopaths have to be in possession of a recognised qualification from a course of training accredited by the General Osteopathic Council. The General Osteopathic Council is responsible for regulating, developing, and promoting the profession.

GENERAL OSTEOPATHIC COUNCIL, Osteopathy House, 176 Tower Bridge Road, London SE1 3LU. Tel: 020-7357 6655; Email: info@osteopathy.org.uk; Web: www.osteopathy.org.uk.

## PHARMACY

The Royal Pharmaceutical Society of Great Britain is the professional statutory body for practising pharmacists in Great Britain. It maintains the Register of Pharmaceutical Chemists where all pharmacists must be registered before being able to practice.

FACULTY OF PHARMACEUTICAL MEDICINE, 1 St Andrew's Place, London NW1 4LB. Tel: 020-7224 0343; Email: fpm@f-pharm-med.org.uk; Web: www.fpm.org.uk. *Faculty Administrator*, Mrs K. Swanston

## PHOTOGRAPHY

The professional body is:

BRITISH INSTITUTE OF PROFESSIONAL PHOTOGRAPHY, Fox Talbot House, Amwell End, Ware, Herts SG12 9HN. Tel: 01920-464011; Email: bipp@compuserve.com; Web: www.bipp.com. *Chief Executive*, A. Mair

## PRINTING

Details of training courses in printing can be obtained from the Institute of Printing and the British Printing Industries Federation. In addition to these examining and organising bodies, examinations are held by various independent regional examining boards in further education.

BRITISH PRINTING INDUSTRIES FEDERATION, Farringdon Point, 29–35 Farringdon Rd, London EC1M 3JF. Tel: 020-7915 8300; Email: info@bpif.org.uk; Web: www.bpif.org.uk.

INSTITUTE OF PRINTING, The Mews, Hill House, Clanricarde Road, Tunbridge Wells, Kent TN1 1PJ. Tel: 01892-538118; Email: david@iop.ftech.co.uk; Web: www.instituteofprinting.org.

## SCIENCE

Professional qualifications are awarded by:

THE INSTITUTE OF BIOLOGY, 20–22 Queensberry Place, London SW7 2DZ. Tel: 020-7581 8333; Email: info@iob.org; Web: www.iob.org. *Chief Executive*, Prof. A. D. B. Malcolm

THE ROYAL SOCIETY OF CHEMISTRY, Burlington House, Piccadilly, London W1J 0BA. Tel: 020-7437 8656; Email: rsc@rsc.org; Web: www.rsc.org. *Secretary-General and Chief Executive*, Dr D. Giachardi

## SPEECH AND LANGUAGE THERAPY

The Royal College of Speech and Language Therapists accredits education and training courses leading to qualification as a speech and language therapist.

ROYAL COLLEGE OF SPEECH AND LANGUAGE THERAPISTS, 2 White Hart Yard, London SE1 1NX. Tel: 020-7378 1200; Email: info@rcslt.org.uk; Web: www.rcslt.org.uk.

## SURVEYING

The qualifying professional bodies include:

ARCHITECTURE AND SURVEYING INSTITUTE, St Mary House, 15 St Mary Street, Chippenham, Wilts SN15 3WD. Tel: 01249-444505; Email: mail@asi.org.uk; Web: www.asi.org.uk. *Chief Executive*, I. N. Norris

ASSOCIATION OF BUILDING ENGINEERS, Lutyens House, Billing Brook Road, Weston Favell, Northampton NN3 8NW. Tel: 01604-404121; Email: building.engineers@abe.org.uk; Web: www.abe.org.uk. *Chief Executive*, D. R. Gibson

INSTITUTE OF REVENUES, RATING AND VALUATION, 41 Doughty Street, London WC1N 2LF. Tel: 020-7831 3505; Email: enquiries@irrv.org.uk; Web: www.irrv.org.uk. *Director*, Ms K. Aldred

THE ROYAL INSTITUTION OF CHARTERED SURVEYORS, 12 Great George Street, London SW1P 3AD. Tel: 020-7222 7000; Email: info@rics.org.uk; Web: www.rics.org. *Chief Executive*, J. H. A. J. Armstrong

## TEACHING

Teachers in maintained schools must acquire Qualified Teacher Status (QTS) by completing a programme of Initial Teacher Training. Those without a first degree may take a Bachelor of Education (BEd) or a Bachelor of Arts/Science (BA/BSc) with QTS, full-time for three or four years, depending on the programme followed. These degrees combine subject and professional studies with teaching practice. Shortened courses of these degrees are available for those who have successfully completed one or two years of higher education. Flexible routes into teaching are increasing, including part-time, distance learning and modular courses. Alternatively, teachers can gain QTS through employment-based training, following individual training plans while in post.

For those who already have a first degree, the most common route is through a one-year Postgraduate Certificate of Education (PGCE). This may be taken full-time or part-time, or as a distance-learning programme. Postgraduates may also gain QTS through training in a school (School-Centred Initial Teacher Training). Since January 1998, graduates have been able to join the Graduate Teacher Programme which provides teaching and training for one year.

Details of courses in England and Wales are contained in the *NATFHE Handbook of Initial Teacher Training in England and Wales 2000*, in *University and College Entrance: 2000* (*The Big Book*) published by UCAS and on the UCAS website. Further information about teaching in England and Wales is available from the Teaching Information Line, 0845 600 0991. Details of courses in Scotland can be obtained from universities and the Graduate Teacher Training Registry (GTTR). Details of courses in Northern Ireland can be obtained from the Department of Education for Northern Ireland. Applications for teacher training courses in Northern Ireland are made to the institutions direct.

TEACHER TRAINING AGENCY, Portland House, Stag Place, London SW1E 5TT. Tel: 020-7925 3700; Web: www.canteach.gov.uk.

## TEXTILES

THE TEXTILE INSTITUTE, 4th Floor, St James's Buildings, Oxford Street, Manchester M1 6FQ. Tel: 0161-237 1188; Email: tiihq@textileinst.org.uk; Web: www.texi.org.uk. *Director-General*, T. D. Hennessey

## THEOLOGICAL COLLEGES

### ANGLICAN

COLLEGE OF THE RESURRECTION, Mirfield, W. Yorks WF14 0BW. Tel: 01924-490441; Email: registrar@mirfield.org.uk; Web: www.mirfield.org.uk. *Principal*, Revd C. Irvine

CRANMER HALL, St John's College, Durham DH1 3RJ. Tel: 0191-374 3579; Web: www.dur.ac.uk/cranmer. *Principal*, The Rt. Revd S. W. Sykes

OAK HILL COLLEGE, Chase Side, Southgate, London N14 4PS. Tel: 020-8449 0467; Email: mailbox@oakhill.ac.uk; Web: www.oakhill.ac.uk. *Principal*, Revd Dr D. Peterson

RIDLEY HALL, Cambridge CB3 9HG. Tel: 01223-741080; Email: ridley-pa@lists.cam.ac.uk; Web: www.ridley.cam.ac.uk. *Principal*, The Revd Canon Dr Christopher Cocksworth

RIPON COLLEGE, Cuddesdon, Oxford OX44 9EX. Tel: 01865-874427; Email: admin@ripon-cuddesdon.ac.uk; Web: www.ripon-cuddesdon.ac.uk. *Principal*, Canon J. Clarke

ST JOHN'S COLLEGE, Chilwell Lane, Bramcote, Nottingham NG9 3DS. Tel: 0115-925 1114; Email: principal@stjohns-nottm.ac.uk; Web: www.stjohns-nottm.ac.uk. *Principal*, Canon Dr C. Baxter

ST MICHAEL'S THEOLOGICAL COLLEGE, Llandaff, Cardiff CF5 2YJ. Tel: 029-2056 3379; Email: stmichael@nildram.co.uk. *Principal*, Revd Dr J. Holdsworth

ST STEPHEN'S HOUSE, 16 Marston Street, Oxford OX4 1JX. Tel: 01865-247874; Email: jeremy.sheehy@theology.oxford.ac.uk. *Principal*, Revd Dr J. P. Sheehy

THEOLOGICAL INSTITUTE OF THE SCOTTISH EPISCOPAL CHURCH, Old Coates House, 32 Manor Place, Edinburgh EH3 7EB. Tel: 0131-220 2272; Email: office@stisec.scotland.anglican.org. *Principal*, Revd Canon Dr M. Fuller

TRINITY COLLEGE, Stoke Hill, Bristol BS9 1JP. Tel: 0117-968 2803; Email: principal@trinity-bris.ac.uk; Web: www.trinity-bris.ac.uk. *Principal*, Revd Dr F. Bridger

WESTCOTT HOUSE, Jesus Lane, Cambridge CB5 8BP. Tel: 01223-741000; Email: westcott.house@lists.cam.ac.uk; Web: www.ely.anglican.org/westcott. *Principal*, Revd M. Roberts

WYCLIFFE HALL THEOLOGICAL COLLEGE, 54 Banbury Road, Oxford OX2 6PW. Tel: 01865-274200; Email: enquiries@wycliffe.ox.ac.uk; Web: www.wycliffe.ox.ac.uk. *Principal*, Revd Prof. A. E. McGrath

### BAPTIST

BRISTOL BAPTIST COLLEGE, The Promenade, Clifton, Bristol BS8 3NF. Tel: 0117-946 7050; Email: admin@bristol-baptist.ac.uk Web: www.bristol-baptist.ac.uk. *Principal*, Revd C. Ellis

NORTHERN BAPTIST COLLEGE, Luther King House, Brighton Grove, Rusholme, Manchester M14 5JP. Tel: 0161-224 6404; Email: richard.kidd@appleonline.net. *Principal*, Revd Dr R. Kidd

NORTH WALES BAPTIST COLLEGE, Ffordd Ffriddoedd, Bangor LL57 2EH. Tel: 01248-362608; Web: www.bangor.ac.uk/rs/gttest.html. *Warden*, Revd Dr D. D. Morgan

REGENT'S PARK COLLEGE, Oxford OX1 2LB. Tel: 01865-288120; Email: postmaster@regents.ox.ac.uk; Web: www.rpc.ox.ac.uk/rpc. *Principal*, Revd Dr P. S. Fiddes

THE SCOTTISH BAPTIST COLLEGE, 12 Aytoun Road, Glasgow G41 5RN. Tel: 0141-424 0747; Web: www.scottishbaptistcollege.org.uk. *Principal*, Dr K. B. E. Roxburgh

SOUTH WALES BAPTIST COLLEGE, 54 Richmond Road, Cardiff CF24 3UR. Tel: 029-2025 6066; Email: swbc@cardiff.ac.uk; Web: www.welshbaptists.com. *Principal*, Revd Dr J. Weaver

CHURCH OF SCOTLAND

NEW COLLEGE, Mound Place, Edinburgh EH1 2LX. Tel: 0131-650 8916/8900; Email: lyalld@div.ed.ac.uk; Web: www.divinity.ed.ac.uk. *Principal*, Revd Dr D. Lyall

TRINITY COLLEGE, Faculty of Divinity, University of Glasgow, Glasgow G12 8QQ. Tel: 0141-330 6840; Email: d.murray@arts.gla.ac.uk. *Principal*, Revd Dr D. M. Murray

CONGREGATIONAL

THE QUEEN'S FOUNDATION FOR ECUMENICAL THEOLOGICAL INFORMATION, Somerset Road, Edgbaston, Birmingham B15 2QH. Tel: 0121-454 1527; Email: enquire@queens.ac.uk; Web: www.queens.ac.uk. *Principal*, Revd Canon P. Fisher

METHODIST

EDGHILL THEOLOGICAL COLLEGE, 9 Lennoxvale, Belfast BT9 5BY. Tel: 028-9066 5870. *Principal*, Revd Dr D. Cooke

HARTLEY VICTORIA COLLEGE, Luther King House, Brighton Grove, Rusholme, Manchester M14 5JP. Tel: 0161-249 2516. *Principal*, Revd Dr J. A. Harrod

WESLEY COLLEGE, College Park Drive, Henbury Road, Bristol BS10 7QD. Tel: 0117-959 1200; Email: admin@wescoll.demon.co.uk; Web: www.wescoll.demon.co.uk. *Principal*, Revd Dr N. Richardson

WESLEY THEOLOGICAL COLLEGE, Wesley House, Jesus Lane, Cambridge CB5 8BJ. Tel: 01223-741033; Email: bursar@wesley.org.uk; Web: www.wesley.org.uk. *Principal*, Revd Dr P. Luscombe

WESLEY STUDY CENTRE, 55 The Avenue, Durham DH1 4EB. Tel: 0191-374 3580. *Director*, Revd R. Walton

NON-DENOMINATIONAL

CHRIST'S College, 25 High Street, Old Aberdeen, Aberdeen AB24 3EE. Tel: 01224-272138. *Master*, Revd Prof. Iain R. Torrance

ST MARY'S COLLEGE, The University, St Andrews, Fife KY16 9JU. Tel: 01334-462850; Email: divinity@st-andrews.ac.uk; Web: www.st-andrews.ac.uk. *Principal*, Prof. R. A. Piper

SPURGEON'S COLLEGE, South Norwood Hill, London SE25 6DJ. Tel: 020-8653 0850; Email: enquiries@spurgeons.ac.uk; Web: www.spurgeons.ac.uk. *Principal*, Revd Dr N. Wright

PRESBYTERIAN

UNION THEOLOGICAL COLLEGE, 108 Botanic Avenue, Belfast BT7 1JT. Tel: 028-9020 5080; Email: admin@union.ac.uk; Web: www.union.ac.uk. *Principal*, Revd J. C. McCullough

PRESBYTERIAN CHURCH OF WALES

UNITED THEOLOGICAL COLLEGE, Aberystwyth, Ceredigion SY23 2LT. Tel: 01970-624574; Web: www.ebcpcw.org.uk.

ROMAN CATHOLIC

ALLEN HALL, 28 Beaufort Street, London SW3 5AA. Tel: 020-7351 1296; Email: secretary@allenhall.co.uk. *Rector*, Revd P. McGinn

CAMPION HOUSE COLLEGE, 112 Thornbury Road, Isleworth, Middx TW7 4NN. Tel: 020-8560 1924; Email: campionhouseosterley@compuserve.com; Web: www.campionhouse.org.uk. *Principal*, Revd M. Barrow

OSCOTT COLLEGE, Chester Road, Sutton Coldfield, West Midlands B73 5AA. Tel: 0121-321 5000; Email: oscott@dial.pipex.com. *Rector*, Monsignor K. McDonald

ST JOHN'S SEMINARY, Wonersh, Guildford, Surrey GU5 0QX. Tel: 01483-892217. *Rector*, Revd K. Haggerty

SCOTUS COLLEGE, 2 Chesters Road, Bearsden, Glasgow G61 4AG. Tel: 0141-942 8384. *Rector*, Revd N. Donnachie

USHAW COLLEGE, Durham DH7 9RH. Tel: 0191-373 8501; Email: j.p.o'keefe@dur.ac.uk; Web: www.dur.ac.uk/ushaw. *President*, Revd J. O'Keefe

UNITARIAN

*Unitarian College*, Luther King House, Brighton Grove, Rusholme, Manchester M14 5JP. Tel: 0161-224 2849; Email: ucm@ptem.freeserve.co.uk. *Principal*, Revd Dr L. Smith

UNITED REFORMED

NORTHERN COLLEGE, Luther King House, Brighton Grove, Rusholme, Manchester M14 5JP. Tel: 0161-249 2506; Email: reception@lkh.co.uk. *Principal*, Revd Dr D. R. Peel

WESTMINSTER COLLEGE, Madingley Road, Cambridge CB3 0AA. Tel: 01223-741084; Email: mr258@cam.ac.uk; Web: www.westminster.cam.ac.uk. *Principal*, Revd Dr S. Orchard

JEWISH

LEO BAECK COLLEGE, Sternberg Centre for Judaism, 80 East End Road, London N3 2SY. Tel: 020-8349 5600; Email: info@lbc.ac.uk; Web: www.lbc.ac.uk. *Principal*, Rabbi Prof. J. Magonet

LONDON SCHOOL OF JEWISH STUDIES, Schaller House, 44a Albert Road, London NW4 2SJ. Tel: 020-8203 6427; Email: enquiries@lsjs.ac.uk; Web: www.lsjs.ac.uk. *Principal*, Dr A. Weiss

## VETERINARY MEDICINE

The regulatory body for veterinary medicine is the Royal College of Veterinary Surgeons, which keeps the register of those entitled to practise veterinary medicine. In order to be registered, a person must complete a five-year undergraduate degree (BVetMed, BVSc., BVMS, BVM and S) at one of the six authorised institutions in the UK.

The British Veterinary Association is the professional body representing veterinary surgeons. The British Veterinary Nursing Association is the professional body representing veterinary nurses who are also registered with the Royal College of Veterinary Surgeons.

BRITISH VETERINARY NURSING ASSOCIATION, Level 15, Terminus House, Terminus Street, Harlow, Essex CM20 1XA. Tel: 01279-450567; Email: bvna@bvna.co.uk; Web: www.bvna.org.uk.

ROYAL COLLEGE OF VETERINARY SURGEONS, Belgravia House, 62-64 Horseferry Road, London SW1P 2AF. Tel: 020-7222 2001; Email: admin@rcvs.org.uk; Web: www.rcvs.org.uk.

# Health

## Selected Causes of Death, by Gender and Age 1999 (United Kingdom)

| | Under 1* | 1–14 | 15–24 | 25–34 | 35–54 | 55–64 | 65–74 | 75 and over | All ages |
|---|---|---|---|---|---|---|---|---|---|
| Males | | | | | | | | | |
| Circulatory diseases | 28 | 64 | 90 | 368 | 6,969 | 13,097 | 31,293 | 67,821 | 119,730 |
| Cancer | 6 | 195 | 207 | 426 | 6,109 | 12,320 | 24,727 | 34,820 | 78,810 |
| Respiratory diseases | 94 | 93 | 76 | 143 | 1,245 | 2,944 | 9,675 | 34,640 | 48,910 |
| Injury and poisoning | 39 | 280 | 1,613 | 2,387 | 3,666 | 1,156 | 1,056 | 2,175 | 12,372 |
| Infectious diseases | 77 | 64 | 54 | 100 | 386 | 222 | 395 | 805 | 2,103 |
| Other causes | 2074 | 336 | 598 | 1,092 | 4,420 | 3,599 | 6,590 | 19,734 | 38,443 |
| All males (number) | 2,318 | 1,032 | 2638 | 4516 | 22,795 | 33,338 | 73,763 | 159,995 | 300,368 |
| Females | | | | | | | | | |
| Circulatory diseases | 23 | 44 | 90 | 214 | 2,629 | 5,365 | 18,852 | 103,349 | 130,566 |
| Cancer | 8 | 137 | 132 | 509 | 7,285 | 10,304 | 18,887 | 36,404 | 73,666 |
| Respiratory diseases | 51 | 70 | 62 | 97 | 929 | 2118 | 7,525 | 50,024 | 60,876 |
| Injury and poisoning | 30 | 153 | 414 | 543 | 1,134 | 499 | 719 | 3,712 | 7,204 |
| Infectious diseases | 69 | 50 | 51 | 42 | 168 | 165 | 327 | 1,183 | 2,055 |
| Other causes* | 1,546 | 319 | 277 | 519 | 2,654 | 2,594 | 5,930 | 43,485 | 57,327 |
| All females (number) | 1,727 | 773 | 1,026 | 1,924 | 14,802 | 21,045 | 52,240 | 238,157 | 331,694 |

* Deaths at under 28 days are not assigned a specific cause and are entered under 'other'.
*Source:* Office for National Statistics, Mortality Statistics Section, GRO Scotland and NISRA

## Notifications of Infectious Diseases (UK) 1999

| | |
|---|---|
| Measles | 2,953 |
| Mumps | 2,005 |
| Rubella | 2,581 |
| Whooping cough | 1,461 |
| Scarlet fever | 2,951 |
| Dysentery | 1,627 |
| Food poisoning | 96,944 |
| Typhoid and paratyphoid fevers | 278 |
| Hepatitis | 4,346 |
| Tuberculosis | 6,703 |
| Malaria | 1,039 |

*Source:* The Stationery Office – *Annual Abstract of Statistics 2001* (Crown copyright)

## HIV/AIDS and Sexually Transmitted Diseases (England)

| | 1987 | 2000 |
|---|---|---|
| HIV cases diagnosed | 1,917 | 3,551 |
| Exposure category | | |
| Homosexual intercourse | 73% | 39% |
| Heterosexual intercourse | 9% | 49% |
| Injecting drug use | 12% | 2.6% |
| Blood products | 2% | 0.6% |
| Mother to infant | — | 2.4% |
| Other/undetermined | 4% | 6.4% |
| Aids cases diagnosed | 640 | 718 |

*Source:* Public Health Laboratory Service

## Current Smokers (United Kingdom)

*By gender and socio-economic group*

Percentage

| | 1982 | 1998-99 |
|---|---|---|
| Males | | |
| Professional | 20 | 13 |
| Employers and managers | 29 | 20 |
| Intermediate and junior non-manual | 30 | 23 |
| Skilled manual | 42 | 34 |
| Semi-skilled manual | 47 | 39 |
| Unskilled manual | 49 | 44 |
| Females | | |
| Professional | 21 | 14 |
| Employers and managers | 29 | 24 |
| Intermediate and junior non-manual | 30 | 23 |
| Skilled manual | 39 | 28 |
| Semi-skilled manual | 36 | 34 |
| Unskilled manual | 41 | 33 |

*Source:* The Stationery Office - *Social Trends 31* (Crown copyright)

## Adults Consuming Over Selected Weekly Limits of Alcohol, by Gender and Age

*Percentage*

| | 1998 | 1998-99 |
|---|---|---|
| Men | | |
| 16-24 | 31 | 37 |
| 25-44 | 34 | 28 |
| 45-64 | 24 | 17 |
| 65 and over | 13 | 4 |
| All aged 16 and over | 26 | 21 |
| Women | | |
| 16-24 | 15 | 23 |
| 25-44 | 14 | 11 |
| 45-64 | 9 | 4 |
| 65 and over | 4 | 1 |
| All aged 16 and over | 10 | 8 |

*Source:* The Stationery Office - *Social Trends 31* (Crown copyright)

# Social Welfare

## National Health Service

The National Health Service (NHS) came into being on 5 July 1948 under the National Health Service Act 1946, covering England and Wales, and under separate legislation for Scotland and Northern Ireland. The NHS is now administered by the Secretary of State for Health (in England), the National Assembly for Wales, the Scottish Executive and the Secretary of State for Northern Ireland.

The function of the NHS is to provide a comprehensive health service designed to secure improvement in the physical and mental health of the people and to prevent, diagnose and treat illness. It was founded on the principle that treatment should be provided according to clinical need rather than ability to pay, and should be free at the point of delivery. However, prescription charges were provided for by legislation in 1949 and implemented in 1952, and charges for some dental and ophthalmic treatment have also been introduced.

The NHS covers a comprehensive range of hospital, specialist, family practitioner (medical, dental, ophthalmic and pharmaceutical), artificial limb and appliance, ambulance, and community health services. Everyone normally resident in the UK is entitled to use any of these services.

### STRUCTURE

The structure of the NHS remained relatively stable for the first 30 years of its existence. In 1974, a three-tier management structure comprising Regional Health Authorities, Area Health Authorities and District Management Teams was introduced in England, and the NHS became responsible for community health services. In 1979 Area Health Authorities were abolished and District Management Teams were replaced by District Health Authorities.

The National Health Service and Community Care Act 1990 provided for more streamlined Regional Health Authorities and District Health Authorities, and for the establishment of Family Health Services Authorities (FHSAs) and NHS Trusts. The concept of the 'internal market' was introduced into health care, whereby care was provided through NHS contracts where health authorities or boards and GP fundholders (the purchasers) were responsible for buying health care from hospitals, non-fundholding GPs, community services and ambulance services (the providers).

NHS Trusts operate as self-governing health care providers independent of health authority control and responsible to the Secretary of State. Until 1999 they derived their income principally from contracts to provide services to health authorities and fund-holding GPs. In Northern Ireland, 20 health and social services trusts are responsible for providing health and social services in an organisational model unique to Northern Ireland.

The Act also paved the way for the Community Care reforms, which were introduced in April 1993 and changed the way care is administered for elderly people, the mentally ill, the physically handicapped and people with learning disabilities.

The eight Regional Health Authorities in England were abolished in April 1996 and replaced by eight regional offices which, together with the headquarters in Leeds, form the NHS Executive. The regional offices are part of the Department of Health, and their functions include financial and performance monitoring of local purchasers and providers, public health, regional research and development, and education programmes.

In April 1996 the District Health Authorities and Family Health Service Authorities were merged to form 100 unified Health Authorities (HAs) in England. The HAs are responsible for health and health services in their areas. They are also responsible for assessing the health care needs of the local population and developing integrated strategies for meeting these needs in partnership with GPs and in consultation with the public, hospitals and others. HAs' resources are allocated by the NHS Executive headquarters, to which they are also accountable for their performance. HA chairmen are appointed by the Health Secretary and non-executive members by the regional offices of the NHS Executive.

In Wales the chairman and non-executive members of the five HAs which replaced the former 17 HAs and FHSAs in April 1996 are appointed by the First Secretary. Health Solutions Wales provides a range of specialist services to the NHS in Wales. In Scotland there are 15 Health Boards with similar responsibilities to those of HAs. In Northern Ireland there are four Health and Social Services Boards.

There are also Community Health Councils (called Local Health Councils in Scotland and Health and Social Services Councils in Northern Ireland) throughout the UK; their role is to represent the interests of the public to health authorities and boards. The Government announced in March 1998 that public consultation and patient representation in the NHS would be increased.

Under the Health Act 1999 the NHS internal market in England was replaced by teams of GPs and community nurses working together in primary care groups (*see* pages 481–2) from 1 April 1999. Long-term service agreements are beginning to replace annual contracts between primary care groups, health authorities, and NHS Trusts. A National Institute for Clinical Excellence has been established to produce new national guidelines and National Service Frameworks are being prepared to guarantee consistency in access to services. The first of these, published in late 1999, addressed mental health and coronary heart disease services. A Commission for Health Improvement was established in autumn 1999 to promote best practice. In Scotland, the Act replaced the internal market with Local Health Care Co-operatives (see page 482) from 1 April 1999. The NHS Trusts were reorganised into 13 primary care trusts and 15 acute care trusts, responsible to the Health Boards. In Wales the internal market was replaced by a system of Local Health Groups (see page 482). In Scotland the Scottish Health Technology Assessment Centre provide guidelines to promote best practice.

In March 2000 the government launched The NHS Plan, an extensive programme of reforms intended to modernise the NHS. Under a system of 'earned autonomy' power over spending will be devolved to local health organisations that achieve the government's targets for providing healthcare and they will have access to a £500 million performance fund. Increased overlap between the social services and the NHS will be co-ordinated by the care trusts, with a focus on providing care for the elderly in their own homes. The Plan also outlines a concordat with private healthcare providers whereby the NHS will pay for the use of facilities in private hospitals. In 2000 the NHS spent £1.25 billion on healthcare from the private sector.

The implementation of The Plan is to be overseen by The Modernisation Board which meets on a quarterly basis and is chaired by the Secretary of State.

## FINANCE

### UNITED KINGDOM

The NHS is still funded mainly through general taxation, although in recent years more reliance has been placed on the NHS element of National Insurance contributions, patient charges and other sources of income. In 2000–01 80.4 per cent of NHS expenditure was financed from general taxation and 12.1 per cent from National Insurance Contributions. Forecast UK Gross Expenditure on the NHS in 2000–01 is 6.2 per cent of GDP and is set to rise to 6.3 per cent in 2001–02. The Government announced in July 1998 that an additional £21,000 million would be spent on the NHS between 1999 and 2002. In the March 2000 Budget the Government unveiled its plans to put extra funding into the NHS in order for it to grow by one half in cash terms and by one third in real terms by 2005. Their objectives include 7,000 extra beds in hospitals and intermediate care; over 100 new hospitals by 2010 and 500 new one-stop primary care centres; over 3,000 GP premises modernised and 250 new scanners; cleaner wards and better hospital food; more IT systems in every hospital and GP surgery; 7,500 more consultants and 2,000 more GPs; 20,000 extra nurses and 6,500 extra therapists; 1,000 more medical school places and childcare support for NHS staff with 100 on-site nurseries.

#### National Health Current Expenditure 1999–2000

| | *£ million* |
|---|---|
| National Health Service: | |
| Hospitals, Community Health Services and Family Health Services | 48,279 |
| Departmental administration | 231 |
| Other central services | 1,601 |
| Less payments by patients | –1,089 |
| Total | 49,022 |

#### Personal Social Services Current Expenditure 1999–2000

| | *£ million* |
|---|---|
| Central government | 50 |
| Local authorities running expenses | 11,563 |
| Capital expenditure | 145 |
| Total | 11,758 |

*Source:* The Stationery Office – *Annual Abstract of Statistics 2001* (Crown copyright)

#### Total NHS Expenditure Per Head Of Population 2000–1

| | Net £ | Gross £ |
|---|---|---|
| UK | 967 | 906 |
| England | 949 | 885 |
| Scotland | 1,094 | 1,026 |
| Wales | 976 | 958 |
| Northern Ireland | 912 | 898 |

*Source:* Department of Health

## ORGANISATIONS

### HEALTH AUTHORITIES (ENGLAND)

There are 100 health authorities in England. For details, contact the relevant NHS Executive regional office (*see* below).

#### NHS Executive Regional Offices

Eastern, Capital Park, Fulbourn, Cambridge CB1 5XB. Tel: 01223 597500. *Regional Director*, P. Houghton

London, 40 Eastbourne Terrace, London W2 3QR. Tel: 020-7725 5300. *Regional Director*, J. Bacon

Northern and Yorkshire, John Snow House, Durham University Science Park, Durham DH1 3YG. Tel: 0191-301 1325. *Regional Director*, P. Garland

North West, 930–932 Birchwood Boulevard, Millennium Park, Birchwood, Warrington WA3 7QN. Tel: 01925-704000. *Regional Director*, Prof. R. Tinston

South East, 40 Eastbourne Terrace, London W2 3QR. Tel: 020-7725 2500. *Regional Director*, R. Cavnall

South West, Westward House, Lime Kiln Close, Stoke Gifford, Bristol BS34 8SR. Tel: 0117-984 1750. *Regional Director*, T. Laurance

Trent, Fulwood House, Old Fulwood Road, Sheffield S10 3TH. Tel: 0114-263 0300. *Regional Director*, D. Nicholson

West Midlands, Bartholomew House, 142 Hagley Road, Birmingham B16 9PA. Tel: 0121-224 4600. *Regional Director*, S. Day

### HEALTH BOARDS (SCOTLAND)

Argyll and Clyde, Ross House, Hawkhead Road, Paisley PA2 7BN. Tel: 0141-842 7200. *Chairman*, J. Mullin; *Chief Executive*, N. McConachie

Ayrshire and Arran, Boswell House, 10 Arthur Street, Ayr KA7 1QJ. Tel: 01292-611040. *Chairman*, Dr J. Morrow; *Chief Executive*, Mrs W. Hatton

Borders, Newstead, Melrose, Roxburghshire TD6 9TD. Tel: 01896-825500. *Chairman*, T. Keeler, OBE; *Chief Executive*, Dr L. Burley

Dumfries and Galloway, Grierson House, The Crichton Royal, Bankend Road, Dumfries DG1 4ZG. Tel: 01387-272700. *Chairman*, J. Ross, CBE; *Chief Executive*, M. Wright

Fife, Springfield House, Cupar KY15 5UP. Tel: 01334-656200. *Chairman*, Ms E. Roberton; *Chief Executive*, T. Ranzetta

Forth Valley, 33 Spittal Street, Stirling FK8 1DX. Tel: 01786-463031. *Chairman*, F. Clark; *General Manager*, D. Hird

Grampian, Summerfield House, 2 Eday Road, Aberdeen AB15 6RE. Tel: 01224-663456. *Chairman*, Dr C. E. MacLeod, CBE; *General Manager*, F. E. L. Hartnett, OBE

Greater Glasgow, Dalian House, 350 St Vincent Street, Glasgow G3 8YZ. Tel: 0141-201 4444. *Chairman*, Prof. D. Hamblen; *Chief Executive*, C. J. Spry

Highland, Assynt House, Beechwood Park, Inverness IV2 3HG. Tel: 01463-717123. *Chairman*, Mrs C. Thomson; *General Manager*, R. Gibbins

Lanarkshire, 14 Beckford Street, Hamilton, Lanarkshire ML3 0TA. Tel: 01698-281313. *Chairman*, I. Livingstone, CBE; *General Manager*, Prof. T. A. Divers

Lothian, Deaconess House, 148 Pleasance, Edinburgh EH8 9RS. Tel: 0131-536 9000. *Chairman*, R. Findlay; *Chief Executive*, J. Barbour

Orkney, Garden House, New Scapa Road, Kirkwall, Orkney KW15 1BQ. Tel: 01856-885400. *Chairman*, I. Leslie; *General Manager*, J. Wellden

SHETLAND, Brevik House, South Road, Lerwick ZE1 0TG. Tel: 01595-696767. *Chairman*, J. Telford; *Chief Executive*, Miss S. Laurenson

TAYSIDE, Gateway House, Luna Place, Dundee Technology Park, Dundee DD2 1TP. Tel: 01382-561818. *Chairman*, P. Bates; *General Manager*, T. Brett

WESTERN ISLES, 37 South Beach Street, Stornoway, Isle of Lewis HS1 2BN. Tel: 01851-702997. *Chairman*, A. Matheson; *General Manager*, M. Maclennan

## HEALTH AUTHORITIES (WALES)

BRO TAF, 17 Churchill House, Churchill Way, Cardiff CF10 2TW. Tel: 029-2040 2402. *Chairman*, S. Jones; *Chief Executive*, Mrs J. Williams

DYFED POWYS, PO Box 13, St David's Hospital, Carmarthen SA31 3YH. Tel: 01267-225225. *Chairman*, Ms M. Price; *Chief Executive*, S. Gray

GWENT, Mamhilad House, Mamhilad Park Estate, Pontypool NP4 0YP. Tel: 01495-765065. *Chairman*, Mrs F. Peel; *Chief Executive*, B. Hudson

IECHYD MORGANNWG, 41 High Street, Swansea SA1 1LT. Tel: 01792-458066. *Chairman*, D. H. Thomas; *Chief Executive*, Ms J. Perrin

NORTH WALES, Preswylfa, Hendy Road, Mold CH7 1PZ. Tel: 01352-700227. *Chairman*, Mrs P. Wood; *Chief Executive*, D. Hands

HEALTH SOLUTIONS WALES, Brunnell House, 2 Fitzellen Road, Cardiff CF24 0HA. Tel: 029-2050 0500.

## NORTHERN IRELAND HEALTH AND SOCIAL SERVICES BOARDS

EASTERN, Champion House, 12–22 Linenhall Street, Belfast BT2 8BS. Tel: 028-9032 1313. *Chairman*, D. Russell; *Chief Executive*, Dr M. P. J. Kilbane, FRCP

NORTHERN, County Hall, 182 Galgorm Road, Ballymena BT42 1QB. Tel: 028-2565 3333. *Chairman*, M. A. Wood; *Chief Executive*, J. S. MacDonell

SOUTHERN, Tower Hill, Armagh BT61 7DR. Tel: 028-3741 0041. *Chairman*, W. Gillespie; *Chief Executive*, B. P. Cunningham

WESTERN, 15 Gransha Park, Clooney Road, Londonderry BT47 6FN. Tel: 028-7186 0086. *Chairman*, J. Bradley; *Chief Executive*, S. Lindsay

## HEALTH PROMOTION AUTHORITIES

HEALTH PROMOTION ENGLAND, 40 Eastbourne Terrace, London W2 3QR. Tel: 020-7725 9030. *General Manager*, Mrs D. Ashdon

HEALTH EDUCATION BOARD FOR SCOTLAND, Woodburn House, Canaan Lane, Edinburgh EH10 4SG. Tel: 0131-536 5500. *Chairman*, D. R. Campbell; *Chief Executive*, Prof. A. Tannahill

HEALTH PROMOTION AGENCY FOR NORTHERN IRELAND, 18 Ormeau Avenue, Belfast BT2 8HS. Tel: 028-9031 1611; *Chief Executive*, Dr B. Gaffney

# EMPLOYEES AND SALARIES

## EMPLOYEES

NHS HOSPITAL AND COMMUNITY HEALTH SERVICES – ALL NON-MEDICAL STAFF (*England*) *as at September 1999**

| | |
|---|---|
| Ambulance service | 15,910 |
| Administration and estates | 204,617 |
| Healthcare assistants and other support staff | 115,024 |
| Nursing, midwifery and health visiting | 431,103 |
| Nursing, midwifery and health visiting learners | 1,945 |
| Scientific, therapeutic and technical | 128,293 |
| Other non-medical staff | 675 |
| All non-medical staff | 897,567 |

* Figures exclude agency staff
*Source:* The Department of Health – *1999 Non-medical Workforce Census*

### SALARIES *as at 1 April 2001*

General Practitioners (GPs), dentists, optometrists and pharmacists are self-employed, and are employed by the NHS under contract. GPs are paid for their NHS work in accordance with a scheme of remuneration which includes a basic practice allowance, capitation fees, reimbursement of certain practice expenses and payments for out-of-hours work. Dentists receive payment for items of treatment for individual adult patients and, in addition, a continuing care payment for those registered with them. Optometrists receive approved fees for each sight test they carry out. Pharmacists receive professional fees from the NHS and are refunded the cost of prescriptions supplied.

| | |
|---|---|
| Consultant | £50,810–£66,120 |
| Specialist Registrar | £25,015–£36,460 |
| Registrar | £25,015–£30,340 |
| Senior House Officer | £22,380–£29,880 |
| House Officer | £17,935–£20,245 |
| GP | *£54,220 |
| Nursing Grades G–I (Senior Ward Sister) | £21,605–£30,720 |
| Nursing Grade F (Ward Sister) | £18,310–£22,865 |
| Nursing Grade E (Senior Staff Nurse) | £16,510–£19,935 |
| Nursing Grade D (Staff Nurse) | £15,445–£17,055 |
| Nursing Grade C (Enrolled Nurse) | £12,585–£15,445 |
| Nursing Grades A–B (Nursing Auxiliary) | £9,335–£12,585 |

*average intended net remuneration

# HEALTH SERVICES

## PRIMARY AND COMMUNITY HEALTH CARE

Primary and community health care services comprise the family health services (i.e. the general medical, personal medical, pharmaceutical, dental, and ophthalmic services) and community services (including preventive activities such as vaccination, immunisation and fluoridation) commissioned by HAs and provided by NHS Trusts, health centres and clinics. Nursing services including practice nurses, district nurses and health visitors, community psychiatric nurses, school nurse and ante- and post-natal care are also an integral part of primary and community health care.

### FAMILY DOCTOR SERVICE

In England and Wales the Family Doctor Service (or General Medical Service) is now the responsibility of the HAs. In late 1999 a pilot scheme of 19 walk-in centres, where people may consult a doctor without an appointment between the hours of 7 a.m. and 10 p.m., was introduced. The scheme has since been expanded to cover 43 walk-in centres around the country. They are responsible to HAs and work closely with primary care groups.

Any doctor may take part in the Family Doctor Service (provided the area in which he/she wishes to practise has not already an adequate number of doctors) and 27,700 GPs in England do so. The distribution of GPs is controlled by the Medical Practices Committee, a statutory body. The average number of patients on a doctor's list in the UK as at August 2001 was 1,853.GPs may also have private fee-paying patients.

The Government has replaced the fundholding system by allowing the new primary care groups and trusts to assume one of four levels of responsibility. In April 1999 481 primary care groups became operational in England, covering populations of between 46,000 and 257,000. They operate as a committee of a Health Authority and are responsible for health improvement, primary and community health service development and commissioning secondary care services where appropriate. Primary care groups operate at one of two levels of responsibility. At level one, the group advises the Health Authority and is responsible for less than 40 per cent of the group's unified budget. Level two primary care groups are responsible for 40 per cent of the group's unified budget, rising to 60 per cent in their second year of operation. A board consisting of GPs, nurses, a social services officer, a health authority representative and a local member of the public administers each group.

From 1 April 2000, Primary Care Trusts became operational in England. They are free-standing statutory bodies undertaking many of the functions previously exercised by Health Authorities. They operate at one of two levels. Level three Trusts are able to commission services with greater scope than a level two primary care group, but not directly provide them. Those at level four are able to commission and directly provide services and run community hospitals and health services.

In Scotland, fundholding was replaced by over 70 Local Health Care Co-operatives on 1 April 1999. These, consisting of GPs and others involved in primary care, are responsible for developing health care in their area.

In Wales 22 Local Health Groups were set up by the Health Authorities and began work in April 1999. They are coterminous with local authority areas. At present, they advise Health Authorities but in the future they will assume responsibility for commissioning services and devising strategies for improved health. They will also integrate the delivery of primary and community care. A governing body including GPs and other health professionals, social services and community representatives administers each group.

Everyone aged 16 or over can choose their doctor (parents or guardians choose for children under 16); the doctor is free to accept or refuse an individual. Should a patient have difficulty in registering with a doctor, HAs have powers to assign the patient to a GP. A person may change their doctor if they wish, by going to the surgery of a GP of their choice who is willing to accept them, and either handing in their medical card to register or filling in a form. When people are away from home they can still use the Family Doctor Service if they ask to be treated as temporary residents, and in an emergency, any doctor in the service will give treatment and advice. A number of drop-in medical centres are being set up where anyone can consult a doctor.

### Pharmaceutical Service

Patients may obtain medicines, appliances and oral contraceptives prescribed under the NHS from any pharmacy whose owner has entered into arrangements with the HA to provide this service; the number of these pharmacies in England and Wales in December 2000 was 12,257. There are also some appliance suppliers who only provide special appliances. In rural areas, where access to a pharmacy may be difficult, patients may be able to obtain medicines, etc., from their doctor.

Except for contraceptives (for which there is no charge), a charge of £6.10 is payable for each item supplied unless the patient is exempt and the declaration on the back of the prescription form is completed. Prepayment certificates (£31.90 valid for four months, £87.60 valid for a year) may be purchased by those patients not entitled to exemption who require frequent prescriptions.

The following people are exempt from prescription charges:

- children under 16
- full-time students under 19
- men and women aged 60 and over
- pregnant women who hold an exemption certificate
- women who have had a baby in the last 12 months and who hold an exemption certificate
- people suffering from certain medical conditions who hold an exemption certificate
- people who receive income support, full working families' tax credit or credit reduced by up to £70, full disabled person's tax credit or credit reduced by up to £70 or income-based jobseeker's allowance, and their partners
- people who are named on an HC2 certificate issued by the Health Benefits Division
- war pensioners (for their accepted disablements)

Booklet HC11, available from main post offices and local social security offices, gives further details.

The number of prescriptions dispensed in the community in 2000 was:

| | |
|---|---|
| England and Wales | 551,800,000 |
| Scotland | 60,900,000 |
| Northern Ireland | 22,171,000* |

*1998 figure

### Dental Service

Dentists, like doctors, may take part in the NHS and also have private patients. About 17,000 dentists in England provide NHS general dental services. They are responsible to the HAs in whose areas they provide services.

Patients may go to any dentist who is taking part in the NHS and is willing to accept them. Patients are required to pay 80 per cent of the cost of NHS dental treatment. Since 1 April 1999 the maximum charge for a course of treatment has been £348. There is no charge for arrest of bleeding or repairs to dentures; home visits by the dentist or re-opening a surgery in an emergency are charged for as treatment given in the normal way. The following people are exempt from dental charges or have charges remitted:

- people under 18
- full-time students under 19
- women who were pregnant when accepted for treatment
- women who have had a child in the previous 12 months
- people who receive income support, full working families' tax credit or credit reduced by up to £70, full disabled person's tax credit or credit reduced by up to £70, or income-based jobseeker's allowance, and their partners
- people who are named on an HC2 certificate issued by the Health Benefits Division

Booklet HC11, available from main post offices and local social security offices, gives further details.

### General Dental Service 2000–1 (England)

| | |
|---|---|
| Number of dentists | 18,107 |
| Number of patients registered | |
| Adults | 16,900,000 |
| Children | 6,800,000 |

| | |
|---|---|
| Number of courses of treatment | |
| Adults | 26,400,000 |
| Expenditure (£ million) | |
| Gross expenditure | 1,550 |
| Paid by patients | 450 |
| Paid out of public funds | 1,100 |

*Source:* Department of Health

### General Ophthalmic Services

General Ophthalmic Services are administered by HAs. Testing of sight may be carried out by any ophthalmic medical practitioner or ophthalmic optician (optometrist). The optician must give the prescription to the patient, who can take this to any supplier of glasses to have them dispensed. Only registered opticians can supply glasses to children and to people registered as blind or partially sighted. At the end of March 2001 there were 7,548 practising Optometrists in Great Britain. 16.5 million sight tests were carried out in 2000–1.

The NHS sight test costs £15.01. Those on a low income may qualify for help with the cost. The test is available free to:

- people aged 60 or over
- children under 16*
- full-time students under 19*
- people who receive income support, income-based jobseeker's allowance, full working families' tax credit or credit reduced by up to £70, full disabled person's tax credit or credit reduced by up to £70, and their partners*
- people who are named on an HC2 certificate issued by the Health Benefits Division*
- people prescribed complex lenses*
- people registered as blind or partially sighted
- diagnosed diabetic and glaucoma patients
- people advised by an ophthalmologist that they are at risk of glaucoma

The categories indicated by * above are automatically entitled to help with the purchase of glasses under an NHS voucher scheme, as are people whose spectacles are lost or damaged as a result of illness. Booklet HC11, available from main post offices and local social security offices, gives further details.

### Community Child Health Services

Pre-school services at GP surgeries or child health clinics provide regular monitoring of children's physical, mental and emotional health and development, and advice to parents on their children's health and welfare.

The School Health Service provides for the medical and dental examination of schoolchildren, and advises the local education authority, the school, the parents and the pupil of any health factors which may require special consideration during the pupil's school life. GPs are increasingly undertaking child health monitoring in order to improve the preventive health care of children.

### Health Action Zones

Health Action Zones aim to improve health services and tackle health inequalities in certain areas, working with the primary care groups in their area. The first 11 zones were set up in April 1998 and there are currently a total of 26 in existence. Each zone receives funding for seven years.

## HOSPITALS AND OTHER SERVICES

Hospital, medical, dental, nursing, ophthalmic and ambulance services are provided by the NHS to meet all reasonable requirements. Facilities for the care of expectant and nursing mothers and young children, and other services required for the diagnosis and treatment of illness, are also provided. Rehabilitation services (occupational therapy, physiotherapy and speech therapy) may also be provided, and surgical and medical appliances are supplied where appropriate. Specialists and consultants who work in NHS hospitals can also engage in private practice, including the treatment of their private patients in NHS hospitals although, under the terms of the NHS plan, newly qualified consultants are unable to do private work for up to seven years.

### Private Finance Initiative

The Private Finance Initiative (PFI) was launched in 1992, and involves the private sector in designing, building, financing and operating new hospitals, which are then leased to the NHS. In July 1997 a new programme of hospital building under the PFI was announced by the Government.

### Charges

Certain hospitals have accommodation in single rooms or small wards which, if not required for patients who need privacy for medical reasons, may be made available to patients who desire it as an amenity for a small charge. These patients are still NHS patients and are treated as such.

In a number of hospitals, accommodation is available for the treatment of private in-patients who undertake to pay the full costs of hospital accommodation and services and (usually) separate medical fees to a specialist as well. The amount of the medical fees is a matter for agreement between doctor and patient. Hospital charges for private in-patients are set locally at a commercial rate.

There is no charge for drugs supplied to NHS hospital in-patients, but out-patients pay £6.10 an item unless they are exempt. With certain exceptions, hospital out-patients have to pay fixed charges for dentures, contact lenses and certain appliances. Glasses may be obtained either from the hospital or an optician, and the charge will be related to the type of lens prescribed and the choice of frame.

### Ambulance Service

The NHS provides emergency ambulance services free of charge via the 999 emergency telephone service. There are 35 ambulance services in the UK. Helicopter ambulances are used in some areas where access may be difficult or heavy traffic could hinder road progress, and an air ambulance service is available throughout Scotland. Non-emergency ambulance services are provided free of charge to patients who are deemed to require them on medical grounds.

In 2000–01 in England approximately 4,140,000 emergency calls were made to the ambulance service, an increase of 6 per cent on the previous year. There were about 2,900,000 emergency patient journeys. The Patients' Charter requires emergency ambulances to respond to 95 per cent of calls within 14 minutes in urban areas and 19 minutes in rural areas, and to reach 50 per cent of cases within eight minutes. In 2000–01, of the 31 ambulance services that had introduced call prioritisation by 1 January 2001, 26 ambulance services met the Charter standard for responding to life-threatening emergencies and 13 met the standard for non-life threatening emergencies.

### NHS Direct

NHS Direct is a telephone service staffed by nurses which gives patients advice on how to look after themselves as well as directing them to the appropriate part of the NHS for treatment if necessary. Tel: 0845-4647.

### Blood Services

There are four national bodies which co-ordinate the blood donor programme in each constituent country of the UK. About two million donations of blood are given each year; donors give blood at local centres on a voluntary basis.

National Blood Authority, Oak House, Reeds Crescent, Watford, Herts WD24 4GN. Tel: 01923-486800. *Chairman*, M. Fogden, CB; *Chief Executive*, M. Gorham

Scottish National Blood Transfusion Service, 21 Ellens Glen Road, Edinburgh EH17 7QT. Tel: 0131-536 5700. *National Director*, Dr D. Perry

Welsh Blood Service, Ely Valley Road, Talbot Green, Pontyclun CF72 9WB. Tel: 01443-622000. *Director*, Dr F. G. Williams

Northern Ireland Blood Transfusion Service, Belfast City Hospital Complex, Lisburn Road, Belfast BT9 7TS. Tel: 028-9032 1414

### Hospices

Hospice or palliative care may be available for patients with life-threatening illnesses. It may be provided at the patient's home or in a voluntary or NHS hospice or in hospital, and is intended to ensure the best possible quality of life for the patient during their illness, and to provide help and support to both the patient and the patient's family. The National Council for Hospices and Specialist Palliative Care Services co-ordinates NHS and voluntary services in England, Wales and Northern Ireland; the Scottish Partnership Agency for Palliative and Cancer Care performs the same function in Scotland.

National Council for Hospice and Specialist Palliative Care Services, 1st Floor, 34–44 Britannia Street, London WC1X 9JG. Tel: 020-7520 8299. *Executive Director*, Ms E. S. Richardson

Scottish Partnership Agency for Palliative and Cancer Care, 1A Cambridge Street, Edinburgh EH1 2DY. Tel: 0131-229 0538. *Director*, Mrs M. Stevenson

### Number Of Beds And Patient Activity 1999

| | *England** | *Wales* |
|---|---|---|
| In-patients: | | |
| Average daily available beds | 190,000 | 14,700 |
| Average daily occupation of beds | 157,000 | 11,800 |
| Persons waiting for admission at 31 March | 1,298,000 | 75,400 |
| Day-case admissions | 3,421,000 | 342,200 |
| Ordinary admissions | 8,563,000 | 516,300 |
| Out-patient attendances: | | |
| New patients | 11,778,000 | 694,100 |
| Total attendances | 42,154,000 | 2,706,200 |
| Accident and emergency: | | |
| New patients | 12,811,000 | 868,000 |
| Total attendances | 14,280,000 | 026,400 |
| Ward attendances | 1,068,000 | n/a |

* 1998 figures
n/a not available

### Scotland

| | |
|---|---|
| In-patients: | |
| Average available staffed beds | 35,200 |
| Average occupied beds | 28,200 |
| Out-patient attendances: | |
| New patients | 2,734,000 |
| Total attendances | 6,424,000 |

*Source:* The Stationery Office – *Annual Abstract of Statistics 2001* (Crown copyright)

### Waiting Lists

At the end of June 2001 the total number of patients waiting to be admitted to NHS hospitals in England was 1,037,900, a decrease of 1.0 per cent on the previous year. The number of patients who had been waiting more than one year was 46,000, an increase of 9.2 per cent on the previous year. Under the Patient's Charter, patients are guaranteed admission within 18 months of being placed on a waiting list however, 356 patients had been waiting longer than 18 months at the end of June 2001.

### COMPLAINTS

The Patient's Charter includes the right to have any complaint about the service provided by the NHS dealt with quickly, with a full written reply being provided by a relevant chief executive. There are two levels to the NHS complaints procedure: the first level involves resolution of a complaint locally, following a direct approach to the relevant service provider; the second level involves an independent review procedure if the complaint is not resolved locally. As a final resort, patients may approach the Health Service Commissioner or Ombudsman (*see* page 350) (in Northern Ireland, the Commissioner for Complaints if they are dissatisfied with the response of the NHS to a complaint.

In 1999–2000 there were 86,536 written complaints about hospital and community health services, of which 60 per cent were resolved locally within the target period of four weeks; just over two per cent of complainants requested an independent review. Hospital and Community Trusts received 93 per cent of the total number of complaints with Ambulance Trusts receiving four per cent and Health Authorities three per cent.

### RECIPROCAL ARRANGEMENTS

Citizens of countries in the European Economic Area (EEA *see* European Union) are entitled to receive emergency health care either free of charge or for a reduced charge when they are temporarily visiting other member states of the EEA. Form E111, available at post offices, should be obtained before travelling. Non-EEA nationals, or visitors receiving routine, non-emergency care, are normally required to pay for treatment in Britain. There are bilateral agreements with several other countries, including Australia and New Zealand, for the provision of urgent medical treatment either free of charge or for a reduced charge.

## Personal Social Services

The Secretary of State for Health is responsible, under the Local Authority Social Services Act 1970, for the provision of social services for elderly people, disabled people, families and children, and those with mental disorders. Personal Social Services are administered by local authorities according to policies and standards set by central government. Each authority has a Director of Social Services and a Social Services Committee responsible for the social services functions placed upon them. Local authorities provide, enable and commission care after assessing the needs of their population.

The Community Care reforms introduced in 1993 were intended to enable vulnerable groups to live in the community rather than in residential homes wherever possible, and to offer them as independent a lifestyle as possible.

At 31 March 2000, there were 345,600 residential places in 24,800 residential and nursing care homes in England. About 267,500 residents were supported by local authorities (compared to 216,000 in 1996).

## FINANCE

The Personal Social Services programme is financed partly by central government, with decisions on expenditure allocations being made at local authority level.

## STAFF

STAFF OF LOCAL AUTHORITY SOCIAL SERVICES DEPARTMENTS 2000 (ENGLAND)

*Full-time equivalents*

| | |
|---|---|
| Area office/field work staff | 108,800 |
| Residential care staff | 56,600 |
| Day care staff | 30,800 |
| Central/strategic HQ staff | 19,400 |
| Other staff | 1,500 |
| Total staff | 217,200 |

*Source:* Department of Health

## ELDERLY PEOPLE

Services for elderly people are designed to enable them to remain living in their own homes for as long as possible. Local authority services include advice, domestic help, meals in the home, alterations to the home to aid mobility, emergency alarm systems, day and/or night attendants, laundry services and the provision of day centres and recreational facilities. Charges may be made for these services. Respite care may also be provided in order to allow carers temporary relief from their responsibilities.

Local authorities and the private sector also provide 'sheltered housing' for elderly people, sometimes with resident wardens.

If an elderly person is admitted to a residential home, charges are made according to a means test; if the person cannot afford to pay, the costs are met by the local authority.

In line with the recommendations made by The Royal Commission on Long-Term Care the government has created a National Care Standards Commission to oversee the registration, regulation and enforcement of care standards. It is due to assume its powers in April 2002.

## DISABLED PEOPLE

Services for disabled people are designed to enable them to remain living in their own homes wherever possible. Local authority services include advice, adaptations to the home, meals in the home, help with personal care, occupational therapy, educational facilities and recreational facilities. Respite care may also be provided in order to allow carers temporary relief from their responsibilities.

Special housing may be available for disabled people who can live independently, and residential accommodation for those who cannot.

## FAMILIES AND CHILDREN

Local authorities are required to provide services aimed at safeguarding the welfare of children in need and, wherever possible, allowing them to be brought up by their families. Services include advice, counselling, help in the home and the provision of family centres. Many authorities also provide short-term refuge accommodation for women and children.

### DAY CARE

In allocating day-care places to children, local authorities give priority to children with special needs, whether in terms of their health, learning abilities or social needs. They also provide a registration and inspection service in relation to childminders, play groups and private day nurseries in the local authority area. In England in August 2000 there were approximately 7,000 day nurseries providing 170,000 places, 98,500 registered child-minders providing 365,000 places, and 14,500 play groups providing 362,000 places.

A national child care strategy is being developed by the Government, under which day care and out-of-school child care facilities will be extended to match more closely the needs of working parents.

### CHILD PROTECTION

Children considered to be at risk of physical injury, neglect or sexual abuse are placed on the local authority's child protection register. Local authority social services staff, school nurses, health visitors and other agencies work together to prevent and detect cases of abuse. In England at 31 March 2000 there were 30,300 children on child protection registers, a five per cent decrease from March 1999. This figure represents 28 children per 10,000 of population aged under 18. Of these, 46 per cent were at risk of neglect, 29 per cent of physical injury, 18 per cent of sexual abuse and 18 per cent of emotional abuse.

### LOCAL AUTHORITY CARE

Local authorities are required to provide accommodation for children who have no parent or guardian or whose parents or guardians are unable or unwilling to care for them. A family proceedings court may also issue a care order in cases where a child is being neglected or abused, or is not attending school; the court must be satisfied that this would positively contribute to the well-being of the child.

The welfare of children in local authority care must be properly safeguarded. Children may be placed with foster families, who receive payments to cover the expenses of caring for the child or children, or in residential care. Children's homes may be run by the local authority or by the private or voluntary sectors; all homes are subject to inspection procedures. In England at 31 June 2000, 58,100 children were in the care of local authorities. Of these, 65 per cent were placed with foster parents and four per cent were placed for adoption.

### ADOPTION

Local authorities are required to provide an adoption service, either directly or via approved voluntary societies. In England and Wales in 1998, 4,387 children (2,214 boys and 2,173 girls) were adopted.

## PEOPLE WITH LEARNING DISABILITIES

Services for people with learning disabilities (i.e. mental handicap) are designed to enable them to remain living in the community wherever possible. Local authority services include short-term care, support in the home, the provision of day care centres, and help with other activities outside the home. Residential care is provided for the severely or profoundly disabled.

## MENTALLY ILL PEOPLE

Under the Care Programme Approach, mentally ill people should be assessed by specialist services and receive a care plan, and a key worker should be appointed for each patient. Regular reviews of the patient's progress should be conducted. Local authorities provide help and advice to mentally ill people and their families, and places in day centres and social centres. Social workers can apply for a mentally disturbed person to be compulsorily detained in hospital. Where appropriate, mentally ill people are

LOCAL AUTHORITY PERSONAL SOCIAL SERVICES GROSS EXPENDITURE BY CLIENT GROUP 1998–9 (ENGLAND)

*£ million*

| | Elderly | Children | Learningdisability | Adults | Mental health | Other | Total |
|---|---|---|---|---|---|---|---|
| HQ costs | — | — | — | — | — | 149 | 149 |
| Area officers/senior managers | 103 | 161 | 26 | 29 | 28 | — | 348 |
| Care management/care assessment | 329 | 505 | 76 | 101 | 126 | — | 1,136 |
| Residential care | 3,180 | 724 | 838 | 218 | 224 | — | 5184 |
| Non-residential care | 1,605 | 1,074 | 555 | 402 | 186 | — | 3,822 |
| Other | — | — | — | — | — | 208 | 208 |
| TOTAL | 5,216 | 2,465 | 1,495 | 750 | 564 | 357 | 10,847 |

Source: *The Department of Health* – Health and Personal Social Services Statistics for England 2000 *(Crown copyright)*

provided with accommodation in special hospitals, local authority accommodation, or homes run by private or voluntary organisations. Patients who have been discharged from hospitals may be placed on a supervision register. In July 1998 the Government announced that the system of care for mentally ill people would be replaced. A Mental Health National Service Framework was published in September 1999 setting the first ever national standards on how to prevent and treat mental illness. The government has pledged £700 million in the next two years in a drive to build modern and dependable mental health services.

LOCAL AUTHORITY-SUPPORTED RESIDENTS IN STAFFED RESIDENTIAL AND NURSING CARE (ENGLAND)
*as at 31 March 2000*

| | |
|---|---|
| All staffed homes | 261,139 |
| Local authority staffed | 47,611 |
| Independent residential care | 139,150 |
| Independent nursing care | 74,378 |
| People aged 65 and over | 210,638 |
| People aged under 65 | |
| Physically/sensorily disabled adults | 9,876 |
| People with mental health problems | 10,969 |
| People with learning disabilities | 30,931 |
| Other people | 2,111 |

*Source:* Department of Health

# National Insurance and Related Cash Benefits

The state insurance and assistance schemes, comprising schemes of national insurance and industrial injuries insurance, national assistance, and non-contributory old age pensions, came into force from 5 July 1948. The Ministry of Social Security Act 1966 replaced national assistance and non-contributory old age pensions with a scheme of non-contributory benefits. These and subsequent measures relating to social security provision in Great Britain were consolidated by the Social Security Act 1975, the Social Security (Consequential Provisions) Act 1975, and the Industrial Injuries and Diseases (Old Cases) Act 1975. Corresponding measures were passed for Northern Ireland. The Social Security Pensions Act 1975 introduced a new state pensions scheme in 1978, and the graduated pension scheme 1961 to 1975 has been wound up, existing rights being preserved. Under the Pensions Act 1995 the age of retirement is to be 65 for both men and women, this being phased in between 2010 and 6 April 2020. The Pensioners' Payments and Social Security Act 1979 provided for a Christmas bonus for pensioners in 1979 and in succeeding years. The Child Benefit Act 1975 replaced family allowances (introduced 1946) with child benefit and one-parent benefit. Some of this legislation has been superseded by the provisions of the Social Security Acts 1969 to 1992. The Government is reforming the social security system. The Welfare Reform and Pensions Act became law on 11 November 1999. Changes in benefits came into effect from April 2001.

## NATIONAL INSURANCE SCHEME

The National Insurance (NI) scheme operates under the Social Security Contributions and Benefits Act 1992 and the Social Security Administration Act 1992, and orders and regulations made thereunder. The scheme is financed by contributions payable by earners, employers and others (*see* below) and by a Treasury grant. Money collected under the scheme is used to finance the National Insurance Fund (from which contributory benefits are paid) and to contribute to the cost of the National Health Service.

National Insurance Fund
Receipts and payments of the National Insurance Fund for the year ended 31 March 2000 were:

| *Receipts* | £'000 |
|---|---|
| National Insurance contributions | 50,592,578 |
| Grant from Inland Revenue | 2,200 |
| Compensation from Consolidated Fund for Statutory Sick Pay and Statutory Maternity Pay recoveries | 607,000 |
| Income from investments | 714,737 |
| State scheme premiums | 126,294 |
| Other receipts | 123,211 |
| Redundancy receipts | 20,685 |
| | 52,186,705 |

| *Payments* | £'000 |
|---|---|
| Benefits | 46,215,093 |
| Personal pensions | 2,573,715 |
| Transfers to Northern Ireland | 230,000 |
| Administration | 816,694 |
| Redundancy payments (net) | 170,895 |
| Other payments | 19,159 |
| | 50,025,556 |

| *Balances* | £'000 |
|---|---|
| Opening balance | 12,277,381 |
| Excess of receipts over payments | 2,161,149 |
| Closing balance, 31 March 2000 | 14,438,530 |

## CONTRIBUTIONS

There are six classes of NI contributions:

| | |
|---|---|
| Class 1 | paid by employees and their employers |
| Class 1A | paid by employers who provide employees with cars/fuel for private use |
| Class 1B | paid by employers in value of any items included on a PAYE settlement with the Inland Revenue |
| Class 2 | paid by self-employed people |
| Class 3 | voluntary contributions paid to protect entitlement to certain benefits |
| Class 4 | paid by the self-employed on their taxable profits over a set limit |

The lower and upper earnings limits and the percentage rates referred to below apply from 3 April 2001 to 2 April 2002 unless otherwise stated.

### CLASS 1

Class 1 contributions are paid where a person:

- is an employed earner (employee) or office holder (e.g. company director)
- is 16 or over and under state pension age
- earns at or above £76.00 per week (including overtime pay, bonus, commission, etc., without deduction of superannuation contributions)

Class 1 contributions are made up of primary and secondary contributions. Primary contributions are those paid by the employee and these are deducted from earnings by the employer. From 6 April 2001 the employee's earnings threshold has been raised to the same level as the employer's earnings threshold, they will now be referred to as the earnings threshold. Primary contributions are not paid on earnings below the earnings threshold of £87.00. Contributions are payable at the rate of ten per cent on earnings between the earnings threshold and the upper earnings limit of £575.00 per week (8.4 per cent for contracted-out employment, *see* page 496).

Some married women or widows pay a reduced rate of 3.85 per cent on earnings between the lower and upper earnings limits. It is no longer possible to elect to pay the reduced rate but those who had reduced liability before 12 May 1977 may retain it so long as certain conditions are met. *See* leaflet CA09 (widows) or leaflet CA13 (married women).

Secondary contributions are paid by employers of employed earners at the rate of 11.9 per cent on all earnings at or above the earnings threshold of £87.00 per week. Employers operating contracted-out salary related schemes (*see* page 489) pay reduced contributions of 8.9 per cent; those with contracted-out money-purchase schemes (*see* page 489) pay 11.3 per cent. There is no upper earnings limit for employers' contributions. The contracted-out rate applies only to that portion of earnings between the earnings threshold and the upper earnings limits. Employers' contributions below and above those respective limits are assessed at the appropriate not contracted-out rate.

### CLASS 2

Class 2 contributions are paid where a person is self-employed and is 16 or over and under state pension age. Contributions are paid at a flat rate of £2.00 per week regardless of the amount earned. However, those with earnings of less than £3,955 a year can apply for Small Earnings Exception, e.g. exemption from liability to pay Class 2 contributions. Those granted exemption from Class 2 contributions may pay Class 2 or Class 3 contributions voluntarily. Self-employed earners (whether or not they pay Class 2 contributions) may also be liable to pay Class 4 contributions based on profits. There are special rules for those who are concurrently employed and self-employed.

Married women and widows can no longer choose not to pay Class 2 contributions but those who elected not to pay Class 2 contributions before 12 May 1977 may retain the right so long as certain conditions are met.

Class 2 contributions are collected by the National Insurance Contributions Office (NICO), an executive agency of the Inland Revenue, by direct debit or quarterly bills. *See* leaflets CA03 and CA02.

### CLASS 3

Class 3 contributions are voluntary flat-rate contributions of £6.75 per week payable by persons over the age of 16 who would otherwise be unable to qualify for retirement pension and certain other benefits because they have an insufficient record of Class 1 or Class 2 contributions. This may include those who are not working, those not liable for Class 1 or Class 2 contributions or those excepted from Class 2 contributions. Married women and widows who on or before 11 May 1977 elected not to pay Class 1 (full rate) or Class 2 contributions cannot pay Class 3 contributions while they retain this right.

Class 3 contributions are collected by the NICO by quarterly bills or direct debit. *See* leaflet CA08.

### CLASS 4

Self-employed people whose profits and gains are over £4,535 a year pay Class 4 contributions in addition to Class 2 contributions. This applies to self-employed earners over 16 and under the state pension age. Class 4 contributions are calculated at seven per cent of annual profits or gains between £4,535 and £29,900. The maximum Class 4 contribution payable on £29,900 or more is £2,093.00.

Class 4 contributions are assessed and collected by the Inland Revenue together with Schedule D tax. It is possible, in some circumstances, to apply for exceptions from liability to pay Class 4 contributions or to have the amount of contribution reduced (where Class 1 contributions are payable on earnings assessed for Class 4 contributions). *See* leaflet CA03.

## PENSIONS

The Social Security Pensions Act came into force in 1978. It aimed to:

- reduce reliance on means-tested benefit in old age, widowhood and chronic ill-health
- ensure that occupational pension schemes which are contracted out of the state scheme fulfil the conditions of a good scheme
- ensure that pensions are adequately protected against inflation
- ensure that men and women are treated equally in state and occupational schemes

Legislation and regulations introduced since 1978 go further towards fulfilling these aims and more changes came into effect in April 1997 (*see* below). One of the changes is to equalise the state pension age for men (currently 65 years) and women (currently 60 years) from 6 April 2020. The change will be phased in over the ten years leading up to 6 April 2020. As a result the state pension age is as follows:

- the pension age for men remains at 65
- the pension age for women born on or before 5 April 1950 remains at 60

- the pension age for women born on or after 6 April 1955 is now 65
- for women born after 5 April 1950 and before 6 April 1955, the pension age is 60 plus one month for every month, or part of a month, that their date of birth fell after 5 April 1950.

The Welfare Reform and Pensions Bill provides for the sharing of pensions between divorcing couples.

### State Pension Scheme

The state pension scheme consists of the basic flat-rate pension and the state earnings-related pension scheme (SERPS), also known as additional pension.

The amount of basic pension paid is dependent on the number of 'qualifying years' a person has in their 'working life'. A 'qualifying year' is a tax year in which a person pays Class 1 (at the standard rate), 2 or 3 NI contributions for the whole year (*see* above). Those in receipt of invalid care allowance, disabled person's tax credit, jobseeker's allowance, incapacity benefit, severe disablement allowance or approved training have contributions credited to them for each week they receive benefit or fulfil certain other conditions. For those reaching pensionable age on or after 6 April 1999, a Class 3 credit of earnings will be awarded for each week from 6 April 1995 that family credit or, subsequently, working families tax credit, has been received. 'Working life' is counted from the start of the tax year in which a person reaches 16 to the end of the tax year before the one in which they reach pensionable age: for men this is normally 49 years and for women this varies between 44 and 49 years because the pension ages vary (*see* above). To get the full rate (100 per cent) basic pension a person must have qualifying years for about 90 per cent of their working life. To get the minimum basic pension (25 per cent) a person will need ten or eleven qualifying years. Married women who are not entitled to a pension on their own contributions may get a pension on their husband's contributions. It is possible for people who are unable to work because they care for children or a sick or disabled person at home to reduce the number of qualifying years required. This is called home responsibilities protection (HRP) and can be given for any tax year since April 1978; the number of years for which HRP is given is deducted from the number of qualifying years needed.

The amount of SERPS or additional pension paid depends on the amount of earnings a person has between the lower and upper earnings limits (*see* page 487) for each complete tax year between 6 April 1978 (when the scheme started) and the tax year before they reach state pension age. The right to additional pension does not depend on the person's right to basic pension. The amount of additional pension paid also depends on when a person reaches retirement; changes phased in from 6 April 1999 mean that pensions are calculated differently from that date. Men or Women widowed before 5 October 2002 inherit all their late spouse's additional pension. Those widowed on or after this date will inherit a proportion of their spouse's additional pension, up to weekly maximum of £131.35, in line with the table below:

| Maximum % SERPS entitlement for surviving spouse | Date when contributor reaches state pension age |
|---|---|
| 100% | 5/10/2002 or earlier |
| 90% | 6/10/2002–5/10/04 |
| 80% | 6/10/2004–5/10/06 |
| 70% | 6/10/2006–5/10/08 |
| 60% | 6/10/2008–5/10/10 |
| 50% | 6/10/2010 or later |

There are four categories of state pension provided under the Social Security Contributions and Benefits Act 1992:

- Category A, a contributory pension made up of basic and additional elements, payable to those of pensionable age who satisfy the entitlement conditions described above (*see* pages 491–2)
- Category B, a contributory pension made up of basic and additional elements, payable to married women and widows and based on their husband's contributions. This category of pension is to be extended to men whose wives were born after 5 April 1950 from 6 April 2010 (*see* pages 491–2)
- Category C, a non-contributory pension payable to those who reached pensionable age before 5 July 1948 (*see* page 493)
- Category D, a non-contributory pension for those over 80 (*see* page 493)

Graduated retirement benefit is also available to those who paid graduated NI contributions into the scheme when it existed between April 1961 and April 1975.

It is possible to find out how much basic and additional pension a person might receive by filling in form BR19, available from local social security offices or by telephoning the Retirement Pensions Forecasting and Advice Unit on 0191-218 7585.

The Welfare Reform and Pensions Bill will make changes to pensions. SERPS will be replaced by a second state pension from 2002. This will initially be earnings-related, but will subsequently be paid at a flat rate, targeted towards low earners. It will provide a guaranteed minimum income. Under certain circumstances, people not working (such as disabled people and those caring for children or sick relatives) will receive credits into the scheme as though they had earned £9,000 per year. As with SERPS, a person will be entitled to contract out into an occupational, personal or new stakeholder pension scheme.

### Contracted-out Occupational and Personal Pension Schemes

Under the Pensions Schemes Act 1993, an employer can contract out of SERPS those employees who are members of an occupational scheme, so long as the occupational scheme satisfies certain conditions. The occupational pension took the place of the additional pension from April 1997 (previously it took the place of part of the additional pension); the state remains responsible for the flat rate state basic pension. Until April 1997 members of contracted-out occupational and personal pension schemes accrued additional pension in the same way as someone who is not contracted-out but the rate payable was reduced by contracted-out deductions. Since 5 April 1997, it has not been possible to accrue any SERPS while being a member of a contracted-out occupational or personal pension scheme. Members are still entitled to those rights earned before April 1997. Since April 1997 there have been age-related NI contribution rebates for people who leave SERPS and become members of either a COMP (*see* below), a stakeholder or an appropriate personal pension scheme; these will be lower for younger people and higher for older people.

There are three types of contracted-out occupational schemes.

#### *Contracted-Out Salary-Related Scheme (COSR)*

- this scheme must provide a pension related to earnings
- the pension provided must not be less than a person's guaranteed minimum pension (GMP), i.e. worth

about the same as the additional pension provided by the state scheme had the member remained in the State scheme
- any notional additional pension earned from 6 April 1978 to 5 April 1997 will be reduced by the amount of GMP earned during that period (the contracted-out deduction)
- from 6 April 1997 these schemes no longer provide a GMP but do have to satisfy a new scheme-based test, certified by an actuary, before a contracting-out certificate can be issued

*Contracted-Out Money Purchase Scheme (COMP)*
- this scheme must provide a pension based on the value of the fund built up, i.e. the money paid in, along with returns from investment
- part of the pension, known as protected rights, takes the place of the additional pension. A contracted-out deduction, which may be more or less than the pension provided by the scheme, will be made from any additional pension earned from 6 April 1987 to 5 April 1997

In contracted-out occupational pension schemes, both the employee and employer pay lower NI contribution rates in recognition that SERPS will not be paid.

*Contracted-Out Mixed Benefit Scheme (COMBS)*
A mixed benefit scheme has two active sections, one salary-related and the other money purchase. Scheme rules set out which section individual employees may join and the circumstances (if any) in which members may move between sections. Each section must satisfy the respective contracting-out conditions for COSRs and COMPs.

*Appropriate Personal Pension Schemes*
The option of a personal pension scheme is open to all employees, even if their employer has an occupational pension scheme. A personal pension scheme must provide a pension based on the value of the fund built up, i.e. the money paid in, along with returns from investment. Part of the pension, known as protected rights, takes the place of the additional pension. A contracted-out deduction, which may be more or less than the pension provided by the scheme, will be made from any additional pension earned from 6 April 1987 to 5 April 1997.

Employees who are members of a personal pension plan and their employers pay NI contributions at the full rate and the Inland Revenue pays the difference between the full rate and the contracted-out rate into the personal pension scheme.

A Pensions Ombudsman deals with complaints about maladministration of pensions schemes. The Occupational Pensions Board, which supervised contracting-out and approved personal pension schemes, was abolished in April 1997 and replaced by the Occupational Pensions Regulatory Authority (OPRA). *See* leaflet NP46.

*Stakeholder Pensions*
Stakeholder pensions became available in April 2001. They are targeted at those earning between £9,000 and £20,000 who have no occupational or appropriate personal scheme to join although higher earners are able to join a stakeholder scheme if they wish. It is possible to invest up to £3,600 (including tax relief) annually in a stakeholder pension scheme without evidence of earnings. The minimum contribution cannot be set higher than £20 and providers are prohibited from levying a charge of more than 1%. People who are already members of occupational pension schemes may also contribute to a stakeholder pension scheme and it is possible to contribute to a scheme that is not your own, for example that of a non-working partner.

Normally there will be tax relief on any payments made into a stakeholder pension. If an individual contracts out of SERPS using a stakeholder pension plan, a rebate of National Insurance contributions is paid into their stakeholder plan. *See* leaflet PSO2.

For further information contact the Office of the Pensions Advisory Service on 020-7233 8080.

## BENEFITS

Leaflets relating to the various benefits and contribution conditions for different benefits are available from local social security offices; leaflets NI196 *Social Security Benefit Rates*, FB2 *Which Benefit?* and MG1 *A Guide to Benefits* are general guides to benefits, benefit rates and contributions.

The benefits payable under the Social Security Acts are:

### CONTRIBUTORY BENEFITS

Jobseeker's allowance (contribution-based)
Incapacity benefit
Maternity allowance
Widow's benefit (comprising widow's payment, widowed mother's allowance and widow's pension)
Retirement pensions, categories A and B

### NON-CONTRIBUTORY BENEFITS AND TAX CREDITS

Child benefit
Guardian's allowance
Jobseeker's allowance (income-based)
Invalid care allowance
Severe disablement allowance
Attendance allowance
Disability living allowance
Disabled person's tax credit
Retirement pensions, categories C and D
Income support
Working families tax credit
Housing benefit
Council tax benefit
Social fund

### BENEFITS FOR INDUSTRIAL INJURIES AND DISABLEMENT

Other
Statutory sick pay
Statutory maternity pay

## TAX CREDITS

Under the Tax Credits Act 1999, Family Credit and Disability Working Allowance (both non-contributory benefits) were replaced by Working Families Tax Credit and Disabled Person's Tax Credit from 5 October 1999. Both of these are administered by the Inland Revenue. The first payments were made from April 2000. People receiving Family Credit or Disability Working Allowance on 5 October 1999 continue to receive their benefits until the award expires, when they will be able to change to the new tax credits. From April 2000 employees will receive the credits from their employer along with their wages or salary. Self-employed applicants will be paid direct by the Inland Revenue. Further information and application forms are available from Inland Revenue Tax Enquiry Centres, Benefits Agency offices, Jobcentres, post offices and Citizens' Advice Bureaux.

### WORKING FAMILIES TAX CREDIT

Working Families Tax Credit is a system of tax credits paid to couples (married or unmarried) or lone parents who have at least one child living with them and where at least one partner works at least 16 hours per week. The credit is not payable if any savings exceed £8,000.

Working Families Tax Credit will usually be paid at the same rate for 26 weeks. There are four elements:

- a basic credit of £59.00 per family per week
- a credit of £11.45 per week where one earner works at least 30 hours per week
- a credit for each child at the rate of £26.00 per week from birth and £26.75 from the September following their 16th birthday up to the day before their 19th birthday
- a childcare credit (in certain circumstances) of up to 70 per cent of eligible childcare costs up to a maximum of £135 per week for one child and £200 per week for two or more children.

If net income is below £92.90 per week, the maximum tax credit is payable. If net income exceeds £92.90 per week, the total tax credit is reduced by 55p for each £1.00 above £92.90.

### Disabled Person's Tax Credit

Disabled Person's Tax Credit is a system of tax credits for people who are working at least 16 hours per week but have an illness or disability which puts them at a disadvantage in getting a job. To qualify, a person must have one of the 'qualifying benefits' or have had them up to 182 days before applying. The credit is not payable if any savings exceed £16,000.

Disabled Person's Tax Credit will usually be paid at the same rate for 26 weeks. There are six elements:

- a basic credit of £61.05 per week for a single person or £91.25 for a couple or lone parent
- enhanced disability tax credit (where applicant or partner is entitled to the highest rate care component of Disability Living Allowance) £11.05 or £16.00 for a couple or lone parent
- a credit of £11.45 per week where one applicant works at least 30 hours per week
- a credit for each child at the rate of £26.00 from birth and £26.75 from the September following their 16th birthday up to the day before their 19th birthday
- a disabled child's tax credit of £30.00 per week or an enhanced disabled child's credit of £41.05 for each severely disabled child
- a childcare credit (in certain circumstances) of up to 70 per cent of eligible childcare costs up to a maximum of £135 per week for one child and £200 per week for two or more children.

If net income is below £70 per week for a single person or £90 per week for a couple or lone parent, the maximum tax credit is payable. If net income exceeds these thresholds, the total tax credit is reduced by 55p for each £1.00 above the threshold.

## CONTRIBUTORY BENEFITS

Entitlement to contributory benefits depends on contribution conditions being satisfied either by the claimant or by some other person (depending on the kind of benefit). The class or classes of contribution which for this purpose are relevant to each benefit are:

| | |
|---|---|
| Jobseeker's allowance (contribution-based) | Class 1 |
| Incapacity benefit | Class 1 or 2 |
| Maternity allowance | Class 1 or 2 |
| Widow's benefits | Class 1, 2 or 3 |
| Retirement pensions, categories A and B | Class 1, 2 or 3 |

The system of contribution conditions relates to yearly levels of earnings on which contributions have been paid.

### Jobseeker's Allowance

Jobseeker's allowance (JSA) replaced unemployment benefit and income support for unemployed people under pension age from 7 October 1996. There are two routes of entitlement. Contribution-based JSA is paid as a personal rate (i.e. additional benefit for dependants is not paid) to those who have made sufficient NI contributions in two particular tax years. Savings and partner's earnings are not taken into account and payment can be made for up to six months. Those who do not qualify for contribution-based JSA, those who have exhausted their entitlement to contribution-based JSA or those for whom contribution-based JSA provides insufficient income may qualify for income-based JSA. The amount paid depends on age and number of dependants and income and savings are taken into account. Income-based JSA may comprise three parts: a personal allowance for the jobseeker and his/her partner and one for each child or young person for whom they are responsible; premiums for groups of people with special needs; and housing costs. This is payable for the claimant and their dependants for as long as they satisfy the rules. Rates of jobseeker's allowance correspond to income support rates.

Claims for this benefit are made through Employment Service Jobcentres. A person wishing to claim jobseeker's allowance must be unemployed, capable of work and available for any work which they can reasonably be expected to do, usually for at least 40 hours per week. They must agree and sign a 'jobseeker's agreement', which will set out each claimant's plans to find work, and must actively seek work. If they refuse work or training their benefit may be suspended for between two and six weeks.

A person will be disqualified from jobseeker's allowance if they have left a job voluntarily or through misconduct, if they refuse to take up an offer of employment or if they fail to attend a training scheme or employment programme. In these circumstances, it may be possible to receive hardship payments, particularly where the claimant or their family is vulnerable, e.g. if sick or pregnant, or for those with children or caring responsibilities. *See* leaflet JSAL5.

### Incapacity Benefit

Incapacity benefit is available to those who are incapable of work but cannot get statutory sick pay from their employer. It is not payable to those over state pension age. However, people who are already in receipt of short-term incapacity benefit when they reach state pension age may continue to receive this benefit for up to 52 weeks. The Welfare Reform and Pensions Bill 1999 restricts eligibility for incapacity benefit to people who have paid National Insurance contributions for one of the previous three years. The Bill also provides for the reduction of the amount of incapacity benefit payable where a claimant receives more than a specified amount of occupational or personal pension. Severely disabled people aged between 16 and 19 should receive incapacity benefit without meeting the national insurance contribution conditions under the Government's proposals. There are three rates of incapacity benefit:

- short-term lower rate for the first 28 weeks of sickness
- short-term higher rate from weeks 29 to 52
- long-term rate after week 52

The terminally ill and those entitled to the highest rate care component of disability living allowance are paid the long-term rate after 28 weeks. Incapacity benefit is taxable after 28 weeks.

Two rates of age addition are paid with long-term benefit based on the claimant's age when incapacity started. The higher rate is payable where incapacity for work commenced before the age of 35; and the lower rate where incapacity commenced before the age of 45. Increases for dependants are also payable with short and long-term incapacity benefit.

There are two medical tests of incapacity: the 'own occupation' test and the 'all work' test. Those who worked before becoming incapable of working will be assessed, for the first 28 weeks of incapacity, on their ability to do their own job. After 28 weeks (or from the start of incapacity for those who were not working) claimants are assessed on their ability to carry out a range of work-related activities. The 'all work' test applies to most former sickness and invalidity benefit claimants. The Government plans to replace the 'all work' test with a new 'personal capability assessment.' *See* leaflets IB202 and SD1.

### MATERNITY ALLOWANCE

The maternity allowance (MA) scheme covers women who are self-employed or otherwise do not qualify for statutory maternity pay (*see* page 496). In order to qualify, the woman must have been working and paying standard rate NI contributions for at least 26 weeks in the 66-week period which ends with the week before the week in which the baby is due. A woman can choose to start receiving MA between the beginning of the 11th week before the week in which the baby is due and the Sunday after the baby is born, depending on when she stops working. MA is paid for a period of up to 18 weeks. MA is only paid while the woman is not working. *See* leaflet NI17A.

### BEREAVEMENT BENEFITS

Bereavement benefits replaced widows' benefits on 9 April 2001. Those claiming widows' benefits before this date will continue to receive them under the old scheme for as long as they qualify. The new system provides bereavement benefits for widows and widowers providing that their deceased spouse paid National Insurance contributions. The new system offers benefits in three forms:

*Bereavement payment* – may be received by a man or woman who is under the state pension age at the time of their spouse's death, or whose husband or wife was not entitled to a Category A retirement pension when he or she died. It is a single tax-free lump sum of £2,000 payable immediately on becoming a widow or widower.

*Widowed parent's allowance* – a taxable benefit payable to the surviving partner if he or she is entitled or treated as entitled to child benefit, or to a widow if she is expecting her husband's baby

*Bereavement allowance* – a taxable weekly benefit paid for 52 weeks after the spouse's death. A widow or widower may receive this pension if aged 45 or over at the time of his or her spouse's death (40 or over if widowed before 11 April 1988) or when his or her widowed parent's allowance ends. If aged 55 or over he or she will receive the full bereavement allowance

It is not possible to receive widowed parent's allowance and bereavement allowance at the same time, and bereavement benefit in any form ceases upon remarriage or during a period of cohabitation as man and wife without being legally married. *See* leaflet NP45.

### RETIREMENT PENSION: CATEGORIES A AND B

A Category A pension is payable for life to men and women who reach state pension age and who satisfy the contributions conditions (*see* page 488). A Category B pension is payable for life to a spouse and is based on their wife or husband's contributions. It becomes payable only when the wife or husband has claimed their pension and the spouse has reached state pension age. It is also payable on widowhood after the state retirement age regardless of whether the wife or husband had qualified for their pension. There are special rules for those who are widowed before reaching pensionable age.

A person may defer claiming their pension for five years after state pension age. In doing so they may earn increments which will increase the weekly amount paid when they claim their pension. If a married man defers his Category A pension, his wife cannot claim a Category B pension on his contributions but she may earn increments on her pension during this time. A woman can defer her Category B pension, and earn increments, even if her husband is claiming his Category A pension.

The basic state pension is £72.50 per week plus any additional (earnings-related) pension the person may be entitled to (*see* page 488). An increase of £43.40 is paid for an adult dependant, providing the dependant's earnings do not exceed the rate of jobseeker's allowance for a single person (*see* below). It is also possible to get an increase of Category A and B pensions for a child or children. An age addition of 25p per week is payable if a retirement pensioner is aged 80 or over.

Since 1989 pensioners have been allowed to have unlimited earnings without affecting their retirement pension. Income support is payable on top of a pension where a pension does not give the person enough to live on and to those who are entitled to retirement pension but who have not claimed it. Pensioners may also be entitled to housing and council tax benefits.

### GRADUATED RETIREMENT BENEFIT

Graduated NI contributions were first payable from 1961 and were calculated as a percentage of earnings between certain bands. They were discontinued in 1975. Any graduated pension which an employed person over 18 and under 70 (65 for a woman) had earned by paying graduated contributions will be paid when the contributor claims retirement pension or at 70 (65 for a woman), in addition to any retirement pension for which he or she qualifies. A wife can get a graduated pension in return for her own graduated contributions, but not for her husband's.

Graduated retirement benefit is at a weekly rate for each 'unit' of graduated contributions paid by the employee (half a unit or more counts as a whole unit); the rate varies from person to person. A unit of graduated pension can be calculated by adding together all graduated contributions and dividing by 7.5 (men) or 9.0 (women). If a person defers making a claim beyond 65 (60 for a woman), entitlement may be increased by one seventh of a penny per £1 of its weekly rate for each complete week of deferred retirement, as long as the retirement is deferred for a minimum of seven weeks.

### WEEKLY RATES OF BENEFIT

*from April 2001*

| | |
|---|---|
| *Jobseeker's allowance (contribution-based)* | |
| Person under 18 | £31.95 |
| Person aged 18–24 | 42.00 |
| Person over 25 | 53.05 |
| *Short-term incapacity benefit* | |
| Person under pension age – lower rate | 52.60 |
| *Person under pension age – higher rate | 62.20 |
| Increase for adult dependant | 32.55 |
| *Person over pension age | 66.90 |
| Increase for adult dependant | 32.55 |
| **Long-term incapacity benefit* | |
| Person (under or over pension age) | 69.75 |
| Increase for adult dependant | 41.75 |
| Age addition – lower rate | 7.35 |
| Age addition – higher rate | 14.65 |

| | | |
|---|---|---|
| *Invalidity allowance: maximum amount payable* | | |
| Higher rate | | 14.65 |
| Middle rate | | 9.30 |
| Lower rate | | 4.65 |
| *Maternity allowance* | | |
| Employed | | 62.20 |
| Maternity rate threshold | | 30.00 |
| *Widow's benefits (before 9 April 2001)* | | |
| Widow's payment (lump sum) | | 1,000.00 |
| Widowed mother's allowance | | 72.50 |
| Widow's pension | | 72.50 |
| *Bereavement benefit (from 9 April 2001)* | | |
| Bereavement payment (lump sum) | | 2,000.00 |
| *Widowed parents allowance | | 72.50 |
| *Bereavement allowance | | 72.50 |
| *Age related | 54 | 67.43 |
| | 53 | 62.35 |
| | 52 | 57.28 |
| | 51 | 52.20 |
| | 50 | 47.13 |
| | 49 | 42.05 |
| | 48 | 36.98 |
| | 47 | 31.90 |
| | 46 | 26.83 |
| | 45 | 21.75 |
| **Retirement pension: categories A and B* | | |
| Single person | | 72.50 |
| Increase for wife/other adult dependant | | 43.40 |

*These benefits attract an increase for each dependent child (in addition to child benefit) of £9.70 for the first or only child and £11.35 for each subsequent child

## NON-CONTRIBUTORY BENEFITS

These benefits are paid from general taxation and are not dependent on NI contributions. Unless otherwise stated, a benefit is tax-free and is not means tested.

### Child Benefit

Child benefit is payable for virtually all children aged under 16, and for those aged 16 to 18 who are studying full-time up to and including A-level or equivalent standard. It is also payable for a short period if the child has left school recently and is registered for work or work-based training for young people at a careers office.

A higher rate of benefit (child benefit (lone parent)) may be paid to a person who is responsible for bringing up one or more children on his/her own. It is a flat rate benefit payable for the eldest child only. Since 6 July 1998 child benefit (lone parent) has not been available to new lone parents but it may still be payable in certain circumstances. *See* leaflets CH1 and CH11.

### Guardian's Allowance

Where the parents of a child are dead, the person who has the child in his/her family may claim a guardian's allowance in addition to child benefit. In exceptional circumstances the allowance is payable on the death of only one parent. *See* leaflet NI14.

### Invalid Care Allowance

Invalid care allowance (ICA) is a taxable benefit payable to people of working age who give up the opportunity of full-time paid employment because they are regularly and substantially engaged (spending at least 35 hours per week) in caring for a severely disabled person. To qualify for ICA a person must be caring for someone in receipt of one of the following benefits:

- the middle or highest rate of disability living allowance care component
- either rate of attendance allowance
- constant attendance allowance, paid at not less than the normal maximum rate, under the industrial injuries or war pension schemes

*See* leaflets FB31 and SD1.

### Severe Disablement Allowance

From April 2001 Severe Disablement Allowance (SDA) has not been available to new claimants. Those claiming SDA before that date will continue to receive it for as long as they qualify. *See* leaflet NI252.

### Attendance Allowance

This is payable to disabled people who claim after the age of 65 and who need a lot of care or supervision because of physical or mental disability for a period of at least six months. People not expected to live for six months because of an illness do not have to wait six months. The allowance has two rates: the lower rate is for day or night care, and the higher rate is for day and night care. *See* leaflets DS702 and SD1.

### Disability Living Allowance

This is payable to disabled people who claim before the age of 65 who have personal care and mobility needs because of an illness or disability for a period of at least three months and are likely to have those needs for a further six months or more. People not expected to live for six months because of an illness do not have to wait three months. The allowance has two components: the care component, which has three rates, and the mobility component, which has two rates. The rates depend on the care and mobility needs of the claimant. *See* leaflets DS704 and SD1.

### Retirement Pension: Categories C and D

A Category C pension is provided, subject to a residence test, for persons who were over pensionable age on 5 July 1948, and for the wives and widows of men who qualified if they are over pension age. A Category D pension is provided for people aged 80 and over if they are not entitled to another category of pension or are entitled to less than the Category D rate.

### Weekly Rates of Benefit

| *from April 2001* | |
|---|---|
| *Child benefit* | |
| Eldest child | £15.50 |
| Eldest child of certain lone parents | 17.35 |
| Each subsequent child | 10.35 |
| *Guardian's allowance* | |
| Eldest child | 9.85 |
| Each subsequent child | 11.35 |
| **Invalid care allowance* | 41.75 |
| Increase for wife/other adult dependant | 24.95 |
| **Severe disablement allowance* | |
| †Basic rate | 42.15 |
| Under 40 | 14.65 |
| 40–49 | 9.30 |
| 50–59 | 4.65 |
| Increase for wife/other adult dependant | 25.00 |
| *Attendance allowance* | |
| Higher rate | 55.30 |
| Lower rate | 37.00 |
| *Disability living allowance* | |
| Care component | |
| Higher rate | 55.30 |
| Middle rate | 37.00 |
| Lowest rate | 14.65 |

| | |
|---|---|
| Mobility component | |
| Higher rate | 38.65 |
| Lower rate | 14.65 |
| *Retirement pension: categories *C and D* | |
| Single person | 43.40 |
| Increase for wife/other adult dependant (not payable with Category D pension) | 24.95 |

*These benefits attract an increase for each dependent child (in addition to child benefit) of £9.85 for the first or only child and £11.35 for each subsequent child
†The age addition applies to the age when incapacity began

## INCOME SUPPORT

Income support is a benefit for those aged 16 and over whose income is below a certain level. It can be paid to people who are not expected to sign on as unemployed (income support for unemployed people was replaced by jobseeker's allowance in October 1996) and who are:

- incapable of work due to sickness or disability
- bringing up children alone
- 60 or over
- looking after a person who has a disability
- registered blind

Some people who are not in these categories may also be able to claim income support.

Income support is also payable to people who work for less than 16 hours a week on average (or 24 hours for a partner). Some people can claim income support if they work longer hours.

Income support is not payable if the claimant, or claimant and partner, have capital or savings in excess of £8,000. For capital and savings in excess of £3,000, a deduction of £1 is made for every £250 or part of £250 held. Different limits apply to people permanently in residential care and nursing homes: the upper limit is £16,000 and deductions apply for capital in excess of £10,000.

Sums payable depend on fixed allowances laid down by law for people in different circumstances. If both partners are entitled to income support, either may claim it for the couple. People receiving income support may be able to receive housing benefit, help with mortgage or home loan interest and help with health care. They may also be eligible for help with exceptional expenses from the Social Fund. Special rates may apply to some people living in residential care or nursing homes. Leaflet IS20 gives a detailed explanation of income support.

In October 1998 the Government's voluntary New Deal for Lone Parents programme became available throughout the UK. All lone parents receiving income support are assigned a personal adviser at a jobcentre who will provide guidance and support with a view to enabling the claimant to find work.

## INCOME SUPPORT PREMIUMS

Income support premiums are additional weekly payments for those with special needs. People qualifying for more than one premium will normally only receive the highest single premium for which they qualify. However, family premium, disabled child premium, severe disability premium and carer premium are payable in addition to other premiums.

People with children may qualify for:

- the family premium if they have at least one child (a higher rate is paid to lone parents, although from 6 April 1998 it has not generally been available to new claimants)
- the disabled child premium if they have a child who receives disability living allowance or is registered blind

Carers may qualify for:

- the carer premium if they or their partner are in receipt of invalid care allowance

Long-term sick or disabled people may qualify for:

- the disability premium if they or their partner are receiving certain benefits because they are disabled or cannot work; are registered blind; or if the claimant has been incapable of work or receiving statutory sick pay for at least 364 days (196 days if the person is terminally ill), including periods of incapacity separated by eight weeks or less
- the severe disability premium if the person lives alone and receives attendance allowance or the middle or higher rate of disability living allowance care component and no one receives invalid care allowance for caring for that person. This premium is also available to couples where both partners meet the above conditions

People aged 60 and over may qualify for:

- the pensioner premium if they or their partner are aged 60 to 74
- the enhanced pensioner premium if they or their partner are aged 75 to 79
- the higher pensioner premium if they or their partner are aged 80 or over. This is also available to people over 60 who receive attendance allowance, disability living allowance, long-term incapacity benefit or severe disablement allowance, or who are registered blind

### WEEKLY RATES OF BENEFIT

| | |
|---|---|
| *from April 2001* | |
| *Income support* | |
| Single person | |
| under 18 | £31.95 |
| under 18 (higher) | 42.00 |
| aged 18–24 | 42.00 |
| aged 25 and over | 53.05 |
| aged under 18 and a single parent (lower) | 31.95 |
| aged under 18 and a single parent (higher) | 42.00 |
| aged 18 and over and a single parent | 53.05 |
| Couples* | |
| Both under 18 | 63.35 |
| one or both aged 18 or over | 83.25 |
| For each child in a family from birth | |
| until September following 16th birthday | 31.45 |
| †from September following 16th birthday to day before 19th birthday | 32.25 |
| *Premiums* | |
| Family premium | 14.50 |
| Family (lone parent) premium | 15.90 |
| Disabled child premium | 30.00 |
| Carer premium | 24.40 |
| Disability premium | |
| Single | 22.60 |
| Couple | 32.25 |
| Enhanced disability premium | |
| Single | 11.05 |
| Disabled child rate | 11.05 |
| Couple | 32.25 |
| Severe disability premium | |
| Single | 41.55 |
| Couple (one person qualified) | 41.55 |
| Couple (both qualified) | 83.10 |
| Pensioner premium | |
| Single | 39.10 |
| Couple | 57.30 |

| | |
|---|---|
| Higher pensioner premium | |
| Single | 39.10 |
| Couple | 57.30 |
| Enhanced pensioner premium | |
| Single | 39.10 |
| Couple | 57.30 |
| Bereavement premium | 19.45 |

*Where one or both partners are aged under 18, their personal allowance will depend on their situation
†If in full-time education up to A-level or equivalent standard

## HOUSING BENEFIT

Housing benefit is designed to help people with rent (including rent for accommodation in guest houses, lodgings or hostels). It does not cover mortgage payments. The amount of benefit paid depends on:

- the income of the claimant, and partner if there is one, including earned income, unearned income (any other income including some other benefits) and savings
- number of dependants
- certain extra needs of the claimant, partner or any dependants
- number and gross income of people sharing the home who are not dependent on the claimant
- how much rent is paid

Housing benefit is not payable if the claimant, or claimant and partner, have savings of over £16,000. The amount of benefit is affected if savings held exceed £3,000. Housing benefit is not paid for meals, fuel or certain service charges that may be included in the rent. Deductions are also made for most non-dependants who live in the same accommodation as the claimant (and their partner).

The maximum amount of benefit (which is not necessarily the same as the amount of rent paid) may be paid where the claimant is in receipt of income support or income-based jobseeker's allowance or where the claimant's income is less than the amount allowed for their needs. Any income over that allowed for their needs will mean that their benefit is reduced.

Claims for housing benefit are made to the local council. Those who are also claiming income support or income-based jobseeker's allowance may claim housing benefit at the local benefits or employment services office. *See* leaflets RR1 and RR2.

## COUNCIL TAX BENEFIT

Nearly all the rules which apply to housing benefit apply to council tax benefit, which helps people on low incomes to pay council tax bills. The amount payable depends on how much council tax is paid and who lives with the claimant. The benefit may be available to those receiving income support or income-based jobseeker's allowance or to those whose income is less than that allowed for their needs. Any income over that allowed for their needs will mean that their council tax benefit is reduced. Deductions are made for non-dependants.

The maximum amount that is payable for those living in properties in council tax bands A to E is 100 per cent of the claimant's council tax liability. This also applies to those living in properties in bands F to H who were in receipt of the benefit at 31 March 1998 if they have remained in the same property. From 1 April 1998 council tax benefit for new claimants living in property bands F to H (or existing claimants moving into these bands) was restricted to the level payable for band E.

If a person shares a home with one or more adults (not their partner) who are on a low income, it may be possible to claim a second adult rebate. Those who are entitled to both council tax benefit and second adult rebate will be awarded whichever is the greater. Second adult rebate may be claimed by those not in receipt of council tax benefit.

## THE SOCIAL FUND

The Social Fund helps people with expenses which are difficult to meet from regular income. Regulated maternity and funeral payments are decided by Decision Makers; cold weather payments and winter fuel payments are made automatically. These payments are not limited by the district's Social Fund budget. Discretionary community care grants, and budgeting and crisis loans are decided by Social Fund Officers and come out of a yearly budget which is allocated to each district (1999–2000, grants £98 million; loans £436.7 million; £0.5 million set aside as a contingency reserve). *See* leaflet SB16.

### REGULATED PAYMENTS

*Maternity Payments*

From April 2000 the Maternity Payment Scheme was replaced by the State Maternity Grant Scheme. A payment of up to £200 for each baby expected, born, adopted or the subject of a parental order (in the case of surrogacy), will be linked to the claimant seeking advice on the welfare of the baby. It is payable to people on income support, income-based jobseeker's allowance, disabled person's tax credit and working families tax credit and does not have to be repaid.

*Funeral Payments*

Payable for the necessary cost of burial or cremation, plus other funeral expenses reasonably incurred up to £600, to people receiving income support, income-based jobseeker's allowance, disabled person's tax credit, working families' tax credit, council tax benefit or housing benefit who have good reason for taking responsibility for the funeral expenses. These payments are recoverable from any estate of the deceased.

*Cold Weather Payments*

A payment of £8.50 when the average temperature over seven consecutive days is recorded as or forecast to be 0°C or below in their area. Payments are made to people on income support or income-based jobseeker's allowance and who have a child under five or whose benefit includes a pensioner or disability premium. They do not have to be repaid.

*Winter Fuel Payments*

An annual payment of £100 per household paid automatically to eligible pensioners. Payments are made before Christmas and do not have to be repaid.

### DISCRETIONARY PAYMENTS

*Community Care Grants*

These are intended to help people on income support or income-based jobseeker's allowance (or those likely to receive these benefits on leaving residential or institutional accommodation) to live as independently as possible in the community; ease exceptional pressures on families; care for a prisoner or young offender released on temporary licence; help people set up home as part of a resettlement programme and/or assist with certain travelling expenses. They do not have to be repaid.

*Budgeting Loans*

These are interest-free loans to people who have been receiving income support or income-based jobseeker's allowance for at least 26 weeks, for intermittent expenses that may be difficult to budget for.

*Crisis Loans*
These are interest-free loans to anyone, whether receiving benefit or not, who is without resources in an emergency, where there is no other means of preventing serious damage or serious risk to their health or safety.

### SAVINGS

Savings over £500 (£1,000 for people aged 60 or over) are taken into account for maternity and funeral payments, community care grants and budgeting loans. All savings are taken into account for crisis loans. Savings are not taken into account for cold weather or winter fuel payments.

## INDUSTRIAL INJURIES AND DISABLEMENT BENEFITS

The industrial injuries scheme, administered under the Social Security Contributions and Benefits Act 1992, provides a range of benefits designed to compensate for disablement resulting from an industrial accident (i.e. an accident arising out of and in the course of an employed earner's employment) or from a prescribed disease due to the nature of a person's employment. Those who are self-employed are not covered by this scheme.

### INDUSTRIAL INJURIES DISABLEMENT BENEFIT

A person must be at least 14 per cent disabled (except for certain respiratory diseases) in order to qualify for this benefit. The amount paid depends on the degree of disablement:

- those assessed as 14–19 per cent disabled are paid at the 20 per cent rate
- those with disablement of over 20 per cent will have the percentage rounded up or down to the nearest ten per cent, e.g. a disablement of 44 per cent will be paid at the 40 per cent rate while a disablement of 45 per cent will be paid at the 50 per cent rate

Benefit is payable 15 weeks (90 days) after the date of the accident or onset of the disease and may be payable for a limited period or for life. The benefit is payable whether the person works or not and those who are incapable of work are entitled to draw statutory sick pay or incapacity benefit in addition to industrial injuries disablement benefit. It may also be possible to claim the following allowances:

- reduced earnings allowance for those who are unable to return to their regular work or work of the same standard and who had their accident (or whose disease started) before 1 October 1990
- retirement allowance for those who were entitled to reduced earnings allowance who have reached state pension age
- constant attendance allowance for those with a disablement of 100 per cent who need constant care. There are four rates of allowance depending on how much care the person needs
- exceptionally severe disablement allowance for those who are entitled to constant care attendance allowance at one of the higher rates and who need constant care permanently

*See* leaflets NI6 and N12.

### OTHER BENEFITS

People who are disabled because of an accident or disease that was the result of work that they did before 5 July 1948 are not entitled to industrial injuries disablement benefit. They may, however, be entitled to payment under the workmen's compensation scheme or the pneumoconiosis, byssinosis and miscellaneous diseases benefit scheme. *See* leaflets WS1 and PN1.

### WEEKLY RATES OF BENEFIT

*from April 2001*

| | |
|---|---|
| *Disablement benefit/pension | |
| Degree of disablement | |
| 100 per cent | £112.90 |
| 90 | 101.61 |
| 80 | 90.32 |
| 70 | 79.03 |
| 60 | 67.74 |
| 50 | 56.45 |
| 40 | 45.16 |
| 30 | 33.87 |
| 20 | 22.58 |
| †Unemployability supplement | 69.75 |
| Addition for adult dependant (subject to earnings rule) | 40.40 |
| Reduced earnings allowance (maximum) | 45.16 |
| Retirement allowance (maximum) | 11.29 |
| Constant attendance allowance (normal maximum rate) | 45.20 |
| Exceptionally severe disablement allowance | 45.20 |

*There is a weekly benefit for those under 18 with no dependants which is set at a lower rate

†This benefit attracts an increase for each dependent child (in addition to child benefit) of £9.85 for the first child and £11.35 for each subsequent child

## CLAIMS AND QUESTIONS

With a few exceptions, claims and questions relating to social security benefits are decided in agencies. The decision makers act impartially. *See* leaflets GL24 and NI260(DMA).

Entitlement to benefit (including disablement questions) and regulated Social Fund payments is determined by decision makers. A claimant who is dissatisfied with that decision can ask for an explanation and review of the decision. If they are still dissatisfied they can go to the Appeals Service, an independent tribunal. There is a further right of appeal to a Social Security Commissioner against the tribunal's decision but leave to appeal must first be obtained. Appeals to the Commissioner must be on a point of law. Provision is also made for the determination of certain questions by the Secretary of State for Social Security.

Decisions on applications to the discretionary Social Fund are made by Social Fund Officers. Applicants can ask for a review within 28 days of the date on the decision letter. The Social Fund Review Officer will review the case and there is a further right of review to an independent Social Fund Inspector.

Reviews of housing and council tax benefit decisions are dealt with initially by the council. The claimant must ask for a review within six weeks of being told how much benefit they will receive. Further reviews are dealt with by an independent review board.

## OTHER BENEFITS

### STATUTORY SICK PAY

Employers usually pay statutory sick pay (SSP) to their employees for up to 28 weeks of sickness in any period of incapacity for work that lasts longer than four days. SSP is paid at £62.20 per week and is subject to PAYE tax and NI deductions. Employees who cannot obtain SSP may be able to claim incapacity benefit. Employers may be able to recover some SSP costs. *See* leaflets NI244 and NI245.

### Statutory Maternity Pay

In general, employers pay statutory maternity pay (SMP) to pregnant women who have been employed by them full or part-time for at least 26 weeks before the end of the 'qualifying week', which is 15 weeks before the week the baby is due, and whose earnings on average at least equal the lower earnings limit applied to NI contributions. All women who meet these conditions receive payment of 90 per cent of their average earnings for six weeks, followed by a maximum of 12 weeks at £62.20. SMP can be paid from the beginning of the 11th week before the week in which the baby is due but women can decide to begin maternity leave later than this. SMP is not payable for any week in which the woman works. Employers are reimbursed for 92 per cent of the SMP they pay (105 per cent for those whose annual NI liability (excluding Class 1A) is £20,000 or less). *See* Leaflet NI17A.

# War Pensions

The War Pensions Agency, which became an executive agency of the Ministry of Defence in June 2001, awards war pensions under The Naval, Military and Air Forces, Etc. (Disablement and Death) Service Pensions Order 1983 to members of the armed forces in respect of service after 4 August 1914. There is also a scheme for civilians and civil defence workers in respect of the 1939–45 war, and other schemes for groups such as merchant seamen and Polish armed forces who served under British command.

### Pensions

War disablement pension is awarded for the disabling effects of any injury, wound or disease which is the result of, or has been aggravated by, conditions of service in the armed forces. It can only be paid once the person has left the armed forces. The amount of pension paid depends on the severity of disablement, which is assessed by comparing the health of the claimant with that of a healthy person of the same age and sex. The person's earning capacity or occupation are not taken into account in this assessment. A pension is awarded if the person has a disablement of 20 per cent or more and a lump sum is usually payable to those with a disablement of less than 20 per cent. No award is made for noise-induced sensorineural hearing loss where the assessment of disablement is less than 20 per cent.

War widow's pension is payable where the husband's death was due to, or hastened by, his service in the armed forces or where the husband was in receipt of a war disablement pension constant attendance allowance (or would have been had he not been in hospital). A war widow's pension is also payable if the husband was getting unemployability supplement at the time of his death and his pensionable disablement was at least 80 per cent. Most war widows receive a standard rank-related rate but a lower weekly rate is payable to war widows of men below the rank of Lieutenant-Colonel who are under the age of 40, without children and capable of maintaining themselves. This is increased to the standard rate at age 40. Allowances are paid for children (in addition to child benefit) and adult dependants. An age allowance may also be given when the woman reaches 65 and increased at age 70 and age 80.

A war widower's pension may be payable to a man whose wife died because of service in the armed forces, if he was dependent on his wife before her death and cannot support himself.

All war pensions and war widow's pensions are tax-free and pensioners living overseas receive the same amount as those resident in the UK.

### Supplementary Allowances

A number of supplementary allowances may be awarded to a war pensioner which are intended to meet various needs which may result from disablement or death and take account of its particular effect on the pensioner or spouse. The principal supplementary allowances are unemployability supplement, allowance for lowered standard of occupation and constant attendance allowance. Others include exceptionally severe disablement allowance, severe disablement occupational allowance, treatment allowance, mobility supplement, comforts allowance, clothing allowance, age allowance and widow's age allowance. There is a rent allowance available on a war widow's pension.

## DEPARTMENT FOR WORK AND PENSIONS BENEFITS

Benefits formerly administered by the Department of Social Services are now overseen by the Department of Work and Pensions. Most benefits are paid in addition to the basic war disablement pension or war widow's pension. Any retirement pension for which a war widow qualifies on her own NI contribution record can be paid in addition to her war widow's pension.

A war pensioner or war widow who claims income support, working families tax credit or disabled person's tax credit has the first £10 a week of pension disregarded. A similar provision operates for housing benefit and council tax benefit; but the local authority may, at its discretion, disregard any or all of the balance.

### Claims and Questions

To claim a war pension it is necessary to contact the nearest war pensioners' welfare service office, the address of which is available from local social security offices, or to write to the War Pensions Agency, Norcross, Blackpool FY5 3WP. Claims can also be made through authorised agents, usually ex-service organisations such as the RBL, BLESMA etc. Claim forms are also available from the WPA website listed below.

The war pensioners' welfare service advises and assists war pensioners and widows on any matters affecting their welfare. General advice on any war pensions matter can be obtained by ringing the War pensions Freeline (UK only) on 0800-169 2277. If living overseas ring 00 44 1253 866043; E-mail warpensions@gtnet.gov.uk; Web: www.dss.gov.uk/wpa

# The Water Industry

## ENGLAND AND WALES

The water industry supplies 58 million people 18,000 million litres of water every day. Around 2.8 million tests are carried out to check water quality every year and 99.82 per cent of samples meet all British/European standards. In England and Wales the Secretary of State for Environment, Food and Rural Affairs and the National Assembly for Wales have overall responsibility for water policy and set the environmental and health and safety standards for the water industry. The Drinking Water Inspectorate acts on their behalf as the regulator of drinking water quality.

The Director-General of Water Services, as the independent economic regulator, is responsible for ensuring that the private water companies are able to fulfil their statutory obligation to provide water supply and sewerage services, and for protecting the interests of consumers.

The Secretary of State for Environment, Food and Rural Affairs and the National Assembly for Wales are responsible for policy relating to land drainage, flood protection, sea defences and the protection and development of fisheries.

The Environment Agency is responsible for water quality and the control of pollution, the management of water resources and nature conservation.

### THE WATER COMPANIES

Until 1989, nine regional water authorities in England and the Welsh Water Authority in Wales were responsible for water supply and the development of water resources, sewerage and sewage disposal, pollution control, freshwater fisheries, flood protection, water recreation, and environmental conservation. The Water Act 1989 provided for the creation of a privatised water industry under public regulation, and the functions of the regional water authorities were taken over by ten holding companies and the regulatory bodies and has since been consolidated into the Water Industry Act 1991.

Of the 99 per cent of the population of England and Wales who are connected to a public water supply, 78 per cent are supplied by the water companies (through their principal operating subsidiaries, the water service companies). The remaining 22 per cent are supplied by statutory water companies which were already in the private sector. Most of these have public limited company (PLC) status and many are now in foreign ownership or are part of larger multi-utility companies. They are represented by Water UK, which also represents the ten water service companies responsible for sewerage and sewage disposal in England and Wales, and the state-owned water authorities of Scotland and Northern Ireland. Water UK is the trade association for all the water service companies except Mid Kent Water.

Limited competition exists in the water industry, with large industrial customers being able to negotiate separate supply arrangements. Discussions are underway to determine the feasibility and future extent of competition.

WATER UK, 1 Queen Anne's Gate, London, SW1H 9BT. Tel: 020-7344 1844 Web: www.water.org.uk. *Chief Executive*, Ms P. Taylor

*Water Service Companies*

ANGLIAN WATER SERVICES LTD, Anglian House, Ambury Road, Huntingdon, Cambs PE18 6NZ

DWR CYMRU (WELSH WATER), Pentwyn Road, Nelson, Treharris, Mid Glamorgan CF46 6LY

NORTHUMBRIAN WATER LTD, Abbey Road, Pity Me, Durham DH1 5FJ

SEVERN TRENT WATER LTD, 2297 Coventry Road, Sheldon, Birmingham B26 3PU

## WATER SUPPLY AND CONSUMPTION 1999–2000

| | Supply | | Consumption | | | |
|---|---|---|---|---|---|---|
| | Supply from treatment works (*Ml/day*) | Total leakage (*Ml/day*) | Household (*l/head/day*) Unmetered | Non-household (*l/prop/day*) Metered | Unmetered | Metered |
| WATER SERVICE COMPANIES | | | | | | |
| Anglian | 1,140.3 | 189.9 | 165.8 | 143.4 | 542.3 | 3,282.4 |
| Dwr Cymru (Welsh) | 929.8 | 228.4 | 158.8 | 149.4 | 744.7 | 2,627.1 |
| North West | 1,947.2 | 487.1 | 152.1 | 137.4 | 698.9 | 2,690.2 |
| Northumbrian | 757.6 | 167.8 | 167.0 | 148.7 | 922.4 | 4,935.8 |
| Severn Trent | 1,878.0 | 340.1 | 155.8 | 142.6 | 600.0 | 2,352.9 |
| South West | 431.4 | 83.7 | 175.2 | 127.3 | 859.9 | 1,659.1 |
| Southern | 584.8 | 92.7 | 171.8 | 150.7 | 816.3 | 2,597.6 |
| Thames | 2,553.3 | 661.9 | 189.4 | 164.1 | 976.6 | 3,640.8 |
| Wessex | 376.2 | 88.3 | 161.0 | 137.6 | 2,266.1 | 2,579.4 |
| Yorkshire | 1,283.3 | 316.5 | 154.9 | 138.4 | 147.1 | 2,726.3 |
| Total | 11,881.9 | 2,716.3 | — | — | — | — |
| Average | — | — | 164.8 | 145.5 | 783.0 | 2,844.0 |
| WATER COMPANIES | | | | | | |
| Total | 3,175.9 | 589.9 | — | — | — | — |
| Average | — | — | 177.6 | 151.7 | 852.2 | 2,962.6 |

*Source:* Office of Water Services

SOUTHERN WATER SERVICES LTD, Southern House, Yeoman Road, Worthing, W. Sussex BN13 3NX
SOUTH WEST WATER SERVICES LTD, Peninsula House, Rydon Lane, Exeter EX2 7HR
THAMES WATER UTILITIES LTD, Reading Bridge House, c/o Blake House, Manor Farm Road, Reading RG2 0JN
UNITED UTILITIES WATER LTD (formerly NORTH WEST WATER), Dawson House, Liverpool Road, Great Sankey, Warrington WA5 3LW
WESSEX WATER SERVICES LTD, Claverton Down Road, Claverton Down, Bath BA2 7WW
YORKSHIRE WATER SERVICES LTD, Western House, Western Way, Halifax Road, Bradford BD6 2LZ

### REGULATORY BODIES

The Office of Water Services (Ofwat) was set up under the Water Act 1989 and is the independent economic regulator of the water and sewerage companies in England and Wales. Ofwat's main duty is to ensure that the companies can finance and carry out their statutory functions and to protect the interests of water customers. Ofwat is a non-ministerial government department headed by the Director-General of Water Services, who is appointed by the Secretary of State for Environment, Food and Rural Affairs and the Secretary of State for Wales. Under the Competition Act 1998, from 1 March 2000 the Competition Commission has heard appeals against the regulator's decisions regarding anti-competitive agreements and abuse of a dominant position in the marketplace. The Environment Agency has statutory duties and powers in relation to water resources, pollution control, flood defence, fisheries, recreation, conservation and navigation in England and Wales.

The Drinking Water Inspectorate is responsible for assessing the quality of the drinking water supplied by the water companies, inspecting the companies themselves and investigating any accidents affecting drinking water quality. The Chief Inspector presents an annual report to the Secretary of State for the Environment, Food and Rural Affairs and to the National Assembly for Wales.

### METHODS OF CHARGING

In England and Wales, most domestic customers still pay for domestic water supply and sewerage services through charges based on the old rateable value of their property, although about 20 per cent of householders are now charged according to consumption, which is recorded by meter. Industrial and most commercial customers are charged according to consumption.

Under the Water Industry Act 1999, water companies can continue basing their charges on the old rateable value of property. Domestic customers can continue paying on an unmeasured basis unless they choose to pay according to consumption. After having a meter installed (which is free of charge), a customer can revert to unmeasured charging within 12 months. Domestic, school and hospital customers cannot be disconnected for non-payment.

In November 1999 Ofwat decided to set new price limits for the period 2000-5. The average reduction in prices for the first year, 2000-1, was 12.3 per cent.

## SCOTLAND

Overall responsibility for national water policy in Scotland rested with the Secretary of State for Scotland until July 1999 when it was devolved to the Scottish Ministers.

Until The Local Government etc. (Scotland) Act 1994, water supply and sewerage services were local authority responsibilities. The Central Scotland Water Development Board had the function of developing new sources of water supply for the purpose of providing water in bulk to water authorities whose limits of supply were within the board's area. Under the Act, three new public water authorities, covering the north, east and west of Scotland respectively, took over the provision of water and sewerage services from April 1996. The Central Scotland Water Development Board was then abolished. The new authorities were accountable to the Secretary of State for Scotland, and since July 1999 have been accountable to the Scottish Ministers. The Act also established the Scottish Water and Sewerage Customers Council representing consumer interests. It monitored the performance of the authorities; approved charges schemes; investigated complaints; and advised the Secretary of State. The Water Industry Act 1999, whose Scottish provisions were accepted by the Scottish Executive, abolished the Scottish Water and Sewerage Customers Council and replaced it in November 1999 by a Water Industry Commissioner who promotes the interests of customers. The Commissioner makes long-term recommendations about charging and efficiency to the Scottish Ministers and is advised by three water industry consultative committees (one for each water authority).

The Scottish Environment Protection Agency (SEPA) is responsible for promoting the cleanliness of Scotland's rivers, lochs and coastal waters. SEPA is also responsible for controlling pollution.

### WATER RESOURCES 1999

| | *No.* | *Yield (Ml/day)* |
|---|---|---|
| Reservoirs and lochs | 322 | 3,099 |
| Feeder intakes | 23 | — |
| River intakes | 249 | 452 |
| Bore-holes | 45 | 100 |
| Underground springs | 84 | 27 |
| TOTAL | *723 | 3,678 |

* Including compensation reservoirs

### WATER CONSUMPTION 1999

| | |
|---|---|
| TOTAL (*Ml/day*) | 2,363 |
| Potable | 2,352.3 |
| Unmetered | 1,912.3 |
| Metered | 520.2 |
| Non-potable† | 10.7 |
| TOTAL (*l/head/day*) | 474.4 |
| Unmetered | 383.9 |
| Metered and non-potable† | 106.3 |

† 'Non-potable' supplied for industrial purposes. Metered supplies in general relate to commercial and industrial use and unmetered to domestic use

*Source:* The Scottish Office; *Public Water Supplies in Scotland 1999-2000*

EAST OF SCOTLAND WATER AUTHORITY, 55 Buckstone Terrace, Edinburgh EH10 6XH. Tel: 0131-453 7500. *Chief Executive*, J. Hargreaves
NORTH OF SCOTLAND WATER AUTHORITY, Cairngorm House, Beechwood Business Park, Inverness IV2 3ED. Tel: 01463-245400. *Chief Executive*, K. Bryan
WATER INDUSTRY COMMISSIONER FOR SCOTLAND, Ochil House, Springkerse Business Park, Stirling FK7 7XE. Tel: 01786-430200. *Commissioner*, A. D. A. Sutherland
WEST OF SCOTLAND WATER AUTHORITY, 419 Balmore Road, Glasgow G22 6NU. Tel: 0141-355 5333. *Chief Executive*, C. Cornish

### METHODS OF CHARGING

The water authorities set charges for domestic and non-domestic water and sewerage provision through charges schemes which have to be approved by the Water

Industries Commissioner. The authorities must publish a summary of their charges schemes.

## NORTHERN IRELAND

In Northern Ireland ministerial responsibility for water services lies with The Minister of the Department for Regional Development. The Water Service, which is an executive agency of the Department for Regional Development, is responsible for policy and co-ordination with regard to supply, distribution and cleanliness of water, and the provision and maintenance of sewerage services.

The Water Service is divided into four regions, the Eastern, Northern, Western and Southern Divisions. These are based in Belfast, Ballymena, Londonderry and Craigavon respectively.

### METHODS OF CHARGING

Until last year Water Service was funded mainly through the regional rate (part of which was appropriated in-aid of the Department) and direct charges principally for metered water. However, the regional rate is no longer appropriated-in-aid and following Devolution the Water service is now funded by Parliamentary Vote and direct charges.

All properties, which are not exclusively domestic, are metered. The are, however, granted an allowance of 200 cubic metres per annum to reflect domestic usage - this is known as the domestic usage allowance. Customers are charged only for water used in excess of the domestic usage allowance together with a standing charge, which is intended to cover the costs of meter provision, maintenance, reading and billing. This allowance is not granted if rates are not paid on the property. Traders operating from rated premises are required to pay for the treatment and disposal of trade effluent which they discharge into the public sewer.

# Energy

The main primary sources of energy in Britain are oil, natural gas, coal, nuclear power and water power. The main secondary sources (e.g. sources derived from the primary sources) are electricity, coke and smokeless fuels, and petroleum products. The Department for the Environment, Food and Rural Affairs (DEFRA) is responsible for promoting energy efficiency.

### INDIGENOUS PRODUCTION OF PRIMARY FUELS

*Million tonnes of oil equivalent*

| | 1999 | 2000p |
|---|---|---|
| Coal | 25.2 | 21.9 |
| Petroleum | 150.3 | 138.4 |
| Natural gas | 99.3 | 108.5 |
| Primary electricity | | |
| Nuclear | 22.68 | 20.26 |
| Natural flow hydro | 0.54 | 0.52 |
| Total | 298.0 | 289.6 |

p provisional

### INLAND ENERGY CONSUMPTION BY PRIMARY FUEL

*Million tonnes of oil equivalent, seasonally adjusted*

| | 1999 | 2000p |
|---|---|---|
| Coal | 38.3 | 40.6 |
| Petroleum | 7.4 | 73.1 |
| Natural gas | 92.6 | 96.2 |
| Primary electricity | 24.45 | 22.0 |
| Nuclear | 22.68 | 20.26 |
| Natural flow hydro | 0.54 | 0.52 |
| Net imports | 1.23 | 1.22 |
| Total | 229.9 | 231.9 |

p provisional

### TRADE IN FUELS AND RELATED MATERIALS 2000

| | *Quantity** | *Value†* |
|---|---|---|
| IMPORTS | | |
| Coal and other solid fuel | 16.5 | 696 |
| Crude petroleum | 40.5 | 5,026 |
| Petroleum products | 20.7 | 3,424 |
| Natural gas | 1.2 | 91 |
| Electricity | 1.2 | 373 |
| Total | 78.8 | 9,610 |
| Total (fob)‡ | — | 8,886 |
| EXPORTS | | |
| Coal and other solid fuel | 0.2 | 73 |
| Crude petroleum | 83.4 | 10,287 |
| Petroleum products | 32.4 | 4,842 |
| Natural gas | 6.9 | 507 |
| Electricity | — | 5 |
| Total | 122.9 | 15,714 |
| Total (fob)‡ | — | 15,714 |

* Million tonnes of oil equivalent
† *£ million*
‡ Adjusted to exclude estimated costs of insurance, freight, etc.
Source: *Department of Trade and Industry*

## OIL

Until the 1960s Britain imported almost all its oil supplies. In 1969 oil was discovered in the Arbroath field of the UK Continental Shelf (UKCS). The first oilfield to be brought into production was the Argyll field in 1975, and since the mid-1970s Britain has been a major producer of crude oil.

Licences for exploration and production are granted to companies by the Department of Trade and Industry; the leading British oil companies are British Petroleum (BP) and Shell Transport and Trading. At the end of 1998, 1,021 offshore licences and 150 onshore licences had been awarded, and there were 121 offshore oilfields in production. In 1998 there were 10 oil refineries and four smaller refining units processing crude and process oils. There are estimated to be reserves of 1,800 million tonnes of oil in the UKCS. Royalties are payable on fields approved before April 1982 and petroleum revenue tax is levied on fields approved between 1975 and March 1993.

### DRILLING ACTIVITY 2000

| *Number of wells started* | *Offshore* | *Onshore* |
|---|---|---|
| Exploration and appraisal | 59 | 14 |
| Exploration | 26 | — |
| Appraisal | 33 | — |
| Development | 216 | 11 |

### VALUE OF UKCS OIL AND GAS PRODUCTION AND INVESTMENT

*£ million*

| | 1999 | 2000 |
|---|---|---|
| Total income | 19,427 | 27,009 |
| Operating costs | 4,249 | 4,288 |
| Exploration expenditure | 457 | 377 |
| Gross trading profits* | 13,493 | 21,196 |
| Percentage contribution to GVA | 1.9 | 2.7 |
| Capital investment | 3,116 | 2,848 |
| Percentage contribution to industrial investment | 13 | 12 |

* Net of stock appreciation

### INDIGENOUS PRODUCTION AND REFINERY RECEIPTS

| | 1999 | 2000 |
|---|---|---|
| *Indigenous production (thousand tonnes)* | 137,125 | 126,245 |
| Crude oil | 128,286 | 128,262 |
| NGLs* | 8,839 | 8,363 |
| *Refinery receipts (thousand tonnes)* | | |
| Indigenous | 50,886 | 34,519 |
| Other† | 2,113 | 3,493 |
| Net foreign imports | 36,346 | 45,771 |

* Natural gas liquids: condensates and petroleum gases derived at onshore treatment plants
† Mainly recycled products

Deliveries of Petroleum Products for Inland Consumption by Energy Use

*Thousand tonnes*

| | 1999 | 2000 |
|---|---|---|
| Electricity generators | 1,018 | 798 |
| Gas works | 47 | 40 |
| Iron and steel industry | 485 | 429 |
| Other industries | 5,638 | 5,690 |
| Transport | 48,486 | 49,203 |
| Domestic | 2,874 | 2,279 |
| Other | 3,060 | 2,866 |
| Total | 61,608 | 61,305 |

*Source:* Department of Trade and Industry

## GAS

From the late 18th-century gas in Britain was produced from coal. In the 1960s town gas began to be produced from oil-based feedstocks using imported oil. In 1965 gas was discovered in the North Sea in the West Sole field, which became the first gasfield in production in 1967, and from the late 1960s natural gas began to replace town gas. Britain is now the world's fourth largest producer of gas and in 1998 only 1.5 per cent of gas available for consumption in the UK was imported. From October 1998 Britain was connected to the continental European gas system via a pipeline from Bacton, Norfolk to Zeebrugge, Belgium.

By the end of 1998 there were 80 offshore gasfields producing natural gas and associated gas (mainly methane). There is estimated to be 1,795,000 million cubic metres of recoverable gas reserves. There are about 9,419km of major submarine pipelines for transporting hydrocarbons, and onshore pipelines for carrying refined products and chemicals. Natural gas is transported around Britain by about 273,000km of pipelines supplied by seven coastal terminals. This pipeline system is owned by Transco and licensed gas shippers are allowed access under a network code. New arrangements for trading within the pipeline system were introduced on 1 October 1999. Greater efficiency in balancing supply and demand is expected to achieve savings which will be reflected in lower prices.

The Office of Gas and Electricity Markets is the regulator for the gas industry. It was formed in 1999 by the merger of the Office of Gas Supply and the Office of Electricity Regulation. Under the Competition Act 1998, from 1 March 2000 the Competition Commission has heard appeals against the regulator's decisions regarding anti-competitive agreements and abuse of a dominant position in the marketplace.

The gas industry in Britain was nationalised in 1949 and operated as the Gas Council. The Gas Council was replaced by the British Gas Corporation in 1972 and the industry became more centralised. The British Gas Corporation was privatised in 1986 as British Gas PLC.

In 1993 the Monopolies and Mergers Commission found that British Gas's integrated business in Great Britain as a gas trader and the owner of the gas transportation system could be expected to operate against the public interest. In February 1997, British Gas demerged its trading arm and became two separate companies: BG PLC, which was responsible for the Transco pipeline business in Britain and oil and gas exploration and production in the UK and abroad; and Centrica PLC, which runs the trading and services operations under the British Gas brand name in Great Britain. In October 2000 Transco demerged from BG PLC and became part of Lattice Group PLC.

Competition was gradually introduced into the industrial gas market from 1986. Supply of gas to the domestic market was opened to companies other than British Gas, starting in April 1996 with a pilot project in the West Country and Wales. From spring 1997 competition was progressively introduced throughout the rest of Britain in stages which were completed in May 1998. With the electricity market also open, many suppliers now offer their customers both gas and electricity. Some gas companies have become part of larger multi-utility companies, often operating internationally.

BG PLC, 100 Thames Valley Park Drive, Reading RG6 1PT. Tel: 0118-935 3222. *Chairman*, R. V. Giordano; *Chief Executive*, F. Chapman

Centrica PLC, Charter Court, 50 Windsor Road, Slough, Berks SL1 2HA. Tel: 01753-758000. *Chief Executive*, R. Gardner

Lattice Group PLC, 130 Jermyn Street, London SW14 4UR. Tel: 020 7389 3200. *Chairman*, J. Parker

Natural Gas Production and Supply

*GWh*

| | 1999 | 2000 |
|---|---|---|
| Gross gas production | 1,152,154 | 1,258,549 |
| Exports | 84,433 | 146,342 |
| Imports | 12,862 | 26,032 |
| Gas available | 1,011,157 | 1,062,187 |
| Gas transmitted‡ | 1,011,284 | 1,061,953 |

‡ Figures differ from gas available mainly because of stock changes

Natural Gas Consumption

*GWh*

| | 1999 | 2000 |
|---|---|---|
| Electricity generators | 313,319 | 323,371 |
| Iron and steel industry | 22,664 | 22,383 |
| Other industries | 180,950 | 193,244 |
| Domestic | 356,067 | 373,400 |
| Public administration, commerce and agriculture | 121,560 | 122,277 |
| Total | 994,560 | 1,034,675 |

*Source:* Department of Trade and Industry

## COAL

Coal has been mined in Britain for centuries and the availability of coal was crucial to the industrial revolution of the 18th- and 19th-centuries. Mines were in private ownership until 1947 when they were nationalised and came under the management of the National Coal Board, later the British Coal Corporation. In addition to producing coal at its own deep-mine and opencast sites, of which there were 850 in 1955, British Coal was responsible for licensing private operators.

Under the Coal Industry Act 1994, the Coal Authority was established to take over ownership of coal reserves and to issue licences to private mining companies as part of the privatisation of British Coal. The Coal Authority also deals with the physical legacy of mining, e.g. subsidence damage claims, and is responsible for holding and making available all existing records. The mines were sold as five separate businesses in 1994 and coal production in the UK is now undertaken entirely in the private sector. At the end of 2000 there were 17 large deep mines in operation.

The main UK customer for coal is the electricity supply industry. A review of energy policy was undertaken during 1998 and the Government announced measures in its October 1998 Energy White Paper which included a freeze on new applications to build gas-fired power stations in order to increase opportunities for coal-fired power stations. The moratorium on new gas-fired power stations was lifted in 2000 in the light of two measures to improve the competitiveness of coal fired generation. Firstly the government reached agreement with the European Commission to make available temporary state aid for the coal industry; such aid to end with the termination of the European Coal and Steel Community Treaty in 2002. Secondly there was the reform of the electricity wholesale market and the replacement of The Pool with the New Electricity Trading Arrangement (NETA) which took effect from 27 March 2001.

### Coal Production and Foreign Trade

*Thousand tonnes*

| | 1999 | 2000p |
|---|---|---|
| Total production | 37,077 | 31,972 |
| Deep-mined | 20,888 | 17,611 |
| Opencast | 15,275 | 13,564 |
| Imports | 20,758 | 23,446 |
| Exports | 762 | 660 |

p provisional

### Inland Coal Use

*Thousand tonnes*

| | 1999 | 2000 |
|---|---|---|
| *Fuel producers* | | |
| Collieries | 10 | 12 |
| Electricity generators | 40,471 | 46,052 |
| Coke ovens | 8,558 | 8,697 |
| Other conversion industries | 643 | 540 |
| *Final users* | | |
| Industry | 2,836 | 1,449 |
| Domestic | 2,693 | 1,919 |
| Public administration, commerce and agriculture | 318 | 355 |
| Total | 55,529 | 59,024 |

p provisional
*Source:* Department of Trade and Industry

## ELECTRICITY

The first power station in Britain generating electricity for public supply began operating in 1882. In the 1930s a national transmission grid was developed, and it was reconstructed and extended in the 1950s and 1960s. Power stations were operated by the Central Electricity Generating Board.

Under the Electricity Act 1989, 12 regional electricity companies (RECs), which are responsible for the distribution of electricity from the national grid to consumers, were formed from the former area electricity boards in England and Wales. Four companies were formed from the Central Electricity Generating Board: three generating companies (National Power PLC, Nuclear Electric PLC and PowerGen PLC) and the National Grid Company PLC, which owns and operates the transmission system. National Power and PowerGen were floated on the stock market in 1991. National Power was demerged in October 2000 to form two separate companies: International Power PLC and Innogy PLC, which manages the bulk of National Power's UK assets. Nuclear Electric was split into two parts in 1995; the part comprising the more modern nuclear stations was incorporated into a new company, British Energy, which was floated on the stock market in 1996. Magnox Electric, which owns the magnox nuclear reactors, remained in the public sector and was integrated into British Nuclear Fuels (BNFL) in 1999. Ownership of the National Grid Company was transferred to the RECs and it was subsequently floated in 1995.

Generators and suppliers participate in a competitive wholesale trading market known as NETA (New Electricity Trading Arrangements) which began in March 2001, replacing the Electricity Pool. The introduction of competition into the domestic electricity market was completed in May 1999. With the gas market also open, many suppliers now offer their customers both gas and electricity.

Electricity companies can now also sell gas to their customers. Similarly, gas companies can also offer electricity. Some electricity companies have bought others, and there is a trend towards larger multi-utility companies, often operating internationally.

In Scotland, three new companies were formed under the Electricity Act 1989: Scottish Power PLC and Scottish Hydro-Electric PLC, which are responsible for generation, transmission, distribution and supply; and Scottish Nuclear Ltd. Scottish Power and Scottish Hydro-Electric were floated on the stock market in 1991 (the latter merged with Southern Electric in 1998 to become Scottish and Southern Energy PLC); Scottish Nuclear was incorporated into British Energy in 1995.

In Northern Ireland, Northern Ireland Electricity PLC was set up in 1993 under a 1991 Order in Council. It is responsible for transmission, distribution and supply and has been floated on the stock market. There is no Pool in Northern Ireland; three private companies are responsible for electricity generation and the electricity is sold to Northern Ireland Electricity under a series of power purchase agreements.

The Office of Gas and Electricity Markets is the regulator for the electricity industry. It was formed in 1999 by the merger of the Office of Electricity Regulation and the Office of Gas Supply. Under the Competition Act 1998, the Competition Commission hears appeals against the regulator's decisions regarding anti-competitive agreements and abuse of a dominant position in the marketplace.

The Electricity Association is the electricity industry's main trade association, providing representational and professional services for the electricity companies. EA Technology Ltd provides distribution and utilisation research, development and technology transfer.

### Nuclear Power

Nuclear reactors began to supply electricity to the national grid in 1956. It is generated at six magnox reactors, seven advanced gas-cooled reactors (AGRs) and one pressurised water reactor (PWR), Sizewell 'B' in Suffolk. Nuclear stations now generate about 29 per cent of the UK's electricity.

In preparation for privatisation, the nuclear industry was restructured in December 1995. A holding company, British Energy PLC, was formed with two operational subsidiaries, Nuclear Electric Ltd and Scottish Nuclear Ltd. Nuclear Electric operates the five AGRs and the PWR in England and Wales; Scottish Nuclear operates the two AGRs in Scotland. British Energy was floated on the stock market in 1996. The Magnox reactors were transferred to Magnox Electric PLC, and later to British

Nuclear Fuels Ltd (BNFL). BNFL is in public ownership, providing reprocessing, waste management and effluent treatment services. The UK Atomic Energy Authority is responsible for the decommissioning of nuclear reactors and other nuclear facilities used in research and development. UK Nirex, which is owned by the nuclear generating companies and the Government, is responsible for the disposal of intermediate and some low-level nuclear waste. The Nuclear Installations Inspectorate of the Health and Safety Executive is the nuclear industry's regulator.

ELECTRICITY UTILITIES

BRITISH ENERGY PLC, 10 Lochside Place, Edinburgh EH12 9DF. Tel: 0131-527 2000

BNFL MAGNOX GENERATION PLC, Berkeley Centre, Berkeley, Glos GL13 9PB. Tel: 01453-810451

EAST MIDLANDS ELECTRICITY PLC, PO Box 44, Wollaton, Nottingham NG8 1EZ. Tel: 0115-929 1151

EASTERN ENERGY PLC, PO Box 40, Wherstead Park, Wherstead, Ipswich IP9 2AQ. Tel: 01473-688688

FIRST HYDRO COMPANY, Bala House, Lakeside Business Village, St David's Park, Ewloe CH5 3XJ. Tel: 01244-520234

GENERAL PUBLIC UTILITIES, Whittington Hall, Whittington WR5 2RB. Tel: 0845-735 3637.

GUERNSEY ELECTRICITY, PO Box 4, Electricity House, North Side, Vale, Guernsey GY1 3AD. Tel: 01481-46931

HYDER PLC, Newport Road, St Mellons, Cardiff CF3 9XW. Tel: 029-2079 2111

INNOGY PLC (formerly NATIONAL POWER), Windmill Hill Business Park, Whitehill Way, Swindon, Wilts SN5 9FH. Tel: 01793-877777

JERSEY ELECTRICITY, PO Box 45, Queens Road, St Helier, Jersey JE4 8NY. Tel: 01534-505000

LONDON ELECTRICITY PLC, Templar House, 81–87 High Holborn, London WC1V 6NU. Tel: 020-7242 9050

MANWEB PLC, Manweb House, Kingsfield Court, Chester Business Park, Chester CH4 9RF. Tel: 0845-272 3636

MANX ELECTRICITY AUTHORITY, PO Box 177, Douglas, Isle of Man IM99 1PS. Tel: 01624-687687

NATIONAL GRID COMPANY PLC, National Grid House, Kirby Corner Road, Coventry CV4 8JY. Tel: 024-7642 3000

NIGEN Ltd., AES Kilroot Power Station, Larne Road, Carrickfergus, Co. Antrim BT38 7LX. Tel: 028-9335 1644

NORTHERN ELECTRIC PLC, Carliol House, Market Street, Newcastle upon Tyne NE1 6NE. Tel: 0191-210 2000

NORTHERN IRELAND ELECTRICITY PLC, 120 Malone Road, Belfast BT9 5HT. Tel: 028-9066 1100

NORWEB ENERGI PLC, Oakland House, Talbot Road, Old Trafford, Manchester M16 0HQ. Tel: 0161-873 8000

POWERGEN PLC, Westwood Way, Westwood Business Park, Coventry CV4 8LG. Tel: 024-7642 4000

PREMIER POWER LTD, Ballylumford, Islandmagee, Larne, Co. Antrim BT40 3RS. Tel: 028-9335 1644

SCOTTISH AND SOUTHERN ENERGY PLC, 10 Dunkeld Road, Perth PH1 5WA. Tel: 01738-452100

SCOTTISHPOWER PLC, 1 Atlantic Quay, Glasgow G2 8SP. Tel: 0141-248 8200

SEEBOARD PLC, Forest Gate, Brighton Road, Crawley, W. Sussex RH11 9BH. Tel: 01293-565888

SWEB PLC, 300 Park Avenue, Aztec West, Almondsbury, Bristol BS32 4SE. Tel: 01454-201101

YORKSHIRE ELECTRICITY GROUP PLC, Wetherby Road, Scarcroft, Leeds LS15 3HS. Tel: 0113-289 2123

ELECTRICITY ASSOCIATION LTD, 30 Millbank, London SW1P 4RD. Tel: 020-7963 5700

EA TECHNOLOGY LTD, Capenhurst, Chester CH1 6ES. Tel: 0151-339 4181

ELECTRICITY GENERATION, SUPPLY AND CONSUMPTION

*GWh*

| | 1998 | 1999 |
|---|---|---|
| *Electricity generated: total* | 362,014 | 366,798 |
| Major power producers: total | 335,145 | 337,142 |
| Conventional steam stations | 134,317 | 118,453 |
| Nuclear stations | 100,140 | 96,281 |
| Gas turbines and oil engines | 229 | 196 |
| Combined cycle gas turbine stations | 93,832 | 114,242 |
| Hydro-electric stations: | | |
| Natural flow | 4,357 | 4,422 |
| Pumped storage | 1,624 | 2,902 |
| Renewables other than hydro | 646 | 646 |
| Other generators | 26,870 | 29,656 |
| *Electricity used on works: total* | 17,686 | 17,456 |
| Major generating companies | 16,471 | 16,182 |
| Other generators | 1,215 | 1,215 |
| *Electricity supplied (gross): total* | 344,328 | 349,342 |
| Major power producers: total | 318,674 | 320,960 |
| Conventional steam stations | 127,581 | 112,552 |
| Nuclear stations | 91,186 | 87,672 |
| Gas turbines and oil engines | 210 | 186 |
| Combined cycle gas turbine stations | 93,005 | 112,763 |
| Hydro-electric stations: | | |
| Natural flow | 4,344 | 4,409 |
| Pumped storage | 1,569 | 2,804 |
| Renewables other than hydro | 572 | 574 |
| Other generators | 25,655 | 28,302 |
| *Electricity used in pumping* | | |
| Major power producers | 2,594 | 3,774 |
| *Electricity supplied (net): total* | 341,734 | 345,568 |
| Major power producers | 316,080 | 317,186 |
| Other generators | 25,655 | 28,382 |
| Net imports | 12,468 | 14,244 |
| Electricity available | 354,202 | 359,812 |
| Losses in transmission, etc. | 29,161 | 29,842 |
| *Electricity consumption: total* | 325,040 | 329,940 |
| Fuel industries | 8,130 | 8,315 |
| Final users: total | 316,910 | 321,625 |
| Industrial sector | 106,810 | 109,710 |
| Domestic sector | 109,610 | 110,408 |
| Other sectors | 100,490 | 101,430 |

*Source:* The Stationery Office – Annual Abstract of Statistics 2001

## RENEWABLE SOURCES

Renewable sources of energy principally include biofuels, hydro, wind and solar. Renewable sources accounted for 3.0 million tonnes of oil equivalent of primary energy use in 2000; of this, about 2.2 million tonnes was used to generate electricity and about 0.8 million tonnes to generate heat.

The Non-Fossil Fuel Obligation (NFFO) Renewables Orders have, to date, been the Government's principal mechanism for developing renewable energy sources. NFFO Renewables Orders require the regional electricity companies to buy specified amounts of electricity from specified non-fossil fuel sources. The technologies covered by NFFO Orders have included landfill gas, municipal and industrial waste, small-scale hydro, onshore wind and energy crops. The fifth NFFO Renewables Order was made in September 1998. In Scotland a similar system of Scottish Renewables Orders exists. The third Order was made in February 1999 and covers wave energy, the first time that this technology has been supported by a Renewables Order.

Since February 2000 the United Kingdom's renewables policy has consisted of four key strands:

- a new obligation for all electricity suppliers to supply a specific proportion of electricity from renewables
- the exemption of renewable electricity sources from the Climate Change Levy
- an expanded support programme for new and renewble energy, including capital grants and an expanded research and development programme
- development of a regional strategic approach to planning and targets for renewables

The Government intends to achieve 10 per cent of the UK's electricity needs from renewables by 2010.

RENEWABLE ENERGY SOURCES 2000

| | *Percentages* |
|---|---|
| Biofuels | 82.3 |
| Landfill gas | 24.4 |
| Sewage gas | 5.4 |
| Wood combustion | 16.8 |
| Straw combustion | 2.4 |
| Refuse combustion | 21.2 |
| Other biofuels | 12.1 |
| Hydro | 14.6 |
| Large-scale | 14.02 |
| Small-scale | 0.6 |
| Wind | 2.7 |
| Active solar heating | 0.4 |
| Total | 100 |

*Source:* Department of Trade and Industry

# Transport

## CIVIL AVIATION

Since the privatisation of British Airways in 1987, UK airlines have been operated entirely by the private sector. In 2000, total capacity on British airlines amounted to 43 billion tonne-km, of which 33 billion tonne-km was on scheduled services. British airlines carried 103.7 million passengers, 70.3 million on scheduled services and 33.4 million on charter flights.

Leading British airlines include British Airways, Britannia Airways, British Midland, Air 2000, Airtours, JMC and Virgin Atlantic.

There are 142 licensed civil aerodromes in Britain, with Heathrow and Gatwick handling the highest volume of passengers. BAA PLC owns and operates the seven major airports: Heathrow, Gatwick, Stansted, Southampton, Glasgow, Edinburgh and Aberdeen, which between them handle about 70 per cent of air passengers and 81 per cent of air cargo traffic in Britain. Many other airports, including Manchester, are controlled by local authorities or private companies.

The Civil Aviation Authority (CAA), an independent statutory body, is responsible for the economic regulation of UK airlines and for the safety regulation of the UK civil aviation industry.

The CAA is responsible for ensuring that UK airlines meet stringent safety standards. It is also responsible for the economic regulation of the larger airports.

All commercial airline companies must be granted an Air Operator's Certificate, which is issued by the CAA to operators meeting the required safety standards. The CAA also issues airport safety licences, which must be obtained by any airport used for public transport and training flights. All British-registered aircraft must be granted an airworthiness certificate, and the CAA also issues professional licences to pilots, flight crew, ground engineers and air traffic controllers.

The Transport Act, passed by parliament on 29 November 2000, separated the CAA from its subsidiary, National Air Traffic Services (NATS), which plans and provides air traffic control services throughout the United Kingdom and over the North Atlantic - more than a million square miles - and at most of Britain's major airports. In March 2001, the Airline Group, comprising 7 of Britain's major airlines, was selected by the government as its strategic partner for NATS. The Airline Group plans to invest 1 billion of private capital in NATS over 10 years. Under the terms of a Public Private Partnership 46 per cent of shares in NATS were sold to The Airline Group, 5 per cent to staff and 49 per cent were retained by the government.

### AIR PASSENGERS 2000*

| | |
|---|---|
| ALL UK AIRPORTS: TOTAL | 181,178,687 |
| LONDON AREA AIRPORTS: TOTAL | 116,528,429 |
| Battersea Heliport | 6,452 |
| Gatwick (BAA) | 32,068,540 |
| Heathrow (BAA) | 64,620,286 |
| London City | 1,583,843 |
| Luton | 6,190,499 |
| Southend | 3,568 |
| Stansted (BAA) | 11,879,693 |
| OTHER UK AIRPORTS: TOTAL | 64,805,826 |
| Aberdeen (BAA) | 2,488,597 |
| Barra | 7,796 |
| Barrow-in-Furness | 77 |
| Belfast City | 1,290,566 |
| Belfast International | 3,148,577 |
| Benbecula (HIAL) | 35,805 |
| Biggin Hill | 6,168 |
| Birmingham | 7,596,893 |
| Blackpool | 108,806 |
| Bournemouth | 275,198 |
| Bristol | 2,142,626 |
| Cambridge | 20,094 |
| Campbeltown (HIAL) | 8,369 |
| Cardiff | 1,519,920 |
| Carlisle | 456 |
| Coventry | 3,993 |
| Dundee | 49,682 |
| East Midlands | 2,234,494 |
| Edinburgh (BAA) | 5,523,559 |
| Exeter | 328,450 |
| Glasgow (BAA) | 6,965,500 |
| Gloucestershire | 2,038 |
| Hawarden | 2,490 |
| Humberside | 447,738 |
| Inverness (HIAL) | 360,698 |
| Islay (HIAL) | 20,813 |
| Isle of Man | 728,846 |
| Kent International | 7,594 |
| Kirkwall (HIAL) | 94,093 |
| Leeds/Bradford | 1,585,039 |
| Lerwick (Tingwall) | 4,650 |
| Liverpool | 1,982,714 |
| Londonderry | 162,704 |
| Lydd | 1,522 |
| Manchester | 18,568,709 |
| Newcastle upon Tyne | 3,208,734 |
| Norwich | 367,457 |
| Penzance Heliport | 126,409 |
| Plymouth | 151,874 |
| Prestwick | 910,023 |
| St Mary's, Isles of Scilly | 128,269 |
| Scatsta | 240,489 |
| Sheffield City | 60,636 |
| Shoreham | 1,379 |
| Southampton (BAA) | 856,957 |
| Stornoway (HIAL) | 90,490 |
| Sumburgh (HIAL) | 129,918 |
| Teesside | 751,839 |
| Tiree (HIAL) | 5,011 |
| Tresco, Isles of Scilly (H) | 39,789 |
| Unst | 1,429 |
| Wick (HIAL) | 29,832 |
| CHANNEL IS. AIRPORTS: TOTAL | 2,681,695 |
| Alderney | 75,199 |
| Guernsey | 931,894 |
| Jersey | 1,674,602 |

*Total terminal, transit, scheduled and charter passengers

*Source:* Civil Aviation Authority

## RAILWAYS

Britain pioneered railways and a railway network was developed across Britain by private companies in the course of the 19th century. In 1948 the main railway companies were nationalised and were run by a public authority, the British Transport Commission. The Commission was replaced by the British Railways Board in 1963, operating as British Rail. On 1 April 1994, responsibility for managing the railway infrastructure passed to a newly-formed company, Railtrack; the British Railways Board continued as operator of all train services until they were sold or franchised to the private sector. All passenger activities have now been franchised and all British Rail's freight, technical support and specialist function businesses have been sold. The Board still has certain functions, including overall responsibility for the British Transport Police.

### PRIVATISATION

Since 1 April 1994, ownership of operational track and land has been vested in Railtrack, which was floated on the Stock Exchange in 1996. Railtrack manages the track and charges for access to it and is responsible for signalling and timetables. It does not operate train services. It owns the stations, and leases most of them out to the train operating companies. Infrastructure support functions are now provided by private sector companies. Railtrack invests in infrastructure principally using finance raised by track charges, and takes investment decisions in consultation with rail operators. Railtrack is also responsible for overall safety on the railways.

### OTHER RAIL SYSTEMS

The government announced plans for a public-private partnership for London Underground on 20 March 1998. London underground will remain responsible for all aspects of operations and safety, in the public sector. Three long-term contracts for maintainance and renewal of infrastructure will be awarded to private sector companies. There are two groupings of 'deep tube' lines and one group for the sub-surface lines. London Underground announced preferred bidders for the two deep tube contracts on 2 May 2001. A preferred bidder for the sub-surface lines is expected to be announced in summer 2001. In 2000-1 there were 972 million passenger journeys on the London Underground, up 5 per cent on the previous year.

Light rail and metro systems in Great Britain contributed to the growth in public transport, with 109 million passenger journeys in 1999-2000, up 9 per cent on the previous year. The Government's 10-year Transport Plan announced up to 25 new rapid transit lines and set a target to double light rail use in England over the next decade.

### RAIL REGULATOR

The independent Rail Regulator is responsible for the licensing of new railway operators, approving access agreements, promoting the use and development of the network, preventing anti-competitive practices (in conjunction with the Director-General of The Office of Fair Trading) and protecting the interests of rail users.

Regulations, which took effect on 28 June 1998, established licensing and access arrangements for certain international train services in Great Britain. These are overseen by the International Rail Regulator.

The White Paper *New Deal for Transport*, published in July 1998, announced plans to establish a Strategic Rail Authority (SRA) to manage passenger railway franchising, take responsibility for increasing the use of the railways for freight transport, and lead strategic planning of passenger and freight rail services. The SRA began work in shadow form in July 1999, using the existing powers of the Franchising Director and British Rail, and became a fully operational authority in February 2001 when its shadow status was dropped.

### SERVICES

For privatisation, domestic passenger services were divided into 25 train-operating units, which have been franchised to private sector operators via a competitive tendering process overseen by the Strategic Rail Authority (SRA). The franchise agreements were for between five and 15 years. The Government continues to subsidise loss-making but socially necessary rail services. The SRA is responsible for monitoring the performance of the franchisees, allocating and administering government subsidy payments, proposing closures to the Rail Regulator and designating experimental services.

There are currently 25 train operating companies (TOCs): Anglia Railways; Arriva Trains Merseyside; Arriva Trains Northern; C2C; Cardiff Railway; Central Trains; Chiltern Railways; Connex South Eastern; Gatwick Express; GO-Via; Great Eastern Railway; Great North Eastern Railway; Great Western Trains; Island Line (Isle of Wight); Midland Mainline; North Western Trains; Scotrail Railways; Silverlink Train Services (North London); South West Trains; Thameslink Rail; Thames Trains; Virgin Crosscountry; Virgin West Coast; Wales and West Passenger Trains; and West Anglia Great Northern Railway (WAGN).

In addition to these 25 franchised TOCs, Eurostar and Eurotunnel provide services through the channel tunnel, but are not subject to the franchise process. The first phase of the Channel Tunnel high speed link through Kent is due open in 2003. The Heathrow Express service is a subsidiary of the airports group BAA and is also exempt from the franchise process.

The SRA is currently replacing the short term franchises that are due to expire on or before 2004 with the aim of completing the process by the end of 2001. New, long term franchises lasting 15-20 years will take their place.

Railtrack publishes a national timetable which contains details of rail services operated over the Railtrack network, coastal shipping information and connections with Ireland, the Isle of Man, the Isle of Wight, the Channel Islands and some European destinations.

The national rail enquiries service offers information about train times and fares for any part of the country:

National Rail Enquiries 08457-484950;
Web: www.nationalrail.co.uk
Transport for London 020-7941 4500
Eurostar 0345-303030;
Web: www.eurostar.com

Rail Users' Consultative Committees monitor the policies and performance of train and station operators in their area (there are nine, covering Britain). They are statutory bodies and have a legal right to make recommendations for changes. The London Regional Passengers Committee represents users of buses, the Underground and the Docklands Light Railway as well as the users of rail services in the London area. In summer 2000 the Greater London Assembly and Mayor established Transport for London with a view to developing a strategy for transport in the capital.

British Rail's passenger rolling stock was divided between three subsidiary companies, which were privatised in 1996. The companies lease rolling stock to passenger service operators. On privatisation, British Rail's bulk freight haulage companies and Rail Express Systems, which carries Royal Mail traffic, were sold to English, Welsh and Scottish Railways, which also purchased Railfreight Distribution (international freight) in 1997. In 1999–2000 102.9 million tonnes of freight was transported by an average of 1,600 trains a day.

RAILTRACK, Railtrack House, Euston Square, London NW1 2EE. Tel: 020-7557 8000.
Web: www.railtrack.co.uk *Chairman*, J. Robinson. *Chief Executive*, S. Marshall

ASSOCIATION OF TRAIN OPERATING COMPANIES, 40 Bernard Street, London WC1N 1BY. Tel: 020-7904 3010.
*Chairman*, R. Brown

OFFICE OF THE RAIL REGULATOR (ORR) 1 Waterhouse Square, 138–142 Holborn, London EC1N 2TQ. Tel: 020-7282 2000. Web: www.rail-reg.gov.uk
*Rail Regulator*, T. Winsor

STRATEGIC RAIL AUTHORITY, 55 Victoria Street, London, SW1H 0EU. Tel: 020-7654 6000 Web: www.sra.gov.uk
*Chairman*, Sir Alastair Morton

### RAILTRACK

At 31 March 2001, Railtrack had about 20,000 miles of standard gauge lines and sidings in use, representing 10,343 miles of route of which 3,208 miles were electrified. Standard rail on main line has a weight of 110 lb per yard. Railtrack owns 2,495 stations, 90 light maintenance depots, about 40,000 bridges, viaducts and tunnels, and over 9,000 level crossings.

Passenger journeys made in 1999–2000 totalled 947 million, including 404 million made by holders of season tickets. This national total was the largest since the early 1960s. Passenger kilometres in the year totalled 38.3 billion, earning a total revenue of £3,368 million.

In 1999–2000 Railtrack showed an operating profit of £471 million and a pre-tax profit of £428 million. In 1999-2000 Railtrack employed over 10,000 people.

### RAIL SAFETY

The Railways (Safety Case) Regulations 1994 require infrastructure controllers (e.g. Railtrack, London Underground) to have systems in place to manage safety on the railway networks for which they are responsible.

Each infrastructure controller is required to present a Railway Safety Case (RSC) to the Railway Inspectorate (part of the Health and Safety Executive). The RSC must be accepted by the Inspectorate, and is subject to regular compliance audits.

The infrastructure controllers require companies wishing to operate services to present an RSC. The RSC must be accepted by the infrastructure controller before a train or station operator can receive a licence and begin to provide services. If any revision is required, the RSC must be re-presented. RSCs must be thoroughly reviewed at least every three years. The Inspectorate may examine the RSC of train and service operators as part of its general inspection activities.

Following consultation the Railways (Safety Case) Regulations were amended to transfer the responsibility for acceptance of RSCs of train and station operators from the infrastructure controllers to the Health and Safety Executive. The new regulations and guidance came into force on 31 December 2000.

### ACCIDENTS ON RAILWAYS

| | 1998-9 | 1999-2000 |
|---|---|---|
| *Train accidents: total* | 1,835 | 1,895 |
| Persons killed: total | 3 | 33 |
| Passengers | 0 | 29 |
| Railway staff | 0 | 2 |
| Others | 3 | 2 |
| Persons injured: total | 84 | 332 |
| Passengers | 40 | 290 |
| Railway staff | 31 | 23 |
| Others | 13 | 19 |
| *Other accidents through movement of railway vehicles* | | |
| Persons killed | 27 | 27 |
| Persons injured | 962 | 906 |
| *Other accidents on railway premises* | | |
| Persons killed | 7 | 5 |
| Passengers | 3 | 4 |
| Railway staff | 3 | 1 |
| Others | 1 | 0 |
| Persons injured | 4,172 | 3,992 |
| *Trespassers and suicides* | | |
| Persons killed | 249 | 274 |
| Persons injured | 149 | 144 |

## THE CHANNEL TUNNEL

The earliest recorded scheme for a submarine transport connection between Britain and France was in 1802. Tunnelling has begun simultaneously on both sides of the Channel three times: in 1881, in the early 1970s, and on 1 December 1987, when construction workers began to bore the first of the three tunnels which form the Channel Tunnel. They 'holed through' the first tunnel (the service tunnel) on 1 December 1990 and tunnelling was completed in June 1991. The tunnel was officially inaugurated by The Queen and President Mitterrand of France on 6 May 1994.

The submarine link comprises three tunnels. There are two rail tunnels, each carrying trains in one direction, which measure 24.93 ft (7.6 m) in diameter. Between them lies a smaller service tunnel, measuring 15.75 ft (4.8 m) in diameter. The service tunnel is linked to the rail tunnels by 130 cross-passages for maintenance and safety purposes. The tunnels are 31 miles (50 km) long, 24 miles (38 km) of which is under the sea-bed at an average depth of 132 ft (40 m). The rail terminals are situated at Folkestone and Calais, and the tunnels go underground at Shakespeare Cliff, Dover, and Sangatte, west of Calais.

Eurostar is the high speed passenger train connecting London with Paris in three hours and Brussels in two hours 40 minutes, via the Channel Tunnel. There are up to 24 trains each way per day on the Paris route and ten each way per day on the Brussels route. Some trains stop en route at Ashford (Kent), Calais and Lille. Connecting services from Edinburgh and Manchester via London began in 1997. Vehicle shuttle services operate between Folkestone and Calais.

### RAIL LINKS

The route for the British Channel Tunnel Rail Link will run from Folkestone to a new terminal at St Pancras station, London, with new intermediate stations at Ebbsfleet, Kent, and Stratford, east London; at present services run into a terminal at Waterloo station, London.

Construction of the rail link is being financed by the private sector with a substantial government contribution. A private sector consortium, London and Continental Railways Ltd (LCR), is responsible for the design, construction and ownership of the rail link, and comprises Union Railways and the UK operator of Eurostar. Construction was expected to be completed in 2003, but on 28 January 1998 LCR informed the Government that it was unable to fulfil its obligations. On 3 June 1998 the Government announced a new funding agreement with LCR. The rail link will be constructed in two phases: phase one, from the Channel Tunnel to Fawkham Junction (where an existing connection allows trains to continue to Waterloo), began in October 1998 and will be completed in 2003; phase two, from Fawkham Junction to St Pancras, will be built between 2001 and 2007. Railtrack will buy phase one when it is completed and has an option to buy phase two by 2003.

Infrastructure developments in France have been completed and high-speed trains run from Calais to Paris, linking the Channel Tunnel with the high-speed European network.

## ROADS

### HIGHWAY AUTHORITIES

The powers and responsibilities of highway authorities in England and Wales are set out in the Highways Acts 1980; for Scotland there is separate legislation.

Responsibility for trunk road motorways and other trunk roads in Great Britain rests in England with the Secretary of State for Transport, Local Government and the Regions, in Scotland with the Scottish Parliament, and in Wales with the National Assembly for Wales. The costs of construction, improvement and maintenance are paid for by central government. The White Paper *New Deal for Transport*, published in July 1998, restated and revised the Highways Agency's responsibility for operating, maintaining and improving the trunk road network.

The highway authority for non-trunk roads in England, Wales and Scotland is, in general, the unitary authority, county council or London borough council in whose area the roads lie.

In Northern Ireland the Department of Regional Development is the statutory road authority responsible for public roads and their maintenance and construction; the Roads Service executive agency carries out these functions on behalf of the Department.

### FINANCE

The Government contributes towards capital expenditure through grants and credit approvals in England and Transport Grant (TG) in Wales. Grant rates are determined by the Secretary of State for Transport, Local Government and the Regions in England, the Scottish Ministers and the National Assembly for Wales in each country respectively. Grant is paid at 50 per cent of expenditure accepted for grant in England and Wales.

In England Transport Supplementary Grant (TSG) is paid towards capital spending on highways and the regulation of traffic; other capital spending is financed by credit approvals and specific grants. Current expenditure is funded by revenue support grant (i.e. central government grants to local authorities for non-specific services). From 2000 all bridge assessment and strengthening, and structural maintenance of principal road carriageways has been funded entirely through credit approvals. In Wales TG is paid towards capital expenditure only; current expenditure is funded by revenue support grant.

For the financial year 2000–1 local authorities in England received £22 million in TSG and £720 million in credit approvals. Total estimated expenditure on building and maintaining motorways and trunk roads in England in 1999–2000 was £1,389 million; estimated outturn for 2000–1 was £1,430 million.

In Wales total expenditure on trunk roads, motorways, and transport services in 2000–01 was £117.9 million and estimated expenditure in 2001–02 is £131.2 million.

Until 1999, the Scottish Office received a block vote from Parliament, and the Secretary of State for Scotland determined how much was spent on roads. Since 1 July 1999 all decisions on transport expenditure have been devolved to the Scottish Ministers. Total expenditure on building and maintaining trunk roads in Scotland was estimated at £17 million in 1998–9.

In Northern Ireland estimated expenditure on roads for 2000-1 was £176.0 million and £190.5 million has been allocated for expenditure in 2001–2.

The Government is considering the possibility of introducing tolls on certain roads. The Transport Bill currently before Parliament contains proposals to enable local authorities to levy charges for driving cars in congested areas or for workplace charging. In 2000–1, £18 million was allocated to a number of pilot authorities to develop charging schemes.

### PRIVATE FINANCE

Private finance is being increasingly used to help finance road schemes. The current targeted programme of road improvements contains two design, build, finance and operate road contracts with a capital value of £360 million which will deliver five of the road schemes in the Government's targeted programme of improvements.

### TARGETED PROGRAMME OF IMPROVEMENTS (TPI)

The 1998 Roads Review increased the emphasis given to making better use of the existing road network and improving road maintenance. It resulted in a carefully targeted £1,400 million programme of 37 trunk road improvements to be started by 2005. In February 2000, the Government announced the acceleration of the TPI with the result that 13 rather than seven schemes were started in 2000-1. A series of studies are also underway looking at traffic problems not addressed by the TPI. Road schemes that emerge from these studies will be progressed through the regional planning guidance (RPG) system. This is now the method by which truck road schemes will enter the TPI. Four additional schemes with a value of £100 million were added to the TPI in March 2000.

### ROAD LENGTHS
(in miles) *2000*

| | *Total roads* | *Trunk roads (including Motorways)* | *Motorways** |
|---|---|---|---|
| England | 230,958 | 6,290 | 1,705 |
| Wales | 20,917 | 1,062 | 82 |
| Scotland | 33,115 | 2,154 | 229 |
| N. Ireland | 15,374 | 765† | 83 |

*There were in addition 26.1 miles of local authority motorway in England

† Including motorways and slip roads

### Motorways

England and Wales:

M1 London to Yorkshire
M2 London to Faversham
M3 London to Southampton
M4 London to South Wales
M5 Birmingham to Exeter
M6 Catthorpe to Carlisle
M10 St Albans spur
M11 London to Cambridge
M18 Rotherham to Goole
M20 London to Folkestone
M23 London to Gatwick
M25 London orbital
M26 M20 to M25 spur
M27 Southampton bypass
M32 M4 to Bristol spur
M40 London to Birmingham
M41 London to West Cross
M42 South-west of Birmingham to Measham
M45 Dunchurch spur
M50 Ross spur
M53 Chester to Birkenhead
M54 M6 to Telford
M55 Preston to Blackpool
M56 Manchester to Chester
M57 Liverpool outer ring
M58 Liverpool to Wigan
M60 Manchester ring road
M61 Manchester to Preston
M62 Liverpool to Hull
M65 Calder Valley
M67 Manchester Hyde to Denton
M69 Coventry to Leicester
M180 South Humberside

Scotland:

M8 Edinburgh-Newhouse, Baillieston-West Ferry Interchange
M9 Edinburgh to Dunblane
M73 Maryville to Mollinsburn
M74 Glasgow-Gretna,
M77 Ayr Road Route
M80 Stirling to Haggs/Glasgow (M8) to Stepps
M90 Inverkeithing to Perth
M876 Dennyloanhead (M80) to Kincardine Bridge

Northern Ireland:

M1 Belfast to Dungannon
M2 Belfast to Antrim
M2 Ballymena bypass
M3 Belfast Cross Harbour Bridge
M5 M2 to Greencastle
M12 M1 to Craigavon
M22 Antrim to Randalstown

## ROAD USE

### Estimated Traffic on all Roads (Great Britain) 1999

*Million vehicle kilometres*

| | |
|---|---|
| All motor vehicles | 467,100 |
| Cars and taxis | 380,300 |
| Two-wheeled motor vehicles | 4,000 |
| Buses and coaches | 5,000 |
| Light vans | 44,400 |
| Other goods vehicles | 32,800 |
| Total goods vehicles | 77,200 |
| Pedal cycles | 4,200 |

### Road Goods Transport (Great Britain) 1999

*Analysis by mode of working and by gross weight of vehicle*

| | |
|---|---|
| *Estimated tonne kilometres (thousand million)* | 149.2 |
| Own account | 38.3 |
| Public haulage | 110.9 |
| *By gross weight of vehicle (billion tonne kilometres)* | |
| Estimated tonnes carried (millions) | 1,567.0 |
| Own account | 576.0 |
| Public haulage | 991.0 |
| *By gross weight of vehicle (million tonnes)* | |
| Not over 25 tonnes | 346.0 |
| Over 25 tonnes | 1,221.0 |

### Road Passenger Services

Until 1988 most road passenger transport services in Great Britain were provided by the public sector; the National Bus Company was the largest bus and coach operator in England and Wales and the Scottish Bus Group the largest operator in Scotland. The privatisation of the National Bus Company was completed in 1988 and that of the Scottish Bus Group in 1991. London Transport's bus operating subsidiaries were privatised by the end of 1994. Almost all bus and coach services in Great Britain are now provided by private sector companies.

Bus services outside London were deregulated in 1986, although local authorities can subsidise the provision of socially necessary services after competitive tendering. In London, Transport for London retains overall responsibility for the running of the bus network.

The largest bus operators in Great Britain are Stagecoach Holdings, FirstGroup (formerly FirstBus) and Arriva (formerly Cowie British Bus), which between them account for over 50 per cent of all bus services (by turnover). There are also 17 municipal bus companies in England and Wales, and thousands of smaller private sector operators. National Express runs a national network of coach routes, operating through a number of contractors.

In Northern Ireland, almost all passenger transport services are provided by Ulsterbus Limited and Citybus Limited, two wholly owned subsidiaries of the Northern Ireland Transport Holding Company. Along with Northern Ireland Railways, Ulsterbus and Citybus operate under the brand name of Translink and are publicly owned. Ulsterbus operates long distance, rural, town and Londonderry City bus services while Citybus provide the bulk of internal bus services in Greater Belfast. There are also 136 small private sector operators.

The transport White Paper and the subsequent 10-year transport plan intend to promote bus use, primarily through agreements between local authorities and bus operators to improve the standard and efficiency of services. The 10-year plan sets targets for bus patronage and reliability of services in England.

There are about 70,000 licensed taxis in Great Britain, of which about 20,000 are in London. There are also around 76,000 licensed private hire vehicles in England and Wales outside London, and an estimated 60,000 in London (where there has been no licensing system). The Greater London Assembly and Mayor control the licensing of taxis and private hire vehicles, through the Public Carriage Office. Licensing of private hire vehicle operators in London is in progress.

### Buses and Coaches (Great Britain) 1999–2000

| | |
|---|---|
| Number of vehicles (31 March 2000) | 80,000 |
| Vehicle kilometres (millions) | 4,016 |
| Local bus passenger journeys (millions) | 4,279 |
| Passenger receipts (£ million) | 4,043 |

### Road Safety

The Government in 1987 set a target of reducing road traffic casualties by a third by the year 2000 compared to the average for 1981–5. Measures to achieve this were successful in reducing the number of deaths on the road by 39 per cent by 1998, and the number of serious casualties by 45 per cent. Over the same period the number of slight casualties increased by 16 per cent, but as road traffic increased by 55 per cent, the number of casualties per 100 km travelled has increased by only 1 per cent. In 1998, fatalities were reduced by 5 per cent from 1997, and all casualties decreased by 1 per cent.

In March 2000, the Government published a new road safety strategy, Tomorrow's Roads - Safer for Everyone which set new casualty reduction targets for 2010. The new targets include a 40 per cent reduction in the overall number of people killed or seriously injured in road accidents, a 50 per cent reduction in the number of children killed or seriously injured and a 10 per cent reduction in the slight casualty rate, all compared with the average for 1994-8.

The previous target was to reduce casualties by a third by 2000 compared to the average for 1981-5. Measures to achieve this were successful in reducing the number of deaths on the road by 39 per cent by 1998 and the number of seriously injured by 45 per cent. Both figures represent a 5 per cent reduction compared to 1997. The total number of casualties rose by 1 per cent taking into account a 16 per cent rise in slight casualties although this is considerably less than the 55 per cent rise in traffic between the average for 1981-9 and 1998.

### Road Accident casualties 2000

| | *Fatal* | *Serious* | *Slight* | *All Severities* |
|---|---|---|---|---|
| England | 2,915 | 32,951 | 249,855 | 285,721 |
| Wales | 169 | 1,652 | 12,266 | 13,918 |
| Scotland | 325 | 3,552 | 16,598 | 20,150 |
| Great Britain | 3,409 | 38,155 | 278,719 | 320,283 |

| | *Killed* | *Injured* |
|---|---|---|
| 1965 | 7,952 | 389,985 |
| 1970 | 7,499 | 355,869 |
| 1975 | 6,366 | 318,584 |
| 1980 | 6,010 | 323,000 |
| 1985 | 5,165 | 312,359 |
| 1990 | 5,217 | 335,924 |
| 1995 | 3,621 | 306,885 |
| 1996 | 3,598 | 316,704 |
| 1997 | 3,599 | 323,945 |
| 1998 | 3,421 | 321,791 |
| 1999 | 3,429 | 316,887 |

*Source:* Department of Transport, Local Government and the Regions

## DRIVING LICENCES

It is necessary to hold a valid full licence in order to drive unaccompanied on public roads in the UK. Learner drivers must obtain a provisional driving licence before starting to learn to drive and must then pass theory and practical tests to obtain a full driving licence.

There are separate tests for driving motor cycles, cars, passenger-carrying vehicles (PCVs) and large goods vehicles (LGVs). Drivers must hold full car entitlement before they can apply for PCV or LGV entitlements.

The Driver and Vehicle Licensing Agency (DVLA) no longer issues paper licenses, however, those currently in circulation will remain valid until they expire or the details on them change. The photocard driving license was introduced to comply with the second EC directive on driving licenses. This requires a photograph of the driver to be included on all UK licenses issued from July 2001. In March 2000 the DVLA ceased issuing paper licenses and over 10 million photocards have since been issued. Some 39 million people in the UK (21 million male, 18 million female) hold either a valid provisional or full driving license.

To apply for a first photocard driving license, individuals are required to complete the forms *Application for a Driving License* (D1) and *Application for a Photocard Driving License* (D 750). Application forms are available from post offices.

The minimum age for driving motor cars, light goods vehicles up to 3.5 tonnes and motor cycles is 17 (moped, 16). Since June 1997, drivers who collect six or more penalty points within two years of qualifying lose their licence and are required to take another test. A leaflet, *What You Need to Know About Driving Licences* (form D100), is available from post offices.

The DVLA is responsible for issuing driving licences, registering and licensing vehicles, and collecting excise duty in Great Britain. In Northern Ireland the Driver and Vehicle Licensing Agency (Northern Ireland) has similar responsibilities.

### Driving Licence Fees *as at 1 April 2001*

| | |
|---|---|
| First provisional licence | £27.50 |
| Changing a provisional to a full licence after passing a driving test | £12.50 |
| Renewal of licence | £6.00 |
| Renewal of licence including PCV or LGV entitlements | £32.50 |
| Renewal after disqualification | £27.50 |
| Renewal after drinking and driving disqualification | £37.50 |
| Medical renewal | Free |
| Medical renewal (over 70) | Free |
| Duplicate Licence | £17.50 |
| Exchange licence | £17.50 |
| Removing endorsements | £17.50 |
| Replacement (change of name or address) | Free |

### Driving Tests

The Driving Standards Agency is responsible for carrying out driving tests and approving driving instructors in Great Britain. In Northern Ireland the Driver and Vehicle Testing Agency (Northern Ireland) is responsible for testing drivers and vehicles.

In 1999-2000, almost 1.2 million driving tests, nearly 55,500 vocational tests (lorries and buses) and over 96,500 motorcycle tests were conducted in Great Britain. In the same period, 1.1 million theory tests were conducted. In 1998–9, almost 1.2 million car driving tests were conducted in Great Britain of which 45.9 per cent resulted in a pass. In addition over 49,000 lorry tests were undertaken, of which 51.9 per cent were successful. Over 83,000 motorcycle tests were undertaken, of which 67.9 per cent were successful. There were more than 7,600 bus tests, with a pass rate of 47.8 per cent. In the same period, 1.2 million theory tests were conducted. A new, longer driving test was introduced on 4 May 1999.

Since 1 March 1997 driving test candidates have been required to produce photographic confirmation of their identity.

### *Driving Test Fees (weekday rate/evening and Saturday rate) *as at 1 July 2001*

| | |
|---|---|
| For cars | £36.75/£46 |
| †For motor cycles | £45/£55 |
| For lorries, buses | £73.50/£92 |

*Since 1 July 1996 most candidates for car and motor cycle tests have also been required to take a written driving theory test, for which there is a separate fee of £15.50. Theory tests for lorry and bus drivers were introduced on 1 January 1997
†Before riding on public roads, learner motor cyclists and learner moped riders are required to have completed Compulsory Basic Training, provided by DSA-approved training bodies. The Compulsory Basic Training certificate costs £8.00. All exemptions from CBT were removed on 1 January 1997

An extended driving test was introduced in 1992 for those convicted of dangerous driving. The fee is £73.50/£92 (car) or £90/£110 (motorcycle).

## MOTOR VEHICLES

Vehicles must be licensed by the DVLA or the DVLNI before they can be driven on public roads. They must also be approved as roadworthy by the Vehicle Certification Agency. The Vehicle Inspectorate carries out annual testing and inspection of goods vehicles, buses and coaches.

There were approximately 27 million vehicles registered at the DVLA at March 2001: (approximate figures)

| | |
|---|---|
| Private and light goods | 23,900,000 |
| Motor cycles, scooters, mopeds | 800,000 |
| Coaches and buses | 83,500 |
| Large goods vehicles | 450,000 |
| Electric vehicles | 10,200 |
| Others | 1,750,000 |
| TOTAL: | 27,000,000 |

*Source:* DVLA

### VEHICLE LICENCES

Registration and first licensing of vehicles is through local offices of the Driver and Vehicle Licensing Agency in Swansea. Local facilities for relicensing are available at any post office which deals with vehicle licensing. Applicants will need to take their vehicle registration document; if this is not available the applicant must complete form V62 which is held at post offices. Postal applications can be made to the post offices shown on form V100, available at any post office. This form also provides guidance on registering and licensing vehicles.

Details of the present duties chargeable on motor vehicles are available at post offices and Vehicle Registration Offices. The Vehicle Excise and Registration Act 1994 provides *inter alia* that any vehicle kept on a public road but not used on roads is chargeable to excise duty as if it were in use. All non-commercial vehicles constructed before 1 January 1973 are exempt from vehicle excise duty.

### VEHICLE EXCISE DUTY RATES *from 1 July 2001*

REGISTERED BEFORE 1 MARCH 2001

| | Twelve months £ | Six Months £ |
|---|---|---|
| *Motor Cars* | | |
| Light vans, cars, taxis, etc. | | |
| Under 1549cc | 105.00 | 57.75 |
| Over 1549cc | 160.00 | 88.00 |
| *Motor Cycles* | | |
| With or without sidecar, not over 150 cc | 15.00 | — |
| With or without sidecar, 150–250 cc | 40.00 | — |
| **Others** | 65.00 | 35.75 |
| Electric motorcycles (including tricycles) | 15.00 | — |
| *Tricycles (not over 450 kg)* | | |
| Not over 150 cc | 15.00 | — |
| Others | 65.00 | 35.75 |
| *Buses** | | |
| Seating 9–16 persons | 165.00 (160.00) | 90.75 (88.00) |
| Seating 17–35 persons | 220.00 (160.00) | 121.00 (88.00) |
| Seating 36–60 persons | 330.00 (160.00) | 181.00 (88.00) |
| Seating over 60 persons | 500.00 (160.00) | 275.00 (88.00) |

* Figures in parentheses refer to reduced pollution vehicles.

REGISTERED ON OR AFTER 1 MARCH 2001

| Band | $CO^2$ Emissions (g/km) | Diesel Car 12 month rate £ | Diesel Car 6 month rate £ |
|---|---|---|---|
| A | Up to 150 | 110.00 | 60.50 |
| B | 151-165 | 130.00 | 71.50 |
| C | 166-185 | 150.00 | 82.50 |
| D | Over 185 | 160.00 | 88.00 |

| Petrol Car 12 month rate £ | Petrol Car 6 month rate £ | Alternative Fuel Car 12 month rate £ | Alternative Fuel Car 6 month rate £ |
|---|---|---|---|
| 100.00 | 55.00 | 90.00 | 49.50 |
| 120.00 | 66.00 | 110.00 | 60.50 |
| 140.00 | 77.00 | 130.00 | 71.50 |
| 155.00 | 85.25 | 150.00 | 82.50 |

### MOT TESTING

Cars, motor cycles, motor caravans, light goods and dual-purpose vehicles more than three years old must be covered by a current MoT test certificate. However, some vehicles i.e. minibuses may require a certificate at one year old. All certificates must be renewed annually. The MoT testing scheme is administered by the Vehicle Inspectorate on behalf of the Secretary of State for Transport.

A fee is payable to MoT testing stations, which must be authorised to carry out tests. The maximum fees, which are prescribed by regulations, are:

| | | |
|---|---|---|
| For cars and light vans | £34.00 | |
| For solo motor cycles | £13.70 | |
| For motor cycle combinations | £22.70 | |
| For three-wheeled vehicles | £24.60 | |
| Private passenger vehicles and ambulance Including seat-belt installation check | | |
| With 9-12 passenger seats | £36.90 | £40.75* |
| 13-16 passenger seats | £41.70 | £50.60* |
| Over 16 passenger seats | £54.15 | £80.80* |
| For light goods vehicles between 3,000 and 3,500 kg | £35.75 | |

* including seatbelt installation check

### METHOD OF TRAVEL TO WORK, *Great Britain (percentage*)*

| | 1993 | 1997 |
|---|---|---|
| Car, van, minibus, works van | 68 | 71 |
| Bus, coach, private bus | 9 | 8 |
| Train (incl. Underground and light rail) | 5 | 6 |
| Walk | 12 | 11 |
| Other | 5 | 5 |
| All | 100 | 100 |

* All figures are rounded

*Source:* DETR/The Stationery Office – *Focus on Personal Travel 1998* (Crown copyright)

## SHIPPING AND PORTS

Since earliest times sea trade has played a central role in Britain's economy. By the 17th century Britain had built up a substantial merchant fleet and by the early 20th century it dominated the world shipping industry. In recent years the size and tonnage of the UK-registered trading fleet have declined; the UK-flagged merchant fleet now constitutes about 1 per cent of the world fleet. In December 1998 the Government published a document, *British Shipping: Charting a New Course*, which outlined strategies to promote the long-term interests of British shipping.

Freight is carried by liner and bulk services, almost all scheduled liner services being containerised. About 95 per cent by weight of Britain's overseas trade is carried by sea; this amounts to 75 per cent of its total value. Passengers and vehicles are carried by roll-on, roll-off ferries, hovercraft, hydrofoils and high-speed catamarans. There are about 53 million ferry passengers a year, of whom 32 million travel internationally. The leading British operators of passenger services are P&O Stena, Stena Line (which has a Swedish parent company) and P&O European Ferries.

Lloyd's of London provides the most comprehensive shipping intelligence service in the world. *Lloyd's Shipping Index*, published daily, lists some 25,000 ocean-going vessels and gives the latest known report of each.

### PORTS

There are about 70 commercially significant ports in Great Britain, including such ports as London, Dover, Forth, Tees and Hartlepool, Grimsby and Immingham, Sullom Voe, Milford Haven, Southampton, Felixstowe and Liverpool. Belfast is the principal freight port in Northern Ireland.

Broadly speaking, ports are owned and operated by private companies, local authorities or trusts. The largest operator is Associated British Ports (formerly the British Transport Docks Board, privatised in 1981), which owns 23 ports. Total traffic through UK ports in 2000 amounted to 577 million tonnes, an increase of 2 per cent on the previous year's figure of 566 million tonnes.

### MARINE SAFETY

By 1 October 2002 all roll-on, roll-off ferries operating to and from the UK will be required to meet the new international safety standards on stability established by the Stockholm Agreement.

The Maritime and Coastguard Agency (MCA) was established on 1 April 1998 by the merger of the Coastguard Agency and the Marine Safety Agency. It is an executive agency of the Department for Transport, Local Government and the Regions. The Agency's aims are to minimise loss of life amongst seafarers and coastal users, respond to maritime emergencies 24 hours a day, develop, promote and enforce high standards of marine safety and to minimise the risk of pollution of the marine environment from ships and where pollution occurs, minimise the impact on UK interests. Each year HM Coastguard co-ordinate Search and Rescue for around 11,000 incidents saving around 250 lives. Locations hazardous to shipping in coastal waters are marked by lighthouses and other lights and buoys. The lighthouse authorities are the Corporation of Trinity House (for England, Wales and the Channel Islands), the Northern Lighthouse Board (for Scotland and the Isle of Man), and the Commissioners of Irish Lights (for Northern Ireland and the Republic of Ireland). Trinity House maintains 72 lighthouses, 13 major floating aids to navigation and more than 429 buoys; and the Northern Lighthouse Board 84 lighthouses, 116 minor lights and many buoys.

Harbour authorities are responsible for pilotage within their harbour areas; and the Ports Act 1991 provides for the transfer of lights and buoys to harbour authorities where these are used for mainly local navigation.

### UK-REGISTERED TRADING VESSELS OF 500 GROSS TONS AND OVER *as at end 1999*

| *Type of vessel* | *No.* | *Gross tonnage* |
|---|---|---|
| Tankers[1] | 67 | 552,000 |
| Bulk carriers[2] | 3 | 29,000 |
| Specialised carriers[3] | 10 | 54,000 |
| Container (fully cellular)[4] | 32 | 1,151,000 |
| Ro-Ro[5] | 78 | 937,000 |
| Other general cargo[6] | 63 | 85,000 |
| Passenger[7] | 11 | 363,000 |
| TOTAL | 264 | 3,171,000 |

1 Includes oil, gas, chemical and other specialised tankers
2 Includes combination bulk carriers: ore/oil and ore/bulk/oil carriers
3 Includes livestock, car and chemical carriers
4 Fully cellular container ships only.
5 Ro-Ro passenger and cargo vessels
6 Reefer vessels, general cargo/passenger vessels, and single and multi-deck general cargo vessels.
7 Cruise liner and other passenger

*Source:* The Department of Transport, Local Government and the Regions

### PASSENGER MOVEMENT BY SEA 1999

*Arrivals plus departures at UK seaports by place of embarkation or landing**

| | |
|---|---|
| All passenger movements | 31,382,000 |
| Irish Republic | 4,343,000 |
| Belgium | 1,592,000 |
| France† | 22,454,000 |
| Netherlands | 1,939,000 |
| Other EU countries | 843,000 |
| Other European and Mediterranean countries‡ | 211,000 |

* Passengers are included at both departure and arrival if their journeys begin and end at a UK seaport
† Includes hovercraft passengers
‡ Includes North Africa and Middle East Mediterranean countries

*Source:* The The Department of Transport, Local Government and the Regions

# Communications

## Postal Services

On the 26 March 2001 the Post Office became a public limited company and adopted a new name, Consignia plc. Responsibility for running postal services in the UK remains with Consignia. While the company has signalled its eagerness to expand into the global market, domestic services including Royal Mail, Parcelforce and the local branches of the Post Office remain unchanged. An independent postal services regulator, The Postal Services Commission (Postcomm), has been appointed by the Government to oversee Consignia's operation. The Secretary of State for Trade and Industry has powers to suspend Consignia's letter monopoly in certain areas and to issue licences to other bodies to provide an alternative service.

For further details please contact the relevant service provider, i.e Royal Mail or Parcelforce. For a quick reference guide to the price of postal services consult the Royal Mail's postal calculator at www.royalmail.com.

### INLAND POSTAL SERVICES AND REGULATIONS

#### Inland Letter Post Rates*

| *Not over* | *1st class*† | *2nd class*† |
|---|---|---|
| 60 g | 27p | 19p |
| 100 g | 41p | 33p |
| 150 g | 57p | 44p |
| 200 g | 72p | 54p |
| 250 g | 84p | 66p |
| 300 g | 96p | 76p |
| 350 g | £1.09 | 87p |
| 400 g | £1.24 | £1.00 |
| 450 g | £1.41 | £1.14 |
| 500 g | £1.58 | £1.30 |
| 600 g | £1.90 | £1.52 |
| 700 g | £2.39 | £1.74 |
| 750 g | £2.56 | £1.85 (not Admissible over 750 g) |
| 800 g | £2.77 | |
| 900 g | £3.05 | |
| 1,000 g | £3.32 | |
| Each extra 250 g or part thereof | 81p | |

#### UK Parcel Rates

Parcel Force Standard Tariff

| *Not over* | |
|---|---|
| 1 kg | £3.10 |
| 2 kg | £4.30 |
| 4 kg | £6.50 |
| 6 kg | £7.05 |
| 8 kg | £8.05 |
| 10 kg | £8.65 |

*Postcards travel at the same rates as letter post

† First class letters are normally delivered the following day and second class post within three days

#### Overseas Surface Mail Rates

*Letters*

| *Not over* | | *Not over* | |
|---|---|---|---|
| 20 g | 36p | 450 g | £3.14 |
| 60 g | 58p | 500 g | £3.47 |
| 100 g | 83p | 750 g | £5.12 |
| 150 g | £1.16 | 1,000 g | £6.77 |
| 200 g | £1.49 | 1,250 g | £8.42 |
| 250 g | £1.82 | 1,500 g | £10.07 |
| 300 g | £2.15 | 1,750 g | £11.72 |
| 350 g | £2.48 | 2,000 g | £13.77 |
| 400 g | £2.81 | | |

Postcards travel at 20 g letter rate

#### Airmail Letter Rates

*Europe: Letters*

| *Not over* | | *Not over* | |
|---|---|---|---|
| 20 g | 36p | 280 g | £2.30 |
| 40 g | 50p | 300 g | £2.45 |
| 60 g | 65p | 320 g | £2.60 |
| 80 g | 80p | 340 g | £2.75 |
| 100 g | 95p | 360 g | £2.90 |
| 120 g | £1.10 | 380 g | £3.05 |
| 140 g | £1.25 | 400 g | £3.20 |
| 160 g | £1.40 | 420 g | £3.35 |
| 180 g | £1.55 | 440 g | £3.50 |
| 200 g | £1.70 | 460 g | £3.65 |
| 220 g | £1.85 | 480 g | £3.80 |
| 240 g | £2.00 | 500 g | £3.95 |
| 260 g | £2.15 | 1,000 g | £7.70 |
| | | *2,000 g | £15.20 |

* Max. 2 kg

Postcards to Europe travel at 20 g letter rate

*Outside Europe: Letters*

| | *Not over 10 g* | *Not over 20 g* | *Over 20 g* |
|---|---|---|---|
| Zones 1 & 2 | 45p | 65p | Varies |

For airmail letter zones outside Europe, *see* pages 515-7

#### Stamps

Postage stamps are sold in values of 1p, 2p, 4p, 5p, 8p, 10p, 19p, 20p, 27p, 33p, 41p, 45p, 50p, 65p, £1, £2.00, £3.00 and £5.00.

#### Prepaid Stationery

Airletters to all destinations are 40p, with a packet of six costing £2.20. Pictorial aerogrammes are 49p; a packet of six, £2.70. Forces aerogrammes are free to certain destinations.

Special Delivery prepaid envelopes:

| *Not over* | |
|---|---|
| 500 g (C4 and C5 size) | £3.80 |
| 1 kg | £4.95 |

Printed postage stamps cut from envelopes, postcards, newspaper wrappers, etc., may be used as stamps in payment of postage, provided that they are not imperfect or defaced.

#### Restrictions

Advice at to what articles may not be sent through the post is available from Royal Mail (Tel: 08457-950950) for letters and small packets; Parcelforce (Tel: 0800-224466) for parcels; or local post office counter staff.

The exportation of some goods by post is prohibited except under Department of Trade licence. Enquiries should be addressed to the Export Data Branch, Overseas Trade Divisions, Department of Trade and Industry, 1 Victoria Street, London SW1H 0ET Tel: 020-7215 5000.

## SPECIAL DELIVERY SERVICES

### DATAPOST

A guaranteed service for the delivery of documents and packages: (i) Datapost Sameday offers same working day collection and delivery in many areas; (ii) Datapost 10 (for delivery before 10 a.m.) and Datapost 12 (for delivery before noon) offer next working day delivery nationwide and are available only to certain destinations.

### ROYAL MAIL SPECIAL DELIVERY

A guaranteed next working day delivery service by 12.00 p.m. to most UK destinations for first class letters and packets. The fee is £3.50. Compensation of up to £250 can be awarded for an item if next working day delivery is not achieved, provided that items are posted before latest recommended posting times. Details of other compensation levels can be obtained by telephoning 08457-950950.

### SWIFTAIR

An express airmail service. Items are placed on the first available flight to the destination country. Although Swiftair mail receives priority treatment, delivery times are not guaranteed.

## OTHER SERVICES

### CERTIFICATE OF POSTING

Issued free on request at time of posting.

### COMPENSATION (INLAND AND INTERNATIONAL)

Inland: compensation up to a maximum of £27 may be paid where it can be shown that a letter was damaged or lost in the post due to the fault of the Post Office, its employees or agents. The Post Office does not accept responsibility for loss or damage arising from faulty packing.

International: if a certificate of posting is produced, compensation up to a maximum of £27 may be given for loss or damage in the UK to uninsured parcels to or from most overseas countries. No compensation will be paid for any loss or damage due to the action of the Queen's Enemies.

### NEWSPAPER POST

Copies of newspapers registered at the Post Office may be posted only by the publisher or their agents in open-ended wrappers or unsealed envelopes approved by the Post Office, or tied with string removable without cutting. Wrappers and envelopes must be prominently marked 'newspaper post' in the top left-hand corner.

### POSTE RESTANTE

Poste Restante is solely for travellers and is for three months in any one town. A packet may be addressed to any post office, except town sub-offices, and should state 'Poste Restante' or 'to be called for' in the address. Redirection from a Poste Restante is undertaken for up to three months. Letters for an expected ship at a port are kept for two months, otherwise letters are kept for two weeks, or one month if from abroad.

### PRIVATE BOX

Provides an alternative address (e.g. PO Box 123) and mail is held at the local delivery office for collection.

### RECORDED MAIL

Provides a record of posting and delivery of letters and ensures a signature on delivery. This service is recommended for items of little or no monetary value. All packets must be handed to the post office and a certificate of posting issued. Charges: 63p plus postage (inland); £2.60 plus postage (international).

### REDIRECTION

By agent of addressee: mail other than parcels, business reply and freepost items may be reposted free not later than the day after delivery (not counting Sundays and public holidays) if unopened and if original addressee's name is unobscured. Parcels may be redirected free within the same time limits only if the original and substituted address are in the same local parcel delivery area (or the London postal area). Registered packets must be taken to a post office and are re-registered free up to the day after delivery.

By the Post Office: a printed form obtainable from the Post Office must be signed by the person to whom the letters are to be addressed. A fee is payable for each different surname on the application form. Charges: up to 1 calendar month, £6.30 (abroad via airmail, £12.60); up to 3 calendar months, £13.65 (£27.30); up to 12 calendar months, £31.50 (£63.00).

### REGISTERED MAIL (INTERNATIONAL)

All packets must be handed to the post office and a certificate of posting obtained. Charges (plus postage):

| *Compensation up to* | *Registered fee plus postage* |
|---|---|
| £500 | £3.15 |

Compensation in respect of currency or other forms of monetary worth is given only if money is sent by registered letter post. Compensation is only paid for well-packed fragile articles and not for exceptionally fragile or perishable articles.

### SMALL PACKETS POST AND PRINTED PAPERS (INTERNATIONAL)

Permits the transmission of goods up to 2 kg to all countries, in the same mails as printed papers. Packets can be sealed and can contain personal correspondence relating to the contents. Registration is allowed as insurance as long as the item is packed in a way complying with any insurance regulations. A customs declaration is required and the packet must be marked with 'small packet' and a return address. Instructions for the disposal of undelivered packets must be given at the time of posting. An undeliverable packet will be returned to the sender at his/her expense.

*Surface mail: worldwide*

| *Not over* | | *Not over* | |
|---|---|---|---|
| 100 g | 57p | 450 g | £1.90 |
| 150 g | 76p | 500 g | £2.09 |
| 200 g | 95p | 750 g | £3.04 |
| 250 g | £1.14 | 1,000 g | £3.99 |
| 300 g | £1.33 | 1,500 g | £5.89 |
| 350 g | £1.52 | 2,000 g | £7.79 |
| 400 g | £1.71 | | |

UNDELIVERED AND UNPAID MAIL

Undelivered mail is returned to the sender provided the return address is indicated either on the outside of the envelope or inside. If the sender's address is not available items not containing property are destroyed. If the packet contains something of value it is retained for up to three months. Undeliverable second class mail containing newspapers, magazines or commercial advertising is destroyed.

# Airmail and IDD Codes

AIRMAIL ZONES (AZ)

The table includes airmail letter zones for countries outside Europe, and destinations to which European and European Union airmail letter rates apply (*see also* page 513).
(*Source:* Post Office)
1 airmail zone 1
2 airmail zone 2
*e* Europe

INTERNATIONAL DIRECT DIALLING (IDD)

International dialling codes are composed of four elements which are dialled in sequence:
(i) the international code
(ii) the country code (*see* below)
(iii) the area code
(iv) the customer's telephone number

Calls to some countries must be made via the international operator. (*Source:* BT)
*p* A pause in dialling is necessary whilst waiting for a second tone
* Varies in some areas
** Varies depending on carrier

| *Country* | AZ | IDD from UK | IDD to UK |
|---|---|---|---|
| Afghanistan | 1 | 00 93 | 00 44 |
| Albania | *e* | 00 355 | 00 44 |
| Algeria | 1 | 00 213 | 00*p*44 |
| Andorra | *e* | 00 376 | 00 44 |
| Angola | 1 | 00 244 | 00 44 |
| Anguilla | 1 | 00 1 264 | 011 44 |
| Antigua and Barbuda | 1 | 00 1 268 | 011 44 |
| Argentina | 1 | 00 54 | 00 44 |
| Armenia | *e* | 00 374 | 810 44 |
| Aruba | 1 | 00 297 | 00 44 |
| Ascension Island | 1 | 00 247 | 00 44 |
| Australia | 2 | 00 61 | 00 11 44 |
| Austria | *e* | 00 43 | 00 44 |
| Azerbaijan | *e* | 00 994 | 810 44 |
| Azores | *e* | 00 351 | 00 44 |
| Bahamas | 1 | 00 1 242 | 011 44 |
| Bahrain | 1 | 00 973 | 0 44 |
| Bangladesh | 1 | 00 880 | 00 44 |
| Barbados | 1 | 00 1 246 | 011 44 |
| Belarus | *e* | 00 375 | 810 44 |
| Belgium | *e* | 00 32 | 00 44 |
| Belize | 1 | 00 501 | 00 44 |
| Benin | 1 | 00 229 | 00*p*44 |
| Bermuda | 1 | 00 1 441 | 011 44 |
| Bhutan | 1 | 00 975 | 00 44 |
| Bolivia | 1 | 00 591 | 00 44 |
| Bosnia-Hercegovina | *e* | | |
| Muslim-Croat Federation | | 00 387 | 00 44 |
| Republika Srpska | | 00 381 | 00 44 |
| Botswana | 1 | 00 267 | 00 44 |
| Brazil | 1 | 00 55 | 00 44 |
| British Virgin Islands | 1 | 00 1 284 | 011 44 |
| Brunei | 1 | 00 673 | 00 44 |
| Bulgaria | *e* | 00 359 | 00 44 |
| Burkina Faso | 1 | 00 226 | 00 44 |
| Burundi | 1 | 00 257 | 90 44 |
| Cambodia | 1 | 00 855 | 00 44 |
| Cameroon | 1 | 00 237 | 00 44 |
| Canada | 1 | 00 1 | 011 44 |
| Canary Islands | *e* | 00 34 | 00 44 |
| Cape Verde | 1 | 00 238 | 0 44 |
| Cayman Islands | 1 | 00 1 345 | 011 44 |
| Central African Republic | 1 | 00 236 | 19 44 |
| Chad | 1 | 00 235 | 15 44 |
| Chile | 1 | 00 56 | 00 44 |
| China | 2 | 00 86 | 00 44 |
| Hong Kong | 1 | 00 852 | 001 44 |
| Macao | 1 | 00 853 | 00 44 |
| Colombia | 1 | 00 57 | 009 44 |
| Comoros | 1 | 00 269 | 00 44 |
| Congo, Dem. Rep. of | 1 | 00 243 | 00 44 |
| Congo, Republic of | 1 | 00 242 | 00 44 |
| Cook Islands | 2 | 00 682 | 00 44 |
| Costa Rica | 1 | 00 506 | 00 44 |
| Côte d'Ivoire | 1 | 00 225 | 00 44 |
| Croatia | *e* | 00 385 | 00 44 |
| Cuba | 1 | 00 53 | 119 44 |
| Cyprus | *e* | 00 357 | 00 44 |
| Czech Republic | *e* | 00 420 | 00 44 |
| Denmark | *e* | 00 45 | 00 44 |
| Djibouti | 1 | 00 253 | 00 44 |
| Dominica | 1 | 00 1 767 | 011 44 |
| Dominican Republic | 1 | 00 1 809 | 011 44 |
| Ecuador | 1 | 00 593 | 00 44 |
| Egypt | 1 | 00 20 | 00 44 |
| Equatorial Guinea | 1 | 00 240 | 00 44 |
| Eritrea | 1 | 00 291 | 00 44 |
| Estonia | *e* | 00 372 | 800 44 |
| Ethiopia | 1 | 00 251 | 00 44 |
| Falkland Islands | 1 | 00 500 | 0 44 |
| Faroe Islands | *e* | 00 298 | 009 44 |
| Fiji | 2 | 00 679 | 05 44 |
| Finland | *e* | 00 358 | 00 44** |
| France | *e* | 00 33 | 00 44 |
| French Guiana | 1 | 00 594 | 00 44 |
| French Polynesia | 2 | 00 689 | 00 44 |
| Gabon | 1 | 00 241 | 00 44 |
| The Gambia | 1 | 00 220 | 00 44 |
| Georgia | *e* | 00 995 | 810 44 |
| Germany | *e* | 00 49 | 00 44 |
| Ghana | 1 | 00 233 | 00 44 |
| Gibraltar | *e* | 00 350 | 00 44 |
| Greece | *e* | 00 30 | 00 44 |
| Greenland | *e* | 00 299 | 009 44 |
| Grenada | 1 | 00 1 473 | 011 44 |
| Guadeloupe | 1 | 00 590 | 00 44 |
| Guam | 2 | 00 1 671 | 001 44 |
| Guatemala | 1 | 00 502 | 00 44 |
| Guinea | 1 | 00 224 | 00 44 |
| Guinea-Bissau | 1 | 00 245 | 099 44 |
| Guyana | 1 | 00 592 | 001 44 |
| Haiti | 1 | 00 509 | 00 44 |

| *Country* | AZ | IDD from UK | IDD to UK |
|---|---|---|---|
| Honduras | 1 | 00 504 | 00 44 |
| Hungary | *e* | 00 36 | 00 44 |
| Iceland | *e* | 00 354 | 00 44 |
| India | 1 | 00 91 | 00 44 |
| Indonesia | 1 | 00 62 | 001 44** |
| | | | 00844** |
| Iran | 1 | 00 98 | 00 44 |
| Iraq | 1 | 00 964 | 00 44 |
| Ireland, Republic of | *e* | 00 353 | 00 44 |
| Israel | 1 | 00 972 | 00 44** |
| Italy | *e* | 00 39 | 00 44 |
| Jamaica | 1 | 00 1 876 | 011 44 |
| Japan | 2 | 00 81 | 001 44** |
| | | | 004144** |
| | | | 006144** |
| Jordan | 1 | 00 962 | 00 44* |
| Kazakhstan | *e* | 00 7 | 810 44 |
| Kenya | 1 | 00 254 | 00 44 |
| Kiribati | 2 | 00 686 | 00 44 |
| Korea, North | 2 | 00 850 | 00 44 |
| Korea, South | 2 | 00 82 | 001 44** |
| | | | 00244** |
| Kuwait | 1 | 00 965 | 00 44 |
| Kyrgystan | *e* | 00 996 | 00 44 |
| Laos | 1 | 00 856 | 00 44 |
| Latvia | *e* | 00 371 | 00 44 |
| Lebanon | 1 | 00 961 | 00 44 |
| Lesotho | 1 | 00 266 | 00 44 |
| Liberia | 1 | 00 231 | 00 44 |
| Libya | 1 | 00 218 | 00 44 |
| Liechtenstein | *e* | 00 423 | 00 44 |
| Lithuania | *e* | 00 370 | 810 44 |
| Luxembourg | *e* | 00 352 | 00 44 |
| Macedonia | *e* | 00 389 | 99 44 |
| Madagascar | 1 | 00 261 | 00 44 |
| Madeira | *e* | 00 351 91 | 00 44* |
| Malawi | 1 | 00 265 | 101 44 |
| Malaysia | 1 | 00 60 | 00 44 |
| Maldives | 1 | 00 960 | 00 44 |
| Mali | 1 | 00 223 | 00 44 |
| Malta | *e* | 00 356 | 00 44 |
| Mariana Islands, Northern | 2 | 00 1 670 | 011 44 |
| Marshall Islands | 2 | 00 692 | 011 44 |
| Martinique | 1 | 00 596 | 00 44 |
| Mauritania | 1 | 00 222 | 00 44 |
| Mauritius | 1 | 00 230 | 00 44 |
| Mayotte | 1 | 00 269 | 10 44 |
| Mexico | 1 | 00 52 | 98 44 |
| Micronesia, Federated States of | 2 | 00 691 | 011 44 |
| Moldova | *e* | 00 373 | 810 44 |
| Monaco | *e* | 00 377 | 00 44 |
| Mongolia | 2 | 00 976 | 00 44 |
| Montenegro | *e* | 00 381 | 99 44 |
| Montserrat | 1 | 00 1 664 | 011 44 |
| Morocco | 1 | 00 212 | 00*p*44 |
| Mozambique | 1 | 00 258 | 00 44 |
| Myanmar | 1 | 00 95 | 00 44 |
| Namibia | 1 | 00 264 | 00 44 |
| Nauru | 2 | 00 674 | 00 44 |
| Nepal | 1 | 00 977 | 00 44 |
| Netherlands | *e* | 00 31 | 00 44 |
| Netherlands Antilles | 1 | 00 599 | 00 44 |
| New Caledonia | 2 | 00 687 | 00 44 |
| New Zealand | 2 | 00 64 | 00 44 |
| Nicaragua | 1 | 00 505 | 00 44 |
| Niger | 1 | 00 227 | 00 44 |

| *Country* | AZ | IDD from UK | IDD to UK |
|---|---|---|---|
| Nigeria | 1 | 00 234 | 009 44 |
| Niue | 2 | 00 683 | 00 44 |
| Norfolk Island | 2 | 00 672 | 0101 44 |
| Norway | *e* | 00 47 | 00 44 |
| Oman | 1 | 00 968 | 00 44 |
| Pakistan | 1 | 00 92 | 00 44 |
| Palau | 2 | 00 680 | 011 44 |
| Panama | 1 | 00 507 | 00 44 |
| Papua New Guinea | 2 | 00 675 | 05 44 |
| Paraguay | 1 | 00 595 | 00 44** |
| | | | 003 44** |
| Peru | 1 | 00 51 | 00 44 |
| Philippines | 2 | 00 63 | 00 44 |
| Poland | *e* | 00 48 | 00 44 |
| Portugal | *e* | 00 351 | 00 44 |
| Puerto Rico | 1 | 00 1 787 | 011 44 |
| Qatar | 1 | 00 974 | 00 44 |
| Réunion | 1 | 00 262 | 00 44 |
| Romania | *e* | 00 40 | 00 44 |
| Russia | *e* | 00 7 | 810 44 |
| Rwanda | 1 | 00 250 | 00 44 |
| St Christopher and Nevis | 1 | 00 1 869 | 011 44 |
| St Helena | 1 | 00 290 | 0 44 |
| St Lucia | 1 | 00 1 758 | 011 44 |
| St Pierre and Miquelon | 1 | 00 508 | 00 44 |
| St Vincent and the Grenadines | 1 | 00 1 784 | 001 44 |
| El Salvador | 1 | 00 503 | 0 44 |
| Samoa | 2 | 00 685 | 0 44 |
| Samoa, American | 2 | 00 684 | 00 44 |
| San Marino | *e* | 00 378 | 00 44 |
| São Tomé and Princípe | 1 | 00 239 | 00 44 |
| Saudi Arabia | 1 | 00 966 | 00 44 |
| Senegal | 1 | 00 221 | 00*p*44 |
| Serbia | *e* | 00 381 | 99 44 |
| Seychelles | 1 | 00 248 | 00 44 |
| Sierra Leone | 1 | 00 232 | 00 44 |
| Singapore | 1 | 00 65 | 001 44 |
| Slovak Republic | *e* | 00 421 | 00 44 |
| Slovenia | *e* | 00 386 | 00 44 |
| Solomon Islands | 2 | 00 677 | 00 44 |
| Somalia | 1 | 00 252 | 16 44 |
| South Africa | 1 | 00 27 | 09 44 |
| Spain | *e* | 00 34 | 00 44 |
| Sri Lanka | 1 | 00 94 | 00 44 |
| Sudan | 1 | 00 249 | 00 44 |
| Suriname | 1 | 00 597 | 00 44 |
| Swaziland | 1 | 00 268 | 00 44 |
| Sweden | *e* | 00 46 | 007 44** |
| | | | 00944** |
| | | | 008744** |
| Switzerland | *e* | 00 41 | 00 44 |
| Syria | 1 | 00 963 | 00 44 |
| Taiwan | 2 | 00 886 | 002 44 |
| Tajikistan | *e* | 00 7 | 810 44 |
| Tanzania | 1 | 00 255 | 00 44 |
| Thailand | 1 | 00 66 | 001 44 |
| Tibet | 1 | 00 86 | 00 44 |
| Togo | 1 | 00 228 | 00 44 |
| Tonga | 2 | 00 676 | 00 44 |
| Trinidad and Tobago | 1 | 00 1 868 | 011 44 |
| Tristan da Cunha | 1 | 00 2 897 | ‡ |
| Tunisia | 1 | 00 216 | 00 44 |
| Turkey | *e* | 00 90 | 00 44 |
| Turkmenistan | *e* | 00 993 | 810 44 |
| Turks and Caicos Islands | 1 | 00 1 649 | 0 44 |

| *Country* | AZ | IDD from UK | IDD to UK |
|---|---|---|---|
| Tuvalu | 2 | 00 688 | 00 44 |
| Uganda | 1 | 00 256 | 00 44 |
| Ukraine | *e* | 00 380 | 810 44 |
| United Arab Emirates | 1 | 00 971 | 00 44 |
| Uruguay | 1 | 00 598 | 00 44 |
| USA | 1 | 00 1 | 011 44 |
| Alaska | | 00 1 907 | 011 44 |
| Hawaii | | 00 1 808 | 011 44 |
| Uzbekistan | *e* | 00 998 | 810 44 |
| Vanuatu | 2 | 00 678 | 00 44 |
| Vatican City State | *e* | 00 390 66982 | 00 44 |
| Venezuela | 1 | 00 58 | 00 44 |
| Vietnam | 1 | 00 84 | 00 44 |
| Virgin Islands (US) | 1 | 00 1 340 | 011 44 |
| Yemen | 1 | 00 967 | 00 44 |
| Yugoslav Fed. Rep. | *e* | 00 381 | 99 44 |
| Zambia | 1 | 00 260 | 00 44 |
| Zimbabwe | 1 | 00 263 | 00 44 |

# The UK Mobile Communications Industry

## General Introduction

The UK's mobile market has historically been among the most mature of the world's mobile markets. Liberalisation was introduced early and competition has been actively encouraged by a progressive regulator. The UK now boasts one of the world's most competitive markets with a range of services offered through a number of forward-thinking suppliers.

### Regulation

The Regulator is responsible for setting the controls for the UK mobile market and ensuring that none of the industry players indulge in anti-competitive behaviour.

The two government bodies covering the regulation of the mobile industry in the UK are the Radiocommunications Agency and Oftel. The Radiocommunications Agency is part of the Department of Trade and Industry (DTI) and is responsible for radio frequency allocation. The greater part of regulation falls under the jurisdiction of Oftel. Oftel was created by the 1984 Telecommunications Act and empowered to ensure competition in the UK market. It was therefore given authority over licensing procedures, tariffing, interconnection (where one operator has access to another's infrastructure) as well as acting as an arbitrator between operators in disputes. Oftel has authority over the UK's other communications sectors as well.

The policies adopted and enforced by Oftel are largely driven by the European Commission (with the support of the Parliament and Council of Ministers). This follows the European Court of Justice's ruling allowing the European Commission to apply the competition rules of the Treaty of Rome to telecommunications (in 1985). This ruling also prompted the formation of DGXIII (Telecommunications, Information Industries and Innovation) in 1986.

In general policy has been aimed at providing access to networks and public services and guarantee harmonised, objective, transparent and non-discriminatory conditions based on the so called 'Open Network Provision' (ONP) principles which endeavour to ensure fair competition and access for new entrants. Among other things that have impacted on the mobile industry, the Commission has addressed:

- *Universal Service*
  This is the stipulation by which services must be provided to all customers irrespective of their location. New entrants often have to contribute to the cost of universal service provision. In the UK in 1996, the government and the EU agreed to offer grants to Vodafone and BT Cellnet to extend their mobile telephony coverage to sparsely populated areas of Scotland.
- *Number Portability*
  This allows the customer to keep his or her telephone number even if they change service provider so the telephone number is seen to belong to the customer not the service provider. Number portability was introduced to the UK's fixed line communications industry in June 1997 and to the mobile industry in January 1999.
- *Licensing*
  The provision of and requirements of the licensing process.
- *Incumbent's Tariffs*
  This provision is to stop incumbent operators abusing their positions as providers of both local, national and long distance services by cross-subsidising one with another.

In the UK the two major pieces of legislation that have shaped the communications industry are the 1981 and the 1984 Telecommunications Acts. The former divided the General Post Office (which prior to this had provided both telecommunications and postal services) into British Telecommunications and the Post Office and made provision for the introduction of competition. The latter established BT as a public limited company and created Oftel as the industry watchdog.

Since its creation, Oftel has licensed hundreds of companies to compete in the various sectors of the UK communications industry. These licenses are divided into the following four categories:

- PTO or Public Telecommunications Operator (a total of 39 licensed to date)
- IFS or International Facilities Based Service Provider (110 licensed to date)
- ISVR or International Simple Voice Reseller (179 licensed to date)
- Satellite Services Provider (36 licensed to date)

It must be noted that not all these licenses are current, some operators may have ceased to exist or may never have begun operations.

PTOs can provide either fixed or mobile services and will own their network (the physical infrastructure over which the call is routed). IFS providers also own infrastructure although this is limited by the nature of the services they offer i.e. international calls only. ISR providers do not own any infrastructure but buy capacity from other operators. Finally, as the name suggests, Satellite Services Providers offer satellite-based services.

Much of the early regulation of the UK telecommunications industry was concerned with the promotion of competition and since this has by and large been achieved in most of the sectors covered by Oftel, the regulator has announced that it intends to take a much 'softer' approach in the future. In light of this, Oftel's activities can now broadly be described as:

- Continuing to review its current customer protection policies to promote the interests of consumers
- Policing the regulation of licenses
- Conducting separate twice yearly reviews of each sector – fixed, mobile, Internet access and interactive broadcasting – to monitor for anti-competitive behaviour, excessive profits and market share

Oftel's three directorates – Regulatory Policy, Compliance and Business Support – conduct these activities. The Regulatory Policy Directorate is responsible for developing telecommunications policies. The Compliance Directorate makes sure phone companies meet the obligations of their licenses and existing telecoms regulations. Finally, the Business Support Directorate supports the entire organisation.

One aspect of the mobile sector which is currently not covered by Oftel regulation is mobile Internet access.

### Industry Players

The provision of mobile services in the UK is offered through Network Operators, Service Providers and MVNOs.

The Network Operator owns the license to provide cellular services as well as the physical network. Network operators are responsible for billing and maintaining the networks, can set tariffs and have a direct billing relationship with the end users. There are currently four Network Operators in the UK (*see table below*).

The Service Providers were introduced into the UK market at the very beginning when their role was to increase competition within the market. They buy airtime wholesale from the network operators and sell it onto the end users. This agreement means that they can set their own tariff structures and they have a billing relationship with the end users.

The incumbent operators (those who have been operating since the start) BT Cellnet and Vodafone, have an obligation under the terms of their licenses to offer wholesale minutes of airtime to Service Providers. The next two entrants Orange and One2One were never obliged to offer this and although this came up for review in April 1998, both these operators were considered at this time to have insignificant market share. There are around 50 Service Providers still operating in the market including One.Tel, Sainsbury's, Sony Cellular Services and Martin Dawes. In order to maintain a viable business operation, many of these Service Providers have diversified their product offer away from pure mobile service offering to other telecom or Internet-based services.

Finally, the newest entrants to the market are MVNOs, Mobile Virtual Network Operators. Unlike the Service Providers there is no obligation for the Network operators to open their networks to MVNOs rather it is an entirely commercial agreement where the Network Operator allows the MVNO access to their network. This differs from the Service Provider in that a true MVNO that has its own mobile network code, issues its own SIM cards (Subscriber Identity Module card – the 'brain' of the handset), operates its own mobile switching centre and has a pricing structure fully independent from the network operator. As these are commercial agreements there are as yet no regulations covering MVNOs, but, as with mobile Internet access, the regulator is currently observing development closely and may step in as MVNOs become a more important force. To date, the most successful MVNO is Virgin which operates on the One2One network although others are emerging including Energis (operating on the Orange network) and Carphone Warehouse which claims to operate on all four networks.

### Current Mobile Market

| *Operator* | *Ownership* | *Technology* | *Launch Date* |
|---|---|---|---|
| BT Cellnet | 100% BT | Tacs-900<br>GSM | January 1985<br>January 1994 |
| Vodafone | 100% Vodafone AirTouch | Tacs-900<br>GSM | January 1985<br>July 1992 |
| One2One | 100% Deutsche Telekom | GSM 1800 | September 1993 |
| Orange | 100% France Telecom | GSM 1800 | April 1994 |
| Hutchison 3G | 65% Hutchison Whampoa, 20% DoCoMo & 15% KPN | UMTS | To begin operations 2002 |

### Market Share

| | *BT Cellnet* | *Vodafone* | *One2One* | *Orange* |
|---|---|---|---|---|
| Current Subscriber Base | 11,158,000 | 12,279,000 | 8,981,000 | 11,030,000 |
| Total Market Share | 25.7% | 28.3% | 20.7% | 25.3% |

### Subscriber Growth

| Date | Jan 1997 | Jan 1998 | Jan 1999 | Jan 2000 | Mar 2001 |
|---|---|---|---|---|---|
| Subscriber Base | 6,810,000 | 8,344,000 | 13,001,000 | 23,944,000 | 43,448,000 |
| Penetration Rate | 11.7% | 14.3% | 22.3% | 41% | 73.8% |

Subscriber growth in the UK has been driven by a number of factors. The most important of these are

- Promotion of prepaid services
- Subsidised handsets
- Number portability

### Prepaid Services

There are two methods of paying for mobile services in the UK, monthly contracts or pre-paid cards. With monthly contracts, the end user pays a fixed subscription fee each month which entitles them to a number of basic services (for example voicemail) and gives them a certain amount of 'airtime' each month. Prepaid subscribers have access to the same services but pay in advance. Initially this allowed industry players to target additional consumer groups in particular the youth market and those people who would normally not pass the credit checks necessary for a contract. It has proved to be a very popular option as it allows people to control their spend and is a low entry cost method to mobile services.

### Number Portability

All UK operators have been obliged to provide number portability since the beginning of 1999. This means that any end user who wishes to change Network Operator (or service provider) must be given the option of retaining their existing number i.e. taking their mobile number with them to the new service provider. This was considered to be a barrier to competition. The regulator is currently looking at how the administrative system for number portability can be improved in order to enforce this obligation.

### Technology

Services were introduced to the UK in 1985 using an analogue technology called TACS. In 1992 Vodafone launched a new digital 'GSM' network. The introduction of GSM was therefore referred to as 2G or second-generation services. BT Cellnet and two more entrants launched GSM services in the following two years making the UK one of Europe's most competitive markets.

The UK was the third European country to license 3G operators after Finland and Spain but was the first to auction its licenses. Auctions are not new to the European communications industry. Many of the second and third entrants had to bid for their license, what is spectacular about the UK's 3G auction is the height of the bids. While industry observers has speculated that the auction might reach £4 billion, in the event a total of £22 billion was raised from the sale of spectrum.

There is continued speculation about the impact of the UK's 3G spectrum auction. Since operators must recoup the investment in the license it is expected that this will result in higher costs for the consumer thus hindering the UK's migration to 3G services.

### UK 3G License Winners and Total Cost

| | | | |
|---|---|---|---|
| Hutchison 3G UK | License A | 2 x 15MHz paired 5MHz unpaired | 7 billion |
| Vodafone | License B | 2 x 15MHz paired | 9.6 billion |
| BT Cellnet | License C | 2 x 10 MHz paired 5MHz unpaired | 6.5 billion |
| One2One | License D | 2 x 10 MHz paired 5MHz unpaired | 6.4 billion |
| Orange | License E | 2 x 10 MHz paired 5MHz unpaired | 6.6 billion |
| TOTAL | | | 36.1 billion |

### Data Services

As in the fixed line communications, mobile operators are no longer content to offer connection, voice telephony and standard applications i.e. voicemail, bundled airtime and so on. Competition has driven down price and therefore revenue from the basic services and operators are now seeking to differentiate themselves by offering innovative value added services. The most important of these to date is the development of SMS and WAP applications.

SMS (Short Messaging Services) or 'text messaging' as it is more commonly referred to allows consumers to send and receive text messages up to 160 characters long on their mobile phones. These messages can be personal messages sent from one user to another or can be information based services specified by the end user and sent by the network operator. Most popular SMS information services are sports results and news headlines. Due to its simplicity and popularity among young users, the number of SMS messages being sent each day has increased dramatically (*see table below*).

### Total Number of SMS Sent in the UK

| Date | December '98 | December '99 | December '00 | March '01 |
|---|---|---|---|---|
| Number of Messages | 170 million | 271 million | 756 million | 864 million |

SMS is a relatively simple technology but the more complicated offering is WAP, or Wireless Application Protocol. WAP is a language that allows Internet-style data to be viewed from a mobile phone. To date, applications have be uninspiring, news and weather reports, sports information, horoscopes etc and uptake much slower than anticipated. However, it is key to Operators' future business plans that users accept and use more sophisticated services to prepare them for the changes that 3G services are expected to herald.

*3G* will offer much faster data transfer rates (up to 2Mbps is commonly quoted) which will expand the facility of the network to include full Internet browsing and streamed video content. The question remains as to whether ordinary consumers will want or use these enhanced services.

### PMR

There is a fifth operational national mobile network which must be mentioned in a discussion of the communications industry in the UK. Dolphin Telecom operates a national mobile network based on the TETRA standard. PMR (Public Mobile Radio) or PAMR (Public Access Mobile Radio) as it is also referred to differs from other mobile networks in its ability to allow group communication, a single user has the ability to push a button which allows him to broadcast to members of a pre-selected group. Most often PMR is used by the emergency services but the Dolphin network interconnects with the fixed network and is offered primarily to business users as the UK's fifth mobile network. However, the take up of services has been much slower than anticipated.

OFTEL
50 Ludgate Hill, London EC4M 7JJ
Tel: 020-7634 8700; Fax: 020-7634 8943
Web: www.oftel.co.uk

Department of Trade and Industry (DTI)
Telecommunications Division, 151 Buckingham Palace Road, London SW1W 9SS
Tel: 020-7215 5000; Fax: 020-7215 2909

BT Cellnet
260 Bath Road Slough, Berkshire SL1 4DX
Tel: 01753 565000; Fax: 01753 565010
Web: www.cellnet.co.uk

Dolphin Telecom
The Crescent, Jays Close, That Viables, Basingstoke Hampshire RG22 4BS
Tel: 01256 811822; Fax: 01256 474537
Web: www.dolphin-telecom.co.uk

Hutchison 3G UK
43 New Bond Street, London W1Y 9HB
Tel: 020-7499 1886; Fax: 020-7491 7266

Orange Plc
The Economist Building, 25 St James Street, London SW1A 1HA
Tel: 020-7766 1766; Fax: 020-7766 1767
Web: www.orange.co.uk

One2One
Imperial Place, Maxwell Road, Borehamwood WD6 1EA
Tel: 020-8214 2121; Fax: 020-8214 3601
Web: www.one2one.co.uk

Vodafone Group
The Courtyard, 2–4 London Road, Newbury, Berkshire RG14 1JX
Tel: 01635 33251; Fax: 01635 45713
Web: www.vodafone.co.uk

# Information Technology and Computer Science

It can be asserted that there have been three marvels of the twentieth century: modern medicine, nuclear fusion and the computer. It can be further asserted that modern medicine and nuclear fusion might not have so advanced were it not for the invention of the computer.
This article provides an overview of the rapid and broad development of computers and computer science.

### Ancestry

The ancestors of the modern century computer are the Difference Engine and Analytical Engine devised by mathematician Charles Babbage. Designed in 1820 to automatically compute mathematical tables, construction of his mechanical, clockwork-like Difference Engine was abandoned by Babbage in the 1840s due to financial problems, personal tragedy and a disagreement with head engineer Joseph Clement.

In 1834 Babbage began work on his Analytical Engine. Unlike the Difference Engine, the Analytical Engine was designed as a general purpose tool with a store to hold information and a mill to take information input on punched cards and translate it into results, or output, on similar punched cards.

Following the financial problems with the incomplete Difference Engine project, Babbage was unable to secure further government funding for his Analytical Engine and it was not until 1991 that an actual engine was built by a group of historical enthusiasts.

### First Generation

Babbage's work relied heavily on mechanics and physical machinery. It was not until the twentieth century invention of the electrical vacuum tube and then the transistor that computers became a feasible means to solving problems.

War has been a significant factor in the development of the computer. In 1943, during World War II, the British and Americans developed electronic computers. Colossus, a British effort, was specifically developed to crack the German coding cipher Lorenz whilst an American effort, Harvard Mark I, was developed as a more general purpose electromechanical programmable computer.

Regarded as early 'first generation' computers, these machines primarily comprised wired circuits and vacuum valves. Punched cards were employed as the input, output and main storage systems.

Following on from initial developments, ENIAC (Electronic Numerical Integrator and Computer) was completed in 1946 by the Americans. Capable of carrying out 100,000 calculations a second, it was remarkable for its day. Like all first generation machines, ENIAC was huge and power hungry (weighing 30 tonnes and consuming 25 kilowatts of electricity).

### Second Generation

Similar to light bulbs, valves were prone to failure, requiring tedious checks to resolve problems (ENIAC alone contained 18,000 vacuum valves). In 1947, the transistor was invented. Performing the same role as a vacuum valve but less prone to failure, smaller and more efficient, the transistor allowed smaller 'second generation' computers to be developed throughout the 1950s and early 1960s.

Computers remained the province of government and universities due to their scale of cost and size. Their use was significant in nuclear weapon and power generation research and development.

### Third Generation

In 1958 Jack St Claire Kilby produced the first integrated circuit, or 'micro-chip'. A micro-chip is comprised of a large number of transistors and other components bonded to a single substrate – typically a wafer of silicon, interconnected by a surface film of conductive material rather than by wires. By reducing distance between components, savings are made in both size and electricity. In 1963 the first 'third generation' computers based on 'micro-chip' technology appeared.

### Fourth Generation

In 1971 Intel produced the first 'microprocessor' heralding a 'fourth generation' of computers. The Intel 4004 (capable of 60,000 instructions per second) grouped much of the processing functions onto a single micro-chip.
Around the same time, Intel invented the RAM (random access memory) chip which grouped significant amounts of memory onto a single chip. Intel remains today a leading chip manufacturer. Successive microprocessors had ever-increasing calculating ability while the capacity of RAM also increased. Supercomputers and mainframes utilising scores of microprocessors had terrific power in the order of 150 million instructions per second.

The power of the computer has exponentially increased as science has scaled down the size and electrical consumption of the core component (the transistor) from thumb size to far smaller than the thickness of a human hair, allowing a greater density and thus increasing the total power of the computer. Developments such as multiple-layer circuits and the use of copper instead of gold continue to yield gains in size and performance through miniaturisation.

The microprocessor facilitated the advent of immensely powerful supercomputers and also allowed small and affordable micro or personal computers. Early micro computers included the Altair 8800 in 1974, the Apple I & II, Commodore PET through to the IBM PC based on Intel's 8086 in 1981. The 8086 chip began a dynasty of hugely successful microprocessors for Intel that continues today with the Pentium III range.

IBM's original PC set a standard which was effectively wrestled from IBM by companies making clones or copies of the IBM design. IBM designed the initial PC only to see other companies take the lion's share of the market. The operating system supplier Microsoft made thousands of times more money out of the IBM PC than IBM ever did.

In the mid 1980s Apple Computer abandoned its highly successful Apple II computer range to produce the Apple Lisa and Apple Macintosh computers utilising the Motorola 68000 processor. Being the first widely available commercial computers with a graphical mouse/pointer driven interface they were relatively expensive compared to the command line (text only) operated IBM PC clones.

The Lisa was abandoned but the Apple Macintosh today ranks as the second largest personal computer system.

In the early 1990s RISC (reduced instruction set computing) became common. Compared with conventional CISC (complex instruction set computing) chips, a RISC processor uses a small set of highly efficient instruction types in combinations to achieve the same result as one CISC instruction. Because of performance optimisation the RISC chip can often perform some tasks more quickly than a CISC chip.

The first RISC chips were installed in UNIX servers and workstations. In the mid-1990s Apple Computer teamed up with IBM and Motorola to produce the PowerPC chip. Apple stopped shipping personal computers with the ageing 68040 CISC chip and instead utilised the PowerPC chip. Around that time Intel began shipping the Pentium CISC chip. Successive releases have produced ever faster versions of the PowerPC and Intel chip sets. For example: from an initial speed of 66 MHz in the mid-1990s, the PowerPC chip was released at 1,000 MHz in 2000.

### Next Generation

Most modern computers are still regarded as 'fourth generation' as they use essentially the same technology, albeit highly miniaturised. The future of computer technology is widely thought to be dependent on the physics of light. Already used extensively in the computer industry for high speed communications, laser light offers possibilities for both calculation and storage.

As has been seen, there is huge diversity in the field of computer science and processor types are no exception – there have been literally hundreds of design families and thousands of processor models.

### Programming Languages

A multitude of programming languages have been devised with the common purpose of devising a program of instructions for computers to follow to achieve a task. Programming languages are categorised by generation:

1GL or first-generation language is the machine language that the processor chips execute. Instructions and arguments are in binary form (strings of zeros and ones). For the very early computers, machine language was the only choice as there was often insufficient resources to support assembly language or even an operating system. Machine language tends to be highly specific to a particular processor or processor family.

2GL or second-generation language. Assembly language is a human-understandable language insofar as it uses names instead of numbers. An assembler program takes assembly language and turns it into a machine code program. Very common on early systems where resources (speed, storage) were at a premium, it is typically only used today as an output from 3GL and higher systems. It is rare for the assembly language of two different processor families to be identical but they all share similar syntax. Assembly language programs do not lend themselves to being used on different hardware platforms.

3GL or third-generation language is a 'high-level' programming language. Typically more readable and concise than assembly language, 3GL programs are converted by a compiler program into either machine or assembly language for later execution. 3GL languages allow programs to be converted or ported from one operating system or hardware platform to another (with varying degrees of effort) and allow more complex data structures and program flows than 2GLs. 4GL or fourth generation language is designed to be closer to natural language than a 3GL language. Languages for accessing databases are often described as 4GLs.

5GL or fifth-generation language programming uses graphical development environments to create source language to be compiled with a 3GL or 4GL language compiler. Often 5GLs are used to develop prototype applications which have the look and feel of a final application but often without the underlying power provided by a 3GL or 4GL. Often a mix of generations is used, with a high level language (4 or 5GL) used to produce interface elements and a lower level language used to provide the processing power.

### Operating Systems

An operating system (OS) is a set of utility programs that acts as the liaison between the computer user, the computer hardware (processor unit, memory) and its peripherals (hard disk, mouse, display, printer, network etc) and the program that a user is running (e.g. a spreadsheet).

The first computers had no operating system, and each program had to directly control the hardware on its own adding greatly to the burden of programming a computer. Initial input was by setting dials and switches (or even plugging cables), with calculation results shown on dials. The input was in the form of elementary machine language encoded in binary.

The early code-breaking systems utilised teletype paper tape. Then came punched cards – where instructions were laboriously encoded onto cardboard cards that were fed through the machine telling it both what to do and giving it the information or data to compute. The result was either produced onto further punched cards or output on to rudimentary display panels.

The use of punched cards allowed some routine components or programs to be re-used (by re-using routines on sets of cards). Later, the development of memory chips, magnetic tape and hard disks has allowed more extensive programs and information to be stored, executed and re-executed.

Early OS were hardware and vendor-specific with assembly language or machine code as the programming language. Each computer model or series tended to have its own specific operating system.

In 1969 a major mainstream operating systems, UNIX, was first released. Originated at Bell Labs in the USA, it was based on 'Multics', an earlier time-sharing system.

UNIX was one of the first operating systems that could be ported (converted) to a variety of system hardware. This ability was made largely through the use of the 'C' programming language which was first defined and developed around the same time.

UNIX has evolved into many different versions or 'strains' due in part to the fact that the source code is largely free and written in C. UNIX systems were keystones in the development of the Internet and a large proportion of Internet servers today are UNIX-driven. UNIX is available on more hardware platforms than any other OS, although there is no dominant version of UNIX with a dozen or so major versions.

In 1979 Digital Equipment Corporation (DEC) released VMS (Virtual Memory System) as the operating system for the DEC VAX mini-computer. The main features of VMS was the adoption of a 32-bit virtual memory system that allowed use of hard disk as virtual memory in place of actual RAM chips. There have been many operating systems devised and abandoned over the years.

### Personal Computer Operating Systems

Throughout the 1990s the personal computer world has been dominated by two main players: Microsoft and Apple Computer. Although not a significant manufacturer of computer equipment itself, Microsoft Corporation has built on its market share secured in the 1980s with MSDOS to become the market leading operating system provider. Microsoft's MS Windows range of personal computer operating systems are installed on more computers than any other commercial operating system.

Concern over the market dominance of Microsoft has led to legislatures in the US and European Union bringing anti-trust (anti-monopoly) lawsuits against the company. Success or failure for Microsoft in such litigation is likely to significantly shape the future of computing over the first decade of the new millennium.

Microsoft's main rival is Apple Computer. Established in the 1970s, Apple became highly successful with its Apple I, II and III range of personal computers and is one of the few of a flock of personal computer companies from that time that has continued to manufacture both its own operating system and hardware to run upon it.

Unlike Microsoft, Apple's strategy has been to control both the hardware and software of its systems. The Apple Macintosh operating system (MacOS) can only be run on Apple Macintosh hardware. This has resulted in a benefit that is also a curse: the Macintosh is a quality product but quality tends to cost. Microsoft benefited from the production of a huge volume of less expensive PCs, while Apple sells on quality and features. Both have significant benefits and downfalls. Many other operating systems exist but tend to be brand or hardware-specific.

## 'The Net'

Prior to the Internet or 'the Net' as it is known colloquially, computers tended to be connected together by hardware and protocols that were peculiar to each particular connection. Typically, links were point-to-point (a link had to be directly and physically established between the two computers).

As in other areas of computing, the military had an important influence on the development of what was to become 'the Net'. In 1969 ARPANET was formed by the US Department of Defence. A main concern was to establish a way for the computer capability of the military to be dispersed so that no one centre was critical to the operation of the network as a whole. This was achieved by interconnecting computers both directly and by way of other intermediary computers; thus if one link or 'node' computer was hit by a nuclear bomb, other pathways of communication could be established. The interconnections, when drawn, appeared as a mesh or net or web.

ARPANET was extended to non-military users such as universities early in the 1970s, with initial international links appearing in 1972. Early network research lead to the protocol of request for comments (RFC) whereby ideas in development can be adopted and studied by other computer users, who will comment on it, expand it and improve on it allowing a de facto standard to quickly evolve. The collaboration ethos instilled in the RFC protocol has fuelled development of the Internet and related computer fields. RFC number 1 was written in 1969 and there are well over 2,000 today.

Early Internet was merely a means for computers rather than people to communicate and was a side-effect of research into networking. It was not 'the Web', and web pages and email as we know it did not exist – these were the days of command line, text-only green screens (if not Teletype printer/keyboards).

The introduction of domain names (e.g. ditdit.co.uk) in 1984 offered an easier means of using the Web. Prior to domain names one had to remember IP numbers (e.g.192.168.1.100) for accessing destination computers. The use of email increased and implementations improved as various RFCs were adopted as standards; however, the Internet was primarily limited to government agencies, the military, academic and research organisations and some big businesses.

In 1989 what most people perceive as 'the Net' was born. It was effectively invented at CERN (the European Particle Physics Laboratory) by Tim Berners-Lee as a way for scientists to share information by placing it in a prescribed format (defined in an RFC) on a server. Initially text only, development of computer capability allowed inclusion of images through use of a program called NCSA Mosaic – the first graphical 'browser' (*see glossary*).

By 1993 a whole new industry of ISPs (Internet Service Providers) had begun, allowing computer users to dial up via a modem and access the Internet and to view the Web through their browser of choice. The leading two browsers today, Netscape and Microsoft Explorer, were both based on the open source code of NCSA Mosaic.

In the mid 1990s the term 'information superhighway' was coined to refer to the Internet. Sadly, the Internet is not a superhighway – it suffers from rush hours, traffic jams and link closures despite the fact that new connections are added at a frantic pace.

Developments of the late 1990s have allowed music, video, games, text, graphics and even telephone conversations to co-exist on the same Internet. The core technologies underpinning the Internet are TCP/IP, routers and domain names (*see glossary*).

The future of the Internet is likely to see the majority of telephone calls and probably video being transmitted over the Internet for at least part of its journey. Expansion of fibre-optic cable networks to homes and businesses will underpin this. The advent of high-capacity mobile phones will also facilitate and demand expansion of the Internet.

Simple but successful virus attacks like the 'love bug' computer virus of early 2000 show how much the world depends on and is affected by Internet technology. With no central governing body or legal jurisdiction, the legal implications of the Internet will continue to puzzle for years to come.

## Glossary of IT Terms

The following is a selected list of modern computing terms. It is by no means exhaustive but is intended to cover those that the average computer user might encounter.

*Kbps:* kilo bits per second – measure of transmission speed, denoting 1,000 bits transmitted per second.

*Mbps:* mega bits per second – denoting 1 million bits transmitted per second.

*Gbps:* giga bits per second – denoting 1,000 million bits transmitted per second.

*10-BaseT:* 10 Mbps Ethernet. *See also* Ethernet.

*100-BaseT:* 100 Mbps Ethernet. *See also* Ethernet.

*1000-BaseT:* 1000 Mbps or 1 Gbps Ethernet also known as Gigabit Ethernet. *See also* Ethernet.

*10-Base2:* 2 Mbps Ethernet over co-axial cable. (*See* Ethernet).

*ADB:* a defunct proprietary standard formerly built into Apple Macintosh computers to connect keyboard and mice and other input peripherals, ADB has now been supplanted by USB. *See also* USB.

*ADSL:* Asymmetric Digital Subscriber Line – a high speed digital protocol that allows continuous connection over standard copper wire to the Internet at over 265 kbps for sending and at least twice as fast for receiving. First available in the United Kingdom in 2000, ADSL is ideal for receiving streamed video and audio and is seen as the replacement for modems and ISDN. *See also* DSL, SDSL and ISDN.

*Animated Gif:* a multi-layered Gif file that allows simple animations to be created by transitions between the layers. Banner advertising on the Internet tends to utilise animated Gifs. *See also* Gif.

*Applet:* a very small application that is run in a special environment to provide a specialised function. For example Java applets provide special functions to web pages and are run in the Java virtual machine environment from which they derive their functionality.

*ATA:* Advanced Technology Attachment – ANSI name for IDE. *See also* IDE.

*Browser:* typically referring to a 'web browser' that allows a computer user to view web page content on their computer. Browsers can be designed for different specialist functions such as presenting image libraries, databases or computer code to users in a friendly format.

*BASIC:* Beginners All Purpose Symbolic Instruction Code – was designed for mainframe computers in 1963. Included on many personal computers in the 1970s (due to its minimal memory requirements) it became popular for beginners and non-professional programmers. Available on most operating systems, BASIC has been further popularised by Microsoft Visual Basic (an object-oriented graphical language).

*Bluetooth:* a de facto standard for wireless connectivity between devices. Bluetooth is based on short-range (10 metre) radio link and allows devices such as laptops, cellphones and printers to interact without wires. Developed primarily by joint initiatives between several of the large telecommunication and computer companies as a way for applicances of any type (including household applicances) to interact.

*Burn:* to 'Burn' or 'toast' a file or files to a CD-ROM or similar media means to copy the files to the media from hard disk (or other source). Derived from the fact that CD-ROMs are burnt by a laser during the process of writing to the disk.

*Bytecode:* file format which is the product of a compiler. Bytecode allows programs written in Java or PERL to be executed on virtual machines on any supporting platform.

*Cat-5:* an electrical performance and cable quality standard prescribed to support high-speed Ethernet networks. There are higher category specifications denoted by higher numbers but Cat-5 is the most commonly installed today.

*C:* a 3GL programming language developed in the late 1960s in parallel with the UNIX operating systems. Primarily limited to UNIX until the mid 1980s when standards emerged (the POSIX standard among others) allowing C to be widely adopted on many operating systems. UNIX used C as its core programming language.

*C++:* 3GL programming language invented by Bell Labs in 1985 with a final standard ratified in the late 1990s. Hugely popular, it has overthrown C as the language of choice for professional operating system and application developers. Based on C, it uses the object-oriented programming model.

*CD:* Compact Disc – a digital disk format capable of storing 650 megabytes of information on each of its two sides. Information is read by a laser head that detects pits etched into the substrate of the spinning disk and interprets them as information. Widely used in an audio format for storing recorded music. The computer format CD-ROM is likely to be superseded by the higher capacity DVD in the next few years. CD-RAM/CD-RW is a modifiable version and CD-R is a write once, read many format – both use lasers to alter the disk substrate to make the pits interpreted later as information. (CD-ROM is pressed by machine and die). *See also* DVD.

*CGI:* Common Gateway Interface – specification for how a web server and web page interact with applications on the server to accept, process and return web content dynamically. Typically, CGI handles form submission and searches, converting user input into database entries etc.

*COBOL:* Common Business Oriented Language – was released in 1960. Its authors aimed to produce a programming language that was easy to understand and use, more like English and less like code. COBOL in all its versions has been widely adopted for the development of business and financial systems. Millennium preparation for many organisations involved replacing legacy COBOL systems with more modern solutions using standard relational database and Internet tools. COBOL is still commercially available today.

*DNS:* Domain Name Server – a server that translates domain names into the IP numbers used by programs to directly access computers on the Internet. Each server has a telephone number and a name and DNS is analogous to the directory enquiries service, providing a means of locating a computer connected to the Internet.

*Domain:* a set of words, numbers and letters separated by dots used to identify an Internet server or group of servers, e.g. www.whitakers-almanack.co.uk, where 'www' denotes a web (http) server, 'whitakers-almanack' denotes the organisation name, 'co' denotes that the organisation is a company and 'uk' denotes United Kingdom (there are alternates for every country but 'us' is seldom used for United States). Alternatives include: org - organisation; net - network; gov - government; co/com - company (and many more).

*DVD:* Digital Versatile Disc – DVD-ROM is a high capacity (read only) disk format that has the same form factor as CD-ROM. Unlike the CD-ROM, however, DVD-ROM can store several Gigabytes of information on each surface and can have four readable surfaces (through laser focusing technology) compared with CD-ROM's two surfaces of 650 Megabytes. DVD-RAM is a modifiable version of DVD. Various formats of DVD are available, the most common being that used to store high-quality digital video, an alternative to the laser disk or video tape. *See also* CD.

*DSL:* Digital Subscriber Line – A family of high speed digital technologies for connection to the Internet over ordinary copper telephone cable. *See also* ADSL and SDSL.

*Email:* Electronic mail – An email message is a document that is addressed to one or more persons from an individual. Usually containing a message, it can also include other documents and email is the modern version of the telex, telegram, postcard and letter for exchanging information electronically. The advent of the Internet has seen an explosion in the use of email in modern life. Without encryption or digital signature, an Internet email is not secure.

*Ethernet:* a local area network type that typically utilises twisted pair cables directly between a central switch or hub. Utilising simple, standard and relatively cheap cable and connectors (RJ-45) Ethernet has become the standard for local area networks. Speeds of 10 Mbps (10-BaseT) and 100 Mbps (100-BaseT) are common with 1000 Mbps (1000-BaseT) also available. Ethernet employs a system whereby each computer listens for information addressed to its own unique address. Before transmitting, each computer waits for silence on the line; if multiple computers start transmitting simultaneously, they each detect the 'collision' and wait a random period of time before listening for silence and retransmitting, thus allowing communications to resume much like polite society. Ethernet reliability depends on the hub or switch rather than on one individual computer. Ethernet is also available over co-axial (television style) cable typically at 2 Mbps (10-Base2); although higher speeds are available, they are less common as co-axial cable is less resilient than twisted pair. 10-Base2 does not typically employ hubs or switches and comprises an open ended 'daisy-chain' of computers connected to the network. A break in the chain will divide the network into two or ever cause it to fail.

*Extranet:* secure subset of the Internet, using Internet protocols. Common today for exchanging information and services between a specific group or organisation. Security prevents outsiders from accessing the Extranet.

*File Server:* a computer on a network that stores computer files that users can access from other computers on the network. Popular modern systems include Windows NT, UNIX, Novell NetWare and AppleShare IP.

*Fire Wall:* computer or device to protect a network from security risks posed by the Internet, just as a firewall or fire-door protects parts of a building from a fire raging on the other side.

*Firewire:* Apple Computer trade mark for their implementation of the IEEE 1394 standard. *See also* SCSI, IEEE 1394, iLink.

*Flash:* a de facto standard for providing online animated web content from something as simple as an animated logo or button to an online video game. Flash is primarily produced by Macromedia Director and can be programmed with the logo language.

*FORTRAN:* FORmula TRANslation is a 3GL programming language designed for users and creators of scientific algorithms rather than business solutions. Today it has been succeeded by C for most applications but many legacy FORTRAN applications still exist and many developers still use it.

*FTP:* File Transfer Protocol – an Internet protocol whereby an FTP client program can request listings of files on a remote server and exchange files with that server. Publicly accessible FTP servers allow Anonymous FTP which does not require a password or user name, whereas private ones do.

*GIF:* Graphics Interchange Format – compressed graphic format most suitable for logos and non-photographic images. Invented by Unisys to allow images to be electronically sent in an efficient manner. Royalties due to Unisys for any implementation of GIF have lead to the development of a replacement format, PNG.

*Hot-plugable:* adjective to describe the ability of a protocol or device to be connected and disconnected as required without restarting the computer or device.

*HTML:* HyperText Mark-up Language – A small programming language used to denote or mark-up how an Internet page should be presented to a user from a HTTP server via a web browser. HTTP is an evolving standard that has grown greatly from its first version in order to accommodate new types of web content and features provided by the different web browsers (e.g. Netscape and Internet Explorer).

*HTTP:* Hypertext Transfer Protocol – an Internet protocol whereby a web server sends web pages, images and files to a web browser. HTTP is a perpetually evolving application protocol.

*HUB:* An Ethernet HUB connects a 10/100-BaseT network together with each machine or network device connected to the hub by a cable, with the hub linking them all together. Any traffic on any HUB 'Port' (connection) is echoed to all Ports. A USB hub performs a similar function allowing multiple USB devices to be connected to a single Computer via the HUB. *See also* Ethernet, 10/100-BaseT, USB. *See also* Switch.

*IDE:* Integrated Drive Electronics – a standard electronic interface used between computer disk storage devices. The IDE interface is based on the IBM PC ISA 16-bit bus standard. *See also* ATA.

*IEEE 1394:* developed primarily by Apple Computer (as FireWire) and Sony (as iLink), IEEE 1394 is a high-performance hot-plugable replacement for SCSI for connection of hard disks, scanners and digital video and still cameras. *See also* SCSI, FireWire, iLink.

*iLink:* Sony Corporation trade mark for their implementation of the IEEE 1394 standard. *See also* SCSI, IEEE 1394, iLink.

*IMAP:* Internet Mail Access Protocol – an Internet protocol offered as a replacement for POP3. IMAP allows a user to review, manipulate and store email on a central server from one or more workstations without necessitating message removal from the server. Advanced versions such as IMAP4 allow multiple users to have shared mailboxes or folders on the email server.

*Internet:* an abstract concept applied to describe the global network of INTER-connected computer NET-works of computers. *See body of article.*

*Intranet:* subset of the Internet, using Internet protocols but on a local area network. Common today for publishing information and services within a company or office.

*IP Address/IP Number:* typically in number form e.g. 192.168.1.100, an IP Address is unique to the computer that possesses it. Its purpose is similar to that of a telephone number, each digit allowing an Internet or network connection to be made between computers. When transmitting, a computer quotes the destination address and its own address and the information is routed accordingly using those numbers. *See also* Router. The widely used IP Address scheme is running out of unique numbers and an extended scheme is being phased in to replace it, although this is likely to take many years.

*IRC:* Internet Relay Chat – protocol that allows users to 'chat' online with other users using their keyboards. Under IRC a user can log into various chat rooms under their own name or an alias and have a text 'conversation' in real time with other users. IRC spans the globe and allows a person to build a persona based entirely on what they type.

*ISDN:* Integrated Services Digital Network – widely adopted in the United Kingdom and Europe but not North America, ISDN allows both digital computer data and voice telephony to coexist simultaneously on the same cable circuits. Data can be digitally exchanged at 64 kbps on one pair of copper wires, and at 128 kbps for a typical installation of two pairs. Typically used for point-to-point file transfer of large documents when first introduced, more recently it has been used for 'dialup' Internet for small to medium-sized business. In the UK, widespread adoption has been hampered by pricing structures (a 128 kbps connection incurs call charges for two lines per minute). Introduction of ADSL is likely to limit or reduce market penetration of ISDN.

*Java:* a development environment that allows development of cross-platform applications or applets typically utilised by web sites or Intranets. Java applications are compiled into Java Virtual Machine code in the same way as normal programs and thus cannot be modified by end users and is relatively efficient when compared to Java Script. Java is related to C++, an object-oriented development language used to develop many modern operating systems and as such can be used to develop sophisticated web-based programs.

*Java Script:* Netscape version of Java code that is executed or interpreted on the web user's machine each time it is run and is thus less efficient than compiled Java applets. Unlike Java, Java Script is typically provided in source form and is modifiable by the end user.

*Java Virtual Machine (JVM):* Java applets are required by Java standard to be able to run on any operating system that has a Java Virtual Machine which must provide a standard suite of facilities to the Java program. Microsoft, among others, has produced its own extensions to Java that are outside the standard, causing problems to MacOS users and others who do not have access to the Microsoft extensions.

*JPEG:* Joint Photographic Experts Group – compressed graphic format most suitable for compression of photographic images. Image data is compressed in manner that simplifies the image, losing definition in the process. As the level of compression increases so too does the image degradation.

*MacOS:* operating system developed by Apple Computer for use on their own Macintosh personal and server computers. A co-operative multi-tasking system up to version 9.1, it has become a more powerful operating system with MacOS X (10) which is a preemptive multi-tasking operating system based on UNIX.

*Novell NetWare*: introduced in the late 1980s, NetWare was one of the first network server operating systems and until MS Windows NT4 overtook it in the mid-to late1990s it was the market leader.

*Modem:* modulator/demodulator – a device that modulates digital signals from a computer into analogue signals for transmission over a standard telephone line and demodulates an incoming analogue signal and converts it to a digital signal for the computer.

*MP3:* motion picture group 1 layer 3 – popular format for compressing audio information for transmission over the Internet for later playback on personal computers and hand-held music players and other devices.

*MPEG:* Motion Picture Encoding Group – popular format standards for compressing video and audio information for transmission over the Internet for later playback on personal computers and on some hand-held devices.

*MS-DOS:* Microsoft Corporation's Disk Operating System – an early OS developed but not invented by Microsoft for use on early Intel-based personal computers. MS-DOS is believed by many to still be a core for Microsoft's more modern operating systems. *See also* PC-DOS; Operating System.

*Name Server: see* DNS Network Server: both Print Servers and File Servers are types of network server. Other types of network service include provision of configuration or security controls.

*News: see* NNTP.

*News Group: see* NNTP.

*NNTP:* Network News Transfer Protocol – an Internet protocol that implements a bulletin board, but on a global scale. Using a NNTP browser one can subscribe to one or more news groups of a huge diversity of topics from Archaeology to Zebras. Messages are posted to a virtual notice board by users through their news browser software to a news group on their local server which in turn passes it to other servers higher up in the hierarchy. To simplify, the hierarchy ends at a server for each country which passes the messages back down the chain in its own country and to its peers abroad (in actuality countries are irrelevant and network boundaries are important). Network News generates huge volumes each day and messages are discarded off servers after an amount of time specified by the individual server manager for each specific group. This period could be minutes, hours or days. Moderated news requires a news group administrator to approve each message before it is posted to a moderated news group. News groups can be specific to a particular organisation, country or network. There is no central store for news and no central control of content.

*Operating System (OS):* computer software developed to provide computer programs with standard facilities to interact with users and with computer hardware (via drivers). *See also* MS-DOS, PC-DOS, UNIX, MacOS, MS Windows.

*PERL:* Practical Extraction and Reporting Language – powerfull text processing language typically used to develop CGI's for web servers. Compiled into Byte-code, a PERL program can be run on any computer supporting the PERL virtual machine.

*Parallel:* adjective to describe a communications type to denote that bits of information are sent in groups simultaneously side by side over multiple pairs within a single cable. Commonly used to connect PCs and printers.

*PC-DOS:* very closely related to MS-DOS and providing the same functionality. Initially adopted by IBM as the operating system for their personal computers but was effectively abandoned as MS-DOS became ubiquitous. *See also* PC-DOS; Operating System.

*PGP:* Pretty Good Privacy – an implementation of the Public Key System of data encryption. Available on many different platforms PGP is a widely used program. Developed by Philip R Zimmermann in 1991 it is typically used for email security and digital signatures. There are two versions Rivest-Shamire-Adleman (RSA) and Diffie-Hellman. The RSA version incurs a licence fee to RSA. PGP is available in restricted shareware and commercial versions. Availability of PGP has until recently been heavily restricted by the US government (via classification as a war munition). *See also* Public Key System.

*PNG:* an improved royalty-free graphics file replacement for GIF.

*POP3:* Post Office Protocol 3 – an Internet protocol whereby a workstation can collect email from a personal mailbox on an email server and move it to a mailbox typically on a user's own machine. Mail collection typically copies the messages from the server to the local machine before deleting them from the server.

*Public Key:* a virtual key generated and publicly available from a destination (e.g. email or web site) for use in encryption of information sent to that destination. Akin to a recipient providing unlocked padlocks for which only the recipient has the key. The sender uses the key (padlock) to encrypt (secure) the contents of the message or web submission (cargo) for the recipient to receive and unlock.

*Print Server:* a computer or device on a network that manages the sharing of one or more printers between multiple computers over a network. Many modern printers have a print server built in, although early printers almost always needed a print server to be actively shared.

*RJ-45:* a standard for cable connectors in Ethernet networks.

*RIP:* Raster Image Processor – Hardware and/or Software product that generates a raster graphic (or bitmap) from images in vector graphic format.

*Router:* where multiple networks are joined together, a router acts like a very fast sorting office, examining the destination address of each information packet and passing or routing it to the appropriate network.

Routers select the most efficient general route for packets of information based on current system demands.

*SCSI:* Small Computer System Interface – available in a variety of performance specifications. Typically used for connection of high speed hard disks, scanners, specialist printers and removable drives, SCSI was until recently shipped as standard on all Apple Macintosh computers and is common on UNIX servers and workstations. SCSI has been replaced by Firewire on Apple Macintosh and is becoming more common on other platforms.

*SDSL:* Symetric Digital Subscriber Line – Form of DSL providing high speed connection to the Internet over ordinary copper telephone cables. Unlike ADSL, SDSL offers the same transfers in each direction. Common in North America and Europe but not in the United Kingdom. *See also* DSL, ADSL.

*Serial:* adjective to describe a communication type to denote that bits of information are sent one after another down a single wire pair as opposed to being sent in parallel. Commonly used for mice and keyboards, and on Macintosh computers for printers (*see* Parallel).

*SMTP:* Simple Mail Transfer Protocol – an Internet protocol whereby a workstation can send email to a server or whereby two servers can exchange email.

*SNMP:* Simple Network Management Protocol – Widely used protocol for remotely monitoring and managing network device status and function.

*Stuffit:* popular Apple Macintosh mechanism to compress information for transmission and later expansion without loss of information. Stuffit is a proprietary brand name of Aladdin Systems. *See also* Zip.

*Switch:* Unlike an Ethernet HUB the Ethernet switch only passes network traffic between the parties to a connection. For example when printing from Workstation A to Printer B, the switch only passes information to the switch ports (connections) for the workstation and the printer, not all ports. Typically a good switch is more expensive and provides better performance on average than a HUB. *See also* HUB.

*TCP/IP:* Transmission Control Protocol/Internet Protocol – a protocol which is the lifeblood of the Internet, TCP/IP defines how information and requests generated by all other protocols are transmitted and received over the Internet. The majority of information on the Internet is chopped up into small chunks or packets of information which are addressed with a destination and origination address. It sometimes happens that a packet gets lost and TCP/IP dictates how such a loss is handled.

*Token ring:* historically popular but less so today, a token ring is a form of network that takes the form of a ring connecting each computer. An electronic token (or tokens) is passed around the ring to each computer in turn. Possession of the token allows a computer to transmit for a limited period of time. Token ring is less resilient than Ethernet as any break or flaw in the ring can seriously degrade performance or cause it to fail completely.

*USB:* Universal Serial Bus – new standard for connecting serial devices such as scanners, mice, keyboards, modems and printers to computers. With USB, speeds of 10 Mbps and higher are possible. Has replaced standard serial ports and ADB connections on Apple Macintosh computers. USB devices can be hot-plugged as required. *See also* ADB.

*URL:* Uniform Resource Locator – address of an Internet file accessible on the Internet. Typically the server and path to an image, HTML page, CGI, Java applet or other Internet content available to web browsers.

*Virus:* a computer program or script written for the express purpose of replicating itself onto as many machines as possible (much like its biological namesake) often with negative side effects to the host computer and computer network. Such effects vary from harmless screen messages to deletion or corruption of document integrity, network overload or compromising of security or privacy. A typical motive is notoriety for the author. Most viruses are not particularly sophisticated and tend to capitalise on specific flaws or features of a particular operating system or program. Very few viruses are truly self-modifying and simply robotically clone themselves. Historically transmitted by floppy disk between offices and over networks within offices, the prevalence of email means viruses can spread globally within hours.

*WAP:* Wireless Application Protocol – a set of standards to defined how portable devices connected via radio waves (such as cell phones) can access Internet services. Launched in 2000 into the United Kingdom, WAP has not been as widely used as expected.

*Windows ME:* Windows Millennium Edition – operating system successor to Windows 98 for Pentium compatible personal computers. *See also* Windows 98.

*Windows 3.1.1:* Microsoft's first credible implementation of an graphical user interface operating system (GUI OS) implementation. Still used by many companies but superseded by successive MS Windows releases.

*Windows 2000 Professional:* Replacement for Windows NT Workstation. *See also* Windows NT.

*Windows 2000 Server:* Replacement for Windows NT Server. Available in various optimised and targeted versions. *See also* Windows NT.

*Windows 95:* Microsoft's highly successful upgrade to 3.1.1 providing more features but consuming more resources.

*Windows 98:* essentially a bug-fix, correcting problems with Windows 95.

*Windows NT 3:* appearing to the user as a 32 bit implementation of Windows 3.1.1, Windows NT was marketed as a stable and powerful business operating system. NT was mainly adopted by organisations as a server operating system and thus competing with Novell NetWare. Subsequently has been superseded by Windows NT 4.

*Windows NT 4:* this evolution of Windows NT 3 was marketed as Windows NT 4 Workstation for business machines and as NT4 Workstation for network servers. Significant in-built network administration and work group features coupled with the highly successful graphical interface of Windows 95 led to Windows NT being a leading operating system.

*XML:* Extensible Mark-up Language; similar to HTML but more powerful, XML allows pages of information to be encoded for publishing on the web and for traditional paper publishing. It is extensible insomuch as XML primaries can be combined to extend the language providing greater functionality.

*Zip:* compression – a popular mechanism on PCs to compress information for transmission and later expansion without loss of information. *See also* Stuffit.

*Zip DRIVE:* a popular 3.5" inexpensive removable disk format capable of storing either 100 or 250 Megabytes of information depending on format. Zip is a proprietary brand name of Iomega.

# Local Government

Major changes in local government were introduced in England and Wales in 1974 and in Scotland in 1975 by the Local Government Act 1972 and the Local Government (Scotland) Act 1973. Further significant alterations were made in England by the Local Government Acts of 1985, 1992 and 2000.

The structure in England was based on two tiers of local authorities (county councils and district councils) in the non-metropolitan areas; and a single tier of metropolitan councils in the six metropolitan areas of England and London borough councils in London.

Following reviews of the structure of local government in England by the Local Government Commission, 46 unitary (all-purpose) authorities were created between April 1995 and April 1998 to cover certain areas in the non-metropolitan counties. The remaining county areas continue to have two tiers of local authorities. The county and district councils in the Isle of Wight were replaced by a single unitary authority on 1 April 1995; the former counties of Avon, Cleveland, Humberside and Berkshire have been replaced by unitary authorities; and Hereford and Worcester was replaced by a new county council for Worcestershire (with district councils) and a unitary authority for Herefordshire.

The Local Government (Wales) Act 1994 and the Local Government etc. (Scotland) Act 1994 abolished the two-tier structure in Wales and Scotland with effect from 1 April 1996, replacing it with a single tier of unitary authorities.

Local authorities are empowered or required by various Acts of Parliament to carry out functions in their areas. The legislation concerned comprises public general Acts and 'local' Acts which local authorities have promoted as private bills.

## ELECTIONS

Local elections are normally held on the first Thursday in May. Generally, all British subjects, citizens of the Republic of Ireland, Commonwealth and other European Union citizens who are 18 years or over and resident on the qualifying date in the area for which the election is being held, are entitled to vote at local government elections. A register of electors is prepared and published annually by local electoral registration officers.

A returning officer has the overall responsibility for an election. Voting takes place at polling stations, arranged by the local authority and under the supervision of a presiding officer specially appointed for the purpose. Candidates, who are subject to various statutory qualifications and disqualifications designed to ensure that they are suitable persons to hold office, must be nominated by electors for the electoral area concerned.

In England, the Local Government Commission is responsible for carrying out periodic reviews of electoral arrangements and making recommendations to the Secretary of State for changes found necessary. In Wales and Scotland these matters are the responsibility of the Local Government Boundary Commission for Wales and the Local Boundary Commission for Scotland respectively. The Local Government Act 2000 provided for the Secretary of State to change the frequency and phasing of elections.

LOCAL GOVERNMENT COMMISSION FOR ENGLAND, Dolphyn Court, 10–11 Great Turnstile, Lincoln's Inn Fields, London WC1V 7JU. Tel: 020-7430 8400

LOCAL GOVERNMENT BOUNDARY COMMISSION FOR WALES, Caradog House, 1–6 St Andrew's Place, Cardiff CF1 3BE. Tel: 029-2039 5031

LOCAL GOVERNMENT BOUNDARY COMMISSION FOR SCOTLAND, 3 Drumsheugh Gardens, Edinburgh EH3 7QJ. Tel: 0131-538 7510

## INTERNAL ORGANISATION

The council as a whole is the final decision-making body within any authority. Councils are free to a great extent to make their own internal organisational arrangements. The Local Government Act, given Royal assent on 28 July 2000, allows councils to adopt one of three broad categories of a new constitution which include a separate executive. These three categories are:

- A directly elected mayor with a cabinet selected by that mayor.
- A cabinet, either elected by the council or appointed by its leader.
- A directly elected mayor and council manager.

Normally, questions of policy are settled by the full council, while the administration of the various services is the responsibility of committees of councillors. Day-to-day decisions are delegated to the council's officers, who act within the policies laid down by the councillors.

## FINANCE

Local government in England, Wales and Scotland is financed from four sources: the council tax, non-domestic rates, government grants, and income from fees and charges for services.

### COUNCIL TAX

Under the Local Government Finance Act 1992, from 1 April 1993 the council tax replaced the community charge (which had been introduced in April 1989 in Scotland and April 1990 in England and Wales in place of domestic rates).

The council tax is a local tax levied by each local council. Liability for the council tax bill usually falls on the owner-occupier or tenant of a dwelling which is their sole or main residence. Council tax bills may be reduced because of the personal circumstances of people resident in a property, and there are discounts in the case of dwellings occupied by fewer than two adults.

In England, each county council, each district council and each police authority sets its own council tax rate. The district councils collect the combined council tax, and the county councils and police authorities claim their share from the district councils' collection funds. In Wales, each unitary authority and each police authority sets its own council tax rate. The unitary authorities collect the combined council tax and the police authorities claim their share from the funds. In Scotland, each island council and unitary authority sets its own rate of council tax.

The tax relates to the value of the dwelling. Each dwelling is placed in one of eight valuation bands, ranging from A to H, based on the property's estimated market value as at 1 April 1991.

The valuation bands and ranges of values in England, Wales and Scotland are:

*England*

| | | | |
|---|---|---|---|
| A | Up to £40,000 | E | £88,001–£120,000 |
| B | £40,001–£52,000 | F | £120,001–£160,000 |
| C | £52,001–£68,000 | G | £160,001–£320,000 |
| D | £68,001–£88,000 | H | Over £320,000 |

*Wales*

| | | | |
|---|---|---|---|
| A | Up to £30,000 | E | £66,001–£90,000 |
| B | £30,001–£39,000 | F | £90,001–£120,000 |
| C | £39,001–£51,000 | G | £120,001– £240,000 |
| D | £51,001–£66,000 | H | Over £240,000 |

*Scotland*

| | | | |
|---|---|---|---|
| A | Up to £27,000 | E | £58,001–£80,000 |
| B | £27,001–£35,000 | F | £80,001–£106,000 |
| C | £35,001–£45,000 | G | £106,001–£212,000 |
| D | £45,001–£58,000 | H | Over £212,000 |

The council tax within a local area varies between the different bands according to proportions laid down by law. The charge attributable to each band as a proportion of the Band D charge set by the council is approximately:

| | | | |
|---|---|---|---|
| A | 67% | E | 122% |
| B | 78% | F | 144% |
| C | 89% | G | 167% |
| D | 100% | H | 200% |

The band D rate is given in the tables on the following pages. There may be variations from the given figure within each district council area because of different parish or community precepts being levied.

### Non-Domestic Rates

Non-domestic (business) rates are collected by billing authorities; these are the district councils in those areas of England with two tiers of local government and unitary authorities in other parts of England, in Wales and in Scotland. In respect of England and Wales, the Local Government Finance Act 1988 provides for liability for rates to be assessed on the basis of a poundage (multiplier) tax on the rateable value of property (hereditaments). Separate multipliers are set by the Secretary of State for Transport, Local Government and the Regions in England, the National Assembly for Wales and the Scottish Executive, and rates are collected by the billing authority for the area where a property is located. Rate income collected by billing authorities is paid into a national non-domestic rating (NNDR) pool and redistributed to individual authorities on the basis of the adult population figure as prescribed by the Secretary of State for Transport, Local Government and the Regions, the National Assembly for Wales or the Scottish Executive. The rates pools are maintained separately in England, Wales and Scotland. Actual payment of rates in certain cases is subject to transitional arrangements, to phase in the larger increases and reductions in rates resulting from the effects of the 2000 revaluation.

Rates are levied in Scotland in accordance with the Local Government (Scotland) Act 1975. For 1995–6, the Secretary of State for Scotland prescribed a single non-domestic rates poundage to apply throughout the country at the same level as the uniform business rate (UBR) in England. Rate income is pooled and redistributed to local authorities on a per capita basis. For the year 1995–6 payment of rates was subject to transitional arrangements to phase in the effect of the 1995 revaluation.

Rateable values for the 2000 rating lists came into force on 1 April 2000. They are derived from the rental value of property as at 1 April 1993 and determined on certain statutory assumptions by the Valuation Office Agency in England and Wales, and by Regional Assessors in Scotland. New property which is added to the list, and significant changes to existing property, necessitate amendments to the rateable value on the same basis. Rating lists (valuation rolls in Scotland) remain in force until the next general revaluation. Such revaluations take place every five years, the next being in 2005.

Certain types of property are exempt from rates, e.g. agricultural land and buildings, certain businesses and places of public religious worship. Charities and other non-profit-making organisations may receive full or partial relief. Empty property is liable to pay rates at 50 per cent, except for certain specified classes which are exempt entirely.

### Government Grants

In addition to specific grants in support of revenue expenditure on particular services, central government pays revenue support grant to local authorities. This grant is paid to each local authority so that if each authority spends at the level of its standard spending assessment, all authorities in the same class can set broadly the same council tax.

## COMPLAINTS

Commissioners for Local Administration in England, Wales and Scotland are responsible for investigating complaints from members of the public who claim to have suffered injustice as a consequence of maladministration in local government or in certain local bodies.

The Northern Ireland Commissioner for Complaints fulfils a similar function in Northern Ireland, investigating complaints about local authorities and certain public bodies.

Complaints are made to the relevant local authority in the first instance and complainants may approach the Commissioners if not satisfied. Complaints may also be made directly to the Commissioners.

The Local Government Act 2000 established a Standards Board and Adjudication Panel in England. The Standards Board investigates any allegations that councillors have breached the council's Code of Conduct and if there is evidence of wrongdoing the Adjudication Panel will consider the report of investigations and if it is upheld, impose a penalty. In Wales the Commission for Local Administration in Wales undertakes the role of the Standards Board.

## THE QUEEN'S REPRESENTATIVES

The Lord-Lieutenant of a county is the permanent local representative of the Crown in that county. The appointment of Lord-Lieutenants is now regulated by the Lieutenancies Act 1997. They are appointed by the Sovereign on the recommendation of the Prime Minister. The retirement age is 75. The office of Lord-Lieutenant dates from 1551, and its holder was originally responsible for the maintenance of order and for local defence in the county. The duties of the post include attending on royalty during official visits to the county, performing certain duties in connection with armed forces of the Crown (and in particular the reserve forces), and making presentations of honours and awards on behalf of the Crown. In England, Wales and Northern Ireland, the Lord-Lieutenant usually also holds the office of *Custos Rotulorum*. As such, he or she acts as head of the county's commission of the peace (which recommends the appointment of magistrates).

The office of Sheriff (from the Old English shire-reeve) of a county was created in the tenth century. The Sheriff was the special nominee of the Sovereign, and the office reached the peak of its influence under the Norman kings. The Provisions of Oxford (1258) laid down a yearly tenure of office. Since the mid-16th century the office has been purely civil, with military duties taken over by the Lord-Lieutenant of the county. The Sheriff (commonly known as 'High Sheriff') attends on royalty during official visits to the county, acts as the returning officer during parliamentary elections in county constituencies, attends the opening ceremony when a High Court judge goes on circuit, executes High Court writs, and appoints under-sheriffs to act as deputies. The appointments and duties of the High Sheriffs in England and Wales are laid down by the Sheriffs Act 1887.

The serving High Sheriff submits a list of names of possible future sheriffs to a tribunal which chooses three names to put to the Sovereign. The tribunal nominates the High Sheriff annually on 12 November and the Sovereign picks the name of the Sheriff to succeed in the following year. The term of office runs from 25 March to the following 24 March (the civil and legal year before 1752). No person may be chosen twice in three years if there is any other suitable person in the county.

## CIVIC DIGNITIES

District councils in England may petition for a royal charter granting borough or 'city' status to the district. Local councils in Wales may petition for a royal charter granting county borough or 'city' status to the council.

In England and Wales the chairman of a borough or county borough council may be called a mayor, and the chairman of a city council a Lord Mayor. Parish councils in England and community councils in Wales may call themselves 'town councils', in which case their chairman is the town mayor.

In Scotland the chairman of a local council may be known as a convenor; a provost is the equivalent of a mayor. The chairmen of the councils for the cities of Aberdeen, Dundee, Edinburgh and Glasgow are Lord Provosts.

## ENGLAND

There are currently 34 non-metropolitan counties; all are divided into non-metropolitan districts. In addition, there are 45 unitary authorities (13 created in April 1996, 13 in April 1997 and 19 in April 1998). At present there are 238 non-metropolitan districts. The populations of most of the new unitary authorities are in the range of 100,000 to 300,000. The non-metropolitan districts have populations broadly in the range of 60,000 to 100,000; some, however, have larger populations, because of the need to avoid dividing large towns, and some in mainly rural areas have smaller populations.

The main conurbations outside Greater London – Tyne and Wear, West Midlands, Merseyside, Greater Manchester, West Yorkshire and South Yorkshire – are divided into 36 metropolitan districts, most of which have a population of over 200,000.

There are also about 10,000 parishes, in 219 of the non-metropolitan and 18 of the metropolitan districts.

### ELECTIONS

For districts, non-metropolitan counties and for about 8,000 parishes, there are elected councils, consisting of directly elected councillors. The councillors elect annually one of their number as chairman.

Generally, councillors serve four years and there are no elections of district and parish councillors in county election years. In metropolitan districts, one-third of the councillors for each ward are elected each year except in the year when county elections take place elsewhere. Non-metropolitan districts can choose whether to have elections by thirds or whole council elections. In the former case, one-third of the council, as nearly as may be, is elected in each year of metropolitan district elections. If whole council elections are chosen, these are held in the year midway between county elections.

### FUNCTIONS

In non-metropolitan areas, functions are divided between the districts and counties, those requiring the larger area or population for their efficient performance going to the county. The metropolitan district councils, with the larger population in their areas, already had wider functions than non-metropolitan councils, and following abolition of the metropolitan county councils were given most of their functions also. A few functions continue to be exercised over the larger area by joint bodies, made up of councillors from each district.

The allocation of functions is as follows:

*County councils:* education; strategic planning; traffic, transport and highways; fire service; consumer protection; refuse disposal; smallholdings; social services; libraries

*Non-metropolitan district councils:* local planning; housing; highways (maintenance of certain urban roads and off-street car parks); building regulations; environmental health; refuse collection; cemeteries and crematoria

*Unitary councils:* their functions are all those listed above, except that the fire service is exercised by a joint body

*Concurrently by county and district councils:* recreation (parks, playing fields, swimming pools); museums; encouragement of the arts, tourism and industry

The Police and Magistrates Court Act 1994 set up police authorities in England and Wales separate from the local authorities.

### PARISH COUNCILS

Parishes with 200 or more electors must generally have parish councils, which means that over three-quarters of the parishes have councils. A parish council comprises at least five members, the number being fixed by the district council. Elections are held every four years, at the time of the election of the district councillor for the ward including the parish. All parishes have parish meetings, comprising the electors of the parish. Where there is no council, the meeting must be held at least twice a year.

Parish council functions include: allotments; encouragement of arts and crafts; community halls, recreational facilities (e.g. open spaces, swimming pools), cemeteries and crematoria; and many minor functions. They must also be given an opportunity to comment on planning applications. They may, like county and district councils, spend limited sums for the general benefit of the parish. They levy a precept on the district councils for their funds.

The Local Government and Rating Act 1997 gave additional powers to parish councils to spend money on community transport initiatives and crime prevention equipment.

### FINANCE

Aggregate external finance for 2001-2002 was originally determined at £44,520 million. Of this, specific and special grants were estimated at £9,229 million; £21,122 million was in respect of revenue support grant and £15,137 million was support from the national non-domestic rate pool. Total standard spending by local authorities considered for grant purposes was £57,133 million.

In England, the average council tax per dwelling in 2000-2001 was £697, an increase of 6.2 per cent from the 1999-2000 level. The average council tax was £710 in shire areas, £713 in London and £650 in metropolitan areas. In England, the average council tax bill for a band D dwelling (occupied by two adults) for 2000-2001 was £847, an increase of 6.1 per cent from the 1999-2000 level. The average band D council tax was £843 in shire areas, £778 in London and £919 in metropolitan areas.

The provisional amount estimated to be raised from national non-domestic rates from central and local lists is £15,068 million. Total rateable value held on draft local authority lists at 30 December 2000 was £41,351 million. The amount of national non-domestic rates to be redistributed to authorities from the pool in 2001-2002 was £15,137 million. The national non-domestic rate multiplier, or poundage, for 2001-2002 is 43.0p. Under the Local Government and Housing Act 1989, local authorities have four main ways of paying for capital expenditure: borrowing and other forms of extended credit; capital grants from central government towards some types of capital expenditure; 'usable' capital receipts from the sale of land, houses and other assets; and revenue.

The amount of capital expenditure which a local authority can finance by borrowing (or other forms of credit) is effectively limited by the credit approvals issued to it by central government. Most credit approvals can be used for any kind of local authority capital expenditure; these are known as basic credit approvals. Others (supplementary credit approvals) can be used only for the kind of expenditure specified in the approval, and so are often given to fund particular projects or services.

Local authorities can use all capital receipts from the sale of property or assets for capital spending, except in the case of sales of council houses. Generally, the 'usable' part of a local authority's capital receipts consists of 25 per cent of receipts from the sale of council houses and 50 per cent of other housing assets such as shops or vacant land. The balance has to be set aside as provision for repaying debt and meeting other credit liabilities.

### Expenditure

Local authority budgeted net revenue expenditure for 2001–2002 was (2001–2002 cash prices):

| *Service* | £m |
|---|---|
| Education | 25,813 |
| Personal social services | 11,076 |
| Police | 7,861 |
| Highway maintenance | 1,615 |
| Fire | 1,842 |
| Emergency Planning and other Home Office services | 105 |
| Magistrates courts | 324 |
| Public transport and parking | 972 |
| Housing benefit administration | 6,167 |
| Non-housing revenue account housing | 434 |
| Libraries, culture and heritage | 1,201 |
| Sport | 557 |
| Local environmental services | 4,696 |
| Other services | 2,427 |
| *Net current expenditure* | 65,073 |
| Capital charges | 2,050 |
| Capital charged to revenue | 699 |
| Other non-current expenditure | 2,378 |
| Interest receipts | –809 |
| *Gross revenue expenditure* | 69,390 |
| Specific and special grants outside AEF | –8,119 |
| *Revenue expenditure* | 61,270 |
| Specific and special grants inside AEF | –5,431 |
| *Net revenue expenditure* | 55,839 |

AEF = aggregate external finance

## London

Since the abolition of the Greater London Council in 1986, the Greater London area has not had a single local government body. The area is divided into 32 borough councils, which have a status similar to the metropolitan district councils in the rest of England, and the Corporation of the City of London.

In March 1998 the Government announced proposals for a Greater London Authority (GLA) covering the area of the 32 London boroughs and the City of London, which would comprise a directly elected mayor and a 25-member assembly. A referendum was held in London on 7 May 1998; the turnout was approximately 34 per cent, of whom 72 per cent voted in favour of the GLA. The independent candidate for London Mayor, Ken Livingstone, was elected on 4 May 2000 and the Authority assumed its responsibilities on 3 July 2000. The GLA is responsible for transport, economic development, strategic planning, culture, health, the environment, the police and fire and emergency planning. The separately elected assembly scrutinise the mayor's activities and approve plans and budgets. There are 14 Constituency Assembly members, each representing a separate area of London (each constituency is made up of two or three complete London boroughs). Eleven additional members, making up the total Assembly complement of 25 members, are elected on a Londonwide basis, either as independents or from party political lists on the basis of proportional representation. Parties or independent candidates must secure at least five per cent of the vote to be entitled to additional seats.

### London Borough Councils

The London boroughs have whole council elections every four years, in the year immediately following the county council election year. The next elections will be in 2002.

The borough councils have responsibility for the following functions: building regulations; cemeteries and crematoria; consumer protection; education; youth employment; environmental health; electoral registration; food; drugs; housing; leisure services; libraries; local planning; local roads; museums; parking; recreation (parks, playing fields, swimming pools); refuse collection and street cleansing; social services; town planning; and traffic management.

### The Corporation of London

The Corporation of London is the local authority for the City of London. Its legal definition is 'The Mayor and Commonalty and Citizens of the City of London'. It is governed by the Court of Common Council, which consists of the Lord Mayor, 24 other aldermen, and 130 common councilmen. The Lord Mayor and two sheriffs are nominated annually by the City guilds (the livery companies) and elected by the Court of Aldermen. Aldermen and councilmen are elected from the 25 wards into which the City is divided; councilmen must stand for re-election annually. The Council is a legislative assembly, and there are no political parties.

The Corporation has the same functions as the London borough councils. In addition, it runs the City of London Police; is the health authority for the Port of London; has health control of animal imports throughout Greater London, including at Heathrow airport; owns and manages public open spaces throughout Greater London; runs the Central Criminal Court; and runs Billingsgate, Smithfield and Spitalfields markets.

### The City Guilds (Livery Companies)

The livery companies of the City of London grew out of early medieval religious fraternities and began to emerge as trade and craft guilds, retaining their religious aspect, in the 12th century. From the early 14th century, only members of the trade and craft guilds could call themselves citizens of the City of London. The guilds began to be called livery companies, because of the distinctive livery worn by the most prosperous guild members on ceremonial occasions, in the late 15th century.

By the early 19th century the power of the companies within their trades had begun to wane, but those wearing the livery of a company continued to play an important role in the government of the City of London. Liverymen still have the right to nominate the Lord Mayor and sheriffs, and most members of the Court of Common Council are liverymen.

### Greater London Services

After the abolition of the Greater London Council (GLC) in 1986, the London boroughs took over most of its functions. Successor bodies have also been set up for certain functions. The London Residuary Body (LRB) was set up in 1986 to deal with residual matters of the GLC. It completed its work and was wound up in 1995.

## WALES

The Local Government (Wales) Act 1994 abolished the two-tier structure of eight county and 37 district councils which had existed since 1974, and replaced it, from 1 April 1996, with 22 unitary authorities. The new authorities were elected in May 1995. Each unitary authority has inherited all the functions of the previous county and district councils, except fire services (which are provided by three combined fire authorities, composed of representatives of the unitary authorities) and National Parks (which are the responsibility of three independent National Park authorities).

The Police and Magistrates Courts Act 1994 set up four police authorities with effect from 1 April 1995: Dyfed-Powys, Gwent, North Wales, and South Wales.

### Community Councils

In Wales community councils are the equivalent of parishes in England. Unlike England, where many areas are not in any parish, communities have been established for the whole of Wales, approximately 865 communities in all. Community meetings may be convened as and when desired.

Community councils exist in 735 communities and further councils may be established at the request of a community meeting. Community councils have broadly the same range of powers as English parish councils. Community councillors are elected for a term of four years.

### Finance

Aggregate external finance for 2001-2002 (excluding specific grants) is £2,848 million. This comprises revenue support grant of £2,147 million, support from the national non-domestic rate pool of £697 million, and £4 million in council tax reduction grants. Total standard spending by local authorities considered for grant purposes is £3,495 million.

The average Band D council tax levied in Wales for 2001-02 is £710, comprising unitary authorities £606, police authorities £86, community councils £18 and an average grant reduction of £4.

### Expenditure

Local authority budgeted net revenue expenditure for 2001–2 was:

| *Service* | £m |
|---|---|
| Education | 1,585.0 |
| Personal social services | 716.5 |
| Police | 426.2 |
| Fire | 102.9 |
| Other law, order and protective services | 34.8 |
| Roads and Transport | 192.3 |
| Council tax benefit and administration | 124.4 |
| Non-housing revenue account housing, including housing benefit | 280.0 |
| Libraries, culture, heritage, sport and recreation | 122.8 |
| Local environmental services | 293.7 |
| National Parks | 9.6 |
| Debt financing costs | 256.8 |
| Other services | 196.7 |
| *Gross Revenue Expenditure* | 4,342.2 |
| Less specific government grants | –578.0 |
| *Net revenue expenditure* | 3,763.7 |

## SCOTLAND

The Local Government etc. (Scotland) Act 1994 abolished the two-tier structure of nine regional and 53 district councils which had existed since 1975 and replaced it, from 1 April 1996, with 29 unitary authorities on the mainland; the three islands councils remained. The new authorities were elected in April 1995. Each unitary authority has inherited all the functions of the regional and district councils, except water and sewerage (now provided by three public bodies whose members were appointed by the Secretary of State for Scotland; this power has now been devolved to the Scottish Executive) and reporters panels (now a national agency).

In July 1999 the Scottish Parliament assumed responsibility for legislation on local government. The Government had established a Commission on Local Government and the Scottish Parliament (the McIntosh Commission) to make recommendations on the relationship between local authorities and the new Parliament and on increasing local authorities' accountability. The Commission reported to the First Minister of the Scottish Parliament in June 1999. Following this, the Scottish Executive established the 'Renewing Local Democracy' working group to consider ways in which council membership could be made more attractive and councils could become more representative of the make-up of the community and advise on the appropriate numbers of members for each council, taking account of new management arrangements and characteristics. They also investigated which method of election would be most appropriate, taking account of the following criteria; proportionality and the councillor-ward link, fair provision for independents, allowance for geographical diversity and a close fit between council wards and natural communities, and advise on an appropriate system of remuneration for councillors, taking account of available resources.

The Scottish Executive also set up the Leadership Advisory Panel in October 1999 following the recommendations of the McIntosh Report. The panel is working closely with all Scottish local authorities conducting reviews of their policy development and decision-making structures.

### Elections

The unitary authorities consist of directly elected councillors. Elections take place every three years; the next elections are in 2002. In 2001 the register showed 3,984,306 electors in Scotland.

### Functions

The functions of the councils and islands councils are: education; social work; strategic planning; the provision of infrastructure such as roads; consumer protection; flood prevention; coast protection; valuation and rating; the police and fire services; civil defence; electoral registration; public transport; registration of births, deaths and marriages; housing; leisure and recreation; development control and building control; environmental health; licensing; allotments; public conveniences; and the administration of district courts.

### Community Councils

Unlike the parish councils and community councils in England and Wales, Scottish community councils are not local authorities. Their purpose as defined in statute is to ascertain and express the views of the communities they represent, and to take in the interests of their communities such action as appears to be expedient or practicable. Over 1,000 community councils have been established under schemes drawn up by district and islands councils in Scotland.

Since April 1996 community councils have had an enhanced role, becoming statutory consultees on local planning issues and on the decentralisation schemes which the new councils have to draw up for delivery of services.

### Finance

Figures for 2000–01 show total receipts from non-domestic rates of £1,535,173,000 (provisional). The unified business rate for 2001–2 was 45p for property with a rateable value of less than £10,000 and 47p otherwise. The average Band D council tax payable in 2001–2 was £929.

### Expenditure

The 2001–2 budget estimates for local authorities in Scotland were:

| *Service* | £m |
|---|---|
| Education | 3,245.9 |
| Arts and Libraries | 126.5 |
| Social Work Services | 1,334.0 |
| Law, order and protective services | 1,011.8 |
| Roads and transport | 365.3 |
| Other environmental services | 758.2 |
| Tourism | 9.1 |
| Housing | 3.3 |
| Sub-total | 6,854.6 |
| Sheltered employment | 9.6 |
| Housing benefit administration | 42.7 |
| Consumer protection | 70.8 |
| Total | 6,925.3 |

## NORTHERN IRELAND

For the purpose of local government Northern Ireland has a system of 26 single-tier district councils.

### Elections

There are 582 members of the councils, elected for periods of four years at a time on the principle of proportional representation.

### Functions

The district councils have three main roles. These are:

*Executive:* responsibility for a wide range of local services including building regulations; community services; consumer protection; cultural facilities; environmental health; miscellaneous licensing and registration provisions, including dog control; litter prevention; recreational and social facilities; refuse collection and disposal; street cleansing; and tourist development

*Representative:* nominating representatives to sit as members of the various statutory bodies responsible for the administration of regional services such as drainage, education, fire, health and personal social services, housing, and libraries

*Consultative:* acting as the medium through which the views of local people are expressed on the operation in their area of other regional services, notably conservation (including water supply and sewerage services), planning and roads, provided by those departments of central government which have an obligation, statutory or otherwise, to consult the district councils about proposals affecting their areas

### Finance

Local government in Northern Ireland is funded by a system of rates (a local property tax calculated by using the rateable value of a property multiplied by an amount per pound of rateable value). Rates are collected by the Rate Collection Agency, an executive agency within the Department of the Environment for Northern Ireland. A general revaluation of non-domestic properties became effective on 1 April 1997. As a result of this, separate regional rates are now made at standard uniform amounts by the Department of Finance and Personnel for both domestic and non-domestic sectors. District councils now make their individual district rates on the same basis.

In 2000–01 approximately £607.9 million was raised in rates. The average domestic poundage levied was 227.83p and the average non-domestic rate poundage was 47.13p.

# Political Composition of Local Councils

AS AT END JUNE 2001

*Abbreviations:*

| | |
|---|---|
| *C.* | Conservative |
| *Com.* | Communist |
| *Dem.* | Democrat |
| *Green* | Green |
| *Ind.* | Independent |
| *Lab.* | Labour |
| *Lib.* | Liberal |
| *LD* | Liberal Democrat |
| *MK* | Mebyon Kernow |
| *NP* | Non-political/Non-party |
| *PC* | Plaid Cymru |
| *RA* | Ratepayers'/Resident's Associations |
| *SD* | Social Democrat |
| *SNP* | Scottish National Party |

## ENGLAND

### COUNTY COUNCILS

| | |
|---|---|
| Bedfordshire | *C.* 25, *Lab.* 14, *LD* 10 |
| Buckinghamshire | *C.* 40, *Lab.* 5, *LD* 9 |
| Cambridgeshire | *C.* 34, *Lab.* 9, *LD* 16 |
| Cheshire | *C.* 28, *Ind.* 1, *Lab.* 17, *LD* 5 |
| Cornwall | *C.* 9, *Ind.* 25, *Lab.* 9, *LD* 35, *Lib.* 1 |
| Cumbria | *C.* 33, *Ind.* 1, *Lab.* 40, *LD* 10 |
| Derbyshire | *C.* 13, *Ind.* 1, *Lab.* 43, *LD* 7 |
| Devon | *C.* 22, *Ind.* 3, *Lab.* 5, *LD* 21, *Lib.* 2, *Other* 1 |
| Dorset | *C.* 23, *Ind.* 1, *Lab.* 4, *LD* 14 |
| Durham | *C.* 2, *Ind.* 2, *Lab.* 53, *LD* 4 |
| East Sussex | *C.* 20, *Lab.* 7, *LD* 17 |
| Essex | *C.* 40, *Ind.* 1, *Lab.* 24, *LD* 14 |
| Gloucestershire | *C.* 24, *Ind.* 3, *Lab.* 15, *LD* 20, *Others* 1 |
| Hampshire | *C.* 46, *Lab.* 9, *LD* 19 |
| Hertfordshire | *C.* 40, *Lab.* 27, *LD* 10 |
| Kent | *C.* 52, *Lab.* 22, *LD* 10 |
| Lancashire | *C.* 26, *Green* 1, *Lab.* 44, *LD* 6, *Other* 1 |
| Leicestershire | *C.* 25, *Lab.* 17, *LD* 11, *Other* 1 |
| Lincolnshire | *C.* 49, *Ind.* 3, *Lab.* 21, *LD* 4 |
| Norfolk | *C.* 37, *Ind.* 1, *Lab.* 33, *LD* 13 |
| Northamptonshire | *C.* 33, *Lab.* 39, *LD* 1 |
| Northumberland | *C.* 17, *Ind.* 3, *Lab.* 38, *LD* 9 |
| North Yorkshire | *C.* 37, *Ind.* 5, *Lab.* 11, *LD* 21 |
| Nottinghamshire | *C.* 20, *Lab.* 40, *LD* 3 |
| Oxfordshire | *C.* 26, *Green* 2, *Lab.* 24, *LD* 18 |
| Shropshire | *C.* 18, *Lab.* 11, *LD* 9, *Others* 6 |
| Somerset | *C.* 24, *Lab.* 5, *LD* 29 |
| Staffordshire | *C.* 24, *Lab.* 36, *LD* 2 |
| Suffolk | *C.* 31, *Ind.* 1, *Lab.* 36, *LD* 12 |
| Surrey | *C.* 51, *Lab.* 6, *LD* 13, *Others* 6 |
| Warwickshire | *C.* 20, *Ind.* 1, *Lab.* 28, *LD* 13 |
| West Sussex | *C.* 42, *Lab.* 11, *LD* 18 |
| Wiltshire | *C.* 28, *Ind.* 3, *Lab.* 3, *LD* 13 |
| Worcestershire | *C.* 26, *Ind.* 6, *Ind. Lib.* 3, *Lab* 14, *LD* 8 |

### UNITARY COUNCIL

| | |
|---|---|
| Barnsley | *C.* 3, *Ind.* 7, *Lab.* 52, *LD* 3 *Others* 1 |
| Bath and North-East Somerset | *C.* 16, *Ind.Lab.* 2, *Lab.* 17, *LD* 30, |
| Birmingham | *C.* 28, *Lab.* 66, *LD* 18, *Others* 5 |
| Blackburn with Darwen | *C.* 19, *Lab.* 37, *LD* 6 |
| Blackpool | *C.* 15, *Lab.* 25, *LD* 4 |
| Bolton | *C.* 15, *Lab.* 34, *LD* 11 |
| Bournemouth | *C.* 27, *Ind.* 6, *Lab.* 6, *LD* 18 |
| Bracknell Forest | *C.* 30, *Lab.* 9, *Lab.* 1 |
| Bradford | *C.* 37, *Green* 1, *Lab.* 40, *LD* 11, *vacant* 1 |
| Brighton and Hove | *C.* 26, *Green* 3, *Lab.* 45, *LD* 3, *vacant* 1 |
| Bristol | *C.* 10, *Lab.* 35, *LD* 24, *Other* 1 |
| Bury | *C.* 13, *Lab.* 31, *LD* 3, *vacant* 1 |
| Calderdale | *C.* 28, *Ind.* 1, *Lab.* 8, *LD* 17 |
| Coventry | *C.* 15, *Lab.* 35, *SD* 1, *Others* 3 |
| Darlington | *C.* 15, *Lab.* 35 *LD* 2 |
| Derby | *C.* 9, *Lab.* 29, *LD* 6 |
| Doncaster | *C.* 6, *Ind.* 4, *Lab.* 40, *LD* 7, *Others* 6 |
| Dudley | *C.* 18, *Lab.* 43, *LD* 11 |
| East Riding of Yorkshire | *C.* 27, *Ind.* 6, *Lab.* 12, *LD* 22 |
| Gateshead | *Lab.* 47, *LD* 18, *Lib.* 1 |
| Halton | *C.* 2, *Lab.* 43, *LD* 7, *Others* 4 |
| Hartlepool | *C.* 9, *Ind.* 3, *Lab.* 21, *LD* 14 |
| Herefordshire | *C.* 22, *Ind.* 13, *Lab.* 5, *LD* 20 |
| Isle of Wight | *C.* 15, *Ind.* 8, *Lab.* 4, *LD* 17, *Lib.* 2, *Others* 1 |
| Kingston upon Hull | *C.* 2, *Ind. Lab.* 2, *Lab.* 44, *LD* 10, *Others* 2 |
| Kirklees | *C.* 15, *Green* 3, *Lab.* 25, *LD* 29 |
| Knowsley | *Lab.* 60, *LD* 4, *Others* 2 |
| Leeds | *C.* 16, *Green* 2, *Ind.* 1, *Lab.* 61, *LD* 19 |
| Leicester | *C.* 10, *Lab.* 30, *LD* 16 |
| Liverpool | *Ind.* 1, *Lab.* 20, *Ind. Lab.* 3, *LD* 70, *Lib.* 3, *Others* 2 |
| Luton | *C.* 3, *Lab.* 36, *LD* 9 |
| Manchester | *Lab.* 77, *LD* 21, *Other* 1 |
| Medway | *C.* 38, *Lab.* 25, *LD* 15, *Others* 2 |
| Middlesbrough | *C.* 4, *Ind.* 1, *Lab.* 42, *LD* 6 |
| Milton Keynes | *C.* 8, *Ind.* 1, *Lab.* 22, *LD* 20 |
| Newcastle upon Tyne | *Lab.* 62, *LD* 16 |
| North East Lincolnshire | *C.* 11, *Ind.* 4, *Lab.* 23, *LD* 5 |
| North Lincolnshire | *C.* 19, *Lab.* 23 |
| North Somerset | *C.* 32, *Green* 1, *Ind.* 3, *Lab.* 13, *LD* 11, *Others* 1 |
| North Tyneside | *C.* 17, *Lab.* 35, *LD* 8 |
| Nottingham City | *C.* 11, *Lab.* 40, *LD* 4 |
| Oldham | *C.* 2, *Green* 2, *Ind.* 2, *Lab.* 24, *LD* 30 |
| Peterborough | *C.* 27, *Lab.* 22, *LD* 3, *Lib.* 3, *Other* 2 |
| Plymouth | *C.* 39, *Lab.* 21 |
| Poole | *C.* 17, *Lab.* 3, *LD* 19 |
| Portsmouth | *C.* 16, *Lab.* 15, *LD* 8 |
| Reading | *C.* 3, *Lab.* 36, *LD* 5 |
| Redcar and Cleveland | *C.* 14, *Lab.* 31, *LD* 10, *Others* 4 |
| Rochdale | *C.* 8, *Lab.* 31, *LD* 21 |
| Rotherham | *C.* 4, *Ind.* 4, *Lab.* 57, *LD* 1 |
| Rutland | *C.* 1, *Green* 1, *Ind.* 10, *Lab.* 2, *LD* 4, *Others* 2 |
| St Helens | *C.* 4, *Lab.* 35, *LD* 15 |
| Salford | *C.* 3, *Lab.* 52, *LD* 5 |
| Sandwell | *C.* 6, *Ind.* 1, *Lab.* 55, *Lib.* 10 |
| Sefton | *C.* 19, *Lab.* 22, *LD* 25 |
| Sheffield | *Ind.* 1, *Lab.* 37, *LD* 48, *Lib.* 1 |
| Slough | *C.* 8, *Ind.* 1, *Lab.* 26, *LD* 1, *Lib.* 4, *Other* 1 |
| Solihull | *C.* 29, *Lab.* 11, *LD* 8, *Others* 3 |
| Southampton | *C.* 7, *Lab.* 22, *LD* 16 |

| | |
|---|---|
| South Gloucestershire | *C.* 10, *Lab.* 23, *LD* 37 |
| Southend | *C.* 32, *Lab.* 11, *LD* 7 |
| South Tyneside | *Lab.* 50, *LD* 6, *Others* 4 |
| Stockport | *C.* 6, *Ind.* 3, *Lab.* 22, *LD* 32 |
| Stockton-on-Tees | *C.* 12, *Lab.* 38, *LD* 5 |
| Stoke-on-Trent | *C.* 6, *Ind.* 15, *Lab.* 32, *LD* 7 |
| Sunderland | *C.* 10, *Lab.* 61, *LD* 3 |
| Swindon | *C.* 23, *Lab.* 28, *LD* 8 |
| Tameside | *C.* 6, *Lab.* 47, *LD* 2, *Others* 2 |
| Telford and Wrekin | *C.* 15, *Ind.* 4, *Lab.* 30, *LD* 4, *RA* 1 |
| Thurrock | *C.* 10, *Ind.* 3, *Lab.* 36 |
| Torbay | *C.* 31, *LD* 5 |
| Trafford | *C.* 27, *Lab.* 33, *LD* 3 |
| Wakefield | *C.* 6, *Ind. Lab.* 1, *Lab.* 55, *Lib. Dem.* 1 |
| Walsall | *C.* 26, *Lab.* 27, *Lib.* 7 |
| Warrington | *C.* 4, *Lab.* 43, *LD* 13 |
| West Berkshire | *C.* 25, *Ind.* 1, *LD* 28 |
| Wigan | *C.* 1, *Lab.* 69, *LD* 2 |
| Windsor and Maidenhead | *C.* 29, *Lab.* 1, *LD* 21, *Others* 7 |
| Wirral | *C.* 20, *Lab.* 34, *LD* 12 |
| Wokingham | *C.* 27, *LD* 27 |
| Wolverhampton | *C.* 24, *Lab.* 33, *LD* 3 |
| York | *C.* 3, *Ind.* 1, *Lab.* 25, *LD* 24 |

DISTRICT COUNCILS

*Denotes councils where one-third of Councillors retire each year except in the year of county council elections

| | |
|---|---|
| *Adur, W. Sussex | *C.* 18, *Ind.* 2, *Lab.* 12, *LD* 7 |
| Allerdale, Cumbria | *C.* 10, *Ind.* 2, *Lab.* 36, *LD* 7, *vacant* 1 |
| Alnwick, Northumberland | *C.* 2, *Ind.* 13, *Lab.* 2, *LD* 12, *Others* 1 |
| Amber Valley, Derbys | *C.* 32, *Ind.* 1, *Lab.* 12 |
| Arun, W. Sussex | *C.* 36, *Ind.*3, *Lab.* 8, *LD* 9 |
| Ashfield, Notts | *C.* 1, *Ind.* 2, *Lab.* 30 |
| Ashford, Kent | *C.* 24, *Ind.* 2, *Ind. C.* 1, *Lab.* 10, *LD* 9, *Others* 3 |
| Aylesbury Vale, Bucks | *C.* 25, *Ind.* 7, *Lab.* 1, *LD* 25 |
| Babergh, Suffolk | *C.* 10, *Ind.* 13, *Lab.* 5, *LD* 13, *Others* 1 |
| *Barrow-in-Furness, Cumbria | *C.* 16, *Lab.* 18, *Others* 4 |
| *Basildon, Essex | *C.* 18, *Lab.* 19, *LD* 4, *vacant* 1 |
| *Basingstoke and Deane, Hants | *C.* 25, *Ind.* 2, *Lab.* 15, *LD* 15 |
| *Bassetlaw, Notts | *C.* 14 *Ind.* 2, *Lab.* 31 *LD* 3 |
| *Bedford, Beds | *C.* 7, *Ind. C.* 6,*Ind.*6, *Lab.* 18, *LD* 16 |
| Berwick-upon-Tweed, Northumberland | *C.* 3, *Ind.* 5, *Lab.* 1, *LD* 16, *Others* 4 |
| Blaby, Leics | *C.* 25, *Lab.* 6, *LD* 8 |
| Blyth Valley, Northumberland | *C.* 2, *Ind.* 3, *Lab.* 35, *LD* 9, *vacant* 1 |
| Bolsover, Derbys | *Ind.* 4, *Lab.* 32, *RA* 1 |
| Boston, Lincs | *C.* 14, *Ind.* 5, *Lab.* 10, *LD* 3 |
| Braintree, Essex | *Lab.* 31, *LD* 3, *Others* 3 |
| Breckland, Norfolk | *C.* 34, *Ind.* 3, *Lab.* 14, *LD* 2 |
| *Brentwood, Essex | *C.* 11, *Ind.C.* 1, *Lab.* 2, *LD* 24, *Lib.* 1 |
| Bridgnorth, Shrops | *C.* 8, *Ind.* 10, *Ind. Al.* 9, *LD* 4, *Others* 2 |
| Broadland, Norfolk | *C.* 25, Ind. *8*, Lab. *7*, LD *9* |
| Bromsgrove, Worcs | *C.* 30, *Ind C.* 1, *Lab.* 6, *RA* 2 |
| *Broxbourne, Herts | *C.* 35, *Lab.* 3 |
| Broxtowe, Notts | *C.* 12, *Ind.* 1, *Lab.* 25, *LD* 11 |
| *Burnley, Lancs | *C.* 3, *Ind.* 11, *Lab.* 24, *LD* 9, *Others* 1 |
| *Cambridge, Cambs | *C.* 3, *Ind.* 1, *Lab.* 15, *LD* 23 |
| *Cannock Chase, Staffs | *C.* 8, *Lab.* 27, *LD* 7 |
| Canterbury, Kent | *C.* 18, *Lab.* 13, *LD* 17, *Other* 1 |
| Caradon, Cornwall | *C.* 1, *Ind.* 20, *Lab.* 2, *LD* 18 |
| *Carlisle, Cumbria | *C.* 29, *Ind.* 2, *Lab.* 16, *LD* 5 |
| Carrick, Cornwall | *C.* 15, *Ind.* 6, *Lab.* 2, *LD* 18 *Ind. LD* 1 |
| Castle Morpeth, Northumberland | *C.* 4, *Green* 1, *Ind.* 10, *Lab.* 9, *LD* 8 |
| Castle Point, Essex | *C.* 15, *Lab.* 22, *Others* 2 |
| Charnwood, Leics | *C.* 20, *Ind. C* 1, *Lab.* 24, *LD* 6, *Other* 1 |
| Chelmsford, Essex | *C.* 23, *Ind.* 2, *Lab.* 5, *LD* 26 |
| *Cheltenham, Glos | *C.* 23, *Lab.* 2, *LD* 11, *Others* 5 |
| *Cherwell, Oxon | *C.* 33, *Ind.* 3, *Lab.* 12, *LD* 4 |
| Chesterfield, Derbys | *Lab.* 28, *LD* 19 |
| Chester-le-Street, Co. Durham | *C.* 1, *Ind.* 1, *Lab.* 30, *LD* 1 |
| *Chester, Cheshire | *C.* 18, *Ind.* 2, *Lab.* 22, *LD* 18 |
| Chichester, W. Sussex | *C.* 30, *Ind.* 2 *LD* 18 |
| Chiltern, Bucks | *C.* 29, *LD* 19, *RA* 2 |
| *Chorley, Lancs | *C.* 15, *Ind.* 2, *Lab.* 24, *LD* 7 |
| Christchurch, Dorset | *C.* 17, *Ind.* 3, *LD* 5 |
| *Colchester, Essex | *C.* 22, *Lab.* 14, *LD* 23, *RA* 1 |
| *Congleton, Cheshire | *C.* 14, *Lab.* 2, *LD* 32 |
| Copeland, Cumbria | *C.* 17, *Ind.* 3, *Lab.* 30, *LD* 1 |
| Corby, Northants | *C.* 2, *Ind.* 1, *Lab.* 26 |
| Cotswold, Glos | *C.* 11, *Ind.* 25, *Lab.* 2, *LD* 7 |
| *Craven, N. Yorks | *C.* 18, *Ind.* 12, *LD* 4 |
| *Crawley, W. Sussex | *C.* 6, *Lab.* 24, *LD* 2 |
| *Crewe and Nantwich, Cheshire | *C.* 21, *Ind.* 1, *Lab.* 26, *LD* 5, *Others* 3 |
| Dacorum, Herts | *C.* 27, *Ind.* 1, *Lab.* 20, *LD* 4 |
| Dartford, Kent | *C.* 13, *Ind.* 5, *Lab.* 29 |
| *Daventry, Northants | *C.* 20, *Ind.* 2, *Lab.* 13, *LD* 3 |
| Derbyshire Dales, Derbys | *C.* 21, *Ind.* 3, *Lab.* 6, *LD* 9 |
| Derwentside, Co. Durham | *Ind.* 7, *Lab.* 47, *Others* 1 |
| Dover, Kent | *C.* 26, *Ind.* 1, *Lab.* 28, *LD* 1 |
| Durham, Co. Durham | *Ind.* 3, *Lab.* 32, *Ind. Lab.* 1, *LD* 13 |
| Easington, Co. Durham | *Ind.* 5, *Lab.* 45, *LD* 1 |
| *Eastbourne, E. Sussex | *C.* 17, *LD* 13 |
| East Cambridgeshire, Cambs | *Ind.* 13, *Lab.* 4, *LD* 20 |
| East Devon, Devon | *C.* 37, *Ind.* 6, *Lab.* 1, *LD* 15, *Lib.* 1 |
| East Dorset, Dorset | *C.* 26, *Ind.* 1, *LD* 9 |
| East Hampshire, Hants | *C.* 22, *Ind.* 3, *LD* 17 |
| East Hertfordshire, Herts | *C.* 32, *Ind.* 2, *Lab.* 7, *LD* 9 |
| *Eastleigh, Hants | *C.* 9, *Lab.* 7, *LD* 28 |
| East Lindsey, Lincs | *C.* 7, *Lab.* 9, *LD* 8, *Others* 36 |
| East Northamptonshire, Northants | *C.* 21, *Lab.* 15 |
| East Staffordshire, Staffs | *C.* 15, *Lab.* 28, *LD* 3 |
| Eden, Cumbria | *C.* 4, *Ind.* 30, *Lab.* 1, *LD* 3 |
| *Ellesmere Port and Neston, Cheshire | *C.* 6, *Lab.* 36, *LD* 1 |
| *Elmbridge, Surrey | *C.* 22, *Lab.* 1, *LD* 9, *RA* 28 |
| *Epping Forest, Essex | *C.* 20, *Ind. C.* 3, *Lab.* 12, *LD* 16, *Others* 8 |
| Epsom and Ewell, Surrey | *Lab.* 3, *LD* 9, *RA* 27 |
| Erewash, Derbys | *C.* 16, *Ind.* 3, *Lab.* 29, *LD* 3, *vacant* 1 |
| *Exeter, Devon | *C.* 6, *Lab.* 22, *LD* 8, *Lib.* 4 |
| *Fareham, Hants | *C.* 29, *Lab.* 2, *LD* 11 |
| Fenland, Cambs | *C.* 27, *Ind.* 3, *Lab.* 7, *LD* 1, *vacant* 2 |
| Forest Heath, Suffolk | *C.* 21, *Ind.* 1, *Lab.* 1, *LD* 2 |
| Forest of Dean, Glos | *Con.* 2, *Ind.* 14, *Lab.* 28, *LD* 6 |
| Fylde, Lancs | *C.* 20, *Ind.* 13, *Lab.* 2, *LD* 3, *Others* 11 |
| Gedling, Notts | *C.* 29, *Ind.* 2, *Lab.* 19, *LD* 7 |
| *Gloucester, Glos | *C.* 11, *Ind.* 1, *Lab.* 19, *LD* 8 |
| *Gosport, Hants | *C.* 13, *Lab.* 12, *LD*5 |
| Gravesham, Kent | *C.* 15, *Lab.* 29 |
| *Great Yarmouth, Norfolk | *C.* 26, *Lab.* 22 |
| Guildford, Surrey | *C.* 17, *Ind.* 3, *Lab.* 6, *LD* 19 |
| Hambleton, N. Yorks | *C.* 35, *Ind.* 6, *Lab.* 2, *LD* 4 |
| Harborough, Leics | *C.* 17, *Ind.* 3, *Lab.* 3, *LD* 14 |
| *Harlow, Essex | *C.* 8, *Ind.* 1, *Lab.* 25, *LD* 8 |
| *Harrogate, N. Yorks | *C.* 18, *Lab.* 1, *LD* 40 |
| *Hart, Hants | *Ind.* 17, *Con.* 18 |

| | |
|---|---|
| *Hastings, E. Sussex | C. 6, *Lab.* 18, *LD* 8 |
| *Havant, Hants | C. 19, *Ind.* 3, *Lab.* 11, *LD* 8 |
| *Hertsmere, Herts | C. 22, *Lab.* 12, *LD* 5 |
| High Peak, Derbys | C. 10, *Ind.* 2, *Lab.* 27, *LD* 5 |
| Hinckley and Bosworth, Leics | C. 11, *Lab.* 9, *LD* 14 |
| Horsham, W. Sussex | C. 24, *Ind.* 3, *LD* 16 |
| *Huntingdonshire, Cambs | C. 37, *Ind.* 3, *LD* 13 |
| *Hyndburn, Lancs | C. 31, *Lab.* 16 |
| *Ipswich, Suffolk | C. 15, *Lab.* 31, *LD* 2 |
| Kennet, Wilts | C. 23, *Ind.* 11, *Lab.* 4, *LD* 2 |
| Kerrier, Cornwall | C. 4, *Ind.* 21, *Lab.* 9, *LD* 10 |
| Kettering, Northants | C. 18, *Ind.* 4, *Lab.* 22, *LD* 1 |
| King's Lynn and West Norfolk, Norfolk | C. 27, *Lab.* 27, *LD* 5, *Others* 1 |
| Lancaster, Lancs | C. 9, *Green* 6, *Ind.* 23, *Lab.* 15, *LD* 7 |
| Lewes, E. Sussex | C. 16, *Ind.* 1, *LD* 30, *RA* 1 |
| Lichfield, Staffs | C. 29, *Lab.* 25, *LD* 2 |
| *Lincoln, Lincs | C. 4, *Lab.* 29 |
| *Macclesfield, Cheshire | C. 36, *Lab.* 6, *LD* 15, *Others* 3 |
| *Maidstone, Kent | C. 16, *Ind.* 5, *Lab.* 12, *LD* 22 |
| Maldon, Essex | C. 18, *Ind.* 6, *Lab.* 6 |
| Malvern Hills, Worcs | C. 24, *LD* 13, *Others* 5 |
| Mansfield, Notts | C. 5, *Lab.* 39, *LD* 2 |
| Melton, Leics | C. 9, *Ind.* 6, *Lab.* 11 |
| Mendip, Somerset | C. 18, *Ind.* 2, *Lab.* 10, *LD* 16 |
| Mid Bedfordshire, Beds | C. 35, *Ind.* 5, *Lab.* 7, *LD* 6 |
| Mid Devon, Devon | C. 2, *Ind.* 18, *Lab.* 1, *LD* 18, *Lib.* 1 |
| Mid Suffolk, Suffolk | C. 18, *Ind. Lab.* 2, *Lab.* 6, *LD* 13, *Ind. Lib.* 1 |
| *Mid Sussex, W. Sussex | C. 29, *Ind.* 2, *Lab.* 2, *LD* 21 |
| *Mole Valley, Surrey | C. 19, *Ind.* 7, *Lab.* 1, *LD* 14 |
| Newark and Sherwood, Notts | C. 21, *Ind.* 2, *Lab.* 26, *LD* 5 |
| *Newcastle under Lyme, Staffs | C. 9, *Ind.* 1, *Lab.* 30, *Lib.* 16 |
| New Forest, Hants | C. 33, *Ind.* 3, *LD* 22 |
| Northampton, Northants | C. 8, *Lab.* 28, *LD* 11 |
| North Cornwall, Cornwall | C. 3, *Ind.* 27, *LD* 11 |
| North Devon, Devon | C. 5, *Ind.* 10, *LD* 27, *Others* 2 |
| North Dorset, Dorset | C. 15, *Ind.* 8, *LD* 10 |
| North East Derbyshire, Derbys | C. 9, *Ind.* 2, *Lab.* 39, *LD* 3 |
| *North Hertfordshire, Herts | C. 27, *Lab.* 19, *LD* 3 |
| North Kesteven, Lincs | C. 17, *Ind.* 4, *Lab.* 6, *LD* 6, *Others* 7 |
| North Norfolk, Norfolk | *Ind.* 7, *Lab.* 7, *Ind. Lab.* 3, *LD* 12, *Others* 17 |
| North Shropshire, Shrops | C. 12, *Ind.* 9, *Lab.* 5, *LD* 1, *Others* 13 |
| North Warwickshire, Warks | C. 9, *Ind.* 1, *Lab.* 22, *LD* 2 |
| North West Leicestershire, Leics | C. 8, *Ind. C.* 1, *Lab.* 31 |
| North Wiltshire, Wilts | C. 20, *Ind.* 2, *Lab.* 4, *LD* 26 |
| *Norwich, Norfolk | C. 1, *Lab.* 26, *LD* 21 |
| *Nuneaton and Bedworth, Warks | C. 10, *Lab.* 35 |
| *Oadby and Wigston, Leics | C. 5, *LD* 21 |
| Oswestry, Shrops | C. 4, *Ind.* 13, *Lab.* 5, *LD* 6, *vacant* 1 |
| *Oxford, Oxon | C. 1, *Green* 8, *Lab.* 22, *LD* 20 |
| *Pendle, Lancs | C.9, *Lab.* 23, *LD* 19 |
| *Penwith, Cornwall | C. 11, *Ind.* 9, *Lab.* 3, *LD* 7, *Others* 5 |
| *Preston, Lancs | C. 17, *Ind.* 1, *Ind. Lab.* 4, *Lab.* 25, *LD* 10 |
| *Purbeck, Dorset | C. 16, *Ind. C.* 4, *Ind.* 4 |
| *Redditch, Worcs | C. 10, *Lab.* 17, *LD* 2 |
| *Reigate and Banstead, Surrey | C. 33, *Lab.* 8, *LD* 4, *RA* 6 |
| Restormel, Cornwall | C. 13, *Ind.* 11, *Lab.* 1, *LD* 17, *Others* 1, *vacant* 1 |
| Ribble Valley, Lancs | C. 19, *Ind.* 2, *Lab.* 1, *LD* 17 |
| Richmondshire, N. Yorks | C. 6, *Ind.* 17, *LD* 9 |
| *Rochford, Essex | C. 19, *Lab.* 9, *LD* 9, *Others* 3 |
| *Rossendale, Lancs | C. 24, *Lab.* 12 |
| Rother, E. Sussex | C. 29, *Ind.* 4, *Lab.* 4, *LD* 8 |
| *Rugby, Warks | C. 14, *Ind.* 6, *Lab.* 17, *LD* 10, *vacant* 1 |
| *Runnymede, Surrey | C. 33, *Ind.* 6, *Lab.* 3 |
| Rushcliffe, Notts | C. 30, *Ind.* 1, *Lab.* 11, *LD* 12 |
| *Rushmoor, Hants | C. 24, *Ind.* 1, *Lab.* 10, *LD* 10 |
| Ryedale, N. Yorks | C. 11, *Ind.* 6, *Lab.* 1, *LD* 5 |
| *St Albans, Herts | C. 19, *Ind.* 1, *Lab.* 15, *LD* 23 |
| St Edmundsbury, Suffolk | C. 22, *Ind.* 4, *Lab.* 15, *LD* 2, *vacant* 1 |
| Salisbury, Wilts | C. 29, *Ind.* 3, *Lab.* 11, *LD* 15 |
| Scarborough, N. Yorks | C. 19, *Ind.* 14, *Lab.* 11, *LD* 5 |
| Sedgefield, Co. Durham | *Ind.* 3, *Lab.* 44, *LD* 2 |
| Sedgemoor, Somerset | C. 31, *Lab.* 16, *LD* 3 |
| Selby, N. Yorks | C. 15, *Ind.* 6, *Lab.* 20 |
| Sevenoaks, Kent | C. 33, *Ind.* 2, *Lab.* 9, *LD* 9 |
| Shepway, Kent | C. 29, *Lab.* 11, *LD* 16 |
| *Shrewsbury and Atcham, Shrops | C. 16, *Ind.* 4, *Lab.* 18, *LD* 10 |
| *South Bedfordshire, Beds | C. 26, *Ind.* 3, *Lab.* 7, *LD* 17 |
| South Bucks, Berks | C. 28, *Ind.* 10, *LD* 2 |
| *South Cambridgeshire, Cambs | C. 20, *Ind.* 5, *Lab.* 13, *LD* 15, *Other* 1 |
| South Derbyshire, Derbys | C. 10, *Lab.* 24 |
| South Hams, Devon | C. 29, *Ind.* 4, *Lab.* 3, *LD* 4 |
| South Holland, Lincs | C. 19, *Ind.* 10, *Lab.* 3, *LD* 1, *Others* 7 |
| South Kesteven, Lincs | C. 30, *Ind.* 12, *Lab.* 12, *LD* 3, *Other* 1 |
| *South Lakeland, Cumbria | C. 16, *Ind.* 4, *Lab.* 9, *LD* 22, *vacant* 1 |
| South Norfolk, Norfolk | C. 16, *Ind.* 2, *Lab.* 2, *LD* 27 |
| South Northamptonshire, Northants | C. 29, *Ind.* 4, *Lab.* 6, *LD* 3 |
| South Oxfordshire, Oxon | C. 20, *Ind.* 3, *Lab.* 7, *LD* 20 |
| South Ribble, Lancs | C. 18, *Lab.* 21, *LD* 12, *Others* 3 |
| South Shropshire, Shrops | *Green* 2, *Ind.* 16, *LD* 16, *Others* 6 |
| South Somerset, Somerset | C. 13, *Ind.* 6, *LD* 41 |
| South Staffordshire, Staffs | C. 37, *Ind.* 2, *Lab.* 10, *LD* 1 |
| Spelthorne, Surrey | C. 27, *Lab.* 9, *LD* 4 |
| *Stafford Moorlands, Staffs | C. 17, *Ind.* 3, *Lab.* 14, *LD* 10, *Others* 10 |
| Staffordshire, Staffs | C. 23, *Ind.* 1, *Lab.* 28, *LD* 8 |
| *Stevenage, Herts | C. 3, *Lab.* 33, *LD* 3 |
| *Stratford, Warks | C. 28, *Ind.* 5, *Lab.* 2, *LD* 18, *Others* 2 |
| *Stroud, Glos | C. 24, *Green* 4, *Ind.* 4, *Lab.* 18, *LD* 5 |
| Suffolk Coastal, Suffolk | C. 35, *Ind.* 2, *Lab.* 7, *LD* 10 |
| Surrey Heath, Surrey | C. 22 *Lab.* 6, *LD* 7 |
| *Swale, Kent | C. 15, *Lab.* 12, *LD* 22 |
| *Tamworth, Staffs | C. 13, *Ind.* 1, *Lab.* 16 |
| *Tandridge, Surrey | C. 29, *Lab.* 3, *LD* 10 |
| Taunton Deane, Somerset | C. 21, *Green* 1, *Ind.* 4, *Lab.* 5, *LD* 23 |
| Teesdale, Co. Durham | C. 2, *Ind.* 12, *Lab.* 8, *Others* 9 |
| Teignbridge, Devon | C. 20, *Ind.* 20, *Lab.* 1, *LD* 17 |
| Tendring, Essex | C. 16, *Ind.*8, *Lab.* 23, *LD* 9, *RA* 4 |
| Test Valley, Hants | C. 28, *Ind.* 2, *LD* 14 |
| Tewkesbury, Glos | C. 16, *Ind.* 5, *Lab.* 8, *LD* 4, *Others* 3 |
| Thanet, Kent | C. 18, *Ind.* 3, *Lab.* 33 |
| *Three Rivers, Herts | C. 15, *Lab.* 7, *LD* 26 |
| *Tonbridge and Malling, Kent | C. 27, *Lab.* 7, *LD* 21 |
| Torridge, Devon | C. 1, *Green* 1, *Ind.* 13, *Lab.* 2, *LD* 12, *Others* 6, *vacant* 1 |
| *Tunbridge Wells, Kent | C. 31, *Ind.* 1, *Lab.* 5, *LD* 11 |
| Tynedale, Northumberland | C. 23, *Ind.* 6, *Lab.* 12, *LD* 11 |

| | |
|---|---|
| Uttlesford, Essex | *C.* 6, *Ind.* 8, *Lab.* 2, *LD* 29 |
| Vale of White Horse, Oxon | *C.* 15, *Ind.* 1, *Lab.* 2, *LD* 33 |
| Vale Royal, Cheshire | *C.* 16, *Lab.* 32, *LD* 8 |
| Wansbeck, Northumberland | *Lab.* 25, *LD* 20 |
| Warwick, Warks | *C.* 10, *Ind.* 6, *Lab.* 16, *LD* 13 |
| *Watford, Herts | *C.* 8, *Lab.* 18, *LD* 10 |
| *Waveney, Suffolk | *C.* 13, *Ind.* 3, *Lab.* 27, *LD* 4, *Others* 1 |
| Waverley, Surrey | *C.* 31, *Lab.* 2, *LD* 24 |
| Wealden, E. Sussex | *C.* 34, *Ind.* 2, *LD* 22 |
| Wear Valley, Co. Durham | *Ind.* 6, *Lab.* 30, *LD* 4 |
| Wellingborough, Northants | *C.* 14, *Ind. C.* 1, *Ind.* 1, *Lab.* 20 |
| *Welwyn Hatfield, Herts | *C.* 23, *Lab.* 25 |
| West Devon, Devon | *C.* 10, *Ind.* 12, *LD* 8 |
| West Dorset, Dorset | *C.* 22, *Lab.* 4, *LD* 15, *Others* 14 |
| *West Lancashire, Lancs | *C.* 23, *Ind.* 1, *Lab.* 24, *Others* 7 |
| *West Lindsey, Lincs | *C.* 9, *Ind.* 9, *Lab.* 3, *LD* 16 |
| *West Oxfordshire, Oxon | *C.* 26, *Ind.* 8, *Lab.* 2, *LD* 13 |
| West Somerset, Somerset | *C.* 19, *Ind.* 7, *Lab.* 4, *LD* 1 |
| West Wiltshire, Wilts | *C.* 11, *Ind.* 2, *Lab.* 2, *LD* 25, *Others* 3 |
| *Weymouth and Portland, Dorset | *C.* 5, *Lab.* 13, *LD* 12, *Others* 5 |
| *Winchester, Hants | *C.* 11, *Ind.* 5, *Lab.* 4, *LD* 35 |
| *Woking, Surrey | *C.* 14, *Ind.* 1, *Lab.* 5, *LD* 16 |
| *Worcester, Worcs | *C.* 15, *Ind. C.* 1, *Ind.* 4, *Lab.* 15, *LD* 1 |
| *Worthing, W. Sussex | *C.* 20, *LD* 16 |
| Wychavon, Worcs | *C.* 32, *Ind.* 2, *Lab.* 4, *LD* 11 |
| Wycombe, Bucks | *C.* 42, *Ind.* 2, *Lab.* 9, *LD* 7 |
| Wyre, Lancs | *C.* 35, *Lab.* 19, *LD* 2 |
| *Wyre Forest, Worcs | *C.* 5, *Lab.* 11, *LD* 4, *Others* 22 |

GREATER LONDON COUNCILS

| | |
|---|---|
| Barking and Dagenham | *Lab.* 47, *LD* 1, *RA* 3 |
| Barnet | *C.* 28, *Lab.* 26, *LD* 6 |
| Bexley | *C.* 32, *Lab.* 24, *LD* 6 |
| Brent | *C.* 19, *Lab.* 43, *LD* 4 |
| Bromley | *C.* 30, *Lab.* 7, *LD* 23 |
| Camden | *C.* 11, *Lab.* 42, *LD* 6 |
| City of Westminster | *C.* 47, *Lab.* 13 |
| Croydon | *C.* 31, *Lab.* 38, *LD* 1 |
| Ealing | *C.* 16, *Lab.* 52, *LD* 3 |
| Enfield | *C.* 22, *Ind.* 1, *Lab.* 42 |
| Greenwich | *C.* 8, *Lab.* 52, *LD* 2 |
| Hackney | *C.* 10, *Green* 2, *Ind.* 1, *Lab.* 30, *LD* 15 |
| Hammersmithand Fulham | *C.* 14, *Ind.* 1, *Lab.* 35 |
| Haringey | *C.* 2, *Lab.* 52, *LD* 3 |
| Harrow | *C.* 20, *Ind.* 2, *Lab.* 32, *Lib.* 9 |
| Havering | *C.* 13, *Lab.* 31, *LD* 3, *RA* 16 |
| Hillingdon | *C.* 33, *Lab.* 32, *LD* 4 |
| Hounslow | *C.* 11, *Lab.* 43, *LD* 5, *Others* 1 |
| Islington | *Lab.* 25, *LD* 27 |
| Kensington and Chelsea | *C.* 39, *Lab.* 15 |
| Kingston upon Thames | *C.* 20, *Ind. C.* 1, *Lab.* 10, *LD* 19 |
| Lambeth | *C.* 5, *Lab.* 41, *LD* 18 |
| Lewisham | *C.* 2, *Ind.* 1, *Lab.* 58, *LD* 4, *Other* 2 |
| Merton | *C.* 13, *Ind. Lab.* 3, *Lab.* 35, *LD* 2, *Other* 1 |
| Newham | *Lab.* 59, *Other* 1 |
| Redbridge | *C.* 25, *Lab.* 28, *LD* 9 |
| Richmond upon Thames | *C.* 14, *Lab.* 4, *LD* 34 |
| Southwark | *C.* 4, *Ind.* 1, *Lab.* 31, *LD* 27 |
| Sutton | *C.* 5, *Lab.* 5, *LD* 46 |
| Tower Hamlets | *Ind.* 1, *Lab.* 41, *LD* 8 |
| Waltham Forest | *C.* 14, *Ind.* 1, *Lab.* 30, *LD* 12 |
| Wandsworth | *C.* 50, *Lab.* 11 |

WALES

| | |
|---|---|
| Anglesey | *Ind.* 27, *Lab.* 4, *PC* 7 |
| Blaenau Gwent | *Ind.* 2, *Ind. Lab.* 1, *Lab.* 34, *LD* 1, *Others* 4 |
| Bridgend | *C.* 1, *Ind.* 4, *Ind. Lab.* 1, *Lab.* 40, *LD* 6, *PC* 2 |
| Caerphilly | *Ind.* 3, *Lab.* 28, *LD* 4, *PC* 38 |
| Cardiff | *C.* 5, *Ind.* 1, *Lab.* 50, *LD* 18, *PC* 1 |
| Carmarthenshire | *Ind.* 28, *Ind. Lab* 2, *Lab.* 27, *LD* 1, *PC* 15, *RA* 1 |
| Ceredigion | *Ind.* 22, *Lab.* 1, *LD* 7, *PC* 13, *Others* 1 |
| Conwy | *C.* 5, *Ind.* 14, *Lab.* 19, *LD* 13, *PC* 8 |
| Denbighshire | *C.* 2, *Ind.* 17, *Lab.* 14, *LD* 1, *NP* 1, *PC* 8, *Others* 4 |
| Flintshire | *Lab.* 42, *LD* 7, *PC* 2, *Others* 19 |
| Gwynedd | *Ind.* 21, *Lab.* 13, *LD* 6, *Others* 2, *PC* 41 |
| Merthyr Tydfil | *Ind.* 13, *Lab.* 16, *PC* 4 |
| Monmouthshire | *C.* 19, *Ind.* 3, *Lab.* 18, *LD* 1, *Others* 1 |
| Neath Port Talbot | *Ind.* 3, *Ind. Lab.* 1, *Lab.* 40, *LD* 2, *PC* 10, *RA* 5, *Others* 3 |
| Newport | *C.* 5, *Ind.* 2, *Lab.* 39, *LD* 1 |
| Pembrokeshire | *C.* 4, *Ind.* 38, *Lab.* 13, *LD* 3, *PC* 2 |
| Powys | *C.* 1, *Ind.* 59, *Lab.* 6, *LD* 7 |
| Rhondda, Cynon, Taff | *Ind.* 5, *Lab.* 26, *LD* 2, *PC* 42 |
| Swansea | *C.* 5, *Ind.* 7, *Lab.* 46, *LD* 11, *PC* 2, *Others* 1 |
| Torfaen | *C.* 1, *Ind.* 3, *Lab.* 39, *LD* 1 |
| Vale of Glamorgan | *C.* 22, *Lab.* 18, *LD* 1, *PC* 6 |
| Wrexham | *C.* 4, *Ind.* 11, *Lab.* 24, *Others* 13 |

SCOTLAND

| | |
|---|---|
| Aberdeen City | *C.* 6, *Lab.* 22, *LD* 12, *SNP* 3 |
| Aberdeenshire | *Com.* 7, *Ind.* 10, *LD* 28, *SNP* 23 |
| Angus | *C.* 2, *Ind.* 3, *Lab.*1, *LD* 2, *SNP* 21 |
| Argyll and Bute | *C.* 4, *Ind.* 3, *LD* 6, *NP* 19, *SNP* 4 |
| City of Edinburgh | *C.* 13, *Lab.* 31, *LD* 13, *SNP* 1 |
| Clackmannanshire | *C.*1*Lab.* 7, *SNP* 10 |
| Dumfries and Galloway | *C.* 8, *Ind.* 15, *Lab.* 13, *LD* 6, *SNP* 5 |
| Dundee City | *C.* 4, *Ind.* 1, *Ind. Lab.* 1, *Lab.* 13, *SNP* 11 |
| East Ayrshire | *C.* 1, *Lab.* 17, *SNP* 14 |
| East Dunbartonshire | *C.* 3, *Lab.* 11, *LD* 10 |
| East Lothian | *C.* 5, *Lab.* 16, *SNP* 2 |
| East Renfrewshire | *C.* 8, *Lab.* 9, *LD* 2, *RA* 1 |
| Eilean Siar/Western Isles | *Ind.* 23, *Lab.* 5, *SNP* 3 |
| Falkirk | *C.* 2, *Ind.* 2, *Lab.* 14, *SNP* 10, *Others* 4 |
| Fife | *C.* 2, *Lab.* 42, *LD* 21, *SNP* 10, *Others* 3 |
| Glasgow City | *C.* 1, *Lab.* 74, *LD* 1, *SNP* 2, *SSP* 1 |
| Highland | *Ind.* 50, *Lab.* 11, *LD* 10, *SNP* 9 |
| Inverclyde | *C.* 1, *Lab.* 10, *LD* 9 |
| Midlothian | *Lab.* 17, *LD* 1 |
| Moray | *C.* 1, *Ind.* 13, *Lab.* 6, *LD* 2, *SNP* 2, *Others* 2 |
| North Ayrshire | *C.* 2, *Ind.* 1, *Lab.* 25, *SNP* 2 |
| North Lanarkshire | *Ind.* 2, *Lab.* 56, *SNP* 12 |
| Orkney Islands | *Ind.* 21 |
| Perth and Kinross | *C.* 11, *Ind.* 2, *Lab.* 6, *LD* 6, *SNP* 16 |
| Renfrewshire | *C.* 1, *Lab.* 21, *LD* 3, *SNP* 15 |
| Scottish Borders | *C.* 1, *Ind.* 15, *Lab.* 1, *LD* 14, *SNP* 3 |
| Shetland Islands | *Ind.* 13, *LD* 9 |
| South Ayrshire | *C.* 13, *Lab.* 15, *NP* 2 |
| South Lanarkshire | *C.* 2, *Lab.* 53, *LD* 1, *SNP* 11 |
| Stirling | *C.* 10, *Lab.* 11, *SNP* 1 |
| West Dunbartonshire | *Lab.* 13, *SNP* 7, *Others* 2 |
| West Lothian | *C.* 1, *Ind.* 1, *Lab.* 20, *SNP* 10 |

# England

The Kingdom of England lies between 55° 46′ and 49° 57′ 30″ N. latitude (from a few miles north of the mouth of the Tweed to the Lizard), and between 1° 46′ E. and 5° 43′ W. (from Lowestoft to Land's End). England is bounded on the north by the Cheviot Hills; on the south by the English Channel; on the east by the Straits of Dover (Pas de Calais) and the North Sea; and on the west by the Atlantic Ocean, Wales and the Irish Sea. It has a total area of 50,351 sq. miles (130,410 sq. km): land 50,058 sq. miles (129,652 sq. km); inland water 293 sq. miles (758 sq. km).

## Population

The population at the 1991 census was 47,055,204. The average density of the population in 1991 was 3.6 persons per hectare.

## Flag

The flag of England is the cross of St George, a red cross on a white field (cross gules in a field argent). The cross of St George, the patron saint of England, has been used since the 13th century.

## Relief

There is a marked division between the upland and lowland areas of England. In the extreme north the Cheviot Hills (highest point, The Cheviot, 2,674 ft) form a natural boundary with Scotland. Running south from the Cheviots, though divided from them by the Tyne Gap, is the Pennine range (highest point, Cross Fell, 2,930 ft), the main orological feature of the country. The Pennines culminate in the Peak District of Derbyshire (Kinder Scout, 2,088 ft). West of the Pennines are the Cumbrian mountains, which include Scafell Pike (3,210 ft), the highest peak in England, and to the east are the Yorkshire Moors, their highest point being Urra Moor (1,490 ft).

In the west, the foothills of the Welsh mountains extend into the bordering English counties of Shropshire (the Wrekin, 1,334 ft; Long Mynd, 1,694 ft) and Hereford and Worcester (the Malvern Hills –Worcestershire Beacon, 1,394 ft). Extensive areas of highland and moorland are also to be found in the south-western peninsula formed by Somerset, Devon and Cornwall: principally Exmoor (Dunkery Beacon, 1,704 ft), Dartmoor (High Willhays, 2,038 ft) and Bodmin Moor (Brown Willy, 1,377 ft). Ranges of low, undulating hills run across the south of the country, including the Cotswolds in the Midlands and south-west, the Chilterns to the north of London, and the North (Kent) and South (Sussex) Downs of the south-east coastal areas.

The lowlands of England lie in the Vale of York, East Anglia and the area around the Wash. The lowest-lying are the Cambridgeshire Fens in the valleys of the Great Ouse and the River Nene, which are below sea-level in places. Since the 17th century extensive drainage has brought much of the Fens under cultivation. The North Sea coast between the Thames and the Humber, low-lying and formed of sand and shingle for the most part, is subject to erosion and defences against further incursion have been built along many stretches.

## Hydrography

The Severn is the longest river in Great Britain, rising in the north-eastern slopes of Plynlimon (Wales) and entering England in Shropshire with a total length of 220 miles (354 km) from its source to its outflow into the Bristol Channel, where it receives on the east the Bristol Avon, and on the west the Wye, its other tributaries being the Vyrnwy, Tern, Stour, Teme and Upper (or Warwickshire) Avon. The Severn is tidal below Gloucester, and a high bore or tidal wave sometimes reverses the flow as high as Tewkesbury (13½ miles above Gloucester). The scenery of the greater part of the river is very picturesque and beautiful, and the Severn is a noted salmon river, some of its tributaries being famous for trout. Navigation is assisted by the Gloucester and Berkeley Ship Canal (16¾ miles), which admits vessels of 350 tons to Gloucester. The Severn Tunnel was begun in 1873 and completed in 1886 at a cost of £2 million and after many difficulties from flooding. It is 4 miles 628 yards in length (of which 2¼ miles are under the river). The Severn road bridge between Haysgate, Gwent, and Almondsbury, Glos, with a centre span of 3,240 ft, was opened in 1966.

The longest river wholly in England is the Thames, with a total length of 215 miles (346 km) from its source in the Cotswold hills to the Nore, and is navigable by ocean-going ships to London Bridge. The Thames is tidal to Teddington (69 miles from its mouth) and forms county boundaries almost throughout its course; on its banks are situated London, Windsor Castle, the oldest royal residence still in regular use, Eton College and Oxford, the oldest university in the kingdom.

Of the remaining English rivers, those flowing into the North Sea are the Tyne, Wear, Tees, Ouse and Trent from the Pennine Range, the Great Ouse (160 miles), which rises in Northamptonshire, and the Orwell and Stour from the hills of East Anglia. Flowing into the English Channel are the Sussex Ouse from the Weald, the Itchen from the Hampshire Hills, and the Axe, Teign, Dart, Tamar and Exe from the Devonian hills. Flowing into the Irish Sea are the Mersey, Ribble and Eden from the western slopes of the Pennines and the Derwent from the Cumbrian mountains.

The English Lakes, noteworthy for their picturesque scenery and poetic associations, lie in Cumbria, the largest being Windermere (10 miles long), Ullswater and Derwent Water.

## Islands

The Isle of Wight is separated from Hampshire by the Solent. The capital, Newport, stands at the head of the estuary of the Medina, Cowes (at the mouth) being the chief port. Other centres are Ryde, Sandown, Shanklin, Ventnor, Freshwater, Yarmouth, Totland Bay, Seaview and Bembridge.

Lundy (the name means Puffin Island), 11 miles north-west of Hartland Point, Devon, is about two miles long and about half a mile wide on average, with a total area of about 1,116 acres, and a population of about 20. It became the property of the National Trust in 1969 and is now principally a bird sanctuary.

The Isles of Scilly consist of about 140 islands and skerries (total area, 6 sq. miles/10 sq. km) situated 28 miles south-west of Land's End. Only five are inhabited: St Mary's, St Agnes, Bryher, Tresco and St Martin's. The population is 1,978. The entire group has been designated a Conservation Area, a Heritage Coast, and an Area of Outstanding Natural Beauty, and has been given National Nature Reserve status by the Nature Conservancy Council because of its unique flora and fauna. Tourism and the winter/spring flower trade for the home market form the basis of the economy of the Isles. The island group is a recognised rural development area.

## EARLY HISTORY

Archaeological evidence suggests that England has been inhabited since at least the Palaeolithic period, though the extent of the various Palaeolithic cultures was dependent upon the degree of glaciation. The succeeding Neolithic and Bronze Age cultures have left abundant remains throughout the country, the best-known of these being the henges and stone circles of Stonehenge (ten miles north of Salisbury, Wilts) and Avebury (Wilts), both of which are believed to have been of religious significance. In the latter part of the Bronze Age the Goidels, a people of Celtic race, and in the Iron Age other Celtic races of Brythons and Belgae, invaded the country and brought with them Celtic civilisation and dialects, place names in England bearing witness to the spread of the invasion over the whole kingdom.

### THE ROMAN CONQUEST

The Roman conquest of Gaul (57–50 BC) brought Britain into close contact with Roman civilisation, but although Julius Caesar raided the south of Britain in 55 BC and 54 BC, conquest was not undertaken until nearly 100 years later. In AD 43 the Emperor Claudius dispatched Aulus Plautius, with a well-equipped force of 40,000, and himself followed with reinforcements in the same year. Success was delayed by the resistance of Caratacus (Caractacus), the British leader from AD 48–51, who was finally captured and sent to Rome, and by a great revolt in AD 61 led by Boudicca (Boadicea), Queen of the Iceni; but the south of Britain was secured by AD 70, and Wales and the area north to the Tyne by about AD 80.

In AD 122, the Emperor Hadrian visited Britain and built a continuous rampart, since known as Hadrian's Wall, from Wallsend to Bowness (Tyne to Solway). The work was entrusted by the Emperor Hadrian to Aulus Platorius Nepos, legate of Britain from AD 122 to 126, and it was intended to form the northern frontier of the Roman Empire.

The Romans administered Britain as a province under a Governor, with a well-defined system of local government, each Roman municipality ruling itself and its surrounding territory, while London was the centre of the road system and the seat of the financial officials of the Province of Britain. Colchester, Lincoln, York, Gloucester and St Albans stand on the sites of five Roman municipalities, and Wroxeter, Caerleon, Chester, Lincoln and York were at various times the sites of legionary fortresses. Well-preserved Roman towns have been uncovered at or near Silchester (*Calleva Atrebatum*), ten miles south of Reading, Wroxeter (*Viroconium Cornoviorum*), near Shrewsbury, and St Albans (*Verulamium*) in Hertfordshire.

Four main groups of roads radiated from London, and a fifth (the Fosse) ran obliquely from Lincoln through Leicester, Cirencester and Bath to Exeter. Of the four groups radiating from London, one ran south-east to Canterbury and the coast of Kent, a second to Silchester and thence to parts of western Britain and south Wales, a third (later known as Watling Street) ran through Verulamium to Chester, with various branches, and the fourth reached Colchester, Lincoln, York and the eastern counties.

In the fourth century Britain was subject to raids along the east coast by Saxon pirates, which led to the establishment of a system of coastal defences from the Wash to Southampton Water, with forts at Brancaster, Burgh Castle (Yarmouth), Walton (Felixstowe), Bradwell, Reculver, Richborough, Dover, Lympne, Pevensey and Porchester (Portsmouth). The Irish (Scoti) and Picts in the north were also becoming more aggressive; from about AD 350 incursions became more frequent and more formidable. As the Roman Empire came under attack increasingly towards the end of the fourth century, many troops were removed from Britain for service in other parts of the empire. The island was eventually cut off from Rome by the Teutonic conquest of Gaul, and with the withdrawal of the last Roman garrison early in the fifth century, the Romano-British were left to themselves.

### SAXON SETTLEMENT

According to legend, the British King Vortigern called in the Saxons to defend him against the Picts, the Saxon chieftains being Hengist and Horsa, who landed at Ebbsfleet, Kent, and established themselves in the Isle of Thanet; but the events during the one and a half centuries between the final break with Rome and the re-establishment of Christianity are unclear. However, it would appear that in the course of this period the raids turned into large-scale settlement by invaders traditionally known as Angles (England north of the Wash and East Anglia), Saxons (Essex and southern England) and Jutes (Kent and the Weald), which pushed the Romano-British into the mountainous areas of the north and west, Celtic culture outside Wales and Cornwall surviving only in topographical names. Various kingdoms were established at this time which attempted to claim overlordship of the whole country, hegemony finally being achieved by Wessex (capital, Winchester) in the ninth century. This century also saw the beginning of raids by the Vikings (Danes), which were resisted by Alfred the Great (871–899), who fixed a limit to the advance of Danish settlement by the Treaty of Wedmore (878), giving them the area north and east of Watling Street, on condition that they adopt Christianity.

In the tenth century the kings of Wessex recovered the whole of England from the Danes, but subsequent rulers were unable to resist a second wave of invaders. England paid tribute (*Danegeld*) for many years, and was invaded in 1013 by the Danes and ruled by Danish kings from 1016 until 1042, when Edward the Confessor was recalled from exile in Normandy. On Edward's death in 1066, Harold Godwinson (brother-in-law of Edward and son of Earl Godwin of Wessex) was chosen King of England. After defeating (at Stamford Bridge, Yorkshire, 25 September) an invading army under Harald Hadraada, King of Norway (aided by the outlawed Earl Tostig of Northumbria, Harold's brother), Harold was himself defeated at the Battle of Hastings on 14 October 1066, and the Norman conquest secured the throne of England for Duke William of Normandy, a cousin of Edward the Confessor.

### CHRISTIANITY

Christianity reached the Roman province of Britain from Gaul in the third century (or possibly earlier); Alban, traditionally Britain's first martyr, was put to death as a Christian during the persecution of Diocletian (22 June 303), at his native town Verulamium; and the Bishops of Londinium, Eboracum (York), and Lindum (Lincoln) attended the Council of Arles in 314. However, the Anglo-Saxon invasions submerged the Christian religion in England until the sixth century when conversion was undertaken in the north from 563 by Celtic missionaries from Ireland led by St Columba, and in the south by a mission sent from Rome in 597 which was led by St Augustine, who became the first archbishop of Canterbury. England appears to have been converted again by the end of the seventh century and followed, after the Council of Whitby in 663, the practices of the Roman Church, which brought the kingdom into the mainstream of European thought and culture.

## PRINCIPAL CITIES

### BIRMINGHAM

Birmingham is Britain's second city. It is a focal point in national communications networks with a rapidly expanding international airport. The generally accepted derivation of 'Birmingham' is the *ham* (dwelling-place) of the *ing* (family) of *Beorma*, presumed to have been Saxon. During the Industrial Revolution the town grew into a major manufacturing centre and in 1889 was granted city status.

Despite the decline in manufacturing, Birmingham is still a major hardware trade and motor component industry centre. As well as the National Exhibition Centre and the Aston Science Park, recent developments include the International Convention Centre, the National Indoor Arena and Brindleyplace.

The principal buildings are the Town Hall (1834–50); the Council House (1879); Victoria Law Courts (1891); Birmingham University (1906–9); the 13th-century Church of St Martin-in-the-Bull-Ring (rebuilt 1873); Our Lady, Help of Christians Church; the Cathedral (formerly St Philip's Church) (1711) and the Roman Catholic Cathedral of St Chad (1839–41).

### BRADFORD

Bradford lies on the southern edge of the Yorkshire Dales National Park, including within its boundaries the village of Haworth, home of the Brontë sisters, and Ilkley Moor.

Originally a Saxon township, Bradford received a market charter in 1251 but developed only slowly until the industrialisation of the textile industry brought rapid growth during the 19th century; it was granted its city charter in 1897. The prosperity of that period is reflected in much of the city's architecture, particularly the public buildings: City Hall (1873), Wool Exchange (1867), St George's Hall (Concert Hall, 1853), Cartwright Hall (Art Gallery, 1904) and the Technical College (1882). Other chief buildings are the Cathedral (15th century) and Bolling Hall (14th century).

Textiles still play an important part in the city's economy but industry is now more broadly based, including engineering, micro-electronics, printing and chemicals. The city has a strong financial services sector, and a growing tourism industry.

### BRIGHTON AND HOVE

Brighton and Hove was granted city status in December 2000. Originally a small fishing village, the city was transformed into a fashionable seaside retreat in the mid 18th century when Dr Richard Russell popularised the area with his 'sea-water' cure. The Prince Regent (later King George IV) visited Brighton in 1783 and the city's most prominent architectural feature, the Royal Pavilion, is the legacy of his love of the city.

The Pavilion, built on the sight of a farmhouse rented for the Prince's initial visit, is the result of a succession of projects carried out between 1787 and 1823. The architect William Porden initiated the buildings' famous Indo-Saracenic style when he designed the royal stables. The Indian conceit was extended by John Nash in 1813 when he added the large central dome and the tent-like roofs over the banqueting hall and music room.

The city has numerous other examples of Regency architecture including Adelaide Crescent and Brunswick and Palmeira Squares in Hove, as well as hundreds of townhouses designed by Amon Wilds and Augustin Busby. There are also striking examples of Victorian design including Brighton's two piers.

### BRISTOL

Bristol was a Royal Borough before the Norman Conquest. The earliest form of the name is *Bricgstow*. In 1373 Edward III granted Bristol county status.

The chief buildings include the 12th-century Cathedral (with later additions), with Norman chapter house and gateway, the 14th-century Church of St Mary Redcliffe, Wesley's Chapel, Broadmead, the Merchant Venturers' Almshouses, the Council House (1956), Guildhall, Exchange (erected from the designs of John Wood in 1743), Cabot Tower, the University and Clifton College. The Roman Catholic Cathedral at Clifton was opened in 1973.

The Clifton Suspension Bridge, with a span of 702 feet over the Avon, was projected by Brunel in 1836 but was not completed until 1864. Brunel's SS *Great Britain*, the first ocean-going propeller-driven ship, is now being restored in the City Docks from where she was launched in 1843. The docks themselves have been extensively restored and redeveloped and are becoming a focus for the arts and recreation.

### CAMBRIDGE

Cambridge, a settlement far older than its ancient University, lies on the River Cam or Granta. The city is a county town and regional headquarters. Its industries include electronics, high technology research and development, and biotechnology. Among its open spaces are Jesus Green, Sheep's Green, Coe Fen, Parker's Piece, Christ's Pieces, the University Botanic Garden, and the Backs, or lawns and gardens through which the Cam winds behind the principal line of college buildings. East of the Cam, King's Parade, upon which stand Great St Mary's Church, Gibbs' Senate House and King's College Chapel with Wilkins' screen, joins Trumpington Street to form one of the most beautiful throughfares in Europe.

University and college buildings provide the outstanding features of Cambridge architecture but several churches (especially St Benet's, the oldest building in the city, and St Sepulchre's, the Round Church) are also notable. The Guildhall (1939) stands on a site of which at least part has held municipal buildings since 1224.

### CANTERBURY

Canterbury, the Metropolitan City of the Anglican Communion, dates back to prehistoric times. It was the Roman *Durovernum Cantiacorum* and the Saxon *Cant-wara-byrig* (stronghold of the men of Kent). Here in 597 St Augustine began the conversion of the English to Christianity, when Ethelbert, King of Kent, was baptised.

Of the Benedictine St Augustine's Abbey, burial place of the Jutish Kings of Kent (whose capital Canterbury was), only ruins remain. St Martin's Church, on the eastern outskirts of the city, is stated by Bede to have been the place of worship of Queen Bertha, the Christian wife of King Ethelbert, before the advent of St Augustine.

In 1170 the rivalry of Church and State culminated in the murder in Canterbury Cathedral, by Henry II's knights, of Archbishop Thomas Becket. His shrine became a great centre of pilgrimage, as described in Chaucer's *Canterbury Tales*. After the Reformation pilgrimages ceased, but the prosperity of the city was strengthened by an influx of Huguenot refugees, who introduced weaving. The poet and playwright Christopher Marlowe was born and reared in Canterbury, and there are also literary associations with Defoe, Dickens, Joseph Conrad and Somerset Maugham.

The Cathedral, with architecture ranging from the 11th to the 15th centuries, is world famous. Modern pilgrims are attracted particularly to the Martyrdom, the Black Prince's Tomb, the Warriors' Chapel and the many examples of medieval stained glass.

The medieval city walls are built on Roman foundations and the 14th-century West Gate is one of the finest buildings of its kind in the country.

The 1,000-seat Marlowe Theatre is a centre for the Canterbury Arts Festival each autumn.

## CARLISLE

Carlisle is situated at the confluence of the River Eden and River Caldew, 309 miles north-west of London and about ten miles from the Scottish border. It was granted a charter in 1158.

The city stands at the western end of Hadrian's Wall and dates from the original Roman settlement of *Luguvalium*. Granted to Scotland in the tenth century, Carlisle is not included in the Domesday Book. William Rufus reclaimed the area in 1092 and the castle and city walls were built to guard Carlisle and the western border; the citadel is a Tudor addition to protect the south of the city. Border disputes were common until the problem of the Debateable Lands was settled in 1552. During the Civil War the city remained Royalist; in 1745 Carlisle was besieged for the last time by the Young Pretender.

The Cathedral, originally a 12th-century Augustinian priory, was enlarged in the 13th and 14th centuries after the diocese was created in 1133. To the south is a restored Tithe Barn and nearby the 18th-century church of St Cuthbert, the third to stand on a site dating from the seventh century.

Carlisle is the major shopping, commercial and agricultural centre for the area, and industries include the manufacture of metal goods, biscuits and textiles. However, the largest employer is the services sector, notably in central and local government, retailing and transport. The city has an important communications position at the centre of a network of major roads, as a stage on the main west coast rail services, and with its own airport at Crosby-on-Eden.

## CHESTER

Chester is situated on the River Dee, and was granted borough and city status in 1974. Its recorded history dates from the first century when the Romans founded the fortress of *Deva*. The city's name is derived from the Latin *castra* (a camp or encampment). During the Middle Ages, Chester was the principal port of north-west England but declined with the silting of the Dee estuary and competition from Liverpool. The city was also an important military centre, notably during Edward I's Welsh campaigns and the Elizabethan Irish campaigns. During the Civil War, Chester supported the King and was besieged from 1643 to 1646. Chester's first charter was granted *c.* 1175 and the city was incorporated in 1506. The office of Sheriff is the earliest created in the country (*c.* 1120s), and in 1992 the Mayor was granted the title of Lord Mayor. He/she also enjoys the title 'Admiral of the Dee'.

The city's architectural features include the city walls (an almost complete two-mile circuit), the unique 13th-century Rows (covered galleries above the street-level shops), the Victorian Gothic Town Hall (1869), the Castle (rebuilt 1788 and 1822) and numerous half-timbered buildings. The Cathedral was a Benedictine abbey until the Dissolution. Remaining monastic buildings include the chapter house, refectory and cloisters and there is a modern free-standing bell tower. The Norman church of St John the Baptist was a cathedral church in the early Middle Ages.

Chester is a thriving retail, business and tourist centre.

## COVENTRY

Coventry is an important industrial centre, producing vehicles, machine tools, agricultural machinery, man-made fibres, aerospace components and telecommunications equipment. New investment has come from financial services, power transmission, professional services, leisure and education.

The city owes its beginning to Leofric, Earl of Mercia, and his wife Godiva who, in 1043, founded a Benedictine monastery. The guildhall of St Mary dates from the 14th century, three of the city's churches date from the 14th and 15th centuries, and 16th-century almshouses may still be seen. Coventry's first cathedral was destroyed at the Reformation, its second in the 1940 blitz (the walls and spire remain) and the new cathedral designed by Sir Basil Spence, consecrated in 1962, now draws numerous visitors.

Coventry is the home of the University of Warwick and its Science Park, Coventry University, the Westwood Business Park, the Cable and Wireless College, the Museum of British Road Transport and the Coventry Arena.

## DERBY

Derby stands on the banks of the River Derwent, and its name dates back to 880 when the Danes settled in the locality and changed the original Saxon name of *Northworthy* to *Deoraby*.

Derby has a wide range of industries including aero engines, cars, pipework, specialised mechanical engineering equipment, textiles, chemicals, plastics and the Royal Crown Derby porcelain. The city is an established railway centre with rail research, engineering, safety testing, infrastructure and train-operating companies.

Buildings of interest include St Peter's Church and the Old Abbey Building (14th century), the Cathedral (1525), St Mary's Roman Catholic Church (1839) and the Industrial Museum, formerly the Old Silk Mill (1721). The traditional city centre is complemented by the Eagle Centre and 'out-of-centre' retail developments. In addition to the Derby Playhouse, the Assembly Rooms are a multi-purpose venue.

The first charter granting a Mayor and Aldermen was that of Charles I in 1637. Previous charters date back to 1154. It was granted city status in 1977.

## DURHAM

The city of Durham is a district in the county of Durham and a major tourist attraction because of its prominent Norman Cathedral and Castle set high on a wooded peninsula overlooking the River Wear. The Cathedral was founded as a shrine for the body of St Cuthbert in 995. The present building dates from 1093 and among its many treasures is the tomb of the Venerable Bede (673–735). Durham's Prince Bishops had unique powers up to 1836, being lay rulers as well as religious leaders. As a palatinate Durham could have its own army, nobility, coinage and courts. The Castle was the main seat of the Prince Bishops for nearly 800 years; it is now used as a college by the University. The University, founded on the initiative of Bishop William Van Mildert, is England's third oldest.

Among other buildings of interest is the Guildhall in the Market Place which dates originally from the 14th century. Work has been carried out to conserve this area as part of the city's contribution to the Council of Europe's Urban Renaissance Campaign. Annual events include Durham's Regatta in June (claimed to be the oldest rowing event in Britain) and the Annual Gala (formerly Durham Miners' Gala) in July.

The economy has undergone a significant change with the replacement of mining as the dominant industry by 'white collar' employment. Although still a predominantly rural area, the industrial and commercial sector is growing and a wide range of manufacturing and service industries are based on industrial estates in and around the city. A research and development centre, linked to the University, also plays an important role in the local economy.

## EXETER

Exeter lies on the River Exe ten miles from the sea. It was granted a charter by Henry II. The Romans founded *Isca Dumnoniorum* in the first century AD, and in the third century a stone wall (much of which remains) was built, providing protection against Saxon, and then Danish invasions. After the Conquest, the city led resistance to William in the west until reduced by siege. The Normans built the ringwork castle of Rougemont, the gatehouse and one tower of which remain, although the rest was pulled down in 1784. The first bridge across the Exe was built in the early 13th century. The city's main port was situated downstream at Topsham until the construction in the 1560s of the first true canal in England, the redevelopment of which in 1700 brought seaborne trade direct to the city. Exeter was the Royalist headquarters in the west during the Civil War.

The diocese of Exeter was established by Edward the Confessor in 1050, although a minster existed near the Cathedral site from the late seventh century. A new cathedral was built in the 12th century but the present building, which incorporates the Norman Towers, was begun *c.* 1275 and completed about a century later. The Guildhall dates from the 12th century and there are many other medieval buildings in the city, as well as architecture in the Georgian and Regency styles, and the Custom House (1680). Damage suffered by bombing in 1942 led to the redevelopment of the city centre.

Exeter's prosperity from medieval times was based on trade in wool and woollen cloth (commemorated by Tuckers Hall), which flourished until the late 18th century when export trade was hit by the French wars. Subsequently Exeter has developed as an administrative and commercial centre, notably in the distributive trades, light manufacturing industries and tourism.

## KINGSTON UPON HULL

Hull (officially Kingston upon Hull) lies at the junction of the River Hull with the Humber, 22 miles from the North Sea. It is one of the major seaports of the United Kingdom, comprising 2,000 acres in four main dock installations. The port provides a wide range of cargo services, including ro-ro and container traffic, and handles a million passengers annually on daily sailings to Rotterdam and Zeebrugge. There is a variety of manufacturing and service industries, as well as increasing tourism and conference business.

The city, restored after heavy air raid damage during the Second World War, has good office and administrative buildings, its municipal centre being the Guildhall, its educational centres the University of Hull and the University of Lincolnshire and Humberside and its religious centre the Parish Church of the Holy Trinity. The old town area has been renovated and includes a marina and shopping complex. Just west of the city is the Humber Bridge, the world's longest single-span suspension bridge.

Kingston upon Hull was so named by Edward I. City status was accorded in 1897 and the office of Mayor raised to the dignity of Lord Mayor in 1914.

## LEEDS

Leeds, situated in the lower Aire Valley, is a junction for road, rail, canal and air services and an important manufacturing and commercial centre. Seventy-three per cent of employment is in services, notably the distributive trades, public administration, medical services and business services. The main manufacturing industries are mechanical engineering, printing and publishing, metal goods and furniture.

The principal buildings are the Civic Hall (1933), the Town Hall (1858), the Municipal Buildings and Art Gallery (1884) with the Henry Moore Gallery (1982), the Corn Exchange (1863) and the University. The Parish Church (St Peter's) was rebuilt in 1841; the 17th-century St John's Church has a fine interior with a famous English Renaissance screen; the last remaining 18th-century church in the city is Holy Trinity in Boar Lane (1727). Kirkstall Abbey (about three miles from the centre of the city), founded by Henry de Lacy in 1152, is one of the most complete examples of Cistercian houses now remaining. Temple Newsam, birthplace of Lord Darnley, was acquired by the Council in 1922. The present house was largely rebuilt by Sir Arthur Ingram in about 1620. Adel Church, about five miles from the centre of the city, is a fine Norman structure. The new Royal Armouries Museum houses the collection of antique arms and armour formerly held at the Tower of London.

Leeds was first incorporated by Charles I in 1626. The earliest forms of the name are *Loidis* or *Ledes*, the origins of which are obscure.

## LEICESTER

Leicester is situated geographically in the centre of England. It dates back to pre-Roman times and was one of the Five Danish Boroughs of the Danelaw. In 1589 Queen Elizabeth I granted a charter to the city and the ancient title was confirmed by letters patent in 1919.

The principal industries are hosiery, knitwear, footwear manufacturing and engineering. The growth of Leicester as a hosiery centre increased rapidly from the introduction there of the first stocking frame in 1670 and today it has some of the largest hosiery factories in the world.

The principal buildings are the Town Hall, the New Walk Centre, the University of Leicester, De Montfort University, De Montfort Hall, one of the finest concert halls in the provinces seating over 2,750 people, and the Granby Halls, an indoor sports facility. The ancient churches of St Martin (now Leicester Cathedral), St Nicholas, St Margaret, All Saints, St Mary de Castro, and buildings such as the Guildhall, the 14th-century Newarke Gate, the Castle and the Jewry Wall Roman site still exist. The Haymarket Theatre was opened in 1973 and The Shires shopping centre in 1992.

## LINCOLN

Situated 40 miles inland on the River Witham, Lincoln derives its name from a contraction of *Lindum Colonia*, the settlement founded in AD 48 by the Romans to command the crossing of Ermine Street and Fosse Way. Sections of the third-century Roman city wall can be seen, including an extant gateway (Newport Arch), and excavations have discovered traces of a sewerage system unique in Britain.

The Romans also drained the surrounding fenland and created a canal system, laying the foundations of Lincoln's agricultural prosperity and also of the city's importance in the medieval wool trade as a port and Staple town.

As one of the Five Boroughs of the Danelaw, Lincoln was an important trading centre in the ninth and tenth centuries and medieval prosperity from the wool trade lasted until the 14th century, enabling local merchants to build parish churches (of which three survive), and attracting in the 12th century a Jewish community (Jew's House and Court, Aaron's House). However, the removal of the Staple to Boston in 1369 heralded a decline from which the city only recovered fully in the 19th century when improved fen drainage made Lincoln agriculturally important and improved canal and rail links led to industrial development, mainly in the manufacture of machinery, components and engineering products.

The castle was built shortly after the Conquest and is unusual in having two mounds; on one motte stands a Keep (Lucy's Tower) added in the 12th century. It currently houses one of the four surviving copies of the Magna Carta. The Cathedral was begun *c.* 1073 when the first Norman bishop moved the *See* of Lindsey to Lincoln, but was mostly destroyed by fire and earthquake in the 12th century. Rebuilding was begun by St Hugh and completed over a century later. Other notable architectural features are the 12th-century High Bridge, the oldest in Britain still to carry buildings, and the Guildhall situated above the 15th–16th-century Stonebow gateway.

## LIVERPOOL

Liverpool, on the right bank of the River Mersey, three miles from the Irish Sea, is the United Kingdom's foremost port for the Atlantic trade. Tunnels link Liverpool with Birkenhead and Wallasey.

There are 2,100 acres of dockland on both sides of the river and the Gladstone and Royal Seaforth Docks can accommodate Panamax-sized vessels. Approximately 31 million tonnes of cargo is handled annually. The main cargoes are crude oil, grain, fossil fuels, edible oils, timber, scrap metal, containers and break-bulk cargo. Liverpool Free Port, Britain's largest, was opened in 1984.

Liverpool was created a free borough in 1207 and a city in 1880. From the early 18th century it expanded rapidly with the growth of industrialisation and the Atlantic trade. Surviving buildings from this period include the Bluecoat Chambers (1717, formerly the Bluecoat School), the Town Hall (1754, rebuilt to the original design 1795), and buildings in Rodney Street, Canning Street and the suburbs. Notable from the 19th and 20th centuries are the Anglican Cathedral, built from the designs of Sir Giles Gilbert Scott (the foundation stone was laid in 1904, and the building was completed only in 1980), the Catholic Metropolitan Cathedral (designed by Sir Frederick Gibberd, consecrated 1967) and St George's Hall (1838–54), regarded as one of the finest modern examples of classical architecture. The refurbished Albert Dock (designed by Jesse Hartley) contains the Merseyside Maritime Museum and Tate Gallery, Liverpool.

In 1852 an Act was obtained for establishing a public library, museum and art gallery; as a result Liverpool had one of the first public libraries in the country. The Brown, Picton and Hornby libraries now form one of the country's major libraries. The Victoria Building of Liverpool University, the Royal Liver, Cunard and Mersey Docks & Harbour Company buildings at the Pier Head, the Municipal Buildings and the Philharmonic Hall are other examples of the city's fine buildings.

## MANCHESTER

Manchester (the *Mamucium* of the Romans, who occupied it in AD 79) is a commercial and industrial centre with a population engaged in the engineering, chemical, clothing, food processing and textile industries and in education. Banking, insurance and a growing leisure industry are among the prime commercial activities. The city is connected with the sea by the Manchester Ship Canal, opened in 1894, 35½ miles long, and accommodating ships up to 15,000 tons. Manchester Airport handles 15 million passengers yearly.

The principal buildings are the Town Hall, erected in 1877 from the designs of Alfred Waterhouse, with a large extension of 1938; the Royal Exchange (1869, enlarged 1921); the Central Library (1934); Heaton Hall; the 17th-century Chetham Library; the Rylands Library (1900), which includes the Althorp collection; the University precinct; the 15th-century Cathedral (formerly the parish church) and G-MEX exhibition centre. Recent developments include the Manchester Arena, the largest indoor arena in Europe, and the Bridgewater Hall. Manchester is the home of the Hallé Orchestra, the Royal Northern College of Music, the Royal Exchange Theatre and seven public art galleries. Metrolink, the light rail system, opened in 1992.

The Commonwealth Games are to be held in Manchester in 2002 and new sports facilities include a stadium, a swimming pool complex and the National Cycling Centre.

The town received its first charter of incorporation in 1838 and was created a city in 1853.

## NEWCASTLE UPON TYNE

Newcastle upon Tyne, on the north bank of the River Tyne, is eight miles from the North Sea. A cathedral and university city, it is the administrative, commercial and cultural centre for north-east England and the principal port. It is an important manufacturing centre with a wide variety of industries.

The principal buildings include the Castle Keep (12th century), Black Gate (13th century), Blackfriars (13th century), West Walls (13th century), St Nicholas's Cathedral (15th century, fine lantern tower), St Andrew's Church (12th–14th century), St John's (14th–15th century), All Saints (1786 by Stephenson), St Mary's Roman Catholic Cathedral (1844), Trinity House (17th century), Sandhill (16th-century houses), Guildhall (Georgian), Grey Street (1834–9), Central Station (1846–50), Laing Art Gallery (1904), University of Newcastle Physics Building (1962) and Medical Building (1985), Civic Centre (1963), Central Library (1969) and Eldon Square Shopping Development (1976). Open spaces include the Town Moor (927 acres) and Jesmond Dene. Nine bridges span the Tyne at Newcastle.

The city's name is derived from the 'new castle' (1080) erected as a defence against the Scots. In 1400 it was made a county, and in 1882 a city.

## NORWICH

Norwich grew from an early Anglo-Saxon settlement near the confluence of the Rivers Yare and Wensum, and now serves as provincial capital for the predominantly agricultural region of East Anglia. The name is thought to relate to the most northerly of a group of Anglo-Saxon villages or *wics*. The city's first known charter was granted in 1158 by Henry II.

Norwich serves its surrounding area as a market town and commercial centre, banking and insurance being prominent among the city's businesses. From the 14th century until the Industrial Revolution, Norwich was the regional centre of the woollen industry, but now the biggest single industry is financial services and principal trades are engineering, printing, shoemaking, double glazing, the production of chemicals and clothing, food processing and technology. Norwich is accessible to seagoing vessels by means of the River Yare, entered at Great Yarmouth, 20 miles to the east.

Among many historic buildings are the Cathedral (completed in the 12th century and surmounted by a 15th-century spire 315 feet in height), the keep of the Norman castle (now a museum and art gallery), the 15th-century flint-walled Guildhall (now a tourist information centre), some thirty medieval parish churches, St Andrew's and Blackfriars' Halls, the Tudor houses preserved in Elm Hill and the Georgian Assembly House. The University of East Anglia is on the city's western boundary.

## NOTTINGHAM

Nottingham stands on the River Trent and is connected by canal with the Atlantic Ocean and the North Sea. *Snotingaham* or *Notingeham*, literally the homestead of the people of Snot, is the Anglo-Saxon name for the Celtic settlement of *Tigguocobauc*, or the house of caves. In 878, Nottingham became one of the Five Boroughs of the Danelaw. William the Conqueror ordered the construction of Nottingham Castle, while the town itself developed rapidly under Norman rule. Its laws and rights were later formally recognised by Henry II's charter in 1155. The Castle became a favoured residence of King John. In 1642 King Charles I raised his personal standard at Nottingham Castle at the start of the Civil War.

Nottingham is home to Notts County FC (the world's oldest football league side), Nottingham Racecourse and the National Watersports Centre. The principal industries include textiles, pharmaceuticals, food manufacturing, engineering and telecommunications. There are two universities within the city boundaries.

Architecturally, Nottingham has a wealth of notable buildings, particularly those designed in the Victorian era by T. C. Hine and Watson Fothergill. The City Council owns the Castle, of Norman origin but restored in 1878, Wollaton Hall (1580–8), Newstead Abbey (home of Lord Byron), the Guildhall (1888) and Council House (1929). St Mary's, St Peter's and St Nicholas's Churches are of interest, as is the Roman Catholic Cathedral (Pugin, 1842–4).

Nottingham was granted city status in 1897.

## OXFORD

Oxford is a university city, an important industrial centre, and a market town. Industry played a minor part in Oxford until the motor industry was established in 1912.

It is for its architecture that Oxford is of most interest to the visitor, its oldest specimens being the reputedly Saxon tower of St Michael's church, the remains of the Norman castle and city walls, and the Norman church at Iffley. It is chiefly famous, however, for its Gothic buildings, such as the Divinity Schools, the Old Library at Merton College, William of Wykeham's New College, Magdalen College and Christ Church and many other college buildings. Later centuries are represented by the Laudian quadrangle at St John's College, the Renaissance Sheldonian Theatre by Wren, Trinity College Chapel, and All Saints Church; Hawksmoor's mock-Gothic at All Souls College, and the 18th-century Queen's College. In addition to individual buildings, High Street and Radcliffe Square, just off it, both form architectural compositions of great beauty. Most of the Colleges have gardens, those of Magdalen, New College, St John's and Worcester being the largest.

## PLYMOUTH

Plymouth is situated on the borders of Devon and Cornwall at the confluence of the Rivers Tamar and Plym. The city has a long maritime history; it was the home port of Sir Francis Drake and the starting point for his circumnavigation of the world, as well as the last port of call for the *Mayflower* when the Pilgrim Fathers sailed for the New World in 1620. Today Plymouth is host to many international yacht races. The Barbican harbour area has many Elizabethan buildings and on Plymouth Hoe stands Smeaton's lighthouse, the third to be built on the Eddystone Rocks 13 miles offshore.

The city centre was rebuilt following extensive war damage, and comprises a large shopping centre, municipal offices, law courts and public buildings. The main employment is provided at the naval base, though many industrial firms and service industries have become established in the post-war period and the city is a growing tourism centre. In 1982 the Theatre Royal was opened. In conjunction with the Cornwall County Council, the Tamar Bridge was constructed linking the city by road with Cornwall.

## PORTSMOUTH

Portsmouth occupies Portsea Island, Hampshire, with boundaries extending to the mainland. It is a centre of industry and commerce, including many high technology and manufacturing industries. It is the British headquarters of several major international companies. The Royal Navy base still has a substantial work-force, although this has decreased in recent years. The commercial port and continental ferry port is owned and run by the City Council, and carries passengers and vehicles to France and northern Spain.

A major port since the 16th century, Portsmouth is also a thriving seaside resort catering for thousands of visitors annually. Among many historic attractions are Lord Nelson's flagship, HMS *Victory*, the Tudor warship *Mary Rose*, Britain's first 'ironclad' warship, HMS *Warrior*, the D-Day Museum, Charles Dickens' birthplace at 393 Old Commercial Road, the Royal Naval and Royal Marine museums, Southsea Castle (built by Henry VIII), Fort Nelson on Portsdown Hill, the Sealife Centre and the Round Tower and Point Battery, which for hundreds of years have guarded the entrance to Portsmouth Harbour.

## ST ALBANS

The origins of St Albans, situated on the River Ver, stem from the Roman town of *Verulamium*. Named after the first Christian martyr in Britain, who was executed here, St Albans has developed around the Norman Abbey and Cathedral Church (consecrated 1115), built partly of materials from the old Roman city. The museums house Iron Age and Roman artefacts and the Roman Theatre, unique in Britain, has a stage as opposed to an amphitheatre. Archaeological excavations in the city centre have revealed evidence of pre-Roman, Saxon and medieval occupation.

The town's significance grew to the extent that it was a signatory and venue for the drafting of the Magna Carta. It was also the scene of riots during the Peasants' Revolt, the French King John was imprisoned there after the Battle of Poitiers, and heavy fighting took place there during the Wars of the Roses.

Previously controlled by the Abbot, the town achieved a charter in 1553 and city status in 1877. The street market, first established in 1553, is still an important feature of the city, as are many hotels and inns which survive from the days when St Albans was an important coach stop. Tourist attractions include historic churches and houses, and a 15th-century clock tower.

The city now contains a wide range of firms, with special emphasis on information and legal services. In addition, it is the home of the Royal National Rose Society, and of Rothamsted Park, the agricultural research centre.

## SHEFFIELD

Sheffield, the centre of the special steel and cutlery trades, is situated at the junction of the Sheaf, Porter, Rivelin and Loxley valleys with the River Don. Though its cutlery, silverware and plate have long been famous, Sheffield has other and now more important industries: special and alloy steels, engineering, tool-making, medical equipment and media-related industries (in its new Cultural Industries Quarter). Sheffield has two universities and is an important research centre.

The parish church of St Peter and St Paul, founded in the 12th century, became the Cathedral Church of the Diocese of Sheffield in 1914. The Roman Catholic Cathedral Church of St Marie (founded 1847) was created Cathedral for the new diocese of Hallam in 1980. Parts of the present building date from *c.*1435. The principal buildings are the Town Hall (1897), the Cutlers' Hall (1832), City Hall (1932), Graves Art Gallery (1934), Mappin Art Gallery, the Crucible Theatre and the restored 19th-century Lyceum theatre, which dates from 1897 and was reopened in 1990. Three major sports venues were opened in 1990 to 1991. The National Centre for Popular Music was opened in 1999. Sheffield was created a city in 1893.

## SOUTHAMPTON

Southampton is the leading British deep-sea port on the Channel and is situated on one of the finest natural harbours in the world. The first charter was granted by Henry II and Southampton was created a county of itself in 1447. In 1964 it was granted city status.

There were Roman and Saxon settlements on the site of the city, which has been an important port since Anglo-Saxon times due to its natural deep-water harbour. The oldest church is St Michael's (1070) which has an unusually tall spire built in the 18th century as a landmark for navigators of Southampton Water. Other buildings and monuments within the city walls are the Bargate, the Tudor House Museum, God's House Tower, the Tudor Merchants Hall, the Weigh-house, West Gate, King John's House, Long House, Wool House, the ruins of Holy Rood Church, St Julien's Church and the Mayflower Memorial. The medieval town walls, built for artillery, are among the most complete in the UK. Public open spaces total over 1,000 acres and comprise 9 per cent of the city's area.

## STOKE-ON-TRENT

Stoke-on-Trent, standing on the River Trent and familiarly known as The Potteries, is the main centre of employment for the population of North Staffordshire. The city is the largest clayware producer in the world (china, earthenware, sanitary goods, refractories, bricks and tiles) and also has a wide range of other manufacturing industry, including steel, chemicals, engineering and tyres. Extensive reconstruction has been carried out in recent years.

The city was formed by the federation of the separate municipal authorities of Tunstall, Burslem, Hanley, Stoke, Fenton, and Longton in 1910 and received its city status in 1925.

## WINCHESTER

Winchester, the ancient capital of England, is situated on the River Itchen. The city is rich in architecture of all types but the Cathedral takes pride of place. The longest Gothic cathedral in the world, it was built in 1079–93 and exhibits examples of Norman, Early English and Perpendicular styles. The author Jane Austen is buried in the Cathedral. Winchester College, founded in 1382, is one of the most famous public schools, the original building (1393) remaining largely unaltered. St Cross Hospital, another great medieval foundation, lies one mile south of the city. The almshouses were founded in 1136 by Bishop Henry de Blois, and Cardinal Henry Beaufort added a new almshouse of 'Noble Poverty' in 1446. The chapel and dwellings are of great architectural interest, and visitors may still receive the 'Wayfarer's Dole' of bread and ale.

Excavations have done much to clarify the origins and development of Winchester. Part of the forum and several of the streets of the Roman town have been discovered; excavations in the Cathedral Close have uncovered the entire site of the Anglo-Saxon cathedral (known as the Old Minster) and parts of the New Minster which was built by Alfred's son Edward the Elder and is the burial place of the Alfredian dynasty. The original burial place of St Swithun, before his remains were translated to a site in the present cathedral, was also uncovered.

Excavations in other parts of the city have thrown much light on Norman Winchester, notably on the site of the Royal Castle (adjacent to which the new Law Courts have been built) and in the grounds of Wolvesey Castle, where the great house built by Bishops Giffard and Henry de Blois in the 12th century has been uncovered. The Great Hall, built by Henry III between 1222 and 1236 survives and houses the Arthurian Round Table.

## WOLVERHAMPTON

Wolverhampton was awarded 'Millennium City' status by the Queen in December 2000. The city's first known charter was awarded in AD 985 by the Saxon King Aethelred to the Lady Wulfruna, grandmother of King Harold. The charter referred to the area as Heantun, or High Town, and it is from Wulfrun Heantun that the city's current name is derived.

Wolverhampton has long been an industrial centre. Initially a focus for the medieval wool trade, from the 17th century the city has been famous for the quality of its metalwork.

The city's notable features include the municipal gardens and conservatory at West Park and St Peter's Collegiate Church.

## YORK

The city of York is an archiepiscopal seat. Its recorded history dates from AD 71, when the Roman Ninth Legion established a base under Petilius Cerealis which later became the fortress of *Eburacum*. In Anglo-Saxon times the city was the royal and ecclesiastical centre of Northumbria, and after capture by a Viking army in AD 866 it became the capital of the Viking kingdom of Jorvik. By the 14th century the city had become a great mercantile centre, mainly because of its control of the wool trade, and was used as the chief base against the Scots. Under the Tudors its fortunes declined, though Henry VIII made it the headquarters of the Council of the North. Excavations on many sites, including Coppergate, have greatly expanded knowledge of Roman, Viking and medieval urban life.

The city is rich in examples of architecture of all periods. The earliest church was built in AD 627 and, in the 12th to 15th centuries, the present Minster was built in a succession of styles. Other examples within the city are the medieval city walls and gateways, churches and guildhalls. Domestic architecture includes the Georgian mansions of The Mount, Micklegate and Bootham.

# English Counties and Shires

## LORD-LIEUTENANTS AND HIGH SHERIFFS

| *County/Shire* | *Lord-Lieutenant* | *High Sheriff, 2001–2* |
|---|---|---|
| Bedfordshire | S. C. Whitbread | Hon. Mrs Fiona Chapman |
| Berkshire | P. L. Wroughton | D. J. M. Roberts, MC |
| Bristol | J. Tidmarsh, MBE | Dr M. Campbell |
| Buckinghamshire | Sir Nigel Mobbs | M. H. T. Jourdan |
| Cambridgeshire | J. G. P. Crowden | W. H. Proby |
| Cheshire | W. A. Bromley-Davenport | A. W. A. Spiegelberg |
| Cornwall | Lady Mary Holborow | Lady Frances Banham |
| Cumbria | J. A. Cropper | R. B. Hassell-McCosh |
| Derbyshire | J. K. Bather | Miss J. K. Walker-Okeover, LVO |
| Devon | E. Dancer, CBE | Lt.-Col. A. Drake |
| Dorset | Capt. M. Fulford-Dobson, RN | C. A. G. Perry |
| Durham | Sir Paul Nicholson | T. M. Swan |
| East Riding of Yorkshire | R. Marriott, TD | Hon. Elizabeth Susan Cunliffe-Lister |
| East Sussex | P. Stewart-Roberts. | A. R. P. Carden |
| Essex | The Lord Braybrooke | G. Courtauld |
| Gloucestershire | H. W. G. Elwes | Mrs Jane Jenner-Fust |
| Greater London | The Lord Imbert, QPM | A. H. Scott |
| Greater Manchester | Col. J. B. Timmins, OBE, TD | Major J. N. Abbott, TD, DL |
| Hampshire | Mrs F. M. Fagan | A. R. C. B. Cooke |
| Herefordshire | Sir Thomas Dunne, KCVO | A. W. D. Perrins |
| Hertfordshire | S. A. Bowes Lyon | C. M. Laing |
| Isle of Wight | C. D. J. Bland | Capt. H. Wrigley |
| Kent | The Lord Kingsdown, KG, PC | R. H. B. Neame, CBE |
| Lancashire | The Lord Shuttleworth | R. N. Swarbrick, CBE, DL |
| Leicestershire | T. G. M. Brooks | M. C. C. Sandell |
| Lincolnshire | Mrs B. K. Cracroft-Eley | C. G. Rowles Nicholson |
| Merseyside | A. W. Waterworth | W. D. Fulton, JP, DL |
| Norfolk | Sir Timothy Colman, KG | Mrs Theresa Caroline Courtauld |
| Northamptonshire | Lady Juliet Townsend, LVO | Lady Robinson |
| Northumberland | Sir John Riddel, CVO | J. P. P. Anderson |
| North Yorkshire | The Lord Crathorne | D. G. H. Nelson, OBE |
| Nottinghamshire | Sir Andrew Buchanan, Bt. | Sir John Whitaker, Bt. |
| Oxfordshire | H. L. J. Brunner | Lady McLintock |
| Rutland | Air Chief Marshal Sir Thomas Kennedy, GCB, AFC | M. M. Allen |
| Shropshire | A. E. H. Heber-Percy | J. R. Ravenscroft |
| Somerset | Lady Gass | T. H. R. Poole, TD |
| South Yorkshire | The Earl of Scarbrough | A. M. C. Staniforth |
| Staffordshire | J. A. Hawley, TD | The Countess of Shrewsbury and Waterford |
| Suffolk | The Lord Belstead, PC | D. W. Barclay |
| Surrey | Mrs S. J. F. Goad | C. W. Biddell |
| Tyne and Wear | N. Sherlock | Mrs Anne Darling |
| Warwickshire | M. Dunne | Miss Sarah Holman |
| West Midlands | R. R. Taylor, OBE | Mrs Tessa King-Farlow |
| West Sussex | H. Wyatt | G. G. Ferguson |
| West Yorkshire | J. Lyles, CBE | J. D. N. Stoddart-Scott |
| Wiltshire | Lt.-Gen. Sir Maurice Johnston, KCB, OBE | R. D. Stratton, OBE |
| Worcestershire | Sir Thomas Dunne, KCVO | A. W. D. Perrins |

## COUNTY COUNCILS: Area, Population, Finance

| *Council* | *Administrative Headquarters* | *Area (Hectares)* | *Population* | *Net current expenditure 2000-1* |
|---|---|---|---|---|
| Bedfordshire | County Hall, Bedford | 119,220 | 380,500 | £307,412,000.00 |
| Buckinghamshire | County Hall, Aylesbury | 156,538 | 476,200 | £346,501,000.00 |
| Cambridgeshire | Shire Hall, Cambridge | 305,399 | 573,500 | £397,377,000.00 |
| Cheshire | County Hall, Chester | 208,344 | 677,300 | £523,362,000.00 |
| Cornwall | County Hall, Truro | 354,810 | 493,900 | £367,006,000.00 |
| Cumbria | The Courts, Carlisle | 681,000 | 492,900 | £398,563,000.00 |
| Derbyshire | County Hall, Matlock | 262,858 | 740,200 | £546,862,000.00 |
| Devon | County Hall, Exeter | 670,343 | 692,400 | £512,509,000.00 |
| Dorset | County Hall, Dorchester | 254,375 | 392,800 | £279,328,000.00 |
| Durham | County Hall, Durham | 223,180 | 490,100 | £407,210,000.00 |
| East Sussex | Pelham House, St Andrew's Lane, Lewes | 172,500 | 497,500 | £373,393,000.00 |
| Essex | County Hall, Chelmsford | 344,781 | 1,295,000 | £1,008,446,000.00 |
| Gloucestershire | Shire Hall, Gloucester | 265,535 | 565,200 | £405,063,000.00 |
| Hampshire | The Castle, Winchester | 367,915 | 1,255,900 | £485,995,000.00 |
| Hertfordshire | County Hall, Hertford | 164,306 | 1,051,300 | £813,694,000.00 |
| Kent | County Hall, Maidstone | 354,296 | 1,332,000 | £1,082,458,000.00 |
| Lancashire | County Hall, Preston | 289,780 | 1,147,300 | £929,012,000.00 |
| Leicestershire | County Hall, Glenfield, Leicester | 208,380 | 602,000 | £430,852,000.00 |
| Lincolnshire | County Offices, Newland, Lincoln | 588,000 | 635,300 | £461,788,000.00 |
| Norfolk | County Hall, Norwich | 537,234 | 801,000 | £578,212,000.00 |
| Northamptonshire | County Hall, Northampton | 236,737 | 622,800 | £478,753,000.00 |
| Northumberland | County Hall, Morpeth | 502,594 | 312,000 | £261,318,000.00 |
| North Yorkshire | County Hall, Northallerton | 830,399 | 572,200 | £412,921,000.00 |
| Nottinghamshire | County Hall, Nottingham | 208,510 | 744,400 | £593,807,000.00 |
| Oxfordshire | County Hall, Oxford | 260,595 | 625,400 | £423,595,000.00 |
| Shropshire | The Shirehall, Shrewsbury | 319,736 | 283,000 | £193,867,000.00 |
| Somerset | County Hall, Taunton | 345,233 | 494,600 | £349,079,000.00 |
| Staffordshire | County Buildings, Stafford | 262,355 | 807,000 | £589,598,000.00 |
| Suffolk | County Hall, Ipswich | 380,207 | 670,000 | £475,480,000.00 |
| Surrey | County Hall, Kingston upon Thames | 167,011 | 1,055,400 | £717,320,000.00 |
| Warwickshire | Shire Hall, Warwick | 198,054 | 510,000 | £362,587,000.00 |
| West Sussex | County Hall, Chichester | 199,025 | 759,600 | £535,143,000.00 |
| Wiltshire | County Hall, Trowbridge | 348,070 | 431,000 | £306,454,000.00 |
| Worcestershire | County Hall, Worcester | 173,529 | 545,000 | £374,950,000.00 |

Source of population statistics and net expenditure figures, CIPFA

## COUNTY COUNCILS: OFFICERS AND CHAIRMEN

| *Council* | *Chief Executive* | *County Treasurer* | *Chairman of County Council* |
|---|---|---|---|
| Bedfordshire | D. Bell | B. Dodds | A. P. Hendry |
| Buckinghamshire | C. Williams | S. Nolan | D. Shakespeare |
| Cambridgeshire | A. Barnish | M. Parsons | J. Eddy |
| Cheshire | C. Cheesman | A. Cope | B. Grange |
| Cornwall | P. Davies | F. P. Twyning | J. M. Philp |
| Cumbria | L. Victory | R. F. Mather | R. S. J. Edgar |
| Derbyshire | A. R. N. Hodgson | P. Swaby | Mrs K. M. Trueman |
| Devon | P. Jenkinson | Mrs J. Stanhope | S. Day |
| Dorset | D. H. Jenkins | A. P. Peel | J. C. Peake, MBE |
| Durham | K. W. Smith | J. Kirkby | C. Megee |
| East Sussex | Mrs C. Miller | J. Howes | M. Tunwell |
| Essex | S. Ashurst | K. D. Neale | J. Pike |
| Gloucestershire | J. Redfearn | R. Potter | Dr J. Cardwell |
| Hampshire | P. C. B. Robertson | J. C. Pittam | A. W. Rice |
| Hertfordshire | W. D. Ogley | Chris Sweeney | K. Gray |
| Kent | M. Pitt | D. Lewis | C. Thorton |
| Lancashire | M. B. Winterbottom | B. Aldred | D. Westell |
| Leicestershire | J. B. Sinnott | A. Youd | J. F. Howard |
| Lincolnshire | D. Bowles | P. Moore | Mrs H. D. Judge |
| Norfolk | T. J. Byles | R. D. Summers | Dr J. Norris |
| Northamptonshire | P. Gould | S. Wood | J. Gardner |
| Northumberland | A. Clarke | C. Burns | Dr G. H. Fisher |
| North Yorkshire | J. Walker | J. S. Moore | G. Rennie |
| Nottinghamshire | P. J. Housden | R. Latham | J. T. Napier |
| Oxfordshire | R. Shaw | C. Gray | C. Scholar |
| Shropshire | N. T. Pursey | L. Rowly | Maj. A. Coles, MBE, TD |
| Somerset | Dr D. Radford | C. N. Bilsland | R. J. E. Bush |
| Staffordshire | B. A. Price, CBE | R. G. Tettenborn, OBE | Dr. D. Mole |
| Suffolk | Mrs L. Homer | W. Banks | R. Sudds |
| Surrey | P. Coen | N. W. Skelett | Dr B. J. Coffin |
| Warwickshire | I. G. Caulfield | D. Clarke | M. Singh |
| West Sussex | D. P. Rigg | Mrs H. Kilpatrick | Mrs M. Johnson |
| Wiltshire | Dr K. Robinson | D. Chalker | J. P. Johnson |
| Worcestershire | R. Sykes | M. Weaver | P. Fallows |

# Unitary Councils

SMALL CAPTIALS denote CITY status
§ Denotes Borough status

| Council | *Population* | *Band D charge 2001* | *Chief Ececutive* | *Mayor (a) Lord Mayor (b) Chairman 2001–2* |
|---|---|---|---|---|
| §Barnsley | 227,213 | 899.31 | P. J. Coppard | C. Evans |
| Bath and North-East Somerset | 158,692 | 923.00 | J. Everitt | M. McVeir |
| §BIRMINGHAM | 961,041 | 978.94 | Sir Michael Lyons | (*a*) J. Wormwood |
| §Blackburn with Darwen | 139,490 | 1,010.52 | P. S. Watson | J. Williams |
| §Blackpool | 154,000 | 810.47 | G. E. Essex-Crosby | Mrs S. E. Wright |
| §Bolton | 226,100 | 978.15 | B. Knight | K. Helsby |
| §Bournemouth | 162,000 | 839.93 | D. Newell | D. Eyre |
| §Bracknell Forest | 110,000 | 799.00 | G. S. Mitchell | Mrs D. Hayes |
| BRADFORD | 457,344 | 882.25 | I. Stewart | (*a*) G. Khaliq |
| §Brighton and Hove | 258,100 | 828.11 | G. Jones | H. Steer |
| BRISTOL | 399,600 | 1,004.00 | R. Weston | (*a*) Mrs B. Hughill |
| §Bury | 182,400 | 910.89 | D. Taylor | P. Nesbit |
| §Calderdale | 193,000 | 959.00 | P. Sheehan | C. O'Connor |
| §COVENTRY | 305,000 | 1,065.00 | Mrs S. Manzie | (*a*) D. Chater |
| §Darlington | 100,500 | 829.77 | B. Keel | Mrs I. Harley |
| DERBY | 235,000 | 873.16 | R. H. Cowlishaw | J. Till |
| §Doncaster | 288,854 | 842.18 | D. Marlow | Mrs B. Roberts |
| §Dudley | 311,468 | 896.00 | A. Sparke | J. Walters |
| East Riding of Yorkshire | 315,717 | 992.00 | D. Stephenson | (*b*) Ms M. Kingston |
| §Gateshead | 199,600 | 1,056.91 | L. N. Elton | J. Hatton |
| §Halton | 123,038 | 801.14 | M. Cuff | Ms J. Devaney |
| Hartlepool | 90,000 | 1,068.21 | B. J. Dinsdale | D. Ferriday |
| Herefordshire | 167,000 | 852.29 | N. Pringle | R. Thomas |
| Isle of Wight | 126,000 | 859.00 | B. Quoroll | (*b*) V. J. Morey |
| KINGSTON UPON HULL | 257,873 | 892.32 | I. Crookham | (*a*) F. Beedle |
| §Kirklees | 392,300 | 948.00 | A. Elson | T. Elson |
| §Knowsley | 153,252 | 1,027.17 | S. Gallagher | T. Russell |
| §LEEDS | 727,000 | 845.00 | P. Rogerson | (*a*) D. Hudson |
| LEICESTER | 290,900 | 920.68 | R. Green | (*a*) J. Allen |
| §LIVERPOOL | 468,000 | 1,171.54 | D. Henshaw | (*a*) G. Scott |
| §Luton | 180,600 | 805.14 | D. Singh | B. Devenish |
| §MANCHESTER | 431,052 | 1,027.42 | H. Bernstein | (*a*) H. Barrett |
| Medway | 250,000 | 745.02 | Ms J. Armitt | T. Goulden |
| Middlesbrough | 145,000 | 880.00 | N. Sayer | P. Walker |
| §Milton Keynes | 210,000 | 853.46 | H. Miller | Mrs Pat Seymour |
| §NEWCASTLE UPON TYNE | 273,000 | 1,049.43 | K. G. Lavery | (*a*) Mrs M. J. Carr |
| North East Lincolnshire | 156,243 | 984.53 | J. Leivers | N. Lincoln |
| North Lincolnshire | 152,287 | 1,051.00 | M. Garnett | Mrs M. Simpson |
| North Somerset | 189,776 | 818.00 | G. Turner | (*b*) P. Bryant |
| §North Tyneside | 198,000 | 1,009.57 | *vacant* | C. Gambling |
| NOTTINGHAM CITY | 284,000 | 983.00 | E. F. Cantle | (*a*) R. Greensmith |
| §Oldham | 220,000 | 1,069.97 | A. W. Kilburn | C. Wheeler |
| PETERBOROUGH | 159,900 | 858.30 | P. Martin | R. Pobgee, MBE |
| PLYMOUTH | 250,000 | 789.60 | Mrs A. Stone | (*a*) D. Viney |
| §Poole | 139,000 | 837.00 | J. Brooks | R. Parker |
| PORTSMOUTH | 188,800 | 744.00 | N. Gurney | (*a*) Mrs E. Baker |
| §Reading | 143,520 | 962.00 | Ms J. Markham | T. Jones |
| Redcar and Cleveland | 138,200 | 1,080.99 | C. Moore | V. Collins |
| §Rochdale | 202,000 | 972.00 | R. Ellis | Ms I. Davidson |
| §Rotherham | 251,637 | 940.22 | G. B. Fitzgerald | R. Littleboy |
| Rutland | 35,000 | 1,299.00 | K. Franklin | (*b*) Mrs J. Bews |
| §St Helens | 180,000 | 1,063.00 | Mrs C. Hudson | K. Roberts |
| §SALFORD | 229,300 | 1,084.00 | J. C. Willis | J. King |
| §Sandwell | 290,500 | 964.00 | F. N. Summers | Lord Tarsem King |
| §Sefton | 289,542 | 950.15 | G. J. Haywood | A. Hill |
| §SHEFFIELD | 529,000 | 999.78 | R. W. Kerslake | (*a*) D. Baker |
| §Slough | 108,000 | 760.12 | Ms C. Coppell | J. Jones |
| §Solihull | 205,600 | 852.00 | Ms K. Kerswell | Mrs L. Kellie |
| SOUTHAMPTON | 210,352 | 831.90 | B. Roynton | Mrs C. Kelly |
| South Gloucestershire | 252,000 | 906.00 | M. Robinson | (*b*) A. Bracey |

| Council | Population | Band D charge 2001 | Chief Ececutive | Mayor (a) Lord Mayor (b) Chairman 2001–2 |
|---|---|---|---|---|
| §Southend | 176,000 | 770.36 | J. K. M. Krawiec | H. Briggs |
| §South Tyneside | 154,057 | 972.36 | P. J. Haigh | A. Kerr |
| §Stockport | 292,000 | 1,018.74 | J. R. Schultz | E. Pyle |
| §Stockton-on-Tees | 178,300 | 952.90 | G. Garlick | W. T. Bean |
| STOKE-ON-TRENT | 254,400 | 853.05 | B. Smith | (a) W. F. Austin |
| §SUNDERLAND | 290,700 | 911.16 | C. W. Sinclair | J. K. Murray |
| Swindon | 177,500 | 793.00 | P. Doherty | D. Cox |
| §Tameside | 219,400 | 987.84 | M. J. Greenwood | S. Poole |
| Telford and Wrekin | 153,000 | 899.89 | M. Frater | (b) A. Mackenzie |
| §Thurrock | 150,000 | 769.00 | E. Nath | B. Lawrence |
| §Torbay | 124,100 | 848.84 | A. J. Hodgkiss | B. Pudner |
| §Trafford | 230,000 | 771.28 | Ms C. Hassan | H. Faulkner |
| WAKEFIELD | 319,600 | 819.46 | M. Pullan | D. Kitchen |
| §Walsall | 261,600 | 923.55 | H. Bhogal | C. Belby |
| §Warrington | 188,000 | 823.00 | S. Broomhead | J. Richards |
| West Berkshire | 145,000 | 940.00 | Ms S. Manzie | (b) Mrs M. Lock |
| §Wigan | 310,000 | 960.52 | S. M. Jones | J. E. Hilton |
| §Windsor and Maidenhead | 140,500 | 794.41 | D. C. Lunn | J. Tryon |
| §Wirral | 326,000 | 1,077.00 | S. Maddox | J. Cocker |
| Wokingham | 146,252 | 948.00 | Ms J. Earl | (b) D. Swindells |
| §WOLVERHAMPTON | 240,900 | 1,043.00 | D. B. Anderson | Mrs J. Hill |
| YORK | 178,000 | 790.65 | D. Atkinson | (a) I. Waubby |

# District Councils

SMALL CAPITALS denote CITY status
§ Denotes Borough status

| Council | Population | Band D charge 2001 | Chief Ececutive | Chairman (a) Mayor (b) Lord Mayor 2001–2 |
|---|---|---|---|---|
| Adur, W. Sussex | 58,400 | 897.00 | I. Lowrie | D. Philips |
| §Allerdale, Cumbria | 96,000 | 952.71 | P. J. Leonard | (a) A. Barry |
| Alnwick, Northumberland | 31,400 | 956.25 | L. A. B. St Ruth | V. Vaggs |
| Amber Valley, Derbys | 115,000 | 990.00 | P. M. Carney | (a) J. Nelson |
| Arun, W. Sussex | 143,800 | 775.94 | I. Sumnall | Mrs J. Maconachie |
| Ashfield, Notts | 107,000 | 1,042.00 | E. N. Bernasconi | Mrs Y. White |
| §Ashford, Kent | 102,177 | 842.67 | A. Baker | (a) L. G. Lawrie |
| Aylesbury Vale, Bucks | 156,597 | 853.12 | R. Carr | Mrs C. Lambert |
| Babergh, Suffolk | 80,790 | 872.00 | M. Hammond | Mrs S. Carpendale |
| §Barrow-in-Furness, Cumbria | 71,000 | 987.00 | T. O. Campbell | (a) Mrs P. J. M. Smith |
| Basildon, Essex | 162,800 | 933.75 | J. Robb | Mrs L. Gordon |
| §Basingstoke and Deane, Hants | 156,700 | 843.52 | Mrs K. E. P. Sporle | (a) Mrs R. Wellman |
| Bassetlaw, Notts | 106,600 | 1,026.87 | J. Molloy | Avril Borsley |
| §Bedford, Beds | 140,700 | 959.98 | S. Field | (a) P. Olney |
| §Berwick-upon-Tweed, Northumberland | 26,731 | 1,002.55 | P. Rutherford (Acting) | (a) W. R. Huntly |
| Blaby, Leics | 86,400 | 920.00 | E. Hemsley | R. Berrington |
| §Blyth Valley, Northumberland | 79,900 | 995.61 | G. Paul | (a) J. Newman |
| Bolsover, Derbys | 71,000 | 1,020.02 | J. R. Fotherby | B. W. Hendry |
| §Boston, Lincs | 54,140 | 879.00 | M. James | (a) S. Bakewell |
| Braintree, Essex | 132,300 | 879.20 | Ms A. F. Ralph | K. Boylan |
| Breckland, Norfolk | 120,000 | 837.78 | R. N. Garnett | Mrs S. Matthews |
| §Brentwood, Essex | 71,400 | 886.00 | B. McLintock | (a) A. Davies |
| Bridgnorth, Shrops | 52,300 | 871.00 | R. Heath | L. Jones |
| Broadland, Norfolk | 116,000 | 882.00 | C. Bland | D. Thompson |
| Bromsgrove, Worcs | 85,210 | 873.00 | R. F. Lewis | M. H. Gill |
| §Broxbourne, Herts | 81,500 | 804.22 | M. J. Walker | (a) D. C. Smith |
| §Broxtowe, Notts | 110,319 | 1,007.14 | M. Brown | (a) T. Syson |
| §Burnley, Lancs | 89,900 | 1,043.42 | Dr G. Taylor | (a) J. Alston |
| CAMBRIDGE, CAMBS | 122,900 | 850.00 | R. Hammond | (a) C. Lakin |

| Council | Population | Band D charge 2001 | Chief Ececutive | Chairman (a) Mayor (b) Lord Mayor 2001–2 |
|---|---|---|---|---|
| Cannock Chase, Staffs | 91,000 | 908.00 | M. G. Kemp | M. Holder |
| CANTERBURY, KENT | 123,900 | 867.71 | C. Carmichael | (b) F. Whitemore |
| Caradon, Cornwall | 81,280 | 861.00 | Dr J. Neal | E. J. Lewis |
| CARLISLE, CUMBRIA | 102,317 | 975.00 | P. Stybelski | (a) Mrs D. H. Parsons |
| Carrick, Cornwall | 85,300 | 872.35 | J. P. Winskill | L. Brokenshire |
| §Castle Morpeth, Northumberland | 50,000 | 1,021.00 | P. Wilson | (a) C. Cuthbertson |
| §Castle Point, Essex | 84,800 | 935.00 | B. Rollinson | (a) E. Brett |
| §Charnwood, Leics | 155,400 | 910.67 | S. M. Peatfield | (a) A. W. Stott |
| §Chelmsford, Essex | 156,000 | 898.27 | M. Easteal | (a) C. Rycroft |
| §Cheltenham, Glos | 103,115 | 888.68 | L. Davison | (a) Ms D. Pennell |
| Cherwell, Oxon | 132,578 | 836.38 | G. J. Handley | Mrs C. A. Fulljames |
| §Chesterfield, Derbys | 101,000 | 960.02 | D. R. Shaw | (a) J. McManus |
| Chester-le-Street, Co. Durham | 53,000 | 907.20 | M. W. Waterson | J. Tinnion |
| CHESTER, CHESHIRE | 118,700 | 986.47 | P. F. Durham | (b) G. Proctor |
| Chichester, W. Sussex | 110,110 | 815.80 | J. S. Marsland | B. B. Trinkwoh |
| Chiltern, Bucks | 91,682 | 878.17 | A. Goodrum | Ian Gomm |
| §Chorley, Lancs | 98,075 | 987.10 | J. W. Davies | (a) D. Edgerley |
| §Christchurch, Dorset | 44,327 | 904.10 | M. A. Turvey | (a) Mrs J. Spencer |
| §Colchester, Essex | 159,000 | 882.99 | J. Cobley | (a) M. Hogg |
| §Congleton, Cheshire | 88,400 | 972.55 | P. Cooper | (a) R.Giltrap |
| §Copeland, Cumbria | 69,800 | 985.00 | Dr J. Stanforth | (a) N. Williams |
| §Corby, Northants | 53,000 | 856.00 | N. Rudd | (a) Mrs B. Wade |
| Cotswold, Glos | 83,000 | 893.00 | N. C. Abbott | B. I. Evans |
| Craven, N. Yorks | 52,100 | 838.01 | Miss R. Mann | S. Butcher |
| §Crawley, W. Sussex | 97,000 | 796.59 | M. D. Sander | (a) C. Mullins |
| §Crewe and Nantwich, Cheshire | 116,800 | 922.19 | A. Wenham | (a) W. T. Beard |
| §Dacorum, Herts | 130,000 | 839.00 | P. Walker | (a) D. Pownsend |
| §Dartford, Kent | 86,000 | 809.00 | G. Harris | (a) T. A. Maddison |
| Daventry, Northants | 69,000 | 820.08 | S. Atkinson | A. Compling |
| Derbyshire Dales, Derbys | 71,300 | 989.17 | D. Wheatcroft | T. Boam |
| Derwentside, Co. Durham | 87,300 | 981.20 | L. Vaux | A. Watson |
| Dover, Kent | 109,400 | 853.20 | J. P. Moir, TD | W. Hansell |
| DURHAM, CO. DURHAM | 80,669 | 931.44 | C. Shearsmith | (a) J. G. Cowper |
| Easington, Co. Durham | 97,824 | 1,041.00 | P. Wilding | Mrs A. E. Laing |
| §Eastbourne, E. Sussex | 90,000 | 926.00 | *vacant* | (a) D. Stevens |
| East Cambridgeshire, Cambs | 66,200 | 828.08 | J. Hill | V. Leake |
| East Devon, Devon | 130,600 | 861.00 | F. J. Vallender | Dr W. H. Waterworth |
| East Dorset, Dorset | 82,400 | 944.00 | A. Breakwell | R. Daw |
| East Hampshire, Hants | 112,432 | 883.14 | P. Burton | P. Rodgers |
| East Hertfordshire, Herts | 124,000 | 852.60 | R. J. Bailey | R. Gilbert |
| §Eastleigh, Hants | 113,500 | 882.00 | C. Tapp | (a) Mrs M. A. Sollitt |
| East Lindsey, Lincs | 124,160 | 843.12 | P. Haigh | G. Allan |
| East Northamptonshire, Northants | 76,750 | 864.00 | G. Wise | A. Campbell |
| §East Staffordshire, Staffs | 103,400 | 908.60 | F. W. Saunders | (a) P. Davies |
| Eden, Cumbria | 45,581 | 957.56 | I. W. Bruce | J. Banks |
| §Ellesmere Port and Neston, Cheshire | 81,200 | 980.00 | S. Ewbank | (a) Mrs M. Andrews |
| §Elmbridge, Surrey | 114,479 | 856.00 | M. Lockwood | (a) Mrs M. Sheldrick |
| Epping Forest, Essex | 118,000 | 904.00 | J. Burgess | J. Gilliham |
| §Epsom and Ewell, Surrey | 67,007 | 841.16 | D. J. Smith | (a) A. C. Carlson |
| §Erewash, Derbys | 108,160 | 974.00 | Tony Harris | (a) P. Trueman |
| EXETER, DEVON | 111,264 | 849.96 | P. Bostock | (a) M. G. Baldwin |
| Fareham, Hants | 107,000 | 845.00 | A. A. Davies | (a) A. Mandry |
| Fenland, Cambs | 81,900 | 854.00 | N. R. Topliss | A. Carlisle |
| Forest Heath, Suffolk | 69,200 | 827.70 | D. W. Burnip | W. E. Sadler |
| Forest of Dean, Glos | 75,351 | 911.11 | Ms M. Holborow | D. Clarke |
| §Fylde, Lancs | 74,900 | 967.00 | K. Lee | (a) P. Fieldhouse |
| §Gedling, Notts | 110,133 | 953.20 | *vacant* | (a) M. Roach |
| GLOUCESTER, GLOS | 101,608 | 889.00 | P. Smith | (a) T. L. Haines |
| §Gosport, Hants | 78,040 | 880.34 | M. C. Crocker | (a) D. F. Wright |
| §Gravesham, Kent | 92,454 | 846.00 | E. C. Anderson | (a) V. Ashenden |
| §Great Yarmouth, Norfolk | 89,900 | 880.73 | R. W. Packham | D. W. Thompson |
| §Guildford, Surrey | 129,200 | 850.00 | D. T. Watts, FRSA | (a) Mrs J. E. Powell |
| Hambleton, N. Yorks | 86,500 | 797.53 | P. Simpson | M. J. Prest |
| Harborough, Leics | 75,300 | 916.00 | M. C. Wilson | P. Callis |
| Harlow, Essex | 74,629 | 986.00 | D. Patterson | R. Long |

| Council | *Population* | *Band D charge 2001* | *Chief Ececutive* | *Chairman (a) Mayor (b) Lord Mayor 2001–2* |
|---|---|---|---|---|
| §Harrogate, N. Yorks | 143,000 | 879.00 | P. M. Walsh | (*a*) P. Nash |
| Hart, Hants | 80,921 | 869.00 | G. R. Jelbart | S. Band |
| §Hastings, E. Sussex | 84,500 | 953.63 | R. Mawford | (*a*) J. Dowling |
| §Havant, Hants | 120,113 | 862.82 | R. D. Smith | (*a*) R. V. Bellinger |
| §Hertsmere, Herts | 97,314 | 851.00 | R. Higgins | (*a*) W. Hogan |
| §High Peak, Derbys | 87,900 | 987.16 | P. Sloman | (*a*) R. Priestly |
| §Hinckley and Bosworth, Leics | 97,699 | 882.24 | J. Corry | (*a*) W. G. Joy |
| Horsham, W. Sussex | 122,405 | 837.35 | M. J. Pearson | Mrs C. Vickers |
| Huntingdonshire, Cambs | 153,000 | 860.00 | D. Monks | K. Reynolds |
| §Hyndburn, Lancs | 78,390 | 1,026.48 | M. J. Chambers | (*a*) D. Parkins |
| §Ipswich, Suffolk | 116,956 | 946.70 | J. D. Hehir | (*a*) Mrs M. Corrington-Brown |
| Kennet, Wilts | 79,500 | 894.00 | M. J. Boden | K. R. F. Beard |
| Kerrier, Cornwall | 87,566 | 879.75 | G. G. Cox | Mrs B. Godolphin |
| §Kettering, Northants | 81,320 | 860.30 | D. Cook | (*a*) R. Civil |
| §King's Lynn and West Norfolk, Norfolk | 133,420 | 886.16 | G. Chilton | (*a*) G. Pratt |
| LANCASTER, LANCS | 137,000 | 978.86 | M. Cullinan | (*a*) Mrs P. Quinton |
| Lewes, E. Sussex | 85,859 | 956.00 | J. N. Crawford | P. R. Harper |
| Lichfield, Staffs | 92,699 | 881.00 | J. T. Thompson | J. R. T. Mercer |
| LINCOLN, LINCS | 170,000 | 851.85 | A. Taylor | (*a*) P. McGinley |
| §Macclesfield, Cheshire | 151,590 | 959.71 | D. W. Parr | (*a*) Mrs M. Clampett |
| §Maidstone, Kent | 137,000 | 910.74 | D. Petford | (*a*) Mrs P. Stockell |
| Maldon, Essex | 57,300 | 885.64 | S. W. Packham | Mrs P. A. Channer |
| Malvern Hills, Worcs | 74,011 | 844.86 | C. J. Bocock | Mrs B. Williams |
| Mansfield, Notts | 100,300 | 1,055.00 | R. P. Goad | M. Sage |
| §Melton, Leics | 46,861 | 907.00 | P. M. Murphy | (*a*) T. P. Cullen |
| Mendip, Somerset | 100,000 | 887.00 | G. Jeffs | T. O'Connel |
| Mid Bedfordshire, Beds | 109,800 | 969.00 | J. Salsbury | R. A. Holden |
| Mid Devon, Devon | 68,600 | 880.96 | P. Edwards | Mrs J. Campbell |
| Mid Suffolk, Suffolk | 77,100 | 833.61 | A. Good | T. Fowler |
| Mid Sussex, W. Sussex | 126,000 | 854.00 | W. J. H. Hatton | C. A. C. Hersey |
| Mole Valley, Surrey | 79,220 | 826.97 | Mrs H. Kerswell | M. Homewood |
| Newark and Sherwood, Notts | 104,010 | 1,080.00 | R. G. Dix | Ms. J. Dawn |
| §Newcastle under Lyme, Staffs | 123,300 | 883.63 | F. Harley | (*a*) Mrs G. Williams |
| New Forest, Hants | 170,610 | 889.00 | D. Yates | Ms. A. Drake |
| §Northampton, Northants | 198,300 | 881.77 | R. J. B. Morris | (*a*) T. Hadland |
| North Cornwall, Cornwall | 81,000 | 873.56 | D. Brown | E. T. Denholm |
| North Devon, Devon | 87,740 | 894.00 | D. T. Cunliffe | D. Paul |
| North Dorset, Dorset | 62,000 | 910.40 | A. Greaves | Mrs D. L. Jones |
| North East Derbyshire, Derbys | 99,000 | 1,024.00 | Ms C. A. Gilby | Mrs M. Treweek |
| North Hertfordshire, Herts | 113,500 | 843.15 | S. Philp | P. Burt |
| North Kesteven, Lincs | 78,400 | 893.00 | Mrs R. Marlow | B. Drain |
| North Norfolk, Norfolk | 100,900 | 887.00 | B. A. Barrell | V. Woodcock |
| North Shropshire, Shrops | 54,100 | 905.71 | R. J. Hughes | F. J. Udale |
| §North Warwickshire, Warks | 60,747 | 977.00 | J. Hutchinson | (*a*) M. E. Stanley |
| North West Leicestershire, Leics | 86,000 | 921.71 | M. J. Diaper | Mrs A. Harrop |
| North Wiltshire, Wilts | 126,829 | 924.26 | R. Marshall | B. Atfield |
| NORWICH, NORFOLK | 123,500 | 934.00 | Ms A. Seex | (*b*) K. Ratcliffe |
| §Nuneaton and Bedworth, Warks | 117,052 | 951.00 | Ms C. Kerr | (*a*) W. Hancox |
| §Oadby and Wigston, Leics | 53,570 | 924.88 | Mrs R. E. Hyde | (*a*) G. A. Boulter |
| §Oswestry, Shrops | 33,508 | 907.00 | P. Shevlin | (*a*) L. Dennis |
| OXFORD, OXON | 146,100 | 955.25 | M. Headicar | (*b*) P. Moss |
| §Pendle, Lancs | 83,000 | 1,034.47 | S. Barnes | (*a*) F. M. Hartley |
| Penwith, Cornwall | 60,107 | 848.00 | J. A. R. McKenna | R. A. Mann |
| §Preston, Lancs | 135,000 | 1,050.00 | J. E. Carr | (*a*) A. Hackett |
| Purbeck, Dorset | 46,140 | 934.24 | P. B. Croft | R. Anderson |
| §Redditch, Worcs | 77,000 | 906.00 | C. Smith | (*a*) D. Dudley |
| §Reigate and Banstead, Surrey | 119,000 | 863.80 | N. Clifford | (*a*) S. A. Gates |
| §Restormel, Cornwall | 91,000 | 847.51 | Mrs P. Crowson | (*a*) Mrs E. J. Vincent |
| §Ribble Valley, Lancs | 52,444 | 978.31 | D. G. Morris | (*a*) Mrs G. Pye |
| Richmondshire, N. Yorks | 49,300 | 864.68 | H. Tabiner | Mrs J. Metcalfe |
| Rochford, Essex | 78,273 | 911.62 | P. Warren | Mrs S. J. Lemmon |
| §Rossendale, Lancs | 65,681 | 1,027.57 | J. S. Hartley | (*a*) J. Grogan |
| Rother, E. Sussex | 90,100 | 906.65 | D. Stevens | W. H. Clements |
| §Rugby, Warks | 87,000 | 938.00 | Mrs D. M. Colley | (*a*) R. Kirby |

| Council | Population | Band D charge 2001 | Chief Eecutive | Chairman (a) Mayor (b) Lord Mayor 2001–2 |
|---|---|---|---|---|
| §Runnymede, Surrey | 76,629 | 781.00 | T. N. Williams | (a) J. R. Ashmore |
| §Rushcliffe, Notts | 105,000 | 1,008.00 | K. Beaumont | (a) T. D. Barlow |
| §Rushmoor, Hants | 86,000 | 863.49 | J. A. Lloyd | (a) C. S. Choudhary |
| Ryedale, N. Yorks | 49,000 | 883.98 | H. W. Mosley | C. R. Wainwright |
| ST ALBANS, HERTS | 128,700 | 858.06 | P. Learner | (a) J. Peters |
| §St Edmundsbury, Suffolk | 97,000 | 850.00 | G. R. N. Toft | (a) B. Bagnall |
| Salisbury, Wilts | 115,000 | 891.06 | R. Sheard | I. Tomes |
| §Scarborough, N. Yorks | 106,067 | 796.54 | J. M. Trebble | (a) Mrs L. Haycock |
| §Sedgefield, Co. Durham | 89,500 | 1,055.49 | N. Vaulks | (a) A. Gray |
| Sedgemoor, Somerset | 104,000 | 865.00 | K. Rickards | (a) K. Richards |
| Selby, N. Yorks | 89,428 | 844.47 | M. Connor | W. Norton |
| Sevenoaks, Kent | 111,000 | 887.25 | N. Howells | P. Deans |
| Shepway, Kent | 96,460 | 899.00 | R. J. Thompson | (a) D. Dickinson |
| §Shrewsbury and Atcham, Shrops | 97,400 | 877.00 | R. Hooper | (a) C. Forshaw |
| South Bedfordshire, Beds | 111,250 | 1,019.53 | J. Ruddick | Mrs Staples |
| South Bucks, Berks | 62,482 | 858.79 | C. R. Furness | J. R. A. Kennedy |
| South Cambridgeshire, Cambs | 126,500 | 819.00 | J. S. Ballantyne | G. Elsbury |
| South Derbyshire, Derbys | 81,200 | 972.00 | F. McArdle | C. H. Rose |
| South Hams, Devon | 82,600 | 875.60 | Miss R. E. Bagley | I. Longrigg |
| South Holland, Lincs | 74,095 | 833.22 | C. J. Simpkins | E. J. Poll |
| South Kesteven, Lincs | 120,000 | 855.05 | C. Farmer | A. Parkin |
| South Lakeland, Cumbria | 103,240 | 956.00 | P. J. Cunliffe | R. Bingham |
| South Norfolk, Norfolk | 104,334 | 900.00 | G. Rivers | Mrs P. Dore |
| South Northamptonshire, Northants | 78,800 | 883.38 | R. Tinlin | L. Richards |
| South Oxfordshire, Oxon | 125,000 | 904.26 | D. Buckle | Mrs E. Haros |
| §South Ribble, Lancs | 104,300 | 974.82 | Ms J. Hunter | (a) N. Crossley |
| South Shropshire, Shrops | 282,500 | 908.00 | G. C. Biggs, MBE | M. R. Williams |
| South Somerset, Somerset | 155,000 | 891.47 | Ms E. Peters | Mrs H. Merrifield |
| South Staffordshire, Staffs | 105,487 | 823.60 | L. T. Barnfield | R. Williams |
| §Spelthorne, Surrey | 89,748 | 836.65 | M. B. Taylor | (a) Ms J. Wood-Dow |
| Stafford Moorlands, Staffs | 95,000 | 903.00 | B. J. Preedy | R. Plant |
| §Staffordshire, Staffs | 127,000 | 808.70 | D. Rawlings | (a) P. Bruce |
| §Stevenage, Herts | 77,000 | 856.26 | I. Paske | (a) H. C. L. Tessier |
| Stratford, Warks | 109,400 | 891.70 | I. B. Prosser | L. Topham |
| Stroud, Glos | 108,000 | 944.26 | D. Hagg | Mrs S. M. Bruce |
| Suffolk Coastal, Suffolk | 121,000 | 858.65 | T. K. Griffin | Mrs D. Savage |
| §Surrey Heath, Surrey | 85,000 | 846.00 | B. R. Catchpole | (a) R. Christie |
| §Swale, Kent | 120,000 | 874.00 | C. Edwards | (a) Mrs B. Simpson |
| §Tamworth, Staffs | 77,000 | 853.00 | D. Weatherley | (a) M. Cooper |
| Tandridge, Surrey | 76,316 | 846.76 | J. D. Thomas | E. Morgan |
| §Taunton Deane, Somerset | 100,000 | 857.00 | S. Fletcher | (a) Mrs M. Whitmarsh |
| Teesdale, Co. Durham | 24,992 | 913.89 | C. M. Anderson | N. Wood |
| Teignbridge, Devon | 116,500 | 886.00 | H. Davies | D. Tracy |
| Tendring, Essex | 130,328 | 885.00 | J. Hawkins | Miss C. Jessop |
| §Test Valley, Hants | 111,000 | 837.00 | A. Jones | (a) J. E. Taylor |
| §Tewkesbury, Glos | 74,478 | 851.79 | T. Turner | (a) Mrs F. M. Ogden |
| Thanet, Kent | 127,000 | 898.52 | D. Ralls, CBE | W. E. Palmer |
| Three Rivers, Herts | 84,000 | 865.00 | A. Robertson | G. Emery |
| §Tonbridge and Malling, Kent | 106,300 | 880.03 | T. Thompson | (a) Mrs J. Oxely |
| Torridge, Devon | 55,440 | 893.00 | R. K. Brasington | P. Waters |
| §Tunbridge Wells, Kent | 102,738 | 816.22 | R. J. Stone | (a) M. Howell |
| Tynedale, Northumberland | 58,181 | 987.14 | P. A. Kemp | Mrs A. Hutchinson |
| Uttlesford, Essex | 69,796 | 901.00 | Mrs E. Forbes | D. Gregory |
| Vale of White Horse, Oxon | 113,940 | 870.00 | T. A. Stock | V. Butt |
| §Vale Royal, Cheshire | 118,300 | 984.88 | A. Bingham-Holmes | (a) S. Gough |
| Wansbeck, Northumberland | 63,171 | 1,016.25 | R. A. Stephenson | D. Armstrong |
| Warwick, Warks | 124,500 | 900.07 | Miss J. M. Barrett | H. Thomas |
| §Watford, Herts | 81,000 | 926.49 | A. Clarke | (a) Mrs S. Tuckwood |
| Waveney, Suffolk | 108,163 | 839.00 | Mrs M. McLean | Ms M. Rodgers |
| §Waverley, Surrey | 113,212 | 865.77 | Ms C. L. Pointer | (a) M. R. Goodridge |
| Wealden, E. Sussex | 130,214 | 963.79 | Ms S. Douglas | N. Buck |
| Wear Valley, Co. Durham | 62,746 | 943.36 | I. Phillips | W. Dobinson |
| §Wellingborough, Northants | 70,400 | 805.66 | A. D. W. McArdle | (a) Mrs P. Beirne |
| Welwyn Hatfield, Herts | 92,366 | 863.06 | M. Saminaden | T. Wilder |
| §West Devon, Devon | 47,716 | 906.54 | D. J. Incoll | (a) R. Pike |

| Council | Population | Band D charge 2001 | Chief Ececutive | Chairman (a) Mayor (b) Lord Mayor 2001–2 |
|---|---|---|---|---|
| West Dorset, Dorset | 91,100 | 934.00 | R. C. Rennison | Mrs N. M. Penfold |
| West Lancashire, Lancs | 110,200 | 1,010.00 | W. J. Taylor | R. Hodge |
| West Lindsey, Lincs | 77,560 | 879.75 | R. W. Nelsey | R. Rainforth |
| West Oxfordshire, Oxon | 99,000 | 840.90 | G. Bonner | A. Walker |
| West Somerset, Somerset | 32,700 | 851.00 | T. Howes | E. S. Taylor |
| West Wiltshire, Wilts | 108,000 | 830.50 | J. Ligo | Mrs A. Irving |
| §Weymouth and Portland, Dorset | 63,000 | 936.90 | T. Grainger | (a) Mrs J. Stanley |
| WINCHESTER, HANTS | 110,000 | 863.00 | D. H. Cowan | (a) Ms T. Evans |
| §Woking, Surrey | 86,765 | 877.05 | P. Russell | (a) B. J. Pope |
| WORCESTER, WORCS | 95,500 | 864.91 | D. Wareing | (a) D. Clark |
| §Worthing, W. Sussex | 100,000 | 849.51 | Miss S. Grady | (a) Mrs V. Sutton |
| Wychavon, Worcs | 101,716 | 864.00 | S. Pritchard | A. Hotham |
| Wycombe, Bucks | 162,000 | 870.00 | R. J. Cummins | R. W. Jennings |
| §Wyre, Lancs | 105,010 | 974.60 | M. Brown | (a) F. Baillie |
| Wyre Forest, Worcs | 94,814 | 904.00 | W. Delin | F. Bailly |

Northumberland
Newcastle upon Tyne
North Tyneside
Gateshead
South Tyneside
Sunderland
Durham
Cumbria
Hartlepool
Darlington
1
2
Redcar and Cleveland
North Yorkshire
York
3
Lancashire
Bradford
East Riding of Yorkshire
Leeds
4
Calderdale
Wakefield
Kingston upon Hull
Sefton
Wigan
Kirklees
N Lincs
Barnsley
Doncaster
NE Lincs
Wirral
Sheffield
Rotherham
Cheshire
Derbyshire
Lincolnshire
Stoke-on-Trent
Nottinghamshire
Derby
Staffordshire
Leicestershire
Shropshire
Rutland
Leicester
Norfolk
Worcestershire
Northants
Cambridgeshire
Warwickshire
Herefordshire
Milton Keynes
Suffolk
Beds
Gloucestershire
Luton
Bucks
Herts
Essex
Oxfordshire
Swindon
NW Somerset
LONDON (see box)
W Berks
Wiltshire
Surrey
Somerset
Hampshire
Kent
Southampton
West Sussex
East Sussex
Devon
Dorset
Poole
Portsmouth
Brighton and Hove
Bournemouth
Isle of Wight
Cornwall
1 Stockton-on-Tees
2 Middlesbrough
3 Blackpool
4 Blackburn with Darwen
5 Bolton
6 Bury
7 Rochdale
8 Salford
9 Oldham
10 Liverpool
11 Knowsley
12 St Helens
13 Halton
14 Warrington
15 Trafford
16 Manchester
17 Tameside
18 Stockport
19 Nottingham
20 Telford and Wrekin
21 Wolverhampton
22 Walsall
23 Sandwell
24 Dudley
25 Birmingham
26 Solihull
27 Coventry
28 Peterborough
29 South Glos
30 Bristol
31 Bath and NE Somerset
32 Windsor and Maidenhead
33 Slough
34 Reading
35 Wokingham
36 Bracknell Forest
37 Thurrock
38 Southend
39 Medway
40 Plymouth
41 Torbay
LONDON
1 Hillingdon
2 Harrow
3 Barnet
4 Enfield
5 Waltham Forest
6 Redbridge
7 Barking and Dagenham
8 Havering
9 Ealing
10 Brent
11 Camden
12 Haringey
13 Islington
14 Hackney
15 Newham
16 Hounslow
17 Hammersmith and Fulham
18 Kensington and Chelsea
19 City of Westminster
20 City of London
21 Tower Hamlets
22 Richmond upon Thames
23 Wandsworth
24 Lambeth
25 Southwark
26 Lewisham
27 Greenwich
28 Bexley
29 Kingston upon Thames
30 Merton
31 Sutton
32 Croydon
33 Bromley

# London

## THE CORPORATION OF LONDON

The City of London is the historic centre at the heart of London known as 'the square mile' around which the vast metropolis has grown over the centuries. The City's residential population is 5,500. The civic government is carried on by the Corporation of London through the Court of Common Council.

The City is an international financial centre, generating over £20 billion a year for the British economy. It includes the head offices of the principal banks, insurance companies and mercantile houses, in addition to buildings ranging from the historic Roman Wall and the 15th-century Guildhall, to the massive splendour of St Paul's Cathedral and the architectural beauty of Wren's spires.

The City of London was described by Tacitus in AD 62 as 'a busy emporium for trade and traders'. Under the Romans it became an important administration centre and hub of the road system. Little is known of London in Saxon times, when it formed part of the kingdom of the East Saxons. In 886 Alfred recovered London from the Danes and reconstituted it a burgh under his son-in-law. In 1066 the citizens submitted to William the Conqueror who in 1067 granted them a charter, which is still preserved, establishing them in the rights and privileges they had hitherto enjoyed.

### THE MAYORALTY

The Mayoralty was probably established about 1189, the first Mayor being Henry Fitz Ailwyn who filled the office for 23 years and was succeeded by Fitz Alan (1212–14). A new charter was granted by King John in 1215, directing the Mayor to be chosen annually, which has ever since been done, though in early times the same individual often held the office more than once. A familiar instance is that of 'Whittington, thrice Lord Mayor of London' (in reality four times, 1397, 1398, 1406, 1419); and many modern cases have occurred. The earliest instance of the phrase 'Lord Mayor' in English is in 1414. It was used more generally in the latter part of the 15th century and became invariable from 1535 onwards. At Michaelmas the liverymen in Common Hall choose two Aldermen who have served the office of Sheriff for presentation to the Court of Aldermen, and one is chosen to be Lord Mayor for the following mayoral year.

### LORD MAYOR'S DAY

The Lord Mayor of London was previously elected on the feast of St Simon and St Jude (28 October), and from the time of Edward I, at least, was presented to the King or to the Barons of the Exchequer on the following day, unless that day was a Sunday. The day of election was altered to 16 October in 1346, and after some further changes was fixed for Michaelmas Day in 1546, but the ceremonies of admittance and swearing-in of the Lord Mayor continued to take place on 28 and 29 October respectively until 1751. In 1752, at the reform of the calendar, the Lord Mayor was continued in office until 8 November, the 'New Style' equivalent of 28 October. The Lord Mayor is now presented to the Lord Chief Justice at the Royal Courts of Justice on the second Saturday in November to make the final declaration of office, having been sworn in at Guildhall on the preceding day. The procession to the Royal Courts of Justice is popularly known as the Lord Mayor's Show.

### REPRESENTATIVES

Aldermen are mentioned in the 11th century and their office is of Saxon origin. They were elected annually between 1377 and 1394, when an Act of Parliament of Richard II directed them to be chosen for life.

The Common Council, elected annually on the first Friday in December, was, at an early date, substituted for a popular assembly called the *Folkmote*. At first only two representatives were sent from each ward, but the number has since been greatly increased. The Corporation is reducing the number of Common Councilmen from 130 to 100 through natural wastage. The Government has introduced legislation to remove anomalies from the election system and to extend the non-resident franchise.

### OFFICERS

Sheriffs were Saxon officers; their predecessors were the *wic-reeves* and *portreeves* of London and Middlesex. At first they were officers of the Crown, and were named by the Barons of the Exchequer; but Henry I (in 1132) gave the citizens permission to choose their own Sheriffs, and the annual election of Sheriffs became fully operative under King John's charter of 1199. The citizens lost this privilege, as far as the election of the Sheriff of Middlesex was concerned, by the Local Government Act 1888; but the liverymen continue to choose two Sheriffs of the City of London, who are appointed on Midsummer Day and take office at Michaelmas.

The office of Chamberlain is an ancient one, the first contemporary record of which is 1237. The Town Clerk (or Common Clerk) is mentioned in 1274.

### ACTIVITIES

The work of the Corporation is assigned to a number of committees which present reports to the Court of Common Council. These Committees are: City Lands and Bridge House Grants Estates, Policy and Resources, Finance, Planning and Transportation, Central Markets, Billingsgate and Leadenhall Markets, Spitalfields Market, Police, Port and City of London Health and Social Services, Libraries, Art Galleries and Records, Board of Governors of City of London Freemen's School, Music and Drama (Guildhall School of Music and Drama), Establishment, Housing and Sports Development, Gresham (City side), Hampstead Heath Management, Epping Forest and Open Spaces, West Ham Park, Privileges, Barbican Residential and Barbican Centre (Barbican Arts and Conference Centre).

The City's estate, in the possession of which the Corporation of London differs from other municipalities, is managed by the City Lands and Bridge House Grants Estates Committee, the chairmanship of which carries with it the title of Chief Commoner.

The Honourable the Irish Society, which manages the Corporation's estates in Ulster, consists of a Governor and five other Aldermen, the Recorder, and 19 Common Councilmen, of whom one is elected Deputy Governor.

### THE LORD MAYOR 2000–2001*

*The Rt. Hon. the Lord Mayor*, Alderman Sir David Howard, TD *Private Secretary*, P. Tribe

* The Lord Mayor for 2001–2002 was elected on Michaelmas Day. *See* Stop-press

THE SHERIFFS 2001-2

Michael Savory (*Alderman Bread Street*) and David Mauleverer

OFFICERS, ETC

*Town Clerk*, T. Simmons
*Chamberlain*, P. Derrick
*Chief Commoner (2001)*, A. Eskenzi
*Clerk, The Honourable the Irish Society*, S. Waley, The Irish Chamber, 1st Floor, 75 Watling Street, London EC4M 9BJ

## THE ALDERMEN

| *Name and Ward* | *CC* | *Ald.* | *Shff.* | *Lord Mayor* |
|---|---|---|---|---|
| Sir Christopher Leaver, GBE, *Dowgate* | 1973 | 1974 | 1979 | 1981 |
| Sir Alan Traill, GBE, *Langbourn* | 1970 | 1975 | 1982 | 1984 |
| Sir David Rowe-Ham, GBE, *Bridge* and *Bridge Wt.* | — | 1976 | 1984 | 1986 |
| Sir Christopher Collett, GBE, *Broad Street* | 1973 | 1979 | 1985 | 1988 |
| Sir Alexander Graham, GBE, *Queenhithe* | 1978 | 1979 | 1986 | 1990 |
| Sir Brian Jenkins, GBE, *Cordwainer* | — | 1980 | 1987 | 1991 |
| Sir Paul Newall, TD, *Walbrook* | 1980 | 1981 | 1989 | 1993 |
| Sir Christopher Walford, *Farringdon Wn.* | — | 1982 | 1990 | 1994 |
| Sir John Chalstrey, *Vintry* | 1981 | 1984 | 1993 | 1995 |
| Sir Roger Cork, *Tower* | 1978 | 1983 | 1992 | 1996 |
| Richard Nichols, *Candlewick* | 1983 | 1984 | 1994 | 1997 |
| Lord Levene of Portsoken, KBE, *Portsoken* | 1983 | 1984 | 1995 | 1998 |
| Clive Martin, Aldgate | — | 1985 | 1996 | 1999 |

*All the above have passed the Civic Chair*

| | | | | |
|---|---|---|---|---|
| Michael Oliver, *Bishopsgate* | 1980 | 1987 | 1997 | |
| Anthony Bull, *Cheap* | 1968 | 1984 | | |
| Gavyn Arthur, *Cripplegate* | 1988 | 1991 | 1998 | |
| Robert Finch, *Coleman Street* | — | 1992 | 1999 | |
| Richard Agutter, *Castle Baynard* | — | 1995 | 1999 | |
| Michael Savory, *Bread Street* | 1980 | 1996 | | |
| David Brewer, *Bassishaw* | 1992 | 1996 | | |
| Nicholas Anstee, *Aldersgate* | 1987 | 1996 | | |
| Michael Everard, CBE, *Lime Street* | — | 1996 | | |
| John Hughesdon, *Billingsgate* | 1991 | 1997 | | |
| Simon Walsh, *Farringdon Wt.* | 1989 | 2000 | | |

## THE COMMON COUNCIL

*Deputy:* Each Common Councilman so described serves as deputy to the Alderman of her/his ward.

| | |
|---|---|
| Abrahams, G. (2000) | *Farringdon Wt* |
| Absalom, J. D. (1994) | *Farringdon Wt.* |
| Altman, L. P., CBE (1996) | *Cripplegate Wn.* |
| Angell, E. H. (1991) | *Cripplegate Wt.* |
| Archibald, *Deputy* W. W. (1986) | *Cornhill* |
| Ayers, K. E. (1996) | *Bassishaw* |
| Balls, H. D. (1970) | *Castle Baynard* |
| Barker, *Deputy* J. A. (1981) | *Cripplegate Wn.* |
| Barter, S. (1999) | *Langbourn* |
| Beale, *Deputy* M. J. (1979) | *Lime Street* |
| Bird, J. L., OBE (1977) | *Bridge* |
| Bradshaw, D. J. (1991) | *Cripplegate Wn.* |
| Bramwell, F. M. (1983) | *Langbourn* |
| Brewster, J. W., OBE (1994) | *Bassishaw* |
| Brighton, R. L. (1984) | *Portsoken* |
| Brooks, W. I. B. (1988) | *Billingsgate* |
| Byllam-Barnes, J. C. F. B. (1997) | *Cheap* |
| Caspi, D. R. (1994) | *Bridge* |
| Cassidy, *Deputy* M. J. (1989) | *Coleman Street* |
| Catt, B. F. (1982) | *Farringdon Wn.* |
| Chadwick, R. A. H. (1994) | *Tower* |
| Charkham, J. P. (1996) | *Farringdon Wt.* |
| Cohen, Mrs C. M. (1986) | *Lime Street* |
| Cotgrove, D. (1991) | *Lime Street* |
| Currie, *Deputy* Miss S. E. M. (1985) | *Cripplegate Wt.* |
| Daily-Hunt, R. B. (1989) | *Cripplegate Wt.* |
| Darwin, G. E. (1995) | *Farringdon Wt.* |
| Davis, C. B. (1991) | *Bread Street* |
| Dove, W. H., MBE (1993) | *Bishopsgate* |
| Duckworth, S. (2000) | *Bishopsgate* |
| Dunitz, A. A. (1984) | *Portsoken* |
| Eskenzi, *Deputy* A. N. (1970) | *Farringdon Wn.* |
| Eve, R. A. (1980) | *Cheap* |
| Everett, K. M. (1984) | *Candlewick* |
| Falk, F. A., TD (1997) | *Broad Street* |
| Farr, M. C. (1998) | *Walbrook* |
| Farrow, M. W. W. (1996) | *Farringdon Wt.* |
| Farthing, R. B. C. (1981) | *Aldgate* |
| FitzGerald, *Deputy* R. C. A. (1981) | *Bread Street* |
| Forbes, G. B. (1993) | *Bishopsgate* |
| Fraser, S. J. (1993) | *Coleman Street* |
| Fraser, W. B. (1981) | *Vintry* |
| Galloway, A. D. (1981) | *Broad Street* |
| Gillon, G. M. F. (1995) | *Cordwainer* |
| Ginsburg, S. (1990) | *Bishopsgate* |
| Gowman, *Deputy* Miss A. J. (1991) | *Dowgate* |
| Graves, A. C. (1985) | *Bishopsgate* |
| Green, C. (1994) | *Aldersgate* |
| Hall, B. R. H. (1995) | *Farringdon Wn.* |
| Halliday, Mrs P. (1992) | *Walbrook* |
| Hardwick, Dr P. B. (1987) | *Aldgate* |
| Harris, B. N. (1996) | *Broad Street* |
| Hart, *Deputy* M. G. (1970) | *Bridge* |
| Haynes, J. E. H. (1986) | *Cornhill* |
| Henderson-Begg, M. (1977) | *Coleman Street* |
| Holland, *Deputy* J., CBE (1972) | *Aldgate* |
| Holliday, Mrs E. H. L. (1987) | *Vintry* |
| Hook, J. W. (2000) | *Walbrook* |
| Jackson, L. St J. T. (1978) | *Bread Street* |
| Kellett, Mrs M. W. F. (1986) | *Tower* |
| Kemp, D. L. (1984) | *Coleman Street* |
| King, A. (1999) | *Queenhithe* |
| Knowles, S. K. (1984) | *Candlewick* |
| Lawrence, G. A. (1994) | *Farringdon Wt.* |
| Lawson, G. C. H. (1971) | *Portsoken* |
| Leck, P. (1998) | *Aldersgate* |
| Littlechild, Mrs V. (1998) | *Cripplegate Wt.* |
| Lord, C. E. (2000) | *Coleman Street* |
| Luder, I. D. (1998) | *Farringdon Wt.* |
| McGuinness, C. (1997) | *Castle Baynard* |
| McNeil, I. D. (1977) | *Lime Street* |
| Malins, *Deputy* J. H., QC (1981) | *Farringdon Wt.* |
| Martinelli, *Deputy* P. J. (1994) | *Bassishaw* |
| Mayhew, Miss J. (1986) | *Queenhithe* |
| Mayhew, J. P. (1996) | *Aldersgate* |
| Mead, Mrs W. (1997) | *Farringdon Wt.* |
| Mitchell, *Deputy* C. R. (1971) | *Castle Baynard* |
| Mobsby, *Deputy* D. J. L. (1985) | *Billingsgate* |

Montgomery, B. (1999) *Dowgate*
Mooney, B. D. F. (1998) *Queenhithe*
Moss, A. D. (1989) *Tower*
Moys, Mrs S. (2000) *Aldgate*
Nash, *Deputy* Mrs J. C. (1983) *Aldersgate*
Newman, Mrs P. B. (1989) *Aldersgate*
Owen, Mrs J. (1975) *Langbourn*
Owen-Ward, J. R. (1983) *Bridge*
Parmley, A. C., Ph.D. (1992) *Vintry*
Pembroke, *Deputy* Mrs A. M. F. (1978) *Cheap*
Platts-Mills, J. F. F., QC *Farringdon Wt.*
Price, E. E. (1996) *Farringdon Wt.*
Pulman, *Deputy* G. A. G. (1983) *Tower*
Punter, C. (1993) *Cripplegate Wn.*
Quilter, S. D. (1998) *Cripplegate Wt.*
Regan, R. D. (1998) *Farringdon Wn.*
Rigby, P. P., CBE (1972) *Farringdon Wn.*
Robinson, Mrs D. C. (1989) *Bishopsgate*
Roney, E. P. T., CBE (1974) *Bishopsgate*
Samuel, *Deputy* Mrs I., MBE (1971) *Portsoken*
Sargant, K. A. (1991) *Cornhill*
Scott, J. (1999) *Broad Street*
Scriven, R. G., CBE (1984) *Candlewick*
Shalit, D. M. (1972) *Farringdon Wn.*
Sherlock, M. R. C. (1992) *Dowgate*
Snyder, *Deputy* M. J. (1986) *Cordwainer*
Stevenson, F. P. (1994) *Cripplegate Wn.*
Taylor, J. A. F., TD (1991) *Bread Street*
Thorp, C. R. (1996) *Billingsgate*
Thorp, D. (2000) *Farringdon Wt.*
Trotter, J. (1993) *Billingsgate*
Warner, D. W. (1994) *Cripplegate Wn.*
Willoughby, P. J. (1985) *Bishopsgate*
Wilmot, R. T. D. (1973) *Cordwainer*

# The City Guilds (Livery Companies)

The constitution of the livery companies has been unchanged for centuries. There are three ranks of membership: freemen, liverymen and assistants. A person can become a freeman by patrimony (through a parent having been a freeman); by servitude (through having served an apprenticeship to a freeman); or by redemption (by purchase).

Election to the livery is the prerogative of the company, who can elect any of its freemen as liverymen. Assistants are usually elected from the livery and form a Court of Assistants which is the governing body of the company. The Master (in some companies called the Prime Warden) is elected annually from the assistants.

As at June 1998, 22,923 liverymen of the guilds were entitled to vote at elections at Common Hall.

The order of precedence, omitting extinct companies, is given in parenthesis after the name of each company in the list below. In certain companies the election of Master or Prime Warden for the year does not take place until the autumn. In such cases the Master or Prime Warden for 2000–1 is given.

## THE TWELVE GREAT COMPANIES

*In order of civic precedence*

MERCERS *(1)*. Hall, Ironmonger Lane, London EC2V 8HE. *Livery*, 229. *Clerk*, C. H. Parker. *Master*, A. E. Hodson

GROCERS *(2)*. Hall, Princes Street, London EC2R 8AD. *Livery*, 319. *Clerk*, Brig. P. P. Rawlins. *Master*, J. G. Tregoning

DRAPERS *(3)*. Drapers' Hall, Throgmorton Avenue, London EC2N 2DQ. *Livery*, 262. *Clerk*, Rear-Admiral A. B. Ross. *Master*, Lord Luke, DL

FISHMONGERS *(4)*. Hall, London Bridge, London EC4R 9EL. *Livery*, 355. *Clerk*, K. S. Waters. *Prime Warden*, Sir Thomas Stockdale, BT

GOLDSMITHS *(5)*. Hall, Foster Lane, London EC2V 6BN. *Livery*, 293. *Clerk*, R. D. Buchanan-Dunlop. *Prime Warden*, B. L. Schroder

MERCHANT TAYLORS *(6/7)*. 30 Threadneedle Street, London EC2R 8JB. *Livery*, 323. *Clerk*, D. A. Peck. *Master*, David Brewer, CMG

SKINNERS *(6/7)*. Hall, 8 Dowgate Hill, London EC4R 2SP. *Livery*, 390. *Clerk*, Capt. D. Hart Dyke. *Master*, G. B. Thompson

HABERDASHERS *(8)*. 39-40 Bartholomew Close, London EC1A 7JN. *Livery*, 320. *Clerk*, Capt. R. J. Fisher. *Master*, (from 23 November 2001) H. N. Lund

SALTERS *(9)*. Salters Hall, 4 Fore Street, London EC2Y 5DE. *Livery*, 170. *Clerk*, Col. M. P. Barneby. *Master*, J. C. Russell

IRONMONGERS *(10)*. Hall, Shaftesbury Place, Barbican, London EC2Y 8AA. *Livery*, 129. *Clerk*, J. A. Oliver. *Master*, W. L. Weller, DL

VINTNERS *(11)*. Hall, Upper Thames Street, London EC4V 3BG. *Livery*, 290. *Clerk*, Brig. M. Smythe. *Master*, H. J. Newton

CLOTHWORKERS *(12)*. Hall, Dunster Court, Mincing Lane, London EC3R 7AH. *Livery*, 210. *Clerk*, A. C. Blessly. *Master*, R. Saunders

## OTHER CITY GUILDS

*In alphabetical order*

ACTUARIES *(91)*. 81 Worrin Road, Shenfield, Brentwood, Essex CM15 8JN. *Livery*, 198. *Clerk*, Mrs J. V. Evans. *Master*, P. J. Derby

AIR PILOTS AND AIR NAVIGATORS, GUILD OF *(81)*. Cobham House, 9 Warwick Court, Gray's Inn, London WC1R 5DJ. *Livery*, 500. *Clerk*, Capt. J. G. F. Stoy. *Master*, H. Greyburn. *Grand Master*, HRH The Prince Philip, Duke of Edinburgh, KG, KT, OM, GBE, PC

APOTHECARIES, SOCIETY OF *(58)*. Hall, 14 Black Friars Lane, London EC4V 6EJ. *Livery*, 1700. *Clerk*, Lt.-Col. R. J. Stringer. *Master*, J. H. D. Briscoe

ARBITRATORS *(93)*. 13 Hall Gardens, Colney Heath, St Albans, Herts AL4 0QF. *Livery*, 220. *Clerk*, Mrs G. Duffy. *Master*, Miss Victoria Russell

ARMOURERS AND BRASIERS *(22)*. Hall, 81 Coleman Street, London EC2R 5BJ. *Livery*, 120. *Clerk*, Cdr. T. J. K. Sloane. *Master*, Rear-Admiral J. P. W. Middleton, CB

BAKERS *(19)*. Hall, Harp Lane, London EC3R 6DP. *Livery*, 380. *Clerk*, R. E. B. Sawyer. *Master*, A. G. Cavan

BARBERS *(17)*. Barber-Surgeons' Hall, Monkwell Square, Wood Street, London EC2Y 5BL. *Livery*, 225. *Clerk*, Brig. A. F. Eastburn. *Master*, W. S. Shand, MA, MD, FRCS, FRCS (ED)

BASKETMAKERS *(52)*. 48 Seymour Walk, London SW10 9NF. *Livery*, 308. *Clerk*, Maj. G. J. Flint-Shipman. *Prime Warden*, N. E. Woolley

BLACKSMITHS *(40)*. 48 Upwood Road, London SE12 8AN. *Livery*, 224. *Clerk*, C. Jeal. *Prime Warden*, P. R. Allcard

BOWYERS *(38)*. 11 Aldermans Hill, London N13 4YD. *Livery*, 103. *Clerk*, J. R. Owen-Ward. *Master*, E. J. Burnett

BREWERS *(14)*. Hall, Aldermanbury Square, London EC2V 7HR. *Livery*, 133. *Clerk*, Brig. D. J. Ross. *Master*, W. R. Lees-Jones, TD, DL

BRODERERS *(48)*. Ember House, 35–37 Creek Road, East Molesey, Surrey KT8 9BE. *Livery*, 175. *Clerk*, P. J. C. Crouch. *Master*, I. M. Brackenbury

BUILDERS MERCHANTS *(88)*. 4 College Hill, London EC4R 2RB. *Livery*, 200. *Clerk*, Miss S. M. Robinson. *Master*, C. G. Bence

BUTCHERS *(24)*. Hall, 87 Bartholomew Close, London EC1A 7EB. *Livery*, 582. *Clerk*, G. J. Sharp. *Master*, D. J. Noakes, MBE

CARMEN *(77)*. 8 Little Trinity Lane, London EC4V 2AN. *Livery*, 453. *Clerk*, Cdr. R. M. H. Bawtree. *Master*, B. H. Owen

CARPENTERS *(26)*. Hall, 1 Throgmorton Avenue, London EC2N 2JJ. *Livery*, 150. *Clerk*, Maj.-Gen. P. T. Stevenson. *Master*, R. S. Miller

CHARTERED ACCOUNTANTS *(86)*. The Rustlings, Valley Close, Studham, Dunstable LU6 2QN. *Livery*, 340. *Clerk*, C. Bygrave. *Master*, P. Brennan, OBE

CHARTERED ARCHITECTS *(98)*. 82A Muswell Hill Road, London N10 3JR. *Livery*, 161. *Clerk*, D. Cole-Adams. *Master*, M. P. West

CHARTERED SECRETARIES AND ADMINISTRATORS *(87)*. Sadler's Hall, 3rd Floor, 40 Gutter Lane, London EC2V 6BR. *Livery*, 240. *Clerk*, G. E. L. Lintott. *Master*, P. M. Marcell, FCIS, FFA

CHARTERED SURVEYORS *(85)*. 16 St Mary-at-Hill, London EC3R 8EF. *Livery*, 350. *Clerk*, Mrs A. L. Jackson. *Master*, M. P. L. Baker

CLOCKMAKERS *(61)*. Room 66-67 Albert Buildings, 49 Queen Victoria Street, London EC4N 4SE. *Livery*, 230. *Clerk*, Gp Capt. P. H. Gibson. *Master*, M. M. Smith

COACHMAKERS AND COACH-HARNESS MAKERS *(72)*. 8 Chandlers Court, Burwell, Cambridge CB5 0AZ. *Livery*, 400. *Clerk*, Gp Capt. G. Bunn. *Master*, Hon. Roy Constantine

CONSTRUCTORS *(99)*. 181 Fentiman Road, London SW8 1JY. *Livery*, 136. *Clerk*, L. L. Brace. *Master*, J. M. Burrell

COOKS *(35)*. Registry Chambers, The Old Deanery, Deans Court, London EC4V 5AA. *Livery*, 75. *Clerk*, M. C. Thatcher. *Master*, P. A. P. Wright

COOPERS *(36)*. Hall, 13 Devonshire Square, London EC2M 4TH. *Livery*, 260. *Clerk*, J. A. Newton. *Master*, J. W. S. Clarke, RD

CORDWAINERS *(27)*. 8 Warwick Court, Gray's Inn, London WC1R 5DJ. *Livery*, 161. *Clerk*, Lt.-Col. J. R. Blundell. *Master*, D. M. B. Skinner

CURRIERS *(29)*. Kestrel Cottage, East Knoyle, Salisbury SP3 6AD. *Livery*, 95. *Clerk*, Gp Capt. F. J. Hamilton. *Master*, P. D. MacCorkindale

CUTLERS *(18)*. Hall, Warwick Lane, London EC4M 7BR. *Livery*, 100. *Clerk*, J. P. Allen. *Master*, D. Barnes

DISTILLERS *(69)*. 71 Lincoln's Inn Fields, London WC2A 3JF. *Livery*, 270. *Clerk*, C. V. Hughes. *Master*, R. R. Howell

DYERS *(13)*. Hall, 10 Dowgate Hill, London EC4R 2ST. *Livery*, 121. *Clerk*, J. R. Chambers. *Prime Warden*, E. R. Verney, BA, FRICS

ENGINEERS *(94)*. Kiln Bank, Bodle Street Green, Hailsham, E. Sussex BN27 4UA. *Livery*, 290. *Clerk*, Cdr. B. D. Gibson. *Master*, A. G. Jackson

ENVIRONMENTAL CLEANERS *(97)*. Woodside Cottage, 44 New Road, Bengeo, Herts SG14 3JL. *Livery*, 245. *Clerk*, J. C. M. Chapman. *Master*, M. G. O'Connor

FAN MAKERS *(76)*. 2 Bolts Hill, Castle Camps, Cambridge CB1 6TL. *Livery*, 210. *Clerk*, Lt.-Col. I. R. P. Green. *Master*, R. I. Simpson

FARMERS *(80)*. Farmers' and Fletchers' Hall, 3 Cloth Street, London EC1A 7LD. *Livery*, 300. *Clerk*, Miss M. L. Winter. *Master*, H. R. H. The Princess Royal

FARRIERS *(55)*. 19 Queen Street, Chipperfield, Kings Langley, Herts WD4 9BT. *Livery*, 345. *Clerk*, Mrs C. C. Clifford. *Master*, S. J. Curtis, FWCF

FELTMAKERS *(63)*. Providence Cottage, Chute Cadley, Andover, Hants SP11 9EB. *Livery*, 170. *Clerk*, Lt.-Col. C. J. Holroyd. *Master*, W. Horsham

FIREFIGHTERS *(No livery)*. The Insurance Hall, 20 Aldermanbury, London EC2V 7GF. *Freemen*, 130. *Clerk*, Mrs M. Holland-Prior. *Master*, W. W. A. Redford, QFSM

FLETCHERS *(39)*. Farmers' and Fletchers' Hall, 3 Cloth Street, London EC1A 7LD. *Livery*, 130. *Clerk*, J. R. Owen-Ward. *Master*, C. J. Brown

FOUNDERS *(33)*. Founders' Hall, Number One, Cloth Fair, London EC1A 7JQ. *Livery*, 175. *Clerk*, A. J. Gillett. *Master*, A. C. Newman

FRAMEWORK KNITTERS *(64)*. Whitegarth Chambers, 37 The Uplands, Loughton, Essex IG10 1NQ. *Livery*, 211. *Clerk*, H. W. H. Ellis. *Master*, B. A. F. Smith

FRUITERERS *(45)*. Chapelstones, 84 High Street, Codford St Mary, Warminster BA12 0ND. *Livery*, 262. *Clerk*, Lt.-Col. L. G. French. *Master*, H. E. B. Kelsey

FUELLERS *(95)*. 22 Broadfields, Headstone Lane, Hatch End, Middx HA2 6NH. *Livery*, 85. *Clerk*, R. A. Riley. *Master*, R. J. Budge

FURNITURE MAKERS *(83)*. Painters' Hall, 9 Little Trinity Lane, London EC4V 2AD. *Livery*, 296. *Clerk*, Mrs J. A. Wright. *Master*, P. G. Keen

GARDENERS *(66)*. 25 Luke Street, London EC2A 4AR. *Livery*, 249. *Clerk*, Col. N. G. S. Gray. *Master*, A. H. K. Edwards

GIRDLERS *(23)*. Hall, Basinghall Avenue, London EC2V 5DD. *Livery*, 80. *Clerk*, Lt.-Col. R. Sullivan. *Master*, F. M. French

GLASS-SELLERS *(71)*. 43 Aragon Avenue, Thames Ditton, Surrey KT7 0PY. *Livery*, 180. *Hon. Clerk*, B. J. Rawles. *Master*, R. Long FCA, ATII

GLAZIERS AND PAINTERS OF GLASS *(53)*. Glaziers' Hall, 9 Montague Close, London SE1 9DD. *Livery*, 248. *Clerk*, Col. D. W. Eking. *Master*, R. A. Stone

GLOVERS *(62)*. 71 Ifield Road, London SW10 9AU. *Livery*, 275. *Clerk*, Mrs M. Hood. *Master*, J. D. H. Clarke, BEM

GOLD AND SILVER WYRE DRAWERS *(74)*. 'Twizzletwig', The Ballands South, Fetcham, Leatherhead, Surrey KT22 9EP. *Livery*, 310. *Clerk*, T. J. Waller. *Master*, Sir Peter G. Yarranton

GUNMAKERS *(73)*. The Proof House, 48-50 Commercial Road, London E1 1LP. *Livery*, 238. *Clerk*, J. M. Riches. *Master*, S. Duckworth

HORNERS *(54)*. c/o St. Saviours Church, Warwick Avenue, London W9 2QB. *Livery*, 238. *Clerk*, A. R. Layard. *Master*, Miles St. C. Baird

INFORMATION TECHNOLOGISTS *(100)*. 39A Bartholomew Close, London EC1A 7JN. *Livery*, 265. *Clerk*, Mrs G. Davies. *Master*, J. C. Carrington

INNHOLDERS *(32)*. Innholders' Hall, 30 College Street, London EC4R 2RH. *Livery*, 139. *Clerk*, D. E. Bulger. *Master*, A. G. Fisher

INSURERS *(92)*. The Hall, 20 Aldermanbury, London EC2V 7HY. *Livery*, 375. *Clerk*, L. J. Walters. *Master*, M. J. Bright

JOINERS AND CEILERS *(41)*. 75 Meadway Drive, Horsell, Woking, Surrey GU21 4TF. *Livery*, 124. *Clerk*, Mrs A. L. Jackson. *Master*, J. P. T. Brown

LAUNDERERS *(89)*. Hall, 9 Montague Close, London Bridge, London SE1 9DD. *Livery*, 250. *Clerk*, Mrs J. Polek. *Master*, D. A. Hargreaves

LEATHERSELLERS *(15)*. The Hall, 15 St Helen's Place, London EC3A 6DQ. *Livery*, 150. *Clerk*, Capt. J. G. F. Cooke. *Master*, D. R. Curtis

LIGHTMONGERS *(96)*. Crown Wharf, 11a Coldharbour, Blackwall Reach, London E14 9NS. *Livery*, 145. *Clerk*, D. B. Wheatley. *Master*, B. Hurst

LORINERS *(57)*. 8 Portland Square, London E1W 2QR. *Livery*, 355. *Clerk*, G. B. Forbes. *Master*, R. H. Walker-Arnott

MAKERS OF PLAYING CARDS *(75)*. 6 The Priory, Godstone, Surrey RH9 8NL. *Livery*, 140. *Clerk*, M. J. Smyth. *Master*, Y. Beresiner

MARKETORS *(90)*. 13 Hall Gardens, Colney Heath, St Albans, Herts AL4 0PF. *Livery*, 220. *Clerk*, Mrs G. Duffy. *Master*, W. S. C. Kennett

MASONS *(30)*. 22 Cannon Hill, Southgate, London N14 6LG. *Livery*, 122. *Clerk*, P. F. Clark. *Master*, T. F. Ackland

MASTER MARINERS, HONOURABLE COMPANY OF *(78)*. HQS Wellington, Temple Stairs, Victoria Embankment, London WC2R 2PN. *Livery*, 210. *Clerk*, J. A. V. Maddock. *Master*, Commadore A. D. Barrett, CBE, RD, DL, RNR. *Admiral*, HRH The Prince Philip, Duke of Edinburgh, KG, KT, OM, GBE, PC

MUSICIANS *(50)*. 75 Watling Street, London EC4M 9BJ. *Livery*, 365. *Clerk*, Mrs M. Alford. *Master*, D. R. Hill

NEEDLEMAKERS *(65)*. 5 Staple Inn, London WC1V 7QH. *Livery*, 230. *Clerk*, M. G. Cook. *Master*, M. Copsey

PAINTER-STAINERS *(28)*. Painters' Hall, 9 Little Trinity Lane, London EC4V 2AD. *Livery*, 320. *Clerk*, Col. W. J. Chesshyre. *Master*, Rev. G. Blacktop

PARISH CLERKS *(No livery)*. c/o 1 Dean Trench Street, London SW1P 3HB. *Members*, 95. *Clerk*, Lt. Col. B. J. N. Coombes. *Master*, S. J. Murray

PATTENMAKERS *(70)*. Vanguard House, Sutton Valence, Kent ME17 3JA. *Livery*, 200. *Clerk*, Lt. Col. R. W. Murfin. *Master*, M. P. Fincham

PAVIORS *(56)*. 3 Ridgemount Gardens, Enfield, Middx EN2 8QL. *Livery*, 230. *Clerk*, J. L. White. *Master*, K. C. White

PEWTERERS *(16)*. Hall, Oat Lane, London EC2V 7DE. *Livery*, 120. *Clerk*, Cdr. A. St J. Steiner. *Master*, M. M. Sutcliffe FRCS

PLAISTERERS *(46)*. 6th Floor, 19 Great Winchester Street, London EC2N 2BH. *Livery*, 213. *Clerk*, R. Vickers. *Master*, A. J. Turner

PLUMBERS *(31)*. Room 28, 49 Queen Victoria Street, London EC4N 4SA. *Livery*, 339. *Clerk*, Lt.-Col. R. J. A. Paterson-Fox. *Master*, A. K. Woollaston

POULTERS *(34)*. 53 Sandersfield Road, Banstead, Surrey 8M7 2DH. *Livery*, 178. *Clerk*, Mrs G. W. Butcher. *Master*, D. M. Jackson

SADDLERS *(25)*. Hall, 40 Gutter Lane, London EC2V 6BR. *Livery*, 75. *Clerk*, Gp Capt. W. S. Brereton Martin. *Master*, M. A. C. Lawrie

SCIENTIFIC INSTRUMENT MAKERS *(84)*. 9 Montague Close, London SE1 9DD. *Livery*, 240. *Clerk*, N. J. Watson. *Master*, Dr D. Cornish

SCRIVENERS *(44)*. HQS Wellington, Temple Stairs, Victoria Embankment, London WC2R 2PN. *Livery*, 228. *Clerk*, G. A. Hill. *Master*, D. M. F. Scott

SHIPWRIGHTS *(59)*. Ironmongers Hall, Barbican, London EC2Y 8AA. *Livery*, 400. *Clerk*, Capt. R. F. Channon. *Prime Warden*, Vice-Adm. Sir James Weatherall KCVO, KBE

Permanent Master, HRH The Prince Philip, Duke of Edinburgh, KG, KT, OM, GBE, PC

SOLICITORS *(79)*. 4 College Hill, London EC2R 2RB. *Livery*, 260. *Clerk*, N. Cameron. *Master*, M. J. Cassidy

SPECTACLE MAKERS *(60)*. Apothecaries' Hall, Black Friars Lane, London EC4V 6EL. *Livery*, 325. *Clerk*, Lt.-Col. J. A. B. Salmon. *Master*, G. W. D, McLaren FBDO, FLUSTD, MIMGT

STATIONERS AND NEWSPAPER MAKERS *(47)*. Stationers' Hall, Ave Maria Lane, London EC4M 7DD. *Livery*, 452. *Clerk*, Brig. D. G. Sharp. *Master*, R. J. Russell

TALLOW CHANDLERS *(21)*. Tallow Chandlers' Hall, 4 Dowgate Hill, London EC4R 2SH. *Livery*, 180. *Clerk*, Brig. W. K. L. Prosser. *Master*, C. P. Tootal

TAX ADVISERS *(No Livery)*. 504 Bryer Court, Barbican, London EC2Y 8DE. *Freemen*, 120. *Clerk*, E. Lord. *Master*, M. B. Squires

TIN PLATE WORKERS (ALIAS WIRE WORKERS) *(67)*. Bartholomew House, 66 Westbury Road, New Malden, Surrey KT3 5AS. *Livery*, 190. *Clerk*, M. Henderson-Begg. *Master*, J. H. Perry

TOBACCO PIPE MAKERS AND TOBACCO BLENDERS *(82)*. Hackhurst Farm, Lower Dicker, Hailsham, E. Sussex BN27 4BP. *Livery*, 156. *Clerk*, N. J. Hallings-Pott. *Master*, J. A. G. Murray

TURNERS *(51)*. 182 Temple Chambers, Temple Avenue, London EC4Y 0HP. *Livery*, 160. *Clerk*, E. A. Windsor Clive. *Master*, A. M. Sherred

TYLERS AND BRICKLAYERS *(37)*. Hawthorns, Claygate Lane, Thames Ditton, Surrey KT7 0DT. *Livery*, 128. *Clerk*, J. A. Norris. *Master*, A. P. Wallace

UPHOLDERS *(49)*. Hall in the Wood, 46 Quail Gardens, Selsdon Vale, Croydon CR2 8TF. *Livery*, 225. *Clerk*, J. P. Cody. *Master*, R. C. Olney

WATER CONSERVATORS *(102)*. Watermen's Hall, 16 St Mary-at-Hill, London EC2R 8EF. *Livery*, 148. *Hon. Clerk*, R. A. Riley. *Master*, P. N. Paul

WATERMEN AND LIGHTERMEN *(No livery)*. Watermen's Hall, 16 St Mary-at-Hill, London EC3R 8EF. *Craft Owning Freemen*, 362. *Clerk*, C. Middlemiss. *Master*, C. G. Newens

WAX CHANDLERS *(20)*. Hall, Gresham Street, London EC2V 7AD. *Livery*, 125. *Clerk*, J. R. Williamson. *Master*, His Hon. W. N. Denison QC

WEAVERS *(42)*. Saddlers' House, Gutter Lane, London EC2V 6BR. *Livery*, 125. *Clerk*, Mrs F. Newcombe. *Upper Bailiff*, P. Littlewood

WHEELWRIGHTS *(68)*. Ember House, 35–37 Creek Road, East Molesey, Surrey KT8 9BE. *Livery*, 212. *Clerk*, P. J. C. Crouch. *Master*, N. A. Joseph

WOOLMEN *(43)*. Hollands, Hedsor Road, Bourne End, Bucks SL8 5EE. *Livery*, 138. *Clerk*, F. Allen. *Master*, J. W. Bishop

WORLD TRADERS *(101)*. 36 Ladbroke Grove, London W11 2PA. *Livery*, 143. *Clerk*, N. R. Pullman. *Master*, B. K. Whalley TD

## LONDON BOROUGH COUNCILS

| *Council* | *Municipal offices* | *Population* | *Band D charge 2001* | *Chief Executive* | *Mayor (a) Lord Mayor 2001–2* |
|---|---|---|---|---|---|
| Barking and Dagenham | °Dagenham, RM10 7BN | 156,000 | £848.43 | G. Farrant | P. Twomey |
| Barnet | †The Burroughs, Hendon, NW4 4BG | 293,500 | £874.29 | L. Boland | Mrs A. Campbell |
| Bexley | ‡Bexleyheath, Kent DA6 7LB | 219,000 | £882.00 | C. Duffield | Mrs A. Beckwith |
| Brent | †Forty Lane, Wembley, HA9 9EZ | 243,025 | £779.00 | G. Daniel | R. Patel |
| Bromley | °Bromley, BR1 3UH | 297,600 | £826.00 | Dr M. Blanch | J. Holbrook |
| §Camden | †Judd Street, WC1H 9JE | 192,000 | £950.00 | S. Bundred | R. Robinson |
| §City of Westminster | City Hall, Victoria Street, SW1E 6QP | 175,000 | £410.00 | P. Rogers | (a) H. Marshall |
| Croydon | Taberner House, Park Lane, Croydon, CR9 3JS | 337,500 | £824.00 | D. Wechsler | P. Hopson |
| Ealing | †Uxbridge Road, W5 2HL | 298,000 | £823.00 | Ms G. Guy | R. Dheer |
| Enfield | °Enfield, EN1 3XA | 257,417 | £884.73 | D. Plank | Y. Brett |
| §Greenwich | †Wellington Street, SE18 6PW | 207,700 | £911.00 | Ms M. Ney | T. Malone |
| §Hackney | †Mare Street, E8 1EA | 195,000 | £923.00 | M. Caller | S. Siddiqui |
| §Hammersmithand Fulham | †King Street, W6 9JU | 157,000 | £923.00 | R. Harbord | A. Slaughter |
| Haringey | °Wood Green, N22 4LE | 223,700 | £960.00 | D. Warwick | H. Brown |
| Harrow | °Harrow, HA1 2UJ | 220,000 | £938.95 | T. Redmond | B. Currie |
| Havering | †Romford, RM1 3BD | 229,800 | £959.00 | H. W. Tinworth | D. O'Flynn |
| Hillingdon | °Uxbridge, UB8 1UW | 231,600 | £911.71 | D. Leatham | C. Dann |
| Hounslow | °Lampton Road, Hounslow, TW3 4DN | 205,000 | £955.00 | M. Gilks | M. Gill |
| §Islington | †Upper Street, N1 2UD | 176,393 | £877.00 | Ms L. Fullick | J. Trotter |
| §Kensington and Chelsea (RB) | †Hornton Street, W8 7NX | 140,000 | £688.86 | D. Myers | T. Holt |
| Kingston upon Thames (RB) | Guildhall, Kingston upon Thames, KT1 1EU | 144,000 | £946.60 | B. McDonald | J. Thorn |
| §Lambeth | †Brixton Hill, SW2 1RW | 272,500 | £741.00 | L. Casey | Ms C. Hewitt |
| §Lewisham | †Catford, SE6 4RU | 241,500 | £876.77 | Dr B. Quirk, CBE | D. Sullivan |
| Merton | °London Road, Morden, SM4 5DX | 182,000 | £952.00 | R. Paine | S. Pickover |
| §Newham | †East Ham, E6 2RP | 230,000 | £827.66 | D. Burbage | S. Marway |
| Redbridge | †Ilford, IG1 1DD | 232,500 | £870.00 | M. Frater | L. Weinberg |
| Richmond upon Thames | °Richmond Road, Twickenham, TW1 3AA | 182,700 | £999.00 | Mrs G. Norton | Ms E. Stanier |
| §Southwark | †Peckham Road, SE5 8UB | 237,300 | £845.00 | R. A. Coomber | Ms H. Wines |
| Sutton | ‡St Nicholas Way, Sutton, SM1 1EA | 180,000 | £872.64 | Mrs J. Simons | J. Leach |
| §Tower Hamlets | 107A Commercial Street, E1 6BG | 176,000 | £781.00 | Ms E. Kelly | Ms L. Melvin |
| Waltham Forest | †Forest Road, Walthamstow, E17 4JF | 219,000 | £928.00 | S. White | Mrs M. Broadley |
| §Wandsworth | †Wandsworth, SW18 2PU | 266,300 | £451.71 | G. K. Jones | R. Smith |

§ Inner London Borough
RB Royal Borough
° Civic Centre
† Town Hall
‡ Civic Offices

# Wales

The Principality of Wales (Cymru) occupies the extreme west of the central southern portion of the island of Great Britain, with a total area of 8,015 sq. miles (20,758 sq. km): land 7,965 sq. miles (20,628 sq. km); inland water 50 sq. miles (130 sq. km). It is bounded on the north by the Irish Sea, on the south by the Bristol Channel, on the east by the English counties of Cheshire, Shropshire, Worcestershire and Gloucestershire, and on the west by St George's Channel.

Across the Menai Straits is the island of Anglesey (Ynys Môn) (276 sq. miles), communication with which is facilitated by the Menai Suspension Bridge (1,000 ft long) built by Telford in 1826, and by the tubular railway bridge (1,100 ft long) built by Stephenson in 1850. Holyhead harbour, on Holy Isle (north-west of Anglesey), provides accommodation for ferry services to Dublin (70 miles).

### Population

The population at the 1991 census was 2,835,073 (males 1,370,104; females 1,464,969). The average density of population in 1991 was 1.36 persons per hectare.

### Relief

Wales is a country of extensive tracts of high plateau and shorter stretches of mountain ranges deeply dissected by river valleys. Lower-lying ground is largely confined to the coastal belt and the lower parts of the valleys. The highest mountains are those of Snowdonia in the north-west (Snowdon, 3,559 ft), Berwyn (Aran Fawddwy, 2,971 ft), Cader Idris (Pen y Gadair, 2,928 ft), Dyfed (Plynlimon, 2,467 ft), and the Black Mountain, Brecon Beacons and Black Forest ranges in the south-east (Carmarthen Van, 2,630 ft, Pen y Fan, 2,906 ft, Waun Fâch, 2,660 ft).

### Hydrography

The principal river rising in Wales is the Severn, which flows from the slopes of Plynlimon to the English border. The Wye (130 miles) also rises in the slopes of Plynlimon. The Usk (56 miles) flows into the Bristol Channel, through Gwent. The Dee (70 miles) rises in Bala Lake and flows through the Vale of Llangollen, where an aqueduct (built by Telford in 1805) carries the Pontcysyllte branch of the Shropshire Union Canal across the valley. The estuary of the Dee is the navigable portion, 14 miles in length and about five miles in breadth, and the tide rushes in with dangerous speed over the 'Sands of Dee'. The Towy (68 miles), Teifi (50 miles), Taff (40 miles), Dovey (30 miles), Taf (25 miles) and Conway (24 miles), the last named broad and navigable, are wholly Welsh rivers.

The largest natural lake is Bala (Llyn Tegid) in Gwynedd, nearly four miles long and about one mile wide. Lake Vyrnwy is an artificial reservoir, about the size of Bala, and forms the water supply of Liverpool; Birmingham is supplied from reservoirs in the Elan and Claerwen valleys.

### Welsh Language

According to the 1991 census results, the percentage of persons of three years and over able to speak Welsh was:

| | | | |
|---|---|---|---|
| Clwyd | 18.2 | Powys | 20.2 |
| Dyfed | 43.7 | S. Glamorgan | 6.5 |
| Gwent | 2.4 | W. Glamorgan | 15.0 |
| Gwynedd | 61.0 | | |
| Mid Glamorgan | 8.5 | Wales | 18.7 |

The 1991 figure represents a slight decline from 18.9 per cent in 1981 (1971, 20.8 per cent; 1961, 26 per cent).

### Flag

The flag of Wales, the Red Dragon (Y Ddraig Goch), is a red dragon on a field divided white over green (per fess argent and vert a dragon passant gules). The flag was augmented in 1953 by a royal badge on a shield encircled with a riband bearing the words *Ddraig Goch Ddyry Cychwyn* and imperially crowned, but this augmented flag is rarely used.

## EARLY HISTORY

The earliest inhabitants of whom there is any record appear to have been subdued or exterminated by the Goidels (a people of Celtic race) in the Bronze Age. A further invasion of Celtic Brythons and Belgae followed in the ensuing Iron Age. The Roman conquest of southern Britain and Wales was for some time successfully opposed by Caratacus (Caractacus or Caradog), chieftain of the Catuvellauni and son of Cunobelinus (Cymbeline). South-east Wales was subjugated and the legionary fortress at Caerleon-on-Usk established by about AD 75–77; the conquest of Wales was completed by Agricola about AD 78. Communications were opened up by the construction of military roads from Chester to Caerleon-on-Usk and Caerwent, and from Chester to Conwy (and thence to Carmarthen and Neath). Christianity was introduced during the Roman occupation, in the fourth century.

### Anglo-Saxon Attacks

The Anglo-Saxon invaders of southern Britain drove the Celts into the mountain stronghold of Wales, and into Strathclyde (Cumberland and south-west Scotland) and Cornwall, giving them the name of *Waelisc* (Welsh), meaning 'foreign'. The West Saxons' victory of Deorham (AD 577) isolated Wales from Cornwall and the battle of Chester (AD 613) cut off communication with Strathclyde and northern Britain. In the eighth century the boundaries of the Welsh were further restricted by the annexations of Offa, King of Mercia, and counter-attacks were largely prevented by the construction of an artificial boundary from the Dee to the Wye (Offa's Dyke).

In the ninth century Rhodri Mawr (844–878) united the country and successfully resisted further incursions of the Saxons by land and raids of Norse and Danish pirates by sea, but at his death his three provinces of Gwynedd (north), Powys (mid) and Deheubarth (south) were divided among his three sons, Anarawd, Mervyn and Cadell. Cadell's son Hywel Dda ruled a large part of Wales and codified its laws but the provinces were not united again until the rule of Llewelyn ap Seisyllt (husband of the heiress of Gwynedd) from 1018 to 1023.

### The Norman Conquest

After the Norman conquest of England, William I created palatine counties along the Welsh frontier, and the Norman barons began to make encroachments into Welsh territory. The Welsh princes recovered many of their losses during the civil wars of Stephen's reign and in the early 13th century Owen Gruffydd, prince of Gwynedd, was the dominant figure in Wales. Under Llywelyn ap Iorwerth (1194–1240) the Welsh united in powerful resistance to English incursions and Llywelyn's privileges and *de facto* independence were recognised in

Magna Carta. His grandson, Llywelyn ap Gruffydd, was the last native prince; he was killed in 1282 during hostilities between the Welsh and English, allowing Edward I of England to establish his authority over the country. On 7 February 1301, Edward of Caernarvon, son of Edward I, was created Prince of Wales, a title which has subsequently been borne by the eldest son of the sovereign.

Strong Welsh national feeling continued, expressed in the early 15th century in the rising led by Owain Glyndŵr, but the situation was altered by the accession to the English throne in 1485 of Henry VII of the Welsh House of Tudor. Wales was politically assimilated to England under the Act of Union of 1535, which extended English laws to the Principality and gave it parliamentary representation for the first time.

### EISTEDDFOD

The Welsh are a distinct nation, with a language and literature of their own, and the national bardic festival (Eisteddfod), instituted by Prince Rhys ap Griffith in 1176, is still held annually. These *Eisteddfodau* (sessions) form part of the *Gorsedd* (assembly), which is believed to date from the time of Prydian, a ruling prince in an age many centuries before the Christian era.

## PRINCIPAL CITIES

### CARDIFF

Cardiff, at the mouth of the Rivers Taff, Rhymney and Ely, is the capital city of Wales and a major administrative, commercial and business centre. The National Assembly for Wales was opened in Cardiff in 1999. It has many industries, including steel, and its flourishing port is within the Cardiff Bay area, subject of a major redevelopment continuing until the year 2000.

The many fine buildings include the City Hall, the National Museum of Wales, University Buildings, Law Courts, Welsh Office, County Hall, Police Headquarters, the Temple of Peace and Health, Llandaff Cathedral, the Welsh National Folk Museum at St Fagans, Cardiff Castle, the New Theatre, the Sherman Theatre and the Welsh College of Music and Drama. More recent buildings include St David's Hall, Cardiff International Arena and World Trade Centre, and the Welsh National Ice Rink. The Millennium Stadium is under construction for the 1999 rugby World Cup and the Centre for Visual Arts opened in 1999.

### SWANSEA

Swansea (*Abertawe*) is a city and a seaport. The Gower peninsula was brought within the city boundary under local government reform in 1974. The trade of the port includes coal, steel products, containerised goods, petroleum products and petrochemicals.

The principal buildings are the Norman Castle (rebuilt *c.*1330), the Royal Institution of South Wales, founded in 1835 (including Library), the University of Wales Swansea at Singleton, and the Guildhall, containing Frank Brangwyn's British Empire panels. The Dylan Thomas Centre, formerly the old Guildhall, was restored in 1995. More recent buildings include the County Hall, the new Maritime Quarter and Marina and the leisure centre.

Swansea was chartered by the Earl of Warwick, *c.* 1158–84, and further charters were granted by King John, Henry III, Edward II, Edward III and James II, Cromwell (two) and the Marcher Lord William de Breos.

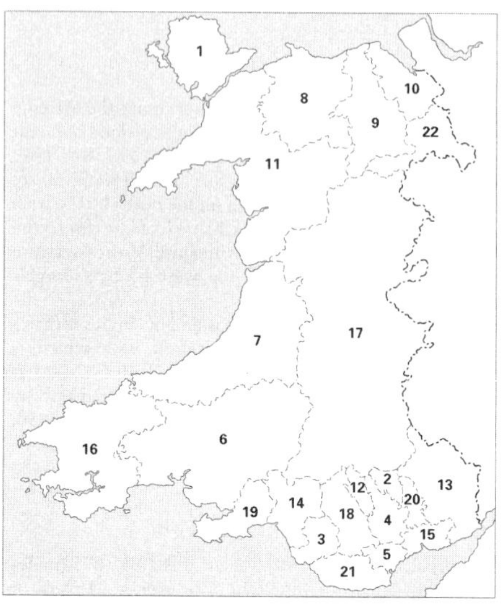


## LOCAL COUNCILS

| *Key* | *County* |
|---|---|
| 1 | Anglesey |
| 2 | Blaenau Gwent |
| 3 | Bridgend |
| 4 | Caerphilly |
| 5 | Cardiff |
| 6 | Carmarthenshire |
| 7 | Ceredigion |
| 8 | Conwy |
| 9 | Denbighshire |
| 10 | Flintshire |
| 11 | Gwynedd |
| 12 | Merthyr Tydfil |
| 13 | Monmouthshire |
| 14 | Neath Port Talbot |
| 15 | Newport |
| 16 | Pembrokeshire |
| 17 | Powys |
| 18 | Rhondda, Cynon, Taff |
| 19 | Swansea |
| 20 | Torfaen |
| 21 | Vale of Glamorgan |
| 22 | Wrexham |

## LORD-LIEUTENANTS AND HIGH SHERIFFS

| *County/Shire* | *Lord-Lieutenant* | *High Sheriff, 2001–2* |
|---|---|---|
| Clwyd | T. Jones, CBE | R. J. Best |
| Dyfed | Sir David Mansel Lewis, KCVO | R. H. James |
| Gwent | Vacant | J. W. H. Tenison |
| Gwynedd | Prof. E. Sunderland, OBE | Mrs Bettina Harden |
| Mid Glamorgan | M. A. McLaggan | M. E. McGrane |
| Powys | The Hon. Mrs E. S. Legge-Bourke, LVO | D. P. Trant |
| S. Glamorgan | Capt. N. Lloyd-Edwards | Lt.-Col. Rhodri Llewellyn Traherne |
| W. Glamorgan | R. C. Hastie, CBE | D. P. Ll. Davies |

## LOCAL COUNCILS

SMALL CAPITALS denote CITY status
§ Denotes Borough status

| *Council* | *Administrative headquaters* | *Population* | *Band D charge 2000* | *Chief Executive* | *Chairman 2001–2 (a) Mayor (b) Lord Mayor* |
|---|---|---|---|---|---|
| Anglesey | Llangefni | 68,500 | £647.10 | G. F. Edwards | J. Williams |
| Blaenau Gwent | Ebbw Vale | 73,000 | £796.40 | R. Leadbeter, OBE | (*a*) B. Clements |
| Bridgend | Bridgend | 131,000 | £768.40 | I. K. Lewis | (*a*) D. Buttle |
| §Caerphilly | Hengoed | 69,100 | £696.60 | M. Davies | A. Donaldson |
| CARDIFF | Cardiff | 324,500 | £691.40 | B. Davies | (*b*) R. Goodway |
| Carmarthenshire | Carmarthen | 170,000 | £607.00 | A. Howells | E. Williams |
| Ceredigion | Aberaeron | 71,700 | £760.60 | O. Watkin | G. Edwards |
| §Conwy | Conwy | 111,000 | £599.73 | C. D. Barker | A. Barrett |
| Denbighshire | Ruthin | 90,000 | £666.50 | M. Hughes (Acting) | D. Jones |
| Flintshire | Mold | 147,000 | £702.39 | P. McGreevy | Mrs A. Slowick |
| Gwynedd | Caernarfon | 116,000 | £694.70 | G. R. Jones | I. L. Jones |
| §Merthyr Tydfil | Merthyr Tydfil | 58,100 | £869.30 | G. W. Meredith | (*a*) R. Thomas |
| Monmouthshire | Cwmbran | 86,000 | £679.54 | Mrs E. Raikes | D. Spencer |
| §Neath Port Talbot | Port Talbot | 139,500 | £884.19 | K. R. Sawyers | (*a*) D. Davies |
| §Newport | Newport | 139,000 | £582.18 | C. Freegard | (*a*) R. J. Morris |
| Pembrokeshire | Haverfordwest | 114,000 | £499.00 | B. Parry-Jones | Mrs R. Hayes |
| Powys | Llandrindod Wells | 126,000 | £673.40 | Miss J. Tonge | E. Jones |
| §Rhondda, Cynon, Taff | Tonypandy | 240,000 | £809.60 | K. Ryley | Mrs L. Jones |
| SWANSEA | Swansea | 231,000 | £674.61 | Ms V. Sugar | (*b*) R. Francis-Davies |
| §Torfaen | Pontypool | 90,000 | £646.09 | Dr C. Grace | (*a*) Mrs C. Thomas |
| Vale of Glamorgan | Barry | 121,300 | £654.80 | J. Maitland-Evans | M. Nugent |
| §Wrexham | Wrexham | 125,000 | £728.64 | D. Griffin | (*a*) Mrs S. Mewies |

# Scotland

The Kingdom of Scotland occupies the northern portion of the main island of Great Britain and includes the Inner and Outer Hebrides, and the Orkney, Shetland, and many other islands. It lies between 60° 51′ 30″ and 54° 38′ N. latitude and between 1° 45′ 32″ and 6° 14′ W. longitude, with England to the south, the Atlantic Ocean on the north and west, and the North Sea on the east.

The greatest length of the mainland (Cape Wrath to the Mull of Galloway) is 274 miles, and the greatest breadth (Buchan Ness to Applecross) is 154 miles. The customary measurement of the island of Great Britain is from the site of John o' Groats house, near Duncansby Head, Caithness, to Land's End, Cornwall, a total distance of 603 miles in a straight line and approximately 900 miles by road.

The total area of Scotland is 30,420 sq. miles (78,789 sq. km); land 29,767 sq. miles (77,097 sq. km), inland water 653 sq. miles (1,692 sq. km).

### Population

The population at the 1991 census was 4,998,567 (males 2,391,961; females 2,606,606). The average density of the population in 1991 was 0.65 persons per hectare.

### Relief

There are three natural orographic divisions of Scotland. The southern uplands have their highest points in Merrick (2,766 ft), Rhinns of Kells (2,669 ft), and Cairnsmuir of Carsphairn (2,614 ft), in the west; and the Tweedsmuir Hills in the east (Hartfell 2,651 ft, Dollar Law 2,682 ft, Broad Law 2,756 ft).

The central lowlands, formed by the valleys of the Clyde, Forth and Tay, divide the southern uplands from the northern Highlands, which extend almost from the extreme north of the mainland to the central lowlands, and are divided into a northern and a southern system by the Great Glen.

The Grampian Mountains, which entirely cover the southern Highland area, include in the west Ben Nevis (4,406 ft), the highest point in the British Isles, and in the east the Cairngorm Mountains (Cairn Gorm 4,084 ft, Braeriach 4,248 ft, Ben Macdui 4,296 ft). The north-western Highland area contains the mountains of Wester and Easter Ross (Carn Eige 3,880 ft, Sgurr na Lapaich 3,775 ft).

Created, like the central lowlands, by a major geological fault, the Great Glen (60 miles long) runs between Inverness and Fort William, and contains Loch Ness, Loch Oich and Loch Lochy. These are linked to each other and to the north-east and south-west coasts of Scotland by the Caledonian Canal, providing a navigable passage between the Moray Firth and the Inner Hebrides.

### Hydrography

The western coast is fragmented by peninsulas and islands, and indented by fjords (sea-lochs), the longest of which is Loch Fyne (42 miles long) in Argyll. Although the east coast tends to be less fractured and lower, there are several great drowned inlets (firths), e.g. Firth of Forth, Firth of Tay, Moray Firth, as well as the Firth of Clyde in the west.

The lochs are the principal hydrographic feature. The largest in Scotland and in Britain is Loch Lomond (27 sq. miles), in the Grampian valleys; the longest and deepest is Loch Ness (24 miles long and 800 feet deep), in the Great Glen; and Loch Shin (20 miles long) and Loch Maree in the Highlands.

The longest river is the Tay (117 miles), noted for its salmon. It flows into the North Sea, with Dundee on the estuary, which is spanned by the Tay Bridge (10,289 ft) opened in 1887 and the Tay Road Bridge (7,365 ft) opened in 1966. Other noted salmon rivers are the Dee (90 miles) which flows into the North Sea at Aberdeen, and the Spey (110 miles), the swiftest flowing river in the British Isles, which flows into Moray Firth. The Tweed, which gave its name to the woollen cloth produced along its banks, marks in the lower stretches of its 96-mile course the border between Scotland and England.

The most important river commercially is the Clyde (106 miles), formed by the junction of the Daer and Portrail water, which flows through the city of Glasgow to the Firth of Clyde. During its course it passes over the picturesque Falls of Clyde, Bonnington Linn (30 ft), Corra Linn (84 ft), Dundaff Linn (10 ft) and Stonebyres Linn (80 ft), above and below Lanark. The Forth (66 miles), upon which stands Edinburgh, the capital, is spanned by the Forth (Railway) Bridge (1890), which is 5,330 feet long, and the Forth (Road) Bridge (1964), which has a total length of 6,156 feet (over water) and a single span of 3,000 feet.

The highest waterfall in Scotland, and the British Isles, is Eas a'Chùal Aluinn with a total height of 658 feet (200 m), which falls from Glas Bheinn in Sutherland. The Falls of Glomach, on a head-stream of the Elchaig in Wester Ross, have a drop of 370 feet.

### Gaelic Language

According to the 1991 census, 1.4 per cent of the population of Scotland, mainly in the Highlands and western coastal regions, were able to speak the Scottish form of Gaelic.

### Lowland Scottish Language

Several regional Lowland Scottish dialects, known variously as Scots, Scotch, Lallans or Doric, are widely spoken. The General Register Office (Scotland) has estimated that 1.5 million people, or 30 per cent of the population, are Scots speakers.

### Flag

The flag of Scotland is known as the Saltire. It is a white diagonal cross on a blue field (saltire argent in a field azure) and represents St Andrew, the patron saint of Scotland.

## THE SCOTTISH ISLANDS

### Orkney

The Orkney Islands (total area 375½ sq. miles) lie about six miles north of the mainland, separated from it by the Pentland Firth. Of the 90 islands and islets (holms and skerries) in the group, about one-third are inhabited.

The total population at the 1991 census was 19,612; the 1991 populations of the islands shown here include those of smaller islands forming part of the same civil parish.

Mainland, 15,128
Burray, 363
Eday, 166
Flotta and Fara, 126
Graemsay and Hoy, 477
North Ronaldsay, 92
Papa Westray, 85
Rousay, 291
Sanday, 533
Shapinsay, 322
South Ronaldsay, 943
Stronsay, 382
Westray, 704

The islands are rich in prehistoric and Scandinavian remains, the most notable being the Stone Age village of Skara Brae, the burial chamber of Maeshowe, the many brochs (towers) and the 12th-century St Magnus Cathedral. Scapa Flow, between the Mainland and Hoy, was the war station of the British Grand Fleet from 1914 to 1919 and the scene of the scuttling of the surrendered German High Seas Fleet (21 June 1919).

Most of the islands are low-lying and fertile, and farming (principally beef cattle) is the main industry. Flotta, to the south of Scapa Flow, is the site of the oil terminal for the Piper, Claymore and Tartan fields in the North Sea.

The capital is Kirkwall (population 6,881) on Mainland.

### SHETLAND

The Shetland Islands have a total area of 551 sq. miles and a population at the 1991 census of 22,522. They lie about 50 miles north of the Orkneys, with Fair Isle about half-way between the two groups. Out Stack, off Muckle Flugga, one mile north of Unst, is the most northerly part of the British Isles (60° 51′ 30″ N. lat.).

There are over 100 islands, of which 16 are inhabited. Populations at the 1991 census were:

| | |
|---|---|
| Mainland, 17,596 | Muckle Roe, 115 |
| Bressay, 352 | Trondra, 117 |
| East Burra, 72 | Unst, 1,055 |
| Fair Isle, 67 | West Burra, 857 |
| Fetlar, 90 | Whalsay, 1,041 |
| Housay, 85 | Yell, 1,075 |

Shetland's many archaeological sites include Jarlshof, Mousa and Clickhimin, and its long connection with Scandinavia has resulted in a strong Norse influence on its place-names and dialect.

Industries include fishing, knitwear and farming. In addition to the fishing fleet there are fish processing factories, while the traditional handknitting of Fair Isle and Unst is supplemented now with machine-knitted garments. Farming is mainly crofting, with sheep being raised on the moorland and hills of the islands. Latterly the islands have become a centre of the North Sea oil industry, with pipelines from the Brent and Ninian fields running to the terminal at Sullom Voe, the largest of its kind in Europe. Lerwick is the main centre for supply services for offshore oil exploration and development.

The capital is Lerwick (population 7,901) on Mainland.

### THE HEBRIDES

Until the late 13th century the Hebrides included other Scottish islands in the Firth of Clyde, the peninsula of Kintyre (Argyll), the Isle of Man, and the (Irish) Isle of Rathlin. The origin of the name is stated to be the Greek *Eboudai*, latinised as *Hebudes* by Pliny, and corrupted to its present form. The Norwegian name *Sudreyjar* (Southern Islands) was latinised as *Sodorenses*, a name that survives in the Anglican bishopric of Sodor and Man.

There are over 500 islands and islets, of which about 100 are inhabited, though mountainous terrain and extensive peat bogs mean that only a fraction of the total area is under cultivation. Stone, Bronze and Iron Age settlement has left many remains, including those at Callanish on Lewis, and Norse colonisation influenced language, customs and place-names. Occupations include farming (mostly crofting and stock-raising), fishing and the manufacture of tweeds and other woollens. Tourism is also an important factor in the economy.

The Inner Hebrides lie off the west coast of Scotland and relatively close to the mainland. The largest and best-known is Skye (area 643 sq. miles; pop. 8,868; chief town, Portree), which contains the Cuillin Hills (Sgurr Alasdair 3,257 ft), the Red Hills (Beinn na Caillich 2,403 ft), Bla Bheinn (3,046 ft) and The Storr (2,358 ft). Skye is also famous as the refuge of the Young Pretender in 1746. Other islands in the Highland council area include Raasay (pop. 163), Rum, Eigg and Muck.

Further south the Inner Hebridean islands include Arran (pop. 4,474) containing Goat Fell (2,868 ft); Coll and Tiree (pop. 940); Colonsay and Oronsay (pop. 106); Islay (area 235 sq. miles; pop. 3,538); Jura (area 160 sq. miles; pop. 196) with a range of hills culminating in the Paps of Jura (Beinn-an-Oir, 2,576 ft, and Beinn Chaolais, 2,477 ft); and Mull (area 367 sq. miles; pop. 2,708; chief town Tobermory) containing Ben More (3,171 ft).

The Outer Hebrides, separated from the mainland by the Minch, now form the Eilean Siar Western Isles Islands Council area (area 1,119 sq. miles; population at the 1991 census 29,600). The main islands are Lewis with Harris (area 770 sq. miles, pop. 21,737), whose chief town, Stornoway, is the administrative headquarters; North Uist (pop. 1,404); South Uist (pop. 2,106); Baleshare (55); Benbecula (pop. 1,803) and Barra (pop. 1,244). Other inhabited islands include Bernera (262), Berneray (141), Eriskay (179), Grimsay (215), Scalpay (382) and Vatersay (72).

## EARLY HISTORY

There is evidence of human settlement in Scotland dating from the third millennium BC, the earliest settlers being Middle Stone Age hunters and fishermen. Early in the second millennium BC, New Stone Age farmers began to cultivate crops and rear livestock; their settlements were on the west coast and in the north, and included Skara Brae and Maeshowe (Orkney). Settlement by the Early Bronze Age 'Beaker folk', so-called from the shape of their drinking vessels, in eastern Scotland dates from about 1800 BC. Further settlement is believed to have occurred from 700 BC onwards, as tribes were displaced from further south by new incursions from the Continent and the Roman invasions from AD 43.

Julius Agricola, the Roman governor of Britain AD 77–84, extended the Roman conquests in Britain by advancing into Caledonia, culminating with a victory at Mons Graupius, probably in AD 84; he was recalled to Rome shortly afterwards and his forward policy was not pursued. Hadrian's Wall, mostly completed by AD 30, marked the northern frontier of the Roman empire except for the period between about AD 144 and 190 when the frontier moved north to the Forth–Clyde isthmus and a turf wall, the Antonine Wall, was manned.

After the Roman withdrawal from Britain, there were centuries of warfare between the Picts, Scots, Britons, Angles and Vikings. The Picts, believed to be a non-Indo-European race, occupied the area north of the Forth. The Scots, a Gaelic-speaking people of northern Ireland, colonised the area of Argyll and Bute (the kingdom of Dalriada) in the fifth century AD and then expanded eastwards and northwards. The Britons, speaking a Brythonic Celtic language, colonised Scotland from the south from the first century BC; they lost control of south-eastern Scotland (incorporated into the kingdom of Northumbria) to the Angles in the early seventh century but retained Strathclyde (south-western Scotland and Cumbria). Viking raids from the late eighth century were followed by Norse settlement in the western and northern isles, Argyll, Caithness and Sutherland from the mid-ninth century onwards.

### UNIFICATION

The union of the areas which now comprise Scotland began in AD 843 when Kenneth mac Alpin, king of the Scots from *c.*834, became also king of the Picts, joining the two lands to form the kingdom of Alba (comprising Scotland north of a line between the Forth and Clyde rivers). Lothian, the eastern part of the area between the Forth and the Tweed, seems to have been leased to Kenneth II of Alba (reigned 971–995) by Edgar of England *c.*973/4, and Scottish possession was confirmed by Malcolm II's victory over a Northumbrian army at Carham *c.*1016. At about this time Malcolm II (reigned 1005–34) placed his grandson Duncan on the throne of the British kingdom of Strathclyde, bringing under Scots rule virtually all of what is now Scotland.

The Norse possessions were incorporated into the kingdom of Scotland from the 12th century onwards. An uprising in the mid-12th century drove the Norse from most of mainland Argyll. The Hebrides were ceded to Scotland by the Treaty of Perth in 1266 after a Norwegian expedition in 1263 failed to maintain Norse authority over the islands. Orkney and Shetland fell to Scotland in 1468–9 as a pledge for the unpaid dowry of Margaret of Denmark, wife of James III, though Danish claims of suzerainty were relinquished only with the marriage of Anne of Denmark to James VI in 1590.

From the 11th century, there were frequent wars between Scotland and England over territory and the extent of England's political influence. The failure of the Scottish royal line with the death of Margaret of Norway in 1290 led to disputes over the throne which were resolved by the adjudication of Edward I of England. He awarded the throne to John Balliol in 1292 but Balliol's refusal to be a puppet king led to war. Balliol surrendered to Edward I in 1296 and Edward attempted to rule Scotland himself. Resistance to Scotland's loss of independence was led by William Wallace, who defeated the English at Stirling Bridge (1297), and Robert Bruce, crowned in 1306, who held most of Scotland by 1311 and routed Edward II's army at Bannockburn (1314). England recognised the independence of Scotland in the Treaty of Northampton in 1328. Subsequent clashes include the disastrous battle of Flodden (1513) in which James IV and many of his nobles fell.

### The Union

In 1603 James VI of Scotland succeeded Elizabeth I on the throne of England (his mother, Mary Queen of Scots, was the great-granddaughter of Henry VII), his successors reigning as sovereigns of Great Britain. Political union of the two countries did not occur until 1707.

### The Jacobite Revolts

After the abdication (by flight) in 1688 of James VII and II, the crown devolved upon William III (grandson of Charles I) and Mary II (elder daughter of James VII and II). In 1689 Graham of Claverhouse roused the Highlands on behalf of James VII and II, but died after a military success at Killiecrankie.

After the death of Anne (younger daughter of James VII and II), the throne devolved upon George I (great-grandson of James VI and I). In 1715, armed risings on behalf of James Stuart (the Old Pretender, son of James VII and II) led to the indecisive battle of Sheriffmuir, and the Jacobite movement died down until 1745, when Charles Stuart (the Young Pretender) defeated the Royalist troops at Prestonpans and advanced to Derby (1746). From Derby, the adherents of 'James VIII and III' (the title claimed for his father by Charles Stuart) fell back on the defensive and were finally crushed at Culloden (16 April 1746).

## PRINCIPAL CITIES

### ABERDEEN

Aberdeen, 130 miles north-east of Edinburgh, received its charter as a Royal Burgh in 1179. Scotland's third largest city, Aberdeen is the second largest Scottish fishing port and the main centre for offshore oil exploration and production. It is also an ancient university town and distinguished research centre. Other industries include engineering, food processing, textiles, paper manufacturing and chemicals.

Places of interest include King's College, St Machar's Cathedral, Brig o' Balgownie, Duthie Park and Winter Gardens, Hazlehead Park, the Kirk of St Nicholas, Mercat Cross, Marischal College and Marischal Museum, Provost Skene's House, Art Gallery, Gordon Highlanders Museum, Satrosphere Hands-On Discovery Centre, and Aberdeen Maritime Museum in Provost Ross's House.

### DUNDEE

Dundee, a Royal Burgh, is situated on the north bank of the Tay estuary. The city's port and dock installations are important to the offshore oil industry and the airport also provides servicing facilities. Principal industries include textiles, computers and other electronic industries, lasers, printing, tyre manufacture, food processing, carpets, engineering, clothing manufacture and tourism.

The unique City Churches – three churches under one roof, together with the 15th-century St Mary's Tower – are the most prominent architectural feature. Dundee has two historic ships: the Dundee-built RRS *Discovery* which took Capt. Scott to the Antarctic lies alongside Discovery Quay, and the frigate *Unicorn*, the only British-built wooden warship still afloat, is moored in Victoria Dock. Places of interest include Mills Public Observatory, the Tay road and rail bridges, McManus Galleries, Barrack Street Museum, Claypotts Castle, Broughty Castle and Verdant Works (Textile Heritage Centre).

### EDINBURGH

Edinburgh is the capital of and seat of government in Scotland. The city is built on a group of hills and contains in Princes Street one of the most beautiful thoroughfares in the world.

The principal buildings are the Castle, which now houses the Stone of Scone and also includes St Margaret's Chapel, the oldest building in Edinburgh, and near it, the Scottish National War Memorial; the Palace of Holyroodhouse; Parliament House, the present seat of the judicature; three universities (Edinburgh, Heriot-Watt, Napier); St Giles' Cathedral; St Mary's (Scottish Episcopal) Cathedral (Sir George Gilbert Scott); the General Register House (Robert Adam); the National and the Signet Libraries; the National Gallery; the Royal Scottish Academy; the National Portrait Gallery; and the Edinburgh International Conference Centre, opened in 1995. A new Scottish Parliament building is under construction at Holyrood.

### GLASGOW

Glasgow, a Royal Burgh, is the principal commercial and industrial centre in Scotland. The city occupies the north and south banks of the Clyde, formerly one of the chief commercial estuaries in the world. The principal industries include engineering, electronics, finance, chemicals and printing. The city has also developed recently as a tourism and conference centre.

The chief buildings are the 13th-century Gothic Cathedral, the University (Sir George Gilbert Scott), the City Chambers, the Royal Concert Hall, St Mungo Museum of Religious Life and Art, Pollok House, the School of Art (Mackintosh), Kelvingrove Art Galleries, the Gallery of Modern Art, the Burrell Collection museum and the Mitchell Library. The city is home to the Scottish National Orchestra, Scottish Opera and Scottish Ballet.

## INVERNESS

Inverness was granted city status in January 2001. The city's name is derived from the Gaelic for 'the mouth of the Ness', referring to the river on which it lies. Inverness is recorded as being at the junction of the old trade routes since 565AD. Today the city is the main administrative centre for the north of Scotland and is the capital of the Highlands. Tourism is one of the city's main industries

Among the city's most notable buildings is Abertarff House, built in 1593 and the oldest secular building remaining in Inverness. Balnain House, built as a town house in 1726 is a fine example of early Georgian architecture. Once a hospital for Hanoverian soldiers after the battle of Culloden and as billets for the Royal Engineers when completing the 1st Ordnance Survey, today Balnain House is the National Trust of Scotland's regional HQ. The Old High Church, on St Michael's Mount, is the original Parish Church of Inverness and is built on the sight of the earliest Christian church in the city. Parts of the church date back to the 14th century.

## LORD-LIEUTENANTS

| *Title* | *Name* |
|---|---|
| Aberdeenshire | A. D. M. Farquharson, OBE |
| Angus | Mrs G. L. Osborne |
| Argyll and Bute | Vacant |
| Ayrshire and Arran | Maj. R. Y. Henderson, TD |
| Banffshire | J. A. S. McPherson, CBE |
| Berwickshire | Maj. A. Trotter |
| Caithness | Maj. G. T. Dunnett, TD |
| Clackmannan | Mrs S. G. Cruickshank |
| Dumfries | Capt. R. C. Cunningham-Jardine |
| Dunbartonshire | Brig. D. D. G. Hardie, TD |
| East Lothian | W. Garth Morrison, CBE |
| Eilean Siar/ Western Isles | A. Matheson, OBE |
| Fife | Mrs C. M. Dean |
| Inverness | Rt. Hon. The Lord Gray of Contin, PC |
| Kincardineshire | J. D. B. Smart |
| Lanarkshire | G. Cox, MBE |
| Midlothian | Capt. G. W. Burnet, LVO |
| Moray | Air Vice-Marshal G. A. Chesworth, CB, OBE, DFC |
| Nairn | E. J. Brodie |
| Orkney | G. R. Marwick |
| Perth and Kinross | Sir David Montgomery, Bt. |
| Renfrewshire | C. H. Parker, OBE |
| Ross and Cromarty | Capt. R. W. K. Stirling of Fairburn, TD |
| Roxburgh, Ettrick and Lauderdale | Dr June Paterson-Brown, CBE |
| Shetland | J. H. Scott |
| Stirling and Falkirk | Lt.-Col. J. Stirling of Garden, CBE, TD |
| Sutherland | Maj.-Gen. D. Houston, CBE |
| The Stewartry of Kirkcudbright | Lt.-Gen. Sir Norman Arthur, KCB |
| Tweeddale | Capt. D. Younger |
| West Lothian | *vacant* |
| Wigtown | Maj. E. S. Orr-Ewing |

The Lord Provosts of the four city districts of Aberdeen, Dundee, Edinburgh and Glasgow are Lord-Lieutenants for those districts *ex officio*.

## LOCAL COUNCILS

| *Council* | *Administrative headquaters* | *Population (latest estimate)* | *Band D charge 2001* | *Chief Executive* | *Chairman (a) Convenor (b) Provost (c) Lord Provost* |
|---|---|---|---|---|---|
| Aberdeen City | Aberdeen | 217,200 | £934.00 | D. Paterson | (*c*) Ms M. Smith |
| Aberdeenshire | Aberdeen | 228,000 | £855.00 | A. G. Campbell | (*a*) R. Bisset, OBE |
| Angus | Forfar | 110,200 | £821.00 | A. B. Watson | (*b*) Mrs F. M. Duncan, OBE |
| Argyll and Bute | Lochgilphead | 88,790 | £984.00 | J. A. McLellan | (*a*) W. Petrie |
| City of Edinburgh | Edinburgh | 449,000 | £960.00 | T. N. Aitchison | (*c*) Rt. Hon. E. Milligan |
| Clackmannanshire | Alloa | 48,500 | £951.00 | K. Bloom | (*b*) W. McAdam |
| Dumfries and Galloway | Dumfries | 148,000 | £857.00 | P. N. Jones | (*a*) A. Campbell, OBE |
| Dundee City | Dundee | 146,690 | £1,046.00 | A. Stephen | (*c*) Rt. Hon. H. W. Wright |
| East Ayrshire | Kilmarnock | 124,000 | £828.00 | D. Montgomery | (*b*) J. Boyd |
| East Dunbartonshire | Glasgow | 110,000 | £872.00 | Dr V. Nash | (*b*) R. McSkimming |
| East Lothian | Haddington | 85,600 | £909.00 | J. Lindsay | (*b*) P. O'Brien |
| East Renfrewshire | Giffnock | 89,280 | £859.00 | P. Daniels | (*b*) A. Steele |
| Eilean Siar/Western Isles | Stornoway | 27,560 | £765.00 | W. Howat | (*a*) A. A. Macdonald |

| *Council* | *Administrative headquaters* | *Population (latest estimate)* | *Band D charge 2001* | *Chief Executive* | *Chairman (a) Convenor (b) Provost (c) Lord Provost* |
|---|---|---|---|---|---|
| Falkirk | Falkirk | 144,688 | £813.00 | Mrs M. Pitcaithly | (*b*) J. Johnson |
| Fife | Glenrothes | 352,000 | £891.00 | D. Sinclair | (*a*) J. MacDougall |
| Glasgow City | Glasgow | 611,500 | £1,120.00 | J. Andrews | (*c*) A. Mosson |
| Highland | Inverness | 208,700 | £889.00 | A. D. McCourt | (*a*) D. Green |
| Inverclyde | Greenock | 85,000 | £894.00 | R. Cleary | (*b*) R. Jackson |
| Midlothian | Dalkeith | 81,680 | £1,001.00 | T. Muir | (*b*) S. Campbell |
| Moray | Elgin | 86,000 | £825.00 | A. Keddie | (*a*) E. Aldridge |
| North Ayrshire | Irvine | 140,000 | £877.00 | B. Devine | (*a*) S. Taylor |
| North Lanarkshire | Motherwell | 327,000 | £844.00 | G. Whitefield | (*b*) B. McCulloch |
| Orkney Islands | Kirkwall | 19,817 | £754.00 | A. Buchan | (*a*) H. Halcro-Johnston |
| Perth and Kinross | Perth | 134,000 | £875.00 | H. Robertson | (*b*) M. O'Malley |
| Renfrewshire | Paisley | 177,000 | £896.40 | T. Scholes | (*b*) J. McDowell |
| Scottish Borders | Newtown St Boswells | 106,400 | £785.00 | A. M. Croall | (*a*) A. L. Tulley |
| Shetland Islands | Lerwick | 23,000 | £747.00 | M. Goodlad | (*a*) T. Stove |
| South Ayrshire | Ayr | 114,000 | £1,140.00 | G. W. F. Thorley | (*b*) Ms E. Foulkes |
| South Lanarkshire | Hamilton | 301,000 | £924.40 | M. Docherty | (*b*) A. Dick |
| Stirling | Stirling | 85,200 | £954.00 | K. Yates | (*b*) T. Brookes |
| West Dunbartonshire | Dumbarton | 93,977 | £1,024.00 | T. Huntingford | (*b*) A. Macdonald |
| West Lothian | Livingston | 152,000 | £919.00 | A. M. Linkston | (*b*) J. Thomas |

## LOCAL COUNCILS

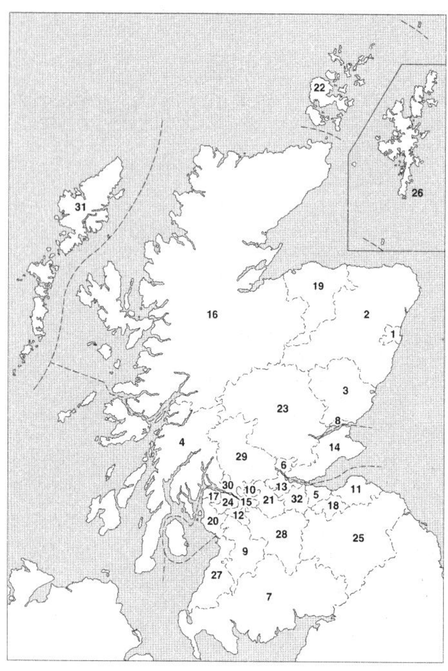


| *Key* | *Council* |
|---|---|
| 1 | Aberdeen City |
| 2 | Aberdeenshire |
| 3 | Angus |
| 4 | Argyll and Bute |
| 5 | City of Edinburgh |
| 6 | Clackmannanshire |
| 7 | Dumfries and Galloway |
| 8 | Dundee City |
| 9 | East Ayrshire |
| 10 | East Dunbartonshire |
| 11 | East Lothian |
| 12 | East Renfrewshire |
| 13 | Falkirk |
| 14 | Fife |
| 15 | Glasgow City |
| 16 | Highland |
| 17 | Inverclyde |
| 18 | Midlothian |
| 19 | Moray |
| 20 | North Ayrshire |
| 21 | North Lanarkshire |
| 22 | Orkney |
| 23 | Perth and Kinross |
| 24 | Renfrewshire |
| 25 | Scottish Borders |
| 26 | Shetland |
| 27 | South Ayrshire |
| 28 | South Lanarkshire |
| 29 | Stirling |
| 30 | West Dunbartonshire |
| 31 | Western Isles (Eilean Siar) |
| 32 | West Lothian |

# Northern Ireland

Northern Ireland has a total area of 5,467 sq. miles (14,144 sq. km): land, 5,225 sq. miles (13,532 sq. km); inland water and tideways, 249 sq. miles (628 sq. km).

The population of Northern Ireland at the 1991 census was 1,577,836 (males, 769,071; females, 808,765). The average density of population in 1991 was 1.11 persons per hectare.

In 1991 the number of persons in the various religious denominations (expressed as percentages of the total population) were: Roman Catholic, 38.4; Presbyterian, 21.4; Church of Ireland, 17.7; Methodist, 3.8; others 7.7; none, 3.7; not stated, 7.3.

### FLAG

The official national flag of Northern Ireland is now the Union Flag. The flag formerly in use (a white, six-pointed star in the centre of a red cross on a white field, enclosing a red hand and surmounted by a crown) has not been used since the imposition of direct rule.

## PRINCIPAL CITIES

### BELFAST

Belfast, the administrative centre of Northern Ireland, is situated at the mouth of the River Lagan at its entrance to Belfast Lough. The city grew, owing to its easy access by sea to Scottish coal and iron, to be a great industrial centre.

The principal buildings are of a relatively recent date and include the Parliament Buildings at Stormont, the City Hall, Waterfront Hall, the Law Courts, the Public Library and the Museum and Art Gallery.

Belfast received its first charter of incorporation in 1613 and was created a city in 1888; the title of Lord Mayor was conferred in 1892.

### LONDONDERRY

Londonderry (originally Derry) is situated on the River Foyle, and has important associations with the City of London. The Irish Society was created by the City of London in 1610, and under its royal charter of 1613 it fortified the city and was for long closely associated with its administration. Because of this connection the city was incorporated in 1613 under the new name of Londonderry.

The city is famous for the great siege of 1688–9, when for 105 days the town held out against the forces of James II until relieved by sea. The city walls are still intact and form a circuit of almost a mile around the old city.

Interesting buildings are the Protestant Cathedral of St Columb's (1633) and the Guildhall, reconstructed in 1912 and containing a number of beautiful stained glass windows, many of which were presented by the livery companies of London.

## CONSTITUTIONAL DEVELOPMENTS

Northern Ireland is subject to the same fundamental constitutional provisions which apply to the rest of the United Kingdom. It had its own parliament and government from 1921 to 1972, but after increasing civil unrest the Northern Ireland (Temporary Provisions) Act 1972 transferred the legislative and executive powers of the Northern Ireland parliament and government to the UK Parliament and a Secretary of State. The Northern Ireland Constitution Act 1973 provided for devolution in Northern Ireland through an assembly and executive, but a power-sharing executive formed by the Northern Ireland political parties in January 1974 collapsed in May 1974; since then Northern Ireland has been governed by direct rule under the provisions of the Northern Ireland Act 1974. This allows Parliament to approve all laws for Northern Ireland and places the Northern Ireland department under the direction and control of the Secretary of State for Northern Ireland.

Attempts were made by successive governments to find a means of restoring a widely acceptable form of devolved government to Northern Ireland. In 1985 the governments of the United Kingdom and the Republic of Ireland signed the Anglo-Irish Agreement, establishing an inter-governmental conference in which the Irish government may put forward views and proposals on certain aspects of Northern Ireland affairs.

Discussions between the British and Irish governments and the main Northern Ireland parties began in 1991. It was agreed that any political settlement would need to address relationships within Northern Ireland, within the island of Ireland (north/south) and between the British and Irish governments (east/west). Although round table talks ended in 1992 the process continued from September 1993 as separate bilateral discussions with three of the Northern Ireland parties (the DUP declined to participate).

In December 1993 the British and Irish governments published the Joint Declaration complementing the political talks, and making clear that any settlement would need to be founded on principles of democracy and consent. The declaration also stated that all democratically mandated parties could be involved in political talks as long as they permanently renounced paramilitary violence.

The provisional IRA and loyalist paramilitary groups announced cease-fires on 31 August and 13 October 1994 respectively. The Government initiated exploratory meetings with Sinn Fein and loyalist representatives in December 1994.

In February 1995 the then Prime Minister (John Major) launched *A Framework for Accountable Government in Northern Ireland* and, with the Irish Prime Minister, *A New Framework for Agreement*. These outlined what a comprehensive political settlement might look like. The ideas were intended to facilitate multilateral dialogue involving the Northern Ireland parties and the British government.

In autumn 1995 the Prime Minister said that Sinn Fein would not be invited to all-party talks until the IRA had decommissioned its arms; the IRA ruled out any decommissioning of weapons in advance of a political settlement. An international body chaired by a former US senator, George Mitchell, reported in January 1996 that no weapons would be decommissioned before the start of all-party talks and that a compromise agreement was necessary under which weapons would be decommissioned during negotiations. The Prime Minister accepted the report and proposed the election of representatives to conduct all-party talks. On 9 February 1996 the IRA called off its cease-fire.

### PEACE TALKS

Following elections on 30 May 1996, all-party talks opened at Stormont Castle on 10 June 1996 which included nine of the ten parties returned at the election;

Sinn Fein representatives were turned away because the IRA had failed to reinstate its cease-fire. On 29 July 1996 the all-party talks were suspended after disagreements over the issue of decommissioning arms. An opening agenda for the talks was agreed in October 1996.

On 25 June 1997 the newly-elected Labour Government said that substantive negotiations should begin in September 1997 with a view to reaching conclusions by May 1998. The British and Irish governments issued a joint paper outlining their proposals for resolving the decommissioning issue. The Government also indicated that if the IRA were to call a cease-fire, it would assess whether it was genuine over a period of six weeks, and if satisfied that it was so, would then invite Sinn Fein to the talks. An IRA cease-fire was declared on 20 July 1997.

When the UK Government announced in August 1997 that Sinn Fein would be present when the substantive talks opened on 15 September, the Unionist and loyalist parties, unhappy at the terms on which Sinn Fein had been admitted, boycotted the opening session. The Ulster Unionist Party, the Progressive Unionist Party and the Ulster Democratic Party re-entered the negotiations on 17 September. Full-scale peace talks began on 7 October. The parties had agreed to concentrate on constitutional issues, with the issue of decommissioning terrorist weapons to be handled by a new independent commission.

On 12 January 1998 the British and Irish governments issued a joint document, *Propositions on Heads of Agreement*, proposing the establishment of various new cross-border bodies; further proposals were presented on 27 January. A draft peace settlement was issued by the talks' chairman, Sen. George Mitchell, on 6 April 1998 but was rejected by the Unionists the following day. On 10 April agreement was reached between the British and Irish governments and the eight Northern Ireland political parties still involved in the talks (the Good Friday/Belfast Agreement). The agreement provided for an elected New Northern Ireland Assembly; a North/South Ministerial Council, and a British-Irish Council comprising representatives of the British, Irish, Channel Islands and Isle of Man governments and members of the new assemblies for Scotland, Wales and Northern Ireland. Further points included the abandonment of the Republic of Ireland's constitutional claim to Northern Ireland; the decommissioning of weapons; the release of paramilitary prisoners; and changes in policing. Referendums on the agreement were held in Northern Ireland and the Republic of Ireland on 22 May 1998. In Northern Ireland the turnout was 81 per cent, of which 71.12 per cent voted in favour of the agreement. In the Republic of Ireland, the turnout was about 55 per cent, of which 94.4 per cent voted in favour of both the agreement and the necessary constitutional change. In the UK, the Northern Ireland Act 1998, enshrining the provisions of the Agreement, received Royal Assent in November 1998.

For details of the *Northern Ireland Assembly and the further political developments in Northern Ireland, see* Regional Government section.

### Other Bodies

Consultations between the First Minister and Deputy First Minister, the British and Irish Governments and the political parties concluded in early 1999 with an agreement to establish six areas for cross-border bodies and a further six areas for co-operation. Treaties between the British and Irish governments establishing the bodies and parallel domestic legislation to underpin them are now in place.

The intergovernmental conference established by the 1985 Anglo-Irish Agreement was replaced by a new British-Irish Intergovernmental Conference which will discuss all areas of mutual bilateral interest.

The British-Irish Council will operate on the basis of consensus and may reach agreements and pursue common policies in areas of mutual interest.

## ECONOMY

### Finance

Northern Ireland's expenditure is funded by the Northern Ireland Consolidated Fund (NICF). Up to date of devolution on 2 December 1999, the NICF was largely financed by Northern Ireland's attributed share of UK taxation and supplemented by a grant-in-aid. From devolution, these separate elements have been subsumed into a single Block Grant. In 2000–1 the provisional outturn for public expenditure falling within the Northern Ireland Departmental Expenditure Limit was £5,245 million. For 2001–2 the provisional estimate of required funds was £5,758 million.

### Production

The products of the engineering and allied industries, which employed 28,800 persons in 1997, were valued at £2,093 million. The textiles industry (manufacture of textiles and textile products), employing about 22,500 persons, produced goods valued at approximately £936 million. The food products, beverages and tobacco industry, employing about 20,700 persons, produced goods valued at £3,836 million.

In 1999, 1,724 persons were employed in mining and quarrying operations in Northern Ireland and the minerals raised (28,555,000 tonnes) were valued at £58,433,000.

### Communications

The total tonnage handled by Northern Ireland ports in 2000 was 22.8 million. Regular ferry, freight and container services operate to ports in Great Britain and Europe from a number of ports, with most trade passing through Belfast (58 per cent of the total), Larne and Warrenpoint.

The Northern Ireland Transport Holding Company is largely responsible for the supervision of the subsidiary companies, Ulsterbus and Citybus (which operate the public road passenger services) and Northern Ireland Railways (collectively known as Translink). Road freight services are also provided by a large number of hauliers operating competitively under licence.

Belfast International Airport, owned by TBI International, provides scheduled and chartered services on domestic and international routes. In 2000–1 the airport handled approximately 3 million passengers and 26,000 tonnes of freight. Scheduled services also operate from Belfast City Airport (BCA, owned by Shorts Bombardier Aerospace) to 16 UK destinations. In 2000–1 the airport handled approximately 1.2 million passengers. City of Derry Airport (Londonderry, owned and operated by Derry City Council) provides services to 3 UK and European destinations and to Belfast, providing links to many of the locations serviced by BCA. In 2000–1 City of Derry Airport served approximately 103,000 passengers.

## NORTHERN IRELAND COUNTIES

| *County* | *Area** *(sq. miles)* | *Lord-Lieutenant* | *High Sheriff, 2001* |
|---|---|---|---|
| Antrim | 1,093 | The Lord O'Neill, TD | J. W. Wallace |
| Armagh | 484 | The Earl of Caledon | P. S. Kellet |
| ‡Belfast City | 25 | Lady Carswell, OBE | A. R. Crow |
| Down | 945 | W. J. Hall | R. J. Gordon |
| Fermanagh | 647 | The Earl of Erne | Mrs E. G. Thompson |
| †Londonderry | 798 | J. Thompson Eaton, CBE, TD | Mrs F. M. Sloan, MBE |
| ‡Londonderry City | 3.4 | D. F. Desmond, CBE | Mrs F. M. O'Kane |
| Tyrone | 1,211 | The Duke of Abercorn, KG | Mr J. G. Ferguson, OBE |

* Excluding inland waters and tideways
‡ Denotes County Borough
† Excluding the City of Londonderry

## DISTRICT COUNCILS

SMALL CAPITALS denotes CITY status
§ Denotes Borough Council

| *Council* | *Population (May 2000)* | *Net Annual Value £* | *Council Clerk* | *Chairman* *† Mayor 2000* |
|---|---|---|---|---|
| §Antrim, Co. Antrim | 49,100 | 32,562,784 | S. J. Magee | † M. Rea |
| §Ards, Co. Down | 72,300 | 29,416,655 | D. J. Fallows | † Mrs M. Craig |
| §ARMAGH, Co. Armagh | 54,200 | 21,485,083 | V. Brownlees | † Mrs S. McRoberts |
| §Ballymena, Co. Antrim | 59,500 | 34,649,252 | M. G. Rankin | † T. Nicholl |
| §Ballymoney, Co. Antrim | 26,200 | 8,977,431 | J. Dempsey | † B. Kennedy |
| Banbridge, Co. Down | 40,500 | 15,706,117 | R. Gilmore | W. J. Martin |
| BELFAST, Co. Antrim and Co. Down | 281,700 | 297,090,024 | B. Hanna | † J. Rodgers |
| §Carrickfergus, Co. Antrim | 38,400 | 16,236,190 | A. Cardwell | † W. Ash |
| §Castlereagh, Co. Down | 67,000 | 35,575,626 | A. Donaldson | † K. Morton |
| §Coleraine, Co. Londonderry | 55,900 | 30,201,937 | W. Moore | † J. Dallot |
| Cookstown, Co. Tyrone | 31,600 | 15,744,017 | M. J. McGuckin | P. McAleer |
| §Craigavon, Co. Armagh | 80,300 | 45,917,344 | T. Reaney | † S. Gardner |
| DERRY, Co. Londonderry | 106,100 | 60,041,828 | C. Logue *(acting)* | † Mrs M. Garfield |
| Down, Co. Down | 64,000 | 24,106,390 | J. McGrillen | Mrs A. Aleenan |
| Dungannon, Co. Tyrone | 48,500 | 25,842,535 | W. J. Beattie | W. Beattie |
| Fermanagh, Co. Fermanagh | 57,600 | 28,899,077 | R. Connor | R. Martin |
| §Larne, Co. Antrim | 31,000 | 17,539,967 | C. McGarry | † D. Fleck |
| §Limavady, Co. Londonderry | 31,300 | 12,369,586 | J. K. Stevenson | † L. Lowry |
| §Lisburn, Co. Antrim and Co. Down | 109,700 | 58,400,242 | N. Davidson | † J. Dillon |
| Magherafelt, Co. Londonderry | 39,200 | 15,485,660 | J. A. McLaughlin | A. Hughes |
| Moyle, Co. Antrim | 15,400 | 4,964,065 | R. G. Lewis | R. McDonald |
| Newry and Mourne, Co. Down and Co. Armagh | 87,800 | 39,082,703 | T. McCall | D. Hyland |
| §Newtownabbey, Co. Antrim | 81,800 | 44,591,040 | N. Dunn | † Mrs V. McWilliams |
| §North Down, Co. Down | 75,300 | 39,774,190 | T. Polley | † I. Henry |
| Omagh, Co. Tyrone | 47,200 | 23,326,205 | D. McSorley | B. McElduss |
| Strabane, Co. Tyrone | 37,800 | 13,591,913 | J. Stewart (Acting) | I. Barr |

# The Isle of Man

*Ellan Vannin*

The Isle of Man is an island situated in the Irish Sea, in latitude 54° 3′–54° 25′ N. and longitude 4° 18′–4° 47′ W., nearly equidistant from England, Scotland and Ireland. Although the early inhabitants were of Celtic origin, the Isle of Man was part of the Norwegian Kingdom of the Hebrides until 1266, when this was ceded to Scotland. Subsequently granted to the Stanleys (Earls of Derby) in the 15th century and later to the Dukes of Atholl, it was brought under the administration of the Crown in 1765. The island forms the bishopric of Sodor and Man.

The total land area is 221 sq. miles (572 sq. km). The report on the 1991 census showed a resident population of 69,788 (males, 33,693; females, 36,095). The main language in use is English. There are no remaining native speakers of Manx Gaelic but 643 people are able to speak the language.

CAPITAL – ΨDouglas; population (1991), 22,214.
ΨCastletown (3,152) is the ancient capital; the other towns are ΨPeel (3,829) and ΨRamsey (6,496)

FLAG – A red flag charged with three conjoined armoured legs in white and gold

TYNWALD DAY – 5 July

## GOVERNMENT

The Isle of Man is a self-governing Crown dependency, having its own parliamentary, legal and administrative system. The British Government is responsible for international relations and defence. Under the UK Act of Accession, Protocol 3, the island's relationship with the European Union is limited to trade alone and does not extend to financial aid. The Lieutenant-Governor is The Queen's personal representative in the island.

The legislature, Tynwald, is the oldest parliament in the world in continuous existence. It has two branches: the Legislative Council and the House of Keys. The Council consists of the President of Tynwald, the Bishop of Sodor and Man, the Attorney-General (who does not have a vote) and eight members elected by the House of Keys. The House of Keys has 24 members, elected by universal adult suffrage. The branches sit separately to consider legislation and sit together, as Tynwald Court, for most other parliamentary purposes.

The presiding officer of Tynwald Court is the President of Tynwald, elected by the members, who also presides over sittings of the Legislative Council. The presiding officer of the House of Keys is Mr Speaker, who is elected by members of the House.

The principal members of the Manx Government are the Chief Minister and nine departmental ministers, who comprise the Council of Ministers.

*Lieutenant-Governor*, HE Air-Marshal I. MacFadyen, CB, OBE
*ADC to the Lieutenant-Governor*, C. J. Tummon
*President of Tynwald*, The Hon. N. Q. Cringle
*Speaker, House of Keys*, The Hon. J. D. Q. Cannan
*The First Deemster and Clerk of the Rolls*, His Honour T. W. Cain, QC
*Clerk of Tynwald, Secretary to the House of Keys and Counsel to the Speaker*, Mr Malachy Cornwell-Kelly
*Clerk of the Legislative Council and Deputy Clerk of Tynwald*, Mrs M. Cullen
*Attorney-General*, W. J. H. Corlett, QC
*Chief Minister*, The Hon. D. J. Gelling
*Chief Secretary*, J. F. Kissack
*Chief Financial Officer*, Mrs M. Williams

## ECONOMY

Most of the income generated in the island is earned in the services sector with financial and professional services accounting for just over half of the national income. Tourism and manufacturing are also major generators of income whilst the island's other traditional industries of agriculture and fishing now play a smaller role in the economy.

Under the terms of Protocol 3, the island has tariff-free access to EU markets for its goods.

The island's unemployment rate is approximately 0.5 per cent and price inflation is around 2.5 per cent per annum.

## FINANCE

The budget for 2000–2001 provided for net revenue expenditure of £317 million. The principal sources of government revenue are taxes on income and expenditure. Income tax is payable at a rate of 14 per cent on the first £10,000 of taxable income for single resident individuals and 20 per cent on the balance, after personal allowances of £7,535. These bands are doubled for married couples. The rate of income tax is 14 per cent on the first £125,000 of taxable income of companies, rising to 20 per cent on the balance. Non-residents are charged tax at the rate of 20 per cent. By agreement with the British Government, the island keeps most of its rates of indirect taxation (VAT and duties) the same as those in the United Kingdom, but this agreement may be terminated by either party. However, VAT on tourist accommodation, property, repairs and renovations is charged at 5 per cent. A reciprocal agreement on national insurance benefits and pensions exists between the governments of the Isle of Man and the United Kingdom. Taxes are also charged on property (rates), but these are comparatively low.

The major government expenditure items are health, social security and education, which account for 60 per cent of the government budget. The island makes a voluntary annual contribution to the United Kingdom for defence and other external services.

The island has a special relationship with the European Union and neither contributes money to nor receives funds from the EU budget.

# The Channel Islands

The Channel Islands, situated off the north-west coast of France (at distances of from ten to 30 miles), are the only portions of the Dukedom of Normandy still belonging to the Crown, to which they have been attached since the Norman Conquest of 1066. They were the only British territory to come under German occupation during the Second World War, following invasion on 30 June to 1 July 1940. The islands were relieved by British forces on 9 May 1945, and 9 May (Liberation Day) is now observed as a bank and public holiday.

The islands consist of Jersey (28,717 acres/11,630 ha), Guernsey (15,654 acres/6,340 ha), and the dependencies of Guernsey: Alderney (1,962 acres/795 ha), Brechou (74/30), Great Sark (1,035/419), Little Sark (239/97), Herm (320/130), Jethou (44/18) and Lihou (38/15) – a total of 48,083 acres/19,474 ha, or 75 sq. miles/194 sq. km. In 1996 the population of Jersey was 85,150; and of Guernsey, 58,681; Alderney, 2,147 and Sark, 575. The official languages are English and French but French is being supplanted by English, which is the language in daily use. In country districts of Jersey and Guernsey and throughout Sark a Norman-French *patois* is also in use, though to a declining extent.

## GOVERNMENT

The islands are Crown dependencies with their own legislative assemblies (the States in Jersey, Guernsey and Alderney, and the Court of Chief Pleas in Sark), and systems of local administration and of law, and their own courts. Acts passed by the States require the sanction of The Queen-in-Council. The British Government is responsible for defence and international relations. The Channel Islands have trading rights alone within the European Union; these rights do not include financial aid.

In both Bailiwicks the Lieutenant-Governor and Commander-in-Chief, who is appointed by the Crown, is the personal representative of The Queen and the channel of communication between the Crown (via the Privy Council) and the island's government.

The government of each Bailiwick is conducted by committees appointed by the States. Justice is administered by the Royal Courts of Jersey and Guernsey, each consisting of the Bailiff and 12 elected Jurats. The Bailiffs of Jersey and Guernsey, appointed by the Crown, are President of the States and of the Royal Courts of their respective islands.

Each Bailiwick constitutes a deanery under the jurisdiction of the Bishop of Winchester (*see* Index).

## ECONOMY

A mild climate and good soil have led to the development of intensive systems of agriculture and horticulture, which form a significant part of the economy. Equally important are invisible earnings, principally from tourism and banking and finance, the low rate of income tax (20p in the £ in Jersey and Guernsey; no tax of any kind in Sark) and the absence of super-tax and death duties making the islands a popular tax-haven.

Principal exports are agricultural produce and flowers; imports are chiefly machinery, manufactured goods, food, fuel and chemicals. Trade with the UK is regarded as internal.

British currency is legal tender in the Channel Islands but each Bailiwick issues its own coins and notes (*see* page 617). They also issue their own postage stamps; UK stamps are not valid.

## JERSEY

*Lieutenant-Governor and Commander-in-Chief of Jersey*, Chief Marshall Sir John Cheshire, KBE, CB, *apptd* 2001
*Secretary and ADC*, Lt.-Col. A. J. C. Woodrow, OBE, MC
*Bailiff of Jersey*, Sir Philip Bailhache, Kt.
*Deputy Bailiff*, M. C. St J. Birt, Esq
*Attorney-General*, W. J. Bailhache, QC, Esq
*Receiver-General*, Gp Capt. R. Green, OBE
*Solicitor-General*, Miss S. C. Nicolle, QC
*Greffier of the States*, Miss C. M. Newcombe
*States Treasurer*, Mr I. Black

### FINANCE

| *Year to 31 Dec.* | 1999 | 2000 |
|---|---|---|
| Revenue income | £478,161,000 | £518,177,000 |
| Revenue expenditure | 405,162,000 | 446,605,000 |
| Capital expenditure | 79,687,000 | 51,861,000 |
| Public debt | 0 | 0 |

CHIEF TOWN – ΨSt Helier, on the south coast of Jersey
FLAG – A white field charged with a red saltire cross, and the arms of Jersey in the upper centre

## GUERNSEY AND DEPENDENCIES

*Lieutenant-Governor and Commander-in-Chief of the Bailiwick of Guernsey and its Dependencies*, HE Lieutenant-General. Sir John Foley, KCB, OBE, MC, *apptd 2000*
*Secretary and ADC*, Colonel R. H. Graham, MBE
*Bailiff of Guernsey*, de V. G. Carey
*Deputy Bailiff*, A. C. K. Day, QC
*HM Procureur and Receiver-General*, G. R. Rowland, QC
*HM Comptroller*, H. E. Roberts, QC
*States Supervisor*, M. J. Brown

### FINANCE

| *Year to 31 Dec.* | 1999 | 2000 |
|---|---|---|
| Revenue | £238,216,000 | £257,600,000 |
| Expenditure | 190,846,000 | 204,400,000 |

CHIEF TOWNS – ΨSt Peter Port, on the east coast of Guernsey; St Anne on Alderney
FLAG – White, bearing a red cross of St George, with a gold cross overall in the centre

### ALDERNEY

*President of the States*, J. Kay-Mouat, OBE
*Clerk of the States*, D. V. Jenkins
*Clerk of the Court*, Mrs S. Kelly

### SARK

*Seigneur of Sark*, J. M. Beaumont, OBE
*The Seneschal*, Lieutenant-Colonel R. J. Guille, MBE
*The Greffier*, J. P. Hamon

### OTHER DEPENDENCIES

Herm and Lihou are owned by the States of Guernsey; Herm is leased. Jethou is leased by the Crown to the States of Guernsey and is sub-let by the States. Brecqhou is within the legislative and judicial territory of Sark.

# The Environment

INTERNATIONAL CONVENTIONS

Legislation and strategies to protect the environment in the UK are driven by the requirements of international conventions and protocols (of which there are over 50) and European Directives (of which there are over 300), as well as the desires of the UK government. The Environment Agency, the Scottish Environment Protection Agency and the Environment and Heritage Service for Northern Ireland are responsible for regulation.

EUROPEAN UNION MEASURES

The European Union's (EU) work is developed based on its Environmental Action Programme. The Sixth Environmental Action Programme, *Environment 2010: Our Future, Our Choice*, sets the programme to 2010. It proposes five priority areas: improving the implementation of existing legislation; integration of environmental concerns into other policies; working more closely with the market; empowering private citizens and helping them to change behaviour; and taking account of the environment in land-use planning and management decisions.

SUSTAINABLE DEVELOPMENT AND LOCAL AGENDA 21

The environmental agenda in the UK, both at a business and government level is moving forward to address sustainability which incorporates social, environmental and economic development. The most commonly used definition is 'development that meets the needs of the present without compromising the ability of future generations to meet their own needs'.

The UK published its first national sustainable development strategy in 1994 and its first set of sustainable development indicators in 1996. The latest strategy *A Better Quality of Life* was published in May 1999. It establishes a framework for integrating social, environmental and economic policies to meet four objectives: social progress, to protect the environment, prudent use of natural resources, and to maintain high and stable levels of economic growth and employment. The strategy contains 14 headline indicators, which are backed by a further 150, against which progress in the UK is measured. Leading businesses are beginning to use the indicators in assessing and reporting their own progress towards achieving sustainability. Sustainable development indicators are also being developed for Scotland.

Local authorities also have a role to play in sustainable development. Under Local Agenda 21, which came out of the UN Conference on Environment and Development in Rio, Brazil in 1992, local authorities are to draw up sustainable development strategies for their areas. Although not a statutory obligation, the government wants all councils to have adopted Local Agenda 21 by the end of 2000. Currently some 93% have adopted it. Partnership between regional and local councils is needed. Regional Development Agencies will take Local Agenda 21 strategies into account in sustainable development frameworks for each English region. The EU is also developing a sustainable development strategy.

WASTE

Waste policy in the UK follows a number of principles: the waste hierarchy of reduce, reuse, recycle, dispose; the proximity principle of disposing of waste close to its generation; and national self sufficiency.

Directives from Europe are playing an increasingly important role in driving UK policy particularly regarding commercial and industrial waste: the recent Landfill Directive sets stringent targets for reducing the amount of waste sent to landfill and the planned integrated products policy aims to internalise the environmental costs of products throughout their life-cycle through market forces, by focusing on eco-design and incentives to ensure increased demand for greener products. Greater responsibility for end-of-life products is already being addressed with the producer responsibility directives for packaging waste, which came into force in the UK in 1997, and the end-of-life-vehicle directive, which entered into force in December last year.

In May 2000, the Waste Strategy for England and Wales was published. It aims to tackle the amount of waste produced; increase recycling rates through statutory targets for local authorities; reduce the amount of waste sent to landfill; and develop markets and end-uses for secondary materials. To meet the targets the public and local authorities will have to vastly increase their current recycling rates.

Scotland also has a national waste strategy which aims to encourage more effective use of natural resources through greater efficiency, waste minimisation, recycling and increased value recovery from waste. The Northern Ireland waste strategy is a framework to help achieve the goal of sustainable waste management and meet the targets for the diversion of waste from landfill.

CLIMATE CHANGE AND AIR POLLUTION

The UK's response to climate change is driven by the Framework Convention on Climate Change. This is a binding agreement that has been signed and ratified by 184 countries. It was ratified in the UK in December 1993 and came into force in March 1994. It is intended to reduce the risks of global warming by limiting 'greenhouse' gas emissions.

Progress towards the convention's targets are assessed at regular conferences. At Kyoto in 1997, a protocol (the Kyoto Protocol) to the convention was adopted. It covers the six main greenhouse gases - carbon dioxide, methane, nitrous oxide, hydrofluorocarbons (HFCs), perfluorocarbons (PFCs), and sulphur hexafloride. Under the protocol industrialised countries agreed to legally binding targets for cutting emissions of greenhouse gases by 5.2% below 1990 levels by 2008-2012. EU members agreed to an 8% reduction and the UK's target is a 12.5% cut.

The protocol set three ways (Kyoto mechanisms) for countries to increase the flexibility and reduce the cost of making emission cuts: the clean development mechanism, emissions trading and joint implementation. The sixth Conference of the Parties in The Hague, Netherlands in November 2000 was suspended. It had been hoped that the methodology of using sinks (such as offsetting emissions by growing forests) and a compliance regime to ensure countries meet their targets would be clarified. The talks are to resume in Bonn, Germany in July. Informal talks have been held since the failure of the November meeting, including a meeting in April that focused on the US statement that the Bush administration opposed the Kyoto Protocol.

In November 2000, a climate change programme was published which sets out how the UK intends to meet its Kyoto target and progress towards its domestic goal of a 20% cut in carbon dioxide emissions by 2010, some of the policies mentioned are already in place. The proposed measures include: a climate change levy which came into effect in April applied to sales of electricity, coal, natural gas, and liquified petroleum gas to the business and public sectors; agreements with energy intensive sectors to meet targets; integrated pollution prevention and control (see below); cutting transport congestion and pollution; energy efficiency standards of performance requiring electricity and gas suppliers to help domestic consumers save energy; better countryside management; cuts in fertiliser use; new targets for improving energy management of public buildings; and emissions trading.

The voluntary greenhouse gas emissions trading scheme is expected to start this year. Participants will agree to cap on emissions and can meet that cap, or reduce emission to below the cap and sell the excess allowance, or let emissions remain over the cap and buy allowances.

The government has also committed £50m to support offshore wind and biomass, while the EU is proposing a directive on renewable energy sources. This would expect the UK to increase its share of renewable energy sources from 1.7% to 10%. The Scottish climate change programme was published in November.

Other conventions covering air pollution include the Convention on Long Range Transboundary Air Pollution which was adopted in 1979 and came into force in 1993. Protocols to this convention cover various pollutants, such as sulphur and nitrogen oxides.

The UK has also developed its own policy on air pollution. The Environmental Protection Act 1990 established two regimes: integrated pollution control (IPC) to regulate emissions to any environmental medium from certain industrial processes and local air pollution control to regulate emissions to air from smaller processes. The recent European Integrated Pollution Prevention and Control (IPPC) Directive was largely based on the UK's IPC regime. This new regime came into force in the UK in August 2000 (and Scotland in September) after much delay and wrangling over details. Although IPPC is very similar to the UK's IPC it will cover many more installations and will include returning sites to a satisfactory state on closure, using energy efficiently and noise and vibration regulation.

The first National Air Quality Strategy was published in 1997 and was revised in January 2000. The strategy sets air quality objectives for the main pollutants (benzene, 1-3, butadiene, carbon monoxide, lead, nitrogen dioxide, sulphur dioxide, ozone, and particulates) to be met by 2003-2008.

Under the strategy, all district and unitary authorities have a duty to review air quality, including likely future air quality, in their areas. This is accompanied by an assessment of whether air quality objectives (set in the strategy) are being, or are likely to be, met. If authorities find that any part of their area breaches the objectives, an air quality management area must be declared and an action plan drawn up for improvements.

### Water

Water quality targets are set at both EU and UK levels for drinking water sources, wastewater discharges, rivers, coastal water and bathing water.

The EU's water framework directive, which entered into force in December, has an objective to achieve 'good water status' throughout the EU by 2015. Consultations later this year and next year will focus on how the directive will be implemented in the UK and on some initial draft regulations.

The EC Bathing Water Directive sets standards for bathing waters. This applies to 391 coastal and nine inland bathing waters in the UK. This directive is over 25 years old and a new version is being drafted.

The Environment Agency sets river quality objectives for each stretch of river. A survey, published last year, shows that 92% of rivers and canals are classified as of 'good' or 'fair' quality.

Water quality is currently protected through licensing abstraction and regulating discharges. Consents to discharge sewage and industrial effluent are regulated under the Water Resources Act 1991 and the Environmental Protection Act 1990 through its IPC regime and the IPPC regime. Discharge consents are based on the river quality objectives and relevant EU directives and specify the concentration and quantity permitted.

The European Urban Waste Water Treatment Directive sets minimum standards for sewage treatment before discharge into coastal waters with the levels of treatment needed depending on the sensitivity of the receiving water. In 1999 the government set more stringent UK targets for all significant coastal discharges to have a minimum of secondary treatment by 2005.

### Selected UK Targets

#### *Global atmosphere*

- Reduce greenhouse gas emissions to 12.5% below 1990 levels by 2010
- Reduce carbon dioxide emissions to 20% below 1990 levels by 2010

#### *Air quality*

- Reduce sulphur dioxide emissions by 63% based on 1990 levels by 2010
- Reduce emissions of nitrogen oxides by 41% based on 1990 levels by 2010
- Reduce emissions of volatile organic compounds by 40% based on 1990 levels by 2010
- Reduce ammonia emissions by 17% based on 1990 levels by 2010

#### *Fresh water and sea*

- 97% of bathing waters to meet European directive standards consistently by 2005
- Provide secondary treatment for discharges above 15,000 population equivalent by 31 March 2002
- Provide secondary treatment for all significant coastal discharges (over 2,000 population equivalent) by 2005

#### *Waste*

- Reduce industrial and commercial waste going to landfill by 85% of 1998 levels by 2005
- Recover 40% of municipal waste by 2005, 45% by 2010 and 67% by 2015
- Recycle or compost 25% of household waste by 2005, 30% by 2010 and 33% by 2015
- Reduce biodegradable waste sent to landfill to 75% of 1995 levels by 2010, 50% by 2013 and 35% by 2020

- Ensure 60% of UK newspaper feedstock content is waste paper by end of 2001, 65% by end of 2003 and 70% by end of 2006
- The 2001 recovery and recycling target for packaging waste set at 56%, up from the 2000 target of 45%
- Proposed re-use and recovery of 85% of the mass of end-of-life vehicles with a minimum of 80% recycling by 2006, 95% and 85% by 2015
- EU target to reduce the amount of waste going to final disposal by 20% by 2010 and 50% by 2050

*Land*

- Ensure 60% of all new housing is built on re-used sites

CONTACTS

ADVISORY COMMITTEE ON BUSINESS AND THE ENVIRONMENT, Zone 6/D12, Ashdown House, 123 Victoria Street, London SW1E 6DE. Tel: 020-7890 6278
Web: www.environment.detr.gov.uk/acbe/index.htm

DEPARTMENT FOR ENVIRONMENT, FOOD AND RURAL AFFAIRS, Nobel House, 17 Smith Square, London SW1P 3JR. Tel: 020-7238 3000
Web: www.defra.gov.uk

ENVIRONMENT AGENCY, Rivers House, Waterside Drive, Aztec West, Almondsbury, Bristol BS12 4UD
Tel: 01454-624400
Web: www.environment-agency.gov.uk

ENVIROWISE, THE ENVIRONMENT AND ENERGY HELPLINE. Tel: 0800 585794
Web: www.environwise.gov.uk

EUROPEAN ENVIRONMENT AGENCY, Kongens Nytorv 6, DK-1050 Copenhagen K, Denmark
Tel: Copenhagen 3336 7100
Web: www.eea.eu.int

LOCAL AGENDA 21, Improvement and Development Agency, Layden House, 76-78 Turnmill Street, London EC1M 5QU
Tel: 020-7296 6599
Web: www.la21-uk.org.uk

ROYAL COMMISSION ON ENVIRONMENTAL POLLUTION, Steel House, 11 Tothill Street, London SW1H 9RE
Tel: 020-7273 6635
Web: www.rcep.org.uk

SCOTTISH ENVIRONMENTAL PROTECTION AGENCY, Erskine Court, Castle Business Park, Stirling FK9 4TR
Tel: 01786-457700
Web: www.sepa.org.uk

SUSTAINABLE DEVELOPMENT COMMISSION, 5th Floor, Romney House, Tufton Street, London SW1P 3RA
Tel: 020-7944 4964
Web: www.sd-commission.gov.uk

SUSTAINABLE DEVELOPMENT UNIT, 5/B2 Ashdown House, 123 Victoria Street, London SW1E 6DE
Tel: 020-7944 6485
Web: www.sustainable-development .gov.uk

UN COMMISSION ON SUSTAINABLE DEVELOPMENT, Division for Sustainable Development, 2 UN Plaza, Room DC2-2220, New York, NY 10017, USA.
Tel: New York 963 3170
Web: www.un.org/esa/sustdev

# Conservation and Heritage

## Conservation of the Countryside

### NATIONAL PARKS

#### ENGLAND AND WALES

The ten National Parks of England and Wales were set up under the provisions of the National Parks and Access to the Countryside Act 1949 to conserve and protect scenic landscapes from inappropriate development and to provide access to the land for public enjoyment.

The Countryside Agency (established on 1 April 1999 from the merger of the Countryside Commission and the Rural Development Commission) is the statutory body which has the power to designate National Parks in England, and the Countryside Council for Wales is responsible for National Parks in Wales. Designations in England are confirmed by the Secretary of State for Environment, Food and Rural Affairs and those in Wales by the National Assembly for Wales. The designation of a National Park does not affect the ownership of the land or remove the rights of the local community. The majority of the land in the National Parks is owned by private landowners (74 per cent) or by bodies such as the National Trust (7 per cent) and the Forestry Commission (7 per cent). The National Park Authorities own only 2.3 per cent of the land.

The Environment Act 1995 replaced the existing National Park boards and committees with free-standing National Park Authorities (NPAs). NPAs are the sole local planning authorities for their areas and as such influence land use and development, and deal with planning applications. Their duties include conserving and enhancing the natural beauty, wildlife and cultural heritage of the National Parks; promoting opportunities for public understanding and enjoyment of the National Parks; and fostering the economic and social well-being of the communities within National Parks. The NPAs publish management plans as statements of their policies and appoint their own officers and staff.

Membership of the NPAs differs slightly between England and Wales. In England membership is split between representatives of the constituent local authorities and members appointed by the Secretary of State (of whom one half, minus one, are nominated by the parish councils in the park), with the local authority representatives in a majority of one. The Countryside Agency advises the Secretary of State on appointments not nominated by the parish councils. In Wales two-thirds of NPA members are appointed by the constituent local authorities and one-third by the National Assembly for Wales, advised by the Countryside Council for Wales.

Central government provides 75 per cent of the funding for the parks through the National Park Grant. The remaining 25 per cent is supplied by the local authorities concerned. Approved net expenditure for all National Parks in 2000–1 was £27,920,800 for England and £8,712,000 for Wales.

The National Parks (with date designation confirmed) are:

BRECON BEACONS (1957), Powys (66 per cent)/Carmarthenshire/Rhondda, Cynon and Taff/Merthyr Tydfil/Blaenau Gwent/Monmouthshire, 1,351 sq. km/522 sq. miles – The park is centred on the Beacons, Pen y Fan, Corn Du and Cribyn, but also includes the valley of the Usk, the Black Mountains to the east and the Black Mountain to the west. There are information centres at Brecon, Craig-y-nos Country Park, Abergavenny and Llandovery, a study centre at Danywenallt and a day visitor centre near Libanus.
*Information Office*, 7 Glamorgan Street, Brecon, Powys LD3 7DP. Tel: 01874-624437. *National Park Officer*, C. Gledhill

DARTMOOR (1951 and 1994), Devon, 954 sq. km/368 sq. miles – The park consists of moorland and rocky granite tors, and is rich in prehistoric remains. There are information centres at Newbridge, Tavistock, Bovey Tracey, Steps Bridge, Princetown and Postbridge.
*Information Office*, Parke, Haytor Road, Bovey Tracey, Devon TQ13 9JQ. Tel: 01626-832093. *National Park Officer*, N. Atkinson

EXMOOR (1954), Somerset (71 per cent)/Devon, 693 sq. km/268 sq. miles – Exmoor is a moorland plateau inhabited by wild ponies and red deer. There are many ancient remains and burial mounds. There are information centres at Lynmouth, County Gate, Dulverton and Combe Martin.
*Information Office*, Exmoor House, Dulverton, Somerset TA22 9HL. Tel: 01398-322322. *National Park Officer*, N. Stone

LAKE DISTRICT (1951), Cumbria, 2,292 sq. km/885 sq. miles – The Lake District includes England's highest mountains (Scafell Pike, Helvellyn and Skiddaw) but it is most famous for its glaciated lakes. There are information centres at Keswick, Waterhead, Hawkshead, Seatoller, Bowness, Grasmere, Coniston, Glenridding and Pooley Bridge, an information van at Gosforth and a park centre at Brockhole, Windermere.
*Information Office*, Murley Moss, Oxenholme Road, Kendal, Cumbria, LA9 7RL. Tel: 01539-724555. *National Park Officer*, P. Tiplady

NORTHUMBERLAND (1956), Northumberland, 1,049 sq. km/405 sq. miles – The park is an area of hill country stretching from Hadrian's Wall to the Scottish Border. There are information centres at Ingram, Once Brewed, Rothbury, Housesteads, Harbottle and Kielder, and an information caravan at Cawfields.
*Information Office*, Eastburn, South Park, Hexham, Northumberland NE46 1BS. Tel: 01434-605555. *National Park Officer*, G. Taylor

NORTH YORK MOORS (1952), North Yorkshire (96 per cent)/Redcar and Cleveland, 1,436 sq. km/554 sq. miles – The park consists of woodland and moorland, and includes the Hambleton Hills and the Cleveland Way. There are information centres at Danby, Pickering, Sutton Bank, Ravenscar, Helmsley and Hutton-le-Hole, and a day study centre at Danby.
*Information Office*, The Old Vicarage, Bondgate, Helmsley, York YO6 5BP. Tel: 01439-770657. *National Park Officer*, D. Arnold-Forster

PEAK DISTRICT (1951), Derbyshire (64 per cent)/ Staffordshire/South Yorkshire/Cheshire/West Yorkshire/Greater Manchester, 1,438 sq. km/555 sq. miles – The Peak District includes the gritstone moors of the 'Dark Peak' and the limestone dales of the 'White Peak'. There are information centres at Bakewell, Edale, Fairholmes and Castleton, and information points at Torside (in the Longdendale Valley) and at Hartington (former station).
*Information Office*, Aldern House, Baslow Road, Bakewell, Derbyshire DE45 1AE. Tel: 01629-816200. *National Park Officer*, C. Harrison

PEMBROKESHIRE COAST (1952 and 1995), Pembrokeshire, 584 sq. km/225 sq. miles – The park includes cliffs, moorland and a number of islands, including Skomer. There are information centres at Tenby, St David's, Pembroke, Kilgetty and Haverfordwest.
*Information Office*, Winch Lane, Haverfordwest, Pembrokeshire SA61 1PY. Tel: 01437-764636. *National Park Officer*, N. Wheeler

SNOWDONIA (1951), Gwynedd/Conwy, 2,142 sq. km/827 sq. miles – Snowdonia is an area of deep valleys and rugged mountains. There are information centres at Aberdyfi, Bala, Betws y Coed, Blaenau Ffestiniog, Conwy, Harlech, Dolgellau and Llanberis.
*Information Office*, Penrhyndeudraeth, Gwynedd LL48 6LF. Tel: 01766-770274. *National Park Officer*, I. Huws

YORKSHIRE DALES (1954), North Yorkshire (88 per cent)/ Cumbria, 1,769 sq. km/683 sq. miles – The Yorkshire Dales are composed primarily of limestone overlaid in places by millstone grit. The three peaks of Ingleborough, Whernside and Pen-y-Ghent are within the park. There are information centres at Clapham, Grassington, Hawes, Aysgarth Falls, Malham and Sedbergh.
*Information Office*, Yorebridge House, Bainbridge, Leyburn, N. Yorks DL8 3EE. Tel: 01969-650456. *National Park Officer*, H. Hancock

Two other areas considered to have equivalent status to national parks are the Broads and the New Forest. The Broads Authority, a special statutory authority, was established in 1989 to develop, conserve and manage the Norfolk and Suffolk Broads. The Government declared in 1992 its intention of giving the New Forest a status equivalent to that of a National Park by declaring it an 'area of national significance'.

THE BROADS (1989), Norfolk, 303 sq. km/117 sq. miles – The Broads are located between Norwich and Great Yarmouth on the flood plains of the five rivers flowing through the area to the sea. The area is one of fens, winding waterways, woodland and marsh. The 40 or so broads are man-made, and are connected to the rivers by dykes, providing over 200 km of navigable waterways. There are information centres at Beccles, Hoveton, North-west Tower (Yarmouth), Ranworth and Toad Hole.
*Broads Authority*, Thomas Harvey House, 18 Colegate, Norwich NR3 1BQ. Tel: 01603-610734. *Chief Executive*, J. Packman

THE NEW FOREST, Hampshire, 376 sq. km/145 sq. miles – The forest has been protected since 1079 when it was declared a royal hunting forest. The area consists of forest, ancient woodland and heathland. Much of the Forest is managed by the Forestry Commission, which provides several camp-sites. The main villages are Brockenhurst, Burley and Lyndhurst, which has a visitor centre.
*The New Forest Committee*, 4 High Street, Lyndhurst, Hants SO43 7BD. Tel: 023-8028 2249. *Chief Executive*, Ted Johnson

### SCOTLAND AND NORTHERN IRELAND

The National Parks and Access to the Countryside Act 1949 dealt only with England and Wales and made no provision for Scotland or Northern Ireland.

On 9 August 2000, The National Parks (Scotland) Bill received Royal Assent, providing the Parliament with the ability to create National Parks in Scotland in any area deemed to be appropriate. The first Scottish National Park, Loch Lomond and the Trossachs, is expected to be operational by May 2002, with the Cairngorms following a year later.

There is power to designate National Parks in Northern Ireland under the Amenity Lands Act 1965 and the Nature Conservation and Amenity Lands Order (Northern Ireland) 1985.

## AREAS OF OUTSTANDING NATURAL BEAUTY

### ENGLAND AND WALES

Under the National Parks and Access to the Countryside Act 1949, provision was made for the designation of Areas of Outstanding Natural Beauty (AONBs) by the Countryside Commission. The Countryside Agency is now responsible for AONBs in England and since April 1991 the Countryside Council for Wales has been responsible for the Welsh AONBs. Designations in England are confirmed by the Secretary of State for Environment, Food and Rural Affairs and those in Wales by the National Assembly for Wales. The Countryside and Rights of Way Act 2000 provided for the creation of conservation boards for individual AONBs and placed greater responsibility on local authorities to protect them.

Although less emphasis is placed upon the provision of open-air enjoyment for the public than in the national parks, AONBs are areas which are no less beautiful and require the same degree of protection to conserve and enhance the natural beauty of the countryside. This includes protecting flora and fauna, geological and other landscape features. In AONBs planning and management responsibilities are split between county and district councils and the newly established conservation boards (where they exist); where unitary authorities exist in Wales, they have sole responsibility for planning and management. Several AONBs cross local authority boundaries. Finance for the AONBs is provided by grant-aid.

The 41 Areas of Outstanding Natural Beauty (with date of designation confirmed) are:

ANGLESEY (1967), Anglesey, 221 sq. km/85 sq. miles

ARNSIDE AND SILVERDALE (1972), Cumbria/Lancashire, 75 sq. km/29 sq. miles

BLACKDOWN HILLS (1991), Devon/Somerset, 370 sq. km/ 143 sq. miles

CANNOCK CHASE (1958), Staffordshire, 68 sq. km/26 sq. miles

CHICHESTER HARBOUR (1964), Hampshire/West Sussex, 74 sq. km/29 sq. miles

CHILTERNS (1965; extended 1990), Bedfordshire/ Hertfordshire/Buckinghamshire/Oxfordshire, 833 sq. km/322 sq. miles

CLWYDIAN RANGE (1985), Denbighshire/Flintshire, 157 sq. km/60 sq. miles
CORNWALL (1959; Camel estuary 1983), 958 sq. km/370 sq. miles
COTSWOLDS (1966; extended 1990), Gloucestershire/ Wiltshire/Warwickshire/ Worcestershire/Somerset, 2,038 sq. km/787 sq. miles
CRANBORNE CHASE AND WEST WILTSHIRE DOWNS (1983), Dorset/Hampshire/Somerset/Wiltshire, 983 sq. km/379 sq. miles
DEDHAM VALE (1970; extended 1978, 1991), Essex/ Suffolk, 90 sq. km/35 sq. miles
DORSET (1959), 1,129 sq. km/436 sq. miles
EAST DEVON (1963), 268 sq. km/103 sq. miles
EAST HAMPSHIRE (1962), 383 sq. km/148 sq. miles
FOREST OF BOWLAND (1964), Lancashire/North Yorkshire, 802 sq. km/310 sq. miles
GOWER (1956), Swansea, 188 sq. km/73 sq. miles
HIGH WEALD (1983), Kent/Surrey/East Sussex/West Sussex, 1,460 sq. km/564 sq. miles
HOWARDIAN HILLS (1987), North Yorkshire, 204 sq. km/ 79 sq. miles
ISLE OF WIGHT (1963), 189 sq. km/73 sq. miles
ISLES OF SCILLY (1976), 16 sq. km/6 sq. miles
KENT DOWNS (1968), 878 sq. km/339 sq. miles
LINCOLNSHIRE WOLDS (1973), 558 sq. km/215 sq. miles
LLEYNN (1957), Gwynedd, 161 sq. km/62 sq. miles
MALVERN HILLS (1959), Herefordshire/Worcestershire/ Gloucestershire, 105 sq. km/40 sq. miles
MENDIP HILLS (1972; extended 1989), Somerset, 198 sq. km/76 sq. miles
NIDDERDALE (1994), North Yorkshire, 603 sq. km/233 sq. miles
NORFOLK COAST (1968), 451 sq. km/174 sq. miles
NORTH DEVON (1960), 171 sq. km/66 sq. miles
NORTH PENNINES (1988), Cumbria/Durham/ Northumberland, 1,983 sq. km/766 sq. miles
NORTHUMBERLAND COAST (1958), 135 sq. km/52 sq. miles
QUANTOCK HILLS (1957), Somerset, 99 sq. km/38 sq. miles
SHROPSHIRE HILLS (1959), 804 sq. km/310 sq. miles
SOLWAY COAST (1964), Cumbria, 115 sq. km/44 sq. miles
SOUTH DEVON (1960), 337 sq. km/130 sq. miles
SOUTH HAMPSHIRE COAST (1967), 77 sq. km/30 sq. miles
SUFFOLK COAST AND HEATHS (1970), 403 sq. km/156 sq. miles
SURREY HILLS (1958), 419 sq. km/162 sq. miles
SUSSEX DOWNS (1966), 983 sq. km/379 sq. miles
TAMAR VALLEY (1995), Cornwall/Devon, 195 sq. km/115 sq. miles
NORTH WESSEX DOWNS (1972), Berkshire/Hampshire/ Oxfordshire/Wiltshire, 1,730 sq. km/668 sq. miles
WYE VALLEY (1971), Monmouthshire/Gloucestershire/ Herefordshire, 326 sq. km/126 sq. miles

### NORTHERN IRELAND

The Department of the Environment for Northern Ireland, with advice from the Council for Nature Conservation and the Countryside, designates Areas of Outstanding Natural Beauty in Northern Ireland. At present there are nine and these cover a total area of approximately 284,948 hectares (704,121 acres).

ANTRIM COAST AND GLENS, Co. Antrim, 70,600 ha/ 174,452 acres
CAUSEWAY COAST, Co. Antrim, 4,200 ha/10,378 acres
LAGAN VALLEY, Co. Down, 2,072 ha/5,119 acres
LECALE COAST, Co. Down, 3,108 ha/7,679 acres
MOURNE, Co. Down, 57,012 ha/140,876 acres
NORTH DERRY, Co. Londonderry, 12,950 ha/31,999 acres
RING OF GULLION, Co. Armagh, 15,353 ha/37,938 acres
SPERRIN, Co. Tyrone/Co. Londonderry, 101,006 ha/ 249,585 acres
STRANGFORD LOUGH, Co. Down, 18,647 ha/46,077 acres

## NATIONAL SCENIC AREAS

In Scotland, National Scenic Areas have a broadly equivalent status to AONBs. Scottish Natural Heritage recognises areas of national scenic significance. At mid 1999 there were 40, covering a total area of 1,001,800 hectares (2,475,448 acres).

Development within National Scenic Areas is dealt with by local authorities, who are required to consult Scottish Natural Heritage concerning certain categories of development. Disagreements between Scottish Natural Heritage and local authorities are referred to the Scottish Executive. Land management uses can also be modified in the interest of scenic conservation.

ASSYNT-COIGACH, Highland, 90,200 ha/222,884 acres
BEN NEVIS AND GLEN COE, Highland/Argyll and Bute/ Perth and Kinross, 101,600 ha/251,053 acres
CAIRNGORM MOUNTAINS, Highland/Aberdeenshire/ Moray, 67,200 ha/166,051 acres
CUILLIN HILLS, Highland, 21,900 ha/54,115 acres
DEESIDE AND LOCHNAGAR, Aberdeenshire/Angus, 40,000 ha/98,840 acres
DORNOCH FIRTH, Highland, 7,500 ha/18,532 acres
EAST STEWARTRY COAST, Dumfries and Galloway, 4,500 ha/11,119 acres
EILDON AND LEADERFOOT, Scottish Borders, 3,600 ha/ 8,896 acres
FLEET VALLEY, Dumfries and Galloway, 5,300 ha/13,096 acres
GLEN AFFRIC, Highland, 19,300 ha/47,690 acres
GLEN STRATHFARRAR, Highland, 3,800 ha/9,390 acres
HOY AND WEST MAINLAND, Orkney Islands, 14,800 ha/ 36,571 acres
JURA, Argyll and Bute, 21,800 ha/53,868 acres
KINTAIL, Highland, 15,500 ha/38,300 acres
KNAPDALE, Argyll and Bute, 19,800 ha/48,926 acres
KNOYDART, Highland, 39,500 ha/97,604 acres
KYLE OF TONGUE, Highland, 18,500 ha/45,713 acres
KYLES OF BUTE, Argyll and Bute, 4,400 ha/10,872 acres
LOCH NA KEAL, MULL, Argyll and Bute, 12,700 ha/31,382 acres
LOCH LOMOND, Argyll and Bute/Stirling/West Dunbartonshire, 27,400 ha/67,705 acres
LOCH RANNOCH AND GLEN LYON, Perth and Kinross/ Stirling, 48,400 ha/119,596 acres
LOCH SHIEL, Highland, 13,400 ha/33,111 acres
LOCH TUMMEL, Perth and Kinross, 9,200 ha/22,733 acres
LYNN OF LORN, Argyll and Bute, 4,800 ha/11,861 acres
MORAR, MOIDART AND ARDNAMURCHAN, Highland, 13,500 ha/33,358 acres
NORTH-WEST SUTHERLAND, Highland, 20,500 ha/ 50,655 acres
NITH ESTUARY, Dumfries and Galloway, 9,300 ha/22,980 acres
NORTH ARRAN, North Ayrshire, 23,800 ha/58,810 acres
RIVER EARN, Perth and Kinross, 3,000 ha/7,413 acres
RIVER TAY, Perth and Kinross, 5,600 ha/13,838 acres
ST KILDA, Western Isles, 900 ha/2,224 acres
SCARBA, LUNGA AND THE GARVELLACHS, Argyll and Bute, 1,900 ha/4,695 acres

SHETLAND, Shetland Islands, 11,600 ha/28,664 acres
SMALL ISLES, Highland, 15,500 ha/38,300 acres
SOUTH LEWIS, HARRIS AND NORTH UIST, Western Isles, 109,600 ha/270,822 acres
SOUTH UIST MACHAIR, Western Isles, 6,100 ha/15,073 acres
THE TROSSACHS, Stirling, 4,600 ha/11,367 acres
TROTTERNISH, Highland, 5,000 ha/12,355 acres
UPPER TWEEDDALE, Scottish Borders, 10,500 ha/25,945 acres
WESTER ROSS, Highland, 145,300 ha/359,036 acres

## THE NATIONAL FOREST

The National Forest is being planted across 200 square miles of Derbyshire, Leicestershire and Staffordshire. About 30 million trees, of mixed species but mainly broadleaved, will be planted, and will eventually cover about one-third of the designated area. The project is funded by the Department for Environment, Food and Rural Affairs. It was developed in 1992–5 by the Countryside Commission and is now run by the National Forest Company, which was established in April 1995. Since then 4 million trees have been planted on 2,500 hectares of land across 480 sites. Under the National Forest Tender Scheme, anybody wishing to undertake a project can submit a competitive bid to the National Forest Company.

NATIONAL FOREST COMPANY, Enterprise Glade, Bath Lane, Moira, Swadlincote, Derbys DE12 6BD. Tel: 01283-551211. *Chief Executive*, Miss S. Bell, OBE

# Nature Conservation Areas

## SITES OF SPECIAL SCIENTIFIC INTEREST

Site of Special Scientific Interest (SSSI) is a legal notification applied to land in England, Scotland or Wales which English Nature (EN), Scottish Natural Heritage (SNH), or the Countryside Council for Wales (CCW) identifies as being of special interest because of its flora, fauna, geological or physiographical features. In some cases, SSSIs are managed as nature reserves.

EN, SNH and CCW must notify the designation of a SSSI to the local planning authority, every owner/occupier of the land, and the Secretary of State for Environment, Food and Rural Affairs, the First Minister in Scotland or the National Assembly for Wales. Forestry and agricultural departments and a number of other bodies are also informed of this notification.

Objections to the notification of a SSSI can be made and ultimately considered at a full meeting of the Council of EN or CCW. In Scotland an objection will be dealt with by the appropriate area board or the main board of SNH, depending on the nature of the objection. Unresolved objections on scientific grounds must be referred to the Advisory Committee on SSSI.

The protection of these sites depends on the co-operation of individual landowners and occupiers. Owner/occupiers must consult EN, SNH or CCW and gain written consent before they can undertake certain listed activities on the site. Funds are available through management agreements and grants to assist owners and occupiers in conserving sites' interests. As a last resort a site can be purchased.

The number and area of SSSIs in Britain as at 1 March 2001 was:

| | *no.* | *Hectares* | *Acres* |
|---|---|---|---|
| England | 4,115 | 1,089,260 | 2,690,472 |
| Scotland | 1,449 | 957,710 | 2,366,469 |
| Wales | 1,008 | 224,733 | 555,090 |

NORTHERN IRELAND

In Northern Ireland 161 Areas of Special Scientific Interest (ASSIs) have been established by the Department of the Environment for Northern Ireland. These cover a total area of 83,465.476 hectares (206,243.19 acres).

## NATIONAL NATURE RESERVES

National Nature Reserves are defined in the National Parks and Access to the Countryside Act 1949 as land designated for the study and preservation of flora and fauna, or of geological or physiographical features.

English Nature (EN), Scottish Natural Heritage (SNH) or the Countryside Council for Wales (CCW) can designate as a National Nature Reserve land which is being managed as a nature reserve under an agreement with one of the statutory nature conservation agencies; land held and managed by EN, SNH or CCW; or land held and managed as a nature reserve by another approved body. EN, SNH or CCW can make by-laws to protect reserves from undesirable activities; these are subject to confirmation by the Secretary of State for Environment, Food and Rural Affairs, the National Assembly for Wales or the Scottish Ministers in Scotland.

The number and area of National Nature Reserves in Britain as at 1 March 2001 was:

| | *no.* | *Hectares* | *Acres* |
|---|---|---|---|
| England | 208 | 83,560 | 206,393 |
| Scotland | 72 | 114,327 | 282,498 |
| Wales | 65 | 19,269 | 47,594 |

NORTHERN IRELAND

National Nature Reserves are established and managed by the Department of the Environment for Northern Ireland, with advice from the Council for Nature Conservation and the Countryside. There are 46 National Nature Reserves covering 4,322.1 hectares (10,676 acres).

## LOCAL NATURE RESERVES

Local Nature Reserves are defined in the National Parks and Access to the Countryside Act 1949 as land designated for the study and preservation of flora and fauna, or of geological or physiographical features. The Act gives local authorities in England, Scotland and Wales the power to acquire, declare and manage local nature reserves in consultation with English Nature, Scottish Natural Heritage and the Countryside Council for Wales. Conservation trusts can also own and manage non-statutory local nature reserves.

The number and area of designated Local Nature Reserves in Britain as at 1 March 2001 was:

| | *no.* | *hectares* | *Acres* |
|---|---|---|---|
| England | 665 | 30,702 | 75,834 |
| Scotland | 34 | 9,382 | 23,183 |
| Wales | 51 | 4,701 | 11,611 |

An additional 38 km of linear trails are designated as Local Nature Reserves.

## FOREST NATURE RESERVES

Forest Enterprise (an executive agency of the Forestry Commission) is responsible for the management of the Commission's forests. It has created 46 Forest Nature Reserves with the aim of protecting and conserving special forms of natural habitat, flora and fauna. There are about 300 SSSIs on the estates, some of which are also Nature Reserves.

Forest Nature Reserves extend in size from under 50 hectares (124 acres) to over 500 hectares (1,236 acres). The largest include the Black Wood of Rannoch, by Loch Rannoch; Cannop Valley Oakwoods, Forest of Dean; Culbin Forest, near Forres; Glen Affric, near Fort Augustus; Kylerhea, Skye; Pembrey, Carmarthen Bay; Starr Forest, in Galloway Forest Park; and Wyre Forest, near Kidderminster.

Forest Enterprise also manages 18 Caledonian Forest Reserves in Scotland. These reserves are intended to protect and expand 16,000 hectares of native oak and pine woods in the Scottish highlands.

### NORTHERN IRELAND

There are 35 Forest Nature Reserves in Northern Ireland, covering 1,637 hectares (4,043 acres). They are designated and administered by the Forest Service, an agency of the Department of Agriculture and Rural Development for Northern Ireland. There are also 16 National Nature Reserves on Forest Service-owned property.

## MARINE NATURE RESERVES

The Secretary of State for Environment, Food and Rural Affairs, the National Assembly for Wales and the Scottish Executive have the power to designate Marine Nature Reserves. English Nature, Scottish Natural Heritage and the Countryside Council for Wales select and manage these reserves. Marine Nature Reserves may be established in Northern Ireland under a 1985 Order.

Marine Nature Reserves provide protection for marine flora and fauna, and geological and physiographical features on land covered by tidal waters or parts of the sea in or adjacent to the UK. Reserves also provide opportunities for study and research.

The three statutory Marine Nature Reserves are:

LUNDY (1986), Bristol Channel
SKOMER (1990), Dyfed
STRANGFORD LOUGH (1995), Northern Ireland

Two other areas proposed for designation as reserves are: the Menai Strait, and Bardsey Island and part of the Llŷn peninsula, both in Wales.

A number of non-statutory marine reserves have been set up by conservation groups.

### EUROPEAN MARINE SITES

The 1992 EC Habitats Directive and the 1979 Birds Directive allow the UK government to establish Special Areas of Conservation (SACs) on Special Protection Areas (SPA) for birds on land and at sea. Where the designated area includes sea or seashore it is described as a European marine site. The UK Marine SACs project is a demonstration initiative, funded partly by the EU, to establish management schemes for twelve of the marine SACs in the UK.

# World Heritage Sites

The Convention Concerning the Protection of the World Cultural and Natural Heritage was adopted by UNESCO in 1972 and ratified by the UK in 1984. By May 2000 the convention had been ratified by 156 states. The convention provides for the identification, protection and conservation of cultural and natural sites of outstanding universal value.

Cultural sites may be:
- monuments
- groups of buildings
- sites of historic, aesthetic, archaeological, scientific, ethnologic or anthropologic value
- historic areas of towns
- 'cultural landscapes', i.e. sites whose characteristics are marked by significant interactions between human populations and their natural environment

Natural sites may be:
- those with remarkable physical, biological or geological formations
- those with outstanding universal value from the point of view of science, conservation or natural beauty
- the habitat of threatened species and plants

Governments which are party to the convention nominate sites in their country for inclusion in the World Cultural and Natural Heritage List. Nominations are considered by the World Heritage Committee, an intergovernmental committee composed of 21 representatives of the parties to the convention. The committee is advised by the International Council on Monuments and Sites (ICOMOS) and the International Union for the Conservation of Nature (IUCN). ICOMOS evaluates and reports on proposed cultural sites and IUCN on proposed natural sites. The International Centre for the Study of the Preservation and Restoration of Cultural Property (ICCROM) provides the committee with expert advice on monument restoration. The Department for Culture, Media and Sport represents the UK government in matters relating to the convention.

A prerequisite for inclusion in the World Cultural and Natural Heritage List is the existence of an effective legal protection system in the country in which the site is situated (e.g. listing, conservation areas and planning controls in the United Kingdom) and a detailed management plan to ensure the conservation of the site. Inclusion in the list does not confer any greater degree of protection on the site than that offered by the national protection framework.

If a site is considered to be in serious danger of decay or damage the committee may add it to a complementary list, the World Heritage in Danger List. Sites on this list may benefit from particular attention or emergency measures.

Financial support for the conservation of sites on the World Cultural and Natural Heritage List is provided by the World Heritage Fund. This is administered by the World Heritage Committee, which determines the financial and technical aid to be allocated. The fund's income is derived from the obligatory contributions of the parties to the convention, amounting to 1 per cent of their contribution to UNESCO. The fund may also receive voluntary contributions from the parties to the convention, donations from institutions or individuals, and income from national and international promotional activities.

## Designated Sites

As at December 2000 there were 690 sites in 122 countries on the World Cultural and Natural Heritage List. Of these, 17 were in the United Kingdom and three in British overseas territories; 15 were listed for their cultural significance (†) and five for their natural significance (*).

*United Kingdom*

†Bath – the city
†Blaenarvon, Wales
†Blenheim Palace and park, Oxfordshire
†Canterbury Cathedral, St Augustine's Abbey, St Martin's Church, Kent
†Castle and town walls of King Edward I, north Wales – Beaumaris, Anglesey, Caernarfon Castle, Conwy Castle, Harlech Castle
†Durham Cathedral and Castle
†Edinburgh Old and New Towns
*Giant's Causeway and Causeway coast, Co. Antrim
†Greenwich, London – maritime Greenwich, including the Royal Naval College, Old Royal Observatory, Queen's House, town centre
†Hadrian's Wall, northern England
†Heart of Neolithic Orkney
†Ironbridge Gorge, Shropshire – the world's first iron bridge and other early industrial sites
*St Kilda, Western Isles
†Stonehenge, Avebury and related megalithic sites, Wiltshire
†Studley Royal Park, Fountains Abbey, St Mary's Church, N. Yorkshire
†Tower of London
†Westminster Abbey, Palace of Westminster, St Margaret's Church, London

*British Overseas Territories*

*Henderson Island, Pitcairn Islands, South Pacific Ocean
*Gough Island wildlife reserve (part of Tristan da Cunha), South Atlantic Ocean
*St George town and related fortifications, Bermuda

Buildings, Monuments and Sites Division, Department for Culture, Media and Sport, 2-4 Cockspur Street, London SW1Y 5DH. Tel: 020-7211 6909

World Heritage Centre, UNESCO, 7 place de Fontenoy, 75352 Paris, France. Tel: Paris 4568 1876; Email wh-info@unesco.org

International Centre for the Study of the Preservation and Restoration of Cultural Property (ICCROM), Via di San Michele 13, I-00153 Rome, Italy. Tel: Rome 585531

International Council on Monuments and Sites (ICOMOS), 10 Barley Mow Passage, London W4 4PH. Tel. 020-8994 6477

International Union for the Conservation of Nature (IUCN), UK Committee, c/o 36 Kingfisher Court, Hambridge Road, Newbury, Berks RG14 5SJ. Telephone: 01635-522925

# Conservation of wildlife and habitats

The UK is party to a number of international conventions.

RAMSAR CONVENTION

The 1971 Ramsar Convention on Wetlands of International Importance especially as Waterfowl Habitat, entered into force in the UK in May 1976. By May 2001 124 countries were party to the convention.

The aim of the convention is the conservation and wise use of wetlands and their flora and fauna, especially waterfowl. Governments that are party to the convention must designate wetlands and include wetland conservation considerations in their land-use planning. A total of 1,069 wetland sites, totalling 81.2 million hectares have been designated for inclusion in the List of Wetlands of International Importance. The UK currently has 161 designated sites covering 805,669 hectares. The member countries meet every three years to assess the progress of the convention. The next meeting will be held in Spain next November.

The UK has set targets under its Ramsar Strategic Plan, 1997-2002. Progress towards these is monitored by the UK Ramsar Committee, known as the Joint Working Party. The UK and the Republic of Ireland have established a formal protocol to ensure common monitoring standards for waterbirds in the two countries.

RAMSAR CONVENTION BUREAU, Rue Mauverney 28, CH-1196 Gland, Switzerland. Tel: Gland 9990170. Web: www.ramsar.org

BIODIVERSITY

There is much synergy between the Ramsar Convention and the 1992 Convention on Biological Diversity. In 1996 the Ramsar Secretariat became a lead partner in implementing activities under the Convention on Biological Diversity with joint work plans. The UK ratified the Convention on Biological Diversity in June 1994. There are 180 parties to the convention.

The objectives are the conservation of biological diversity, the sustainable use of its components and the fair and equitable sharing of the benefits arising out of the use of genetic resources. There are thematic work programmes addressing marine and coastal, forest, inland waters, dry land, and sub-humid land.

The UK published its own Biodiversity Action Plan in 1994. A report from the UK Biodiversity Steering Group, published in 1995, identified some 400 priority species and 38 priority habitats, requiring urgent action.

A report on the plan's first five years, published in March, made a number of recommendations including to support actions for conservation of species and habitats at UK, county and local levels, and to enhance access to biological information. Individual action plans have been published for most areas of the UK.

THE BIODIVERSITY ACTION PLAN SECRETARIAT, European Wildlife Division, Department of the Environment Transport and the Regions, Room 902D, Tollgate House, Houlton Street, Bristol, BS2 9DJ. Tel: Bristol 987 8974. Web: www.ukbap.org.uk

CITIES

The 1973 Convention on International Trade in Endangered Species of Wild Fauna and Flora (CITES) came into force in the UK in July 1975. Currently 152 countries are members. The countries party to the convention ban commercial international trade in an agreed list of endangered species and regulate and monitor trade in others species that might become endangered. The convention covers around 30,000 species.

The Conference of the Parties to CITES meets every two to three years to review the convention's implementation

The Global Wildlife Division at the Department of the Environment, Transport and the Regions carries out the government's responsibilities under CITES and the Bonn Convention on the Conservation of Migratory Species of Wild Animals

CITES SECRETARIAT, 15 Chemin des Anemones, CH-1219 Châtelaine, Geneva, Switzerland. Tel: Geneva 917 8139/8140. Web: www:international.fws.gov/cites/cites.html

BONN CONVENTION

The 1979 Convention on Conservation of Migratory Species of Wild Animals came into force in the UK in October 1979. By May 2001 70 parties were party to the convention.

It requires the protection of listed endangered migratory species and encourages international agreements covering these and other threatened species. International agreements can range from legally-binding treaties to less formal memoranda of understanding.

Nine agreements have been concluded to date under the convention. They aim to conserve: bats in Europe; cetaceans of the Mediterranean and Black Seas; small cetaceans of the Baltic and North Seas; seals in the Wadden Sea; African-Eurasian migratory waterbirds; the Siberian Crane; the Slender-billed Curlew; marine turtles; and middle-European great bustards.

Further agreements are being developed for a wide range of migratory species, including Sahelo-Saharan ungulates and albatrosses of the southern hemisphere.

UNEP/CMS SECRETARIAT, United Nations Premises in Bonn, Martin-Luther-King Strasse 8, D-53175. Tel: Bonn 815 2401/2. Web: www.wcmc.org.uk/cms

BERN CONVENTION

The 1979 Bern Convention on the Conservation of European Wildlife and Natural Habitats came into force in the UK in June 1982. Over 40 countries are party to the convention and a number of other states attend meetings as observers.

The aims are to conserve wild flora and fauna and their natural habitats, especially where this requires the cooperation of several countries, and to promote such cooperation. The convention gives particular emphasis to endangered and vulnerable species.

All parties to the convention must promote national conservation policies and take account of the conservation of wild flora and fauna when setting planning and development policies.

SECRETARIAT OF THE BERN CONVENTION STANDING COMMITTEE, Council of Europe, F-67075 Strasbourg Cedex, France. Tel: Strasbourg 8841 3476. Web: www.nature.coe.int

EUROPEAN WILDLIFE TRADE REGULATION

The Council (EC) Regulation on the Protection of Species of Wild Fauna and Flora by Regulating Trade Therein came into force in the UK on 1 June 1997. It is intended to standardise wildlife trade regulations across Europe and to improve the application of CITES. Approximately 30,000 plant and animal species are protected under the regulation.

UK Legislation

The Wildlife and Countryside Act 1981 gives legal protection to a wide range of wild animals and plants. Subject to parliamentary approval, the Secretary of State for the Environment, Food and Rural Affairs may vary the animals and plants given legal protection. The most recent variation of Schedules 5 and 8 came into effect in March and April 1998.

Under Section 9 and Schedule 5 of the Act it is illegal without a licence to kill, injure, take, possess or sell any of the listed animals (whether alive or dead) and to disturb its place of shelter and protection or to destroy that place.

Under Section 13 and Schedule 8 of the Act it is illegal without a licence to pick, uproot, sell or destroy any of the listed plants and, unless authorised, to uproot any wild plant.

The Act lays down a close season for wild birds (other than game birds) from 1 February to 31 August inclusive, each year. Exceptions to these dates are made for:

*Capercaillie* and (except Scotland) *Woodcock* – 1 February to 30 September
*Snipe* – 1 February to 11 August
*Wild Duck* and *Wild Goose* (below high water mark) – 21 February to 31 August

Birds which may be killed or taken outside the close season (except on Sundays and on Christmas Day in Scotland, and on Sundays in prescribed areas of England and Wales) are the above-named, plus coot, certain wild duck (gadwall, goldeneye, mallard, pintail, pochard, shoveler, teal, tufted duck, wigeon), certain wild geese (Canada, greylag, pink-footed, white-fronted (in England and Wales only)), moorhen, golden plover and woodcock.

Certain wild birds may be killed or taken subject to the conditions of a general licence at any time by authorised persons: crow, collared dove, gull (great and lesser black-backed or herring), jackdaw, jay, magpie, pigeon (feral or wood), rook, sparrow (house), and starling. Conditions usually apply where the birds pose a threat to agriculture, public health, air safety, other bird species, and to prevent the spread of disease.

All other British birds are fully protected by law throughout the year.

*Animals*

‡*Adder* (Vipera berus)
Anemone, Ivell's Sea (*Edwardsia ivelli*)
Anemone, Starlet Sea (*Nematosella vectensis*)
Apus, Tadpole shrimp (*Triops cancriformis*)
Bat, Horseshoe (*Rhinolophidae*, all species)
Bat, Typical (*Vespertilionidae*, all species)
Beetle (*Graphoderus zonatus*)
Beetle (*Hypebaeus flavipes*)
Beetle, Lesser Silver Water (*Hydrochara caraboides*)
§§Beetle, Mire Pill (*Curimopsis nigrita*)
Beetle, Rainbow Leaf (*Chrysolina cerealis*)
*Beetle, Stag (*Lucanus cervus*)
Beetle, Violet Click (*Limoniscus violaceus*)
Beetle, Water (*Graphoderus zonatus*)
Beetle, Water (*Paracymus aeneus*)
Burbot (*Lota lota*)
*Butterfly, Adonis Blue (*Lysandra bellargus*)
*Butterfly, Black Hairstreak (*Strymonidia pruni*)
*Butterfly, Brown Hairstreak (*Thecla betulae*)
*Butterfly, Chalkhill Blue (*Lysandra coridon*)
*Butterfly, Chequered Skipper (*Carterocephalus palaemon*)
*Butterfly, Duke of Burgundy Fritillary (*Hamearis lucina*)
*Butterfly, Glanville Fritillary (*Melitaea cinxia*)
Butterfly, Heath Fritillary (*Mellicta athalia* (or *Melitaea athalia*))
Butterfly, High Brown Fritillary (*Argynnis adippe*)
Butterfly, Large Blue (*Maculinea arion*)
Butterfly, Large Copper (*Lycaena dispar*)
*Butterfly, Large Heath (*Coenonympha tullia*)
*Butterfly, Large Tortoiseshell (*Nymphalis polychloros*)
*Butterfly, Lulworth Skipper (*Thymelicus acteon*)
Butterfly, Marsh Fritillary (*Eurodryas aurinia*)
*Butterfly, Mountain Ringlet (*Erebia epiphron*)
*Butterfly, Northern Brown Argus (*Aricia artaxerxes*)
*Butterfly, Pearl-bordered Fritillary (*Boloria euphrosyne*)
*Butterfly, Purple Emperor (*Apatura iris*)
*Butterfly, Silver Spotted Skipper (*Hesperia comma*)
*Butterfly, Silver-studded Blue (*Plebejus argus*)
*Butterfly, Small Blue (*Cupido minimus*)
Butterfly, Swallowtail (*Papilio machaon*)
*Butterfly, White Letter Hairstreak (*Stymonida w-album*)
*Butterfly, Wood White (*Leptidea sinapis*)
Cat, Wild (*Felis silvestris*)
Cicada, New Forest (*Cicadetta montana*)
**Crayfish, Atlantic stream (*Austropotamobius pallipes*)
Cricket, Field (*Gryllus campestris*)
Cricket, Mole (*Gryllotalpa gryllotalpa*)
Damselfly, Southern (*Coenagrion mercuriale*)
Dolphin (*Cetacea*)
Dormouse (*Muscardinus avellanarius*)
Dragonfly, Norfolk Aeshna (*Aeshna isosceles*)
*Frog, Common (*Rana temporaria*)
Goby, Couch's (*Gobius couchii*)
Goby, Giant (*Gobius cobitis*)
Grasshopper, Wart-biter (*Decticus verrucivorus*)
Hatchet Shell, Northern (*Thyasira gouldi*)
Hydroid, Marine (*Clavopsella navis*)
Lagoon Snail (*Paludinella littorina*)
Lagoon Snail, De Folin's (*Caecum armoricum*)
Lagoon Worm, Tentacled (*Alkmaria romijni*)
Leech, Medicinal (*Hirudo medicinalis*)
Lizard, Sand (*Lacerta agilis*)
‡Lizard, Viviparous (*Lacerta vivipara*)
Marten, Pine (*Martes martes*)
Moth, Barberry Carpet (*Pareulype berberata*)
Moth, Black-veined (*Siona lineata* (or *Idaea lineata*))
Moth, Essex Emerald (*Thetidia smaragdaria*)
Moth, Fiery clearwing (*Bembecia chrysidiformis*)
Moth, Fisher's estuarine (*Gortyna borelii*)
Moth, New Forest Burnet (*Zygaena viciae*)
Moth, Reddish Buff (*Acosmetia caliginosa*)
Moth, Sussex Emerald (*Thalera fimbrialis*)
††Mussel, Fan (*Atrina fragilis*)
†Mussel, Freshwater Pearl (*Margaritifera margaritifera*)
Newt, Great Crested (or Warty) (*Triturus cristatus*)
*Newt, Palmate (*Triturus helveticus*)
*Newt, Smooth (*Triturus vulgaris*)
Otter, Common (*Lutra lutra*)
Porpoise (*Cetacea*)
Sandworm, Lagoon (*Armandia cirrhosa*)
††Sea Fan, Pink (*Eunicella verrucosa*)
Sea-Mat, Trembling (*Victorella pavida*)
Sea Slug, Lagoon (*Tenellia adspersa*)
‡‡Shad, Allis (*alosa alosa*)
§§Shad, Twaite (*alosa fallax*)
Shark, Basking (*Cetorhinus maximus*)
Shrimp, Fairy (*Chirocephalus diaphanus*)
Shrimp, Lagoon Sand (*Gammarus insensibilis*)

‡Slow-worm (*Anguis fragilis*)
Snail, Glutinous (*Myxas glutinosa*)
Snail, Sandbowl (*Catinella arenaria*)
‡Snake, Grass (*Natrix natrix* (*Natrix helvetica*))
Snake, Smooth (*Coronella austriaca*)
Spider, Fen Raft (*Dolomedes plantarius*)
Spider, Ladybird (*Eresus niger*)
Squirrel, Red (*Sciurus vulgaris*)
Sturgeon (*Acipenser sturio*)
*Toad, Common (*Bufo bufo*)
Toad, Natterjack (*Bufo calamita*)
Turtle, Marine (*Dermochelyidae* and *Cheloniidae*, all species)
Vendace (*Coregonus albula*)
§§Vole, Water (*Arvicola terrestris*)
Walrus (*Odobenus rosmarus*)
Whale (*Cetacea*)
Whitefish (*Coregonus lavaretus*)

* The offence relates to 'sale' only
** The offence relates to 'taking' and 'sale' only
† The offence relates to 'killing and injuring' only
‡ The offence relates to 'killing, injuring and sale'
§ The offence relates to 'killing, injuring and taking'
§§ The offence relates only to damaging, destroying or obstructing access to a shelter or protection
†† The offence relates to killing, injuring, taking, possession and sale
‡‡ The offence relates to killing, injuring, taking and damaging, etc., a shelter

*Plants*

Adder's tongue, Least (*Ophioglossum lusitanicum*)
Alison, Small (*Alyssum alyssoides*)
Blackwort (*Southbya nigrella*)
°Bluebell (*Hyacinthoides non-scripta*)
Broomrape, Bedstraw (*Orobanche caryophyllacea*)
Broomrape, Oxtongue (*Orobanche loricata*)
Broomrape, Thistle (*Orobanche reticulata*)
Cabbage, Lundy (*Rhynchosinapis wrightii*)
Calamint, Wood (*Calamintha sylvatica*)
Caloplaca, Snow (*Caloplaca nivalis*)
Catapyrenium, Tree (*Catapyrenium psoromoides*)
Catchfly, Alpine (*Lychnis alpina*)
Catillaria, Laurer's (*Catellaria laureri*)
Centaury, Slender (*Centaurium tenuiflorum*)
Cinquefoil, Rock (*Potentilla rupestris*)
Cladonia, Upright Mountain (*Cladonia stricta*)
Clary, Meadow (*Salvia pratensis*)
Club-rush, Triangular (*Scirpus triquetrus*)
Colt's-foot, Purple (*Homogyne alpina*)
Cotoneaster, Wild (*Cotoneaster integerrimus*)
Cottongrass, Slender (*Eriophorum gracile*)
Cow-wheat, Field (*Melampyrum arvense*)
Crocus, Sand (*Romulea columnae*)
Crystalwort, Lizard (*Riccia bifurca*)
Cudweed, Broad-leaved (*Filago pyramidata*)
Cudweed, Jersey (*Gnaphalium luteoalbum*)
Cudweed, Red-tipped (*Filago lutescens*)
Cut-grass (*Leersia oryzoides*)
Diapensia (*Diapensia lapponica*)
Dock, Shore (*Rumex rupestris*)
Earwort, Marsh (*Jamesoniella undulifolia*)
Eryngo, Field (*Eryngium campestre*)
Fern, Dickie's bladder (*Cystopteris dickieana*)
Fern, Killarney (*Trichomanes speciosum*)
Flapwort, Norfolk (*Leiocolea rutheana*)
Fleabane, Alpine (*Erigeron borealis*)
Fleabane, Small (*Pulicaria vulgaris*)
Fleawort, South stack (*Tephroseris integrifolia (ssp maritima)*)
Frostwort, Pointed (*Gymnomitrion apiculatum*)
Fungus, Hedgehog (*Hericium erinaceum*)
Fungus, Oak polypore (*Buglossoporus pulvinus*)
Fungus, Royal bolete (*Boletus regius*)
Fungus, Sandy stilt puffball (*Battarraea phalloides*)
Galingale, Brown (*Cyperus fuscus*)
Gentian, Alpine (*Gentiana nivalis*)
Gentian, Dune (*Gentianella uliginosa*)
Gentian, Early (*Gentianella anglica*)
Gentian, Fringed (*Gentianella ciliata*)
Gentian, Spring (*Gentiana verna*)
Germander, Cut-leaved (*Teucrium botrys*)
Germander, Water (*Teucrium scordium*)
Gladiolus, Wild (*Gladiolus illyricus*)
Goosefoot, Stinking (*Chenopodium vulvaria*)
Grass-poly (*Lythrum hyssopifolia*)
Grimmia, Blunt-leaved (*Grimmia unicolor*)
Gyalecta, Elm (*Gyalecta ulmi*)
Hare's-ear, Sickle-leaved (*Bupleurum falcatum*)
Hare's-ear, Small (*Bupleurum baldense*)
Hawk's-beard, Stinking (*Crepis foetida*)
Hawkweed, Northroe (*Hieracium northroense*)
Hawkweed, Shetland (*Hieracium zetlandicum*)
Hawkweed, Weak-leaved (*Hieracium attenuatifolium*)
Heath, Blue (*Phyllodoce caerulea*)
Helleborine, Red (*Cephalanthera rubra*)
Helleborine, Young's (*Epipactis youngiana*)
Horsetail, Branched (*Equisetum ramosissimum*)
Hound's-tongue, Green (*Cynoglossum germanicum*)
Knawel, Perennial (*Scleranthus perennis*)
Knotgrass, Sea (*Polygonum maritimum*)
Lady's-slipper (*Cypripedium calceolus*)
Lecanactis, Churchyard (*Lecanactis hemisphaerica*)
Lecanora, Tarn (*Lecanora archariana*)
Lecidea, Copper (*Lecidea inops*)
Leek, Round-headed (*Allium sphaerocephalon*)
Lettuce, Least (*Lactuca saligna*)
Lichen, Alpine sulphur-tresses (*Alectoria ochroleuca*)
Lichen, Arctic kidney (*Nephroma arcticum*)
Lichen, Ciliate strap (*Heterodermia leucomelos*)
Lichen, Convoluted cladonia (*Cladonia convoluta*)
Lichen, Coralloid rosette (*Heterodermia propagulifera*)
Lichen, Ear-lobed dog (*Peltigera lepidophora*)
Lichen, Forked hair (*Bryoria furcellata*)
Lichen, Goblin lights (*Catolechia wahlenbergii*)
Lichen, Golden hair (*Teloschistes flavicans*)
Lichen, New Forest beech-lichen (*Enterographa elaborata*)
Lichen, Orange fruited Elm (*Caloplaca luteoalba*)
Lichen, River jelly (*Collema dichotomum*)
Lichen, Scaly breck (*Squamarina lentigera*)
Lichen, Stary breck (*Buellia asterella*)
Lily, Snowdon (*Lloydia serotina*)
Liverwort, Leafy (*Petallophyllum ralfsi*)
Liverwort, Lindenberg's (*Adelanthus lindenbergianus*)
Marsh-mallow, Rough (*Althaea hirsuta*)
Marshwort, Creeping (*Apium repens*)
Milk-parsley, Cambridge (*Selinum carvifolia*)
Moss (*Drepanocladius vernicosus*)
Moss, Alpine copper (*Mielichoferia mielichoferi*)
Moss, Anomodon, long-leaved (*Anomodon longifolius*)
Moss, Baltic bog (*Sphagnum balticum*)
Moss, Blue dew (*Saelania glaucescens*)
Moss, Blunt-leaved bristle (*Orthotrichum obtusifolium*)
Moss, Bright green cave (*Cyclodictyon laetevirens*)
Moss, Cordate beard (*Barbula cordata*)
Moss, Cornish path (*Ditrichum cornubicum*)
Moss, Derbyshire feather (*Thamnobryum angustifolium*)
Moss, Dune thread (*Bryum mamillatum*)
Moss, Flamingo (*Desmatodon cernuus*)
Moss, Glaucous beard (*Barbula glauca*)

Moss, Green shield (*Buxbaumia viridis*)
Moss, Hair silk (*Plagiothecium piliferum*)
Moss, Knothole (*Zygodon forsteri*)
Moss, Large yellow feather (*Scorpidium turgescens*)
Moss, Millimetre (*Micromitrium tenerum*)
Moss, Multifruited river (*Cryphaea lamyana*)
Moss, Nowell's limestone (*Zygodon gracilis*)
Moss, Polar feather-moss (*Hygrohypnum polare*)
Moss, Rigid apple (*Bartramia stricta*)
Moss, Round-leaved feather (*Rhyncostegium rotundifolium*)
Moss, Schleicher's thread (*Bryum schleicheri*)
Moss, Threadmoss, long-leaved (*Bryum neodamense*)
Moss, Triangular pygmy (*Acaulon triquetrum*)
Moss, Vaucher's feather (*Hypnum vaucheri*)
Mudwort, Welsh (*Limosella austeralis*)
Naiad, Holly-leaved (*Najas marina*)
Naiad, Slender (*Najas flexilis*)
Orache, Stalked (*Halimione pedunculata*)
Orchid, Early spider (*Ophrys sphegodes*)
Orchid, Fen (*Liparis loeselii*)
Orchid, Ghost (*Epipogium aphyllum*)
Orchid, Lapland marsh (*Dactylorhiza lapponica*)
Orchid, Late spider (*Ophrys fuciflora*)
Orchid, Lizard (*Himantoglossum hircinum*)
Orchid, Military (*Orchis militaris*)
Orchid, Monkey (*Orchis simia*)
Panneria, Caledonia (*Panneria ignobilis*)
Parmelia, New Forest (*Parmelia minarum*)
Parmentaria, Oil stain (*Parmentaria chilensis*)
Pear, Plymouth (*Pyrus cordata*)
Penny-cress, Perfoliate (*Thlaspi perfoliatum*)
Pennyroyal (*Mentha pulegium*)
Pertusaria, Alpine moss (*Pertusaria bryontha*)
Physcia, Southern grey (*Physcia tribacioides*)
Pigmyweed (*Crassula aquatica*)
Pine, Ground (*Ajuga chamaepitys*)
Pink, Cheddar (*Dianthus gratianopolitanus*)
Pink, Childing (*Petroraghia nanteuilii*)
Pink, Deptford (*Dianthus armeria*) (England and Wales only)
Plantain, Floating water (*Luronium natans*)
Pseudocyphellaria, Ragged (*Pseudocyphellaria lacerata*)
Psora, Rusty Alpine (*Psora rubiformis*)
Ragwort, Fen (*Senecio paludosus*)
Ramping-fumitory, Martin's (*Fumaria martinii*)
Rampion, Spiked (*Phyteuma spicatum*)
Restharrow, Small (*Ononis reclinata*)
Rock-cress, Alpine (*Arabis alpina*)
Rock-cress, Bristol (*Arabis stricta*)
Rustwort, Western (*Marsupella profunda*)
Sandwort, Norwegian (*Arenaria norvegica*)
Sandwort, Teesdale (*Minuartia stricta*)
Saxifrage, Drooping (*Saxifraga cernua*)
Saxifrage, Marsh (*Saxifrage hirulus*)
Saxifrage, Tufted (*Saxifraga cespitosa*)
Solenopsora, Serpentine (*Solenopsora liparina*)
Solomon's-seal, Whorled (*Polygonatum verticillatum*)
Sow-thistle, Alpine (*Cicerbita alpina*)
Spearwort, Adder's-tongue (*Ranunculus ophioglossifolius*)
Speedwell, Fingered (*Veronica triphyllos*)
Speedwell, Spiked (*Veronica spicata*)
Spike rush, Dwarf (*Eleocharis parvula*)
Star-of-Bethlehem, Early (*Gagea bohemica*)
Starfruit (*Damasonium alisma*)
Stonewort, Bearded (*Chara canescens*)
Stonewort, Foxtail (*Lamprothamnium papulosum*)
Strapwort (*Corrigiola litoralis*)
Turpswort (*Geocalyx graveolens*)
Violet, Fen (*Viola persicifolia*)
Viper's-grass (*Scorzonera humilis*)
Water-plantain, Ribbon-leaved (*Alisma gramineum*)
Wood-sedge, Starved (*Carex depauperata*)
Woodsia, Alpine (*Woodsia alpina*)
Woodsia, Oblong (*Woodsia ilvenis*)
Wormwood, Field (*Artemisia campestris*)
Woundwort, Downy (*Stachys germanica*)
Woundwort, Limestone (*Stachys alpina*)
Yellow-rattle, Greater (*Rhinanthus serotinus*)

° The sale of plants taken from the wild is prohibited; the sale of cultivated plants is still permitted

### Most Under Threat

The animals and birds considered to be most under threat in Great Britain by the Joint Nature Conservation Committee are the high brown fritillary butterfly; violet click beetle; new forest burnet moth; corncrake; aquatic warbler; tree sparrow; wryneck; water vole; red squirrel; allis shad; and twaite shad.

# Historic Buildings and Monuments

## LISTING

Under the Planning (Listed Buildings and Conservation Areas) Act 1990, the Secretary of State for Culture, Media and Sport has a statutory duty to compile lists of buildings or groups of buildings in England which are of special architectural or historic interest. Under the Ancient Monuments and Archaeological Areas Act 1979 as amended by the National Heritage Act 1983, the Secretary of State is also responsible for compiling a schedule of ancient monuments. Decisions are taken on the advice of English Heritage (*see* page 332).

Listed buildings are classified into Grade I, Grade II* and Grade II. There are currently about 500,000 individual listed buildings in England, of which about 95 per cent are Grade II listed. Almost all pre-1700 buildings are listed, and most buildings of 1700 to 1840. English Heritage is carrying out thematic surveys of particular types of buildings with a view to making recommendations for listing, and members of the public may propose a building for consideration. The main purpose of listing is to ensure that care is taken in deciding the future of a building. No changes which affect the architectural or historic character of a listed building can be made without listed building consent (in addition to planning permission where relevant). Applications for listed building consent are normally dealt with by the local planning authority, although English Heritage is always consulted about proposals affecting Grade I and Grade II* properties. It is a criminal offence to demolish a listed building, or alter it in such a way as to affect its character, without consent.

There are currently about 22,500 scheduled monuments in England. English Heritage is carrying out a Monuments Protection Programme assessing archaeological sites with a view to making recommendations for scheduling, and members of the public may propose a monument for consideration. All monuments proposed for scheduling are considered to be of national importance. Where buildings are both scheduled and listed, ancient monuments legislation takes precedence. The main purpose of scheduling a monument is to preserve it for the future and to protect it from damage, destruction or any unnecessary interference. Once a monument has been scheduled, scheduled monument consent is required before any works are carried out. The scope of the control is more extensive and more detailed than that applied to listed buildings, but certain minor works, as detailed in the Ancient Monuments (Class Consents) Order 1994, may be carried out without consent. It is a criminal offence to carry out unauthorised work to scheduled monuments.

Under the Planning (Listed Buildings and Conservation Areas) Act 1990 and the Ancient Monuments and Archaeological Areas Act 1979, the Secretary of State for Wales is responsible for listing buildings and scheduling monuments in Wales on the advice of Cadw (*see* Regional Government section), the Historic Buildings Council for Wales (*see* page 336) and the Royal Commission on the Ancient and Historical Monuments of Wales (*see* page 359). The criteria for evaluating buildings are similar to those in England and the same listing system is used. There are approximately 19,200 listed buildings and approximately 3,000 scheduled monuments in Wales.

Under the Planning (Listed Buildings and Conservation Areas) (Scotland) Act 1997 and the Ancient Monuments and Archaeological Areas Act 1979, Scottish Ministers are responsible for listing buildings and scheduling monuments in Scotland on the advice of Historic Scotland (*see* Regional Government section), the Historic Buildings Council for Scotland (*see* page 336) and the Royal Commission on the Ancient and Historical Monuments of Scotland (*see* page 358). The criteria for evaluating buildings are similar to those in England but an A, B, C categorisation is used. There are 45,498 listed buildings and 7,439 scheduled monuments in Scotland.

Under the Planning (Northern Ireland) Order 1991 and the Historic Monuments and Archaeological Objects (Northern Ireland) Order 1995, the Department of the Environment of the Northern Ireland Executive (*see* Regional Government section) is responsible for listing buildings and scheduling monuments in Northern Ireland on the advice of the Historic Buildings Council for Northern Ireland and the Historic Monuments Council for Northern Ireland. The criteria for evaluating buildings are similar to those in England but no statutory grading system is used. In March 1999 there were 8,563 listed buildings and 1,365 scheduled monuments in Northern Ireland.

## OPENING TO THE PUBLIC

The following is a selection of the many historic buildings and monuments open to the public. Admission charges and opening hours vary. Many properties are closed in winter and some are also closed in the mornings. Most properties are closed on Christmas Eve, Christmas Day, Boxing Day and New Year's Day, and many are closed on Good Friday. During the winter season, most English Heritage monuments are closed on Mondays and Tuesdays and monuments in the care of Cadw are closed on Sunday mornings. In Northern Ireland most monuments are closed on Mondays except on bank holidays. Information about a specific property should be checked by telephone.

*Closed in winter (usually November-March)
†Closed in winter, and in mornings in summer

---

## ENGLAND

---

For more information on any of the English Heritage properties listed below, the official website is: www.english-heritage.org.uk. For more information on any of the National Heritage properties lited below, the official website is: www.nationaltrust.org.uk

EH English Heritage property
NT National Trust property

*A LA RONDE (NT), Summer Lane, Exmouth, Devon. Tel: 01395-265514.
Unique 16-sided house completed *c.*1796

†ALNWICK CASTLE, Northumberland. Tel: 01665-510777. Seat of the Dukes of Northumberland since 1309; Italian Renaissance-style interior

ALTHORP, Northants. Tel: 01604-770107, ticket reservations 01604-592020.
Spencer family seat. Diana, Princess of Wales memorabilia

†ANGLESEY ABBEY (NT), Cambs. Tel: 01223-811200. House built *c.*1600. Outstanding grounds with unique statuary

APSLEY HOUSE, London W1. Tel: 020-7499 5676. Built by Robert Adam 1771–8, home of the Dukes of Wellington since 1817 and known as 'No. 1 London'. Collection of fine and decorative arts

†ARUNDEL CASTLE, W. Sussex. Tel: 01903-883136. Castle dating from the Norman Conquest. Seat of the Dukes of Norfolk

AVEBURY (NT), Wilts. Tel: 01672-539250. Remains of stone circles constructed 4,000 years ago surrounding the later village of Avebury. Also *Alexander Keiller Museum*.

BANQUETING HOUSE, Whitehall, London SW1. Tel: 020-7930 4179. Designed by Inigo Jones; ceiling paintings by Rubens. Site of the execution of Charles I

†BASILDON PARK (NT), Berks. Tel: 0118-984 3040. Palladian house built in 1776–83

BATTLE ABBEY (EH), E. Sussex. Tel: 01424-773792. Remains of the abbey founded by William the Conqueror on the site of the Battle of Hastings

BEAULIEU, Hants. Tel: 01590-612345. House and gardens, Beaulieu Abbey and exhibition of monastic life, National Motor Museum

BEESTON CASTLE (EH), Cheshire. Tel: 01829-260464. Thirteenth-century inner ward with gatehouse and towers, and remains of outer ward

†BELTON HOUSE (NT), Grantham, Lincs. Tel: 01476-566116. Fine 17th-century house in landscaped park

*BELVOIR CASTLE, nr Grantham, Lincs. Tel: 01476-870262. Seat of the Dukes of Rutland; 19th-century Gothic-style castle

*BERKELEY CASTLE, Glos. Tel: 01453-810332. Completed 1153; site of the murder of Edward II (1327)

*BLENHEIM PALACE, Woodstock, Oxon. Tel: 01993-811325. Seat of the Dukes of Marlborough and Winston Churchill's birthplace; designed by Vanbrugh

†BLICKLING HALL (NT), Norfolk. Tel: 01263-738030. Jacobean house with state rooms, temple and 18th-century orangery

BODIAM CASTLE (NT), E. Sussex. Tel: 01580-830436. Well-preserved medieval moated castle

BOLSOVER CASTLE (EH), Derbys. Tel: 01246-823349. Notable 17th-century buildings

BOSCOBEL HOUSE (EH), Shropshire. Tel: 01902-850244. Timber-framed 17th-century hunting lodge, refuge of fugitive Charles II

†BOUGHTON HOUSE, Northants. Tel: 01536-515731. A 17th-century house with French-style additions

*BOWOOD HOUSE, Wilts. Tel: 01249-812102. An 18th-century house in Capability Brown park, with lake, temple and arboretum

†BROADLANDS, Hants. Tel: 01794-505010. Palladian mansion in Capability Brown parkland. Mountbatten exhibition

BRONTË PARSONAGE, Haworth, W. Yorks. Tel: 01535-642323. Home of the Brontë sisters; museum and memorabilia

BUCKFAST ABBEY, Devon. Tel: 01364-642519. Benedictine monastery on medieval foundations

*BUCKINGHAM PALACE, London SW1. Tel: 020-7839 1377. Purchased by George III in 1762, and the Sovereign's official London residence since 1837. Eighteen state rooms, including the Throne Room, and Picture Gallery

BUCKLAND ABBEY (NT), Devon. Tel: 01822-853607. A 13th-century Cistercian monastery. Home of Sir Francis Drake

BURGHLEY HOUSE, Stamford, Lincs. Tel: 01780-752451. Late Elizabethan house; vast state apartments

†CALKE ABBEY (NT), Derbys. Tel: 01332-863822. Baroque 18th-century mansion

CARISBROOKE CASTLE (EH), Isle of Wight. Tel: 01983-522107. Norman castle; prison of Charles I 1647-8

CARLISLE CASTLE (EH), Cumbria. Tel: 01228-606000. Medieval castle, prison of Mary Queen of Scots

*CARLYLE'S HOUSE (NT), Cheyne Row, London SW3. Tel: 020-7352 7087. Home of Thomas Carlyle

CASTLE ACRE PRIORY (EH), Norfolk. Tel: 01760-755394. Remains include 12th-century church and prior's lodgings

*CASTLE DROGO (NT), Devon. Tel: 01647-433306. Granite castle designed by Lutyens

*CASTLE HOWARD, N. Yorks. Tel: 01653-648444. Designed by Vanbrugh 1699–1726; mausoleum designed by Hawksmoor

CASTLE RISING CASTLE (EH), Norfolk. Tel: 01553-631330. A 12th-century keep in a massive earthwork with gatehouse and bridge

*CHARTWELL (NT), Kent. Tel: 01732-866368. Home of Sir Winston Churchill

*CHATSWORTH, Derbys. Tel: 01246-582204. Tudor mansion in magnificent parkland

CHESTERS ROMAN FORT (EH), Northumberland. Tel: 01434-681379. Roman cavalry fort

*CHYSAUSTER ANCIENT VILLAGE (EH), Cornwall. Tel: 0831-757934. Romano-Cornish village, 2nd and 3rd century AD, on a probably late Iron Age site

CLIFFORD'S TOWER (EH), York. Tel: 01904-646940. A 13th-century tower built on a mound

†CLIVEDEN (NT), Berks. Tel: 01628-605069. House open Thurs. and Sun. only, gardens daily. Former home of the Astors, now an hotel set in garden and woodland

CORBRIDGE ROMAN SITE (EH), Northumberland. Tel: 01434-632349. Excavated central area of a Roman town and successive military bases

CORFE CASTLE (NT), Dorset. Tel: 01929-481294. Ruined former royal castle dating from 11th-century

†CROFT CASTLE (NT), Herefordshire. Tel: 01568-780246. Pre-Conquest border castle with Georgian-Gothic interior

DEAL CASTLE (EH), Kent. Tel: 01304-372762. Largest of the coastal defence forts built by Henry VIII

DICKENS HOUSE, Doughty Street, London WC1. Tel: 020-7405 2127. House occupied by Dickens 1837–9; manuscripts, furniture and portraits

DR JOHNSON'S HOUSE, 17 Gough Square, London EC4. Tel: 020-7353 3745. Web: www.drjh.dircon.co.uk. Home of Samuel Johnson

DOVE COTTAGE, Grasmere, Cumbria. Tel: 01539-435544. Wordsworth's home 1799-1808; museum

DOVER CASTLE (EH), Kent. Tel: 01304-201628. Castle with Roman, Saxon and Norman features; wartime operations rooms

DUNSTANBURGH CASTLE (EH), Northumberland. Tel: 01665-576231. A 14th-century castle on a cliff, with a substantial gatehouse-keep

ELTHAM PALACE (EH), Court Yard, Eltham, London SE9 . Tel: 020-8294 2548. Combines a 1930s country house and remains of medieval palace set in moated gardens.

FARLEIGH HUNGERFORD CASTLE (EH), Somerset. Tel: 01225-754026. Late 14th-century castle with two courts; chapel with tomb of Sir Thomas Hungerford

*FARNHAM CASTLE KEEP (EH), Surrey. Tel: 01252-713393. Large 12th-century shell-keep

FOUNTAINS ABBEY (NT), nr Ripon, N. Yorks. Tel: 01765-608888. Deer park visitor centre, deer park and St Mary's Church. Ruined Cistercian monastery; 18th-century landscaped gardens of Studley Royal estate

FRAMLINGHAM CASTLE (EH), Suffolk. Tel: 01728-724189. Castle (*c.*1200) with high curtain walls enclosing an almshouse (1639)

FURNESS ABBEY (EH), Cumbria. Tel: 01229-823420. Remains of church and conventual buildings founded in 1123

GLASTONBURY ABBEY, Somerset. Tel: 01458-832267. Ruins of a 12th-century abbey rebuilt after fire. Site of an early Christian settlement

GOODRICH CASTLE (EH), Herefordshire. Tel: 01600-890538. Remains of 13th- and 14th-century castle with 12th-century keep

GREENWICH, London SE10. *Royal Observatory*. Tel: 020-8858 6575. Web: www.rof.nmm.ac.uk. Former Royal Observatory (founded 1675) housing the time ball and zero meridian of longitude. *The Queen's House*. Tel: 020-8858 4422. Designed for Queen Anne, wife of James I, by Inigo Jones. *Painted Hall and Chapel* (Royal Naval College). Visitors admitted to Sunday service (11 a.m.) in the chapel during college term

GRIME'S GRAVES (EH), Norfolk. Tel: 01842-810656. Neolithic flint mines. One shaft can be descended

GUILDHALL, London EC2. Tel: 020-7332 1460. Centre of civic government of the City. Built *c*.1441; facade built 1788-9

*HADDON HALL, Derbys. Tel: 01629-812855. Well-preserved 12th-century manor house

HAILES ABBEY (EH), Glos. Tel: 01242-602398. Ruins of a 13th-century Cistercian monastery

†HAM HOUSE (NT), Richmond, Surrey. Tel: 020-8940 1950. Garden open all year except Thurs. and Fri. Stuart house with fine interiors

HAMPTON COURT PALACE, East Molesey, Surrey. Tel: 020-8781 9500. A 16th-century palace with additions by Wren. Gardens with maze; Tudor tennis court (summer only)

†HARDWICK HALL (NT), Derbys. Tel: 01246-850430. Built 1591–7 for Bess of Hardwick; notable furnishings

*HARDY'S COTTAGE (NT), Dorset. Tel: 01305-262366. Higher Bockhampton, Dorset. Birthplace of Thomas Hardy

*HAREWOOD HOUSE, W. Yorks. Tel: 0113-288 6331. An 18th-century house designed by John Carr and Robert Adam; park by Capability Brown

†HATFIELD HOUSE, Herts. Tel: 01707-262823. Jacobean house built by Robert Cecil; surviving wing of Royal Palace of Hatfield (1497)

HELMSLEY CASTLE (EH), N. Yorks. Tel: 01439-770442. A 12th-century keep and curtain wall with 16th-century buildings. Spectacular earthwork defences

†HEVER CASTLE, Kent. Tel: 01732-865224. A 13th-century double-moated castle, childhood home of Anne Boleyn

*HOLKER HALL, Cumbria. Tel: 015395-58328. Former home of the Dukes of Devonshire; award-winning gardens

†HOLKHAM HALL, Norfolk. Tel: 01328-710227. Fine Palladian mansion

HOUSESTEADS ROMAN FORT (EH), Northumberland. Tel: 01434-344363. Excavated infantry fort on Hadrian's Wall with extra-mural civilian settlement

†HUGHENDEN MANOR (NT), High Wycombe. Tel: 01494-755565. Home of Disraeli; small formal garden

JANE AUSTEN'S HOUSE, Chawton, Hants. Tel: 01420-83262. Jane Austen's home 1809–17

KEDLESTON HOUSE (NT), Derby. Tel: 01332-842191. A classical Palladian mansion built 1759-65; complete Robert Adam interiors.

*KELMSCOTT MANOR, nr Lechlade, Oxon. Tel: 01367-252486. Summer home of William Morris, with products of Morris and Co.

KENILWORTH CASTLE (EH), Warks. Tel: 01926-852078. Castle with building styles from 1155 to 1649

KENSINGTON PALACE, London W8. Tel: 020-7937 7079. Built in 1605 and enlarged by Wren; bought by William and Mary in 1689. Birthplace of Queen Victoria. Royal Ceremonial Dress Collection

KENWOOD (EH), Hampstead Lane, London NW3. Tel: 020-8348 1286. Adam villa housing the Iveagh bequest of paintings and furniture. Open-air concerts in summer

*KEW, Surrey. Tel: 020-8332 5189. *Queen Charlotte's Cottage*

†KINGSTON LACY HOUSE (NT), Dorset. Tel: 01202-883402. A 17th-century house with 19th-century alterations; important art collection

†KNEBWORTH HOUSE, Herts. Tel: 01438-812661. Tudor manor house concealed by 19th-century Gothic decoration; Lutyens gardens

*KNOLE (NT), Kent. Tel: 01732-450608. House dating from 1456 set in parkland; fine art treasures

LAMBETH PALACE, London SE1. Tel: 020-7898 1200. Web: www.archbishopofcanterbury.org. Official residence of the Archbishop of Canterbury. A 19th-century house with parts dating from the 12th century

*LANERCOST PRIORY (EH), Cumbria. Tel: 01697-73030. The nave of the Augustinian priory church, *c*.1166, is still used; remains of other claustral buildings

*LANHYDROCK (NT), Cornwall. Tel: 01208-73320. House dating from the 17th century; 45 rooms, including kitchen and nursery

LEEDS CASTLE, Kent. Tel: 01622-765400. Castle dating from 9th century, on two islands in lake

†LEVENS HALL, Cumbria. Tel: 01539-560321. Elizabethan house with unique topiary garden (1694). Steam engine collection

LINCOLN CASTLE. Tel: 01522-511068. Built by William the Conqueror in 1068

LINDISFARNE PRIORY (EH), Northumberland. Tel: 01289-389200. Bishopric of the Northumbrian kingdom destroyed by the Danes; re-established in the 11th-century as a Benedictine priory, now ruined

LITTLE MORETON HALL (NT), Cheshire. Tel: 01260-272018. Timber-framed moated manor house with knot garden

LONGLEAT HOUSE, Warminster, Wilts. Tel: 01985-844400. Elizabethan house in Italian Renaissance style

LULLINGSTONE ROMAN VILLA (EH), Kent. Tel: 01322-863467. Large villa occupied for much of the Roman period; fine mosaics

MANSION HOUSE, London EC4. Tel: 020-7626 2500. The official residence of the Lord Mayor of London

MARBLE HILL HOUSE (EH), Twickenham, Middx. Tel: 020-8892 5115. English Palladian villa with Georgian paintings and furniture

*MICHELHAM PRIORY, E. Sussex. Tel: 01323-844224. Tudor house built onto an Augustinian priory

MIDDLEHAM CASTLE (EH), N. Yorks. Tel: 01969-623899. A 12th-century keep within later fortifications. Childhood home of Richard III

†MONTACUTE HOUSE (NT), Somerset. Tel: 01935-823289. Elizabethan house with National Portrait Gallery portraits from period

MOUNT GRACE PRIORY (EH), N. Yorks. Tel: 01609-883494. Carthusian monastery, with remains of monastic buildings

NETLEY ABBEY (EH), Hants. Tel: 023-8045 3076. Remains of Cistercian abbey, used as house in Tudor period

OLD SARUM (EH), Wilts. Tel: 01722-335398. Earthworks enclosing remains of the castle and the 11th-century cathedral

ORFORD CASTLE (EH), Suffolk. Tel: 01394-450472. Circular keep of *c.*1170 and remains of coastal defence castle built by Henry II

*OSBORNE HOUSE (EH), Isle of Wight. Tel: 01983-200022. Queen Victoria's seaside residence

†OSTERLEY PARK HOUSE (NT), Isleworth, Middx. Tel: 020-8568 7714. Elizabethan mansion set in parkland

PENDENNIS CASTLE (EH), Cornwall. Tel: 01326-316594. Well-preserved coastal defence castle built by Henry VIII

†PENSHURST PLACE, Kent. Tel: 01892-870307. House with medieval Baron's Hall and 14th-century gardens

†PETWORTH (NT), W. Sussex. Tel: 01798-343929. Late 17th-century house set in deer park

PEVENSEY CASTLE (EH), E. Sussex. Tel: 01323-762604. Walls of a 4th-century Roman fort; remains of an 11th-century castle

PEVERIL CASTLE (EH), Derbys. Tel: 01433-620613. A 12th-century castle defended on two sides by precipitous rocks

†POLESDEN LACEY (NT), Surrey. Tel: 01372-458203. Regency villa remodelled in the Edwardian era. Fine paintings and furnishings

PORTCHESTER CASTLE (EH), Hants. Tel: 023-9237 8291. Walls of a late Roman fort enclosing a Norman keep and an Augustinian priory church

*POWDERHAM CASTLE, Devon. Tel: 01626-890243. Medieval castle with 18th- and 19th-century alterations

†RABY CASTLE, Co. Durham. Tel: 01833-660202. A 14th-century castle with walled gardens

*RAGLEY HALL, Warks. Tel: 01789-762090. A 17th-century house with gardens, park and lake

RICHBOROUGH ROMAN FORT (EH), Kent. Tel: 01304-612013. Landing-site of the Claudian invasion in AD 43, with 3rd-century stone walls

RICHMOND CASTLE (EH), N. Yorks. Tel: 01748-822493. A 12th-century keep with 11th-century curtain wall and domestic buildings

RIEVAULX ABBEY (EH), N. Yorks. Tel: 01439-798228. Remains of a Cistercian abbey founded *c.*1131

ROCHESTER CASTLE (EH), Kent. Tel: 01634-402276. An 11th-century castle partly on the Roman city wall, with a square keep of *c.*1130

†ROCKINGHAM CASTLE, Northants. Tel: 01536-770240. Built by William the Conqueror

ROYAL PAVILION, Brighton. Tel: 01273-290900. Palace of George IV, in Chinese style with Indian exterior and Regency gardens

†RUFFORD OLD HALL (NT), Lancs. Tel: 01704-821254. A 16th-century hall with unique screen

ST AUGUSTINE'S ABBEY (EH), Canterbury, Kent. Tel: 01227-767345. Remains of Benedictine monastery, with Norman church, on site of abbey founded AD 598 by St Augustine

ST MAWES CASTLE (EH), Cornwall. Tel: 01326-270526. Coastal defence castle built by Henry VIII

ST MICHAEL'S MOUNT (NT), Cornwall. Tel: 01736-710507. A 12th-century castle with later additions, off the coast at Marazion

*SANDRINGHAM, Norfolk. Tel: 01553-772675. The Queen's private residence; a neo-Jacobean house built in 1870

SCARBOROUGH CASTLE (EH), N. Yorks. Tel: 01723-372451. Remains of 12th-century keep and curtain walls

†SHERBORNE CASTLE, Dorset. Tel: 01935-813182. Web: www.sherbournecastle.com. Sixteenth-century castle built by Sir Walter Raleigh

*SHUGBOROUGH (NT), Staffs. Tel: 01889-881388. House set in 18th-century park with monuments, temples and pavilions in the Greek Revival style

SKIPTON CASTLE, N. Yorks. Tel: 01756-792442. D-shaped castle with six round towers and beautiful inner courtyard

†SMALLHYTHE PLACE (NT), Kent. Tel: 01580-762334. Half-timbered 16th-century house; home of Ellen Terry 1899-1928

†STANFORD HALL, Leics. Tel: 01788-860250. William and Mary house with Stuart portraits. Motorcycle museum

STONEHENGE (EH), Wilts. Tel: 01980-624715. Prehistoric monument consisting of concentric stone circles surrounded by a ditch and bank

†STONOR PARK, Oxon. Tel: 01491-638587. Medieval house with Georgian facade. Centre of Roman Catholicism after the Reformation

†STOURHEAD (NT), Wilts. Tel: 09001-335205. English Palladian mansion with famous gardens

*STRATFIELD SAYE HOUSE, Hants. Tel: 01256-882882. Web: www.stratfield-saye.co.uk. House built 1630-40; home of the Dukes of Wellington since 1817

STRATFORD-UPON-AVON, Warks. *Shakespeare's Birthplace* with Shakespeare Centre; *Anne Hathaway's Cottage*, home of Shakespeare's wife; *Mary Arden's House*, home of Shakespeare's mother; *Nash's House and New Place*, where Shakespeare died; and *Hall's Croft*, home of Shakespeare's daughter. Tel: 01789-204016. Web: www.shakespeare.org.uk. Also *Grammar School* attended by Shakespeare, *Holy Trinity Church*, where Shakespeare is buried, *Royal Shakespeare Theatre* (burnt down 1926, rebuilt 1932) and *Swan Theatre* (opened 1986)

*SUDELEY CASTLE, Glos. Tel: 01242-602308. Castle built in 1442; restored in the 19th century

SYON HOUSE, Brentford, Middx. Tel: 020-8560 0883. Built on the site of a former monastery; Adam interior

TILBURY FORT (EH), Essex. Tel: 01375-858489. A 17th-century coastal fort

TINTAGEL CASTLE (EH), Cornwall. Tel: 01840-770328. A 12th-century cliff-top castle and Dark Age settlement site

TOWER OF LONDON, London EC3N 4AB. Tel: 020-7709 0765. Web: www.hrp.org.uk. Royal palace and fortress begun by William the Conqueror in 1078. Houses the Crown Jewels

*TRERICE (NT), Cornwall. Tel: 01637-875404. Elizabethan manor house

TYNEMOUTH PRIORY AND CASTLE (EH), Tyne and Wear. Tel: 0191-257 1090. Remains of a Benedictine priory, founded *c.*1090, on Saxon monastic site

†UPPARK (NT), W. Sussex. Tel: 01730-825857. Late 17th-century house, completely restored after fire. Fetherstonhaugh art collection

WALMER CASTLE (EH), Kent. Tel: 01304-364288. One of Henry VIII's coastal defence castles, now the residence of the Lord Warden of the Cinque Ports

WALTHAM ABBEY (EH), Essex. Tel: 01992-702200. Ruined abbey including the nave of the abbey church, 'Harold's Bridge' and late 14th-century gatehouse. Traditionally the burial place of Harold II (1066)

WARKWORTH CASTLE (EH), Northumberland. Tel: 01665-711423. A 15th-century keep amidst earlier ruins, with 14th-century hermitage upstream

WARWICK CASTLE. Tel: 01926-406600. Medieval castle with Madame Tussaud's waxworks, in Capability Brown parkland

WHITBY ABBEY (EH), N. Yorks. Tel: 01947-603568. Remains of Norman church on the site of a monastery founded in AD 657

*WILTON HOUSE, Wilts. Tel: 01722-746720. A 17th-century house on the site of a Tudor house and Saxon abbey

WINDSOR CASTLE, Berks. Tel: 01753-831118. Official residence of The Queen; oldest royal residence still in regular use. Also *St George's Chapel*

*WOBURN ABBEY, Beds. Tel: 01525-290666. Built on the site of a Cistercian abbey; seat of the Dukes of Bedford. Important art collection; antiques centre

WROXETER ROMAN CITY (EH), Shropshire. Tel: 01743-761330. Second-century public baths and part of the forum of the Roman town of Viroconium

## WALES

For more information on any of the National Trust properties listed below, the official website is: www.nationaltrust.org.uk. For more information on any of the Cadw properties listed below, the official website is: www.cadw.wales.gov.uk

(C) Property of Cadw: Welsh Historic Monuments
(NT) National Trust property

BEAUMARIS CASTLE (C), Anglesey. Tel: 01248-810361. Concentrically-planned castle, still almost intact

CAERLEON ROMAN BATHS AND AMPHITHEATRE (C), nr Newport. Tel: 01633-890104. Rare example of a legionary bath-house and late 1st-century arena surrounded by bank for spectators

CAERNARFON CASTLE (C). Tel: 01286-677617. Important Edwardian castle built, with the town wall, between 1283 and 1330

CAERPHILLY CASTLE (C). Tel: 029 2088 3143. Concentrically-planned castle (*c*.1270) notable for its scale and use of water defences

CARDIFF CASTLE. Tel: 029-2087 8100. Castle built on the site of a Roman fort; spectacular towers and rich interior

CASTELL COCH (C), nr Cardiff. Tel: 029-2081 0101. Rebuilt 1875-90 on medieval foundations

CHEPSTOW CASTLE (C). Tel: 01291-624065. Rectangular keep amid extensive fortifications

CONWY CASTLE (C). Tel: 01492-592358. Built by Edward I, 1283-7

*CRICCIETH CASTLE (C). Tel: 01766-522227. Native Welsh 13th-century castle, altered by Edward I

DENBIGH CASTLE (C). Tel: 01745-813385. Remains of the castle (begun 1282), including triple-towered gatehouse

HARLECH CASTLE (C). Tel: 01766-780552. Well-preserved Edwardian castle, constructed 1283-90, on an outcrop above the former shoreline

PEMBROKE CASTLE. Tel: 01646-681510. Web: www.pembrokecastle.co.uk. Castle founded in 1093; Great Tower built 1200; birthplace of King Henry VII

*PENRHYN CASTLE (NT), Bangor. Tel: 01248-353084. Neo-Norman castle built in the 19th-century. Industrial railway museum

PORTMEIRION, Penrhyndeudraeth. Tel: 01766-770228. Village in Italianate style

†POWIS CASTLE (NT), nr Welshpool. Tel: 01938-557018. Medieval castle with interior in variety of styles; 17th-century gardens and Clive of India museum

RAGLAN CASTLE (C). Tel: 01291-690228. Remains of 15th-century castle with moated hexagonal keep

ST DAVIDS BISHOP'S PALACE (C), St Davids. Tel: 01437-720517. Remains of residence of Bishops of St Davids built 1328–47

TINTERN ABBEY (C), nr Chepstow. Tel: 01291-689251. Remains of 13th-century church and conventual buildings of a Cistercian monastery

*TRETOWER COURT AND CASTLE (C), nr Crickhowell. Tel: 01874-730279. Medieval house with remains of 12th-century castle nearby

## SCOTLAND

For more information on any of the Historic Scotland properties listed below, the official website is: www.historic-scotland.gov.uk
For more information on any of the National Trust For Scotland properties listed below, the official website is: www.nts.org.uk

(HS) Historic Scotland property
(NTS) National Trust for Scotland property

ANTONINE WALL, between the Clyde and the Forth. Built about AD 142, consists of ditch, turf rampart and road, with forts every two miles

BALMORAL CASTLE, nr Braemar. Tel: 013397-42334. Web: www.balmoralcastle.com. Baronial-style castle built for Victoria and Albert. The Queen's private residence

BLACK HOUSE, ARNOL (HS), Lewis, Western Isles. Tel: 01851-710395. Traditional Lewis thatched house

*BLAIR CASTLE, Blair Atholl. Tel: 01796-481207. Mid 18th-century mansion with 13th-century tower; seat of the Dukes of Atholl

*BONAWE IRON FURNACE (HS), Argyll and Bute. Tel: 01866-822432. Charcoal-fuelled ironworks founded in 1753

†BOWHILL, Selkirk. Tel: 01750-22204. Seat of the Dukes of Buccleuch and Queensberry; fine collection of paintings, including portrait miniatures

BROUGH OF BIRSAY (HS), Orkney. Remains of Norse church and village on the tidal island of Birsay

CAERLAVEROCK CASTLE (HS), nr Dumfries. Tel: 01387-770244. Fine early classical Renaissance building

CALANAIS STANDING STONES (HS), Lewis, Western Isles. Tel: 01851-621422. Standing stones in a cross-shaped setting, dating from 3000 BC

CATHERTUNS (BROWN AND WHITE) (HS), nr Brechin. Two large Iron Age hill forts

*CAWDOR CASTLE, Inverness. Tel: 01667-404615. A 14th-century keep with 15th- and 17th-century additions

CLAVA CAIRNS (HS), Highland. Late Neolithic or early Bronze Age cairns

*CRATHES CASTLE (NTS), nr Banchory. Tel: 01330-844525. A 16th-century baronial castle in woodland, fields and gardens

*CULZEAN CASTLE (NTS), S. Ayrshire. Tel: 01655-760274. An 18th-century Adam castle with oval staircase and circular saloon

DRYBURGH ABBEY (HS), Scottish Borders. Tel: 01835-822381. A 12th-century abbey containing tomb of Sir Walter Scott

*DUNVEGAN CASTLE, Skye. Tel: 01470-521206. A 13th-century castle with later additions; home of the chiefs of the Clan MacLeod; trips to seal colony

EDINBURGH CASTLE (HS). Tel: 0131-225 9846. Includes the Scottish National War Memorial, Scottish United Services Museum and historic apartments

EDZELL CASTLE (HS), nr Brechin. Tel: 01356-648631. Medieval tower house; unique walled garden

*EILEAN DONAN CASTLE, Wester Ross. Tel: 01599-555202. A 13th-century castle with Jacobite relics

ELGIN CATHEDRAL (HS), Moray. Tel: 01343-547171. A 13th-century cathedral with fine chapterhouse

*FLOORS CASTLE, Kelso. Tel: 01573-223333. Largest inhabited castle in Scotland; seat of the Dukes of Roxburghe

FORT GEORGE (HS), Highland. Tel: 01667-462777. An 18th-century fort

*GLAMIS CASTLE, Angus. Tel: 01307-840393. Seat of the Lyon family (later Earls of Strathmore and Kinghorne) since 1372

GLASGOW CATHEDRAL (HS). Tel: 0141-552 6891. Medieval cathedral with elaborately vaulted crypt

GLENELG BROCH (HS), Highlands. Two broch towers with well-preserved structural features

*HOPETOUN HOUSE, nr Edinburgh. Tel: 0131-331 2451. House designed by Sir William Bruce, enlarged by William Adam

HUNTLY CASTLE (HS). Tel: 01466-793191. Ruin of a 16th- and 17th-century house

*INVERARAY CASTLE, Argyll. Tel: 01499-302203. Gothic-style 18th-century castle; seat of the Dukes of Argyll

IONA ABBEY, Inner Hebrides. Tel: 01681-700 793. Monastery founded by St Columba in AD 563

*JARLSHOF (HS), Shetland. Tel: 01950-460112. Remains from Stone Age

JEDBURGH ABBEY (HS), Scottish Borders. Tel: 01835-863925. Romanesque and early Gothic church founded *c.*1138

KELSO ABBEY (HS), Scottish Borders. Remains of great abbey church founded 1128

LINLITHGOW PALACE (HS). Tel: 01506-842896. Ruin of royal palace in park setting. Birthplace of Mary, Queen of Scots

MAES HOWE (HS), Orkney. Tel: 01856-761606. Neolithic tomb

*MEIGLE SCULPTURED STONES (HS), Angus. Tel: 01828-640612. Celtic Christian stones

MELROSE ABBEY (HS), Scottish Borders. Tel: 01896-822562. Ruin of Cistercian abbey founded *c.*1136

MOUSA BROCH (HS), Shetland. Finest surviving Iron Age broch tower

NETHER LARGIE CAIRNS (HS), Argyll and Bute. Bronze Age and Neolithic cairns

NEW ABBEY CORN MILL (HS), nr Dumfries. Tel: 01387-850260. Water-powered mill

PALACE OF HOLYROODHOUSE, Edinburgh. Tel: 0131-556 7371. The Queen's official Scottish residence. Main part of the palace built 1671-9

RING OF BROGAR (HS), Orkney. Neolithic circle of upright stones with an enclosing ditch

RUTHWELL CROSS (HS), Dumfries and Galloway. Seventh-century Anglian cross

ST ANDREWS CASTLE AND CATHEDRAL (HS), Fife. Tel: 01334-477196 (castle); 01334-472563 (cathedral). Ruins of 13th-century castle and remains of the largest cathedral in Scotland

*SCONE PALACE, Perth. Tel: 01738-552300. House built 1802-13 on the site of a medieval palace

SKARA BRAE (HS), Orkney. Tel: 01856-841815. Stone-Age village with adjacent 17th-century house

*SMAILHOLM TOWER (HS), Scottish Borders. Tel: 01573-460365. Well-preserved tower-house

STIRLING CASTLE (HS). Tel: 01786-450000. Great Hall and gatehouse of James IV, palace of James V, Chapel Royal remodelled by James VI

TANTALLON CASTLE (HS), E. Lothian. Tel: 01620-892727. Fortification with earthwork defences and a 14th-century curtain wall with towers

*THREAVE CASTLE (HS), Dumfries and Galloway. Tel: 0831-168512. Late 14th-century tower on an island; reached by boat, long walk to castle

URQUHART CASTLE (HS), Loch Ness. Tel: 01456-450551. Castle remains with well-preserved tower

## NORTHERN IRELAND

For more information on any of the National Trust properties listed below, the official website is: www.nationaltrust.org.uk

DE Property in the care of the Northern Ireland Department of the Environment

NT National Trust property

CARRICKFERGUS CASTLE (DE), Co. Antrim. Tel: 01960-351273. Castle begun in 1180 and garrisoned until 1928

†CASTLE COOLE (NT), Enniskillen. Tel: 01365-322690. An 18th-century mansion by James Wyatt in parkland

†CASTLE WARD (NT), Co. Down. Tel: 01396-881204. An 18th-century house with Classical and Gothic facades

*DEVENISH ISLAND (DE), Co. Fermanagh. Island monastery founded in the 6th century by St Molaise

DOWNHILL CASTLE (NT), Co. Londonderry. Tel: 01265-848728. Ruins of palatial house in landscaped estate including Mussenden Temple.

DUNLUCE CASTLE (DE), Co. Antrim. Tel: 012657-31938. Ruins of 16th-century stronghold of the MacDonnells

†FLORENCE COURT (NT), Co. Fermanagh. Tel: 01365-348249. Mid–18th-century house with rococo plasterwork

*GREY ABBEY (DE), Co. Down. Tel: 01247-788585. Substantial remains of a Cistercian abbey founded in 1193

HILLSBOROUGH FORT (DE), Co. Down. Built in 1650

†MOUNT STEWART (NT), Co. Down. Tel: 012477-88387. An 18th-century house, childhood home of Lord Castlereagh

NENDRUM MONASTERY (DE), Mahee Island, Co. Down. Founded in the 5th century by St Machaoi

*TULLY CASTLE (DE), Co. Fermanagh. Fortified house and bawn built in 1613

*WHITE ISLAND (DE), Co. Fermanagh. Tenth-century monastery and 12th-century church. Access by ferry

# Presidents of the Royal Academy

The President is elected by members of the Royal Academy from among their number and is subject only to the authority of the Sovereign. The post was usually held for life until the early 20th century. The President now retires at his own discretion.

Sir Joshua Reynolds (1723–92), appointed 1768
Benjamin West (1738–1820), appointed 1792
James Wyatt (1746–1813), appointed 1805
Benjamin West (1738–1820), appointed 1806
Sir Thomas Lawrence (1769–1830), appointed 1820
Sir Martin Shee (1770–1850), appointed 1830
Sir Charles Eastlake (1793–1865), appointed 1850
Sir Francis Grant (1803–78), appointed 1866
Lord Leighton (1830–96), appointed 1878
Sir John Millais (1829–96), appointed 1896
Sir Edward Poynter (1836–1919), appointed 1896
Sir Aston Webb (1849–1930), appointed 1919
Sir Francis Dicksee (1853–1928), appointed 1924
Sir William Llewellyn (1863–1941), appointed 1928
Sir Edwin Lutyens (1869–1944), appointed 1938
Sir Alfred Munnings (1878–1959), appointed 1944
Sir Gerald Kelly (1879–1972), appointed 1949
Sir Albert Richardson (1880–1964), appointed 1954
Sir Charles Wheeler (1892–1974), appointed 1956
Sir Thomas Monnington (1902–76), appointed 1966
Sir Hugh Casson (1910–), appointed 1976
Sir Roger de Grey (1918–95), appointed 1984
Sir Philip Dowson (1924–), appointed 1993
Prof. Philip King (1934–), appointed 1999

# Museums and Galleries

There are more than 2,500 museums and galleries in the United Kingdom. Over 1,800 are registered with Resource: The Council for Museums, Archives and Libraries, formerly the Museums and Galleries Commission, which indicates that they have an appropriate constitution, are soundly financed, have adequate collection management standards and public services, and have access to professional curatorial advice. Museums must achieve full or provisional registration status in order to be eligible for grants from Resource and from Area Museums Councils. Over 700 of the registered museums are run by a local authority.

The national museums and galleries receive direct government grant-in-aid. These are: British Museum; Imperial War Museum; National Army Museum; National Galleries of Scotland; National Gallery; National Maritime Museum; National Museums and Galleries on Merseyside; National Museum of Wales; National Museums of Scotland; National Portrait Gallery; Natural History Museum; RAF Museum; Royal Armouries; Science Museum; Tate Gallery; Ulster Folk and Transport Museum; Ulster Museum; Victoria and Albert Museum; Wallace Collection. An online art museum (Web: www.24hourmuseum.org.uk) has also been awarded national collection status.

Local authority museums are funded by the local authority and may also receive grants from Resource. Independent museums and galleries mainly rely on their own resources but are also eligible for grants from the Museums and Galleries Commission.

The former Museums and Galleries Commission identified 26 non-national museum bodies which have pre-eminent collections of more than local or regional importance. Some of those designated are museum services with a wide variety of collections; others are small and more focused in a particular field. Ten Area Museum Councils in the UK, which are independent charities, give advice and support to the museums in their area and may offer improvement grants. They also circulate exhibitions and assist with training and marketing.

### Opening to the Public

The following is a selection of the museums and art galleries in the United Kingdom. Opening hours and admission charges vary. Most museums are closed on Christmas Eve, Christmas Day, Boxing Day and New Year's Day; many are closed on Good Friday, and some are closed on May Day Bank Holiday. Some smaller museums close at lunchtimes. Information about a specific museum or gallery should be checked by telephone.

## ENGLAND

* Local authority museum/gallery
† Museum/gallery contains a collection designated pre-eminent

Barnard Castle, Co. Durham – *†*The Bowes Museum*, Westwick Road DR12 8NP. Tel: 01833-690606; Web: www.barnard-castle.co.uk
European art from the late medieval period to the 19th century; music and costume galleries; English period rooms from Elizabeth I to Victoria; local archaeology

Bath – *American Museum in Britain*, Claverton Manor BA2 7BD. Tel: 01225-460503; Web: www.americanmuseum.org
American decorative arts from the 17th to 19th century
**Museum of Costume*, Bennett Street BA1 2EW. Tel: 01225-477752; Web: www.museumofcostume.co.uk
Fashion from the 16th century to the present day
**Roman Baths Museum*, Abbey Church Yard BA1 1LZ. Tel: 01225-477774; Web: www.romanbaths.co.uk
Museum adjoins the remains of a Roman baths and temple complex
**Victoria Art Gallery*, Bridge Street BA2 4AT. Tel: 01225-477772; Web: www.victoria.gal.org.uk
European Old Masters and British art since the 18th century

Beamish, Co. Durham – *†*Beamish, The North of England Open Air Museum*, DH9 0RG Tel: 0191-370 4000; Web: www.countydurham.com/beamish.
Recreated northern town *c.*1900, with rebuilt and furnished local buildings, colliery village, farm, railway station, tramway, Pockerley Manor and horse-yard (set *c.*1800)

Beaulieu, Hants – †*National Motor Museum*. SO42 7ZN. Tel: 01590-612345; Web: www.beaulieu.co.uk
Displays of over 250 vehicles dating from 1895 to the present day

Birmingham – *†*Aston Hall*, Trinity Road, B6 6JD. Tel: 0121-327 0062.
Jacobean House containing paintings, furniture and tapestries from 17th to 19th century
*†*Barber Institute of Fine Arts*, off Edgbaston Park Road, B15 2TS. Tel: 0121-472 0962; Web: www.barber.org.uk
Fine arts, including Old Masters
**Birmingham Nature Centre*, Edgbaston, B5 7RL. Tel: 0121-472 7775.
Indoor and outdoor enclosures displaying wildlife, especially British and European
*†*City Museum and Art Gallery*, Chamberlain Square. Tel: 0121-303 2834; Web: www.bmag.org.uk/museum_and_art_gallery
Includes notable collection of Pre-Raphaelites
*†*Museum of the Jewellery Quarter*, Vyse Street, Hockley. Tel: 0121-554 3598; Web: www.bmag.org.uk/jewellery_quarter
Built around a real jewellery workshop
*†*Soho House*, Soho Avenue. Tel: 0121-554 9122; Web: www.bmag.org.uk/soho_house
Eighteenth-century home of industrialist Matthew Boulton

Bovington Camp, Dorset – †*Tank Museum* BH20 6JD. Tel: 01929-405096; Web: www.tankmuseum.org.uk
Collection of 300 tanks from the earliest days of tank warfare to the present

Bradford – **Cartwright Hall Art Gallery*, Lister Park BD9 4NS. Tel: 01274-493313.
British 19th- and 20th-century fine art
**Industrial Museum and Horses at Work*, Moorside Road BD2 3HP. Tel: 01274-631756; Web: www.bradford.gov.uk
Engineering, textiles, transport and social history exhibits, including recreated back-to-back cottages, shire horses and horse tram-rides
*National Museum of Photography, Film and Television* BD1 1NQ. Tel: 01274-202030; Web: www.nmpft.org.uk

Photography, film and television interactive exhibits. Features the UK's first IMAX cinema and the only public Cinerama screen in the world

BRIGHTON – *†*Booth Museum of Natural History*, Dyke Road. Tel: 01273-292777.
Zoology, botany and geology collections; British birds in recreated habitats

*†*Brighton Museum and Art Gallery*, Church Street, BN1 1UE. Tel: 01273-290900;
Web: www.royalpavilion.brighton.co.uk
Includes fine art and design, fashion, non-Western art, Brighton history

BRISTOL – *Arnolfini Gallery*, Narrow Quay BS1 4QA. Tel: 0117-929 9191; Web: www.arnolfini.demon.co.uk
Contemporary visual arts, dance, performance, music, talks and workshops

*†*Blaise Castle House Museum*, Henbury BS10 7QS. Tel: 0117-950 6789; Web: www.bristol-city.gov.uk
Agricultural and social history collections in an 18th-century mansion

*†*Bristol Industrial Museum*, Prince Street BS1 4RN. Tel: 0117-925 1470; Web: www.bristol-city.gov.uk
Industrial, maritime and transport collections

*†*City Museum and Art Gallery*, Queen's Road B58 1RL Tel: 0117-922 3571;
Web: www.bristol-city.gov.uk/museums
Includes fine and decorative art, oriental art, Egyptology and Bristol ceramics and paintings

CAMBRIDGE – *Duxford Airfield*, Duxford CB2 4QR Tel: 01223-835000; Web: www.lwm.org.uk
Displays of military and civil aircraft, tanks, guns and naval exhibits

†*Fitzwilliam Museum*, Trumpington Street CB2 1RB. Tel: 01223-332900; Web: www.fitzmuseum.cam.ac.uk
Antiquities, fine and applied arts, clocks, ceramics, manuscripts, furniture, sculpture, coins and medals, temporary exhibitions

†*Sedgwick Museum of Geology*, Downing Street, CB2 3EQ. Tel: 01223-333456;
Extensive geological collection

†*University Museum of Archaeology and Anthropology*, Downing Street CB2 3EJ. Tel: 01223-333516;
Web: www.cumaa.archanth.cam/museum.htm
Archaeology and anthropology from all parts of the world

†*University Museum of Zoology*, Downing Street CB2 3EJ. Tel: 01223-336650; Web: www.zoo.cam.ac.uk
Extensive zoological collection

†*Whipple Museum of the History of Science*, Free School Lane CB2 3RH. Tel: 01223-330906
Scientific instruments from the 14th century to the present

CARLISLE – **Tullie House Museum and Art Gallery*, Castle Street CA3 8TP. Tel: 01228-534781.
Prehistoric archaeology, Hadrian's Wall, Viking and medieval Cumbria, and the social history of Carlisle; also British 19th- and 20th-century art and English porcelain

CHATHAM - *World Naval Base* ME4 4TZ Tel: 01634-823800;
Web: www.worldnavalbase.org.uk
Maritime attractions including HMS *Cavalier*, the UK's last World War II destroyer

†*Royal Engineers Museum*, Brompton Barracks ME4 4U9. Tel: 01634-406397; Web: www.royalengineers.org.uk
Regimental history, ethnography, decorative art and photography

CHELTENHAM – *Art Gallery and Museum*, Clarence Street GL50 3JT. Tel: 01242-237431;
Web: www.cheltenhammuseum.org.uk
Paintings, arts and crafts

CHESTER – **Grosvenor Museum*, Grosvenor Street CH1 2DD. Tel: 01244-321616;
Web: www.chestercc.gov.uk
Roman collections, natural history, art, Chester silver, local history and costume

CHICHESTER – †*Weald and Downland Open Air Museum*, Singleton PO18 0EU. Tel: 01243-811348;
Web: www.wealddown.co.uk
Rebuilt vernacular buildings from south-east England; includes medieval houses, agricultural and rural craft buildings and a working watermill

COLCHESTER – *†*Colchester Castle Museum*, Castle Park CO1 1YG. Tel: 01206-282931;
Web: www.colchestercastle.co.uk
Largest Norman keep in Europe standing on foundations of roman Temple of Claudius; tours of the Roman vaults, castle walls and chapel with medieval and prison displays

COVENTRY – **Herbert Art Gallery and Museum*, Jordan Well CV1 5QP. Tel: 024-7683 2565;
Web: www.coventrymuseum.org.uk
Local history, archaeology and industry, and fine and decorative art

*†*Museum of British Road Transport*, Hales Street CV1 1PN. Tel: 024-7683 2425; Web: www.mbrt.co.uk
Hundreds of motor vehicles and bicycles

CRICH, nr Matlock, Derbys – †*National Tramway Museum* BE4 5DP. Tel: 01773-852565; Web: www.tramway.co.uk
Open-air working museum with tram rides

DERBY – **Derby Museum and Art Gallery*, The Strand DE1 1BS. Tel: 01332-716659;
Web: www.derby.gov.uk/museums
Includes paintings by Joseph Wright of Derby and Derby porcelain

**Industrial Museum*, off Full Street DE1 3AR. Tel: 01332-255308;
Web: www.derby.gov.uk/museums
Rolls-Royce aero engine collection and a railway engineering gallery

DEVIZES – †Wiltshire Heritage *Museum*, Long Street SN10 1NS. Tel: 01380-727369;
Web: www.devizes-dc.gov.uk/museums
Natural and local history, art gallery, archaeological finds from Bronze Age, Iron Age, Roman and Saxon sites

DORCHESTER – *Dorset County Museum*, High West Street, DT1 1XA. Tel: 01305-262735
Includes a collection of Thomas Hardy's manuscripts, books, notebooks and drawings

DOVER - *Dover Museum*, Market Square CT16 1PB. Tel: 01304-201066; Web: www.dovermuseum.co.uk
Contains Dover Bronze Age Boat Gallery and archaeological finds from the Bronze Age, Roman and Saxon sites.

ELLESMERE PORT – *Boat Museum*, South Pier Road CH65 4FW. Tel: 0151-355 5017;
Web: www.boatmuseum.co.uk
Craft and boating history

EXETER – *†*Royal Albert Memorial Museum*, Queen Street EX4 3RX. Tel: 01392-265858; Web: www.exeter.gov.uk
Natural history, archaeology, worldwide fine and decorative art including Exeter silver

GATESHEAD – *Shipley Art Gallery*, Prince Consort Road NE8 4JB. Tel: 0191-477 1495.
Contemporary crafts

GAYDON, Warwick – *British Motor Industry Heritage Trust*, Heritage Motor Centre, Banbury Road CB35 0BJ. Tel: 01926-641188; Web; www.heritage.org.uk

History of British motor industry from 1895 to present; classic vehicles; engineering gallery; Corgi and Lucas collections

GLOUCESTER, – †*National Waterways Museum*, Llanthony Warehouse, Gloucester Docks GL1 2EH. Tel: 01452-318054; Web: www.nwm.org.uk
Two-hundred-year history of Britain's canals and inland waterways

GOSPORT, Hants – *Royal Navy Submarine Museum*, Haslar Jetty Road PO12 2AS. Tel: 023-9252 9217; Web: www.rnsbmus.co.uk
Underwater warfare, including the submarine *Alliance*; historical and nuclear galleries; and first Royal Navy submarine

GRASMERE, Cumbria – †*Dove Cottage* and the *Wordsworth Museum* LA22 9SH. Web: www.wordsworth.org.uk

HALIFAX – *Eureka! The Museum for Children*, Discovery Road HX1 2NE. Tel: 01426-983191; Web: www.eureka.org.uk
Hands-on museum designed for children up to age 12

HULL – **Ferens Art Gallery*, Queen Victoria Square HU1 3RA. Tel: 01482-613902; Web: www.hullcc.gov.uk/museums/index.htm
European art, especially Dutch 17th-century paintings, British portraits from 17th- to 20th-century, and marine paintings

**Town Docks Museum*, Queen Victoria Square HU1 3DX. Tel: 01482-613902; Web: www.hullcc.gov.uk/museums
Whaling, fishing and navigation exhibits

HUNTINGDON – **Cromwell Museum*, Grammar School Walk P29 3LS. Tel: 01480-375830; Web:www.cromwell.argonet.co.uk.
Portraits and memorabilia relating to Oliver Cromwell

IPSWICH – **Christchurch Mansion and Wolsey Art Gallery*, Christchurch Park IP4 2BE. Tel: 01473-253246.
Tudor house with paintings by Gainsborough, Constable and other Suffolk artists; furniture and 18th-century ceramics. Art gallery for temporary exhibitions

LEEDS – *†*City Art Gallery*, The Headrow LS1 3AA. Tel: 0113-247 8248.
British and European paintings including English watercolours, modern sculpture, Henry Moore gallery, print room

**Leeds Industrial Museum* at Armley Mills, Canal Road, Armley LS12 2QF. Tel: 0113-263 7861; Web: www.leeds.gov.uk.
Largest woollen mill in world

*†*Lotherton Hall*, Aberford. Tel: 0113-281 3259.
Costume and oriental collections in furnished Edwardian house; deer park and bird garden

*Royal Armouries Museum*, Armouries Drive. Tel: 0113-220-1940.
National collection of arms and armour from BC to present; demonstrations of foot combat in museum's five galleries; falconry and mounted combat in the tiltyard

*†*Temple Newsam House* LS15 7SE. Tel: 0113-264 7321.
Old Masters and 17th- and 18th-century decorative art in furnished Jacobean/Tudor house

LEICESTER – **Jewry Wall Museum*, St Nicholas Circle. Tel: 0116-247 3021
Archaeology, Roman Jewry Wall and baths, and mosaics

**New Walk Museum and Art Gallery*, New Walk LE1 7EA. Tel: 0116-255 4100; Web: www.leicestermuseums.ac.uk
Natural history, geology, ancient Egypt gallery, European art and decorative arts

**Snibston Discovery Park*, Coalville LE67 3LN. Tel: 01530-510851.
Open-air science and industry museum on site of a coal mine; country park with nature trail

LINCOLN – **Museum of Lincolnshire Life*, Burton Road LN1 3LY. Tel: 01522-528448.
Social history and agricultural collection

**Usher Gallery*, Lindum Road LN2 1NN. Tel: 01522-527980.
Watches, miniatures, porcelain, silver; collection of Peter de Wint works; Lincolnshire topography and Royal Lincs Regiment memorabilia

LIVERPOOL – *Lady Lever Art Gallery*, Wirral CH62 4EQ. Tel: 0151-478 4136; Web: www.portsunlight.org.uk
Paintings, furniture and porcelain

*Liverpool Museum*, William Brown Street L3 8EN. Tel: 0151-478 4399; Web: www.nmgm.org.uk.
Includes Egyptian mummies, weapons and classical sculpture; planetarium, aquarium, vivarium and natural history centre

*Merseyside Maritime Museum*, Albert Dock L3 4AQ. Tel: 0151-478 4499; Web: www.nmgm.org.uk.
Floating exhibits, working displays and craft demonstrations; incorporates *HM Customs and Excise National Museum*

*Museum of Liverpool Life*, Mann Island L3 4AA. Tel: 0151-478 4080; Web: www.nmgm.org.uk.
The history of Liverpool

*Sudley House*, Mossley Hill Road. Tel: 0151-724 3245.
Late 18th- and 19th-century British paintings in former shipowner's home

*Tate Gallery Liverpool*, Albert Dock L3 4BB. Tel: 0151-709 3223; Web: www.tate.org.uk.
Twentieth-century painting and sculpture

*Walker Art Gallery*, William Brown Street. Tel: 0151-478 4199.
Paintings from the 14th to 20th century

LONDON: GALLERIES – **Barbican Art Gallery*, Barbican Centre EC2Y 8DS. Tel: 020-7382 7105; Web: www.barbican.org.uk.
Temporary exhibitions

†*Courtauld Gallery*, Somerset House, Strand, WC2. Tel: 020-7848 2526.
The University of London galleries

†*Dulwich Picture Gallery*, College Road, SE21 7AD. Tel: 020-8693 5254; Web: www.dulwichpicturegalleryorg.uk.
Built by Sir John Soane to house 17th- and 18th-century paintings

*Hayward Gallery*, Belvedere Road, SE18 XE2. Tel: 020-7928 3144; Web: www.haywardgallery.org.uk
Temporary exhibitions

*National Gallery*, Trafalgar Square, WC2N 5DN. Tel: 020-7839 3321; Web: www.nationalgallery.org.uk.
Western painting from the 13th to 20th century; early Renaissance collection in the Sainsbury wing

*National Portrait Gallery*, St Martin's Place, WC2H 0HE. Tel: 020-7306 0055; Web: www.npg.org.uk.
Portraits of eminent people in British history

*Percival David Foundation of Chinese Art*, Gordon Square, WC1H 0PD. Tel: 020-7387 3909.
Chinese ceramics from tenth to 18th-century

*Photographers Gallery*, Great Newport Street, WC2. Tel: 020-7831 1772; Web: www.photonet.org.uk
Temporary exhibitions

*The Queen's Gallery*, Buckingham Palace, SW1A 1AA. Tel: 020-7839 1377; Web: www.royal.org.uk
Art from the Royal Collection

*Royal Academy of Arts*, Piccadilly, W1V 0DS.
Tel: 020-7300 8000; Web: www.royalacademy.org.uk.
British art since 1750 and temporary exhibitions; annual Summer Exhibition
*Saatchi Gallery*, Boundary Road, NW8 0RH.
Tel: 020-7624 8299; Web: www.saatchigallery.org.uk
Contemporary art including paintings, photographs, sculpture and installations
*Serpentine Gallery*, Kensington Gardens, W2 3XA.
Tel: 020-7298 1515;
Web: www.serpentinegallery.org.uk.
Temporary exhibitions of British and international contemporary art
*Tate Britain*, Millbank, SW1P 4RG. Tel: 020-7887 8000;
Web: www.tate.org.uk.
British painting and 20th-century painting and sculpture. In 2000 the Millbank site became the Tate Gallery of British Art, and the Tate Gallery of Modern Art opened on the South Bank, London SE1
*Wallace Collection*, Manchester Square, W1 U3BN.
Tel: 020-7935 0687;
Web: www.the-wallace-collection.org.uk.
Paintings and drawings, French 18th-century furniture, armour, porcelain, clocks and sculpture
*Whitechapel Art Gallery*, Whitechapel High Street, E1 7QZ. Tel: 020-7522 7878;
Web: www.whitechapel.org.uk
Temporary exhibitions of modern art

LONDON: MUSEUMS – *Bank of England Museum*, Threadneedle Street, EC2 (entrance from Bartholomew Lane).
Tel: 020-7601 5545.
History of the Bank since 1694
*Bethnal Green Museum of Childhood*, Cambridge Heath Road, E2 1PA. Tel: 020-8983 5200;
Web: www.museumofchildhood.org.uk.
Toys, games and exhibits relating to the social history of childhood
*British Museum*, Great Russell Street, WC1 B3DG.
Tel: 020-7636 1555;
Web: www.thebritishmuseum.ac.uk
Antiquities, coins, medals, prints and drawings
*Cabinet War Rooms*, King Charles Street, SW1A TAQ.
Tel: 020-7930 6961; Web: www.iwm.org.uk.
Underground rooms used by Churchill and the Government during the Second World War
*Commonwealth Experience*, Kensington High Street W8 6NQ. Tel: 020-7603 4535;
Web: www.commonwealth.org.uk
Exhibitions on Commonwealth nations, visual arts and crafts; Interactive World
*Cutty Sark*, Greenwich, SE10 9HT. Tel: 020-8858 3445;
Web: www.cuttysark.org.uk
Restored and re-rigged tea clipper with exhibits on board.
*Design Museum*, Shad Thames, SE1.
Tel: 020-7378 6055; Web: www.designmuseum.org.uk
The development of design and the mass-production of consumer objects
*Estorick Collection*, Canonbury Square, N1 2AN
Tel: 020-7704 9522;
Web: www.estorickcollection.com.
Stages the main Estorick Collection of modern Italian art together with temporary loan exhibitions.
*Geffrye Museum*, Kingsland Road, E2 8EA.
Tel: 020-7739 9893;
Web: www.geffrye-museum.org.uk.
English urban domestic interiors from 1600 to present day; also paintings, furniture, decorative arts, walled herb garden and period garden rooms
*Firepower! The Royal Artillery Museum*, Royal Arsenal, Woolwich, SE18 6ST. Tel: 020-8855 7755;
Web: www.firepower.org.uk
The history and development of artillery over the last 700 years including the collections of the Royal Regiment of Artillery
*Gilbert Collection*, The Strand WC2R 1LN.
Tel: 020-7240 4080;
Web: www.gilbert-collection.org.uk
The collection comprises some 800 works of art including European silver, gold snuff boxes and Italian mosaics.
*HMS Belfast*, Morgans Lane, Tooley Street, SE1 2TH.
Tel: 020-7940 6300; Web: www.hmsbelfast.org.uk
Life on a warship, illustrated on World War II warship
†*Horniman Museum and Gardens*, London Road SE23 3PQ.
Tel: 020-8699 1872;
Web: www.horniman.demon.co.uk
Museum of ethnography, musical instruments, natural history and aquarium; reference library; sunken, water and flower gardens
*Imperial War Museum*, Lambeth Road SE1 6HZ.
Tel: 020-7416 5000; Web: www.iwm.org.uk
All aspects of the two world wars and other military operations involving Britain and the Commonwealth since 1914
†*Jewish Museum, Camden Town*, Albert Street NW1 7NB.
Tel: 020-7284 1997.
Jewish life, history and religion
†*Jewish Museum, Finchley*, East End Road N3 2SY.
Tel: 020-8349 1143; Web: www.jewmusm.ort.org.
Jewish life in London and Holocaust education
†*London Transport Museum*, Covent Garden WC2E 7BB.
Tel: 020-7379 6344;
Web: www.londontransport.co.uk/ltmuseum.
Vehicles, photographs and graphic art relating to the history of transport in London
*MCC Museum*, Lord's NW8 8QN. Tel: 020-7289 1611;
Web: www.lords.org
Cricket museum. Conducted tours by appointment with Tours Manager.
*Museum of Garden History*, Lambeth Palace Road SE1 7LB. Tel: 020-7401 8865;
Web: www.museumgardenhistory.org
Exhibition of aspects of garden history and re-created 17th-century garden
†*Museum of London*, London Wall, EC2Y 5HN
Tel: 020-7600 3699;
Web: www.museumoflondon.org.uk
History of London from prehistoric times to present day
*National Army Museum*, Royal Hospital Road SW3 4HT.
Tel: 020-7730 0717; Web: www.faille.com/nam
Five-hundred-year history of the British soldier; exhibits include model of the Battle of Waterloo and *Army for Today* gallery
*National Maritime Museum*, Greenwich SE10 9NF.
Tel: 020-8858 4422; Web; www.port.nmm.ac.uk
Comprises the main building, the Royal Observatory and the Queen's House. Maritime history of Britain; collections include globes, clocks, telescopes and paintings
*Natural History Museum*, Cromwell Road SW7 5BD.
Tel: 020-7938 9123; Web: www.nhm.ac.uk
Natural history collections
†*Petrie Museum of Egyptian Archaeology*, University College London. Tel: 020-7504 2884.
Egyptian archaeology collection
*Royal Air Force Museum*, Colindale, NW9 5LL.
Tel: 020-8205 2266; Web: www.rafmuseum.org.uk

National museum of aviation with over 70 full-size aircraft; aviation from before the Wright brothers to the present-day RAF; flight simulator
*Royal Mews*, Buckingham Palace SW1A 1AA.
Tel: 020-7839 1377.
Carriages, coaches, stables and horses
*Science Museum*, Exhibition Road, SW7 2DD.
Tel: 020-7942 4454;
Web: www.science museum.org.uk
Science, technology, industry and medicine collections
*Shakespeare Globe Exhibition*, Bankside SE1 9DT.
Tel: 020-7902 1500;
Web: www.shakespeares-globe.org
Recreation of Elizabethan theatre using 16th-century techniques
*Sherlock Holmes Museum*, Baker Street NW1 6XE.
Tel: 020-7935 8866;
Web: www.sherlock-holmes.co.uk
Recreated rooms of the fictional detective
*Sir John Soane's Museum*, Lincoln's Inn Fields WC2A 3BP.
Tel: 020-7430 0175; Web: www.soane.org
Art and antiques
*Theatre Museum*, Russell Street WC2.
Tel: 020-7836 2330.
History of the performing arts
**Tower Bridge Experience*, SE1. Tel: 020-7940 3985.
History of the bridge and display of Victorian steam machinery; panoramic views from walkways
*Victoria and Albert Museum*, Cromwell Road SW7 2RL.
Tel: 020-7938 8500; Web: www.varn.ac.uk
Includes National Art Library and Print Room. Fine and applied art and design, including furniture, glass, textiles, dress collections (British Galleries closed for refurbishment)
*Wellington Museum*, Apsley House, W1
*Wimbledon Lawn Tennis Museum*, Church Road SW19.
Tel: 020-8946 6131.
Tennis trophies, fashion and memorabilia; view of Centre Court

MANCHESTER – **Gallery of Costume*, Rusholme M14 5LL
Tel: 0161-224 5217.
Exhibits from the 16th- to 20th-century
†*Manchester Museum*, Oxford Road M13 9PL
Tel: 0161-275 2634; Web: www.museum.man.ac.uk.
Archaeology, archery, botany, Egyptology, entomology, ethnography, geology, natural history, numismatics, oriental and zoology collections
†*Museum of Science and Industry*, Castlefield M3 4SP.
Tel: 0161-832 2244; Web: www.msim.org.uk
On site of world's oldest passenger railway station; galleries relating to space, energy, power, transport, aviation, textiles and social history; interactive science centre
†*Pump House People's History Museum*, for *National Museum of Labour History*, Left Bank M3 3ER.
Tel: 0161-228 7212; Web: www.nmlhweb.org
Political and and working life history
†*Whitworth Art Gallery*, Oxford Road M15 6ER.
Tel: 0161-275 7450; Web: www.whitworth.ac.uk
Watercolours, drawings, prints, textiles, wallpapers and 20th-century British art

MONKWEARMOUTH – *†*Monkwearmouth Station Museum*, North Bridge Street SR5 1AP. Tel: 0191-567 7075.
Victorian train station

NEWCASTLE UPON TYNE – *†*Hancock Museum*, Barras Bridge. Tel: 0191-222 7418.
Natural history
*†*Laing Art Gallery*, New Bridge Street.
Tel: 0191-232 7734.
British and European art, ceramics, glass, silver, textiles and costume; *Art on Tyneside* display
*†*Newcastle Discovery Museum*, Blandford Square NE1 4JA.
Tel: 0191-232 6789;
Web: www.thenortheast.com/museums/news.htm
Science and industry, local history, fashion and Tyneside's maritime history; *Turbinia* (first steam-driven vessel) gallery

NEWMARKET – *National Horseracing Museum*, High Street CB8 8JL. Tel: 01638-667333; Web: www.nhrm.co.uk
The Essential Horse Millennium Exhibition, horse-racing exhibits and tours of local trainers' yards and studs

NORTHAMPTON – *†*Central Museum and Art Gallery*, Guildhall Road NN1 1DP. Tel: 01604-238548;
Web: www.northampton.gov.uk/museums
Boot and shoe collection

NORTH SHIELDS – †*Stephenson Railway Museum*, Middle Engine Lane. Tel: 0191-200 7144.
Locomotive engines and rolling stock

NOTTINGHAM – **Brewhouse Yard Museum*,
Castle Boulevard NG7 1FB. Tel: 0115-915 3600.
Daily life from the 17th to 20th century
**Castle Museum and Art Gallery* NG1 6EL.
Tel: 0115-915 3700.
Paintings, ceramics, silver and glass; history of Nottingham
**Industrial Museum*, Wollaton Park. Tel: 0115-915 3910.
Lacemaking machinery, steam engines and transport exhibits
**Museum of Costume and Textiles*, Castle Gate NG1 6AF.
Tel: 0115-915 3500.
Costume displays from 1790 to the mid-20th century in period rooms
**Natural History Museum*, Wollaton Park.
Tel: 0115-915 3900.
Local natural history and wildlife dioramas

OXFORD – †*Ashmolean Museum*, Beaumont Street OX1 2PH.
Tel: 01865-278000; Web: www.ashmol.ox.ac.uk
European and Oriental fine and applied arts, archaeology, Egyptology and numismatics
*Museum of Modern Art*, Pembroke Street OX1 1BP.
Tel: 01865-722733; Web: www.moma.org.uk
Temporary exhibitions
†*Museum of the History of Science*, Broad Street OX1 3AZ.
Tel: 01865-277280; Web: www.mhs.ox.ac.uk
Displays include early scientific instruments, chemical apparatus, clocks and watches
†*Oxford University Museum of Natural History*, Parks Road. Tel: 01865-272950.
Entomology, geology, mineralogy and zoology
†*Pitt Rivers Museum*, South Parks Road OX1 3PP.
Tel: 01865-270927; Web: www.prm.ox.ac.uk
Ethnographic and archaeological artefacts.

PLYMOUTH – *†*City Museum and Art Gallery*, Drake Circus PL4 8AJ. Tel: 01752-304774;
Web: www.plymouth.gov.co.uk
Local and natural history, ceramics, silver, Old Masters, temporary exhibitions
**The Dome*, The Hoe. Tel: 01752-603300.
Maritime history museum

PORTSMOUTH – **Charles Dickens Birthplace Museum*, Old Commercial Road PO1 4QL. Tel: 023-9282 7261.
Dickens memorabilia
**D-Day Museum*, Clarence Esplanade PO1 2LJ.
Tel: 023-9282 7261;
Web: www.portsmouthmuseums.co.uk
Includes the Overlord Embroidery

*Flagship Portsmouth*, HM Naval Base. Incorporates the *Royal Naval Museum* (Tel: 023-9272 7562), HMS *Victory* (Tel: 023-9282 2034), HMS *Warrior* (Tel: 023-9229 1379), the †*Mary Rose* (Tel: 023-9275 0521) and the *Dockyard Museum*. History of the Royal Navy and of the dockyard and the trades in it

PRESTON – **Harris Museum and Art Gallery*, Market Square PR1 2PP. Tel: 01772-258248;
Web: www.preston.gov.uk/harris
British art since the 18th century, ceramics, glass, costume and local history; also contemporary exhibitions

READING – †*Rural History Museum*, University of Reading. Tel: 0118-931 8660.
History of farming and the countryside over the last 200 years

ST ALBANS – **Verulamium Museum*, St Michael's AL3 4SW. Tel: 01727-866100;
Web: www.stalbansmuseums.org.uk.
Iron Age and Roman Verulamium, including wall plasters, jewellery, mosaics and room reconstructions

ST IVES, Cornwall – *Tate Gallery St Ives*, Porthmeor Beach TR26 1TG. Tel: 01736-796226; Web: www.tate.org.uk
Painting and sculpture by artists associated with St Ives

SALISBURY – *Salisbury and South Wiltshire Museum*, The Close SP1 2EN Tel: 01722-332151.
Archaeology collection

SHEFFIELD – **City Museum and Mappin Art Gallery*, Weston Park. Tel: 0114-276 8588.
Includes applied arts, natural history, Bronze Age archaeology and ethnography, 19th- and 20th-century art

**Graves Art Gallery*, Surrey Street. Tel: 0114-273 5158.
Twentieth-century British art, Grice Collection of Chinese ivories

**Kelham Island Industrial Museum*, off Alma Street. Tel: 0114-272 2106.
Local industrial and social history

**Ruskin Gallery and Ruskin Craft Gallery*, Norfolk Street LA21 8DU. Tel: 0114-273 5299/203 9416;
Web: www.coniston.org.uk.

SOUTHAMPTON – City Art Gallery, Civic Centre SO14 7LP. Tel: 023-8083 2277;
Web: www.southampton.gov.uk/leisure/arts
Fine art, especially 20th-century British

*†*Maritime Museum*, Town Quay SO14 2NY. Tel: 023-8022 3941. Southampton maritime history

*†*Museum of Archaeology*, Town Quay SO14 2NY. Tel: 023-8063 5904.
Roman, Saxon and medieval archaeology

*†*Tudor House Museum and Garden*, Bugle Street S014 2AD. Tel: 023-8033 2513.
Restored 16th century garden; social history exhibitions

SOUTH SHIELDS – *Arbeia Roman Fort*, Baring Street. Tel: 0191-456 6612.
Excavated ruins

*South Shields Museum and Art Gallery*, Ocean Road NE33 2JA. Tel: 0191-456 8740.
South Tyneside history, including reconstructed street

STOKE-ON-TRENT – **Etruria Industrial Museum*, Etruria ST4 7AS. Tel: 01782-233144.
Britain's sole surviving steam-powered potter's mill

**Gladstone Pottery Museum*, Longton ST3 1PQ. Tel: 01782-319232;
Web: www.stoke.gov.uk/gladstone
A working Victorian pottery

*†*Potteries Museum and Art Gallery*, Hanley ST1 3DE. Tel: 01782-232323;
Web: www.stoke.gov.uk/citymuseum
Pottery, china and porcelain collections and a Mark XVI Spitfire. Pottery factory tours are available by arrangement, at the following: *Royal Doulton*, Burslem; *Spode*, Stoke; *Wedgwood*, Barlaston; *W. Moorcroft*, Cobridge; *Staffordshire Enamels*, Longton; *Royale Stratford China*, Fenton

STYAL, Cheshire – *Quarry Bank Mill* FK9 4LA.
Tel: 01625-527468; Web: www.quarrybankmill.org.uk
Working mill illustrating history of cotton industry; costumed guides at restored Apprentice House

SUNDERLAND – †*Sunderland Art Gallery*, Borough Road SO1 1PP. Tel: 0191-553 2323.
Fine and decorative art

WASHINGTON – †*Washington 'F' Pit Museum*, Albany Way
Colliery-related collection

TELFORD – *†*Ironbridge Gorge Museums* TF8 7AW. Tel: 01952-432166; Web: www.ironbridge.org.uk
Includes first iron bridge; Blists Hill (late Victorian working town); Museum of Iron; Jackfield Tile Museum; Coalport China Museum; Tar Tunnel; Broseley Pipeworks

TRING, Herts – *Tring Zoological Museum*, Akeman Street HP23 6AT. Tel: 01442-824181.
Display of more than 4,000 animal species

WAKEFIELD – *Yorkshire Sculpture Park*, West Bretton WS4 4LG. Tel: 01924-830302.
Open-air sculpture gallery including works by Moore, Hepworth, Frink and others in 300 acres of parkland

WORCESTER – **City Museum and Art Gallery*, Foregate Street WR1 1DT. Tel: 01905-25371.
Includes a military museum, River Severn Gallery and changing art exhibitions

*Museum of Worcester Porcelain and Royal Worcester Visitor Centre*, Severn Street WR1 2NE. Tel: 01905-23221.
Factory tours

WROUGHTON, nr Swindon, Wilts – *Science Museum*, Wroughton Airfield. Tel: 01793-814466.
Aircraft displays and some of the Science Museum's transport and agricultural collection

YEOVIL, Somerset – *Fleet Air Arm Museum*, Royal Naval Air Station, Yeovilton BA22 8HT. Tel: 01935-840565;
Web: www.fleetairarm.com
History of naval aviation; historic aircraft, including Concorde 002

*Montacute House*, Montacute. Elizabethan and Jacobean portraits from the National Portrait Gallery

YORK – *Beningbrough Hall*, Shipton-by-Beningbrough YO6 1DD. Tel: 01904-470666.
Portraits from the National Portrait Gallery

*†*Castle Museum*. Tel: 01904-653611.
Reconstructed streets; costume and military collections

*†*City Art Gallery*, Exhibition Square YO1 7EW.
Tel: 01904-551861; Web: www.york.gov.uk.
European and British painting spanning seven centuries; modern pottery

*Jorvik Viking Centre*, Coppergate YO1 9WT.
Tel: 01904-643211; Web: www.vikingyorvik.com
Reconstruction of Viking York

*National Railway Museum*, Leeman Road YO2 4XJ.
Tel: 01904-621261; Web: www.nmsi.ac.uk/nrm
Includes locomotives, rolling stock and carriages

*†*Yorkshire Museum*, Museum Gardens WO1 7FR.
Tel: 01904-551800;
Web: www.theyorkshiremuseum.com.
Yorkshire life from Roman to medieval times; geology gallery

## WALES

BODELWYDDAN, Denbighshire – *Bodelwyddan Castle* LL18 5YA. Tel: 01745-584060.
Portraits from the National Portrait Gallery, furniture from the Victoria and Albert Museum and sculptures from the Royal Academy

CAERLEON – *Roman Legionary Museum*. Tel: 01633-423134.
Material from the site of the Roman fortress of Isca and its suburbs

CARDIFF – *National Museum and Gallery Cardiff*, Cathays Park CF1 3NP. Tel: 029-2039 7951; Web: www.nmgw.ac.uk/index.htm
Includes natural sciences, archaeology and Impressionist paintings

*Museum of Welsh Life*, St Fagans CF5 6XB. Tel: 029-2057 3500; Web: www.nmgw.ac.uk
Open-air museum with re-erected buildings, agricultural equipment and costume

DRE-FACH FELINDRE, nr Llandysul – *Museum of the Welsh Woollen Industry* SA44 5UP. Tel: 01559-370929; Web: www.nmgw.ac.uk
Exhibitions, a working woollen mill and craft workshops

LLANBERIS, nr Caernarfon – *Welsh Slate Museum* WL55 4TY. Tel: 01286-870630; Web: www.nmgw.ac.uk.
Former slate quarry with original machinery and plant slate crafts demonstrations

LLANDRINDOD WELLS – *National Cycle Exhibition*, Automobile Palace, Temple Street. Tel: 01597-825531.
Over 200 bicycles on display, from 1818 to the present day

SWANSEA – **Glynn Vivian Art Gallery and Museum*, Alexandra Road. Tel: 01792-655006.
Paintings, ceramics, Swansea pottery and porcelain, clocks, glass and Welsh art

**Swansea Maritime and Industrial Museum*, Museum Square SA1 1SN. Tel: 01792-650351.
Includes a working woollen mill and historic boats afloat

**Swansea Museum*, Victoria Road SA1 1SN. Tel: 01792-653763; Web: www.swansea.gov.uk.
Archaeology, social history, Swansea pottery

## SCOTLAND

ABERDEEN – **Aberdeen Art Gallery*, Schoolhill AB10 1FQ. Tel: 01224-523700.
Art from the 18th to 20th century

**Aberdeen Maritime Museum*, Shiprow AB11 5BY. Tel: 01224-337700; Web: www.aagm.co.uk
Maritime history, incl. shipbuilding and North Sea oil

EDINBURGH – *Britannia*, Leith docks. Tel: 0131-555 5566; Web: www.royal.gov.uk/faq/hmy.htm
Former royal yacht with royal barge and royal family picture gallery. Tickets must be pre-booked

**City Art Centre*, Market Street. Tel: 0131-529 3993.
Late 19th- and 20th-century art and temporary exhibitions

**Huntly House Museum*, Canongate EH8 8DD. Tel: 0131-529 4143; Web: www.cac.org.uk
Local history, silver, glass and Scottish pottery

**Museum of Childhood*, High Street EH1 1TG. Tel: 0131-529 4142; Web: www.cac.org.uk
Toys, games, clothes and exhibits relating to the social history of childhood

*Museum of Flight*, East Fortune Airfield, nr North Berwick. Tel: 01620-880308.
Display of aircraft

*Museum of Scotland*, Chambers Street EH1 1JF. Tel: 0131-247 4422; Web: www.nms.ac.uk
Scottish history from prehistoric times to the present

*National Gallery of Scotland*, The Mound EH2 2EL. Tel: 0131-624 6200; Web: www.natgalscot.ac.uk
Paintings, drawings and prints from the 16th- to 20th-century, and the national collection of Scottish art

**The People's Story*, Canongate EH8 8BN. Tel: 0131-529 4057.
Edinburgh life since the 18th-century

*Royal Museum of Scotland*, Chambers Street EH1 1JF. Tel: 0131-225 7534; Web: www.nms.ac.uk
Scottish and international collections from prehistoric times to the present

*Scottish Agricultural Museum*, Ingliston. Tel: 0131-333 2674.
History of agriculture in Scotland

*Scottish National Gallery of Modern Art*, Belford Road EH4 3DR. Tel: 0131-624 6200; Web: www.natgalscot.ac.uk
Twentieth-century painting, sculpture and graphic art

*Scottish National Portrait Gallery*, Queen Street EH2 1JD. Tel: 0131-624 6200; Web; www.natgalscot.ac.uk
Portraits of eminent people in Scottish history, and the national collection of photography

**The Writers' Museum*, Lawnmarket EH1 2PA. Tel: 0131-529 4901; Web: www.edinburgh.gov.uk
Robert Louis Stevenson, Walter Scott and Robert Burns exhibits

FORT WILLIAM – *West Highland Museum*, Cameron Square PH33 6AJ. Tel: 01397-702169.
Includes tartan collections and exhibits relating to 1745 uprising

GLASGOW – **Burrell Collection*, Pollokshaws Road G43 1AT. Tel: 0141-287 2550.
Paintings, textiles, furniture, ceramics, stained glass and silver from classical times to the 19th century

**Gallery of Modern Art*, Queen Street G1 3AZ. Tel: 0141-229 1996.
Collection of contemporary Scottish and world art

**Glasgow Art Gallery and Museum*, Kelvingrove Tel: 0141-287 2699.
Includes Old Masters, 19th-century French paintings and armour collection

*Hunterian Art Gallery*, Hillhead Street G12 8QQ. Tel: 0141-330 5431; Web: www.hunterian.ac.uk
Rennie Mackintosh and Whistler collections; Old Masters, Scottish paintings and modern paintings, sculpture and prints

**McLellan Galleries*, Sauchiehall Street Tel: 0141-331 1854.
Temporary exhibitions

**Museum of Transport*, Bunhouse Road G3 8DP. Tel: 0141-287 2720; Web: www.clyde-valley.com/glasgow/transmus.htm
Includes a reproduction of a 1938 Glasgow street, cars since the 1930s, trams and a Glasgow subway station

**People's Palace Museum*, Glasgow Green G3 8AG. Tel: 0141-554 0223; Web: www.glasgow.gov.uk
History of Glasgow since 1175

**St Mungo Museum of Religious Life and Art*, Castle Street G4 0RH. Tel: 0141-553 2557.
Explores universal themes through objects of all the main world religions

## NORTHERN IRELAND

BELFAST – *Ulster Museum*, Botanic Gardens BT9 5AB. Tel: 028-9038 3000; Web: www.ulstermuseum.org.uk
Irish antiquities, natural and local history, fine and applied arts

HOLYWOOD, Co. Down – *Ulster Folk and Transport Museum*, Cultra. Tel: 028-9042 8428.
Open-air museum with original buildings from Ulster town and rural life *c.*1900; indoor galleries including Irish rail and road transport and *Titanic* exhibitions

LONDONDERRY – *The Tower Museum*, Union Hall Place P248 6LU. Tel: 028-7137 2411.
Tells the story of Ireland through the history of Londonderry

OMAGH, Co. Tyrone – *Ulster American Folk Park*, Castletown BT78 5QY. Tel: 028-8224 3292.
Open-air museum telling the story of Ulster's emigrants to America; restored or recreated dwellings and workshops; ship and dockside gallery

# Royal Academicians (as at August 2001)

Date of appointment in parentheses

### PAINTERS

*Senior Academicians*

Diana Armfield (1989)
Jeffery Camp (1974)
John Craxton (1993)
Bernard Dunstan (1959)
Anthony Eyton (1976)
Mary Fedden (1992)
Sir Terry Frost (1992)
Frederick Gore, CBE (1964)
Colin Hayes (1963)
Albert Irvin (1998)
Flavia Irwin (1996)
Leonard Rosoman (1960)
Sir Kyffin Williams, OBE (1970)

*Academicians*

Norman Adams (1967)
Craigie Aitchison, CBE (1978)
Gillian Ayres (1991) (re-elected following resignation in 2000)
John Bellany, CBE (1986)
Adrian Berg, (1992)
Elizabeth Blackadder, OBE (1971)
Peter Blake, CBE (1974)
Sandra Blow (1971)
Olwyn Bowey (1970)
William Bowyer (1974)
Patrick Caulfield (1993)
Maurice Cockrill (1999)
Peter Coker (1965)
Jean Cooke (1965)
Frederick Cuming (1969)
Gus Cummins (1992)
Jennifer Durrant (1994)
Stephen Farthing (1998)
Donald Hamilton Fraser (1975)
Anthony Green (1971)
David Hockney, CH (1985)
Ken Howard (1983)
John Hoyland (1983)
Paul Huxley (1987)
William Jacklin (1989)
R. B. Kitaj (1984)
Sonia Lawson (1982)
Ben Levene (1975)
Patrick Procktor (1996)
Barbara Rae,CBE (1996)
Michael Rooney (1990)
Philip Sutton (1977)
David Tindle (1973)
Anthony Whishaw (1980)

### SCULPTORS

*Senior Academicians*

Kenneth Armitage (1994)
Prof. Sir Eduardo Paolozzi, CBE (1979)

*Academicians*

Ivor Abrahams (1989)
Ralph Brown (1968)
James Butler (1964)
Ann Christopher (1980)
Geoffrey Clarke (1970)
Robert Clatworthy (1968)
Prof. Tony Cragg (1994)
Richard Deacon (1998)
Ken Draper (1990)
Barry Flanagan, OBE (1987)
Anish Kapoor, (1990)
Prof. Phillip King, CBE (1977)
Prof. Bryan Kneale (1970)
David Mach (1998)
John Maine (1995)
Dhruva Mistry (1991)
David Nash (1999)
William Tucker (1992)
Alison Wilding (1999)
John Wragg (1983)

### ARCHITECTS

*Senior Academicians*

Prof. H.T. Cadbury-Brown, OBE (1971)
Prof. Trevor Dannatt (1977)
Sir Philip Dowson, CBE (1979)
Leonard Manasseh, OBE (1976)
John Partridge, CBE (1980)
Sir Philip Powell, CH, OBE (1972)
Prof. Sir Colin St John Wilson (1990)

*Academicians*

Will Alsop (2000)
Gordon Benson (2000)
Edward Cullinan, CBE (1989)
Lord Foster of Thames Bank, OM (1983)
Nicholas Grimshaw, CBE (1994)
Sir Michael Hopkins, CBE (1992)
Eva Jiricna, CBE (1997)
Paul Koralek, CBE (1986)
Richard MacCormac, CBE (1993)
Michael Manser, CBE (1994)
Ian Ritchie (1998)
Lord Rogers of Riverside (1978)

### ENGRAVERS, PRINTMAKERS, AND DRAFTSMEN

*Senior Academicians*

Paul Hogarth, OBE (1974)

*Academicians*

Prof. Norman Ackroyd (1988)
Jennifer Dickson (1970)
Peter Freeth (1990)
Allen Jones (1981)
Christopher Le Brun (1996)
Leonard McComb (1987)
Mick Moon (1994)
Prof. Brendan Neiland (1992)
Prof. Chris Orr (1995)
Tom Phillips (1984)
Joe Tilson (1985)

*Honorary Academicians*

Georg Baselitz (1999)
Eduardo Chillida (1983)
Ralph Erskine (1984)
Frank O. Gehry (1998)
Arata Isozaki (1994)
Jasper Johns (1989)
Elsworth Kelly (2001)
Anselm Kiefer (1996)
Matta (1997)
Mimmo Paladino (1999)
Ieoh Ming Pei (1993)
Robert Rauschenberg (2000)
Richard Serra (1995)
Frank Stella (1993)
Antoni Tàpies (1992)
Cy Twombly (1998)
Jørn Utzon (1985)
Andrew Wyeth (1996)

# Sights of London

For historic buildings and museums and galleries, *see* pages 587–592 and 594–601

ALEXANDRA PALACE, Alexandra Palace Way, Wood Green, London N22 7AY. Tel: 020-8365 2121. The Victorian Palace was severely damaged by fire in 1980 but was restored, and reopened in 1988. Alexandra Palace now provides modern facilities for exhibitions, conferences, banquets and leisure activities. There is an ice rink, open daily, a boating lake, the Phoenix Bar and a conservation area.

BARBICAN CENTRE, Silk Street, London EC2Y 8DS. Tel: 020-7638 4141. Web: www.barbican.org.uk. Owned, funded and managed by the Corporation of London, the Barbican Centre opened in 1982 and houses the 1,156-seat Barbican Theatre, a 200-seat studio theatre (The Pit), and the 1,989-seat Barbican Hall. There are also three cinemas, two art galleries, a sculpture court, a lending library, conference, trade and banqueting facilities, conservatory, shops, restaurants, cafés and bars.

BRIDGES. The bridges over the Thames (from east to west) are:

*The Queen Elizabeth II Bridge*, opened 1991, from Dartford to Thurrock

*Tower Bridge*, opened 1894

*London Bridge*, opened after rebuilding by Rennie, 1831; the new London Bridge opened 1973

*Alexandra Bridge* (railway bridge), built 1863–6

*Southwark Bridge* (Rennie), built 1814–19; rebuilt 1912-21

*Millennium Bridge*, opened June 2000

*Blackfriars Railway Bridge*, completed 1864

*Blackfriars Bridge*, built 1760–9; rebuilt 1860–9; widened 1907–10

*Waterloo Bridge* (Rennie), opened 1817; rebuilt 1937–42

*Hungerford Railway Bridge* (Brunel), suspension bridge built 1841–5; replaced by present railway and footbridge 1863

*Westminster Bridge* (width 84ft), opened 1750; rebuilt 1854–62

*Lambeth Bridge*, built 1862; rebuilt 1929–32

*Vauxhall Bridge*, built 1811–16; rebuilt 1895–1906

*Grosvenor Bridge* (railway bridge), built 1859–60; rebuilt 1963–7

*Chelsea Bridge*, built 1851–8; replaced by suspension bridge 1934; widened 1937

*Albert Bridge*, opened 1873; restructured (Bazalgette) 1884; strengthened 1971–3

*Battersea Bridge* (Holland), opened 1772; rebuilt (Bazalgette) 1890

*Battersea Railway Bridge*, opened 1863

*Wandsworth Bridge*, opened 1873; rebuilt 1940

*Putney Railway Bridge*, opened 1889

*Putney Bridge*, built 1727–9; rebuilt (Bazalgette) 1882–6; starting point of Oxford and Cambridge Boat Race

*Hammersmith Bridge*, built 1824–7; rebuilt (Bazalgette) 1883–7; closed in 1997 for safety work

*Barnes Railway Bridge* (also pedestrian), built 1846–9; restructured 1893

*Chiswick Bridge*, opened 1933

*Kew Railway Bridge*, opened 1869

*Kew Bridge*, built 1758–9; rebuilt and renamed King Edward VII Bridge 1903

*Richmond Lock*; lock, weir and footbridge opened 1894

*Twickenham Bridge*, opened 1933

*Richmond Railway Bridge*, opened 1848; restructured 1906–8

*Richmond Bridge*, built 1774–7; widened 1937

*Teddington Lock*, footbridge opened 1889; marks the end of the tidal reach of the Thames

*Kingston Bridge*, built 1825–8; widened 1914

*Hampton Court Bridge*, built 1753; replaced by iron bridge 1865; present bridge built 1933

A new footbridge is under construction; it is being constructed alongside the railway on Hungerford Bridge

CEMETERIES. *Abney Park*, Stamford Hill, N16 (35 acres), tomb of General Booth, founder of the Salvation Army, and memorials to many Nonconformist divines. *Brompton*, Old Brompton Road, SW10 (40 acres), graves of Sir Henry Cole, Emmeline Pankhurst, John Wisden. *City of London Cemetery and Crematorium*, Aldersbrook Road, E12 (200 acres). *Golders Green Crematorium*, Hoop Lane, NW11 (12 acres), with Garden of Rest and memorials to many famous men and women. *Hampstead*, Fortune Green Road, NW6 (36 acres), graves of Kate Greenaway, Lord Lister, Marie Lloyd. *Highgate*, Swains Lane, N6 (38 acres), tombs of George Eliot, Faraday and Marx; guided tours only, west side. *Kensal Green*, Harrow Road, W10 (70 acres), tombs of Thackeray, Trollope, Sydney Smith, Wilkie Collins, Tom Hood, George Cruikshank, Leigh Hunt, I. K. Brunel and Charles Kemble. Churchyard of the former *Marylebone Chapel*, Marylebone High Street, W1, Charles Wesley and his son Samuel Wesley buried; chapel demolished in 1949, now Garden of Rest. *Nunhead*, Linden Grove, SE15 (26 acres), closed in 1969, recently restored and opened for burials. *St Marylebone Cemetery and Crematorium*, East End Road, N2 (47 acres). *West Norwood Cemetery and Crematorium*, Norwood High Street, SE27 (42 acres), tombs of Sir Henry Bessemer, Mrs Beeton, Sir Henry Tate and Joseph Whitaker (*Whitaker's Almanack*).

CENOTAPH, Whitehall, London SW1. The word 'cenotaph' means 'empty tomb'. The monument, erected 'To the Glorious Dead', is a memorial to all ranks of the sea, land and air forces who gave their lives in the service of the Empire during the First World War. Designed by Sir Edwin Lutyens and erected as a temporary memorial in 1919, it was replaced by a permanent structure unveiled by George V on Armistice Day 1920. An additional inscription was made after the Second World War to commemorate those who gave their lives in that conflict.

CHARTERHOUSE, Charterhouse Square, London EC1M 6AN. Tel: 020-7253 9503. A Carthusian monastery from 1371 to 1537, purchased in 1611 by Thomas Sutton, who endowed it as a residence for aged men 'of gentle birth' and a school for poor scholars (removed to Godalming in 1872).

CHELSEA PHYSIC GARDEN, 66 Royal Hospital Road, London SW3 4HS. Tel: 020-7352 5646. A garden of general botanical research and education, maintaining a wide range of rare and unusual plants. The garden was established in 1673 by the Society of Apothecaries. All enquiries to the Curator.

DOWNING STREET, London SW1. Number 10 Downing Street is the official town residence of the Prime Minister, No. 11 of the Chancellor of the Exchequer and No. 12 is the office of the Government Whips. The street was named after Sir George Downing, Bt., soldier and diplomatist, who was MP for Morpeth from 1660 to 1684.

*Chequers*, a Tudor mansion in the Chilterns near Princes Risborough, was presented by Lord and Lady Lee of Fareham in 1917 to serve, from 1921, as a country residence for the Prime Minister of the day.

GEORGE INN, Borough High Street, London SE1. The last galleried inn in London, built in 1677. Now run as an ordinary public house.

GREENWICH, London SE10. *The Royal Naval College* Tel: 020-8269 4791 was until 1873 the Greenwich Hospital. It was built by Charles II, largely from designs by John Webb, and by Queen Mary II and William III, from designs by Wren. It stands on the site of an ancient abbey, a royal house and Greenwich Palace which was constructed by Henry VII. Henry VIII, Mary I and Elizabeth I were born in the royal palace and Edward VI died there. *Greenwich Park* (196½ acres) was enclosed by Humphrey, Duke of Gloucester, and laid out by Charles II from the designs of Le Nôtre. On a hill in Greenwich Park is the Royal Observatory (founded 1675). Its buildings are now managed by the National Maritime Museum and the earliest building is named Flamsteed House, after John Flamsteed (1646–1719), the first Astronomer Royal. *The Cutty Sark*, the last of the famous tea clippers, has been preserved as a memorial to ships and men of a past era. Sir Francis Chichester's round-the-world yacht, *Gipsy Moth IV*, can also be seen.

HORSE GUARDS, Whitehall, London SW1. Archway and offices built about 1753. The mounting of the guard takes place at 11a.m. (10a.m. on Sundays) and the dismounted inspection at 4p.m. Only those with the Queen's permission may drive through the gates and archway into *Horse Guards' Parade* (230,000 sq. ft), where the Colour is 'trooped' on The Queen's official birthday.

THE HOUSE OF COMMONS, Westminster, London SW1A 2TT. Tel: 020-7219 4272. E-mail: hcinfo@parliament.uk. The royal palace of Westminster, originally built by Edward the Confessor, was the normal meeting place of Parliament from about 1340. St Stephen's Chapel was used from about 1550 for the meetings of the House of Commons, which had previously been held in the Chapter House or Refectory of Westminster Abbey. The House of Lords met in an apartment of the royal palace.

The fire of 1834 destroyed much of the palace and the present Houses of Parliament were erected on the site from the designs of Sir Charles Barry and Augustus Welby Pugin between 1840 and 1867. The chamber of the House of Commons was destroyed by bombing in 1941 and a new Chamber designed by Sir Giles Gilbert Scott was used for the first time in 1950.

*Lord Chancellor's Residence*, Lord Chancellor's Office, House of Lords, London, SW1A 0PW. Tel: 020-7219 3107.

*Westminster Hall and the Crypt Chapel* was the only part of the old palace of Westminster to survive the fire of 1834. It was built by William Rufus (1097–9) and altered by Richard II (1394–9). The hammerbeam roof of carved oak dates from 1396–8. The Hall was the scene of the trial of Charles I.

*The Victoria Tower* of the House of Lords is about 330 ft high, and when Parliament is sitting the Union flag flies by day from its flagstaff. *The Clock Tower* of the House of Commons is about 320 ft high and contains 'Big Ben', the hour bell said to be named after Sir Benjamin Hall, First Commissioner of Works when the original bell was cast in 1856. This bell, which weighed 16 tons 11 cwt, was found to be cracked in 1857. The present bell (13½ tons) is a recasting of the original and was first brought into use in 1859. The dials of the clock are 23 ft in diameter, the hands being 9 ft and 14 ft long (including balance piece). A light is displayed from the Clock Tower at night when Parliament is sitting.

For security reasons tours of the Houses of Parliament are available only to those who have made advance arrangements through an MP or peer. The Palace is open during the summer recess for line of route tours which should be booked via Ticketmaster on 020-7344 9966 or www.ticketmaster.co.uk. Tickets are also on sale at the palace.

Admission to the Strangers' Gallery of the House of Lords is arranged by a peer or by queue via St Stephen's Entrance. Admission to the Strangers' Gallery of the House of Commons is by Members' order (Members' orders should be sought several weeks in advance), or by queue via St Stephen's Entrance. The House does not always sit on Fridays. Overseas visitors may write to the Parliamentary Education Unit to obtain a permit to tour the Houses of Parliament, or obtain cards of introduction from their Embassy or High Commission to attend the public gallery.

INNS OF COURT. The *Inner* and *Middle Temple*, Fleet Street/Victoria Embankment, London EC4. Tel: 020-7797 8250. Have occupied since the early 14th century the site of the buildings of the Order of Knights Templars. *Inner Temple Hall* is open by appointment on application to the Treasury Office. *Middle Temple Hall* (1562–70) is open when not in use. In the Temple Gardens Shakespeare (Henry VI, Part I) places the incident which led to the 'Wars of the Roses' (1455–85). *Temple Church*, London EC4, has a nave which forms one of five remaining round churches in England. *Master of the Temple*, Revd R. Griffith-Jones

*Lincoln's Inn*, Chancery Lane/Lincoln's Inn Fields, London WC2. Tel: 020-7405 1393. Occupies the site of the palace of a former Bishop of Chichester and of a Black Friars monastery. The hall and library buildings are of 1845, although the library is first mentioned in 1474; the old hall (late 15th century) and the chapel were rebuilt *c.* 1619–23. Halls open by appointment, chapel and gardens, Monday–Friday 12–2.30. Chapel services Sunday 11.30 a.m. during law terms. *Lincoln's Inn Fields* (7 acres). The square was laid out by Inigo Jones.

*Gray's Inn*, Holborn/Gray's Inn Road, London WC1. Tel: 020-7458 7800. Web: www.greysinn.org.uk. Founded early 14th century; Hall 1556–8.

No other 'Inns' are active, but there are remains of *Staple Inn*, a gabled front on Holborn (opposite Gray's Inn Road). *Clement's Inn* (near St Clement Danes Church), *Clifford's Inn*, Fleet Street, and *Thavies Inn*, Holborn Circus, are all rebuilt. *Serjeants' Inn*, Fleet Street, and another (demolished 1910) of the same name in Chancery Lane, were composed of Serjeants-at-Law, the last of whom died in 1922.

LLOYD'S, Lime Street, London EC3M 7HA. Tel: 020-7327 1000; E-mail: lloyds-external-enquiries@lloyds.com; Web: www.lloyds.com. International insurance market which evolved during the 17th-century from Lloyd's Coffee House. The present building was opened for business in May 1986, and houses the Lutine Bell. Underwriting is on three floors with a total area of 114,000 sq. ft.

LONDON EYE, The Thames South Bank. Opened in February 2000 as London's millennium landmark, this 450ft observation wheel is the capital's fourth largest structure. The wheel provides a 30 minute ride offering spectacular panoramic views of the capital.

LONDON PARKS, ETC.

Royal Parks

*Bushy Park* (1,099 acres), Middx. Adjoining Hampton Court, contains avenue of horse-chestnuts enclosed in a fourfold avenue of limes planted by William III. 'Chestnut Sunday' (when the trees are in full bloom with their 'candles') is usually about 1 to 15 May

*Green Park* (49 acres), London W1. Between Piccadilly and St James's Park, with Constitution Hill leading to Hyde Park Corner

*Greenwich Park* (196½ acres), London SE10

*Hyde Park* (341 acres), London W1/W2. From Park Lane to Kensington Gardens, containing the Serpentine. Fine gateway at Hyde Park Corner, with Apsley House, the Achilles Statue, Rotten Row and the Ladies' Mile. To the north-east is the Marble Arch, originally erected by George IV at the entrance to Buckingham Palace and re-erected in the present position in 1851

*Kensington Gardens* (275 acres), London W2/W8. From the western boundary of Hyde Park to Kensington Palace, containing the Albert Memorial and Peter Pan statue

*Kew, Royal Botanic Gardens, see* page 358

*Regent's Park* and *Primrose Hill* (464 acres), London NW1. From Marylebone Road to Primrose Hill surrounded by the Outer Circle and divided by the Broad Walk leading to the Zoological Gardens

*Richmond Park* (2,469 acres), Middx

*St James's Park* (93 acres), London SW1. From Whitehall to Buckingham Palace. Ornamental lake of 12 acres. The original suspension bridge built in 1857 was replaced in 1957. The Mall leads from the Admiralty Arch to Buckingham Palace, Birdcage Walk from Storey's Gate to Buckingham Palace. Maintained by the Royal Parks Agency

*Ashtead Common* (500 acres), Surrey

*Burnham Beeches* and *Fleet Wood* (540 acres), Bucks. Purchased by the Corporation for the benefit of the public in 1880, Fleet Wood (65 acres) being presented in 1921

*Coulsdon Common* (133 acres), Surrey

*Epping Forest* (6,000 acres), Essex. Purchased by the Corporation and opened to the public in 1882. The present forest is 12 miles long by 1 to 2 miles wide, about one-tenth of its original area

*Farthing Downs* (121 acres), Surrey

*Hampstead Heath* (789 acres), London NW3. Including Golders Hill (36 acres) and Parliament Hill (271 acres)

*Highgate Wood* (70 acres), London N6/N10

*Kenley Common* (138 acres), Surrey

*Queen's Park* (30 acres), London NW6

*Riddlesdown* (90 acres), Surrey

*Spring Park* (51 acres), Kent

*West Ham Park* (77 acres), London E15

*West Wickham Common* (25 acres), Kent

*Woodredon and Warlies Park Estate* (740 acres), Waltham Abbey

Also smaller open spaces within the City of London, including *Finsbury Circus Gardens* which are maintained by Historic Royal Palaces

*Hampton Court Gardens* (54 acres), Middx

*Hampton Court Green* (17 acres), Middx

*Hampton Court Park* (622 acres), Middx

LONDON PLANETARIUM, Marylebone Road, London NW1 5LR. Tel: 0890 4003000. Star show and interactive exhibits.

LONDON ZOO, Regent's Park, London NW1. Tel: 020-7722 3333. Opened in 1826.

MADAME TUSSAUD'S, Marylebone Road, London NW1 5LR. Tel: 0870-400 3000.
Web: www.madame-tussauds.com. Waxwork exhibition.

MARKETS. The London markets are mostly administered by the Corporation of London. *Billingsgate* (fish), Thames Street site dating from 1875, a market site for over 1,000 years, moved to the Isle of Dogs in 1982. *Borough*, SE1 (vegetables, fruit, flowers, etc.), established on present site 1756, privately owned and run. *Covent Garden* (vegetables, fruit, flowers, etc.), established in 1661 under a charter of Charles II, moved in 1973 to Nine Elms. *Leadenhall*, EC3 (meat, poultry, fish, etc.), built 1881, part recently demolished. *London Fruit Exchange*, Brushfield Street, built by Corporation of London 1928–9 as buildings for Spitalfields market; not connected with the market since it moved in 1991. *Petticoat Lane*, Middlesex Street, E1, a market has existed on the site for over 500 years, now a Sunday morning market selling almost anything. *Portobello Road*, W11, originally for herbs and horse-trading from 1870; became famous for antiques after the closure of the Caledonian Market in 1948. *Smithfield, Central Meat, Fish, Fruit, Vegetable and Poultry Markets*, built 1851–66, the site of St Bartholomew's Fair from 12th to 19th century, new hall built 1963, market refurbished 1993–4. *Spitalfields*, E1 (vegetables, fruit, etc.), established 1682, modernised 1928, moved to Leyton in 1991. A much smaller market is still on the original site on Commercial Street, selling arts, crafts, books, clothes and antiques, Sundays.

MARLBOROUGH HOUSE, Pall Mall, London SW1A 5HX. Tel: 020-7839 3411. E-mail: info@commonwealth.int. Web: www.thecommonwealth.org. Built by Wren for the first Duke of Marlborough and completed in 1711, the house reverted to the Crown in 1835. In 1863 it became the London house of the Prince of Wales and was the London home of Queen Mary until her death in 1953. In 1959 Marlborough House was given by The Queen as the headquarters for the Commonwealth Secretariat and it was opened as such in 1965. The Queen's Chapel, Marlborough Gate was begun in 1623 from the designs of Inigo Jones for the Infanta Maria of Spain, and completed for Queen Henrietta Maria.

LONDON MONUMENT (commonly called The Monument), Monument Street, London EC3. Built from designs of Wren, 1671–7, to commemorate the Great Fire of London, which broke out in Pudding Lane on 2 September 1666. The fluted Doric column is 120 ft high; the moulded cylinder above the balcony supporting a flaming vase of gilt bronze is an additional 42 ft; and the column is based on a square plinth 40 ft high (with fine carvings on the west face) making a total height of 202 ft. Splendid views of London from gallery at top of column (311 steps).

MONUMENTS (sculptor's name in parenthesis). *Albert Memorial* (Durham), Kensington Gore; *Royal Air Force* (Blomfield), Victoria Embankment; *Viscount Alanbrooke*, Whitehall; *Beaconsfield*, Parliament Square; *Beatty* (Macmillan), Trafalgar Square; *Belgian Gratitude* (setting by Blomfield, statue by Rousseau), Victoria Embankment; *Boadicea* (or Boudicca), Queen of the Iceni (Thornycroft), Westminster Bridge; *Brunel* (Marochetti), Victoria Embankment; *Burghers of Calais* (Rodin), Victoria Tower Gardens, Westminster; *Burns* (Steel), Embankment Gardens; *Canada Memorial* (Granche), Green Park; *Carlyle* (Boehm), Chelsea

Embankment; *Cavalry* (Jones), Hyde Park; *Edith Cavell* (Frampton), St Martin's Place; *Cenotaph* (Lutyens), Whitehall; *Charles I* (Le Sueur), Trafalgar Square; *Charles II* (Gibbons), South Court, Chelsea Hospital; *Churchill* (Roberts-Jones), Parliament Square; *Cleopatra's Needle* (68½ ft high, *c*.1500 BC, erected on the Thames Embankment in 1877–8; the sphinxes are Victorian); *Clive* (Tweed), King Charles Street; *Captain Cook* (Brock), The Mall; *Crimean*, Broad Sanctuary; *Oliver Cromwell* (Thornycroft), outside Westminster Hall; *Cunningham* (Belsky), Trafalgar Square; *Gen. Charles de Gaulle*, Carlton Gardens; *Lord Dowding* (Faith Winter), Strand; *Duke of Cambridge* (Jones), Whitehall; *Duke of York* (124 ft), Carlton House Terrace; *Edward VII* (Mackennal), Waterloo Place; *Elizabeth I* (1586, oldest outdoor statue in London; from Ludgate), Fleet Street; *Eros* (Shaftesbury Memorial) (Gilbert), Piccadilly Circus; *Marechal Foch* (Mallisard, copy of one in Cassel, France), Grosvenor Gardens; *Charles James Fox* (Westmacott), Bloomsbury Square; *George III* (Cotes Wyatt), Cockspur Street; *George IV* (Chantrey), riding without stirrups, Trafalgar Square; *George V* (Reid Dick), Old Palace Yard; *George VI* (Macmillan), Carlton Gardens; *Gladstone* (Thornycroft), Strand; *Guards'* (Crimea) (Bell), Waterloo Place; (Great War) (Ledward, figures, Bradshaw, cenotaph), Horse Guards' Parade; *Haig* (Hardiman), Whitehall; *Sir Arthur (Bomber) Harris* (Faith Winter), Strand; *Irving* (Brock), north side of National Portrait Gallery; *James II* (Gibbons and/or pupils), Trafalgar Square; *Jellicoe* (Wheeler), Trafalgar Square; *Samuel Johnson* (Fitzgerald), opposite St Clement Danes; *Kitchener* (Tweed), Horse Guards' Parade; *Abraham Lincoln* (Saint-Gaudens, copy of one in Chicago), Parliament Square; *Milton* (Montford), St Giles, Cripplegate; *The Monument* (*see* above); *Mountbatten*, Foreign Office Green; *Nelson* (170 ft 2 in), Trafalgar Square, with Landseer's lions (cast from guns recovered from the wreck of the *Royal George*); *Florence Nightingale* (Walker), Waterloo Place; *Palmerston* (Woolner), Parliament Square; *Peel* (Noble), Parliament Square; *Pitt* (Chantrey), Hanover Square; *Portal* (Nemon), Embankment Gardens; *Prince Consort* (Bacon), Holborn Circus; *Queen Elizabeth Gate*, Hyde Park Corner; *Raleigh* (Macmillan), Whitehall; *Richard I (Coeur de Lion)* (Marochetti), Old Palace Yard; *Roberts* (Bates), Horse Guards' Parade; *Franklin D. Roosevelt* (Reid Dick), Grosvenor Square; *Royal Artillery* (South Africa) (Colton), The Mall; (Great War), Hyde Park Corner; *Captain Scott* (Lady Scott), Waterloo Place; *Shackleton* (Sarjeant Jagger), Kensington Gore; *Shakespeare* (Fontana, copy of one by Scheemakers in Westminster Abbey), Leicester Square; *Smuts* (Epstein), Parliament Square; *Sullivan* (Goscombe John), Victoria Embankment; *Trenchard* (Macmillan), Victoria Embankment; *Victoria Memorial*, in front of Buckingham Palace; *Raoul Wallenberg* (Phillip Jackson), Great Cumberland Place; *George Washington* (Houdon copy), Trafalgar Square; *Wellington* (Boehm), Hyde Park Corner, (Chantrey) riding without stirrups, outside Royal Exchange; *John Wesley* (Adams Acton), City Road; *William III* (Bacon), St James's Square; *Wolseley* (Goscombe John), Horse Guards' Parade.

PORT OF LONDON. Port of London Authority, Bakers Hall, 7 Harp Lane, London EC3R 6LB. Tel: 020-7743 7900. The Port of London covers the tidal section of the River Thames from Teddington to the seaward limit (the outer Tongue buoy and the Sunk light vessel), a distance of 150km. The governing body is the Port of London Authority (PLA). Each year over 52 million tonnes of cargo is handled at privately operated riverside terminals between Fulham and Canvey Island, including the enclosed dock at Tilbury, 40km below London Bridge. Passenger vessels and cruise liners can be handled at moorings at Greenwich, Tower Bridge and Tilbury.

ROMAN REMAINS. The city wall of Roman *Londinium* was largely rebuilt during the medieval period but sections may be seen near the White Tower in the Tower of London; at Tower Hill; at Coopers' Row; at All Hallows, London Wall, its vestry being built on the remains of a semi-circular Roman bastion; at St Alphage, London Wall, showing a succession of building repairs from the Roman until the late medieval period; and at St Giles, Cripplegate. Sections of the great forum and basilica, more than 165 $m^2$, have been encountered during excavations in the area of Leadenhall, Gracechurch Street and Lombard Street. Traces of Roman activity along the river include a massive riverside wall built in the late Roman period, and a succession of Roman timber quays along Lower and Upper Thames Street. Finds from these sites can be seen at the Museum of London (*see* page 598).

Other major buildings are the amphitheatre at Guildhall; remains of bath-buildings in Upper and Lower Thames Street; and the temple of Mithras in Walbrook.

ROYAL ALBERT HALL, Kensington Gore, London SW7 2AP. Tel: 020-7589 3203. E-mail: sales@royalalberthall.com. Web: www.royalalberthall.com. The elliptical hall, one of the largest in the world, was completed in 1871, and since 1941 has been the venue each summer for the Promenade Concerts founded in 1895 by Sir Henry Wood. Other events include pop and classical music concerts, dance, opera, sporting events, conferences and banquets.

ROYAL HOSPITAL, CHELSEA, Royal Hospital Road, London SW3 4SR. Tel: 020-7881 5204.
Web: www.chelseapensioner.org.uk. Founded by Charles II in 1682, and built by Wren; opened in 1692 for old and disabled soldiers. The extensive grounds include the former Ranelagh Gardens and are the venue for the Chelsea Flower Show each May. *Governor*, Gen. Sir Jeremy Mackenzie, GCB, OBE.

ROYAL OPERA HOUSE, Covent Garden, London WC2E 9DD. Home of The Royal Ballet (1931) and The Royal Opera (1946). The Royal Opera House is the third theatre to be built on the site, opening 1858; the first was opened in 1732.

ST JAMES'S PALACE, Pall Mall, London SW1. Tel: 020-7 930 4832. Web: www.royal.gov.uk. Built by Henry VIII; the Gatehouse and Presence Chamber remain; later alterations were made by Wren and Kent. Representatives of foreign powers are still accredited 'to the Court of St James's'. *Clarence House* (1825) in the palace precinct is the home of The Queen Mother.

ST PAUL'S CATHEDRAL, St Paul's Churchyard, London EC4M 8AD. Tel: 020-7246 8348.
E-mail: chapterhouse@stpaulscathedral.org.uk.
Web: www.stpauls.co.uk Built 1675–1710, cost £747,660. The cross on the dome is 365 ft above the ground level, the inner cupola 218 ft above the floor. 'Great Paul' in the south-west tower weighs nearly 17 tons. The organ by Father Smith (enlarged by Willis and rebuilt by Mander) is in a case carved by Grinling Gibbons, who also carved the choir stalls.

SOMERSET HOUSE, Strand and Victoria Embankment, London WC2. The river façade (600 ft long) was built in 1776–86 from the designs of Sir William Chambers; the eastern extension, which houses part of King's

College, was built by Smirke in 1829. Somerset House was the property of Lord Protector Somerset, at whose attainder in 1552 the palace passed to the Crown, and it was a royal residence until 1692.

SOUTH BANK, London SE1. Tel: 020-7960 4242. E-mail: boxoffice@rfh.org.uk. Web: www.rfh.org.uk The arts complex on the south bank of the River Thames which consists of the 2,903-seat *Royal Festival Hall* (opened in 1951 for the Festival of Britain), the adjacent 1,056-seat *Queen Elizabeth Hall*, the 368-seat *Purcell Room*, and the 77-seat Voice Box.

The *National Film Theatre* (Opened 1952) Tel: 020-7928 3232. Web: www.bfi.org.uk/nft. Administered by the British Film Institute, has three auditoria showing over 2,000 films a year. The London Film Festival is held here every November. There is an IMAX cinema with 500 seats.

The *Royal National Theatre* Tel: 020-7452 3000. Web: www.nationaltheatre.org.uk. Opened in 1976 and stages classical, modern, new and neglected plays in its three auditoria: the 1,160-seat Olivier theatre, the 890-seat Lyttelton theatre and the Cottesloe theatre which seats up to 400.

SOUTHWARK CATHEDRAL, London SE1 9DA. Tel: 020-7367 6700. E-mail: cathedral@dswark.org.uk. Web: www.dswark.org. Mainly 13th century, but the nave is largely rebuilt. The tomb of John Gower (1330–1408) is between the Bunyan and Chaucer memorial windows in the north aisle; Shakespeare's effigy, backed by a view of Southwark and the Globe Theatre, is in the south aisle; the tomb of Bishop Andrewes (died 1626) is near the screen. The lady chapel was the scene of the consistory courts of the reign of Mary (Gardiner and Bonner) and is still used as a consistory court. John Harvard, after whom Harvard University is named, was baptised here in 1607, and the chapel by the north choir aisle is his memorial chapel.

THAMES EMBANKMENTS. The *Victoria Embankment*, on the north side from Westminster to Blackfriars, was constructed by Sir Joseph Bazalgette (1819–91) for the Metropolitan Board of Works, 1864–70; the seats, of which the supports of some are a kneeling camel, laden with spicery, and of others a winged sphinx, were presented by the Grocers' Company and by W. H. Smith, MP, in 1874; the *Albert Embankment*, on the south side from Westminster Bridge to Vauxhall, 1866–9; the *Chelsea Embankment*, 1871–4. The total cost exceeded £2,000,000. Bazalgette also inaugurated the London main drainage system, 1858–65. A medallion (*Flumini vincula posuit*) has been placed on a pier of the Victoria Embankment to commemorate the engineer.

THAMES FLOOD BARRIER. Officially opened in May 1984, though first used in February 1983, the barrier consists of ten rising sector gates which span 570 yards from bank to bank of the Thames at Woolwich Reach. When not in use the gates lie horizontally, allowing shipping to navigate the river normally; when the barrier is closed, the gates turn through 90 degrees to stand vertically more than 50 feet above the river bed. The barrier took eight years to complete and can be raised within about 30 minutes.

THAMES TUNNELS. The *Rotherhithe Tunnel*, opened 1908, connects Commercial Road, London E14, with Lower Road, Rotherhithe; it is 1 mile 332 yards long, of which 525 yards are under the river. The first *Blackwall Tunnel* (northbound vehicles only), opened 1897, connects East India Dock Road, Poplar, with Blackwall Lane, East Greenwich. The height restriction on the northbound tunnel is 13ft 4in. A second tunnel (for southbound vehicles only) opened 1967. The lengths of the tunnels measured from East India Dock Road to the Gate House on the south side are 6,215 ft (old tunnel) and 6,152 ft. *Greenwich Tunnel* (pedestrians only), opened 1902, connects the Isle of Dogs, Poplar, with Greenwich; it is 406 yards long. The *Woolwich Tunnel* (pedestrians only), opened 1912, connects North and South Woolwich below the passenger and vehicular ferry from North Woolwich Station, London E16, to High Street, Woolwich, London SE18; it is 552 yards long.

WALTHAM CROSS, Herts. At Waltham Cross is one of the crosses (partly restored) erected by Edward I to mark a resting place of the corpse of Queen Eleanor on its way to Westminster Abbey. Ten crosses were erected, but only those at Geddington, Northampton and Waltham survive; 'Charing' Cross originally stood near the spot now occupied by the statue of Charles I at Whitehall.

WESTMINSTER ABBEY, Broad Sanctuary, London, SW1P. Tel: 0207-7222 5152.
E-mail: info@westminster-abbey.org.
Web: www.westminster-abbey.org. The original abbey was a Benedictine monastery founded around 960 by St Dunstan, and re-founded by Edward the Confessor in 1065. It has been the coronation church since 1066. The present structure was begun by Henry III in 1245 and contains Edward the Confessor's shrine, the tombs of kings and queens and several hundred monuments and memorials, including the Tomb of the Unknown Warrior. Numerous literary figures are buried or commemorated in Poet's Corner. Among its other treasures are the Coronation Chair and the 13th-century Cosmati pavement

WESTMINSTER CATHEDRAL, Ashley Place, London SW1P 1QW. Tel: 020-7798 9055.
Web:www.westminstercathedral.org.uk
Roman Catholic cathedral built 1895–1903 from the designs of J. F. Bentley. The campanile is 283 feet high.

LONDON TOURIST BOARD AND CONVENTION BUREAU, Glen House, Stag Place, London, SW1E 5LT. Tourist information: 0839-123456

# Hallmarks

Hallmarks are the symbols stamped on gold, silver or platinum articles to indicate that they have been tested at an official Assay Office and that they conform to one of the legal standards. With certain exceptions, all gold, silver or platinum articles are required by law to be hallmarked before they are offered for sale. Hallmarking was instituted in England in 1300 under a statute of Edward I.

## MODERN HALLMARKS

Since 1 January 1999, UK hallmarks have consisted of three compulsory symbols – the sponsor's mark, the fineness (standard) mark and the assay office mark. Traditional marks such as the year date letter, the Britannia for 958 silver, the lion passant for 925 silver (lion rampant in Scotland) and the orb for 950 platinum may be added voluntarily. The distinction between UK and foreign articles has been removed, and more finenesses are now legal, reflecting the more common finenesses elsewhere in Europe.

### Sponsor's Mark

Instituted in England in 1363, the sponsor's mark was originally a device such as a bird or fleur-de-lis. Now it consists of the initial letters of the name or names of the manufacturer or firm. Where two or more sponsors have the same initials, there is a variation in the surrounding shield or style of letters.

### Fineness (Standard) Mark

The fineness (standard) mark indicates that the content of the precious metal in the alloy from which the article is made, is not less than the legal standard. The legal standard is the minimum content of precious metal by weight in parts per thousand, and the standards are:

| | | |
|---|---|---|
| Gold | 999 | |
| | 990 | |
| | 916.6 | (22 carat) |
| | 750 | (18 carat) |
| | 585 | (14 carat) |
| | 375 | (9 carat) |
| Silver | 999 | |
| | 958.4 | (Britannia) |
| | 925 | (sterling) |
| | 800 | |
| Platinum | 999 | |
| | 950 | |
| | 900 | |
| | 850 | |

### Assay Office Mark

This mark identifies the particular assay office at which the article was tested and marked. The British assay offices are:

London, Goldsmith's Hall, London EC2V 8AQ.
Tel: 020-7606 8975

Birmingham, Newhall Street, Birmingham B3 1SB.
Tel: 0121-236 6951

Sheffield, 137 Portobello Street, Sheffield S1 4DS.
Tel: 0114-275 5111

Edinburgh, 24 Broughton Street, Edinburgh EH1 3RH.
Tel: 0131-556 1144

Assay offices formerly existed in other towns, e.g. Chester, Exeter, Glasgow, Newcastle, Norwich and York, each having its own distinguishing mark.

### Date Letter

The date letter shows the year in which an article was assayed and hallmarked. Each alphabetical cycle has a distinctive style of lettering or shape of shield. The date letters were different at the various assay offices and the particular office must be established from the assay office mark before reference is made to tables of date letters. Date letter marks became voluntary from 1 January 1999.

The table on page 608 shows specimen shields and letters used by the London Assay Office on silver articles in each period from 1498. The same letters are found on gold articles but the surrounding shield may differ. Since 1 January 1975, each office has used the same style of date letter and shield for all articles.

## OTHER MARKS

### Foreign Goods

Foreign goods imported into the UK are required to be hallmarked before sale, unless they already bear a convention mark (*see* below) or a hallmark struck by an independent assay office in the European Economic Area which is deemed to be equivalent to a UK hallmark.

The following are the assay office marks used for gold until the end of 1998. For silver and platinum the symbols remain the same but the shields differ in shape.

 *London*

 *Birmingham*

 *Sheffield*

*Edinburgh*

### Convention Hallmarks

Special marks at authorised assay offices of the signatory countries of the International Convention on Hallmarking (Austria, the Czech Republic, Denmark, Finland, Ireland, the Netherlands, Norway, Portugal, Sweden, Switzerland and the UK) are legally recognised in the United Kingdom as approved hallmarks. These consist of a sponsor's mark, a common control mark, a fineness mark (arabic numerals showing the standard in parts per thousand), and an assay office mark. There is no date letter.

The fineness marks are:

| | | |
|---|---|---|
| Gold | 750 | (18 carat) |
| | 585 | (14 carat) |
| | 375 | (9 carat) |
| Silver | 925 | (sterling) |
| Platinum | 950 | |

The common control marks are:

*Gold (18 carat)*

*Silver*

*Platinum*

### Duty Marks

In 1784 an additional mark of the reigning sovereign's head was introduced to signify that the excise duty had been paid. The mark became obsolete on the abolition of the duty in 1890.

### Commemorative Marks

There are three other marks to commemorate special events: the silver jubilee of King George V and Queen Mary in 1935, the coronation of Queen Elizabeth II in 1953, and her silver jubilee in 1977. During 1999 and 2000 there is a voluntary additional Millennium Mark.

## LONDON (GOLDSMITHS' HALL) DATE LETTERS FROM 1498

| | | |
|---|---|---|
| Black letter, small | 1498–9 | 1517–8 |
| Lombardic | 1518–9 | 1537–8 |
| Roman and other capitals | 1538–9 | 1557–8 |
| Black letter, small | 1558–9 | 1577–8 |
| Roman letter, capitals | 1578–9 | 1597–8 |
| Lombardic, external cusps | 1598–9 | 1617–8 |
| Italic letter, small | 1618–9 | 1637–8 |
| Court hand | 1638–9 | 1657–8 |
| Black letter, capitals | 1658–9 | 1677–8 |
| Black letter, small | 1678–9 | 1696–7 |
| Court hand | 1697 | 1715–6 |
| Roman letter, capitals | 1716–7 | 1735–6 |
| Roman letter, small | 1736–7 | 1738–9 |
| Roman letter, small | 1739–40 | 1755–6 |
| Old English, capitals | 1756–7 | 1775–6 |
| Roman letter, small | 1776–7 | 1795–6 |
| Roman letter, capitals | 1796–7 | 1815–6 |
| Roman letter, small | 1816–7 | 1835–6 |
| Old English, capitals | 1836–7 | 1855–6 |
| Old English, small | 1856–7 | 1875–6 |
| Roman letter, capitals[A to M *square* shield N to Z as shown] | 1876–7 | 1895–6 |
| Roman letter, small | 1896–7 | 1915–6 |
| Black letter, small | 1916–7 | 1935–6 |
| Roman letter, capitals | 1936–7 | 1955–6 |
| Italic letter, small | 1956–7 | 1974 |
| Italic letter, capitals | 1975 | |

# Economic Statistics

## The Budget 2001

GOVERNMENT RECEIPTS £ *billion*

| | Outturn 1999-2000 | Estimate 2000–2001 | Forecast 2001-2002 |
|---|---|---|---|
| Inland Revenue | 138.8 | 149.1 | 156.4 |
| Income tax (gross) | 95.7 | 106.7 | 111.5 |
| Income tax credits | –3.2 | –4.9 | –7.4 |
| Corporation tax[1] | 34.4 | 32.1 | 37.8 |
| Petroleum revenue tax | 0.9 | 1.9 | 1.6 |
| Capital gains tax | 2.1 | 2.9 | 2.5 |
| Inheritance tax | 2.0 | 2.2 | 2.3 |
| Stamp duties | 6.9 | 8.2 | 8.0 |
| Customs and Excise | 97.3 | 102.8 | 105.9 |
| Value added tax | 56.4 | 59.0 | 61.3 |
| Fuel duties | 22.5 | 23.0 | 22.5 |
| Tobacco duties | 5.7 | 7.5 | 7.6 |
| Spirits duties | 1.8 | 1.8 | 1.8 |
| Wine duties | 1.7 | 1.8 | 1.9 |
| Beer and cider duties | 3.0 | 3.0 | 3.0 |
| Betting and gaming duties | 1.5 | 1.5 | 1.5 |
| Air passenger duty | 0.9 | 1.0 | 1.0 |
| Insurance premium tax | 1.4 | 1.7 | 1.8 |
| Landfill tax | 0.4 | 0.5 | 0.5 |
| Customs duties and levies | 2.0 | 2.1 | 2.1 |
| Vehicle excise duties | 4.8 | 4.5 | 4.5 |
| Oil royalties | 0.4 | 0.6 | 0.6 |
| Business rates[2] | 15.8 | 17.2 | 17.5 |
| Social security contributions | 56.4 | 60.1 | 62.6 |
| Council tax | 13.0 | 13.9 | 14.7 |
| Other taxes and royalties[3] | 8.4 | 8.9 | 9.5 |
| Net taxes and social security contributions[4] | 334.9 | 357.0 | 371.6 |
| Interest and dividends | 3.8 | 5.3 | 4.8 |
| Accural adjustments on taxes | 4.8 | 3.1 | 1.7 |
| *Less* own resources contribution to EU budget | –5.6 | -6.3 | –5.9 |
| Less PC corporation tax payments | –0.3 | –0.2 | –0.2 |
| Income tax credits[5] | 3.2 | 4.9 | 5.8 |
| Other receipts | 17.9 | 19.4 | 20.5 |
| CURRENT RECEIPTS | 358.7 | 383.2 | 398.4 |
| North Sea revenues[6] | 2.5 | 4.8 | 5.9 |

1. Includes advance corporation tax (net of payment). Also includes North Sea corporation tax after ACT set-off and corporation tax on gains
2. Includes district council rates in Northern Ireland
3. Includes money paid into the National Lottery Distribution Fund
4. Includes VAT and 'traditional own resources' contributions to EU budget. Net of income tax credits. Cash basis
5. Excludes Children's Tax Credit, which scores as a tax repayment in the national accounts
6. North Sea corporation tax (before ACT set-off), petroleum revenue tax and royalties

*Source*: The Stationery Office – *Budget 2001*

GOVERNMENT EXPENDITURE

The Economic and Fiscal Strategy Report in June 1998 introduced changes to the public expenditure control regime. Three-year departmental expenditure limits (DELs) now apply to most government departments. Spending which cannot easily be subject to three-year planning is reviewed annually in the Budget as annually managed expenditure (AME). Current and capital expenditure are treated separately.

DEPARTMENTAL EXPENDITURE LIMITS
CURRENT BUDGET £ *billion*

| | Outturn 1999-2000 | Estimate 2000-2001 | Plans 2001-2002 |
|---|---|---|---|
| Education and Employment | 14.2 | 17.0 | 18.9 |
| Health | 40.0 | 44.0 | 47.7 |
| of which NHS | 39.4 | 43.2 | 46.7 |
| DETR – main programmes | 4.0 | 4.7 | 5.1 |
| DETR – local government and regional policy | 33.9 | 35.3 | 36.9 |
| Home Office | 7.1 | 8.2 | 8.7 |
| Legal departments | 2.7 | 3.0 | 3.1 |
| Defence | 18.2 | 18.1 | 18.5 |
| Foreign and Commonwealth Office | 1.0 | 1.1 | 1.2 |
| International Development | 2.2 | 2.6 | 2.7 |
| Trade and Industry[1] | 2.8 | 3.2 | 4.0 |
| Agriculture, Fisheries and Food[2] | 1.0 | 1.1 | 1.1 |
| Culture, Media and Sport | 0.9 | 1.0 | 1.0 |
| Social Security (administration) | 3.2 | 3.6 | 3.8 |
| Scotland[3] | 12.0 | 12.7 | 13.7 |
| Wales[3] | 6.2 | 6.9 | 7.6 |
| Northern Ireland[3] | 5.3 | 5.9 | 6.0 |
| Chancellor of the Exchequer's departments | 3.5 | 3.8 | 3.9 |
| Cabinet Office | 1.2 | 1.2 | 1.3 |
| Employment Opportunities Fund[4] | 0.5 | 0.7 | 0.9 |
| Invest to save budget | 0 | 0 | 0 |
| Reserve | 0 | 0 | 1.2 |

| | | | |
|---|---|---|---|
| Allowance for shortfall | 0 | –2.0 | 0 |
| TOTAL CURRENT BUDGET | 159.9 | 172.3 | 187.0 |

1. Including capital expenditure of the Export Credits Guarantee Department
2. Includes spending on BSE related programmes.
3. For Scotland and Wales, the split between current and capital budgets is decided by the respective Executives. For Northern Ireland, during any period when the assembly ceases to operate, this is a matter for the Secretary of State.4 Formerly Welfare to Work expenditure financed by the Windfall Tax
*Source:* The Stationery Office - *Budget 2001*

## ANNUALLY MANAGED EXPENDITURE (FORECASTS) £ *billion*

| | 1999–2000 | 2000-2001 | 2001-02 |
|---|---|---|---|
| Departmental expenditure limits | 179.3 | 194.2 | 212.3 |
| Social security benefits | 97.2 | 99.1 | 104.9 |
| Housing revenue account subsidies | 3.4 | 3.2 | 4.6 |
| Common agricultural policy | 2.9 | 2.8 | 2.6 |
| Export Credits Guarantee Department | 0.9 | 1.1 | 0.8 |
| Net payment to EC institutions | 2.9 | 3.5 | 2.7 |
| Self-financing public corporations | 1.4 | 1.4 | 1.0 |
| Locally financed expenditure | 17.2 | 18.0 | 19.1 |
| Net public service pensions | 5.2 | 5.4 | 5.6 |
| National Lottery | 1.9 | 2.0 | 2.3 |
| Central government gross debt interest | 25.3 | 26.6 | 23.1 |
| Accounting and other adjustments | –18.0 | –11.5 | –7.5 |
| AME margin | 0.0 | 0.0 | 1.0 |
| Annually managed expenditure | 164.1 | 174.0 | 181.4 |

*Source:* The Stationery Office - *Budget 2001*

## SUMMARY OF LOCAL AUTHORITY 1999/2000 BUDGETS (OUTTURN PRICES) AND 2000/01 BUDGETS (OUTTURN PRICES) £ *billion*

| | Budget Estimates 1999/2000* | Budget Estimates 2000/01 | Change % |
|---|---|---|---|
| | £m | £m | |
| Total Service Expenditure | 54,177 | 57,943 | 7.0 |
| Mandatory Student Awards, Rent Allowances, Levies & Other Adjustments | 6,919 | 7,025 | 1.5 |
| Net Current Expenditure | 61,096 | 64,968 | 6.3 |
| Capital Financing, Interest Receipts, Dividends And Other Items | 4,761 | 4,627 | (2.8) |
| Gross Revenue Expenditure | 65,857 | 69,595 | 5.7 |
| *Funded By:* | | | |
| Specific Grants outside Aggregate External Finance | (8,404) | (8,889) | 5.8 |
| Specific Grants inside Aggregte External Finance | (2,691) | (3,748) | 39.3 |
| Net Revenue Expenditure (all services) | 54,762 | 56,958 | 4.0 |
| Met From: | | | |
| Reserves | (878) | (592) | (32.6) |
| Budget Requirement | 53,884 | 56,366 | 4.6 |
| SSA Reduction Grant/ Council Tax Reduction Grant | (90) | (35) | (61.1) |
| Police Grant | (3,686) | (3,813) | 3.4 |
| Revenue Support Grant | (21,765) | (21,468) | (1.4) |
| Central Support Protection Grant | (51) | (34) | (33.3) |
| Council Tax Benefit Subsidy Limitation Scheme | 31 | 51 | 64.5 |
| National Non-Domestic Rates | (14,268) | (16,042) | 12.4 |
| General Greater London Authority Grant | — | (22) | — |
| Council Tax | (11,708) | (12,652) | 8.1 |
| Gross Expenditure on Council Tax Benefits and Expenditure funded by Council Tax Transitional Reduction Scheme Grant | (2,166) | (2,219) | 2.4 |
| Other Items | (181) | (132) | (27.1) |

* The following adjustments were made to the 1999/2000 budget estimates to enable comparison with 2000/01
*Source:* CIPFA — *Finance and General Statistics 2000-01*

## PUBLIC SECTOR FINANCES £ *billion*

| | Outturn 1999–2000 | Estimate 2000-2001 | Forecast 2001-2002 |
|---|---|---|---|
| Current receipts | 358.7 | 383.2 | 398.0 |
| Current expenditure | 325.3 | 346.0 | 367.0 |
| Depreciation | 14.6 | 14.9 | 15.0 |
| Surplus on current budget* | 19.2 | 23.1 | 17 |
| Net investment | 3.5 | 7.4 | 11.0 |
| Public sector net borrowing | –16.0 | –16.4 | –6.0 |

### AS A PERCENTAGE OF GDP

| | Outturn 1999-2000 | Estimate 2000-2001 | Forecast 2001-2002 |
|---|---|---|---|
| Current receipts | 39.6 | 40.5 | 40.2 |
| Current expenditure | 35.9 | 36.6 | 37.1 |
| Depreciation | 1.6 | 1.6 | 1.6 |
| Surplus on current budget* | 2.1 | 2.4 | 1.7 |
| Net investment | 0.4 | 0.8 | 1.1 |
| Public sector net borrowing | –1.8 | –1.7 | -0.6 |
| Public sector net debt | 36.8 | 31.8 | 30.3 |

* Excluding windfall tax receipts and associated spending
*Source:* The Stationery Office – *Budget 2001*

GROSS VALUE ADDED AT BASIC PRICES BY INDUSTRY 1999 *£ *million*

| | |
|---|---|
| Agriculture, hunting, forestry and fishing | 9,332 |
| Mining and quarrying, including oil and gas extraction | 17,976 |
| Manufacturing (revised definition) | 147,699 |
| Electricity, gas and water supply | 17,944 |
| Construction | 41,273 |
| Wholesale and retail trade | 117,554 |
| Transport and communication | 69,208 |
| Financial intermediation | 220,601 |
| Adjustment for financial services | -30,411 |
| Public administration, defence | 40,199 |
| Education; health; social work | 93,241 |
| Other services | 41,498 |
| ALL INDUSTRIES | 787,863 |

*At basic prices, not market prices, and excluding taxes on products
*Source:* The Stationery Office – *Annual Abstract of Statistics 2001* (Crown copyright)

BALANCE OF PAYMENTS 1999 £ *million*

CURRENT ACCOUNT

| | |
|---|---|
| Trade in goods | |
| Exports | 165,667 |
| Imports | 192,434 |
| Trade in goods balance | -26,767 |
| Services balance | 11,538 |
| Investment income | 8,131 |
| Transfers balance | -4,084 |
| CURRENT BALANCE | -10,981 |

*Source:* The Stationery Office – *Annual Abstract of Statistics 2001* (Crown copyright)

UK TRADE ON A BALANCE OF PAYMENTS BASIS £ *million*

| | *Exports* | *Imports* | *Balance* |
|---|---|---|---|
| 1989 | 92,611 | 117,335 | -24,724 |
| 1990 | 102,313 | 121,020 | -18,707 |
| 1991 | 103,939 | 114,162 | -10,223 |
| 1992 | 107,863 | 120,913 | -13,050 |
| 1993 | 122,039 | 135,358 | -13,319 |
| 1994 | 135,260 | 146,351 | -11,091 |
| 1995 | 153,725 | 165,449 | -11,724 |
| 1996 | 167,403 | 180,489 | -13,086 |
| 1997 | 171,798 | 183,590 | -11,792 |
| 1998 | 171,798 | 184,897 | -20,765 |
| 1999 | 165,667 | 192,434 | -26,767 |

*Source:* The Stationery Office – *Annual Abstract of Statistics 20001* (Crown copyright)

VALUE OF UK EXPORTS 2000
BY DESTINATION £ *million*

| | |
|---|---|
| European Community | 105,524.6 |
| Other western Europe | 7,692.4 |
| Eastern Europe | 5,086.3 |
| North America | 33,909.0 |
| Other America | 2,668.4 |
| Middle East and North Africa | 8,107.6 |
| Sub-Saharan Africa | 3,170.2 |
| Asia and Oceania | 19,794.9 |
| Low-value exports | 485.5 |
| Total non-EC exports | 80,914.8 |
| Total exports | 186,439.4 |

*Source:* HM Customs and Excise

VALUE OF UK IMPORTS 2000
BY SOURCE £ *million*

| | |
|---|---|
| European Community | 109,295.4 |
| Other western Europe | 13,702.1 |
| Eastern Europe | 5,990.4 |
| North America | 34,458.6 |
| Other America | 3,677.9 |
| Middle East and North Africa | 5,324.1 |
| Sub-Saharan Africa | 4,201.3 |
| Asia and Oceania | 43,600.5 |
| Low-value imports | 587.9 |
| Total non-EC imports | 111,543.1 |
| Total imports | 220,838.5 |

*Source:* HM Customs and Excise

EMPLOYMENT

LABOUR FORCE BY AGE 1999 (UK)

| *Age* | *Male* | *Female* |
|---|---|---|
| 16-24 | 2,400,000 | 2,000,000 |
| 25-44 | 8,300,000 | 6,600,000 |
| 45-59 | 4,600,000 | 3,800,000 |
| 60-64 | 700,000 | 400,000 |
| 65 and over | 300,000 | 200,000 |
| Total | 16,200,000 | 13,000,000 |

*Source:* The Stationery Office – *Social Trends 31* (Crown copyright)

ECONOMIC STATUS OF PEOPLE OF WORKING AGE (UK) *as at spring 2000*

| | *Male* | *Female* |
|---|---|---|
| All in employment | 15,000,000 | 11,900,000 |
| Working full-time | 11,800,000 | 6,300,000 |
| Working part-time | 1,000,000 | 4,700,000 |
| Self-employed | 2,200,000 | 800,000 |
| Others in employment | 100,000 | 100,000 |
| Unemployed | 1,000,000 | 600,000 |
| All economically active | 16,000,000 | 12,500,000 |
| Economically inactive | 3,000,000 | 4,800,000 |
| TOTAL | 19,000,000 | 17,300,000 |

*Source*: The Stationery Office – *Social Trends 31* (Crown copyright)

THE WORKFORCE IN EMPLOYMENT (UK)
SEASONALLY ADJUSTED, AT DECEMBER 2000

| | |
|---|---|
| Employees in employment | 25,380,000 |
| Self-employed | 3,397,000 |
| *HM Forces | 206,000 |
| *Work-related government-supported training | 112,000 |
| Total workforce in employment | 29,095,000 |

* not seasonally adjusted

## Employees in Employment, by Main Sector (UK)seasonally adjusted, at December 2000

| | |
|---|---|
| Service industries | 22,409,000 |
| Manufacturing industries | 4,131,000 |
| Energy and water supply | 195,000 |
| Other industries | 1,721,000 |
| Total employees in employment | 29,095,000 |

## Average Gross Weekly Earnings of Full-Time Employees (Great Britain) 2000

| | |
|---|---|
| All adults | £390 |
| All men | 428 |
| Men, manual | 311 |
| Men, non-manual | 529 |
| All women | 319 |
| Women, manual | 202 |
| Women, non-manual | 350 |

*Source:* Office for National Statistics, Labour Force Survey

## Unemployment By Regions seasonally adjusted, December 2000 to February 2001

| | *Total* | *% of total economically active* |
|---|---|---|
| United Kingdom | 1,535,000 | 5.2 |
| England: | 1,253,000 | 5.0 |
| Eastern | 96,000 | 3.4 |
| East Midlands | 97,000 | 4.6 |
| London | 252,000 | 6.9 |
| North East | 95,000 | 8.0 |
| North West | 173,000 | 5.2 |
| South East | 146,000 | 3.4 |
| South West | 98,000 | 3.9 |
| West Midlands | 157,000 | 6.0 |
| Yorkshire and the Humber | 139,000 | 5.6 |
| Wales | 83,000 | 6.2 |
| Scotland | 152,000 | 6.0 |
| Northern Ireland | 46,000 | 6.1 |

*Source:* Office for National Statistics

## Unemployment Rates By Age 2000 (UK)

*Percentages*

| *Age* | *Male* | *Female* |
|---|---|---|
| 16–17 | 20.1 | 16.9 |
| 18–24 | 11.8 | 8.5 |
| 25–44 | 4.8 | 4.5 |
| 45–54 | 4.8 | 2.9 |
| 55–59 | 5.4 | 3.1 |
| 60–64 | 5.8 | — |
| 60 and over | — | — |
| All ages | 6.1 | 4.8 |

*Source:* The Stationery Office – *Social Trends 31* (Crown copyright)

## Industrial Stoppages 1999 (UK)

| *Duration* | |
|---|---|
| Not more than 5 days | 179,000 |
| 6–10 days | 8,000 |
| 11–20 days | 9,000 |
| 21–30 days | 4,000 |
| 31–50 days | 3,000 |
| More than 50 days | 2,000 |
| Total number of stoppages | 205,000 |

*Source:* The Stationery Office – *Annual Abstract of Statistics 20001*(Crown copyright)

## Trade Unions (UK)

| *Year* | *No. of unions at end of year* | *Total membership at end of year* |
|---|---|---|
| 1970 | 543 | 11,187,000 |
| 1975 | 470 | 12,026,000 |
| 1980 | 438 | 12,947,000 |
| 1985 | 370 | 10,821,000 |
| 1990 | 287 | 9,947,000 |
| 1995 | 238 | 8,089,000 |
| 1997* | 233 | 7,795,000 |
| 1998* | 221 | 7,807,000 |

* Figures for Great Britain only

*Source:* Office for National Statistics; Department of Trade and Industry

# HOUSEHOLDS AND THEIR EXPENDITURE 1999–2000[1]

## Number of Households Supplying Data

| | |
|---|---|
| Number of households supplying data | 7,079 |
| Total number of persons | 16,786 |
| Total number of adults[2] | 12,432 |

## Distribution by Tenure

| | |
|---|---|
| Rented unfurnished | 28% |
| Rented furnished | 3.% |
| Rent-free | 1% |
| Owner-occupied | 67% |

## Average Number of Persons per Household

| | |
|---|---|
| All persons | 2.3 |
| Males | 1.1 |
| Females | 1.2 |
| Adults[2] | 1.8 |
| Persons under 65 | 1.4 |
| Persons 65 and over | 0.3 |
| Children[2] | 0.5 |
| Children under 2 | 0.1 |
| Children 2 and under 5 | 0.1 |
| Children 5 and under 18 | 0.4 |
| Persons economically active | 1.1 |
| Persons not economically active | 1.2 |
| Men 65 and over, women 60 and over | 0.4 |
| Others | 0.8 |

## Household Expenditure on Commodities and Services – Weekly Average

| | £ | *As % of total* |
|---|---|---|
| Housing | 57.00 | 16 |
| Fuel and power | 11.30 | 3 |
| Food | 59.60 | 17 |
| Alcoholic drink | 15.30 | 4 |
| Tobacco | 6.00 | 2 |
| Clothing and footwear | 21.00 | 6 |
| Household goods | 30.70 | 9 |
| Household services | 18.90 | 5 |
| Personal goods and services | 13.90 | 4 |
| Motoring expenditure | 52.60 | 15 |
| Fares and other travel costs | 9.20 | 3 |
| Leisure goods | 18.50 | 5 |
| Leisure services | 43.90 | 12 |
| Miscellaneous | 1.40 | |
| *Total* | 359.40 | 100.0 |

1. Information derived from the Family Expenditure Survey; relates to the UK
2. Adults = all persons 18 and over and married persons under 18
Children = all unmarried persons under 18
*Source:* The Stationery Office – *Annual Abstract of Statistics 2001* (Crown copyright)

## SOURCES OF HOUSEHOLD INCOME 1999–2000*

| AVERAGE WEEKLY INCOME BY SOURCE (£) | |
|---|---|
| Wages and salaries | 315.40 |
| Self-employment | 46.00 |
| Investments | 21.80 |
| Annuities and pensions (other than social security benefits) | 32.80 |
| Social security benefits | 58.00 |
| Other sources | 5.90 |
| *Total* | 479.90 |

| SOURCES AS A PERCENTAGE OF TOTAL HOUSEHOLD INCOME (%) | |
|---|---|
| Wages and salaries | 66.0 |
| Self-employment | 10.0 |
| Investments | 5.0 |
| Annuities and pensions (other than social security benefits) | 7.0 |
| Social security benefits | 12.0 |
| Other sources | 1.0 |
| *Total* | 100.0 |

* Information derived from the Family Expenditure Survey; relates to the UK. Number of households supplying data, 7,097
*Source:* The Stationery Office – *Annual Abstract of Statistics 2001* (Crown copyright)

## AVAILABILITY OF CERTAIN DURABLE GOODS 1999–2000*

| | *% of households* |
|---|---|
| Car | 71 |
| One | 43 |
| Two | 21 |
| Three or more | 6 |
| Central heating, full or partial | 90 |
| Washing machine | 91 |
| Fridge/freezer or deep freezer | 91 |
| Refrigerator | 53 |
| Television | 98† |
| Telephone | 95 |
| Home computer | 38 |
| Internet Access | 19 |
| Video recorder | 86 |

* Information derived from the Family Expenditure Survey; relates to the UK. Number of households supplying data, 7,097
† 1992 figure
*Source:* The Stationery Office – *Annual Abstract of Statistics* 2001 (Crown copyright)

# Cost of Living and Inflation Rates

The first cost of living index to be calculated took July 1914 as 100 and was based on the pattern of expenditure of working-class families in 1914. The cost of living index was superseded in 1947 by the general index of retail prices (RPI), although the older term is still popularly applied to it.

## General Index of Retail Prices

The general index of retail prices measures the changes month by month in the average level of prices of goods and services purchased by most households in the United Kingdom. The spending pattern on which the index is based is revised each year, mainly using information from the Family Expenditure Survey. The expenditure of certain higher income households and of households mainly dependent on state pensions is excluded.

The index is compiled using a selection of over 600 goods and services, and the prices charged for these items are collected at regular intervals in about 146 locations throughout the country. For the index, the price changes are weighted in accordance with the pattern of consumption of the average family.

## Inflation Rate

The twelve-monthly percentage change in the 'all items' index of the RPI is usually referred to as the rate of inflation. The percentage change in prices between any two months/years can be obtained using the following formula:

$$\frac{\text{Later date RPI} - \text{Earlier date RPI}}{\text{Earlier date RPI}} \times 100$$

e.g. to find the rate of inflation for 1988, using the annual averages for 1987 and 1988:

$$\frac{106.9 - 101.9}{101.9} \times 100 = 4.9\%$$

## Purchasing Power of the Pound

Changes in the internal purchasing power of the pound may be defined as the 'inverse' of changes in the level of prices; when prices go up, the amount which can be purchased with a given sum of money goes down. To find the purchasing power of the pound in one month or year, given that it was 100p in a previous month or year, the calculation would be:

$$100\text{p} \times \frac{\text{Earlier month/year RPI}}{\text{Later month/year RPI}}$$

Thus, if the purchasing power of the pound is taken to be 100p in 1975, the comparable purchasing power in 1997 would be:

$$100\text{p} \times \frac{34.2}{157.5} = 21.71\text{p}$$

For longer term comparisons, it has been the practice to use an index which has been constructed by linking together the RPI for the period 1962 to date; an index derived from the consumers expenditure deflator for the period from 1938 to 1962; and the prewar 'cost of living' index for the period 1914 to 1938. This long-term index enables the internal purchasing power of the pound to be calculated for any year from 1914 onwards. It should be noted that these figures can only be approximate.

| | Long-term index of consumer goods and services (Jan. 1987 = 100) | Comparable purchasing power of £1 in 1998 | Rate of inflation (annual average) |
|---|---|---|---|
| 1914 | 2.8 | 58.18 | |
| 1915 | 3.5 | 46.54 | |
| 1920 | 7.0 | 23.27 | |
| 1925 | 5.0 | 32.58 | |
| 1930 | 4.5 | 36.20 | |
| 1935 | 4.0 | 40.72 | |
| 1938 | 4.4 | 37.02 | |
| *There are no official figures for 1939–45* | | | |
| 1946 | 7.4 | 22.01 | |
| 1950 | 9.0 | 18.10 | |
| 1955 | 11.2 | 14.54 | |
| 1960 | 12.6 | 12.93 | |
| 1965 | 14.8 | 11.00 | |
| 1970 | 18.5 | 8.80 | |
| 1975 | 34.2 | 4.76 | |
| 1980 | 66.8 | 2.44 | 18.0 |
| 1981 | 74.8 | 2.18 | 11.9 |
| 1982 | 81.2 | 2.01 | 8.6 |
| 1983 | 84.9 | 1.92 | 4.6 |
| 1984 | 89.2 | 1.83 | 5.0 |
| 1985 | 94.6 | 1.72 | 6.1 |
| 1986 | 97.8 | 1.67 | 3.4 |
| 1987 | 101.9 | 1.60 | 4.2 |
| 1988 | 106.9 | 1.52 | 4.9 |
| 1989 | 115.2 | 1.41 | 7.8 |
| 1990 | 126.1 | 1.29 | 9.5 |
| 1991 | 133.5 | 1.22 | 5.9 |
| 1992 | 138.5 | 1.18 | 3.7 |
| 1993 | 140.7 | 1.16 | 1.6 |
| 1994 | 144.1 | 1.13 | 2.4 |
| 1995 | 149.1 | 1.09 | 3.5 |
| 1996 | 152.7 | 1.07 | 2.4 |
| 1997 | 157.5 | 1.03 | 3.1 |
| 1998 | 162.9 | 1.00 | 3.4 |
| 1999 | 165.4 | 0.98 | 1.5 |
| 2000 | 170.3 | 0.96 | 3.0 |

The RPI figures are published around the middle of each month. They are available as a recorded message which can be heard by telephoning 020-7533 5866. Each month an updated Consumer Price Indices bulletin is published by the Office of National Statistics.

Office of National Statistics, 1 Drummond Gate, London SW1V 2QQ.
Public Enquiries Line: 020-7533 5874
Web: www.statistics.gov.uk

# Lotteries and Gaming

Gaming and lotteries in the UK are officially regulated and may only be run by licensed operators or in licensed premises. Responsibility for policy and the laws on gaming and lotteries rests with the Home Secretary. The National Lottery is regulated by the National Lottery Commission, which replaced the Office of the National Lottery in April 1999. Supervision of other lottery operations and gaming is mostly the responsibility of the Gaming Board of Great Britain.

Most betting is on horseracing and greyhound racing, and may take place at racecourses and greyhound tracks, or at off-course betting offices. The amount spent on on-course betting is estimated to be about 10 per cent of the figures for off-course betting.

OFF-COURSE BETTING (UK)

| | £ million |
|---|---|
| 1996–7 | 6,718 |
| 1997–8 | 6,851 |
| 1998–9 | 7,109 |
| 1999-2000 | 7,293 |
| 2000-2001 | 7,221p |

p provisional
*Source:* Horserace Totalisator Board

Other forms of gaming and lotteries include the following:

| | |
|---|---|
| Number of casinos operating | 118 |
| Total drop (1998-9) | 3.1billion |
| Bingo clubs holding gaming licences | 727 |
| Amount staked (1998–9) | £1.08billion |
| Gaming machines licensed | 250,000 |
| Society lottery schemes registered | 646 |
| Total ticket sales (£ million) | *c.*£104m |

In 1999–2000 sales of society lottery tickets declined by 35 per cent to £103.5 million. Of this, £28 million (27 per cent) was spent on prizes, £27 million (26 per cent) on expenses and £48.5 million (47 per cent) went to good causes.
*Source:* Report of the Gaming Board for Great Britain 1999-2000

## THE NATIONAL LOTTERY

The National Lottery is currently run by a private company, Camelot Group PLC. The initial seven-year licence granted to Camelot expired on 30 September 2001 but the company has been awarded an interim licence from 1 October 2001 to 26 January 2002 and a new seven-year licence commencing on 27 January 2002.

The National Lottery Commission is responsible for the granting, varying and enforcing of licences to run the National Lottery. The Commission's duties are to ensure that the National Lottery is run with all due care and attention, that the interests of players are protected and, subject to these two points, to maximise the money raised for good causes.

The first National Lottery tickets draw was made on 19 November 1994, with a mid week draw introduced on Wednesday 5 February 1997. Instants (scratchcards) were introduced on 21 March 1995. Camelot has also introduced two other draws; the weekly Thunderball draw, launched on 12 June 1999, and the bi-weekly Lottery Extra, introduced on 13 November 2000. Tickets for the main lottery game cost £1. To play, players must choose six numbers from 1 to 49. If the jackpot prize is not won, it is 'rolled over' to the next draw. The highest win on a single ticket to date was £22,590,829 on 10 June 1995. By June 2001, 1,167 millionaires had been created.

SALES 1999–2000

| | |
|---|---|
| Average number of tickets (on-line and instants) sold per week | 90–95m |
| Average number of people playing weekly | *c.*29m |
| % of adult population buying tickets regularly | *c.*61% |
| Amount raised by ticket sales, 1994 to June 2001 | *c.*£32.5 billion |

*Sources:* Camelot, National Lottery Commission

DISTRIBUTION OF PROCEEDS

*over the seven-year licence period*

| *Allocated to:* | % |
|---|---|
| Prize money | 50 |
| Tax | 12 |
| Retailer commission | 5 |
| Camelot (operating costs and profit) | 5 |
| Good causes | 28 |

The 'good causes' originally benefiting from lottery funds were the arts, sport, heritage, charities and Millennium projects. In July 1998 the National Lottery Act created a sixth good cause, the New Opportunities Fund, to fund health, education and environmental initiatives. The New Opportunities Fund announced its first awards in summer 1999. The Act also created a National Endowment for Science, Technology and the Arts (NESTA), a non-departmental public body whose objectives are: to help talented individuals; to enable inventions and ideas to be commercially exploited; and to promote public knowledge of science, technology and the arts. NESTA received an initial £200 million from LotteryFunds but thereafter is to generate its own income.

The percentage of all the funds allocated to the good causes received by each cause is as follows: the arts, sport, heritage and charities 16.66 per cent each; the Millennium projects 20 per cent; and the New Opportunities Fund 13.33 per cent. On 21 August 2001 the share going to the Millennium Commission will be transferred to the New Opportunities Fund.

The cumulative amount allocated to the good causes from November 1994 to April 2001 was £10,924 million.

AWARDS 2000-2001

Most awards are conditional on partnership funding being obtained from other sources.

| | *Number* | *Total value £* |
|---|---|---|
| Total | 22,004 | 1,206,498,915 |
| Arts, total | 3,744 | 145,977,983 |
| Arts Council of England | 2,563 | 91,678,516 |
| Arts Council of Wales | 491 | 13,904,385 |
| Scottish Arts Council | 482 | 7,767,125 |
| Arts Council of Northern Ireland | 71 | 1,768,609 |
| Film Council | 80 | 27,504,348 |
| Scottish Screen | 57 | 3,355,000 |
| Millennium Commission | 681 | 36,116,049 |
| Heritage Lottery Fund | 2,349 | 224,567,433 |
| Community Fund | 9,724 | 374,501,878 |
| New Oppertunities Fund | 2,215 | 215,190,716 |
| Sport, total | 3,291 | 210,144,856 |
| Sport England | 312 | 107,027,298 |
| Sports Council for Wales | 1,535 | 14,706,758 |
| Sportscotland | 898 | 20,021,846 |
| Sports Council for Northern Ireland | 190 | 6,846,024 |
| UK Sport | 356 | 61,542,930 |

# Finance

## British Currency

The unit of currency is the pound sterling (£) of 100 pence. The decimal system was introduced on 15 February 1971.

### COIN

*Gold Coins*
*One hundred pounds £100
*Fifty pounds £50
*Twenty-five pounds £25
*Ten pounds £10
Five pounds £5
Two pounds £2
Sovereign £1
Half-Sovereign 50p

*Silver Coins*
(*Britannia coins)
*Two pounds £2*
One pound £1
50 pence 50p
Twenty pence 20p
(†*Maundy Money*)
Fourpence 4p
Threepence 3p
Twopence 2p
Penny 1p

‡*Bi-colour Coins*
Two pounds £2

*Nickel-Brass Coins*
§Two pounds £2
One pound £1

*Cupro-Nickel Coins*
Crown £5 (since 1990)
50 pence 50p
Crown 25p (pre-1990)
20 pence 20p
10 pence 10p
5 pence 5p

*Bronze Coins*
2 pence 2p
1 penny 1p

*Copper-plated Steel Coins*
2 pence 2p
1 penny 1p

*Britannia coins: gold bullion coins introduced 1987; silver coins introduced 1997
†Gifts of special money distributed by the Sovereign annually on Maundy Thursday to the number of aged poor men and women corresponding to the Sovereign's own age
‡Cupro-nickel centre and nickel-brass outer ring
§Commemorative coins; not intended for general circulation

#### GOLD COIN

Gold ceased to circulate during the First World War. Since then controls on buying, selling and holding gold coin have been imposed at various times but subsequently have been revoked. Under the Exchange Control (Gold Coins Exemption) Order 1979, gold coins may now be imported and exported without restriction, except gold coins which are more than 50 years old and valued at a sum in excess of £8,000; these cannot be exported without specific authorisation from the Department of Trade and Industry.

Value Added Taxation on the sale of gold coins was revoked in 2000.

#### SILVER COIN

Prior to 1920 silver coins were struck from sterling silver, an alloy of which 925 parts in 1,000 were silver. In 1920 the proportion of silver was reduced to 500 parts. From 1 January 1947 all 'silver' coins, except Maundy money, have been struck from cupro-nickel, an alloy of copper 75 parts and nickel 25 parts, except for the 20p, composed of copper 84 parts, nickel 16 parts. Maundy coins continue to be struck from sterling silver.

#### BRONZE COIN

Bronze, introduced in 1860 to replace copper, is an alloy of copper 97 parts, zinc 2.5 parts and tin 0.5 part. These proportions have been subject to slight variations in the past. Bronze was replaced by copper-plated steel in September 1992 and reintroduced in April 1997.

#### LEGAL TENDER

| | |
|---|---|
| Gold (dated 1838 onwards, if not below least current weight) to any amount | |
| £5 (Crown since 1990) | to any amount |
| £2 | to any amount |
| £1 | to any amount |
| 50p | up to £10 |
| 25p (Crown pre-1990) | up to £10 |
| 20p | up to £10 |
| 10p | up to £5 |
| 5p | up to £5 |
| 2p | up to 20p |
| 1p | up to 20p |

The £1 coin was introduced in 1983 to replace the £1 note.

These coins ceased to be legal tender on the following dates:

| | |
|---|---|
| Farthing | 31 December 1960 |
| Halfpenny ($\frac{1}{2}$d) | 1 August 1969 |
| Half-crown | 1 January 1970 |
| Threepence | 31 August 1971 |
| Penny (1d) | 31 August 1971 |
| Sixpence | 30 June 1980 |
| Halfpenny ($\frac{1}{2}$p) | 31 December 1984 |
| old 5 pence | 31 December 1990 |
| old 10 pence | 30 June 1993 |
| old 50 pence | 28 February 1998 |

Since 1982 the word 'new' in 'new pence' displayed on decimal coins has been dropped.

The Channel Islands and the Isle of Man issue their own coinage, which are legal tender only in the island of issue. For denominations, *see* page 617.

| | *Metal* | *Standard weight* (g) | *Standard diameter* (cm) |
|---|---|---|---|
| Penny | bronze | 3.564 | 2.032 |
| Penny | copper-plated steel | 3.564 | 2.032 |
| 2 pence | bronze | 7.128 | 2.591 |
| 2 pence | copper-plated steel | 7.128 | 2.591 |
| 5p | cupro-nickel | 3.25 | 1.80 |
| 10p | cupro-nickel | 6.5 | 2.45 |
| 20p | cupro-nickel | 5.0 | 2.14 |
| 25p Crown | cupro-nickel | 28.28 | 3.861 |
| 50p | cupro-nickel | 13.5 | 3.0 |
| 50p | cupro-nickel | 8.00 | 2.73 |
| £1 | nickel-brass | 9.5 | 2.25 |
| £2 | nickel-brass | 15.98 | 2.84 |
| ‡£2 | cupro-nickel, nickel-brass | 12.00 | 2.84 |
| £5 Crown | cupro-nickel | 28.28 | 3.861 |

The 'remedy' is the amount of variation from standard permitted in weight and fineness of coins when first issued from the Mint.

The Trial of the Pyx is the examination by a jury to ascertain that coins made by the Royal Mint, which have been set aside in the pyx (or box), are of the proper weight, diameter and composition required by law. The trial is held annually, presided over by the Queen's Remembrancer (the Senior Master of the Supreme Court), with a jury of freemen of the Company of Goldsmiths.

## BANKNOTES

Bank of England notes are currently issued in denominations of £5, £10, £20 and £50 for the amount of the fiduciary note issue, and are legal tender in England and Wales. No £1 notes have been issued since 1984 and in March 1998 the outstanding notes were written off in accordance with the provision of the Currency Act 1983.

The current E series of notes was introduced from June 1990, replacing the D series (*see* below). The historical figures portrayed in this series are:

| | | |
|---|---|---|
| £5 | June 1990– | George Stephenson |
| £10 | November 2000– | Charles Darwin* |
| £20 | June 1991– | Michael Faraday† |
| £20 | June 1999– | Sir Edward Elgar |
| £50 | April 1994– | Sir John Houblon |

*The version of the Bank of England £10 banknote issued in April 1992, bearing a portrait of Charles Dickens, remains legal tender. No plans have been announced to remove it from circulation.

†Withdrawn from circulation on 28 February 2001.

### NOTE CIRCULATION

Note circulation is highest at the two peak spending periods of the year, around Christmas and during the summer holiday period. The total value of notes in circulation at 3 January 2001 was £29,360 million, compared to £25,991 million at 23 December 1998.

The value of notes in circulation at the end of February 2000 and 2001 was:

| | 2000 | 2001 |
|---|---|---|
| £5 | £1,045m | £1,041m |
| £10 | £5,684m | £6,107m |
| £20 | £13,197m | £14,381m |
| £50 | £4,195m | £4,657m |
| Other notes† | £1,014m | £1,009m |
| Total | £25,135m | £27,195m |

† Includes higher value notes used internally in the Bank of England, e.g. as cover for the note issues of banks in Scotland and Northern Ireland in excess of their permitted issue

### LEGAL TENDER

Banknotes which are no longer legal tender are payable when presented at the head office of the Bank of England in London.

The white notes for £10, £20, £50, £100, £500 and £1,000, which were issued until April 1943, ceased to be legal tender in May 1945, and the white £5 note in March 1946.

The white £5 note issued between October 1945 and September 1956, the £5 notes issued between 1957 and 1963 (bearing a portrait of Britannia) and the first series to bear a portrait of The Queen, issued between 1963 and 1971, ceased to be legal tender in March 1961, June 1967 and September 1973 respectively.

The series of £1 notes issued during the years 1928 to 1960 and the 10 shilling notes issued from 1928 to 1961 (those without the royal portrait) ceased to be legal tender in May and October 1962 respectively. The £1 note first issued in March 1960 (bearing on the back a representation of Britannia) and the £10 note first issued in February 1964 (bearing a lion on the back), both bearing a portrait of The Queen on the front, ceased to be legal tender in June 1979. The £1 note first issued in 1978 ceased to be legal tender on 11 March 1988. The 10 shilling note was replaced by the 50p coin in October 1969, and ceased to be legal tender on 21 November 1970.

The D series of banknotes was introduced from 1970 and ceased to be legal tender from the dates shown below. The predominant identifying feature of each note was the portrayal on the back of a prominent figure from British history:

| | | |
|---|---|---|
| £1 | Feb. 1978–March 1988 | Sir Isaac Newton |
| £5 | Nov. 1971–Nov. 1991 | The Duke of Wellington |
| £10 | Feb. 1975–May 1994 | Florence Nightingale |
| £20 | July 1970–March 1993 | William Shakespeare |
| £50 | March 1981–Sept. 1996 | Sir Christopher Wren |

The £1 coin was introduced on 21 April 1983 to replace the £1 note.

### OTHER BANKNOTES

SCOTLAND – Banknotes are issued by three Scottish banks. The Royal Bank of Scotland issues notes for £1, £5, £10, £20 and £100. The Bank of Scotland and the Clydesdale Bank issue notes for £5, £10, £20, £50 and £100. Scottish notes are not legal tender in Scotland but they are an authorised currency and enjoy a status comparable to that of Bank of England notes.

NORTHERN IRELAND – Banknotes are issued by four banks in Northern Ireland. The Bank of Ireland, the Northern Bank and the Ulster Bank issue notes for £5, £10, £20, £50 and £100. The First Trust Bank issues notes for £10, £20, £50 and £100. Northern Ireland notes are not legal tender in Northern Ireland but they circulate widely and enjoy a status comparable to that of Bank of England notes.

CHANNEL ISLANDS – The States of Guernsey issues its own currency notes and coinage. The notes are for £1, £5, £10, £20 and £50, and the coins are for 1p, 2p, 5p, 10p, 20p, 50p, £1, £2 and £5. The States of Jersey issues its own currency notes and coinage. The notes are for £1, £5, £10, £20 and £50, and the coins are for 1p, 2p, 5p, 10p, 20p, 50p, £1 and £2.

THE ISLE OF MAN – The Isle of Man Government issues notes for £1, £5, £10, £20 and £50. Although these notes are only legal tender in the Isle of Man, they are accepted at face value in branches of the clearing banks in the UK. The Isle of Man issues coins for 1p, 2p, 5p, 10p, 20p, 50p, £1, £2 and £5.

Although none of the series of notes specified above is legal tender in the UK, they are generally accepted by the banks irrespective of their place of issue. At one time the banks made a commission charge for handling Scottish and Irish notes but this was abolished some years ago.

# Banking

There are two main types of deposit-taking institutions: banks and building societies, although National Savings also provides savings products. Banks and building societies are supervised by the Financial Services Authority although National Savings is not. As a result of the conversion of several building societies into banks in recent years, the size of the banking sector, which was already substantially greater than the non-bank deposit-taking sector, has increased further.

The main institutions within the British banking system are the Bank of England (the central bank), the retail banks, the investment banks and the overseas banks. In its role as the central bank, the Bank of England acts as banker to the Government and as a note-issuing authority; it also oversees the efficient functioning of payment and settlement systems.

Since May 1997, the Bank of England has had operational responsibility for monetary policy. At monthly meetings of its monetary policy committee the Bank sets the interest rate at which it will lend to the money markets.

OFFICIAL INTEREST RATES 2000–2001

| | |
|---|---|
| 14 January2000 | 5.75% |
| 10 February 2000 | 6.00% |
| 8 February 2001 | 5.75% |
| 5 April 2001 | 5.50% |
| 10 May 2001 | 5.25% |
| 2 August 2001 | 5.00% |

## RETAIL BANKS

The major retail banks are Abbey National, Alliance and Leicester, Bank of Scotland, Barclays (including the Woolwich), Bradford and Bingley, Halifax, HSBC, Lloyds/TSB, National Westminster, Northern Rock, Royal Bank of Scotland (including National Westminster).

Retail banks offer a wide variety of financial services to companies and individuals, including current and deposit accounts, loan and overdraft facilities, automated teller (cash dispenser) machines, cheque guarantee cards, credit cards and debit cards. Many banks also now offer telephone and Internet banking facilities.

The Financial Ombudsman Service provides independent and impartial arbitration in disputes between a bank and its customer (*see also* page 637).

Banking hours differ throughout the UK. Many banks now open longer hours and some at weekends, and hours vary from branch to branch. Current core opening hours are:

ENGLAND AND WALES: Monday–Friday, 9.30–4.30
SCOTLAND: Monday–Friday, 9.00–5.00
NORTHERN IRELAND: Monday–Friday, 9.30–4.30 (Wednesdays 10.00–4.30, except Ulster Bank Ltd); Northern Bank, 10.00–3.30, Saturdays 9.30–12.30

## PAYMENT CLEARINGS

The Association for Payment Clearing Services (APACS) is an umbrella organisation for payment clearings in the UK. It manages three clearing companies:

- BACS Ltd is the UK's automated clearing house for bulk clearing of electronic debits and credits (e.g. direct debits and salary credits)
- the Cheque and Credit Clearing Company Ltd operates bulk clearing systems for inter-bank cheques and paper credit items in Great Britain
- CHAPS Clearing Company Ltd provides same-day clearing for electronic funds transfers throughout the UK in sterling and globally in euro

Membership of APACS and the clearing companies is open to any appropriately regulated financial institution providing payment services and meeting the relevant membership criteria. As at May 2001, APACS had 31 members, comprising the major banks, building societies and The Post Office.

ASSOCIATION FOR PAYMENT CLEARING SERVICES (APACS), Mercury House, Triton Court, 14 Finsbury Square, London EC2A 1LQ. Tel: 020-7711 6200. *Head of Public Affairs*, R. Tyson-Davies

BACS LTD, De Havilland Road, Edgware, Middx HA8 5QA. Tel: 0870 165 0019. *Chief Executive*, G. Younger

CHEQUE AND CREDIT CLEARING COMPANY LTD, Mercury House, Triton Court, 14 Finsbury Square, London EC2A 1LQ. Tel: 020-7711 6200

CHAPS CLEARING COMPANY LTD, Mercury House, Triton Court, 14 Finsbury Square, London EC2A 1LQ. Tel: 020-7711 6200

MAJOR RETAIL BANKS: FINANCIAL RESULTS 2000

| *Bank Group* | *Profit before taxation £m* | *Profit after taxation £m* | *Total assets £m* | *Number of UK branches* |
|---|---|---|---|---|
| Abbey National | 1,975 | 1,416 | 204,391 | 755 |
| Alliance and Leicester | 447 | 336 | 34,716 | 310 |
| Bank of Scotland | 965 | 588 | 71,813 | 330 |
| †Barclays (incorporating Woolwich plc) | 3,496 | 2,552 | 316,190 | 2,129 |
| Halifax | 1,892 | – | 183,000 | 762 |
| Lloyds/TSB Group | 3,886 | 2,773 | 217,982 | 2,400 |
| HSBC | 2,046 | 1,345 | 104,846 | 1,663 |
| Northern Rock | 250.1 | 182 | 22,544 | 76 |
| § Royal Bank of Scotland Group (incorporating NatWest Group) | 3,373 | 2,216 | 320,004 | 2,298 |

†Statutory results for 2000 including Woolwich plc from the date of its acquisition on 25 October 2000.
§ Statutory results for the 15 months ended 31 December 2000 including Natwest from the date of its acquisition on 6 March 2000.

# Stamp Duties and Stamp Duty Reserve Tax

Stamp duty is a tax on documents; Stamp duty reserve tax is charged upon agreements for the sale of shares and securities where there is no stamped stock transfer form.

For the majority of people, contact with Stamp duty arises when they purchase a property. Stamp duty is payable by the buyer through a solicitor upon completion as a way of raising money for the government based on the purchase price of a property. Stamp duty on share dealing is levied at 0.5 per cent or, in special circumstances 1.5 per cent.

Where stamp duty is not paid or deposited with the Stamp Office within 30 days after execution, interest accrues. This applies where the instrument is executed offshore. For agreements for leases the interest commences from 30 days after the execution of the lease. A stampable instrument may be stamped without penalty if presented for stamping within 30 days after its date of first execution. Where wholly executed abroad, the period begins to run from the date of arrival in the UK.

Instruments presented after the proper time may be subject to a penalty.

Under the Finance Act 1999, a person dissatisfied with a decision of the Commissioners as to the issuing or the appropriate level of stamp duty may appeal within thirty days of their decision.

### Agreement for Sale of Property

Charged with *ad valorem* duty as if an actual conveyance on sale, with certain exceptions, e.g. agreements for the sale of legal interests in land, stocks and shares, goods, wares or merchandise, a ship or foreign property. If *ad valorem* duty is paid on an agreement in accordance with this provision, the subsequent conveyance or transfer is not chargeable with any *ad valorem* duty and the Commissioners will upon application either place a denoting stamp on such conveyance or transfer or will transfer the *ad valorem* duty thereto. Further, if such an agreement is not performed the *ad valorem* duty paid will be returned.

### Conveyance or Transfer on Sale

"Sale" includes transfers for cash, shares and debt and in the case of land exchanges, any other property.

Value not exceeding £60,000, *nil*
Value of £60,001–£250,000, 1 per cent
Value of £250,001–£500,000, 3 per cent
Value exceeding £500,000, 4 per cent

Stamp duty for shares and marketable securities is levied at a rate of 0.5 per cent.

### Conveyance or Transfer of Any Other Kind

There is a fixed duty, however, under the Stamp Duty (Exempt Instruments) Regulations 1987, instruments which would otherwise fall under this head are exempt from stamp duty provided that the document is duly certified.

### Leases (including Agreements for Leases)

Lease or tack for any definite term less than a year of any furnished dwelling-house or apartments where the rent for such term exceeds £500, £5

Of any lands, tenements etc. in consideration of any rent, according to the following:

Term not exceeding seven years or indefinite (and rent not exceeding £500 p.a.), 1 per cent
Term not exceeding 35 years, 2 per cent
Term not exceeding 100 years, 12 per cent
Term exceeding 100 years, 24 per cent

Where a consideration other than rent is payable e.g. a premium in cash or other property, the same rule applies where the consideration does not exceed £60,000 as under conveyance or transfer on sale (except stock or marketable securities), provided that any rent payable does not exceed £600 a year and a certificate of value is included in the conveyance or transfer and the reduced rates of 1 per cent and 3 per cent for consideration not exceeding £500,000 apply.

Where a lease is granted pursuant to a prior written agreement for lease, the agreement itself is liable to duty. Credit for any duty paid on the agreement will be given against the duty payable on the lease and the Commissioners will place a denoting stamp on the lease. Where there is no prior written agreement for lease, the lease must contain a certificate that it has not been made in pursuance of such an agreement.

### Stamp Duties

### Unit Trust Instrument

Duty was abolished in the Finance Act 1988. Transfer of property to a unit trust or agreement to transfer units is generally subject to Conveyance on Sale duty or Stamp Duty Reserve Tax. By the Finance Act 1989, the transfer of units in certain authorised unit trusts is no longer subject to duty.

### Voluntary Disposition, *Inter Vivos*

There is a fixed duty, however, under the Stamp Duty (Exempt Instruments) Regulations 1987, instruments which would otherwise fall under this head are exempt provided that the document is certified as falling within category L in the schedule to the Regulations.

### Stamp Duty Reserve Tax

This is charged where there is a contract for the transfer of chargeable securities unless the charge is cancelled. The tax is payable by or on behalf of the buyer who is required to report the transaction and pay the tax on the seventh day of the month following that in which the contract is made or becomes unconditional. Penalties and interest are imposed for late payment or reporting.

For further information, the Inland Revenue Stamp Offices can be contacted. They have offices in Belfast, London, Birmingham, Bristol, Worthing, Manchester, Edinburgh and Newcastle. Visit the Inland Revenue site at www.inlandrevenue.co.uk

# Mutual Societies

Shortly after the 1997 General Election the new Government announced the creation of a single financial regulatory authority for the UK. The financial regulation of mutual societies – building societies and credit unions – currently the responsibility of the Building Societies Commission (BSC), the Friendly Societies Commission (FSC) and the Chief Registrar of the Friendly Societies (CR) were to be included amongst other bodies in the remit of the new organisation.

The Financial Services Authority (FSA) has since been developed under the Chairmanship of Sir Howard Davies, former Deputy Governor of the Bank of England. On 1 January 1999 staff of the Registry of Friendly Societies (RFS) supporting the functions of the BSC, the FSC and (in relation to the Credit Unions) the CR were transferred with their work to the FSA. Mutual Societies registration and records work, on which a decision had earlier been deferred, was transferred to FSA with the relevant staff on 1 February 2001.

FSA provides services and support to the Commissions, the CR and the RFS under formal service level agreements. These lay down the requirements to be met in carrying out the contracted work until the responsibilities are subsumed into those of FSA when the provisions of the Financial Services and Markets Act 2000 are brought into force. This final stage in the transition process, the transfer of statutory functions to FSA, is planned to become effective from 1 December 2001.

## FRIENDLY SOCIETIES IN BRITAIN

Friendly societies are voluntary mutual organisations, where the main purposes are assisting members during sickness, unemployment or retirement, and the provision of life assurance. Many of the older traditional societies complement their business activities by social activity and a general care for individual members in ways normally outside the scope of a purely commercial organisation. There are three main categories of friendly societies: societies with separately registered branches, commonly called orders; centralised societies, which conduct business directly with members (having no separately registered branches); and collecting societies which conduct industrial assurance business (commonly known as home service assurance). Collecting societies will benefit from a number of deregulatory measures included in the Financial Services and Markets Act 2000 involving relaxation for the future administration of existing contracts and by the removal of special requirements, in the industrial assurance legislation, concerning the selling of future contracts. Such business will be subject to the general conduct of business rules governing the marketing and selling of investment products.

The Friendly Societies Act 1992 created a new legislative framework for friendly societies, enabling them to provide a wider range of services to their members and allowing them to compete on more equal terms with other financial institutions. At the same time it provided for more flexible prudential supervision to safeguard members of societies.

The Act enables friendly societies to incorporate and establish subsidiaries to provide various financial and other services to their members and the public. The activities which subsidiaries are able to conduct include those to establish and manage unit trust schemes and personal equity plans; to arrange for the provision of credit, whether as agents or providers; to carry on long-term or general insurance business; to provide insurance intermediary services; to provide fund management services for trustees of pension funds; to administer estates and execute trusts of wills; and to establish and manage sheltered housing, residential homes for the elderly, hospitals and nursing homes.

The Act established a new framework to oversee friendly societies, including a Friendly Societies Commission, whose principal functions are to regulate the activities of friendly societies, promote their financial stability and protect members' funds. All friendly societies carrying on insurance or non-insurance business require authorisation by the Commission, which has a broad range of prudential powers. Friendly societies were also to be brought within the scope of the Policyholders Protection Act 1975, the statutory investor protection scheme covering insurance policyholders.

At the end of May 2001 there were 104 societies authorised to write new business. In all there were 40 incorporated societies. Of these, 37 were previously registered under the 1974 Act and three were new registrations under the Friendly Societies Act 1992. Twenty-two of the societies had active subsidiaries.

Over half of all registered friendly societies are not authorised to write new business, many being small and with a declining membership. At the end of March 2001 there were 247 friendly societies on the register compared to 259 a year earlier. The 42 Life Directive and Incorporated Societies, with assets of over £15 billion accounted for over 97 per cent of the total funds of the movement as at 31 December 1999. Contribution income paid by their members in that year amounted to £907 million. Statistics for these societies are set out in the table below:

Life Directive and Incorporated Societies

| | *1999* | *1998* |
|---|---|---|
| No. of societies | 42 | 42 |
| Membership (000s) | 4,736 | 4,681 |
| Contribution income (£000s) | 906,624 | 787,305 |
| Investment income (£000s) | 1,375,616 | 1,137,073 |
| Benefits paid (£000s) | 959,308 | 945,789 |
| Management expenses (£000s) | 332,276 | 314,920 |
| Total assets (£000s) | 15,088,479 | 12,894,769 |

The Friendly Societies Act 1974 allowed three other main classes of society to be registered: benevolent societies, working men's clubs and specially authorised societies. Benevolent societies are established for any charitable or benevolent purpose, to provide the same type of benefits as would be permissible for a friendly society, but in contrast the benefits must be for persons who are not members instead of, or in addition to, members. Working men's clubs provide social and recreational facilities for members. Specially authorised societies are registered for any purpose authorised by the Treasury as a purpose to which some or all of the provisions of the 1974 Act ought to be extended. Examples are societies for the promotion of science, literature and the fine arts, or to enable members to pursue an interest in sports and games. No new societies of any type may now be registered under this Act.

The numbers of the various types of bodies registered under the Friendly Societies Acts at the end of 1999 were:

| | |
|---|---|
| FRIENDLY SOCIETIES | |
| Orders* | 13 |
| Collecting societies | 14 |
| Other centralised societies | 238 |
| OTHER BODIES | |
| Benevolent societies* | 64 |
| Working men's clubs | 2,039 |
| Specially authorised societies | 117 |

* With 698 branches

## INDUSTRIAL AND PROVIDENT SOCIETIES IN BRITAIN

The familiar 'Co-op' societies are amongst the wide variety which are registered under the Industrial and Provident Societies Act 1965. This consolidating Act, provides for the registration of societies and lays down the broad framework within which they must operate. Internal relations of societies are governed by their registered rules.

Registration under the Act confers upon a society corporate status by its registered name with perpetual succession and a common seal, and limited liability. A society qualifies for registration if it is carrying on an industry, business or trade, and it satisfies the Registrar either (a) that it is a bona fide co-operative society, or (b) that in view of the fact that its business is being, or is intended to be, conducted for the benefit of the community, there are special reasons why it should be registered under the Act rather than as a company under the Companies Act.

The Credit Unions Act 1979 added a new class of society registrable under the 1965 Act. It also made provision for the supervision of these savings and loan bodies. Unlike other classes, where the role of the Registry remains solely that of a registration authority, it became for credit unions the financial regulator, a role now carried out for it by the FSA.

During 1999, the Housing sector was overtaken by the General Service sector as the largest single class of society in terms of asset holdings. It was also overtaken by the Clubs sector in terms of the number or registered societies. The total number of societies on the register (excluding credit unions) fell by 880 to 8,907 during the year. These shifting patterns and the overall reduction in numbers were partly the result of a programme or deregistrations of defunct societies. The number of new credit unions has been growing steadily at an average rate in excess of 50 new registrations a year since 1988. In 1999 there were 50 new registrations and in the period to end-September 2000 a further 34. The principle statistics for all classes on industrial and provident society at the end of 1999 are given in the table below:

| | *No. of societies* | *No. of members 000s* | *Funds of members £000s* | *Total assets £000s* |
|---|---|---|---|---|
| Retail | 90 | 5,800 | 1,639,182 | 3,507,318 |
| Wholesale and productive | 104 | 45 | 693,735 | 1,668,683 |
| Agricultural | 855 | 408 | 213,948 | 573,674 |
| Fishing | 74 | 3 | 8,766 | 18,701 |
| Clubs | 3,417 | 3,486 | 355,830 | 511,960 |
| General service | 1,059 | 560 | 2,129,612 | 26,027,926 |
| Housing | 3,308 | 163 | 8,868,305 | 24,393,160 |
| Credit unions | 666 | 296 | 170,394 | 180,633 |
| TOTAL | 9,573 | 10,761 | 14,079,772 | 56,822,055 |

## BUILDING SOCIETIES IN THE UK

The Building Societies Act 1997, which received royal assent on 21 March 1997, made substantive amendments to, but did not replace, the Building Societies Act 1986. It liberalised the statutory regime for building societies to enable them to compete on more level terms with other financial institutions without having to forego their mutual status.

The Building Societies Act 1986 gave building societies a completely new legal framework for the first time since the initial comprehensive building society legislation in 1874. The 1986 Act sets out detailed provisions in relation to:

- the constitution of building societies
- building societies' powers in relation to raising funds, advances, loans, other assets and the provision of services
- the powers of control of the Building Societies Commission
- protection of investors, and complaints and disputes
- management of building societies, accounts and audit
- mergers and transfers of business

The 1986 Act was prescriptive in respect of building societies' powers and the way in which they were exercised. However, it gave numerous powers to the Building Societies Commission and/or the Treasury to make statutory instruments which, subject to parliamentary approval, can amend, extend and supplement the provisions of the Act. Since it came into force on 1 January 1987 the Act had been amended and extended considerably, especially in respect of building societies' powers.

The main purposes of the Building Societies Act 1997 are:

- remove the prescriptive powers' regime relating to building societies and to replace it with a permissive regime with appropriately revised balance-sheet 'nature limits', thus increasing the commercial freedom of societies and allowing increased competition and wider choice for customers
- enhance the powers of control of the Building Societies Commission
- introduce a package of measures to enhance the accountability of building societies' boards to their members
- make changes to the provisions relating to the transfer of a building society's business to a company

The Act came fully into force on 21 October 1997. Under it a building society may pursue any activities set out in its memorandum, subject only to:

- principal purpose: its purpose or principal purpose must be that of making loans which are secured on residential properties and are funded substantially by its members
- lending limit: at least 75 per cent of its business assets must be loans fully secured on residential property
- funding limit: at least 50 per cent of its funds must be raised in the form of shares held by individual members
- restrictions: subject to certain exceptions, it must not act as a market maker in securities, commodities or currencies; trade in commodities or currencies; enter into transactions involving derivatives, except in relation to hedging; nor create a floating charge over its assets
- prudential: it must comply with the criteria of prudential management

All authorised building societies, after making the necessary changes to their memoranda and rules, are now operating under the more liberal statutory regime set out in the 1997 Act.

### Conversions and Take-Overs

During the year ending 31 March 2000 two building societies transferred their business to other societies. There were no transfers in the year to 31 March 2001 but Bradford and Bingley Building Society completed the process of change to PLC status. The requisite transfer resolutions were passed by a special general meeting of the society on 17 July 2000 and the Building Societies Commission confirmed the transfer on the 28 September 2000. The transfer of its business to Bradford and Bingley PLC was completed on 4 December 2000. The following table shows how the number of societies has reduced through mergers, conversions and take-overs, over the five years 1996–2001 and the amount of the assets involved.

| *Year* | *Authorised societies* | | *Societies transferring their engagements within the sector* | | *Societies transferring their business out of the sector* | |
|---|---|---|---|---|---|---|
| | *No.* | *Assets £bn* | *No.* | *Assets £bn* | *No.* | *Assets £bn* |
| 1996 | 80 | 292 | 2 | 0.14 | 1 | 13.89 |
| 1997 | 77 | 297 | 1 | 0.18 | 5 | 176.80 |
| 1998 | 71 | 131 | – | – | – | – |
| 1999 | 71 | 148 | 1 | 0.02 | 1 | 7.83 |
| 2000 | 69 | 155 | 1 | 0.06 | 1 | 23.71 |
| 2001 (first half) | 67 | 151 | – | – | – | – |

### Ombudsman Scheme

Complaints about the actions of building societies may be resolved through societies' own internal complaints procedures. All authorised building societies are, in addition, members of the Building Societies Ombudsmen scheme which provides an independent service to consider and determine complaints which are within its remit. The Financial Services and Markets Act 2000 brings together the Building Societies Ombudsman and seven others including the Banking Ombudsman and the Insurance Ombudsman, in a single Financial Ombudsman Service. This new complaints-handling organisation provides consumers with a free, informal and independent service for resolving disputes with most providers of financial products and services. From 1 April 2000 this new body has provided a complaints handling service on behalf of each of the existing schemes. The arrangements will continue until the Financial Ombudsman Service receives powers in its own right when the legislation is brought into force from 1 December 2001. In the year to 31 March 2001 a total of 1,400 new building society references were made to the Ombudsman, compared to 971 in the previous year, an increase of 44 per cent. Complainants can write to the Financial Ombudsman Service at South Quay Plaza, 183 Marsh Wall, London E14 9SR. Tel: 020-7964 1000.

The principal statistics for building society activity for 1999–2000 are given in the table below:

### Building Societies 1999–2000

| | 1999 | 2000 |
|---|---|---|
| No. of societies – total | 72 | 68 |
| – authorised | 69 | 67 |
| No. of shareholders (000s) | 21,774 | 22,237 |
| No. of depositors (000s) | 722 | 740 |
| No. of borrowers (000s) | 3,044 | 3,107 |
| Share balances (£m) | 109,138 | 119,299 |
| Deposit balances (£m) | 34,579 | 43,579 |
| Mortgage balances (£m) | 120,410 | 134,100 |
| Total assets (£m) | 157,141 | 177,747 |
| Advances during year | | |
| No. (000s) | 519 | 548 |
| Amount (£m) | 26,555 | 31,514 |

## INTEREST RATES: Mortgage and Share 1996–2001

The interest rates prevailing on mortgage lending and share investment vary from society to society and in relation to the type or amount of loan or investment.

The interval between the payments or compounding of interest is crucial in determining the competitiveness of particular societies' accounts. In order to make a true comparison of interest rates, the annual percentage rate or APR, which should appear in all advertisements and leaflets, must be used.

| | *1996* | *1997* | *1998* | *1999* | *2000* | *2001 1st quarter* |
|---|---|---|---|---|---|---|
| Average bank base rate | 5.96 | 6.56 | 7.24 | 5.34 | 5.97 | 5.86 |
| Building societies average mortgage rate | 6.72 | 7.03 | 7.76 | 6.47 | 6.79 | 6.56 |
| Building societies average share rate | 4.54 | 5.49 | 6.34 | 4.89 | 5.41 | 5.38 |

AUTHORISED SOCIETIES AT END OF JULY 2001

| *Name of Building Society(a) and principal office address* | *Members(b)* | *Total assets (c)* £'000 |
|---|---|---|
| Barnsley, Regent Street, Barnsley, S. Yorks S70 2EH | 38,415 | 269,194 |
| Bath Investment, 20 Charles Street, Bath BA1 1HY | 22,500 | 103,838 |
| Beverley, 57 Market Place, Beverley, E. Yorks HU17 8AA | 13,000 | 60,283 |
| Britannia, Britannia House, Cheadle Road, Leek, Staffs ST13 5RG | 2,162,542 | 15,114,569 |
| Buckinghamshire, High Street, Chalfont St Giles, Bucks HP8 4QB | 9,818 | 104,264 |
| Cambridge, 51 Newmarket Road, Cambridge CB5 8FF | 49,060 | 528,556 |
| Catholic, 7 Strutton Ground, London SW1P 2HY | 4,755 | 32,140 |
| Century, 21 Albany Street, Edinburgh EH1 3QW | 3,862 | 16,264 |
| Chelsea, Thirlestaine Hall, Thirlestaine Road, Cheltenham, Glos GL53 7AL | 548,000 | 5,304,483 |
| Chesham, 12 Market Square, Chesham, Bucks HP5 1ER | 21,610 | 179,132 |
| Cheshire, Castle Street, Macclesfield, Cheshire SK11 6AF | 350,000 | 2,605,400 |
| Chorley and District, Key House, Foxhole Road, Chorley, Lancs PR7 1NZ | 18,041 | 103,378 |
| City of Derry, 31A Carlisle Road, Londonderry BT24 6JJ | 1,386 | 14,245 |
| Clay Cross, Eyre Street, Clay Cross, Chesterfield S45 9NS | 5,216 | 20,465 |
| Coventry, PO Box 9, High Street, Coventry CV1 5QN | 850,000 | 6,429,023 |
| Cumberland, Cumberland House, Castle Street, Carlisle CA3 8RX | 178,000 | 830,006 |
| Darlington, Sentinel House, Lingfield Way, Darlington, Co. Durham DL1 4PR | 94,003 | 445,414 |
| Derbyshire, Duffield Hall, Duffield, Derby DE56 1AG | 377,561 | 3,178,894 |
| Dudley, Dudley House, Stone Street, Dudley DY1 1NP | 23,000 | 130,204 |
| Dunfermline, Caledonia House, Carnegie Avenue, Dunfermline, Fife KY11 8PJ | 343,000 | 1,654,497 |
| Earl Shilton, 22 The Hollow, Earl Shilton, Leicester LE9 7NB | 13,081 | 77,839 |
| Ecology, 18 Station Road, Cross Hills, Keighley, W. Yorks BD20 7EH | 7,500 | 33,545 |
| Furness, 51–55 Duke Street, Barrow-in-Furness LA14 1RT | 111,724 | 504,303 |
| Gainsborough, 9 Lord Street, Gainsborough, Lincs DN21 2DD | 7,372 | 33,521 |
| Hanley Economic, Granville House, Festival Park, Hanley, Stoke-on-Trent, Staffs ST1 5TB | 42,000 | 254,447 |
| Harpenden, 14 Station Road, Harpenden, Herts AL5 4SE | 16,824 | 77,253 |
| Hinckley and Rugby, Upper Bond Street, Hinckley, Leics LE10 1DG | 98,000 | 464,817 |
| Holmesdale, 43 Church Street, Reigate, Surrey RH2 0AE | 9,429 | 109,480 |
| Ilkeston Permanent, 3 South Street, Ilkeston, Derby DE7 5HQ | 3,250 | 17,006 |
| Ipswich, 44 Upper Brook Street, Ipswich IP4 1DP | 31,541 | 258,559 |
| Kent Reliance, Reliance House, Manor Road, Chatham, Kent ME4 6AF | 69,000 | 367,595 |
| Lambeth, 118–120 Westminster Bridge Road, London SE1 7XE | 78,875 | 687,795 |
| Leeds and Holbeck, 105 Albion Street, Leeds LS1 5AS | 553,387 | 3,799,160 |
| Leek United, 50 St Edward Street, Leek, Staffs ST13 5DH | 72,112 | 500,122 |
| Loughborough, 6 High Street, Loughborough, Leics LE11 2QB | 29,292 | 165,209 |
| Manchester, 24 Queen Street, Manchester M2 5AH | 22,421 | 243,967 |
| Mansfield, Regent House, Regent Street, Mansfield, Notts NG18 1SS | 27,233 | 152,414 |
| Market Harborough, Welland House, The Square, Market Harborough, Leics LE16 7PD | 63,876 | 307,509 |
| Marsden, 6–20 Russell Street, Nelson, Lancs BB9 7NJ | 77,510 | 291,223 |
| Melton Mowbray, 39 Nottingham Street, Melton Mowbray, Leics LE13 1NR | 63,456 | 274,172 |
| Mercantile, Mercantile House, Silverlink Business Park, Wallsend, Tyne and Wear NE28 9NY | 35,962 | 187,192 |
| Monmouthshire, John Frost Square, Newport, Gwent NP20 1PX | 42,985 | 299,570 |
| National Counties, National Counties House, Church Street, Epsom, Surrey KT17 4NL | 41,547 | 654,100 |
| Nationwide, Nationwide House, Pipers Way, Swindon SN38 1NW | 10,400,000 | 71,133,900 |
| Newbury, 17–20 Bartholomew Street, Newbury, Berks RG14 5LY | 67,396 | 353,840 |
| Newcastle, Portland House, New Bridge Street, Newcastle upon Tyne NE1 8AL | 416,004 | 2,414,176 |
| Norwich and Peterborough, Peterborough Business Park, Lynch Wood, Peterborough PE2 6WZ | 343,409 | 2,334,758 |
| Nottingham, 5–13 Upper Parliament Street, Nottingham NG1 2BX | 231,693 | 1,550,179 |
| Penrith, 7 King Street, Penrith, Cumbria CA11 7AR | 7,279 | 59,665 |
| Portman, Portman House, Richmond Hill, Bournemouth, Dorset BH2 6EP | 1,211,057 | 6,853,541 |
| Principality, PO Box 89, Principality Buildings, Queen Street, Cardiff CF10 1UA | 370,000 | 2,347,205 |
| Progressive, 33–37 Wellington Place, Belfast BT1 6HH | 105,167 | 739,786 |
| Saffron Walden, Herts and Essex, 1A Market Street, Saffron Walden, Essex CB10 1HX | 67,931 | 373,737 |
| Scarborough, Prospect House, PO Box 6, Scarborough, N. Yorks YO12 6EQ | 149,781 | 1,187,940 |
| Scottish, 23 Manor Place, Edinburgh EH3 7XE | 28,201 | 158,838 |
| Shepshed, Bull Ring, Shepshed, Loughborough, Leics LE12 9QD | 9,352 | 47,234 |
| Skipton, The Bailey, Skipton, N. Yorks BD23 1DN | 550,000 | 5,867,061 |
| Stafford Railway, 4 Market Square, Stafford ST16 2JH | 12,878 | 73,711 |
| Staffordshire, Jubilee House, PO Box 66, 84 Salop Street, Wolverhampton WV3 0SA | 240,000 | 1,534,722 |
| Stroud and Swindon, Rowcroft, Stroud, Glos GL5 3BG | 212,071 | 1,439,728 |
| Swansea, 11 Cradock Street, Swansea SA1 3EW | 5,005 | 34,034 |
| Teachers, Allenview House, Hanham Road, Wimborne, Dorset BH21 1AG | 20,364 | 180,428 |
| Tipton and Coseley, 70 Owen Street, Tipton, W. Midlands DY4 8HG | 35,071 | 180,442 |

| *Name of Building Society(a) and principal office address* | *Members(b)* | *Total assets (c)* £'000 |
|---|---|---|
| Universal, Universal House, Kings Manor, Newcastle upon Tyne NE1 6PA | 62,000 | 406,746 |
| Vernon, 19 St Petersgate, Stockport, Cheshire SK1 1HF | 39,463 | 170,576 |
| West Bromwich, 374 High Street, West Bromwich, W. Midlands B70 8LR | 517,206 | 3,324,600 |
| Yorkshire, Yorkshire House, Yorkshire Drive, Bradford BD5 8LJ | 1,825,552 | 11,435,710 |

(a) Building Society are the last words in every society's name
(b) Includes both investing and borrowing members. Some totals are estimated or the latest available
(c) At 31 December 2000

# National Savings

## Investment and Ordinary Accounts

Interest is earned at 1.10 per cent per year on each ordinary account for every complete calendar month in which the balance is £500 or more. The minimum deposit is £10; maximum balance £10,000 plus interest credited.

The investment account pays a higher rate of interest depending on the account balance (the current rate can be found at any post office). The minimum deposit is £20; maximum balance £100,000 plus interest credited.

Since April 1999 Individual Savings Accounts (ISAs) have been offered by National Savings. An ISA can be opened with £10. Interest is calculated daily on balances of over £1 and is free of tax. The same regulations apply as for ISAs offered by all companies.

## Premium Bonds

Premium Bonds are a government security which were first introduced in 1956. Premium Bonds enable savers to enter a regular draw for tax-free prizes, while retaining the right to get their money back. A sum equivalent to interest on each bond is put into a prize fund and distributed by monthly prize draws. (The rate of interest is 3.50 per cent a year from 1 September 2001). The prizes are drawn by ERNIE (electronic random number indicator equipment) and are free of all UK income tax and capital gains tax.

Bonds are in units of £1, with a minimum purchase of £100; above this, purchases must be in multiples of £10, up to a maximum holding limit of £20,000 per person. The scheme offers a facility to reinvest prize wins automatically. Upon completion of an automatic prize reinvestment mandate, holders receive new bonds which are immediately eligible for future prize draws. Bonds can only be held in the name of an individual and not by organisations.

Bonds become eligible for prizes once they have been held for one clear calendar month following the month of purchase. Each £1 unit can win only one prize per draw, but it will be awarded the highest for which it is drawn. Bonds remain eligible for prizes until they are repaid. When a holder dies, bonds remain eligible for prizes up to and including the twelfth monthly draw after the month in which the holder dies.

By the June 2001 prize draw, 86 million prizes totalling £5.5 billion had been distributed since the first prize draw in June 1957.

## Income Bonds

National Savings Income Bonds were introduced in 1982. They are suitable for those who want to receive regular monthly payments of interest while preserving the full cash value of their capital. The bonds are sold in multiples of £500. The minimum holding is £500 and the maximum £1,000,000 (sole or joint holding).

Interest is calculated on a day-to-day basis and paid monthly. Interest is taxable but is paid without deduction of tax at source. The bonds have a guaranteed life of ten years, but may be repaid at par before maturity on giving three months' notice. Repayment is also possible without giving notice but incurs a penalty. If the sole or sole surviving holder dies, however, no fixed period of notice is required and there is no loss of interest for repayment made within the first year.

## Pensioners Guaranteed Income Bonds

Pensioners Guaranteed Income Bonds were introduced in January 1994 and are designed for people aged 60 and over who wish to receive regular monthly payments with a rate of interest that is fixed for a five-year period whilst preserving the full cash value of their investment. A two-year fixed rate term bond was introduced in May 1999. In October 2000 a new one-year fixed rate term bond was also introduced.

The minimum limit for each purchase is £500. The maximum holding is £1,000,000 (sole or joint holding); within those limits bonds can be bought for any amount in pounds and pence. The rate of interest is fixed and guaranteed for the first one, two or five years, depending on the term invested in. Interest is taxable but is paid without deduction of tax at source.

Holders can apply for repayment (or part repayment of a bond subject to the minimum holding limits) by giving 60 days' notice (if repayment is before the fifth anniversary date). No interest is earned during the notice period. If repayment is requested within two weeks of any fifth anniversary of purchase, there is no formal period of notice. Repayment is possible without giving notice but a penalty is incurred. On the death of a holder or sole surviving investor in a joint holding, repayment will be made without notice. Interest will be paid in full up to the date of repayment.

## Children's Bonus Bonds

Children's Bonus Bonds were introduced in 1991. The latest issue, Issue W, was introduced in May 2001. They can be bought for any child under 16 and will go on growing in value until he or she is 21. The bonds are sold in multiples of £25. The minimum holding is £25. The maximum holding in Issue W is £1,000 per child. This is in addition to holdings of earlier issues of the bond (excluding interest and bonuses). Bonds for children under 16 must be held by a parent or guardian.

Children's Bonus Bonds (Issue W) earn 3.0 per cent a year over five years. A bonus (9.32 per cent) of the purchase price is added at the fifth anniversary. This is equal to 4.60 per cent a year compound. All returns are totally exempt from UK income tax. No interest is earned on bonds cashed in before the first anniversary of purchase. Bonuses are only payable if the bond is held until the next bonus date. Bonds over five years old continue to earn interest and bonuses until the holder is 21, when they should be cashed in. If bonds are not cashed in on the holder's 21st birthday, they earn no interest after that birthday.

## Fixed Rate Savings Bond

Fixed Rate Savings Bonds are lump sum investments that earn guaranteed rates of interest over set periods of time from six months to three years. Interest, from which basic rate tax is deducted at source, can be paid out or reinvested into the bond monthly, annually or at the end of the term. Holders can also choose where the interest is paid.

## Capital Bonds

National Savings Capital Bonds were introduced in 1989. The latest series, Series Z, was introduced in May 2001. Capital Bonds offer capital growth over five years with guaranteed returns at fixed rates. The interest is taxable each year (for those who pay income tax) but is not deducted at source. The minimum purchase is £100. There is a maximum holding limit of £250,000 from Series B onwards.

Capital Bonds will be repaid in full with all interest gained at the end of five years. No interest is earned on bonds repaid in the first year. Reinvestment or extension terms may also be available.

### National Savings Treasurer's Account

The Treasurer's Account, introduced in September 1996, offers attractive rates and security to non-profit making organisations such as charities, friendly societies, clubs, etc. The minimum holding is £10,000 and the maximum is £2 million. Interest is paid at the rate of 4.25 per cent a year on holdings of £10,000 to £24,999, 4.55 per cent a year on holdings of £25,000 to £99,999, and 4.95 per cent a year on holdings of £100,000 and above.

## NATIONAL SAVINGS CERTIFICATES

### Recent Issues

Interest, index-linked increase, bonus or other sum payable is free of UK income tax (including investment income surcharge) and capital gains tax.

From June 1982, savings certificates of the 7th to 54th Issues have been extended on general extension rates as they reach the end of their existing extension periods. The percentage interest rate is determined by the Treasury and any change in this general extension rate will be applicable from the first of the month following its announcement. Under the system, a certificate earns interest for each complete period of three months beyond the expiry of the previous extension terms. Within each three-month period, interest is calculated separately for each month at the rate applicable from the beginning of that month. The interest for each month is one-twelfth of the annual rate (i.e. it does not vary with the number of days in the month) and is capitalised annually on the anniversary of the date of purchase. The current rate of interest under the general extension rate is given in leaflets available at post offices.

# Insurance

## AUTHORISATION

The Insurance Companies Act 1982 initially empowered the Department of Trade and Industry, Insurance Division to authorise corporate bodies to transact insurance in the United Kingdom provided they comply with the financial and other regulations detailed in the Act. In January 1998 an interim transfer of this function to the Insurance Directorate of HM Treasury was completed. The Financial Services and Markets Act transferred this function to the Insurance and Friendly Societies Division of the Financial Services Authority, (FSA), 25 The North Colonnade, London E14 5HS Web: www.fsa.gov.uk

At the end of 2000 there were over 829 insurance companies with authorisation from the FSA to transact one or more classes of insurance business. However, with the establishment of the single European insurance market on 1 July 1994 an insurer authorised in any of the European Union (EU) countries can now transact insurance in the UK without further formality; this creates a potential market of over 5,000 insurance companies.

## REGULATION

Over 23,000 firms are authorised to conduct a wide variety of investment business in the UK. The overall regulator for investment business of any kind is the Financial Services Authority. The FSA does not undertake all the regulatory work itself. Instead it recognises a number of specialist bodies to carry out the frontline regulation. The bulk of this work is undertaken by three Self Regulating Organisations (SROs).

The main regulator of firms advising on and arranging deals in life insurance and pensions, friendly society investments, unit trusts and investment trusts is one of the SROs, the Personal Investment Authority (PIA). (25 The North Colonnade, Canary Wharf, London E14 5HS)

Disputes between policy holders and life or general insurers can be referred to the Financial Ombudsman Service administered by the FSA. The Chief Ombudsman is Walter Merricks .

Private policy holders with a complaint against their insurer must firstly take the matter to the highest level within the company. Thereafter, if it remains unresolved, they can refer their problem, free of charge to the Ombudsman who examines the facts of a complaint and delivers a decision which is binding on the insurer (but not the policy holder). Small businesses with a turnover of up to £1m also have access to the scheme. The Financial Ombudsman Service also covers other areas of the industry including banks, building societies and investment firms.

## ASSOCIATION OF BRITISH INSURERS

Over 98 per cent of the world-wide business of UK insurance companies is transacted by the 400 members of the Association of British Insurers (ABI). 51 Gresham Street, London EC2V 7HQ Web: www.abi.org.uk. ABI is a trade association which represents both life and general insurers.

*Chairman*, Mike Ross
*Chief Executive*, Mary Francis

## GENERAL INSURANCE STANDARDS COUNCIL

On 3rd July 2000, the General Insurance Standards Council, 110 Cannon Street London EC4N 6EU, www.gisc.co.uk, a non-statutory regulatory organisation for the general insurance industry, was launched. GISC will regulate the sales, advisory and service standards of Members which will include insurers, intermediaries and brokers. Following completion of the formation of GISC, the Insurance Brokers Registration Act will be repealed and the voluntary General Insurance Selling Code produced by the Association of British Insurers will be withdrawn.

## BALANCE OF PAYMENTS

The insurance industry contributes just over 2% to the UK's Gross Domestic Product (GDP). In 1999 the overseas earnings of the UK insurance sector was £6,798m

## TAKE-OVERS AND MERGERS

The year 2000 saw further take-overs and mergers although the activity in this area has died down somewhat from its peak in 1999.

During 2000 the newly formed company CGU, formed from the merger of Commercial Union and General Accident, merged again with the newly demutualised Norwich Union to form the UK's largest general insurer, CGNU.

Having sold their Life operation, GAN merged with Lombard General to form Groupama.

Take-overs included Lloyds TSB's purchase of Scottish Widows following their demutualisation, Royal London Group's purchase of United Assurance and the purchase of NIG by Winterthur Insurance.

## GENERAL INSURANCE

The year 2000 began with relief that the millennium date change had caused few problems in the UK. However, the possibility of IT problems resurfaced with suggestions that the additional leap year brought about by the millennium might still cause software to crash. In the event no serious problems were experienced.

There was no such relief for the policy holders of Drake Insurance which went into liquidation in July 2000. Its financial problems were partly caused by the very competitive private motor insurance market. In addition, Drake specialised in offering cover for the non-standard and high risk end of the market which meant other insurers were not anxious to take over their business. Private policy holders with outstanding claims are, of course protected by the Policy Holders' Protection Act.

The UK motor insurance market as a whole suffered a loss of £1,310m in 1999, a slight improvement on the 1998 figure of £1,479m. Premium increases are inevitable but may be mitigated by the competitive market which may force insurers to reconsider the level of increase if they wish to maintain market share.

In June 2000 and again at the end of the year, Britain was hit by severe flooding. This pushed the weather damage claims figure for 2000 up by 40% to £857m from £614m in 1999. This flooding and the consequent disruption and financial losses raised the question of the adequacy of UK flood defences and the willingness of insurers to continue cover in areas prone to flooding.

To complete the misery, there was a period of bad publicity for the liability insurers following the insolvency of an insurer called Chester Street Securities. This company was originally part of the Iron Trades Insurance Group but in January 2000 most of the group was sold to QBE Insurance. However, a small number of employers' liability policies were not included in the deal. These reverted to Chester Street and without the security of the rest of the Iron Trades Group the company quickly became insolvent. This insolvency hit a number of people suffering from asbestosis as they were in the process of claiming compensation and as these claims arose before employers' liability became compulsory by law, the Policy Holders Protection Act did not apply. These cases have been taken up by both the press and Members of Parliament and the insurance industry's refusal to offer some form of compensation has brought widespread criticism.

There were also changes during the year in the way general insurance is regulated. The General Insurance Standards Council was launched in July and will eventually take over all responsibility for the voluntary regulation of general insurers, intermediaries and brokers.

### London Insurance Market

The London Insurance Market is a distinct, separate sector of the UK insurance and reinsurance industry. It is the world's leading market for internationally traded insurances and reinsurance, its business comprising mainly overseas non-life large and high-exposure risks. The market is centred on the City of London, which provides the required international financial, banking, legal and other support services. Currently there are 123 Lloyd's syndicates, about 96 insurance companies and 39 Marine Protection and Indemnity Clubs active in the market. In 1999 the market had a written gross premium income of £14,208 million. Most of the business is brought to the market by the 127 firms of Lloyd's brokers.

The trade association for the international insurance and reinsurance companies writing primarily non-marine insurance and all classes of reinsurance business in the London Market is the International Underwriting Association (IUA) London Underwriting Centre, 3 Minster Court, Mincing Lane, London EC3R 7DD Web: www.iua.co.uk

### British Insurance Companies

The following insurance company figures refer to members and certain non-members of the ABI.

### Claims Statistics (£ million)

| | 1999 | 2000 |
|---|---|---|
| Domestic claims | | |
| Theft | 535 | 542 |
| Fire | 286 | 334 |
| Weather | 614 | 857 |
| Subsidence | 364 | 350 |
| Business interruption | n/a | n/a |
| *Total* | 1,799 | 2,083 |
| Commercial claims | | |
| Theft | 172 | 198 |
| Fire | 579 | 521 |
| Weather | 247 | 438 |
| Subsidence | n/a | n/a |
| Business interruption | 123 | 215 |
| *Total* | 1,121 | 1,372 |

### World-wide General Business Trading Result

| | 1998 £m | 1999 £m |
|---|---|---|
| Net written premiums | 36,089 | 34,870 |
| Underwriting profit (loss) for one year account business | (4,038) | (3,156) |
| Transfer to profit and loss account for 3 year business | | |
| Marine, Aviation, Transport | (212) | (177) |
| Other | (96) | (186) |
| Total underwriting result | (4,347) | (3,519) |
| Net investment income | 5,202 | 4,414 |
| Overall trading profit | 855 | 895 |
| Profit as % of premium income | 2.4 | 2.6 |

### World-wide General Business Underwriting Result

| | 1998 | | | | | 1999 | | | | |
|---|---|---|---|---|---|---|---|---|---|---|
| | UK | Other EU | USA | Other | Total | UK | Other EU | USA | Other | Total |
| Motor | | | | | | | | | | |
| Premiums: £m | 6,512 | 1,915 | 1,591 | 1,786 | 11,804 | 7,044 | 1,592 | 1,425 | 1,587 | 11,648 |
| Profit (loss): £m | (1,479) | (333) | (93) | (88) | (1,993) | (1,310) | (352) | (93) | (56) | (1,811) |
| % of premiums | (22.7) | (17.4) | (5.8) | (4.9) | (16.9) | (18.6) | (22.1) | (6.5) | (3.5) | (15.5) |
| Non-motor | | | | | | | | | | |
| Premiums: £m | 13,125 | 2,415 | 2,008 | 1,821 | 19,369 | 12,794 | 2,549 | 2,114 | 1,627 | 19,084 |
| Profit (loss): £m | (563) | (17) | (859) | (218) | (1,657) | (433) | (51) | (195) | (178) | (857) |
| % of premiums | (4.3) | (0.7) | (42.7) | (12) | (8.55) | (3.38) | (2) | (9.22) | (10.9) | (4.5) |

### Net Premium Income by Territory 1999

| | UK £m | Other EU £m | USA £m | Other £m | Total £m |
|---|---|---|---|---|---|
| Motor | 7,044 | 1,592 | 1,425 | 1,587 | 11,165 |
| Non-motor | 12,794 | 2,549 | 2,114 | 1,627 | 19,084 |
| Marine, Aviation and Transport | 657 | 128 | 153 | 114 | 1,052 |
| Non-MAT reinsurance | 1,378 | 462 | 36 | 207 | 2,083 |
| Other funded business | 341 | 14 | 1 | 0 | 356 |
| *Total general business* | 22,214 | 4,745 | 3,729 | 3,535 | 34,223 |
| Ordinary long-term | 90,917 | 8,243 | 4,834 | 5,837 | 109,831 |
| Industrial long-term | 858 | — | — | — | 58 |
| *Total long-term business* | 91,775 | 8,243 | 4,834 | 5,837 | 110,689 |

## LLOYD'S OF LONDON

Lloyd's of London is an international market for almost all types of general insurance. Lloyd's currently has a capacity to accept insurance premiums of over £10,000 million. Much of this business comes from outside Great Britain and makes a valuable contribution to the balance of payments.

A policy is underwritten at Lloyd's by a mixture of private and corporate members, corporate members having been admitted for the first time in 1992. Specialist underwriters accept insurance risks at Lloyd's on behalf of members (referred to as 'Names') grouped in syndicates. There are currently around 122 syndicates of varying sizes, some with up to 2,000 names, each managed by an underwriting agent approved by the Council of Lloyd's.

Individual members are still in the majority at Lloyd's with a total of 3,296 individuals as opposed to 853 corporate members. In 2000 the market capacity of the corporate sector was £8,062 while individuals represented £2,003 million of capacity.

Lloyd's is incorporated by an Act of Parliament (Lloyd's Acts 1971 onwards) and is governed by a council of 19 members. Market management is handled by a Market Board of 18 members (comprising three working members and three external members of the Council, three Corporation executives (including the chief executive officer), eight additional market practitioners and one external member. Regulation is supervised by a Board of 15 members Chaired by John Young who is also Deputy Chairman of the Council of Lloyd's.

The Corporation is a non-profit making body chiefly financed by its members' subscriptions. It provides the premises, administrative staff and services enabling Lloyd's underwriting syndicates to conduct their business. It does not, however, assume corporate liability for the risks accepted by its members, who remain responsible to the full extent of their personal means for their underwriting affairs.

At present, Lloyd's syndicates have no direct contact with the public. All business is transacted through insurance brokers accredited by the Corporation of Lloyd's. In addition, non-Lloyd's brokers in the UK, when guaranteed by Lloyd's brokers, are able to deal directly with Lloyd's motor syndicates, a facility which has made the Lloyd's market more accessible to the insuring public.

Following the enactment of the Financial Services and Markets Act, the Financial Services Authority will be responsible for the regulation of the Lloyd's market. However, in situations where Lloyd's internal regulatory and compensation arrangements are deemed to be more far-reaching, as for example with the Lloyd's Central Fund, which safeguards claim payments to policy holders, the existing arrangements remain in force.

Lloyd's also provides the most comprehensive shipping intelligence service in the world. The shipping and other information received from Lloyd's agents, shipowners, news agencies and other sources throughout the world is collated and distributed to the media as well as to the maritime and commercial sectors in general. *Lloyd's List* is London's oldest daily newspaper and contains news of general commercial interest as well as shipping information. *Lloyd's Shipping Index*, also published daily, lists some 25,000 ocean-going vessels in alphabetical order and gives the latest known report of each.

### DEVELOPMENTS IN 2000

Losses within the Lloyd's market continued to grow for the 1998 year of account. The overall market loss was £1,065m which was substantially greater than the figure of £176m for 1997. It is expected that these heavy losses will continue for 1999 and these years will mark the bottom of an extremely severe loss cycle.

Some good news for Lloyd's of London came in November 2000 when the UK High Court rejected allegations of fraud made in The Jaffray case. The case centred on a counterclaim by Sir William Jaffray and a group of over 200 former Names, to actions by Lloyd's for the collection of debts relating to the 1996 restructuring of the market. In his Judgement Mr Justice Cresswell said there had been no fraud or misrepresentation and that the Committee of Lloyd's had, at all times, acted honestly. The Names are seeking permission from the Court of Appeal, the judge having denied leave, to appeal.

In July 2000 Lloyd's announced a change in the role of Chairman of the Council of Lloyd's. Since 1992 the issues facing the market have demanded the role of Chairman be a full-time position but it was confirmed that it would revert to a part-time role from December. At that time Max Taylor ended his term as Chairman and was replaced by Saxon Riley who agreed to act as Chairman for one year while a candidate for the chairmanship in its new form was sought.

*Chairman*, Saxon Riley
*Chief Executive*, Nick Prettejohn

### LLOYD'S MEMBERSHIP

| | 1998 | 1999 | 2000 |
|---|---|---|---|
| Total no. of underwriting members participating | | | |
| Individuals | 6,825 | 4,503 | 3,296 |
| Corporate | 435 | 668 | 853 |

### TOTAL MARKET CAPACITY

| | 1998 £m | 1999 £m | 2000 £m |
|---|---|---|---|
| Individual | 4,105 | 2,700 | 2,003 |
| Corporate | 6,064 | 7,170 | 8,062 |
| Total | 10,169 | 9,870 | 10,065 |

### LLOYDS RESULTS 1998 (BY OECD CATEGORY)

| | Accident & Health | Aircraft damage & liability | Ships damage & liability | Motor vehicle damage & liability | Goods in transit | Property damage | General liability | Pecuniary loss | Life |
|---|---|---|---|---|---|---|---|---|---|
| | £m | £m | £m | £m | £m | £m | £m | £m | £m |
| Net Premiums | 253.9 | 438.0 | 666.9 | 967.7 | 214.1 | 1223.0 | 830.3 | 177.4 | 24.3 |
| Net Claims | 208.6 | 235.5 | 360.2 | 963.8 | 164.8 | 739.6 | 478.0 | 127.8 | 19.6 |
| Overall profit (loss) | 11.7 | 137.3 | 232.1 | (105.2) | 45.9 | 426.3 | 41.1 | (45.2) | 4.8 |

## Lloyd's Global Accounts

| | 1997 and prior years of account £m | 1998 pure year result £m |
|---|---|---|
| Gross premiums written (net of brokerage) | 6,863 | 7,605 |
| Outward reinsurance premiums | 2,154 | 2,736 |
| Net premiums | 4,709 | 4,869 |
| Reinsurance to close premiums received from earlier years of account | 4,352 | 5,060 |
| Amounts retained to meet all known and unknown outstanding liabilities brought forward | 254 | 465 |
| | 9,061 | 9,929 |
| Gross claims paid | 5,456 | 7,790 |
| Reinsurers' share | 1,709 | 3,051 |
| Net claims | 3,747 | 4,739 |
| Other reinsurance premiums paid to close the year of account | 4,863 | 5,456 |
| Amounts retained to meet all known and unknown outstanding liabilities carried forward | 254 | 465 |
| | 8,864 | 10,660 |
| Underwriting result | 197 | (731) |
| Other profit (loss) on exchange | 13 | 1 |
| Syndicate operating expenses | (433) | (493) |
| Balance on technical account | (223) | (1,223) |
| Investment income | 487 | 463 |
| Investment expenses and charges | (8) | (9) |
| Investment gains less losses | (91) | 40 |
| Result before personal expenses | 165 | (729) |
| Personal expenses | (341) | (302) |
| Result after personal expenses | (176) | (1,031) |

# LIFE AND LONG-TERM INSURANCE AND PENSIONS

## Lloyds, Life Insurance

The total individual long-term new business in the UK fell by 6.4 per cent in 2000 to £3,489 million for annual contracts. Coincidentally, single premium business rose by exactly the same amount, 6.4 per cent, to £49,623 over the same period.

The continuing period of low interest rates and lower investment returns were thought to be the reason for the decline in the sales of new regular premium business. However a number of highly publicised problems facing the life insurance industry may have also contributed.

Poor investment returns were certainly a contributing factor in the problems of one of the UK's oldest life insurance companies, Equitable Life. In July 2000 the House of Lords ruled that the company was obliged to pay around 90,000 holders of guaranteed annuities the full amounts they had been promised. Equitable had argued that the marked change in economic climate since the annuities were sold made it impossible for them to honour the agreements. Following the defeat Equitable firstly closed to new business and subsequently appeared doomed before it was eventually purchased by Halifax plc.

Perhaps the most controversial issue of the year was the ongoing debate over whether life and health insurers should be entitled to see the results of genetic tests conducted on prospective policy holders. The insurers argued that if they are not allowed access to such test results they will be unable to underwrite properly. Pressure groups however fear that if such data were to be made available to insurers it could lead to people identified by the tests as potential sufferers becoming uninsurable. At present, insurers have agreed not to request genetic tests of any kind for potential policy holders where the level of cover is below £300,000. This is not considered adequate by some groups who point to the total ban on insurers using data of this kind which applies in some European countries and some states of the USA. The debate is likely to continue for some time.

Much of the year was also taken up with preparations for the launch in 2001 of Stakeholder Pensions. Although initially not well received by the industry because of the limit of 1% on charges, many companies have now devised and launched products which comply with the stakeholder requirements.

## New Non-Linked Personal Pension Business

| | Regular premium policies | | Single premium policies | |
|---|---|---|---|---|
| | No. new policies | New premiums £m | No. new policies | New premiums £m |
| 1996 | 307,000 | 391 | 114,000 | 1,865 |
| 1997 | 330,000 | 424 | 144,000 | 2,173 |
| 1998 | 419,000 | 555 | 125,000 | 1,419 |
| 1999 | 316,000 | 443 | 109,000 | 1,273 |
| New Linked Personal Pension Business | | | | |
| 1996 | 573,000 | 582 | 165,000 | 2,169 |
| 1997 | 693,000 | 768 | 196,000 | 2,913 |
| 1998 | 730,000 | 919 | 173,000 | 2,989 |
| 1999 | 750,000 | 1,000 | 184,000 | 3,241 |

NET PREMIUM INCOME FOR WORLDWIDE LONG-TERM INSURANCE BUSINESS

| | 1998 £m | 1999 £m |
|---|---|---|
| *Ordinary Branch* | | |
| Business written in UK | | |
| Annual premiums | | |
| Life | 12,567 | 13,073 |
| Annuities | 50 | 45 |
| Pensions | 11,976 | 12,493 |
| Income protection | 656 | 795 |
| Industrial business | 952 | 858 |
| Single premiums | | |
| Life | 17,539 | 23,471 |
| Annuities | 373 | 156 |
| Pensions | 26,548 | 34,989 |
| Income protection | 56 | 85 |
| Business written overseas | | |
| Annual premiums | 4,872 | 5,112 |
| Single premiums | 10,113 | 12,943 |
| *Total* | 87,171 | 106,442 |

PAYMENTS TO POLICYHOLDERS

| | 1998 £m | 1999 £m |
|---|---|---|
| Payments to UK policyholders | 55,150 | 60,676 |
| Payments to overseas policyholders | 10,284 | 10,831 |
| *Total* | 65,433 | 71,507 |

INVESTMENTS OF INSURANCE COMPANIES 1999

| Investment of funds | Long-term business £m | General business £m |
|---|---|---|
| Index-linked British Government securities | 22,056 | 3,631 |
| Non-index-linked British Government securities | 99,729 | 11,673 |
| Other UK public sector debt securities | 6,258 | 1,465 |
| Overseas government, provincial and municipal securities | 30,710 | 13,624 |
| Debentures, loan shares, preference and guaranteed stocks and shares | | |
| UK | 79,965 | 6,843 |
| Overseas | 38,979 | 9,348 |
| Ordinary stocks and shares | | |
| UK | 371,208 | 16,788 |
| Overseas | 125,104 | 11,656 |
| Unit trusts | | |
| Equities | 71,644 | 1,637 |
| Fixed interest | 3,770 | 149 |
| Loans secured on property | 14,011 | 2,905 |
| Real property and ground rents | 50,406 | 3,987 |
| Other invested assets | 60,407 | 31,194 |
| *Total invested assets* | 977,248 | 114,901 |
| *Net investment income* | 35,485 | 4,414 |

NEW NON-LINKED PERSONAL PENSION BUSINESS

| | Regular premium policies: No. new policies | Regular premium policies: New premiums £m | Single premium policies: No. new policies | Single premium policies: New premiums £m |
|---|---|---|---|---|
| 1996 | 307,000 | 391 | 114,000 | 1,865 |
| 1997 | 330,000 | 424 | 144,000 | 2,173 |
| 1998 | 419,000 | 555 | 125,000 | 1,419 |
| 1999 | 316,000 | 443 | 109,000 | 1,273 |

## DIRECTORY OF INSURANCE COMPANIES

INSURANCE COMPANIES

*Classes of insurance undertaken*

| | |
|---|---|
| G | General |
| L | Life |
| M | Marine |
| Re | Reinsurance |

*Group membership*

| | |
|---|---|
| (CGNU) | CGNU |
| (Z) | Zurich Financial Group |
| (A) | AXA Group Union |
| (RSA) | Royal & SunAlliance |

| *Nature of business* | *Name of company* | *Head Office address* |
|---|---|---|
| L | Abbey Life | Abbey Life House, PO Box 33, Bournemouth BH8 8AL |
| G | Abbey National Healthcare | 9 Nelson Street, Bradford BD1 5AN |
| L | Abbey National Life | 287 St Vincent Street, Glasgow, G2 5NB |
| G | Ace Insurance SANV | CIGNA House, 8 Lime Street, London EC3M 7NA |
| L | AIG Life (UK) | Alico House, 22 Addiscombe Road, Croydon CR9 5AZ |
| L | Alba Life Limited | Britannia Court, 50 Bothwell Steet, Glasgow G2 6HR |
| GM Re | Albion | Whittaker House, Whittaker Avenue, Richmond, TW9 1EH |
| L | Alico | Alico House, 22 Addiscombe Road, Croydon CR9 5AZ |
| GL | Alliance & Leicester Insurance | Carlton Park, Narborough, LE9 5XX |
| L | Allied Dunbar (Z) | UK Life Centre, Swindon SN1 1EL |
| G | Ansvar | 31 St Leonards Road, Eastbourne BN21 3UR |
| GL | Assicurazioni Generali | 117 Fenchurch Street, EC3M 5DY |
| L | Australian Mutual Provident | Spectrum, Bond Street, Bristol BS1 3AL |
| LGM | Avon Insurance | Arden Street, Stratford-upon-Avon CV37 6WA |
| G | AXA General Insurance (A) | Civic Drive, Ipswich, IP1 2AN |
| G | AXA Insurance (A) | 107 Cheapside, London EC2V 6DU |
| Medical | AXA PPP Healthcare (A) | PPP House, Vale Road, Tunbridge Wells TN1 1BJ |
| L | AXA Sun Life (A) | Sun Life Centre, PO Box 1810, Bristol BS99 5SN |

| *Nature of business* | *Name of company* | *Head Office address* |
|---|---|---|
| LG | Bankers | St Johns Place, Easton St, High Wycombe, HP11 1NL |
| G | Baptist | 1 Merchant Street, London E3 4LY |
| L | Barclays Life | 9 Fleetway House, 25 Farringdon Street, London EC4 A4JA |
| G | British Reserve | Adriatic Hose, 6 Vale Avenue, Tunbridge Wells TN1 1EH |
| M | Bradford (RSA) | Bowling Mill, Dean Clough, Halifax HX3 5WA |
| GL | Britannic Assurance | 1 Wythall Green Way, Wythall, Birmingham B47 6WG |
| L | British Life Office | Reliance House, Mount Ephraim, Tunbridge Wells, Kent TN4 8BL |
| PM | BUPA | BUPA House, 15-19 Bloomsbury Way, London WC1A 2BA |
| L | Caledonian (A) | Royal Exchange, London EC3V 3LS |
| GM | Cambrian (A) | Royal Exchange, London EC3V 3LS |
| L | Canada Life | Canada Life House, Potters Bar EN6 5BA |
| L | Century Life | Century House, 5 Old Bailey, London EC4M 7BA |
| G | CGNU Insurance (CGNU) | St Helens, 1 Undershaft, London EC3P 3DQ |
| L | CGNU Life | 2 Rougier Street, York YO90 1UU |
| L | CIGNA Healthcare & Group Life | PO Box 42, Greenock, PA15 1AB |
| L | Clerical, Medical Group | Narrow Plain, Bristol BS2 0JH |
| L | Colonial Life | Colonial House, Chatham Maritime ME14 4YY |
| G | Congregational and General | Currer House, Currer Street, Bradford BD1 5BA |
| GLM Re | Co-operative | Miller Street, Manchester M60 0AL |
| GLM Re | Cornhill | 57 Ladymead, Guildford GU1 1DB |
| GL | Direct Line Insurance | 3 Edridge Road, Croydon CR9 1AG |
| GLM Re | Eagle Star (Z) | 60 St Mary Axe, London EC3A 8JQ |
| GL Re | Ecclesiastical | Beaufort House, Brunswick Road, Gloucester GL1 1JZ |
| G | Equine and Livestock | PO Box 100, Ouseburn, York YO5 9SZ |
| L | Equitable Life | Walton Street, Aylesbury HP21 7QW |
| G | Fortis Insurance | Fortis House, Tollgate, Eastleigh, SO53 3YA |
| L | Friends' Provident | Pixham End, Pixham Lane, Dorking RH4 1QA |
| L | GE Life | Stalwart House, Station Road, Dorking, RH4 1HL |
| G | Gresham Fire and Accident | 11 Queen Victoria Street, London EC4N 4XP |
| G | Groupama Insurance | Groupama House, Arthur Street, London EC4R 9AT |
| G | Groupama General Insurance | Groupama House, Arthur Street, London EC4R 9AT |
| GLMRe | Guardian Insurance (A) | Civic Drive, Ipswich IP1 2AN |
| GLM Re | Hibernian | Haddington Road, Dublin 4, Republic of Ireland |
| L | Hill Samuel Life | NLA Tower, 12-16 Addiscombe Road, Croydon CR9 6DR |
| G | Hiscox Insurance Co. | 52 Leadenhall Street, London EC3A 2BJ |
| GL | Ideal | Pitmaston, Moseley, Birmingham B13 8NG |
| L | Irish Life | Irish Life Centre, Victoria Street, St Albans AL1 5TS |
| GF | Iron Trades | Iron Trades House, 21–24 Grosvenor Place, London SW1X 7JA |
| L | J P Morgan Fleming Life | 10 Aldermanbury, London EC2V 7RF |
| L | J Rothscild | Dollar Street, Cirencester, GL7 2AQ |
| GLM Re | Legal and General | Temple Court, 11 Queen Victoria Street, London EC4N 4TP |
| L | Lincoln | Barnett Way, Barnwood, Gloucester, GL4 3RZ |
| GM | Liverpool Marine and General (RSA) | 1 Bartholomew Lane, London EC2N 2AB |
| GL | Liverpool Victoria | 135 Poole Road, Bournemouth BH4 9BG |
| GM | Local Government Guarantee (A) | Royal Exchange, London EC3V 3LS |
| L | London Life | Spectrum, Bond Street, Bristol BS1 3AL |
| G | MMA Insurance | Norman Insurance House, Kings Road, RG1 4LL |
| L | M and G Life | Three Quays, Tower Hill, London EC3R 6BQ |
| L | Manulife | Broadstreet House, 55 Old Broad Street, London EC2N 1TL |
| M | Marine (RSA) | 1 Cornhill, London EC3V 3QR |
| M Re | Maritime (CGNU) | PO Box 6, Surrey Street, Norwich NR1 3NS |
| L | Medical Sickness Society | Colmore Circus, Birmingham B4 6AR |
| Re | Mercantile and General | Moorfields House, Moorfields, London EC4R 9BJ |
| L | Merchant Investors | St Bartholomew's House, Lewins Mead, Bristol BS1 2NH |
| G Re | Methodist | Brazennose House, Brazennose Street, Manchester M2 5AS |
| L | MGM Assurance | MGM House, Heene Road, Worthing BN11 2DY |
| L | National Mutual Life | The Priory, Hitchin SG5 2DW |
| GM | Navigators and General (Z) | Lanchester House, Trafalgar Place, Trafalgar Street, Brighton BN1 4DA |
| GL Re | NFU Mutual | Tiddington Road, Stratford-upon-Avon CV37 7BJ |
| G | NIG | Crown House, 145 City Road, London EC1V 1LP |
| L | NM Financial Management | Enterprise House, Isambard Brunel Road, Portsmouth PO1 2AW |
| L | NPI | NPI House, 55 Calverley Road, Tunbridge Wells TN1 2UE |
| GLM Re | Pearl | The Pearl Centre, Lynchwood, Peterborough PE2 6FY |
| L Sickness | Permanent | Pynes Hill House, Rydon Lane, Exeter EX2 5SP |

| *Nature of business* | *Name of company* | *Head Office address* |
|---|---|---|
| GLM | Phoenix (RSA) | 1 Bartholomew Lane, London EC2N 2AB |
| L | Property Growth (RSA) | Phoenix House, Redcliff Hill, Bristol BS1 6SX |
| GLM Re | Prudential | Laurence Pountney Hill, London EC4R 0EU |
| GL | Refuge | Refuge House, Alderley Road, Wilmslow, Cheshire SK9 1PF |
| L | Reliance Mutual | Reliance House, Mount Ephraim, Tunbridge Wells, Kent TN4 8BL |
| G | Road Transport and General (CGNU) | Pitheavlis, Perth PH2 0NH |
| G | Royal Exchange (A) | Royal Exchange, London EC3V 3LS |
| L | Royal Heritage Life (RSA) | Royal Insurance House, Business Park, Peterborough PE2 6GG |
| GLM Re | Royal & SunAlliance (RSA) | 30 Berkeley Square, London, W1X 5AN |
| Engineering | Royal & SunAlliance Engineering (RSA) | 17 York Street, Manchester M2 3RS |
| L | Royal Liver | Royal Liver Building, Pier Head, Liverpool L3 1HT |
| GL | Royal London | Royal London House, 27 Middleborough, Colchester CO1 1RA |
| L | Royal National Pension Fund for Nurses | Burdett House, 15 Buckingham Street, Strand, London WC2N 6ED |
| F | Salvation Army | 117–121 Judd Street, London WC1H 9NN |
| L | Save and Prosper | Hexagon House, 28 Western Road, Romford RM1 3LB |
| L | Scottish Amicable | Craigforth, PO Box 25, Stirling FK9 4UE |
| Engineering | Scottish Boiler (CGNU) | PO Box 131, 825 Wilmslow Road, Didsbury, Manchester M20 8GS |
| L | Scottish Equitable | 28 St Andrew Square, Edinburgh EH2 2QZ |
| L | Scottish Friendly | 16 Blythswood Square, Glasgow G2 6HJ |
| M | Scottish General (CGNU) | PO Box 896, 103 Westerhill Road, Bishopbriggs, Glasgow G64 2QX |
| L | Scottish Legal Life | 95 Bothwell Street, Glasgow G2 7HY |
| L | Scottish Life | 19 St Andrew Square, Edinburgh EH2 1YE |
| L | Scottish Mutual | 301 St Vincent Street, Glasgow G2 5HN |
| L | Scottish Provident Life | 6 St Andrew Square, Edinburgh EH2 2YA |
| L | Scottish Widows' | 15 Dalkeith Road, Edinburgh EH16 5BU |
| GM | Sea (RSA) | 1 Bartholomew Lane, London EC2N 2AB |
| L | Standard Life | 30 Lothian Road, Edinburgh EH1 2DH |
| GLM | Sun Alliance (RSA) | 1 Bartholomew Lane, London EC2N 2AB |
| GM | Sun Insurance Office (RSA) | 1 Bartholomew Lane, London EC2N 2AB |
| L Re | Sun Life of Canada | Basing View, Basingstoke RG21 2DZ |
| L | Swiss Life | Swiss Life House, South Park, Sevenoaks TN13 1BG |
| GL | Teacher's Provident Soc | Deansleigh Road, Bournemouth BH7 7DT |
| L | Tunstall Assurance | Station Chambers, The Boulevard, Tunstall, Stoke-on-Trent ST6 6DU |
| M | Ulster Marine (CGNU) | Pitheavlis, Perth PH2 0NH |
| GL | UIA Insurance | Kings Court, London Road, Stevenage SG1 2TP |
| GM | Union Insurance Society of Canton (CGNU) | Royal Exchange, London EC3V 3LS |
| L | United Friendly | Refuge House, Alderley Road, Wilmslow SK9 1PF |
| L | UNUM | Milton Court Dorking, RH4 3LZ |
| GL Re | Wesleyan Assurance | Colmore Circus, Birmingham B4 6AR |
| L | Windsor Life | Windsor House, Telford TF3 4NB |
| L | Winterthur Life | Winterthur Way, Basingstoke RG21 6SZ |
| GM Re | Zurich (Z) | Zurich House, Stanhope Road, Portsmouth PO1 1DU |
| L | Zurich Life (Z) | The Zurich Centre, 3000 Parkway, Whiteley, Fareham PO15 7JY |

# Slang Terms for Money

(Reproduced from *Whitaker's Almanack* 1891)
In addition to the ordinary terms there are others which, although puzzling to a foreigner, are tolerably well understood in this country. In Scotland, a man who flies 'kites' may not be worth a 'bodle', and in England not worth a 'mag' – coins which no one ever saw. Such a man will toss you for a 'bob'. He, of course, would be shunned by the lady who lost a 'pony' on last year's Oaks, and by her husband who lost a 'monkey' on the Derby at Epsom a day or two previously. A gentleman who is worth a 'plum' (£100,000) need never be short of 'tin'; while the outcast who begs a few 'coppers' in order to procure a bed generally has no 'blunt'. The following words are commonly in use:

A Joey = 4*d.*
A Tanner = 6*d.*
A Bob = 1*s.*
Half a Bull = 2*s.* 6*d.*
A Bull = 5*s.*
A Quid = £1
A Pony = £25
A Monkey = £500
A Kite = An accommodation Bill
Browns = Copper or bronze
Tin = Money generally
Blunt = Silver, or money in general

# The London Stock Exchange

The London Stock Exchange plc serves the needs of industry and investors by providing facilities for raising capital and a central market-place for securities trading. This market-place covers government stocks (called gilts), UK and overseas company shares (called equities and fixed interest stocks), and traditional options.

### Primary Markets

The Exchange enables companies to raise capital for development and growth through the issue of securities. For a company entering the market for the first time there is a choice of Exchange markets, depending upon the size, history and requirements of the company. The first is the main market, which exists for well-established companies; these must comply with stringent criteria relating to all aspects of their operations.

A company's securities are admitted to the Official List by the UK Listing Authority (UKLA), a division of the Financial Services Authority, and also admitted to trading by the Exchange. In parallel to the UKLA's listing process, the Exchange has its own set of admission and disclosure standards which are designed to sit alongside the UKLA's listing rules.

The Alternative Investment Market (AIM) began trading in June 1995. It enables small, young and growing companies to raise capital, widen their investor base and have their shares traded on a regulated market without the expense of a full Exchange listing. Many companies use AIM as a stepping-stone to a full listing.

Once admitted to the Exchange, all companies are obliged to keep their shareholders informed of their progress, making announcements of a price-sensitive nature through the Exchange's company announcement department.

At the end of 2000 there were 2,428 UK companies listed on the London Stock Exchange; their equity capital had a total market value of £1,812 billion. In addition, 501 international companies were listed, with a total equity market value of £3,526 billion. By the end of 2000 AIM had attracted 524 companies, with a total capitalisation of £14,935 million.

UK equity turnover in 2000 was £1,895,534 million with an average 115,000 bargains a day. International equity turnover in 2000 totalled £3,519,722 million.

### Big Bang

During 1986 the London Stock Exchange went through the greatest period of change in its 200-year history. In March 1986 it opened its doors for the first time to overseas and corporate membership of the Exchange, allowing banks, insurance companies and overseas securities houses to become members of the Exchange and to buy existing member firms. On 27 October 1986, three major reforms took place, changes which became known as 'Big Bang'.

- the abolition of scales of minimum commissions, allowing clients to negotiate freely with their brokers about the charge for their services
- the abolition of the separation of member firms into brokers and jobbers: firms are now broker/dealers, able to act as agents on behalf of clients; to act as principals buying and selling shares for their own account; and to become registered market makers, making continuous buying and selling prices in specific securities
- the introduction of the Stock Exchange automated quotations (SEAQ) system

Since the introduction of SEAQ in 1986, dealing in stocks and shares has taken place by telephone in the firms' own dealing rooms, rather than face to face on the floor of the Exchange. The Stock Exchange Electronic Trading Service (SETS), launched in 1997, introduced over-driven trading in which deals are executed electronically on an electronic order book. SETS runs alongside SEAQ and allows remote control access to the Exchange. The new systems also provide increased investor protection. All deals taking place via the Exchange systems are recorded on a database which can be used to resolve disputes or to carry out investigations.

Members of the London Stock Exchange buy and sell shares on behalf of the public, as well as institutions such as pension funds or insurance companies. In return for transacting the deal, the broker will charge a commission, which is usually based upon the value of the transaction. The market makers, or wholesalers, in each security do not charge a commission for their services, but will quote the broker two prices, a price at which they will buy and a price at which they will sell. It is the middle of these two prices which is published in lists of Stock Exchange prices in newspapers.

### Regulatory Bodies

The London Stock Exchange and the Securities and Futures Authority are the two main regulatory bodies. They were formed under the provisions of the Financial Services Act 1986, which requires investment businesses to be authorised and regulated by a self-regulating organisation (SRO), of which the Securities and Futures Authority is one. The Act also requires business to be conducted through a recognised investment exchange (RIE). The London Stock Exchange is an RIE, regulating three main markets: UK equities, international equities and gilts. In May 2000 the UKLA, which regulates the flotation of UK companies on public markets, transferred to the Financial Services Authority.

### Demutualisation and Listing

On 15 March 2000, the 298 members voted to become shareholders in a demutualised London Stock Exchange, making possible the further commercialisation of the company.

At the end of May 2001 the exchange announced its intention to list on its own main market. The exchange listed on 20 July following an annual general meeting on 19 July 2001. The full listing is intended to enable the Exchange to exploit business opportunities with greater flexibility.

London Stock Exchange Ltd, Old Broad Street, London EC2N 1HP. Tel: 020-7797 1000; Web: www.londonstockexchange.com

*Chairman*, D. Cruickshank

*Chief Executive*, C. Furse

*Executive Directors*, M. Wheatley, J. Howell

*Non-Executive Directors*, G. Allen, CBE; Baroness Cohen, O. Fanjul; M. Marks; P. Meinertzhagen; I. Salter; N. Stapleton; R. Webb, QC.

# Financial Services Regulation

## The Financial Services Authority

A major reform of financial services regulation in the UK has recently been undertaken. The first stage was completed in June 1998 when responsibility for banking supervision was transferred from the Bank of England to the Financial Services Authority (FSA). The second stage occurred in June 2000 when the Financial Services and Markets Act 2000 (FSMA) received Royal Assent. The third stage took place on 1 December 2001, when the FSA assumed its full powers under the FSMA and became the single regulator directly responsible for deposit-taking, insurance and investment business.

The FSA has taken on responsibility, under a range of service agreements and other arrangements, for carrying out regulatory activities on behalf of other organisations - the self-regulating organisations which regulate firms doing investment business, the Building Societies Commission, the Friendly Societies Commission and the Treasury (in relation to the supervision of insurance companies).

The FSA also supervises the recognised professional bodies and recognised clearing houses, ensuring that they continue to fulfil their regulatory responsibilities. On 1 May 2000 the FSA took over from the London Stock Exchange the role of the UK's listing authority.

Under the new legislation the FSA has certain responsibilities not carried out by previous regulatory bodies. The FSA is required to pursue four statutory objectives:

- maintaining market confidence
- raising of public awareness
- protection of consumers
- reduction of financial crime

The legislation will require the FSA to carry out its general functions, whilst having regard to:

- the need to use its resources in the most efficient way
- the responsibilities of regulated firms' own management
- being proportionate in imposing burdens or restrictions on the industry.
- facilitating innovation
- the international character of financial services and the competitive position of the United Kingdom
- the need to facilitate, and not have unnecessarily adverse effect, on competition

## The FSA as an Organisation

The FSA is a company limited by guarantee, financed by levies on the industry. It receives no funds from the public purse. It is accountable to Treasury Ministers and, through them, to Parliament. Under the new legislation the FSA must report annually on the achievement of its statutory objectives to the Treasury, which is required to lay the report before Parliament.

The FSA's governing body is a board, consisting of a chairman, three executive directors and eleven non-executives, all appointed by the Treasury. The Board sets overall FSA policy. Day-to-day operational decisions and management of the staff are the responsibility of the Executive. The Chairman is responsible for the overall strategic direction and management of the FSA. Three Managing Directors and a Chief Operating Officer report to the chairman. Together they constitute the executive management of the FSA.

The FSA currently has over 2000 staff. Its budget for 2001-2 is £187.7million. Under the new legislation it will regulate approximately 10,000 institutions. This total includes over 7,500 investment firms, over 650 banks, around 70 building societies, almost 1000 insurance companies and friendly societies and the Lloyds insurance market. In addition the FSA will regulate about 180,000 approved individuals. From mid-2002, the FSA will also regulate about 700 credit unions.

## FSA Central Register/Consumer Helpline

The FSA maintains a Central Register of all firms that are, or were, authorised to carry on investment business and authorised deposit takers. The entry for each firm gives its name, address and telephone number; a reference number; its authorisation status; and states which organisation regulates it; and whether it can handle client money.

The Consumer Helpline is available to members of the public seeking information about firms listed on the register. In addition the Helpline explains complaints procedures and provides information on what is and is not regulated by the FSA.

Consumer Helpline: 0845-606 1234

Web: www.fsa.gov.uk

Financial Services Authority, 25 The North Colonade, Canary Wharf, London E14 5HS. Tel: 020 7676 1000. Fax: 020 7676 1099.
*Chairman*, Howard Davies

## Compensation

Under the new legislation the Financial Services Compensation Scheme (FSCS) replaced the six previous compensation schemes. It provides compensation if a firmcollapses owing money to investors, depositors or policyholders. The FSA appoints their boards and makes their rules.

The FSCS is operationally independent from the FSA, with separate staff and premises. However, the FSA appoints the board of the FSCS and dictates its procedures.

The financial services Compensation Scheme, 7th Floor Lloyds Chambers, 1 Portsoken Street, E1 8BN. Tel: 020-7892 7300. Fax: 020-7892 7301.
*Chairman*, Susan McCarthy

## AUTHORISED DEPOSIT-TAKING INSTITUTIONS

For deposit-taking institutions, *see* Banking

## DESIGNATED PROFESSIONAL BODIES

Under the FSMA legislation the FSA is responsible for regulating a number of firms previously regulated by Designated Professional Bodies (DPBs). These firms are members of certain professions (e.g. solicitors, accountants) whose main activity is the practice of their profession but who, in addition, carry on investment business. The DPBs are:

Institute of Chartered Accountants in England and Wales, Chartered Accountants' Hall, PO Box 433, Moorgate Place, London EC2P 2BJ. Tel: 020-7920 8100

Institute of Chartered Accountants of Scotland, CA House, 21 Haymarket Yards, Edinburgh EH12 5BH. Tel: 0131-347 0100

THE ULSTER SOCIETY OF THE INSTITUTE OF CHARTERED ACCOUNTANTS IN IRELAND, 11 Donegall Square South, Belfast BT1 5JE. Tel: 028-9032 1600

ASSOCIATION OF CHARTERED CERTIFIED ACCOUNTANTS, 29 Lincoln's Inn Fields, London WC2A 3EE. Tel: 020-7242 6855

INSTITUTE OF ACTUARIES, Staple Inn Hall, High Holborn, London WC1V 7QJ. Tel: 020-7632 2100

THE LAW SOCIETY OF ENGLAND AND WALES, 113 Chancery Lane, London WC2A 1PL. Tel: 020-7242 1222

LAW SOCIETY OF NORTHERN IRELAND, Law Society House, 98 Victoria Street, Belfast BT1 3JT. Tel: 028-9023 1614

LAW SOCIETY OF SCOTLAND, Law Society's Hall, 26 Drumsheugh Gardens, Edinburgh EH3 7YR. Tel: 0131-226 7411

## RECOGNISED INVESTMENT EXCHANGES

The FSA supervises eight Recognised Investment Exchanges (RIEs). These are organised markets on which member firms can trade investments such as equities and derivatives. Examples are the London Stock Exchange and the London Metal exchange. As a regulator the FSA must also focus on the impact of changes brought about by the continued growth in electronic trading by exchanges and other organisations. Issues such as how these changes affect market quality, reliability and access are important and the FSA works with the exchanges to ensure that new systems meet regulatory requirements. The RIEs are:

COREDEAL, Seven Limeharbour, Docklands, London E14 9NQ. Tel: 020-7510 2700

INTERNATIONAL PETROLEUM EXCHANGE (IPE), International House, 1 St Katharine's Way, London E1 9UN. Tel: 020-7481 0643

JIWAY LTD, Old Change House, 128 Queen Victoria Street, London EC4V 4BJ. Tel: 020-7651 3900

LONDON INTERNATIONAL FINANCIAL FUTURES AND OPTIONS EXCHANGE (LIFFE), Cannon Bridge, London EC4R 3XX. Tel: 020-7623 0444

LONDON METAL EXCHANGE LTD (LME), 56 Leadenhall Street, London EC3A 2DX. Tel: 020-7264 5555

LONDON STOCK EXCHANGE (LSE), Old Broad Street, London EC2N 1HP. Tel: 020-7797 1000

OM LONDON EXCHANGE LTD, 131 Finsbury Pavement, London EC2A 1NT. Tel: 020-7065 8000

VIRT-X, 35 King Street, London WC2E 8JD. Tel: 020-7240 8000

## RECOGNISED CLEARING HOUSES

The FSA is also responsible for recognising and supervising Recognised Clearing Houses. These are bodies which organise the settlement of transactions on Recognised Investment Exchanges. These are:

CREST CO LTD, 33 Cannon Street, London EC4M 5SB. Tel: 020-7849 0000

LONDON CLEARING HOUSE LTD (LCH), Aldgate House, 33 Aldgate High Street, London EC3N 1EA. Tel: 020-7426 7000

## OMBUDSMAN SCHEMES

The Financial Ombudsman Service has been set up by the Financial Services and Markets Act to provide consumers with a free, independent service for resolving disputes with financial firms. It brought together eight existing complaints-handling schemes within the financial sector including the Banking Ombudsman, the Insurance Ombudsman, the Investment Ombudsman and the Personal Investment Authority Ombudsman.

The Financial Ombudsman Service can help with most financial complaints about:

- Banking services
- Endowment Policies
- Financial and investment advice
- Mortgages
- Health and loan protection insurance
- Household and buildings insurance
- Investment portfolio management
- Life assurance
- Motor insurance
- Personal pension plans (but not occupational pensions - *see* Pensions Ombudsman)
- Private medical insurance
- Saving plans and accounts
- Stocks and shares
- Travel insurance
- Unit trusts and income bonds

Complainants must first complain to the firm involved. They do not have to accept the ombudsman's decision and are free to go to court if they wish.

The Pensions Ombudsman is appointed and operates under the Pension Schemes Act 1993 as amended by the Pensions Act 1995; he is responsible to Parliament. He investigates and decides complaints and disputes concerning occupational pension schemes, primarily alleged maladministration by the persons responsible for managing an occupational pension scheme. Personal pension complaints are normally dealt with only if outside the jurisdiction of the Personal Investment Authority.

FINANCIAL OMBUDSMAN SERVICE, South Quay Plaza, 183 Marsh Wall, London, E14 9SR Tel: 020-7964 1000 Fax: 020-7964 1001 Web: www.financial-ombudsman.org.uk *Chief Ombudsman:* W. Merricks *Principle Ombudsmen: Banking and Loans:* D. Thomas; *Insurance:* T. Boorman; *Investment:* J. Whittles

THE PENSIONS OMBUDSMAN, 6th Floor, 11 Belgrave Road, London SW1V 1RB. Tel: 020-7834 9144. *Pensions Ombudsman*, Dr J. T. Farrand

## THE TAKEOVER PANEL

The Takeover Panel was set up in 1968 in response to concern about practices unfair to shareholders in takeover bids for public and certain private companies. Its principal objective is to ensure equality of treatment, and fair opportunity for all shareholders to consider on its merits an offer that would result in the change of control of a company. It is a non-statutory body that operates the City code on take-overs and mergers.

The chairman, deputy chairmen and three lay members of the panel are appointed by the Bank of England. The remainder are representatives of the banking, insurance, investment, pension fund and accountancy professional bodies, the CBI, IMRO and the Stock Exchange.

THE PANEL ON TAKEOVERS AND MERGERS, PO Box 226, The Stock Exchange Building, London, EC2P 2JX. Tel: 020-7382 9026. Web: www.takeoverpanel.org.uk; *Chairman*, Peter Scott, QC

# Taxation

## INCOME TAX

Income tax is charged on the taxable income of individuals for a year of assessment commencing on 6 April and ending on the following 5 April. Many changes have been introduced during recent years which affect both the calculation of income chargeable to tax and the rate or rates at which the amount of tax due must be determined. In view of these changes the following information is confined to the year of assessment 2001–2 ending on 5 April 2002 and has only limited application to earlier years. However, some changes affecting future years are also noted where the information is available.

An individual's liability to satisfy income tax for 2001–2 is determined by establishing the level of taxable income for the year. This income must then be allocated between three different headings, namely: (a) all income excluding that arising from savings and dividends; (b) income from savings; (c) company dividends, including distributions.

Once this allocation has been completed the first calculation must be limited to taxable income excluding that arising from both savings and dividends. This income will be reduced by an individual's personal allowance and any other available allowances. The first £1,880 of taxable income remaining is assessed to income tax at the starting rate of 10 per cent. The next £27,520 is taxable at the basic rate of 22 per cent. Should any excess over £29,400 (£1,880 plus £27,520) remain, this will be taxable at the higher rate of 40 per cent.

The second calculation is limited to income from savings, if any. Liability may arise at the starting rate of 10 per cent, the lower rate of 20 per cent or the higher rate of 40 per cent. There is no liability to income tax at the basic rate of 22 per cent. The appropriate rate which must be used is determined by adding income from savings to other taxable income, excluding dividends. To the extent that the addition does not increase taxable income above £1,880, income from savings is taxed at the starting rate of 10 per cent. Should this level be exceeded but total income does not reach £29,400 any excess remains taxable at the lower rate of 20 per cent. In those situations where the addition of savings extends total income above £29,400 the excess is taxed at the higher rate of 40 per cent.

Finally, any company dividends are taxed at either the Schedule F ordinary rate of 10 per cent or the Schedule F upper rate of 32.5 per cent. The amount of dividends (with the addition of any tax credit) must be added to taxable income comprising general income together with income from savings. If this addition does not increase total taxable income above £29,400 dividends remain taxable at the ordinary rate of 10 per cent only. However, if or to the extent that the addition discloses dividends exceeding the £29,400 level the excess is taxed at the upper rate of 32.5 per cent.

It is assumed that the entire married couple's allowance will be given to the husband only. Persons over the age of 74 years may pay less tax, unless their income is substantial. Some taxpayers may be entitled to further allowances and reliefs which reduce the tax payable below the amount shown by the tables. These tables have been structured on the assumption that none of the income arises from savings or dividends. Should income of this nature be received, less tax may be due.

Trustees administering settled property and personal representatives dealing with the estate of a deceased person are chargeable to income tax at the basic rate of 22 per cent. Where trustees retain discretionary powers or income from settled property is accumulated, liability may be increased to 34 per cent. Companies residing in the UK are not liable to income tax but suffer corporation tax on income, profits and gains (*see* pages 649–651).

Income arising overseas will often incur liability to foreign taxation. If that income is also chargeable to UK income tax, excessive liability could arise. The UK has concluded double taxation agreements with the governments of many overseas territories and these ensure that the same slice of income is not doubly taxed.

### Husband and Wife

A husband and wife are separately taxed, with each entitled to his or her personal allowance. A married man 'living with' his wife can only obtain a married couple's allowance if one party to the marriage was over the age of 64 years before 6 April 2000. In the absence of any claim, this allowance must be used by the husband but where any balance remains the surplus may be transferred to the wife. It is possible for a married woman to claim half the basic married couple's allowance as of right. In addition, the entire basic allowance may be claimed by the wife, if her husband so agrees.

Each spouse may obtain other allowances and reliefs where the required conditions are satisfied. Income must be accurately allocated between the couple by reference to the individual beneficially entitled to that income. Where income arises from jointly-held assets, this must be apportioned equally between husband and wife. However, in those cases where the beneficial interests in jointly-held assets are not equal, a special declaration can be made to apportion income by reference to the actual interests in that income.

### Self-Assessment

Self-assessment for income tax purposes affects individuals, trustees and personal representatives. Central to self-assessment is the requirement to deliver a completed tax return. This must normally be submitted by 31 January following the end of the year of assessment to which the return relates. In addition to completing the return, the taxpayer must calculate the amount of income tax due. If a taxpayer wishes the Inland Revenue to calculate the tax due, the return must be forwarded to the Inland Revenue not later than the previous 30 September.

It is the responsibility of the taxpayer to submit payments of income tax on time. There are three different dates on which payments may fall due:

(a) an interim payment due on 31 January in the year of assessment itself

(b) a second interim payment due on the following 31 July

(c) a balancing payment, or possibly a repayment, on the following 31 January

The two interim payments will be based on tax payable for the previous year of assessment but liability may be reduced where income has fallen or even avoided entirely where the amounts are not substantial.

The impact of self-assessment is largely restricted to some nine million persons receiving tax returns. These comprise self-employed individuals, those receiving income from the exploitation of land in the UK, company directors, others with investment income liable to higher rate income tax, trustees and personal representatives. Elderly persons receiving untaxed income may be excluded from the need to complete a tax return. Separate tax return forms are issued to a husband and wife, where such forms are needed.

Failure to submit completed tax returns by 31 January or to discharge payments of income tax on time will incur a liability to interest, surcharges and penalties.

## Income Taxable

Income tax is assessed under several Schedules. Each Schedule determines the extent of liability and establishes the amount to be included in taxable income. In some instances the actual income arising in a year of assessment will be charged to income tax for that year.

A different basis must be used for business profits taxable under Case I or Case II of Schedule D. This basis requires taxable profits to be those for the business accounting period ending in the year of assessment, with special adjustments for the opening and closing years of a business. Other income assessable under Schedule D will be that which arises in the actual year of assessment.

Following the withdrawal of income tax liability for most commercial woodlands in the UK, Schedule B no longer applies. Schedule C has also been withdrawn as the result of further changes. The contents of the remaining schedules are shown below.

### *Schedule A*

Tax is charged under Schedule A on the annual profits or gains arising from a business carried on for the exploitation of land in the UK. The determination of profits from a Schedule A business adopts principles identical to those used when establishing the profits or gains of a trade, profession or vocation. Rents and other income from the exploitation of land are included in the calculation, and outgoings incurred wholly and exclusively for the purposes of the Schedule A business may be deducted from income.

Schedule A does not extend to profits from farming, market gardening or woodlands, nor does it apply to mineral rents and royalties. Premiums arising on the grant of a lease for a period not exceeding 50 years in duration are treated as rents. However, the amount of the taxable premium may be reduced by 2 per cent for each complete year, after the first 12 months, of the leasing period. Income arising from the provision of certain furnished holiday accommodation attracts a number of tax advantages not otherwise available for most income chargeable under Schedule A.

Receipts not exceeding £4,250 annually and accruing to an individual from letting property furnished in his or her own home are usually excluded from liability to income tax.

### *Schedule D*

This Schedule is divided into six Cases:

*Cases I and II* – profits arising from trades, professions and vocations, including farming and market gardening. Profits must now be calculated on an accounting basis which provides 'a true and fair view' of business results. This remains subject to any statutory adjustment which may be required. For example, only sums laid out 'wholly and exclusively' for the purposes of a business may be subtracted from receipts, notwithstanding that those outgoings may reflect a proper accounting charge. Capital expenditure incurred on assets used for business purposes will often produce an entitlement to capital allowances which reduce the profits chargeable. These profits may also be reduced by claims for loss relief and other matters.

*Case III* – interest on government stocks not taxed at source, interest on National Savings Bank deposits and discounts. Interest up to £70 on ordinary National Savings Bank deposits is exempt from income tax. The exemption applies to both husband and wife separately. Interest on National Savings Bank special investment accounts is not exempt. Interest and other items of savings income incur liability at the starting rate, lower rate or the higher rate depending on the level of the recipients income.

*Cases IV and V* – interest from overseas securities, rents, dividends and all other income accruing outside the UK. Assessment is based on the full amount of income arising, whether remitted to the UK or retained overseas, but individuals who are either not domiciled in the UK or who are ordinarily resident overseas may be taxed on a remittance basis. Overseas pensions are taxable but the amount arising may be reduced by 10 per cent for assessment purposes. Interest received on most overseas investments is chargeable at the same rates as those which apply to interest from sources within the UK. Overseas dividends are usually taxed at 10 per cent or 32.5 per cent.

*Case VI* – sundry profits and annual receipts not assessed under any other Case or Schedule. These may include insurance commissions, post-cessation receipts from a discontinued business and numerous other receipts specifically charged under Case VI.

### *Schedule E*

All earnings from an office or employment are assessable under this Schedule. There are three Cases:

*Case I* – applies to all earnings of an individual resident and ordinarily resident in the UK.

*Case II* – of application where the individual is not resident or not ordinarily resident and extends to earnings for duties undertaken in the UK.

*Case III* – applies in rare situations to other earnings remitted to the UK.

A 'receipts basis' applies for determining the year of assessment to which earnings must be allocated and taxed. Where earnings are assessable under Case I or Case II, the date of receipt will comprise the earlier of the date of payment, or the date entitlement arises. In the case of company directors it is the earlier of these two dates, with the addition of the following three which establish the time of receipt: the date earnings are credited in the company's books; where earnings for a period are determined after the end of that period, the date of determination; where earnings for a period are determined in that period, the last day of that period.

The earnings assessable under Schedule E include all salaries, wages, director's fees and other money sums. In addition, the value of a wide range of benefits must be added to taxable earnings. These include the provision of living accommodation on advantageous terms and advantages arising from the use of vouchers.

Further taxable benefits accrue to directors and also to employees receiving earnings of £8,500 or more in the year of assessment. Such benefits include the reimbursement of expenses, the availability of motor cars for private motoring, the provision of petrol or other fuel for private motoring, the use of vans, the provision of interest-free loans, and other benefits provided at the employer's expense. The cost of providing a limited range of child care facilities and a works bus for the transportation of employees may be excluded. Mileage allowances paid to employees who provide their own motor vehicles or cycles for business travel may also be excluded unless they exceed stated limits.

In arriving at the amount to be assessed under Schedule E, all expenses incurred wholly, exclusively and necessarily in the performance of the duties, together with the cost of business travel, may be deducted. Fees and subscriptions paid to certain professional bodies and learned societies may also be deducted. Fees paid to managers by entertainers, actors and others assessable under Schedule E may be deducted, up to a maximum of 17.5 per cent of earnings.

Compensation for loss of office and other sums received on the termination of an office or employment are assessable to tax. However, the first £30,000 may be excluded with only the balance remaining chargeable, unless the compensatory payment is linked with the retirement of the recipient or the performance of their duties.

*Schedule F*

This Schedule is concerned with dividends and distributions received from a UK resident company.

### Income From Savings

Many payments of interest made by building societies and banks are received after the deduction of income tax at the lower rate of 20 per cent. However, investors not liable to income tax may arrange to receive interest gross with no tax being deducted on payment.

Interest of this nature represents 'income from savings'; an expression which also extends to interest on government securities, interest on a restricted range of National Savings products and the income element of purchased life annuities. In addition, 'income from savings' may extend to other income of a similar nature arising outside the United Kingdom. Not all forms of investment income are included in the list, notable exceptions comprising income from letting property and company dividends.

A great deal of interest arising from sources in the United Kingdom will be received after deduction of income tax at the lower rate of 20 per cent. Although this interest is not taxable at the basic rate it remains chargeable at the starting rate of 10 per cent, the lower rate of 20 per cent or the higher rate of 40 per cent. Where such interest when added to other income, excluding dividends, falls within the starting rate band tax will be due at 10 per cent. As tax will have been suffered by deduction at the lower rate of 20 per cent a repayment of the excess may well be obtained from the Inland Revenue. To the extent that interest from savings when added to other income exceeds £1,880 but does not exceed £29,400 liability arises at the lower rate of 20 per cent. In those situations where, or to the extent that, income from savings when added to other income produces a combined total exceeding £29,400 liability arises at the higher rate of 40 per cent. As income tax will usually have been deducted at source at the rate of 20 per cent higher rate liability arises at a further 20 per cent (40 per cent less 20 per cent).

### Dividends

Dividends and other distributions paid by a UK resident company have a tax credit attached equal to one-ninth of the sum received in 2001–2. Therefore a recipient shareholder also residing in the UK who receives a cash dividend of £90 will have a tax credit of £10. The gross dividend or distribution (sum received plus tax credit) is regarded as having suffered income tax, equal to the tax credit, at the rate of 10 per cent. Where the shareholder is not liable, or not fully liable, to income tax it is not possible to claim a repayment of the tax credit. However, for 2001–2 dividends are taxed at the Schedule F ordinary rate of 10 per cent or the Schedule F upper rate of 32.5 per cent. Where the total income of an individual is not unduly substantial the amount of the tax credit, namely 10 per cent, will be offset against the Schedule F ordinary rate of income tax, which is also 10 per cent, leaving no further liability. Should the gross amount of dividends or distributions when added to other taxable income exceed £29,400 the excess is chargeable at the Schedule F upper rate of 32.5 per cent. The amount of the tax credit will then reduce tax otherwise payable at the upper rate. Although the rates of 10 per cent and 32.5 per cent apply to dividends and distributions from United Kingdom companies, they also extend to income of a similar nature arising outside the UK.

### Income Not Taxable

Income which is not taxable in 2001–2 includes interest on National Savings certificates, most scholarship income, bounty payments to members of the armed services and annuities payable to the holders of certain awards. Dividend income arising from qualifying investments in personal equity plans (PEPs) and venture capital trusts is exempt from tax. Although tax credits on dividends from trust can no longer be recovered it is possible for PEP managers to obtain repayment of credits during a five year period ending on 5 April 2004. Income received under maintenance agreements and court orders made after will not be liable to tax. Nor will payments made under many deeds of covenant be recognised for tax purposes, unless the recipient is a charity. Interest arising on a tax exempt special savings account (TESSA) opened with a building society or bank will be exempt from tax if the account is maintained throughout a five-year period.

A popular investment, the individual savings account (ISA), is available to United Kingdom residents aged 18 years and over. The ISA may have three components, namely cash, stocks and shares and life assurance. Interest on the cash component, usually comprising bank or building society deposits, is exempt from income tax. Dividends on most quoted buildings in the stocks and shares component are also immune from liability to income tax, with tax credits being repaid for years up to and including that ending on 5 April 2004. Income and gains accruing to the provider of the life assurance component will be free of all liability to taxation.

A maximum subscription of £7,000 can be made by an individual to an ISA during 2001–2. Of this sum no more than £3,000 can be allocated to the cash component and £1,000 to the life assurance component. Potential investors are provided with the choice of whether to invest in a maxi-ISA or in mini-ISAs. Should a maxi-ISA be selected the entire £7,000 can be invested in stocks and share, but the use of a mini-ISA limits such an investment to £3,000 with the balance of £4,000 capable of being used to invest in the cash and life assurance components.

Although no new TESSA accounts can now be opened, where an existing TESSA matures at the end of a five-year period the capital (but not the income) proceeds can be separately invested in the cash component of an ISA. This is in addition to the normal limits governing investment in an ISA.

### Social Security Benefits

Many social security benefits are not liable to income tax. These include income support, maternity allowance, child benefit, war widow's pension and disability living allowance. The benefits which are taxable include the retirement pension, widow's pension, widowed mother's allowance and jobseeker's allowance. Short-term sick pay and maternity pay payable by an employer are also chargeable to tax. Incapacity benefit is chargeable to tax but no liability arises on most short term benefit.

A working families' tax credit and a disabled persons tax credit may be payable to many individuals (*see* Social Welfare section).

## Pay As You Earn

The Pay As You Earn (PAYE) system is not an independent form of taxation but is designed to collect income tax by deduction from most earnings. When paying earnings to employees, an employer is usually required to deduct income tax and account for that tax to the Inland Revenue. In many cases this deduction procedure will fully exhaust the individual's liability to income tax, unless there is other income. The date of 'receipt' used for assessment purposes also identifies the date of 'payment' when establishing liability for PAYE.

The PAYE system is used to collect tax on certain payments made 'in kind'. The system is also used when collecting tax on many pensions, jobfinders benefits, some incapacity benefits and maternity pay.

## Allowances

Several allowances which were previously available for individuals ceased to apply after 5 April 2000. Those allowances which can be obtained for 2001–2 are shown below.

### *Personal allowance*

| | |
|---|---|
| Basic personal allowance | £4,535 |
| Those over 64 on 5 April 2002 | £5,990 |
| Those over 74 on 5 April 2002 | £6,260 |

The increased allowance for older individuals is available for those who died during the year of assessment but who would otherwise have achieved the appropriate age not later than 5 April 2002.

The amount of the increased personal allowance for older taxpayers will be reduced by one-half of total income in excess of £17,600. This reduction in the allowance will continue until it has been reduced to the basic personal allowance of £4,535.

The personal allowance is given as a deduction in calculating taxable income and may therefore produce relief at the rate of 10, 23 or 40 per cent, as appropriate.

### *Married couple's allowance*

A married man who was 'living with' his wife at any time in the year ending on 5 April 2002 may be entitled to a married couple's allowance. It is a requirement before this allowance can be obtained that at least one party to the marriage reached the age of 65 years before 6 April 2000. The allowance cannot be obtained where both parties were below this age on that date, nor will it be forthcoming where a husband or wife reaches 65 on some future date.

The allowance is £5,365 if the husband or the wife satisfies the 65 year requirement. It may, however, be increased to £5,435 where either party to the marriage was 75 or over on 5 April 2002. Where an individual would otherwise have reached the age of 75 by 5 April 2002 but who died earlier in the year the increased allowance is given.

The amount of the married couple's allowance will be reduced where the income of the husband (excluding the income of the wife) exceeds £17,600. The deduction will comprise:

(a) one-half of the husband's total income in excess of £17,600, less
(b) the amount of any reduction made when calculating the husband's increased personal allowance.

This reduction in the married couple's allowance cannot reduce that allowance below the basic allowance of £2,070.

If husband and wife were married during 2001–2 the married couple's allowance must be reduced by one-twelfth for each complete month commencing on 6 April 2001 and preceding the date of marriage.

Unlike the personal allowance, the married couple's allowance does not reduce taxable income. Relief is granted by reducing the tax otherwise payable by 10 per cent of the allowance. Should the amount of the reductions exceed tax otherwise payable, no tax will be due, nor will any repayment arise.

In the absence of any further action, the married couple's allowance will be given to the husband. If he is unable to utilise all or any part of that allowance due to an absence of income, the husband may transfer the unused portion to his wife. The decision whether or not to transfer remains at the discretion of the husband.

However, a wife may file an election to obtain one-half of the basic married couple's allowance of £2,070 as of right, leaving the husband with the balance of that allowance. Alternatively, the couple may jointly elect that the entire basic allowance should be allocated to the wife only. Should either spouse be unable to utilise his or her share of the total married couple's allowance the unused part may be transferred to the other spouse.

### *Blind person's allowance*

An allowance of £1,450 is available to an individual if at any time during the year ending on 5 April 2002, he or she was registered as blind on a register maintained by a local authority. If the individual is 'living with' a wife or husband, any unused part of the blind person's allowance can be transferred to the other spouse. The allowance reduces taxable income and may therefore give rise to relief at the taxpayer's highest rate of tax suffered.

### *Children's Tax Credit*

A new allowance, the children's tax credit, is available for 2001-2 and future years. The credit can be claimed by an individual who has one or more qualifying children resident which him or her during all or part of the tax year. The credit for 2001-2 is £5,200 and is given at the rate of 10 per cent as a deduction from income tax otherwise payable. This may achieve a maximum deduction of £520. However, where the income of the claimant incurs liability to income tax at the higher rate of 40 per cent the credit allowance of £5,200 is reduced by two-thirds to the income changeable at the higher rate.

An adjustment is necessary where a husband and wife are 'living together; or a man and woman are 'living together' as a husband and wife. In this situation the credit will be given to whichever of the two individuals has the higher taxable income. This allocation will determine whether any reduction is necessary due to income tax liability at a higher rate. Where neither individual has sufficient income to incur liability at the higher rate the children's tax credit may be allocated between the couple.

An addition to the children's tax credit is to be introduced for 2002-3 and future years. This addition will be available for the year of assessment in which a baby is born. This assumes that after birth the child resides with the claimant. The amount of the 'baby rate' credit is £5,200 and will be added to the normal children's tax credit mentioned above. This will increase the aggregate credit to £10,400, which continues to be given at the rate of 10 per cent as a deduction from income tax otherwise payable.

### Maintenance Payments

Relief for maintenance payments made in 2001-2 to a separated spouse or a divorced former spouse is limited to £2,070 or the amount of the payment, whichever is smaller. A further requirement before relief can be obtained is that at least one of the parties to the transaction has reached his or her 65th birthday before 6 April 2000. No relief is available to younger parties. Relief is given at the rate of 10 per cent and subtracted from the amount of tax otherwise due by the payer.

The maintenance payment is exempt from liability to income tax in the hands of the recipient.

### Interest

In some instances, interest paid by a business proprietor may be included when calculating profits chargeable to income tax under Case I or Case II of Schedule D. In addition, relief for interest paid on a loan applied to acquire or develop land and buildings for letting may be obtained by including the outlay in the calculation of income chargeable under Schedule A. However, many private individuals cannot obtain relief in this manner and must satisfy stringent requirements before relief will be forthcoming. In general terms it is a requirement that before interest can qualify for relief it must be paid for a qualifying purpose. Relief will not be available to the extent that interest exceeds a reasonable commercial rate and no relief is forthcoming for interest on an overdraft.

Interest paid in 2001-2 which can be treated as laid out for a qualifying purpose will include the following payments:

(a) Interest on a loan used to acquire an interest in a close company or in a partnership, or to advance money to such a person
(b) Interest on a loan to a member of a partnership to acquire machinery or plant for use in the partnership business
(c) Interest on a loan to an employed person to acquire machinery or plant for the purposes of his or her employment
(d) Interest on a loan made for the purpose of contributing capital to an industrial co-operative
(e) Interest on a loan applied for investment in an employee-controlled company
(f) Interest on a loan to personal representatives to provide funds for the payment of inheritance tax
(g) Interest on a loan made to elderly persons for the purchase of an annuity where the loan is secured on land. If the loan exceeds £30,000, relief is limited to interest on this amount. This relief is restricted to income tax at the basic rate of 22 per cent. Whilst the relief remains for existing borrowers, it cannot be obtained for interest only new loans taken out after 8 March 1999

Relief under headings (a) to (f) is given by deducting interest from taxable income. This enables the taxpayer to obtain relief at his or her top rate of tax suffered.

### Other Outgoings

Many employees pay contributions to an approved occupational pension scheme. The amount of their contributions may be deducted when calculating earnings assessable under Schedule E. Relief should also be available for any additional voluntary contributions paid.

Self-employed individuals and those receiving earnings not covered by an occupational pension scheme may contribute under personal pension scheme arrangements or under stakeholder schemes. Individuals may also pay premiums under retirement annuity schemes if the arrangements were concluded before 1 July 1988. Contributions paid under all headings and which do not exceed upper limits may obtain income tax relief by deduction from taxable income.

Subject to a maximum of £150,000 in 2001–2, the cost of subscribing for shares in an unquoted trading company or companies may qualify for relief under the Enterprise Investment Scheme. Many requirements must be satisfied before this relief can be obtained, but a husband and wife may each take advantage of the £150,000 maximum. Relief is given by reducing tax payable at the rate of 20 per cent of the share subscription cost. Further relief on an outlay, up to a maximum of £100,000 and also given at the rate of 20 per cent, is available for a subscription of shares in a venture capital trust company.

## CAPITAL GAINS TAX

An individual is potentially chargeable to capital gains tax on chargeable gains which accrue from disposals made by her during a year of assessment ending on 5 April. The application of the tax and the calculation of liability has been the subject of numerous changes in recent years. In recognition of these changes the following information is largely confined to the year of assessment 2001–2, ending on 5 April 2002.

Liability extends to individuals who are either resident or ordinarily resident for the year but special rules apply where a person permanently leaves the UK or comes to this territory for the purpose of acquiring residence. Non-residents are not usually liable to capital gains tax unless they carry on a business in the UK through a branch or agency. However, individuals who left the UK after 16 March 1998 and who have been resident or ordinarily resident in at least four of the seven years preceding departure may remain liable to capital gains tax unless they reside overseas throughout a period of five complete tax years. Exceptions from this may apply where there is a disposal of assets acquired in the period of absence.

Trustees residing in the UK, together with personal representatives are chargeable to capital gains tax at the rate of 34 per cent but chargeable gains accruing to companies are assessable to corporation tax.

For 1997–8 and earlier years, capital gains tax was chargeable on the net chargeable gains accruing to a person in a year of assessment after subtracting the annual exemption for that year. Net chargeable gains represented capital gains less capital losses arising from disposals carried out during the year. Unused losses brought forward from an earlier year could be offset against current net chargeable gains, but in the case of individuals were not to reduce the net gains below the annual exemption limit. It was possible to utilise trading losses against chargeable gains where those losses had not been offset against income.

### Taper Relief

The calculation of net gains chargeable to capital gains tax since 1998–9 is frequently governed by taper relief. The purpose of this relief, which replaced the former indexation allowance, is to require that only a percentage of gains become chargeable to capital gains tax.

Taper relief draws a distinction between business assets and non-business assets. The expression 'business asset' broadly identifies an asset used for business purposes in addition to some holdings of shares in both trading and non-trading companies. Where the nature of an asset has changed during the period of ownership from a business asset to a non-business asset, or vice versa, the asset must be effectively broken down into two parts. This may be particularly relevant where the period overlaps 5 April 2000 when some previously non-business assets were re-classified as business assets.

The percentage which must be used to calculate taper relief is governed by the number of complete years of ownership falling after 5 April 1998. Initially an additional 'bonus year' could be added for most assets acquired before 17 March 1998. This 'bonus year' continues to apply to non-business assets but has been withdrawn where the disposal of a business asset takes place after 5 April 2000.

The maximum percentage attributable to business assets was previously achieved after an ownership period extending throughout 10 years. This was reduced to one of four years only where the disposal takes place after 5 April 2000. No corresponding change was made in the percentages attributable to non-business assets. The percentages which must be used for disposals taking place after 5 April 2000 are as follows:

| | Percentage of gain chargeable | |
|---|---|---|
| No. of whole years of ownership | Business assets | Non-business assets |
| | % | % |
| 1 | 87.5 | 100 |
| 2 | 75.0 | 100 |
| 3 | 50.0 | 95 |
| 4 | 25.0 | 90 |
| 5 | 25.0 | 85 |
| 6 | 25.0 | 80 |
| 7 | 25.0 | 75 |
| 8 | 25.0 | 70 |
| 9 | 25.0 | 65 |
| 10 | 25.0 | 60 |

It has been indicated that where the disposal of business assets takes place on or after 6 April 2002, the ownership period will be further reduced. As a result of this reduction once that period exceeds one year, only 50 per cent of the gain will be chargeable falling to 25 per cent where two whole years are exceeded.

If only chargeable gains arise from disposals carried out in 2001–2, the taper relief, if any, must be calculated by reference to each disposal. The aggregate sum will of taper relief then be subtracted from the total chargeable gains to produce the net gains for the year.

Where disposals in 2001–2 give rise to both gains and losses, the losses must be subtracted from the gains and taper relief calculated on the net sum remaining. It is necessary to allocate the losses between the gains where there are two or more disposals, with the allocation being carried out in the most tax efficient manner. Losses brought forward from an earlier year must also be subtracted when calculating the net gains qualifying for taper relief. However, losses brought forward are not to reduce the net gains below the annual exemption of £7,500 which applies for 2001-2.

### Annual Exemption

The initial slice of net gains arising in a tax year is exempt from liability to capital gains tax. This slice, comprising the annual exemption, is £7,500 for 2001-2. Should any part of the exemption remain unused, this cannot be carried forward to a future year.

### Rates of Tax

The next gains remaining, if any, calculated after subtracting the annual exemption, incur liability to capital gains tax for 2001–2. Although income tax rates are used for this purpose, liability arises only at the starting rate of 10 per cent, the lower rate of 20 per cent, the higher rate of 40 per cent, or a combination of the three rates. Unlike some income tax commitments, there is no liability at the basic rate of 22 per cent.

The first step is to calculate the amount of taxable income chargeable to income tax. This will include income from savings, company dividends and all other forms of taxable income. The second step is to add the amount of net chargeable gains to the taxable income chargeable to income tax. To the extent that this does not increase the aggregate total above £1,880, capital gains tax will be charged at the rate of 10 per cent. If the aggregate total exceeds £1,880 but does not exceed £29,400 any balance needed to reach £1,880 is chargeable at 10 per cent and the excess at 20 per cent. If, or to the extent that, any part of the chargeable gains exceed the limit of £29,400 the excess is chargeable at 40 per cent. Although some income tax rates are used, capital gains tax remains an entirely separate tax.

Capital gains tax for 2001–2 falls due for payment in full on 31 January 2003. If payment is delayed beyond that date, interest or surcharges may be imposed.

### Husband and Wife

Independent taxation requires that a husband and wife 'living together' are separately assessed to capital gains tax. Each spouse must independently calculate his or her gains and losses, with each entitled to the benefit of taper relief, if any, and the annual exemption of £7,500 for 2001–2002. No liability to capital gains tax arises from the transfer of assets between husband and wife 'living together'.

### Disposal of Assets

Before chargeable gains potentially liable to capital gains tax can arise, a disposal or deemed disposal of an asset must take place. This occurs not only where assets are sold or exchanged but applies on the making of a gift. There is also a disposal of assets where any capital sum is derived from assets, e.g. where compensation is received for loss or damage to an asset.

The date on which a disposal must be treated as having taken place will determine the year of assessment into which the chargeable gain or allowable loss falls. In those cases where a disposal is made under an unconditional contract, the time of disposal will be that when the contract was entered into and not the subsequent date of conveyance or transfer. A disposal under a conditional contract or option is treated as taking place when the contract becomes unconditional or the option is exercised. Disposals by way of gift are undertaken when the gift becomes effective.

### Valuation of Assets

The amount actually received as consideration for the disposal of an asset will be the sum from which very limited outgoings must be deducted for the purpose of establishing the gain or loss. In cases where the consideration does not accurately reflect the value of the asset, a different basis must be used. This applies, in particular, where an asset is transferred by way of gift or otherwise than by a bargain made at arm's length. Such transactions are deemed to take place for a consideration representing market value, which will determine both the disposal proceeds accruing to the transferor and the cost of acquisition to the transferee.

Market value represents the price which an asset might reasonably be expected to fetch on a sale in the open market. In the case of unquoted shares or securities, it is to be assumed that the hypothetical purchaser in the open market would have available all the information which a prudent prospective purchaser of shares or securities might reasonably require if that person were proposing to purchase them from a willing vendor by private treaty and at arm's length. The market value of unquoted shares or securities will often be established following negotiations with the Shares Valuation Division of the Capital Taxes Office. The valuation of land and interests in land in the UK will be dealt with by the District Valuer. Special rules apply to determine the market value of shares quoted on the Stock Exchange.

### Deduction for Outgoings

Once the actual or notional disposal proceeds have been determined, it only remains to subtract eligible outgoings for the purpose of computing the gain or loss. There is the general rule that any outgoings deducted, or which are available to be deducted, when calculating income tax liability must be ignored. Subject to this, deductions will usually be limited to:

(a) the cost of acquiring the asset, together with incidental costs wholly and exclusively incurred in connection with the acquisition
(b) expenditure incurred wholly and exclusively on the asset in enhancing its value, being expenditure reflected in the state or nature of the asset at the time of the disposal, and any other expenditure wholly and exclusively incurred in establishing, preserving or defending title to, or a right over, the asset
(c) the incidental costs of making the disposal

Where the disposal concerns a leasehold interest having less than 50 years to run, any expenditure falling under (a) and (b) must be written off throughout the duration of the lease using a 'curved line' approach.

### Indexation Allowance

For many years an indexation allowance could be inserted when calculating a gain on the disposal of an asset. The allowance was based on percentage increases in the retail prices index between the month of March 1982, or the month in which expenditure was incurred if later, and the month of disposal. The indexation allowance established on this basis entered into the calculation of chargeable gain arising on the disposal of an asset. It was not possible to use the allowance to increase or to create an allowable loss.

Taper relief has largely replaced the indexation allowance for disposals made after 5 April 1998. However, where an asset was acquired before this date, the indexation allowance will be calculated to the month of April 1998 and frozen. The frozen allowance then enters into the calculation of chargeable gain, if any, when the asset is disposed of at some later date. The adjustment for the indexation allowance must be made before calculating taper relief on the net sum remaining.

### Exemptions

There is a general exemption from liability to capital gains tax where the net gains of an individual for 2001–2 do not exceed £7,500. This general exemption applies separately to a husband and wife whether or not the parties are 'living together'.

The disposal of many assets will not give rise to chargeable gains or allowable losses and these assets include:

(a) private motor cars
(b) government securities
(c) loan stock and other securities (but not shares)
(d) options and contracts relating to securities within (b) and (c)
(e) National Savings Certificates, Premium Bonds, Defence Bonds and National Development Bonds
(f) currency of any description acquired for personal expenditure outside the UK
(g) decorations awarded for valour
(h) betting wins and pools, lottery or games prizes
(i) compensation or damages for any wrong or injury suffered by an individual in his or her person, profession or vocation
(j) life assurance and deferred annuity contracts where the person making the disposal is the original beneficial owner
(k) dwelling-houses and land enjoyed with the residence which is an individual's only or main residence
(l) tangible movable property, the consideration for the disposal of which does not exceed £6,000
(m) certain tangible movable property which is a wasting asset having a life not exceeding 50 years
(n) assets transferred to charities and other bodies
(o) works of art, historic buildings and similar assets
(p) assets used to provide maintenance funds for historic buildings
(q) assets transferred to trustees for the benefit of employees
(r) assets held in a Personal Equity Plan or Individual Savings Account

### Dwelling-Houses

Exemption from capital gains tax will usually be available for any gain which accrues to an individual from the disposal of, or of an interest in, a dwelling-house or part of a dwelling-house which has been his or her only or main residence. The exemption extends to land which has been occupied and enjoyed with the residence as its garden or grounds. Some restriction may be necessary where the land exceeds half a hectare.

The gain will not be chargeable to capital gains tax if the dwelling-house, or part, has been the individual's only or main residence throughout the period of ownership, or throughout the entire period except for all or any part of the final three years. A proportionate part of the gain will be exempt in other cases if the dwelling-house has been the individual's only or main residence for part only of the period of ownership. In the case of property acquired before 31 March 1982, the period of ownership is treated as commencing on this date.

Where part of the dwelling-house has been used exclusively for business purposes, that part of the gain attributable to business use will not be exempt.

In those cases where part of a qualifying dwelling-house has been used to provide rented residential accommodation, this non-personal use may frequently be ignored when calculating exemption from capital gains tax, unless relatively substantial sums are involved.

Dwellings occupied by dependent relatives, separated spouses or divorced former spouses, may also qualify for the exemption, but only where occupation commenced before 6 April 1988.

### Roll-over Relief

Persons carrying on business will often undertake the disposal of an asset and use the proceeds to finance the acquisition of a replacement asset. Where this situation arises, a claim for roll-over relief may be available. The broad effect of such a claim is that all or part of the gain arising on the disposal of the old asset may be disregarded.

The gain or part is then subtracted from the cost of acquiring the replacement asset. As this cost is reduced, any gain arising from the future disposal of the replacement asset will be correspondingly increased, unless a further roll-over situation then develops.

It remains a requirement that both the old and the replacement asset must be used for the purpose of the taxpayer's business. Relief will only be available if the acquisition of the replacement asset takes place within a period commencing twelve months before, and ending three years after, the disposal of the old asset, although the Inland Revenue retain a discretion to extend this period where the circumstances were such that it was impossible for the taxpayer to acquire the replacement asset before the expiration of the normal time limit.

Whilst many business assets qualify for roll-over relief there are exceptions.

Roll-over relief may also be available where a gain arises on the disposal of land or buildings to an authority capable to exercising compulsory purchase powers. Similar relief may be forthcoming where shares in a company are transferred to trustees administering an employees' share ownership plan for the benefit of persons employed by that company or group of companies of which the company is a member.

### Deferral Relief

A form of roll-over relief, known as 'deferral relief' enables gains arising on the disposal of an asset to be matched, in whole or in part, with a subscription for shares in a restricted range of unquoted companies, including certain companies whose shares are dealt in on the Alternative Investment Market. Where matching can be achieved any part of the gain arising on disposal, not exceeding the cost of the qualifying share subscription, may become the subject of a claim. Unlike the usual form of roll-over relief, this claim for deferral relief does not eliminate or reduce the chargeable gain. It has the effect of deferring that gain until the time of some future event, which will usually be identified by the disposal of the newly acquired shares or the loss of UK residential status.

A similar form of deferral relief is available for gains arising on other disposals which are matched with a qualifying share investment in a venture capital trust company. To the extent of the gain arising, which must not exceed the amount of the investment qualifying for income tax relief, that gain is deferred until the time of a future event, which will normally comprise the disposal of shares in the venture capital trust or the loss of UK residential status.

### Hold-over Relief – Gifts

The gift of an asset is treated as a disposal made for a consideration equal to market value, with a corresponding acquisition by the transferee at an identical value. In the case of gifts made by individuals and a limited range of trustees to a transferee resident in the UK, a form of hold-over relief may be available. Relief, which must be claimed, is limited to the transfer of certain assets, including the following:

(a) assets used for the purposes of a trade or similar activity carried on by the transferor or his/her personal company
(b) shares or securities of a trading company which is not listed on a stock exchange
(c) shares or securities of a trading company which is listed but which is the transferor's personal company
(d) many interests in agricultural property qualifying for agricultural property relief for inheritance tax purposes
(e) assets involved in transactions which are lifetime transfers for inheritance tax purposes, other than potentially exempt transfers

The transfer of shares or securities to a company is precluded from obtaining relief where the transaction takes place after 8 November 1999. The effect of a valid claim for hold-over relief is similar to that following a claim for roll-over relief on the disposal of business assets, but adjustments may be necessary where some consideration is given for the transfer, the asset has not been used for business purposes throughout the period of ownership, or not all assets of a company are used for business purposes.

### Retirement Relief

Retirement relief is available to an individual who disposes by way of sale or gift of the whole or part of a business. The isolated disposal of assets used for the purpose of a business will not necessarily represent the disposal of the whole or part of a business. The main condition for granting this relief is that throughout a period of at least one year the business has been owned either by the individual or by a trading company in which the individual retained a sufficient shareholding interest. The relief extends also to cases where an individual disposes by way of sale or gift of shares or securities of a company. It must be demonstrated that the company was a trading company, that the individual retained a sufficient shareholding interest, and that he or she was engaged as a full-time working officer or employee.

An individual who has attained the age of 50 years at the time of a disposal may obtain substantial retirement relief which shelters gains from liability to capital gains tax. No retirement relief will be forthcoming if the disposal occurs before the individual's 50th birthday, except where an individual is compelled to retire early on the grounds of ill-health.

Maximum relief was available for disposals taking place not later than 5 April 1999. The amount of relief then reduces on an annual basis before being abolished entirely for disposals taking place on and after 6 April 2003. Retirement relief must be subtracted from the net gains arising on disposal, leaving the balance, if any, chargeable to capital gains tax in the normal manner. Taper relief applies only to this balance of net gains and not to the calculation of gains eliminated by retirement relief.

### Death

No capital gains tax is chargeable on the value of assets retained at the time of death. However, the personal representatives administering the deceased's estate are deemed to acquire those assets for a consideration representing market value on death. This ensures that any increase in value occurring before the date of death will not be chargeable to capital gains tax. If a legatee or other person acquires an asset under a will or intestacy no chargeable gain will accrue to the personal representatives, and the person taking the asset will also be treated as having acquired it at the time of death for its then market value.

## INHERITANCE TAX

Liability to inheritance tax may arise on a limited range of lifetime gifts and other dispositions and also on the value of assets retained, or deemed to be retained, at the time of death. An individual's domicile at the time of any gift or on death is an important matter. Domicile will generally be determined by applying normal rules, although special considerations may be necessary where an individual was previously domiciled in the UK but subsequently acquired a domicile of choice overseas. In addition, individuals who have been resident in the UK for at least 17 of the previous 20 years at the time of an event are treated as domiciled in the UK for this purpose.

Where a person was domiciled, or treated as domiciled, in the UK at the time of a disposition or on death the location of assets is immaterial and full liability to inheritance tax arises. Individuals domiciled outside the UK are, however, chargeable to inheritance tax only on transactions affecting assets located in the UK.

The assets of husband and wife are not merged for inheritance tax purposes. Each spouse is treated as a separate individual entitled to receive the benefit of his or her exemptions, reliefs and rates of tax. Where husband and wife retain similar assets, e.g. shares in the same family company, special 'related property' provisions may require the merger of those assets for valuation purposes only.

## Lifetime Gifts and Dispositions

Gifts and dispositions made during lifetime fall under four broad headings, namely:

(a) dispositions which are not transfers of value
(b) exempt transfers
(c) potentially exempt transfers
(d) chargeable transfers

### *Dispositions which are not transfers of value*

Several lifetime transactions are not treated as transfers of value and may be entirely disregarded for inheritance tax purposes. These include transactions not intended to confer gratuitous benefit, the provision of family maintenance, the waiver of the right to receive remuneration or dividends, and the grant of agricultural tenancies for full consideration.

### *Exempt transfers*

Certain transfers are treated as exempt transfers and incur no liability to inheritance tax. The main exempt transfers are listed below:

*Transfers between spouses* – Transfers between husband and wife are usually exempt. However, if the transferor is, but the transferee spouse is not, domiciled in the UK, transfers will be exempt only to the extent that the total does not exceed £55,000. Unlike the requirement used for income tax and capital gains tax purposes, it is immaterial whether husband and wife are living together.

*Annual exemption* – The first £3,000 of gifts and other dispositions made in a year ending on 5 April is exempt. If the exemption is not used, or not wholly used, in any year the balance may be carried forward to the following year only. The annual exemption will only be available for a potentially exempt transfer if that transfer becomes chargeable by reason of the donor's subsequent death.

*Small gifts* – Outright gifts of £250 or less to any person in one year ending on 5 April are exempt.

*Normal expenditure* – A transfer made during lifetime and comprising normal expenditure is exempt. To obtain this exemption it must be shown that:

(a) the transfer was made as part of the normal expenditure of the transferor;
(b) taking one year with another, the transfer was made out of income; and
(c) after allowing for all transfers of value forming part of normal expenditure the transferor was left with sufficient income to maintain his or her usual standard of living

*Gifts in consideration of marriage* – These are exempt if they satisfy certain requirements. The amount allowed will be governed by the relationship between the donor and a party to the marriage. The allowable amounts comprise:

(a) gifts by a parent, £5,000
(b) gifts by a grandparent, £2,500
(c) gifts by a party to the marriage, £2,500
(d) gifts by other persons, £1,000

*Gifts to charities* – These are exempt from liability.

*Gifts to political parties* – Gifts which satisfy certain requirements are generally exempt.

*Gifts for national purposes* – Gifts made to certain bodies are exempt from liability. These bodies include, among others, the National Gallery, the British Museum, the National Trust, the National Art Collections Fund, the National Heritage Memorial Fund, the Historic Buildings and Monuments Commission for England (English Heritage), any local authority, and any university or university college in the UK.

A number of other gifts made for the public benefit are also exempt.

### *Potentially exempt transfers*

Lifetime gifts and dispositions which are neither to be ignored nor comprise exempt transfers incur possible liability to inheritance tax. However, relief is available for a range of potentially exempt transfers. These comprise gifts made by an individual to:

(a) a second individual
(b) trustees administering an accumulation and maintenance trust
(c) trustees administering a disabled person's trust

The accumulation and maintenance trust mentioned in (b) must provide that on reaching a specified age, not exceeding 25 years, a beneficiary will become absolutely entitled to trust assets or obtain an interest in possession in the income from those assets.

Additions to the above list affect settled property administered by trustees where an individual, or individuals, retain an interest in possession. The transfer of assets to, the removal of assets from, or the rearrangement of interests in such property comprise potentially exempt transfers if the person transferring an interest and the person benefiting from the transfer are both individuals.

No immediate liability to inheritance tax will arise on the making of a potentially exempt transfer. Should the donor survive for a period of seven years, immunity from liability will be confirmed. However, the donor's death within the seven-year *inter vivos* period produces liability if the amounts involved are sufficiently substantial (*see* below).

### *Chargeable transfers*

Any remaining lifetime gifts or dispositions which are neither to be ignored nor represent exempt transfers or potentially exempt transfers, incur liability to inheritance tax.

## Gifts with Reservation

A lifetime gift of assets made at any time after 17 March 1986 may incur additional liability to inheritance tax if the donor retains some interest in the subject matter of the gift. This may arise, for example, where a parent transfers a dwelling-house to a son or daughter and continues to occupy the property or to enjoy some benefit from that property. The retention of a benefit may be ignored where it is enjoyed in return for full consideration, perhaps a commercial rent, or where the benefit arises from changed circumstances which could not have been foreseen at the time of the original gift. The gift with reservation provisions will not usually apply to most exempt transfers.

There are three possibilities which may arise where the donor reserves or enjoys some benefit from the subject matter of a previous gift and subsequently dies, namely:

(a) if no benefit is enjoyed within a period of seven years before death there can be no further liability
(b) if the benefit ceased to be enjoyed within a period of seven years before the date of death, the original donor is deemed to have made a potentially exempt transfer representing the value of the asset at the time of cessation
(c) if the benefit is enjoyed at the time of death, the value of the asset must be included in the value of the deceased's estate on death

It must be emphasised that the existence of a benefit enjoyed at any time within a period of seven years before death will establish liability to tax on gifts with reservation, notwithstanding that the gift may have been made many years earlier, providing it was undertaken after 17 March 1986.

### Death

Immediately before the time of death an individual is deemed to make a transfer of value. This transfer will comprise the value of assets forming part of the deceased's estate after subtracting most liabilities. Any exempt transfers may, however, be excluded. These include transfers for the benefit of a surviving spouse, a charity and a qualifying political party, together with bequests to approved bodies and for national purposes.

Death may also trigger three additional liabilities:

(a) A potentially exempt transfer made within the period of seven years ending on death loses its potential status and becomes chargeable to inheritance tax
(b) The value of gifts made with reservation may incur liability if any benefit was enjoyed within a period of seven years preceding death
(c) Additional tax may become payable for chargeable lifetime transfers made within seven years before death

### Valuations

The valuation of assets establishes the value transferred for lifetime dispositions and also the value of a person's estate at the time of death. The value of property will represent the price which might reasonably be expected from a sale in the open market.

In some cases it may be necessary to incorporate the value of 'related property'. This will include property comprised in the estate of the transferor's spouse and certain property previously transferred to charities. The purpose of the related property valuation rules is not to add the value of the property to the estate of the transferor. Related property must be merged to establish the aggregate value of the respective interests and this value is then apportioned, usually on a *pro rata* basis, to the separate interests.

The value of shares and securities listed on the Stock Exchange will be determined by extracting figures from the daily list of official prices.

Where quoted shares and securities are sold or the quotation is suspended within a period of 12 months following the date of death, a claim may be made to substitute the proceeds or subsequent value for the value on death. This claim will only be beneficial if the gross proceeds realised are lower or the value has fallen below market value at the time of death. A similar claim may be available for interests in land sold within a period of four years following death.

### Relief for Selected Assets

Special relief is made available for certain assets, notably:

#### *Woodlands*

Where woodlands pass on death the value will usually be included in the deceased's estate. However, an election may be made in respect of land in the UK on which trees or underwood is growing to delete the value of those assets. Relief is confined to the value of trees or underwood and does not extend to the land on which they are growing. Liability to inheritance tax will arise if and when the trees or underwood are sold.

#### *Agricultural property*

Relief is available for the agricultural value of agricultural property. Such property must be occupied and used for agricultural purposes and relief is confined to the agricultural value only.

The value transferred, either on a lifetime gift or on death, must be determined. This value may then be reduced by a percentage. For events taking place after 9 March 1992, a 100 per cent deduction will be available if the transferor retained vacant possession or could have obtained that possession within a period of 12 months following the transfer. In other cases, notably including land let to tenants, a lower deduction of 50 per cent is usually available. However, this lower deduction may be increased to 100 per cent if the letting was made after 31 August 1995.

It remains a requirement that the agricultural property was either occupied by the transferor for the purposes of agriculture throughout a two-year period ending on the date of the transfer, or was owned by him or her throughout a period of seven years ending on that date and also occupied for agricultural purposes.

#### *Business property*

Where the value transferred is attributable to relevant business property, that value may be reduced by a percentage. The reduction in value applies to:

(a) property consisting of a business or an interest in a business (i.e. a partnership)
(b) securities of an unquoted company which, together with any unquoted shares in the same company provided the transferor with control
(c) other unquoted shares in a company
(d) shares or securities of a quoted company which provided the transferor with control
(e) any land, building, machinery or plant which, immediately before the transfer, was used wholly or mainly for the purposes of a business carried on by a company of which the transferor had control
(f) any land, building, machinery or plant which, immediately before the transfer, was used wholly or mainly for the purposes of a business carried on by a partnership of which the transferor was a partner
(g) any land, building, machinery or plant which, immediately before the transfer, was used wholly or mainly for the purposes of a business carried on by the transferor and was then settled property in which he/she retained an interest in possession

The percentage deduction has changed from time to time but for events occurring after 5 April 1996, a deduction of 100 per cent is available for assets falling within (a), (b) and (c). A deduction of 50 per cent remains for assets within (d) to (g).

It is a general requirement that the property must have been retained for a period of two years before the transfer or death and restrictions may be necessary if the property has not been used wholly for business purposes. The same property cannot obtain both business property relief and the relief available for agricultural property.

### Calculation of Tax Payable

The calculation of inheritance tax payable adopts the use of a cumulative total. Each chargeable lifetime transfer is added to the total with a final addition made on death. The top slice added to the total for the current event determines the rate at which inheritance tax must be paid. However, the cumulative total will only include transfers made within a period of seven years before the current event and those undertaken outside this period must be excluded.

#### *Lifetime chargeable transfers*

The value transferred by the limited range of lifetime chargeable transfers must be added to the seven-year cumulative total to calculate whether any inheritance tax is due. Should the nil rate band be exceeded, tax will be imposed on the excess at the rate of 20 per cent. However, if the donor dies within a period of seven years from the date of the chargeable lifetime transfer, additional tax may be due. This is calculated by applying tax at the full rate or 40 per cent in substitution for the rate of 20 per cent previously used. The amount of tax is then reduced to a percentage by applying tapering relief. This percentage is governed by the number of years from the date of the lifetime gift to the date of death, as follows:

| Period of years before death | |
|---|---|
| Not more than 3 | 100% |
| More than 3 but not more than 4 | 80% |
| More than 4 but not more than 5 | 60% |
| More than 5 but not more than 6 | 40% |
| More than 6 but not more than 7 | 20% |

Should this exercise produce liability greater than that previously paid at the 20 per cent rate on the lifetime transfer, additional tax, representing the difference, must be discharged. Where the calculation shows an amount falling below tax paid on the lifetime transfer, no additional liability can arise nor will the shortfall become repayable.

Tapering relief will, of course, only be available if the calculation discloses a liability to inheritance tax. There can be no liability to the extent that the lifetime transfer falls within the nil rate band.

#### *Potentially exempt transfers*

Where a potentially exempt transfer loses immunity from liability due to the donor's death within the seven-year *inter vivos* period, the value transferred by that transfer enters into the cumulative total. Any liability to inheritance tax will be calculated by applying the full rate of 40 per cent, reduced to the percentage governed by tapering relief if the original transfer occurred more than three years before death. Liability can only arise to the extent, if any, that the nil rate band is exceeded.

#### *Death*

The final addition to the seven-year cumulative total will comprise the value of an estate on death. Inheritance tax will be calculated by applying the full rate of 40 per cent to the extent the nil rate band is exceeded. No tapering relief can be obtained.

### Rates of Tax

In earlier times there were several rates of inheritance tax which progressively increased as the value transferred grew in size. However, since 1988 there have been only three rates, namely:

(a) a nil rate
(b) a lifetime rate of 20 per cent
(c) a full rate of 40 per cent

The nil rate band usually changes on an annual basis and for events taking place after 5 April 2001 applies to the first £242,000. Any excess over this level is taxable at 20 per cent or 40 per cent as the case may be.

### Payment of Tax

Inheritance tax usually falls due for payment six months after the end of the month in which the chargeable transaction takes place. Where a transfer other than that made on death occurs after 5 April and before the following 1 October, tax falls due on the following 30 April, although there are some exceptions to this.

Inheritance tax attributable to the transfer of certain land, controlling shareholding interests, unquoted shares, businesses and interests in businesses, together with agricultural property, may usually be satisfied by instalments spread over ten years. Except in the case of non-agricultural land, where interest is charged on outstanding instalments, no liability to interest arises where tax is paid on the due date. In all cases, delay in the payment of tax may incur a liability to discharge interest.

### Settled Property

Complex rules apply to establish inheritance tax liability on settled property. Where a person is beneficially entitled to an interest in possession, that person is effectively deemed to own the property in which the interest subsists. It follows that where the interest comes to an end during the beneficiary's lifetime and some other person becomes entitled to the property or interest, the beneficiary is treated as having made a transfer of value. However, this will usually comprise a potentially exempt transfer. In addition, no liability will arise where the property vests in the absolute ownership of the beneficiary retaining the interest in possession. The death of a person entitled to an interest in possession will require the value of the underlying property to be added to the value of the deceased's estate.

In the case of other settled property where there is no interest in possession (e.g. discretionary trusts), liability to tax will arise on each ten-year anniversary of the trust. There will also be liability if property ceases to be held on discretionary trusts before the first ten-year anniversary date is reached or between anniversaries. The rate of tax suffered will be governed by several considerations, including previous dispositions made by the settlor of the trust, transactions concluded by the trustees, and the period throughout which property has been held in trust.

Accumulation and maintenance settlements which require assets to be distributed, or interests in income to be created, not later than a beneficiary's 25th birthday may be exempt from any liability to inheritance tax.

## CORPORATION TAX

Profits, gains and income accruing to companies resident in the UK incur liability to corporation tax. Non-resident companies are immune from this tax unless they carry on a trade in the UK through a permanent establishment, branch or office. Companies residing outside the UK may be liable to income tax at the basic rate on other income arising in the UK, perhaps from letting property. The following comments are confined to companies resident in the UK.

Liability to corporation tax is governed by the profits, gains or income for an accounting period. This is usually the period for which financial accounts are made up, and in the case of companies preparing accounts to the same accounting date annually will comprise successive periods of 12 months.

### Rate of Tax

The amount of profits or income for an accounting period must be determined on normal taxation principles. The special rules which apply to individuals where a source of income is acquired or discontinued are ignored and consideration is confined to the actual profits or income for an accounting period.

The rate of corporation tax is fixed for a financial year ending on 31 March. Where the accounting period of a company overlaps this date and there is a change in the rate of corporation tax, profits and income must be apportioned.

The full rate of corporation tax for each of the financial years ending on the 31 March 2000, 31 March 2001 and 31 March 2002 is 30 per cent. This may be reduced to a lower level where profits fall within the small companies' rate or companies' starting rate bands.

### Small Companies' Rate

Where the profits of a company do not exceed stated limits, corporation tax becomes payable at the small companies' rate. This may be replaced by a lower starting rate where profits are very small, as discussed later. It is the amount of profits and not the size of the company which governs the application of both the small companies' rate and the starting rate.

For each of the financial years ending on 31 March 2000, 31 March 2001 and 31 March 2002 the small companies' rate has remained at 20 per cent.

The level of profits which a company may derive without losing the benefit of the small companies' rate is £300,000 for each of the three years. However, if profits exceed £300,000 but fall below £1,500,000, marginal small companies' rate relief applies. The effect of marginal relief is that the average rate of corporation tax imposed on all profits steadily increases from the lower small companies' rate to the full rate of 30 per cent, with tax being imposed on profits in the margin at an increased rate. Where a change in the rate of tax is introduced and the accounting period of a company overlaps 31 March, profits must be apportioned to establish the appropriate rate for each part of those profits.

The lower limit of £300,000 and the upper limit of £1,500,000 apply to a period of 12 months and must be proportionately reduced for shorter periods. Some restriction in the small companies' rate and the marginal rate may be necessary if there are two or more associated companies, namely companies under common control.

The small companies' rate is not available for close investment-holding companies.

### Companies' Starting Rate

A new companies' starting rate was introduced for the financial years ending on 31 March 2001 and 31 March 2002. This requires that where profits of a 12-month period do not exceed £10,000 a starting rate of 10 per cent will apply. Marginal relief is available where profits exceed £10,000 but do not exceed £50,000. Here also restrictions apply where the accounting period is less than 12 months, there are associated companies or a company retains close investment-holding status.

It has been indicated that the £50,000 band is likely to be widened for the financial year commencing on 1 April 2002.

### Payment of Tax

Corporation tax charged on profits for an accounting period usually falls due for payment in a single lump sum nine months after the end of that period. Most companies discharge corporation tax on this basis but other arrangements concern large companies for accounting periods ending on or after 1 July 1999. These companies must discharge their liability by four instalments. The receipt of annual profits amounting to £1,500,000 or more is sufficient to identify a large company. Where a company is a member of a group the profits of the entire group must be merged to establish whether the company is large.

### Capital Gains

Chargeable gains arising to a company are calculated in a manner similar to that used for individuals. However, the withdrawal of the indexation allowance after April 1998 and the introduction of taper relief from the same date have no application to companies. Nor are companies entitled to the annual exemption of £7,500. Companies do not suffer capital gains tax on chargeable gains but incur liability to corporation tax. Tax is due on the full chargeable gain of an accounting period after subtracting relief for losses, if any.

### Distributions

Dividends and other qualifying distributions made by a UK resident company on or after 6 April 1999 are not satisfied after deduction of income tax. Similar outgoings made by a company previously required the payment of advance corporation tax but this obligation no longer applies. The only effect which the payment of a dividend or the making of a distribution now has on a company is that the outlay cannot form an ingredient in the calculation of profits.

### Interest

On making many payments of interest a company is required to deduct income tax at the lower rate of 20 per cent and account for the tax deducted to the Inland Revenue. The gross amount of interest paid will usually be included in the calculation of profits on which corporation tax becomes payable.

### Groups of Companies

Each company within a group is separately charged to corporation tax on profits, gains and income. However, where one group member realises a loss, other than a capital loss, a claim may be made to offset the deficiency against profits of some other member of the same group.

Claims are also available to avoid the deduction of income tax on most payments of interest for transactions between members of a group of companies. The transfer of capital assets from one member of a group to a fellow member will usually incur no liability to tax on chargeable gains.

### Compliance

For several years a 'pay and file' system affected all companies. A feature of this system required that tax should be payable nine months following the end of the accounting period involved with accounts and returns being submitted three months later. Failure to satisfy corporation tax or to submit documents within these time limits could result in a liability to discharge interest and penalties. This system has been replaced following the introduction of self-assessment which now extends to all companies for accounting periods ending after 30 June 1999.

## VALUE ADDED TAX

Value added tax (VAT) is charged on the value of the supplies made by a registered trader and extends to both the supply of goods and the supply of services. It is administered by Customs and Excise.

Liability to account for VAT arises on the value of goods imported into the UK from sources outside the European Community. In contrast goods imported by a trader from a second trader in a member state of the European Community attract no VAT on importation. Instead there is an acquisition tax whereby a trader who acquires goods must include the acquisition in his normal VAT return and account for the tax due. A UK trader who exports goods to a member state will not be required to account for VAT on the supply, if that trader observes the requirements laid down by regulations.

### REGISTRATION

All traders, including professional men and women and companies, making taxable supplies of a value exceeding stated limits are required to register for VAT purposes. Taxable supplies represent the supply of goods and services potentially chargeable with VAT. The limits which govern mandatory registration are amended periodically, and from 1 April 2001 an unregistered trader must register:

(a) at any time, if there are reasonable grounds for believing that the value of taxable supplies in the next 30 days will exceed £54,000
(b) at the end of any month if the value of taxable supplies in the 12 months then ending has exceeded £54,000.

Liability to register under (b) may be avoided if it can be shown that the value of supplies in the period of 12 months then beginning will not exceed £52,000. There may, however, be liability to register immediately where a business is taken over from another trader as a 'going concern'. Other limits apply where goods are acquired from within the European Community.

Where the limits governing mandatory registration have been exceeded, the trader must notify Customs and Excise. In the event of failure to provide prompt notification, the person concerned will be required to account for VAT from the proper registration date.

A trader whose taxable supplies do not reach the mandatory registration limits may apply for voluntary registration. This step may be thought advisable to recover input tax or to compete with other registered traders.

A registered trader may submit an application for deregistration if the value of taxable supplies subsequently falls. From 1 April 2001, an application for deregistration can be made if the value of taxable supplies for the year beginning on the application date is not expected to exceed £52,000.

### INPUT TAX

A registered trader will both suffer tax (input tax) when obtaining goods or services for the purposes of his business and also become liable to account for tax (output tax) on the value of goods and services which he or she supplies. Relief can usually be obtained for input tax suffered, either by setting that tax against output tax due or by repayment. Most items of input tax can be relieved in this manner but there are exceptions, including the prohibition of relief for the cost of business entertaining. Where a registered trader makes both exempt supplies and taxable supplies to his customers or clients, there may be some restriction in the amount of input tax which can be recovered.

### OUTPUT TAX

When making a taxable supply of goods or services, a registered trader must account for output tax, if any, on the value of the supply. Usually the price charged by the registered trader will be increased by adding VAT but failure to make the required addition will not remove liability to account for output tax.

The liability to account for output tax, and also relief for input tax, may be affected where a trader is using a special second-hand goods scheme.

### EXEMPT SUPPLIES

No VAT is chargeable on the supply of goods or services which are treated as exempt supplies. These include the provision of burial and cremation facilities, insurance, finance and education. The granting of a lease to occupy land or the sale of land will usually comprise an exempt supply, but there are numerous exceptions. In particular, the sale of new non-domestic buildings or certain buildings used by charities cannot be treated as exempt supplies.

A taxable person may elect to tax rents and other supplies relating to buildings and agricultural land not used for residential or charitable purposes.

Exempt supplies do not enter into the calculation of taxable supplies which governs liability to mandatory registration. Such supplies made by a registered trader may, however, limit the amount of input tax which can be relieved. It is for this reason that the election may be useful.

### RATES OF TAX

Two main rates of VAT have applied for many years, namely:

(a) a zero, or nil, rate
(b) a standard rate of 17.5 per cent

In addition, a special reduced rate of 5 per cent applies to supplies of domestic fuels, installation of energy saving materials in domestic premises and children's car seats.

### ZERO-RATING

A large number of supplies are zero-rated. The following list is not exhaustive but indicates the wide range of supplies which may be included under this heading:

(a) the supply of many items of food and drink for human consumption. This does not include ice creams, chocolates, sweets, potato crisps and alcoholic drinks. Nor does it extend to supplies made in the course of catering or to items supplied for consumption in a restaurant or café. Whilst the supply of cold items, e.g. sandwiches for consumption away from the supplier's premises, is zero-rated, the supply of hot food, e.g. fish and chips, is not
(b) animal feeding stuffs
(c) sewerage and water, unless for industrial purposes
(d) books, brochures, pamphlets, leaflets, newspapers, maps and charts
(e) talking books for the blind and handicapped, and wireless sets for the blind
(f) supplies of services, other than professional services, when constructing a new domestic building or a building to be used by a charity. The supply of materials for such a building is zero-rated, together

with the sale or the grant of a long lease. Alterations to some protected buildings are zero-rated

(g) the transportation of persons in a vehicle, ship or aircraft designed to carry not less than 10 persons
(h) supplies of drugs, medicines and other aids for the handicapped
(i) supplies of clothing and footwear for young persons
(j) supplies of pedal cycle helmets
(k) exports

Although no tax is due on a zero-rated supply, this does comprise a taxable supply which must be included in the calculation governing liability to register.

### Collection of Tax

Registered traders submit VAT returns for accounting periods usually of three months in duration but arrangements can be made to submit returns on a monthly basis. Very large traders must account for tax on a monthly basis but this does not affect the three-monthly return. The return will show both the output tax due for supplies made by the trader in the accounting period and also the input tax for which relief is claimed. If the output tax exceeds input tax the balance must be remitted with the VAT return. Where input tax suffered exceeds the output tax due the registered trader may claim recovery of the excess from Customs and Excise.

This basis for collecting tax explains the structure of VAT. Where supplies are made between registered traders the supplier will account for an amount of tax which will usually be identical to the tax recovered by the person to whom the supply is made. However, where the supply is made to a person who is not a registered trader there can be no recovery of input tax and it is on this person that the final burden of VAT eventually falls.

Where goods are acquired by a UK trader from a supplier within a member state of the European Community, the trader must also account for the tax due on acquisition.

An optional scheme is available for registered traders having an annual turnover of taxable supplies not exceeding £600,000. The previous limit of £300,000 was doubled to the new level on 1 April 2001. Such traders may render returns annually. Nine interim payments of VAT will be made on account, with a final balancing payment accompanying submission of the return. The number of interim payments may be reduced if turnover is small.

### Bad Debts

Many retailers operate special retail schemes for calculating the amount of VAT due. These schemes are based on the volume of consideration received in an accounting period. Should a customer fail to pay for goods or services supplied, there will be no consideration on which to calculate VAT.

To avoid the problem of bad debts incurred by traders not operating a special retail scheme, an optional system of cash accounting is available. This scheme, confined to traders with annual taxable supplies not exceeding £600,000, enables returns to be made on a cash basis, in substitution for the normal supply basis. Here also the revised level applies from April 2001. Traders using such a scheme will not include bad debts in the calculation of cash receipts.

Where neither the cash accounting arrangements nor a special retail scheme applies, output tax falls due on the value of the supply and liability is not affected by failure to receive consideration. However, where a debt is more than six months old, relief for bad debts will be forthcoming. The calculation of the six-month period commences from the date on which payment for the supply falls due.

In those cases where a supplier obtains relief for a bad debt, the person to whom the supply has been made must refund to Customs and Excise any input tax relief which may have been granted.

### Other Special Schemes

In addition to the schemes for retailers, there are several special schemes applied to calculate the amount of VAT due and which also limit the ability to recover input tax. The supply of virtually all second-hand goods has now been brought with special margin schemes.

### Farmers

Farmers may elect to apply a special flat rate scheme. This scheme is available to farmers who are not registered traders. Under the scheme a flat-rate addition of 4 per cent may be made on sales, with the amount of the addition being retained by the farmer. Registered traders to whom such a supply is made may treat the 4 per cent as recoverable input tax.

# Legal Notes

## IMPORTANT

These notes outline certain aspects of the law as they might affect the average person. They are intended only as a broad guideline and are by no means definitive. The law is constantly changing so expert advice should always be taken. In some cases, sources of further information are given in these notes.

It is always advisable to consult a solicitor without delay; timely advice will set your mind at rest but sitting on your rights can mean that you lose them. Anyone who does not have a solicitor already can contact the Citizens' Advice Bureau, the Community Legal Service (www.legalservices.gov.uk), the Law Society of England and Wales (113 Chancery Lane, London WC2A 1PL) or the Law Society of Scotland (26 Drumsheugh Gardens, Edinburgh EH3 7YR) for assistance in finding one.

The community legal service fund and legal aid and assistance schemes exist to make the help of a lawyer available to those who would not otherwise be able to afford one. Entitlement depends on an individual's means but a solicitor or Citizens' Advice Bureau will be able to advise about entitlement.

## ADOPTION OF CHILDREN

In England and Wales the adoption of children is mainly governed by the Adoption Act 1976 and the Children Act 1989.

Anyone over 21 (or 18 if the natural birth parent wants to adopt with a partner who must be over 21) can legally adopt a child. Married couples must adopt 'jointly', unless one partner cannot be found, is incapable of making an application, or if a separation is likely to be permanent. Unmarried couples may not adopt 'jointly' although one partner in that couple may adopt. The only organisations allowed to arrange adoptions are the social services departments of local authorities or voluntary agencies which are registered with the local authorities.

Once an adoption has been arranged, a court order is necessary to make it legal. These are obtained from the High Court (Family Division) or from a magistrates, county or family proceedings court. The child's natural parents (or guardians) must consent to the adoption, unless the court dispenses with the consent, e.g. where the natural parent has neglected the child or is incapable of giving consent. Once adopted, the child has the same status as a child born to the adoptive parents and the natural parents cease to have any rights or responsibilities where the child is concerned. The adopted child will be treated as the natural child of the adoptive parents for the purposes of intestate succession, national insurance, family allowances, etc. The adopted child ceases to have any rights to the estates of his/her natural parents.

It is an offence for a person other than an adoption agency to make arrangements for the adoption of a child or place a child for adoption unless the proposed adopter is a relative or is acting according to a court order. It is also an offence to receive a child who is placed in breach of this rule and it is an offence to make or receive payments for adoption.

### Registration and Certificates

All adoptions in England and Wales are registered in the Adopted Children Register kept by the Office of National Statistics, and by the General Register Office for Scotland. Certificates from the registers can be obtained in a similar way to birth certificates.

### Tracing Natural Parents or Children Who Have Been Adopted

An adult adopted person may apply to the Registrar-General for information to enable him/her to obtain a full birth certificate. For those adopted before 12 November 1975 it is obligatory to receive counselling services before this information is given; for those adopted after that date counselling services are optional. There is also an Adoption Contact Register (created after the 1989 Act) in which details of adult adopted people and of their relatives may be recorded. The BAAF can provide addresses of organisations which offer advice, information and counselling to adopted people, adoptive parents and people who have had their children adopted.

### Scotland

The relevant legislation is the Adoption (Scotland) Act 1978 (as amended by the Children Act 1995) and the provisions are similar to those described above. In Scotland, petitions for adoption are made to the Sheriff Court or the Court of Session.

Further information can be obtained from:

British Agencies for Adoption and Fostering (BAAF), Skyline House, 200 Union Street, London SE1 0LX. Tel: 020-7593 2000

Scottish Adoption Advice Service 16 Sandyford Place, Glasgow G3 7NB Tel: 0141-339 0772

## BIRTHS (REGISTRATION)

The birth of a child must be registered within 42 days of birth at the register office of the district in which the baby was born. In England and Wales it is possible to give the particulars to be registered at any other register office. Responsibility for registering the birth rests with the parents, except in the case of an illegitimate child, when the mother is responsible for registration. Responsibility rests firstly with the parents (in Scotland, if the father of the child is not married to the mother and has not been married to her since the child's conception, the mother alone is responsible for registration) but if they fail, particulars may be given to the registrar by:

- a relative of either parent (in Scotland only)
- the occupier of the house in which the baby was born
- a person present at the birth
- the person having who is responsible for the child

Failure to register the birth within 42 days without reasonable cause may leave the parents liable to a penalty in England and Wales and may lead to a court decree being granted by a sheriff in Scotland.

If the parents were married at the time of the birth, either parent may register the birth and details about both parents will be entered on the register. If the parents were unmarried at the time of the birth, the father's details are entered only if both parents attend or if the parents have made a statutory declaration confirming the identity of the father. Copies of the forms necessary to make such a declaration are available at the register offices. A short birth certificate is issued free when the birth is registered.

### Re-registration

In certain circumstances it may be necessary to re-register a birth, e.g. where the birth of an illegitimate child is legitimated by the subsequent marriage of the parents. It is also possible to re-register the birth of an illegitimate child so that the father's name is entered on the register.

### Birth Abroad

Births of British subjects occurring abroad are registered with consular officers and certificates of birth are subsequently available from the Registrar-General.

### SCOTLAND

In Scotland the birth of a child must be registered within 21 days at the register office of either the district in which the baby was born or the district in which the mother was resident at the time of the birth.

If the child is born, either in or out of Scotland, on a ship, aircraft or land vehicle that ends its journey at any place in Scotland, the child, in most cases, will be registered as if born in that place.

## CERTIFICATES OF BIRTHS, DEATHS OR MARRIAGES

Certificates of births, deaths or marriages that have taken place in England and Wales since 1837 can be obtained from the Office of National Statistics (General Register Office). Applications can be made:

- by a personal visit
- by postal application

Certificates are also available from the Superintendent Registrar for the district in which the event took place or, in the case of marriage certificates, from the minister of the church in which the marriage took place. Any register office can advise about the best way to obtain certificates.
The fees for certificates (from 1 April 2001) are:

*Obtained from Registrar who registered the birth, death or marriage*
Standard certificate, £3.50
Short certificate of birth (other than the first issued at the time of birth registration), death, marriage and adoption, £5.00

*Obtained from Superintendent Registrar*
Standard certificate, £6.50
Short certificate of birth, death, marriage and adoption, £5.00

*From the Family Records Centre, London/by post from the General Register Office, Southport*
Standard certificate of birth, death or marriage
Personal application, £6.50
Standard certificate of adoption
Personal application, £6.50
Short certificate of birth
Personal application, £6.50
Short certificate of adoption
Personal application, £5.00
for postal application fees, please contact the General Register Office

Indexes prepared from the registers are available for searching by the public at the Family Records Centre in London or at a Superintendent Registrar's Office; indexes at the latter relate only to births, deaths and marriages which occurred in that registration district. There is no charge for searching the indexes in the Public Search Room at the Family Records Centre but a general search fee is charged for searches at a Superintendent Registrar's Office. A fee is charged for verifying index references against the records.

The Society of Genealogists has many records of baptisms, marriages and deaths prior to 1837.

### SCOTLAND

Certificates of births, deaths or marriages that have taken place in Scotland since 1855 can be obtained from the General Register Office for Scotland or from the appropriate local registrar. The General Register Office for Scotland also keeps the Register of Divorces (including decrees of declaration of nullity of marriage), and holds parish registers dating from before 1855.
Fees for certificates (from 1 April 2001) are:

*Certificates (full or abbreviated) of birth, death, marriage or adoption:*
Personal application: £11.00
Postal or telephone ordering system: £13.00
A priority service is available for an additional fee of £10.00

*General search in the indexes to the statutory registers and parochial registers, per day or part thereof:*
Full day search (i.e. 9 a.m. to 4.30 p.m.), £17.00
Afternoon (i.e. 1 p.m. to 4.30 p.m.) search £10.00
Full day (i.e. 9 a.m. to 4.30 p.m.) search with payment being made not less than 14 days in advance, £13.00 (only available for the period November 2001 to January 2002)
One week search, £65.00
Four week search, £220.00
One quarter search, £500.00
One year search, £1,500.00

Further information can be obtained from:
The General Register Office, Office for National Statistics, Smedley Hydro, Trafalgar Road, Birkdale, Southport, Merseyside PR8 2HH. Tel: 01704-569824
Family Records Centre, 1 Myddelton Street, London EC1R 1UW. Opens 9 a.m. on Monday, Wednesday, Thursday, Friday, 10 a.m. Tuesday, 9.30 a.m. Saturday. Closes 5 p.m. Monday, Wednesday, Friday, Saturday, 7 p.m. Tuesday, Thursday
The General Register Office For Scotland, New Register House, Edinburgh EH1 3YT. Tel: 0131-334 0380
The Society of Genealogists, 14 Charterhouse Buildings, Goswell Road, London EC1M 7BA. Tel: 020-7251 8799

## BRITISH CITIZENSHIP

The British Nationality Act 1981 which came into force on 1 January 1983 established three types of citizenship to replace the single form of Citizenship of the UK and Colonies created by the British Nationality Act 1948. The three forms of citizenship are: British Citizenship; British Dependent Territories Citizenship; and British Overseas Citizenship. Three residual categories were created: British Subjects; British Protected Persons; and British Nationals (Overseas).

### British Citizenship

Almost everyone who was a citizen of the UK and colonies and had a right of abode in the UK prior to the 1981 Act became British citizens when the Act came into force. British citizens have the right to live permanently in the UK and are free to leave and re-enter the UK at any time.

A person born on or after 1 January 1983 in the UK (including, for this purpose, the Channel Islands and the Isle of Man) is entitled to British citizenship if he/she falls into one of the following categories:

- he/she has a parent who is a British citizen
- he/she has a parent who is settled in the UK
- he/she is a newborn infant found abandoned in the UK
- his/her parents subsequently settle in the UK
- he/she lives in the UK for the first ten years of his/her life and is not absent for more than 90 days in each of those years
- he/she is adopted in the UK and one of the adopters is a British Citizen

A person born outside the UK may acquire British citizenship if he/she falls into one of the following categories:

- he/she has a parent who is a British citizen otherwise than by descent, e.g. a parent who was born in the UK
- he/she has a parent who is a British citizen serving the Crown overseas
- the Home Secretary consents to his/her registration while he/she is a minor
- he/she is a British Dependent Territories citizen, a British Overseas citizen, a British subject or a British protected person and has been lawfully resident in the UK for five years
- he/she is a British Dependent Territories citizen who acquired that citizenship from a connection with Gibraltar
- he/she is adopted or naturalised

Where parents are married, the status of either may confer citizenship on their child. If a child is illegitimate, the status of the mother determines the child's citizenship.

Under the 1981 Act, Commonwealth citizens and citizens of the Republic of Ireland were entitled to registration as British citizens before 1 January 1988. In 1985, citizens of the Falkland Islands were granted British citizenship.

Renunciation of British citizenship must be registered with the Home Secretary and will be revoked if no new citizenship or nationality is acquired within six months. If the renunciation was required in order to retain or acquire another citizenship or nationality, the citizenship may be reacquired once.

### British Dependent Territories Citizenship

Under the 1981 Act, this type of citizenship was conferred on citizens of the UK and colonies by birth, naturalisation or registration in British Dependent Territories. British Dependent Territories citizens may be entitled to registration as British citizens on completion of five years' legal residence in the UK.

On 1 July 1997 citizens of Hong Kong who did not qualify to register as British citizens under the British Nationality (Hong Kong) Act 1990 lost their British Dependent Territories citizenship on the handover of sovereignty to China; they may, however, have applied to register as British Nationals (Overseas).

Eligibility for British Dependent Territories citizenship is determined by similar rules to those for acquiring British citizenship, except that the connection is with the dependent territory rather than with the UK.

### British Overseas Citizenship

Under the 1981 Act, this type of citizenship was conferred on any UK and colonies citizens who did not qualify for British citizenship or citizenship of the British Dependent Territories. British Overseas citizenship may be acquired by the wife and minor children of a British Overseas citizen in certain circumstances. British Overseas citizens may be entitled to registration as British citizens on completion of five years' legal residence in the UK.

### Residual Categories

British subjects, British protected persons and British Nationals (Overseas) may be entitled to registration as British citizens on completion of five years' legal residence in the UK.

Citizens of the Republic of Ireland who were also British subjects before 1 January 1949 can retain that status if they fulfil certain conditions.

### European Union Citizenship

British citizens (including Gibraltarians who are registered as such) are also EU citizens and are entitled to travel freely to other EU countries to work, study, reside and set up a business. EU citizens have the same rights with respect to the United Kingdom.

### Naturalisation

Naturalisation is granted at the discretion of the Home Secretary. The basic requirements are five years' residence (three years if the applicant is married to a British citizen), good character, adequate knowledge of the English, Welsh or Scottish Gaelic language, and an intention to reside permanently in the UK.

### Status of Aliens

Aliens may not hold public office or vote in Britain and they may not own a British ship or aircraft. Citizens of the Republic of Ireland are not deemed to be aliens. Certain provisions of the Immigration and Asylum Act 1999 make provision about immigration and asylum and about procedures in connection with marriage by superintendent registrar's certificate.

## CONSUMER LAW

### Sale of Goods

A sale of goods contract is the most common type of contract. It is governed by the Sale of Goods Act 1979 (as amended by the Sale and Supply of Goods Act 1994). The Act provides protection for buyers by implying terms into every sale of goods contract. These terms are:

- a condition that the seller will pass good title to the buyer (unless the seller agrees to transfer only such title as he has)
- where the seller sells goods by reference to a description, a condition that the goods will match that description and, where the sale is by sample and description, a condition that the bulk of the goods will correspond with such sample and description
- where goods are sold by a business seller, a condition that the goods will be of satisfactory quality if they meet the standard that a reasonable person would regard as satisfactory taking into account any description of the goods, the price, and all other relevant circumstances. The quality of the goods includes their state and condition, relevant aspects being whether they are

suitable for their common purpose, their appearance and finish, freedom from minor defects and their safety and durability. This term will not be implied, however, if a buyer has examined the goods and should have noticed the defect or if the seller specifically drew the buyer's attention to the defect
- where goods are sold by a business seller, a condition that the goods are reasonably fit for any purpose made known to the seller by the buyer, unless the buyer does not rely on the seller's judgement, or it is not reasonable for him/her to do so
- where goods are sold by sample, conditions that the bulk of the sample will correspond with the sample in quality, that the buyer will have a reasonable opportunity of comparing the two and that the goods are free from any defect rendering them unsatisfactory which would not be obvious from the sample

Some of the above terms can be excluded from contracts by the seller. The seller's right to do this is, however, restricted by the Unfair Contract Terms Act 1977. The Act offers more protection to a buyer who 'deals as a consumer', that is where the sale is a business sale, the goods are of a type ordinarily bought for private use and the goods are bought by a buyer who is not a business buyer. In a sale by auction or competitive tender, a buyer never deals as consumer. Also, a seller can never exclude the implied term as to title mentioned above.

## Hire-purchase Agreements

Terms similar to those implied in contracts of sales of goods are implied into contracts of hire-purchase, under the Supply of Goods (Implied Terms) Act 1973. The 1977 Act limits the exclusion of these implied terms as before.

## Supply of Goods and Services

Under the Supply of Goods and Services Act 1982, similar terms are also implied in other types of contract under which ownership of goods passes, e.g. a contract for 'work and materials' such as supplying new parts while servicing a car, and contracts for the hire of goods. These types of contracts have additional implied terms:
- that the supplier will use reasonable care and skill
- that the supplier will carry out the service in a reasonable time (unless the time has been agreed)
- that the supplier will make a reasonable charge (unless the charge has already been agreed)

The 1977 Act limits the exclusion of these implied terms in a similar manner as before.

## Unfair Terms

The Unfair Terms in Consumer Contracts Regulations 1999 apply to contracts between business sellers (or suppliers of goods and services) and consumers, where the terms have not been individually negotiated, i.e where the terms were drafted in advance so that the consumer was unable to influence those terms. An unfair term is one which operates to the detriment of the consumer. An unfair term does not bind the consumer but the contract will continue to bind the parties if it is capable of existing without the unfair term. The regulations contain a non-exhaustive list of terms which are regarded as unfair. Whether a term is regarded as fair or not will depend on many factors, including the nature of the goods or services, the surrounding circumstances (such as the bargaining strength of both parties) and the other terms in the contract.

## Trade Descriptions

It is a criminal offence under the Trade Descriptions Act 1968 for a business seller to apply a false trade description of goods or to supply or offer to supply any goods to which a false description has been applied. A 'trade description' includes descriptions of quality, size, composition, fitness for purpose and method, and place and date of manufacture of the goods. It is also an offence to give a false indication of the price of goods.

## Fair Trading

The Fair Trading Act 1973 is designed to protect the consumer. It provides for the appointment of a Director-General of Fair Trading, one of whose duties is to review commercial activities in the UK relating to the supply of goods and services to consumers. An example of a practice which has been prohibited by a reference made under this Act is that of business sellers posing in advertisements as private sellers.

## Consumer Protection

Under the Consumer Protection Act 1987, producers of goods are liable for any injury or for any damage exceeding £275 caused by a defect in their product (subject to certain defences).

The Consumer Protection (Cancellation of Contracts Concluded Away from Business Premises) Regulations 1987 allow consumers a seven-day period in which to cancel contracts for the supply of goods and services, where the contracts were made during an unsolicited visit to the consumer's home or workplace. This only applies to contracts where the cost exceeds £35.

## Consumer Credit

In matters relating to the provision of credit (or the supply of goods on hire or hire-purchase), consumers are also protected by the Consumer Credit Act 1974. Under this Act a licence, issued by the Director-General of Fair Trading, is required to conduct a consumer credit or consumer hire business or to deal in credit brokerage, debt adjusting, counselling or collecting. Any 'fit' person may apply to the Director-General of Fair Trading for a licence, which is normally renewable after ten years. A licence is not necessary if such types of business are only transacted occasionally, or if only exempt agreements are involved. The provisions of the Act only apply to 'regulated' agreements, i.e. those that are with individuals or partnerships, those that are not exempt (such as certain local authority and building society loans), and those where the total credit does not exceed £25,000. Provisions include:
- the terms of the regulated agreement can be altered by the creditor provided the agreement gives him/her the right to do so; in such cases the debtor must be given proper notice of this
- in order for a creditor to enforce a regulated agreement, the agreement must comply with certain formalities and must be properly executed. The debtor must also be given specified information by the creditor or his/her broker or agent during the negotiations which take place before the signing of the agreement. The agreement must state certain information such as the amount of credit, the annual interest rate, the amount and timing of repayments
- if an agreement is signed other than at the creditor's (or credit broker's or negotiator's) place of business and oral representations were made in the debtor's presence during discussions pre-agreement, the debtor has a

right to cancel the agreement. Time for cancellation expires five clear days after the debtor receives a second copy of the agreement. The agreement must inform the debtor of his right to cancel and how to cancel
- if the debtor is in arrears (or otherwise in breach of the agreement), the creditor must serve a default notice before taking any action such as repossessing the goods
- if the agreement is a hire-purchase or conditional sale agreement, the creditor cannot repossess the goods without a court order if the debtor has paid one-third of the total price of the goods
- in agreements where the debtor is required to make grossly exorbitant payments or where the agreement grossly contravenes the ordinary principles of fair trading, the debtor may request that the court alter or set aside some of the terms of the agreement. The agreement can also be reopened during enforcement proceedings by the court itself

Where a credit reference agency has been used to check the debtor's financial standing, the creditor must give the agency's name to the debtor, who is entitled to *See* the agency's file on him. A fee of £1 is payable to the agency.

### SCOTLAND

The legislation governing the sale and supply of goods applies to Scotland as follows:
- the Sale of Goods Act 1979 applies with some modifications and it has been amended by the Sale and Supply of Goods Act 1994
- the Supply of Goods (Implied Terms) Act 1973 applies
- the Supply of Goods and Services Act 1982 does not extend to Scotland but some of its provisions were introduced by the Sale and Supply of Goods Act 1994
- only Parts II and III of the Unfair Contract Terms Act 1977 apply
- the Trade Descriptions Act 1968 applies with minor modifications
- the Consumer Credit Act 1974 applies

## PROCEEDINGS AGAINST THE CROWN

Until 1947, proceedings against the Crown were generally possible only by a procedure known as a petition of right, which put the litigant at a considerable disadvantage. The Crown Proceedings Act 1947 placed the Crown (not the Sovereign in his/her private capacity, but as the embodiment of the State) largely in the same position as a private individual. The Act did not, however, extinguish or limit the Crown's prerogative or statutory powers, and it granted immunity to HM ships and aircraft. It also left certain Crown privileges unaffected. The Act largely abolished the special procedures which previously applied to civil proceedings by and against the Crown. Civil proceedings may be instituted against the appropriate government department or against the Attorney-General.

In Scotland proceedings against the Crown founded on breach of contract could be taken before the 1947 Act and no special procedures applied. The Crown could, however, claim certain special pleas. The 1947 Act applies in part to Scotland and brings the practice of the two countries as closely together as the different legal systems permit. Civil proceedings may be instituted against the Lord Advocate where proceedings are against the Scottish Administration of the Scottish Parliament or against the Advocate General for Scotland representing the appropriate government department in any other case.

## DEATHS

### When a Death Occurs

If the death (including stillbirth) was expected, the doctor who attended the deceased during their final illness should be contacted. If the death was sudden or unexpected, the family doctor (if known) and police should be contacted. If the cause of death is quite clear the doctor will provide:
- a medical certificate that shows the cause of death
- a formal notice that states that the doctor has signed the medical certificate and that explains how to get the death registered

If the death was known to be caused by a natural illness but the doctor wishes to know more about the cause of death, he/she may ask the relatives for permission to carry out a post-mortem examination. This should not delay the funeral.

In England and Wales a coroner is responsible for investigating deaths occurring in the following circumstances:
- where there is no doctor who can issue a medical certificate of cause of death
- when no doctor has treated the deceased during his or her last illness or when the doctor attending the patient did not *See* him or her within 14 days before death, or after death; or
- when the death occurred during an operation or before recovery from the effect of an anaesthetic; or
- when the death was sudden and unexplained or attended by suspicious circumstances; or
- when the death might be due to an industrial injury or disease, or to accident, violence, neglect or abortion, or to any kind of poisoning; or
- the death occurred in prison or in police custody

The doctor will write on the formal notice that the death has been referred to the coroner; if the post mortem shows that death was due to natural causes, the coroner may issue a notification which gives the cause of death so that the death can be registered. If the cause of death was violent or unnatural, the coroner is obliged to hold an inquest.

In Scotland the office of coroner does not exist. The local procurator fiscal inquires into sudden or suspicious deaths. A fatal accident inquiry will be held before the sheriff where the death has resulted from an accident during the course of the employment of the person who has died, or where the person who has died was in legal custody, or where the Lord Advocate deems it in the public interest that an inquiry be held.

### Registering a Death

In England and Wales the death must be registered by the registrar of births and deaths for the district in which it occurred; details can be obtained from the telephone directory (under registration of births and deaths and marriages), from the doctor or local council, or at a post office or police station. From April 1997, information concerning a death can be given before any registrar of births and deaths in England and Wales. The registrar will pass the relevant details to the registrar for the district where the death occurred, who will then register the death or, if different in the registration district in which the death took place. In England and Wales the death must normally be registered within five days; in Scotland it must be registered within eight days. If the death has been referred to the coroner/local procurator fiscal it cannot be registered until the registrar has received authority from the coroner/local procurator fiscal to do so. Failure to register a death involves a penalty in England and Wales and may lead to a court decree being granted by a sheriff in Scotland.

If the death occurred at a house, the death may be registered by:

- any relative of the deceased
- any person present at the death
- the occupier or any inmate of the house or hospital if he/she knew of the occurrence of the death
- any person making the funeral arrangements

The person registering the death should take the medical certificate of the cause of death with them; it is also useful, though not essential, to take the deceased's birth and marriage certificates, medical card (if possible), pension documents and life assurance details. The registrar will issue a certificate for burial or cremation and a certificate of registration of death; both are free of charge. A death certificate is a certified copy of the entry in the death register; these can be provided on payment of a fee and may be required for the following purposes:

- the will
- bank and building society accounts
- savings bank certificates and premium bonds
- insurance policies
- pension claims

If the death occurred abroad or on a foreign ship or aircraft, the death should be registered according to the local regulations of the relevant country and a death certificate should be obtained. The death can also be registered with the British Consul in that country and a record will be kept at the General Register Office. This avoids the expense of bringing the body back.

After 12 months of death or the finding of a dead body, no death can be registered without the consent of the Registrar-General.

### Burial and Cremation

In most circumstances in England and Wales a certificate for burial or cremation must be obtained from the registrar before the burial or cremation can take place. If the death has been referred to the coroner, an order for burial or a certificate for cremation must be obtained. In Scotland a body may be buried (but not cremated) before the death is registered.

Funeral costs can normally be repaid out of the deceased's estate and will be given priority over any other claims. If the deceased has left a will it may contain directions concerning the funeral; however, these directions need not be followed by the executor.

The deceased's papers should also indicate whether a grave space had already been arranged. Most town churchyards and many suburban churchyards are no longer open for burial because they are full. Most cemeteries are non-denominational and may be owned by local authorities or private companies; fees vary.

If the body is to be cremated, an application form, two cremation certificates (for which there is a charge) or a certificate for cremation if the death was referred to the coroner, and a certificate signed by the medical referee must be completed in addition to the certificate for burial or cremation (the form is not required if the coroner has issued a certificate for cremation). All the forms are available from the funeral director or crematorium. Most crematoria are run by local authorities; the fees usually include the medical referee's fee and the use of the chapel. Ashes may be scattered, buried in a churchyard or cemetery, or kept.

The registrar must be notified of the date, place and means of disposal of the body within 96 hours (England and Wales) or three days (Scotland).

If the death occurred abroad or on a foreign ship or aircraft, a local burial or cremation may be arranged. If the body is to be brought back to England or Wales, a death certificate from the relevant country or an authorisation for the removal of the body from the country of death from the coroner or relevant authority will be required. To arrange a funeral in England or Wales an authenticated translation of a foreign death certificate or a death certificate issued in Scotland or Northern Ireland which must show the cause of death, is needed, together with a certificate of no liability to register from the registrar in England and Wales in whose sub-district it is intended to bury or cremate the body. If it is intended to cremate the body a cremation order will be required from the Home Office or a certificate for cremation.

Further information can be obtained from:

The General Register Office, Office for National Statistics, Smedley Hydro, Trafalgar Road, Birkdale, Southport, Merseyside PR8 2HH. Tel: 01704-569824

The General Register Office for Scotland, New Register House, Edinburgh EH1 3YT. Tel: 0131-334 0380

---

## DIVORCE AND RELATED MATTERS

---

## ENGLAND AND WALES

There are two types of matrimonial suit: those seeking the annulment of a marriage, and those seeking a judicial separation or divorce. To obtain an annulment, judicial separation or divorce in England and Wales, one or both of the parties must have their permanent home in England and Wales when the petition is started, or have been living in England and Wales for at least a year on the day the petition is started. All cases are commenced in divorce county courts or in the Divorce Registry in London. If a suit is defended it may be transferred to the High Court.

### Nullity of Marriage

Various circumstances will render a marriage invalid from the beginning including if: the marriage has not been consumated; one partner had a venereal disease at the time of the marriage and the other did not know about it; the female partner was pregnant at the time of marriage with another person's child and the male partner did not know of the pregnancy; the parties were within the prohibited degrees of consanguinity, affinity or adoption; the parties were not male and female; either of the parties was already married; either of the parties was under the age of 16; the formalities of the marriage were defective, e.g. the marriage did not take place in an authorised building, and both parties knew of the defect. Declarations of nullity are sought in very few cases.

### Separation

A couple may enter into an agreement to separate by consent but for the agreement to be valid it must be followed by an immediate separation; a solicitor should be contacted.

Judicial separation does not dissolve a marriage and it is not necessary to prove that the marriage has irretrievably broken down. Either party can petition for a judicial separation at any time; the grounds listed below as grounds for divorce are also grounds for judicial separation. To petition for judicial separation the parties do not have to prove that they have been married for 12 months or more.

### Divorce

Neither party can petition for divorce until at least one year after the date of the marriage. The sole ground for divorce is the irretrievable breakdown of the marriage; this must be proved on one or more of the following grounds:

- the respondent has committed adultery and the petitioner finds it intolerable to live with him/her; however the petitioner cannot rely on an act of adultery by the other party if they have lived together for more than six months after the discovery that adultery had been committed
- the respondent has behaved in such a way that the petitioner cannot reasonably be expected to continue living with him/her
- the respondent deserted the petitioner for two years immediately before the petition. Desertion may be defined as a voluntary withdrawal from cohabitation by the respondent without just cause and against the wishes of the petitioner; where one party is guilty of serious misconduct which forces the other party to leave, the party at fault is said to be guilty of constructive desertion
- the respondent and the petitioner have lived separately for two years immediately before the petition and the respondent consents to the decree
- the respondent and the petitioner have lived separately for five years immediately before the petition

A total period of less than six months during which the parties have resumed living together is disregarded in determining whether the prescribed period of separation or desertion has been continuous (but cannot be included as part of the period of separation).

The Matrimonial Causes Act 1973 requires the solicitor for the petitioner in certain cases to certify whether the possibility of a reconciliation has been discussed with the petitioner.

### The Decree Nisi

A decree nisi does not dissolve or annul the marriage but must be obtained before a divorce or annulment can take place.

Where the suit is undefended, the evidence normally takes the form of a sworn written statement made by the petitioner which is considered by a district judge. If the judge is satisfied that the petitioner has proved the contents of the petition, he/she will set a date for the pronouncement of the decree nisi in open court; neither party need attend.

If the judge is not satisfied that the petitioner has proved the contents of the petition, or if the suit is defended, the petition will be heard in open court with the parties giving oral evidence.

### The Decree Absolute

The decree nisi is usually made absolute after six weeks and on the application of the petitioner. If the judge thinks it may be necessary to exercise any of his/her powers under the Children Act 1989, he/she can in exceptional circumstances delay the granting of the decree absolute. The decree absolute dissolves or annuls the marriage.

### Children

Neither parent is now awarded 'custody' of any children of the marriage in England and Wales. Both parents, if married, have 'parental responsibility'. Either parent can exercise this, independently of the other. Any dispute between the parents can be resolved by the courts. In all court cases concerning children, whether connected to a matrimonial suit or not, the welfare of the child is the paramount consideration.

### Maintenance, etc.

Either party may be liable to pay maintenance to their former spouse. If there were any children of the marriage, both parents have a legal responsibility to support them financially if they can afford to do so. These so-called ancillary matters, including any property settlements, may be settled before the divorce goes through but currently can go on long after the marriage is dissolved.

The courts are responsible for assessing maintenance for the former spouse, taking into account each party's income and essential outgoings and other aspects of the case. The court also deals with any maintenance for a child which has been treated by the spouses as a 'child of the family', e.g. a stepchild, and any property settlements.

The Child Support Agency (CSA) was set up under the Child Support Act 1991 and is now responsible for assessing the maintenance that absent parents should pay for their natural or adopted children (whether or not a marriage has taken place). The CSA accepts applications only when all the people involved are habitually resident in the UK; the courts will continue to deal with cases where one of the people involved lives abroad. The CSA deals with all new cases, and is gradually taking on cases where the parent with care (or his/her new partner) was already receiving income support, family credit or disability working allowance before 5 April 1993. People with existing court orders or written maintenance agreements made before 5 April 1993 should continue to use the courts. Where it is already collecting child maintenance, the CSA has the power to offer a collection and enforcement service for certain other payments of maintenance.

A formula is used to work out how much child maintenance is payable. The formula ensures that after the payment of child maintenance the absent parent's income, and that of any second family he/she may now have, remains significantly above basic income support rates. Also, no absent parent will normally be assessed to pay more than 30 per cent of his/her net income in current child maintenance, or more than 33 per cent if he/she is also liable for any arrears. Absent parents are normally expected to pay at least a minimum amount of child maintenance.

A scheme has begun to be introduced since the end of 1996 which allows departures from the formula in certain tightly defined circumstances, e.g. the high costs of travel to maintain contact with a child, or to have a property and capital transfer ('clean break' settlement) entered into before April 1993 taken into account; there will also be some additional grounds which may result in liability being increased.

Some cases involving unusual circumstances are treated as special cases and the assessment is modified. Where there is financial need (e.g. because of disability or continuing education), maintenance may be ordered by the court for children even beyond the age of 18.

The level of maintenance is reviewed automatically every two years. Either parent can report a change of circumstances and request a review at any time. An independent complaints examiner for the CSA was appointed in early 1997.

If the absent parent does not pay the child maintenance, the CSA may make an order for payments to be deducted directly from his/her salary or wages; if all other methods fail, the CSA may take court action to enforce the payment.

### COURT ORDERS

Magistrates' courts used for domestic proceedings are now called family proceedings courts. A spouse can apply to the family proceedings court for a court order on the grounds that the other spouse:

- has failed to pay reasonable maintenance for the applicant
- has failed to make a proper contribution towards the reasonable maintenance of a 'child of the family'
- has deserted the applicant
- has behaved in such a way that the applicant cannot reasonably be expected to live with the respondent

If the case is proved, the court can order:

- periodical payments for the applicant and/or a 'child of the family'
- a lump sum payment to the applicant and/or a 'child of the family'

In deciding what orders (if any) to make, the court must consider guidelines which are similar to those governing financial orders in divorce cases. There are also special provisions relating to consent orders and separation by agreement. An order may be enforceable even if the parties are living together, but in some cases it will cease to have effect if they continue to do so for six months.

### MATRIMONIAL PROPERTY

Married couples can own property in two ways. The first is according to the title deeds (joint ownership) and the second relates to contributions to the property (beneficial interest). Just because a couple jointly own a property does not mean that in the event of divorce that the proceeds of matrimonial property will be distributed evenly. When deciding on what financial orders to make the court will take into consideration the length of marriage, the parties' ages, the parties' needs, the parties' earning capacity and the needs of the children to the marriage.

### COHABITING COUPLES

Rights of unmarried couples are not the same as for married couples. By virtue of this it may be worth considering entering into a contract which establishes how money and property should be divided in the event that 'separation deeds' or 'cohabitation contracts'.

### DOMESTIC VIOLENCE

If one spouse has been subjected to violence at the hands of the other, it is now possible to obtain a court order very quickly to restrain further violence and if necessary to have the other spouse excluded from the home. Such orders may also relate to unmarried couples and to a range of other relationships.

## SCOTLAND

Although there is separate legislation for Scotland covering nullity of marriage, judicial separation, divorce and ancillary matters, the provisions are in most respects the same as those for England and Wales. The following is confined to major points on which the law in Scotland differs.

An action for 'declarator of nullity' can be brought only in the Court of Session. Where a spouse is capable of sexual intercourse but refuses to consummate the marriage, this is not a ground of nullity in Scots law, though it could be a ground for divorce. The fact that a spouse was suffering from venereal disease at the time of marriage and the other spouse did not know this is not a ground of nullity in Scots law, neither is the fact that a wife was pregnant by another man at the time of marriage and her husband did not know this.

An action for judicial separation or divorce may be raised in the Court of Session; it may also be raised in the Sheriff Court if either party was resident in the sheriffdom for 40 days immediately before the date of the action or for 40 days ending not more than 40 days before the date of the action. The fee for starting a divorce petition in the Sheriff Court is £72.

When adultery is cited as proof that the marriage has broken down irretrievably, it is not necessary in Scotland to prove also that it is intolerable for the pursuer to live with the defender. In the case of desertion, irretrievable breakdown is not established if, after the two year desertion period has expired, the parties resume living together at any time after the end of three months from the date when they first resume living together.

Where a divorce action has been raised, it may be sisted or put on hold for a variety of reasons.

If the parties do cohabit during such postponement, no account is taken of the cohabitation if the action later proceeds.

In actions for divorce and separation, the court has the power to award a residence order in respect of any children of the marriage. The welfare of the children is of paramount importance, and the fact that a spouse has caused the breakdown of the marriage does not in itself preclude him/her from being awarded residence.

A simplified procedure for 'do-it-yourself' divorce was introduced in 1983 for certain divorces. If the action is based on two or five years' separation and will not be opposed, and if there are no children under 16 and no financial claims, and there is no sign that the applicant's spouse is unable to manage his or her affairs through mental illness or handicap, the applicant can write directly to the local sheriff court or to the Court of Session for the appropriate forms to enable him or her to proceed. The fee is £57, unless the applicant receives income support, family credit or legal advice and assistance, in which case there is no fee.

An extract decree, which dissolves or annuls marriage, will be made available 14 days after the divorce has been granted.

Further information can be obtained from any divorce county court, solicitor or Citizens' Advice Bureau, the Lord Chancellor's Department or the Lord Advocate's Office, or the following:

THE PRINCIPAL REGISTRY, First Avenue House, 42–49 High Holborn, London WC1V 6NP. Tel: 020-7936 6000

THE COURT OF SESSION, Parliament House, Parliament Square, Edinburgh EH1 1HQ. Tel: 0131-225 2595

THE CHILD SUPPORT AGENCY, Longbenton, Newcastle upon Tyne NE98 1YX. Tel: 0191-213 5000

---

# EMPLOYMENT LAW

---

## PAY AND CONDITIONS

The Employment Rights Act 1996 consolidates the statutory provisions relating to employees' rights. Employers must give each employee employed for more than one month a written statement containing the following information:

- names of employer and employee
- date when employment began
- remuneration and intervals at which it will be paid
- job title or description of job
- hours and place(s) of work
- holiday entitlement and holiday pay

- entitlement to sick leave and sick pay
- details of pension scheme(s)
- length of notice period that employer and employee need to give to terminate employment, or the end date for a fixed-term contract
- details of any collective agreement which affects the terms of employment
- details of disciplinary and grievance procedures
- if the employee is to work outside the UK for more than one month, the period of such work and the currency in which payment is made

This must be given to the employee within two months of the start of their employment. The Working Time Regulation 1998, the National Minimum Wage Act 1998 and the Employment Relations Act 1999 now supplement the 1996 Act.

### Sick Pay

Employees absent from work through illness or injury are entitled to receive Statutory Sick Pay (SSP) from the employer for a maximum period of 28 weeks in any three-year period. This applies to all employees, both men and women, up to the age of 65.

### Deductions From Pay

Employers may not make deductions from an employee's wages without the employee's prior written consent or unless authorised by statute (e.g. deductions for national insurance or tax).

### Sunday Trading

The Sunday Trading Act 1994 gave new rights to shop workers. They have the right not to be dismissed, selected for redundancy or to suffer any detriment (such as the denial of overtime, promotion or training) if they refuse to work on Sundays. This does not apply to those who, under their contracts, are employed to work on Sundays.

### Disputes

Where it has not been possible to settle a dispute in the workplace, it may be possible for employees to make a complaint to an industrial tribunal. ACAS offers advice and conciliation in employment disputes.

## TERMINATION OF EMPLOYMENT

An employee may be dismissed without notice if guilty of gross misconduct but in other cases a period of notice must be given by the employer. The minimum periods of notice specified in the Employment Rights Act 1996 are:

- at least one week if the employee has been continuously employed for one month or more but for less than two years
- at least two weeks if the employee has been continuously employed for two years or more. A week is added for every complete year of continuous employment up to 12 years
- at least 12 weeks for those who have been continuously employed for 12 years or more
- longer periods apply if these are specified in the contract of employment

If an employee is dismissed with less notice than he/she is entitled to, the employer is generally liable to pay wages for the period of proper notice (or for the period of the contract for those on fixed-term contracts). Generally, no notice needs to be given of the expiry of a fixed-term contract.

### Redundancy

An employee dismissed because of redundancy may be entitled to a lump sum. This applies if:

- the employee has at least two years' continuous service
- the employee is actually dismissed by the employer (even in cases of voluntary redundancy)
- dismissal is due to a reduction in the work force

An employee may not be entitled to a redundancy payment if offered a new job by the same employer. The amount of payment depends on the length of service, the salary and the age of the employee. The redundancy payment is guaranteed by the State in cases where the employer becomes insolvent (subject to the conditions above).

### Unfair Dismissal

Complaints about unfair dismissal are dealt with by an employment tribunal. Any employee, with one years' continuous service subject to exceptions, regardless of their hours of work, can make a complaint to the tribunal. At the tribunal the employer must prove that the dismissal was due to one or more of the following reasons:

- the employee's capability for the job
- the employee's conduct
- redundancy
- a legal restriction preventing the continuation of the employee's contract
- some other substantial reason (including breaking the law)

If so, the tribunal must decide whether the employer acted reasonably in dismissing the employee for that reason. If the employee is found to have been unfairly dismissed, the tribunal can order that he/she be reinstated or compensated.

## DISCRIMINATION

Discrimination in employment on the grounds of sex, race, colour, nationality, ethnic or national origins, married status or (subject to wide exceptions) disability is unlawful. Discrimination also includes sexual harassment and gender reassignment. The following legislation applies to those employed in Great Britain but not to employees in Northern Ireland or (subject to EC exceptions) to those who work mainly abroad:

- The Equal Pay Act 1970 (as amended) entitles men and women to equality in matters related to their contracts of employment. Those doing like work for the same employer are entitled to the same pay and conditions regardless of their sex
- The Sex Discrimination Act 1975 (as amended by the Sex Discrimination Act 1986) makes it unlawful to discriminate on grounds of sex or marital status. This covers all aspects of employment, including advertising for recruits, terms offered, opportunities for promotion and training, and dismissal procedures
- The Race Relations Act 1976 gives individuals the right not to be discriminated against in employment matters on the grounds of race, colour, nationality, or ethnic or national origins. It applies to all aspects of employment
- The Disability Discrimination Act 1995 makes discrimination against a disabled person in all aspects of employment unlawful. Unlike sex and race discrimination, an employer may show that the treatment is justified and that the employer acted reasonably.

  Employers with fewer than 15 employees are exempt.

The Equal Opportunities Commission, the Commission for Racial Equality and the Disability Rights Commission have the function of eliminating such discriminations in the workplace and can provide further information and assistance.

In Northern Ireland similar provisions exist but are constituted in separate legislation which also provides protection against religious discrimination.

## RECENT CHANGES

The Employment Relations Act 1999 has made a number of important changes to the existing law. The main changes are:

- a right of accompaniment. A worker attending a serious disciplinary or grievance hearing will have a right to be accompanied by a trade union representative or co-worker of their choice
- a new scheme of compulsory trade union recognition following a workplace ballot
- greater protection from dismissal for striking employees
- more 'family friendly' measures, including greater rights to maternity leave and parental leave
- the maximum award for unfair dismissal is £51,700 which relates to dismissals occurring on or after 1 February 2001.

## HUMAN RIGHTS

On 2 October 2000 the Human Rights Act 1998 came into force. This Act incorporates the European Convention on Human Rights into the law of the United Kingdom and it is expected to have a wide impact.

The main principles of the Act are as follows:

- all legislation must be interpreted by the courts as compatible with the Convention so far as it is possible to do so
- subordinate legislation (e.g. statutory instruments) which are incompatible with the Convention can be struck down by the courts
- primary legislation (e.g. Acts of Parliament) which is incompatible with the Convention cannot be struck down by a court, but the higher courts can make a declaration of incompatibility which is a signal to Parliament to change the law
- all public authorities (including courts and tribunals) must not act in a way which is incompatible with the Convention;
- individuals whose Convention rights have been infringed by a public authority may bring proceedings against that authority, but the Act is not intended to create new rights as between individuals.

The main human rights protected by the Convention are the right to life (article 2); protection from torture and inhuman or degrading treatment (article 3); protection from slavery or forced labour (article 4); the right to liberty and security of the person (article 5); right to a fair trial (article 6); the right not to be subject to retrospective criminal offences (article 7); right to private and family life (article 8); freedom of thought, conscience and religion (article 9); freedom of expression (article 10); freedom of association and assembly (article 11); right to marry and found a family (article 12); protection from discrimination (article 14); the right to property (article 1 Protocol No.1) and the right to education (article 2 Protocol No.1). Most of the Convention rights are subject to limitations which are 'necessary in a democratic society'.

## ILLEGITIMACY AND LEGITIMATION

The Children Act 1989 gives the mother parental responsibility for the child when she is not married to the father. The unmarried father can acquire parental responsibility either by agreement with her (in prescribed form) or by applying to the court. If an illegitimate child is to be adopted, the father's consent is required only where he has been awarded parental rights by the court.

Every child born to a married woman during marriage is presumed to be legitimate, unless the couple are separated under court order when the child is conceived, in which case the child is presumed not to be the husband's child. It is possible to challenge the presumption of legitimacy or illegitimacy through civil proceedings.

In Scotland, the relevant legislation is the Children (Scotland) Act 1995, which also gives the mother parental responsibility for her child when she is not married to the child's father. The Act also provides that a father has no automatic parental rights when unmarried to the mother, but can acquire parental responsibility by applying to the court.

### Legitimation

Under the Legitimacy Act 1976, an illegitimate person automatically becomes legitimate when his/her parents marry. This applies even where one of the parents was married to a third person at the time of the birth. In such cases it is necessary to re-register the birth of the child. In Scotland, the relevant legislation is the Legitimation (Scotland) Act 1968.

## JURY SERVICE

In England and Wales a person charged with any but the most minor offences is entitled to be tried by jury (However the right to trial by jury will be restricted if the Criminal Justice (Mode of Trial) (No.2) Bill presently before Parliament becomes law). No such right exists in Scotland, although more serious offences are heard before a jury. In England and Wales there are 12 members of a jury in a criminal case and eight members in a civil case. In Scotland there are 12 members of a jury in a civil case in the Court of Session (the civil jury being confined to the Court of Session and a restricted number of actions), and 15 in a criminal trial. Jurors are normally asked to serve for ten working days, although jurors selected for longer cases are expected to sit for the duration of the trial.

Every parliamentary or local government elector between the ages of 18 and 70 who has lived in the UK (including, for this purpose, the Channel Islands and the Isle of Man) for any period of at least five years since reaching the age of 13 is qualified to serve on a jury unless he/she is ineligible or disqualified.

### England and Wales

Those ineligible for jury service include:

- those who have at any time been judges, magistrates or senior court officials
- Those who have within the previous ten years been concerned with the administration of justice
- priests of any religion and vowed members of religious communities
- certain sufferers from mental illness

Those disqualified from jury service include:

- those who have at any time been sentenced by a court in the UK (including, for this purpose, the Channel Islands and the Isle of Man) to a term of imprisonment or custody of five years or more
- those who have within the previous ten years served any part of a sentence of imprisonment, youth custody or detention, been detained in a young offenders' institution, received a suspended sentence of imprisonment or order for detention, or received a community service order
- those who have within the previous five years been placed on probation

- those who are on bail in criminal proceedings

Those who may be excused as of right from jury service include:

- persons over the age of 65
- members and officers of the Houses of Parliament
- members of the National Assembly for Wales
- representatives to the European Parliament
- full-time serving members of the armed forces
- registered and practising members of the medical, dental, nursing, veterinary and pharmaceutical professions
- those who have served on a jury in the previous two years

The court has the discretion to excuse a juror from service, or defer the date of service, if the service would be a hardship to the juror. If a person serves on a jury knowing himself/herself to be ineligible or disqualified, he/she is liable to be fined up to £5,000 if disqualified and up to £1,000 for all other offences. The defendant can object to any juror if he/she can show cause.

A juror may claim travelling expenses, a subsistence allowance and an allowance for other financial loss (e.g. loss of earnings or benefits, fees paid to carers or child-minders) up to a stated limit.

It is an offence for a juror to disclose what happened in the jury room even after the trial is over. A jury's verdict must normally be unanimous, but if no verdict has been reached after two hours' consideration (or such longer period as the court deems to be reasonable) a majority verdict is acceptable if ten jurors agree to it.

### Scotland

Qualification criteria for jury service in Scotland are similar to those in England and Wales, except that the maximum age for a juror is 65, members of the judiciary are ineligible for ten years after ceasing to hold their post, and others concerned with the administration of justice are only eligible for service five years after ceasing to hold office. Ministers of religion, persons in holy orders and those who have served on a jury in the previous five years are excusable as of right.

The maximum fine for a person serving on a jury knowing himself/herself to be ineligible is £1,000. The maximum fine for failing to attend without good cause is also £1,000.

Further information can obtained from:

The Court Service, Southside, 105 Victoria Street, London SW1E 6QT. Tel: 020-7210 2266

The Clerk of Justiciary, High Court of Justiciary, Lawnmarket, Edinburgh EH2 2NS. Tel: 0131-225 2595

## LANDLORD AND TENANT

When a property is rented to a tenant, the rights and responsibilities of the landlord and the tenant are determined largely by the tenancy agreement but also by statutory provisions. Some of the main provisions are outlined below but it is advisable to contact the Citizens' Advice Bureau or the local authority housing department for further information.

## RESIDENTIAL LETTINGS

The provisions outlined here apply only where the tenant lives in a separate dwelling from the landlord and where the dwelling is the tenant's only or main home. It does not apply to licensees such as lodgers, guests or service occupiers.

The 1996 Housing Act radically changes certain aspects of the legislation referred to below, in particular the grant of assured and assured shorthold tenancies under the Housing Act 1988. It is advisable to check whether the new legislation has come into force before relying on the provisions set out below.

### Assured Shorthold Tenancies

If a tenancy was granted on or after 15 January 1989 and before 28 February 1997, the tenant may have an assured tenancy giving that tenant greater rights. The tenant could, for example, stay in possession of the dwelling for as long as the tenant observed the terms of the tenancy. The landlord cannot obtain possession from such a tenant unless the landlord can establish a specific ground for possession (set out in the Housing Act 1988) and obtains a court order. The rent payable is that agreed with the landlord unless the rent has been fixed by the rent assessment committee of the local authority. The tenant or the landlord may request that the committee set the rent in line with open market rents for that type of property. Any rent increases that are to take place should be written into the agreement but failing that, the landlord must give advance notice of the increase.

Under the Housing Act 1996, most new lettings entered into on or after 28 February 1997 will be assured shorthold tenancies. This means that tenants are given limited rights. The landlord must obtain a court order, however, to obtain possession if the tenant refuses to vacate at the end of the tenancy.

### Regulated Tenancies

Before the Housing Act 1988 came into force (15 January 1989) there were regulated tenancies; some are still in existence and are protected by the Rent Act 1977. Under this Act it is possible for the landlord or the tenant to apply to the local rent officer to have a 'fair' rent registered. The fair rent is then the maximum rent payable.

### Secure Tenancies

Secure tenancies are generally given to tenants of local authorities, housing associations and certain other bodies. This gives the tenant lifelong tenure unless the terms of the agreement are broken by the tenant. In certain circumstances those with secure tenancies may have the right to buy their property. In practice this right is generally only available to council tenants.

### Agricultural Property

Tenancies in agricultural properties are governed by the Agricultural Holdings Act 1986 and the Rent (Agricultural) Act 1976, which give similar protections to those described above, e.g. security of tenure, right to compensation for disturbance, etc. The Agricultural Holdings (Scotland) Act 1991 applies similar provisions to Scotland.

### Eviction

Under the Protection from Eviction Act 1977 (as amended by the Housing Act 1988), a landlord must give reasonable notice that he/she is to evict the tenant, and in most cases a possession order, granted in court, is necessary. Notice is generally to be at least four weeks and in prescribed statutory form (notices are available from law stationers). It is illegal for a landlord to evict a person by putting their belongings onto the street, by changing the locks and so on. It is also illegal for a landlord to harass a tenant in any way in order to persuade him/her to give up the tenancy.

LANDLORD RESPONSIBILITIES

Under the Landlord and Tenant Act 1985, where the term of the lease is less than seven years the landlord is responsible for maintaining the structure and exterior of the property and all installations for the supply of water, gas and electricity, for sanitation, and for heating and hot water.

## LEASEHOLDERS

Legally leaseholders have bought a long lease rather than a property and in certain limited circumstances the landlord can end the tenancy. Under the Leasehold Reform Act 1967 (as amended by the Housing Acts 1969, 1974 and 1980), leaseholders of houses may have the right to buy the freehold or to take an extended lease for a term of 50 years. This applies to leases where the term of the lease is over 21 years and where the leaseholder has occupied the house as his/her main residence for the last three years, or for a total of three years over the last ten.

The Leasehold Reform, Housing and Urban Development Act came into force in 1993 and allows the leaseholders of flats in certain circumstances to buy the freehold of the building in which they live.

Responsibility for maintenance of the structure, exterior and interior of the building should be set out in the lease. Usually the upkeep of the interior of his/her part of the property is the responsibility of the leaseholder, and responsibility for the structure, exterior and common interior areas is shared between the freeholder and the leaseholder(s).

If leaseholders are in any way dissatisfied with treatment from their landlord or with charges made in respect of lease extensions, they are entitled to have their situation evaluated by the Leasehold Valuation Tribunal.

## BUSINESS LETTINGS

The Landlord and Tenant Acts 1927 and 1954 (as amended) give security of tenure to the tenants of most business premises. The landlord can only evict the tenant on one of the grounds laid down in the 1954 Act, and in some cases where the landlord repossesses the property the tenant may be entitled to compensation.

## SCOTLAND

In Scotland assured and short assured tenancies exist for lettings after 2 January 1989 and are similar to assured tenancies in England and Wales. The relevant legislation is the Housing (Scotland) Act 1988.

Most tenancies created before 2 January 1989 were regulated tenancies and the Rent (Scotland) Act 1984 still applies where these exist. The Act defines, among other things, the circumstances in which a landlord can increase the rent when improvements are made to the property. The provisions of the Rent Act do not apply to tenancies where the landlord is the Crown, a local authority, the development corporation of a new town or a housing corporation.

The Housing (Scotland) Act 1987 and its provisions relate to local authority responsibilities for housing, the right to buy, and local authority secured tenancies. The provisions are broadly similar to England and Wales.

In Scotland, business premises are not controlled by statute to the same extent as in England and Wales, although the Shops (Scotland) Act 1949 gives some security to tenants of shops. Tenants of shops can apply to the sheriff for a renewal of tenancy if threatened with eviction. This application may be dismissed on various grounds including where the landlord has offered to sell the property to the tenant at an agreed price or, in the absence of agreement as to price, at a price fixed by a single arbiter appointed by the parties or the sheriff. The Act extends to properties where the Crown or government departments are the landlords or the tenants.

Under the Leases Act 1449 the landlord's successors (either purchasers or creditors) are bound by the agreement made with any tenants so long as the following conditions are met:

- the lease, if for more than one year, must be in writing
- there must be a rent
- there must be a term of expiry
- the tenant must have entered into possession

Many leases contain references to term and quarter days.

# LEGAL AID

The Access to Justice Act 1999 has transformed what used to known as the Legal Aid system. The Legal Aid Board has been abolished and replaced from 1 April 2000 with the Legal Services Commission (85 Gray's Inn Road, London, WC1X 8TX. Tel: 020-7759 0000). The changeover from the Legal Aid system is set to continue until 2002 with the latest major change being the introduction of the Criminal Defence Service in April 2001 to replace the old system of criminal legal aid. Up-to-date information and further guidance can be obtained from the Legal Services Commission website www.legalservices.gov.uk. The Legal Services Commission administers the Community Legal Service fund under which (like the former legal aid) people on low or moderate incomes may qualify for help with the costs of legal advice or representation. Further advice about entitlement to assistance should be sought from a solicitor or Citizens' Advice Bureau. A key element of the reforms has been the introduction of the Community Legal Service which is designed to increase access to legal information and advice by involving a much wider network of funders and providers in giving publicly funded legal services. In Scotland, provision of legal aid is governed by the Legal Aid (Scotland) Act 1986.

## CIVIL LEGAL AID

From 1 January 2000, only organisations (solicitors or Citizens' Advice Bureau) with a contract with the Legal Services Commission have been able to give initial help in any civil matter. Moreover, from that date decisions about funding were devolved from the Legal Services Commission to contracted organisations in relation to any level of publicly funded service in family and immigration cases. For other types of case, applications for public funding are made through a solicitor (or other contracted legal services providers) in much the same way as the former Legal Aid. From 1 April 2001 the so-called civil contracting scheme will be extended to cover all levels of service for all types of cases.

Under the new civil funding scheme there are broadly seven levels of service available:

- legal help
- help at court (the first two types of service are limited to advice and assistance with preparing a case, but do not include representation)
- approved family help – either general family help or help with mediation (special levels of service for family cases)
- legal representation – either investigative help or full representation (this covers assistance with representation in court)

- support funding – either investigative support or litigation support (this is a new type of assistance which allows the costs of a privately funded case to be topped up from public funds. It is only available for personal injury claims)
- family mediation
- such other services as are specifically authorised by the Lord Chancellor

In general, public funding is not available for the following type of cases:

- personal injury (except for the availability of support funding and clinical negligence claims)
- allegations of negligent damage to property
- conveyancing
- boundary disputes
- the making of wills
- matters of trust law
- defamation proceedings
- partnership disputes and company law
- other matters arising out of the carrying on of a business.

### ELIGIBILITY

Eligibility for funding from the Community Legal Service depends broadly on 5 factors:

- the level of service sought (see above)
- whether the applicant qualifies financially
- the merits if the applicant's case
- a costs-benefits analysis (if the costs are likely to outweigh any benefit that might be gained from the proceedings, funding may be refused)
- whether there is any public interest in the case being litigated (i.e. whether the case has a wider public interest beyond that of the parties involved – for example, a human rights case)

The limits on capital and income above which a person is not entitled to public funding vary with the type of service sought.

### CONTRIBUTIONS

Some of those who qualify for Community Legal Service funding will have to contribute towards their legal costs. Contributions must be paid by anyone who has a disposable income or disposable capital exceeding a prescribed amount. The rules relating to applicable contributions is complex and detailed information can be obtained from the Legal Services Commission. Tel: 020-7759 0000; Web: www.legalservices.gov.uk

### STATUTORY CHARGE

A statutory charge is made if a person receives money or property in a case for which they have received legal aid. This means that the amount paid by the Community Legal Service fund on their behalf is deducted from the amount that the person receives. This does not apply if the court has ordered that the costs be paid by the other party (unless the amount paid by the other party does not cover all of the costs) or if the payments are for maintenance.

### CONTINGENCY OR CONDITIONAL FEES

This system was introduced by the Courts and Legal Services Act 1990. It offers legal representation on a "no win, no fee" basis. It provides an alternative form of assistance, especially for those cases which are ineligible for funding by the Community Legal Service. The main area for such work is in the field of personal injuries which claims are now largely exempt from public funding (except for clinical negligence claims).

Not all solicitors offer such a scheme and different solicitors may well have different terms. The effect of the agreement is that solicitors will not make any charges until the case is concluded successfully. The charges are usually linked to a percentage of the amount recovered. The merits of a case are usually assessed before the scheme is offered to potential litigants. Should the case be accepted, then the percentage charges will be linked to the risks involved: the higher the risks, the higher the percentage. Any agreement should be in writing and set out the exact terms of the agreement and the effects of success and failure.

### SCOTLAND

Civil legal aid is available for cases in the following:

- the House of Lords
- the Court of Session
- the Lands Valuation Appeal Court
- the Scottish Land Court
- sheriff courts
- the Lands Tribunal for Scotland
- the Employment Appeal Tribunals
- the Restrictive Practices Court

Civil legal aid is not available for defamation actions, small claims or simplified divorce procedures.

Eligibility for civil legal aid is assessed in a similar way to that in England and Wales, though the financial limits differ in some respects and are as follows:

- a person is eligible if disposable income is £9,034 or less and disposable capital is £8,560 or less
- if disposable income is between £2,767 and £9,034, contributions are payable
- if disposable capital exceeds £3,000, contributions are payable
- those receiving income support or income related job seeker's allowance qualify automatically.

## CRIMINAL LEGAL AID

Criminal legal aid is now administered by the Legal Services Commission. As part of the changes under the Access to Justice Act 1999, in April 2001 the Criminal Defence Service replaced the old system of criminal legal aid under the Legal Aid Act 1988. Up-to-date information and further guidance can be obtained from the Legal Services Commission website www.legalservices.gov.uk or from a solicitor or Citizens' Advice Bureau.

The courts will grant criminal legal aid if it is desirable in the interests of justice (e.g. if there are important questions of law to be argued or the case is so serious that if found guilty the person may go to prison) and the person needs help to pay their legal costs.

Criminal legal aid covers the cost of preparing a case and legal representation (including the cost of a barrister) in criminal proceedings. It is also available for appeals against verdicts or sentences in magistrates' courts, the Crown Court or the Court of Appeal. It is not available for bringing a private prosecution in a criminal court.

If granted criminal legal aid, either the person may choose their own solicitor or the court will assign one. Contributions to the legal costs must be paid by anyone who has a disposable income or disposable capital which exceeds a prescribed amount. The rules relating to applicable contributions are complex and detailed information can be obtained from the Legal Services Commission. Tel: 020-7759 0000; Web: www.legalservices.gov.uk.

### DUTY SOLICITORS

The Legal Aid Act 1988 also provides free advice and assistance to anyone questioned by the police (whether under arrest or helping the police with their enquiries). No means test or contributions are required for this. The advice or assistance can be from the duty solicitor at the police station, from a person's own solicitor or from any local solicitor (a list is available at police stations).

Duty solicitors are usually available at the magistrates' court, in criminal cases, for advice and/or representation on first appearances. This assistance is not means-tested.

### Scotland

Legal advice and assistance operates in a similar way in Scotland. A person is eligible:

- if disposable income does not exceed £186 a week. If disposable income is between £79 and £186 a week, contributions are payable
- if disposable capital does not exceed £1,000 (£1,335 if the person has one dependant, £1,535 if two dependants with an additional £100 for every other dependant). There are no contributions from capital. The procedure for application for criminal legal aid depends on the circumstances of each case. In solemn cases (more serious cases, such as homicide) heard before a jury, a person is automatically entitled to criminal legal aid until they are given bail or placed in custody. Thereafter, it is for the court to decide whether to grant legal aid. The court will do this if the person accused cannot meet the expenses of the case without undue hardship on him or his dependants. In less serious cases the procedure depends on whether the person is in custody:
- anyone taken into custody has the right to free legal aid from the duty solicitor up to and including the first court appearance
- if the person is not in custody and wishes to plead guilty, they are not entitled to criminal legal aid but may be entitled to legal advice and assistance, including assistance by way of representation
- if the person is not in custody and wishes to plead not guilty, they can apply for criminal legal aid. This must be done within 14 days of the first court appearance at which they made the plea

The criteria used to assess whether or not criminal legal aid should be granted is similar to the criteria for England and Wales.

## MARRIAGE

Any two persons may marry provided that:

- they are at least 16 years old on the day of the marriage (in England and Wales persons under the age of 18 must generally obtain the consent of their parents; if consent is refused an appeal may be made to the High Court, the county court or a court of summary jurisdiction)
- they are not related to one another in a way which would prevent their marrying
- they are unmarried (a person who has already been married must produce documentary evidence that the previous marriage has been ended by death, divorce or annulment)
- they are not of the same sex
- they are capable of understanding the nature of a marriage ceremony and of consenting to marriage
- the marriage would be regarded as valid in any foreign country of which either party is a citizen

### Degrees of Relationship

A marriage between persons within the prohibited degrees of consanguinity, affinity or adoption is void.

A man may not marry his mother, daughter, grandmother, granddaughter, sister, aunt, niece, great-grandmother, great-granddaughter, adoptive mother, former adoptive mother, adopted daughter or former adopted daughter. In some circumstances he may now be allowed to marry his former wife's daughter, former wife's granddaughter, father's former wife or grandfather's former wife.

A woman may not marry her father, son, grandfather, grandson, brother, uncle, nephew, great-grandfather, great-grandson, adoptive father, former adoptive father, adopted son or former adopted son. In some circumstances she may now be allowed to marry her former husband's son, former husband's grandson, mother's former husband or grandmother's former husband.

## ENGLAND AND WALES

### Types of Marriage Ceremony

It is possible to marry by either religious or civil ceremony. A religious ceremony can take place at a church or chapel of the Church of England or the Church in Wales, or at any other place of worship which has been formally registered by the Registrar-General.

A civil ceremony can take place at a register office, a registered building or any other premises approved by the local authority.

An application for an approved premises licence must be made by the owners or trustees of the building concerned; it cannot be made by the prospective marriage couple. Approved premises must be regularly open to the public so that the marriage can be witnessed; the venue must be deemed to be a permanent and immovable structure. Open-air ceremonies are prohibited.

Non-Anglican marriages may also be solemnised following the issue of a Registrar-General's licence in unregistered premises where one of the parties is seriously ill, is not expected to recover, and cannot be moved to registered premises. Detained and housebound persons may be married at their place of residence.

### Marriage in the Church of England or the Church in Wales

#### *Marriage by banns*

The marriage must take place in a parish in which one of the parties lives, or in a church in another parish if it is the usual place of worship of either or both of the parties. The banns must be called in the parish in which the marriage is to take place on three Sundays before the day of the ceremony; if either or both of the parties lives in a different parish the banns must also be called there. After three months the banns are no longer valid.

#### *Marriage by common licence*

The vicar who is to conduct the marriage will arrange for a common licence to be issued by the diocesan bishop; this dispenses with the necessity for banns. One of the parties must have lived in the parish for 15 days immediately before the issuing of the licence or must usually worship at the church. Affidavits are prepared from the personal instructions of one of the parties and the licence will be given to the applicant in person.

### *Marriage by special licence*

A special licence is granted by the Archbishop of Canterbury in special circumstances for the marriage to take place at any place, with or without previous residence in the parish, or at any time. Application must be made to the Faculty Office of the Archbishop of Canterbury, 1 The Sanctuary, London SW1P 3JT. Tel: 020-7222 5381.

### *Marriage by certificate*

The marriage can be conducted on the authority of the superintendent registrar's certificate, provided that the vicar's consent is obtained. One of the parties must live in the parish or must usually worship at the church.

## Marriage by Other Religious Ceremony

One of the parties must normally live in the registration district where the marriage is to take place. In addition to giving notice to the superintendent registrar it may also be necessary to book a registrar to be present at the ceremony.

## Civil Marriage

A marriage may be solemnised at any register office, registered building or approved premises in England and Wales. The superintendent registrar of the district should be contacted, and, if the marriage is to take place at approved premises, the necessary arrangements at the venue must also be made.

## Notice of Marriage

Unless it is to take place by banns or under common or special licence in the Church of England or the Church in Wales, a notice of the marriage must be given in person to the superintendent registrar. Notice of marriage may be given in the following ways:

- by certificate. Both parties must have lived in a registration district in England or Wales for at least seven days immediately before giving notice at the local register office. If they live in different registration districts, notice must be given in both districts. The marriage can take place in any register office in England and Wales 21 days after notice has been given
- by licence (often known as 'special licence'). One of the parties must have lived in a registration district in England or Wales for at least 15 days before giving notice at the register office; the other party need only be a resident of, or be physically in, England and Wales on the day notice is given. The marriage can take place one clear day (other than a Sunday, Christmas Day or Good Friday) after notice has been given

A notice of marriage is valid for 12 months. It is not therefore possible to give formal notice of a marriage more than three months before it is to take place, but it should be possible to make an advance (provisional) booking 12 months before the ceremony. In this case it is still necessary to give formal notice three months before the marriage. When giving notice of the marriage it is necessary to produce official proof, if relevant, that any previous marriage has ended in divorce or death by producing a decree absolute or death certificate; it is also useful, but not necessary, to take birth certificates or passports as proof of age and identity.

## Solemnisation of the Marriage

On the day of the wedding there must be at least two other people present who are prepared to act as witnesses and sign the marriage register. A registrar of marriages must be present at a marriage in a register office or at approved premises, but an authorised person may act in the capacity of registrar in a registered building.

If the marriage takes place at approved premises, the room must be separate from any other activity on the premises at the time of the ceremony, and no food or drink can be sold or consumed in the room during the ceremony or for one hour beforehand.

The marriage must be solemnised between 8 a.m. and 6 p.m., with open doors. At some time during the ceremony the parties must make a declaration that they know of no legal impediment to the marriage and they must also say the contracting words; the declaratory and contracting words may vary according to the form of service in use but the most basic forms are:

- (*declaratory words*) 'I declare that I know of no legal reason why I, A. B., may not be joined in marriage to C. D.' Alternatively, the couple may answer 'I am' to the question 'Are you, A. B., free lawfully to marry C. D.?'
- (*contracting words*) 'I, A. B., take you, C. D., to be my wedded wife [or husband]'

A civil marriage cannot contain any religious aspects, but it may be possible for non-religious music and/or poetry readings to be included. It may also be possible to embellish the marriage vows taken by the couple.

If both parties are Jewish, they may be married in a synagogue, in a private house or elsewhere. The wedding may take place at any time of day and must be registered by the secretary of the synagogue of which the man is a member. The presence of a registrar of marriages is not necessary.

If both parties are members of the Society of Friends (Quakers), they may be married in a Friends' meeting-house. The marriage must be registered by the registering officer of the Society appointed to act for the district in which the meeting-house is situated. The presence of a registrar of marriages is not necessary.

## Civil Fees *from 1 April 2001*

*Marriage at a Register Office (the fees below include a fee of £34.00 for the registrar's attendance on the day of the wedding)*

By superintendent registrar's certificate, £94.00

Marriage on Approved Premises (in addition to the fees below a fee will also be payable for the superintendent registrar's and registrar's attendance at the marriage which is set locally by the local authority responsible. A further charge is likely to be made by the owners of the building for the use of the premises) AND Marriage in a religious building other than in the Church of England or Church in Wales (in addition to the fees below a fee of £40.00 will also be payable for the registrar's attendance at the marriage unless an "Authorised Person" appointed by the trustees of the building has agreed to register to marriage. Additional fees may also be charged by the trustees of the building for the wedding, and by the person who performs the ceremony)

By superintendent registrar's certificate, £60.00

## Ecclesiastical Fees *since 1 January 2001*

(Church of England and Church in Wales*)

*Marriage by banns*

For publication of banns, £15.00

For certificate of banns issued at time of publication, £8.00

For marriage service, £142.00

*Marriage by common licence*

Fee for licence, £55.00

*Marriage by special licence*

Fee for licence, £125.00

Further fees may be payable for additional facilities at the marriage, e.g. the organist's fee.

*Some of these fees may not apply to the Church in Wales

## SCOTLAND

### Regular Marriages

A regular marriage is one which is celebrated by a minister of religion or authorised registrar or other celebrant. Each of the parties must complete a marriage notice form and return it to the district registrar for the area in which they are to be married, irrespective of where they live, at least 15 days before the ceremony is due to take place. The district registrar must then enter the date of receipt and certain details in a marriage book kept for this purpose, and must also enter the names of the parties and the proposed date of marriage in a list which is displayed in a conspicuous place at the registration office until the date of the marriage has passed. All persons wishing to enter into a regular marriage in Scotland must follow the same preliminary procedure regardless of whether they intend to have a religious or civil ceremony.

A marriage schedule, which is prepared by the registrar, will be issued to one or both of the parties in person up to seven days before a religious marriage; for a civil marriage the schedule will be available at the ceremony. The schedule must be handed to the celebrant before the ceremony starts; it must be signed immediately after the wedding and the marriage must be registered within three days.

The authority to conduct a religious marriage is deemed to be vested in the authorised celebrant rather than the building in which it takes place; open-air religious ceremonies are therefore permissible in Scotland.

### Marriage by Cohabitation With Habit and Repute

If two people live together constantly as husband and wife and are generally held to be such by the neighbourhood and among their friends and relations, there may arise a presumption from which marriage can be inferred. Before such a marriage can be registered, however, a decree of declarator of marriage must be obtained from the Court of Session.

### Civil Fees

The basic statutory fee is £79.00, comprising a £13.00 per person fee for a statutory notice of intention to marry, a £45.00 fee for solemnisation of the marriage in a register office, and an £8.00 fee for a copy of the marriage certificate.

Further information can be obtained from:

The General Register Office, Office for National Statistics, Smedley Hydro, Trafalgar Road, Birkdale, Southport, Merseyside PR8 2HH. Tel: 01704-569824

The General Register Office for Scotland, New Register House, Edinburgh EH1 3YT. Tel: 0131-334 0380

## TOWN AND COUNTRY PLANNING

The planning system is important in helping to protect the environment, as well as assisting individuals in assessing their land rights. There are a number of Acts governing the development of land and buildings in the UK and advice should always be sought from a Citizen's Advice Bureau or local planning authority before undertaking building works to any land or property. If building takes place which requires planning permission without permission being sought in advance, the situation may need to be rectified.

## PLANNING PERMISSION

Planning permission is needed if the work involves:

- making a material change in use, such as dividing off part of the house so that it can be used as a separate home or dividing off part of the house for commercial use, e.g. for a workshop
- going against the terms of the original planning permission, e.g. there may be a restriction on fences in front gardens on an open-plan estate
- building, engineering for mining, except for the permissions below
- new or wider access to a main road
- additions or extensions to flats or maisonettes

Planning permission is not needed to carry out internal alterations or work which does not affect the external appearance of the building.

There are certain types of development for which the Secretary of State for the Environment has granted general permissions (permitted development rights). These include:

- house extensions and additions (including conservatories, loft conversions, garages and dormer windows). Up to 10 per cent or up to 50 cubic metres (whichever is the greater) can be added to the original house for terraced houses. Up to 15 per cent or 70 cubic metres (whichever is the greater) to other kinds of houses. The maximum that can be added to any house is 115 cubic metres
- buildings such as garden sheds and greenhouses so long as they are no more than 3 metres high (or 4 metres if the roof is ridged), are no nearer to a highway than the house, and at least half the ground around the house remains uncovered by buildings
- adding a porch with a ground area of less than 3 square metres and that is less than 3 metres in height
- putting up fences, walls and gates of under 1 metre in height if next to a road and under 2 metres elsewhere
- laying patios, paths or driveways for domestic use

## OTHER RESTRICTIONS

It may be necessary to obtain other types of permissions before carrying out any development. These permissions are separate from planning permission and apply regardless of whether or not planning permission is needed, e.g.:

- building regulations will probably apply if a new building is to be erected, if an existing one is to be altered or extended, or if the work involves building over a drain or sewer The building control department of the local authority will advise on this
- any alterations to a listed building or the grounds of a listed building must be approved by the local authority
- local authority approval is necessary if a building (or, in some circumstances, gates, walls, fences or railings) in a conservation area is to be demolished; each local authority keeps a register of all local buildings that are in conservation areas
- many trees are protected by tree preservation orders and must not be pruned or taken down without local authority consent
- bats and other species are protected and English Nature, the Countryside Council for Wales or Scottish Natural Heritage must be notified before any work is carried out that will affect the habitat of protected species, e.g. timber treatment, renovation or extensions of lofts

- any development in areas designated as a National Park, an Area of Outstanding National Beauty, a National Scenic Area or in the Norfolk or Suffolk Broads is subject to greater restrictions. The local planning authority will advise or refer enquirers to the relevant authority

If you think you require planning permission, contact your local planning authority. They will advise you and provide the correct form for your application. For further information, contact the Department for Transport, Local Government and the Regions.

## VOTERS' QUALIFICATIONS

Those entitled to vote at parliamentary, European Union (EU) and local government elections are those who are:

- on the electoral role. Local authorities administer the roll and non-registration can lead to a fine of up to £1,000
- over 18 years old
- Commonwealth (which includes British) citizens or citizens of the Republic of Ireland

British citizens resident abroad are entitled to vote, for 20 years after leaving Britain, as overseas electors in parliamentary and EU elections in the constituency in which they were last resident. Members of the armed forces, Crown servants and employees of the British Council who are overseas and their spouses are entitled to vote regardless of how long they have been abroad.

European Union citizens resident in the UK may vote in EU and local government elections.

The main categories of people who are not entitled to vote are:

- sitting peers in the house of lords
- patients detained under mental health legislation who have criminal convictions
- those serving prison sentences
- those convicted within the previous five years of corrupt or illegal election practices

Under the Representation of the Peoples Act 2000, several new groups of people are permitted to vote for the first time. These include: people who live on barges; unconvicted or remand prisoners; people in mental health hospitals (other than those with criminal convictions) and homeless people who have made a 'declaration of local connection'.

### Registering to Vote

Voters must be entered on an electoral register, which runs from 16 February in one year to 15 February in the following year. The registration officer for each constituency is responsible for preparing and publishing the register. A registration form is sent to all households in the autumn of each year and the householder is required to provide details of all occupants who are eligible to vote, including ones who will reach their 18th birthday in the year covered by the register. Those who fail to give the required information or who give false information are liable to be fined. A draft register is usually published at the end of November. Any person whose name has been omitted may ask to be registered and should contact the registration officer. Anyone on the register may object to the inclusion of another person's name, in which case he/she should notify the registration officer, who will investigate that person's eligibility. Supplementary electors lists are published throughout the duration of the register.

### Voting

Voting is not compulsory in the UK. Those who wish to vote must generally vote in person at the allotted polling station. Those who will be away at the time of the election, those who will not be able to attend in person due to physical incapacity or the nature of their occupation, and those who have changed address during the period for which the register is valid, may apply for a postal vote or nominate a proxy to vote for them. Overseas electors who wish to vote must do so by proxy.

Further information can be obtained from the local authority's electoral registration officer in England and Wales or the electoral registration office in Scotland, or the Chief Electoral Officer in Northern Ireland (3rd Floor, St Anne's House, 15 Church Street, Belfast BT1 1ER. Tel: 028-9024 5353).

## WILLS AND INTESTACY

In a will a person leaves instructions as to the disposal of their property after they die. A will is also used to appoint executors (who will administer the estate), give directions as to the disposal of the body, appoint guardians for children and, for larger estates, can operate to reduce the level of inheritance tax. It is best to have a will drawn up by a solicitor but if a solicitor is not employed, the following points must be taken into account:

- if possible the will must not be prepared on behalf of another person by someone who is to benefit from it or who is a close relative of a major beneficiary
- the language used must be clear and unambiguous and it is better to avoid the use of legal terms where the same thing can be expressed in plain language
- it is better to rewrite the whole document if a mistake is made. If necessary, alterations can be made by striking through the words with a pen, and the signature or initials of the testator and the witnesses must be put in the margin opposite the alteration. No alteration of any kind should be made after the will has been executed
- if the person later wishes to change the will or part of it, it is better to write a new will revoking the old. The use of codicils (documents written as supplements or containing modifications to the will) should be left to a solicitor
- the will should be typed or printed, or if handwritten be legible and preferably in ink. Commercial will forms can be obtained from some stationers.

The form of a will varies to suit different cases; the following is an example of how a will might be written. The notes after this example explain the terms used and procedures that need to be followed in drawing up a will.

This is the last will and testament of me [*Thomas Smith*] of [*Heather Cottage, Prospero Road, Manchester* M1 4DK] which I make this [*seventeenth*] day of [*May* 2000] and I revoke all previous wills and testamentary dispositions.

1. I appoint as my executors and trustees [*Ann Green of ___________ and Richard Brown of ___________*]. In my will the expression 'my Trustees' means any executors and trustees for the time being of my will and of any trust arising under it.

2. I give all my property to [*such of my children as shall survive me by 28 days and if more than one in equal shares* or as the case may be].

*or*

2. I give to [*Pamela Henderson of* ________] the sum of [£___] and to [*Michael Broadbent of* ________] the sum of [£___] and to [*Ruth Walker of* ________] all of my [*jewellery, books* or as the case may be]
*and*
3. I give everything not otherwise disposed of to [*Richard Black of* ______]
Signed by the testator in our joint presence and then by us in his.
Thomas Smith
[*Signature of the person making the will*]
Elizabeth Wall
[*Signature of witness*] of 67 Beatrice Lane, Manchester M1 4DK, journalist
William Jones
[*Signature of witness*] of 17 Paris Road, Manchester M1 4EN, tailor

### Specific Gifts and Legacies

Gifts of specific items usually fail if the property is not owned by the person making the will on their death. This problem can be avoided by making a gift of any property fulfilling a particular description, e.g. a car, which is owned at the date of death. It is better in all cases where such gifts are made, to insert a clause which reads 'I give everything not otherwise disposed of to [*Richard Black of* ________], even if it seems that all property has already been disposed of in the will.

### Lapsed Legatees

If a person who has been left property in a will dies before the person who made the will, the gift fails and will pass to the person entitled to everything not otherwise disposed of (the residuary estate).

If the person left the residuary estate dies before the person who made the will, their share will generally pass to the closest relative(s) of the person who made the will (as in intestacy) unless the will names a beneficiary such as a charity who will take as a 'long stop' if this gift is unable to take effect for any reason.

It is always better to draw up a new will if a beneficiary predeceases the person who made the will.

### Executors

It is usual to appoint two executors, although one is sufficient. No more than four persons can deal with the estate of the person who has died. The name and address of each executor should be given in full (the addresses are not essential but including them adds clarity to the document).

Executors should be 18 years of age or over. An executor may be a beneficiary of the will.

### Witnesses

A person who is a beneficiary of a will, or the spouse of a beneficiary at the time the will is signed, must not act as a witness or else he/she will be unable to take his/her gift. Husband and wife can both act as witnesses provided neither benefits from the will. It is better that a person does not act as an executor and as a witness, as he/she can take no benefit under a will to which he/she is witness. The identity of the witnesses should be made as explicit as possible.

### Execution of a Will

The person making the will should sign his/her name at the foot of the document, in the presence of the two witnesses. The witnesses must then sign their names while the person making the will looks on. If this procedure is not adhered to, the will will be considered invalid. There are certain exceptional circumstances where these rules are relaxed, e.g. where the person may be too ill to sign, and in these cases the attestation clause which normally reads 'signed by the testator in our joint presence and then by us in his/hers' should be reworded as follows:

'The will was read over to Thomas Smith in our presence when he stated that he understood it. It was then signed on his behalf by Thomas Brown in the presence of the testator and by his direction in our joint presence and then by us in his'.

### Capacity to Make a Will

Anyone aged 18 or over can make a will. However, if there is any suspicion that the person making the will is not, through reasons of infirmity or age, fully in command of his/her faculties, it is advisable to arrange for a medical practitioner to examine the person making the will at the time it is to be executed to verify his/her mental capacity and to record that medical opinion in writing, and to ask the examining practitioner to act as a witness. If a person is not mentally able to make a will, the Court may do this for him/her by virtue of the Mental Health Act 1983.

### Revocation

A will may be revoked or cancelled in a number of ways:
- a later will revokes an earlier one if it says so; otherwise the earlier will is impliedly revoked by the later one to the extent that it contradicts or repeats the earlier one
- a will is also revoked if the physical document on which it is written is destroyed by the person whose will it is. There must be an intention to revoke the will. It may not be sufficient to obliterate the will with a pen
- a will is revoked when the person marries, unless it is clear from the will that the person intended the will to stand after the marriage
- where a marriage ends in divorce or is annulled or declared void, gifts to the spouse and the appointment of the spouse as executor fail unless the will says that this is not to happen. A former spouse is treated as having predeceased the testator. A separation does not change the effect of a married person's will.

### Probate and Letters of Administration

Probate is granted to the executors named in a will and once granted, the executors are obliged to carry out the instructions of the will. Letters of administration are granted where no executor is named in a will or is willing or able to act or where there is no will or no valid will; this gives a person, often the next of kin, similar powers and duties to those of an executor.

Applications for probate or for letters of administration can be made to the Principal Registry of the Family Division, to a district probate registry or to a probate sub-registry. Applicants will need the following documents: the original will (if any); a certificate of death; oath for executors or administrators; particulars of all property and assets left by the deceased; a list of debts and funeral expenses. Certain property, up to the value of £5,000, may be disposed of without a grant of probate or letters of administration.

### Where to Find a Proved Will

Since 1858 wills which have been proved, that is wills on which probate or letters of administration have been granted, must have been proved at the Principal Registry of the Family Division or at a district probate registry. The Lord Chancellor has power to direct where the original documents are kept but most are filed where they were proved and may be inspected there and a copy obtained. The Principal Registry also holds copies of all wills proved at district probate registries and these may be inspected at

Somerset House. An index of all grants, both of probate and of letters of administration, is compiled by the Principal Registry and may be seen either at the Principal Registry or at a district probate registry.

It is also possible to discover when a grant of probate or letters of administration is issued by requesting a standing search. In response to a request and for a small fee, a district probate registry will supply the names and addresses of executors or administrators and the registry in which the grant was made, of any grant in the estate of a specified person made in the previous 12 months or following six months. This is useful for applicants who may be beneficiaries to a will but who have lost contact with the deceased and for creditors of the deceased.

## SCOTLAND

In Scotland any person over 12 and of sound mind can make a will. The person making the will can only freely dispose of the heritage and what is known as the 'dead's part' of the estate because:

- the spouse has the right to inherit one-third of the moveable estate if there are children or other descendants, and one-half of it if there are not
- children are entitled to one-third of the moveable estate if there is a surviving spouse, and one-half of it if there is not

The remaining portion is the dead's part, and legacies and bequests are payable from this. Debts are payable out of the whole estate before any division.

From August 1995, wills no longer needed to be 'holographed' and it is now only necessary to have one witness. The person making the will still needs to sign each page. It is better that the will is not witnessed by a beneficiary although the attestation would still be sound and the beneficiary would not have to relinquish the gift.

Subsequent marriage does not revoke a will but the birth of a child who is not provided for may do so. A will may be revoked by a subsequent will, either expressly or by implication, but in so far as the two can be read together both have effect. If a subsequent will is revoked, the earlier will is revived.

Wills may be registered in the sheriff court Books of the Sheriffdom in which the deceased lived or in the Books of Council and Session at the Registers of Scotland.

### CONFIRMATION

Confirmation (the Scottish equivalent of probate) is obtained in the sheriff court of the sheriffdom in which the deceased was resident at the time of death. Executives are either 'nominate' (named by the deceased in the will) or 'dative' (appointed by the court in cases where no executor is named in a will or in cases of intestacy). Applicants for confirmation must first provide an inventory of the deceased's estate and a schedule of debts, with an affidavit. In estates under £25,000 gross, confirmation can be obtained under a simplified procedure at reduced fees, with no need for a solicitor. The local sheriff clerk's office can provide assistance.

Further information can be obtained from:

PRINCIPAL REGISTRY (FAMILY DIVISION), First Avenue House, 42–49 High Holborn, London, WC1V 6NP. Tel: 020-7947 6000

REGISTERS OF SCOTLAND, Meadowbank House, 153 London Road, Edinburgh, EH8 7AU. Tel: 0131-659 6111

## INTESTACY

Intestacy occurs when someone dies without leaving a will or leaves a will which is invalid or which does not take effect for some reason. In such cases the person's estate (property, possessions, other assets following the payment of debts) passes to certain members of the family. The relevant legislation is the Administration of Estates Act 1925, as amended by various legislation including the Intestates Estates Act 1952, the Law Reform (Succession) Act 1995, and the Trusts of Land and Appointment of Trustees Act 1996 and Orders made there under. Some of the provisions of this legislation are described below. If a will has been written that disposes of only part of a person's property, these rules apply to the part which is undisposed of.

If the person (intestate) leaves a spouse who survives for 28 days and children (legitimate, illegitimate and adopted children and other descendants), the estate is divided as follows:

- the spouse takes the 'personal chattels' (household articles, including cars, but nothing used for business purposes), £125,000 free of tax (with interest payable at 6 per cent from the time of the death until payment) and a life interest in half of the rest of the estate (which can be capitalised by the spouse if he/she wishes)
- the rest of the estate goes to the children*

If the person leaves a spouse who survives for 28 days but no children:

- the spouse takes the personal chattels, £200,000 free of tax (interest payable as before) and full ownership of half of the rest of the estate
- the other half of the rest of the estate goes to the parents (equally, if both alive) or, if none, to the brothers and sisters of the whole blood*
- if there are no parents or brothers or sisters of the whole blood or their children, the spouse takes the whole estate

If there is no surviving spouse, the estate is distributed among those who survive the intestate as follows:

- to surviving children*, but if none to
- parents (equally, if both alive), but if none to
- brothers and sisters of the whole blood*, but if none to
- brothers and sisters of the half blood*, but if none to
- grandparents (equally, if more than one), but if none to
- aunts and uncles of the whole blood*, but if none to
- aunts and uncles of the half blood*, but if none to
- the Crown, Duchy of Lancaster or the Duke of Cornwall (*bona vacantia*)

* To inherit, a member of these groups must survive the intestate and attain 18, or marry under that age. If they die under 18 (unless married under that age), their share goes to others, if any, in the same group. If any member of these groups predeceases the intestate leaving children, their share is divided equally among their children.

In England and Wales the provisions of the Inheritance (Provision for Family and Dependants) Act 1975 may allow other people to claim provision from the deceased's assets. This Act also applies to cases where a will has been made and allows a person to apply to the Court if they feel that the will or rules of intestacy or both do not make adequate provision for them. The Court can order payment from the deceased's assets or the transfer of property from them if the applicant's claim is accepted. The application must be made within six months of the grant of probate or letters of administration and the following people can make an application:

- the spouse
- a former spouse who has not remarried
- a child of the deceased
- someone treated as a child of the deceased's family
- someone maintained by the deceased
- someone who has cohabited for two years before the death in the same household as the deceased and as the husband or wife of the deceased

SCOTLAND

Under the Succession (Scotland) Act 1964, no distinction is made between 'moveable' and 'heritable' property in intestacy cases.

A surviving spouse is entitled to 'prior rights'. This means that from 1 April 1999 the spouse has the right to inherit:

- the matrimonial home up to a value of £130,000, or one matrimonial home if there is more than one, or, in certain circumstances, the value of the matrimonial home
- the furnishings and contents of that home, up to the value of £22,000
- a cash sum of £35,000 if the deceased left children or other descendants, or £58,000 if not

These figures are increased from time to time by regulations.

Once prior rights have been satisfied, what remains of the estate is generally divided between the surviving spouse and children (legitimate and illegitimate) according to 'legal' rights. Legal rights are:

*Jus relicti(ae)* – the right of a surviving spouse to one-half of the net moveable estate, after satisfaction of prior rights, if there are no surviving children; if there are surviving children, the spouse is entitled to one-third of the net moveable estate

*Legitim* – the right of surviving children to one-half of the net moveable estate if there is no surviving spouse; if there is a surviving spouse, the children are entitled to one-third of the net moveable estate after the satisfaction of prior rights

Where there are no surviving spouse or children, half of the estate is taken by the parents and half by the brothers and sisters. Failing that, the lines of succession, in general, are:

- to descendants
- if no descendants, then to collaterals (i.e. brothers and sisters) and parents
- surviving spouse
- if no collaterals or parents or spouse, then to ascendants collaterals (i.e. aunts and uncles), and so on in an ascending scale
- if all lines of succession fail, the estate passes to the Crown

Relatives of the whole blood are preferred to relatives of the half blood. The right of representation, i.e. the right of the issue of a person who would have succeeded if he/she had survived the intestate, also applies.

# Crime Statistics

## ENGLAND AND WALES

RECORDED CRIME 1999

| | |
|---|---|
| Violence against the person | 581,000 |
| Sexual offences | 37,800 |
| Burglary | 906,500 |
| Robbery | 84,300 |
| Theft and handling stolen goods | 2,223,600 |
| Fraud and forgery | 334,800 |
| Criminal damage | 945,700 |
| Drug offences | 121,900 |
| Other offences | 65,700 |
| Total offences | 5,301,200 |

*Source:* The Stationery Office – *Annual Abstract of Statistics 2001* (Crown copyright)

CRIMINAL JUSTICE STATISTICS 1999

| | |
|---|---|
| Number of arrests | 1,300,000 |
| Notifiable offences cleared up | 1,321,000 |
| Clear-up rate | 25% |
| †Number of offenders cautioned | 266,000 |
| Defendants proceeded against at magistrates' courts | 1,882,000 |
| Defendants found guilty at magistrates' courts | 1,351,000 |
| Defendants tried at Crown Courts | 77,000 |
| Defendants found guilty at Crown Courts | 57,000 |
| Defendants sentenced at Crown Courts after summary conviction | 20,000 |
| Total offenders found guilty at both courts | 1,408,000 |
| †Total offenders found guilty or cautioned | 1,675,000 |

†Excludes motoring offences

OFFENDERS SENTENCED BY TYPE OF SENTENCE OR ORDER 1999

| | |
|---|---|
| Absolute discharge | 15,900 |
| Conditional discharge | 114,100 |
| Fine | 993,300 |
| Probation order | 58,400 |
| Supervision order | 12,700 |
| Community service order | 49,600 |
| Attendance sentence order | 8,700 |
| Combination order | 20,800 |
| Curfew order | 1,600 |
| Young offender institution | 24,900 |
| Imprisonment: | |
| Suspended | 3,200 |
| Unsuspended | 79,900 |
| Otherwise dealt with | 25,600 |
| All sentences or orders: total | 1,409,200 |

## SCOTLAND

CRIMES AND OFFENCES RECORDED 1999

| | |
|---|---|
| Non-sexual crimes of violence against the person | 23,440 |
| Crimes involving indecency | 5,982 |
| Crimes involving dishonesty | 276,189 |
| Fire-raising, vandalism, etc. | 79,568 |
| Other crimes | 50,524 |
| Miscellaneous offences | 151,045 |
| Motor vehicle offences | 353,405 |
| Total crimes and offences | 940,153 |

*Source:* The Scottish Executive

PERSONS WITH CHARGE PROVED BY MAIN PENALTY 1999

| | |
|---|---|
| Absolute discharge | 985 |
| Remit to children's hearing | 136 |
| Admonition or caution | 12,914 |
| Compensation order | 1,154 |
| Fine | 83,479 |
| Probation | 7,340 |
| Community service order | 4,888 |
| Insanity or hospital order | 135 |
| Detention of child | 17 |
| Young offender institution | 4,483 |
| Prison | 11,591 |
| All penalties: total | 127,435 |

*Source:* The Scottish Executive

# Intellectual Property

## COPYRIGHT

Copyright protects all original literary, dramatic, musical and artistic works (including photographs, maps and plans), published editions of works, computer programs, sound recordings, films (including video), broadcasts (including satellite broadcasts) and cable programmes (including on-line information services). Under copyright the creators of these works can control the various ways in which their material may be exploited, the rights broadly covering copying, adapting, issuing (including renting and lending) copies to the public, performing in public, and broadcasting the material.

Copyright protection in the United Kingdom is automatic and there is no registration system. The main legislation is the Copyright, Designs and Patents Act 1988, which has been amended by other Acts and by Statutory Instrument to take account of EC Directives. As a result of an EC Directive effective from January 1996, the term of copyright protection for literary, dramatic, musical and artistic works lasts until 70 years after the death of the author, and for film now lasts for 70 years after the death of the last to survive of the director, author of the screenplay, author of the dialogue and composer of music specially created for the film. Sound recordings are protected for 50 years after their publication, and broadcasts and cable programmes for 50 years from the end of the year in which the first broadcast/transmission is made. Published editions remain under copyright protection for 25 years from the end of the year in which the edition was published. An EC Directive effective from January 1998 created a 15-year non-copyright called 'database right' to protect substantial investment in obtaining, verifying or presenting the contents of a database.

The main international treaties protecting copyright are the Bern Convention for the Protection of Literary and Artistic Works, the Rome Convention for the Protection of Performers, Producers of Phonograms and Broadcasting Organisations, and the Universal Copyright Convention (UCC); the UK is a signatory to these conventions. Copyright material created by UK nationals or residents is protected in each country which is a member of the conventions by the national law of that country. A list of participating countries may be obtained from the Patent Office. The World Trade Organisation Trade-Related Aspects of Intellectual Property Agreement (TRIPS) also confers reciprocal obligations on signatory states to protect copyright works.

Two new treaties were agreed in December 1996, but have yet to enter into force. These are WIPO (World Intellectual Property Organisation) Copyright Treaty, and the WIPO Performance and Phonograms Treaty, which strengthen and update international standards of protection, particularly in relation to new technologies.

### LICENSING

Use of copyright material without seeking permission in each instance may be permitted under "blanket" licences available from copyright licensing agencies.The International Federation of Reproduction Rights Organisations facilitates agreements between its member licensing agencies and on behalf of its members with organisations such as the WIPO, UNESCO, the European Union and the Council of Europe.

## PATENTS

A patent is a document issued by the Patent Office relating to an invention and giving the proprietor monopoly rights, effective within the United Kingdom (including the Isle of Man). In return the patentee pays a fee to cover the costs of processing the patent and publicly discloses details of the invention.

To qualify for a patent an invention must be new, must exhibit an inventive step, and must be capable of industrial application. The patent is valid for a maximum of 20 years from the date on which the application was filed, subject to payment of annual fees from the end of the fourth year.

The Patent Office, established in 1852, is responsible for ensuring that all stages of an application comply with the Patents Act 1977, and that the invention meets the criteria for a patent. Patent Office Examiners check that the invention is new and innovative by searching previously published documents on the Patent Office databank, which contains details of some two million British patents and published international and European patents via online databases. The contents of the databank and of the Science Reference Library, which developed from the library established at the Patent Office, are available to the public.

The WIPO is responsible for administering many of the international conventions on intellectual property. The Patent Co-operation Treaty allows inventors to file a single application for patent rights in some or all of the contracting states. This application is searched by an International Searching Authority and published by the International Bureau of WIPO. It may also be the subject of an (optional) international preliminary examination. Applicants must then deal directly with the patent offices in the countries where they are seeking patent rights.

The European Patent Convention, linked to the Patent Co-operation Treaty, allows inventors to obtain patent rights in all the contracting states by filing a single European patent application which is processed by the European Patent Office (EPO). Once granted, the patent is subject to national laws in each signatory country. To comply with security requirements, an applicant resident in the UK must file a European patent application with the UK Patent Office unless the Patent Office gives permission for it to be filed directly with the EPO.

## TRADE MARKS

Trade marks are a means of identification, whether a word or device or a combination of both, a logo, or the shape of goods or their packaging, which enable traders to make their goods or services readily distinguishable from those supplied by other traders. Registration prevents other traders using the same or a similar trade mark for similar products or services for which the mark is registered.

In the UK trade marks are registered at the Trade Marks Registry in the Patent Office. In order to qualify for registration a mark must be capable of distinguishing its proprietor's goods or services from those of other undertakings. It should be non-deceptive and not easily confused with a mark that has already been registered for the same or similar goods or services. The relevant current legislation is the Trade Marks Act 1994.

It is possible to obtain an international trade mark registration, effective in 68 countries, under the Madrid Agreement. UK companies cannot take advantage of this because the UK is not a party to this agreement. Following revision of UK trade marks law, however, the UK has ratified the protocol to the Madrid Agreement, and British companies can now obtain international trade mark registration through a single application to WIPO in those countries party to the protocol.

EC trade mark regulation is now in force and is administered by the Office for Harmonisation in the Internal Market (Trade Marks and Designs) in Alicante, Spain. The office registers EC trade marks, which are a unitary right valid throughout the European Union.

## DESIGN PROTECTION

Design protection covers the outward appearance of an article and takes two forms in the UK, registered design and design right, which are not mutually exclusive. Registered design protects the aesthetic appearance of an article, including shape, configuration, pattern or ornament, although artistic works such as sculptures are excluded, being generally protected by copyright. In order to qualify for protection, a design must be new and materially different from earlier UK published designs. The owner of the design must apply to the Designs Registry at the Patent Office. Initial registration lasts for five years and is extendible in five-yearly steps to a maximum of 25 years. The current legislation is the Registered Designs Act 1949 (as amended).

There is no international design registry currently available to UK applicants; in general, separate applications must be made in each country in which protection is sought. However, the EC Directive for the Legal Protection of Designs was adopted in 1998 to harmonise laws on certain aspects of design protection throughout the European Union. Member states are to amend their laws to comply with the Directive by 28 October 2001.

Design right is an automatic right which applies to the shape or configuration of articles and does not require registration. Designs must be original and non-commonplace. The term of design right is ten years from first marketing of the design and the right is effective only in the UK. The current legislation is Part 3 of the Copyright, Designs and Patents Act 1988.

## LEGAL DEPOSIT

Publishers are legally obliged to send one copy of a new publication to each of the legal deposit libraries within one month of publication. The aim of legal deposit is to keep a complete national archive of published works as a current reference and information source. The legal deposit libraries are the British Library, the Bodleian Library in Oxford, Cambridge University Library, the National Library of Scotland, the National Library of Wales, and Trinity College Library in Dublin.

In 1998 the Report of the Working Party on Legal Deposit recommended that legislation should be introduced establishing legal deposit for certain electronically published materials (mainly CD-ROMs). The Government agreed in principle, but called for a voluntary scheme to be established first. In mid-1999 negotiations between publishers and the copyright libraries to agree a code of practice were still under way.

## ORGANISATIONS

COPYRIGHT LIBRARIES AGENCY, 100 Euston Street, London NW1 2HQ. Tel: 020-7388 5061.

CHARTERED INSTITUTE OF PATENT AGENTS, Staple Inn Buildings, High Holborn, London WC1V 7PZ. Tel: 020-7405 9450, *Secretary and Registrar:* M. Ralph

DESIGNS REGISTRY, The Patent Office, Cardiff Road, Newport NP10 8QQ. Tel: 0845-950-0505

EUROPEAN PATENT OFFICE, *Headquarters*, Erhardtstrasse 27, D-8000, Munich 2, Germany. Tel: 49-399 4538

INTERNATIONAL FEDERATION OF REPRODUCTION RIGHTS ORGANISATIONS (IFRRO), rue du Prince Royal 87, B-1050 Brussels, Belgium. Tel: 32-551 0899

LEGAL DEPOSIT OFFICE, The British Library, Boston Spa, Wetherby, W. Yorks LS23 7BY. Tel: 01937-546267

NEWSPAPER LEGAL DEPOSIT OFFICE, The British Library, Newspaper Library, Colindale Avenue, London NW9 5LF. Tel: 020-7412 7378

OFFICE FOR HARMONISATION IN THE INTERNAL MARKET (TRADE MARKS AND DESIGNS), Avenida de Europa 4, Aptdo de Correos 77, E-03080 Alicante, Spain, Tel: 34 139459

THE PATENT OFFICE, Cardiff Road, Newport NP10 8QQ. Tel: 0845-950 0505

SCIENCE REFERENCE LIBRARY, 96 Euston Road, London NW1 2DB. Tel: 020-7412 7494

STATIONERS' HALL REGISTRY LTD, The Registrar, Stationers' Hall, Ave Maria Lane, London EC4M 7DD. Tel: 020-7248 2934

TRADE MARKS REGISTRY, The Patent Office, Cardiff Road, Newport NP10 8QQ. Tel: 0845-950 0505

WORLD INTELLECTUAL PROPERTY ORGANISATION (WIPO), 34 chemin des Colombettes, 1211 Geneva 20, Switzerland. Tel: 41-338 9111

### COPYRIGHT LICENSING/COLLECTING AGENCIES

AUTHORS' LICENSING AND COLLECTING SOCIETY, Marlborough Court, 14–18 Holborn, London EC1N 2LE. Tel: 020-7395 0600

CHRISTIAN COPYRIGHT LICENSING (EUROPE) LTD, PO Box 1339, Eastbourne, E. Sussex BN21 4YF. Tel: 01323-417711

COPYRIGHT LICENSING AGENCY LTD, 90 Tottenham Court Road, London W1P 0LP. Tel: 020-7631 5555.

DESIGN AND ARTISTS COPYRIGHT SOCIETY, Parchment House, 13 Northburgh Street, London EC1V 0JP. Tel: 020-7336 8811

EDUCATIONAL RECORDING AGENCY LTD, New Premier House, 150 Southampton Row, London WC1B 5AL. Tel: 020-7837 3222

INTERNATIONAL FEDERATION OF THE PHONOGRAPHIC INDUSTRIES, 54 Regent Street, London W1B 5RE. Tel: 020-7878 7900. Fax: 020-7878 7950.

MCPS-PRS ALLIANCE, Copyright House, 29–33 Berners Street, London W1T 3AB. Tel: 020-7580 5544

NEWSPAPER LICENSING AGENCY, Wellington Gate, Church Road, Tunbridge Wells, Kent TN1 1NL. Tel: 01892-525274

PHONOGRAPHIC PERFORMANCE LTD, 1 Upper James Street, London W1F 9DE. Tel: 020-7534 1000.

PUBLISHERS LICENSING SOCIETY, 5 Dryden Street, London WC2E 9NW. Tel: 020-7829 8486.

VIDEO PERFORMANCE LTD, 1 Upper James Street, London W1R 3HG. Tel: 020-7534 1400

# The Media

### Cross-Media Ownership

There are rules on cross-media ownership to prevent undue concentration of ownership. These were amended by the Broadcasting Act 1996. Radio companies are now permitted to own one AM, one FM and one other (AM or FM) service; ownership of the third licence is subject to a public interest test. Local newspapers with a circulation under 20 per cent in an area are also allowed to own one AM, one FM and one other service, and may control a regional Channel 3 television service subject to a public interest test. Local newspapers with a circulation between 20 and 50 per cent in an area may own one AM and one FM service, subject to a public interest test, but may not control a regional Channel 3 service. Those with a circulation over 50 per cent may own one radio service in the area (provided that more than one independent local radio service serves the area) subject to a public interest test.

Ownership controls on the number of television or radio licences have been removed; holdings are now restricted to 15 per cent of the total television audience or 15 per cent of the total points available in the radio points scheme. Ownership controls on cable operators have also been removed. National newspapers with less than 20 per cent of national circulation may apply to control any broadcasting licences, subject to a public interest test. National newspapers with more than 20 per cent of national circulation may not have more than a 20 per cent interest in a licence to provide a Channel 3 service, Channel 5 or national and local analogue radio services.

## Broadcasting

The British Broadcasting Corporation is responsible for public service broadcasting in the UK. Its constitution and finances are governed by royal charter and agreement. On 1 May 1996 a new royal charter came into force, establishing the framework for the BBC's activities until 2006.

The Independent Television Commission and the Radio Authority were set up under the terms of the Broadcasting Act 1990. The ITC is the regulator and licensing authority for all commercially-funded television services, including cable and satellite services. The Radio Authority is the regulator and licensing authority for all independent radio services.

### Complaints

The Broadcasting Standards Commisson was set up in April 1997 under the Broadcasting Act 1996 and was formed from the merger of the Broadcasting Complaints Commission and the Broadcasting Standards Council. The Commission considers and adjudicates upon complaints of unfair treatment or unwarranted infringement of privacy in all broadcast programmes and advertisements on television, radio, cable, satellite and digital services. It also monitors the portrayal of violence and sex, and matters of taste and decency. Its new code of practice came into force on 1 January 1998.

Broadcasting Standards Commission, 7 The Sanctuary, London SW1P 3JS. Tel: 020-7808 1000. *Chairman*, Lord Dubs of Battersea; *Deputy Chairman*, Lady Suzanne Warner; *Director*, Paul Bolt

## TELEVISION

All channels are broadcast in colour on 625 lines UHF from a network of transmitting stations. The BBC's transmission network was sold to the Castle Tower Consortium in February 1997; ITV transmission services are owned and operated by National Transcommunications Ltd. Transmissions are available to more than 99 per cent of the population.

The total number of television licences in force in the UK at the end of March 2001 was 22,814,000, of which 99.3 per cent were for colour televisions. Annual television licence fees until 1 April 2002 are: monochrome £36.50; colour £109.00.

No overall statistics are available for subscriptions in the UK to satellite television services; British Sky Broadcasting had 9.5 million subscribers at the end of June 2001 (5.5 million via digital and analogue satellite, 2.7 million via cable and 1.1 million via digital terrestrial television).

### Digital Television

Digital broadcasting will increase the number and quality of television channels. It uses digital modulation to improve reception and digital compression to make more effective use of the frequency channels available than PAL, the analogue system currently used.

The Broadcasting Act 1996 provided for the licensing of 20 or more digital terrestrial television channels (on six frequency channels or 'multiplexes'). Analogue broadcasting will eventually be discontinued, with the frequencies being sold to mobile telephone companies.

In June 1997 the licences to run the remaining digital multiplexes were awarded by the ITC to British Digital Broadcasting (now called ONdigital), a consortium led by Carlton Communications and Granada. The first digital services went on air in autumn 1998. A set-top digital decoder or an integrated digital television set is required to convert the digital signals into analogue sound and picture waves in order to watch the digital channels. Digital television services are also offered by cable and satellite companies.

Estimated Audience Share *for 12 months to 31 March 2001*

| | Percentage (rounded) |
|---|---|
| ITV companies | 28.5 |
| BBC 1 | 26.7 |
| BBC 2 | 11.0 |
| Cable, satellite and digital channels | 17.4 |
| Channel 4 | 9.9 |
| Channel 5 | 5.6 |
| S4C Wales | 0.3 |

*Source*: Independent Television Commission

### BBC TELEVISION

Television Centre, Wood Lane, London W12 7RJ. Tel: 020-8743 8000. Web: www.bbc.co.uk/info

The BBC's experiments in television broadcasting started in 1929 and in 1936 the BBC began the world's first public service of high-definition television from Alexandra Palace. The BBC broadcasts two UK-wide terrestrial television services, BBC One and BBC Two; outside

England these services are designated BBC Scotland on One, BBC Scotland on Two, BBC One Northern Ireland, BBC Two Northern Ireland, BBC Wales on One and BBC Wales on Two. The BBC's digital services include BBC One, BBC Two, BBC Choice, BBC Knowledge and BBC News. The services are funded by the licence fee.

BBC WORLDWIDE LTD
Woodlands, 80 Wood Lane, London W12 0TT
Tel 020-8433 2000; Fax: 020-8749 0538
Web: www.bbcworldwide.com

BBC Worldwide Limited is the commercial arm, and a wholly owned subsidiary, of the British Broadcasting Corporation. The company was formed in 1994 to develop a co-ordinated approach to the BBC's commercial activities; television, publishing, product licensing, Internet and interactive media. BBC Worldwide exists to maximise the value of the BBC's programme and publishing assets for the benefit of the licence payer, and re-invest in public service programming.

## INDEPENDENT TELEVISION

The ITV franchises for the 15 regional companies and for breakfast television were allocated new ten-year licences from January 1993. Since 1998 licensees have had several opportunities to apply for renewal of their licence; the last such opportunity was in 2001. The ITC received bids for the licence for a new independent national television channel in May 1995. The winner was Channel 5 Broadcasting Ltd and the new channel was launched on 30 March 1997.

ITV NETWORK CENTRE/ITV ASSOCIATION
200 Gray's Inn Road, London WC1X 8HF.
Tel: 020-7843 8000

The ITV Network Centre is wholly owned by the ITV companies and undertakes the commissioning and scheduling of those television programmes which are shown across the ITV network. Through its sister organisation, the ITV Association, it also provides a range of services to the ITV companies where a common approach is required.

In December 1998 ITV launched an addition digital channel called ITV2.
*Chairman*, Leslie Hill

### INDEPENDENT TELEVISION NETWORK COMPANIES

ANGLIA TELEVISION LTD (owned by United Broadcasting and Entertainment) (*eastern England*), Anglia House, Norwich NR1 3JG. Tel: 01603-615151 Web: www.anglia.tv.co.uk

BORDER TELEVISION PLC (*the Borders*), The Television Centre, Carlisle CA1 3NT. Tel: 01228-525101 Web: www.border-tv.com

CARLTON UK TELEVISION (*London* (*weekdays*)), 101 St Martin's Lane, London WC2N 4AZ. Tel: 020-7240 4000 Web: www.carlton.com

CENTRAL INDEPENDENT TELEVISION LTD (owned by Carlton Communications) (*the Midlands*), Central Court, Gas Street, Birmingham B1 2JT. Tel: 0121-643 9898

CHANNEL TELEVISION LTD (*Channel Islands*), The Television Centre, St Helier, Jersey JE1 3ZD. Tel: 01534-816816 Web: www.channeltv.co.uk

GMTV LTD (*breakfast television*), The London Television Centre, Upper Ground, London SE1 9TT. Tel: 020-7827 7000 Web: www.gmtv.co.uk

GRAMPIAN TELEVISION PLC (owned by Scottish Media) (*northern Scotland*), Queen's Cross, Aberdeen AB15 2XJ. Tel: 01224-846846 Web: www.grampiantv.co.uk

GRANADA TELEVISION LTD (owned by Granada Media) (*north-west England*), Quay Street, Manchester M60 9EA. Tel: 0161-832 7211 Web: www.granadatv.co.uk

HTV GROUP PLC (owned by United Broadcasting and Entertainment ) (*Wales and western England*), HTV Wales, The Television Centre, Culverhouse Cross, Cardiff CF5 6XJ. Tel: 029-2059 0590; HTV West, The Television Centre, Bath Road, Bristol BS4 3HG. Tel: 0117-977 8366

LONDON WEEKEND TELEVISION LTD (owned by Granada Media) (*London* (*weekends*)), The London Television Centre, Upper Ground, London SE1 9LT. Tel: 020-7620 1620 Web: www.lwt.co.uk

MERIDIAN BROADCASTING LTD (owned by United Broadcasting and Entertainment) (*south and south-east England*), The Television Centre, Southampton SO14 0PZ. Tel: 023-8022 2555 Web: www.meridian.co.uk

SCOTTISH TELEVISION PLC (owned by Scottish Media) (*central Scotland*), Cowcaddens, Glasgow G2 3PR. Tel: 0141-300 3000 Web: www.scottishtv.co.uk

TYNE TEES TELEVISION LTD (owned by Granada Media) (*north-east England*), The Television Centre, City Road, Newcastle upon Tyne NE1 2AL. Tel: 0191-261 0181

ULSTER TELEVISION PLC (*Northern Ireland*), Havelock House, Ormeau Road, Belfast BT7 1EB. Tel: 028-9032 8122 Web: www.utvlive.com

WESTCOUNTRY TELEVISION LTD (owned by Carlton Communications) (*south-west England*), Langage Science Park, Plymouth PL7 5BG. Tel: 01752-333333

YORKSHIRE TELEVISION LTD (owned by Granada Media) (*Yorkshire*), The Television Centre, Kirkstall Rd, Leeds LS3 1JS. Tel: 0113-243 8283

### OTHER INDEPENDENT TELEVISION COMPANIES

CHANNEL 5 BROADCASTING LTD, 22 Long Acre, London WC2E 9LY. Tel: 020-7550 5555

CHANNEL FOUR TELEVISION CORPORATION, 124 Horseferry Road, London SW1P 2TX. Tel: 020-7396 4444. Provides a service to the UK except Wales and is charged to cater for interests under-represented by the ITV network companies. Channel 4 sells its own advertising.

INDEPENDENT TELEVISION NEWS LTD, 200 Gray's Inn Road, London WC1X 8XZ. Tel: 020-7833 3000

TELETEXT LTD, 101 Farm Lane, London SW6 1QJ. Tel: 020-7386 5000. Provides teletext services for the ITV companies and Channel 4

WELSH FOURTH CHANNEL AUTHORITY (Sianel Pedwar Cymru), Parc Ty Glas, Llanishen, Cardiff CF4 5DU. Tel: 029-2074 7444. S4C schedules Welsh language and most Channel 4 programmes.

## DIRECT BROADCASTING BY SATELLITE TELEVISION

BRITISH SKY BROADCASTING LTD, 6 Centaurs Business Park, Grant Way, Isleworth, Middx TW7 5QD. Tel: 020-7705 3000.

British Sky Broadcasting is the UK's broadband entertainment company, delivering sports, movies, entertainment and news to nearly 10 million households throughout the UK and Eire (5.5 via digital and analogue satellite, 2.9 via cable and 1.1 via digital terrestrial television).

Sky Digital, launched on 1 October 1998, offers over 200 channels, pay-per-view services and interactive entertainment (including the launch of Open... in October 1999, Sky Sports Active in August 1999 and Sky News Live in June 2000). It has attracted more than 5 million customers to date.

British Sky Broadcasting is one of the largest private sector employers in Scotland with more than 6000 individuals, the majority employed at Sky's call centres in Livingston and Dumfermline.

## RADIO

UK domestic radio services are broadcast across three wavebands: FM (or VHF), medium wave (also referred to as AM) and long wave (used by BBC Radio 4). In the UK the FM waveband extends in frequency from 87.5 MHz to 108 MHz and the medium wave band extends from 531 kHz to 1602 kHz. Some radios are still calibrated in wavelengths rather than frequency. To convert frequency to wavelength, divide 300,000 by the frequency in kHz.

### DIGITAL RADIO

Digital radio allows more services to be broadcast to a higher technical quality and provides the data facility for text and pictures. It improves the robustness of high fidelity radio services, especially compared with current FM and AM radio transmissions. It was developed in a collaborative research project under the pan-European EUREKA initiative and has been adopted as a world standard for new digital radio systems. The frequencies allocated for terrestrial digital radio in the UK are 217.5 to 230 MHz.

The Broadcasting Act 1996 provided for the licensing of digital radio services (on seven frequency channels or 'multiplexes'). The BBC has been allocated a multiplex capable of broadcasting six to eight national stereo services; BBC digital broadcasts began in the London area in September 1995. A national digital multiplex has also been made available to the three independent national radio stations, and local and regional services (BBC and commercial) will use the remaining five multiplexes. The Radio Authority is responsible for awarding licences for capacity on the non-BBC multiplexes. The first national independent radio digital licence was awarded to Digital One, which began broadcastingin November 1999. The first local multiplex licence was awarded in May 1999 (to CE Digital, for Birmingham) and commenced broadcasting in May 2000. It is necessary to buy a new digital radio set in order to receive digital radio broadcasts.

### ESTIMATED AUDIENCE SHARE *Ending June 2001*

| | Percentage |
|---|---|
| BBC Radio 1 | 9.6 |
| BBC Radio 2 | 14.3 |
| BBC Radio 3 | 1.1 |
| BBC Radio 4 | 10.7 |
| BBC Radio 5 Live | 4.2 |
| BBC Local/Regional | 11.4 |
| Atlantic 252 | 0.5 |
| Classic FM | 4.3 |
| talkSport (wasTalk Radio) | 1.5 |
| Virgin Radio (AM only) | 1.6 |
| Local commercial | 38.6 |
| Other | 2.1 |

*Source:* RAJAR/RSL

## BBC RADIO

Broadcasting House, Portland Place, London W1A 1AA.
Tel: 020-7580 4468

BBC Radio broadcasts five network services to the UK, Isle of Man and the Channel Islands. There is also a tier of national services in Wales, Scotland and Northern Ireland and 39 local radio stations in England and the Channel Islands. In Wales and Scotland there are also dedicated language services in Welsh and Gaelic respectively.

### BBC NETWORK RADIO SERVICES

RADIO 1 (Contemporary pop music, social action campaigns and entertainment news) – 24 hours a day. *Frequencies:* 97.6–99.8 FM, coverage 99%

RADIO 2 (Popular music, entertainment, comedy and the arts) – 24 hours a day. *Frequencies:* 88–90.2 FM, coverage 99%

RADIO 3 (Classical music, classic drama, documentaries and features) – 24 hours a day. *Frequencies:* 90.2–92.4 FM, coverage 99%

RADIO 4 (News, documentaries, drama, entertainment, and cricket on long wave in season) – 5.55a.m.–1.00a.m. daily, with BBC World Service overnight. *Frequencies:* 92.4–94.6 FM, and 198 LW, coverage 99%

RADIO 5 LIVE (News and sport) – 24 hours a day. *Frequencies:* 693 and 909 MW

### BBC NATIONAL RADIO SERVICES

RADIO SCOTLAND *Frequencies:* 810 MW plus two local fillers; 92.4–94.7 FM, coverage 99%. Local programmes on FM as above: HIGHLANDS; NORTH-EAST; BORDERS; SOUTH-WEST (also 585 MW); ORKNEY; SHETLAND

RADIO NAN GAIDHEAL (Gaelic service) *Frequencies:* 103.5–105 FM, 990 MW in Aberdeen, coverage 90%.

RADIO ULSTER *Frequencies:* 1341 MW (873 MW Enniskillen), plus two local fillers; 92.4–95.4 FM, coverage 96%. Local programmes on RADIO FOYLE *Frequencies:* 792 AM; 93.1 MW

RADIO WALES *Frequencies:* 882 MW plus two local fillers; 95.1 FM, 95.9 FM (*Gwent*), 103.9 FM (Cardiff), 95.4 FM (Wrexham), coverage 97%

RADIO CYMRU (Welsh-language) *Frequencies:* 92.4–94.6 FM, 95.7 FM (*Llanfyllin*), 96.1 FM (*Llandinam*), 96.8 FM and 103.5–105 FM, coverage 97%

### BBC LOCAL RADIO STATIONS

There are 40 local stations serving England and the Channel Islands:

ASIAN NETWORK, Epic House, Charles Street, Leicester LE1 3SH. Tel: 0116-251 6688. *Frequencies:* 828/837/1458 MW

BERKSHIRE, BBC Radio Berkshire, PO Box 1044, Reading RG94 8FH. Tel: 0645 311444. *Frequencies*: 94.6, 95.4, 104.1, 104.4 FM

BRISTOL/SOMERSET SOUND, PO Box 194, Bristol BS99 7QT. Tel: 0117-974 1111; *Frequencies:* 94.9, 95.5, 104.6, 1548 MW

CAMBRIDGESHIRE, PO Box 96, Hills Road, Cambridge CB2 1LD. Tel: 01223-259696. *Frequencies:* 95.7/96.0 FM, 1026/1449 MW

CLEVELAND, PO Box 95FM, Newport Road, Middlesbrough TS1 5DG. Tel: 01642-225211. *Frequencies:* 95.0/95.8 FM

CORNWALL, Phoenix Wharf, Truro, Cornwall TR1 1UA. Tel: 01872-275421. *Frequencies:* 95.2/96.0/103.9 FM, 630/657 MW

COVENTRY AND WARWICKSHIRE, Holt Court, 1 Greyfriars Road, Coventry CV1 2WR. Tel: 024-7623 1231. *Frequencies:* 94.8/103.7/104.0 FM
CUMBRIA, Annetwell Street, Carlisle CA3 8BB. Tel: 01228-592444. *Frequencies:* 95.2/95.6/96.1/104.1 FM, 756/837/1458 MW
DERBY, PO Box 269, Derby DE1 3HL. Tel: 01332-361111. *Frequencies:* 94.2/95.3/104.5 FM, 1116 MW
DEVON, PO Box 5, Plymouth PL1 1XT. Tel: 01752-260323. *Frequencies:* 103.4/96.0/95.8/94.8 FM, 801, 855, 990, 1458 MW
ESSEX, 198 New London Road, Chelmsford CM2 9XB. Tel: 01245-616000. *Frequencies:* 95.3/103.3 FM, 729/765/1530 MW
GLOUCESTERSHIRE, London Road, Gloucester GL1 1SW. Tel: 01452-308585. *Frequencies:* 95/95.8/104.7 FM
GMR (GREATER MANCHESTER RADIO), PO Box 951, Oxford Road, Manchester M60 1SD. Tel: 0161-200 2000. *Frequencies:* 95.1/104.6 FM
GUERNSEY, Commerce House, Les Banques, St Peter Port, Guernsey GY1 2HS. Tel: 01481-728977. *Frequencies:* 1116 AM, 93.2 FM
HEREFORD AND WORCESTER, Hylton Road, Worcester WR2 5WW. Tel: 01905-748485. *Frequencies:* 94.7/104.0/104.6 FM, 818/738 MW
HUMBERSIDE, 9 Chapel Street, Hull HU1 3NU. Tel: 01482-323232. *Frequency:* 95.9 FM, 1485 MW
JERSEY, 18 Parade Road, St Helier, Jersey JE2 3PL. Tel: 01534-870000. *Frequencies:* 1026 AM, 88.8 FM
KENT, Sun Pier, Chatham, Kent ME4 4EZ. Tel: 01634-830505. *Frequencies:* 96.7/97.6/104.2 FM, 774/1602 MW
LANCASHIRE, 26 Darwen Street, Blackburn BB2 2EA. Tel: 01254-262411. *Frequencies:* 95.5/103.9/104.5 FM, 855/1557 MW
LEEDS, Broadcasting House, Woodhouse Lane, Leeds LS2 9PN. Tel: 0113-244 2131. *Frequencies:* 774 AM, 92.4/95.3/103.9 FM, 774 MW
LEICESTER, Epic House, Charles Street, Leicester LE1 3SH. Tel: 0116-251 6688. *Frequency:* 104.9 FM
LINCOLNSHIRE, PO Box 219, Newport, Lincoln LN1 3XY. Tel: 01522-511411. *Frequencies:* 94.9 FM, 1368 MW
LONDON, BBC London Live, 35C Marylebone High Street, London W1A 4LG. Tel: 020-7224 2424. *Frequency:* 94.9 FM
MERSEYSIDE, 55 Paradise Street, Liverpool L1 3BP. Tel: 0151-708 5500. *Frequency:* 95.8 FM, 1485 MW
NEWCASTLE, Broadcasting Centre, Barrack Road, Newcastle upon Tyne NE99 1RN. Tel: 0191-232 4141. *Frequencies:* 95.4/96.0/103.7/104.4 FM, 206 MW
NORFOLK, Norfolk Tower, Surrey Street, Norwich NR1 3PA. Tel: 01603-617411. *Frequencies:* 95.1/104.4 FM, 855/873 MW
NORTHAMPTON, Broadcasting House, Abington Street, Northampton NN1 2BH. Tel: 01604-239100. *Frequencies:* 103.6/104.2 FM, 1107 MW
NOTTINGHAM, York House, Mansfield Road, Nottingham NG1 3JB. Tel: 0115-955 0500. *Frequencies:* 95.5/103.8 FM, 1584 MW
OXFORD, BBC Radio Oxford, 269 Banbury Road, Oxford OX2 7DW. Tel: 01865-311444. *Frequency:* 95.2 FM
SHEFFIELD, Ashdell Grove, 60 Westbourne Road, Sheffield S10 2QU. Tel: 0114-268 6185. *Frequencies:* 88.6/94.7/104.1 FM
SHROPSHIRE, 2–4 Boscobel Drive, Shrewsbury SY1 3TT. Tel: 01743-248484. *Frequencies:* 95.0/96.0 FM, 1584 MW
SOLENT, Broadcasting House, Havelock Road, Southampton SO14 7PW. Tel: 023-8063 1311. *Frequencies:* 96.1/ FM, 999 MW
SOMERSET SOUND 14–15 Paul street, Taunton TA1 3PF. Tel: 01823-252437. *Frequency:* 1323 MW
SOUTHERN COUNTIES, Broadcasting Centre, Guildford GU2 5AP. Tel: 01483-306306. *Frequencies:* 95–95.3/104–104.8 FM
STOKE, Cheapside, Hanley, Stoke-on-Trent ST1 1JJ. Tel: 01782-208080. *Frequencies:* 94.6/104.1 FM, 1503 MW
SUFFOLK, Broadcasting House, St Matthew's Street, Ipswich IP1 3EP. Tel: 01473-250000. *Frequencies:* 95.5/103.9/104.6 FM
THREE COUNTIES RADIO, PO Box 3CR, Luton, Beds LU1 5XL. Tel: 01582-637400. *Frequencies:* 95.5/103.8/104.5 FM, 630/1161 MW
WILTSHIRE SOUND, Broadcasting House, Prospect Place, Swindon SN1 3RW. Tel: 01793-513626. *Frequencies:* 103.5/103.6/104.3/104.9 FM, 1332/1368 MW
WM (WEST MIDLANDS), Pebble Mill Road, Birmingham B5 7SD. Tel: 0121-432 8484 *Frequency:* 95.6 FM.
YORK, 20 Bootham Row, York YO3 7BR. Tel: 01904-641351. *Frequencies:* 95.5/103.7/104.3 FM, 666/1260 MW

BBC WORLD SERVICE
Bush House, Strand, London WC2B 4PH.
Tel 020-7240 3456

The BBC World Service broadcasts over 1,000 hours of programmes a week in 43 languages including English. It has a weekly audience of 153 million globally, of whom 42 million listen to English language services. Many services are also available by satellite and on the internet. *UK frequencies:* 648 AM in Southern England and on BBC Radio 4 at night.

The World Service is organised into five world regions, each responsible for programmes in English as well as regional languages.

AFRICA AND THE MIDDLE EAST, Arabic, French, Hausa, Kinyarwanda/Kirundi, Portuguese, Somali and Swahili; English programmes including *Network Africa* and *Focus on Africa*
ASIA AND THE PACIFIC, Bengali, Burmese, Cantonese, Hindi, Indonesian, Mandarin, Nepali, Sinhala, Tamil, Thai, Urdu and Vietnamese; English programmes including *East Asia Today*
EUROPE, Albanian, Bulgarian, Croatian, Czech, Greek, Hungarian, Macedonian, Polish, Romanian, Serbian, Slovak and Slovene; English programmes including *The World Today*
FORMER SOVIET UNION AND SOUTH-WEST ASIA, Azeri, Kazakh, Kyrgyz, Pashto, Persian, Russian, Turkish, Ukrainian and Uzbek
THE AMERICAS, Portuguese for Brazil, Spanish; English programmes including *The World* (a global news magazine for American listeners), *Caribbean Report* and *Calling the Falklands*
BBC ENGLISH teaches English world-wide through radio, television and a wide range of published courses
BBC MARKET INTELLIGENCE carries out audience research and sells printed publications and data
BBC MONITORING supplies news and information from the output of overseas radio and television stations and news agency sources
BBC WORLD SERVICE TRAINING runs journalism, management and skills training courses for overseas broadcasters

## INDEPENDENT RADIO

The Radio Authority began advertising new licences for the development of commercial radio in January 1991. Since then it has awarded three national licences, 101 new local radio licences (including ten regional licences) and one additional service licence (to use the spare capacity in an existing channel which is not used by the programme service). The Authority has also issued about 2,000 restricted service licences (for temporary low-powered radio services). In 2000–2001 the Authority advertised one new analogue licence a month. It also advertised one digital multiplex licence a month and re-advertise existing analogue licences.

COMMERCIAL RADIO COMPANIES ASSOCIATION, 77 Shaftesbury Avenue, London W1V 7AD. Tel: 020-7306 2603. Email: info@crca.co.uk. Web: www.crca.co.uk. *Chief Executive*, P. Brown

### INDEPENDENT NATIONAL RADIO STATIONS

CLASSIC FM, 7 Swallow Place, London W1R 7AA. Tel: 020-7343 9000. 24 hours a day. *Frequencies:* 99.9/101.9 FM

TALK SPORT, 18 Hatfields, London SE1 8DJ . Tel: 020-7959 7900. 24 hours a day. *Frequencies:* 1053/1089 AM

VIRGIN RADIO, 1 Golden Square, London W1R 4DJ. Tel: 020-7434 1215. 24 hours a day. *Frequencies:* 1215/1197/1233/1242/1260 AM

### INDEPENDENT REGIONAL LOCAL RADIO STATIONS

100.7 HEART FM (*west Midlands*), 1 The Square, 111 Broad Street, Birmingham B15 1AS. Tel: 0121-626 1007. *Frequency:* 100.7 FM

CENTURY 105 *(north-west)*, Century House, Waterfront Quay, Salford Quays, Manchester M5 2XW. Tel: 0161-400 0105. *Frequency:* 105.4 FM

CENTURY 106 *(east Midlands)*, City Link, Nottingham NG2 4NG. Tel: 0115-910 6100. *Frequency:* 106.0 FM

CENTURY RADIO (*north-east*), Century House, PO Box 100, Gateshead NE8 2YX. Tel: 0191-477 6666. *Frequencies:* 100.7/101.8/96.2/96.4 FM

GALAXY 101 (*Severn estuary*), Millennium House, 26 Baldwin Street, Bristol BS1 1SE. Tel: 0117-901 0101. *Frequencies:* 101.0/97.2 FM (Bristol)

GALAXY 105 *(Yorkshire)*, Joseph's Well, Westgate, Leeds LS3 1AB. Tel: 0113-213 0105. *Frequencies*: 105.1 FM (Leeds); 105.6 FM (Bradford and Sheffield); 105.8 FM (Hull)

GALAXY 105-106 *(north-east)*, Kingfisher Way, Silverlink Business Park, Tyne and Wear NE28 9ND. Tel: 0191-206 8000. *Frequencies:* 105.3/105.6/106.4 FM

JAZZ FM 100.4 (*north-west*), The World Trade Centre, Exchange Quay, Manchester M5 3EJ. Tel: 0161-877 1004. *Frequency*: 100.4 FM

SCOT FM (*central Scotland*), 1 Albert Quay, Leith EH6 7DN. Tel: 0131-554 6677. *Frequencies:* 100.3/101.1 FM

VIBE FM (*east*), Reflection House, The Anderson Centre, Olding Road, Bury St Edmunds, Suffolk IP33 3TA. Tel: 01284-718800. *Frequencies:* 107.7 FM (Peterborough); 105.6 FM (Cambridge); 106.1 FM (Norwich); 106.4 FM (Ipswich)

WAVE 105 FM *(Solent)*, 5 Manor Court, Barnes Wallis Road, Segensworth East, Fareham, Hants PO15 5TH. Tel: 01489-481050. *Frequencies:* 105.2 FM (Solent); 105.8 FM (Poole)

### INDEPENDENT LOCAL RADIO STATIONS

*England*

2-TEN FM, PO Box 2020, Reading RG31 7FG. Tel: 0118-945 4400. *Frequencies:* 97.0/102.9/103.4 FM

2BR FM, Imex Lomeshaye Business Village, Nelson, Lancs BB9 7DR. Tel: 01282 690000. *Frequency*: 99.8 FM

2CR FM, 5 Southcote Road, Bournemouth BH1 3LR. Tel: 01202-259259. *Frequency:* 102.3 FM

96 TRENT FM 29–31 Castle Gate, Nottingham NG1 7AP. Tel: 0115-952 7000. *Frequencies:* 96.2/96.5 FM

96.3 AIRE FM, 51 Burley Road, Leeds LS3 1LR. Tel: 0113-283 5500. *Frequency:* 96.3 FM

96.4 FM BRMB, Nine Brindleyplace, 4 Oozells Square, Birmingham B1 2DJ. Tel: 0121-245 5000. *Frequency:* 96.4 FM

96.4 THE EAGLE, Dolphin House, North Street, Guildford, Surrey GU1 4AA. Tel: 01483-300964. *Frequency:* 96.4 FM

96.9 VIKING FM, Commercial Road, Hull HU1 2SG. Tel: 01482-325141. *Frequency:* 96.9 FM

97.2 STRAY FM, PO Box 972, Station Parade, Harrogate HG1 5YF. Tel: 01423-522972. *Frequency:* 97.2 FM

97.4 VALE FM, Longmead, Shaftesbury, Dorset SP7 8QQ. Tel: 01747-855711. *Frequency:* 97.4 FM

102.4 WISH FM, Orrell Lodge, Orrell Road, Orrell, Wigan WN5 8HJ. Tel: 01942-761024. *Frequency:* 102.4 FM

102.7 HEREWARD FM, PO Box 225, Queensgate Centre, Peterborough PE1 1XJ. Tel: 01733-460460. *Frequency:* 102.7 FM

103.2 POWER FM, Radio House, Whittle Avenue, Segensworth West, Fareham, Hants PO15 5SH. Tel: 01489-589911. *Frequency:* 103.2 FM

103.4 THE BEACH, PO Box 103.4, Lowestoft, Suffolk NR32 2TL. Tel: 07000-001035. *Frequency:* 103.4 FM

106 CTFM RADIO, 16 Lower Bridge Street, Canterbury, Kent CT1 2HQ. Tel: 01227-789106. *Frequency:* 106.0 FM

106.9 SILK FM, Radio House, Bridge Street, Macclesfield, Cheshire SK11 6DJ. Tel: 01625-268000. *Frequency:* 106.9 FM

107 OAK FM, 7 Waldron Court, Prince William Road, Loughborough, Leics LE11 5GD. Tel: 01509-211711. *Frequency:* 107.0 FM

107.2 WIRE FM, Warrington Business Park, Long Lane, Warrington WA2 8TX. Tel: 01925-445545. *Frequency:* 107.2 FM

107.3 THE EAGLE, Bristol Evening Post Building, Temple Way, Bristol BS99 7HD. Tel: 0117-910 6600. *Frequency:* 107.3 FM

107.4 TELFORD FM, PO Box 1074, Telford TF3 3WG. Tel: 01952-280011. *Frequency:*107.4 FM

107.5 CAT FM, Regent Arcade, Cheltenham, Glos GL50 1JZ. Tel: 01242-699555. *Frequency:* 107.5 FM

107.6 KESTREL FM, 2nd Floor, Paddington House, The Walks Shopping Centre, Basingstoke, Hants RG21 7LJ. Tel: 01256-694000. *Frequency:* 107.6 FM

107.7 CHELMER FM, Cater House, High Street, Chelmsford, Essex CM1 1AL. Tel: 01245-259400. *Frequency:* 107.7 FM

107.7 THE WOLF, 10th Floor, Mander House, Wolverhampton WV1 3NB. Tel: 01902-571070. *Frequency:* 107.7 FM

107.7 WFM, 11 Beaconsfield Road, Weston-super-Mare, Somerset BS23 1YE. Tel: 01934-624455. *Frequency:* 107.7FM

107.8 ARROW FM, Priory Meadow Centre, Hastings, E. Sussex TN34 1PJ. Tel: 01424-461177. *Frequency:* 107.8 FM

107.8 FM THAMES RADIO, Brentham House, 45C High Street, Hampton Wick, Kingston upon Thames KT1 4DG. Tel: 020-8288 1300. *Frequency:* 107.8 FM

107.9 THE EAGLE, Radio House, Sturton Street, Cambridge CB1 2QF. Tel: 01223-722300. *Frequency:* 107.9 FM

963/972 LIBERTY RADIO, 7th Floor, Trevor House, 100 Brompton Road, London SW3 1ER. Tel: 020-7893 8966. *Frequency:* 963/972 AM

1458 LITE AM, PO Box 1458, Quay West, Trafford Park, Manchester M17 1FL. Tel: 0161-872 1458. *Frequency:* 1458 AM

ACTIVE 107.5 FM, Lambourne House, 7 Western Road, Romford, Essex RM1 3LD. Tel: 01708-731643. *Frequency:* 107.5 FM

ALPHA 103.2, Radio House, 11 Woodland Road, Darlington DL3 7BJ. Tel: 01325-255552. *Frequency:* 103.2 FM

ASIAN SOUND RADIO, Globe House, Southall Street, Manchester M3 1LG. Tel: 0161-288 1000. *Frequencies:* 1377/963 AM

B97 Chiltern FM, 55 Goldington Road, Bedford MK40 3LT. Tel: 01234-272400. *Frequency:* 96.9 FM

BATH FM, Station House, Ashley Avenue, Lower Weston, Bath BA1 3DS. Tel: 01225-471571. *Frequency:* 107.9 FM

THE BAY, PO Box 969, St George's Quay, Lancaster LA1 3LD. Tel: 01524-848747. *Frequencies:* 96.9/102.3/103.2 FM

BCR FM, 33 Manor Road, Bridgwater, Somerset TA6 4RJ. Tel: 01278 444211. *Frequencies*: to be announced.

BEACON FM, 267 Tettenhall Road, Wolverhampton WV6 0DQ. Tel: 01902-461300. *Frequencies:* 97.2 FM (Wolverhampton and Black Country); 103.1 FM (Shrewsbury and Telford)

BIG AM, Forster Square, Bradford, Yorks BD1 5NE. Tel: 01274 203040. *Frequencies*: 1278/1530 AM

BIG 1170, Stoke Road, Stoke-on-Trent ST4 2SR. Tel: 01782-747047. *Frequency*: 1170 AM

BIG 1458 AM, 4th Floor, Quay West, Trafford Park, Manchester M17 1FL. Tel: 0161-607 0420. *Frequency*: 1458 AM

THE BREEZE, Radio House, Clifftown Road, Southend-on-Sea, Essex SS1 1SX. Tel: 01702-333711. *Frequencies:* 1359 AM (Chelmsford); 1431 AM (Southend)

BREEZE 1521, The Stanley Centre, Kelvin Way, Crawley, W. Sussex RH10 2SE. Tel: 01293-519161. *Frequency:* 1521 AM

BROADLAND 102, St George's Plain, 47–49 Colegate, Norwich NR3 1DB. Tel: 01603-630621. *Frequency:* 102.4 FM

THE BUZZ 97.1, Media House, Claughton Road, Birkenhead CH41 6EY. Tel: 0151-650 1700. *Frequency:* 97.1 FMCAPITAL FM 30 Leicester Square, London WC2H 7LA. Tel: 020-7766 6000. *Frequency*: 95.8 FM

CAPITAL GOLD (1152), Nine Brindleyplace, 4 Oozells Square, Birmingham B1 2DJ. Tel: 0121-245 5000. *Frequency*: 1152 AM

CAPITAL GOLD (1170 AND 1557), Radio House, Whittle Avenue, Segensworth West, Fareham, Hants PO15 5SH. Tel: 01489-589911. *Frequencies:* 1170/1557 AM

CAPITAL GOLD (1242 AND 603), Radio House, John Wilson Business Park, Whitstable, Kent CT5 3QX. Tel: 01227-772004. *Frequencies:* 603 AM (East Kent); 1242 AM (Maidstone and Medway)

CAPITAL GOLD (1323 AND 945), Radio House, PO Box 2000, Brighton BN41 2SS. Tel: 01273-430111. *Frequencies*: 945/1323 AM

CAPITAL GOLD (1548), 30 Leicester Square, London WC2H 7LA. Tel: 020-7766 6000. *Frequency*: 1548 AM

CENTRE FM, 5–6 Aldergate, Tamworth, Staffs B79 7DJ. Tel: 01827-318000. *Frequencies:* 101.6/102.4 FM

CENTURY (105), Century House, Waterfront Quay, Salford Quays, Manchester M5 2XW. Tel: 0161-400 0105. *Frequency*: 105.4 FM

CENTURY (106), City Link, Nottingham NG2 4NG. Tel: 0115-910 6100. *Frequency*: 106 FM

CENTURY RADIO, Century House, PO Box 100, Gateshead NE8 2YY. Tel: 0191-477 6666. *Frequencies*: 96.2/96.4/100.7/101.8 FM

CFM, PO Box 964, Carlisle, Cumbria CA1 3NG. Tel: 01228-818964. *Frequencies:* 96.4 FM (Penrith); 102.5 FM (Carlisle); 102.2 FM (Workington); 103.4 FM (Whitehaven)

CHANNEL (103), 6 Tunnell Street, St Helier, Jersey JE2 4LU. Tel: 01534-888103. *Frequency*: 103.7 FM

CHANNEL TRAVEL RADIO, Main Control Building, Folkestone, Kent CT18 8XY. Tel: 01303-283873. *Frequency:* 107.6 FM

CHELMER FM (107.7), Cater House, High Street, Chelmsford CM1 1AL. Tel: 01245-259400. *Frequency*: 107.7FM

CHILTERN FM (96.9), 55 Goldington Road, Bedford, Beds MK40 3LT. Tel: 01234-272400. *Frequency:* 96.9 FM

CHILTERN FM (97.6), Chiltern Road, Dunstable, Beds LU6 1HQ. Tel: 01582-676200. *Frequency*: 97.6 FM

CHOICE FM, 291–299 Borough High Street, London SE1 1JG. Tel: 020-7378 3969. *Frequency:* 96.9 FM

CHOICE (107.1), 291-299 Borough High Street, London SE1 1JG. Tel: 020-8348 1033. *Frequency*: 107.1 FM

RADIO CITY 96.7, 8–10 Stanley Street, Liverpool L1 6AF. Tel: 0151-227 5100. *Frequency:* 96.7 FM

CLASSIC GOLD 666/954, Hawthorn House, Exeter Business Park, Exeter EX1 3QS. Tel: 01392-444444. *Frequencies:666/954* AM

CLASSIC GOLD 774, Bridge Studios, Eastgate Centre, Gloucester GL1 1SS. Tel: 01452-313200. *Frequency:* 774 AM

CLASSIC GOLD 792/828, Chiltern Road, Dunstable, Beds LU6 1HQ. Tel: 01582-676200. *Frequencies:* 792 AM (Bedford); 828 AM (Luton)

CLASSIC GOLD 828, 5 Southcote Road, Bournemouth, Dorset BH1 3LR. Tel: 01202-259259. *Frequency:* 828 AM

CLASSIC GOLD 936/1161 AM, PO Box 2000, Swindon SN4 7EX. Tel: 01793-842600. *Frequencies:* 936 AM (West Wilts); 1161 AM (Swindon)

CLASSIC GOLD RADIO 954/1530, The Old Smithy, Post Office Lane, Kempsey, Worcs WR5 3NS. Tel: 01905-820659. *Frequencies:* 954 AM (Hereford); 1530 AM (Worcester)

CLASSIC GOLD 1260, PO Box 2020, Watershed, Canons Road, Bristol BS99 7SN. Tel: 0117-984 3200. *Frequency:* 1260 AM

CLASSIC GOLD 1332 AM, PO Box 2020, Queensgate Centre, Peterborough PE1 1LL. Tel: 01733-460460. *Frequency:* 1332 AM

CLASSIC GOLD 1359, Hertford Place, Coventry CV1 3TT. Tel: 024-7686 8200. *Frequency:* 1359 AM

CLASSIC GOLD 1431/1485, PO Box 2020, Reading RG31 7FG. Tel: 0118-945 4400. *Frequencies:* 1431/1485 AM

CLASSIC GOLD 1557, 19–21 St Edmunds Road, Northampton NN1 5DY. Tel: 01604-795600. *Frequency:* 1557 AM

CLASSIC GOLD AMBER, St George's Plain, 47–49 Colegate, Norwich NR3 1DB. Tel: 01603-630621. *Frequency:* 1152 AM

CLASSIC GOLD AMBER (SUFFOLK), Alpha Business Park, 6–12 White House Road, Ipswich IP1 5LT. Tel: 01473-461000. *Frequency:* 1170 AM (Ipswich); 1251 AM (Bury St Edmunds)

CLASSIC GOLD GEM, 29–31 Castle Gate, Nottingham NG1 7AP. Tel: 0115-952 7000. *Frequencies:* 945/999 AM
CLASSIC GOLD WABC, 267 Tettenhall Road, Wolverhampton WV6 0DQ. Tel: 01902-461300. *Frequencies:* 990 AM (Wolverhampton); 1017 AM (Shrewsbury and Telford)
CONNECT FM, Unit 1, Centre 2000, Kettering, Northants, NN16 8PU. Tel: 01536-412413. *Frequency:* 97.2 FM/107.4 FM
COUNTY SOUND RADIO 1566 MW, Dolphin House, North Street, Guildford GU1 4AA. Tel: 01483-300964. *Frequency:* 1566 MW
DELTA FM 97.1, 65 Weyhill, Haslemere, Surrey GU27 1HN. Tel: 01428-651971. *Frequency:* 97.1/101.6/102 FM
Dream 100 FM, Northgate House, St Peter's Street, Colchester, CO1 1HT. Tel: 01206-764466. *Frequency:* 100.2 FM
DUNE FM, The Power Station, Victoria Way, Southport PR8 1RR. Tel: 01704-502500. *Frequency:* 107.9 FM
ELEVEN SEVENTY, PO Box 1170, High Wycombe, Bucks HP13 6YT. Tel: 01494-446611. *Frequency:* 1170 FM
ESSEX FM, Radio House, Clifftown Road, Southend-on-Sea, Essex SS1 1SX. Tel: 01702-333711. *Frequencies:* 96.3 FM (Southend); 97.5 FM (Southend Centre); 102.6 FM (Chelmsford)
FLR 107.3, Astra House, Arklow Road, London SE14 6EB. Tel: 020-8691 9202. *Frequency:* 107.3 FM
FM 102 – THE BEAR, The Guard House Studios, Banbury Road, Stratford-upon-Avon, Warks CV37 7HX. Tel: 01789-262636. *Frequency:* 102.0 FM
FM 103 HORIZON, The Broadcast Centre, Vincent Avenue, Crownhill, Milton Keynes MK8 0AB. Tel: 01908-269111. *Frequency:* 103.3 FM
FM 107 THE FALCON, Brunel Mall, London Road, Stroud, Glos GL5 2BP. Tel: 01453-767369. *Frequency:* 107.2/107.9 FM
FOSSEWAY RADIO, PO Box 107, Hinckley, Leics LE10 1WR. Tel: 01455-614151. *Frequency:* 107.9 FM
FOX FM, Brush House, Pony Road, Oxford OX4 2XR. Tel: 01865-871000. *Frequencies:* 102.6/97.4 FM
FRESH AM, Gargrave Road, Skipton, N. Yorks BD23 1YD. Tel: 01756-799991. *Frequencies*: 936 MW (Hawes); 1413 MW (Skipton)
GALAXY 101, Millennium House, 26 Baldwin Street, Bristol BS1 1SE. Tel: 0117-901 0101. *Frequencies*: 97.2 FM (Bristol); 101 FM (Severn Estuary)
GALAXY 102, 127–129 Portland Street, Manchester M1 6ED. Tel: 0161-228 0102. *Frequency:* 102.0 FM
GALAXY 102.2, 1 The Square, 111 Broad Street, Birmingham B15 1AS. Tel: 0121-695 0000. *Frequency:* 102.2 FM
GALAXY 105, Joseph's Well, Westgate, Leeds LS3 1AB. Tel: 0113-213 0105. *Frequencies*: 105.1 FM (Leeds); 105.6 FM (Bradford and Sheffield); 105.8 FM (Hull)
GALAXY 105-106, Kingfisher Way, Silverlink Business Park, Tyne and Wear NE28 9ND. Tel: 0191-206 8000. *Frequencies*: 105.3/105.6/106.4 FM
GEMINI FM, Hawthorn House, Exeter Business Park, Exeter EX1 3QS. Tel: 01392-444444. *Frequencies:* 96.4/97.0/103.0 FM
GWR FM (BRISTOL AND BATH), PO Box 2000, Watershed, Canon's Road, Bristol BS99 7SN. Tel: 0117-984 3200. *Frequencies:* 96.3 FM (Bristol); 103.0 FM (Bath)
GWR FM (SWINDON AND WEST WILTSHIRE), PO Box 2000, Swindon SN4 7EX. Tel: 01793-842600. *Frequencies:* 97.2 FM (Swindon); 102.2 FM (West Wilts); 96.5 FM (Marlborough)
HALLAM FM, Radio House, 900 Herries Road, Sheffield S6 1RH. Tel: 0114-285 3333. *Frequencies:* 97.4 FM (Sheffield); 102.9 FM (Barnsley); 103.4 FM (Doncaster)
HEART 106.2 The Chrysalis Building, Bramley Road, London W10 6SP. Tel: 020-7468 1062. *Frequency:* 106.2 FM
HEART FM, 1 The Square, 111 Broad Street, Birmingham B15 1AS. Tel: 0121-695 0000. *Frequency*: 100.7 FM
HERTBEAT 106.9 FM, PO Box 299, Herts, Gertfordshire SG14 3XN. Tel: 01992-505362. *Frequencies*: 106.7/106.9 FM
HOME, The Old Stableblock, Lockwood Park, Huddersfield HD1 3UR. Tel: 01484-321107. *Frequency*: 107.9 FM
IMAGINE FM, Regent House, Heaton Lane, Stockport SK4 1BX. Tel: 0161-285 4545. *Frequencies*: 96.4 FM (Cheshire); 104.9 FM (Stockport)
INVICTA FM, Radio House, John Wilson Business Park, Whitstable, Kent CT5 3QX. Tel: 01227-772004. *Frequencies:* 103.1 FM (Maidstone and Medway); 102.8 FM (Canterbury); 95.9 FM (Thanet); 97.0 FM (Dover); 96.1 FM (Ashford)
ISLAND FM, 12 Westerbrook, St Sampsons, Guernsey GY2 4QQ. Tel: 01481-242000. *Frequencies*: 93.7 FM (Alderney); 104.7 FM (Guernsey)
ISLE OF WIGHT RADIO, Dodnor Park, Newport, Isle of Wight PO30 5XE. Tel: 01983-822557. *Frequencies:* 102.0/107.0 FM
JAZZ FM 102.2, 26–27 Castlereagh Street, London W1H 6DJ. Tel: 020-7706 4100. *Frequency:* 102.2 FM
JAZZ FM 100.4, The World Trade Centre, Exchange Quay, Manchester M5 3EJ. Tel: 0161-877 1004. *Frequency*: 100.4 FM
JUICE 107.2, PO Box 107, Brighton BN1 1QG. Tel: 01273-386107. Frequency: 107.2 FM
JUICE 107.6, 27 Fleet Street, Liverpool L1 4AR. Tel: 0151-707 3107. *Frequency*: 107.6 FM
KCR, PO Box 106, Prescot, Merseyside L35 0RN. Tel: 0151-2901501. Expected on air early 2001. *Frequency*: 106.7 FM
KICK FM, The Studios, 42 Bone Lane, Newbury, Berks RG14 5SD. Tel: 01635-841600. *Frequencies*: 105.6/107.4 FM
KISS 100 FM, Kiss House, 80 Holloway Road, London N7 8JG. Tel: 020-7700 6100. *Frequency:* 100.0 FM
KIX 96, Watch Close, Spon Street, Coventry CV1 3LN. Tel: 024-7652 5656. *Frequency:* 96.2 FM
KL.FM 96.7, PO Box 77, 18 Blackfriars Street, King's Lynn, Norfolk PE30 1NN. Tel: 01553772777. *Frequency:* 96.7 FMLANTERN FM, 2B Lauder Lane, Roundswell Business Park, Barnstaple EX31 3TA. Tel: 01271-340340. *Frequency:* 96.2 FM
LBC 1152 AM, 200 Gray's Inn Road, London WC1X 8XZ. Tel: 020-7973 1152. *Frequency:* 1152 AM
LEICESTER SOUND, Granville House, Granville Road, Leicester LE1 7RW. Tel: 0116-256 1300. *Frequency:* 105.4 FM
LINCS FM, Witham Park, Waterside South, Lincoln LN5 7JN. Tel: 01522-549900. *Frequencies:* 102.2/96.7 FM (Grantham Relay)/97.6 FM (Scunthorpe Relay)
LITE FM, 5 Church Street, Peterborough PE1 1XJ. Tel: 01733-898106. *Frequency:* 106.8 FM
LONDON GREEK RADIO, Florentia Village, Vale Road, London N4 1TD. Tel: 020-8800 8001. *Frequency:* 103.3 FM
LONDON TURKISH RADIO LTR, 185B High Road, Wood Green, London N22 6BA. Tel: 020-8881 0606. *Frequency:* 1584 AM

MAGIC 105.4 FM, The Network Building, 97 Tottenham Court Road, London W1P 9HF. Tel: 020-7504 7000. *Frequency:* 105.4 FM

MAGIC 828, 51 Burley Road, Leeds LS3 1LR. Tel: 0113-283 5500. *Frequency:* 828 AM

MAGIC 999, PO Box 999, Preston, Lancs PR1 1XR. Tel: 01772-556301. *Frequency:* 999 AM

MAGIC 1152, Castle Quay, Castlefield, Manchester M15 4PR. Tel: 0161-288 5000. *Frequency:* 1152 AM

MAGIC 1152 AM, Newcastle upon Tyne NE99 1BB. Tel: 0191-420 3040. *Frequency:* 1152 AM

MAGIC 1161 AM, Commercial Road, Hull HU1 2SG. Tel: 01482-325141. *Frequency:* 1161 AM

MAGIC 1170, Radio House, Yales Crescent, Thornaby, Stockton-on-Tees, Cleveland TS17 6AA. Tel: 01642-888222. *Frequency:* 1170 AM

MAGIC 1548, 8–10 Stanley Street, Liverpool L1 6AF. Tel: 0151-227 5100. *Frequency:* 1548 AM

MAGIC AM, Radio House, 900 Herries Road, Sheffield S6 1RH. Tel: 0114-285 2121. *Frequencies:* 990/1305/1548 AM

MANCHESTER'S MAGIC (1152), Castle Quay, Castlefield, Manachester M15 4PR. Tel: 0161-288 5000. *Frequency:* 1152 AM

MANSFIELD 103.2, The Media Suite, Brunts Business Centre, Samuel Brunts Way, Mansfield, Notts NG18 2AH. Tel: 01623-646666.. *Frequency:* 103.2 FM

MARCHER GOLD, The Studios, Mold Road, Wrexham LL11 4AF. Tel: 01978-752202. *Frequency:* 1260 AM

MEDWAY FM, Berkeley House, 186 High Street, Rochester ME1 1EY. Tel: 01634-841111. *Frequencies:* 107.9/100.4 FM

MERCIA FM, Hertford Place, Coventry CV1 3TT. Tel: 024-7686 8200. *Frequencies:* 97.0/102.9 FM

MERCURY 96.2 FM, 1 East Street, Tonbridge, Kent TN9 1AR. Tel: 01732-369200. *Frequencies*: 96.2 FM (South); 101.6 FM (North)

MERCURY 96.6 FM, 9 Christopher Place, Shopping Centre, St Albans, Herts AL3 5DQ. Tel: 01727-831966. *Frequency*: 96.6 FM

MERCURY 102.7 FM, The Stanley Centre, Kelvin Way, Crawley, W. Sussex RH10 2SE. Tel: 01293-519161. *Frequencies:* 97.5/102.7 FM

MERCURY 107.9 FM, Berkeley House, 186 High Street, Rochester ME1 1EY. Tel: 01634-841111. *Frequencies*: 100.4/107.9 FM

METRO RADIO, Newcastle upon Tyne NE99 1BB. Tel: 0191-420 0971. *Frequencies:* 97.1 FM (Northumberland, Tyne and Wear, Durham); 103.0 FM (Tyne Valley); 102.6 FM (Alnwick); 103.2 FM (Hexham)

MFM 103.4, The Studios, Mold Road, Gwersyllt, Nr Wrexham LL11 4AF. Tel: 01978-752202. *Frequency:* 103.4 FM

MILLENNIUM RADIO, Harrow Manor Way, Thamesmead, London SE2 9XH. Tel: 020-8311 3112. *Frequency:* 106.8 FM

MINSTER FM, PO Box 123, Dunnington, York YO1 5ZX. Tel: 01904-488888. *Frequencies:* 104.7 FM (York); 102.3 FM (Thirsk)

MIX 96, Friars Square Studios, 11 Bourbon Street, Aylesbury, Bucks HP20 2PZ. Tel: 01296-399396. *Frequency:* 96.2 FM

NEPTUNE RADIO, PO Box 1068, Dover CT16 1GB; PO Box 964, Folkestone CT18 8GG. Tel: 01304-202505. *Frequencies:* 96.4 FM (Folkestone); 106.8 FM (Dover)

NEWS DIRECT 97.3 FM, 200 Gray's Inn Road, London WC1X 8XZ. Tel: 020-7973 1152. *Frequency:* 97.3 FM

NORTHANTS 96, 19–21 St Edmunds Road, Northampton NN1 5DY. Tel: 01604-795601. *Frequency:* 96.6 FM

THE NRG, PO Box 1234, Bournemouth BH1 3YH. Tel: 01202-318100. *Frequency:* 107.6 FM

OCEAN FM, Radio House, Whittle Avenue, Segensworth West, Fareham, Hants PO15 5SH. Tel: 01489-589911. *Frequencies:* 96.7/97.5 FM

ORCHARD FM, Haygrove House, Taunton, Somerset TA3 7BT. Tel: 01823-338448. *Frequencies:* 96.5 FM (Taunton); 97.1 FM (Yeovil); 102.6 FM (Somerset)

OXYGEN 107.9 FM, Suite 41, Westgate Centre, Oxford OX1 1PD. Tel: 01865-724442. *Frequency:* 107.9 FM

PEAK 107 FM, Radio House, Foxwood Road, Chesterfield, Derbys S41 9RF. Tel: 01246-269107. *Frequencies:* 107.4 FM (Chesterfield and NE Derbyshire); 102.0 FM (Matlock and Bakewell)

PICCADILLY KEY, Castle Quay, Castlefield, Manchester M15 4PR. Tel: 0161-288 5000. *Frequency*: 103 FM

PIRATE FM 102, Carn Brea Studios, Wilson Way, Redruth, Cornwall TR15 3XX. Tel: 01209-314400. *Frequencies:* 102.2 FM (East Cornwall and West Devon); 102.8 FM (West Cornwall and Isles of Scilly)

PLYMOUTH SOUND FM, Earl's Acre, Plymouth PL3 4HX. Tel: 01752-227272. *Frequencies:* 96.6/97.0 FM

PREMIER CHRISTIAN RADIO, Glen House, Stag Place, London SW1E 5AG. Tel: 020-7316 1300. *Frequencies:* 1305/1332/1413 AM

THE PULSE, Pennine House, Forster Square, Bradford BD1 5NE. Tel: 01274-203040. *Frequencies:* 97.5 FM (Bradford); 102.5 FM (Huddersfield and Halifax)

Q103 FM, Enterprise House, The Vision Park, Chivers Way, Histon, Cambridge CB4 4WW. Tel: 01223-235255. *Frequencies:* 103.0 FM (Cambridge); 97.4 FM (Newmarket)

QUAY WEST RADIO, Harbour Studios, The Esplanade, Watchet, Somerset TA23 0AJ. Tel: 01984-634900. *Frequency:* 102.4 FM

RADIO XL 1296 AM, KMS House, Bradford Street, Birmingham B12 0JD. Tel: 0121-753 5353. *Frequency:* 1296 AM

RAM FM, 35-36 Irongate, Derby DE1 3GA. Tel: 01332-205599. *Frequency:* 102.8 FM

REVOLUTION, PO Box 962, Oldham OL1 1FE. Tel: 0161-628 8787. *Frequency:* 96.2 FM

RIDINGS FM, 2 Thornes Office Park, Monckton Road, Wakefield WF2 7AN. Tel: 01924-367177. *Frequency:* 106.8 FM

RITZ 1035 AM, 33–35 Wembley Hill Road, London HA9 8RT. Tel: 020-8733 1300. *Frequency:* 1035 AM

ROCK FM, PO Box 974, Preston PR1 1XS. Tel: 01772-556301. *Frequency:* 97.4 FM

RUTLAND RADIO, Rutland Business Centre, Gaol Street, Oakham, Rutland LE15 6AY. Tel: 01572-757868. *Frequency:* 107.2 FM (Rutland); 97.4 FM (Stamford)

SABRAS RADIO, Radio House, 63 Melton Road, Leicester LE4 6PN. Tel: 0116-261 0666. *Frequency:* 1260 AM

SEVERN SOUND FM, Bridge Studios, Eastgate Centre, Gloucester GL1 1SS. Tel: 01452-313200. *Frequencies:* 103.0/102.4 FM

SGR COLCHESTER, Abbeygate Two, 9 Whitewell Road, Colchester CO2 7DE. Tel: 01206-575859. *Frequency:* 96.1 FM

SGR-FM, Radio House, Alpha Business Park, White House Road, Ipswich IP1 5LT. Tel: 01473-461000. *Frequencies:* 97.1 FM (Ipswich); 96.4 FM (Bury St Edmunds)

SIGNAL ONE FM, Stoke Road, Stoke-on-Trent ST4 2SR. Tel: 01782-747047. *Frequencies:* 96.9/102.6 FM

SOUTHCITY FM, City Studios, Marsh Lane, Southampton, SO14 3ST. Tel: 023-8022 0020. *Frequency:* 107.8 FM

SOUTHERN FM, Radio House, PO Box 2000, Brighton BN41 2SS. Tel: 01273-430111. *Frequencies:* 102.0 FM (Hastings); 102.4 FM (Eastbourne); 96.9 FM (Newhaven); 103.5 FM (Brighton)

SOUTH HAMS RADIO, Unit 9, South Hams Business Park, Churchstow, Knightsbridge, Devon TQ7 3QR. Tel: 01548-854595. *Frequency:* 100.5 FM (Totnes); 100.8 FM (Dartmouth); 101.2 FM (South Hams); 101.9 FM (Ivybridge)

SOVEREIGN RADIO, 14 St Mary's Walk, Hailsham, E. Sussex BN27 1AF. Tel: 01323-442700. *Frequency:* 107.5 FM

SPECTRUM INTERNATIONAL RADIO, International Radio Centre, 204–206 Queenstown Road, London SW8 3NR. Tel: 020-7627 4433. *Frequency:* 558 AM

SPIRE FM, City Hall Studios, Malthouse Lane, Salisbury, Wilts SP2 7QQ. Tel: 01722-416644. *Frequency:* 102.0 FM

SPIRIT FM, Dukes Court, Bognor Road, Chichester, W. Sussex PO19 2FX. Tel: 01243-773600. *Frequencies:* 96.6/102.3 FM

STAR FM, The Observatory Shopping Centre, Slough, Berks SL1 1LH. Tel: 01753-551066. *Frequency:* 106.6 FM

SUN FM, PO Box 1034, Sunderland SR5 2YL. Tel: 0191-548 1034. *Frequency:* 103.4 FM

SUNRISE FM, Sunrise House, 30 Chapel Street, Little Germany, Bradford BD1 5DN. Tel: 01274-735043. *Frequency:* 103.2 FM

SUNRISE RADIO, Sunrise House, Sunrise Road, Southall, Middx UB2 4AU. Tel: 020-8574 6666. *Frequency:* 1458 AM

SUNSHINE 855, Sunshine House, Waterside, Ludlow, Shropshire SY8 1PE. Tel: 01584-873795. *Frequency:* 855 AM

TEN 17, Latton Bush Centre, Southern Way, Harlow, Essex CM18 7BU. Tel: 01279-431017. *Frequency:* 101.7 FM

TFM, Radio House, Yale Crescent, Thornaby, Stockton-on-Tees TS17 6AA. Tel: 01642-888222. *Frequency:* 96.6 FM

TLR, Imperial House, 2–14 High Street, Margate, Kent CT9 1DH. Tel: 01843-220222. *Frequency:* 107.2 FM

TOWER FM, The Mill, Brownlow Way, Bolton BL1 2RA. Tel: 01204-387000. *Frequency*: 107.4 FM

TRAX FM, PO Box 444, Worksop, Notts S81 9YW. Tel: 01909-500611. *Frequency:* 107.9AM

TRAX FM, PO Box 444, Doncaster DN3 3GB. Tel: 01302-341166. *Frequency:* 107.1 FM

VIBE FM, Reflection House, The Anderson Centre, Olding Road, Bury, St Edmunds IP33 3TA. Tel: 01284-718800. *Frequencies*: 105.6 FM (Cambridge); 106.1 FM (Norwich); 106.4 FM (Ipswich); 107.7 FM (Peterborough)

VICTORY 107.4, Media House, Tipner Wharf, Twyford Avenue, Portsmouth PO2 8PE. Tel: 023-9263 9922. *Frequency*: 107.4 FM

VIRGIN 105.8, 1 Golden Square, London W1R 4DJ. Tel: 020-7434 1215. *Frequency:* 105.8 FM

THE WAVE 96.5, 965 Mowbray Drive, Blackpool FY3 7JR. Tel: 01253-304965. *Frequency:* 96.5 FM

WAVE 105 FM, 5 Manor Court, Barnes Wallis Road, Segensworth East, Fareham, Hampshire PO15 5[TH]. Tel: 01489-481050. *Frequencies*: 105.2 FM (Solent); 105.8 FM (Poole)

WESSEX FM, Radio House, Trinity Street, Dorchester DT1 1DJ. Tel: 01305-250333. *Frequencies:* 97.2/96.0 FM

WIN 107.2, PO Box 1072, The Brooks, Winchester SO23 8FT. Tel: 01962-841071. *Frequency:* 107.2 FM

WYVERN FM, 5-6Barbourne Terrace, Worcester WR1 3JZ. Tel: 01905-612212. *Frequencies:* 97.6 FM (Hereford); 102.8 FM (Worcester); 96.7 FM (Kidderminster)

X-CEL FM, 46 Camel Road, Littleport, Cambs CB6 1EW. Tel: 01353-865102. *Frequencies:* 107.1/107.5 FM

XFM, 30 Leicester Square, London WC2H 7LA. Tel: 020-7766 6600. *Frequency:* 104.9 FM

YORKSHIRE COAST RADIO, PO Box 962, Scarborough, N. Yorks YO12 5YX. Tel: 01723-500962. *Frequencies:* 96.2/103.1 FM

YORKSHIRE COAST RADIO BRIDLINGTON'S BEST, Old Harbour Master's Office, Harbour Road, Bridlington,E. Yorks YO15 5NR. Tel: 01262-404400. *Frequency*: 102.4 FM

*Wales*

BRIDGE FM, 25 Wyndham Street, Bridgend CF31 1EB. Tel: 01656-647777. *Frequency*: 106.3 FM

CAPITAL GOLD, West Canal Wharf, Cardiff CF10 5XL. Tel: 029-2023 7878. *Frequencies:* 1359 AM (Cardiff); 1305 AM (Newport)

CHAMPION FM, Llys y Dderwen, Parc Menai, Bangor LL57 4BN. Tel: 01248-671888. *Frequency:* 103.0 FM

COAST FM, 41 Conwy Road, Colwyn Bay LL28 5AB. Tel: 01492-533733. *Frequency:* 96.3 FM

RADIO CEREDIGION, Yr Hen Ysgol Gymraeg, Ffordd Alexandra, Aberystwyth SY23 1LF. Tel: 01970-627999. *Frequencies:* 96.6/97.4/103.3/FM

RADIO MALDWYN, The Studios, The Park, Newtown, Powys SY16 2NZ. Tel: 01686-623555. *Frequency:* 756 AM

REAL RADIO, PO Box 6105, Ty-Nant Court, Cardiff CF15 8YF. Tel: 029-2031 5100. *Frequency*: 105/106 FM.

RED DRAGON FM, Radio House, West Canal Wharf, Cardiff CF10 5XL. Tel: 029-2038 4041. *Frequencies:* 103.2 FM (Cardiff); 97.4 FM (Newport)

SWANSEA SOUND, PO Box 1170, Victoria Road, Gowerton, Swansea SA4 3AB. Tel: 01792-511170. *Frequency:* 1170 AM

VALLEYS RADIO, Festival Park, Victoria, Ebbw Vale NP3 6XW. Tel: 01495-301116. *Frequencies:* 999/1116 AM

THE WAVE 96.4 FM, PO Box 964, Victoria Road, Gowerton, Swansea SA4 3AB. Tel: 01792-511964. *Frequency:* 96.4 FM

*Scotland*

96.3 QFM, 26 Lady Lane, Paisley PA1 2LG. Tel: 0141-887 9630. *Frequency:* 96.3 FM

ARGYLL FM, 27-29 Longrow, Campbelltown, Argyll PA28 6ER. Tel: 01586-551800. *Frequency:* 107.1/107.7/106.5 FM

BEAT 106, Four Winds Pavilion, Pacific Quay, Glasgow G51 1EB. Tel: 0141-566 6106. *Frequencies:* 105.7/106.1 FM

CENTRAL FM, 201 High Street, Falkirk FK1 1DU. Tel: 01324-611164. *Frequency:* 103.1 FM

CLAN FM, Radio House, Rowantree Avenue, Newhouse Industrial Estate, Newhouse ML1 5RX. Tel: 01689-733107. *Frequency:* 107.5/107.9 FM

CLYDE 1 (FM) AND 2 (AM), Clydebank Business Park, Clydebank, Glasgow G81 2RX. Tel: 0141-565 2200. *Frequencies:* 102.5 FM; 103.3 FM (Firth of Clyde); 97.0 FM (Vale of Leven); 1152 AM

FORTH AM AND FM, Forth House, Forth Street, Edinburgh EH1 3LF. Tel: 0131-556 9255. *Frequencies:* 1548 AM, 97.3/97.6/102.2 FM

HEARTLAND FM, Atholl Curling Rink, Lower Oakfield, Pitlochry, Perthshire PH16 5HQ. Tel: 01796-474040. *Frequency:* 97.5 FM

ISLES FM, PO Box 333, Stornoway, Isle of Lewis HS1 2PU. Tel: 01851-703333. *Frequency:* 103.0 FM

KINGDOM FM, Haig House, Haig Business Park, Markinch, Fife KY7 6AQ. Tel: 01592-753753. *Frequencies:* 95.2/96.1 FM

LOCHBROOM FM, Radio House, Mill Street, Ullapool, Wester Ross IV26 2UN. Tel: 01854-613131. *Frequency:* 102.2 FM

MORAY FIRTH RADIO, Scorguie Place, Inverness IV3 8UJ. Tel: 01463-224433. *Frequencies:* 97.4 FM, 1107 AM; *local opt-outs:* MFR Speysound 96.6 FM, MFR Keith Community Radio 102.8 FM; MFR Kinnaird Radio 96.7 FM; MFR Caithness 102.5 FM

NECR (NORTH-EAST COMMUNITY RADIO), Town House, Kintore, Inverurie, AB51 0US. Tel: 01467-632909. *Frequencies:* 97.1 FM (Braemar); 102.1 FM (Meldrum and Inverurie); 102.6 FM (Kildrummy); 103.2 FM (Colpy)

NEVIS RADIO, Inverlochy, Fort William, Inverness-shire PH33 6LU. Tel: 01397-700007. *Frequencies:* 96.6 FM (Fort William); 97.0 FM (Glencoe); 102.3 FM (Skye); 102.4 FM (Loch Leven)

NORTHSOUND ONE (FM) AND TWO (AM), 45 Kings Gate, Aberdeen AB15 4EL. Tel: 01224-337000. *Frequencies:* 1035 AM, 96.9/97.6/103.0 FM

OBAN FM, 132 George Street, Oban, Argyll PA34 5NT. Tel: 01631-570057. *Frequency:* 103.3 FM

RADIO BORDERS, Tweedside Park, Galashiels TD1 3TD. Tel: 01896-759444. *Frequencies:* 96.8/97.5/103.1/103.4 FM

RADIO TAY AM AND TAY FM, 6 North Isla Street, Dundee DD3 7JQ. Tel: 01382-200800. *Frequencies:* 1161 AM, 102.8 FM (Dundee); 1584 AM, 96.4 FM (Perth)

RNA FM, Arbroath Infirmary, Rosemount Road, Arbroath, Angus DD11 2AT. Tel: 01241-879660. *Frequency:* 96.6 FM

SCOT FM, 1 Albert Quay, Leith EH6 7DN. Tel: 0131-625 8400. *Frequencies*: 100.3 FM (West); 101.1 FM (East)

SIBC, Market Street, Lerwick, Shetland ZE1 0JN. Tel: 01595-695299. *Frequencies:* 96.2/102.2 FM

SOUTH WEST SOUND, Campbell House, Bankend Road, Dumfries DG1 4TH. Tel: 01387-250999. *Frequencies:* 96.5/97.0/103.0 FMWAVE 102, 8 South Tay Street, Dundee DD1 1PA. Tel: 01382-901000. *Frequency*: 102 FM

WAVES RADIO PETERHEAD,Unit 2, Blackhouse Industrial Estate, Peterhead AB42 1BW. Tel: 01779-491012. *Frequency:* 101.2 FM

WEST SOUND AM AND WEST FM, Radio House, 54A Holmston Road, Ayr KA7 3BE. Tel: 01292-283662. *Frequencies:* 1035 AM, 96.7 FM (Ayr); 97.5 FM (Girvan)

*Northern Ireland*

CITY BEAT 96.7, Lamont Buildings, Stranmillis Embankment, Belfast BT9 5FN. Tel: 028-9020 5967. *Frequency:* 96.7 FM

COOL FM, PO Box 974, Belfast BT1 1RT. Tel: 028-9081 7181. *Frequency:* 97.4 FM

DOWNTOWN RADIO, Newtownards, Co. Down BT23 4ES. Tel: 028-9181 5555. *Frequencies:* 1026 AM (Belfast); 96.4 FM (Limavady); 96.6 FM (Enniskillen); 97.1 FM (Larne); 102.3 FM (Ballymena); 102.4 FM (Londonderry); 103.1 FM (Newry); 103.4 FM (Newcastle); 102.6 AM (Belfast)

Q97.2 FM, 24 Clafin Road, Coleraine BT52 2NU. Tel: 028-7035 9100. *Frequency*: 97.2 FM

Q102.9 FM, The Riverside Suite, Old Waterside Railway Station, Duke Street, Londonderry BT47 6DH. Tel: 028-7134 4449. *Frequency:* 102.9 FM

*Channel Islands*

104.7 ISLAND FM, 12 Westerbrook, St Sampsons, Guernsey GY2 4QQ. Tel: 01481-242000. *Frequencies:* 104.7 FM (Guernsey); 93.7 FM (Alderney)

CHANNEL 103 FM, 6 Tunnell Street, St Helier, Jersey JE2 4LU. Tel: 01534-888103. *Frequency:* 103.7 FM

# The Press

The newspaper and periodical press in the UK is large and diverse, catering for a wide variety of views and interests. There is no state control or censorship of the press, though it is subject to the laws on publication and the Press Complaints Commission was set up by the industry as a means of self-regulation.

The press is not state-subsidised and receives few tax concessions. The income of most newspapers and periodicals is derived largely from sales and from advertising; the press is the largest advertising medium in Britain.

### SELF-REGULATION

The Press Complaints Commission was founded by the newspaper and magazine industry in January 1991 to replace the Press Council (established in 1953). It is a voluntary, non-statutory body set up to operate the press's self-regulation system following the Calcutt report in 1990 on privacy and related matters, when the industry feared that failure to regulate itself might lead to statutory regulation of the press. The performance of the Press Complaints Commission was reviewed after 18 months of operation (the *Calcutt Review of Press Self-Regulation*, presented to Parliament in January 1993) to determine whether statutory measures were required. No proposals for replacing the self-regulation system have been made to date.

The Commission is funded by the industry through the Press Standards Board of Finance.

### COMPLAINTS

The Press Complaints Commission's objectives are to consider, adjudicate, conciliate, and resolve complaints of unfair treatment by the press; and to ensure that the press maintains the highest professional standards with respect for generally recognised freedoms, including freedom of expression, the public's right to know, and the right of the press to operate free from improper pressure. The Commission judges newspaper and magazine conduct by a code of practice drafted by editors, agreed by the industry and ratified by the Commission.

Seven of the Commission's members are editors of national, regional and local newspapers and magazines, and nine, including the chairman, are drawn from other fields. One member has been appointed Privacy Commissioner with special powers to investigate complaints about invasion of privacy.

PRESS COMPLAINTS COMMISSION, 1 Salisbury Square, London EC4Y 8JB Tel: 020-7353 1248. Fax: 020-7353 8355. Email: complaints@pcc.org.uk;
Web: www.pcc.org.uk
*Chairman*, Lord Wakeham, PC *Director*, G. Black

## NEWSPAPERS

Newspapers are usually financially independent of any political party, though most adopt a political stance in their editorial comments, usually reflecting proprietorial influence. Ownership of the national and regional daily newspapers is concentrated in the hands of large corporations whose interests cover publishing and communications. The rules on cross-media ownership, as amended by the Broadcasting Act 1996, limit the extent to which newspaper organisations (with over 20 per cent of national circulation) may become involved in broadcasting.

There are about 15 daily and 17 Sunday national papers, about 84 regional daily papers, and several hundred local papers that are published weekly or twice-weekly. Scotland, Wales and Northern Ireland all have at least one daily and one Sunday national paper.

### Circulation (*as at June 2001*)

*National Daily Newspapers*

| | |
|---|---|
| Daily Mail | 2,415,273 |
| Daily Sport | 258,000 |
| Daily Star | 595,236 |
| Daily Telegraph | 1,020,363 |
| Daily Express | 956,239 |
| Financial Times | 486,725 |
| The Guardian | 403,210 |
| The Independent | 226,433 |
| The Mirror | 2,193,228 |
| Racing Post | 80,944 |
| The Scotsman | 88,133 |
| The Sun | 3,447,499 |
| The Times | 706,733 |

*National Sunday Newspapers*

| | |
|---|---|
| Sunday Express | 899,977 |
| Independent on Sunday | 252,672 |
| Mail on Sunday | 2,328,604 |
| News of the World | 3,899,417 |
| The Observer | 453,095 |
| Sunday People | 1,372,032 |
| Scotland on Sunday | 91,760 |
| Sunday Mirror | 1,865,943 |
| Sunday Sport | 195,768 |
| Sunday Telegraph | 794,653 |
| Sunday Times | 1,361,281 |

*Source: Audit Bureau of Circulations Ltd, May 2001. For further information please see www.abc.org.uk*

## NATIONAL DAILY NEWSPAPERS

DAILY MAIL Northcliffe House, 2 Derry Street, London W8 5TT. Tel: 020-7938 6000. Fax: 020-7937 3745

DAILY SPORT 19 Great Ancoats Street, Manchester M60 4BT. Tel: 0161-236 4466. Fax: 0161-236 4535.
Email: sport@globalnet.co.uk;
Web: www.dailysport.co.uk

DAILY STAR Ludgate House, 245 Blackfriars Road, London SE1 9UX. Tel: 020-7928 8000.
Fax: 020-7633 0244. Web: www.megastar.co.uk

DAILY TELEGRAPH 1 Canada Square, Canary Wharf, London E14 5DT. Tel: 020-7538 5000.
Fax: 020-7513 2506. Email: dtnews@telegraph.co.uk;
Web: www.telegraph.co.uk

FINANCIAL TIMES 1 Southwark Bridge, London SE1 9HL.
Tel: 020-7873 3000. Fax: 020-7873 3072.
Email: readersenquiries@ft.com; Web: www.ft.com

MORNING STAR Cape House, 787 Commercial Road, London E14 7HG. Tel: 020-7538 5181.
Fax: 020-7538 5125.
Email: morsta@geo2.poptel.org.uk;
Web: www.poptel.org.uk/morning-star/

RACING POST 1 Canada Square, Canary Wharf, London E14 5AP. Tel: 020-7293 3000. Fax: 020-7293 3758.
Email: editor@racingpost.co.uk;
Web: www.racingpost.co.uk

THE EXPRESS Ludgate House, 245 Blackfriars Road, London SE1 9UX. Tel: 020-7928 8000. Fax: 020-7633 0244. Web: www.express.co.uk

THE GUARDIAN 119 Farringdon Road, London EC1R 3ER. Tel: 020-7278 2332. Fax: 020-7837 2114. Email: letters@guardian.co.uk; Web: www.guardian.co.uk

THE HERALD 200 Renfield Street, Glasgow G2 3PR. Tel: 0141-302 7000. Fax: 0141-333 1147. Email: heraldmail@cims.co.uk; Web: www.theherald.co.uk

THE INDEPENDENT Independent House, 191 Marsh Wall, London E14 9RS. Tel: 020-7005 2000. Fax: 020-7005 2999. Email: letterspage@independent.co.uk; Web: www.independent.co.uk

THE MIRROR 1 Canada Square, Canary Wharf, London E14 5AP. Tel: 020-7293 3000. Fax: 020-7293 3405. Email: ic24@mgn.co.uk; Web: www.mirror.co.uk

THE SCOTSMAN Barclay House, 108 Holyrood Road, Edinburgh EH8 8AS. Tel: 0131-620 8620. Fax: 0131-620 8615/6. Email: newsdesk_ts@scotsman.com; Web: www.scotsman.com

THE SUN 1 Virginia Street, London E1 9XR. Tel: 020-7782 4000. Fax: 020-7782 5605. Web: www.the-sun.co.uk

THE TIMES The Times House, 1 Pennington Street, London E98 1TT. Tel: 020-7782 5000. Fax: 020-7782 5988. Email: home.news@thetimes.co.uk; Web: www.thetimes.co.uk

## REGIONAL DAILY NEWSPAPERS

### BERKSHIRE

READING EVENING POST 8 Tessa Road, Reading RG1 8NS. Tel: 0118-918 3000. Fax: 0118-959 9363. Email: editorial@reading-epost.co.uk; Web: www.getreading.co.uk

### CAMBRIDGESHIRE

CAMBRIDGE EVENING NEWS Winship Road, Milton, Cambridge CB4 6PP. Tel: 01223-434434. Fax: 01223-434415. Email: colingrant@cambridge-news.co.uk; Web: www.cambridge-news.co.uk

PETERBOROUGH EVENING TELEGRAPH New Priestgate House, 57 Priestgate, Peterborough PE1 1JW. Tel: 01733-555111. Fax: 01733-555188.

### CUMBRIA

NEWS AND STAR Newspaper House, Dalston Road, Carlisle CA2 5UA. Tel: 01228-612600. Fax: 01228-612601. Email: news@cumbrian-newspapers.co.uk; Web: www.news-and-star.co.uk

### DERBYSHIRE

DERBY EVENING TELEGRAPH Northcliffe House, Meadow Road, Derby DE1 2DW. Tel: 01332-291111. Fax: 01332-253011. Web: www.thisisderbyshire.co.uk

### DEVON

EVENING HERALD 17 Brest Road, Derriford Business Park, Plymouth PL6 5AA. Tel: 01752-765500. Fax: 01752-765515. Email: news@westcountrypublications.co.uk; Web: www.thisisplymouth.co.uk

EXPRESS AND ECHO Heron Road, Sowton, Exeter EX2 7NF. Tel: 01392-442211. Fax: 01392-442294. Email: echonews@westcountrypublications.co.uk; Web: www.thisisexeter.co.uk

HERALD EXPRESS Harmsworth House, Barton Hill Road, Torquay TQ2 8JN. Tel: 01803-676000. Fax: 01803-676228. Email: editor@thisissouthdevon.co.uk; Web: www.thisissouthdevon.co.uk

WESTERN MORNING NEWS 17 Brest Road, Derriford Business Park, Plymouth PL6 5AA. Tel: 01752-765500. Fax: 01752-765515

### DORSET

DORSET ECHO Fleet House, Hampshire Road, Granby Industrial Estate, Weymouth, Dorset DT4 9XD. Tel: 01305-830930. Fax: 01305-830802. Web: www.dorsetecho.co.uk

THE DAILY ECHO Richmond Hill, Bournemouth BH2 6HH. Tel: 01202-554601. Fax: 01202-293676. Email: newsdesk@bournemouthecho.co.uk; Web: www.daily-echo.co.uk

### DURHAM

NORTHERN ECHO PO Box 14, Priestgate, Darlington DL1 1NF. Tel: 01325-381313. Fax: 01325-380539. Email: echo@nen.co.uk; Web: www.thisisthenortheast.co.uk

### EAST SUSSEX

THE ARGUS/EVENING ARGUS Argus House, Crowhurst Road, Hollingury, Brighton BN1 8AR. Tel: 01273-544544. Fax: 01273-566114. Web: www.thisisbrightonandhove.co.uk

### ESSEX

EVENING ECHO Newspaper House, Chester Hall Lane, Basildon SS14 3BL. Tel: 01268-522792. Fax: 01268-532060

EVENING GAZETTE Oriel House, 43-44 North Hill, Colchester CO1 1TZ. Tel: 01206-506000. Fax: 01206-508274

### GLOUCESTERSHIRE

GLOUCESTERSHIRE ECHO 1 Clarence Parade, Cheltenham GL50 3NY. Tel: 01242-271900. Fax: 01242-271792

### HAMPSHIRE

SOUTHERN DAILY ECHO Newspaper House, Test Lane, Retbridge, Southampton SO16 9JX. Tel: 023-8042 4777. Fax: 023-8042 4770

THE NEWS The News Centre, Hilsea, Portsmouth PO2 9SX. Tel: 023-9266 4488. Fax: 023-9267 3363. Web: www.portsmouth.co.uk

### KENT

MEDWAY TODAY 395 High Street, Chatham, Kent ME4 4PQ. Tel: 01634-830600. Fax: 01634-829484. Email: medwaytoday@thekmgroup.co.uk; Web: www.kent-online.co.uk

### LANCASHIRE

BOLTON EVENING NEWS Newspaper House, Churchgate, Bolton BL1 1DE. Tel: 01204-522345. Fax: 01204-365068. Email: ben_editorial@newsquest.co.uk; Web: www.thisisbolton.co.uk

LANCASHIRE EVENING POST Oliver's Place, Fulwood, Preston PR2 9ZA. Tel: 01772-254841. Fax: 01772-880173

LANCASHIRE EVENING TELEGRAPH Newspaper House, High Street, Blackburn BB1 1HT. Tel: 01254-678678. Fax: 01254-682185

MANCHESTER EVENING NEWS 164 Deansgate, Manchester M3 3RN. Tel: 0161-832 7200. Fax: 0161-832 5351. Email: newsdesk@mcr-evening-news.co.uk; Web: www.manchesteronline.co.uk

OLDHAM EVENING CHRONICLE 172 Union Street, Oldham OL1 1EQ. Tel: 0161-633 2121. Fax: 0161-652 2111. Email: editorial@oldham-chronicle.co.uk; Web: www.oldham-chronicle.co.uk

THE GAZETTE Avroe House, Avroe Crescent, Blackpool Business Park, Blackpool FY4 2DP. Tel: 01253-400888. Fax: 01253-694152

WIGAN EVENING POST Mart Land Mill, Mart Land Mill Lane, Wigan, WN5 0LX. Tel: 01772-254841. Fax: 01772-880173

LEICESTERSHIRE

LEICESTER MERCURY St George Street, Leicester LE1 9FQ. Tel: 0116-251 2512. Fax: 0116-262 4687

LINCOLNSHIRE

GRIMSBY EVENING TELEGRAPH 80 Cleethorpe Road, Grimsby DN31 3EH. Tel: 01472-360360. Fax: 01472-352272

LINCOLNSHIRE ECHO Brayford Wharf East, Lincoln LN5 7AT. Tel: 01522-820000. Fax: 01522-804492. Email: editor@thisislincolnshire.co.uk; Web: www.thisislincolnshire.co.uk

SCUNTHORPE EVENING TELEGRAPH Telegraph House, Doncaster Road, Scunthorpe DN15 7RE. Tel: 01724-273273. Fax: 01724-853495

LONDON

THE EVENING STANDARD Northcliffe House, 2 Derry Street, London W8 5TT. Tel: 020-7938 6000. Fax: 020-7937 3745

MERSEYSIDE

DAILY POST, AND LIVERPOOL ECHO PO Box 48, Old Hall Street, Liverpool L69 3EB. Tel: 0151-227 2000. Fax: 0151-236 4682

NORFOLK

EASTERN DAILY PRESS, AND EVENING NEWS Prospect House, Rouen Road, Norwich NR1 1RE. Tel: 01603-628311. Fax: 01603-612930

NORTHAMPTONSHIRE

CHRONICLE AND ECHO Upper Mounts, Northampton NN1 3HR. Tel: 01604-467000. Fax: 01604-467190

NORTHAMPTONSHIRE EVENING TELEGRAPH Newspaper House, Ise Park, Rothwell Road, Kettering NN16 8GA. Tel: 01536-506100. Fax: 01536-506196

NOTTINGHAMSHIRE

NOTTINGHAM EVENING POST Castle Wharf House, Nottingham NG1 7EU. Tel: 0115-948 2000. Fax: 0115-964 4032. Email: nep.editorial@dial.pipex.com; Web: www.thisisnottingham.co.uk

OXFORDSHIRE

THE OXFORD MAIL Newspaper House, Osney Mead, Oxford OX2 0EJ. Tel: 01865-425262. Fax: 01865-425554. Email: news@nqo.com

SHROPSHIRE

SHROPSHIRE STAR Ketley, Telford TF1 5HU. Tel: 01743-248428. Fax: 01743-222451

SOMERSET

BRISTOL EVENING POST, AND WESTERN DAILY PRESS Temple Way, Bristol BS99 7HD. Tel: 0117-934 3000. Fax: 0117-934 3571. Web: www.epost.co.uk

THE BATH CHRONICLE Windsor House, Windsor Bridge, Bath BA2 3AU. Tel: 01225-322322. Fax: 01225-322291. Web: www.thisisbath.com

SUFFOLK

EAST ANGLIAN DAILY TIMES, AND EVENING STAR 30 Lower Brook Street, Ipswich IP4 1AN. Tel: 01473-230023. Fax: 01473-211391 Email: eadt@ecng.co.uk; Web: www.suffolk-now.co.uk

TYNE AND WEAR

NEWCASTLE EVENING CHRONICLE, AND THE JOURNAL Groat Market, Newcastle upon Tyne NE1 1ED. Tel: 0191-232 7500. Fax: 0191-230 4144

SHIELDS GAZETTE Chapter Row, South Shields NE33 1BL. Tel: 0191-455 4661. Fax: 0191-456 8270

SUNDERLAND ECHO Echo House, Pennywell, Sunderland SR4 9ER. Tel: 0191-5015800. Fax: 0191-5345975. Email: echo.news@northeast.press.co.uk; Web: www.sunderlandecho.com

WEST MIDLANDS

COVENTRY EVENING TELEGRAPH Corporation Street, Coventry CV1 1FP. Tel: 024-7663 3633. Fax: 024-7663 1736. Email: editorial@go2coventry.co.uk; Web: www.iccoventry.co.uyk

THE BIRMINGHAM POST, AND BIRMINGHAM EVENING MAIL 28 Colmore Circus, Queensway, Birmingham B4 6AX. Tel: 0121-236 3366. Fax: 0121-233 3958

WILTSHIRE

SWINDON EVENING ADVERTISER Newspaper House, 100 Victoria Road, Swindon SN1 3BE. Tel: 01793-528144. Fax: 01793-523883. Web: www.thisiswiltshire.co.uk

WORCESTERSHIRE

WORCESTER EVENING NEWS Hylton Road, Worcester WR2 5JX. Tel: 01905-748200. Fax: 01905-748009. Email: wen@newsquestmidlands.co.uk; Web: www.thisisworcester.co.uk

YORKSHIRE

EVENING GAZETTE Gazette Buildings, Borough Road, Middlesbrough TS1 3AZ. Tel: 01642-234242. Fax: 01642-249843

EVENING PRESS PO Box 29, 76–86 Walmgate, York YO1 9YN. Tel: 01904-653051. Fax: 01904-612853 Email: editor@ycp.co.uk; Web: www.thisisyork.co.uk

HALIFAX EVENING COURIER PO Box 19, Courier Buildings, King Cross Street, Halifax HX1 2SF. Tel: 01422-260200. Fax: 01422-260341. Email: editor@halifaxcourier.co.uk; Web: www.halifaxtoday.co.uk

HULL DAILY MAIL Blundell's Corner, Beverley Road, Hull HU3 1XS. Tel: 01482-327111. Fax: 01482-584353. Email: news@hulldailymail.co.uk; Web: www.thisishull.co.uk

SCARBOROUGH EVENING NEWS 17–23 Aberdeen Walk, Scarborough YO11 1BB. Tel: 01723-363636. Fax: 01723-354092. Email: editorial@scarborougheveningnews.co.uk; Web: www.scarborougheveningnews.co.uk

SHEFFIELD STAR York Street, Sheffield S1 1PU. Tel: 0114-276 7676. Fax: 0114-272 5978. Web: www.thisissheffield.net

TELEGRAPH AND ARGUS Hall Ings, Bradford BD1 1JR. Tel: 01274-729511. Fax: 01274-723634

YORKSHIRE EVENING POST PO Box 168, Wellington Street, Leeds LS1 1RF. Tel: 0113-243 2701. Fax: 0113-244 3430. Email: eped@ypn.co.uk; Web: www.yorkshire-evening-post.co.uk

YORKSHIRE POST PO Box 168, Wellington Street, Leeds LS1 1RF. Tel: 0113-243 2701. Fax: 0113-238 8525. Email: yp.editor@ypn.co.uk; Web: www.yorkshirepost.co.uk

### WALES

EVENING LEADER Mold Business Park, Wrexham Road, Mold CH7 1XY. Tel: 01352-707707. Fax: 01352-700048

SOUTH WALES ARGUS Cardiff Road, Maesglas, Newport NP9 1QW. Tel: 01633-810000. Fax: 01633-462121

SOUTH WALES ECHO Thomson House, Havelock Street, Cardiff CF1 1XR. Tel: 029-2058 3583. Fax: 029-2058 3451

SOUTH WALES EVENING POST PO Box 14, Adelaide Street, Swansea SA1 1QT. Tel: 01792-510000. Fax: 01792-514697. Email: postbox@swwp.co.uk; Web: www.thisissouthwales.co.uk

WESTERN MAIL Thomson House, Havelock Street, Cardiff CF1 1XR. Tel: 029-2058 3583. Fax: 029-2058 3451

### SCOTLAND

COURIER AND ADVERTISER 80 Kingsway East, Dundee DD4 8SL. Tel: 01382-223131. Fax: 01382-454590. Email: courier@dcthomson.co.uk; Web: www.thecourier.co.uk

DAILY RECORD 1 Central Quay, Glasgow G3 8DA. Tel: 0141-248 7000. Fax: 0141-242 3340. Web: www.record-mail.co.uk

EDINBURGH EVENING NEWS 108 Holyrood Road, Edinburgh EH8 8AS. Tel: 0131-620 8620. Fax: 0131-225 7302. Web: www.scotsman.com

EVENING EXPRESS PO Box 43, Lang Stracht, Mastrick, Aberdeen AB15 6DF. Tel: 01224-690222. Fax: 01224-344106. Email: ee.editor@ajl.co.uk; Web: www.thisisnorthscotland.co.uk

EVENING TELEGRAPH AND POST 80 Kingsway east, Dundee DD4 8SL. Tel: 01382-223131. Fax: 01382-454590. Email: general@eveningtelegraph.co.uk; Web: www.eveningtelegraph.co.uk

EVENING TIMES 200 Renfield Street, Glasgow G2 3PR. Tel: 0141-302700. Fax: 0141-302660. Email: times@eveningtimes.co.uk; Web: www.eveningtimes.co.uk

GREENOCK TELEGRAPH 2 Crawford Street, Greenock PA15 1LH. Tel: 01383-728201.

PAISLEY DAILY EXPRESS 14 New Street, Paisley, PA1 1YA. Tel: 0141-8877744. Fax: 0141-8897149. Web: www.inside-scotland.co.uk

PRESS AND JOURNAL PO Box 43, Lang Stracht, Mastrick, Aberdeen AB15 6DF. Tel: 01224-690222. Fax: 01224-694613.

### NORTHERN IRELAND

BELFAST TELEGRAPH 124–144 Royal Avenue, Belfast BT1 1EB. Tel: 028-9026 4000. Fax: 028-9055 4506

### CHANNEL ISLANDS

GUERNSEY PRESS AND STAR PO Box 57, Guernsey GY1 3BW. Tel: 01481-240240. Fax: 01481-240235. Email: newsroom@guernsey-press.com; Web: www.guernsey-press.com

JERSEY EVENING POST PO Box 582, Five Oaks, St Saviour, Jersey JE4 8XQ. Tel: 01534-611611. Fax: 01534-611622. Email: editorial@jerseyevening post.com; Web: www.thisisjersey.com

## WEEKLY NEWSPAPERS

INDEPENDENT ON SUNDAY Independent House, 191 Marsh Wall, London E14 9RS. Tel: 020-7005 2000. Fax: 020-7005 2628. Email: sundayletters@independent.co.uk; Web: www.independent.co.uk

NEWS OF THE WORLD 1 Virginia Street, London E98 1NW. Tel: 020-7782 4000. Fax: 020-7583 9504

SCOTLAND ON SUNDAY 108 Holyrood Road, Edinburgh EH8 8AS. Tel: 0131-620 8620. Fax: 0131-523 0313. Email: letters-sos@scotlandonsunday.com; Web: www.scotlandonsunday.com

SUNDAY BUSINESS 3 Waterhouse Square, 142 Holborn Bars, London EC1N 2NP. Tel: 020-7961 0000. Fax: 020-7961 0102

SUNDAY EXPRESS Ludgate House, 245 Blackfriars Road, London SE1 9UX. Tel: 020-7928 8000. Fax: 020-7633 0244. Email: sundaynews@express.co.uk; Web: www.express.co.uk

SUNDAY MAIL 1 Central Quay, Glasgow G3 8DA. Tel: 0141-248 7000. Fax: 0141-242 3340. Web: www.sundaymail.co.uk

SUNDAY MIRROR 1 Canada Square, Canary Wharf, London E14 5AP. Tel: 020-7293 3000. Fax: 020-7293 3405. Web: www.mirror.co.uk

SUNDAY PEOPLE 1 Canada Square, Canary Wharf, London E14 5AP. Tel: 020-7293 3000. Fax: 020-7293 3405. Web: www.mirror.co.uk

SUNDAY POST Courier Place, Dundee DD1 9QJ. Tel: 01382-223131. Fax: 01382-201064. Email: mail@sundaypost.com; Web: www.sundaypost.com

SUNDAY SPORT 840B Melton Road, Thurmaston, Leicester LE4 8BJ. Tel: 0116-269 4892. Fax: 0116-264 0948. Email: sport@globalnet.co.uk; Web: www.sundaysport.com

THE MAIL ON SUNDAY Northcliffe House, 2 Derry Street, London W8 5TS. Tel: 020-7938 6000. Fax: 020-7937 7896. Web: www.smos.co.uk

THE OBSERVER 119 Farringdon Road, London EC1R 3ER. Tel: 020-7278 2332. Fax: 020-7713 4250. Web: www.observer.co.uk

THE SUNDAY HERALD 200 Renfield Street, Glasgow G2 3PR. Tel: 0141-3027802. Fax: 0141-3027808. Email: editor@sundayherald.com; Web: www.sundayherald.com

THE SUNDAY TELEGRAPH 1 Canada Square, Canary Wharf, London E14 5DT. Tel: 020-7538 5000. Fax: 020-7512 2504. Web: www.telegraph.co.uk

THE SUNDAY TIMES 1 Pennington Street, London E1 9XN. Tel: 020-7782 5000. Fax: 020-7782 5988. Web: www.sunday-times.co.uk

WALES ON SUNDAY Thomson House, Havelock Street, Cardiff CF1 1XR. Tel: 029-2058 3721. Fax: 029-2058 3725. Email: wosmail@wme.co.uk; Web: www.icwales.co.uk

WEEKLY NEWS Courier Place, Dundee DD1 9QJ. Tel: 01382-223131. Fax: 01382-201390. Email: weeklynews@dcthomson.co.uk; Web: www.dcthomson.co.uk

## RELIGIOUS PAPERS

ACCOUNTANCY ABG Professional Information, 40 Bernard Street, London WC1N 1LD. Tel: 020-7833 3291. Fax: 020-7833 2085. Email: postmaster@theabg.demon.co.uk; Web: www.accountancymagazine.com

BAPTIST TIMES PO Box 54, 129 The Broadway, Didcot, Oxon OX11 8XB. Tel: 01235-517670. Fax: 01235-517678. Email: btadmin@buecom.net

CATHOLIC HERALD Herald House, Lambs Passage, Bunhill Row, London EC1Y 8TQ. Tel: 020-7588 3101. Fax: 020-7256 9728. Email: catholic@atlas.co.uk; Web: www.catholicherald.co.uk

CHURCH OF IRELAND GAZETTE 36 Bachelor's Walk, Lisburn, Co. Antrim BT28 1XN. Tel: 028-9267 5743. Fax: 028-9267 5743. Web: www.gazette.ireland.anglican.org

CHURCH TIMES 33 Upper Street, London N1 0PN. Tel: 020-7359 4570. Fax: 020-7226 3073. Email: editor@churchtimes.co.uk; Web: www.churchtimes.co.uk

ENGLISH CHURCHMAN 22 Fitch drive, Brighton BN2 4HU. Tel: 01273-818555. Fax: 01273-386362

GOOD NEWS PAPER 50 Loxwood Avenue, Worthing, W. Sussex BN14 7RA. Tel: 01903-824174. Fax: 01903-824174

JEWISH CHRONICLE 25 Furnival Street, London EC4A 1JT. Tel: 020-7415 1500. Fax: 020-7405 9040

JEWISH TELEGRAPH Telegraph House, 11 Park Hill, Bury Old Road, Prestwich, Manchester M25 0HH. Tel: 0161-740 9321. Fax: 0161-740 9325. Email: mail@jewishtelegraph.com; Web: www.jewishtelegraph.com

LIFE AND WORK Church of Scotland, 121 George Street, Edinburgh EH2 4YN. Tel: 0131-225 5722. Fax: 0131-240 2207. Email: lifework@dial.pipex.com; Web: www.lifeandwork.org

METHODIST RECORDER 122 Golden Lane, London EC1Y 0TL. Tel: 020-7251 8414. Fax: 020-7608 3490. Email: editorial@methodistrecorder.co.uk; Web: www.methodistrecorder.co.uk

MIDDLE WAY Buddhist Society, 58 Eccleston Square, London SW1V 1PH. Tel: 020-7834 5858. Fax: 020-7976 5238. Web: www.buddsoc.org.uk

ORTHODOX OUTLOOK 42 Withens Lane, Wallasey, Wirral CH45 7NN. Tel: 0151-639 6509. Fax: 0151-200 6359. Email: pancratios.outlook@mcmail.com

PRESBYTERIAN HERALD Church House, Fisherwick Place, Belfast BT1 6DW. Tel: 028-9032 2284. Fax: 028-9024 8377. Email: herald@presbyterianireland.org; Web: www.presbyterianireland.org

QUAKER MONTHLY Friends House, Euston Road, London NW1 2BJ. Tel: 020-7663 1000. Fax: 020-7663 1001

REFORM United Reformed Church, 86 Tavistock Place, London WC1H 9RT. Tel: 020-7916 8630. Fax: 020-7916 2021. Email: reform@urc.org.uk; Web: www.urc.org.uk

THE CHURCH OF ENGLAND NEWSPAPER 20-26 Brunswick Place, London N1 6DZ. Tel: 020-747 5800. Fax: 020-7216 6410. Email: cen@parlicom.com; Web: www.churchnewspaper.com

THE FRIEND New Premier House, 150 Southampton Row, London WC1B 5BQ. Tel: 020-7387 7549. Fax: 020-7387 9382. Email: editorial@thefriend.org; Web: www.thefriend.org

THE SIKH COURIER INTERNATIONAL World Sikh Foundation, 33 Wargrave Road, Harrow, Middx HA2 8LL. Tel: 020-8864 9228.

THE SIKH MESSENGER 43 Dorset Road, London SW19 3EZ. Tel: 020-8540 4148.

THE TABLET 1 King Street Cloisters, Clifton Walk, London W6 0QZ. Tel: 020-8748 8484. Fax: 020-8748 1550. Email: publisher@thetablet.co.uk; Web: www.thetablet.co.uk

THE UNIVERSE 1st Floor, St James Building, Oxford Street, Manchester M1 6FP. Tel: 0161-236 8856. Fax: 0161-236 8530

THE WAR CRY 101 Newington Causeway, London SE1 6BN. Tel: 020-7367 4900. Fax: 020-7367 4710. Email: warcry@salvationarmy.org.uk; Web: www.salvationarmy.org.uk/warcry

---

# PERIODICALS

---

There are about 6,500 periodicals published in Britain. These are classified as consumer, e.g. general interest, or as trade, professional or academic.

## CONSUMER PERIODICALS

19 King's Reach Tower, Stamford Street, London SE1 9LS. Tel: 020-7261 5000. Fax: 020-7261 7634

ANGLING TIMES Bushfield House, Orton Centre, Peterborough PE2 5UW. Tel: 01733-232600. Fax: 01733-465844. Email: richard.lee@emap.com

ARENA 3rd Floor, Block A, Exmouth House, Pine Street, London EC1R 0JL. Tel: 020-7689 9999. Fax: 020-7689 0901. Email: editorial@arenamag.co.uk

ART MONTHLY 4th Floor, 28 Charing Cross Road, London WC2H 0DG. Tel: 020-7240 0389. Fax: 020-7240 0389. Email: info@artmonthly.co.uk; Web: www.artmonthly.co.uk

ASTRONOMY NOW PO Box 175, Tonbridge, Kent TN10 4ZY. Tel: 01903-266165. Fax: 01732-356230. Web: www.astronomynow.com

BBC GARDENER'S WORLD Woodlands, 80 Wood Lane, London W12 0TT. Tel: 020-8576 3959. Fax: 020-8576 3986. Email: adam.pasco@bbc.co.uk; Web: www.gardenersworld.co.uk

BBC GOOD FOOD MAGAZINE Woodlands, 80 Wood Lane, London W12 0TT. Tel: 020-8433 2000. Fax: 020-8433 3931. Email: good.food.magazine@bbc.co.uk

BBC HOMES AND ANTIQUES BBC Worldwide, Woodlands, 80 Wood Lane, London W12 0TT. Tel: 020-8433 3490. Fax: 020-8433 3867

BBC WILDLIFE MAGAZINE Broadcasting House, Whiteladies Road, Bristol, BS8 2LR. Tel: 0117-973 8402. Fax: 0117-946 7075 Email: wildlife.magazine@bbc.co.uk;

BELFAST GAZETTE (OFFICIAL) The Stationery Office, 16 Arthur Street, Belfast BT1 4GD. Tel: 028-9089 5135. Fax: 028-9023 5401. Email: roy.dubois@theso.co.uk; Web: www.thestationeryoffice.com

BIRDS RSPB, The Lodge, Sandy, Beds SG19 2DL. Tel: 01767-680551. Fax: 01767-683262. Web: www.rspb.org.uk

BRIDES Vogue House, Hanover Square, London W1S 1JU. Tel: 020-7499 9080. Fax: 020-7460 6369. Email: ccurry@msmail.condenast.co.uk; Web: www.bridesuk.net

BRITISH PHILATELIC BULLETIN Royal Mail, 2–14 Bunhill Row, London EC1Y 8HQ. Fax: 020-7847 3359. Web: www.royalmail.com

CAR Angel House, 338–346 Goswell Road, London EC1V 7QP. Tel: 020-7477 7399. Fax: 020-7477 7279. Email: car@emap.com

CLASSIC & SPORTS CAR Somerset House, Somerset Road, Teddington, Middx TW11 8RT. Tel: 020-8267 5399. Fax: 020-8267 5318. Email: letters.classicandsportscar@haynet.com

COMPUTER AND VIDEO GAMES Priory Court, 30–32 Farringdon Lane, London EC1R 3AU. Tel: 020-7972 6700. Fax: 020-7972 6710

COSMOPOLITAN National Magazine House, 72 Broadwick Street, London W1V 2BP. Tel: 020-7439 5000. Fax: 020-7439 5016. Email: cosmo.mail@natmags.co.uk; Web: www.natmags.co.uk

COUNTRY LIFE King's Reach Tower, Stamford Street, London SE1 9LS. Tel: 020-7261 7058. Fax: 020-7261 5139. Web: www.countrylife.co.uk

COUNTRY LIVING MAGAZINE National Magazine House, 72 Broadwick Street, London W1V 2BP. Tel: 020-7439 5000. Fax: 020-7439 5093. Web: www.natmags.co.uk

CYCLING WEEKLY Focus House, Dingwall Avenue, Croydon CR9 2TA. Tel: 020-8774 0811. Fax: 020-8686 0952. Email: cycling@ipcmedia.com

DANCING TIMES Clerkenwell House, 45–47 Clerkenwell Green, London EC1R 0EB. Tel: 020-7250 3006. Fax: 020-7253 6679. Email: DT@dancing-times.co.uk; Web: www.dancing-times.co.uk

EDINBURGH GAZETTE (OFFICIAL) The Stationery Office, PO Box 276, London SW8 5DT. Tel: 020-7873 9090. Fax: 020-7873 8200

ELLE Endeavour House, 189 Shaftesbury Avenue, London WC2H 8JG. Tel: 020-7437 9011. Fax: 020-7208 3599

EMPIRE Mappin House, 4 Winsley Street, London W1N 7AR. Tel: 020-7437 9011. Fax: 020-7859 8613. Email: empire@ecm.emap.com; Web: www.empireonline.co.uk

ESQUIRE National Magazine House, 72 Broadwick Street, London W1V 2BP. Tel: 020-7439 5000. Fax: 020-7312 3920. Web: www.esquire.co.uk

EXCHANGE AND MART Link House, 25 West Street, Poole, Dorset BH15 1LL. Tel: 01202-445000. Fax: 01202-445245. Web: www.ixm.co.uk

FAMILY CIRCLE King's Reach Tower, Stamford Street, London SE1 9LS. Tel: 020-7261 6195. Fax: 020-7261 5929 Email: familycircle@ipc.co.uk;

FHM The Network Building, 97 Tottenham Court Road, London W1T 4TP. Tel: 020-7504 6000. Fax: 020-7504 6300. Web: ww.fhm.com

FILM REVIEW 9 Blades Court, Deodar Road, London SW15 2NU. Tel: 020-8875 1520. Fax: 020-8875 1588. Email: filmreview@visimag.com; Web: www.visimag.com

GAY TIMES Ground Floor, Worldwide House, 116–134 Bayham Street, London NW1 0BA. Tel: 020-7482 2576. Fax: 020-7284 0329. Email: edit@gaytimes.co.uk; Web: www.gaytimes.co.uk

GEOGRAPHICAL JOURNAL Royal Geographical Society, 1 Kensington Gore, London SW7 2AR. Tel: 020-7591 3026. Fax: 020-7591 3001. Email: g.lowman@rgs.org; Web: www.rgs.org

GOLF WORLD Bushfield House, Orton Centre, Peterborough PE3 8DZ. Tel: 01733-237111. Fax: 01733-288025

GOOD HOUSEKEEPING National Magazine House, 72 Broadwick Street, London W1V 2BP. Tel: 020-7439 5000. Fax: 020-7439 5591. Web: www.goodhousekeeping.co.uk

GQ Vogue House, Hanover Square, London W1R 0AD. Tel: 020-7499 9080. Fax: 020-7493 1345. Email: djones@condenast.co.uk

GRAMOPHONE Haymarket Magazines Ltd, 38–42 Hampton Road, Teddington, Middx TW11 0JE. Tel: 020-8943 5000. Fax: 020-8267 5844. Email: editor@gramophone.co.uk; Web: www.gramophone.co.uk

GUIDING MAGAZINE 17–19 Buckingham Palace Road, London SW1W 0PT. Tel: 020-7592 821. Fax: 020-7828 5791. Email: guiding@guides.org.uk; Web: www.guides.org.uk

HANSARD The Stationery Office, PO Box 29, Norwich NR3 1GN. Tel: 0870-600 5522. Fax: 0870-600 5533

HARPERS AND QUEEN National Magazine House, 72 Broadwick Street, London W1V 2BP. Tel: 020-7439 5000. Fax: 020-7439 5482

HELLO! 69–71 Upper Ground, London SE1 9PQ. Tel: 020-7667 8700. Fax: 020-7667 8716

HISTORY TODAY 20 Old Compton Street, London W1D 4TW. Tel: 020-7534 8000. Email: editorial@historytoday.com; Web: www.historytoday.com

HOMES & GARDENS King's Reach Tower, Stamford Street, London SE1 9LS. Tel: 020-7261 5678. Fax: 020-7261 6247

HORSE AND HOUND Room 2018, King's Reach Tower, Stamford Street, London SE1 9LS. Tel: 020-7261 6315. Fax: 020-7261 5429. Email: jenny_sims@ipcmedia.com; Web: www.horseandhound.co.uk

ILLUSTRATED LONDON NEWS 20 Upper Ground, London SE1 9PF. Tel: 020-7805 5555. Fax: 020-7805 5911

IRISH POST Cambridge House, Cambridge Grove, London W6 0LE. Tel: 020-8741 0649. Fax: 020-8741 3382. Email: info@irishpost.co.uk; Web: www.irishpost.co.uk

J17 Endeavour House, 189 Shaftesbury Avenue, London WC2H 8JG. Tel: 020-7208 3408. Fax: 020-7208 3590. Email: sara.williams@emap.co.uk

JAZZ JOURNAL INTERNATIONAL 3 & 3A Forest Road, Loughton, Essex, IG10 1DR. Tel: 020-8532 0456. Fax: 020-8532 0440

LABOUR RESEARCH 78 Blackfriars Road, London SE1 8HF. Tel: 020-7928 3649. Fax: 020-7928 0621. Email: info@lrd.org.uk; Web: www.lrd.org.uk

LITERARY REVIEW 44 Lexington Street, London W1R 3LH. Tel: 020-7437 9392. Fax: 020-7734 1844. Email: litrev@dircon.co.uk

LOADED King's Reach Tower, Stamford Street, London SE1 9LS. Tel: 020-7261 5000. Fax: 020-7261 5640. Web: www.uploaded.com

LONDON GAZETTE (OFFICIAL) The Stationery Office, PO Box 7923, London SE1 5ZH. Tel: 020-7394 4580. Fax: 020-7394 4581. Web: www.london-gazette.co.uk

LONDON REVIEW OF BOOKS 28 Little Russell Street, London WC1A 2HN. Tel: 020-7209 1101. Fax: 020-7209 1102. Email: edit@lrb.co.uk; Web: www.lrb.co.uk

MAJESTY 26–28 Hallam Street, London W1N 6NP. Tel: 020-7436 4006. Fax: 020-7436 3458 Email: majestymagazine@aol.com

MARIE CLAIRE 2 Hatfields, London SE1 9PG. Tel: 020-7261 5177. Fax: 020-7261 5277

METEOROLOGICAL MAGAZINE The Stationery Office, PO Box 276, London SW8 5DT. Tel: 0870-600 5522. Fax: 020-7873 8200

MONEYWISE 11 Westferry Circus, Canary Wharf, London E14 4HE. Tel: 020-7715 8000. Fax: 020-7715 8181. Web: www.moneywise.co.uk

MORE! Endeavour House, 189 Shaftesbury Avenue, London WC2H 8JG. Tel: 020-7208 3165. Fax: 020-7208 3595. Email: more.letters@ecm.emap.com

NEEDLECRAFT Future Publishing, 30 Monmouth Street, Bath BA1 2BW. Tel: 01225-442244. Fax: 01225-732398. Email: needlecraft@futurenet.co.uk; Web: www.futurenet.co.uk

NEW INTERNATIONALIST 55 Rectory Road, Oxford OX4 1BW. Tel: 01865-728181. Fax: 01865-793152. Email: ni@newint.org; Web: www.newint.org

NEW MUSICAL EXPRESS (NME) King's Reach Tower, Stamford Street, London SE1 9LS. Tel: 020-7261 6472. Fax: 020-7261 5185

NEW SCIENTIST 151 Wardour Street, London W1F 8WE. Tel: 020-7331 2702. Fax: 020-7331 2777. Email: enquiries@newscientist.com; Web: www.newscientist.com

NEW STATESMAN 7th Floor, Victoria Station House, 191 Victoria Street, London SW1E 5NE. Tel: 020-7828 1232. Fax: 020-7828 1881. Email: info@newstatesman; Web: www.newstatesman.co.uk

NEWSWEEK 18 Park Street, London W1Y 4HH. Tel: 020-7629 8361. Fax: 020-7408 1403. Web: www.newsweek.msnbc.com

OK! Ludgate House, 245 Blackfriars Road, London SE1 9UX. Tel: 020-7928 8000. Fax: 020-7579 4607

OPERA 36 Black Lion Lane, London W6 9BE. Tel: 020-8563 8893. Fax: 020-8563 8635. Email: editor@operamag.clara.co.uk; Web: www.opera.co.uk

PARLIAMENTARY DEBATES (COMMONS) (HANSARD) The Stationery Office, PO Box 29, Norwich NR3 1GN. Tel: 0870-600 5522. Fax: 0870-600 5533

PARLIAMENTARY DEBATES (LORDS) (HANSARD) The Stationery Office, PO Box 29, Norwich NR3 1GN. Tel: 0870-600 5522. Fax: 0870-600 5533

PHILOSOPHY NOW 25 Blansfield Road, London SW12 8BQ. Tel: 020-8673 7310. Fax: 020-8675 5539. Email: info@philososphy now.demon.co.uk; Web: www.philosophynow.org

POETRY REVIEW 22 Betterton Street, London WC2H 9BU. Tel: 020-7420 9880. Fax: 020-7240 4818. Email: poetryreview@poetrysoc.com; Web: www.poetrysoc.com

PRACTICAL BOAT OWNER Westover House, West Quay Road, Poole, Dorset BH15 1JG. Tel: 01202-440820. Fax: 01202-440860. Email: pbo@ipcmedia.com; Web: www.pbo.co.uk

PRACTICAL PARENTING King's Reach Tower, Stamford Street, London SE1 9LS. Tel: 020-7261 5058. Fax: 020-7261 6542

PRACTICAL PHOTOGRAPHY Bretton Court, Bretton, Peterborough, PE3 8DZ. Tel: 01733-264666. Fax: 01733-465246. Email: practical.photography@emap.com

PRIMA 197 Marsh Wall, London E14 9SG. Tel: 020-7519 5500.

PRIVATE EYE 6 Carlisle Street, London W1D 3BN. Tel: 020-7437 4017. Fax: 020-7437 0705. Web: www.private-eye.co.uk

PROSPECT 4 Bedford Square, London WC1B 3RA. Tel: 020-7255 1281. Fax: 020-7255 1279. Email: editorial@prospect-magazine.co.uk; Web: www.prospect-magazine.co.uk

Q Mappin House, 4 Winsley Street, London W1V 8HF. Tel: 020-7436 1515. Fax: 020-7312 8247. Email: q@emap.com; Web: www.q4music.com

RUGBY WORLD King's Reach Tower, Stamford Street, London SE1 9LS. Tel: 020-7261 6810. Fax: 020-7261 5419. Email: Paul_Morgan@ipc.co.uk; Web: www.rugbyworld.com

SEA ANGLER Emap Active, Bushfield House, Orton Centre, Peterborough PE2 5UW. Tel: 01733-237111. Fax: 01733-465658

SHOOTING TIMES AND COUNTRY MAGAZINE King's Reach Tower, Stamford Street, London SE1 9LS. Tel: 020-7261 6180. Fax: 020-7261 7179. Email: julian_murray-evans@ipcmedia.co.uk

SLIMMING MAGAZINE Endeavour House, 189 Shaftesbury Avenue, London WC2H 8JG. Tel: 020-7437 1854. Fax: 020-7347 1863. Email: claire.selsby@emap.com

SMASH HITS Mappin House, 4 Winsley Street, London W1N 7AR. Tel: 020-7436 1515. Fax: 020-7636 0276.

TATLER Vogue House, Hanover Square, London W1R 0AD. Tel: 020-7499 9080. Fax: 020-7495 0451. Web: www.tatler.co.uk

THE BIG ISSUE 1/3 Rivington Street, London EC2A 3DT. Tel: 020-7526 3200. Fax: 020-7739 6734. Email: london@bigissue.com; Web: www.thebigissue.co.uk

THE COUNTRYMAN Sheep Street, Burford, Ofxordshire, London OX18 4LS. Tel: 01993-824424. Fax: 01993-822012

THE CRICKETER INTERNATIONAL Beech Hanger, Ashurst, Tunbridge Wells, Kent TN3 9ST. Tel: 01892-740256. Fax: 01892-740588

THE ECOLOGIST Unit 18, Chelsea Wharf, 15 Lots Road, London SW10 0QJ. Tel: 020-7351 3578. Fax: 020-7351 3617. Email: kate@theecologist.org; Web: www.theecologist.org

THE ECONOMIST 25 St James's Street, London SW1A 1HG. Tel: 020-7830 7000. Fax: 020-7839 2968. Web: www.economist.com

THE FACE 2nd Floor, Block A, Exmouth House, Pine Street, London EC1R 0JL. Tel: 020-7689 9999. Fax: 020-7689 0900

THE GOOD SKI GUIDE 145-147 Ewell Road, Surbiton, Surrey KT6 6AW. Tel: 020-8786 2950. Fax: 020-87862 2951. Email: info@goodskiguide.com; Web: www.goodskiguide.com

THE LADY 39–40 Bedford Street, London WC2E 9ER. Tel: 020-7379 4717. Fax: 020-7836 4620. Web: www.lady.co.uk

THE RACING CALENDAR British Horseracing Board Publications, c/o Weatherbys Group Ltd, Sanders Road, Wellingborough, Northants NN8 4BX. Tel: 01933-440077. Fax: 01933-270300. Email: pubsdept@weatherbys-group.com; Web: www.weatherbys-group.com

THE RAILWAY MAGAZINE King's Reach Tower, Stamford Street, London SE1 9LS. Tel: 020-7261 5821. Fax: 020-7261 5269. Email: railway@ipcmedia.co.uk

THE SPECTATOR 56 Doughty Street, London WC1N 2LL. Tel: 020-7405 1706. Fax: 020-7242 0603. Email: editor@spectator.co.uk; Web: www.spectator.co.uk

THE STRAD 3 Waterhouse Square, 138-142 Holbron, London EC1N 2NY. Tel: 020-7882 1040. . Email: thestrad@orpheuspublications.com; Web: www.thestrad.com

THE VOICE Blue Star House, 234-244 Stockwell Road, London SW9 9SP. Tel: 020-7737 7377. Fax: 020-7274 8994. Email: thevoicenewspaper@the-voice.co.uk; Web: www.voice-online.co.uk

THIS ENGLAND Alma House, 73 Rodney Road, Cheltenham, Glos GL50 1HT. Tel: 01242-537900. Fax: 01242-537901. Email: sales@thisengland.co.uk; Web: www.thisengland.co.uk

TIME MAGAZINE Brettenham House, Lancaster Place, London WC2E 7TL. Tel: 020-7490 4080. Fax: 020-7322 1230. Web: www.timeinc.com

TIME OUT Universal House, 251 Tottenham Court Road, London W1P 0AB. Tel: 020-7813 3000. Fax: 020-7813 6001. Web: www.timeout.com

TRIBUNE 9 Arkwright Road, London NW3 6AN. Tel: 020-7433 6410. Email: george@tribpub.demon.co.uk; Web: www.tribuneuk.co.uk

VACHER'S PARLIAMENTARY COMPANION 1 Douglas Street, London SW1P 4PA. Tel: 020-7828 7256. Fax: 020-7828 7269. Email: politics@vacherdod.co.uk; Web: www.politicallinks.co.uk

VANITY FAIR Vogue House, Hanover Square, London W1S 1JU. Tel: 020-7499 9080. Fax: 020-7493 1962

VIZ MAGAZINE The New Boathouse, 136–142 Bramley Road, London W10 6SR. Tel: 020-7565 3000. Fax: 020-7565 3055. Email: viz.comic@virgin.net; Web: www.viz.co.uk

VOGUE Vogue House, Hanover Square, London W1S 1JU. Tel: 020-7499 9080. Fax: 020-7408 0559. Web: www.vogue.co.uk

WEATHER Royal Meteorological Society, 104 Oxford Road, Reading RG1 7LL. Tel: 0118-956 8500. Fax: 0118-956 8571. Email: weather@royal-met-soc.org.uk; Web: www.royal-met-soc.org.uk

WHAT CAR? 60 Waldegrave Road, Teddington, Middx TW11 8LG. Tel: 020-8267 5688. Fax: 020-8267 5750. Email: whatcar@haynet.com; Web: www.whatcar.co.uk

WOMAN King's Reach Tower, Stamford Street, London SE1 9LS. Tel: 020-7261-7023. Fax: 020-7261 5997

WOMAN'S OWN King's Reach Tower, Stamford Street, London SE1 9LS. Tel: 020-7261 5500. Fax: 020-7261 5346

WOMAN'S WEEKLY King's Reach Tower, Stamford Street, London SE1 9LS. Tel: 0870 444 5000. Fax: 020-7261 5322

YACHTING MONTHLY King's Reach Tower, Stamford Street, London SE1 9LS. Tel: 020-7261 6040. Fax: 020-7261 7555. Email: yachting@ipcmedia.com; Web: www.yachtingmonthly.com

ZEST National Magazine House, 72 Broadwick Street, London W1V 2BP. Tel: 020-7439 5000. Fax: 020-7312 3750. Web: www.zest.co.uk

## TRADE, PROFESSIONAL AND ACADEMIC PERIODICAL

ACCOUNTANCY AGE VNU House, 32–34 Broadwick Street, London W1A 2HG. Tel: 020-7316 9000. Fax: 020-7316 9250. Email: accountancy.age@vnu.co.uk; Web: www.accountancyage.com

ANTIQUARIAN BOOK MONTHLY (ABM) PO Box 97, High Wycombe, Bucks HP14 4GH. Tel: 01494-562266. Fax: 01494-565533. Email: editor@abmr.co.uk; Web: www.abmr.co.uk

ANTIQUE DEALER AND COLLECTORS GUIDE PO Box 805, London SE10 8TD. Tel: 020-8691 4820. Fax: 020-8691 2489. Email: antiquedealercollectorsguide@ukbusiness.com; Web: www.antiquecollectorsguide.co.uk

ANTIQUES TRADE GAZETTE 115 Shaftesbury Avenue, London WC2H 8AD. Tel: 020-7420 6600. Fax: 020-7420 6605. Email: editorial@antiquestradegazette.com; Web: www.antiquestradegazette.com

THE ARCHITECTS' JOURNAL 151 Rosebery Avenue, London EC1R 4QW. Tel: 020-7505 6700. Fax: 020-7505 6701. Web: www.ajplus.co.uk

THE ARCHITECTURAL REVIEW 151 Rosebery Avenue, London EC1R 4GB. Tel: 020-7505 6725. Fax: 020-7505 6701. Web: www.arplus.com

THE AUTHOR Society of Authors, 84 Drayton Gardens, London SW10 9SB. Tel: 020-7373 6642. Fax: 020-7373 5768. Email: Dparker@societyofauthors.org; Web: www.societyofauthors.org

BIOLOGIST Institute of Biology, 20–22 Queensberry Place, London SW7 2DZ. Tel: 020-7581 8333. Fax: 020-7823 9409. Email: biologist@iob.org; Web: www.iob.org

THE BOOKSELLER 5th Floor, Endeavor House, 189 Shaftesbury Avenue, London WC2H 8TJ. Tel: 020-7420 6000. Fax: 020-7420 6177. Email: letters.to.editor@bookseller.co.uk; Web: www.thebookseller.com

BREWING AND DISTILLING INTERNATIONAL 52 Glenhouse Road, London SE9 1JQ. Tel: 020-8859 4300. Fax: 020-8859 5813. Email: bdilondon@dial.pipex.com; Web: www.bdinews.com

BRITISH BAKER Quantum House, 19 Scarbrook Road, Croydon CR9 1LX. Tel: 020-8565 4285. Fax: 020-8565 4303. Email: britishbaker@qpp.co.uk; Web: www.britishbaker.net

BRITISH DENTAL JOURNAL 64 Wimpole Street, London W1G 8YS. Tel: 020-7535 5830. Fax: 020-7535 5843. Email: bdj@bda-dentistry.co.uk; Web: www.bdj.co.uk

BRITISH JOURNAL OF PSYCHIATRY Royal College of Psychiatrists, 17 Belgrave Square, London SW1X 8PG. Tel: 020-7235 2351. Fax: 020-7259 6507. Web: www.repsych.ac.uk

BRITISH MEDICAL JOURNAL British Medical Association, BMA House, Tavistock Square, London WC1H 9JR. Tel: 020-7387 4499. Fax: 020-7383 6418. Email: bmj@bmj.com; Web: www.bmj.com

BRITISH TAX REVIEW 100 Avenue Road, London NW3 3PF. Tel: 020-7393 7000. Fax: 020-7393 7020.

BUILDING Exchange Tower, 2 Harbour Exchange Square, London E14 9GE. Tel: 020-7560 4000.

CAMPAIGN 174 Hammersmith Road, London W6 7JP. Tel: 020-8267 4656. Fax: 020-8267 4915. Email: campaign@haynet.com; Web: www.campaignlive.com

CHEMISTRY AND INDUSTRY 15 Belgrave Square, London SW1X 8PS. Tel: 020-7235 3681. Fax: 020-7235 9410. Email: enquiries@soci.org; Web: www.chemind.org

CHILD EDUCATION Villiers House, Clarendon Avenue, Leamington Spa, Warks CV32 5PR. Tel: 01926-887799. Fax: 01926-883331. Email: childed@scholastic.co.uk; Web: www.scholastic.co.uk

CLASSICAL MUSIC 241 Shaftesbury Avenue, London WC2H 8TF. Tel: 020-7333 1742. Fax: 020-7333 1736

COMPUTER WEEKLY Quadrant House, The Quadrant, Sutton, Surrey SM2 5AS. Tel: 020-8652 8642. Fax: 020-8652 8979. Email: computer.weekly@rbi.co.uk; Web: www.computerweekly.com

CONSTRUCTION NEWS 151 Rosebery Avenue, London EC1R 4GB. Tel: 020-7505 6868. Fax: 020-7505 6867. Web: www.onplus.co.uk

CRAFTS MAGAZINE Crafts Council, 44a Pentonville Road, London N1 9BY. Tel: 020-7806 2538. Fax: 020-7837 6891. Email: crafts@craftscouncil.org.uk; Web: www.craftscouncil.org.uk

DAIRY INDUSTRIES INTERNATIONAL Wilmington House, Maidstone Road, Foots Cray, Sidcup DA14 5HZ. Tel: 020-8269 7700. Fax: 020-8269 7874. Email: foodgroup@wilmington.co.uk; Web: www.connectingdairy.com

THE DENTIST Unit 2, Riverview Business Park, Walnut Tree Close, Guildford, Surrey GU1 4QT. Tel: 01483-304944. Fax: 01483-303191. Email: geowarman@aol.com

DESIGN WEEK St Giles House, 49–50 Poland Street, London W1F 7AX. Tel: 020-7970 6666. Fax: 020-7970 6430. Email: design-week@centaur.co.uk; Web: www.design-week.co.uk

THE DIRECTOR (Magazine of the Institute of Directors), 116 Pall Mall, London SW1Y 5ED. Tel: 020-7766 8950. Fax: 020-7766 8840. Email: director-ed@iod.co.uk; Web: www.iod.co.uk

DRAPERS RECORD Angel House, 338-346 Goswell Road, London EC1V 7QP. Tel: 020-7520 1534. Fax: 020-7837 4699. Email: dr@fashion.emap.co.uk

THE ECONOMIC JOURNAL 108 Cowley Road, Oxford OX4 1JF. Tel: 01865-791100. Fax: 01865-791347

EDUCATION TODAY Datateam Publishing Ltd, London Road, Maidstone, Kent ME16 8LY. Tel: 01622-687031. Fax: 01622-757646. Email: education@datateam.co.uk; Web: www.datateam.co.uk

ELECTRICAL AND RADIO TRADING Queensway House, 2 Queensway, Redhill, Surrey RH1 1QS. Tel: 01737-855271. Fax: 01737-855460. Email: ert@dmg.co.uk; Web: www.dmg.co.uk

THE ENGINEER St Giles House, 50 Poland Street, London W1F 7AX. Tel: 020-7970 4100. Fax: 020-7970 4189. Email: pcarslake@centaur.co.uk; Web: www.e4engineering.com

EQUITY JOURNAL Guild House, Upper St Martin's Lane, London WC2H 9EG. Tel: 020-7379 6000. Fax: 020-7379 6074. Email: mbrown@equity.org.uk; Web: www.equity.org.uk

ESTATES GAZETTE 151 Wardour Street, London W1V 4BN. Tel: 020-7437 0141. Fax: 020-7437 2432. Email: peter.bill@rbi.co.uk

FARMERS WEEKLY Quadrant House, The Quadrant, Sutton, Surrey SM2 5AS. Tel: 020-8652 4911. Fax: 020-8652 4005. Email: famers.weekly@rbi.co.uk; Web: www.fwi.co.uk

FINANCIAL MANAGEMENT Chartered Institute of Management Accountants, 63 Portland Place, London W1N 4AB. Tel: 020-7637 2311. Fax: 020-7580 6916

FIRE PREVENTION Fire Protection Association, Bastille Court, 2 Paris Garden, London SE1 8ND. Tel: 020-7902 5308. Fax: 020-7902 5301. Email: fpa@thefpa.co.uk; Web: www.thefpa.co.uk

FLIGHT INTERNATIONAL Quadrant House, The Quadrant, Sutton, Surrey SM2 5AS. Tel: 020-8652 3842. Fax: 020-8652 3840. Email: flight.international@rbi.co.uk; Web: www.flightinternational.com

FORESTRY AND BRITISH TIMBER Sovereign House, Sovereign Way, Tonbridge, Kent TN9 1RW. Tel: 01732-364422. Fax: 01732-361534

FOUNDRY TRADE JOURNAL Queensway House, 2 Queensway, Redhill, Surrey RH1 1QS. Tel: 01737-855164. Fax: 01737-855469. Web: www.dmg.co.uk/castings/

GEOGRAPHY Geographical Association, 160 Solly Street, Sheffield S1 4BF. Tel: 0114-296 0088. Fax: 0114-296 7176. Email: ga@geography.org.uk; Web: www.geography.org.uk

GEOLOGICAL MAGAZINE Cambridge University Press, The Edinburgh Building, Shaftesbury Road, Cambridge CB2 2RU. Tel: 01223-325757. Fax: 01223-315052

THE GROCER Broadfield Park, Crawley, W. Sussex RH11 9RT. Tel: 01293-613400. Fax: 01293-610333. Email: grocer.editorial@william.reed.co.uk; Web: www.foodanddrink.co.uk

GROWER Nexus House, Azalea Drive, Swanley, Kent BR8 8HU. Tel: 01322-660070. Fax: 01322-667633

HAIRDRESSERS' JOURNAL INTERNATIONAL Quadrant House, The Quadrant, Sutton, Surrey SM2 5AS. Tel: 020-8652 8251. Fax: 020-8652 8937

INTERNATIONAL AFFAIRS RIIA, 10 St. James's Square, London SW1Y 4LE. Tel: 020-7957 5700. Fax: 020-7957 5710. Email: c.soper@riia.org; Web: www.riia.org

JANE'S DEFENCE WEEKLY Sentinel House, 163 Brighton Road, Coulsdon, Surrey CR5 2YH. Tel: 020-8700 3700. Fax: 020-8763 1007. Email: jdw@janes.co.uk; Web: www.jdw.janes.com

JOURNAL OF THE BRITISH ASTRONOMICAL ASSOCIATION Burlington House, Piccadilly, London W1J 0BQ. Tel: 020-7734 4145. Fax: 020-7439 4629. Web: www.star.ucl.ac.uk

JUSTICE OF THE PEACE REPORTS Butterworths Tolley, Halsbury House, 35 Chancery Lane, London WC2A 1EL. Tel: 020-7400 2828. Fax: 020-8686 3155. Email: jpr@tolley.co.uk

THE LANCET 84 Theobalds Road, London WC1X 8RR. Tel: 020-7611 4100. Fax: 020-7611 4101. Web: www.thelancet.com

THE LAW REPORTS Megarry House, 119 Chancery Lane, London WC2A 1PP. Tel: 020-7242 6741. Fax: 020-7831 5247. Email: postmaster@iclr.co.uk; Web: www.lawreports.co.uk

LEISURE AND HOSPITALITY BUSINESS St Giles House, 49–50 Poland Street, London W1F 7AX. Tel: 020-7970 4588. Fax: 020-7970 4891. Email: mels@centaur.co.uk; Web: www.leisureandhospitalitybusiness.co.uk

LIBRARY ASSOCIATION RECORD 7 Ridgmount Street, London WC1E 7AE. Tel: 020-7255 0500. Fax: 020-7255 0581. Email: record@la-hq.org.uk; Web: www.la-hq.org.uk/record

LOCAL GOVERNMENT CHRONICLE Greater London House, Hampstead Rd, London NW1 7EJ. Tel: 020-7347 1837. Fax: 020-7347 1831. Email: lgc@lgc.emap.com; Web: www.lgcnet.com

MANAGEMENT TODAY 174 Hammersmith Road, London W6 7JP. Tel: 020-7413 4360. Fax: 020-7413 4515. Email: management.today@haynet.com; Web: www.clickmt.com

MANAGING INFORMATION Aslib-IMI, Staple Hall, Stone House Court, London EC3A 7PB. Tel: 020-7903 0000. Fax: 020-7903 0011. Email: graham.coult@aslib.com; Web: www.managinginformation.com

MARKETING 174 Hammersmith Road, London W6 7JP. Tel: 020-8267 4150. Fax: 020-8267 4504. Email: marketing@haynet.com; Web: www.marketing.haynet.com

MARKETING WEEK St Giles House, 49–50 Poland Street, London W1F 7AX. Tel: 020-7970 4000. Fax: 020-7970 6721. Web: www.marketing-week.co.uk

MATERIALS WORLD Institute of Materials, 1 Carlton House Terrace, London SW1Y 5DB. Tel: 020-7451 7321. Fax: 020-7451 7319. Email: materials_world@materials.org.uk; Web: www.materials.org.uk

MEDIA WEEK Quantum House, 19 Scarbrook Road, Croydon, Surrey CR9 1LX. Tel: 020-8565 4323. Fax: 020-8565 4394. Email: mweeked@qpp.co.uk; Web: www.mediaweek.co.uk

MINING JOURNAL 60 Worship Street, London EC2A 2HD. Tel: 020-7216 6060. Fax: 020-7216 6050. Email: editorial@mining-journal.com; Web: www.mining-journal.com/mj

MUNICIPAL JOURNAL 32 Vauxhall Bridge Road, London SW1V 2SS. Tel: 020-7973 6400. Fax: 020-7233 5053

MUSIC JOURNAL Incorporated Society of Musicians, 10 Stratford Place, London W1C 1AA. Tel: 020-7629 4413. Fax: 020-7408 1538. Email: membership@ism.org; Web: www.ism.org

MUSICIAN 241 Shaftesbury Avenue, London WC2H 8TF. Tel: 020-7333 1733. Fax: 020-7333 1736. Web: www.musiciansunion.org.uk

NUCLEAR ENGINEERING INTERNATIONAL Maidstone Road, Foots Cray, Sidcup, Kent DA14 5HZ. Tel: 020-8269 770. Fax: 020-8269 7878. Email: energy-advertising@wilmington.co.uk; Web: www.connectingpower.com

OPTICIAN Quadrant House, The Quadrant, Sutton, Surrey SM2 5AS. Tel: 020-8652 8243. Fax: 020-8652 8993

PATENT WORLD Informa Professional, 69–77 Paul Street, London EC2A 4LQ. Tel: 020-7553 1000. Fax: 020-7553 1107. Email: Iquraishi@informa.com; Web: www.ipworldonline.com

PEOPLE MANAGEMENT 17 Britton Street, London EC1M 5TP. Tel: 020-7880 6200. Fax: 020-7336 7635. Email: editorial@peoplemanagement.co.uk; Web: www.peoplemanagement.co.uk

PHARMACEUTICAL JOURNAL Royal Pharmaceutical Society of Great Britain, 1 Lambeth High Street, London SE1 7JN. Tel: 020-7735 9141. Fax: 020-7582 7327. Email: editor@pharmj.org.uk; Web: www.pharmj.com

PHILOSOPHY (JOURNAL OF THE ROYAL INSTITUTE OF PHILOSOPHY) The Royal Institute of Philosophy, 14 Gordon Square, London WC1H 0AG. Tel: 020-7387 4130. Fax: 020-7383 4061. Email: j.garvey@royalinstitutephilosophy.org; Web: www.royalinstitutephilosophy.org

THE PHOTOGRAPHER British Institute of Professional Photography, Fox Talbot House, Amwell End, Ware, Herts SG12 9HN. Tel: 01920-464011. Fax: 01920-487056. Email: bipp@compuserve.com; Web: www.bipp.com

PHYSICS WORLD Dirac House, Temple Back, Bristol BS1 6BE. Tel: 0117-929 7481. Fax: 0117-930 1178

POLICE REVIEW Jane's Information Group, 180 Wardour Street, London W1F 8FS. Tel: 020-7851 9700.

PRINTING WORLD Sovereign House, Sovereign Way, Tonbridge, Kent TN9 1RW. Tel: 01732-377391. Fax: 01732-377552. Email: printing.world@cmpinformation.com; Web: www.dotprint.com

PROBATION JOURNAL 217A Balham High Road, London SW17 7BP. Tel: 020-8671 0640. Fax: 020-8671 0640. Email: prbjournal@aol.com

THE PSYCHOLOGIST British Psychological Society, St Andrews House, 48 Princess Road East, Leicester LE1 7DR. Tel: 0116-254 9568. Fax: 0116-247 0787. Email: psychologist@bps.org.uk; Web: www.bps.org.uk

RUSI JOURNAL Royal United Services Institute for Defence Studies, Whitehall, London SW1A 2ET. Tel: 020-7930 5854. Fax: 020-7321 0943. Web: www.rusi.org

SOCIOLOGICAL REVIEW 108 Cowley Road, Oxford OX4 1JF. Tel: 01865-791100. Fax: 01865-791347

SOLICITORS JOURNAL 100 Avenue Road, London NW3 3PG. Tel: 020-7393 7000. Fax: 020-7393 7780. Email: solicitors.journal@sweetandmaxwell.co.uk; Web: www.sweetandmaxwell.co.uk

THE STAGE 47 Bermondsey Street, London SE1 3XT. Tel: 020-7403 1818. Fax: 020-7357 9287. Email: editor@thestage.co.uk; Web: www.thestage.co.uk

TAX ADVISER The Chartered Institute of Taxation, 12 Upper Belgrave Street, London SW1X 8BB. Tel: 020-7235 9381. Fax: 020-7235 2562. Email: post@tax.org.uk; Web: www.tax.org.uk

TAXI Taxi House, 7–11 Woodfield Road, London W9 2BA. Tel: 020-7432 1429. Fax: 020-7266 2297. Email: spessok@comcab.co.uk

THE TEACHER National Union of Teachers, Hamilton House, Mabledon Place, London WC1H 9BD. Tel: 020-7380 4708. Fax: 020-7387 8458. Email: teacher@netcomuk.co.uk; Web: www.teachers.org.uk

TELEVISION Royal Television Society, Holborn Hall, 100 Gray's Inn Road, London WC1X 8AL. Tel: 020-7430 1000. Fax: 020-7430 0924. Email: publications@rts.org.uk; Web: www.rts.org.uk

TEXTILE MONTH Perkin House, 1 Longlands Street, Bradford, W. Yorks BD1 2TB. Tel: 01274-378800. Fax: 01274-378811. Email: adrianw@aol.com; Web: www.world-textile.com

TOWN AND COUNTRY PLANNING Town and Country Planning Association, 17 Carlton House Terrace, London SW1Y 5AS. Tel: 020-7930 8903. Fax: 020-7930 3280. Email: editor@tcpa.org.uk; Web: www.tcpa.org.uk

TRAVEL TRADE GAZETTE (UK AND IRELAND) 1st Floor, City Reach, 5 Greenwich View Place, Millharbour, London E14 9NN. Tel: 020-7861 6096. Fax: 020-7861 6227. Email: phil.davies@unmf.com

VETERINARY RECORD 7 Mansfield Street, London W1G 9NQ. Tel: 020-7636 6541.

THE WEEKLY LAW REPORTS Megarry House, 119 Chancery Lane, London WC2A 1PP. Tel: 020-7242 6471. Fax: 020-7831 5247. Email: postmaster@iclr.co.uk; Web: www.lawreports.co.uk

# Book Publishers

AA PUBLISHING
Fanum House, Basingstoke, Hants RG21 4EA.
Tel: 08705-448866; Fax: 01256-322575;
Web: www.theaa.co.uk

AGE CONCERN ENGLAND
Astral House, 1268 London Road, London SW16 4ER.
Tel: 020-8765 7200; Fax: 020-8765 7211;
Email: ace@ace.org.uk; Web: www.ageconcern.org.uk

ALLEN & UNWIN
PO Box 30474, London NW6 7FQ.
Tel: 020-8537 1531; Fax: 020-8621 3701;
Email: allenunwin@compuserve.com;
Web: www.allen-unwin.com.au

ALLISON & BUSBY
Suite 111, The Bon Marche Centre, 241 Ferndale Rd, London SW9 8BJ. Tel: 020-7636 2942; Fax: 020-7323 2023; Email: all@allisonbusby.co.uk;
Web: www.allisonandbusby.ltd.uk

APPLE PRESS
The Old Brewery, 6 Blundell Street, London N7 9BH.
Tel: 020-7700 2929; Fax: 020-7609 6695;
Email: apple@quarto.com

ARNOLD
338 Euston Road, London NW1 3BH.
Tel: 020-7873 6000; Fax: 020-7873 6325;
Email: arnold@hodder.co.uk;
Web: www.arnoldpublishers.com

ARROW BOOKS
Random House UK, 20 Vauxhall Bridge Road, London SW1V 2SA.
Tel: 020-7840 8400; Fax: 020-7932 0761;
Email: enquiries@randomhouse.co.uk;
Web: www.randomhouse.co.uk

ASLIB, THE ASSOCIATION FOR INFORMATION MANAGEMENT
Staple Hall, Stone House Court, London EC3A 7PB.
Tel: 020-7903 0000; Fax: 020-7903 0011;
Email: aslib@aslib.com; Web: www.aslib.com

AURUM PRESS
25 Bedford Avenue, London WC1B 3AT.
Tel: 020-7637 3225; Fax: 020-7580 2469;
Email: editorial@aurumpress.co.uk;
Web: www.aurumpress.co.uk

BANTAM BOOKS
61-63 Uxbridge Road, London W5 5SA.
Tel: 020-8579 2652; Fax: 020-8231 6612;
Web: www.booksattransworld.co.uk

A. & C. BLACK
35 Bedford Row, London WC1R 4JH.
Tel: 020-7242 0946; Fax: 020-7831 8478;
Email: enquiries@acblack.com;
Web: www.acblack.co.uk

BLACKWELL PUBLISHERS
108 Cowley Road, Oxford OX4 1JF.
Tel: 01865-791100; Fax: 01865-791347;
Web: www.blackwellpublishers.co.uk

BLOOMSBURY PUBLISHING
38 Soho Square, London W1D 3HB.
Tel: 020-7494 2111; Fax: 020-7434 0151;
Web: www.bloomsbury.com

BRIMAX CHILDREN'S BOOKS
2–4 Heron Quays, London E14 4JP.
Tel: 020-7531 8598; Fax: 020-7531 8607;
Web: www.brimax.co.uk

BUTTERWORTH TOLLEY
Halsbury House, 35 Chancery Lane, London WC2A 1EL.
Tel: 020-7400 2500; Fax: 020-7400 2842

CADOGAN BOOKS
Network House, 1 Ariel Way, London W12 7SL.
Tel: 020-8600 3550; Fax: 020-8600 3599;
Email: guides@morrispub.co.uk;
Web: www.cadoganguides.com

CAMBRIDGE UNIVERSITY PRESS
The Edinburgh Building, Shaftesbury Road, Cambridge CB2 2RU. Tel: 01223-325566;
Web: www.uk.cambridge.org

JONATHAN CAPE
20 Vauxhall Bridge Road, London SW1V 2SA.
Tel: 020-7840 8400; Fax: 020-7233 6117;
Email: enquiries@randomhouse.co.uk;
Web: www.randomhouse.co.uk

CASSELL & CO
Wellington House, 125 Strand, London WC2R 0BB.
Tel: 020-7420 5555; Fax: 020-7240 7261

CAVENDISH PUBLISHING
The Glass House, Wharton Street, London WC1X 9PX.
Tel: 020-7278 8000; Fax: 020-7278 8080;
Email: info@cavendishpublishing.com;
Web: www.cavendishpublishing.com

CENTURY
Random House Group Ltd, 20 Vauxhall Bridge Road, London SW1V 2SA.
Tel: 020-7840 8400; Fax: 020-7233 6127;
Email: enquiries@randomhouse.co.uk;
Web: www.randomhouse.co.uk

CHAMBERS HARRAP PUBLISHERS LTD
7 Hopetoun Crescent, Edinburgh EH7 4AY.
Tel: 0131-556 5929; Fax: 0131-556 5313;
Email: enquiries@chambersharrap.co.uk;
Web: www.chambersharrap.com

CHIVERS PRESS
Windsor Bridge Road, Bath BA2 3AX.
Tel: 01225-335336; Fax: 01225-310771;
Email: sales@chivers.co.uk; Web: www.chivers.co.uk

CHURCH HOUSE PUBLISHING
Church House, Great Smith Street, London SW1P 3NZ.
Tel: 020-7898 1451; Fax: 020-7898 1449;
Email: publishing@c-of-e.org.uk;
Web: www.chpublishing.co.uk

DARTON, LONGMAN & TODD
1 Spencer Court, 140–142 Wandsworth High Street, London SW18 4 JJ. Tel: 020-8875 0155; Fax: 020-8875 0133; Email: mail@darton-longman-todd.co.uk

DEBRETT'S PEERAGE LTD
Kings Court, 2–16 Goodge Street, London W1T 2QA.
Tel: 020-7753 4213; Fax: 020-7753 4212;
Email: people@debretts.co.uk;
Web: www.debretts.co.uk

ANDRE DEUTSCH
20 Mortimer Street, London W1T 3JW.
Tel: 020-7612 0400; Fax: 020-7612 0401

DORLING KINDERSLEY
80 Strand, London WC2R 0RL.
Tel: 020-7010 3000; Web: www.dk.com

DOUBLEDAY
61–63 Uxbridge Road, London W5 5SA.
Tel: 020-8579 2652; Fax: 020-8579 5479;
Web: www.booksattransworld.co.uk

EBURY PRESS
20 Vauxhall Bridge Road, London SW1V 2SA.
Tel: 020-7840 8400; Web: www.randomhouse.co.uk

ELSEVIER SCIENCE
The Boulevard, Langford Lane, Kidlington, Oxon OX5 1GB. Tel: 01865-843000; Web: www.elsevier.co.uk

ENCYCLOPAEDIA BRITANNICA INTERNATIONAL
16 Golden Square, London W1F 9JQ.
Tel: 020-7851 1000; Fax: 020-7861 1040;
Email: enq@britannica.co.uk;
Web: www.britannica.co.uk

EPWORTH PRESS
SCM Press, 9–17 St Albans Place, London N1 0NX.
Tel: 020-7359 8033; Fax: 020-7359 0049;
Email: scmpress@btinternet.com

FABER & FABER
3 Queen Square, London WC1N 3AU.
Tel: 020-7465 0045; Fax: 020-7465 0034;
Email: mailbox@faber.co.uk; Web: www.faber.co.uk

FOURTH ESTATE
77-85 Fulham Palace Road, London W6 8JB.
Tel: 020-8741 4414; Fax: 020-8307 4466;
Email: general@4thestate.co.uk;
Web: www.4thestate.co.uk

SAMUEL FRENCH LTD
52 Fitzroy Street, London W1T 5JR.
Tel: 020-7387 9373; Fax: 020-7387 2161;
Email: theatre@samuelfrench-london.co.uk;
Web: www.samuelfrench-london.co.uk

GALE RESEARCH INTERNATIONAL
2nd Floor, 110 St Martin's Lane, London WC2N 4AZ.
Tel: 020-7257 2930; Web: www.galegroup.com

GINN & CO.
Linacre House, Jordan Hill, Oxford OX2 8DP.
Tel: 01865-888000; Fax: 01865-314116;
Email: services@ginn.co.uk; Web: www.ginn.co.uk

GOWER PUBLISHING LTD
Gower House, Croft Road, Aldershot, Hants GU11 3HR. Tel: 01252-331551; Fax: 01252-344405;
Email: info@gowerpub.com;
Web: www.gowerpub.com

ROBERT HALE
45 Clerkenwell Green, London EC1R 0HT.
Tel: 020-7251 2661; Fax: 020-7490 4958;
Email: enquire@halebooks.com;
Web: www.halebooks.com

HAMLYN
2–4 Heron Quays, London E14 4JP.
Tel: 020-7531 8400; Fax: 020-7531 8650;
Email: info-ho@hamlyn.co.uk;
Web: www.hamlyn.co.uk

HARCOURT BRACE
32 Jamestown Road, London NW1 7BY.
Tel: 020-7424 4200

HARPERCOLLINS PUBLISHERS
77–85 Fulham Palace Road, London W6 8JB.
Tel: 020-8741 7070; Fax: 020-8307 4440;
Web: www.fireandwater.com

R. HAZELL & CO
PO Box 39, Henley on Thames, Oxfordshire RG9 5UA.
Tel: 01491-641018

HEINEMANN (WILLIAM)
The Random House Group, 20 Vauxhall Bridge Road, London SW1V 2SA.
Tel: 020-7840 8400; Fax: 020-7233 6127;
Web: www.randomhouse.co.uk

HERBERT PRESS
35 Bedford Row, London WC1R 4JH.
Tel: 020-7242 0946; Fax: 020-7831 7489;
Email: llambert@acblack.co.uk

ISIS PUBLISHING
24 Nutford Place, London W1H 6DQ.
Tel: 0171-724 7773

JARROLD PUBLISHING
Whitefriars, Norwich NR3 1TR.
Tel: 01603-763300; Fax: 01603-662748;
Email: publishing@jarrold.com;
Web: www.jarrold-publishing.co.uk

JORDAN PUBLISHING
21 St Thomas Street, Bristol BS1 6JS.
Tel: 0117-923 0600; Fax: 0117-925 0486;
Email: webmaster@jordanpublishing.co.uk;
Web: www.jordanpublishing.co.uk

KINGFISHER PUBLICATIONS PLC
New Penderel House, 283–288 High Holborn, London WC1V 7HZ.
Tel: 020-7903 9999; Fax: 020-7242 4979;
Email: jhudron@kingfisherpub.co.uk;
Web: www.kingfisherpub.com

KINGSWAY PUBLICATIONS
Lottbridge Drove, Eastbourne BN23 6NT.
Tel: 01323-437700; Fax: 01323-411970;
Email: books@kingsway.co.uk;
Web: www.kingsway.co.uk

KOGAN PAGE
120 Pentonville Road, London N1 9JN.
Tel: 020-7278 0433; Fax: 020-7837 6348;
Email: kpinfo@kogan-page.co.uk;
Web: www.kogan-page.co.uk

LETTS EDUCATIONAL
Aldine House, Aldine Place, London W12 8AW.
Tel: 020-8740 2266; Fax: 020-8743 8451;
Email: mail@lettsed.co.uk;
Web: www.letts-education.com

FRANCES LINCOLN
4 Torriano Mews, Torriano Avenue, London NW5 2RZ.
Tel: 020-7284 4009; Fax: 020-7485 0490;
Email: reception@frances-lincoln.com

LITTLE, BROWN & CO.
Brettenham House, Lancaster Place, London WC2E 7EN.
Tel: 020-7911 8000; Fax: 020-7911 8100;
Email: email.uk@littlebrown.com;
Web: www.littlebrown.co.uk

LUTTERWORTH PRESS
PO Box 60, Cambridge CB1 2NT.
Tel: 01223-350865; Fax: 01223-366951;
Email: sales@jamesclarke.co.uk;
Web: www.jamesclarke.co.uk

MACMILLAN PUBLISHERS
25 Eccleston Place, London SW1W 9NF.
Tel: 020-7881 8000Web: www.macmillan.com

MAINSTREAM PUBLISHING CO.
7 Albany Street, Edinburgh EH1 3UG.
Tel: 0131-557 2959; Fax: 0131-556 8720;
Email: enquiries@mainstreampublishing.com;
Web: www.mainstreampublishing.com

MCGRAW-HILL
Shoppenhangers Road, Maidenhead, Berks SL6 2QL.
Tel: 01628-502500; Fax: 01628-770224;
Email: sales@mcgraw-hill.com;
Web: www.mcgraw-hill.co.uk

METHUEN PUBLISHING LTD
215 Vauxhall Bridge Road, London SW1V 1EJ.
Tel: 020-7798 1600; Fax: 020-7828 2098;
Web: www.methuen.co.uk

JOHN MURRAY
50 Albemarle Street, London W1S 4BD.
Tel: 020-7493 4361; Fax: 020-7499 1792;
Web: www.johnmurray.co.uk

OCTOPUS PUBLISHING GROUP
2–4 Heron Quays, London E14 4JP.
Tel: 020-7531 8400; Fax: 020-7531 8650

MICHAEL O'MARA BOOKS LTD
9 Lion Yard, Tremadoc Road, London SW4 7NQ.
Tel: 020-7720 8643; Fax: 020-7627 8953;
Email: enquiries@michaelomarabooks.com;
Web: www.mombooks.com

OXFORD UNIVERSITY PRESS
Great Clarendon Street, Oxford OX2 6DP.
Tel: 01865-556767; Fax: 01865-556646;
Email: enquiry@oup.co.uk; Web: www.oup.co.uk

PAVILION BOOKS LTD
London House, Great Eastern Wharf, Parkgate Road, London SW11 4NQ.
Tel: 020-7350 1230; Fax: 020-7350 1261;
Email: info@pavilionbooks.co.uk;
Web: www.pavilionbooks.co.uk

PEARSON EDUCATION
Edinburgh Gate, Harlow CM20 2JE.
Tel: 01279-623928

PENGUIN BOOKS
27 Wrights Lane, London W8 5TZ.
Tel: 020-7416 3000; Fax: 020-7416 3099;
Email: penguin@penguin.co.uk;
Web: www.penguin.co.uk

PHAIDON PRESS
Regent's Wharf, All Saints Street, London N1 9PA.
Tel: 020-7843 1234; Fax: 020-7843 1111;
Email: sales@phaidon.com

PITMAN PUBLISHING
128 Long Acre, London WC2E 9AN.
Tel: 020-7447 2000; Web: www.pearson-ema.com

QUARTET BOOKS
27 Goodge Street, London W1P 2LD.
Tel: 020-7636 3992; Fax: 020-7637 1866;
Email: quartetbooks@easynet.co.uk

QUILLER PRESS
46 Lillie Road, London SW6 1TN.
Tel: 020-7499 6529; Fax: 020-7381 8941;
Email: greenwood@quiller.conx.co.uk

RANDOM HOUSE UK
20 Vauxhall Bridge Road, London SW1V 2SA.
Tel: 020-7840 8400

REED BUSINESS INFORMATION
Quadrant House, The Quadrant, Sutton, Surrey SM2 5AS. Tel: 020-8652 3500; Fax: 020-8652 8932;
Web: www.reedbusiness.com

ROUGH GUIDES
62–70 Shorts Gardens, London WC2H 9AH.
Tel: 020-7556 5000; Fax: 020-7556 5050;
Email: mail@roughguides.co.uk;
Web: www.roughguides.com

ROUTLEDGE
11 New Fetter Lane, London EC4P 4EE.
Tel: 020-7583 9855; Fax: 020-7842 2298

SAINT ANDREW PRESS
121 George Street, Edinburgh EH2 4YN.
Tel: 0131-225 5722; Fax: 0131-200 3113

SCHOLASTIC CHILDREN'S BOOKS
Commonwealth House, 1–19 New Oxford Street, London WC1A 1NU.
Tel: 020-7421 9000; Fax: 020-7421 9001;
Email: publicity@scholastic.co.uk;
Web: www.scholastic.co.uk

SCM PRESS
9-17 St Albans Place, London N1 0NX.
Tel: 020-7359 8033; Fax: 020-7359 0049;
Email: scmpress@btinternet.com;
Web: www.scm-canterburypress.co.uk

SECKER & WARBURG
20 Vauxhall Bridge Road, London SW1V 2SA.
Tel: 020-7840 8570; Fax: 020-7233 6117;
Web: www.randomhouse.co.uk

SERPENT'S TAIL
4 Blackstock Mews, London N4 2BT.
Tel: 020-7354 1949; Fax: 020-7704 6467;
Email: info@serpentstail.com

SPCK
Holy Trinity Church, Marylebone Road, London NW1 4DU. Tel: 020-7643 0382; Fax: 020-7643 0391;
Email: publishing@spck.org.uk;
Web: www.spck.org.uk

THE STATIONERY OFFICE LTD
PO Box 29, Norwich NR3 1GN.
Tel: 0870-600 5522;
Web: www.thestationeryoffice.com

SWEET & MAXWELL
100 Avenue Road, London NW3 3PF.
Tel: 020-7393 7000; Fax: 020-7393 7010;
Web: www.sweetandmaxwell.co.uk

TAYLOR & FRANCIS
Routledge, 11 New Fetter Lane, London EC4P 4EE.
Tel: 020-7842 2001; Fax: 020-7842 2298

USBORNE PUBLISHING
Usborne House, 83–85 Saffron Hill, London EC1N 8RT.
Tel: 020-7430 2800; Fax: 020-7430 1562;
Email: mail@usborne.co.uk; Web: www.usborne.com

VIKING
27 Wrights Lane, London W8 5TZ.
Tel: 020-7416 3000; Fax: 020-7416 3290;
Web: www.penguin.co.uk

VIRAGO PRESS
Brettenham House, Lancaster Place, London WC2E 7EN. Tel: 020-7911 8000; Fax: 020-7911 8100;
Email: email.uk@littlebrown.com;
Web: www.virago.co.uk

VIRGIN PUBLISHING
Units 5 and 6, Thames Wharf, Rainville Road, London W6 9HT. Tel: 020-7386 3300
Email: publicity@virgin-pub.co.uk;
Web: www.virgin-books.com

WALKER BOOKS
87 Vauxhall Walk, London SE11 5HJ.
Tel: 020-7793 0909; Fax: 020-7587 1123

WATTS PUBLISHING GROUP
96 Leonard Street, London EC2A 4XD.
Tel: 020-7739 2929; Fax: 020-7739 2318;
Email: gm@wattspub.co.uk;
Web: www.wattspub.co.uk

J. WHITAKER
Woolmead House West, Bear Lane, Farnham GU9 7LG. Tel: 01252-742500; Fax: 01252-742501;
Email: custserv@whitaker.co.uk;
Web: www.whitaker.co.uk

# Annual Reference Books

ADVERTISER'S ANNUAL (£247)
Harlequin House, 7 High Street, Teddington TW11 8EL
Tel: 020-8977 7711; Fax: 020-8977 1133;
Web: www.hollis-pr.co.uk

ANNUAL ABSTRACT OF STATISTICS (£39.50)
PO Box 29, Norwich NR3 1GN
Tel: 0870-600 5522

ASTRONOMICAL ALMANAC (£32.50)
PO Box 29, Norwich NR3 1GN
Tel: 0870-600 5522

BAILY'S HUNTING DIRECTORY (£34.95)
Chesterton Mill, French's Road, Cambridge CB4 3NP
Tel: 01223-350555; Fax: 01223-356484;
Email: info@pearson.co.uk

BENEDICTINE AND CISTERCIAN MONASTIC YEAR BOOK (£2.50)
Ampleforth Abbey, York YO62 4EN
Tel: 01257-463248;
Email: osbyearbook@hotmail.com;
Web: www.benedictines.org.uk

BRITAIN: THE OFFICIAL HANDBOOK OF THE UNITED KINGDOM (£37.50)
PO Box 29, Norwich NR3 1GN
Tel: 0870-600 5522

BRITISH THEATRE DIRECTORY (£40.95)
Douglas House, 3 Richmond Buildings, London W1D 3HE
Tel: 020-7437 9556; Fax: 020-7287 3463;
Email: sales@rhpco.co.uk; Web: www.rhpco.co.uk

BROWN'S NAUTICAL ALMANAC DAILY TIDE TABLES (£45)
4–10 Darnley Street, Glasgow G41 2SD
Tel: 0141-429 1234; Fax: 0141-420 1694;
Email: info@skipper.co.uk; Web: www.skipper.co.uk

CHRISTIES' REVIEW OF THE YEAR (£45)
1 Langley Lane, London SW8 1TH
Tel: 020-7389 2242; Fax: 020-7820 9659;
Email: christiesbooks@christies.com;
Web: www.christies.com

COMMONWEALTH UNIVERSITIES YEARBOOK (£180)
36 Gordon Square, London WC1H 0PF
Tel: 020-7380 6700; Fax: 020-7387 2655;
Email: acusales@acu.ac.uk; Web: www.acu.ac.uk

DEBRETT'S PEOPLE OF TODAY (£140)
Kings Court, 2-16 Goodge Street, London W1T 2QA
Tel: 020-7753 4213; Fax: 020 7753 4212

THE EDUCATION AUTHORITIES' DIRECTORY AND ANNUAL (£75)
Darby House, Bletchingley Road, Merstham, Redhill, Surrey RH1 3DN
Tel: 01737-642223; Fax: 01737-644283;
Email: ead@schoolgovernment.co.uk;
Web: www.schoolgovernment.co.uk/pages/pub/ead.htm

ELECTRONICS AND ELECTRICAL BUYER'S GUIDE (£82)
Riverbank House, Angle Lane, Tonbridge, Kent TN9 1SE
Tel: 01732-377556; Fax: 01732-377454;
Email: industry@cmpinformation.com;
Web: www.electronics-electrical.co.uk

EUROPA WORLD YEAR BOOK (£495)
11 New Fetter Lane, London EC4P 4EE
Tel: 020-7842 2110; Fax: 020-842 2249;
Email: info.europa@tandf.co.uk

THE EUROPA DIRECTORY OF INTERNATIONAL ORGANISATIONS (£150)
11 New Fetter Lane, London EC4P 4EE
Tel: 020-7842 2110; Fax: 020-7842 2249;
Email: info.europa@tandf.co.uk

GUINNESS BOOK OF RECORDS (£18)
Brunel Road, Houndsmills, Basingstoke, Hants RG21 2XS
Tel: 01256-329242; Fax: 01256-327961

HOLLIS SPONSORSHIP AND DONATIONS YEARBOOK (£110)
Harlequin House, 7 High Street, Teddington TW11 8EL
Tel: 020-8977 7711; Fax: 020-8977 1133

HOLLIS UK PRESS AND PR ANNUAL (£132.50)
Harlequin House, 7 High Street, Teddington TW11 8EL
Tel: 020-8977 7711; Fax: 020-8977 1133;
Email: orders@hollis-pr.co.uk; Web: www.hollis-pr.com

INTERNATIONAL WHO'S WHO (£210)
11 New Fetter Lane, London EC4P 4EE
Tel: 020-7822 4300; Fax: 020-7842 2249;
Email: sales.europa@tandf.co.uk;
Web: www.europapublications.co.uk

JANE'S ARMOUR AND ARTILLERY (£360)
Sentinel House, 163 Brighton Road, Coulsdon, Surrey CR5 2YH
Tel: 020-8700 3803; Fax: 020-8700 3715

JANE'S ALL THE WORLD'S AIRCRAFT (£360)
Sentinel House, 163 Brighton Road, Coulsdon, Surrey CR5 2NH

JOHANSENS HISTORIC HOUSES, CASTLES AND GARDENS INCORPORATING MUSEUMS AND GALLERIES (£7.95)
Johansens, 5th Floor, Therese House, Glasshouse Yard, London EC1A 4JN
Tel: 020-7566 9700; Fax: 020-7490 2538;
Email: info@johansens.com;
Web: www.johansens.com

NAUTICAL ALMANAC (£28)
PO Box 29, Norwich NR3 1GN
Tel: 0870-600 5522

THE PRIMARY EDUCATION DIRECTORY (£55)
Darby House, Bletchingley Road, Merstham, Redhill RH1 3DN
Tel: 01737-642223; Fax: 01737-644283;
Email: ped@schoolgovernment.co.uk;
Web: www.schoolgovernment.co.uk/pages/pub/PED2002.htm

REGIONAL TRENDS (£39.50)
PO Box 29, Norwich NR3 1GN
Tel: 0870-600 5522

ROYAL AND ANCIENT GOLFER'S HANDBOOK (£50)
Pan Macmillan Ltd, 20 New Wharf Road, London N1 9RR
Tel: 020-7014 6000; Fax: 020-7014 6001;
Web: www.panmacmillan.com

ROYAL SOCIETY YEAR BOOK (£22)
6 Carlton House Terrace, London SW1Y 5AG
Tel: 020-7451 2500; Fax: 020-7930 2170;
Email: info@royalsoc.ac.uk;
Web: www.royalsoc.ac.uk

SALVATION ARMY YEAR BOOK ( £5.50)
101 Queen Victoria Street, London EC4P 4EP
Tel: 020-7332 0101; Fax: 020-7236 4981;
Web: www.salvationarmy.org

SOCIAL TRENDS (£39.50)
PO Box 29, Norwich NR3 1GN
Tel: 0870-600 5522

THE SPECIAL EDUCATION DIRECTORY (£50)
Darby House, Bletchingley Road, Merstham, Redhill RH1 3DN
Tel: 01737-642223; Fax: 01737-644283;
Email: sed@schoolgovernment.co.uk;
Web: www.schoolgovernment.co.uk/pages/sped.htm

SPINK STANDARD CATALOGUE OF BRITISH COINAGE (£18)
69 Southampton Row, Bloomsbury, London WC1B 4ET
Tel: 020-7563 4045; Fax: 020-7563 4068;
Email: info@spinkandson.com; Web: www.spink-online.com

STATESMAN'S YEARBOOK (£60)
Porters South, Crinan Street, London N1 9XW
Tel: 020-7843 4665; Fax: 020-7843 4650;
Email: syb@palgrave.com; Web: www.palgrave.com

STONE'S JUSTICES' MANUAL (£310)
Halsbury House, 35 Chancery Lane, London WC2A 1EL
Tel: 020-7400 2500; Fax: 020-7400 2842;
Email: customer_services@Butterworths.com

UNITED KINGDOM MINERALS YEARBOOK (£35)
Onshore Mineral and Energy Resources, British Geological Survey, Keyworth, Notts NG12 5GG
Tel: 0115-936 3100; Fax: 0115-936 3200;
Email: minerals@bgs.ac.uk;
Web: www.mineralsUK.com

WHITAKER'S BOOKS IN PRINT (£449)
Woolmead House West, Bear Lane, Farnham, Surrey GU9 7LG
Tel: 01252-742500; Web: www.whitaker.co.uk

WHITAKER'S RED BOOK - the Directory of Publishers (£18)
Woolmead House West, Bear Lane, Farnham, Surrey GU9 7LG
Tel: 01252-742500; Fax: 01252-742501;
Email: custserv@whitaker.co.uk;
Web: www.whitaker.co.uk

WILLING'S PRESS GUIDE (£245)
Chess House, 34 Germain Street, Chesham, Bucks HP5 1ST
Tel: 0870-736 0015; Fax: 0870-736 0011;
Email: willings@waymaker.co.uk;
Web: www.willingspressguide.com

WISDEN CRICKETERS' ALMANACK (£29.99)
25 Down Road, Merrow, Guildford, Surrey GU1 2PY
Tel: 01483-570358; Email: wisden@ndirect.co.uk;
Web: www.wisden.com

WORLD OF LEARNING (£300)
11 New Fetter Lane, London EC4P 4EE
Tel: 020-7822 4300; Fax: 020-7842 2249;
Email: saleseuropa@tandf.co.uk;
Web: www.europapublications.co.uk

WRITERS' AND ARTISTS' YEARBOOK (£12.99)
PO Box 19, St Neots, Cambs PE19 8SF
Tel: 01480-212379; Fax: 01480-405014;
Email: sales@acblack.com

# Employers' and Trade Associations

Most national employers' associations are members of the Confederation of British Industry (CBI).

CONFEDERATION OF BRITISH INDUSTRY
Centre Point, 103 New Oxford Street, London WC1A 1DU Tel 020-7395 8247; Fax: 020-7240 1578; Email: enquiry.desk@cbi.org.uk; Web: www.cbi.org.uk

The Confederation of British Industry was founded in 1965 and is an independent non-party political body financed by industry and commerce. It exists primarily to ensure that the Government understands the intentions, needs and problems of British business. It is the recognised spokesman for the business viewpoint and is consulted as such by the Government.

The CBI represents, directly and indirectly, some 250,000 companies, large and small, from all sectors.

The governing body of the CBI is the 200-strong Council, which meets four times a year in London under the chairmanship of the President. It is assisted by 17 expert standing committees which advise on the main aspects of policy. There are 13 regional councils and offices, covering the administrative regions of England, Wales, Scotland and Northern Ireland. There is also an office in Brussels.

*President*, Sir Iain Vallance
*Director-General*, Digby Jones
*Secretary*, P. Forder

WALES: Capital Tower, Greyfriars Road Cardiff CF1 3JR. Tel: 029-2045 3710.
*Regional Director*, David Rosser

SCOTLAND: 16 Robertson Street, Glasgow G2 8DS. Tel: 0141-222 2184.
*Regional Director*, I. McMillan

NORTHERN IRELAND: Fanum House, 108 Great Victoria Street, Belfast BT2 7PD. Tel: 028-9032 6658.
*Regional Director*, N. Smyth

ASSOCIATIONS

ADVERTISING ASSOCIATION, Abford House, 15 Wilton Road, London SW1V 1NJ. Tel: 020-7828 2771; Fax: 020-7931 0376; Email: aa@adassoc.org.uk; Web: www.adassoc.org.uk

SOCIETY OF BRITISH AEROSPACE COMPANIES LTD, Duxbury House, 60 Petty France, London SW1H 9EU. Tel: 020-7227 1000; Fax: 020-7227 1067; Email: post@sbac.co.uk; Web: www.sbac.co.uk

ASSOCIATION OF BRITISH INSURERS, 51 Gresham Street, London EC2V 7HQ. Tel: 020-7600 3333; Fax: 020-7696 8999; Email: info@abi.org.uk; Web: www.abi.org.uk

ASSOCIATION OF PRIVATE MARKET OPERATORS, 4 Worrygoose Lane, Rotherham S. Yorks S60 4AD. Tel: 01709-700072; Fax: 01709-703648; Email: market-planuk@LineOne.net

BLC LEATHER TECHNOLOGY CENTRE LTD, Leather Trade House, Kings Park Road, Moulton Park, Northampton NN3 6JD. Tel: 01604-679999; Fax: 01604-679998; Email: info@blcleathertech.com; Web: www.blcleathertech.com

BOSS FEDERATION, 6 Wimpole Street, London W1G 9SL. Tel: 020-7637 7692; Fax: 020-7436 3137; Email: info@bossfed.co.uk; Web: www.bossfed.co.uk

BREWERS AND LICENSED RETAILERS ASSOCIATION, 42 Portman Square, London W1H 0BB. Tel: 020-7486 4831; Fax: 020-7935 3991; Email: mailbox@blra.co.uk; Web: www.blra.co.uk

BRITISH APPAREL AND TEXTILE CONFEDERATION, 5 Portland Place, London W1B 1PW. Tel: 020-7636 7788; Fax: 020-7636 7515; Email: batc@dial.pipex.com; Web: www.batc.co.uk

BRITISH BANKERS' ASSOCIATION, Pinners Hall, 105–108 Old Broad Street, London EC2N 1EX. Tel: 020-7216 8800; Fax: 020-7216 8811; Web: www.bba.org.uk

BRITISH CLOTHING INDUSTRY ASSOCIATION LTD, 5 Portland Place, London W1B 1PW. Tel: 020-7636 7788; Fax: 020-7636 7515; Email: bcia@dial.pipex.com

BRITISH MARINE INDUSTRIES FEDERATION, Marine House, Thorpe Lea Road, Egham, Surrey TW20 8BF. Tel: 01784-223600; Fax: 01784-439678; Email: bmif@bmif.co.uk; Web: www.bmif.co.uk

BRITISH PLASTICS FEDERATION, 6 Bath Place, Rivington Street, London EC2A 3JE. Tel: 020-7457 5000; Fax: 020-7457 5045

BRITISH PORTS ASSOCIATION, Africa House, 64–78 Kingsway, London WC2B 6AH. Tel: 020-7242 1200; Fax: 020-7405 1069; Email: info@britishports.org.uk; Web: www.britishports.org.uk

BRITISH PRINTING INDUSTRIES FEDERATION, Farringdon Point, 29-35 Farringdon Road, London EC1M 3JF. Tel: 020-7915 8300; Fax: 020-7405 7784; Email: info@bpif.org.uk; Web: www.bpif.org.uk

BRITISH PROPERTY FEDERATION, 7th Floor, 1 Warwick Row, London SW1E 5ER. Tel: 020-7828 0111; Fax: 020-834 3442; Email: info@bpf.org.uk; Web: www.bpf.org.uk

BRITISH RETAIL CONSORTIUM, 5 Grafton Street, London W1X 3LB. Tel: 020-7647 1500; Fax: 020-7647 1599; Email: info@brc.org.uk

BRITISH RUBBER MANUFACTURERS' ASSOCIATION LTD, 6 Bath Place, Rivington Street, London EC2A 3JE. Tel: 020-7457 5040; Fax: 020-7972 9008; Email: mail@brma.co.uk

INSTITUTE OF CHARTERED FORESTERS, 7a Sidcolme Street, Edinburgh, EH3 6AA. Tel: 0131-225 2705; Email: icfor@btinternet.com

THE CHAMBER OF SHIPPING LTD, Carthusian Court, 12 Carthusian Street, London EC1M 6EZ. Tel: 020-7417 2800; Fax: 020-7726 2080; Email: postmaster@british-shipping.org; Web: www.british-shipping.org

CHEMICAL INDUSTRIES ASSOCIATION LTD, Kings Buildings, Smith Square, London SW1P 3JJ. Tel: 020-7963 6701; Fax: 020-7834 4470; Email: finere@cia.org.uk

COMMERCIAL RADIO COMPANIES ASSOCIATION (CRCA), 77 Shaftesbury Avenue, London W1D 5DU. Tel: 020-7306 2603; Fax: 020-7470 0062; Email: info@crca.co.uk; Web: www.crca.co.uk

CONFEDERATION OF PASSENGER TRANSPORT UK, Imperial House, 15–19 Kingsway, London WC2B 6UN. Tel: 020-7240 3131; Fax: 020-7240 6565; Email: info@cpt-uk.org; Web: www.cpt-uk.org/cpt

CONSTRUCTION CONFEDERATION, Construction House, 56–64 Leonard Street, London EC2A 4JX. Tel: 020-7608 5004; Fax: 020-7608 5008; Email: enquiries@constructionconfederation.co.uk; Web: www.constructionconfederation.co.uk

CONSTRUCTION PRODUCTS ASSOCIATION, 26 Store Street, London WC1E 7BT. Tel: 020-7323 3770; Fax: 020-7323 0307; Email: enquiries@constprod.org.uk; Web: www.constprod.org.uk

DAIRY INDUSTRY FEDERATION, 19 Cornwall Terrace, London NW1 4QP. Tel: 020-7486 7244; Fax: 020-7935 3920; Email: mailbox@dif.org.uk

ENGINEERING EMPLOYERS' FEDERATION, Broadway House, Tothill Street, London SW1H 9NQ. Tel: 020-7222 7777; Fax: 020-7222 0792; Email: enquiries@eef-fed.org.uk; Web: www.eef.org.uk

THE FEDERATION OF BAKERS, 6 Catherine Street, London WC2B 5JW. Tel: 020-7420 7190; Fax: 020-7379 0542; Email: info@bakersfederation.org.uk; Web: www.bakersfederation.org.uk

FEDERATION OF BRITISH ELECTROTECHNICAL AND ALLIED MANUFACTURERS' ASSOCIATIONS (BEAMA), Westminster Tower, 3 Albert Embankment, London SE1 7SL. Tel: 020-7793 3000; Fax: 020-7793 3003; Email: info@beama.org.uk; Web: www.beama.org.uk

FEDERATION OF MASTER BUILDERS, Gordon Fisher House, 14–15 Great James Street, London WC1N 3DP. Tel: 020-7242 7583; Fax: 020-7404-0296; Email: central@fmb.org.uk; Web: www.fmb.org.uk

FINANCE AND LEASING ASSOCIATION, 15–19 Imperial House, Kingsway, London WC2B 6UN. Tel: 020-7836 6511; Fax: 020-7420 9600; Email: info@fla.org.uk; Web: www.fla.org.uk

FOOD AND DRINK FEDERATION, 6 Catherine Street, London WC2B 5JJ. Tel: 020-7836 2460; Fax: 020-7836 0580; Web: www.fdf.org.uk

FREIGHT TRANSPORT ASSOCIATION, Hermes House, St John's Road, Tunbridge Wells Kent TN4 9UZ. Tel: 01892-526171; Fax: 01892-534989; Email: inquiries@fta.org.uk; Web: www.fta.co.uk

KNITTING INDUSTRIES' FEDERATION, 12 Beaumanor Road, Leicester LE4 5QA. Tel: 0116-266 3332; Fax: 0116-266 3335; Email: directorate@knitfed.co.uk

LEATHER PRODUCERS' ASSOCIATION, 8 Queensberry Road, Kettering Northants NN15 7HL. Tel: 01536-483668; Fax: 01536-416771; Email: jaklpa@globalnet.co.uk

MANAGEMENT CONSULTANCIES ASSOCIATION, 11 West Halkin Street, London SW1X 8JL. Tel: 020-7235 3897; Fax: 020-7235 0825; Email: will@mca.org.uk; Web: www.mca.org.uk

THE NATIONAL FARMERS' UNION (NFU), Agriculture House, 164 Shaftesbury Avenue, London WC2H 8HL. Tel: 020-7331 7200; Fax: 020-7331 7313; Email: nfu@nfu.org.uk; Web: www.nfu.org.uk

NATIONAL FEDERATION OF RETAIL NEWSAGENTS, Yeoman House, Sekforde Street, London EC1R 0HD. Tel: 020-7253 4225; Fax: 020-7250 0927; Email: info@nfrn.org.uk; Web: www.nfrn.org.uk

NATIONAL MARKET TRADERS' FEDERATION, Hampton House, Hawshaw Lane, Hoyland, Barnsley S74 0HA. Tel: 01226-749021; Fax: 01226-740329; Email: enquiries@nmtf.co.uk; Web: www.nmtf.co.uk

NEWSPAPER PUBLISHERS ASSOCIATION, 34 Southwark Bridge Road, London SE1 9EU. Tel: 020-7207 2200; Fax: 020-7928 2067

NEWSPAPER SOCIETY, Bloomsbury House, 74–77 Great Russell Street, London WC1B 3DA. Tel: 020-7636 7014; Fax: 020-7580 1972; Email: directorate@newspapersoc.org.uk; Web: www.newspapersoc.org.uk

THE PAPER FEDERATION OF GREAT BRITAIN, Papermakers House, Rivenhall Road, Swindon SN5 7BD. Tel: 01793-889600; Fax: 01793-878700; Email: fedn@paper.org.uk; Web: www.paper.org.uk

THE PUBLISHERS ASSOCIATION, 1 Kingsway, London WC2B 6XD. Tel: 020-7565 7474; Fax: 020-7836 4543; Email: mail@publishers.org.uk; Web: www.publishers.org.uk

ROAD HAULAGE ASSOCIATION, Roadway House, 35 Monument Hill, Weybridge Surrey KT13 8RN. Tel: 01932-841515; Fax: 01932-852516; Email: weybridge@rha.net; Web: www.rha.net

SOCIETY OF MOTOR MANUFACTURERS AND TRADERS, Forbes House, Halkin Street, London SW1X 7DS. Tel: 020-7235 7000; Fax: 020-7235 7112; Email: membership@smmt.co.uk; Web: www.smmt.co.uk

THE SPORT INDUSTRIES FEDERATION, Federation House, National Agricultural Centre, Stoneleigh Park, Kenilworth Warks CV8 2RF. Tel: 02476-414999; Fax: 02476-414990; Email: admin@sportslife.org.uk; Web: www.sportslife.org.uk

THE TIMBER TRADE FEDERATION, Clareville House, 26–27 Oxendon Street, London SW1Y 4EL. Tel: 020-7839 1891; Fax: 020-7930 0094; Email: ttf@ttf.co.uk; Web: www.ttf.co.uk

UK OFFSHORE OPERATORS ASSOCIATION, Second Floor, 232-242 Vauxhall Bridge Road, London SW1V 1AY. Tel: 020-7802 2400; Fax: 020-7802 2401; Email: info@ukooa.co.uk; Web: www.oilandgas.org.uk

UK PETROLEUM INDUSTRY ASSOCIATION, 9 Kingsway, London WC2B 6XF. Tel: 020-7240 0289; Fax: 020-7379 3102; Email: ukpia@aol.com; Web: www.ukpia.com

ULSTER FARMERS' UNION, 475 Antrim Road, Belfast BT15 3DA. Tel: 028-9037 0222; Fax: 028-9037 1231; Email: info@ufuhq.com; Web: www.ufuni.org

# Trade Unions

Nearly 80 per cent of trade union members belong to unions affiliated to the TUC .

The Central Arbitration Committee arbitrates on trade disputes, adjudicates on disclosure of information complaints, determines claims for statutory recognition under the Employment Relations Act 1999 and certain issues relating to the implementation of the European Works Council Directive.

THE CENTRAL ARBITRATION COMMITTEE, 3rd Floor, Discovery House, 28–42 Banner Street, London EC1Y 8QE. Tel: 020-7251 9747; Fax: 020-7251 3114; Web: www.cac.gov.uk

*Chairman*, Sir Michael Burton; *Secretary*, C. Johnston

## TUC-AFFILIATED TRADE UNIONS

### TRADES UNION CONGRESS (TUC)

Congress House, 23-28 Great Russell Street, London WC1B 3LS. Tel: 020-7636 4030; Fax: 020-7636 0632 Web: www.tuc.org.uk

The Trades Union Congress, founded in 1868, is an independent association of trade unions. The TUC promotes the rights and welfare of those in work and helps the unemployed. It helps its member unions promote membership in new areas and industries, and campaigns for rights at work for all employees, including part-time and temporary workers, whether union members or not. TUC representatives sit on many public bodies at national and international level. It makes representations to government, political parties, employers and international bodies such as the European Union.

The governing body of the TUC is the annual Congress. Between Congresses, business is conducted by a General Council, which meets five times a year, and an Executive Committee, which meets monthly. The full-time staff is headed by the General Secretary who is elected by Congress and is a permanent member of the General Council.

Affiliated unions in 2000–2001 totalled 76 with a total membership of over 6,800,000.

*President* (2000–2001), Bill Morris (TGWU).

(The President for 2001–2 was elected in September 2001; *see* Stop-press)

*General Secretary*, J. Monks, *elected* 1993

### SCOTTISH TRADES UNION CONGRESS

333 Woodlands Road, Glasgow G3 6NG Tel: 0141-337 8100; fax 0141-337 8101 Email: info@stuc.org.uk

The Congress was formed in 1897 and acts as a national centre for the trade union movement in Scotland. The STUC promotes the rights and welfare of those in work and helps the unemployed. It helps its member unions to promote membership in new areas and industries, and campaigns for rights at work for all employees, including part time and temporary workers, whether union members or not. It makes representations to government and employers. In 2000 it consisted of 46 unions with a membership of 628,159 and 34 directly affiliated Trade Councils.

The Annual Congress in April elects a 39-member General Council on the basis of six industrial sections.

*Chairperson*, David Bleiman

*General Secretary*, B. Speirs

### AFFILIATED UNIONS AS AT AUGUST 2001

ALLIANCE AND LEICESTER GROUP UNION OF STAFF (ALGUS), Croft, Carlton Park, Narborough, Leicester LE9 5XX. Tel: 0116-200 2259; Fax: 0116-200 3240

AMALGAMATED ENGINEERING AND ELECTRICAL UNION (AEEU), Hayes Court, West Common Road, Bromley, Kent BR2 7AU. Tel: 020-8462 7755; Fax: 020-8315 8215; Web: www.aeeu.org.uk

ANSA (INDEPENDENT UNION FOR ABBEY NATIONAL STAFF), 2nd Floor, 16-17 High Street, Tring, Herts HP23 5AH. Tel: 01442-891122; Fax: 01442-891133; Email: info@ansa.org.uk; Web: www.ansa.org.uk

ASSOCIATED METALWORKERS UNION (AMU), 92 Worsley Road North, Worsley, Manchester M28 5QW. Tel: 01204-793245; Fax: 01204-793245

ASSOCIATION OF EDUCATIONAL PSYCHOLOGISTS, 26 The Avenue, Durham DH1 4ED. Tel: 0191-384 9512; Fax: 0191-386 5287

ASSOCIATED SOCIETY OF LOCOMOTIVE ENGINEERS AND FIREMEN (ASLEF), 9 Arkwright Road, London NW3 6AB. Tel: 020-7317 8600; Fax: 020-7794 6406; Email: info@ascef.org.uk;

ASSOCIATION OF FIRST DIVISION CIVIL SERVANTS (FDA), 2 Caxton Street, London SW1H 0QH. Tel: 020-7343 1111; Fax: 020-7343 1105; Email: head-office@fda.org.uk; Web: www.fda.org.uk

ASSOCIATION OF FLIGHT ATTENDANTS (AFA), COUNCIL 7, United Airlines Cargo Centre, Shoreham Road East, Heathrow Airport, Hounslow TW6 3UA. Tel: 020-8276 6723; Fax: 020-8276 6706; Email: 75452.2427@compuserve.com; Web: www.unitedafa.org/councils/7-london.html

ASSOCIATION OF MAGISTERIAL OFFICERS (AMO), 1 Sellmongers Path, 176 Tower Bridge Road, London SE1 3LY. Tel: 020-7403 2244; Fax: 020-7403 2274; Email: helen@amo.org.uk; Web: www.amo-online.org.uk

ASSOCIATION OF UNIVERSITY TEACHERS (AUT), Egmont House, 25-31 Tavistock Place, London WC1H 9UT. Tel: 020-7670 9700; Fax: 020-7670 9799; Email: hq@aut.org.uk; Web: www.aut.org.uk

ASSOCIATION OF TEACHERS AND LECTURERS (ATL), 7 Northumberland Street, London WC2N 5RD. Tel: 020-7930 6441; Fax: 020-7930 1359; Email: info@atl.org.uk; Web: www.askate.org.uk

BAKERS, FOOD AND ALLIED WORKERS' UNION, Stanborough House, Great North Road, Stanborough, Welwyn Garden City, Herts AL8 7TA. Tel: 01707-260150; Fax: 01707-261570; Email: bfawu@aol.com;

BFSA (BRITANNIC FIELD STAFF ASSOCIATION), 286 Oxford Road, Gomersal, Cleckheaton, West Yorkshire BD19 4PY. Tel: 01274-851360; Fax: 01274-852742; Email: jhg-tp@bfsa75.freeserve.co.uk

BRITISH AIR LINE PILOTS ASSOCIATION (BALPA), 81 New Road, Harlington, Hayes, Middx UB3 5BG. Tel: 020-8476 4000; Fax: 020-8476 4077; Email: balpa@balpa.org; Web: www.balpa.org

BRITISH ASSOCIATION OF COLLIERY MANAGEMENT–TECHNICAL, ENERGY AND ADMINISTRATIVE MANAGEMENT (BACM-TEAM), 17 South Parade, Doncaster, S. Yorks DN1 2DR. Tel: 01302-815551; Fax: 01302-815552; Email: bacmteam@aol.com

BRITISH ORTHOPTIC SOCIETY, Tavistock House North, Tavistock Square, London WC1H 9HX. Tel: 020-7387 7992; Fax: 020-7383 2584; Email: bos@orthoptics.org.uk; Web: www.orthoptics.org.uk

BROADCASTING, ENTERTAINMENT, CINEMATOGRAPH AND THEATRE UNION (BECTU), 111 Wardour Street, London W1F 0AY. Tel: 020-7437 8506; Fax: 020-7437 8268Web: www.bectu.org.uk

CARD SETTING MACHINE TENTERS' SOCIETY, 48 Scar End Lane, Staincliffe, Dewsbury, W. Yorks WF13 4NY. Tel: 01924-400206; Fax: 01924-400206

CERAMIC AND ALLIED TRADES UNION, Hillcrest House, Garth Street, Hanley, Stoke-on-Trent ST1 2AB. Tel: 01782-272755; Fax: 01782-284902

THE CHARTERED SOCIETY OF PHYSIOTHERAPY (CSP), 14 Bedford Row, London WC1R 4ED. Tel: 020-7306 6666; Fax: 020-7306 6611; Email: ceo@csphysio.org.uk; Web: www.csp.org.uk

COMMUNICATION WORKERS UNION (CWU), 150 The Broadway, Wimbledon, London SW19 1RX. Tel: 020-8971 7200; Fax: 020-8971 7300; Email: cproctor@cwu.org; Web: www.cwu.org

COMMUNITY AND DISTRICT NURSING ASSOCIATION (CDNA), Thames Valley University, 32–38 Uxbridge Road, Ealing, London W5 2BS. Tel: 020-8280 5342; Fax: 020-8280 5341; Email: cdna@tvu.ac.uk; Web: www.cdna.tvu.ac.uk

COMMUNITY AND YOUTH WORKERS UNION (CYWU), Unit 302, The Argent Centre, 60 Frederick Street, Birmingham B1 3HS. Tel: 0121-244 3344; Fax: 0121-244 3345; Email: dougnic@email.msn.com

CONNECT, THE UNION FOR PROFESSIONALS IN COMMUNICATIONS, 30 St George's Road, London SW19 4BD. Tel: 020-8971 6000; Fax: 020-8971 6002; Email: birmingham1@connectuk.org; Web: www.connectuk.org

EDUCATIONAL INSTITUTE OF SCOTLAND (EIS), 46 Moray Place, Edinburgh EH3 6BH. Tel: 0131-225 6244; Fax: 0131-220 3151; Email: membership@eis.org.uk; Web: www.eis.org.uk

ENGINEERING AND FASTENER TRADE UNION (EFTU), 42 Galton Road, Warley, West Midlands B67 5JU. Tel: 0121-429 2594; Fax: 0121-429 2594

ENGINEERS' AND MANAGERS' ASSOCIATION (EMA), Flaxman House, Gogmore Lane, Chertsey, Surrey KT16 9JS. Tel: 01932-577007; Fax: 01932-567166; Email: gs@ema.org.uk; Web: www.ema.org.uk

EQUITY, Guild House, Upper St Martin's Lane, London WC2H 9EG. Tel: 020-7379 6000; Fax: 020-7379 7001; Email: info@equity.org.uk; Web: www.equity.org.uk

THE FIRE BRIGADES UNION (FBU), Bradley House, 68 Coombe Road, Kingston upon Thames, Surrey KT2 7AE. Tel: 020-8541 1765; Fax: 020-8546 5187; Email: office@fbu-ho.org.uk; Web: www.fbu-ho.org.uk

GENERAL UNION OF LOOM OVERLOOKERS (GULO), 9 Wellington Street, St Johns, Blackburn, Lancs BB1 8AF. Tel: 01254-51760; Fax: 01254-51760

GMB 22-24 Worple Road, London SW19 4DD. Tel: 020-8947 3131; Fax: 020-8944 6552; Email: john.edmonds@gmb.org.uk; Web: www.gmb.org.uk

GRAPHICAL, PAPER AND MEDIA UNION (GPMU), Keys House, 63-67 Bromham Road, Bedford MK40 2AG. Tel: 01234-351521; Fax: 01234-270580; Email: general@gpmu.org.uk; Web: www.gpmu.org.uk

GUINNESS STAFF ASSOCIATION (GSA), Sun Works Cottage, Park Royal Brewery, London NW10 7RR. Tel: 020-8965 7700; Fax: 020-8963 5184

HOSPITAL CONSULTANTS AND SPECIALISTS ASSOCIATION (HCSA), 1 Kingsclere Road, Overton, Basingstoke, Hants RG25 3JA. Tel: 01256-771777; Fax: 01256-770999; Email: conspec@hcsa.com; Web: www.hcsa.com

INDEPENDENT UNION OF HALIFAX STAFF (IUHS), Simmons House, 46 Old Bath Road, Charvil, Reading RG10 9QR. Tel: 0118-934 1808; Fax: 0118-932 0208

INSTITUTION OF PROFESSIONALS, MANAGERS AND SPECIALISTS (IPMS), 75-79 York Road, London SE1 7AQ. Tel: 020-7239 1200; Fax: 020-7278 8378; Email: ipmshq@ipms.org.uk; Web: www.ipms.org.uk

IRON AND STEEL TRADES CONFEDERATION (ISTC), Swinton House, 324 Gray's Inn Road, London WC1X 8DD. Tel: 020-7239 1200; Fax: 020-7278 8378; Email: istc@istc-tu.org

MANUFACTURING, SCIENCE AND FINANCE UNION (MSF), MSF Centre, 33-37 Moreland Street, London EC1V 8BB. Tel: 020-7505 3000; Fax: 020-7505 3020; Email: info@msf.org.uk; Web: www.msf.org.uk

MILITARY AND ORCHESTRAL MUSICAL INSTRUMENT MAKERS TRADE SOCIETY (MOMIMTS), 2 Whitehouse Avenue, Borehamwood, Herts WD6 1HD.

MUSICIANS' UNION (MU), 60-62 Clapham Road, London SW9 0JJ. Tel: 020-7582 5566; Fax: 020-7582 9805; Email: info@musiciansunion.org.uk; Web: www.musiciansunion.org.uk

NATIONAL ASSOCIATION OF COLLIERY OVERMEN, DEPUTIES AND SHOTFIRERS, 37 Church Street, Barnsley S70 2AR. Tel: 01226-203743; Fax: 01226-295563

NASUWT (NATIONAL ASSOCIATION OF SCHOOLMASTERS/ UNION OF WOMEN TEACHERS), Hillscourt Education Centre, Rednal, Birmingham B45 8RS. Tel: 0121-453 6150; Fax: 0121-457 6208; Email: nasuwt@nasuwt.org.uk; Web: www.teachersunion.org.uk

NATFHE (UNIVERSITY AND COLLEGE LECTURERS UNION), 27 Britannia Street, London WC1X 9JP. Tel: 020-7837 3636; Fax: 020-7837 4403; Email: hq@natfhe.org.uk; Web: www.natfhe.org.uk

NATIONAL ASSOCIATION OF CO-OPERATIVE OFFICIALS (NACO), 6A Clarendon Place, Hyde, Cheshire, SK14 2QZ. Tel: 0161-351 7900; Fax: 0161-366 6800; Email: lwe@nacoco-op.org

NATIONAL ASSOCIATION OF PROBATION OFFICERS (NAPO), 4 Chivalry Road, London SW11 1HT. Tel: 020-7223 4887; Fax: 020-7223 3503; Email: napo@ukonline.co.uk

NATIONAL UNION OF DOMESTIC APPLIANCES AND GENERAL OPERATIVES (NUDAGO), 1st Floor, 7-8 Imperial Buildings, Corporation Street, Rotherham, S. Yorks S60 1PB. Tel: 01709-382820; Fax: 01709-362826

NATIONAL UNION OF JOURNALISTS (NUJ), Headland House, 308-312 Gray's Inn Road, London WC1X 8DP. Tel: 020-7278 7916; Fax: 020-7278 1812; Email: acorn.house@nuj.org.uk; Web: www.nuj.org.uk

NATIONAL UNION OF KNITWEAR, FOOTWEAR AND APPAREL TRADES (KFAT), 55 New Walk, Leicester LE1 7EA. Tel: 0116-255 6703; Fax: 0116-254 4406; Email: head-office@kfat.org.uk; Web: www.kfat.org.uk

NATIONAL UNION OF LOCK AND METAL WORKERS (NULMW), Bellamy House, Wilkes Street, Willenhall, W. Midlands WV13 2BS. Tel: 01902-366651; Fax: 01902-368035

NATIONAL UNION OF MARINE, AVIATION AND SHIPPING TRANSPORT OFFICERS (NUMAST), Oceanair House, 750-760 High Road, London E11 3BB. Tel: 020-8989 6677; Fax: 020-8530 1015; Email: info@numust.org; Web: www.numast.org

NATIONAL UNION OF MINEWORKERS (NUM), Miners' Offices, 2 Huddersfield Road, Barnsley, S. Yorks S70 2LS. Tel: 01226-215555; Fax: 01226-215561

NATIONAL UNION OF RAIL, MARITIME AND TRANSPORT WORKERS (RMT), Unity House, 39 Chalton Street, London NW1 1JD. Tel: 020-7387 4771; Fax: 020-7387 4123; Email: jknapp@rmt-hq.demon.co.uk; Web: www.rmt.org.uk

NATIONAL UNION OF TEACHERS (NUT), Hamilton House, Mabledon Place, London WC1H 9BD. Tel: 020-7388 6191; Fax: 020-7387 8458; Web: www.teachers.org.uk

Nationwide Group Staff Union (NGSU), Middleton Farmhouse, 37 Main Road Middleton Cheney, Banbury, Oxfordshire OX17 2QT. Tel: 01295-710767; Fax: 01295-712580; Email: ngsu@ngsu.org.uk; Web: www.ngsu.org.uk

Northern Carpet Trades' Union (NCTU), 22 Clare Road, Halifax HX1 2HX. Tel: 01422-360492; Fax: 01422-321146

Prison Officers' Association (POA), Cronin House, 245 Church Street, London N9 9HW. Tel: 020-8803 0255; Fax: 020-8803 1761

Professional Footballers Association (PFA), 20 Oxford Court, Bishopsgate, Manchester M2 3WQ. Tel: 0161-236 0575; Fax: 0161-228 7229; Email: info@thepfa.co.uk; Web: www.givemefootball.com

Public and Commercial Services Union (PCS), 160 Falcon Road, London SW11 2LN. Tel: 020-7924 2727; Fax: 020-7924 1847; Email: jim@pcs.org.uk; Web: www.pcs.org.uk

Sheffield Wool Shear Workers' Union (SWSWU), 17 Galsworthy Road, Sheffield S5 8QX. Tel: 07718-559 439

Society of Chiropodists and Podiatrists (SCP), 1 Fellmongers Path, Tower Bridge Road, London SE1 3LY. Tel: 020-7234 8620; Fax: 020-7234 8621; Email: eng@scpod.org; Web: www.feetforlife.org

The Society of Radiographers (SOR), 207 Providence Square, Mill Street, London SE1 2EW. Tel: 020-7740 7200; Fax: 020-7740 7204; Email: info@sor.org; Web: www.sor.org

Transport and General Workers' Union (TGWU), Transport House, 128 Theobalds Road, London WC1X 8TN. Tel: 020-7611 2500; Fax: 020-7611 2555; Email: tgwu@tgwu.org.uk; Web: www.tgwu.org.uk

Transport Salaried Staffs' Association (TSSA), Walkden House, 10 Melton Street, London NW1 2EJ. Tel: 020-7387 2101; Fax: 020-7383 0656; Email: enquiries@tssa.org.uk; Web: www.tssa.org.uk

UBAC (Representing Staff in the Bradford and Bingley Group and Alltel Mortgage Solutions), 18D Market Place, Malton, N. Yorks YO17 7LX. Tel: 01653-697634; Fax: 01653-695222

Undeb Cenedlaethol Athrawon Cymru (National Association of Teachers of Wales), Pen Roc, Rhodfa'r Mr, Aberystwyth, Ceredigion SY23 2AZ. Tel: 01970-615577; Fax: 01970-626765; Email: swyddfa@ucac.cymru.org; Web: www.ucac.cymru.org

UNIFI, Sheffield House, 1b Amity Grove, London SW20 0LG. Tel: 020-8946 9151; Fax: 020-8879 7916; Email: amity@bifu.org.uk; Web: www.unifi.org.uk

Union of Construction, Allied Trades and Technicians (UCATT), UCATT House, 177 Abbeville Road, London SW4 9RL. Tel: 020-7622 2362; Fax: 020-7720 4081; Email: info@ucatt.org.uk; Web: www.ucatt.org.uk

Union of Shop, Distributive and Allied Workers (USDAW), Oakley, 188 Wilmslow Road, Fallowfield, Manchester M14 6LJ. Tel: 0161-224 2804; Fax: 0161-257 2566; Email: enquiries@usdaw.org.uk; Web: www.usdaw.org.uk

Union of Textile Workers (UTW), 18 West Street, Leek, Staffs ST13 8AA. Tel: 01538-382068; Fax: 01538-384270;

UNISON, 1 Mabledon Place, London WC1H 9AJ. Tel: 020-7388 2366; Fax: 020-7387 6692Web: www.unison.org.uk

The Union for Woolwich Staff, 40 High Street, Swanley, Kent, BR8 8BQ. Tel: 01322-614957; Fax: 01322-614947; Email: enquiries@wisa-union.org

Writers' Guild of Great Britain, 430 Edgware Road, London W2 1EH. Tel: 020-7723 8074; Fax: 020-7706 2413; Email: admin@writersguild.org.uk; Web: www.writers.org.uk/guild

Yorkshire Independent Staff Association, Principal Offices, 32 Conniston Road, Dewsbury, West Yorkshire WF12 7EA. Tel: 01274-740740; Fax: 01274-741730

## NON-AFFILATED UNIONS as at August 2001

British Dental Association, 64 Wimpole Street, London W1G 8YS. Tel: 020-7935 0875; Fax: 020-7487 5232; Email: enquiries@bda-dentistry.org.uk; Web: www.bda-dentistry.org.uk

Chartered Institute of Journalists, 2 Dock Offices, Surrey Quays Road, London SE16 2XU. Tel: 020-7252 1187; Fax: 020-7232 2302; Email: memberservices@ioj.co.uk; Web: www.ioj.co.uk

National Association of Head Teachers (NAHT), 1 Heath Square, Boltro Road, Haywards Heath, W. Sussex RH16 1BL. Tel: 01444-472472; Fax: 01444-472473; Email: info@naht.org.uk

National Society for Education in Art and Design, The Gatehouse, Corsham Court, Corsham, Wilts SN13 0BZ. Tel: 01249-714825; Fax: 01249-716138; Email: AnneIngall@compuserve.com; Web: www.nsead.org

Prison Governors Association, Room 718, Horseferry House, Dean Ryle Street, London SW1P 2AW. Tel: 020-7217 8591; Fax: 020-7217 8923; Email: prisgvuk@waverider.co.uk; Web: www.wavespace.waverider.co.uk/~prisgvuk/

Retail Book, Stationery and Allied Trades Employees' Association, 8-9 Commercial Road, Swindon SN1 5RB. Tel: 01793-615811; Fax: 01793-421319; Email: rba@rba-union.demon.co.uk

Royal College of Midwives, 15 Mansfield Street, London W1M 0BE. Tel: 020-7312 3535; Fax: 020-7312 3536; Email: info@rcm.org; Web: www.rcm.org.uk

Secondary Heads Association, 130 Regent Road, Leicester LE1 7PG. Tel: 0116-299 1122; Fax: 0116-299 1123; Email: info@sha.org.uk; Web: www.sha.org.uk

Society of Authors, 84 Drayton Gardens, London SW10 9SB. Tel: 020-7373 6642; Fax: 020-7373 5768; Email: authorsoc@writers.org.uk; Web: www.writers.org.uk/society

United Road Transport Union, 76 High Lane, Chorlton-cum-Hardy, Manchester M21 9EF. Tel: 0161-881 6245; Fax: 0161-861 0976; Email: info@urtu.com; Web: www.urtu.com

# National Academies of Scholarship

## THE BRITISH ACADEMY (1901)

10 Carlton House Terrace, London SW1Y 5AH
Tel 020-7969 5200

The British Academy is an independent, self-governing learned society for the promotion of the humanities and social sciences. It supports advanced academic research and is a channel for the Government's support of research in those disciplines.

The Fellows are scholars who have attained distinction in one of the branches of study that the Academy exists to promote. Candidates must be nominated by existing Fellows. At 5 May 2001 there were 720 Fellows, 16 Honorary Fellows, and 317 Corresponding Fellows overseas.

*President*, The Viscount Runciman, PBA
*Vice-President, Treasurer*, Prof. R. J. P. Kain, FBA
*Foreign Secretary*, Prof. C. N. J. Mann, FBA
*Publications Secretary*, Dr D. J. McKitterick, FBA
*Secretary*, P. W. H. Brown, CBE

## ROYAL ACADEMY (1768)

Burlington House, Picaddilly, London W1J OBD
Tel 020-7300 8000

The Royal Academy of Arts is an independent, self-governing society devoted to the encouragement and promotion of the fine arts.

Membership of the Academy is limited to 80 Royal Academicians, all being painters, engravers, sculptors or architects. Candidates are nominated and elected by the existing Academicians. There is also a limited class of honorary membership and there were 19 honorary members in 2001.

*President*, Prof. Phillip King, CBE, PRA
*Treasurer*, Prof. P. Huxley, RA
*Keeper*, Prof. B. Neiland, RA
*Secretary*, D. Gordon

## THE ROYAL ACADEMY OF ENGINEERING (1976)

29 Great Peter Street, London SW1P 3LW
Tel 020-7222 2688

The Royal Academy of Engineering was established as the Fellowship of Engineering in 1976. It was granted a royal charter in 1983 and its present title in 1992. It is an independent, self-governing body whose object is the pursuit, encouragement and maintenance of excellence in the whole field of engineering, in order to promote the advancement of the science, art and practice of engineering for the benefit of the public.

Election to the Fellowship is by invitation only from nominations supported by the body of Fellows. Fellows are chosen from among 9 engineers of all disciplines. At July 2001 there were 1,175 Fellows, 22 Honorary Fellows and 82 Foreign Members. The Duke of Edinburgh is the Senior Fellow and the Duke of Kent is a Royal Fellow.

*President*, Sir Alec Broers, FRS, FREng
*Senior Vice-President*, Dr J. R. Forrest, FREng
*Vice-Presidents*, Mr G. A. Campbell, FREng; FRS; Prof. A. P. Dowling, CBE, FREng; Prof. P. J. Dowling, FREng, FRS; B. V. George, CBE, FREng; Sir Duncan Michael, FREng; Prof. R. W. E. Shannon, FREng
*Hon. Treasurer*, J. W. Herbert, FREng
*Hon. Secretaries*, Prof. J. M. Brady FRS, FREng (*Electrical Engineering*); Prof. P. Braiden, FREng (*Mechanical Engineering*); J. R. Darley, FREng (*Process Engineering*); Prof. R. W. E. Shannon, FREng (*International Activities*); Prof. G. F. Hewitt, FREng, FRS (*Education and Training*)
Executive Secretary, *J. Burch*

## THE ROYAL SCOTTISH ACADEMY (1838)

17 Waterloo Place, The Mound, Edinburgh EH1 3BG
Tel 0131-558 7097

The Scottish Academy was founded in 1826 to arrange exhibitions of contemporary paintings and to establish a society of fine art in Scotland. The Academy was granted a royal charter in 1838.

Members are elected from the disciplines of painting, sculpture, architecture and printmaking. Elections are from nominations put forward by the existing membership. At mid-2001 there were four Senior Academicians, six Senior Associates, 36 Academicians, 39 Associates, four non-resident Associates and 28 Honorary Members.

The administrative offices have temporarily moved to 17 Waterloo Place while the R.S.A. building undergoes major refurbishment.

*President*, Ian McKenzie Smith, OBE, PRSA
*Secretary*, W. Scott, RSA
*Treasurer*, I. Metzstein, RSA
*Librarian*, P. Collins, RSA
*Administrative Secretary*, B. Laidlaw, ACIS

## ROYAL SOCIETY (1660)

6 Carlton House Terrace, London SW1Y 5AG
Tel 020-7839 5561

The Royal Society is an independent academy promoting the natural and applied sciences. Founded in 1660, the Society has three roles, as the UK academy of science, as a learned Society, and as a funding agency. It responds to individual demand with select by merit, not by field. The Society's objectives are to recognise excellence in science; support leading-edge scientific research and its applications; stimulate international interaction; further the role of science, engineering and technology in society; promote education and the public's understanding of science, provide independent authoritative advice on matters relating to science, engineering and technology and to encourage research into the history of science.

Fellows are elected for their contributions to science, both in fundamental research resulting in greater understanding, and also in leading and directing scientific and technological progress in industry and research establishments. A maximum of 42 new Fellows, who must be citizens or residents of the British Commonwealth countries or Ireland, may be elected annually.

Up to 6 Foreign Members, who are selected from those not eligible to become Fellows because of citizenship or residency, are elected annually for their contributions to science.

One Honorary Fellow may be elected each year from those not eligible for election as Fellows or Foreign Members but who have rendered signal service in the cause of science, or whose election would significantly benefit the a Society by their experience in other walks of life.

*President*, Sir Robert May
*Treasurer*, Sir Eric Ash, Kt., CBE, FRSEng, FRS
*Biological Secretary*, Prof. P. Bateson, FRS
*Physical Secretary*, Prof. J. Enderby, CBE, FRS,
*Foreign Secretary*, Prof. B.. Heap, CBE, FRS
*Executive Secretary*, S. Cox, CVO

---

THE ROYAL SOCIETY OF EDINBURGH (1783)
22–26 George Street, Edinburgh EH2 2PQ
Tel 0131-240 5000

---

The Royal Society of Edinburgh (RSE) is Scotland's National Academy. A wholly independent, non party-political body with charitable status, the RSE is a knowledge resource for the people of Scotland. Organising conferences and lectures both for the specialist and for the general public, the RSE is a forum for informed debate on issues of national and international importance.

Scotland's foremost think-tank, the society draws upon the expertise of its multidisciplinary fellowship of men and women of international standing, to provide independent, expert advice to key decision making bodies, including Government and Parliament. Strengthening links between academia and industry and boosting wealth generation at home, the Society's Research Awards programme annually awards well over half a million pounds to exceptionally talented young academics and potential entrepreneurs. Today, operating a successful programme of inspiring lectures and hands on workshops for primary and secondary school pupils, the RSE is also active in classrooms from the Borders to the Northern Isles.

At May 2001 there were 1,203 Ordinary Fellows, 69 Honorary Fellows and 10 Corresponding Fellows.

*President*, Prof. Sir William Stewart, FRS, FRSE
*Vice-Presidents*, Sir David Carter, FRSE; Prof. R. J. Donovan, FRSE; The Rt. Hon. Lord Ross, FRSE
*Treasurer*, Prof. Sir Laurence Hunter, CBE, FRSE
*General Secretary*, Prof. P. N. Wilson, CBE, FRSE
*Executive Secretary*, Dr W. Duncan

# The Research Councils

The Government funds basic and applied civil science research, mostly through the seven research councils, which are supported by the Department of Trade and Industry. The councils support research and training in universities and other higher education establishments. They also receive income for research commissioned by government departments and the private sector. In July 2000, the Government announced additional funding for research of £725 million over the three years 2001-04.

The Government science budget for 2000-01 was £1,594,753 million in total and included the following allocations:

| | 2000-01 £m | 2001-02 £m |
|---|---|---|
| BBSRC | 213.491 | 213.987 |
| ESRC | 71.800 | 74.447 |
| EPSRC | 413.552 | 436.202 |
| MRC | 319.651 | 349.614 |
| NERC | 185.350 | 192.865 |
| PPARC | 205.774 | 206.289 |
| CCLRC | 4.075 | 7.421 |
| Pensions | 25.620 | 26.970 |
| Royal Society | 24.622 | 25.945 |
| Royal Academy of Engineering | 4.025 | 4.270 |
| OST initiatives | 3.842 | 3.000 |
| Joint Research Equipment Initiative | 4.330 | 10.000 |
| University Challenge | 0.586 | - |
| Joint Infrastructure Fund | 88.116 | 125.000 |
| Science Enterprise Challenge | 15.750 | - |
| The Synchrotron Radiation Source | 4.069 | 20.000 |
| Cambridge/Massachusetts Institute of Technology | 10.100 | 14.000 |
| Higher Education Innovation Fund | - | 20.000 |
| Exploitation of Discoveries at PSREs | - | 10.000 |

---

## BIOTECHNOLOGY AND BIOLOGICAL SCIENCES RESEARCH COUNCIL (BBSRC)

Polaris House, North Star Avenue, Swindon SN2 1UH
Tel: 01793-413200

---

The BBSRC promotes and supports research and postgraduate training relating to the understanding and exploitation of biological systems; advances knowledge and technology; provides trained scientists to meet the needs of biotechnological-related industries; and provides advice, disseminates knowledge, and promotes public understanding of biotechnology and the biological sciences.

*Chairman*, Dr P. Doyle, CBE, FRSE
*Chief Executive*, Prof. R. Baker, FRS

### INSTITUTES

BABRAHAM INSTITUTE
*Director*, Dr R. G. Dyer, Babraham Hall, Babraham, Cambridge CB2 4AT. Tel: 01223-496000

INSTITUTE FOR ANIMAL HEALTH
*Director*, Dr C. J. Bostock, Compton, Newbury, Berks RG20 7NN. Tel: 01635-578411

BBSRC AND MRC NEUROPATHOGENESIS UNIT, Ogston Building, West Mains Road, Edinburgh EH9 3JF. Tel: 0131-667 5204/5.

COMPTON LABORATORY, Compton, Newbury, Berks RG20 7NN. Tel: 01635-578411.

PIRBRIGHT LABORATORY, Ash Road, Pirbright, Woking, Surrey GU24 0NF. Tel: 01483-232441. *Head*, Dr A. I. Donaldson

INSTITUTE OF ARABLE CROPS RESEARCH
*Director*, Prof. I. R. Crute, Rothamsted, Harpenden, Herts AL5 2JQ. Tel: 01582-763133

IACR – BROOM'S BARN, Higham, Bury St Edmunds, Suffolk IP28 6NP. Tel: 01284-812200. *Director*, Dr J. D. Pidgeon

IACR – LONG ASHTON RESEARCH STATION, Long Ashton, Bristol BS41 9AF. Tel: 01275-392181. *Director*, Prof. P. R. Shewry

IACR – ROTHAMSTED, Harpenden, Herts AL5 2JQ. Tel: 01582-763133. *Director*, Prof. I. R. Crute

INSTITUTE OF FOOD RESEARCH
Norwich Research Park, Colney Lane, Norwich NR4 7UA. Tel: 01603-255000. *Director*, Prof. Alisatair Robertson

INSTITUTE OF GRASSLAND AND ENVIRONMENTAL RESEARCH
*Director*, Prof. C. J. Pollock, Plas Gogerddan, Aberystwyth, Ceredigion SY23 3EB. Tel: 01970-828255

ABERYSTWYTH RESEARCH CENTRE, Plas Gogerddan, Aberystwyth, Ceredigion SY23 3EB. Tel: 01970-828255

BRONYDD MAWR RESEARCH STATION, Trecastle, Brecon, Powys LD3 8RD. Tel: 01874-636480

NORTH WYKE RESEARCH STATION, Okehampton, Devon EX20 2SB. Tel: 01837-82558. *Head*, Prof. R. J. Wilkins

TRAWSGOED RESEARCH FARM, Trawsgoed, Aberystwyth, Ceredigion SY23 4LL. Tel: 01974-261615

JOHN INNES CENTRE
*Director*, Prof. C. Lamb, Norwich Research Park, Colney, Norwich NR4 7UH. Tel: 01603-452571

ROSLIN INSTITUTE
*Director*, Prof. G. Bulfield, FRSE, Roslin, Midlothian EH25 9PS. Tel: 0131-527 4200

SILSOE RESEARCH INSTITUTE
*Director*, Prof. B. Day, , Wrest Park, Silsoe, Bedford MK45 4HS. Tel: 01525-860000

---

## SCOTTISH AGRICULTURAL AND BIOLOGICAL RESEARCH INSTITUTES

---

HANNAH RESEARCH INSTITUTE, Ayr KA6 5HL. Tel: 01292-674000. *Director*, Prof. M. Peaker, FRS

MACAULAY LAND USE RESEARCH INSTITUTE, Craigiebuckler, Aberdeen AB15 8QH. Tel: 01224-318611. *Director*, Prof. E. M. Gill, Ph.D.

MOREDUN RESEARCH INSTITUTE, Pentlands Science Park, Bush Loan, Penicuik, Midlothian EH26 0PZ. Tel: 0131-445 5111. *Director*, Prof. Q. A. McKellar

ROWETT RESEARCH INSTITUTE, Greenburn Road, Bucksburn, Aberdeen AB21 9SB. Tel: 01224-712751. *Director*, Prof. P. J. Morgan

SCOTTISH CROP RESEARCH INSTITUTE (SCRI), Invergowrie, Dundee DD2 5DA. Tel: 01382-562731.

BIOMATHEMATICS AND STATISTICS SCOTLAND (BioSS) (administered by SCRI), University of Edinburgh, James Clerk Maxwell Building, The King's Buildings, Mayfield Road, Edinburgh EH9 3JZ. Tel: 0131-650 4901. *Director*, R. A. Kempton

## CENTRAL LABORATORY OF THE RESEARCH COUNCILS (CLRC)

Chilton, Didcot, Oxon OX11 0QX
Tel: 01235-821900

The CLRC was formed in April 1995. CLRC comprises Daresbury, Chilbolton and Rutherford Appleton Laboratories, which provide advanced facilities and specialist expertise to support academic and industrial research in the physical and life sciences. It is operated by the Council for the Central Laboratory of the Research Councils (CCLRC), an independent, non departmental public body of the Office of Science and Technology, which is itself part of the Department of Trade and Industry.

*Chairman*, Prof. B. Eyre, CBE
*Chief Executive*, Prof. J Wood

DARESBURY LABORATORY, Daresbury, Warrington, Cheshire WA4 4AD. Tel: 01925-603000

RUTHERFORD APPLETON LABORATORY, Chilton, Didcot, Oxon OX11 0QX. Tel: 01235-821900

CHILBOLTON OBSERVATORY, Stockbridge, Hampshire SO20 6BJ. Tel: 01264-860391

## ECONOMIC AND SOCIAL RESEARCH COUNCIL (ESRC)

Polaris House, North Star Avenue, Swindon SN2 1UJ
Tel: 01793-413000

The purpose of the ESRC is to promote and support research and postgraduate training in the social sciences; to advance knowledge and provide trained social scientists; to provide advice on, and disseminate knowledge and promote public understanding of, the social sciences.

*Chief Executive*, Dr G. Marshall, FBA

### RESEARCH CENTRES

CENTRE FOR THE ANALYSIS OF SOCIAL EXCLUSION, London School of Economics, Houghton Street, London WC2A 2AE. Tel: 020-7955 7419.

CENTRE FOR BUSINESS RESEARCH, Department of Applied Economics, University of Cambridge, Sidgwick Avenue, Cambridge CB3 9DE. Tel: 01223-335248. *Director*, A. Hughes

CENTRE FOR ECONOMIC LEARNING AND SOCIAL EVOLUTION, Department of Economics, University College London, Gower Street, London WC1E 6BT. Tel: 020-7387 7050. *Research Director*, Prof. K. Binmore

CENTRE FOR ECONOMIC PERFORMANCE, London School of Economics, Houghton Street, London WC2A 2AE. Tel: 020-7955 7048. *Director*, Prof. R. Layard

CENTRE FOR FISCAL POLICY, Institute for Fiscal Studies, 7 Ridgmount Street, London WC1E 7AE. Tel: 020-7636 3784. *Director*, Prof. R. Blundell

CENTRE FOR ORGANISATION AND INNOVATION, Institute of Work Psychology, University of Sheffield, Sheffield S10 2TN. Tel: 0114-222 3287. *Director*, Prof. T. Wall

CENTRE FOR RESEARCH IN DEVELOPMENT, INSTRUCTION AND TRAINING, Department of Psychology, University of Nottingham, Nottingham NG7 2RD. Tel: 0115-951 5312. *Director*, Prof. D. J. Wood

CENTRE FOR RESEARCH INTO ELECTIONS AND SOCIAL TRENDS, Social and Community Planning Research, 35 Northampton Square, London EC1V 0AX. Tel: 020-7250 1866. *Director*, Prof. R. Jowell

CENTRE FOR RESEARCH ON INNOVATION AND COMPETITION, Faculty of Economic and Social Studies, University of Manchester M13 9PL. Tel: 0161-275 2000. *Director*, Prof. S. Metcalfe; Manchester School of Management, UMIST, Manchester M60 1QD. Tel: 0161-236 3311. *Director*, Prof. R. Coombs

CENTRE FOR SKILLS, KNOWLEDGE AND ORGANISATIONAL PERFORMANCE (SKOPE), University of Oxford, Department of Economics, Manor Road, Oxford, OX1 3UP. Tel: 01865-271087

CENTRE FOR SOCIAL AND ECONOMIC RESEARCH ON THE GLOBAL ENVIRONMENT, School of Environmental Sciences, University of East Anglia, Norwich NR4 7TJ. Tel: 01603-593176. *Director*, Prof. K. Turner

CENTRE FOR THE STUDY OF AFRICAN ECONOMIES, Department of Economics, University of Oxford, Manor Road, Oxford, OX1 3UQ. Tel: 01865-271084 OX1 3UL. Tel: 01865-271084. *Director*, Prof. J. Toye

CENTRE FOR THE STUDY OF GLOBALISATION AND REGIONALISATION, Department of Political Science, University of Warwick, Coventry CV4 7AL. Tel: 024-7652 3916. *Directors*, Prof. R. Higgott, Prof. J. Whalley

COMPLEX PRODUCT SYSTEM INNOVATION CENTRE, SPRU, Mantell Building, University of Sussex, Brighton BN1 9RF. Tel: 01273-686758. *Director*, Dr M. Hobday; CENTRIM, University of Brighton, Brighton BN1 9PH. Tel: 01273-642188.

FINANCIAL MARKETS CENTRE, London School of Economics, Houghton Street, London WC2A 2AE. Tel: 020-7955 7002. *Director*, Prof. D. Webb

RESEARCH CENTRE ON MICRO-SOCIAL CHANGE, University of Essex, Wivenhoe Park, Colchester, Essex CO4 3SQ. Tel: 01206-872957. *Director*, Prof. J. Gershuny

TRANSPORT STUDIES UNIT, Centre for Transport Studies, University College London, Gower Street, London WC1E 6BT. Tel: 020-7380 7009.

### RESOURCE CENTRES

BUSINESS PROCESS RESOURCE CENTRE, Warwick Manufacturing Group, University of Warwick, Coventry CV4 7AL. Tel: 024-7652 4173.

CENTRE FOR APPLIED SOCIAL SURVEYS, Social and Community Planning Research, 35 Northampton Square, London EC1V 0AX. Tel: 020-7250 1866.

CENTRE FOR ECONOMIC POLICY RESEARCH, 90–98 Goswell Road, London EC1V 7DB. Tel: 020-7878 2900.

ESRC DATA ARCHIVE, University of Essex, Wivenhoe Park, Colchester, Essex CO4 3SQ. Tel: 01206-872001.

ESRC UK CENTRE FOR EVIDENCE BASED POLICY Queen Mary University London, Department of Politics, Mile End Road, London, E1 4NS. *Director*, Prof. K. Young

INTERNATIONAL BIBLIOGRAPHY OF THE SOCIAL SCIENCES, British Library of Political and Economic Science, London School of Economics, Houghton Street, London WC2A 2AE. Tel: 020-7955 7000.

INTERNATIONAL BIBLIOGRAPHY OF THE SOCIAL SCIENCES: ON-LINE RESOURCE CENTRE
LSE, 10 Portugal Street, London, WC2A 2HD. Tel: 020-7955 7455. *Director*, Ms. L. Brindley

QUALITATIVE DATA ARCHIVAL RESOURCE CENTRE, Department of Sociology, University of Essex, Colchester, Essex CO4 3SQ. Tel: 01206-873058.

RESOURCE CENTRE FOR ACCESS TO DATA IN EUROPE, Department of Geography, University of Durham, Durham DH1 3HP. Tel: 0191-374 7350.

ENGINEERING AND PHYSICAL SCIENCES RESEARCH COUNCIL (EPSRC)
Polaris House, North Star Avenue, Swindon SN2 1ET
Tel: 01793-444000

The EPSRC promotes and supports basic, strategic and applied research and training in UK higher education institutions in the physical sciences and engineering.
*Chief Executive*, Prof. R. Brook, OBE, FREng.

MEDICAL RESEARCH COUNCIL (MRC)
20 Park Crescent, London W1BA 1AL
Tel: 020-7636 5422; Fax: 020-7436 2663;
Web:wwwmrc.ac.uk

The purpose of the MRC is to promote medical and related biological research. The council employs its own research staff and funds research by other institutions and individuals, complementing the research resources of the universities and hospitals.
*Chairman*, Sir Anthony Cleaver
*Chief Executive*, Prof. G. K. Radda, CBE, D.Phil., FRS
*Chairman, Neurosciences and Mental Health Board*, Prof. E. Johnston, MD, FRCP, FRCPsych
*Chairman, Molecular and Cellular Medicine Board*, Prof. I. C. MacLennan
*Chairman, Physiological Medicine and Infections Board*, Prof. N. J. Rothwell
*Chairman, Health Services and Public Health Research Board*, Prof. R. Fitzpatrick, Ph.D.
LABORATORY OF MOLECULAR BIOLOGY, Hills Road, Cambridge CB2 2QH. Tel: 01223-248011.

RESEARCH UNITS
BIOCHEMICAL AND CLINICAL MAGNETIC RESONANCE UNIT, Magnetic Resonance Spectroscopy, John Radcliffe Hospital, Headington, Oxford OX3 9DU. Tel: 01865-221111. *Hon. Director*, P. Styles, D.Phil.
CELL MUTATION UNIT, University of Sussex, Falmer, Brighton BN1 9RR. Tel: 01273-678123. *Director*, Prof. B. A. Bridges, Ph.D., FIBiol.
CELLULAR IMMUNOLOGY UNIT, Sir William Dunn School of Pathology, Oxford OX1 3RE. Tel: 01865-275594. *Director (acting)*, D. W. Mason
CENTRE FOR BRAIN REPAIR (MRC CAMBRIDGE), Ed Brian Building, University Forvie Site, Robinson Way, Cambridge CB2 2PY. Tel: 01223-331160.
CENTRE FOR COGNITIVE NEURO-SCIENCE (MRC IRC), Department of Experimental Psychology, University of Oxford, Oxford OX1 3UD. Tel: 01865-271444. *Director*, Prof. C. Blakemore, FRS
CENTRE FOR MECHANISMS OF HUMAN TOXICITY, Hodgkin Building, University of Leicester, PO Box 138, Lancaster Road, Leicester LE1 9HN. Tel: 0116-252 5600. *Director*, Prof. G. C. K. Roberts, Ph.D.
CENTRE FOR PROTEIN ENGINEERING, MRC Centre, Hills Road, Cambridge CB2 2QH. Tel: 01223-248011. *Director*, Prof. A. Fersht, Ph.D., FRS
CYCLOTRON UNIT, MRC Clinical Sciences Centre, RPMS Hammersmith Hospital, Du Cane Road, London W12 0NN. Tel: 020-8383 3161. *Director*, Prof. C. Higgins, Ph.D., FRSE
HUMAN GENOME MAPPING PROJECT RESOURCE CENTRE, Hinxton Hall, Hinxton, Cambridge CB10 1RQ. Tel: 01223-494500. *Director*, D. Campbell, Ph.D.
HUMAN MOVEMENT AND BALANCE UNIT, Institute of Neurology, National Hospital for Neurology and Neuro-surgery, Queen Square, London WC1 3BG. Tel: 020-7837 3611. *Hon. Director*, Dr J. C. Rothwell
INSTITUTE OF MOLECULAR MEDICINE, John Radcliffe Hospital, Headington, Oxford OX3 9DU. Tel: 01865-222359. *Director*, Prof. Sir David Weatherall, MD, FRCP, FRCPath., FRS
INTERDISCIPLINARY RESEARCH CENTRE IN CELL BIOLOGY, MRC Laboratory for Molecular Cell Biology, University College London, Gower Street, London WC1E 6BT. Tel: 020-7380 7806. *Director*, Dr Jane Cope
MAMMALIAN GENETICS UNIT, Harwell Site, Chilton, Didcot, Oxon OX11 0RD. Tel: 01235-834393. *Director*, Prof. S. Brown, Ph.D.
MRC ANATOMICAL NEUROPHARMACOLOGY UNIT, Mansfield Road, Oxford OX1 3TH. Tel: 01865-271865. *Director*, Prof. P. Somogyi, Ph.D.
MRC BIOSTATISTICS UNIT, Institute of Public Health, University Forvie Site, Robinson Way, Cambridge CB2 2SR. Tel: 01223-330366.
MRC CELL BIOLOGY UNIT, University College London, Gower Street, London, WC1E 6BT. *Director*, Prof. A. Hall
MRC CLINICAL TRIALS UNIT, 222 Euston Road, London NW1 2DA. Tel: 020-7380 9991. *Director*, Prof. J. H. Darbyshire
MRC FUNCTIONAL GENETICS UNIT, The Department of Human Anatomy, South Parks Road, Oxford OX1 3QX.
MRC CANCER CELL UNIT, HUTCHINSON/MRC RESEARCH CENTRE, Hills Road, Cambridge, CB2 2XZ. Tel: 01223-248011
MRC CENTRE, OXFORD, Manor House, John Radcliffe Hospital, Headington, Oxford OX3 9DU. Tel: 01865-222124. *Head of Centre*, D. McLaren, Ph.D.
MRC CLINICAL SCIENCES CENTRE, Imperial College of Medicine, Hammersmith Hospital, Du Cane Road, London, W12 0NN.
MRC COGNITION AND BRAIN SCIENCES UNIT, 15 Chaucer Road, Cambridge CB2 2EF. Tel: 01223-355294. *Director*, Prof. W. Marslen-Wilson, FBA
MRC DUNN HUMAN NUTRITION UNIT, The Wellcome Trust, MRC Building, Addenbrooks Site, Hill Road, Cambridge CB2 2XY. Tel: 01223-415695. *Director*, Prof. Sir John Walker, D.Phil., FRS
MRC ENVIRONMENTAL EPIDEMIOLOGY UNIT, Southampton General Hospital, Southampton SO16 6YD. Tel: 023-8077 7624. *Director*, Prof. D. J. P. Barker, MD, Ph.D., FRCP, FRCOG
MRC EPIDEMIOLOGY AND MEDICAL CARE UNIT, Wolfson Institute of Preventive Medicine, Charterhouse Square, London EC1M 6BQ. Tel: 020-7982 6253. *Director*, Prof. T. W. Meade, CBE, DM, FRCP
MRC HEALTH SERVICES RESEARCH COLLABORATION, University of Bristol, Canynge Hall, Whiteladies Road, Bristol BS8 2PR. Tel: 0117-928 9000. *Director*, Prof. P. Dieppe
MRC HUMAN GENETICS UNIT, Western General Hospital, Crewe Road, Edinburgh EH4 2XU. Tel: 0131-322 2471. *Director*, Prof. N. D. Hastie, Ph.D., FRSE
MRC HUMAN IMMUNOLOGY UNIT, Weatherfield Institute of Molecular Science, John Radcliffe Hospital, Headington, Oxford OX1 9DS. Tel: 01865-222443. *Director*, Prof. A. McMichael
MRC HUMAN REPRODUCTION SCIENCE UNIT, Centre for Reproductive Biology, 37 Chalmers Street, Edinburgh EH3 9EW. Tel: 0131-229 2575. *Director*, Prof. R. P. Millar, Ph.D., FRCPath.

MRC IMMUNOCHEMISTRY UNIT, University Department of Biochemistry, South Parks Road, Oxford OX1 3QU. Tel: 01865-275354. *Director*, Prof. K. B. M. Reid, Ph.D.
MRC INSTITUTE FOR ENVIRONMENT AND HEALTH, University of Leicester, 94 Regent Road, Leicester LE1 7DD. Tel: 0116-223 1600. *Director*, Dr P. Harrison
MRC INSTITUTE OF HEARING RESEARCH, University of Nottingham, Nottingham NG7 2RD. Tel: 0115-922 3431. *Director*, Prof. M. P. Haggard, Ph.D.
MRC LABORATORIES, THE GAMBIA, Atlantic Road, Fajara, Near Banjul, The Gambia, W. Africa. *Director*, Prof. K. McAdam, FRCP
MRC LABORATORIES, JAMAICA, University of the West Indies, Mona, Kingston 7, Jamaica. *Director*, Prof. G. R. Serjeant, CMG, MD, FRCP
MRC LABORATORIES OF MOLECULAR BIOLOGY, Hills Road, Cambridge CB2 2QH. Tel: 01223-248011
MRC MOUSE GENOME CENTRE, MRC Mammalian Genetics Unit, Harwell, Didcot, Oxon OX11 0RD. Tel: 01235-834393. *Director*, Prof. S. Brown, Ph.D.
MRC MOLECULAR HAEMATOLOGY UNIT, Weatherall Institute of Molecular Medicine, John Radcliffe Hospital, Headington, Oxford OX3 9DU. Tel: 01865-222359. *Hon. Director*, Prof. D. Higgs
MRC MUSCLE AND CELL MOTILITY UNIT, The Randall Centre, Kings College London, New Hunts House, Guy's Campus, London SE1 1UL. Tel: 020-7848 6434.
MRC NATIONAL INSTITUTE FOR MEDICAL RESEARCH, The Ridgeway, Mill Hill, London NW7 1AA. Tel: 020-8959 3666.
MRC PRION UNIT, Imperial College School of Medicine at St Mary's, Norfolk Place, London W2 1PG. Tel: 020-7594 3760. *Director*, Prof. J. Collinge
MRC PROTEIN PHOSPHORYLATION UNIT, Department of Biochemistry, Medical Sciences Institute, University of Dundee, Dundee DD1 5EH. Tel: 01382-344241. *Hon. Director*, Prof. Sir Philip Cohen, Ph.D., FRS, FRSE
MRC RADIATION AND GENOME STABILITY UNIT, Harwell Site, Chilton, Didcot, Oxon OX11 0RD. Tel: 01235-834393. *Director*, Prof. D. Goodhead, D.Phil.
MRC RESOURCE CENTRE FOR HUMAN NUTRITION RESEARCH, Elsie Widdowson Labororatory, Fulbourn Road, Cambridge CB1 9LR. Tel: 01223-426356.
MRC SOCIAL AND PUBLIC HEALTH SCIENCES UNIT, 6 Lilybank Gardens, Glasgow G12 8QQ. Tel: 0141-357 3949. *Director*, Prof. S. Macintyre, OBE, Ph.D., FRSE
MRC TOXICOLOGY UNIT, Hodgkin Building, University of Leicester, PO Box 138, Lancaster Road, Leicester LE1 9HN. Tel: 0116-252 5600. *Director (acting)*, Prof. G. Cohen
MRC VIROLOGY UNIT, Institute of Virology, Church Street, Glasgow G11 5JR. Tel: 0141-330 4017. *Director*, Prof. D. J. McGeoch
SOCIAL, GENETIC AND DEVELOPMENTAL PSYCHIATRY RESEARCH CENTRE, Institute of Psychiatry, De Crespigny Park, Denmark Hill, London SE5 8AF. Tel: 020-7919 3873. *Director*, Prof. P. McGuffin
SYNAPATIC PLASTICITY CENTRE, School of Medical Sciences, University of Bristol, University Walk, Bristol BS8 1TD. Tel: 0117-928 7420. *Director*, Prof. G. L. Collingridge

## NATURAL ENVIRONMENT RESEARCH COUNCIL (NERC)

Polaris House, North Star Avenue, Swindon SN2 1EU
Tel: 01793-411500

The UK's Natural Environment Research Council (NERC) funds and carries out impartial scientific research in the sciences of the environment. Its work covers the full range of atmospheric, earth, terrestrial and aquatic sciences, from the depth of the oceans to the upper atmosphere. Its mission is to gather and apply knowledge, create understanding and predict the behaviour of the natural environment and its resources.
*Chairman*, R. Margetts, CBE, FREng
*Chief Executive*, Prof. J. Lawton, CBE, FRS

### RESEARCH CENTRES

ATMOSPHERIC CHEMISTRY MODELLING SUPPORT UNIT, University Chemical Laboratory, University of Cambridgeshire, Lensfield Road, Cambridge, CB2 1EP. Tel: 01223-336473. *Director*, Dr J. A. Pyle
BRITISH ANTARCTIC SURVEY, High Cross, Madingley Road, Cambridge, CB3 0ET. Tel: 01233-221400. *Director*, Dr C. Rapley
BRITISH GEOLOGICAL SURVEY, Kingsley Dunham Centre, Keyworth, Nottingham, NG12 5GG. Tel: 0115-936 3100. *Director*, Dr D. Fawley
CENTRE FOR ECOLOGY AND HYDROLOGY (CEH) *Director (Acting Head)*, Prof. J. Wallace
CEH WINDERMERE, The Ferry House, Far Sawrey, Ambleside, Cumbria, LA22 0LP. Tel: 01539-42468. *Director*, Prof. A. D. Pickering
CEH WALLINGFRORD, Maclean Building, Crowmarsh Gifford, Wallingford, Oxon, OX10 8BB. Tel: 01491-838800. *Director*, Prof. J. Wallace
CEH MONKSWOOD, Abbots Reipton, Huntington, PE17 2LS. Tel: 01487-772400. *Director*, Prof. B. Wyatt
CEH Oxford, Mansfield Road, Oxford, OX1 3SR. Tel: 01865-281630. *Director*, Dr P. Nuttal
CENTRE FOR GLOBAL ATMOSPHERIC MODELLING, Department of Meteorology, University of Reading, 2 Earley Gate, Whiteknights, Reading, RG6 2AU. Tel: 0118-931 8315. *Director*, Prof. A. O'Neill
CENTRE FOR POPULATION BIOLOGY, Imperial College, Silwood Park, Ascot, SL5 7PY. Tel: 020-7594 2346. *Director*, Prof. C. Godfray
DUNSTAFFNAGE MARINE LABORATORY, PO Box 3, Oban, Argyll, PA34 4AD. Tel: 0161-559000. *Director*, Prof. G. Shimmield
ENVIRONMENTAL SYSTEMS SCIENCE CENTRE, University of Reading, Harry Pitt Building, 3 Earley Gate, PO Box 238, Reading, RG6 6AL. Tel: 0118-931 8741. *Director*, Prof. R. Gurney
PLYMOUTH MARINE LABORATORY, Prospect Place, West Hoe, Plymouth, PL1 3DH. Tel: 01752-633100. *Director*, Prof. N. Owens
PROUDMAN OCEANOGRAPHIC LABORATORY, Bidston Observatory, Birkenhead, L43 7RA. Tel: 0151-653 8633. *Director*, Dr E. Hill
SEA MAMMAL RESEARCH UNIT, Gatty Marine Laboratory, University of St Andrews, Fife, KY16 8LB. Tel: 01334-462630
SOUTHAMPTON OCEANOGRAPHY CENTRE, University of Southampton, Empress Dock, Southampton, SO14 3ZH. Tel: 023-8059 6666. *Director*, Prof. H. Roe
TYNDALL CENTRE FOR CLIMATE CHANGE RESEARCH, University of East Anglia, Norwich, NR4 7TJ. Tel: 01603-593162. *Director*, Dr M. Hulme

CENTRES/SURVEYS

CENTRE FOR COASTAL AND MARINE SCIENCE *Director*, Prof. J. McGlade (based at Plymouth Marine Laboratory)

INSTITUTE OF FRESHWATER ECOLOGY, The Ferry House, Far Sawrey, Ambleside, Cumbria LA22 0LP. Tel: 015394-42468. *Director*, Dr P. Mathesion

INSTITUTE OF TERRESTRIAL ECOLOGY, Monks Wood, Abbots Ripton, Huntingdon PE17 2LS. Tel: 01487-773381. *Director*, Dr P. Nuttall

INSTITUTE OF VIROLOGY AND ENVIRONMENTAL MICROBIOLOGY, Mansfield Road, Oxford OX1 3SR. Tel: 01865-281630. Acting *Director*, Dr E. Gould

PROUDMAN OCEANOGRAPHIC LABORATORY, Bidston Observatory, Birkenhead L43 7RA. Tel: 0151-653 8633. *Director*, Dr E. Hill

SCOTTISH ASSOCIATION FOR MARINE SCIENCE Dunstaffnage Marine Laboratory, Dunbeg, By-opan, Argyll, PA34 4AD. Tel: 01631-562244. *Director*, Prof. G. Shimmield

SOUTHAMPTON OCEANOGRAPHY CENTRE, University of Southampton, Empress Dock, Southampton SO14 3ZH. Tel: 023-8059 6888. *Director*, Dr J. Shepherd

UNITS

ATMOSPHERIC CHEMISTRY MODELLING SUPPORT UNIT, University Chemical Laboratory, University of Cambridge, Lensfield Road, Cambridge CB2 1EP. Tel: 01223-336473. *Director*, Dr J. A. Pyle

CENTRE FOR GLOBAL ATMOSPHERIC MODELLING, Department of Meteorology, University of Reading, 2 Earley Gate, Whiteknights, Reading RG6 2AU. Tel: 0118-931 8315. *Director*, Prof. A. O'Neill

ENVIRONMENTAL SYSTEMS SCIENCE CENTRE, Harry Pitt Building, PO Box 238, Reading University, Reading RG6 6AL. Tel: 0118-931 8741. *Director*, Prof. R. Gurney

SEA MAMMAL RESEARCH UNIT, Gatty Marine Laboratory, University of St Andrews, St Andrews, Fife KY16 8LB. Tel: 01334-462630. *Head*, Prof. I. Boyd

---

PARTICLE PHYSICS AND ASTRONOMY RESEARCH COUNCIL (PPARC)

Polaris House, North Star Avenue, Swindon SN2 1SZ
Tel: 01793-442000; Fax: 01793-442002;
Email: pr.pus@pparc.ac.uk

---

The Particle Physics and Astronomy Research Centre (PPARC) is the UK's strategic science investment agency. It funds research, education and public understanding in four broad areas of science – particle physics, astronomy, cosmology and space sciences.

PPARC is government funded and provides research grants and studentships to scientists in British universities, gives researchers access to world-class facilities and funds the UK membership of international bodies such as the European Laboratory for Particle Physics (CERN), the European Space Agency. It also contributes money to the UK telescopes overseas on La Palma, Hawaii, Australia and in Chile, the UK Astronomy Technology Centre at the Royal Observatory, Edinburgh and the MERLIN/VLBI National Facility.

*Chairman*, Dr R. Hawley, CBE, FRSE, FREng.
*Chief Executive*, Prof. I. Halliday

ISAAC NEWTON GROUP OF TELESCOPES, Apartado de Coreos 321, Santa Cruz de la Palma, Tenerife 38780, Canary Islands. Tel: 00 3422-411048. *Director*, R. Rutten

JOINT ASTRONOMY CENTRE, 660 N A'ohoku Place, University Park, Hilo, Hawaii 96720. Tel: Hawaii 961 3756. *Head*, Prof. I. Robson

UK ASTRONOMY TECHNOLOGY CENTRE, Blackford Hill, Edinburgh EH9 3HJ.Tel: 0131-668 8100. *Director*, Dr A. Russell

---

# Research and Technology Organisations

The following industrial and technological research bodies are members of the Association of Independent Research and Technology Organisations (AIRTO). Members' activities span a wide range of disciplines from life sciences to engineering. Their work includes basic research, development and design of innovative products or processes, instrumentation testing and certification, and technology and management consultancy. AIRTO publishes a directory to help clients identify the organisations which might be able to assist them.

ADVANCED MANUFACTURING TECHNOLOGY RESEARCH INSTITUTE, Hulley Road, Macclesfield, Cheshire SK10 2NE. Tel: 01625-425421. *Managing Director*, D. Palethorpe

AIRCRAFT RESEARCH ASSOCIATION LTD, Manton Lane, Bedford MK41 7PF. Tel: 01234-350681. *Chief Executive*, B. Timmins

AIRTO, PO Box 85, Leatherhead, Surrey KT22 7RY Tel: 01372-374153. *President*, Dr B. Blunden, OBE

BHR GROUP LTD (*Fluid mechanics and process technology*), The Fluid Engineering Centre, Cranfield, Bedford MK43 0AJ. Tel: 01234-750422. *Chief Executive*,

BLC (THE LEATHER TECHNOLOGY CENTRE), Leather Trade House, Kings Park Road, Moulton Park, Northants NN3 6JD. Tel: 01604-679999. *Chief Executive*, Dr K. Alexander

BRE, Gartson, Watford, Hertfordshire, WD2 7JR. Tel: 01923-664000. *Chief Executive*, Dr M. Wyatt

BRITISH GLASS TECHNOLOGY, Northumberland Road, Sheffield S10 2UA. Tel: 0114-268 6201. *Director-General*, Mr D. Workman

BRITISH MARITIME TECHNOLOGY LTD, Orlando House, 1 Waldegrave Road, Teddington, Middx TW11 8LZ. Tel: 020-8943 5544. *Chief Executive*, D. Goodrich

BREWING RESEARCH INTERNATIONAL (*Alcoholic beverages*), Lyttel Hall, Coopers Hill Road, Nutfield, Surrey RH1 4HY. Tel: 01737-822272. *Director-General*, Dr M. Kierstan

BRITISH TEXTILE TECHNOLOGY GROUP, Wira House, West Park Ring Road, Leeds LS16 6QL. Tel: 0113-259 1999; Shirley House, Wilmslow Road, Didsbury, Manchester M20 2RB. Tel: 0161-445 8141. *Chief Executive*, A. King

BUILDING RESEARCH ESTABLISHMENT, Garston, Watford WD2 7JR. Tel: 01923-664000. *Managing Director*, Dr M. Wyatt

BUILDING SERVICES RESEARCH AND INFORMATION ASSOCIATION, Old Bracknell Lane West, Bracknell, Berks RG12 7AH. Tel: 01344-426511. *Chief Executive*, A. Eastwell

CAMBRIDGE REFRIGERATION TECHNOLOGY (CRT), 140 Newmarket Road, Cambridge CB5 8HE. Tel: 01223-365101. *Managing Director*, R. Heap, MBE

CAMPDEN AND CHORLEYWOOD FOOD RESEARCH ASSOCIATION, Chipping Campden, Glos GL55 6LD. Tel: 01386-842000. *Director-General*, Prof. C. Dennis

CENTRAL LABORATORY OF THE RESEARCH COUNCILS, Chilton, Didcot, Oxfordshire, OX11 0QX. Tel: 01235-821900. *Chairman*, Prof. B. Eyre

CERAM RESEARCH (BRITISH CERAMIC RESEARCH LTD), Queen's Road, Penkhull, Stoke-on-Trent ST4 7LQ. Tel: 01782-764444. *Chief Executive*, Dr N. E. Sanderson

CIRIA (CONSTRUCTION INDUSTRY RESEARCH AND INFORMATION ASSOCIATION), 6 Storey's Gate, London SW1P 3AU. Tel: 020-7222 8891. *Director-General*, Dr P. L. Bransby

CRL (*Specialist products, technology licences, research and development*), Dawley Road, Hayes, Middx UB3 1HH. Tel: 020-8848 9779. *Managing Director*, Dr J. White

ERA TECHNOLOGY LTD (*Electronic, electrical, materials and structural engineering*), Cleeve Road, Leatherhead, Surrey KT22 7SA. Tel: 01372-367000. *Financial and Commercial Director*, C. Perks

FIRA INTERNATIONAL LTD (FURNITURE INDUSTRY RESEARCH ASSOCIATION), Maxwell Road, Stevenage, Herts SG1 2EW. Tel: 01438-313433. *Managing Director*, H. Davies

HR WALLINGFORD GROUP LTD (*Hydroinformatics and engineering*), Howbery Park, Wallingford, Oxon OX10 8BA. Tel: 01491-835381. *Chief Executive*, Dr S. W. Huntington

INSPECTORATE PLC, 2 Perry Road, Witham, Essex, CM8 3TU. Tel: 01376-515081

LABORATORY OF THE GOVERNMENT CHEMIST, Queens Road, Teddington, Middx TW11 0LY. Tel: 020-8943 7300. *Chief Executive and Government Chemist*, Dr R. Worswick

LEATHERHEAD FOOD RESEARCH ASSOCIATION, Randalls Road, Leatherhead, Surrey KT22 7RY. Tel: 01372-376761. *Director*, Dr R. Pugh

MATERIALS ENGINEERING RESEARCH LABORATORY LTD, Tamworth Road, Hertford SG13 7DG. Tel: 01992-500120. *Managing Director*, Dr R. H. Martin

MINERAL INDUSTRY RESEARCH ORGANISATION, Expert House, Sandford Street, Lichfield, Staffs WS13 6QA. Tel: 01543-262957. *Director*, N. Roberts

MOTOR INDUSTRY RESEARCH ASSOCIATION, Watling Street, Nuneaton, Warks CV10 0TU. Tel: 024-7635 5000. *Managing Director*, J. R. Wood

MOTOR INSURANCE REPAIR RESEARCH CENTRE, Colthorp Lane, Thatcham, Berks, RG19 4NP. Tel: 01635-868855. *Chief Executive*, P. Roberts

THE NATIONAL COMPUTING CENTRE LTD, Oxford House, Oxford Road, Manchester M1 7ED. Tel: 0161-228 6333. *Chief Executive*, M. Gough

NATIONAL PHYSICAL LABORATORY, Queens Road, Teddington, Middx TW11 0LW. Tel: 020-8977 3222. *Deputy Director*, Dr A. Wallard

PAINT RESEARCH ASSOCIATION, 8 Waldegrave Road, Teddington, Middx TW11 8LD. Tel: 020-8977 4427. Acting *Managing Director, Company Secretary and Finance Director*, J. Marshall

PERA GROUP (*Multi-disciplinary research, design, development and consultancy*), Middle Aston House, Middle Aston, Oxon OX6 3PT. Tel: 01869-347755. *Chief Executive*, Dr P.Davies

PIRA INTERNATIONAL (*Paper and board, printing, publishing and packaging*), Randalls Road, Leatherhead, Surrey KT22 7RU. Tel: 01372-802000. *Managing Director*, M. Hancock

RAPRA TECHNOLOGY LTD (*Rubber and plastics*), Shawbury, Shrewsbury SY4 4NR. Tel: 01939-250383; North East Centre, 18 Belasis Court, Belasis Technology Park, Billingham TS23 4AZ. Tel: 01642-370406. *Managing Director*, A. Ward

SATRA TECHNOLOGY CENTRE (*Footwear, apparel, safety products and furniture*), Satra House, Rockingham Road, Kettering, Northants NN16 9JH. Tel: 01536-410000. *Chief Executive*, Dr R. E. Whittaker

SCOTCH WHISKY RESEARCH INSTITUTE, The Robertson Trust Building, Research Park North, Riccarton, Edinburgh, EH14 4AP. Tel: 0131 449-8900. *Director*, Dr G. M. Steele

SIRA LTD (*Measurement, instrumentation, control and optical systems technology*), South Hill, Chislehurst, Kent BR7 5EH. Tel: 020-8467 2636. *Managing Director*, Prof. R. A. Brook

SMITH INSTITUTE (*Mathematics and computing*), PO Box 183, Guildford, Surrey GU2 5GG. Tel: 01483-579108. *Chairman of the Council*, Dr B. Smith

SPORTS TURF RESEARCH INSTITUTE, St Ives Estate, Bingley, W. Yorks BD16 1AU. Tel: 01274-565131. *Chief Executive*, Dr G. McKillop

STEEL CONSTRUCTION INSTITUTE, Silwood Park, Ascot, Berks SL5 7QN. Tel: 01344-623345. *Director*, Dr G. Owens

TNO BIBRA INTERNATIONAL LTD, Woodmansterne Road, Carshalton, Surrey SM5 4DS. Tel: 020-8652 1000, *Director*, Dr G. van der Veek

TRADA TECHNOLOGY LTD (*Timber and wood-based products*), Chiltern House, Stocking Lane, Hughenden Valley, High Wycombe, Bucks HP14 4ND. Tel: 01494-563091. *Managing Director*, A. Abbott

TRANSPORT RESEARCH LABORATORY, Old Wokingham Road, Crowthorne, Berks RG45 6AU. Tel: 01344-773131. *Chief Executive*, G. Clarke

TRW AUTOMOTIVE TECHNICAL CENTRE, Stratford Road, Solihull, W. Midlands B90 4GW. Tel: 0121-627 4141. *Director*, Mr D. Chew

TWI, Abington Hall, Abington, Cambridge CB1 6AL. Tel: 01223-891162. *Chief Executive*, A. B. M. Braithwaite, OBE

# Sports Bodies

*Sports Councils*

CENTRAL COUNCIL OF PHYSICAL RECREATION, Francis House, Francis Street, London SW1P 1DE. Tel: 020-7828 3163; Fax: 020-7630 8820; *General Secretary*, M. Denton

SPORT ENGLAND, 16 Upper Woburn Place, London WC1H 0QP. Tel: 020-7273 1500; Fax: 020-7383 5740; Email: info@english.sports.gov.uk; Web: www.sportsengland.org; *Chief Executive*, D. Casey. *Chairman*, T. Brooking

SPORTSCOTLAND, Caledonia House, South Gyle, Edinburgh EH12 9DQ. Tel: 0131-317 7200; Fax: 0131-317 7202; Email: library@sportscotland.org.uk; Web: www.sportscotland.org.uk; *Chief Executive*, I. Robson. *Chairman*, A. Dempster

SPORTS COUNCIL FOR NORTHERN IRELAND, House of Sport, Upper Malone Road, Belfast BT9 5LA. Tel: 028-9038 1222; Fax: 028-9068 2757; Web: www.sportni.com; *Chief Executive*, E. McCartan. *Chairman*, Prof. E. Saunders

SPORTS COUNCIL FOR WALES, Sophia Gardens, Cardiff CF11 9SW. Tel: 029-2030 0500; Fax: 029-2030 0600; Email: scw@scw.co.uk; Web: www.sports-council-wales.co.uk; *Chief Executive*, Dr H. Jones. *Chairman*, G. Davies

UK SPORTS COUNCIL, 40 Bernard Street, London WC1N 1LE. Tel: 020-7841 9500; Fax: 020-7841 8850; Email: info@uksport.gov.uk; Web: www.uksport.gov.uk; *Chief Executive*, R. Callicott. *Chairman*, Sir Rodney Walker

*Angling*

NATIONAL FEDERATION OF ANGLERS, Halliday House, Egginton Junction, Derbys DE65 6GU. Tel: 01283-734735; Fax: 01283-734799; Email: office@nfahq.freeserve.co.uk; Web: www.the.nfa.org.uk; *Administration Manager*, Mrs J. A. Price. *President*, K. W. Ball

*Archery*

GRAND NATIONAL ARCHERY SOCIETY, Lilleshall National Sports Centre, Newport, Shropshire TF10 9AT. Tel: 01952-677888; Fax: 01952-606019; Email: enquiries@gnas.org; Web: www.gnas.org; *Chief Executive*, D. Sherratt

*Association Football*

THE FOOTBALL ASSOCIATION, 25 Soho Square, London W1D 4FA. Tel: 020-7745 4545; Fax: 020-7745 4546; Web: www.the-fa.org; *Chief Executive*, A. Crozier. *Chairman*, G. Thompson

FOOTBALL ASSOCIATION OF WALES, Plymouth Chambers, 3 Westgate Street, Cardiff CF10 1DP. Tel: 029-2037 2325; Fax: 029-2034 3961; Email: hburlace@faw.co.uk; Web: www.faw.org.uk; *Secretary-General*, D. G. Collins. *President*, D. W. Shantlin

THE FOOTBALL LEAGUE LTD, Edward VII Quay, Navigation Way, Preston, Lancs PR2 2YF. Tel: 01772-325800; Fax: 01772-325801; Email: fl@football-league.co.uk; Web: www.football-league.co.uk; *Secretary*, vacant

IRISH FOOTBALL ASSOCIATION, 20 Windsor Avenue, Belfast BT9 6EE. Tel: 028-9066 9458; Fax: 028-9066 7620; Email: enquiries@irishfa.com; Web: www.irishfa.com; *General Secretary*, D. I. Bowen

IRISH FOOTBALL LEAGUE, 96 University Street, Belfast BT7 1HE. Tel: 028-9024 2888; Fax: 028-9033 0773; Email: mail@irish-league.co.uk; Web: www.irish-league.co.uk; *Secretary*, H. Wallace. *President*, J. Semple

SCOTTISH FOOTBALL ASSOCIATION, Hampden Park, Glasgow G42 9AY. Tel: 0141-661 6000; Fax: 0141-661 6001; Email: info@scottishfa.co.uk; Web: www.scottishfa.co.uk; *Chief Executive*, D. Taylor. *President*, J. McGinn

SCOTTISH FOOTBALL LEAGUE, The National Stadium, Hampden Park, Glasgow G42 9EB. Tel: 0141-620 4160; Fax: 0141-620 4161; Email: info@scottishfootball.com; Web: www.scottishfootball.com; *Secretary*, Peter Donald

*Athletics*

ATHLETICS ASSOCIATION OF WALES, Catsash Road, Catsash, Newport NP18 1WA. Tel: 01633-423833; Fax: 01633-430654; Email: walesathletics@lineone.net; Web: www.welshathletics.org; *Chairman*, Ms L. Harries

NORTHERN IRELAND ATHLETIC FEDERATION, Athletics House, Old Coach Road, Belfast BT9 5PR. Tel: 028-9060 2707; Fax: 028-9030 9939; Email: info@niathletics.org; Web: www.niathletics.org; *Secretary*, J. Allen

SCOTTISH ATHLETICS FEDERATION, Caledonia House, South Gyle, Edinburgh EH12 9DQ. Tel: 0131-317 7320; Fax: 0131-317 7321; Email: admin@saf.org.uk; Web: www.saf.org.uk; *General Manager*, N. F. Park. *President*, Mrs J. Watt *Chief Executive*, D. Joy

UK ATHLETICS, Athletics House, 10 Harborne Road, Edgbaston, Birmingham B15 3AA. Tel: 0121-456 5098; Fax: 0121-456 8752; Email: information@ukathletics.org.uk; Web: www.ukathletics.org; *Chief Executive*, D. Moorcroft, OBE. *Information Officer*, W. Adcocks

*Badminton*

BADMINTON ASSOCIATION OF ENGLAND LTD, National Badminton Centre, Bradwell Road, Loughton Lodge, Milton Keynes MK8 9LA. Tel: 01908-268400; Fax: 01908-268412; Email: enquiries@baofe.co.uk; Web: www.baofe.co.uk; *Chief Executive*, S. Baddeley. *Chairman*, J. Havers *President*, W. Andrew

SCOTTISH BADMINTON UNION, Cockburn Centre, 40 Bogmoor Place, Glasgow G51 4TQ. Tel: 0141-445 1218; Fax: 0141-425 1218; Web: www.scotbadminton.demon.co.uk; *Chief Executive*, Miss A. Smillie. *Hon. Secretary*, I. E. Brown

WELSH BADMINTON UNION, Fourth Floor, 3 Westgate Street, Cardiff CF10 1DP. Tel: 029-2022 2082; Fax: 029-2039 4282; Email: wbu@btclick.com; Web: www.welshbadminton.net; *Director of Badminton*, L. Williams

*Baseball*

BASEBALLSOFTBALL UK, Ariel House, 74A Charlotte Street, London W1P 1LR. Tel: 020-7453 7055; Fax: 020-7453 7007; Email: info@baseballsoftballuk.com; Web: www.baseballsoftballuk.com; *Chief Executive*, B. Fromer

*Basketball*

BASKETBALL SCOTLAND, Caledonia House, South Gyle, Edinburgh EH12 9DQ. Tel: 0131-317 7260; Fax: 0131-317 7489; Email: sba@basketball-scotland.com; Web: www.basketball-scotland.com; *Chief Executive Officer*, Mr R. Thompson. *Chairman*, W. D. McInnes

ENGLISH BASKETBALL ASSOCIATION, 48 Bradford Road, Stanningley, Leeds LS28 6DF. Tel: 0113-236 1166; Fax: 0113-236 1022; Email: enquiries@ebbaonline.net; Web: www.basketballengland.org.uk; *Chief Executive*, S. Kirkland. *President*, K. Mitchell OBE

*Billiards*

WORLD LADIES BILLIARDS AND SNOOKER ASSOCIATION, The Ground Floor, Albert House, 111-117 Victoria Street, Bristol BS1 6AX. Tel: 0117-317 8200; *Company Secretary*, Ms E. Walker. *Chairman*, M. Wildman

WORLD PROFESSIONAL BILLIARDS AND SNOOKER ASSOCIATION, Ground Floor, Albert House, 111-117 Victoria Street, Bristol BS1 6AX. Tel: 0117-317 8200; Fax: 0117-317 8300; Email: enq@worldsnooker.com; Web: www.worldsnooker.com; *Chief Executive*, J. McKenzie. *Chairman*, M. Wildman

*Bobsleigh*

BRITISH BOBSLEIGH ASSOCIATION, Department of Sports Development and Recreation, University of Bath, Claverton Down, Bath BA2 7AY. Tel: 01225-826826; Email: bba@dial.pipex.com; Web: www.british-bobsleigh.com; *Chairman*, R. B. B. Ropner. *Administrator*, G. C. Fraser

*Bowls*

BRITISH ISLES BOWLS COUNCIL, 23 Laysland Avenue, Countesthorpe, Leics LE8 5XX. Tel: 0116-277 3234; *Hon. Secretary*, Mr Swatland

BRITISH ISLES WOMEN'S BOWLING COUNCIL, 2 Case Gardens, Seaton, Devon EX12 2AP. Tel: 01297-21317; Fax: 01297-21317; *Hon. Secretary*, Mrs N. Colling, MBE

BRITISH ISLES WOMEN'S INDOOR BOWLS COUNCIL, 39-7 Murrayburn Park, Edinburgh EH14 2PQ. *Secretary*, Mrs Muriel Old

ENGLISH BOWLING ASSOCIATION, Lyndhurst Road, Worthing, W. Sussex BN11 2AZ. Tel: 01903-820222; Fax: 01903-820444; Email: ebaqueries@bowlsengland.com; Web: www.bowlsengland.com; *Secretary*, G. D. Shaw

ENGLISH INDOOR BOWLING ASSOCIATION, David Cornwell House, Bowling Green, Leicester Road, Melton Mowbray, Leics LE13 0DA. Tel: 01664-481900; Fax: 01664-428888; Email: info@eiba.co.uk; Web: www.eiba.co.uk; *Secretary*, D. N. Brown

ENGLISH WOMEN'S BOWLING ASSOCIATION, 2 Case Gardens, Seaton, Devon EX12 2AP. Tel: 01297-21317; Fax: 01297-21317; *Hon. Secretary*, Mrs N. Colling, MBE. *President*, J. Tait

ENGLISH WOMEN'S INDOOR BOWLING ASSOCIATION, 3 Scirocco Close, Moulton Park, Northampton NN3 6AP. Tel: 01604-494163; Fax: 01604-494434; Email: ewiba@talk21.com; *Secretary*, Mrs M. E. Ruff

*Boxing*

THE AMATEUR BOXING ASSOCIATION OF ENGLAND LTD, Crystal Palace National Sports Centre, London SE19 2BB. Tel: 020-8778 0251; Fax: 020-8778 9324; Email: hq@abae.org.uk; . *Chairman*, J. Smart

BRITISH BOXING BOARD OF CONTROL LTD, Jack Petersen House, 52A Borough High Street, London SE1 1XN. Tel: 020-7403 5879; Fax: 020-7378 6670; Web: www.bbbofc.com; *General Secretary*, S. J. Block

*Canoeing*

BRITISH CANOE UNION, John Dudderidge House, Adbolton Lane, West Bridgford, Nottingham NG2 5AS. Tel: 0115-982 1100; Fax: 0115-982 1797; Email: info@bcu.org.uk; Web: www.bcu.org.uk; *Chief Executive*, P. Owen

*Chess*

BRITISH CHESS FEDERATION, The Watch Oak, Chain Lane, Battle, E. Sussex TN33 0YD. Tel: 01424-775222; Fax: 01424-775904; Email: office@bcf.org.uk; Web: www.bcf.ndirect.co.uk; *Manager*, Mrs G. White

*Cricket*

ENGLAND AND WALES CRICKET BOARD, Lord's Cricket Ground, London NW8 8QZ. Tel: 020-7432 1200; Fax: 020-7289 5619; Web: www.ecb.co.uk; *Chief Executive*, T. Lamb

MCC, Lord's Cricket Ground, London NW8 8QN. Tel: 020-7289 1611; Fax: 020-7289 9100; *Secretary and Chief Executive*, R. D. V. Knight. *President*, The Rt. Hon. The Lord Alexander of Weedon QC

*Croquet*

CROQUET ASSOCIATION, c/o The Hurlingham Club, Ranelagh Gardens, London SW6 3PR. Tel: 020-7736 3148; Fax: 020-7736 3148; Email: caoffice@croquet.org.uk; Web: www.croquet.org.uk; *Secretary*, N. R. Graves

*Cycling*

BRITISH CYCLING FEDERATION, National Cycling Centre, Stuart Street, Manchester M11 4DQ. Tel: 0161-230 2301; Fax: 0161-231 0591; Email: info@bcf.uk.com; Web: www.bcf.uk.com; *Chief Executive*, P. King. *President*, B. Cookson

ROAD TIME TRIALS COUNCIL, 77 Arlington Drive, Pennington, Leigh, Lancs WN7 3QP. Tel: 01942-603976; Fax: 01942-262326; Email: nationalsecretary@rttchq.freeserve.co.uk; Web: www.rttc.org.uk; *National Secretary*, P. Heaton. *Chairman*, P. McGrath

*Darts*

BRITISH DARTS ORGANISATION, 2 Pages Lane, Muswell Hill, London N10 1PS. Tel: 020-8883 5544; Fax: 020-8883 0109; Email: 101776.666@compuserve.com; Web: www.bdodarts.com; *Director*, O. A. Croft

*Equestrianism*

BRITISH EQUESTRIAN FEDERATION, National Agricultural Centre, Stoneleigh Park, Kenilworth, Warks CV8 2RH. Tel: 024-7669 8871; Email: mary.kelly@bef.co.uk; Web: www.bef.co.uk; *Secretary-General*, A. Finding

BRITISH EVENTING, National Agricultural Centre, Stoneleigh Park, Kenilworth, Warks CV8 2RN. Tel: 024-7669 8856; Fax: 024-7669 7235; Email: info@britisheventing.com; Web: www.britisheventing.com; *Chief Executive*, P. Durrant

*Eton Fives*

ETON FIVES ASSOCIATION, 3 Bourchier Close, Sevenoaks, Kent TN13 1PD. Tel: 01732-458775; Fax: 01732-743112; Email: mike.fenn@etonfives.co.uk; Web: www.etonfives.co.uk; *Secretary*, M. R. Fenn

*Fencing*

BRITISH FENCING ASSOCIATION, 1 Baron's Gate, 33–35 Rothschild Road, London W4 5HT. Tel: 020-8742 3032; Fax: 020-8742 3033; Email: british_fencing@compuserve.com; Web: www.britishfencing.com; *General Secretary*, Miss G. Kenneally

*Gliding*

BRITISH GLIDING ASSOCIATION, Kimberley House, Vaughan Way, Leicester LE1 4SE. Tel: 0116-253 1051; Fax: 0116-251 5939; Email: bga@gliding.co.uk; Web: www.gliding.co.uk; *Secretary*, B. Rolfe

*Golf*

LADIES' GOLF UNION, The Scores, St Andrews, Fife KY16 9AT. Tel: 01334-475811; Fax: 01334-472818; Web: www.lgu.org; *Secretary*, Greg Mills

THE ROYAL AND ANCIENT GOLF CLUB OF ST ANDREWS, Golf Place, St Andrews, Fife KY16 9JD. Tel: 01334-460000; Fax: 01334-460001; Email: thesecretary@randagc.org; Web: www.randa.org; *Secretary*, P. Dawson

*Greyhound Racing*

NATIONAL GREYHOUND RACING CLUB LTD, Twyman House, 16 Bonny Street, London NW1 9QD. Tel: 020-7267 9256; Fax: 020-7482 1023; Email: ngrc@clara.net; Web: www.thedogs.co.uk; *Chief Executive*, F. Melville

*Gymnastics*

BRITISH GYMNASTICS, Ford Hall, Lilleshall National Sports Centre, Newport, Shropshire TF10 9NB. Tel: 01952-820300; Fax: 01952-820306; Email: information@british-gymnastics.org; Web: www.baga.co.uk; *Chief Executive*, Alan Sommerville

*Hockey*

ENGLISH HOCKEY ASSOCIATION, The National Hockey Stadium, The Stadium, Silbury Boulevard, Milton Keynes MK9 1HA. Tel: 01908-544644; Fax: 01908-241106; Email: info@englishhockey.org; Web: www.hockeyonline.co.uk; *Chief Executive*, R. F. Wyatt. *President*, Mrs M. Pickersgill

SCOTTISH HOCKEY UNION, 34 Cramond Road North, Edinburgh EH4 6JD. Tel: 0131-312 8870; Fax: 0131-312 7829; Email: info@scottish-hockey.org.uk; Web: www.scottish-hockey.org.uk; *Chairman*, G. Ralph

WELSH HOCKEY UNION, 80 Woodville Road, Cathays, Cardiff CF24 4ED. Tel: 029-2023 3257; Fax: 029-2023 3258; Email: welsh.hockey@whu.softnet.co.uk; Web: www.welsh-hockey.co.uk; *Chairman*, A. J. Rookes

*Horse-racing*

BRITISH HORSERACING BOARD, 42 Portman Square, London W1H 0EN. Tel: 020-7396 0011; Fax: 020-7935 3626; Email: info@bhb.co.uk; Web: www.bhb.co.uk; *Managing Director*, C. Reynolds

THE JOCKEY CLUB, 42 Portman Square, London W1H 0EN. Tel: 020-7486 4921; Fax: 020-7935 8703; Email: info@thejockeyclub.co.uk; Web: www.thejockeyclub.co.uk; *Senior Steward*, C. Spence

*Ice Hockey*

ICE HOCKEY UK, The Galleries of Justice, Shire Hall, High Pavement, The Lace Market, Nottingham NG1 1HN. Tel: 0115-915 9204; Fax: 0115-915 1376; Email: hockey@icehockeyuk.co.uk; Web: www.icehockeyuk.co.uk; *Directors*, J. Anderson; A. Montrey; N. Moralee; G. Stefan; R. Stirling; R. Zeller

*Ice Skating*

NATIONAL ICE SKATING ASSOCIATION OF THE UK Ltd, National Ice Centre, Lower Parliament Street, Nottingham NG1 1LA. Email: nisa@iceskating.org.uk; Web: www.iceskating.org.uk; *Chairman*, Haig Oundjian

*Judo*

BRITISH JUDO ASSOCIATION, 7A Rutland Street, Leicester LE1 1RB. Tel: 0116-255 9669; Fax: 0116-255 9660; Email: britjudo@aol.com; Web: www.britishjudo.org.uk; *Head of Corporate Affairs*, Donald Steel

*Lacrosse*

ENGLISH LACROSSE ASSOCIATION, PO Box 2041, Reading, RG4 7GJ. Tel: 0161-834 4582; Fax: 0161-834 4582; Email: info@englishlacrosse.co.uk; Web: www.englishlacrosse.co.uk; *President*, T. Malkin

*Lawn Tennis*

LAWN TENNIS ASSOCIATION, The Queen's Club, London W14 9EG. Tel: 020-7381 7000; Fax: 020-7381 3773; *Secretary*, J. C. U. James

*Martial Arts*

MARTIAL ARTS DEVELOPMENT COMMISSION, No 3, Brockley Cross Business Centre, Endwell Road, London SE4 2PD. Tel: 020-7639 5005; Fax: 020-7639 5065; Email: office@madec.org; Web: www.madec.org; *Office Administrator*, Mrs E. Jewell. *Chairman*, R. Thomas

*Motor Sports*

MOTORCYCLE GREAT BRITAIN, Auto-Cycle Union, ACU House, Wood Street, Rugby, Warks CV21 2YX. Tel: 01788-566400; Fax: 01788-573585; Email: admin@acu.org.uk; Web: www.acu.org.uk, www.motorcyclinggb.com; *Chief Executive*, G. Wilson. *Chairman*, E. P. Bartlett

THE MOTOR SPORTS ASSOCIATION, Motor Sports House, Riverside Park, Colnbrook, Berks SL3 0HG. Tel: 01753-765000; Fax: 01753-682938; Email: msa_mail@compuserve.com; Web: www.msauk.org; *Chief Executive*, Colin Hilton

SCOTTISH AUTO CYCLE UNION LTD, 28 West Main Street, Uphall, W. Lothian EH52 5DW. Tel: 01506-858354; Fax: 01506-855792; Email: office@sacu.co.uk; Web: www.sacu.co.uk;

*Mountaineering*

BRITISH MOUNTAINEERING COUNCIL, 177–179 Burton Road, West Didsbury, Manchester M20 2BB. Tel: 0161-445 4747; Fax: 0161-445 4500; Email: office@thebmc.co.uk; Web: www.thebmc.co.uk; *General Secretary*, R. Payne

*Multi-Sport Bodies*

British Olympic Association, 1 Wandsworth Plain, London SW18 1EH. Tel: 020-8871 2677; Fax: 020-8871 9104; Web: www.olympics.org.uk; *Chief Executive*, S. Clegg

British Universities Sports Association, 8 Union Street, London SE1 1SZ. Tel: 020-7357 8555; Fax: 020-7403 0127; Web: www.busa.org.uk; *Chief Executive*, G. Gregory-Jones

Commonwealth Games Council for England, Tavistock House South, Tavistock Square, London WC1H 9JZ. Tel: 020-7388 6643; Fax: 020-7388 6744; Email: info@cgce.co.uk; Web: www.cgce.co.uk; *Chief Executive*, Miss A. Hogbin

Commonwealth Games Federation, Walkden House, 3–10 Melton Street, London NW1 2EB. Tel: 020-7383 5596; Fax: 020-7383 5506; Email: office@thecgf.com; Web: www.thecgf.com; *Hon. Secretary*, Ms L. Martin

*Netball*

All England Netball Association Ltd, Netball House, 9 Paynes Park, Hitchin, Herts SG5 1EH. Tel: 01462-442344; Fax: 01462-442343; Email: info@aena.co.uk; Web: www.england-netball.co.uk; *Chief Executive*, Miss C. Alcock. *President*, Mrs J. Jack

Netball Scotland, 24 Ainslie Road, Hillington Business Park, Hillington, Glasgow G52 4RU. Tel: 0141-570 4016; Fax: 0141-570 4017; Email: netballscotland@btinternet.com; Web: www.netballscotland.freeserve.co.uk;

Welsh Netball Association, 2nd Floor, 33–35 Cathedral Rd, Cardiff CF11 9HB. Tel: 029-2023 7048; Fax: 029-2022 6430; Email: welshnetball@mcmail.com; Web: www.welshnetball.org.uk; *Chief Executive Officer*, Mrs S. J. Holvey. *President*, Miss P. Nicholas

*Orienteering*

British Orienteering Federation, Riversdale, Dale Road North, Darley Dale, Matlock, Derbys DE4 2HX. Tel: 01629-734042; Fax: 01629-733769; Email: bof@bof.cix.co.uk; Web: www.britishorienteering.org.uk; *Secretary-General*, D. Locke

*Polo*

The Hurlingham Polo Association, Manor Farm, Little Coxwell, Faringdon, Oxfordshire SN7 7LW. Tel: 01367-242828; Fax: 01367-242829; Email: enquiries@hpa-polo.co.uk; Web: www.hpa-polo.co.uk; *Chief Executive*, D. J. B. Woodd

*Rackets and Real Tennis*

Tennis and Rackets Association, c/o The Queen's Club, Palliser Road, London W14 9EQ. Tel: 020-7386 3447/8; Fax: 020-7385 7424; Email: cpo@tennis-rackets.net; Web: www.rackets.co.uk, www.real-tennis.com; *Chief Executive and Secretary*, James D. Wyatt. *Chairman*, C. J. Swallow *President*, The Rt. Hon. Lord Aberdare, KBE, DL

*Rifle Shooting*

National Rifle Association, Bisley Camp, Brookwood, Woking, Surrey GU24 0PB. Tel: 01483-797777; Fax: 01483-797285; Email: info@nra.org.uk; Web: www.nra.org.uk; *Chief Executive*, Col. C. C. C. Cheshire, OBE. *Chairman*, J. A. de Havilland

National Small-bore Rifle Association, Lord Roberts House, Bisley Camp, Brookwood, Woking, Surrey GU24 0NP. Tel: 0845-130 6772; Fax: 01483-476392; Email: info@nsra.co.uk; Web: www.nsra.co.uk; *Secretary*, Lt.-Col. J. D. Hoare. *Chairman*, G. D. Pound

*Rowing*

Amateur Rowing Association Ltd, The Priory, 6 Lower Mall, London W6 9DJ. Tel: 020-8748 3632; Fax: 020-8741 4658; Web: www.ara-rowing.org; *National Manager*, Mrs R. Napp

Henley Royal Regatta, Regatta Headquarters, Henley-on-Thames, Oxon RG9 2LY. Tel: 01491-572153; Fax: 01491-575509; Web: www.hrr.co.uk; *Secretary*, R. S. Goddard

*Rugby Fives*

Rugby Fives Association, The Old Forge, Sutton Valence, Maidstone, Kent ME17 3AW. Tel: 01622-842278; Email: rugbyfives@aol.com; Web: www.rfa.org.uk; *General Secretary*, M. F. Beaman. *President*, D. J. Hebden

*Rugby League*

British Amateur Rugby League Association, West Yorkshire House, 4 New North Parade, Huddersfield HD1 5JP. Tel: 01484-544131; Fax: 01484-519985; Email: info@barla.org.uk; Web: www.barla.org.uk; *Chief Executive*, I. Cooper. *Chairman*, T. Parle

The Rugby Football League, Red Hall, Red Hall Lane, Leeds LS17 8NB. Tel: 0113-232 9111; Fax: 0113-232 3666; Email: rfl@rfl.uk.com; Web: www.rfl.uk.com; *Executive Management Committee*, D. B. Callaghan, G. J. McCallum, P. D. Webster. *Chairman*, Sir Rodney Walker

*Rugby Union*

Irish Rugby Football Union, 62 Lansdowne Road, Ballsbridge, Dublin 4 Tel: 00 353-1-647 3800; Fax: 00 353-1-647 3801; Web: www.irfu.ie; *Chief Executive*, P. R. Browne. *President*, R Loughead

Rugby Football Union, Rugby House, Rugby Road, Twickenham TW1 1DS. Tel: 020-8892 2000; Fax: 020-8892 9816; Web: www.rfu.com; *Chief Executive*, F. Baron. *Chairman of the Management Board*, B. Baister

Rugby Football Union for Women, Newbury Sports Arena, Monks Lane, Newbury RG14 7RW. Tel: 01635-42333; Fax: 01635-43016; *Secretary*, Ms D. Lintonbon

Scottish Rugby Union, Murrayfield, Roseburn Street, Edinburgh EH12 5PJ. Tel: 0131-346 5000; Fax: 0131-346 5001; Email: feedback@sru.org.uk; Web: www.sru.org.uk; *Chief Executive*, W. S. Watson. *Secretary*, I. A. L. Hogg

Scottish Women's Rugby Union, Scottish Rugby Union, Roseburn Terrace, Murrayfield, Edinburgh EH12 5PJ. Tel: 0131-346 5163; Fax: 0131-346 5001; Email: barb@shawltd.demon.co.uk; *Chairwoman*, Miss B. Wilson

Welsh Rugby Union, Custom House, Custom House Street, Cardiff CF10 1RF. Tel: 029-2078 1700; Fax: 029-2022 5601; Web: www.wru.co.uk; *Secretary*, D. Gethin. *Chairman*, G. S. Griffiths *President*, Sir Tasker Watkins, VC, GBE, DL

*Shooting*

CLAY PIGEON SHOOTING ASSOCIATION LTD, Bisley Camp, Brookwood, Woking, Surrey GU24 0NP. Tel: 01536-443566; Fax: 01536-443438; Email: info@cpsa.co.uk; Web: www.cpsa.co.uk; *Director*, E. G. Orduna

*Skiing*

BRITISH SKI AND SNOWBOARD FEDERATION, Hillend, Biggar Road, Midlothian EH10 7EF. Tel: 0131-445 7676; Fax: 0131-445 7722; Email: britski@easynet.co.uk; Web: www.ifyouski.com/bssf; *Operations Director*, Mrs F. McNeilly

*Snooker*

WORLD LADIES BILLIARDS AND SNOOKER ASSOCIATION, PO Box 16, Wisbech, PE13 2ZX. Tel: 01945-588598; Fax: 01945-588598; Email: worldladiessnooker@cwcom.net; Web: www.wpbsa.com; *Chairman and Administrator*, Mandy Fisher

WORLD PROFESSIONAL BILLIARDS AND SNOOKER ASSOCIATION, Ground Floor, Albert House, 111-117 Victoria Street, Bristol BS1 6AX. Tel: 0117-317 8200; Fax: 0117-317 8300; Email: wsa@wpbsa.com; Web: www.wpbsa.com; *Chief Executive*, Jim McKenzie

*Speedway*

SPEEDWAY CONTROL BOARD LTD, ACU Headquarters, Wood Street, Rugby, Warks CV21 2YX. Tel: 01788-565603; Fax: 01788-552308; Email: office.scb@lineone.net; *General Secretary*, R. Allan. *Chairman*, J. Quenby

*Squash Rackets*

SCOTTISH SQUASH, Caledonia House, South Gyle, Edinburgh EH12 9DQ. Tel: 0131-317 7343; Fax: 0131-317 7734; Email: scottishsquash@aol.com; *Administration Manager*, Derek Welch

SQUASH RACKETS ASSOCIATION, Ground Floor, Bellevue Athletics Centre, Pink Bank Lane, Manchester M12 5GL. Tel: 0161-231 4499; Fax: 0161-231 4231; Email: sra@squash.uk.com; Web: www.squash.co.uk; *Chief Executive*, S. H. Courtney. *President*, M. Corby

SQUASH WALES, St Mellons Country Club, St Mellons, Cardiff CF3 2XR. Tel: 01633-682108; Fax: 01633-680998; Email: squash.wales@tesco.net; *Administrator*, Ms D. Selley. *Chairman*, D. Jenkins *President*, A. James

*Sub-Aqua*

BRITISH SUB-AQUA CLUB, Telfords Quay, South Pier Road, Ellesmere Port, Cheshire CH65 4FL. Tel: 0151-350 6200; Fax: 0151-350 6215; Email: postmaster@bsac.com; Web: www.bsac.com; *Chairman*, P. Harrison

*Swimming*

AMATEUR SWIMMING ASSOCIATION, Harold Fern House, Derby Square, Loughborough, Leics LE11 5AL. Tel: 01509-618700; Fax: 01509-618701; Email: cserv@asagb.org.uk; Web: www.britishswimming.org; *Chief Executive*, D. Sparkes

SCOTTISH AMATEUR SWIMMING ASSOCIATION, Holmhills Farm, Greenlees Road, Cambuslang, Glasgow G72 8DT. Tel: 0141-641 8818; Fax: 0141-641 4443; Email: scotswim@aol.com; *Chief Executive*, P. Bush

WELSH AMATEUR SWIMMING ASSOCIATION, Roath Park House, Ninian Road, Cardiff CF23 5ER. Tel: 029-2048 8820; Fax: 029-2048 8820; Email: brynwilliams@welshasa.co.uk; Web: www.welshasa.co.uk; *Director of Swimming*, B. Williams. *Head of Administration*, Julie Tyler

*Table Tennis*

ENGLISH TABLE TENNIS ASSOCIATION, Queensbury House, Havelock Road, Hastings, E. Sussex TN34 1HF. Tel: 01424-722525; Fax: 01424-422103; Email: admin@ettahq.freeserve.co.uk; Web: www.etta.co.uk; *Chief Executive*, R. Yule. *Chairman*, A. E. Ransome OBE

*Volleyball*

ENGLISH VOLLEYBALL ASSOCIATION, 27 South Road, West Bridgford, Nottingham NG2 7AG. Tel: 0115-981 6324; Fax: 0115-945 5429; Email: general@eng-volleyball.demon.co.uk; Web: www.volleyballengland.org; *Chief Executive Officer*, T. Ojasoo

SCOTTISH VOLLEYBALL ASSOCIATION, 48 The Pleasance, Edinburgh EH8 9TJ. Tel: 0131-556 4633; Fax: 0131-557 4314; Email: sva@callnetuk.com; *Director*, N. S. Moody

*Walking*

RACE WALKING ASSOCIATION, Hufflers, Heard's Lane, Shenfield, Brentwood, Essex CM15 0SF. Tel: 01277-220687; Fax: 01277-212380; Email: racewalkingassociation@btinternet.com; Web: www.racewalkingassociation.btinternet.co.uk; *Hon. General Secretary*, P. J. Cassidy. *President*, P. Nihill MBE

*Water Skiing*

BRITISH WATER SKI FEDERATION, 390 City Road, London EC1V 2QA. Tel: 020-7833 2855; Fax: 020-7837 2855; Email: info@bwsf.co.uk; Web: www.britishwaterski.co.uk; *Executive Officer*, Ms G. Hill

*Weightlifting*

BRITISH WEIGHTLIFTERS ASSOCIATION (BWLA), 131 Hurst Street, Oxford OX4 1HE. Tel: 01865-200339; Fax: 01865-790096; Email: twister@clara.co.uk; Web: www.bawla.com; *Chief Executive*, S. Cannon. *President*, H. Binder *Chairman*, B. Barton

*Wrestling*

BRITISH AMATEUR WRESTLING ASSOCIATION, 12 Westwood Lane, Brimington, Chesterfield, Derbyshire S43 1PA. Tel: 01246-236443; Fax: 01246-236443; Web: www.britishwrestling.org; *Chairman*, M. Morley. *Treasurer*, S. McNeil

*Yachting*

ROYAL YACHTING ASSOCIATION, RYA House, Romsey Road, Eastleigh, Hants SO50 9YA. Tel: 023-8062 7400; Fax: 023-8062 9924; Email: admin@rya.org.uk; Web: www.rya.org.uk; *Secretary-General*, R. P. Carr. *Chairman*, K. Ellis

# Clubs

## LONDON CLUBS

ALPINE CLUB (1857), 55 Charlotte Road, London EC2A 3QF. Tel: 020-7613 0755; Fax: 020-7613 0755; Email: sec@alpine-club.org.uk; Web: www.alpine-club.org.uk; *Hon. Secretary*, G. D. Hughes

AMERICAN WOMEN'S CLUB (1899), 68 Old Brompton Road, London SW7 3LQ. Tel: 020-7589 8292; Fax: 020-7283 9006; Email: mail@awc-london.demon.co.uk; Web: www.london.fawco.org; *President*, T. Erzmoneit

ANGLO-BELGIAN CLUB (1955), 60 Knightsbridge, London SW1X 7LF. Tel: 020-7235 2121; Fax: 020-7245 9470; Email: secretary@ra-bc.com; *Chairman*, Sir John Gray, KBE, CMG

ARMY AND NAVY CLUB (1837), 36 Pall Mall, London SW1Y 5JN. Tel: 020-7930 9721; Fax: 020-7930 9720; Email: secretary@therag.co.uk; Web: www.armynavyclub.co.uk; *Secretary*, Cdr. J. A. Holt, MBE, RN

ARTS CLUB (1863), 40 Dover Street, London W1S 4NP. Tel: 020-7499 8581; Fax: 020-7409 0913; *Secretary*, I. Campbell

THE ATHENAEUM (1824), 107 Pall Mall, London SW1Y 5ER. Tel: 020-7930 4843; Fax: 020-7839 4114; Email: library@hellenist.org.uk; *Secretary*, J. Ford

AUTHORS' CLUB (1892), 40 Dover Street, London W1S 4NP. Tel: 020-7499 8581; Fax: 020-7409 0913; *Club Secretary*, Mrs A. de La Grange

BEEFSTEAK CLUB (1876), 9 Irving Street, London WC2H 7AT. Tel: 020-7930 5722; Fax: 020-7925 2325; *Secretary*, Sir John Lucas-Tooth, BT.

BOODLE'S (1762), 28 St James's Street, London SW1A 1HJ. Tel: 020-7930 7166; *Secretary*, R. R. T. Smith

BROOKS'S (1764), St James's Street, London SW1A 1LN. Tel: 020-7493 4411; Fax: 020-7499 3736; *Secretary*, G. Snell

BUCK'S CLUB (1919), 18 Clifford Street, London W1X 1RG. Tel: 020-7734 6896; Fax: 020-7287 2097; Email: secretary@bucksclub.co.uk; *Secretary*, Capt. P. G. J. Murison, RN

CALEDONIAN CLUB (1891), 9 Halkin Street, London SW1X 7DR. Tel: 020-7235 5162; Fax: 020-7235 4635; Email: secy@caledonian-club.org.uk; Web: www.caledonian-club.org.uk; *Secretary*, P. J. Varney

CANNING CLUB (1910), 4 St James's Square, London SW1Y 4JU. Tel: 020-7827 5757; Fax: 020-7827 5758; Email: canningclub@compuserve.com; *Secretary*, T. M. Harrington

CARLTON CLUB (1832), 69 St James's Street, London SW1A 1PJ. Tel: 020-7493 1164; Fax: 020-7495 4090; Email: secretary@carltonclub.co.uk; Web: www.carltonclub.co.uk; *Secretary*, A. E. Telfer

CAVALRY AND GUARDS CLUB (1893), 127 Piccadilly, London W1J 7PX. Tel: 020-7499 1261; Fax: 020-7495 5956; *Secretary*, Cdr. I. R. Wellesley-Harding, RN

CITY LIVERY CLUB (1914), 20 Aldermanbury, London EC2V 7HP. Tel: 020-7814 0200; Fax: 020-7814 0201; Email: citylivery club@btclick.com; Web: www.citylivery club.com; *Hon. Secretary*, W. C. Hammond

CITY OF LONDON CLUB (1832), 19 Old Broad Street, London EC2N 1DS. Tel: 020-7588 7991; Fax: 020-7374 2020; Email: cityclub@dial.pipex.com; Web: www.cityclub.uk.com; *Secretary*, G. Jones

CITY UNIVERSITY CLUB (1895), 50 Cornhill, London EC3V 3PD. Tel: 020-7626 8571; Fax: 020-7626 8572; Email: secretary@city-university-club.demon.co.uk; Web: www.city-university-club.demon.co.uk; *Secretary*, Miss R. C. Graham

THE CRUISING ASSOCIATION (1908), CA House, 1 Northey Street, Limehouse Basin, London E14 8BT. Tel: 020-7537 2828; Fax: 020-7537 2266; Email: office@cruising.org.uk; Web: www.cruising.org.uk; *General Secretary*, Mrs. L. Hammett

EAST INDIA CLUB (1849), 16 St James's Square, London SW1Y 4LH. Tel: 020-7930 1000; Fax: 020-7321 0217; Email: eastindi@globalnet.co.uk; *Secretary*, M. Howell

FARMERS CLUB (1842), 3 Whitehall Court, London SW1A 2EL. Tel: 020-7930 3751; Fax: 020-7839 7864; *Secretary*, Gp Capt. G. P. Carson

FLYFISHERS' CLUB (1884), 69 Brook Street, London W1K 4ER. Tel: 020-7629 5958; *Secretary*, Cdr. T. H. Boycott, OBE, RN

GARRICK CLUB (1831), 15 Garrick Street, London WC2E 9AY. Tel: 020-7379 6478; Fax: 020-7379 5966; *Secretary*, M. J. Harvey

GREEN ROOM CLUB (1877), 4-5 Greek Street, London W1D 4DD. Tel: 020-7381 4287 (temporary); Email: info@greenroomclub.co.uk; Web: www.greenroomclub.co.uk; *Secretary*, D. Lamden

THE KENNEL CLUB (1873), 1–5 Clarges Street, London W1J 8AB. Tel: 0870-606 6750; Fax: 020-7518 1058; Email: info@the-kennel-club.org.uk; Web: www.the-kennel-club.org.uk; *Chief Executive*, R. French

LANSDOWNE CLUB (1934), 9 Fitzmaurice Place, London W1J 5JD. Tel: 020-7629 7200; Fax: 020-7409 7839; Email: info@lansdowne-club.co.uk; Web: www.lansdowne-club.co.uk; *Secretary*, M. Anderson

LONDON ROWING CLUB (1856), Embankment, Putney, London SW15 1LB. Tel: 020-8788 1400; Fax: 020-8874 9056; Email: metregatta@compuserve.com; Web: www.londonrc.org.uk; *Hon. Secretary*, N. A. Smith

MCC (MARYLEBONE CRICKET CLUB) (1787), Lord's Cricket Ground, London NW8 8QN. Tel: 020-7289 1611; Fax: 020-7289 9100; Web: www.lords.org; *Secretary and Chief Executive*, R. D. V. Knight

THE NATIONAL CLUB (1845), c/o Carlton Club, 69 St James's Street, London SW1A 1PJ. Tel: 020-8579 0874; Fax: 020-8363 2269; Email: suezdm@aol.com; *Hon. Secretary*, I. A. Sowton

NATIONAL LIBERAL CLUB (1882), Whitehall Place, London SW1A 2HE. Tel: 020-7930 9871; Fax: 020-7839 4768; Web: www.nlc.org.uk; *Secretary*, S. J. Roberts

NAVAL CLUB (1946), 38 Hill Street, London W1J 5NS. Tel: 020-7493 7672; Fax: 020-7629 7995; Email: reservations@navalclub.co.uk; Web: www.navalclub.co.uk; *Chief Executive*, Cdr. J. L. L. Prichard

NAVAL AND MILITARY CLUB (1862), 4 St James's Square, London SW1Y 4JU. Tel: 020-7827 5757; Fax: 020-7827 5758; Email: admin@navalandmilitaryclub.co.uk; Web: www.navalandmilitaryclub.co.uk; *Secretary*, M. G. G. Ebbitt

NEW CAVENDISH CLUB (1920), 44 Great Cumberland Place, London W1H 7BS. Tel: 020-7723 0391; Fax: 020-7262 8411; *General Manager*, J. P. Dauvergne

ORIENTAL CLUB (1824), Stratford House, Stratford Place, London W1C 1ES. Tel: 020-7629 5126; Fax: 020-7629 0494; Email: sec@orientalclub.org.uk; *Secretary*, S. C. Doble

PORTLAND CLUB (1816), 69 Brook Street, London W1Y 2ER. Tel: 020-7499 1523; *Secretary*, J. Burns, CBE

PRATT'S CLUB (1841), 14 Park Place, London SW1A 1LP. Tel: 020-7493 0397; Fax: 020-7499 3736; Email: secretary@prattsclub.org; *Secretary*, G. Snell

THE QUEEN'S CLUB (1886), Palliser Road, London W14 9EQ. Tel: 020-7385 3421; Fax: 020-7386 8295; Email: admin@queensclub.co.uk; Web: www.queensclub.co.uk; *Secretary*, J. A. S. Edwardes

RAILWAY CLUB (1899), Room 208, 25 Marylebone Road, London NW1 5JS. Tel: 01737-812175; *Hon. Secretary*, A. G. Wells

REFORM CLUB (1836), 104–105 Pall Mall, London SW1Y 5EW. Tel: 020-7930 9374; Fax: 020-7930 1857; Email: reform.club@msn.com; *Secretary*, R. A. M. Forrest

ROEHAMPTON CLUB (1901), Roehampton Lane, London SW15 5LR. Tel: 020-8480 4200; Fax: 020-8480 4265; *Chief Executive*, M. Yates

ROYAL AIR FORCE CLUB (1918), 128 Piccadilly, London W1J 7PY. Tel: 020-7399 1000; Fax: 020-7355 1516; Email: admin@rafclub.org.uk; Web: www.rafclub.org.uk; *Secretary*, P. N. Owen

ROYAL AUTOMOBILE CLUB (1897), 89–91 Pall Mall, London SW1Y 5HS. Tel: 020-7930 2345; Fax: 020-7976 1086; Email: secretary@royalautomobileclub.co.uk; Web: www.royalautomobileclub.co.uk; *Secretary*, A. I. G. Kennedy

ROYAL OCEAN RACING CLUB (1925), 20 St James's Place, London SW1A 1NN. Tel: 020-7493 2248; Fax: 020-7493 5252; Email: rorc@saintjames.demon.co.uk; Web: www.rorc.org; *General Manager*, D. J. Minords, OBE

ROYAL OVER-SEAS LEAGUE (1910), Over-Seas House, Park Place, St James's Street, London SW1A 1LR. Tel: 020-7408 0214; Fax: 020-7499 6738; Email: info@rosl.org.uk; Web: www.rosl.org.uk; *Director-General*, R. F. Newell

ROYAL THAMES YACHT CLUB (1775), 60 Knightsbridge, London SW1X 7LF. Tel: 020-7235 2121; Fax: 020-7245 9470; Email: club@royalthames.com; Web: www.royalthames.com; *Secretary*, Capt. D Goldson, RN

ST STEPHEN'S CONSTITUTIONAL CLUB (1870), 34 Queen Anne's Gate, London SW1H 9AB. Tel: 020-7222 1382; Fax: 020-7222 8740; Web: www.ststephensclub.co.uk; *Secretary*, L. D. Mawby

SAVAGE CLUB (1857), 1 Whitehall Place, London SW1A 2HD. Tel: 020-7930 8118; Fax: 020-7839 4768; Email: info@savageclub.com; Web: www.savageclub.com; *Hon. Secretary*, The Ven. B. H. Lucas, CB

SAVILE CLUB (1868), 69 Brook Street, London W1K 4ER. Tel: 020-7629 5462; Fax: 020-7499 7087; Email: admin@savileclub.co.uk; Web: www.savileclub.co.uk; *Secretary*, N. Storey

SKI CLUB OF GREAT BRITAIN (1903), The White House, 57–63 Church Road, Wimbledon SW19 5DQ. Tel: 020-8410 2000; Fax: 020-8410 2001; Email: skiers@skiclub.co.uk; Web: www.skiclub.co.uk; *Managing Director*, Ms C. Stuart-Taylor

THAMES ROWING CLUB (1860), Embankment, Putney, London SW15 1LB. Tel: 020-8788 0798; Fax: 020-8788 0798; Email: contact@thamesrc.demon.co.uk; Web: www.thamesrc.co.uk; *Hon. Secretary*, J. R. Elder

TRAVELLERS CLUB (1819), 106 Pall Mall, London SW1Y 5EP. Tel: 020-7930 8688; Fax: 020-7930 2019; Email: secretary@thetravellersclub.org.uk; Web: www.csma.org.uk; *Secretary*, M. S. Allcock

TURF CLUB (1868), 5 Carlton House Terrace, London SW1Y 5AQ. Tel: 020-7930 8555; *Secretary*, Lt. Col. O. R. StJ. Breakwell, MBE

UNITED OXFORD AND CAMBRIDGE UNIVERSITY CLUB (1972), 71 Pall Mall, London SW1Y 5HD. Tel: 020-7930 5151; Fax: 020-7930 9490; Email: uocuc@uocuc.demon.co.uk; Web: www.uocuc.co.uk; *Secretary*, G. R. Buchanan

THE UNIVERSITY WOMEN'S CLUB (1886), 2 Audley Square, London W1K 1DB. Tel: 020-7499 2268; Fax: 020-7499 7046; Email: wwc@uwc-london.com; Web: www.univeristywomensclub.com; *Acting Secretary*, Ms S. McCue

VICTORY SERVICES CLUB (1907), 63–79 Seymour Street, London W2 2HF. Tel: 020-7723 4474; Fax: 020-7402 9496; Email: res@vsc.co.uk; Web: www.vsc.co.uk; *General Manager*, G. F. Taylor

WHITE'S (1693), 37–38 St James's Street, London SW1A 1JG. Tel: 020-7493 6671; Fax: 020-7495 6674; *Secretary*, D. A. Anderson

WIG AND PEN CLUB (1908), 229–230 Strand, London WC2R 1BA. Tel: 020-7583 7255; Fax: 020-8293 4321; *Chairman*, E. Ertan

## CLUBS OUTSIDE LONDON AND YACHT CLUBS

THE ATHENAEUM (1797), Church Alley, Liverpool L1 3DD. Tel: 0151-709 7770; Fax: 0151-709 0418; Email: library@athena.force9.net; *Honorary Secretary*, B. H. Denton

BATH AND COUNTY CLUB (1858), Queen's Parade, Bath BA1 2NJ. Tel: 01225-423732; Fax: 01225-423732; Email: secretary@bathandcountyclub.com; Web: www.bathandcountyclub.com; *Secretary*, R. M. Lockert

BEMBRIDGE SAILING CLUB (1886), Embankment Road, Bembridge, Isle of Wight PO35 5NR. Tel: 01983-872237; Fax: 01983-874950; Email: bsc@clara.net; Web: www.bembridgesailingclub.co.uk; *Secretary*, Lt.-Col. M. J. Samuelson, RM

BRISTOL CHANNEL YACHT CLUB (1875), 744 Mumbles Road, Mumbles, Swansea SA3 4EL. Tel: 01792-366000; Fax: 01792-366000; *Hon. Secretary*, R. L. Morgan

CARDIFF AND COUNTY CLUB (1866), Westgate Street, Cardiff CF10 1DA. Tel: 029-2022 0846; Fax: 029-2037 3393; *Hon. Secretary*, Cdr. J. E. Payn, RD

CASTLE CLUB (1865), 3 The Esplanade, Rochester, Kent ME1 1QE. Tel: 01634-281227; *Hon. Secretary*, S. M. Dixon

CHICHESTER YACHT CLUB (1965), Chichester Marina, Birdham, Chichester, W. Sussex PO20 7EJ. Tel: 01243-512918; Fax: 01243-512627; Email: secretary@cyc.co.uk; Web: www.cyc.co.uk; *Secretary*, I. M. Clarke

CLIFTON CLUB (1882), 22 The Mall, Clifton, Bristol BS8 4DS. Tel: 0117-973 5527; Fax: 0117-974 3910; Email: cliftonclub@hotmail.com; *Secretary*, P. J. Organ

FREWEN CLUB (1869), 98 St Aldate's, Oxford OX1 1BT. Tel: 01865-243816; *Hon. Secretary*, B. R. Boyt

HOVE CLUB (1882), 28 Fourth Avenue, Hove, E. Sussex BN3 2PJ. Tel: 01273-730872; Fax: 01273-732481; *Secretary*, G. J. L. Gordon

KENT AND CANTERBURY CLUB (1873), The Elms, 17 Old Dover Road, Canterbury CT1 3JB. Tel: 01227-462181; Email: kentandcanterburyclub@btinternet.com; *Secretary*, K. D. Bassey

THE KINGSWAY CLUB (1868), Lightfoot Institute, Kingsway, Bishop Auckland, Co. Durham DL14 7JN. Tel: 01388-603219; *Hon. Secretary*, A. Heatherington

LEANDER CLUB (1818), Henley-on-Thames, Oxon RG9 2LP. Tel: 01491-575782; Fax: 01491-410291; Email: leander@globalnet.co.uk; *Hon. Secretary*, I. Codrington

THE LEEDS CLUB (1849), 3 Albion Place, Leeds LS1 6JL. Tel: 0113-242 1591; Fax: 0113-245 0755; *Administrator*, Mrs I. Sigsworth

NEW CLUB (1874), 2 Montpellier Parade, Cheltenham GL50 1UD. Tel: 01242-523285; *Hon. Secretary*, N. S. Parrack

THE NORFOLK CLUB (1770), 17 Upper King Street, Norwich NR3 1RB. Tel: 01603-610652; *Secretary*, G. G. Hardaker

NORTH BAILEY CLUB (1842), 24 North Bailey, Durham DH1 3EW. Tel: 0191-384 3724; Fax: 0191-384 7060; Email: Union.Society@durham.ac.uk; Web: www.dur.ac.uk/DUS; *Permanent Secretary*, Mrs E. M. Hardcastle

NORTHERN CONSTITUTIONAL CLUB (1882), 37 Pilgrim Street, Newcastle upon Tyne NE1 6QE. Tel: 0191-232 0884; *Hon. Secretary*, D. Blake

NORTHERN COUNTIES CLUB (1880), 24 Bishop Street, Londonderry BT48 6PP. Tel: 028-7126 2012; *Hon. Secretary*, N. Dykes

OLD BOYS' AND PARK GREEN CLUB (1771), 7 Churchside, Macclesfield, Cheshire SK10 1HG. Tel: 01625-423292; *Hon. Secretary*, J. G. P. van der Feltz

PAIGNTON CLUB (1882), The Esplanade, Paignton, Devon TQ4 6ED. Tel: 01803-559682; Fax: 01803-559043; Email: pgrafton@freenet.co.uk; *Hon. Secretary*, P. Grafton

PARKSTONE YACHT CLUB (1895), Pearce Avenue, Poole, Dorset BH14 8EH. Tel: 01202-743610; Fax: 01202-716394; Email: office@parkstoneyc.co.uk; Web: www.parkstoneyc.co.uk; *General Manager*, M. Simms

PENARTH YACHT CLUB (1880), The Esplanade, Penarth, Vale of Glamorgan CF64 3AU. Tel: 029-2070 8196; *Hon. Secretary*, R. S. McGregor

PHYLLIS COURT CLUB (1906), Marlow Road, Henley-on-Thames, Oxon RG9 2HT. Tel: 01491-570500; Fax: 01491-570528; Email: phyllisc@globalnet.co.uk; Web: www.phylliscourt.co.uk; *Secretary*, R. Edwards

POOLE HARBOUR YACHT CLUB (1949), 38 Salterns Way, Lilliput, Poole, Dorset BH14 8JR. Tel: 01202-707321; Fax: 01202-700398; Email: marina@salterns.co.uk; Web: www.salterns.co.uk; *Managing Director*, J. N. J. Smith

THE POOLE YACHT CLUB (1865), New Harbour Road West, Hamworthy, Poole, Dorset BH15 4AQ. Tel: 01202-672687; Fax: 01202-661174; Email: secretary@pooleyc.co.uk; Web: www.polleyc.co.uk; *Secretary/Manager*, Miss L. Clark

REGNUM CLUB (1862), 45A South Street, Chichester, W. Sussex PO19 1DS. Tel: 01243-780219; *Hon. Secretary*, A. H. Murray

ROYAL ANGLESEY YACHT CLUB (1802), 5–6 Green Edge, Beaumaris, Anglesey LL58 8BY. Tel: 01248-810295; Email: info@royalanglesey.marine.co.uk; Web: www.royalanglesey.marine.co.uk; *Hon. Secretary*, J. E. de Leyland-Berry

ROYAL CANOE CLUB (1866), Trowlock Island, Teddington, Middx TW11 9QZ. Tel: 020-8977 5269; Fax: 020-8977 5269; Email: dawdy@btinternet.com; *Hon. Secretary*, Mrs J. S. Evans

ROYAL CHANNEL ISLANDS YACHT CLUB (1862), Le Mont du Boulevard, St Aubin, Jersey JE3 8AD. Tel: 01534-745783; Fax: 01534-490042; Email: rciyc@localdial.com; *Hon. Secretary*, B. Murray

ROYAL CINQUE PORTS YACHT CLUB (1872), 5 Waterloo Crescent, Dover, Kent CT16 1LA. Tel: 01304-206262; Fax: 01304-202641; *Secretary*, Ms L. Powell

ROYAL CORINTHIAN YACHT CLUB (1872), The Quay, Burnham-on-Crouch, Essex CM0 8AX. Tel: 01621-782105; Fax: 01621-784965; Email: info@royalcorinthian.co.uk; Web: www.royalcorinthian.co.uk; *Hon. Secretary*, D. Horn

ROYAL DART YACHT CLUB (1866), Priory Street, Kingswear, Dartmouth, Devon TQ6 0AB. Tel: 01803-752272; Fax: 01803-752496; Email: office@royaldart.co.uk; Web: www.royaldart.co.uk; *Hon. Secretary*, M. D. Deeley

ROYAL DORSET YACHT CLUB (1875), 11 Custom House Quay, Weymouth, Dorset DT4 8BG. Tel: 01305-786258; Fax: 01305-786258; Email: rdyc@weymouthharbour.fsnet.co.uk; *Secretary*, Mrs M. Tye

ROYAL FOWEY YACHT CLUB (1881), Whitford Yard, Fowey, Cornwall PL23 1BH. Tel: 01726-833573; Fax: 01726-833573; Email: honsec@rfyc-fowey.org.uk; Web: www.rfyc.fowey.org.uk; *Hon. Secretary*, P. J. Selbie

ROYAL HARWICH YACHT CLUB (1843), Woolverstone, Ipswich IP9 1AT. Tel: 01473-780319; Fax: 01473-780919; Email: secretary@rhyc.demon.co.uk; Web: www.rhyc.demon.co.uk; *Secretary*, Cdr. J. A. Adams, RD

ROYAL LYMINGTON YACHT CLUB (1922), Bath Road, Lymington, Hants SO41 3SE. Tel: 01590-672677; Fax: 01590-671642; Email: sail@rlymyc.org.uk; Web: www.rlymyc.org.uk; *Secretary*, I. Gawn

ROYAL NAVAL CLUB AND ROYAL ALBERT YACHT CLUB (1867), 17 Pembroke Road, Portsmouth PO1 2NT. Tel: 023-9282 5924; Email: rncrayc@aol.com; *Secretary*, Cdr. P. Bolas

ROYAL NORFOLK AND SUFFOLK YACHT CLUB (1859), Royal Plain, Lowestoft, Suffolk NR33 0AQ. Tel: 01502-566726; Fax: 01502-517981; Email: rnsyc@ctc-net.co.uk; *Commodore*, B. Falat

ROYAL PLYMOUTH CORINTHIAN YACHT CLUB (1877), Madeira Road, Plymouth PL1 2NY. Tel: 01752-664327; Fax: 01752-256140; Email: admin@rpcyc.com; Web: www.rpcyc.com; *Hon. Secretary*, A. L. Cooper

ROYAL SOUTHERN YACHT CLUB (1837), Rope Walk, Hamble, Southampton SO31 4HB. Tel: 023-8045 0300; Fax: 023-8045 0310; *Secretary*, M. G. Long, TD

ROYAL TEMPLE YACHT CLUB (1857), 6 Westcliff Mansions, Ramsgate, Kent CT11 9HY. Tel: 01843-591766; Fax: 01843-583211; Email: info@rtyc.com; Web: www.rtyc.com; *Hon. Secretary*, R. Green

ROYAL TORBAY YACHT CLUB (1863), 12 Beacon Terrace, Torquay, Devon TQ1 2BH. Tel: 01803-292006; Fax: 01803-200297; Email: admin@royaltorbayyc.org.uk; Web: www.royaltorbay.org; *Secretary*, R. M. Porteous

ROYAL ULSTER YACHT CLUB (1866), 101 Clifton Road, Bangor, Co. Down BT20 5HY. Tel: 028-9127 0568; Fax: 028-9127 3525; Email: info@ruyc.co.uk; Web: www.royalulsteryachtclub.org; *Commodore*, HRH The Duke of Gloucester

ROYAL WESTERN YACHT CLUB OF ENGLAND (1827), Queen Anne's Battery, Plymouth PL4 0TW. Tel: 01752-660077; Fax: 01752-224299; Email: admin@rwyc.org; Web: www.rwyc.org; *Chief Executive*, Major J. Lewis, RM

ROYAL YACHT SQUADRON (1815), The Castle, Cowes, IOW PO31 7QT. Tel: 01983-292191; Fax: 01983-200253; Email: rys@btinternet.com; Web: www.rys.org.uk; *Secretary*, Captain P. D. Mansfield, RN

ROYAL YORKSHIRE YACHT CLUB (1847), 1 Windsor Crescent, Bridlington, E. Yorks YO15 3HX. Tel: 01262-672041; Fax: 01262-678319; Email: sec@ryyc.org.uk; Web: www.ryyc.org.uk; *Secretary*, J. H. Evans

ROYAL WELSH YACHT CLUB (1847), Porth-Yr-Aur, Caernarfon LL55 1SN. Tel: 01286-672599; *Commodore*, Mrs C. Sotherland

ROYAL WINDERMERE YACHT CLUB (1860), Fallbarrow Road, Bowness-on-Windermere, Windermere, Cumbria LA23 3DJ. Tel: 015394-43106; *Hon. Secretary*, Mrs M. A. Kirk

STOURBRIDGE OLD EDWARDIAN CLUB (1898), Drury Lane, Stourbridge, W. Midlands DY8 1BL. Tel: 01384-395635; *Hon. Secretary*, C. M. Bowden-Davies

TENNIS COURT CLUB (1846), 50 Bedford Street, Leamington Spa, Warks CV32 5DT. Tel: 01926-424977; Fax: 01926 435724; *Hon. Secretary*, P. J. Lloyd

THAMES ESTUARY YACHT CLUB (1895), 3 The Leas, Westcliff-on-Sea, Essex SS0 7ST. Tel: 01702-345967; Email: djb64b@aol.com; *Hon. Secretary*, D. G. Brown

ULSTER REFORM CLUB (1885), 4 Royal Avenue, Belfast BT1 1DA. Tel: 028-9032 3411; Fax: 028-9031 2833; Email: info@ulsterreformclub.com; Web: www.ulsterreformclub.com; *General Manager*, A. W. Graham

VICTORIA CLUB (1853), Beresford Street, St Helier, Jersey JE2 4WN. Tel: 01534-723381; Fax: 01534-874700; Email: victoriaclub@jerseymail.co.uk; *Secretary*, C. J. Blackstone

# Societies and Institutions

This list is in alphabetical order and contains a selection of societies and insitiutions. The date in parenthesis is the year of foundation.

2care (1929), 11 Harwood Road, London SW6 4QP. Tel: 020-7371 0118; Fax: 020-7371 7519; *Chief Executive*, Miss E. C. R. O'Sullivan

ACE STUDY TOURS (1958), Babraham, Cambridge CB2 4AP. Tel: 01223-835055; Fax: 01223-837394; Email: ace@study-tours.org; Web: www.study-tours.org; *General Secretary*, Hugh Barnes

ACTION FOR BLIND PEOPLE (1857), 14–16 Verney Road, London SE16 3DZ. Tel: 020-7635 4800; Fax: 020-7635 4900; Email: central@afbp.org; Web: www.afbp.org; *Chief Executive*, S. Remington

ACTION RESEARCH (1952), Vincent House, Horsham, W. Sussex RH12 2DP. Tel: 01403-210406; Fax: 01403-210541; Email: info@actionresearch.co.uk; Web: www.actionresearch.co.uk; *Chief Executive*, Simon Moore

ACTORS' BENEVOLENT FUND (1882), 6 Adam Street, London WC2N 6AD. Tel: 020-7836 6378; Fax: 020-7836 8978; Email: office@abf.org.uk; *General Secretary*, Mrs J. Skerrett

ACTORS' CHARITABLE TRUST (1896), 255–256 Africa House, 64–78 Kingsway, London WC2B 6BD. Tel: 020-7242 0111; Fax: 020-7242 0234; Email: tact.actors@virgin.net; *General Secretary*, B. Batchelor

ACTORS' CHURCH UNION (1899), St Paul's Church, Bedford Street, London WC2E 9ED. Tel: 020-7240 0344; *Senior Chaplain*, Canon W. Hall

ADAM SMITH INSTITUTE (1977), 23 Great Smith Street, London SW1P 3BL. Tel: 020-7222 4995; Fax: 020-7222 7544; Email: info@adamsmith.org.uk; Web: www.adamsmith.org.uk; *President*, Dr M. Pirie

ADVERTISING STANDARDS AUTHORITY (1962), 2 Torrington Place, London WC1E 7HW. Tel: 020-7580 5555; Fax: 020-7631 3051; Email: inquiries@asa.org.uk; Web: www.asa.org.uk; *Director/General*, C. Graham

AFRICAN MEDICAL AND RESEARCH FOUNDATION (1961), 4 Grosvenor Place, London SW1X 7HJ. Tel: 020-7201 6070; Fax: 020-7201 6170; Email: amref.uk@amref.org; Web: www.amref.org; *Executive Director*, A. Heroys

AGE CONCERN ENGLAND (1940), Astral House, 1268 London Road, London SW16 4ER. Tel: 020-8765 7200; Helpline: 0800-009966; Fax: 020-8765 7211; Email: ace@ace.org.uk; Web: www.ageconcern.org.uk; *Director General*, G. Lishman

AGE CONCERN SCOTLAND (1943), 113 Rose Street, Edinburgh EH2 3DT. Tel: 0131-220 3345; Fax: 0131-220 2779; Email: enquiries@acscot.org.uk; Web: www.ageconcernscotland.org.uk; *Director*, Ms M. O'Neill

THE AIR LEAGUE (1909), Broadway House, Tothill Street, London SW1H 9NS. Tel: 020-7222 8463; Fax: 020-7222 8462; Email: exec@airleague.co.uk; Web: www.airleague.co.uk; *Director*, E. Cox

ACOHOLICS ANONYMOUS (1947), PO Box 1, Stonebow House, Stonebow, York YO1 2NJ. Tel: 01904-644026. National Helpline: 0845-769 7555; Fax: 01904-629091; Web: www.alcoholics-anonymous.org.uk; *General-Secretary*, J. Keeney

ALEXANDRA ROSE DAY (1912), 2A Ferry Road, London SW13 9RX. Tel: 020-8748 4824; Fax: 020-8748 3188; *National Director*, Mrs G. Greenwood

ALLIANCE PARTY OF NORTHERN IRELAND (1970), 88 University Street, Belfast BT7 1HE. Tel: 028-9032 4274; Fax: 028-9033 3147; Email: alliance@allianceparty.org; Web: www.allianceparty.org; *Party Leader*, S. Neeson

ALZHEIMER'S SOCIETY (1979), Gordon House, 10 Greencoat Place, London SW1P 1PH. Tel: 020-7306 0608. Helpline: 0845-300 0336; Fax: 020-7306 0608; Email: info@alzheimers.org.uk; Web: www.alzheimers.org.uk; *Chief Director*, H. Cayton

AMNESTY INTERNATIONAL UNITED KINGDOM (1961), 99–119 Rosebery Avenue, London EC1R 4RE. Tel: 020-7814 6200; Fax: 020-7833 1510; Email: info@amnesty.org.uk; Web: www.amnesty.org.uk; *Director*, Ms K. Allan

ANCIENT MONUMENTS SOCIETY (1924), St Ann's Vestry Hall, 2 Church Entry, London EC4V 5HB. Tel: 020-7236 3934; Fax: 020-7329 3677; Email: ancientmonuments@talk21.com; Web: www.ancientmonumentssociety.org.uk; *Secretary*, M. J. Saunders

ANGLO-BELGIAN SOCIETY (1982), 5 Hartley Close, Bickley, Kent BR1 2TP. Tel: 020-8467 8442; Fax: 020-8467 8442; *Hon. Secretary*, P. R. Bresnan

ANGLO-BRAZILIAN SOCIETY (1943), 32 Green Street, London W1K 7AU. Tel: 020-7493 8493; Fax: 020-7493 8493; Email: anglo@braziliansociety.freeserve.com; *Secretary*, J. Wright

ANGLO-DANISH SOCIETY (1924), Hillgate House, 26 Old Bailey, London EC4M 7HW. Tel: 01753-883510; *Chairman*, Mr P. J. Willoughby

ANGLO-NORSE SOCIETY (1918), 25 Belgrave Square, London SW1X 8QD. Tel: 020-7591 5500/09; Fax: 020-7245 6993; *Chairman*, Sir John Robson

ANIMAL CONCERN, PO Box 3982, Glasgow G51 4WD. Tel: 0141-445 3570; Fax: 0141-445 6470; Email: animals@jfrobins.force9.co.uk; *Organising Secretary*, Dr M. Daly

ANTHROPOSOPHICAL SOCIETY IN GREAT BRITAIN (1923), Rudolf Steiner House, 35 Park Road, London NW1 6XT. Tel: 020-7723 4400; Fax: 020-7724 4364; Email: rsh@cix.compulink.co.uk; Web: www.anth.org.uk; *General Secretary*, N. C. Thomas

ANTIQUARIAN HOROLOGICAL SOCIETY (1953), New House, High Street, Ticehurst, Wadhurst, E. Sussex TN5 7AL. Tel: 01580-200155; Fax: 01580-201323; Email: secretary@ahsoc.demon.co.uk; Web: www.ahsoc.demon.co.uk; *Secretary*, Mrs W. B. Barr

ANTI-SLAVERY INTERNATIONAL (1839), Thomas Clarkson House, The Stableyard, Broomgrove Road, London SW9 9TL. Tel: 020-7501 8920; Fax: 020-7738 4110; Email: antislavery@antislavery.org; Web: www.antislavery.org; *Director*, M. Dottridge

ARCHITECTS BENEVOLENT SOCIETY (1850), 43 Portland Place, London W1N 3AG. Tel: 020-7580 2823; Fax: 020-7580 7075; Email: mail@theabs.org.uk; *Secretary*, K. Robinson

ARCHITECTS REGISTRATION BOARD (1931 and 1997), 8 Weymouth Street, London W1W 5BU. Tel: 020-7580 5861; Fax: 020-7436 5269; Email: info@arb.org.uk; Web: www.arb.org.uk; *Chief Executive and Registrar*, Robin Vaughan

ARCHITECTURAL ASSOCIATION INC. (1847), 34–36 Bedford Square, London WC1B 3ES. Tel: 020-7887 4000; Fax: 020-7414 0782; Email: arch-assoc@arch-assoc.org.uk; Web: www.aaschool.ac.uk; *Chief Executive*, Mohsen Mostafari

ARCHITECTURAL HERITAGE FUND (1976), Clareville House, 26–27 Oxendon Street, London SW1Y 4EL. Tel: 020-7925 0199; Fax: 020-7930 0295; Email: ahf@ahfund.org.uk; Web: www.ahfund.org.uk; *Director*, J. Thompson

ARLIS/UK AND IRELAND (THE ART LIBRARIES SOCIETY) (1969), 18 College Road, Bromsgrove, Worcs B60 2NE. Tel: 01527-579298; Fax: 01527-579298; Email: sfrench@arlis.demon.co.uk; Web: www.arlis.nal.vam.ac.uk; *Administrator*, Ms S. French

ARMY BENEVOLENT FUND (1944), 41 Queen's Gate, London SW7 5HR. Tel: 020-7591 2000; Fax: 020-7589 0889; *Controller*, Maj.-Gen. M. D. Regan

ARMY CADET FORCE ASSOCIATION (1930), Duke of York's HQ, London SW3 4RR. Tel: 020-7730 9733; Fax: 020-7730 8264; Email: acfa@armycadets.com; Web: www.armycadets.com; *General Secretary*, Brig. J. E. Neeve

ARTHRITIS CARE (1949), 18 Stephenson Way, London NW1 2HD. Tel: 020-7380 6500; Fax: 020-7380 6505; Web: www.arthritiscare.org.uk; *Chief Executive*, R. Gutch

ASIAN FAMILY COUNSELLING SERVICE, 76 Church Road, London W7 1LB. Tel: 020-8567 5616; Fax: 020-8567 5616; Email: afcs99@hotmail.com; *Director*, R. Atma

ASLIB (THE ASSOCIATION FOR INFORMATION MANAGEMENT) (1924), Staple Hall, Stone House Court, London EC3A 7PB. Tel: 020-7903 0000; Fax: 020-7903 0011; Email: aslib@aslib.com; Web: www.aslib.com; *Chief Executive*, R. Bowes

ASSOCIATION FOR SCIENCE EDUCATION (1901), College Lane, Hatfield, Herts AL10 9AA. Tel: 01707-283000; Fax: 01707-266532; Email: davidmoore@ase.org.uk; Web: www.ase.org.uk; *Chief Executive*, Dr D. S. Moore

ASSOCIATION FOR THE PROTECTION OF RURAL SCOTLAND (1926), 3rd Floor, Gladstone's Land, 483 Lawnmarket, Edinburgh EH1 2NT. Tel: 0131-225 7012/3; Fax: 0131-225 6592; Email: aprs@aprs.org.uk; Web: www.aprs.org.uk; *Director*, Mrs J. Geddes

ASSOCIATION OF ACCOUNTING TECHNICIANS (1980), 154 Clerkenwell Road, London EC1R 5AD. Tel: 020-7837 8600; Fax: 020-7837 6970; Email: aatuk@dial.pipex.com; Web: www.aat.co.uk; *Chief Executive*, Ms J. Scott Paul

ASSOCIATION OF ANAESTHETISTS OF GREAT BRITAIN AND IRELAND, 9 Bedford Square, London WC1B 3RA. Tel: 020-7631 1650; Fax: 020-7631 4352; Email: info@aagbi.org; Web: www.aagbi.org; *Chief Executive*, Kevin Horlock

ASSOCIATION OF BRITISH CORRESPONDENCE COLLEGES (1955), PO Box 17926, London SW19 3WB. Tel: 020-8544 9559; Fax: 020-8540 7657; Email: abcc@msn.com; Web: www.homestudy.org.uk; *Secretary*, Mrs H. Owen

ASSOCIATION OF BRITISH DISPENSING OPTICIANS (1925), 199 Gloucester Terrace, London W2 6HX. Email: general@abdo.org.uk; *Registrar*, D. G. Baker

ASSOCIATION OF BRITISH INSURERS (1985), 51 Gresham Street, London EC2V 7HQ. Tel: 020-7600 3333; Fax: 020-7696 8999; Email: info@abi.org.uk; Web: www.abi.org.uk; *Director General*, Mrs M. Francis

ASSOCIATION OF BRITISH TRAVEL AGENTS (1950), 68–71 Newman Street, London W1T 3AH. Tel: 020-7637 2444; Fax: 020-7637 0713; Email: abta@abta.co.uk; Web: www.abtanet.com; *Chief Executive*, I. Reynolds

ASSOCIATION OF CHARTERED CERTIFIED ACCOUNTANTS (1904), 29 Lincoln's Inn Fields, London WC2A 3EE. Tel: 020-7242 6855; Fax: 020-7831 8054; Web: www.accaglobal.org.uk; *Chief Executive*, Mrs A. L. Rose

ASSOCIATION OF CONSULTING ENGINEERS (1913), Alliance House, 12 Caxton Street, London SW1H 0QL. Tel: 020-7222 6557; Fax: 020-7222 0750; Email: consult@acenet.co.uk; Web: www.acenet.co.uk; *Chief Executive*, N. Bennett

ASSOCIATION OF CONVENIENCE STORES LTD (1995), Federation House, 17 Farnborough Street, Farnborough, Hants GU14 8AG. Tel: 01252-515001; Fax: 01252-515002; Email: acs@acs.org.uk; Web: www.cstoreretailing.co.uk; *Chief Executive*, T. Dixon

ASSOCIATION OF CORPORATE TREASURERS (1979), Ocean House, 10–12 Little Trinity Lane, London EC4V 2DJ. Tel: 020-7213 9728; Fax: 020-7248 2591; Email: enquiries@treasurers.co.uk; Web: www.treasurers.org; *Director General*, Dr D. Creed

ASSOCIATION OF CORPORATE TRUSTEES (1974), 3 Brackerne Close, Cooden, Bexhill on Sea, East Sussex TN39 3BT. Tel: 01424-844144; Fax: 01424-844144; Email: tact@cooden.fsbusiness.co.uk; Web: www.trustees.org.uk; *Secretary*, W. J. Stevenson

ASSOCIATION OF COUNCIL SECRETARIES AND SOLICITORS (1974, merged 1996), Foxcroft, Gill Lane, Longton, Preston PR4 4SR. Tel: 01772-611167; Fax: 01772-611167; Email: acssny@cybase.co.uk; Web: www.acses.org.uk; *Executive Officer*, N. Yates

ASSOCIATION OF COUNTY CHIEF EXECUTIVES (1974), Office of the Chief Executive, County Hall, West Bridgford, Nottingham NG2 7QP. Tel: 0115-977 3582; Fax: 0115-977 2419; Email: peter.housden@nottscc.gov.uk; *Hon. Secretary*, P. Housden

ASSOCIATION OF DRAINAGE AUTHORITIES (1937), The Mews, 3 Royal Oak Passage, High Street, Huntingdon, Cambs PE29 3EA. Tel: 01480-411123; Fax: 01480-431107; Email: drainage@ada.org.uk; Web: www.ada.org.uk; *Chief Executive*, D. Noble

ASSOCIATION OF FRIENDLY SOCIETIES (1995), 10–13 Lovat Lane, London EC3R 8DT. Tel: 020-7397 9550; Fax: 020-7397 9551; Email: friendly@afs.org.uk; *General Secretary*, Miss M. Poole

ASSOCIATION OF INTER VARSITY CLUBS (1946), 2nd Floor, Grosvenor House, 94–96 Grosvenor Square, Manchester M1 7HL. Tel: 0161-273 2316; Email: aivc_secretary@bigfoot.com; Web: www.ivc.org.uk; *Chairman*, R. Clifford

ASSOCIATION OF ROYAL NAVY OFFICERS (1920), 70 Porchester Terrace, London W2 3TP. Tel: 020-7402 5231; Fax: 020-7402 5533; Email: ARNO@eurosurf.com; Web: www.eurosurf.com/ARNO; *Secretary*, Lt.-Cdr. I. M. P. Coombes

ATS AND WRAC ASSOCIATION BENEVOLENT FUND (1944), AGC Centre, Worthy Down, Winchester, Hants SO21 2RG. Tel: 01962-887612; Fax: 01962-887612; *Secretary*, Maj. D. M. McElligott

THE AUTOMOBILE ASSOCIATION LTD (1905), Norfolk House, Priestley Road, Basingstoke, Hants RG24 9NY. Tel: 0990-500600; Fax: 01256-493389; Email: customer.services@theaa.com; Web: www.theaa.com; *Director General*, Roy Gardner

AYRSHIRE ARCHAEOLOGICAL AND NATURAL HISTORY SOCIETY (1947), 10 Longlands Park, Ayr KA7 4RJ. Tel: 01292-441915; *Hon. Secretary*, Dr T. Mathews

AYRSHIRE CATTLE SOCIETY OF GREAT BRITAIN AND IRELAND (1877), 1 Racecourse Road, Ayr KA7 2DE. Tel: 01292-267123; Fax: 01292-611973; Email: society@ayrshires.org; Web: www.ayrshires.org; *General Manager*, D. Sayce

BACKCARE, 16 Elmtree Road, Teddington, Middx TW11 8ST. Tel: 020-8977 5474; Fax: 020-8943 5318; Email: Back_Pain@compuserve.com; Web: www.backpain.org; *Chief Executive*, Ms Alison Mills

BALTIC AIR CHARTER ASSOCIATION (1949), The Baltic Exchange, St Mary Axe, London EC3A 8BH. Tel: 020-7623 5501; Fax: 020-7369 1623; Web: www.baca.org.uk; *Chairman*, Colin Bailey

THE BALTIC EXCHANGE (1903), St Mary Axe, London EC3A 8BH. Tel: 020-7623 5501; Fax: 020-7369 1622; Email: enquiries@balticexchange.co.uk; Web: www.balticexchange.com; *Chief Executive*, J. Buckley

BALTIC EXCHANGE CHARITABLE SOCIETY (1978), 13 Norton Folgate, Bishopsgate, London E1 6DB. Tel: 020-7247 6863; Email: douglas_painter@talk21.com; *Secretary*, D. A. Painter

BAR ASSOCIATION FOR LOCAL GOVERNMENT AND THE PUBLIC SERVICE (1945), c/o Birmingham City Council, Ingleby House, 11–14 Cannon Street, Birmingham B2 5EN. Tel: 0121-303 9991; Fax: 0121-303 1312; Email: chairman@balgps.freeserve.co.uk; Web: www.balgps.freeserve.co.uk; *Chairman*, M. F. N. Ahmad

BARNARDO'S (1866), Tanners Lane, Barkingside, Ilford, Essex IG6 1QG. Tel: 020-8550 8822; Fax: 020-8551 6870; Web: www.barnardos.org.uk; *Senior Director*, R. Singleton

BARRISTERS' BENEVOLENT ASSOCIATION (1873), 14 Gray's Inn Square, London WC1R 5JP. Tel: 020-7242 4761; Fax: 020-7831 5366; Email: linda@thebba.swinternet.co.uk; *Secretary*, Mrs L. C. Carlier

BCB (BRITISH CONSULTANTS BUREAU) (1965), One Westminster Palace Gardens, 1–7 Artillery Row, London SW1P 1RJ. Tel: 020-7222 3651; Fax: 020-7222 3664; Email: mail@bcb.co.uk; Web: www.bcbforum.demon.co.uk; *Director*, C. Adams

BESO (BRITISH EXECUTIVE SERVICE OVERSEAS) 164 Vauxhall Bridge Road, London SW1V 4RB. Tel: 020-7630 0644; Fax: 020-7630 0624; *Chief Executive*, G. Ramsey

BEVIN BOYS ASSOCIATION (1989), 28 Sir Christopher Court, Hythe, Southampton, Hampshire SO45 6JR. Tel: 023-8087 9766; Fax: 023-8087 9766; *Vice President and Public Relations Officer*, W. H. Taylor

BIBLIOGRAPHICAL SOCIETY (1892), c/o The Wellcome Library, 183 Euston Road, London NW1 2BE. Tel: 020-7611 7244; Fax: 020-7611 8703; Email: jm93@dial.pipex.com; *Hon. Secretary*, D. Pearson

THE BIOCHEMICAL SOCIETY (1911), 59 Portland Place, London W1B 1QW. Tel: 020-7580 5530; Fax: 020-7637 3626; Email: genadmin@biochemistry.org; Web: www.biochemistry.org; *Executive Secretary*, G. D. Jones

BIRMINGHAM AND MIDLAND INSTITUTE AND LIBRARY (1954), Margaret Street, Birmingham B3 3BS. Tel: 0121-236 3591; Fax: 0121-212 4577; Web: www.bmi.org.uk; *Administrator and General Secretary*, P. A. Fisher

THE BLUE CROSS (1897), Shilton Road, Burford, Oxon OX18 4PF. Tel: 01993-822651; Fax: 01993-823083; Email: info@bluecross.org.uk; Web: www.bluecross.org.uk; *Chief Executive*, A. Kennard

BOOK AID INTERNATIONAL (1954), 39–41 Coldharbour Lane, London SE5 9NR. Tel: 020-7733 3577; Fax: 020-7978 8006; Email: info@bookaid.org; Web: www.bookaid.org; *Director*, Mrs S. Harrity

BOOK TRUST (1926), Book House, 45 East Hill, London SW18 2QZ. Tel: 020-8516 2977; Fax: 020-8516 2978; Web: www.booktrust.org.uk; *Executive Director*, C. Meade

BOOKSELLERS ASSOCIATION OF THE UK & IRELAND LTD (1895), Minster House, 272 Vauxhall Bridge Road, SW1V 1BA. 020-7834 5477; Fax: 020-7834 8812; Email: mail@booksellers.org.uk; Web: www.booksellers.org.uk; *Chief Executive*, T. E. Godfray

BOTANICAL SOCIETY OF SCOTLAND, c/o Royal Botanic Garden, Inverleith Row, Edinburgh EH3 5LR. Tel: 0131-552 7171; Fax: 0131-248 2901; *Hon. General Secretary*, R. Galt

BOTANICAL SOCIETY OF THE BRITISH ISLES (1836), c/o Department of Botany, The Natural History Museum, Cromwell Road, London SW7 5BD. Tel: 020-7942 5002; Email: bsbihgs@aol.com; Web: www.members.aol.com/bsbihgs; *Acting Hon. General Secretary*, Miss A. Burns

BOY'S BRIGADE (1883), Felden Lodge, Hemel Hempstead, Herts HP3 0BL. Tel: 01442-231681; Fax: 01442-235391; Email: bbhq@boys-brigade.org.uk; Web: www.boys-brigade.org.uk; *Brigade Secretary*, S. Jones

BRIDEWELL ROYAL HOSPITAL (1553), Witley, Godalming, Surrey GU8 5SG. Tel: 01428-686700; Fax: 01428-682850; Web: www.kesw.surrey.sch.uk; *Clerk*, D. W. Hanson

BRITAIN-NEPAL SOCIETY, 3C Gunnersbury Avenue, London W5 3NH. Tel: 020-8992 0173; *Hon. Secretary*, Mrs P. Mellor

THE BRITAIN-RUSSIA CENTRE (1959), 1 Nine Elms Lane, London SW8 5NQ. Tel: 020-7498 6640; Fax: 020-7498 4660; Web: www.briteastwest.org.uk; *Director*, G. Cromwell

BRITISH ACADEMY OF COMPOSERS AND SONGWRITERS, 2nd Floor, 25–27 Berners Street, London W1P 3DB. Tel: 020-7636 2929; Fax: 020-7636 2212; Email: info@britishacademy.com; Web: www.britishacademy.com; *Chief Executive*, C. Green

BRITISH ACADEMY OF FORENSIC SCIENCES, Anaesthetic Unit, The Royal London Hospital, Whitechapel, London E1 1BB. Tel: 020-7377 9201; Fax: 020-7377 7126; *Secretary-General*, Dr P. J. Flynn

BRITISH AND FOREIGN SCHOOL SOCIETY (1808), Croudace House, Godstone Road, Caterham, Surrey CR3 6RE. Tel: 01883-331177; *Director*, J. Kidd

BRITISH ANTIQUE DEALERS' ASSOCIATION (1918), 20 Rutland Gate, London SW7 1BD. Tel: 020-7589 4128; Fax: 020-7581 9083; Email: enquiry@bada.demon.co.uk; Web: www.bada.org; *Secretary-General*, Mrs E. J. Dean

BRITISH ASSOCIATION FOR EARLY CHILDHOOD EDUCATION (1923), 136 Cavell Street, London E1 2JA. Tel: 020-7539 5400; Fax: 020-7539 5409; Email: office@early-education.org.uk; Web: www.early-education.org.uk

BRITISH ASSOCIATION FOR LOCAL HISTORY (1952), PO Box 1576, Salisbury, Wilts SP2 8SY. Tel: 01722-322158; Fax: 01722-413242; Web: www.balh.co.uk; *General Secretary*, M. Cowan

BRITISH ASSOCIATION FOR THE ADVANCEMENT OF SCIENCE (1831), 23 Savile Row, London W1S 2EZ. Tel: 020-7973 3500; Fax: 020-7973 3063; Email: info@britassoc.org.uk; Web: www.britassoc.org.uk; *Chief Executive*, Dr P. Briggs

BRITISH ASSOCIATION OF COMMUNICATORS IN BUSINESS (1949), 42 Borough High Street, London SE1 1XW. Tel: 020-7378 7139; Fax: 020-7378 7140; Email: enquiries@bacb.org; Web: www.bacb.org; *Secretary-General*, Mrs K. Jones

BRITISH ASTRONOMICAL ASSOCIATION (1890), Burlington House, Piccadilly, London. Web: www.ast.cam.ac.uk/~baa; *Assistant Secretary*, Miss P. M. Barber

BRITISH BOARD OF FILM CLASSIFICATION (1912), 3 Soho Square, London W1D 3HD. Tel: 020-7440 1570; Fax: 020-7287 0141; Email: webmaster@bbfc.co.uk; Web: www.bbfc.co.uk; *Director*, R. Duval

BRITISH COMMONWEALTH EX-SERVICES LEAGUE (1921), 48 Pall Mall, London SW1Y 5JG. Tel: 020-7973 7263; Fax: 020-7973 7308; Web: www.bcel.org.uk; *Secretary-General*, Colonel B. G. G. Nicholson

BRITISH COPYRIGHT COUNCIL (1965), 29–33 Berners Street, London W1T 3AB. Tel: 01986-788122; Fax: 01986-788847; Email: copyright@bcc2.demon.co.uk; *Secretary*, Ms J. Ibbotson

BRITISH DEAF ASSOCIATION (1890), 1 Worship Street, London EC2A 2AB. Tel: 020-7588 3520; Fax: 020-7588 3527; Email: info@bda.org.uk; Web: www.bda.org.uk; *Chief Executive*, J. McWhinney

BRITISH DRIVING SOCIETY (1957), 27 Dugard Place, Barford, Warwick CV35 8DX. Tel: 01926-624420; Fax: 01926-624633; Email: brit.driving.soc@care4free.net; Web: www.carriage-driving.com; *Secretary*, Mrs J. M. Dillon

BRITISH EPILEPSY ASSOCIATION (1950), New Anstey House, Gate Way Drive, Yeadon, Leeds LS19 7XY. Tel: 0113-210 8800. Helpline: 0808-800 5050; Fax: 0113-391 0300; Email: epilepsy@bea.org.uk; Web: www.epilepsy.org.uk; *Chief Executive*, P. Lee

British False Memory Society (1993),Bradford on Avon, Wilts BA15 1NF. Tel: 01225-868682; Fax: 01225-862251; Email: BFMS@compuserve.com; Web: www.bfms.org.uk; *Director*, M. Greenhalgh

British Federation of Women Graduates (1907), 4 Mandeville Courtyard, 142 Battersea Park Road, London SW11 4NB. Tel: 020-7498 8037; Fax: 020-7498 8037; Email: bfwg@bfwg.demon.co.uk; *Secretary*, Mrs A. B. Stein

British Goat Society, 34–36 Fore Street, Bovey Tracey, Newton Abbot, Devon TQ13 9AD. Tel: 01626-833168; Fax: 01626-833168; Email: goats@charity.ufree.com; Web: www.allgoats.com; *Secretary*, Ms S. Knowles

British Health Care Association (1930), 24A Main Street, Garforth, Leeds LS25 1AA. Tel: 0113-232 0903; Fax: 0113-232 0904; Email: cbell@bhca.org.uk; Web: www.bhca.org.uk; *Chief Executive*, Mrs C. Bell

British Heart Foundation, 14 Fitzhardinge Street, London W1H 6DH. Tel: 020-7487 7186; Fax: 020-7486 5820; Email: directorate@bhf.org.uk; Web: www.bhf.org.uk; *Director General*, Maj.-Gen. L. F. H. Busk

British Hedgehog Preservation Society (1982), Knowbury House, Knowbury, Ludlow, Shropshire SY8 3LQ. Tel: 01584-890801; Fax: 01584-891313; Email: bhps@dhustone.fsbusiness.co.uk; Web: www.software-technics.com/bhps; *Chief Executive and Founder*, Maj. A. H. Coles

British Herpetological Society, c/o Zoological Society of London, Regent's Park, London NW1 4RY. Tel: 020-8452 9578; *Secretary*, Mrs M. Green

British Homeopathic Association, 15 Clerkenwell Close, London EC1R 0AA. Tel: 020-7566 7800; Fax: 020-7566 7815; Email: info@trusthomeopathy.org; Web: www.trusthomeopathy.org

British Horological Institute (1858), Upton Hall, Upton, Newark, Notts NG23 5TE. Tel: 01636-813795; Fax: 01636-812258; Email: clocks@bhi.co.uk; Web: www.bhi.co.uk; *Secretary*, Martin Taylor

British Horse Society (1947), Stoneleigh Deer Park, Kenilworth, Warks CV8 2XZ. Tel: 01926-707700; Fax: 01926-707800; Email: enquiry@bhs.org.uk; Web: www.bhs.org.uk; *Chief Executive*, Mrs Kay Driver

British Hospitality Association (1906), Queens House, 55–56 Lincoln's Inn Fields, London WC2A 3BH. Tel: 020-7404 7744; Fax: 020-7404 7799; Email: bha@bha.org.uk; Web: www.bha-online.org.uk; *Chief Executive*, Bob Cotton

British Humanist Association (1896), 47 Theobald's Road, London WC1X 8SP. Tel: 020-7430 0908; Fax: 020-7430 1271; Email: info@humanism.org.uk; Web: www.humanism.org.uk; *Executive Director*, Robert Ashby

British Institute in Eastern Africa (1959), 10 Carlton House Terrace, London SW1Y 5AH. Tel: 020-7969 5201; Fax: 020-7969 5401; Email: biea@britac.ac.uk; Web: www.britac.ac.uk/institutes/eafrica; *London Secretary*, Mrs J. Moyo

British Institute of Archaeology at Ankara (1948), 10 Carlton House Terrace, London SW1Y 5AH. Tel: 020-7969 5204; Fax: 020-7969 5401; Email: biaa@britac.ac.uk; *Director*, Dr R. J. Matthews

British Institute of Graphologists, 24–26 High Street, Hampton Hill, Hampton, Middx TW12 1PD. Tel: 01753-891241; Email: text@virgin.net; *Chairman*, E. Rees

British Institute of Human Rights (1970), 8th Floor, Kings College London, 75–79 York Road, London SE1 7AW. Tel: 020-7401 2712; Fax: 020-7401 2695; Email: bihr@kcl.ac.uk; Web: www.bihr.org; *Director*, Ms S. Cooke

British Institute of Persian Studies, c/o The British Academy, 10 Carlton House Terrace, London SW1Y 5AH. Tel: 020-7969 5203; Fax: 020-7226 1318; *Secretary and Joint Hon. Editor*, Dr Vesta S. Curtis

British Insurance Brokers' Association (1978), BIBA House, 14 Bevis Marks, London EC3A 7NT. Tel: 020-7623 9043; Fax: 020-7626 9676; Email: enquiries@biba.org.uk; Web: www.biba.org.uk; *Chief Executive*, R. M. Williams

British Israel World Federation (1919), 8 Blades Court, Deodar Road, London SW15 2NU. Tel: 020-8877 9010; Fax: 020-8871 4770; Email: admin@britishisrael.co.uk; Web: www.britishisrael.co.uk; *Hon. Secretary*, M. A. Clark

British Lung Foundation (1984), 78 Hatton Garden, London EC1N 8LD. Tel: 020-7831 5831; Fax: 020-7831 5832; Email: blf@britishlungfoundation.com; Web: www.lunguk.org; *Chief Executive*, B. Walden

British Music Hall Society, 82 Fernlea Road, London SW12 9RW. Tel: 020-8673 2175; *Hon. Secretary*, Mrs D. Masterton

British Music Information Centre, 10 Stratford Place, London W1C 1BA. Tel: 020-7499 8567; Fax: 020-7499 4795; Email: bmic@bmic.co.uk; Web: www.bmic.co.uk; *Director*, M. Greenall

British National Party (1982), PO Box 14, Welshpool, Powys SY21 0WE. Tel: 0700-900 2671; Fax: 01938-820560; Email: letters@bnp.net; Web: www.bnp.net; *Chairman*, N. Griffin

British Naturalists' Association (1905), 1 Bracken Mews, London E4 7UT. Web: www.bna-naturalists.org; *Hon. Membership Secretary*, Mrs Y. H. Griffiths

British Nuclear Energy Society, 1–7 Great George Street, London SW1P 3AA. Tel: 020-7665 2241; Fax: 020-7799 1325; Email: andrew.tillbrook@ice.org.uk; Web: www.bnes.org.uk; *Secretary*, A. Tillbrook

British Nutrition Foundation, High Holborn House, 52–54 High Holborn, London WC1V 6RQ. Tel: 020-7404 6504; Fax: 020-7404 6747; Email: british_nutrition@compuserve.com; Web: www.nutrition.org.uk; *Director General*, Prof. R. S. Pickard

BRITISH PHARMACOLOGICAL SOCIETY (1931), 16 Angel Gate, City Road, London EC1V 2SG. Tel: 020-7417 0110; Fax: 020-7417 0114; Email: pjc@bps.ac.uk; Web: www.bps.ac.uk; *President*, Prof. N. G. Bowery

BRITISH PIG ASSOCIATION, Scotsbridge House, Scots Hill, Rickmansworth, Herts WD3 3BB. Tel: 01923-695295; Fax: 01923-695347; Email: bpa@britishpigs.org; Web: www.britishpigs.org; *General Manager*, M. Bates

BRITISH POLIO FELLOWSHIP (1939), Ground Floor, Unit A, Eagle Office Centre, The Runway, South Ruislip, Middx HA4 6SE. Tel: 0800-018 0586; Fax: 020-8842 0555; Email: info@britishpolio.org; Web: www.britishpolio.org; *Chief Executive*, A. Kemp

THE BRITISH PSYCHOLOGICAL SOCIETY (1901), St Andrews House, 48 Princess Road East, Leicester LE1 7DR. Tel: 0116-254 9568; Fax: 0116-247 0787; Email: mail@bps.org.uk; Web: www.bps.org.uk; *Chief Executive*, B. A. Brooking

BRITISH RED CROSS (1870), 9 Grosvenor Crescent, London SW1X 7EJ. Tel: 020-7235 5454; Fax: 020-7245 6315; Email: information@redcross.org.uk; Web: www.redcross.org.uk and www.redcrossdonations.org.uk; *Director General*, S. Younger

BRITISH SAFETY COUNCIL (1957), 70 Chancellor's Road, London W6 9RS. Tel: 020-8741 1231; Fax: 020-8741 4555; Email: mail@britsafe.org; Web: www.britishsafetycouncil.org; *Director General*, Sir Neville Purvis

BRITISH SOCIETY OF DOWSERS (1933), Sycamore Barn, Hastingleigh, Ashford, Kent TN25 5HW. Tel: 01233-750253; Fax: 01233-750253; Email: bsd@dowsers.demon.co.uk; Web: www.dowsers.demon.co.uk; *General Secretary*, M. D. Rust

BRITISH TRUST FOR ORNITHOLOGY, The Nunnery, Thetford, Norfolk IP24 2PU. Tel: 01842-750050; Fax: 01842-750030; Email: general@bto.org; Web: www.bto.org; *Director*, Dr J. J. D. Greenwood

BRITISH UNION FOR THE ABOLITION OF VIVISECTION (1898), 16A Crane Grove, London N7 8NN. Tel: 020-7700 4888; Fax: 020-7700 0252; Email: info@buav.org; *Chief Executive*, Ms M. Thew

BRITISH VETERINARY ASSOCIATION (1883), 7 Mansfield Street, London W1G 9NQ. Tel: 020-7636 6541; Fax: 020-7436 2970; Email: bvahq@bva.co.uk; Web: www.bva.co.uk and www.vetrecord.co.uk; *Chief Executive*, J. H. Baird

BTBS THE BOOK TRADE CHARITY (1837), Dillon Lodge, The Retreat, Kings Langley, Herts WD4 8LT. Tel: 01923-263128; Fax: 01923-270732; Email: btbs@booktradecharity.demon.co.uk; Web: www.booktradecharity.demon.co.uk; *Chief Executive*, D. Hicks

BTCV (1959), 36 St Mary's Street, Wallingford, Oxon OX10 0EU. Tel: 01491-821600; Fax: 01491-839646; Email: information@btcv.org.uk; Web: www.btcv.org; *Chief Executive*, T. O. Flood

THE BUDGERIGAR SOCIETY (1925), Spring Gardens, Northampton NN1 1DR. Tel: 01604-624549; Fax: 01604-627108; Web: www.budgerigarsociety.com; *General Secretary*, D. Whittaker

BUILDING SOCIETIES ASSOCIATION, 3 Savile Row, London W1S 3PB. Tel: 020-7437 0655; Fax: 020-7734 6416; Web: www.bsa.org.uk; *Director General*, A. Coles

BUSINESS AND PROFESSIONAL WOMEN UK LTD (1938), PO Box 26166, London SW8 4WG. Tel: 020-7627 5040; Fax: 020-7627 5085; Email: HQ@bpwuk.org.uk; Web: www.bpwuk.org.uk

BUSINESS IN THE COMMUNITY (1981), 137 Shepherdess Walk, London N1 7RQ. Tel: 0870-600 2482; Fax: 020-7253 1877; Email: information@bitc.org.uk; Web: www.bitc.org.uk; *Chief Executive*, Ms J. Cleverdon

CAFOD (CATHOLIC FUND FOR OVERSEAS DEVELOPMENT) (1962), Romero Close, Stockwell Road, London SW9 9TY. Tel: 020-7733 7900; Fax: 020-7274 9630; Email: hq@cafod.org.uk; Web: www.cafod.org.uk; *Director*, J. Filochowski

CALOUSTE GULBENKIAN FOUNDATION (1956), 98 Portland Place, London W1B 1ET. Tel: 020-7636 5313; Fax: 020-7908 7580; Email: info@gulbenkian.org.uk; *Director*, Ms P. Ridley

CAMERON FUND, Tavistock House North, Tavistock Square, London WC1H 9HR. Tel: 020-7388 0796; *Secretary*, Mrs J. Martin

CAMPAIGN FOR AN INDEPENDENT BRITAIN, 81 Ashmole Street, London SW8 1NF. Tel: 020-8340 0314; Fax: 020-7582 7021; Email: info@cibhq.co.uk; Web: www.cibhq.co.uk; *Hon. Secretary*, Sir Robin Williams

CAMPAIGN FOR NUCLEAR DISARMAMENT (CND) (1958), 162 Holloway Road, London N7 8DQ. Tel: 020-7700 2393; Fax: 020-7700 2357; Email: cnd@gn.apc.org; Web: www.cnduk.org; *Chair*, D. Knight

CANADA-UNITED KINGDOM CHAMBER OF COMMERCE, 38 Grosvenor Street, London W1K 4DP. Tel: 020-7258 6572; Fax: 020-7258 6594; Email: info@canada-uk.org; Web: www.canada-uk.org; *Executive Director*, M. Newton

CANCER RESEARCH CAMPAIGN (1923), 10 Cambridge Terrace, London NW1 4JL. Tel: 020-7224 1333; Fax: 020-7487 4310; Email: cancerinfo@crc.org.uk; Web: www.crc.org.uk; *Director General*, Prof. J. G. McVie

CARERS UK (1988), Ruth Pitter House, 20–25 Glasshouse Yard, London EC1A 4JT. Tel: 020-7490 8818; Fax: 020-7490 8824; Email: info@ukcarers.org; Web: www.carersuk.demon.co.uk; *Chief Executive*, Ms D. Whitworth

CARNEGIE DUNFERMLINE TRUST (1903), Abbey Park House, Dunfermline, Fife KY12 7PB. Tel: 01383-723638; Fax: 01383-721862; Email: admin@carnegietrust.com; *Secretary and Treasurer*, W. C. Runciman

CARNEGIE HERO FUND TRUST (1908), Abbey Park House, Dunfermline, Fife KY12 7PB. Tel: 01383-723638; Fax: 01383-721862; *Secretary and Treasurer*, W. C. Runciman

CATHEDRALS FABRIC COMMISSION FOR ENGLAND (1991), Church House, Great Smith Street, London SW1P 3NZ. Tel: 020-7898 1863; Fax: 020-7898 1881; Email: enquiries@cfce.c-of-e.org.uk; *Secretary*, Dr R. Gem

CATHOLIC ENQUIRY OFFICE (1902), The Chase Centre, 114 West Heath Road, London NW3 7TX. Tel: 020-8458 3316; Fax: 020-8905 5780; Email: cms@cms.org.uk; Web: www.cms.org.uk; *Director*, Fr P. Billington

CATHOLIC HOUSING AID SOCIETY, 209 Old Marylebone Road, London NW1 5QT. Tel: 020-7723 7273; Fax: 020-7723 5943; Email: info@chasnat.demon.co.uk; Web: www.chasnat.demon.co.uk; *Director*, Ms R. Rafferty

CATHOLIC TRUTH SOCIETY (1868), 40–46 Harleyford Road, London SE11 5AY. Tel: 020-7640 0042; Fax: 020-7640 0046; Email: info@cts-online.org.uk; Web: www.cts-online.org.uk; *General Secretary*, F. Martin

CATHOLIC UNION OF GREAT BRITAIN (1872), St Maxmilian Kolbe House, 63 Jeddo Road, London W12 9EE. Tel: 020-8749 1321; Fax: 020-8735 0816; *Secretary*, P. H. Higgs

CENTRAL BUREAU FOR EDUCATIONAL VISITS AND EXCHANGES, 10 Spring Gardens, London SW1A 2BN. Tel: 020-7389 4487; Fax: 020-7389 4497; Email: peter.upton@britishcouncil.org; Web: www.britishcouncil.org/cbiet; *Director*, P. Upton

CENTRAL COUNCIL OF CHURCH BELL RINGERS, The Cottage, School Hill, Warnham, Horsham RH12 3QN. Tel: 01403-269743; Web: www.cccbr.org.uk; *Secretary*, Mr I. H. Oram

CENTREPOINT, Neil House, 7 Whitechapel Road, London E1 1DU. Tel: 020-7426 5300; Fax: 020-7426 5301; Web: www.centrepoint.org.uk; *Chief Executive*, V. O. Adebowale

CHADWICK TRUST, Department of Civil and Environmental Engineering, University College, Gower Street, London WC1E 6BT. Tel: 020-7679 5774; Fax: 020-7679 5789; Email: h.fisher@ucl.ac.uk; *Secretary to the Trustee*, Helen Fisher

CHARITIES AID FOUNDATION (1924), Kings Hill, West Malling, Kent ME19 4TA. Tel: 01732-520000; Fax: 01732-520001; Email: enquiries@caf.charitynet.org; Web: www.cafonline.org; *Chief Executive*, M. Brophy

CHARTERED INSTITUTE OF ARBITRATORS (1915), 12 Bloomsbury Square, London WC1A 2LP. Tel: 020-7421 7444; Fax: 020-7404 4023; Email: info@arbitrators.org; Web: www.arbitrators.org; *Secretary-General*, D. Farrar-Hockley

CHARTERED INSTITUTE OF ENVIRONMENTAL HEALTH, Chadwick Court, 15 Hatfields, London SE1 8DJ. Tel: 020-7928 6006; Fax: 020-7827 5866; Email: cieh@dial.pipex.com; Web: www.cieh.org.uk; *Director of Professional Services*, G. Jukes

CHARTERED INSTITUTE OF PATENT AGENTS (1882), Staple Inn Buildings, High Holborn, London WC1V 7PZ. Tel: 020-7405 9450; Fax: 020-7430 0471; Email: mail@cipa.org.uk; Web: www.cipa.org.uk; *Secretary and Registrar*, M. C. Ralph

CHARTERED INSTITUTE OF PUBLIC FINANCE AND ACCOUNTANCY (1885), 3 Robert Street, London WC2N 6BH. Tel: 020-7543 5600; Fax: 020-7543 5700; Web: www.cipfa.org.uk; *Chief Executive*, S. Freer

CHARTERED INSTITUTION OF BUILDING SERVICES ENGINEERS, Delta House, 222 Balham High Road, London SW12 9BS. Tel: 020-8675 5211; Fax: 020-8675 5449; *Chief Executive*, R. John

CHARTERED INSTITUTION OF WATER AND ENVIRONMENTAL MANAGEMENT, 15 John Street, London WC1N 2EB. Tel: 020-7831 3110; Fax: 020-7405 4967; *Executive Director*, N. Reeves

CHILDREN 1ST (ROYAL SCOTTISH SOCIETY FOR PREVENTION OF CRUELTY TO CHILDREN) (1884), 41 Polwarth Terrace, Edinburgh EH11 1NU. Tel: 0131-337 8539; Fax: 0131-346 8284; Email: info@children1st.org.uk; Web: www.children1st.org.uk; *Chief Executive*, Margaret McKay

THE CHILDREN'S SOCIETY, Edward Rudolf House, Margery Street, London WC1X 0JL. Tel: 020-7841 4000; Fax: 020-7841 4500; Web: www.the-childrens-society.org.uk; *Chief Executive*, I. Sparks

CHINA ASSOCIATION (1891), Swire House, 59 Buckingham Gate, London SW1E 6AJ. Tel: 020-7963 9446/45; Fax: 020-7630 0353; *Executive Director*, D. F. L. Turner

CHRISTIAN AID SCOTLAND, 41 George IV Bridge, Edinburgh EH1 1EL. Tel: 0131-220 1254; Fax: 0131-225 8861; Email: edinburgh@christian-aid.org; Web: www.christian-aid.org.uk; *National Secretary*, Revd J. Wylie

CHURCH ARMY (1882), Independents Road, London SE3 9LG. Tel: 020-8318 1226; Fax: 020-8318 5258; Email: information@churcharmy.org.uk; Web: www.churcharmy.org.uk; *Chief Secretary*, Capt. P. Johanson

CHURCH EDUCATION CORPORATION (1903), Bedgebury School, Goudhurst, Cranbrook, Kent TN17 2SH. Tel: 01580-211221; Fax: 01580-212252; Email: info@bedgebury.ndirect.co.uk; Web: www.bedgebury.ndirect.co.uk; *Secretary*, J. N. Willoughby

CHURCH LADS' AND CHURCH GIRLS' BRIGADE (1891), 2 Barnsley Road, Wath upon Dearne, Rotherham, S. Yorks S63 6PY. Tel: 01709-876535; Fax: 01709-878089; Email: general-secretary@church-brigade.syol.com; Web: www.church-brigade.syol.com; *General Secretary*, A. J. Reed Screen

CHURCH MONUMENTS SOCIETY, c/o Society of Antiquaries, Burlington House, Piccadilly, London W1J 0BE. Tel: 020-7734 0193; Fax: 020-7287 6967; Email: john@bromilow.screaming.net; Web: freespace.virgin.net/john.bromilow/links.html; *Hon. Secretary*, Dr Sophie Oosterwijk

CHURCH OF ENGLAND PENSIONS BOARD (1926), 29 Great Smith Street, London SW1P 3PS. Tel: 020-7898 1800; Fax: 020-7898 1801; Email: enquiries@capbc-of-e.org.uk; *Secretary*, R. G. Radford

CHURCH UNION (1859), Faith House, 7 Tufton Street, London SW1P 3QN. Tel: 020-7222 6952; Fax: 020-7976 7180; Email: churchunion@care4free.net; Web: www.churchunion.care4free.net; *House Manager*, Mrs J. Miller

CHURCHES MAIN COMMITTEE (1941), Elizabeth House, 39 York Road, London SE1 7NQ. Tel: 020-7898 1878; Fax: 020-7898 1798; Email: cmc@c-of-e.org.uk; Web: www.cmainc.org.uk; *Secretary*, D. Taylor Thompson

CHURCH'S MINISTRY AMONG JEWISH PEOPLE (1809), 30C Clarence Road, St Albans, Herts AL1 4JJ. Tel: 01727-833114; Fax: 01727-848312; Email: enquiries@cmj.org.uk; Web: www.cmj.org.uk; *General Director*, Revd T. Higton

THE CHURCHILL SOCIETY – LONDON (1990), c/o 18 Grove Lane, Ipswich, Suffolk IP4 1NR. Tel: 01473-413533; Fax: 01473-413533; Email: secretary@churchill-society-london.org.uk; Web: www.churchill-society-london.org.uk/index.htm; *General Secretary*, N. H. Rogers

CITY BUSINESS LIBRARY (1970), Corporation of London, Brewers' Hall Garden, London EC2V 5BX. Tel: 020-7332 1812; Fax: 020-7332 1847; Web: www.cityoflondon.gov.uk; *Business Librarian*, G. P. Humphreys

CITY OF COVENTRY FREEMEN'S GUILD, 47 Brownshill Green Road, Coventry CV6 2AP. Tel: 024-7627 4321; *Hon. Clerk*, K. Talbot

THE CIVIC TRUST (1957), 17 Carlton House Terrace, London SW1Y 5AW. Tel: 020-7930 0914; Fax: 020-7321 0180; Email: pride@civictrust.org.uk; Web: www.civictrust.org.uk; *Chief Executive*, Martin Bacon

CLERGY ORPHAN CORPORATION, 1 Dean Trench Street, London SW1P 3HB. Tel: 020-7799 3696; Fax: 020-7233 1913; *Registrar*, R. A. M. Welsford

COMMONWEALTH SOCIETY FOR THE DEAF 'SOUND SEEKERS' (1959), 34 Buckingham Palace Road, London SW1W 0RE. Tel: 020-7233 5700; Fax: 020-7233 5800; Email: sound.seekers@btinternet.com; Web: www.sound-seekers.org.uk; *Chief Executive*, Brig. J. A. Davis

CONSUMERS' ASSOCIATION (1957), c/o The Association for Consumer Research, 2 Marylebone Road, London NW1 4DF. Tel: 020-7770 7000; Fax: 020-7770 7600; Email: which@which.net; Web: www.which.net; *Director*, Ms S. McKechnie

CONTEMPORARY APPLIED ARTS (1948), 2 Percy Street, London W1T 1DD. Tel: 020-7436 2344; Fax: 020-7436 2446; Web: www.caa.org.uk; *Director*, Ms M. La Trobe-Bateman

CO-OPERATIVE GROUP (CWS) LTD. (1863), PO Box 53, New Century House, Manchester M60 4ES. Tel: 0161-834 1212; Fax: 0161-834 4507; Web: www.co-op.co.uk; *Chief Executive*, G. J. Melmoth

CO-OPERATIVE PARTY, Victory House, 10–14 Leicester Square, London WC2H 7QH. Tel: 020-7439 0123; Fax: 020-7439 3434; *Secretary*, P. Hunt

CORAM FAMILY (1739), 49 Mecklenburgh Square, London WC1N 2QA. Tel: 020-7520 0300; Fax: 020-7520 0301; Email: reception@coram.org.uk; Web: www.coram.org.uk; *Chief Executive*, Dr G. Pugh

CORONER'S SOCIETY OF ENGLAND AND WALES (1846), 44 Ormond Avenue, Hampton, Middx TW12 2RX. Tel: 020-8979 6805; Fax: 020-8979 6805; Email: honsec.corsoc@btinternet.com; *Hon. Secretary*, M. J. C. Burgess

CORPORATION OF CHURCH HOUSE (1888), Church House, Dean's Yard, London SW1P 3NZ. Tel: 020-7898 1310; Fax: 020-7898 1321; *Secretary*, C. D. L. Menzies

COUNCIL FOR BRITISH ARCHAEOLOGY (1944), Bowes Morrell House, 111 Walmgate, York YO1 9WA. Tel: 01904-671417; Fax: 01904-671384; Email: info@britarch.ac.uk; Web: www.britarch.ac.uk; *Director*, G. Lambrick

COUNCIL FOR LICENSED CONVEYANCERS, 16 Glebe Road, Chelmsford, Essex CM1 1QG. Tel: 01245-349599; Fax: 01245-341300; Email: clc@theclc.gov.uk; *Director*, Mrs V. Eden

COUNCIL FOR THE CARE OF CHURCHES (1921), Church House, Great Smith Street, London SW1P 3NZ. Tel: 020-7898 1866; Fax: 020-7898 1881; Email: enquiries@ccc.c-of-e.org.uk; *Secretary*, Dr T. Cocke

COUNCIL FOR WORLD MISSION, Ipalo House, 32–34 Great Peter Street, London SW1P 2DB. Tel: 020-7222 4214; Fax: 020-7233 1747; Email: council@csmission.org.uk; Web: www.cwmission.org.uk; *General Secretary*, Dr D. P. Niles

COUNCIL OF CHRISTIANS AND JEWS (1942), 5th Floor, Camelford House, 87–89 Albert Embankment, London SE1 7TP. Tel: 020-7820 0090; Fax: 020-7820 0504; Email: cjrelations@ccj.org.uk; Web: www.ccj.org.uk; *Director*, Sr M. Shepherd

COUNSEL AND CARE (1954), Twyman House, 16 Bonny Street, London NW1 9PG. Tel: 020-7485 1550; Fax: 020-7267 6877; Email: advice@counselandcare.org.uk; Web: www.counselandcare.org.uk; *Chief Executive*, M. Green

COUNTRY LAND AND BUSINESS ASSOCIATION (1907), 16 Belgrave Square, London SW1X 8PQ. Tel: 020-7235 0511; Fax: 020-7235 4696; Email: mail@cla.org.uk; Web: www.cla.org.uk; *President*, A. Bosanquet

COUNTRYSIDE ALLIANCE (1998), Old Town Hall, 367 Kennington Road, London SE11 4PT. Tel: 020-7582 5432; Fax: 020-7793 8484; Email: info@countryside-alliance.org; Web: www.countryside-alliance.org; *Chairman*, J. Jackson

CPRE (COUNCIL FOR THE PROTECTION OF RURAL ENGLAND), Warwick House, 25 Buckingham Palace Road, London SW1W 0PP. Tel: 020-7976 6433; Fax: 020-7976 6373; Email: info@cpre.org.uk; Web: www.cpre.org.uk; *Director*, Ms K. Parminter

CRAFTS COUNCIL (1971), 44A Pentonville Road, London N1 9BY. Tel: 020-7278 7700; Fax: 020-7837 6891; Email: reference@craftscouncil.org.uk; Web: www.craftscouncil.org.uk; *Director*, Ms J. Barnes

CRISIS (1967), 1st Floor, Challenger House, 42 Adler Street, London E1 1EE. Tel: 020-7655 8300; Fax: 020-7247 1525; Email: enquiries@crisis.org.uk; Web: www.crisis.org.uk; *Chief Executive*, S. Ghosh

CROSSLINKS (1922), 251 Lewisham Way, London SE4 1XF. Tel: 020-8691 6111; Fax: 020-8694 8023; Email: mail@crosslinks.org; *General Secretary*, Revd A. Lines

CRUSE BEREAVEMENT CARE, 126 Sheen Road, Richmond, Surrey TW9 1UR. Tel: 020-8940 4818. Helpline: 0845-758 5565; Fax: 020-8940 7638; Web: www.crusebereavementcare.org.uk; *Executive Director*, Dr C. Easton

CTC (CYCLISTS' TOURING CLUB), 69 Meadrow, Godalming, Surrey GU7 3HS. Tel: 01483-417217; Fax: 01483-426994; Email: cycling@ctc.org.uk; Web: www.ctc.org.uk; *Director*, K. Mayne

CWMNI URDD GOBAITH CYMRU (1922), Swyddfa'r Urdd, Aberystwyth, Sir Ceredigion SY23 1EN. Tel: 01970-613100; Fax: 01970-626120; Email: urdd@urdd.org; Web: www.urdd.org; *Chief Executive*, J. O'Rourke

CYSTIC FIBROSIS TRUST (1964), 11 London Road, Bromley, Kent BR1 1BY. Tel: 020-8464 7211; Fax: 020-8313 0472; Email: info@cftrust.org.uk; Web: www.cftrust.org.uk; *Chief Executive*, Ms R. Barnes

DESIGN AND INDUSTRIES ASSOCIATION, 2 Lawford Road, Grove Park, Chiswick, London W4 3HS. Tel: 020-8747 0766; Email: info@dia.org.uk; Web: www.dia.org.uk; *Chairman*, Paul Williams

DIANA, PRINCESS OF WALES MEMORIAL FUND (1997), County Hall, Westminster Bridge Road, London SE1 7PB. Tel: 020-7902 5500; Fax: 020-7902 5511; Email: memorial.fund@memfund.org.uk; Web: www.theworkcontinues.org.uk; *Chief Executive*, Dr A. Purkis

DICKENS FELLOWSHIP (1902), Dickens House, 48 Doughty Street, London WC1N 2LX. Tel: 020-7405 2127; Fax: 020-7831 5175; Email: arwilliams33@compuserve.com; Web: www.dickens.fellowship.btinternet.co.uk; *Joint Hon. General Secretaries*, Mrs T. Grove; Dr T. Williams

DIRECTORY & DATABASE PUBLISHERS ASSOCIATION (1970), PO Box 23034, London W6 0RJ. Tel: 020-8846 9707; Fax: 0870 168 0552; Web: www.directory-publisher.co.uk; *Secretary*, Ms R. Pettit

DITCHLEY FOUNDATION (1958), Ditchley Park, Enstone, Chipping Norton, Oxon OX7 4ER. Tel: 01608-677346; Fax: 01608-677399; Email: mail@ditchley.co.uk; Web: www.ditchley.co.uk; *Director*, Sir Nigel Broomfield

DOWNS SYNDROME ASSOCIATION (1970), 155 Mitcham Road, London SW17 9PG. Tel: 020-8682 4001; Fax: 020-8682 4012; Email: info@downs-syndrome.org.uk; Web: www.downs-syndrome.org.uk; *Director*, Ms C. Boys

DRUGSCOPE 32–36 Loman Street, London SE1 0EE. Tel: 020-7928 1211; Fax: 020-7928 1771; Email: services@drugscope.org.uk; Web: www.drugscope.org.uk; *Chief Executive*, R. Howard

DUKE OF EDINBURGH'S AWARD, Gulliver House, Madeira Walk, Windsor, Berks SL4 1EU. Tel: 01753-727400; Fax: 01753-810666; Email: info@theaward.org; Web: www.theaward.org; *Director*, Vice-Adm. M. P. Gretton

DYSLEXIA INSTITUTE, 133 Gresham Road, Staines, Middx TW18 2AJ. Tel: 01784-463851; Fax: 01784-460747; Email: info@dyslexia-inst.org.uk; Web: www.dyslexia-inst.org.uk; *Chief Executive*, Shirley Cramer

EATING DISORDERS ASSOCIATION, First Floor, Wensum House, 103 Prince of Wales Road, Norwich NR1 1DW. Tel: Helpline: 01603-621414. Youthline: 01603-765050; Fax: 01603-664915; Email: info@edauk.com; Web: www.edauk.com; *Chief Executive*, Mrs N. Bryant

ECCLESIASTICAL HISTORY SOCIETY, Department of History (Medieval), University of Glasgow, Glasgow G12 8QQ. Tel: 0141-330 4087; Fax: 0141-330 5056; Email: M.Kennedy@medhist.arts.gla.ac.uk; *President*, Prof. Henry Mayr-Harting

EDITH CAVELL AND NATION'S FUND FOR NURSES (1920), Flints, Petersfield Road, Winchester, Hants SO23 0JD. Tel: 01962-860900; Fax: 01962-860900; Email: natnurses.fund@virgin.net; *Administrator*, Mrs A. Rich

EDWINA MOUNTBATTEN TRUST (1960), Estate Office, Broadlands, Romsey, Hants SO51 9ZE. Tel: 01794-518885; *Trust Secretary*, J. Moss

EGYPT EXPLORATION SOCIETY, 3 Doughty Mews, London WC1N 2PG. Tel: 020-7242 1880; Fax: 020-7404 6118; Email: eeslondon@talk21.com; Web: www.ees.ac.uk; *Secretary*, Dr P. A. Spencer

ELECTORAL REFORM SOCIETY (1884), 6 Chancel Street, London SE1 0UU. Tel: 020-7928 1622; Fax: 020-7401 7789; Email: ers@reform.demon.co.uk; Web: www.electoral-reform.org.uk; *President*, Rt Hon. Prof. The Earl Russell

ELGAR FOUNDATION, The Elgar Birthplace Museum, Lower Broadheath, Worcester WR2 6RH. Tel: 01905-333224; Fax: 01905-333224; Email: birthplace@elgar.org; Web: www.elgar.org; *Administrator*, John Lowles

ELGAR SOCIETY (1951), c/o 29 Van Diemens Close, Chinnor, Oxon OX39 4QE. Tel: 01844-354096; Fax: 01844-354459; Email: elgar@music.com; Web: www.elgar.org; *Hon. Secretary*, Ms W. Hillary

EMERGENCY PLANNING SOCIETY (1993), Northumberland House, 11 The Pavement, Popes Lane, London W5 4NG. Tel: 020-8579 7971; Fax: 020-8579 7972; Email: headquarters@emergplansoc.org.uk; Web: www.emergplansoc.org.uk; *Hon. Secretary*, I. Hoult

ENABLE (SCOTTISH SOCIETY FOR THE MENTALLY HANDICAPPED) (1954), 7 Buchanan Street, Glasgow G1 3HL. Tel: 0141-226 4541; Fax: 0141-204 4398; Email: enable@enable.org.uk; *Director*, N. Dunning

THE ENGINEERING COUNCIL, 10 Maltravers Street, London WC2R 3ER. Tel: 020-7240 7891; Fax: 020-7240 7517; Email: mcshirley@engc.org.uk; Web: www.engc.org.uk; *Director General*, M. Shirley

ENGINEERING INDUSTRIES ASSOCIATION (1940), Broadway House, Tothill Street, London SW1H 9NS. Tel: 020-7222 2367; Fax: 020-7799 2206; Email: info@eia.co.uk; Web: www.eia.co.uk; *Director*, C. J. Mason

THE ENGLISH ASSOCIATION (1906), University of Leicester, University Road, Leicester LE1 7RH. Tel: 0116-252 3982; Fax: 0116-252 2301; Email: engassoc@le.ac.uk; Web: www.le.ac.uk/engassoc; *Chief Executive*, Ms H. Lucas

ENGLISH FOLK DANCE AND SONG SOCIETY (1932), Cecil Sharp House, 2 Regent's Park Road, London NW1 7AY. Tel: 020-7485 2206; Fax: 020-7284 0534; Web: www.efdss.org.com; *Chief Executive*, T. Walker

ENGLISH NATIONAL BOARD FOR NURSING, MIDWIFERY AND HEALTH VISITING, Victory House, 170 Tottenham Court Road, London W1P 0HA. Tel: 020-7391 6229; Fax: 020-7383 4031; Email: ceo@enb.org.uk; Web: www.enb.org.uk; *Chief Executive*, A. P. Smith

ENGLISH-SPEAKING UNION OF THE COMMONWEALTH (1918), Dartmouth House, 37 Charles Street, London W1J 5ED. Tel: 020-7529 1550; Fax: 020-7495 6108; Email: esu@esu.org; Web: www.esu.org; *Director General*, Mrs V. Mitchell

THE ENVIRONMENT COUNCIL, 212 High Holborn, London WC1V 7BF. Tel: 020-7836 2626; Fax: 020-7242 1180; Web: www.the-environment-council.org.uk; *Chief Executive*, S. Robinson

ERSKINE HOSPITAL (1916),Bishopton, Renfrewshire PA7 5PU. Tel: 0141-812 1100; Fax: 0141-812 3733; Email: enquiries@erskine.org.uk; Web: www.erskine.org/welcome.htm; *Chief Executive*, Col. M. F. Gibson

ESPERANTO ASSOCIATION OF BRITAIN, Wedgwood Memorial College, Barlaston, Stoke-on-Trent ST12 9DG. Tel: 01782-372105; Fax: 01782-372393; Email: eabo@esperanto.demon.co.uk; Web: www.esperanto.demon.co.uk; *Hon. Secretary*, E. Walker

EVANGELICAL LIBRARY, 78A Chiltern Street, London W1U 5HB. Tel: 020-7935 6997; Email: stlibrary@aol.com; Web: www.elib.org.uk; *Librarian*, S. J. Taylor

EX-SERVICES MENTAL WELFARE SOCIETY (1919), Hollybush House, Hollybush, nr Ayr KA6 7EA. Tel: 01292-560214; Fax: 01292-560871; Web: www.combatstress.com; *Regional Director Scotland and Ireland*, Wg Cdr D. Devine

F.A.N.Y. (PRINCESS ROYAL'S VOLUNTEER CORPS) (1907), Right Wing, Duke of York's HQ, Turks Row, London SW3 4RY. Tel: 020-7730 2058; Fax: 020-7414 5399; Email: fanyhq@cwcom.net; Web: www.fany.org.uk; *Corps Commander*, Mrs L. Rose

FABIAN SOCIETY, 11 Dartmouth Street, London SW1H 9BN. Tel: 020-7227 4900; Fax: 020-7976 7153; Email: info@fabian-society.org.uk; Web: www.fabian-society.org.uk; *General Secretary*, M. Jacobs

FACULTY OF ROYAL DESIGNERS FOR INDUSTRY, RSA, 8 John Adam Street, London WC2N 6EZ. Tel: 020-7451 6801; Fax: 020-7839 5805; Email: rdi@rsa-uk.demon.co.uk; Web: www.rsa.org.uk

FAIR ISLE BIRD OBSERVATORY TRUST (1948), Fair Isle Bird Observatory, Fair Isle, Shetland ZE2 9JU. Tel: 01595-760258; Fax: 01595-760258; Email: fairisle.birdobs@zetnet.co.uk; Web: www.fairislebirdobs.co.uk

FEDERATION OF BRITISH ARTISTS (1961), 17 Carlton House Terrace, London SW1Y 5BD. Tel: 020-7930 6844; Fax: 020-7839 7830; Web: www.mallgalleries.org.uk; *Chairman*, T. Muir

FEDERATION OF FAMILY HISTORY SOCIETIES (1974), PO Box 2425, Coventry, CV5 6YX. Tel: 07041-492032; Fax: 07041-492032; Email: info@ffhs.org.uk; Web: www.ffhs.org.uk; *Administrator*, Maggie Loughran

FIELD STUDIES COUNCIL (1943), Preston Montford, Montford Bridge, Shrewsbury SY4 1HW. Tel: 01743-852100; Fax: 01743-852101; Email: fsc.headoffice@ukonline.co.uk; Web: www.field-studies-council.org; *Chief Executive*, A. D. Thomas

FIRE PROTECTION ASSOCIATION (1946), Bastille Court, 2 Paris Garden, London SE1 8ND. Tel: 020-7902 5300; Fax: 020-7902 5301; Email: fpa@thefpa.co.uk; Web: www.thefpa.co.uk; *Managing Director*, Chris Mounsey

FLEET AIR ARM OFFICERS' ASSOCIATION (1957), 4 St James's Square, London SW1Y 4JU. Tel: 020-7930 7722; Fax: 020-7930 7728; Email: faaoa@fleetairarmoa.org; Web: www.fleetairarmoa.org; *Administration Director*, Cdr J. D. O. Macdonald

FOLEY HOUSE RESIDENTIAL HOME FOR DEAF PEOPLE, Foley House, 115 High Garrett, Braintree, Essex CM7 5NU. Tel: 01376-326652; Fax: 01376-553350; Email: info@foleyhouse.org.uk; Web: www.foleyhouse.org.uk; *Director*, J. Bethell

FOOD FROM BRITAIN, 123 Buckingham Palace Road, London SW1W 9SA. Tel: 020-7233 3111; Fax: 020-7233 9515; Email: jfletcher@foodfrombritain.co.uk; Web: www.foodfrombritain.com; *Chief Executive*, D. McNair

FORCES PENSION SOCIETY (1946), 68 South Lambeth Road, London SW8 1RL. Tel: 020-7820 9988; Fax: 020-7820 7583; Email: memsec@forpen.co.uk; Web: www.forpen.co.uk; *General Secretary*, Maj.-Gen. J. C. M. Gordon

FOREIGN PRESS ASSOCIATION IN LONDON (1888), 11 Carlton House Terrace, London SW1Y 5AJ. Tel: 020-7930 0445; Fax: 020-7925 0469; Email: secretariat@foreign-press.org.uk; Web: www.foreign-press.org.uk; *Secretary*, Ms D. Crole

FOUNDATION FOR THE STUDY OF INFANT DEATHS, 11–19 Artillery Row, London SW1P 1RT. Tel: 020-7222 8001. Helpline: 020-7233 2090; Fax: 020-7222 8002; Email: fsid@sids.org.uk; Web: www.sids.org.uk/fsid; *Director*, Mrs J. Epstein

FRANCO-BRITISH SOCIETY, Room 623, Linen Hall, 162–168 Regent Street, London W1R 5TB. Tel: 020-7734 0815; Fax: 020-7734 0815; *Executive Secretary*, Mrs K. Brayn

FREEMEN OF ENGLAND AND WALES (1966), Glenrise, Churchfields, Stonesfield, Witney, Oxon OX8 8PP. Tel: 01993-891414; *Immediate Past President*, R. J. M. Bishop

FRIENDS OF CATHEDRAL MUSIC (1956), Aeron House, Llangeitho, Tregaron, Ceredigion SY25 6SU. Email: info@fcm.org.uk; Web: www.fcm.org.uk; *Secretary*, M. J. Cooke

FRIENDS OF FRIENDLESS CHURCHES (1957), St Ann's Vestry Hall, 2 Church Entry, London EC4V 5HB. Tel: 020-7236 3934; Fax: 020-7329 3677; Email: ancientmonuments@talk21.com; *Hon. Director*, M. Saunders

FRIENDS OF THE BODLEIAN (1925), Bodleian Library, Oxford OX1 3BG. Tel: 01865-277022/277234; Fax: 01865-277182/277187; Email: fob@bodley.ox.ac.uk; Web: www.bodley.ox.ac.uk/friends; *Secretary*, G. Groom

FRIENDS OF THE EARTH SCOTLAND (1978), 72 Newhaven Road, Edinburgh EH6 5QG. Tel: 0131-554 9977; Fax: 0131-554 8656; Email: info@foe-scotland.org.uk; Web: www.foe-scotland.org.uk; *Director*, K. Dunion

FRIENDS OF THE ELDERLY (1905), 40–42 Ebury Street, London SW1W 0LZ. Tel: 020-7730 8263; Fax: 020-7259 0154; *Chief Executive*, Geoffrey Dennis

FRIENDS OF THE NATIONAL LIBRARIES, c/o Department of Manuscripts, The British Library, 96 Euston Road, London NW1 2DB. Tel: 020-7412 7559; *Chairman*, Lord Egremont

FURNITURE HISTORY SOCIETY (1964), 1 Mercedes Cottages, St John's Road, Haywards Heath, W. Sussex RH16 4EH. Tel: 01444-413845; Fax: 01444-413845; *Membership Secretary*, Dr B. Austen

GALLIPOLI ASSOCIATION (1969), Earleydene Orchard, Earleydene, Ascot, Berks SL5 9JY. Tel: 01344-626523; Email: webmaster@gallipoli-association.org; Web: www.gallipoli-association.org; *Hon. Secretary*, J. C. Watson Smith

GALTON INSTITUTE (1907), 19 Northfields Prospect, London SW18 1PE. *General Secretary*, Mrs B. Nixon

GARDEN HISTORY SOCIETY, 70 Cowcross Street, London EC1M 6EJ. Tel: 020-7608 2409; Fax: 020-7490 2974; Email: gardenhistorysociety@compuserve.com; *Director*, Ms L. Wigley

GARDENERS' ROYAL BENEVOLENT SOCIETY (1839), Bridge House, 139 Kingston Road, Leatherhead, Surrey KT22 7NT. Tel: 01372-373962; Fax: 01372-362575; Email: info@gardeners-grbs.org.uk; Web: www.gardeners-grbs.org.uk; *Chief Executive*, R. T. Capewell

GEMMOLOGICAL ASSOCIATION AND GEM TESTING LABORATORY OF GREAT BRITAIN (1931), 27 Greville Street, (Saffron Hill entrance), London EC1N 8TN. Tel: 020-7404 3334; Fax: 020-7404 8843; Email: gagtl@btinternet.com; Web: www.gagtl.com; *Director*, Dr R. R. Harding

GENERAL DENTAL COUNCIL, 37 Wimpole Street, London W1G 8DQ. Tel: 020-7887 3800; Fax: 020-7224 3294; *Chief Executive & Registrar*, Anthony Townsend

GENERAL OPTICAL COUNCIL (1959), 41 Harley Street, London W1G 8DJ. Tel: 020-7580 3898; Fax: 020-7436 3525; Email: goc@optical.org; Web: www.optical.org; *Chief Executive and Registrar*, P. C. Coe

GENERAL OSTEOPATHIC COUNCIL (1993), Osteopathy House, 176 Tower Bridge Road, London SE1 3LU. Tel: 020-7357 6655; Fax: 020-7357 0011; Email: info@osteopathy.org.uk; Web: www.osteopathy.org.uk; *Chief Executive & Registrar*, Miss M. J. Craggs

GEOLOGICAL SOCIETY (1807), Burlington House, Piccadilly, London W1V 0JU. Tel: 020-7434 9944; Fax: 020-7439 8975; Email: enquiries@geolsoc.org.uk; Web: www.geolsoc.org.uk; *Executive Secretary*, E. Nickless

GEOLOGISTS' ASSOCIATION, Burlington House, Piccadilly, London W1V 9AG. Tel: 020-7434 9296; Fax: 020-7287 0280; Email: geol.assoc@btinternet.com; *Executive Secretary*, Mrs S. Stafford

GEORGIAN GROUP (1937), 6 Fitzroy Square, London W1T 5DX. Tel: 020-7387 1720; Fax: 020-7387 1721; Email: office@georgian-group.org.uk; *Secretary*, N. Burton

GILBERT AND SULLIVAN SOCIETY, 1 Nethercourt Avenue, London N3 1PS. Hon. Secretary, *Ms M. Bowden*

GILD OF FREEMEN OF THE CITY OF YORK (1953), 29 Albermarle Road, York YO23 1EW. Tel: 01904-653698; Fax: 0870-052 9911; Email: gild@bedern.demon.co.uk; Web: www.bedern.demon.co.uk; *Hon. Clerk*, R. Lee

GLASGOW CHAMBER OF COMMERCE AND MANUFACTURES (1783), 30 George Square, Glasgow G2 1EQ. Tel: 0141-204 2121; Fax: 0141-221 2336; Email: chamber@glasgowchamber.org; Web: www.glasgowchamber.org; *Chief Executive*, Duncan Tannahill

THE GOOD GARDENERS' ASSOCIATION (1966), 4 Lisle Place, Wotton-under-Edge, Glos GL12 7AZ. Tel: 01453-520322; Web: www.goodgardeners.org.uk; *Hon. Director*, M.C. Adams

GRAND LODGE OF ANCIENT FREE AND ACCEPTED MASONS OF SCOTLAND (1736), Freemasons' Hall, 96 George Street, Edinburgh EH2 3DH. Tel: 0131-225 5304; Fax: 0131-225 3953; Web: www.grandlodgescotland.com; *Grand Master Mason*, A. D. Orr Ewing

GRAND LODGE OF MARK MASTER MASONS, Mark Masons' Hall, 86 St James's Street, London SW1A 1PL. Tel: 020-7839 5274; Fax: 020-7930 9750; *Grand Secretary*, T. J. Lewis

GREEK INSTITUTE, 34 Bush Hill Road, London N21 2DS. Tel: 020-8360 7968; Fax: 020-8360 7698; *Director*, Dr K. Tofallis

GREENPEACE UK, Canonbury Villas, London N1 2PN. Tel: 020-7865 8100; Fax: 020-7865 8200; Email: info@uk.greenpeace.org; Web: www.greenpeace.org.uk; *Executive Director*, Stephen Tindale

THE GUIDE ASSOCIATION (1910), 17–19 Buckingham Palace Road, London SW1W 0PT. Tel: 020-7834 6242; Fax: 020-7828 8317; Email: chq@guides.org.uk; Web: www.guides.org.uk; *Chief Guide*, Miss B. E. Towle

GUILD OF AID FOR GENTLEPEOPLE, 10 St Christopher's Place, London W1U 1HZ. Tel: 020-7935 0641; *Secretary*, Miss N. E. Inkson

GUILD OF FREEMEN OF THE CITY OF LONDON, PO Box 153, 40A Ludgate Hill, London EC4M 7DE. *Clerk*, Col. D. Ivy

GUILD OF GLASS ENGRAVERS (1975), 35 Ossulton Way, London N2 0JY. Tel: 020-8731 9352; Fax: 020-8731 9352; Email: admin.gge@talk21.com; *Secretary*, Ms C. Weatherhead

GUILD OF HEALTH, PO Box 227, Epsom KT19 9WQ. Tel: 020-8786 0517; Fax: 020-8786 0517; Email: gohealth@freeserve.com; Web: www.gohealth.org.uk; *General Secretary and Chaplain*, Revd A. Lynn

GUILD OF PASTORAL PSYCHOLOGY (1937), PO Box 1107, London W3 6ZP. Tel: 020-8993 8366; Fax: 020-8993 3148; Email: nvs@gpp.ndo.co.uk; Web: www.guildofpastoralpsychology.org.uk; *Chairman*, Revd Lyn Phillips

GURKHA WELFARE TRUST (1969), 2nd Floor, 1 Old Street, London EC1V 9XB. Tel: 020-7251 5234; Fax: 020-7251 5248; Email: secretary@gwt.org.uk; Web: www.gwt.org.uk; *Director*, E. D. Powell-Jones

HAEMOPHILIA SOCIETY, Chesterfield House, 385 Euston Road, London NW1 3AU. Tel: 020-7380 0600; Fax: 020-7387 8220; Email: info@haemophilia.org.uk; Web: www.haemophilia.org.uk; *Chief Executive*, Ms K. Pappenheim

HAIG HOMES, Alban Dobson House, Green Lane, Morden, Surrey SM4 5NS. Tel: 020-8685 5777; Fax: 020-8685 5778; Email: haig@haighomes.org.uk; Web: www.haighomes.org.uk; *Director*, A. N. Carlier

THE HAKLUYT SOCIETY, c/o Map Library, The British Library, 96 Euston Road, London NW1 2DB. Tel: 01986-788359; Fax: 01986-788181; Email: office@hakluyt.com; Web: www.hakluyt.com; *Hon. Secretary*, Dr A. Cook

THE HANSARD SOCIETY FOR PARLIAMENTARY GOVERNMENT, St Philips Building North, Sheffield Street, London WC2A 2EX. Tel: 020-7955 7459; Fax: 020-7955 7492; Email: hansard@hansard.lse.ac.uk; Web: www.hansardsociety.org.uk; *Director*, Mrs S. Diplock

HARVEIAN SOCIETY OF LONDON (1831), Lettsom House, 11 Chandos Street, London W1M 0EB. Tel: 020-7580 1043; Fax: 020-7580 5793; *Executive Secretary*, Col. R. Kinsella-Bevan

HAWICK ARCHAEOLOGICAL SOCIETY, Orrock House, Stirches Road, Hawick, Roxburghshire TD9 7HF. Tel: 01450-375546; *Hon. Secretary*, I. W. Landles

HELP THE AGED (1961), 207-221 Pentonville Road, London N2 9UZ. Tel: 020-7278 1114; Fax: 020-7278 1116; Email: info@helptheaged.org.uk; Web: www.helptheaged.org.uk; *Director General*, C. M. Lake

THE HERALDRY SOCIETY (1947), PO Box 32, Maidenhead, Berks SL6 3FD. Tel: 0118-932 0210; Fax: 0118-932 0210; Email: heraldry-society@cwcom.net; *Secretary*, Mrs M. Miles

HISPANIC AND LUSO BRAZILIAN COUNCIL (1943), Canning House, 2 Belgrave Square, London SW1X 8PJ. Tel: 020-7235 2303; Fax: 020-7235 3587; Email: enquiries@canninghouse.com; Web: www.canninghouse.com; *Director General*, P. A. McLean

HISTORIC HOUSES ASSOCIATION, 2 Chester Street, London SW1X 7BB. Tel: 020-7259 5688; Fax: 020-7259 5590; Email: hha@compuserve.com; Web: www.hha.org.uk; *Director General*, R. C. Wilkin

THE HISTORICAL ASSOCIATION (1906), 59A Kennington Park Road, London SE11 4JH. Tel: 020-7735 3901; Fax: 020-7582 4989; Email: enquiry@history.org.uk; Web: www.history.org.uk; *Chief Executive*, Mrs M. Stiles

HONG KONG ASSOCIATION, Swire House, 59 Buckingham Gate, London SW1E 6AJ. Tel: 020-7963 9445/47; Fax: 020-7630 0353; *Executive Director*, D. F. L. Turner

HONOURABLE SOCIETY OF CYMMRODORION (1751), 30 Eastcastle Street, London W1N 7PD. Tel: 020-7631 0502; Email: cymmrodorion@tinyworld.co.uk; Web: www.cymmrodorion1751.org.uk; *Hon. Secretary*, J. Samuel

THE HOSPITAL SATURDAY FUND (1873), 24 Upper Ground, London SE1 9PD. Tel: 020-7928 6662; Fax: 020-7928 0446; Email: sales@hsf.co.uk; Web: www.hsf.co.uk; *Chief Executive*, K. R. Bradley

HOSTELLING INTERNATIONAL NORTHERN IRELAND, 22–32 Donegall Road, Belfast BT12 5JN. Tel: 028-9032 4733; Fax: 028-9043 9699; Email: info@hini.org.uk; Web: www.hini.org.uk; *Hon. Secretary*, D. Forsythe

HOTEL AND CATERING INTERNATIONAL MANAGEMENT ASSOCIATION, 191 Trinity Road, London SW17 7HN. Tel: 020-8772 7400; Fax: 020-8772 7500; Email: library@hcima.org.uk; Web: www.hcima.org.uk; *Chief Executive*, D. Wood

HOUSE OF ST BARNABAS-IN-SOHO, 1 Greek Street, London W1V 6NQ. Tel: 020-7434 1846; Fax: 020-7434 1746; *Director*, Ms W. Taylor

THE HOVERCRAFT SOCIETY AND MUSEUM TRUST, c/o 15 St Mark's Road, Alverstoke, Gosport, Hants PO12 2DA. Tel: 02392-552090; Fax: 02392-552090; Email: chris@hovercraft-museum.org; Web: www.hovercraft-museum.org; *Chairman*, S. Syrad

THE HOWARD LEAGUE FOR PENAL REFORM, 1 Ardleigh Road, London N1 4HS. Tel: 020-7249 7373; Fax: 020-7249 7789; Email: howard.league@ukonline.co.uk; Web: www.howardleague.org; *Director*, Ms F. Crook

HUGUENOT SOCIETY OF GREAT BRITAIN AND IRELAND (1885), The Huguenot Library, University College, Gower Street, London WC1E 6BT. Tel: 020-7679 7094; Email: s.massil@ucl.ac.uk; Web: www.ucl.ac.uk/UCL-INFO/Divisions/Library/Huguenot.htm; *Hon. Secretary*, Mrs M. Bayliss

HUMANE RESEARCH TRUST, Brook House, 29 Bramhall Lane South, Bramhall, Stockport, Cheshire SK7 2DN. Tel: 0161-439 8041; Fax: 0161-439 3713; Email: members@humane.freeserve.co.uk; *Chairman*, K. Cholerton

HYDROGRAPHIC SOCIETY (1972), c/o University of East London, Longbridge Road, Dagenham, Essex RM8 2AS. Tel: 020-8597 1946; Fax: 020-8590 9730; Email: hydrosoc@compuserve.com; Web: www.hydrographicsociety.org; *Hon. Secretary*, P. J. H. Warden

HYMN SOCIETY OF GREAT BRITAIN AND IRELAND (1936), 7 Paganel Road, Minehead, Somerset TA24 5ET. Tel: 01643-703530; Fax: 01643-703530; Email: g.wrayford@breathemail.net; *Secretary*, Revd G. Wrayford

ICAN (THE NATIONAL EDUCATIONAL CHARITY FOR CHILDREN WITH SPEECH AND LANGUAGE DIFFICULTIES), 4 Dyers Buildings, Holborn, London EC1N 2QP. Tel: 0870-010 4066; Fax: 0870-010 4067; Email: ican@ican.org.uk; *Chief Executive*, Ms G. Edelman

IMMIGRATION ADVISORY SERVICE (1970), County House, 190 Great Dover Street, London SE1 4YB. Tel: 020-7357 7511; Fax: 020-7403 5875; Email: advice@iasuk.org; Web: www.iasuk.org; *Chief Executive*, Keith Best

IMPERIAL CANCER RESEARCH FUND, Scottish Fundraising Centre, Wallace House, Maxwell Place, Stirling FK8 1JU. Tel: 01786-446689; Fax: 01786-446691; Email: l.brady@icrf.icnet.uk; Web: www.imperialcancer.co.uk; *Fundraising Director*, L. J. Brady

INCORPORATED CHURCH BUILDING SOCIETY, Fulham Palace, London SW6 6EA. Tel: 020-7736 3054; *Secretary*, M. W. Tippen

INCORPORATED COUNCIL OF LAW REPORTING FOR ENGLAND AND WALES (1865), Megarry House, 119 Chancery Lane, London WC2A 1PP. Tel: 020-7242 6471; Fax: 020-7831 5247; Email: postmaster@iclr.co.uk; Web: www.lawreports.co.uk; *Secretary*, J. Cobbett

INCORPORATED SOCIETY OF MUSICIANS (1882), 10 Stratford Place, London W1N 9AE. Tel: 020-7629 4413; Fax: 020-7408 1538; Email: membership@ism.org; Web: www.ism.org; *Chief Executive*, N. Hoyle

INDEPENDENT SCHOOLS' BURSARS ASSOCIATION (1932), 5 Chapel Close, Old Basing, Basingstoke, Hants RG24 7BZ. Tel: 01256-330369; Fax: 01256-330376; Email: office@isba.uk.com; Web: www.isba.uk.com; *General Secretary*, M. J. Sant

INDEPENDENT SCHOOLS CAREERS ORGANISATION (1973), 12A Princess Way, Camberley, Surrey GU15 3SP. Tel: 01276-21188; Fax: 01276-691833; Email: info@isco.org.uk; Web: www.isco.org.uk; *National Director*, J. D. Stuart

INDEPENDENT SCHOOLS COUNCIL (1986), Grosvenor Gardens House, 35–37 Grosvenor Gardens, London SW1W 0BS. Tel: 020-7798 1590; Fax: 020-7798 1591; Email: isc@isc.org.uk; Web: www.isc.org.uk; *General Secretary*, Dr A. B. Cooke

INDEPENDENT SCHOOLS INFORMATION SERVICE (1972), Grosvenor Gardens House, 35–37 Grosvenor Gardens, London SW1W 0BS. Tel: 020-7798 1500; Fax: 020-7798 1501; Email: national@isis.org.uk; Web: www.isis.org.uk; *Director*, D. J. Woodhead

INDUSTRIAL CHRISTIAN FELLOWSHIP, c/o St Matthews House, 100 George Street, Croydon CR0 1PE. Tel: 020-8656 1644; Fax: 020-8656 1644; *Chairman*, Revd M. Fass

INDUSTRIAL SOCIETY, Robert Hyde House, 48 Bryanston Square, London W1M 7LN. Tel: 020-7479 2000; Fax: 020-7479 2222; Web: www.indsoc.co.uk; *Chief Executive*, T. Morgan

INSTITUTE OF ACTUARIES (1848), Staple Inn Hall, High Holborn, London WC1V 7QJ. Tel: 020-7632 2100; Fax: 020-7632 2111; Email: institute@actuaries.org.uk; Web: www.actuaries.org.uk; *President*, P. N. S. Clark

INSTITUTE OF ADMINISTRATIVE MANAGEMENT (1915), 40 Chatsworth Parade, Petts Wood, Orpington, Kent BR5 1RW. Tel: 01689-875555; Fax: 01689-891541; Email: enquiries@instam.org; Web: www.instam.org; *Chief Executive*, Alan King

INSTITUTE OF CANCER RESEARCH: ROYAL CANCER HOSPITAL (1909), 123 Old Brompton Road, London SW7 3RP. Tel: 020-7352 8133; Fax: 020-7370 5261; Web: www.icr.ac.uk; *Chief Executive*, Dr P. W. J. Rigby

INSTITUTE OF CAST METAL ENGINEERS, Bordesley Hall, The Holloway, Alvechurch, Birmingham B48 7QA. Tel: 01527-596100; Fax: 01527-596102; Email: info@icme.org.uk; Web: www.icme.org.uk; *Secretary*, A. M. Turner

INSTITUTE OF CHARTERED ACCOUNTANTS IN ENGLAND AND WALES (1880), Chartered Accountants' Hall, PO Box 433, Moorgate Place, London EC2P 2BJ. Tel: 020-7920 8100; Fax: 020-7920 0547; *Secretary-General*, J. S. Collier

INSTITUTE OF CHARTERED SECRETARIES AND ADMINISTRATORS (1891), 16 Park Crescent, London W1N 4AH. Tel: 020-7580 4741; Fax: 020-7323 1132; Email: icsa@dial.pipex.com; Web: www.icsa.org.uk; *Chief Executive*, M. J. Ainsworth

INSTITUTE OF CHARTERED SHIPBROKERS, 3 St Helen's Place, London EC3A 6EJ. Tel: 020-7628 5559; Fax: 020-7628 5445; Email: info@ics.org.uk; Web: www.ics.org.uk; *Director*, Ms B. Fletcher

INSTITUTE OF CLERKS OF WORKS OF GREAT BRITAIN (1882), 41 The Mall, London W5 3TJ. Tel: 020-8579 2917; Fax: 020-8579 0554; Email: gensec@lcwgb.sagehost.co.uk; Web: www.lcwgb.com; *General Secretary*, D. McGeorge

INSTITUTE OF COMPANY ACCOUNTANTS (1928), 40 Tyndalls Park Road, Bristol BS8 1PL. Tel: 0117-973 8261; Fax: 0117-923 8292; *Director General*, B. T. Banks

INSTITUTE OF COMPLEMENTARY MEDICINE (1982), PO Box 194, London SE16 7QZ. Tel: 020-7237 5165; Fax: 020-7237 5175; Email: icm@icmedicine.co.uk; Web: www.icmedicine.co.uk; *Director*, A. Baird

INSTITUTE OF DIRECTORS, 116 Pall Mall, London SW1Y 5ED. Tel: 020-7839 1233; Fax: 020-7930 1949; *Chief Executive*, A. Mainwilson

INSTITUTE OF ECONOMIC AFFAIRS (1955), 2 Lord North Street, London SW1P 3LB. Tel: 020-7799 8900; Fax: 020-7799 2137; Email: iea@iea.org.uk; Web: www.iea.org.uk; *General Director*, J. Blundell

THE INSTITUTE OF ENERGY (1927), 18 Devonshire Street, London W1G 7AU. Tel: 020-7580 7124; Fax: 020-7580 4420; Email: info@instenergy.org.uk; Web: www.instenergy.org.uk; *Chief Executive and Secretary*, Ms L. Kingham

INSTITUTE OF EXPORT (1935), Minerva Business Park, Lynchwood, Peterborough PE2 6FT. Tel: 01733-404400; Email: institute@export.org.uk; Web: www.export.org.uk; *Director General*, I. J. Campbell

INSTITUTE OF FIELD ARCHAEOLOGISTS (1982), University of Reading, 2 Earley Gate, PO Box 239, Reading RG6 6AU. Tel: 0118-931 6446; Fax: 0118-931 6448; Email: admin.ifa@virgin.net; Web: www.archaeologists.net; *Director*, P. Hinton

INSTITUTE OF FOOD SCIENCE AND TECHNOLOGY (1964), 5 Cambridge Court, 210 Shepherd's Bush Road, London W6 7NJ. Tel: 020-7603 6316; Email: info@ifst.org; Web: www.ifst.org; *Chief Executive*, Ms H. G. Wild

INSTITUTE OF HEALTH PROMOTION AND EDUCATION, Department of Oral Health and Development, University Dental Hospital, Higher Cambridge Street, Manchester M15 6FH. Tel: 0161-275 6610; Fax: 0161-275 6299; Web: www.ihpe.org.uk; *Hon. Secretary*, Prof. A. S. Blinkhorn

INSTITUTE OF INFORMATION SCIENTISTS, 39–41 North Road, London N7 9DP. Tel: 020-7619 0624/5; Fax: 020-7619 0627; *Director*, M. F. Shearer

INSTITUTE OF LEGAL EXECUTIVES (1963), Kempston Manor, Kempston, Bedford MK42 7AB. Tel: 01234-841000; Fax: 01234-840373; Email: info@ilex.org.uk; Web: www.ilex.org.uk; *Secretary General*, Ms D. Burleigh

INSTITUTE OF LINGUISTS (1910), Saxon House, 48 Southwark Street, London SE1 1UN. Tel: 020-7940 3100; Fax: 020-7940 3101; Email: info@iol.org.uk; Web: www.iol.org.uk; *Director*, H. Pavlovich

INSTITUTE OF MARINE ENGINEERS (1889), 80 Coleman Street, London EC2R 5BJ. Tel: 020-7382 2600; Fax: 020-7382 2670; Email: imare@imare.org.uk; Web: www.imare.org.uk; *Director General*, K. F. Read

INSTITUTE OF MASTERS OF WINE (1955), Five Kings House, 1 Queen Street Place, London EC4R 1QS. *Executive Director*, Jane Carr

INSTITUTE OF MATERIALS, 1 Carlton House Terrace, London SW1Y 5DB. Tel: 020-7451 7300; Fax: 020-7839 1702; *Chief Executive*, Dr B. A. Rickinson

INSTITUTE OF MATHEMATICS AND ITS APPLICATIONS (1964), Catherine Richards House, 16 Nelson Street, Southend-on-Sea, Essex SS1 1EF. Tel: 01702-354020; Fax: 01702-354111; Email: post@ima.org.uk; Web: www.ima.org.uk; *Executive Secretary*, Dr A. M. Lepper

INSTITUTE OF MEASUREMENT AND CONTROL (1944), 87 Gower Street, London WC1E 6AF. Tel: 020-7387 4949; Fax: 020-7388 8431; Email: m.yates@instmc.org.uk; Web: www.instmc.org.uk; *Secretary*, M. J. Yates

INSTITUTE OF PATENTEES AND INVENTORS (1919), Suite 505A, Triumph House, 189 Regent Street, London W1B 4JY. Tel: 020-7434 1818; Fax: 020-7434 1727; Email: ipi@invent.org.uk; Web: www.invent.org.uk; *Chairman*, P. Ambridge

INSTITUTE OF PETROLEUM (1913), 61 New Cavendish Street, London W1G 7AR. Tel: 020-7467 7100; Fax: 020-7255 1472; Email: ip@petroleum.co.uk; Web: www.petroleum.co.uk; *Director General*, J. Pym

INSTITUTE OF PRACTITIONERS IN ADVERTISING (1917), 44 Belgrave Square, London SW1X 8QS. Tel: 020-7235 7020; Fax: 020-7245 9904; Email: mark@ipa.co.uk; Web: www.ipa.co.uk; *Director General*, Nick Phillips

INSTITUTE OF QUARRYING (1917), 7 Regent Street, Nottingham NG1 5BS. Tel: 0115-941 1315; Fax: 0115-948 4035; Email: iq@qmj.co.uk; Web: www.inst-of-quarrying.org/iq; *Secretary*, Mrs L. Bryden

INSTITUTE OF REFRIGERATION (1899), Kelvin House, 76 Mill Lane, Carshalton, Surrey SM5 2JR. Tel: 020-8647 7033; Fax: 020-8773 0165; Email: ior@ior.org.uk; Web: www.ior.org.uk; *Secretary*, M. J. Horlick

INSTITUTE OF SPORTS MEDICINE (1965), Department of Surgery, Royal Free and University College Medical School, 67/73 Riding House Street, London W1W 7EJ. Tel: 020-7813 2832; Fax: 020-7813 2832; Email: m.hobsley@ucl.ac.uk; *Hon. Secretary*, Dr W. T. Orton

INSTITUTE OF TRADE MARK ATTORNEYS (1934), Canterbury House, 2–6 Sydenham Road, Croydon CR0 9XE. Tel: 020-8686 2052; Fax: 020-8680 5723; Email: tm@itma.org.uk; Web: www.itma.org.uk; *Secretary*, Mrs M. J. Tyler

INSTITUTE OF TRANSLATION AND INTERPRETING (1986), 377 City Road, London EC1V 1ND. Tel: 020-7713 7600; Fax: 020-7713 7650; Email: info@iti.org.uk; Web: www.iti.org.uk; *Chairman*, Dr C. Greensmith

INSTITUTION OF CIVIL ENGINEERS, 1 Great George Street, London SW1P 3AA. Tel: 020-7222 7722; Fax: 020-7222 7500; Email: mike.casebourne@ice.org.uk; *Chief Executive*, M. Casebourne

INSTITUTION OF ELECTRICAL ENGINEERS, Savoy Place, London WC2R 0BL. Tel: 020-7240 1871; Fax: 020-7240 7735; Email: postmaster@iee.org.uk; Web: www.iee.org.uk; *Secretary*, Dr A. Roberts

INSTITUTION OF ENGINEERING DESIGNERS (1945), Courtleigh, Westbury Leigh, Westbury, Wilts BA13 3TA. Tel: 01373-822801; Fax: 01373-858085; Email: ied@inst-engg-design.demon.co.uk; Web: www.ied.org.uk; *Acting Secretary*, E. Brodhurst

INSTITUTION OF GAS ENGINEERS, 21 Portland Place, London W1B 1PY. Tel: 020-7636 6603; Fax: 020-7636 6602; Email: general@igaseng.demon.co.uk; Web: www.igaseng.com; *Chief Executive*, C. J. Bleach

INSTITUTION OF MECHANICAL ENGINEERS (1847), 1 Birdcage Walk, London SW1H 9JJ. Tel: 020-7222 7899; Fax: 020-7222 4557; Web: www.imeche.org.uk; *Director General*, Sir Michael Moore

INTERCONTINENTAL CHURCH SOCIETY (1823), 1 Athena Drive, Tachbrook Park, Warwick CV34 6NL. Tel: 01926-430347; Fax: 01926-888092; Email: enquiries@ics-uk.org; Web: www.ics-uk.org; *Chief Executive*, The Revd Ian Watson

INTERNATIONAL AFRICAN INSTITUTE (1926), SOAS, Thornhaugh Street, Russell Square, London WC1H 0XG. Tel: 020-7898 4420; Fax: 020-7898 4419; Email: iai@soas.ac.uk; Web: www.oneworld.org/iai; *Hon. Director*, Prof. P. Spencer

INTERNATIONAL CONSULTING ECONOMISTS' ASSOCIATION (1986), c/o Capricorn Business Services, 50 London End, Beaconsfield, Bucks HP9 2JH. Tel: 01494-670372; Fax: 01494-675426; *Chairman*, G. Todd

INTERNATIONAL FINANCIAL SERVICES, LONDON (1968), Windsor House, 39 King Street, London EC2V 8DQ. Tel: 020-7600 1198; Fax: 020-7606 4248; Email: enquiries@ifsl.org.uk; Web: www.ifsl.org.uk; *Acting Chief Executive*, John Nichols

INTERNATIONAL FRIENDSHIP LEAGUE, 3 Creswick Road, London W3 9HE. Tel: 020-8752 0055; Fax: 020-8752 0066; Email: bookings@ifl-peacehaven.co.uk; *Chairman*, M. J. A. Prowse

INTERNATIONAL HOSPITAL FEDERATION, 4 Abbot's Place, London NW6 4NP. Tel: 020-7372 7181; Fax: 020-7328 7433; Web: www.hospitalmanagement.net and www.ihf.co.uk; *Director General*, Dr E. N. Pickering

INTERNATIONAL INSTITUTE FOR CONSERVATION OF HISTORIC AND ARTISTIC WORKS (1950), 6 Buckingham Street, London WC2N 6BA. Tel: 020-7839 5975; Fax: 020-7976 1564; Email: iicon@compuserve.com; Web: www.iiconservation.org; *Secretary-General*, D. Bomford

INTERNATIONAL INSTITUTE FOR STRATEGIC STUDIES (1958), Arundel House, 13–15 Arundel Street, Temple Place, London WC2R 3DX. Tel: 020-7395 9120; Fax: 020-7395 9186; Email: iiss@iiss.org.uk; Web: www.isn.ethz.ch/iiss; *Director*, Dr J. Chipman

INTERNATIONAL PEN (1921), 9–10 Charterhouse Buildings, Goswell Road, London EC1M 7AT. Tel: 020-7253 4308; Fax: 020-7253 5711; Email: intpen@dircon.co.uk; Web: www.oneworld.org/internatpen; *International Secretary*, T. Carlbom

INTERNATIONAL POLICE ASSOCIATION (BRITISH SECTION) (1950), 1 Fox Road, West Bridgford, Nottingham NG2 6AJ. Tel: 0115-981 3638; Email: mail@ipa-uk.org; Web: www.ipa-uk.org; *Executive Officer*, Mrs E. Jones

INTERNATIONAL STUDENTS HOUSE, 1 Park Crescent, London W1B 1SH. Tel: 020-7631 8300; Fax: 020-7631 8315; Email: general@ish.org.uk; Web: www.ish.org.uk; *Executive Director*, P. Anwyl

INTERNATIONAL UNION FOR LAND-VALUE TAXATION AND FREE TRADE (1926), Room 427, London Fruit Exchange, Brushfield Street, London E1 6EL. Tel: 020-7377 8885; Fax: 020-7377 8686; Email: in@interunion.org.uk; Web: www.interunion.org.uk; *Hon. Secretary*, Mrs B. P. Sobrielo

INTERSERVE, 325 Kennington Road, London SE11 4QH. Tel: 020-7735 8227; Fax: 020-7587 5362; Web: www.interserve.org/ew; *National Director*, R. Clark

INVALIDS-AT-HOME (1965), 17 Lapstone Gardens, Kenton, Harrow, Middx HA3 0EB. Tel: 020-8907 1706; *Executive Officer*, Mrs S. Lomas

INVOLVEMENT AND PARTICIPATION ASSOCIATION (1884), 42 Colebrooke Row, London N1 8AF. Tel: 020-7354 8040; Fax: 020-7354 8041; Email: involved@ipa-involve.com; Web: www.ipa-involve.com; *Director*, W. Coupar

IRAN SOCIETY, 2 Belgrave Square, London SW1X 8PJ. Tel: 020-7235 5122; Fax: 020-7259 6771; Email: iransoc@rsaa.org.uk; Web: www.iransoc.dircon.co.uk

IRISH GENEALOGICAL RESEARCH SOCIETY (1936), c/o The Irish Club, 82 Eaton Square, London SW1W 9AJ. Tel: 020-7235 4164; *Hon. Librarian*, T. G. Chartres

ITRI LTD, Kingston Lane, Uxbridge, Middx UB8 3PJ. Tel: 01895-272406; Fax: 01895-251841; Email: postmaster@itri.co.uk; Web: www.itri.co.uk; *Director*, D. Bishop

JACQUELINE DU PRÉ MUSIC BUILDING LTD, St Hilda's College, Oxford OX4 1DY. Tel: 01865-276821; Fax: 01865-286674; Email: jdp@st-hildas.ox.ac.uk; Web: www.sthildas.ox.ac.uk/jdp; *Manager*, Ms M. A. Frappat

THE JAPAN ASSOCIATION, Swire House, 59 Buckingham Gate, London SW1E 6AJ. Tel: 020-7963 9446/45; Fax: 020-7630 0353; *Executive Director*, D. F. L. Turner

JERUSALEM AND THE MIDDLE EAST CHURCH ASSOCIATION, 1 Hart House, The Hart, Farnham, Surrey GU9 7HJ. Tel: 01252-726994; Fax: 01252-735558; Email: jmeca@lineone.net; *Secretary*, Mrs V. Wells

JEWISH HISTORICAL SOCIETY OF ENGLAND (1983), 33 Seymour Place, London W1H 5AP. Tel: 020-7723 5852; Fax: 020-7723 5852; Email: jhse@dircon.co.uk; Web: www.jhse.org; *Hon. Secretary*, Dr Gerry Black

JUSTICE (1957), 59 Carter Lane, London EC4V 5AQ. Tel: 020-7329 5100; Fax: 020-7329 5055; Email: admin@justice.org.uk; Web: www.justice.org.uk; *Director*, Ms A. Owers

KING'S FUND (1897), 11–13 Cavendish Square, London W1G 0AN. Tel: 020-7307 2400; Fax: 020-7307 2801; Web: www.kingsfund.org.uk; *Chief Executive*, Rabbi Julia Neuberger

KIPLING SOCIETY (1927), 6 Clifton Road, London W9 1SS. Tel: 020-7286 0194; Fax: 020-7286 0194; Email: sharadkeskar@hotmail.com; Web: www.kipling.org.uk; *Hon. Secretary*, S. Keskar

LCIA (LONDON COURT OF INTERNATIONAL ARBITRATION), The International Dispute Resolution, 8 Breams Buildings, Chancery Lane, London EC4A 1HP. Tel: 020-7405 8008; Fax: 020-7405 8009; Email: lcia@lcia-arbitration.com; Web: www.icia-arbitration.com/lcia; *Director General and Registrar*, Adrian Winstanley

THE LEAGUE OF WELLDOERS (1893), 119–133 Limekiln Lane, Liverpool L5 8SN. Tel: 0151-207 1984; Fax: 0151-207 4445; Email: Welldoers@lineone.net; *Finance Officer*, Mrs L. A. Black

LEAGUE AGAINST CRUEL SPORTS LTD, 83–87 Union Street, London SE1 1SG. Tel: 020-7403 6155; Fax: 020-7357 6749; *Chief Officer*, G. Sirl

LEAGUE OF THE HELPING HAND, Petersham Hollow, 226 Petersham Road, Petersham, Richmond, Surrey TW10 7AL. Tel: 020-8940 7303; Fax: 020-8940 7303; Email: lnga@lhh.org.uk; *Secretary*, Mrs I. Goodlad

LEPROSY MISSION (ENGLAND AND WALES) (1874), Goldhay Way, Orton Goldhay, Peterborough PE2 5GZ. Tel: 01733-370505; Fax: 01733-404880; Email: post@tlmew.org.uk; Web: www.leprosymission.org

LEUKAEMIA RESEARCH FUND (1960), 43 Great Ormond Street, London WC1N 3JJ. Tel: 020-7405 0101; Fax: 020-7405 3139; Email: info@lrf.org.uk; Web: www.lrf.org.uk; *Chief Executive*, D. L. Osborne

THE LIBERAL PARTY (1877), PO Box 263, Southport, Lancs PR9 9WS. Tel: 01704-500115; Fax: 01704-500115; Email: libparty@libparty.demon.co.uk; Web: www.liberal.org.uk; *Communications Director*, D. Green

LIBERTY (NATIONAL COUNCIL FOR CIVIL LIBERTIES) (1934), 21 Tabard Street, London SE1 4LA. Tel: 020-7403 3888; Fax: 020-7407 5354; Email: info@liberty-human-rights.org.uk; Web: www.liberty-human-rights.org.uk; *Director*, J. Wadham

THE LIBRARY ASSOCIATION, 7 Ridgmount Street, London WC1E 7AE. Tel: 020-7255 0500; Textphone 020-7255 0505; Fax: 020-7255 0501; *Chief Executive*, Dr R. A. McKee

LINNEAN SOCIETY OF LONDON, Burlington House, Piccadilly, London W1J 0BF. Tel: 020-7434 4479; Fax: 020-7287 9364; Email: john@linnean.org; Web: www.linnean.org; *President*, Prof. Sir Ghillean Prance

LIONS CLUBS INTERNATIONAL (BRITISH ISLES AND IRELAND) (1950), 257 Alcester Road South, Kings Heath, Birmingham B14 6DT. Tel: 0121-441 4544; Fax: 0121-441 4510; *Office Manager*, Mrs J. Davis

LLOYD'S OF LONDON, 1 Lime Street, London EC3M 7HA. Tel: 020-7327 1000; Fax: 020-7327 6512; Email: caroline.d.krantz@lloyds.com; Web: www.lloyds.com; *Chief Executive*, N. E. Prettejohn

LLOYD'S REGISTER OF SHIPPING, 71 Fenchurch Street, London EC3M 4BS. Tel: 020-7709 9166; Fax: 020-7488 4796; Email: mipg@lr.org; Web: www.lr.org; *Chairman*, D. Moorhouse

LOCAL GOVERNMENT ASSOCIATION (1997), Local Government House, Smith Square, London SW1P 3HZ. Tel: 020-7664 3000; Fax: 020-7664 3030; Email: info@lga.gov.uk; Web: www.lga.gov.uk; *Chief Executive*, B. Briscoe

LOCAL GOVERNMENT INTERNATIONAL BUREAU (1989), 35 Great Smith Street, London SW1P 3BJ. Tel: 020-7664 3100; Fax: 020-7664 3128; Email: enquiries@lgib.gov.uk; Web: www.lgib.gov.uk; *Director*, J. Smith

LONDON APPRECIATION SOCIETY (1932), 45 Friars Avenue, Friern Barnet, London N20 0XG. *Chairman*, Anthea H. Gray

LONDON CITY MISSION, 175 Tower Bridge Road, London SE1 2AH. Tel: 020-7407 7585; *General Secretary*, Revd J. McAllen

THE LONDON LIBRARY (1841), 14 St James's Square, London SW1Y 4LG. Tel: 020-7930 7705; Fax: 020-7766 4766; Email: membership@londonlibrary.co.uk; Web: www.londonlibrary.co.uk; *Librarian*, A. S. Bell

LONDON PLAYING FIELDS SOCIETY (1890), Fraser House, 29 Albermarle Street, London W1S 4JB. Tel: 020-7493 3211; Fax: 020-7409 3405; Email: lonplayingfields@aol.com; *Chief Executive*, Dr C. Goodson-Wickes

THE LONDON SOCIETY (1912), 4th Floor, Senate House, Malet Street, London WC1E 7HU. Tel: 020-7580 5537; Email: londonsociety@hotmail.com; Web: www.lonsoc.org.uk/lonsoc; *Hon. Secretary*, Mrs B. Jones

LORD'S DAY OBSERVANCE SOCIETY (1831), 3 Epsom Business Park, Kiln Lane, Epsom, Surrey KT17 1JF. Tel: 01372-728300; Fax: 01372-722400; Email: info@dayone.co.uk; Web: www.lordsday.co.uk; *General Secretary*, J. G. Roberts

THE LOTTERIES COUNCIL (1979), Woodlands, High Grove Road, Grasscroft, Saddleworth OL4 4HG. Tel: 01457-872988; Fax: 01457-872988; Email: sue@lotco.freeserve.co.uk; Web: www.lotteriescouncil.co.uk; *Chairman*, A. Austin

MACA - PARTNERS IN MENTAL HEALTH (1859), 2 Bedford Square, London WC1B 3HW. Tel: 020-7436 6194; Fax: 020-7637 1980; Email: maca-bs@maca.org.uk; Web: www.maca.org.uk; *Chief Executive*, G. Hitchon

MACMILLAN CANCER RELIEF (1911), 89 Albert Embankment, London SE1 7UQ. Tel: 020-7840 7840; Fax: 020-7840 7841; Email: information_line@macmillan.org.uk; Web: www.macmillan.org.uk; *Chief Executive*, N. Young

MAILING PREFERENCE SERVICE, 5th Floor, Haymarket House, 1 Oxendon Street, London SW1Y 4EE. Tel: 020-7766 4410; Fax: 020-7976 1886; Email: mps@dma.org.uk; Web: www.mpsonline.org.uk; *Director of Compliance Operations*, Ms T. Kelly

MAKOR-AYJ (1899), Balfour House, 741 High Road, London N12 0BQ. Tel: 020-8446 8020; Fax: 020-8343 9037; Email: info@makor.org.uk; *Deputy Director*, E. Finestone

MANIC DEPRESSION FELLOWSHIP (1983), Castle Works, 21 St George's Road, London SE1 6ES. Tel: 020-7793 2600; Fax: 020-7793 2639; Email: mdf@mdf.org.uk; Web: www.mdf.org.uk; *Chief Executive*, Ms K. Campbell

MANORIAL SOCIETY OF GREAT BRITAIN (1906), 104 Kennington Road, London SE11 6RE. Tel: 020-7735 6633; Fax: 020-7582 7022; Email: msgb@manor.net; *Hon. Chairman*, R. A. Smith

MARIE CURIE CANCER CARE (1948), 89 Albert Embankment, London SE1 7TP. Tel: 020-7599 7777; Fax: 020-7599 7788; Email: info@mariecurie.org.uk; Web: www.mariecurie.org.uk; *Chief Executive*, Thomas Hughes-Hallett

MARIO LANZA EDUCATIONAL FOUNDATION (1976), 7 Lionfields Avenue, Allesley Village, Coventry CV5 9GN. *Hon. Secretary*, Miss Patricia Barrow

MARRIAGE CARE, Clitherow House, 1 Blythe Mews, Blythe Road, London W14 0NW. Tel: 020-7371 1341; Fax: 020-7371 4921; Email: info@marriagecare.org.uk; Web: www.marriagecare.org.uk; *Chief Executive*, Terry Prendergast

MASONIC TRUST FOR GIRLS AND BOYS (1978), 31 Great Queen Street, London WC2B 5AG. Tel: 020-7405 2644; Fax: 020-7831 4094; Web: www.mtgb.org; *Secretary*, Lt.-Col. J. C. Chambers

MEDICAL SOCIETY OF LONDON (1773), Lettsom House, 11 Chandos Street, London W1M 0EB. Tel: 020-7580 1043; Fax: 020-7580 5793; *Registrar*, Col. R. Kinsella-Bevan

MEDICAL WOMEN'S FEDERATION, Tavistock House North, Tavistock Square, London WC1H 9HX. Tel: 020-7387 7765; Fax: 020-7387 7765; Email: MWF@m-w-f.demon.co.uk; Web: www.medicalwomensfederation.com; *President*, Prof. Llora Finlay

MEDIC-ALERT FOUNDATION, 1 Bridge Wharf, 156 Caledonian Road, London N1 9UU. Tel: 020-7833 3034; Fax: 020-7278 0647; Email: info@medicalert.co.uk; Web: www.medicalert.co.uk; *Chief Executive*, Miss J. Friend

MENCAP (ROYAL SOCIETY FOR MENTALLY HANDICAPPED CHILDREN AND ADULTS) (1946), 123 Golden Lane, London EC1Y 0RT. Tel: 020-7454 0454; Fax: 020-7608 3254; Email: information@mencap.org.uk; Web: www.mencap.co.uk; *Chief Executive*, F. Heddell

THE MENTAL HEALTH FOUNDATION, 20–21 Cornwall Terrace, London NW1 4QL. Tel: 020-7535 7400; Fax: 020-7535 7474; Email: mhf@mentalhealth.org.uk; Web: www.mentalhealth.org.uk; *Director*, Ms J. McKerrow

MERCHANT NAVY WELFARE BOARD, 19–21 Lancaster Gate, London W2 3LN. Tel: 020-7723 3642; Fax: 020-7723 3643; Email: enquiries@mnwb.org.uk; Web: www.mnwb.org.uk; *General Secretary*, Capt. D. A. Parsons

METROPOLITAN HOSPITAL-SUNDAY FUND (1873), 45 Westminster Bridge Road, London SE1 7JB. Tel: 020-7922 0200; Fax: 020-7401 3641; Email: mhsf@peabody.org.uk; Web: www.mhsf.org.uk; *Secretary*, H. F. Doe

THE MIDDLE EAST ASSOCIATION, Bury House, 33 Bury Street, London SW1Y 6AX. Tel: 020-7839 2137; Fax: 020-7839 6121; Email: mail@the-mea.co.uk; Web: www.the-mea.co.uk; *Director General*, B. P. Constant

MIGRAINE ACTION ASSOCIATION (1958), 178A High Road, Byfleet, West Byfleet, Surrey KT14 7ED. Tel: 01932-352468; Fax: 01932-351257; Email: info@migraine.org.uk; Web: www.migraine.org.uk; *Director*, Mrs A. Turner

THE MIGRAINE TRUST (1965), 45 Great Ormond Street, London WC1N 3HZ. Tel: 020-7831 4818; Fax: 020-7831 5174; Email: info@migrainetrust.org; Web: www.migrainetrust.org; *Director*, Ms A. Rush

MILITARY HISTORICAL SOCIETY, National Army Museum, Royal Hospital Road, London SW3 4HT. Tel: 01980-615689; Fax: 01980-618746; Email: pjjobson@hotmail.com; *Secretary*, P. Jobson

MIND (NATIONAL ASSOCIATION FOR MENTAL HEALTH) (1946), Granta House, 15–19 Broadway, London E15 4BQ. Tel: 020-8519 2122; Fax: 020-8522 1725; Email: contact@mind.org.uk; Web: www.mind.org.uk; *Chief Executive*, Ms J. Clements

MINERALOGICAL SOCIETY (1876), 41 Queen's Gate, London SW7 5HR. Tel: 020-7584 7516; Fax: 020-7823 8021; Email: info@minersoc.org; Web: www.minersoc.org; *General Secretary*, Ms F. Wall

MODERN CHURCHPEOPLE'S UNION (1898), MCU Office, 25 Birch Grove, London W3 9SP. Tel: 020-8932 4379; Fax: 020-8993 5812; Email: modchurchunion@btinternet.com; Web: www.modchurchunion.org; *General Secretary*, Revd N. P. Henderson

MONUMENTAL BRASS SOCIETY, Lowe Hill House, Stratford St Mary, Colchester, Essex CO7 6JX. Tel: 020-8520 5249; Fax: 020-8521 8387; *Hon. Secretary*, H. M. Stuchfield

THE MOTHERS' UNION (1876), Mary Sumner House, 24 Tufton Street, London SW1P 3RB. Tel: 020-7222 5533; Fax: 020-7222 1591; Email: mu@themothersunion.org; Web: www.themothersunion.org; *Chief Executive*, R. Bailey

MOUNTBATTEN MEMORIAL TRUST (1979), Estate Office, Broadlands, Romsey, Hants SO51 9ZE. Tel: 01794-518885; *Trust Secretary*, J. B. Moss

MUSICIANS' BENEVOLENT FUND (1921), 16 Ogle Street, London W1W 6JA. Tel: 020-7636 4481; Fax: 020-7637 4307; Email: hfaulkner@mbf.org.uk; Web: www.mbf.org.uk; *Secretary*, Ms H. Faulkner

NABS, 32 Wigmore Street, London W1U 2RP. Tel: 020-7299 2888; Fax: 020-7299 2887; Email: nabs@nabs.org.uk; Web: www.nabs.org.uk; *Director*, Miss K. Harris

NACRO (THE CRIME REDUCTION CHARITY) (1966), 169 Clapham Road, London SW9 0PU. Tel: 020-7582 6500; Fax: 020-7735 4666; Email: office@narco.org.uk; Web: www.narco.org; *Chief Executive*, Ms H. Edwards

NATIONAL ADULT SCHOOL ORGANISATION (1899), Riverton, 370 Humberstone Road, Leicester LE5 0SA. Tel: 0116-253 8333; Fax: 0116-251 3626; Email: gensec@naso.org.uk; Web: www.naso.org.uk; *General Secretary*, Mrs P. C. Dean

NATIONAL ART COLLECTIONS FUND (1903), Mallais House, 7 Cromwell Place, London SW7 2JN. Tel: 020-7225 4800; Fax: 020-7225 4848; Email: info@art-fund.org; Web: www.art-fund.org; *Director*, D. Barrie

NATIONAL ASSOCIATION FOR COLITIS AND CROHN'S DISEASE (1979), 4 Beaumont House, Sutton Road, St Albans, Herts AL1 5HH. Tel: 01727-830038; Fax: 01727-862550; Email: nacc@nacc.org.uk; Web: www.nacc.org.uk; *Director*, R. Driscoll

NATIONAL ASSOCIATION FOR GIFTED CHILDREN (1967), Elder House, Milton Keynes MK9 1LR. Tel: 01908-673677; Fax: 01908-673679; Email: amazingchildren@nagcbritain.org.uk; Web: www.nagcbritain.org.uk; *Director*, K. Bore

NATIONAL ASSOCIATION OF CITIZENS ADVICE BUREAUX (1939), Myddelton House, 115–123 Pentonville Road, London N1 9LZ. Tel: 020-7833 2181; Fax: 020-7833 4371; Web: www.nacab.org.uk; *Chief Executive*, D. Harker

NATIONAL ASSOCIATION OF CLUBS FOR YOUNG PEOPLE (1925), 371 Kennington Lane, London SE11 5QY. Tel: 020-7793 0787; Fax: 020-7820 9815; Email: office@nacyp.org.uk; Web: www.nacyp.org.uk; *National Director*, C. Groves

NATIONAL ASSOCIATION OF LOCAL COUNCILS (1947), 109 Great Russell Street, London WC1B 3LD. Tel: 020-7637 1865; Fax: 020-7436 7451; Web: www.nalc.gov.uk; *Chief Executive*, John Finlay

NATIONAL ASSOCIATION OF PRISON VISITORS, 29 Kimbolton Road, Bedford MK40 2PB. Tel: 01234-359763; Fax: 01234-359763; *General Secretary*, Mrs A. G. McKenna

NATIONAL ASTHMA CAMPAIGN (1990), Providence House, Providence Place, London N1 0NT. Tel: 020-7226 2260; Fax: 020-7704 0740; Web: www.asthma.org.uk; *Chief Executive*, Anne Smith

NATIONAL BLOOD AUTHORITY, Oak House, Reeds Crescent, Watford, Herts WD1 1QH. Tel: 01923-486800; Fax: 01923-486801; Web: www.blood.co.uk; *Chairman*, M. Fogden

NATIONAL CAMPAIGN FOR THE ARTS LTD (1985), Pegasus House, 37–43 Sackville Street, London W1S 3EH. Tel: 020-7333 0375; Fax: 020-7333 0660; Email: nca@artscampaign.org.uk; Web: www.artscampaign.org.uk; *Director*, Ms V. Todd

NATIONAL CHILDBIRTH TRUST (1956), Alexandra House, Oldham Terrace, Acton, London W3 6NH. Tel: Administration 020-8992 2616. Enquiries: 0870 444 8707; Fax: 020-8992 5929; Web: www.nctpregnancyandbabycare.com; *Chief Executive*, Ms B. Phipps

NATIONAL CHRISTIAN EDUCATION COUNCIL (1803), 1020 Bristol Road, Selly Oak, Birmingham B29 6LB. Tel: 0121-472 4242; Fax: 0121-472 7575; Email: ncec@ncec.org.uk; Web: www.ncec.org.uk; *General Manager*, Mrs S. Sharman

NATIONAL COUNCIL FOR ONE PARENT FAMILIES (1918), 255 Kentish Town Road, London NW5 2LX. Tel: 020-7428 5400; Fax: 020-7482 4851; Email: info@oneparentfamilies.org.uk; Web: www.oneparentfamilies.org.uk; *Director*, K. Green

NATIONAL COUNCIL OF WOMEN OF GREAT BRITAIN, 36 Danbury Street, London N1 8JU. Tel: 020-7354 2395; Fax: 020-7354 9214; Email: ncwgb@danburystreet.freeserve.co.uk; Web: www.ncwgb.org; *President*, Ms Marie Birkenhead

NATIONAL EXTENSION COLLEGE (1963), Michael Young Centre, Purbeck Road, Cambridge CB2 2HN. Tel: 01223-400200; Fax: 01223-400399; Email: info@nec.ac.uk; Web: www.nec.ac.uk; *Director*, Dr R. Morpeth

NATIONAL FEDERATION OF RETIREMENT PENSIONS ASSOCIATIONS (1940), Thwaites House, Railway Road, Blackburn BB1 5AX. Tel: 01254-52606; Fax: 01254-52606; *General Secretary*, R. Stansfield

NATIONAL FEDERATION OF WOMEN'S INSTITUTES, 104 New Kings Road, London SW6 4LY. Tel: 020-7371 9300; Fax: 020-7736 3652; Email: cspa@nfwi.org.uk; Web: www.womens-insitute.co.uk; *General Secretary*, Mrs J. Osborne

NATIONAL FOUNDATION FOR EDUCATIONAL RESEARCH IN ENGLAND AND WALES (1946), The Mere, Upton Park, Slough SL1 2DQ. Tel: 01753-574123; Fax: 01753-691632; Email: enquiries@nfer.ac.uk; Web: www.nfer.ac.uk; *Director*, Dr S. Hegarty

NATIONAL GARDENS SCHEME CHARITABLE TRUST (1927), Hatchlands Park, East Clandon, Guildford, Surrey GU4 7RT. Tel: 01483-211535; Fax: 01483-211537; Email: ngs@ngs.org.uk; Web: www.ngs.org.uk; *Director*, C. Barham Carter

NATIONAL MISSING PERSONS HELPLINE (1992), Roebuck House, 284-286 Upper Richmond Road West, London SW14 7JE. Tel: 020-8392 4590; Helpline: 0500-700700; Fax: 020-8878 7752; Email: admin@missingpersons.org; Web: www.missingpersons.org; *Co-Founders*, Mrs M. Asprey, OBE; Mrs J. Newman, OBE

NATIONAL OPERATIC AND DRAMATIC ASSOCIATION (1899), NODA House, 1 Crestfield Street, London WC1H 8AU. Tel: 020-7837 5655; Fax: 020-7833 0609; Email: everyone@noda.org.uk; Web: www.noda.org.uyk; *Chief Executive*, M. Pemberton

NATIONAL OSTEOPOROSIS SOCIETY, Manor Farm, Skinners Hill, Camerton, Bath BA2 0PJ. Tel: 01761-471771; Fax: 01761-471104; Email: info@nos.org.uk; Web: www.nos.org.uk; *Communications Manager*, Deborah Wearing

NATIONAL PLAYING FIELDS ASSOCIATION (1925), Stanley House, St Chads Place, London WC1X 9HH. Tel: 020-7833 5360; Fax: 020-7833 5365; Email: npfa@npfa.co.uk; Web: www.npfa.co.uk; *Director*, Ms E. Davies

NATIONAL SCHIZOPHRENIA FELLOWSHIP (1972), 30 Tabernacle Street, London EC2A 4DD. Tel: 020-7330 9100; Fax: 020-7330 9102; Email: info@nsf.org.uk; Web: www.nsf.org.uk; *Chief Executive*, C. Prior

NATIONAL SCHIZOPHRENIA FELLOWSHIP SCOTLAND (1984), Claremont House, 130 East Claremont Street, Edinburgh EH7 4LB. Tel: 0131-557 8969; Fax: 0131-557 8968; Email: info@nsfscot.org.uk; Web: www.nsfscot.org.uk; *Chief Executive*, Ms M. Weir

NATIONAL SECULAR SOCIETY LTD (1866), 25 Red Lion Square, London WC1R 4RL. Tel: 020-7404 3126; Fax: 020-7404 3126; Email: kpw@secularism.org.uk; Web: www.secularism.org.uk; *General Secretary*, K. P. Wood

NATIONAL SOCIETY FOR EPILEPSY (1892), Chesham Lane, Chalfont St Peter, Bucks SL9 0RJ. Tel: 01494-601300; Fax: 01494-871927; Web: www.epilepsynse.org.uk; *Chief Executive*, Graham Faulkner

THE NATIONAL SOCIETY (1811), Church House, Great Smith Street, London SW1P 3NZ. Tel: 020-7898 1518; Fax: 020-7898 1493; Email: info@natsoc.c-of-e.org.uk; Web: www.natsoc.org.uk; *General Secretary*, Canon J. Hall

NATIONAL SOCIETY OF ALLOTMENT AND LEISURE GARDENERS LTD, O'Dell House, Hunters Road, Corby, Northants NN17 5JE. Tel: 01536-266576; Fax: 01536-264509; Email: natsoc@nsalg.demon.co.uk; Web: www.nsalg.demon.co.uk; *National Secretary*, G. W. Stokes

THE NATIONAL TRUST, 36 Queen Anne's Gate, London SW1H 9AS. Tel: 020-7222 9251; Fax: 020-7222 5097; Web: www.nationaltrust.org.uk; *Director General*, Fiona Reynolds

THE NATIONAL TRUST FOR SCOTLAND (1931), Wemyss House, 28 Charlotte Square, Edinburgh EH2 4ET. Tel: 0131-243 9300; Fax: 0131-243 9301; Email: information@nts.org.uk; Web: www.nts.org.uk; *Director*, T. Croft

NATIONAL UNION OF STUDENTS (1922), Nelson Mandela House, 461 Holloway Road, London N7 6LJ. Tel: 020-7272 8900; Fax: 020-7263 5713; Email: nusuk@nus.org.uk; Web: www.nusonline.co.uk; *National President*, O. James

NATIONAL WOMEN'S REGISTER, 3A Vulcan House, Vulcan Road North, Norwich NR6 6AQ. Tel: 01603-406767; Fax: 01603-407003; Email: office@nwr.org; Web: www.nwr.og; *Marketing and Membership Co-ordinators*, Mrs M. Dodkins; Mrs E. Thorn

NAVAL, MILITARY AND AIR FORCE BIBLE SOCIETY (1780), Radstock House, 3 Eccleston Street, London SW1W 9LZ. Tel: 020-7463 1468; Fax: 020-7730 0240; Email: nma@sgm.org; *Director*, J. M. Hines

NAVY RECORDS SOCIETY, c/o Department of War Studies, King's College, The Strand, London WC2R 2LS. Web: www.navyrecordssociety.com; *Hon. Secretary*, Dr A. D. Lambert

NCH ACTION FOR CHILDREN, 85 Highbury Park, London N5 1UD. Tel: 020-7704 7000; Fax: 020-7226 2537; *Chief Executive*, D. Mead

NEW POLITICS NETWORK, 6 Cynthia Street, London N1 9JF. Tel: 020-7278 4443; Fax: 020-7278 4425; Email: info@new-politics.net; Web: www.new-politics.net; *Director*, A. Pakes

NEWSPAPER PRESS FUND (1864), Dickens House, 35 Wathen Road, Dorking, Surrey RH4 1JY. Tel: 01306-887511; Fax: 01306-888212; *Director*, D. Ilott

THE NHS CONFEDERATION, 1 Warwick Row, London SW1E 5ER. Tel: 020-7959 7272; Fax: 020-7959 7273; Web: www.nhsconfed.net; *Chief Executive*, S. Thornton

NORWOOD RAVENSWOOD, Broadway House, 80–82 The Broadway, Stanmore, Middx HA7 4HB. Tel: 020-8954 4555; Fax: 020-8420 6800; *Executive Directors*, Ms N. Brier; S. Brier

THE NOTARIES SOCIETY (1882), 23 New Street, Woodbridge, Suffolk IP12 1DN. Tel: 01394-384134; Fax: 01394-382906; Web: www.thenotariessociety.org.uk; *Secretary*, A. G. Dunford

THE NUFFIELD FOUNDATION (1943), 28 Bedford Square, London WC1B 3JS. Tel: 020-7631 0566; Fax: 020-7323 4877; Web: www.nuffieldfoundation.org; *Director*, A. Tomei

NUFFIELD TRUST (1940), 59 New Cavendish Street, London W1G 7LP. Tel: 020-7631 8450; Fax: 020-7631 8451; Email: mail@nuffieldtrust.org.uk; Web: www.nuffieldtrust.org.uk; *Secretary*, J. Wyn Owen

NUTRITION SOCIETY, 10 Cambridge Court, 210 Shepherds Bush Road, London W6 7NJ. Tel: 020-7602 0228; Fax: 020-7602 1756; *Hon. Secretary*, Dr J. D. Oldham

THE OFFICERS' ASSOCIATION, 48 Pall Mall, London SW1Y 5JY. Tel: 020-7930 0125; Fax: 020-7930 9053; Email: postmaster@oaed.org.uk; Web: www.officersassociation.org.uk; *General Secretary*, Brig. J. M. A. Nurton

OPAS (THE PENSIONS ADVISORY SERVICE), 11 Belgrave Road, London SW1V 1RB. Tel: 020-7233 8080; Fax: 020-7233 8016; Email: opas@iclwebkiv.co.uk; Web: www.opas.org.uk; *Chief Executive*, M. McLean

THE OPEN-AIR MISSION (1853), 19 John Street, London WC1N 2DL. Tel: 020-7405 6135; Fax: 020-7405 6135; Email: oamission@btinternet.com; Web: www.btinternet.com/~oamission; *Secretary*, A. N. Banton

OPEN SPACES SOCIETY (1865), 25A Bell Street, Henley-on-Thames, Oxon RG9 2BA. Tel: 01491-573535; Fax: 01491-573051; Email: hq@oss.org.uk; Web: www.oss.org.uk; *General Secretary*, Miss K. Ashbrook

OPSIS (1992), c/o Queen Alexandra College, Court Oak Road, Birmingham B17 9TG. Tel: 0121-428 5037; Fax: 0121-428 5048; Email: opsis@dircon.co.uk; *Executive Manager*, C. Gregory

ORDERS AND MEDALS RESEARCH SOCIETY (1942), PO Box 1904, Southam CV47 2ZX. Tel: 01295-690009; Web: www.omrs.org.uk; *General Secretary*, P. M. R. Helmore

THE ORIENTAL CERAMIC SOCIETY (1921), 30B Torrington Square, London WC1E 7LJ. Tel: 020-7636 7985; Fax: 020-7580 6749; Email: ocs-london@beeb.net; Web: www.ocs-london.com; *President*, Ross Kerr

OUTWARD BOUND TRUST (1941), Loch Eil Centre, Achdalieu, Corpach, Fort William PH33 7NN. Tel: 01397-772866; Fax: 01397-773905; Web: www.outwardbound-uk.org; *Director*, Sir Michael Hobbs

OVERSEAS DEVELOPMENT INSTITUTE, 111 Westminster Bridge Road, London SE1 7JD. Tel: 020-7922 0300; Fax: 020-7922 0399; Email: odi@odi.org.uk; Web: www.odi.org.uk; *Director*, S. Maxwell

OVERSEAS SERVICE PENSIONERS' ASSOCIATION (1960), 138 High Street, Tonbridge, Kent TN9 1AX. Tel: 01732-363836; *Secretary*, D. F. B. Le Breton

OXFAM GREAT BRITAIN (1943), 274 Banbury Road, Oxford OX2 7DZ. Tel: 01865-311311; Email: oxfam@oxfam.org.uk; Web: www.oxfam.org.uk; *Director*, B. Stocking

OXFORD PRESERVATION TRUST (1927), 10 Turn Again Lane, St Ebbes, Oxford OX1 1QL. Tel: 01865-242918; Fax: 01865-251022; Email: info@oxfordpreservation.org.uk; *Secretary*, Mrs D. Dance

OXFORD UNIVERSITY SOCIETY, Oxfenford House, Magdalen Street, Oxford OX1 3AB. Tel: 01865-288088; Fax: 01865-288086; Email: oxforduniversitysociety@admin.ox.ac.uk; *Secretary*, T. J. Lewis

PARENTS AT WORK, 45 Beech Street, Barbican, London EC2Y 8AD. Tel: 020-7628 3578; Fax: 020-7628 3591; Email: info@parentsatwork.org.uk; Web: www.parentsatwork.org.uk; *Joint Chief Executives*, Ms S. Jackson; Ms S. Monk

PARLIAMENTARY AND SCIENTIFIC COMMITTEE (1939), 48 Westminster Palace Gardens, 1–7 Artillery Row, London SW1P 1RR. Tel: 020-7222 7085; Fax: 020-7222 5355; *Administrative Secretary*, Dr A. Whitehouse

PEARSON'S HOLIDAY FUND (1892), PO Box 3017, South Croydon, Surrey CR2 9PN. Tel: 020-8657 3053; Fax: 020-8657 3053; *General Secretary*, B. K. H. Rogers

THE PEDESTRIANS ASSOCIATION (1929), 31–33 Bondway, London SW8 1SJ. Tel: 020-7820 1010; Fax: 020-7820 8208; Email: info@pedestrians.org.uk; Web: www.pedestrians.org.uk; *Director*, B. Plowden

PERFORMING RIGHT SOCIETY LTD, Copyright House, 29–33 Berners Street, London W1T 3AB. Tel: 020-7580 5544; Fax: 020-7306 4450; Web: www.prs.co.uk; *Chief Executive*, J. Hutchinson

PERIODICAL PUBLISHERS ASSOCIATION LTD, Queens House, 28 Kingsway, London WC2B 6JR. Tel: 020-7404 4166; Fax: 020-7404 4167; Email: info@ppa.co.uk; *Chief Executive*, I. Locks

PESTALOZZI CHILDREN'S VILLAGE TRUST (1957), Sedlescombe, Battle, E. Sussex TN33 0RR. Tel: 01424-870444; Fax: 01424-870655; Email: office@pestalozzi.org.uk; Web: www.pestalozzi.org.uk; *Director*, Ms P. Rogers

PHILOLOGICAL SOCIETY (1842), School of Oriental and African Studies, University of London, Thornhaugh Street, London WC1H 0XG. *Hon. Secretary*, Prof. N. Sims-Williams

THE PHYSIOLOGICAL SOCIETY (1876), PO Box 11319, London WC1E 7JF. Tel: 020-7631 1458; Fax: 020-7631 1462; Email: admin@physoc.org; Web: www.physoc.org; *Executive Secretary*, Mrs M. Lewis

THE PILGRIM TRUST (1930), Cowley House, 9 Little College Street, London SW1P 3XS. Tel: 020-7222 4723; Fax: 020-7976 0461; *Director*, Miss G. Nayler

THE PILGRIMS OF GREAT BRITAIN (1902), Allington Castle, Maidstone, Kent ME16 0NB. Tel: 01622-606404; Fax: 01622-606402; Email: sec@pilgrimsoc.freeserve.co.uk; *Chairman*, R. M. Worcester

THE POETRY SOCIETY, 22 Betterton Street, London WC2H 9BU. Tel: 020-7420 9880; Email: info@poetrysoc.com; Web: www.poetrysoc.com; *Director*, Ms C. Patterson

POLICY STUDIES INSTITUTE (1978), 100 Park Village East, London NW1 3SR. Tel: 020-7468 0468; Fax: 020-7388 0914; Web: www.psi.org.uk; *Director*, Prof. J. Skea

THE PONY CLUB (1928), National Agricultural Centre, Stoneleigh Park, Kenilworth, Warks CV8 2RW. Tel: 024-7669 8300; Fax: 024-7669 6836; Email: enquiries@pony-club.org.uk; Web: www.pony-club.org.uk; *Chief Executive*, D. Robb

THE PRAYER BOOK SOCIETY (1975), St James Garlickhythe, Garlick Hill, London EC4V 2AF. Tel: 01923-824278; Web: www.prayerbookuk.com; *Chairman*, C. A. A. Kilmister

THE PRINCE'S TRUST (1976), 18 Park Square East, London NW1 4LH. Tel: 0800-842842; Email: info@princes-trust.org.uk; Web: www.princes-trust.org.uk; *Chief Executive*, T. Shebbeare

PRINCESS ROYAL TRUST FOR CARERS (1991), 142 Minories, London EC3N 1LB. Tel: 020-7480 7788; Fax: 020-7481 4729; Email: info@carers.org; Web: www.carers.org; *Chief Executive*, Ms A. Ryan

PRINTING HISTORICAL SOCIETY, St Bride Institute, Bride Lane, London EC4Y 8EE; *Hon. Secretary*, P. Wickens

PRISONERS ABROAD (1978), 89–93 Fonthill Road, London N4 3JH. Tel: 020-7561 6820; Fax: 020-7561 6821; Email: info@prisonersabroad.org.uk; Web: www.prisonersabroad.org.uk; *Director*, C. Laurenzi

PRIVATE LIBRARIES ASSOCIATION, Ravelston, South View Road, Pinner, Middx HA5 3YD. Web: www.the-old-school.demon.co.uk/PLA.htm; *Hon. Secretary*, F. Broomhead

PROFESSIONAL CLASSES AID COUNCIL, 10 St Christopher's Place, London W1U 1HZ. Tel: 020-7935 0641; *Secretary*, Miss N. E. Inkson

PROFESSIONAL FOOTBALLERS' ASSOCIATION (1907), 20 Oxford Court, Bishopsgate, Manchester M2 3WQ. Tel: 0161-236 0575; Fax: 0161-228 7229; Email: info@thepfa.co.uk; Web: www.givemefootball.com; *Chief Executive*, G. Taylor

PSORIASIS ASSOCIATION (1968), 7 Milton Street, Northampton NN2 7JG. Tel: 01604-711129; Fax: 01604-792894; Email: mail@psoriasis.demon.co.uk; *Chief Executive*, Gladys Edwards

QUAKER SOCIAL RESPONSIBILITY AND EDUCATION, Friends House, 173–177 Euston Road, London NW1 2BJ. Tel: 020-7663 1000; Fax: 020-7663 1001; Email: qps@quaker.org.uk; Web: www.quaker.org.uk; *General Secretary*, Ms L. Fielding

QUEEN ELIZABETH'S FOUNDATION FOR DISABLED PEOPLE (1934), Leatherhead Court, Leatherhead, Surrey KT22 0BN. Tel: 01372-841100; Fax: 01372-844072; Web: www.qefd.org; *Director*, Dr C. Robinson

QUEEN VICTORIA CLERGY FUND (1897), Church House, Dean's Yard, London SW1P 3NZ. Tel: 020-7898 1310; Fax: 020-7898 1321; *Secretary*, C. D. L. Menzies

QUEEN VICTORIA SCHOOL (1908),Dunblane, Perthshire FK15 0JY. Tel: 01786-822288; Fax: 0131-310 2955; Email: enquiries@qvs.org.uk; Web: www.qvs.pkc.org.uk; *Headmaster*, B. Raine

THE QUEEN'S ENGLISH SOCIETY (1973), 20 Jessica Road, London SW18 2QN. Tel: 020-8874 2200; Web: www.queens-english-society.co.uk; *Hon. Secretary*, Miss P. Raper

QUEEN'S NURSING INSTITUTE (1887), 3 Albemarle Way, London EC1V 4RQ. Tel: 020-7490 4227; Fax: 020-7490 1269; Email: mail@qni.org.uk; Web: www.qni.org.uk; *Director*, Mrs J. Hesketh

QUEKETT MICROSCOPICAL CLUB, Flat 3, Romagna, 101 Truro Road, London W1T 7NR. *Hon. Business Secretary*, Miss P. Hamer

RADAR (ROYAL ASSOCIATION FOR DISABILITY AND REHABILITATION) (1977), 12 City Forum, 250 City Road, London EC1V 8AF. Tel: 020-7250 3222; Fax: 020-7250 0212; Email: radar@radar.org.uk; Web: www.radar.org.uk; *Chief Executive*, Angela Rice

RAILWAY AND CANAL HISTORICAL SOCIETY (1954), 3 West Court, West Street, Oxford OX2 0NP. Tel: 01865-240514; Email: ms@bodley.ox.ac.uk; Web: www.bodley.ox.ac.uk/external/rchs/index.html; *Hon. Secretary*, M. Searle

RAILWAY BENEVOLENT INSTITUTION, Elcetra Way, Crewe Business Park, Crewe, Cheshire CW1 6HS. Tel: 01270-251316; Fax: 01270-503966; *Director*, B. R. Whitnall

RAMBLERS' ASSOCIATION (1935), 2nd Floor, Camelford House, 87–90 Albert Embankment, London SE1 7TW. Tel: 020-7339 8500; Fax: 020-7339 8501; Email: ramblers@london.ramblers.org.uk; Web: www.ramblers.org.uk; *Chief Executive*, Nick Barrett

RED POLL CATTLE SOCIETY (1888), 52 Border Cot Lane, Wickham Market, Woodbridge, Suffolk IP13 0EZ. Tel: 01728-747230; Fax: 01728-748226; Email: secretary@redpoll.co.uk; *Secretary*, Mrs T. J. Booker

REGIONAL STUDIES ASSOCIATION (1965), PO Box 2058, Seaford BN25 4QU. Tel: 01323-899698; Fax: 01323-899798; Email: rsa@mailbox.ulcc.ac.uk; Web: www.regional-studies-assoc.ac.uk; *Chief Executive*, Mrs S. Hardy

REGULAR FORCES EMPLOYMENT ASSOCIATION LTD (1885), 49 Pall Mall, London SW1Y 5JG. Tel: 020-7321 2011; Fax: 020-7839 0970; Email: ghall@ctp.org.uk; Web: www.rfea.org.uk; *Chief Executive*, Maj.-Gen. M. F. L. Shellard

RESEARCH DEFENCE SOCIETY, 58 Great Marlborough Street, London W1V 1DD. Tel: 020-7287 2818; Fax: 020-7287 2627; *Executive Director*, Dr M. Matfield

RESEARCH INTO AGEING (1976), PO Box 32833, London N1 9ZQ. Tel: 020-7843 1550; Fax: 020-7843 1559; Email: ria@ageing.org; Web: www.ageing.org; *Director*, Mrs E. Mills

RESERVE FORCES ASSOCIATION (1972), Duke of York's HQ, London SW3 4SG. Tel: 020-7414 5588; Fax: 020-7414 5589; Email: reserveforces.assoc@btinternet.com; *Secretary-General*, Air Vice-Marshall A. J. Stables

RETIRED NURSES' NATIONAL HOME, Riverside Avenue, Bournemouth BH7 7EE. Tel: 01202-396418; Fax: 01202-302530; *Chairman*, Ms J. Deacon

RICHARD III SOCIETY (1924), 4 Oakley Street, London SW3 5NN. Email: neil_trump@richardiii.net; Web: www.richardiii.net; *Secretary*, Miss E. M. Nokes

ROOM: THE NATIONAL COUNCIL FOR HOUSING AND PLANNING (1900), 14–18 Old Street, London EC1V 9BH. Tel: 020-7251 2363; Fax: 020-7608 2830; *Director*, Prof. K. MacDonald

ROYAL AERONAUTICAL SOCIETY, 4 Hamilton Place, London W1J 7BQ. Tel: 020-7670 4302; Fax: 020-7499 6230; *Director*, K. Mans

ROYAL AGRICULTURAL SOCIETY OF THE COMMONWEALTH (1957), 2 Grosvenor Gardens, London SW1W 0DH. Tel: 020-7259 9678; Fax: 020-7259 9675; Email: rasc@commagshow.org; Web: www.commagshow.org; *Hon. Secretary*, C. Runge

ROYAL AIR FORCE BENEVOLENT FUND (1919), 67 Portland Place, London W1B 1AR. Tel: 020-7580 8343; Fax: 020-7307 3374; Email: michael.vearncombe@rafbf.org.uk; Web: www.raf-benfund.org; *Controller*, Air Chief Marshal Sir David Cousins

ROYAL ANTHROPOLOGICAL INSTITUTE (1843), 50 Fitzroy Street, London W1T 5BT. Tel: 020-7387 0455; Fax: 020-7383 4235; Email: admin@therai.org.uk; Web: www.therai.org.uk; *Director*, Ms H. Callan

ROYAL ARCHAEOLOGICAL INSTITUTE (1844), c/o Society of Antiquaries of London, Burlington House, Piccadilly, London W1J 0BE. Tel: 020-7479 7092; *Secretary*, J. G. Coad

ROYAL ARTILLERY ASSOCIATION, Artillery House, Front Parade, Royal Artillery Barracks, Woolwich, London SE18 4BH. Tel: 020-8781 3003; Fax: 020-8854 3617; Email: gensec.fhqra@mod.uk.net; Web: www.raa.uk.com; *General Secretary*, Lt.-Col. M. G. Felton

ROYAL ASIATIC SOCIETY, 60 Queen's Gardens, London W2 3AF. Tel: 020-7724 4742; Fax: 020-7706 4008; Email: royalasiaticsociety@btinternet.com; Web: www.royalasiaticsociety.co.uk; *Publications Officer*, A. P. A. Belloli

ROYAL BRITISH LEGION (1921), 48 Pall Mall, London SW1Y 5JY. Tel: 0345-725725; Fax: 020-7973 7399; Email: info@britishlegion.org.uk; Web: www.britishlegion.org.uk; *Secretary-General*, Brig. I. G. Townsend

ROYAL CALEDONIAN SCHOOLS TRUST (1815), 80A High Street, Bushey, Watford, Herts WD2 3DE. Tel: 020-8421 8845; Fax: 020-8421 8845; Email: rcst@caleybushey.demon.co.uk; *Chief Executive*, J. Horsfield

ROYAL CAMBRIAN ACADEMY OF ARTS (1882), Crown Lane, Conwy LL32 8AN. Tel: 01492-593413; Fax: 01492-593413; Email: rca@rcaconwy.co.uk; Web: www.rcaconwy.co.uk; *Curator and Secretary*, Ms G. Jones

ROYAL CELTIC SOCIETY (1820), 23 Rutland Street, Edinburgh EH1 2RN. Tel: 0131-228 6449; Fax: 0131-229 6987; Email: gcameron@stuartandstuart.co.uk; *Secretary*, J. G. Camerson

ROYAL CHORAL SOCIETY (1872), Studio 9, 92 Lots Road, London SW10 0QD. Tel: 020-7376 3718; Fax: 020-7376 3719; Email: royalchoralsociety@compuserve.com; *Administrator*, Helen Body

ROYAL COLLEGE OF GENERAL PRACTITIONERS (1952), 14 Princes Gate, London SW7 1PU. Tel: 020-7581 3232; Fax: 020-7225 3047; Email: info@rcgp.org.uk; Web: www.rcgp.org.uk; *Hon. Secretary*, Dr M. Baker

ROYAL COLLEGE OF MIDWIVES, 15 Mansfield Street, London W1M 0BE. Tel: 020-7312 3535; Fax: 020-7312 3536; Email: info@rcm.org.uk; Web: www.rcm.org.uk; *General Secretary*, Mrs K. Davis

ROYAL COLLEGE OF NURSING, 20 Cavendish Square, London W1G 0RN. Tel: 020-7409 3333; Fax: 020-7647 3434; Email: corpaffairs.dept@rcn.org.uk; Web: www.rcn.org.uk; *General Secretary*, Beverly Malone

ROYAL COLLEGE OF OBSTETRICIANS AND GYNAECOLOGISTS (1929), 27 Sussex Place, Regent's Park, London NW1 4RG. Tel: 020-7772 6200; Fax: 020-7723 0575; Email: coll.sec@rcog.org.uk; Web: www.rcog.org.uk; *College Secretary*, P. A. Barnett

ROYAL COLLEGE OF PAEDIATRICS AND CHILD HEALTH, 5 St Andrews Place, Regent's Park, London NW1 4LB. Tel: 020-7486 6151; Fax: 020-7486 6009; *Hon. Secretary*, Dr K. Dodd

ROYAL COLLEGE OF PATHOLOGISTS, 2 Carlton House Terrace, London SW1Y 5AF. Tel: 020-7451 6700; Fax: 020-7451 6701; *Chief Executive*, K. Lockyer

ROYAL COLLEGE OF PHYSICIANS (1518), 11 St Andrews Place, Regent's Park, London NW1 4LE. Tel: 020-7935 1174; Fax: 020-7487 5218; Web: www.rcplondon.ac.uk; *Chief Executive*, P. Masterton-Smith

ROYAL COLLEGE OF PSYCHIATRISTS (1841), 17 Belgrave Square, London SW1X 8PG. Tel: 020-7235 2351; Fax: 020-7245 1231; Email: rcpsych@rcpsych.ac.uk; Web: www.rcpsych.ac.uk; *Secretary*, Mrs V. Cameron

ROYAL COLLEGE OF RADIOLOGISTS (1975), 38 Portland Place, London W1N 4JQ. Tel: 020-7636 4432; Fax: 020-7323 3100; Email: enquiries@rcr.ac.uk; Web: www.rcr.ac.uk; *General Secretary*, A. J. Cowles

ROYAL COLLEGE OF VETERINARY SURGEONS (1844), Belgravia House, 62–64 Horseferry Road, London SW1P 2AF. Tel: 020-7222 2001; Fax: 020-7222 2004; Email: admin@rcvs.org.uk; Web: www.rcvs.org.uk; *Registrar*, Miss J. C. Hern

ROYAL GEOGRAPHICAL SOCIETY (WITH THE INSTITUTE OF BRITISH GEOGRAPHERS) (1830), 1 Kensington Gore, London SW7 2AR. Tel: 020-7591 3000; Fax: 020-7591 3001; Email: info@rgs.org; Web: www.rgs.org; *Director*, Dr R. Gardner

ROYAL HIGHLAND AND AGRICULTURAL SOCIETY OF SCOTLAND (1784), Royal Highland Centre, Ingliston, Edinburgh EH28 8NF. Tel: 0131-335 6200; Fax: 0131-333 5236; Email: rayj@rhass.org.uk; Web: www.rhass.org.uk; *Chief Executive*, R. Jones

ROYAL HISTORICAL SOCIETY (1868), University College London, Gower Street, London WC1E 6BT. Tel: 020-7387 7532; Fax: 020-7387 7532; Email: royalhistsoc@ucl.ac.uk; Web: www.rhs.ac.uk; *Executive Secretary*, Mrs J. N. McCarthy

ROYAL HORTICULTURAL SOCIETY (1804), 80 Vincent Square, London SW1P 2PE. Tel: 020-7834 4333; Fax: 020-7630 6060; Web: www.rhs.org.uk; *Director General*, Dr A. Colquhoun

ROYAL HOSPITAL FOR NEURO-DISABILITY, West Hill, Putney, London SW15 3SW. Tel: 020-8780 4500; Fax: 020-8780 4501; Email: info@neuro-disability.org.uk; Web: www.neuro-disability.org.uk; *Chief Executive*, Peter Franklyn

ROYAL HUMANE SOCIETY (1774), Brettenham House, Lancaster Place, London WC2E 7EP. Tel: 020-7836 8155; Fax: 020-7836 8155; Email: rhs@supanet.co.uk; *Secretary*, Maj.-Gen. C. Tyler

ROYAL INCORPORATION OF ARCHITECTS IN SCOTLAND (1916), 15 Rutland Square, Edinburgh EH1 2BE. Tel: 0131-229 7545; Fax: 0131-228-2188; Email: stombs@rias.org.uk; Web: www.rias.org.uk; *Secretary*, S. Tombs

ROYAL INSTITUTE OF INTERNATIONAL AFFAIRS, Chatham House, 10 St James's Square, London SW1Y 4LE. Tel: 020-7957 5700; Fax: 020-7957 5710; Email: contact@riia.org; Web: www.riia.org; *Director*, Dr C. Gamble

ROYAL INSTITUTE OF NAVIGATION (1947), 1 Kensington Gore, London SW7 2AT. Tel: 020-7591 3130; Fax: 020-7591 3131; Email: info@rin.org.uk; Web: www.rin.org.uk; *Director*, Gp Capt. D. W. Broughton

ROYAL INSTITUTE OF OIL PAINTERS (1882), 17 Carlton House Terrace, London SW1Y 5BD. Tel: 020-7930 6844; Fax: 020-7839 7830; Web: www.mallgalleries.org.uk; *Secretary*, Ms J. Easterling

ROYAL INSTITUTE OF PAINTERS IN WATER COLOURS (1831), 17 Carlton House Terrace, London SW1Y 5BD. Tel: 020-7930 6844; Fax: 020-7839 7830; Web: www.mallgalleries.org.uk; *Secretary*, T. Hunt

THE ROYAL INSTITUTE OF PHILOSOPHY (1925), 14 Gordon Square, London WC1H 0AR. Tel: 020-7387 4130; Fax: 020-7383 4061; Email: i.purkiss@mailbox.ulcc.ac.uk; *Director*, Prof. A. O'Hear

ROYAL INSTITUTION OF CHARTERED SURVEYORS 12 Great George Street, London SW1P 3AD. Tel: 020-7222 7000; Fax: 020-7222 5074; Email: info@rics.org.uk; Web: www.rics.org; *Chief Executive*, J. H. A. J. Armstrong

THE ROYAL INSTITUTION OF GREAT BRITAIN (1799), 21 Albemarle Street, London W1S 4BS. Tel: 020-7409 2992; Fax: 020-7629 3569; Email: ri@ri.ac.uk; Web: www.ri.ac.uk; *Director*, Prof. S. Greenfield

ROYAL INSTITUTION OF NAVAL ARCHITECTS, 10 Upper Belgrave Street, London SW1X 8BQ. Tel: 020-7235 4622; Fax: 020-7259 5912; Email: hq@rina.org.uk; Web: www.rina.org.uk; *Chief Executive*, T. Blakeley

ROYAL LITERARY FUND, 3 Johnson's Court, off Fleet Street, London EC4A 3EA. Tel: 020-7353 7150; Fax: 020-7353 1300; Email: egunnflf@globalnet.co.uk; *General Secretary*, Ms E. M. Gunn

ROYAL MASONIC BENEVOLENT INSTITUTION (1842), 20 Great Queen Street, London WC2B 5BG. Tel: 020-7405 8341; Fax: 020-7404 0724; Email: enquiries@rmbi.org.uk; *Chief Executive*, Peter Gray

ROYAL MEDICAL BENEVOLENT FUND, 24 King's Road, London SW19 8QN. Tel: 020-8540 9194; Fax: 020-8542 0494; Email: rm.bf@virgin.net; Web: www.rmbf.co.uk; *Chief Executive*, M. Baber

ROYAL MICROSCOPICAL SOCIETY (1839), 37–38 St Clements, Oxford OX4 1AJ. Tel: 01865-248768; Fax: 01865-791237; Email: info@rms.org.uk; Web: www.rms.org.uk; *Administrator*, P. B. Hirst

ROYAL NATIONAL COLLEGE FOR THE BLIND (1872), College Road, Hereford HR1 1EB. Tel: 01432-265725; Fax: 01432-353478; Email: ss@rncb.ac.uk; Web: www.rncb.ac.uk; *Principal*, Mrs R. Burge

ROYAL NATIONAL INSTITUTE FOR DEAF PEOPLE, 19–23 Feathersone Street, London EC1Y 8SL. Tel: 020-7296 8000; Fax: 020-7296 8199; Email: helpline@rnid.org.uk; Web: www.rnid.org.uk; *Chief Executive*, J. Strachan

ROYAL NATIONAL INSTITUTE FOR THE BLIND, 224 Great Portland Street, London W1W 5AA. Tel: 0845-669999; Fax: 020-7388 2034; Email: helpline@rnib.org.uk; Web: www.rnib.org.uk; *Director General*, I. Bruce

ROYAL NATIONAL LIFEBOAT INSTITUTION (1824), West Quay Road, Poole, Dorset BT15 1HZ. Tel: 01202-663000; Fax: 01202-663167; Email: info@rnli.org.uk; Web: www.rnli.org.uk; *Chief Executive*, A. Freemantle

ROYAL NAVAL ASSOCIATION, 82 Chelsea Manor Street, London SW3 5QJ. Tel: 020-7352 6764; Fax: 020-7351 0610; Email: rna@netcomuk.co.uk; *General Secretary*, Capt. R. McQueen

ROYAL NAVAL BENEVOLENT SOCIETY FOR OFFICERS (1739), 1 Fleet Street, London EC4Y 1BD. Tel: 020-7427 7471; Fax: 020-7427 7471; *Secretary*, Capt. I. B. Sutherland

ROYAL PATRIOTIC FUND CORPORATION (1854), 40 Queen Anne's Gate, London SW1H 9AP. Tel: 020-7233 1894; Fax: 020-7233 1799; *Secretary*, Brig. T. G. Williams

ROYAL PHARMACEUTICAL SOCIETY OF GREAT BRITAIN (1841), 1 Lambeth High Street, London SE1 7JN. Tel: 020-7735 9141; Fax: 020-7735 7629; Email: enquiries@rpsgb.org.uk; Web: www.rpsgb.org.uk; *Secretary and Registrar*, Ms A. M. Lewis

ROYAL PHILATELIC SOCIETY LONDON (1869), 41 Devonshire Place, London W1G 6JY. Tel: 020-7486 1044; Fax: 020-7486 0803; Email: secretary@rpsl.org.uk; Web: www.rpsl.org.uk; *Hon. Secretary*, D. Gurney

ROYAL PINNER SCHOOL FOUNDATION, 110 Old Brompton Road, London SW7 3RB. Tel: 020-7373 6168; *Secretary*, D. Crawford

ROYAL SCHOOL FOR DEAF CHILDREN MARGATE (1792), Victoria Road, Margate, Kent CT9 1NB. Tel: 01843-227561; Fax: 01843-227637; Email: enquiries@royalschoolfordeaf.kent.sch.uk; Web: www.royalschoolfordeaf.kent.sch.uk; *Secretary*, J. C. Gunnell

ROYAL SCHOOL OF CHURCH MUSIC (1927), Cleveland Lodge, Westhumble, Dorking, Surrey RH5 6BW. Tel: 01306-872800; Fax: 01306-887260; Email: cl@rscm.com; Web: www.rscm.com; *Director General*, Prof. J. Harper

ROYAL SCHOOL OF NEEDLEWORK, Apartment 12A, Hampton Court Palace, East Molesey, Surrey KT8 9AU. Tel: 020-8943 1432; Fax: 020-8943 4910; Web: www.royal-needlework.co.uk; *Principal*, Mrs E. Elvin

ROYAL SCOTTISH AGRICULTURAL BENEVOLENT INSTITUTION (1897), Ingliston, Edinburgh EH28 8NB. Tel: 0131-333 1023/1027; Fax: 0131-333 1027; Email: rsabi@charity.vfree.com; *Director*, I. C. Purves-Hume

THE ROYAL SOCIETY FOR ASIAN AFFAIRS (1901), 2 Belgrave Square, London SW1X 8PJ. Tel: 020-7235 5122; Fax: 020-7259 6771; Email: sec@rsaa.org.uk; Web: www.rsaa.org.uk; *Secretary*, D. J. Easton

ROYAL SOCIETY FOR THE ENCOURAGEMENT OF ARTS, MANUFACTURES AND COMMERCE (RSA) (1754), 8 John Adam Street, London WC2N 6EZ. Tel: 020-7930 5115; Email: general@rsa-uk.demon.co.uk; Web: www.rsa.org.uk; *Director*, Penny Egan

ROYAL SOCIETY FOR THE PREVENTION OF ACCIDENTS (1917), ROSPA House, Edgbaston Park, 353 Bristol Road, Birmingham B5 7ST. Tel: 0121-248 2000; Fax: 0121-248 2001; Email: HELP@rospa.co.uk; Web: www.rospa.co.uk; *Chief Executive*, Dr J. Hooper

ROYAL SOCIETY FOR THE PREVENTION OF CRUELTY TO ANIMALS (1824), Wilberforce Way, Horsham, W. Sussex RH13 7WN. Tel: 0870-010 1181; Web: www.rspca.org.uk; *Director General*, P. R. Davies

THE ROYAL SOCIETY FOR THE PROMOTION OF HEALTH (1876), 38a St George's Drive, London SW1V 4BH. Tel: 020-7630 0121; Fax: 020-7976 6847; Email: rshealth@rshealth.org.uk; Web: www.rsph.org; *Chief Executive*, H. Lowson

ROYAL SOCIETY FOR THE PROTECTION OF BIRDS (RSPB) (1889), The Lodge, Sandy, Beds SG19 2DL. Tel: 01767-680551; Fax: 01767-692365; Web: www.rspb.org.uk; *Chief Executive*, G. R. Wynne

ROYAL SOCIETY OF LITERATURE (1820), Somerset House, Strand, London WC2R 0RN. Tel: 020-7845 4676; Fax: 020-7845 4679; Email: info@rslit.org; Web: www.rslit.org; *Secretary*, Ronald Harwood

ROYAL SOCIETY OF MARINE ARTISTS (1945), 17 Carlton House Terrace, London SW1Y 5BD. Tel: 020-7930 6844; Fax: 020-7839 7830; Web: www.mallgalleries.org.uk; *Secretary*, D. Howell

THE ROYAL SOCIETY OF MEDICINE, 1 Wimpole Street, London W1G 0AE. Tel: 020-7290 2900; Fax: 020-7290 2992; Email: membership@roysocmed.ac.uk; Web: www.rsm.ac.uk; *Executive Director*, Dr A. Grocock

THE ROYAL SOCIETY OF MUSICIANS OF GREAT BRITAIN (1738), 10 Stratford Place, London W1C 1BA. Tel: 020-7629 6137; Fax: 020-7629 6137; *Secretary*, Mrs M. Gibb

ROYAL SOCIETY OF PAINTER-PRINTMAKERS (1880), Bankside Gallery, 48 Hopton Street, London SE1 9JH. Tel: 020-7928 7521; Fax: 020-7928 2820; Email: bankside@freeuk.com; *President*, Prof. D. Carpanini

ROYAL SOCIETY OF PORTRAIT PAINTERS (1891), 17 Carlton House Terrace, London SW1Y 5BD. Tel: 020-7930 6844; Fax: 020-7839 7830; Web: www.mallgalleries.org.uk; *Secretary*, D. Cobley

ROYAL SOCIETY OF TROPICAL MEDICINE AND HYGIENE (1907), Manson House, 26 Portland Place, London W1B 1EY. Tel: 020-7580 2127; Fax: 020-7436 1389; Email: mail@rstmh.org; Web: www.rstmh.org; *Hon. Secretary*, Prof. R. D. Ward

THE ROYAL STAR AND GARTER HOME FOR DISABLED SAILORS, SOLDIERS AND AIRMEN (1916), Richmond Hill, Richmond upon Thames, Surrey TW10 6RR. Tel: 020-8940 3314; Fax: 020-8940 1953; Email: ian.lashbrooke@starandgarter.org; Web: www.starandgarter.org; *Chief Executive*, I. A. Lashbrooke

ROYAL STATISTICAL SOCIETY (1834), 12 Errol Street, London EC1Y 8LX. Tel: 020-7638 8998; Fax: 020-7256 7598; Email: rss@rss.org.uk; Web: www.rss.org.uk; *Executive Secretary*, I. J. Goddard

ROYAL THEATRICAL FUND, 11 Garrick Street, London WC2E 9AR. Tel: 020-7836 3322; Fax: 020-7379 8273; Email: admin@trtf.com; Web: www.trtf.com; *Secretary*, Mrs R. M. Foster

ROYAL ULSTER AGRICULTURAL SOCIETY, The King's Hall, Balmoral, Belfast BT9 6GW. Tel: 028-9066 5225; Fax: 028-9066 1264; Email: general@kingshall.co.uk; Web: www.balmoralshow.co.uk; *Chief Executive*, W. H. Yarr

THE ROYAL UNITED KINGDOM BENEFICENT ASSOCIATION (1863), 6 Avonmore Road, London W14 8RL. Tel: 020-7605 4200; Fax: 020-7605 4201; Email: charity@rukba.org.uk; Web: www.rukba.org.uk; *Director*, W. Rathbone

ROYAL UNITED SERVICES INSTITUTE FOR DEFENCE STUDIES, Whitehall, London SW1A 2ET. Tel: 020-7930 5854; Fax: 020-7321 0943; Email: defence@rusi.org; Web: www.rusi.org; *Director*, Rear-Adm. R. Cobbold

ROYAL WATERCOLOUR SOCIETY (1804), Bankside Gallery, 48 Hopton Street, London SE1 9JH. Tel: 020-7928 7521; Fax: 020-7928 2820; Email: bankside@freeuk.com; *President*, F. Bowyer

SALMON AND TROUT ASSOCIATION (1903), Fishmongers' Hall, London Bridge, London EC4R 9EL. Tel: 020-7283 5838; Fax: 020-7626 5137; Email: salmon.trout@virgin.net; Web: www.salmon-trout.org; *Director*, C. W. Poupard

SANE (1986), 1st Floor, Cityside House, 40 Alder Street, London E1 1EE. Tel: 020-7375 1002; Fax: 020-7375 2162; Email: info@sane.org.uk; Web: www.sane.org.uk; *Chief Executive*, Ms M. Wallace

SAVE BRITAIN'S HERITAGE (1975), 70 Cowcross Street, London EC1M 6EJ. Tel: 020-7253 3500; Fax: 020-7253 3400; Email: save@btinternet.com; Web: www.savebritainsheritage.org; *Secretary*, A. Wilkinson

SAVE THE CHILDREN FUND, 17 Grove Lane, London SE5 8RD. Tel: 020-7703 5400; Fax: 020-7703 2278; Web: www.savethechildren.org.uk; *Director General*, M. Aaronson

SCHOOL LIBRARY ASSOCIATION (1937), Unit 1, Lotmead Business Village, Lotmead Farm, Wanborough, nr Swindon SN4 0UY. Tel: 01793-791787; Fax: 01793-791786; Email: info@sla.org.uk; Web: www.sla.org.uk; *Chief Executive*, Ms K. Lemaire

SCHOOLMISTRESSES AND GOVERNESSES BENEVOLENT INSTITUTION (1848), Queen Mary House, Manor Park Road, Chislehurst, Kent BR7 5PY. Tel: 020-8468 7997; *Director*, L. I. Baggott

SCOPE (1952), 6 Market Road, London N7 9PW. Tel: 0808-800 3333; Fax: 01908-321051; Email: cphelpline@scope.org.uk; Web: www.scope.org.uk; *Chief Executive*, R. P. Brewster

SCOTTISH ASSOCIATION FOR MARINE SCIENCE, Dunstaffnage Marine Laboratory, Oban, Argyll PA34 4AD. Tel: 01631-559000; Fax: 01631-559001; Email: mail@dml.ac.uk; Web: www.sams.ac.uk; *Director*, Prof. G. B. Shimmield

SCOTTISH ASSOCIATION FOR MENTAL HEALTH, Cumbrae House, 15 Carlton Court, Glasgow G5 9JP. Tel: 0141-568 7000; Fax: 0141-568 7001; Email: enquire@samh.org.uk; *Chief Executive*, Ms S. M. Barcus

SCOTTISH CHAMBERS OF COMMERCE (1948), 12 Broughton Place, Edinburgh EH1 3RX. Tel: 0131-557 9500; Fax: 0131-558 3257; Email: mail@scottishchambers.org.uk; Web: www.scottishchambers.org.uk; *Director*, L. Gold

SCOTTISH CHURCH HISTORY SOCIETY (1927), Crown Manse, 39 Southside Road, Inverness IV2 4XA. Tel: 01463-231140; Fax: 01463-230537; *Hon. Secretary*, Revd Dr P. H. Donald

SCOTTISH LANDOWNERS' FEDERATION, Stuart House, Eskmills Business Park, Musselburgh EH21 7PB. Tel: 0131-653 5400; Fax: 0131-653 5401; Email: slfinfo@slf.org.uk; Web: www.slf.org.uk; *Director*, Dr M. S. Hankey

SCOTTISH WILDLIFE TRUST (1964), Cramond House, Kirk Cramond, Cramond Glebe Road, Edinburgh EH4 6NS. Tel: 0131-312 7765; Fax: 0131-312 8705; Web: www.swt.org.uk; *Chief Executive*, S. Sankey

SCOTTISH YOUTH HOSTELS ASSOCIATION, 7 Glebe Crescent, Stirling FK8 2JA. Tel: 01786-891400; Fax: 01786-891333; Email: enquiries@syha.org.uk; Web: www.syha.org.uk; *General Secretary*, W. Forsyth

THE SCOUT ASSOCIATION (1907), Gilwell Park, Chingford, London E4 7QW. Tel: 020-8443 7100; Fax: 020-8443 7103; Email: info.centre@scout.org.uk; Web: www.scoutbase.org.uk; *Chief Executive*, D. M. Twine

SCRIPTURE GIFT MISSION INCORPORATED (1888), Radstock House, 3 Eccleston Street, London SW1W 9LZ. Tel: 020-7730 2155; Fax: 020-7730 0240; Email: int@sgm.org; *International Director*, H. Q. Davies

THE SEA CADET ASSOCIATION, 202 Lambeth Road, London SE1 7JF. Tel: 020-7928 8978; Fax: 020-7928 8914; Email: schq@sea-cadets.org; Web: www.sea-cadets.org; *Chief Executive*, Cdre. R. M. Parker

SELDEN SOCIETY (1887), Faculty of Laws, Queen Mary and Westfield College, Mile End Road, London E1 4NS. Tel: 020-7882 5136; Fax: 020-8981 8733; Email: selden-society@qmw.ac.uk; Web: www.selden-society.qmw.ac.uk; *Secretary*, V. Tunkel

SENSE (THE NATIONAL DEAFBLIND AND RUBELLA ASSOCIATION), 11–13 Clifton Terrace, London N4 3SR. Tel: 020-7272 7774; Fax: 020-7272 6012; Email: enquiries@sense.org.uk; Web: www.sense.org.uk; *Chief Executive*, R. Clark

SHAFTESBURY HOMES AND ARETHUSA, The Chapel, Royal Victoria Patriotic Building, Trinity Road, London SW18 3SX. Tel: 020-8875 1555; Fax: 020-8875 1954; *Chief Executive*, Ms A. Chesney

THE SHAFTESBURY SOCIETY, 16 Kingston Road, London SW19 1JZ. Tel: 020-8239 5555; Fax: 020-8239 5580; *Chief Executive*, Ms F. Beckett

SHELLFISH ASSOCIATION OF GREAT BRITAIN, Fishmongers' Hall, London Bridge, London EC4R 9EL. Tel: 020-7283 8305; Fax: 020-7929 1389; *Director*, Dr P. Hunt

SIR OSWALD STOLL FOUNDATION, 446 Fulham Road, London SW6 1DT. Tel: 020-7385 2110; Fax: 020-7381 7485; Email: stoll44b@aol.com; *Chief Executive*, R. C. Brunwin

THE SOCIALIST PARTY (1904), 52 Clapham High Street, London SW4 7UN. Tel: 020-7622 3811; Fax: 020-7720 3665; Email: spgb@worldsocialism.org; Web: www.worldsocialism.org

THE SOCIETY FOR OPERATIONS ENGINEERS, 22 Greencoat Place, London SW1P 1PR. Tel: 020-7630 1111; Fax: 020-7630 6677; Email: soe@soe.org.uk; Web: www.soe.org.uk; *Chief Executive*, P. J. G. Corp

SOCIETY FOR PROMOTING CHRISTIAN KNOWLEDGE (SPCK) (1698), Holy Trinity Church, Marylebone Road, London NW1 4DU. Tel: 020-7643 0382; Fax: 020-7643 0391; Email: spck@spck.org.uk; Web: www.spck.org.uk; *General Secretary*, P. Chandler

SOCIETY FOR PSYCHICAL RESEARCH (1882), 49 Marloes Road, London W8 6LA. Tel: 020-7937 8984; Fax: 020-7937 8984; Web: www.spr.ac.uk; *Secretary*, P. M. Johnson

SOCIETY FOR THE ASSISTANCE OF LADIES IN REDUCED CIRCUMSTANCES (1886), Lancaster House, 25 Hornyold Road, Malvern, Worcs WR14 1QQ. Tel: 01684-574645; *Secretary*, Miss H. C. Grahamslaw

SOCIETY FOR THE PROMOTION OF ROMAN STUDIES (1910), Senate House, Malet Street, London WC1E 7HU. Tel: 020-7643 0382; Fax: 020-7643 0391; Email: romansoc@sas.ac.uk; Web: www.sas.ac.uk/icls/roman; *Secretary*, Dr H. M. Cockle

SOCIETY FOR THE PROTECTION OF ANCIENT BUILDINGS (1877), 37 Spital Square, London E1 6DY. Tel: 020-7377 1644; Fax: 020-7247 5296; Email: info@spab.org.uk; Web: www.spab.org.uk; *Secretary*, P. Venning

SOCIETY FOR THEATRE RESEARCH (1948), c/o The Theatre Museum, 1E Tavistock Street, London WC2E 7PA. ; Email: e.cottis@btinternet.com; Web: www.str.org.uk; *Joint Hon. Secretaries*, Ms E. Cottis; Ms F. Dann

SOCIETY OF ANTIQUARIES OF LONDON (1707), Burlington House, Piccadilly, London W1J 0BE. Tel: 020-7734 0193; Fax: 020-7287 6967; Email: admin@sal.org.uk; Web: www.sal.org.uk; *General-Secretary*, D. Morgan Evans

SOCIETY OF ANTIQUARIES OF SCOTLAND (1780), Royal Museum, Chambers Street, Edinburgh EH1 1JF. Tel: 0131-247 4115/4133; Fax: 0131-247 4163; Email: f.ashmore@nms.ac.uk; *Director*, Mrs F. Ashmore

SOCIETY OF APOTHECARIES OF LONDON (1617), 14 Black Friars Lane, London EC4V 6EJ. Tel: 020-7236 1189; Fax: 020-7329 3177; Email: clerk@apothecaries.org; Web: www.apothecaries.org; *Clerk*, R. J. Stringer

SOCIETY OF ARCHIVISTS (1947 and 1954), 40 Northampton Road, London EC1R 0HB. Tel: 020-7278 8630; Fax: 020-7278 2107; Email: societyofarchivists@archives.org.uk; Web: www.archives.org.uk; *Executive Secretary*, P. S. Cleary

SOCIETY OF AUTHORS, 84 Drayton Gardens, London SW10 9SB. Tel: 020-7373 6642; Fax: 020-7373 5768; Email: info@societyofauthors.org; Web: www.societyofauthors.org; *General Secretary*, M. Le Fanu

SOCIETY OF COUNTY TREASURERS, East Sussex County Council, PO Box 3, County Hall, St Anne's Crescent, Lewes, East Sussex BN7 1SF. Tel: 01273-481406; Fax: 01273-482848; *Hon. Secretary*, S. J. Nolan

SOCIETY OF EDITORS (1999), University Centre, Granta Place, Cambridge CB2 1RU. Tel: 01223-304080; Fax: 01223-304090; Email: society@ukeditors.com; Web: www.ukeditors.com; *Executive Director*, R. Satchwell

SOCIETY OF EDUCATION OFFICERS (1972), Manchester House, 84–86 Princess Street, Manchester M1 6NG. Tel: 0161-236 5766; Fax: 0161-236 6742; Email: office@seo.org.uk; *General Secretary*, Chris Waterman

SOCIETY OF GENEALOGISTS ENTERPRISES LTD (1911 and 1999), 14 Charterhouse Buildings, Goswell Road, London EC1M 7BA. Tel: 020-7251 8799; Fax: 020-7250 1800; Email: info@sog.org.uk; Web: www.sog.org.uk; *Managing Director*, R. I. N. Gordon

SOCIETY OF GLASS TECHNOLOGY (1916), Don Valley House, Savile Street East, Sheffield S4 7UQ. Tel: 0114-263 4455; Fax: 0114-263 4411; Email: info@sgt.org; Web: www.sgt.org

SOCIETY OF INDEXERS (1957), Globe Centre, Penistone Road, Sheffield S6 3AE. Tel: 0114-281 3060; Fax: 0114-281 3061; Email: admin@socind.demon.co.uk; Web: www.socind.demon.co.uk; *Secretary*, Ms L. Weinkove

SOCIETY OF NAUTICAL RESEARCH, c/o National Maritime Museum, Greenwich, London SE10 9NF. Tel: 020-8312 6712; Fax: 020-8312 6722; Email: lxveri@nmm.ac.uk; Web: www.snr.org.uk; *Hon. Secretary*, Liza Verity

SOCIETY OF PUBLIC TEACHERS OF LAW (1908), School of Law, Kings College London, Strand, London WC2R 2LS. Tel: 020-7848 2849; Fax: 020-7848 2465; Email: peter.niven@kcl.ac.uk; Web: www.law.warwick.ac.uk/sptl; *Hon. Secretary*, Prof. N. J. Wikely

SOCIETY OF SCHOOLMASTERS AND SCHOOLMISTRESSES (1798), The King's School, Canterbury, Kent CT1 2ES. Tel: 01227-595546; Fax: 01227-595589; Email: rbma@kings-school.co.uk; *Hon. Secretary*, Dr R. B. Mallion

SOCIETY OF SCRIBES AND ILLUMINATORS (1922), 6 Queen Square, London WC1N 3AT. Tel: 01524-251534; Fax: 01524-251534; Email: scribe@calligraphy.org; Web: www.calligraphy.org; *Hon. Secretary*, Mrs G. Hazeldine

SOCIETY OF SOLICITORS IN THE SUPREME COURT OF SCOTLAND (1784), SSC Library, Parliament House, 11 Parliament Square, Edinburgh EH1 1RF. Tel: 0131-225 6268; Fax: 0131-225 2270; Email: ssc.library@dial.pipex.com; *Secretary*, I. L. S. Balfour

SOCIETY OF WRITERS TO HM SIGNET (1594), Signet Library, Parliament Square, Edinburgh EH1 1RF. Tel: 0131-220 3426; Fax: 0131-220 4016; Email: wssoc@dial.pipex.com; Web: www.signetlibrary.co.uk; *General Manager*, M. R. McVittie

SONS OF TEMPERANCE FRIENDLY SOCIETY, 176 Blackfriars Road, London SE1 8ET. Tel: 020-7928 7384; Fax: 020-7928 7384; Web: www.sonsoftemperance.co.uk; *Chief Executive*, Mrs M. C. Scroby

SSAFA FORCES HELP, 19 Queen Elizabeth Street, London SE1 2LP. Tel: 020-7403 8783; Fax: 020-7403 8815; Email: info@ssafa.org.uk; Web: www.ssafa.org.uk; *Controller*, Maj.-Gen. P. Sheppard

ST DUNSTAN'S (CARING FOR BLIND EX-SERVICE MEN AND WOMEN) (1915), 12-14 Harcourt Street, London W1H 4DD. Tel: 020-7723 5021; Fax: 020-7262 6199; *Chief Executive*, Robert Leader

ST JOHN AMBULANCE (1099), 1 Grosvenor Crescent, London SW1X 7EF. Tel: 020-7235 5231; Fax: 020-7235 0796; Email: pr@nhq.sja.org.uk; Web: www.sja.org.uk; *Chief Executive*, L. Martin

STANDING COUNCIL OF THE BARONETAGE (1903), 3 Eastcroft Road, West Ewell, Epsom, Surrey KT19 9TX. Tel: 020-8393 6620; Fax: 020-8393 6620; *Chairman*, Sir Brian Barttelot

THE STRATEGIC PLANNING SOCIETY, 17 Portland Place, London W1B 1PU. Tel: 020-7636 7737; Fax: 020-7323 1692; Email: enquiries@sps.org.uk; Web: www.sps.org.uk; *General Manager*, D. Lambert

THE STROKE ASSOCIATION, Stroke House, Whitecross Street, London EC1Y 8JJ. Tel: 020-7566 0300; Fax: 020-7490 2686; Web: www.stroke.org.uk; *Chief Executive Office*, Miss M. Goose

SURREY ARCHAEOLOGICAL SOCIETY (1854), Castle Arch, Guildford, Surrey GU1 3SX. Tel: 01483-532454; Fax: 01483-532454; Email: surreyarch@compuserve.com; *Hon. Secretary*, Miss A. J. Monk

SURVIVAL INTERNATIONAL (1969), 11–15 Emerald Street, London WC1N 3QT. Tel: 020-7242 1441; Fax: 020-7424 1771; Email: info@survival-international.org; Web: www.survival-international.org; *Director*, S. Corry

SUZY LAMPLUGH TRUST (1986), 14 East Sheen Avenue, London SW14 8AS. Tel: 020-8392 1839; Fax: 020-8392 1830; Email: trust@suzylamplugh.org; Web: www.suzylamplugh.org; *Director, Administration and Development*, Ms A. Mortlock

SWEDENBORG SOCIETY, 20–21 Bloomsbury Way, London WC1A 2TH. Tel: 020-7405 7986; Fax: 020-7831 5848; Email: swed.soc@netmatters.co.uk; Web: www.swedenborg.org.uk; *Secretary*, Miss Sarah Harding

THE TAVISTOCK INSTITUTE, 30 Tabernacle Street, London EC2A 4UE. Tel: 020-7417 0407; Fax: 020-7417 0566; Web: www.tavistockinstitute.org

TELECOMMUNICATIONS USERS' ASSOCIATION (1965), Woodgate Studios, 2–8 Games Road, Cockfosters, Barnet, Herts EN4 9HN. Tel: 020-8449 8844; Fax: 020-8447 4901; Email: tua@dial.pipex.com; Web: www.tua.co.uk; *Executive Chairman*, W. E. Mieran

TERRENCE HIGGINS TRUST, 52–54 Grays Inn Road, London WC1X 8JU. Tel: 020-7831 0330; Fax: 020-7242 0121; Email: info@tht.org.uk; Web: www.tht.org.uk; *Chief Executive*, N. Partridge

THE THEATRES TRUST (1976), 22 Charing Cross Road, London WC2H 0QL. Tel: 020-7836 8591; Fax: 020-7836 3302; Email: info@theatrestrust.org.uk; Web: www.theatrestrust.org.uk; *Director*, P. Longman

THEOSOPHICAL SOCIETY IN ENGLAND (1875), 50 Gloucester Place, London W1U 8EA. Tel: 020-7935 9261; Fax: 020-7935 9543; Email: theosophical@freenetname.co.uk; Web: www.theosophical-society.org.uk; *National President*, C. Price

TOWN AND COUNTRY PLANNING ASSOCIATION (1899), 17 Carlton House Terrace, London SW1Y 5AS. Tel: 020-7930 8903/4/5; Fax: 020-7930 3280; Email: tcpa@tcpa.org.uk; Web: www.tcpa.org.uk; *Director*, Gideon Amos

THE TREE COUNCIL (1974), 51 Catherine Place, London SW1E 6DY. Tel: 020-7828 9928; Fax: 020-7828 9060; Web: www.treecouncil.org.uk; *Director*, R. Osborne

TURNER SOCIETY (1975), BCM Box Turner, London WC1N 3XX. Email:: turner@equinox.demon.co.uk; Web: www.turnersociety.org.uk; *Chairman*, Eric Shanes

UK INDEPENDENCE PARTY, Triumph House, 189 Regent Street, London W1B 4JX. Tel: 020-7434 4559; Fax: 020-7439 4659; Email: mail@ukip.org; Web: www.ukip.org; *Secretary*, Michael Harvey

UK YOUTH (1911), 2nd Floor, Kirby House, 20–24 Kirby Street, London EC1N 8TS. Tel: 020-7242 4045; Fax: 020-7242 4125; Email: info@ukyouth.org.uk; Web: www.ukyouth.org.uk; *Chief Executive*, J. Bateman

UNITED NATIONS ASSOCIATION OF GREAT BRITAIN AND NORTHERN IRELAND, 3 Whitehall Court, London SW1A 2EL. Tel: 020-7930 2931; Fax: 020-7930 5893; Email: info@UNA-UK.org; *Director*, M. C. Harper

UNITED SOCIETY FOR THE PROPAGATION OF THE GOSPEL (1701), Partnership House, 157 Waterloo Road, London SE1 8XA. Tel: 020-7928 8681; Fax: 020-7928 2371; Email: enquiries@uspg.org.uk; Web: www.uspg.org.uk; *Secretary*, Rt Revd M. Rumalshah

VEGETARIAN SOCIETY OF THE UNITED KINGDOM LTD (1847), Parkdale, Dunham Road, Altrincham, Cheshire WA14 4QG. Tel: 0161-925 2000; Fax: 0161-926 9182; Email: info@vegsoc.org; Web: www.vegsoc.org; *Chief Executive*, Ms T. Fox

VICTIM SUPPORT (NATIONAL ASSOCIATION OF VICTIMS SUPPORT SCHEMES) (1979), National Office, Cranmer House, 39 Brixton Road, London SW9 6DZ. Tel: 020-7735 9166. Helpline: 0845-3030 900; Fax: 020-7582 5712; Email: contact@victimsupport.org.uk; *Chief Executive*, Ms H. Reeves

VICTORIA CROSS AND GEORGE CROSS ASSOCIATION, Horse Guards, Whitehall, London SW1A 2AX. Tel: 020-7930 3506; *Secretary*, Mrs D. Grahame

THE VICTORIAN SOCIETY (1958), 1 Priory Gardens, Bedford Park, London W4 1TT. Tel: 020-8994 1019; Fax: 020-8995 4895; Email: admin@victorian-society.org; Web: www.victorian-society.org.uk; *Director*, Dr Ian Dungavell

VICTORY (SERVICES) ASSOCIATION LTD AND CLUB, 63–79 Seymour Street, London W2 2HF. Tel: 020-7723 4474; Fax: 020-7724 1134; Email: office@vsc.co.uk; Web: www.vsc.co.uk; *General Manager*, G. F. Taylor

VIKING SOCIETY FOR NORTHERN RESEARCH, Department of Scandinavian Studies, University College, Gower Street, London WC1E 6BT. Tel: 020-7679 7176; Fax: 020-7380 7750; Email: s.rust@ucl.ac.uk; *Hon. Secretaries*, Prof. M. P. Barnes; Dr J. Jesh

VSO (VOLUNTARY SERVICE OVERSEAS) (1958), 317 Putney Bridge Road, London SW15 2PN. Tel: 020-8780 7200; Fax: 020-8780 7300; Web: www.vso.org.uk; *Chief Executive*, M. Goldring

WAR ON WANT, Fenner Brockway House, 37–39 Great Guildford Street, London SE1 0ES. Tel: 020-7620 1111; Fax: 020-7261 9291; *Director*, Ms M. Lynch

WELLBEING – HEALTH RESEARCH CHARITY FOR WOMEN AND BABIES (1965), 27 Sussex Place, Regent's Park, London NW1 4SP. Tel: 020-7772 6400; Fax: 020-7724 7725; Email: wellbeing@rcog.org.uk; Web: www.wellbeing.org.uk; *Director*, Mrs J. Arnell

THE WELLCOME TRUST (1936), The Wellcome Building, 183 Euston Road, London NW1 2BE. Tel: 020-7611 8888; Fax: 020-7611 8545; Email: director@wellcome.ac.uk; Web: www.wellcome.ac.uk; *Director*, Dr Michael Dexter

WES WORLD-WIDE EDUCATION SERVICE LTD, Canada House, 272 Field End Road, Eastcote, Ruislip, Middx HA4 9NA. Tel: 020-8582 0317; Fax: 020-8429 4838; Email: wes@wesworldwide.com; Web: www.wesworldwide.com; *Director*, Mrs T. Mulder-Reynolds

WEST LONDON MISSION, 19 Thayer Street, London W1V 2QJ. Tel: 020-7935 6179; Fax: 020-7487 3965; Email: office@westlondonmission.freeserve.co.uk; Web: www.methodist.org.uk/west.london.mission; *Superintendent*, Revd D. S. Cruise

WESTMINSTER FOUNDATION FOR DEMOCRACY (1992), 2nd Floor, 125 Pall Mall, London SW1Y 5EA. Tel: 020-7930 0408; Fax: 020-7930 0449; Email: wfd@wfd.org; Web: www.wfd.org; *Chairman*, Trevor Williams

WILLIAM MORRIS SOCIETY AND KELMSCOTT FELLOWSHIP, Kelmscott House, 26 Upper Mall, London W6 9TA. Tel: 020-8741 3735; Fax: 020-8748 5207; Email: williammorris@care4free.net; Web: www.morrissociety.org; *Hon. Secretary*, P. Faulkner

THE WINE AND SPIRIT ASSOCIATION (1824), Five Kings House, 1 Queen Street Place, London EC4R 1XX. Tel: 020-7248 5377; Fax: 020-7489 0322; Email: wsa@wsa.org.uk; Web: www.wsa.org.uk; *Director*, Q. Rappoport

WOMEN'S ENGINEERING SOCIETY (1919), 2 Queen Anne's Gate Buildings, Dartmouth Street, London SW1H 9BP. Tel: 020-7233 1974; Email: info@wes.org.uk; Web: www.wes.org.uk; *Secretary*, Mrs C. MacGillivray

WOMEN'S NATIONWIDE CANCER CONTROL CAMPAIGN, 1st Floor, Charity House, 14-15 Perseverance Works, London E2 8DD. Tel: 020-7729 4688; Fax: 020-7613 0771; Email: admin@wnccc.org.uk; Web: www.wnccc.org.uk; *Chief Executive*, Ms J. Cohen

WORKERS' EDUCATIONAL ASSOCIATION, Temple House, 17 Victoria Park Square, London E2 9PB. Tel: 020-8983 1515; Fax: 020-8983 4840; Email: nationaloffice@wea.org.uk; Web: www.wea.org.uk; *General Secretary*, R. Lochrie

WORLD ENERGY COUNCIL, Regency House, 1–4 Warwick Street, London W1B 5LT. Tel: 020-7734 5996; Fax: 020-7734 5926; Email: info@worldenergy.org; Web: www.worldenergy.org; *Secretary-General*, G. W. Doucet

ZOOLOGICAL SOCIETY OF LONDON (1826), Regent's Park, London NW1 4RY. Tel: 020-7722 3333; Fax: 020-7586 5743; Web: www.zsl.org; *Director General*, Dr Michael Dixon

# International Organisations

## ANDEAN COMMUNITY

General Secretariat, Paseo de la República 3895, esq. Aramburú, San Isidro, Lima 27, Peru
Tel: (00 51) (1) 411 1400;
Fax: (00 51) (1) 221 3329
E-mail: contacto@comunidadandina.org
Web: www.comunidadandina.org

The Andean Community came into being on 1 August 1997. It facilitates the development of the member countries through economic and social integration and co-operation, acceleration of the economic growth of the Andean countries, the promotion of job creation, furthering the aim of creating a Latin American common market, strengthening the position of the member states in the international economic context, and reducing the differences in development that exist between the member states.

It aims to achieve its objectives by a programme of complete trade liberalisation, a common external tariff, the reduction of border controls, the progressive harmonisation of economic and social policies, the co-ordination of national legislation in relevant fields, promoting industrialisation and agricultural development, and supporting technological development programmes.

It comprises the five member states, Bolivia, Colombia, Ecuador, Peru and Venezuela, and the bodies of the Andean Integration System (AIS). The General Secretariat of the Andean Community is its executive body, which is responsible for administration, ensuring that member states comply with their obligations, and resolving disputes. The General Secretariat is under the direction of the Secretary-General, who is elected by the Andean Council of Foreign Ministers (ACFM). The General Secretariat can propose decisions or suggestions to the ACFM and to the Commission. It also manages the integration process, ensures that Community commitments are fulfilled, and maintains relations with the member countries and the executive bodies of other international bodies.

The Andean Presidential Council is the highest-level body of the AIS and comprises the presidents of the member states; it meets at least once a year and decides on new policies, evaluates the integration process and makes decisions on reports and suggestions from other bodies. The chairmanship is rotated among the members of the council on a calendar year basis. The ACFM co-ordinates the positions of the member states in international issues, signs international agreements on behalf of its member states and can issue decisions that are legally binding in the member states. The Commission of the Andean Community is composed of a plenipotentiary representative from each member state and makes, implements and evaluates policies in the field of trade and investment in the region. The Court of Justice of the Andean Community comprises one judge from each member state. It ensures the uniform implementation of decisions and settles disputes. The Andean Development Corporation aims to support the sustainable development of the member states by promoting trade and investment. The Andean Parliament is presently composed of representatives of the national legislatures of the member states, but is due to become directly elected in 2003. It submits proposals to other bodies and promotes the harmonisation of legislation.

*Secretary-General*, Sebastián Alegrett

## ARAB MAGHREB UNION

27 Avenue Okba, Rabat, Morocco
Tel: (00 212) (7) 777 2668; fax: (00 212) (7) 777 2693
E-mail: sg.uma@maghrebarabe.org
Web: www.maghrebarabe.org

The treaty establishing the Arab Maghreb Union (AMU) was signed on 17 February 1989 by the heads of state of the five member states, Algeria, Libya, Mauritania, Morocco and Tunisia. The AMU aims to strengthen ties between the member states, who share strong historical, cultural and linguistic affinities, by developing agriculture and commerce, introducing the free circulation of goods and services, and establishing joint projects and economic co-operation programmes.

Decisions are made by the Council of Heads of State, which meets annually, and must be unanimous. A Council of Foreign Affairs Ministers meets regularly to prepare for the sessions of the Council of Heads of State. The Secretariat is based in Rabat and there is a Consultative Assembly, which consists of 30 representatives from each member state, based in Algiers, and a Court of Justice, with two judges from each country, based in Nouakchott, Mauritania.

*Secretary-General*, Mohamed Amamou

## ASIA-PACIFIC ECONOMIC CO-OPERATION

438 Alexandra Road, #14–00 Alexandra Point, Singapore 119958
Tel: (00 65) 276 1880; fax: (00 65) 276 1775
E-mail: info@mail.apecsec.org.sg
Web: www.apecsec.org.sg

Asia-Pacific Economic Co-operation (APEC) was founded in 1989 in response to the growing interdependence among Asia-Pacific economies. The 1994 Declaration of Common Resolve envisaged a free trade zone, to be established by 2010 by the industrialised countries and by 2020 by the developing member states. There are three pillars of APEC activities: trade and investment liberalisation, business facilitation, and economic and technical co-operation. Members define and fund work programmes for APEC's three committees, one sub-committee, 11 working groups and other APEC fora.

The members are: Australia, Brunei, Canada, Chile, China (People's Republic), China (Hong Kong), Indonesia, Japan, Republic of Korea, Malaysia, Mexico, New Zealand, Papua New Guinea, Peru, the Philippines, Russia, Singapore, Taiwan, Thailand, the USA and Vietnam.

The APEC chairman is responsible for hosting the annual ministerial meeting of foreign and economic ministers. The chairmanship rotates annually among member states. Senior officials of the organisation make recommendations to the ministers and carry out their decisions. They oversee and co-ordinate budgets and work programmes. In addition, there are many advisory groups.

ASSOCIATION OF SOUTH EAST ASIAN NATIONS
70 A. Jalan Sisingamangaraja, Jakarta 12110, Indonesia Tel: (00 62) (21) 726 2991;
fax: (00 62) (21) 739 8234
E-mail: public@asean.or.id
Web: www.asean.or.id

The Association of South East Asian Nations (ASEAN) was formed in 1967 with the aims of accelerating economic growth, social progress and cultural development, and ensuring regional stability. The founding members are Indonesia, Malaysia, the Philippines, Singapore and Thailand. Brunei and Vietnam joined in 1984 and 1995 respectively. Laos and Myanmar were admitted in July 1997. Cambodia was admitted on 30 April 1999.

The ASEAN Summit, a meeting of the heads of government, which convenes every three years, is ASEAN's highest authority, but informal summits are held annually. The ASEAN Ministerial Meeting (AMM) is an annual meeting of ASEAN foreign ministers and is responsible for the formulation of policy guidelines and the co-ordination of activities, although other relevant ministers are included in the AMM depending on the subject under discussion. The ASEAN Economic Ministers (AEM) meet annually to co-ordinate economic policy. The AMM and AEM usually hold a joint ministerial meeting before an ASEAN summit.

The 1992 Summit agreed to set up the ASEAN Free Trade Area (AFTA), which is due to be fully implemented by 2003. A common preferential tariff was introduced in 1993. At the annual summit in 1995, a South East Asia nuclear weapon-free zone was declared.

The Secretary-General of ASEAN is appointed on merit by the heads of government and can initiate, advise on, co-ordinate and implement ASEAN activities. In addition to the ASEAN Secretariat based in Jakarta, each member state has a national secretariat in its foreign ministry which organises and implements activities at national level.

*Secretary-General*, Rodolfo C. Severino (Philippines)

ASEAN COMMITTEE IN THE UK, Indonesian Embassy, 38 Grosvenor Square, London W1X 9AD Tel 020-7499 7661; fax 020-7491 4993

*Chairman*, H.E. Nana S. Sutresna

BALTIC ASSEMBLY Basteja bulvaris 12, LV-1050 Riga, Latvia
Tel: (00 371) 770 1795; fax: (00 371) 770 1796
E-mail: baltasam@parks.lv
Web: www.saeima.lv/baltasam/

The Baltic Assembly (BA) is an international organisation for co-operation between the parliaments of Estonia, Latvia and Lithuania, established in November 1991.

The legislature of each member state appoints 20 parliamentarians to the BA, including a head and deputy head of the national delegation. The BA holds two sessions per year, which are held in each of the member states in rotation.

The Presidium of the BA comprises the head and deputy head of each national delegation. It selects a Chairman, who is the head of the delegation of the member state which will host the following session, and the heads of the two other delegations become Deputy Chairmen. The Presidium is responsible for co-ordinating the activities of BA institutions, organises the sessions, supervises the budget and maintains relations with international organisations and the member states' national legislatures. In addition, there are permanent and ad-hoc committees.

The Baltic Assembly meets once a year with the Baltic Council of Ministers, which comprises the heads of government and ministers of the Baltic states and which carries out intergovernmental and regional co-operation between the Baltic States; the joint sessions are known as the Baltic Council.

*Chairman of the Presidium*, Romualds Rauks (Latvia)

*Deputy Chairmen*, Trivimi Velliste (Estonia); Audrius KliÞonis (Lithuania)

BANK FOR INTERNATIONAL SETTLEMENTS
Centralbahnplatz 2, CH-4002 Basel, Switzerland
Tel: (00 41) (61) 280 8080; fax: (00 41) (61) 280 9100
E-mail: email@bis.org
Web: www.bis.org

The Bank for International Settlements (BIS), which was founded in 1930, fosters international monetary and financial co-operation by acting as a forum to promote discussion and facilitate decision-making processes among central banks and within the international financial community. It also acts as a centre for economic and monetary research and an agent in connection with international financial operations.

The statutory organs of the BIS are the General Meeting and the Board of Directors. Forty-nine central banks have rights of voting and representation at General Meetings. Administrative control is vested in the Board of Directors which comprises 17 members including the Governor of the Bank of England.

*Chairman of the Board of Directors and President of the Bank for International Settlements*, Urban Bäckström (Sweden)

CAB INTERNATIONAL
Wallingford, Oxon OX10 8DE
Tel: 01491-832111; fax: 01491-833508
E-mail: cabi@cabi.org
Web: www.cabi.org

CAB International (formerly the Commonwealth Agricultural Bureaux) was founded in 1929. It generates, disseminates and applies scientific knowledge in support of sustainable development, with an emphasis on agriculture, forestry and natural resources, and the needs of developing countries. The organisation is owned and governed by its 41 member governments, each represented on an Executive Council. A Governing Board provides guidance to management on policy issues.

CABI has three divisions: bioscience, information and publishing. These undertake research and consultancy aimed at raising agricultural productivity, conserving biological resources, protecting the environment and controlling disease. The organisation publishes books, journals and newsletters and produces bibliographic databases on agriculture, health and allied disciplines. It also undertakes contracted scientific research and provides consultancy services and information support to developing countries.

*Director-General*, Dr Denis Blight

## CARIBBEAN COMMUNITY AND COMMON MARKET

PO Box 10827, Georgetown, Guyana
Tel: (00 592) (2) 69281; fax: (00 592) (2) 67816
E-mail: carisec2@caricom.org
Web: www.caricom.org

The Caribbean Community and Common Market (CARICOM) was established in 1973 with three objectives: economic co-operation through the Caribbean Common Market, the co-ordination of member states' foreign policy, and the provision of common services and co-operation in health, education, culture, communications and industrial relations.

The supreme organ is the Conference of Heads of Government, which determines policy, takes strategic decisions and is responsible for resolving conflicts and all matters relating to the founding treaty. The Community Council of Ministers consists of ministers of government responsible for CARICOM affairs and any other ministers designated by member states, and is responsible for strategic planning in the areas of economic integration, functional co-operation and external relations. The principal administrative arm is the Secretariat, based in Guyana. The Bureau of the Conference of Heads of Government is the executive body. It comprises the Chairman of the Conference, the outgoing Chairman and the Secretary-General, who are authorised to initiate proposals and to secure the implementation of CARICOM decisions. In addition, there are four ministers' councils dealing with trade and economic development, foreign and community relations, human and social development, and finance and planning.

The 14 member states are Antigua and Barbuda, the Bahamas (which is not a member of the Common Market), Barbados, Belize, Dominica, Grenada, Guyana, Jamaica, Montserrat, St Christopher and Nevis, St Lucia, St Vincent and the Grenadines, Suriname, and Trinidad and Tobago. Anguilla, the British Virgin Islands and the Turks and Caicos Islands are associate members. Aruba, Bermuda, the Cayman Islands, Colombia, the Dominican Republic, Mexico, the Netherlands' Antilles, Puerto Rico and Venezuela have observer status. Following a successful application for membership, Haiti is to be admitted as a full member of the Caribbean Community upon depositing an instrument of accession.

*Secretary-General*, Edwin W. Carrington

## THE COMMONWEALTH

The Commonwealth is a voluntary association of 54 sovereign independent states together with their associated states and dependencies. All of the states were formerly parts of the British Empire or League of Nations (later UN) mandated territories, except for Mozambique which was admitted as a unique case because of its history of co-operation with neighbouring Commonwealth nations.

The status and relationship of member nations were first defined by the Inter-Imperial Relations Committee of the 1926 Imperial Conference, when the six existing dominions (Australia, Canada, the Irish Free State, Newfoundland, New Zealand and South Africa) were described as 'autonomous Communities within the British Empire, equal in status, in no way subordinate one to another in any aspect of their domestic or external affairs, though united by a common allegiance to the Crown and freely associated as Members of the British Commonwealth of Nations'. This formula was given legal substance by the Statute of Westminster 1931.

This concept of a group of countries owing allegiance to a single Crown changed in 1949 when India decided to become a republic. Her continued membership of the Commonwealth was agreed by the other members on the basis of her 'acceptance of The King as the symbol of the free association of its independent member nations and as such the head of the Commonwealth'. This paved the way for other republics to join the association in due course. Member nations agreed at the time of the accession of Queen Elizabeth II to recognise Her Majesty as the new Head of the Commonwealth. However, the position is not vested in the British Crown.

### The Modern Commonwealth

As the UK's former colonies joined, initially with India and Pakistan in 1947, the Commonwealth was transformed from a grouping of all-white dominions into a multiracial association of equal, sovereign nations. It increasingly focused on promoting development and racial equality and effectively expelled South Africa in 1961 over its policy of apartheid.

The new goals of advocating democracy, the rule of law, good government and social justice were enshrined in the Harare Commonwealth Declaration (1991), which formed the basis of new membership guidelines agreed in Cyprus in 1993. Following the adoption of measures at the New Zealand summit in 1995 against serious or persistent violations of these principles, Nigeria was suspended in 1995 and Sierra Leone was suspended in 1997 for anti-democratic behaviour. Sierra Leone's suspension was revoked in March 1998 when the legitimate government was returned to power. Similarly, Nigeria's suspension was lifted on 29 May 1999, the day a newly elected civilian president took office. The heads of government meeting in Edinburgh in 1997 established a set of economic principles for the Commonwealth, promoting economic growth whilst protecting smaller member states from the negative effects of globalisation.

### Membership

Membership of the Commonwealth involves acceptance of the association's basic principles and is subject to the approval of existing members. There are 54 members at present. (The date of joining the Commonwealth is shown in parenthesis.)

*Antigua and Barbuda (1981)
*Australia (1931)
*The Bahamas (1973)
Bangladesh (1972)
*Barbados (1966)
*Belize (1981)
Botswana (1966)
Brunei (1984)
Cameroon (1995)
*Canada (1931)
Cyprus (1961)
Dominica (1978)
‡Fiji (1970, 1997)
The Gambia (1965)
Ghana (1957)
*Grenada (1974)
Guyana (1966)
India (1947)
*Jamaica (1962)
Kenya (1963)
Nauru (1968)
*New Zealand (1931)
Nigeria (1960)
†Pakistan (1947)
*Papua New Guinea (1975)
*St Christopher and Nevis (1983)
*St Lucia (1979)
*St Vincent and the Grenadines (1979)
Samoa (1970)
Seychelles (1976)
Sierra Leone (1961)
Singapore (1965)
*Solomon Islands (1978)
South Africa (1931)
Sri Lanka (1948)
Swaziland (1968)
Tanzania (1961)
Tonga (1970)

Kiribati (1979)
Lesotho (1966)
Malawi (1964)
Malaysia (1957)
The Maldives (1982)
Malta (1964)
Mauritius (1968)
Mozambique (1995)
Namibia (1990)
Trinidad and Tobago (1962)
*Tuvalu (1978)
Uganda (1962)
*United Kingdom
Vanuatu (1980)
Zambia (1964)
Zimbabwe (1980)

*Realms of Queen Elizabeth II; †Suspended 18 October 1999; ‡ Suspended 6 June 2000

Tuvalu became a full member on 1 September 2000. Pakistan's membership was suspended on 18 October 1999, following a military coup. Fiji's membership was suspended on 6 June 2000 following the overthrow of its democratically elected government.

*Countries which have left the Commonwealth*
Fiji (1987, rejoined 1997, suspended 2000)
Republic of Ireland (1949)
Pakistan (1972, rejoined 1989, suspended 1999)
South Africa (1961, rejoined 1994)

Of the 54 member states, 16 have Queen Elizabeth II as head of state, 33 are republics, and five have national monarchies.

In each of the realms where Queen Elizabeth II is head of state (except for the UK), she is personally represented by a Governor-General, who holds in all essential respects the same position in relation to the administration of public affairs in the realm as is held by Her Majesty in Britain. The Governor-General is appointed by The Queen on the advice of the government of the state concerned.

### Intergovernmental and Other Links

The main forum for consultation is the Commonwealth heads of government meetings held biennially to discuss international developments and to consider co-operation among members. Decisions are reached by consensus, and the views of the meeting are set out in a communiqué. There are also annual meetings of finance ministers and frequent meetings of ministers and officials in other fields, such as education, health, women's affairs, agriculture, and science. Intergovernmental links are complemented by the activities of some 300 Commonwealth non-governmental organisations linking professionals, sportsmen and sportswomen, and interest groups, forming a 'people's Commonwealth'. The Commonwealth Games take place every four years.

Assistance to other Commonwealth countries normally has priority in the bilateral aid programmes of the association's developed members (Australia, Britain, Canada and New Zealand), who direct about 30 per cent of their aid to other member countries. Developing Commonwealth nations also assist their poorer partners, and many Commonwealth voluntary organisations promote development.

### Commonwealth Secretariat

The Commonwealth has a secretariat, established in 1965 in London, which is funded by all member governments. This is the main agency for multilateral communication between member governments on issues relating to the Commonwealth as a whole. It promotes consultation and co-operation, disseminates information on matters of common concern, organises meetings including the biennial summits, co-ordinates Commonwealth activities, and provides technical assistance for economic and social development through the Commonwealth Fund for Technical Co-operation.

The Commonwealth Foundation was established by Commonwealth governments in 1966 as an autonomous body with a board of governors representing Commonwealth governments that fund the Foundation. It promotes and funds exchanges and other activities aimed at strengthening the skills and effectiveness of professionals and non-governmental organisations. It also promotes culture, rural development, social welfare and the role of women.

Commonwealth Secretariat, Marlborough House, Pall Mall, London SW1Y 5HX. Tel: 020-7839 3411; fax: 020-7839 9081; E-mail: info@commonwealth.int;
Web: www.thecommonwealth.org
*Secretary-General*, Rt. Hon. Don McKinnon (New Zealand)
Commonwealth Foundation, Marlborough House, Pall Mall, London SW1Y 5HY. Tel: 020-7930 3783. *Director*, Colin Ball (UK)
Commonwealth Institute, Kensington High Street, London W8 6NQ. Tel: 020-7603 4535. *Director-General*, David French

---

## COMMONWEALTH OF INDEPENDENT STATES

Ul. Kirava 17, Minsk, Belarus
Tel: (00 375) (17) 222 3517
fax: (00 375) (17) 227 2339
E-mail: webmaster@www.cis.minsk.by
Web: www.cis.minsk.by

---

The Commonwealth of Independent States (CIS) is a multilateral grouping of 12 sovereign states that were formerly constituent republics of the USSR (Armenia, Azerbaijan, Belarus, Georgia, Kazakhstan, Kyrgyzstan, Moldova, Russia, Tajikistan, Turkmenistan, Ukraine and Uzbekistan). It was formed in 1991. Georgia joined in 1993. The CIS charter, signed in 1993 by seven states (Armenia, Belarus, Kazakhstan, Kyrgyzstan, Russia, Tajikistan, Uzbekistan) and open for signing by the other states, formally established the functions of the organisation and the obligations of its member states.

The CIS acts as a co-ordinating mechanism for foreign, defence and economic policies, and is a forum for addressing problems which have specifically arisen from the break-up of the USSR. These matters are addressed in more than 70 inter-state, intergovernmental co-ordinating and consultative statutory bodies. However, member states have criticised the CIS for operating ineffectively, and for failing to carry through decisions made by CIS organs.

### Structure

The two supreme CIS bodies are the Council of Heads of State and the Council of Heads of Government. The Council of Heads of State is the highest organ of the CIS and there are various ministerial, parliamentary, banking, economic and security councils. The Executive Committee, based in Minsk and Moscow, provides administrative support.

### Defence Co-operation

On becoming member states of the CIS, the member states agreed to recognise their existing borders, respect one another's territorial integrity and reject the use of military force or other forms of coercion to settle disputes between them.

A Treaty on Collective Security was signed in 1992 by six states and a joint peacemaking force, to intervene in CIS conflicts, was agreed upon by nine states. Russia concluded bilateral and multilateral agreements with other CIS states under the supervision of the Council of Heads of Collective Security (established 1993). These were gradually upgraded into CIS agreements under the umbrella of the Treaty on Collective Security, enabling Russia to station troops in nine of the other 11 CIS states (not Moldova, Turkmenistan or Ukraine), and giving Russian forces *de facto* control of virtually all of the former USSR's external borders. Only Ukraine and Moldova remained outside the defence co-operation framework and did not sign the Treaty on Collective Security, from which Azerbaijan, Georgia and Uzbekistan withdrew in 1999, forming a new defensive grouping with Moldova and Ukraine. Russian border guards were also withdrawn from Georgia, Kyrgyzstan and Turkmenistan in 1999.

### Economic Co-operation

In 1991, 11 republics signed a treaty forming an economic community. The principles of the treaty were embodied within the CIS and formed the basis of its economic co-operation. Members agreed to refrain from economic actions that would damage each other and to co-ordinate economic and monetary policies. A Co-ordinating Consultative Committee, an economic arbitration court and an inter-state bank were established. A single monetary unit, the rouble, was originally agreed upon by all member states, and the members recognised that the basis of recovery for their economies was private ownership, free enterprise and competition.

The 11 CIS members who signed the Treaty on the Establishment of an Economic Union in September 1993 (Ukraine is an associate member of the economic union) committed themselves to a common economic space with free movement of goods, services, capital and labour. Belarus, Kazakhstan, Kyrgyzstan and Russia signed the Treaty on the Establishment of a Customs Union in March 1996; the treaty was later signed by Tajikistan and on 10 October 2000, the presidents of the five countries approved a treaty establishing the Eurasian Economic Community.

*Executive Secretary*, Yuri Yarov

---

## COUNCIL OF THE BALTIC SEA STATES

Secretariat, Strömsborg, P.O Box 2010, S-103 11 Stockholm, Sweden
Tel: (00 46) (8) 440 1936; fax: (00 46) (8) 440 1944
E-mail: cbss@baltinfo.org Web: www.baltinfo.org

---

The Council of the Baltic Sea States (CBSS) was founded in March 1992 with the aim of creating a regional forum to increase co-operation and co-ordination among the states which border on the Baltic Sea in assisting new democratic institutions, economic and technical development, humanitarian aid and health, energy and the environmental issues, cultural programmes, education, tourism, transportation and communication.

There are 12 members: Denmark, Estonia, Finland, Germany, Iceland, Latvia, Lithuania, Norway, Poland, Russia, Sweden and the European Commission.

The Council consists of the foreign ministers of each member state and a member of the European Commission. Chairmanship of the Council rotates on an annual basis, and the annual session is held in the country currently in the chair. The foreign minister of the presiding country is responsible for co-ordinating activities between the sessions.

*Chairmanship July 2001-June 2002*, Russia; *July 2002-June 2003*, Finland

---

## THE COUNCIL OF EUROPE

F-67075 Strasbourg, France
Tel: (00 33) (3) 8841 2033; fax: (00 33) (3) 8841 2745
E-mail: point_i@coe.int Web: www.coe.int

---

The Council of Europe was founded in 1949. Its aim is to achieve greater unity between its members, to safeguard their European heritage and to facilitate their progress in economic, social, cultural, educational, scientific, legal and administrative matters, and in the furtherance of pluralist democracy, human rights and fundamental freedoms.

The 43 members are Albania, Andorra, Armenia, Austria, Azerbaijan, Belgium, Bulgaria, Croatia, Cyprus, Czech Republic, Denmark, Estonia, Finland, France, Georgia, Germany, Greece, Hungary, Iceland, Republic of Ireland, Italy, Latvia, Liechtenstein, Lithuania, Luxembourg, Macedonia, Malta, Moldova, the Netherlands, Norway, Poland, Portugal, Romania, Russia, San Marino, Slovakia, Slovenia, Spain, Sweden, Switzerland, Turkey, the UK and Ukraine. 'Special guest status' has been granted to Bosnia-Hercegovina, Monaco and Yugoslavia. Canada, Japan, Mexico, the USA , and the Vatican City State have observer status. The organs are the Committee of Ministers, consisting of the foreign ministers of member countries, who meet twice yearly, and the Parliamentary Assembly of 301 members, elected or chosen by the national parliaments of member countries in proportion to the relative strength of political parties. There is also a Joint Committee of Ministers and Representatives of the Parliamentary Assembly.

The Committee of Ministers is the executive organ. The majority of its conclusions take the form of international agreements (known as European Conventions) or recommendations to governments. Decisions of the Ministers may also be embodied in partial agreements to which a limited number of member governments are party. Member governments accredit Permanent Representatives to the Council in Strasbourg, who are also the Ministers' Deputies. The Committee of Deputies meets every month to transact business and to take decisions on behalf of Ministers.

The Parliamentary Assembly holds three week-long sessions a year. Its 13 permanent committees meet once or twice between each public plenary session of the Assembly. The Congress of Local and Regional Authorities of Europe each year brings together mayors and municipal councillors in the same numbers as the members of the Parliamentary Assembly.

One of the principal achievements of the Council of Europe is the European Convention on Human Rights (1950) under which was established the European Commission and the European Court of Human Rights, which were merged in 1993. The reorganised European Court of Human Rights sits in chambers of seven judges or exceptionally as a grand chamber of 17 judges. Litigants must exhaust legal processes in their own country before bringing cases before the court.

Among other conventions and agreements are the European Social Charter, the European Cultural Convention, the European Code of Social Security, the European Convention on the Protection of National Minorities, and conventions on extradition, the legal status of migrant workers, torture prevention, conservation, and the transfer of sentenced prisoners. Most recently, the specialised bodies of the Venice Commission and Demosthenes have been set up to assist in developing legislative, administrative and constitutional reforms in central and eastern Europe.

Non-member states take part in certain Council of Europe activities on a regular or *ad hoc* basis; thus the Holy See participates in all the educational, cultural and sports activities. The European Youth Centre is an educational residential centre for young people. The European Youth Foundation provides youth organisations with funds for their international activities.

*Secretary-General*, Walter Schwimmer (Austria)

*Permanent UK Representative*, HE Andrew Carter, CMG, *apptd* 1997

---

THE ECONOMIC COMMUNITY OF WEST AFRICAN STATES

Secretariat Building, 60 Yakubu Gowon Crescent, PMB 401, Abuja, Nigeria

Tel: (00 234) (9) 314 7647 9;

fax: (00 234) (9) 314 3005/6

E-mail: info@ecowasmail.net Web: www.ecowas.int

---

The Economic Community of West African States (ECOWAS) was founded in 1975 and came into operation in 1977. It aims to promote the cultural, economic and social development of West Africa through mutual co-operation. A revised ECOWAS Treaty was signed in 1993 and came into effect in July 1995. It makes the prevention and control of regional conflicts an aim of ECOWAS and provides for the imposition of a community tax and for the establishment of a regional parliament, an economic and social council, and a court of justice.

The supreme authority of ECOWAS is vested in the annual summit of heads of government of all 15 member states. A Council of Ministers, two from each member state, meets biannually to monitor the organisation and make recommendations to the summit. ECOWAS operates through a Secretariat, headed by the Executive Secretary. In addition there are four Deputy Executive Secretaries.

The ECOWAS Parliament was inaugurated in November 2000 and justices for the Court of Justice were sworn in in January 2001.

The Fund for Co-operation, Compensation and Development, situated at Lomé, Togo, has been restructured into three funds: the ECOWAS Regional Development Fund, the ECOWAS Bank for Investment and Development and the ECOWAS Regional Investment Bank. The funds finance development projects and provide compensation to member states who have suffered losses as a result of ECOWAS's policies, particularly trade liberalisation.

The members of ECOWAS are: Benin, Burkina Faso, Cape Verde, Côte d'Ivoire, Gambia, Ghana, Guinea, Guinea-Bissau, Liberia, Mali, Niger, Nigeria, Senegal, Sierra Leone and Togo. Mauritania left the organisation in December 2000.

An ECOWAS Monitoring Group (ECOMOG) peace-keeping force has been involved in attempts to restore peace in Liberia (1990–6), in Guinea-Bissau (1998-9) and in Sierra Leone since 1997.

*Executive Secretary*, Lansana Kouyate (Guinea)

---

THE EUROPEAN BANK FOR RECONSTRUCTION AND DEVELOPMENT

One Exchange Square, London EC2A 2JN

Tel: 020-7338 6000; fax: 020-7338 6100

Web: www.ebrd.com

---

The European Bank for Reconstruction and Development (EBRD), established in 1991, is an international institution with 62 members (60 countries, the European Community and the European Investment Bank).

The aim of the EBRD is to facilitate the transition of the countries of central and eastern Europe and the former USSR from centrally planned to free-market economies, and to promote multi-party democracy, entrepreneurial initiative, and environmentally sound development.

The EBRD finances projects in 27 countries, in both the private and public sectors, providing direct funding for financial institutions, infrastructure, and industry and commerce. The main forms of EBRD financing are loans, equity investments and guarantees. No more than 40 per cent of the EBRD's investment can be made in state-owned concerns. The bank is the largest foreign investor in the region's private sector, paying particular attention to strengthening the financial sector and to promoting small and medium-sized enterprises. It works in co-operation with national governments, private companies, and international organisations such as the OECD, the IMF, the World Bank and the UN specialised agencies.

The EBRD has a subscribed capital of 20 billion. The EBRD is also able to borrow on world capital markets. Its major subscribers are the USA, 10 per cent; Britain, France, Germany, Italy and Japan, 8.5 per cent each. As of 31 December 2000, the EBRD had signed 708 projects with a total net value of 12.2 billion.

The highest authority is the Board of Governors; each member appoints one Governor and one Alternate. The Governors delegate most powers to a 23-member Board of Directors; the Directors are responsible for the EBRD's operations and budget, and are elected by the Governors for three-year terms. The Governors also elect the President of the Board of Directors, who acts as the Bank's president for a four-year term.

*President of the Board of Directors*, Jean Lemierre (France)

*Chairman of the Board of Governors*, Laurent Fabius (France)

---

EUROPEAN FREE TRADE ASSOCIATION

Headquarters: 9–11 rue de Varembé, CH-1211 Geneva 20, Switzerland

Tel: (00 41) (22) 749 1111; fax: (00 41) (22) 733 9291

Web: www.efta.int

EEA matters: Trierstraat 74, B-1040 Brussels, Belgium

Tel: (00 32) (2) 286 1711; fax: (00 32) (2) 286 1750

E-mail: efta-mailbox@secrbru.efta.be

---

The European Free Trade Association (EFTA) was established in 1960 by Austria, Denmark, Norway, Portugal, Sweden, Switzerland and the UK, and was subsequently joined by Finland (associate member 1961, full member 1986), Iceland (1970) and Liechtenstein (1991). Six members have left to join the European Union: Denmark and the UK (1972), Portugal (1985), Austria, Finland and Sweden (1995). The existing members are Iceland, Liechtenstein, Norway and Switzerland.

The first objective of EFTA was to establish free trade in industrial products between members; this was achieved in 1966. Its second objective was the creation of a single market in western Europe and in 1972 EFTA signed free trade agreements with the EC covering trade in industrial goods; the remaining tariffs on industrial products were abolished in 1977 and the Luxembourg Declaration on broader co-operation between EFTA and the European Community was signed in 1984.

An agreement on the creation of the European Economic Area (EEA), an extension of the EC single market to the EFTA states, was signed in 1992 and entered into force on 1 January 1994. Switzerland rejected EEA membership in a referendum in 1992 and Liechtenstein joined on 1 May 1995 after adapting its customs union with Switzerland. The implementation of the agreement is supervised by the EEA Council, composed of EFTA and EU ministers, and the EFTA Surveillance Authority. The three EFTA EEA members also participate in a wide range of other EC programmes including research and development, environmental matters, and education and training.

EFTA has expanded its relations with other non-EU states in recent years, signing free trade agreements with Turkey (1991), Israel, Poland and Romania (1992), Bulgaria, the Czech Republic, Hungary and Slovakia (1993), Estonia, Latvia, Lithuania and Slovenia (1995), Morocco (1997), the PLO (1998), Macedonia and Mexico (2000) and Croatia (2001). In addition, EFTA has signed declarations of economic co-operation with Albania (1992), Egypt and Tunisia (1995), and Jordan and Lebanon (1997).

The EFTA Council is the principal organ of the Association. It meets regularly at the level of ambassadors to the EFTA Secretariat in Geneva.

*Secretary-General*, William Rossier (Switzerland)
*Deputy Secretary-General (Geneva)*, Grétar Már Sigurdsson (Iceland)
*Deputy Secretary-General (Brussels)*, Per Mannes (Norway)

---

## EUROPEAN ORGANISATION FOR NUCLEAR RESEARCH (CERN)

CH-1211 Geneva 23, Switzerland
Tel: (00 41) (22) 767 4101; fax: (00 41) (22) 785 0247
Web: www.cern.ch

---

The Convention establishing the European Organisation for Nuclear Research (CERN) came into force in 1954. CERN promotes European collaboration in high energy physics of a scientific, rather than a military nature.

The member countries are Austria, Belgium, Bulgaria, the Czech Republic, Denmark, Finland, France, Germany, Greece, Hungary, Italy, the Netherlands, Norway, Poland, Portugal, Slovakia, Spain, Sweden, Switzerland and the UK. Israel, Japan, Russia, Turkey, the USA, the EU Commission and UNESCO have observer status.

The Council is the highest policy-making body and comprises two delegates from each member state. There is also a Committee of the Council comprising a single delegate from each member state (who is also a Council member) and the chairmen of the scientific policy and finance advisory committees. The Council is chaired by the President who is elected by the Council in Session. The Council also elects the Director-General, who is responsible for the internal organisation of CERN. The Director-General heads a workforce of approximately 3,000, including physicists, craftsmen, technicians and administrative staff. At present over 6,500 physicists use CERN's facilities.

The member countries contribute to the budget in proportion to their net national revenue. The 2001 budget was SFr 1,050 million.

*President of the Council*, Maurice Bourquin (Switzerland)
*Director-General* (1999–2004), Prof. Luciano Maiani (Italy)

---

## EUROPEAN SPACE AGENCY

8–10 rue Mario Nikis, F-75738 Paris Cedex 15, France

---

Tel: (00 33) (1) 5369 7654; fax: (00 33) (1) 5369 7560
Web: www.esa.int

The European Space Agency (ESA) was created in 1975 by the merger of the European Space Research Organisation (ESRO) and the European Launcher Development Organisation (ELDO). Its aims include the advancement of space research and technology and the implementation of a long-term European space policy.

The member countries are Austria, Belgium, Denmark, Finland, France, Germany, Republic of Ireland, Italy, the Netherlands, Norway, Portugal, Spain, Sweden, Switzerland and the UK. Canada is a co-operating state.

The agency is directed by a Council composed of the representatives of the member states; its chief officer is the Director-General.

*Director-General*, Antonio Rodotà, *apptd* 1997

---

## FOOD AND AGRICULTURE ORGANISATION OF THE UNITED NATIONS

Viale delle Terme di Caracalla, I-00100 Rome, Italy
Tel: (00 39) (6) 57051; fax: (00 39) (6) 5705 3152
E-mail: fao-hq@fao.org; Web: www.fao.org

---

The Food and Agriculture Organisation (FAO) is a specialised UN agency, established in 1945. It assists rural populations by raising levels of nutrition and living standards, and by encouraging greater efficiency in food production and distribution. It analyses and disseminates information on agriculture and natural resources. The FAO also advises governments on national agricultural policy and planning; its Investment Centre, together with the World Bank and other financial institutions, helps to prepare development projects. The FAO's field programme covers a range of activities, including strengthening crop production, rural and livestock development, and conservation.

The FAO's top priorities are sustainable agriculture, rural development and food security. The Organisation attempts to ensure the availability of adequate food supplies, stability in the flow of supplies and the securing of access to food by the poor. The FAO monitors potential famine areas. The Special Relief Operations Service channels emergency aid from governments and other agencies, and assists in rehabilitation. The Technical Co-operation Programme responds to urgent or unforeseen requests for technical assistance.

The FAO had 181 members (180 states and the EU) as at April 2001. It is governed by a biennial conference of its members which sets a programme and budget. The budget for 2000–1 was US$650million, funded by member countries in proportion to their gross national products. The FAO is also funded by the UN Development Programme, donor governments and other institutions.

The Conference elects a Director-General and a 49-member Council which governs between conferences. The Regular and Field Programmes are administered by a Secretariat, headed by the Director-General. Five regional, five sub-regional and 80 national offices help administer the Field Programme.

*Director-General*, Jacques Diouf (Senegal)

*UK Representative*, Anthony Beattie, British Embassy, Rome

## INTERNATIONAL ATOMIC ENERGY AGENCY

Vienna International Centre, Wagramerstrasse 5, PO Box 100, A-1400 Vienna, Austria
Tel: (00 43) (1) 26000; fax: (00 43) (1) 26007
E-mail: Official.Mail@iaea.org
Web: www.iaea.org/worldatom

The International Atomic Energy Agency (IAEA) was established in 1957. It is an intergovernmental organisation that reports to, but is not a specialised agency of, the UN.

The IAEA aims to enhance the contribution of atomic energy to peace, health and prosperity, and to ensure that any assistance that it provides is not used for military purposes. It establishes atomic energy safety standards and offers services to its member states for the safe operation of their nuclear facilities and for radiation protection. It is the focal point for international conventions on the early notification of a nuclear accident, assistance in the case of such an accident, civil liability for nuclear damage, physical protection of nuclear material, nuclear safety and the safety of spent fuel and radioactive waste management. The IAEA also encourages research and training in nuclear power. It is additionally charged with drawing up safeguards and verifying their use in accordance with the Nuclear Non-Proliferation Treaty (NPT) 1968, the Treaty for the Prohibition of Nuclear Weapons in Latin America (Tlatelolco Treaty) 1968, the Treaty on a South Pacific Nuclear Free Zone (Rarotonga Treaty), the South East Asia Nuclear Weapon-Free Zone Treaty (Bangkok Treaty) and the African Nuclear Weapon-Free Zone Treaty (Pelindaba Treaty) 1996. Together with the Food and Agriculture Organisation and the World Health Organisation, the IAEA established an International Consultative Group on Food Irradiation in 1983.

The IAEA concluded a safeguards agreement with North Korea in April 1992 and began inspections to verify that its nuclear programme was for peaceful purposes only. In 1993 the IAEA informed the UN Security Council that North Korea had violated its NPT obligations and all technical aid to North Korea was suspended. North Korea resigned from the IAEA in 1994, but permitted IAEA inspections under the terms of an agreement with the USA which enabled the IAEA to resume safeguards inspections.

The IAEA had 130 members as at May 2001. A General Conference of all its members meets annually to decide policy, a programme and a budget (2000, US$226.3 million), as well as electing a Director-General and a 35-member Board of Governors. The Board meets four times a year to formulate policy which is implemented by the Secretariat under a Director-General.

*Director-General*, Mohamed El Baradei (Egypt)
*Permanent UK Representative*, Dr John Freeman, Jaurèsgasse 12, A-1030 Vienna, Austria

## INTERNATIONAL CIVIL AVIATION ORGANISATION

999 University Street, Montréal, Québec, Canada H3C 5H7
Tel: (00 1) (514) 954 8219; fax: (00 1) (514) 954 6077
E-mail: icaohq@icao.int; Web: www.icao.int

The International Civil Aviation Organisation (ICAO) was founded with the signing of the Chicago Convention on International Civil Aviation in 1944, and became a specialised agency of the United Nations in 1947. It sets international technical standards and recommended practices for all areas of civil aviation, including airworthiness, air navigation, air traffic control and pilot licensing. It encourages uniformity and simplicity in ground regulations and operations at international airports, including immigration and customs control. The ICAO also promotes regional air navigation, plans for ground facilities, and collects and distributes air transport statistics world-wide. It is dedicated to improving safety and to the orderly development of civil aviation throughout the world.

The ICAO had 187 members as at April 2001. It is governed by an assembly of its members which meets at least once every three years. A Council of 33 members is elected, which represents leading air transport nations as well as less developed countries. The Council elects the President, appoints the Secretary-General and supervises the organisation through subsidiary committees, serviced by a Secretariat.

*President of the Council*, Dr Assad Kotaite (Lebanon)
*Secretary-General*, R. C. Costa Pereira (Brazil)
*UK Representative*, D. S. Evans, CMG, 999 University Street, Montréal, Québec, Canada H3C 5H7

## INTERNATIONAL CONFEDERATION OF FREE TRADE UNIONS

Koning Albert II laan 5, Bus 1, B-1210 Brussels, Belgium
Tel: (00 32) (2) 224 0211; fax: (00 32) (2) 201 5815
E-mail: internetpo@icftu.org; Web: www.icftu.org

The International Confederation of Free Trade Unions (ICFTU) was created in 1949. It aims to establish, maintain and promote free trade unions, and to promote peace with economic security and social justice.

Affiliated to the ICFTU are 221 individual unions and representative bodies in 148 countries and territories. There were 156 million members in November 2000.

The Congress, the supreme authority of the ICFTU, convenes at least every four years. It is composed of delegates from the affiliated trade union organisations. The Congress elects an Executive Board of 53 members, including five nominated by the Women's Committee and one representing young workers, which meets not less than once a year. The Board establishes the budget and receives suggestions and proposals from affiliates as well as acting on behalf of the Confederation. The Congress also elects the General Secretary.

*General Secretary*, Bill Jordan (UK)
*UK Affiliate*, TUC, Congress House, 23–28 Great Russell Street, London WC1B 3LS. Tel: 020-7636 4030

## INTERNATIONAL CRIMINAL POLICE ORGANISATION (INTERPOL)

200 Quai Charles de Gaulle, F-69006 Lyon, France
Tel: (00 33) (4) 7244 7000; fax: (00 33) (4) 7244 7163
E-mail: compr@interpol.int; Web: www.interpol.com

Interpol was set up in 1923 to establish an international criminal records office and to harmonise extradition procedures. As of 1 April 2001, the organisation comprised 178 member states.

Interpol's aims are to promote co-operation between criminal police authorities, and to support government agencies concerned with combating crime, whilst respecting national sovereignty. It is financed by annual contributions from the governments of member states.

Interpol's policy is decided by the General Assembly which meets annually; it is composed of delegates appointed by the member states. The 13-member Executive Committee is elected by the General Assembly from among the member states' delegates, and is chaired by the President, who has a four-year term of office. The permanent administrative organ is the General Secretariat, headed by the Secretary-General, who is appointed by the General Assembly.

*Secretary-General*, Ronald Noble (USA)

UK OFFICE, NCIS Interpol, PO Box 8000, London SE11 5EN. Tel: 020-7238 8000.

*UK Representative*, J. M. Abbott, QPM

---

INTERNATIONAL ENERGY AGENCY
9 rue de la Fédération, F-75739 Paris Cedex 15, France
Tel: (00 33) (1) 4057 6551; fax: (00 33) (1) 4057 6559
E-mail: info@iea.org Web: www.iea.org

---

The International Energy Agency (IEA), founded in 1974, is an autonomous agency within the framework of the Organisation for Economic Co-operation and Development (OECD). The IEA had 25 member countries as at April 2001.

The IEA's objectives include improvement of energy co-operation world-wide, increased efficiency, development of alternative energy sources and the promotion of relations between oil producing and oil consuming countries. The IEA also maintains an emergency system to alleviate the effects of severe oil supply disruptions.

The main decision-making body is the Governing Board, composed of senior energy officials from member countries. Various standing groups and special committees exist to facilitate the work of the Board. The IEA Secretariat, with a staff of energy experts, carries out the work of the Governing Board and its subordinate bodies. The Executive Director is appointed by the Board.

*Executive Director*, Robert Priddle (UK)

---

INTERNATIONAL FRANCOPHONE ORGANISATION Cabinet du Secrétaire général, 28 rue de Bourgogne, F-75007 Paris, France
Tel: (00 33) (1) 44111250; fax: (00 33) (1) 441112 76
E-mail: webmaitre@francophonie.org
Web: www.francophonie.org

---

The International Francophone Organisation (known as La Francophonie) is an intergovernmental organisation founded in 1970 by 21 French-speaking countries. It aims to prevent conflict and promote development and co-operation between the Francophone countries, to represent its member states internationally and to promote French culture and the use of the French language.

The Conference of Heads of State and Heads of Government of Countries using French as a Common Language, also known as the Francophone Summit, takes place biennially. Other institutions include the Ministerial Conference of La Francophonie, the Permanent Council of La Francophonie and the Secretariat.

The Ministerial Conference of La Francophonie, which consists of the foreign minister or the minister responsible for Francophone affairs of each member state, implements decisions made at the summits and makes preparations for the following summit. It also puts forward prospective new members.

The Permanent Council of La Francophonie, which is chaired by the Secretary-General and consists of representatives of the member states, oversees the execution of decisions made by the Ministerial Conference, allocates funds, and reviews and approves projects. It has 18 members, chosen in advance of each summit, in rotation from among the member states.

La Francophonie has a current membership of 55 member states and regional governments (Albania (observer), Belgium, the Francophone Community of Belgium, Benin, Bulgaria, Burkina Faso, Burundi, Cambodia, Cameroon, Canada, Canada (New Brunswick), Canada (Québec), Cape Verde, Central African Republic, Chad, the Comoros, Czech Republic (observer), Democratic Republic of Congo, Republic of Congo-Brazzaville, Côte d'Ivoire, Djibouti, Dominica, Egypt, Equatorial Guinea, France, Gabon, Guinea, Guinea-Bissau, Haiti, Laos, Lebanon, Lithuania (observer), Luxembourg, Macedonia (observer), Madagascar, Mali, Mauritania, Mauritius, Moldova, Monaco, Morocco, Niger, Poland (observer), Romania, Rwanda, St Lucia, São Tomé e Princípe, Senegal, Seychelles, Slovenia (observer), Switzerland, Togo, Tunisia, Vanuatu and Vietnam).

*Secretary-General*, Boutros Boutros-Ghali

---

INTERNATIONAL FUND FOR AGRICULTURAL DEVELOPMENT
107 Via del Serafico, I-00142 Rome, Italy
Tel: (00 39) (6) 54591; fax: (00 39) (6) 5459 2143
E-mail: ifad@ifad.org Web: www.ifad.org

---

The establishment of the International Fund for Agricultural Development (IFAD) was proposed by the 1974 World Food Conference and IFAD began operations as a UN specialised agency in 1977. Its purpose is to mobilise additional funds for agricultural and rural development projects in developing countries that benefit the poorest rural populations; provide employment and additional income for poor farmers; reduce malnutrition; and improve food distribution systems.

IFAD had 161 members as at April 2001. Membership is divided into three lists: List A (OECD countries), List B (OPEC countries), and List C (developing countries) which is subdivided into C1 (Africa), C2 (Africa, Asia and the Pacific) and C3 (Latin America and the Caribbean). All powers are vested in a Governing Council of all member countries. It elects an 18-member Executive Board (with 18 alternate members) responsible for IFAD's operations. The Council meets annually and elects a President who is also chairman of the Board. The President serves a four-year term that is renewable once and is assisted by a Vice-President and three Assistant Presidents.

Between 1978 and 2000, IFAD has committed a total of US$6.9 billion in loans and grants for 578 approved projects in 115 developing countries.

*President*, Lennart Båge (Sweden), *apptd* 2001

---

INTERNATIONAL LABOUR ORGANISATION
4 route des Morillons, CH-1211 Geneva 22, Switzerland
Tel: (00 41) (22) 799 6111; fax: (00 41) (22) 798 8685
Web: www.ilo.org

---

The International Labour Organisation (ILO) was established in 1919 as an autonomous body of the League of Nations and became the UN's first specialised agency in 1946. The ILO aims to increase employment, improve working conditions, raise living standards and encourage democratic development. It sets minimum international labour standards through the drafting of international conventions. Member countries are obliged to submit these to their domestic authorities for ratification, and thus undertake to bring their domestic legislation in line with the conventions. Members must report to the ILO periodically on how these regulations are being implemented. The ILO plays a major role in helping developing countries achieve economic stability and job expansion through its wide-ranging programme of technical co-operation. The ILO is also the world's principal resource centre for information, analysis and guidance on labour and employment. The organisation aims to improve working and living conditions throughout the world and to support the transition to democracy and market economics under way in many states.

The ILO had 175 members as at January 2001. It is composed of the International Labour Conference, the Governing Body and the International Labour Office. The Conference of members meets annually, and is attended by national delegations comprising two government delegates, one worker delegate and one employer delegate. It formulates international labour conventions and recommendations, provides a forum for discussion of world employment and social issues, and approves the ILO's programme and budget (2000–1, US$467 million).

The 56-member Governing Body, composed of 28 government, 14 worker and 14 employer members, acts as the ILO's executive council. Ten governments, including the UK, hold permanent seats on the Governing Body because of their industrial importance. There are also various regional conferences and advisory committees. The International Labour Office acts as a secretariat and as a centre for operations, publishing and research.

*Director-General*, Juan Somavia (Chile)

UK OFFICE, Millbank Tower, 21-24 Millbank, London SW1P 4QP. Tel: 020-7828 6401; fax: 020-7233-5925. E-mail: london@ilo-london.org.uk

---

## INTERNATIONAL MARITIME ORGANISATION

4 Albert Embankment, London SE1 7SR
Tel: 020-7753 7611; fax: 020-7587 3210
E-mail: info@imo.org; Web: www.imo.org

---

The International Maritime Organisation (IMO) was established as a UN specialised agency in 1948. Owing to delays in treaty ratification it did not commence operations until 1958. Originally it was called the Inter-Governmental Maritime Consultative Organisation (IMCO) but changed its name in 1982.

The IMO fosters intergovernmental co-operation in technical matters relating to international shipping, especially with regard to safety at sea, efficiency in navigation and protecting the marine environment by preventing and controlling marine pollution caused by shipping. The IMO is responsible for convening maritime conferences and drafting marine conventions. It also provides technical aid to countries wishing to develop their activities at sea.

The IMO had 158 members and two associate members as at May 2001. It is governed by an Assembly comprising delegates of all its members. It meets biennially to formulate policy, set a budget (2000–1, £36.6 million), vote on specific recommendations on pollution and maritime safety and elect the Council. The Council, which meets twice a year, fulfils the functions of the Assembly between sessions and appoints the Secretary-General. It consists of 32 members: eight from the world's largest shipping nations, eight from the nations most dependent on seaborne trade, and 16 other members to ensure a fair geographical representation. The Maritime Safety, Marine Environment Protection, Legal, Technical Co-operation and Facilitation Committees make reports and recommendations to the Council and the Assembly. There are a number of other specialist subsidiary committees.

The IMO acts as the secretariat for the London Convention (1972) which regulates the disposal of land-generated waste at sea.

*Secretary-General*, William A. O'Neil (Canada)

---

## INTERNATIONAL MONETARY FUND

700 19th Street NW, Washington DC 20431, USA
Tel: (00 1) (202) 623 7300; fax: (00 1) (202) 623 6278
E-mail: publicaffairs@imf.org
Web: www.imf.org

---

The International Monetary Fund (IMF) was established in 1944, at the UN Monetary and Financial Conference held at Bretton Woods, New Hampshire. Its Articles of Agreement entered into force in 1945 and it began operations in 1947.

The IMF exists to promote international monetary co-operation, the expansion of world trade, and exchange stability. It advises members on their economic and financial policies; promotes policy co-ordination among the major industrial countries; and gives technical assistance in central banking, balance of payments accounting, taxation, and other financial matters. The IMF serves as a forum for members to discuss important financial and monetary issues and seeks the balanced growth of international trade and, through this, high levels of employment, income and productive capacity. As at April 2001 the IMF had 183 members.

Upon joining the IMF, a member is assigned a 'quota', based on the member's relative standing in the world economy and its balance of payments position, that determines its capital subscription to the Fund, its access to IMF resources, its voting power, and its share in the allocation of Special Drawing Rights (SDRs). Quotas are reviewed every five years and adjusted accordingly. Since the 11th General Review of quotas in 1999, total Fund quotas stand at SDR 212 billion. The SDR, an international reserve asset issued by the IMF, is calculated daily on a basket of usable currencies and is the IMF's unit of account; on 22 June 2001, SDR 1 equalled US$1.24877. SDRs are allocated at intervals to supplement members' reserves and thereby improve international financial liquidity.

IMF financial resources derive primarily from members' capital subscriptions, which are equivalent to their quotas. In addition, the IMF is authorised to borrow from official lenders. It may also draw on a line of credit of SDR 18.5 billion from various countries under the so-called General Arrangements to Borrow (GAB). Periodic charges are also levied on financial assistance. At the end of May 2001, total outstanding IMF credits amounted to SDR 51.5 billion.

The IMF is not a bank and does not lend money; it provides temporary financial assistance by selling a member's SDRs or other members' currencies in exchange for the member's own currency. The member can then use the purchased currency to alleviate its balance of payments difficulties. The IMF's credit under its regular facilities is made available to members in tranches or segments of 25 per cent of quota. For first credit tranche purchases, members are required to demonstrate reasonable efforts to overcome their balance of payments difficulties. There are no performance criteria. Upper credit tranche purchases are normally associated with stand-by arrangements and are aimed at overcoming balance of payment difficulties and are required to meet certain performance criteria. Repurchases are made in three and a quarter to five years.

The IMF supports long-term efforts at economic reform and transformation as well as medium-term programmes under the extended Fund facility, which runs for three to four years and is aimed at overcoming balance of payments difficulties stemming from macroeconomic and structural problems. Members experiencing a temporary balance of payments shortfall have access to the compensatory and contingency financing facility.

The IMF is headed by a Board of Governors, comprising representatives of all members, which meets annually. The Governors delegate powers to 24 Executive Directors, who are appointed or elected by member countries. The Executive Directors operate the Fund on a daily basis under a Managing Director, whom they elect.

*Managing Director*, Michel Camdessus (France)

*UK Executive Director*, Gus O'Donnell, Room 11-120, IMF, 700 19th Street NW, Washington DC 20431, USA

---

INTERNATIONAL RED CROSS AND RED CRESCENT MOVEMENT

17 avenue de la Paix, CH-1211 Geneva, Switzerland

Web: www.icrc.org

---

The International Red Cross and Red Crescent Movement is composed of three elements. The International Committee of the Red Cross (ICRC), the organisation's founding body, was formed in 1863. It aims to negotiate between warring factions and to protect and assist victims of armed conflict. It also seeks to ensure the application of the Geneva Conventions with regard to prisoners of war and detainees.

The International Federation of Red Cross and Red Crescent Societies was founded in 1919 to contribute to the development of the humanitarian activities of national societies, to co-ordinate their relief operations for victims of natural disasters, and to care for refugees outside areas of conflict. There are Red Cross and Red Crescent Societies in 175 countries, with a total membership of 250 million.

The International Conference of the Red Cross and Red Crescent meets every four years, bringing together delegates of the ICRC, the International Federation and the national societies, as well as representatives of nations bound by the Geneva Conventions.

*President of the ICRC*, Jakob Kellenberger

British Red Cross, 9 Grosvenor Crescent, London SW1X 7EJ. Tel: 020-7235 5454; fax: 020-7245 6315.

E-mail: information@redcross.org.uk

Web: www.redcross.org.uk.

*Director-General*, Sir Nicholas Young

---

INTERNATIONAL TELECOMMUNICATIONS SATELLITE ORGANISATION

3400 International Drive NW, Washington DC 20008, USA

Tel: (00 1) (202) 944 6800; fax: (00 1) (202) 944 7898

E-mail: customer.service@intelsat.int

Web: www.intelsat.int

---

The International Telecommunications Satellite Organisation (Intelsat) was formed in 1964. It owns and operates the world-wide commercial communications satellite system which is composed of 20 satellites and more than 4,000 antennas which connect over 200 countries, territories and dependencies. Intelsat provides international and domestic voice/data and video services.

Each of the 143 member states contributes to the capital costs of the organisation in proportion to its investment share, which is based on its relative usage of the system.

There is a four-tier hierarchy. The Assembly of Parties to the agreement meets every two years to consider long-term objectives and is composed of representatives of the member governments. The Meeting of Signatories annually considers the financial, technical and operational aspects of the system. The Board of Governors has 28 members; Intelsat Management is the permanent staff of the organisation and is headed by a Director-General who reports to the Board of Governors.

*Director-General*, Conny Kullman (Sweden)

---

INTERNATIONAL TELECOMMUNICATION UNION

Place des Nations, CH-1211 Geneva 20, Switzerland

Tel: (00 41) (22) 730 5111; fax: (00 41) (22) 733 7256

E-mail: itumail@itu.int; Web: www.itu.int

---

The International Telecommunication Union (ITU) was founded in Paris in 1865 as the International Telegraph Union and became a UN specialised agency in 1947.

ITU is an intergovernmental organisation for the development of telecommunications and the harmonisation of national telecommunication policies. ITU comprises 189 member states and some 661 members who represent public and private organisations involved in telecommunications. ITU's mission is to promote the development of telecommunications and information and communication technologies; to promote and offer technical assistance to developing countries; and to promote at international level the adoption of a broader approach to the issues of telecommunications.

ITU fulfils its mission through initiatives aimed at promoting the growth and expansion of electronic commerce; a programme of strategic workshops; the adoption of international regulations and treaties governing uses of the frequency spectrum; the adoption of technical standards that foster global interconnectivity and interoperability; and the provision of policy advice and technical assistance to developing countries.

ITU also organises world-wide and regional exhibitions and forums to exchange ideas, knowledge and technology.

*Secretary-General*, Yoshio Utsumi (Japan)

---

LEAGUE OF ARAB STATES

Maidane Al-Tahrir, Cairo, Egypt

Tel: (00 20) (2) 575 0511; fax: (00 20) (2) 574 0331

---

The purpose of the League of Arab States, founded in 1945, is to ensure co-operation among member states and protect their independence and sovereignty, to supervise the affairs and interests of Arab countries, to control the execution of agreements concluded among the member states, and to promote the process of integration among them. The League considers itself a regional organisation and has observer status at the United Nations.

Member states are Algeria, Bahrain, the Comoros, Djibouti, Egypt, Iraq, Jordan, Kuwait, Lebanon, Libya, Mauritania, Morocco, Oman, Palestine, Qatar, Saudi Arabia, Somalia, Sudan, Syria, Tunisia, the UAE and Yemen.

Member states participate in various specialised agencies of the League whose role is to develop specific areas of co-operation between Arab states. These include: the Arab Organisation for Mineral Resources; the Arab Monetary Fund; the Arab Satellite Communications Organisation; the Arab Academy of Maritime Transport; the Arab Bank for Economic Development in Africa; the Arab League Educational, Cultural and Scientific Organisation and the Council of Arab Economic Unity.

*Secretary-General*, Dr Ahmed Esmat Abdul-Maguid (Egypt)

UK OFFICE, 52 Green Street, London W1Y 3RH. Tel: 020-7629 0044; fax: 020-7493 7943

---

MERCOSUR Dr. Luis Piera 1992, piso 1, 11200-Montevideo, Uruguay
Tel: (00 598) (2) 402 9024 fax: (00 598) (2) 400 0958
E-mail: webmaster@mercosur.org
Web: www.mercosur.org

---

Brazil and Argentina signed a Treaty for Integration, Co-operation and Development in 1988 which aimed to created a common market between the two countries within ten years, with the elimination of all tariff barriers and harmonisation of macroeconomic policies; the agreement was to be open to other Latin American countries. Paraguay and Uruguay expressed their interest and MERCOSUR (the Southern Common Market) was created by the Treaty of Asunción, which was signed by the four countries on 26 March 1991. Chile became an associate member in 1996 and Bolivia in 1997.

The Common Market Council (CMC) is the highest-level agency of MERCOSUR, with authority to conduct its policy, and responsibility for compliance with the objects and time frames set forth in the Asunción Treaty. It comprises the ministers of foreign affairs and the economy of the member states. Each country presides over the council for a period of six months, in rotating alphabetical order. The CMC meets at least once a year. The presidents of the member states can take part whenever possible.

The Common Market Group (CMG) is the executive body of MERCOSUR and is co-ordinated by the foreign ministries of the member states. Its function is to ensure compliance with the Asunción Treaty and to implement decisions made by the CMC, and where necessary, to help resolve disputes. It can establish work subgroups to work on particular issues. It is composed of four permanent members and four substitutes from each country. It normally meets at least four times a year.

Other bodies include a Joint Parliamentary Committee, a Trade Commission and a Socio-economic Advisory Forum.

---

## THE NORDIC COUNCIL

---

The Nordic Council was established in March 1952 as an advisory body on economic and social co-operation, comprising parliamentary delegates from Denmark, Iceland, Norway and Sweden. It was subsequently joined by Finland (1956), and representatives from the Færøes (1970), the Åland Islands (1970), and Greenland (1984).

Co-operation is regulated by the Treaty of Helsinki signed in 1962. This was amended in 1971 to create the Nordic Council of Ministers, which discusses all matters except defence and foreign affairs. Matters are given preparatory consideration by a Committee of Co-operation Ministers' Deputies and joint committees of officials. Decisions of the Council of Ministers, which are taken by consensus, are binding, although if ratification by member parliaments is required, decisions only become effective following parliamentary approval. The Council of Ministers is advised by the Nordic Council, to which it reports annually. There are Ministers for Nordic Co-operation in every member government.

The Nordic Council, comprising 87 voting delegates nominated from member parliaments and about 80 non-voting government representatives, meets at least once a year in plenary sessions. The full Council chooses a 13-member Praesidium, which conducts business between sessions. A Secretariat, headed by a Secretary-General, liaises with the Council of Ministers and provides administrative support. The Council of Ministers has a separate Secretariat.

SECRETARIAT OF THE NORDIC COUNCIL, PO Box 3043, DK-1021 Copenhagen K, Denmark. Tel: (00 45) 3396 0400; fax: (00 45) 3311 1870. E-mail: nordisk-rad@nordisk-rad.dk; Web: www.norden.org. *Secretary-General*, Frida Nokken (Norway)

SECRETARIAT OF THE NORDIC COUNCIL OF MINISTERS, Store Strandstræede 18, DK-1255 Copenhagen K, Denmark. Tel: (00 45) 3396 0400; fax: (00 45) 3311 1870. Web: www.norden.org. *Secretary-General*, Søren Christensen (Denmark)

---

## NORTH AMERICAN FREE TRADE AGREEMENT

NAFTA Secretariat, Canadian Section, 90 Sparks Street, Suite 705, Ottawa, OntarioK1P 5B4, Canada
Tel: (00 1) (613) 992 9388; fax: (00 1) (613) 992 9392

NAFTA Secretariat, Mexican Section, Blvd. Adolfo López Mateos 3025, 2° Piso, Col. Héroes de Padierna, C.P. 10700, Mexico, D.F. Tel: (00 52) (5) 629 9630; fax: (00 52) (5) 629 9637

NAFTA Secretariat, US Section, 14th Street and Constitution Avenue, NW, Room 2061, Washington DC, 20230, USA Tel: (00 1) (202) 482 5438; fax: (00 1) (202) 482 0148; E-mail: webmaster@nafta-sec-alena.org
Web: www.nafta-sec-alena.org

---

The leaders of Canada, Mexico and the USA signed the North American Free Trade Agreement (NAFTA) on 17 December 1992 in their respective capitals; it came into force on 1 January 1994 after being ratified by the legislatures of the three member states.

NAFTA aims to eliminate barriers to trade in goods and services, promote fair competition within the free trade area, protect and enforce intellectual property rights and create a framework for further co-operation. To achieve these aims, import tariffs and quotas are being removed, with the aim of achieving a free trade zone by 2008 at the latest.

The NAFTA Secretariat is composed of Canadian, Mexican and US sections. It is responsible for the administration of the dispute settlement provisions of the agreement, provides assistance to the Free Trade

Commission and support for various committees and working groups, and facilitates the operation of the agreement.

---

NORTH ATLANTIC TREATY ORGANISATION

Leopold III laan, Brussels B-1110, Belgium
Tel: (00 32) (2) 707 4111; fax: (00 32) (2) 707 4579
E-mail: natodoc@hq.nato.int
Web: www.nato.int

---

The North Atlantic Treaty (Treaty of Washington) was signed in 1949 by Belgium, Canada, Denmark, France, Iceland, Italy, Luxembourg, the Netherlands, Norway, Portugal, the UK and the USA. Greece and Turkey acceded to the Treaty in 1952, the Federal Republic of Germany in 1955 (the reunited Germany acceded in October 1990), Spain in 1982, and the Czech Republic, Hungary and Poland in 1999.

The North Atlantic Treaty Organisation (NATO) is the structural framework for a defensive political and military alliance designed to provide common security for its members through co-operation and consultation in political, military and economic as well as scientific and other non-military fields.

STRUCTURE

The North Atlantic Council (NAC), chaired by the Secretary-General, is the highest authority of the Alliance and is composed of permanent representatives of the 19 member countries. It meets at ministerial level (foreign and/or defence ministers) at least twice a year. The permanent representatives (ambassadors) head national delegations of advisers and experts. The Defence Planning Committee (DPC), composed of representatives of all member countries, deals with defence matters. The DPC also meets at ministerial level (defence ministers) at least twice a year. Nuclear matters are dealt with in the Nuclear Planning Group (NPG), composed of representatives of all countries except for France. The NPG meets regularly at Permanent Representative level and twice a year at ministerial level (defence ministers). The NATO Secretary-General chairs the Council, the DPC and the NPG.

The Council and DPC are forums for constant intergovernmental consultation and are the main decision-making bodies within the Alliance. They are assisted by an International Staff, divided into five divisions: political affairs; defence planning and operations; defence support; security investment, logistics and civil emergency planning; scientific and environmental affairs.

The senior military authority in NATO, under the Council and DPC, is the Military Committee composed of the Chief of Defence Staffs of each member country except Iceland, which has no military and may be represented by a civilian. The Military Committee, which is assisted by an integrated international military staff, also meets in permanent session with permanent military representatives and is responsible for making recommendations to the Council and DPC on measures considered necessary for the common defence of the NATO area and for supplying guidance on military matters to the major NATO commanders. The Chairman of the Military Committee, elected for a period of two to three years, represents the committee on the Council.

The strategic area covered by the North Atlantic Treaty is divided between two major NATO commands (MNCs), European and Atlantic; and three major subordinate commands (MSCs) within Allied Command Europe, South, Central and North-West. There is also a Regional Planning Group (Canada and the United States).

The major NATO commanders are responsible for the development of defence plans for their respective areas, for the determination of force requirements and for the deployment and exercise of the forces under their command. The major NATO commanders report to the Military Committee. The integrated military structure of the Alliance has been reorganised. The new structure, based on reduced numbers of permanent headquarters and more flexible and mobile forces, is expected to be fully in place by 2003.

POST-COLD WAR DEVELOPMENTS

In response to the new security environment arising from the demise of the Warsaw Pact and the end of the Cold War in 1990, NATO issued a Declaration on Peace and Co-operation in 1991, and published a new strategic concept which introduced organisational changes and force reductions of around 30 per cent. The strategic concept was subsequently revised and updated and a new edition was published in April 1999.

The Euro-Atlantic Partnership Council (EAPC) was established in 1997 to develop closer security links with eastern European and former Soviet states. It focuses on defence planning, defence industry conversion, defence management and force structuring, and the democratic concepts of civilian-military relations. Its membership comprises the 19 NATO members and Albania, Armenia, Austria, Azerbaijan, Belarus, Bulgaria, Croatia, Estonia, Finland, Georgia, Ireland, Kazakhstan, Kyrgyzstan, Latvia, Lithuania, Macedonia, Moldova, Romania, Russia, Slovakia, Slovenia, Sweden, Switzerland, Tajikistan, Turkmenistan, Ukraine and Uzbekistan. The EAPC provides the framework for consultations and co-operation under the Partnership for Peace (PFP) programme, a form of association with NATO launched in 1994. All EAPC members are members of PFP with the exception of Tajikistan. NATO will consult with any PFP partner that perceives a direct threat to its territorial integrity, political independence or security. Most of the 27 PFP partners send liaison officers to NATO headquarters in Brussels and to the Partnership Co-ordination Cell in Mons, Belgium, and participate in joint military exercises co-ordinated by NATO. EAPC meets monthly at ambassadorial level in Brussels and twice a year at foreign minister and defence minister level.

In 1994, NATO announced that it would consider admitting new members, and in March 1999, Poland, the Czech Republic and Hungary acceded to the Treaty. The NATO-Ukraine Charter, signed in July 1997, recognised the importance to European security of a democratic and independent Ukraine, and set up a programme for further co-operation in the future. Russian opposition to NATO's enlargement was tempered by the signing of a Founding Act on Mutual Relations, Co-operation and Security in May 1997, which provided for the creation of a Permanent Joint Council, which meets at foreign minister level at least twice a year. The strengthening of the European Security and Defence Identity (ESDI) was one of several objectives developed in the new strategic concept issued by the Alliance at the Washington summit, which was held on 23-24 April 1999.

From 1992 until the end of 1995, NATO provided support for UN peacekeeping efforts in the former Yugoslavia. With the signing of the Bosnian peace agreement in 1995, a NATO-led multinational Implementation Force (IFOR) was formed, which was replaced by the Sustaining Force (SFOR) in December 1996.

In March 1999, NATO began air operations against military and industrial targets in Yugoslavia following the repression and ethnic cleansing of ethnic Albanians in Kosovo. Yugoslavia accepted a peace plan drawn up by NATO and Russia on 3 June 1999 and the withdrawal of Yugoslav forces from Kosovo took place between 10–20 June. NATO ended its air operations on 10 June and on 12 June 1999, the NATO-led security force (KFOR) entered Kosovo to oversee the demilitarisation of the Kosovo Liberation Army, facilitate the return of refugees and provide humanitarian support. By May 2000, KFOR had overseen the disbanding and demilitarisation of the Kosovo Liberation Army and the return of over 850,000 refugees.

At the Washington summit a Defence Capabilities Initiative (DCI) was launched, which aims to improve defence capabilities and interoperability among Alliance forces to ensure the effectiveness of future multinational operations. A temporary High Level Steering Group (HLSG) was established to oversee the implementation of the DCI.

*Secretary-General and Chairman of the North Atlantic Council, of the DPC and of the NPG*, Lord Robertson (UK)

*UK Permanent Representative on the North Atlantic Council*, Sir John Goulden, GCMG

*Chairman of the Military Committee*, Adm. Guido Venturoni (Italy)

*Supreme Allied Commander, Europe*, Gen. Joseph Ralston (USA)

*Supreme Allied Commander, Atlantic*, Lt. Gen. William. F. Kernan (USA)

---

## ORGANISATION FOR ECONOMIC CO-OPERATION AND DEVELOPMENT

2 rue André-Pascal, F-75116 Paris
Tel: (00 33) (1) 4524 8200; fax: (00 33) (1) 4524 8500
E-mail: webmaster@oecd.org Web: www.oecd.org

---

The Organisation for Economic Co-operation and Development (OECD) was formed in 1961 to replace the Organisation for European Economic Co-operation. It is the instrument for international co-operation among industrialised member countries on economic and social policies. Its objectives are to assist its member governments in the formulation and co-ordination of policies designed to achieve high, sustained economic growth while maintaining financial stability, to contribute to world trade on a multilateral basis and to stimulate members' aid to developing countries.

The members are Australia, Austria, Belgium, Canada, Czech Republic, Denmark, Finland, France, Germany, Greece, Hungary, Iceland, Republic of Ireland, Italy, Japan, Republic of Korea, Luxembourg, Mexico, the Netherlands, New Zealand, Norway, Poland, Portugal, Slovakia, Spain, Sweden, Switzerland, Turkey, the UK and the USA.

The Council is the supreme body of the organisation. It is composed of one representative for each member country and meets at permanent representative level under the chairmanship of the Secretary-General, and at ministerial level (usually once a year) under the chairmanship of a minister elected annually. Decisions and recommendations are adopted by the unanimous agreement of all members. Most of the OECD's work is undertaken in over 200 specialised committees and working parties. Five autonomous or semi-autonomous bodies are associated in varying degrees to the Organisation: the Nuclear Energy Agency, the International Energy Agency, the Development Centre, the Centre for Educational Research and Innovation, and the European Conference of Ministers of Transport. These bodies, the committees and the Council are serviced by an international Secretariat headed by the Secretary-General.

*Secretary-General*, Donald J. Johnston (Canada)

*UK Permanent Representative*, HE Christopher Crabbie, 19 rue de Franqueville, Paris F-75116

---

## ORGANISATION FOR SECURITY AND CO-OPERATION IN EUROPE

Kärntner Ring 5–7, A-1010 Vienna, Austria
Tel: (00 43) (1) 514 36 180;
fax: (00 43) (1) 514 36 105
E-mail: info@osce.org; Web: www.osce.org

---

The Organisation for Security and Co-operation in Europe (OSCE) was launched in 1975 (as the Conference on Security and Co-operation in Europe (CSCE)) under the Helsinki Final Act. This established agreements between NATO members, Warsaw Pact members, and neutral and non-aligned European countries covering security, co-operation and human rights.

The Charter of Paris for a New Europe, signed on 21 November 1990, committed members to support multi-party democracy, free-market economics, the rule of law, and human rights. The signatories also agreed to regular meetings of heads of government, ministers and officials. The first institutionalised heads of state and government summit was held in Helsinki in December 1992, at which the Helsinki Document was adopted. This declared the CSCE to be a regional organisation and defined the structures of the organisation. The summit also appointed a High Commissioner on National Minorities. At its December 1994 summit the CSCE was renamed the Organisation for Security and Co-operation in Europe.

Three structures have been established: the Ministerial Council, which comprises the foreign ministers of participating states and is the central decision-making and governing body, and which meets at least once a year; the Senior Council, which prepares work for the Ministerial Council, carries out its decisions and is responsible for the overview, management and co-ordination of OSCE activities and meets at least three times a year; and the Permanent Council, which is responsible for the day-to-day operational tasks of the OSCE and is the regular body for political consultation, meeting weekly. The chairmanship of the Ministerial Council, Senior Council and Permanent Council rotates among participating states with the Senior Council meeting in Prague and the Permanent Council in Vienna.

The OSCE is also underpinned by five permanent institutions: a Secretariat (Vienna); a Forum for Security Co-operation (Vienna), which meets weekly to discuss arms control, disarmament and security-building measures; an Office for Democratic Institutions and Human Rights (Warsaw), which is charged with furthering human rights, democracy and the rule of law; an office of the High Commissioner on National Minorities (The Hague), which identifies ethnic tensions that might endanger peace and promotes their resolution; and a Representative on Freedom of the Media (Vienna), which is responsible for assisting governments in the furthering of free, independent and pluralistic media. There is also a documentation and conference centre in Prague, an

OSCE Parliamentary Assembly with a secretariat based in Copenhagen, and a Court of Conciliation and Arbitration in Geneva.

The OSCE has monitoring missions in ten OSCE countries, and has sent an assistance group to Chechnya. It is also organising a peacekeeping force in Nagorno-Karabakh. The OSCE supervised all elections in Bosnia-Hercegovina between 1996 and 2000. A Joint Consultative Group of the OSCE promotes the objectives and implementation of the Conventional Armed Forces in Europe (CFE) Treaty (1990) which limits conventional ground and air forces. In November 1999, the Charter on European Security committed the OSCE to co-operate with other organisations and institutions concerned with the promotion of security within the OSCE area.

The OSCE has 55 participating states: Albania, Andorra, Armenia, Austria, Azerbaijan, Belarus, Belgium, Bosnia-Hercegovina, Bulgaria, Canada, Croatia, Cyprus, Czech Republic, Denmark, Estonia, Finland, France, Georgia, Germany, Greece, Hungary, Iceland, Republic of Ireland, Italy, Kazakhstan, Kyrgyzstan, Latvia, Liechtenstein, Lithuania, Luxembourg, Macedonia, Malta, Moldova, Monaco, the Netherlands, Norway, Poland, Portugal, Romania, Russia, San Marino, Slovakia, Slovenia, Spain, Sweden, Switzerland, Tajikistan, Turkey, Turkmenistan, the UK, Ukraine, the USA, Uzbekistan, the Vatican and Yugoslavia (suspended from activities July 1992).

*Chair of the OSCE*, Romania (2001); Portugal (2002)
*Secretary-General of the OSCE*, Ján Kubiš (Slovakia)
*Director of the Office for Democratic Institutions and Human Rights*, Gérard Stoudmann (Switzerland)
*OSCE High Commissioner on National Minorities*, Max van der Stoel (Netherlands)
*Representative on Freedom of the Media*, Freimut Duve (Germany)

---

## ORGANISATION OF AFRICAN UNITY

PO Box 3243, Addis Ababa, Ethiopia
Tel: (00 251) (1) 517700; fax: (00 251) (1) 513036
Web: www.oau-oua.org

---

The Organisation of African Unity (OAU) was established in 1963 and has 53 members; Morocco suspended its participation in 1985 in protest at the Polisario-proclaimed Saharan Arab Democratic Republic (SADR), representing Western Sahara, being admitted as a member. The OAU aims to further African unity and solidarity, to co-ordinate political, economic, social and defence policies, and to eliminate colonialism in Africa.

The chief organs are the Assembly of heads of state or government, which is the supreme organ of the OAU and meets once a year to consider matters of common African concern and to co-ordinate the Organisation's policies; the Council of foreign ministers, which is the Organisation's executive body responsible for the implementation of the Assembly's policies, and which meets twice a year; and the Commission of Mediation, Conciliation and Arbitration which promotes the peaceful settlement of disputes between member countries. The main administrative body is the General Secretariat, based in Addis Ababa, headed by a Secretary-General who is elected by the Assembly for a four-year term.

Substantial budgetary arrears due to delays in the payment of national contributions has meant that the OAU continually faces difficulties in furthering its aims. Its budget for 2001 is about US$31 million; several OAU programmes have been suspended since November 1994 after unpaid contributions reached US$77 million, although by June 1995 arrears had dropped to US$38.3 million. In June 1991 the Assembly adopted an African Economic Community Treaty which envisages establishment of the Economic Community after ratification by two-thirds of the OAU's membership. In June 1993 a mechanism was created for conflict prevention, management and resolution, and a peace fund was established.

*Secretary-General*, Salim Ahmed Salim (Tanzania)

---

## ORGANISATION OF AMERICAN STATES

17th Street and Constitution Avenue NW, Washington DC 20006, USA
Tel: (00 1) (202) 458 3000; fax: (00 1) (202) 458 6421
E-mail: pi@oas.org; Web: www.oas.org

---

Originally founded in 1890 for largely commercial purposes, the Organisation of American States (OAS) adopted its present name and charter in 1948. The charter entered into force in 1951 and was amended in 1967, 1985 and 1996; the 1992 Protocol of Washington will enter into force upon ratification by two-thirds of member states.

The OAS aims to strengthen the peace and security of the continent; to promote and consolidate representative democracy with due respect for the principle of non-intervention; to prevent possible causes of difficulties and to ensure the peaceful resolution of disputes arising among its member states; to provide for common action on the part of those states in the event of aggression; to seek the resolution of political, judicial and economic problems that may arise among them; to promote, by co-operative action, their economic, social and cultural development; and to achieve an effective limitation of conventional weapons so that resources can be devoted to economic and social development.

The Declaration of Principles and the Plan of Action resulting from the 1994 Miami summit and signed by all the members except Cuba, envisage the establishment of a free trade area, in which barriers to trade and investment will be progressively eliminated.

Policy is determined by the annual General Assembly, which is the supreme authority and elects the Secretary-General for a five-year term. The Meeting of Consultation of ministers of foreign affairs considers urgent problems on an *ad hoc* basis. The Permanent Council, comprising one representative from each member state, promotes friendly inter-state relations, acts as an intermediary in case of disputes arising between states and oversees the General Secretariat, the main administrative body. The Inter-American Council for Integral Development was created in 1996 by the ratification of the Protocol of Managua to promote sustainable development.

The 35 member states are Antigua and Barbuda, Argentina, the Bahamas, Barbados, Belize, Bolivia, Brazil, Canada, Chile, Colombia, Costa Rica, Cuba, Dominica, Dominican Republic, Ecuador, El Salvador, Grenada, Guatemala, Guyana, Haiti, Honduras, Jamaica, Mexico, Nicaragua, Panama, Paraguay, Peru, St Christopher and Nevis, St Lucia, St Vincent and the Grenadines, Suriname, Trinidad and Tobago, Uruguay, the USA and Venezuela. The European Union and 39 non-American states have permanent observer status.

*Secretary-General*, Dr César Gaviria Trujillo (Colombia)

## ORGANISATION OF ARAB PETROLEUM EXPORTING COUNTRIES

PO Box 20501, Safat 13066, Kuwait
Tel: (00 965) 484 4500; fax: (00 965) 481 5747
E-mail: oapec@qualitynet.net
Web: www.oapecorg.org

The Organisation of Arab Petroleum Exporting Countries (OAPEC) was founded in 1968. Its objectives are to promote co-operation in economic activities, to safeguard members' interests, to unite efforts to ensure the flow of oil to consumer markets, and to create a favourable climate for the investment of capital and expertise.

The Ministerial Council is composed of oil ministers from the member countries and meets twice a year to determine policy and to approve the budgets and accounts of the General Secretariat and the Judicial Tribunal. The Judicial Tribunal is composed of seven part-time judges who rule on disputes between member countries and disputes between countries and oil companies. The executive organ of OAPEC is the General Secretariat.

The members are Algeria, Bahrain, Egypt, Iraq, Kuwait, Libya, Qatar, Saudi Arabia, Syria and the United Arab Emirates. Tunisia's membership has been inactive since 1987.

*Secretary-General*, Abdel-Aziz A. Al-Turki

## ORGANISATION OF THE BLACK SEA ECONOMIC CO-OPERATION

Permanent International Secretariat, Istinye Caddesi, Müsir Fuad Pasa Yalisi, Eski Tersane, 80860 Istinye-Istanbul, Turkey Tel: (00 90) (212) 229 6330/6335; fax: (00 90) (212) 229 6336;
E-mail: bsec@turk.net; Web: www.bsec.gov.tr

The Black Sea Economic Co-operation (BSEC) resulted from the Istanbul Summit Declaration and the adoption of the Bosporus Statement on 25 June 1992. BSEC acquired a permanent secretariat in 1994. Following the Yalta Summit of the Heads of State or Government in June 1998, a charter was drawn up to found the Organisation of the Black Sea Economic Co-operation, which was inaugurated on 1 May 1999.

The organisation aims to promote closer political and economic co-operation in the context of the European integration process between the countries in the Black Sea region and to foster security, regional initiatives, social justice, economic liberty and respect for human rights.

The Council of the Ministers of Foreign Affairs, the highest decision-making authority, meets twice yearly. The meetings rotate among the member states and the chairman is the foreign minister of the state in which the meeting is held. There is also a Committee of Senior Officials and 15 working groups, which deal with specific areas of co-operation.

There are 11 member states: Albania, Armenia, Azerbaijan, Bulgaria, Georgia, Greece, Moldova, Romania, Russia, Turkey and Ukraine.

## ORGANISATION OF THE ISLAMIC CONFERENCE

PO Box 178, Jeddah 21411, Saudi Arabia
Tel: (00 966) (2) 680 0800; fax: (00 966) (2) 687 3568
E-mail: oiccabinet@oic-un.org;
Web: www.oic-oci.org

The Organisation of the Islamic Conference (OIC) was established in 1969 with the purpose of promoting solidarity and co-operation between Islamic countries. It also has the specific aims of co-ordinating efforts to safeguard the Muslim holy places, supporting the formation of a Palestinian state, assisting member states to maintain their independence, co-ordinating the views of member states in international forums such as the UN, and improving co-operation in the economic, cultural and scientific fields.

The OIC has three central organs, supreme among them the Conference of the Heads of State which meets once every three years to discuss issues of importance to Islamic states. The Conference of Foreign Ministers meets annually to prepare reports for the Conference of Heads of State. The General Secretariat carries out administrative tasks. It is headed by a Secretary-General who is elected by the Conference of Foreign Ministers for a non-renewable four-year term.

In addition to this structure, the OIC has several subsidiary bodies, specialised institutions, affiliated bodies and standing committees. These include the Islamic Solidarity Fund, to aid Islamic institutions in member countries, the Islamic Development Bank, to finance development projects in poorer member states and the Islamic Educational, Scientific and Cultural Organisation. The OIC runs various offices to organise the economic boycott of Israel.

The achievement of the OIC's aims has often been prevented by political rivalry and conflicts between member states, such as the Iran-Iraq war and the Iraqi invasion of Kuwait. Egypt's membership was suspended from 1979 to 1984 because of its peace treaty with Israel. Saudi Arabia, the main source of funding, exercises great influence within the OIC. Since 1991 the OIC has become more united and has spoken out against violence against Muslims in India, the Occupied Territories and Bosnia-Hercegovina. From 1993 to 1995 the OIC co-ordinated the offering of troops to the UN by Muslim states to protect Muslim areas of Bosnia-Hercegovina.

The Organisation has 56 members (55 sovereign Muslim states in Africa, the Middle East, central and south-east Asia and Europe, plus the Palestine Liberation Organisation) and three observers, the Central African Republic, Turkish Northern Cyprus and Côte d'Ivoire. It has an annual budget of US$11 million.

*Secretary-General*, Dr Abdelouahed Belkeziz (Morocco)

## ORGANISATION OF THE PETROLEUM EXPORTING COUNTRIES

Obere Donaustrasse 93, A-1020 Vienna, Austria
Tel: (00 43) (1) 21112 279; fax: (00 43) (1) 214 9827
E-mail: prid@opec.org
Web: www.opec.org

The Organisation of the Petroleum Exporting Countries (OPEC) was created in 1960 as a permanent intergovernmental organisation with the principal aims of unifying and co-ordinating the petroleum policies of its members, determining ways of protecting their interests individually and collectively, and ensuring the stabilisation of prices in international oil markets with a view to eliminating unnecessary fluctuations. Since 1982 OPEC has attempted (only partially successfully) to impose overall production limits and production quotas in an attempt to maintain stable oil prices. An OPEC summit in Caracas on 27-28 September 2000 produced agreement to stabilise oil prices, which had been rising sharply.

The supreme authority is the Conference of Ministers of oil, mines and energy of member countries, which meets at least twice a year to formulate policy. The Board of Governors, nominated by member countries, directs the management of OPEC and implements conference resolutions. The Secretariat carries out executive functions under the direction of the Board of Governors.

The member states are Algeria, Indonesia, Iran, Iraq, Kuwait, Libya, Nigeria, Qatar, Saudi Arabia, the UAE and Venezuela. Ecuador withdrew in 1992 and Gabon in 1995.

*Secretary-General*, HE Dr Alí Rodríguez-Araque (Venezuela)

---

THE SECRETARIAT OF THE PACIFIC COMMUNITY
BP D5, 98848 Nouméa Cedex, New Caledonia
Tel: (00 687) 262000; fax: (00 687) 263818
E-mail: spc@spc.int; Web: www.spc.int

---

The Secretariat of the Pacific Community (formerly the South Pacific Commission) was established in 1947 by Australia, France, the Netherlands, New Zealand, the UK and the USA with the aim of promoting the economic and social stability of the islands in the region. The Community now numbers 27 member states and territories: the five remaining founder states (the Netherlands has withdrawn), in which no programmes are run, and the other 22 states and territories of Melanesia, Micronesia and Polynesia.

The Secretariat of the Pacific Community (SPC) is a technical assistance agency with programmes in marine resources (coastal and oceanic fisheries; maritime programme), land resources (agriculture, animal health and plant protection; forestry) and social resources (community health; socio-economic and statistical services; community education services).

The governing body is the Conference of the Pacific Community, which meets every two years. The Director-General is the chief executive.

*Director-General*, Lourdes Pangelinan (Guam)

*Deputy Directors-General*, Dr Jimmie Rodgers (Solomon Islands); Yves Corbel (France)

---

SOUTH ASIAN ASSOCIATION FOR REGIONAL CO-OPERATION
PO Box 4222, Kathmandu, Nepal
Tel: (00 977) (1) 221794/221785; fax: (00 977) (1) 227033/223991 E-mail: saarc@saarc-sec.org
Web: www.saarc-sec.org

---

The South Asian Association for Regional Co-operation (SAARC) was established in 1985 by Bangladesh, Bhutan, India, the Maldives, Nepal, Pakistan and Sri Lanka. Its main aim is to promote the acceleration of economic and social development in member states through collective action in agreed areas of co-operation. These include agriculture and rural development, human resource development, environment, meteorology and forestry, science and technology, transport and communications, energy, and social development.

A SAARC preferential trading arrangement (SAPTA), which is designed to reduce tariffs on trade between SAARC member states, was signed in 1993 and entered into force in December 1995. A committee of experts was established in 1998 to draft a comprehensive treaty to create a free trade area. The text of the treaty was due to be finalised by 2001.

The highest authority rests with the heads of state or government of each member state. The Council of Ministers, which meets twice a year, is made up of the foreign ministers of the member states; it is responsible for formulating policy and considering new projects. The Standing Committee is composed of the foreign secretaries of the member states and monitors and co-ordinates SAARC programmes; it meets twice a year. Technical committees are responsible for individual areas of SAARC's activities. The Secretariat co-ordinates, monitors, facilitates and promotes SAARC's activities and serves as a channel of communication between the association and other regional and intergovernmental institutions.

*Secretary-General*, Nihal Rodrigo (Sri Lanka)

---

SOUTHERN AFRICAN DEVELOPMENT COMMUNITY
Private Bag 0095, Gaborone, Botswana
Tel: (00 267) 351 863; fax: (00 267) 372 848
E-mail: sadcsec@sadc.int
Web: www.saep.org/sadc/sadc.html

---

The Southern African Development Community (SADC) was formed in August 1992 by the members of its predecessor, the Southern African Development Co-ordination Conference, founded in 1980 to harmonise economic development among the countries in Southern Africa and reduce their dependence on South Africa. The SADC now comprises 14 countries, including South Africa, and works on a regional basis to increase economic integration and regional security.

It aims to evolve common political values, systems and institutions, to promote development and economic growth, regional security, self-sustaining development and the interdependence of member states, and to maximise production and strengthen and consolidate the historical, social and cultural links among the peoples of the region.

The original ten members, Angola, Botswana, Lesotho, Malawi, Mozambique, Namibia, Swaziland, Tanzania, Zambia and Zimbabwe, were joined by South Africa in 1994, Mauritius in 1995 and the Democratic Republic of Congo and the Seychelles in 1997.

The headquarters of the SADC are in Gaborone, Botswana, but member states each have a responsibility for an area of economic activity.

*Executive Secretary*, Dr Prega Ramsamy

---

THE UNITED NATIONS
UN Plaza, New York, NY 10017, USA
Tel: (00 1) (212) 963 1234
Web: www.un.org

---

The United Nations (UN) is an intergovernmental organisation of member states, dedicated through signature of the UN Charter to the maintenance of international peace and security and the solution of economic, social and political problems through international co-operation.

The UN was founded as a successor to the League of Nations and inherited many of its procedures and institutions. The name 'United Nations' was first used in the Washington Declaration 1942 to describe the 26 states that had allied to fight the Axis powers. The UN Charter developed from discussions at the Moscow Conference of the foreign ministers of China, the UK, the USA and the Soviet Union in 1943. Further progress was made at Dumbarton Oaks, Washington, in 1944 during talks involving the same states. The role of the Security Council was formulated at the Yalta Conference in 1945. The Charter was formally drawn up by 50 allied nations at the San Francisco Conference between April and 26 June 1945, when it was signed. Following ratification the UN came into effect on 24 October 1945, which is celebrated annually as United Nations Day. The UN flag is light blue with the UN emblem centred in white.

The principal organs of the UN are the General Assembly, the Security Council, the Economic and Social Council, the Trusteeship Council, the Secretariat and the International Court of Justice. The Economic and Social Council and the Trusteeship Council are auxiliaries, charged with assisting and advising the General Assembly and Security Council. The official languages used are Arabic, Chinese, English, French, Russian and Spanish. Deliberations at the International Court of Justice are in English and French only.

A Millennium summit was held in New York on 6-8 September 2000 at which the reform of the UN was debated and an attempt was made to redefine its role.

### Membership

Membership is open to all countries which accept the Charter and its principle of peaceful co-existence. New members are admitted by the General Assembly on the recommendation of the Security Council. The original membership of 51 states has grown to 189: *Original member (i.e. from 1945)

From 25 October 1971 'China' was taken to mean the People's Republic of China. Czechoslovakia was an original member in 1945 and a member until 31 December 1992; the successor states of the Czech Republic and Slovakia were admitted as members in January 1993.

The Russian Federation took over the membership of the Soviet Union in the Security Council and all other UN organs on 24 December 1991. Belarus (formerly Belorussia) and Ukraine on becoming independent sovereign states continued their existing memberships of the UN, both having been granted separate UN membership in 1945 as a concession to the Soviet Union.

### Observers

Permanent observer status is held by the Holy See and Switzerland. The Palestine Liberation Organisation has special observer status.

### Non-Members

A number of countries are not members, usually due to their small size and limited financial resources. Notable exceptions include Switzerland, which follows a policy of absolute neutrality, and Taiwan, which was replaced by the People's Republic of China in 1971. The others are Kiribati, Nauru, Tonga and the Holy See.

## THE GENERAL ASSEMBLY
UN Plaza, New York, NY 10017, USA

The General Assembly is the main deliberative organ of the UN. It consists of all members, each entitled to five representatives but having only one vote. The annual session begins on the third Tuesday of September, when the President is elected, and usually continues until mid-December. Special sessions are held on specific issues and emergency special sessions can be called within 24 hours.

The Assembly is empowered to discuss any matter within the scope of the Charter, except when it is under consideration by the Security Council, and to make recommendations. Under the 'uniting for peace' resolution, adopted in 1950, the Assembly may also take action to maintain international peace and security when the Security Council fails to do so because of a lack of unanimity of its permanent members. Important decisions, such as those on peace and security, the election of officers, the budget, etc., need a two-thirds majority. Others need a simple majority. The Assembly has effective power only over the internal operations of the UN itself; external recommendations are not legally binding.

The work of the General Assembly is divided among six main committees, on each of which every member has the right to be represented: disarmament and international security; economic and financial; social, humanitarian and cultural; special political issues and decolonisation (including non-self governing territories); administrative and budgetary; and legal. In addition, the General Assembly appoints *ad hoc* committees to consider special issues, such as human rights, peacekeeping, disarmament and international law. All committees consider items referred to them by the Assembly and recommend draft resolutions to its plenary meeting.

The Assembly is assisted by a number of functional committees. The General Committee co-ordinates its proceedings and operations, while the Credentials Committee verifies the credentials of representatives. There are also two standing committees, the Advisory Committee on Administration and Budgetary Questions and the Committee on Contributions, which suggests the scale of members' payments to the UN.

*President of the General Assembly* (2001), Harri Holkeri (Finland)

The Assembly has created a large number of specialised bodies over the years, which are supervised jointly with the Economic and Social Council. They are supported by UN and voluntary contributions from governments, non-governmental organisations and individuals. These organisations include:

### The Conference on Disarmament (CD)

Palais des Nations, CH-1211 Geneva 10, Switzerland
Established by the UN as the Committee on Disarmament in 1962, the CD is the single multilateral disarmament negotiating forum. The present title of the organisation was adopted in 1984. There were 40 members as at June 1994.

A Chemical Weapons Convention was agreed in Paris in 1993 and came into force in April 1997 after being ratified by 87 countries. It bans the use, production, stockpiling and transfer of all chemical weapons. All US and Russian weapons must be destroyed within 15 years of the Convention entering into force and all other states' weapons must be destroyed within ten years.

*Secretary-General*, Vladimir Petrovsky (Russia)
*UK Representative*, I. Soutar, 37–39 rue de Vermont, CH-1211 Geneva 20, Switzerland

### The United Nations Children's Fund (UNICEF)

3 UN Plaza, New York, NY 10017, USA
Established in 1947 to assist children and mothers in the immediate post-war period, UNICEF now concentrates

on developing countries. It provides primary health-care and health education. In particular, it conducts programmes in oral hydration, immunisation against leading diseases, child growth monitoring, and the encouragement of breast-feeding. Its operations are often conducted in co-operation with the World Health Organisation (WHO).
*Executive Director*, Carol Bellamy (USA)

### The United Nations Development Programme (UNDP)

1 UN Plaza, New York, NY 10017, USA
Established in 1966 from the merger of the UN Expanded Programme of Technical Assistance and the UN Special Fund, UNDP is the central funding agency for economic and social development projects around the world. Much of its annual expenditure is channelled through UN specialised agencies, governments and non-governmental organisations.
*Administrator*, James G. Speth (USA)

### The United Nations High Commissioner for Refugees (UNHCR)

Centre William Rappard, 154 rue de Lausanne, PO Box 2500, CH-1211 Geneva 2, Switerland
Established in 1951 to protect the rights and interests of refugees, UNHCR organises emergency relief and longer-term solutions, such as voluntary repatriation, local integration or resettlement.
*High Commissioner*, Ruud Lubbers (Netherlands)
UK Office, 76 Westminster Palace Gardens, London SW1P 1RL. Tel: 020-7828 9191

### The UN Relief and Works Agency for Palestine Refugees in the Near East (UNRWA)

Vienna International Centre, Wagramerstrasse 5, PO Box 100, A-1400 Vienna, Austria
Established in 1949 to bring relief to the Palestinians displaced by the Arab-Israeli conflict.
*Commissioner-General*, Peter Hansen (Denmark)

### The United Nations High Commissioner for Human Rights

Established in 1993 to secure respect for, and prevent violations of human rights by engaging in dialogue with governments and international organisations. Responsible for the co-ordination of all UN human rights activities.
*High Commissioner*, Mary Robinson (Ireland)

*Other bodies include*:

The UN Centre for Human Settlements (Habitat), PO Box 30030, Nairobi, Kenya
The UN Conference on Trade and Development (UNCTAD), Palais des Nations, CH-1211 Geneva 10, Switzerland
The Department of Humanitarian Affairs (DHA), Palais des Nations, CH-1211 Geneva 10, Switzerland
The International Seabed Authority, Kingston, Jamaica
The UN Environment Programme (UNEP), PO Box 30552, Nairobi, Kenya
The UN Population Fund (UNFPA), 220 East 42nd Street, New York, NY 10017, USA
The UN Institute for the Advancement of Women (INSTRAW), PO Box 21747, Santo Domingo, Dominican Republic
The UN University (UNU), Toho Seimei Building, 15-1, Shibuya, 2-Chome, Shibuya-ku, Tokyo 150, Japan
The World Food Council (WFC), Via delle Terme di Caracalla, I-00100 Rome, Italy
The World Food Programme (WFP), Via delle Terme di Caracalla, I-00100 Rome, Italy

### Budget of the United Nations

The budget adopted for the biennium 1998–9 was US$2,387 million. The scale of assessment contributions of 88 UN members is set at the minimum 0.01 per cent. The ten largest assessments are: USA, 25 per cent; Japan, 12.45; Germany, 8.93; Russia, 6.91; France, 6.00; UK, 5.02; Italy, 4.29; Canada, 3.11; Spain, 1.98; Australia, 1.51.

## THE SECURITY COUNCIL
## UN Plaza, New York, NY 10017, USA

The Security Council is the senior arm of the UN and has the primary responsibility for maintaining world peace and security. It consists of 15 members, each with one representative and one vote. There are five permanent members, China, France, Russia, the UK and the USA, and ten non-permanent members. Each of the non-permanent members is elected for a two-year term by a two-thirds majority of the General Assembly and is ineligible for immediate re-election. Five of the elective seats are allocated to Africa and Asia, one to eastern Europe, two to Latin America and two to western Europe and remaining countries. Procedural questions are determined by a majority vote. Other matters require a majority inclusive of the votes of the permanent members; they thus have a right of veto. The abstention of a permanent member does not constitute a veto. The presidency rotates each month by state in (English) alphabetical order. Parties to a dispute, other non-members and individuals can be invited to participate in Security Council debates but are not permitted to vote.

The Security Council is empowered to settle or adjudicate in disputes or situations which threaten international peace and security. It can adopt political, economic and military measures to achieve this end. Any matter considered to be a threat to or breach of the peace or an act of aggression can be brought to the Security Council's attention by any member state or by the Secretary-General. The Charter envisaged members placing at the disposal of the Security Council armed forces and other facilities which would be co-ordinated by the Military Staff Committee, composed of military representatives of the five permanent members. The Security Council is also supported by a Committee of Experts, to advise on procedural and technical matters, and a Committee on Admission of New Members.

Owing to superpower disunity, the Security Council rarely played the decisive role set out in the Charter; the Military Staff Committee was effectively suspended from 1948 until 1990, when a meeting was convened during the Gulf Crisis on the formation and control of UN-supervised armed forces. However, at an extraordinary meeting of the Security Council in January 1992, heads of government laid plans to transform the UN in light of the changed post-Cold War world. The Secretary-General was asked to draw up a report on enhancing the UN's preventive diplomacy, peacemaking and peacekeeping ability. The report, *An Agenda for Peace*, was produced in June 1992 and centred on the establishment of a UN army composed of national contingents on permanent standby, as envisaged at the time of the UN's formation.

PEACEKEEPING FORCES

The Security Council has established a number of peacekeeping forces since its foundation, comprising contingents provided mainly by neutral and non-aligned UN members. Current forces include: the UN Truce Supervision Organisation (UNTSO), Israel, 1948; the UN Military Observer Group in India and Pakistan (UNMOGIP), 1949; the UN Peacekeeping Force in Cyprus (UNFICYP), 1964; the UN Disengagement Observer Force (UNDOF), Golan Heights, Syria, 1974; the UN Interim Force in Lebanon (UNIFIL), 1978; the UN Iraq-Kuwait Observation Mission (UNIKOM), 1991; the UN Mission for the Referendum in Western Sahara (MINURSO), 1991; the UN Observer Mission in Georgia (UNOMIG), 1993; the UN Observer Mission in Liberia (UNOMIL), 1993; the UN Observer Mission in Guatemala (MINUGA), 1994; the UN Observer Mission in Tajikistan (UNMOT), 1994; the UN Preventive Deployment Force (UNPREDEP), Macedonia, 1995; the UN Mission in Bosnia-Hercegovina (UNMIBH), 1995; the UN Mission of Observers in Prevlaka (UNMOP), 1996.

## THE ECONOMIC AND SOCIAL COUNCIL
UN Plaza, New York, NY 10017, USA

The Economic and Social Council is responsible under the General Assembly for the economic and social work of the UN and for the co-ordination of the activities of the 15 specialised agencies and other UN bodies. It makes reports and recommendations on economic, social, cultural, educational, health and related matters, often in consultation with non-governmental organisations, passing the reports to the General Assembly and other UN bodies. It also drafts conventions for submission to the Assembly and calls conferences on matters within its remit.

The Council consists of 54 members, 18 of whom are elected annually by the General Assembly for a three-year term. Each has one vote and can be immediately re-elected on retirement. A President is elected annually and is also eligible for re-election. One substantive session is held annually and decisions are reached by simple majority vote of those present.

The Council has established a number of standing committees on particular issues and several commissions. Commissions include: Statistical, Human Rights, Social Development, Sustainable Development, Status of Women, Crime Prevention and Criminal Justice, Narcotic Drugs, Science and Technology for Development, and Population; and Regional Economic Commissions for Europe, Asia and the Pacific, Western Asia, Latin America and Africa.

## THE TRUSTEESHIP COUNCIL
UN Plaza, New York, NY10017, USA

The Trusteeship Council supervised the administration of territories within the UN Trusteeship system inherited from the League of Nations. It consists of the five permanent members of the Security Council. With the independence of the Republic of Palau in October 1994, all eleven trusteeships have now progressed to independence or merged with neighbouring states and the Trusteeship Council suspended its operations on 1 November 1994.

## THE SECRETARIAT
UN Plaza, New York, NY 10017, USA

The Secretariat services the other UN organs and is headed by a Secretary-General elected by a majority vote of the General Assembly on the recommendation of the Security Council. He is assisted by an international staff, chosen to represent the international character of the organisation. The Secretary-General is charged with bringing to the attention of the Security Council any matter which he considers poses a threat to international peace and security. He may also bring other matters to the attention of the General Assembly and other UN bodies and may be entrusted by them with additional duties. As chief administrator to the UN, the Secretary-General is present in person or via representatives at all meetings of the other five main organs of the UN. He may also act as an impartial mediator in disputes between member states.

The power and influence of the Secretary-General has been determined largely by the character of the office-holder and by the state of relations between the superpowers. The thaw in these relations since the mid-1980s has increased the effectiveness of the UN, particularly in its attempts to intervene in international disputes. It helped to end the Iran-Iraq war and sponsored peace in Central America. Following Iraq's invasion of Kuwait in 1990 the UN took its first collective security action since the Korean War. UN action to protect the Kurds in northern Iraq has widened its legal authority by breaching the prohibition on its intervention in the essentially domestic affairs of states. Currently the UN is involved in peacekeeping, aid distribution and negotiations in the former Yugoslavia; and is addressing the global problems of AIDS and environmental destruction.

*Secretary-General*, Kofi Annan, apptd 1996 (Ghana)
*Deputy Secretary-General*, Louise Frechette, apptd 1998 (Canada)

UNDER-SECRETARIES-GENERAL

*Administration and Management*, Joseph Connor (USA)
*Chef de Cabinet*, Iqbqal Riza (Pakistan)
*Development Support and Management Services*, Jin Yongjian (China)
*Humanitarian Affairs*, Sergio Vieira de Mello (Brazil)
*Legal Affairs and UN Legal Counsel*, Hans Corell (Sweden)
*Peacekeeping Operations*, Bernard Miyet (France)
*Policy Co-ordination and Sustainable Development*, Nitin Desai (India)
*Political Affairs*, Sir Kieran Prendergast (UK)

FORMER SECRETARIES-GENERAL

| | |
|---|---|
| 1946–53 | Trygve Lie (Norway) |
| 1953–61 | Dag Hammarskjöld (Sweden) |
| 1961–71 | U Thant (Burma) |
| 1971–81 | Kurt Waldheim (Austria) |
| 1981–91 | Javier Pérez de Cuéllar (Peru) |
| 1991–96 | Boutros Boutros-Ghali (Egypt) |

## INTERNATIONAL COURT OF JUSTICE
The Peace Palace, NL-2517 KJ The Hague, The Netherlands

The International Court of Justice is the principal judicial organ of the UN. The Statute of the Court is an integral part of the Charter and all members of the UN are *ipso facto* parties to it. The Court is composed of 15 judges, elected by both the General Assembly and the Security Council for nine-year terms which are renewable. Judges may deliberate over cases in which their country is involved. If no judge on the bench is from a country which is a party to a dispute under consideration, that party may designate a judge to participate *ad hoc* in that particular deliberation. If any party to a case fails to adhere to the judgement of the Court, the other party may have recourse to the Security Council.

*President*, Gilbert Guillaume (France) (2006)
*Vice-President*, Shi Jiuyong (China) (2003)
*Judges*, Carl-August Fleischhauer (Germany) (2003); Géza Herczegh (Hungary) (2003); Rosalyn Higgins (UK) (2009); Pieter H. Kooijmans (Netherlands) (2006); Abdul G. Koroma (Sierra Leone) (2003); Shigeru Oda (Japan) (2003); Gonzalo Parra-Aranguren (Venezuela) (2009); Raymond Ranjeva (Madagascar) (2009); José Francisco Rezek (Brazil) (2006); Vladlen S. Vereshchetin (Russia) (2006); Mohammed Bedjaoui; (Algeria) (2006); Akin Shawkat Al-Khasawneh (Jordan) (2009); Thomas Buergenthal (USA) (2009)

### INTERNATIONAL CRIMINAL TRIBUNAL FOR THE FORMER YUGOSLAVIA

Churchill Plein 1, PO Box 13888, NL-2501 EW The Hague, The Netherlands

In February 1993, the Security Council voted to establish a war crimes tribunal for the former Yugoslavia to hear cases covering grave breaches of the Geneva Conventions and crimes against humanity. The Court was inaugurated in November 1993 in The Hague with 11 judges elected by the UN General Assembly from 11 states, divided into two trial chambers of three judges each and an appeal chamber of five judges. The court is unable to force suspects to stand trial but is empowered to pass verdicts in the absence of suspects and can put suspects under an 'act of accusation' which prevents them from leaving their own country.

In October 1995, the tribunal formally charged the Bosnian Serb leaders Radovan Karadzić and Gen. Ratko Mladić, and the Croatian Serb President Milan Martić and 21 others with genocide and crimes against humanity. As at January 1997 only one of the 75 suspected war criminals to be indicted has been imprisoned. In May 1999, the tribunal formally charged the Yugoslav president Slobodan Milošević, the Serbian president Milan Milutinović, two other Serb politicians and the Yugoslav armed forces chief of staff Dragoljub Ojdanić.
*President*, Antonio Cassese (Italy)
*Chief Prosecutor*, Louise Arbour (Canada)

### INTERNATIONAL CRIMINAL TRIBUNAL FOR RWANDA

In November 1994, the UN Security Council voted to establish a tribunal to try those responsible for genocide and other violations of international humanitarian law in Rwanda between 1 January and 31 December 1994. The tribunal, based in Arusha, Tanzania, is empowered to try the most senior people responsible for the massacre. It formally opened in November 1995 to consider 463 indictments.
*Chief Prosecutor*, Carla del Ponte (Switzerland)

### UNITED NATIONS MONITORING, VERIFICATION AND INSPECTION COMMISSION

Room S-3120, New York, NY 10017, USA
Tel: (00 1) (212) 963 3017; fax: (00 1) (212) 963 3922
Web: www.unmovic.org

The United Nations Monitoring, Verification and Inspection Commission (UNMOVIC), was created by UN Security Council Resolution 1284, adopted in December 1999. It replaced the former United Nations Special Commission for the Elimination of Iraq's Weapons of Mass Destruction (UNSCOM).

UNMOVIC is mandated to verify Iraq's compliance with its obligation not to possess or acquire weapons of mass destruction (atomic, biological or chemical weapons of mass destruction, together with ballistic missiles with a target distance of more than 150 km), to destroy all research, development and production facilities and to desist from the future development or acquisition of such weapons and operate a monitoring and verification programme to ensure that prohibited items and programmes are not reactivated.

The lifting of sanctions on the export of goods to Iraq was linked to its co-operation with UNMOVIC.

To date, UNMOVIC has not been permitted to enter Iraq and fulfil its mandate.
*Executive Chairman*, Dr Hans Blix (Sweden)

## SPECIALISED AGENCIES

Fifteen independent international organisations, each with its own membership, budget and headquarters, carry out their responsibilities in co-ordination with the UN under agreements made with the Economic and Social Council. An entry for each appears elsewhere in the International Organisations section. They are: the Food and Agriculture Organisation of the UN; International Civil Aviation Organisation; International Fund for Agricultural Development; International Labour Organisation; International Maritime Organisation; the International Monetary Fund; International Telecommunications Union; UN Educational, Scientific and Cultural Organisation; UN Industrial Development Organisation; Universal Postal Union; World Bank (International Bank for Reconstruction and Development, International Development Agency, International Finance Corporation); World Health Organisation; World Intellectual Property Organisation; and World Meteorological Organisation. The International Atomic Energy Agency and the World Trade Organisation are linked to the UN but are not specialised agencies.

### UK MISSION TO THE UNITED NATIONS

1 Dag Hammarskjöld Plaza, 885 Second Avenue, New York, NY 10017, USA
Tel: (00 1) (212) 745 9250; fax: (00 1) (212) 745 9316
Web: www.ukun.org
*Permanent Representative to the United Nations and Representative on the Security Council*, Sir Jeremy Greenstock, KCMG, *apptd* 1998
*Deputy Permanent Representative*, S. G. Eldon, CMG, OBE

### UK MISSION TO THE OFFICE OF THE UN AND OTHER INTERNATIONAL ORGANISATIONS IN GENEVA

37–39 rue de Vermont, CH-1211 Geneva 20, Switzerland
Tel: (00 41) (22) 918 2300; fax: (00 41) (22) 918 2333
E-mail: mission.uk@ties.itu.int
*Permanent UK Representative*, S. W. J. Fuller, CMG, *apptd* 2000
*Deputy Permanent Representative*, N. M. McMillan, CMG

### UK MISSION TO THE UN IN VIENNA

Jaurèsgasse 12, A-1030 Vienna, Austria
*UK Permanent Representative*, Dr J. P. G. Freeman, *apptd* 1997
*Deputy Permanent Representative*, M. R. Etherton

### UN OFFICE AND INFORMATION CENTRE

Millbank Tower, 21–24 Millbank, London, SW1P 4QH
Tel: 020-7630 1981; fax: 020-7976 6478

UNITED NATIONS EDUCATIONAL, SCIENTIFIC AND CULTURAL ORGANISATION
7 place de Fontenoy, F-75352 Paris 07 SP, France
Tel: (00 33) (1) 4568 1000; fax: (00 33) (1) 4567 1690
Web: www.unesco.org

The United Nations Educational, Scientific and Cultural Organisation (UNESCO) was established in 1946. It promotes collaboration among its member states in education, science, culture and communication. It aims to further a universal respect for human rights, justice and the rule of law, without distinction of race, sex, language or religion, in accordance with the UN Charter.

UNESCO runs a number of programmes to improve education and extend access to it. It provides assistance to ensure the free flow of information and its wider and better balanced dissemination without any obstacle to freedom of expression, and to maintain cultural heritage in the face of development. It fosters research and study in all areas of the social and environmental sciences.

UNESCO had 189 member states as at April 2001. The General Conference, consisting of representatives of all the members, meets biennially to decide the programme and the budget (2000–1, US$544,400,000). It elects the 58-member Executive Board, which supervises operations, and appoints a Director-General who heads a Secretariat responsible for carrying out the organisation's programmes. In most member states national commissions liaise with UNESCO to execute its programme.

The UK withdrew from UNESCO in 1985; it rejoined on 1 July 1997.

*Director-General*, Koichiro Matsuura (Japan)

UNITED NATIONS INDUSTRIAL DEVELOPMENT ORGANISATION
Vienna International Centre, Wagramerstrasse 5, PO Box 300, A-1400 Vienna, Austria
Tel: (00 43) (1) 260 260; fax: (00 43) (1) 269 2669
E-mail: unido-press@unido.org
Web: www.unido.org

The United Nations Industrial Development Organisation (UNIDO) was established in 1966 by the UN General Assembly to act as the central co-ordinating body for industrial activities within the UN. It became a UN specialised agency in 1985. UNIDO aims to help developing countries and those with economies in transition to develop sustainable industrialisation by concentrating on economic competitiveness, environmental awareness and employment issues both in the public and private sectors. UNIDO designs and implements programmes to support industrial development in individual member states and offers specialised support for programme development.

UNIDO had 169 members as at May 2001. It is funded by the UN, member states and non-governmental organisations. A General Conference of all the members meets biennially to discuss strategy and policy, approve the budget (2000–1, US$133.3 million) and elect the Director-General. The Industrial Development Board is composed of members from 53 member states and reviews the work programme and the budget, which is prepared by the Programme and Budget Committee.

*Director-General*, Carlos Magariños (Argentina)

*Permanent UK Representative*, Peter Jenkins, British Embassy, Vienna

UNIVERSAL POSTAL UNION
Weltpoststrasse 4, CH-3000 Bern 15, Switzerland
Tel: (00 41) (31) 350 3111; fax: (00 41) (31) 350 3110
E-Mail: info@upu.int; Web: www.upu.int

The Universal Postal Union (UPU) was established by the Treaty of Bern 1874, taking effect from 1875, and became a UN specialised agency in 1948. The UPU is an intergovernmental organisation that exists to form and regulate a single postal territory of all member countries for the reciprocal exchange of correspondence without discrimination. It also assists and advises on the improvement of postal services.

The UPU had 189 members as at April 2001. A Universal Postal Congress of all its members is the UPU's supreme authority and meets every five years to review the Treaty. A Council of Administration composed of 41 members was established by the 1994 Congress. It meets annually to ensure continuity between congresses, study regulatory developments and broad policies, approve the budget and examine proposed Treaty changes. A Postal Operations Council also meets annually to deal with specific technical and operational issues. The three UPU bodies are served by the International Bureau, a secretariat headed by a Director-General.

Funding is provided by members according to a scale of contributions drawn up by the Congress. The Council sets the biennial budget (2001–2002, SFr71,400,000) within a five-year figure decided by the Congress.

*Director-General*, Thomas E. Leavey (USA)

UNREPRESENTED NATIONS AND PEOPLES ORGANISATION 40A Javastraat, NL-2585 AP, The Hague, The Netherlands
Tel: (00 31) (70) 360 3318; fax: (00 31) (70) 360 3346
E-mail: unponl@unpo.orgWeb: www.unpo.org

The Unrepresented Nations and Peoples Organisation (UNPO) was founded in 1991 to offer an international forum for occupied nations, indigenous peoples and national minorities who are not represented in other international organisations.

UNPO does not aim to represent these nations and peoples, but rather to assist and empower them to represent themselves more effectively, and provides professional services and facilities as well as education and training in the fields of diplomacy, international and human rights law, democratic processes, institution building, conflict management and resolution, and environmental protection.

Participation is open to all nations and peoples who are inadequately represented at the United Nations and who declare allegiance to five principles relating to the right of self-determination of all peoples, human rights, democracy, non-violence and the rejection of terrorism, and protection of the natural environment. Applicants must show that they constitute a 'nation or people' and that the organisation applying for membership is representative of that nation or people.

As at December 1999, there were 52 full members and five supporting members, who are all former full members who have achieved full independence.

*Interim General Secretary*, Erkin Alptekin (Eastern Turkestan)

WESTERN EUROPEAN UNION
Regentschapsstraat 4, B-1000 Brussels, Belgium
Tel: (00 32) (2) 500 4411; fax: (00 32) (2) 511 3270
E-mail: ueo.presse@skynet.be
Web: www.weu.int

The Western European Union (WEU) originated as the Brussels Treaty Organisation (BTO) established under the Treaty of Brussels, signed in 1948 by Belgium, France, Luxembourg, the Netherlands and the UK, to provide collective self-defence and economic and social collaboration amongst its signatories. The BTO was modified to become the WEU in 1954 with the admission of West Germany and Italy. From the late 1970s onwards efforts were made to add a security dimension to the EC's European Political Co-operation. Opposition to these efforts from Denmark, Greece and Ireland led the remaining EC countries, all WEU members, to decide to reactivate the Union in 1984. Members committed themselves to harmonising their views on defence and security and developing a European security identity, while bearing in mind the importance of transatlantic relations. Portugal and Spain joined the WEU in 1988, and Greece became a full member in 1995.

In 1991, the EU Maastricht Treaty committed the European Community to the establishment of a Common Foreign and Security Policy (CFSP). The WEU was designated as the future defence component of the European Union and member states of the EU who were not already members of the WEU were invited to join or become observers. In November 1992 the WEU's role as the common security dimension of the EU was enhanced when WEU ministers signed a declaration with remaining European NATO members to give them various forms of WEU membership. Iceland, Norway and Turkey became associate members; the Republic of Ireland, Denmark, Austria, Finland and Sweden became observer members. In 1994 the WEU reached agreements with Estonia, Latvia, Lithuania, Poland, the Czech Republic, Slovakia, Hungary, Romania and Bulgaria, under which they all became associate partners; Slovenia became an associate partner in 1996. The Czech Republic, Hungary and Poland, who had been associate partners, became associate members in 1999, following their accession to NATO.

The WEU has worked in close co-operation with the Atlantic Alliance, and relations between the WEU and NATO were developed on the basis of transparency and complementarity. The 1993 Luxembourg Declaration states that the WEU is ready to participate in the future work of the NATO Alliance as its European pillar, and at the Atlantic Alliance summit in January 1994, NATO expressed its readiness to make Alliance assets and capabilities available for WEU operations. In June 1996, NATO foreign and defence ministers approved the Combined Joint Task Force (CJTF) concept and the elaboration of multinational European command arrangements for WEU-led operations.

A Council of Ministers (foreign and defence) has met biannually in the capital of the presiding country; the presidency rotates biannually, and from 1999 the sequence of WEU presidencies has been harmonised with those of the EU Council of Ministers. A Permanent Council of the member states' permanent representatives meets in Brussels. The Permanent Council is chaired by the Secretary-General and serviced by the Secretariat. The WEU military staff is responsible for the implementation of policies and decisions as directed by the council and the military committee. It prepares plans, carries out studies and recommends policy on matters of an operational nature for the WEU. It comprises a planning cell and a situation centre.

In 1999, NATO and the EU decided to establish a direct relationship; the EU committed itself to ensuring that it was able to take decisions on conflict prevention and crisis management and NATO agreed to give the EU access to its collective assets and capabilities for operations in which NATO as a whole was not engaged. The WEU's crisis management functions were transferred to the EU in June 2001.

The Assembly of the WEU is composed of 115 parliamentarians of member states and meets twice annually in Paris to debate matters within the scope of the revised Brussels Treaty.

*Presidency* (2001) Netherlands, Belgium; (2002) Spain, Portugal
*Secretary-General*, Javier Solana Madariaga (Spain)
*UK Representative on the Permanent Council*, David Richmond
ASSEMBLY, 43 avenue du Président Wilson, F-75775 Paris Cedex 16, France

THE WORLD BANK
1818 H Street NW, Washington 20433, USA
Tel: (00 1) (202) DC 477 1234; fax: (00 1) (202) 477 6391; E-mail: feedback@worldbank.org;
Web: www.worldbank.org

The World Bank, more formally known as the International Bank for Reconstruction and Development (IBRD), is a specialised agency of the UN. It developed from the international monetary and financial conference held at Bretton Woods, New Hampshire, in 1944 and was established by 44 nations in 1945 to encourage economic growth in developing countries through the provision of loans and technical assistance to their respective governments. The IBRD now has 182 members.

The Bank is owned by the governments of member countries and its capital is subscribed by its members. It finances its lending primarily from borrowing in world capital markets, and derives a substantial contribution to its resources from its retained earnings and the repayment of loans. The interest rate on its loans is calculated in relation to its cost of borrowing. Loans generally have a grace period of five years and are repayable within 20 years. The loans made by the Bank since its inception to 30 June 1997 totalled US$295,263.9 million to 131 countries. Total capital is US$182,426 million.

Originally directed towards post-war reconstruction in Europe, the Bank has subsequently turned towards assisting less-developed countries with the establishment of two affiliates, the International Finance Corporation (IFC) in 1956 and the International Development Association (IDA) in 1960. The IFC promotes the growth of the private sector in developing member countries by mobilising domestic and foreign capital. The IFC's subscribed share capital was US$2.36 million at 30 June 1997. It is also empowered to borrow up to two and a half times the amount of its unimpaired subscribed capital and accumulated earnings for use in its lending programme. At 30 June 1997, the IFC had committed financing totalling more than US$6.7 billion in 129 countries.

The IDA performs the same function as the World Bank but primarily to less-developed countries and on terms that bear less heavily on their balance of payments than IBRD loans. Eligible countries typically have a per capita gross national product of less than US$925 (1996). Funds (called credits to distinguish them from IBRD loans) come mostly in the form of subscriptions and contributions from the IDA's richer members and transfers from the net income of the IBRD. The terms for IDA credits, which bear no interest and are made to governments only, are ten-year grace periods and 35- or 40-year maturities. By 30 June 1997, the IDA had extended development credits totalling US$101,563.4 million to 100 countries.

The IBRD and its affiliates are financially and legally distinct but share headquarters. The IBRD is headed by a Board of Governors, consisting of one Governor and one alternate Governor appointed by each member country. Twenty-four Executive Directors exercise all powers of the Bank except those reserved to the Board of Governors. The President, elected by the Executive Directors, conducts the business of the Bank, assisted by an international staff. Membership in both the IFC (162 members) and the IDA (160 members) is open to all IBRD countries. The IDA is administered by the same staff as the Bank; the IFC has its own personnel but draws on the IBRD for administrative and other support. All share the same President.

In 1988 a third affiliate, the Multilateral Investment Guarantee Agency (MIGA) was formed. MIGA encourages foreign investment in developing states by providing investment guarantees to potential investors and advisory services to developing member countries. At 30 December 1994, 128 countries were members of MIGA.

*President (IBRD, IFC, IDA, MIGA)*, James D. Wolfensohn (USA)

*UK Executive Director*, A. O'Donnell, Room 11-120, IMF, 700 19th Street NW, Washington DC 20431

EUROPEAN OFFICE, 66 avenue d'Iéna, F-75116 Paris, France

JAPAN OFFICE, 10F, Fukoku Seimei Building, 2-2-2 Uchisaiwai-cho, Chiyoda-ku, Tokyo 100-0011, Japan

UK OFFICE, New Zealand House, Haymarket, London SW1Y 4TQ. Tel: 020-7930 8511; fax: 020-7930 8515

---

## THE WORLD COUNCIL OF CHURCHES

PO Box 2100, CH-1211 Geneva 2, Switzerland
Tel: (00 41) (22) 791 6111; fax: (00 41) (22) 791 0361
E-mail: info@mail.wcc-coe.org
Web: www.wcc-coe.org

---

The World Council of Churches (WCC) was constituted in 1948 to promote unity among Christian churches. The 342 member churches have adherents in more than 120 countries. With the exception of Roman Catholicism, virtually all Christian traditions are represented.

The policies of the Council are determined by delegates of the member churches meeting in Assembly, roughly every seven years; the seventh Assembly was held in Canberra, Australia, in February 1991 and the eighth Assembly was held in Harare, Zimbabwe, in December 1998. More detailed decisions are taken by a 156-member Central Committee which is elected by the Assembly and meets, with the eight WCC Presidents, annually. The Central Committee in turn appoints a smaller Executive Committee and also nominates commissions to guide the various programmes.

*General Secretary*, Dr Konrad Raiser (Germany)

---

## WORLD HEALTH ORGANISATION

20 avenue Appia, CH-1211 Geneva 27, Switzerland
Tel: (00 41) (22) 791 2111; fax: (00 41) (22) 791 0746
E-mail: info@who.ch; Web: www.who.ch

---

The UN International Health Conference, held in 1946, established the World Health Organisation (WHO) as a UN specialised agency, with effect from 1948. It is dedicated to attaining the highest possible level of health for all. It collaborates with member governments, UN agencies and other bodies to improve health standards, control communicable diseases and promote all aspects of family and environmental health. It seeks to raise the standards of health teaching and training, and promotes research through collaborating research centres world-wide. Its other services include the *International Pharmacopoeia*, epidemiological surveillance, and the collation and publication of statistics. WHO activities are orientated to achieving 'Health for All'.

WHO had 191 members as at April 2001. It is governed by the annual World Health Assembly of members which meets to set policy, approve the budget (1998–9, US$1,801 million), appoint a Director-General, and adopt health conventions and regulations. It also elects 32 members who designate one expert to serve on the Executive Board. The Board effects the programme, suggests initiatives and is empowered to deal with emergencies. A Secretariat, headed by the Director-General, supervises the activities of six regional offices.

*Director-General*, Gro Harlem Bruntland (Norway)

---

## WORLD INTELLECTUAL PROPERTY ORGANISATION

34 chemin des Colombettes, CH-1211 Geneva 20, Switzerland
Tel: (00 41) (22) 338 9111; fax: (00 41) (22) 733 5428
E-mail: publicinf.mail@wipo.int
Web: www.wipo.int

---

The World Intellectual Property Organisation (WIPO) was established in 1967 by the Stockholm Convention, which entered into force in 1970. In addition to that Convention, WIPO administers 19 treaties, the principal ones being the Paris Convention for the Protection of Industrial Property and the Bern Convention for the Protection of Literary and Artistic Works. WIPO became a UN specialised agency in 1974.

WIPO promotes the protection of intellectual property throughout the world through co-operation among states, and the administration of various 'Unions', each founded on a multilateral treaty and dealing with the legal and administrative aspects of intellectual property.

Intellectual property comprises two main branches: industrial property (inventions, trademarks, industrial designs and appellations of origin); and copyright (literary, musical, photographic, audiovisual and artistic works, etc.). WIPO also assists creative intellectual activity and facilitates technology transfer, particularly to developing countries.

WIPO had 177 members as at April 2001. The biennial session of all its governing bodies sets policy, a programme and a budget (1998–9, SFr400 million). WIPO has three governing bodies: the General Assembly, composed of WIPO members who are also members of the Paris or Bern conventions; the Conference, composed of all WIPO members; and the Co-ordination Committee, composed of member states elected by members of WIPO and the Paris and Bern conventions. The General Assembly elects a Director-General, who heads the International Bureau (secretariat).

A separate International Union for the Protection of New Varieties of Plants (UPOV), established by convention in 1961, is linked to WIPO. It has 46 members.

*Director-General*, Dr Kamil Idris (Sudan)

## WORLD METEOROLOGICAL ORGANISATION

7 bis, avenue de la Paix, PO Box 2300, CH-1211 Geneva 2, Switzerland
Tel: (00 41) (22) 730 8111; fax: (00 41) (22) 730 8181
E-mail: ipa@gateway.wmo.ch Web: www.wmo.ch

The World Meteorological Organisation (WMO) was established in 1950 and became a UN specialised agency in 1951, succeeding the International Meteorological Organisation founded in 1873. It facilitates co-operation in the establishment of networks for making meteorological, climatological, hydrological and geophysical observations, as well as their exchange, processing and standardisation, and assists technology transfer, training and research. It also fosters collaboration between meteorological and hydrological services, and furthers the application of meteorology to aviation, shipping, environment, water problems, agriculture and the mitigation of natural disasters.

The WMO had 179 member states and six member territories as at April 2001. Six regional associations are responsible for the co-ordination of activities within their own regions, There are also eight technical commissions, which study meteorological and hydrological problems, establish methodology and procedures, and make recommendations to the Executive Council and the Congress. The supreme authority is the World Meteorological Congress of member states and member territories, which meets every four years to determine general policy, make recommendations and set a budget (2000–3, SFr252.3 million). It also elects 26 members of the 36-member Executive Council, the other members being the President and three Vice-Presidents of the WMO, and the Presidents of the six regional associations, who are ex-officio members. The Council supervises the implementation of Congress decisions, initiates studies and makes recommendations on matters needing international action. The Secretariat is headed by a Secretary-General, appointed by the Congress.

*Secretary-General*, G. O. P. Obasi (Nigeria)

## WORLD TRADE ORGANISATION

Centre William Rappard, 154 rue de Lausanne, 1211 CH-Geneva 21, Switzerland
Tel: (00 41) (22) 739 5111; fax: (00 41) (22) 739 5458
E-mail: enquiries@wto.org; Web: www.wto.org

The World Trade Organisation was established on 1 January 1995 as the successor to the General Agreement on Tariffs and Trade (GATT). GATT was established in 1948 as an interim agreement until the charter of a new international trade organisation could be drafted by a committee of the UN Economic and Social Council and ratified by member states. The charter was never ratified and GATT became the only regime for the regulation of world trade, evolving its own rules and procedures.

GATT was dedicated to the expansion of non-discriminatory international trade and progressively extended free trade via 'rounds' of multilateral negotiations. Eight rounds were concluded: Geneva (1947), Annecy (1948), Torquay (1950), Geneva (1956), Dillon (1960–1), Kennedy (1964–7), Tokyo (1973–9) and Uruguay (1986–94). By the time the measures of the Uruguay Round are fully implemented in 2002, the average duties on manufactured goods will have been reduced from 40 per cent in the 1940s to 3 per cent. The Final Act of the Uruguay Round was signed by trade ministers from the 128 GATT negotiating states and the EU in Marrakesh, Morocco, on 15 April 1994. It established the World Trade Organisation (WTO) to supersede GATT and implement the Uruguay Round agreements. A summit held in Seattle, USA, in December 1999 was unable to reach agreement on further integration of the international trading system.

The WTO is the legal and institutional foundation of the multilateral trading system. It provides the contractual obligations determining how governments frame and implement trade policy and provides the forum for the debate, negotiation and adjudication of trade problems. The WTO's principal aims are to liberalise world trade and place it on a secure basis, and it seeks to achieve this partly by an agreed set of trade rules and market access agreements and partly through further trade liberalisation negotiations. The WTO also administers and implements a further 29 multilateral agreements in fields such as agriculture, textiles and clothing, services, government procurement, rules of origin and intellectual property.

The highest authority of the WTO is the Ministerial Conference composed of all members, which meets at least once every two years. The General Council meets as required and acts on behalf of the Ministerial Conference in regard to the regular working of the WTO. Composed of all members, the General Council also convenes in two particular forms: as the Dispute Settlement Body, dealing with disputes between members arising from the Uruguay Round Final Act; and as the Trade Policy Review Body, conducting regular reviews of the trade policies of members. A secretariat of 500 staff headed by a Director-General services WTO bodies and provides trade performance and trade policy analysis.

As at November 2000 there were 140 WTO members, and a further 31 governments had applied to join. The WTO budget for 2000 was SFr127 million, with members' contributions calculated on the basis of their share of the total trade conducted by WTO members. The official languages of the WTO are English, French and Spanish.

*Acting Director-General*, Mike Moore

*Permanent UK Representative*, R. M. J. Lyne, 37–39 rue de Vermont, CH-1211 Geneva 20

# Travel Overseas

## PASSPORT REGULATIONS

Applications for United Kingdom passports must be made on the forms obtainable from UK Passport Service's general telephone enquiry line, regional passport offices (*see* below), or website and also from main post offices and WorldChoice travel agents.

DURHAM - Passport Office, Millburngate House, Durham DN97 1PA

LONDON – Passport Office, Globe House, 89 Eccleston Square, London SW1V 9PN

LIVERPOOL – Passport Office, 5th Floor, India Buildings, Water Street, Liverpool L2 0QZ

NEWPORT – Passport Office, Olympia House, Upper Dock Street, Newport, Gwent NP20 1XA

PETERBOROUGH – Passport Office, Aragon Court, Northminster Road, Peterborough PE1 1QG

GLASGOW – Passport Office, 3 Northgate, 96 Milton Street, Cowcaddens, Glasgow G4 0BT

BELFAST – Passport Office, Hampton House, 47–53 High Street, Belfast BT1 2QS

Central telephone number: 0870-521 0410
Central fax number: 0901-4700 130
Web site: www.passport.gov.uk

The passport offices are open Monday-Saturday on an appointment-only basis (appointments should be arranged by calling the central telephone number listed above

Straightforward, properly completed applications are processed within 10 working days throughout the year. Applying in person does not guarantee that an application will be given priority.

The completed application form should be submitted via a partner or posted, with the appropriate documents and fee, to the regional passport office indicated on the addressed envelope which is provided with each application form (an exception to this is the London office which is a calling-in office only). Accompanying cheques and postal orders should be crossed and made payable to 'The Passport Office'.

A passport cannot be issued or extended on behalf of a person already abroad; such persons should apply to the nearest British High Commission or Consulate.

UK passports are granted to:

(i) British citizens
(ii) British Dependent Territories citizens
(iii) British Nationals (Overseas)
(iv) British Overseas citizens
(v) British Subjects
(vi) British Protected Persons

### ADULTS

A passport granted to a person over 16 will normally be valid for ten years and will not be renewable.

The issue of passports including details of the holder's spouse has been discontinued, but existing family passports may be used until expiry. A spouse who is included in a family passport cannot travel on the passport without the holder.

### CHILDREN

Since 5 October 1998 all children under the age of 16 are required to have their own passport. This is primarily to help prevent child abductions. The passports are normally valid for five years, after which point a new passport application must be made. This replaces the system whereby children under the age of 16 could either have their own document or be added to their parents' passports.

A passport granted to a child prior to this date is still valid for five years, although the free, five-year extension option no longer exists. On expiry, a new application must be made. Children included in their parents' passports when the new regulations came into force are not affected and, can continue to travel on them until they reach the age of 16 or the passport expires or is amended.

### COUNTERSIGNATURES

The completed application form should be countersigned by an MP, justice of the peace, minister of religion, a professionally qualified person (e.g. doctor, engineer, lawyer, teacher), bank officer, military officer, established Civil Servant, police officer, graduate or a person of similar standing who has known the applicant for at least two years, and who is either a British citizen, British Dependent Territories citizen, British National (Overseas), British Overseas citizen, British Subject or a citizen of a Commonwealth country. A relative must not countersign the application.

If the application is for a child under the age of 16, the countersignature should be by someone of relevant standing who has known the parent or person with parental responsibility who signs the declaration of consent, rather than the child.

### PHOTOGRAPHS

Two identical unmounted photographs of the applicant must be sent. These photographs should be printed on normal thin photographic paper. They should measure 45 mm35 mm (1.77 in1.38 in) and should be taken full face against a white background. The person who countersigns the application form should certify one photograph as a true likeness of the applicant.

### DOCUMENTATION

The applicant's birth certificate or previous British passport, must be produced at the time of applying. Details of which documents are required are in the notes accompanying the application form.

If the applicant for a passport is a British national by naturalisation or registration, the certificate proving this must be produced with the application, unless the applicant holds a previous UK passport issued after registration or naturalisation.

### 48-PAGE PASSPORTS

The 48-page passport is intended to meet the needs of frequent travellers who fill standard passports well before the validity has expired. It is valid for ten years.

### PASSPORT FEES* *from December 1999*

| | |
|---|---|
| New adult passport | £28 |
| New child passport | £14.80 |
| Renewal of passport | £28 |
| Amendment of passport | £17 |
| 48-page passport | £38 |

* postal applications only. A £12 charge is added for applications made in person at a passport office in the UK or made abroad

# The European Union

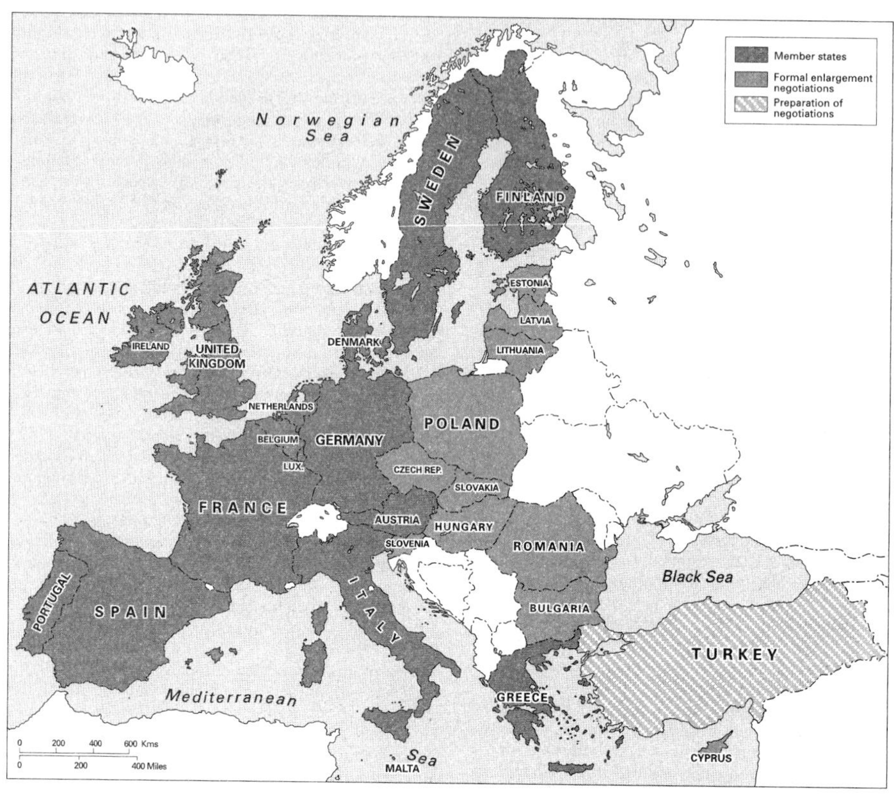


MEMBERS

| State | Accession Date | Population (million) (2000) | GNP (US$ million) (1999) | GDP per Head in PPS (ECU) (1999) | Council Votes | EP Seats |
|---|---|---|---|---|---|---|
| Austria | 1 January 1995 | 8.10 | 209,972 | 23,484 | 4 | 21 |
| Belgium | 1 January 1958* | 10.24 | 250,619 | 23,446 | 5 | 25 |
| Denmark | 1 January 1973 | 5.33 | 170,327 | 25,026 | 3 | 16 |
| Finland | 1 January 1995 | 5.17 | 122,874 | 21,442 | 3 | 16 |
| France | 1 January 1958* | 59.30 | 1,427,164 | 20,861 | 10 | 87 |
| Germany | 1 January 1958*† | 82.16 | 2,079,227 | 22,712 | 10 | 99 |
| Greece | 1 January 1981 | 10.55 | 124,010 | 14,198 | 5 | 25 |
| Ireland | 1 January 1973 | 3.78 | 71,405 | 24,133 | 3 | 15 |
| Italy | 1 January 1958* | 57.68 | 1,135,986 | 21,158 | 10 | 87 |
| Luxembourg | 1 January 1958* | 0.44 | 19,285 | 38,773 | 2 | 6 |
| Netherlands | 1 January 1958* | 15.86 | 384,325 | 23,838 | 5 | 31 |
| Portugal | 1 January 1986 | 10.00 | 105,917 | 16,065 | 5 | 25 |
| Spain | 1 January 1986 | 39.44 | 551,560 | 17,319 | 8 | 64 |
| Sweden | 1 January 1995 | 8.86 | 221,764 | 21,620 | 4 | 22 |
| UK | 1 January 1973 | 59.62 | 1,338,079 | 21,598 | 10 | 87 |
| Total | | 376.53 | 8,212,514 | | 87 | 626 |

*Sources*: Eurostat Yearbook 2001, World Bank World Development Indicators database

*Acceded to the European Coal and Steel Community (ECSC) on its formation in 1952

†Federal Republic of Germany (West) 1952/1958; German Democratic Republic (East) acceded on German reunification (3 October 1990)

EP European Parliament PPS - purchasing power standards

## DEVELOPMENT

1950 Robert Schuman (French foreign minister) proposes that France and West Germany pool their coal and steel industries under a supranational authority (Schuman Plan)
1951 Paris Treaty signed by France, West Germany, Belgium, Italy, Luxembourg and the Netherlands establishes the European Coal and Steel Community (ECSC)
1952 ECSC Treaty enters into force
1957 25 March: Treaty of Rome signed by the six, establishes the European Economic Community (EEC) and the European Atomic Energy Authority (EURATOM). Treaty aims to create a customs union; remove obstacles to free movement of capital, goods, people and services; establish common external trade policy and common agricultural and fisheries policies; co-ordinate economic policies; harmonise social policies; promote co-operation in nuclear research
1958 1 January: EEC and EURATOM begin operation. Joint Parliament and Court of Justice established for all three communities, and the Commission, Council of Ministers, Economic and Social Committee and Investment Bank for the EEC established.
1962 Common Agricultural Policy (CAP) agreed (*see* page 781)
1967 EEC, ECSC and EURATOM merge to form the European Communities (EC), with a single Council of Ministers and Commission
1968 EEC customs union completed
Implementation of CAP completed
1974 Regular heads of governments summits begin
1975 'Own resources' funding of EC budget introduced (*see* page 781)
UK renegotiates its terms of accession
European Regional Development Fund created
1979 European Monetary System (EMS) comes into operation (*see* page 780)
First direct elections to European Parliament (June)
1984 Fontainebleau summit settles UK annual budget rebate and agrees first major CAP reform
1986 Single European Act (SEA) signed (*see* page 780)
European Political Co-operation (EPC) established
1988 Second major CAP reform
1991 Maastricht Treaty agreed (*see* page 782)
1992 31 December: Single internal market programme completed
1993 September: the exchange rate mechanism (ERM) of the EMS effectively suspended
1 November: The Maastricht Treaty enters into force, establishing the European Union (EU)
1994 1 January: European Economic Area (EEA) agreement comes into operation (*see* page 782)
Norway rejects EU membership in referendum
1997 Amsterdam Treaty agreed
1998 11 states chosen to enter first round of EMU
European Central Bank replaces European Monetary Institute
1999 1 January: Euro launched
March: 'Agenda 2000' financial and policy reform agreed
1 May: The Amsterdam Treaty enters into force
2000 9 December: Treaty of Nice agreed
2001 7 June: Ireland rejects Treaty of Nice in referendum

## ENLARGEMENT AND EXTERNAL RELATIONS

The procedure for accession to the EU is laid down in the Treaty of Rome; states must be stable European democracies governed by the rule of law with free market economies. A membership application is studied by the Commission, which produces an Opinion. If the Opinion is positive, negotiations may be opened leading to an Accession Treaty which must be approved by all member state governments and parliaments, the European Parliament, and the applicant state's government and parliament.

*Applicants:* Morocco (applied 1987/rejected 1987), Turkey (applied 1987/negative Opinion 1989/offered accession partnership 1999), Cyprus (applied 1990/ negotiations begun 1998), Malta (applied 1990/reapplied following a change of government 1998/negotiations begun 2000), Switzerland (applied 1992/application put on hold 1994), Hungary (applied 1994/negotiations begun 1998), Poland (applied 1994/negotiations begun 1998), Bulgaria (applied 1995/offered partnership 1998/negotiations begun 2000), Estonia (applied 1995/negotiations begun 1998), Latvia (applied 1995/offered partnership 1998/ negotiations begun 2000), Lithuania (applied 1995/ offered partnership 1998/negotiations begun 2000), Romania (applied 1995/offered partnership 1998/negotiations begun 2000), Slovakia (applied 1995/offered partnership 1998/negotiations begun 2000), the Czech Republic (applied 1996/negotiations begun 1998), Slovenia (applied 1996/negotiations begun 1998).

Apart from the EEA Agreement (*see* page 782), the EU has three types of agreements with other European and CIS states. 'Europe' Agreements commit the EU and signatory states to long-term political and economic integration, a free trade zone (apart from agriculture and labour movement) and eventual EU membership. Government representatives from the signatory states are entitled to attend one summit and two finance and foreign council meetings a year. Agreements have been signed with Bulgaria (1993), the Czech Republic (1993), Estonia (1995), Hungary (1991), Latvia (1995), Lithuania (1995), Poland (1991), Romania (1993), Slovakia (1993) and Slovenia (1996). Association agreements include a commitment to EU financial aid and to eventual membership; agreements have been signed with Malta (1970), Cyprus (1972) and Turkey (1963). Partnership and co-operation agreements are based on regulating and improving political and economic relations and mutual trade concessions but exclude any possibility of membership. Agreements have been implemented with Russia (1997), Ukraine (1998) and Georgia, Kazakhstan, Kyrgyzstan, Moldova and Uzbekistan (1999). Agreements have been signed with Belarus (1995) and Turkmenistan (1998) but are not yet in force.

Agenda 2000, a document issued by the Commission in 1997, addressed both the challenges posed by further enlargement of the Union, the institutional reforms that would be required to enable the Union to function effectively with additional members, and also evaluated each applicant in relation to the accession criteria, establishing a new financial framework for the period 2000-2006.

In March 1998, formal accession negotiations were begun with Hungary, Poland, Estonia, the Czech Republic, Slovenia and Cyprus; they were begun with Bulgaria, Romania, Latvia, Lithuania, Malta and Slovakia in 2000, following the Helsinki Summit in December 1999, when it was also agreed that an accession partnership should be offered to Turkey.

The Göteborg Summit in June 2001 agreed on a timetable for accession for the first group of countries to complete negotiations.

## THE COUNCIL OF THE EUROPEAN UNION
Wetstraat 175, B-1048 Brussels, Belgium

The Council of the European Union (Council of Ministers) formally comprises the foreign ministers of the member states but in practice the ministers attending depend on the subject under discussion. Council decisions are taken by qualified majority vote (in which members' votes are weighted), by a simple majority, or by unanimity. The Council is assisted by a General Secretariat, whose head has since 1999 been the High Representative for the Common Foreign and Security Policy.

Unanimity votes are taken on sensitive issues such as taxation and constitutional matters; in preparation for an expanded Union, the Amsterdam Treaty extended areas where qualified majority votes may be taken, to areas such as Single Market laws and harmonisation, environment policy, health and safety, transport policy, overseas aid, research and development, culture, consumer protection, education and training, the development of a single currency and some aspects of social policy. Member states have weighted votes in the Council loosely proportional to their relative population sizes (*see* introductory table), with a total of 87 votes. For a proposal from the Commission to be passed, it must receive 62 votes; 26 votes are necessary to block a proposal, and 23 votes constitute a temporary blocking minority. For other proposals to be passed they must receive 62 votes cast by at least ten member states.

The Treaty of Nice, which was agreed on 7-9 December 2000 and signed on 26 February 2001, agreed amendments to the treaties in relation to the size and composition of the European Commission, the weighting of votes and the extension of qualified majority voting in the Council of Ministers and other issues relating to the Treaty of Amsterdam. The extension of qualified majority voting to external border controls, the EU budget, the composition of the European Courts and certain committees, visa rules and, by 2007, structural funds, was also agreed.

The European Council, comprising the heads of state or government of the member states and the President of the European Commission, meets twice a year to provide overall policy direction. The presidency of the EC is held in rotation for six-month periods, setting the agenda for and chairing all Council meetings. The European Council holds a summit in the country holding the presidency at the end of its period in office. The holders of the presidency for the years 2001–2002 are:
2001 Sweden, Belgium
2002 Spain, Denmark

### GENERAL SECRETARIAT OF THE COUNCIL OF THE EUROPEAN UNION
Wetstraat 175, B-1048 Brussels, Belgium
E-mail: public.info@consilium.eu.int

*Secretary-General of the Council of the European Union and High Representative for the Common Foreign and Security Policy*, Javier Solana Madariaga (Spain)
*Deputy Secretary-General of the Council of the European Union*, Pierre de Boissieu (France)

### OFFICE OF THE UNITED KINGDOM PERMANENT REPRESENTATIVE TO THE EUROPEAN UNION
Oudergemselaan 10, B-1040 Brussels, Belgium

*Ambassador and UK Permanent Representative*, HE Sir Nigel Sheinwald, KCMG, *apptd* 2000
*Deputy Permanent Representative*, W. Stow

## THE EUROPEAN COMMISSION
Wetstraat 200, B-1049 Brussels, Belgium

The Commission consists of 20 Commissioners, two each from France, Germany, Italy, Spain and the UK, and one each from the remaining member states. The members of the Commission are appointed for five-year renewable terms by the agreement of the member states; the terms run concurrently with the terms of the European Parliament. The President and the other Commissioners are nominated by the governments of the member states, and, under the terms of the Amsterdam Treaty, the appointments are approved by the European Parliament. The Commissioners pledge sole allegiance to the EC. The Commission initiates and implements EC legislation and is the guardian of the EC treaties. It is the exponent of Community-wide interests rather than the national preoccupations of the Council. Each Commissioner is supported by advisers and oversees whichever of the departments, known as Directorates-General (DGs), is assigned to him. Each Directorate-General is headed by a Director-General.

President Romano Prodi was nominated by the governments of the member states on 24 March 1999, and under the terms of the Amsterdam Treaty, his appointment was approved by the European Parliament on 15 September 1999, having already announced his new Commission in June. The previous commission had resigned *en masse* after a committee of experts appointed by the European Parliament had concluded that lax management had allowed fraud and nepotism in the Commission's services. The new Commission has restructured the Directorates-General to reflect the priorities of the new administration.

The Commission has a total staff of around 16,000 permanent civil servants.

### COMMISSIONERS *as at March 2001*

*President*, Romano Prodi (Italy)
*Vice-President for Administrative Reform; Administrative Reform; Personnel and Administration; Linguistic Services*, Neil Kinnock (UK)
*Vice-President for Relations with the European Parliament, and for Transport and Energy*, Loyola de Palacio (Spain)

*Members*
*Agriculture, Rural Development and Fisheries*, Franz Fischler (Austria)
*Budget, Financial Control, European Anti-Fraud Office*, Michaele Schreyer (Germany)
*Competition*, Mario Monti (Italy)
*Development, Humanitarian Aid, Chief Executive of EuropeAid*, Poul Nielson (Denmark)
*Economic and Monetary Affairs*, Pedro Solbes Mira (Spain)
*Education and Culture*, Viviane Reding (Luxembourg)
*Employment and Social Affairs*, Anna Diamantopoulou (Greece)
*Enlargement*, Günter Verheugen (Germany)
*Enterprise and Information Society*, Erkki Liikanen (Finland)
*Environment*, Margot Wallström (Sweden)
*External Relations, Chairman of EuropeAid*, Chris Patten (UK)
*Internal Market, Taxation and Customs Union*, Frits Bolkestein (Netherlands)

## EUROPEAN PARLIAMENT POLITICAL GROUPINGS

| | PES | EPP-ED | UEN | ELDR | EUL/NGL | Green/EFA | TGI | EDD | Ind. | Total |
|---|---|---|---|---|---|---|---|---|---|---|
| Austria | 7 | 7 | – | – | – | 2 | – | – | 5 | 21 |
| Belgium | 5 | 6 | – | 5 | – | 7 | 2 | – | – | 25 |
| Denmark | 3 | 1 | 1 | 6 | 1 | – | – | 4 | – | 16 |
| Finland | 3 | 5 | – | 5 | 1 | 2 | – | – | – | 16 |
| France | 22 | 21 | 5 | – | 11 | 9 | 5 | 7 | 7 | 87 |
| Germany | 35 | 53 | – | – | 6 | 5 | – | – | – | 99 |
| Greece | 9 | 9 | – | – | 7 | – | – | – | – | 25 |
| Ireland | 1 | 5 | 6 | 1 | – | 2 | – | – | – | 15 |
| Italy | 16 | 34 | 9 | 8 | 6 | 2 | 12 | – | – | 87 |
| Luxembourg | 2 | 2 | – | 1 | – | 1 | – | – | – | 6 |
| Netherlands | 6 | 9 | – | 8 | 1 | 4 | – | 3 | – | 31 |
| Portugal | 12 | 9 | 2 | – | 2 | – | – | – | – | 25 |
| Spain | 24 | 28 | – | 3 | 4 | 4 | – | – | 1 | 64 |
| Sweden | 6 | 7 | – | 4 | 3 | 2 | – | – | – | 22 |
| UK | 30 | 36 | – | 11 | – | 6 | – | 3 | 1 | 87 |
| TOTAL | 181 | 232 | 23 | 52 | 42 | 46 | 19 | 17 | 14 | 626 |

| | |
|---|---|
| PES | Party of European Socialists (including the British, Irish and Dutch Labour Parties, Northern Ireland Social Democratic and Labour Party, Austrian, Danish, Finnish, German, Italian and Swedish Social Democrats, Belgian, French, Greek, Portuguese, and Spanish Socialists, Italian Democratic Left Party, Luxembourg Socialist Workers' Party), Socialist, Social Democratic and Labour parties |
| EPP-ED | European People's Party and European Democrats (including British and Danish Conservative Parties, Spanish Popular Party, French Nouvelle UDF, RPR and DL, Irish Fine Gael, Swedish Moderate Party, Finnish National Coalition Party, Austrian People's Party, Greek New Democracy, Belgian Christian Socialists, Italian Christian Democrats, Pensioners' Party and People's Party, Luxembourg Christian Socialists, Portuguese Social Democrats), Christian Democrats, Christian Socialists and Conservatives |
| UEN | Union for a Europe of Nations |
| ELDR | European Liberal, Democrat and Reform Party (including British Liberal Democrats, Danish Left and Radical Left Parties, Dutch Democrats '66 and People's Party for Freedom and Democracy, Belgian Liberals, Italian and Luxembourg Democrats, Swedish Liberal People's Party, Finnish Swedish People's Party and Centre Party), centre and liberal parties |
| EUL/ NGL | Confederal Group of the European United Left/Nordic Green Left (French, Greek, Italian and Portuguese Communist Parties, Italian Refounded Communist Party, Danish, Dutch, Swedish, Finnish, Greek and Spanish Socialist/Left parties) |
| Green/ EFA | Greens/European Free Alliance Group (Austrian, British, Danish, Finnish, French, German, Greek, Irish, Italian, Luxembourgish, Portuguese, Spanish and Swedish Green Parties, Dutch Green Left Party, Belgian Ecological Parties, Plaid Cymru and Scottish National Parties), green and nationalist parties |
| TGI | Technical Group of Independent Members (Belgian Flemish Block, Italian National Alliance, French National Front), technical group allowing independents group privileges |
| EDD | Group for a Europe of Democracies and Diversities (French Hunting, Fishing, Nature and Traditions, Dutch Calvinists and Christians, UK Independence Party, Danish June Movement and Movement Against the EU), anti-EU, anti-federalist and religious parties |
| Ind. | Independents (Austrian Freedom Party, Northern Ireland Democratic Unionist Party) |

*Justice and Home Affairs*, António Vitorino (Portugal)
*Public Health, Consumer Protection*, David Byrne (Ireland)
*Regional Policy and Institutional Reform, Inter-Governmental Conference*, Michel Barnier (France)
*Research*, Philippe Busquin (Belgium)
*Trade*, Pascal Lamy (France)

## THE EUROPEAN PARLIAMENT

E-mail: civis@europarl.eu.int
Web: www.europarl.eu.int

The European Parliament (EP) originated as the Common Assembly of the ECSC; it acquired its present name in 1962. Members (MEPs) were initially appointed from the membership of national parliaments; direct elections to the Parliament were first held in 1979 and take place at five-year intervals. Elections to the Parliament are held on differing bases throughout the EC; in June 1999, British

MEPs were elected for the first time by a 'regional list' system of proportional representation. The Parliament comprises 626 seats. The most recent elections were held in June 1999. For total number of seats per member and political groupings, *see* table on previous page. MEPs serve on committees which scrutinise draft EC legislation and the activities of the Commission. A minimum of 12 plenary sessions a year are held in Strasbourg and Brussels, committees meet in Brussels, and the Secretariat's headquarters is in Luxembourg.

The EP has gradually expanded its influence within the EU through the Single European Act, which introduced the co-operation procedure, the Maastricht Treaty, which extended the co-operation procedure and introduced the co-decision procedure (*see* Legislative Process), and the Amsterdam Treaty, which effectively extended co-decision to all areas except economic and monetary union. It has general powers of supervision over the Commission, and consultation and co-decision with the Council; it votes to approve a newly appointed Commission and can dismiss it at any time by a two-thirds majority (as it threatened to do in January 1999). Under the Maastricht Treaty it has the right to be consulted on the appointment of the new Commission and can veto its appointment. It can reject the EU budget as a whole, alter non-compulsory expenditure not specified in the EU primary legislation, and can question the Commission's management of the budget and call in the Court of Auditors. Although the EP cannot directly initiate legislation, its reports can spur the Commission into action. In accordance with the Maastricht Treaty the EP appointed an ombudsman in October 1995, to provide citizens with redress against maladministration by EU institutions.

The Parliament's organisation is deliberately biased in favour of multi-national political groupings, recognition of a political grouping in the parliament entitling it to offices, funding, representation on committees and influence in debates and legislation. A political grouping with members from only one country needs a minimum of 29 members for recognition, whereas one with members from two countries needs 23 members, a grouping with members from three countries needs 18 members, and a grouping with members from four or more countries needs only 14 members.

PARLIAMENT, Palais de l'Europe, Allée du Printemps, BP 1024/F, F-67070 Strasbourg Cedex, France. Tel: (00 33) (3) 8817 4001; Fax: (00 33) (3) 8825 6501; Wiertzstraat, Postbus 1047, B-1047 Brussels, Belgium. Tel: (00 32) (2) 284 2111; Fax: (00 32) (2) 284 9075/9077

SECRETARIAT, Centre Européen, Plateau du Kirchberg, BP 1601, L-2929 Luxembourg. Tel: (00 352) 43001; Fax: (00 352) 4300 29393/29292

*President*, Nicole Fontaine (France)

*Ombudsman*, Jacob Söderman (Finland), 1 avenue du Président Robert Schuman, BP 403, F-67001, Strasbourg, France.
E-mail: euro-ombudsman@europarl.eu.int.
Web: www.euro-ombudsman.eu.int

(For a full list of British MEPs, *see* European Parliament Section)

## THE LEGISLATIVE PROCESS

The core of the EU policymaking process is a dialogue between the Commission, which initiates and implements policy, and the Council of Ministers, which takes policy decisions. An increasing degree of democratic control is exercised by the European Parliament.

The original legislative process is known as the consultative procedure. The Commission drafts a proposal which it submits to the Council and to the Parliament. The Council then consults the Economic and Social Committee (ESC), the Parliament and the Committee of the Regions; the Parliament may request that amendments are made. With or without these amendments, the proposal is then adopted by the Council and becomes law.

Under the Single European Act (SEA), the role of the Parliament was strengthened by the introduction of the co-operation procedure. The Parliament now has a second reading of proposals in some fields, and after the second reading its rejection of a proposal can only be overturned by a unanimous decision of the Council. The Maastricht Treaty extended the scope of the co-operation procedure, which was applied to Single Market laws and harmonisation, trans-European networks, development policy, the social fund, and some aspects of transport, environment, research, social policy and competition policy.

The SEA introduced the assent procedure, whereby an absolute majority of the Parliament must vote to approve laws in certain fields before they are passed. Issues covered by the assent procedure include foreign treaties, accession treaties, international agreements with budgetary implications, citizenship, residence rights, the CAP, and regional and structural funds.

The Maastricht Treaty introduced the co-decision procedure; if, after the Parliament's second reading of a proposal, the Council and Parliament fail to agree, a conciliation committee of the two will reach a compromise. If a compromise is not reached, the Parliament can reject the legislation by the vote of an absolute majority of its members. The Amsterdam Treaty extended co-decision to all areas covered by qualified majority voting, with the exception of measures related to European Monetary Union (EMU).

The Council issues the following legislation:

- Regulations, which are binding in their entirety and directly applicable to all member states; they do not need to be incorporated into national law to come into effect
- Directives, which are less specific, binding as to the result to be achieved but leaving the method of implementation open to member states; a directive thus has no force until it is incorporated into national law
- Decisions, which are also binding but are addressed solely to one or more member states or individuals in a member state
- Recommendations
- Opinions, which are merely persuasive

The Council also has certain budgetary powers, including the power to reject the budget as a whole and to increase expenditure or redistribute money within sectors. However, the final decision on whether the budget should be adopted or rejected lies with the Parliament.

The Council may delegate legislative powers to the Commission. These consist of implementing powers and technical updating of existing legislation.

The European Central Bank has legislative powers within its field of competence. The Commission also has limited legislative powers, where it has been delegated the power to implement or revise legislation by the Council.

## THE COMMUNITY BUDGET

The principles of funding the European Community budget were established by the Treaty of Rome and remain with modifications to this day. There is a legally binding limit on the overall level of resources (known as 'own resources') that the Community can raise from its member states; this limit is defined as a percentage of gross national product (GNP). Budget revenue and expenditure must balance and there is therefore no deficit financing. The own resources decision, which came into effect in 1975 and has been regularly updated, states that there are four sources of Community funding under which each member state makes contributions: levies charged on agricultural imports into the Community from non-member states; customs duties on imports from non-member states; contributions based on member states' shares of a notional Community harmonised VAT base; and contributions based on member states' shares of Community GNP. The latter is the budget-balancing item and covers the difference between total expenditure and the revenue from the other three sources. Since 1984 the UK has had an annual rebate equivalent to 66 per cent of the difference between what the UK contributes to the budget and what it receives. This was introduced to compensate the UK for disproportionate contributions caused by its high proportion of agricultural and non-agricultural imports from non-member states and its relatively small receipts from the Common Agricultural Policy, the most important portion of Community expenditure.

BUDGET 2001

| | Billion Euro* | As % of total |
|---|---|---|
| Agriculture | 43.3 | 45.0 |
| Regional and Social | 32.7 | 34.0 |
| External Action | 4.9 | 5.1 |
| Pre-accession Aid | 3.2 | 3.3 |
| Research and Technology | 3.9 | 4.1 |
| Other internal policies | 2.3 | 2.4 |
| Administration | 4.9 | 5.1 |
| Reserves | 0.9 | 0.9 |
| TOTAL | 96.2 | 99.9 |

*Source*: General Budget of the European Union for the Financial Year 2001

EC BUDGET BY MEMBER STATE 1999 (*Billion Euro**)

| | Contributions | Receipts | Net gain‡ |
|---|---|---|---|
| Germany | 21.07 (25.5%) | 9.71 | -11.36 |
| France | 13.99 (17.0%) | 12.83 | -1.16 |
| UK | 11.08 (13.4%) | 5.79 | -5.29 |
| Italy | 10.77 (13.0%) | 9.01 | -1.76 |
| Spain | 6.23 (7.5%) | 12.89 | +6.66 |
| Netherlands | 5.09 (6.2%) | 1.73 | -3.36 |
| Belgium | 3.20 (3.9%) | 1.92 | -1.28 |
| Sweden | 2.35 (2.8%) | 1.12 | -1.23 |
| Austria | 2.05 (2.5%) | 1.22 | -0.83 |
| Denmark | 1.66 (2.0%) | 1.51 | -0.15 |
| Greece | 1.35 (1.6%) | 4.99 | +3.64 |
| Portugal | 1.23 (1.6%) | 3.90 | +2.67 |
| Finland | 1.21 (1.5%) | 0.90 | -0.31 |
| Ireland | 1.06 (1.3%) | 2.88 | +1.82 |
| Luxembourg | 0.19 (0.2%) | 0.08 | -0.11 |
| TOTAL | 82.53 (100%) | 75.8 | — |

*Source*: Official Journal of the European Communities C series 1.12.2000

* 1 euro = £0.619 as at 11 April 2001

‡ Net contributor/net recipient (+)

Under the Edinburgh summit agreement (December 1992) the EC budget rose to a maximum of 1.27 per cent of the EU's GNP in 1999. The agreed budget for 2000–2006 will keep the 1.27 per cent ceiling, but resources devoted to the existing member states will fall to 0.98 per cent, with the remaining resources devoted to enlargement.

## THE COMMON AGRICULTURAL POLICY

The Common Agricultural Policy (CAP) was established to increase agricultural production, provide a fair standard of living for farmers and ensure the availability of food at reasonable prices. This aim was achieved by a number of mechanisms:

- import levies
- intervention purchase
- export subsidies

These measures stimulated production but also placed increasing demands on the EC budget which were exacerbated by the increase in EC members and yields enlarged by technological innovation; CAP now accounts for over 40 per cent of EC expenditure. To surmount these problems reforms were agreed in 1984, 1988, 1992, 1997 and 1999.

### REFORMS

The 1984 reforms created the system of co-responsibility levies: farm payments to the EC by volume of product sold. This system was supplemented by national quotas for particular products, such as milk. The 1988 reforms emphasised 'set-aside', whereby farmers are given direct grants to take land out of production as a means of reducing surpluses. The set-aside reforms were extended in 1993 for another five years and to every farm in the EC. The 1999 reforms will further reduce surpluses of cereals, beef and milk by cutting the intervention prices by up to 20 per cent and compensating producers by making area payments. Under the reforms, CAP rules will also be simplified, eliminating inconsistencies between policies.

Under the Uruguay round agreement of GATT concluded in 1993, the EU must, over a six-year period from 1 January 1995, reduce its import levies by 36 per cent, reduce its domestic subsidies by 20 per cent, reduce its export subsidies by 36 per cent in value, and reduce its subsidised exports by 21 per cent in volume. Agenda 2000, the programme to overhaul the policies of the EU and prepare it for the accession of new member states, will temporarily increase the cost of the CAP by 1,000 million a year in compensation payments, but leave it broadly stable by the end of the current planning period in 2006.

## THE SINGLE MARKET

Even after the removal of tariffs and quotas between member states in the 1970s and 1980s, the EC was still separated into a number of national markets by a series of non-tariff barriers. It was to overcome these internal barriers to trade that the concept of the Single Market was developed. The measures to be undertaken were codified in the Commission's 1985 White Paper on completing the internal market.

The White Paper included articles removing obstacles that distorted the internal market: the elimination of frontier controls; the mutual recognition of professional qualifications; the harmonisation of product specifications, largely by the mutual recognition of national standards; open tendering for public procurement contracts; the free movement of capital; the harmonisation of VAT and excise duties; and the reduction of state aid to particular industries. The target date for the completion of this process was 31 December 1992. The Single European Act aided the completion of the Single Market by changing the legislative process within the EC, particularly with the introduction of qualified majority voting in the Council of Ministers for some policy areas, and the introduction of the assent procedure in the European Parliament. The SEA also extends EC competence into the fields of technology, the environment, regional policy, monetary policy and external policy. The Single Market came into effect on 1 January 1993. The full implementation of the elimination of frontier controls and the harmonisation of taxes have, however, been repeatedly delayed.

## THE EUROPEAN ECONOMIC AREA (*see also* EFTA)

The EC Single Market programme spurred European non-member states to open negotiations with the EC on preferential access for their goods, services, labour and capital to the Single Market. Principal among these states were European Free Trade Association (EFTA) members who opened negotiations on extending the Single Market to EFTA by the formation of the European Economic Area (EEA) encompassing all 19 EC and EFTA states. Agreement was reached in May 1992 but the operation of the EEA was delayed by its rejection in a Swiss referendum, necessitating an additional protocol agreed by the remaining 18 states. The EEA came into effect on 1 January 1994 after ratification by 17 member states (Liechtenstein joined on 1 May 1995 after adapting its customs union with Switzerland).

Austria, Finland and Sweden joined the EU itself on 1 January 1995, leaving only Norway, Iceland and Liechtenstein as the non-EU EEA members. Under the EEA agreement, the three states are to adopt the EU's *acquis communautaire*, apart from in the fields of agriculture, fisheries, and coal and steel.

The EEA is controlled by regular ministerial meetings and by a joint EU-EFTA committee which extends relevant EU legislation to EEA states. Apart from single market measures, there is co-operation in education, research and development, consumer policy and tourism.

An EFTA Court of Justice has been established in Luxembourg and an EFTA Surveillance Authority in Brussels to supervise the implementation of the EEA Agreement.

## THE EUROPEAN MONETARY SYSTEM AND THE SINGLE CURRENCY

The European monetary system (EMS) began operation in March 1979 with three main purposes. The first was to establish monetary stability in Europe, initially in exchange rates between EC member state currencies through the exchange rate mechanism (ERM), and in the longer term to be part of a wider stabilisation process, overcoming inflation and budget and trade deficits. The second purpose was to overcome the constraints resulting from the interdependence of EC economies, and the third was to aid the long-term process of European monetary integration.

The Maastricht Treaty set in motion timetables for achieving economic and monetary union (EMU) and a single currency (the euro). At the Brussels summit in May 1998, 11 member states were judged to fulfil or be close to fulfilling the necessary convergence criteria for participation in the first stage of EMU: Austria, Belgium, Finland, France, Germany, Ireland, Italy, Luxembourg, the Netherlands, Portugal and Spain.

The criteria were that:

- the budget deficit should be 3 per cent or less of gross domestic product (GDP)
- total national debt must not exceed 60 per cent of GDP
- inflation should be no more than 1.5 per cent above the average rate of the three best performing economies in the EU
- long-term interest rates should be no more than 2 per cent above the average of the three best performing economies in the EU in the previous 12 months
- applicants must have been members of the ERM for two years without having realigned or devalued their currency

Under the terms of a stability and growth pact agreed in Dublin in December 1996, penalties may be imposed on EMU members with high budget deficits. Governments with deficits exceeding 3 per cent of GDP will receive a warning and will be obliged to pay up to 0.5 per cent of their GDP into a fund after ten months. This will become a fine if the budget deficit is not rectified within two years. A member state with negative growth will be allowed to apply for an exemption from the fine in 'exceptional circumstances', e.g. a recession whereby GDP had fallen by 0.75 per cent or more during one year.

On 1 January 1999, the qualifying member states adopted the euro at irrevocably fixed exchange rates (*see* table below), the European Central Bank (ECB) took charge of the single monetary policy, and the euro replaced the ECU on a one-for-one basis.

On 19 June 2000, Greece was judged to have fulfilled the criteria for participation and adopted the euro on 1 January 2001. A referendum on the adoption of the euro was held in Denmark on 28 September 2000, but participation was rejected by the electorate. The euro is now the legal currency in the participating states. Euro notes and coins will be introduced from 1 January 2002 and will circulate alongside national currencies for a maximum of six months, after which time national notes and coins will cease to be legal tender.

## THE CONVERSION RATES BETWEEN THE EURO AND THE CURRENCIES OF THE MEMBER STATES ADOPTING THE EURO ARE:

| | |
|---|---|
| 1_ euro = | 13.7603 Austrian Schilling |
| | 40.3399 Belgian Francs |
| | 2.20371 Dutch Gulden |
| | 5.94573 Finnish Markka |
| | 6.55957 French Francs |
| | 1.95583 German Deutsche Mark |
| | 340.750 Greek Drachma |
| | 0.787564 Irish Punts |
| | 1,936.27 Italian Lire |
| | 40.3399 Luxembourg Francs |
| | 200.482 Portuguese Escudos |
| | 166.386 Spanish Pesetas |

*Source*: The Official Journal of the European Communities

The ECB (*see also* page 784) meets every two weeks to set interest rates for the countries participating in the euro. Its governing council has 17 members, being the six members of the ECB's executive board and the 11 governors of the national central banks of the participating states.

The UK, Denmark and Sweden chose not to take part in the first stage of EMU; Greece was unable to meet the criteria. With the advent of EMU, the ERM was revised and Denmark became a member of ERM II, which requires it to maintain its currencies within set margins of the euro. Membership of ERM II is voluntary, although all member states outside the euro zone are encouraged to take part. Sweden and the UK are currently not members.

## THE MAASTRICHT TREATY

The Treaty on European Union was agreed at a meeting of the European Council in Maastricht, the Netherlands, in December 1991. It came into effect in November 1993 following ratification by the member states.

Three 'pillars' formed the basis of the new treaty:
- the European Community with its established institutions and decision-making processes
- a Common Foreign and Security Policy (*see* below) with the Western European Union as the potential defence component of the EU
- co-operation in justice and home affairs, with the Council of Ministers to co-ordinate policies on asylum, immigration, conditions of entry, cross-border crime, drug trafficking and terrorism

The Treaty established a common European citizenship for nationals of all member states and introduced the principle of subsidiarity whereby decisions are taken at the most appropriate level: national, regional or local. It extended EC competency into the areas of environmental and industrial policies, consumer affairs, health, and education and training, and extended qualified majority voting in the Council of Ministers to some areas which had previously required a unanimous vote. The powers of the European Parliament over the budget and over the Commission were also enhanced and a co-decision procedure enabled the Parliament to override decisions made by the Council of Ministers in certain policy areas (*see* pages 778). A separate protocol to the Maastricht Treaty on social policy was agreed by 11 states and was incorporated into the Amsterdam Treaty in 1997 following adoption by the UK.

## THE AMSTERDAM TREATY

The treaties of Rome and Maastricht were again amended through the Treaty of Amsterdam, which came into effect on 1 May 1999. It extends the scope of qualified majority voting and the powers of the European Parliament.

## COMMON FOREIGN AND SECURITY POLICY

The Common Foreign and Security Policy (CFSP) was created as a pillar of the EU by the Maastricht Treaty (*see* above). It adopted the machinery of the European Political Co-operation (EPC) framework which it replaced and was charged with providing a forum for member states and EU institutions to consult on foreign affairs.

The CFSP system is headed by the Council of the European Union, which provides general lines of policy. Specific policy decisions are taken by the Council of Foreign Ministers, which meets at least four times a year to determine areas for joint action. The High Representative of the CFSP initiates action, manages the CFSP and represents it abroad. The Council of Ministers is supported by the Political Committee which meets monthly, or within 48 hours if there is a crisis, to prepare for ministerial discussions. A group of correspondents, designated diplomats in each member's foreign ministry, provides day-to-day contact.

The Amsterdam Treaty introduced qualified majority voting for foreign affairs and created a high representative on CFSP to act as a spokesperson. It also established a new policy planning and early warning unit to monitor international developments. The unit is to consist of specialists from the member states, the Council and the Commission, as well as from the WEU.

## THE SCHENGEN AGREEMENT

The Schengen Agreement was signed by France, Germany, Belgium, Luxembourg and the Netherlands in 1985. The Agreement committed the five states to abolishing internal border controls and erecting external frontiers against illegal immigrants, drug traffickers, terrorists and organised crime.

Subsequently signed by Spain and Portugal, the Agreement was ratified by the seven signatory states and entered into force in March 1995 with the removal of internal frontier, passport, customs and immigration controls. Italy and Austria became full members in April 1998 and Greece achieved full membership on 1 January 2000. Provisional agreement was reached in June 1995 between the signatory states and the Nordic Union on a merger of the two frontier-free zones, and Denmark, Finland, Sweden, Iceland and Norway became full members of the Schengen Agreement on 1 April 2001. The UK and the Republic of Ireland have not signed the Agreement, but have expressed their intention to join in some aspects of its work.

The Schengen Agreement originated as an intergovernmental agreement but became part of the EU following the signing of the Amsterdam Treaty.

## THE TREATY OF NICE

The Treaty of Nice aims to enable the EU to accommodate up to 13 new member states. It extends qualified majority voting to 30 further articles of the treaties that previously required unanimity. The weighting of votes in the EU Council is to be altered from 1 January 2005 in preparation for the new member states, whose numbers of votes have been set. To obtain a qualified majority, a decision will require a specified number of votes (to be reviewed following each accession); the decision will have to be approved by a majority of member states and represent at least 62 per cent of the total population of the EU. The Treaty also sets the number of MEPs that both existing and new member states will have following enlargement.

The Treaty of Maastricht had established the right of groups of member states to work together without requiring the participation of all (enhanced co-operation); the Treaty of Nice removes the right of individual member states to veto the launch of enhanced co-operation and establishes a minimum number of eight member states for establishing enhanced co-operation in the field of common foreign and security policy (CFSP).

The European Commission will be limited to one member per member state from 2005, with a maximum of 27 commissioners; a rotation system is to be introduced once EU membership exceeds 27 states.

The Treaty also adds to the powers of the President of the Commission and amends the rules of the operation of the Court of Justice.

The Treaty was rejected by 54 per cent of voters in a referendum in Ireland, the only country to put the issue to its electorate.

---

## COURT OF JUSTICE OF THE EUROPEAN COMMUNITIES

Palais de la Cour de justice, Boulevard Konrad Adenauer, Kirchberg, L–2925 Luxembourg
Web: www.curia.eu.int

---

The Court of Justice is common to the three European Communities. It exists to safeguard the law in the interpretation and application of the Community treaties, to decide on the legality of decisions of the Council of Ministers or the Commission, and to determine infringements of the treaties. Cases may be brought to it by the member states, the Community institutions, firms or individuals. Its decisions are directly binding in the member countries, and the Maastricht Treaty enhanced the Court's powers by permitting it to impose fines on member states. The 15 judges and eight advocates-general of the Court are appointed for renewable six-year terms by the member governments in concert. During 2000, 503 new cases were lodged at the court and 526 cases were concluded.

Composition of the Court, in order of precedence, with effect from 7 October 2000:
G. C. Rodríguez Iglesias (*President*); C. Gulmann (*President of the 3rd and 6th Chambers*); A. M. La Pergola (*President of the 4th and 5th Chambers*); D. Ruíz-Jarabo Colomer (*First Advocate-General*); M. Wathelet (*President of the 1st Chamber*); V. Skouris (*President of the 2nd Chamber*); F. G. Jacobs (*Advocate-General*); D. A. O. Edward (*Judge*); J.-P. Puissochet (*Judge*); P. Léger (*Advocate General*); P. Jann (*Judge*); L. Sevón (*Judge*); R. Schintgen (*Judge*); S. Alber (*Advocate-General*); J. Mischo (*Advocate-General*); F. Macken (*Judge*); N. Colneric (*Judge*); S. von Bahr (*Judge*); A. Tizzano (*Advocate-General*); J. N. da Cunha Rodrigues (*Judge*); C. W. A. Timmermans (*Judge*); L. A. Geelhoed (*Advocate-General*); C. Stix-Hackl (*Advocate-General*); R. Grass (*Registrar*)

### Court of First Instance
Palais de la Cour de justice, Boulevard Konrad Adenauer, Kirchberg, L-2925 Luxembourg

Established under powers conferred by the Single European Act, the Court of First Instance has jurisdiction to hear and determine all actions brought by natural or legal persons. It is composed of 15 judges, appointed for renewable six-year terms by the governments of the member states. During 2000, 398 new cases were lodged at the court and 344 cases were concluded.

Composition of the Court, in order of precedence, for the judicial year 2000–2001:
B. Vesterdorf (*President of the Court of First Instance*); P. Lindh (*President of the 5th Chamber*); J. Azizi (*President of the 3rd Chamber*); P. Mengozzi (*President of the 4th Chamber*); A. Meij (*President of the 2nd Chamber*); R. García-Valdecasas y Fernández (*Judge*); K. Lenaerts (*Judge*); V. Tiili (*Judge*); A. Potocki (*Judge*); R. Moura Ramos (*Judge*); J. Cooke (*Judge*); M. Jaeger (*Judge*); J. Pirrung (*Judge*); M. Vilaras (*Judge*); N. Forwood (*Judge*); H. Jung (*Registrar*)

## THE COMMITTEE OF THE REGIONS
Montoyerstraat 92/102, B-1000 Brussels, Belgium
E-mail: info@cor.eu.int Web: www.cor.eu.int

The Committee of the Regions (COR) is an advisory and consultative body established to redress the lack of a role for regional and local authorities in the EU democratic system. The COR is composed of 222 appointed and indirectly elected members, of whom half are from large regions and half are from small local authorities, who meet five times each year for two days. The COR has eight commissions which deliver opinions on policies affecting regions, such as trans-border transport links, economic and social cohesion, education and training, social policy, culture and regional policy.
*President*, Jos Chabert (Belgium)

## THE ECONOMIC AND SOCIAL COMMITTEE
Ravensteinstraat 2, B-1000 Brussels, Belgium
Web: www.ces.eu.int

The Economic and Social Committee (ESC) is an advisory and consultative body. It has 222 members, nominated by member states, and is divided into three groups: employers, workers, and other interest groups such as consumers, farmers and the self-employed. It issues opinions on draft EC legislation and can bring matters to the attention of the Commission, Council and Parliament. Consultation of the ESC by the Parliament is enshrined in the Amsterdam Treaty, formally recognising the importance of the opinions of the EU's economic and social partners.
*President*, Göke Daniel Frerichs (Germany)

## THE EUROPEAN CENTRAL BANK
29 Kaiserstrasse, D-60311 Frankfurt-am-Main, Germany E-mail: info@ecb.int Web: www.ecb.int

The European Central Bank (ECB), which superseded the European Monetary Institute, was established on 1 July 1998. Its governing bodies are the Executive Board, the Governing Council and the General Council. The Executive Board consists of the President, the Vice-President and four other members, who are appointed by the governments of the states participating in the single currency, from people with recognised standing and professional experience; the Governing Council comprises the six members of the Executive Board and the 12 governors of the national central banks of the participating states; the General Council comprises the President and Vice-President and the 15 governors of the national central banks, the other members of the Executive Board being entitled to participate but not to vote. The ECB is independent of national governments and of all other EU institutions. It became fully operational on 1 January 1999, and defines and implements the single monetary policy necessary for EMU. It operates as part of the European System of Central Banks (ESCB), which consists of the ECB and the national central banks of the EU member states.
*President*, Willem Duisenberg (Netherlands)
*Vice-President*, Christian Noyer (France)

## THE EUROPEAN COURT OF AUDITORS
12 rue A. De Gasperi, L-1615 Luxembourg
E-mail: euraud@eca.eu.int Web: www.eca.eu.int

The European Court of Auditors, established in 1977, examines the accounts of all revenue and expenditure of the European Communities and Community bodies and evaluates whether all revenue has been received and all expenditure incurred in a lawful and regular manner and in accordance with the principles of sound financial management. The Court issues an annual report and a statement of assurance as to the reliability of the accounts and the legality and regularity of the underlying transactions. It also publishes special reports on specific topics and delivers opinions on financial matters. The Court has 15 members appointed for six-year terms by the Council of Ministers following consultation with the European Parliament.
*President*, Jan O. Karlsson (Sweden)

THE EUROPEAN INVESTMENT BANK
100 boulevard Konrad Adenauer, L-2950 Luxembourg E-mail: info@eib.org
Web: www.eib.eu.int

The European Investment Bank (EIB) was set up in 1958 under the terms of the Treaty of Rome to finance capital investment projects promoting the balanced development of the European Community.

It grants long-term loans to private and public enterprises, public authorities and financial institutions, to finance projects which further the economic development of less advanced regions (Assisted Areas); improvement of European transport and telecommunications infrastructure; environmental protection; attainment of the EU's energy policy objectives; modernisation of enterprises, and promotion of industrial competitiveness and integration at EU level.

Outside the EU, the EIB participates in the implementation of the EU's development policy, through long-term loans from own resources or subordinated loans and risk capital from EU or member states' budgetary funds, in some 150 non-EU countries: in pre-accession countries and, under the terms of different association or co-operation agreements, with countries in the Mediterranean region, in the Balkans, in Latin America, Asia and South Africa, in Africa, the Caribbean and the Pacific.

The Bank's total financing operations in 2000 amounted to 36 billion, of which 30.6 billion was for investment within the EU. On 31 December 2000, total outstanding borrowings totalled 160 billion and outstanding loans 199 billion.

In June 2000, the EIB launched the Innovation 2000 Initiative, under which 12,000-15,000 million would be available over a three-year period to invest in the provision of new technologies in education, co-finance research and development, finance information and communications technology networks, make use of information technology to increase access to public services and assist SMEs to acquire and use information technologies.

The members of the EIB are the 15 member states of the EU, who have all subscribed to the Bank's capital of 100,000 million. The bulk of the funds required by the Bank to carry out its tasks are borrowed on the capital markets of the EU and non-member countries, and on the international market.

As it operates on a non-profit-making basis, the interest rates charged by the EIB reflect the cost of the Bank's borrowings and closely follow conditions on world capital markets.

The Board of Governors of the EIB consists of one government minister nominated by each of the member countries, usually the finance, economic affairs or treasury minister, who lay down general directives on the credit policy of the Bank and appoint members to the Board of Directors (24 nominated by the member states, one by the European Commission), which takes decisions on the granting and raising of loans and the fixing of interest rates. A Management Committee, composed of the Bank's President and seven Vice-Presidents, also appointed by the Board of Governors, is responsible for the day-to-day operations of the Bank. The President and Vice-Presidents also preside as Chairman and Vice-Chairmen at meetings of the Board of Directors.

*President*, Philippe Maystadt

*Vice-Presidents*, Wolfgang Roth; Massimo Ponzellini; Ewald Nowotny; Francis Mayer; Peter Sedgwick; Isabel Martín Castellá; Michael Tutty

UK OFFICE: 68 Pall Mall, London SW1Y 5ES. Tel: 020-7343 1200

THE EUROPEAN POLICE OFFICE
PO Box 90850, NL-2509 LW The Hague, The Netherlands E-mail: info@europol.eu.int
Web: www.europol.eu.int

The European Police Office (Europol), came into being on 1 October 1998 and assumed its full powers on 1 July 1999. It superseded the Europol Drugs Unit and exists to improve police co-operation between member states and to combat terrorism, illicit traffic in drugs and other serious forms of international crime. It is ultimately responsible to the Council. Each member state has set up a national unit to liaise with Europol, and the units send at least one liaison officer to represent its interests at Europol headquarters. Europol maintains a computerised information system, designed to facilitate the exchange of information between member states; the system is maintained by the national units and may be consulted by Europol agents. The computerised database may contain both personal and non-personal data; individuals are entitled to request access to data concerning themselves. Europol has a Management Board comprising one senior police representative from each member state. All Europol activities are monitored by an independent joint supervisory body, to ensure the rights of the individual are upheld.

*Director*, Jürgen Storbeck (Germany)

*Deputy Directors*, Willy Bruggeman (Belgium); Gilles Leclair (France); Emanuele Marotta (Italy); Georges Rauchs (Luxembourg); David Valls-Russell (UK)

Other bodies:

THE EUROPEAN MEDICINE EVALUATION AGENCY (EMEA), 7 Westferry Circus, London E14 4HB; E-mail: mail@emea.eudra.org

THE EUROPEAN ENVIRONMENT AGENCY (EEA), Kongens Nytorv 6, DK- 1050, København, Denmark; E-mail: eea@eea.eu.int

THE EUROPEAN TRAINING FOUNDATION, Villa Gualino, Viale Settimio Severo 65, I-10133 Torn, Italy; E-mail: info@etf.eu.int

THE EUROPEAN CENTRE FOR THE DEVELOPMENT OF VOCATIONAL TRAINING (CEDEFOP), PO Box 22427, GR-55102 Thessaloniki (Finikas), Greece; E-mail: webmaster@cedefop.gr

THE EUROPEAN MONITORING CENTRE FOR DRUGS AND DRUG ADDICTION, Rua da Cruz de Santa Apolónia 23-25, P-1149-045 Lisboa, Portugal; E-mail: info@emcdda.org

THE EUROPEAN FOUNDATION FOR THE IMPROVEMENT OF LIVING AND WORKING CONDITIONS, Wyattville Road, Loughlinstown, Co. Dublin, Ireland; E-mail: postmaster@eurofound.ie

THE OFFICE FOR HARMONISATION IN THE INTERNAL MARKET (OHIM), Avenida de Europa 4, AC 77, E-03080 Alicante, Spain; E-mail: information@oami.eu.int

THE COMMUNITY PLANT VARIETY RIGHTS OFFICE (CPVO), BP 2141, F- 49021 Angers Cédex 02, France; E-mail: cpvo@cpvo.eu.int

THE EUROPEAN AGENCY FOR RECONSTRUCTION (EAR), PO Box 10177, GR-54626 Thessaloniki, Greece; E-mail: huges.mingarelli@ear.eu.int

The European Agency for Safety and Health at Work, Gran Vía 33, E-48009 Bilbao, Spain; E-mail: information@osha.eu.int

The Translation Centre for Bodies in the European Union, Bâtiment Nouvel Hémicycle, niveau 4, 1 rue du Fort Thüngen, L-1499 Luxembourg; E-mail: cdt@eu.int

The European Monitoring Centre on Racism and Xenophobia, Rahlgasse 3, A-1060 Wien, Austria; E-mail: office@eumc.eu.int

## EUROPEAN COMMUNITY INFORMATION

European Commission Representation Offices

England, 8 Storey's Gate, London SW1P 3AT. Tel: 020-7973 1992

Wales, 4 Cathedral Road, Cardiff CF11 9SG. Tel: 029-2037 1631

Scotland, 9 Alva Street, Edinburgh EH2 4HP. Tel: 0131-225 2058

Northern Ireland, Windsor House, 9–15 Bedford Street, Belfast BT2 7EG. Tel: 028-9024 0708

Republic of Ireland, 18 Dawson Street, Dublin 2

European Commission Delegations

Australia, 18 Arkana Street, Yarralumla, ACT 2600, and a number of other cities

Canada, Inn of the Provinces, Office Tower (Suite 1110), 350 Sparks Street, Ottawa, Ontario K1R 7SA

USA, 2300 M Street NW (Suite 707), Washington DC 20037; 1 Dag Hammarskjöld Plaza, 254 East 47th Street, New York, NY 10017

UK Office of the European Parliament 2 Queen Anne's Gate, London SW1H 9AA. Tel: 020-7227 4300

There are European Information Centres, set up to give information and advice to small and medium-sized businesses, in 25 British towns and cities. A number of universities maintain European Documentation Centres. Many local authorities also maintain European Public Information Centres, which provide information to the general public.

# Countries of the World

## WORLD AREA AND POPULATION

The total population of the world in mid-1990 was estimated at 5,292 million, compared with 3.019 million in 1960 and 2.070 million in 1930.

| Continent, etc. | Area sq. miles '000 | sq. km '000 | Estimated population mid-1990 |
|---|---|---|---|
| Africa | 11,704 | 30,313 | 642,000,000 |
| North America[1] | 8,311 | 21,525 | 276,000,000 |
| Latin America[2] | 7,933 | 20,547 | 448,000,000 |
| Asia[3] | 10,637 | 27,549 | 3,113,000,000 |
| Europe[4] | 1,915 | 4,961 | 498,000,000 |
| Former USSR | 8,649 | 22,402 | 289,000,000 |
| Oceania[5] | 3,286 | 8,510 | 26,500,000 |
| TOTAL | 52,435 | 135,807 | 5,292,000,000 |

[1]Includes Greenland and Hawaii
[2]Mexico and the remainder of the Americas south of the USA
[3]Includes European Turkey, excludes former USSR
[4]Excludes European Turkey and former USSR
[5]Includes Australia, New Zealand and the islands inhabited by Micronesian, Melanesian and Polynesian peoples.
*Source: UN Demographic Yearbook 1990* (pub. 1992)

A United Nations report *The Sex and Age Distribution of the World Populations* (revised 1994) puts the world's population in the late 20th and the 21st centuries at the following levels (medium variant data):

| | | | |
|---|---|---|---|
| 1995 | 5,176.4m | 2030 | 8,670.6m |
| 2000 | 6,158.0m | 2040 | 9,318.2m |
| 2010 | 7,032.3m | 2050 | 9,833.2m |
| 2020 | 7,887.8m | | |

The population forecast for the years 2000 and 2050 is:

| Continent, etc. | Estimated population (million) 2000 | 2050 |
|---|---|---|
| Africa | 831.596 | 2,140.844 |
| North America[1] | 306.280 | 388.997 |
| Latin America[2] | 523.875 | 838.527 |
| Asia | 3,753.846 | 5,741.005 |
| Europe | 729.803 | 677.764 |
| Oceania | 30,651 | 46,070 |
| TOTAL | 6,158.051 | 9,833.207 |

[1]Includes Bermuda, Greenland, and St Pierre and Miquelon
[2]Mexico and the remainder of the Americas south of the USA

### AREA AND POPULATION BY CONTINENT

No complete survey of many countries has yet been achieved and consequently accurate area figures are not always available. Similarly, may countries have not recently, or have never, taken a census. The areas of countries given below are derived from estimate figures published by the United Nations. The conversion factors used are:

(i) to convert square miles to square km, multiply by 2.589988

(ii) to convert square km to square miles, multiply by 0.3861022

Population figures for countries are derived from the most recent estimates available. Accurate and up-to-date data for the populations of capital cities are scarce, and definitions of cities' extent differ. The figures given below are the latest estimates available.

Ψ seaport

## AFRICA

| COUNTRY/TERRITORY | AREA Sq. miles | Sq. Km | POPULATION | CAPITAL | POPULATION OF CAPITAL |
|---|---|---|---|---|---|
| Algeria | 919,595 | 2,381,741 | 29,050,000 | Ψ Algiers (El Djazaïr) | 1,507,241 |
| Angola | 481,354 | 1,246,700 | 11,569,000 | Ψ Luanda | 475,328 |
| Benin | 43,484 | 112,622 | 5,828,000 | Ψ Porto Novo | 179,138 |
| Botswana | 224,607 | 581,730 | 1,533,000 | Gaborone | 286,779 |
| Burkina Faso | 105,792 | 274,000 | 11,087,000 | Ouagadougou | 634,479 |
| Burundi | 10,747 | 27,834 | 6,194,000 | Bujumbura | 235,440 |
| Cameroon | 183,569 | 475,442 | 13,937,000 | Yaoundé | 653,670 |
| Cape Verde | 1,557 | 4,033 | 406,000 | Ψ Praia | 61,644 |
| Central African Republic | 240,535 | 622,984 | 3,245,000 | Bangui | 473,817 |
| Chad | 495,755 | 1,284,000 | 6,702,000 | N'Djaména | 179,000 |
| Comoros | 863 | 2,235 | 651,000 | Moroni | 17,267 |
| Congo, Democratic Republic of | 905,355 | 2,344,858 | 48,040,000 | Kinshasa | 2,664,309 |
| Congo-Brazzaville, Rep. of | 132,047 | 342,000 | 2,745,000 | Brazzaville | 596,200 |
| Côte d'Ivoire | 124,504 | 322,463 | 14,300,000 | Yamoussoukro | 126,191 |
| Djibouti | 8,958 | 23,200 | 634,000 | Ψ Djibouti | 62,000 |
| Egypt | 386,662 | 1,001,449 | 67,974,000 | Cairo | 6,800,000 |
| Equatorial Guinea | 10,831 | 28,051 | 420,000 | Ψ Malabo | 30,418 |
| Eritrea | 45,406 | 117,600 | 3,409,000 | Asmara | 358,100 |
| Ethiopia | 426,373 | 1,104,300 | 63,495,000 | Addis Ababa | 2,495,000 |
| Gabon | 103,347 | 267,668 | 1,138,000 | Ψ Libreville | 251,000 |
| Gambia | 4,361 | 11,295 | 1,169,000 | Ψ Banjul | 109,986 |

| COUNTRY/TERRITORY | AREA Sq. miles | Sq. Km | POPULATION | CAPITAL | POPULATION OF CAPITAL |
|---|---|---|---|---|---|
| Ghana | 92,098 | 238,533 | 18,885,616 | Ψ Accra | 1,445,515 |
| Guinea | 94,926 | 245,857 | 7,614,000 | Ψ Conakry | 763,000 |
| Guinea–Bissau | 13,948 | 36,125 | 1,112,000 | Ψ Bissau | 109,214 |
| Kenya | 224,081 | 580,367 | 33,144,000 | Nairobi | 1,400,000 |
| Lesotho | 11,720 | 30,355 | 2,131,000 | Maseru | 367,000 |
| Liberia | 43,000 | 111,369 | 2,879,000 | Ψ Monrovia | 421,053 |
| Libya | 679,362 | 1,759,540 | 4,389,739 | Ψ Tripoli (Tarābulus) | 1,000,000 |
| Madagascar | 226,658 | 587,041 | 15,845,000 | Antananarivo | 1,052,835 |
| Malaŵi | 45,747 | 118,484 | 10,441,000 | Lilongwe | 233,973 |
| Mali | 478,841 | 1,240,192 | 11,480,000 | Bamako | 809,552 |
| Mauritania | 395,956 | 1,025,520 | 2,392,000 | Nouakchott | 850,000 |
| Mauritius | 788 | 2,040 | 1,160,000 | Ψ Port Louis | 146,499 |
| Mayotte (*Fr.*) | 144 | 372 | 94,410 | Mamoudzou | 12,000 |
| Morocco | 172,414 | 446,550 | 27,310,000 | Ψ Rabat | 1,220,000 |
| Western Sahara | 102,703 | 266,000 | 265,000 | El-Aaiūn | 20,010 |
| Mozambique | 309,494 | 801,590 | 16,916,600 | Ψ Maputo | 1,039,700 |
| Namibia | 318,261 | 824,292 | 1,613,000 | Windhoek | 147,056 |
| Niger | 489,191 | 1,267,000 | 9,788,000 | Niamey | 392,169 |
| Nigeria | 356,669 | 923,768 | 118,369,000 | Abuja | 378,671 |
| Réunion (*Fr.*) | 969 | 2,510 | 673,000 | St Denis | 121,999 |
| Rwanda | 10,169 | 26,338 | 5,883,000 | Kigali | 116,227 |
| Saint Helena (*UK*) | 47 | 122 | 6,000 | Ψ Jamestown | 884 |
| Ascension (*UK*) | 34 | 88 | 1,051 | Ψ Georgetown | — |
| Tristan Da Cunha (*UK*) | 38 | 98 | 288 | Ψ Edinburgh of the Seven Seas | — |
| São Tomé And Príncipe | 372 | 964 | 138,000 | Ψ São Tomé | 43,420 |
| Senegal | 75,955 | 196,722 | 8,802,000 | Ψ Dakar | 1,641,358 |
| Seychelles | 176 | 455 | 78,846 | Ψ Victoria | 24,324 |
| Sierra Leone | 27,699 | 71,740 | 4,428,000 | Ψ Freetown | 469,776 |
| Somalia | 246,201 | 637,657 | 10,217,000 | Ψ Mogadishu | 230,000 |
| South Africa | 471,445 | 1,221,037 | 43,336,000 | { Pretoria<br>Ψ Cape Town;<br>Bloemfontein | 822,925;<br>1,911,521;<br>300,150 |
| Sudan | 967,500 | 2,505,813 | 27,889,000 | Khartoum (Al-Khartūm) | 947,483 |
| Swaziland | 6,704 | 17,364 | 906,000 | Mbabane | 38,290 |
| Tanzania | 341,216 | 883,749 | 31,507,000 | Dodoma | 85,000 |
| Togo | 21,925 | 56,785 | 4,317,000 | Ψ Lomé | 366,476 |
| Tunisia | 63,170 | 163,610 | 9,215,000 | Ψ Tunis | 1,830,634 |
| Uganda | 93,065 | 241,038 | 20,438,000 | Kampala | 750,000 |
| Zambia | 290,587 | 752,618 | 8,478,000 | Lusaka | 982,362 |
| Zimbabwe | 150,872 | 390,757 | 12,294,000 | Harare | 1,189,103 |
| AMERICA | | | | | |
| *North America* | | | | | |
| Canada | 3,849,674 | 9,970,610 | 30,491,294 | Ottawa | 1,010,498 |
| Greenland (*Den.*) | 840,004 | 2,175,600 | 56,000 | Ψ Godthåb (Nuuk) | 12,483 |
| Mexico | 756,066 | 1,958,201 | 96,400,000 | Mexico City | 15,047,685 |
| Saint Pierre and Miquelon (*Fr.*) | 93 | 242 | 6,316 | Ψ St Pierre | 5,416 |
| United States Of America | 3,536,382 | 9,156,119 | 274,520,000 | Washington DC | 7,285,206 |
| *Central America and the West Indies* | | | | | |
| Anguilla (*UK*) | 37 | 96 | 12,394 | The Valley | 2,400 |
| Antigua And Barbuda | 171 | 442 | 67,000 | Ψ St John's | 22,342 |
| Aruba (Neth) | 75 | 193 | 87,000 | Ψ Oranjestad | 25,000 |
| Bahamas | 5,358 | 13,878 | 289,000 | Ψ Nassau | 172,196 |
| Barbados | 166 | 430 | 262,000 | Ψ Bridgetown | 108,000 |
| Belize | 8,763 | 22,696 | 230,000 | Belmopan | 44,087 |
| Bermuda (*UK*) | 20 | 53 | 60,000 | Ψ Hamilton | 2,277 |
| Cayman Islands (*UK*) | 102 | 264 | 38,000 | Ψ George Town | 20,000 |
| Costa Rica | 19,730 | 51,100 | 3,464,000 | San José | 1,220,412 |
| Cuba | 42,804 | 110,861 | 11,059,000 | Ψ Havana | 2,184,990 |
| Dominica | 290 | 751 | 71,000 | Ψ Roseau | 16,243 |
| Dominican Republic | 18,730 | 48,511 | 8,097,000 | Ψ Santo Domingo | 2,134,779 |

| Country/Territory | Area Sq. miles | Sq. Km | Population | Capital | Population of Capital |
|---|---|---|---|---|---|
| El Salvador | 8,124 | 21,041 | 5,928,000 | San Salvador | 1,200,000 |
| Grenada | 133 | 344 | 93,000 | Ψ St George's | 4,788 |
| Guadeloupe *(Fr.)* | 658 | 1,705 | 437,000 | Ψ Basse Terre | 29,522 |
| Guatemala | 42,042 | 08,889 | 10,517,000 | Guatemala City | 1,675,589 |
| Haïti | 10,714 | 27,750 | 7,492,000 | Ψ Port-au-Prince | 884,472 |
| Honduras | 43,277 | 112,088 | 6,338,000 | Tegucigalpa | 670,100 |
| Jamaica | 4,243 | 10,990 | 2,590,400 | Ψ Kingston | 524,638 |
| Martinique *(Fr.)* | 425 | 1,102 | 388,000 | Ψ Fort de France | 133,920 |
| Montserrat *(UK)* | 39 | 102 | 4,500 | Ψ Plymouth | 1,478 |
| Netherlands Antilles (Neth) | 309 | 800 | 207,333 | Ψ Willemstad | 50,000 |
| Nicaragua | 50,193 | (130,000 | 4,351,000 | Managua | 608,020 |
| Panama | 29,157 | 75,517 | 2,719,000 | Ψ Panama City | 464,928 |
| Puerto Rico *(USA)* | 3,427 | 8,875 | 3,771,000 | Ψ San Juan | 1,222,316 |
| Saint Kitts – Nevis | 101 | 261 | 41,000 | Ψ Basseterre | 12,200 |
| Saint Lucia | 240 | 622 | 146,000 | Ψ Castries | 51,994 |
| Saint Vincent And The Grenadines | 150 | 388 | 112,000 | Ψ Kingstown | 15,466 |
| Trinidad And Tobago | 1,981 | 5,130 | 1,307,000 | Ψ Port of Spain | 43,396 |
| Turks And Caicos Islands *(UK)* | 166 | 430 | 23,000 | Ψ Grand Turk | 3,691 |
| Virgin Islands, | | | | | |
| British *(UK)* | 58 | 151 | 20,000 | Ψ Road Town | 3,983 |
| Virgin Islands, US *(USA)* | 134 | 347 | 114,483 | Ψ Charlotte Amalie | 11,842 |
| *South America* | | | | | |
| Argentina | 1,073,518 | 2,780,400 | 35,672,000 | Ψ Buenos Aires | 11,298,030 |
| Bolivia | 424,165 | 1,098,581 | 8,140,000 | La Paz | 739,453 |
| Brazil | 3,300,171 | 8,547,403 | 159,884,000 | Brasília | 1,737,813 |
| Chile | 292,135 | 756,626 | 14,622,000 | Santiago | 4,640,635 |
| Colombia | 439,737 | 1,138,914 | 36,162,000 | Bogotá | 5,398,998 |
| Ecuador | 109,484 | 283,561 | 11,937,000 | Quito | 1,444,363 |
| Falkland Islands *(UK)* | 4,700 | 12,173 | 2,221 | Ψ Stanley | 1,636 |
| French Guiana *(Fr.)* | 34,749 | 90,000 | 159,000 | Ψ Cayenne | 41,164 |
| Guyana | 83,000 | 214,969 | 847,000 | Ψ Georgetown | 250,000 |
| Paraguay | 157,048 | 406,752 | 5,085,000 | Asunción | 718,690 |
| Peru | 496,225 | 1,285,216 | 25,015,000 | Lima | 6,321,173 |
| South Georgia *(UK)* | 1,580 | 4,092 | — | — | — |
| Suriname | 63,037 | 163,265 | 437,000 | Ψ Paramaribo | 265,000 |
| Uruguay | 67,574 | 175,016 | 3,221,000 | Ψ Montevideo | 1,303,182 |
| Venezuela | 352,145 | 912,050 | 22,777,000 | Caracas | 3,672,779 |
| ASIA | | | | | |
| Afghanistan | 251,773 | 652,090 | 22,132,000 | Kābol (Kabul) | 1,424,400 |
| Bahrain | 268 | 694 | 620,000 | Ψ Manama (Al-Manāmah) | 140,401 |
| Bangladesh | 55,598 | 143,998 | 122,013,000 | Dhaka | 3,397,187 |
| Bhutan | 18,147 | 47,000 | 1,862,000 | Thimphu | 15,000 |
| Brunei Darussalam | 2,226 | 5,765 | 307,000 | Bandar Seri Begawan | 49,902 |
| Cambodia | 69,898 | 181,035 | 10,516,000 | Ψ Phnom Penh | 832,000 |
| China[1] | 3,705,408 | 9,596,961 | 1,248,100,000 | Beijing | 7,362,426 |
| Hong Kong *(China)* | 415 | 1,075 | 6,687,200 | — | — |
| Macao *(China)* | 7 | 18 | 440,000 | Ψ Macao | 241,413 |
| East Timor | 5,743 | 14,874 | 839,719 | Ψ Dili | 62,000 |
| India | 1,269,213 | 3,287,263 | 970,930,000 | New Delhi | 301,297 |
| Indonesia | 735,358 | 1,904,569 | 199,867,000 | Ψ Jakarta | 9,160,500 |
| Iran | 630,574 | 1,633,188 | 60,694,000 | Tehran | 6,750,043 |
| Iraq | 169,235 | 438,317 | 21,177,000 | Baghdād | 3,841,268 |
| Israel[2] | 8,130 | 21,056 | 6,100,000 | Tel Aviv | 1,919,700 |
| West Bank And Gaza Strip | 2,406 | 6,231 | 1,635,000 | Gaza City | 120,000 |
| Japan | 145,880 | 377,829 | 125,638,000 | Tokyo | 11,680,296 |
| Jordan | 37,738 | 97,740 | 5,774,000 | Ammān | 1,270,000 |
| Kazakhstan | 1,052,085 | 2,724,900 | 15,671,000 | Astana | 275,100 |
| Korea, Democratic People's Republic | 46,540 | 120,538 | 22,082,000 | Pyongyang | 2,741,260 |
| Korea, Republic of | 38,327 | 99,268 | 46,858,460 | Seoul | 10,321,000 |

| Country/Territory | Area Sq. miles | Sq. Km | Population | Capital | Population of Capital |
|---|---|---|---|---|---|
| Kuwait | 6,880 | 17,818 | 1,866,104 | Ψ Kuwait City (Al-Kuwayt) | 388,663 |
| Kyrgyzstan | 77,181 | 199,900 | 4,856,000 | Bishkek | 589,400 |
| Laos | 91,429 | 236,800 | 5,035,000 | Vientiane | 132,253 |
| Lebanon | 4,015 | 10,400 | 3,144,000 | Ψ Beirut | 1,500,000 |
| Malaysia | 127,320 | 329,758 | 21,667,000 | Kuala Lumpur; Putrajaya | 1,145,342 |
| Maldives | 115 | 298 | 273,000 | Ψ Malé | 62,973 |
| Mongolia | 604,829 | 1,566,500 | 2,313,000 | Ulaanbaatar | 515,100 |
| Myanmar | 261,228 | 676,578 | 46,402,000 | Ψ Yangon (Rangoon) | 2,513,023 |
| Nepal | 56,827 | 147,181 | 22,591,000 | Kathmandu | 421,258 |
| Oman | 82,030 | 212,457 | 2,302,000 | Ψ Muscat (Masqat) | 400,000 |
| Pakistan | 307,374 | 796,095 | 138,150,000 | Islamabad | 350,000 |
| Philippines | 115,831 | 300,000 | 73,527,000 | Ψ Manila | 8,594,150 |
| Qatar | 4,247 | 11,000 | 569,000 | Ψ Doha (Ad-Dawhah) | 217,294 |
| Saudi Arabia | 830,000 | 2,149,690 | 19,494,000 | Riyadh (Ar-Riyād) | 3,100,000 |
| Singapore | 239 | 618 | 3,737,000 | — | — |
| Sri Lanka | 25,332 | 65,610 | 18,552,000 | Ψ Colombo | 615,000 |
| Syria | 71,498 | 185,180 | 14,951,000 | Damascus | 1,549,000 |
| Taiwan | 13,800 | 35,742 | 21,854,273 | Taipei | 2,638,565 |
| Tajikistan | 55,251 | 143,100 | 5,513,400 | Dushanbe | 528,600 |
| Thailand | 198,115 | 513,115 | 60,206,000 | Ψ Bangkok | 5,882,000 |
| Turkey[3] | 314,508 | 814,578 | 63,745,000 | Ankara | 3,258,026 |
| Turkmenistan | 188,456 | 488,100 | 3,808,900 | Ashgabat | 407,000 |
| United Arab Emirates | 32,278 | 83,600 | 2,940,000 | Abu Dhabi (Abu Żaby) | 450,000 |
| Uzbekistan | 172,742 | 447,400 | 21,206,800 | Tashkent | 2,200,000 |
| Vietnam | 128,066 | 331,689 | 76,548,000 | Hanoi | 1,073,760 |
| Yemen | 203,850 | 527,968 | 15,919,000 | Sana'ā' | 926,595 |

[1]Including Tibet
[2]Including East Jerusalem, the Golan Heights and Israeli citizens on the West Bank
[3]Including Turkey in Europe

## EUROPE

| Country/Territory | Area Sq. miles | Sq. Km | Population | Capital | Population of Capital |
|---|---|---|---|---|---|
| Albania | 11,099 | 28,748 | 3,731,000 | Tirana | 244,153 |
| Andorra | 181 | 468 | 65,877 | Andorra la Vella | 21,721 |
| Armenia | 11,506 | 29,800 | 3,798,400 | Yerevan | 1,254,400 |
| Austria | 32,378 | 83,859 | 8,086,000 | Vienna | 1,806,737 |
| Azerbaijan | 33,436 | 86,600 | 7,625,000 | Ψ Baku | 1,149,000 |
| Belarus | 80,155 | 207,600 | 10,179,000 | Minsk | 1,708,308 |
| Belgium | 11,787 | 30,528 | 10,188,000 | Brussels | 953,175 |
| Bosnia-Hercegovina | 19,767 | 51,197 | 3,784,000 | Sarajevo | 529,021 |
| Bulgaria | 42,823 | 110,912 | 8,306,000 | Sofia | 1,192,735 |
| Croatia | 21,824 | 56,538 | 4,498,000 | Zagreb | 867,717 |
| Cyprus | 3,572 | 9,251 | 766,000 | Nicosia | 193,000 |
| Czech Republic | 30,450 | 78,866 | 10,304,000 | Prague | 1,200,458 |
| Denmark | 16,639 | 43,094 | 5,284,000 | Ψ Copenhagen | 1,362,264 |
| Færoe Islands | 540 | 1,399 | 48,000 | Ψ Tórshavn | 16,218 |
| Estonia | 17,413 | 45,100 | 1,453,844 | Tallinn | 415,299 |
| Finland | 130,559 | 338,145 | 5,140,000 | Ψ Helsinki | 905,555 |
| France | 212,935 | 551,500 | 58,607,000 | Paris | 9,319,367 |
| Georgia | 26,911 | 69,700 | 5,434,000 | Tbilisi | 1,268,000 |
| Germany | 137,846 | 357,022 | 82,071,000 | Berlin | 3,472,009 |
| Gibraltar *(UK)* | 2.3 | 6.0 | 28,000 | Ψ Gibraltar | — |
| Greece | 50,949 | 131,957 | 10,522,000 | Athens | 3,072,922 |
| Hungary | 35,920 | 93,032 | 10,153,000 | Budapest | 1,896,507 |
| Iceland | 39,769 | 103,000 | 275,277 | Ψ Reykjavík | 107,764 |
| Ireland, Republic of | 27,132 | 70,273 | 3,626,087 | Ψ Dublin | 952,692 |
| Italy | 116,339 | 301,318 | 57,523,000 | Rome | 2,648,843 |
| Latvia | 24,942 | 64,600 | 2,474,000 | Riga | 805,997 |
| Liechtenstein | 62 | 160 | 32,015 | Vaduz | 5,106 |
| Lithuania | 25,174 | 65,200 | 3,701,300 | Vilnius | 580,099 |
| Luxembourg | 998 | 2,586 | 417,000 | Luxembourg | 77,400 |
| Macedonia | 9,928 | 25,713 | 2,190,000 | Skopje | 429,964 |
| Malta | 122 | 316 | 378,518 | Ψ Valletta | 7,100 |

| Country/Territory | Area Sq. miles | Sq. Km | Population | Capital | Population of Capital |
|---|---|---|---|---|---|
| Moldova | 13,012 | 33,700 | 4,335,000 | Chişinău | 655,940 |
| Monaco | 0.4 | 1 | 32,000 | Monaco | 27,063 |
| Netherlands | 16,033 | 41,526 | 15,604,000 | Ψ Amsterdam | 1,102,323 |
| Norway[1] | 125,050 | 323,877 | 4,445,460 | Ψ Oslo | 499,693 |
| Poland | 124,808 | 323,250 | 38,650,000 | Warsaw | 1,632,534 |
| Portugal[2] | 35,514 | 91,982 | 9,920,760 | Ψ Lisbon | 2,561,225 |
| Romania | 92,043 | 238,391 | 22,520,000 | Bucharest | 2,027,500 |
| Russia[3] | 6,592,850 | 17,075,400 | 146,100,000 | Moscow | 8,598,896 |
| San Marino | 24 | 61 | 26,000 | San Marino | 4,357 |
| Slovakia | 18,923 | 49,012 | 5,383,000 | Bratislava | 452,278 |
| Slovenia | 7,821 | 20,256 | 1,987,000 | Ljubljana | 273,000 |
| Spain[4] | 195,365 | 505,992 | 39,270,000 | Madrid | 3,084,673 |
| Sweden | 173,732 | 449,964 | 8,846,000 | Ψ Stockholm | 1,148,953 |
| Switzerland | 15,940 | 41,284 | 7,114,600 | Bern | 321,932 |
| Ukraine | 233,090 | 603,700 | 50,500,000 | Kiev (Kyiv) | 2,630,000 |
| United Kingdom[5] | 93,784 | 242,900 | 58,784,000 | Ψ London | 7,074,265 |
| England | 50,351 | 130,410 | 48,903,000 | — | — |
| Northern Ireland | 5,467 | 14,160 | 1,649,000 | Ψ Belfast | 297,300 |
| Scotland | 30,420 | 78,789 | 5,137,000 | Ψ Edinburgh | 448,850 |
| Wales | 8,015 | 20,758 | 2,917,000 | Ψ Cardiff (Caerdydd) | 315,040 |
| Vatican City State | 0.2 | 0.44 | 1,000 | Vatican City | 766 |
| Yugoslavia | 39,449 | 102,173 | 10,597,000 | Belgrade | 1,338,856 |

[1]Excludes Svalbard and Jan Mayen Islands (approx. 24,101 sq. miles (62,422 sq. km) and 3,000 population)
[2]Includes Madeira (314 sq. miles) and the Azores (922 sq. miles)
[3]Includes Russia in Asia
[4]Includes Balearic Islands, Canary Islands, Ceuta and Melilla
[5]Excludes Isle of Man (221 sq. miles (572 sq. km), 69,788 population), and Channel Islands (75 sq. miles (194 sq. km), 142,949 population)

## OCEANIA

| Country/Territory | Area Sq. miles | Sq. Km | Population | Capital | Population of Capital |
|---|---|---|---|---|---|
| American Samoa *(USA)* | 77 | 199 | 58,000 | Ψ Pago Pago | 3,519 |
| Australia | 2,988,902 | 7,741,220 | 19,104,600 | Canberra | 309,500 |
| Norfolk Island | 14 | 36 | 1,772 | Ψ Kingston | — |
| Fiji | 7,056 | 18,274 | 809,000 | Ψ Suva | 141,273 |
| French Polynesia *(Fr.)* | 1,544 | 4,000 | 227,000 | Ψ Papeete | 36,784 |
| Guam *(USA)* | 212 | 549 | 145,780 | Agana | 1,139 |
| Kiribati | 280 | 726 | 81,000 | Tarawa | 17,921 |
| Marshall Islands | 70 | 181 | 61,000 | Dalap-Uliga-Darrit | 20,000 |
| Micronesia, Federated States Of | 271 | 702 | 130,000 | Palikir | — |
| Nauru | 8 | 21 | 11,000 | Ψ Nauru | — |
| New Caledonia *(Fr.)* | 7,172 | 18,575 | 193,000 | Ψ Noumea | 97,581 |
| New Zealand | 104,454 | 270,534 | 3,811,000 | Ψ Wellington | 346,700 |
| Cook Islands | 91 | 236 | 20,000 | Rarotonga | 9,281 |
| Niue | 100 | 260 | 2,000 | Alofi | — |
| Ross Dependency[1] | 175,000 | 453,248 | — | — | — |
| Tokelau | 5 | 12 | 2,000 | — | — |
| Northern Mariana Islands *(USA)* | 179 | 464 | 49,000 | Saipan | 52,706 |
| Palau *(USA)* | 177 | 459 | 17,000 | Koror | 10,493 |
| Papua New Guinea | 178,704 | 462,840 | 4,500,000 | Ψ Port Moresby | 173,500 |
| Pitcairn Islands *(UK)* | 2 | 5 | 54 | — | — |
| Samoa | 1,093 | 2,831 | 168,000 | Ψ Apia | 36,000 |
| Solomon Islands | 11,157 | 28,896 | 404,000 | Ψ Honiara | 40,000 |
| Tonga | 288 | 747 | 99,000 | Ψ Nuku'alofa | 29,018 |
| Tuvalu | 10 | 26 | 10,000 | Ψ Fongafale | 2,856 |
| Vanuatu | 4,706 | 12,189 | 178,000 | Ψ Port Vila | 26,100 |
| Wallis And Futuna Islands *(Fr.)* | 77 | 200 | 15,000 | Ψ Mata-Utu | — |

[1] Includes permanent ice shelf

# Time Zones

Standard time differences from the Greenwich meridian

- \+ hours ahead of GMT
- – hours behind GMT
- * may vary from standard time at some part of the year (Summer Time or Daylight Saving Time)
- ‡ some areas may keep another time zone
- *h* hours
- *m* minutes

| | *h* | *m* |
|---|---|---|
| Afghanistan | + 4 | 30 |
| *Albania | + 1 | |
| Algeria | + 1 | |
| *Andorra | + 1 | |
| Angola | + 1 | |
| Anguilla | – 4 | |
| Antigua and Barbuda | – 4 | |
| Argentina | – 3 | |
| *Armenia | + 4 | |
| Aruba | – 4 | |
| Ascension Island | 0 | |
| *Australia | +10 | |
| ACT, NSW (except Broken Hill area) Qld, Tas., Vic, Whitsunday Islands | | |
| *Broken Hill area (NSW) | + 9 | 30 |
| *Lord Howe Island | +10 | 30 |
| Northern Territory | + 9 | 30 |
| *South Australia | + 9 | 30 |
| Western Australia | + 8 | |
| *Austria | + 1 | |
| *Azerbaijan | + 4 | |
| *Bahamas | – 5 | |
| Bahrain | + 3 | |
| Bangladesh | + 6 | |
| Barbados | – 4 | |
| *Belarus | + 2 | |
| *Belgium | + 1 | |
| Belize | – 6 | |
| Benin | + 1 | |
| *Bermuda | – 4 | |
| Bhutan | + 6 | |
| Bolivia | – 4 | |
| *Bosnia-Hercegovina | + 1 | |
| Botswana | + 2 | |
| Brazil | | |
| western states | – 5 | |
| central states | – 4 | |
| N. and NE coastal states | – 3 | |
| *S. and E. coastal states, including Brasilia | – 3 | |
| Fernando de Noronha Island | – 2 | |
| British Antarctic Territory | – 3 | |
| British Indian Ocean Territory | + 5 | |
| Diego Garcia | + 6 | |
| British Virgin Islands | – 4 | |
| Brunei | + 8 | |
| *Bulgaria | + 2 | |
| Burkina Faso | 0 | |
| Burundi | + 2 | |

| | *h* | *m* |
|---|---|---|
| Cambodia | + 7 | |
| Cameroon | + 1 | |
| Canada | | |
| *Alberta | – 7 | |
| *‡British Columbia | – 8 | |
| *‡Labrador | – 4 | |
| *Manitoba | – 6 | |
| *New Brunswick | – 4 | |
| *Newfoundland | – 3 | 30 |
| *Northwest Territories | | |
| east of 85° W. | – 5 | |
| 85° W.–102° W. | – 6 | |
| *Nunavut | – 7 | |
| *Nova Scotia | – 4 | |
| Ontario | | |
| *east of 90° W. | – 5 | |
| west of 90° W. | – 5 | |
| *Prince Edward Island | – 4 | |
| Québec | | |
| east of 63° W. | – 4 | |
| *west of 63° W. | – 5 | |
| ‡Saskatchewan | – 6 | |
| *Yukon | – 8 | |
| Cape Verde | – 1 | |
| Cayman Islands | – 5 | |
| Central African Republic | + 1 | |
| Chad | + 1 | |
| *Chatham Islands | +12 | 45 |
| *Chile | – 4 | |
| China (inc. Hong Kong and Macao) | + 8 | |
| Christmas Island (Indian Ocean) | + 7 | |
| Cocos (Keeling) Islands | + 6 | 30 |
| Colombia | – 5 | |
| Comoros | + 3 | |
| Congo (Dem. Rep.) | | |
| Haut-Zaïre, Kasai, Kivu, Shaba | + 2 | |
| Kinshasa, Mbandaka | + 1 | |
| Congo-Brazzaville | + 1 | |
| Costa Rica | – 6 | |
| Côte d'Ivoire | 0 | |
| *Croatia | + 1 | |
| *Cuba | – 5 | |
| *Cyprus | + 2 | |
| *Czech Republic | + 1 | |
| *Denmark | + 1 | |
| *Færøe Islands | 0 | |
| *Greenland | – 3 | |
| Danmarkshavn, Mesters Vig | 0 | |
| *Scoresby Sound | – 1 | |
| *Thule area | – 4 | |
| Djibouti | + 3 | |
| Dominica | – 4 | |
| Dominican Republic | – 5 | |
| East Timor | + 9 | |
| Ecuador | – 5 | |
| Galápagos Islands | – 6 | |
| *Egypt | + 2 | |
| El Salvador | –6 | |
| Equatorial Guinea | + 1 | |
| Eritrea | + 3 | |
| Estonia | + 2 | |

| | *h* | *m* |
|---|---|---|
| Ethiopia | + 3 | |
| *Falkland Islands | – 4 | |
| Fiji | +12 | |
| *Finland | + 2 | |
| *France | + 1 | |
| French Guiana | – 3 | |
| French Polynesia | –10 | |
| Guadeloupe | – 4 | |
| Martinique | – 4 | |
| Réunion | + 4 | |
| Marquesas Islands | – 9 | 30 |
| Gabon | + 1 | |
| The Gambia | 0 | |
| *Georgia | + 3 | |
| *Germany | + 1 | |
| Ghana | 0 | |
| *Gibraltar | + 1 | |
| *Greece | + 2 | |
| Grenada | – 4 | |
| Guam | +10 | |
| Guatemala | – 6 | |
| Guinea | 0 | |
| Guinea-Bissau | 0 | |
| Guyana | – 4 | |
| Haïti | – 5 | |
| Honduras | – 6 | |
| *Hungary | + 1 | |
| Iceland | 0 | |
| India | + 5 | 30 |
| Indonesia | | |
| Java, Kalimantan (west and central), Madura, Sumatra | + 7 | |
| Bali, Flores, Kalimantan (south and east), Lombok, Sulawesi, Sumbawa, West Timor | + 8 | |
| Irian Jaya, Maluku, | + 9 | |
| *Iran | + 3 | 30 |
| *Iraq | + 3 | |
| *Ireland, Republic of | 0 | |
| *Israel | + 2 | |
| *Italy | + 1 | |
| Jamaica | – 5 | |
| Japan | + 9 | |
| *Jordan | + 2 | |
| *Kazakhstan | | |
| western | + 4 | |
| central | + 5 | |
| eastern | + 6 | |
| Kenya | + 3 | |
| Kiribati | +12 | |
| Line Islands | +14 | |
| Phoenix Islands | +13 | |
| Korea, North | + 9 | |
| Korea, South | + 9 | |
| Kuwait | + 3 | |
| *Kyrgyzstan | + 5 | |
| Laos | + 7 | |
| Latvia | + 2 | |
| *Lebanon | + 2 | |
| Lesotho | + 2 | |
| Liberia | 0 | |
| Libya | + 2 | |
| *Liechtenstein | + 1 | |

| | h | m |
|---|---|---|
| Line Islands not part of Kiribati | –10 | |
| Lithuania | + 1 | |
| *Luxembourg | + 1 | |
| *Macedonia | + 1 | |
| Madagascar | + 3 | |
| Malawi | + 2 | |
| Malaysia | + 8 | |
| Maldives | + 5 | |
| Mali | 0 | |
| *Malta | + 1 | |
| Marshall Islands | +12 | |
| Ebon Atoll | –12 | |
| Mauritania | 0 | |
| Mauritius | + 4 | |
| *Mexico | – 6 | |
| *Nayarit, Sinaloa, S. Baja California | – 7 | |
| Sonora | – 7 | |
| N. Baja California | – 8 | |
| Micronesia | | |
| Caroline Islands | +10 | |
| Kosrae, Pingelap, Pohnpei | +11 | |
| *Moldova | + 2 | |
| *Monaco | + 1 | |
| Mongolia | + 8 | |
| Montserrat | – 4 | |
| Morocco | 0 | |
| Mozambique | + 2 | |
| Myanmar | + 6 | 30 |
| *Namibia | + 1 | |
| Nauru | +12 | |
| Nepal | + 5 | 45 |
| *Netherlands | + 1 | |
| Netherlands Antilles | – 4 | |
| New Caledonia | +11 | |
| *New Zealand | +12 | |
| *Cook Islands | –10 | |
| Nicaragua | – 6 | |
| Niger | + 1 | |
| Nigeria | + 1 | |
| Niue | –11 | |
| Norfolk Island | +11 | 30 |
| Northern Mariana Islands | +10 | |
| *Norway | + 1 | |
| Oman | + 4 | |
| Pakistan | + 5 | |
| Palau | + 9 | |
| Panama | – 5 | |
| Papua New Guinea | +10 | |
| *Paraguay | – 4 | |
| Peru | – 5 | |
| Philippines | + 8 | |
| *Poland | + 1 | |
| *Portugal | 0 | |
| *Azores | – 1 | |
| kern;*Madeira | 0 | |
| Puerto Rico | – 4 | |
| Qatar | + 3 | |
| Réunion | + 4 | |
| *Romania | + 2 | |
| *Russia | | |
| Zone 1 | + 2 | |
| Zone 2 | + 3 | |
| Zone 3 | + 4 | |
| Zone 4 | + 5 | |
| Zone 5 | + 6 | |
| Zone 6 | + 7 | |
| Zone 7 | + 8 | |
| Zone 8 | + 9 | |
| Zone 9 | +10 | |
| Zone 10 | +11 | |
| Zone 11 | +12 | |
| Rwanda | + 2 | |
| St Helena | 0 | |
| St Christopher and Nevis | – 4 | |
| St Lucia | – 4 | |
| *St Pierre and Miquelon | – 3 | |
| St Vincent and the Grenadines | – 4 | |
| Samoa | –11 | |
| Samoa, American | –11 | |
| *San Marino | + 1 | |
| São Tomé and Princípe | 0 | |
| Saudi Arabia | + 3 | |
| Senegal | 0 | |
| Seychelles | + 4 | |
| Sierra Leone | 0 | |
| Singapore | + 8 | |
| *Slovakia | + 1 | |
| *Slovenia | + 1 | |
| Solomon Islands | +11 | |
| Somalia | + 3 | |
| South Africa | + 2 | |
| South Georgia | – 2 | |
| *Spain | + 1 | |
| *Canary Islands | 0 | |
| Sri Lanka | + 6 | |
| Sudan | + 3 | |
| Suriname | – 3 | |
| Swaziland | + 2 | |
| *Sweden | + 1 | |
| *Switzerland | + 1 | |
| *Syria | + 2 | |
| Taiwan | + 8 | |
| Tajikistan | + 5 | |
| Tanzania | + 3 | |
| Thailand | + 7 | |
| Togo | 0 | |
| *Tonga | +13 | |
| Trinidad and Tobago | – 4 | |
| Tristan da Cunha | 0 | |
| Tunisia | + 1 | |
| *Turkey | + 2 | |
| Turkmenistan | + 5 | |
| *Turks and Caicos Islands | – 5 | |
| Tuvalu | +12 | |
| Uganda | + 3 | |
| *Ukraine | + 2 | |
| United Arab Emirates | + 4 | |
| *United Kingdom | 0 | |
| *United States of America | | |
| Alaska | – 9 | |
| Aleutian Islands, east of 169° 30′ W. | – 9 | |
| Aleutian Islands, west of 169° 30′ W. | –10 | |
| eastern time | – 5 | |
| central time | – 6 | |
| Hawaii | –10 | |
| mountain time | – 7 | |
| Pacific time | – 8 | |
| Uruguay | – 3 | |
| Uzbekistan | + 5 | |
| Vanuatu | +11 | |
| *Vatican City State | + 1 | |
| Venezuela | – 4 | |
| Vietnam | + 7 | |
| Virgin Islands (US) | – 4 | |
| Yemen | + 3 | |
| *Yugoslavia (Fed. Rep. of) | + 1 | |
| Zambia | + 2 | |
| Zimbabwe | + 2 | |

*Source:* reproduced with permission from data produced by HM Nautical Almanac Office

## THE ANTARCTIC

The Antarctic is generally defined as the area lying within the Antarctic Convergence, the zone where cold northward-flowing Antarctic sea water sinks below warmer southward-flowing water. This zone is at about latitude 50° S. in the Atlantic Ocean and latitude 55°–62° S. in the Pacific Ocean. The continent itself lies almost entirely within the Antarctic Circle, an area of about 13.66 million sq. km (5.3 million sq. miles), 99.67 per cent of which is permanently ice-covered. The average thickness of the ice is 2,450 m (7,100 ft) but in places exceeds 4,500 m (14,500 ft). Some mountains protrude, the highest being Vinson Massif, 4,897 m (16,067 ft). The ice amounts to some 30 million cubic km (7.2 million cubic miles) and represents more than 90 per cent of the world's fresh water. Much of the sea freezes in winter, forming fast ice which breaks up in summer and drifts north as pack ice.

The most conspicuous physical features of the continent are its high inland plateau (much of it over 3,000 m (10,000 ft)), the Transantarctic Mountains and the mountainous Antarctic Peninsula and off-lying islands which extend northwards towards South America.

### CLIMATE

On land, summer temperatures range from just above freezing around the coast to –34° C (about –30° F) on the plateau, and in winter from –20° C (about –4° F) on the coast to –65° C (about –85° F) inland. Over a large area the maxima do not exceed –15° C (+5° F).

Precipitation is scant over the plateau but amounts to 25–76 cm (10–30 in) (water equivalent) along the coast and some scientific stations are permanently buried by snow. Some rain falls over the more northerly areas in summer. Gravity winds on the plateau slopes and cyclonic storms further north can both exceed 160 km/h (100 m.p.h.) and visibility can be reduced to zero in blizzards.

### FLORA AND FAUNA

Although a small number of flowering plants, ferns and clubmosses occur on the sub-Antarctic islands, only two (a grass and a pearlwort) extend south of 60° S. Antarctic vegetation is dominated by lichens and mosses, with a few liverworts, algae and fungi. Most of these occur around the coast or on islands.

The only land animals are tiny insects and mites with nematodes, rotifers, and tardigrades in the mosses, but large numbers of seals, penguins and other sea-birds go ashore to breed in the summer. The emperor penguin is the only species which breeds ashore throughout the winter. By contrast, the Antarctic seas abound with life, a wide variety of invertebrates (including krill) and fish providing food for the seals, penguins and other birds, and a residual population of whales.

In 1994 the International Whaling Commission agreed to establish a whale sanctuary around Antarctica in which commercial whaling will be banned for ten years.

### POTENTIAL RESOURCES

Minerals may be present in great variety but not in commercially exploitable concentrations in accessible localities. There are indications that off-shore hydrocarbons may be present but mostly below great depths of stormy, ice-infested seas. A 50-year ban on Antarctic mineral exploitation came into effect in January 1998 (*see* below).

Currently, the chief interest is in marine protein, including the shrimp-like krill already fished commercially by Japan and Poland. It is estimated that these could sustain a yield equal to the present total annual world fish catch.

### THE ANTARCTIC TREATY

The co-operative 12 nations (Argentina, Australia, Belgium, Chile, France, Japan, New Zealand, Norway, South Africa, the Soviet Union, the UK and the USA) pledged themselves to promote scientific and technical co-operation unhampered by politics, and the Antarctic Treaty was signed by the 12 states in 1959. The signatories agreed to establish free use of the Antarctic continent for peaceful scientific purposes; to freeze all territorial claims and disputes in the Antarctic; to ban all military activities in the area; and to prohibit nuclear explosions and the disposal of radioactive waste. Since then additional agreements have been reached to promote conservation and regulate tourism, waste disposal and pollution.

The Antarctic Treaty was defined as covering areas south of latitude 60° S., excluding the high seas but including the ice shelves, and came into force in 1961. It has since been signed by a further 31 states, 14 of which are active in the Antarctic and have therefore been accorded consultative status, bringing the number of consultative parties to 26. In 1998 an extension to the treaty came into effect, placing a 50-year ban on mining, oil exploration and mineral extraction in Antarctica. Furthermore, all tourists, explorers and expeditions will now need permission to enter the Antarctic.

### TERRITORIAL CLAIMS

Under the provisions of the Antarctic Treaty all territorial claims and disputes were frozen without the acceptance or denial of the claims of the various claimants. The US and Soviet governments also made it clear that although they had not made any specific territorial claims, they did not relinquish the right to make such claims.

Seven states have made claims in the Antarctic: Argentina claims the part of Antarctica between 74° W. and 25° W.; Chile that part between 90° W. and 53° W.; Britain claims the British Antarctic Territory, an area of 1,709,340 sq. km (660,000 sq. miles) between 20° and 80° W. longitude; France claims Terre Adélie, 432,000 sq. km (166,800 sq. miles) between 136° and 142° E.; Australia claims the Australian Antarctic Territory, 6,120,000 sq. km (2,320,000 sq. miles) between 160° and 45° E. longitude excluding Terre Adélie; Norway claims Queen Maud Land between 20° W. and 45° E.; and New Zealand claims the Ross Dependency, 450,000 sq. km (175,000 sq. miles) between 160° E. and 150° W. longitude. The Argentinian, British and Chilean claims overlap; the part of the continent between 90° W. and 150° W. is unclaimed by any state.

### SCIENTIFIC RESEARCH

There were 37 permanently occupied stations in 2000–1 operated by the following nations: Argentina (6), Australia (3), Brazil (1), Chile (4), China (2), France (1), Germany (1), India (1), Japan (2), New Zealand (1), Poland (1), Republic of Korea (1); Russia (4), South Africa (1), UK (2), Ukraine (1), Uruguay (2), USA (3, including one at the South Pole).

The staff of these stations and summer field-workers are the only people present on the continent and off-lying islands. There are no indigenous inhabitants.

# Currencies of the World

AND EXCHANGE RATES AGAINST £ STERLING

| Country/Territory | Monetary Unit | Average Rate to £ 14 September 2000 | Average Rate to £ 19 September 2001 |
|---|---|---|---|
| Afghanistan | Afghani (Af) of 100 puls | Af 6936.19 | Af 6945.45 |
| Albania | Lek (Lk) of 100 qindraka | Lk 215.387 | Lk 207.486 |
| Algeria | Algerian dinar (DA) of 100 centimes | DA 112.936 | DA 109.808 |
| American Samoa | Currency is that of the USA | US$ 1.4603 | US$ |
| Andorra* | French and Spanish currencies in use | – | Francs – 10.6435 |
| | | – | Peseta – 269.976 |
| Angola | Readjusted kwanza (Krzl) of 100 lwei | Krzl 10.7745 | Kzrl 34.3712 |
| Anguilla | East Caribbean dollar (EC$) of 100 cents | EC$ 3.9427 | EC$ |
| Antigua and Barbuda | East Caribbean dollar (EC$) of 100 cents | EC$ 3.9427 | EC$ 3.9480 |
| Argentina | Peso of 10,000 australes | Pesos 1.4593 | Pesos 1.4617 |
| Armenia | Dram of 100 louma | Dram 775.539 | Dram 809.898 |
| Aruba | Aruban florin | Florins 2.6139 | Florins 2.6174 |
| Ascension Island | Currency is that of St Helena | at parity with £ sterling | |
| Australia | Australian dollar ($A) of 100 cents | $A 2.5365 | $A 2.9507 |
| Norfolk Island | Currency is that of Australia | $A 2.5365 | $A 2.9507 |
| Austria* | Euro (€) of 100 cents/ Schilling of 100 Groschen | Schilling 22.3274 | € 1.5864/Schilling 21.8284 |
| Azerbaijan | Manat of 100 gopik | Manat 6391.52 | Manat 6862.10 |
| The Bahamas | Bahamian dollar (B$) of 100 cents | B$ 1.4603 | B$ 1.4622 |
| Bahrain | Bahraini dinar (BD) of 1,000 fils | BD 0.5505 | BD 0.5513 |
| Bangladesh | Taka (Tk) of 100 poisha | Tk 78.9266 | Tk 83.2724 |
| Barbados | Barbados dollar (BD$) of 100 cents | BD$ 2.9205 | BD$ 2.9098 |
| Belarus | Belarusian rouble of 100 kopeks | BYR 1486.54 (market rate) | BYR 2152.36 (market rate) |
| Belgium* | Euro (€) of 100 cents/ Belgian franc (or frank) of 100 centimes (centiemen) | Francs 65.4551 | € 1.5864/Francs 63.9924 |
| Belize | Belize dollar (BZ$) of 100 cents | BZ$ 2.9205 | BZ$ 2.8952 |
| Benin | Franc FCA | Francs 1064.35 | Francs 1040.57 |
| Bermuda | Bermuda dollar of 100 cents | $ 1.4603 | $ 1.4622 |
| Bhutan | Ngultrum of 100 chetrum (Indian currency is also legal tender) | Ngultrum 66.8065 | Ngultrum 70.1417 |
| Bolivia | Boliviano ($b) of 100 centavos | $b 9.0244 | $b 9.8260 |
| Bosnia-Hercegovina | Convertible marka | Marka 3.1735 | Marka 3.1026 |
| Botswana | Pula (P) of 100 thebe | P 7.5290 | P 8.5609 |
| Brazil | Real of 100 centavos | Real 2.6628 (floating rate) | Real 3.9136 (floating rate) |
| Brunei | Brunei dollar (B$) of 100 sen (fully interchangeable with Singapore currency) | B$ 2.5123 | $ 2.5386 |
| Bulgaria | Lev of 100 stotinki | Leva 3.1583 | Leva 3.0878 |
| Burkina Faso | Franc CFA | Francs 1064.35 | Francs 1040.57 |
| Burundi | Burundi franc of 100 centimes | Francs 1133.37 | Francs 1230.44 |
| Cambodia | Riel of 100 sen | Riel 5621.96 | Riel 5607.54 |
| Cameroon | Franc CFA | Francs 1064.35 | Francs 1040.57 |
| Canada | Canadian dollar (C$) 100 cents | C$ 2.1517 | C$ 2.2974 |
| Cape Verde | Escudo Caboverdiano of 100 centavos | Esc 181.384 | Esc 175.099 |
| Cayman Islands | Cayman Islands dollar (CI$) of 100 cents | CI$ 1.2168 | CI$ 1.1990 |
| Central African Republic | Franc CFA | Francs 1064.35 | Francs 1040.57 |
| Chad | Franc CFA | Francs 1064.35 | Francs 1040.57 |
| Chile | Chilean peso of 100 centavos | Pesos 822.632 | Pesos 1009.65 |
| China | Renminbi Yuan of 10 jiao or 100 fen | Yuan 12.0890 | Yuan 12.1024 |
| Hong Kong | Hong Kong (HK$) of 100 cents | HK$ 11.3886 | HK$ 11.4051 |
| Macao | Pataca of 100 avos | Pataca 11.7346 | Pataca 11.7459 |
| Colombia | Colombian peso of 100 centavos | Pesos 3234.45 | Pesos 3419.65 |
| The Comoros | Comorian franc (KMF) of 100 centimes | Francs 796.139 | Francs 804.423 |
| Congo, Dem. Rep. of | Congolese franc | CFr 6.5711 | Francs 1040.57 |
| Congo, Rep. of | Franc CFA | Francs 1064.35 | CFr 6.57980 |
| Costa Rica | Costa Rican colón (₡) of 100 céntimos | ₡ 447.275 | ₡ 485.845 |
| Côte d'Ivoire | Franc CFA | Francs 1064.35 | Francs 1040.57 |
| Croatia | Kuna of 100 lipa | Kuna 12.2506 | Kuna 11.9834 |
| Cuba | Cuban peso of 100 centavos | Pesos 30.6653 | Pesos 30.7062 |
| Cyprus | Cyprus pound (C£) of 100 cents | C£ 0.9289 | C£ 0.9085 |
| Czech Republic | Koruna (Kčs) of 100 haléřu | Kčs 57.3711 | Kčs 54.3953 |

| | | | |
|---|---|---|---|
| Denmark | Danish krone of 100 øre | Kroner 12.1033 | Kroner 11.8059 |
| Færøe Islands | Currency is that of Denmark | Kroner 12.1033 | Kroner 11.8059 |
| Dijbouti | Dijbouti franc of 100 centimes | Francs 253.646 | Francs 250.767 |
| Dominica | East Caribbean dollar (EC$) of 100 cents | EC$ 3.9427 | EC$ 3.9480 |
| Dominican Republic | Dominican Republic peso (RD$) of 100 centavos | RD$ 26.6350 | RD$ 23.8339 |
| East Timor | Currency is that of the USA | – | US$ 1.4622 |
| Ecuador | Currency is that of the USA (formerly sucre of 100 centavos) | Sucres 36506.3 (official rate) | US$ 1.4622 |
| Egypt | Egyptian pound (£E) of 100 piastres or 1,000 millièmes | £E 5.1365 | £E 6.2144 |
| El Salvador | El Salvador colón (₡) of 100 centavos | ₡ 12.7334 | ₡ 12.7972 |
| Equatorial Guinea | Franc CFA | Francs 1064.35 | Francs 1040.57 |
| Eritrea | Nakfa | – | – |
| Estonia | Kroon of 100 sents | Kroons 25.3740 | Kroons 24.8343 |
| Ethiopia | Ethiopian birr (EB) of 100 cents | EB 11.8894 | EB 12.2869 |
| Falkland Islands | Falkland pound of 100 pence | at parity with £ sterling | |
| Fiji | Fiji dollar (F$) of 100 cents | F$ 3.1608 | F$ 33.3461 |
| Finland* | Euro (€) of 100 cents/ Markka (Mk) of 100 penniä | Mk 9.6475 | € 1.5864/Mk 9.4319 |
| France* | Euro (€) of 100 cents/ Franc of 100 centimes | Francs 10.6435 | € 1.5864/Francs 10.4057 |
| French Guiana* | Currency is that of France | Francs 10.6435 | € 1.5864/Francs 10.4057 |
| French Polynesia | Franc CFP | Francs 195.498 | Francs 191.038 |
| Gabon | Franc CFA | Francs 1064.35 | Francs 1040.57 |
| The Gambia | Dalasi (D) of 100 butut | D 19.1294 | D 24.8940 |
| Georgia | Laria of 100 tetri | Laria 2.8986 | Laria 3.0412 |
| Germany* | Euro (€) of 100 cents/ Deutsche Mark (DM) of 100 Pfennige | DM 3.1735 | € 1.5864/DM 3.1026 |
| Ghana | Cedi of 100 pesewas | Cedi 10294.8 | Cedi 10367.0 |
| Gibraltar | Gibraltar pound of 100 pence | at parity with £ sterling | |
| Greece* | Euro (€) of 100 cents/ Drachma of 100 leptae | Drachmae 547.754 | € 1.5864/Drachmae 540.542 |
| Greenland | Currency is that of Denmark | Kroner 12.1033 | Kroner 11.8059 |
| Grenada | East Caribbean dollar (EC$) of 100 cents | EC$ 3.9427 | EC$ 3.9480 |
| Guadeloupe* | Currency is that of France | Francs 10.6435 | € 1.5864/Francs 10.4057 |
| Guam | Currency is that of the USA | US$ 1.4603 | US$ 1.4622 |
| Guatemala | Quetzal (Q) of 100 centavos | Q 11.4170 | Q 11.5390 |
| Guinea | Guinea franc of 100 centimes | Francs 2381.67 | Francs 2865.92 |
| Guinea-Bissau | Franc CFA | Francs 1064.35 | Francs 1040.57 |
| Guyana | Guyana dollar (G$) of 100 cents | G$ 266.204 | G$ 263.196 |
| Haiti | Gourde of 100 centimes | Gourdes 32.1255 | Gourdes 34.7273 |
| Honduras | Lempira of 100 centavos | Lempiras 21.7870 | Lempiras 22.7665 |
| Hungary | Forint of 100 fillér | Forints 424.071 | Forints 408.005 |
| Iceland | Icelandic króna (Kr) of 100 aurar | Kr 117.930 | Kr 146.220 |
| India | Indian rupee (Rs) of 100 paisa | Rs 66.8065 | Rs 70.1417 |
| Indonesia | Rupiah (Rp) of 100 sen | Rp 12083.6 | Rp 14000.6 |
| Iran | Rial | Rials 2551.79 (official rate) | Rials 2558.85 (official rate) |
| Iraq | Iraqi dinar (ID) of 1,000 fils | ID 0.4540 | ID 0.4548 |
| Ireland, Republic of* | Euro (€) of 100 cents/ Punt (IR£) of 100 pence | IR£ 1.2779 | € 1.5864/IR£ 1.2494 |
| Israel | Shekel of 100 agora | Shekels 5.8629 | Shekels 6.3767 |
| Italy* | Euro (€) of 100 cents/ Lira of 100 centesimi | Lire 3141.77 | € 1.5864/Lire 3071.56 |
| Jamaica | Jamaican dollar (J$) of 100 cents | J$ 61.3305 | J$ 66.6032 |
| Japan | Yen | Yen 154.422 | Yen 171.699 |
| Jordan | Jordanian dinar (JD) of 1,000 fils | JD 1.0382 | JD 1.0393 |
| Kazakhstan | Tenge | Tenge 208.356 | Tenge 215.989 |
| Kenya | Kenya shilling (Ksh) of 100 cents | Ksh 112.804 | Ksh 115.368 |
| Kiribati | Australian dollar ($A) of 100 cents | $A 2.5365 | $A 2.9507 |
| Korea, Dem. People's Rep. of | Won of 100 chon | Won 3.2126 | Won 3.2169 |
| Korea, Republic of | Won | Won 1614.53 | Won 1896.47 |
| Kuwait | Kuwaiti dinar (KD) of 1,000 fils | KD 0.4493 | KD 0.4458 |
| Kyrgyzstan | Som | Som 70.1436 | Som 69.7818 |
| Laos | Kip (K) of 100 at | K 11046.8 | K11112.7 |
| Latvia | Lats of 100 santims | Lats 0.8872 | Lats 0.9031 |
| Lebanon | Lebanese pound (L£) of of 100 piastres | L£ 2210.82 | L£ 2214.14 |
| Lesotho | Loti (M) of 100 lisente | M 10.1670 | M 12.6772 |
| Liberia | Liberian dollar (L$) of 100 cents | L$ 1.4603 | L$ 1.4622 |

| | | | |
|---|---|---|---|
| Libya | Libyan dinar (LD) of 1,000 dirhams | LD 0.737 | LD 0.9411 |
| Liechtenstein | Swiss franc of 100 rappen (or centimes) | Francs 2.5143 | Francs 2.3486 |
| Lithuania | Litas of 100 centas | Litas 5.8425 | Litas 5.8474 |
| Luxembourg* | Euro (€) of 100 cents/ Luxembourg franc (LF) of 100 centimes (Belgian currency is also legal tender) | LF 65.4551 | € 1.5864/LF 63.9924 |
| Macedonia | Denar of 100 deni | Den 95.4931 | Den 96.2675 |
| Madagascar | Franc malgache(FMG) of 100 centimes | FMG 9588.00 | FMG 9011.54 |
| Malaŵi | Kwacha (K) of 100 tambala | MK 89.1265 | MK 90.0204 |
| Malaysia | Malaysian dollar (ringgit) (M$) of 100 sen | M$ 5.5490 (official rate) | M$ 5.5564 (official rate) |
| Maldives | Rufiyaa of 100 laaris | Rufiyaa 17.1872 | Rufiyaa 17.2101 |
| Mali | Franc CFA | Francs 1064.35 | Francs 1040.57 |
| Malta | Maltese lira (LM) of 100 cents of 1,000 mils | LM 0.6534 | LM 0.6461 |
| Marshall Islands | Currency is that of the USA | US$ 1.4603 | US$ 1.4622 |
| Martinique* | Currency is that of France | Francs 10.6435 | € 1.5864/Francs 10.4057 |
| Mauritania | Ouguiya (UM) of 5 khoums | UM 352.490 | UM 374.353 |
| Mauritius | Mauritius rupee of 100 cents | Rs 38.1856 | Rs 43.2446 |
| Mayotte* | Currency is that of France | Francs 10.6435 | € 1.5864/Francs 10.4057 |
| Mexico | Peso of 100 centavos | Pesos 13.4343 | Pesos 13.8105 |
| Micronesia, Federated States of | Currency is that of the USA | US$ 1.4603 | US$ 1.4622 |
| Moldova | Moldovan leu of 100 bani | MDL 18.0706 | MDL 18.8258 |
| Monaco* | Currency is that of France | Francs 10.6435 | € 1.5864/Francs 10.4057 |
| Mongolia | Tugrik of 100 möngö | Tugriks 1565.87 | Tugriks 1608.42 |
| Montserrat | East Caribbean dollar (EC$) of 100 cents | EC$ 3.9427 | EC$ 3.9480 |
| Morocco | Dirham (DH) of 100 centimes | DH 15.7328 | DH 16.3950 |
| Mozambique | Metical (MT) of 100 centavos | MT 23510.1 | MT 31645.7 |
| Myanmar | Kyat (K) of 100 pyas | K 9.1290 | K 9.66380 |
| Namibia | Namibian dollar of 100 cents | at parity with SA Rand | |
| Nauru | Australian dollar ($A) of 100 cents | $A 2.5365 | $A 2.9507 |
| Nepal | Nepalese rupee of 100 paisa | Rs 106.774 | Rs 111.595 |
| The Netherlands* | Euro (€) of 100 cents/ Gulden (guilder) of florin of 100 cents | Guilders 3.5757 | € 1.5864/Guilders 3.4959 |
| Netherlands Antilles | Netherlands Antilles guilder of 100 cents | Guilders 2.5847 | Guilders 2.6027 |
| New Caledonia | Franc CFP | Francs 195.498 | Francs 191.038 |
| New Zealand | New Zealand dollar (NZ$) of 100 cents | NZ$ 3.4130 | NZ$ 3.5703 |
| Cook Islands | Currency is that of New Zealand | NZ$ 3.4130 | NZ$ 3.5703 |
| Niue | Currency is that of New Zealand | NZ$ 3.4130 | NZ$ 3.5703 |
| Tokelau | Currency is that of New Zealand | NZ$ 3.4130 | NZ$ 3.5703 |
| Nicaragua | Córdoba (C$) of 100 centavos | C$ 17.0192 | C$ 19.9152 |
| Niger | Franc CFA | Francs 1064.35 | Francs 1040.57 |
| Nigeria | Naira (N) of 100 kobo | N 151.355 | N 164.732 |
| Northern Mariana Islands | Currency is that of the USA | US$ 1.4603 | US$ 1.4622 |
| Norway | Krone of 100 øre | Kroner 13.1471 | Kroner 12.6693 |
| Oman | Rial Omani (OR) of 1,000 baisas | OR 0.5622 | OR 0.5630 |
| Pakistan | Pakistan rupee of 100 paisa | Rs 79.9560 | Rs 93.9829 |
| Palau | Currency is that of the USA | US$ 1.4603 | US$ 1.4622 |
| Panama | Balboa of 100 centésimos (US notes are also in circulation) | Balboa 1.4603 | Balboa 1.4622 |
| Papua New Guinea | Kina (K) of 100 toea | K 3.8916 | K 5.0640 |
| Paraguay | Guarani (Gs) of 100 céntimos | Gs 5117.45 | Gs 6465.12 |
| Peru | New Sol of 100 cénts | New Sol 5.0693 | New Sol 5.1155 |
| The Philippines | Philippine peso (P) of 100 centavos | P 65.9303 | P 75.2302 |
| Pitcairn Islands | Currency is that of New Zealand | NZ$ 3.4130 | NZ$ 3.5703 |
| Poland | Złoty of 100 groszy | Złotych 6.3915 | Złotych 6.1832 |
| Portugal* | Euro (€) of 100 cents/ Escudo (Esc) of 100 centavos | Esc 325.300 | € 1.5864/Esc 318.031 |
| Puerto Rico | Currency is that of the USA | US$ 1.4603 | US$ 1.4622 |
| Qatar | Qatar riyal of 100 dirhams | Riyals 5.3157 | Riyals 5.3234 |
| Réunion* | Currency is that of France | Francs 10.6435 | € 1.5864/Francs 10.4057 |
| Romania | Leu of 100 bani | Lei 33666.1 | Lei 44238.9 |
| Russia | Rouble of 100 kopeks | Rbl 40.5468 | Rbl 43.0764 |
| Rwanda | Rwanda franc of 100 centimes | Francs 524.271 | Francs 638.981 |
| St Christopher and Nevis | East Caribbean dollar (EC$) of 100 cents | EC$ 3.9427 | EC$ 3.9480 |
| St Helena | St Helena pound (£) of 100 pence | at parity with £ sterling | |

| | | | |
|---|---|---|---|
| St Lucia | East Caribbean dollar (EC$) of 100 cents | EC$ 3.9427 | EC$ 3.9480 |
| St Pierre and Miquelon* | Currency is that of France | Francs 10.6435 | € 1.5864/Francs 10.4057 |
| St Vincent and the Grenadines | East Caribbean dollar (EC$) of 100 cents | EC$ 3.9427 | EC$ 3.9480 |
| Samoa | Tala (S$) of 100 sene | S$ 45.112 | S$ 5.0507 |
| San Marino* | San Marino and Italian currencies are in circulation | Lire 3141.77 | € 1.5864/Lire 3071.56 |
| São Tomé and Princípe | Dobra of 100 centavos | Dobra 3490.00 | Dobra 13068.0 |
| Saudi Arabia | Saudi riyal (SR) of 20 qursh or 100 halala | SR 5.4769 | SR 5.4842 |
| Senegal | Franc CFA | Francs 1064.35 | Francs 1040.57 |
| Seychelles | Seychelles rupee of 100 cents | Rs 8.3660 | Rs 8.0531 |
| Sierra Leone | Leone (Le) of 100 cents | Le 2976.21 | Le 2846.90 |
| Singapore | Singapore dollar (S$) of 100 cents | S$ 2.5123 | S$ 2.5386 |
| Slovakia | Koruna (Sk) of 100 halierov | Kčs 69.3437 | Kčs 69.3560 |
| Slovenia | Tolar (SIT) of 100 stotin | Tolars 339.107 | Tolars 348.749 |
| Solomon Islands | Solomon Islands dollar (SI$) of 100 cents | SI$ 7.3836 | SI$ 7.8402 |
| Somalia | Somali shilling of 100 cents | Shillings 3825.86 | Shillings 3830.96 |
| South Africa | Rand (R) of 100 cents | R 10.1670 | R 12.6772 |
| Spain* | Euro (€) of 100 cents/ Peseta of 100 céntimos | Pesetas 269.976 | € 1.5864/Pesetas 263.943 |
| Sri Lanka | Sri Lankan rupee of 100 cents | Rs 114.119 | Rs 131.795 |
| Sudan | Sudanese dinar (SD) of 100 piastres | SD 377.913 | SD 378.271 |
| Suriname | Surinamese guilder of 100 cents | Guilders 1182.07 | Guilders 1434.42 |
| Swaziland | Lilangeni (E) of 100 cents (South African currency is also in circulation) | at parity with SA Rand | |
| Sweden | Swedish krona of 100 öre | Kronor 13.6183 | Kronor 15.4366 |
| Switzerland | Swiss franc of 100 rappen (or centimes) | Francs 2.5143 | Francs 2.3486 |
| Syria | Syrian pound (S£) of 100 piastres | S£ 76.6632 | S£ 75.8151 |
| Taiwan | New Taiwan dollar NT$) of 100 cents | NT$ 45.3846 | NT$ 50.5483 |
| Tajikistan | Somoni of 100 dirams | – | TJS 3.5341 |
| Tanzania | Tanzanian shilling of 100 cents | Shillings 1166.74 | Shillings 1302.82 |
| Thailand | Baht of 100 satang | Baht 59.6878 | Baht 64.5854 |
| Togo | Franc CFA | Francs 10.6435 | Francs 1040.57 |
| Tonga | Pa'anga (T$) of 100 seniti | T$ 2.5365 | T$ 2.9507 |
| Trinidad and Tobago | Trinidad and Tobago dollar (TT$) of 100 cents | TT$ 9.0828 | TT$ 8.8463 |
| Tristan da Cunha | Currency is that of the UK | – | |
| Tunisia | Tunsian dinar of 1,000 millimes | Dinars 2.0456 | Dinars 2.0712 |
| Turkey | Turkish lira (TL) of 100 kurus | TL 952995.7 | TL 2186722 |
| Turkmenistan | Manat of 100 tenge | – | – |
| Turks and Caicos Islands | US dollar (US$) | US$ 1.4603 | US$ 1.4622 |
| Tuvalu | Australian dollar ($A) of 100 cents | $A 2.5365 | $A 2.9507 |
| Uganda | Uganda shilling of 100 cents | Shilling 2507.98 | Shillings 2554.46 |
| Ukraine | Hryvna of 100 kopiykas | UAH 7.9620 | UAH 7.8115 |
| United Arab Emirates | UAE dirham (Dh) of 100 fils | Dirham 5.3635 | Dirham 5.3705 |
| United Kingdom | Pound sterling (£) of 100 pence | | |
| United States of America | US dollar (US$) of 100 cents | US$ 1.4603 | US$ 1.4622 |
| Uruguay | Uruguayan peso of 100 centésimos | Pesos 18.0487 | Pesos 20.0066 |
| Uzbekistan | Sum of 100 tiyin | Sum 1131.69 | Sum 617.341 |
| Vanatu | Vatu of 100 centimes | Vatu 204.654 | Vatu 213.335 |
| Vatican City State* | Italian currency is legal tender | Lire 3141.77 | € 1.5864/Lire 3071.56 |
| Venezuela | Bolívar (Bs) of 100 céntimos | Bs 1005.46 | Bs 1088.61 |
| Vietnam | Dông of 10 hào or 100 xu | Dông 20618.7 | Dông 21928.6 |
| Virgin Islands, British | US dollar (US$) (£ sterling and EC$ also circulate) | US$ 1.4603 | US$ 1.4622 |
| Virgin Islands, US | Currency is that of the USA | US$ 1.4603 | US$ 1.4622 |
| Wallis and Futuna Islands | Franc CFP | Francs 195.498 | Francs 191.038 |
| Yemen | Riyal of 100 fils | Riyals 237.145 | Riyals 247.594 |
| Yugoslavia | New dinar of 100 paras | New Dinars 17.7813 | New Dinars 98.4090 |
| Zambia | Kwacha (K) of 100 ngwee | K 4840.74 | K 5468.64 |
| Zimbabwe | Zimbabwe dollar (Z$) of 100 cents | Z$ 60.8129 | Z$ 80.8963 |

* The euro is now the legal currency in these countries. Euro notes and coins will be introduced from 1 January 2002 and will circulate alongside national currencies for between four weeks and two months, after which time national notes and coins will cease to be legal tender.

# Countries of the World: A–Z

## AFGHANISTAN

*Dı Afgānistān Islāmī Dawlat (Pushtu)/*
*Dowlat-e Eslâmî-ye Afqânestân (Dari)*
The Islamic Republic of Afghanistan

AREA – 251,773 sq. miles (652,090 sq. km). Neighbours: Iran (west), Pakistan (south), Tajikistan, Uzbekistan and Turkmenistan (north), Pakistan and China (east)
POPULATION – 25,869,000 (1997 UN estimate): Pushtuns (38 per cent) predominate in the south and west; Tajiks (25 per cent); Hazaras (19 per cent) in the centre; Uzbeks (6 per cent) in the north; Aimaqs (4 per cent); Baluchis (0.5 per cent). The principal languages are Dari (a form of Persian) and Pushtu
CAPITAL – Kābol (Kabul) (population, 1,424,400, 1988)
MAJOR CITIES – Herāt (177,300); Jalālābād (55,000); Qandahār (225,500); Mazār-i-Sharīf (130,600) (1988 UN estimates)
CURRENCY – Afghani (Af) of 100 puls
NATIONAL ANTHEM – Sorūd-e-Melli
NATIONAL DAY – 19 August
NATIONAL FLAG – Three horizontal stripes of green, white, black with the national arms in the centre in gold
LIFE EXPECTANCY (years) – male 45.3; female 47.2
POPULATION GROWTH RATE – 4.5 per cent (1999)
POPULATION DENSITY – 33 per sq. km (1998)
URBAN POPULATION – 21.9 per cent (2000 estimate)

Mountains, chief among which are the Hindu Kush, cover three-quarters of the country. There are three great river basins, the Oxus, Helmand, and Kābol. The climate is dry, with extreme temperatures.

### HISTORY AND POLITICS

In December 1979 Soviet troops invaded Afghanistan and installed Babrak Karmal as head of state. Armed Islamic resistance groups, the mujahidin, fought against Soviet and Afghan forces until the government collapsed in April 1992. Mujahidin forces overran Kābol and declared an Islamic state.

The new government appointed Burhanuddin Rabbani as interim president, but infighting between factions of the mujahidin resumed in December 1992. In the winter of 1994–5, divided mujahidin forces suffered heavy defeats at the hands of the Taliban (armed Islamic students), which extended its power across half of the country and seized Kābol in September 1996. The forces of the former government were forced northwards. The United Islamic Front for the Salvation of Afghanistan (UIFSA) or Northern Alliance was formed by the four main mujahidin factions. The Taliban, thought to be backed by Pakistan and Saudi Arabia, imposed strict Shari'ah law.

Peace talks between the Taliban and UIFSA resumed in March 1999, but soon collapsed; a further round was conducted in May 2000. Fighting continues throughout the country.

The United Nations imposed limited sanctions on Afghanistan on 19 December 2000 for refusing to extradite Osama bin Laden, an Islamic terrorist. On 8 March 2001 troops began the destruction of statues deemed idolatrous by the Taliban, among them the world's largest standing Buddha in Bamiyan.

#### POLITICAL SYSTEM

The National Assembly was abolished in 1992 and no new legislature has been established. While most countries continue to recognise the government of Burhanuddin Rabbani, the Taliban form the de facto government of more than nine-tenths of the country.

Afghanistan is divided into 29 provinces; those under Taliban control are governed through an interim council (*shura*).

#### DE FACTO HEAD OF STATE

*Leader of the Taliban*, Mohammad Omar

SUPREME COUNCIL *as at July 2001*
Chair, *vacant*
*Vice-Chair*, Mohammad Hasan Akhond
*Agriculture*, Ahmadollah Moti
*Borders*, Habibollah Mangal
*Central Statistics*, Mohammad Omar Faruqi
*Civil Aviation*, Akhtar Mohammad Mansur
*Communications*, Ahmadollah Nanai
*Construction Affairs*, Agha Lalay
*Defence*, Obeydollah Akhond
*Director-General of the Administrative Affairs Department*, Mohammad Sayd Haqqani
*Director-General of Alms-giving Department*, Hafez Mohebollah
*Education*, Amir Khan Motaqi
*Finance*, Abdol Wasay Aghajan Motasem
*Foreign Affairs*, Wakil Ahmad Motawakkil
*Hajj and Endowment Affairs*, Sayd Ghaysoddin Agha
*Health*, Mohammad Abas Akhond
*Higher Education*, Din Mohammad Hanif
*Information, Culture*, Qodratollah Jamal Akhond
*Internal Affairs*, Abdul Razzaq Akhond
*Justice*, Nuroddin Torabi
*Labour and Social Affairs*, Mohammad Mir
*Martyrs and Refugee Affairs*, Abdol Raqib
*Mines and Industries*, Ahmed Jan
*Planning*, Mohammad Taher Anwari
*Public Works*, Sadoddin Sayed
*Rural Development*, Sediqollah
*Security*, Mohammad Fazel
*Telecommunications*, Ahmadollah Motee

EMBASSY OF THE ISLAMIC STATE OF AFGHANISTAN
31 Prince's Gate, London SW7 1QQ
Tel: 020-7589 8891
*Ambassador Extraordinary and Plenipotentiary*, new appointment awaited
*Minister-Counsellor and Chargé d'Affaires*, Ahmad Wali Masud

BRITISH EMBASSY

Karte Parwan, Kābol
Staff were withdrawn from post in February 1989.

### ECONOMY

The economy has been devastated by the political upheavals of the last 20 years. Traditional industries have diminished as the narcotics trade has grown. In 1999 around 4,600 tonnes of opium were produced; following a Taliban *fatwa* (religious edict) in July 2000 decreeing that the cultivation of the opium poppy was unislamic, production fell to 3,200 tonnes in 2000, which accounted for three-quarters of total world production.

By the end of 2000 one million people were thought to be close to starvation due to continuing fighting and crop failures caused by three successive years of drought. Strained relations with the Taliban authorities have hampered international aid efforts.

Agriculture and sheep raising were traditionally the principal industries. Silk, woollen and hair cloths and carpets were manufactured. Salt, silver, copper, coal, iron, lead, rubies, lapis lazuli, gold, chrome, barite, uranium, and talc are found.

There are thought be considerable fuel reserves. US and Saudi Arabian companies have attempted to negotiate with the Taliban and mujahidin for permission to construct an oil pipeline from Pakistan to Turkmenistan crossing Afghanistan.

GDP – US$5,976 million (1997); US$523 per capita (1998)
ANNUAL AVERAGE GROWTH OF GDP – 6.0 per cent (1996)
INFLATION RATE – 56.7 per cent (1991); estimated to be 400 per cent in 1996

### TRADE

Trade is now largely limited to narcotics, but in the past exports have been Persian lambskins (Karakul), dried fruits, nuts, cotton, raw wool, carpets, spice and natural gas, while the imports are chiefly oil, cotton yarn and piece goods, tea, sugar, machinery and transport equipment.

The UN sanctions imposed in December 2000 banned arms sales to the Taliban and halted international flights by the national air carrier, Ariana. In 1995 imports totalled US$50 million and exports US$26 million.

| *Trade with UK* | 1999 | 2000 |
|---|---|---|
| Imports from UK | £3,624,000 | £3,251,000 |
| Exports to UK | 1,769,000 | 8,493,000 |

## COMMUNICATIONS

Main roads run from Kābol to Kandahar, Herat, Maimana via Mazār-ī-Sharīf and Faizabad via Khanabad. Roads cross the border with Pakistan at Chaman and via the Khyber Pass, and there are roads from Herat to the borders of Central Asia and Iran. Much of the country's road system has been damaged during the fighting.

In 1982 the Afghan and Uzbek shores of the River Oxus were linked by a road and rail bridge which joins the Afghan port of Hairatan and the Uzbek port of Termez.

## EDUCATION

Education is free and nominally compulsory, elementary schools having been established in most centres; there are secondary schools in large urban areas and four universities, in Kābol (established 1932), Jalālābād (established 1962), Balkh and Herāt (both established 1988). Kābol's 26 newspapers were closed by the Taliban and women were prohibited from teaching or studying at schools and universities; in late 1999, the Taliban allowed schooling for girls under the age of 12.

ILLITERACY RATE – 63.7 per cent (2000)
ENROLMENT (percentage of age group) – primary 29 per cent (1993); secondary 14 per cent (1993); tertiary 1.8 per cent (1990)

---

## ALBANIA
*Republika e Shqipërisë*

---

AREA – 11,099 sq. miles (28,748 sq. km). Neighbours: Montenegro (north), Kosovo and Macedonia (east), Greece (south)
POPULATION – 3,375,000 (1997 UN estimate). Muslim (70 per cent), Greek Orthodox (20 per cent), Roman Catholic (10 per cent). The language is Albanian
CAPITAL – Tirana (population, 244,153, 1990)
CURRENCY – Lek (Lk) of 100 qindarka
NATIONAL ANTHEM -Rreth flamurit të për bashkuar (The flag that united us in the struggle)
NATIONAL DAY – 28 November
NATIONAL FLAG – Black two-headed eagle on a red field
LIFE EXPECTANCY (years) – male 65.1; female 72.7
POPULATION GROWTH RATE – 0.6 per cent (1999)
POPULATION DENSITY – 132 per sq. km (1998)
URBAN POPULATION – 41.6 per cent (2000 estimate)
ENROLMENT (percentage of age group) – primary 100 per cent (1996); tertiary 12.0 per cent (1996)

## HISTORY AND POLITICS

Albania was under Turkish suzerainty from 1468 until 1912, when independence was declared. After a period of unrest, a republic was declared in 1925, and in 1928 a monarchy. The King went into exile in 1939 when the country was occupied by the Italians; Albania was liberated in November 1944. Elections in 1945 resulted in a Communist-controlled Assembly; the King was deposed in absentia and a republic declared in January 1946.

From 1946 to 1991 Albania was a one-party, Communist state. In March 1991 multiparty elections took place. Rioting broke out in January 1997 following the collapse of several pyramid investment schemes. Anti-government protests, taking the form of armed rebellion, spread throughout the country.

Following the abandonment of the Rambouillet peace talks on the future of Kosovo, NATO commenced air operations against Yugoslavia in March 1999. Yugoslavia responded by actively expelling hundreds of thousands of Kosovar Albanians, with the majority fleeing to Albania. In April 1999, Albania granted NATO unrestricted access to Albania's airspace, ports and military infrastructure. There were several incursions into Albanian territory by Serb troops. By mid-May 1999, over 400,000 Kosovar Albanians had taken refuge in Albania and over 10,000 NATO troops were stationed there. In June 1999 the refugees began returning home following the end of air operations and the entry of NATO forces into Kosovo. By the end of 1999, nearly all of the refugees had left Albania and the number of NATO troops stationed in the country had fallen to 2,000.

The most recent general election took place on 24 June and 8 July 2001.

### HEAD OF STATE

*President*, Prof. Rexhep Mejdani, *elected by parliament* 24 July 1997

### COUNCIL OF MINISTERS *as at July 2001*

Prime Minister, *Ilir Meta (SP)*
*Deputy PM, Labour and Social Affairs*, Makbule Ceco
*Agriculture and Food*, Lufter Xhuveli (AP)
*Culture, Youth and Sport*, Esmeralda Uruci
*Defence*, Ismail Lleshi (SP)
*Economic Co-operation and Trade*, Ermelinda Meksi (SP)
*Education and Science*, Et'hem Ruka (SP)
*Finance*, Anastas Angjeli (SP)
*Foreign Affairs*, Paskal Milo (SDP)
*Health*, Leonard Solis (HRUP)
*Interior*, Ilir Gjoni
*Justice*, Arben Imami
*Local Government*, Bashkim Fino
*Minister of State to the Prime Minister*, Ndre Legisi
*Public Economy and Privatisation*, Mustafa Muci
*Public Works*, Spartak Poci (SP)
*Transport*, Viktor Doda (Ind.)

AP Agrarian Party; HRUP Human Rights Union Party; SP Socialist Party; SDP Social Democratic Party; Ind. Independent

### EMBASSY OF THE REPUBLIC OF ALBANIA

2nd Floor, 24 Buckingham Gate, London SW1E 6LB
Tel: 020-7828 8897
*Ambassador Extraordinary and Plenipotentiary*, HE Agim Besim Fagu, apptd 1997

BRITISH EMBASSY
Rruga Skenderbeg 12, Tirana
Tel: (00 355) (42) 34973/4/5
*Ambassador Extraordinary and Plenipotentiary*, HE Dr Peter January, apptd 1999
BRITISH COUNCIL CENTRE MANAGER, E. Agolli, c/o The British Embassy; e-mail: evis@icc.al.eu.org

## DEFENCE

The Army has 600 main battle tanks and 103 armoured personnel carriers. The Navy has 21 patrol and coastal combatant vessels at four bases. The Air Force has 98 combat aircraft.

MILITARY EXPENDITURE – 3.6 per cent of GDP (1999)
MILITARY PERSONNEL – Armed Forces yet to be reconstituted following civil unrest: Army c.40,000, Navy 2,500, Air Force 4,500

## ECONOMY

Much of the country is mountainous and nearly a half is covered by forest. The main crops are wheat, maize, sugar beet, potatoes and fruit. There are large chromium deposits. The principal industries are agricultural product processing, textiles, oil products and cement.

Since April 1992, the government has imposed austerity measures in an attempt to reduce the budget deficit and to cut inflation. Up to US$1,200 million worth of personal savings were lost in the collapse of several fraudulent pyramid savings schemes in January 1997, and the value of the lek fell heavily.

Remittances from 500,000 overseas workers remain an important source of revenue.

GNP – US$3,146 million (1999); US$870 per capita (1999)
GDP – US$2,264 million (1997); US$972 per capita (1998)
ANNUAL AVERAGE GROWTH OF GDP – 9.1 per cent (1996)
INFLATION RATE – 0.4 per cent (1999)
UNEMPLOYMENT – 9.1 per cent (1991)
TOTAL EXTERNAL DEBT – US$821 million (1998)

### TRADE

Exports include crude oil, minerals (bitumen, chrome, nickel, copper), tobacco, fruit and vegetables. In 1999 imports totalled US$829 million and exports US$205 million. In 1999 Albania had a trade deficit of US$663 million and a current account deficit of US$155 million.

| *Trade with UK* | 1999 | 2000 |
|---|---|---|
| Imports from UK | £12,062,000 | £6,994,000 |
| Exports to UK | 793,000 | 2,915,000 |

## ALGERIA

*Al-Jumhūriyya al-Jazā'iriyya ad-Dimuqratiyya ash-Sha'-biyya*

AREA – 919,595 sq. miles (2,381,741 sq. km). Neighbours: Morocco and Western Sahara (west), Mauritania and Mali (south-west), Niger (south-east), Libya and Tunisia, (east)
POPULATION – 29,950,000 (1997 UN estimate); 22,971,558 (1987 census).
Arabic is the official language although French and Berber languages are also spoken. The state religion is Sunni Islam
CAPITAL – ΨAlgiers (Al-Jazā'ir) (population, 1,507,241, 1987). It is one of the principal ports of the Mediterranean

MAJOR CITIES – ΨAnnaba; ΨBejaia; Blida (El Boulaida); Constantine (Qacentina); ΨMostaganem; ΨOran (Wahran); Setif; Sidi-Bel-Abbès; ΨSkikda; Tizi Ouzou; Tlemcen
CURRENCY – Algerian dinar (DA) of 100 centimes
NATIONAL ANTHEM – Qassaman bin nazilat il-mahiqat (We swear by the lightning that destroys)
NATIONAL DAY – 1 November
NATIONAL FLAG – Divided vertically green and white with a red crescent and star over all in the centre
LIFE EXPECTANCY (years) – male 68.2; female 68.8
POPULATION GROWTH RATE – 2.4 per cent (1999)
POPULATION DENSITY – 13 per sq. km (1998)
ILLITERACY RATE – 36.7 per cent (2000)
ENROLMENT (percentage of age group) – primary 94 per cent (1996); secondary 56 per cent (1996); tertiary 12.0 per cent (1996)

## HISTORY AND POLITICS

Algeria was annexed to France from 1830until gaining its independence in 1962 following an eight-year armed liberation struggle by the Front de Libération Nationale (FLN). Ben Bella was elected president in 1963, but was deposed in 1965 by Col. Houari Boumediène, who was formally elected president in 1976. Boumediène died in 1978 and was succeeded by Chadli Bendjedid.

A new constitution agreed by referendum in 1988 moved Algeria towards pluralism. However, the 1991 legislative elections were abandoned in anticipation of the success of the opposition Islamic Salvation Front (FIS), which had campaigned on a radical 'Islamist' platform. President Bendjedid resigned and a Higher Committee of State (HCS), headed by former FLN veteran Mohammed Boudiaf, took power. Gen. Liamine Zeroual was elected president for a five-year term in November 1995, but announced his intention to stand down from office in September 1998. Abdelaziz Bouteflika was elected president on 15 April 1999. The other candidates decided to boycott the election some days before it took place, saying that the military had intervened to rig the vote in his favour.

Multiparty elections on 5 June 1997 were won by the newly-formed National Democratic Rally (RND), which captured 155 seats. Hamas (Movement for a Society of Peace) (MSP) won 69 seats; the FLN 64 seats; Annahda (Renaissance Movement) 34; Rally for Culture and Democracy 19; Socialist Forces Front 19. Elections to the National Council (the upper house) took place in December 1997 and were dominated by RND, which won 80 of the 96 elected seats.

### INSURGENCY

Since the abortive elections in 1992, the FIS-backed Islamic Salvation Army (AIS) and the more extreme Armed Islamic Group (GIA) have waged an armed campaign against the regime in favour of an Islamic state. The two groups have targeted the military and security forces, their secular supporters in the population, and foreign expatriates, resulting in up to 100,000 deaths since 1992. The AIS announced in June 1999 that it was renouncing the armed struggle following negotiations with the government; the resulting peace plan was approved by 98 per cent of the electorate in a referendum which was held on 16 September 1999. On 5 January 2000, the AIS announced that it had agreed to disband. Attacks have continued, however, and it was estimated that around 2,500 civilians were killed in 2000.

Rioting broke out in the Berber-populated Kabyle region in April and May 2001, resulting in about 80 deaths.

### POLITICAL SYSTEM

The legislature is bicameral. The National Assembly (the lower chamber) has 380 members, directly elected for a five-year term. The *Majlis el-Umma* (Council of the Nation) is the upper chamber, with a third of its 144 members appointed by the president; two-thirds are indirectly elected for six-year terms, of which half are re-elected every three years.

### HEAD OF STATE

*President*, Abdelaziz Bouteflika, *elected* April 1999

### COUNCIL OF MINISTERS *as at July 2001*

*Head of Government*, Ali Benflis
*Agriculture*, Said Barkat
*Commerce*, Abdelhamid Temmar
*Communications and Culture*, Mohamed Abbou
*Defence*, The President
*Energy and Mines*, Chakib Khelil
*Finance*, Mourad Medelci
*Fisheries and Marine Resources*, Omar Ghoul
*Health and Population*, Abdelhamid Aberkane
*Higher Education and Scientific Research*, Ammar Sakhri
*Housing and Construction*, Abdelmadjid Tebboune
*Industry and Restrucuturing*, Abdelmajid Menasra (MSP)
*Institutions and Small and Medium-Sized Enterprises*, Abdelkadar Semari
*Labour and Social Security*, Mohamed Larbi
*Ministers delegate*, Abdelkader Messahel (*African Affairs*); Abdelaziz
Ziari (*Algerian Expatriate Community and Regional Co-operation*); Mohamed Terbache
(*Budget*); Amine Kherbi (*Foreign Affairs*); Daho Ould-Kablia (*Local*
Communities*); Mohamed-Ali Boughazi (*Scientific Research*); Abdelouahabe Keramane*
*(Treasury and Financial Reform)*
*Ministers of State*, Abdelaziz Belkhadem (*Foreign Affairs*); Noureddine Zerhouni (*Interior and Local Communities*); Ahmed Ouyahia (*Justice*)
*National Education*, Boubekeur Benbouzid (RND)
*Participation and Co-ordination of Reforms*, Noureddine Boukrouh
*Post and Telecommunications*, Mohamed Maghlaoui
*Public Works*, Abdelmalek Sellal
*Regional Development and the Environment*, Cherif Rahmani
*Relations with Parliament*, Abdelwahab Derbal
*Religious Affairs and Endowments*, Bouabdellah Ghalamallah (RND)
*Secretary-General*, Ahmed Noui (RND)
*Small and Medium-sized Enterprises*, Abdelkader Semari
*Social Action and National Solidarity*, Djamel Ould Abbès
*Tourism and Handicrafts*, Lakhdar Dorbani (MSP)
*Trade*, Abdelhamid Temmar
*Transport*, Salim Saâdi
*Vocational Training*, Karim Younès (FLN)
*War Veterans*, Mohamed Cherif Abbas
*Water Resources*, Aïssa Abdellaoui
*Youth and Sports*, Abdelhamid Berchiche

### ALGERIAN EMBASSY

54 Holland Park, London W11 3RS
Tel: 020-7221 7800
*Ambassador Extraordinary and Plenipotentiary*, HE Ahmed Attaf, apptd 2001

### BRITISH EMBASSY

7 Chemin des Glycines,
BP 08, Alger-Gare 16000, Algiers
Tel: (00 213) (2) 230092
*Ambassador Extraordinary and Plenipotentiary*, HE William Sinton, OBE, apptd 1999

### BRITISH COUNCIL,

c/o The British Embassy, e-mail: hafida.gabouze@algiers.mail.fco.gov.uk

## DEFENCE

The Army has 1,006 main battle tanks and 680 armoured personnel carriers. The Navy has two submarines, three frigates and 17 patrol and coastal vessels. The Air Force has 214 combat aircraft and 65 armed helicopters.
MILITARY EXPENDITURE – 6.6 per cent of GDP (1999)
MILITARY PERSONNEL – 124,000: Army 107,000, Navy 7,000, Air Force 10,000, Paramilitaries 181,200
CONSCRIPTION DURATION – 18 months

## ECONOMY

The main industry is the hydrocarbons industry. Oil and natural gas are pumped from the Sahara to terminals on the coast before being exported; the gas is first liquefied at liquefaction plants at Skikda and Arzew, although pipelines serve Libya and Italy direct. In November 1996 a 750-mile gas pipeline to Spain was opened, enabling Algeria to double its gas exports to Morocco, Spain, Germany and France. Its initial annual capacity of 8,000 million cubic metres was projected to rise to 20,000 million cubic metres a year by 2000.

Other major industries include a steel industry, motor vehicles, building materials, paper making, chemical products and metal manufactures. Most major industrial enterprises are still under state control.

Prior to 1989 the economy was centrally planned and state-controlled in most sectors. Economic reform, begun in 1987, was speeded up in 1988 and now includes industrial and financial sectors. In 1994 the government finally accepted full economic reform and liberalisation under a reform programme agreed with the IMF. The government has cut the budget deficit, devalued the currency and freed price controls. The first stock exchange in Algiers opened on 15 December 1997.
GNP – US$46,548 million (1999); US$1,550 per capita (1999)
GDP – US$32,255 million (1997); US$1,689 per capita (1998)
ANNUAL AVERAGE GROWTH OF GDP – 4.0 per cent (1996)
INFLATION RATE – 2.5 per cent (1999)
UNEMPLOYMENT – 26.3 per cent (1998)
TOTAL EXTERNAL DEBT – US$30,665 million (1998)

### TRADE

Export earnings come mainly from crude oil and liquefied natural gas sales. Algeria's main trading partners are France, Italy, USA, Spain and Germany.

In 1991 Algeria had a trade surplus of US$5,468 million and a current account surplus of US$2,367 million. In 1996 imports totalled US$8,840 million and exports US$12,620 million.

| *Trade with UK* | 1999 | 2000 |
|---|---|---|
| Imports from UK | £110,780,000 | £105,025,000 |
| Exports to UK | 162,388,000 | 442,343,000 |

## ANDORRA
*Principat d'Andorra*

AREA – 181 sq. miles (468 sq. km). Neighbours: Spain and France
POPULATION – 65,000 (1998); less than one-quarter of the population are native Andorrans. The official language is Catalan, but French and Spanish (Castilian) are also spoken. The established religion is Roman Catholicism
CAPITAL – Andorra la Vella (population, 21,721, 1996)
CURRENCY – French and Spanish currencies in use
NATIONAL ANTHEM - El gran Carlemany, mon pare (Great Charlemagne, my father)
NATIONAL DAY – 8 September
NATIONAL FLAG – Three vertical bands, blue, yellow, red; Andorran coat of arms frequently imposed on central (yellow) band but not essential
POPULATION GROWTH RATE – 4.3 per cent (1999)
POPULATION DENSITY – 154 per sq. km (1998)
URBAN POPULATION – 93.0 per cent (2000 estimate)

### HISTORY AND POLITICS

Andorra is a small, neutral principality formed by a treaty in 1278. The first elections under the new constitution were held in December 1993, and on 20 January 1994 the first sovereign government of Andorra took office.

#### POLITICAL SYSTEM

Under a new constitution promulgated in May 1993, Andorra became an independent, democratic parliamentary co-principality, with sovereignty vested in the people rather than in the two co-princes, as had previously been the case. The constitution enables Andorra to establish an independent judiciary and to carry out its own foreign policy, whilst its people may now join trade unions and political parties. The two co-princes, the President of the French Republic and the Spanish Bishop of Urgel, remain heads of state but now only have the power to veto treaties with France and Spain which affect the state's borders and security. The co-princes are represented by Permanent Delegates of whom one is the French Prefect of the Pyrénées Orientales department at Perpignan and the other is the Spanish Vicar-General of the diocese of Urgel.

Andorra has a unicameral legislature of 28 members known as the *Consell General de las Valls d'Andorra* (Valleys of Andorra General Council). Fourteen members are elected on a national list basis and 14 in seven dual-member constituencies based on Andorra's seven parishes. The Council appoints the head of the executive government, who designates the members of his government.

*Permanent French Delegate*, Pierre Steinmetz
*Permanent Episcopal Delegate*, Nemesi Marqués Oste

#### EXECUTIVE GOVERNMENT *as at July 2001*

Prime Minister, *Marc Forné Molné*
*Agriculture and the Environment*, Olga Adellach Coma
Chef de Cabinet, *Jordi Guillamet Anton*
*Economy*, Miquel Alvarez Marfany
*Education, Youth and Sports*, Pere Cervós Cardona
*Finance*, Mireia Maestre Cortadella
*Foreign Affairs*, Juli Minoves Triquell
*Health and Social Security*, Mònica Codina Tort
*Justice and Home Affairs*, Jordi Visent Guitart
*Public Works*, Jordi Serra Malleu
*Secretary-General*, Joaquima Sol Ordis
*Tourism and Culture*, Enric Pujal Areny

ANDORRAN DELEGATION, 63 Westover Road, London SW18 2RF. Tel: 020-8874 4806
BRITISH AMBASSADOR – HE Peter Torry, resident at Madrid

### ECONOMY

Potatoes are produced in the highlands and tobacco in the valleys. The economy is largely based on tourism, banking, commerce, tobacco, construction and forestry; a third of the country is classified as forest. Andorra has negotiated a customs union with the European Union which came into force in 1991. The economy is now diversifying rapidly into offshore financial services.
GDP – US$951 million (1997); US$14,690 per capita (1998)
ANNUAL AVERAGE GROWTH OF GDP - 2.3 per cent (1996)

| *Trade with UK* | 1999 | 2000 |
|---|---|---|
| Imports from UK | £10,966,000 | £10,584,000 |
| Exports to UK | 340,000 | 93,000 |

### COMMUNICATIONS

A road into the valleys from Spain is open all year round, and that from France is closed only occasionally in winter. There are two radio stations in Andorra, one privately owned and Radio Andorra, operated by the government, as well as a state-owned television station.

## ANGOLA
*República de Angola*

AREA – 481,354 sq. miles (1,246,700 sq. km). Neighbours: Democratic Republic of Congo (north and east), Zambia (east), Namibia (south). The enclave of Cabinda is separated from the rest of Angola by the Democratic Republic of Congo and also borders on the Republic of Congo–Brazzaville
POPULATION – 12,352,000 (1997 UN estimate). Main ethnic groups are Ovimbundu (37 per cent); Kimbundu (25 per cent); Bakongo (13 per cent). The official language is Portuguese
CAPITAL – ΨLuanda (population, 475,328, 1970; now estimated at 3,000,000)
CURRENCY – Readjusted kwanza (Kzrl) of 100 lwei
NATIONAL ANTHEM – Angola Avante (Advance Angola)
NATIONAL DAY – 11 November (Independence Day)
NATIONAL FLAG – Red and black with a yellow star, machete and cog-wheel
LIFE EXPECTANCY (years) – male 46.3; female 49.1
POPULATION GROWTH RATE - 3.4 per cent (1999)
POPULATION DENSITY – 10 per sq. km (1998)
URBAN POPULATION – 34.2 per cent (2000 estimate)
ENROLMENT (percentage of age group) – tertiary 0.7 per cent (1991)

### HISTORY AND POLITICS

After a Portuguese presence of five centuries, and an anti-colonial war since 1961, Angola became independent on 11 November 1975 in the midst of civil war. The Popular Movement for the Liberation of Angola (MPLA) took control early in 1976, but remained under pressure from the National Union for the Total Independence of Angola

(UNITA). A peace agreement was signed between the government and UNITA in 1991 and multiparty legislative and presidential elections took place in 1992, which were won by the MPLA and its leader, José Eduardo dos Santos. UNITA refused to accept the results and the civil war resumed in 1993.

UNITA and the MPLA government signed a peace agreement (the Lusaka Protocol) in 1994. A government of national reconciliation was formed in April 1997 and 70 UNITA legislators took up their seats in parliament, although UNITA's leader, Dr Jonas Savimbi, rejected an offer of the vice-presidency. UNITA also refused to allow central state administration to be restored in key areas and fighting resumed in May 1997.

On 31 October 1997 the UN Security Council ordered sanctions against UNITA for failing to meet its obligations under the Lusaka Protocol. UNITA returned much of its territory to government control in December, and in March 1998 UNITA became a legitimate political party. Three of its representatives were appointed governors of provinces of Angola.

Fighting continued and the UN Security Council adopted a resolution in September 1998 which urged the rejection of military force by all parties and named UNITA as 'the primary cause of the crisis in Angola'. In February 1999 the UN Security Council voted to withdraw the UN Observer Mission in Angola, the UN Secretary-General Kofi Annan having declared that the country was on the verge of a catastrophic breakdown and that there was no more peace to keep. In December 1999 Namibia allowed the Angolan government to use its territory and armed forces for a joint operation against the UNITA rebels. The UN Security Council adopted a further resolution on 13 April 2000, which called for an investigation into allegations that several countries had violated sanctions imposed on UNITA. Government forces succeeded in capturing large tracts of UNITA-controlled territory in late 2000.

### SECESSION

In the northern enclave of Cabinda, the Front for the Liberation of the Cabinda Enclave (FLEC) fought a 20-year war of independence until the signing of a cease-fire with the government in September 1995, which was followed by the initialling of a peace agreement in April 1996.

### POLITICAL SYSTEM

The MPLA, formerly a Marxist-Leninist party, was the sole legal party until early 1991 when a multiparty system was adopted. The constitution declares Angola to be a democratic state and provides for a president, who appoints a Council of Ministers to assist him, and a 223-member National Assembly. In November 1996 the National Assembly adopted a constitutional amendment extending its mandate for between two and four years.

### HEAD OF STATE

*President*, José Eduardo dos Santos, *re-elected* 30 September 1992

### COUNCIL OF MINISTERS *as at July 2001*

*Prime Minister*, vacant
*Agriculture and Rural Development*, Gilberto Buta Lutukuta (MPLA)
*Assistance and Social Reintegration*, Albino Malungo (MPLA)
*Commerce*, Victorino Domingos Hossi (UNITA)
*Defence*, Gen. Kundi Paihama (MPLA)
*Education and Culture*, Antonio Burity da Silva Neto (MPLA)
*Energy and Water*, Luis Felipe da Silva (MPLA)
*Ex-Servicemen and War Veterans*, Pedro José van Dúnem (MPLA)
*Family and Women's Advancement*, Cândida Celeste da Silva (MPLA)
*Finance*, Julio Bessa (MPLA)
*Fisheries and Environment*, Maria de Fatima Monteiro Jardim (MPLA)
*Foreign Affairs*, João Bernardo de Miranda (MPLA)
*Geology and Mines*, Manuel Antonio Africano (MPLA)
*Governor of the National Bank*, Aguinaldo Jaime (MPLA)
*Health*, Albertina Julia Hamukuya (UNITA)
*Hotel Industry and Tourism*, Jorge Alicerces Valentim (UNITA)
*Industry*, Joaquim Duarte da Costa David (MPLA)
*Information*, Pedro Hendrick vaal Neto (MPLA)
*Interior*, Fernando da Piedade Dias dos Santos (MPLA)
*Justice*, Paulo Tjipilica (FDA)
*Oil*, José Maria Botelho de Vasconcelos (MPLA)
*Planning*, Ana Dias Lourenço (MPLA)
*Posts and Telecommunications*, Licinio Tavares Ribeiro (MPLA)
*Public Administration, Employment and Social Welfare*, Antonio Pitra Costra Neto (MPLA)
*Public Works and Town Planning*, António Henriques da Silva (MPLA)
*Science and Technology*, João Baptista Ngandagina (MPLA)
*Territorial Administration*, Fernando Faustino Muteka (MPLA)
*Transport*, André Luis Brandão (MPLA)
*Youth and Sports*, José Marcos Barrica (MPLA)

FDA Angolan Democratic Forum; MPLA Popular Movement for the Liberation of Angola; UNITA National Union for the Total Independence of Angola

EMBASSY OF THE REPUBLIC OF ANGOLA
98 Park Lane, London W1Y 3TA
Tel: 020-7495 1752
*Ambassador Extraordinary and Plenipotentiary*, HE Antonio da Costa Fernandes, apptd 1993

BRITISH EMBASSY
Rua Diogo Cão 4 (Caixa Postal 1244), Luanda
Tel: (00 244) (2) 334582
*Ambassador Extraordinary and Plenipotentiary*, HE Caroline Elmes, CMG, apptd 1998

## DEFENCE

The Army has 560 main battle tanks and 100 armoured personnel carriers. The Navy has seven patrol vessels. The Air Force has 104 combat aircraft and 40 armed helicopters.

MILITARY EXPENDITURE - 16.5 per cent of GDP (1999)
MILITARY PERSONNEL – 107,500: Army 100,000, Navy 1,500, Air Force 6,000, Paramilitaries 10,000

## ECONOMY

Angola has valuable oil and diamond deposits and exports of these two commodities account for over 90 per cent of total exports. Principal agricultural crops are cassava, maize, bananas, coffee, palm oil and kernels, cotton and sisal. Coffee, sisal, maize and palm oil are exported; exports also include mahogany and other hardwoods from the tropical rain forests in the north of the country.

The government is attempting to reform the socialist economy by free market reforms but is making little progress, with high inflation and a collapsing economy.

The government raised fuel prices by 1,600 per cent in February 2000 in response to IMF demands to remove state subsidies on petroleum products.

In 1996 Angola had a trade surplus of US$3,055 million and a current account surplus of US$3,266 million.

GNP – US$3,276 million (1999); US$220 per capita (1999)
GDP – US$7,768 million (1997); US$528 per capita (1998)
ANNUAL AVERAGE GROWTH OF GDP - 8.6 per cent (1996)
INFLATION RATE – 286.1 per cent (1999)
TOTAL EXTERNAL DEBT – US$12,173 million (1998)

| *Trade with UK* | 1999 | 2000 |
|---|---|---|
| Imports from UK | £66,353,000 | £76,252,000 |
| Exports to UK | 10,818,000 | 5,556,000 |

## ANTIGUA AND BARBUDA
*State of Antigua and Barbuda*

AREA – 171 sq. miles (442 sq. km); Antigua 108 sq. miles (279 sq. km); Barbuda 62 sq.miles (160 sq. km); Redonda $^{1}/_{2}$ sq. mile (1.2 sq. km)
POPULATION – 67,000 (1997 UN estimate); 65,962, Antigua 64,562, Barbuda 1,400 (official census 1991); the official language is English
CAPITAL – ΨSt John's (population, 22,342, 1991)
MAJOR TOWNS – The town of Barbuda is Codrington
CURRENCY – East Caribbean dollar (EC$) of 100 cents
NATIONAL ANTHEM – Fair Antigua and Barbuda
NATIONAL DAY – 1 November (Independence Day)
NATIONAL FLAG – Red with an inverted triangle divided black over blue over white, with a rising gold sun on the white band
LIFE EXPECTANCY (years) – male 71.4; female 76.8
POPULATION GROWTH RATE – 0.6 per cent (1999)
POPULATION DENSITY – 151 per sq. km (1998)
URBAN POPULATION – 36.8 per cent (2000 estimate)
MILITARY EXPENDITURE – 0.6 per cent of GDP (1999)
MILITARY PERSONNEL – 150: Army 125, Navy 45

Antigua is part of the Leeward Islands in the eastern Caribbean. It is distinguished from the rest of the Leeward group by its absence of high hills and forest, and a drier climate than most of the West Indies. Barbuda is very flat with a large lagoon.

### HISTORY AND POLITICS

Antigua was first settled by the English in 1632, and was granted to Lord Willoughby by Charles II. It became internally self-governing in 1967 and fully independent on 1 November 1981.

The Antigua Labour party won the general election of 9 March 1999 and a sixth successive term of office with 12 seats in the House of Representatives compared to four seats for the United Progressive Party.

#### POLITICAL SYSTEM

Antigua and Barbuda is a constitutional monarchy with Queen Elizabeth II as Head of State, represented by the Governor-General. There is a Senate of 17 appointed members and a House of Representatives of 17 members elected every five years. The Attorney-General may be appointed.
*Governor-General*, HE Sir James Carlisle, GCMG

#### CABINET *as at July 2001*

*Prime Minister, Finance, Foreign Affairs*, Lester Bird
*Agriculture, Lands and Fisheries*, Vere Bird Jr
*Attorney-General*, Gertel Thorn
Economic Development, Trade, Industry,Commerce, *Hilroy Humphreys*
*Education, Culture and Technology*, Dr Rodney Williams
*Health and Social Improvementt*, John E. St Luce
*Home Affairs, Urban Renewal and Rural Development*, Bernard Percival
*Information, Broadcasting, Sports, Carnivals*, Guy Yearwood
*Labour and Co-operatives, Public Safety*, Steadroy Benjamin
*Ministers of State*, Jeremy Longford (*Economic Development*); George B. Walker (*Information, Broadcasting and Public Works*)
*Planning, Implementation and Public Service Affairs*, Gaston Browne
*Public Utilities, Housing, Transportation and Aviation*, Robin Yearwood
*Public Works, Communications and Insurance, Minister of State for Finance*, Asot Michael
*Tourism and Environment*, Molwyn Joseph

#### HIGH COMMISSION FOR ANTIGUA AND BARBUDA

15 Thayer Street, London W1U 3JT
Tel: 020-7486 7073
*High Commissioner*, HE Sir Ronald M. Sanders, KCN, CMG, apptd 1995

#### BRITISH HIGH COMMISSION

11 Old Parham Road (PO 483), St John's
Tel: (00 1 268) 462 0008/9
*High Commissioner*, HE John White, resident at Bridgetown, Barbados
*Resident Acting High Commissioner*, Sandra Murphy

### ECONOMY

The economy is largely based on tourism and related services, and offshore financial services. Agricultural production includes livestock, sea island cotton, mixed market gardening and fishing.

In 1996 Antigua and Barbuda had a trade deficit of US$263 million and a current account deficit of US$40 million. In 1998 imports totalled US$388 million and exports US$15 million.
GNP – US$606 million (1999); US$8,450 per capita (1998)
GDP – US$584 million (1997); US$9,370 per capita (1998)
ANNUAL AVERAGE GROWTH OF GDP – 6.0 per cent (1996)
INFLATION RATE – 1.0 per cent (1985)
UNEMPLOYMENT – 6.0 per cent (1991)

| *Trade with UK* | 1999 | 2000 |
|---|---|---|
| Imports from UK | £32,387,000 | £24,419,000 |
| Exports to UK | 1,628,000 | 2,601,000 |

## ARGENTINA
*República Argentina*

AREA – 1,073,518 sq. miles (2,780,400 sq. km). Neighbours: Bolivia (north), Paraguay, Brazil and Uruguay (north-east), Chile (west) from which it is separated by the Cordillera de los Andes
POPULATION – 36,571,000 (1997 UN estimate); 32,370,298 (1991 census). The language is Spanish
CAPITAL – ΨBuenos Aires (population, 11,298,030, 1991; metropolitan area 2,965,403)
MAJOR CITIES – Córdoba (1,208,554); ΨLa Plata (642,979); ΨMar del Plata (512,880); Mendoza (773,113); ΨRosario (1,118,905); San Miguel de Tucumán (622,324)
CURRENCY – Peso of 10,000 australes
NATIONAL ANTHEM – Oid Mortales! (Hear, oh mortals!)
NATIONAL DAY – 25 May
NATIONAL FLAG – Horizontal bands of blue, white, blue; gold sun in centre of white band
LIFE EXPECTANCY (years) – male 70.6; female 77.8
POPULATION GROWTH RATE – 1.3 per cent (1999)
POPULATION DENSITY – 13 per sq. km (1998)

URBAN POPULATION – 89.9 per cent (2000 estimate)

Argentina occupies the greater portion of the southern part of the South American continent, and extends from Bolivia to Cape Horn.

## HISTORY AND POLITICS

The estuary of La Plata was discovered in 1515 by Juan Díaz de Solís and the region was subsequently colonised by the Spanish. Spain ruled the territory from the 16th century until 1810. In 1816, after a long campaign of liberation conducted by General José de San Martín, independence was declared by the Congress of Tucumán.

President Juan Domingo Perón was overthrown in 1955, and there followed 18 years of instability until 1973 when he was recalled from exile. Perón died within a year and was succeeded by his widow, Vice-President María Estela Martínez de Perón. A coup led to the establishment of a military junta in 1976. Following the Falkland Islands defeat in 1982, the President, Gen. Galtieri, resigned and the Army appointed Gen. Bignone. A civilian president was elected in 1983. In the October 1999 general election the Radical Civic Union-National Solidarity Front (UCR-Frepaso) Alliance became the largest party in the Chamber of Deputies and took office on 10 December 1999.

Vice-President Carlos Alvárez resigned in October 2000 in protest at the president's decision not to dismiss two senior officials involved in a bribery allegation.

### POLITICAL SYSTEM

The 1853 constitution was amended in 1994. Power is vested in the president who appoints the Cabinet and is directly elected for a once-renewable four-year term. A presidential candidate must win at least 45 per cent of the vote, or 40 per cent with a 10 per cent lead over the nearest challenger, to gain victory in the first round of voting; if no candidate meets these criteria, a second round must be held. The legislature consists of a 72-member (three for each province) Senate and a 257-member Chamber of Deputies. A half of the Chamber of Deputies is elected every two years. Deputies serve for a four-year term. Senators have served for a nine-year term, with a third being elected every three years, but the terms of all sitting senators will end in December 2001, after which all members will be directly elected by the provinces for a six-year term, with one-third renewable every two years.

### FEDERAL STRUCTURE

The republic is divided into 23 provinces, each with an elected Governor and legislature, and one federal district (Buenos Aires), with an elected mayor and autonomous government.

| *Province* | *Area (sq. km)* | *Population (1991 census)* | *Capital* |
|---|---|---|---|
| Buenos Aires | 307,571 | 12,594,974 | La Plata |
| Catamarca | 102,602 | 264,234 | Catamarca |
| Chaco | 99,633 | 839,677 | Resistencia |
| Chubut | 224,686 | 357,189 | Rawson |
| Córdoba | 165,321 | 2,766,683 | Córdoba |
| Corrientes | 88,199 | 795,594 | Corrientes |
| Entre Ríos | 78,781 | 1,020,257 | Paraná |
| Federal Capital | 200 | 2,965,403 | Buenos Aires |
| Formosa | 72,066 | 398,413 | Formosa |
| Jujuy | 53,219 | 512,329 | San Salvador de Jujuy |
| La Pampa | 143,440 | 259,996 | Santa Rosa |
| La Rioja | 89,680 | 229,729 | La Rioja |
| Mendoza | 148,827 | 1,412,481 | Mendoza |
| Misiones | 29,801 | 788,915 | Posadas |
| Neuquén | 94,078 | 388,833 | Neuquén |
| Rio Negro | 203,013 | 506,772 | Viedma |
| Salta | 155,488 | 866,153 | Salta |
| San Juan | 89,651 | 528,715 | San Juan |
| San Luis | 76,748 | 286,458 | San Luis |
| Santa Cruz | 243,943 | 159,839 | Rio Gallegos |
| Santa Fé | 133,007 | 2,798,422 | Santa Fé |
| Santiago del Estero | 136,351 | 671,988 | Santiago del Estero |
| Tierra del Fuego | 21,571 | 69,369 | Ushuaia |
| Tucumán | 22,524 | 1,142,105 | San Miguel de Tucumán |

### HEAD OF STATE

*President*, Fernando de la Rúa, *elected* 24 October 1999, *sworn in* 10 December 1999
*Vice-President*, vacant

### CABINET *as at July 2001*

*Cabinet Chief*, Chrystian Gabriel Colombo
*Defence*, José Horacio Jaunarena
*Economy and Finance*, Domingo Cavallo
*Education*, Andrés Guillermo Delich
*Foreign Affairs, International Trade, Culture*, Adalberto Rodríguez Giavarini
*Infrastructure and Housing*, Carlos Manuel Bastos
*Interior*, Ramón Bautista Mestre
*Justice*, Jorge Enrique de la Rua
*Labour*, Patricia Bullrich
*Public Health*, Héctor Lombardo
*Social Affairs*, Juan Pablo Cafiero

### EMBASSY OF THE ARGENTINE REPUBLIC

65 Brook Street, London W1Y 1YE
Tel: 020-7318 1300
*Ambassador Extraordinary and Plenipotentiary*, HE Vicente Berasategui, apptd 2000
*Defence Attaché*, Col. Juan Manuel Durante
*Counsellor (Economic and Commercial Affairs)*, Gustavo Martino
*Cultural Attaché, Secretary*, Marcos Bednarski

### BRITISH EMBASSY

Dr Luis Agote 2412/52, 1425 Buenos Aires
Tel: (00 54) (11) 4576 2222
*Ambassador Extraordinary and Plenipotentiary*, HE Sir Robin Christopher, KBE, CMG, apptd 2000
*Deputy Head of Mission and Minister*, Dominic Asquith
*Air Attaché*. Gp Capt. T. Brewer, OBE
*Defence, Naval and Military Attaché*, Col. P. A. Reynolds
*First Secretary (Commercial)*, H. Deas
*Cultural Attaché and British Council Director*, P. Dick, Marcelo T. de Alvear 590, C1058AAF Buenos Aires; e-mail: info@britishcouncil.org.ar
BRITISH CHAMBER OF COMMERCE, Av. Corrientes 457, 10 piso, 1043 Buenos Aires

## DEFENCE

The Army has 200 main battle tanks, 160 armoured infantry fighting vehicles, 449 armoured personnel carriers and 41 helicopters. The Navy has three submarines, six destroyers, seven frigates, 15 patrol and coastal vessels, 21 combat aircraft and 14 armed helicopters. The Air Force has 133 combat aircraft and 27 armed helicopters.
MILITARY EXPENDITURE – 1.9 per cent of GDP (1999)
MILITARY PERSONNEL – 71,100: Army 41,400, Navy 17,200, Air Force 12,500, Paramilitaries 31,240

## ECONOMY

A large proportion of the land is still held in large estates devoted to cattle raising but the number of small farms is increasing. The principal crops are wheat, maize, oats, barley, rye, linseed, sunflower seed, alfalfa, sugar, fruit and cotton. Argentina is pre-eminent in the production of beef, mutton and wool. There is an oil refinery in San Lorenzo (Santa Fé province). Natural gas is also produced. Coal, lead, zinc, tungsten, iron ore, sulphur, mica and salt are the other chief minerals being exploited. There are small worked deposits of beryllium, manganese, bismuth, uranium, antimony, copper, kaolin, arsenate, gold, silver and tin. Coal is produced at the Rio Turbio mine in the province of Santa Cruz.

Meat-packing is one of the principal industries; flour-milling, sugar-refining, and the wine industry are also important. In recent years progress has been made by the textile, plastic and machine tool industries and engineering, especially in the production of motor vehicles and steel manufactures.

Measures were taken in July 2000 to stimulate the economy and reduce the rising unemployment rate. A bill passed in October declared an economic state of emergency in the country and in December 2000 a package of economic austerity measures was introduced in an attempt to tackle the budget deficit.

GNP – US$276,097 million (1999); US$7,600 per capita (1999)
GDP – US$323,548 million (1997); US$8,257 per capita (1998)
Annual Average Growth of GDP – 4.3 per cent (1996)
Inflation Rate – 1.2 per cent (1999)
Unemployment – 15.4 per cent (2000)
Total External Debt – US$144,050 million (1998)

### Trade

The chief imports are machinery, industrial and transport equipment, chemicals, metals and plastics. The chief exports are vegetable products, processed foods, minerals, live animals and oils. Argentina's main trading partners are Brazil and the USA.

In 1999 Argentina had a trade deficit of US$829 million and a current account deficit of US$12,152 million. Imports totalled US$25,538 million and exports US$23,309 million.

| *Trade with UK* | 1999 | 2000 |
|---|---|---|
| Imports from UK | £295,880,000 | £286,270,000 |
| Exports to UK | 196,977,000 | 185,184,000 |

## COMMUNICATIONS

The 25,386 miles of railway are state-owned. The combined national and provincial road network totals approximately 137,000 miles of which 23,180 miles are surfaced.

## CULTURE AND EDUCATION

The literature of Spain is part of the culture. There is little indigenous literature before the break from Spain, but all branches have flourished since the latter half of the 19th century. About 450 daily newspapers are published in Argentina, including seven major ones in the city of Buenos Aires. The English language newspaper is the *Buenos Aires Herald* (daily).

Education is compulsory for the seven grades of primary school (six to 13). Secondary schools (14 to 17+) are available in and around Buenos Aires and in most of the important towns in the interior of the country. Most secondary schools are administered by the Central Ministry of Education in Buenos Aires, while primary schools are administered by the Central Ministry or by Provincial Ministries of Education. Private schools, of which there are many, are also loosely controlled by the Central Ministry. The total number of universities is over 50 with 24 national, 25 private and a small number of provincial universities.

Illiteracy Rate – 3.1 per cent (2000)
Enrolment (percentage of age group) – primary 95 per cent (1991); secondary 59 per cent (1991); tertiary 36.2 per cent (1996)

---

# ARMENIA
*Hayastany Hanrapetoutioun*

---

Area – 11,506 sq. miles (29,800 sq. km). Neighbours: Azerbaijan (east and south-west), Georgia (north), Iran (south), Turkey (west)
Population – 3,798,400 (2000). Armenians 93.8 per cent, Kurds 1.7 per cent and Russians 1.6 per cent. Azeris formed 2.6 per cent of the population, but most fled or were expelled after the outbreak of war with Azerbaijan. There are also Ukrainians, Greeks and Assyrians. The Armenian diaspora numbers some 5,300,000. Armenian is the official language, though Russian is widely spoken and understood. The main religion is Armenian Orthodox Christian (Armenian Church centred in Etchmiadzin). Armenia adopted Christianity as its official religion in AD 301, the first state in the world to do so
Capital – Yerevan (population, 1,249,700, 1996 estimate)
Currency – Dram of 100 louma
National Anthem – Mer Hayrenik azat, ankakh (Land of our fathers)
National Day – 21 September (Independence Day)
National Flag – Three horizontal stripes of red, blue and orange
Life Expectancy (years) – male 72.3; female 77.1
Population Growth Rate – 0.1 per cent (1999)
Population Density – 119 per sq. km (1998)
Urban Population – 70.0 per cent (2000 estimate)

Armenia lies between the Black and Caspian Seas, occupying the south-western part of the Caucasus region of the former Soviet Union. It is very mountainous, consisting of several vast tablelands surrounded by ridges. The climate is continental, dry and cold, but the Ararat valley has a long, hot and dry summer.

## HISTORY AND POLITICS

Armenia was first unified in 95 BC but was divided between the Persian and Byzantine Empires in AD 387 and then conquered in the 11th century by the Seljuk Turks and the Mongols. In the 16th century most of Armenia was incorporated into the Ottoman Empire. In 1639 the country was divided again, the easternmost portions, now the republic of Armenia, becoming part of the Persian Empire. In 1828 eastern Armenia became part of the Russian Empire while western Armenia remained under Ottoman rule. The Ottomans launched pogroms against the Armenians from 1894 onwards, and in 1915 to 1918 massacred 1,500,000 Armenians.

Armenia declared its independence on 28 May 1918, but was crushed and divided between Turkish and Soviet forces in 1920, with the area under Soviet control proclaimed a Soviet Socialist Republic on 29 November 1920. The Soviet government was overthrown by a nationalist revolt in 1921 but reinstated by the Red Army a few months later. In early 1922 Armenia acceded to the USSR.

An Armenian nationalist movement swept to power in national elections in mid-1990. In a referendum in 1991, 99 per cent of the electorate voted for independence, which was declared on 21 September 1991.

Prime Minister Vazgen Sarkissian and six other politicians were shot dead in the National Assembly during an attempted coup on 27 October 1999; Aram

Sarkissian, the younger brother of Vazgen Sarkissian, was appointed prime minister on 5 November 1999, but was replaced by Andranik Markarian in May 2000.

### Foreign Relations

The dispute between the (ethnic Armenian) Nagorno-Karabakh forces supported by Armenia and the Azeri government over Nagorny-Karabakh erupted into all-out war in May 1992, when Nagorno-Karabakh forces breached Azerbaijan's defences to form a land bridge to Armenia. By the end of summer 1992 all of Nagorny-Karabakh was under Armenian control, and by the end of 1993 all Azeri territory that separated Nagorny-Karabakh from Armenia and all mountainous Azeri territory around Nagorny-Karabakh was under the control of Nagorno-Karabakh Armenians. Armenia claims this territory as historically Armenian land arbitrarily given to Azerbaijan by Stalin in 1921–2. A cease-fire agreement between Armenia, Azerbaijan and Nagorny-Karabakh was reached in May 1994, and talks mediated by the OSCE continue to seek a peaceful resolution to the dispute.

In August 1997 Armenia and Russia renewed a Treaty of Friendship, Co-operation and Mutual Assistance in effect since 1991.

### Political System

There is a 131-member unicameral National Assembly (*Azgayin Joghov*), directly elected every four years.. A new constitution was approved by a referendum in July 1995. Armenia is divided into 11 Administrative Regions.

Since the 1999 election, Unity, an alliance of the Republican Party and the People's Party, has been the dominant grouping in the National Assembly.

### Head of State

*President*, Robert Kocharian, *elected* 30 March 1998, *sworn in* 9 April 1998

### Cabinet *as at July 2001*

*Prime Minister*, Andranik Markarian
*Agriculture*, Zaven Gevorkian
*Culture, Youth and Sport*, Roland Sharoian
*Defence*, Serge Sarkissian
*Ecology*, Murad Muradian
*Education and Science*, Eduard Kazarian
*Energy*, Karen Galustyan
*Finance and Economy*, Vardan Khachatryan
*Foreign Affairs*, Vardan Oskanian
*Head of the Government Executive*, Manuk Topuzyan
*Health*, Ararat Mkrtchian
*Internal Affairs*, Haik Haroutiounian
*Justice*, David Haroutiounian
*National Security*, Karlos Petrosian
*Prime Minister's Chief of Staff*, Karine Kirakosian
*Production Infrastructures*, David Zadoyan
*Social Security*, Razmik Martirosian
*State Income*, Andranik Manukian
*State Property*, David Vardanian
*Territorial Administration*, Hovik Abrahamian
*Trade, Services, Tourism and Industry*, Karen Chshmaritian
*Transport and Communications*, Yervand Zakaryan
*Urban Development*, David Lokian

### Embassy of the Republic of Armenia

25A Cheniston Gardens, London W8 6TG
Tel: 020-7938 5435
*Ambassador Extraordinary and Plenipotentiary*, HE Dr Vahram Abadijian, apptd 2001

### British Embassy

28 Charents Street, Yerevan
Tel: (00 374) (1) 151 841
*Ambassador Extraordinary and Plenipotentiary*, HE T. A. Jones, apptd 2000

## DEFENCE

The Army has 102 main battle tanks, 168 armoured infantry fighting vehicles and 36 armoured personnel carriers, six combat aircraft and 12 armed helicopters.

Russia maintains 3,100 army personnel in Armenia. An agreement on military co-operation with Russia was signed in 1996 which paved the way for joint military exercises. A protocol was also signed on the establishment of coalition troops in Transcaucasia and the planned use of Russian and Armenian armed forces as part of coalition troops in cases of mutual interest.

Military Expenditure – 8.6 per cent of GDP (1999)
Military Personnel – 42,300: Army 41,300, Paramilitaries 1,000
Conscription Duration – 24 months

## ECONOMY

The Armenian economy has been badly affected by the Azeri and Turkish economic embargoes which have been in place since 1988. The main trade and transportation routes now lie via Georgia and Iran.

Armenia has a strong agricultural sector in low-lying areas, where industrial and fruit crops are grown. Grain is grown in the hills and the country is also noted for its wine and brandy. There are large copper ore and molybdenum deposits and other minerals. The country also has developed chemicals, industrial vehicles and textiles industries.

The government introduced a programme of economic reforms in November 1994 with IMF support, including the liberalisation of prices, stabilisation of the currency and privatisation.

In 1999 Armenia had a trade deficit of US$474 million and a current account deficit of US$319 million. Imports totalled US$800 million and exports US$232 million.

GNP – US$1,878 million (1999); US$490 per capita (1999)
GDP – US$1,627 million (1997); US$533 per capita (1998)
Annual Average Growth of GDP – 4.1 per cent (1996)
Inflation Rate – 0.7 per cent (1999)
Unemployment – 9.3 per cent (1998)
Total External Debt – US$800 million (1998)

| *Trade with UK* | 1999 | 2000 |
|---|---|---|
| Imports from UK | £4,571,000 | £3,870,000 |
| Exports to UK | 871,000 | 547,000 |

## CULTURE AND EDUCATION

The Armenian alphabet was established in AD 405. Major cultural figures include the poets Narekatsi (10th century), Frick (13th century), Nahapet Kuchak (16th century) and Sayat-Nova (18th century), the composer Aram Khachaturian (1903–78), and the film director Sergei Parajanov.

Enrolment (percentage of age group) – tertiary 12.2 per cent (1996)

## AUSTRALIA
*The Commonwealth of Australia*

AREA – 2,988,902 sq. miles (7,741,220 sq. km)
POPULATION – 19,157,037 (2000 estimate): 386,049 of Aboriginal and Torres Strait Islander origin (1996 estimate). The language is English
CAPITAL – Canberra, in the Australian Capital Territory (population, 309,500, 1997 estimate). It has been the seat of government since 1927
MAJOR CITIES – ΨAdelaide (1,088,400); ΨBrisbane (1,574,600); ΨHobart (195,000); ΨMelbourne (3,371,300); ΨPerth, including Fremantle (1,341,900); ΨSydney (3,986,700), 1998 estimates
CURRENCY – Australian dollar ($A) of 100 cents
NATIONAL ANTHEM – Advance Australia Fair
NATIONAL DAY – 26 January (Australia Day)
NATIONAL FLAG – The British Blue Ensign with five stars of the Southern Cross in the fly and the white Commonwealth Star of seven points beneath the Union Flag
LIFE EXPECTANCY (years) – male 76.8; female 82.2
POPULATION GROWTH RATE – 1.1 per cent (1999)
POPULATION DENSITY – 2 per sq. km (1998)
URBAN POPULATION – 84.7 per cent (2000 estimate)

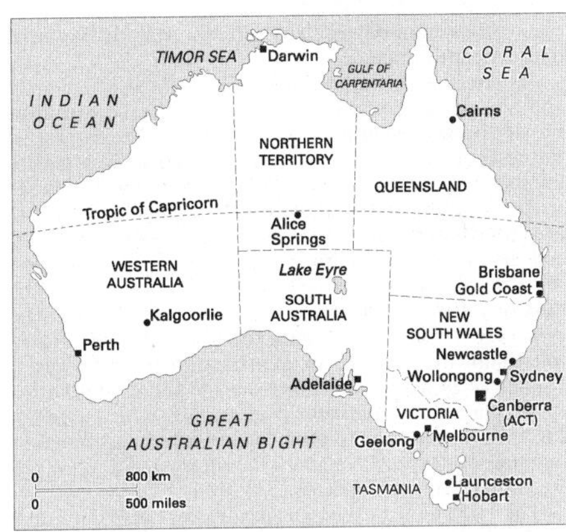


Australia is a continent in the southern hemisphere. The highest point is Mt. Kosciusko (2,228 m) and the lowest, Lake Eyre (–15 m). Climatic conditions range from the alpine to the tropical. Two-thirds of the continent is arid or semi-arid although good rainfalls (over 800 mm annually) occur in the northern monsoonal belt and along the eastern and southern highland regions.

## HISTORY AND POLITICS

Australia was discovered by Europeans in the 17th century. Its eastern coast was claimed by Capt. James Cook on behalf of Britain in 1770 and became a penal colony; Tasmania, Western Australia, South Australia, Victoria and Queensland were established as colonies between 1825 and 1859. The colonies were federated as the Commonwealth of Australia on 1 January 1901, at which time Australia gained dominion status within the British Empire. Australia became independent within the British Commonwealth by the 1931 Statute of Westminster. Following a referendum in 1967, the Aboriginal population was granted full political rights. In 1986, the Australia Act was passed, which abolished the remaining legislative, executive and judicial links to the UK, while retaining the British monarch as head of state.

On 13 February 1998, the Constitutional Convention voted by 89 votes to 52 to sever constitutional links with the United Kingdom monarchy. A national referendum was held on the issue on 6 November 1999; the proposition to make Australia a republic was defeated, with 45.3 per cent voting in favour and 54.7 per cent against.

The general election in October 1998 was won by the ruling Liberal Party-National Party coalition, though with a much reduced majority.

### POLITICAL SYSTEM

The government is that of a federal commonwealth within the Commonwealth, the executive power being vested in the Sovereign (through the Governor-General), assisted by a federal government. Under the constitution the powers of the federal government are defined, and residuary legislative power remains with the states. The right of a state to legislate on any matter is not abrogated except in connection with matters exclusively under federal control, but where a state law is inconsistent with

## STATES AND TERRITORIES

| | *Area (sq. km)* | *Resident population 31 December 2000p* | *Capital* | *Governor* | *Premier* |
|---|---|---|---|---|---|
| Australian Capital Territory (ACT) | 2,360 | 312,384 | Canberra | — | Gary Humphries (LP)‡ |
| New South Wales (NSW) | 801,600 | 6,502,615 | Sydney | HE Prof. Marie Bashir, AO | Bob Carr (Lab) |
| Northern Territory (NT) | 1,349,130 | 196,308 | Darwin* | John Anictomatis, OAM† | Denis Burke (LP)‡ |
| Queensland (Qld) | 1,730,650 | 3,597,203 | Brisbane | HE Maj.-Gen. Peter Arnison, AO | Peter Beattie (Lab) |
| South Australia (SA) | 983,480 | 1,500,491 | Adelaide | HE Sir Eric Neal, AC, CVO | John Olsen (LP) |
| Tasmania (Tas.) | 68,400 | 470,142 | Hobart | HE Sir Guy Green, AC, KBE, CVO | Jim Bacon (Lab) |
| Victoria (Vic.) | 227,420 | 4,797,366 | Melbourne | HEJohn Landy, AC, MBE | Steve Bracks (Lab) |
| Western Australia (WA) | 2,529,880 | 1,897,381 | Perth | HE Lt.-Gen. John M. Sanderson, AC | Dr Geoff Gallop, MLA (LP) |

*p* preliminary
* Seat of administration
† Administrator
‡ Chief Minister

a law of the Commonwealth the latter prevails to the extent of the inconsistency.

Parliament consists of Queen Elizabeth II, the Senate and the House of Representatives. The constitution provides that the number of members of the House of Representatives shall be, as nearly as practicable, twice the number of senators. Members of the Senate are elected for six years by universal suffrage, half the members retiring every third year, except in the Australian Capital Territory and the Northern Territory, where members are elected for a three-year term. Each of the six states returns 12 senators, and the Australian Capital Territory and the Northern Territory two each. The House of Representatives, similarly elected for a maximum of three years, contains members proportionate to the population, with a minimum of five members for each state. There are now 148 members in the House of Representatives, including one member for the Northern Territory and two for the Australian Capital Territory.

The High Court exercises jurisdiction over all matters arising under the constitution, all matters arising between the states and between residents of different states, matters to which the Commonwealth of Australia is a party, matters arising under any treaty, and matters affecting foreign representatives in Australia. The High Court also hears appeals from the Federal Court and from the Supreme Courts of states and territories.

The Federal Court of Australia has jurisdiction over important industrial, trade practices, intellectual property, administrative law, admiralty law and bankruptcy matters. It also acts as a court of appeal for decisions from the Australian Capital Territory Supreme Court and certain decisions of state Supreme Courts exercising federal jurisdiction. Each state has its own judicature of supreme, superior and minor courts for criminal and civil cases.

### FEDERAL STRUCTURE

In the states, executive authority is vested in a Governor (appointed by the Crown), assisted by a Council of Ministers or Executive Council. Each state has a legislature comprising a Legislative Council and a Legislative Assembly or House of Assembly which are elected for four-year terms, except Queensland, which has a Legislative Assembly only.

The Northern Territory and Australian Capital Territory have a Legislative Assembly only.

### GOVERNOR-GENERAL

*Governor-General*, HE The Hon. Peter Hollingworth, *assumed office* 29 June 2001

### CABINET *as at July 2001*

*Prime Minister*, John Howard (LP)
*Deputy Prime Minister, Transport and Regional Development*, John Anderson (NP)
*Agriculture, Fisheries and Forestry*, Warren Truss (NP)
*Attorney-General*, Daryl Williams (LP)
*Communications, Information Technology and the Arts*, Sen. Richard Alston (LP)
*Defence*, Peter Reith (LP)
*Education, Training and Youth Affairs*, David Kemp (LP)
*Employment, Workplace Relations and Small Business, Leader of the House*, Tony Abbott (LP)
*Environment and Heritage, Leader of the Government in the Senate*, Sen. Robert Hill (LP)
*Family and Community Services*, Amanda Vanstone (LP)
*Finance and Administration*, John Fahey (LP)
*Foreign Affairs*, Alexander Downer (LP)
*Health and Aged Care*, Dr Michael Wooldridge (LP)
*Immigration and Multicultural Affairs, Aboriginal and Torres Strait Islander Affairs*, Philip Ruddock (LP)
*Industry, Science and Resources*, Sen. Nick Minchin (LP)
*Trade*, Mark Vaile (NP)
*Treasurer*, Peter Costello (LP)
*President of the Senate*, Sen. Margaret Reid (LP)
*Speaker, House of Representatives*, Neil Andrew (LP)

Lab Labor Party; LP Liberal Party; NP National Party

### AUSTRALIAN HIGH COMMISSION

Australia House, Strand, London WC2B 4LA
Tel: 020-7379 4334
*High Commissioner*, HE Michael L'Estrange, apptd 2000
*Deputy High Commissioner*, D. A. Ritchie
*Minister*, M. B. Jenkins *(Commercial)*
*Head of Defence Staff*, Cdre Geoffrey Geraghty
NEW SOUTH WALES GOVERNMENT OFFICE, The Australia Centre, Strand, London WC2B 4LG. Tel: 020-7887 5871. *Director*, Gary Offner
AGENT-GENERAL FOR QUEENSLAND, 392 Strand, London WC2R 0LZ. Tel: 020-7836 1333. *Agent-General*, John Dawson
AGENT-GENERAL FOR SOUTH AUSTRALIA, Australia Centre, Strand, London WC2B 4LG. Tel: 020-7836 3455. *Agent-General*, Maurice de Rohan
AGENT-GENERAL FOR VICTORIA, Victoria House, Melbourne Place, Strand, London WC2B 4LG. Tel: 020-7836 2656. *Agent-General*, Peter A. Hansen
AGENT-GENERAL FOR WESTERN AUSTRALIA, Australia Centre, Strand, London WC2B 4LG. Tel: 020-7240 2881. *Agent-General*, Clive E. Griffiths

### BRITISH HIGH COMMISSION

Commonwealth Avenue, Yarralumla, Canberra, ACT 2600
Tel: (00 61) (2) 6270 6666
*High Commissioner*, HE Sir Alistair Goodlad, KCMG, apptd 1999
*Deputy High Commissioner*, Dr A. J. Pocock
*First Secretary*, J. Harrod *(Political)*
*First Secretary (Defence/Research) and Head of British Defence Research and Supply Staff*, Dr G. Stott
*Consuls-General*, S. J. Hiscock (*Brisbane*); P. M. Innes (*Melbourne*); H. Dunnachie (*Perth*); P. Beckingham (*Sydney*)
*Cultural Adviser and British Council Director*, Simon Gammell, Suite 401, Edgecliff Centre, 203–233 New South Head Road (PO Box 88), Edgecliff, Sydney, NSW 2027; e-mail: enquiries@britishcouncil.org.au

## DEFENCE

The Army has 71 main battle tanks, 463 armoured personnel carriers, 111 light assault vehicles, six aircraft and 123 armed helicopters. The Navy has three submarines, one destroyer, eight frigates, 15 patrol and coastal vessels and 16 armed helicopters. There are bases at Sydney, Stirling, Cairns and Darwin. The Air Force has 148 combat aircraft.

MILITARY EXPENDITURE – 1.9 per cent of GDP (1999)
MILITARY PERSONNEL – 50,600: Army 24,150, Navy 12,500, Air Force 13,950

## ECONOMY

The wide range of climatic and soil conditions has resulted in a diversity of crops. Generally, cereal crops (excluding rice and sorghum) are widely grown, while other crops are confined to specific locations in a few states. However, scant or erratic rainfall, limited potential for irrigation and unsuitable soils or topography have restricted intensive agriculture.

Livestock ranching is widespread, primarily cattle and sheep; meat, meat derivatives, wool and dairy products are significant agricultural products. Significant mineral resources include bauxite, coal, copper, crude petroleum, gems, gold, ilmenite, iron ore, lead, limestone, manganese, nickel, rutile, salt, silver, tin, tungsten, uranium, zinc and zircon. In 1998 287,620,000 tonnes of coal, 28,000,000 tonnes of crude oil, 30,361,000 cubic metres of natural gas, 153,243,000 tonnes of iron ore, 618,000 tonnes of lead, and 309,600 kilograms of gold were produced.

GNP – US$397,345 million (1999); US$20,050 per capita (1999)

GDP – US$402,787 million (1997); US$21,432 per capita (1999)

ANNUAL AVERAGE GROWTH OF GDP – 2.1 per cent (2000)

INFLATION RATE – 5.8 per cent (2000)

UNEMPLOYMENT – 6.9 per cent (2001)

### TRADE

In 1999-2000 the main exports were metalliferous ores and metal scrap (11.6 per cent); coal, coke and briquettes (8.6 per cent); non-ferrous metals (7.6 per cent); gold (5.2 per cent); and cereals and cereal preparations (5.1 per cent). The major imports were manufactured articles (14.1 per cent); motor vehicles and parts (11.6 per cent); computer technology (6.9 per cent); petroleum and related products (6.9 per cent); telecommunications equipment (6.2 per cent); electrical machinery (5.7 per cent); and general industrial machinery and parts (4.9 per cent).

Australia's main trading partners are Japan, the USA, New Zealand, China, Korea, Germany, Taiwan and the UK.

In 1999 Australia had a trade deficit of US$9,771 million and a current account deficit of US$22,526 million. Imports totalled US$69,135 million and exports US$56,087 million.

| *Trade with UK* | 1999 | 2000 |
|---|---|---|
| Imports from UK | £2,163,073,000 | £2,682,828,000 |
| Exports to UK | 1,399,032,000 | 1,587,084,000 |

## COMMUNICATIONS

There are six government-owned railway systems, operated by the State Rail Authority of NSW, VicRail, Queensland Government Railways, Western Australian Government Railways, the State Transport Authority of Southern Australia, and the National Rail Corporation (NRC). The NRC incorporates the former Commonwealth Railways system, and the Tasmanian and non-metropolitan South Australian railways (urban rail services in Southern Australia remain the responsibility of the State Transport Authority). In 1999 there was a total of 39,930 km of railway track.

The Northern Territory has three main ports: Darwin, and the private mining ports of Gove and Groote Eylandt. Most freight in the Territory is moved by road trains. These are massive trucks hauling two or three trailers, having a net capacity of about 100 tonnes and measuring up to 45 metres in length.

## EDUCATION

Education is administered by the state governments and is compulsory between the ages of five or six and 15 years. It is available at government schools controlled by the state education department and at private or independent schools, some of which are denominational. Tertiary education is available through universities, and technical and further education colleges. There are 39 universities in Australia; the Australian Capital Territory has two universities, New South Wales 11, Queensland seven, Northern Territory one, South Australia three, Tasmania one, Victoria nine and Western Australia five.

ENROLMENT (percentage of age group) – primary 95 per cent (1997); secondary 89 per cent (1996); tertiary 80 per cent (1997)

## EXTERNAL TERRITORIES

### ASHMORE AND CARTIER ISLANDS

Ashmore Islands (known as Middle, East and West Islands) and Cartier Island are situated in the Indian Ocean 850 km and 790 km west of Darwin respectively. The islands are uninhabited. The territory has been administered by the Australian Government since 1933.

### THE AUSTRALIAN ANTARCTIC TERRITORY

The Australian Antarctic Territory was established in 1933 and comprises all the islands and territories, other than Adélie Land, which are situated south of the latitude 60° S. and lying between 160° E. longitude and 45° E. longitude. The territory is administered by the Antarctic Division of the Department of the Environment and Heritage. There are nine scientific research stations.

### CHRISTMAS ISLAND

AREA – 52 sq. miles (135 sq. km)

POPULATION – 1,906 (1996 census)

Christmas Island is situated in the Indian Ocean about 1,408 km NW of North West Cape in Western Australia. The island became an Australian territory in 1958 and is managed by the Department of Transport and Regional Services. The Shire of Christmas Island (SOCI) has nine elected members. SOCI is responsible for municipal functions and services on the island.

*Administrator*, W. Taylor

### Cocos (Keeling) Islands

AREA – 5.4 sq. miles (14 sq. km)

POPULATION – 655 (1996 census)

The Cocos (Keeling) Islands are two separate atolls (North Keeling Island and, 24 km to the south, the main atoll) comprising some 27 small coral islands, situated in the Indian Ocean. The main islands of the southern atoll are West Island (about 9 km in length); Home Island, where the Cocos Malay community lives; Direction Island, Horsburgh and South Island.

The islands were declared a British possession in 1857. All land in the islands was granted to George Clunies-Ross and his heirs by Queen Victoria in 1886. In 1978 the Australian Government purchased all Clunies-Ross land and property interests except for the family home and grounds; the last of the remaining grounds were purchased in 1993. Between 1979 and 1984 most of the land was transferred to trusts with the Cocos (Keeling) Islands Council as trustee, the local government body established in 1979 which was replaced by the Shire of the Cocos (Keeling) Islands in July 1992.

On 6 April 1984 the Cocos community, in a UN-supervised Act of Self-Determination, chose to integrate with Australia. The islands are managed by the Australian Government through the Department of Transport and Regional Services.

*Administrator*, W. Taylor

### CORAL SEA ISLANDS TERRITORY

The Coral Sea Islands Territory lies east of Queensland between the Great Barrier Reef and longitude 156° 06′ E., and between latitudes 12° and 24° S. It comprises scattered islands, spread over a sea area of 780,000 sq. km. The islands are formed mainly of coral and sand, and most are extremely small. There is a manned meteorological station in the Willis Group but the remaining islands are uninhabited.

The territory is managed by the Department of Transport and Regional Services.

## HEARD ISLAND AND McDONALD ISLANDS

The Territory of the Heard and McDonald Islands, about 4,100 km south-west of Perth, comprises all the islands and rocks lying between 52° 30′ and 53° 30′ S. latitude and 72° and 74° 30′ E. longitude. The islands are administered by the Antarctic Division of the Department of the Environment and Heritage.

## NORFOLK ISLAND

AREA – 13.3 sq. miles (34.5 sq. km)
POPULATION – 1,772 (1996 census)
SEAT OF GOVERNMENT – Kingston

Norfolk Island is situated in the South Pacific Ocean. It is about 8 km long by 5 km wide. The climate is mild and subtropical.

The island, discovered by Captain Cook in 1774, served as a penal colony from 1788 to 1814 and 1825 to 1855. In 1856, 194 descendants of the *Bounty* mutineers accepted an invitation to leave Pitcairn and settle on Norfolk Island. Norfolk Island is an Australian external territory.

In 1979 Norfolk Island gained a substantial degree of self-government. Wide powers are exercised by a nine-member Legislative Assembly. The Administrator is responsible to the Australian Minister for Regional Services, Territories and Local Government.

*Administrator*, A. J. Messner
Source: for demographic, economic and education statistics, Australian Bureau of Statistics. Copyright in ABS data resides with the Commonwealth of Australia. Used with permission.

---

# AUSTRIA
*Republik Österreich*

---

AREA – 32,378 sq. miles (83,859 sq. km). Neighbours: the Czech Republic and Slovakia (north), Italy and Slovenia (south), Hungary (east), Germany (north-west), Switzerland and Liechtenstein (west)
POPULATION – 8,086,000 (1997 estimate); 7,813,000 (1991 census). The language is German, but the rights of the Slovene- and Croat-speaking minorities in Carinthia, Styria and Burgenland are protected. The predominant religion is Roman Catholicism
CAPITAL – Vienna, on the Danube (population, 1,806,737, 1995 estimate)
MAJOR CITIES – Graz (271,017); Innsbruck (136,516); Klagenfurt (89,415); Linz (281,566); Salzburg (162,908)
CURRENCY – Euro (€) of 100 cents/Schilling of 100 Groschen
NATIONAL ANTHEM – Land der Berge, Land am Strome (Land of mountains, land on the river)
NATIONAL DAY – 26 October
NATIONAL FLAG – Three equal horizontal stripes of red, white, red
LIFE EXPECTANCY (years) – male 74.4; female 80.4
POPULATION GROWTH RATE – 0.7 per cent (1999)
POPULATION DENSITY – 96 per sq. km (1998)
URBAN POPULATION – 64.7 per cent (2000 estimate)

## HISTORY AND POLITICS

The Austrian state dates back to the eighth century AD when Emperor Charlemagne conquered the territory and founded the *Ostmark*, the eastern march of the Holy Roman Empire. The Habsburg dynasty established an empire which united much of central Europe, including present-day Austria and Hungary. The Republic of Austria was established in 1918 on the break-up of the Austro-Hungarian Empire. In March 1938 Austria was incorporated into Nazi Germany under the name *Ostmark*. After the liberation of Vienna in 1945, the Republic of Austria was reconstituted within the 1937 frontiers and a freely-elected government took office in December 1945. The country was divided into four zones occupied respectively by the UK, USA, USSR and France, while Vienna was jointly occupied by the four Powers. In 1955 the Austrian State Treaty was signed by the foreign ministers of the four Powers and of Austria. This treaty recognised the re-establishment of Austria as a sovereign, independent and democratic state, having the same frontiers as on 1 January 1938. Austria acceded to the European Union on 1 January 1995.

After the general election of 17 December 1995 the Social Democrats and the People's Party formed a coalition government. In the general election of 3 October 1999, the Social Democrats won 65 seats and the People's Party and the Freedom Party won 52 seats each. Attempts to form a coalition between the Social Democrats and the People's Party were unsuccessful. A coalition government between the People's Party and the Freedom Party, which had stood on an anti-immigration platform and whose leader, Jörg Haider, had expressed support for some aspects of the wartime Nazi regime, was sworn in on 5 February 2000 after the signing by both parties of a document expressing the commitment of the new government to the European Union and condemning discrimination and intolerance. International opposition to the inclusion of the Freedom Party in the government resulted in the suspension of bilateral relations between the governments of the other EU members and Austria. On 1 May, Jörg Haider resigned as leader of the Freedom Party in an attempt to calm the situation. The suspension of relations between the EU members and Austria was lifted in September 2000 following an investigation into the Austrian government which cleared it of any wrongdoing.

### POLITICAL SYSTEM

There is a bicameral national assembly; the lower house (*Nationalrat*) has 183 members and the upper house (*Bundesrat*) has 64 members. There is a 4 per cent qualification for parliamentary representation.

### FEDERAL STRUCTURE

There are nine provinces:

| *Provinces* | *Area (sq. km)* | *Population* | *Capital* |
|---|---|---|---|
| Burgenland | 3,965 | 274,334 | Eisenstadt |
| Carinthia | 9,533 | 560,994 | Klagenfurt |
| Lower Austria | 19,174 | 1,518,254 | St Pölten |
| Salzburg | 7,154 | 506,850 | Salzburg |
| Styria | 16,388 | 1,206,317 | Graz |
| Tirol | 12,648 | 658,312 | Innsbruck |
| Upper Austria | 11,980 | 1,385,769 | Linz |
| Vienna | 415 | 1,592,596 | Vienna |
| Vorarlberg | 2,601 | 343,109 | Bregenz |

### HEAD OF STATE

*President of the Republic of Austria*, Dr Thomas Klestil, *took office* 8 July 1992, *re-elected* 19 April 1998

### CABINET *as at July 2001*

*Chancellor*, Wolfgang Schüssel (ÖVP)
*Vice-Chancellor, Public Affairs and Sports*, Susanne Riess-Passer (FPÖ)
*Agriculture and Environment*, Wilhelm Molterer (ÖVP)
*Economic Affairs and Labour*, Martin Bartenstein (ÖVP)
*Education, Science and Cultural Affairs*, Elisabeth Gehrer (ÖVP)
*Finance*, Karl-Heinz Grasser (FPÖ)
*Foreign Affairs*, Benita Ferrero-Waldner (ÖVP)

*Interior*, Ernst Strasser (ÖVP)
*Justice*, Dieter Böhmdorfer (Ind.)
*National Defence*, Herbert Scheibner (FPÖ)
*Social Security and Generations*, Herbert Haupt (FPÖ)
*Transport, Innovation and Technology*, Monika Forstinger (FPÖ)

ÖVP People's Party; FPÖ Freedom Party; Ind. Independent

AUSTRIAN EMBASSY
18 Belgrave Mews West, London SW1X 8HU
Tel: 020-7235 3731
*Ambassador Extraordinary and Plenipotentiary*, Alexander Christiani, apptd 2000
*Minister and Chargé d'Affaires*, B. Öppinger-Walchshofer
*Defence Attaché*, Brig.-Gen. W. Plasche
*Consul-General*, S.Bagyura
*Commercial Counsellor and Trade Commissioner*, Dr R. J. Engel

BRITISH EMBASSY
Jaurèsgasse 12, 1030 Vienna
Tel: (00 43) (1) 716130
*Ambassador Extraordinary and Plenipotentiary*, HE Anthony Ford, CMG, apptd 2000
*Deputy Head of Mission, Counsellor and Consul-General*, I. C. Cliff, OBE
*Defence Attaché*, Lt.-Col. J. A. Bourne
*First Secretaries*, P. J. Seymour; H. D. Marcelin; J. Hall

BRITISH CONSULAR OFFICES – There is a consular office at Vienna, and Honorary Consulates at Bregenz, Graz, Innsbruck and Salzburg.

BRITISH COUNCIL DIRECTOR, Dr Simon Cole, Schenkenstrasse 4, A–1010 Vienna; e-mail: bc.vienna@bc-vienna.at

## DEFENCE

The Army has 283 main battle tanks and 533 armoured personnel carriers. The Air Force has 52 combat aircraft and 11 armed helicopters.

Women were permitted to join the army for the first time in February 1998.

MILITARY EXPENDITURE – 0.8 per cent of GDP (1999)
MILITARY PERSONNEL – Army 35,500, of which Air Force 6,500
CONSCRIPTION DURATION – Eight months including refresher training

## ECONOMY

Austria produces wheat, rye, barley, oats, maize, potatoes, sugar beet and turnips. Timber forms a valuable source of Austria's indigenous wealth, about 47 per cent of the total land area consisting of forest areas. Foreign exchange receipts from tourism were a major contribution to the balance of payments.

GNP – US$205,743 million (1999); US$25,970 per capita (1999)
GDP – US$206,236 million (1997); US$25,948 per capita (1999)
ANNUAL AVERAGE GROWTH OF GDP – 1.9 per cent (2000)
INFLATION RATE – 2.7 per cent (2001)
UNEMPLOYMENT – 3.7 per cent (2001)

### TRADE

Main exports are processed goods (iron and steel, other metal goods, textiles, paper and cardboard products), machinery and transport equipment, other finished goods (including clothing), raw materials, chemical products and foodstuffs. Main imports are machinery and transport equipment, processed goods, chemical products, foodstuffs, fuel and energy. Austria's main trading partners are Germany, Italy, France and Switzerland.

In 1999, Austria had a trade deficit of US$3,560million and a current account deficit of US$5,701 million. Imports totalled US$68,755 million and exports US$63,407 million.

| *Trade with UK* | 1999 | 2000 |
|---|---|---|
| Imports from UK | £1,092,800,000 | £1,081,500,000 |
| Exports to UK | 1,392,900,000 | 1,341,200,000 |

## COMMUNICATIONS

Internal communications are partly restricted because of the mountainous nature of the country, although there is now a network of 1,567 km of *Autobahn* between major cities which also links up with the German and Italian networks. The railways are state-owned and in 1993 had 5,605 km of track, 58.8 per cent of which is electrified. Of the 425 km of waterways, 350 km are navigable and there is considerable trade through the Danube ports by both local and foreign shipping. There are six commercial airports catering for 5,527,600 passengers in 1995.

There are four national radio and two national television channels, together with three national and twelve regional newspapers.

## CULTURE AND EDUCATION

In the late 18th and 19th centuries, Vienna became the centre of classical music and the city attracted composers from many countries. Austrian composers include Joseph Haydn (1732-1809), Wolfgang Amadeus Mozart (1756-1791), Franz Peter Schubert (1797-1828), Johann Strauss II (1825-1899), Gustav Mahler (1860-1911) and Arnold Schönberg (1874-1951). Important artists include Gustav Klimt (1862-1918), Egon Schiele (1890-1918) and Oskar Kokoschka (1886-1980). Austrian literary figures include the novelists Arthur Schnitzler (1862-1931), Stefan Zweig (1881-1942) and Franz Kafka (1883-1924), the poet and novelist Rainer Maria Rilke (1875-1926), and the dramatists Franz Grillparzer (1791-1872) and Johann Nestroy (1801-1862)

In the field of architecture, famous Austrians include Fischer von Erlach (1656-1723), Otto Wagner (1841-1918), Adolf Loos (1870-1933) and Friedensreich Hundertwasser (1928-2000).

Education is free and compulsory between the ages of six and 15 and there are good facilities for secondary, technical and professional education. There are 12 state-maintained universities and six colleges of art.

ENROLMENT (percentage of age group) – primary 87 per cent (1996); secondary 88 per cent (1996); tertiary 48.3 per cent (1996)

---

# AZERBAIJAN
*Azərbaycan Respublıkası*

---

AREA – 33,436 sq. miles (86,600 sq. km). Neighbours: Iran (south), Armenia (west), Georgia and Russia (north)
POPULATION – 7,980,000 (1998): 83 per cent Azeri, 6 per cent Russian and 6 per cent Armenian. There are also Kurds, Jews, Georgians and Turks. There are more Azeris in Iran than in Azerbaijan. The population is predominantly Shia Muslim although it was heavily secularised during the Soviet era. The language is Azeri
CAPITAL – ΨBaku (population, 1,712,800, 1997 estimate)
CURRENCY – Manat of 100 gopik
NATIONAL ANTHEM - Azerbaijan! Azerbaijan!
NATIONAL DAY – 28 May (Independence Day)

NATIONAL FLAG – Three horizontal stripes of blue, red and green with a white crescent and eight-pointed star in the centre
LIFE EXPECTANCY (years) – male 67.8; female 75.3
POPULATION GROWTH RATE – 0.8 per cent (1999)
POPULATION DENSITY – 89 per sq. km (1998)
URBAN POPULATION – 57.3 per cent (2000 estimate)

Azerbaijan occupies the eastern part of the Caucasus region of the former Soviet Union, on the shore of the Caspian Sea. The north-eastern part of the republic is taken up by the south-eastern end of the main Caucasus ridge, its south-western part by the smaller Caucasus hills, and its south-eastern corner by the spurs of the Talysh Ridge. Its central part is a depression irrigated by the River Kura and the lower reaches of its tributary the Araks. Azerbaijan has a continental climate.

Azerbaijan has 64 administrative districts and also includes the Nakhichevan Autonomous Republic, which is geographically separated from the rest of Azerbaijan by Armenia and borders on Iran and Turkey, and the Nagorno-Karabakh Autonomous Province.

## HISTORY AND POLITICS

The Turkic Azeri people formed an independent state in the first century BC. Invading Arabs introduced Islam in the seventh century. In the 16th century Azerbaijan was again invaded by Persia and became a Persian province. The country was divided during the Russo-Persian wars of the early 19th century, the northern portion (the present-day Azerbaijan) becoming part of the Russian Empire and the southern portion remaining Persian and subsequently Iranian.

In 1918 the Azerbaijan Democratic Republic was established. It was overthrown by Communists in 1918 and Azerbaijan acceded to the USSR in 1922.

In January 1990, the Azeri Popular Front took power from the local Communist Party and declared independence from the Soviet Union. Soviet troops overthrew the Popular Front and restored the Communist regime, which declared Azerbaijan's independence in August 1991. At the presidential election in June 1992 the Popular Front leader Abulfaz Elchibey was elected.

Popular discontent at military defeats caused Elchibey to flee Baku in June 1993 and the former Azeri Communist Party First Secretary Heydar Aliyev took over the presidency. The new regime was confirmed in office in a referendum in August and Aliyev won the presidential election in October 1993.

The *Milli Majlis* (parliament) has 125 seats, of which 100 are directly elected and 25 are allocated by proportional representation.

Presidential elections were held on 11 October 1998. The incumbent President Aliyev won 76.1 per cent of the vote, but the elections were criticised by the OSCE and other international monitoring groups. A general election was held on 5 November 2000. The New Azerbaijan party, founded by Aliyev, won 62.5 per cent of the vote and 78 seats. The election was boycotted by several parties, who alleged that electoral fraud had been committed; their claims were supported by OSCE observers.

### SECESSION

In 1988 fighting broke out in the predominantly Armenian-populated region of Nagorny-Karabakh between Soviet Azeri forces and ethnic Armenians demanding unification with Armenia. In late 1993 Nagorno-Karabakh forces captured all of the region, together with all Azeri territory separating the region from Armenia (20 per cent of Azeri territory). Azeri forces pushed back the Nagorno-Karabakh forces in early 1994 before a cease-fire agreement was signed in May 1994. Between 500,000 and one million Azeris have been displaced by the fighting, which briefly flared up again along the Azeri-Armenian border in April and May 1997. Peace talks, held under the auspices of the OSCE, have yet to yield any significant results, although both sides reaffirmed their commitment to finding a peaceful solution at a meeting in October 1997, in which both sides rejected the idea of full independence for Nagorny-Karabakh as 'unrealistic'. President Aliyev held talks with President Kocharian of Armenia in March and April 2001, but the leaders failed to reach an agreement on the future of Nagorny-Karabakh.

### POLITICAL SYSTEM

A new constitution was approved by a referendum in November 1995, which created a presidential republic with executive power to be exercised by the president and with legislative power vested in the unicameral *Milli Majlis* (National Assembly). The president appoints the prime minister and the Cabinet. Both the president and the National Assembly are directly elected for five-year terms.

### HEAD OF STATE

*President*, Heydar Alirza ogly Aliyev, *assumed office* 18 June 1993, *elected* 3 October 1993, *re-elected* 11 October 1998

### GOVERNMENT *as at July 2001*

*Prime Minister*, Artur Rasi-Zade
*First Deputy PM*, Abbas Abbasov
*Deputy Prime Ministers*, Abid Shazifov; Ali Gasanov (*Chair of State Refugee Committee*); Yagub Abdulla oglu Eyyubov; Hajibula Abutalibov; Elehin Efendiyev
*Agriculture*, Irshad Aliyev
*Communications*, Nadir Akhmedov
*Culture*, Polad Bulbuloglu
*Defence*, Lt.-Gen. Safar Abiyev
*Ecology and Natural Resources*, Hoseun Bagirov
*Economic Development*, Farhad Aliyev
*Education*, Misir Mardanov
*Finance*, Avaz Alekperov
*Foreign Affairs*, Vilayat Mukhtar oglu Guliyev
*Fuel and Energy*, Mejid Kerimov
*Health*, Ali Insanov
*Interior*, Lt.-Gen. Ramil Usubov
*Justice*, Fikrat Farrukh Mammadov
*Labour and Social Security*, Ali Nagiyev
*National Security*, Namiq Abbasov
*Taxation*, Fazil Mamedov
*Youth and Sports*, Abdulfaz Karayev

### EMBASSY OF THE AZERBAIJAN REPUBLIC

4 Kensington Court, London W8 5DL
Tel: 020-7938 5482/3412
*Ambassador Extraordinary and Plenipotentiary*, HE Mahmud Mamed-Kuliyev, apptd 1994

### BRITISH EMBASSY

2 Izmir Street, AZ-370065 Baku
Tel: (00 994) (12) 924813
E-mail: office@britemb.baku.az
*Ambassador Extraordinary and Plenipotentiary*, HE Andrew Tucker, apptd 2000

BRITISH COUNCIL DIRECTOR, Margaret Jack, 1 Vali Mammadov Street, AZ-370004 Baku; E-mail: enquiries@britishcouncil.az

## DEFENCE

The Army has 220 main battle tanks, 135 armoured infantry fighting vehicles and 355 armoured personnel carriers. The Navy is based at Baku, with a share of the former Soviet Caspian Fleet Flotilla, comprising nine

patrol and coastal vessels. The Air Force has 50 combat aircraft and 15 attack helicopters.
MILITARY EXPENDITURE – 4.4 per cent of GDP (1999)
MILITARY PERSONNEL – 72,100: Army 61,800, Navy 2,200, Air Force 8,100, Paramilitaries 15,000
CONSCRIPTION DURATION – 17 months

## ECONOMY

Azerbaijan was heavily industrialised as part of the Russian Empire. Industry is dominated by oil and natural gas extraction and related industries centred on Baku and Sumgait and the large oil deposits in the Caspian Sea, estimated at more than 6,000 million barrels. Natural gas reserves are estimated to be more than 1,200,000 million cubic metres. Five contracts to explore and exploit oilfields in the Caspian Sea have been signed since 1994.

The republic is also rich in mineral resources, with iron, copper, aluminium, lead and zinc, and is important as a cotton-growing area and a silkworm-breeding area.

Around 90 per cent of agricultural land has been privatised. Grapes, cereals (primarily wheat, barley, maize and rice), cotton, vegetables and fruit are the major agricultural products.

The Azeri economy was devastated by the war although it is now showing signs of recovery.

In 1999 Azerbaijan had a trade deficit of US$408 million and a current account deficit of US$600 million. In 1998 imports totalled US$1,077 million and exports US$606 million
GNP – US$3,705 million (1999); US$550 per capita (1999)
GDP – US$3,790 million (1997); US$537 per capita (1998)
ANNUAL AVERAGE GROWTH OF GDP – 1.4 per cent (2000)
INFLATION RATE – 8.6 per cent (1999)
UNEMPLOYMENT – 1.5 per cent (1998)
TOTAL EXTERNAL DEBT – US$693 million (1998)

| *Trade with UK* | 1999 | 2000 |
|---|---|---|
| Imports from UK | £27,756,000 | £35,544,000 |
| Exports to UK | 9,566,000 | 9,908,000 |

## COMMUNICATIONS

There are 2,200 km of railway track, much of it electrified, and over 25,000 km of roads. There are ferry links to Turkmenistan. Oil pipelines link the Azeri oilfields to the Russian Black Sea port of Novorossiysk and the Georgian port of Supsa.

## CULTURE AND EDUCATION

Azerbaijan was the birthplace of the prophet Zoroaster, who founded one of the first monotheistic religions in the world. The country has witnessed a succession of three religions: Zoroastrianism, Christianity and Islam.

Azeri is one of the Turkic languages. Previously written in the Russian script, Azeri in the Latin script was adopted as the official language in December 1992. In the 18th and 19th centuries Azerbaijani literature produced the poets and dramatists Vagif, Vazekhi, Zakir, Akhundov and Vezirov.

Education up to university level is free. There are several universities and colleges of higher education.
ENROLMENT (percentage of age group) – tertiary 17.4 per cent (1996)

# THE BAHAMAS

*The Commonwealth of The Bahamas*

AREA – 5,383 sq. miles (13,942 sq. km)
POPULATION – 310,000 (2001 estimate). The language is English
CAPITAL – ΨNassau (population, 172,196, 1996 estimate)
CURRENCY – Bahamian dollar (B$) of 100 cents
NATIONAL ANTHEM – March on, Bahamaland
NATIONAL DAY – 10 July (Independence Day)
NATIONAL FLAG – Horizontal stripes of aquamarine, gold and aquamarine, with a black equilateral triangle on the hoist
LIFE EXPECTANCY (years) – male 67.0; female 73.6
POPULATION GROWTH RATE – 1.6 per cent (1999)
POPULATION DENSITY – 21 per sq. km (1998)
URBAN POPULATION – 88.5 per cent (2000 estimate)

The Bahamas extend from the coast of Florida on the north-west almost to Hispaniola on the south-east. The group consists of more than 4,000 islands, islets and cays. The 14 major islands are inhabited, as are a few of the smaller islands. The principal islands include: Abaco, Acklins, Andros, Berry Islands, Bimini, Cat Island, Crooked Island, Eleuthera, Exuma, Grand Bahama, Harbour Island, Inagua, Long Island, Mayaguana, New Providence (on which is located the capital, Nassau), Ragged Island, Rum Cay, San Salvador and Spanish Wells. San Salvador was the first landfall in the New World of Christopher Columbus on 12 October 1492.

## HISTORY AND POLITICS

The Bahamas were settled by the British and became a Crown colony in 1717. Taken over in 1782 by the Spanish, the Treaty of Versailles in 1783 restored them to the British. The Bahamas gained independence on 10 July 1973.

A general election held in March 1997 was won by the Free National Movement which defeated the Progressive Liberal Party. The Free National Movement holds 35 seats in the House of Assembly and the Progressive Liberal Party five seats.

### POLITICAL SYSTEM

The head of state is Queen Elizabeth II who is represented in the islands by a Governor-General. There is an appointed Senate of 16 members and an elected House of Assembly of 40 members.

*Governor-General*, HE Sir Orville Turnquest, GCMG, QC, apptd 1995

### CABINET *as at July 2001*

*Prime Minister*, Hubert Ingraham
*Deputy Prime Minister, National Security*, Frank Watson
*Agriculture and Industry*, James Knowles
*Attorney-General, Justice*, Carl Bethel
*Economic Development*, Zhivargo Laing
*Education and Youth, Sports and Culture*, Dion Foulkes
*Finance*, William Allen, KCMG
*Foreign Affairs*, Janet Bostwick
*Health*, Ronald Knowles
*Labour and Immigration*, Earl Deveaux
*Social Development and Housing*, Algernon Allen
*Tourism*, Orville Turnquest
*Transport and Local Government*, Cornelius Smith
*Works*, Kenneth Russell

*President of the Court of Appeal*, Kenneth George
*Chief Justice*, Dame Joan Sawyer

BAHAMAS HIGH COMMISSION
Bahamas House, 10 Chesterfield Street, London W1J 5JL
Tel: 020-7408 4488
*High Commissioner*, HE Basil O'Brien, CMG, apptd 1999

BRITISH HIGH COMMISSION
PO Box N-7516, Nassau
Tel: (00 1 242) 325 7471
*High Commissioner*, HE P. Heigl, apptd 2000

## DEFENCE

The Navy has seven patrol and coastal vessels, four harbour patrol units and four light aircraft.
MILITARY EXPENDITURE – 0.7 per cent of GDP (1999)
MILITARY PERSONNEL – 860: Royal Bahamian Defence Force

## ECONOMY

Tourism employs about 40 per cent of the labour force and provides about half of the country's GDP. International banking and finance are also important, accounting for about 15 per cent of GDP. The absence of direct taxation coupled with internal stability have enabled the country to become one of the world's leading offshore financial centres. A securities exchange was opened in May 2000.

Manufacturing and agriculture account for less than 10 per cent of GDP. Agricultural production is mainly of fresh vegetables, fruit, meat and eggs. Crawfish, other seafood, vegetables, fruit and salt are exported. Reserves of aragonite and limestone are being commercially exploited. Freeport is the country's leading industrial centre, with a pharmaceutical and chemicals plant, an oil trans-shipment and storage terminal, and port and bunkering facilities. There are also a brewery and a rum distillery on New Providence.
GNP – US$3,297 million (1995); US$11,940 per capita (1995)
GDP – US$3,795 million (1997); US$11,395 per capita (1998)
ANNUAL AVERAGE GROWTH OF GDP – 5.2 per cent (1996)
INFLATION RATE – 1.3 per cent (1999)
UNEMPLOYMENT – 9.8 per cent (1997)

### TRADE

The imports are chiefly vehicles, manufactured articles, chemicals and petroleum. The chief exports are machinery and transport equipment, foodstuffs and livestock, raw materials, chemicals, manufactured goods, and beverages and tobacco.

In 1999 the Bahamas had a trade deficit of US$1,428 million and a current account deficit of US$672 million. Imports totalled US$1,810 million and exports US$380 million.

| *Trade with UK* | 1999 | 2000 |
|---|---|---|
| Imports from UK | £31,498,000 | £25,264,000 |
| Exports to UK | 66,724,000 | 45,983,000 |

## COMMUNICATIONS

The main ports are Nassau (New Providence), Freeport (Grand Bahama) and Matthew Town (Inagua). International air services are operated from Abaco, Bimini, Eleuthera, Exuma, Grand Bahama and New Providence. More than 60 smaller airports and landing strips facilitate services between the islands, the services being mainly provided by Bahamasair, the national carrier. In 1997 there were 2,693 km of roads. There are no railways.

## EDUCATION

Education is compulsory between the ages of five and 16. More than 66,000 students are enrolled in Ministry of Education and independent schools in New Providence and the Family Islands.
ILLITERACY RATE – 3.9 per cent (2000)
ENROLMENT (percentage of age group) – primary 98 per cent (1993); secondary 86 per cent (1993); tertiary 17.7 per cent (1985)

---

# BAHRAIN
*Dawlat al-Bahrayn*

---

AREA – 268 sq. miles (694 sq. km)
POPULATION – 665,000 (1997 UN estimate); about 70 per cent are Bahraini; about 40 per cent of the Bahrainis are Sunni Muslims, the remaining 60 per cent being Shias; the ruling family and many of the most prominent merchants are Sunnis. The official language is Arabic; English is often used for business, and Farsi, Hindi and Urdu are also spoken
CAPITAL – ΨManama (Al-Manāmah) (population, 140,401, 1991 census)
CURRENCY – Bahraini dinar (BD) of 1,000 fils
NATIONAL ANTHEM - Bahrayn ona, baladolaman (Our Bahrain, secure)
NATIONAL DAY – 16 December
NATIONAL FLAG – Red, with vertical serrated white bar next to staff
LIFE EXPECTANCY (years) – male 70.6; female 73.6
POPULATION GROWTH RATE – 2.4 per cent (1999)
POPULATION DENSITY – 927 per sq. km (1998)
URBAN POPULATION – 92.2 per cent (2000 estimate)
ILLITERACY RATE – 12.4 per cent (2000)
ENROLMENT (percentage of age group) – primary 98 per cent (1996); secondary 83 per cent (1996); tertiary 20.2 per cent (1993)

Bahrain consists of a group of low-lying islands situated about half-way down the Gulf, some 20 miles off the east coast of Saudi Arabia. The largest of these, Bahrain Island, is about 30 miles long and 10 miles wide at its broadest, with the capital, Manama, situated on the north shore. The second largest, Al-Muharraq, with the town and Bahrain International Airport, is connected to Manama by a causeway 1½ miles long.

### INSURGENCIES

Since 1994 Shi'ite protestors demanding the re-establishment of the National Assembly have regularly clashed with security forces and Shi'ite leaders have been detained. Opponents of the government have engaged in a sustained bombing campaign.

### POLITICAL SYSTEM

Bahrain is a constitutional monarchy and has been fully independent since 1971, when British protectorate status was ended. The 1973 constitution provides for a National Assembly but this was dissolved in 1975. A 40-member Consultative Council, the Majlis al-Shura, was appointed in September 1996; it is an advisory body with no legislative powers.

On 14-15 February 2001, a referendum on constitutional change was held, in which over 98 per cent of the electorate approved plans for the introduction of elections for some of the members of the Consultative Council, the establishment of an independent judiciary and a constitutional monarchy. Women were able to vote for the first time in the referendum.

HEAD OF STATE

*HH The Amir of Bahrain, C.–in –C., Bahrain Defence Force*, Shaikh Hamad bin Isa al-Khalifa, KCMG

CABINET *as at July 2001*

*Prime Minister*, HH Shaikh Khalifa bin Sulman al-Khalifa
*Commerce and Industry*, Ali Saleh Abdulla al-Saleh
*Communications*, Shaikh Ali bin Khalifa bin Sulman al-Khalifa
*Defence*, Maj.-Gen. Shaikh Khalifa bin Ahmed al-Khalifa
*Education*, Mohammad Jassem al-Ghatam
*Electricity and Water*, Shaikh Deij bin Khalifa al-Khalifa
*Finance and National Economy*, Abdulla Hassan Seif
*Foreign Affairs*, Shaikh Mohammed bin Mubarak al-Khalifa
*Health*, Faisal Radhi al-Mousawi
*Housing and Agriculture*, Shaikh Khalid bin Abdullah al-Khalifa
*Information*, Nabil Yacub al-Hamar
*Interior*, Shaikh Mohammed bin Khalifa al-Khalifa
*Justice and Islamic Affairs*, Shaikh Abdullah bin Khalid al-Khalifa
*Labour and Social Affairs*, Abdul-Nabi Abdullah al-Shoala
*Ministers of State*, Mohammed Ibrahim al-Mutawwa (*Cabinet Affairs*); Brig.-Gen. Abdul-Aziz Mohammed al-Fadhil (*Consultative Council Affairs*); Mohammad Abdul Ghaffar Abdullah (*Foreign Affairs*); Jawad Salim al-Arrayed (*Municipal and Environmental Affairs*); Majed Jawad al-Jeshi (*PM's Office*); Mohammad Hassan Kamaledin (*Without Portfolio*)
*Oil*, Shaikh Isa bin Ali bin Hamad al-Khalifa
*Public Works*, Fahmi Ali al-Jouder

EMBASSY OF THE STATE OF BAHRAIN
98 Gloucester Road, London SW7 4AU
Tel: 020-7370 5132/3
*Ambassador Extraordinary and Plenipotentiary*, HE Shaikh Abdul-Aziz bin Mubarak al-Khalifa, apptd 1996

BRITISH EMBASSY
21 Government Avenue, Manama 306, PO Box 114
Tel: (00 973) 534404
E-mail: britemb@batelco.com.bh
*Ambassador Extraordinary and Plenipotentiary*, HE Peter Ford, apptd 1999

BRITISH COUNCIL DIRECTOR, Amanda Burrell, AMA Centre, 146 Shaikh Salman Highway, PO Box 452, Manama 356; e-mail: bc.enquiries@britishcouncil.org.bh

## DEFENCE

The Army has 106 main battle tanks and 340 armoured personnel carriers. The Navy, based at Mina Sulman, has one frigate and 10 patrol and coastal vessels. The Air Force has 34 combat aircraft and 40 armed helicopters.
MILITARY EXPENDITURE – 7.7 per cent of GDP (1999)
MILITARY PERSONNEL – 11,000: Army 8,500, Navy 1,000, Air Force 1,500, Paramilitaries 10,150

## ECONOMY

The largest sources of revenue are oil production and refining. The Bahrain field, discovered in 1932, is wholly owned by the Bahrain National Oil Co. The Sitra refinery derives about 70 per cent of its crude oil by submarine pipeline from Saudi Arabia. Bahrain also has a half share with Saudi Arabia in the profits of the offshore Abu Sa'afa field. A reservoir of unassociated gas has recently been developed on Bahrain Island.

There is some heavy industry on the islands and a number of small to medium-sized industrial units.

The state has developed as a financial centre. Apart from several commercial banks, many international banks have been licensed as offshore banking units; there are also money brokers and merchant banks.
GNP – US$4,909 million (1998); US$7,640 per capita (1998)
GDP – US$5,547 million (1997); US$9,684 per capita (1998)
ANNUAL AVERAGE GROWTH OF GDP – 3.8 per cent (1996)
INFLATION RATE – 0.4 per cent (1998)

TRADE

In 1999 the government had a trade surplus of US$719 million and a current account deficit of US$420 million. Imports totalled US$3,588 million and exports US$4,088 million..

| *Trade with UK* | 1999 | 2000 |
|---|---|---|
| Imports from UK | £118,133,000 | £124,882,000 |
| Exports to UK | 39,076,000 | 83,401,000 |

## COMMUNICATIONS

Bahrain International airport is one of the main air traffic centres of the Gulf; it is the headquarters of Gulf Air, and a stopping point on routes between Europe and Australia and the Far East for other airlines. A causeway links Bahrain to Saudi Arabia.

A worldwide telephone and telex service, by satellite and cable, is operated by Bahrain Telecommunications Company.

---

# BANGLADESH
*Ghana Praja Tantri Bangladesh*

---

AREA – 55,598 sq. miles (143,998 sq. km). Neighbours: India (west, north and east), Myanmar (east)
POPULATION – 127,669,000 (1997 UN estimate). The state language is Bengali. Use of Bengali is compulsory in all government departments. English is understood and is used widely as an unofficial second language. The faith of 88 per cent of the population is Islam and 10.5 per cent Hinduism. Islam has been declared the state religion
CAPITAL – Dhaka (population, 3,397,187, 1991 census)
CURRENCY – Taka (Tk) of 100 poisha
NATIONAL ANTHEM – Amar Sonar Bangla (My golden Bengal)
NATIONAL DAY – 26 March (Independence Day)
NATIONAL FLAG – Red circle on a bottle-green ground
LIFE EXPECTANCY (years) – male 57.5; female 58.1
POPULATION GROWTH RATE – 1.7 per cent (1999)
POPULATION DENSITY – 866 per sq. km (1998)
URBAN POPULATION – 24.5 per cent (2000 estimate)

The country is crossed by a network of rivers, including the eastern arms of the Ganges, the Jamuna (Brahmaputra) and the Meghna, flowing into the Bay of Bengal. The climate is tropical and monsoon; hot and extremely humid during the summer, and mild and dry during the short winter.

## HISTORY AND POLITICS

Prior to becoming East Pakistan, Bangladesh had been the province of East Bengal and the Sylhet district of Assam of British India. The territory acceded to Pakistan in August 1947, which became a republic on 23 March 1956. Bangladesh achieved its independence from Pakistan on 16 December 1971, following a civil war. Pakistan and Bangladesh accorded one another mutual recognition in 1974.

In 1975 a one-party presidential system was introduced, but this was replaced by a multiparty presidential system of government in 1978. President Justice Abdus Sattar was overthrown in 1982 in a coup led by the then Chief of Army Staff, Gen. Ershad. Following parliamentary elections in 1986, Gen. Ershad was elected president. Popular unrest forced his resignation in December 1990; the Bangladesh Nationalist Party (BNP) won the subsequent parliamentary elections. In August 1991 a constitutional amendment returned Bangladesh to parliamentary rule.

In December 1994, the opposition parties resigned from parliament, demanding fresh elections. Public disorder persisted despite a general election in February 1996 which was won by the BNP, although turnout was a mere five per cent. In March 1996, Prime Minister Zia agreed to new elections; these elections in June 1996 produced a majority for the Awami League under Prime Minister Sheikh Hasina Wajed. In November 1997, the BNP walked out of parliament, accusing the government of repression. They returned in March 1998 after signing a memorandum of understanding with the government.

Border clashes occurred between Bangladeshi and Indian troops on the northern border in April 2001.

### POLITICAL SYSTEM

There is a unicameral parliament (*Jatiya Sangsad*) of 330 members, of whom 300 are directly elected and 30 reserved for women, which can amend the constitution by a two-thirds majority. The country is divided into six administrative divisions, sub-divided into 64 districts.

### HEAD OF STATE

*President*, Shahabuddin Ahmed, *sworn in* 9 October 1996

### CABINET *as at July 2001*

*Prime Minister, Armed Forces Division, Cabinet Division, Special Affairs, Defence, Establishment, Energy and Minerals*, Shaikh Hasina Wajed
*Agriculture*, Matia Choudhury
*Chittagong Hill Tracts Affairs*, Kalpa Ranjan Chakma
*Civil Aviation, Tourism, Housing, Public Works*, Mosharraf Hossain
*Commerce*, Abdul Jalil
*Communications*, Anwar Hossain
*Education, Primary and Mass Education Division*, A. S. H. K. Sadek
*Environment and Forests*, Syeda Sajeda Chowdhury
*Finance*, Shah A. M. S. Kibria
*Fisheries and Livestock*, A. S. M. Abdur Rab
*Food*, Amir Hossain Amu
*Foreign Affairs*, Abdus Samad Azad
*Health and Family Welfare*, Sheikh Fazlul Karim Selim
*Home Affairs, Post and Telecommunications*, Mohammad Nasim
*Industry*, Tofael Ahmed
*Labour and Manpower*, Abdul Mannan
*Law, Justice and Parliamentary Affairs*, Abdul Matin Khasru
*Local Government*, Mohammad Zillur Rahman
*Science and Technology*, Lt.-Gen. Nooruddin Khan
*Water Resources, Irrigation and Flood Control*, Abdur Razzak

There are 22 Ministers of State.

### BANGLADESH HIGH COMMISSION

28 Queen's Gate, London SW7 5JA
Tel: 020-7584 0081
*High Commissioner*, vacant
*Defence Adviser*, Brig. M. A. Yusuf Farazi
*First Secretary (Commerce)*, Mohammed Mahmud Reza Khan

### BRITISH HIGH COMMISSION

United Nations Road, Baridhara, Dhaka
PO Box 6079, Dhaka-1212
Tel: (00 880) (2) 882 2705
E-mail: immbhcd@citechco.net
*High Commissioner*, HE Dr D. Carter, CVO
*Deputy High Commissioner*, S. E. Turner
*Defence Adviser*, Brig. S. M. A. Lee, OBE

### BRITISH COUNCIL DIRECTOR,

Carl Reuter, 5 Fuller Road, PO Box 161, Dhaka 1000; e-mail: dhaka.enquiries@bd.britishcouncil.org. There is a regional director in Chittagong

## DEFENCE

The army has 200 main battle tanks and 130 armoured personnel carriers. The Navy has four frigates and 33 patrol and coastal vessels. The Air Force has 83 combat aircraft.
MILITARY EXPENDITURE – 1.9 per cent of GDP (1999)
MILITARY PERSONNEL – 137,000: Army 120,000, Navy 10,500, Air Force 6,500, Paramilitaries 55,200

## ECONOMY

Bangladesh is self-sufficient in food production. Agricultural products include rice, wheat, tobacco, tea, oil seeds, pulses and sugar cane. The chief industries are jute, cotton, tea, leather, pharmaceuticals, fertiliser, sugar, prawn fishing and natural gas. Garment manufacturing is the main export. Remittances sent home by Bangladeshis abroad are of considerable significance to the economy.

Heavy flooding during the summer of 1998 left 23 million people homeless and killed 1,500; two-thirds of the country was under water and 800,000 hectares of farmland was destroyed.

International donors agreed in April 2000 to provide around US$2,000 million in additional aid over a 20-year period dependent on the introduction of free-market economic reforms.

GNP – US$47,071 million (1999); US$370 per capita (1999)
GDP – US$35,107 million (1997); US$299 per capita (1998)
ANNUAL AVERAGE GROWTH OF GDP – 5.6 per cent (1996)
INFLATION RATE – 6.3 per cent (1999)
UNEMPLOYMENT – 2.5 per cent (1996)
TOTAL EXTERNAL DEBT – US$16,376 million (1998)

### TRADE

In 1999 Bangladesh had a current account deficit of US$292 million and a trade deficit of US$1,962 million. Imports totalled US$7,694 million and exports US$3,922 million.

| *Trade with UK* | 1999 | 2000 |
|---|---|---|
| Imports from UK | £63,685,000 | £74,494,000 |
| Exports to UK | 272,266,000 | 381,937,000 |

## COMMUNICATIONS

Principal seaports are Chittagong and Mongla. The Bangladesh Shipping Corporation was set up by the Government to operate the Bangladesh merchant fleet. The principal airports are Dhaka (Zia International) and Chittagong. The international airline, Bangladesh Biman, serves Europe, the Middle East, South and South-East Asia, and an internal network. A railway line links the Bangladeshi town of Benapol with Petrapol in India.

## EDUCATION

Primary education is free and was planned to be universal by 2000. There are 18 universities.

ILLITERACY RATE – 59.2 per cent (2000)
ENROLMENT (percentage of age group) – primary 64 per cent (1990); secondary 18 per cent (1990); tertiary 4.2 per cent (1990)

## BARBADOS

AREA – 166 sq. miles (430 sq. km); nearly 21 miles long by 14 miles broad
POPULATION – 267,000 (1997 UN estimate). The official language is English
CAPITAL – ΨBridgetown in the parish of St Michael (population, 108,000, 1990)
MAJOR TOWNS – Holetown in St James, Oistins in Christ Church and Speightstown in St Peter
CURRENCY – Barbados dollar (BD$) of 100 cents
NATIONAL ANTHEM – In Plenty and in Time of Need
NATIONAL DAY– 30 November (Independence Day)
NATIONAL FLAG – Three vertical stripes, aquamarine, gold and aquamarine, with a trident head on gold stripe
LIFE EXPECTANCY (years) – male 72.7; female 77.8
POPULATION GROWTH RATE – 0.5 per cent (1999)
POPULATION DENSITY – 624 per sq. km (1998)
URBAN POPULATION – 50.0 per cent (2000 estimate)
MILITARY EXPENDITURE – 0.5 per cent of GDP (1999)
MILITARY PERSONNEL – 610: Army 500, Navy 110

Barbados is the most easterly of the Caribbean islands. The land rises in a series of terraced tablelands to the highest point, Mt Hillaby (1,116 ft). The annual average temperature is 26.6°C (79.8°F) with rainfall varying from a yearly average of 75 inches in the high central district to 50 inches in the low-lying coastal areas.

### HISTORY AND POLITICS

The first inhabitants of Barbados were Arawak Indians but the island was uninhabited when first settled by the British in 1627. It was a Crown Colony from 1652 until it became an independent state within the Commonwealth on 30 November 1966.

The last general election took place on 20 January 1999 and seats in the House of Assembly were distributed as follows: Barbados Labour Party 26, Democratic Labour Party 2.

#### POLITICAL SYSTEM

The head of state is the British sovereign. The legislature consists of the Governor-General, a Senate and a House of Assembly. The Senate comprises 21 Senators appointed by the Governor-General, of whom 12 are appointed on the advice of the prime minister, two on the advice of the Leader of the Opposition and seven by the Governor-General at his/her discretion to represent religious, economic or social interests. The House of Assembly comprises 28 members elected every five years by adult suffrage.

There are 11 administrative areas (parishes): St Michael, Christ Church, St Andrew, St George, St James, St John, St Joseph, St Lucy, St Peter, St Philip and St Thomas.

*Governor-General*, HE Sir Clifford Husbands, GCMG, KA, apptd 1996

#### CABINET *as at July 2001*

*Prime Minister, Defence and Security, Finance and Economic Affairs*, Owen Arthur
*Deputy Prime Minister, Foreign Affairs, Foreign Trade*, Billie Miller
*Agriculture and Rural Development*, Anthony Wood
*Attorney-General and Home Affairs*, David Simmons, QC
*Consumer Affairs and Business Development*, Ronald Toppin
*Education, Youth Affairs and Culture*, Mia Mottley
*Environment, Energy and Natural Resources*, Rawle Eastmond
*Health*, Philip Goddard
*Housing and Lands*, Gline Clarke
*Industry and International Business*, Reginald Farley
*Labour, Sports and Public Sector Reform*, Rudolph Greenidge
*Minister of State, Prime Minister's Office*, Glyne Murray
*Public Works and Transport*, Rommel Marshall
*Social Transformation*, Hamilton Lashley
*Tourism and International Transport*, Noel Anderson Lynch

#### BARBADOS HIGH COMMISSION

1 Great Russell Street, London WC1B 3JY
Tel: 020-7631 4975
*High Commissioner*, HE Peter Simmons, apptd 1995
*Deputy High Commissioner*, Herbert Yearwood
*First Secretary (Commercial)*, Jannette Babb

#### BRITISH HIGH COMMISSION

Lower Collymore Rock, PO Box 676, Bridgetown
Tel: (00 1 246) 430 7800
E-mail: britishhc@sunbeach.net
*High Commissioner*, HE John White, apptd 2001
*Deputy High Commissioner*, M. J. E. Mayhew
*Defence Adviser*, Capt. P. Jackson
*First Secretary (Chancery)*, P. Curwen

### ECONOMY

The economy is based on tourism, sugar and light manufacturing. In 1995, 442,107 tourists visited Barbados and 484,670 cruise ship passengers. Chief exports are sugar, chemicals, electronic components and clothing.
GNP – US$2,294 million (1999); US$6,560 per capita (1995)
GDP – US$2,183 million (1997); US$8,717 per capita (1998)
ANNUAL AVERAGE GROWTH OF GDP – 5.5 per cent (1996)
INFLATION RATE – 1.6 per cent (1999)
UNEMPLOYMENT – 14.5 per cent (1997)
TOTAL EXTERNAL DEBT – US$608 million (1998)

#### TRADE

In 1998 Barbados had a current account deficit of US$57 million and a trade deficit of US$644 million. In 1999 exports totalled US$229 million and imports US$1,021 million.

| *Trade with UK* | 1999 | 2000 |
|---|---|---|
| Imports from UK | £43,407,000 | £51,191,000 |
| Exports to UK | 21,526,000 | 24,496,000 |

### COMMUNICATIONS

Barbados has some 965 miles of roads, of which about 917 miles are asphalted. The Grantley Adams International airport is situated at Seawell, 12 miles from Bridgetown. Bridgetown, the only port of entry, has a deep-water harbour with berths for eight ships; oil is pumped ashore at Spring Garden and at an Esso installation on the West Coast.

### EDUCATION

Education is free in government schools at primary and secondary levels. There are 105 primary schools, 22 government secondary schools and 10 private secondary schools.
ENROLMENT (percentage of age group) – primary 78 per cent (1991); secondary 75 per cent (1989); tertiary 28.7 per cent (1996)

## BELARUS
*Respublika Belarus*

AREA – 80,155 sq. miles (207,600 sq. km). Neighbours: Latvia and Lithuania (north), Russia (east), Ukraine (south), Poland (west)
POPULATION – 9,999,600 (2001 estimate): 78 per cent Belarusian, 13 per cent Russian, 4 per cent Polish and 3 per cent Ukrainian, with smaller numbers of Jews and Lithuanians. Belarusian and Russian have equal official language status. Most of the population are Belarusian Orthodox with a minority of Roman Catholics
CAPITAL – Minsk (population, 1,716,757, 1998 UN estimate); the administrative centre of the CIS
MAJOR CITIES – Brest (297,235); Homyel' (501,926); Hrodna (306,296); Mahilyow (368,886); Vitsyebsk (355,829), 1998 estimates
CURRENCY – Belarusian rouble
NATIONAL ANTHEM – The former Soviet national anthem but with the words omitted
NATIONAL DAY – 3 July (Independence Day)
NATIONAL FLAG – Red with a green strip along the lower edge, and in the hoist a vertical red and white ornamental pattern
LIFE EXPECTANCY (years) – male 62.4; female 74.6
POPULATION GROWTH RATE – 0.0 per cent (1999)
POPULATION DENSITY – 49 per sq. km (1998)
URBAN POPULATION – 71.2 per cent (2000 estimate)

Belarus is situated in the western part of the European area of the former USSR. The main rivers are the upper reaches of the Dnieper, of the Niemen and of the Western Dvina. Much of the land is a plain, with many lakes, swamps and marshy areas. The climate is continental with mild, humid winters and relatively cool and rainy summers.

### HISTORY AND POLITICS

After being absorbed into Lithuania in the 13th and 14th centuries, the Belarusian nationality, language and culture flourished until Belarus came under Polish rule in the mid-16th century. Two hundred years of Polish rule followed until Belarus was re-absorbed into the Russian Empire.

Belarus was devastated by the German invasion in the Second World War; 25 per cent of the population was killed and thousands deported.

Belarus issued a Declaration of State Sovereignty on 27 July 1990 and declared its independence from the Soviet Union after the failed coup in Moscow in August 1991. Stanislav Shuskevich became Belarusian leader at the head of a coalition of Communists and democrats, but he was forced to resign in January 1994 and was replaced by Gen. Mecheslav Grib who pursued closer political, economic and trade relations with Russia. The presidential election in June 1994 was won by Alexandr Lukashenka.

The most recent legislative election was held on 15 October 2000, with a second round on 29 October. The election was condemned as neither free nor fair by opposition groups and international observers from OSCE, the European Parliament and the Council of Europe. Most opposition parties boycotted the election and many opposition candidates were prevented from standing or intimidated into withdrawing by the authorities.

#### FOREIGN RELATIONS

An agreement was signed with Russia in April 1996 to form a Commonwealth of Independent States (CIS). In April 1997 a treaty of union was signed with Russia. The presidents of Belarus and Russia signed documents in December 1998 which called for the adoption of a common budget and single currency and for joint defence and security policies. On 8 December 1999, they signed the Treaty on the Creation of a Union State, which committed the two countries to eventually becoming a confederal state. In April 2001, the National Assembly ratified an agreement to introduce the Russian rouble as the currency of the Russia-Belarus Union State from 2005, with a new union currency from 2008.

#### POLITICAL SYSTEM

The president's term of office is five years, although two referendums in 1996 and 1997 extended Lukashenka's term until 2002; the president has authority to appoint half the members of the constitutional court and the electoral commission. The legislature is the bicameral National Assembly, comprising a 110-member House of Representatives (lower chamber) and a 64-member Council of the Republic (upper chamber). Eight members of the upper chamber are appointed by the president, the rest are indirectly elected by members of the local soviets in each region.

The republic is divided into six regions (*oblasts*): Brest, Homyel', Hrodna, Minsk, Mahilow and Vitsyebsk.

#### HEAD OF STATE

*President*, Alyaksandr Lukashenka, *elected* 10 July 1994

#### COUNCIL OF MINISTERS *as at July 2001*

*Prime Minister*, Uladzimir Yermoshin
*First Deputy Prime Minister*, Andrey Kabyakou
*Deputy Prime Ministers*, Alyaksandr Popkou (*Agro-industrial Complex*); Mikhail Khvastou (*Foreign Affairs*); Valery Kokoreu (*Industrial Development, Fuel and Energy*); Mikhail Dzyamchuk (*Science, Education and Healthcare*); Uladzimir Zamyatalin (*Social and Cultural Policy*); Leanid Kozik (*Taxation, State Property, Privatisation, Agriculture and Food*), Mikhail Rusy
*Architecture and Construction*, Genadz Kurachkin
*Communications and Information Technology*, Uladzimir Hancharenkai
*Culture*, Leonid Hulyaka
*Defence*, Lt.-Gen. Leanid Maltsau
*Economy*, Uladzimir Shymou
*Education*, Vasil Strazhau
*Emergency Situations*, Valery Astapou
*Enterprise and Investments*, Alyaksandr Sazonau
*Finance*, Nikolai Korbut
*Forestry*, Valentin Zorin
*Health*, Igor Zelenkevich
*Housing and Communal Services*, Boris Batura
*Industry*, Anatol Kharlap
*Internal Affairs (acting)*, Maj.-Gen. Uladzimir Navumau
*Justice*, Genadz Varantsou
*Labour*, Ivan Lyakh
*Natural Resources and Environmental Protection*, Lyavontsiy Kharuzhyk
*Social Security*, Volga Dargel
*Sport and Tourism*, Yawhen Vorsin
*State Property and Privatisation*, Vasil Novak
*Statistics and Analysis*, Uladzimir Zinavsky
*Trade*, Pyotr Kazlo
*Transport*, Alyaksandr Lukashou

#### EMBASSY OF THE REPUBLIC OF BELARUS

6 Kensington Court, London W8 5DL
Tel: 020-7937 3288
*Ambassador Extraordinary and Plenipotentiary*, HE Dr Valery Sadokho, apptd 2000

#### BRITISH EMBASSY

37 Karl Marx Street, BY-220030 Minsk
Tel: (00 375) (172) 105920
E-mail: pia@bepost.belpak.minsk.by
*Ambassador Extraordinary and Plenipotentiary*, HE Iain Kelly, apptd 1999

## DEFENCE

The Army has 1,724 main battle tanks, 1,560 armoured infantry fighting vehicles and 918 armoured personnel carriers. The Air Force has 230 combat aircraft and 60 armed helicopters.

MILITARY EXPENDITURE – 5.0 per cent of GDP (1999)
MILITARY PERSONNEL – 83,100: Army 43,500, Air Force 22,500, Paramilitaries 110,000
CONSCRIPTION DURATION – 18 months

## ECONOMY

Agricultural productivity was severely affected by nuclear fallout from the Chernobyl disaster in 1986 although Belarus is now self-sufficient in the production of foodstuffs. As a result of the collapse of the Soviet centrally planned economic system, the country lost cheap supplies of energy and raw materials. Energy from Russia is still the largest import.

Economic reform and privatisation have been introduced and in May 1995 a customs union agreement with Russia took effect. A treaty was signed with Kazakhstan, Kyrgyzstan and Russia in March 1996 aimed at the establishment of a single customs territory. In December 1997 the first Russia-Belarus joint budget was endorsed, with projects estimated to cost US$100 billion. Industrial output increased by 9.7 per cent in 1999.

In 1999 Belarus had a trade deficit of US$599 million and a current account deficit of US$257 million. Imports totalled US$6,664 million and exports US$5,922 million.

GNP – US$26,299 million (1999); US$2,630 per capita (1999)
GDP – US$13,779 million (1997); US$1,360 per capita (1998)
INFLATION RATE – 293.7 per cent (1999)
UNEMPLOYMENT – 2.3 per cent (1998)
TOTAL EXTERNAL DEBT – US$1,120 million (1998)

| *Trade with UK* | 1999 | 2000 |
|---|---|---|
| Imports from UK | £26,946,000 | £36,251,000 |
| Exports to UK | 21,104,000 | 34,158,000 |

## CULTURE AND EDUCATION

Belarusian is an Eastern Slavonic language, closely related to Russian and Ukrainian and written in the Cyrillic script. Important cultural figures include the poet Yanka Kupala (1882-1942), the writer Yakub Kolas (1882-1956) and the painter Marc Chagall (1887-1985).

The national education system comprises pre-school, general secondary, out-of-school, vocational training and trade schools, secondary specialised and higher education. General secondary education begins at the age of six. There are also 22 private educational institutions.

ILLITERACY RATE – 0.6 per cent (2000)
ENROLMENT (percentage of age group) – primary 85 per cent (1996); tertiary 43.8 per cent (1996)

---

# BELGIUM
*Koninkrijk België*

---

AREA – 11,787 sq. miles (30,528 sq. km). Neighbours: the Netherlands (north), France (south), Germany and Luxembourg (east)
POPULATION – 10,239,085 (2000 estimate). Greater Brussels 959,318; Flanders 5,940,251; Wallonia 3,339,516, of whom 70,831 are German-speaking. Roman Catholicism is the religion of 86 per cent of the population. The official languages are Flemish, French and German
CAPITAL – Brussels (population, 959,318, 2000 estimate)
MAJOR CITIES – ΨAntwerp, the chief port (931,718); Bruges (269,158); Charleroi (424,515); ΨGhent (493,329); Liège (588,312); Leuven (453,772); Mons (250,748); Namur (279,675), 1998 estimates
CURRENCY – Euro (€) of 100 cents/Belgian franc (or frank) of 100 centimes (centiemen)
NATIONAL ANTHEM – O Vaderland, o edel land der Belgen (Oh Fatherland, oh noble land of the Belgians)
NATIONAL DAY – 21 July (Accession of King Leopold I, 1831)
NATIONAL FLAG – Three vertical bands, black, yellow, red
LIFE EXPECTANCY (years) – male 74.5; female 81.3
POPULATION GROWTH RATE – 0.2 per cent (1999)
POPULATION DENSITY – 335 per sq. km (1998)
URBAN POPULATION – 97.3 per cent (2000 estimate)

The Maas and its tributary, the Sambre, divide Belgium into two distinct regions, that in the west being generally level and fertile, while the tableland of the Ardennes, in the east, has mostly poor soil. The polders near the coast, which are protected by dykes against floods, cover an area of 193 sq. miles. The principal rivers are the Schelde and the Maas.

Belgium is divided between those who speak Dutch (the Flemings) and those who speak French (the Walloons). Dutch is recognised as the official language in the northern areas and French in the southern (Walloon) area and there are guarantees for the respective linguistic minorities. Brussels is officially bilingual. There is a small German-speaking area (Eupen and Malmédy) along the German border, east of Liège.

## HISTORY AND POLITICS

The kingdom formed part of the Low Countries (Netherlands) from 1815 until 14 October 1830, when a National Congress proclaimed its independence. Belgium was invaded by Germany in 1914 and Eupen and Malmédy were ceded to Belgium by Germany under the Versailles Treaty of 1919. The kingdom was again invaded by Germany in 1940 and was occupied by Nazi troops until liberated by the Allies in September 1944. In 1977 Belgium was divided into three administrative regions: Flanders, Wallonia and Brussels.

The last general election was held on 13 June 1999. The results were as follows (seats):

*Chamber of Deputies:* Christian Social Party (CVP) (Flemish) 22; Socialist Party (PS) (Francophone) 19; Flemish Liberals and Democrats (VLD) 23; Socialist Party (SP) (Flemish) 14; Liberal Reform Party-Democratic Front (PRL-FDF) (Francophone) 18; Christian Social Party (PSC) (Francophone) 10; Vlaams Blok (Flemish Nationalist Party) 15; Ecolo (Francophone Ecology Party) 11; Agalev (Flemish Environmental Party) 9; Flemish People's Union (VU) 8; Front National (FN) 1.

*Senate:* of the 40 seats directly elected, CVP 6; SP 4; VLD 6; PRL-FDF 5; PS 4; PSC 3; Vlaams Blok 4; VU 2; Ecolo 3; Agalev 3. A further 31 Senators are indirectly elected or co-opted (*see* below).

### POLITICAL SYSTEM

Belgium is a constitutional representative and hereditary monarchy with a bicameral legislature, consisting of the King, the Senate and the Chamber of Deputies. The parliamentary term is four years. Amendments to the constitution enacted since 1968 have devolved power to the regions. The national government retains competence only in foreign and defence policies, the national budget and monetary policy, social security, and the judicial, legal and penal systems. The Senate has 71 seats, of which 40 are directly elected, 21 indirectly elected and ten co-opted by the Flemish and Francophone Communities. The Chamber of Deputies has 150 seats. There are four levels of sub-national government: community, regional, provincial, and communal.

### Federal Structure

There are three communities: Flemish; Francophone; Germanophone. Each community has its own assembly, which elects the community government. At this level, Flanders is covered by the Flemish Community Assembly; most of Wallonia is covered by the Francophone Community Assembly, and the areas of Wallonia in the German-speaking communities of Eupen and Malmédy are covered by the Germanophone Community Assembly; Brussels is covered by a Joint Community Commission of the Flemish and Francophone Community Assemblies.

At regional level, Belgium is divided into the three regions of Wallonia, Brussels and Flanders. Each region has its own assembly and government.

There are ten provinces; five French-speaking in Wallonia (Hainaut, Liège, Luxembourg, Namur and French Brabant); and five Dutch-speaking in Flanders (Antwerp, East Flanders, West Flanders, Limburg and Flemish Brabant). In addition, Belgium has 589 communes as the lowest level of local government.

*Minister-President of the Flemish Government*, Patrick Dewael (VLD)
*Minister-President of the Walloon Regional Government*, Jean-Claude Van Cauwenberghe (PS)
*Head of City Government in Brussels*, François-Xavier de Donnéa

### Head of State

*HM The King of the Belgians*, King Albert II, *born* 6 June 1934; *succeeded* 9 August 1993; *married* 2 July 1959, Donna Paola Ruffo di Calabria, and has *issue* Prince Philippe (*see* below); Princess Astrid, *b.* 5 June 1962; Prince Laurent, *b.* 19 October 1963
*Heir*, HRH Prince Philippe Léopold Louis Marie, *born* 15 April 1960

### Cabinet *as at July 2001*

*Prime Minister*, Guy Verhofstadt (VLD)
*Deputy PM, Budget, Social Integration and Social Economy*, Johan Vande Lanotte (SP)
*Deputy PM, Foreign Affairs*, Louis Michel (PRL)
*Deputy PM, Labour and Equal Opportunities*, Laurette Onkelinx (PS)
*Deputy PM, Mobility and Transport*, Isabelle Durant (Ecolo)
*Agriculture and Small and Medium-sized Enterprises*, Jaak Gabriels (VLD)
*Civil Service and Modernisation of Public Administration*, Luc Van Den Bossche (SP)
*Consumer Protection, Public Health and Environment*, Magda Aelvoet (Agalev)
*Defence*, André Flahaut (PS)
*Economic Affairs and Scientific Research*, Charles Picqué (PS)
*Finance*, Didier Reynders (PRL)
*Interior*, Antoine Duquesne (PRL)
*Justice*, Mark Verwilghen (VLD)
*Social Affairs and Pensions*, Frank Vandenbroucke (SP)
*Telecommunications, Public Enterprises and Participation*, Rik Daems (VLD)

Agalev Green Party (Flemish); Ecolo Green Party (Francophone); PS Socialist Party (Francophone); SP Socialist Party (Flemish); PRL Liberal Reform Party (Francophone); VLD Liberal Democrats (Flemish)

### Belgian Embassy

103-105 Eaton Square, London SW1W 9AB
Tel: 020-7470 3700
*Ambassador Extraordinary and Plenipotentiary*, HE Lode Willems, apptd 1997
*Minister-Counsellors*, P. Roland (*Political*); F. De Sutter (*Economic*)
*Defence Attaché*, Capt. A. Kockx

### British Embassy

Aarlenstraat 85, B-1040 Brussels
Tel: (00 32) (2) 287 6211
*Ambassador Extraordinary and Plenipotentiary*, HE David Colvin, CMG, apptd 1993
*Deputy Head of Mission, Counsellor (Commercial and Economic) and Consul-General*, J. Smith
*Defence Attaché*, Col. T. Hall, CBE
There are British Consular Offices at Brussels, Antwerp and Liège.

British Council Director for Belgium and Luxembourg - M.Rose, Liefdadigheidstraat 15, B-1210 Brussels; e-mail: bc.brussels@britishcouncil.be
British Chamber of Commerce for Belgium and Luxembourg (Inc.), Egmontstraat 15, B-1000 Brussels

## DEFENCE

The Army has 140 main battle tanks, 468 armoured personnel carriers, 283 armoured infantry fighting vehicles and 76 helicopters. The Navy is based at Ostend and Zeebrugge and has three frigates. The Air Force has 90 combat aircraft.

The headquarters of NATO, SHAPE and the Western European Union Military Planning Cell are in Belgium; 790 US personnel are stationed in the country.

Military Expenditure – 1.5 per cent of GDP (1999)
Military Personnel – 39,250: Army 26,800, Navy 2,600, Air Force 8,600, Medical Service 1,250

## ECONOMY

The service sector accounts for more than half of Belgium's GDP. With no natural resources except coal, production of which has now ceased, industry is based

| *Province* | *Area (sq. km)* | *Population (2000)* | *Main Town* | *Population (1998)* |
|---|---|---|---|---|
| Flanders | | | | |
| Antwerp | 2,867 | 1,643,972 | Antwerp | 931,718 |
| East Flanders | 2,982 | 1,361,623 | Ghent | 493,329 |
| Flemish Brabant | 2,106 | 1,014,704 | Leuven | 453,772 |
| Limburg | 2,422 | 791,178 | Hasselt | 67,456 |
| West Flanders | 3,144 | 1,128,774 | Bruges | 269,158 |
| Wallonia | | | | |
| Hainaut | 3,786 | 1,279,467 | Mons | 92,260 |
| Liège | 3,862 | 1,019,442 | Liège | 588,312 |
| Luxembourg | 4,440 | 246,820 | Arlon | 15,000 |
| Namur | 3,666 | 443,903 | Namur | 279,675 |
| Walloon Brabant | 1,091 | 349,884 | Wavre | 27,000 |

largely on the processing for re-export of imported raw materials. Principal industries are steel and metal products, chemicals and petrochemicals, textiles, glass, and foodstuffs.

Belgium has participated in the European Single Currency since 1 January 1999.

In 1999 there was a budget deficit of 0.9 per cent of GDP and public debt was 112.5 per cent of GDP.

GNP – US$252,051 million (1999); US$24,510 per capita (1999)
GDP – US$242,508 million (1997); US$24,347 per capita (1999)
ANNUAL AVERAGE GROWTH OF GDP – 3.2 per cent (2000)
INFLATION RATE – 2.1 per cent (2001)
UNEMPLOYMENT – 6.8 per cent (2001)

### TRADE

External trade figures relate to Luxembourg as well as Belgium since the two countries formed an economic union in 1921. The main trading partners are Germany, France, the Netherlands and the UK.

In 1999 Belgium and Luxembourg had a trade surplus of US$7,486 million and a current account surplus of US$11,961 million. Exports from Belgium totalled US$160,818 million and imports US$176,198 million.

| *Trade with UK* | 1999 | 2000 |
|---|---|---|
| Imports from UK | £8,680,100,000 | £9,570,300,000 |
| Exports to UK | 9,022,000,000 | 9,688,400,000 |

## COMMUNICATIONS

The railways are operated by the Belgian National Railways. Major ports include Antwerp, Zeebrugge, Ghent and Ostend. There are 1,586 km of inland waterways; ship canals link Ghent with Terneuzen in the Netherlands, Willebroek Rupel with Brussels, Zeebrugge with Bruges, Liège with Antwerp and Charleroi with Brussels. The rivers Maas, Sambre and Schelde form an integral part of the network.

There are 14,421 km of trunk road, of which 1,631 km are motorways.

## CULTURE AND EDUCATION

The literature of France and the Netherlands is supplemented by an indigenous Belgian literary activity in both French and Dutch. Flemish literary figures include Guido Gezelle (1830-1899) and Karel van de Woestijne (1878-1929). Francophone authors include Maurice Maeterlinck (1862–1949), who was awarded the Nobel Prize for Literature in 1911, the poet Émile Verhaeren (1855–1916) and Georges Simenon (1903–1989).

Nursery schools provide free education for children from two and a half to six years. There are over 4,000 primary schools (6 to 12 years), more than 1,000 secondary schools offering a general academic education slightly over half of which are free institutions (predominantly Roman Catholic but subsidised by the state) and the remainder official institutions. The official school-leaving age is 18.

ENROLMENT (percentage of age group) – primary 98 per cent (1996); secondary 88 per cent (1996); tertiary 56.3 per cent (1996)

---

# BELIZE

---

AREA – 8,763 sq. miles (22,696 sq. km). Neighbours: Mexico (north and north-west), Guatemala (west and south)
POPULATION – 247,000 (1997 UN estimate): 44 per cent Mestizo (Maya-Spanish); 26 per cent Creole; 11 per cent Maya; plus a number of East Indian and Spanish descent. The races are now inter-mixed. The majority of the population is Christian, about 58 per cent Catholic and 34 per cent Protestant. The official language and language of instruction is English. Spanish is also widely spoken and English Creole is the vernacular. There are also Garifuna and Maya speakers
CAPITAL – Belmopan (population, 44,087, 1991)
MAJOR CITIES – ΨBelize City (1993 census 46,342), the former capital; Corozal (7,420); Dangriga (6,761); Orange Walk (11,573); San Ignacio (9,417)
CURRENCY – Belize dollar (BZ$) of 100 cents. The Belize dollar is tied to the US dollar, BZ$2=US$1
NATIONAL ANTHEM – Land of the Free
NATIONAL DAY – 21 September (Independence Day)
NATIONAL FLAG – Blue ground with red band along top and bottom edges, and in centre a white disc containing the coat of arms surrounded by a green garland
LIFE EXPECTANCY (years) – male 69.6; female 75.0
POPULATION GROWTH RATE – 2.6 per cent (1999)
POPULATION DENSITY – 11 per sq. km (1998)
URBAN POPULATION – 54.2 per cent (2000 estimate)
MILITARY EXPENDITURE – 2.5 per cent of GDP (1999)
MILITARY PERSONNEL – Army 1,050

The coastal areas are mostly flat and swampy with many islets but the country rises gradually towards the interior, which is mainly forest. The northern and western districts are hilly, and in the south the Maya Mountains and the Cockscombs form the backbone of the country, reaching a height of 3,700 feet at Victoria Peak. The climate is sub-tropical.

## HISTORY AND POLITICS

Numerous ruins in the area indicate that Belize was heavily populated by the Maya Indians. The first British settlement was established in 1638 but was subject to repeated attacks by the Spanish, who claimed sovereignty until defeated by the Royal Navy and settlers in 1798. In 1871 the area was recognised by Britain as a colony and called British Honduras. The colony became self-governing in 1964, with the UK retaining control of foreign policy, internal security and defence. In 1973 the colony was renamed Belize, and was granted independence on 21 September 1981.

The 1998 elections were won by the People's United Party, who took 26 out of the 29 seats in the House of Representatives.

### FOREIGN RELATIONS

A long-standing territorial dispute with Guatemala was provisionally resolved in 1992 when the Guatemalan Congress and Supreme Court voted to recognise Belize and establish diplomatic relations. Guatemala still retains its claim, subject to arbitration by the International Court of Justice.

### POLITICAL SYSTEM

Queen Elizabeth II is head of state, represented in Belize by a Governor-General. There is a National Assembly, comprising a House of Representatives (29 members elected for five years) and a Senate (eight members appointed by the Governor-General on the advice of the prime minister and the leader of the opposition). Executive power is vested in the Cabinet, which is responsible to the National Assembly.

*Governor-General*, HE Sir Colville Norbert Young, GCMG, apptd 17 November 1993

CABINET *as at July 2001*

*Prime Minister, Finance and Foreign Affairs*, Said Musa
*Deputy PM, Natural Resources, Environment and Industry*, John Briceño
*Senior Minister*, George Price*Agriculture, Fisheries and Co-operatives*, Daniel Silva
*Attorney-General, Information*, Godfrey Smith
*Budget Management, Investment and Trade*, Ralph Fonseca
*Education and Sports*, Cordel Hyde
*Health and Public Services*, José Coye
*Housing, Urban Renewal and Home Affairs*, Richard Bradley
*Human Development, Women and Civil Society*, Dolores Balderamos García
*National Security and Economic Development*, Jorge Espat
*Public Utilities, Energy, Communications and Immigration*, Maxwell Samuels
*Rural Development and Culture*, Marcial Mes
*Sugar Industry, Local Government and Labour*, Valdemar Castillo
*Tourism and Youth*, Mark Espat
*Works, Transport, Citrus and Banana Industries*, Henry Canton

BELIZE HIGH COMMISSION
22 Harcourt House, 19 Cavendish Square, London W1M 9AD
Tel: 020-7499 9728
*High Commissioner*, HE Assad Shoman, apptd 1999

BRITISH HIGH COMMISSION
PO Box 91, Belmopan
Tel: (00 501) (8) 22146/7
E-mail: brithicom@btl.net
*High Commissioner*, HE Philip Priestley, apptd 2001

## ECONOMY

About 30 per cent of the population is engaged in agriculture. The country is more or less self-sufficient in fresh beef, pork and poultry, but processed meat and dairy products are imported. About 25 per cent of timber production (mostly mahogany) is exported, and there is a large US market for lobster, conch and scale fish. Tourism is also a valuable source of income.

In 1999 Belize had a trade deficit of US$129 million and a current account deficit of US$77 million. Imports totalled US$366 million and exports US$166 million.

GNP – US$673 million (1999); US$2,730 per capita (1999)
GDP – US$625 million (1997); US$2,741 per capita (1998)
ANNUAL AVERAGE GROWTH OF GDP – 3.5 per cent (1996)
INFLATION RATE – 1.2 per cent (1999)
UNEMPLOYMENT – 12.7 per cent (1997)
TOTAL EXTERNAL DEBT – US$338 million (1998)

| *Trade with UK* | 1999 | 2000 |
|---|---|---|
| Imports from UK | £11,658,000 | £11,460,000 |
| Exports to UK | 43,229,000 | 39,565,000 |

## COMMUNICATIONS

There is a government-operated radio service and six privately-owned radio stations but no official television service in the country. An automatic telephone service operated by Belize Telecommunications Ltd covers the whole country.

The principal airport is at Belize City and various airlines operate international flights to the USA and other Central American states. The main port is also Belize City, which has deep water quays. Several inland waterways are also navigable. There are 1,865 miles of road, including four main highways, but there is no railway system.

## EDUCATION

Education is compulsory from six to 14 years of age. In 1992 primary education was provided by 241 schools, most of which are government-aided. Secondary education is provided by 40 secondary and post-secondary institutions. A University College of Belize has been established. There is an extra-mural faculty of the University of the West Indies, with a resident tutor.

ENROLMENT (percentage of age group) – primary 99 per cent (1994); secondary 36 per cent (1992)

# BENIN
*République du Benin*

AREA – 43,484 sq. miles (112,622 sq. km). Neighbours: Togo (west), Burkina Faso and Niger (north), Nigeria (east)
POPULATION – 6,114,000 (1997 UN estimate). The official language is French
CAPITAL – ΨPorto Novo (population, 179,138, 1992)
MAJOR TOWNS – ΨCotonou (487,020, 1992) is the principal commercial town and port
CURRENCY – Franc CFA of 100 centimes
NATIONAL ANTHEM - L'aube nouvelle (The new dawn)
NATIONAL DAY – 30 November
NATIONAL FLAG – Two horizontal stripes of yellow over red with a vertical green band in the hoist
LIFE EXPECTANCY (years) – male 51.3; female 53.3
POPULATION GROWTH RATE – 2.7 per cent (1999)
POPULATION DENSITY – 54 per sq. km (1998)
URBAN POPULATION - 42.3 per cent (2000 estimate))
MILITARY EXPENDITURE – 1.4 per cent of GDP (1999)
MILITARY PERSONNEL – 4,750: Army 4,500, Navy 100, Air Force 150, Paramilitaries 2,500
CONSCRIPTION DURATION – 18 months (selective)
ILLITERACY RATE – 62.5 per cent (2000)
ENROLMENT (percentage of age group) – primary 63 per cent (1996); tertiary 3.1 per cent (1996)

Benin (formerly known as Dahomey) has a short coastline of 78 miles on the Gulf of Guinea but extends northwards inland for 437 miles. The four main regions, running horizontally, are a narrow sandy coastal strip, a succession of inter-communicating lagoons, a clay belt and a sandy plateau in the north.

## HISTORY AND POLITICS

Benin was placed under French administration in 1892 and became an independent republic within the French Community in December 1958; full independence outside the Community was proclaimed on 1 August 1960. Between 1963 and 1972 successive governments were overthrown by the military until a coup d'état in 1972 brought to power a Marxist-Leninist military government headed by Lt.-Col. Kérékou.

A pluralistic constitution was adopted in December 1990 and legislative and presidential elections were held in 1991. Nicéphore Soglo was sworn in as president and appointed a Benin Renaissance Party (PRB)-dominated provisional government. He was defeated by Gen. Kérékou in a presidential election in March 1996. Legislative elections to the 83-seat National Assembly in March 1999 gave the PRB and allies 27 seats and opposition parties 42 seats. Gen. Kérékou won a second term of office in presidential elections held on 4 and 22 March 2001.

### POLITICAL SYSTEM

The president is head of government as well as head of state, and is directly elected for a five-year term, renewable once only. The president appoints and presides over the Council of Ministers. The National Assembly has 83 members, directly elected for a maximum of four years.

HEAD OF STATE

*President and Head of the Armed Forces*, HE Gen. Mathieu Kérékou, *elected* 1996, *re-elected* 22 March 2001, *sworn in* 3 April 2001

CABINET *as at July 2001*

*State Minister in charge of Co-ordination of Government Action, Planning, Employment Promotion and Expansion*, Bruno Amoussou
*Minister Delegate to the Presidency, Defence*, Pierre Osho
*Civil Service, Administrative Reform*, Ousmane Batoko
*Commerce, Industry, Community Development and Employment Promotion*, Lazare Sehoueto
*Culture, Handicrafts, Tourism*, Amos Elegbe
*Communications and the Promotion of New Information Technologies*, Gaston Zossou
*Environment, Housing and Town Planning*, Luc-Marie Constant Gnancadja
*Family Affairs, Social Welfare and Solidarity*, Claire Hougan Ayemona
*Finance and Economy*, Abdoulaye Bio Tchane
*Foreign Affairs and Co-operation*, Antoine Idji Kolawole
*Health*, Marina d'Almeida-Massougbodji
*Higher Education and Scientific Research*, Dorothée Sossa
*Industry, Small and Medium-sized Enterprises*, John Igue
*Interior, Security and Territorial Administration*, Daniel Tawema
*Justice, Legislation and Human Rights*, Joseph Gnonlonfou
*Mines, Energy and Water Resources*, Kamarou Fassassi
*National Education and Scientific Research*, Damien Alahassa
*Primary and Secondary Education*, Jean Bio Tchabi Orou
*Public Health*, Céline Seignon Kandissounon
*Public Works and Transport*, Joseph Attin
*Relations with Institutions, Civilian Society and Benin Nationals Abroad*, Adekpedjou Sylvain Akindes
*Rural Development*, Théophile Nata
*Social Welfare and Women's Affairs*, Ramatou Baba-Moussa
*Trade, Tourism and Handicrafts*, Séverin Adjovi
*Vocational Training*, Dominique Sohounhloue
*Youth, Sports and Leisure*, Valentin Aditi House

EMBASSY OF THE REPUBLIC OF BENIN
87 Avenue Victor Hugo, F-75116 Paris, France
Tel: (00 33) (1) 4500 9882
*Ambassador Extraordinary and Plenipotentiary*, HE André-Guy Ologoudou, apptd 1998
HONORARY CONSULATE, Dolphin House, 16 The Broadway, Stanmore, Middx HA7 4DW. Tel: 020-8954 8800. *Honorary Consul*, Lawrence Landau

BRITISH AMBASSADOR, HE Sir Graham Burton, KCMG, resident at Lagos, Nigeria
BRITISH CONSULATE, Lot 24, Patte d'Oie, Contonou, Benin. Tel: (00 229) 301120. *Honorary Consul*, C. Barnes

## ECONOMY

The principal exports are cotton, palm products, groundnuts, shea-nuts, and coffee. Small deposits of gold, iron and chrome have been found. Oil production started in 1983.

In July 2000 the IMF and the International Development Association agreed to a US$460 million debt reduction package for Benin.

In 1997 Benin had a trade surplus of US$153 million and a current account surplus of US$154 million. In 1999 imports totalled US$643 million and exports US$389 million.

GNP – US$2,320 million (1999); US$380 per capita (1999)
GDP – US$2,048 million (1997); US$399 per capita (1998)
ANNUAL AVERAGE GROWTH OF GDP – 5.5 per cent (1996)
INFLATION RATE – 0.3 per cent (1999)
TOTAL EXTERNAL DEBT – US$1,647 million (1998)

| *Trade with UK* | 1999 | 2000 |
|---|---|---|
| Imports from UK | £59,394,000 | £43,430,000 |
| Exports to UK | 1,049,000 | 703,000 |

## BHUTAN
*Druk-yul*

AREA – 18,147 sq. miles (47,000 sq. km). Neighbours: Tibet (north), India (west, south and east)
POPULATION – 782,000 (1997 UN estimate): about 80 per cent are Buddhists, the remainder (mostly the Nepali Bhutanese) are Hindu. The official language, for administrative and religious purposes, is Dzongkha, a variant of Tibetan, which functions as a lingua franca amongst a variety of languages and dialects. Nepali remains a recognised language and English remains the medium of instruction and the working language of the administration
CAPITAL – Thimphu (population, 15,000, 1987 estimate)
CURRENCY – Ngultrum of 100 chetrum (Indian currency is also legal tender)
NATIONAL ANTHEM - Druk tsendhen koipi gyelknap na (In the Thunder Dragon Kingdom)
NATIONAL DAY – 17 December
NATIONAL FLAG – Saffron yellow and orange-red divided diagonally, with dragon device in centre
LIFE EXPECTANCY (years) – male 59.6; female 60.8
POPULATION GROWTH RATE – 2.2 per cent (1999)
POPULATION DENSITY – 43 per sq. km (1998)
URBAN POPULATION – 7.1 per cent (2000 estimate)
MILITARY EXPENDITURE – 5.3 per cent of GDP (1999)
ILLITERACY RATE – 52.7 per cent (2000)

There is a mountainous northern region which is infertile and sparsely populated, a central zone of upland valleys where most of the population and cultivated land is found, and in the south the densely forested foothills of the Himalayas, which are mainly inhabited by Nepalese settlers and indigenous tribespeople.

INSURGENCIES

In January 1989 the King introduced a code of national etiquette designed to protect the national culture and language from Nepali encroachment. These measures, together with the granting of citizenship only to Nepalis settled in Bhutan before 1958, led to an exodus of ethnic Nepalis to Nepal, where about 96,000 live in camps. A low-level insurgency has been waged in the south of the country against the King's policies by ethnic Nepalis since 1990. Talks between the Nepali and Bhutanese governments continue in an attempt to resolve the fate of the refugees.

FOREIGN RELATIONS

Under a 1949 treaty Bhutan is guided by the advice of India in regard to its external relations. It retains its own diplomatic representatives and is a member of the UN. It also receives from India an annual payment of Rs500,000 as compensation for portions of its territory annexed by the British Government in India in 1864.

### Political System

Bhutan has a 154-member unicameral *Tshogdu* (National Assembly), 105 of whom are directly elected and serve three-year terms, 12 are representatives of religious bodies and 37 are nominated by the government. The National Assembly meets twice a year. The ten-member Royal Advisory Council, nominated by the King and the National Assembly, acts as a consultative body when the National Assembly is not in session. The King is also assisted by the *Lhengyal Shungtshog* (Cabinet). There are no political parties.

In July 1998 the King introduced reforms giving the legislature the right to dismiss the King and to nominate the members of the cabinet, although the King retains the right to assign their portfolios.

### Head of State

*HM The King of Bhutan*, Jigme Singye Wangchuk, *born* 11 November 1955; *succeeded his father* July 1972; *crowned* 2 June 1974
*Heir*, Crown Prince Jigme Gesar Namgyal Wangchuk, *designated* 31 October 1988

### Cabinet *as at July 2001*

*Cabinet Chairman, Finance*, Yeshey Zimba
*Chair of the Royal Advisory Council*, Kungang Tsangbi
*Chair of the Third Committee (Social, Humanitarian, Cultural)*, Ugyen Tsering
*Agriculture*, Kinzang Dorji
*Education and Health*, Sangay Ngedup
*Foreign Affairs*, Jigme Thinley
*Home Affairs*, Thinley Gyamtsho
*Law*, Sonam Tobgye
*Trade and Industry*, Khandu Wangchuk

## ECONOMY

The economy is based on industry, which in 1998 accounted for 35 per cent of GDP, and agriculture (37 per cent of GDP). Agriculture and animal husbandry engage around 94 per cent of the workforce in what is largely a self-sufficient rural society. The principal food crops are rice, wheat, maize and barley. Vegetables and fruit are also produced. Bhutan is the world's largest producer of cardamom, which forms its principal export to countries other than India. Agriculture is, however, limited by the country's mountainous topography and 60 per cent forest cover.

The mountains contain rich deposits of limestone, gypsum, dolomite and graphite and small amounts of coal, which are exported to India. A distillery and cement, chemicals and food-processing plants are in production; a forestry industries complex is being expanded. Tourism and postage stamps are increasingly important sources of foreign exchange.

In 1997 imports totalled US$137 million and exports US$118 million.

GNP – US$399 million (1999); US$510 per capita (1999)
GDP – US$383 million (1997); US$199 per capita (1998)
Annual Average Growth of GDP – 6.4 per cent (1996)
Inflation Rate – 8.5 per cent (1998)
Total External Debt – US$120 million (1998)

### Trade

Trade with India accounted for 71 per cent of imports and 95 per cent of exports in 1997. Principal exports are electricity, calcium carbide and timber; main imports are rice, machinery and diesel oil. Bhutan's airline, Druk Air, flies between Paro, New Delhi and Calcutta.

| *Trade with UK* | 1999 | 2000 |
|---|---|---|
| Imports from UK | £1,876,000 | £1,208,000 |
| Exports to UK | 534,000 | 1,662,000 |

## BOLIVIA
*República de Bolivia*

Area – 424,165 sq. miles (1,098,581 sq. km). Neighbours: Brazil (north and east), Paraguay and Argentina (south), Chile and Peru (west)
Population – 8,135,000 (1999 estimate): 12 per cent is of white European descent, 30 per cent Mestizo (mixed European-Indian), 25 per cent Quechua Indian and 17 per cent Aymará Indian. The official language is Spanish; Quechua and Aymará are also spoken. Roman Catholicism was the state religion until disestablishment in 1961
Capital – La Paz, the seat of government (population, 940,281, 1998 estimate)
Major Cities – Cochabamba (565,395); El Alto (534,466); Oruro (223,553); Potosí (140,642); Santa Cruz (935,361); Sucre, the legal capital and seat of the judiciary (178,426)
Currency – Boliviano ($b) of 100 centavos
National Anthem – Bolivianos, El Hado Propicio (Oh Bolivia, our long-felt desires)
National Day – 6 August (Independence Day)
National Flag – Three horizontal bands, red, yellow, green
Life Expectancy (years) – male 60.7; female 62.2
Population Growth Rate – 2.4 per cent (1999)
Population Density – 7 per sq. km (1998)
Urban Population – 62.5 per cent (2000 estimate)

The chief topographical feature is the great central plateau over 500 miles in length, at an average altitude of 12,500 feet above sea level, between the two great chains of the Andes, which traverse the country from south to north. The total length of the navigable rivers is about 12,000 miles, the principal rivers being the Itenez, Beni, Mamore and Madre de Dios.

## HISTORY AND POLITICS

Bolivia won its independence from Spain in 1825 after a war of liberation led by Simon Bolivar (1783–1830), from whom the country derives its name. From 1964 to 1982 Bolivia was ruled by military juntas until civilian rule was restored.

Congressional and presidential elections were held in June 1997. No party won an outright majority in Congress and a multiparty government was formed. Following a period of protests and strikes which had been prompted by proposed increases in water rates, a state of emergency was declared between 8-20 April 2000. The Cabinet resigned on 24 April 2000; a new Cabinet, which included most of the members of the previous one, was appointed the following day.

A new wave of protests and strikes took place in September and October 2000, but ended after the government made concessions to public sector workers and promised investment in areas where coca was produced. In April 2001 the protestors claimed that the government had failed to deliver the promised concessions and recommenced the campaign of demonstrations and strikes.

### Political System

The constitution provides for a directly elected executive president who appoints the Cabinet. The legislature (Congress) consists of a 27-member Senate and a 130-

member Chamber of Deputies; both chambers are elected for five-year terms, and the president also for five years.

HEAD OF STATE

*President of the Republic*, Gen. (retd) Hugo Bánzer Suárez, *inaugurated* 6 August 1997
*Vice-President*, Jorge Quiroga Ramírez

CABINET *as at July 2001*

*Agriculture, Livestock and Rural Development*, Hugo Carvajal
*Defence*, Gen. Oscar Vargas Lorenzetti (NDA)
*Economic Development*, Carlos Saavedra Bruno (RLM)
*Education, Culture and Sport*, Tito Hoz de Vila (NDA)
*Finance*, José Luis Lupo Flores (NDA)
*Foreign Affairs and Worship*, Javier Murillo de la Rocha (NDA)
*Housing and Basic Services*, Rubén Poma Rojas (CSU)
*International Trade and Investment*, Claudio Mancilla
*Interior*, Guillermo Fortún (NDA)
*Justice and Human Rights*, Luis Vásquez Villamor (RLM)
*Labour and Small Businesses*, Jorge Pacheco
*Presidency*, Marcelo Perez Monasterios (NDA)
*Social Welfare and Health*, Guillermo Cuentas Yanez (RLM)
*Sustainable Development and Environment*, Ronald MacLean Abaroa (NDA)
*Without Portfolio*, Manfredo Kempff (NDA) (*Government Information*); Wieberto Rivero (*Peasants' and Indigenous Peoples' Affairs*)

CSU Civil Solidarity Union; NDA National Democratic Action; RLM Revolutionary Leftist Movement

BOLIVIAN EMBASSY
106 Eaton Square, London SW1W 9AD
Tel: 020-7235 2257/4248
*Ambassador Extraordinary and Plenipotentiary*, Jaime Quiroga Matos, apptd 1998

BRITISH EMBASSY
Avenida Arce 2732, (Casilla 694) La Paz
Tel: (00 591) (2) 433424
E-mail: ppa@mail.megalink.com
*Ambassador Extraordinary and Plenipotentiary*, HE Graham Minter, LVO, apptd 1998
*Deputy Head of Mission and Consul*, P. Hogarth
BRITISH COUNCIL DIRECTOR, E.Lawrie, Avenida Arce 2708 (esq. Campos), Casilla 15047, La Paz; e-mail: information@britishcouncil.org.bo

## DEFENCE

The Army has 72 armoured personnel carriers. The Navy has 18 patrol vessels. The Air Force has 62 combat aircraft and 10 armed helicopters.
MILITARY EXPENDITURE – 1.7 per cent of GDP (1999)
MILITARY PERSONNEL – 32,500: Army 25,000, Navy 3,500, Air Force 3,000, Paramilitaries 37,100
CONSCRIPTION DURATION – 12 months (selective)

## ECONOMY

Mining, natural gas, petroleum and agriculture are the principal industries. The ancient silver mines of Potosí are now worked chiefly for tin, but gold is obtained on the Eastern Cordillera of the Andes. Tin output, together with other minerals (copper, tungsten, antimony, lead, zinc, asbestos, wolfram, bismuth salt and sulphur), provides over one-third of exports. Following a decline in the price of tin, many workers have taken to growing coca, which has become a significant export. A government plan to reduce coca production by offering growers alternative means of support has only been of limited success. New incentives to coca growers to abandon its production were announced in October 2000. Small quantities of oil are produced for internal consumption, and gas (currently providing about a quarter of export income) is piped to Argentina; in December 1997 the World Bank approved financing for the 3,150 km Bolivia-Brazil gas pipeline, estimated to cost around US$2 billion.

The economy deteriorated badly in the late 1970s and early 1980s; in the mid-1980s economic reforms were introduced with privatisation of some state-owned firms and the encouragement of foreign investment. The peso was replaced in 1987 with the Boliviano of 1,000,000 old pesos in a successful effort to stem hyperinflation. The economy and currency have stabilised.

In 1996 the government signed an agreement with the South American Common Market (Mercosur) to create a free trade zone within 18 years.
GNP – US$8,092 million (1999); US$1,010 per capita (1999)
GDP – US$7,740 million (1997); US$1,077 per capita (1998)
ANNUAL AVERAGE GROWTH OF GDP – 3.9 per cent (1996)
INFLATION RATE – 2.2 per cent (1999)
UNEMPLOYMENT – 4.4 per cent (1998)
TOTAL EXTERNAL DEBT – US$6,077 million (1998)

TRADE

Mineral exports represent about 40 per cent of total trade. Bolivia has now developed its own smelters and is exporting metals. The chief imports are wheat and flour, iron and steel products, machinery, vehicles and textiles.

In 1999 Bolivia had a trade deficit of US$488 million and a current account deficit of US$556 million. Imports totalled US$1,227 million and exports US$1,033 million.

| *Trade with UK* | 1999 | 2000 |
|---|---|---|
| Imports from UK | £9,755,000 | £7,660,000 |
| Exports to UK | 21,010,000 | 14,693,000 |

## COMMUNICATIONS

There are 4,300 km of railways in operation. Communication with Peru is by road from La Paz via Copacabana and thence to the railhead at Puno. In 1993 Bolivia and Peru signed an agreement granting Bolivia a concession of 162 hectares at the southern Peruvian port of Ilo for 98 years to construct a free trade zone.

Commercial aviation is conducted by the national airline, Lloyd Aereo Boliviano and Transporte Aereo Militar between the major towns; Lloyd Aereo Boliviano and a number of foreign airlines provide international flights to the USA, South and Central America and Europe.

Most towns have radio, telephone or telegraph communication with the main cities. There are nine principal daily newspapers.

## EDUCATION

Elementary education is compulsory and free and there are secondary schools in urban centres. Provision is also made for higher education; in addition to St Francisco Xavier's University at Sucre, founded in 1624, there are seven other universities, the largest being the University of San Andrés at La Paz, and ten private universities.
ILLITERACY RATE – 14.4 per cent (2000)
ENROLMENT (percentage of age group) – primary 91 per cent (1990); secondary 29 per cent (1990); tertiary 22 per cent (1991)

## BOSNIA-HERCEGOVINA

AREA – 19,767 sq. miles (51,197 sq. km). Neighbours: Serbia (east), Montenegro (south-east), Croatia (north and west)
POPULATION – 3,881,000 (1997 UN estimate); 4.4 million (1991 census): 44 per cent Bosniac, 33 per cent Serbs and 17 per cent Croats. The languages are Bosnian (spoken by Bosniacs and written in the Latin script), Serbian (spoken by Serbs and written in the Cyrillic alphabet) and Croatian (spoken by Croats and written in the Latin script)
CAPITAL – Sarajevo (population, 529,021, 1991 estimate)
MAJOR CITIES – Banja Luka (195,994); Mostar (127,034); Tuzla (131,866); Zenica (145,837)
CURRENCY – Convertible marka
NATIONAL DAY – 1 March (anniversary of 1992 declaration of independence)
NATIONAL FLAG – Blue, bearing a yellow triangle above a line of white stars
LIFE EXPECTANCY (years) – male 71.2; female 75.0
POPULATION GROWTH RATE – 1.3 per cent (1999)
POPULATION DENSITY – 82 per sq. km (1998)
URBAN POPULATION – 43.0 per cent (2000 estimate)
MILITARY EXPENDITURE – 8.4 per cent of GDP (1999)
MILITARY PERSONNEL – Bosniac Army (BiH): 30,000; Croat Defence Council (HVO): 10,000; Bosnian Serb Army: 30,000
GDP – US$3,300 million (1997); US$1,061 per capita (1998)

## HISTORY AND POLITICS

The country was settled by Slavs in the seventh century and conquered by the Ottoman Turks in 1463. Ruled by the Turks for over 400 years, the country came under Austro-Hungarian control in 1878. The assassination of the heir to the Austro-Hungarian throne in Sarajevo by an ethnic Serb precipitated the First World War, after which Bosnia-Hercegovina became part of the 'Kingdom of Serbs, Croats and Slovenes' (renamed Yugoslavia in 1929). It was occupied by German and Axis forces between 1941 and 1945. At the end of the war Bosnia-Hercegovina became part of the Socialist Federal Republic of Yugoslavia, which eventually collapsed with the secession of Slovenia and Croatia in 1991.

The Bosnia-Hercegovina government issued a declaration of sovereignty in October 1991 against the wishes of the ethnic Serb Democratic Party. Independence was declared on 1 March 1992 following a referendum which was boycotted by the Bosnian Serbs. Bosnia-Hercegovina was recognised as an independent state by the EC and USA in April 1992 and admitted to UN membership in May 1992.

### THE WAR

Fighting broke out in March 1992 between the pro-independence Muslims and Bosnian Serbs who wanted to merge with the Serbian republic to form a Greater Serbia. The Bosnian Serbs, assisted by the Federal Yugoslav Army (JNA), gained control of 70 per cent of Bosnia and in August 1992 declared their own 'Republika Srpska' with its capital at Pale.

The Bosnian government (Muslim) forces formed an alliance with Bosnian Croat and Croat forces in early 1992 which collapsed in 1993. The Muslims then came under fire from both Bosnian Serb and Bosnian Croat forces.

In August 1993 the Bosnian Croats declared a 'Republic of Herceg-Bosna', with its capital in Mostar, and following a cease-fire in February 1994 joined the government forces in a Muslim-Croat Federation.

NATO galvanised the USA, Britain, France, Germany and Russia to form the Contact Group (CG) to co-ordinate peace efforts. The CG brought about a cease-fire in June 1994 and presented a peace plan, which was rejected by the Bosnian Serbs.

Fighting intensified in 1995, climaxing in a land-grab during the final months of the war. Bosnian Serb forces overran the UN safe areas of Zepa and Srebrenica in July, allegedly massacring thousands of fleeing Muslims, and then laid siege to the Bihac 'safe area' together with Croatian Serbs and rebel Muslims. Bosnian government and Croatian forces lifted the siege of Bihac in August, enabling a joint attack on Serb-held central Bosnia.

The foreign ministers of Bosnia, Croatia and Serbia (rump Yugoslavia) met in Geneva in September 1995 and agreed to a US-sponsored peace accord. A cease-fire agreement was signed on 5 October and observed from 22 October, delayed by a Federation advance in the west and north-west, and Bosnian Serbs overrunning Tuzla.

### THE PEACE AGREEMENT

The Dayton Peace Treaty was signed in Paris on 14 December 1995. It was agreed to preserve Bosnia as a single state with a 51:49 division of territory between the Bosnian and Croat Federation and the Republika Srpska (Bosnian Serbs). A Republican (national) government, presidency and democratically elected institutions, based in Federation-controlled Sarajevo, were provided for.

The Dayton agreement provided for the deployment of a NATO-led Peace Implementation Force (IFOR) which took over from UNPROFOR on 20 December 1995 and was mandated until December 1996. IFOR was replaced by a NATO-led Stabilisation Force (SFOR).

Mostar, which had been divided during the war between the Muslims and Croats of the Federation and administered by the EU, held elections in June 1996. The EU withdrew in December 1996, when the Bosnian Croat state of Herceg-Bosna ceased to exist. Following a decision by international arbitrators, the northern town of Brcko, which had been under Bosnian Serb control, was merged into a self-governing neutral district in March 1999.

Elections were held for the presidency of the Republika Srpska, the House of Representatives and the legislative assemblies of the Bosniac-Croat Federation and the Republika Srpska on 11 November 2000. The non-nationalist Alliance for Change coalition became the largest grouping in the House of Representatives.

On 3 March 2001 the Croat National Congress, a grouping of Croatian parties, resolved to boycott the government and set up parallel institutions in mainly Croat areas, a decision which led to violent clashes between Croats and SFOR troops determined to preserve the unity of the Federation.

### POLITICAL SYSTEM

Under the Dayton peace agreement, the Bosnian republican (national) government was made responsible for foreign affairs, currency, citizenship and immigration. Executive authority was vested in a democratically elected rotating presidential triumvirate comprising a representative from each community, but in March 2001 the Assembly of Bosnia-Hercegovina nominated two members of a multi-ethnic party.

Legislative authority is vested in a bicameral parliament, the Assembly of Bosnia-Hercegovina, comprising a House of Peoples and a House of Representatives. Both houses have two-year terms. The House of Peoples has 15 members, 10 from the Bosniac-Croat Federation and 5 from the Republika Srpska, who are selected by the House of Representatives. The House of Representatives has 42 members who are directly elected to the two constituent chambers, the Chamber of Deputies of the Federation, which has 28 members, and the Chamber of Deputies of the Republika Srpska, which has 14 members. Within the Bosniac-Croat Federation there is a 140-member House of Representatives and ten cantonal assemblies; in the Republika Srpska there is an 83-member People's Assembly.

The Dayton peace agreement uses the term 'Bosniac' to refer to Bosnian Muslims.

### HEADS OF STATE (FOR ALL BOSNIA)

*Current President*, Jozo Krizanović; *Presidency Members*, Živko Radišić; Beriz Belkić

### HEAD OF THE FEDERATION

*President*, Karlo Filipović
*Vice-President*, Safet Halilović

### HEAD OF REPUBLIKA SRPSKA

*President*, Mirko Sarović
*Vice-President*, Dragan Cavić

### COUNCIL OF MINISTERS (FOR ALL BOSNIA) *as at July 2001*

*Prime Minister, Treasury*, Bozidar Matić
*Civil Works and Communications*, Svetozar Mihajlović
*European Integration*, Dragan Mikerević
*Foreign Affairs*, Zlatko Lagumdzija
*Foreign Trade and Economic Relations*, Azra Hadziahmetović
*Human Rights and Refugees*, Kresimir Zubak

### FEDERATION CABINET *as at July 2001*

*Prime Minister*, Alija Behmen
*Deputy PM, Finance*, Nikola Grabovac
*Agriculture, Water Power and Forestry*, Behija Hadžihajdarevic
*Defence*, Mijo Anic
*Education, Science, Culture and Sport*, Mujo Demirović
*Health*, Zeljko Mišanović
*Industry, Energy and Mining*, Hasan Becirović
*Interior*, Muhamed Bešic
*Justice*, Zvonko Mijan
*Labour, Social Affairs, Displaced People and Refugees*, Gen. Sefer Halilović
*Trade*, Andrija Jurković
*Transport and Communications*, Besim Mehmedić
*Urban Planning and Environment*, Ramiz Mehmedović
*Veterans and Disabled from the War of Freedom*, Suada Hadović
*Without Portfolio*, Mladen Ivanković; Gavrilo Grahovac

### REPUBLIKA SRPSKA GOVERNMENT *as at July 2001*

*Prime Minister*, Mladen Ivanić
*Deputy PM, Local Administration*, Petar Kunić
*Agriculture, Forestry and Water Management*, Rajko Latinović
*Defence*, Slobodan Bilić
*Education*, Gojko Savanović
*External Economic Affairs*, Fuad Turalić
*Finance*, Milenko Vracar
*Health and Social Care*, Milorad Balaban
*Industry*, Pero Bukejlović
*Interior*, Dragomir Jovicić
*Justice*, Biljana Marić
*Mining and Energy*, Bosko Lemez
*Refugees and Displaced Persons*, Mico Micić
*Religion*, Dušan Antelj
*Science*, Mitar Novaković
*Sport*, Zoran Tesanović
*Town Planning*, Nedjo Djurić
*Trade and Tourism*, Zeljko Tadić
*Transport and Communications*, Branko Dokić
*War Veterans*, Dragan Solaja

EMBASSY OF BOSNIA-HERCEGOVINA
4th Floor, Morley House, 320 Regent Street, London W1R 5AB
Tel: 020-7255 3758
*Ambassador Extraordinary and Plenipotentiary*, HE Osman Topcagić, apptd 1998

BRITISH EMBASSY
8 Tina Ujevica, Sarajevo
Tel: (00 387) (71) 204781/2/3
E-mail: britemb@bih.net.ba
*Ambassador Extraordinary and Plenipotentiary*, HE Graham Hand, apptd 1998

BRITISH COUNCIL DIRECTOR, Clare Newton, 2nd Floor, Obala Kulina Bana 4, Sarajevo 71000; e-mail: British.Council@britishcouncil.ba

## ECONOMY

Wheat, maize, potatoes and cabbage are among the major crops; crude steel and lignite are among the principal mineral products.

| *Trade with UK* | 1999 | 2000 |
|---|---|---|
| Imports from UK | £16,077,000 | £20,654,000 |
| Exports to UK | 5,321,000 | 2,936,000 |

## BOTSWANA
*The Republic of Botswana*

AREA – 224,607 sq. miles (581,730 sq. km). Neighbours: South Africa (south and east), Zimbabwe (north and north-east), Namibia (west)
POPULATION – 1,588,000 (1997 UN estimate): Batswana (95 per cent); the remainder are Kalanga, Basarwa, Kgalagadi and Europeans. The national language is Setswana and the official language is English
CAPITAL – Gaborone (population, 183,487, 1997 UN estimate)

MAJOR CITIES – Francistown (55,244); Lobatse (26,052); Selebi-Phikwe (39,772)
CURRENCY – Pula (P) of 100 thebe
NATIONAL ANTHEM – Fatshe La Rona (Blessed be this noble land)
NATIONAL DAY – 30 September
NATIONAL FLAG – Light blue with a horizontal black stripe fimbriated in white across the centre
LIFE EXPECTANCY (years) – male 39.5; female 39.3
POPULATION GROWTH RATE – 2.5 per cent (1999)
POPULATION DENSITY – 3 per sq. km (1998)
URBAN POPULATION – 50.3 per cent (2000 estimate)

A plateau at a height of about 4,000 feet divides Botswana into two main topographical regions. To the east of the plateau streams flow into the Marico, Notwani and Limpopo rivers; to the west lies a flat region comprising the Kgalagadi Desert, the Okavango Swamps and the Northern State Lands area. The climate is generally sub-tropical.

## HISTORY AND POLITICS

The Tswana people were dominant in the area now known as Botswana from the 17th century. In 1885, at the request of indigenous chiefs fearing invasion by the Boers, Britain formally took control of Bechuanaland, and the northern part of the territory was formally declared a British protectorate, while land to the south of the Molopo river became British Bechuanaland, which was later incorporated into the Cape Colony. On 30 September 1966 the British Protectorate of Bechuanaland became a republic within the Commonwealth under the name Botswana.

The last general election on 16 October 1999 was won by the Botswana Democratic Party with 33 seats to the Botswana National Front's 7 seats.

### POLITICAL SYSTEM

The president is head of state and is elected by an absolute majority in the National Assembly. He appoints as vice-president a member of the National Assembly who is leader of government business in the National Assembly. The Assembly consists of the president, 40 members elected on a basis of universal adult suffrage, four co-opted members, and the Attorney-General (non-voting). Presidential and legislative elections are held every five years. There is also a 15-member House of Chiefs which considers legislation affecting the constitution and chieftaincy matters. In August 1997 the minimum voting age was lowered from 21 to 18.

### HEAD OF STATE

*President*, HE Festus Mogae, *sworn in* 2 April 1998
*Vice President*, Lt.-Gen. Ian Khama Seretse Khama

### CABINET *as at July 2001*

The President
*Agriculture*, Johnnie Swartz
*Assistant Ministers*, Pelokgale Seloma *(Agriculture)*; Boyce Sebetela *(Finance and Development Planning)*; Gladys Kokorwe *(Local Government, Lands and Housing)*
*Commerce and Industry*, Tebekelo Seretse
*Education*, George Kgoroba
*Finance and Development Planning*, Baledzi Gaolathe
*Foreign Affairs*, Lt.-Gen. Mompati Merafhe
*Health*, Joy Phumaphi
*Labour and Home Affairs*, Daniel Kwelagobe
*Lands and Housing*, Jacob Nkate
*Local Government*, Margaret Nasha
*Mineral Resources, Energy and Water Affairs*, Boometswe Mokgothu
*Presidential Affairs and Public Administration*, Thebe Mogami
*Works, Transport and Communications*, David Magang

BOTSWANA HIGH COMMISSION
6 Stratford Place, London W1C 1AY
Tel: 020-7499 0031
*High Commissioner*, HE Roy Warren Blackbeard, apptd 1998

BRITISH HIGH COMMISSION
Private Bag 0023, Gaborone
Tel: (00 267) 352841/2/3
E-mail: british@britishcouncil.org.bw
*High Commissioner*, HE J. Wilde, apptd 1998

BRITISH COUNCIL DIRECTOR, Dr Phil Mitchell, British High Commission Building, Queen's Road, The Mall, PO Box 439, Gaborone; e-mail: general.enquiries@bc.bw

## DEFENCE

The Army has 36 armoured personnel carriers. The Air Wing has 32 combat aircraft.
MILITARY EXPENDITURE – 5.2 per cent of GDP (1999)
MILITARY PERSONNEL – 9,000: Army 8,500, Air Wing 500, Paramilitaries 1,000

## ECONOMY

Agriculture is predominantly pastoral and accounts for around 3 per cent of GDP. The national herd is around 2.2 million cattle and one million sheep and goats. Cattle rearing accounts for about 85 per cent of agricultural output.

Mineral extraction and processing is now the major source of income following the opening of large mines for diamonds, copper and nickel. Botswana is one of the largest producers of diamonds in the world, with diamonds accounting for 74 per cent of export revenue. Large deposits of coal have been discovered and are now being mined.

Service industries account for nearly half of GDP. Tourism is the third largest industry, generating about 7 per cent of GDP. Main imports are motor vehicles, machinery and electrical equipment and foodstuffs; main exports are diamonds, motor vehicles and cupro-nickel.

In 1998 the government had a trade surplus of US$77 million and a current account surplus of US$170 million. Imports totalled US$2,387 million and exports US$1,948 million.

GNP – US$5,139 million (1999); US$3,240 per capita (1999)
GDP – US$4,944 million (1997); US$3,069 per capita (1998)
ANNUAL AVERAGE GROWTH OF GDP – 7.0 per cent (1996)
INFLATION RATE – 7.1 per cent (1999)
UNEMPLOYMENT – 21.5 per cent (1995)
TOTAL EXTERNAL DEBT – US$548 million (1998)

| *Trade with UK* | 1999 | 2000 |
|---|---|---|
| Imports from UK | £21,874,000 | £19,944,000 |
| Exports to UK | 177,638,000 | 353,250,000 |

## COMMUNICATIONS

The railway from Cape Town to Zimbabwe passes through eastern Botswana. The main roads are the north-south road, which closely follows the railway, and the road running east-west that links Francistown and Maun. Air services are provided on a scheduled basis between the main towns.

## EDUCATION

There are 657 primary schools, 163 community junior secondary schools and 23 government and government-aided senior secondary schools. Total enrolment in the tertiary sector (teacher training establishments, colleges of education and the University of Botswana) numbers 6,923.

ILLITERACY RATE – 22.8 per cent (2000)

ENROLMENT (percentage of age group) – primary 81 per cent (1996); secondary 44 per cent (1996); tertiary 5.8 per cent (1996)

---

# BRAZIL

*República Federativa do Brasil*

---

AREA – 3,300,171 sq. miles (8,547,403 sq. km). Neighbours: Guyana, Suriname, French Guiana, Colombia and Venezuela (north), Peru, Bolivia, Paraguay and Argentina (west), Uruguay (south)

POPULATION – 169,590,693 (2000 census. Portuguese is the national language. Spanish and English are widely spoken

CAPITAL – Brasília (population, 2,043,169, 2000 census)

MAJOR CITIES – Belo Horizonte (2,232,747); ΨFortaleza (2,138,234); Ψ Porto Alegre (1,360,033); Ψ Recife (1,421,993); ΨRio de Janeiro (5,851,914), the former capital; ΨSalvador (2,440,828); São Paulo (10,405,867)

CURRENCY – Real of 100 centavos

NATIONAL ANTHEM – Ouviram do Ipiranga às Margens Plácidas (From peaceful Ypiranga's banks)

NATIONAL DAY – 7 September (Independence Day)

NATIONAL FLAG – Green with a yellow lozenge containing a blue sphere studded with white stars, and crossed by a white band with the motto *Ordem e Progresso*

LIFE EXPECTANCY (years) – male 63.7; female 71.7

POPULATION GROWTH RATE – 1.4 per cent (1999)

POPULATION DENSITY – 19 per sq. km (1998)

URBAN POPULATION – 81.3 per cent (2000 estimate)

The north is mainly wide, low-lying, forest-clad plains. The central areas are principally plateau land and the east and south are traversed by successive mountain ranges interspersed with fertile valleys. The principal ranges are the Serra do Mar, the Serra da Mantiqueira and the Serra do Espinhaco along the east coast. The River Amazon flows from the Peruvian Andes to the Atlantic.

## HISTORY AND POLITICS

Brazil was discovered by the Portuguese navigator Pedro Álvares Cabral in 1500 and colonised by Portugal in the early 16th century. In 1822 it became independent under Dom Pedro I, son of King João VI of Portugal, who had been forced to flee to Brazil during the Napoleonic Wars. In 1889, Dom Pedro II was dethroned and a republic was proclaimed. In 1985 Brazil returned to democratic rule after two decades of military government.

Fernando Henrique Cardoso of the Social Democratic Party won the presidential election of October 1994 and was returned for a second term on 4 October 1998. In simultaneous legislative elections, the five-party coalition which supported him won 377 seats in the Chamber of Deputies and 21 state governorships. The coalition ceased to be the largest block in the legislature when the Brazilian Labour Party left the coalition in August 2000, but remained in power.

### POLITICAL SYSTEM

The Federative Republic of Brazil is composed of the federal district and 26 states. Under the 1988 constitution the president, who heads the executive, is directly elected for a four-year term; in June 1997 the constitution was amended to allow the president to stand for a second term. The Congress consists of an 81-member Senate (three senators per state elected for an eight-year term) and a 513-member Chamber of Deputies which is elected every four years; the number of deputies per state depends upon the state's population. Each state has a Governor, and a Legislative Assembly with a four-year term.

### FEDERAL STRUCTURE

| *Federal Unit* | *Area (sq. km)* | *Population (2000 census)* | *Capital* |
|---|---|---|---|
| *Central west* | | 11,616,745 | |
| Distrito Federal | 5,822 | 2,043,169 | Brasília |
| Goiás | 341,290 | 4,996,439 | Goiânia |
| Mato Grosso | 906,807 | 2,502,260 | Cuiabá |
| Mato Grosso do Sul | 358,159 | 2,074,877 | Campo Grande |
| *North* | | 12,841,299 | |
| Acre | 153,150 | 557,226 | Rio Branco |
| Amapá | 143,454 | 423,581 | Macapá |
| Amazonas | 1,577,820 | 2,813,085 | Manaus |
| Pará | 1,253,165 | 6,189,550 | Belém |
| Rondônia | 238,513 | 1,377,792 | Pôrto Velho |
| Roraima | 225,116 | 324,152 | Boa Vista |
| Tocantins | 278,421 | 1,155,913 | Palmas |
| *North-east* | | 47,693,254 | |
| Alagoas | 27,933 | 2,819,172 | Maceió |
| Bahia | 567,295 | 13,066,910 | Salvador |
| Ceará | 146,348 | 7,418,476 | Fortaleza |
| Maranhão | 333,366 | 5,642,960 | São Luís |
| Paraíba | 56,585 | 3,439,344 | João Pessoa |
| Pernambuco | 98,938 | 7,911,937 | Recife |
| Piauí | 252,378 | 2,841,202 | Teresina |
| Rio Grande do Norte | 53,307 | 2,771,538 | Natal |
| Sergipe | 22,050 | 1,781,714 | Aracajú |
| *South* | | 25,089,783 | |
| Paraná | 199,709 | 9,558,454 | Curitiba |
| Rio Grande do Sul | 282,062 | 10,181,749 | Pôrto Alegre |
| Santa Catarina | 95,443 | 5,349,580 | Florianópolis |
| *South-east* | | 72,297,351 | |
| Espírito Santo | 46,184 | 3,094,390 | Vitória |
| Minas Gerais | 588,384 | 17,866,402 | Belo Horizonte |
| Rio de Janeiro | 43,910 | 14,367,083 | Rio de Janeiro |
| São Paulo | 248,809 | 36,969,476 | São Paulo |

### HEAD OF STATE

*President*, Fernando Henrique Cardoso, *sworn in* 1 January 1995

*Vice-President*, Marco Maciel

### CABINET *as at July 2001*

*Agrarian Development*, Raul Jungmann Pinto
*Agriculture and Supply*, Marcus Vinícius Pratini de Moraes
*Air Force Chief of Staff*, Carlos Damasceno
*Army Chief of Staff*, Gleuber Vieira
*Civilian Household of the Presidency*, Pedro Parente
*Communications*, João Pimenta da Veiga Filho
*Culture*, Francisco Corrêa Weffort
*Defence*, Geraldo Magela Quintão
*Development, Industry and Commerce*, Alcides Tápias
*Education*, Paulo Souza
*Energy and Mines*, José Lima
*Environment*, José Sarney Filho
*Finance*, Pedro Malan
*Foreign Affairs*, Celso Lafer
*Government Communication*, Andrea Matarazzo
*Health*, José Serra
*Justice*, José Gregori

*Labour and Employment*, vacant
*Military Household of the Presidency*, Gen. Alberto Cardoso
*National Integration*, Ramez Tebet
*Navy Chief of Staff*, Sérgio Chagasteles
*Planning, Budget and Management*, Martus Tavares
*Presidential Spokesman*, Georges Lamazière
*Science and Technology*, Ronaldo Sardenberg
*Secretariat of the Presidency*, Aloysio Nunes Ferreira
*Social Security and Assistance*, Roberto Brant
*Sport and Tourism*, Carlos Melles
*Transport*, Eliseu Padilha

BRAZILIAN EMBASSY
32 Green Street, London W1K 7AT
Tel: 020-7499 0877
*Ambassador Extraordinary and Plenipotentiary*, HE Sergio Silva Do Amaral, KBE, apptd 1999
*Military Attachés*, Col. Luiz de Castro (*Army*), Capt. Arlei Caetano Franco (*Defence and Navy*), Gp. Capt. Antonio Biasus (*Air Force*)
*Counsellor (Commercial Affairs)*, João de Mendonça Lima Neto

There is also a Brazilian Consulate-General in London and honorary consular offices at Cardiff and Glasgow.

BRITISH EMBASSY
Setor de Embaixadas Sul, Quadra 801, Conjunto K, CEP 70.408–900, Brasília DF
Tel: (00 55) (61) 225 2710
E-mail: britemb@zaz.com.br
*Ambassador Extraordinary and Plenipotentiary*, HE Roger Bone, CMG, apptd 1999
*Deputy Head of Mission, Consul-General, Minister/ Counsellor*, S. Gillett, MVO
*Defence Attaché*, Col. J. M. Bowles, MBE
*First Secretary*, J. F. Jarvie

There are British Consulates-General at Rio de Janeiro and São Paulo.

BRITISH COUNCIL DIRECTOR, Howard Thompson, OBE, Edificio Centro Empresarial Varig, SCN Quadra 04, Bloco B, Torre Oeste Conjunto 202, 70710-926-Brasília DF; e-mail: brasilia@britishcouncil.org.br. Regional directors in Curitiba, Recife, Rio de Janeiro and São Paulo

BRITISH CHAMBER OF COMMERCE, Rua Ferreira de Araujo, 741-1 Andar Pinheiros, 05428-002 São Paulo and Av. Graça Aranha, 01-4 andar, 20030-002 Rio de Janeiro

## DEFENCE

The Army has 178 main battle tanks, 803 armoured personnel carriers and 73 helicopters. The Navy has bases at Rio de Janeiro, Salvador, Recife, Belém, Florianópolis and Ladario. It is equipped with five submarines, one aircraft carrier, 14 frigates and 50 patrol and coastal vessels. Naval aviation has 22 combat aircraft and 54 armed helicopters; the Marines have 33 armoured personnel carriers. The Air Force has 268 combat aircraft and 29 armed helicopters.
MILITARY EXPENDITURE – 2.7 per cent of GDP (1999)
MILITARY PERSONNEL – 287,600: Army 189,000, Navy 48,600, Air Force 50,000, Paramilitaries 385,600
CONSCRIPTION DURATION – 12 months (can be extended to 18)

## ECONOMY

There are large mineral deposits including iron ore (hematite), manganese, bauxite, beryllium, chrome, nickel, tungsten, cassiterite, lead, gold, monazite (containing rare earths and thorium) and zirconium. Diamonds and precious and semi-precious stones are also found. Brazil is the world's largest producer of coffee; the other main agricultural products are cassava, maize, soya, rice, wheat, sugar, potatoes, cotton, cocoa, tobacco and peanuts. Tourism is a growing industry; Brazil attracted 5.1 million visitors in 2000.

In 1994 the government introduced the Real Plan. The plan introduced a new currency, the real, doubled interest rates, increased taxes and cut budgets, and succeeded in bringing inflation under control and stabilising the economy.
GNP – US$730,424 million (1999); US$4,420 per capita (1999)
GDP – US$806,972 million (1997); US$4,673 per capita (1998)
ANNUAL AVERAGE GROWTH OF GDP – 10.7 per cent (2000)
INFLATION RATE – 6.0 per cent (2000)
UNEMPLOYMENT – 6.8 per cent (1998)
TOTAL EXTERNAL DEBT – US$232,004 million (1998)

TRADE

Principal imports are machinery, fuel and lubricants, mineral products, transport equipment and chemicals. Principal exports are industrial goods, coffee, iron ore and soya. In 2001 the Brazilian automobile industry was expected to produce 1,500,000 vehicles. The main trading partners are the USA, Argentina and the EU.

In 1998 Brazil had a trade deficit of US$6,603 million and a current account deficit of US$33,829 million. In 1997 imports totalled US$65,007 million and in 1999 exports totalled US$48,011 million.

| *Trade with UK* | 1999 | 2000 |
|---|---|---|
| Imports from UK | £744,930,000 | £774,953,000 |
| Exports to UK | 948,956,000 | 1,158,389,000 |

## COMMUNICATIONS

There are 1,670,148 km of highways, of which 161,503 km are paved, and the route-length of railways is 30,129 km, of which 2,150 km are electrified. There are ten international airports and internal air services are highly developed. There are some 50,000 km of navigable inland waterways. Rio de Janeiro and Santos are the two leading ports. A 3,415 km gas pipeline running from Santa Cruz, Bolivia, to São Paolo, was opened in 2000.

## EDUCATION

The education system includes both public and private institutions. Public education is free at all levels.
ILLITERACY RATE – 14.7 per cent (2000)
ENROLMENT (percentage of age group) – primary 90 per cent (1996); secondary 19 per cent (1994); tertiary 14.5 per

---

## BRUNEI
*Negara Brunei Darussalam*

---

AREA – 2,226 sq. miles (5,765 sq. km). Neighbour: Malaysia
POPULATION – 322,000 (1997 UN official estimate): 66.9 per cent Malay, 15.2 per cent Chinese, 5.9 per cent indigenous races and 12 per cent European, Indian and other races. The majority are Sunni Muslims. The official language is Malay; English and dialects of Chinese are also spoken
CAPITAL – Bandar Seri Begawan (population, 49,902, 1994 estimate)
CURRENCY – Brunei dollar (B$) of 100 sen (fully interchangeable with Singapore currency)

NATIONAL ANTHEM – Allah Peliharakan Sultan (God Bless His Majesty)
NATIONAL DAY – 23 February
NATIONAL FLAG – Yellow with diagonal stripes of white over black and the arms in red all over the centre
LIFE EXPECTANCY (years) – male 74.5; female 79.8
POPULATION GROWTH RATE – 2.5 per cent (1999)
POPULATION DENSITY – 55 per sq. km (1998)
URBAN POPULATION – 72.2 per cent (2000 estimate)
ILLITERACY RATE – 8.4 per cent (2000)
ENROLMENT (percentage of age group) – primary 91 per cent (1996); secondary 68 per cent (1996); tertiary 6.6 per cent (1996)

Brunei is situated on the north-west coast of the island of Borneo. It has a humid tropical climate.

## HISTORY AND POLITICS

Formerly a powerful Muslim sultanate, Brunei was reduced to its present size by the mid-19th century and became a British Protectorate in 1888. In 1959 the Sultan promulgated the first written constitution, and on 1 January 1984 Brunei resumed full independence from Britain.

### POLITICAL SYSTEM

Supreme executive authority rests with the Sultan, who presides over and is advised by the Privy Council, the Religious Council and the Council of Ministers. The Sultan effectively rules by decree as a state of emergency has been in effect since a revolt in 1962; there are no political parties and no elections.

### HEAD OF STATE

*HM The Sultan of Brunei*, HM Sultan Haji Hassanal Bolkiah Mu'izzaddin Waddaullah, Sultan and Yang Di-Pertuan, GCB, *acceded* 1967, *crowned* 1 August 1968

### COUNCIL OF MINISTERS *as at July 2001*

*Prime Minister, Defence, Finance*, HM The Sultan
*Communications*, Pehin Dato Zakaria
*Development*, Pengiran Dato Haji Ismail
*Education; Health (acting)*, Pehin Dato Haji Abdul Aziz
*Foreign Affairs*, Prince Mohamed Bolkiah
*Home Affairs, Special Adviser to the Sultan*, Pehin Dato Haji Isa Umar
*Industry and Primary Resources*, Pehin Dato Haji Abdul Rahman
*Law*, Pengiran Haji Bahrin
*Religious Affairs*, Pehin Dato Haji Mohammad Zain
*Youth, Sports and Culture*, Pehin Dato Haji Hussein

BRUNEI DARUSSALAM HIGH COMMISSION
19–20 Belgrave Square, London SW1X 8PG
Tel: 020-7581 0521
*High Commissioner*, HE Dato Haji Yusof Hamid, apptd 1999

BRITISH HIGH COMMISSION
PO Box 2197, Bandar Seri Begawan 8674
E-mail: brithc@brunet.bn
Tel: (00 673) (2) 222231
*High Commissioner*, Stuart Laing, apptd 1998

BRITISH COUNCIL DIRECTOR, Ben Harris, 45 Simpang 100, Gadong BE3619, Bandar Seri Begawan 3192; e-mail: all.enquiries@bn.britishcouncil.org

## DEFENCE

The Army has 50 armoured personnel carriers. The Navy, based in Muara, has six patrol and coastal vessels. The Air Force has five armed helicopters.
MILITARY EXPENDITURE – 6.7 per cent of GDP (1999)
MILITARY PERSONNEL – 5,000: Army 3,900, Navy 700, Air Force 400, Paramilitaries 3,750

## ECONOMY

The economy is based on the production of oil and natural gas, which accounted for about 36 per cent of GDP in 1996 and 90 per cent of exports. Royalties and taxes from these operations form the bulk of government revenue and have enabled the construction of free health, education and welfare services.

The country has eight hospitals, 350 schools and one university. Royal Brunei Airlines operates scheduled flights to the UK, Australia and throughout the Far East. Radio Television Brunei broadcasts one television and three radio channels from the capital.

In 1998 Brunei produced 7,800,000 tonnes of crude petroleum and 10,700 million cubic metres of natural gas. In 1994 imports totalled US$1,634 million and exports US$2,215 million.
GNP – US$7,753 million (1998); US$24,630 per capita (1999 estimate)
GDP – US$5,517 million (1997); US$13,719 per capita (1998)
ANNUAL AVERAGE GROWTH OF GDP – 4.6 per cent (1996)

| *Trade with UK* | 1999 | 2000 |
|---|---|---|
| Imports from UK | £132,042,000 | £97,206,000 |
| Exports to UK | 76,118,000 | 102,256,000 |

## COMMUNICATIONS

There are two main ports, at Muara and Kuala Belait, and an international airport at Bandar Seri Begawan.

---

# BULGARIA
*Republika Balgarija*

---

AREA – 42,823 sq. miles (110,912 sq. km). Neighbours: Romania (north), Serbia and the Former Yugoslav Republic of Macedonia (west), Greece and Turkey (south)
POPULATION – 8,216,000 (1997 estimate): 85.7 per cent Bulgarian, 9.4 per cent Turkish, 3.7 per cent Roma, 1.2 per cent others. The language is Bulgarian, a Southern Slavonic tongue closely allied to Serbo-Croat and Russian with local admixtures of modern Greek, Albanian and Turkish words. The alphabet is Cyrillic. The predominant religion is the Bulgarian Orthodox Church (85.7 per cent of the population); Islam is the second largest religion (13.1 per cent).
CAPITAL – Sofia (population, 1,189,794, 1997 estimate)
MAJOR CITIES – ΨBurgas (212,369); Plovdiv (340,142); ΨVarna (305,516), 1997 estimates
CURRENCY – Lev of 100 stotinki
NATIONAL ANTHEM - Gorda stara planina (Proud and ancient mountains)
NATIONAL DAY – 3 March
NATIONAL FLAG – Three horizontal bands, white, green, red
LIFE EXPECTANCY (years) – male 67.4; female 74.7
POPULATION GROWTH RATE – 0.6 per cent (1999)
POPULATION DENSITY – 74 per sq. km (1998)
URBAN POPULATION – 69.6 per cent (2000 estimate)

## HISTORY AND POLITICS

A principality of Bulgaria was created by the Treaty of Berlin in 1878, and in 1908 the country was declared an independent kingdom. A coup d'état in September 1944 gave power to the Fatherland Front, a coalition of Communists, Agrarians and Social Democrats. In August 1945, the main body of Agrarians and Social Democrats left the government. A referendum in September 1946 led to the abolition of the monarchy and the establishment of a republic.

The post-war period was dominated by the Communist Party (BCP), led by Todor Zhivkov. In January 1990 the National Assembly voted to abolish the BCP's constitutional guarantee of power and establish a multiparty democracy.

In November 1996 the Union of Democratic Forces' (UDF) candidate, Petar Stoyanov, became president. The general election held on 17 June 2001 was won by the National Movement for Simeon II, a movement founded in April 2001 by the former king, which won 43.74 per cent of the vote and 120 of the 240 seats in the legislature.

### POLITICAL SYSTEM

A new constitution enshrining democracy and the free market was adopted in 1991. It provides for a directly-elected president who serves for no more than two five-year terms. The chief executive is the prime minister who is appointed by the president, and is usually the leader of the largest party in the legislature. There is a unicameral National Assembly of 240 members who are directly elected by proportional representation for four-year terms.

### HEAD OF STATE

*President*, Petar Stoyanov, *elected* 3 November 1996

### COUNCIL OF MINISTERS *as at July 2001*

*Prime Minister, State Administration*, Ivan Kostov
*Deputy PM, Economy*, Petar Zhotev
*Agriculture, Forests and Land Reform*, Ventsislav Vurbanov
*Culture*, Ema Moskova
*Defence*, Boiko Noev
*Education and Science*, Dimitar Dimitrov
*Environment and Water*, Evdokia Maneva
*Finance*, Mouravei Radev
*Foreign Affairs*, Nadezhda Mihailova
*Health*, Ilko Semerdjiev
*Internal Affairs*, Emanouil Yordanov
*Justice and Legal Affairs*, Teodossi Simeonov
*Labour and Social Affairs*, Ivan Neikov
*National and Regional Development and Urbanisation*, Yevgeni Chachev
*Transport and Communications*, Antoni Slavinski
*Without Portfolio*, Aleksander Pramatarski

### EMBASSY OF THE REPUBLIC OF BULGARIA

186–188 Queen's Gate, London SW7 5HL
Tel: 020-7584 9400/9433
*Ambassador Extraordinary and Plenipotentiary*, HE Valentin Dobrev, apptd 1998
*Counsellor (Commercial/Economic)*, Christo Charenkov

### BRITISH EMBASSY

38 Boulevard Vassil Levski, Sofia
Tel: (00 359) (2) 2980 1220
E-mail: britembsof@mbox.cit.bg
*Ambassador Extraordinary and Plenipotentiary*, HE Richard Stagg, CMG, apptd 1998
*Deputy Head of Mission and First Secretary*, T. J. Colley
*Defence Attaché*, Col. R. E. Fielding
*First Secretary (Commercial)*, D. Leith

BRITISH COUNCIL DIRECTOR, Kevin Lewis, 7 Tulovo Street, BG-1504, Sofia; e-mail: bc.sofia@britishcouncil.bg

## DEFENCE

The Army has 1,475 main battle tanks, 214 armoured infantry fighting vehicles and 1,750 armoured personnel carriers. The Navy has one submarine, one frigate, 23 patrol and coastal vessels, and nine armed helicopters. The Air Force has 181 combat aircraft and 43 armed helicopters.
MILITARY EXPENDITURE – 3.3 per cent of GDP (1999)
MILITARY PERSONNEL – 79,760: Army 42,400, Navy 5,260, Air Force 18,300, Paramilitaries 34,000
CONSCRIPTION DURATION – 12 months

## ECONOMY

The principal crops are wheat, maize, beet, tomatoes, tobacco, oleaginous seeds, fruit, vegetables and cotton. Around 24 per cent of the population is engaged in agriculture, which accounted for 19 per cent of GDP in 1998. Cadmium, coal, copper, pig iron, kaolin, lead, silver and zinc are produced.

The government adopted a radical reform package in 1997 in order to stimulate the economy and bring inflation under control. The package included pegging the lev to the Deutsche Mark.
GNP – US$11,572million (1999); US$1,380 per capita (1999)
GDP – US$10,169 million (1997); US$1,470 per capita (1998)
ANNUAL AVERAGE GROWTH OF GDP – 5.7 per cent (2000)
INFLATION RATE – 8.5 per cent (2001)
UNEMPLOYMENT – 14.4 per cent (1997)
TOTAL EXTERNAL DEBT – US$9,907 million (1998)

### TRADE

The principal imports are fuels, industrial equipment, chemicals, textiles and clothing, and foodstuffs and beverages. The principal exports are textiles and clothing, iron and steel products, foodstuffs and beverages, industrial equipment, oil derivatives and non-ferrous metals.

In 1993 Bulgaria signed an Association Agreement with the EU, and EU duties on many Bulgarian industrial goods were abolished by 1995 and levies on agricultural goods significantly lowered.

In 1999 Bulgaria had a trade deficit of US$1,064 million and a current account deficit of US$660 million. Imports totalled US$5,409 million and exports US$3,925 million. The principal trading partners are Russia, Germany and Italy.

| *Trade with UK* | 1999 | 2000 |
|---|---|---|
| Imports from UK | £78,032,000 | £86,313,000 |
| Exports to UK | 68,567,000 | 88,215,000 |

## EDUCATION

Education is free and compulsory for children from six to 16 years inclusive. There are three universities (at Sofia, Plovdiv and Veliko Turnovo), an American University and 21 higher education establishments.
ILLITERACY RATE – 1.5 per cent (2000)
ENROLMENT (percentage of age group) – primary 92 per cent (1996); secondary 74 per cent (1996); tertiary 41.2 per cent (1996)

## BURKINA FASO
*République Démocratique du Burkina Faso*

AREA – 105,792 sq. miles (274,000 sq. km). Neighbours: Mali (west), Niger and Benin (east), Togo, Ghana and Côte d'Ivoire (south)
POPULATION – 10,996,000 (1997 UN estimate). The official language is French. Mossi, More, Dioula and Gourmantché are indigenous languages
CAPITAL – Ouagadougou (population, 634,479, 1991 estimate)
MAJOR CITIES – Bobo-Dioulasso (228,668); Koudougou (30,000)
CURRENCY – Franc CFA of 100 centimes
NATIONAL ANTHEM – Ditanyé
NATIONAL DAY – 11 December
NATIONAL FLAG – Equal bands of red over green, with a yellow star in centre
LIFE EXPECTANCY (years) – male 44.1; female 45.7
POPULATION GROWTH RATE – 2.8 per cent (1999)
POPULATION DENSITY – 39 per sq. km (1998)
URBAN POPULATION – 18.5 per cent (2000 estimate)
MILITARY EXPENDITURE – 2.1 per cent of GDP (1999)
MILITARY PERSONNEL – 10,000: Army 5,600, Air Force 200, Paramilitaries 49,450
ILLITERACY RATE – 77.0 per cent (2000)
ENROLMENT (percentage of age group) – primary 31 per cent (1996); secondary 7 per cent (1993); tertiary 0.9 per cent (1996)

Burkina Faso (formerly Upper Volta) is an inland savannah state in West Africa. The largest tribe is the Mossi whose king, the Moro Naba, still wields a certain moral influence.

### HISTORY AND POLITICS

Burkina Faso was annexed by France in 1896 and between 1932 and 1947 was administered as part of the Colony of the Ivory Coast. It decided on 11 December 1958 to remain an autonomous republic within the French Community; full independence outside the Community was proclaimed on 5 August 1960.

Following a number of military coups, Capt. Blaise Compaoré seized power in 1987. A new constitution was adopted in 1991. A general election was held in May 1997 and won by the Congress for Democracy and Progress group (CDP); since October 1999 the government has included members of the Burkina Greens and the Movement for Tolerance and Progress. Presidential elections were held in November 1998 and won by Compaoré, the CDP candidate, in the face of a boycott by the opposition parties.

#### HEAD OF STATE

*President*, Capt. Blaise Compaoré, *assumed office* October 1987, *elected* December 1991, *re-elected* November 1998

#### COUNCIL OF MINISTERS *as at July 2001*

*Prime Minister, Economy and Finance*, Paramanga Ernest Yonli
*Agriculture*, Salif Diallo
*Animal Resources*, Alphonse Bonou
*Basic Education and Literacy*, Fidèle Kientga
*Civil Service and Institutional Development*, Jean Émile Somda
*Culture and Arts*, Mahmadou Ouédraogo
*Defence*, Kouamé Lougué
*Employment, Labour, Social Security*, Alain Ludovic Tou
*Energy and Mines*, Abdoulayé Abdul Kader Cissé
*Environment and Water*, Fidèle Hien
*Foreign Affairs*, Youssouf Ouédraogo
*Health*, Pierre Joseph Emmanuel Tapsoba
*Information, Government Spokesman*, Kilimité Théodore Hien
*Infrastructure, Housing, Urban Planning*, Hyppolite Lingani
*Justice, Keeper of the Seals, Promotion of Human Rights*, Boureima Badini
*Ministers of State*, Ram Ouédraogo; Monique Ilboudo (*Human Rights*); Jeanne Somé (*Literacy and Non-formal Education*); Bassirou Ly (*Youth*)
*Post and Telecommunications*, Justin Tièba Thombiano
*Regional Administration and Decentralisation*, Bernard T. Nabare
*Regional Integration*, Nayabtigungu Congo Kaboré
*Relations with Parliament*, Sané Mohamed Topan
*Secondary and Higher Education, Scientific Research*, Laya Sawadogo
*Security*, Djibril Yipéné Bassole
*Social Action and National Solidarity*, Gilbert Ouédraogo
*Trade, Industry and Crafts*, Bedouma Alain Yoda
*Transport and Tourism*, Salvador Yaméogo
*Women's Promotion*, Gisèle Guigma
*Youth and Sports*, René Émile Kaboré

EMBASSY OF THE REPUBLIC OF BURKINA FASO
Guy d'Arezzoplein 16, B-1180 Brussels, Belgium
Tel: (00 32) (2) 345 9912
*Ambassador Extraordinary and Plenipotentiary*, Kadré Désiré Ouédraogo

HONORARY CONSULATE, 5 Cinnamon Row, Plantation Wharf, London SW11 3TW. Tel: 020-7738 1800.
*Honorary Consul*, S. G. Singer

BRITISH AMBASSADOR, HE Haydon Warren-Gash, CMG, resident at Abidjan, Côte d'Ivoire

### ECONOMY

The principal industry is cattle and sheep rearing. Agriculture employs over 90 per cent of the workforce and contributes 33 per cent of GDP. The chief exports are cotton, livestock and animal feed, and gold.. The chief imports are capital goods, foodstuffs and fuel oils.

In 1994 Burkina Faso had a trade deficit of US$129 million and a current account surplus of US$15 million. In 1999 imports totalled US$696 million and exports US$254 million.

GNP – US$2,602 million (1999); US$240 per capita (1999)
GDP – US$1,758 million (1997); US$221 per capita (1998)
ANNUAL AVERAGE GROWTH OF GDP – 5.6 per cent (1996)
INFLATION RATE – 1.1 per cent (1999)
TOTAL EXTERNAL DEBT – US$1,399 million (1998)

| *Trade with UK* | 1999 | 2000 |
|---|---|---|
| Imports from UK | £6,711,000 | £5,702,000 |
| Exports to UK | 824,000 | 1,364,000 |

### COMMUNICATIONS

There are 12,349 km of roads, of which 1,988 km are bituminised, and 617 km of railway track in operation. There are two main airports, Ouagadougou and Bobo-Dioulasso.

## BURUNDI
*République du Burundi*

AREA – 10,747 sq. miles (27,834 sq. km). Neighbours: Rwanda (north), Tanzania (east and south), Democratic Republic of Congo (west)

POPULATION – 6,678,000 (1997 UN estimate): 83 per cent Hutu, 15 per cent Tutsi. The official languages are Kirundi, a Bantu language, and French. Kiswahili is also used
CAPITAL – Bujumbura (formerly Usumbura) (population, 235,440, 1990)
MAJOR CITIES – Kitega (18,000)
CURRENCY – Burundi franc of 100 centimes
NATIONAL DAY – 1 July
NATIONAL FLAG – Divided diagonally by a white saltire into red and green triangles; on a white disc in the centre three red six-pointed stars edged in green
NATIONAL ANTHEM – Burundi Bwacu (Dear Burundi)
LIFE EXPECTANCY (years) – male 43.2; female 43.8
POPULATION GROWTH RATE – 2.1 per cent (1999)
POPULATION DENSITY – 226 per sq. km (1998)
URBAN POPULATION – 9.0 per cent (2000 estimate)
MILITARY EXPENDITURE – 6.4 per cent of GDP (1999)
MILITARY PERSONNEL – 45,500: Army 40,000, Paramilitaries 6,500
ILLITERACY RATE – 51.9 per cent (2000)
ENROLMENT (percentage of age group) – primary 52 per cent (1992); secondary 5 per cent (1992); tertiary 0.9 per cent (1995)

## HISTORY AND POLITICS

Formerly a Belgian trusteeship under the United Nations, Burundi became independent as a constitutional monarchy on 1 July 1962. However, the monarchy was overthrown in 1966 and the country became a republic.

Although most of the population is Hutu, political and military power has traditionally rested with the Tutsi minority. Since the 1960s, Hutu attempts to overthrow Tutsi rule have resulted in ethnic massacres. The Tutsi-dominated army attempted a coup in 1993 in which President Melchior Ndadaye was killed. The government regained control in December but two months of inter-racial fighting left more than 50,000 dead and 500,000 refugees.

The Front for Democracy in Burundi (FRODEBU) and the National Unity and Progress Party (UPRONA) agreed to form a coalition government in 1994 with a Tutsi prime minister and Hutu president. However, the government was unable to halt attacks by the Tutsi-dominated army and Hutu militias on each other's communities. The fighting claimed 200,000 lives in 1993–5.

In July 1996 the army again seized power and installed Maj. Buyoya as president. Political parties were banned and the National Assembly was suspended until October 1996 when fewer than half its deputies attended. A multi-ethnic government of national unity was formed in August 1996. More than 300,000 refugees remain in camps in Tanzania and the Democratic Republic of Congo. In April 2000, President Buyoya promised to dismantle the 'regroupment camps' into which over 800,000 Hutus had been placed to stabilise the security situation.

A new transitional constitution, designed to provide for a political partnership between Hutus and Tutsis, came into being in June 1998 and a 117-member Transitional National Assembly was inaugurated in July 1998.

A partial peace accord was formally signed in Nairobi on 20 September 2000 by President Buyoya, the Tutsi political parties and the moderate Hutu parties, but the two main Hutu rebel groups refused to sign the accord. On 18 April 2001 an attempted coup by Tutsi soldiers opposed to the peace agreement was ended peaceably. Clashes between the army and Hutu militias, and massacres of civilians have continued.

### HEAD OF STATE

*President*, Maj. Pierre Buyoya, *appointed* 25 July 1996, *sworn in* 11 June 1998
*Vice-Presidents*, Frédéric Bamvunginyumvira; Mathias Sinamenye

### COUNCIL OF MINISTERS *as at July 2001*

*Agriculture and Livestock*, Salvator Ntihabose
*Communal Development and Handicrafts*, Denis Nshimirimana
*Defence*, Col. Cyrille Ndayirukiye
*Development Planning and Reconstruction*, Léon Nimbona
*Education*, Prosper Mpawenayo
*Energy and Mines*, Bernard Barandereka
*External Relations and Co-operation*, Séverin Ntahomvukiye
*Finance*, Charles Nihangaza
*Health*, Stanislas Ntahobari
*Human Rights, Institutional Reforms and Relations with National Assembly*, Eugène Nindorera
*Information and Government Spokesman*, Luc Rukingama
*Internal Affairs and Public Security*, Col. Ascension Twagiramungu
*Justice*, Térence Sinunguruza
*Labour, Civil Service and Professional Training*, Emmanuel Tungamwese
*Land and Environment*, Jean-Pacifique Nsengiyumva
*Peace Process*, Ambroise Niyonsaba
*Public Works and Housing*, Gaspard Ntirampeba
*Reintegration and Resettlement of Displaced Persons and Repatriates*, Pascal Nkurunziza
*Trade, Industry and Tourism*, Joseph Ntanyotora
*Transport, Posts and Telecommunications*, Cyprien Mbonigaba
*Women, Welfare and Social Affairs*, Romaine Ndorimana
*Youth, Sports and Culture*, Gérard Nyamwiza

### EMBASSY OF THE REPUBLIC OF BURUNDI

Maria-Louizaplein 46, B-1040 Brussels, Belgium
Tel: (00 32) (2) 2304535
*Ambassador Extraordinary and Plenipotentiary*, HE Jonathas Niyungeko, apptd 1999
BRITISH AMBASSADOR, HE G. Loten, resident at Kigali, Rwanda

## ECONOMY

The chief crops are coffee and tea, accounting for around 98 per cent of export earnings. Mineral, hide and skin exports are also important. Agriculture accounted for 54 per cent of GDP and employed over 90 per cent of the workforce in 1998.

In 1999 there was a trade surplus of US$42 million and a current account surplus of US$27 million. Imports totalled US$118 million and exports US$54 million.

GNP – US$823 million (1999); US$120 per capita (1999)
GDP – US$803 million (1997); US$103 per capita (1998)
ANNUAL AVERAGE GROWTH OF GDP – 3.6 per cent (1996)
INFLATION RATE – 3.4 per cent (1999)
TOTAL EXTERNAL DEBT – US$1,119 million (1998)

| *Trade with UK* | 1999 | 2000 |
|---|---|---|
| Imports from UK | £2,110,000 | £1,968,000 |
| Exports to UK | 973,000 | 1,252,000 |

---

# CAMBODIA

*Preăh Réachéanachâkr Kâmpŭchéa - The Kingdom of Cambodia*

---

AREA – 69,898 sq. miles (181,035 sq. km). Neighbours: Laos (north), Thailand (north and west), Vietnam (east)
POPULATION – 11,757,000 (1997 UN estimate). The language is Khmer. Chinese, Vietnamese and French are also spoken

CAPITAL – ΨPhnom Penh (population, 570,155, 1998 census)
CURRENCY – Riel of 100 sen
NATIONAL ANTHEM – Nokoreach
NATIONAL DAY – 9 November (Independence Day)
NATIONAL FLAG – Three horizontal stripes of blue, red, blue, with the blue of double width and containing a representation of the temple of Angkor in white
LIFE EXPECTANCY (years) – male 52.2; female 55.4
POPULATION GROWTH RATE – 2.6 per cent (1999)
POPULATION DENSITY – 59 per sq. km (1998)
URBAN POPULATION – 15.9 per cent (2000 estimate)
ILLITERACY RATE – 34.7 per cent
ENROLMENT (percentage of age group) – primary 100 per cent (1997); tertiary 1 per cent (1997)

## HISTORY AND POLITICS

Cambodia became a French protectorate in 1863 and was granted independence within the French Union as an Associate State in 1949. Full independence was proclaimed in 1953, and Prince Norodom Sihanouk became head of state. In 1970 Prince Sihanouk was deposed and a Khmer Republic was declared.

In 1975, Phnom Penh fell to the North Vietnamese-backed Khmer Rouge. During Khmer Rouge rule hundreds of thousands of Cambodians fled into exile and an estimated two million were killed.

In 1978, Vietnamese troops invaded Cambodia and the state was renamed The People's Republic of Kampuchea (PRK); in 1989 it became the State of Cambodia (SOC). Following the Vietnamese withdrawal in 1989, the resistance forces regained ground.

In September 1990, the government and the resistance forces established a Supreme National Council and peace agreements were signed in October 1991. In March 1992 the United Nations Transitional Authority for Cambodia (UNTAC) assumed authority from the government in the run-up to the multiparty elections, which were held in May 1993. In September 1993 a new constitution was adopted under which Cambodia became a pluralist liberal democracy with a constitutional monarchy. Prince Sihanouk was elected king and he appointed a new government.

In November 1998 a coalition government was formed with Hun Sen as prime minister and Prince Ranariddh as chairman of the National Assembly.

### INSURGENCIES

In July 1994 the Royal Government outlawed the Khmer Rouge, which responded by declaring a provisional government. Large numbers of Khmer Rouge defected to the Royal Government. Khmer Rouge leader Pol Pot was captured by a group of defectors in June 1997 and died in captivity on 15 April 1998. The remaining 4,332 Khmer Rouge soldiers surrendered on 9 February 1999.

On 15 January 2001 the Royal Government approved legislation creating an international tribunal composed of Cambodians and UN appointees to prosecute former leaders of the Khmer Rouge regime for atrocities committed during its rule.

### POLITICAL SYSTEM

Legislative power is vested in the National Assembly, which has 122 members elected for five-year terms, and the Senate, which has 61 appointed members and was formed on 25 March 1999, following an amendment to the constitution by the National Assembly. Executive power rests in the Royal Government, with the King having the power only to make appointments and declare a state of emergency, in consultation with the government.

### HEAD OF STATE

*HM The King of Cambodia*, Norodom Sihanouk, *elected by the Council of the Throne* 24 September 1993

### ROYAL GOVERNMENT OF CAMBODIA *as at July 2001*

*Prime Minister*, Hun Sen (CPP)
*Deputy Prime Minister, Co-Minister of Interior*, Sar Kheng (CPP)
*Deputy Prime Minister, Education, Youth and Sports*, Tol Loah (F)
*Agriculture, Forestry and Fishing*, vacant
*Co-Minister of National Defence*, Prince Sisowath Sereiroat (F)
*Commerce*, Cham Prasit (CPP)
*Culture and Fine Arts*, Princess Norodom Bophadevi (F)
*Environment*, Mok Maret (CPP)
*Foreign Affairs and International Co-operation*, Hor Namhong (CPP)
*Health*, Hong Sun-huot (F)
*Industry, Mines and Energy*, Suy Sem (CPP)
*Information and Press*, Loe Laysreng (F)
*Justice*, Uk Vithun (F)
*Landscaping, Urbanism and Construction*, Im Chhunlim (CPP)
*Planning*, Chhay Than (CPP)
*Post and Telecommunications*, So Khun (CPP)
*Public Works and Transport*, Khi Tanglim (F)
*Relations with National Assembly and Inspection*, Khun Hang (F)
*Religious Affairs*, Chea Savoeun (F)
*Rural Development*, Chhim Siekleng (F)
*Social Affairs, Labour, Vocational Training and Youth Rehabilitation*, It Sam-heng (CPP)
*State Minister, Co-Minister of Interior*, Yu Hokkri (F)
*State Minister, Co-Minister of National Defence*, Gen. Tie Banh (CPP)
*State Minister, Economy and Finance*, Keat Chong (CPP)
*State Minister, Office of the Council of Ministers*, Sok An (CPP)
*State Ministers*, Loe Laysreng (F); Hor Namhong (F)
*Tourism*, Veng Sereivut (F)
*Water Resources*, Lim Kean-hao (CPP)

*Women's and Veterans' Affairs* Mu Sok-huo (F)

CPP Cambodian People's Party; F United National Front for an Independent, Neutral, Peaceful and Co-operative Cambodia (FUNCINPEC)

ROYAL EMBASSY OF CAMBODIA
4 rue Adolph Yvon, F-75116 Paris, France
Tel: (00 33) (1) 45 03 47 20
*Ambassador Extraordinary and Plenipotentiary*, HE Park Sokhonn, apptd 2000

BRITISH EMBASSY
29, Street 75, Phnom Penh
Tel: (00 855) (23) 427124
*Ambassador Extraordinary and Plenipotentiary*, HE George Edgar, apptd 1997

## DEFENCE

The Army has 150 main battle tanks and 190 armoured personnel carriers. The Navy has 4 patrol and coastal vessels. The Air Force has 24 combat aircraft.

MILITARY EXPENDITURE – 5.1 per cent of GDP (1999)
MILITARY PERSONNEL – 140,000: Army 90,000, Navy 3,000, Air Force 2,000, Provincial Forces 45,000, Paramilitaries 67,000
CONSCRIPTION DURATION – conscription authorised but not implemented since 1993

## ECONOMY

The economy is largely based on agriculture, fishing and forestry. Agriculture employs over 70 per cent of the workforce and produced 51 per cent of GDP in 1998. In addition to rice, which is the staple crop, the major products are rubber, livestock, maize, timber, pepper, palm sugar, fresh and dried fish, kapok, beans, soya and tobacco. Textiles, leather goods, furnishings, timber and rubber are the main exports; the main imports are cigarettes, gold, diesel and oil.

Under the Khmer Rouge, the urban population was forced to work on the land, and re-establish plantations producing such crops as cotton, rubber and bananas. Following the Vietnamese invasion of 1978 the towns were repopulated and factories, in particular textile mills, iron smelting works and cement works, were put back in production.

In 1999 there was a trade deficit of US$240 million and a current account deficit of US$96 million.

GNP – US$3,023 million (1999); US$260 per capita (1999)
GDP – US$1,666 million (1997); US$255 per capita (1998)
ANNUAL AVERAGE GROWTH OF GDP - 6.5 per cent (1996)
INFLATION RATE – 4.0 per cent (1999)
TOTAL EXTERNAL DEBT – US$2,210 million (1998)

| *Trade with UK* | 1999 | 2000 |
|---|---|---|
| Imports from UK | £4,184,000 | £4,099,000 |
| Exports to UK | 42,798,000 | 54,510,000 |

## COMMUNICATIONS

The country has about 34,100 kilometres of roads, although most are now in a state of disrepair. There are two railways, one from Phnom Penh to the Thai border, the other from Phnom Penh to Kampot and Sihanoukville (Kompong Som). Phnom Penh is on a river capable of receiving ships of up to 2,500 tons all the year round. The deep water port at Sihanoukville (Kompong Som) on the Gulf of Thailand can receive ships of up to 10,000 tons. The port is linked to Phnom Penh by a modern highway.

# CAMEROON
*République du Cameroun*

AREA – 183,569 sq. miles (475,442 sq. km). Neighbours: Nigeria (north and west), Chad and Central African Republic (east), Republic of Congo-Brazzaville, Gabon and Equatorial Guinea (south)
POPULATION – 14,691,000 (1997 UN estimate). French and English are both official languages and enjoy equal status
CAPITAL – Yaoundé (population, 653,670, 1986 estimate)
MAJOR CITIES – ΨDouala (1,029,731) is the commercial centre
CURRENCY – Franc CFA of 100 centimes
NATIONAL ANTHEM – O Cameroun, Berceau de Nos Ancêtres (O Cameroon, thou cradle of our forefathers)
NATIONAL DAY – 20 May
NATIONAL FLAG – Vertical stripes of green, red and yellow with single five-pointed yellow star in centre of red stripe
LIFE EXPECTANCY (years) – male 49.9; female 52.0
POPULATION GROWTH RATE – 2.8 per cent (1999)
POPULATION DENSITY – 30 per sq. km (1998)
URBAN POPULATION – 48.9 per cent (2000 estimate)
MILITARY EXPENDITURE – 1.5 per cent of GDP (1999)
MILITARY PERSONNEL – 22,100: Army 11,500, Navy 1,300, Air Force 300, Paramilitaries 9,000
ILLITERACY RATE – 24.6 per cent (2000)
ENROLMENT (percentage of age group) – secondary 15 per cent (1980); tertiary 3.3 per cent (1990)

## HISTORY AND POLITICS

The German colony of the Cameroons, established in 1884, was captured by British and French forces in 1916 and divided into the League of Nations-mandated territories (later UN trusteeships) of East (French) and West (British) Cameroon. On 1 January 1960 East Cameroon became independent as the Republic of Cameroon. This was joined on 1 October 1961 by the southern part of West Cameroon after a plebiscite held under United Nations auspices; the northern part joined Nigeria. Cameroon became a federal republic with separate East and West Cameroon state governments. After a plebiscite held in 1972, Cameroon became a unitary republic and a one-party state.

After extensive unrest, multiparty elections were held in March 1992. The ruling People's Democratic Movement formed a coalition government with a small opposition party, the Movement for the Defence of the Republic.

A legislative election held in May 1997 was dominated by the ruling Cameroon People's Democratic Movement (CPDM) which won 109 of the 180 seats, though Commonwealth observers reported widespread fraud and voter intimidation.

### INTERNATIONAL RELATIONS

There have been armed clashes with Nigeria over the disputed Bakassi peninsula. The dispute is under consideration at the International Court of Justice.

### POLITICAL SYSTEM

The president is directly elected for a seven-year term, and appoints the prime minister and Cabinet. The National Assembly comprises 180 members, directly elected for a five-year term. Under the 1995 constitutional amendments a Senate is to be created.

HEAD OF STATE

*President and Commander-in-Chief of the Armed Forces*, Paul Biya, *acceded* 6 November 1982, *elected* 14 January 1984, *re-elected* 24 April 1988, 10 October 1992, 12 October 1997

CABINET *as at July 2001*

*Prime Minister*, Peter Mafany Musonge
*Agriculture*, Zacharie Perevet
*City Affairs*, Claude Joseph Mbafou
*Civil Service and Administrative Reform*, René Ze Nguele
*Communication*, Jacques Famé Ndongo
*Culture*, Ferdinand Leopold Oyono
*Delegate at the Presidency in charge of Defence*, Laurent Esso
*Economy and Finance*, Michel Meva'a Meboutou
*Employment, Labour and Social Causes*, Pius Ondoua
*Environment and Forests*, Sylvester Naah Ondoua
*Foreign Affairs*, François-Xavier Goubeyou
*Higher Education*, Jean-Marie Atangana Mebara
*Industrial and Commercial Development*, Bello Bouba Maigari
*Justice, Keeper of the Seals*, Ali Amadou
*Livestock, Fisheries and Animal Industries*, Ajoudji Hamadjoda
*Mines, Water Resources and Energy*, Yves Mbelle
*National Education*, Joseph Owona
*Post and Telecommunications*, Maximin Koué Kongo
*Public Health*, Urbain Olanguena Awono
*Public Investment and Regional Planning*, Martin Okouda
*Public Works*, Jérome Etah
*Scientific and Technical Research*, Henri Hogbe Nlend
*Social Affairs*, Marie Madeleine Fouda
*Territorial Administration*, Ferdinand Koungou Edima
*Tourism*, Pierre Hele
*Town Planning and Housing*, Boubakary Yerima Halilou
*Transport*, Christopher Nsalai
*Women's Affairs*, Catherine Bakang Mbock
*Youth and Sports*, Bidoung Mkpatt

HIGH COMMISSION FOR THE REPUBLIC OF CAMEROON
84 Holland Park, London W11 3SB
Tel: 020-7727 0771
*Ambassador Extraordinary and Plenipotentiary*, HE Samuel Libock Mbei, apptd 1995

BRITISH HIGH COMMISSION
Avenue Winston Churchill, BP 547 Yaoundé
Tel: (00 237) 220545
*High Commissioner*, HE Peter Boon, MBE, apptd 1998
There is also a British Consulate at Douala.

BRITISH COUNCIL DIRECTOR, June Rollinson, Avenue Charles de Gaulle, BP 818, Yaoundé; e-mail: bc.yaounde@bc-yaounde.iccnet.cm

## ECONOMY

Principal products are cocoa, coffee, bananas, cotton, timber, groundnuts, aluminium, rubber and palm products. Crude petroleum is also one of Cameroon's principal products.

France, Italy and other European Union states are Cameroon's main trading partners. In 1995 there was a trade surplus of US$627 million and a current account surplus of US$90 million. In 1997 exports totalled US$1,860 million and imports US$1,359 million.

GNP – US$8,798 million (1999); US$580 per capita (1999)
GDP – US$8,596 million (1997); US$702 per capita (1998)
ANNUAL AVERAGE GROWTH OF GDP – 5.1 per cent (1996)
INFLATION RATE – 0.1 per cent (1998)
TOTAL EXTERNAL DEBT – US$9,829 million (1998)

| *Trade with UK* | 1999 | 2000 |
|---|---|---|
| Imports from UK | £23,866,000 | £23,534,000 |
| Exports to UK | 42,854,000 | 47,364,000 |

## CANADA

AREA – 3,855,101 sq. miles (9,984,670 sq. km). Neighbours: USA (south), Alaska (USA) (west)
POPULATION – 30,871,957 (2001 estimate). The languages are English and French
CAPITAL – Ottawa (population, 1,045,249, 1997 estimate).
MAJOR CITIES - Calgary (885,130); Edmonton (899,466); Hamilton (663,587); ΨMontréal (3,384,233); Québec (700,197); Toronto (4,511,966); ΨVancouver (1,927,998); Winnipeg (677,291), 1997 estimates
CURRENCY – Canadian dollar (C$) of 100 cents
NATIONAL ANTHEM – O Canada
NATIONAL DAY – 1 July (Canada Day)
NATIONAL FLAG – Red maple leaf with 11 points on white square, flanked by vertical red bars one-half the width of the square
LIFE EXPECTANCY (years) – male 76.2; female 81.9
POPULATION GROWTH RATE – 1.2 per cent (1999)
POPULATION DENSITY – 3 per sq. km (1998)
URBAN POPULATION – 77.1 per cent (2000 estimate)

Canada occupies the whole of the northern part of the North American continent, with the exception of Alaska. In eastern Canada, the southernmost point is Middle Island in Lake Erie. Canada has six main physiographic divisions: the Appalachian-Acadian region, the Canadian shield, which comprises more than half the country, the St Lawrence-Great Lakes lowland, the interior plains, the Cordilleran region and the Arctic archipelago.

The climate of the eastern and central portions presents greater extremes than in corresponding latitudes in Europe, but in the south-western portion of the prairie region and the southern portions of the Pacific slope the climate is milder.

## HISTORY AND POLITICS

Canada was originally discovered by Cabot in 1497 and the French took possession of the country in 1534. The first permanent settlement at Port Royal (now Annapolis), Nova Scotia, was founded in 1605, and Québec was founded in 1608. In 1759 Québec was captured by British forces under General Wolfe and in 1763 the whole territory of Canada became a possession of Great Britain by the Treaty of Paris 1763. Nova Scotia was ceded in 1713 by the Treaty of Utrecht, the provinces of New Brunswick and Prince Edward Island being subsequently formed out of it. British Columbia was formed into a Crown colony in 1858, having previously been a part of the Hudson Bay Territory, and was united to Vancouver Island in 1866.

The constitution of Canada has its source in the British North America Act of 1867 which formed a Dominion, under the name of Canada, of the four provinces of Ontario, Québec, New Brunswick and Nova Scotia. To this federation the other provinces and territories have subsequently been admitted: Manitoba and Northwest Territories (1870), British Columbia (1871), Prince Edward Island (1873), Yukon (1898), Alberta and Saskatchewan (1905) and Newfoundland (1949). In 1982, the constitution was patriated (severed from the British parliament) with the approval of all provinces except Québec. In 1985, the federal prime minister and the provincial premiers concluded the Meech Lake Accord which provided for Québec to be recognised as a distinct society within Canada. However, two provincial legislatures withheld approval and the accord did not come into force. In Québec, a referendum calling for sovereignty and a new political and economic partnership was defeated in

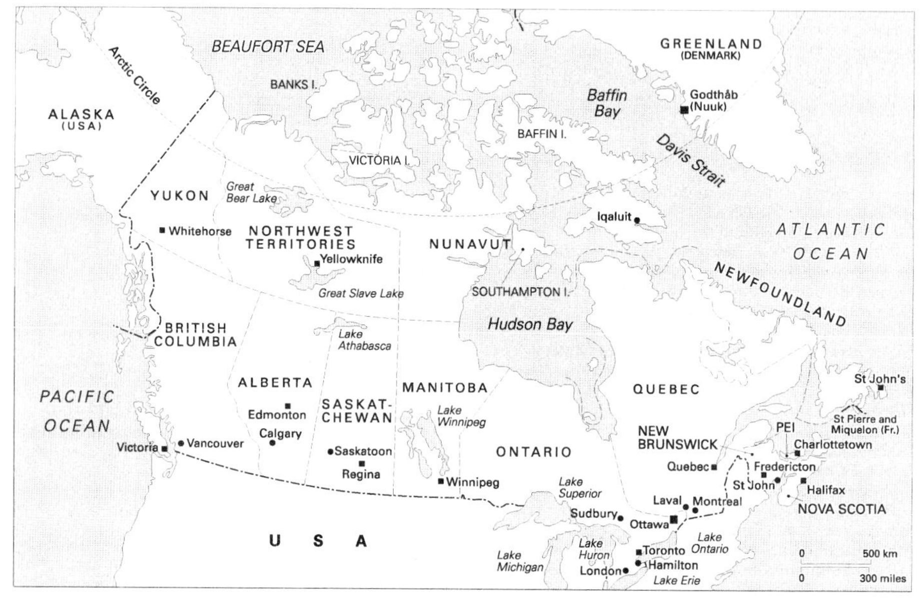


FEDERAL STRUCTURE

| *Provinces or Territories (with official contractions)* | *Area (sq. kilometres)* | *Population, 1 January 2001* | *Capital* | *Lieutenant-Governor* | *Premier* |
|---|---|---|---|---|---|
| Alberta (AB) | 661,848 | 3,022,861 | Edmonton | Lois Hole | Ralph Klein |
| British Columbia (BC) | 944,735 | 4,077,369 | ΨVictoria | Garde Gardom | Gordon Campbell |
| Manitoba (MB) | 647,797 | 1,149,220 | Winnipeg | Peter Liba | Gary Doer |
| New Brunswick (NB) | 72,908 | 757,267 | Fredericton | Marilyn Trenholme Counsell | Bernard Lord |
| Newfoundland and Labrador (NF) | 405,212 | 537,797 | ΨSt John's | Arthur House | Roger Grimes |
| Northwest Territories (NT) | 1,346,106 | 42,105 | *Yellowknife | †Daniel Marion | |
| Nova Scotia (NS) | 55,284 | 942,322 | ΨHalifax | Myra Freeman | John Hamm |
| Nunavut (NT)§ | 2,093,190 | 27,978 | *Iqaluit | †Peter Irniq | Paul Okalik |
| Ontario (ON) | 1,076,395 | 11,741,793 | ΨToronto | Hilary Weston | Michael Harris |
| Prince Edward Island (PE) | 5,660 | 139,078 | ΨCharlottetown | J. Léonce Bernard | Patrick Binns |
| Québec (QC) | 1,542,056 | 7,383,300 | ΨQuébec | Lise Thibeault | Bernard Landry |
| Saskatchewan (SK) | 651,036 | 1,020,650 | Regina | Dr Lynda Haverstock | Lorne Calvert |
| Yukon Territory (YT) | 482,443 | 30,194 | *Whitehorse | †Judy Gingell | ‡Pat Duncan |

Area figures include land and water area
* seat of government
§ Nunavut was created in 1999 from the Northwest Territories
† Commissioner
‡ Government Leader

October 1995. In September 1997 Québec was recognised as having a 'unique character' by leaders of the other provinces and territories. A new territory, Nunavut, which means 'our land' in the Inuit language of Inuktitut, was created on 1 April 1999 by partitioning the Northwest Territories.

In the federal election on 27 November 2000 the Liberal Party won a third consecutive term of office. The state of parties in the House of Commons following the election was Liberals 172, Canadian Alliance 66, Bloc Québécois 38, New Democrats 13, and Progressive Conservatives 12.

POLITICAL SYSTEM

Executive power is vested in a Governor General appointed by the Sovereign on the advice of the prime minister.

Parliament consists of a Senate and a House of Commons. The Senate consists of 105 members, nominated by the Governor General on the advice of the prime minister, the seats being distributed between the various provinces. The House of Commons has 301 members directly elected for a five-year term. Representation is proportional to the population of each province.

The judicature is administered by judges following the civil law in Québec province and common law in other provinces. Each province has a Court of Appeal. All superior, county and district court judges are appointed by the Governor General, the others by the Lieutenant-Governors of the provinces.

The highest federal court is the Supreme Court of Canada, which exercises general appellate jurisdiction throughout Canada in civil and criminal cases. There is one other federally constituted court, the Federal Court of

Canada, which has jurisdiction on appeals from its trial division, from federal tribunals and reviews of decisions and references by federal boards and commissions.

GOVERNOR GENERAL

*Governor General and Commander-in-Chief*, HE Adrienne Clarkson

FEDERAL CABINET *as at July 2001*

*Prime Minister*, Jean Chrétien
*Deputy Prime Minister*, Herbert Gray
*Agriculture and Agri-Food*, Lyle Vanclief
*Citizenship and Immigration*, Elinor Caplan
*Environment*, David Anderson
*Finance*, Paul Martin
*Fisheries and Oceans*, Herb Dhaliwal
*Foreign Affairs*, John Manley
*Health*, Allan Rock
*Heritage*, Sheila Copps
*Human Resources Development*, Jane Stewart
*Indian Affairs and Northern Development*, Robert Nault
*Industry*, Brian Tobin
*Infrastructure, President of the Treasury Board*, Lucienne Robillard
*Intergovernmental Affairs, President of the Privy Council*, Stéphane Dion
*International Co-operation*, Maria Minna
*International Trade*, Pierre Pettigrew
*Justice and Attorney-General*, Anne McLellan
*Labour and the Homeless*, Claudette Bradshaw
*Leader of the Government in the House of Commons*, Don Boudria
*Leader of the Government in the Senate*, Sharon Carstairs
*National Defence*, Arthur C. Eggleton
*National Revenue*, Martin Cauchon
*Natural Resources, Canadian Wheat Board*, Ralph Goodale
*Public Works and Government Services*, Alfonso Gagliano
*Solicitor-General*, Lawrence MacAulay
*Transport*, David Collenette
*Veterans' Affairs*, Ronald Duhamel

CANADIAN HIGH COMMISSION
Macdonald House, 1 Grosvenor Square, London W1K 4AB
Tel: 020-7258 6600
Canada House, Pall Mall East, London SW1Y 5BJ
*High Commissioner*, HE Jeremy Kinsman, apptd 2000
*Deputy High Commissioner*, R. Rochon
*Minister*, T. MacDonald (*Commercial/Economic*)
*Commander and Defence Adviser*, Brig.-Gen. W. Richard

BRITISH HIGH COMMISSION
80 Elgin Street, Ottawa K1P 5K7
Tel: (00 1) (613) 237 1530
*High Commissioner*, HE Sir Andrew Burns, KCMG, apptd 2000
*Deputy High Commissioner*, R. Codrington
*Counsellor*, M. Uden (*Economic*)
*Defence and Military Adviser*, Brig. E. Springfield, CBE
CONSULATES-GENERAL – Montréal, Toronto, Vancouver
CONSULATES – Halifax/Dartmouth, Québec City, St John's, Winnipeg
BRITISH COUNCIL DIRECTOR, Peter Chenery, c/o British High Commission; e-mail: ottawa.enquiries@ca.britishcouncil.org
BRITISH COUNCIL REPRESENTATIVE IN QUÉBEC, Sarah Dawbarn, 1000 ouest rue de La Gauchetière, Montréal, Québec H3B 4W5; e-mail: montreal.enquiries@ca.britishcouncil.org

## DEFENCE

The Canadian armed forces are unified and organised into three functional commands: Land Force Command; Maritime Command; Air Command.

The Army (Land Forces) has 114 main battle tanks and 1,790 armoured personnel carriers. The Navy (Maritime Forces) has four destroyers, 12 frigates and 14 patrol and coastal vessels. The Air Force has 140 combat aircraft and 30 armed helicopters.

MILITARY EXPENDITURE – 1.2 per cent of GDP (1999)
MILITARY PERSONNEL – 59,100: Army 20,900, Navy 9,000, Air Force 13,500, Paramilitaries 9,350

## ECONOMY

About 68 million hectares of land is farmed, about 7.3 per cent of the total land area. Over 60 per cent of this is under cultivation, the remainder being predominantly classified as unimproved pasture. More than 80 per cent of the cultivated land is in the prairie region of western Canada. In 1996, there were 274,955 farms in Canada, with a total land area of 168 million acres. The farm sector accounts for about 3 per cent of GDP and employs about 3.7 per cent of the labour force.

Almost half of Canada's land area is forest, making it the world's largest exporter of timber, pulp and newsprint.

The fishing industry contributed C$1,657 million in 1998.

In 1997, Canada was the world's largest producer of potash and uranium, the second largest of nickel, asbestos, cadmium, zinc and elemental sulphur. The country is also rich in gold, copper, lead, molybdenum, platinum group metals, gypsum, cobalt, titanium concentrates, and aluminium. The total value of mineral production in 1996 was C$49,171.8 million.

Production of gold was 157,790 kg in 1999 and of silver 1,173,000 kg. Uranium production in 1999 was 9,892 tonnes.

There were 18.8 million foreign tourists in 1998, who accounted for receipts of C$11.2 billion.

GNP – US$614,003 million (1999); US$19,320 per capita (1999)
GDP – US$607,702 million (1997); US$20,822 per capita (1999)
ANNUAL AVERAGE GROWTH OF GDP – 4.0 per cent (2000)
INFLATION RATE – 2.9 per cent (2001)
UNEMPLOYMENT – 6.9 per cent (2001)

### TRADE

The main exports in 1999 were automotive products, including cars, trucks and parts, machinery and equipment, industrial products and raw materials, forestry products, including wood, wood pulp and paper products, agricultural products (chiefly wheat and meat products), fishery products, and energy products, including crude petroleum and natural gas.

Agricultural exports amounted to C$21.7 billion in 1999.

Trade with the USA accounts for about 84 per cent of Canada's exports and 77 per cent of its imports.

In 1999 imports totalled US$220,183 million and exports US$238,446 million. There was a trade surplus of US$22,756 million and a current account deficit of US$2,273 million.

| *Trade with UK* | 1999 | 2000 |
|---|---|---|
| Imports from UK | £2,556,271,000 | £3,507,718,000 |
| Exports to UK | 3,137,050,000 | 4,057,600,000 |

## COMMUNICATIONS

In 1999 there were 901,902 km of roads, of which 318,371 km were paved, and 36,114 km of railway track in operation.

The registered shipping on 1 January 1991 including inland vessels, was 43,787 vessels with gross tonnage 4,956,845. The bulk of canal shipping in Canada is handled through the two sections of the St Lawrence Seaway, which provide access to the Great Lakes for ocean-going ships.

## EDUCATION

Education is under the control of the provincial governments, the cost of the publicly controlled schools being met by local taxation, aided by provincial grants. Education is compulsory between the ages of five or six and fifteen or sixteen.

In 1995–6 there were 16,096 elementary and secondary schools with 5,899,943 pupils. There were 70 degree-granting universities.

ENROLMENT (percentage of age group) – primary 95 per cent (1996); secondary 91 per cent (1996); tertiary 87.3 per cent (1996)

---

# CAPE VERDE

*República de Cabo Verde*

---

AREA – 1,557 sq. miles (4,033 sq. km). Comprising the Windward Islands (Santo Antão, São Vicente, Santa Luzia, São Nicolau, Bõa Vista and Sal) and Leeward Islands (Maio, São Tiago, Fogo and Brava)
POPULATION – 429,000 (1997 estimate), the majority of whom are Roman Catholic. The official language is Portuguese; a creole is spoken by most of the population
CAPITAL – ΨPraia (population, 61,644, 1995 estimate)
CURRENCY – Escudo Caboverdiano of 100 centavos
NATIONAL ANTHEM - É patria amada (This is our beloved country)
NATIONAL DAY – 5 July (Independence Day)
NATIONAL FLAG – Blue with three horizontal stripes of white, red, white near the bottom; over all on these near the hoist a ring of ten yellow stars
LIFE EXPECTANCY (years) – male 64.2; female 71.8
POPULATION GROWTH RATE – 2.3 per cent (1999)
POPULATION DENSITY – 103 per sq. km (1998)
URBAN POPULATION – 62.2 per cent (2000 estimate)
MILITARY EXPENDITURE – 2.7 per cent of GDP (1999)
MILITARY PERSONNEL – 1,150: Army 1,000, Air Force 100, Coast Guard 50
CONSCRIPTION DURATION – Selective conscription
ILLITERACY RATE – 26.5 per cent (2000)
ENROLMENT (percentage of age group) – primary 100 per cent (1989); secondary 48 per cent (1996)

## HISTORY AND POLITICS

The islands, colonised *c.*1460, achieved independence from Portugal on 5 July 1975 under the Partido Africano da Independência da Guiné e Cabo Verde (PAIGC). A federation of the islands with Guinea Bissau was planned but this was dropped following the 1980 coup in Guinea Bissau.

The republic was a one-party state under the African Party for the Independence of Cape Verde (PAICV) until the constitution was amended in 1990. Multiparty elections, held in January 1991, were won by the opposition Movement for Democracy (MPD), which was re-elected in December 1995. President António Mascarenhas Monteiro of the MPD was elected in February 1991 and re-elected unopposed in February 1996. The general election held on 14 January 2001 returned the PAICV to power with 40 of the 72 seats in the National Assembly. The MPD won 30 seats and the Democratic Alliance for Change won two seats. Pedro Pires of the PAICV narrowly won the second round of the presidential election held on 25 February 2001 by 164 votes. The MPD candidate, Carlos Veiga, appealed to the Supreme Court, citing irregularities in the conduct of the elections; the court upheld some of the appeals, which reduced Pires's winning margin to just 12 votes. .

### HEAD OF STATE

*President*, Pedro Pires, *elected* 25 February 2001, *assumed office* 22 March 2001

### COUNCIL OF MINISTERS *as at July 2001*

*Prime Minister, Defence*, José Maria Neves
*Agriculture and Fisheries*, Mario Anselmo Couto de Matos
*Education*, Victor Borges
*Finance*, Carlos Augusto Duarte Burgo
*Foreign Affairs and Communities*, Manuel Inocencio Sousa
*Health, Employment and Solidarity*, Dario Laval Rezende Dantas Dos Reis
*Infrastructure and Transport*, Jorge Lima Delgado Lopes
*Justice and Interior*, Cristina Fontes
*Secretary of State for Foreign Affairs*, Fatima Lima Veiga
*Secretary of State for Parliamentary Affairs and Defence*, Armindo Cipriano Mauricio
*Secretary of State for State Reforms, Public Administration and Local Government*, Edeltrudes Pires Neves
*Secretary of State for Youth Affairs*, Maria de Jesus Veiga Miranda Mascarenhas
*Tourism, Industry and Trade*, José Armando Duarte

### EMBASSY OF THE REPUBLIC OF CAPE VERDE

Jeannelaan 29, B-1050 Brussels, Belgium
Tel: (00 32) (2) 646 9025
*Ambassador Extraordinary and Plenipotentiary*, HE Fernando Wahnon Ferreira, apptd 2001

BRITISH AMBASSADOR, HE Alan Burner, resident at Dakar, Senegal
There is a British Consulate on São Vicente.

## ECONOMY

The islands have little rain and agriculture is mostly confined to irrigated inland valleys. The chief products are bananas and coffee (for export), maize, sugar cane and nuts. Fish and shellfish are important exports. Salt is obtained on Sal, Bõa Vista and Maio; volcanic rock is also mined for export.

In 1998 there was a trade surplus of US$186 million and a current account deficit of US$58 million. In 1995 imports totalled US$252 million and exports US$9 million.

The main ports are Praia and Mindelo, and there is an international airport on Sal.

GNP – US$569 million (1999); US$1,330 per capita (1999)
GDP – US$332 million (1997); US$1,085 per capita (1998)
ANNUAL AVERAGE GROWTH OF GDP – 4.0 per cent (1996)
TOTAL EXTERNAL DEBT – US$244 million (1998)

| *Trade with UK* | 1999 | 2000 |
|---|---|---|
| Imports from UK | £5,498,000 | £4,077,000 |
| Exports to UK | 2,424,000 | 1,684,000 |

## CENTRAL AFRICAN REPUBLIC
*République Centrafricaine/Ködrö tî Bê-Afrîka*

AREA – 240,535 sq. miles (622,984 sq. km). Neighbours: Chad (north), Sudan (east), Democratic Republic of Congo and Congo-Brazzaville (south), Cameroon (west)
POPULATION – 3,540,000 (1997 UN estimate). French is the official language; the national language is Sangho.
CAPITAL – Bangui (population, 473,817, 1984 estimate)
CURRENCY – Franc CFA of 100 centimes
NATIONAL ANTHEM - La Renaissance
NATIONAL DAY – 1 December
NATIONAL FLAG – Four horizontal stripes, blue, white, green, yellow, crossed by central vertical red stripe with a yellow five-pointed star in top left-hand corner
LIFE EXPECTANCY (years) – male 43.3; female 44.9
POPULATION GROWTH RATE – 2.1 per cent (1999)
POPULATION DENSITY – 6 per sq. km (1998)
URBAN POPULATION – 41.2 per cent (2000 estimate)
MILITARY EXPENDITURE – 4.0 per cent of GDP (1999)
MILITARY PERSONNEL – 4,150: Army 3,000, Air Force 150, Paramilitaries 1,000
CONSCRIPTION DURATION – Two years (selective)
ILLITERACY RATE – 53.5 per cent (2000)
ENROLMENT (percentage of age group) – primary 53 per cent (1990); tertiary 1.4 per cent (1991)

### HISTORY AND POLITICS

In December 1958 the French colony of Ubanghi Shari elected to remain within the French Community and adopted the title of the Central African Republic. It became fully independent on 17 August 1960. The first president, David Dacko, was overthrown in 1966 by the then Col. Bokassa, who in 1976 proclaimed himself Emperor and renamed the country the Central African Empire. In 1979 Bokassa was deposed by Dacko in a bloodless coup and the country reverted to a republic. President Dacko surrendered power in 1981 to Gen. André Kolingba, who instituted military rule until 1985, when a civilian-dominated Cabinet was appointed. In November 1986 a referendum was held which approved a new constitution and the establishment of a one-party state.

Multiparty presidential and legislative elections were held in October 1992 but were annulled due to irregularities. President Kolingba formed a coalition government in February 1993. Presidential elections held in 1993 were won by Ange-Félix Patasse of the Central African People's Liberation Party (MLPC); he was re-elected in September 1999. Legislative elections were held on 22 November and 13 December 1998. The MLPC emerged as the largest party with 47 of 109 seats and formed a multiparty coalition government.

#### POLITICAL SYSTEM

Constitutional reforms were passed in a national referendum in December 1994 which created a constitutional court, introduced elected local assemblies, extended the presidential mandate to a maximum of two six-year terms and subordinated the government to the president.

#### INSURGENCY

The army is divided between southerners loyal to former President Gen. Kolingba and northerners loyal to President Patasse. The 1,100 French troops stationed near Bangui have been called upon to quell frequent mutinies by Gen. Kolingba's supporters; in March 1998 the French troops were replaced by the UN MINURCA peacekeeping force, which withdrew on 15 February 2000.

#### HEAD OF STATE

*President*, Ange-Félix Patasse, *elected* 19 September 1993, *re-elected* 19 September 1999

#### COUNCIL OF MINISTERS *as at July 2001*

*Prime Minister*, Martin Ziguele (MLPC)
*Civil Service, Employment and Social Security*, Laurent Ngon Baba (ADP)
*Energy and Mines*, André Nalke Dorogo (MLPC)
*Foreign Affairs*, Agba Otikpo Mezode (Ind.)
*Interior and Territorial Administration*, Théodore Bikoo (PLD)
*Justice*, Marcel Metefara (MLPC)
*Minister of State, Finance and Budget*, Eric Sorongope (MLPC)
*Minister of State, Posts and Telecommunications*, Gabriel Jean-Édouard Koyambounou (MLPC)
*Ministers-Delegate*, Michel Doyene (MLPC) (*Disarmament*); Lazarre Dokoula (MLPC) (*Finance and Budget*); Victor Boucher (MLPC) (*Foreign Affairs*); Clément Eregani (MLPC) (*Planning and International Co-operation*); Robert Zana (MLPC) (*Public Security*)
*National and Higher Education*, Timoléon M'baikoua (MLPC)
*National Defence*, Jean-Jacques Demafouth (MLPC)
*Planning and International Co-operation*, Alexis N'gomba (PLD)
*Promotion of Rural Life*, Salomon Namkoserena (MLPC)
*Public Health and Population*, Joseph Kalite (MLPC)
*Relations with Parliament*, Michel Doko (PLD)
*Social Affairs, Promotion of Women, Children and the Disabled*, Françoise Ibrahim N'doma (CN)
*Trade, Industry and Private Sector Promotion*, Jacob M'baitadjim (MLPC)
*Transport and Civil Aviation*, Désiré Pendémou (MLPC)
*Water Resources, Forestry, Fisheries, Environment and Tourism*, Constance Nathalie Gounebana (PLD)
*Youth and Sports*, Jean Dominique N'darata (UDR/FK)

CN National Convention; MLPC Central African People's Liberation Party; ADP Alliance for Democracy and Progress ; PLD Liberal Democratic Party; ; UDR/FK Democratic Union for Renewal - Fini Ködrö; Ind. Independent

EMBASSY OF THE CENTRAL AFRICAN REPUBLIC
30 rue des Perchamps, F-75016, Paris
Tel: (00 33) (1) 4224 4256
*Ambassador Extraordinary and Plenipotentiary*, vacant
*First Counsellor*, G. Gresenguet
BRITISH AMBASSADOR, HE Peter Boon, resident at Yaoundé, Cameroon

### ECONOMY

Cotton, diamonds, coffee and timber are the major exports. Industrial goods, machinery and transport equipment, foodstuffs and fuels are the main imports.

In 1994 there was a trade surplus of US$15 million and a current account deficit of US$25 million. In 1997 exports totalled US$154 million and imports US$145 million.
GNP – US$1,035 million (1999); US$290 per capita (1999)
GDP – US$1,245 million (1997); US$296 per capita (1998)
ANNUAL AVERAGE GROWTH OF GDP – 0.9 per cent (1996)
INFLATION RATE – 1.9 per cent (1998)
TOTAL EXTERNAL DEBT – US$921 million (1998)

| *Trade with UK* | 1999 | 2000 |
|---|---|---|
| Imports from UK | £748,000 | £550,000 |
| Exports to UK | 576,000 | 215,000 |

## CHAD
*République du Tchad*

AREA – 495,755 sq. miles (1,284,000 sq. km). Neighbours: Niger, Nigeria and Cameroon (west), Libya (north), Sudan (east), Central African Republic (south)
POPULATION – 7,486,000 (1997 UN estimate); French and Arabic are the official languages; there are more than 50 indigenous languages, of which the most widely spoken is Sara
CAPITAL – N'Djaména (population, 179,000, 1972 estimate)
CURRENCY – Franc CFA of 100 centimes
NATIONAL ANTHEM - Peuple tchadien, debout et à l'ouvrage (People of Chad, arise and to work)
NATIONAL DAY – 1 December
NATIONAL FLAG – Vertical stripes, blue, yellow and red
LIFE EXPECTANCY (years) – male 47.3; female 50.1
POPULATION GROWTH RATE – 2.9 per cent (1999)
POPULATION DENSITY – 6 per sq. km (1998)
URBAN POPULATION – 23.8 per cent (2000 estimate)
MILITARY EXPENDITURE – 2.9 per cent of GDP (1999)
MILITARY PERSONNEL – 30,350: Army 25,000, Air Force 350, Paramilitaries 4,500
ILLITERACY RATE – 46.4 per cent (2000)
ENROLMENT (percentage of age group) – primary 46 per cent (1996); secondary 6 per cent (1995); tertiary 0.6 per cent (1996)

### HISTORY AND POLITICS

Chad became a member state of the French Community in 1958, and was proclaimed fully independent on 11 August 1960. The constitution was suspended in 1975 when President Tombalbaye was killed in a coup by Gen. Félix Malloum; following a succession of further coups, Idriss Déby came to power in 1990 and announced the adoption of a multiparty system, allowing the legalisation of political parties in 1991 and 1992. A Higher Transitional Council (CST) was elected in 1993 to serve as the transitional legislature and appointed a transitional government in conjunction with President Déby. The CST has twice extended the transitional period by one year to allow sufficient time to organise elections. In March 1996, the government concluded the Franceville agreement with opposition parties which provided for a national cease-fire and an independent commission to oversee the election. A new constitution, establishing a unified, democratic state, was confirmed by a referendum. Déby won the first multiparty presidential elections in 1996. Elections to the 125-member National Assembly in January and February 1997 were won by the pro-Déby Patriotic Salvation Movement (MPS).

#### INSURGENCIES

Three rebel movements, the Movement for Unity and the Republic (MUR), the Movement for Democracy and Justice in Chad (MDJT), and the Democratic Revolutionary Council (DRC), announced that they had formed an alliance in February 2000.

In July 2000, the government came to an agreement with the Armed Resistance against Anti-Democratic Forces (RAFAD) movement and agreed to integrate its members into the armed forces.

#### HEAD OF STATE

*President*, Idriss Déby, *took power* December 1990, *elected* 3 July 1996

#### GOVERNMENT *as at July 2001*

*Prime Minister*, Nagoum Yamassoum
*Agriculture*, Moctar Moussa
*Civil Service, Labour, Employment, Promotion and Modernisation*, Gen. Routouang Yoma Golom
*Communications, Government Spokesman*, Nadjo Abdel Kerim
*Culture, Youth and Sport*, Moussa Wayor
*Development and Economic Promotion*, Mahamat Ali Hassane
*Education*, Abderahim Bireme Hamid
*Environment and Water*, Oumar Boukar Kadjallami
*Finance*, Mahamat Loani
*Foreign Affairs*, Mohamat Saleh Annadif
*Higher Education*, Ramat Issaka
*Industry, Commerce and Handicrafts*, Kalzeude Tahini
*Interior, Security and Decentralisation*, Abderrahmane Moussa
*Justice, Guardian of the Seals*, Mahamat Ahmat Alabo
*Livestock*, Gen. Weiding Assi-Assoue
*Mines, Energy and Oil*, Albert Pahimi
*Minister-Delegate to the PM for Decentralisation*, Djimtedaye Lapia
*National Defence and Rehabilitation*, Mahamat Nouri
*Posts and Telecommunications*, Salibou Garba
*Public Health*, Fatime Kimto
*Public Works, Transport and Urban Development*, Moussa Moustapha
*Secretary-General to the Government*, David Houdeingar
*Social Action and Family*, Mariam Atahir
*Tourism Development*, Mahamat Ahmat Choukou

EMBASSY OF THE REPUBLIC OF CHAD
Lambermontlaan 52, B-1030 Brussels, Belgium
Tel: (00 32) (2) 215 1975
*Ambassador Extraordinary and Plenipotentiary*, HE Abderahim Yacoub Ndiaye, apptd 2000

BRITISH AMBASSADOR, HE Peter Boon, resident at Yaoundé, Cameroon
*Honorary Consulate*, BP877, Avenue Charles de Gaulle, N'Djaména

### ECONOMY

About 90 per cent of the workforce is occupied in agriculture, fishing and forestry. There is an oilfield in Kanem and salt is mined around Lake Chad, but the most important activities are cotton growing and animal husbandry. Raw cotton, meat and groundnuts are the main exports. Chad's main trading partners are France and Cameroon.

On 7 January 2000 the IMF approved a loan facility of about US$26.5 million to support the government's 1999-2002 economic programme.

In 1994 Chad had a trade surplus of US$77 million and a current account deficit of US$38 million. In 1998 imports totalled US$264 million and exports US$261 million.
GNP – US$1,555 million (1999); US$200 per capita (1999)
GDP – US$1,059 million (1997); US$150 per capita (1998)
ANNUAL AVERAGE GROWTH OF GDP – 2.7 per cent (1996)
INFLATION RATE – 6.8 per cent (1999)
TOTAL EXTERNAL DEBT – US$1,091 million (1998)

| *Trade with UK* | 1999 | 2000 |
|---|---|---|
| Imports from UK | £917,000 | £2,452,000 |
| Exports to UK | 259,000 | 62,000 |

## CHILE
*República de Chile*

AREA – 292,135 sq. miles (756,626 sq. km). Neighbours: Peru (north), Bolivia and Argentina (east)

POPULATION – 15,018,000 (1997 UN estimate). The main groups are: indigenous Araucanian Indians, Fuegians, Rapanui and Changos; Spanish settlers and their descendants; mixed Spanish Indians; and European immigrants. Because of extensive intermarriage only a few indigenous Indians are racially separate. The language is Spanish, with admixtures of local words of Indian origin. The main religion is Roman Catholicism
CAPITAL – Santiago (population, 4,690,684, 1998 UN estimate)
MAJOR CITIES – ΨAntofagasta (246,023); Concepción (368,428); Puente Alto (384,016); ΨValparaíso (284,086); ΨPunta Arenas (121,533), on the Straits of Magellan, is the southernmost city in the world (1998 UN estimates)
CURRENCY – Chilean peso of 100 centavos
NATIONAL ANTHEM – Canción Nacional de Chile
NATIONAL DAY – 18 September (National Anniversary)
NATIONAL FLAG – Two horizontal bands, white, red; in top sixth a white star on blue square, next staff
LIFE EXPECTANCY (years) – male 73.4; female 79.9
POPULATION GROWTH RATE – 1.5 per cent (1999)
POPULATION DENSITY – 20 per sq. km (1998)
URBAN POPULATION – 85.7 per cent (2000 estimate)

Chile lies between the Andes (5,000 to 15,000 feet above sea level) and the shores of the South Pacific, extending coastwise from the arid north around Arica to Cape Horn. The extreme length of the country is about 2,800 miles, with an average breadth, north of 41°, of 100 miles.

Island possessions include the Juan Fernández group (three islands) about 360 miles from Valparaíso; one of these islands is the reputed scene of Alexander Selkirk's (Robinson Crusoe) shipwreck. Easter Island, about 2,000 miles away in the South Pacific Ocean, contains stone platforms and hundreds of stone figures.

## HISTORY AND POLITICS

Chile was discovered by Spanish adventurers in the 16th century and remained under Spanish rule until 1810, when the first autonomous government was established. Full independence was consolidated in 1818 after a revolutionary war.

A Marxist, Salvador Allende, was elected president in 1970, but was overthrown in a military coup in 1973.

Gen. Pinochet, who led the coup, assumed the presidency until presidential and congressional elections were held in 1989, beginning the transition to full democracy.

Gen. Pinochet was arrested in London on 16 October 1998 following a request by the Spanish government for his extradition, but extradition proceedings were dropped on the grounds of poor health on 2 March 2000, and he was freed and allowed to return to Chile. The Chilean Supreme Court lifted his immunity from prosecution in August 2000 and on 1 December he was put under house arrest pending trial on charges relating to the kidnapping and murder of more than 70 political opponents. The charges were dismissed by the Court of Appeals, but formally reinstated on 31 January 2001 after it had been determined that Gen. Pinochet was fit to stand trial. On 8 March the charges were reduced to conspiracy to conceal the actions of military death squads.

Presidential and legislative elections were held in 1993. Eduardo Frei won the presidential election and his ruling Coalition for Democracy (CPD) (centre and centre-left parties) won 70 seats in the Chamber of Deputies and 22 in the Senate. In the 1997 legislative election the CPD maintained its 70-seat majority in the Chamber of Deputies. The most recent presidential elections were held in December 1999 and January 2000 and were won by the CPD candidate, Ricardo Lagos Escobar.

### POLITICAL SYSTEM

Executive power is held by the president. Legislative power is exercised by a Congress which comprises a Senate of 47 Senators (38 elected and nine appointed) and a Chamber of Deputies of 120 elected members. Senators serve eight-year terms and deputies serve four-year terms. The presidential term is six years with no possibility of re-election.

Chile is divided into 12 regions and the Metropolitan Area.

### HEAD OF STATE

*President of the Republic*, Ricardo Lagos Escobar, *elected* 16 January 2000, *sworn in* 11 March 2000

### CABINET *as at July 2001*

*Agriculture*, Jaime Campos (PRSD)
*Defence*, Mario Fernández (PDC)
*Economy, Energy and Mining*, José de Gregorio (PDC)
*Education*, Mariana Aylwin (PDC)
*Finance*, Nicolás Eyzaguirre (PPD)
*Foreign Affairs*, María Soledad Alvear (PDC)
*Health*, Michelle Bachelet (PS)
*Housing and Social Assets*, Jaime Ravinet (PDC)
*Interior*, José Miguel Insulza (PS)
*Justice*, José Antonio Gómez (PRSD)
*Labour*, Ricardo Solari (PS)
*National Women's Secretariat*, Adriana Delpiano (PPD)
*Planning*, Alejandra Krauss (PDC)
*Public Works, Transport and Telecommunications*, Carlos Cruz (PS)
*Secretary-General of the Government*, Claudio Huepe (PDC)
*Secretary-General of the Presidency*, Alvaro García Hurtado (PPD)
PDC Christian Democratic Party; PS Socialist Party; PPD Party for Democracy; PRSD Social Democratic Radical Party

### EMBASSY OF CHILE

12 Devonshire Street, London W1N 2DS
Tel: 020-7580 6392
*Ambassador Extraordinary and Plenipotentiary*, HE Cristián Barros, apptd 2000

### BRITISH EMBASSY

Avenida El Bosque 0125, Casilla 72-D, Santiago
Tel: (00 56) (2) 370 4100
E-mail: consulate@santiago.mail.fco.gov.uk
*Ambassador Extraordinary and Plenipotentiary*, HE Greg Faulkner, apptd 2000
*Deputy Head of Mission, Counsellor and Consul-General*, P. Whiteway
*Defence Attaché*, Col. R. Rollo-Walker
*First Secretary (Commercial)*, T. Torlot
CONSULAR OFFICES – Punta Arenas, Valparaíso.

BRITISH COUNCIL DIRECTOR, David Stokes (*Cultural Attaché*), Eliodoro Yáñez 832, Providencia, Santiago; e-mail: info@britcoun.cl
BRITISH-CHILEAN CHAMBER OF COMMERCE, Av. Suecia 155-C, Casilla 536, Santiago

## DEFENCE

The Army has 251 main battle tanks, 20 armoured infantry fighting vehicles and 565 armoured personnel carriers. The Navy has three submarines, two destroyers, three frigates, 26 patrol and coastal vessels, and 20 armed helicopters. The Air Force has 88 combat aircraft.
MILITARY EXPENDITURE – 4.0 per cent of GDP (1999)

MILITARY PERSONNEL – 87,000: Army 51,000, Navy 24,000, Air Force 12,000; Paramilitaries 29,500
CONSCRIPTION DURATION – 12–22 months

## ECONOMY

Economic reforms during the late 1970s and the 1980s, with large-scale privatisation and deregulation, have made Chile one of the most successful economies in Latin America. Cereals, vegetables, fruit, tobacco, hemp and vines are grown extensively and livestock accounts for nearly 40 per cent of agricultural production. Sheep farming predominates in the extreme south. There are large timber tracts in the central and southern zones which produce timber, cellulose and wood for export. Fishing is also a major industry.

Chile is rich in copper-ore, iron-ore and nitrates, and has the only commercial production of nitrate of soda (Chile saltpetre) from natural resources in the world. There are large deposits of high grade sulphur. Oil and natural gas are produced in the Magallanes area, but domestic production is now declining.

In 1999 there was a trade surplus of US$1,664 million and a current account deficit of US$80 million.

GNP – US$69,602 million (1999); US$4,740 per capita (1999)
GDP – US$77,084 million (1997); US$4,921 per capita (1998)
ANNUAL AVERAGE GROWTH OF GDP – 7.2 per cent (1996)
INFLATION RATE – 3.3 per cent (1999)
UNEMPLOYMENT – 6.4 per cent (1998)
TOTAL EXTERNAL DEBT – US$36,302 million (1998)

### TRADE

The principal exports are minerals, timber and metal products, fish products and vegetables. The principal imports are food products, industrial raw materials, machinery, and equipment and spares. The main trade partners are Japan and the USA; in 1996 Chile joined the Mercosur Free Trade Zone, and in March 1998 signed an extension to a free trade agreement with Mexico. In 1999 imports totalled US$15,137 million and exports US$15,616 million.

| *Trade with UK* | 1999 | 2000 |
|---|---|---|
| Imports from UK | £113,884,000 | £115,230,000 |
| Exports to UK | 342,730,000 | 469,708,000 |

## COMMUNICATIONS

With the improvement of the roads an increasing share of internal transportation is moving by road and rail, although shipping is still important. The road system is about 80,000 km in length, of which around 11,000 km is paved.

There are 6,782 km of railway track. A railway line runs from Valparaíso through La Calera and Santiago to Puerto Montt. With the completion of a section of 435 miles from Corumba, Brazil, to Santa Cruz, Bolivia, the Trans-Continental Line will link the Chilean Pacific port of Arica with Rio de Janeiro on the Atlantic. A line runs from Antofagasta to Salta (Argentina).

Domestic air traffic is carried by Línea Aérea Nacional (LAN) and LADECO, which also operate internationally, and smaller regional carriers.

## CULTURE AND EDUCATION

Chilean Nobel Prize winners include the writers Gabriela Mistral (1945) and Pablo Neruda (1971).

Elementary education is free and compulsory. There are eight state universities (three in Santiago, two in Valparaíso, one each in Antofagasta, Concepción and Valdivia), and many private universities.

ILLITERACY RATE – 4.3 per cent (2000)
ENROLMENT (percentage of age group) – primary 89 per cent (1996); secondary 58 per cent (1996); tertiary 31 per cent (1997)

---

# CHINA

*Zhonghua Renmin Gongheguo – The People's Republic of China*

---

AREA – 3,705,408 sq. miles (9,596,961 sq. km). Neighbours: Russia and Mongolia (north), North Korea (east), Vietnam, Laos, Myanmar, India, Bhutan and Nepal (south), India, Pakistan, Afghanistan, Tajikistan, Kyrgyzstan and Kazakhstan (west)
POPULATION – 1,295,330,000 (2001 census). Han Chinese make up 91.9 per cent of the population and the remainder of the population belongs to around 55 ethnic minorities. Among the largest are the Zhuang of Guangxi, the Hui of Ningxia, the Miao of southern China, the Manchu of Heilongjiang, the Uygurs and Kazakhs of Xinjiang, the Tibetans and the Mongols. The indigenous religions are Confucianism, Taoism and Buddhism. There are also Muslims (officially estimated at about 12 million) and Christians (unofficially estimated at about 50 million). The official language is Mandarin Chinese; of the many local dialects the largest are Cantonese, Fukienese, Xiamenhua and Hakka. The autonomous regions of Mongolia, Tibet and Xinjiang have their own languages
CAPITAL – Beijing (population, 7,362,426, 1990)
MAJOR CITIES – Chengdu (2,954,872); Chongqing (3,172,178); Dalian (2,483,776); Guangzhou (Canton) (3,935,193); Harbin (2,990,921); Qingdo (2,101,808); ΨShanghai (8,214,384); Shenyang (4,669,737); Tianjin (5,855,044); Wuhan (4,040,113); Wuxi (1,013,606); Yantai (847,285); Zaozhuang (1,793,103)
CURRENCY – Renminbi Yuan of 10 jiao or 100 fen
NATIONAL ANTHEM – March of the Volunteers
NATIONAL DAY – 1 October (Founding of People's Republic)
NATIONAL FLAG – Red, with large gold five-point star and four small gold stars in crescent, all in upper quarter next staff
LIFE EXPECTANCY (years) – male 68.1; female 71.3
POPULATION GROWTH RATE – 1.0 per cent (1999)
POPULATION DENSITY – 131 per sq. km (1998)
URBAN POPULATION – 32.1 per cent (2000 estimate)

## HISTORY AND POLITICS

China was ruled by imperial dynasties for over 20 centuries until revolutionaries led by Sun Yat-sen forced the Emperor to abdicate on 10 October 1911. Neither the new Nationalist Party (Kuomintang (KMT)) government nor the emergent Chinese Communist Party (CCP) were able to unify China, or to agree on the basis for further reform. Warlord infighting rendered China weak, enabling Japan to occupy Manchuria and all the important northern and coastal areas of China by 1939. Japan's occupation was ended by its defeat by the allies in 1945.

The Communists established control over large areas of China in the early 1940s, seizing the territory abandoned by Japan in 1945. Civil war lasted until 1949 when the CCP, led by Mao Zedong (Mao Tse-tung), inaugurated the People's Republic of China (PRC), and the KMT under Chiang Kai-shek went into exile in Taiwan. The USA continued to recognise the Chiang Kai-shek regime as the rightful government of China until 1971, when the PRC took over China's membership of the United Nations from Taiwan.

Under Mao Zedong China was ruled on the basis of four 'cardinal principles': Marxist–Leninist–Maoist thought, the Socialist Road, the dictatorship of the proletariat, and the leadership of the CCP. Mao's 'Great Leap Forward' (1958–61) was an attempt to industrialise rural areas which resulted in a famine in which 30–40 million people died. China was plunged into chaos during the Cultural Revolution (1966–70) when the Red Guards were used to rid the country of 'rightist elements'.

Following the death of Mao Zedong in 1976, the disgraced Deng Xiaoping was recalled. In 1977 he was elected Vice-Chairman of the CCP, becoming the dominant force within the party by eliminating leftist influence, rehabilitating fallen leaders and promoting an 'open door' policy of economic liberalisation. The Congresses of 1982 and 1987 reaffirmed Deng's policies, and in 1987 most of the revolutionary generation were replaced in the top posts by younger, more liberal supporters of reform.

Student-led pro-democracy demonstrations in April and May 1989, centred on Tiananmen Square in Beijing, ended on 3–4 June when the army took control of Beijing, killing thousands of protesters. This strengthened the position of hardliners within the leadership, who readopted policies of centralisation based on Marxist ideology. Deng retired from his last official post in November 1989 but retained effective control until late 1994.

At Deng's instigation during 1992 the emphasis switched back to economic reform and the power of the hardliners waned. The 14th Party Congress in 1992 endorsed Deng's calls for faster, bolder economic reforms and his 'socialist market economy'. Deng died on 19 February 1997 and Jiang Zemin assumed the mantle of leader.

In addition to continuing economic reforms, Jiang has sought to improve China's standing in the international community.

The plenary session of the Central Committee of the Communist Party declared in September 1999 that the reform of the state sector was the country's most pressing task. A ten-year restructuring programme is due to be completed by 2010.

## Insurgencies

Separatists from the Uygur Muslim minority group in Xinjiang Autonomous Region have demonstrated against Han rule. They have claimed responsibility for bomb attacks in the provincial capital, Ürümqi, and in Beijing. Two Muslim separatists were executed in January 1999 as part of an effort to tighten control of the region and in February 2001, the death sentence was passed on the founder of an underground Islamic party.

The government banned the Falun gong cult on 22 July 1999, which had claimed to have 70 million followers; the government had become worried after it was revealed that a large number of Chinese Communist Party officials and senior officers in the People's Liberation Army had joined the cult. Falun gong members continued to protest against the banning of the organisation and there were reports that thousands of its members had been sent to labour camps.

## Political System

Under the 1982 constitution, the National People's Congress is the highest organ of state power. It is elected for a term of five years and is supposed to hold one session a year. It is empowered to amend the constitution, make laws, select the president and vice-president and other

leading officials of the state, approve the national economic plan, the state budget and the final state accounts, and to decide on questions of war and peace. The State Council is the highest organ of the state administration. It is composed of the Premier, the Vice-Premiers, the State Councillors, heads of Ministries and Commissions, the Auditor-General and the Secretary-General. Command over the armed forces is vested in the Central Military Commission.

Deputies to Congresses at the primary level are 'directly elected' by the voters 'through a secret ballot after democratic consultation'. This is now extended to county level. These Congresses elect the deputies to the Congress at the next higher level. Deputies to the National People's Congress are elected by the People's Congresses of the provinces, autonomous regions and municipalities directly under the central government, and by the armed forces.

Local government is conducted through People's Governments at provincial, municipal and county levels. Autonomous regions, prefectures and counties exist for national minorities and are described as self-governing.

### HEAD OF STATE

*President of the People's Republic of China*, Jiang Zemin, *elected* March 1993, *re-elected* 16 March 1998
*Vice-President*, Hu Jintao
*Chairman of the Standing Committee of the National People's Congress*, Li Peng
*Chairman of the Central Military Committee*, Jiang Zemin
*Deputy Chairmen of the Central Military Committee*, Chi Haotian; Hu Jintao; Zhang Wannian

### STATE COUNCIL *as at July 2001*

*Premier*, Zhu Rongji
*Vice-Premiers*, Qian Qichen; Li Lanqing; Wen Jiabao; Wu Bangguo
*State Councillors*, Gen. Chi Haotian; Ismail Amat; Luo Gan; Wu Yi; Wang Zhongyu

### MINISTERS

*Agriculture*, Chen Yaobang
*Civil Affairs*, Doje Cering
*Communications*, Huang Zhendong
*Construction*, Yu Zhengsheng
*Culture*, Sun Jiazheng
*Defence*, Gen. Chi Haotian
*Education*, Chen Zhili
*Finance*, Xiang Huaicheng
*Foreign Affairs*, Tang Jiaxuan
*Foreign Trade and Economic Co-operation*, Shi Guansheng
*Health*, Zhang Wenkang
*Information Industry*, Wu Jichuan
*Justice*, Zhang Fusen
*Labour and Social Security*, Zhang Zuoji
*Land and Natural Resources*, Tian Fengshan
*Personnel*, Zhang Xuezhong
*Public Security*, Jia Chunwang
*Railways*, Fu Zhihuan
*Science Technology*,
*State Security*, Xu Yongyue
*Supervision*, He Yong
*Water Resources*, Wang Shucheng

### MINISTERS IN CHARGE OF STATE COMMISSIONS

*Development Planning*, Zeng Peiyan
*Economics and Trade*, Sheng Huaren
*Ethnic Affairs*, Li Dezhu
*Family Planning*, Zhang Weiqing
*Science, Technology and Industry for National Defence*, Liu Jibin
*Auditor-General*, Li Jinhua
*Governor of the People's Bank of China*, Dai Xianglong

### CHINESE PEOPLE'S POLITICAL CONSULTATIVE CONFERENCE

*Chair*, Li Ruihan

### THE CHINESE COMMUNIST PARTY

*General Secretary*, Jiang Zemin
*Politburo Standing Committee*, Jiang Zemin; Li Peng; Zhu Rongji; Li Ruihuan; Hu Jintao; Wei Jiangxing; Li Lanqing
*Politburo of the Central Committee*, Tian Jiyun; Jiang Zemin; Li Tieying; Li Ruihuan; Zhu Rongji; Hu Jintao; Ding Guangen; Qian Qichen; Li Lanqing; Wei Jianxing; Wu Bangguo; Li Peng; Huang Ju; Wen Jiabao; Li Changchun; Wu Guanzheng; Chi Haotian; Zhang Wannian; Luo Gan; Jia Qinglin; Jiang Chunyun (*full members*); Zeng Qinghong; Wu Yi (*alternate members*)
*Secretariat of the Central Committee*, Zeng Qinghong (*Director*); Ding Guangen; Hu Jintao; Wei Jianxing; Wen Jiabao; Luo Gan (*full members*)
*Membership*, 52,000,000 (1993)

### EMBASSY OF THE PEOPLE'S REPUBLIC OF CHINA

49-51 Portland Place, London W1N 4JL
Tel: 020-7636 5197
*Ambassador Extraordinary and Plenipotentiary*, HE Ma Zhengang, apptd 1997
*Minister-Counsellor*, Zhao Jun
*Defence Attaché*, Maj.-Gen. Yan Kunsheng

### BRITISH EMBASSY

11 Guang Hua Lu, Jian Guo Men Wai, Beijing 100600
Tel: (00 86) (10) 6532 1961/2/3/4
E-mail: beinfo@public.bta.net.cn
*Ambassador*, HE Anthony Galsworthy, KCMG, apptd 1997
*Minister, Consul-General and Deputy Head of Mission*, N. J. Cox
*Counsellors*, J. V. Everard (*Political and Economic*); C. Segar (*Commercial*)*Defence, Military and Air Attaché*, Brig. J. G. Kerr, OBE, QGM

BRITISH CONSULATES-GENERAL - Chongqing, Shanghai and Guangzhou

BRITISH COUNCIL DIRECTOR - Michael O'Sullivan (*Cultural Counsellor*), Cultural and Education Section, British Embassy, Landmark Building, 8 North Dongsanhuan Road, Chaoyang District, Beijing 100004; e-mail: bc.beijing@britishcouncil.org.cn. Regional directors in Chengdu, Guangzhou and Shanghai

BRITISH CHAMBER OF COMMERCE, 3i Technical Club, 15 Guanghuali, Jianguomenwai, Beijing 100020

## DEFENCE

All three military arms are parts of the People's Liberation Army (PLA). China has at least 20 intercontinental and 100 intermediate range land-based, and 13 submarine-launched nuclear ballistic missiles. The Army has about 7,060 main battle tanks and 4,800 armoured personnel carriers and armoured infantry fighting vehicles.

The Navy has 65 submarines, 20 destroyers, 40 frigates, 368 patrol and coastal vessels, 507 combat aircraft and 37 armed helicopters. The Air Force has over 3,000 combat aircraft and some armed helicopters.

MILITARY EXPENDITURE – 5.4 per cent of GDP (1999)
MILITARY PERSONNEL – 2,470,000: Army 1,700,000, Navy 220,000, Air Force 420,000; Strategic Missile Forces 100,000; Paramilitaries 1,100,000
CONSCRIPTION DURATION – Two years (selective)

## ECONOMY

Economic liberalisation in the early 1980s reduced central planning and broadened the role of the market, which led to an explosion in manufacturing, concentrated in China's coastal regions. Foreign direct investment, especially from Hong Kong and Taiwan, has enabled the construction of a significant industrial base and transport infrastructure. In the coastal regions the economy has become a free market in all but name, with several stock markets and Shanghai's emergence as a financial centre. Since 1980, special economic zones have been established in Guangdong, Fujian and Hainan provinces. In addition, there are free trade and development zones throughout the country, designed to stimulate both foreign trade and internal economic development. The reforms have enabled the economy to grow more than fivefold since 1980. China has become the third-largest beneficiary of foreign investment in the world, primarily into its export industries.

Agriculture remains of great importance, employing nearly half the working population and accounting for about 18 per cent of GDP. Cereals, with peas and beans, are grown in the northern provinces, and rice, tea and sugar in the south. Rice is the staple food of the inhabitants. Cotton (mostly in valleys of the Yangtze and Yellow Rivers), tea (in the west and south), with hemp, jute and flax, are the most important crops. Livestock is raised in large numbers. Sericulture is one of the oldest industries. Cottons, woollens and silks are manufactured in large quantities.

Coal, iron ore, tin, antimony, wolfram, bismuth and molybdenum are abundant. Oil is produced in several northern provinces, particularly in Heilongjiang and Shandong, and off-shore deposits are being sought in co-operation with western and Japanese companies. In November 1997, a deal was reached with Russia over the construction of a US$12 billion liquefied natural gas (LNG) pipeline to take LNG from Siberia to China's Pacific coast. In March 1998, China announced the construction of a US$2.3 billion 1,875-mile oil pipeline along the Silk Road to Kazakhstan.

Overcapacity in some of the traditional industries is being tackled, with the closure of 26,000 coal mines and 2,500 steel smelters. The more successful state-owned enterprises are being prepared for listing on the stock-market, others are being prepared for sale, and failing companies are being wound up. Tourism has become a major industry, with 7.11 million foreign visitors in 1998.

GNP – US$979,894 million (1999); US$780 per capita (1999)
GDP – US$901,981 million (1997); US$777 per capita (1998)
ANNUAL AVERAGE GROWTH OF GDP – 9.2 per cent (2000)
INFLATION RATE – 1.4 per cent (2001)
UNEMPLOYMENT – 3.3 per cent (1998)
TOTAL EXTERNAL DEBT – US$154,599 million (1998)

### TRADE

Foreign trade and external economic relations have grown enormously since 1978. In 1995, import tariffs were cut to an average 23 per cent in line with China's attempts to join the World Trade Organisation. The principal exports are clothing, electronics, machine plant, yarns and fabrics, chemicals, footwear, travel goods, and iron and steel. The principal imports are machinery, electronics, raw materials, yarns and fabrics, plastics and motor vehicles. The main trading partners are Japan, the USA, Hong Kong, South Korea, Taiwan and Germany.

In 1999 China had a trade surplus of US$36,207 million and a current account surplus of US$15,667 million. Imports totalled US$165,788 million and exports US$195,150 million.

| *Trade with UK* | 1999 | 2000 |
|---|---|---|
| Imports from UK | £1,216,253,000 | £1,468,692,000 |
| Exports to UK | 3,530,789,000 | 5,005,763,000 |

## COMMUNICATIONS

There are 57,600 km of railway lines, of which 13,022 km are electrified, and 1,278,000 km of highway, of which 6,258 km are motorways (1998). In addition, internal civil aviation has been developed, with routes totalling more than 1,506,000 km.

In the past the principal means of communication east to west was by the rivers, the most important of which are the Yangtze (Changjiang) (3,400 miles), the Yellow River (Huanghe) (2,600 miles) and the West River (Xihe) (1,650 miles). These, together with the network of canals connecting them, are still much used but their overall importance has declined. Coastal port facilities are being improved and the merchant fleet expanded.

Postal services and telecommunications have developed in recent years and it is claimed that 95 per cent of all rural townships are on the telephone and that postal routes reach practically every production brigade headquarters.

## EDUCATION

Primary education lasts six years and secondary education lasts six years (three years in junior middle school and three years in senior middle school). In 1998 there were 1,022 universities and colleges.

ILLITERACY RATE – 15.0 per cent
ENROLMENT (percentage of age group) – primary 100 per cent (1996); tertiary 6 per cent (1997)

## CULTURE

The Chinese language has many dialects, notably Cantonese, Hakka, Amoy, Foochow, Changsha, Nanchang, Wu (Shanghai) and the northern dialect. The Common Speech or *putonghua* (often referred to as Mandarin) is based on the northern dialect. The Communists have promoted it as the national language and it is taught throughout the country. As *putonghua* encourages the use of the spoken language in writing, the old literary style and ideographic form of writing has fallen into disuse. Since 1956 simplified characters have been introduced to make reading and writing easier. In 1958 the National People's Congress adopted a system of romanisation known as pinyin.

Chinese literature is one of the richest in the world. Paper has been employed for writing and printing for nearly 2,000 years. The Confucian classics which formed the basis of traditional Chinese culture date from the Warring States period (fourth to third centuries BC), as do the earliest texts of Taoism. Histories, philosophical and scientific works, poetry, literary and art criticism, novels and romances survive from most periods.

Important newspapers and magazines include the *People's Daily* and the twice-monthly *Qiushi*, which replaced *Red Flag* as the CCP's mouthpiece in 1989.

## TIBET

AREA – 463,000 sq. miles (1,199,164 sq. km)
POPULATION – 2,260,000 (1993)
CAPITAL – Lhasa

Tibet is a plateau seldom lower than 10,000 feet, which forms the northern frontier of India (boundary imperfectly demarcated), from Kashmir to Myanmar, but is separated therefrom by the Himalayas.

From 1911 to 1950, Tibet was virtually an independent country though its status was never officially so recognised. In 1950 Chinese Communist forces invaded eastern Tibet. In 1951 an agreement was reached whereby the Chinese army was allowed entry into Tibet, and a

Communist military and administrative headquarters was set up. A series of revolts against Chinese rule culminated in 1959 in a rising in Lhasa, the capital. Fighting continued for several days before the rebellion was crushed and military rule was imposed. The Dalai Lama fled to India where he and his followers were granted political asylum and established a government in exile.

In 1964 the Dalai Lama and the Panchen Lama were dismissed, marking the end of co-operation between the Chinese government and the traditional religious authorities. Tibet became an Autonomous Region of China in 1965. Martial law was declared in Tibet in 1989 after serious unrest, and sporadic outbursts of unrest continue.

The Panchen Lama died in 1989. China rejected the Dalai Lama's choice of successor, who is believed to have been executed, and enthroned its own candidate.

In December 1997, the International Commission of Jurists issued a report declaring that Tibet was 'under alien subjugation' and called for a UN-managed referendum to decide its future status. China contested that the report failed to acknowledge its historical claims to the region.

The 17th Karmapa Lama, the first reincarnation of a living Buddha to be recognised by both China and the Dalai Lama, defected from Tibet in late December 1999 and fled to India, where he appealed for political asylum. On 16 January 2000, the 7th Reting Lama was ordained in Tibet; the Dalai Lama had refused to recognise him as the reincarnation of the previous Reting Lama.

In May 2001 the government published details of a modernisation programme for Tibet which aimed to improve the low standard of living by promoting market reforms and extensive public construction projects.

## SPECIAL ADMINISTRATIVE REGIONS

### HONG KONG

AREA – 424 sq. miles (1,098 sq. km)
POPULATION – 6,975,000 (1999)
CURRENCY – Hong Kong dollar (HK$) of 100 cents
FLAG – Red, with a white bauhinia flower of five petals each containing a red star
LIFE EXPECTANCY (years) – male 77.2; female 82.6
POPULATION GROWTH RATE – 1.9 per cent (1997)
POPULATION DENSITY – 6,221 per sq. km (1998)
URBAN POPULATION – 100.0 per cent (2000 estimate)

Hong Kong, consisting of more than 230 islands and of a portion of the mainland (Kowloon and the New Territories) on the south-east coast of China, is situated at the eastern side of the mouth of the Pearl River. Hong Kong Island is about 11 miles (18 km) long and from two to five miles (three to eight km) broad. It is separated from the mainland by a narrow strait.

The climate is sub-tropical, tending towards the temperate for nearly half the year. The mean monthly temperature ranges from 16° C to 29° C. The average annual rainfall is 2,214 mm, of which nearly 80 per cent falls between May and September. Tropical cyclones occur between May and November, causing high winds and heavy rain.

### HISTORY AND POLITICS

Hong Kong Island was first occupied by Great Britain in 1841 and formally ceded by the Treaty of Nanking in 1842. Kowloon was acquired by the Beijing Convention of 1860 and the New Territories, consisting of a peninsula in the southern part of the Guangdong province together with adjacent islands, by a 99-year lease signed on 9 June 1898.

On 19 December 1984 the UK and China signed a Joint Declaration in which it was agreed that China would resume sovereignty over Hong Kong on 1 July 1997. In the run-up to the 1997 handover, the Chinese government's insistence on a greater say in the running of the colony and Governor Patten's plan for an extension of democracy prompted acrimonious disputes. The Chinese government refused to accept the reforms and replaced the Legislative Council.

Hong Kong became, with effect from 1 July 1997, a Special Administrative Region (SAR) of the People's Republic of China.

The Joint Declaration which took effect in May 1985 guarantees: the free movement of goods and capital; the retention of Hong Kong's free port status, separate customs territory and freely convertible currency; the protection of property rights and foreign investment; the right of free movement to and from Hong Kong; Hong Kong's autonomy in the conduct of its external commercial relations and its own monetary and financial policies; and judicial independence. Hong Kong's constitution is the Basic Law, which was passed by China's National People's Congress in 1990 and guarantees that the SAR's social and economic systems will remain unchanged for 50 years.

A Legislative Council election was held on 10 September 2000. The Democratic Party, a pro-democracy opposition party, remained the largest in the legislature with 12 seats and the pro-China Democratic Alliance for the Betterment of Hong Kong won 11 seats; 20 seats were won by independent candidates.

### POLITICAL SYSTEM

Hong Kong is administered by the Hong Kong SAR government, headed by the Chief Executive, who is aided by an Executive Council and a Legislative Council. The Executive Council consists of three ex-officio members (the Chief Secretary, the Financial Secretary and the Attorney-General) together with ten other members, including the President of the Legislative Council.

The Legislative Council consists of 60 members, of whom 24 are directly elected. Thirty members are elected by functional constituencies composed of professional and business groups and six more by an election committee.

*Chief Executive*, Tung Chee-hwa, *sworn in* 1 July 1997

### EXECUTIVE COUNCIL *as at July 2001*

*Non-official Members*, Leung Chun-ying *(Convenor)*; Dr Raymond Ch'ien Kuo-fung; Chung Shui-ming; Nellie Fong Wong; Lee Yeh-kwong; Tam Yiu-chung; Henry Tang; Rosanna Wong; Yang Ti-liang
*Ex-officio Members*, Anthony Leung; Donald Tsang; Elsie Leung

### GOVERNMENT SECRETARIAT *as at July 2001*

*Administrative Secretary*, Donald Tsang
*Financial Secretary*, Antony Leung
*Justice*, Elsie Leung
*Civil Service*, Joseph Wong
*Commerce and Industry*, Chau Tak-hay
*Constitutional Affairs*, Michael Suen
*Economic Services*, Sandra Lee
*Education and Manpower*, Fanny Law
*Environment and Food*, Lily Yam Kwan
*Financial Services*, Stephen Ip
*Health and Welfare*, Dr E. Yeoh
*Home Affairs*, Lam Woon-kwong
*Housing*, Dominic Wong
*Information, Technology and Broadcasting*, Carrie Yau
*Planning and Lands*, John Tsang
*Security*, Regina Ip
*Transport*, Nicholas Ng
*Treasury*, Denise Yue
*Works*, Li Cheng-shi
*President of the Legislative Council*, Rita Fan

CONSUL-GENERAL, Sir James Hodge, KCVO, CMG, 1 Supreme Court Road, Central, (PO Box 528), Hong Kong. Tel: (00 852) 2901 3000

BRITISH COUNCIL DIRECTOR, Desmond Lauder, 3 Supreme Court Road, Admiralty, Hong Kong; e-mail: info@britishcouncil.org.hk

HONG KONG ECONOMIC AND TRADE OFFICE, 6 Grafton Street, London W1X 3LB. Tel: 020-7499 9821. *Commissioner*, Sandra Lee, apptd 1999

BRITISH CHAMBER OF COMMERCE, Room 1712, Shui On Centre, 8 Harbour Road, Wan Chai, Hong Kong

## ECONOMY

The main economic sector is the services industry, especially financial services. It employed 85 per cent of the workforce and contributed 84.7 per cent of GDP in 1998. Principal exports are clothing, electrical machinery and apparatus, and textiles.

Diversification in terms of products and markets continues to be the main feature of recent industrial development, as are industrial partnerships with overseas companies. The economy is based on export rather than the domestic market. Tourism is very important to the economy; 13 million people visited Hong Kong in 2000.

GNP – US$165,122 million (1999); US$23,520 per capita (1999)

GDP – US$172,963 million (1997); US$24,581 per capita (1998)

ANNUAL AVERAGE GROWTH OF GDP – 5.0 per cent (1996)

INFLATION RATE – 4.0 per cent (1999)

## TRADE

In 1999 Hong Kong had a trade deficit of US$3,159 million and a current account surplus of US$9,281 million. Imports totalled US$179,520 million and exports US$173,885 million. Hong Kong's principal customers for its domestic products, in order of value of trade, were China, USA, Japan and Germany. China was its principal supplier. About 40 per cent of China's foreign trade passes through Hong Kong.

| *Trade with UK* | 1999 | 2000 |
|---|---|---|
| Imports from UK | £2,319,999,000 | £2,673,859,000 |
| Exports to UK | 5,121,330,000 | 6,138,486,000 |

## COMMUNICATIONS

Hong Kong has one of the world's finest natural harbours, and it is the busiest container port in the world, with eight terminals, as well as large modern cargo and liner terminals. Dockyard facilities include eight floating drydocks, the largest being capable of docking vessels up to 150,000 tonnes deadweight. A new 17-berth container port will open in stages between 1997 and 2003.

An international airport built on reclaimed land at Chek Lap Kok opened in July 1998. When fully operational, it will be capable of handling 35 million passengers and 1.5 million tonnes of cargo annually.

## EDUCATION

Free education for children up to the age of 15 is compulsory. Post-secondary education is provided by six universities and one college. The Open Learning Institute of Hong Kong provides university education. There are also seven technical institutes and the Hong Kong Institute of Education.

ILLITERACY RATE – 6.6 per cent

ENROLMENT (percentage of age group) – primary 90 per cent (1996); secondary 69 per cent (1996); tertiary 21.9 per cent (1993)

## MACAO (AOMEN)

AREA – 7 sq. miles (18 sq. km)

POPULATION - 469,000 (1997)

Macao, situated at the mouth of the Pearl River, comprises a peninsula and the islands of Coloane and Taipa.

Macao became a Portuguese colony in 1557; in a Sino-Portuguese treaty of 1887 China recognised Portugal's sovereignty over Macao. An agreement to transfer the administration of Macao to the Chinese authorities was signed on 13 April 1987. Macao became the Macao Special Administrative Region (MSAR) of China when power was transferred by the outgoing Portuguese governor Vasco Rocha Vieira to the new chief executive on 19 December 1999. The final session of the Macao SAR Basic Law Drafting Committee had been held in Beijing in January 1993 and had approved the Basic Law which was to serve as Macao's constitution after 1999.

On 10 April 1999, a 200-member committee of Macao residents was established to determine the composition of the first government of the Macao SAR. They elected Edmund Ho Hao Wah to be its first chief executive. The Chief Executive announced in September 1999 that he had appointed the 10 members of his Executive Council, a body intended to assist the chief executive in policy-making. In addition, he appointed seven legislators to the 23-member MSAR First Legislative Council, which included 15 members of the previous 16-member Legislative Assembly; a replacement was chosen for the member who had not wished to continue.

*Chief Executive*, Edmund Ho Hao Wah

EXECUTIVE COUNCIL SECRETARIAT *as at July 2001*

*Administration and Justice*, Florinda da Rosa Silva Chan

*Economy and Finance*, Francis Tam Pak Yuen

*Security*, Cheong Kuoc Va

*Social Affairs and Culture*, Fernando Chui Sai On

*Transport and Public Works*, Ao Man Long

CONSUL-GENERAL, Sir James Hodge, KCVO, CMG, resident at Hong Kong

## ECONOMY

Service industries comprise the greatest part of the economy, providing 71.2 per cent of employment in 1997. In 1998, gambling provided 43 per cent of GNP and there were 6.9 million foreign visitors. Imports totalled US$1,937 million and exports US$2,122 million.

The main trading partners are the EU, the USA, China, Hong Kong and Japan.

| *Trade with UK* | 1999 | 2000 |
|---|---|---|
| Imports from UK | £19,598,000 | £39,337,000 |
| Exports to UK | 42,636,000 | 41,134,000 |

---

# COLOMBIA
*República de Colombia*

---

AREA – 439,737 sq. miles (1,138,914 sq. km). Neighbours: Venezuela (north and east), Brazil (south-east), Peru (south), Ecuador (south-west), Panama (north-west)

POPULATION – 41,539,000 (1997 UN estimate): 58 per cent mestizo, 20 per cent white, 14 per cent mulatto, 4 per cent black, 3 per cent mixed black-Amerindian, 1 per cent Amerindian. The language is Spanish. Roman Catholicism is the established religion

CAPITAL – Bogotá (population, 5,398,998, 1993)

MAJOR CITIES – ΨBarranquilla (1,328,833), the major port on the Caribbean; Bucaramanga (759,651); ΨBuenaventura (227,478), the major port on the Pacific; Cali (2,063,867); ΨCartagena (656,632); Medellín (2,556,357)
CURRENCY – Colombian peso of 100 centavos
NATIONAL ANTHEM – Oh gloria inmarcesible (Oh glory unfading!)
NATIONAL DAY – 20 JULY (National Independence Day)
NATIONAL FLAG – Broad yellow band in upper half, surmounting equal bands of blue and red
LIFE EXPECTANCY (years) – male 68.1; female 74.1
POPULATION GROWTH RATE – 1.9 per cent (1999)
POPULATION DENSITY – 32 per sq. km (1998)
URBAN POPULATION – 73.9 per cent (2000 estimate)

Colombia lies in the extreme north-west of South America, having a coastline on both the Caribbean Sea and Pacific Ocean.

The country is divided by the Cordillera de los Andes into a coastal region in the north and west and extensive plains in the east. The eastern range of the Colombian Andes is a series of vast tablelands. This temperate region is the most densely peopled portion of the country. The principal rivers are the Magdalena, Guaviare, Cauca, Atrato, Caquetá, Putumayo and Patia.

## HISTORY AND POLITICS

The Colombian coast was visited in 1502 by Columbus, and in 1536 a Spanish expedition penetrated the interior and established a government. The country remained under Spanish rule until 1819 when Simón Bolivar established the Republic of Colombia, consisting of the territories now known as Colombia, Panama, Venezuela and Ecuador. In 1829–30 Venezuela and Ecuador withdrew, and in 1831 the remaining territories formed the Republic of New Granada. The name was changed to the Granadine Confederation in 1858, to the United States of Colombia in 1861 and to the Republic of Colombia in 1866. Panama seceded in 1903.

From 1957 to 1974 the country was governed under the 'National Front' agreement with an alternating presidency and equal numbers of ministerial posts. The alternation of the presidency ended in 1974 and parity in appointments in 1978.

A new constitution was promulgated in 1991. The March 1998 legislative elections were won by the Liberal Party, but some of its members defected to join the Great Alliance for Change (GAC), a Conservative-led coalition which now commands an overall majority in the House of Representatives. The presidential election in June 1998 was won by the GAC candidate Andrés Pastrana Arango.

### INSURGENCIES

Colombia is dogged by insurgency from left-wing guerrillas. The main active guerrilla factions are the Revolutionary Armed Forces of Colombia (FARC) and the National Liberation Army (ELN). Formal peace talks began on 9 November 1998, but fighting has continued.

In December 2000, the United Self-Defence Forces of Colombia (AUC), a right-wing paramilitary organisation, began to attack civilians in towns and villages which were suspected of being pro-FARC. ELN and FARC were also reported to have carried out joint actions against the AUC.

### POLITICAL SYSTEM

The Congress is a bicameral legislature. The lower house (the House of Representatives) has 161 members directly elected for a four-year term. The upper house (the Senate) has 102 members, directly elected for four years; two seats are reserved for representatives of indigenous people. The president, who appoints the Cabinet, is directly elected for a four-year term.

### HEAD OF STATE

*President*, Andrés Pastrana Arango, *elected* 21 June 1998
*Vice-President, Defence*, Gustavo Bell

### CABINET *as at July 2001*

*Agriculture and Rural Development*, Rodrigo Villalba Mosquera
*Communications*, María del Rosario Sintes Ulloa
*Culture*, Aracely Morales López
*Economic Development*, Eduardo Pizano de Narvaez (PSC)
*Education*, Francisco José Lloreda Mera
*Environment*, Juan Mayr Maldonado (Ind.)
*Finance and Public Credit*, Juan Manuel Santos Calderón (LP)
*Foreign Affairs*, Guillermo Fernández de Soto (PSC)
*Foreign Trade*, Marta Lucia Ramírez de Rincon (LP)
*Health*, Sara Ordonez Noriega
*Interior*, Armando Estrada Villa
*Justice*, Rómulo González Trujillo
*Labour and Social Security*, vacant
*Mines and Energy*, Luis Ramiro Valencia Cossio (PSC)
*Transport*, Gustavo Adolfo Canal Mora
LP Liberal Party; PSC Social Conservative Party; Ind. Independent

### COLOMBIAN EMBASSY

Flat 3A, 3 Hans Crescent, London SW1X 0LN
Tel: 020-7589 9177/5037
*Ambassador Extraordinary and Plenipotentiary*, HE Victor G. Ricardo-Piñeros, apptd 2000

### BRITISH EMBASSY

Edificio Ing Barings, Carrera 9 No 76-49 Piso 9, Bogotá
Tel: (00 57) (1) 317 6690/6310/6321
E-mail: britain@cable.net.co
*Ambassador Extraordinary and Plenipotentiary*, HE Jeremy W. Thorp, CMG, apptd 1998
BRITISH CONSULAR OFFICES – Cali and Medellín

BRITISH COUNCIL DIRECTOR, Joe Docherty, Calle 87 No. 12–79, Bogotá; e-mail: brit.council@bc-bogota.bcouncil.orgCOLOMBO-BRITISH CHAMBER OF COMMERCE, Calle 106, No. 25-41, Apartado Aereo 054 728, Bogotá D. E.

## DEFENCE

The Army has 30 light tanks and 160 armoured personnel carriers. The Navy has four submarines, four corvettes, 27 patrol and coastal vessels, six aircraft and two helicopters at nine bases. The Air Force has 72 combat aircraft and 60 armed helicopters.
MILITARY EXPENDITURE – 2.8 per cent of GDP (1999)
MILITARY PERSONNEL – 153,000: Army 130,000, Navy 15,000, Air Force 8,000; Paramilitaries 95,000
CONSCRIPTION DURATION – 12–18 months

## ECONOMY

Coal, natural gas and hydroelectricity resources are largely unexploited, although development of coal is being given priority. The hydrocarbon sector accounts for over half of the mining output, precious metals (gold, platinum and silver) and iron ore accounting for the remainder. Other mineral deposits include nickel, bauxite, copper, gypsum, limestone, phosphates, sulphur and uranium. Colombia is also the world's largest producer of emeralds.

Major cash crops are coffee, sugar, bananas, cut flowers and cotton. Cattle are raised in large numbers, and meat and cured skins and hides are also exported.

The government has encouraged diversification to reduce dependence on coffee as the major export and this has led to the growth of new export-orientated industries, particularly textiles, paper products and leather goods. Stimulus to the economy has been provided by loans from the World Bank and IADB for project development.

Since the late 1980s the government has introduced trade liberalisation and privatisation measures which have effectively freed foreign exchange transactions, increased foreign competition, ended protectionism and reduced inflation.

In 1999 there was a trade surplus of US$1,734 million and a current account deficit of US$979 million. In 1996 and 1997 Colombia was blacklisted by the USA for failing to curb levels of drug production sufficiently. These sanctions were ended in March 1998.

GNP – US$90,007 million (1999); US$2,250 per capita (1999)

GDP – US$95,455 million (1997); US$2,523 per capita (1998)

ANNUAL AVERAGE GROWTH OF GDP – 2.2 per cent (1996)

INFLATION RATE – 11.2 per cent (1999)

UNEMPLOYMENT – 12.1 per cent (1998)

TOTAL EXTERNAL DEBT – US$33,263 million (1998)

### TRADE

Principal exports are petroleum and derivatives, coffee, bananas, cut flowers, clothing and textiles, ferro-nickel and coal. Principal trading partners are the USA, the EU and Latin America.

In 1999 imports totalled US$10,659 million and exports US$11,576 million.

| *Trade with UK* | 1999 | 2000 |
|---|---|---|
| Imports from UK | £106,961,000 | £102,243,000 |
| Exports to UK | 200,008,000 | 241,555,000 |

## COMMUNICATIONS

The Andes make surface transport difficult so air transport is used extensively. There are daily air services between Bogotá and all the principal towns, as well as frequent services to other countries. The road network consists of 106,600 km of roads of all types, of which 21,800 km are classified as main trunk and transversal roads. A canal to link the Pacific Ocean and the Caribbean Sea has been planned.

There are five national television channels.

## CULTURE AND EDUCATION

There is a flourishing press in urban areas and a national literature supplements the rich inheritance from the time of Spanish colonial rule. Gabriel García Márquez was awarded the Nobel prize for Literature in 1982. State education is free.

ILLITERACY RATE – 8.2 per cent (2000)

ENROLMENT (percentage of age group) – primary 85 per cent (1996); secondary 46 per cent (1996); tertiary 16.7 per cent (1996)

---

# THE COMOROS

*République Fédérale Islamique des Comores*

---

AREA – 863 sq. miles (2,235 sq. km). The Comoro archipelago includes the islands of Great Comoro, Anjouan, Mayotte and Moheli and certain islets in the Indian Ocean

POPULATION – 544,000 (1997 UN estimate), mostly Muslim. French and Arabic are the official languages; the majority of the population speak Comoran, a blend of Arabic and Swahili

CAPITAL – Moroni (population, 17,267, 1980 estimate), on Great Comoro

CURRENCY – Comorian franc (KMF) of 100 centimes. The Franc CFA of 100 centimes is also used

NATIONAL ANTHEM - Udzima wa ya Masiwa (The union of the islands)

NATIONAL DAY – 6 July (Independence Day)

NATIONAL FLAG – Green ground, with a white crescent and four white stars, horns towards the fly. The name of *Allah*, in Arabic script in the upper fly and the name of *Mohammed* in the lower hoist

LIFE EXPECTANCY (years) – male 56.0; female 58.1

POPULATION GROWTH RATE – 2.8 per cent (1999)

POPULATION DENSITY – 294 per sq. km (1998)

URBAN POPULATION – 33.2 per cent (2000 estimate)

ILLITERACY RATE – 43.8 per cent

ENROLMENT (percentage of age group) – primary 52 per cent (1993); tertiary 0.6 per cent (1996)

## HISTORY AND POLITICS

The islanders voted for independence from France in December 1974 and three islands became independent on 6 July 1975. The island of Mayotte opposed independence and has remained under French administration.

An election in 1993 brought President Djohar's National Rally for Development party (RND) to power. Djohar was temporarily ousted in a coup in 1995 which was thwarted by French troops. While Djohar was abroad for medical attention, Prime Minister Caabiel Yachroutou declared himself interim president and refused to acknowledge Djohar's authority, resulting in the formation of a rival government. Djohar returned to the Comoros in January 1996 but was prohibited from contesting the March 1996 presidential election, which was won by Mohammad Taki Abdoulkarim of the National Union for Democracy in the Comoros. Taki dissolved the National Assembly and legislative elections were held in December 1996 although boycotted by the opposition Forum for National Recovery party (FRN).

President Taki died in office on 6 November 1998 and Tajiddine Ben Said Massonde took over as interim president. He and the government he had appointed were deposed in a coup on 30 April 1999 by Col. Assoumani Azzali, who was sworn in as president on 6 May. On 2 September 1999, an unsuccessful coup was launched while Col. Azzali was overseas. He announced that he would retain power until a presidential election was held, which was due to take place by 14 April 2000. The election did not take place and Col. Azzali declared that he would not restore civilian rule due to the issue of Anjouan separatism. However, in March 2001, he announced that the country would be restored to civilian rule in 2002 and that he would not contest the presidential election.

### INSURGENCIES

In August 1997 separatists on the islands of Anjouan and Moheli demanded independence from the Comoros and a return to French rule. Following a failed attempt to resolve the situation by force, President Taki assumed absolute power and established a State Transition Commission to function as a Cabinet. In a referendum in October 1997, the inhabitants of Anjouan voted overwhelmingly for independence. Talks mediated by the OAU began in December 1997 and an agreement drawn up with OAU support, which would have given each island considerable autonomy, was signed by Grand Comore and Moheli, but was rejected by Anjouan. Anjouan citizens voted by a large majority against reincorporation into the Comoros in a referendum held on 23 January 2000.

In March 1998, Anjouan's self-proclaimed President Abdallah Ibrahim appointed a prime minister and Cabinet, though their legitimacy has not been recognised internationally. Fighting broke out between President Ibrahim's forces and those of a previous Anjouan prime minister, Chamassi Said Omar, on 5 December 1998. On 1

August 1999, President Ibrahim resigned and transferred most of his powers to Col. Said Abeid. A general election was held in Anjouan in August 1999.

President Assoumani and the leader of Anjouan, Lt.-Col. Abderemane, signed an agreement on national reconciliation on 17 February 2001, which would have given Anjouan considerable autonomy. The Anjouan government withdrew from the reconciliation process on 15 April, alleging that the conditions of the agreement had not been met.

### POLITICAL SYSTEM

In October 1996 a new constitution was approved by referendum. The president may be elected for an unlimited number of six-year terms and has the authority to appoint a prime minister and Governors, and reports to the Federal Assembly.

Each island is administered by a Governor, assisted by up to four Commissioners whom he appoints, and has an elected Legislative Council.

### HEAD OF STATE

*President, Defence*, Col. Assoumani Azzali

### COUNCIL OF MINISTERS *as at July 2001*

*Prime Minister*, Hamada Madi Bolero
*Civil Service, Employment and Labour*, Milisaani Hamdia
*Culture, Youth, Sport and Information*, Ahmed Sidi
*Economy, Commerce, Industry and Crafts*, Assumani Abdou
*Equipment and Energy*, Djaffar Mmadi
*Finance and Budget*, Soundi Abdou Toybou
*Foreign Affairs*, Soeuf Mohamed Elamine
*Interior and Establishment of Institutions*, Mohamed Abdou Soimadou
*Justice and Islamic Affairs*, Abdoulbar Youssouf
*National Education, Professional Training and Francophone Issues*, Moinaecha Cheikh Yahaya
*Production and Environment*, Charif Abdallah
Public Health, Population and Women's Affairs, *Mlahali Mistoihi*
*Tourism, Transport, Posts and Telecommunications*, Said Dhoifir Bounou

EMBASSY OF THE FEDERAL ISLAMIC REPUBLIC OF THE COMOROS
20 rue Marbeau, F-75016 Paris, France
Tel: (00 33) (1) 4067 9054

BRITISH AMBASSADOR, HE C. F. Mochan, resident at Antananarivo, Madagascar

## ECONOMY

The most important products are vanilla, copra, cloves and essential oils, which are the principal exports; cacao, sisal and coffee are also cultivated. Great Comoro is well forested and produces some timber.

GNP – US$189 million (1999); US$350 per capita (1999)
GDP – US$214 million (1997); US$305 per capita (1998)
ANNUAL AVERAGE GROWTH OF GDP – 7.0 per cent (1996)
TOTAL EXTERNAL DEBT – US$203 million (1998)

| *Trade with UK* | 1999 | 2000 |
|---|---|---|
| Imports from UK | £1,008,000 | £877,000 |
| Exports to UK | 74,000 | 460,000 |

## DEMOCRATIC REPUBLIC OF CONGO
*République Démocratique du Congo*

AREA – 905,355 sq. miles (2,344,858 sq. km). Neighbours: Central African Republic (north), Sudan (north-east), Uganda, Rwanda, Burundi and Tanzania (east), Zambia (south), Angola (south-west), Republic of Congo-Brazzaville (north-west)
POPULATION – 49,776,000 (1997 UN estimate). The population was 34,671,607 at the 1985 census, composed of Bantu, Hamitic, Nilotic, Sudanese and Pygmoid groups, divided into 365 300 semi-autonomous tribes. More than 400 languages are spoken. Swahili, a Bantu language with an admixture of Arabic, is the nearest approach to a common language in the east and south, while Lingala is the language of a large area along the river and in the north, and Kikongo of the region between Kinshasa and the sea. French is the language of administration. Roman Catholicism is the predominant religion; there are also Protestants, Muslims and Kimbanguists
CAPITAL – Kinshasa (population, 2,664,309, 1984)
MAJOR CITIES – Kananga (298,693); Kisangani (317,581); Likasi (213,862); Lubumbashi (564,830); ΨMatadi (138,798); Mbandaka (137,291)
CURRENCY – Congolese franc
NATIONAL DAY - 30 June (Independence Day)
NATIONAL FLAG – Blue with a large yellow five-pointed star in the centre and five small yellow five-pointed stars in a vertical line down the hoist
LIFE EXPECTANCY (years) – male 45.1; female 46.5
POPULATION GROWTH RATE – 3.4 per cent (1999)
POPULATION DENSITY – 21 per sq. km (1998)
URBAN POPULATION – 30.3 per cent (2000 estimate)
MILITARY EXPENDITURE – 7.8 per cent of GDP (1999)
MILITARY PERSONNEL – 55,900: Army 55,000, Navy 900
ILLITERACY RATE – 22.7 per cent
ENROLMENT (percentage of age group) – primary 61 per cent (1994); secondary 23 per cent (1994); tertiary 2.3 per cent (1996)

The Democratic Republic of Congo (formerly Zaïre) is Africa's third largest state. Apart from the coastal district in the west which is fairly dry, the rainfall averages between 60 and 80 inches a year. The average temperature is about 27°C, but in the south the winter temperature can fall nearly to freezing point. Extensive forest covers the central districts.

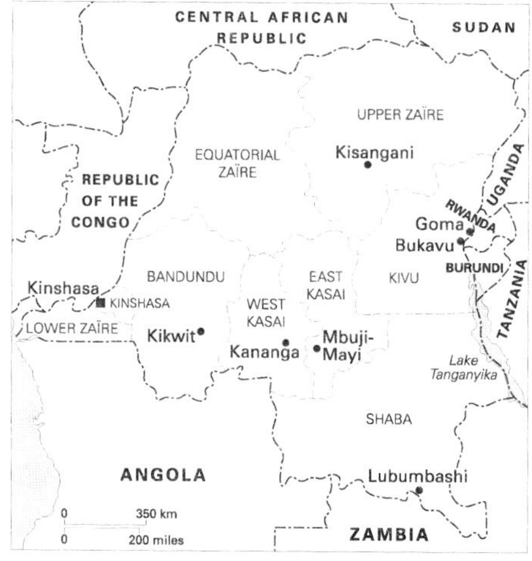

## HISTORY AND POLITICS

The state of the Congo, founded in 1885, became a Belgian colony in 1908 and gained its independence in 1960. Mobutu Sésé Seko came to power in a coup in 1965 and was elected president in 1970. Legislative power was vested in a unicameral National Legislative Council, with candidates proposed by the sole legal political party, Mouvement Populaire de la Révolution (MPR).

Political reforms were announced in April 1990 and President Mobutu accepted an opposition-dominated government under Prime Minister Etienne Tshisekedi in October 1991.

In January 1994 President Mobutu dissolved the government and in April promulgated a Transitional Constitutional Act which regulated a period of transition to democracy.

In October 1996 fighting broke out between Zaïrean Tutsis (*Banyamulenge*) and the Zaïrean army in North and South Kivu provinces which had received an influx of Hutu refugees from Rwanda. The pro-Hutu army attempted to expel the Tutsis from the region but found themselves outgunned by the rebels, under the leadership of Laurent Kabila, who were backed by the Rwandan and Ugandan governments. Kabila's Alliance of Democratic Forces for the Liberation of Congo-Zaïre (AFDL) captured Kinshasa in May 1997 and President Mobutu fled. Zaïre was renamed the Democratic Republic of Congo.

A rebellion against the government of Laurent Kabila began in Kivu on 2 August 1998 and by the end of the month the rebels had seized large areas in the east and west of the country. Angola, Chad, Kenya, Namibia and Zimbabwe promised President Kabila military support. The Angolan army quickly recaptured several towns in the south-west, but the rebels maintained their grip on the eastern regions. The rebel movement, the Congolese Democratic Rally (RCD), was supported by Uganda and Rwanda. On 17 May 1999, Ernest Wamba dia Wamba, the RCD leader, was ousted, splitting the movement into two distinct factions, that led by Wamba dia Wamba being called the Congolese Democratic Rally - Liberation Movement (RCD-LM). A cease-fire signed on 31 August 1999 between the government and the two rebel groups has remained largely intact, although localised clashes have been frequent. The main rebel groups, the RCD, the RCD-LM and the Congolese Liberation Movement (MLC) reached agreement on 20 December 1999 to form an umbrella organisation to defeat the government. A new rebel group, the Congolese Democratic Rally-National (RCD-N), was founded in October 2000 and in January 2001, the RCD and the RCD-LM were reunited as the Congolese Liberation Front.

On 6 December 2000, the government and the rebel groups signed an agreement to withdraw troops from the front line in preparation for the arrival of the United Nations Organisation Monitoring Mission in the Democratic Republic of Congo (MONUC). Foreign governments who had troops in the country agreed to withdraw their forces.

President Laurent Désiré Kabila died on 18 January 2001, having been shot by his bodyguard two days previously. His son, Maj.-Gen. Joseph Kabila, was sworn in as president on 26 January.

All the parties to the civil war had withdrawn their troops 15 km from their frontline positions by 26 March 2001, as had been stipulated in the agreement signed in December 2000.

### POLITICAL SYSTEM

A 300-member Constituent and Legislative Council was established on 21 August 2000 to draft a new constitution, which is to be put to a referendum.

There are 11 regions, each under a Governor and provincial administration: Bas-Zaïre (provincial capital, Matadi); Bandundu (Bandundu); Equateur (Mbandaka); Haut-Zaïre (Kisangani); Kinshasa (Kinshasa); Maniema (Kindu); North Kivu (Goma); South Kivu (Bukavu); Shaba (Katanga) (Lubumbashi); East Kasai (Mbuji-Mayi); West Kasai (Kananga).

### HEAD OF STATE

*President and Minister of Defence*, Maj.-Gen. Joseph Kabila, *sworn in* 26 January 2001

### CABINET *as at July 2001*

*Agriculture, Fisheries and Animal Husbandry*, André Philip Futa
*Civil Service*, Benjamin Mukulungu
*Communication and Press*, Kikaya bin Karubi
*Culture and the Arts*, Marthe Ngalula Wakuana
*Delegate for National Defence*, Irong Awan
*Economy, Finance and Budget*, Matungulu Nguyamu
*Education*, Kutumisa Tshioka
*Energy*, George Buse Talai
*Foreign Affairs and International Co-operation*, Leonard She Okitundu
*Health*, Masako Mamba
*Human Rights*, Ntumba Luaba
*Industry, Commerce and SMEs*, Helen Mateibo
*Interior*, Mira Ndjoku
*Justice and Keeper of the Seals*, Ngele Masudi
*Labour and Social Security*, Marie-Ange Lukiana
*Land Affairs, Environment and Tourism*, Salomo Banamuwere
*Mines and Hydrocarbons*, Simon Bawangamio Tumawako
*Minister at the Presidency*, Augustin Katumba Mwanke
*National Security and Public Order*, Mwenze Kongolo
*Planning and National Reconstruction*, Maj. Denis Kalume Nunbi
*Post and Telecommunications*, Philippe Kohotama Mawuoko
*Public Works, Territorial Administration, Urban Development and Housing*, Nkodi Mbaki
*Social Affairs*, Jeanne Ebamba Boboto
*Transport*, Dakahu Dino Wakale Minada
*Youth and Sports*, Timote Moleka Ngulama

### EMBASSY OF THE DEMOCRATIC REPUBLIC OF CONGO

38 Holne Chase, London N2 0QQ
Tel: 020-8458 0254
*Chargé d'Affaires*, Henri N'Swana

### BRITISH EMBASSY

Avenue du Roi Baudouin, Kinshasa
Tel: (00 243) 88 46102
E-mail: ambrit@ic.cd
*Ambassador Extraordinary and Plenipotentiary*, HE James Atkinson, apptd 2000

## ECONOMY

Palm oil is the most important agricultural cash product though it is no longer exported. Coffee, rubber, cocoa and timber are the most important agricultural exports. The production of cotton, pyrethrum and copal is increasing. Copper is widely exploited, and industrial diamonds and cobalt are also produced. Oil deposits are exploited off the Zaïre estuary and reef-gold is mined in the north-east of the country.

The main industrial products are foodstuffs, beverages, tobacco, textiles, leather, wood products, cement and building materials, metallurgy, small river craft and bicycles. There are reserves of hydroelectric power and the Inga dam on the river Zaïre supplies electricity to Matadi, Kinshasa and Shaba.

Whilst the country has many natural resources, civil war has led to the collapse of the economy, with total debt amounting to more than twice the GNP.

GNP – US$4,985 million (1998); US$110 per capita (1998)
GDP – US$2,474 million (1997); US$98 per capita (1998)
ANNUAL AVERAGE GROWTH OF GDP – 1.3 per cent (1996)
INFLATION RATE – 175.5 per cent (1997)
TOTAL EXTERNAL DEBT – US$12,929 million (1998)

### TRADE

The chief exports are copper, crude oil, coffee, diamonds, rubber, cobalt, gold, zinc and other metals.

In 1996 imports totalled US$424 million and exports US$592 million.

| *Trade with UK* | 1999 | 2000 |
|---|---|---|
| Imports from UK | £2,657,000 | £4,146,000 |
| Exports to UK | 3,359,000 | 911,000 |

## COMMUNICATIONS

There are approximately 145,000 km of roads, of which 20,500 km are earth-surfaced, and 6,000 km of railways. The country has four international and 40 principal airports.

# REPUBLIC OF CONGO-BRAZZAVILLE
*République du Congo-Brazzaville*

AREA – 132,047 sq. miles (342,000 sq. km). Neighbours: Gabon (west), Cameroon and Central African Republic (north), Angola (Cabinda) (south-west), the Democratic Republic of Congo (east and south)
POPULATION – 2,859,000 (1997 UN estimate). The official language is French; Lingala, Monokutuba and Kikongo are widely spoken
CAPITAL – Brazzaville (population, 596,200, 1984)
MAJOR CITIES – ΨPointe Noire (298,014), the main commercial centre
CURRENCY – Franc CFA of 100 centimes
NATIONAL ANTHEM – La Congolaise
NATIONAL DAY – 15 August
NATIONAL FLAG – Divided diagonally into green, yellow and red bands
LIFE EXPECTANCY (years) – male 53.6; female 55.2
POPULATION GROWTH RATE – 2.9 per cent (1999)
POPULATION DENSITY – 8 per sq. km (1998)
URBAN POPULATION – 62.5 per cent (2000 estimate)
MILITARY EXPENDITURE – 3.4 per cent of GDP (1999)
MILITARY PERSONNEL – 10,000: Army 8,000, Navy 800, Air Force 1,200, Paramilitaries 2,000
ILLITERACY RATE – 19.3 per cent
ENROLMENT (percentage of age group) – primary 96 per cent (1980); tertiary 7 per cent (1992)

## HISTORY AND POLITICS

Formerly the French colony of Middle Congo, Congo-Brazzaville became a member state of the French Community on 28 November 1958 and fully independent on 17 August 1960.

In 1968, a National Council of army officers took power and created the Parti Congolais du Travail (PCT) and the People's Republic of the Congo. After popular pressure, the PCT abandoned its monopoly of power and renounced Marxism in 1990. In 1992 the country adopted a new multiparty constitution with a directly elected president and a bicameral parliament. The lack of a parliamentary majority forced President Lissouba to call fresh elections in 1993. These were won by the Pan-African Union for Social Democracy (UPADS) but the results were disputed by opposition groups and violence broke out between rival parties. A new UPADS-dominated government was appointed in January 1995. In June 1997, fighting broke out between forces of President Lissouba and followers of former president Sassou-Nguesso, who was reinstalled as president in October 1997. Elections scheduled for July 1997 were called off and a National Forum for Unity and Democracy was set up to schedule legislative elections. It declared a three-year transition period after which democratic elections will be held. A constitutional committee was inaugurated on 19 November 1998, charged with drafting a constitution to be approved by referendum in 1999.

In April 1999, supporters of former prime minister Bernard Kolelas formed themselves into a political party, the Patriotic Union of Ninja Forces. Following a period of intense fighting, negotiations between the government and the rebels began on 13 November 1999; an accord was reached in which the two sides agreed to an unconditional end to hostilities and the demilitarisation of political parties. President Omar Bongo of Gabon was appointed as mediator on 29 December.

A 'non-exclusive national dialogue' was held between 17 March and14 April 2001, but was boycotted by many opposition groups; the process consisted of public debates in regional capitals and ended with a national conference in Brazzaville, at which rebel leaders and the government adopted a draft constitution, which aimed to establish a directly elected executive presidency and bicameral legislature.

### HEAD OF STATE

*President*, Denis Sassou-Nguesso, *sworn in* 25 October 1997

### CABINET *as at July 2001*

*Agriculture and Livestock*, Nkoua Celestin Gongara
*Civil Service, Administrative Reform and Women's Affairs*, Jeanne Dambenze
*Commerce, Small and Medium-sized Enterprises*, Pierre Damien Boussoukou Boumba
*Communication and Government Spokesman*, François Ibovi
*Culture and Tourism*, Mambou Elie Niamy
*Energy and Water Resources*, Jean-Marie Tassoua
*Finance and Budget*, Mathias Dzon
*Foreign Affairs and Co-operation*, Rodolphe Adada
*Forestry*, Henri Djombo
*Health and National Solidarity*, Leon Alfred Opimba
*Industrial Development*, Alphonse Mbamba
*Industry and Mines*, Michel Mampoya
*Interior, Security and Territorial Administration*, Col. Pierre Oba
*Keeper of the Seals, Justice*, Jean-Martin M'bemba
*Labour and Social Security*, Lambert Ndouane
*Minister in the President's Office in charge of Defence*, Itihi Lekounzou Ossetoumba
*Petroleum Affairs*, Jean-Baptiste Taty-Loutard
*Posts and Telecommunications*, Jean-Félix Demba Dello
*Primary and Secondary Education*, Pierre Tsiba
*Social Amenities and Public Works, Reconstruction and Urban Development*, Col. Florent Tsiba
*Technical Education and Vocational Training*, André Okombi Salissan
*Territorial and Regional Development*, Pierre Moussa
*Transport, Civil Aviation and Merchant Navy*, Isidore Mvouba

EMBASSY OF THE REPUBLIC OF CONGO-BRAZZAVILLE
37 bis rue Paul Valéry, F-75116 Paris, France

Tel: (00 33) (1) 4500 6057
*Ambassador Extraordinary and Plenipotentiary*, HE Henri Marie Joseph Lopes, apptd 1999

HONORARY CONSULATE, 4 Wendle Court, 131–137 Wandsworth Road, London SW8 2LH. Tel: 020-7622 0419. *Honorary Consul*, L. Muzzu

BRITISH AMBASSADOR, HE James Atkinson,resident at Kinshasa, Democratic Republic of Congo
HONORARY CONSULATE – Brazzaville

## ECONOMY

Congo-Brazzaville has its own oil deposits, producing about 9 million tonnes annually. It also produces lead, zinc and gold. The principal agricultural products are timber, cassava and yams. Imports are mainly of machinery.

In 1997 Congo-Brazzaville had a trade surplus of US$941 million and a current account deficit of US$252 million. Imports in 1996 totalled US$1,551 million and exports US$1,555 million.

GNP – US$1,571 million (1999); US$670 per capita (1999)
GDP – US$1,903 million (1997); US$691 per capita (1998)
ANNUAL AVERAGE GROWTH OF GDP – 6.8 per cent (1996)
INFLATION RATE – 0.2 per cent (1996)
TOTAL EXTERNAL DEBT – US$5,119 million (1998)

| *Trade with UK* | 1999 | 2000 |
|---|---|---|
| Imports from UK | £12,230,000 | £18,991,000 |
| Exports to UK | 8,463,000 | 5,272,000 |

# COSTA RICA
*República de Costa Rica*

AREA – 19,730 sq. miles (51,100 sq. km). Neighbours: Nicaragua, Panama
POPULATION – 3,588,000 (1997 UN estimate), mainly of European origin. The language is Spanish
CAPITAL – San José (population, 1,273,504, 1998 estimate)
MAJOR CITIES – Alajuela (183,232); Cartago (125,799), 1998 UN estimates
CURRENCY – US dollar (US$) of 100 cents/ Costa Rican colón (₡) of 100 céntimos
NATIONAL ANTHEM – Himno Nacional de Costa Rica
NATIONAL DAY – 15 September
NATIONAL FLAG – Five horizontal bands, blue, white, red, white, blue (the red band twice the width of the others with emblem near staff)
LIFE EXPECTANCY (years) – male 74.2; female 78.9
POPULATION GROWTH RATE – 2.9 per cent (1999)
POPULATION DENSITY – 65 per sq. km (1998)
URBAN POPULATION – 47.8 per cent (2000 estimate)
MILITARY EXPENDITURE – 0.6 per cent of GDP (1999)
MILITARY PERSONNEL – Paramilitaries 8,400
ILLITERACY RATE – 4.4 per cent
ENROLMENT (percentage of age group) – primary 89 per cent (1996); secondary 40 per cent (1996); tertiary 30.3 per cent (1996)

The coastal lowlands have a tropical climate but the interior plateau, with a mean elevation of 4,000 feet, enjoys a temperate climate.

## HISTORY AND POLITICS

For nearly three centuries (1530–1821) Costa Rica was under Spanish rule. In 1821 the country obtained its independence, although from 1824 to 1839 it was one of the United States of Central America.

In 1948 the Army was abolished, the President declaring it unnecessary. The main political parties are the Social Christian Unity Party (PUSC) and the National Liberation Party (PLN). The last presidential and legislative elections were held on 1 February 1998, when PUSC candidate Miguel Angel Rodríguez won the presidential election, and the PUSC won 27 seats in the Legislative Assembly.

### POLITICAL SYSTEM

Executive power is vested in the president, who is head of state and government, with legislative power vested in the 57-member Legislative Assembly. Under the constitution both the president and the members of the Legislative Assembly are elected for a single four-year term and may not be re-elected.

### HEAD OF STATE

*President*, Miguel Angel Rodríguez , *elected* 1 February 1998
*First Vice-President*, Astrid Fischel
*Second Vice-President, Minister of Environment*, Elizabeth Odio

### CABINET *as at July 2001*

*Agriculture and Livestock*, Alberto Dent
*Culture*, Enrique Granados
*Economy, Industry and Commerce*, Gilberto Barrantes
*Finance*, Leonel Baruch
*Foreign Affairs*, Roberto Rojas
*Foreign Trade*, Tomás Dueñas
*Health*, Rogelio Pardo
*Housing*, Alexander Salas
*Interior, Police and Public Security*, Rogelio Ramos
*Justice*, Mónica Nágel
*Labour and Social Security*, Bernardo Benavides
*Presidency and Planning*, Danilo Chaverri
*President of the Central Bank*, Eduardo Lizano
*Public Education*, Guillermo Vargas
*Public Security*, Rogelio Ramos
*Public Works and Transport*, Mario Fernández
*Science and Technology*, Guy de Terramond
*Women's Affairs*, Gloria Valerín

### COSTA RICAN EMBASSY

Flat 1, 14 Lancaster Gate, London W2 3LH
Tel: 020-7706 8844
*Ambassador Extraordinary and Plenipotentiary*, HE Rodolfo Gutiérrez, apptd 1998

### BRITISH EMBASSY

Apartado 815, Edificio Centro Colón (Eleventh Floor), San José 1007
Tel: (00 506) 258 2025
E-mail: britemb@sol.racsa.co.cr
*Ambassador Extraordinary and Plenipotentiary and Consul-General*, HE Peter Spiceley, MBE, apptd 1998

## ECONOMY

Tourism is the largest single industry, with ecotourism a growing area; one third of the country is national parkland or nature reserve. In 1999, there were more than one million foreign visitors. Industrial activity is principally in the manufacturing sector and manufactured goods include computer components, foodstuffs, textiles and clothing, plastic goods and pharmaceuticals. The principal agricultural products are coffee, bananas, sugar and cattle (for meat).

GNP – US$12,828 million (1999); US$2,740 per capita (1999)
GDP – US$9,519 million (1997); US$2,793 per capita (1998)
ANNUAL AVERAGE GROWTH OF GDP – 0.5 per cent (1996)
INFLATION RATE – 10.0 per cent (1999)

UNEMPLOYMENT – 5.6 per cent (1998)
TOTAL EXTERNAL DEBT – US$3,971 million (1998)

### TRADE

The chief exports are manufactured goods, bananas, coffee, fish and shellfish, machinery and tropical fruits. The chief imports are raw materials for industry, consumer goods, capital equipment, and fuel and mineral oils. The USA accounts for around 40 per cent of imports and exports. Other major trading partners are Japan, Germany, Mexico and the UK. In 1998 there was a trade deficit of US$245 million and a current account deficit of US$460 million. In 1999 imports totalled US$6,320 million and exports US$6,577 million.

| *Trade with UK* | 1999 | 2000 |
|---|---|---|
| Imports from UK | £37,561,000 | £33,829,000 |
| Exports to UK | 359,671,000 | 544,453,000 |

## COMMUNICATIONS

The chief ports are Limón on the Atlantic coast, through which passes most of the coffee exported, and Caldera on the Pacific coast. LACSA is the national airline, operating flights throughout Central and South America, the Caribbean and the USA, besides internal flights to local airports by SANSA.

---

## CÔTE D'IVOIRE
*République de la Côte d'Ivoire*

---

AREA – 124,504 sq. miles (322,463 sq. km). Neighbours: Guinea and Liberia (west), Mali and Burkina Faso (north), Ghana (east)
POPULATION – 14,729,000 (1997 UN estimate): 39 per cent Muslim, 28 per cent Christian (mainly Roman Catholic) and 17 per cent maintain traditional beliefs. The official language is French, but Agni, Baoulé, Dioula, Senoufo and Yacouba are spoken
CAPITAL – Yamoussoukro (population, 126,191, 1988), the political and administrative capital since 1983
MAJOR CITIES – ΨAbidjan (1,929,079), the economic and financial centre
CURRENCY – Franc CFA of 100 centimes
NATIONAL ANTHEM – L'Abidjanaise
NATIONAL DAY – 7 August
NATIONAL FLAG – Three vertical stripes, orange, white and green
LIFE EXPECTANCY (years) – male 47.2; female 48.3
POPULATION GROWTH RATE – 2.5 per cent (1999)
POPULATION DENSITY – 44 per sq. km (1998)
URBAN POPULATION – 46.4 per cent (2000 estimate)
MILITARY EXPENDITURE – 1.0 per cent of GDP (1999)
MILITARY PERSONNEL – 13,900: Army 6,800, Navy 900, Air Force 700, Paramilitaries 7,000
CONSCRIPTION DURATION – Six months (selective)
ILLITERACY RATE – 53.2 per cent (2000)
ENROLMENT (percentage of age group) – primary 55 per cent (1996); tertiary 6.2 per cent (1996)

The climate is equatorial in the south and west, which are mainly forested; tropical in the centre and east, which are savannah regions with trees; dry and tropical in the north, which is a grassy savannah region.

## HISTORY AND POLITICS

Although French contact was made in the first half of the 19th century, Côte d'Ivoire became a colony only in 1893 and was finally pacified in 1912. It decided on 5 December 1958 to remain an autonomous republic within the French Community; full independence outside the Community was proclaimed on 7 August 1960.

After having been president since independence in 1960, President Houphouët-Boigny died in December 1993 and was replaced by the parliamentary speaker Henri Konan-Bédié. The President was deposed by Gen. Robert Guëi in a military coup on 24–25 December 1999, who announced a transitional government on 4 January 2000.

A referendum on a new constitution was held on 23-24 July 2000, which was approved by 86.58 per cent of those who voted.

On 22 October 2000 a presidential election was held. President Guëi dissolved the electoral commission following early results which indicated that Laurent Gbagbo of the Ivorian Popular Front (FPI) was leading, and it was announced that Guëi had won. Demonstrations and mounting violence led to Guëi fleeing the country on 26 October and Gbagbo was inaugurated as president.

A general election held in 196 of the 225 constituencies on 10 December 2000 resulted in the FPI becoming the largest party. Following polling on 14 January 2001 in 28 of the remaining 29 seats, the FPI had won 96 seats and the Democratic Party of Côte d'Ivoire (PDCI) had won 94 seats. The election was boycotted by the Rally of Republicans (RDR), the strongest party in the north of the country.

### POLITICAL SYSTEM

The Côte d'Ivoire has a presidential system of government and a single-chamber National Assembly of 225 members, directly elected for a five-year term. It has been a multiparty system since 1990. The president's term of office is seven years.

### HEAD OF STATE

*President*, Laurent Gbagbo, *elected* 22 October 2000, *sworn in* 26 October 2000

### CABINET *as at July 2001*

*Prime Minister, Planning and Development*, Pascal N'Guessan Affi (FPI)
*Agriculture and Animal Resources*, Alphonse Douati (FPI)
*Commerce*, Eric Victor Kahe Kplohourou (Ind.)
*Communication and New Technologies*, Lia Bi Douayoua (FPI)
*Construction and Urbanism*, Dr Assoa Adou (FPI)
*Culture and Francophone Affairs*, Dramane Kone (FPI)
*Economic Infrastructure and Government Spokesman*, Patrick Achi (PDCI)
*Economy and Finance*, Bohoun Bouabre (FPI)
*Education*, Michel N'Guessan Amani (FPI)
*Environment and Standard of Living*, Gilbert Bleu-Laine (Ind.)
*Family, Women and Children*, Henriette Lagou (PDCI)
*Health*, Raymond Abouo N'dori (FPI)
*Higher Education and Scientific Research*, Seri Bailly (FPI)
*Industry and Promotion of the Private Sector*, Alain Cocauthreh (PDCI)
*Justice and Civil Rights, Keeper of the Seals*, Siéné Oulai (FPI)
*Mining and Energy*, Léon Emmanuel Monnet (FPI)
*Minister in the PM's Office charged with the Fight against HIV/AIDS and other Pandemics*, Assana Sangare (PDCI)
*Ministers of State*, Kouassi Moïse Lida (FPI) (*Defence and Civil Protection*); Abou Drahamane Sangare (FPI) (*Foreign Affairs*); Doudou Émile Boga (FPI) (*Interior and Decentralisation*)
*Relations with Parliament and other Institutions*, Sébastien Dano Djedje (FPI)
*Social Security and National Solidarity*, Clothilde Ohouochi (PDCI)
*Sport and Leisure*, Grébé Geneviève Bro (PDCI)
*Tourism and Crafts*, Odette Likikouet (FPI)

*Transport*, Appiah Aimé Kabran (PIT)
*Water and Forestry*, Angèle Boka (PIT)
*Works, Civil Service and Administrative Reform*, Hubert Oulaye (FPI)
*Youth, Employment and Professional Training*, Lazare Koffi Koffi (FPI)

FPI Ivorian Popular Front; PDCI Democratic Party of Côte d'Ivoire; PIT Ivorian Labour Party; Ind. Independent

EMBASSY OF THE REPUBLIC OF CÔTE D'IVOIRE
2 Upper Belgrave Street, London SW1X 8BJ
Tel: 020-7235 6991
*Ambassador Extraordinary and Plenipotentiary*, HE Kouadio Adjoumani, apptd 1997

BRITISH EMBASSY
Immeuble 'Les Harmonies', 01 BP 2581 01, Abidjan
Tel: (00 225) 226850
E-mail: britemb.a@africaonline.co.ci
*Ambassador Extraordinary and Plenipotentiary*, HE François Gordon, apptd 2001

## ECONOMY

Côte d'Ivoire became wealthy in the 1970s because of the high prices of its two principal export earners, coffee and cocoa. In the late 1980s the economy contracted considerably as its exports deteriorated in competitiveness and its rivals devalued their currencies while the franc CFA remained pegged to the French franc. An economic reform and stabilisation programme began in 1989 under IMF auspices and has brought down inflation, increased investment and led to GDP growth. The devaluation of the CFA franc in January 1994 has increased exports considerably and restored a trade surplus. In February 1998 a further economic reform programme began.

The principal exports are coffee, cocoa, timber, palm oil, sugar, rubber, pineapples, bananas, and cotton. There are a few deposits of diamonds and minerals including manganese and iron. Oil and gas deposits began to be exploited in 1995.

There was a trade surplus of US$1,870 million in 1998 and a current account deficit of US$313 million. In 1999 imports totalled US$3,270 million and exports US$4,077 million.

GNP – US$10,387 million (1999); US$710 per capita (1999)
GDP – US$10,284 million (1997); US$889 per capita (1998)
ANNUAL AVERAGE GROWTH OF GDP – 6.8 per cent (1996)
INFLATION RATE – 0.8 per cent (1999)
TOTAL EXTERNAL DEBT – US$14,852 million (1998)

| *Trade with UK* | 1999 | 2000 |
|---|---|---|
| Imports from UK | £47,733,000 | £53,147,000 |
| Exports to UK | 80,025,000 | 78,549,000 |

## CROATIA
*Republika Hrvatska*

AREA – 21,824 sq. miles (56,538 sq. km). Neighbours: Slovenia, Hungary (north), the rump Federal Yugoslav state (east), Bosnia-Hercegovina (south, and east of Adriatic coastal strip)
POPULATION – 4,464,000 (1997 UN estimate); 4,784,265 (1991 census): 78 per cent Croat, 12 per cent Serb, 2 per cent Yugoslav; also Hungarians, Italians, Albanians, Czechs, Ukrainians and Jews. Roman Catholic 76.5 per cent, Eastern Orthodox 11.1 per cent, Protestant 1.4 per cent, Muslim 1.2 per cent. The language is Croatian in the Latin script
CAPITAL – Zagreb (population, 867,717, 1991)
MAJOR CITIES – Osijek (129,792); Rijeka (167,964); Split (200,459), 1991
CURRENCY – Kuna of 100 lipa
NATIONAL ANTHEM – Lijepa naša domovina (Our Beautiful Homeland)
NATIONAL DAY – 30 May (Statehood Day)
NATIONAL FLAG – Three horizontal stripes of red, white, blue, with the national arms over all in the centre
LIFE EXPECTANCY (years) – male 69.3; female 77.3
POPULATION GROWTH RATE – 0.1 per cent (1999)
POPULATION DENSITY – 81 per sq. km (1998)
URBAN POPULATION – 57.7 per cent (2000 estimate)
ILLITERACY RATE – 1.7 per cent
ENROLMENT (percentage of age group) – primary 82 per cent (1996); secondary 66 per cent (1996); tertiary 27.9 per cent (1996)

Croatia is divided into three major geographic regions: the Pannonian region in the north, the central mountain belt, and the Adriatic coast region of Istria and Dalmatia which has 1,185 islands and islets and 1,104 miles (1,778 km) of coastline.

## HISTORY AND POLITICS

Croatia was part of the Austro-Hungarian Empire from 1526 to 1918. On 29 October 1918 the Croatian parliament declared Croatia independent and soon after Croatia joined with Slovenia, Bosnia-Hercegovina, Serbia and Montenegro to form the 'Kingdom of Serbs, Croats and Slovenes' (renamed Yugoslavia in 1929). From 1941 to 1945 Yugoslavia was occupied by the Axis powers, with Italy and Hungary annexing parts of Croatia and a pro-Nazi Croat puppet state being established in the remainder of Croatia and Bosnia-Hercegovina. The armed extremists of this state (Ustaše) engaged in fierce fighting with Serbian royalists, Communist partisans and pro-Allied Croat partisans.

At the end of the war Yugoslavia was re-established as a federal republic under Communist rule but gradually disintegrated following the death of the wartime partisan leader Josep Tito in 1980.

In April and May 1990 Croatia's first free, democratic elections were won by the Croatian Democratic Union (HDZ) of Dr Franjo Tudjman. A referendum in May 1991 backed independence from Yugoslavia, which was declared on 30 May 1991. Croatia's ethnic Serb minority, which rejected Croatia's independence, began fighting with the Croat defence forces and by September 1991 this had escalated into war between Croatia and Serbia. The war in Croatia continued until January 1992 when a cease-fire was declared. The Federal Yugoslav Army (JNA) and Serb forces had secured control of virtually all ethnic Serb areas in Croatia.

President Tudjman was re-elected in June 1997. but was temporarily replaced by Vlatko Pavletić on 26 November 1999 after he fell ill; he died on 10 December. Stipe Mesić was elected in presidential elections held on 7 February 2000. In the general election held on 3 January 2000, the opposition coalition of the Social Democratic Party of Croatia (SPH) and the Croatian Social Liberal Party (HSLS) scored a decisive victory, winning a total of 68 seats.

### SECESSION

Croatia's ethnic Serbs voted to establish a Republic of Serbian Krajina (RSK) in 1993.

The government seized Western Slavonia in May 1995 and the whole of Krajina in August 1995 prompting the withdrawal of 10,000 UNCRO peacekeepers and the flight of 150,000 Serbs. The last Croatian Serb-held area of Eastern Slavonia agreed in November 1995 to its eventual reintegration into Croatia, which was achieved on 15 January 1998.

### Foreign Relations

An agreement to normalise relations with Yugoslavia was signed in August 1996. Croatia was sworn in as a member of the Council of Europe in November 1996.

### Political System

Executive power is vested in a president and government. The president is directly elected for five-year terms. Legislative power is vested in the 151-member Chamber of Representatives, whose members are directly elected for a four-year term.

The constitution was amended in November 2000 to reduce the powers of the presidency. A further amendment was agreed in March 2001, when the Chamber of Representatives voted to abolish the Chamber of Counties, the upper house of the legislature.

Croatia is divided into 21 counties. Counties are composed of groups of districts and function both as units of local government and as regional offices for the central administration. There are 102 districts.

### Head of State

*President*, Stipe Mesić, *elected* 7 February 2000

### Cabinet *as at July 2001*

*Prime Minister*, Ivica Racan (SPH)
*First Deputy Prime Minister*, Goran Granić (HSLS)
*Deputy PMs*, Slavko Linić (SPH) (*Economy*); Željka Antunović (SPH) (*Social Affairs*)
*Agriculture and Forestry*, Božidar Pankretić (HSS)
*Crafts, Small and Medium Businesses*, Željko Pecek (HSLS)
*Croatian Homeland War Defenders*, Ivica Pančić
*Culture*, Anton Vujić (SPH)
*Defence*, Jozo Radoš (HSLS)
*Economy*, Goranko Fižulić (HSLS)
*Education and Sport*, Vladimir Strugar (HSS)
*Environmental Protection and Zoning*, Božo Kovačević (LS)
*European Integration*, vacant
*Finance*, Mato Crkvenac (SPH)
*Foreign Affairs*, Tonino Picula (SPH)
*Government Secretary*, Jagoda Premužić
*Health*, Ana Stavljević-Rukavina
*Interior*, Šime Lučin (SPH)
*Justice, Administration and Local Self-Government*, vacant
*Labour and Social Welfare*, Davorko Vidović (SPH)
*Maritime Affairs, Transport and Telecommunications*, Alojz Tušek (HSLS)
*Public Works, Reconstruction and Construction*, Radimir Čačić (HNS)
*Science and Technology*, Žrvoje Kraljević (HSLS)
*Tourism*, Pave Župan Rusković

HNS Croatian People's Party; HSLS Croatian Social Liberal Party; HSS Croatian Peasants' Party; LS Liberal Party; SPH Social Democratic Party of Croatia

### Embassy of the Republic of Croatia

21 Conway Street, London W1T 6BN
Tel: 020-7387 2022
*Ambassador Extraordinary and Plenipotentiary*, HE Andrija Kojaković, apptd 1997

### British Embassy

Vlaska 121/III Floor, PO Box 454, 10001 Zagreb
Tel: (00 385) (1) 455 5310
E-mail: british-embassy@zg.tel.hr
*Ambassador Extraordinary and Plenipotentiary*, HE Nicholas Jarrold, apptd 2000
British Consulates – Split and Dubrovnik

British Council Director, Robin Evans, Ilica 12, PO Box 55, 10001 Zagreb; e-mail: zagreb.info@britishcouncil.hr

## DEFENCE

The Army has 305 main battle tanks, 45 armoured personnel carriers and 109 armoured infantry fighting vehicles. The Air Force has 41 combat aircraft and 10 armed helicopters. The Navy has one submarine and 8 patrol and coastal combatants at five bases.
Military Expenditure – 4.1 per cent of GDP (1999)
Military Personnel – 101,000: Army 53,000, Navy 3,000, Air Force 5,000; Paramilitaries 40,000
Conscription Duration – Nine months

## ECONOMY

Production was severely hampered during the conflict in 1991–5; the material damage was estimated by the government to be US$27 billion, with the loss of 13,583 lives. Large areas of farmland were destroyed and the tourist industry, which provided one third of total foreign exchange earnings in 1990, was decimated.

Shipbuilding and fishing are major industries on the Adriatic coast. Inland there is a light manufacturing sector, food-processing industries, bauxite deposits, thermal mineral springs, hydroelectric potential, and agriculture based on grain, horticulture, livestock and tobacco. Textiles is one of the most important industries employing more than 17 per cent of the population. In April 1996, Croatia agreed to pay 29.5 per cent of Yugoslavia's debt, totalling US$1.45 billion.

In 1999 Croatia had a trade deficit of US$3,301 million and a current account deficit of US$1,468 million. Imports totalled US$7,777 million and exports US$4,280 million.
GNP – US$20,222 million (1999); US$4,580 per capita (1999)
GDP – US$19,514 million (1997); US$4,758 per capita (1998)
Annual Average Growth of GDP – 4.3 per cent (1996)
Inflation Rate – 6.4 per cent (1998)
Unemployment – 11.4 per cent (1998)
Total External Debt – US$8,297 million (1998)

### Trade

| *Trade with UK* | 1999 | 2000 |
|---|---|---|
| Imports from UK | £79,413,000 | £74,650,000 |
| Exports to UK | 41,630,000 | 42,183,000 |

## CUBA

*República de Cuba*

Area – 42,804 sq. miles (110,861 sq. km)
Population – 11,150,000 (1997 UN estimate). The language is Spanish
Capital – ΨHavana (population, 2,204,333, 1996 UN estimate)
Major Cities – Camagüey (298,726); Guantánamo (205,078); Holguín (249,492); Santa Clara (207,350); ΨSantiago (433,180), 1996 UN estimates
Currency – Cuban peso of 100 centavos
National Anthem – Al Combate, Corred Bayameses (To battle, men of Bayamo)
National Day – 1 January (Day of Liberation)
National Flag – Five horizontal bands, blue and white (blue at top and bottom) with red triangle, close to staff, charged with five-point star
Life Expectancy (years) – male 73.5; female 77.4
Population Growth Rate – 0.5 per cent (1999)
Population Density – 100 per sq. km (1998)
Urban Population – 75.3 per cent (2000 estimate)

## HISTORY AND POLITICS

The island was visited by Columbus in 1492. Early in the 16th century the island was conquered by the Spanish, and for almost four centuries remained under Spanish rule. Separatist agitation culminated in the closing years of the 19th century in open warfare. In 1898 the USA intervened and demanded the evacuation of Cuba by Spanish forces. The Spanish–American war led to the abandonment of the island, which came under American military rule from 1899 until 1902, when an autonomous government was inaugurated with an elected president, and bicameral legislature.

A revolution led by Dr Fidel Castro overthrew the government of Gen. Batista in 1959. In 1965 the Communist Party of Cuba (PCC) was formed to succeed the United Party of the Socialist Revolution; it is the only authorised political party. A new Socialist constitution came into force in 1976 and indirect elections to the National Assembly of People's Power were subsequently held. The first direct elections to the National Assembly were held in February 1993; all candidates were officially approved by the Communist Party and ran for election unopposed. The 14 provincial assemblies were elected in the same manner. The fifth congress of the PCC was held in October 1997. At the election of deputies to the National Assembly in January 1998, all 601 PCC candidates received the required 50 per cent of the vote, and in February the National Assembly confirmed Dr Castro as president for a further five-year term.

HEAD OF STATE

*President of Council of State and Council of Ministers*, Dr Fidel Castro Ruz, *appointed* 2 November 1976, *re-elected* 15 March 1993, 24 February 1998

### COUNCIL OF STATE *as at July 2001*

*President*, Dr Fidel Castro Ruz
*First Vice-President*, Gen. Raúl Castro Ruz
*Vice-Presidents*, Carlos Lage Dávila; Juan Almeida Bosque; Abelardo Colomé Ibarra; Esteban Lazo Hernández; José Ramón Machado Ventura
*Secretary*, José Miyar Barrueco

### COUNCIL OF MINISTERS *as at July 2001*

*President*, Dr Fidel Castro Ruz
*First Vice-President, Revolutionary Armed Forces*, Gen. Raúl Castro Ruz
*Vice-Presidents*, Osmany Cienfuegos Gorriaran; Pedro Miret Prieto; José Ramón Fernández Alvárez; Adolfo Diaz Suárez
*Secretary*, Carlos Lage Dávila
*Ministers*, Alfredo Jordán Morales (*Agriculture*); Lina Pedraza Rodríguez (*Auditing and Control*); Roberto Ignacio González Planas (*Communications*); Juan Mario Junco del Pino (*Construction*); vacant (*Construction Materials Industry*); Abel Prieto Jiménez (*Culture*); Barbara Castillo Cuesta (*Domestic Trade*); José Luis Rodríguez García (*Economy and Planning*); Luís Ignacio Gómez Gutiérrez (*Education*); Manuel Millares Rodríguez (*Finance and Prices*); Alfredo López Valdez (*Fishing Industry*); Alejandro Rocas Iglesias (*Food Industry*); Marta Lomas Morales (*Foreign Investment and Economic Co-operation*); Felipe Pérez Roque (*Foreign Relations*); Raúl de la Nuez Ramírez (*Foreign Trade*); Marcos J. Portal León (*Heavy Industries*); Fernando Vecino Alegret (*Higher Education*); Gen. Abelardo Colomé Ibarra (*Interior*); Roberto Díaz Sotolongo (*Justice*); Alfredo Morales Cartaya (*Labour and Social Security*); Jesús Pérez Othon (*Light Industry*); Fernando Acosta Santana (*Metalworking and Electronics Industries*); Carlos Dotres Martínez (*Public Health*); Rosa Eleana Simeón Negrín (*Science, Technology and Environment*); Div.-Gen. Ulises Rosales del Toro (*Sugar Industry*); Ibrahim Ferradaz García (*Tourism*); Alvaro Pérez Morales (*Transport*); Wilfredo López Rodríguez; Ricardo Cabrisas Ruiz (*Without Portfolio*)

EMBASSY OF THE REPUBLIC OF CUBA
167 High Holborn, London WC1V 6PA
Tel: 020-7240 2488
*Ambassador Extraordinary and Plenipotentiary*, HE Dr José Fernández de Cossío, apptd 2000

BRITISH EMBASSY
Calle 34 No. 702/4, entre 7ma Avenida y 17, Miramar, Havana.
Tel: (00 53) (7) 241 771
*Ambassador Extraordinary and Plenipotentiary*, HE Paul Hare, apptd 2001
BRITISH COUNCIL DIRECTOR, Michael White, Calle 34 No 702, 7ma Avenida, Miramar, Havana; e-mail: britcoun@ip.etecsa.cu

## DEFENCE

The Army has about 900 main battle tanks and 700 armoured personnel carriers. The Navy has five patrol and coastal vessels at six bases. The Air Force has 130 combat aircraft and 45 armed helicopters.

The last former Soviet combat personnel left Cuba in 1993, but 810 Russian military advisers remain to operate military intelligence facilities. The United States has 1,080 naval personnel at Guantánamo Bay Naval Base, which has been leased since before the 1959 revolution.
MILITARY EXPENDITURE – 4.8 per cent of GDP (1999)
MILITARY PERSONNEL – 58,000: Army 45,000, Navy 3,000, Air Force 10,000; Paramilitaries 26,500
CONSCRIPTION DURATION – Two years

## ECONOMY

After the revolution virtually all land and industrial and commercial enterprises were nationalised. Following the curtailing of Cuba's privileged trading relationships with the Soviet bloc in 1989, the economy deteriorated sharply. GDP fell by 75 per cent between 1989 and 1994, and the government was forced to introduce reforms. Since 1993, the government has legalised the holding of US dollars by private individuals, permitted private enterprise, cut subsidies to loss-making state industries, allowed prices for some goods and services to rise, and introduced income tax. State farms have been transformed into co-operatives run by private individuals and permitted to sell 20 per cent of produce on the open market, but remain relatively unproductive. In 1995, foreign investors were permitted to buy property and own Cuban-based companies, with British and Canadian firms becoming involved in the oil and mining industries.

Following austerity measures imposed in 1993, the economy has slowly started to grow; output has risen by 15 per cent since 1994. Sugar is still the mainstay of the economy and the principal source of foreign exchange; production dropped from 8.04 million tons in 1989–90 to 4.4 million tons in 1996–7. Domestic oil production is rising and reached 1,680,000 tonnes in 1998. Lack of external finance has been a major obstacle to economic recovery, as has the long-standing trade and economic embargo imposed by the USA, which has been criticised repeatedly by the UN and was condemned by the European Parliament in November 1998.

The tourism industry has expanded since 1986 to become the country's largest foreign exchange earner. In 1999 1.6 million tourists visited Cuba, generating some US$1,900 million.
GDP – US$23,248 million (1997); US$2,150 per capita (1998)
ANNUAL AVERAGE GROWTH OF GDP – 7.8 per cent (1996)

### Trade

Cuba's exports dropped from US$8.1 billion in 1989 to US$1.7 billion in 1993 while imports declined by 73 per cent. Trade between Cuba and the former socialist economies of Europe is now less than 10 per cent of pre-1989 levels. A trade deal was signed with Russia in 1995 providing for the exchange of sugar for oil. The US trade and economic embargo remains in force, in spite of it having been repeatedly condemned by the UN General Assembly, though it was relaxed in March 1998 to allow food and medicine into the country. Principal exports are sugar, nickel, seafood, citrus fruits, tobacco and rum.

| *Trade with UK* | 1999 | 2000 |
|---|---|---|
| Imports from UK | £21,825,000 | £21,657,000 |
| Exports to UK | 16,671,000 | 9,644,000 |

## COMMUNICATIONS

There are 12,700 km of railway track, of which 5,000 km are in public service. In 1986 there were 13,247 km of road. Scheduled international air services run to Central and South American countries and Europe. In March 1998 the ban on direct flights between Cuba and the USA was lifted. Direct telephone links between Cuba and the USA were suspended in December 2000.

## CULTURE AND EDUCATION

The press and broadcasting are under the control of the government. Education is compulsory and free. In 1964 illiteracy was officially declared to be eliminated.

ILLITERACY RATE – 3.6 per cent

ENROLMENT (percentage of age group) – primary 100 per cent (1996); secondary 59 per cent (1993); tertiary 12.4 per cent (1996)

---

# CYPRUS

*Kypriaki Dimokratía/Kıbrıs Çumhuriyeti*

---

AREA – 3,572 sq. miles (9,251 sq. km)

POPULATION – 754,800 (2000 estimate): 85 per cent Greek, 12 per cent Turkish. Greek and Turkish are official languages

CAPITAL – Nicosia (Lefkosía/Lefkosa) ( population, (195,300, 2000 estimate)

MAJOR CITIES – ΨFamagusta (34,300); ΨLarnaca (110,900); ΨLimassol (191,500); Paphos (57,400), 1998 estimates

CURRENCY – Cyprus pound (C£) of 100 cents

NATIONAL ANTHEM – Ode to Freedom

NATIONAL DAY – 1 October (Independence Day)

NATIONAL FLAG – White with a gold map of Cyprus above a wreath of olive

LIFE EXPECTANCY (years) – male 75.3; female 80.4

POPULATION GROWTH RATE – 1.5 per cent (1999)

POPULATION DENSITY – 81 per sq. km (1998)

URBAN POPULATION – 56.8 per cent (2000 estimate)

ENROLMENT (percentage of age group) – primary 97 per cent (1996); secondary 92 per cent (1996); tertiary 23.0 per cent (1996)

The climate is Mediterranean, with a hot dry summer and a variable warm winter.

## HISTORY AND POLITICS

Cyprus came under British administration from 1878, and was formally annexed to Britain in 1914 on the outbreak of war with Turkey. From 1925 to 1960 it was a Crown Colony. Following the launching in 1955 of an armed campaign by EOKA in support of union with Greece, a state of emergency was declared which lasted for four years. An agreement was signed on 19 February 1959 between the United Kingdom, Greece, Turkey, and the Greek and Turkish Cypriots which provided that Cyprus would be an independent republic.

The island became independent on 16 August 1960. The constitution provided for a Greek Cypriot president and a Turkish Cypriot vice-president. The constitution proved unworkable and led to intercommunal trouble. The UN Peacekeeping Force in Cyprus (UNFICYP) was set up in 1964.

In February 1998, Glafcos Clerides of the Democratic Rally-Liberal Party was re-elected president with 51 per cent of the vote. On 30 March 1998, formal accession talks with the EU began. A general election was held for the House of Representatives (56 Greek Cypriot and 24 vacant Turkish Cypriot seats) on 27 May 2001, resulting in the parties gaining the following seats: AKEL (Left-wing) 20; DISY (Liberal) 19; Democratic Party (DIKO) 9; KISOS (Social Democrats) 4; others 4.

### Head of State

*President*, Glafcos Clerides, *elected* 14 February 1993, *re-elected* 15 February 1998

### Council of Ministers *as at July 2001*

*Agriculture, Environment and Natural Resources*, Konstantinos Themistokleous
*Commerce, Industry and Tourism*, Nikolaos Rolandis
*Communications and Works*, Averof Neophytou
*Defence*, Socrates Hassikos
*Education and Culture*, Ouranios Ioannides
*Finance*, Takis Klerides
*Foreign Affairs*, Ioannis Kasoulides
*Health*, Frixos Savvides
*Interior*, Christodoulos Christodoulou
*Justice and Public Order*, Nikolaos Kosis
*Labour and Social Insurance*, Andreas Mousiouttas

### Cyprus High Commission

93 Park Street, London W1K 7ET
Tel: 020-7499 8272
*High Commissioner*, HE Myrna Kleopas, apptd 2000
*Deputy High Commissioner*, P. Kestoras
*First Counsellor, Consul-General*, Yannis Iacovou
*Counsellors*, K. Pillas (*Cultural Affairs*); A. Georgiades (*Commerce*), S. Georgiallis (*Press Counsellor*)

### British High Commission

Alexander Pallis Street (PO Box 1978), CY-1587 Nicosia
Tel: (00 357) (2) 2-861100
*High Commissioner*, HE Lyn Parker, apptd 2001
*Counsellor and Deputy High Commissioner*, P. R. Barton
*Defence Adviser*, Col. C. S. Wakelin, OBE
*First Secretary (Commercial)*, W. Ross

BRITISH COUNCIL DIRECTOR, Peter Skelton, 3 Museum Street, CY-1097 Nicosia; e-mail: enquiries@britishcouncil.org.cy

### British Sovereign Areas

The UK retained full sovereignty and jurisdiction over two areas of 99 square miles in all: Akrotiri–Episkopi–Paramali and Dhekelia–Pergamos–Ayios Nicolaos–Xylophagou. The British Administrator of these areas is appointed by The Queen and is responsible to the Secretary of State for Defence. The combined total of army and RAF personnel stationed in the areas is 3,200.

*Administrator of the British Sovereign Areas*, Air Vice-Marshal T. W. Rimmer, OBE

## DEFENCE

The National Guard has 145 main battle tanks, 70 armoured infantry fighting vehicles and 402 armoured personnel carriers. Turkey has about 36,000 troops in northern Cyprus.

In January 1998, a military airfield in Paphos was completed. It is intended to provide a base for Greek military aircraft, as Cyprus does not possess its own air force.

MILITARY EXPENDITURE – 6.1 per cent of GDP (1999)
MILITARY PERSONNEL – 10,000 National Guard, Paramilitaries 750, Northern Cyprus Army 5,000
CONSCRIPTION DURATION – 26 months (24 months Northern Cyprus)

## ECONOMY

In 1997, 9.9 per cent of the workforce were employed in agriculture, 23.5 per cent in industry and 66.6 per cent in the services sector.. Main products are citrus fruits, grapes and vine products, meat, milk, potatoes and other vegetables. Manufacturing, construction, distribution and other service industries are other major employers. Tourism is the main growth industry with over two million tourists producing C£878 million in foreign exchange earnings in 1998, accounting for 18.9 per cent of GDP. 1,055 foreign firms were registered as offshore companies in Cyprus in 1998, and 20 per cent of the world's ships are Cypriot registered.

GNP - US$9,086 million (1999); US$11,960 per capita (1999)
GDP – US$8,478 million (1997); US$11,631 per capita (1998)
ANNUAL AVERAGE GROWTH OF GDP – 4.1 per cent (1996)
INFLATION RATE – 1.6 per cent (1999)
UNEMPLOYMENT – 3.3 per cent (1998)

### TRADE

The UK is the main trading partner, taking 15 per cent of exports in 1998 and supplying 11 per cent of imports. In 1999 there was a trade deficit of US$2,309 million and a current account deficit of US$234 million. Imports totalled US$3,618 million and exports US$997 million.

| *Trade with UK* | 1999 | 2000 |
|---|---|---|
| Imports from UK | £259,513,000 | £320,153,000 |
| Exports to UK | 190,550,000 | 213,853,000 |

## TURKISH REPUBLIC OF NORTHERN CYPRUS

In 1974, mainland Greek officers under instructions from the military junta in Athens launched a coup and installed a former EOKA member, Nikos Sampson, as president. Turkey invaded northern Cyprus and occupied over a third of the island. In 1975 a 'Turkish Federated State of Cyprus' under Rauf Denktaş was declared in this area and in 1983 a 'Declaration of Statehood' was issued which purported to establish the 'Turkish Republic of Northern Cyprus'. The declaration was condemned by the UN Security Council and only Turkey has recognised the new 'state'. In 1985, Denktaş was elected president and a general election was held. Denktaş was re-elected in 1990, 1995 and on 15 April 2000. A UN plan for the reunification of the island was formally rejected by him on 31 August 1998. On 6 December 1998, elections to the 50-seat Republican Assembly resulted in a coalition government between the National Unity Party, who gained 24 seats, and the Democrat Party, who gained 13 seats. UN-sponsored proximity talks were held on 3-14 December 1999 between representatives of the Greek and Turkish communities, but no agreement was reached; a further round was planned.

### DE FACTO HEAD OF STATE

*President*, Rauf Denktaş, *elected* 1985, *re-elected* 1990, 1995, 15 April 2000
*Prime Minister*, Dervis Eroglu

---

# CZECH REPUBLIC
*Česká Republika*

---

AREA – 30,450 sq. miles (78,866 sq. km). Neighbours: Poland (north-east), Germany (west and north-west), Austria (south), Slovakia (east)
POPULATION – 10,280,000 (1997 UN estimate), 10,302,000 (1991 census): 95 per cent Czech, 3 per cent Slovak. Czech is the official language. The majority of the population is Roman Catholic, with a small Protestant minority
CAPITAL – Prague (Praha) on the Vltava (Moldau) (population, 1,202,552, 1998 UN estimate)
MAJOR CITIES – Brno (Brünn) (386,566); Ostrava (323,539); Plžeň (Pilsen); (169,946),1998 UN estimates
CURRENCY – Koruna (Kčs) of 100 haléru
NATIONAL ANTHEM – Kde Domov Můj (Where is my Motherland)
NATIONAL DAY – 28 October
NATIONAL FLAG – White over red horizontally with a blue triangle extending from the hoist to the centre of the flag
LIFE EXPECTANCY (years) – male 71.3; female 78.2
POPULATION GROWTH RATE – 0.0 per cent (1999)
POPULATION DENSITY – 131 per sq. km (1998)
URBAN POPULATION – 74.7 per cent (2000 estimate)

The Czech Republic is composed of Bohemia and Moravia. Bohemia is surrounded by mountain ranges while Moravian land stretches to the Danubian basin.

## HISTORY AND POLITICS

The area which is now the Czech Republic came under the rule of the Habsburg dynasty in 1526 and remained part of the Austro-Hungarian Empire until 1918. The rise of Czech nationalism in the late 19th century led to the proclamation of the independence of Czechoslovakia on 28 October 1918 following an amalgamation of Bohemia, Moravia, Slovakia and Ruthenia and was confirmed by the Versailles Peace Conference in 1919.

Czechoslovakia was forced to cede the ethnic German Sudetenland to Nazi Germany in 1938 after the Munich Agreement. German forces invaded the Czech Republic in March 1939 and incorporated it into Germany while Slovakia became a puppet state. The Czech Republic was liberated by Soviet and American forces in May 1945. The pre-war democratic Czechoslovak state was re-established in 1945, having ceded Ruthenia to the Soviet Union. The Communists took power in a coup in 1948 and remained in power until 1989.

In 1968 the Communist Party under Alexander Dubček embarked on a political and economic reform programme (the Prague Spring). The reforms were suppressed following an invasion by Warsaw Pact troops on the night of 20 August 1968, and were abandoned when Gustáv Husák became leader of the Communist Party in 1969.

Mass protests in November 1989 led to the resignation of the Communist Party Central Committee. The Party was forced to concede its monopoly of power and on 10 December a new government was appointed in which only half the ministers were Communists. Husák resigned as president and was replaced by the dissident writer Václav Havel. Free elections were held in June 1990 in which the Communist Party was defeated.

In late 1992 the leaders of the Czech and Slovak republics agreed to dissolve the federation and form two sovereign states; this took effect on 1 January 1993.

The general election in June 1998 produced no outright winner. Miloš Zeman, leader of the Czech Social Democratic Party (ČSSD), formed a coalition government. As of July 2001, the ČSSD had 74 seats, the Civic Democratic Party (ODS) 63 seats, the Communists 24 seats, the Christian Democratic Union-Czech People's Party (KDU-ČSL) 20 seats, the Freedom Union 18 seats, and there was one independent.

Following the election for 26 of the 81 seats in the Senate held in November 2000, the KDU-ČSL had 21 seats and its ally the Freedom Union/Civic Democratic Alliance group had 18 seats. The ODS had 22 seats and the ČSSD had 15 seats.

### Political System

The constitution vests legislative power in the bicameral parliament, comprising a 200-member Chamber of Deputies elected for a four-year term and an 81-member Senate elected for a six-year term, one-third being renewed every two years. The president is elected by parliament for a five-year term. Executive power is held by the prime minister and Council of Ministers. A two-thirds majority in parliament is necessary to amend the constitution, and federal laws remain in place unless superseded by Czech ones. A Constitutional Court has been established comprising 15 judges nominated by the president for ten-year terms with Senate approval.

### Head of State

*President*, Václav Havel , *elected* 26 January 1993, *re-elected* 20 January 1998

### Council of Ministers *as at July 2001*

*Prime Minister*, Miloš Zeman (ČSSD)
*Deputy Prime Minister, Commerce and Industry*, Miroslav Grégr (ČSSD)
*Deputy Prime Minister in charge of Foreign Affairs and Security Policy*, Jan Kavan (ČSSD)
*Deputy Prime Minister in charge of Legislative Affairs*, Pavel Rychetský (ČSSD)
*Deputy Prime Minister in charge of Labour and Social Affairs*, Vladimír Špidla (ČSSD)
*Agriculture*, Jan Fencl (ČSSD)
*Culture*, Pavel Dostál (ČSSD)
*Defence*, Jaroslav Tvrdík (ČSSD)
*Education*, Eduard Zeman (ČSSD)
*Environment*, Miloš Kužvart (ČSSD)
*Finance*, Jiří Rusnok (ČSSD)
*Health*, Bohumil Fišer
*Interior*, Stanislav Gross (ČSSD)
*Justice*, Jaroslav Bureš
*Regional Development*, Petr Lachnit
*Transport and Communications*, Jaromír Schling
*Without Portfolio*, Karel Březina

### Embassy of the Czech Republic

26 Kensington Palace Gardens, London W8 4QY
Tel: 020-7243 1115
*Ambassador Extraordinary and Plenipotentiary*, HE Pavel Seifter, apptd 1997
*Minister-Counsellor*, Milan Čoupek
*Military Attaché*, Col. Pavel Zuna

### British Embassy

Thunovská 14, CZ-11800 Prague 1
Tel: (00 420) (2) 5732 0278
E-mail: info@britishcouncil.cz
*Ambassador Extraordinary and Plenipotentiary*, HE David Broucher, apptd 1997
*Counsellor and Deputy Head of Mission*, D. E. P. P. Keefe
*Defence Attaché*, Col. A. F. Davidson, MBE
*First Secretary (Commercial)*, M. C. Day
British Council Director, Paul Docherty (*Cultural Attaché*), Narodni 10, CZ-12501 Prague 1; e-mail: info@britcoun.cz. Regional offices in Brno, České Budějovice, Olomouc, Ostrava, Pardubice, Plžeň and Ustí Nad Labem
British Chamber of Commerce, Pobrezeni 3, CZ-186-00 Prague 8

## DEFENCE

The army has 792 main battle tanks, 801 armoured infantry fighting vehicles and 403 armoured personnel carriers. The Air Force has 110 combat aircraft and 34 attack helicopters. The Czech Republic became a member of NATO on 12 March 1999.
Military Expenditure – 2.3 per cent of GDP (1999)
Military Personnel – 57,700: Army 25,100, Air Force 13,400, Paramilitaries 5,600, Others 13,600
Conscription Duration – 12 months

## ECONOMY

Under Communist rule industry and most agricultural land was state-owned. An economic reform programme began in 1990 to produce a free-market economy. This has necessitated a restrictive monetary policy to stem inflation and a restructuring of industry to be competitive, and these were major reasons for the break with Slovakia. As a result, foreign investment (about US$4,500 million in 2000) and private enterprises have grown, over 90 per cent of the economy had been privatised, and reliance on trade with the former Soviet bloc countries has ended. Foreign-owned firms accounted for nearly half of all exports in 2000.

A trade-liberalising association agreement with the EU is in operation, and formal EU accession talks began in March 1998.

A customs union between the Czech and Slovak Republics is in place but separate currencies were introduced in February 1993 following speculation. The Koruna was made fully convertible in October 1995.

Principal agricultural products are sugar beet, potatoes and cereal crops; the timber industry is also very important. Having been the major industrial area of the Austro-Hungarian Empire, the country has long been industrialised, and machinery, industrial consumer goods and raw materials are major exports.

In 1999 there was a trade deficit of US$2,069 million and a current account deficit of US$1,071 million. In 1998 imports totalled US$30,258 million and exports US$26,418 million.
GNP – US$51,623 million (1999); US$5,060 per capita (1999)
GDP – US$52,038 million (1999); US$5,156 per capita (1999)
Annual Average Growth of GDP – 3.9 per cent (2000)
Inflation Rate – 4.1 per cent (2001)
Unemployment – 8.6 per cent (2000)
Total External Debt – US$25,301 million (1998)

| *Trade with UK* | 1999 | 2000 |
|---|---|---|
| Imports from UK | £739,158,000 | £930,940,000 |
| Exports to UK | 597,354,000 | 824,113,000 |

## EDUCATION

Education is compulsory and free for all children from the ages of six to 15. There are nine universities of which the oldest and most famous is Charles University in Prague (founded 1348).

ENROLMENT (percentage of age group) – primary 91 per cent (1996); secondary 87 per cent (1996); tertiary 23.5 per cent (1996)

## CULTURE

The Reformation gave a widespread impetus to Czech literature, the writings of Jan Hus (martyred in 1415 as a religious and social reformer) familiarising the people with Wyclif's teaching. This lasted until the close of the 17th century when Jan Amos Komenský or Comenius (1592–1670) was expelled from the country. There was a period of stagnation until the national revival in the 19th century. Authors of international reputation include Jaroslav Hašek (1883–1923), Jaroslav Seifert (1901–86, Nobel Prize for Literature, 1985), Václav Havel (b. 1936) and Milan Kundera (b. 1929).

---

# DENMARK
*Kongeriget Danmark*

---

AREA – 16,639 sq. miles (43,094 sq. km). Neighbour: Germany (south)
POPULATION – 5,317,000 (1997 UN estimate). The majority of the population is Lutheran. The language is Danish
CAPITAL – ΨCopenhagen (population, 1,379,413, 1998 projection)
MAJOR CITIES – ΨÅlborg (160,937); ΨÅrhus (283,673); ΨOdense (183,584), 1997 UN estimates
CURRENCY – Danish krone of 100 øre
NATIONAL ANTHEMS – Kong Kristian stod ved højen mast (King Christian stood by the lofty mast); Det er et yndigt land (There is a lovely land)
NATIONAL DAY – 5 June (Constitution Day)
NATIONAL FLAG – Red, with white cross
LIFE EXPECTANCY (years) – male 72.9; female 78.1
POPULATION GROWTH RATE – 0.3 per cent (1999)
POPULATION DENSITY – 123 per sq. km (1998)
URBAN POPULATION – 85.3 per cent (2000 estimate)

Denmark is a kingdom, consisting of the islands of Zealand (Sjælland), Funen (Fyn), Lolland, etc., the peninsula of Jutland (Jylland), the outlying island of Bornholm in the Baltic, and the Færøes and Greenland.

## HISTORY AND POLITICS

The Danes were at the forefront of Viking expansionism and briefly united England and Scandinavia under Knut (Canute) (995– 1035).

The Union of Kalmar (1397) brought Norway and Sweden (including Finland) under Danish rule. Danish power waned during the 16th century, however, enabling Sweden to re-establish its independence in 1523. In the 19th century Norway was ceded to Sweden under the Treaty of Kiel (1814) and both Schleswig and Holstein, which had been subsumed in 1460, were surrendered to Germany.

Denmark remained neutral during the First World War, and in a plebiscite held in accordance with the Versailles Treaty (1919), northern Schleswig voted to return to Danish sovereignty. In 1939 Denmark signed a non-aggression pact with Germany but was invaded on 9 April 1940 and coerced into contributing to the German war effort. Iceland declared its independence from Denmark in 1944 and the Færøe Islands were granted home rule in 1948. Greenland, which had had the status of a colony, was integrated into Denmark in 1953 and granted home rule in 1979. Social Democrat-led coalitions dominated the post-war era until 1982 when a right-wing government was elected. Denmark joined the European Community in 1973.

On 21 September 1994, a new coalition government of the Social Democrat, Social Liberal and Centre Democrat parties was formed. On 12 March 1998, Poul Nyrup Rasmussen's centre-left coalition was re-elected, winning 90 of the 179 seats in the parliament, giving a majority of a single seat.

A referendum was held on 28 September 2000 on membership of the European single currency. Membership was rejected by 53.1 per cent of those who voted.

### POLITICAL SYSTEM

The legislature consists of one chamber, the *Folketing*, of 179 members, including two for the Færøes and two for Greenland, which is elected for a four-year term. The voting age is 18 with voting based on a proportional representation system with a 2 per cent threshold for parliamentary representation.

### HEAD OF STATE

*HM The Queen of Denmark*, Queen Margrethe II, KG, *born* 16 April 1940, *succeeded* 14 January 1972, *married* 10 June 1967, Count Henri de Monpezat (Prince Henrik of Denmark), and *has issue* Crown Prince Frederik (*see below*); Prince Joachim, *born* 7 June 1969, *married* 18 November 1995, Miss Alexandra Manley (Princess Alexandra of Denmark)
*Heir*, HRH Crown Prince Frederik, *born* 26 May 1968

### CABINET *as at July 2001*

*Prime Minister*, Poul Nyrup Rasmussen (SD)
*Deputy Prime Minister, Economic Affairs and Nordic Co-operation*, Marianne Jelved (RV)
*Culture*, Elsebeth Gerner Nielsen (RV)
*Defence*, Jan Trøjborg (SD)
*Development Co-operation*, Anita Bay Bundesgaard (RV)
*Education*, Margrethe Vestager (RV)
*Environment and Energy*, Svend Auken (SD)
*Finance*, Pia Gjellerup (SD)
*Food, Agriculture and Fisheries*, Ritt Bjerregaard (SD)
*Foreign Affairs*, Mogens Lykketoft (SD)
*Health*, Arne Rolighed (SD)
*Housing and Urban Affairs, Gender Equality*, Lotte Bundesgaard (SD)
*Interior*, Karen Jespersen (SD)
*Justice*, Frank Jensen (SD)
*Labour*, Ove Hygum (SD)
*Religious Affairs*, Johannes Lebech (RV)
*Research and Information Technology*, Birte Weiss (SD)
*Social Affairs*, Henrik Dam Kristensen (SD)
*Taxation*, Frode Sørensen (SD)
*Trade and Industry*, Ole Stavad (SD)
*Transport and Communications*, Jacob Buksti (SD)

SD Social Democrat Party; RV Social Liberal Party

### ROYAL DANISH EMBASSY

55 Sloane Street, London SW1X 9SR
Tel: 020-7333 0200
*Ambassador Extraordinary and Plenipotentiary*, HE Ole Lønsmann Poulsen, GCVO, apptd 1996
*Counsellor (Commercial)*, Gunner Tetler
*Defence Attaché*, Capt. Uffe Haagen Olsen, CBE

### BRITISH EMBASSY

36–40 Kastelsvej, DK-2100 Copenhagen Ø
Tel: (00 45) 3544 5200
E-mail: www.brit-emb@post6.tele.dk
*Ambassador Extraordinary and Plenipotentiary*, HE Philip Astley, LVO, apptd 1999
*Counsellor and Deputy Head of Mission*, P. B. Yaghmourian
*Defence Attaché*, Cmdr. A. Gordon-Lennox, RN
*First Secretary (Commercial)*, F. J. Martin

BRITISH CONSULATES – Åbenrå, Ålborg, Århus, Esbjerg, Fredericia, Herning, Odense, Rønne (Bornholm), Tórshavn (Færøe Islands)

BRITISH COUNCIL DIRECTOR, Dr Michael Sørensen-Jones, Gammel Mønt 12.3, DK-1117 Copenhagen K; e-mail: british.council@britishcouncil.dk

## DEFENCE

The Army has 248 main battle tanks, 315 armoured personnel carriers and 12 attack helicopters. The Navy has three submarines, three corvettes and 27 patrol and coastal vessels at two bases. The Air Force has 69 combat aircraft.
MILITARY EXPENDITURE – 1.6 per cent of GDP (1999)
MILITARY PERSONNEL – 21,800: Army 12,850, Navy 4,060, Air Force 4,900
CONSCRIPTION DURATION – Four to 12 months

## ECONOMY

Of the labour force in 1996, 45 per cent was employed in the professional services and administration; 18 per cent in commerce; 19 per cent in manufacturing and 5 per cent in agriculture. The chief agricultural products are pigs, dairy products, poultry and eggs, seeds and cereals; manufactures are mostly based on imported raw materials but there are also considerable imports of finished goods. Denmark is self-sufficient in oil and natural gas.
GNP – US$170,685 million (1999); US$32,030 per capita (1999)
GDP – US$161,455 million (1997); US$33,124 per capita (1999)
ANNUAL AVERAGE GROWTH OF GDP – 2.3 per cent (2000)
INFLATION RATE – 2.4 per cent (2001)
UNEMPLOYMENT – 4.7 per cent (2001)

### TRADE

The principal imports are industrial raw materials, consumer goods, construction inputs, machinery, raw materials, vehicles and textile products. The chief exports are manufactured articles, and agricultural and dairy products. Germany and Sweden are Denmark's main trading partners.

In 1999 Denmark had a trade surplus of US$6,537 million and a current account surplus of US$2,176 million. Imports totalled US$43,971 million and exports US$48,342 million.

| *Trade with UK* | 1999 | 2000 |
|---|---|---|
| Imports from UK | £1,913,700,000 | £2,181,900,000 |
| Exports to UK | 2,125,300,000 | 2,276,700,000 |

## COMMUNICATIONS

In 1996, the Danish mercantile fleet numbered 584 ships of more than 100 gross tonnage. There were 3,000 km of railway, 85 per cent of which belonged to the state and 15 per cent to privately-owned companies. A rail tunnel and bridge linking the islands of Sjælland and Fyn was opened in 1997, and a road and rail tunnel and bridge across the Øresund, linking Copenhagen with the Swedish city of Malmö, was opened on 1 July 2000.

## CULTURE AND EDUCATION

The Danish language is akin to Swedish and Norwegian. Danish literature, ancient and modern, embraces all forms of expression, familiar names being Hans Christian Andersen (1805–75), Søren Kierkegaard (1813–55), Karen Blixen (1885–1962) and Peter Høeg (b. 1957). Some 38 newspapers are published in Denmark; eight daily papers are published in Copenhagen.

Education is free and compulsory. Special schools are numerous, commercial, technical and agricultural predominating. There are universities at Copenhagen (founded in 1479), Århus (1928), Odense (1966), Roskilde (1972) and Ålborg (1974).
ENROLMENT (percentage of age group) – primary 99 per cent (1996); secondary 88 per cent (1996); tertiary 48.2 per cent (1996)

## THE FÆRØE ISLANDS

AREA – 540 sq. miles (1,399 sq. km)
POPULATION – 44,000 (1997 UN estimate)
CAPITAL – Tórshavn (population, 16,218, 1992)

Since 1948 the Færøes or Sheep Islands have had a degree of home rule. The islands are governed by a *Løgting* of between 27 and 32 members and a *Landsstýri* of three to six members which deals with special Færøes affairs, and send two representatives to the *Folketing* at Copenhagen. The Færøes are not part of the EU.

Prime Minister, Anfinn Kallsberg

| *Trade with UK* | 1999 | 2000 |
|---|---|---|
| Imports from UK | £7,050,000 | £7,094,000 |
| Exports to UK | 85,132,000 | 76,213,000 |

## GREENLAND

AREA – 840,004 sq. miles (2,175,600 sq. km) of which about 16 per cent is ice-free
POPULATION – 56,000 (1997)
CAPITAL – Godthåb (Nuuk) (population, 12,483, 1997 estimate)

Greenland attained a status of internal autonomy in May 1979 and a government (*Landsstyret*) was established. It has a *Landsting* (parliament) of 31 members and sends two representatives to the *Folketing* at Copenhagen. Greenland negotiated its withdrawal from the EU, without discontinuing relations with Denmark, and left on 1 February 1985.

The USA has acquired certain rights to maintain air bases in Greenland.

*Prime Minister*, Jonathan Motzfeldt

| *Trade with UK* | 1999 | 2000 |
|---|---|---|
| Imports from UK | £2,087,000 | £3,108,000 |
| Exports to UK | 1,171,000 | 351,000 |

---

# DJIBOUTI
*Jumhūriyya Jībūtī*

---

AREA – 8,958 sq. miles (23,200 sq. km). Neighbours: Eritrea (north), Ethiopia (west and south), Somalia (south-east)
POPULATION – 648,000 (1997 UN estimate), 520,000 (1991 census), mostly Afar or Issas. The official languages are Arabic and French; Afar and Somali are also spoken
CAPITAL – ΨDjibouti (population, 62,000, 1991)
CURRENCY – Djibouti franc of 100 centimes
NATIONAL ANTHEM – Hinjinne u sara kaca (Arise with strength)
NATIONAL DAY – 27 June (Independence Day)
NATIONAL FLAG – Blue over green with white triangle in the hoist containing a red star
LIFE EXPECTANCY (years) – male 45.0; female 45.0
POPULATION GROWTH RATE – 2.2 per cent (1999)
POPULATION DENSITY – 27 per sq. km (1998)
URBAN POPULATION – 83.3 per cent (2000 estimate)
MILITARY EXPENDITURE – 5.0 per cent of GDP (1999)
MILITARY PERSONNEL – 9,600: Army 8,000, Navy 200, Air Force 200, Paramilitaries 3,000
GNP – US$511 million (1999); US$790 per capita (1999)

GDP – US$604 million (1997); US$800 per capita (1998)
ANNUAL AVERAGE GROWTH OF GDP – 0.2 per cent (1996)
TOTAL EXTERNAL DEBT – US$288 million (1998)
ILLITERACY RATE – 48.6 per cent
ENROLMENT (percentage of age group) – primary 32 per cent (1996); secondary 12 per cent (1996); tertiary 0.3 per cent (1996)

The climate is harsh and much of the country is semi-arid desert.

## HISTORY AND POLITICS

Formerly French Somaliland and then the French Territory of the Afars and the Issas, the Republic of Djibouti became independent on 27 June 1977. A multiparty constitution was adopted by referendum in 1992 and subsequent multiparty elections held in December 1992 were won by the *Rassemblement Populaire pour le Progrès* (RPP, the Popular Rally for Progress). President Aptidon was re-elected for a fourth six-year term in 1993. However, less than half the electorate voted in either election and the Front for the Restoration of Unity and Democracy (FRUD) boycotted both. In December 1997, in the first elections since the 1994 peace accord, the RPP and the FRUD formed an alliance and won all 65 seats in the Chamber of Deputies. On 9 April 1999, President Ismael Omar Guelleh was elected, gaining approximately three-quarters of the votes cast; about 60 per cent of the electorate were estimated to have voted. On 7 February 2000, the government signed a peace agreement with a breakaway faction of the FRUD, which had continued its armed opposition to the government after the 1994 peace accord.

On 7 December 2000, an attempted coup by a group of police officers was quickly put down by the armed forces.

### HEAD OF STATE

*President*, Ismael Omar Guelleh, *elected* 9 April 1999

### COUNCIL OF MINISTERS *as at July 2001*

*Prime Minister, National and Regional Development*, Dilleita Mohamed Dilleita
*Agriculture, Livestock and Marine Affairs*, Ali Muhammad Daoud
*Communication and Culture, Posts and Telecommunications, Government Spokesman*, Rifki Abdoulkader Bamakhrama
*Defence*, Ougoure Kifle Ahmed
*Economy, Finance and Privatisation*, Yacin Elmi Bouh
*Energy and Natural Resources*, Muhammad Ali Muhammad
*Foreign Affairs and International Co-operation, Relations with Parliament*, Ali Abdi Farah
*Housing, Town Planning, Environment and Regional Development*, Saleiban Omar Oudine
*Interior*, Abdallah Abdillahi Miguil
*Justice, Human Rights, Islamic Affairs and Prisons*, Ibrahim Idriss Djibril
*Labour and Vocational Training*, Mohamed Barkat Abdillahi
*Ministers-Delegate*, Ahmed Guirreh Waberi *(Decentralisation)*; Cheikh Mogueh Dirir Samatar *(Religious Affairs and Islamic Affairs)*; Hawa Ahmad Yousouf *(Women, Families and Social Welfare)*;
*National Education*, Abdi Ibrahim Absieh
*Presidential Affairs and Promotion of Investments*, Osman Ahmad Moussa
*Public Health*, Mohamed Dini Farah
*Trade, Industry and Handicrafts*, Elmi Obsieh Waiss
*Transport and Equipment*, Osman Idriss Djama
*Youth, Sport, Leisure and Tourism*, Dini Abdallah Bililis

EMBASSY OF THE REPUBLIC OF DJIBOUTI
26 rue Emile Ménier, F-75116 Paris, France
Tel: (00 33) (1) 4727 4922
*Ambassador Extraordinary and Plenipotentiary*, HE Djama Omar Idleh, apptd 1998

BRITISH AMBASSADOR, HE M. A. Wickstead, resident at Addis Ababa, Ethiopia

BRITISH CONSULATE
PO Box 169, Rue de Djibouti, Djibouti
*Honorary Consul*, A. Martinet

## ECONOMY AND TRADE

The economy depends mainly on the operation of the free port, which accounts for about three-quarters of Djibouti's GDP. Agriculture accounts for less than 4 per cent of GDP, but employs three-quarters of the workforce. The main imports are foodstuffs, machinery, clothing, and oil and oil derivatives. The main exports are foodstuffs and livestock. Djibouti's primary trading partners are Ethiopia, Somalia, Yemen and France.

| *Trade with UK* | 1999 | 2000 |
|---|---|---|
| Imports from UK | £19,971,000 | £18,330,000 |
| Exports to UK | 386,000 | 109,000 |

## COMMUNICATIONS

Djibouti has an excellent port, an international airport, and a railway line runs to Addis Ababa in Ethiopia.

---

# DOMINICA
*The Commonwealth of Dominica*

---

AREA – 290 sq. miles (751 sq. km)
POPULATION – 73,000 (1997 UN estimate). English is the official language although Creole French is more commonly used
CAPITAL – ΨRoseau (population, 16,243, 1991)
CURRENCY – East Caribbean dollar (EC$) of 100 cents
NATIONAL ANTHEM – Isle of Beauty
NATIONAL DAY – 3 November (Independence Day)
NATIONAL FLAG – Green ground with a cross overall of yellow, black and white stripes, and in the centre a red disc charged with a Sisserou parrot in natural colours within a ring of ten green stars
LIFE EXPECTANCY (years) – male 74.0; female 80.2
POPULATION GROWTH RATE – 0.1 per cent (1999)
POPULATION DENSITY – 101 per sq. km (1998)
URBAN POPULATION – 71.0 per cent (2000 estimate)

Dominica, in the Lesser Antilles, lies in the Windward Islands group 95 miles south of Antigua. It is about 29 miles long and 16 miles wide. The island is of volcanic origin and very mountainous, and the soil is very fertile. The temperature varies, according to the altitude, from 13° to 29°C.

## HISTORY AND POLITICS

The island was discovered by Columbus in 1493, when it was a stronghold of the Caribs, who remained virtually the sole inhabitants until the French established settlements in the 18th century. It was captured by the British in 1759 but passed back and forth between France and Britain until 1805, after which British possession was not challenged. From 1871 to 1939 Dominica was part of the Leeward Islands Colony, then from 1940 the island was a unit of the Windward Islands group. Internal self-government from

1967 was followed on 3 November 1978 by independence as a republic.

The most recent general election was held on 31 January 2000 and won by the Dominica Labour Party, which captured 10 seats, with nine seats going to the United Workers' Party and two seats to the Dominica Freedom Party.

Pierre Charles was appointed as prime minister following the sudden death of his predecessor, Roosevelt Douglas, on 1 October 2000.

### POLITICAL SYSTEM

Executive authority is vested in the president, who is elected by the House of Assembly for not more than two terms of five years. Parliament consists of the president and the House of Assembly (21 representatives elected by universal adult suffrage for a five-year term) and nine senators, five of whom are appointed on the advice of the prime minister and the other four on the advice of the Leader of the Opposition.

### HEAD OF STATE

*President*, HE Vernon Shaw, *elected* 2 October 1998, *took office* 6 October 1998

### CABINET *as at July 2001*

*Prime Minister, Foreign Affairs, Banana Industry*, Pierre Charles
*Agriculture and the Environment*, Vince Henderson
*Attorney-General,Legal Affairs, Immigration and Labour*, David Bruney
*Communications and Works, Aviation and Telecommunications, Housing*, Reginald Austrie
*Community Development and Women's Affairs*, Matthew Walters
*Finance and Planning*, Ambrose George
*Health and Social Security*, Herbert Sabaroche
*Ministers of State*, Loreen Bannis-Robert (*Education*); Urban Baron (*Fishing*)
*Tourism, Ports and Employment*, Charles Savarin
*Trade, Industry and Marketing*, Osborne Riviere
*Without Portfolio*, Urban Baron
*Youth and Sports, Education, Science and Technology*, Roosevelt Skerrit

### HIGH COMMISSION FOR THE COMMONWEALTH OF DOMINICA

1 Collingham Gardens, London SW5 0HW
Tel: 020-7370 5194/5
*High Commissioner*, HE George Williams, apptd 1996

BRITISH HIGH COMMISSIONER, HE Gordon Baker, resident at Bridgetown, Barbados

### BRITISH CONSULATE

PO Box 2269, Roseau
*Honorary Consul*, P. Fletcher

## ECONOMY

Agriculture is the principal occupation, with tropical and citrus fruits the main crops. Products for export are bananas, fruit juices, lime oil, bay oil, copra and rum. Forestry, fisheries and agro-processing are being encouraged. The only commercially exploitable mineral is pumice, used chiefly for building purposes. Manufacturing consists largely of the processing of agricultural products although there have been attempts to diversify into light industry. In 1998 Dominica had a trade deficit of US$37 million and a current account deficit of US$18 million. In 1999 imports totalled US$141 million and exports US$54 million.

GNP – US$238 million (1999); US$3,170 per capita (1999)
GDP – US$243 million (1997); US$3,690 per capita (1999)
ANNUAL AVERAGE GROWTH OF GDP – 3.2 per cent (1996)
INFLATION RATE – 1.2 per cent (1999)
UNEMPLOYMENT – 23.1 per cent (1997)
TOTAL EXTERNAL DEBT – US$109 million (1998)

| *Trade with UK* | 1999 | 2000 |
|---|---|---|
| Imports from UK | £13,294,000 | £9,357,000 |
| Exports to UK | 15,556,000 | 13,928,000 |

## DOMINICAN REPUBLIC
*República Dominicana*

AREA – 18,730 sq. miles (48,511 sq. km). Neighbour: Haiti (west)
POPULATION – 8,404,000 (1997 UN estimate). The language is Spanish
CAPITAL – ΨSanto Domingo (population, 2,134,779, 1993)
MAJOR CITIES – Duarte (272,227); La Vega (335,140); Puerto Plata (255,061); San Cristóbal (409,381); San Juan (247,029); Santiago de los Caballeros (690,458), 1993 UN estimates
CURRENCY – Dominican Republic peso (RD$) of 100 centavos
NATIONAL FLAG – Divided into blue and red quarters by a white cross
NATIONAL ANTHEM – Quisqueyanos Valientes, Alcemos (Brave men of Quisqueya, let's raise our song)
NATIONAL DAY – 27 February (Independence Day 1844)
LIFE EXPECTANCY (years) – male 71.4; female 72.8
POPULATION GROWTH RATE – 1.8 per cent (1999)
POPULATION DENSITY – 167 per sq. km (1998)
URBAN POPULATION – 65.0 per cent (2000 estimate)
MILITARY EXPENDITURE – 0.9 per cent of GDP (1999)
MILITARY PERSONNEL – 24,500: Army 15,000, Navy 4,000, Air Force 5,500, Paramilitaries 15,000
ILLITERACY RATE – 16.2 per cent (2000)
ENROLMENT (percentage of age group) – primary 81 per cent (1994); secondary 22 per cent (1996); tertiary 22.9 per cent (1996)

The Dominican Republic, the eastern part of the island of Hispaniola (Haiti is the western part), is the oldest European settlement in America. The climate is tropical in the lowlands and semi-tropical to temperate in the higher altitudes.

## HISTORY AND POLITICS

Santo Domingo was discovered by Columbus in 1492, and was a Spanish colony until 1797, when it passed to France. It was restored to Spanish rule in 1809. Independence was proclaimed in 1821, but in 1822 it was subjugated by the neighbouring Haitians who remained in control until 1844, when the Dominican Republic was proclaimed. The country was occupied by American marines from 1916 until 1924, and ruled by Gen. Rafael Trujillo from 1930 until 1961.

The general election on 16 May 1998 resulted in the Dominican Revolutionary Party (PRD) winning 83 seats in the Chamber of Deputies and 24 seats in the Senate. The presidential election on 16 May 2000 was won by Hipólito Mejía, the PRD candidate.

### POLITICAL SYSTEM

Executive power is vested in the president, who is directly elected for a single four-year term and appoints the Cabinet. Legislative power is exercised by the Congress, which has a term of four years. The Congress comprises the Senate of 30 senators, one for each province and one for Santo Domingo, and the 149-member Chamber of Deputies.

### HEAD OF STATE

*President*, Hipólito Mejía Domingues, *elected* 16 May 2000, *sworn in* 16 August 2000
*Vice-President, Minister of Education*, Milagros Ortiz Bosch

### CABINET *as at July 2001*

*Agriculture*, Eligio Jaquez
*Attorney-General*, Virgilio Bello Rosa
*Culture*, Tony Raful
*Defence*, José Miguel Soto Jiménez
*Environment*, Frank Moya Pons
*Finance*, Fernanado Álvarez Bogaert
*Foreign Affairs*, Hugo Tolentino Dipp
*Health*, José Rodríguez Soldevilla
*Industry and Commerce*, Angel Lockward
*Interior*, Rafael Suberví Bonilla
*Labour*, Milton Ray Guevara
*Presidency*, Sergio Grullón
*Public Works*, Miguel Vargas
*Sports, Physical Education and Recreation*, César Cedeño
*Tourism*, Ramón Alfredo Bordas
*Women*, Yadira Henríquez
*Youth*, Antonio Pena Guaba

EMBASSY OF THE DOMINICAN REPUBLIC
139 Inverness Terrace, London, W2 6JF
Tel: 020-7727 6285
*Ambassador Extraordinary and Plenipotentiary*, HE Rafael Ludovino Fernández, apptd 2000

BRITISH EMBASSY
Edificio Corominas Pepin, Ave 27 de Febrero No 233, Santo Domingo
Tel: (00 1 809) 472 7111/7905
*Ambassador Extraordinary and Plenipotentiary*, HE David Ward, apptd 1999
BRITISH CONSULAR OFFICE – Puerto Plata

## ECONOMY

Since 1990 the government has successfully reduced inflation and increased output. Large amounts of foreign debt have been paid off but unemployment remains high.

Sugar, cocoa, coffee, bananas, rice and tobacco are the most important crops. Other products are maize, molasses, beans, tomatoes, cement, ferro-nickel, gold, silver and cattle. Light industry produces beer, tinned foodstuffs, glass products, textiles, soap, cigarettes, construction materials, plastic articles, paint, rum, matches and peanut oil. Tourism is an important part of the economy, with 2.3 million foreign visitors to the Dominican Republic in 1998.

GNP – US$16,130 million (1999); US$1,910 per capita (1999)
GDP – US$14,907 million (1997); US$1,925 per capita (1998)
ANNUAL AVERAGE GROWTH OF GDP – 7.0 per cent (1996)
INFLATION RATE – 6.5 per cent (1999)
UNEMPLOYMENT – 15.9 per cent (1997)
TOTAL EXTERNAL DEBT – US$4,451 million (1998)

### TRADE

The chief imports are fuel oils, foodstuffs, motor vehicles, pharmaceuticals and machinery components. The chief exports are minerals, sugar and sugar by-products, coffee and cocoa. The USA is the main trading partner.

In 1998 there was a trade deficit of US$2,617 million and a current account deficit of US$336 million. Imports totalled US$5,631 million and exports US$795 million.

| *Trade with UK* | 1999 | 2000 |
|---|---|---|
| Imports from UK | £36,900,000 | £48,343,000 |
| Exports to UK | 26,621,000 | 29,669,000 |

## COMMUNICATIONS

There are over 4,000 miles of roads and a direct road from Santo Domingo to Port-au-Prince, the capital of Haiti, but that part of it in the border area has fallen into disuse. The frontier has been closed since 1967, except for the section crossed by the main road linking the two capitals. A telephone system connects all the principal towns. There are more than 90 commercial broadcasting stations and six television stations.

---

# EAST TIMOR
*Timor Lorosae*

---

AREA – 5,743 sq. miles (14,874 sq. km). Neighbour: Indonesia (west). The exclave of Oekussi is separated from the rest of East Timor by the Indonesian province of West Timor
POPULATION – 839,719 (1995 Intercensal census): 78 per cent Timorese, 20 per cent Indonesian, 2 per cent Chinese. Tetum is the national language and is spoken by about 60 per cent of the population, although Mambai, Tokodede, Kemak, Galoli, Idate, Waima'a, Naueti, Bunak, Makasae and Fatuluku are also spoken. Portuguese and Bahasa Indonesia are widely understood. The population is predominantly Roman Catholic
CAPITAL – ΨDili (population, 62,000, 1996 estimate)
MAJOR CITY – Lautem (17,850, 1996 estimate)
CURRENCY – US dollar of 100 cents
NATIONAL ANTHEM – Funu Nain Falintil
NATIONAL FLAG – Red with a yellow triangle based on the hoist and surmounted by a black triangle containing a white star
POPULATION DENSITY – 58 per sq. km (1998)

East Timor comprises the eastern half of the island of Timor and the Oekussi exclave in the western half. Parallel mountain ranges cross Timor. Tata Mailau (9,679 ft/ 2,950 m) is the highest mountain.

## HISTORY AND POLITICS

East Timor was a Portuguese colony from 1702 until Portuguese control collapsed following the 1974 coup in Portugal. Local elections were held in early 1975, in which the left-wing, pro-independence Fretilin (Revolutionary Front for an Independent East Timor) emerged as the strongest party. Indonesia had supported Apodeti (Popular Democratic Association of Timor), which urged the integration of the territory into Indonesia, but following its failure to gain a substantial proportion of the vote, Indonesia encouraged the pro-autonomy Democratic Union of Timor (UDT) to attempt a coup in August 1975, but this was convincingly suppressed by the better equipped and disciplined Fretilin. The Portuguese administration withdrew without formally handing over power. Indonesia began to infiltrate the border and attack villages in the frontier regions to create the illusion that the civil war was still continuing in order to justify an invasion. Fretilin proclaimed the Democratic Republic of East Timor on 28 November 1975, which was recognised by Portugal. The following day the leaders of Apodeti and UDT, who had fled to Indonesia following the failed coup, were coerced into signing a request for Indonesian assistance to restore order in East Timor. Indonesian forces began to invade East Timor on 7 December 1975 and declared East Timor Indonesia's 27th province on 17 July 1976 following their establishment of a provisional East Timorese government consisting of Apodeti ministers, which signed a petition requesting integration with Indonesia. Fretilin forces resisted strongly, but by 1979 most of East Timor was under Indonesian control. Resistance and atrocities committed by Indonesian troops left at least 200,000 East Timorese dead, predominantly civilians. About 150,000 Muslims were settled in East Timor alongside the predominantly Roman Catholic population (80 per cent in 1975). The UN did not recognise the annexation.

Following negotiations between Indonesia and Portugal, an agreement was reached to conduct a plebiscite on 30 August 1999, which would offer East Timor autonomy within Indonesia or independence. The plebiscite resulted in a turnout of 98.6 per cent of the electorate, with 78.5 per cent voting for independence for East Timor.

After extensive violence and intimidation by pro-Indonesian militias and Indonesian troops against the civilian population, and the forcible evacuation of many towns and villages, the UN voted to send in peacekeeping troops after having gained the agreement of the Indonesian government; the first UN peacekeepers arrived on 20 September 1999 and Indonesian troops began to withdraw. On 19 October, the Indonesian Consultative Assembly unanimously ratified the result of the referendum on the independence of East Timor. By early October, the UN-established International Force for East Timor (INTERFET) had managed to install its forces on the border with West Timor with the aim of preventing cross-border attacks by pro-Indonesia militias. INTERFET also managed to land troops in the East Timorese enclave of Oekussi. The commander of Indonesian forces in West Timor signed an agreement with INTERFET on the repatriation of refugees on 22 November 1999. In December 2000, it was estimated that about 120,000 East Timorese remained in Indonesian refugee camps.

The UN Security Council voted unanimously on 25 October 1999 to replace INTERFET with a UN force of up to 8,950 troops and 1,600 police to support the establishment of a UN Transitional Administration in East Timor (UNTAET). On 27 November, the pro-independence activist José Xanana Gusmão visited Jakarta to establish relations with the Indonesian government. The East Timor National Council (ETNC), which was established to make policy recommendations to UNTAET, held its first meeting on 11 December.

In December 1999, international donors pledged US$520 million in aid for the reconstruction of East Timor.

Two reports which were published on 31 January 2000 concluded that the Indonesian authorities had co-operated with the pro-Indonesian militias in wide-ranging human rights abuses and called for the establishment of an international war crimes tribunal. The ETNC adopted the US dollar as the country's transitional currency on 24 January 2000.

President Wahid signed a memorandum of understanding with UNTAET on 29 February, to allow the resumption of cross-border trade and transport between East Timor and Indonesia.

In December 2000, UN prosecutors began issuing indictments for crimes against humanity against those responsible for the violence that had accompanied the referendum; the first trials began soon after.

José Xanana Gusmão resigned as president of the ETNC on 28 March 2001 and was replaced by Manuel Carrascalão.

### Political System

In October 2000 a 36-member transitional legislative body, the East Timor National Council, was established. It was replaced by a Constituent Assembly which was elected on 30 August 2001.

East Timor is divided into 13 administrative districts.

Transitional Administrator, Sergio Vieira de Mello (Brazil)
Deputy Transitional Administrators, Jean-Christian Cady (France) (*Governance and Public Administration*); Akira Takahashi (Japan) (*Humanitarian Assistance and Emergency Rehabilitation*)

British Representation Office
PO Box 194, the Post Office, Dili
Tel: (00 61) 408 101 991; e-mail: dili.fco@gtnet.gov.uk

## ECONOMY

The main commercially grown crops include coffee, coconuts, cloves and cocoa. Rice, maize and candlenuts are also widely cultivated. There is some commercial forestry.

The main exports are coffee, copra, rubber, wax and sandalwood.

## COMMUNICATIONS

There is only one major road, which links the main townships along the northern coast to the east of Dili.

---

## ECUADOR
*República del Ecuador*

---

Area – 109,484 sq. miles (283,561 sq. km). Neighbours: Colombia (north), Peru (east and south)
Population – 12,409,000 (1997 UN estimate), descendants of the Spanish, Amerindians, and mestizos. Spanish is the principal language but Quechua is also a recognised language and is spoken by most Indians
Capital – Quito (population, 1,573,458, 1998 estimate)
Major Cities – Cuenca (270,353); ΨGuayaquil (2,070,040), the chief port (1998 UN estimates)
Currency – Currency is that of the USA
National Anthem - Salve, oh patria, mil veces, oh patria (Hail, oh fatherland, a thousand times, oh fatherland)
National Day – 10 August (Independence Day)
National Flag – Three horizontal bands, yellow, blue and red (the yellow band twice the width of the others); emblem in centre
Life Expectancy (years) – male 67.4; female 70.3
Population Growth Rate – 2.1 per cent (1999)
Population Density – 43 per sq. km (1998)
Urban Population – 65.3 per cent (2000 estimate)
Military Expenditure – 2.9 per cent of GDP (1999)
Military Personnel – 57,500: Army 50,000, Navy 4,500, Air Force 3,000, Paramilitaries 270
Conscription Duration – 12 months (selective)

Ecuador is an equatorial state of South America. It extends across the Western Andes, the highest peaks being Chimborazo (20,408 ft) and Ilinza (17,405 ft) in the Western Cordillera; and Cotopaxi (19,612 ft) and Cayambe (19,160 ft) in the Eastern Cordillera. Ecuador is watered by the Upper Amazon, and by the rivers Guayas, Mira, Santiago, Chone and Esmeraldas on the Pacific coast. There are extensive forests.

## HISTORY AND POLITICS

The former kingdom of Quito was conquered by the Incas of Peru in the 15th century. Early in the 16th century

Pizarro's conquests led to the inclusion of the present territory of Ecuador in the Spanish viceroyalty of Quito. Independence was achieved in a revolutionary war which culminated in the battle of Mount Pichincha (1822).

After seven years of military rule, Ecuador returned to democracy in 1979. In the July 1996 elections the ruling Social Christian Party (PSC) won a majority of seats. Abdala Bucaram was elected president in July 1996, and appointed a coalition government. Bucaram was ousted by the legislature on the grounds of insanity and replaced firstly by Vice-President Arteaga and then by the Speaker of the National Congress Fabián Alarcón. In the May 1998 election the Popular Democracy Party (DP) replaced the PSC as the largest party in the National Congress. The presidential elections in July 1998 were won by Jamil Mahaud, the former Mayor of Quito, who gained 51 per cent of the vote.

A series of strikes and protests caused disruption throughout July 1999 and led to mass demonstrations calling for the removal of the president. Proposed tax increases led to another wave of protest in November, which again called for the removal of the president. On 18 January 2000, Quito and most provincial capitals were occupied by thousands of Indians. President Mahaud was deposed in a coup by a military junta on 21 January 2000, which was dissolved by the military just five hours after taking office and Vice-President Noboa was elevated to the presidency.

A tax reform bill to reduce the budget deficit, which would have increased value added tax and fuel costs, provoked widespread demonstrations and strikes by an alliance of indigenous farmers and public sector workers and students in January 2001. The government and the protestors reached a compromise agreement on 7 February, but on 8 May the National Congress refused to pass the bill.

### Foreign Relations

The border with Peru was demarcated by a 1942 treaty that was partly revoked by Ecuador in 1960 in relation to a disputed 50-mile stretch. An inconclusive four-week border war was fought with Peru in February 1995 until a cease-fire was signed on 1 March 1995. A 54-mile demilitarised zone was agreed in July 1995. An agreement was signed on 26 October 1998 by the presidents of the two countries formally ending the territorial dispute after mediation by Argentina, Brazil, Chile and the USA.

### Political System

The 1998 constitution provides for an elected president and vice-president who serve for a single four-year term. There is a unicameral National Congress which meets for two months a year and has 121 members, 20 of whom are elected on a national basis and 101 on a provincial basis, all for four-year terms. Voting is compulsory for all literate and voluntary for all illiterate citizens over the age of 18. The republic is divided into 21 provinces.

### Head of State

*President*, Gustavo Noboa Bejarano, *sworn in* 22 January 2000
*Vice-President*, Pedro Pinto Rubianes

### Cabinet *as at July 2001*

*Agriculture and Livestock*, vacant
*Education*, Roberto Hanze Salem
*Energy and Mines*, Pablo Terán
*Finance and Economy*, Jorge Gallardo
*Foreign Relations*, Heinz Moeller
*Foreign Trade, Industry, Fisheries*, Richard Moss
*Interior*, Juan Manrique Martínez
*Labour and Human Resources*, Martin Insua Chang
*National Defence*, Adm. Hugo Unda
*Public Health*, Fernando Bustamante Riofrio
*Public Works*, José Machiavello Almeida
*Secretary-General of the Administration*, Marcelo Santos
*Social Welfare*, Raúl Patino Aroca
*Tourism and Environment*, María Lourdes Luque de Jaramillo Vázquez
*Urban Development and Housing*, Nelson Murgueytio Penaherrera

### Embassy of Ecuador

Flat 3B, 3 Hans Crescent, London SW1X 0LS
Tel: 020-7584 1367/2648/8084
*Ambassador Extraordinary and Plenipotentiary*, HE Osvaldo Ramírez-Landázuri, apptd 1998

### British Embassy

Citiplaza Building, Av. Naciones Unidas y República de El Salvador, PO Box 17-17-830, Quito
Tel: (00 593) (2) 970 800/1
E-mail: britemcom@impsat.net.ec
*Ambassador Extraordinary and Plenipotentiary*, HE Ian Gerken, LVO, apptd 2000
British Consular Offices – Cuenca, Galápagos and Guayaquil

British Council Director, John Knagg, OBE, Av. Amazonas 1646 y La Niña, Casilla 17-07-8829, Quito; e-mail: info@britishcouncil.org.ec

## ECONOMY

Agriculture is the most important sector of the economy. The main products for export are fish, bananas, which provide a third of agricultural exports, cocoa and coffee. Other important crops are sugar, soya, rice, cotton, African palm, vegetables, fruit and timber. The main imports are manufactured goods and machinery.

The economy was transformed by the discovery in 1972 of major oil fields in the Oriente area.

The US dollar was adopted in 1999 in order to stabilise the economy.

In 1999 there was a trade surplus of US$1,665 million and a current account surplus of US$955 million. Imports totalled US$3,017 million and exports US$4,451 million.
GNP – US$16,841 million (1999); US$1,310 per capita (1999)
GDP – US$19,673 million (1997); US$1,620 per capita (1998)
Annual Average Growth of GDP – 2.0 per cent (1996)
Inflation Rate – 52.2 per cent (1999)
Unemployment – 8.4 per cent (1998)
Total External Debt – US$15,140 million (1998)

| *Trade with UK* | 1999 | 2000 |
|---|---|---|
| Imports from UK | £25,929,000 | £26,619,000 |
| Exports to UK | 29,644,000 | 30,599,000 |

## COMMUNICATIONS

There are 23,256 km of permanent roads and 5,044 km of roads which are only open during the dry season. Ten commercial airlines operate international flights and there are internal services between all important towns. Two daily newspapers are published at Quito and four at Guayaquil.

## EDUCATION

Elementary education is free and compulsory. There are ten universities (three at Quito, three at Guayaquil, and one each at Cuenca, Machala, Loja and Portoviejo), polytechnic schools at Quito and Guayaquil and eight technical colleges in other provincial capitals.

ILLITERACY RATE – 8.1 per cent
ENROLMENT (percentage of age group) – primary 97 per cent (1996); tertiary 20.0 per cent (1990)

## GALÁPAGOS ISLANDS

The Galápagos (Giant Tortoise) Islands, forming the province of the Archipelago de Colón, were annexed by Ecuador in 1832. The archipelago lies in the Pacific, about 500 miles from the mainland. There are 12 large and several hundred smaller islands with a total area of about 3,000 sq. miles and an estimated population (1982) of 6,119. The capital is Puerto Baquerizo Moreno, on San Cristóbal Island. Although the archipelago lies on the equator, the temperature of the surrounding water is well below equatorial average owing to the Humboldt current. The province consists for the most part of National Park Territory, where unique marine birds, iguanas, and the giant tortoises are conserved. There is some local subsistence farming; the main industry, apart from tourism, is tuna and lobster fishing.

---

# EGYPT

*Al-Jumhūriyya al-Misriyya al-'Arabiyya*

---

AREA – 386,662 sq. miles (1,001,449 sq. km). Neighbours: Sudan (south), Libya (west), Gaza Strip and Israel (east)
POPULATION – 67,974,000 (1999 estimate). The largest, or 'Egyptian' element, is a Hamito-Semite race. A second element is the *Bedouin*, or nomadic Arabs of the Western and Eastern deserts, who are now mainly semi-sedentary tent-dwellers. The third element is the *Nubian* of the Nile Valley of mixed Arab and Negro blood. Over 90 per cent of the population are Muslims of the Sunni denomination, and most of the rest are Coptic Christians. Arabic is the official language
CAPITAL – Cairo (Al-Qāhirah) (population, 6,800,992, 1996 estimate) stands on the Nile about 14 miles from the head of the delta
MAJOR CITIES – ΨAlexandria (Al-Iskandarīya) (3,328,196, 1997 estimate), founded 332 BC by Alexander the Great, was the capital for over 1,000 years; Asyūt (2,802,185); Faiyūm (1,989,881); Ismailia (715,009); ΨPort Said (Būr Sa'īd) (469,533); ΨSuez (As-Suways) (417,610)
CURRENCY – Egyptian pound (£E) of 100 piastres or 1,000 millièmes
NATIONAL ANTHEM - Biladi (My homeland)
NATIONAL DAY – 23 July (Anniversary of Revolution in 1952)
NATIONAL FLAG – Horizontal bands of red, white and black, with an eagle in the centre of the white band
LIFE EXPECTANCY (years) – male 64.2; female 65.8
POPULATION GROWTH RATE – 2.0 per cent (1999)
POPULATION DENSITY – 66 per sq. km (1998)
URBAN POPULATION – 45.2 per cent (2000 estimate)
ILLITERACY RATE – 44.7 per cent (2000)
ENROLMENT (percentage of age group) – primary 93 per cent (1996); secondary 67 per cent (1996); tertiary 20.2 per cent (1996)

Egypt comprises Egypt proper, the peninsula of Sinai and a number of islands in the Gulf of Suez and Red Sea, of which the principal are Jubal, Shadwan, Gafatin and Zeberged (or St John's Island).

The country is mainly flat but there are mountainous areas in the south-west, along the Red Sea coast and in the south of the Sinai peninsula; the highest peak is Mt Catherina (8,668 ft). Most of the land is desert and the Nile valley and delta were the only fertile areas until the opening of the Aswan Dam allowed areas of desert to be reclaimed. West of the Nile Valley is the Western Desert, containing some depressions whose springs irrigate oases. The Eastern Desert between the Nile and the mountains along the Red Sea coast is mostly plateaux dissected by wadis (dry water-courses).

## HISTORY AND POLITICS

The unification of the kingdoms of Lower and Upper Egypt under the Pharaohs *c.*3100 BC marked the establishment of the Egyptian state, with Memphis as its capital. Egypt was ruled for nearly 2,800 years by a succession of 31 Pharaonic dynasties which built the pyramids at Gizeh. A period of Hellenic rule began in 332 BC, followed by a period of rule by Rome (30 BC to AD 324) and then by the Byzantine Empire. In AD 640 Egypt was subjugated by Arab Muslim invaders. In 1517 the country was incorporated in the Ottoman Empire, under which it remained until the early 19th century. A British Protectorate over Egypt lasted from 1914 to 1922, when Sultan Ahmed Fuad was proclaimed King of Egypt. In 1953 the monarchy was deposed and Egypt became a republic.

In 1956 President Nasser seized the assets of the Suez Canal Company. Egyptian occupation of the Canal Zone was used as a pretext for military action by Britain and France in support of their Suez Canal Company interests. A cease-fire and Anglo-French withdrawal were negotiated by the UN.

The Israeli invasion of 1956 overran the Sinai peninsula but six months later Israel withdrew. However, mounting tension culminated in a second invasion of Sinai (the Six Day War in June 1967) and occupation of the peninsula by Israel. Sinai was returned to Egypt in 1982 under the treaty of 1979 which resulted from the Camp David talks and formally terminated a 31-year-old state of war between the two countries.

President Mubarak was nominated by the legislature to run unopposed for a fourth six-year term in June 1999, and was endorsed by a national referendum held on 26 September..

A general election was held in three rounds between 18 October and 14 November 2000. The ruling National Democratic Party (NDP) won 388 of the 444 elective seats, which included some 218 independent candidates who joined the party immediately after the election.

### INSURGENCY

Militant Islamist fundamentalists re-emerged in 1992, carrying out attacks on tourists, Coptic Christians, government ministers, civil servants and the security forces. On 27 March 1999, the largest fundamentalist organisation, Gamaat-i-Islamiya, announced that it had given up its violent campaign to overthrow the government.

### POLITICAL SYSTEM

The constitution of 1971 provides for an executive president who appoints the Council of Ministers and determines government policy. The president is elected by the legislature every six years. The legislature is the People's Assembly which has 454 members, 444 of whom are elected, the remaining ten nominated by the president. The Shura Council or Consultative Assembly (210 members) has an advisory role. A state of emergency, which was first introduced following the assassination of President Sadat in 1981, remains in force.

### HEAD OF STATE

*President*, Mohammed Hosni Mubarak, *elected* 1981, *re-elected* 1987, 1993, 2 June 1999, *confirmed by national referendum* 26 September 1999

### COUNCIL OF MINISTERS *as at July 2001*

*Prime Minister*, Atef Mohammad Obeid

*Deputy PM, Agriculture and Land Reclamation*, Yousef Amin Wali
*Communications and Information Technology*, Ahmed Muhammad Nazif
*Culture*, Farouk Hosni Abdel Aziz
*Defence and Military Production*, Field Marshal Mohammad Hussein Tantawi
*Economy and Foreign Trade*, Yussef Boutros Ghali
*Education*, Hussein Kamel Bahaeddin
*Electricity and Energy*, Ali Fahmi Ibrahim al-Sa'idi
*Finance*, Mohammed Midhat Hasanayn
*Foreign Affairs*, Ahmed Maher
*Health and Population*, Ismail Awadallah Sallam
*Higher Education and Scientific Research*, Mufid Shehab
*Information*, Muhammad Safwat El-Sherif
*Interior*, Maj.-Gen. Habib al-Adli
*Justice*, Farouk Seif El-Nasr
*Labour and Emigration*, Ahmed al-Amawi
*Ministers of State*, Mahmoud Zaki Abu Amer *(Administrative Development)*; Nadia Makram Obeid *(Environment)*; Gen. Sayyid Abduh Mustafa Mash'al *(Military Production)*; Kamal Mohammed Al Shazli *(People's National Assembly and Consultative Council Affairs)*; Mustafa Abdel Qader *(Rural Development)*
*Oil and Mineral Resources*, Amin Sameh Fahmi
*Planning and International Co-operation*, Ahmed Mahrus al-Darsh
*Public Enterprise*, Mukhtar Khattab
*Public Works and Irrigation*, Mahmoud Abdul Halim Abu Zaid
*Reconstruction, New Urban Zones and Environment*, Mohammed Ibrahim Soliman
*Religious Affairs and Wakfs (Endowments)*, Mahmoud Hamdi Zakzouk
*Secretary-General to the Council of Ministers*, Ahmed Hassan Abu Taleb
*Social Insurance and Social Affairs*, Amina Hamzah al-Jundi
*Supply and Internal Trade*, Hassan Ali Khedr
*Technological Development and Industry*, Mustafa al-Rifai
*Tourism*, Mamdouh Ahmed Al-Beltagui
*Transport*, Ibrahim al-Dumeiri
*Youth*, Ali al-Din Hilal al-Dasuqi

EMBASSY OF THE ARAB REPUBLIC OF EGYPT
26 South Street, London W1K 1DW
Tel: 020-7499 2401/3304
*Ambassador Extraordinary and Plenipotentiary*, HE Abdel El-Gazzar, apptd 1997
*Consul-General*, M. Ebeid
*Minister Plenipotentiary and Deputy Chief of Mission*, E. Elessawi
*Defence Attaché*, Col. M. Hegab
Minister Plenipotentiary (*Commercial*), M. Zidan

BRITISH EMBASSY
Ahmed Ragheb Street, Garden City, Cairo
Tel: (00 20) (2) 794 0852
E-mail: information@cairo.mail.fco.gov.uk
*Ambassador Extraordinary and Plenipotentiary*, HE Graham Boyce, KCMG, apptd 1999
*Counsellor and Deputy Head of Mission*, G. D. Adams
*Defence and Military Attaché*, Col. P. Dennison, OBE
*First Secretaries*, P. Byrde (*Consul*); D. G. Reader (*Commercial*)
BRITISH CONSULAR OFFICES – *Consulate-General*, Alexandria; *Consulates*, Luxor, Suez

BRITISH COUNCIL DIRECTOR, David Marler OBE (*Cultural Counsellor*), 192 Sharia el Nil, Agouza, Cairo; e-mail: british.council@eg.britishcouncil.org. Regional directors in Alexandria and Heliopolis

## DEFENCE

The Army has 3,960 main battle tanks, 750 armoured infantry fighting vehicles and 4,230 armoured personnel carriers. The Navy has one destroyer, ten frigates, four submarines, 40 patrol and coastal vessels and 24 armed helicopters at six bases. The Air Force has 580 combat aircraft and 129 armed helicopters.
MILITARY EXPENDITURE – 3.4 per cent of GDP (1999)
MILITARY PERSONNEL – 448,500: Army 320,000, Navy 18,500, Air Force 30,000, Air Defence Command 80,000, Paramilitaries 230,000
CONSCRIPTION DURATION – 18 months to three years (selective)

## ECONOMY

Despite increasing industrialisation, agriculture remains the most important economic activity, employing 35 per cent of the labour force and producing 17 per cent of GDP in 1998. Egypt is still a net importer of foodstuffs, especially grain, and a food security programme has been set up with the aim of achieving self-sufficiency. The main cash crop is cotton, of which Egypt is one of the world's main producers. Other important crops are maize, rice, sugar cane, wheat and potatoes. Other fruits and vegetables are also grown.

With its considerable reserves of petroleum and natural gas, and the hydroelectric power produced by the Aswan and High Dams, Egypt is self-sufficient in energy. The major manufacturing industries are food processing, motor cars, electrical goods, steel, chemical products, yarns and textiles. In 1998 3.5 million foreign tourists visited Egypt, generating US$4,063 million in revenue.

The government transferred control over exchange rates to the central bank in January 2001.

In 1999 the government had a trade deficit of US$9,928 million and a current account deficit of US$1,635 million.
GNP – US$86,544 million (1999); US$1,400 per capita (1999)
GDP – US$75,635 million (1997); US$1,211 per capita (1998)
ANNUAL AVERAGE GROWTH OF GDP – 6.5 per cent (1999)
INFLATION RATE – 3.1 per cent (1999)
UNEMPLOYMENT – 8.3 per cent (1998)
TOTAL EXTERNAL DEBT – US$31,964 million (1998)

### TRADE

The main imports are wheat, maize, chemicals and motor vehicles and parts. The main exports are crude petroleum, cotton, cotton yarn, oranges, rice and cotton textiles.

In 1999 Egypt's imports totalled US$16,022 million and exports US$3,559 million.

| *Trade with UK* | 1999 | 2000 |
|---|---|---|
| Imports from UK | £540,790,000 | £499,990,000 |
| Exports to UK | 266,940,000 | 426,511,000 |

## COMMUNICATIONS

There are international airports at Cairo and Luxor. The road and rail networks link the Nile valley and delta with the main development areas east and west of the river. The Suez Canal was reopened in 1975 and a two-stage development project begun to widen and deepen the canal to allow the passage of larger shipping and to permit two-way traffic. Port Said and Suez have been reconstructed and the port of Alexandria is being improved. There are two nationwide terrestrial television channels and five regional channels and 11 satellite channels.

## EL SALVADOR
*República de El Salvador*

AREA – 8,124 sq. miles (21,041 sq. km). Neighbours: Guatemala (north-west), Honduras (north-east and east)
POPULATION – 6,189,000 (1997 UN estimate): 94 per cent mestizo, 5 per cent Amerindian, 1 per cent European. The language is Spanish
CAPITAL – San Salvador (population, 1,200,000, 1998)
MAJOR CITIES – San Miguel (127,696); Santa Ana (139,389)
CURRENCY –US dollar (US$) of 100 cents/El Salvador colón (₡) of 100 centavos
NATIONAL ANTHEM – Saludemos La Patria Orgullosos (Let us proudly hail the Fatherland)
NATIONAL DAY – 15 September
NATIONAL FLAG – Three horizontal bands, sky blue, white, sky blue; coat of arms on white band
LIFE EXPECTANCY (years) – male 66.9; female 73.0
POPULATION GROWTH RATE – 2.1 per cent (1999)
POPULATION DENSITY – 287 per sq. km (1998)
URBAN POPULATION – 46.6 per cent (2000 estimate)
MILITARY EXPENDITURE – 1.1 per cent of GDP (1999)
MILITARY PERSONNEL – 16,800: Army 15,000, Navy 700, Air Force 1,100; Paramilitaries 12,000
CONSCRIPTION DURATION – 12 months (selective)

El Salvador extends along the Pacific coast of Central America for 160 miles. The surface of the country is very mountainous, many of the peaks being extinct volcanoes. Much of the interior has an average altitude of 2,000 feet. The climate varies from tropical to temperate. There is a wet season from May to October, and a dry season from November to April. Earthquakes are frequent, the most recent being in October 1986.

### HISTORY AND POLITICS

El Salvador was conquered in 1526 by Pedro de Alvarado, and formed part of the Spanish viceroyalty of Guatemala until 1821. It is divided into 14 Departments.

Decades of military rule ended in October 1979; a Constituent Assembly was elected in 1982. Subsequent presidential and parliamentary elections were boycotted by the FMLN (Farabundo Martí National Liberation Front) guerrilla movement. Conflict between the guerrillas and the government continued throughout the 1980s until negotiations culminated in a peace plan signed in January 1992. In December 1992 the FMLN disarmed and became a political party.

On 7 March 1999, Francisco Flores of the ruling right-wing National Republican Alliance (ARENA) party won the presidential election; he took office on 1 June. ARENA won 29 of the Legislative Assembly's 84 seats and formed a government with other right-wing parties in legislative elections on 12 March 2000; the FMLN became the largest party, winning 31 seats.

#### HEAD OF STATE

*President*, Francisco Flores Pérez, *elected* 7 March 1999, *took office* 1 June 1999
*Vice-President*, *Minister of the Presidency*, Carlos Quintanilla Schmidt
*Secretary of the Presidency*, Juan José Daboub

#### COUNCIL OF STATE *as at July 2001*

*Agriculture and Livestock*, Salvador Urrutia Loucel
*Defence*, Gen. Juan Antonio Martínez Varela
*Director of the Salvadorean Institute of Tourism*, Arturo Morales
*Economy*, Miguel Lacayo
*Education*, Ana Evelyn Jacir de Lovo
*Environment and Natural Resources*, Ana María Majano Guerrero
*Foreign Affairs*, María Eugenia Brizuela de Avila
*Interior*, Mario Acosta Oertel
*Justice and Public Security*, Francisco Bertrand Galindo
*Labour and Social Security*, Jorge Nieto Menéndez
*Public Health*, José López Beltrán
*Public Works*, José Angel Quiroz
*Treasury*, José Luis Trigueros

#### EMBASSY OF EL SALVADOR

Mayfair House, 39 Great Portland Street, London W1W 7JZ
Tel: 020-7436 8282
*Ambassador Extraordinary and Plenipotentiary*, HE Mauricio Castro-Aragón, apptd 1999

#### BRITISH EMBASSY

PO Box 1591, San Salvador
Tel: (00 503) 263 6520/7/9
E-mail: britemb@sal.gbm.net
*Ambassador Extraordinary and Plenipotentiary*, HE Patrick Morgan, apptd 1999

### ECONOMY

The principal agricultural products are coffee, cotton, sugar cane, maize, shrimps and balsam. In the lower altitudes towards the east, sisal is produced and used in the manufacture of coffee and cereal bags. Existing factories make textiles, clothing, constructional steel, furniture, cement and household items.

The US dollar was adopted on 1 January 2001; the colón remained in use for a transitional period.

Nearly one million people were made homelesss in two major earthquakes in January and February 2001.

GNP – US$11,806 million (1999); US$1,900 per capita (1999)
GDP – US$11,435 million (1997); US$1,941 per capita (1998)
ANNUAL AVERAGE GROWTH OF GDP – 2.5 per cent (1998)
INFLATION RATE – 0.5 per cent (1999)
UNEMPLOYMENT – 8.0 per cent (1997)
TOTAL EXTERNAL DEBT – US$3,633 million (1998)

#### TRADE

Chief exports are coffee, cotton, sugar, shrimps, sisal, balsam, meat, towels, hides and skins. The chief imports are chemicals, petroleum, manufactured goods, industrial and electronic machinery, pharmaceutical goods, vehicles and consumer goods.

In 1998 there was a trade deficit of US$1,267 million and a current account deficit of US$84 million. In 1999 imports totalled US$3,130 million and exports US$1,164 million.

| *Trade with UK* | 1999 | 2000 |
|---|---|---|
| Imports from UK | £12,727,000 | £16,258,000 |
| Exports to UK | 12,044,000 | 14,581,000 |

### COMMUNICATIONS

The principal ports are Cutuco, La Unión and Acajutla. There are more than 12,000 km of roads and 600 km of railways. The Pan-American Highway from the Guatemalan frontier passes through San Salvador and Santa Ana, and continues to the Honduran frontier. Comalapa international airport has daily flights to other Central American capitals, Mexico and the USA. There are 100 broadcasting stations and nine television stations. Five daily newspapers are published in San Salvador.

## EDUCATION

Primary education is free and compulsory. There are 38 universities.

ILLITERACY RATE – 21.3 per cent

ENROLMENT (percentage of age group) – primary 78 per cent (1996); secondary 22 per cent (1996); tertiary 17.8 per cent (1996)

# EQUATORIAL GUINEA

*República de Guinea Ecuatorial*

AREA – 10,831 sq. miles (28,051 sq. km). Neighbours: Cameroon (north), Gabon (east and south)

POPULATION – 443,000 (1997 UN estimate). The official languages are Spanish and French; Bubi, Fang, Ibo and pidgin English are also spoken

CAPITAL – ΨMalabo on the island of Bioko (population, 30,418, 1983 estimate)

MAJOR TOWN – ΨBata is the principal town and port of Rio Muni

CURRENCY – Franc CFA of 100 centimes

NATIONAL ANTHEM - Himno Nacional

NATIONAL DAY – 12 October

NATIONAL FLAG – Three horizontal bands, green over white over red; blue triangle next staff; coat of arms in centre of white band

LIFE EXPECTANCY (years) – male 51.4; female 55.4

POPULATION GROWTH RATE – 2.6 per cent (1999)

POPULATION DENSITY – 15 per sq. km (1998)

URBAN POPULATION – 48.2 per cent (2000 estimate)

MILITARY EXPENDITURE – 1.8 per cent of GDP (1999)

MILITARY PERSONNEL – 1,320: Army 1,100, Navy 120, Air Force 100

ILLITERACY RATE – 16.8 per cent

Equatorial Guinea consists of the island of Bioko, in the Bight of Biafra about 20 miles from the west coast of Africa, Annonbón Island in the Gulf of Guinea, the Corisco Islands (Corisco, Elobey Grande and Elobey Chico), and Rio Muni, a mainland area between Cameroon and Gabon.

## HISTORY AND POLITICS

Formerly colonies of Spain, the territories now forming Equatorial Guinea were constituted as two provinces of Metropolitan Spain in 1959, became autonomous in 1963 and fully independent in 1968.

In 1979 President Macias was deposed by a revolutionary military council headed by Col. Obiang Nguema. Constitutional amendments in 1982 provided for legislative elections, which were held in 1983 and 1988, but all candidates were chosen by the president.

A multiparty political system under a new constitution was approved by a referendum in 1991 and ten opposition parties have been legalised, operating alongside the ruling Equatorial Guinea Democratic Party (PDGE). A National Pact was agreed and signed in March 1993 but legislative elections in November, which were won by the PDGE, were boycotted by most of the electorate and opposition parties. In the February 1996 election, the president claimed to have won more than 99 per cent of the vote. Most opposition parties boycotted the ballot. In June 1997 the Progress Party, the largest opposition party, was banned by the government, and in February 1998 opposition party coalitions were deemed illegal. The PDGE won 75 of the 80 seats in the National Assembly elections on 7 March 1999 amid allegations of electoral malpractice. Prime Minister Angel Serafín Seriche Dougan resigned on 23 February 2001 due to his growing unpopularity. He was replaced by Cándido Muatetema Rivas on 26 February.

### HEAD OF STATE

*President of the Supreme Military Council and Minister of Defence*, Brig.-Gen. Teodoro Obiang Nguema Mbasogo, *took office* August 1979, *re-elected* June 1989, 25 February 1996

### MINISTERS *as at July 2001*

*Prime Minister*, Cándido Muatetema Rivas

*Deputy PM, Civil Service and Administrative Reforms*, Ignacio Milam Tang

*Minister of State, Agriculture, Fisheries and Animal Husbandry*, Gregorio Boho Camo

*Minister of State, Education and Science, Government Spokesman*, Antonio Fernando Nve Ngu

*Minister of State, Forestry, Fisheries and Environment*, Teodoro Nguema Obiang

*Minister of State, Health and Social Welfare*, Marcelino Nguema Onguene

*Minister of State, Information, Tourism and Culture*, Lucas Nguema Esono

*Minister of State, Labour and Social Security*, Ricardo Mangue Obama Nfube

*Minister of State, Presidency*, Alejandro Evuna Owono Asangono

*Minister of State, Relations with Assemblies and Legal Matters*, vacant

*Minister of State, Secretary-General of the Government*, Francisco Pascual Eyegue Obama

*Minister of State, Transport and Communications*, Marcelino Oyono Ntutumu

*Economic Affairs and Finance*, Baltasar Engonga Edjo

*Foreign Affairs, International Co-operation, Francophone Affairs*, Santiago Nsobeya Efuman

*Industry, Commerce, Small Enterprises*, Constantino Ekong Nsue

*Interior and Local Corporations*, Clemente Engonga Nguema Onguene

*Justice and Religion*, Rubén Maye Nsue

*Mines and Energy*, Cristóbal Menana Ela

*Planning and Economic Development*, Fortunato Ofa Mbo

*Public Works, Housing and Urban Affairs*, Florentino Nkogo Ndong

*Social Affairs, Women's Development*, Teresa Efua Asangono

*Youth and Sports*, Juan Antonio Bibang Ntutumu

### EMBASSY OF THE REPUBLIC OF EQUATORIAL GUINEA

6 rue Alfred de Vigny, F-75008 Paris

Tel: (00 33) (1) 4766 4433

*Ambassador Extraordinary and Plenipotentiary*, vacant

BRITISH AMBASSADOR, HE Peter Boon, resident at Yaoundé, Cameroon

## ECONOMY

The chief products are cocoa, coffee and wood. Production has declined and except for cocoa there is little commercial agriculture. The economy is heavily dependent on outside aid, principally from Spain. Oil and gas production is increasing. Equatorial Guinea entered the 'franc zone' in 1985.

In 1996, there was a trade surplus of US$117 million and a current account deficit of US$344 million. In 1998 imports totalled US$32 million and exports US$423 million.

GNP – US$516 million (1999); US$1,170 per capita (1999)

GDP – US$147 million (1997); US$377 per capita (1998)

ANNUAL AVERAGE GROWTH OF GDP – 5.0 per cent (1996)

INFLATION RATE – 7.8 per cent (1998)

TOTAL EXTERNAL DEBT – US$306 million (1998)

| *Trade with UK* | 1999 | 2000 |
|---|---|---|
| Imports from UK | £6,386,000 | £28,075,000 |
| Exports to UK | 781,000 | 1,074,000 |

## ERITREA

AREA – 45,406 sq. miles (117,600 sq. km). Neighbours: Sudan (north and north-west), Ethiopia (south and south-west), Djibouti (south-east)
POPULATION – 3,991,000 (1997 UN estimate), roughly half Coptic Christian (mainly highlanders) and half Muslim (mainly lowlanders). Arabic and Tigrinya are official languages, but English and Italian are widely spoken. There are nine indigenous language groups: Afar; Bilen; Hadareb; Kunama; Nara; Rashida; Saho; Tigre; Tigrinya
CAPITAL – Asmara (population, 358,100, 1990 estimate)
MAJOR TOWNS – ΨAssab; ΨMassawa
CURRENCY – Nakfa
NATIONAL DAY – 24 May (Independence Day)
NATIONAL FLAG – Divided into three triangles; the one based on the hoist is red and bears a gold olive wreath; the upper triangle is green and the lower one light blue
LIFE EXPECTANCY (years) – male 46.6; female 46.5
POPULATION GROWTH RATE – 2.8 per cent (1999)
POPULATION DENSITY – 30 per sq. km (1998)
URBAN POPULATION – 18.7 per cent (2000 estimate)
ENROLMENT (percentage of age group) – primary 30 per cent (1996); secondary 16 per cent (1996); tertiary 1 per cent (1997)

### HISTORY AND POLITICS

Eritrea was colonised by Italy in the late 19th century and was the base for the 1936 Italian invasion of Abyssinia (Ethiopia). After the Italian defeat in East Africa in 1941 by British and Commonwealth forces, Eritrea became a British protectorate. This lasted until 15 September 1952 when Eritrea was federated with Ethiopia. The Ethiopian Emperor Haile Selassie incorporated Eritrea as a province of Ethiopia in 1962. An armed campaign for independence began in the 1970s, first against Emperor Haile Selassie's forces and from 1974 against the Mengistu regime.

In 1991 the Mengistu government was overthrown by the Eritrean People's Liberation Front (EPLF) and the Ethiopian People's Revolutionary Democratic Front (EPRDF). The new EPRDF-led government in Ethiopia agreed to an Eritrean referendum on independence which was held in April 1993 and recorded a 99 per cent vote in favour. Independence was declared on 24 May 1993.

#### FOREIGN RELATIONS

Eritrea had claimed the Hanish and Mohabaka Islands in the Red Sea, which they seized from Yemen in December 1995; however, on 9 October 1998, the International Court of Justice ruled that the Hanish Islands belonged to Yemen and Eritrea formally handed them over to Yemen on 1 November 1998. The land border with Djibouti is also disputed.

In May 1998 sporadic fighting flared up on the border with Ethiopia, with both countries accusing the other of sending troops across the border. Proposals for a resolution of the conflict drawn up by the Organisation for African Unity (OAU) in November 1998, which called on Eritrea to hand back the disputed town of Badme pending adjudication, were rejected by Eritrea. Full-scale fighting broke out on 6 February 1999 and Ethiopia had recaptured the town by 28 February. Eritrea accepted the OAU's proposals on 9 March, but fighting continued. A further proposal to end the fighting was brokered by the OAU in July 1999, which envisaged a return to the original borders and was provisionally accepted by both sides, but Ethiopia later rejected some of the provisions. Fighting resumed on 23 February 2000. On 12 May, Ethiopia launched a full-scale invasion, which ended in early June after Ethiopian forces had captured much of Eritrea's western lowlands. An interim peace plan was signed by both countries on 18 June, which envisaged the international demarcation of the border and, in the interim period, a UN force to monitor the border in a 25 km-wide buffer zone in Eritrean territory.

UN observers began to deploy on 15 September 2000. Direct talks between Eritrea and Ethiopia opened on 23 October and on 12 December a comprehensive peace agreement was signed in Algeria; UN peacekeeping troops moved into the buffer zone in April 2001 and on 21 May Eritrea and Ethiopia agreed to set up regional military commissions to solve local security issues.

#### POLITICAL SYSTEM

Under the 1997 constitution, the head of state is the president, elected for a five-year term by the National Assembly, of which he is chair. The 150-member unicameral legislature (the *Hagerawi Baito*) is directly elected for four years. The president is head of government and presides over a State Council, which includes ten provincial governors.

#### HEAD OF STATE

*President, Chairman of the National Assembly*, Issaias Afewerki, *elected by National Assembly* 22 May 1993
*Vice-President*, Ahmed Sherifo Mahmud

#### STATE COUNCIL *as at July 2001*

*Chairman*, The President
*Agriculture*, Arefaine Berhe
*Defence*, Gen. Sehat Efrem
*Education*, Osman Saleh
*Energy and Mines*, Tesfai Gebresselassie
*Eritrean Relief, Refugee Commission*, Hiwot Zemichael
*Finance and Development*, Berhane Abrehe
*Fisheries*, Ahmed Hajj Ali
*Foreign Affairs*, Ali Said Abdellah
*Health*, Saleh Meki
*Industry and Trade*, Gergish Teklemikael
*Information*, vacant
*Justice*, Fawzia Hashim
*Labour and Human Welfare*, Askalu Menkerios
*Land, Water and Environment*, Weldenkiel Ghebremariam
*Local Government*, vacant
*Public Works*, Abraha Asfaha
*Tourism*, vacant
*Transport (acting)*, Stifanos Aferwerki

#### EMBASSY OF THE STATE OF ERITREA

96 White Lion Street, London N1 9PF
Tel: 020-7713 0096.
*Ambassador Extraordinary and Plenipotentiary*, HE Ghirmai Ghebremariam, apptd 2000

BRITISH AMBASSADOR, HE Gordon Wetherell, resident at Addis Ababa, Ethiopia

#### BRITISH EMBASSY

Emperor Yohannes Avenue, House no 24, PO Box 5584, Asmara
Tel: (00 291) (1) 120145
E-mail: alembca@gemel.com.er
*Honorary Consul*, T. Thodensen

BRITISH COUNCIL DIRECTOR, Dr Negusse Araya, PO Box 997, Asmara; e-mail: britcoun@eol.com.er

## DEFENCE

The Navy has ten patrol and coastal combatants. The Air Force has 17 combat aircraft.
MILITARY EXPENDITURE – 44.4 per cent of GDP (1999)
MILITARY PERSONNEL – 200,000: Army 200,000, Navy 1,100, Air Force 1,000
CONSCRIPTION DURATION – 16 months

## ECONOMY

Since 1991 the government has attempted to rebuild industry, agriculture and infrastructure which were devastated by the war of independence. The rebuilding programme has focused on the ports of Massawa and Assab, the roads from the ports to Ethiopia, and the railway from Massawa to Sudan via Asmara. Before 1962 Eritrea was one of the most industrialised areas of Africa and some industry remains, producing textiles and footwear. The government hopes to base the rebuilding of the economy on the return of well-educated exiles, international aid and investment, the development of tourism along the coast, and the diversification of the economy away from agriculture.
GNP – US$779 million (1999); US$200 per capita (1999)
GDP – US$593 million (1997); US$210 per capita (1998)
ANNUAL AVERAGE GROWTH OF GDP – 3.9 per cent (1996)
TOTAL EXTERNAL DEBT – US$149 million (1998)

| *Trade with UK* | 1999 | 2000 |
|---|---|---|
| Imports from UK | £5,737,000 | £4,707,000 |
| Exports to UK | 314,000 | 187,000 |

---

# ESTONIA
*The Republic of Estonia*

---

AREA – 17,413 sq. miles (45,100 sq. km). Neighbours: Russia (east), Latvia (south)
POPULATION – 1,442,000 (1998): 65 per cent Estonian, 28 per cent Russian, 2.5 per cent Ukrainian, 1.5 per cent Belarusian, 1 per cent Finnish, others 2 per cent. The majority religion is Lutheran, with Russian Orthodox and Baptist minorities. Estonian is the first language of 64.2 per cent and Russian of 28.7 per cent
CAPITAL – Tallinn (population, 415,299, 1998 estimate)
MAJOR TOWNS AND CITIES – Kohtla-Järve (70,800); Narva (80,300); Tartu (109,100)
CURRENCY – Kroon of 100 sents
NATIONAL ANTHEM – Mu Isamaa, mu onn ja rõõm (My Native Land, My Joy, Delight)
NATIONAL DAY – 24 February (Independence Day)
NATIONAL FLAG – Three horizontal stripes of blue, black, white
LIFE EXPECTANCY (years) – male 64.4; female 75.3
POPULATION GROWTH RATE – 1.2 per cent (1999)
POPULATION DENSITY – 32 per sq. km (1998)
URBAN POPULATION – 68.6 per cent (2000 estimate)
MILITARY EXPENDITURE – 1.5 per cent of GDP (1999)
MILITARY PERSONNEL – 4,800: Army 4,320, Navy 250, Air Force 140; Paramilitiaries 2,800
CONSCRIPTION DURATION – 12 months

Estonia includes 1,500 islands in the Baltic Sea and the Gulf of Riga. Forests cover roughly 20 per cent of the country, which also has many lakes. The climate is mild and maritime.

## HISTORY AND POLITICS

Estonia, a former province of the Russian Empire, declared its independence on 24 February 1918. A war of independence was fought against the German army until November 1918, and then against Soviet forces until the peace treaty of Tartu was signed in 1920. By this treaty the Soviet Union recognised Estonia's independence.

The Soviet Union annexed Estonia in 1940 under the terms of the Molotov-Ribbentrop pact with Germany. Estonia was occupied when Germany invaded the Soviet Union during the Second World War. In 1944 the Soviet Union recaptured the country from Germany and confirmed its annexation.

The Estonian Supreme Soviet in November 1989 declared the republic to be sovereign and its 1940 annexation by the Soviet Union to be illegal. In February 1990 the leading role of the Communist Party was abolished, and following multiparty elections in March 1990 a period of transition to independence was inaugurated. Independence was declared on 20 August 1991.

After legislative elections held on 7 March 1999, a centre-right coalition government of the Pro Patria Union (I), the Mõõdukad Party (M) and the Reform Party was formed.

### POLITICAL SYSTEM

Legislative power is exercised by the unicameral *Riigikogu* of 101 members elected by proportional representation every four years. The president is elected for a five-year term by the Riigikogu by a two-thirds majority or, if no candidate receives this majority after three rounds of voting, by an electoral body composed of Riigikogu members and local government officials. Executive authority is vested in a prime minister who is nominated by the president and who forms a government. Members of the government need not be members of the Riigikogu.

Estonia is divided into 46 towns and 15 districts for local administration purposes.

### HEAD OF STATE

*President*, Lennart Meri, *elected* 5 October 1992, *re-elected* 20 September 1996

### GOVERNMENT *as at July 2001*

*Prime Minister*, Mart Laar (I)
*Agriculture*, Ivari Padar (M)
*Culture*, Signe Kivi (R)
*Defence*, Jüri Luik (I)
*Economics*, Mihkel Pärnoja (M)
*Education*, Tõnis Lukas (I)
*Environment*, Heiki Kranich (R)
*Ethnic Affairs*, Katrin Saks (M)
*Finance*, Siim Kallas (R)
*Foreign Affairs*, Toomas Hendrik Ilves (M)
*Interior*, Tarmo Loodus (I)
*Justice*, Märt Rask (R)
*Regional Affairs*, Toivo Asmer (R)
*Social Affairs*, Eiki Nestor (M)
*Transport and Communications*, Toivo Jürgenson (I)

### EMBASSY OF THE REPUBLIC OF ESTONIA

16 Hyde Park Gate, London SW7 5DG
Tel: 020-7589 3428
*Ambassador Extraordinary and Plenipotentiary*, HE Raul Mälk, apptd 1996

### BRITISH EMBASSY

Wismari 6, EE-10136 Tallinn
Tel: (00 372) 667 4700
*Ambassador Extraordinary and Plenipotentiary*, HE Sarah Squire, apptd 2000
BRITISH COUNCIL DIRECTOR, Kyllike Tohver, Resource Centre, Vana Posti 7, EE-10146 Tallinn; e-mail: british.council@britishcouncil.ee

## ECONOMY

Since 1992 the government has introduced free-market reforms, privatisation and restructuring. Estonia is still dependent on Russian natural gas supplies.

Ten per cent of the workforce are engaged in agriculture, which accounts for 6 per cent of GDP , the main products being rye, oats, barley, flax, potatoes, meat, milk, butter and eggs.

Industry accounts for 34 per cent of employment and 27 per cent of GDP, concentrating on textiles, clothing and footwear, forestry, wood and paper products, and food and fish processing. Some heavy industry exists, mostly chemicals and the manufacture of power equipment.

The kroon is pegged to the euro.

GNP – US$4,906 million (1999); US$3,480 per capita (1999)

GDP – US$4,688 million (1997); US$3,645 per capita (1998)

ANNUAL AVERAGE GROWTH OF GDP – 6.9 per cent (2000)

INFLATION RATE – 6.0 per cent (2001)

UNEMPLOYMENT – 9.6 per cent (1998)

TOTAL EXTERNAL DEBT – US$782 million (1998). The IMF approved a stand-by credit of US$22 million in December 1997

### TRADE

Although Estonia signed a free trade deal with Russia in 1992, it has greatly reduced its trade with the former Soviet states. Its main trading partners are Finland, Sweden, Russia, Germany and Latvia. The main imports are machinery and equipment, chemicals, clothing and footwear, foodstuffs and vehicles. Exports consist mainly of machinery and equipment, timber and wood products, textiles and clothing, foodstuffs, metals and furniture. Free trade and association agreements with the EU came into effect in 1995 and formal accession negotiations were begun in March 1998.

In 1999 there was a trade deficit of US$878 million and a current account deficit of US$295million. Imports totalled US$4,093 million and exports US$2,939 million.

| *Trade with UK* | 1999 | 2000 |
|---|---|---|
| Imports from UK | £53,126,000 | £65,890,000 |
| Exports to UK | 188,464,000 | 318,822,000 |

## COMMUNICATIONS

Freedom of the press is guaranteed in the constitution, and the state monopoly on television and radio ended soon after independence. All newspapers have been privatised and broadcasting channels are in the process of being privatised. Russian-language news and programmes are provided on Estonian Television. There are five Estonian- and three Russian-language daily newspapers.

## EDUCATION

Estonia has a three-tier education system, consisting of primary level (four years), secondary level (six years) and university level (four to six years). Primary- and secondary-level education is compulsory.

ILLITERACY RATE – 0.2 per cent

ENROLMENT (percentage of age group) – primary 87 per cent (1996); secondary 83 per cent (1996); tertiary 41.8 per cent (1996)

# ETHIOPIA

*Federal Democratic Republic of Ethiopia*

AREA – 426,373 sq. miles (1,104,300 sq. km). Neighbours: Sudan (west), Kenya (south), Djibouti and Somalia (east), Eritrea (north)

POPULATION – 63,495,000 (2000 estimate). About one-third are of Semitic origin (Amharas and Tigreans) and the remainder mainly Oromos (40 per cent), Somalis (6 per cent) and Afar (4 per cent). Amharas, Tigreans and many Oromos are Ethiopian Orthodox Christians. The Afar people in the north and the Somalis in the south-east, as well as some Oromos, are Muslim. Amharic is the most widely used of the 70 languages

CAPITAL – Addis Ababa (population, 2,495,000, 2000 estimate)

MAJOR CITY – Dire Dawa (population, 229,000, 2000 estimate)

CURRENCY – Ethiopian birr (EB) of 100 cents

NATIONAL ANTHEM - Yezeginet Kibir

NATIONAL DAY – 28 May

NATIONAL FLAG – Three horizontal bands: green, yellow, red; in the centre a blue disc, containing a yellow pentagram

LIFE EXPECTANCY (years) – male 41.4; female 43.1

POPULATION GROWTH RATE – 2.7 per cent (1999)

POPULATION DENSITY – 54 per sq. km (1998)

URBAN POPULATION – 17.6 per cent (2000 estimate)

## HISTORY AND POLITICS

The Hamitic culture was heavily influenced by Semitic immigration from Arabia at about the time of Christ. Christianity was introduced in the fourth century. The empire attained its zenith in the sixth century under the Axum rulers but was checked by Islamic expansion from the east. Modern Ethiopia dates from 1855 when Theodros established supremacy over the various tribes. The last emperor was Haile Selassie who reigned from 1930 until 1974, when he was deposed by the armed forces. After ten years of military rule, a Workers' Party on the Soviet model was formed with Lt.-Col. Mengistu Haile Mariam as General Secretary. The People's Democratic Republic of Ethiopia was established under a new constitution in 1987 with Lt.-Col. Mengistu as president. Armed insurgencies by the Eritrean People's Liberation Front (EPLF) and the Ethiopian People's Revolutionary Democratic Front (EPRDF), originating in Tigre, brought down Mengistu's government in May 1991.

A transitional administration comprising the EPRDF and other opposition groups formed a Council of Representatives which governed until 1995 under President Meles Zenawi. In 1994, the Council agreed on a draft federal constitution, which was adopted by an elected Constituent Assembly on 8 December 1994. Multiparty elections in May and June 1995 were won by the EPRDF. The Federal Democratic Republic of Ethiopia was proclaimed on 22 August 1995.

In the general election held on 14 May 2000, the EPRDF won 472 seats.

### FOREIGN RELATIONS

Eritrea, which since 1962 had been a province of Ethiopia, seceded and became independent on 24 May 1993. Relations between the two countries had been good until fighting broke out along the border in June 1998, with each side accusing the other of sending troops across the border. Ethiopia launched an attack on Eritrea in May 2000, capturing much of the west of the country. An interim peace plan was signed in June, and a comprehensive peace agreement was signed in December (*see* Eritrea).

### Political System

The constitution provides for a federal government responsible for foreign affairs, defence and economic policy. The president is elected by both houses of the legislature. The House of People's Representatives (*Yehizb Tewokayoch Mekir Bet*) has 548 directly elected members who serve a five-year term. The House of Federation (*Yefederesh Mekir Bet*) has 108 members, indirectly elected for a five-year term by the nine regional administrations (Tigre, Afar, Amara, Oromia, Somali, Benshangui, Gambela, Harer and Southern), who have considerable autonomy and the right to secede.

### Head of State

*President*, Dr Negaso Gidada, *elected by the Council of People's Representatives* 22 August 1995

### Council of Ministers *as at July 2001*

*Prime Minister*, Meles Zenawi
*Deputy Prime Minister, Economic Affairs*, Kassu Illala
*Deputy Prime Minister, National Defence*, Adisu Legese
*Agriculture*, Mengistu Huluka
*Commerce and Industry*, Kasahun Ayele
*Economic Development and Co-operation*, Girma Birru
*Education*, Genet Zewdie
*Finance*, Sufyan Ahmad
*Foreign Affairs*, Seyoum Mesfin
*Health*, vacant
*Information and Culture*, Wolde Mikael Chamo
*Justice*, Worede-Wold Wolde
*Labour and Social Affairs*, Hassan Abdella
*Mines and Energy*, Ezaddin Ali
*Revenue Board*, Desta Amare
*Transport and Communications*, Mohammed Dirir
*Water Resources*, Shiferaw Jarso
*Works and Urban Development*, Haile Aseged

### Embassy of Ethiopia

17 Prince's Gate, London SW7 1PZ
Tel: 020-7589 7212
*Ambassador Extraordinary and Plenipotentiary*, HE Fisseha Adugna, apptd 2000
*Counsellor*, O. Beshir (*Commercial*)

### British Embassy

Fikre Mariam Abatechan Street (PO Box 858), Addis Ababa
Tel: (00 251) (1) 612354
E-mail: b.emb4@telecom.net.et
*Ambassador Extraordinary and Plenipotentiary*, HE Myles Wickstead, apptd 2000
*Deputy Head of Mission and First Secretary*, F. Guy

British Council Director, Rosemary Arnott, OBE, PO Box 1043, Artistic Building, Adwa Avenue, Addis Ababa; e-mail: bc.addisababa@bc-addis.bcouncil.org

## DEFENCE

The Army has 160 main battle tanks and 200 armoured infantry fighting vehicles and armoured personnel carriers. The Air Force has 53 combat aircraft and 18 armed helicopters.
Military Expenditure – 7.1 per cent of GDP (1999)
Military Personnel – 352,500: Army 350,000, Air Force 2,500

## ECONOMY

The post-Mengistu government implemented a programme of free-market economic reform which reduced government spending and inflation.

Agriculture accounts for approximately 50 per cent of GDP and employs around 80 per cent of the workforce. The major food crops are teff, maize, barley, sorghum, wheat, pulses and oil seeds. Famine conditions in 1984–5 recurred to a lesser extent in 1992, 1997 and 2000. However, agricultural liberalisation has led to dramatic progress in food production.

The economy deteriorated sharply in 1999 and 2000 as a result of drought, a worsening balance of trade, and war with Eritrea. In April 2001 Ethiopia was permitted to reschedule some two-thirds of its US$430 million debt until 2004.

Manufacturing industry accounts for less than 9 per cent of GDP and is heavily dependent on agriculture. Ethiopia's known, but as yet largely unexploited, natural resources include gold, platinum, copper and potash. Traces of oil and natural gas have been found.

In 1998 there was a trade surplus of US$474 million and a current account deficit of US$134 million.
GNP – US$6,524 million (1999); US$100 per capita (1999)
GDP – US$6,075 million (1997); US$107 per capita (1998)
Annual Average Growth of GDP – 6.5 per cent (1996)
Inflation Rate – 8.2 per cent (1998)
Total External Debt – US$10,352 million (1998)

### Trade

The chief imports by value are machinery and transport equipment, manufactured goods and chemicals; the principal exports by value are coffee, oil seeds, hides and skins, and pulses. In 1999 imports totalled US$1,317 million and in 1998 exports totalled US$561 million.

| *Trade with UK* | 1999 | 2000 |
|---|---|---|
| Imports from UK | £33,091,000 | £32,943,000 |
| Exports to UK | 9,989,000 | 14,001,000 |

## COMMUNICATIONS

A network of roads in rural areas links the major cities with each other, with the Sudanese and Kenyan borders and through Eritrea to the Red Sea coast.

There is a railway link from Addis Ababa to Djibouti. Ethiopian Airlines maintains regular services from Addis Ababa to many provincial towns, throughout Africa and to Europe.

## EDUCATION

Elementary and secondary education are provided by government schools in the main centres of population; there are also mission schools. The National University (founded 1961) co-ordinates the institutions of higher education. There are also universities at Alemaya (agricultural), Debub, Mekele, Bashir Dar and Jimma.
Illiteracy Rate – 61.3 per cent (2000)
Enrolment (percentage of age group) – primary 32 per cent (1996); tertiary 0.8 per cent (1996)

---

# FIJI

*Matanitu ko Viti – Republic of Fiji*

---

Area – 7,056 sq. miles (18,274 sq. km)
Population – 801,000 (1997 UN estimate), 715,373 (1986 census): 48.6 per cent Indians, 46.2 per cent Fijians, and 5.2 per cent other races. Since the 1987 coup many ethnic Indians have left and by 1994 Melanesian Fijians formed the largest population group. The main languages are Fijian and Hindi

CAPITAL – ΨSuva (population, 141,273, 1986), on the island of Viti Levu
CURRENCY – Fiji dollar (F$) of 100 cents
NATIONAL ANTHEM – God Bless Fiji
NATIONAL DAY – 10 October (Fiji Day)
NATIONAL FLAG – Light blue ground with Union flag in top left quarter and the shield of Fiji in the fly
LIFE EXPECTANCY (years) – male 64.0; female 69.2
POPULATION GROWTH RATE – 1.2 per cent (1999)
POPULATION DENSITY – 44 per sq. km (1998)
URBAN POPULATION – 49.4 per cent (2000 estimate)
MILITARY EXPENDITURE – 1.9 per cent of GDP (1999)
MILITARY PERSONNEL – 3,500: Army 3,200, Navy 300
ILLITERACY RATE – 7.1 per cent
ENROLMENT (percentage of age group) – primary 99 per cent (1992); tertiary 11.9 per cent (1991)

Fiji is composed of roughly 332 islands (about 100 permanently inhabited) and over 500 islets in the South Pacific, about 1,100 miles north of New Zealand. The group extends 300 miles from east to west and 300 miles north to south. The International Date Line has been diverted to the east of the island group. The largest islands are Viti Levu and Vanua Levu. The main groups of islands are Lomaiviti, Lau and Yasawas. The climate is tropical without extremes of heat.

## HISTORY AND POLITICS

Fiji was a British colony from 1874 until 10 October 1970 when it became an independent state and a member of the Commonwealth. The constitution was changed in 1990 to give greater power to indigenous Melanesian Fijians at the expense of the Indian community, but this was revoked in the 1997 constitution. In the general election on 8–15 May 1999, the Fijian Political Party was swept from power by a coalition of parties led by the Fiji Labour Party. Its leader, Mahendra Chaudhry, became Fiji's first ethnic Indian prime minister.

On 19 May 2000 a group of indigenous Fijian rebels, led by George Speight, stormed parliament and took Prime Minister Mahendra Chaudhry and most of the Cabinet hostage. The army declared martial law on 29 May following the resignation of President Ratu Sir Kamisese Mara. An interim administration was set up on 28 June, following unsuccessful negotiations between the military government and the rebels. The military named an all-indigenous government to replace the multiracial coalition of the deposed premier. The interim government was to rule for two years and prepare for fresh elections. Following the release of the last hostages on 13 July, the Great Council of Chiefs announced the appointment of Ratu Josefa Iloilo as president.

The Fijian High Court ruled on 15 November 2000 that the 1997 Constitution remained in force. Following an appeal by the interim government, the Court of Appeal ruled on 1 March 2001 that the 1997 Constitution was still in force, that the parliament had been suspended rather than dissolved, and that the interim government was not legitimate, but accepted that the then Vice-President Iloilo had the right to exercise presidential powers after the resignation of President Ratu Sir Kamisese Mara. On 7 March the interim government led by Laisenia Qarase offered its collective resignation and Mahendra Chaudhry was reappointed as prime minister, but was dismissed by President Iloilo on 14 March. Qarase was reappointed as interim prime minister the following day. On 8 March 2001 the Great Council of Chiefs rejected the judgement of the Appeal Court and reaffirmed its support for the interim government and again nominated Iloilo as president.

Fiji's membership of the Commonwealth was suspended following the coup.

### INTERIM HEAD OF STATE

*President*, Ratu Josefa Iloilo, *appointed* 13 July 2000; *reappointed* 13 March 2001; *sworn in* 15 March 2001
*Vice-President*, Ratu Jope Naucabalavu Seniloii

### INTERIM CABINET *as at July 2001*

*Prime Minister, National Reconciliation*, Laisenia Qarase
*Deputy Prime Minister, Fijian Affairs*, Ratu Epeli Nailatikau
*Agriculture, Fisheries, Forests and ALTA*, Apisai Tora
*Assistant Minister for Fijian Affairs*, Ratu Suliano Matanitobua
*Attorney-General, Justice*, Alipate Qetaki
*Commerce, Business Development and Investment*, Tomasi Vuetilovoni
*Education*, Nelson Delailomaloma
*Finance and National Planning*, Ratu Jone Kubuabola
*Foreign Affairs, External Trade and Sugar*, Kaliopate Tavola
*Health*, Pita Nacuva
*Home Affairs and Immigration*, Ratu Talemo Ratakele
*Information and Communications*, Ratu Inoke Kubuabola
*Labour and Industrial Relations*, Ratu Tevita Moemoedonu
*Lands and Mineral Resources*, Mitieli Bulanauca
*Local Government, Housing and Urban Development*, Ratu Tuakitau Cokanauto
*Public Enterprises and Public Sector Reform*, Hector Hatch
*Public Works and Energy*, Joketani Cokanasiga
*Regional Development and Multi-Ethnic Affairs*, Ilaitia Tuisese
*Tourism and Transport*, Jone Koroitamana
*Women, Culture and Social Welfare*, Ro Teimumu Kepa
*Youth, Sports and Employment Opportunities*, Keni Dakuidreketi

### HIGH COMMISSION OF THE REPUBLIC OF FIJI

34 Hyde Park Gate, London SW7 5DN
Tel: 020-7584 3661
*Ambassador Extraordinary and Plenipotentiary*, HE Filimone Jitoko, apptd 1996

### BRITISH HIGH COMMISSION

Victoria House, 47 Gladstone Road, PO Box 1355, Suva
Tel: (00 679) 311033
E-mail: ukconsular@bhc.org.fj
*Ambassador Extraordinary and Plenipotentiary*, HE Michael Dibben, apptd 1997

## ECONOMY

Agriculture accounts for 18 per cent of GDP and employs 44 per cent of the workforce. The economy is primarily agrarian. The principal cash crop is sugar cane, which is the main export, followed by coconuts, ginger and copra. A variety of other fruit, vegetables and root crops are also grown, and self-sufficiency in rice is a major aim. Forestry, fishing and beef production are being encouraged in order to diversify the economy. The processing of agricultural, marine and timber products are the main industries, along with gold mining and textiles. Tourism is second only to sugar as a money-earner, but visitor numbers have fallen as a result of the coup, causing widespread job losses. GNP – US$1,848 million (1999); US$2,210 per capita (1999)
GDP – US$2,149 million (1997); US$1,982 per capita (1998)
ANNUAL AVERAGE GROWTH OF GDP – 3.1 per cent (1996)
INFLATION RATE – 2.0 per cent (1999)
UNEMPLOYMENT – 5.4 per cent (1995)
TOTAL EXTERNAL DEBT – US$193 million (1998)

### TRADE

The chief imports are foodstuffs, machinery, mineral fuels, chemicals, beverages, tobacco and manufactured articles. Chief exports are sugar, coconut oil, fish, lumber, molasses and ginger.

In 1998 there was a trade deficit of US$218 million and a current account deficit of US$55 million. Imports totalled US$721 million and exports US$510 million.

| *Trade with UK* | 1999 | 2000 |
|---|---|---|
| Imports from UK | £7,312,000 | £4,216,000 |
| Exports to UK | 66,244,000 | 66,726,000 |

## COMMUNICATIONS

Fiji is one of the main aerial crossroads in the Pacific, providing services to New Zealand, Australia, Tonga, Samoa, Vanuatu, the Solomon Islands, Kiribati, Tuvalu, New Caledonia and American Samoa. Fiji has three ports of entry, at Suva, Lautoka and Levuka. There are 5,100 km of roads.

---

# FINLAND
*Suomen Tasavalta*

---

AREA – 130,559 sq. miles (338,145 sq. km). Neighbours: Norway (north-west and north), Russia (east), Sweden (west)
POPULATION – 5,171,300 (2000 estimate). Finnish and Swedish are both official languages, 93 per cent speaking Finnish as their first language and 5.6 per cent Swedish. Sami is spoken by 1,700 of the 6,500-strong Sami population who live in the far north. The population is predominantly Lutheran
CAPITAL – ΨHelsinki (Helsingfors) (population, 912,782, 1997 estimate)
MAJOR CITIES – Espoo (Esbo) (213,271); ΨOulu (Uleåborg) (120,753); Tampere (Tammerfors) (195,468); ΨTurku (Åbo) (172,561); Vantaa (Vanda) (178,471), 2000 estimates
CURRENCY – Euro () of 100 cents/Markka (Mk) of 100 penniä
NATIONAL ANTHEM - Maame/Vårt land (Our land)
NATIONAL DAY – 6 December (Independence Day)
NATIONAL FLAG – White with blue cross
LIFE EXPECTANCY (years) – male 73.7; female 81.0
POPULATION GROWTH RATE – 2.3 per cent (1999)
POPULATION DENSITY – 17 per sq. km (2000)
URBAN POPULATION – 67.3 per cent (2000 estimate)

The Åland archipelago (Ahvenanmaa), a group of small islands at the entrance to the Gulf of Bothnia, covers about 1,552 square km, with a population (2000) of 25,776 (95.2 per cent Swedish-speaking). The Åland islands are an autonomous province of Finland.

## HISTORY AND POLITICS

Finland was part of the Swedish Empire from the Middle Ages until it was ceded to Russia in 1809 and became an autonomous grand duchy of the Russian Empire. Finland became independent after the Russian revolution of 1917, but was forced to cede around one-tenth of its land to the Soviet Union and to resettle 10 per cent of its population under the Treaty of Paris (1947). A Soviet-Finnish Co-operation Treaty forced Finland to demilitarise its Soviet border, to enter into a barter trade agreement and to adopt a stance of neutrality. These terms lasted until the demise of the Soviet Union in 1991.

Finland joined the European Union on 1 January 1995 following a referendum in October 1994.

The present government took office in April 1999. The five parties in the ruling coalition are the Social Democratic Party, the National Coalition Party (conservative), the Left-wing Alliance, the Swedish People's Party, and the Greens, with a total of 139 out of 200 seats.

### POLITICAL SYSTEM

Under the constitution there is a unicameral legislature, the *Eduskunta*, composed of 200 members elected by universal suffrage for a four-year term. The highest executive power is held by the president who is directly elected for a period of six years. The first direct elections for the presidency were held in 1994, the president having previously been elected by an electoral college.

### HEAD OF STATE

*President*, Tarja Kaarina Halonen, *elected* 6 February 2000, *inaugurated* 1 March 2000

### CABINET *as at July 2001*

*Prime Minister*, Paavo Lipponen (SDP)
*Deputy PM, Finance*, Sauli Niinistö (NCP)
*Agriculture and Forestry*, Kalevi Hemilä (Ind.)
*Culture*, Suvi Lindén (NCP)
*Defence*, Jan-Erik Enestam (SPP)
*Education*, Maija Rask (SDP)
*Environment*, Satu Hassi (Greens)
*Foreign Affairs*, Erkki Tuomioja (SDP)
*Foreign Trade*, Kimmo Sasi (NCP)
*Health and Social Services*, Osmo Soininvaara (Greens)
*Interior*, Ville Itala
*Justice*, Johannes Koskinen (SDP)
*Labour*, Tarja Filatov
*Minister at the Ministry of Finance*, Suvi-Anne Siimes (LA)
*Regional and Municipal Affairs*, Martti Korhonen (LA)
*Social Affairs and Health*, Maija Perho (NCP)
*Trade and Industry*, Sinikka Mönkäre (SDP)
*Transport*, Olli-Pekka Heinonen (NCP)

SDP Social Democratic Party; NCP National Coalition Party; LA Left-wing Alliance; SPP Swedish People's Party; Ind. Independent

### EMBASSY OF FINLAND

38 Chesham Place, London SW1X 8HW
Tel: 020-7838 6200
*Ambassador Extraordinary and Plenipotentiary*, HE Pertti Salolainen, apptd 1996
*Minister*, C. Hartman
*Counsellor (Commercial)*, J. Hietala
*Defence Attaché*, Lt.-Col. J. Tammikivi

### BRITISH EMBASSY

Itäinen Puistotie 17, FIN-00140 Helsinki
Tel: (00 358) (9) 2286 5100
*Ambassador Extraordinary and Plenipotentiary*, HE Alyson J. K. Bailes, CMG, apptd 2000
*Deputy Head of Mission and Counsellor*, R. Cambridge
*First Secretary (Commercial)*, M. Towsey
*Defence Attaché*, Lt.-Col. G. Grant

BRITISH CONSULAR OFFICES – Helsinki, Jyväskylä, Kotka, Kuopio, Oulu, Pori, Tampere, Turku, Vaasa, Mariehamn

BRITISH COUNCIL DIRECTOR, Tuija Talvitie, Hakaniemenkatu 2, FIN-00530 Helsinki; e-mail: office@britishcouncil.fi

## DEFENCE

The Army has 230 main battle tanks, 273 armoured infantry fighting vehicles and 790 armoured personnel carriers. The Navy has 10 patrol and coastal vessels. The Air Force has 64 combat aircraft.
MILITARY EXPENDITURE – 1.4 per cent of GDP (1999)
MILITARY PERSONNEL – 31,700: Army 24,000, Navy 5,000, Air Force 2,700, Paramilitaries 3,400
CONSCRIPTION DURATION – Six to 12 months

## ECONOMY

Finland produces a wide range of capital and consumer goods. The glass, ceramics and furniture industries enjoy international reputations. Other important industries are mobile phones, rubber, plastics, chemicals and pharmaceuticals, footwear, foodstuffs and shipbuilding.

The markka joined the ERM in August 1996, and has participated in the European Single Currency since January 1999.

In 1997 the budget deficit was equivalent to 4.5 per cent of GDP, and public debt was 67.7 per cent of GDP.

GNP – US$127,764 million (1999); US$23,780 per capita (1999)

GDP – US$119,834 million (1997); US$25,046 per capita (1999)

ANNUAL AVERAGE GROWTH OF GDP – 5.5 per cent (2000)

INFLATION RATE – 3.1 per cent (2001) UNEMPLOYMENT – 9.2 per cent (2001)

### TRADE

The principal imports are raw materials, machinery and manufactured goods. The main exports are electronic and electrical goods, paper and wood pulp, machinery, and metal products. Trade with EU countries accounts for more than half of Finland's total trade.

In 1999 there was a trade surplus of US$11,655 million and a current account surplus of US$6,936 million. Imports totalled US$30,726 million and exports US$40,665 million.

| *Trade with UK* | 1999 | 2000 |
|---|---|---|
| Imports from UK | £1,267,100,000 | £1,392,100,000 |
| Exports to UK | 2,246,100,000 | 2,654,600,000 |

## COMMUNICATIONS

There are 5,859 km of railroad, railway connections with Russia, and passenger boat connections with Sweden, Germany and Estonia. There are also passenger/cargo services between Britain and Helsinki, Kotka and other Finnish ports. External air services are maintained by most European airlines.

## CULTURE AND EDUCATION

Newspapers, books, plays and films appear in both Finnish and Swedish. There is a vigorous modern literature. F. E. Sillanpää, who died in 1964, was awarded the Nobel Prize for Literature in 1939. Jean Sibelius (1865-1957) is the most famous composer. In 1999 there were 56 daily newspapers.

Primary education (co-educational comprehensive school) is free and compulsory for children from seven to 16 years.

ENROLMENT (percentage of age group) – primary 98 per cent (1996); secondary 93 per cent (1996); tertiary 74.1 per cent (1996)

---

## FRANCE
*La République française*

---

AREA – 212,935 sq. miles (551,500 sq. km). Neighbours: Belgium and Luxembourg (north-east), Germany, Switzerland and Italy (east), Spain and Andorra (south-west)

POPULATION – 60,794,000 (1999 estimate); 57,218,000 (Metropolitan France), and 58,745,000 including overseas departments (1992 official estimate): 72 per cent Catholic, 8 per cent Muslim, 2 per cent Jewish. The language is French; there are several regional languages including Basque, Breton, Catalan, Corsican, Dutch, German and Occitan

CAPITAL – Paris (population, 9,319,367, 1990), on the Seine

MAJOR CITIES – ΨBordeaux (696,819); Grenoble (404,837); Lille (959,433); Lyon (1,262,342); ΨMarseille (1,230,871); Nantes (495,229); Nice (517,291); Strasbourg (388,466); Toulon (437,825); Toulouse (650,311). The chief towns of Corsica are ΨAjaccio (58,315) and ΨBastia (52,446)

CURRENCY – Euro (€) of 100 cents/Franc of 100 centimes

NATIONAL ANTHEM – La Marseillaise

NATIONAL DAY – 14 July (Bastille Day 1789)

NATIONAL FLAG – The tricolour, three vertical bands, blue, white, red (blue next to flagstaff)

LIFE EXPECTANCY (years) – male 74.9; female 83.6

POPULATION GROWTH RATE – 0.4 per cent (1999)

POPULATION DENSITY – 107 per sq. km (1998)

URBAN POPULATION – 75.6 per cent (2000 estimate)

## HISTORY AND POLITICS

Gaul, the area which is now France, was conquered by Julius Caesar in the 1st century BC and remained a part of the Roman Empire until the Frankish invasions in the 5th and 6th centuries. The Treaty of Verdun (AD 843) divided the Frankish Empire into three parts, of which the western part, *Francia Occidentalis*, became the basis for modern France.

France established itself as the dominant country in Europe in the 17th century. As a result of the French Revolution, a republic was declared in 1792 and the king, Louis XVI, was executed. The republic was overthrown by Napoléon Bonaparte, who established the first French Empire, which ended in 1815. The ensuing Congress of Vienna restored the monarchy, but in 1848 the Second Republic was declared, which lasted only until 1852, when the Second Empire was proclaimed under Napoléon III. He was forced to abdicate after the defeat of France in the Franco-Prussian war (1870–1871) and the Third Republic was established.

In 1940, Germany invaded France, occupying most of the country and establishing a pro-German government in the south. France was liberated in 1944, a provisional government was established under Gen. Charles de Gaulle, and the Fourth Republic was declared in 1946. In 1958, the threat of a military coup following a rebellion in Algeria resulted in the assembly inviting Gen. de Gaulle to return as premier; a new constitution which strengthened the powers of the president was adopted, the Fifth Republic was proclaimed, and Gen. De Gaulle was elected president. France granted its colonies independence between 1954 and 1962.

President Jacques Chirac, the candidate of the Rally for the Republic (RPR), was elected in May 1995. The state of the parties in the Senate at August 2000 was: RPR 99; Socialist Party (PS) 77; Centrist Union (UDC) 52; Republican and Independent Union (RI) 46; Democratic and European Rally (RDE) 23; Communists (PCF) 17; Independents 7.

In the last elections to the National Assembly in May and June 1997 the PS won 241 seats, the Gaullist RPR 134, Union pour la Démocratie Française (UDF) 108, PCF 38, Independent Left 21, Independent Right 14, Radical Socialist Party (PRS) 12, Green Party 7, National Front 1, Independent 1. The government is formed of a coalition of the PS, the PCF, the PRS and the Greens.

### POLITICAL SYSTEM

The head of state is a directly elected president, whose term of office has hitherto been seven years, but will be five years with effect from the presidential election due to be

held in March 2002. The legislature consists of the National Assembly of 577 deputies (555 for Metropolitan France and 22 for the overseas departments and territories) and the Senate of 321 Senators (296 for Metropolitan France, 13 for the overseas departments and territories and 12 for French citizens abroad). Deputies in the National Assembly are directly elected for a five-year term. One-third of the Senate is indirectly elected every three years.

The prime minister is appointed by the president, as is the Council of Ministers on the prime minister's recommendation. They are responsible to the legislature, but as the executive is constitutionally separate from the legislature, ministers may not sit in the legislature and must hand over their seats to a substitute.

France is divided into 22 metropolitan regions and 96 metropolitan and four overseas departments, which are also regions. There are also four overseas territories and two territorial collectivities.

## Head of State

*President of the French Republic*, Jacques Chirac, *elected* 7 May 1995, *took office* 17 May 1995

## Council of Ministers *as at July 2001*

*Prime Minister*, Lionel Jospin (PS)
*Agriculture and Fisheries*, Jean Glavany (PS)
*Capital Works, Transport and Housing*, Jean-Claude Gayssot (PS)
*Civil Service, Administrative Reform and Decentralisation*, Michel Sapin (PS)
*Culture and Communications, Government Spokesperson*, Cathérine Tasca (PS)
*Defence*, Alain Richard (PS)
*Economy, Finance and Industry*, Laurent Fabius (PS)
*Employment and Solidarity*, Elisabeth Guigou (PS)
*Foreign Affairs*, Hubert Védrine (PS)
*Interior*, Daniel Vaillant (PS)
*Justice, Keeper of the Seals*, Marylise Lebranchu (PS)
*National Education*, Jack Lang (PS)
*Relations with Parliament*, Jean-Jack Queyranne (PS)
*Research*, Roger-Gérard Schwartzenberg (PRS)
*Town and Country Planning and the Environment*, Dominique Voynet (Greens)
*Youth and Sport*, Marie-George Buffet (PCF)

## French Embassy

58 Knightsbridge, London SW1X 7JT
Tel: 020-7201 1000
*Ambassador Extraordinary and Plenipotentiary*, HE Daniel Bernard, CMG, CBE, apptd 1998
*Minister-Counsellor*, S. Gompertz
*Defence Attaché*, Contre-Amiral P. Sabatie-Garat
*Cultural Counsellor*, X. North
*Minister-Counsellor (Economic and Commercial Affairs)*, P. O'Quin

## British Embassy

35 rue du Faubourg St Honoré, F-75383 Paris Cedex 08
Tel: (00 33) (1) 4451 3100
*Ambassador Extraordinary and Plenipotentiary*, HE Sir Michael Jay, KCMG, apptd 1996
*Minister*, S. F. Howarth
*Defence and Air Attaché*, Air Cdre D. N. Adams
*Counsellor*, V. Caton (*Finance and Economic*)
*First Secretary and Consul-General*, S. Gregson

British Consular Offices – Amiens, Biarritz, Bordeaux, Boulogne, Calais, Cherbourg, Dunkerque, Le Havre, Lille, Lorient, Lyon, Marseille, Montpellier, Nantes, Nice, Paris, Perpignan, St Malo-Dinard, Saumur, Toulouse, Tours; overseas in Cayenne (French Guiana), Noumea (New Caledonia), Papeete (French Polynesia), Fort de France (Martinique) and Pointe à Pitre (Guadeloupe)

British Council Director, John Tod, OBE, 9 rue de Constantine, F-75340 Paris Cédex 07; e-mail: information@britishcouncil.fr. Regional office in Bordeaux

Franco-British Chamber of Commerce, 31 rue Boissy d'Anglas, F-75008 Paris. *President*, R. Lyon. *Vice-President*, B. Cordery, OBE

## DEFENCE

The Army has 834 main battle tanks, 3,900 armoured personnel carriers, 713 armoured infantry fighting vehicles and 498 helicopters.

The Navy has 11 submarines, one aircraft carrier, one cruiser, four destroyers, 29 frigates and 40 patrol and coastal vessels, 52 combat aircraft and 32 armed helicopters. The Navy has four domestic and five overseas bases.

The Air Force has 517 combat aircraft.

France deploys 35,460 armed forces personnel abroad; 2,700 in Germany (including members of Eurocorps); 17,450 in French Overseas Departments and Territories; 6,540 in former French colonies in Africa; and 8,770 on UN and peacekeeping duties.

Military Expenditure – 2.7 per cent of GDP (1999)

Military Personnel – 194,430: Army 169,300, Strategic Nuclear Forces 8,400, Navy 49,490, Air Force 60,500, Paramilitaries 94,950

Conscription Duration – Ten months. Conscription is to be phased out over six years, beginning in 1997

## ECONOMY

Viniculture is extensive, regions famous for their wines including Bordeaux, Burgundy and Champagne. Production of wine in 2000 was 59 million hectolitres. Cognac, liqueurs and cider are also produced. Other important agricultural products include sugar beet, dairy products, cereals and oilseeds. In 1998, 2.9 per cent of the workforce was engaged in agriculture. Nearly 55 per cent of the land area of metropolitan France is utilised for agricultural production and a further quarter is accounted for by forests.

Oil is produced from fields in the Landes area, but France is a net importer of crude oil, for processing by its important oil-refining industry. Natural gas is produced in the foothills of the Pyrenees.

Heavy industries include oil-refining and the production of iron and steel, and aluminium. In 2000 production of pig iron was 13.9 million tonnes and steel 21 million tonnes. Other important industries are construction and civil engineering, chemicals, rubber and plastics, pharmaceuticals, vehicle production and telecommunications services..

The Banque de France was made independent in 1994 with the formation of a nine-member monetary policy council to define and implement monetary policy independent of the government.

France has participated in the European Single Currency since January 1999.

GNP – US$1,453,211 million (1999); US$23,480 per capita (1999)
GDP – US$1,394,124 million (1997); US$23,764 per capita (1999)
ANNUAL AVERAGE GROWTH OF GDP – 2.8 per cent (2000)
INFLATION RATE – 1.4 per cent (2001) UNEMPLOYMENT – 8.6 per cent (2001)

### TRADE

The principal imports are raw materials for the heavy and manufacturing industries (e.g. oil, minerals, chemicals), machinery and precision instruments, agricultural products, chemicals and vehicles. Agricultural products, chemicals, pharmaceuticals and vehicles are also the principal exports. Most of France's trade is done with other EU countries. There are around 45 million hectares of farmland.

In 1999 there was a trade surplus of US$20,065 million and a current account surplus of US$37,231 million. Imports totalled US$289,927 million and exports US$300,162 million.

| *Trade with UK* | 1999 | 2000 |
|---|---|---|
| Imports from UK | £15,834,700,000 | £17,587,500,000 |
| Exports to UK | 17,235,800,000 | 17,155,800,000 |

## COMMUNICATIONS

The length of roads in 1998 was 965,916 km, of which 9,011 km were motorways.

The railroad system is extensive. The length of lines open for traffic in 1998 was 31,852 km.

The French mercantile marine consisted in 1998 of 210 ships of a total of 4,100,000 tonnes which transported 91,500,000 tonnes of freight.

## CULTURE AND EDUCATION

French is the official language. The work of the French Academy, founded in 1635, has established *le bon usage*, equivalent to 'The Queen's English' in Britain. French authors have been awarded the Nobel Prize for Literature on 12 occasions and include R. F. A. Sully-Prudhomme (1901), Anatole France (1921), André Gide (1947), François Mauriac (1952), Albert Camus (1957), Jean-Paul Sartre (1964) and Claude Simon (1985).

Education is compulsory, free and secular from six to 16. Schools may be single-sex or co-educational. Primary education is given in nursery schools, primary schools and *collèges d'enseignement général* (four-year secondary modern course); secondary education in *collèges d'enseignement technique*, *collèges d'enseignement secondaire* and *lycées* (seven-year course leading to one of the five *baccalauréats*). Special schools are numerous.

There are many *grandes écoles* in France which award diplomas in many subjects not taught at university, especially applied science and engineering. Most of these are state institutions but have a competitive system of entry, unlike universities. There are universities in 24 towns including 13 in Paris and the immediate area.

In 1993 the government gave German official parity with French in Alsace schools.

ENROLMENT (percentage of age group) – primary 100 per cent (1996); secondary 95 per cent (1996); tertiary 51.0 per cent (1996)

## OVERSEAS DEPARTMENTS

Greater powers of self-government were granted to French Guiana, Guadeloupe, Martinique and Réunion in 1982. These former colonies had enjoyed departmental status since 1946. Their directly elected Assemblies operate in parallel with the existing, indirectly constituted Regional Councils. The French government is represented by a Prefect in each.

## FRENCH GUIANA

AREA – 34,749 sq. miles (90,000 sq. km)
POPULATION - 157,213 (1999 census)
CAPITAL – ΨCayenne (41,659, 1990 census)

Situated on the north-eastern coast of South America, French Guiana is flanked by Suriname on the west and by Brazil on the south and east. Under the administration of French Guiana is a group of islands (St Joseph, Île Royal and Île du Diable), known as Îles du Salut.

*Prefect*, P. Dartout

## GUADELOUPE

AREA – 658 sq. miles (1,705 sq. km)
POPULATION - 422,496 (1999 census)
CAPITAL – ΨBasse-Terre (14,107, 1990 census) on Guadeloupe

A number of islands in the Leeward Islands group of the West Indies, consisting of the two main islands of Guadeloupe (or Basse-Terre) and Grande-Terre, with the adjacent islands of Marie-Galante, La Désirade and Îles des Saintes, and islands of St-Barthélemy and the part of St-Martin under French administration, which lie over 150 miles to the north-west. The main towns are ΨLes Abymes (62,605); ΨSt-Martin (28,518); ΨPointe-à-Pitre (26,029) in Grande-Terre and ΨGrand Bourg (6,611) in Marie-Galante.

*Prefect*, M. Diefenbacher

## MARTINIQUE

AREA – 425 sq. miles (1,102 sq. km)
POPULATION - 381,427 (1999 census)
CAPITAL – ΨFort-de-France (100,072, 1990 census)

An island situated in the Windward Islands group of the West Indies, between Dominica in the north and St Lucia in the south. The main towns are ΨLe Lamentin (30,026) and ΨSchoelcher (19,813).

*Prefect*, J.-F. Cordet

## RÉUNION

AREA – 969 sq. miles (2,507 sq. km)
POPULATION - 706,300 (1999 census)
CAPITAL - St-Denis (121,999, 1990 census)

Réunion, which became a French possession in 1638, lies in the Indian Ocean, about 569 miles east of Madagascar and 110 miles south-west of Mauritius. Other towns are Saint-Paul (71,669) and Saint-Pierre (58,846). The smaller, uninhabited islands of Bassas da India, Europa, Îles Glorieuses, Juan de Nova and Tromelin are administered from Réunion.

*Prefect*, H. Fournier

## TERRITORIAL COLLECTIVITIES

### MAYOTTE

AREA – 144 sq. miles (372 sq. km)
POPULATION - 131,320 (1997 census)
CAPITAL – Dzaoudzi (8,257)

Part of the Comoros Islands group, Mayotte remained a French dependency when the other three islands became independent as the Comoros Republic in 1975. Since 1976 the island has been a *collectivité territoriale*, an intermediate status between Overseas Department and Overseas Territory. The main town is Mamoudzou (20,450).

*Prefect*, P. Boisadam

| *Trade with UK* | 1999 | 2000 |
|---|---|---|
| Imports from UK | £5,549,000 | £1,358,000 |
| Exports to UK | 476,000 | 643,000 |

### ST PIERRE AND MIQUELON

AREA – 93 sq. miles (242 sq. km)
POPULATION – 6,316 (1999)
CAPITAL – ΨSt-Pierre (5,683, 1990 census)

These two small groups of islands off the coast of Newfoundland became a *collectivité territoriale* in 1985.

*Prefect*, R. Thuau

| *Trade with UK* | 1999 | 2000 |
|---|---|---|
| Imports from UK | £311,000 | £345,000 |
| Exports to UK | 6,000 | 20,000 |

## OVERSEAS TERRITORIES

### FRENCH POLYNESIA

AREA – 1,544 sq. miles (4,000 sq. km)
POPULATION - 231,000 (1997 UN estimate)
CAPITAL – ΨPapeete (36,784), in Tahiti

Five archipelagos in the south Pacific, comprising the Society Islands (Windward Islands group includes Tahiti, Moorea, Makatea, Mehetia, Tetiaroa, Tubuai Manu; Leeward Islands group includes Huahine, Raiatea, Tahaa, Bora-Bora, Maupiti), the Tuamotu Islands (Rangiroa, Hao, Turéia, etc.), the Gambier Islands (Mangareva, etc.), the Tubuai Islands (Rimatara, Rurutu, Tubuai, Raivavae, Rapa, etc.) and the Marquesas Islands (Nuku-Hiva, Hiva-Oa, Fatu-Hiva, Tahuata, Ua Huka, etc.).

*High Commissioner*, P. Roncière

| *Trade with UK* | 1999 | 2000 |
|---|---|---|
| Imports from UK | £3,816,000 | £3,511,000 |
| Exports to UK | 96,000 | 308,000 |

### NEW CALEDONIA

AREA – 7,172 sq. miles (18,575 sq. km)
POPULATION – 213,000 (1997 UN estimate)
CAPITAL – ΨNoumea (97,581)

New Caledonia is a large island in the western Pacific, 700 miles east of Queensland. Dependencies are the Isles of Pines, the Loyalty Islands (Mahé, Lifou, Urea, etc.), the Bélep Archipelago, the Chesterfield Islands, the Huon Islands and Walpole.

New Caledonia was discovered in 1774 and annexed by France in 1854; from 1871 to 1896 it was a convict settlement. In 1995, the territory was divided into three provinces, each with a provincial assembly which combined to form the Territorial Assembly. In elections in July 1995, Kanaks won majorities in North province and the Loyalty Islands, whereas pro-French settlers won a majority in the South province.

A referendum in 1987 on the question of independence was boycotted by the indigenous Kanaks, and New Caledonia therefore voted to remain French. In April 1998 an agreement was reached between the pro-independence Kanak Socialist National Liberation Front, the anti-independence Rally for Caledonia in the Republic and the French government to hold a referendum on independence in 15–20 years' time, and for greater autonomy for the indigenous people in the intervening period. A referendum on the agreement, the Noumea Accord, was held on 8 November 1998. It was supported by 71.9 per cent of voters; more than 74 per cent of registered voters took part.

*High Commissioner*, D. Bur

| *Trade with UK* | 1999 | 2000 |
|---|---|---|
| Imports from UK | £9,924,000 | £9,942,000 |
| Exports to UK | 94,000 | 199,000 |

### SOUTHERN AND ANTARCTIC TERRITORIES

Created in 1955 from former Réunion dependencies, the territory comprises the islands of Amsterdam (25 sq. miles) and St Paul (2.7 sq. miles), the Kerguelen Islands (2,700 sq. miles) and Crozet Islands (116 sq. miles) archipelagos and Adélie Land (116,800 sq. miles) in the Antarctic continent. The only population are members of staff of the scientific stations.

### WALLIS AND FUTUNA ISLANDS

AREA – 77 sq. miles (200 sq. km)
POPULATION – 15,000 (1997 UN estimate)
CAPITAL – Mata-Utu on Uvea, the main island of the Wallis group

Two groups of islands (the Wallis Archipelago and the Îles de Hoorn) in the central Pacific, north-east of Fiji.

*Prefect*, L. Legrand

| *Trade with UK* | 1999 | 2000 |
|---|---|---|
| Imports from UK | £120,000 | £44,000 |
| Exports to UK | — | 1,000 |

## THE FRENCH COMMUNITY

The constitution of the Fifth French Republic, promulgated in 1958, envisaged the establishment of a French Community of States. A number of the former French states in Africa have seceded from the Community but for all practical purposes continue to enjoy the same close links with France as those that remain formally members. Most former French African colonies are closely linked to France by financial, technical and economic agreements.

---

# GABON
*République Gabonaise*

---

AREA – 103,347 sq. miles (267,668 sq. km). Neighbours: Equatorial Guinea and Cameroon (north), Republic of Congo-Brazzaville (east and south)
POPULATION – 1,208,000 (1997 UN estimate). The official language is French; Fang is widely spoken
CAPITAL – ΨLibreville (population, 251,000)
CURRENCY – Franc CFA of 100 centimes
NATIONAL ANTHEM – La Concorde
NATIONAL DAY – 17 August

NATIONAL FLAG – Horizontal bands, green, yellow and blue
LIFE EXPECTANCY (years) – male 54.6; female 57.5
POPULATION GROWTH RATE – 2.8 per cent (1999)
POPULATION DENSITY – 4 per sq. km (1998)
URBAN POPULATION – 81.4 per cent (2000 estimate)
MILITARY EXPENDITURE – 2.1 per cent of GDP (1999)
MILITARY PERSONNEL – 4,700: Army 3,200, Navy 500, Air Force 1,000; Paramilitaries 2,000
ILLITERACY RATE – 29.2 per cent
ENROLMENT (percentage of age group) – tertiary 8.0 per cent (1996)

## HISTORY AND POLITICS

The first Europeans to visit the region were the Portuguese in the 15th century, and Dutch, French and English traders arrived over the following decades. In 1849 a slave ship was captured by the French, and the freed slaves formed a settlement which they called Libreville, the current capital. The territory was annexed to French Congo in 1888.

Gabon elected on 28 November 1958 to remain an autonomous republic within the French Community and gained full independence on 17 August 1960.

Multiparty elections held in autumn 1990 were won by the ruling Parti Démocratique Gabonais (PDG), amid allegations of fraud. The PDG formed a coalition government, although the other parties left the government in 1991 in protest at PDG domination. In September 1994, the government and opposition parties signed the Paris Agreement, which provided for a new coalition government and parliamentary elections. The elections, held in December 1996, returned the PDG to power. President Bongo of the PDG, who first took office in 1967, was re-elected for a fifth term of office in December 1998.

### POLITICAL SYSTEM

The constitution provides for an executive president, directly elected for a seven-year term, who appoints the Council of Ministers. There is a 120-member National Assembly, directly elected for a five-year term, and a 91-member Senate, elected by municipal and regional councillors for a six-year term.

### HEAD OF STATE

*President*, El Hadj Omar Bongo, *assumed office* December 1967, *re-elected* 1973, 1979, 1986, 1993 and 6 December 1998
*Vice-President*, Didjob Divungi-di-Ndinge

### COUNCIL OF MINISTERS *as at July 2001*

*Prime Minister*, Jean-François Ntoutoume-Emane
*Deputy Prime Minister, National Unity, Social Affairs*, Emmanuel Ondo Metgoho
*Minister of State, Communications, Posts and Information Technology*, Jean-Rémy Pendy-Bouyiki
*Minister of State, Equipment and Construction*, Egide Boundono-Simangoye
*Minister of State, Foreign Affairs, Co-operation and Francophone Affairs*, Jean Ping
*Minister of State, Housing, Urban Affairs, Land Survey, Welfare and Cities*, Jacques Adiahénot
*Minister of State, Interior, Public Security, Decentralisation*, Antoine Mboumbou-Miyakou
*Minister of State, Labour, Employment, Professional Training*, Paulette Moussavou Missambo
*Minister of State, Planning, Development, Regional Development*, Casimir Oyé Mba
*Minister of State, Tourism*, Jean Massima
*Agriculture, Livestock and Rural Development*, Fabien Owono-Essono
*Civil Service, Administrative Reform and Modernisation of the State*, Patrice Nziengui
*Commerce, Tourism, Handicrafts and Industrial Development*, Alfred Mabicka
*Culture, Art, Mass Education, Youth, Sport and Leisure*, Daniel Ona-Ondo
*Defence*, Ali Bongo
*Family and the Advancement of Women*, Angélique Ngoma
*Finance, Economy, Budget and Privatisation*, Emile Doumba
*Higher Education, Scientific Research and Technology*, André Dieudonné Berre
*Justice, Keeper of the Seals, Human Rights*, Pascal Désiré Missongo
*Mines, Energy, Oil and Hydraulic Resources*, Paul Toungui
*National Education, Government Spokesperson*, André Mba-Obame
*Public Health and Population*, Faustin Boukoubi
*Small and Medium-sized Enterprises and Industries*, Paul Biyighe-Mba
*Transport and Merchant Marine*, Gen. Idriss Ngari
*Water, Forests, Fishing, Re-afforestation, Environment and Protection of Nature*, Richard Onouviet

### EMBASSY OF THE REPUBLIC OF GABON

27 Elvaston Place, London SW7 5NL
Tel: 020-7823 9986
*Ambassador Extraordinary and Plenipotentiary*, HE Honorine Dossou-Naki, apptd 1996

BRITISH AMBASSADOR, HE Peter Boon, OBE, resident at Yaoundé, Cameroon

## ECONOMY

The economy is heavily dependent on oil and, to a lesser extent, other mineral resources, including manganese and uranium. Gabon has considerable timber reserves with 80 per cent of the country still forested, although production has stagnated in recent years.

France and the USA are the main trading partners. In 1997 imports totalled US$1,104 million and exports US$3,110 million.

GNP – US$3,987 million (1999); US$3,350 per capita (1999)
GDP – US$5,242 million (1997); US$4,787 per capita (1998)
ANNUAL AVERAGE GROWTH OF GDP – 3.3 per cent (1996)
INFLATION RATE – 4.0 per cent (1997)
TOTAL EXTERNAL DEBT – US$4,425 million (1998)

| *Trade with UK* | 1999 | 2000 |
|---|---|---|
| Imports from UK | £16,080,000 | £17,099,000 |
| Exports to UK | 4,768,000 | 4,557,000 |

---

## THE GAMBIA
*The Republic of the Gambia*

---

AREA – 4,361 sq. miles (11,295 sq. km). Neighbour: Senegal, which surrounds the Gambia except at the coast
POPULATION – 1,251,000 (1997 UN estimate), mainly Wollof, Mandinka and Fula peoples who originally migrated from the north and east. The official language is English; Fula, Jola, Mandinka, Serahule and Wollof are indigenous languages
CAPITAL – ΨBanjul (population, 109,986, 1980 estimate)
CURRENCY – Dalasi (D) of 100 butut
NATIONAL ANTHEM – For The Gambia, Our Homeland
NATIONAL DAY – 18 February (Independence Day)
NATIONAL FLAG – Horizontal stripes of red, blue and green, separated by narrow white stripes
LIFE EXPECTANCY (years) – male 56.0; female 58.9

POPULATION GROWTH RATE – 3.6 per cent (1999)
POPULATION DENSITY – 109 per sq. km (1998)
MILITARY EXPENDITURE – 3.5 per cent of GDP (1999)
MILITARY PERSONNEL – Army 800

The Gambia is named after the Gambia River, which it straddles for over 200 miles inland from the west coast of Africa. There is a dry season between October and May and heavy rainfall in July and August.

## HISTORY AND POLITICS

The Gambia River basin was part of the region dominated in the tenth to 16th centuries by the Songhai and Mali kingdoms centred on the upper Niger. The Portuguese reached the Gambia River in 1447; English merchants began to trade along the river from 1588. Merchants from France, Courland (now Latvia) and the Netherlands also established trading posts. In 1816 the British stationed a garrison on an island at the river mouth which became the capital of a small British-administered colony. In 1889 France agreed that the British rights along the upper river should extend to 10 km from the river on either bank. British administration was extended from the Colony to this Protectorate. The Gambia became independent within the Commonwealth on 18 February 1965, and a republic on 24 April 1970.

In July 1994 junior army officers launched a coup which ousted the president and the government, and a military council was formed. The coup leader, Lt. (later Capt.) Jammeh, assumed the presidency, the constitution was suspended and a civilian-military government was formed to rule in conjunction with the Ruling Military Council. A referendum approved a new constitution in August 1996, Jammeh was elected president the following month and the Ruling Military Council was dissolved. A pro-presidential party won 33 of the 49 seats in the new parliament in a legislative election in January 1997.

### FOREIGN RELATIONS

The relationship with Senegal remains an important factor in political and economic policy. Moves towards a closer association were accelerated after an abortive coup in 1981 was put down with the help of Senegalese troops. In 1982 the Senegambia Confederation was instituted but following disagreements it was dissolved in 1989. A treaty of friendship and co-operation was signed with Senegal in 1991.

### POLITICAL SYSTEM

The constitution gives enhanced powers to the president who is elected for an indefinite term. The National Assembly has 49 members, of whom 45 are directly elected, and four appointed by the president, for a five-year term.

### HEAD OF STATE

*President, Defence*, Capt. Yahya Jammeh, *took power* 23 July 1994, *elected* 26 September 1996
*Vice-President, Women and Social Affairs*, Isatou Njie-Saidy

### CABINET *as at July 2001*

*Agriculture*, Hassan Sallah
*Education*, Thérèse Ndong-Jatta
*External Affairs*, Lamine Sedat Jobe
*Finance and Economic Affairs*, Famara Jatta
*Fisheries and Natural Resources*, Susan Waffa-Ogooh
*Health*, Yankuba Gassama
*Interior*, Ousman Badjie
*Justice, Attorney-General*, Joseph Joof
*Local Government and Lands*, Momodou Nai Ceesay
*Public Works, Communications and Information, Presidential Affairs*, Capt. Edward Singhateh
*Tourism and Culture*, Capt. Yankuba Touray
*Trade, Industry and Employment*, Musa Sillah
*Youth and Sports*, Sarjo Jallow

GAMBIA HIGH COMMISSION
57 Kensington Court, London W8 5DG
Tel: 020-7937 6316/7/8
*High Commissioner*, HE Gibril Seman Joof, apptd 2000

BRITISH HIGH COMMISSION
48 Atlantic Road, Fajara (PO Box 507), Banjul
Tel: (00 220) 495133/4
E-mail: bhcbanjul@gamtel.gm
*High Commissioner*, HE John Perrott, apptd 2000

## ECONOMY

Agriculture accounts for 79.9 per cent of employment and contributes 29.1 per cent of GDP. The chief product, groundnuts, forms over 80 per cent of exports. Other crops are cotton, rice, millet, sorghum and maize.

Manufactures are limited to groundnut processing, minor metal fabrications, paints, furniture, soap and bottling. Tourism is developing quickly with more than 80,000 visitors in 1996–7. Trade through the Gambia, re-exporting imported goods to neighbouring countries, is an important element in the economy. The main exports are groundnuts, cotton, and fish and fish products. The main imports are foodstuffs and live animals, industrial goods, machinery and transport equipment, and fuels. In 1997 there was a trade surplus of US$85 million and a current account deficit of US$23 million. Imports in 1999 totalled US$192 million and exports US$7 million.

GNP – US$415 million (1999); US$340 per capita (1999)
GDP – US$385 million (1997); US$355 per capita (1998)
ANNUAL AVERAGE GROWTH OF GDP – 3.2 per cent (1996)
INFLATION RATE – 3.8 per cent (1999)
TOTAL EXTERNAL DEBT – US$477 million (1998)

| *Trade with UK* | 1999 | 2000 |
|---|---|---|
| Imports from UK | £16,654,000 | £14,434,000 |
| Exports to UK | 2,844,000 | 3,506,000 |

## COMMUNICATIONS

There is an international airport at Yundum, 17 miles from Banjul, with scheduled services flying to other West African states and to the UK and Belgium. Banjul is the main port. Internal communication is by road and river. In 1996 there were 2,700 km of roads, of which 956 km were paved. There are seven radio broadcasting stations and a UHF telephone service linking Banjul with the principal towns in the provinces. There is one television station.

## EDUCATION

There are 24 secondary schools (eight high and 16 technical). Two high schools provide A-level education. Gambia College provides post-secondary courses in education, agriculture, public health and nursing. There are seven vocational training institutions. Higher education and advanced training courses are taken outside The Gambia, currently by over 200 students.

ILLITERACY RATE – 63.5 per cent (1997)
ENROLMENT (percentage of age group) – primary 65 per cent (1996); secondary 20 per cent (1992); tertiary 1.7 per cent (1996)

## GEORGIA
*Sakartvelos Respublikis*

AREA – 26,911 sq. miles (69,700 sq. km). Neighbours: Russia (north), Azerbaijan (south-east), Armenia (south), Turkey (south-west)
POPULATION – 5,401,000 (2001 estimate): 70 per cent Georgian, 8 per cent Armenian, 6 per cent Russian, 6 per cent Azerbaijani, 3 per cent Ossetian and 2 per cent Abkhazian, with smaller groups of Greeks, Ukrainians, Jews and Kurds. Georgian is the sole official language, except in Abkhazia where Abkhazian is also officially recognised. Russian and Armenian are commonly spoken. About 65 per cent of the population are adherents of the Georgian Orthodox Church, 11 per cent are Muslims, 10 per cent are Russian Orthodox and 8 per cent are Armenian Orthodox. .
CAPITAL – Tbilisi (population, 1,268,000, 1990 estimate)
MAJOR CITIES – Batumi (137,000); Kutaisi (236,000); Rustavi (160,000); Sukhumi (capital of Abkhazia) (122,000), 1990 UN estimates
CURRENCY – Lari of 100 tetri
NATIONAL ANTHEM - Dideba zetsit kurtheuls (Praise be to the Heavenly Bestower of Blessings)
NATIONAL DAY – 26 May (Independence Day)
NATIONAL FLAG – Cherry red with a canton in the upper hoist divided black over white
LIFE EXPECTANCY (years) – male 69.4; female 76.7
POPULATION GROWTH RATE – 1.0 per cent (1999)
POPULATION DENSITY – 73 per sq. km (1998)
URBAN POPULATION – 60.7 per cent (2000 estimate)
MILITARY EXPENDITURE – 2.4 per cent of GDP (1999)
MILITARY PERSONNEL – 26,900: Army 23,800, Navy 800, Air Force 1,870; Paramilitaries 6,500
CONSCRIPTION DURATION – Two years
ILLITERACY RATE – 0.5 per cent
ENROLMENT (percentage of age group) – primary 90 per cent (1996); secondary 74 per cent (1996); tertiary 42.0 per cent (1996)

Georgia occupies the north-western part of the Caucasus region of the former Soviet Union. It contains the two autonomous republics of Abkhazia and Adjaria and the disputed region of South Ossetia (Tskhinvali).

Georgia is mountainous, with the Greater Caucasus in the north and the Lesser Caucasus in the south. Western Georgia has a mild and damp climate, eastern Georgia is more continental and dry. The Black Sea shore and the Rioni lowland are subtropical.

### HISTORY AND POLITICS

The Georgians formed two states, Colchis and Iberia, on the edge of the Black Sea around 1000 BC. After centuries of invasions by Arabs, Turks and Khazars, Georgia entered its 'Golden Age' in the 12th century AD when trade, irrigation and communications were developed. Invasions by the Khazars and Mongols led to the division of Georgia into several states. These struggled against the Turkish and the Persian empires from the 16th to the 18th centuries, gradually turning to the Russian Empire for protection and support. Eastern Georgia signed a treaty of alliance with Russia which recognised Russian supremacy in 1783 and joined the Russian Empire in 1801, followed soon after by Western Georgia.

In the late 19th century, nationalist and Marxist movements competed for limited political influence under autocratic Russian rule. One of the most prominent Marxist activists was Iosif Dzhugashvili (Josef Stalin). After the Russian revolution of 1917, a nationalist government came to power in Georgia supported by allied intervention forces. In 1921 Soviet forces occupied Tbilisi, and in 1922 Georgia joined the Soviet Union as part of the Transcaucasian Soviet Socialist Republic.

In March 1990 the Georgian Supreme Soviet declared illegal the treaties of 1921–2 by which Georgia had joined the Soviet Union. The Communist Party's monopoly on power was abolished and in multiparty elections held in October and November 1990 the nationalist leader Zviad Gamsakhurdia was elected president. Georgia declared its independence from the Soviet Union in May 1991 and was admitted to UN membership on 31 July 1992.

Gamsakhurdia's government faced armed opposition from 1991 onwards. Defeat in the ensuing civil war in Tbilisi led to Gamsakhurdia's overthrow in January 1992, and in March 1992 a state council was appointed with the former Soviet foreign minister Eduard Shevardnadze as chairman. Fighting continued throughout 1992 and 1993. In October 1992 Shevardnadze was elected head of state and Chairman of the Parliament, and a loose alliance of pro-Shevardnadze parties formed a government.

Gamsakhurdia returned to western Georgia in September 1993. President Shevardnadze failed to prevent the advance of Gamsakhurdia's rebels as most government forces were engaged in Abkhazia. Shevardnadze was forced to accept Russian armaments and troops to defeat the rebellion and in return agreed to join the CIS. Georgia rescinded its participation in the CIS Collective Security treaty in February 1999 and Russian troops, who had been guarding Georgia's frontier with Turkey, began to withdraw. The legislative election held on 31 October and 14 November 1999 was won by the Union of Citizens of Georgia, which gained 130 of the 235 seats. In the presidential election held on 9 April 2000, President Shevardnadze was re-elected, gaining 78.8 per cent of the votes cast.

#### SECESSION

In late 1990 the South Ossetians took up arms against Georgian rule in an attempt to join North Ossetia, itself part of Russia. The South Ossetian provincial parliament voted in November 1992 to secede from Georgia and join Russia. Fighting ceased in June 1992 and a joint Russian-Georgian-Ossetian peacekeeping force was dispatched. Representatives of the South Ossetian and Georgian governments met in April 1996 to agree security and confidence-building measures. Presidential elections in South Ossetia were won by Ludvig Chibirov, the chair of the Supreme Council, in November 1996. Legislative elections were held in May 1999.

In July 1992 the Abkhazian republican parliament declared Abkhazia independent. Fighting broke out between Georgian forces and Abkhazian separatists supported by Russian arms and irregulars; Georgian forces were defeated and were forced to withdraw in September 1993. Negotiations under Russian auspices led to an Abkhaz-Georgian cease-fire and separation of forces agreement being signed in May 1994 and the deployment of 2,500 Russian UN peacekeepers on the Abkhaz-Georgian border. In November 1994 the Abkhaz Supreme Soviet declared Abkhazia's independence again and elected Vladislav Ardzinba as president. Abkhazia was given autonomous republic status under the 1995 constitution; this was rejected by the republican parliament. Elections to the self-declared Abkhaz People's Assembly were held in November 1996. Following a guarantee of security from President Ardzinba, ethnic Georgians who had fled Abkhazia during the fighting began returning in March 1999. A referendum held in Abkhazia in October 1999 approved a new constitution which held Abkhazia to be a sovereign state. On 11 July 2000, Georgia and Abkhazia signed a UN-sponsored protocol on stabilisation measures, agreeing to refrain from the use of force and to establish groups to combat cross-border crime.

### FOREIGN RELATIONS

Georgia and Russia agreed on 18 November 1999 on the closure of two of the four remaining Russian military bases on Georgian territory; in December 2000 they agreed that the two remaining bases would remain operational for an indefinite period.

Georgia has signed a Partnership and Co-operation Agreement with the European Union.

### POLITICAL SYSTEM

The 1995 constitution provides for a federal republic with a unicameral legislature, to become bicameral 'following the creation of appropriate conditions'; and a popularly elected president who serves a maximum of two five-year terms. The present parliament has 235 members, directly elected for a four-year term.

### HEAD OF STATE

*President*, Eduard Shevardnadze, *elected* 11 October 1992, *re-elected* 1995, 9 April 2000

### CABINET *as at July 2001*

*Minister of State, Head of Chancellery*, Giorgi Arsenishvili
*Deputy Minister of State, Economics and Banking Issues, State Property Management*, Levan Dzneladze
*Agriculture and Food*, Davit Kirvalidze
*Culture*, Sesili Gogiberidze
*Defence*, Maj.-Gen. Davit Tevzadze
*Economy, Industry and Trade*, Vano Chakhartishvili
*Education*, Alexandre Kartozia
*Finance*, Zurab Noghaideli
*Foreign Affairs*, Irakli Menagarishvili
*Fuel and Energy*, Davit Mirtskhulava
*Health and Social Security*, Avtandil Jorbenadze
*Internal Affairs*, Kakha Targamadze
*Justice*, Mikheil Saakashvili
*Natural Resources and Environment*, Nino Chkobadze
*Refugees and Resettlement*, Valeri Vashakidze
*State Security*, Vakhtang Kutateladze
*Tax Revenue*, Mikheil Machavariani
*Transport and Communications*, Merab Adeishvili
*Urban Planning and Construction*, Merab Chkhenkeli
*Without Portfolio*, Malkhaz Kakabadze

### EMBASSY OF THE REPUBLIC OF GEORGIA

3 Hornton Place, London, W8 4LZ
Tel: 020-7937 8233
*Ambassador Extraordinary and Plenipotentiary*, HE Teimuraz Mamatsashvili, apptd 1995

### BRITISH EMBASSY

Sheraton Metechi Palace Hotel, GE-380003 Tbilisi
Tel: (00 995) (32) 955497
E-mail: britishembassy@caucasus.net
*Ambassador Extraordinary and Plenipotentiary*, HE Deborah Barnes-Jones, apptd 2001
BRITISH COUNCIL DIRECTOR, Jo Bakowski, 13 Chavchavadze Avenue, GE-380079 Tbilisi; e-mail: office@britishcouncil.org.ge

## ECONOMY

The economy was brought to the brink of collapse by civil and secessionist wars and the ending of former Soviet trading relationships. Although Georgia has deposits of coal, they have not been exploited and it is desperately short of energy supplies. A large proportion of production is stolen by black marketeers, whilst the tourist industry on the Black Sea coast has been destroyed by the fighting. The only productive sector of the economy is agriculture, which employs 30 per cent of the workforce and generates 38 per cent of GDP, with a concentration on viniculture, tea and tobacco-growing and citrus fruits. The main exports are iron alloys, wine, nuts, chemical fertilisers, and oil and oil products. The main imports are oil and oil products, gas, automobiles, pharmaceuticals and wheat. In January 2001 the IMF approved a three-year loan to Georgia, amounting to some US$141 million. In 1998 exports totalled US$192 million and imports US$887 million. GNP – US$3,362 million (1999); US$620 per capita (1999)
GDP – US$4,947 million (1997); US$974 per capita (1998)
ANNUAL AVERAGE GROWTH OF GDP – 10.8 per cent (1996)
INFLATION RATE – 19.1 per cent (1999)
TOTAL EXTERNAL DEBT – US$1,674 million (1998)

| *Trade with UK* | 1999 | 2000 |
|---|---|---|
| Imports from UK | £14,681,000 | £12,204,000 |
| Exports to UK | 3,665,000 | 14,220,000 |

## CULTURE

Famous Georgians include the 12th-century writer Shota Rustaveli, who composed the epic poem *Knight in a Tiger's Skin*, and the film director Tengiz Abuladze (b. 1924), who directed the film *Repentance*.

---

## GERMANY

*Bundesrepublik Deutschland – Federal Republic of Germany*

---

AREA – 137,846 sq. miles (357,022 sq. km). Neighbours: Denmark (north), Poland (east), Czech Republic (east and south-east), Austria (south-east and south), Switzerland (south), France, Luxembourg, Belgium and the Netherlands (west)
POPULATION - 82,027,000 (1997 UN estimate). Approximately 80 per cent of the population live in the former West Germany. In 1994 there were 28,197,000 Protestants, 27,909,797 Roman Catholics, 2,700,000 Muslims and 53,797 Jews. The language is German; there are Danish- and Frisian-speaking minorities in Schleswig-Holstein and a Sorbian-speaking minority in Saxony
CAPITAL – Berlin (population, 3,425,759, 1997 estimate). The seat of government and parliament was transferred from Bonn to Berlin in 2000
MAJOR CITIES – Bremen (546,968); Cologne (964,311); Dortmund (594,866); Dresden (459,222); Duisburg (529,062); Düsseldorf (570,969); Essen (608,732); Frankfurt am Main (643,469); Hamburg (1,704,731); Hannover (520,670); Leipzig (446,491); Munich (1,205,923); Nuremberg (489,758); Stuttgart (585,274), 1998 estimates
CURRENCY – Euro (€) of 100 cents/Deutsche Mark (DM) of 100 Pfennig
NATIONAL ANTHEM – Einigkeit und Recht und Freiheit (Unity and right and freedom)
NATIONAL DAY – 3 October (Anniversary of 1990 Unification)
NATIONAL FLAG – Horizontal bars of black, red and gold
LIFE EXPECTANCY (years) – male 73.7; female 80.1
POPULATION GROWTH RATE – 0.4 per cent (1999)
POPULATION DENSITY – 230 per sq. km (1998)
URBAN POPULATION – 87.5 per cent (2000 estimate)

## HISTORY AND POLITICS

The first German realm was the Holy Roman Empire, established in AD 962 when Otto I of Saxony was crowned Emperor. The Empire endured until 1806, but the achievement of a national state was prevented by fragmentation into small principalities and dukedoms.

The Empire was replaced by a loose association of sovereign states known as the German Confederation, which was dissolved in 1866 and replaced by the Prussian-dominated North German Federation. The south German principalities united with the northern federation to form a second German Empire in 1871 and the King of Prussia was proclaimed Emperor.

Defeat in the First World War led to the abdication of the Emperor, and the country became a republic. The Treaty of Versailles (1919) ceded Alsace-Lorraine to France, and large areas in the east were lost to Poland. The world economic crisis of 1929 contributed to the collapse of the Weimar Republic and the subsequent rise to power of the National Socialist movement of Adolf Hitler, who became Chancellor in 1933.

After concluding a Treaty of Non-Aggression with the Soviet Union in August 1939, Germany invaded Poland (1 September 1939), precipitating the Second World War, which lasted until 1945. Hitler committed suicide on 30 April 1945. On 8 May 1945, Germany unconditionally surrendered.

## The Post-War Period

Germany was divided into American, French, British and Soviet zones of occupation. The territories to the east of the Oder and Neisse rivers were placed under Polish and Russian administration and some 7.75 million Germans were deported.

The Federal Republic of Germany (FRG) was created out of the three western zones in 1949. A Communist government was established in the Soviet zone (henceforth the German Democratic Republic (GDR)). In 1961 the Soviet zone of Berlin was sealed off, and the Berlin Wall was built along the zonal boundary, partitioning the western sectors of the city from the eastern.

Soviet-initiated reform in eastern Europe during the late 1980s led to unrest in the GDR, culminating in the opening of the Berlin Wall in November 1989 and the collapse of Communist government. The 'Treaty on the Final Settlement with Respect to Germany', concluded between the FRG, GDR and the four former occupying powers in September 1990, unified Germany with effect from 3 October 1990 as a fully sovereign state. Economic and monetary union preceded formal union on 1 July 1990. Unification is constitutionally the accession of Berlin and the five reformed *Länder* of the GDR to the FRG, which remains in being. Berlin was declared to be

the capital of the unified Germany and parliament and government departments were transferred from Bonn.

The distribution of seats following the last election for the Bundestag on 27 September 1998 was: Social Democrats, 298; Christian Democratic Union, 198; Christian Social Union, 47; The Greens, 47; Free Democrats, 44; Democratic Socialists, 35. A coalition of Social Democrats and Greens forms the present government.

## Political System

The Basic Law provides for a president, elected by a Federal Convention (electoral college) for a five-year term, a lower house (*Bundestag*) of 669 members elected by direct universal suffrage for a four-year term of office, and an upper house (*Bundesrat*) composed of 69 members appointed by the governments of the *Länder* in proportion to *Länder* populations, without a fixed term of office.

| *Land* | *Area (sq. km)* | *Population (1998)* | *Capital* | *Minister-President (July 2001)* |
|---|---|---|---|---|
| Baden-Württemberg | 35,752 | 10.4m | Stuttgart | Erwin Teufel (CDU) |
| Bavaria | 70,548 | 12.1m | Munich | Dr Edmund Stoiber (CSU) |
| Berlin | 891 | 3.4m | — | Klaus Wowereit (CDU)* |
| Brandenburg | 29,476 | 2.6m | Potsdam | Dr Manfred Stolpe (SPD) |
| Bremen | 404 | 0.7m | — | Dr Henning Scherf (SPD)* |
| Hamburg | 755 | 1.7m | — | Ortwin Runde (SPD)* |
| Hesse | 21,115 | 6.0m | Wiesbaden | Roland Koch (CDU) |
| Lower Saxony | 47,613 | 7.9m | Hannover | Sigmar Gabriel (SPD) |
| Mecklenburg-Western Pomerania | 23,170 | 1.8m | Schwerin | Dr Harald Ringstorff (SPD) |
| North Rhine-Westphalia | 34,079 | 18.0m | Düsseldorf | Wolfgang Clement (SPD) |
| Rhineland-Palatinate | 19,847 | 4.0m | Mainz | Kurt Beck (SPD) |
| Saarland | 2,570 | 1.1m | Saarbrücken | Peter Müller (SPD) |
| Saxony | 18,412 | 4.5m | Dresden | Prof. Kurt Biedenkopf (CDU) |
| Saxony-Anhalt | 20,447 | 2.7m | Magdeburg | Dr Reinhard Höppner (SPD) |
| Schleswig-Holstein | 15,770 | 2.8m | Kiel | Heide Simonis (SPD) |
| Thuringia | 16,172 | 2.5m | Erfurt | Dr Bernhard Vogel (CDU) |

*Berlin, *Governing Mayor*; Bremen, *Mayor*; Hamburg, *First Mayor*
CDU Christian Democratic Union; CSU Christian Social Union; SPD Social Democratic Party

Judicial authority is exercised by the Federal Constitutional Court, the federal courts provided for in the Basic Law and the courts of the *Länder*.

### Federal Structure

Germany is a federal republic composed of 16 states (*Länder*) (ten from the former West, five from the former East and Berlin). Each *Land* has its own directly elected legislature and government led by Minister-Presidents (prime ministers) or equivalents. The 1949 Basic Law vests executive power in the *Länder* governments except in those areas reserved for the federal government.

### Head of State

*Federal President*, Johannes Rau, *elected* 24 May 1999

### Cabinet *as at July 2001*

*Federal Chancellor*, Gerhard Schröder (SPD)
*Federal Vice-Chancellor, Foreign Affairs*, Joschka Fischer (Greens)
*Commissioner for Media and Cultural Affairs*, Julian Nida-Rümelin (SPD)
*Consumer Protection, Nutrition and Agriculture*, Renate Künast (Greens)
*Defence*, Rudolf Scharping (SPD)
*Economic Co-operation and Development*, Heidemarie Wieczorek-Zeul (SPD)
*Economics and Technology*, Werner Müller (Ind.)
*Education and Research*, Edelgard Bulmahn (SPD)
*Environment, Nature Conservation and Reactor Safety*, Jürgen Trittin (Greens)
*Family, Pensioners, Women and Youth*, Dr Christine Bergmann (SPD)
*Finance*, Hans Eichel (SPD)
*Head of Chancellory*, Frank-Walter Steinmeier (SPD)
*Health*, Ulla Schmidt (SPD)
*Interior*, Otto Schily (SPD)
*Justice*, Herta Däubler-Gmelin (SPD)
*Labour and Social Affairs*, Walter Riester (SPD)
*Ministers of State*, Christoph Zöpel (SPD) (*European Affairs*); Hans Martin Bury (SPD); Rolf Schwanitz (SPD)
*Transport, Construction and Housing*, Kurt Bodewig (SPD)

SPD Social Democratic Party Ind. Independent

### Embassy of the Federal Republic of Germany

23 Belgrave Square/Chesham Place, London SW1X 8PZ
Tel: 020-7824 1300
*Ambassador Extraordinary and Plenipotentiary*, HE Dr Hans-Friedrich von Ploetz, apptd 1999
*Minister and Co-ordinator of EU Affairs*, Dr. W. Kischlat
*Defence Attaché*, Rear-Adm. Hubert Hass
*Counsellors*, T. Hanckel (*Cultural Affairs*); J. Ranau (*Economic Affairs*)
*First* Secretary, N. Meyer (*Information*)

### British Embassy

Wilhelmstrasse 70, D-10117 Berlin
Tel: (00 49) (30) 204570
*Ambassador Extraordinary and Plenipotentiary*, HE Sir Paul Lever, KCMG, apptd 1997
*Deputy Head of Mission*, A. Charlton, CMG
*Defence and Military Attaché*, Brig. B. R. Isbell, MBE
*Counsellor (Economic)*, R. L. Turner

### British Embassy Bonn Office

Argelanderstrasse 108a, D-53115 Bonn
Tel: (00 49) (228) 91670

British Consulates-General – Düsseldorf, Frankfurt, Hamburg, Munich, Stuttgart

British Consulates – Bremen, Hannover, Kiel and Nuremberg

British Council Director, Tony Andrews, Hackescher Markt 1, D-10178 Berlin; e-mail: bc.berlin@britcoun.de

British Chamber of Commerce, Severinstrasse 60, D-50678 Köln. *Director*, Herr Heumann; e-mail: generaloffice@bccg.de

## DEFENCE

The Army has 2,815 main battle tanks, 3,026 armoured personnel carriers, 2,253 armoured infantry fighting vehicles, and 204 attack helicopters. The Navy has 14 submarines, two destroyers, 12 frigates, 28 patrol and coastal vessels, 50 combat aircraft and 40 armed helicopters. The Air Force has 457 combat aircraft.

There remain 85,880 NATO personnel in Germany (USA 57,580; UK 20,600; Belgium 2,000; France 2,700; Netherlands 3,000).

Military Expenditure – 1.6 per cent of GDP (1999)
Military Personnel – 321,000: Army 221,100, Navy 26,600, Air Force 73,300. Under the terms of the Treaty of Unification, the German armed forces have been limited to 370,000 active personnel since the end of 1994
Conscription Duration – Ten months

## ECONOMY

Germany has a predominantly industrial economy. Principal industries are coal mining, iron and steel production, machine construction, the electrical industry, the manufacture of steel and metal products, chemicals, automobile production, electronics, textiles and the processing of foodstuffs.

In 1998, Germany produced 207,642,000 tonnes of coal and 2,895,446 tonnes of crude petroleum. The government announced in June 2000 that it was to abolish all 19 of Germany's nuclear power stations over a 32-year period, which currently supplied over 30 per cent of the energy generated in the country.

After a mini-boom generated by new East German demand in 1990 and 1991, Germany entered its most severe recession since the war induced by the costs of reunification. In 1993 a 'Solidarity Pact' was agreed, which lays down the basis of future funding transfers to the East based on a 5.5 per cent rise in income taxes, wage restraint in the West, more private investment in the East, and the distribution of the funding burden between the federal and *Länder* governments. The government was forced to make spending cuts in order to meet the criteria for European monetary union. An austerity package was approved in August 1999, which cut DM30,000 million from public spending in 2000, and in December 1999 it was announced that the basic rate of company tax would fall from 40 per cent to 25 per cent from 1 January 2001. The pension system is to be reformed in 2002, to encourage private pension provision to reduce the cost to the state of an increasingly ageing population.

The rate of economic growth increased in 1999 and 2000, aided by the weakness of the euro, but began to slow in the first quarter of 2001.

In 1999 there was a trade surplus of US$70,503 million and a current account deficit of US$20,901 million. Imports totalled US$472,161 million and exports US$541,076 million.

GNP – US$2,103,804 million (1999); US$25,350 per capita (1999)
GDP – US$2,089,845 million (1997); US$25,729 per capita (1999)
Annual Average Growth of GDP – 2.6 per cent (2000)
Inflation Rate – 2.6 per cent (2001)
Unemployment – 7.8 per cent (2001)

| *Trade with UK* | 1999 | 2000 |
|---|---|---|
| Imports from UK | £19,217,600,000 | £21,456,600,000 |
| Exports to UK | 25,131,000,000 | 26,700,400,000 |

## COMMUNICATIONS

In 1999 the privatised railways measured 41,841 km of which 19,325 km were electrified. Classified roads measured 230,700 km in 2000, of which motorways were 11,500 km. Merchant shipping under the German flag in 1999 amounted to 7,968,000 tonnes gross. Inland waterways are 6,929 km long.

## EDUCATION

School attendance is compulsory between the ages of six and 18 and comprises nine years of full-time education at primary and main schools and three years of vocational education on a part-time basis. The secondary school leaving examination (*Abitur*) entitles the holder to a place of study at a university or another institution of higher education.

Children below the age of 18 who are not attending a general secondary or a full-time vocational school have compulsory day-release at a vocational school.

The largest universities are in Munich, Berlin, Hamburg, Bonn, Frankfurt and Cologne.

ENROLMENT (percentage of age group) – primary 86 per cent (1996); secondary 88 per cent (1996); tertiary 47.2 per cent (1996)

## CULTURE

Modern (or New High) German has developed from the time of the Reformation to the present day, with differences of dialect in Austria, Alsace, Luxembourg, Liechtenstein and the German-speaking cantons of Switzerland.

The literary language is usually regarded as having become fixed by Luther and Zwingli at the Reformation, since which time many great names occur in all branches, notably philosophy, from Leibnitz (1646–1716) to Kant (1724–1804), Schelling (1775–1854) and Hegel (1770–1831); drama, from Goethe (1749–1832) and Schiller (1759–1805) to Gerhart Hauptmann (1862–1946); and poetry, Heinrich Heine (1797–1856). Eight German authors have received the Nobel Prize for Literature: Theodor Mommsen (1902), R. Eucken (1908), P. Heyse (1909), Gerhart Hauptmann (1912), Thomas Mann (1929), N. Sachs (1966), Heinrich Böll (1972) and Gunther Grass (1999).

There are 369 daily newspapers and nearly 10,000 periodicals.

---

# GHANA

*The Republic of Ghana*

---

AREA – 92,098 sq. miles (238,533 sq. km). Neighbours: Burkina Faso (north), Côte d'Ivoire (west), Togo (east)

POPULATION – 18,885,616 (1998 estimate); most are Sudanese Negroes, although Hamitic strains are common in the north. The official language is English. The principal indigenous language group is Akan, of which Twi and Fanti are the most commonly used. Ga, Ewe and languages of the Mole-Dagbani group are common in certain regions. Most Ghanaians are Christians, although there is a substantial Muslim minority in the north

CAPITAL – ΨAccra (population, 1,445,515, 1998), Greater Accra Region (including Tema) 2,384,753 (1998 estimate)

MAJOR CITIES – Koforidua (81,378); Kumasi (577,878); ΨTakoradi (96,897); Tamale (228,827)

CURRENCY – Cedi of 100 pesewas

NATIONAL FLAG – Equal horizontal bands of red over gold over green; five-point black star on gold stripe

NATIONAL ANTHEM – God Bless our Homeland Ghana

NATIONAL DAY – 6 March (Independence Day)

LIFE EXPECTANCY (years) – male 54.2; female 55.6

POPULATION GROWTH RATE – 3.0 per cent (1999)

POPULATION DENSITY – 80 per sq. km (1998)

URBAN POPULATION – 38.4 per cent (2000 estimate)

MILITARY EXPENDITURE – 1.2 per cent of GDP (1999)

MILITARY PERSONNEL – 7,000: Army 5,000, Navy 1,000, Air Force 1,000

ILLITERACY RATE – 29.8 per cent

ENROLMENT (percentage of age group) – tertiary 1.4 per cent (1990)

## HISTORY AND POLITICS

First reached by Europeans in the 15th century, the constituent parts of Ghana came under British administration at various times, the original Gold Coast Colony being constituted in 1874, and Ashanti and the Northern Territories Protectorate in 1901. Trans-Volta-Togoland, part of the former German colony of Togo, was mandated to Britain by the League of Nations after the First World War and was integrated with the Gold Coast Colony in 1956 following a plebiscite. The former Gold Coast Colony and associated territories became the independent state of Ghana on 6 March 1957 and became a republic in 1960.

Since 1966, Ghana has experienced long periods of military rule interspersed with short-lived civilian governments. A coup in 1979 led to the formation of an Armed Forces Revolutionary Council chaired by Flt. Lt. Jerry Rawlings. Civilian rule was restored in 1979 but another coup in December 1981 brought Rawlings back to power.

A referendum in 1992 approved a new multiparty constitution and the legalisation of political parties. The National Democratic Congress (NDC) was established as a political party from the ruling Provisional National Defence Council. The presidential and parliamentary elections in late 1992 were won by Rawlings and the NDC, following a boycott by most opposition parties and most of the electorate. The Fourth Republic was declared on 7 January 1993 and a new government nominated by the president took office in March 1993. In legislative elections in December 1996, the NDC retained its absolute majority; President Rawlings was also re-elected.

The NDC lost power in the general election held on 7 December 2000, which was won by the New Patriotic Party (NPP), who obtained 98 seats; the NDC won 93 seats. The presidential election held on 7 and 28 December 2000 was won by John Kufuor of the NPP.

### POLITICAL SYSTEM

The head of state is an executive president elected for a four-year term, renewable only once. The president appoints the Council of Ministers. The unicameral legislature, the Parliament, has 200 members directly elected for a four-year term.

For political and administrative purposes Ghana is divided into ten regions, each headed by a Regional Minister who is the representative of the central government.

### HEAD OF STATE

*President*, John Kufuor, *elected* 28 December 2000, *sworn in* 7 January 2001

*Vice-President, Youth and Sports*, Aliju Mahama

COUNCIL OF MINISTERS *as at July 2001*

*Communications*, Owusu Agyapong
*Defence*, Kwame Addo-Kufuor
*Education*, Christopher Ameyaw-Akumfi
*Environment, Science and Technology*, Dominic Fobih
*Finance*, Yaw Osafo Maado
*Food and Agriculture*, Maj. Courage Quarshigah
*Foreign Affairs*, Hackman Owusu-Agyemang
*Health*, Richard Anane
*Interior*, Malik Yakubu Alhassan
*Justice and Attorney-General*, Nana Akufo Addo
*Lands and Forestry*, Kwaku Afriyie
*Local Government and Rural Development*, Kwadwo Baah-Wiredu
*Manpower Development and Employment*, Cecilia Bannerman
*Mines and Energy*, Albert Kan-Dapaah
*Ministers of State*, Elizabeth Ohene (*Media Relations*); C. O. Nyanor (*Private Sector Development*)
*Parliamentary Affairs*, J. H. Mensah
*Planning and Regional Economic Co-operation and Integration*, Kwesi Nduom
*Presidential Affairs*, Jake Obetsebi-Lamptey
*Roads and Transport*, Kwadwo Agyei-Darko
*Tourism*, Hawa Yakubu
*Trade and Industry*, Kofi Apraku
*Women's Affairs*, Gladys Asmah
*Works and Housing*, Kwamena Bartels

GHANA HIGH COMMISSION
13 Belgrave Square, London SW1X 8PN
Tel: 020-7235 4142
*High Commissioner*, vacant
*Deputy High Commissioner*, G. C. Kpodo
*Defence Adviser*, Cdre C. B. Puplampu
*Minister-Counsellor*, E. K. Amenuvor (*Trade*)

BRITISH HIGH COMMISSION
PO Box 296, Osu Link, Accra
Tel: (00 233) (21) 221665
E-mail: High.Commission@accra.mail.fco.gov.uk
*High Commissioner*, HE Rod Pullen, apptd 2000
*Deputy High Commissioner*, C. Murray
*Defence Adviser*, Lt.-Col. E. Glover
*First Secretary (Commercial)*, M. A. Ives

BRITISH COUNCIL DIRECTOR, Terence Humphreys, 11 Liberia Road, PO Box 771, Accra.
E-mail: bcaccra@britishcouncil.org.gh.There is also an office in Kumasi.
GHANA-BRITISH CHAMBER OF COMMERCE AND INDUSTRY, Plot No. A132/1 Obedro St Korle Gonno, PO Box GP 21101, Accra

## ECONOMY

Agriculture is the basis of the economy, employing 57.4 per cent of the workforce in 1998. Crops include cocoa, the largest single source of revenue, rice, cassava, plantains, oranges and pineapples, groundnuts, corn, millet, oil palms, yams, maize and vegetables. Livestock is raised in uncultivated areas. Fishing is important in coastal areas and in the Volta lake and river system.

Manganese production ranks among the world's largest, with 384,173 tonnes of ore being produced in 1998. Gold is the main export; production amounted to 74,315 kg in 1998. Diamonds and bauxite are also produced.

Since 1966 the Volta Dams at Akosombo and Kpong have generated hydroelectric power for the processing of bauxite and fed a power transmission network for most of Ghana, Togo and Benin. There is considerable foreign investment in Ghana, and its economy has grown consistently. In 1999 there was a trade deficit of US$1,112 million and a current account deficit of US$766 million. Imports in 1998 totalled US$2,563 million and exports US$1,795 million.

GNP – US$7,451 million (1999); US$390 per capita (1999)
GDP – US$7,434 million (1997); US$346 per capita (1998)
ANNUAL AVERAGE GROWTH OF GDP – 5.2 per cent (1996)
INFLATION RATE – 12.4 per cent (1999)
TOTAL EXTERNAL DEBT – US$6,884 million (1998)

TRADE

Principal exports are gold, cocoa, and timber. Principal imports are capital goods, semi-manufactures, consumables and energy.

| *Trade with UK* | 1999 | 2000 |
|---|---|---|
| Imports from UK | £174,842,000 | £169,365,000 |
| Exports to UK | 153,559,000 | 99,994,000 |

## COMMUNICATIONS

The Kotoka Airport at Accra is an international airport and Ghana Airways is the national airline. There are more than 20,000 miles of motorable roads and 600 miles of railway.

## GREECE
*Elliniki Dimokratia*

AREA – 50,949 sq. miles (131,957 sq. km). Neighbours: Albania, Bulgaria and Macedonia (north), Turkey (east)
POPULATION – 10,536,000 (1997 UN estimate), 10,256,464 (1991 census): 98 per cent Greek Orthodox, 1 per cent Catholic, 1 per cent Muslim. The language is Greek
CAPITAL – Athens (population 3,072,922, 1991); including ΨPiraeus and suburbs, 3,096,775 (1991 census)
MAJOR CITIES – ΨIráklion (Heraklion) (132,117); Lárisa (113,090); ΨPátrai (Patras) (170,452); ΨThessaloníki (Salonika) (749,048); ΨVólos (116,031), 1991
CURRENCY – Drachma of 100 leptae
NATIONAL ANTHEM – Imnos Eis Tin Eleftherian (Hymn to Freedom)
NATIONAL DAY – March 25 (Independence Day)
NATIONAL FLAG – Blue and white stripes with a white cross on a blue field in the canton
LIFE EXPECTANCY (years) – male 75.5; female 80.5
POPULATION GROWTH RATE – 0.4 per cent (1999)
POPULATION DENSITY – 80 per sq. km (1998)
URBAN POPULATION – 60.1 per cent (2000 estimate)

The main areas are: Macedonia, Thrace, Epirus, Thessaly, Continental Greece, Crete and the Peloponnese. The main island groups are the Sporades, the Dodecanese or Southern Sporades, the Cyclades, the Ionian Islands, and the Aegean Islands (Chios, Lesbos, Limnos and Samos). In Crete from about 3000 to 1400 BC a civilisation flourished which spread its influence throughout the Aegean, and the ruins of the palace of Minos at Knossos afford evidence of astonishing comfort and luxury.

## HISTORY AND POLITICS

Greece was under Turkish rule from the mid-15th century until a war of independence (1821–7) led to the establishment of a Greek kingdom in the Peloponnese in 1829. The remainder of Greece gradually became independent until the Dodecanese were returned by Italy in 1947. After the Nazi German occupation of 1941–4, a civil war between monarchist and Communist groups lasted from 1946 to

1949, and tension between right-wing and radical groups continued after 1949. In 1967 right-wing elements in the army seized power and established a military regime (the 'Greek Colonels'). The King went into voluntary exile in 1967. Unrest in Athens in 1973–4 intensified after the government was involved in the overthrow of President Makarios of Cyprus in July 1974, and led the Colonels to surrender power. Konstantinos Karamanlis (prime minister 1955–63) returned from exile to form a provisional government, and the first elections for ten years were held in 1974. The restoration of the monarchy was rejected by referendum on 8 December 1974 and Greece became a republic.

The most recent general election was held on 9 April 2000 with the Panhellenic Socialist Party (PASOK) winning 158 seats, the New Democracy Party (Christian Democrats) 125 seats, the Communist Party 11 seats, and the Coalition of the Left and Progress six seats.

## Political System

In 1986 most executive power was transferred from the president to the government. The unicameral 300-member Chamber of Deputies (*Vouli)* is elected for a four-year term by universal adult suffrage under a system of proportional representation, with a three per cent threshold for parliamentary representation.

## Head of State

*President of the Hellenic Republic*, Constantine Stephanopoulos, *elected by parliament* 1995, *re-elected* 10 March 2000

## Cabinet *as at July 2001*

*Prime Minister*, Costas Simitis
*Aegean*, Nicos Sifounakis
*Agriculture*, Georgios Anomeritis
*Culture*, Evangelos Venizelos
*Development*, Nikos Christodoulakis
*Education and Religious Affairs*, Petros Ephthimiou
*Environment, Town Planning and Public Works*, Costas Laliotis
*Europe*, Elisavet Papazoi
*Foreign Affairs*, George Papandreou
*Health and Welfare*, Alekos Papadopoulos
*Interior, Public Administration and Decentralisation*, Vasso Papandreou
*Justice*, Michalis Stathopoulos
*Labour and Social Affairs*, Anastassios Yiannitsis
*Macedonia and Thrace*, George Pashalidis
*Merchant Marine*, Christos Papoutsis
*Minister of State*, Miltiades Papaioannou
*National Defence*, Apostolis Tsochatzopoulos
*National Economy and Finance*, Yiannos Papandoniou
*Press and Media, Government Spokesman*, Dhimitrios Reppas
*Public Order*, Michalis Chrysohoidis
*Transport and Communications*, Christos Verelis

## Embassy of Greece

1A Holland Park, London W11 3TP
Tel: 020-7229 3850
*Ambassador Extraordinary and Plenipotentiary*, HE Alexandros Sandis, apptd 2000
*Defence Attaché*, Capt. N. Louloudis
*First Counsellor*, C. Bitsios

Honorary Consulates – Belfast, Birmingham, Edinburgh, Falmouth, Glasgow, Leeds and Southampton

## British Embassy

1 Ploutarcou Street, GR-10675 Athens

Tel: (00 30) (1) 727 2600
E-mail: britania@hol.gr
*Ambassador Extraordinary and Plenipotentiary*, HE David C. A. Madden, CMG, apptd 1999
*Deputy Head of Mission, Counsellor and Consul-General*, P. J. Millett
*Defence, Naval and Air Attaché*, Cdre J . L. Milnes
*First Secretary (Commercial)*, G. G. Thomas

British Consular Offices – Athens, Corfu, Iráklion (Crete), Kos, Pátrai, Rhodes, Thessaloníki, Syros and Zakynthos

British Council Director, Chris Hickey, 17 Plateia Philikis Etairias, Athens GR-10673; e-mail: british.council@britishcouncil.gr. There is also an office at Thessaloníki.

British-Hellenic Chamber of Commerce, 25 Vas. Sofias Avenue, GR-10674 Athens. Tel: (00 30) (1) 721 0361

## DEFENCE

The Army has 1,735 main battle tanks, 1,977 armoured personnel carriers and 500 armoured infantry fighting vehicles. The Navy has eight submarines, four destroyers, 12 frigates, 42 patrol and coastal vessels and 20 armed helicopters. The Air Force has a total of 458 combat aircraft.

Greece maintains 1,250 army personnel in Cyprus. There are 420 US military personnel stationed in Greece.
Military Expenditure – 5.0 per cent of GDP (1999)
Military Personnel – 159,170: Army 110,000, Navy 19,000, Air Force 30,170, Paramilitaries 4,000
Conscription Duration – Up to 21 months

## ECONOMY

The principal minerals are nickel, bauxite, iron ore, iron pyrites, manganese magnesite, chrome, lead, zinc and emery. The chief industries are textiles (cotton, woollen and synthetics), chemicals, cement, glass, metallurgy, shipbuilding, domestic electrical equipment and footwear, the production of aluminium, nickel, iron and steel products, tyres, chemicals, fertilisers and sugar (from locally-grown beet). Food processing and ancillary industries are also growing.

The development of the country's electric power resources, irrigation and land reclamation schemes, and the exploitation of lignite resources for fuel and industrial purposes are continuing. Tourism is also a major industry, with nearly 11 million visitors in 1998.

Though there has been substantial industrialisation, agriculture still employs nearly a fifth of the working population and contributes 8.1 per cent of GDP. The most important agricultural products are tobacco, wheat, cotton, sugar, rice, fruit (olives, peaches, vines, oranges, lemons, figs, almonds and currant-vines). Exports of fresh fruit, currants and vegetables are an important contributor to the economy.

In March 1998 the drachma was admitted to the ERM; Greece became a member of EMU on 1 January 2001.

In 1997 there was a trade deficit of US$15,375 million and a current account deficit of US$4,860 million. Imports totalled US$23,644 million and exports US$8,626 million.

GNP – US$127,648 million (1999); US$11,770 per capita (1999)
GDP – US$118,172 million (1997); US$11,848 per capita (1999)
Annual Average Growth of GDP – 3.4 per cent (1999)
Inflation Rate – 3.5 per cent (2001)
Unemployment – 10.3 per cent (1997)

| *Trade with UK* | 1999 | 2000 |
|---|---|---|
| Imports from UK | £1,069,800,000 | £1,164,000,000 |
| Exports to UK | 382,400,000 | 416,200,000 |

## COMMUNICATIONS

The 2,503 km of railways are state-owned, with the exception of the Athens–Piraeus Electric Railway. Roads total over 130,000 km, of which 119,210 km are paved and 116 km are motorways. The Greek mercantile fleet numbers 1,905 ships over 100 tons gross with a total tonnage of 26,769,502 tons gross. Athens has direct airline links with Australasia, North America, most countries in Europe, Africa and the Middle East.

## EDUCATION

Education is free and compulsory from the age of six to 15 and is maintained by state grants. There are eighteen universities and several other institutes of higher learning.

Illiteracy Rate – 2.8 per cent
Enrolment (percentage of age group) – primary 90 per cent (1996); secondary 87 per cent (1996); tertiary 46.8 per cent (1996)

## CULTURE

Greek civilisation emerged *c.*1300 BC and the poems of Homer, which were probably current *c.*800 BC, record the struggle between the Achaeans of Greece and the Phrygians of Troy (1194 to 1184 BC).

The spoken language of modern Greece is descended from the Common Greek of Alexander the Great's empire. *Katharevousa*, a conservative literary dialect evolved by Adamantios Corais (Diamant Coray) (1748–1833) and used for official and technical matters, has been phased out. Novels and poetry are mostly in *dimotiki*, a progressive literary dialect which owes much to John Psycharis (1854–1929). The poets Solomos, Palamas, Cavafy and Sikelianos have won a European reputation. George Seferis (1963) and Odysseus Elytis (1979) have won the Nobel Prize for Literature.

---

# GRENADA
*The State of Grenada*

---

Area – 133 sq. miles (344 sq. km)
Population – 97,000 (1997 UN estimate), 95,000 (1992 census), of which about 75 per cent are of African descent; there are minorities of Europeans and Indians. The language is English
Capital – ΨSt George's (population, 4,788, 1981)
Currency – East Caribbean dollar (EC$) of 100 cents
National Anthem - Hail Grenada, land of ours
National Day – 7 February (Independence Day)
National Flag – Divided diagonally into yellow and green triangles within a red border containing six yellow stars, a yellow star on a red disc in the centre and a nutmeg on the green triangle in the hoist
Life Expectancy (years) – male 69.1; female 75.9
Population Growth Rate – 0.3 per cent (1999)
Population Density – 271 per sq. km (1998)
Urban Population – 37.9 per cent (2000 estimate)

The island is about 21 miles long and 12 miles wide. Also a part of Grenada are some of the Grenadines islets, the largest of which is Carriacou, 13 square miles in area.

## HISTORY AND POLITICS

Discovered by Columbus in 1498, and named Concepción, Grenada was originally colonised by France and was ceded to Great Britain by the Treaty of Versailles in 1783. It became a Crown colony in 1877, an Associated State in 1967 and an independent nation within the Commonwealth on 7 February 1974.

The government was overthrown in 1979 by the New Jewel Movement and a People's Revolutionary Government was set up. In October 1983 disagreements within the PRG led to the death of Prime Minister Maurice Bishop, whose government was replaced by a Revolutionary Military Council. These events prompted the intervention of Caribbean and US forces. The Governor-General installed an advisory council to act as an interim government until a general election was held in December 1984. A phased withdrawal of US forces was completed by June 1985.

The general election held on 18 January 1999 was won by the New National Party led by Dr Keith Mitchell. They won all 15 seats in the House of Representatives.

### Political System

Queen Elizabeth II is head of state and is represented by a Governor-General. Legislative power is vested in a bicameral parliament consisting of an elected 15-member House of Representatives and a 13-member Senate appointed by the Governor-General.

*Governor-General*, HE Sir Daniel Williams, GCMG, QC, apptd 1996

### Cabinet *as at July 2001*

*Prime Minister, National Security and Information*, Keith Mitchell
*Agriculture, Lands, Forestry and Fisheries*, Claris Charles
*Attorney-General, Labour*, Lawrence Joseph
*Communications, Works and Public Utilities*, Gregory Bowen
*Culture, Co-operatives, Housing and Social Services*, Brian McQueen
*Education*, Augustine John
*Finance, Trade, Industry and Planning*, Anthony Boatswain
*Foreign Affairs, Legal Affairs, Labour, Local Government, Carriacou and Petit Martinique Affairs*, Elvin Nimrod
*Health and Environment*, Clarise Modeste-Curwen
*Implementation*, Joslyn Whiteman
*Ministers of State*, Laurina Waldron (*Communications, Works and Public Utilities*); Mark Isaac (*Information*)
*Parliamentary Secretaries*, Einstein Louison (*Agriculture, Forestry, Lands and Fisheries*); Eleuthan Noel (*Carriacou and Petit Martinique Affairs*); Richard McPhail (*Culture*)

*Tourism, Civil Aviation, Social Security and Women's Affairs*, Brenda Hood
*Youth, Sports, Community Development*, Adrian Mitchell

GRENADA HIGH COMMISSION
1 Collingham Gardens, London SW5 0HW
Tel: 020-7373 7809
E-mail: grenada@high-commission.freeserve.co.uk
*High Commissioner*, HE Ruth Elizabeth Rouse, apptd 1999

BRITISH HIGH COMMISSION
14 Church Street, St George's
Tel: (00 1 473) 440 3536/440 3222
E-mail: bhcgrenada@caribsurf.com
*High Commissioner*, HE Gordon Baker, resident at Bridgetown, Barbados
*Resident Acting High Commissioner*, D. R. Miller

## ECONOMY

Services account for 61 per cent of employment and 71 per cent of GDP. The economy was principally agrarian, but agriculture now employs only 17 per cent of the workforce and produces 10 per cent of GDP. Grenada accounts for about a quarter of world nutmeg production. Cocoa and bananas are also major crops. Manufacturing consists of processing agricultural products and the production of textiles, concrete, aluminium and handicrafts. Tourism is the main foreign exchange earner. In 1998 there were 381,669 tourists.

GNP – US$334 million (1999); US$3,450 per capita (1999)
GDP – US$311 million (1997); US$2,997 per capita (1998)
ANNUAL AVERAGE GROWTH OF GDP – 3.0 per cent (1996)
INFLATION RATE – 0.2 per cent (1999)
UNEMPLOYMENT – 17.0 per cent (1996)
TOTAL EXTERNAL DEBT – US$183 million (1998)

### TRADE

The most important exports are nutmegs and cocoa. Imports include machinery and transport equipment, livestock, foodstuffs and beverages, manufactured goods, and fuels. The main trading partners are the USA, the UK and Trinidad and Tobago.

In 1996 there was a trade deficit of US$123 million and a current account deficit of US$58 million. Imports totalled US$152 million and exports US$21 million.

| *Trade with UK* | 1999 | 2000 |
|---|---|---|
| Imports from UK | £7,232,000 | £9,174,000 |
| Exports to UK | 1,266,000 | 1,235,000 |

---

## GUATEMALA
*República de Guatemala*

---

AREA – 42,042 sq. miles (108,889 sq. km). Neighbours: Mexico (north and west), El Salvador, Honduras and Belize (east)
POPULATION – 11,086,000 (1997 UN estimate): 56 per cent mestizo, 44 per cent Amerindian. The language is Spanish, but 40 per cent of the population speak an Indian language
CAPITAL – Guatemala City (population, 1,675,589, 1990 estimate)
MAJOR CITIES – Antigua (30,000); Mazatenango (21,000); ΨPuerto Barrios (23,000); Quezaltenango (100,000)
CURRENCY – Quetzal (Q) of 100 centavos
NATIONAL ANTHEM – Guatemala Feliz (Guatemala be praised)
NATIONAL DAY – 15 September
NATIONAL FLAG – Three vertical bands, blue, white, blue; coat of arms on white stripe
LIFE EXPECTANCY (years) – male 60.2; female 64.7
POPULATION GROWTH RATE – 2.7 per cent (1999)
POPULATION DENSITY – 99 per sq. km (1998)
URBAN POPULATION – 39.7 per cent (2000 estimate)
MILITARY EXPENDITURE – 1.1 per cent of GDP (1999)
MILITARY PERSONNEL – 31,400: Army 29,200, Navy 1,500, Air Force 700; Paramilitaries 19,000
CONSCRIPTION DURATION – 30 months (selective)
ILLITERACY RATE – 31.3 per cent (2000)
ENROLMENT (percentage of age group) – primary 72 per cent (1997); secondary 13 per cent (1980); tertiary 8.5 per cent (1996)

Guatemala is traversed from west to east by mountains containing volcanic summits rising to 13,000 feet above sea level; earthquakes are frequent. There are numerous rivers. The climate is hot and malarial near the coast, temperate in the higher regions.

## HISTORY AND POLITICS

Guatemala was under Spanish rule from 1524 until gaining independence in 1821. It formed part of the Confederation of Central America from 1823 to 1839.

After a series of military coups, civilian rule was restored with the election of a Constituent Assembly in 1984 and the promulgation of a new constitution in 1985. In May 1993 President Serrano partially suspended the constitution and attempted to rule by decree but was effectively ousted by the army on 1 June. Ramiro de León Carpio was elected president by Congress to serve out Serrano's term to January 1996.

The legislative election to the National Congress on 7 November 1999 was won by the Guatemalan Republican Front (FRG) which obtained 63 seats; the National Advancement Party (PAN) won 37 seats. The presidential election on 26 December 1999 was won by Alfonso Portillo of the FRG.

### INSURGENCY

Since 1960 the armed forces had been fighting insurgency by the left-wing, mainly Mayan Indian, guerrillas of the Guatemalan Revolutionary National Unity Movement (URNG). Some 200,000 were killed in the fighting. Government–URNG negotiations began in 1991, leading to a reduction in fighting and agreements in 1993. In March 1994 a human rights accord was reached under which a 300-strong UN Observer Mission (MINUGUA) was established in November 1994 to supervise the implementation of government–URNG accords. An accord recognising the rights of the indigenous population was signed in March 1995, but in a referendum held on 16 May 1999, constitutional reforms which would have amended the constitution to allow for the implementation of peace accords were rejected. Representatives of the four rebel groups comprising the URNG signed a peace treaty with the government in December 1996; an independent commission into the 36-year civil war, set up under the 1996 peace treaty, published a report on 25 February 1999 which concluded that the army had committed acts of genocide against the indigenous Mayan population. In August 2000 President Portillo admitted the state's responsibility for atrocities committed during the civil war and vowed that those responsible would be prosecuted.

### POLITICAL SYSTEM

Executive power is vested in the president, who is directly elected for a single four-year term. He appoints the Cabinet. Legislative authority is vested in the National

Congress, whose 113 members are directly elected for a four-year term.

The republic is divided into 22 departments.

### HEAD OF STATE

*President*, Alfonso Portillo Cabrera, *elected* 26 December 1999, *sworn in* 14 January 2000
*Vice-President*, Juan Francisco Reyes López

### GOVERNMENT *as at July 2001*

*Agriculture, Livestock and Food*, Jorge Escoto
*Communications, Transport and Public Works*, Alvaro Heredia
*Culture and Sport*, Otilia Lux de Coti
*Defence*, Gen. Eduardo Arevalo Lacs
*Economy*, Marco Antonio Ventura
*Education*, Mario Torres
*Energy and Mines*, Raúl Archila
*Environment and Natural Resources*, Leonel Soto Arango
*Foreign Affairs*, Gabriel Orellana Rojas
*Interior*, Byron Barrientos
*Labour and Social Security*, Juan Francisco Alfaro
*Public Finance*, Eduardo Weymann
*Public Health and Social Welfare*, Mario Bolaños

### EMBASSY OF GUATEMALA

13 Fawcett Street, London SW10 9HN
Tel: 020-7351 3042
*Ambassador Extraordinary and Plenipotentiary*, HE Gladys Marithza Ruiz Sanchez De Vielman, apptd 2000

### BRITISH EMBASSY

Avenida La Reforma 16–00, Zona 10, Edificio Torre Internacional, Nivel 11, Guatemala City
Tel: (00 502) (2) 367 5425/6/7/8/9
*Ambassador Extraordinary and Plenipotentiary*, HE Andrew Caie, apptd 1998

## ECONOMY

Agriculture provides 23 per cent of GDP and employs nearly half of the workforce. The principal export is coffee, other articles being manufactured goods, sugar, bananas and cardamom. The chief imports are raw materials and semi-manufactures, capital goods, consumer goods, and fuel oils. The USA, El Salvador and Mexico are the main trading partners.

The chief seaports are San José de Guatemala on the Pacific and Santo Tomás de Castilla and Puerto Barrios on the Atlantic side.

In 1999 there was a trade deficit of US$1,445 million and a current account deficit of US$1,026 million. Imports totalled US$4,382 million and exports US$2,398 million.

GNP – US$18,625 million (1999); US$1,660 per capita (1999)
GDP – US$17,792 million (1997); US$1,760 per capita (1998)
ANNUAL AVERAGE GROWTH OF GDP – 3.1 per cent (1996)
INFLATION RATE – 4.9 per cent (1999)
TOTAL EXTERNAL DEBT – US$4,565 million (1998)

| Trade with UK | 1999 | 2000 |
|---|---|---|
| Imports from UK | £34,145,000 | £27,835,000 |
| Exports to UK | 24,807,000 | 21,093,000 |

---

# GUINEA
*République de Guinée*

---

AREA – 94,926 sq. miles (245,857 sq. km). Neighbours: Guinea-Bissau (east), Senegal and Mali (north), Côte d'Ivoire (west), Sierra Leone and Liberia (south)
POPULATION – 7,247,000 (1997 UN estimate); the official language is French; Fullah, Malinké and Soussou are indigenous languages
CAPITAL – ΨConakry (population, 763,000)
MAJOR CITIES – Kankan; Kindia; Labé; Mamou; N'Zérékoré; Siguiri
CURRENCY – Guinea franc of 100 centimes
NATIONAL ANTHEM – Liberté
NATIONAL DAY – 2 October (Anniversary of the Proclamation of Independence)
NATIONAL FLAG – Three vertical stripes of red, yellow and green
LIFE EXPECTANCY (years) – male 46.2; female 48.9
POPULATION GROWTH RATE – 2.8 per cent (1999)
POPULATION DENSITY – 30 per sq. km (1998)
URBAN POPULATION – 32.8 per cent (2000 estimate)
MILITARY EXPENDITURE – 1.7 per cent of GDP (1999)
MILITARY PERSONNEL –9,700: Army 8,500, Navy 400, Air Force 800, Paramilitaries 2,600
CONSCRIPTION DURATION – Two years
ILLITERACY RATE – 58.9 per cent
ENROLMENT (percentage of age group) – primary 42 per cent (1997); secondary 9 per cent (1985); tertiary 1.3 per cent (1996)

## HISTORY AND POLITICS

Guinea was separated from Senegal in 1891 and administered by France as a separate colony. On 2 October 1958 Guinea became an independent republic.

Ahmed Sékou Touré assumed office as head of the new government, and was elected president in 1961. His death in 1984 was followed by a military coup. Guinea was ruled by a military government directed by a Military Committee for National Recovery (CMRN). A new constitution, providing for the end of military rule, was approved by referendum in 1990.

In January 1991 the CMRN was dissolved and a mixed civilian-military Transitional Committee for National Recovery (CTRN) was established which appointed a new government. Civil disturbances in 1991 caused the government to introduce a full multiparty system in April 1992, since when 40 opposition parties have been legalised. Legislative elections in June 1995 were won by President Conté's Party of Unity and Progress (PUP), which gained 71 of the 114 National Assembly seats. A presidential election held on 14 December 1998 was won by the incumbent President Conté with 54 per cent of the vote. Legislative elections were due on 26 November 2000 but were postponed due to the deteriorating security situation.

### INSURGENCIES

In September 2000, anti-government rebels, believed to be members of the Guinea Liberation Movement (GLM), began a series of incursions into Guinea from Liberia and Sierra Leone. Heavy fighting along the country's southern border hampered international relief efforts aimed at the estimated half million refugees from civil war in Sierra Leone and Liberia who had fled to Guinea.

### HEAD OF STATE

*President*, Maj.-Gen. Lansana Conté, *took power* 3 April 1984, *elected* 19 December 1993, *re-elected* 14 December 1998

COUNCIL OF MINISTERS *as at July 2001*

*Prime Minister*, Lamine Sidimé
*Agriculture and Animal Husbandry*, Jean-Paul Sarr
*Commerce, Industry and Small and Medium-sized Enterprises*, Mariama Dewo Baldé
*Communication*, Mamady Condé
*Defence*, Col. Cande Toure
*Economic Affairs, Finance*, Sheik Amadou Camara
*Employment and Civil Service*, Lamine Camara
*Fishing and Aquaculture*, Mansa Moussa Sidibé
*Foreign Affairs*, Hadja Mahawa Bangoura Camara
*Higher Education and Scientific Research*, Eugène Camara
*Justice, Keeper of the Seals*, Abou Camara
*Mines, Geology and Environment*, Ibrahima Souma
*Pre-University Teaching and Civil Education*, Germain Doualamou
*Public Health*, Mamadou Saliou Diallo
*Public Works, Transport*, Cellou Dalen Diallo
*Secretary-General to the Government*, El Hadj Ousmane Sanoko
*Secretary-General to the President*, El Hadj Fodé Bangoura
*Social Affairs, Promotion of Women and Children*, Mariama Aribot
*Technical Education and Vocational Training*, Almamye Fodé Sylla
*Territorial Administration and Decentralisation*, Moussa Solana
*Tourism, Hotels and Handicrafts*, Sylla Koumba Diakité
*Urbanisation and Housing*, Blaise Ono Foromo
*Water Resources and Energy*, Fassou Sagno
*Youth, Sports and Culture*, Abdel Kader Sangaré

EMBASSY OF THE REPUBLIC OF GUINEA
51 rue de la Faisanderie, F-75016 Paris, France
Tel: (00 33) (1) 4704 8148
*Ambassador Extraordinary and Plenipotentiary*, HE Ibrahima Sylla, apptd 1998

BRITISH CONSULATE
BP 834 Conakry, Guinea
Tel: (00 224) 461 680/446 982/403 523
*British Ambassador*, HE Alan Burner, resident at Dakar, Senegal

## ECONOMY

The principal products are bauxite, alumina, palm kernels, millet, cassava, bananas, plantains and rubber. Deposits of iron ore, gold, diamonds and uranium have been discovered. Principal imports are cotton goods, petroleum products, sugar, flour and salt; exports, bauxite, alumina, iron ore, diamonds, coffee, bananas, palm kernels and pineapples.

In 1999 there was a trade surplus of US$94 million and a current account deficit of US$152 million.

GNP – US$3,556 million (1999); US$510 per capita (1999)
GDP – US$3,916 million (1997); US$515 per capita (1998)
ANNUAL AVERAGE GROWTH OF GDP – 4.5 per cent (1996)
TOTAL EXTERNAL DEBT – US$3,546 million (1998)

| *Trade with UK* | 1999 | 2000 |
|---|---|---|
| Imports from UK | £16,923,000 | £22,726,000 |
| Exports to UK | 4,546,000 | 579,000 |

---

# GUINEA-BISSAU
*Repûblica da Guiné-Bissau*

---

AREA – 13,948 sq. miles (36,125 sq. km). Neighbours: Senegal (north), Guinea (east and south)
POPULATION – 1,185,000 (1997 UN estimate). The main ethnic groups are the Balante, Malinké, Fulani, Mandjako and Pepel. The official language is Portuguese; most of the population speak Guinean Creole
CAPITAL – ΨBissau (population, 109,214, 1979)
CURRENCY – Franc CFA
NATIONAL ANTHEM - É patria amada (This is our beloved country)
NATIONAL DAY – 24 September (Independence Day)
NATIONAL FLAG – Horizontal bands of yellow over green with vertical red band in the hoist charged with a black star
LIFE EXPECTANCY (years) – male 45.0; female 47.0
POPULATION GROWTH RATE – 2.2 per cent (1999)
POPULATION DENSITY – 32 per sq. km (1998)
URBAN POPULATION – 23.7 per cent (2000 estimate)
MILITARY EXPENDITURE – 1.9 per cent of GDP (1999)
MILITARY PERSONNEL – 9,250: Army 6,800, Navy 350, Air Force 100, Paramilitaries 2,000
CONSCRIPTION DURATION – Selective conscription
ILLITERACY RATE – 63.2 per cent
ENROLMENT (percentage of age group) – primary 46 per cent (1986); secondary 3 per cent (1980); tertiary 0.5 per cent (1988)

## HISTORY AND POLITICS

Guinea-Bissau, formerly Portuguese Guinea, achieved independence on 24 September 1974. Following a coup led by Maj. (now Brig.-Gen.) Vieira in 1980, a Revolutionary Council was established. The ruling African Party for the Independence of Guinea and Cape Verde (PAIGC) introduced a multiparty system in January 1991. The PAIGC won the election held in June 1994 and Brig.-Gen. Vieira was elected president in August 1994.

In June 1998, fighting broke out in Bissau between troops loyal to President Vieira and supporters of the sacked army chief Ansumane Mane. Guinea and Senegal sent in troops to support Vieira, and a peace agreement was signed on 1 November, which promised legislative and presidential elections in March 1999. A government of national unity was formed in February 1999 and Guinean and Senegalese troops withdrew in March in accordance with the peace agreement, but no elections took place. Fighting resumed in May 1999, and the government was overthrown on 7 May by rebels loyal to Gen. Mane, who appointed the Speaker of the National Assembly as acting president. Legislative elections held on 28 November 1999 resulted in the Social Renewal Party (PRS) gaining 38 seats in the 102-seat National Assembly. The PRS's ally, the Guinea-Bissau Resistance-Batafa Movement (RGB-Batafa), gained 28 seats. In presidential elections, the founder of the PRS, Kumba Yalla, was elected on 16 January 2000. He resigned his chairmanship of the PRS on 11 May 2000. Gen. Ansumane Mane led an attempted coup in November 2000, during which he was killed. The ruling coalition collapsed on 23 January 2001; on 19 March, President Yalla appointed Faustino Imbali to form a new government which was sworn in on 27 March.

### POLITICAL SYSTEM

A new constitution, which limited the tenure of the presidency to two terms, was adopted in July 1999. Under the constitution, the president is the head of government and appoints the Council of Ministers. There is a unicameral legislature, the Assembleia Nacional Popular (National People's Assembly), composed of 102 members elected by universal suffrage for a four-year term.

HEAD OF STATE

*President, Chairman of the Council of State, C.-in-C. of the Armed Forces*, Kumba Yalla, *elected* 16 January 2000, *took office* 17 February 2000

COUNCIL OF MINISTERS *as at July 2001*

*Prime Minister*, Faustino Fadut Imbali (Ind.)
*Agriculture and Forestry*, Alamara Nhasse (PRS)*Council of Ministers', Media and Parliamentary Issues, Government Spokesperson*, Joaquim Balde (PSD)
*Defence*, Maj. Lucio Soares (Ind.)
*Economy and Finance*, Rui Duarte de Baros (Ind.)
*Education, Science and Technology*, Geraldo Martins (PCD)
*Fisheries*, Oscar Balde (RGB)
*Foreign Affairs*, Antonieta Rosa Gomes (FCG)
*Internal Administration*, Antonio Artur Sanha (PRS)
*Justice*, Dionisio Cabi (PRS)
*Natural Resources and Energy*, Julio Baldé (PCD)
*Public Health*, Francisco Dias (Ind.)
*Public Service and Labour*, Carlos Pinto Pereira (PCD)
*Social Infrastructure*, Carlitos Barai (PRS)
*Social Security, Employment and Poverty Alleviation*, Filomena Mascarenhas Tiopote (PRS)

FCG Guinea-Bissau Civic Forum/Social Democracy; PCD Democratic Convergence Party; PRS Social Renewal Party; PSD Social Democratic Party; RGB Guinea-Bissau Resistance-Batafa Movement; Ind. Independent

EMBASSY OF THE REPUBLIC OF GUINEA-BISSAU

94 rue St Lazare, Paris F-75009, France
Tel: (00 33) (1) 4526 1851
*Chargé d'Affaires*, Fali Embalo

HONORARY CONSULATE

Flat 5, 8 Palace Gate, London W8 5NF
Tel: 020-7589 5253
*Honorary Consul*, Raja Makarem

BRITISH CONSULATE

Mavegro Int., CP100, Bissau
*British Ambassador*, HE Alan Burner, resident at Dakar, Senegal

## ECONOMY

Guinea-Bissau produces rice, coconuts, groundnuts and plantains. Cattle are raised, and there are bauxite and phosphate deposits. In May 1997 Guinea-Bissau joined the French Franc Zone, and the CFA Franc replaced the peso as currency. In December 2000 an international debt reduction package worth US$790 million for Guinea-Bissau was agreed.

In 1997 there was a trade deficit of US$14 million and a current account deficit of US$30 million. In 1999 imports totalled US$95 million and exports US$49 million.

GNP – US$194 million (1999); US$160 per capita (1999)
GDP – US$109 million (1997); US$100 per capita (1998)
ANNUAL AVERAGE GROWTH OF GDP – 5.0 per cent (1996)
INFLATION RATE – 0.7 per cent (1999)
TOTAL EXTERNAL DEBT – US$964 million (1998)

| *Trade with UK* | 1999 | 2000 |
|---|---|---|
| Imports from UK | £1,830,000 | £1,111,000 |
| Exports to UK | — | 1,000 |

## GUYANA

*The Co-operative Republic of Guyana*

AREA – 83,000 sq. miles (214,969 sq. km). Neighbours: Venezuela (west), Brazil (west and south), Suriname (east)
POPULATION – 856,000 (1997 UN estimate): 51 per cent East Indian (mainly rural), 30 per cent African (mainly urban), Amerindians, Europeans, Chinese and people of mixed descent; 50 per cent Christian, 35 per cent Hindu, less than 10 per cent Muslim. Guyana is the only English-speaking country in South America
CAPITAL – ΨGeorgetown (population, 250,000)
MAJOR TOWNS – Corriverton (24,000); Linden (35,000); ΨNew Amsterdam (25,000)
CURRENCY – Guyana dollar (G$) of 100 cents
NATIONAL ANTHEM – Dear Land of Guyana
NATIONAL DAYS – 26 May (Independence Day); 23 February (Republic Day)
NATIONAL FLAG – Green with a yellow, white-bordered triangle based on the hoist and surmounted by a red, black-bordered triangle
LIFE EXPECTANCY (years) – male 65.6; female 72.2
POPULATION GROWTH RATE – 0.8 per cent (1999)
POPULATION DENSITY – 4 per sq. km (1998)
URBAN POPULATION – 38.2 per cent (2000 estimate)
MILITARY EXPENDITURE – 0.9 per cent of GDP (1999)
MILITARY PERSONNEL – 1,600: Army 1,400, Navy 100, Air Force 100

## HISTORY AND POLITICS

Guyana (formerly British Guiana) became independent on 26 May 1966, with a Governor-General appointed by Queen Elizabeth II. It became a republic on 23 February 1970.

In the October 1992 presidential election Dr Cheddi Jagan was elected and his People's Progressive Party (PPP) defeated the People's National Congress (PNC) which had governed since independence. Jagan died in March 1997 and was replaced by former Prime Minister Samuel Hinds. In the December 1997 election, Janet Jagan (who had previously served as prime minister and was the widow of the late president) was elected president and the PPP returned to power. The PNC claimed the result was fixed (in January 2001 a judicial ruling was to declare that the entire election had been null and void) and it was agreed that new elections would be held within three years rather than five. President Janet Jagan resigned on 11 August 1999 on the grounds of ill health and was succeeded by Bharrat Jagdeo, who had previously been the finance minister, but was appointed prime minister just prior to her resignation, the constitution stipulating that if a president left office during his or her term, the prime minister succeeded to the presidency. The general election which was due to be held on 17 January 2001 took place on 19 March 2001; the delay was due to the failure of the National Assembly to pass a bill amending the electoral law. The PPP secured a third consecutive term of office, obtaining 34 seats; the PNC won 27 seats.

POLITICAL SYSTEM

The 1980 constitution provides for an executive president who serves a five-year term, and a National Assembly of 65 members, of which 53 are elected nationally by proportional representation and 12 are regional representatives.

HEAD OF STATE

*President*, Bharrat Jagdeo, *succeeded* 11 August 1999, *elected* 19 March 2001
*Vice-President*, vacant

CABINET *as at July 2001*

*Prime Minister, Public Works*, Sam Hinds
*Agriculture*, Navin Chandarpal
*Amerindian Affairs*, Carolyn Rodrigues
*Attorney-General, Legal Affairs*, Doodnauth Singh
*Economic Planning*, vacant
*Education*, Henry Jeffrey
*Finance, Prime Minister's Office*, Saisnarine Kowlessar
*Fisheries, Crops and Livestock*, Satyadeow Sawh
*Foreign Affairs*, Samuel Rudy Insanally
*Foreign Trade and International Co-operation*, Clement Rohee
*Health*, Leslie Ramsammy
*Home Affairs*, Ronald Gajraj
*Housing and Water*, Shaik Baksh
*Human Services, Social Security and Labour*, Dale Bisnauth; Bibi Shadick
*Local Government*, Harripersaud Nokta; Clinton Collymore
*Parliamentary Affairs*, Reepu Daman Persaud
*Public Service Management*, Jennifer Westford
*Trade, Tourism and Industry*, Manzoor Nadir
*Transport and Hydraulics*, Carl Anthony Xavier
*Youth, Sport and Culture*, Gail Teixeira

GUYANA HIGH COMMISSION
3 Palace Court, Bayswater Road, London W2 4LP
Tel: 020-7229 7684/5/6/7/8
E-mail: ghc.1@ic24.net
*High Commissioner*, HE Laleshwar Singh, apptd 1993

BRITISH HIGH COMMISSION
44 Main Street (PO Box 10849), Georgetown
Tel: (00 592) (2) 65881/2/3/4
*High Commissioner*, HE Edward Glover, MVO, apptd 1998

## ECONOMY

Agriculture is the principal economic activity, accounting for 39 per cent of GDP and employing 19 per cent of the workforce. Main export items include Demerara sugar, gold, rice and bauxite. Diamonds are also mined. There is some cattle ranching in the savanna country, and oil deposits have been found there. Industry is fairly small-scale. Much emphasis is now being placed on eco-tourism. Foreign aid covers much of the government deficit.

In 1997 exports totalled US$596 million and imports US$630 million.

GNP – US$651 million (1999); US$760 per capita (1999)
GDP – US$743 million (1997); US$846 per capita (1998)
ANNUAL AVERAGE GROWTH OF GDP – 7.9 per cent (1996)
INFLATION RATE – 4.6 per cent (1998)
UNEMPLOYMENT – 11.7 per cent (1992)
TOTAL EXTERNAL DEBT – US$1,653 million (1998)

| *Trade with UK* | 1999 | 2000 |
|---|---|---|
| Imports from UK | £21,540,000 | £19,698,000 |
| Exports to UK | 74,136,000 | 64,754,000 |

## COMMUNICATIONS

Georgetown and New Amsterdam are the principal ports, though bauxite ships also sail to Linden, on the Demerara, and Everton, on the Berbice. The few roads are confined mainly to the coastal areas. Paved roads total about 571 km out of a total network of 7,820 km. Air transport is the easiest form of communication between the coast and the interior. The national airline, Guyana Airways 2000, has been privatised.

There is a state-owned radio broadcasting station which operates two channels and a fledgling television service.

## EDUCATION

Education is compulsory between the ages of five and 14; nursery, primary and secondary schooling are free. The government assumed total control of the education system in 1976 and made education free, but instituted fees for study at the University of Guyana in 1994.

There are several technical and vocational institutions, as well as some 30 adult education schools. There are also a number of technical and vocational institutions not under the aegis of the Ministry of Education.

ILLITERACY RATE – 1.5 per cent (2000)
ENROLMENT (percentage of age group) – primary 87 per cent (1996); secondary 66 per cent (1996); tertiary 11.4 per cent (1996)

---

# HAÏTI
*République d'Haïti*

---

AREA – 10,714 sq. miles (27,750 sq. km). Neighbour: Dominican Republic (east)
POPULATION – 7,803,000 (1997 UN estimate) of which 90 per cent are black and 10 per cent mulatto (mixed race). Both French and Creole are regarded as official languages. French is the language of government and the press but it is only spoken by the educated mulatto minority. The usual language is Creole
CAPITAL – ΨPort-au-Prince (population, 884,472, 1996 estimate)
MAJOR CITIES – ΨCap Haïtien (102,233); Carrefour (290,204); Delmas (240,429), 1996 UN estimates
CURRENCY – Gourde of 100 centimes
NATIONAL ANTHEM – La Dessalinienne
NATIONAL DAY – 1 January
NATIONAL FLAG – Horizontally blue over red
LIFE EXPECTANCY (years) – male 50.6; female 55.1
POPULATION GROWTH RATE – 1.8 per cent (1999)
POPULATION DENSITY – 276 per sq. km (1998)
URBAN POPULATION – 35.7 per cent (2000 estimate)
MILITARY EXPENDITURE – 1.3 per cent of GDP (1999)
ILLITERACY RATE – 51.4 per cent (2000)
ENROLMENT (percentage of age group) – primary 22 per cent (1990); tertiary 1.1 per cent (1985)

The Republic of Haïti occupies the western third of the Caribbean island of Hispaniola. The climate is tropical with high humidity and an almost constant temperature.

## HISTORY AND POLITICS

Haïti was a French slave colony under the name of Saint-Domingue from 1697 until 1791, when French rule was overthrown in a revolt led by Toussaint L'Ouverture. French rule was restored by Napoleon in 1802 but in 1803 French forces surrendered to a British naval blockade and on 1 January 1804 the colony was declared independent as Haïti by Jean Jacques Dessalines. Dessalines became Emperor of Haïti but was assassinated in 1806.

Haïti was under US military occupation from 1915 to 1934. Dr François 'Papa Doc' Duvalier was elected in 1957 and became life president in 1964. He was succeeded in 1971 by his son Jean-Claude 'Baby Doc' Duvalier who fled to France in 1986 in the face of sustained popular unrest. Five years of military government followed until Father Jean-Bertrand Aristide, leader of the National Front for Change and Democracy, won a free presidential election in 1990.

Aristide fled to the USA following a military coup in September 1991. The international community imposed sanctions and in September 1994, an agreement was reached on President Aristide's return and the flight of the military junta members abroad. Aristide returned on 15 October 1994 to appoint a new government.

The presidential election in December 1995 was won by Lavalas Family (FL) candidate René Préval. Following the resignation of Prime Minister Rosny Smarth in October 1997, the President and the legislature were unable to agree on a successor and Haïti had no prime minister until 12 January 1999, when the appointment of Jacques Édouard Alexis was confirmed by a presidential decree, after the Senate but not the Chamber of Deputies had approved the appointment. Elections to the 27-member Senate and 83-member Chamber of Deputies on 21 May and 9 July 2000 were won by the pro-Aristide FL, winning 18 and 72 seats respectively; there was much international criticism of the manner in which the elections had been conducted.

The presidential election on 26 November 2000 was won by Jean-Bertrand Aristide, who obtained 92 per cent of the vote; the main opposition parties had refused to contest the election, citing irregularities in the earlier legislative election; in response, Aristide promised to hold a fresh legislative election in November 2002.

### Political System

The head of state is a president, directly elected for a five-year term that may not be renewed immediately. The National Assembly is the bicameral legislature; the lower house, the Chamber of Deputies, has 83 members directly elected for four years. The upper house or Senate has 27 members elected for six years; one third of the senators are elected every two years. The president appoints the prime minister, who must be approved by the National Assembly. The prime minister chooses the Cabinet.

### Head of State

*President*, Jean-Bertrand Aristide, *elected* 26 November 2000, *sworn in* 7 February 2001

### Cabinet *as at July 2001*

*Prime Minister, Interior, Territorial Communities*, Jean-Marie Chérestal
*Agriculture, Natural Resources and Rural Development*, Sébastien Hilaire
*Civil Service*, Webster Pierre
*Commerce and Industry*, Stanley Théard
*Culture and Communication*, Guy Paul
*Economy and Finance*, Gustave Faubert
*Foreign Affairs, Religious Affairs*, Joseph Philippe Antonio
*Haïtians Living Abroad*, Lesly Voltaire
*Interior*, Henri-Claude Ménard
*Justice*, Gary Lissade
*National Education, Youth and Sport*, Gaston Georges Mérisier
*Planning and External Co-operation*, Marc Bazin
*Public Health and Population*, Henri-Claude Voltaire
*Public Works, Transport and Communications*, Ernst Laraque
*Social Affairs*, Eudes Saint-Preux Craan
*Tourism*, Martine Deverson
*Women's Affairs*, Ginette Lubin

British Ambassador, HE David Ward, resident at Santo Domingo, Dominican Republic
British Consulate, Hotel Montana (PO Box 1302), Port-au-Prince
Tel: (00 509) 257 3969
*Vice-Consul*, M. Guercy, MBE

## ECONOMY

Light industrial products account for over 80 per cent of total exports. Coffee is the second largest export earner. Corn, sorghum and rice are also grown. Increased production of tropical fruits and vegetables is being encouraged.

Leather goods, textiles, electronic components and sports equipment are manufactured, using imported raw materials, for re-export. Principal imports are foodstuffs, machinery and transport equipment and fuels.

In 1998 Haïti had a trade deficit of US$341 million and a current account deficit of US$38 million. In 1999 imports totalled US$1,025 million and exports US$196 million.

GNP – US$3,584 million (1999); US$460 per capita (1999)
GDP – US$3,110 million (1997); US$443 per capita (1998)
Annual Average Growth of GDP – 2.8 per cent (1996)
Inflation Rate – 8.7 per cent (1999)
Total External Debt – US$1,048 million (1998)

| *Trade with UK* | 1999 | 2000 |
|---|---|---|
| Imports from UK | £7,003,000 | £6,982,000 |
| Exports to UK | 591,000 | 840,000 |

## COMMUNICATIONS

There are more than 4,000 km of roads. Air services are maintained between the capital and the principal provincial towns and to the USA and Caribbean and South American countries. The principal towns and villages are connected by telephone and/or telegraph. There are several commercial radio stations and two television stations at Port-au-Prince.

HOLY SEE, *see* VATICAN CITY STATE

---

## HONDURAS
*República de Honduras*

---

Area – 43,277 sq. miles (112,088 sq. km). Neighbours: Guatemala (north-west), El Salvador (south-west), Nicaragua (south)
Population – 6,325,000 (1997 UN estimate) of mixed Spanish and Indian blood. The Garifunas in the north are of West Indian origin. The language is Spanish, although English is the first language of many in the islands and on the north coast
Capital – Tegucigalpa (population, 670,100, 1991 estimate)
Major Cities – Choluteca (63,200); ΨLa Ceiba (77,100); ΨPuerto Cortés (32,500); San Pedro Sula (325,900); ΨTela (24,000)
Currency – Lempira of 100 centavos
National Anthem – Tu Bandera Es Un Lampo De Cielo (Your flag is a heavenly light)
National Day – 15 September
National Flag – Three horizontal bands, blue, white, blue (with five blue stars on white band)
Life Expectancy (years) – male 68.2; female 70.8
Population Growth Rate – 2.9 per cent (1999)
Population Density – 55 per sq. km (1998)
Urban Population – 52.7 per cent (2000 estimate)
Military Expenditure – 1.8 per cent of GDP (1999)
Military Personnel – 8,300: Army 5,500, Navy 1,000, Air Force 1,800, Paramilitaries 6,000

The country is mountainous, being traversed by the Cordilleras, with peaks rising to 1,500 and 2,400 metres above sea level. Rainfall is seasonal, May to October being wet and November to April dry.

## HISTORY AND POLITICS

Discovered and settled by the Spanish in the 16th century, Honduras formed part of the Spanish American dominions until 1821 when independence was proclaimed.

Under military government from 1972, Honduras returned to civilian rule in 1981 with an executive presidency, a 128-seat unicameral Congress, and a multi-party system. The most recent legislative elections were held on 30 November 1997 and won by the Liberal Party. A general election was due to be held in November 2001. In October 1997, Congress approved a constitutional amendment reducing the legislature to 80 members. The amendment must also be ratified by the current session of Congress before it becomes law.

The country is divided into 18 departments.

### Head of State

*President of the Republic*, Carlos Roberto Flores Facussé (Liberal), *elected* 30 November 1997
*Vice-Presidents*, William Handal Raudales; Gladys Caballero de Arevalo; Hector Vidal Cerrato

### Cabinet *as at July 2001*

*Agriculture and Livestock*, Guillermo Alvarado
*Culture, Arts and Sports*, Herman Allan Padgett
*Director of the National Agrarian Institute*, Anibal Delgado Fiallos
*Education*, Ramón Calix Figueroa
*Finance*, Gabriela Nuñez López
*Foreign Affairs*, Roberto Flores Bermúdez
*Government and Justice*, Vera Rubi
*Health*, Plutarco Castellanos
*Industry, Commerce*, Oscar Kafati
*Labour and Social Security*, Rosa America de Galo
*Ministers Without Portfolio*, Jorge Arturo Reina; Nahum Valladares; Roberto Leiva
*National Defence and Public Security*, Enrique Flores Valeriano
*Natural Resources and Environment*, Xiomara Gómez
*Presidential Office*, Gustavo Alfaro
*Public Works, Transport and Housing*, Sergio Canales
*Security*, Guatama Fonseca
*Social Investment Fund*, Moises Starkman
*Technical and International Co-operation Secretariat*, Glenda Gallardo
*Tourism*, Ana Abarca

### Embassy of Honduras

115 Gloucester Place, London W1H 3PJ
Tel: 020-7486 4880
*Ambassador Extraordinary and Plenipotentiary*, HE Hernán Antonio Bermúdez-Aguilar, apptd 1999

### British Embassy

Edifíco Financiero Banexpo, 3er Piso, Boulevard San Juan Bosco, Colonia Payaqui, Apartado Postal 290, Tegucigalpa
Tel: (00 504) 232 0612
*Ambassador Extraordinary and Plenipotentiary*, HE David Osborne, apptd 1998
British Consulate – San Pedro Sula

## ECONOMY

Three-quarters of the country is covered by pine forests. Agriculture and cattle raising is mainly confined to the fertile coastal plain on the Caribbean and the extensive valleys in the Comayagua and Olancho regions of the interior. The Mosquitia tropical forest covers the area from the coast to the border with Nicaragua and provides valuable reserves of timber. Lead, zinc and silver are mined on a small scale.

The chief exports are coffee, bananas, frozen meat, shrimps, lobsters and timber, the most important woods being pine, mahogany and cedar. The main imports are machinery and electrical equipment, industrial chemicals and lubricants.

In October 1998 Hurricane Mitch devastated Honduras, killing an estimated 6,500 people and wrecking Tegucigalpa. The cost of repairing the damage was estimated at US$4 billion.

In July 2000, the IMF and the World Bank granted Honduras a debt reduction package worth about US$556 million.

In 1998 Honduras had a trade deficit of US$323 million and a current account deficit of US$333 million. In 1999 imports totalled US$2,728 million and exports US$940 million.

GNP – US$4,829 million (1999); US$760 per capita (1999)
GDP – US$4,698 million (1997); US$870 per capita (1998)
Annual Average Growth of GDP – 3.3 per cent (1996)
Inflation Rate – 11.7 per cent (1999)
Unemployment – 3.9 per cent (1998)
Total External Debt – US$5,002 million (1998)

| *Trade with UK* | 1999 | 2000 |
|---|---|---|
| Imports from UK | £10,043,000 | £11,008,000 |
| Exports to UK | 27,214,000 | 28,104,000 |

## COMMUNICATIONS

There are about 595 km of railway in operation, chiefly to serve the banana plantations and the Caribbean ports. There are 15,100 km of roads, of which 3,050 km are paved. There are over 80 smaller airstrips and four international airports, Tegucigalpa, San Pedro Sula, La Ceiba and Roatún (Bay Island).

The chief ports are Puerto Cortés, Tela and Puerto Castilla on the north coast, through which passes the bulk of the trade with the USA and Europe. Puerto Castilla is being developed as a deep-water container port, and San Lorenzo is also experiencing rapid growth.

## EDUCATION

Primary and secondary education is free, primary education being compulsory from the age of seven to 12, and the government has launched a campaign to eradicate illiteracy.

Illiteracy Rate – 27.8 per cent (2000)
Enrolment (percentage of age group) – primary 90 per cent (1993); secondary 21 per cent (1991); tertiary 10.0 per cent (1996)

---

# HUNGARY
*Magyar Köztársaság*

---

Area – 35,920 sq. miles (93,032 sq. km). Neighbours: Slovakia (north), Ukraine and Romania (east), the rump Yugoslav Federal state and Croatia (south), Slovenia and Austria (west)
Population – 10,068,000 (1997 UN estimate). There are minorities of Romanies (4 per cent), ethnic Germans (3 per cent), Serbs (2 per cent), Romanians (1 per cent) and Slovaks (1 per cent). About two-thirds of the population are Roman Catholic and the remainder mostly Calvinist. The language is Hungarian (Magyar)
Capital – Budapest, (population, 1,873,799, 1997 estimate)
Major Cities – Debrecen (207,666); Miskolc (176,845); Pécs (160,325); Szeged (160,579), 1997 UN estimates
Currency – Forint of 100 fillér
National Anthem – Isten Aldd Meg A Magyart (God Bless the Hungarians)
National Days – 15 March, 20 August, 23 October

NATIONAL FLAG – Red, white, green (horizontally)
LIFE EXPECTANCY (years) – male 66.3; female 75.1
POPULATION GROWTH RATE – 0.3 per cent (1999)
POPULATION DENSITY – 109 per sq. km (1998)
URBAN POPULATION – 64.0 per cent (2000 estimate)

## HISTORY AND POLITICS

The Hungarians settled the Danube basin in 896 AD and in 1000, King Istvan (Stephen) adopted Roman Catholicism and received a crown from the Pope. The Turks invaded Hungary in 1526; the Austrians finally succeeded in expelling them in 1699. Following nationalist unrest, the *Ausgleich* (compromise) of 1867 created the Dual Monarchy of Austria-Hungary, giving Hungary internal autonomy. The defeat of Austria-Hungary in the First World War led to the declaration of Hungarian independence in November 1918.

Hungary joined the Anti-Comintern Pact in February 1939 and entered the Second World War on the side of Germany in 1941. On 20 January 1945 a Hungarian provisional government of liberation signed an armistice under the terms of which the frontiers of Hungary were withdrawn to the 1937 limits.

After the liberation, a coalition of parties carried out land reform and nationalisation. By 1949 the Communists had succeeded in gaining a monopoly of power and by 1952 practically the entire economy had been 'socialised'.

Divisions within the Communist Party and popular demand for free elections and Soviet troop withdrawals grew. An uprising on 23 October 1956 was quelled by Soviet forces the following morning. But a reformist all-party coalition government under Imre Nagy was formed which declared Hungary's withdrawal from the Warsaw pact. This government was suppressed by a renewed attack by Soviet forces on Budapest on 4 November and a new Communist government under János Kádár was announced the same day.

From 1968 the government gradually introduced economic reforms and some political liberalisation. Kádár was forced to resign in May 1989. In October 1989 the National Assembly (*Országgyülés*) approved an amended constitution which described Hungary as an independent, democratic state. The 386-seat National Assembly is elected on a mixed first past the post and proportional representation basis with a 5 per cent threshold for representation. The first free multiparty elections took place in March and April 1990 and were won by the (conservative) Hungarian Democratic Forum.

In the legislative elections in May 1998, no party won an overall majority. The Federation of Young Democrats-Hungarian Civic Party (Fidesz-MPP) won the largest number of seats and its leader, Viktor Orbán, was asked by President Göncz to form a coalition government. The composition of the National Assembly in June 1998 was: Fidesz-MPP 147, Hungarian Socialist Party (HSP) 134, Independent Smallholders Party (FKGP) 48, Alliance of Free Democrats (AFD) 24, Hungarian Democratic Forum (MDF) 18, Hungarian Justice and Life Party 14, others 1. On 6 June 2000, Ferenc Madl, an independent candidate, was elected as president by parliament.

### HEAD OF STATE

*President*, Ferenc Madl, *elected* 6 June 2000, *sworn in* 4 August 2000

### CABINET *as at July 2001*

*Prime Minister, Telecommunications*, Viktor Orbán (F)
*Agriculture and Regional Development*, András Vonza (FKGP)
*Defence*, János Szabó (FKGP)
*Economic Affairs*, György Matolcsi (F)
*Education*, Zoltán Pokorni (F)
*Environmental Protection*, Péter Turi-Kovács (FKGP)
*Finance*, Mihály Varga (F)
*Foreign Affairs*, János Martonyi (F)
*Health*, István Mikola (F)
*Home Affairs*, Sándor Pintér (F)
*Justice*, Ibolya Dávid (MDF)
*National Cultural Heritage*, Zoltán Rockenbauer (F)
*Social and Family Affairs*, Péter Harrach (F)
*Transport and Water Management*, János Fonagy (F)
*Without Portfolio*, Ervin Demeter (F) (*Civilian Intelligence Services*); Imre Boros (FKGP) (*Relations with the EU*); István Stumpf (F) (*Prime Minister's Office, Privatisation*)
*Youth and Sports*, Tamás Deutsch (F)

F Fidesz-MPP; FKGP Independent Smallholders Party; MDF Hungarian Democratic Forum

### EMBASSY OF THE REPUBLIC OF HUNGARY

35 Eaton Place, London SW1X 8BY
Tel: 020-7235 5218
*Ambassador Extraordinary and Plenipotentiary*, HE Gábor Szentiványi, apptd 1997
*Minister Plenipotentiary*, Zsolt Pataki
*Counsellor and Consul-General*, Dr László Takács
*Commercial Counsellor*, András Hirschler
*Defence and Military Attaché*, Col. István Lakatos

### BRITISH EMBASSY

Harmincad Utca 6, H-1051 Budapest
Tel: (00 36) (1) 266 2888
E-mail: info@britemb.hu
*Ambassador Extraordinary and Plenipotentiary*, HE Nigel Thorpe, CVO, RCDS, apptd 1998
*Counsellor and Deputy Head of Mission*, G. B. Reid
*Defence Attaché*, Col. A. T. B. Kimber
*First Secretary (Commercial)*, D. K. Goldthorpe, LVO
*First Secretary (Management) and Consul*, B. Halliwell, MBE

BRITISH COUNCIL DIRECTOR, Dr John Richards, OBE, Benczúr Utca 26, H-1068 Budapest; e-mail: information@britishcouncil.hu. Debrecen, Miskolc, Pécs, Szombathely and Veszprém
BRITISH CHAMBER OF COMMERCE, Bank Utca 6, 2nd floor, H-1054 Budapest

## DEFENCE

The Army has 806 main battle tanks, 572 armoured infantry fighting vehicles and 786 armoured personnel carriers. The Air Force has 68 combat aircraft and 24 attack helicopters. Hungary became a member of NATO in March 1999.
MILITARY EXPENDITURE – 1.6 per cent of GDP (1999)
MILITARY PERSONNEL – 43,790; Army 23,500, Army Maritime Wing 290, Air Force 11,500, Paramilitaries 14,000
CONSCRIPTION DURATION – Nine months

## ECONOMY

Agriculture accounts for around 6 per cent of GDP and employs 7.5 per cent of the workforce. Production is concentrated on maize, wheat, sugar beet, barley, rye and oats.

Industry is mainly based on imported raw materials but Hungary has its own coal, bauxite, considerable deposits of natural gas, some iron ore and oil. Output figures in 1998 were: coal 14,494,299 tonnes; aluminium 33,700 tonnes; crude steel 1,939,784 tonnes; crude petroleum 1,257,830 tonnes. Natural gas production totalled 4,345 million cubic metres.

The economy suffered from the loss of export markets in the Soviet Union and the former Yugoslavia, and the transition to a market economy, but now exports the majority of its goods to the countries of the EU. The economy has benefited from a strong inflow of foreign direct investment.

The main exports are machinery and equipment, manufactures, foodstuffs, beverages and tobacco products, raw materials and energy transmission equipment.

In 1999 Hungary had a trade deficit of US$2,191 million and a current account deficit of US$2,101 million. Imports totalled US$27,923 million and exports US$24,950 million.

GNP – US$46,751 million (1999); US$4,650 per capita (1999)
GDP – US$45,725 million (1997); US$4,790 per capita (1999)
ANNUAL AVERAGE GROWTH OF GDP – 4.4 per cent (1999)
INFLATION RATE – 10.5 per cent (2001)
UNEMPLOYMENT – 6.3 per cent (2000)
TOTAL EXTERNAL DEBT – US$28,580 million (1998)

| *Trade with UK* | 1999 | 2000 |
|---|---|---|
| Imports from UK | £489,481,000 | £610,093,000 |
| Exports to UK | 686,250,000 | 703,309,000 |

## EDUCATION

There are five types of schools under the Ministry of Education: kindergartens for age three to six, general schools for age six to 14 (compulsory), vocational schools (15–18), secondary schools (15–18), universities and adult training schools (over 18).

ILLITERACY RATE – 0.6 per cent (2000)
ENROLMENT (percentage of age group) –
primary 97 per cent (1996); secondary 86 per cent (1996); tertiary 23.6 per cent (1996)

## CULTURE

Magyar, or Hungarian, is one of the Finno-Ugrian languages. Hungarian literature began to flourish in the second half of the 16th century. Among the greatest writers of the 19th and 20th centuries are Mihály Vörösmarty (1800–55), Sándor Petöfi (1823–49), János Arany (1817–82), Imre Madách (1823–64), Kálmán Mikszáth (1847–1910), Endre Ady (1877–1918), Attila József (1905–37), Mihály Babits (1883–1941), Dezsö Kosztolányi (1885–1936), Gyula Illyes (1902–83), János Pilinszky (1921–81) and Sándor Weöres (1913–89).

---

# ICELAND
*Lýðveldið Ísland*

---

AREA – 39,769 sq. miles (103,000 sq. km)
POPULATION – 277,000 (1999). Some 89.4 per cent of the population are members of the (Lutheran) Church of Iceland. The language is Icelandic
CAPITAL – ΨReykjavík (population, 107,764, 1999)
MAJOR CITIES – Akranes; ΨAkureyri; Egilsstaðir; ΨHafnarfjörður; ΨIsafjörður; Kópavogur; Reykjanesbær; ΨSiglufjörður
CURRENCY – Icelandic króna (Kr) of 100 aurar
NATIONAL ANTHEM - Lofsöngur (Song of praise)
NATIONAL DAY – 17 June
NATIONAL FLAG – Blue, with white-bordered red cross
LIFE EXPECTANCY (years) – male 76.1; female 80.4
POPULATION GROWTH RATE – 1.0 per cent (1999)
POPULATION DENSITY – 3 per sq. km (1998)
URBAN POPULATION – 92.5 per cent (2000 estimate)
MILITARY PERSONNEL – 120 Paramilitaries

## HISTORY AND POLITICS

Iceland was uninhabited before the ninth century, when settlers came from Norway. For several centuries a form of republican government prevailed, with an annual assembly of leading men called the *Alþingi (Althingi)*, but in 1262 Iceland became subject to Norway, and later to Denmark. During the colonial period, Iceland maintained its cultural integrity but a deterioration in the climate, together with frequent volcanic eruptions and outbreaks of disease, led to a serious drop in living standards and to a decline in the population to little more than 40,000. In the 19th century a struggle for independence led to home rule in 1918 and to independence as a republic in 1944.

The parliamentary (*Althingi*) elections on 8 May 1999 gave the Independence Party 26 seats, Unified Left 17, Progressives 12, Left-Green Alliance 6 and Liberals 2. A coalition government of the Independence Party and the Progressive Party was formed after the election.

### HEAD OF STATE

*President*, Ólafur Ragnar Grímsson, *elected* 29 June 1996

### CABINET *as at July 2001*

*Prime Minister, Statistical Bureau of Iceland*, Davíð Oddsson (IP)
*Agriculture*, Gudni Ágústsson (PP)
*Education, Culture and Science*, Björn Bjarnason (IP)
*Environment*, Siv Fridleifsdóttir (PP)
*Finance*, Geir Haarde (IP)
*Fisheries*, Árni Mathiesen (IP)
*Foreign Affairs*, Halldór Ásgrímsson (PP)
*Health and Social Security*, Jón Kristjánsson (PP)
*Justice and Ecclesiastical Affairs*, Sólveig Pétursdóttir (IP)
*Social Affairs*, Páll Pétursson (PP)
*Trade and Industry*, Valgerdur Sverrisdóttir (PP)
*Transport*, Sturla Bödvarsson (IP)

IP Independence Party; PP Progressive Party

### EMBASSY OF ICELAND

2A Hans Street, London SW1X 0JE
Tel: 020-7259 3999
*Ambassador Extraordinary and Plenipotentiary*, HE Þorsteinn Pálsson, apptd 1999

### BRITISH EMBASSY

Laufásvegur 31, IS-101 Reykjavík
Tel: (00 354) 550 5100/1/2
E-mail: britemb@centrum.is
*Ambassador Extraordinary and Plenipotentiary and Consul-General*, HE J. Culver, apptd 2000
CONSULATE – Akureyri

## ECONOMY

Iceland has considerable resources of hydroelectric and geothermal energy. Heavy industry includes an aluminium smelter, a nitrogen fertiliser factory, a cement factory, a diatomite plant and a ferro-silicon plant.

The major sectors of the economy are fishing and fish processing, manufacturing, agriculture, energy production and tourism, which is of growing importance with 232,219 visitors in 1998.

As a member of the European Free Trade Association (EFTA), Iceland has become a member of the European Economic Area (EEA) which extends most of the provisions of the EU's single market to EFTA states.

In 1999 Iceland had a trade deficit of US$307 million and a current account deficit of US$591 million. Imports totalled US$2,503 million and exports US$2,005 million.

GNP – US$8,197 million (1999); US$29,280 per capita (1999)
GDP – US$7,435 million (1997); US$31,139 per capita (1999)

ANNUAL AVERAGE GROWTH OF GDP – 4.3 per cent (1999)
INFLATION RATE – 3.9 per cent (2001)
UNEMPLOYMENT – 1.3 per cent (2001)

### TRADE

The principal exports are fish and fish products, which account for nearly three-quarters of exports, ferro-silicon and aluminium; the chief imports are consumer durables, petroleum products, transport equipment, textiles, foodstuffs, animal feeds and timber.

| *Trade with UK* | 1999 | 2000 |
|---|---|---|
| Imports from UK | £164,751,000 | £198,448,000 |
| Exports to UK | 299,319,000 | 337,701,000 |

## COMMUNICATIONS

At 1 January 1999, the mercantile marine consisted of 955 registered vessels (237,379 gross tons). There are regular shipping services between Reykjavík and Felixstowe, the Humber ports, Europe and the USA.

A regular air service is maintained by Icelandair between Glasgow and London and Reykjavík. There are also air services to Scandinavia, the USA, Germany, France, the Netherlands and Canada.

Road communications are adequate in summer but greatly restricted by snow in winter. Only roads in town centres and key highways are metalled, the rest being of gravel, sand and lava dust. The climate and terrain make first-class surfaces for highways out of the question. There are no railways.

There are four television channels (one public, three private) and several private and public radio stations. The government has invested heavily in communications technology.

## CULTURE

The ancient Norræna (or Northern tongue) has close affinities to Anglo-Saxon and as spoken and written in Iceland today differs little from that introduced into the island in the ninth century. There is a rich literature with two distinct periods of development, from the mid-11th to the late 13th century and from the early 19th century to the present.

ENROLMENT (percentage of age group) – primary 98 per cent (1996); secondary 87 per cent (1996); tertiary 37.5 per cent (1996)

---

# INDIA

*The Republic of India/Bhāratīya Ganarājya*

---

AREA – 1,269,213 sq. miles (3,287,263 sq. km). Neighbours: Pakistan (north-west), China, Tibet, Nepal and Bhutan (north), Myanmar (east), Bangladesh
POPULATION – 997,515,000 (1998 estimate), 846,302,688 (1991 census): Hindu (82.41 per cent), the rest being Muslim (11.67 per cent), Christian (2.32 per cent), Sikh (1.99 per cent), Buddhist (0.77 per cent) and Jain (0.41 per cent). The official languages are Hindi in the Devanagari script and English, though 17 regional languages also are recognised for adoption as official state languages
CAPITAL – New Delhi (population, 301,297; 8,419,084 including Delhi/Dilli), 1991
MAJOR CITIES – Ahmedabad (3,312,216); Bangalore (4,130,288); ΨBombay/Mumbai (12,596,243); ΨCalcutta/Kolkata (11,021,918); Hyderabad (4,344,437); Kanpur (2,029,889); Lucknow (1,669,204); ΨMadras/Chennai (5,421,985); Pune (2,493,987) (1991 figures)
CURRENCY – Indian rupee (Rs) of 100 paise
NATIONAL ANTHEM – Jana-gana-mana
NATIONAL DAY – 26 January (Republic Day)
NATIONAL FLAG – A horizontal tricolour with bands of deep saffron, white and dark green in equal proportions. In the centre of the white band appears an Asoka wheel in navy blue
LIFE EXPECTANCY (years) – male 59.6; female 61.2
POPULATION GROWTH RATE – 1.8 per cent (1999)
POPULATION DENSITY – 295 per sq. km (1998)
URBAN POPULATION – 28.4 per cent (2000 estimate)
ILLITERACY RATE – 44.2 per cent (2000)
ENROLMENT (percentage of age group) – tertiary 6.9 per cent (1996)

India has three well-defined regions: the mountain range of the Himalayas, the Indo-Gangetic plain, and the southern peninsula. The main mountain ranges are the Himalayas (over 29,000 feet) and the Western and Eastern Ghats (over 8,000 feet). Major rivers include the Ganges, Indus, Krishna, Godavari and Mahanadi.

Temperatures vary over the country between averages of about 10°C and 33°C, reaching over 38°C in some parts during the hot season. There are similar variations in rainfall, from only a few inches a year falling in the western Thar Desert to over 400 inches in Meghalaya.

## HISTORY AND POLITICS

The Indus civilisation was fully developed by *c.*2500 BC but collapsed *c.*1750 BC, and was replaced by an Aryan civilisation from the west. Arab invasions of the north-west began in the seventh century and Muslim, Hindu and Buddhist states developed until the establishment of the Mughal dynasty in 1526. The British East India Company established settlements throughout the 17th century; clashes with the French and native princes led to the British government taking control of the company in 1784 and gradually extending sovereignty over the whole subcontinent. The separate dominions of India and Pakistan became independent within the Commonwealth on 15 August 1947 and India became a republic in 1950.

Between 1947 and 1996, India was ruled by the Congress (I) Party for all but four years (March 1977–January 1980, November 1989–June 1991). Congress (I) has been led by members of the Nehru-Gandhi dynasty for most of the post-independence period: Prime Ministers Jawaharlal Nehru (1947–64), Indira Gandhi (1966–1977, 1980–84) and Rajiv Gandhi (1984–89). Indira Gandhi was assassinated by Sikh extremists seeking an independent Sikh state in Punjab; her son Rajiv was assassinated by Sri Lankan Tamils.

In November 1997, the United Front government (a coalition of Communist and low-caste parties) collapsed after Congress (I) withdrew its support. The parliamentary elections in February 1998 produced no outright winner; in March 1998, the BJP formed a coalition government under Atal Bihari Vajpayee, which collapsed following the loss of a confidence motion on 17 April 1999. The opposition parties were unable to form a majority government and parliament was dissolved on 26 April 1999 by President Narayanan. The BJP-led 24-party National Democratic Alliance won elections on 3 October 1999 with a majority of 296 seats.

### SECESSION

The Hindu Maharaja of Kashmir signed his state's instrument of accession to India in October 1947, two months after India and Pakistan became independent. This was disputed by Pakistan, on the basis that the majority of the state's population was Muslim. After three Indian-Pakistani wars, a line of control was agreed under the 1972 Simla agreement (China has also occupied some of Kashmir since the 1962 Sino-Indian war). Kashmir was placed under direct rule in 1990. The Islamic militant groups *Hizbul Mujahidin*, *Harakat-ul-Mujahidin* and *Lashkar-e-Tayyeba* continued to launch attacks on Hindu civilians, government officials and security forces. The Indian government announced a unilateral cease-fire during the month of Ramadan, which began on 28 November 2000 and the cease-fire was extended until 24 May 2001. In response, Pakistan announced that its forces would show restraint, but attacks by Islamic militants continued unabated and repeated government offers of talks with the militants were rejected.

### Foreign Relations

In addition to the territory it won as a result of the Sino-Indian war in 1962, China claims Arunachal Pradesh and does not recognise Indian sovereignty over Sikkim.

India and Pakistan have fought three major wars since independence, in 1947–8, 1965 and 1971. Since 1985 they have continued a low-level war at altitude for control of the Siachen glacier in Kashmir.

In May 1998, India conducted five underground nuclear tests, confirming its status as a nuclear power. The tests were condemned by the international community. Within three weeks, Pakistan had conducted its own nuclear tests, leading to fears that border confrontations between the two countries could escalate into nuclear conflict.

In May 1999 India launched air attacks on Muslim insurgents who had occupied mountainous areas within Indian-controlled Kashmir. Small-scale incidents between the Indian and Pakistani troops stationed along the line of control dividing Kashmir continue to occur on a regular basis. The presidents of India and Pakistan held a summit in Agra in July 2001, but failed to agree a joint declaration.

### Political System

Executive power is vested in the president, elected for a five-year term by an electoral college consisting of the elected members of the Union and State legislatures. The president appoints the prime minister and, on the latter's advice, the ministers, and can dismiss them. The Council of Ministers is collectively responsible to the *Lok Sabha* (lower house). The vice-president is ex-officio chairman of the *Rajya Sabha* (upper house).

Legislative power rests with the president, the Rajya Sabha (245 members serving six-year terms) and the Lok Sabha (545 members). Twelve members of the Rajya Sabha are presidential nominees, the rest are indirectly elected representatives of the State and Union Territories. The 543 members of the Lok Sabha representing the States and Union Territories are directly elected by universal adult franchise, and two representatives of the Anglo-Indian community are chosen, for a maximum term of five years.

### Federal Structure

There are 28 States and seven Union Territories. Each state is headed by a Governor, who is appointed by the president and holds office for five years, and by a Council of Ministers. All states have a Legislative Assembly, and some have also a Legislative Council, elected directly by adult suffrage for a maximum period of five years.

The Union Territories are administered, except where otherwise provided by Parliament, by the president acting through an Administrator or Lieutenant-Governor, or other authority appointed by him.

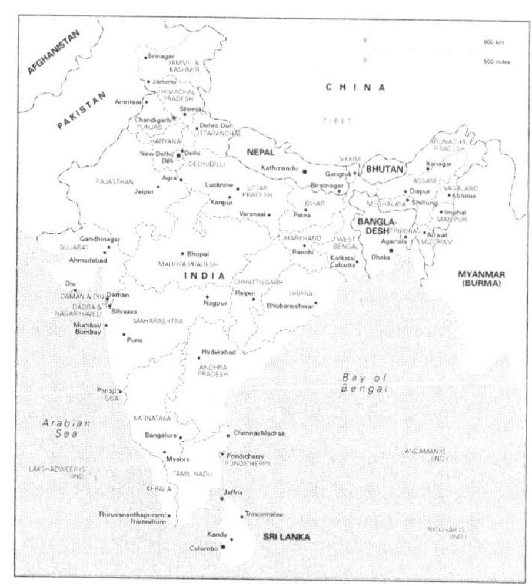


| | *Area (sq. km)* | *Population (1998 estimate)* | *Capital* |
|---|---|---|---|
| **States** | | | |
| Andhra Pradesh | 275,100 | 74,170,000 | Hyderabad |
| Arunachal Pradesh | 83,700 | 1,130,000 | Itanagar |
| Assam | 78,400 | 25,650,000 | Dispur |
| Bihar | 173,900 | 96,960,000 | Patna |
| Jharkhand† | | | Ranchi |
| Goa | 3,700 | 1,510,000 | Panaji |
| Gujarat | 196,000 | 47,100,000 | Gandhinagar |
| Haryana | 44,200 | 19,340,000 | Chandigarh |
| Himachal Pradesh | 55,700 | 6,420,000 | Shimla |
| Jammu and Kashmir* | 222,200 | 9,530,000 | Srinagar/ Jammu |
| Karnataka | 191,800 | 50,980,000 | Bangalore |
| Kerala | 38,900 | 31,780,000 | Trivandrum (Thiruvananthapuram) |
| Madhya Pradesh | 443,500 | 77,400,000 | Bhopal |
| Chhattisgarh‡ | | | Raipur |
| Maharashtra | 307,700 | 89,410,000 | Bombay (Mumbai) |
| Manipur | 22,300 | 2,390,000 | Imphal |
| Meghalaya | 22,400 | 2,310,000 | Shillong |
| Mizoram | 21,100 | 900,000 | Aizawl |
| Nagaland | 16,600 | 1,590,000 | Kohima |
| Orissa | 155,700 | 35,300,000 | Bhubaneswar |
| Punjab | 50,400 | 23,100,000 | Chandigarh |
| Rajasthan | 342,200 | 52,010,000 | Jaipur |
| Sikkim | 7,100 | 530,000 | Gangtok |
| Tamil Nadu | 130,100 | 60,880,000 | Madras (Chennai) |
| Tripura | 10,500 | 3,580,000 | Agartala |
| Uttar Pradesh | 294,400 | 164,040,000 | Lucknow |
| Uttaranchal§ | | | Dehra Dun |
| West Bengal | 88,800 | 77,250,000 | Calcutta (Kolkata) |
| **Union Territories** | | | |
| Andaman and Nicobar Is. | 8,200 | 370,000 | Port Blair |
| Chandigarh | 114 | 840,000 | |
| Dadra and Nagar Haveli | 500 | 180,000 | Silvassa |
| Daman and Diu | 112 | 130,000 | |

| | *Area (sq. km)* | *Population (1998 estimate)* | *Capital* |
|---|---|---|---|
| Delhi/Dilli | 1,500 | 13,040,000 | |
| Lakshadweep | 30 | 70,000 | |
| Kavaratti | | | |
| Pondicherry | 500 | 1,050,000 | |

*The figures include those parts occupied by Pakistan and China, which are claimed by India. The state's capital is at Srinagar in summer and Jammu in winter.
†Jharkhand was created on 15 November 2000 from Bihar; area and population figures given are for both states
‡ Chhattisgarh was created on 1 November 2000 from Madhya Pradesh; area and population figures given are for both states
§ Uttaranchal was created on 9 November 2000 from Uttar Pradesh; area and population figures given are for both states

### HEAD OF STATE

*President of the Republic of India*, Kocheril Raman Narayanan, *elected* 14 July 1997
*Vice-President*, Krishan Kant, *elected* 16 August 1997

### CABINET *as at July 2001*

*Prime Minister, Atomic Energy, Personnel, Public Grievances and Pensions, Space*, Atal Bihari Vajpayee (BJP)
*Agriculture, Railways (acting)*, Nitish Kumar (SP)
*Chemicals and Fertilisers*, Sukhdev Singh Dhindsa
*Civil Aviation*, Sharad Yadav (JDU)
*Commerce and Industry*, Murasoli Maran (DMK)
*Communications*, Ram Vilas Paswan (JDU)
*Consumer Affairs and Public Distribution*, Shanta Kumar
*Culture and Tourism*, Ananth Kumar (BJP)
*Environment and Forests*, T. R. Baalu (DMK)
*Foreign Affairs, Defence (acting)*, Jaswant Singh (BJP)
*Finance*, Yashwant Sinha (BJP)
*Health and Family Welfare*, C. P. Thakur
*Heavy Industries and Public Enterprises*, Manohar Joshi (SS)
*Home Affairs, Jammu and Kashmir Affairs*, Lal Krishna Advani (BJP)
*Human Resource Development, Science and Technology, Ocean Development*, Murli Manohar Joshi (BJP)
*Information and Broadcasting*, Sushma Swaraj (BJP)
*Information Technology, Parliamentary Affairs*, Pramod Mahajan (BJP)
*Labour*, Satya Narayan Jatiya (BJP)
*Law, Justice and Company Affairs*, Arun Jaitley (BJP)
*Mines*, Sunderlal Patwa (BJP)
*Petroleum and Natural Gas*, Ram Naik (BJP)
*Power*, Suresh Prabhakar Prabhu
*Rural Development*,. Venkaiah Naidu (BJP)
*Textiles*, Kashiram Rana (BJP)
*Tribal Affairs*, Jual Oram (BJP)
*Urban Development and Poverty Alleviation*, Jagmohan (BJP)
*Water Resources*, Arjun Sethi
*Youth Affairs and Sports, Mines*, Uma Bharati

BJP Bharatiya Janata Party; DMK Dravida Munnetra Kazhagam; JDU Janata Dal (United); SP Samata Party; SS Shiv Sena

### INDIAN HIGH COMMISSION

India House, Aldwych, London WC2B 4NA
Tel: 020-7836 8484
*High Commissioner*, HE Nareshwar Dayal, apptd 2000
*Deputy High Commissioner*, H. S. Puri
*Ministers*, S. K. Mandal *(Political)*; G. Singh *(Consular)*; G. R. Karnad *(Culture)*
*Counsellor (Economic)*, R. Panday
*Military Adviser*, Brig. S. Sharma
CONSULATES-GENERAL – Birmingham, Edinburgh

### BRITISH HIGH COMMISSION

Chanakyapuri, New Delhi 1100021
Tel: (00 91) (11) 687 2161
*High Commissioner*, HE Sir Rob Young, KCMG, apptd 1998
*Deputy High Commissioner and Minister*, T. T. Macan
*Deputy High Commissioners*, M. C. Bates, OBE *(Bombay/Mumbai)*; S. M. Scaddan *(Calcutta/Kolkata)*; M. E. J. Herridge *(Madras/Chennai)*
*Defence and Military Adviser*, Brig. S. M. A. Lee, OBE
*Counsellor (Economic and Commercial)*, G. C. Gillham
DEPUTY HIGH COMMISSIONERS' OFFICES - Bombay/Mumbai, Calcutta/Kolkata, Madras/Chennai,

BRITISH COUNCIL MINISTER - Edmund Marsden, 17 Kasturba Gandhi Marg, New Delhi 110 001; e-mail: delhi.enquiry@in.britishcouncil.org. Offices at Bombay/Mumbai, Calcutta/Kolkata and Madras/Chennai. British Council libraries at these four centres and British libraries at Ahmedabad, Bangalore, Bhopal, Hyderabad, Lucknow, Patna, Pune and Trivandrum/Triruvananthapuram

## DEFENCE

The Army has 3,414 main battle tanks, 1,350 armoured infantry fighting vehicles and 157 armoured personnel carriers. The Navy has 16 submarines, one aircraft carrier, eight destroyers, 12 frigates, 38 patrol and coastal vessels, 37 combat aircraft and 72 armed helicopters. It has nine bases including one under construction. The Air Force has 774 combat aircraft and 34 armed helicopters.

India exploded its first nuclear weapon in 1974 and is since believed to have acquired a stockpile of nuclear arms. It conducted further nuclear tests in May 1998. In 1993–4 India successfully test-fired its intermediate-range 'Agni' and 'Prithvi' ballistic missiles, and the latter went into production in September 1997.

MILITARY EXPENDITURE – 3.4 per cent of GDP (1999)
MILITARY PERSONNEL – 1,303,000: Army 1,100,000, Navy 53,000, Air Force 150,000; Paramilitaries 1,069,000

## ECONOMY

Agriculture supports about 60 per cent of the population, and contributes 29 per cent of GDP. Production has grown by 2.67 per cent each year since 1951, remaining slightly ahead of the 2 per cent increase necessary to keep pace with the rising population. Food crops occupy three-quarters of the total cultivated area. The main food crops are rice, cereals (principally wheat) and pulses. The major cash crops include sugar cane, jute, cotton and tea. Other products include oil seeds, spices, groundnuts, soya bean, tobacco, rubber and coffee. Livestock is raised, principally for dairy purposes or for the hides.

Industry is based on the exploitation and processing of mineral resources, principally coal, oil and iron, and on the production of textiles. The coal industry reached an output in 1998 of 316,574,000 tonnes; production of crude petroleum was 32,893,000 tonnes. Steel production is mainly in the hands of the public sector, with five public and one private sector integrated steel plants producing 23,863,000 tonnes of ingot steel in 1998. The engineering industry, heavy and light, is increasingly being privatised.

The manufacture of paper, cement, pharmaceuticals, chemicals, fertilisers, petrochemicals, motor vehicles and commercial vehicles has been expanded. Other principal manufactures are those derived from agricultural products, textiles, jute goods, sugar and leather, which along with tea, tobacco, rubber, fish and iron ore are major exports.

Tourism is a major industry, with 167 million domestic tourists and 2,358,609 overseas visitors in 1998, employing 9.8 million people.

The main exports are textiles, gemstones and jewellery, chemical products, agricultural produce, engineering products, leather goods, marine products and ores and minerals.

GDP has been rising by about 6 per cent per annum, but growth has been concentrated in the more prosperous western and southern states, increasing regional inequalities.

Orissa was devastated by a cyclone on 29 October 1999, which left at least 1.5 million people homeless and caused widespread destruction of crops.

In 1999 there was a trade deficit of US$8,029 million and a current account deficit of US$2,784 million. Imports totalled US$44,889 million and exports US$36,316 million.

GNP – US$441,834 million (1999); US$450 per capita (1999)
GDP – US$388,649 million (1997); US$422 per capita (1998)
ANNUAL AVERAGE GROWTH OF GDP – 6.8 per cent (1996)
INFLATION RATE – 4.7 per cent (1999)
TOTAL EXTERNAL DEBT – US$98,232 million (1998)

| *Trade with UK* | 1999 | 2000 |
|---|---|---|
| Imports from UK | £1,454,036,000 | £2,055,698,000,000 |
| Exports to UK | 1,482,350,000 | 1,712,157,000 |

## COMMUNICATIONS

The International Airports Authority manages five international airports: Indira Gandhi (Delhi/Dilli), Sahar (Bombay/Mumbai), Dum Dum (Calcutta/Kolkata), Meenambakkam (Madras/Chennai) and Triruvananthapuram. The other 88 aerodromes are controlled and operated by the Civil Aviation Department of the government. The national airlines are Indian Airlines (internal) and Air India (international).

The railways are grouped into nine administrative zones, Southern, Central, Western, Northern, North-Eastern, North-East Frontier, Eastern, South-Eastern and South-Central; there is also the Konkan Railway which links Bombay/Mumbai and Mangalore. The total track length is 62,495 km, of which 13,490 km is electrified. The total length of the road network is about 3,319,644 km of which 1,334,078 km is surfaced. The national highway system comprises 51,966 km of roads.

The chief seaports are Bombay/Mumbai, Calcutta/Kolkata, Haldia, Madras/Chennai, Mormugao, Cochin, Visakhapatnam, Kandla, Paradip, Mangalore and Tuticorin; these handled a cargo of 179.3 million tonnes in 1993–4. There are 139 minor working ports with varying capacity.

# INDONESIA
*Republik Indonesia*

AREA – 735,358 sq. miles (1,904,569 sq. km). Indonesia shares borders with Malaysia (on Borneo) and Papua New Guinea (on New Guinea)
POPULATION – 207,022,000 (1997 UN estimate): 87 per cent Muslim, with Christian, Buddhist, Hindu and Animist minorities. Bahasa Indonesian, a variant of Malay, is the national language, although more than 250 dialects are spoken
CAPITAL – ΨJakarta (population, 9,112,652, 1995 estimate)
MAJOR CITIES – (Java) Bandung (2,356,120), ΨSemarang (1,104,405), ΨSurabaya (2,663,820); (Kalimantan) Banjarmasin (482,931), ΨPontianak (409,632); (Maluku) Ambon (249,312); (Sulawesi) ΨUjung Pandang (1,060,257); (Sumatra) Medan (1,843,919), Palembang (1,222,764), 1995 estimates
CURRENCY – Rupiah (Rp) of 100 sen
NATIONAL ANTHEM – Indonesia Raya (Great Indonesia)
NATIONAL DAY – 17 August (Anniversary of Proclamation of Independence)
NATIONAL FLAG – Equal bands of red over white
LIFE EXPECTANCY (years) – male 66.6; female 69.0
POPULATION GROWTH RATE – 1.5 per cent (1999)
POPULATION DENSITY – 107 per sq. km (1998)
URBAN POPULATION – 40.9 per cent (2000 estimate)
ILLITERACY RATE – 13.0 per cent (2000)
ENROLMENT (percentage of age group) – primary 95 per cent (1996); secondary 42 per cent (1996); tertiary 11.3 per cent (1996)

Indonesia comprises the islands of Java, Madura, Sumatra, the Riouw-Lingga archipelago, Bangka and Billiton, part of the island of Borneo (Kalimantan), Sulawesi (formerly Celebes), Maluku (formerly Moluccas), the islands of Bali, Lombok, Sumbawa, Sumba, Flores and others comprising the provinces of East and West Nusa Tenggara and the western half of the islands of New Guinea (Irian Jaya) and Timor.

## HISTORY AND POLITICS

From the early part of the 17th century much of the Indonesian archipelago was under Dutch rule. Following the Second World War, during which the archipelago was occupied by the Japanese, a strong nationalistic movement formed and after sporadic fighting all the former Dutch East Indies except western New Guinea became independent as Indonesia on 27 December 1949. Western New Guinea became part of Indonesia in 1963 under the name West Irian (now Irian Jaya), this interpretation being confirmed in an 'Act of Free Choice' in July 1969.

The Army Minister Gen. Suharto assumed effective political power in March 1966. Gen. Suharto was appointed president in 1968 and was reappointed by the People's Consultative Assembly at every subsequent presidential election. The military effectively ruled through its political organisation Golkar.

Rampant inflation and high food and fuel prices provoked civil unrest during 1997, and by April 1998 riots and protests calling for Suharto's resignation were frequent. On 21 May 1998, he announced he would step down. He was replaced by his deputy B. J. Habibie.

The Golkar party was defeated in the general election of 7 June 1999, in which the Indonesian Democratic Struggle Party (DSP) led by Megawati Sukarnoputri, daughter of Indonesia's first president, gained 37.4 per cent of the vote and won the greatest number of seats. The new government elected Abdurrahman Wahid, the leader of the National Awakening Party (NAP), as president and Megawati Sukarnoputri was voted vice-president. A coalition government was formed, consisting of the DSP, NAP, and the National Mandate Party.

President Wahid was formally censured by the House of Representatives on 1 February 2001 and again on 30 April following a report which had implicated him in two financial scandals. Although he was cleared on 28 May of involvement in the scandals, relations between the president and the legislature had become untenable. On 30 May, the House of Representatives voted overwhelmingly to convene a special session of the People's Consultative Assembly to begin impeachment proceedings against President Wahid; the proceedings began on 20 July and resulted in his dismissal from office on 23 July. Megawati Sukarnoputri, who had been the vice-president, was immediately sworn in as his successor.

### FEDERAL STRUCTURE

There are 24 provinces, two special regions and a special capital region.

| | *Area (sq. km)* | *Population (1998 estimate)* | *Capital* |
|---|---|---|---|
| Provinces | | | |
| Aceh* | 55,392 | 3,847,583 | Banda Aceh |
| Sumatera Utara | 70,787 | 11,114,667 | Medan |
| Sumatera Barat | 49,778 | 4,323,170 | Padang |
| Riau | 94,561 | 3,900,534 | Pakanbaru |
| Jambi | 44,800 | 2,369,959 | Jambi |
| Sumatera Selatan | 103,688 | 7,207,545 | Palembang |
| Bengkulu | 21,168 | 1,409,117 | Bengkulu |
| Lampung | 33,307 | 6,657,759 | Tanjungkarang |
| Jakarta Raya† | 661 | 9,112,652 | Jakarta |
| Jawa Barat | 46,229 | 39,206,787 | Bandung |
| Jawa Tengah | 34,206 | 29,653,266 | Semarang |
| Yogyakarta* | 3,169 | 2,916,779 | Yogyakarta |
| Jawa Timur | 47,921 | 33,844,002 | Surabaya |
| Bali | 5,561 | 2,895,649 | Denpasar |
| Nusa Tenggara Barat | 20,177 | 3,645,713 | Mataram |
| Nusa Tenggara Timur | 47,876 | 3,577,472 | Kupang |
| Kalimantan Barat | 146,760 | 3,635,730 | Pontianak |
| Kalimantan Tengah | 152,600 | 1,627,453 | Palangkaraya |
| Kalimantan Selatan | 37,660 | 2,893,477 | Banjarmasin |
| Kalimantan Timur | 210,985 | 2,314,183 | Samarinda |
| Sulawesi Utara | 19,023 | 2,649,093 | Menado |
| Sulawesi Tengah | 69,726 | 1,938,071 | Palu |
| Sulawesi Selatan | 72,781 | 7,558,368 | Ujung Padang |
| Sulawesi Tenggara | 27,686 | 1,586,917 | Kendari |
| Maluku | 74,505 | 2,083,516 | Amboina |
| Irian Jaya | 421,981 | 1,942,627 | Jayapura |

* Special Region
†Special Capital City Region

## Insurgencies

There are two armed secessionist movements based on ethnic and nationalist groups, which are fighting perceived Javanese domination. In Irian Jaya government forces are fighting the Papua Independent Organisation (OPM) guerrillas who claim the 1969 referendum was rigged and oppose Indonesian settlement. In northern Sumatra the Free Aceh Movement (GAM) is active. On 7-8 November 1999, a crowd of at least 500,000 people demonstrated in the provincial capital Banda Aceh calling for independence for Aceh. Following a series of violent incidents between separatists and the armed forces, a cease-fire began on 2 June 2000, which lasted until 15 February 2001.

Periodic outbursts of violence between Christians and Muslims in Maluku province occurred in 1999 and 2000. The violence intensified in May 2000, following the arrival in Maluku of Laskar Jihad, a group of over 2,000 militant Islamic fighters from other parts of Indonesia. The violence had led to at least 5,000 deaths.

In Central Kalimantan province, which had suffered violence between indigenous Dayaks and immigrants from the island of Madura in 1999, a renewed outbreak of attacks on immigrants in February 2001 led to about 42,000 Madurese fleeing the province; another 35,000 were living in refugee camps in Central Kalimantan.
*See also* East Timor, page 000

## Head of State

*President*, Megawati Sukarnoputri, *sworn in* 23 July 2001

## Cabinet *as at July 2001*

*Prime Minister (Acting)*, The President
*Co-ordinating Minister for the Economy*, Burhanuddin Abdullah

*Co-ordinating Minister for Political, Social and Security Affairs*, Gen. Agum Gumelar
*Agriculture and Forestry*, Bungaran Saragih
*Culture and Tourism*, Gede Ardhika
*Defence*, H. Mohamed Mahfud
*Energy and Mineral Resources*, Puronomo Yusgiantoro
*Finance*, Rizal Ramli
*Foreign Affairs*, Alwi Shihab
*Health and Social Welfare*, Ahmad Sujudi
*Home Affairs and Regional Autonomy*, Lt.-Gen. Surjadi Soedirdja
*Housing and Regional Infrastructure*, Erna Anastasjia Witular
*Industry and Trade*, Lt.-Gen. (retd) Luhut Pandjaitan
*Justice and Human Rights*, Marsilam Simanjuntak
*Manpower and Transmigration*, Al Hilal Hamdi
*Maritime Affairs and Fisheries*, Rokhmin Dahuri
*National Education*, Yahya Muhaimin
*Religious Affairs*, K. H. Muhammad Tholchah Hasan
*Transport and Telecommunications*, Budi Mulyawan Suyitno

INDONESIAN EMBASSY
38 Grosvenor Square, London W1X 9AD
Tel: 020-7499 7661
*Ambassador Extraordinary and Plenipotentiary*, HE Nana Sutresna, apptd 1999
*Minister, Deputy Chief of Mission*, R. R. Siahaan
*Trade Attaché*, A. Anugerah

BRITISH EMBASSY
Jalan M. H. Thamrin 75, Jakarta 10310
Tel: (00 62) (21) 315 6264
*Ambassador Extraordinary and Plenipotentiary*, HE Richard Gozney, CMG, apptd 2000
*Deputy Head of Mission and Consul-General*, A. J. Sparkes
*Counsellor (Commercial/Development)*, A. Godson
*Defence Attaché*, Col. A. J. Roberts
BRITISH CONSULAR OFFICES - Bali, Jakarta, Medan, Surabaya

BRITISH COUNCIL DIRECTOR, Dr Richard Phillips, S. Widjojo Centre, Jalan Jenderal Sudirman Kev 71, Jakarta 12190; e-mail: information@britishcouncil.or.id. Offices in Surabaya
BRITISH CHAMBER OF COMMERCE, World Trade Centre, 13th floor, Jl. Jend. Sudirman Kav. 31, Jakarta 12190

## DEFENCE

The Army has 461 armoured personnel carriers, 11 armoured infantry fighting vehicles and 10 aircraft. The Navy has two submarines, 17 frigates, 36 patrol and coastal vessels and 18 armed helicopters. There are five principal naval bases. The Air Force has 108 combat aircraft.
MILITARY EXPENDITURE – 1.1 per cent of GDP (1999)
MILITARY PERSONNEL – 297,000: Army 230,000, Navy 40,000, Air Force 27,000; Paramilitaries 195,000
CONSCRIPTION DURATION – Two years (selective)

## ECONOMY

About 41 per cent of the population is engaged in agriculture and related production. Copra, nutmeg, pepper, palm oil, sugar, fibres, rubber, tea, coffee and tobacco are produced. Rice is a staple food and Java, Sulawesi and Sumatra are important producers.

Oil and liquefied natural gas are the most important assets. Timber is the second largest foreign exchange earner after oil. Indonesia is rich in minerals, particularly tin, of which the country is the world's third biggest producer; coal, nickel and bauxite are the other principal mineral products. There are also considerable deposits of gold, silver, manganese phosphates and sulphur.

Principal exports are petroleum, textiles and clothing, timber, natural gas and rubber. Principal imports are machinery and transport equipment, electrical equipment and chemicals.

Indonesia was one of the countries worst affected by the Asian economic crisis, which began in the latter half of 1997; the ensuing high unemployment and inflation have led to widespread political and inter-ethnic unrest.

In 1999 there was a trade surplus of US$20,644 million and a current account surplus of US$5,785 million. Imports totalled US$24,004 million and exports US$48,665 million.
GNP – US$125,043 million (1999); US$580 per capita (1999)
GDP – US$214,593 million (1997); US$478 per capita (1998)
ANNUAL AVERAGE GROWTH OF GDP – 7.8 per cent (1996)
INFLATION RATE – 20.5 per cent (1999)
UNEMPLOYMENT – 5.0 per cent (1998)
TOTAL EXTERNAL DEBT – US$150,875 million (1998)

| *Trade with UK* | 1999 | 2000 |
|---|---|---|
| Imports from UK | £398,679,000 | £412,332,000 |
| Exports to UK | 1,038,564,000 | 1,169,450,000 |

## COMMUNICATIONS

There are railway systems in Java and Sumatra linking the main towns. There are about 137,060 km of roads.

Sea communications are maintained by the state-run shipping companies Jakarta-Lloyd (ocean-going) and PELNI (coastal and inter-island) and other small concerns. Transport by small craft on the rivers of the larger islands plays an important part in trade.

Air services are operated by Garuda Indonesian Airways and other local airlines, and Jakarta is served by various international services.

---

# IRAN
*Jomhûri-ye-Eslâmi-ye-Îrân*

---

AREA – 630,574 sq. miles (1,633,188 sq. km). Neighbours: Armenia, Azerbaijan, Turkmenistan (north), Afghanistan (north-east), Pakistan (south-east), Iraq (south-west), Turkey (north-west)
POPULATION – 62,977,000 (1996 census): 99 per cent Muslims (Shia 91 per cent and Sunni 8 per cent) with small minorities of Zoroastrians, Jews, and Armenian and Assyrian Christians. The official language is Persian (Farsi). Minority languages are Turkic (26 per cent), Kurdish (9 per cent), Luri (2 per cent), Arabic, Baluchi and Turkish (1 per cent each)
CAPITAL – Tehran (population 6,758,845, 1996 census)
MAJOR CITIES – Ahwaz (804,980); Esfahan (1,266,072); Mashhad (1,887,405); Qom (777,677); Shiraz (1,053,025); Tabriz (1,191,043), 1996 census
CURRENCY – Rial
NATIONAL ANTHEM – Sorûd-e Jomhûri-ye Eslâmi (Anthem of the Islamic Republic of Iran)
NATIONAL DAY – 11 February
NATIONAL FLAG – Three horizontal stripes of green, white, red, with the slogan *Allahu Akbar* repeated 22 times along the edges of the green and red stripes, and the national emblem in the centre
LIFE EXPECTANCY (years) – male 66.8; female 67.9
POPULATION GROWTH RATE – 1.9 per cent (1999)
POPULATION DENSITY – 37 per sq. km (1998)
URBAN POPULATION – 61.6 per cent (2000 estimate)

Iran is mostly an arid tableland, encircled, except in the east, by mountains, the highest in the north rising to 18,934 ft. The central and eastern portion is a vast salt desert.

## HISTORY AND POLITICS

Iran was ruled from the end of the 18th century by Shahs of the Qajar dynasty. In 1925 the last of the dynasty, Sultan Ahmed Shah, was deposed in his absence by the National Assembly, which handed executive power to Prime Minister Reza Khan. Reza Khan was elected Shah as Reza Shah Pahlavi by the Constituent Assembly in December 1925. In 1941 Reza Shah abdicated in favour of the Crown Prince, who ascended the throne as Mohammed Reza Shah Pahlavi.

In January 1979, the Shah left Iran, handing over power to the Prime Minister, who was ousted by Ayatollah Khomeini, the spiritual leader of the Shia Muslims, on his return from exile. Following a national referendum, an Islamic Republic was declared on 1 April 1979. A new constitution, providing for a president, prime minister, Consultative Assembly, and leadership by Ayatollah Khomeini, was approved by referendum in December 1979. In June 1989 Khomeini died and President Khamenei was appointed Leader of the Islamic Republic. Rafsanjani was elected president in July 1989, and the post of prime minister was abolished. The 1997 presidential election was won by Mohammad Khatami, leader of a centre-left coalition. He was seen as a moderate, and since his election has attempted to pursue reformist policies, although these have often been blocked by the conservative clerical establishment. Iran and the UK re-established full diplomatic relations in May 1999. The three rounds of elections to the Majlis held on 18 February, 5 May and 30 May 2000 gave a large majority to reformist candidates. The presidential election on 8 June 2001 resulted in the re-election of Mohammad Khatami, who obtained over 76 per cent of the vote; there were nine other candidates.

### FOREIGN RELATIONS

Iran was at war with Iraq following the Iraqi invasion of Iran in September 1980. International efforts to end the fighting resulted in a cease-fire in August 1988. In August 1990 Iraq accepted Iran's conditions for settling the conflict, including a return to the 1975 border, but a formal peace treaty has not been signed.

Following the murder of nine Iranian diplomats in August 1998 by Taliban militia forces in Afghanistan, Iran held large-scale military manoeuvres on the Afghan frontier. There were border skirmishes on 8 October 1998.

### POLITICAL SYSTEM

The leader of the republic is elected by the Council of Experts whose 83 members are popularly elected every eight years. The president, who is the chief executive, is directly elected for a four-year term, renewable once. Ministers are nominated by the president and must obtain a vote of confidence in the Majlis. The Majlis comprises 290 representatives who are directly elected for a four-year term. Laws passed by the Majlis must be approved by the 12-member Guardian Council. In November 1997, President Khatami announced the establishment of the Committee for the Implementation and Supervision of the Constitution, a five-member body to ensure the constitution was abided by and that people's rights were respected.

*Leader of the Islamic Republic*, Ayatollah Seyed Ali Khamenei, *appointed* June 1989
*President*, Seyed Mohammad Khatami, *elected* 23 May 1997, *re-elected* 8 June 2001
*First Vice-President*, Hassan Ebrahim Habibi

### COUNCIL OF MINISTERS *as at July 2001*

*Vice-Presidents*, Mohammad Baqerian; Mohammed Ali Najafi (*Advisers to the President*); Gholamreza Aqazadeh (*Atomic Energy*); Abdollah Nouri (*Development and Social Affairs*); Masoumeh Ebtekar (*Environmental Protection*); Mohammad Hashemi (*Executive Affairs*); Mohammad Ali Saduqi (*Legal and Parliamentary Affairs*); Mostafa Hashemi-Taba (*Physical Education*)
*Administration and Planning*, Mohammad Reza Aref
*Agricultural Jihad*, Mahmoud Hojjati
*Commerce*, Mohammad Shariatmadari
*Co-operatives*, Morteza Hajji
*Culture and Islamic Guidance*, Ahmad Masjed-Jame'i
*Defence and Logistics*, Adm. Ali Shamkhani
*Economic Affairs and Finance*, Hossain Namazi
*Education*, Hossain Mozafar
*Energy*, Habibollah Bitaraf
*Foreign Affairs*, Kamal Kharrazi
*Health*, Mohammad Farhadi
*Higher Education*, Mostafa Moin
*Housing and Urban Development*, Ali Abdolalizadeh
*Industries and Mines*, Eshaq Jahangiri
*Information*, Ali Yunesi
*Interior, State Security Council*, Abdulvahed Moussavi-Lari
*Justice*, Hojjatolislam Ismail Shostari
*Labour and Social Affairs*, Hossein Kamali
*Oil*, Bijan Namdar Zanganeh
*Posts, Telephones and Telegraphs*, Ahmad Mo'tamedi
*Roads and Transport (acting)*, Sadegh Afshar

EMBASSY OF THE ISLAMIC REPUBLIC OF IRAN
16 Prince's Gate, London SW7 1PT
Tel: 020-7225 3000
*Ambassador Extraordinary and Plenipotentiary*, HE Morteza Sarmadi, *apptd* 2000

BRITISH EMBASSY
143 Ferdowsi Avenue, PO Box 11365–4474, Tehran 11344
Tel: (00 98) (21) 670 5011
*Ambassador Extraordinary and Plenipotentiary*, HE Nicholas W. Browne, CMG
*First Secretary (Commercial)*, E. Jenkinson

## DEFENCE

The Army has around 1,135 main battle tanks, 590 armoured personnel carriers, 440 armoured infantry fighting vehicles and 100 attack helicopters. The Navy has five submarines, three frigates, 63 patrol and coastal vessels, five combat aircraft and 29 armed helicopters. There are six naval bases. The Air Force has some 291 combat aircraft, of which about 60–80 per cent are serviceable.
MILITARY EXPENDITURE – 6.2 per cent of GDP (1999)
MILITARY PERSONNEL – 513,000: Army 350,000, Revolutionary Guard Corps 125,000, Navy 18,000, Air Force 45,000, Paramilitaries 40,000
CONSCRIPTION DURATION – 21 months

## ECONOMY

Iran's alleged support for international terrorism and its suspected nuclear weapons programme prompted the USA to impose a full trade and investment embargo in June 1995. On 17 March 2000, the USA announced that it would lift sanctions on the importation of certain goods, including carpets, caviar and pistachio nuts.

Wheat is the principal agricultural crop; other important crops are barley, rice, cotton, sugar beet, fruit, nuts and vegetables. Wool is also a major product.

The oilfields, which lie in south-western Iran, were nationalised in 1951. In 1979, the National Iranian Oil Company assumed control of the production, refining and sale of oil. Oil production was 187,700,000 tonnes in 1998.

Apart from oil, the principal industrial products are carpets, textiles, sugar, cement and other construction materials, ginned cotton, vegetable oil and other food products, leather and shoes, metal manufactures, pharmaceuticals, motor vehicles, fertilisers and plastics. Privatisation began in 1991.

It was announced in April 2000 that reserves of gas had been found in the Gavband region with an estimated value of US$16,500 million. Natural gas production was 50,000 million cubic metres in 1998.

In 1998 there was a trade deficit of US$626 million and a current account deficit of US$1,897 million. In 1997 imports totalled US$14,165 million and exports US$18,381 million.

GNP – US$113,729 million (1999); US$1,760 per capita (1999)

GDP – US$159,391 million (1997); US$2,850 per capita (1998)

ANNUAL AVERAGE GROWTH OF GDP – 5.9 per cent (1996)

INFLATION RATE – 21.0 per cent (1999)

TOTAL EXTERNAL DEBT – US$14,391 million (1998)

### TRADE

Imports are mainly industrial and agricultural machinery, motor vehicles and components for assembly, iron and steel, electrical machinery and goods, foodstuffs and certain textile fabrics and yarns. The principal exports, apart from oil and gas, are carpets and fruit. Japan, Germany, France, the UAE and Italy are Iran's main trading partners.

| *Trade with UK* | 1999 | 2000 |
|---|---|---|
| Imports from UK | £244,817,000 | £296,052,000 |
| Exports to UK | 36,456,000 | 33,200,000 |

## COMMUNICATIONS

Tehran is the centre of a network of highways linking the major towns, ports, the Caspian Sea and the national frontiers; there are 156,507 km of roads.

The Trans-Iranian Railway runs from Bandar Turcoman, on the Caspian Sea, via Tehran to Bandar Khomeini, on the Persian Gulf. Other lines link Tehran with Tabriz and Mashhad; Tabriz to Julfa; Zahedan to Quetta; Ahvaz to Khorramshahr; Qom to Kerman; and Bandar Turcoman to Gorgan. The rail system is linked to the Turkish system via Van. A track between Mashhad and Tedzhen in Turkmenistan, opened in May 1996, has re-established the ancient Silk Road between China and the Mediterranean; there are 5,612 km of railway track.

There is an international airport at Tehran (Mehrabad), and airports at all the major provincial centres. The national airline, Iranair, is government-owned and operates international and domestic routes.

## EDUCATION AND CULTURE

Since 1943 primary education has been compulsory and free. There are 74 universities in Iran. The educational system has been reformed following the revolution.

Persian or Farsi is an Indo-European language with many Arabic elements added; the alphabet is mainly Arabic, with writing from right to left. Among the great names in Persian literature are those of Abu'l Kásim Mansúr, or Firdausi (AD 939–1020), Omar Khayyám, the astronomer-poet (died AD 1122), Muslihu'd-Din, known as Sa'di (born AD 1184), and Shems-ed-Din Muhammad, or Hafiz (died AD 1389).

ILLITERACY RATE – 23.1 per cent (2000)

ENROLMENT (percentage of age group) – primary 90 per cent (1996); secondary 71 per cent (1996); tertiary 17.6 per cent (1996)

---

# IRAQ

*Al-Jumhūriyya al-'Irāqiyya*

---

AREA – 169,235 sq. miles (438,317 sq. km). Neighbours: Iran (east), Saudi Arabia, Kuwait (south), Jordan (west), Syria (north-west), Turkey (north)

POPULATION – 22,797,000 (1997 UN estimate), 16,278,316 (1987 census). The official language is Arabic. Minority languages include Kurdish (about 15 per cent), Turkic and Aramaic

CAPITAL – Baghdād (population, 3,841,268, 1987)

MAJOR CITIES – ΨAl-Başra (406,296); Kirkūk (418,624); Al-Mawşil (664,221)

CURRENCY – Iraqi dinar (ID) of 1,000 fils

NATIONAL ANTHEM – Land of two rivers

NATIONAL DAY – 17 July (Revolution Day)

NATIONAL FLAG – Three horizontal stripes of red, white, black; on the white stripe three stars and the slogan *Allahu Akbar* all in green

LIFE EXPECTANCY (years) – male 61.6; female 62.8

POPULATION GROWTH RATE – 2.4 per cent (1999)

POPULATION DENSITY – 50 per sq. km (1998)

URBAN POPULATION – 76.8 per cent (2000 estimate)

ILLITERACY RATE – 47.4 per cent (1997)

ENROLMENT (percentage of age group) – primary 76 per cent (1996); secondary 37 per cent (1992); tertiary 11.2 per cent (1995)

In 1993 the border between Iraq and Kuwait was formally demarcated, moving a few hundred metres northwards and giving part of the port of Umm Qasr to Kuwait. The rivers Euphrates (1,700 miles) and Tigris (1,150 miles) rise in Turkey and traverse Iraq to their junction at Qurna, from where the Euphrates flows the 70 miles to the Gulf.

## HISTORY AND POLITICS

Iraq is the site of the remains of several ancient civilisations: one site at Tel Hassuna, near Shura, dates back to 5000 BC; Tel Abu Shahrain near 'Ur of the Chaldees' is the site of the Sumerian city of Eridu; the ancient city of Hillah, 70 miles south of Baghdād, is near the site of Babylon and the Tower of Babel. Al-Mawşil governorate covers a great part of the ancient kingdom of Assyria, the ruins of Nineveh, the Assyrian capital, being visible on the banks of the Tigris, opposite Al-Mawşil. Qurna, at the junction of the Tigris and Euphrates, is traditionally supposed to be the site of the Garden of Eden.

Iraq was part of the Ottoman empire from 1534 until it was captured by British forces in 1916. A provisional government was set up in 1920, and in 1921 the Emir Faisal was elected King of Iraq. The country was a monarchy until July 1958, when King Faisal II was assassinated. From 1958 Iraq has been under the rule of the Ba'ath Party.

The Arab Ba'ath Socialist Party held 165 of the 250 Assembly seats following the most recent election, held on 27 March 2000; the remaining seats were held by independents.

### FOREIGN RELATIONS

Iraq invaded Iran in September 1980 and was at war until the August 1988 cease-fire. A formal peace treaty has not been signed.

Iraq invaded Kuwait on 2 August 1990 and declared Kuwait a province of Iraq. The UN Security Council declared the annexation void and in January 1991, an alliance of NATO and Middle East countries launched an offensive and liberated Kuwait in February 1991.

A United Nations Special Committee (UNSCOM), charged with securing Iraq's full nuclear, biological and chemical disarmament, was frequently hindered in its task by Iraqi officials.

In December 1999, the UN Security Council created a new weapons inspection body, the UN Monitoring, Verification and Inspection Commission (UNMOVIC), to replace UNSCOM. UNMOVIC was to monitor the elimination of Iraq's nuclear, chemical and biological weapons arsenal and was empowered to suspend all sanctions for four-month renewable phases if the Iraqi authorities co-operated fully with UNMOVIC and the IAEA within a whole 120-day period.

On 18 April 2001, Iran launched surface-to-surface missiles against military camps inside Iraq belonging to the main Iranian opposition group, the Mujahidin-i-Khalq and Iraqi aircraft shot down an unmanned Iranian reconnaissance aircraft the following day.

### INSURGENCIES

Following the allied victory in Kuwait in February 1991, rebellion broke out in the Kurdish north and the Shi'ite south. A UN safe haven in northern Iraq to protect the Kurdish population and air exclusion zones north of the 36th parallel and south of the 33rd parallel were also established.

Iraqi aircraft have frequently violated the air exclusion zones; allied forces have responded by attacking Iraqi air defence installations.

### POLITICAL SYSTEM

According to the provisional constitution, the highest state authority is the Revolutionary Command Council (RCC), which elects the president from among its members. A constitutional amendment approved in September 1995 provided for the confirmation of the RCC's choice of president by the National Assembly and by a popular referendum. The president appoints the Council of Ministers. Legislative authority is shared by the RCC and the 250-member National Assembly, which is elected every four years by universal adult suffrage. Following the amendment to the constitution, a referendum on a further seven-year term for President Saddam was approved by a claimed 99.96 per cent of voters on 15 October 1995.

### HEAD OF STATE

*President*, Saddam Hussein, *assumed office* 16 July 1979, *reappointed* 17 October 1995
*Vice-Presidents*, Taha Mohieddin Maarouf, Taha Yassin Ramadan

### REVOLUTIONARY COMMAND COUNCIL

*Chairman*, The President
*Vice-Chairman*, Izzat Ibrahim
*Secretary-General*, Khaled Abdel-Moneim Rasheed
*Members*, Taha Yassin Ramadan; Sa'adoun Shaker; Tariq Aziz; Taha Mohieddin Maarouf; Mizban Khader Hadi

### COUNCIL OF MINISTERS *as at July 2001*

*Prime Minister*, The President
*Deputy Prime Ministers*, Hikmat Mizban Ibrahim al-Azzawi *(Finance)*; Tariq Aziz (*Foreign Affairs*);
*Agriculture*, Abd al-Ilah Hamid Muhammad Salih
*Culture*, Hamid Yusuf Hammadi
*Defence*, Lt.-Gen. Sultan Hashim Ahmad al-Jabburi Tai
*Education*, Fahd Salem al-Shaqra
*Health*, Umid Midhat Mubarak
*Higher Education and Scientific Research*, Humam Abdel Khaliq
*Housing and Reconstruction*, Ma'n Abdullah al-Sarsam
*Industry, Minerals*, Adnan abd al Majid Jasim al-Ani
*Information*, Muhammad Said Kazim al-Sahhaf
*Irrigation*, Rasul Abd-al-Husayn al-Swadi
*Irrigation, Interior (acting)*, Mahmud Dhiyab al-Ahmad
*Justice*, Mondher Ibrahim al-Shawi
*Labour and Social Affairs*, Staff Gen. Sa'di Tu'mah Abbas
*Military Industrialisation*, Abd al-Tawwab al-Mulla Huwaysh
*Oil*, Lt.-Gen. Amir Muhammad Rashid al-Ubaydi
*Religious Endowments and Religious Affairs*, Abd al-Munim Ahmad Salih
*Trade*, Mohammad Mehdi Salih
*Transport and Communications*, Ahmad Murtada Khalil

### IRAQI DIPLOMATIC MISSION IN LONDON

Since Iraq's breach of diplomatic relations with Britain in February 1991, the Jordanian Embassy has handled Iraqi interests in the UK.
*Minister/Head of Interests Section*, Dr Mudhafar Amin

### BRITISH DIPLOMATIC REPRESENTATION

The British Embassy was closed in January 1991. The Russian Embassy has since handled British interests in Iraq.

## DEFENCE

The Army has roughly 2,200 main battle tanks, 2,400 armoured personnel carriers, 1,000 armoured infantry fighting vehicles and 120 armed helicopters. The Navy has six patrol and coastal vessels at two bases.

In 1991, the UN demanded the destruction of all weapons of mass destruction and their means of production as a prerequisite for the lifting of sanctions.
MILITARY EXPENDITURE – 7.6 per cent of GDP (1999)
MILITARY PERSONNEL – 429,000: Army 375,000, Navy 2,000, Air Force 35,000, Air Defence Force 17,000, Paramilitaries 45,000
CONSCRIPTION DURATION – 18–24 months

## ECONOMY

Increasing industrialisation is taking place but production has been hampered by war damage and sanctions. Iraq's major industry is oil production which was nationalised in 1972. Production was 105,300,000 tonnes in 1998.

Agricultural production is important, with two harvests usually gathered in a year, depending on rainfall. Salinity and soil erosion limit productivity.

The UN imposed economic sanctions and a world-wide ban on Iraqi oil exports in August 1990. In May 1996, Iraq agreed to a UN-proposed 'oil-for-food' deal, permitting the sale of oil to buy food and medicine. Limited oil exports resumed in December 1996.
GDP – US$149,036 million (1997); US$3,388 per capita (1998)
ANNUAL AVERAGE GROWTH OF GDP – 0.7 per cent (1996)

### TRADE

The principal imports are normally iron and steel, military equipment, building materials, mechanical and electrical machinery, motor vehicles, textiles and clothing, essential foodstuffs and raw industrial materials. The chief exports are normally crude petroleum, dates, raw wool, raw hides and skins and raw cotton.

Free trade agreements have been signed with Egypt, Syria and Tunisia, which are to be put into effect when UN sanctions are lifted.

| *Trade with UK* | 1999 | 2000 |
|---|---|---|
| Imports from UK | £35,488,000 | £50,990,000 |
| Exports to UK | 412,000 | 62,000 |

## COMMUNICATIONS

The port of Al-Başra has not been used since the outbreak of hostilities with Iran in 1980. Continuous dredging of the Shatt-al-Arab has also been suspended by hostilities and the channel has seriously silted. The port of Umm Qasr on the Kuwaiti border, which was developed for freight and sulphur handling and includes a container terminal, was opened in late 1993.

Iraqi Republican Railways provided regular passenger and goods services between Al-Başra, Baghdād and Al-Mawşil. There is also a metre gauge rail line connecting Baghdād with Khanaqin, Kirkūk and Arbil.

Iraqi communications were greatly affected by the Gulf War; large numbers of bridges were destroyed and the railway system extensively disrupted. Irregular flights primarily from Islamic countries began to fly into Baghdād International Airport in October 2000 in defiance of the sanctions. In November, Iraqi Airlines resumed its internal flights linking Baghdād with Al-Başra and Al-Mawşil.

---

# REPUBLIC OF IRELAND
*Poblacht Na hÉireann*

---

AREA – 27,132 sq. miles (70,273 sq. km). Neighbour: Northern Ireland (north)
POPULATION – 3,727,000 (1996 census). At the 1991 census religious adherence was: Roman Catholic, 3,228,327; Church of Ireland, 89,187; Presbyterians, 13,199; Methodists, 5,037; others, 189,969. Irish is the first official language; English is recognised as a second official language, but is more commonly used
CAPITAL – ΨDublin (*Baile Átha Cliath*) (population, 952,692, 1996 census)
MAJOR CITIES – ΨCork (*Corcaigh*) (180,000); ΨGalway (*Gaillimh*) (57,400); ΨLimerick (*Luimheach*) (79,100); Waterford (*Port Láirge*) (44,200), 1996 census
CURRENCY – Euro (€) of 100 cents/Punt (IR£) of 100 pence
NATIONAL ANTHEM – Amhrán na BhFiann (The Soldier's Song)
NATIONAL DAY – 17 March (St Patrick's Day)
NATIONAL FLAG – Equal vertical stripes of green, white and orange
LIFE EXPECTANCY (years) – male 73.3; female 78.3
POPULATION GROWTH RATE – 0.6 per cent (1999)
POPULATION DENSITY – 53 per sq. km (1998)
URBAN POPULATION – 59.0 per cent (2000 estimate)
MILITARY EXPENDITURE – 0.9 per cent of GDP (1999)
MILITARY PERSONNEL – 11,460: Army 9,300, Navy 1,100, Air Force 1,060

Ireland is separated from Scotland by the North Channel and from England and Wales by the Irish Sea and St George's Channel. The greatest length of the island, from north-east to south-west (Torr Head to Mizen Head), is 302 miles, and the greatest breadth, from east to west (Dundrum Bay to Annagh Head), is 174 miles. On the north coast of Achill Island (Co. Mayo) are the highest cliffs in the British Isles, 2,000 feet sheer above the sea.

The highest point is Carrantuohill (3,414 ft). The principal river is the Shannon (240 miles), which drains the central plain. The Slaney flows into Wexford Harbour, the Liffey to Dublin Bay, the Boyne to Drogheda, the Lee to Cork Harbour, the Blackwater to Youghal Harbour, and the Suir, Barrow and Nore to Waterford Harbour.

The principal hydrographic feature is the loughs; the Shannon chain of Allen, Boderg, Forbes, Ree and Derg, and the Erne chain of Gowna, Oughter, Lower Erne, and Erne; Melvin, Gill, Gara and Conn in the north-west; and Corrib and Mask (joined by a hidden channel) in the west.

The Republic of Ireland is divided into four provinces of 26 counties: Leinster (Carlow, Dublin, Kildare, Kilkenny, Laoighis, Longford, Louth, Meath, Offaly, Westmeath, Wexford and Wicklow); Munster (Clare, Cork, Kerry, Limerick, Tipperary and Waterford); Connacht (Galway, Leitrim, Mayo, Roscommon and Sligo); and part of Ulster (Cavan, Donegal and Monaghan).

## HISTORY AND POLITICS

The first inhabitants of Ireland, hunters from mainland Britain, arrived in 7,000 BC, and were joined by Celts from central Europe from the sixth century BC until about the time of Christ. The introduction of Christianity in the fifth century is traditionally associated with St Patrick and inspired 300 years of rich cultural achievements. The Vikings, who established most of the major towns, including Dublin and Cork, invaded around AD 800 and controlled Ireland until their defeat at the Battle of Clontarf (1014) by Brian Boru, who had become king of all Ireland in 1002.

In the 12th century the Norman English invaded at the invitation of Dermod MacMurrough, the deposed king of Leinster, and established feudal control over most of the island; this lasted for 300 years. King Henry VIII of England reconquered Ireland and in 1541 declared himself king of Ireland, the first English monarch to do so. Protestantism was introduced but failed to take root, except in Ulster where English and Scottish Presbyterians settled during the reign of James I (1603–25). A rebellion initiated by Ulster Catholics in 1641 was ruthlessly crushed by Oliver Cromwell's army. Catholicism was repressed and further Protestant colonisation encouraged. Following the abdication of the Catholic King James II in 1688, Irish Protestants supported William of Orange's accession to the throne. James II was defeated in Ireland, most famously at the Battle of the Boyne (1690), and Protestant ascendancy was restored, enduring throughout the 18th century.

The Irish parliament was granted independence in 1782, although the Dublin administration was still appointed by the king. The parliament was abolished by the Act of Union in 1801 following a rebellion by the Society of the United Irishmen in 1798, and subsequently Irish MPs sat at Westminster. Demands for the restoration of the Irish parliament and home rule for Ireland were successful in 1914, but were delayed when World War I broke out. A rebellion, the Easter Rising of 1916, was suppressed by the British, fuelling support for the *Sinn Féin* party, which won the 1918 election in Ireland and withdrew from the British parliament to form a legislature in Dublin under the leadership of Éamon de Valera. The resulting two-year war of independence between the Irish Republican Army and British forces ended in a truce, followed by negotiations leading to the signing of the Anglo-Irish Treaty in December 1921. The island was partitioned, the 26 counties of the Irish Free State accepting dominion status within the British Empire, while six of the nine counties of Ulster, where the majority Protestant population opposed home rule, remained part of the United Kingdom, governed by a Northern Ireland parliament.

Civil war broke out between the new Irish government and opponents of the treaty until a truce was reached in May 1923. Constitutional links between the Irish Free State and the UK were gradually removed by the Irish parliament and a new constitution enacted in 1937 declared the Irish Free State a sovereign, independent state with a republican government. However, it continued in association with the states of the British Commonwealth until 1949, when constitutional links with Britain were severed and the state was renamed the Republic of Ireland.

Under the terms of the 1998 Belfast Agreement, the Irish Republic gave up its territorial claim to the six counties of Northern Ireland. Additionally, a North-

South Ministerial Council, comprising officials from both countries, would meet to regulate areas of common interest.

The presidential election in October 1997 was won by Mary McAleese with almost 59 per cent of second-round votes. The composition of the Dáil Eireann as of July 1999 was: Fianna Fáil 76; Fine Gael 54; Labour 16; Democratic Left 4; Progressive Democrats 4; Green Party 2; Sinn Fein 1; Socialist 1; others 6. Fianna Fail and the Progressive Democrats formed a coalition government.

### Political System

The president (*Uachtarán na hÉireann*) is directly elected for a term of seven years, and is eligible for a second term. The president is aided and advised by a Council of State.

The National Parliament (*Oireachtas*) consists of the president, House of Representatives (*Dáil Éireann*) and Senate (*Seanad Éireann*). Dáil Éireann is composed of 166 members elected for a five-year term on a basis of proportional representation by means of the single transferable vote. Seanad Éireann is composed of 60 members, of whom 11 are nominated by the prime minister (*Taoiseach*) and 49 are elected, six by institutions of higher education and 43 from panels of candidates established on a vocational basis.

Executive power is vested in the government subject to the constitution. The government is responsible to the Dáil. The taoiseach is appointed by the president on the nomination of the Dáil. The other members of the government are appointed by the president on the nomination of the taoiseach with the previous approval of the Dáil. The taoiseach appoints a member of the government to be his deputy (the *tánaiste*).

The judicial system comprises courts of first instance and a court of final appeal called the Supreme Court (*Cúirt Uachtarach*). The courts of first instance include a High Court (*Ard-Chúirt*) and courts of local and limited jurisdiction, with a right of appeal as determined by law. The High Court alone has original jurisdiction to consider the question of the validity of any law having regard to the provisions of the constitution. The Supreme Court has appellate jurisdiction from decisions of the High Court.

### Head of State

*President*, Mary McAleese, *elected* 30 October 1997, *sworn in* 11 November 1997

### Cabinet *as at July 2001*

*Taoiseach (PM)*, Bertie Ahern
*Tánaiste (Deputy PM), Enterprise, Trade and Employment*, Mary Harney
*Agriculture and Food*, Joe Walsh
*Arts, Heritage, Gaeltachta and Islands*, Síle de Valera
*Defence and European Affairs*, Michael Smith
*Education and Science*, Michael Woods
*Environment and Local Government*, Noel Dempsey
*Finance*, Charlie McCreevy
*Foreign Affairs*, Brian Cowen
*Health and Children*, Michael Martin
*Justice and Equality, Law Reform*, John O'Donoghue
*Marine and Natural Resources*, Frank Fahey
*Public Enterprise*, Mary O'Rourke
*Social, Community and Family Affairs*, Dermot Ahern
*Tourism, Sport and Recreation*, Jim McDaid

### Irish Embassy

17 Grosvenor Place, London SW1X 7HR
Tel: 020-7235 2171
*Ambassador Extraordinary and Plenipotentiary*, HE Edward Barrington, apptd 1995
*Counsellor*, S. Murray (*Economic*)

### British Embassy

29 Merrion Road, IE-Dublin 4
Tel: (00 353) (1) 205 3700
E-mail: bembassy@internet-ireland.ie
*Ambassador Extraordinary and Plenipotentiary*, HE Sir Ivor Roberts, KCMG, apptd 1998
*Counsellor and Deputy Head of Mission*, J. Rankin
*Defence Attaché*, Col. J. D. Wilson
*First Secretary (Commercial)*, R. N. J. Baker

British Council Director, Ann Malamah-Thomas, Newmount House, 22/24 Lower Mount Street, IE-Dublin 2; e-mail: helen.jones@ie.britishcouncil.org

## ECONOMY

Although industry has expanded greatly since Ireland's entry into the European Community in 1973, agriculture remains important; in 2000, 7.8 per cent of the workforce was employed in agriculture, forestry and fisheries. The main crops are wheat, barley, oats, potatoes and sugar beet. Agriculture has benefited considerably from the EU Common Agricultural Policy and support funds but has suffered from the drift of the rural population to urban areas and abroad.

Industry accounted for about 38 per cent of GDP and about 28.3 per cent of employment in 1999. The traditional brewing, spirits and food-processing sectors have expanded and have been joined by the manufacture of textiles, chemicals, pharmaceuticals, electronics, office machinery and transportation equipment. The services sector is currently the fastest-growing sector of the economy and accounted for 57 per cent of GDP and 63.1 per cent of employment in 1999. Tourism is the most important part of the service sector and in recent years has provided substantial revenue, with 6,416,000 visitors in 2000.

The Kinsale gas field off the south coast provided 28 per cent of Ireland's gas needs in 2000, with 72 per cent coming via an undersea pipeline from Moffat, Scotland. There are five government-funded milled peat power-generating stations. Hydroelectric power from the Shannon barrage and other schemes is also important but Ireland still imports 47 per cent of oil and coal for power generation. Metal content of ores raised (2000) was lead, 86,896 tonnes; zinc, 431,426 tonnes.

Computer equipment and organic chemicals are the main exports. The UK, USA, Germany, France and the Netherlands are Ireland's main trading partners.

Following GDP growth of around 9 per cent in 2000, the government proposed a budget for 2001 which aimed to increase spending and reduce taxes. In February 2001 EU finance ministers instructed the Irish Finance Minister, Charlie McCreevy, to amend the budget, claiming that it would raise Ireland's already high inflation rate. He refused, citing statistics showing that the rate of inflation was falling.

Having satisfied the Maastricht convergence criteria, Ireland participates in the European Single Currency.

In 1999 Ireland had a trade surplus of US$24,006 million and a current account surplus of US$305 million. Imports totalled US$46,030 million and exports US$70,281 million.

GNP – US$80,559 million (1999); US$19,160 per capita (1999)

GDP – US$75,358 million (1997); US$24,943 per capita (1999)

ANNUAL AVERAGE GROWTH OF GDP – 9.8 per cent (1999)

INFLATION RATE – 5.3 per cent (1999)

UNEMPLOYMENT – 3.8 per cent (2001)

| *Trade with UK* | 1999 | 2000 |
|---|---|---|
| Imports from UK | £10,100,600,000 | £11,644,200,000 |
| Exports to UK | 8,014,100,000 | 9,165,000,000 |

## COMMUNICATIONS

In 2000 there were 2,812 km of railway operated by *Iarnród Eirann*. In 1999 the number of ships with cargo which arrived at Irish ports was 17,645 (190,818,000 net registered tons), with a total weight of goods handled of 43,928 million tonnes.

Shannon Airport, Co. Clare, is on the main transatlantic air route. In 2000 the airport handled 2.41 million passengers. Dublin Airport serves the cross-channel and European services operated by the Irish national airline Aer Lingus and other airlines. In 2000 the airport handled 13.83 million passengers. In 2000 Cork Airport handled 1.68 million passengers.

## EDUCATION

Primary education is directed by the state, with the exception of 37 private primary schools. There were 3,181 state-aided primary schools in 1998–9.

In 1998–9 there were 432 recognised secondary schools under private management (mainly religious orders), and 245 vocational schools. There were 16 state comprehensive schools and 66 community schools.

Third-level education is catered for by seven university colleges, 13 Institutes of Technology, seven teacher training colleges and a number of other third-level institutions.

ENROLMENT (percentage of age group) – primary 92 per cent (1996); secondary 86 per cent (1996); tertiary 41.0 per cent (1996)

---

# ISRAEL

*Medinat Yisra'el/Dawlat Isrā'īl*

---

AREA – 8,130 sq. miles (21,056 sq. km). Neighbours: Lebanon (north), Syria (north-east), Jordan and the West Bank (east), the Gaza Strip and the Egyptian province of Sinai (south-west)

POPULATION – 6,093,000 (1999 estimate): roughly 82 per cent Jewish, 14 per cent Arab Muslims, 2.5 per cent Christians of which 90 per cent are Arab, and 2 per cent Druze. Since independence Israel has had a policy of granting an immigration visa to every Jew who expresses a desire to settle in Israel. Between 1948 and 1992, 2.3 million immigrants had entered Israel from over 100 different countries. Hebrew and Arabic are the official languages. Arabs are entitled to transact all official business with government departments in Arabic

CAPITAL – Most of the government departments are in Jerusalem, population 617,800 (1997 estimate). A resolution proclaiming Jerusalem as the capital of Israel was adopted by the *Knesset* in 1950. It is not, however, recognised as the capital by the UN because East Jerusalem is part of the Occupied Territories captured in 1967. The UN and international law continues to reject the Israeli annexation of East Jerusalem and considers the pre-1950 capital Tel Aviv (population, 2,566,900) to be the capital

MAJOR CITIES – Beersheba (and district 158,400); ΨHaifa (and district 821,200); Rishon Le'Zion (173,800), 1997 estimates

CURRENCY – Shekel of 100 agora

NATIONAL ANTHEM – Hatikvah (The Hope)

NATIONAL FLAG – White, with two horizontal blue stripes, the Shield of David in the centre

LIFE EXPECTANCY (years) – male 76.2; female 79.3

POPULATION GROWTH RATE – 3.0 per cent (1999)

POPULATION DENSITY – 283 per sq. km (1998)

URBAN POPULATION – 91.2 per cent (2000 estimate)

Israel comprises the hill country of Galilee and parts of Judea and Samaria, rising to heights of nearly 4,000 ft; the coastal plain from the Gaza strip to north of Acre, including the plain of Esdraelon running from Haifa Bay to the south-east which divides the hill region; the Negev, a semi-desert triangular-shaped region, extending from a base south of Beersheba, to an apex at the head of the Gulf of Aqaba; and parts of the Jordan valley, including the Hula region, Tiberias and the south-western extremity of the Dead Sea.

The principal river is the Jordan, which rises from three main sources in Israel, the Lebanon and Syria, and flows through the Hula valley, Lake Tiberias/Kinneret (Sea of Galilee) and the Jordan Valley into the Dead Sea, falling 1,517 ft from Hulata to the Dead Sea. The other principal rivers are the Yarkon and Kishon. The Dead Sea is a lake (shared between Israel, the West Bank and Jordan), 1,286 ft below sea-level; it has no outlet, the surplus being carried off by evaporation.

The climate is variable, modified by altitude and distance from the sea, with hot summers and rainy winters.

## HISTORY AND POLITICS

The Ottoman Empire province of Palestine was captured by British forces in 1917, the same year that the British Government issued the Balfour Declaration which 'viewed with favour the establishment of a national home for the Jewish people in Palestine'. The Balfour Declaration's terms were enshrined in Britain's League of Nations mandate over Palestine, leading to steady Jewish immigration in the inter-war years and a post-1945 flood by Nazi concentration camp survivors. The Arab Palestinian population revolted against Jewish immigration from 1936 onwards, while Jewish groups conducted a terrorist campaign against the British administration from 1945 onwards.

In 1947 Britain announced its withdrawal from Palestine with effect from May 1948, handing over to the UN responsibility for resolving the conflict between Arabs and Jews. Both sides ignored the UN partition plan; on the withdrawal of British forces on 14 May 1948 the State of Israel was proclaimed and the first Arab-Israeli war began.

By the time of the January 1949 cease-fire Israeli forces controlled all of the former mandate territory apart from the West Bank (and East Jerusalem) and the Gaza Strip, which had come under Jordanian and Egyptian control respectively.

During the 1967 Six-Day War Israel captured the West Bank and the Gaza Strip, together with Sinai from Egypt and the Golan Heights from Syria, and annexed East Jerusalem. Israel held on to its gains in the 1973 Yom Kippur War. The Golan Heights were annexed in 1981; Sinai was returned to Egypt in 1982 in accordance with the 1979 Israeli–Egyptian peace treaty, and the South Lebanon Security Zone was established after the 1982–5 invasion of Lebanon, but vacated in June 2000. The annexations of East Jerusalem and the Golan Heights remain unrecognised internationally.

A general election on 29 May 1996, the first to have separate ballots for the prime minister and legislature, was won by Likud leader Binyamin Netanyahu. Ehud Barak, leader of the Labour Party and the One Israel electoral alliance of the Labour, Gesher and Meymad parties, was elected prime minister on 17 May 1999 and formed a six-party coalition government. President Weizman announced that he would resign from office on 10 July 2000 following allegations of fraud. On 31 July, Moshe Katsav was elected president. Ehud Barak resigned as prime minister on 9 December 2000 and called a prime ministerial election, which was held on 6 February 2001; it was won by Likud leader Ariel Sharon, who formed a broad-based eight-party coalition which commanded the support of 72 of the 120 members of the Knesset. Saleh Tarif became the first Israeli Arab to be appointed to the cabinet.

## Foreign Relations

A peace process, started in October 1991 in Madrid, led to agreements with the Palestine Liberation Organisation, and with Jordan on 14 September 1993. A full peace agreement with Jordan was signed on 26 October 1994.

## Political System

Israel is a sovereign democratic republic with executive power vested in a prime minister and Cabinet, and legislative power in a unicameral legislature (*Knesset*) of 120 members elected by proportional representation for a maximum term of four years. The prime minister is elected separately from the legislature. The president is head of state and is elected by the Knesset. Previous presidents have been elected for a maximum of two five-year terms, but under a bill approved by the Knesset in December 1998, the president is to be elected for a seven-year non-renewable term.

## Head of State

*President of Israel*, Moshe Katsav, *elected* 31 July 2000, *sworn in* 1 August 2000

## Cabinet *as at July 2001*

*Prime Minister, Immigrant Absorption*, Ariel Sharon (L)
*Deputy Prime Minister, Finance*, Silvan Shalom (L)
*Deputy Prime Minister, Foreign Affairs*, Shimon Peres (Lab)
*Deputy Prime Minister, Housing and Construction*, Natan Sharansky (YBA)
*Deputy Prime Minister, Interior*, Eli Yishai (S)
*Agriculture and Rural Development*, Shalom Simhon (L)
*Communications*, Reuven Rivlin (L)
*Defence*, Benjamin Ben-Eliezer (Lab)
*Education*, Limor Livnat (L)
*Environment*, Tzachi Hanegbi (L)
*Health*, Nissim Dahan (S)
*Industry and Trade*, Dalia Itzik (Lab)
*Justice*, Meir Sheetrit (L)
*Labour and Social Affairs*, Shlomo Benizri (S)
*National Infrastructures*, Avigdor Lieberman (NU)
*Public Security*, Uzi Landau (L)
*Regional Co-operation*, Tzipi Livni (L)
*Religious Affairs*, Asher Ohana (S)
*Science, Culture and Sport*, Matan Vilnai (Lab)
*Tourism*, Rechavam Ze'evy (NU)
*Transport*, Ephraim Sneh (Lab)
*Without Portfolio*, Dan Naveh (L) (*Co-ordination between the Government and the Knesset*); Eli Suissa (*Jerusalem Affairs*); Shmuel Avital (ON) (*Social Affairs*); Ra'anan Cohen (Lab); Saleh Tarif (Lab)
Lab Labour; L Likud; NU National Union-Yisrael Beytenu; ON One Nation; S Shas; YBA Yisrael B'Aliya

## Embassy of Israel

2 Palace Green, Kensington, London W8 4QB
Tel: 020-7957 9500
*Ambassador Extraordinary and Plenipotentiary*, HE Zvi Shtauber, apptd 2001
*Minister Plenipotentiary*, A. Magid
*Defence and Armed Forces Attaché*, Col. I. Yaar
*Minister*, M. Bar-On (*Consular*)
*Counsellor*, R. Kan (*Commercial*)

## British Embassy

192 Hayarkon Street, Tel Aviv 63405
Tel: (00 972) (3) 725 1222
*Ambassador Extraordinary and Plenipotentiary*, HE Francis Cornish, CMG, LVO, apptd 1998
*Counsellor, Consul-General and Deputy Head of Mission*, S. Pease
*Defence and Military Attaché*, Col. T. M. Fitzalan-Howard, OBE

*First Secretary (Commercial)*, I. Morrison
CONSULATES – Tel Aviv, Eilat

BRITISH COUNCIL DIRECTOR, David Elliott, 140 Hayarkon Street, PO Box 3302, Tel Aviv 61032; e-mail: bc.telaviv@britishcouncil.org.il. Regional offices in Jerusalem and Nazareth
ISRAEL-BRITISH CHAMBER OF COMMERCE, 76 IBN Guirol Street, Tel Aviv 64162

## DEFENCE

Israel is believed to have a nuclear capacity of around 100 warheads which could be delivered by aircraft or Jericho I and II missiles.

The Army has 3,900 main battle tanks and around 9,900 armoured personnel carriers. The Navy has two submarines and 47 patrol and coastal vessels at three bases. The Air Force has 446 combat aircraft and 133 armed helicopters.
MILITARY EXPENDITURE – 8.9 per cent of GDP (1999)
MILITARY PERSONNEL – 172,500: Army 130,000, Navy 6,500, Air Force 36,000, Paramilitaries 8,050
CONSCRIPTION DURATION – men 36 months, women 21 months (Jews and Druze only)

## ECONOMY

The country is generally fertile although water supply for irrigation restricts production. Agriculture accounts for 4 per cent of GDP.

The 'Jaffa' orange is produced in large quantities for export, along with other summer fruits, seasonal vegetables, flowers and glasshouse crops. Olives are cultivated, mainly for the production of oil. The main winter crops are wheat, barley and various kinds of pulses, while in summer sorghum, millet, maize, sesame and summer pulses are grown. Beef, cattle and poultry farming have been developed. Tobacco and cotton are now grown.

Polished diamonds account for about 27.5 per cent of total exports. Amongst the most important industries are textiles, foodstuffs and chemicals (mainly fertilisers and pharmaceuticals). Metal-working and science-based industries are sophisticated and technologically advanced and include the aircraft and military industries. Other important manufacturing industries include plastics, rubber, cement, glass, paper and oil refining. Industry accounts for 38 per cent and services for 58 per cent of GDP.
GNP – US$99,574 million (1999); US$16,180 per capita (1998)
GDP – US$92,587 million (1997); US$17,041 per capita (1998)
ANNUAL AVERAGE GROWTH OF GDP – 5.0 per cent (1996)
INFLATION RATE – 5.2 per cent (1999)
UNEMPLOYMENT – 8.4 per cent (1998)

### TRADE

The principal imports are machinery and transport equipment, semi-manufactures, uncut diamonds, chemicals and chemical products, crude oil, and foodstuffs. The principal exports are semi-manufactures, machinery, polished diamonds, chemicals and chemical products, foodstuffs and uncut diamonds.

In 1999 Israel had a trade deficit of US$4,541 million and a current account deficit of US$2,601 million. Imports totalled US$33,160 million and exports totalled US$25,794 million.

| *Trade with UK* | 1999 | 2000 |
|---|---|---|
| Imports from UK | £1,297,788,000 | £1,518,754,000 |
| Exports to UK | 1,040,915,000 | 1,061,695,000 |

## COMMUNICATIONS

Israel State Railways serves Haifa, Tel Aviv, Jerusalem, Lod, Nahariya, Beersheba, Dimona, Ashdod and intermediate stations with a network of 609 km. There were 15,464 km of paved road in 1997. A major road building programme has been underway in the West Bank since 1992.

The chief ports are Haifa and Ashdod on the Mediterranean, and Eilat on the Red Sea; Acre has an anchorage for small vessels. The chief international airport is Ben Gurion between Tel Aviv and Jerusalem.

## EDUCATION

Education from five to 16 years is free and compulsory. The law also provides for working youth aged 16–18, who for some reason have not completed their education, to be exempted from work in order to do so. There are seven universities including two engineering and technological institutes.
ILLITERACY RATE – 3.9 per cent
ENROLMENT (percentage of age group) – tertiary 40.9 per cent (1996)

## CULTURE

Important historic sites in Israel include: *Jerusalem* – the Church of the Holy Sepulchre, the Al Aqsa Mosque and Dome of the Rock standing on the remains of the Temple Mount of Herod the Great of which the Western (wailing) Wall is a fragment, the Church of the Dormition and the Coenaculum on Mount Zion, Ein Karem, Church of the Visitation, Church of St John the Baptist; *Galilee* – the Sea, Church and Mount of the Beatitudes, ruins of Capernaum and other sites connected with the life of Christ; *Mount Tabor* – Church of the Transfiguration; *Nazareth* – Church of the Annunciation, and other Christian shrines associated with the childhood of Christ; there are also numerous sites dating from biblical and medieval days, such as Ascalon, Caesarea, Atlit, Massada, Megiddo and Hazor.

## PALESTINIAN AUTONOMOUS AREAS

AREA – The total area is 2,406 sq. miles (6,231 sq. km). The area which is fully autonomous is 159 sq. miles (412 sq. km), of which the Gaza Strip is 136 sq. miles (352 sq. km) and the Jericho enclave 23 sq. miles (60 sq. km). The partially autonomous area is the remainder of the West Bank, some 2,247 sq. miles (5,819 sq. km). The UN and the international community also recognise East Jerusalem as part of the Occupied Territories
POPULATION – 2,920,454 (1998 census), of whom 210,209 live in East Jerusalem. In addition there are 141,000 Jewish settlers in the West Bank and 4,000 in the Gaza Strip who remain under Israeli administration and jurisdiction. Some 90 per cent of Palestinians are Muslim (the vast majority Sunni) and 10 per cent are Christians
CAPITAL – Although Palestinians claim East Jerusalem as their capital, the administrative capital has been established in Gaza City (population 120,000)
MAJOR TOWNS – Khan Yunis, Rafah in the Gaza Strip; Nablus, Hebron, Jericho, Ramallah and Bethlehem on the West Bank
FLAG – Three horizontal stripes of black, white, green with a red triangle based on the hoist (the PLO flag)
NATIONAL ANTHEM – Fidai, Fidai (Freedom Fighter, Freedom Fighter)

## HISTORY AND POLITICS

Israel captured the Gaza Strip, East Jerusalem and the West Bank during the 1967 Six-Day War and annexed

East Jerusalem. After the war the Israeli government began to establish settlements in the Occupied Territories. Palestinian resistance to Israeli rule was led by the Palestine Liberation Organisation (PLO) which was established in 1964. Frustration at continued Israeli occupation led to the start of the *intifada*, a campaign of sustained unrest, in 1987. When the 1991 Madrid peace process stalled, Israeli and PLO officials engaged in secret negotiations in Norway which led to the signing of the 'Declaration of Principles on Interim Self-Government Arrangements' on 13 September 1993. Under this agreement the PLO renounced terrorism and recognised Israel's right to exist in secure borders, while Israel recognised the PLO as the legitimate representative of the Palestinian people.

The Declaration of Principles established a timetable for progress towards a final settlement: negotiations leading to an Israeli military withdrawal from the Gaza Strip and Jericho by 13 April 1994, when power was to be transferred to a nominated Palestinian National Authority (PNA); elections to a new Palestinian Council, which would also exercise control over six policy areas in the rest of the West Bank (culture, tourism, health, education, social welfare, direct taxation), and the Israeli military administration dissolved by 13 July 1994; negotiations on a permanent settlement, including Jewish settlers and East Jerusalem, to begin by 13 April 1996; and a permanent settlement to be in place by 13 April 1999.

The 'Oslo B' or Taba Accord was signed on 28 September 1995 and provided for Israeli withdrawal from six towns and 85 per cent of Hebron; the extension of self-rule to most of the West Bank by 1998; the release of 5,300 Palestinian prisoners; and the striking out of the demand for Israel's destruction from the PLO's charter. On 29 December 1995 an agreement was reached on the transfer of 17 areas of civilian power to the PNA in Hebron.

Israeli troops left Ramallah, the last of the six West Bank towns, on 27 December 1995 and the inaugural Palestinian National Council meeting on 23 April 1996 voted to amend the PLO charter. The final element of the Declaration of Principles, the 'final status talks' opened in Taba, Egypt, on 5 May 1996 to decide the final status of the West Bank, Gaza and Jerusalem. The election of a Likud-led government opposed to the establishment of a Palestinian state resulted in a deadlock in negotiations in 1997 and delays in the withdrawal of Israeli troops from Hebron.

Legislative elections on 20 January 1996 were won by the mainstream al-Fatah faction of the PLO, with its leader Yasser Arafat winning 88.1 per cent of the vote to become the president of the Palestinian National Authority.

Yasser Arafat had planned to declare an independent Palestinian state on 4 May 1999, the end of the five-year transitional period which had been agreed in the 1993 Oslo peace accords, but the announcement was postponed in the hope that talks with the new Israeli government would lead to a negotiated settlement.

On 15 May 2000, widespread violence erupted during protests marking *al-Nakba* (the Catastrophe), the anniversary of the founding of the state of Israel in 1948, including exchanges of fire between Palestinian police and Israeli troops. In July, President Clinton hosted talks between Yasser Arafat and Ehud Barak, which aimed to a resolve issues which had thwarted a comprehensive peace settlement, but no agreement was reached.

Following a controversial visit in late September 2000 by Likud leader Ariel Sharon to the Temple Mount, a holy site for both Jews and Muslims, a new intifada broke out. Relations between the Israeli government and the PNA deteriorated further after two Israeli soldiers were lynched by Palestinians; on 12 October Israeli forces launched rocket attacks on the residence and offices of Arafat and declared the peace process to be at an end. A summit was held in Sharm el-Shaikh on 17 October and an agreement was reached to end violence and restart negotiations. However, serious clashes resumed in late October. An agreement was reached on 1 November to call a new ceasefire the following day, but it had broken down by the middle of the month. A new round of talks began on 14 December and a US draft accord was discussed, which envisaged a Palestinian state on 95 per cent of the West Bank and the entire Gaza Strip. Agreement could not be reached and the talks broke down on 27 January 2001. Following the election of Ariel Sharon as Israeli prime minister on 6 February, hopes of a peace agreement faded.

## Political System

The Oslo B accord laid down the political structure of the nascent Palestinian state. Executive authority is vested in the Palestinian National Authority which is headed by a popularly elected leader (*rais*). Legislative authority is vested in the 88-member Palestinian Council which is directly elected by means of a first-past-the-post system, and itself elects the four-fifths of the PNA not appointed by the leader.

## Palestinian National Authority *as at July 2001*

*Leader*, Yasser Arafat
*Agriculture*, Hikmet Zeid
*Cabinet Secretary*, Ahmad Abdel Rahman
*Civil Affairs*, Jamil al-Tarifi
*Culture and Arts, Information*, Yassir Abd ar-Rabbuh
*Detainees' and Freed Detainees' Affairs*, Hisham Abdul Razeq
*Economy and Trade*, Mahir al-Masri
*Education*, vacant
*Environment*, Yusuf Abu-Safiyah
*Finance*, Muhammad Zuhdi al-Nashashibi
*Health*, Riyad al-Za'nun
*Higher Education*, Dr Munther Salah
*Housing*, Dr Abd al-Rahman Hamad
*Industry*, Dr Saad al-Karnaz
*Interior*, vacant
*Justice*, Furayh Abu Middayn
*Labour*, Rafiq al-Natshe
*Local Government*, Dr Sa'ib Urayqat
*Non-governmental Organisations*, Hassan Asfour
*Parliamentary Affairs*, Nabil Amr
*Planning, International Co-operation*, Dr Nabil Sha'ath
*Post and Telecommunications*, Imad al-Faluji
*Public Works*, Azzam al-Ahmad
*Religious Affairs and Waqf*, vacant
*Secretary-General of the Presidency*, Tayeb Abdel Rahim
*Social Affairs*, Intisar al-Wazir
*Supply*, Abd al-Aziz Shahin
*Tourism and Archaeology*, Mitri Abu Ayta
*Transport*, Dr Ali al-Qawasmi
*Without Portfolio*, Faisal Husseini (*Jerusalem*); Ziad Abu Ziad (*Settlements*); Nabil Qsies; Jirar Qudwa; Salah al-Tamari
*Youth and Sport*, vacant

## Palestinian General Delegation

5 Galena Road, London W6 0LT
Tel: 020-8563 0008
*General Delegate*, Afif Safieh
*Deputy Head of Mission*, Naim Samara

## British Consulate-General

19 Nashashibi Street, PO Box 19690, East Jerusalem 97200
*Consul-General*, R. A. Kealy, CMG

BRITISH COUNCIL DIRECTOR, David Martin (*Cultural Attaché*), Al-Nuzha Building, 4 Abu Obeida Street, PO Box 19136, Jerusalem; e-mail: britishcouncil@ej.britishcouncil.org. Regional Offices In Gaza, Hebron, Nablus and Ramallah

| *Trade with UK* | 1999 | 2000 |
|---|---|---|
| Imports from UK | £302,000 | £140,000 |
| Exports to UK | 40,000 | — |

## ITALY
*Repubblica Italiana*

AREA – 116,339 sq. miles (301,318 sq. km). Neighbours: Switzerland and Austria (north), Slovenia (east), France (west)
POPULATION – 57,649,000 (1997 UN estimate): 83 per cent Catholic. The language is Italian, a Romance language derived from Latin. There are several regional languages including Sardinian and Catalan in Sardinia, Friulian in Friuli, German and Ladin in the South Tyrol, French in the Valle d'Aosta, and Slovene in parts of Gorizia
CAPITAL – Rome (population, 2,648,843, 1995 estimate). The Eternal City was founded, according to legend, by Romulus in 753 BC. It was the centre of Latin civilisation and capital of the Roman Republic and Roman Empire
MAJOR CITIES – Bologna (385,813); Florence (381,762); ΨGenoa (655,704); Milan (1,305,591); ΨNaples (1,046,987); Turin (921,485); *Sicily*, ΨPalermo (689,349); *Sardinia*, ΨCagliari (173,564), 1995 estimates
CURRENCY – Euro (€) of 100 cents/Lira of 100 centesimi
NATIONAL ANTHEM – Inno di Mameli
NATIONAL DAY – 2 June
NATIONAL FLAG – Vertical stripes of green, white and red
LIFE EXPECTANCY (years) – male 75.4; female 82.1
POPULATION GROWTH RATE – 0.1 per cent (1999)
POPULATION DENSITY – 190 per sq. km (1998)
URBAN POPULATION – 67.0 per cent (2000 estimate)

Italy consists of a peninsula, the islands of Sicily, Sardinia, Elba and about 70 other small islands. The peninsula is for the most part mountainous, but between the Apennines, which form its spine, and the eastern coastline are two large fertile plains: Emilia-Romagna in the north and Apulia in the south. The Alps divide Italy from France, Switzerland, Austria and Slovenia. Partly within the Italian borders are Monte Rosa (15,217 ft), the Matterhorn (14,780 ft) and several peaks from 12,000 to 14,000 ft. The chief rivers are the Po (405 miles), flowing through Piedmont, Lombardy and the Veneto; the Adige (Trentino and Veneto); the Arno (Florentine plain); and the Tiber (flowing through Rome to Ostia).

### HISTORY AND POLITICS

Italian unity was accomplished under the House of Savoy after a struggle from 1848 to 1870 in which Mazzini (1805–72), Garibaldi (1807–82) and Cavour (1810–61) were the principal figures. It was completed when Lombardy was ceded by Austria in 1859 and Venice in 1866, and through the evacuation of Rome by the French in 1870. In 1871 the King of Italy entered Rome, and that city was declared to be the capital.

A fascist regime came to power in 1922 under Benito Mussolini, known as *Il Duce* (The Leader), who was prime minister from 1922 until 25 July 1943, when the regime was abolished. Mussolini was captured by Italian partisans while attempting to escape across the Swiss frontier and killed on 28 April 1945.

Italy became a republic following a referendum on the future of the monarchy in June 1946.

Political instability and corruption led to public disenchantment with the major political parties, whose support collapsed in the 1992 general election. The so-called 'clean hands' investigation into corruption and Mafia links that began in 1992 has led to the arrest by magistrates of thousands of politicians and businessmen.

The general election on 21 April 1996 was won by the left-wing Olive Tree alliance led by the Democratic Party of the Left, whose leader, Romano Prodi, became prime minister. The government collapsed on 9 October 1998 after the Communist Refoundation party, on whose support it had been dependent, refused to vote for the 1999 budget. Massimo D'Alema was invited by the president to form a new government on 20 October. On 19 December 1999, the government collapsed, but Massimo d'Alema was asked to form a new government the following day; he resigned as prime minister on 17 April 2000 following the defeat of his centre-left coalition in regional elections on 16 April. President Ciampi invited Giuliano Amato to form a new government and Amato was sworn in as prime minister on 26 April 2000.

The general election held on 13 May 2001 was won by the centre-right House of Freedoms alliance, which obtained 368 seats. The alliance was led by Forza Italia and also comprised the Christian Democratic Centre, the Christian Democratic Union, the National Alliance, the New Italian Socialist Party and the Northern League. Silvio Berlusconi, the Forza Italia leader, was sworn in as prime minister.

#### POLITICAL SYSTEM

The constitution provides for the election of the president for a seven-year term by an electoral college which consists of the two houses of the parliament (the Chamber of Deputies and the Senate) sitting in joint session, together with three delegates from each region (one in the case of the Valle d'Aosta). The president, who must be over 50 years of age, has the right to dissolve one or both houses after consultation with the Speakers. Members of both houses were elected wholly by proportional representation until 1993. Now 75 per cent (232) of the 315 elected seats in the Senate are elected on a first-past-the-post basis and the remaining elected seats are filled by proportional representation. There is a variable number of life senators, who are past presidents and senators appointed by incumbent presidents. In the Chamber of Deputies 75 per cent (472) of seats are elected on a first-past-the-post basis, and 25 per cent (158) by proportional representation, with a 4 per cent threshold for parliamentary representation. A referendum on 18 April 1999 on abolishing the seats elected by proportional representation foundered when less than the required 50 per cent of the electorate participated.

#### HEAD OF STATE

*President*, Carlo Azeglio Ciampi, *elected by electoral college* 13 May 1999

#### COUNCIL OF MINISTERS *as at July 2001*

*Prime Minister*, Silvio Berlusconi (FI)
*Deputy Prime Minister*, Gianfranco Fini (AN)
*Agriculture and Forestry*, Giovanni Alemanno (AN)
*Culture*, Giuliano Urbani (FI)
*Defence*, Antonio Martino (FI)
*Economy and Finance*, Giulio Tremonti (FI)
*Education, Higher Education and Scientific Research*, Letizia Moratti (Ind.)
*Employment and Social Welfare*, Roberto Maroni (LN)
*Environment*, Altero Matteoli (AN)
*Foreign Affairs*, Renato Ruggiero (Ind.)
*Health*, Gerolamo Sirchia (Ind.)
*Industry*, Antonio Marzano (FI)

*Infrastructure and Transport*, Pietro Lunardi (Ind.)
*Interior*, Claudio Scajola (FI)
*Justice*, Roberto Castelli (LN)
*Telecommunications*, Maurizio Gasparri (AN)
AN National Alliance; FI Forza Italia; LN Northern League; Ind. Independent

ITALIAN EMBASSY
14 Three Kings Yard, Davies Street, London W1K 4EH
Tel: 020-7312 2200
*Ambassador Extraordinary and Plenipotentiary*, HE Luigi Amaduzzi, apptd 1999
*Ministers (Consular Affairs)*, Dr A. d'Andria; L. Savoia
*Defence and Naval Attaché*, Rear-Admr. A. Campregher
*Cultural Attaché*, M. Fortunato
CONSULAR OFFICES – Bedford, Edinburgh, Manchester

BRITISH EMBASSY
Via XX Settembre 80A, I-00187 Rome
Tel: (00 39) (6) 4220 0001
*Ambassador Extraordinary and Plenipotentiary*, HE Sir John Shepherd, KCVO, CMG, apptd 2000
*Deputy Head of Mission*, A. Leslie
*Defence and Military Attaché*, Brig. A. Mallinson
*Director-General for British Trade Development in Italy and Consul-General*, C. De Chassiron (*Milan*)
*Counsellor (Economic and Commercial)*, M. Hatfull

CONSULATE-GENERAL – Milan
CONSULATES – Rome, Bari, Cagliari, Catania, Florence, Genoa, Messina, Naples, Palermo, Trieste, Turin, Venice

BRITISH COUNCIL DIRECTOR, Richard Alford, OBE, Via Quattro Fontane 20, I-00184 Rome; e-mail: richard.alford@britishcouncil.it
There are British Council Offices at Milan, Bologna, Naples and Turin

BRITISH CHAMBER OF COMMERCE, Via Camperio 9, , I-20123 Milan

## DEFENCE

The Army has 1,301 main battle tanks and 2,647 armoured personnel carriers. The Navy has seven submarines, one aircraft carrier, one cruiser, four destroyers, 24 frigates, nine patrol and coastal vessels, 18 combat aircraft and 80 armed helicopters. There are four naval bases. The Air Force has 336 combat aircraft.
MILITARY EXPENDITURE – 2.0 per cent of GDP (1999)
MILITARY PERSONNEL – 250,600: Army 163,000, Navy 38,000, Air Force 59,600, Paramilitaries 252,500
CONSCRIPTION DURATION – Ten months

## ECONOMY

Deposits of natural methane gas and oil have been discovered, mainly south of Sicily, and have been rapidly exploited. Production of lignite has also increased. Other minerals include iron ores and pyrites, mercury (over one-quarter of the world production), lead, zinc and aluminium. Rich gold veins were discovered in Sardinia in 1996. Marble is a traditional product of the Massa Carrara district.

Agricultural production is concentrated in Tuscany, Emilia-Romagna, Sicily and the whole of the southern third of the country. The principal products are wine, tobacco, citrus fruits, tomatoes, almonds, sugar beet, wheat and maize.

Tourism is a major contributor to the economy; in 1997, around 57 million people visited Italy. The commercial and banking services are concentrated in Rome and in Milan, where the stock market is located.

The state-owned sector of Italian industry is still important, dominated by the holding companies IRI (mechanical, steel, airlines), ENI (petrochemicals), and ENEL (electricity), although in November 1999, the government sold 34.5 per cent of ENEL, and announced in December 2000 that a further tranche of government holdings in ENEL, ENI and Telecom Italia would be sold during 2001. In July 2001, ENEL announced that it was to sell its generation business for €2.6 billion. Industry is centred around Milan (steel, machine tools, motor cars), Turin (motor cars, steel, roller bearings, textiles), Rome (light industries), Venice (shipbuilding, paper, mechanical equipment, electrical goods, woollens), Bologna/Florence (food industry, footwear and textiles, reproduction furniture, glassware, pottery, ceramics), Naples, Bari (valves, vehicle bodies, tyres), Taranto (steel, oil refining), Trieste (shipbuilding) and Cagliari (aluminium production, petrochemicals). Following a programme of severe austerity measures, Italy satisfied the convergence criteria and participated in the European Single Currency from 1 January 1999.

In 1999 there was a trade surplus of US$20,385 million and a current account surplus of US$8,239 million. Imports totalled US$216,621 million and exports US$230,193 million.

Italy's chief exports are industrial and agricultural machinery, textiles and clothing, electrical equipment and chemicals. Chief imports are chemicals, motor vehicles and metals. Italy's main trading partners are Germany, France, the UK and the USA.
GNP – US$1,162,910 million (1999); US$19,710 per capita (1999)
GDP – US$1,145,370 million (1997); US$20,479 per capita (1999)
ANNUAL AVERAGE GROWTH OF GDP – 2.7 per cent (2000)
INFLATION RATE – 2.8 per cent (2001)
UNEMPLOYMENT – 9.9 per cent (2001)

| *Trade with UK* | 1999 | 2000 |
|---|---|---|
| Imports from UK | £7,374,410,000 | £7,973,500,000 |
| Exports to UK | 8,875,600,000 | 9,047,000,000 |

## COMMUNICATIONS

The main railway system is state-run by the *Ferrovia dello Stato*. There are 19,527 km of railway track. A network of motorways (*autostrade*) covers the country, built and operated mainly by the IRI state holding company and

ANAS, the state highway authority. There are 306,445 km of roads. Alitalia, the principal international and domestic airline, is also state-controlled by the IRI group. Other smaller companies, including ATI (an Alitalia subsidiary) and Air Mediterranea, operate on domestic routes. Genoa is the major port, handling about one-third of Italy's foreign trade.

In January 2001, the Italian and French Presidents agreed plans to build a 52-km rail tunnel through the Alps as part of a high-speed rail link between Turin and Lyons.

## EDUCATION

Education is free and compulsory between the ages of six and 14; this comprises five years at primary school and three in 'middle school', of which there are 9,215. Pupils who obtain the middle school certificate may seek admission to any 'senior secondary school', which may be a lyceum with a classical or scientific or artistic bias, or an institute directed at technology (of which there are eight different types), trade or industry (including vocational schools), or teacher-training. Courses at the lyceums and technical institutes usually last for five years and success in the final examination qualifies for admission to university.

There are 62 universities, some of ancient foundation; those at Bologna, Modena, Parma and Padua were started in the 12th century. University education is not free, but entrants with higher qualifications are charged reduced fees according to a sliding scale.

In general, schools, lyceums and universities are financed by local taxation and central government grants.

ILLITERACY RATE – 1.5 per cent (2000)
ENROLMENT (percentage of age group) – primary 100 per cent (1996); tertiary 46.9 per cent (1996)

## CULTURE

Florence, the capital of Tuscany, was one of the greatest cities in Europe from the 11th to the 16th centuries, and the cradle of the Renaissance. Under the Medici family in the 15th century flourished many of the greatest names in Italian art, including Filippo Lippi, Botticelli, Donatello and Brunelleschi, and in the 16th century Michelangelo and Leonardo da Vinci.

Italian literature (in addition to Latin literature, which is the common inheritance of western Europe) is one of the richest in Europe, particularly in its golden age (Dante, 1265–1321; Petrarch, 1304–74; Boccaccio, 1313–75) and in the Renaissance (Ariosto, 1474–1533; Machiavelli, 1469–1527; Tasso, 1544–95). Notable in modern Italian literature are Manzoni (1785–1873), Carducci (1835–1907) and Gabriele d'Annunzio (1864–1938). The Nobel Prize for Literature has been awarded to Italian authors on six occasions: G. Cariducci (1906), Signora G. Deledda (1926), Luigi Pirandello (1934), Salvatore Quasimodo (1959), Eugenio Montale (1975) and Dario Fo (1997).

## ISLANDS

CAPRI, in the Bay of Naples; area 4 sq. miles (10 sq. km); population 12,000
EOLIAN ISLANDS, including Lipari; area 45 sq. miles (116 sq. km); population 18,636
FLEGREAN ISLANDS, including Ischia; area 23 sq. miles (60 sq. km); population 51,883
PANTELLERIA ISLAND (part of Trapani Province) in the Sicilian Narrows; area 31 sq. miles (80 sq. km); population 9,601
THE PELAGIAN ISLANDS (Lampedusa, Linosa and Lampione) are part of the province of Agrigento; area 8 sq. miles (21 sq. km); population 4,811
PONTINE ARCHIPELAGO, including Ponza; area 4 sq. miles (10 sq. km); population 2,515
TREMITI ISLANDS; area 1 sq. mile (3 sq. km); population 426
THE TUSCAN ARCHIPELAGO (including Elba); area 113 sq. miles (293 sq. km); population 31,861

---

# JAMAICA

---

AREA – 4,243 sq. miles (10,990 sq. km)
POPULATION – 2,598,000 (1999estimate). The official language is English; a local patois is also spoken
CAPITAL – ΨKingston (population, 524,638, 1991)
MAJOR CITIES – Mandeville; May Pen; ΨMontego Bay; Ocho Rios; Spanish Town
CURRENCY – Jamaican dollar (J$) of 100 cents
NATIONAL ANTHEM – Jamaica, Land We Love
NATIONAL DAY – 6 August (Independence Day)
NATIONAL FLAG – Gold diagonal cross forming triangles of green at top and bottom, triangles of black at hoist and in fly
LIFE EXPECTANCY (years) – male 75.2; female 77.4
POPULATION GROWTH RATE – 0.9 per cent (1999)
POPULATION DENSITY – 231 per sq. km (1998)
URBAN POPULATION – 56.1 per cent (2000 estimate)
MILITARY EXPENDITURE – 0.8 per cent of GDP (1999)
MILITARY PERSONNEL – 2,830: Army 2,500, Coast Guard 190, Air Wing 140
ILLITERACY RATE – 13.3 per cent (2000)
ENROLMENT (percentage of age group) – primary 100 per cent (1999); secondary 69 per cent (1999); tertiary 13 per cent (1999)

Jamaica is divided into three counties (Surrey, Middlesex and Cornwall) and 14 parishes. The island consists mainly of coastal plains, divided by the Blue Mountain range in the east and the hills and limestone plateaux in the central and western areas of the interior. The central chain of the Blue Mountains is over 6,000 feet above sea level, and the Blue Mountain Peak is 7,402 feet.

## HISTORY AND POLITICS

The island was discovered by Columbus in 1494, and occupied by Spain from 1509 until 1655 when an English expedition under Admiral Penn and General Venables captured the island. In 1670 it was formally ceded to England by the Treaty of Madrid. Jamaica became an independent state within the Commonwealth on 6 August 1962.

At the general election of 18 December 1997, the People's National Party won 50 out of a total of 60 seats, securing a third term for the party and a second term for Prime Minister Percival Patterson.

### POLITICAL SYSTEM

Queen Elizabeth II is the head of state, represented by the Governor-General. The legislature consists of a Senate of 21 nominated members and a House of Representatives consisting of 60 members elected by universal adult suffrage for a five-year term. The prime minister is the leader of the majority party in the House.

*Governor-General*, HE Sir Howard Felix Hanlon Cooke, GCMG, GCVO, apptd 1991

### CABINET *as at July 2001*

*Prime Minister, Defence*, Percival J. Patterson, QC
*Deputy PM, Land and the Environment*, Seymour Mullings
*Agriculture*, Roger Clarke
*Attorney-General*, Arnold Nicholson
*Education, Youth and Culture*, Burchell Whiteman
*Finance and Planning*, Omar Davies

*Foreign Affairs*, Paul Robertson
*Foreign Trade*, Anthony Hylton
*Health*, John Junor
*Industry, Commerce and Technology*, Phillip Paulwell
*Information*, Maxine Henry-Wilson
*Labour and Social Security*, Donald Buchanan
*Local Government, Youth and Community Development*, Arnold Bertram
*Mining and Energy*, Robert Pickersgill
*National Security and Justice*, Keith Desmond Knight
*Tourism and Sports, Gender Affairs*, Portia Simpson Miller
*Transportation and Works*, Peter Phillips
*Water and Housing*, Enoch Carl Blythe

Jamaican High Commission
1–2 Prince Consort Road, London SW7 2BZ
Tel: 020-7823 9911
*High Commissioner*, HE David Muirhead, apptd 1999
*Deputy High Commissioners*, A. Rodriques; J. K. Pringle, CBE, OJ (*Trade*)
*Counsellor and Legal Affairs*, T. Blackwood
*Defence Adviser*, Col. L. Graham

British High Commission
PO Box 575, Trafalgar Road, Kingston 10
Tel: (00 1 876) 926 9050
E-mail: bhckingston@cw.com
*High Commissioner*, HE A. F. Smith, apptd 1999
*Deputy High Commissioner*, J. Malcolm, OBE
*Defence Adviser*, Col. R. Hyde-Bales
*First Secretaries*, M. Bragg (*Chancery*); R. Patten (*Management*)

British Council Manager, Nicola Johnson, British High Commission, 28 Trafalgar Road, Kingston 10; e-mail: bcjamaica@bc-caribbean.org

## ECONOMY

Alumina, bananas, bauxite and sugar are the main exports. Other exports include garments, processed food products, limestone and horticultural products. A task force was established in January 2001 to foster an increase in sugar production. The country's first gold mine became operational in March 2001.

Since 1989 the PNP government has abolished price subsidies, removed foreign exchange controls and introduced a 10 per cent consumption tax. Jamaica is a popular tourist resort, attracting 2,012,738 visitors in 1999.

In February 2000 parliament approved the liberalisation of telecommunications, to be phased in over a three-year period.

The economy has faced many problems, including interest repayments on debt which accounted for 41 per cent of government revenue in 1999, low market prices for many of Jamaica's exports and interest rates of over 30 per cent.

In 1999 Jamaica had a trade deficit of US$1,140 million and a current account deficit of US$273 million. Imports totalled US$2,576 million and exports US$1,127 million.

GNP – US$6,311 million (1999); US$2,330 per capita (1999)
GDP – US$4,280 million (1999); US$2,707 per capita (1998)
Annual Average Growth of GDP – 0.4 per cent (1999)
Inflation Rate – 6.0 per cent (1999)
Unemployment – 15.7 per cent (1999)
Total External Debt – US$3,024 million (1999)

| *Trade with UK* | 1999 | 2000 |
|---|---|---|
| Imports from UK | £92,279,000 | £60,306,000 |
| Exports to UK | 112,995,000 | 124,884,000 |

## COMMUNICATIONS

There are several excellent harbours, Kingston being the principal port. The island has 2,944 miles of main roads and 7,264 miles of subsidiary roads.

There are two international airports, the Norman Manley International Airport on the south coast serving Kingston, and Sangster Airport on the north coast serving the major tourist areas. In addition there are licensed aerodromes at Port Antonio, Ocho Rios, Mandeville and Negril. There are 16 privately owned, seven public and two military airstrips. Air Jamaica, the national airline, operates international services.

---

# JAPAN

*Nihon Koku – Land of the Rising Sun*

---

AREA – 145,880 sq. miles (377,829 sq. km)
POPULATION – 126,570,000 (1997 UN estimate). The principal religions are Mahayana Buddhism and Shinto. About 1 per cent of Japanese are Christians. The language is Japanese
CAPITAL – Tokyo (population, 7,980,230, 1993 estimate)
MAJOR CITIES – ΨFukuoka (1,308,379); ΨKōbe (1,425,139); Kyōto, the ancient capital (1,461,974); ΨNagoya (2,154,376); ΨŌsaka (2,595,674); Sapporo (1,790,886); ΨYokohama (3,339,594), 1997 estimates
CURRENCY – Yen
NATIONAL ANTHEM - Kimigayo (His Majesty's reign)
NATIONAL FLAG – White, charged with sun (red)
LIFE EXPECTANCY (years) – male 77.6; female 84.3
POPULATION GROWTH RATE – 0.3 per cent (1999)
POPULATION DENSITY – 335 per sq. km (1998)
URBAN POPULATION – 78.8 per cent (2000 estimate)

Japan consists of four large islands: *Honshū* (or Mainland) 88,839 sq. miles (230,448 sq. km), *Shikoku*, 7,231 sq. miles (18,757 sq. km), *Kyūshū*, 16,170 sq. miles (42,079 sq. km), *Hokkaidō*, 30,265 sq. miles (78,508 sq. km), and many small islands (including Okinawa).

The interior is very mountainous, and crossing the mainland from the Sea of Japan to the Pacific is a group of volcanoes, mainly extinct or dormant. Mount Fuji, the most sacred mountain of Japan, is 12,370 ft high and has been dormant since 1707, but volcanoes which are active include Mount Aso in Kyūshū. There are frequent earthquakes, mainly along the Pacific coast near the Bay of Tōkyō. The climate varies from sub-tropical in the south to cool temperate in the north.

## HISTORY AND POLITICS

According to tradition, Jimmu, the first Emperor of Japan, ascended the throne on 11 February 660 BC. Under the *Meiji* constitution (1889), the monarchy is hereditary in the male heirs of the Imperial house.

After the unconditional surrender to the Allied nations (14 August 1945), Japan was occupied by Allied forces under General MacArthur. A Japanese peace treaty became effective on 28 April 1952. Japan then resumed her status as an independent power.

The (conservative) Liberal Democratic Party (LDP) governed Japan almost without interruption from the Second World War until 1993.

Following the general election held on 25 June 2000, the Liberal Democratic Party remained the largest party but failed to retain its overall majority, winning 233 seats. The LDP formed a coalition with its previous partners, New Komeito and the New Conservative Party, which accounted for 271 of the 480 seats in the Diet. Prime Minister Yoshiro Mori resigned on 7 April 2001 following mounting criticism of his performance and was replaced by Junichiro Koizumi on 26 April.

### POLITICAL SYSTEM

Legislative authority rests with the bicameral *Diet*, which comprises a 480-member House of Representatives, and a 252-member House of Councillors. The House of Representatives chooses the prime minister from among its ranks, ratifies treaties and passes budget bills. Since January 2000, 180 of its members are elected by proportional representation in 11 regional blocks and 300 in single-member, first-past-the-post constituencies. All members serve four-year terms. The House of Councillors elects half its members every three years for six-year terms. Unlike the lower House it cannot be dissolved by the prime minister. Executive authority is vested in the Cabinet which is responsible to the legislature.

### HEAD OF STATE

*His Imperial Majesty The Emperor of Japan*, Emperor Akihito, *born* 23 December 1933; *succeeded* 8 January 1989; *enthroned* 12 November 1990; *married* 10 April 1959, Miss Michiko Shoda, and has *issue*: the Crown Prince (*see* below); Prince Fumihito, *born* 30 November 1965; and Princess Sayako, *born* 18 April 1969
*Heir*, HRH Crown Prince Naruhito Hironomiya, *born* 23 February 1960, *married* 9 June 1993 Miss Masako Owada

### CABINET *as at July 2001*

*Prime Minister*, Junichiro Koizumi (LDP)
*Agriculture, Forestry and Fisheries*, Tsutomu Takebe (LDP)
*Economy, Trade and Industry*, Takeo Hiranuma (LDP)
*Education, Culture, Sports, Science and Technology*, Atsuko Toyama (Ind.)
*Environment*, Yoriko Kawaguchi (Ind.)
*Finance*, Masajuro Shiokawa (LDP)
*Foreign Affairs*, Makiko Tanaka (LDP)
*Health, Labour and Welfare*, Chikara Sakaguchi (NK)
*Justice*, Mayumi Moriyama (LDP)
*Land, Infrastructure and Transport*, Chikage Ogi (NCP)
*Public Management, Home Affairs, Posts and Telecommunications*, Toranosuke Katayama (LDP)
LDP Liberal Democratic Party; NCP New Conservative Party; NK New Komeito; Ind. Independent

### EMBASSY OF JAPAN

101–104 Piccadilly, London W1V 9FN
Tel: 020-7465 6500
*Ambassador Extraordinary and Plenipotentiary*, HE Sadayuki Hayashi, apptd 1997
*Ministers*, K. Shimanouchi (*Plenipotentiary*); S. Nakamura (*Consul-General*); H. Kuramochi (*Commercial*); T. Shikibu (*Finance*); S. Nishimiya (*Information*); K. Monji (*Political*)

### BRITISH EMBASSY

No. 1 Ichiban-cho, Chiyoda-ku, Tōkyō 102-8381
Tel: (00 81) (3) 5211-1100
E-mail: embassy@tokyo.mail.fco.gov.uk
*Ambassador Extraordinary and Plenipotentiary*, HE Sir Stephen Gomersall, KCMG, apptd 1999
*Counsellors*, P. Bateman (*Commercial*); R. R. Hoggard (*Management and Consul-General*)
*Minister*, S. Jack, CVO
*Defence Attaché*, Capt. J. A. Boyd

CONSULATES-GENERAL – Tōkyō, Ōsaka
HONORARY CONSULATES – Fukuoka, Hiroshima, Nagoya, Sapporo

BRITISH COUNCIL DIRECTOR, Terry Toney, 1-2 Kagurazaka, Shinjuku-ku, Tōkyō 162-0825; e-mail: bctokyo@britishcouncil.or.jp. Regional offices in Fukuoka, Kyōto, Nagoya and Ōsaka

BRITISH CHAMBER OF COMMERCE, 3rd floor, Kenkyusha Eigo Centre Building, 1-2 Kagurazaka, Shinjuku-ku, Tōkyō 162

## DEFENCE

The constitution prohibits the maintenance of armed forces, although internal security forces were created in the 1950s and their mission was extended in 1954 to include the defence of Japan against aggression. In the 1990s legislation was passed permitting the armed forces limited participation in UN peacekeeping missions and allowing them to enter foreign conflicts in order to rescue Japanese nationals. A revision to the USA–Japan defence co-operation guidelines agreed in 1997 permits Japan to play a supporting role in US military operations in areas surrounding Japan.

The Ground Self-Defence Force (GSDF) has 1,070 main battle tanks, around 790 armoured personnel carriers, 60 infantry fighting vehicles, 10 aircraft and 90 attack helicopters. The Maritime Self-Defence Force (MSDF) has 16 submarines, 42 destroyers, 13 frigates, three patrol and coastal vessels, 80 combat aircraft and 80 armed helicopters at five bases. The Air Self-Defence Force (ASDF) has 331 combat aircraft.

The USA has 39,750 personnel stationed in Japan.

MILITARY EXPENDITURE – 0.9 per cent of GDP (1999)

MILITARY PERSONNEL – 236,700: Army 148,500, Navy 42,600, Air Force 44,200, Paramilitaries 12,000

## ECONOMY

Owing to the mountainous nature of the country less than 20 per cent of its area can be cultivated and only 14 per cent is used for agriculture; 67 per cent is wooded. The soil is only moderately fertile but intensive cultivation secures good crops. Tobacco, tea, potatoes, rice, maize, wheat and other cereals are all cultivated. Rice is the staple food of the people. Fruit is abundant and pigs and chickens are widely reared.

Mineral resources include gold, silver, copper, lead, zinc, iron chromite, white arsenic, coal, sulphur, petroleum, salt and uranium. However, iron ore, coal and crude oil are among the principal imports.

Japan is one of the most highly industrialised nations in the world, with the whole range of modern light and heavy industries, including steel, aerospace, computers, office machinery, motor vehicles, electronics, metals, machinery, chemicals, textiles (cotton, silk, wool and synthetics), cement, pottery, glass, rubber, lumber, paper, oil refining and shipbuilding.

Japan's economy was severely affected by the financial crisis in Asia. Its banks had made loans totalling some US$200 billion to tiger economies, and following widespread economic collapse in the region, Japan's financial institutions have suffered. Emergency measures announced by the government were perceived by the markets as inadequate. Japan's economy contracted in 1998; GDP fell by 2.8 per cent. The economy showed signs of recovery in the first half of 1999, but the second half of the year was disappointing. Unemployment reached 4.8 per cent, the highest level since the Second World War. In November 1999, the government announced an economic stimulus package, which was designed to aid economic recovery and restructuring.

On 21 September 2000 the government unveiled a Yen 4,000 billion economic stimulus package. A package of economic reforms was announced on 5 April 2001, which focused on the structural reform of the financial industry.

GNP – US$4,054,545 million (1999); US$32,230 per capita (1999)

GDP – US$4,192,669 million (1997); US$34,313 per capita (1999)

ANNUAL AVERAGE GROWTH OF GDP – 2.8 per cent (2000)

INFLATION RATE – & –:0.1 per cent (2001)

UNEMPLOYMENT – 4.7 per cent (2001)

### TRADE

Being deficient in natural resources, Japan has had to develop a complex foreign trade. Principal imports include mineral fuels, food, raw materials and metal ores. Principal exports include machinery, transport equipment, chemicals, metal products and textiles.

In 1999 Japan had a trade surplus of US$123,325 million and a current account surplus of US$106,865 million. Imports totalled US$311,262 million and exports US$419,367 million. The USA, China, Australia, Hong Kong, South Korea, Taiwan and Singapore are Japan's main trading partners.

| *Trade with UK* | 1999 | 2000 |
|---|---|---|
| Imports from UK | £3,304,346,000 | £3,666,672,000 |
| Exports to UK | 9,542,821,000 | 10,511,063,000 |

## COMMUNICATIONS

There are 27,258 km of railway track and 1,142,308 km of roads. Japan National Railways was privatised in 1987 and is known as Japan Railways (JR). There are six regional companies and one goods company. Shinkansen (bullet train) tracks are currently being expanded. The opening in 1988 of the Seikan rail tunnel and the Seto Ohashi rail bridge means that the four major islands are now linked for the first time. There are six international airports.

## EDUCATION

Education at elementary (six-year course) and lower secondary (three-year course) schools is free, compulsory and co-educational. The (three-year) upper secondary schools are attended by 96.7 per cent of the age group.

There are two- or three-year colleges and four-year universities. Some of the universities have graduate schools. In 1999 there were 622 universities and colleges, most of which are privately maintained. The most prominent universities are the seven state universities of Tōkyō, Kyōto, Tohoku (Sendai), Hokkaidō (Sapporo), Kyūshū (Fukuoka), Ōsaka and Nagoya, and the two private universities of Keio and Waseda.

ENROLMENT (percentage of age group) – primary 100 per cent (1996); secondary 99 per cent (1994); tertiary 40.5 per cent (1996)

## CULTURE

Japanese is said to be one of the Ural-Altaic group of languages and remained a spoken tongue until the fifth to seventh centuries AD, when Chinese characters came into use. Modern Japanese is written in a mixture of Chinese characters (about 1,800) and also the syllabary characters called Kana.

---

# JORDAN

*Al-Mamlaka al-Urdunniyya al-Hashimiyya*

---

AREA – 37,738 sq. miles (97,740 sq. km). Neighbours: Syria (north), Israel and the West Bank (west), Saudi Arabia (south and east), Iraq (east)

POPULATION – 4,693,000 (1997 UN estimate); 4,095,579 (1994 census). The majority are Sunni Muslims and Islam is the religion of the state; however, freedom of belief is guaranteed by the constitution

CAPITAL – 'Amman (population, 1,751,680, 1997 estimate)

MAJOR CITIES – Irbid (231,511); Az-Zarqā' (389,815), 1997 estimates

CURRENCY – Jordanian dinar (JD) of 1,000 fils
NATIONAL ANTHEM - Asha al Malik (Long Live the King)
NATIONAL DAY – 25 May (Independence Day)
NATIONAL FLAG – Three horizontal stripes of black, white, green and a red triangle based on the hoist, containing a seven-pointed white star
LIFE EXPECTANCY (years) – male 66.3; female 67.5
POPULATION GROWTH RATE – 3.8 per cent (1999)
POPULATION DENSITY – 64 per sq. km (1998)
URBAN POPULATION – 74.2 per cent (2000 estimate)
ILLITERACY RATE – 10.2 per cent (2000)
ENROLMENT (percentage of age group) – primary 89 per cent (1992); secondary 42 per cent (1989); tertiary 21.7 per cent (1990)

## HISTORY AND POLITICS

After the defeat of Turkey in the First World War, the Amirate of Transjordan was established in the area east of the River Jordan as a state under British mandate. The mandate was terminated after the Second World War and the Amirate, still ruled by its founder the Amir Abdullah, became the Hashemite Kingdom of Jordan. Following the 1948–9 war between Israel and the Arab states, that part of Palestine remaining in Arab hands (the West Bank and East Jerusalem, but excluding Gaza) was, with Palestinian agreement, incorporated into the Hashemite Kingdom. King Abdullah was assassinated in 1951; his son Talal ruled briefly but abdicated in favour of King Hussein in 1952.

Israel captured the West Bank from Jordan in the 1967 war and annexed East Jerusalem. In 1988 Jordan severed its legal and administrative ties with the occupied West Bank, but did not formally renounce sovereignty over the area. As a result of the wars of 1948–9 and 1967 there are about one million Palestinian refugees and displaced persons living in East Jordan, about 200,000 of whom live in refugee and displaced persons camps established by the UN Relief and Works Agency (UNRWA). In addition there are 300,000 self-supporting Palestinians in East Jordan.

In 1993, multiparty parliamentary elections were held for the first time since 1956. In the most recent elections, held on 4 November 1997, pro-government candidates won 62 out of 80 seats; the main opposition parties boycotted the elections.

### FOREIGN RELATIONS

The Middle East peace process begun in 1991 led to Jordan signing an agreement on a 'common agenda' for peace with Israel in 1993. On 25 July 1994 King Hussein and the Israeli Prime Minister signed a framework agreement for peace which ended the state of war existing since 1948. The first Israeli–Jordanian border crossing was opened between Eilat and Aqaba in August 1994. A full peace treaty was signed on 26 October 1994 which established full diplomatic and economic relations between the two states. It included agreements on sharing water from the Jordan and Yarmouk rivers; co-operating in the fields of commerce, transport, tourism, communications, energy and agriculture; and granted King Hussein custodianship of Islamic holy sites in Jerusalem. Israeli forces completed their withdrawal from Jordanian land in the Arava valley on 9 February 1995.

On 25 January 1999, King Hussein signed a decree naming his eldest son, Abdullah ibn al-Hussein, as his new heir, in place of his youngest brother, Prince Hassan; Prince Abdullah became King following the death of King Hussein on 7 February 1999.

Jordan and Kuwait re-established full diplomatic relations on 3 March 1999, which had been broken off following the 1990 Gulf War.

### POLITICAL SYSTEM

The constitution provides for a Senate of 40 members (all appointed by the King for a four-year term) and an elected House of Representatives which has 104 members, directly elected for a four-year term.

The King appoints the members of the Council of Ministers. In 1991 a new national charter was formulated which lifted the ban on political parties, imposed in 1957.

### HEAD OF STATE

*His Majesty The King of the Jordan*, Abdullah II, *born* 30 January 1962, *succeeded* 7 February 1999
*Crown Prince*, Hamzeh ibn al-Hussein, *born* 29 March 1982, son of King Hussein of Jordan
*Chief of the Royal Court*, Fayez Tarawneh

### COUNCIL OF MINISTERS *as at July 2001*

*Prime Minister, Defence*, Ali Abul Ragheb
*Deputy PM, Economic Affairs*, Muhammad Halaiqa
*Deputy PM, Interior*, Awadh Khleifat
*Deputy PM, Justice*, Faris Nabulsi
Agriculture, *Mahmoud Ayid al-Duwayri*
*Culture*, Mahmoud al-Kayed
*Education*, Khalid Tuqan
*Energy and Mineral Resources*, Muhammad Ali al-Batayinah
*Finance*, Michel Martu
*Foreign Affairs*, Abdul Illah al-Khatib
*Health*, Falih al-Nasir
*Industry and Trade*, Wasif Azar
*Information*, Salih al-Qallab
*Labour*, Eid al-Fayez
*Ministers of State*, Muhammad Thneibat (*Administrative Development*); Salih Irshaydat (*Cabinet Affairs*); Muhammad al-Halayiqah (*Economic Affairs*); Abid al-Shakhanibah (*Legal Affairs*); Shaikh Abd-al-Rahim al-Ukur; Musa Khalaf al-Ma'ani
*Municipal, Rural, and Environmental Affairs*, Abd-al-Razzaq Tubayshat
*Planning*, Jawad Hadid
*Post and Telecommunications*, Fawaz Hatim al-Zu'bi
*Public Works and Housing*, Hosni Abu Gheida
*Religious Endowments (Waqfs), Islamic Affairs*, Ahmad Hulayyil
*Social Development*, Tamam al-Ghoul
*Tourism and Antiquities*, Taleb al-Rifai
*Transport*, Nadir al-Dhahabi
*Water*, Hazim al-Nasir
*Youth and Sport*, Ma'mun Muhammad Nur-al-Din

### EMBASSY OF THE HASHEMITE KINGDOM OF JORDAN

6 Upper Phillimore Gardens, London W8 7HA
Tel: 020-7937 3685
*Ambassador Extraordinary and Plenipotentiary*, HE Timoor Daghistani, apptd 1999
*Counsellor*, M. Qabba'ah
*Defence Attaché*, Brig. Mohammad Quda'h

### BRITISH EMBASSY

Abdoun (PO Box 87), 'Ammān
Tel: (00 962) (6) 592 3100/6592
*Ambassador Extraordinary and Plenipotentiary*, HE Edward Graham Mellish Chaplin, OBE, apptd 2000
*Counsellor*, M. Aron (*Deputy Head of Mission and Consul-General*)
*Defence Attaché*, Col. C. Romberg

BRITISH COUNCIL DIRECTOR, Rebecca Walton, Rainbow Street, Jabal 'Ammān, PO Box 634, 'Ammān 11118; e-mail: bcamman@britishcouncil.org.jo

## DEFENCE

The Army has 1,246 main battle tanks, 1,450 armoured personnel carriers and 32 armoured infantry fighting vehicles. The Navy has six patrol and coastal vessels at its base at Aqaba. The Air Force has 106 combat aircraft and 16 armed helicopters.

MILITARY EXPENDITURE – 7.7 per cent of GDP (1999)
MILITARY PERSONNEL – 103,880: Army 90,000, Navy 480, Air Force 13,400, Paramilitaries 10,000

## ECONOMY

The main agricultural areas are the Jordan valley, the hills overlooking the valley, and the flatter country to the south of 'Ammān and around Madaba and Irbid. However, several large farms, which depend for irrigation on water pumped from deep aquifers, have been established in the southern desert area. The rest of the country is desert and semi-desert. The principal crops are wheat, barley, vegetables, olives and fruit. Agricultural production has increased considerably in recent years due to improvements in production and irrigation techniques.

Important industrial products are raw phosphates (1998, 5,925,000 tonnes) and potash (1998, 916,169 tonnes), most of which is exported, together with fertilisers and pharmaceuticals. The Trans-Arabian oil pipeline (Tapline) runs through north Jordan from Saudi Arabia to the Lebanese port of Sidon. A branch pipeline, together with oil trucked by road from Iraq, feeds a refinery at Zerqa, which meets most of Jordan's requirements for refined petroleum products. Sufficient reserves of natural gas have been discovered in the north-east to produce electricity for the national grid since 1989.

Tourism has developed, principally in 'Ammān, Aqaba, Zerka Ma'in and on the shores of the Dead Sea. In 1996, Jordan had 2,800,000 visitors.

In 1998 there was a trade deficit of US$1,602 million and a current account surplus of US$14 million. In 1999 imports totalled US$3,728 million and exports US$1,782 million.

GNP – US$7,717 million (1999); US$1,500 per capita (1999)
GDP – US$7,463 million (1999); US$1,523 per capita (1999)
ANNUAL AVERAGE GROWTH OF GDP – 1.6 per cent (1999)
INFLATION RATE – 0.6 per cent (1999)
TOTAL EXTERNAL DEBT – US$8,484 million (1998)

| *Trade with UK* | 1999 | 2000 |
|---|---|---|
| Imports from UK | £121,280,000 | £130,953,000 |
| Exports to UK | 24,263,000 | 23,433,000 |

## COMMUNICATIONS

'Ammān is linked to Aqaba, Damascus, Baghdād and Jiddah by roads which are of considerable importance in the overland trade of the Middle East.

The former Hejaz Railway runs from Syria through Jordan, and is used mainly for freight between 'Ammān and Damascus. The Aqaba railway carries phosphate rock from the mines of al-Hasa and al-Abiad to Aqaba.

The Royal Jordanian Airline operates from 'Ammān to Aqaba and has an extensive network of routes to the Middle East, Europe, North America and the Far East.

---

# KAZAKHSTAN
*Kazakstan Respublikasy*

---

AREA – 1,049,150 sq. miles (2,717,300 sq. km). Neighbours: Russia (north and west), Turkmenistan, Uzbekistan and Kyrgyzstan (south), China (east)
POPULATION – 15,438,000 (2000 estimate): Kazakhs (44 per cent), Russians (36 per cent), Ukrainians (5 per cent) and ethnic Germans (4 per cent), with smaller numbers of Tatars, Uzbeks, Koreans and Belarusians. The Russian population is concentrated in the north of the country, where it forms a significant majority, and in Almaty. The majority of ethnic Kazakhs are Sunni Muslims, and this is the main religion of the republic. Kazakh (one of the Turkic languages) became the official language in 1993; a law passed in July 1997 decreed Kazakh as the language of state administration; Russian has a special status as the 'social language between peoples'. Otherwise each ethnic group uses its own language
CAPITAL – Astana (population, 320,000, 2000 estimate. Known as Akmola until May 1998). The capital was moved from Alma-Ata (Almaty) in December 1997
MAJOR CITIES – Almaty (1,061,400); Karaganda (449,200); Pavlodar (341,500); Shimkent (439,800), 1998 estimates
CURRENCY – Tenge
NATIONAL DAY – 25 October (Republic Day)
NATIONAL FLAG – Dark blue with a sun and a soaring eagle in the centre all in gold, and a red vertical ornamentation stripe near the hoist
LIFE EXPECTANCY (years) – male 58.8; female 69.9
POPULATION GROWTH RATE – 0.3 per cent (1999)
POPULATION DENSITY – 6 per sq. km (1998)
URBAN POPULATION – 56.4 per cent (2000 estimate)
ILLITERACY RATE – 2.5 per cent
ENROLMENT (percentage of age group) – tertiary 33.3 per cent (1996)

Kazakhstan occupies the northern part of what was Soviet Central Asia. It stretches from the Volga and the Caspian Sea in the west to the Altai and Tienshan mountains in the east. The country consists of arid steppes and semi-deserts, flat in the west, hilly in the east and mountainous in the south-east (Southern Altai and Tienshan mountains). The main rivers are the Irtysh, the Ural, the Syr-Darya and the Ili. The climate is continental and very dry.

## HISTORY AND POLITICS

Kazakhstan was inhabited by nomadic tribes before being invaded by Ghenghiz Khan and incorporated into his empire in 1218. After his empire disintegrated, feudal towns emerged based on large oases. These towns affiliated and established a Kazakh state in the late 15th century which engaged in almost continuous warfare with the marauding Khanates on its southern border. After appealing to Russia for aid and protection, in 1731 Kazakhstan acceded to the Russian Empire under a voluntary act of accession.

After the 1917 Russian revolution, Kazakhstan came under the control of White Russian forces until 1919. On 26 August 1920 a constitution was signed under which Kazakhstan became a Soviet Socialist Republic. Under Soviet rule in the 1920s and 1930s there was rapid industrial development and the traditional nomadic way of life disappeared. The Kazakhs suffered greatly in the Stalinist purges, the merchant and religious classes being murdered and thousands dying in the desert on collective farms. Other nationalities, such as Tatars and Germans, were forcibly transported to Kazakhstan by Stalin. Kazakhstan declared its independence on 16 December 1991.

The Communist-derived Congress of People's Unity of Kazakhstan (SNEK) won the March 1994 legislative elections which were ruled invalid by the Constitutional Court. The President responded by dissolving parliament in March 1995. Elections to the new legislature were held in December 1995; the requirement for candidates to achieve an absolute majority made run-offs necessary. A referendum on 29 April 1995 extended President Nazarbayev's term until 2000, but constitutional changes unanimously agreed by parliament brought forward presidential elections to 10 January 1999. Elections to the upper chamber of the legislature were held on 17 September 1999 and to the lower house on 10 and 24 October 1999 and were won by the Fatherland Republican Party.

### POLITICAL SYSTEM

Executive power is vested in the president and government. The president must be a Kazakh speaker and has the power to appoint the prime minister, other senior ministers and all ambassadors.

A new constitution approved by referendum on 30 August 1995 granted the president the power to dissolve the legislature and to rule by decree. It also nominated Kazakh as the sole official language; prohibited dual citizenship; and created a new bicameral legislature composed of a 39-member Senate, of whom 32 are indirectly elected and seven appointed, and a 77-member directly elected Majlis (lower house of the legislature). The Constitutional Court, which opposed the new constitution, was replaced by a Constitutional Council which was made subject to presidential veto.

Kazakhstan is divided into 14 administrative regions.

### HEAD OF STATE

*President*, Nursultan Nazarbayev, *elected* 1 December 1991, *confirmed in office by referendum* 29 April 1995, *re-elected* 10 January 1999

### GOVERNMENT *as at July 2001*

*Prime Minister*, Kasymzhomart Tokayev
*First Deputy PM, Economic Affairs*, Daniyal Akhmetov
*Deputy PMs*, Imangali Tasmagambetov (*Cultural and Social Affairs*); Vladimir Shkolnik (*Energy and Natural Resources*); Uraz Dzhandosov (*Tax, Enterprise and State Investment, Relations with International Financial and Economic Organisations*)
*Agriculture*, Akhmetzhan Yesimov
*Culture, Information and Social Harmony*, Mukhtar Kul-Mukhammbed
*Defence*, Lt.-Gen. Sat Tokpakbayev
*Director of the Strategic Planning Agency*, Kairat Kelimbetov
*Economy and Trade*, Zhaksubek Kulyekeyev
*Finance*, Mazhit Yesenbayev
*Foreign Affairs*, Yerlan Idrisov
*Head of Prime Minister's Office*, Altay Tleuberdin
*Interior*, Bulat Iskakov
*Justice*, Igor Rogov
*Labour and Social Security*, Alikhan Baymenov
*National Security*, The President
*Science and Education*, Nuraly Bekturganov
*State Revenues*, Zeynulla Kakimzhanov
*Transport and Communications*, Karim Masimov
*Without Portfolio*, Aitkul Samakova

### EMBASSY OF THE REPUBLIC OF KAZAKHSTAN

33 Thurloe Square, London SW7 2DS
Tel: 020-7581 4646
*Ambassador Extraordinary and Plenipotentiary*, HE Dr Adil Akhmetov, apptd 2000

### BRITISH EMBASSY

U1. Furmanova 173, Almaty
Tel: (00 7) (3272) 506191/2
E-mail: british-embassy@kaznet.kz
*Ambassador Extraordinary and Plenipotentiary*, HE Richard Lewington, apptd 1999

BRITISH COUNCIL DIRECTOR, Louise Coucher, Republic Square, KZ-480013 Almaty; e-mail: general@britishcouncil.or.kz

## DEFENCE

An agreement signed with Russia in January 1995 provides for eventual reunification of the two states' armed forces. The CIS mutual defence treaty of 1993, to which Kazakhstan is a signatory, retains a common air defence force, while Kazakh forces also take part in the CIS peacekeeping force along the Tajikistan–Afghanistan border. By 1996, all nuclear warheads had been returned to Russia although Kazakhstan retained 48 SS-18 intercontinental ballistic missiles. Kazakhstan participates in the NATO Partnership for Peace programme. The Army has 930 main battle tanks and 1,343 armoured combat vehicles. The Caspian Sea Flotilla, which Kazakhstan shares with Russia and Turkmenistan, operates under Russian command. The Air Force has 131 combat aircraft.

MILITARY EXPENDITURE – 3.5 per cent of GDP (1999)
MILITARY PERSONNEL – 64,000: Army 45,000, Air Force 19,000, Paramilitaries 34,500
CONSCRIPTION DURATION – 31 months

## ECONOMY

Kazakhstan is rich in minerals, with copper, lead, gold, uranium, chromium, silver, zinc, iron ore, coal, oil and natural gas. In 1998 production of coal was 68,700,000 tonnes and of iron ore was 18,000,000 tonnes. The oil and gas industry, concentrated in the west of the country, has been expanded by foreign investment, which is also being used to explore the Karachaganak (gas) and Tengiz (oil) fields in the Caspian Sea. Initial exploration of the Kashagan offshore oilfield in 2000 indicated extensive reserves. In November 1997, a deal was signed with the USA that provided for a US$26 billion investment in the energy sector.

Pipelines to Turkey and Russia are in operation and a further pipeline to China is under consideration. Oil production in 1998 was 25.9 million tonnes and gas output was 8.3 billion cubic metres. Industry is dominated by food processing and mining and metals production; textiles, steel and tractors are also produced. The main centres of the metal industry are in the Altai mountains, in Shimkent, north of Lake Balkhash and in central Kazakhstan.

Agriculture, including stock-raising, is highly developed, particularly in the central and south-west of the republic. Grain is grown in the north and north-east, and cotton and wool produced in the south and south-east. 12.5 million tonnes of wheat and 3.5 million tonnes of barley were grown in 1999.

The economy was weakened by the ending of preferential trading links to other CIS states at the break-up of the Soviet Union although a single market was formed with Kyrgyzstan and Uzbekistan in 1994. A treaty on further economic and humanitarian co-operation, as well as a customs union, was signed with Belarus, Kyrgyzstan and Russia in March 1996. A treaty of economic co-operation for 1998–2007 was signed with Russia in October 1998. The tenge was floated on 5 April 1999 in a bid to reduce the trade deficit.

In 1999 the trade surplus was US$344 million and the current account deficit US$171 million. Imports totalled US$3,683 million and exports US$5,592 million.

GNP – US$18,732 million (1999); US$1,230 per capita (1999)
GDP – US$20,553 million (1997); US$1,368 per capita (1998)
ANNUAL AVERAGE GROWTH OF GDP – 0.4 per cent (1996)
INFLATION RATE – 8.2 per cent (1999)
UNEMPLOYMENT – 3.7 per cent (1998)
TOTAL EXTERNAL DEBT – US$5,714 million (1998)

| Trade with UK | 1999 | 2000 |
|---|---|---|
| Imports from UK | £65,782,000 | £65,908,000 |
| Exports to UK | 51,278,000 | 92,088,000 |

## KENYA
*Jamhuri ya Kenya*

AREA – 224,081 sq. miles (580,367 sq. km). Neighbours: Somalia (east), Ethiopia (north), Sudan (north-west), Uganda (west), Tanzania (south)
POPULATION – 29,410,000 (1997 UN estimate). The main tribal groups are the Kikuyu, Luhya, Luo, Kalenjin, Kamba and Masai. The official languages are Swahili, which is generally understood throughout Kenya, and English; numerous indigenous languages are also spoken
CAPITAL – Nairobi (population, 1,400,000, 1989 estimate)
MAJOR CITIES – ΨKisumu (192,733); ΨMombasa (461,753); Nakuru (163,927), 1989 estimates
CURRENCY – Kenya shilling (Ksh) of 100 cents
NATIONAL ANTHEM - Wimbo wa Taifa (National Anthem)
NATIONAL DAY – 12 December (Independence Day)
NATIONAL FLAG – Horizontally black, red and green with the red fimbriated in white, and with a shield and crossed spears all over in the centre
LIFE EXPECTANCY (years) – male 47.3; female 48.1
POPULATION GROWTH RATE – 2.6 per cent (1999)
POPULATION DENSITY – 50 per sq. km (1998)
URBAN POPULATION – 33.1 per cent (2000 estimate)
MILITARY EXPENDITURE – 3.1 per cent of GDP (1999)
MILITARY PERSONNEL – 22,200: Army 18,200, Navy 1,000, Air Force 3,000, Paramilitaries 5,000
ILLITERACY RATE – 17.5 per cent
ENROLMENT (percentage of age group) – primary 91 per cent (1980); tertiary 1.6 per cent (1990)

### HISTORY AND POLITICS

Kenya became an independent state and a member of the British Commonwealth on 12 December 1963 and a republic in 1964. In 1982 the government introduced amendments to the constitution making the country a one-party state, with the Kenya African National Union (KANU) as the ruling party. In December 1991, the government yielded to internal and international pressure and introduced a multiparty democracy.

On 29 December 1997, in elections hampered by heavy flooding and marred by allegations of electoral malpractice, KANU won 109 out of 210 seats in the National Assembly, and President Daniel arap Moi won just over 40 per cent of the vote to win a fifth term in office.

#### POLITICAL SYSTEM

The head of state is a president, directly elected for a five-year term, who is head of government and appoints the Cabinet. The unicameral legislature, the *Bunge* (National Assembly), has 224 members, of whom 210 are directly elected for a five-year term, 12 appointed by the president, and two ex-officio members, the attorney-general and the speaker. In November 1999, an amendment to the constitution was passed which limited the powers of the president over the National Assembly and affirmed the Bunge's supremacy.

The country is divided into eight provinces (Central, Coast, Eastern, Nairobi, Nyanza, North Eastern, Rift Valley, Western).

#### HEAD OF STATE

*President and C.-in-C. Armed Forces*, Daniel T. arap Moi (KANU), *took office* 14 October 1978, *re-elected* 1979, 1983, 1988, 1992 and 29 December 1997
*Vice-President*, George Saitoti

#### CABINET *as at July 2001*

The President
The Vice-President
*Agriculture*, Bonaya Godana
*Attorney-General*, Amos Wako
*Education, Science and Technology*, Henry Kiprono Kosgey
*Energy*, Raila Odinga
*Environment*, Noah Katana Ngala
*Finance*, Chrysanthus Okemo
*Foreign Affairs and International Co-operation*, Chris Mogere Obure
*Heritage and Sport*, Francis Nyenze
*Labour*, Joseph Kimen Ngutu
*Lands and Settlement*, Joseph Nyagah
*Local Government*, Joshua Joseph Kamotho
*Medical Services*, vacant
*Mineral Exploration*, Jackson Kalweo
*Ministers of State in the President's Office*, Maj. Marsden Madoka; Shariff Nassir Taib; William ole Ntimana; Julius Sunkuli
*Planning*, Kiprono Kipyator Nicholas Biwott; Adhu Awiti
*Public Health*, Samson Ongeri
*Roads and Public Works*, William Morogo
*Rural Development*, Yekoyada Francis Masakhalia
*Science and Technology*, Gideon Ndambuki
*Tourism and Information*, Stephen Kalonzo Musyoka
*Transport and Communications*, Wycliffe Musalia Mudavadi
*Vocational Training*, Isaac Ruto
*Water Resources*, Kipng'eno arap Ng'eny

KENYA HIGH COMMISSION
45 Portland Place, London W1N 4AS
Tel: 020-7636 2371/5
*High Commissioner*, HE Nancy Kirui, apptd 2000
*Defence Adviser*, Col. G. L. Okanga
*Commercial Attaché*, D. Mbugua

BRITISH HIGH COMMISSION
Upper Hill Road, PO Box 30465 Nairobi
Tel: (00 254) (2) 714699
E-mail: consular@nairobi.fco.gov.uk
*High Commissioner*, HE Jeffrey James, CMG, KBE, apptd 1997
*Deputy High Commissioner*, C. Harvey
*Defence Adviser*, Col. T. Merritt, OBE
*First Secretary (Commercial)*, J. Chandler
*First Secretary (Consular)*, D. Levoir
CONSULAR OFFICES – Nairobi, Mombasa

BRITISH COUNCIL DIRECTOR, Peter Elborn, ICEA Building, Kenyatta Avenue, PO Box 40751, Nairobi; e-mail: information@britishcouncil.or.ke. There are offices at Kisumu and Mombasa

### ECONOMY

Agriculture provides about a quarter of GDP and employs around three-quarters of the workforce. The great variation in altitude and ecology provides conditions under which a wide range of crops can be grown. These include wheat, barley, pyrethrum, coffee, tea, sisal, coconuts, cashew nuts, cotton, maize and a wide variety of tropical and temperate fruits and vegetables. The total area of well-farmed land on which concentrated mixed farming can be practised is small and the remainder is arid or semi-arid country but population pressure and the need to increase agricultural production for export has led to attempts to develop such areas. Kenya has suffered a prolonged drought that has diminished both food and hydroelectric production.

Mineral production consists of soda ash, salt and limestone. Hydroelectric power has been developed, particularly on the Upper Tana River, and Kenya is now almost self-sufficient in electric power generation.

There has been considerable industrial development over the last 15 years and Kenya has a variety of industries processing agricultural produce and manufacturing products from local and imported raw materials. New industries are steel, textile mills, dehydrated vegetable processing and motor tyre manufacture. Smaller schemes have added to the country's consumer goods manufacturing base. There is an oil refinery in Mombasa supplying both Kenya and Uganda, and a fuel pipeline now connects Mombasa and Nairobi.

In June 2000 the government announced that the state-owned telecommunications company was to be privatised. The government also increased VAT and announced reductions in the number of state employees. Tourism generates some US$400 million per year.

GNP – US$10,696 million (1999); US$360 per capita (1999)
GDP – US$10,134 million (1997); US$373 per capita (1998)
ANNUAL AVERAGE GROWTH OF GDP – 4.2 per cent (1996)
INFLATION RATE – 2.6 per cent (1999)
TOTAL EXTERNAL DEBT – US$7,010 million (1998)

### TRADE

Principal exports are coffee and tea, which account for roughly a third of total export earnings. Also exported are fruit, vegetables, and crude animal and vegetable material. Industrial machinery is the largest single import; other imports are transport equipment, petroleum and petroleum products, metals, pharmaceuticals and chemicals.

In 1998 Kenya had a trade deficit of US$1,016 million and a current account deficit of US$363 million. Imports totalled US$3,197 million and exports US$2,008 million.

| *Trade with UK* | 1999 | 2000 |
|---|---|---|
| Imports from UK | £196,942,000 | 1£65,641,000 |
| Exports to UK | 196,733,000 | 190,267,000 |

## COMMUNICATIONS

The Kenya Railways Corporation has 2,506 km of railway open to traffic. There are also 67,000 km of road, of which 8,900 km are bitumen surfaced.

The principal port is Mombasa, operated by the Kenya Ports Authority. International air services operate from airports at Nairobi and Mombasa. The national airline is Kenya Airways.

---

## KIRIBATI

*Ribaberikin Kiribati – Republic of Kiribati*

---

AREA – 280 sq. miles (726 sq. km)
POPULATION – 88,000 (1997 UN estimate): predominantly Christian. The languages are I-Kiribati and English
CAPITAL – Tarawa (population, 17,921, 1978)
CURRENCY – Australian dollar ($A) of 100 cents
NATIONAL ANTHEM – Teirake Kain Kiribati (Stand Kiribati)
NATIONAL DAY – 12 July (Independence Day)
NATIONAL FLAG – Red, with blue and white wavy lines in base, and in the centre a gold rising sun and a flying frigate bird
LIFE EXPECTANCY (years) – male 61.4; female 65.5
POPULATION GROWTH RATE – 1.7 per cent (1997)
POPULATION DENSITY – 112 per sq. km (1998)
URBAN POPULATION – 39.2 per cent (2000 estimate)

Kiribati (pronounced Kiribas) comprises 36 islands: the Gilberts Group (17) including Banaba (formerly Ocean Island), the Phoenix Islands (8), and the Line Islands (11), which are situated in the south-west central Pacific around the point at which the International Date Line cuts the Equator. The total land area is spread over some 2 million square miles of ocean. Few of the atolls are more than half a mile in width or more than 12 feet high. The vegetation consists mainly of coconut palms, breadfruit trees and pandanus.

## HISTORY AND POLITICS

The Gilbert and Ellice Islands were proclaimed a British protectorate in 1892 and annexed as the Gilbert and Ellice Islands Colony on 10 November 1915 (taking effect 12 January 1916). The Gilbert Islands were occupied by the Japanese army during World War II. Nuclear tests were carried out by the British off Kiritimati (Christmas Island) in 1957. In October 1975 the Ellice Islands seceded to become the independent state of Tuvalu. The Gilbert Islands achieved independence on 12 July 1979 as the Republic of Kiribati.

Legislative elections were held on 23 September 1998 and presidential elections held on 27 November 1998 were won by Teburoro Tito. There are no formal political parties.

### POLITICAL SYSTEM

The president is head of state as well as head of government and is directly elected. There is a House of Assembly of 41 members (39 elected members, the Attorney-General and a representative of the Banaban community from Rabi Island). Executive authority is vested in the Cabinet.

### HEAD OF STATE

*President, Foreign Affairs*, Teburoro Tito, *sworn in* 1 October 1994, *re-elected* 27 November 1998
*Vice-President, Home Affairs, Rural Development*, vacant

### CABINET *as at July 2001*

The President
The Vice-President
*Commerce, Industry and Tourism*, Teaiwa Tenieu
*Education, Training and Technology*, Teambo Keariki
*Environment, Social Development*, Kataotika Tekee
*Finance and Economic Planning*, Beniamina Tinga
*Health and Family Planning*, Baraniko Mooa
*Labour, Employment and Co-operatives*, Teiraoi Tetabea
*Line and Phoenix Islands*, Tim Taekiti
*Natural Resources Development*, Emile Schutz
*Transport, Communications and Information*, Willie Tokataake
*Works and Energy*, Manraoi Kaiea

### KIRIBATI HIGH COMMISSION

c/o Office of the President, P.O Box 68, Bairiki, Tarawa, Kiribati
*High Commissioner*, vacant
*Acting High Commissioner*, Peter Timeon
BRITISH HIGH COMMISSIONER, HE Michael Dibben, apptd 1998, resident at Suva, Fiji

## ECONOMY

Many people still practise a semi-subsistence economy, the main staples of their diet being coconuts and fish.

The principal imports are foodstuffs, consumer goods, machinery and transport equipment. The principal exports are copra and fish.

In May 2000, Japanese-funded improved port facilities at Betio were opened.

GNP – US$81 million (1999); US$910 per capita (1999)
GDP – US$54 million (1997); US$594 per capita (1998)

| *Trade with UK* | 1999 | 2000 |
|---|---|---|
| Imports from UK | £149,000 | £338,000 |
| Exports to UK | 7,000 | 1,000 |

## COMMUNICATIONS

Air communication exists between most of the islands and is operated by Air Kiribati, a statutory corporation. Air Marshall Islands operates a weekly service between Majuro, Tarawa, Funafuti and Nadi, and Air Nauru between Tarawa, Nauru and Nadi. Inter-island shipping is operated by a statutory corporation, the Shipping Corporation of Kiribati.

## EDUCATION AND SOCIAL WELFARE

There are 104 primary schools, eight secondary schools and one high school. There is a teacher training college, a technical institute and a marine training centre.

There is a general hospital at Tarawa. The other inhabited islands have dispensaries.

# KOREA

Korea's southern and western coasts are fringed with innumerable islands, of which the largest, forming a province of its own, is Cheju. The Korean language is of the Ural-Altaic Group. Its script, Hangul, was invented in the 15th century; prior to this Chinese characters alone were used. Despite the great cultural influence of the Chinese, Koreans have developed and preserved their own cultural heritage.

## HISTORY

The Korean peninsula was first unified in AD 668 when Shilla, having emerged as the dominant tribal state, conquered Koguryo and Paekche. The Koryo dynasty ruled from 912 until 1392 and was succeeded by the Choson dynasty, who ruled from 1392 until 1910 when Japan formally annexed Korea. The country remained part of the Japanese Empire until the defeat of Japan in 1945, when it was occupied by troops of the USA and the USSR, the 38th parallel being fixed as the boundary between the two zones of occupation.

The UN in November 1947 resolved that elections should be held for a National Assembly which, when elected, should set up a government. The Soviet government refused to comply and a UN commission was only allowed to operate south of the 38th parallel.

A general election was held on 10 May 1948, and the first National Assembly met in Seoul on 31 May. The Assembly passed a constitution on 12 July and on 15 August 1948 the republic was formally inaugurated and American military government came to an end. Meanwhile, in the Soviet-occupied zone north of the 38th parallel the Democratic People's Republic had been established with its capital at Pyongyang. A Supreme People's Soviet was elected in September 1948, and a Soviet-style constitution adopted.

### THE KOREAN WAR

Korea remained divided along the 38th parallel until June 1950, when North Korean forces invaded South Korea. In response to Security Council recommendations, 16 nations, including the USA and the UK, came to the aid of the Republic of Korea. China entered the war on the side of North Korea in November 1950. The fighting was ended by an armistice agreement signed on 27 July 1953. By this agreement (which was not signed by the Republic of Korea), the line of division between North and South Korea remained close to the 38th parallel.

Talks between North and South Korea on the reunification of the country have taken place intermittently. A non-aggression accord was signed between the North and South in 1991 and an agreement on the denuclearisation of the Korean peninsula was reached in 1992. A summit meeting between the presidents of North and South Korea took place on 13–15 June 2000 at which a communiqué was signed agreeing to promote economic co-operation, achieve reconciliation and eventually reunify the two countries. Construction of a railway line linking the two states began on 18 September 2000.

# DEMOCRATIC PEOPLE'S REPUBLIC OF KOREA

*Chosun Minchu-chui Inmin Kongwa-guk*

AREA – 46,540 sq. miles (120,538 sq. km). Neighbours: China, Russia (north), Republic of Korea (south)
POPULATION – 23,414,000 (1999 estimate). The language is Korean
CAPITAL – Pyongyang (approximate population, 2,741,260)
CURRENCY – Won of 100 chon
NATIONAL ANTHEM – Aegukka (The song of love of country)
NATIONAL DAY – 16 February (Kim Jong-il's birthday)
NATIONAL FLAG – Red with white fimbriations and blue borders at top and bottom; a large red star on a white disc near the hoist
LIFE EXPECTANCY (years) – male 58.0; female 60.6
POPULATION GROWTH RATE – 1.6 per cent (1999)
POPULATION DENSITY – 194 per sq. km (1998)
URBAN POPULATION – 60.2 per cent (2000 estimate)

### POLITICAL SYSTEM

The constitution of the Democratic People's Republic of Korea provides for a Supreme People's Assembly, presently consisting of 687 deputies, which is elected every five years by universal suffrage. The Assembly elects a president for a five-year term, and the Central People's Committee. In turn, the Central People's Committee directs the Administrative Council which implements the policy formulated by the Committee. The Administrative Council (36 members), the government of North Korea, includes the prime minister and various ministers. In practice, however, the country is ruled by the Korean Workers' Party which elects a Central Committee; this in turn appoints a Politburo. The senior ministers of the Administrative Council are all members of the Communist Party Central Committee and the majority are also members of the Politburo. Kim Il-sung, who had been head of the state, party and military since the country's inception in 1948, died on 8 July 1994, but was declared the eternal president in September 1998. His son Kim Jong-il, who had been party general secretary since October 1997, became chair of the National Defence Committee, which is now *de facto* the highest office.

### HEAD OF STATE

*Eternal President*, Kim Il-sung (deceased)
*Chair of the National Defence Committee, General Secretary, Korean Workers' Party; Member of Presidium*, Kim Jong-il
*Chair of the Standing Committee of the Supreme People's Assembly*, Kim Yong-nam

### SPA STANDING COMMITTEE

*Chairman*, Kim Yong-nam
*Vice-Chairmen*, Yang Hyong-sop; Kim Yong-tae
*Secretary-General*, Kim Yun-hyok

*Honorary Vice-Chairmen*, Pak Song-chol; Kim-yong Chu; Yi Chong-ok; Chon Mun-sop
*Members*, Yu Mi-yong; Kang Yong-sop; Yi Kil-song; Yi Chol-pong; Yi Il-hwan; Song Sam-sop

ADMINISTRATIVE COUNCIL *as at July 2001*

*Prime Minister*, Hong Song-nam
*Deputy Prime Ministers*, Kwak Pon-ki; Cho Chang-tok
*Foreign Affairs*, Paek Nam-sun

MINISTERS

*Agriculture*, Kim Chang-sik
*Chair, Physical Culture and Sports Guidance Committee*, Pak Myong-chol
*Chair, State Planning Committee*, Pak Nam-ki
*Chemical Industry*, Pak Pong-chu
*City Management*, Choe Chong-kon
*Commerce*, Yi Yong-son
*Construction and Building Materials Industry*, Cho Yun-hui
*Culture*, Kang Nung-su
*Director of the Central Statistics Bureau*, Kim Chang-su
*Director of the Secretariat and State Administration Council*, Chong Mun-sang
*Education*, Choe Ki-chong
*Finance*, Mun Il-bong
*Fisheries*, Yi Song-un
*Foreign Trade*, Ri Kwang-gun
*Forestry*, Yi Sang-mu
*Labour*, Yi Won-il
*Land and Maritime Transport*, Kim Yong-il
*Land Environmental Protection*, Chang Il-son
*Light Industry*, Yi Yong-su
*Metal and Machine Industry*, Chon Sung-hun
*Mining Industry*, Son Chong-o
*People's Armed Forces*, Vice-Marshall Kim Il-chol
*Posts and Telecommunications*, Yi Kun-pom
*Power and Coal Industry*, Sin Tae-nok
*President of the Academy of Sciences*, Yi Kwang-ho
*President of the Central Bank*, Kim Wan-su
*Procurement and Food Administration*, Paek Chang-yong
*Public Health*, Kim Su-hak
*Public Security*, Lt.-Gen. Paek Hak-nim
*Railways*, Kim Yong-san
*State Construction Commission*, Pae Tal-chun
*State Inspection*, Kim Ui-sun

FULL MEMBERS OF THE POLITBURO

Kim Jong-il; Pak Son-chol; Kim Yong-nam; Kye Ung-tae; Han Song-yong; Kim Yong-ju; Yi Chong-ok; Yon Hyong-muk; Kang Song-san; So Yun-sok; Ho Dam

## DEFENCE

The Army has about 3,500 main battle tanks and 2,500 armoured personnel carriers. The Navy has 26 submarines, three frigates and about 310 patrol and coastal vessels at 15 bases. The Air Force has 621 combat aircraft and 24 armed helicopters.

Between 1992 and 1994 North Korea embarked on a clandestine nuclear weapons programme despite being a signatory of the Nuclear Non-Proliferation Treaty (NPT), but halted the programme in November 1994.

MILITARY EXPENDITURE – 14.3 per cent of GDP (1999)
MILITARY PERSONNEL – 1,082,000: Army 950,000, Navy 46,000, Air Force 86,000, Paramilitaries 189,000
CONSCRIPTION DURATION – Three to ten years

## ECONOMY

North Korea is rich in minerals and industry was developed, but the economy has stagnated owing to poor planning and a shortage of foreign exchange. The current economic crisis was precipitated by the curtailment of barter trade with the Soviet Union after 1991, and the end of subsidised oil and grain from China. Industrial output has collapsed, with industry operating at one-third of capacity. The economy has been sustained by foreign exchange sent by ethnic Koreans in Japan. In April 1998, South Korea lifted its ban on investment in North Korea, allowing South Koreans to send money to their relatives in the north.

In 1995–8, a slump in agricultural production was exacerbated by widespread flooding which devastated the rice harvest. A North Korean survey quoted by South Korean security services stated that up to three million people had died as a result of famine between 1995 and 1998. In January 1998, the UN World Food Programme launched a food aid operation to provide 658,000 tonnes of food to North Korea. The USA increased food aid to North Korea in May 1999.

GDP – US$5,332 million (1997); US$440 per capita (1998)
ANNUAL AVERAGE GROWTH OF GDP 3.7 per cent (1999)

| *Trade with UK* | 1999 | 2000 |
|---|---|---|
| Imports from UK | £13,624,000 | £16,798,000 |
| Exports to UK | 1,518,000 | 2,981,000 |

## REPUBLIC OF KOREA
*Taehanminguk*

AREA – 38,327 sq. miles 99,268 sq. km). Neighbour: Democratic People's Republic of Korea (north)
POPULATION – 47,335,257 (1999 estimate). The largest religions are Buddhism (10.3 million) and Christianity (8.8 million Protestants, 2.9 million Roman Catholics). The language is Korean
CAPITAL – Seoul (population, 10,321,000, 1999 estimate)
MAJOR CITIES – ΨInchon (2,524,000); ΨPusan (3,831,000); Taegu (2,517,000)
CURRENCY – Won
NATIONAL ANTHEM – Aegukka (The Song of Love of Country)
NATIONAL DAY – 15 August (Liberation Day)
NATIONAL FLAG – White with a red and blue yin-yang symbol in the centre, surrounded by four black trigrams
LIFE EXPECTANCY (years) – male 69.2; female 76.3
POPULATION GROWTH RATE – 0.9 per cent (1999)
POPULATION DENSITY – 468 per sq. km (1998)
URBAN POPULATION – 81.9 per cent (2000 estimate)

## HISTORY AND POLITICS

The Republic of Korea was not officially recognised by any former Communist bloc country until 1989, and not by the People's Republic of China until 1992.

The most recent elections to the National Assembly in April 2000 produced no outright majority. The Millennium Democratic Party won 115 seats and formed a coalition with the United Liberal Democrats, who won 17 seats; the opposition Grand National Party won 133 seats. Lee Han-dong was appointed prime minister on 22 May 2000. In the most recent presidential election of 18 December 1997, Kim Dae-jung of the National Congress for New Politics was elected president with just over 40 per cent of the vote.

POLITICAL SYSTEM

A new constitution was adopted in 1988 following a year of political unrest. The president, who is head of state, chief of the executive and commander-in-chief of the armed forces, is directly elected for a single term of five years. He appoints the prime minister with the consent of the National Assembly, and members of the State Council (Cabinet) on the recommendation of the prime minister.

The president is also empowered to take wide-ranging measures in an emergency, including the declaration of martial law, but must obtain the agreement of the National Assembly. The National Assembly of 273 members is directly elected for a four-year term.

### HEAD OF STATE

*President*, Kim Dae-jung, *elected* 18 December 1997, *sworn in* 25 February 1998

### CABINET *as at July 2001*

*Prime Minister*, Lee Han-dong
*Deputy Prime Minister, Education and Human Resources*, Han Wan-sang
*Deputy Prime Minister, Finance and Economy*, Jin Nyum
*Agriculture and Forestry*, Han Kap-soo
*Commerce, Industry and Energy*, Chang Che-shik
*Construction and Transportation*, Oh Jang-seop
*Culture and Tourism*, Kim Han-gill
*Defence*, Kim Dong-shin
*Environment*, Kim Myung-ja
*Foreign Affairs, Trade*, Han Seung-soo
*Gender Equality*, Han Myung-sook
*Government Administration, Home Affairs*, Lee Keun-sik
*Government Policy Co-ordinator*, Na Seung-po
*Health and Welfare*, Kim Won-gil
*Information and Communications*, Yang Seung-taik
*Justice*, Choi Kyung-won
*Labour*, Kin Ho-jin
*Maritime Affairs and Fisheries*, Chung Woo-taik
*Planning and Budget*, Jeon Yun-churl
*Science and Technology*, Kim Young-hwan
*Unification*, Lim Dong-won

### EMBASSY OF THE REPUBLIC OF KOREA

60 Buckingham Gate, London SW1E 6AJ
Tel: 020-7227 5500/2
*Ambassador Extraordinary and Plenipotentiary*, HE Ra Jong-yil, apptd 2001
*Defence Attaché*, Capt. Lee Sun-heung
*Consul*, Chin-Ki-hoon
*First Secretary (Commercial)*, Cheong Seung-il

### BRITISH EMBASSY

No. 4, Chung-dong, Chung-Ku, Seoul 100-120
Tel: (00 82) (2) 735-7341/3;
E-mail: britcom@netsgo.com
*Ambassador Extraordinary and Plenipotentiary*, HE C. Humfrey, CMG, apptd 2000
*Consul-General and Deputy Head of Mission*, D. R. Marsh, CVO
*Defence and Military Attaché*, Brig. J. G. Baker, MBE
*First Secretary (Commercial)*, D. Brown

There is a Trade Office and an Honorary British Consul at Pusan.

BRITISH COUNCIL DIRECTOR, Mark Baumfield, Joongwhoo Building, 61–21 Taepyungro1-ka, Choong-ku, Seoul 100-101; e-mail: info@britishcouncil.or.kr

BRITISH CHAMBER OF COMMERCE, 2nd Floor, Joonghoo Building, 61–21, 1-ka Taepyungro 1-ka, Choong-ku, Seoul 100–101

## DEFENCE

The Army has 2,330 main battle tanks, 2,480 armoured personnel carriers and 117 armed helicopters. The Navy has 19 submarines, six destroyers, 33 frigates, 84 patrol and coastal vessels, 23 combat aircraft, 48 armed helicopters, 60 main battle tanks and 63 armoured personnel carriers. There are eight naval bases. The Air Force has 555 combat aircraft.

The USA maintains 36,630 personnel in the country.

MILITARY EXPENDITURE – 3.0 per cent of GDP (1999)
MILITARY PERSONNEL – 683,000: Army 560,000, Navy 60,000, Air Force 63,000, Paramilitaries 4,500
CONSCRIPTION DURATION – 26–30 months

## ECONOMY

Land redistribution and US aid (US$6,000 million from 1945 to 1978) enabled the rapid industrialisation of South Korea in the 1950s and 1960s. Former land owners formed *chaebols* (industrial conglomerates) which benefited from a highly-educated workforce and import substitution policies. From 1961 to 1979 exports increased by an average of 10 per cent a year. From 1985 to 1997, GDP grew strongly, but fell by 5.8 per cent during 1998; it recovered to grow by 10.7 per cent during 1999. Major industries include shipbuilding, construction, iron and steel, textiles, electrical and electronic goods, semiconductors, passenger vehicles and petrochemicals.

The soil is fertile but arable land is limited by the mountainous nature of the country. Staple agricultural products are rice, barley and other cereals, beans and potatoes. Fruit-growing, sericulture and the growing of the medicinal root ginseng are also practised. The fishing industry is a major contributor to both food supply and exports.

Korea is deficient in mineral resources, except for deposits of coal on the east coast and tungsten. There are some prospects of discovering oil in the sea between Korea and Japan.

Tourism is a growing industry, with 4,650,000 foreign visitors in 1999.

In 1999 there was a trade surplus of US$23,933 million and a current account surplus of US$25,000 million; imports totalled US$119,750 million and exports US$144,745 million. The USA, Japan, the EU and China are the main trading partners. Electronic products, machinery, metal goods, passenger vehicles, chemical products and fabric and clothing are the main exports. Electronic products, petroleum, machinery and chemical products are the main imports.

GNP – US$397,910 million (1999); US$8,490 per capita (1999)
GDP – US$442,543 million (1997); US$8,685 per capita (1999)
ANNUAL AVERAGE GROWTH OF GDP – 5.2 per cent (2000)
INFLATION RATE – 4.4 per cent (2001)
UNEMPLOYMENT – 4.2 per cent (2001)
TOTAL EXTERNAL DEBT – US$ 139,097 million (1998)

| *Trade with UK* | 1999 | 2000 |
|---|---|---|
| Imports from UK | £949,771,000 | £1,350,591,000 |
| Exports to UK | 2,912,110,000 | 3,515,312,000 |

## COMMUNICATIONS

In 1996, there were 3,120 km of railway, of which 577 km were electrified. A high-speed railway line is being constructed between Seoul and Pusan and there are plans to build high-speed rail links between Seoul and Mokp'o and Seoul and Kangnŭng. There were 82,342 km of roads, of which 1,885 km were motorways. There are international airports in Seoul (Kimpo), Kimhae (near Pusan), Taegu and Cheju city. An international airport is under construction at Inch'on. Korean Air and Asiana Airlines operate regular flights to Europe, the USA, the Middle East and south-east Asia. In 1999, 29 foreign airlines operated services to Seoul. Pusan and Inchon are the major ports with Pusan serving the industrial areas of the south-east. The port of Kwangyang is being expanded and a new container terminal is being constructed at

Kadokto. Inch'on, 28 miles from Seoul, serves the capital, but development and operation at Inch'on are hampered by a tidal variation of 9–10 metres.

By the end of 1999, there were 10 million internet users, 23.4 million mobile telephone subscribers and 9.4 million personal computers.

## EDUCATION

Primary education is compulsory for six years from the age of six. Secondary and higher education is extensive with the option of middle school to age 15 and high school to age 18. In 1997 there were 150 universities and colleges of higher education. There were 888 hospitals. Some 108 daily newspapers are published.

ILLITERACY RATE – 2.2 per cent (2000)

ENROLMENT (percentage of age group) – primary 93 per cent (1997); secondary 97 per cent (1996); tertiary 68 per cent (1997)

---

# KUWAIT

*Dawlat al-Kuwayt*

---

AREA – 6,880 sq. miles (17,818 sq. km). Neighbours: Iraq (north and west); Saudi Arabia (south and south-west)

POPULATION – 1,924,000 (1998 estimate): 41.6 per cent were Kuwaiti citizens, the remainder being other Arabs, Iranians, Indians and Pakistanis. The total Western population was 14,240. Islam is the official religion, though religious freedom is constitutionally guaranteed. The official language is Arabic, and English is widely spoken as a second language

CAPITAL – ΨKuwait City (Al-Kuwayt) (population, 388,663, 1998)

CURRENCY – Kuwaiti dinar (KD) of 1,000 fils

NATIONAL DAY – 25 February

NATIONAL FLAG – Three horizontal stripes of green, white and red, with black trapezoid next to staff

LIFE EXPECTANCY (years) – male 71.9; female 75.2

POPULATION GROWTH RATE – 1.3 per cent (1999)

POPULATION DENSITY – 114 per sq. km (1998)

URBAN POPULATION – 97.6 per cent (2000 estimate)

In 1993 the UN settled the dispute between Kuwait and Iraq, moving the border some few hundred metres northwards. Kuwait has since completed a 130-mile ditch, sand wall and barbed wire system along its border.

Kuwait has a dry, desert climate with summer extending from April to September. The mean temperature varies between 29–45°C in summer, and 8–18°C in winter. Humidity rarely exceeds 60 per cent except in July and August.

## HISTORY AND POLITICS

Although Kuwait had been independent for some years, the 'exclusive agreement' of 1899 between the Sheikh of Kuwait and the British government was formally abrogated by an exchange of letters dated 19 June 1961. Iraq invaded Kuwait on 2 August 1990 and it was liberated on 26 February 1991 by an alliance of Western and Arab forces. Iraq built up its armed forces on Kuwait's border in October 1994, until it was deterred by the arrival of US and British forces. Iraq formally recognised the sovereignty and territorial integrity of Kuwait as well as the UN-demarcated border in November 1994. Roughly 600 Kuwaitis are still held in Iraq.

The Amir dissolved the National Assembly on 4 May 1999; elections were held on 3 July 1999. Opposition Liberals won 16 and Islamists won 20 of the 50 seats. The government resigned on 28 January 2001 and a new Cabinet was appointed on 14 February, which included most of the members of the previous Cabinet.

### POLITICAL SYSTEM

Under the constitution legislative power is vested in the Amir and the 50-member National Assembly, and executive power in the Amir and the Cabinet. Following popular pressure after the liberation, elections for the National Assembly were held in October 1992. The electorate consists of all Kuwaiti male nationals over 21 whose families have lived in the Emirate since before 1921. There are no political parties.

There are five governorates: Capital, Hawallī, Ahmadī, Al-Jahrah and Al-Farwaniya.

### HEAD OF STATE

*HH The Amir of Kuwait*, Shaikh Jabir al-Ahmad al-Jabir al-Sabah, *born* 1928, *acceded* 31 December 1977

*Crown Prince*, HH Shaikh Saad al-Abdullah al-Salim al-Sabah

### CABINET *as at July 2001*

*Prime Minister*, HH The Crown Prince

*First Deputy Prime Minister, Foreign Affairs*, Shaikh Sabah al-Ahmed al-Jabir al-Sabah

*Deputy Prime Minister, Cabinet Affairs, National Assembly Affairs*, Mohammed Dhaif Allah Sharar

*Deputy Prime Minister, Defence*, Shaikh Jabir Mubarak al-Sabah

*Deputy Prime Minister, Interior*, Shaikh Mohammad Khaled al-Hamad al-Sabah

*Commerce and Industry*, Salah Abdel Reda Khorshed

*Communications*, Shaikh Ahmad Abdullah al-Sabah

*Education and Higher Education*, Musaed Rashed al-Haroun

*Electricity and Water, Labour and Social Affairs*, Talal Mubarak al-Ayyar

*Finance and Planning*, Yousif Hamad al-Ibrahim

*Foreign Affairs*, Shaikh Mohammad Sabah al-Sabah

*Health*, Dr Mohammad Ahmad al-Jara'Allah

*Information*, Shaikh Ahmad Fahad al-Sabah

*Justice, Awqaf and Islamic Affairs*, Ahmad Yacoub Baqer

*Oil*, Adel Khalid al-Subeeh

*Public Works, Housing Affairs*, Fahad al-Mai al-Azemi

### EMBASSY OF THE STATE OF KUWAIT

2 Albert Gate, London SW1X 7JU
Tel: 020-7590 3400

*Ambassador Extraordinary and Plenipotentiary*, HE Khaled al-Duwaisan, GCVO, apptd 1993

*Cultural Attaché*, Salah al-Mazidi

*Military Attaché*, Ibrahim al-Adwani

### BRITISH EMBASSY

PO Box 2, Safat, 13001 Kuwait
Tel: (00 965) 240 3334/5/6

*Ambassador Extraordinary and Plenipotentiary*, HE Richard Muir, CMG, apptd 1999

*Counsellor and Deputy Head of Mission*, B. E. Stewart

*First Secretaries*, J. Francis (*Management and Consul*); J. Clayton (*Commercial*)

*Defence Attaché*, Col. Hon. A. J. C. Campbell

BRITISH COUNCIL DIRECTOR, John Gildea, 2 Al Arabi Street, Block 2, PO Box 345, 13004 Safat, Mansouriya, Kuwait City; e-mail: bc.kuwait@kw.britishcouncil.org

## DEFENCE

The Army has 385 main battle tanks, 140 armoured personnel carriers and 355 armoured infantry fighting vehicles. The Navy has ten patrol and coastal vessels, based at Ras al-Qalaya. The Air Force has 82 combat aircraft and 20 armed helicopters.

The USA and UK station aircraft and support units in the country to patrol the air exclusion zone in southern Iraq.

MILITARY EXPENDITURE – 11.1 per cent of GDP (1999)
MILITARY PERSONNEL – 15,300: Army 11,000, Navy 1,800, Air Force 2,500, Paramilitaries 5,000
CONSCRIPTION DURATION - Two years

## ECONOMY

Despite the desert terrain, 8.4 per cent of land is under cultivation; tomatoes, onions, melons and dates are the main crops.

The oil industry is run by the Kuwait Petroleum Corporation. Oil installations were extensively damaged when Iraqi forces set light to oil wells prior to their retreat. Oil production was 107,600,000 tonnes in 1998.

There are four power stations capable of generating almost 7,000 MW of electricity. The country depends on desalination plants for its water supply. Both water and power facilities were heavily damaged during the war, although electricity and water distillation capacity were restored to pre-invasion levels in 1995.

The economy is heavily dependent on foreign labour. In 1998 the workforce comprised 211,559 Kuwaitis and 1,040,437 non-Kuwaitis.

GDP – US$30,368 million (1997); US$13,976 per capita (1998)
ANNUAL AVERAGE GROWTH OF GDP – 4.9 per cent (1996)
INFLATION RATE – 0.2 per cent (1998)
UNEMPLOYMENT – 0.4 per cent (1998)

### TRADE

Oil is the major export. Non-oil exports, mainly to Asian countries and the Indian sub-continent, have included chemical fertilisers, ammonia and other chemicals, metal pipes, shrimps and building materials. Re-exports to neighbouring states traditionally accounted for a major proportion of non-oil exports but were brought to a halt by the Iraqi invasion. Major trading partners are Japan, the USA, the UAE, Saudi Arabia and Western Europe.

In 1999 Kuwait had a trade surplus of US$5,571 million and a current account surplus of US$5,062 million. In 1998 imports totalled US$8,619 million and exports US$9,554 million.

| *Trade with UK* | 1999 | 2000 |
|---|---|---|
| Imports from UK | £301,971,000 | £346,934,000 |
| Exports to UK | 134,689,000 | 341,093,000 |

## COMMUNICATIONS

There is a network of dual-carriageway roads and more are under construction; there are 4,741 km of roads. Telecommunications and postal services are conducted by the government.

## SOCIAL WELFARE

The government invested its considerable oil revenues in comprehensive social services. Medical services are free to all residents. In 1998 there were 15 hospitals and 70 clinics. Education is free and compulsory from six to 14 years. In 1999 there were 969 schools (608 government-run, 322 private and 39 vocational) and one university.

ILLITERACY RATE – 17.7 per cent
ENROLMENT (percentage of age group) – primary 62 per cent (1996); secondary 61 per cent (1996); tertiary 19.3 per cent (1996)

# KYRGYZSTAN
*Kyrgyz Respublikasy*

AREA – 76,641 sq. miles (198,500 sq. km). Neighbours: Kazakhstan (north), China (east), Tajikistan (south and south-west), Uzbekistan (west)
POPULATION – 4,856,000 (2001 estimate): 52.4 per cent Kyrgyz (Turkic origin), 21.5 per cent Russian and 12.9 per cent Uzbek, with smaller numbers of Ukrainians, Germans, Tatars and Kazakhs. Islam is the main religion. Kyrgyz, the official language since independence, is a Turkic language, written in the Roman alphabet since 1992. Russian is an equal official language.
CAPITAL – Bishkek (population, 589,400, 1997 estimate; 616,000, 1989 census)
CURRENCY – Som of 100 tyin (introduced on 10 May 1993 at rate of 1:200 against the rouble)
NATIONAL DAY – 31 August (Independence Day)
NATIONAL FLAG – Red with a rayed sun containing a representation of a yurt, all in gold
LIFE EXPECTANCY (years) – male 61.6; female 69.0
POPULATION GROWTH RATE – 0.7 per cent (1999)
POPULATION DENSITY – 24 per sq. km (1998)
URBAN POPULATION – 33.3 per cent (2000 estimate)
MILITARY EXPENDITURE – 4.5 per cent of GDP (1999)
MILITARY PERSONNEL – 9,000: Army 6,600, Air Force 2,400, Paramilitaries 5,000
CONSCRIPTION DURATION – 18 months

Kyrgyzstan (formerly Kyrgyzia) is mountainous, the major part being covered by the ridge of the Central Tienshan, while the Pamir-Altai system occupies its southern part. There are a number of spacious mountain valleys, the Alai, Susamyr and others. Kyrgyzstan is divided into six administrative regions.

## HISTORY AND POLITICS

The Kyrgyz people were first mentioned in Chinese chronicles in the second millennium BC. They are a merger of two ethnic groups, a Turkic-speaking people driven into the area by the Mongols from the River Yenisei area of Central Asia, and indigenous peoples. After a long period under Mongol, Chinese and Persian rule, the Kyrgyz became part of the Russian Empire in the 1860s and 1870s. Kyrgyzstan became part of the Soviet Union in 1920 and underwent some industrialisation.

Kyrgyzstan declared independence just after the failed Moscow coup on 31 August 1991.

Ethnic tensions between the rural nomadic Kyrgyz, the urban Russians and the wealthy Uzbeks who own many businesses and form the majority in the second largest town of Osh, are never far from the surface.

A referendum on amendments to the constitution was held on 17 October 1998, which introduced private ownership of land.

Legislative elections were held on 20 February and 12 March 2000. The largest opposition parties were not allowed to take part on the grounds of supposed minor infractions of the electoral procedures, a decision which was criticised by observers from the Organisation for Security and Co-operation in Europe; their leaders were allowed to stand as independent candidates. The Communist party and the pro-government Union of Democratic Forces emerged as the largest parties. The results were widely condemned by opposition groups amid allegations of widespread electoral fraud.

The presidential election held on 29 October 2000 was won by the incumbent President Askar Akayev, who obtained 74.3 per cent of the votes cast, but the conduct of the poll was criticised by OSCE observers at the time of the election and later by the EU and the USA.

POLITICAL SYSTEM

The head of state is a president directly elected for a five-year term. There is a bicameral legislature composed of a 60-member Legislative Assembly and a 45-member People's Assembly, both of which serve for five-year terms. The president appoints the prime minister and the other members of the government. The Assembly of the People of Kyrgyzstan, which comprises the leaders of the republic's ethnic communities, was designated a consultative body in January 1997.

HEAD OF STATE

*President*, Askar Akayev, *elected* 12 October 1991, *re-elected* 24 December 1995, 29 October 2000

CABINET *as at July 2001*

*Prime Minister*, Kurmanbek Bakiyev
*First Deputy Prime Minister*, Nikolay Tanayev
*Deputy Prime Minister, Trade and Industry*, Arzymat Sulaymankulov
*Agriculture and Water Resources*, Aleksandr Kostyuk
*Communications Agency*, Andrei Titev
*Defence*, Lt.-Gen. Esen Topoyev
*Ecology and Emergencies*, Ratbek Ishmanbetov
*Education, Science and Culture*, Kamila Sharshekeyeva
*Finance*, Temirbek Akmataliyev
*Foreign Affairs*, Muratbek Imanaliyev
*Health*, Tilekbek Meymanaliyev
*Interior*, Tashtemir Aitbaev
*Justice*, Jakyp Abdyrahmanev
*Labour and Social Welfare*, Roza Aknazareva
*Local Government and Regional Development, Director of the State Agency for Registration of Real Estate Rights*, Tolebek Umaraliyev
*Management of State Property and Attraction of Direct Investment*, Nasreddin Biyenbekev
*National Security Council*, Bolot Dzhanuzakev
*Procurement and Material Reserves*, Tashkul Kereksizev
*Science and Copyright*, Roman Umorev
*Transport and Communications*, Kubanychbek Dzhumaliyev

EMBASSY OF THE KYRGYZ REPUBLIC
Ascot House, 119 Crawford Street, London W1H 1AF
Tel: 020-7935 1462
*Ambassador Extraordinary and Plenipotentiary*, HE Roza Otunbayeva, apptd 1997

BRITISH AMBASSADOR, HE Richard Lewington, resident at Almaty, Kazakhstan
BRITISH COUNCIL, 237 Panfilov Street, KS-720000 Bishkek; E-mail: bc@britcoun.elcat.kg

## ECONOMY

Agriculture is the main sector of the economy, with sugar beet, grain and sheep the main products. Private ownership of land was legalised in 1997. Industry is concentrated in the food-processing, textiles, timber and mining fields. Since 1992, some 60 per cent of state-owned enterprises have been privatised. Hydroelectric power is abundant and Kyrgyzstan has reserves of gold, coal, mercury and uranium, although only gold has so far been exploited and is the country's largest export.

The president and government have made the Central Bank independent of government and parliamentary control. In March 1996, a treaty was signed with Belarus, Kazakhstan and Russia enhancing economic co-operation and working towards a single customs territory and in December 2000 an agreement was signed with Russia on the joint production of uranium and non-ferrous and precious metals.

In 1998 there was a trade deficit of US$221 million and a current account deficit of US$371 million. In 1999 imports totalled US$600 million and exports US$454 million.

GNP – US$1,465 million (1999); US$300 per capita (1999)
GDP – US$1,753 million (1997); US$366 per capita (1998)
ANNUAL AVERAGE GROWTH OF GDP – 3.6 per cent (1998)
INFLATION RATE – 35.9 per cent (1999)
TOTAL EXTERNAL DEBT – US$1,148 million (1998)

| *Trade with UK* | 1999 | 2000 |
|---|---|---|
| Imports from UK | £2,494,000 | £4,297,000 |
| Exports to UK | 10,000 | 112,000 |

## CULTURE AND EDUCATION

Until the 1930s the Kyrgyz language had an oral tradition of literature which included the epic poem *Manas*, which tells the history of the Kyrgyz people. Internationally, one of the best-known writers of the former Soviet Union is the Kyrgyz writer Chingiz Aitmatov (1928–).

ENROLMENT (percentage of age group) – primary 95 per cent (1996); tertiary 11.9 per cent (1996)

---

# LAOS

*Satharanarath Pasathipatai Pasason Lao*

---

AREA – 91,429 sq. miles (236,800 sq. km). Neighbours: China (north), Vietnam (north-east and east), Cambodia (south), Thailand (west), Myanmar (north-west)
POPULATION – 5,097,000 (1995 census): 68 per cent Lao Loum (lowland Lao), 22 per cent Lao Theung (upland Lao), 9 per cent Lao Soung (highland Lao, including Hmong and Yau). Lao is the official language; French and English are spoken
CAPITAL – Vientiane (population, 132,253, 1966; 120,000, 1984 estimate)
CURRENCY – Kip (K) of 100 at
NATIONAL ANTHEM - Pheng xat Lao (Laos national anthem)
NATIONAL DAY – 2 December
NATIONAL FLAG – Blue background with a central white circle, framed by two horizontal red stripes
LIFE EXPECTANCY (years) – male 54.0; female 56.6
POPULATION GROWTH RATE – 2.7 per cent (1999)
POPULATION DENSITY – 22 per sq. km (1998)
URBAN POPULATION – 23.5 per cent (2000 estimate)
MILITARY EXPENDITURE – 2.3 per cent of GDP (1999)
MILITARY PERSONNEL – 29,100: Army 25,000, Navy 600, Air Force 3,500; Paramilitaries 100,000
CONSCRIPTION DURATION – 18 months minimum
ILLITERACY RATE – 38.2 per cent
ENROLMENT (percentage of age group) – primary 72 per cent (1996); secondary 22 per cent (1996); tertiary 2.8 per cent (1996)

## HISTORY AND POLITICS

The kingdom of Lane Xang, the Land of a Million Elephants, was founded in the 14th century but broke up at the beginning of the 16th century into the separate kingdoms of Luang Prabang and Vientiane and the principality of Champassac, which together came under French protection in 1893. In 1945 the Japanese staged a coup and suppressed the French administration. In 1947 Laos became a constitutional monarchy under King Sisvang Vong, and an independent sovereign state in 1953. The next 22 years in Laos were marked by power struggles and civil war, eventually won by the North

Vietnamese-backed Pathet Lao, a Communist-dominated organisation.

The Lao People's Democratic Republic was proclaimed in December 1975 following victory by the Pathet Lao and the abdication of the King. A president and Council of Ministers were installed, and a 45-member Supreme People's Council was appointed to draft a constitution, which was approved in 1991. The Lao People's Revolutionary Party (LPRP) is the sole legal political organisation. A general election to the enlarged 99-member National Assembly was held on 21 December 1997; all the candidates were approved by the LPRP. The president, prime minister and Council of Ministers were confirmed in their posts by the National Assembly on 24 February 1998.

### HEAD OF STATE

*President*, Gen. Khamtay Siphandone, *elected by the National Assembly* 24 February 1998
*Vice-President*, Choummali Saignason

### COUNCIL OF MINISTERS *as at July 2001*

*Prime Minister*, Bounnyang Vorachit
*Deputy PMs*, Somsavat Lengsavad (*Foreign Affairs*); Thongloun Sisoulit (*State Planning Committee*)
*Agriculture and Forestry*, Siene Saphangthong
*Commerce and Tourism*, Phoumy Thipphavone
*Communications, Transport, Posts and Construction*, Bouathong Vonglokham
*Defence*, Maj.-Gen. Douangchay Phichit
*Education*, Phimmasone Leuangkhamma
*Finance*, Soukhan Mahalat
*Industry and Handicrafts*, Soulivong Daravong
*Information and Culture*, Phandouangchit Vongsa
*Interior*, Gen. Asang Laoly
*Justice*, Khamouane Boupha
*Labour and Social Welfare*, Somphan Phengkhammy
*Ministers attached to Prime Minister*, Somphavan Inthavong; Somphong Mongkhonvilai; Souly Nanthavong; Bountiam Phitsamai; Saisenglee Tengbliavue
*Permanent Secretary of the President's Office*, Souban Salitthilat
*Public Health*, Ponemek Daraloy

EMBASSY OF THE LAO PEOPLE'S DEMOCRATIC REPUBLIC
74 Avenue Raymond-Poincaré F-75116 Paris
Tel: (00 33) (1) 4553 0298
*Ambassador Extraordinary and Plenipotentiary*, HE Kamphan Simmalavong, apptd 1996

BRITISH AMBASSADOR, HE Lloyd Barnaby Smith, CMG, resident at Bangkok, Thailand

## ECONOMY

A 'new economic mechanism' programme was introduced in 1986 which began the liberalisation of the economy. These reforms have produced a market-orientated economic system which has increased growth and reduced inflation. The economy is dominated by the agricultural sector, which employs about three-quarters of the workforce and contributed 53 per cent of real GDP in 1998. The seventh congress of the LPRP held in March 2001 defined the principal economic goal to be agricultural development. Although Laos is one of the poorest states in the world, there is potential for increased hydroelectric power exports to Thailand and there are deposits of coal, tin, iron ore, gold, bauxite and lignite. Foreign capital investment in infrastructure began with the 1994 opening of the Friendship Bridge over the Mekong river border with Thailand which links road routes from Singapore to China. Clothing, wood and wood products, electricity, coffee and agricultural products are the main exports.

In 1998 Laos had a trade deficit of US$165 million and a current account deficit of US$150 million. In 1999 imports totalled US$525 million and exports US$311 million.

GNP – US$1,476 million (1999); US$280 per capita (1999)
GDP – US$1,753 million (1997); US$250 per capita (1998)
ANNUAL AVERAGE GROWTH OF GDP – 6.9 per cent (1996)
INFLATION RATE – 128.4 per cent (1999)
TOTAL EXTERNAL DEBT – US$2,437 million (1998)

| *Trade with UK* | 1999 | 2000 |
|---|---|---|
| Imports from UK | £4,840,000 | £3,517,000 |
| Exports to UK | 8,514,000 | 5,145,000 |

# LATVIA
*Latvijas Republika*

AREA – 24,942 sq. miles (64,600 sq. km). Neighbours: Estonia (north), Lithuania and Belarus (south), the Russian Federation (east)
POPULATION – 2,430,000 (1997 UN estimate): 55.3 per cent Latvian, 32.5 per cent Russian, 4.0 per cent Belarusian, with small Ukrainian and Polish minorities. The main religions are Lutheran, Roman Catholic and Russian Orthodox. The official language is Latvian; Russian is also spoken. Education is in Latvian and Russian. Public sector employees must pass language tests in Latvian to a level commensurate with the nature of their employment. The right of minorities to use their mother tongue has been acknowledged
CAPITAL – Riga (population, 805,997, 1998 estimate)
MAJOR CITIES – Daugavpils (117,502); Jelgava (70,962); Jūrmala (58,977); Liepāja (97,278); Ventspils (46,564), 1998 estimates
CURRENCY – Lats of 100 santims
NATIONAL ANTHEM – Dievs, svētī Latviju (God bless Latvia)
NATIONAL DAY – 18 November (Independence Day 1918)
NATIONAL FLAG – Crimson, with a white horizontal stripe across the centre
LIFE EXPECTANCY (years) – male 63.6; female 74.6
POPULATION GROWTH RATE – 1.3 per cent (1999)
POPULATION DENSITY – 38 per sq. km (1998)
URBAN POPULATION – 69.0 per cent (2000 estimate)

## HISTORY AND POLITICS

Latvia came under the control of the German Teutonic Knights at the end of the 13th century. During the next few centuries the country endured sporadic invasions by the Swedes, Poles and Russians. By 1795 Latvia was entirely under Russian control. On 18 November 1918, Latvia declared its independence, but was annexed by the Soviet Union in 1940 under the terms of the Molotov–Ribbentrop pact with Germany. Latvia was invaded and occupied when Germany invaded the Soviet Union during the Second World War but recaptured by the Soviet Union in 1944.

In 1988 the Popular Front of Latvia was formed to campaign for greater sovereignty and democracy for Latvia. It won the elections to the Supreme Council in 1989, and on 4 May 1990 the Supreme Council declared the independent republic of Latvia to be, *de jure*, still in existence. A national referendum was held in March 1991 in which 73 per cent voted in favour of independence, and this was declared on 21 August 1991. The State Council of the Soviet Union recognised the independence of Latvia on 10 September 1991.

The last Russian military base in the Baltic states at Skrunda was handed back to Latvian control in 1999.

The general election of 3 October 1998 resulted in the People's Party gaining the most seats, but a coalition of Latvia's Way, the Union for Fatherland and Freedom and the New Party formed a government on 26 November. The Latvian Social Democratic Union joined the coalition on 4 February 1999 and the New Party left the government on 5 February 2001.

## POLITICAL SYSTEM

Executive authority is vested in a prime minister and Cabinet of Ministers. Legislative power is exercised by the unicameral parliament (*Saeima*), which comprises 100 deputies elected for four-year terms by proportional representation, with a 5 per cent threshold for parliamentary representation. The deputies elect a president of state, serving for four years, who in turn appoints the prime minister. The prime minister appoints, and the Saeima approves, the Cabinet of Ministers.

The electorate and citizenship had been restricted to descendants of Latvian citizens before the 1940 Soviet occupation and to those who could pass the required Latvian language tests, until 1994 when a law was passed enabling naturalisation of long-term residents. In October 1998 a referendum to amend the citizenship law was passed which granted citizenship to those children born in Latvia after Latvian independence if their parents requested it and provided for simpler language tests for older residents.

## HEAD OF STATE

*President*, Vaira Vīķe-Freiberga, *elected* 17 June 1999, *sworn in* 8 July 1999

## CABINET *as at July 2001*

*Prime Minister*, Andris Berzins (LC)
*Agriculture*, Atis Slakteris (TP)
*Culture*, Karīna Pētersone (LC)
*Defence*, Ģirts Valdis Kristovskis (TB)
*Economy*, Aigars Kalvitis (TP)
*Education and Science*, Karlis Greiskalns (TP)
*Environment and Regional Development*, Vladimir Makarov (TB)
*Finance*, Gundars Bērziņš (TP)
*Foreign Affairs*, Indulis Bērziņš (LC)
*Interior*, Mareks Segliņš (TP)
*Justice*, Ingrida Labucka
*Special Tasks Minister for Co-operation with International Financial Institutions*, Roberts Zīle (TB)
*Special Tasks Minister for State Administration and Local Government*, Janis Krumins (LC)
*Transport*, Anatolijs Gorbunovs (LC)
*Welfare*, Andrejs Pozarnovs (TB)

TB Union For Fatherland and Freedom; LC Latvia's Way; TP People's Party

## EMBASSY OF THE REPUBLIC OF LATVIA

45 Nottingham Place, London W1M 3FE
Tel: 020-7312 0040
*Ambassador Extraordinary and Plenipotentiary*, HE Normans Penke, apptd 1997

## BRITISH EMBASSY

5, J. Alunana Street, Riga LV-1010
Tel: (00 371) (7) 33 8126-30
E-mail: british.embassy@apollo.lv
*Ambassador Extraordinary and Plenipotentiary*, HE Stephen Nash, CMG, apptd 1999

BRITISH COUNCIL DIRECTOR, Ian Stewart, 5a Blaumana iela, Riga LV-1011; e-mail: mail@britishcouncil.lv

BRITISH LATVIA CHAMBER OF COMMERCE, 3rd floor, Kr. Valdemara Iela 34/8, LV-1010 Riga

## DEFENCE

The Army has three main battle tanks, 13 armoured personnel carriers, the Navy has nine patrol craft at three bases and the Air Force has 19 aircraft and four helicopters.

Russian forces withdrew from Latvia in 1994.

MILITARY EXPENDITURE – 1.0 per cent of GDP (1999)
MILITARY PERSONNEL – 5,050; Army 2,400, Navy 840, Air Force 210, Paramilitaries 3,500
CONSCRIPTION DURATION – 12 months

## ECONOMY

Attempts to move from a command economy to a market economy resulted in low growth and high unemployment in the early 1990s, though economic reforms have begun to show results. By 2001, 97 per cent of previously state-owned enterprises had either been privatised or were assigned for privatisation, and privatised companies accounted for 66 per cent of GDP. A number of energy and telecommunications enterprises were due to be privatised in 2001.

Latvia is an agricultural exporter, specialising in cattle and pig breeding, dairy farming and crops, including sugar beet, flax, cereals and potatoes. In 2000, 16.7 per cent of the population were employed in agriculture, which accounted for 3.4 per cent of GDP. Natural resources include limestone, gypsum, peat and timber.

Industry is specialised in certain areas including the production of food and beverages, motor vehicles, textiles and timber and paper products.

Tourism is being developed, capitalising on Latvia's beach resorts, nature reserves and parks. Latvia is also geographically well-placed for the development of transport services.

GNP – US$5,913 million (1999); US$2,470 per capita (1999)
GDP – US$5,527 million (1997); US$2,638 per capita (1998)

Annual Average Growth of GDP – 5.9 per cent (2000)
Inflation Rate – 1.8 per cent (2000)
Unemployment – 9.1 per cent (1999)
Total External Debt – US$850 million (1999)

### Trade

In 1996, a free trade regime was agreed with the EU and EFTA. The main imports are machinery, chemical goods and transport vehicles, and the main exports are wood and wood products, textiles and base metals and metallic products. The most important import partners are Germany, Russia, Lithuania, Finland and Sweden. The most important export partners are Germany, the UK, Sweden, Lithuania and Denmark.

In 1999 there was a trade deficit of US$1,027 million and a current account deficit of US$641 million. Imports totalled US$2,945 million and exports US$1,723 million.

| *Trade with UK* | 1999 | 2000 |
|---|---|---|
| Imports from UK | £71,153,000 | £84,313,000 |
| Exports to UK | 269,511,000 | 403,396,000 |

## COMMUNICATIONS

Latvia has 2,413 km of railways and some 20,400 km of roads. Many of the exports from former CIS states are transported to Western Europe via Latvia. Latvia is also being developed as a transportation route from Scandinavia to central and southern Europe. Several warm-water ports exist, of which three, Riga, Ventspils and Liepāja, are developed for commercial transport. The national airline, Air Baltic, operates regular flights to Scandinavia and Europe.

## CULTURE AND EDUCATION

The Latvian language belongs to the Baltic branch of the Indo-European languages. The Latin alphabet is used. Latvian literature appeared in the 19th century and played a role in the fight for independence in 1918.

There are 27 higher education institutions, of which five are universities.

Illiteracy Rate – 0.3 per cent (2000)
Enrolment (percentage of age group) – primary 89 per cent (1996); secondary 79 per cent (1996); tertiary 33.3 per cent (1996)

---

# LEBANON
*Al-Jumhūriyya al-Lubnāniyya*

---

Area – 4,015 sq. miles (10,400 sq. km). Neighbours: Syria (north and east), Israel (south)
Population – 4,271,000 (1997 UN estimate): 32 per cent Shi'ite Muslim; 21 per cent Sunni Muslim, 40 per cent Christian, 7 per cent Druze. Arabic is the official language, and French and English are also widely used
Capital – ΨBeirut (Bayrūt) (population, 1,500,000, 1991)
Major Cities – ΨSaydā (Sidon) (100,000); Ψ Tarābulus (Tripoli) (200,000); Ψ Sūr (Tyre) (70,000)
Currency – Lebanese pound (L£) of 100 piastres
National Anthem – Kulluna Lil Watan Lil'ula Lil'alam (We all belong to the homeland)
National Day – 22 November
National Flag – Horizontal bands of red, white and red with a green cedar of Lebanon in the centre of the white band
Life Expectancy (years) – male 66.2; female 67.3
Population Growth Rate – 2.7 per cent (1999)
Population Density – 307 per sq. km (1999)
Urban Population – 89.7 per cent (2000 estimate)

## HISTORY AND POLITICS

Lebanon became an independent state in 1920, administered under French mandate until 22 November 1943. Powers were transferred to the Lebanese government from January 1944 and French troops were withdrawn in 1946.

In 1975, fighting broke out in Beirut between Maronite, Sunni and Shia factions, the latter supported by Palestinian guerrillas based in Lebanon; fighting continued until the end of the civil war in 1990. In 1982 Israeli forces invaded and in 1985 established a buffer zone along the Israeli–Lebanon border controlled by the South Lebanon Army (SLA), a Christian militia.

A new government incorporating the main militia leaders was formed in December 1990. Since 1993 the Lebanese Army has deployed in southern villages alongside UNIFIL forces but has not disarmed Hezbollah forces, who are financed, armed and trained by Syria and Iran.

The Israeli Prime Minister Ehud Barak had committed himself to the withdrawal of Israeli forces from the buffer zone during his election campaign in May 1999 and Israel began its withdrawal in mid-May 2000, initially handing over their positions to the SLA, but a mass movement of exiled civilians, led by Hezbollah forces, effectively routed the SLA. The last Israeli troops left on 24 May 2000 and the SLA troops surrendered to the Lebanese authorities or fled to Israel.

Syrian forces remain in west Beirut and in the north and the east of the country.

The first parliamentary elections since 1972 were held in 1992 and local elections were held in 1998. The general election held on 27 August and 3 September 2000 was won by supporters of Rafik Hariri, who had previously been prime minister between 1992 and 1998. Hariri was appointed prime minister by President Lahoud on 23 October 2000 and named his Cabinet, composed equally of Christians and Muslims, on 26 October.

### Foreign Relations

Resentment has been growing among Christians at the continuing presence of Syrian troops. There has also been tension on the border between Lebanon and Israel over the disputed Shebaa Farms, a 25-sq. km region located between Lebanon, Israel and the Israeli-occupied Golan Heights, which remained under Israeli control following the Israeli withdrawal from southern Lebanon.

### Political System

The National Covenant (1943) is characterised by the division of power between the religious communities. The executive comprises the president, prime minister and Cabinet. The president is elected by the National Assembly for a non-renewable term of six years and must be a Maronite Christian. The prime minister is appointed following consultation between the president and National Assembly and must be a Sunni Muslim. The 128-member unicameral National Assembly comprises equal numbers of Christians and Muslims although the speaker must be a Shia Muslim. Political parties are banned. There are six governorates divided into 26 districts.

The constitution was amended on 15 October 1998 to allow the election of Gen. Lahoud as president. Serving state officials had previously been prohibited from standing for the presidency.

### Head of State

*President of the Republic of Lebanon*, Gen. Émile Lahoud, *elected* 15 October 1998, *sworn in* 24 November 1998

CABINET *as at July 2001*

*Prime Minister*, Rafiq Hariri
*Deputy PM*, Issam Fares
*Agriculture*, Ali Abdallah
*Culture*, Ghassan Salameh
*Displaced Persons*, Marwan Hamadeh
*Economy and Trade*, Basil Fleihan
*Education and Higher Education*, Abdel Rahim Mrad
*Energy and Water Resources*, Mohammad Abdel Hamid Baydoun
*Environment*, Michel Musa
*Finance*, Fouad Siniora
*Foreign Affairs*, Mahmoud Hammud
*Industry*, Georges Frem
*Information*, Ghazi el-Aridi
*Interior and Municipal Affairs*, Elias Murr
*Justice*, Samir Jisr
*Labour*, Ali Kanso
*Ministers of State*, Talal Arslan; Nazih Baydoun; Pierre Helou; Beshara Merhej; Michel Pharaon; Fouad Saad (*Administrative Reform*); Bahij Tabbarah
*National Defence*, Khalil Hrawi
*Post and Telecommunications*, Jean-Louis Qordahi
*Public Health*, Soleiman Franjieh
*Public Works and Transport*, Najib Miqati
*Social Affairs*, Assaad Diab
*Tourism*, Karam Karam
*Youth and Sports*, Sebouh Hovnanian

LEBANESE EMBASSY

21 Kensington Palace Gardens, London W8 4QM
Tel: 020-7229 7265/7727 6696
*Ambassador Extraordinary and Plenipotentiary*, HE Jihad Mortada, apptd 1999

BRITISH EMBASSY

Autostrade Jal El Dib, Coolrite Building (PO Box 60180), Beirut
Tel: (00 961) (4) 715 900–03
E-mail: britemb@cyberia.net.lb
*Ambassador Extraordinary and Plenipotentiary*, HE Richard Kinchen, apptd 2001

BRITISH COUNCIL DIRECTOR, Dr Ken Churchill, OBE, Sidani Street, Azar Building, Beirut; e-mail: general.enquiries@lb.britishcouncil.org

## DEFENCE

The Army has 327 main battle tanks and 1,338 armoured personnel carriers. The Navy has seven patrol and coastal vessels at two bases. There are a 5,619-strong UN peacekeeping force, 22,000 Syrian troops and 150 Iranian Revolutionary Guards operating in Lebanon.

MILITARY EXPENDITURE – 3.4 per cent of GDP (1999)
MILITARY PERSONNEL – 63,570: Army 60,670, Navy 1,200, Air Force 1,700, Paramilitaries 13,000
CONSCRIPTION DURATION – 12 months

## ECONOMY

Fruits are the most important products and include citrus fruit, apples, grapes, bananas and olives. There is some light industry, mostly for the production of consumer goods, but most factories are still in need of reconstruction because of the civil war.

A ten-year plan has been initiated to repair war damage and to restore Lebanon's position as a regional financial services and light industrial centre. The 1993–2002 reconstruction plan is estimated to cost US$12,900 million, of which US$7,600 million is to come from foreign loans and grants and US$5,300 million from budget surpluses. It is to concentrate on rebuilding housing, transport, services, education and health services, and aiding industry and agriculture.

GNP – US$15,796 million (1999); US$3,700 per capita (1999)
GDP – US$14,289 million (1997); US$1,668 per capita (1998)
ANNUAL AVERAGE GROWTH OF GDP – 4.0 per cent (1996)
INFLATION RATE – 6.8 per cent (1994)
TOTAL EXTERNAL DEBT – US$6,725 million (1998)

TRADE

Principal imports are foodstuffs, machinery and electrical equipment, vehicles, chemical products, mineral ores, and metals and metal products. There is a free trade agreement with Syria.

Principal exports include foodstuffs, chemical products, jewellery, machinery and electrical goods, textiles, metals and metal products, paper and paper products, and vehicles.

At one time there was a considerable transit trade through Beirut into the Arab hinterland. Lebanon is the terminal for two oil pipelines, one formerly belonging to the Iraq Petroleum Company, debouching at Tripoli, the other belonging to the Trans Arabian Pipeline Company, at Sidon. These lines have not functioned for some years.

In 1999 imports totalled US$6,207 million and exports US$677 million.

| *Trade with UK* | 1999 | 2000 |
|---|---|---|
| Imports from UK | £157,023,000 | £140,852,000 |
| Exports to UK | 17,121,000 | 16,540,000 |

## COMMUNICATIONS

There are 7,370 km of roads, of which 6,265 km are paved; there is 222 km of railway track. There is an international airport at Beirut, served by the national carrier Middle East Airlines and other airlines. An internal service operates from Beirut to Tripoli.

## EDUCATION

There are 13 universities in Lebanon, among them the American and the French universities, and the Lebanese National University, the Beirut University College, the Kaslik Saint Esprit University and the Arab University in Beirut, with the University of Balamand situated near Tripoli. There are also ten other institutions of higher education and an Academy of Fine Arts. There are several institutions for vocational training, and there is a good provision throughout the country of primary and secondary schools, among which are a great number of private schools.

ILLITERACY RATE – 13.9 per cent
ENROLMENT (percentage of age group) – primary 76 per cent (1996); tertiary 27.0 per cent (1996)

---

# LESOTHO
*'Muso oa Lesotho*

---

AREA – 11,720 sq. miles (30,355 sq. km). Neighbour: South Africa, which completely surrounds Lesotho
POPULATION – 2,105,000 (1997 UN estimate). The languages are Sesotho and English
CAPITAL – Maseru (population, 367,000, 1992 estimate)
CURRENCY – Loti (M) of 100 lisente. The South African rand is also legal tender
NATIONAL ANTHEM – Pina ea Sechaba
NATIONAL DAY – 4 October (Independence Day)

NATIONAL FLAG – Diagonally white over blue over green with the white of double width, and an assegai and knobkerrie on a Basotho shield in brown in the upper hoist
LIFE EXPECTANCY (years) – male 44.1; female 45.1
POPULATION GROWTH RATE – 2.3 per cent (1999)
POPULATION DENSITY – 68 per sq. km (1998)
URBAN POPULATION – 28.0 per cent (2000 estimate)
MILITARY EXPENDITURE – 4.2 per cent of GDP (1999)
MILITARY PERSONNEL – Army 2,000

## HISTORY AND POLITICS

Lesotho (formerly Basutoland) became a constitutional monarchy within the Commonwealth on 4 October 1966. The constitution was suspended in 1970 and the country was governed by a Council of Ministers until the establishment of a National Assembly in 1974.

Leabua Jonathan's government was overthrown in 1986, and executive and legislative powers were conferred on the King. Elections were held in March 1993 and the Basotho Congress Party (BCP) won all 65 seats in the new National Assembly. A BCP government led by Ntsu Mokhele was formed and King Letsie III swore allegiance to a new multiparty democratic constitution .

On 17 August 1994 King Letsie III and sections of the military mounted a coup attempt, but after mediation, the government, which had refused to leave office, was restored by the King. King Letsie also announced his intention to abdicate in favour of his father, Moshoeshoe II, who was restored on 25 January 1995. When King Moshoeshoe II died in a car crash on 15 January 1996, King Letsie III again ascended to the throne.

At the last legislative elections in May 1998, the Lesotho Congress for Democracy won 78 of the 80 seats in the National Assembly. Allegations of electoral fraud, later confirmed by an investigation which said that the election had been marred by irregularities, but that there were insufficient grounds to annul the poll, led to violent protests, which began in August; there were also reports of an alleged army mutiny. The deteriorating situation led to the intervention of South African and Botswanan military forces on 22 September to restore order after a request by the prime minister, Bethuel Pakalitha Mosisili; they withdrew in May 1999.

An Interim Political Authority (IPA) was created in 1998 to enable a new election to be held, free of irregularities. It announced in September 1999 that the first-past-the-post electoral system would be replaced by a new system incorporating a degree of proportional representation and that the number of seats in the National Assembly would be increased by 50 to 130. The general election that had been due in April 2000, was postponed by the IPA to May 2001, and then to early 2002.

On 3 April 2000, the government announced the establishment of a commission of enquiry into the political unrest that had followed the May 1998 general election. Several opposition parties announced that they would boycott the commission.

The country is divided into ten administrative districts. In each district there is a district secretary who co-ordinates all government activity in the area, working in co-operation with hereditary chiefs.

### HEAD OF STATE

HM The King of Lesotho, King Letsie III, *acceded* February 1996, *crowned* 31 October 1997

### COUNCIL OF MINISTERS *as at July 2001*

*Prime Minister, Defence, Public Service*, Bethuel Pakalitha Mosisili
*Deputy Prime Minister, Finance and Development Planning*, Kelebone Albert Maope
*Agriculture*, Vova Bulane
*Education and Manpower Development*, Lesao Lehohla
*Environment, Women, Youth Affairs*, Mathabiso Lepono
*Foreign Affairs*, Motsoahae Thomas Thabane
*Health and Social Welfare*, Tefo Mabote
*Home Affairs, Local Government*, Mopshatla Mabitle
*Industry, Trade and Marketing*, Mpho Malie
*Information, Broadcasting, Post and Telecommunications*, Nyane Mphafi
*Justice, Human Rights, Law and Constitutional Affairs, Rehabilitation*, Shakhane Robong Mokhehle
*Labour and Employment*, Not'si Molopo
*Natural Resources*, Monyane Moleleki
*Prime Minister's Office*, Sephiri Motanyane
*Tourism, Sports and Culture*, Hlalele Motaung
*Works and Transport*, Mofelehetsi Moerane

HIGH COMMISSION FOR THE KINGDOM OF LESOTHO
7 Chesham Place, London SW1 8HN
Tel: 020-7235 5686
E-mail: lesotholondonhighcom@compuserve.com
*High Commissioner*, HE Lebohang Ramohlanka, apptd 2000

### BRITISH HIGH COMMISSION

PO Box Ms 521, Maseru 100
Tel: (00 266) 313961
E-mail: hcmaseru@lesoff.co.za
*High Commissioner*, HE Kaye Oliver, CMG, OBE, apptd 1999

BRITISH COUNCIL DIRECTOR, Paul Feeney, Hobson's Square, PO Box 429, Maseru 100; e-mail: paul.feeney@britishcouncil.org.ls

## ECONOMY

The economy is based on agriculture and animal husbandry, and the adverse balance of trade (mainly consumer and capital goods) is offset by the earnings of the large numbers of the population who work in South Africa. Apart from some diamonds, Lesotho has few natural resources. Agriculture contributes 11 per cent of GDP and the main crops are maize, sorghum and vegetables. Industry contributes 42 per cent and services 47 per cent of GDP. The Lesotho National Development Corporation was set up to promote the development of industry, mining, trade and tourism; a number of light manufacturing and processing industries have recently been established. The main sources of revenue are customs and excise duty.

In 1998 Lesotho had a trade deficit of US$673 million and a current account deficit of US$280 million. Imports totalled US$863 million and exports US$194 million.GNP – US$1,158 million (1999); US$550 per capita (1999)
GDP – US$1,018 million (1997); US$425 per capita (1998)
ANNUAL AVERAGE GROWTH OF GDP – 10.0 per cent (1996)
INFLATION RATE – 7.3 per cent (1999)
TOTAL EXTERNAL DEBT – US$692 million (1998)

| *Trade with UK* | 1999 | 2000 |
|---|---|---|
| Imports from UK | £755,000 | £313,000 |
| Exports to UK | — | 828,000 |

## COMMUNICATIONS

A tarred road links Maseru to several of the main lowland towns, and this is being extended in the south of the country. The mountainous areas are linked by tarred, gravelled and earth roads and tracks. Roads link border towns in South Africa with the main towns in Lesotho. Maseru is also connected by rail with the main Bloemfontein–Natal line of the South African Railways. Scheduled international air services are operated daily between Maseru and Johannesburg, and other scheduled international flights are to Gaborone, Harare, Manzini and Maputo. There are around 30 airstrips. Internal scheduled services are operated by the Lesotho Airways Corporation.

The telephone network is fully automated in all urban centres. Radio telephone communication is used extensively in the remote rural areas.

## EDUCATION

Most schools are mission-controlled, the government providing grants for salaries and buildings. There are over 1,200 primary and over 180 secondary schools, with emphasis being laid on agricultural and vocational education. The National University of Lesotho at Roma was established as a university in 1975.

ILLITERACY RATE – 16.1 per cent

ENROLMENT (percentage of age group) – primary 70 per cent (1996); secondary 18 per cent (1996); tertiary 2.4 per cent (1996)

---

# LIBERIA

*Republic of Liberia*

---

AREA – 43,000 sq. miles (111,369 sq. km). Neighbours: Guinea (north), Côte d'Ivoire (east), Sierra Leone (north-west)

POPULATION – 3,044,000 (1997 UN estimate). The official language is English. The main African languages are Bassa, Kpelle and Kru, though some 16 ethnic languages are spoken

CAPITAL – ΨMonrovia (population, 1,000,000, 1993 estimate

MAJOR CITIES – ΨBuchanan (Grand Bassa); ΨGreenville (Sinoe); ΨHarper (Cape Palmas)

CURRENCY – Liberian dollar (L$) of 100 cents

NATIONAL ANTHEM – All Hail, Liberia, Hail

NATIONAL DAY – 26 July

NATIONAL FLAG – Alternate horizontal stripes (five white, six red), with five-pointed white star on blue field in upper corner next to flagstaff

LIFE EXPECTANCY (years) – male 42.5; female 44.9

POPULATION GROWTH RATE – 1.4 per cent (1999)

POPULATION DENSITY – 24 per sq. km (1998)

URBAN POPULATION – 44.9 per cent (2000 estimate)

MILITARY EXPENDITURE – 5.6 per cent of GDP (1999)

MILITARY PERSONNEL – 11,000 (including militias supporting government forces)

ILLITERACY RATE – 46.6 per cent

## HISTORY AND POLITICS

Liberia was founded by the American Colonisation Society in 1822 as a colony for freed American slaves, and has been recognised since 1847 as an independent state.

William V. S. Tubman, President since 1944, died in 1971 and was succeeded by Dr Tolbert. The constitution was suspended following a military coup in 1980 during which Tolbert was killed. M/Sgt. Samuel Doe assumed power as chairman of a military council. A new constitution was endorsed by a referendum in 1984. Doe and his party, the National Democratic Party of Liberia (NDPL) won the elections held in 1985. Doe was killed in 1990 and civil war ensued. A cease-fire was declared in August 1993 and a council of state governed the country until a general election was held in July 1997, which was won by the National Patriotic Party (NPP), and Charles Taylor was elected president with 75 per cent of the vote in an election deemed free and fair by international observers.

### CIVIL WAR

A rebel incursion in 1989 by the National Patriotic Front of Liberia (NPFL) led by Charles Taylor developed into a full-scale civil war in 1990. A five-nation Economic Community of West African States (ECOWAS) peace-keeping force (known as ECOMOG) landed in Monrovia in an effort to end the conflict but in September 1990 President Doe was killed, having refused to step down.

The Interim Government of National Unity (IGNU) was formed in August 1990. A peace agreement was signed by the IGNU, NPFL and another rebel group, ULIMO, on 25 July 1993, which brought about a cease-fire on 1 August.

In August 1999, President Taylor ordered a state of emergency after rebels from the Joint Forces for the Liberation of Liberia crossed the border from Guinea and briefly seized several towns. In September 1999, Guinea accused Liberia of attacking three Guinean villages, a charge that the Liberian authorities denied. Following talks arranged by Nigeria in September, a commission was established to consider the security problems between Liberia and Guinea.

In July 2000, the USA threatened Liberia with international sanctions if it continued to support insurgency in Sierra Leone.

Liberia accused Guinea of supporting an attack by Liberians United for Reconciliation and Democracy (LURD) rebels on border towns and villages in February 2001 and claimed that Guinea was threatening to invade.

On 7 March 2001 the UN Security Council imposed a diamond embargo on Liberia after discovering that the country exported six times as many diamonds as it produced, and accused Liberia of supporting the Revolutionary United Front, a Sierra Leonean rebel movement. The embargo took effect on 7 May. On 19 March, Liberia expelled the ambassadors of Guinea and Sierra Leone and sealed its border with Sierra Leone.

### POLITICAL SYSTEM

The head of state is an executive president, directly elected for a six-year term, who appoints the Cabinet. There is a bicameral legislature consisting of a 64-member lower chamber, the House of Representatives, which is directly elected for a six-year term, and a 26-member Senate, elected for a nine-year term.

### HEAD OF STATE

*President*, Charles Taylor, *elected* 19 July 1997, *inaugurated* 3 August 1997

*Vice-President*, Moses. Z. Blah

### CABINET *as at July 2001*

*Commerce*, Cora Peabody

*Defence*, Daniel Chea

*Education*, Evelyne Kandakai

*Finance*, Nathaniel Barnes

*Foreign Affairs*, Monie Captan

*Gender Development*, Musuleng Cooper

*Health and Social Welfare*, Peter Coleman

*Information, Culture and Tourism*, Reginald Goodridge

*Internal Affairs*, Richard Flomo

*Justice*, Eddington Varmah

*Labour*, Christian Herbert

*Lands, Mines and Energy*, Jenkins Dunbar

*Ministers of State*, Jonathan Taylor (*Presidential Affairs*); Jonathan Refell (*Without Portfolio*)

*National Security*, Philip Kamah

*Planning and Economic Affairs*, Amelia Ward

*Post and Telecommunications*, Emma Wuor
*Public Works*, Emmet Taylor
*Rural Development*, Hezekiah Bowen
*Transport*, Francis Carbah
*Youth and Sports*, vacant

EMBASSY OF THE REPUBLIC OF LIBERIA
2 Pembridge Place, London W2 4XB
Tel: 020-7221 1036
*Ambassador Extraordinary and Plenipotentiary*, vacant
*Minister-Counsellor (Head of Chancery) and Chargé d'Affaires*, Jeff Gongoer Dowana.

BRITISH AMBASSADOR, HE Haydon Warren-Gash, resident at Abidjan, Côte d'Ivoire

## ECONOMY

Before the civil war began principal exports were iron ore, crude rubber, timber, uncut diamonds, palm kernels, cocoa and coffee, but the civil war has resulted in the suspension of most economic activity.

GDP – US$2,983 million (1997); US$285 per capita (1998)
ANNUAL AVERAGE GROWTH OF GDP – 2.7 per cent (1996)
INFLATION RATE – 9.1 per cent (1989)
TOTAL EXTERNAL DEBT – US$2,103 million (1998)

| *Trade with UK* | 1999 | 2000 |
|---|---|---|
| Imports from UK | £15,273,000 | £16,375,000 |
| Exports to UK | 1,323,000 | 1,712,000 |

## COMMUNICATIONS

The artificial harbour and free port of Monrovia was opened in 1948. There are 10,300 km of roads, of which 628 km are paved, and 490 km of railway track. There are nine ports of entry, including three river ports. Robertsfield International Airport and Spriggs Payne airfield are currently being used for flights to other West African countries.

---

# LIBYA
*Al-Jamāhīriyya Al-'Arabiyya*
*Al-Lībiyya Ash-Sha'biyya Al-Ishtirākiyya*

---

AREA – 679,362 sq. miles (1,759,540 sq. km). Neighbours: Egypt and Sudan (east), Chad and Niger (south), Algeria and Tunisia (west)
POPULATION – 5,419,000 (1997 UN estimate). The people of Libya are principally Arab with some Berbers in the west and some Tuareg tribesmen in the Fezzan. Islam is the official religion but other religions are tolerated. The official language is Arabic
CAPITAL – ΨTripoli (Tarabulus) (population, 1,000,000, 1991 estimate)
MAJOR CITIES – ΨBangāzī (500,000); ΨMisrātah (200,000); Sirte (100,000)
CURRENCY – Libyan dinar (LD) of 1,000 dirhams
NATIONAL DAY – 1 September
NATIONAL FLAG – Libya uses a plain emerald green flag
LIFE EXPECTANCY (years) – male 65.0; female 67.0
POPULATION GROWTH RATE – 2.4 per cent (1999)
POPULATION DENSITY – 3 per sq. km (1998)
URBAN POPULATION – 87.6 per cent (2000 estimate)
ILLITERACY RATE – 20.2 per cent (2000)
ENROLMENT (percentage of age group) – primary 96 per cent (1992); secondary 62 per cent (1980); tertiary 18.4 per cent (1992)

Vast sand and rock deserts, almost completely barren, occupy the greater part of Libya. The southern part of the country lies within the Sahara Desert. There are few rivers and as rainfall is irregular outside parts of Cyrenaica and Tripolitania, good harvests are rare.

The ancient ruins in Cyrenaica, at Cyrene, Ptolemais (Tolmeta) and Apollonia, are outstanding, as are those at Leptis Magna, 70 miles east, and at Sabratha, 40 miles west of Tripoli. An Italian expedition found in the south-west of the Fezzan a series of rock-paintings more than 5,000 years old.

## HISTORY AND POLITICS

From the 16th century Libya was dominated by the Ottoman Empire, until occupied by Italy in 1911–12 in the course of the Italo-Turkish War. Under the 1912 Treaty of Ouchy, sovereignty over the province was transferred by Turkey to Italy, and in 1939 the four provinces of Libya (Tripoli, Misurata, Bangāzī and Derna) were incorporated in the national territory of Italy as *Libia Italiana*. After the Second World War Tripolitania and Cyrenaica were placed provisionally under British and the Fezzan under French administration, and in conformity with a resolution of the UN General Assembly in 1949, Libya became on 24 December 1951 the first independent state to be created by the UN. The monarchy was overthrown by a revolution in 1969 and the country was declared a republic. It was ruled by the Revolutionary Command Council (RCC) under the leadership of Col. Muammar al-Gadhafi.

In 1977, a new form of direct democracy, the 'Jamahiriya' (state of the masses) was promulgated and the official name of the country was changed to Socialist People's Libyan Arab Jamahiriya. Since a reorganisation in 1979, neither Col. Gadhafi nor his former RCC colleagues have held formal posts in the administration. Gadhafi continues to hold the ceremonial title 'Leader of the Revolution'.

### POLITICAL SYSTEM

At local level authority is vested in about 1,500 Basic and 14 Municipal People's Congresses which appoint Popular Committees to execute policy. Officials of these congresses and committees, together with representatives from unions and other organisations, form the 750-member General People's Congress, which normally meets twice each year. In addition, a number of extraordinary sessions are held throughout the year. This is the highest policy-making body in the country.

The General People's Congress appoints its own General Secretariat and the General People's Committee, whose members head the government departments which execute policy at national level. The Secretary of the General People's Committee has functions similar to those of a prime minister.

On 1 March 2000 it was announced that 12 of the ministries run by the General People's Committee had been abolished and that their powers had been devolved to provincial committees.

*Leader of the Revolution and Supreme Commander of the Armed Forces*, Col. Muammar al-Gadhafi

### GENERAL PEOPLE'S COMMITTEE *as at July 2001*

*Secretary-General*, Mubarak al-Shamikh
*Assistant Secretary-General*, Abdullah al-Badri
*Deputy Secretary for Production*, Beshir Bujeneh
*Deputy Secretary for Services*, Bagdadi Mahmudi
*Secretary, African Unity*, Ali Abdel Salam Turayki
*Secretary, Finance*, Al-Ujayli Abd-al-Salam Burayni
*Secretary, Foreign Liaison and International Co-operation*, Abdel Rahman Muhammad Shalgam
*Secretary, Justice and Public Security*, Abdel Rahman al-Abbar

*Co-ordinator of the General Provisional Committee for Defence*, Abu Bakr Jaber Yunes
*Speaker of the General People's Congress*, Mohammad al-Zenati

LIBYAN PEOPLE'S BUREAU
61-62 Ennismore Gardens, London SW7 1NH
Tel 020-7589 6120
*Ambassador Extraordinary and Plenipotentiary*, HE Mohamed Abu Al-Qassim Azwai, apptd 2001
*Deputy Head of Mission*, Taher Ettoumi

BRITISH EMBASSY
Sharia Uahran 1, PO Box 4206, Tripoli
Tel (00 218) (21) 333 1191/2/3
Ambassador Extraordinary and Plenipotentiary, *HE Richard Dalton, CMG, apptd 1999*
BRITISH COUNCIL DIRECTOR, Antony Jones, British Embassy, 24th Floor, Burj al Fatah, Tripoli; e-mail: britishcouncil@lttnet.net

## DEFENCE

The Army has about 2,210 main battle tanks, 1,000 armoured infantry fighting vehicles and 990 armoured personnel carriers. The Navy has two submarines, two frigates, 16 patrol and coastal vessels, and 32 armed helicopters at seven bases. The Air Force has 426 combat aircraft and 52 armed helicopters.

Libya is alleged to have built at least one chemical weapons plant. The USA claims that a plant at Rabta, closed in 1990, was reopened in 1995, and that a plant has been constructed near Tahunah, south of Tripoli.

As part of the UN economic sanctions imposed in April 1992, there is a total embargo on arms sales to Libya.
MILITARY EXPENDITURE – 4.7 per cent of GDP (1999)
MILITARY PERSONNEL – 76,000: Army 45,000, Navy 8,000, Air Force 23,000
CONSCRIPTION DURATION – One to two years (selective)

## ECONOMY

Economic sanctions were imposed on Libya in April 1992 by the UN Security Council following Libya's failure to hand over two suspects in the bombing of Pan-Am flight 103 over Lockerbie, Scotland, in 1988, in which 270 people were killed. The UN imposed additional sanctions in December 1993, including freezing assets abroad and restricting imports of spare parts and equipment for the oil and aviation sectors. Some sanctions were suspended in April 1999, following mediation by President Mandela of South Africa in March 1999, which led to the extradition in April of the two Libyan suspects to the Netherlands to stand trial. Following the conviction of one of the two suspects on 31 January 2001, the lifting of the remaining sanctions has been made dependent on Libya accepting responsibility for the Lockerbie bombing and agreeing to pay compensation to the families of the victims.

Agriculture is confined mainly to the coastal areas of Tripolitania and Cyrenaica, where barley, wheat, olives, citrus fruits and livestock are produced, and to the areas of the oases.

The main industry is oil and gas production. There are pipelines from Zaltan to the terminal at al-Burayqah, from Dahra to as-Sidrah, from Amal to Ras Lanuf, and from the Intisar field to az-Zuwaytīnah. In 1998, 69.2 million tonnes of crude oil was produced. Cement, construction materials and textiles are also produced. Economic constraints have delayed some projects, particularly since Libya decided in 1983 to go ahead with a major irrigation scheme, the 'Great Man-Made River'. The government is now seeking foreign direct investment for the oil and gas industries and to finance improvements to the country's infrastructure.

Libya has technical assistance agreements with a number of countries, and also employs large numbers of foreign labourers and experts.
GDP – US$29,288 million (1997); US$5,930 per capita (1998)
ANNUAL AVERAGE GROWTH OF GDP – 2.0 per cent (1996)

TRADE

Exports are dominated by crude oil, but some wool, cattle, sheep and horses, olive oil, and hides and skins are also exported. Principal imports are machinery and transport equipment, foodstuffs, livestock, and most construction materials and consumer goods. After the revolution the private sector was virtually eliminated and Libya became a state trading country with imports controlled by state monopolies. Since reforms in 1988, however, a small private sector has been re-established.

| *Trade with UK* | 1999 | 2000 |
|---|---|---|
| Imports from UK | £177,050,000 | £186,546,000 |
| Exports to UK | 115,050,000 | 200,824,000 |

## COMMUNICATIONS

There are 25,675 km of roads; the coastal road running from the Tunisian frontier through Tripoli to Bangāzī, Tubruq and the Egyptian border serves the main population centres. Main roads also link the provincial centres, and the oil-producing areas of the south with the coastal towns.

There are airports at Tripoli and Bangāzī (Benina), Kufra, Labrag, Misrātah and Tubruk. Since April 1992 a UN embargo on air links with Libya has been in force.

---

# LIECHTENSTEIN
*Fürstentum Liechtenstein*

---

AREA – 62 sq. miles (160 sq. km). Neighbours: Austria, Switzerland
POPULATION – 32,426 (1999). The language of the principality is Standard German. An Alemannic dialect is in general use. About 65.4 per cent of the population are Liechtensteiners, the remainder being mainly Swiss, Austrians and Germans. Roman Catholicism is the religion of 80.4 per cent of the population; there is a Protestant minority
CAPITAL – Vaduz (population, 5,106, 1998)
CURRENCY – Swiss franc of 100 rappen (or centimes)
NATIONAL ANTHEM – Oben am Jungen Rhein (Up on the young Rhine)
NATIONAL DAY – 15 August
NATIONAL FLAG – Equal horizontal bands of blue over red; gold crown on blue band near staff
LIFE EXPECTANCY (years) – male 66.1; female 72.9
POPULATION GROWTH RATE – 1.4 per cent (1997)
POPULATION DENSITY – 200 per sq. km (1998)
URBAN POPULATION – 22.6 per cent (2000 estimate)

## HISTORY AND POLITICS

The region was settled in the fifth century AD by the West Germanic Alemanni. The Principality of Liechtenstein was established by Emperor Charles VI in 1719. Following the First World War, Liechtenstein severed its ties with Austria and began its association with Switzerland, taking up the Swiss currency in 1921.

In November 1999, the European Court of Human Rights fined Prince Hans Adam II for abusing his subjects' freedom of speech, a development which prompted a constitutional crisis in the principality.

In February 2000, Prince Hans Adam announced that he wished to hold a referendum on constitutional reform, and threatened to abdicate if his proposals were rejected by the electorate.

The Patriotic Union (VU) and the Progressive Citizens' Party (FBP) governed the country in coalition from 1938 until March 1997. The 1997 general election was won by the VU, which lost power to the FBP, who won 13 seats in the general election held on 9 and 11 February 2001. The new government took office on 5 April.

### Political System

Liechtenstein is a constitutional monarchy. The Cabinet is appointed by the Prince on the advice of parliament and consists of a head of government and four ministers. The 25-member *Landtag*, the unicameral parliament, has a four-year term. There is a threshold of 8 per cent for parties to gain representation.

### Head of State

*HSH The Prince of Liechtenstein*, Hans Adam II, *born* 14 February 1945; *succeeded* 13 November 1989; *married* 30 July 1967, Countess Marie Kinsky; and has *issue:* Prince Alois (*see* below); Prince Maximilian, *b.* 16 May 1969; Prince Constantin, *b.* 15 March 1972; Princess Tatjana, *b.* 10 April 1973

*Heir*, HSH Prince Alois, *b.* 11 June 1968, *married* 1993 Duchess Sophie of Bavaria; and has *issue:* Prince Wenzel, *b.* 24 May 1995; Princess Marie, *b.* 17 October 1996; Prince Georg, *b.* 20 April 1999

### Cabinet *as at July 2001*

*Head of Government, Construction, Family Affairs and Equal Opportunities, Finance, General Government Affairs*, Otmar Hasler

*Deputy Head of Government, Education, Justice, Transport*, Rita Kieber-Beck

*Culture and Sports, Environment, Interior*, Alois Ospelt

*Economy, Health, Social Affairs*, Hansjörg Frick

*Foreign Affairs*, Ernst Walch

### Diplomatic Representation

Liechtenstein is represented in diplomatic and consular matters in the United Kingdom by the Swiss Embassy.

British Ambassador, Christopher Hulse, cmg, obe, resident at Bern, Switzerland

## ECONOMY

The main industries are high and ultra-high vacuum engineering, the semiconductor industry, roller bearings, artificial teeth, heating equipment, synthetic fibres, woollen and homespun fabrics. Following international accusations that Liechtenstein was a haven for money-laundering, the country banned anonymous bank accounts in September 2000.

In 1991 Liechtenstein became a member of the European Free Trade Association, and joined the European Economic Area on 1 May 1995.

GDP – US$1,112 million (1997); US$35,910 per capita (1998)

Annual Average Growth of GDP – 0.2 per cent (1996)

| *Trade with UK* | 1999 | 2000 |
|---|---|---|
| Imports from UK | £4,824,000 | £7,287,000 |
| Exports to UK | 21,776,000 | 21,484,000 |

---

# LITHUANIA
*Lietuva*

---

Area – 25,174 sq. miles (65,200 sq. km). Neighbours: Latvia (north), Belarus (east and south), Poland and the Kaliningrad region of the Russian Federation (south-west)

Population – 3,701,300 (1998): 81.6 per cent Lithuanian, 8.2 per cent Russian, 6.9 per cent Polish, 1.5 per cent Belarusian, 1 per cent Ukrainian. The majority are Roman Catholic, with Russian Orthodox and Lutheran minorities. Lithuanian is the state language

Capital – Vilnius (population, 580,099, 1999)

Major Cities – Kaunas (414,199); Klaipėda (202,545), 1999

Currency – Litas of 100 centas, pegged to the dollar, US$1= 4 litas

National Anthem – Tautiška Giesmė (The National Song)

National Day – 16 February (Independence Day)

National Flag – Three horizontal stripes of yellow, green, red

Life Expectancy (years) – male 67.0; female 77.9

Population Growth Rate – 0.2 per cent (1999)

Population Density – 57 per sq. km (1998)

Urban Population – 68.4 per cent (2000 estimate)

Lithuania lies in the middle and lower basin of the river Nemunas. Along the coast is a lowland plain which rises inland to form uplands in east and central Lithuania. These uplands, the Middle Lowlands, give way to the Baltic Highlands in east and south-east Lithuania; the highest point is 294 m (965 ft). There is a network of rivers and over 2,800 lakes, which mainly lie in the east of the country. The climate varies between maritime and continental.

## HISTORY AND POLITICS

The first independent Lithuanian state emerged as the Kingdom of Lithuania in 1251. After forming a joint Commonwealth and Kingdom with Poland in 1569, Lithuania was taken over by the Russian Empire in 1795.

Lithuania declared its independence from the Russian Empire on 16 February 1918 and signed a peace treaty with the Soviet Union on 12 July 1920. The Soviet Union annexed Lithuania in 1940 under the terms of the Molotov–Ribbentrop pact with Germany. Lithuania was invaded and occupied when Germany invaded the Soviet Union during the Second World War. In 1944, the Soviet Union recaptured the country and confirmed its annexation.

In December 1989, public pressure forced the Lithuanian Communist Party to agree to multiparty elections, which were held in February 1990. These were won by the nationalist Sajudis movement, and the Supreme Council (parliament) declared the restoration of independence on 11 March 1990. Over 90 per cent of the population voted for independence in a referendum in February 1991. The Soviet Union recognised the independence of Lithuania on 10 September 1991.

In the general election held on 8 October 2000, the Social Democratic Coalition won 52 seats, the Lithuanian Liberal Union (LLS) won 34 seats, the New Union (Social Liberals) (NS (SL)) won 29 seats, and the Homeland Union, which had formed the previous government, won only nine seats. A coalition government was formed, which comprised the LLS, the (NS (SL)), the Modern Christian Democrats and the Centre Union, with 71 of the 141 seats in the legislature.

### Foreign Relations

Lithuania applied for membership of the EU in December 1995; a treaty of association with the EU entered into force on 1 February 1998 and formal accession negotiations began in 2000.

### Political System

Under the 1992 constitution, the head of state is a directly elected president, whose five-year term of office is renewable once only. Executive authority is vested in the government, consisting of the prime minister, who is appointed by the president with the approval of the *Seimas*, and ministers appointed upon the recommendation of the prime minister. Legislative power is exercised by the Seimas, a unicameral parliament of 141 members directly elected for four-year terms. Seventy-one members are elected in first-past-the-post constituencies and 70 by proportional representation, with a 5 per cent threshold for representation. The constitution bans an alignment of Lithuania with any post-Soviet eastern alliance.

### Head of State

*President*, Valdas Adamkus, *inaugurated* 25 February 1998

### Government *as at July 2001*

*Prime Minister*, Eugenijus Genvilas (LLS)
*Agriculture and Forestry*, Kęstutis Kristinatis (Ind.)
*Culture*, Gintautas Kėvišas (Ind.)
*Defence*, Linas Linkevičius (Ind.)
*Education and Science*, Algirdas Monkevičius (NS (SL))
*Environment*, Henrikas Žukauskas (LLS)
*Finance*, Jonas Lionginas (LLS)
*Foreign Affairs*, Antanas Valionis (Ind.)
*Health*, Konstantinas Romualdas Dobrovolskis (NS (SL))
*Interior*, Vytautas Markevičius (Ind.)
*Justice*, Gintautas Bartkus (Ind.)
*Social Affairs and Labour*, Vilija Blinkevičiūtė (Ind.)
*Transport and Communications*, Dailis Barakauskas (LLS)

LLS Lithuanian Liberal Union; NS (SL) New Union (Social Liberals); Ind. Independent

### Embassy of Lithuania

84 Gloucester Place, London W1U 6AU
Tel: 020-7486 6401/2
E-mail: lralon@globalnet.co.uk
*Ambassador Extraordinary and Plenipotentiary*, HE Justas Vincas Paleckis, apptd 1996

### British Embassy

2 Antakalnio, LT-2055 Vilnius
Tel: (00 370) (2) 222 2070/1
*Ambassador Extraordinary and Plenipotentiary*, HE Christopher Robbins, apptd 1998

British Council Director, Lina Balenaite, Vilnius 39, LT-2001 Vilnius; e-mail: lina.balenaite@britishcouncil.lt

## DEFENCE

The Army has 37 armoured personnel carriers; the Navy has two frigates and four patrol and coastal vessels based at Klaipėda; the Air Force has eight helicopters. The last Russian troops withdrew in 1993.

Military Personnel – 12,700: Army 9,340, Navy 560, Air Force 800, Paramilitaries 3,900
Military Expenditure – 1.7 per cent of GDP (2000)
Conscription Duration – 12 months

## ECONOMY

The economy was largely agricultural prior to rapid industrialisation during the Soviet era. A privatisation programme began in 1991 and progress in the sale of small enterprises has been quick and successful. In 1997, the privatisation of communication, energy and transport companies was begun.

In 1999, agriculture and forestry accounted for 8.8 per cent of GDP, mining and manufacturing industry 23.3 per cent, construction 8 per cent and transport and communications 11 per cent.. The main industries are chemicals and petrochemicals, food processing, wood products, textiles, leather goods, machinery, machine tools and household appliances.

GNP – US$9,751 million (1999); US$2,620 per capita (1999)
GDP – US$9,550 million (1997); US$2,895 per capita (1998)
Annual Average Growth of GDP – 3.4 per cent (2000)
Inflation Rate – 0.2 per cent (2001)
Unemployment – 6.9 per cent (1999)
Total External Debt – US$3,000 million (1999)

### Trade

Lithuania's main trading partners are Germany, Latvia, Russia, Denmark and Belarus. In January 2001, total foreign investment in Lithuania reached US$2.3 billion.

In 2000 there was a trade deficit of US$1,647 million and a current account deficit of US$675 million. Imports totalled US$5,456 million and exports US$3,809 million.

| *Trade with UK* | 1999 | 2000 |
|---|---|---|
| Imports from UK | £95,636,000 | £133,629,000 |
| Exports to UK | 163,125,000 | 254,778,000 |

## COMMUNICATIONS

There are 45,340 km of surfaced roads; there is a relatively well-developed railway system of 2,898 km running east-west and north-south and linking the major towns with Vilnius and Klaipėda, the main international port. Vilnius has an international airport and there are smaller ones at Kaunas, Palanga and Šiauliai.

## CULTURE AND EDUCATION

Lithuanian culture and literature are closely linked to the national liberation movements of the 19th and early 20th centuries, and the literature of Lithuanians who went into exile during the Soviet era.

Lithuania re-established a national education system in 1990. Education is free and compulsory from seven to 16 years, with the system comprising elementary schools (four years), nine-year schools (five years), and secondary schools (three years). The language of instruction is predominantly Lithuanian, but there are also Russian and Polish schools. There are 105 vocational schools and 65 colleges. Lithuania has eight universities and seven other institutes of higher education. Vilnius University, founded in 1579, is one of the oldest universities in eastern Europe.

Illiteracy Rate – 0.5 per cent (2000)
Enrolment (percentage of age group) – secondary 80 per cent (1994); tertiary 31.4 per cent (1996)

---

## LUXEMBOURG
*Groussherzogtom Lëtzebuerg*

---

Area – 998 sq. miles (2,586 sq. km). Neighbours: Germany (east), Belgium (west and north), France (south)

POPULATION – 432,000 (1997 UN estimate), nearly all Roman Catholic. The officially designated 'national language' is Lëtzebuergesch (Luxembourgish), a mainly spoken language. French and German are the official languages for written purposes, and French is the language of administration
CAPITAL – Luxembourg (population, 77,400, 1996)
CURRENCY – Euro (€) of 100 cents/Luxembourg franc (LF) of 100 centimes (Belgian currency is also legal tender)
NATIONAL ANTHEM – Ons Hémécht (Our homeland)
NATIONAL DAY – 23 June
NATIONAL FLAG – Three horizontal bands, red, white and blue
LIFE EXPECTANCY (years) – male 74.5; female 81.4
POPULATION GROWTH RATE – 1.3 per cent (1999)
POPULATION DENSITY – 165 per sq. km (1998)
URBAN POPULATION – 91.5 per cent (2000 estimate)
ENROLMENT (percentage of age group) – primary 81 per cent (1985); secondary 68 per cent (1996); tertiary 9.7 per cent (1996)

## HISTORY AND POLITICS

Established as an independent state under the sovereignty of the King of the Netherlands as Grand Duke by the Congress of Vienna in 1815, Luxembourg formed part of the Germanic Confederation from 1815 to 1866, becoming neutral in 1867.

The territory was invaded by Germany in 1914 but was liberated in 1918. By the Treaty of Versailles (1919), Germany renounced its former agreements with Luxembourg and in 1921 an economic union was formed with Belgium. The Grand Duchy was again invaded and occupied by Germany in 1940, and liberated in 1944.

The constitution was modified in 1948 and the stipulation of permanent neutrality was abandoned.

### POLITICAL SYSTEM

There is a Chamber of 60 deputies, elected by universal suffrage for five years. Legislation is submitted to the Council of State. The last general election was held on 13 June 1999 and a coalition government was installed. In March 1998, Grand Duke Jean passed certain constitutional powers on to his son and heir, Prince Henri, and announced on 25 December 1999 that he would abdicate in favour of Prince Henri in September 2000.

### HEAD OF STATE

*HRH The Grand Duke of Luxembourg*, HRH Grand Duke Henri, *born* 16 April 1955; *succeeded* (on the abdication of his father) 7 October 2000; *married* 14 February 1981, Maria Teresa Mestre, and has *issue*, Prince Guillaume (*see* below); Prince Felix, *b.* 3 June 1984; Prince Louis, *b.* 3 August 1986; Princess Alexandra, *b.* 2 February 1991; Prince Sébastien, *b.* 16 April 1992, Princess Gabriella, *b.* 26 March 1994
*Heir*, HRH Prince Guillaume, *born* 11 November 1981

### CABINET *as at July 2001*

*Prime Minister, Finance*, Jean-Claude Juncker (CSP)
*Deputy PM, Foreign Affairs, Trade, Civil Service and Administrative Reform*, Lydie Polfer (DP)
*Agriculture, Viticulture, Rural Development, Small Businesses, Housing and Tourism*, Fernand Boden (CSP)
*Culture, Higher Education and Research, Public Works*, Erna Hennicot-Schoepges (CSP)
*Development Aid and Defence, Environment*, Charles Goerens (DP)
*Economy, Transport*, Henri Grethen (DP)
*Employment, Religion, Parliamentary Relations*, François Biltgen (CSP)
*Family, Social Solidarity and Youth, Advancement of Women*, Marie-Josée Jacobs (CSP)
*Health and Social Security*, Carlo Wagner (DP)
*Home Affairs*, Michel Wolter (CSP)
*National Education, Vocational Training and Sport*, Anne Brasseur (DP)
*Secretaries of State*, Joseph Schaack (DP) (*Civil Service and Administrative Reform*); Eugène Berger (DP) (*Environment*)
*Treasury and Budget, Justice*, Luc Frieden (CSP)
CSP Christian Social Party; DP Democratic Party

### EMBASSY OF LUXEMBOURG

27 Wilton Crescent, London SW1X 8SD
Tel: 020-7235 6961
*Ambassador Extraordinary and Plenipotentiary*, HE Joseph Weyland, apptd 1993

### BRITISH EMBASSY

14 Boulevard Roosevelt, L-2450 Luxembourg
Tel: (00 352) 229864/5/6
*Ambassador Extraordinary and Plenipotentiary*, HE Gordon Wetherell, apptd 2000
BRITISH CHAMBER OF COMMERCE, 31 Avenue Scheffer, L-2520 Luxembourg

## DEFENCE

For legal reasons, NATO's squadron of E-3A Sentry airborne early warning aircraft is registered in Luxembourg.
MILITARY EXPENDITURE – 0.8 per cent of GDP (1999)
MILITARY PERSONNEL – 899: Army 899, Paramilitaries 612

## ECONOMY

Luxembourg is a member of the Belgium-Netherlands-Luxembourg Customs Union (Benelux 1960). The country has an important iron and steel industry and is an important financial centre. In 1998, 727,000 tourists visited Luxembourg.

The chief exports are metal goods, manufactures, machinery, chemicals, transport equipment, and foodstuffs and livestock. The chief imports are machinery, transport equipment, metal goods, manufactures, chemicals, and foodstuffs and livestock.

In 1999 imports totalled US$10,929 million and exports US$7,888 million.
GNP - US$18,545 million (1999); US$44,640 per capita (1999)
GDP – US$15,760 million (1997); US$44,360 per capita (1999)
ANNUAL AVERAGE GROWTH OF GDP – 7.5 per cent (1999)
INFLATION RATE – 2.9 per cent (2001)
UNEMPLOYMENT – 2.0 per cent (2001)

| Trade with UK | 1999 | 2000 |
|---|---|---|
| Imports from UK | £68,300,000 | £216,700,000 |
| Exports to UK | 121,200,000 | 121,700,000 |

---

# MACEDONIA
*Republika Makedonija*

---

AREA – 9,928 sq. miles (25,713 sq. km). Neighbours: Federal Republic of Yugoslavia (north), Bulgaria (east), Greece (south), Albania (west)
POPULATION – 2,021,000 (1997 UN estimate); 1,936,877 (1994 census): 66.5 per cent Macedonian, 22.9 per cent Albanian, 4.0 per cent ethnic Turks, 2.3 per cent Romanies, 2.0 per cent Serbs and 0.4 per cent Vlachs.

The census results are disputed by the ethnic Albanians and Serbs. Macedonian Orthodox Christianity is the majority religion, with a Muslim minority. The main language is Macedonian (a south Slavic language), which is written in the Cyrillic script

CAPITAL – Skopje (population, 429,964, 1994)

MAJOR CITIES – Bitola (84,002); Kumanov (69,231); Prilep (70,152)

CURRENCY – Denar of 100 deni

NATIONAL ANTHEM – Denes nad Makedonija se radja novo sonce na slobodata (Today a new sun of liberty appears over Macedonia)

NATIONAL FLAG – Red with an eight-rayed sun displayed over the whole field

LIFE EXPECTANCY (years) – male 69.8; female 74.1

POPULATION GROWTH RATE – 0.6 per cent (1999)

POPULATION DENSITY – 78 per sq. km (1998)

URBAN POPULATION – 62.0 per cent (2000 estimate)

MILITARY EXPENDITURE - 2.0 per cent of GDP (1999)

MILITARY PERSONNEL-16,000: Army 15,000, Paramilitaries 7,500

CONSCRIPTION DURATION – Nine months

ENROLMENT (percentage of age group) – primary 95 per cent (1996); secondary 56 per cent (1996); tertiary 19.5 per cent (1996)

## HISTORY AND POLITICS

From the ninth to the 14th centuries AD Macedonia was ruled alternately by the Bulgars and the Byzantine Empire. In the middle of the 14th century the area was conquered by the Turks and remained under the Ottoman Empire for over 500 years. After the defeat of Turkey in the two Balkan wars of 1912–13 the geographical area of Macedonia was divided, the major part becoming Serbian (the areas of the present-day Macedonia) and the remainder given to Greece and Bulgaria. In 1918 Serbian Macedonia was incorporated into Serbia as South Serbia. When Yugoslavia was reconstituted in 1944 as a Communist federal republic under President Tito, Macedonia became a constituent republic.

Multiparty elections for the 120-seat assembly held in November and December 1990 produced the first non-Communist government since the Second World War. The electorate overwhelmingly approved Macedonian sovereignty and independence in a referendum and independence was declared on 8 September 1991.

In elections to the *Sobranje* (National Assembly) held on 18 October and 1 November 1998, the coalition of the Internal Macedonian Revolutionary Organisation-Democratic Party for Macedonian National Unity (RO-DP) and the Democratic Alternative (DA) won 62 of the 120 seats. It invited the National Democratic Party, an ethnic Albanian party, to join the coalition. Presidential elections on 14 November and 5 December 1999 were won by Boris Trajkovski of the RO-DP. A new government of national unity was elected by the Assembly on 13 May 2001, which included the RO-DP, the Democratic Party of Albanians (DPA), the Liberal Party, the Social Democratic Alliance (SDSM) and the (ethnic Albanian) Party for Democratic Prosperity (PDP).

### INSURGENCY

Fighting between ethnic Albanian guerrillas belonging to the National Liberation Army (NLA) and Macedonian security forces began on 26 February 2001 in the village of Tanusevci near the border with Kosovo and by mid-March had spread to Tetovo, the largest ethnic Albanian town. The Macedonian government, which included ethnic Albanians, promised to implement reforms to increase minority rights for ethnic Albanians and moderate Albanian parties called on the guerrillas to surrender their arms. The insurgency was condemned by the UN Security Council on 21 March 2001. On 10 April, President Trajkovski announced the establishment of a commission to investigate discrimination against the Albanian minority.

On 23 May 2001, the two main Albanian parties, the DPA and the PDP, signed an agreement with the NLA, in which the rebels agreed to withdraw in return for an amnesty and NLA participation in discussions with the government. The Macedonian government and international organisations immediately condemned the agreement. President Trajkovski urged the Albanian parties to renounce the agreement, which they refused to do, but it was agreed that discussions should continue in order to preserve the coalition government. On 30 May, the President offered to amend the constitution to recognise the Albanians as a constituent people and make Albanian an official language along with Macedonian.

By early June, fighting had become widespread across the north of the country. On 14 June, President Trajkovski made an official request for NATO assistance to disarm the NLA. A cease-fire declared on 12 June ended after only 11 days when Macedonian forces launched an attack on the village of Aracinovo, but halted their offensive when the NLA agreed to withdraw its forces from the village. On 25 June, Macedonian Slavic nationalists stormed parliament in protest against the government's co-operation with NATO in escorting the besieged NLA rebels from Aracinovo to safety. On 13 August, the leaders of the Slav and Albanian parties signed an agreement that made Albanian an official language, gave Christianity and Islam equal status and cleared the way for the deployment of a NATO disarmament force.

### FOREIGN RELATIONS

A new constitution was adopted in November 1991 and then amended at the EC's request to make it clear that Macedonia had no territorial claim on its neighbours. Macedonia applied for EC recognition in December 1991 but was refused because of Greece's objections to the state's name, flag and currency which, according to the Greek government, amounted to a territorial claim on the Greek province of Macedonia. Macedonia gained UN membership on 8 April 1993 following a compromise with Greece by which it is temporarily known as the 'Former Yugoslav Republic of Macedonia' (FYROM).

Macedonia provided sanctuary to some 300,000 ethnic Albanian Kosovars following the outbreak of hostilities between Yugoslavia and NATO forces on 24 March 1999. The refugees began to return when the conflict ended on 9 June 1999.

A border demarcation agreement was signed with Yugoslavia on 23 February 2001.

### HEAD OF STATE

*President*, Boris Trajkovski, *elected* 5 December 1999

*Vice-Presidents*, Dosta Dimovska (RO-DP); Radmila Kiprijanova Radovanovik (RO-DP); Bedredin Ibrahimi (DPA) (*Labour and Social Policy*)

### CABINET *as at July 2001*

*Prime Minister*, Ljubčo Georgievski (RO-DP)

*Deputy Prime Minister, Labour and Social Policy*, Bedredin Ibrahami (DPA)

*Agriculture, Forestry and Water Resources Management*, Marjan Gjorcev (RO-DP)

*Culture*, Ganka Samoilovask-Cvetanov (RO-DP)

*Defence*, Vlado Buckovski (SDSM)

*Economy*, Besnik Fetai (DPA)

*Education and Science*, Nenad Novkovski (RO-DP)

*Environment and Urban Planning*, Vladimir Dzabirski (RO-DP)

*Finance*, Nikola Grujevski (RO-DP)

*Foreign Affairs*, Ilenka Mitreva (SDSM)

*Health*, Petar Milosevski (LDP)
*Interior*, Ljube Boskovski (RO-DP)
*Justice*, Idzet Memeti (PDP)
*Local Self-government*, Faik Aslani (PDP)
*Transport and Communications*, Ljupco Balkovski (RO-DP)
*Without Portfolio*, Ilija Filipovski (SDSM); Zoran Krstevski (LP); Kemal Musliu (PDP); Xhevdet Nasufi (DPA)

DPA Democratic Party of Albanians; LDP Liberal Democratic Party; LP Liberal Party; PDP Party for Democratic Prosperity; RO-DP Internal Macedonian Revolutionary Organisation-Democratic Party for Macedonian National Unity; SDSM Social Democratic Alliance;

EMBASSY OF THE REPUBLIC OF MACEDONIA
10 Harcourt House, 19A Cavendish Square, London W1M 9AD
Tel: 020-7499 5152/1854
*Ambassador Extraordinary and Plenipotentiary*, HE Stevo Crvenkovski, apptd 1997

BRITISH EMBASSY
Dimitrija Chupovski 26, 4th Floor, MK-9100 Skopje
Tel: (00 389) (91) 116772/109941
*Ambassador Extraordinary and Plenipotentiary*, HE Mark Dickinson, OBE, apptd 1997
BRITISH COUNCIL, British Information Centre, Bulevar Goce Delcev 6, PO Box 562, MK-91000 Skopje; e-mail: borce.nikolovski@britishcouncil.org.mk

## ECONOMY

The economy was decimated by the UN trade sanctions against the rump Yugoslavia (from May 1992 until November 1995), and the Greek economic blockade (from February 1994 until October 1995). Macedonia is attempting to transform its economy to a market-orientated one and to introduce privatisation; by 1997, 45 per cent of the economy was in private hands. In April 2000, the government sold 65 per cent of Macedonia's largest bank, the Stopanska bank, and parliament voted to return property expropriated during the period under Communist rule. An economic co-operation agreement was signed by Macedonia and Albania in July 1999, covering energy, mining and trade.

In 1996 58.3 per cent of GDP was produced by service industries, 28.3 per cent by industry, and 13.4 per cent by agriculture.

The main exports are textiles, tobacco, zinc, wine, iron ore and iron products. The main imports are oil, energy, telecommunications equipment, metal manufactures, foodstuffs and medicines.

In 1999 there was a trade deficit of US$410 million and a current account deficit of US$109 million. Imports totalled US$1,740 million and exports US$1,210 million.
GNP – US$3,348 million (1999); US$1,690 per capita (1999)
GDP – US$3,320 million (1997); US$1,753 per capita (1998)
ANNUAL AVERAGE GROWTH OF GDP – 1.7 per cent (1996)
INFLATION RATE – 1.3 per cent (1999)
UNEMPLOYMENT - 38.8 per cent (1996)
TOTAL EXTERNAL DEBT – US$2,392 million (1998)

| *Trade with UK* | 1999 | 2000 |
|---|---|---|
| Imports from UK | £33,736,000 | £23,029,000 |
| Exports to UK | 18,404,000 | 19,847,000 |

## MADAGASCAR
*Repoblikan'i Madagasikara*

AREA – 226,658 sq. miles (587,041 sq. km)
POPULATION – 15,051,000 (1997 UN estimate). The people are of mixed Malayo-Polynesian, Arab and African origin. There are sizeable French, Chinese and Indian communities. The official languages are Malagasy and French
CAPITAL – Antananarivo (population, 1,052,835, 1993 census)
MAJOR CITIES – ΨAntsiranana (942,410); Fianarantsoa (2,671,150); ΨMahajanga (100,807); ΨToamasina (127,441), the chief port
CURRENCY – Franc malgache (FMG) of 100 centimes
NATIONAL ANTHEM - Ry tanindrazanay malala o (O, our beloved country)
NATIONAL DAY – 26 June (Independence Day)
NATIONAL FLAG – Equal horizontal bands of red (above) and green, with vertical white band by staff
LIFE EXPECTANCY (years) – male 45.0; female 47.7
POPULATION GROWTH RATE – 3.2 per cent (1999)
POPULATION DENSITY – 26 per sq. km (1998)
URBAN POPULATION – 29.6 per cent (2000 estimate)
MILITARY EXPENDITURE – 0.8 per cent of GDP (1999)
MILITARY PERSONNEL – 21,000: Army 20,000, Navy 500, Air Force 500, Paramilitaries 7,500
CONSCRIPTION DURATION – 18 months
ILLITERACY RATE – 54.3 per cent
ENROLMENT (percentage of age group) – primary 61 per cent (1996); tertiary 2.0 per cent (1996)

Madagascar lies 240 miles off the east coast of Africa and is the fourth largest island in the world.

## HISTORY AND POLITICS

Madagascar (known from 1958 to 1975 as the Malagasy Republic) became a French protectorate in 1895, and a French colony in 1896 when the former queen was exiled. Republican status was adopted on 14 October 1958, and independence was proclaimed on 26 June 1960.

The post-independence civilian government was replaced by a military government in 1975 and martial law was declared. A Supreme Council of the Revolution under Didier Ratsiraka was established.

In November 1991, President Ratsiraka relinquished executive power to a new prime minister, Guy Razanamasy. However, the president retained his official position and the main opposition grouping, the *Forces Vives*, established a rival government led by Albert Zafy. In December 1991 a transitional government including Forces Vives and Razanamasy supporters was formed to draft a new constitution, approved by referendum in August 1992. In the presidential election held in November 1992 and February 1993, Albert Zafy became the first president of the Third Republic, which came into being at the same time.

President Zafy was defeated in 1996 by former president Ratsiraka. Following legislative elections held in May 1998, Ratsiraka's *Action de Renouveau de Madagascar* (AREMA) party became the largest party in the National Assembly. The constitution also envisages an upper chamber, but this has yet to be established. Following the senatorial election on 18 March 2001, AREMA held 49 of the 60 elected seats.

### POLITICAL SYSTEM

The president is directly elected and serves a five-year term. The legislature is bicameral. The National Assembly is directly elected and comprises 150 members. The Senate comprises 90 members, of whom two-thirds are elected by an electoral college and one-third are nominated by the president.

HEAD OF STATE

*President*, Didier Ratsiraka, *elected* 29 December 1996, *inaugurated* 9 February 1997

COUNCIL OF MINISTERS *as at July 2001*

*Prime Minister, Finance and Economy*, Tantely Andrianarivo
*Deputy PM, Budget, Development of Autonomous Provinces*, Pierrot Rajaonarivelo
*Agriculture*, Marcel Raveloarijaona
*Armed Forces*, Maj.-Gen. Marcel Ranjeva
*Civil Service, Labour and Social Legislation*, Alice Razafinakanga
*Energy and Mines*, Charles Rasoja
*Environment*, M. Alphonse
*Fishing and Marine Resources*, Abdallah Houssene
*Foreign Affairs*, Lila Ratsifandriamanana
*Health*, Henriette Ratsimbazafimahefa
*Higher Education*, Joseph Sydson
*Industrialisation and Cottage Industry*, Mamy Ratovomalala
*Information, Culture and Communications*, Fredo Betsimifira
*Interior*, Brig.-Gen. Jean-Jacques Rasolondraibe
*Justice, Keeper of the Seals*, Anaclet Imbiky
*Livestock*, M. Rakotondrasoa
*Population, Women's Affairs and Childhood*, Noëline Jaotody
*Posts and Telecommunications*, Ny Hasina Andriamanjato
*Primary and Secondary Education*, Nivoson Jacquit Rosat Simon
*Private Sector Development and Privatisation*, Horace Constant
*Public Works*, Col. Jean Emile Tsaranazy
*Regional and Town Planning*, Herivelona Ramanantsoa
*Scientific Research*, Georges Soalahy Rakotonirainy
*Secretaries of State*, Maj.-Gen. Jean-Paul Bory (*Gendarmerie*); Ben Marofo Azaly (*Public Security*)
*Technical Education and Vocational Training*, Boniface Levelo
*Tourism*, Blandin Razafimanjato
*Trade and Consumption*, Alphonse Randrianambinina
*Transport and Meteorology*, Charles Rasolonahy
*Water and Forests*, Rija Rajohnson
*Youth and Sports*, Cdr. Ndrianasolo

EMBASSY OF THE REPUBLIC OF MADAGASCAR
4 avenue Raphael, F- 75016 Paris, France
Tel: (00 33) (1) 4504 6211
*Ambassador Plenipotentiary and Extraordinary*, HE Malala zo Raolison, apptd 1998

HONORARY CONSULATE OF THE REPUBLIC OF MADAGASCAR
16 Lanark Mansions, Pennard Road, London W12 8DT
Tel: 020-8746 0133
*Honorary Consul*, Stephen Hobbs

BRITISH EMBASSY

Lot II I 164 TER, Alarobia – Ambonilioa,
BP 167, Antananarivo 101
Tel: (00 261) (20) 2249378/9
*Ambassador Extraordinary and Plenipotentiary*, HE C. F. Mochan, apptd 1999

## ECONOMY

The economy is still largely based on agriculture, which employs more than 80 per cent of the workforce. The main products are rice, cassava, sugar cane and sweet potatoes. Development plans have placed emphasis on improving communications, the exploitation of mineral deposits and the creation of small industries. Madagascar was hit by three cyclones in February and April 2000, which caused widespread flooding, resulting in the destruction of much of the rice crop.

In 1998 there was a trade deficit of US$154 million and a current account deficit of US$301 million. Imports totalled US$514 million and exports US$243 million.

GNP – US$3,712 million (1999); US$250 per capita (1999)
GDP – US$1,776 million (1997); US$208 per capita (1998)
ANNUAL AVERAGE GROWTH OF GDP – 2.1 per cent (1996)
INFLATION RATE – 9.9 per cent (1999)
TOTAL EXTERNAL DEBT – US$4,394 million (1998)

| *Trade with UK* | 1999 | 2000 |
|---|---|---|
| Imports from UK | £6,263,000 | £6,787,000 |
| Exports to UK | 21,675,000 | 20,623,000 |

# MALAWI
*Dziko La Malaŵi*

AREA – 45,747 sq. miles (118,484 sq. km). Neighbours: Tanzania (north-east), Zambia (west), Mozambique (south)
POPULATION – 10,788,000 (1997 UN estimate). The official languages are Chichewa and English
CAPITAL – Lilongwe (population, 233,973, 1987)
MAJOR CITIES – Blantyre (331,588), incorporating Blantyre and Limbe, the major commercial and industrial centre; Mzuzu (44,238); Zomba (42,878), the former capital
CURRENCY – Kwacha (K) of 100 tambala
NATIONAL ANTHEM – O God Bless Our Land of Malaŵi
NATIONAL DAY – 6 July (Independence Day)
NATIONAL FLAG – Horizontal stripes of black, red and green, with rising sun in the centre of the black stripe
LIFE EXPECTANCY (years) – male 37.3; female 38.4
POPULATION GROWTH RATE – 1.5 per cent (1999)
POPULATION DENSITY – 87 per sq. km (1998)
URBAN POPULATION – 24.9 per cent (2000 estimate)
MILITARY EXPENDITURE – 1.8 per cent of GDP (1999)
MILITARY PERSONNEL – 5,000: Army 5,000, Paramilitaries 1,000

Malaŵi lies in south-eastern Africa. Much of the eastern border of Malaŵi is formed by Lake Malaŵi (formerly Lake Nyasa), which covers nearly half of the north of the country. The valley of the River Shire runs south from the lake, its watershed with the Zambezi lying on the western border with Mozambique and its tributary, the Ruo, with lakes Chinta and Chirwa, lying on the eastern border with Mozambique. The north and centre are plateaux, and the south highlands.

## HISTORY AND POLITICS

Malaŵi (formerly Nyasaland) assumed internal self-government on 1 February 1963, and became independent on 6 July 1964. It became a republic on 6 July 1966.

In 1991–2 Life President Hastings Banda, who had ruled since independence, came under increasing pressure to introduce a multiparty democratic system of government. In May 1992 aid donors tied new loans to improvements in the human rights record and moves to multiparty democracy. A referendum was held on the adoption of a multiparty democracy in June 1993 and approved by 63 per cent of voters. President Banda and the Malaŵi Congress Party refused to resign but parliament passed a law to amend the constitution to allow multiparty politics and Banda announced a political amnesty to allow exiles to return. Multiparty presidential and legislative elections held in May 1994 were won by Bakili Muluzi and the United Democratic Front (UDF) respectively. Foreign and multilateral aid has since been restored. Former President Banda died on 25 November 1997. Presidential and legislative elections were due to be held on 25 May 1999, but were delayed until 15 June; they were won by the UDF, who won 93 seats. President Muluzi was also re-elected.

### POLITICAL SYSTEM

There is a Cabinet consisting of the president and ministers. The unicameral National Assembly, which usually meets three times a year, consists of 193 members elected by universal suffrage for a five-year term of office.

### HEAD OF STATE

*President, Commander-in-Chief*, Bakili Muluzi, *elected* 17 May 1994, *sworn in* 21 May 1994, *re-elected* 15 June 1999
*Vice-President, Privatisation*, Justin Malewezi

### CABINET *as at July 2001*

The President
The Vice-President
*Agriculture and Irrigation Development*, Leonard Mangulama
*Attorney-General, Justice*, Peter Fachi
*Commerce and Industry*, Peter Kaleso
*Defence*, Rodwell Munyenyembe
*Education, Science and Technology*, George Nga Mtafa
*Finance and Economic Planning*, Mathews Chikaonda
*Foreign Affairs and International Co-operation*, Lilian Patel
*Gender, Youth and Community Services*, Mary Banda
*Health and Population*, Aleke Banda
*Home Affairs and Internal Security*, Mangeza Maloza
*Information*, Clement Stambuli
*Labour and Vocational Training*, Yusufu Mwawa
*Lands, Housing, Physical Planning and Services*, Thengo Maloya
*Natural Resources and Environmental Affairs*, Harry Thomson
*Sports and Culture*, Moses Dossi
*Tourism, National Parks and Wildlife*, Ken Lipenga
*Transport and Public Works*, Samuel Kaliyoma Phumisa
*Water Development*, Lee Mulanga
*Without Portfolio*, Uladi Mussa

### MALAŴI HIGH COMMISSION

33 Grosvenor Street, London W1X 0DE
Tel: 020-7491 4172/7
*High Commissioner*, HE Bright Msaka, apptd 1998

### BRITISH HIGH COMMISSION

PO Box 30042, Lilongwe 3
Tel: (00 265) 772 400
E-mail: bhc@wiss.co.mw
*High Commissioner*, Norman Ling, apptd 2001

BRITISH COUNCIL DIRECTOR, David Higgs, Plot No. 13/20 City Centre, PO Box 30222, Lilongwe 3; e-mail: bc.lilongwe@bc-lilongwe.bcouncil.org

## ECONOMY

The economy is largely agricultural, providing 90 per cent of export earnings; maize is the main subsistence crop, and tobacco, cassava, millet and rice are the main cash crops and principal exports. There are two sugar mills. A number of light manufacturing industries have been established, mainly in agricultural processing, clothing/textiles and building materials.

In 1998 imports totalled US$382 million and exports US$517 million.

GNP – US$1,961 million (1999); US$190 per capita (1999)
GDP – US$2,354 million (1997); US$156 per capita (1998)
ANNUAL AVERAGE GROWTH OF GDP – 8.3 per cent (1996)
INFLATION RATE – 44.9 per cent (1999)
TOTAL EXTERNAL DEBT – US$2,444 million (1998)

| *Trade with UK* | 1999 | 2000 |
|---|---|---|
| Imports from UK | £17,511,000 | £10,878,000 |
| Exports to UK | 10,855,000 | 11,067,000 |

## COMMUNICATIONS

A single-track railway runs from Mchinji on the Zambian border, through Lilongwe and Salima on Lake Malaŵi (itself served by two passenger and a number of cargo boats) through to Blantyre. The route south to the Mozambique port of Beira was severed by the Mozambican civil war, but the route to Nacala in Mozambique is open again; there are 797 km of railway track. There are 14,594 km of roads in Malaŵi of which 2,849 km are bituminised. There is an international airport 26 km from Lilongwe, which handles regional and intercontinental flights, and another airport at Chileka.

## EDUCATION

The Ministry of Education and Culture is responsible for secondary schools, technical education and primary teacher training. Religious bodies, with government assistance, still play an important part in these fields. The University of Malaŵi was opened in 1965; there are also four colleges and one polytechnic.
ILLITERACY RATE – 39.7 per cent
ENROLMENT (percentage of age group) – primary 100 per cent (1996); secondary 2 per cent (1994); tertiary 0.6 per cent (1996)

---

## MALAYSIA
*Persekutuan Tanah Malaysia*

---

AREA – 127,320 sq. miles (329,758 sq. km). Thailand borders the Malay peninsula to the north. On Borneo, Malaysia (Sarawak and Sabah) borders Indonesia to the south, and surrounds Brunei to the north
POPULATION – 22,710,000 (1997 UN estimate); 16,921,300 (1988 census): Malays (58 per cent), Chinese (27 per cent), and those of Indian and Sri Lankan origin, as well as the indigenous races of Sarawak and Sabah. Bahasa Malaysia (Malay) is the official language, but English, various dialects of Chinese, and Tamil are also widely spoken. There are a few indigenous languages widely spoken in Sabah and Sarawak. Islam is the official religion of Malaysia, each ruler being the head of religion in his state (except in Sabah and Sarawak). The Yang di-Pertuan Agong is the head of religion in Melaka and Penang. The constitution guarantees religious freedom
CAPITAL – Kuala Lumpur (population, 1,145,342, 1991); Putrajaya (Administrative Capital) (population 3,000, 1999 estimate)
MAJOR CITIES – Ipoh (382,853); Johore Bharu (328,436); Petaling Jaya (254,350), 1991
CURRENCY – Malaysian dollar (ringgit) (M$) of 100 sen
NATIONAL ANTHEM – Negara-Ku
NATIONAL DAY – 31 August (*Hari Kebangsaan*)
NATIONAL FLAG – Equal horizontal stripes of red (seven) and white (seven); 14-point yellow star and crescent in blue canton
LIFE EXPECTANCY (years) – male 67.6; female 69.9
POPULATION GROWTH RATE – 2.3 per cent (1999)

POPULATION DENSITY – 67 per sq. km (1998)
URBAN POPULATION – 57.4 per cent (2000 estimate)
ILLITERACY RATE – 12.5 per cent (2000)
ENROLMENT (percentage of age group) – primary 100 per cent (1996); tertiary 11.7 per cent (1996)

Malaysia comprises the 11 states of peninsular Malaya plus Sabah and Sarawak. It occupies two distinct regions, the Malay peninsula which extends from the isthmus of Kra to the Singapore Strait, and the north-western coastal area of the island of Borneo. Each is separated from the other by the South China Sea.

The year is commonly divided into the south-west and north-west monsoon seasons. Rainfall averages about 100 inches throughout the year. The average daily temperature varies from 21° C to 32° C, though in higher areas temperatures are lower and vary widely.

## HISTORY AND POLITICS

The Federation of Malaya became an independent country within the Commonwealth on 31 August 1957. On 16 September 1963 the federation was enlarged by the accession of the states of Singapore, Sabah (formerly British North Borneo) and Sarawak, and the name of Malaysia was adopted from that date. On 9 August 1965 Singapore seceded from the federation.

The National Front (Barisan Nasional) Coalition led by Dr Mahathir Mohamed won a fifth term in office in a general election held on 29 November 1999, winning 148 of the 193 seats.

### POLITICAL SYSTEM

The constitution provides for a strong federal government and a degree of autonomy for the state governments. It created a constitutional Supreme Head of the Federation (HM the *Yang di-Pertuan Agong*) and a Deputy Supreme Head (HRH *Timbalan Yang di-Pertuan Agong*) to be elected for a term of five years by the rulers from among their number. The Malay rulers are either chosen or succeed to their position in accordance with the custom of the particular state. In other states of Malaysia, choice of the head of state is at the discretion of the Yang di-Pertuan Agong after consultation with the Chief Minister of the state.

The Federal Parliament consists of two houses, the Senate and the House of Representatives. The Senate (*Dewan Negara*) consists of 69 members who serve a six-year term, 26 being elected by the Legislative Assemblies of the states (two from each) and 43 appointed by the Yang di-Pertuan Agong. The House of Representatives (*Dewan Rakyat*) consists of 193 members elected for a five-year term by universal adult suffrage with a common electoral roll.

### FEDERAL STRUCTURE

According to the constitution, each state shall have its own constitution not inconsistent with the federal constitution, with the ruler or governor acting on the advice of an Executive Council appointed on the advice of the Chief Minister and a single-chamber Legislative Assembly. The Legislative Assemblies are fully elected on the same basis as the federal parliament.

| *State* | *Area (sq. km)* | *Population (1997 estimate)* | *Main Town* |
|---|---|---|---|
| Johor | 18,986 | 2,554,100 | ΨJohor Baharu |
| Kedah | 9,426 | 1,530,100 | Alor Setar |
| Kelantan | 14,943 | 1,447,000 | Kota Baharu |
| Melaka | 1,650 | 582,000 | ΨMelaka |
| Negeri Sembilan | 6,643 | 810,500 | Seremban |
| Pahang | 35,965 | 1,239,000 | ΨKuantan |
| Penang | 1,031 | 1,222,100 | ΨGeorgetown |
| Perak | 21,005 | 2,094,800 | Ipoh |
| Perlis | 795 | 217,400 | Kangar |
| Sabah | 73,711 | 2,593,400 | ΨKota Kinabalu |
| Sarawak | 124,449 | 1,954,300 | ΨKuching |
| Selangor | 7,956 | 2,999,800 | ΨShah Alam |
| Terengganu | 12,955 | 975,800 | ΨKuala Terengganu |
| *Federal Territories* | | | |
| Kuala Lumpur | | 1,231,500 | |
| Labuan | | | |

### HEAD OF STATE

*Supreme Head of State*, HM Salehuddin Abdul Aziz ibni al-Marhum Hisamuddin Alam (Yang di-Pertuan Agong of Selangor), *sworn in* 26 April 1999

### CABINET *as at July 2001*

*Prime Minister, Finance and Special Functions*, Dr Mahathir Mohamed
*Deputy Prime Minister, Home Affairs*, Abdullah Ahmad Badawi
*Agriculture*, Mohamed Effendi Norwani
*Culture, Arts and Tourism*, Abdul Kadir Sheikh Fadzir
*Defence*, Mohamed Najib Tun Razak
*Domestic Trade and Consumer Affairs*, Muhyiddin Yasin
*Education*, Musa Mohamad
*Energy, Telecommunications and Posts*, Leo Moggie Anak Irok
*Entrepreneurial Development*, Mohamed Nazri Abdul Aziz
*Foreign Affairs*, Hamid Albar
*Health*, Chua Jui Meng
*Housing and Local Government*, Ong Ka Ting
*Human Resources*, Fong Chan Ong
*Information*, Mohamad Khalil Yaakob
*International Trade and Industry*, Rafidah Aziz
*Lands and Co-operative Development*, Kasitah Gaddam
*National Unity and Social Development*, Zaharah binti Sulaiman
*Primary Industries*, Dr Lim Keng Yaik
*Prime Minister's Office*, Bernard Dompok; Pandikar Amin Musa; Abdul Hamid Zainal Abidin; Rais Yatim
*Public Works*, S. Samy Vellu
*Rural Development*, Azmi Khalid
*Science, Technology and Environment*, Law Hieng Ding
*Transport*, Dr Ling Liong Sik
*Women's Affairs*, Shahrizat Abdul Jalil
*Youth and Sports*, Hishamuddin Tun Hussein

### MALAYSIAN HIGH COMMISSION

45 Belgrave Square, London SW1X 8QT
Tel: 020-7235 8033
*High Commissioner*, HE Dato Salim bin Hashim, apptd 2001
*Deputy High Commissioner*, Mohamad Daud M. Yusoff
*Defence Adviser*, Col. Kamaruddin Mattan

### BRITISH HIGH COMMISSION

185 Jalan Ampang (PO Box 11030), 50732 Kuala Lumpur
Tel: (00 60) (3) 2148 2122
*High Commissioner*, HE Graham Fry, apptd 1998
*Deputy High Commissioner*, M. Canning
*Counsellor (Commercial)*, M. Horne, OBE
*Defence Adviser*, Col. R. J. Little

BRITISH COUNCIL DIRECTOR, Dr Tom Cameron, Jalan Bukit Aman, PO Box 10539, 50916 Kuala Lumpur; e-mail: kualalumpur@britishcouncil.org.my. There are also offices at Penang, Kota Kinabalu (Sabah) and Kuching (Sarawak).

## DEFENCE

The Army has 816 armoured personnel carriers. The Royal Malaysian Navy has four frigates, 41 patrol and coastal vessels and 17 armed helicopters at three bases. The Royal Malaysian Air Force has 84 combat aircraft.

Australia maintains an infantry company and an air force detachment in Malaysia.

MILITARY EXPENDITURE – 4.0 per cent of GDP (1999)
MILITARY PERSONNEL – 96,000: Army 80,000, Navy 8,000, Air Force 8,000, Paramilitaries 20,100

## ECONOMY

From being an agriculturally-based economy reliant on raw materials exports at independence, Malaysia has undergone an industrialisation programme and now produces clothing, textiles, rubber goods, electronics, office equipment, cars, household appliances, semi-conductors, food processing and chemicals. Under the New Economic Policy of 1970–90, the economy grew at an average rate of 6.7 per cent a year. The National Development Policy 1990–2000 is seen as the second stage in making Malaysia a fully-developed industrial state by 2020; it aims for GDP growth of 8 per cent.per year. There are extensive privatisation programmes involving telecommunications, railways, airports, electricity and shipping. In 1997 40.8 per cent of GDP was produced by services, 47.6 per cent by manufacturing and 11.7 per cent by agriculture.

In October 2000 and March 2001, the government announced measures to stimulate the economy, which included increased spending on schools, agricultural subsidies and incentives to increase spending.

GNP – US$76,944 million (1999); US$3,400 per capita (1999)
GDP – US$97,884 million (1997); US$3,317 per capita (1998)
ANNUAL AVERAGE GROWTH OF GDP – 8.6 per cent (1996)
INFLATION RATE – 2.7 per cent (1999)
UNEMPLOYMENT – 3.2 per cent (1998)
TOTAL EXTERNAL DEBT – US$44,773 million (1998)

### TRADE

Malaysia is the largest exporter of natural rubber, tin, palm oil and tropical hardwoods. Other major export commodities are manufactured and processed products, petroleum, oil and other minerals, palm kernel oil, tea and pepper. Imports consist mainly of machinery and transport equipment, manufactured goods, foods, consumer durables and metal products. Japan, the USA and Singapore are the main trading partners.

In 1997 Malaysia had a trade surplus of US$3,876 million and a current account deficit of US$4,792 million. In 1999 mports totalled US$64,966 million and exports US$84,455 million.

| *Trade with UK* | 1999 | 2000 |
|---|---|---|
| Imports from UK | £940,269,000 | £911,966,000 |
| Exports to UK | 2,039,770,000 | 2,374,441,000 |

## MALDIVES
*Divehi Rājjē ge Jumhūriyyā*

AREA – 115 sq. miles (298 sq. km)
POPULATION – 278,000 (1997 UN estimate). The people are Sunni Muslims and the Maldivian (Dhivehi) language is akin to Elu or old Sinhalese
CAPITAL – ΨMalé (population, 62,973, 1995)
CURRENCY – Rufiyaa of 100 laaris
NATIONAL ANTHEM - Gavmī mi ekuverikan matī tibegen kurīme salām (In national unity we salute our nation)
NATIONAL DAY – 26 July
NATIONAL FLAG – Green field bearing a white crescent, with wide red border
LIFE EXPECTANCY (years) – male 63.3; female 62.6
POPULATION GROWTH RATE – 2.9 per cent (1999)
POPULATION DENSITY – 909 per sq. km (1998)
URBAN POPULATION – 26.1 per cent (2000 estimate)
MILITARY EXPENDITURE – 9.6 per cent of GDP (1999)
ILLITERACY RATE – 3.7 per cent

The Maldives are a chain of coral atolls 400 miles to the south-west of Sri Lanka, stretching north for about 600 miles from just south of the Equator. There are about 19 coral atolls comprising over 1,200 islands, 198 of which are inhabited. No point in the entire chain of islands is more than eight feet above sea-level.

## HISTORY AND POLITICS

Until 1952 the islands were a sultanate under the protection of the British Crown. Internal self-government was achieved in 1948 and full independence in 1965. The Maldives became a special member of the Commonwealth in 1982 and a full member in 1985.

The Maldives form a republic which is elective. The legislature, the Citizens' Assembly (*Majlis*), has 42 representatives elected from all the atolls, and eight appointed by the president, for a five-year term. The government consists of a Cabinet, which is responsible to the Majlis. There are no political parties. Under the 1998 constitution, the president is elected by the Majlis and confirmed by a referendum.

The most recent legislative election took place on 19 November 1999.

### HEAD OF STATE

*President, Defence, National Security, Finance and Treasury*, HE Maumoon Abdul Gayoom, *elected* 1978, *re-elected* 1983, 1989, 1993, 16 October 1998

### CABINET *as at July 2001*

*The President*
*Atolls Administration, Speaker of the Majlis*, Abdullah Hameed
*Attorney-General*, Mohamed Munnawwar
*Chief Justice, President of the Supreme Council on Islamic Affairs*, Mohamed Rashid Ibrahim
*Construction and Public Works*, Umar Zahir
*Education*, Dr Mohamed Latheef
*Fisheries and Agriculture*, Abdul Rasheed Hussain
*Foreign Affairs*, Fathullah Jameel
*Health*, Ahmed Abdulla
*Home Affairs, Housing and Environment*, Ismail Shafeeu
*Human Resources, Employment and Labour*, Abdullah Kamaaludheen
*Information, Arts and Culture*, Ibrahim Manik
*Justice*, Ahmed Zahir
*Minister at the President's Office*, Abdullah Jameel
*Mustashaaru of the Supreme Council on Islamic Affairs*, Moosa Fathuhy
*Planning and National Development*, Ibrahim Hussain Zaki

*Tourism*, Hassan Sobir
*Trade and Industry*, Abdulla Yameen
*Transport and Civil Aviation*, Ilyas Ibrahim
*Women's Affairs and Social Welfare*, Rashida Yoosuf
*Youth and Sports*, Mohamed Zahir Hussain

HIGH COMMISSION OF THE REPUBLIC OF MALDIVES
22 Nottingham Place, London W1M 3FB
Tel: 020-7224 2135
*Acting High Commissioner*, Adam Hassan

BRITISH HIGH COMMISSIONER, HE Linda Duffield, resident at Colombo, Sri Lanka

## ECONOMY

The vegetation of the islands is coconut palms with some scrub. Hardly any cultivation of crops is possible and nearly all food to supplement the basic fish diet has to be imported. Tourism is expanding rapidly (395,700 visitors in 1998). The principal industry is fishing, which together with tourism accounts for about 30 per cent of GDP. The Maldives National Ship Management Ltd (MNSML) has a fleet of nine merchant ships. There is an international airport at Malé.

In 1999 the Maldives had a trade deficit of US$266 million and a current account deficit of US$60 million. Imports totalled US$402 million and exports US$64 million.

GNP – US$322 million (1999); US$1,160 per capita (1999)
GDP – US$349 million (1997); US$1,350 per capita (1998)
ANNUAL AVERAGE GROWTH OF GDP – 6.5 per cent (1996)
INFLATION RATE – 3.0 per cent (1999)
TOTAL EXTERNAL DEBT – US$180 million (1998)

| *Trade with UK* | 1999 | 2000 |
|---|---|---|
| Imports from UK | £4,907,000 | £5,092,000 |
| Exports to UK | 5,460,000 | 6,814,000 |

# MALI
*République du Mali*

AREA – 478,841 sq. miles (1,240,192 sq. km). Neighbours: Senegal (west), Mauritania (north-west), Algeria (north-east), Niger (east), Burkina Faso and Côte d'Ivoire (south), Guinea (south-west)
POPULATION – 10,911,000 (1997 UN estimate): 50 per cent Mande (Bambara, Malinke, Sarakole), 17 per cent Peul, 12 per cent Voltaic, 6 per cent Songhai, 10 per cent Tuareg and Moor. The official language is French; Bambara is the largest local language
CAPITAL – Bamako (population, 809,552, 1996 UN estimate)
MAJOR CITIES – Gao; Kayes; Mopti; Ségou; Sikasso; Timbuktu (all regional capitals)
CURRENCY – Franc CFA of 100 centimes
NATIONAL ANTHEM – A ton appel, Mali (At your call, Mali)
NATIONAL DAY – 22 September
NATIONAL FLAG – Vertical stripes of green (by staff), yellow and red
LIFE EXPECTANCY (years) – male 41.3; female 44.0
POPULATION GROWTH RATE – 2.4 per cent (1999)
POPULATION DENSITY – 9 per sq. km (1998)
URBAN POPULATION – 30.0 per cent (2000 estimate)
MILITARY EXPENDITURE – 1.2 per cent of GDP (1999)
MILITARY PERSONNEL – 7,350: Army 7,350, Paramilitaries 4,800
CONSCRIPTION DURATION – Two years (selective)
ILLITERACY RATE – 59.7 per cent
ENROLMENT (percentage of age group) – primary 31 per cent (1996); secondary 5 per cent (1990); tertiary 1 per cent (1997)

## HISTORY AND POLITICS

Formerly the French colony of Soudan, the territory elected on 24 November 1958 to remain an autonomous republic within the French Community. It associated with Senegal in the Federation of Mali, which was granted full independence on 20 June 1960. The Federation was effectively dissolved in August 1960 by the secession of Senegal. The title of the Republic of Mali was adopted in September 1960.

A new constitution was approved by referendum in January 1992. The new constitution provided for a multiparty political system, and legislative elections were held in February and March 1992 with the Alliance for Democracy in Mali (ADEMA) emerging victorious. Alpha Konaré, the ADEMA leader, won the presidential elections in April 1992 and was re-elected in May 1997. In legislative elections in July and August 1997, ADEMA won 129 out of 147 seats in the National Assembly. On 14 February 2000, the government resigned and a new prime minister and government was formed the following day, comprising members of ADEMA and opposition parties.

### HEAD OF STATE

*President*, Alpha Oumar Konaré, *elected* 1992, *re-elected* 11 May 1997

### CABINET *as at July 2001*

*Prime Minister, Integration*, Mande Sidibé
*Armed Forces and Veterans*, Soumeylou Boubeye Maiga
*Communications*, Ascofaré Tamboura
*Cottage Industry and Tourism*, Zakyatou Oualett Halatine
*Culture*, Pascal Coulibaly
*Economy and Finance*, Bacari Koné
*Education*, Moustapha Dicko
*Environment*, Soumaila Cissé
*Foreign Affairs, Malians Abroad*, Maj. Modibo Sidibé
*Health*, Traore Fatoumata Nafo
*Industry, Commerce, Transport*, Toure Alimata Traoré
*Justice and Keeper of the Seals*, Abdoulaye Ogotembely Poudiougou
*Labour and Professional Training*, Makan Sissoko
*Mines, Energy and Water Resources*, Aboubacary Coulibaly
*Rural Development*, Ahamed El Madani Diallo
*Security and Civil Protection*, Gen. Tiecoura Doumbia
*Social Development, Solidarity and the Elderly*, Diakité Fatoumata N'Diayé
*State Building and Housing*, Bouare Fily Sissoko
*Territorial Administration and Local Communities*, Ousmane Sy
*Women, Children and the Family*, Diarra Afsata Thiero
*Youth and Sports*, Adama Koné

EMBASSY OF THE REPUBLIC OF MALI
Molièrelaan 487, B-1050 Brussels, Belgium
Tel: (00 32) (2) 345 7432
*Ambassador Extraordinary and Plenipotentiary*, Ahmed Mohamed A. G. Hamani, apptd 2001

BRITISH AMBASSADOR, HE E. Alan Burner, resident at Dakar, Senegal
BRITISH CONSULATE – Bamako

## ECONOMY

Mali's principal exports are cotton and gold. Principal imports include machinery and vehicles, petroleum, and foodstuffs. Mali rejoined the CFA Franc Zone in 1984.

The IMF and the International Development Association agreed in September 2000 to provide Mali with US$870 million under the Heavily Indebted Poor Countries initiative.

In 1997 Mali had a trade surplus of US$10 million and a current account deficit of US$178 million. In 1999 imports totalled US$751 million and exports US$536 million.

GNP – US$2,577 million (1999); US$240 per capita (1999)
GDP – US$2,551 million (1997); US$254 per capita (1998)
ANNUAL AVERAGE GROWTH OF GDP – 4.0 per cent (1996)
INFLATION RATE – 4.2 per cent (1999)
TOTAL EXTERNAL DEBT – US$3,201 million (1998)

| *Trade with UK* | 1999 | 2000 |
|---|---|---|
| Imports from UK | £15,965,000 | £17,903,000 |
| Exports to UK | 2,769,000 | 6,851,000 |

## MALTA
*Repubblika ta' Malta*

AREA – 122 sq. miles (316 sq. km)
POPULATION – 379,000 (1998). The Maltese are mainly Roman Catholic. The Maltese language is of Semitic origin and held by some to be derived from the Carthaginian and Phoenician tongues. Maltese and English are the official languages
CAPITAL – ΨValletta (population, 7,100, 1998)
CURRENCY – Maltese lira (LM) of 100 cents or 1,000 mils
NATIONAL ANTHEM – L-Innu Malti
NATIONAL DAYS – 31 March (Freedom Day); 8 September (Our Lady of Victories); 7 June (Sette Giugno Riots); 21 September (Independence Day); 13 December (Republic Day)
NATIONAL FLAG – Two equal vertical stripes, white at the hoist and red at the fly. A representation of the George Cross is carried edged with red in the canton of the white stripe
LIFE EXPECTANCY (years) – male 75.7; female 80.8
POPULATION GROWTH RATE – 1.0 per cent (1999)
POPULATION DENSITY – 1,194 per sq. km (1998)
URBAN POPULATION – 90.5 per cent (2000 estimate)
MILITARY EXPENDITURE – 0.8 per cent of GDP (1999)
MILITARY PERSONNEL – Armed Forces 2,140

Malta lies in the Mediterranean Sea, 93 km (58 miles) from Sicily and about 288 km (180 miles) from the African coast. It is about 27 km (17 miles) in length and 14.5 km (9 miles) in breadth. Malta also includes the islands of Gozo (area 67 sq. km (25.9 sq. miles)), Comino and minor islets.

### HISTORY AND POLITICS

Malta was in turn held by the Phoenicians, Carthaginians, Romans and Arabs. In 1090 it was conquered by Count Roger of Normandy and in 1530 handed over to the Knights of St John. In 1565 it sustained the famous siege, when the Turks were successfully withstood by Grand-master La Valette. The Knights fortified the islands and built Valletta before being expelled by Napoleon in 1798. The Maltese rose against the French garrison soon afterwards and the island was subsequently blockaded by the British fleet. The Maltese people requested the protection of the British Crown in 1802 on condition that their rights would be respected. The islands were finally annexed to the British Crown by the Treaty of Paris in 1814.

Malta was again besieged during the Second World War. From June 1940 to the end of the war, 432 members of the garrison and 1,540 civilians were killed by enemy aircraft. The island was awarded the George Cross for gallantry on 15 April 1942.

On 21 September 1964 Malta became an independent state within the Commonwealth, and on 13 December 1974 a republic within the Commonwealth.

Elections to the unicameral parliament of 65 members are held every five years by a system of proportional representation; to ensure that a party receiving more than 50 per cent of the votes cast obtains a parliamentary majority, extra seats may be allocated to that party.

Elections held in September 1998 were won by the Nationalist Party, who gained 35 seats; Eddie Fenech-Adami, a strong supporter of Malta's accession to the European Union, was appointed prime minister.

#### FOREIGN RELATIONS

Malta applied for EC membership in 1990, but in October 1996 the Labour government announced its intention to withdraw Malta's EU application and its participation in NATO's Partnership for Peace programme. Following the election in 1998, the new government immediately re-activated Malta's application for EU membership. Accession negotiations commenced in February 2000.

#### HEAD OF STATE

*President*, Guido de Marco, *took office* 4 April 1999

#### CABINET *as at July 2001*

*Prime Minister*, Edward Fenech-Adami
*Deputy Prime Minister, Social Policy*, Lawrence Gonzi
*Agriculture and Fisheries*, Ninu Zammit
*Economic Services*, Josef Bonnici
*Education*, Louis Galea
*Environment*, Francis Zammit Dimech
*Finance*, John Dalli
*Foreign Affairs*, Joe Borg
*Gozo*, Giovanna Debono
*Health*, Louis Deguara
*Home Affairs*, Tonio Borg
*Justice and Local Government*, Austin Gatt
*Tourism*, Michael Refalo
*Transport and Communications*, Censu Galea

#### MALTA HIGH COMMISSION

Malta House, 36–38 Piccadilly, London W1V 0PQ
Tel: 020-7292 4800
*High Commissioner*, HE George Bonello Dupuis, apptd 1999

#### BRITISH HIGH COMMISSION

7 St Anne Street, Floriana (PO Box 506), Malta GC
Tel: (00 356) 233134/7
E-mail: bhc@vol.net.mt
*High Commissioner*, HE Howard John Pearce, CVO, apptd 1999

BRITISH COUNCIL DIRECTOR, Ronnie Micallef, c/o British High Commission; e-mail: britcoun@waldonet.net.mt

### ECONOMY

Tourism has assumed primary importance, with 1,214,230 tourists visiting the island in 1999. In 1999 3 3 million passengers passed through Malta International Airport.

Agriculture and fisheries are also important. Principal products are potatoes, tomatoes, animal products, fruit, and other vegetables.

In 1999 manufacturing employed 21.8 per cent of the workforce and accounted for 22.8 per cent of GDP. Industries include communications equipment, food processing, textiles, footwear and clothing, plastics and chemical products, electrical machinery, medical equipment and furniture. Value Added Tax was re-introduced in January 1999.

In 1999 there was a trade deficit of US$574 million and a current account deficit of US$128 million. Imports totalled US$2,860 million and exports US$1,989 million.

GNP – US$3,492 million (1999); US$9,210 per capita (1999)
GDP – US$3,621 million (1999); US$9,350 per capita (1999)
ANNUAL AVERAGE GROWTH OF GDP – 4.6 per cent (1999)
INFLATION RATE – 2.1 per cent (1999)
UNEMPLOYMENT – 5.3 per cent (1999)
TOTAL EXTERNAL DEBT – US$1,034 million (1997)

### TRADE

The principal imports are foodstuffs (mainly wheat, meats, milk and fruit), fodder, beverages and tobacco, fuels, chemicals, textiles and machinery (industrial, agricultural and transport). The chief exports are processed food, electronics, textiles, and other manufactures.

| *Trade with UK* | 1999 | 2000 |
|---|---|---|
| Imports from UK | £199,299,000 | £213,843,000 |
| Exports to UK | 126,184,000 | 129,683,000 |

## EDUCATION

Education is compulsory between the ages of five and 16 and is free at all levels. Secondary education in state schools is provided in secondary schools, junior lyceums and trade schools. There are ten junior lyceums, 18 secondary schools and five centres catering for low achievers.

A Junior College, administered by the University of Malta, prepares students specifically for a university course. Tertiary education is available at the University of Malta. There are also schools administered by the Catholic Church and other private schools.

ILLITERACY RATE – 7.9 per cent (2000)
ENROLMENT (percentage of age group) – primary 100 per cent (1999); secondary 100 per cent (1999); tertiary 21 per cent (1999)

---

## MARSHALL ISLANDS
*Republic of the Marshall Islands*

---

AREA – 70 sq. miles (181 sq. km)
POPULATION – 641,000 (1997 UN estimate): 99 per cent are Micronesian. Over half the population is under 15. About 60 per cent of the population is concentrated on the two atolls of Majuro and Kwajalein. The population is Christian, primarily Protestant but with a substantial Catholic minority. Marshallese and English are the official languages
CAPITAL – Dalap-Uliga-Darrit, on Majuro Atoll (population, 20,000)
MAJOR TOWN – Ebeye (9,200)
CURRENCY – Currency is that of the USA
NATIONAL DAY – 1 May (Independence Day)
NATIONAL FLAG – Blue with a diagonal ray divided white over orange running from the lower hoist to the upper fly; in the canton a white sun
LIFE EXPECTANCY (years) – male 64.0; female 67.1
POPULATION GROWTH RATE – 3.4 per cent (1999)
POPULATION DENSITY – 350 per sq. km (1998)
URBAN POPULATION – 71.9 per cent (2000 estimate)

The Republic of the Marshall Islands consists of 29 atolls and five islands in the central Pacific. The islands and atolls form two parallel chains running north-west to south-east: the Ratak (Sunrise) chain and the Ralik (Sunset) chain. The largest atoll is Kwajalein in the Ralik chain. The atolls are coral and the islands are volcanic. None of the islands rises more than a few metres above sea level. The climate is hot and humid with little seasonal variation in temperature.

## HISTORY AND POLITICS

The Marshall Islands were claimed by Spain in 1592 but were left undisturbed by the Spanish Empire for 300 years. In 1886 the Marshall Islands formally became a German protectorate. On the outbreak of the First World War in 1914, Japan took control of the islands on behalf of the Allied powers, and after the war administered the territory as a League of Nations mandate. During the Second World War US armed forces seized the islands from the Japanese after intense fighting. In 1947 the USA entered into agreement with the UN Security Council to administer the Micronesia area, of which the Marshall Islands are a part, as the UN Trust Territory of the Pacific Islands.

The islands became internally self-governing in 1979, and the US Trusteeship administration came to an end on 21 October 1986, when a Compact of Free Association between the USA and the Republic of the Marshall Islands came into effect. By this agreement the USA recognised the Republic of the Marshall Islands as a fully sovereign and independent state. The UN Security Council terminated the UN Trust Territory of the Pacific in relation to the Marshall Islands and recognised its independence in December 1990.

### FOREIGN RELATIONS

The Republic of the Marshall Islands has no defence forces. The Compact of Free Association places full responsibility for defence of the Marshall Islands on the USA. The US Department of Defense retains control of islands within Kwajalein Atoll where it has a missile test range.

In 2000 the government of the Marshall Islands petitioned the USA for US$2.7 billion to fund medical care for victims of radiation from US nuclear tests in the islands in the 1940s and 1950s and to rectify environmental damage.

### POLITICAL SYSTEM

The republic is a democracy based on a parliamentary system of government. The executive is headed by the president, who is elected by the *Nitijela* from among its members. The president serves for a four-year term. The legislature has two chambers, the Council of Chiefs (*Iroij*) of 12 members and the Nitijela of 33 members. The Nitijela is the law-making chamber, to which the president and government are accountable. The Iroij has an advisory role.

There are 24 local government districts, each of which usually consists of an elected council, a mayor and appointed local officials.

In the general election which took place on 15 November 1999, the United Democratic Party won 18 seats.

### HEAD OF STATE

*President*, Kessai Note, *elected* 4 January 2000

### GOVERNMENT as at *July 2001*

*The President*
*Education*, Wilfred Kendall
*Finance*, Michael Konelious
*Foreign Affairs* Alvin Jacklick

*Health and Environment*, Tadashi Lometo
*Internal Affairs and Welfare*, Nidel Lorak
*Justice*, Witten Philippo
*Minister in Assistance to the Presidents*, Gerald Zackios
*Public Works*, Rien Morris
*Resources and Development*, John Silk
*Transportation and Communications*, Brenson Wase

BRITISH AMBASSADOR, HE Christopher Haslam, resident at Suva, Fiji

## ECONOMY

The economy is a mixture of subsistence and a service-based sector. About half the working population is engaged in agriculture and fishing, with coconut oil and copra production comprising 90 per cent of total exports. Imports include oil, food and machinery. The service sector is based in Majuro and Ebeye and concentrated in banking and insurance, construction, transportation and tourism. Direct US aid under the Compact accounts for two-thirds of the islands' budget. The islands charge foreign fishing fleets licences for fishing tuna in the waters around the islands. Japanese fleets pay some US$3 million a year. The USA, Japan and Australia are the main trading partners.
ANNUAL AVERAGE GROWTH OF GDP – 2.5 per cent (1996)

| *Trade with UK* | 1999 | 2000 |
|---|---|---|
| Imports from UK | £2,606,000 | £7,414,000 |
| Exports to UK | 1,171,000 | 633,000 |

## COMMUNICATIONS

Air Marshall Islands provides air services within the islands and to Hawaii. Continental Air Micronesia serves Majuro and Kwajalein with flights to Hawaii and Guam. Majuro also has shipping links to Hawaii, Australia, Japan and throughout the Pacific.

## SOCIAL WELFARE

Majuro and Ebeye have hospitals run by the government with aid from the US Public Health Service. Each outer island community has a health assistant.

The state school system provides education up to age 18, but only 25 per cent of students proceed beyond elementary level because of inadequate resources.

# MAURITANIA
*Al-Jumhūriyya al-Islāmiyya al-Mawrītāniyya*

AREA – 395,956 sq. miles (1,025,520 sq. km). Neighbours: Senegal (south-west), Mali (east and south), Algeria and Western Sahara (north)
POPULATION – 2,598,000 (1997 UN estimate). The official language is Arabic. Pulaar, Soninke, Wolof and French are also spoken
CAPITAL – Nouakchott (population, 850,000)
CURRENCY – Ouguiya (UM) of 5 khoums
NATIONAL DAY – 28 November
NATIONAL FLAG – Yellow star and crescent on green ground
LIFE EXPECTANCY (years) – male 49.5; female 53.0
POPULATION GROWTH RATE – 2.8 per cent (1999)
POPULATION DENSITY – 2 per sq. km (1998)
UNEMPLOYMENT – 57.7 per cent (2000 estimate)
MILITARY EXPENDITURE – 2.0 per cent of GDP (1999)
MILITARY PERSONNEL – 15,650: Army 15,000, Navy 500, Air Force 150, Paramilitaries 5,000
CONSCRIPTION DURATION – Two years
ILLITERACY RATE – 60.1 per cent (2000)
ENROLMENT (percentage of age group) – primary 57 per cent (1996); tertiary 3.8 per cent (1996)

## HISTORY AND POLITICS

Mauritania elected on 28 November 1958 to remain within the French Community as an autonomous republic. It became fully independent on 28 November 1960. In 1972 Mauritania left the Franc Zone.

Mauritania and Morocco occupied the Western Sahara territory in February 1976 when Spain formally relinquished it and in April 1976 agreed on a new frontier dividing the territory between them. In August 1979, Mauritania relinquished all claim to the southern sector of the Western Sahara after a three-year war against Polisario Front guerrillas.

After a military coup in 1978, Mauritania was ruled by a Military Committee for National Salvation. In April 1991 President ould Taya announced a political amnesty, followed by multiparty elections for a reconvened Senate and National Assembly. The constitution was approved by referendum in July 1991. Multiparty legislative elections were held in March 1992 and won by the Republican Democratic and Social Party (PRDS) led by President ould Taya. The legislative election in October 1996 was won by the PRDS after the opposition grouping, the Union of Democratic Forces (UDF) pulled out after the first round accusing the government of fraud. In the presidential election in December 1997, President ould Taya was re-elected following a boycott by opposition parties. A legislative election was due to be held by October 2001.

### HEAD OF STATE

*President*, Col. Moaouia ould Sidi Mohammed Taya (PRDS), *took power* 12 December 1984, *elected* 17 January 1992, *re-elected* 12 December 1997

### COUNCIL OF MINISTERS *as at July 2001*

*Prime Minister*, Cheik El-Avia ould Mohamed Khouna
*Civil Service, Labour, Youth, Sports*, Baba ould Sidi
*Communications and Relations with Parliament*, Rachid ould Saleh
*Culture, Islamic Orientation*, Salmou ould Sidi Moustaph
*Defence*, Kaba ould Elewa
*Economic and Development Affairs*, Amadou Racine Ba
*Education*, Ahmed ould Hamadi
*Equipment and Transport*, Kamara Ali Gueladio
*Finance*, Mahfoudh ould Mohamed Ali
*Fisheries and Marine Economy*, Mohamed El-Moctar ould Zamel
*Foreign Affairs and Co-operation*, Dah ould Abdi
*Health and Social Affairs*, Biodiel ould Houmeid
*Interior, Post and Telecommunications*, Lemrabet Sidi Mahmoud ould Cheikh Ahmed
*Justice*, Deddoud ould Abdellahi
*Mines and Industry*, Ishagh ould Rajel
*Rural Development and Environment*, Dah ould Abdeljail
*Trade, Handicrafts and Tourism*, Diop Abdul Hame
*Water Power, Energy*, Kane Moustapha

### EMBASSY OF THE ISLAMIC REPUBLIC OF MAURITANIA

1 Chessington Avenue, London N3 3DS
Tel: 020-8343 2829
*Ambassador Extraordinary and Plenipotentiary*, Dr Diagana Youssouf, apptd 1999
BRITISH AMBASSADOR, HE Anthony M. Layden, resident at Rabat, Morocco

## ECONOMY

The main source of potential wealth lies in rich deposits of iron ore around Zouérate, in the north of the country, and rich fishing grounds off the coast.

In 1998 Mauritania had a trade surplus of US$40 million and a current account surplus of US$77 million.

GNP – US$1,001 million (1999); US$380 per capita (1999)
GDP – US$955 million (1997); US$328 per capita (1998)
ANNUAL AVERAGE GROWTH OF GDP – 4.9 per cent (1996)
INFLATION RATE – 4.1 per cent (1999)
TOTAL EXTERNAL DEBT – US$2,589 million (1998)

| *Trade with UK* | 1999 | 2000 |
|---|---|---|
| Imports from UK | £4,964,000 | £8,983,000 |
| Exports to UK | 20,461,000 | 5,397,000 |

## MAURITIUS
*Republic of Mauritius*

AREA – 788 sq. miles (2,040 sq. km)
POPULATION – 1,193,737 (2000 estimate): Asiatic races (Hindus 51.8 per cent, Muslims 16.5 per cent, Chinese 2.8 per cent), and persons of European (mainly French) extraction, mixed and African descent (28.6 per cent). English is the official language but French may be used in the National Assembly and lower law courts. Creole is the most commonly used language and several Asian languages are also used
CAPITAL – ΨPort Louis (population, 148,761, 2000 estimate)
MAJOR TOWNS – Beau Bassin-Rose Hill (102,770); Curepipe (81,233); Quatre Bornes (78,384); Vacoas-Phoenix (101,000), 2000 estimates
CURRENCY – Mauritius rupee of 100 cents
NATIONAL ANTHEM – Glory to thee, Motherland
NATIONAL DAY – 12 March
NATIONAL FLAG – Red, blue, yellow and green horizontal stripes
LIFE EXPECTANCY (years) – male 66.7; female 74.1
POPULATION GROWTH RATE – 0.9 per cent (1999)
POPULATION DENSITY – 579 per sq. km (1999)
URBAN POPULATION – 41.3 per cent (2000 estimate)
MILITARY EXPENDITURE – 2.0 per cent of GDP (1999)
MILITARY PERSONNEL – 1,500 Paramilitaries

Mauritius is an island group lying in the Indian Ocean, 550 miles east of Madagascar. The climate is sub-tropical and maritime, with a wide range of rainfall and temperature resulting from the mountainous nature of the island. Humidity is high throughout the year.

## HISTORY AND POLITICS

Mauritius was discovered in 1511 by the Portuguese; the Dutch visited it in 1598 and named it Mauritius after Prince Maurice of Nassau. From 1638 to 1710 it was held as a Dutch colony; the French took possession in 1715 but did not settle it until 1721. Mauritius was taken by a British force in 1810 and became a Crown Colony. It became an independent state within the Commonwealth on 12 March 1968 and a republic on 12 March 1992.

The general election held on 11 September 2000 resulted in a victory for the coalition of the Mauritian Socialist Movement and the Mauritian Militant Movement, who won 54 of the 62 directly elected seats.

### POLITICAL SYSTEM

The president is head of state and is elected by the National Assembly. The prime minister, appointed by the president, is the member of the National Assembly who appears to the president best able to command the support of the majority of members of the Assembly. Other ministers are appointed by the president acting on the advice of the prime minister.

The National Assembly has a five-year term and consists of 62 elected members (the island of Mauritius is divided into 20 three-member constituencies and Rodrigues returns two members), and eight specially elected members. Of the latter, four seats go to the 'best loser' of whichever communities in the island are under-represented in the Assembly after the general election and the four remaining seats are allocated on the basis of both party and community.

### HEAD OF STATE

*President*, Cassam Uteem, *elected* June 1992, *re-elected* 28 June 1997
*Vice-President*, Angidi Veeriah Chettiar

### COUNCIL OF MINISTERS *as at July 2001*

*Prime Minister, Defence and Home Affairs*, Sir Anerood Jugnauth
*Deputy Prime Minister, Finance*, Paul Berenger
*Agriculture*, Pravind Jugnauth
*Arts and Culture*, Motee Ramdass
*Attorney-General, Justice and Human Rights*, Emmanuel Leung Shing
*Civil Service Affairs and Administrative Reform*, Ahmad Sullivan Jeewah
*Commerce, Industry and International Trade*, Jayen Cuttaree
*Co-operatives*, Premduth Koonjoo
*Education*, Louis Steven Obeegadoo
*Environment*, Rajesh Anand Bhagwan
*Financial Services and Corporate Affairs*, Sushil Kushiram
*Fisheries*, Sylvio Michel
*Foreign Affairs*, Anil Gayan
*Health*, Ashok Jugnauth
*Housing and Lands*, Mookhesswur Choonee
*Labour and Industrial Relations*, Showkatally Soodhun
*Public Infrastructure and Internal Transport*, Anil Kumar Bachoo
*Public Utilities*, Alan Ganoo
*Regional Administration of Rodrigues, Urban and Rural Development*, Joe Lesjongard
*Social Security and Reform Institutions*, Samioullah Lauthan
*Telecommunications and Information Technology*, Pradeep Jeeha
*Tourism*, Nando Bodha
*Training, Skills Development and Productivity*, Sangeet Fowdar
*Women's Rights and Family Welfare*, Marie-Arianne Navarre
*Youth and Sports*, Ravi Yerrigadoo

### MAURITIUS HIGH COMMISSION

32–33 Elvaston Place, London SW7 5NW
Tel: 020-7581 0294/5
*High Commissioner*, HE Mohunlall Goburdhun, apptd 2001

### BRITISH HIGH COMMISSION

Les Cascades Building, Edith Cavell Street, Port Louis (PO Box 1063)
Tel: (00 230) 211 1361
E-mail: bhc@intnet.mu
*High Commissioner*, HE David Snoxell, apptd 2000

BRITISH COUNCIL DIRECTOR, Shoba Ponnappa, OBE, Royal Road, PO Box 111, Rose Hill; e-mail: bcouncil@intnet.mu

## ECONOMY

The major cash crop is sugar cane. Tea and tobacco are grown commercially on a smaller scale. Production in 2000 was: sugar, 569,289 tonnes; tea (manufactured), 1,313 tonnes; in 1999 production of tobacco (leaves) was, air cured 60,238 kg and Virginia flue-cured 662,457 kg. In 1998 production of molasses, mainly for export, was 168,891 tonnes. Other products include alcohol, rum, denatured spirits, perfumed spirits and vinegar.

The bulk of the island's requirements in manufactured products still has to be imported. However, the Mauritius Export Processing Zone (MEPZ) Scheme has attracted investment from overseas and the number of export-orientated enterprises had risen from ten in 1971 to 486 in 1998. The biggest firms are in clothing manufacture, particularly woollen knitwear, but the range of goods produced includes toys, plastic products, leather goods, diamond cutting and polishing, watches, television sets and telephones.

Tourism is a major source of income, with an estimated 656,450 tourists in 2000. France is the most important source of tourists, followed closely by the neighbouring French island of Réunion.

GNP – US$4,157 million (1999); US$3,590 per capita (1999)
GDP – US$4,177 million (1997); US$3,727 per capita (1998)
ANNUAL AVERAGE GROWTH OF GDP – 5.4 per cent (1996)
INFLATION RATE – 6.9 per cent (1999)
UNEMPLOYMENT – 9.8 per cent (1995)
TOTAL EXTERNAL DEBT – US$2,482 million (1998)

### TRADE

Most foodstuffs and raw materials have to be imported from abroad. Apart from local consumption (about 36,500 tonnes a year), the sugar produced is exported, mainly to Britain.

In 1999 Mauritius had a trade deficit of US$660 million and a current account deficit of US$52 million. In 2000 imports totalled US$2,160 million and exports US$1,564 million.

| *Trade with UK* | 1999 | 2000 |
|---|---|---|
| Imports from UK | £54,115,000 | £55,434,000 |
| Exports to UK | 307,638,000 | 290,444,000 |

## COMMUNICATIONS

Port Louis, on the north-west coast, handles the bulk of the island's external trade. A bulk sugar terminal capable of handling the total crop began operating in 1980. The international airport is located at Plaisance, about five miles from Mahébourg. There are five daily newspapers and 15 weeklies, mostly in French. The Mauritius Broadcasting Corporation operates television and radio broadcasting in the country.

## EDUCATION

Primary and secondary education are free and primary education is compulsory. There are a number of training facilities offering vocational training. The Institute of Education is responsible for training primary and secondary school teachers and for curriculum development. The University of Mauritius had about 5,000 students in 1999–2000.

ILLITERACY RATE – 15.7 per cent (2000)
ENROLMENT (percentage of age group) – primary 98 per cent (1997); tertiary 6 per cent (1997)

## RODRIGUES AND DEPENDENCIES

Rodrigues, formerly a dependency but now part of Mauritius, is about 350 miles east of Mauritius, with an area of 40 square miles. Population (1998) 35,332. Cattle, salt fish, sheep, goats, pigs, maize and onions are the principal exports. The island is administered by an Island Secretary.
*Island Secretary*, J. C. Pierre Louis

The islands of Agalega and St Brandon are dependencies of Mauritius. Total population (1996) 170.

---

# MEXICO
*Estados Unidos Mexicanos*

---

AREA – 756,066 sq. miles (1,958,201 sq. km). Neighbours: USA (north), Guatemala and Belize (south-east)
POPULATION – 97,425,000 (2000 census preliminary results). Spanish is the official language and is spoken by about 95 per cent of the population. There are five main groups of Indian languages (Náhuatl, Maya, Zapotec, Otomí, Mixtec) and 59 dialects derived from them
CAPITAL – Mexico City (population, 15,047,685, 1990)
MAJOR CITIES – Ciudad Juárez (797,679); Guadalajara (2,846,000); León (956,070); Monterrey (2,521,697); Puebla (1,454,526); Tijuana (742,686); Toluca (827,339); Torreón (876,456), 1990 census
CURRENCY – Peso of 100 centavos
NATIONAL ANTHEM – Mexicanos, Al Grito De Guerra (Mexicans, to the war cry)
NATIONAL DAY – 16 September (Proclamation of Independence)
NATIONAL FLAG – Three vertical bands in green, white, red, with the Mexican emblem (an eagle on a cactus devouring a snake) in the centre
LIFE EXPECTANCY (years) – male 71.0; female 77.1
POPULATION GROWTH RATE – 1.8 per cent (1999)
POPULATION DENSITY – 49 per sq. km (1998)
URBAN POPULATION – 74.4 per cent (2000 estimate)
ILLITERACY RATE – 9.0 per cent
ENROLMENT (percentage of age group) – primary 100 per cent (1996); secondary 51 per cent (1996); tertiary 16.0 per cent (1996)

The Sierra Nevada, known in Mexico as the Sierra Madre, and Rocky Mountains continue south from the northern border with the USA, running parallel to the west and east coasts. The interior consists of an elevated plateau between the two ranges. In the west is the peninsula of Lower California, separated from the mainland by the Gulf of California. The main rivers are the Rio Grande (Rio Bravo) del Norte, which forms part of the northern boundary and is navigable for about 70 miles from its mouth in the Gulf of Mexico, and the Rio Grande de Santiago, the Rio Balsas and Rio Papaloapan.

## HISTORY AND POLITICS

Present-day Mexico and Guatemala were once the centre of a civilisation which flowered in the periods from AD 500 to 1100 and 1300 to 1500 and collapsed before the Spanish army in the years following 1519. Pre-Columbian Mexico was divided between different Indian cultures, most notably the Mayan, Teotihuacáno, Zapotec, Totonac and Toltec cultures. The last and most famous Indian culture, the Aztec, suffered more than the others at the hands of the Spanish and very few Aztec monuments remain.

After the conquest, the country was largely converted to Christianity and a distinctive colonial civilisation, representing a marriage of Indian and Spanish traditions, developed. In 1810 a revolt began against Spanish rule.

This was finally successful in 1821, when a precarious independence was proclaimed.

Friction with the USA led to the war of 1845–8, at the end of which Mexico was forced to cede the northern provinces of Texas, California and New Mexico. In 1910 began the Mexican Revolution which reformed the social structure and the land system, curbed the power of foreign companies and ushered in the independent industrial Mexico of today.

There are 11 registered political parties; the Partido Revolucionario Institucional (PRI) which constituted the governing party for more than 60 years, until its defeat in July 2000, the Partido de Acción Nacional (PAN) and the Partido de la Revolución Democrática (PRD) are the largest.

In presidential and legislative elections on 2 July 2000, Vicente Fox, the PAN candidate, was elected as president and the PAN-led alliance gained 224 seats, the PRI 209 seats and the PRD 67 seats in the Chamber of Deputies.

## Insurgencies

Two armed revolts of Zapatista peasant Indians in the southern state of Chiapas in January-August 1994 and December 1994-February 1995 caused a political and economic crisis. Negotiations with the Zapatistas produced a preliminary agreement on indigenous rights in February 1996, but talks broke down and were suspended in September 1996. Further talks took place in November 1998.

Following the inauguration of President Fox on 1 December 2000, the Zapatistas announced that peace talks could be resumed on condition that troops were withdrawn from the Chiapas, a bill of indigenous rights was enacted by Congress and an amnesty was declared for Zapatista rebels held by the authorities. On 24 February 2001, the General Staff, the ruling body of the Zapatistas, began a 3,360-km march from Chiapas to Mexico City in support of the bill. They arrived on 11 March, accompanied by hundreds of supporters, and their leaders addressed parliament on 28 March. Congress enacted a bill of indigenous rights on 1 May, but the Zapatistas broke off negotiations with the government, claiming that the provisions of the bill had been watered down.

## Political System

Congress consists of a Senate (*Cámara de Senadores*) of 128 members, elected for six years, and of a Chamber of Deputies (*Cámara de Diputados*), at present numbering 500, elected for three years. The chief executive of the government is the president, who is elected for a six-year term and may not be re-elected.

## Federal Structure

| *State* | *Area (sq. km)* | *Population (2000)* | *Capital* |
|---|---|---|---|
| Federal District | 1,499 | 8,591,309 | Mexico City |
| Aguascalientes | 5,589 | 943,506 | Aguascalientes |
| Baja California | 70,113 | 2,487,700 | Mexicali |
| Baja California Sur | 73,677 | 423,516 | La Paz |
| Campeche | 51,833 | 689,656 | Campeche |
| Coahuila | 151,571 | 2,295,808 | Saltillo |
| Colima | 5,455 | 540,679 | Colima |
| Chiapas | 73,887 | 3,920,515 | Tuxtla Gutiérrez |
| Chihuahua | 247,087 | 3,047,867 | Chihuahua |
| Durango | 119,648 | 1,445,922 | Victoria de Durango |
| Guanajuato | 30,589 | 4,656,761 | Guanajuato |
| Guerrero | 63,794 | 3,075,083 | Chilpancingo |
| Hidalgo | 20,987 | 2,231,392 | Pachuca de Soto |
| Jalisco | 80,137 | 6,321,278 | Guadalajara |
| México | 21,461 | 13,083,359 | Toluca de Lerdo |
| Michoacán | 59,864 | 3,979,177 | Morelia |
| Morelos | 4,941 | 1,552,878 | Cuernavaca |
| Nayarit | 27,621 | 919,739 | Tepic |
| Nuevo León | 64,555 | 3,826,240 | Monterrey |
| Oaxaca | 95,364 | 3,432,180 | Oaxaca de Juárez |
| Puebla | 33,919 | 5,070,346 | Puebla de Zaragoza |
| Querétaro | 11,769 | 1,402,010 | Querétaro |
| Quintana Roo | 50,350 | 873,804 | Chetumal |
| San Luis Potosí | 62,848 | 2,296,363 | San Luis Potosí |
| Sinaloa | 58,092 | 2,534,835 | Culiacán Rosales |
| Sonora | 184,934 | 2,213,370 | Hermosillo |
| Tabasco | 24,661 | 1,889,367 | Villahermosa |
| Tamaulipas | 79,829 | 2,747,114 | Ciudad Victoria |
| Tlaxcala | 3,914 | 961,912 | Tlaxcala |
| Veracruz | 72,815 | 6,901,111 | Jalapa Enríquez |
| Yucatán | 39,340 | 1,655,707 | Mérida |
| Zacatecas | 75,040 | 1,351,207 | Zacatecas |

## Head of State

*President*, Vicente Fox, *elected* 2 July 2000, *sworn in* 1 December 2000

## Cabinet *as at July 2001*

*Agrarian Reform*, María Teresa Herrera Tello
*Agriculture, Livestock, Rural Development, Fisheries and Food*, Javier Usabiaga
*Attorney-General*, Gen. Rafael Macedo de la Concha
*Communications and Transport*, Pedro Cerisola
*Comptroller-General*, Francisco Barrio Terrazas
*Defence*, Gen. Gerardo Clemente Ricardo Vega
*Economy*, Luís Ernesto Derbez
*Education*, Reyes Tamez Guerra
*Energy*, Ernesto Martens
*Environment, Natural Resources*, Victor Lichtinger
*Finance and Public Credit*, Francisco Gil Diaz
*Foreign Affairs*, Jorge Castaneda
*Health*, Julio José Frenk Mora
*Interior*, Santiago Creel Miranda
*Labour and Social Welfare*, Carlos Abascal
*Naval Affairs*, Adm. Marco Antonio Peyrot
*Public Safety*, Alejandro Gertz Manero
*Social Development*, Josefina Vázquez Mota
*Tourism*, Leticia Navarro

## Mexican Embassy

42 Hertford Street, London W1Y 7TF
Tel: 020-7499 8586
*Ambassador Extraordinary and Plenipotentiary*, HE Alma Rosa Moreno Razo, apptd 2001
*Minister, Deputy Head of Mission*, J. Brito-Moncada
*Military Attaché*, Gen. E. Bahena-Pineda
*Consul-General*, R. Xilótl-Ramírez

## British Embassy

Calle Río Lerma 71, Colonia Cuauhtémoc,
06500 Mexico City
Tel: (00 52) (5) 242 8500
E-mail: infogen@mail.embajadabritanica.com.mx

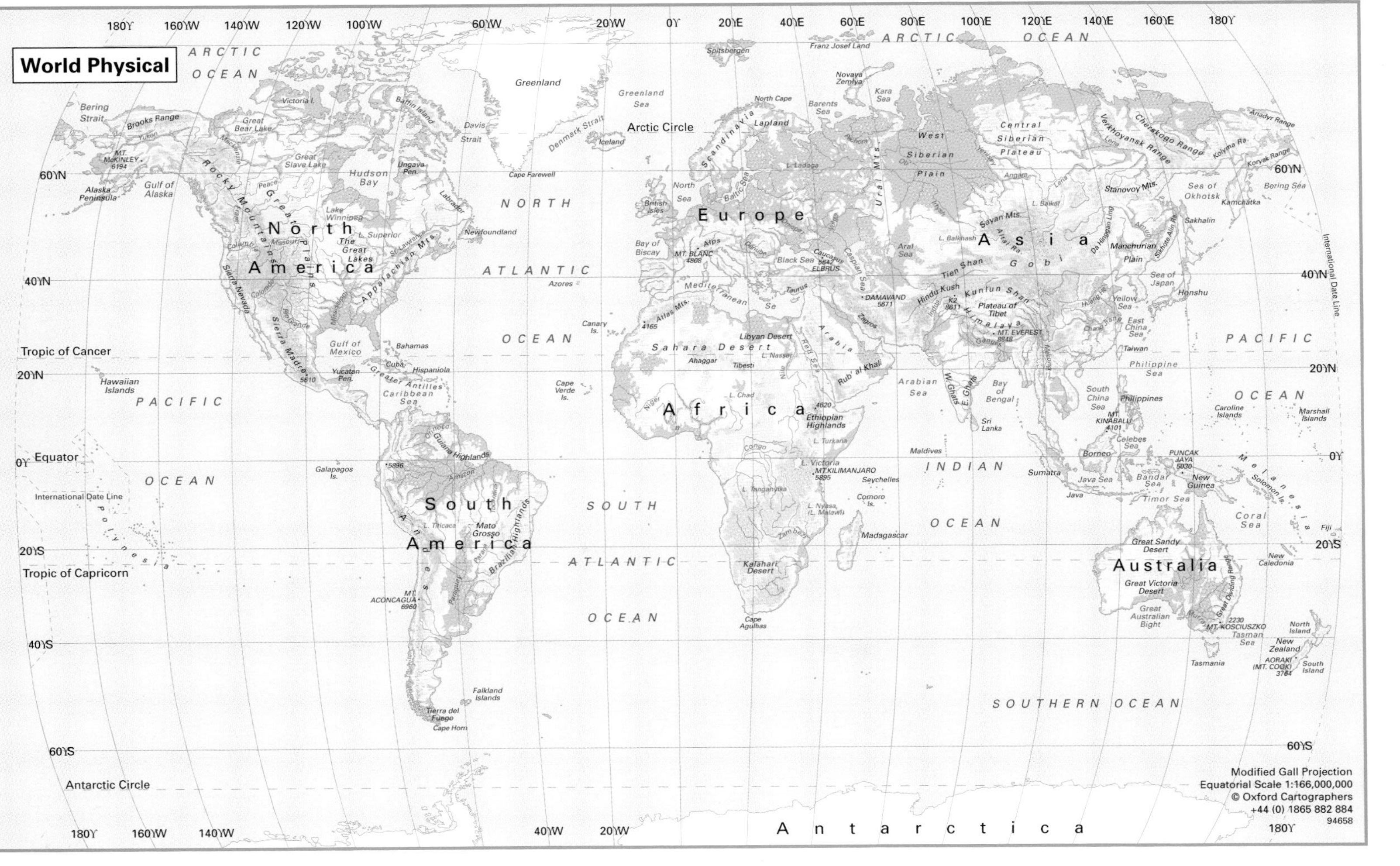
World Physical
ARCTIC OCEAN
Greenland
Greenland Sea
Arctic Circle
Denmark Strait
Iceland
Davis Strait
Baffin Island
Victoria I.
Great Bear Lake
Great Slave Lake
Hudson Bay
Ungava Pen.
Labrador
Newfoundland
Cape Farewell
Bering Strait
Brooks Range
MT. McKINLEY 6194
Alaska Peninsula
Gulf of Alaska
Rocky Mountains
Great Plains
North America
Lake Winnipeg
L. Superior
The Great Lakes
Appalachian Mts.
Sierra Nevada
Sierra Madre
5610
Gulf of Mexico
Yucatan Pen.
Bahamas
Cuba
Hispaniola
Greater Antilles
Caribbean Sea
Hawaiian Islands
Tropic of Cancer
Equator
Tropic of Capricorn
Antarctic Circle
International Date Line
Polynesia
PACIFIC OCEAN
NORTH ATLANTIC OCEAN
Azores
Canary Is.
Cape Verde Is.
Galapagos Is.
Guiana Highlands
Amazon
South America
Andes
L. Titicaca
Mato Grosso
Brazilian Highlands
MT. ACONCAGUA 6960
Falkland Islands
Tierra del Fuego
Cape Horn
SOUTH ATLANTIC OCEAN
Spitsbergen
Franz Josef Land
Novaya Zemlya
North Cape
Lapland
Scandinavia
Barents Sea
Kara Sea
North Sea
British Isles
Baltic Sea
L. Ladoga
Europe
Bay of Biscay
Alps
MT. BLANC 4808
Black Sea
Caucasus
5642 ELBRUS
Caspian Sea
Mediterranean Sea
Atlas Mts.
4165
Sahara Desert
Ahaggar
Tibesti
Libyan Desert
L. Nasser
Red Sea
Arabia
Rub' al Khali
Zagros
DAMAVAND 5671
Africa
L. Chad
Ethiopian Highlands
4620
L. Turkana
Congo
L. Victoria
MT. KILIMANJARO 5895
L. Tanganyika
L. Nyasa (L. Malawi)
Seychelles
Comoro Is.
Madagascar
Kalahari Desert
Cape Agulhas
Ural Mts.
West Siberian Plain
Central Siberian Plateau
Verkhoyansk Range
Cherskogo Range
Kolyma Ra.
Anadyr Range
Koryak Range
Bering Sea
Sea of Okhotsk
Kamchatka
Sakhalin
Stanovoy Mts.
L. Baikal
Sayan Mts.
Altai Ra.
Aral Sea
L. Balkhash
Asia
Gobi
Da Hinggan Ling
Manchurian Plain
Sikhote Alin Ra.
Sea of Japan
Honshu
Tien Shan
Hindu Kush
Kunlun Shan
Plateau of Tibet
K2 8611
Himalaya
MT. EVEREST 8848
Yellow Sea
East China Sea
Taiwan
Philippine Sea
Arabian Sea
W. Ghats
E. Ghats
Bay of Bengal
Sri Lanka
Maldives
South China Sea
Philippines
MT. KINABALU 4101
Celebes Sea
Borneo
Sumatra
Java Sea
Java
Banda Sea
PUNCAK JAYA 5030
New Guinea
Timor Sea
Melanesia
Solomon Is.
Coral Sea
Fiji
New Caledonia
Caroline Islands
Marshall Islands
INDIAN OCEAN
Australia
Great Sandy Desert
Great Victoria Desert
Great Australian Bight
Great Dividing Range
2230 MT. KOSCIUSZKO
Tasmania
Tasman Sea
New Zealand
North Island
South Island
AORAKI (MT. COOK) 3764
SOUTHERN OCEAN
Antarctica
180°
160°W
140°W
120°W
100°W
60°W
40°W
20°W
0°
20°E
40°E
60°E
80°E
100°E
120°E
140°E
160°E
60°N
40°N
20°N
20°S
40°S
60°S
Modified Gall Projection
Equatorial Scale 1:166,000,000
© Oxford Cartographers
+44 (0) 1865 882 884
94658

40°W
30°W
20°W
70°N
10°W
0°
10°E
60°N
50°N
40°N
Arctic Circle
ICELAND
Reykjavík
0 100 200 300 400 Miles
0 100 200 400 500 600 Kms
Conical Orthomorphic Projection
© Oxford Cartographers
+44 (0) 1865 882 884
Faroe Is.
(Denmark)
Shetland Is.
Orkney Is.
Hebrides
ATLANTIC
OCEAN
Trondheim
Bergen
Stavanger
Oslo
Kristiansand
Skagerrak
North
Sea
Gothenburg
Alborg
Arhus
Helsingborg
Malmö
DENMARK
Odense
Inverness
Aberdeen
Dundee
Glasgow
Edinburgh
Londonderry
Belfast
UNITED
KINGDOM
Newcastle
upon Tyne
Galway
Dublin
REP. OF
IRELAND
Cork
Liverpool
Leeds
Manchester
Sheffield
Stoke-
on-Trent
Norwich
Birmingham
Swansea
Cardiff
Bristol
London
Plymouth
Southampton
English Channel
Amsterdam
NETHERLANDS
Rotterdam
Antwerp
Brussels
Lille
BELGIUM
LUX.
Luxembourg
Kiel
Rostock
Hamburg
Bremen
Elbe
Osnabrück
Munster
Hanover
Berlin
Essen
Düsseldorf
Cologne
Leipzig
Dresden
Chemnitz
GERMANY
Frankfurt
Plzeň
Nuremberg
Mannheim
Stuttgart
Regensburg
Munich
Danube
Salzburg
Innsbruck
Rhine
Cherbourg
Le Havre
Rouen
Amiens
Caen
Seine
Reims
Paris
Metz
Strasbourg
Nancy
Brest
Rennes
Nantes
Loire
Orléans
Tours
Dijon
Bay of
Biscay
FRANCE
Limoges
Bordeaux
Clermont-
Ferrand
Lyon
Geneva
Grenoble
Mt. Blanc
4808
Rhône
Zurich
Bern
SWITZERLAND
LIECH.
Trento
Ljubljana
Trieste
Milan
Verona
Venice
Turin
Po
Parma
Genoa
Bologne
La Spezia
SAN
MARINO
Livorno
Florence
Ancona
ITALY
Apennines
Rome
Naples
Corsica
(Fr.)
Ajaccio
Sardinia
(It.)
Sassari
Cagliari
Nice
MONACO
Marseille
Nimes
Montpellier
Toulouse
ANDORRA
Pyrenees
San Sebastian
Pamplona
Bilbao
Burgos
La Coruña
Gijón
Vigo
León
Valladolid
Zaragoza
Lerida
Barcelona
Oporto
Douro
Coimbra
PORTUGAL
Lisbon
Setúbal
Tagus
Salamanca
Madrid
SPAIN
Badajoz
Valencia
Balearic Is.
(Sp.)
Palma
Mallorca
Faro
Huelva
Seville
Córdoba
Granada
Murcia
Cartagena
Cadiz
Málaga
Almeria
Gibraltar(U.K.)
Ceuta(Sp.)
Tangier
Tétouan
Mediterranean
Rabat
Casablanca
Fès
Meknès
Melilla(Sp.)
Oujda
Oran
Sidi Bel Abbès
Algiers
Blida
Bejaia
Skikda
Annaba
Constantine
Tunis
MOROCCO
Atlas
Mountains
ALGERIA
TUNISIA
Sfax
Palermo
Sicily
Valletta
MALTA

30°E
40°E
70°N
50°E
60°E
70°E
orth
Cape
Vadsø
Murmansk
Kola
Peninsula
Ural Mountains
60°N
land
White
Sea
Arkhangel'sk
Syktyvkar
Luleå
Oulu
N. Dvina
Yekaterinburg
Kotlas
Perm
FINLAND
Kuopio
Petrozavodsk
L.
Onega
Sukhona
Kirov
Izevsk
Chelyabinsk
Vaasa
Mikkeli
R U S S I A
Pori
Tampere
Lake
Ladoga
Vologda
Naberezhnyye
Chelny
Ufa
Cherepovets
Magnitogorsk
Turku
Helsinki
St. Petersburg
Kostroma
Cheboksari
Kazan'
Gulf of Finland
Nizhniy
Novgorod
Tallinn
Yaroslavl'
Volga
Ul'yanovsk
ESTONIA
Novgorod
Tartu
Saransk
Orenburg
Pskov
Volga
Samara
Tver'
Velikiye-
Luki
Penza
Ryazan'
50°N
Moscow
Volga Heights
Liepaja
Riga
LATVIA
Ural'sk
Daugavpils
Saratov
Tula
Smolensk
Vitsyebsk
Klaipėda
Ural
LITHUANIA
Kaunas
Tambov
KAZAKHSTAN
Vilnius
RUSSIA
Kaliningrad
Mahilyow
Bryansk
Orel
Minsk
BELARUS
Voronezh
Olsztyn
Grodno
Bobruysk
Kursk
Caspian
Lowlands
Atyrau
Białystok
Baranovich
Homyel'
Volgograd
N D
Don
Brest
Pinsk
Mazyr
Chernihiv
Volga
Astrakhan
Vistula
Łódź
Kharkiv
Kiev
Luhansk
Radom
Poltava
Lublin
Rivne
UKRAINE
Dniprodzerzhinsk
Dnipropetrovsk
Zhytomyr
Częstochowa
Katowice
Rzeszów
Cherkasy
Dnieper
Donetsk
Elista
L'viv
Vinnytsia
Rostov
Kraków
Kirovograd
Zaporozhye
Kryvyi
Rih
Mariupol
Khmel'nitskiy
Caspian
Sea
OVAKIA
Melitopol'
Košice
Carpathians
Beltsy
Mykolaiv
Stavropol'
MOLDOVA
Sea of
Azov
Grozny
Miskolc
Chişinău
Tiraspol
Kherson
Makhachkala
Vladikavkaz
Suceava
Krasnodar
Maykop
Elbrus
5642
Budapest
Debrecen
Iaşi
Odesa
Kerch
Oradea
Caucasus Mountains
GARY
Bacau
Novorossiysk
Cluj-
Napoca
AZERBAIJAN
Baku
GEORGIA
Tbilisi
Szeged
Braşov
Simferopol'
40°N
Sevastopol'
Timişoara
Galaţi
ROMANIA
Ploieşti
Batumi
ARMENIA
Novi Sad
Constanţa
Black Sea
Yerevan
Belgrade
Bucharest
AZER.
Craiova
Trabzon
Ruse
Danube
YUGO-
SLAVIA
Pleven
Varna
Samsun
Tabriz
Niš
BULGARIA
Burgas
Erzurum
L. Van
Van
Priština
Sofia
Stara Zagora
Zonguldak
IRAN
Sivas
L. Urmia
Skopje
Plovdiv
Edirne
Istanbul
TURKEY
Malatya
Diyarbakir
ALBANIA
MACEDONIA
Kocaeli
Ankara
Kirikkale
Tirana
Bitola
Thessaloniki
Bursa
Eskisehir
Kayseri
Kahramanmaraş
Al-Mawşil
Arbil
Çanakkale
Balikesir
Gaziantep
Kirkūk
Tigris
Aegean
Sea
Corfu
Lárissa
Manisa
Konya
Adana
Osmaniye
Raqqah
Euphrates
GREECE
Izmir
Denizli
Isparta
Halab
İçel
SYRIA
Al-Kazimiyah
Baghdad
Aydin
Al-Lādhiqiyah
Patras
Piraeus
Athens
Antalya
Hamah
Hims
IRAQ
Nicosia
Kalamata
Rhodes
Tripoli
CYPRUS
Damascus
Beirut
Syrian
Desert
LEBANON
Iráklion
30°N
Sea
Crete
20°E
30°E
40°E
Ammān
JORDAN

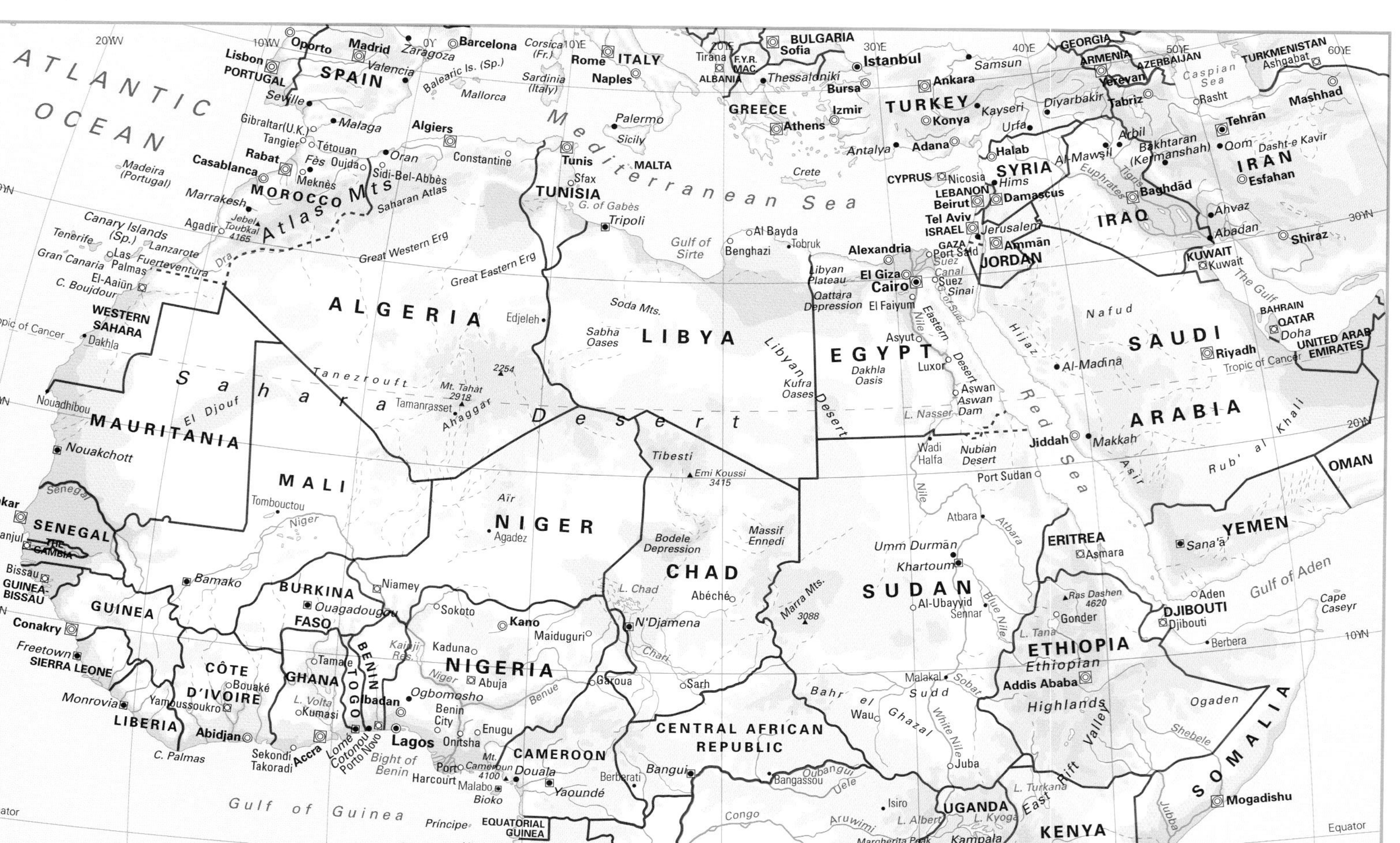
ATLANTIC OCEAN
Mediterranean Sea
Red Sea
Gulf of Aden
Gulf of Guinea
The Gulf
Caspian Sea
Sahara Desert
Libyan Desert
PORTUGAL
Lisbon
Oporto
SPAIN
Madrid
Barcelona
Zaragoza
Valencia
Seville
Malaga
Gibraltar(U.K.)
Balearic Is. (Sp.)
Mallorca
Corsica (Fr.)
Sardinia (Italy)
ITALY
Rome
Naples
Palermo
Sicily
MALTA
ALBANIA
Tirana
F.Y.R. MAC
BULGARIA
Sofia
GREECE
Athens
Thessaloniki
Crete
TURKEY
Istanbul
Ankara
Bursa
Izmir
Konya
Adana
Antalya
Samsun
Kayseri
Urfa
Diyarbakir
GEORGIA
ARMENIA
Yerevan
AZERBAIJAN
TURKMENISTAN
Ashgabat
IRAN
Tehrān
Tabriz
Rasht
Mashhad
Qom
Esfahan
Dasht-e Kavir
Bakhtaran (Kermanshah)
Ahvaz
Abadan
Shiraz
IRAQ
Baghdād
Arbil
Al-Mawşil
Euphrates
Tigris
SYRIA
Halab
Hims
Damascus
CYPRUS
Nicosia
LEBANON
Beirut
ISRAEL
Tel Aviv
Jerusalem
GAZA
JORDAN
Ammān
KUWAIT
Kuwait
BAHRAIN
QATAR
Doha
UNITED ARAB EMIRATES
SAUDI ARABIA
Riyadh
Al-Madina
Makkah
Jiddah
Nafud
Hijaz
Asir
Rub' al Khali
OMAN
YEMEN
Sana'a'
Aden
Tropic of Cancer
MOROCCO
Rabat
Casablanca
Marrakesh
Fès
Meknès
Tangier
Tétouan
Oujda
Agadir
Atlas Mts
Jebel Toubkal 4165
Madeira (Portugal)
Canary Islands (Sp.)
Tenerife
Gran Canaria
Las Palmas
Lanzarote
Fuerteventura
ALGERIA
Algiers
Oran
Constantine
Sidi-Bel-Abbès
Saharan Atlas
Great Western Erg
Great Eastern Erg
Edjeleh
Tanezrouft
Tamanrasset
Ahaggar
Mt. Tahat 2918
2254
TUNISIA
Tunis
Sfax
G. of Gabès
LIBYA
Tripoli
Benghazi
Al Bayda
Tobruk
Gulf of Sirte
Soda Mts.
Sabha Oases
Kufra Oases
EGYPT
Cairo
El Giza
Alexandria
El Faiyum
Asyut
Luxor
Aswan
Aswan Dam
L. Nasser
Port Said
Suez
Suez Canal
Sinai
Libyan Plateau
Qattara Depression
Dakhla Oasis
Eastern Desert
Nile
WESTERN SAHARA
El-Aaiún
C. Boujdour
Dakhla
MAURITANIA
Nouakchott
Nouadhibou
El Djouf
MALI
Bamako
Tombouctou
Niger
NIGER
Niamey
Agadez
Aïr
CHAD
N'Djamena
Abéché
Tibesti
Emi Koussi 3415
Bodele Depression
Massif Ennedi
L. Chad
Chari
SUDAN
Khartoum
Umm Durmān
Port Sudan
Atbara
Wadi Halfa
Nubian Desert
Al-Ubayyid
Sennar
Marra Mts. 3088
Blue Nile
White Nile
Malakal
Sudd
Sobat
Bahr el Ghazal
Wau
Juba
ERITREA
Asmara
DJIBOUTI
Djibouti
ETHIOPIA
Addis Ababa
Ras Dashen 4620
Gonder
L. Tana
Ethiopian Highlands
SOMALIA
Mogadishu
Berbera
Cape Caseyr
Ogaden
Shebele
Jubba
KENYA
East Rift Valley
L. Turkana
UGANDA
Kampala
L. Albert
L. Kyoga
Margherita Peak 5110
Isiro
Aruwimi
Congo
SENEGAL
Dakar
Senegal
THE GAMBIA
Banjul
GUINEA-BISSAU
Bissau
GUINEA
Conakry
SIERRA LEONE
Freetown
LIBERIA
Monrovia
C. Palmas
CÔTE D'IVOIRE
Abidjan
Yamoussoukro
Bouaké
BURKINA FASO
Ouagadougou
GHANA
Accra
Kumasi
Tamale
L. Volta
Sekondi Takoradi
TOGO
Lomé
BENIN
Cotonou
Porto Novo
NIGERIA
Abuja
Lagos
Ibadan
Ogbomosho
Kano
Kaduna
Sokoto
Maiduguri
Benin City
Onitsha
Enugu
Port Harcourt
Kainji Res.
Benue
Bight of Benin
CAMEROON
Yaoundé
Douala
Garoua
Mt. Cameroun 4100
EQUATORIAL GUINEA
Malabo
Bioko
Príncipe
São Tomé
Libreville
CENTRAL AFRICAN REPUBLIC
Bangui
Berberati
Bangassou
Oubangui
Uele
Sarh
Equator
20°W
10°W
0°
10°E
20°E
30°E
40°E
50°E
60°E
30°N
20°N
10°N

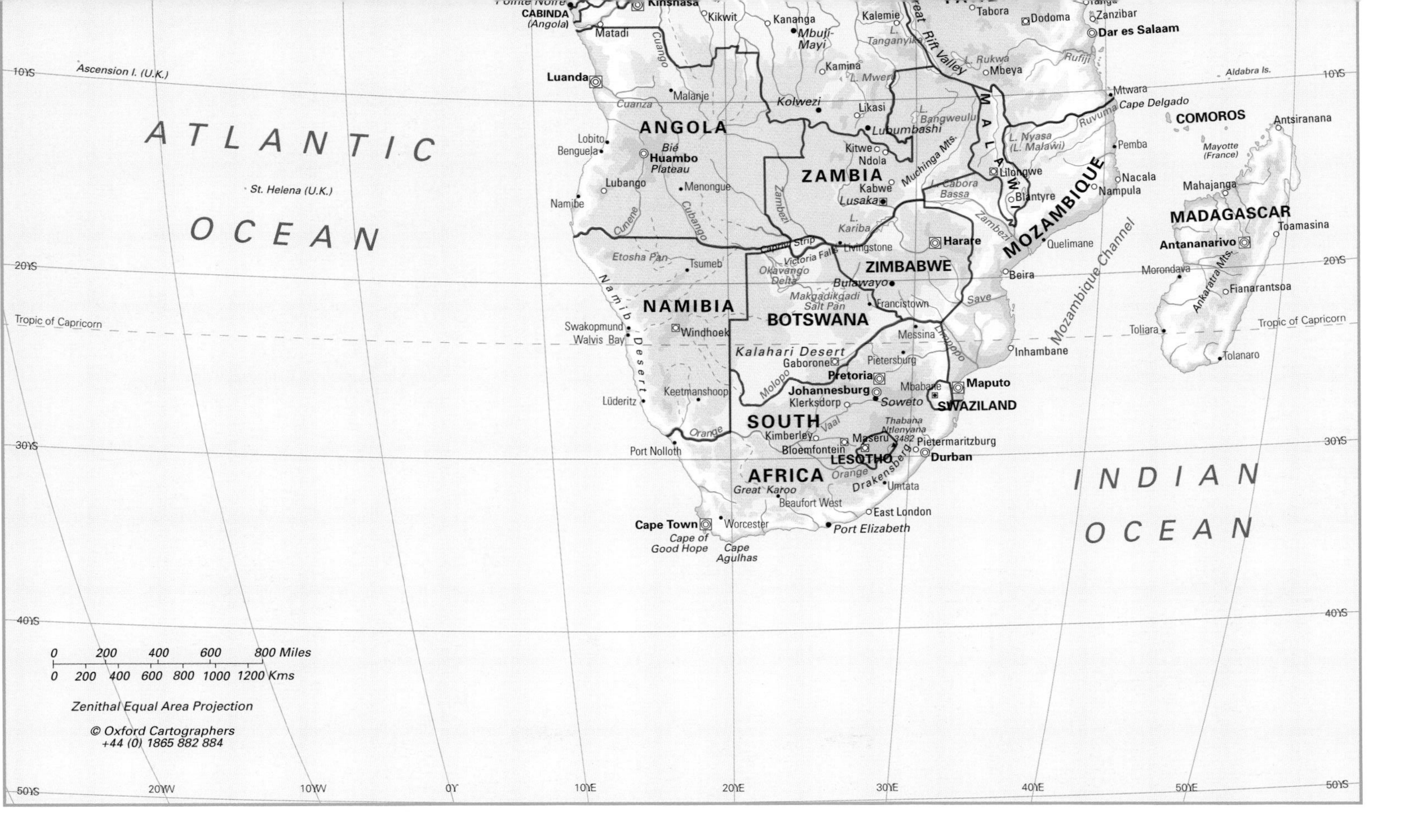
ATLANTIC OCEAN
INDIAN OCEAN
Ascension I. (U.K.)
St. Helena (U.K.)
CABINDA (Angola)
Kinshasa
Matadi
Kikwit
Kananga
Mbuji-Mayi
Kalemie
L. Tanganyika
Rift Valley
Tabora
Dodoma
Zanzibar
Dar es Salaam
Luanda
Malanje
Cuango
Cuanza
Kamina
L. Mweru
Kolwezi
Likasi
Lubumbashi
L. Bangweulu
L. Rukwa
Mbeya
Rufiji
Aldabra Is.
Mtwara
Cape Delgado
Ruvuma
COMOROS
Antsiranana
Mayotte (France)
ANGOLA
Lobito
Benguela
Bié
Huambo
Plateau
Lubango
Menongue
Namibe
Cunene
Cubango
ZAMBIA
Kitwe
Ndola
Kabwe
Lusaka
Muchinga Mts.
Zambezi
L. Kariba
MALAWI
L. Nyasa (L. Malawi)
Lilongwe
Blantyre
Pemba
Nacala
Nampula
MOZAMBIQUE
Mahajanga
MADAGASCAR
Toamasina
Antananarivo
L. Cabora Bassa
Caprivi Strip
Victoria Falls
Livingstone
Harare
Quelimane
Etosha Pan
Tsumeb
Okavango Delta
ZIMBABWE
Bulawayo
Beira
Mozambique Channel
Morondava
Ankaratra Mts.
Fianarantsoa
NAMIBIA
Namib Desert
Makgadikgadi Salt Pan
Francistown
Save
BOTSWANA
Swakopmund
Walvis Bay
Windhoek
Messina
Limpopo
Toliara
Tropic of Capricorn
Inhambane
Tolanaro
Kalahari Desert
Gaborone
Pietersburg
Molopo
Pretoria
Johannesburg
Mbabane
Maputo
Soweto
Klerksdorp
SWAZILAND
Keetmanshoop
Lüderitz
SOUTH AFRICA
Vaal
Thabana Ntlenyana 3482
Kimberley
Maseru
Pietermaritzburg
Orange
Bloemfontein
LESOTHO
Durban
Port Nolloth
Drakensberg
Umtata
Great Karoo
Beaufort West
East London
Cape Town
Worcester
Port Elizabeth
Cape of Good Hope
Cape Agulhas
10°S
20°S
30°S
40°S
50°S
20°W
10°W
0°
10°E
20°E
30°E
40°E
50°E
0 200 400 600 800 Miles
0 200 400 600 800 1000 1200 Kms
Zenithal Equal Area Projection
© Oxford Cartographers
+44 (0) 1865 882 884

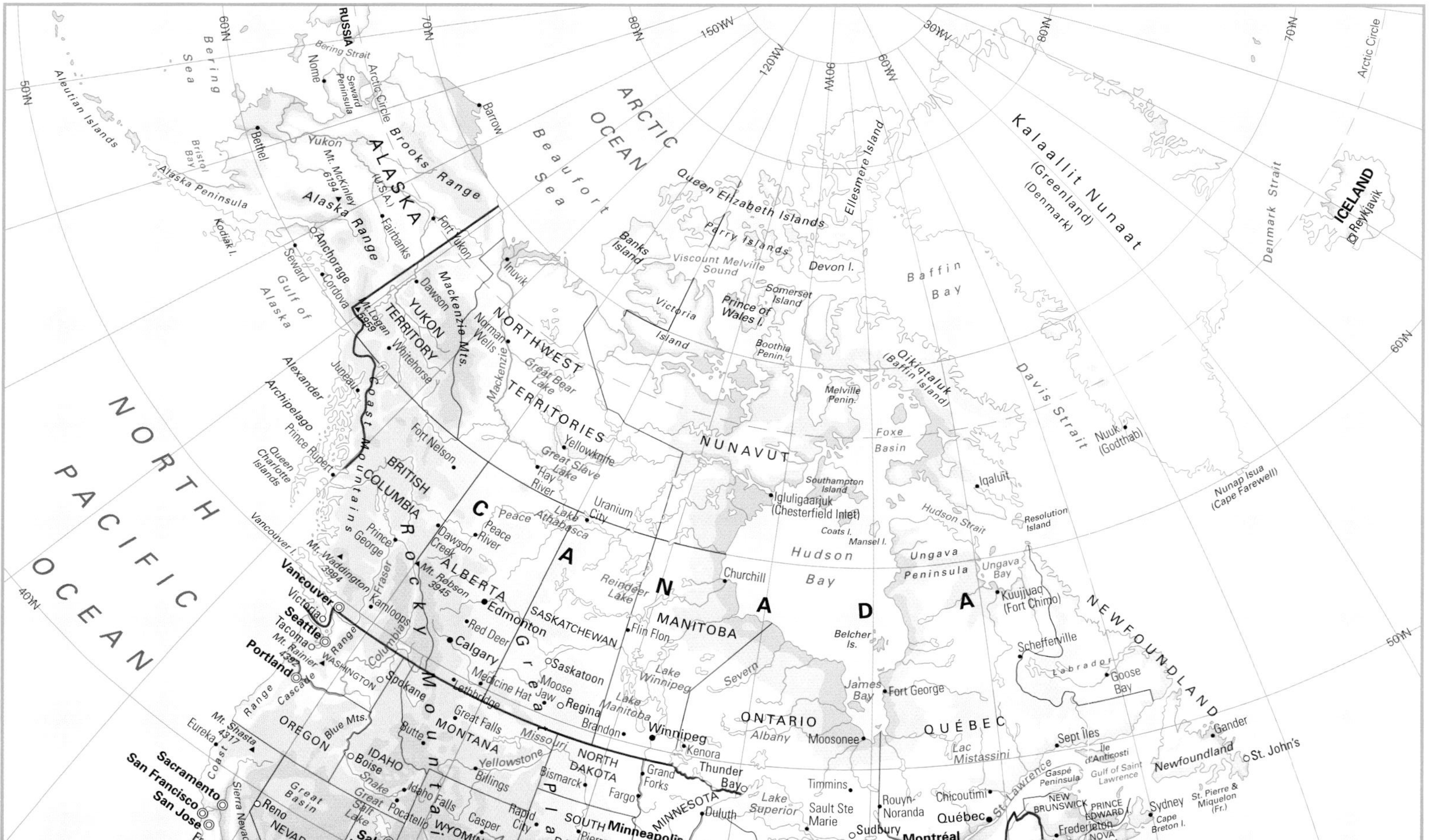

ARCTIC OCEAN
Beaufort Sea
Kalaallit Nunaat (Greenland) (Denmark)
ICELAND
Reykjavik
Arctic Circle
Denmark Strait
Davis Strait
Baffin Bay
Nuuk (Godthab)
Nunap Isua (Cape Farewell)
Ellesmere Island
Devon I.
Queen Elizabeth Islands
Parry Islands
Viscount Melville Sound
Banks Island
Victoria Island
Prince of Wales I.
Somerset Island
Boothia Penin.
Melville Penin.
Qikiqtaaluk (Baffin Island)
Iqaluit
Foxe Basin
Southampton Island
Igluligaarjuk (Chesterfield Inlet)
Coats I.
Mansel I.
Resolution Island
Hudson Strait
Hudson Bay
Ungava Peninsula
Ungava Bay
Kuujjuaq (Fort Chimo)
Schefferville
Labrador
Goose Bay
NEWFOUNDLAND
Newfoundland
Gander
St. John's
St. Pierre & Miquelon (Fr.)
Sydney
Cape Breton I.
Gulf of Saint Lawrence
Île d'Anticosti
Gaspé Peninsula
Sept Îles
St. Lawrence
NEW BRUNSWICK
PRINCE EDWARD
Fredericton
QUÉBEC
Québec
Montréal
Chicoutimi
Lac Mistassini
Fort George
James Bay
Belcher Is.
Rouyn-Noranda
Sudbury
Timmins
Moosonee
Sault Ste Marie
Lake Superior
ONTARIO
Albany
Severn
Thunder Bay
Duluth
Kenora
Winnipeg
Lake Winnipeg
Lake Manitoba
MANITOBA
Churchill
Flin Flon
Brandon
Grand Forks
Fargo
MINNESOTA
Minneapolis
NORTH DAKOTA
Bismarck
SOUTH
Rapid City
Regina
Moose Jaw
Saskatoon
SASKATCHEWAN
Reindeer Lake
Uranium City
Lake Athabasca
NUNAVUT
NORTHWEST TERRITORIES
Great Bear Lake
Great Slave Lake
Yellowknife
Hay River
Inuvik
Norman Wells
Mackenzie
Mackenzie Mts.
Peace
Peace River
C A N A D A
Great Plains
Edmonton
Red Deer
Calgary
Medicine Hat
Lethbridge
ALBERTA
Mt. Robson 3945
Dawson Creek
Fort Nelson
BRITISH COLUMBIA
Prince George
Kamloops
Fraser
Columbia
Rocky Mountains
Coast Mountains
Mt. Waddington 3994
Vancouver
Vancouver I.
Victoria
Seattle
Tacoma
Mt. Rainier 4392
Cascade Range
Portland
WASHINGTON
Spokane
OREGON
Blue Mts.
IDAHO
Boise
Snake
Idaho Falls
Pocatello
Great Salt Lake
Butte
MONTANA
Great Falls
Missouri
Yellowstone
Billings
Casper
WYOMING
Great Basin
Reno
Sierra Nevada
Mt. Shasta 4317
Eureka
Coast Range
Sacramento
San Francisco
San Jose
YUKON TERRITORY
Dawson
Whitehorse
Mt. Logan 5959
Juneau
Prince Rupert
Queen Charlotte Islands
Alexander Archipelago
ALASKA (U.S.A.)
Brooks Range
Fort Yukon
Barrow
Fairbanks
Alaska Range
Mt. McKinley 6194
Anchorage
Cordova
Seward
Yukon
Nome
Seward Peninsula
Bering Strait
RUSSIA
Bethel
Bering Sea
Bristol Bay
Alaska Peninsula
Kodiak I.
Gulf of Alaska
Aleutian Islands
NORTH PACIFIC OCEAN
50°N
60°N
70°N
80°N
40°N
30°W
60°W
90°W
120°W
150°W

NORTH ATLANTIC OCEAN
OF AMERICA
MEXICO
Gulf of Mexico
Caribbean Sea
CUBA
THE BAHAMAS
JAMAICA
HAITI
DOMINICAN REP.
GUATEMALA
BELIZE
HONDURAS
EL SALVADOR
NICARAGUA
COSTA RICA
PANAMA
COLOMBIA
VENEZUELA
GUYANA
SURINAME
French Guiana
ECUADOR
BRAZIL
Greater Antilles
Lesser Antilles
Leeward Is.
Windward Is.
ANTIGUA & BARBUDA
Guadeloupe (Fr.)
DOMINICA
Martinique (Fr.)
ST. LUCIA
BARBADOS
GRENADA
TRINIDAD & TOBAGO
Port of Spain
Aruba (Neth.)
Neth. Antilles
Turks & Caicos Islands (U.K.)
Cayman Is. (U.K.)
Puerto Rico (U.S.A.)
Bermuda (U.K.)
Cocos Is. (C.R.)
Galapagos Is. (Ecuador)
Revilla Gigedo Is. (Mex.)
Guadalupe (Mex.)
Lower California
Gulf of California
C. San Lucas
Sierra Madre Occidental
Sierra Madre Oriental
Sierra Madre del Sur
Yucatan Peninsula
Bay of Campeche
Cape Catoche
Rio Grande
Mississippi
Ohio
Appalachian Mts.
Cape Hatteras
Great Abaco I.
Grand Bahama
Andros I.
Lake Nicaragua
Gulf of Panama
L. Maracaibo
Llanos
Orinoco
Guaviare
Magdalena
Andes
Guiana Highlands
Japurá
Negro
Amazon
Tropic of Cancer
Equator
30°N
20°N
10°N
110°W
100°W
90°W
80°W
70°W
60°W
ARIZONA
NEW MEXICO
TEXAS
OKLAHOMA
KANSAS
MISSOURI
ARKANSAS
LOUISIANA
MISSISSIPPI
ALABAMA
GEORGIA
FLORIDA
TENNESSEE
KENTUCKY
INDIANA
WEST VIRGINIA
VIRGINIA
NORTH CAROLINA
SOUTH CAROLINA
MD.
DE.
N.J.
San Diego
Mexicali
Yuma
Phoenix
Tucson
Nogales
El Paso
Santa Fe
Albuquerque
Amarillo
Lubbock
Wichita Falls
Fort Worth
Dallas
Oklahoma City
Tulsa
Wichita
Dodge City
Kansas City
Springfield
St. Louis
Indianapolis
Cincinnati
Columbus
Pittsburgh
Louisville
Nashville
Memphis
Little Rock
Shreveport
Austin
Houston
San Antonio
Beaumont
Galveston
Corpus Christi
Baton Rouge
New Orleans
Jackson
Mobile
Montgomery
Birmingham
Chattanooga
Atlanta
Macon
Columbus
Columbia
Charleston
Savannah
Jacksonville
Tallahassee
Orlando
Tampa
West Palm Beach
Miami
Greensboro
Charlotte
Wilmington
Norfolk
Washington D.C.
Baltimore
Philadelphia
Newark
New York
Nassau
Havana
Santa Clara
Camagüey
Santiago de Cuba
Guantanamo
Kingston
Port-au-Prince
Santo Domingo
San Juan
Hermosillo
Ciudad Obregón
Chihuahua
Ciudad Juárez
Culiacán
Mazatlán
La Paz
Hidalgo del Parral
Torreón
Durango
Saltillo
Monterrey
Piedras Negras
Nuevo Laredo
Matamoros
Ciudad Victoria
Tampico
Zacatecas
León
Guadalajara
Colima
Morelia
Mexico City
Puebla
Popocatépetl 5452
Pico de Orizaba 5610
Veracruz
Oaxaca
Acapulco
Salina Cruz
Tuxtla Gutiérrez
Villahermosa
Mérida
Belize City
Belmopan
San Pedro Sula
Guatemala City
Santa Ana
San Salvador
Tegucigalpa
Managua
San José
Limón
Colón
Panama City
Barranquilla
Cartagena
Maracaibo
Barquisimeto
Caracas
Cúcuta
Merida
Ciudad Guayana
Ciudad Bolívar
Georgetown
Paramaribo
Cayenne
Boa Vista
Bucaramanga
Medellín
Manizales
Bogotá
Buenaventura
Cali
Tumaco
Quito
Cotopaxi 5896
0 200 400
0 200 400 600 800 1000 Kms
Oblique Mercator Projection
© Oxford Cartographers
+44 (0) 1865 882 884

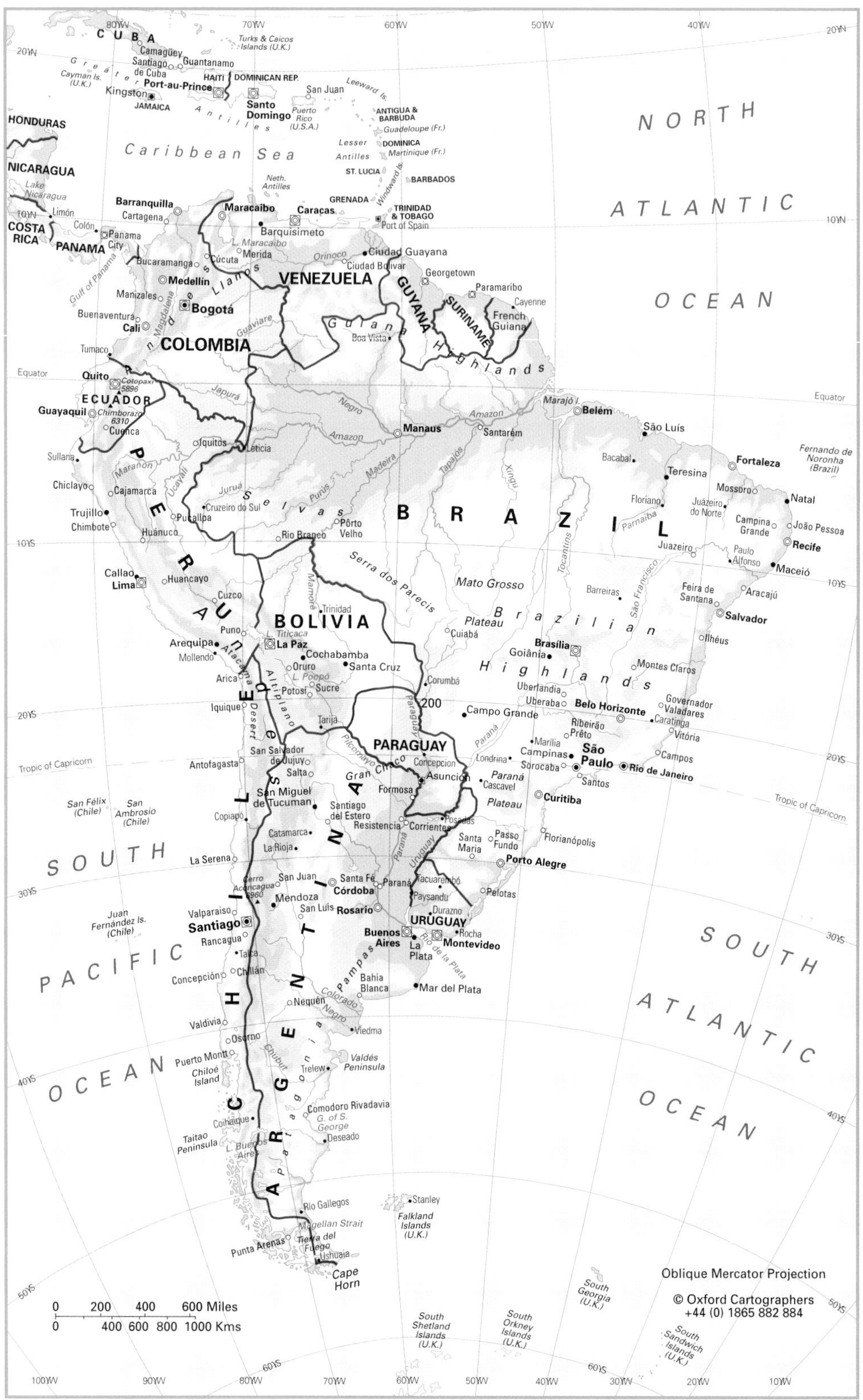

NORTH ATLANTIC OCEAN
SOUTH PACIFIC OCEAN
SOUTH ATLANTIC OCEAN
Caribbean Sea
CUBA
HONDURAS
NICARAGUA
COSTA RICA
PANAMA
COLOMBIA
VENEZUELA
GUYANA
SURINAME
French Guiana
ECUADOR
PERU
BRAZIL
BOLIVIA
PARAGUAY
CHILE
ARGENTINA
URUGUAY
Falkland Islands (U.K.)
South Georgia (U.K.)
South Shetland Islands (U.K.)
South Orkney Islands (U.K.)
South Sandwich Islands (U.K.)
Oblique Mercator Projection
© Oxford Cartographers
+44 (0) 1865 882 884
0 200 400 600 Miles
0 400 600 800 1000 Kms

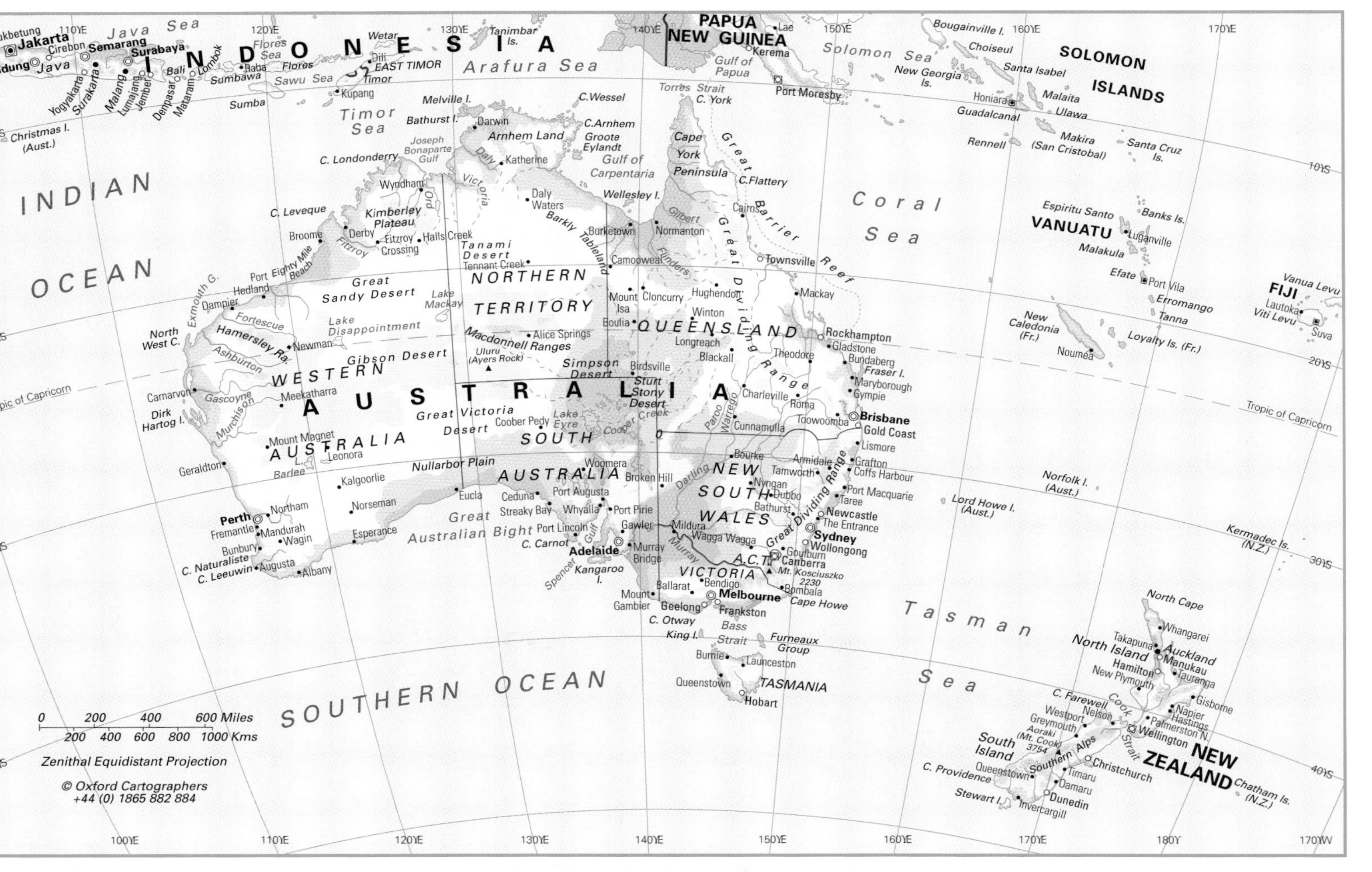

INDONESIA
PAPUA NEW GUINEA
SOLOMON ISLANDS
VANUATU
FIJI
NEW ZEALAND
AUSTRALIA
WESTERN AUSTRALIA
NORTHERN TERRITORY
SOUTH AUSTRALIA
QUEENSLAND
NEW SOUTH WALES
VICTORIA
A.C.T.
TASMANIA
EAST TIMOR
INDIAN OCEAN
SOUTHERN OCEAN
Tasman Sea
Coral Sea
Arafura Sea
Timor Sea
Java Sea
Flores Sea
Sawu Sea
Solomon Sea
Gulf of Carpentaria
Gulf of Papua
Great Australian Bight
Torres Strait
Bass Strait
Cook Strait
Great Barrier Reef
Great Dividing Range
Tropic of Capricorn
Jakarta
Bandung
Telukbetung
Cirebon
Semarang
Surabaya
Yogyakarta
Surakarta
Malang
Lumajang
Jember
Denpasar
Mataram
Java
Bali
Lombok
Raba
Sumbawa
Flores
Sumba
Kupang
Timor
Dili
Wetar
Tanimbar Is.
Christmas I. (Aust.)
Lae
Kerema
Port Moresby
Bougainville I.
Choiseul
Santa Isabel
New Georgia Is.
Honiara
Guadalcanal
Malaita
Ulawa
Makira (San Cristobal)
Rennell
Santa Cruz Is.
Espiritu Santo
Banks Is.
Luganville
Malakula
Efate
Port Vila
Erromango
Tanna
Loyalty Is. (Fr.)
New Caledonia (Fr.)
Noumea
Vanua Levu
Viti Levu
Lautoka
Suva
Norfolk I. (Aust.)
Lord Howe I. (Aust.)
Kermadec Is. (N.Z.)
Chatham Is. (N.Z.)
Melville I.
Bathurst I.
Darwin
C.Wessel
Arnhem Land
C.Arnhem
Groote Eylandt
Joseph Bonaparte Gulf
Katherine
Daly
Victoria
C. Londonderry
Wyndham
Ord
Kimberley Plateau
Daly Waters
Barkly Tableland
Wellesley I.
Burketown
Normanton
Gilbert
Flinders
Cape York Peninsula
C. York
C.Flattery
Cairns
Townsville
Mackay
C. Leveque
Broome
Derby
Fitzroy
Fitzroy Crossing
Halls Creek
Tanami Desert
Tennant Creek
Camooweal
Eighty Mile Beach
Port Hedland
Dampier
Exmouth G.
Great Sandy Desert
Lake Mackay
Mount Isa
Cloncurry
Hughenden
Winton
Boulia
North West C.
Fortescue
Hamersley Ra.
Lake Disappointment
Alice Springs
Macdonnell Ranges
Longreach
Blackall
Rockhampton
Gladstone
Bundaberg
Fraser I.
Maryborough
Gympie
Newman
Ashburton
Gibson Desert
Uluru (Ayers Rock)
Simpson Desert
Birdsville
Sturt Stony Desert
Theodore
Charleville
Roma
Carnarvon
Gascoyne
Meekatharra
Dirk Hartog I.
Murchison
Great Victoria Desert
Coober Pedy
Lake Eyre
Cooper Creek
Paroo
Warrego
Cunnamulla
Toowoomba
Brisbane
Gold Coast
Mount Magnet
Leonora
L. Barlee
Geraldton
Kalgoorlie
Nullarbor Plain
Woomera
Broken Hill
Darling
Bourke
Lismore
Armidale
Grafton
Coffs Harbour
Tamworth
Port Macquarie
Taree
Nyngan
Dubbo
Bathurst
Newcastle
The Entrance
Sydney
Wollongong
Goulburn
Canberra
Mt. Kosciuszko 2230
Bombala
Cape Howe
Eucla
Ceduna
Port Augusta
Streaky Bay
Whyalla
Port Pirie
Port Lincoln
C. Carnot
Spencer Gulf
Kangaroo I.
Adelaide
Gawler
Murray Bridge
Mildura
Murray
Wagga Wagga
Perth
Northam
Fremantle
Mandurah
Wagin
Norseman
Esperance
Bunbury
C. Naturaliste
C. Leeuwin
Augusta
Albany
Mount Gambier
Ballarat
Bendigo
Geelong
Melbourne
Frankston
C. Otway
King I.
Furneaux Group
Burnie
Launceston
Queenstown
Hobart
North Cape
Whangarei
Takapuna
Auckland
Manukau
Tauranga
North Island
Hamilton
New Plymouth
Gisborne
Napier
Hastings
Palmerston N.
Wellington
C. Farewell
Nelson
Westport
Greymouth
Aoraki (Mt. Cook) 3754
Southern Alps
Christchurch
South Island
Timaru
Oamaru
Dunedin
Queenstown
C. Providence
Stewart I.
Invercargill
10°S
20°S
30°S
40°S
100°E
110°E
120°E
130°E
140°E
150°E
160°E
170°E
180°
170°W
0 200 400 600 Miles
200 400 600 800 1000 Kms
Zenithal Equidistant Projection
© Oxford Cartographers
+44 (0) 1865 882 884

0 100 200 300 400 500 Miles
0 100 200 300 500 600 700 800 Kms
Conical Orthomorphic Projection
© Oxford Cartographers
+44 (0) 1865 882 884
70°W
0°
10°E
20°E
30°E
40°E
60°E
Spitsbergen
Svalbard (Norway)
Franz Josef Land
A R C T I
Arctic Circle
Narvik
Tromsø
North Cape
N O R W A Y
Trondheim
Oslo
60°N
S W E D E N
Lapland
Umeå
Luleå
Gulf of Bothnia
Uppsala
Stockholm
Oulu
Vaasa
F I N L A N D
Kandalaksha
Murmansk
Kola Peninsula
Barents Sea
Novaya Zemlya
Kara Sea
Tampere
Helsinki
Gulf of Finland
Tallinn
ESTONIA
LATVIA
Riga
Tartu
White Sea
Severodvinsk
Arkhangel'sk
L. Ladoga
St. Petersburg
L. Onega
Petrozavodsk
Pskov
Daugavpils
Vitsyebsk
BELARUS
Novgorod
Velikiye-Luki
Cherepovets
Konosha
N. Dvina
Pechora
Vorkuta
Gulf of Ob
Dudin
Moscow
Volga
Yaroslavl'
Tver'
Vologda
Kotlas
Ukhta
Pechora
Ob'
Nadym
Smolensk
Bryansk
Tula
Kostroma
Ivanovo
Syktyvkar
R
Ural Mountains
Kaluga
Tula
Vladimir
Nizhniy Novgorod
Kirov (Vyatka)
West Siberian Plain
Orel
Ryazan'
Arzamas
Glazov
Berezniki
Kursk
Don
Cheboksary
Serov
Khanty-Mansiysk
U
Surgut
Belgorod
Lipetsk
Tambov
Saransk
Kazan'
Perm
Kungur
Nizhniy Tagil
Nizhnevartovsk
S
50°N
Voronezh
Borisoglebsk
Penza
Syzran
Simbirsk
Naberezhnyye Chelny
Izhevsk
Sarapul
Yekaterinburg
Tobol'sk
Irtysh
Ob'
Luhansk
Donetsk
Volgograd
Engel's
Saratov
Tol'yatti
Samara
Ufa
Zlatoust
Kamensk-Ural'skiy
Tyumen'
Rostov
Kamyshin
Balakhovo
Orenburg
Magnitogorsk
Chelyabinsk
Kurgan
Ishim
Volga
Troitsk
Tomsk
Elista
Ural
Ural'sk
Kostanay
Omsk
Anzhero-Sudzhensk
Kuybyshev
Kemer
Caspian Lowlands
Rudnyy
Petropavlovsk
Novosibirsk
Aktyubinsk
Orsk
Kokshetau
Leninsk-Kuznetskiy
Novokuznet
Astrakhan
Atyrau
Pavlodar
Barna
Grozny
Kirghiz Steppe
L. Tengiz
Astana
Irtysh
Biy
Makhachkala
Caspian Sea
Karaganda
Rubtsovsk
Aktau
Ust-Urt Plateau
K A Z A K H S T A N
Aral'sk
Semipalatinsk
Zhezkazgan
Kazakh Uplands
Ust'-Kamenogorsk
AZER.
Sumgait
40°N
Aral Sea
Syr Dar'ya
Baku
Kara Bogaz-Gol
Nukus
U Z B E K I S T A N
Kyzyl-Orda
Balkhash
L. Zaysan
Alt
Turkmenbashi
Dashkhovuz
Kyzylkum Desert
Lake Balkhash
Tacheng
Karakum Desert
Muyunkum Desert
Taldy-Kurgan
Karamay
TURKMENISTAN
Chimkent
Dzhambul
Dzungarian B (Junggar Pe
Karaj
Elburz Mts.
Gorgan
Tashkent
Bishkek
Almaty
Yining
Kuytun
Tehrān
Semnan
Ashgabat
Bukhara
Navoi
Dzhizak
KYRGYZSTAN
Pik Pobedy 7439
Issyk-Kul'
Ürüm
Dasht-e Kavir
Mashhad
Samarkand
Chardzhou
Namangan
Tien Shan
I R A N
Mary
Amu Dar'ya
Dushanbe
Khujand
Fergana
Korla
TAJIKISTAN
Aksu
Tarim He
60°E
70°E
Kashi
80°E

East Siberian Sea
Laptev Sea
New Siberia Is.
Lyakhov Is.
Wrangel I.
Severnaya Zemlya
O C E A N
Taymyr Pen.
L. Taymyr
Anadyr Range
Koryak Range
Kolyma Mts.
Cherskogo Range
Verkhoyansk Range
Central Siberian Plateau
Dzhugdzhur Range
Sea of Okhotsk
Sakhalin
Stanovoy Mts.
Yablonovyy Mts.
Lake Baikal
Sayan Mts.
Da Hinggan Ling
Hangayan Mts.
MONGOLIA
Gobi Desert
INNER MONGOLIA
DEM. PEOPLE'S REP. OF KOREA
REP. OF KOREA
Yellow Sea
Korea Bay
Bo Hai
Lena
Yana
Indigirka
Kolyma
Olenek
Vilyuy
Aldan
Amur
Angara
Huang He (Yellow)
Pevek
Anadyr
Tiksi
Magadan
Okhotsk
Yakutsk
Olekminsk
Lensk
Neryungri
Tynda
Skovorodino
Komsomol'sk na-Amure
Khabarovsk
Belogorsk
Blagoveshchensk
Birobidzhan
Ust' Ilimsk
Ust'-Kut
Severobaikal'sk
Krasnoyarsk
Kansk
Tayshek
Bratsk
Tulun
Usol'ye-Sibirskoye
Angarsk
Irkutsk
Abakan
Kyzyl
Chita
Sretensk
Ulan-Ude
Hailar
Manzhouli
Hövsgöl Nuur
Uvs Nuur
Darhan
Ulaanbaatar
Öndörhaan
Saynshand
Hovd
Altay
Hami
Depression
Lop Nur
Yichun
Hegang
Jiamusi
Shuangyashan
Qitaihe
Jixi
Mudanjiang
Bei'an
Qiqihar
Daqing
Harbin
Baicheng
Ulanhot
Jilin
Ussuriysk
Yanji
Vladivostok
Chongjin
Changchun
Liaoyuan
Siping
Tongliao
Fushun
Shenyang
Chifeng
Fuxin
Jinzhou
Anshan
Chengde
Pyongyang
Seoul
Inchon
Tangshan
Dalian
Yantai
Weihai
Zhangjiakou
Beijing (Peking)
Tianjin
Jining
Hohhot
Baotou
Datong
Baoding
Cangzhou
Shijiazhuang
Dezhou
Zibo
Weifang
Qingdao
Jinan
Handan
Taiyuan
Yuci
Linhe
Wuhai
Shizuishan
S
I
A
C H I N A
120°E 140°E 150°E 160°E 170°E 180°
100°E 110°E 120°E
70°N 60°N 50°N 40°N

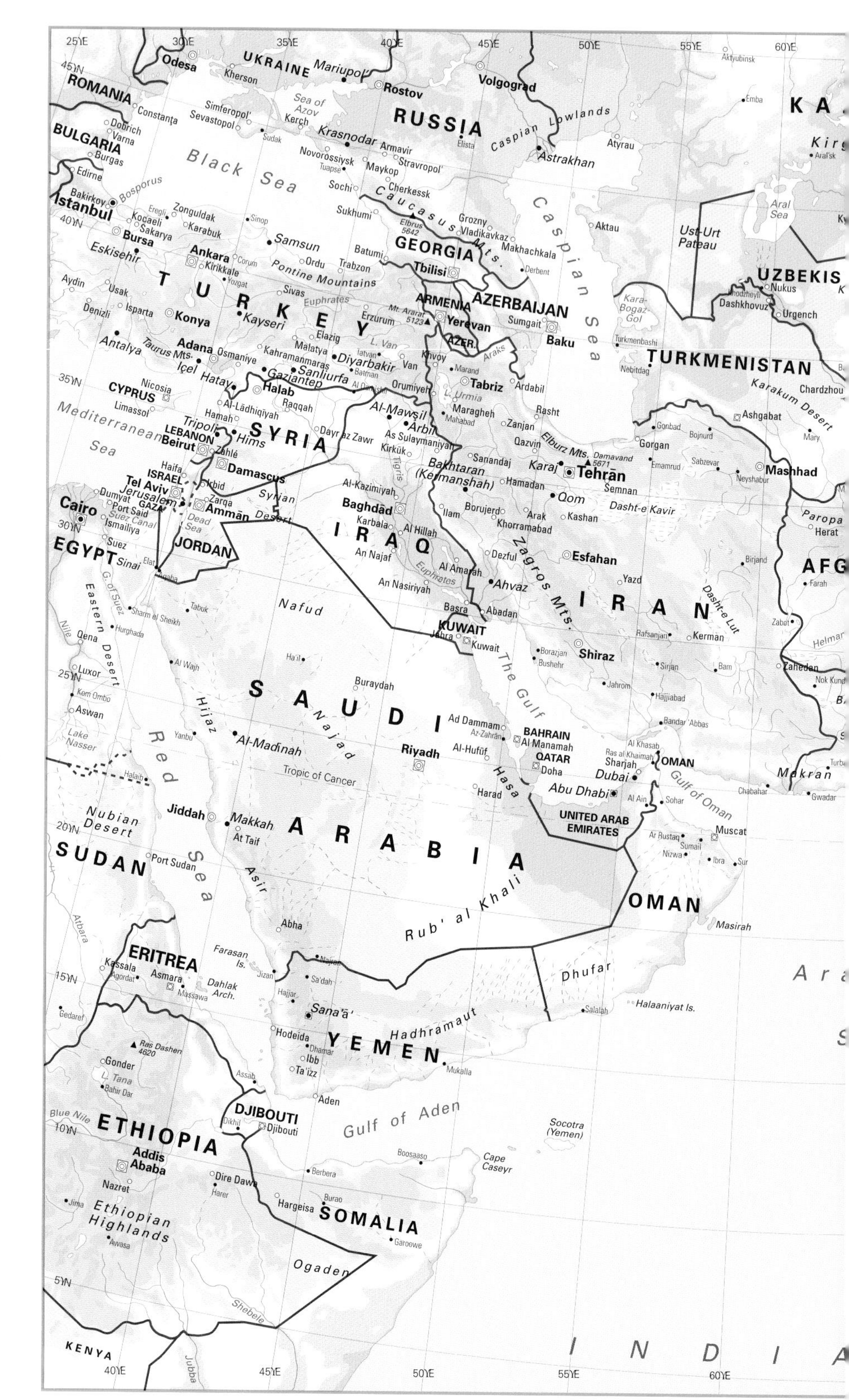

25°E
30°E
35°E
40°E
45°E
50°E
55°E
60°E
45°N
40°N
35°N
30°N
25°N
20°N
15°N
10°N
5°N
UKRAINE
Odesa
Kherson
Mariupol'
Rostov
Volgograd
ROMANIA
Constanța
Sea of Azov
Kerch
Simferopol'
Sevastopol
RUSSIA
Elista
Caspian Lowlands
Astrakhan
Atyrau
Emba
Aktyubinsk
KA
Kirg
Aral'sk
BULGARIA
Dobrich
Varna
Burgas
Edirne
Krasnodar
Armavir
Novorossiysk
Tuapse
Maykop
Stravropol'
Black Sea
Sudak
Sochi
Cherkessk
Caucasus Mts.
Elbrus 5642
Grozny
Vladikavkaz
Makhachkala
Derbent
Sukhumi
Bakirkoy
Bosporus
Istanbul
Eregli
Zonguldak
Kocaeli
Sakarya
Karabuk
Sinop
Bursa
Eskisehir
Samsun
Ankara
Corum
Kirikkale
Yozgat
Ordu
Trabzon
Batumi
GEORGIA
Tbilisi
Aktau
Aral Sea
Ust-Urt Pateau
Caspian Sea
Kara-Bogaz-Gol
UZBEKIS
Nukus
Khodzheyli
Dashkhovuz
Urgench
Aydin
Usak
TURKEY
Pontine Mountains
Sivas
Euphrates
Erzurum
Mt. Ararat 5123
ARMENIA
Yerevan
AZERBAIJAN
Sumgait
Baku
Denizli
Isparta
Konya
Kayseri
Elazig
L. Van
AZER.
Turkmenbashi
Nebitdag
TURKMENISTAN
Antalya
Taurus Mts.
Adana
Osmaniye
Malatya
Kahramanmaras
Diyarbakir
Batman
Van
Khvoy
Araks
Marand
Tabriz
Ardabil
Içel
Hatay
Gaziantep
Sanliurfa
Al Qamishli
Orumiyeh
L. Urmia
Karakum Desert
Chardzhou
Nicosia
CYPRUS
Limassol
Halab
Al-Lādhiqīyah
Raqqah
Al-Mawṣil
Arbīl
Maragheh
Mahabad
Rasht
Ashgabat
Mediterranean Sea
Tripoli
Hamah
LEBANON
Beirut
Hims
SYRIA
Dayr az Zawr
As Sulaymaniyah
Kirkūk
Tigris
Zanjan
Qazvin
Elburz Mts.
Damavand 5671
Gonbad
Bojnurd
Gorgan
Mary
Haifa
ISRAEL
Tel Aviv
Jerusalem
GAZA
Zahlé
Damascus
Irbid
Zarqa
Ammān
Syrian Desert
Sanandaj
Bakhtaran (Kermanshah)
Karaj
Tehrān
Semnan
Emamrud
Sabzevar
Neyshabur
Mashhad
Cairo
Dumyat
Port Said
Suez Canal
Ismailiya
Dead Sea
Al-Kazimiyah
Baghdād
Karbala
Al Hillah
Hamadan
Borujerd
Ilam
Arak
Khorramabad
Qom
Kashan
Dasht-e Kavir
Paropa
Herat
EGYPT
Suez
Sinai
Elat
Aqaba
JORDAN
IRAQ
An Najaf
Euphrates
Al Amarah
Dezful
Ahvaz
Zagros Mts.
Esfahan
Yazd
Birjand
AFG
Farah
G. of Suez
Eastern Desert
Nile
Sharm el Sheikh
Tabuk
Nafud
An Nasiriyah
Basra
Abadan
IRAN
Dasht-e Lut
Qena
Hurghada
KUWAIT
Jahra
Kuwait
Rafsanjan
Kerman
Zabol
Helmand
Luxor
Al Wajh
Ha'il
The Gulf
Borazjan
Bushehr
Shiraz
Sirjan
Bam
Zahedan
Nok Kundi
Kom Ombo
Aswan
Buraydah
SAUDI ARABIA
Jahrom
Hajjiabad
Hijaz
Najd
Ad Dammam
Az-Zahran
BAHRAIN
Al Manamah
Bandar 'Abbas
Lake Nasser
Red Sea
Yanbu
Al-Madinah
Riyadh
Al-Hufuf
Al Khasab
Ras al Khaimah
Sharjah
OMAN
Halaib
Tropic of Cancer
QATAR
Doha
Hasa
Harad
Dubai
Abu Dhabi
Al Ain
Sohar
Gulf of Oman
Chabahar
Makran
Gwadar
Nubian Desert
Jiddah
Makkah
At Taif
UNITED ARAB EMIRATES
Ar Rustaq
Sumail
Muscat
Nizwa
Ibra
Sur
SUDAN
Port Sudan
Asir
Rub' al Khali
OMAN
Masirah
Atbara
Abha
ERITREA
Kassala
Agordat
Asmara
Farasan Is.
Najran
Jizan
Dhufar
Arabian Sea
Dahlak Arch.
Massawa
Sa'dah
Hajjar
Sana'a'
Salalah
Halaaniyat Is.
Gedaref
Ras Dashen 4620
Hodeida
Hadhramaut
YEMEN
Dhamar
Ibb
Ta'izz
Mukalla
Gonder
L. Tana
Bahir Dar
Assab
Aden
Blue Nile
DJIBOUTI
Dikhil
Djibouti
Gulf of Aden
Socotra (Yemen)
ETHIOPIA
Addis Ababa
Boosaaso
Cape Caseyr
Berbera
Dire Dawa
Harer
Nazret
Jima
Ethiopian Highlands
Burao
Hargeisa
SOMALIA
Awasa
Garoowe
Ogaden
Shebele
KENYA
Jubba
INDIA

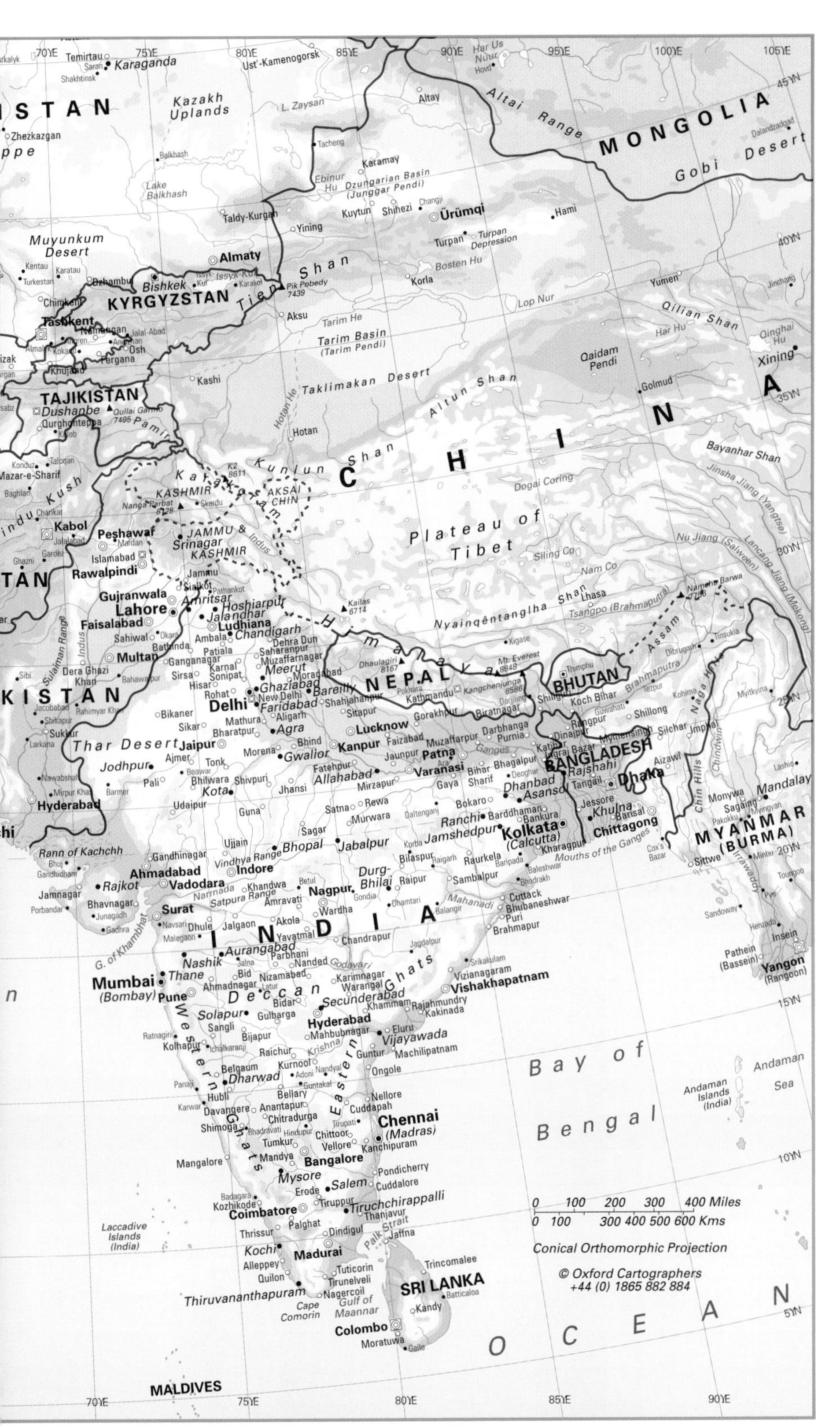

70°E
75°E
80°E
85°E
90°E
95°E
100°E
105°E
45°N
40°N
35°N
30°N
25°N
20°N
15°N
10°N
5°N
Temirtau
Karaganda
Sarah
Shakhtinsk
Ust'-Kamenogorsk
Har Us Nuur
Hovd
STAN
Kazakh Uplands
L. Zaysan
Altay
Altai Range
MONGOLIA
Dalandzadgad
Gobi Desert
Zhezkazgan
ppe
Tacheng
Balkhash
Karamay
Ebinur Hu
Dzungarian Basin (Junggar Pendi)
Lake Balkhash
Kuytun
Shihezi
Changji
Ürümqi
Hami
Taldy-Kurgan
Yining
Turpan
Turpan Depression
Muyunkum Desert
Almaty
Kentau
Karatau
Turkestan
Dzhambul
Bishkek
Issyk-Kul
Karakol
Shan
Pik Pobedy 7439
Bosten Hu
Korla
Yumen
Jinchang
KYRGYZSTAN
Tien
Chimkent
Tashkent
Namangan
Jalal-Abad
Aksu
Lop Nur
Qilian Shan
Tarim He
Tarim Basin (Tarim Pendi)
Har Hu
Qinghai Hu
Almalyk
Andijan
Kokand
Osh
Fergana
Khujand
Qaidam Pendi
Xining
Kashi
Taklimakan Desert
Hotan He
Altun Shan
Golmud
TAJIKISTAN
Dushanbe
Qullai Garmo 7495
Qurghonteppa
Kulob
Pamir
Hotan
CHINA
Bayanhar Shan
Kunlun Shan
K2 8611
Karakoram
Jinsha Jiang (Yangtse)
Konduz
Taloqan
Mazar-e-Sharif
Kush
Baghlan
KASHMIR
Nanga Parbat 8126
Skardu
AKSAI CHIN
Dogai Coring
Plateau of Tibet
Hindu
Charikar
Kabol
Jalalabad
Gardez
Ghazni
Peshawar
Mardan
Islamabad
Rawalpindi
JAMMU & KASHMIR
Srinagar
Indus
Nu Jiang (Salween)
Lancang Jiang (Mekong)
Siling Co
Nam Co
TAN
Jammu
Sialkot
Pathankot
Kailas 6714
Lhasa
Namcha Barwa 7756
Gujranwala
Amritsar
Hoshiarpur
Jalandhar
Ludhiana
Chandigarh
Lahore
Faisalabad
Nyainqêntanglha Shan
Tsangpo (Brahmaputra)
Himalaya
Assam
Sahiwal
Okara
Ambala
Dehra Dun
Xigase
Dibrugarh
Tinsukia
Sulaiman Range
Indus
Multan
Bathinda
Patiala
Saharanpur
Muzaffarnagar
Meerut
Moradabad
Dhaulagiri 8167
Mt. Everest 8848
Thimphu
BHUTAN
Brahmaputra
Tezpur
Naga Hills
Sibi
Dera Ghazi Khan
Bahawalpur
Ganganagar
Sirsa
Karnal
Sonipat
Hisar
Rohtak
Ghaziabad
Bareilly
NEPAL
Pokhara
Kathmandu
Kangchenjunga 8586
Darjiling
Shillong
Koch Bihar
Guwahati
Kohima
Myitkyina
KISTAN
Jacobabad
Shikarpur
Sukkur
Larkana
Rahimyar Khan
Bikaner
Delhi
New Delhi
Faridabad
Shahjahanpur
Aligarh
Sitapur
Gorakhpur
Biratnagar
Darbhanga
Purnia
Rangpur
Dinajpur
Mymensingh
Sylhet
Silchar
Imphal
Sikar
Mathura
Bharatpur
Agra
Lucknow
Faizabad
Muzaffarpur
Patna
Ganges
Katihar
Ingraj Bazar
BANGLADESH
Thar Desert
Jaipur
Ajmer
Morena
Bhind
Gwalior
Kanpur
Jaunpur
Bhagalpur
Rajshahi
Aizawl
Chin Hills
Chindwin
Lashio
Jodhpur
Tonk
Beawar
Bhilwara
Kota
Shivpuri
Jhansi
Fatehpur
Allahabad
Varanasi
Ara
Bihar Sharif
Deoghar
Dhanbad
Asansol
Tangail
Dhaka
Nawabshah
Mirpur Khas
Barmer
Pali
Mirzapur
Gaya
Hyderabad
Udaipur
Guna
Satna
Rewa
Bokaro
Jessore
Khulna
Barisal
Monywa
Mandalay
Sagaing
Pakokku
Myingyan
Murwara
Daltenganj
Ranchi
Barddhaman
Bankura
Ujjain
Sagar
Jabalpur
Jamshedpur
Kolkata (Calcutta)
Chittagong
MYANMAR (BURMA)
Rann of Kachchh
Gandhinagar
Vindhya Range
Bhopal
Korba
Bilaspur
Raigarh
Raurkela
Baripada
Kharagpur
Mouths of the Ganges
Cox's Bazar
Sittwe
Minbu
Bhuj
Gandhidham
Ahmadabad
Indore
Durg-Bhilai
Baleshwar
Irrawaddy
Toungoo
Jamnagar
Rajkot
Vadodara
Narmada
Khandwa
Betul
Nagpur
Raipur
Sambalpur
Bhadrakh
Porbandar
Bhavnagar
Junagadh
Satpura Range
Amravati
Wardha
Gondia
Dhamtari
Mahanadi
Cuttack
Bhubaneshwar
Pye
Surat
Navsari
Dhule
Jalgaon
Akola
INDIA
Balangir
Puri
Brahmapur
Sandoway
Gadhra
Malegaon
Yavatmal
Chandrapur
Henzada
G. of Khambhat
Aurangabad
Parbhani
Jagdalpur
Insein
Nashik
Jalna
Nanded
Godavari
Srikakulam
Pathein (Bassein)
Yangon (Rangoon)
Bid
Nizamabad
Karimnagar
Vizianagaram
Mumbai (Bombay)
Thane
Ahmadnagar
Latur
Warangal
Ghats
Vishakhapatnam
Pune
Deccan
Bidar
Secunderabad
Khammam
Rajahmundry
Kakinada
Solapur
Gulbarga
Hyderabad
Western
Sangli
Ratnagiri
Mahbubnagar
Eluru
Vijayawada
Kolhapur
Ichalkaranji
Bijapur
Krishna
Guntur
Machilipatnam
Bay of Bengal
Andaman Sea
Raichur
Kurnool
Eastern
Belgaum
Dharwad
Adoni
Nandyal
Ongole
Panaji
Hubli
Guntakal
Bellary
Nellore
Andaman Islands (India)
Karwar
Davangere
Anantapur
Cuddapah
Chitradurga
Tirupati
Chennai (Madras)
Shimoga
Bhadravati
Hindupur
Chittoor
Tumkur
Vellore
Kanchipuram
Mandya
Bangalore
Mangalore
Mysore
Pondicherry
Cuddalore
Erode
Salem
Badagara
Kozhikode
Coimbatore
Tiruppur
Tiruchchirappalli
Thanjavur
Laccadive Islands (India)
Thrissur
Palghat
Dindigul
Palk Strait
Jaffna
Kochi
Madurai
Alleppey
Quilon
Tuticorin
Tirunelveli
Trincomalee
SRI LANKA
Batticaloa
Thiruvananthapuram
Nagercoil
Cape Comorin
Gulf of Mannar
Kandy
Colombo
Moratuwa
Galle
OCEAN
MALDIVES
0 100 200 300 400 Miles
0 100 300 400 500 600 Kms
Conical Orthomorphic Projection
© Oxford Cartographers
+44 (0) 1865 882 884

RUSSIA
MONGOLIA
CHINA
JAPAN
INDONESIA
AUSTRALIA
NEW ZEALAND
PHILIPPINES
MICRONESIA
INDIAN OCEAN
Laptev Sea
East Siberian Sea
Bering Sea
Sea of Okhotsk
Philippine Sea
Tasman Sea
Coral Sea
Beijing (Peking)
Tokyo
Seoul
Pyongyang
Manila
Jakarta
Canberra
Wellington
Taipei
Ulaanbaatar
Singapore
Bangkok
Hanoi
Sydney
Melbourne
Brisbane
Perth
Auckland
Shanghai
Hong Kong
Vladivostok
Magadan
Yakutsk
Irkutsk
International Date Line
Tropic of Capricorn
Arctic Circle

Beaufort Sea
Melville Island
McClure Strait
Viscount Melville Sound
Banks Island
Devon Island
Baffin Bay
Somerset I.
Amundsen Gulf
Victoria Island
Gulf of Boothia
Baffin Island
Foxe Basin
Arctic Circle
Cumberland Sound
Frobisher Bay
Hudson Strait
Ungava Peninsula
Ungava Bay
Great Bear Lake
Alaska (USA)
Brooks Range
Yukon
Mackenzie Mts.
Alaska Range
Mt. McKinley 6194
Anchorage
Mt. Logan 5959
Gt. Slave Lake
Hudson Bay
Caribou Mts.
Peace
L. Athabasca
CANADA
Reindeer Lake
Labrador
Gulf of Alaska
Coast Mountains
Rocky Mountains
Queen Charlotte Islands
Mt. Robson 3945
Edmonton
James Bay
Saskatoon
Lake Winnipeg
Calgary
L. Manitoba
Regina
Winnipeg
St. Lawrence
Gulf of St. Lawrence
Vancouver I.
Vancouver
Thunder Bay
Lake Superior
Québec
Seattle
Tacoma
Mt. Rainier 4392
Sudbury
Ottawa
Montréal
Nova Scotia
Portland
Minneapolis
St. Paul
Lake Michigan
Lake Huron
Toronto
Lake Ontario
Halifax
Boise
Milwaukee
Detroit
Lake Erie
Buffalo
Boston
Salt Lake City
Omaha
Missouri
Chicago
Cleveland
New York
Indianapolis
Pittsburgh
Philadelphia
USA
Denver
Kansas City
Cincinnati
Baltimore
Sacramento
St. Louis
Washington DC
San Francisco
San José
Mt. Whitney 4418
Colorado Plateau
Oklahoma City
Norfolk
Las Vegas
Appalachian Mts.
Amarillo
Raleigh
Albuquerque
Memphis
Los Angeles
Phoenix
Fort Worth
Atlanta
ATLANTIC
San Diego
Tucson
Dallas
Columbus
Mississippi
Bermuda (UK)
Ciudad Juárez
Baton Rouge
Tallahassee
Hermosillo
R. Grande
Houston
New Orleans
Gulf of California
Chihuahua
Orlando
Corpus Christi
St. Petersburg
Tampa
OCEAN
BAHAMAS
MEXICO
Monterrey
Gulf of Mexico
Miami
Durango
Nassau
Mazatlán
Ciudad Victoria
Havana
Tropic of Cancer
Tampico
CUBA
Bay of Campeche
Camagüey
Mérida
Guadalajara
Greater Antilles
Port-au-Prince
DOMINICAN REPUBLIC
Revilla Gigedo Is. (Mex.)
Mexico City
Veracruz
Campeche
HAITI
Santo Domingo
Popocatépetl 5452
BELIZE
JAMAICA
Kingston
Acapulco
Belmopan
GUATEMALA
HONDURAS
Caribbean Sea
DOMINICA
Guatemala City
Tegucigalpa
San Salvador
NICARAGUA
EL SALVADOR
Managua
TRINIDAD & TOBAGO
COSTA RICA
Cartegena
Maracaibo
Caracas
San José
Panamá City
PANAMA
VENEZUELA
Orinoco
Medellín
Bogotá
Buenaventura
COLOMBIA
Cali
Guiana Highlands
Galapagos Is. (Ecuador)
Quito
Equator
ECUADOR
Cuenca
Iquitos
Amazon
Selvas
Piura
PERU
Chiclayo
BRAZIL
Trujillo
Marquesas Is. (Fr.)
Lima
Tuamotu Arch.
La Paz
BOLIVIA
Oruro
Arica
Sucre
Society Islands (Fr.)
Potosí
French Polynesia
Gambier Is. (Fr.)
Austral Is. (Fr.)
Antofagasta
Tropic of Capricorn
Gran Chaco
Pitcairn Is. (UK)
Easter I. (Chile)
Salta
Catamarca
Córdoba
Juan Fernández Is. (Chile)
Valparaíso
Aconcagua 6960
Santiago
SOUTH PACIFIC OCEAN
CHILE
ARGENTINA
Concepción
Bahía Blanca
Puerto Montt
Patagonia
Comodoro Rivadavia
0 500 1000 1500 miles
0 500 1000 1500 2000 2500 kms
Miller Projection
© Oxford Cartographers
+44 (0) 1865 882 884
150°W
140°W
130°W
120°W
110°W
100°W
90°W
80°W
70°W
70°N
60°N
50°N
40°N
30°N
20°N
10°N
0°
10°S
20°S
30°S
40°S
50°S

World Political
180° 160°W 140°W 120°W 100°W 60°W 20°W 0° 20°E 40°E 60°E 80°E 100°E 120°E 140°E 160°E 180°
60°N
40°N
20°N
0°
20°S
40°S
60°S
Arctic Circle
Tropic of Cancer
Equator
Tropic of Capricorn
Antarctic Circle
International Date Line
Alaska (USA)
Canada
United States of America
Mexico
Kalaallit Nunaat (Greenland) (Denmark)
Bahamas
Cuba
Haiti
Dom. Rep.
Jamaica
Belize
Guatemala
Honduras
El Salvador
Nicaragua
Costa Rica
Panama
Trinidad and Tobago
Venezuela
Guyana
Sur.
French Guiana
Colombia
Ecuador
Peru
Brazil
Bolivia
Paraguay
Chile
Uruguay
Argentina
Iceland
Norway
Sweden
Finland
Denmark
UK
Rep. of Ireland
Es.
La.
Li.
Rus.
Poland
Belarus
Neth.
Belg.
Lux.
Ger.
France
Sw.
Aust.
Slov.
Ukraine
Mol.
Hungary
Romania
Italy
BH
Bulgaria
Alb.
Ma.
Greece
Spain
Portugal
Gibraltar
Malta
Tunisia
Morocco
Algeria
Libya
Egypt
Western Sahara
Mauritania
Mali
Niger
Chad
Sudan
Eritrea
Djibouti
Ethiopia
Cape Verde
Senegal
Gambia
Guinea Bissau
Gui.
SL
Liberia
Côte
Burkina Faso
Ghana
Benin
Nigeria
Dem. People's
Cam.
Cen. Af. Rep.
Eq. Gui.
Gabon
Congo-Brazz
Dem. Rep. of Congo
Cabinda (Angola)
Uganda
Kenya
Somalia
Rwanda
Burundi
Tanzania
Angola
Zambia
Mal.
Namibia
Zim.
Botswana
Mozambique
Swaziland
South Africa
Lesotho
Madagascar
Mauritius
Seychelles
Turkey
Georgia
Ar.
Azer.
Cyp.
Syria
Leb.
Isr.
Jor.
Iraq
Kuwait
Iran
Saudi Arabia
Q
UAE
Oman
Yemen
Russia
Kazakhstan
Uzbekistan
Turk.
Kyrg.
Taj.
Afghanistan
Pakistan
India
Nepal
Bh.
Bangladesh
Sri Lanka
Maldives
Mongolia
China
Rep. of Korea
Rep. of Korea
Japan
Taiwan
Myanmar
Laos
Thai.
Vietnam
Cam.
Philippines
Malaysia
Brn.
Singapore
Indonesia
East Timor
Papua New Guinea
Micronesia
Australia
Vanuatu
Fiji
New Zealand
Antarctica
Alb. Albania
Ar. Armenia
Aust. Austria
Azer. Azerbaijan
Belg. Belgium
Bh. Bhutan
BH Bosnia-Hercegovina
Brn. Brunei
Cam. Cambodia
Cam. Cameroon
Cen. Af. Rep. Central African Republic
Congo-Brazz Congo-Brazzaville
Cro. Croatia
Cyp. Cyprus
Cz. Rep. Czech Republic
Dom. Rep. Dominican Republic
Eq. Gui. Equatorial Guinea
Es. Estonia
Ger. Germany
Gui. Guinea
Isr. Israel
Jor. Jordan
Kyrg. Kyrgyzstan
La. Latvia
Leb. Lebanon
Li. Lithuania
Lux. Luxembourg
Ma. Macedonia
Mal. Malawi
Mol. Moldova
Neth. Netherlands
Q Qatar
Rus. Russia
SL Sierra Leone
Slov. Slovakia
Slo. Slovenia
Sur. Suriname
Sw. Switzerland
Taj. Tajikistan
Thai. Thailand
T Togo
Turk. Turkmenistan
UAE United Arab Emirates
UK United Kingdom
Yugo. Fed. Rep. Yugoslavia
Zim. Zimbabwe
Modified Gall Projection
Equatorial Scale 1:166,000,000
© Oxford Cartographers
+44 (0) 1865 882 884
94658

*Ambassador Extraordinary and Plenipotentiary*, HE Adrian Thorpe, KCMG, apptd 1999
*Deputy Head of Mission, Minister-Counsellor and Consul-General*, I. Hughes
*Defence Attaché*, Col. I. Blair-Pilling, OBE
*First Secretary (Commercial)*, M. Kent

CONSULAR OFFICES – Mexico City, Acapulco, Cancún, Ciudad Juárez, Guadalajara, Monterrey, Oaxaca, Tampico, Tijuana, Veracruz

BRITISH COUNCIL DIRECTOR, Alan Curry, Lope de Vega 316, Col. Chapultepec Morales, 11570 Mexico DF; e-mail: bc.mexico@britishcouncil.org.mx

BRITISH CHAMBER OF COMMERCE, British Trade Centre, Rio de la Plata 30, Col. Cuauhtémoc, CP 06500, Mexico City DF. *Manager*, Stephen Grant

## DEFENCE

The Army has 862 armoured personnel carriers. The Navy has three destroyers, eight frigates, 109 patrol and coastal vessels, and nine combat aircraft. There are 20 naval bases. The Air Force has 107 combat aircraft and 71 armed helicopters.

MILITARY EXPENDITURE – 0.9 per cent of GDP (1999)
MILITARY PERSONNEL – 192,770: Army 144,000, Navy 37,000, Air Force 11,770
CONSCRIPTION DURATION – 12 months (four hours per week) by lottery

## ECONOMY

The principal crops are maize, beans, sorghum, rice, wheat, barley, sugar cane, coffee, cotton, tomatoes, chillies, tobacco, chick-peas, groundnuts, cocoa and many kinds of fruit. The maguey, or Mexican cactus, yields several fermented drinks, mezcal and tequila (distilled) and pulque (undistilled). Another species of the plant supplies sisal-hemp (henequen). The forests contain mahogany, rosewood, ebony and chicle trees. Agriculture employs an estimated 20 per cent of the working population.

The principal industries are mining and petroleum, although there has been considerable expansion of both light and heavy industries; exports of manufactured goods now average more than 85 per cent of total exports. The steel industry expanded steadily until recently and current production is around 5.8 million tons. More than one million vehicles are exported annually, along with more than two million automotive engines and six million television sets.

The mineral wealth is great, and principal minerals are gold, silver, copper, fluorspar, lead, zinc, quicksilver, iron and sulphur. Substantial reserves of uranium have been found.

Oil production was 164 million tonnes in 1998. Oil reserves have increased substantially due to discoveries in the Gulf of Campeche. A refinery at Tula is the nation's largest; and new refineries in Monterrey, State of Nuevo León, and Salina Cruz, State of Oaxaca, are under construction. The oil industry is state-owned.

The state telephone monopoly, Telmex, was privatised in 1990.

Tariffs on trade between Mexico and the USA and Canada are being reduced and are due to be abolished in 2009 under the North American Free Trade Area agreement.

There is great social inequality; a poverty-alleviation programme guarantees money and food to 2.6 million of the poorest families if they send their children to school.

In 2000, GDP was expected to grow by 5-6 per cent.

Mexico joined GATT in 1986 and the OECD in 1994.

GNP – US$428,877 million (1999); US$4,400 per capita (1999)
GDP – US$402,109 million (1997); US$4,961 per capita (1999)
ANNUAL AVERAGE GROWTH OF GDP – 5.3 per cent (2000)
INFLATION RATE – 7.1 per cent (2001)
UNEMPLOYMENT – 2.1 per cent (2000)
TOTAL EXTERNAL DEBT – US$159,959 million (1998)

### TRADE

Major imports include computers, auto assembly material, electrical parts, auto and truck parts, powdered milk, corn and sorghum, transport, sound-recording and power-generating equipment, chemicals, industrial machinery, pharmaceuticals and specialised appliances. Principal exports include oil, automobiles, auto engines, fruits and vegetables, shrimps, coffee, computers, cattle, glass, iron and steel pipes, and copper. The main trading partners are the USA, EU, Latin America and Japan. The North American Free Trade Agreement, to which Mexico is a signatory, came into effect on 1 January 1994; trade between Mexico, Canada and the USA rose by 17 per cent per year. Mexico has free trade deals with the EU, Bolivia, Chile, Colombia, Costa Rica, Nicaragua and Venezuela, and negotiations are under way to create free trade agreements with other South American countries

In 1999 Mexico had a trade deficit of US$5,360 million and a current account deficit of US$14,016 million. Imports totalled US$148,741 million and exports US$136,703 million.

| *Trade with UK* | 1999 | 2000 |
|---|---|---|
| Imports from UK | £585,016,000 | £674,683,000 |
| Exports to UK | 410,180,000 | 632,867,000 |

## COMMUNICATIONS

Veracruz, Tampico and Coatzacoalcos are the chief ports on the Atlantic, and Guaymas, Mazatlán, Puerto Lázaro Cárdenas and Salina Cruz on the Pacific. Work is proceeding on the reorganisation and re-equipment of the whole rail system. There were 307,142 km of roads in 1994; total track length of the railways was 20,445 km. Mexico City may be reached by at least three highways from the USA, and from the south from Yucatán as well as on two principal highways from the Guatemalan border.

There are 50 international airports and 33 national airports in Mexico. There are many airline companies, including two major, now private, national airlines, Mexicana de Aviación and Aeroméxico.

Teléfonos de México, now privatised, controls about 98 per cent of all telephone services.

---

# FEDERATED STATES OF MICRONESIA

---

AREA – 271 sq. miles (702 sq. km)
POPULATION – 116,000 (1997 UN estimate). Pohnpei: population, 31,000; capital, Kolonia; Chuuk (Truk): population, 52,000; capital, Moen; Yap: population, 12,000; capital, Colonia; Kosrae: population, 6,500; capital, Lelu. The population is Micronesian and predominantly Christian. English (official) and eight other languages are used in different parts of the Federated States: Yapese, Ulithian, Woleaian, Pohnpeian, Nukuoran, Kapingamarangi, Chuukese and Kosraean
FEDERAL CAPITAL – Palikir, on Pohnpei
CURRENCY – Currency is that of the USA
NATIONAL FLAG – United Nations blue with four white stars in the centre
POPULATION GROWTH RATE – 2.1 per cent (1999)
POPULATION DENSITY – 162 per sq. km (1998)

The Federated States of Micronesia comprise more than 600 islands extending 2,900 km (1,800 miles) across the archipelago of the Caroline Islands in the western Pacific Ocean. The islands vary geologically from mountainous islands to low coral atolls. The climate is tropical. Storms are common between August and December, and typhoons between July and November.

## HISTORY AND POLITICS

The Spanish Empire claimed sovereignty over the Caroline Islands until 1899, when Spain withdrew from her Pacific territories and sold her possessions in the Caroline Islands to Germany. The Caroline Islands became a German protectorate until the outbreak of the First World War in 1914, when Japan took control of the islands and given a League of Nations mandate to administer the territory in 1920. During the Second World War, US armed forces took control of the islands from the Japanese. In 1947 the USA entered into agreement with the UN Security Council to administer the Micronesia area, of which the Federated States of Micronesia were a part, as the UN Trust Territory of the Pacific Islands.

The US Trusteeship administration came to an end on 3 November 1986, when a Compact of Free Association between the USA and the Federated States of Micronesia came into effect. By this agreement the USA recognised the Federated States of Micronesia as a fully sovereign and independent state. The independence of the Federated States of Micronesia was recognised by the UN in December 1990.

### POLITICAL SYSTEM

The constitution separates the executive, legislative and judicial branches. There is a bill of rights and provision for traditional rights. The executive comprises a federal president and vice-president, both of whom must be chosen from amongst the four nationally elected senators. There is a single-chamber Congress of 14 members, four members elected on a state-wide basis and ten members elected from congressional districts apportioned by population.

The Compact of Free Association places full responsibility for the defence of the Federated States of Micronesia on the USA.

The judiciary is headed by the Supreme Court, which is divided into trial and appellate divisions. Below this, each state has its own judicial system.

### FEDERAL STRUCTURE

The Federated States of Micronesia is a federal republic of four constituent states: Chuuk, Kosrae, Pohnpei and Yap. Each of the constituent states has its own government and legislative system.

| *State* | *Area (sq. km)* | *Population (1994)* | *Headquarters* |
|---|---|---|---|
| Chuuk | 127 | 52,870 | Weno |
| Kosrae | 109 | 7,354 | Lelu |
| Pohnpei | 344 | 33,372 | Kolonia |
| Yap | 119 | 11,128 | Colonia |

### HEAD OF STATE

*President*, Leo Falcam
*Vice-President*, Redley Killion

### CABINET *as at July 2001*

*Economic Affairs*, Sebastian Anefal
*Finance and Administration*, John Ehsa
*Foreign Affairs*, Ieske Iehsi
*Health, Education and Social Services*, Eliuel Pretrick
*Justice*, Paul McIlraith
*Public Defender*, Beauleen Worswick
*Transportation, Communications and Infrastructure*, Lambert Lokopwe

BRITISH AMBASSADOR, HE Christopher Haslam, resident at Suva, Fiji

## ECONOMY

The economy is dependent mainly on subsistence agriculture, which employs almost half the population, and foreign aid. Copra and fish are the two main exports. The majority of the working population is engaged in government administration, subsistence farming, fishing, copra production and the tourist industry. Pepper is produced for export on Pohnpei and citrus fruits are commercially grown on Kosrae. The government derives a significant income from licensing fees paid by foreign vessels fishing for tuna and tuna processing plants are being constructed in Pohnpei and Kosrae.
In 1994, there were 25,000 visitors.
GNP – US$212 million (1999); US$1,810 per capita (1999)
GDP – US$212 million (1997); US$1,841 per capita (1998)

| Trade with UK | 1999 | 2000 |
|---|---|---|
| Imports from UK | £102,000 | £33,000 |
| Exports to UK | 179,000 | 2,000 |

### COMMUNICATIONS

Continental Air Micronesia connects the islands and provides international flights to Honolulu and, together with Air Nauru, to Guam.

# MOLDOVA
*Republica Moldova*

AREA – 13,012 sq. miles (33,700 sq. km). Neighbours: Ukraine (north, east and south-east), Romania (west)
POPULATION – 4,335,000 (2001 estimate): 65 per cent are Moldovan, 14.2 per cent Ukrainian and 13 per cent Russian, together with smaller numbers of Gagauz (ethnic Turks), Jews and Bulgarians. Most of the population are adherents of the Moldovan Orthodox Church. Moldovan was made the official language (written in the Latin script) in 1989 but the use of Russian in official business is permitted
CAPITAL – Chişinău (population, 746,500, 1997 estimate)
CURRENCY – Moldovan leu of 100 bani (plural lei)
NATIONAL ANTHEM - Lîmbă noastră (Our language)
NATIONAL DAY – 27 August (Independence Day)
NATIONAL FLAG – Vertical stripes of blue, yellow, red, with the national arms in the centre
LIFE EXPECTANCY (years) – male 64.8; female 71.9
POPULATION GROWTH RATE – 0.0 per cent (1999)
POPULATION DENSITY – 108 per sq. km (1998)
URBAN POPULATION – 46.1 per cent (2000 estimate)
MILITARY EXPENDITURE – 0.5 per cent of GDP (1999)
MILITARY PERSONNEL – 9,500: Army 8,500, Air Force 1,000, Paramilitaries 3,400
CONSCRIPTION DURATION – Up to 18 months
ILLITERACY RATE – 1.1 per cent (2000)
ENROLMENT (percentage of age group) – tertiary 26.5 per cent (1996)

## HISTORY AND POLITICS

In the 15th century a Moldovan principality was formed which was absorbed into the Turkish Empire in the 16th century. Moldova became the site of many Russo-Turkish battles and skirmishes in the 18th century before the area between the Dniester and Prut rivers (later known as Bessarabia) was annexed to the Russian Empire by the Bucharest Peace Treaty of 1812.

After the Russian Revolution in 1917, an independent Moldovan state was proclaimed in Bessarabia, which came under the control of White Russian forces and was annexed to Romania under the Versailles Peace Treaty (1919). In 1924 the Moldavian Autonomous Soviet Socialist Republic (ASSR) was established on the east bank of the Dniester river as part of Soviet Ukraine. In August 1940 the Soviet Union forced Romania to cede Bessarabia and the Moldavian Soviet Socialist Republic was formed from the majority of Bessarabia (the southernmost parts were incorporated into the Ukraine) and the Moldavian ASSR.

Moldova (formerly Moldavia) declared its independence from the USSR in August 1991. Reunification with Romania was rejected in a referendum on 6 March 1994, following which the Moldovan parliament voted to join the CIS. President Petru Lucinschi replaced president Mircea Snegur in presidential elections in November–December 1996. In legislative elections in March 1998, no party won an overall majority, and a right-wing coalition government under Ion Ciubuc was formed. Ciubuc resigned on 1 February 1999 and a new government led by Ion Sturza was sworn in on 12 March. On 9 November 1999, Sturza's government lost a vote of confidence and, after six weeks of political turmoil, Parliament approved Dumitri Barghis as prime minister on 21 December 1999.

Following the adoption in September 2000 of constitutional changes giving parliament the power to elect the president, a series of parliamentary votes was held in December 2000, in which none of the candidates were able to obtain the support of the required 61 members. In accordance with the constitutional changes, parliament was dissolved on 12 January 2001 and a general election was held on 25 February, which was won by the Communist Party of Moldova (PCM), who obtained 70 seats. The new parliament elected the PCM leader, Vladimir Voronin, as president on 4 April 2001 and approved a new Cabinet, led by Vasile Tarlev, an independent MP.

### Insurgencies

After independence was declared, the majority ethnic Romanian (Moldovan) population expressed a wish to rejoin Romania. This alienated the ethnic Ukrainian and Russian populations, who formed a majority east of the Dniester, and they declared their independence from Moldova as the Transdniester republic in December 1991. The Moldovan government refused to recognise this and in 1992 a war was waged between government forces and Transdniester forces, who were supported by local Russian soldiers and volunteers.

A mainly Russian CIS peacekeeping force (later changed to a joint Russian-Moldovan-Transdniester force) was deployed in July 1992 and a cease-fire has held since August 1992. The Moldovan government in February 1994 agreed to an OSCE plan for the Transdniester area to have a high degree of autonomy within Moldova but no independent or federal status. A memorandum of understanding on the normalisation of relations between the two sides was signed in May 1997, which committed both parties to hold further talks within 'the framework of a single state'.

A referendum in Transdniester on 24 December 1995 approved independence. President Igor Smirnov was re-elected in presidential elections in Transdniester in December 1996.

A legislative election was held in Transdniester on 10 December 2000 in which the majority of candidates elected were independents.

President Voronin and the leader of Transdniester, Igor Smirnov, agreed on 16 May 2001 to co-ordinate their policies on taxation and remove customs posts along the mutual border.

### Political System

In July 1994 the Moldovan parliament adopted a new constitution which established a presidential parliamentary republic and provided for autonomous status for the Gagauz region, which was given its own elected National Assembly.

Parliament is elected by proportional representation for a four-year term.

On 22 September 2000, the legislature passed a law transforming Moldova into a parliamentary republic. The president is elected by parliament and must obtain the support of at least 61 of the 101 deputies. If no candidate achieves this, parliament must be dissolved and a general election held.

### Head of State

*President*, Vladimir Voronin, *elected* 4 April 2001

### Government *as at July 2001*

*Prime Minister*, Vasile Tarlev
*First Deputy Prime Minister, Economy and Reform*, Andrei Cucu
*Deputy Prime Ministers*, Dmitrii Todoroglo (*Agriculture and Food Industry*); Andrei Cucu (*Economics*); Valerian Cristea (*Without Portfolio*)
*Culture*, Ion Pacuraru
*Defence*, Victor Gaiciuc
*Education and Science*, Ilie Vancea
*Energy*, Ion Lesanu
*Environmental Protection, Construction and Territorial Development*, Gheorghe Duca
*Finance*, Mihail Manoli
*Foreign Affairs*, Nicolae Cernomaz
*Health*, Andrei Gherman
*Industry*, Mihail Garstea
*Interior*, Vasile Draganel
*Justice*, Ion Morei
*Labour, Social Protection and Family Affairs*, Valerian Revenco
*Transport and Communications*, Victor Topa

### Embassy of the Republic of Moldova

Emile Maxlaan 175, B-1030 Brussels, Belgium
Tel: (00 32) (2) 732 9659/9300
*Ambassador Extraordinary and Plenipotentiary*, HE Ion Capatina, apptd 1999

British Ambassador, HE Richard Ralph, CVO, CMG, resident at Bucharest, Romania

## ECONOMY

The main sector is agriculture, especially viniculture, fruit-growing and market gardening. Industry is small and concentrated east of the Dniester. Severe drought in 1992, the severance of most trading ties with former Soviet republics, war damage and reductions in Russian fuel deliveries paralysed the economy from 1992 to 1994. An economic reform programme aiming to attract foreign investment began in 1993; a privatisation programme was completed in 1995. In 1998, telecommunications, power and heating companies were privatised. Moldova is dependent on Russia for energy supplies and owes roughly US$6,000 million.

In 1999 there was a trade deficit of US$123 million and a current account deficit of US$33 million. In 1998 imports totalled US$1,018 million and exports US$644 million.

GNP – US$1,481 million (1999); US$370 per capita (1999)

GDP – US$1,872 million (1997); US$374 per capita (1998)
ANNUAL AVERAGE GROWTH OF GDP – 7.9 per cent (1996)
UNEMPLOYMENT – 1.0 per cent (1995)
TOTAL EXTERNAL DEBT – US$1,035 million (1998)

| *Trade with UK* | 1999 | 2000 |
|---|---|---|
| Imports from UK | £5,926,000 | £5,062,000 |
| Exports to UK | 3,367,000 | 3,942,000 |

## MONACO
*Principauté de Monaco*

AREA – 0.4 sq. miles (1 sq. km). Neighbour: France
POPULATION – 32,000 (1997 UN estimate). Only 6,944 residents have full Monégasque citizenship and thus the right to vote. The official language is French. Monégasque, a mixture of Provençal and Ligurian, is also spoken
CAPITAL – Monaco
CURRENCY – Euro (€) of 100 cents/French franc of 100 centimes
NATIONAL ANTHEM – Hymne Monégasque
NATIONAL DAY – 19 November
NATIONAL FLAG – Two equal horizontal stripes, red over white
LIFE EXPECTANCY (years) – male 74.7; female 83.6
POPULATION GROWTH RATE – 1.2 per cent (1999)
POPULATION DENSITY – 32,894 per sq. km (1998)
URBAN POPULATION – 100.0 per cent (2000 estimate)

A small principality on the Mediterranean, with land frontiers joining France at every point, Monaco is divided into the districts of Monaco-Ville, La Condamine, Fontvieille and Monte Carlo.

### HISTORY AND POLITICS

The principality, ruled by the Grimaldi family since 1297, was abolished during the French Revolution and re-established in 1815 under the protection of the kingdom of Sardinia. In 1861 Monaco came under French protection.

The 1962 constitution, which can be modified only with the approval of the National Council, maintains the traditional hereditary monarchy and guarantees freedom of association, trade union freedom and the right to strike. Legislative power is held jointly by the Prince and a unicameral, 18-member National Council elected by universal suffrage. In the most recent legislative election on 1 and 8 February 1998, all 18 seats were won by the National and Democratic Union. Executive power is exercised by the Prince and a four-member Council of Government, headed by a Minister of State, who is nominated by the Prince from a list of three French diplomats submitted by the French government. The judicial code is based on that of France.

#### HEAD OF STATE

*HSH The Prince of Monaco*, Prince Rainier III Louis-Henri-Maxence Bertrand, *born* 31 May 1923, *succeeded* 9 May 1949; *married* 19 April 1956, Miss Grace Patricia Kelly (died 14 September 1982) and *has issue* Prince Albert (*see* below); Princess Caroline Louise Marguerite, *born* 23 January 1957; and Princess Stephanie Marie Elisabeth, *born* 1 February 1965
*Heir*, HRH Prince Albert Alexandre Louis Pierre, *born* 14 March 1958

*President of the Crown Council*, Charles Ballerio
*President of the National Council*, Dr Jean-Louis Campora
*Minister of State*, Patrick Leclercq
*Finance and Economy*, Franck Biancheri
*Interior*, Philippe Deslandes
*Public Works and Social Affairs*, José Badia

#### CONSULATE-GENERAL OF MONACO
4 Cromwell Place, London SW7 2JE
Tel: 020-7225 2679
*Consul-General*, I. B. Ivanovic

#### BRITISH CONSULATE-GENERAL
33 Boulevard Princesse Charlotte, BP 265, MC-98005 Monaco CEDEX
Tel: (00 377) 93 50 99 66
*Consul-General*, Ian Davies, apptd 1997, resident at Marseille, France
*Honorary Consul*, E. Blair

### ECONOMY

The whole available ground is built over so that there is no cultivation, though there are some notable public and private gardens. The economy is based on real estate revenues, the financial sector and tourism. There is a small harbour (30 ft alongside quay). Monaco has been in a customs union with the European Union since 1984.
GDP – US$776 million (1997); US$24,739 per capita (1998)
ANNUAL AVERAGE GROWTH OF GDP – 1.5 per cent (1996)

## MONGOLIA
*Mongol Uls*

AREA – 604,829 sq. miles (1,566,500 sq. km). Neighbours: Russia (north), China (south)
POPULATION – 2,373,500 (2000 census). Mongolians also live in China and in the neighbouring regions of Russia, especially the Mongolian Buryat Autonomous Region. The official language is Khalkha Mongolian
CAPITAL – Ulaanbaatar (population, 672,882, 1998 estimate)
CURRENCY – Tugrik of 100 möngö
NATIONAL DAY – 11 July
NATIONAL FLAG – Vertical tricolour red, blue, red and in the hoist the traditional Soyombo symbol in gold
LIFE EXPECTANCY (years) – male 58.9; female 64.8
POPULATION GROWTH RATE – 1.9 per cent (1999)
POPULATION DENSITY – 2 per sq. km (1998)
URBAN POPULATION – 63.5 per cent (2000 estimate)
MILITARY EXPENDITURE – 1.9 per cent of GDP (1999)
MILITARY PERSONNEL – 9,100: Army 7,500, Air Defence 800, Paramilitaries 7,200
CONSCRIPTION DURATION – 12 months
ILLITERACY RATE – 0.7 per cent (2000)
ENROLMENT (percentage of age group) – primary 81 per cent (1996); secondary 53 per cent (1996); tertiary 17.0 per cent (1996)

Mongolia, which is almost entirely at least 1,000 metres above sea level, forms part of the central Asiatic plateau and rises towards the west in the mountains of the Mongolian Altai and Hangai ranges. The Hentai range, situated to the north-east of the capital Ulaanbaatar, is lower. The Gobi region covers much of the southern half of the country and contains sand deserts interspersed with semi-desert. There are several long rivers and many lakes but good water is scarce as much of the lake water is salty. The climate is harsh, with a short mild summer giving way to a long winter when temperatures can drop as low as –50°C.

### HISTORY AND POLITICS

Mongolia, under Genghis Khan the conqueror of China and much of Asia, was for many years a buffer state between Tsarist Russia and China, although it was under general Chinese suzerainty. The Mongolian People's

Republic was formally established in 1924. Under the Yalta Agreement, President Chiang Kai-shek of China agreed to a plebiscite, held in 1945, in which the Mongolians declared their desire for independence and this was formally recognised by China.

The Mongolian People's Revolutionary Party (MPRP) was the sole political party from 1924 to 1990. Demonstrations in favour of political and economic reform began in December 1989 and led to changes in the MPRP leadership in March 1990. The MPRP's constitutionally guaranteed monopoly of power was subsequently relinquished, and the introduction of a multiparty system was approved by the Great People's Hural (parliament). The MPRP won the first multiparty elections, held in July 1990. The country's first direct presidential election was held in 1993 and won by the incumbent Punsalmaagiyn Ochirbat, who stood as an opposition candidate after the MPRP refused to endorse him as its candidate; he was ousted in May 1997 by the leader of the MPRP, Natsagyn Bagabandi, who won a second term of office on 20 May 2001, obtaining 58.13 per cent of the votes cast. The June 1996 election was won by the Democratic Union Coalition (Mongolian National Democratic Party and Mongolian Social Democratic Party). The legislative election held on 2 July 2000 resulted in a victory for the MPRP, who gained 72 seats.

The country and three city districts (Ulanbaatar, Darkhan and Erdenet) are divided into 21 *aimaks* (provinces) and beneath these into 258 *somons* (districts), and these form the basis of the state organisation of the country. The last remaining former Soviet armed forces personnel were withdrawn in late 1992.

### Political System

A new constitution was approved in January 1992 which established a democratic parliamentary system of government. The president is directly elected for a term of four years and the unicameral legislature is the State Great Hural (*Ulsyn Ikh Khural*), which has 76 members, elected for four-year terms by a simple majority amounting to at least 25 per cent of the votes cast. In July 2000 a constitutional amendment came into force, which gives the president the right to dissolve the Great State Hural if it is unable to reach agreement on appointing a prime minister.

### Head of State

*President*, Natsagyn Bagabandi, *elected* 18 May 1997, *re-elected* 20 May 2001

### Cabinet *as at July 2001*

*Prime Minister*, Nambariyn Enkhbayar
*Government Secretariat*, Ulziysaihany Enkhtuvshin
*Defence*, Jugderdemidyn Gurragchaa
*Education, Culture and Science*, Ayurzanyn Tsanjid
*Environment*, Ulambaryn Barsbold
*Finance and Economy*, Chultemiyn Ulaan
*Food and Agriculture*, Darjaagyn Nasanjargal
*Foreign Affairs*, Luvsangyn Erdenechuluun
*Health*, Pagvajavyn Nyamdavaa
*Industry and Commerce*, Chimidzorigyn Ganzorig
*Infrastructure*, Byambyn Jigjid
*Justice and Internal Affairs*, Tsendyn Nyamdorj
*Social Welfare and Labour*, Shiylegiyn Batbayar

### Embassy of Mongolia

7 Kensington Court, London W8 5DL
Tel: 020-7937 0150
*Ambassador Extraordinary and Plenipotentiary*, vacant
*Chargé d'Affaires and Counsellor*, C. Battumur

### British Embassy

30 Enkh Taivny Gudamzh (PO Box 703), Ulaanbaatar 13
Tel: (00 976) (1) 458133
E-mail:britemb@magicnet.mn
*Ambassador Extraordinary and Plenipotentiary*, HE Kay Coombs, apptd 1999

## ECONOMY

Traditionally the Mongolians led a nomadic life tending flocks of sheep, goats, horses, cows and camels. Collectivisation at the end of the 1950s into huge *negdels* (co-operatives) and state farms hastened the process of settlement, but within these the herdsmen and their families still move with their traditional *gers*(circular tents) from pasture to pasture as the seasons change.

The semi-desert areas of the Gobi region provide pasture for sheep, goats, camels, horses and some cattle. In the steppe areas to the north of the Gobi pasturage is better and livestock more abundant. Even further north, in the better-watered provinces, grain, fodder and vegetable crops are grown.

Although the economy remains predominantly pastoral, factories have started up, coal, copper and molybdenum are mined and the electricity industry has been developed.

All trade barriers were abolished in May 1997.

A prolonged drought and an exceptionally severe winter in 1999–2000 resulted in the deaths of an estimated two million livestock, affecting 800,000 herders. At least a further 1.3 million livestock were estimated to have died in another severe winter in 2000–2001. In May 2001, international donors promised US$330 million in aid.

GNP – US$927 million (1999); US$350 per capita (1999)
GDP – US$951 million (1997); US$384 per capita (1998)
Annual Average Growth of GDP – 2.6 per cent (1996)
Inflation Rate – 7.6 per cent (1999)
Unemployment – 5.7 per cent (1998)
Total External Debt – US$739 million (1998)

### Trade

Foreign trade was formerly dominated by the Soviet Union and other Eastern bloc countries, but trade with Western countries, Japan and South Korea is now increasing. Since January 1991, trade has been in hard currency, causing particular strain. The principal exports are animal by-products (especially wool, hides and furs) and cattle.

In 1999 there was a trade deficit of US$56 million and a current account deficit of US$112 million. Imports totalled US$1,010 million and exports US$763 million.

| *Trade with UK* | 1999 | 2000 |
|---|---|---|
| Imports from UK | £3,078,000 | £2,117,000 |
| Exports to UK | 4,724,000 | 9,296,000 |

## COMMUNICATIONS

Communication is still difficult as there are only 1,185 km of surfaced roads and horses are still the characteristic means of transport for the rural population. The trans-Mongolian railway links Mongolia with both China and Russia; total track length is 1,928 km.

---

## MOROCCO
*Al-Mamlaka Al-Maghribiyya*

---

Area – 172,414 sq. miles (446,550 sq. km). Neighbours: Algeria (east and south-east), Western Sahara (south-west)

POPULATION – 28,238,000 (1997 UN estimate). Standard Arabic is the official language. Maghrebi Arabic and various Berber languages (Tachelhit, Tamazight and Tarafit) are the vernacular. French and Spanish are also spoken, mainly in the towns. Islam is the state religion.
CAPITAL – ΨRabat (population, 1,220,000, 1993 estimate)
MAJOR CITIES – ΨAgadir (923,000); ΨCasablanca (Ad-Dar-el-Beida) (3,100,000); Fez (554,000); Marrakesh (878,000); Meknès (614,000); Oujda (430,000), 1997 estimates
CURRENCY – Dirham (DH) of 100 centimes
NATIONAL DAY – 3 March (Anniversary of the Throne)
NATIONAL FLAG – Red, with green pentagram (the Seal of Solomon)
LIFE EXPECTANCY (years) – male 65.0; female 66.8
POPULATION GROWTH RATE – 1.7 per cent (1999)
POPULATION DENSITY – 62 per sq. km (1998)
URBAN POPULATION – 56.1 per cent (2000 estimate)

Morocco is traversed in the north by the Rif mountains and, in a south-west to north-east direction, by the Middle Atlas, the High Atlas, the Anti-Atlas and the Sarrho ranges. Much of the country is desert. The north-westerly point of Morocco is the peninsula of Tangier dominated by the Jebel Mousa which, with the rocky eminence of Gibraltar, was known to the ancients as the Pillars of Hercules, the western gateway of the Mediterranean.

## HISTORY AND POLITICS

Morocco became an independent sovereign state in 1956, following joint declarations made with France on 2 March 1956 and with Spain on 7 April 1956. The Sultan of Morocco, Sidi Mohammad ben Youssef, adopted the title of King Mohammad V.

Elections were held on 14 November 1997 to the new House of Representatives; no party won an overall majority, but Abderrahmane El Youssoufi was appointed prime minister as the leader of the Socialist Union of Popular Forces, the largest party in the House of Representatives. On 15 September 2000, elections to the Chamber of Councillors were held.

### POLITICAL SYSTEM

The King nominates the prime minister and, on the latter's recommendation, appoints the members of the Council of Ministers. The government is responsible both to parliament and to the King. There is a bicameral legislature. The Chamber of Representatives (*Majlis an-Nuwab)* has 325 members elected for a five-year term by universal suffrage using a first-past-the-post system. The Chamber of Councillors (*Majlis al-Mustashareen)* has 270 members, 60 per cent of whom are elected by local councils, 20 per cent by employers' associations and 20 per cent by trade unions. One third of its members are elected every three years.

### HEAD OF STATE

*HM The King of Morocco*, King Mohamed VI (Sidi Mohamed Ben Hassan), *born* 21 August 1963, *acceded* 23 July 1999

### COUNCIL OF MINISTERS *as at July 2001*

*Prime Minister*, Abderrahmane El Youssoufi
*Agriculture and Rural Development*, Ismail Alaoui
*Culture and Communications*, Mohamed Achaari
*Economic Estimates and Planning*, Abdelhamid Aouad
*Economy, Finance and Tourism*, Fathallah Oualalou
*Employment, Vocational Training, Social Development and Solidarity*, Abbas Fassi
*Energy and Mining, Industry and Commerce*, Mustapha Mansouri
*Equipment*, Bouamar Tighouane
*Foreign Affairs and Co-operation*, Mohamed Ben Aissa
*General Secretary of the Government*, Abdessadek Rabii
*Health*, Thami Khiari
*Higher Education and Scientific Research*, Najib Zerouali
*Human Rights*, Mohamed Aoujar
*Interior*, Ahmed Midaoui
*Justice*, Omar Azziman
*Marine Fisheries*, Said Chbaatou
*National Education*, Abdallah Saaf
*Public Sector and Privatisation*, Mohamed Khalifa
*Relations with Parliament*, Mohamed Bouzoubaa
*Social Economy, Small and Medium Enterprises and Handicrafts, General Government Affairs*, Ahmed Halimi Alami
*Town and Country Planning, Environment, Housing*, Mohamed el Yazghi
*Transport and Merchant Navy*, Abdeslam Zenined
*Waqf and Islamic Affairs*, Abdelkebir M'Daghri Alaoui
*Youth and Sports*, Ahmed Moussaoui

### EMBASSY OF THE KINGDOM OF MOROCCO

49 Queen's Gate Gardens, London SW7 5NE
Tel: 020-7581 5001/4
*Ambassador Extraordinary and Plenipotentiary*, HE Mohammed Belmahi, apptd 1999

### BRITISH EMBASSY

17 Boulevard de la Tour Hassan (BP 45), Rabat
Tel: (00 212) (7) 729696
E-mail: britemb@mtds.com
*Ambassador Extraordinary and Plenipotentiary*, HE Anthony Layden, apptd 1999
CONSULATE-GENERAL – Casablanca
CONSULATES – Agadir, Marrakesh, Tangier

BRITISH COUNCIL DIRECTOR, Graham McCulloch, MBE, BP 427, 36 rue de Tanger, Rabat; e-mail: britcoun.morocco@britishcouncil.org.ma
BRITISH CHAMBER OF COMMERCE, 1st Floor, 185 Boulevard Zerktouni, Casablanca. Tel: (00 212) (2) 256920

## DEFENCE

The Army has 644 main battle tanks, 115 armoured infantry fighting vehicles, and 785 armoured personnel carriers.

The Navy has one frigate and 27 patrol and coastal combatant vessels at five bases. The Air Force has 89 combat aircraft and 24 armed helicopters.
MILITARY EXPENDITURE – 5.0 per cent of GDP (1999)
MILITARY PERSONNEL – 198,500: Army 175,000, Navy 10,000, Air Force 13,500, Paramilitaries 42,000
CONSCRIPTION DURATION – 18 months

## ECONOMY

Morocco's main sources of wealth are agricultural and mineral. A large-scale privatisation programme has attracted substantial foreign investment. Agriculture contributes 17 per cent of GDP and employs 38.5 per cent of the workforce. The main agricultural exports are fruit and vegetables, with cereals and sugar beet produced and sheep reared for domestic consumption. Cork and wood pulp are the most important commercial forest products. There is a fishing industry and substantial quantities of canned fish are exported.

For a developing country Morocco has a large industrial sector. The main sectors are chemicals, textiles and leather goods, food processing and cement production. Manufacturing industries are centred in Casablanca, Fez, Tangier and Safi.

Morocco's mineral exports are phosphates, fluorite, barite, manganese, iron ore, lead, zinc, cobalt, copper and antimony. Morocco possesses nearly three-quarters of the world's estimated reserves of phosphates. There are oil refineries at Mohammedia and Sidi Kacem handling about four million tonnes of crude oil a year. A new oil and gas deposit was announced in August 2000.

Morocco has a high proportion of public employees; the salaries of its 750,000 civil servants consume about 12 per cent of the country's GDP.

Tourism is of great importance to the economy, with development concentrated in Agadir and Marrakesh. In 1998, about 2 million foreign tourists visited Morocco.

GNP – US$33,715 million (1999); US$1,200 per capita (1999)

GDP – US$33,514 million (1997); US$1,302 per capita (1998)

ANNUAL AVERAGE GROWTH OF GDP – 12.0 per cent (1996)

INFLATION RATE – 0.7 per cent (1999)

UNEMPLOYMENT – 18.4 per cent (1998)

TOTAL EXTERNAL DEBT – US$20,687 million (1998)

### TRADE

The main imports are petroleum products, machinery, chemical products, iron and steel, grain and textiles. The EU, with which an association agreement was signed in November 1995, is Morocco's largest trading partner and in May 1998 awarded Morocco grants totalling US$98 million. The main exports are phosphates and phosphoric acid, textiles and leather, and fish and agricultural products.

In 1998 Morocco had a trade deficit of US$2,319 million and a current account deficit of US$236 million. In 1999 imports totalled US$9,925 million and exports US$7,367 million.

| *Trade with UK* | 1999 | 2000 |
|---|---|---|
| Imports from UK | £357,324,000 | £409,271,000 |
| Exports to UK | 400,219,000 | 470,675,000 |

## COMMUNICATIONS

Railroads cover 1,907 km, linking the major towns. There are 60,449 km of roads; an extensive network of 30,374 km of surfaced roads covers all the main towns. There are air services between Casablanca, Tangier, Agadir (seasonal), Marrakesh and London, and also between Tangier and Gibraltar connecting with London. Royal Air Maroc is the national airline.

## EDUCATION

Education is compulsory between the ages of seven and 16. There are government primary, secondary and technical schools.

ILLITERACY RATE – 51.1 per cent (2000)

ENROLMENT (percentage of age group) – primary 74 per cent (1996); secondary 20 per cent (1980); tertiary 11.1 per cent (1996)

## WESTERN SAHARA

*Al-Jumhūriyya al-'Arabiyya as-Sahrāwiyya ad-Dimuqrātiyya – Sahrawi Arab Democratic Republic*

AREA – 97,344 sq. miles (252,120 sq. km). Neighbours: Morocco (north), Algeria (north-east), Mauritania (east and south)

POPULATION – 244,943 (2000 estimate). Arabic is the official language. Hassaniya and Moroccan Arabic are the main spoken languages; Spanish is widely spoken in the towns. Almost all the population is Sunni Muslim

CAPITAL – El-Aaiūn (population, 139,000 1990 estimate)

NATIONAL FLAG – Three horizontal stripes of black, white and green with a red crescent and five-pointed star in the centre and red triangle based on the hoist

LIFE EXPECTANCY (years) – male 65.0; female 66.8

POPULATION GROWTH RATE – 2.0 per cent (1997)

POPULATION DENSITY – 1 per sq. km (1998)

Formerly the Spanish Sahara, the territory was split between Morocco and Mauritania in 1976 after Spain withdrew in December 1975. In 1976 the Polisario Front (Frente Popular para la Liberación de Saguia y Río de Oro) declared Western Sahara to be an independent state, the Sahrawi Arab Democratic Republic, and formed a government which remains in exile. The Polisario Front has been recognised as the legitimate government of Western Sahara by over 70 states and the Organisation of African Unity. In 1979 Mauritania renounced its claim to its share of the territory, which was added by Morocco to its area.

In 1988, Morocco and the Polisario Front accepted a UN peace plan under which a cease-fire came into effect in September 1991. A referendum to determine the future of the area was to have been held in January 1992 but has not yet taken place because the Moroccan government and Polisario have not agreed on the referendum terms or voter eligibility. Voter identification began in August 1994 but the failure to agree on eligibility prompted the UN to threaten the suspension of the UN Mission for the Referendum in Western Sahara (MINURSO), which had been deployed since 1991. A referendum is not expected before 2002, with MINURSO responsible for identifying voters.

In September 2000, representatives of the Moroccan government and the Polisario Front held negotiations to discuss differences that prevented the implementation of the UN-mediated referendum on the future of the Western Sahara. The talks failed when the Polisario refused to discuss a Moroccan proposal that the territory accept autonomy status within Morocco. Legislative elections to the National Assembly were held in 1995; President Mohamed Abdelaziz, who had been elected president since 1982 by the party congress of the Polisario Front, was re-elected by the National Assembly in 1995. Following a vote of no confidence in the previous incumbent, Bouchraya Hamoudi Bayoun was named Prime Minister on 10 February 1999.

### POLISARIO FRONT OFFICE

138 Tachbrook Street, London SW1V 2ND
Tel: 020-7834 6618
*Representative*, Brahim Mokhtar

## MOZAMBIQUE

*República de Moçambique*

AREA – 309,494 sq. miles (801,590 sq. km). Neighbours: Swaziland (south), South Africa (south and west), Zimbabwe (west), Zambia and Malawi (north-west), Tanzania (north)

POPULATION – 17,264,000 (1998 census). The official language is Portuguese

CAPITAL – ΨMaputo (population, 1,039,700, 1998 census)

MAJOR CITIES – ΨBeira (264,202); ΨNacala (182,505), 1986 estimates

CURRENCY – Metical (MT) of 100 centavos

NATIONAL DAY – 25 June (Independence Day)

NATIONAL FLAG – Horizontally green, black, yellow with white fimbriations; a red triangle based on the hoist containing the national emblem

LIFE EXPECTANCY (years) – male 41.8; female 44.0

POPULATION GROWTH RATE – 3.5 per cent (1999)

POPULATION DENSITY – 21 per sq. km (1998)

URBAN POPULATION – 40.2 per cent (2000 estimate)
MILITARY EXPENDITURE – 4.1 per cent of GDP (1999)
MILITARY PERSONNEL – 6,100: Army 5,000, Navy 100, Air Force 1,000
CONSCRIPTION DURATION – Two to three years
ILLITERACY RATE – 56.2 per cent (2000)
ENROLMENT (percentage of age group) – primary 40 per cent (1996); secondary 6 per cent (1996); tertiary 0.5 per cent (1996)

## HISTORY AND POLITICS

Mozambique, discovered by Vasco da Gama in 1498 and colonised by Portugal, achieved independence on 25 June 1975. It was a Marxist one-party (Frelimo) state until a multiparty system was adopted in 1990.

The Frelimo government and the rebel Mozambican National Resistance (Renamo) signed a peace agreement in October 1992 which ended 16 years of civil war. Demobilisation of government and Renamo troops took place in 1994.

Presidential and legislative elections were held on 3–5 December 1999. The incumbent, Joaquim Chissano of Frelimo, won the presidential election with 52.3 per cent of the vote. Frelimo also won the legislative election, gaining 133 seats to Renamo's 117, amid allegations by Renamo of vote-rigging. No other parties were able to secure the 5 per cent of the total vote necessary to obtain representation.

Mozambique was admitted to the Commonwealth on 12 November 1995 as a special case, because of its close links with Commonwealth countries.

### POLITICAL SYSTEM

The president is directly elected and serves a term of five years, which is renewable no more than twice consecutively. The unicameral legislature, the Assembly of the Republic (*Assembleia Da Republica*), is directly elected for a five-year term and comprises 250 members.

### HEAD OF STATE

*President*, Joaquim Alberto Chissano, *sworn in* November 1986, *elected* 29 October 1994, *re-elected* 5 December 1999

### COUNCIL OF MINISTERS *as at July 2001*

*Prime Minister*, Pascoal Mocumbi
*Agriculture and Rural Development*, Helder Monteiro
*Culture*, Miguel Costa Mkaima
*Education*, Alcido Nguenha
*Environmental Action Co-ordination*, John Katchamila
*Fisheries*, Cadmiel Muthemba
*Foreign Affairs and Co-operation*, Leonardo Simão
*Health*, Francisco Songane
*Higher Education, Science and Technology*, Lidia Brito
*Independence War Veterans*, Gen. (retd) António Hama Thay
*Industry and Commerce*, Carlos Morgado
*Justice*, José Abudo
*Labour*, Mario Sevene
*Mineral Resources and Energy*, Castigo Langa
*Ministers in the President's Office*, Almirinho da Cruz Manhenje (*Defence, Security Affairs and Interior*); Francisco Madeira (*Parliamentary and Diplomatic Affairs*)
*National Defence*, Tobias Dai
*Planning and Finance*, Luisa Diogo
*Public Works and Housing*, Roberto White
*Tourism*, Fernando Sumbane Junior
*Transport and Communications*, Tomas Salomão
*Women's Affairs and Social Welfare Action Co-ordination*, Virginia Matabele
*Youth and Sports*, Joel Libombo

### HIGH COMMISSION FOR THE REPUBLIC OF MOZAMBIQUE

21 Fitzroy Square, London W1P 5HJ
Tel: 020-7383 3800
*High Commissioner*, HE Dr Eduardo José Baciao Koloma, apptd 1996

### BRITISH HIGH COMMISSION

Av. Vladimir I Lenine 310, CP 55, Maputo
Tel: (00 258) (1) 420111/2/5/6/7
E-mail: bhc@virconn.com
*High Commissioner*, HE Bob Dewar, apptd 2000

BRITISH COUNCIL DIRECTOR, Paul Woods, Rua John Issa 226, PO Box 4178, Maputo; e-mail: general.enquiries@-britishcouncil.org.mz

## ECONOMY

The basis of the economy is subsistence agriculture, but there is an industrial sector based mainly in Beira and Maputo. There are substantial coal deposits in Tete province and an offshore gas field at Pande. Economic subsidies have been removed and an IMF reform programme is being implemented. The economy is still heavily dependent on aid. A five-year plan has been launched with the priorities of rural development, education, health and land reform.

Severe flooding in February 2000 caused widespread devastation, destroying a third of the maize crop and up to one million homes. Further flooding in January and February 2001 resulted in some 77,000 people becoming homeless.

GNP – US$3,804 million (1999); US$230 per capita (1999)
GDP – US$1,734 million (1997); US$92 per capita (1998)
ANNUAL AVERAGE GROWTH OF GDP – 6.4 per cent (1996)
INFLATION RATE – 2.0 per cent (1999)
TOTAL EXTERNAL DEBT – US$8,208 million (1998)

### TRADE

The main exports are shellfish, cotton, sugar, cashew nuts, copra, tea and sisal. Mozambique's main trading partners are South Africa, Portugal, Spain and Japan.

In 1998 Mozambique had a trade deficit of US$491 million and a current account deficit of US$429 million. In 1999 imports totalled US$1,161 million and exports US$268 million.

| *Trade with UK* | 1999 | 2000 |
|---|---|---|
| Imports from UK | £11,220,000 | £18,487,000 |
| Exports to UK | 2,550,000 | 5,067,000 |

# MYANMAR

*Pyidaungsu Myanmar Naingngandaw – Union of Myanmar*

AREA – 261,228 sq. miles (676,578 sq. km). Neighbours: Bangladesh (west), India (north-west), China (north-east), Laos and Thailand (east)
POPULATION – 45,029,000 (1997 UN estimate). The indigenous inhabitants are of similar racial types and speak languages of the Tibeto-Burman, Mon-Khmer and Thai groups. The three significant non-indigenous elements are Indians, Chinese and Bangladeshis. Burmese is the official language, but minority languages include Bamar, Chin, Kachin, Kayah, Kayin (Karen), Mon, Rakhine and Shan. English is spoken in educated circles. Buddhism is the religion of 89.3 per cent of the people, with 5.6 per cent Christians, 3.8 per cent Muslims, 0.2 per cent Animists and 0.5 per cent Hindus
CAPITAL – ΨYangon (Rangoon) (population, 2,513,023, 1983)

MAJOR CITIES – Mandalay (532,949); Mawlamyine/ Moulmein (219,961); Pathein/Bassein (144,096)
CURRENCY – Kyat (K) of 100 pyas
NATIONAL ANTHEM - Gba majay Bma (We shall love Burma for ever)
NATIONAL DAY – 4 January
NATIONAL FLAG – Red, with a canton of dark blue, inside which are a cogwheel and two rice ears surrounded by 14 white stars
LIFE EXPECTANCY (years) – male 58.4; female 59.2
POPULATION GROWTH RATE – 1.2 per cent (1999)
POPULATION DENSITY – 66 per sq. km (1998)
URBAN POPULATION – 27.7 per cent (2000 estimate)

## HISTORY AND POLITICS

The Union of Burma (the name was officially changed to the Union of Myanmar in 1989) became an independent republic outside the British Commonwealth on 4 January 1948 and remained a parliamentary democracy for 14 years. In 1962 the army took power, suspended the parliamentary constitution and instituted a socialist state.

After months of popular demonstrations and a series of presidents during 1988, Gen. Saw Maung, leader of the armed forces, assumed power in September 1988. The People's Assembly, the Council of State and the Council of Ministers were abolished and replaced by the State Law and Order Restoration Council (SLORC). The constitution was effectively abrogated.

A People's Assembly Election Law was published in 1989 and multiparty elections were held on 27 May 1990, resulting in a majority for the National League for Democracy (NLD) even though its leader Aung San Suu Kyi had been under house arrest since July 1989. The SLORC refused to transfer power to a civilian government and large numbers of NLD MPs and supporters were detained or fled to Thailand where an exile government was set up. The SLORC released Aung San Suu Kyi (who won the Nobel Peace Prize in 1991) on 10 July 1995, although on several occasions subsequently she has been forcibly prevented from attending political meetings by government troops. Many other opposition figures remain in detention or under house arrest. In November 1997, the SLORC was renamed the State Peace and Development Council (SPDC).

The SPDC detained several hundred NLD members in September 1998 to thwart the NLD's plan to convene a 'People's Parliament' representing the assembly which would have resulted from the 1990 general election; most were released in October and November. Instead, the NLD set up an interim representation committee to act on behalf of the 'People's Parliament', which declared all laws and orders issued by the military government since the general election to be invalid.

Myanmar is comprised of seven states (Chin, Kachin, Kayin (Karen), Kayah, Mon, Rakhine, Shan) and seven divisions (Ayeyarwady (Irrawaddy), Magway (Magwe), Mandalay, Bago (Pegu), Yangon (Rangoon), Sagaing, Tanintharyi (Tenasserim)).

### INSURGENCIES

Since independence in 1948 the government has fought various armed insurgent groups, the largest of which were derived from the Kachin, Kayin (Karen), Karenni, and Wa ethnic groups but the Shan, Mon, Arakan and Chin ethnic minorities have also formed armed groups.

Since 1992, as a result of government offensives, 15 ethnic groups have signed cease-fire agreements with the government. In November 1999, the government launched a military offensive against Kayin (Karen) National Union (KNU) guerrillas and their allies in Karen state.

### STATE PEACE AND DEVELOPMENT COUNCIL *as at July 2001*

*Chairman*, Senior Gen. Than Shwe
*Vice-Chairman*, Gen. Maung Aye
*Members*, Rear-Adml Nyunt Thein; Maj.-Gen. Kyaw Than; Maj.-Gen. Aung Htwe; Maj.-Gen. Ye Myint; Maj.-Gen. Khin Maung Than; Maj.-Gen. Kyaw Win; Maj.-Gen. Thein Sein; Maj.-Gen. Thura Thiha Thura Sit Maung; Brig.-Gen. Thura Shwe Mahn; Brig.-Gen. Myint Aung; Brig.-Gen. Maung Bo; Brig.-Gen. Thiha Thura Tin Aung Myint Oo; Brig.-Gen. Soe Win; Brig.-Gen. Tin Aye
*Secretaries*, Lt.-Gen. Khin Nyunt; Lt.-Gen. Win Myint

### CABINET *as at July 2001*

*Prime Minister, Defence*, Senior Gen. Than Shwe
*Deputy Prime Ministers*, Vice-Adm. Maung Maung Khin; Lt.-Gen. Tin Hla *(Military Affairs)*; Lt.-Gen. Tin Tun
*Agriculture and Irrigation*, Maj.-Gen. Nyunt Tin
*Commerce*, Brig.-Gen. Pyi Sone
*Construction*, Maj.-Gen. Saw Tun
*Co-operatives*, U Aung San
*Culture*, U Win Sein
*Education*, U Than Aung
*Electric Power*, Maj.-Gen. Tin Htut
*Energy*, Brig.-Gen. Lun Thi
*Finance and Revenue*, U Khin Maung Thein
*Foreign Affairs*, U Win Aung
*Forestry*, U Aung Phone
*Health*, Maj.-Gen. Ket Sein
*Home Affairs*, Col. Tin Hlaing
*Hotels and Tourism*, Maj.-Gen. Saw Lwin
*Immigration and Population*, U Saw Tun
*Industry*, U Aung Thaung; Maj.-Gen. Saw Lwin
*Information*, Maj.-Gen. Kyi Aung
*Labour*, Maj.-Gen. Tin Ngwe
*Livestock Breeding and Fisheries*, Brig.-Gen. Maung Maung Thein
*Mines*, Brig.-Gen. Ohn Myint
*Ministers in the Office of the SPDC Chairman*, Lt.-Gen. Min Thein; Brig.-Gen. David Abel
*National Planning and Economic Development*, U Soe Tha
*Prime Minister's Office*, U Tin Win; U Than Shwe; Lt.-Gen. Tin Ngwe
*Progress of Border Area and National Races, Development Affairs*, vacant
*Rail Transport*, U Pan Aung
*Religious Affairs*, U Aung Khin
*Science and Technology*, U Thaung
*Social Welfare, Relief and Resettlement*, Maj.-Gen. Sein Htwa
*Sports*, Brig.-Gen. Thura Aye Myint
*Telecommunications, Posts and Telegraphs*, Brig.-Gen. Thein Zaw
*Transport*, Maj.-Gen. Hla Myint Swe

### EMBASSY OF THE UNION OF MYANMAR

19A Charles Street, Berkeley Square, London W1X 8ER
Tel: 020-7499 8841
*Ambassador Extraordinary and Plenipotentiary*, HE Dr Kyaw Win, apptd 1999

### BRITISH EMBASSY

80 Strand Road (Box No. 638), Yangon
Tel: (00 95) (1) 295300
*Ambassador Extraordinary and Plenipotentiary*, HE Dr John Jenkins, LVO, apptd 1999

BRITISH COUNCIL DIRECTOR, Graham Millington (*Cultural Attaché*), 78 Kanna Road, PO Box 638, Yangon; e-mail: enquiries@britishcouncil.org.mm

## DEFENCE

The Army has some 100 main battle tanks and 270 armoured personnel carriers. The Navy has 68 patrol and coastal vessels at six bases. The Air Force has 83 combat aircraft and 29 armed helicopters.
MILITARY EXPENDITURE – 5.0 per cent of GDP (1999)
MILITARY PERSONNEL – 429,000: Army 325,000, Navy 10,000, Air Force 9,000, Paramilitaries 85,250

## ECONOMY

Agriculture remains the main sector of the economy, accounting for 58.5 per cent of GDP in 1997 and employing 63.4 per cent of the workforce; measures are being taken to increase productivity, promote crop diversification and increase agricultural exports. The chief products are rice, oilseeds (sesame and groundnut), maize, millet, cotton, beans, wheat, grain, tea, sugar cane, tobacco, jute and rubber.

Myanmar is rich in minerals, including petroleum, zinc, nickel, lead, silver, tungsten, wolfram and gemstones. Production of crude petroleum in 1998 totalled 1,177,000 tonnes. There are refineries at Chauk, the main oilfield, Syriam and Mann. Major reserves of natural gas have been discovered in the Martaban Gulf.

Since 1988, Myanmar has moved from a centrally planned economy to a market-oriented economy and has liberalised domestic and external trade, promoted the development of the private sector and encouraged foreign investment.

Myanmar is thought to be the world's leading producer of opium with an estimated annual output of 2,600 tons, although the government claimed to have destroyed 3,800 hectares of opium poppies between November 1998 and March 1999.

The principal exports are agricultural, forestry and fish products, minerals and precious stones. The principle imports are capital goods, chiefly transport equipment, machinery and plant, consumer goods and semi-manufactures.

In July 1997, Myanmar became a member of ASEAN. In 1997 the EU stripped Myanmar of trading privileges and the USA imposed economic sanctions.

In 1999 there was a trade deficit of US$991 million and a current account deficit of US$222 million. Imports totalled US$2,300 million and exports US$1,125 million.
GDP – US$12,041 million (1997); US$282 per capita (1998)
ANNUAL AVERAGE GROWTH OF GDP – 5.8 per cent (1996)
INFLATION RATE – 18.4 per cent (1999)
TOTAL EXTERNAL DEBT – US$5,680 million (1998)

| *Trade with UK* | 1999 | 2000 |
|---|---|---|
| Imports from UK | £7,425,000 | £8,646,000 |
| Exports to UK | 23,835,000 | 49,270,000 |

## COMMUNICATIONS

The Irrawaddy and its chief tributary, the Chindwin, are important waterways, the main stream being navigable 900 miles from its mouth and carrying much traffic. The chief seaports are Yangon (Rangoon), Mawlamyine (Moulmein), Akyab (Sittwe) and Pathein (Bassein).

The railway network covers 3,955 km, extending to Myitkyina on the Upper Irrawaddy. There are 2,452 miles of highways and 14,318 miles of other main roads. The airport at Mingaladon, about 13 miles north of Yangon (Rangoon), handles limited international air traffic.

## EDUCATION

Most children attend primary school, and nearly five million are currently enrolled; in middle and high schools, enrolment is over two million. In 1999 there were 37,627 primary schools, 3,695 middle schools and 1,572 high schools. There are 16 universities, nine degree-awarding colleges and 87 other higher education institutions.
ILLITERACY RATE – 15.3 per cent (2000)
ENROLMENT (percentage of age group) – tertiary 5.4 per cent (1996)

---

# NAMIBIA
*The Republic of Namibia*

---

AREA – 318,261 sq. miles (824,292 sq. km). Neighbours: Angola (north), South Africa (south), Botswana (east), Zambia and Zimbabwe (north-east)
POPULATION – 1,701,000 (1997 UN estimate). The main population groups are: Ovambo (587,000), Kavango (110,000), Damara (89,000), Herero (89,000), whites (78,000), Nama (57,000), coloured (48,000), Caprivians (44,000), Bushmen (34,000), Rehoboth Baster (29,000), Tswana (7,000). English is the official language, with Afrikaans, German and local languages also in use
CAPITAL – Windhoek (population, 147,056, 1995)
MAJOR TOWNS – Ondangwa (33,000); Oshakati (37,000); Rehoboth (21,500); Swakopmund (18,000); Walvis Bay (50,000), 1995
CURRENCY – Namibian dollar of 100 cents at parity to South African rand
NATIONAL ANTHEM - Namibia, land of the brave
NATIONAL DAY – 21 March (Independence Day)
NATIONAL FLAG – Divided diagonally blue, red and green with the red fimbriated in white; a gold twelve-rayed sun in the upper hoist
LIFE EXPECTANCY (years) – male 43.3; female 43.0
POPULATION GROWTH RATE – 2.6 per cent (1999)
POPULATION DENSITY – 2 per sq. km (1998)
URBAN POPULATION – 30.9 per cent (2000 estimate)
MILITARY EXPENDITURE – 4.4 per cent of GDP (1999)
MILITARY PERSONNEL – 9,000: Army 9,000; Coast Guard 100
ILLITERACY RATE – 17.9 per cent
ENROLMENT (percentage of age group) – primary 91 per cent (1996); secondary 36 per cent (1996); tertiary 8.1 per cent (1996)

## HISTORY AND POLITICS

The German protectorate of South West Africa from 1884 to 1915, the territory was entrusted to South Africa by the 1919 Treaty of Versailles. The UN terminated South Africa's mandate in 1967.

An administrator-general was appointed in 1977 to govern the territory until independence and a transitional government was installed in 1985. Elections for Namibia's National Assembly took place under UN supervision on 7–11 November 1989 and independence was declared on 21 March 1990. Namibia joined the Commonwealth on independence.

Previously a British and South African colony separate from German South West Africa/Namibia, Walvis Bay was governed from August 1992 by the joint South African-Namibian Walvis Bay Administrative Body until 28 February 1994, when South Africa renounced its claim to sovereignty over the enclave and it became part of Namibia.

Presidential and legislative elections were held on 30 November–1 December 1999 and were won by the incumbent, Sam Nujoma, and by SWAPO respectively. In the 72-seat National Assembly SWAPO has 55 seats, the Congress of Democrats and the Democratic Turnhalle Alliance 7 seats each, and other parties three seats.

INSURGENCIES

Government officials claimed to have uncovered a plot by Mishake Muyongo, a former leader of the opposition Democratic Turnhalle Alliance, and Mishake Boniface Mamili, a Mafwe chief, to launch a secessionist rebellion in the Caprivi strip in November 1998. An attempted uprising on 9 August 1999, believed to have been led by the Caprivi Liberation Army, was quickly quashed by government forces and 125 of the leaders of the uprising were put on trial for treason.

POLITICAL SYSTEM

Namibia has an executive president as head of state who exercises the functions of government with the assistance of a Cabinet headed by a prime minister. The president is directly elected for a maximum of two five-year terms. There is a bicameral legislature consisting of the 72-member National Assembly, elected for a five-year term, and the National Council, whose 26 members are indirectly elected by the regional councils from among their own members. The National Council is elected for a six-year term, and its main function is to review and consider legislation from the National Assembly. The constitution can only be changed by a two-thirds majority in the National Assembly.

HEAD OF STATE

*President*, Dr Sam Nujoma, *elected* 16 February 1990, *re-elected* 8 December 1994, *re-elected* 1 December 1999

CABINET *as at July 2001*

*Prime Minister*, Hage Geingob
*Deputy Prime Minister*, Revd Hendrik Witbooi
*Agriculture, Water and Rural Development*, Helmut Angula
*Basic Education, Culture and Sport*, John Mutorwa
*Defence*, Erikki Nghimtina
*Environment and Tourism*, Philemon Malima
*Finance*, Nangolo Mbumba
*Fisheries and Marine Resources*, Abraham Iyambo
*Foreign Affairs, Information and Broadcasting*, Theo-Ben Gurirab
*Health and Social Services*, Dr Libertina Amathila
*Higher Education, Training and Employment Creation*, Nahas Angula
*Home Affairs*, Jerry Ekandjo
*Justice, Attorney-General*, Pendukeni Ithana
*Labour*, Andimba Toivo ja Toivo
*Lands, Resettlement, Rehabilitation*, Hifikepunye Pohamba
*Mines and Energy*, Jesaya Nyamu
*Prisons and Correctional Services*, Marco Hausiku
*Regional and Local Government and Housing*, Dr Nick Iyambo
*Trade and Industry*, Hidipo Hamutenya
*Women's Affairs and Child Welfare*, Netumbo Nandi-Ndaitwah
*Works, Transport and Communication*, Moses Amweelo

HIGH COMMISSION OF THE REPUBLIC OF NAMIBIA

6 Chandos Street, London W1M 0LQ
Tel: 020-7636 6244
E-mail: namibia-highcomm@btconnect.com
*High Commissioner*, HE Monica Ndiliawike Nashandi, apptd 1999

BRITISH HIGH COMMISSION

116 Robert Mugabe Avenue, PO Box 22202, Windhoek
Tel: (00 264) (61) 274800
E-mail: bhc@mweb.com.na
*High Commissioner*, HE Brian Donaldson, apptd 1999

BRITISH COUNCIL DIRECTOR, Gillian Belben, 1-4 Peter Muller Street, Windhoek;
e-mail: general.enquiries@britishcouncil.org.na

## ECONOMY

Manufacturing contributes around 31 per cent of GDP, with food production, metals and wooden products the most important areas. Around 44 per cent of the population are engaged in agriculture, primarily livestock. Guano is also exported. Deposits of diamonds along the coast and offshore along the sea bed are estimated at between 1,500 and 3,000 million carats; Namibia accounts for roughly 8 per cent of world diamond production. Walvis Bay and Lüderitz are the main ports. There are 41,815 km of roads, of which 4,572 km are surfaced; there are 2,382 km of railway track.

The principal imports are machinery and transport equipment, foodstuffs, beverages and tobacco, and mineral fuels. The principal exports are diamonds and agricultural products.

In 1998 there was a trade deficit of US$173 million and a current account surplus of US$162 million.

GNP – US$3,211 million (1999); US$1,890 per capita (1999)
GDP – US$3,318 million (1997); US$1,834 per capita (1998)
ANNUAL AVERAGE GROWTH OF GDP – 2.6 per cent (1996)
INFLATION RATE – 8.6 per cent (1999)

| *Trade with UK* | 1999 | 2000 |
|---|---|---|
| Imports from UK | £16,172,000 | £12,554,000 |
| Exports to UK | 78,676,000 | 59,665,000 |

---

## NAURU
*The Republic of Nauru*

---

AREA – 8 sq. miles (21 sq. km)
POPULATION – 11,000 (1997 UN estimate); 8,042 (1983 census): Nauruans 4,964; other Pacific Islanders 2,134; Asians 682; Caucasians 262. About 43 per cent of Nauruans are adherents of the Nauruan Protestant Church and there is a Roman Catholic mission on the island. The main languages are English and Nauruan
CAPITAL – ΨNauru
CURRENCY – Australian dollar ($A) of 100 cents
NATIONAL DAY – 31 January (Independence Day)
NATIONAL FLAG – Twelve-point star (representing the 12 original Nauruan tribes) below a gold bar (representing the Equator), all on a blue background
LIFE EXPECTANCY (years) – male 56.4; female 63.3
POPULATION GROWTH RATE – 1.9 per cent (1999)
POPULATION DENSITY – 529 per sq. km (1998)
URBAN POPULATION – 100.0 per cent (2000 estimate)

## HISTORY AND POLITICS

From 1888 until the First World War Nauru was administered by Germany. In 1920 it became a British Empire-mandated territory under the League of Nations, administered by Australia. A trusteeship superseding the mandate was approved in 1947 by the UN and Nauru continued to be administered by Australia until it became independent on 31 January 1968. Rene Harris was elected president in April 1999 after his predecessor, Bernard Dowiyogo, lost a vote of confidence. Harris resigned on 20 April 2000 and Dowiyogo was re-elected president on 24 April 2000, but lost a vote of confidence on 30 March 2001. Rene Harris was immediately re-elected. Nauru became a full member of the Commonwealth on 1 May 1999; it had been an associate member since 1968.

POLITICAL SYSTEM

Parliament has 18 members including the Cabinet and Speaker. Voting is compulsory for all Nauruans over 20 years of age, except in certain specified instances. Elections are held every three years. The Cabinet is chosen by the president, who is elected by the parliament from amongst its members, and comprises not fewer than five nor more than six members including the president.

HEAD OF STATE

*President, Civil Aviation, Foreign Affairs, Home Affairs, Industry and Investment, Public Service, Works*, Bernard Dowiyogo, *elected by parliament* 29 March 2001

CABINET *as at July 2001*

The President
*Finance, Good Governance*, Aloyisius Amwano
*Health, Sports*, Nimrod Botelanga
*Justice, Marine Resources*, Godfrey Thoma
*Minister assisting the President, Economic Development, Education, Telecommunications, Transport*, Remy Namaduk

HONORARY CONSULATE, Romshed Courtyard, Underriver, Nr. Sevenoaks, Kent TN15 0SD. Tel: 01732-746061. E-mail: nauru@weald.co.uk. *Honorary Consul*, M. Weston

BRITISH HIGH COMMISSIONER, HE Michael Dibben, resident at Suva, Fiji

## ECONOMY

The only fertile areas are in the narrow coastal belt and local requirements of fruit and vegetables are mostly met by imports. The economy is heavily dependent on the extraction of phosphate, of which the island has one of the world's richest deposits. In 1997 541,050 tonnes of phosphate rock was exported. Considerable investments have been made abroad with the royalties on phosphate exports to provide for a time when production declines. A 20-year package of health and education programmes was agreed with Australia in 1993 as part of a compensation package for environmental damage caused by phosphate mining prior to independence. Recent low world phosphate prices have adversely affected the economy.

Air Nauru operates air services throughout the Pacific region and to Australia, New Zealand, Japan, Singapore and the Philippines.

GDP – US$540 million (1997); US$2,900 per capita (1998)
ANNUAL AVERAGE GROWTH OF GDP – 6.0 per cent (1996)

| *Trade with UK* | 1999 | 2000 |
|---|---|---|
| Imports from UK | £1,464,000 | £2,139,000 |
| Exports to UK | 53,000 | 128,000 |

## NEPAL
*Nepāl Adhirājya*

AREA – 56,827 sq. miles (147,181 sq. km). Neighbours: China (north), India (south, west and east)
POPULATION - 23,384,000 (1997 UN estimate). The inhabitants are of mixed stock, with Tibetan characteristics prevailing in the north and Indian in the south. The official religion is Hinduism; 87 per cent of the population are Hindus, 8 per cent Buddhist and 3 per cent Muslim. Gautama Buddha was born in Nepal. The official language is Nepali
CAPITAL – Kathmandu (population, 421,258, 1991)
MAJOR CITIES – Bhadgaon (61,122); Biratnagar (130,129); Patan (117,023), 1991
CURRENCY – Nepalese rupee of 100 paisa
NATIONAL ANTHEM - Sri man gumbhira Nepali prachanda pratapi bhupati (May Glory Crown Our Illustrious Sovereign, the gallant Nepalese)
NATIONAL DAYS – 18 February (National Democracy Day); 28 December (The King's Birthday)
NATIONAL FLAG – Double pennant of crimson with blue border on peaks; white moon with rays in centre of top peak; white quarter sun, recumbent in centre of bottom peak
LIFE EXPECTANCY (years) – male 57.3; female 57.8
POPULATION GROWTH RATE – 2.5 per cent (1999)
POPULATION DENSITY – 148 per sq. km (1998)
URBAN POPULATION – 11.9 per cent (2000 estimate)
MILITARY EXPENDITURE – 0.8 per cent of GDP (1999)
MILITARY PERSONNEL – 46,000: Army 46,000, Paramilitaries 40,000
ILLITERACY RATE – 58.6 per cent
ENROLMENT (percentage of age group) – tertiary 4.8 per cent (1996)

Nepal lies between India and the Tibet Autonomous Region of China on the slopes of the Himalayas, and includes Mount Everest (29,028 ft).

The southern region, the Terai, was covered with jungle but has been more widely cultivated recently. It forms about 23 per cent of the total land area and nearly 44 per cent of the population live there. The central belt is hilly, but with many fertile valleys, leading up to the snowline at about 16,000 feet. The hills account for 42 per cent of the area and about 48 per cent of the population. The remainder of the country, the Himalayan region, consists of high mountains which are sparsely inhabited. The country is drained by three great river systems rising within and beyond the Himalayan mountain ranges and eventually flowing into the Ganges in India.

## HISTORY AND POLITICS

Nepal was originally divided into numerous hill clans and petty principalities but emerged as a nation in the middle of the 18th century when it was unified by the warrior Raja of Gorkha, Prithvi Narayan Shah, who founded the present Nepalese dynasty. In 1846 power was seized by Jung Bahadur Rana after a massacre of nobles, and he was the first of a line of hereditary Rana prime ministers who ruled Nepal for 104 years. During this time the role of the monarchs was mainly ceremonial.

In 1950–1 a revolutionary movement broke the hereditary power of the Ranas and restored the monarchy to its former position. King Mahendra proscribed all political parties and assumed direct powers in 1960. In 1962 he introduced a new constitution embodying a tiered, partyless system of *panchyat* (council) democracy.

Mass agitation for political reform led in April 1990 to the abolition of the panchyat system. A new constitution was promulgated in November 1990 establishing a multiparty, parliamentary system of government and a constitutional monarchy. Elections in May 1991 were won by the Nepali Congress Party.

In October 1997 the government was brought down by a vote of no confidence and several coalition governments ruled until a general election held on 3 and 17 May 1999 gave an absolute majority to the Nepali Congress Party (NCP) who won 110 seats. Prime Minister Krishna Prasad Bhattarai resigned on 16 March 2000, after a motion of no confidence in him was signed by 58 NCP members he was replaced on 20 March by Girija Prasad Koirala. Koirala effectively lost control of the NCP on 28 December 2000 when 56 of the party's 113 MPs signed a no-confidence motion against him, accusing him of having failed to control the Maoist insurgency and administrative corruption. On 5 February 2001, opposition parties called on him to resign over allegations of government corruption and launched a campaign of disruption. In response, King Bihendra prorogued both houses of parliament on 5 April 2001.

On 1 June 2001, King Birendra and Queen Aishwara were shot dead by their son, Crown Prince Dipendra, who then shot himself, but survived long enough to be proclaimed king the following day. King Dipendra was declared dead on 4 June, having never regained consciousness, and Prince Gyanendra, the brother of the late King Birendra, was crowned as king.

Prime Minister Girija Prasad Koirala resigned on 19 July 2001; he was replaced by former prime minister Sher Bahadur Deuba on 22 July 2001.

### INSURGENCIES

Maoist guerrillas from the Communist Party of Nepal, who are opposed to the monarchy, began an armed rebellion in 1996; they organised a campaign to boycott the general election in May 1999 which involved strikes and attacks on government and industrial targets. In November 1999, the government offered an amnesty to the guerrillas if they agreed to abandon violence and enter into dialogue with the government. The guerrillas and the government announced a cease-fire on 23 July 2001 and agreed to hold talks.

### POLITICAL SYSTEM

The King retains joint executive power with the Council of Ministers. The bicameral legislature consists of a 205-member House of Representatives, directly elected for a five-year term, and a 60-member National Council, 50 of whom are indirectly elected for a six-year term and ten royal nominees.

### HEAD OF STATE

*HM The King of Nepal*, King Gyanendra Bir Bikram Shah Dev, *crowned* 4 June 2001

### CABINET *as at July 2001*

*Prime Minister, General Administration, Royal Palace Affairs, Water Resources (acting)*, Sher Bahadur Deuba
*Deputy Prime Minister, Home Affairs*, Khum Bahadur Khadka
*Culture, Tourism and Civil Aviation*, Omkar Shrestha
*Defence*, Mahesh Acharya
*Education and Sports*, Amod Prasad Upadhaya
*Finance*, Ram Sharan Mahat
*Foreign Affairs, Agriculture and Co-operatives (acting)*, Chakara Prasad Bastola
*Forest and Soil Conservation*, Prakesh Koirala
*Health*, Ramkrishna Tamrakar
*Information and Communication*, Shivaraj Joshi
*Labour and Transport Management*, Palten Gurung
*Law, Justice and Parliamentary Affairs, Physical Planning and Public Works*, Mahant Thakur
*Local Development*, Govinda Raj Joshi
*Population and Environment*, Siddharaj Ojha
*Science and Technology*, Surendra Prasad Chaudhary

### ROYAL NEPALESE EMBASSY

12A Kensington Palace Gardens, London W8 4QU
Tel: 020-7229 1594/6231/5352
E-mail: 101642.43@compuserve.com
*Ambassador Extraordinary and Plenipotentiary*, HE Dr Singha Bahadur Basnyat, apptd 1997

### BRITISH EMBASSY

Lainchaur Kathmandu, PO Box 106
Tel: (00 977) (1) 410583/411281/414588/411590
E-mail: britemb@wlink.com.np
*Ambassador Extraordinary and Plenipotentiary*, HE Ronald P. Nash, LVO, apptd 1999

BRITISH COUNCIL DIRECTOR, Brigid O'Connor (*acting*), PO Box 640, Lainchaur, Kathmandu; e-mail: bcnepal@britishcouncil.org.np

## ECONOMY

In 1997, 93.3 per cent of the workforce were engaged in agriculture, which generated 41.6 per cent of GDP. The main exports are carpets, textiles and clothing, hides, jute, handicrafts and agricultural products. The main imports are machinery and transport equipment, and chemical and pharmaceutical products. Tourism is the single largest commercial earner of foreign exchange; 407,300 foreign tourists visited Nepal in 1997. Nepal's main trading partners are India, Germany and the USA.

In 1999 Nepal had a trade deficit of US$861 million and a current account deficit of US$57 million. In 1998 imports totalled US$1,246 million and exports US$474 million.

GNP – US$5,173 million (1999); US$220 per capita (1999)
GDP – US$4,837 million (1997); US$197 per capita (1998)
ANNUAL AVERAGE GROWTH OF GDP – 6.0 per cent (1996)
INFLATION RATE – 8.0 per cent (1999)
TOTAL EXTERNAL DEBT – US$2,646 million (1998)

| *Trade with UK* | 1999 | 2000 |
|---|---|---|
| Imports from UK | £6,988,000 | £7,900,000 |
| Exports to UK | 11,099,000 | 11,797,000 |

## COMMUNICATIONS

The total length of roads is 9,933 km, of which 3,421 km are paved. Kathmandu is connected by road with India and Tibet. Internally, the road network links Kathmandu to Kodari and Pokhara, and Pokhara to Sunauli. There are 155 km of railway track.

Royal Nepal Airlines operates an extensive network of domestic flights, and there are international flights to Europe, the Middle East and throughout Asia. There is an international airport at Kathmandu.

Telecommunication services, both domestic and international, are available. Television was introduced in 1984.

---

# THE NETHERLANDS
*Koninkrijk der Nederlanden*

---

AREA – 16,033 sq. miles (41,526 sq. km). Neighbours: Belgium (south), Germany (east)
POPULATION – 15,802,000 (1997): 36 per cent Catholic, 27 per cent Reformed Church, 8 per cent Muslim. The language is Dutch, a West Germanic language of Low Franconian origin closely akin to Old English and Low German. It is spoken in the Netherlands and the northern part of Belgium (Flanders). Frisian is spoken in Friesland. Dutch is the official language in the Netherlands Antilles and Aruba; Papiamento, a mixture of Dutch and Spanish, is the vernacular
CAPITAL – ΨAmsterdam (population, 1,102,323, 1996 estimate)
SEAT OF GOVERNMENT – The Hague (Den Haag or, in full, 's-Gravenhage), population 695,815, 1996 estimate
MAJOR CITIES – Eindhoven (399,756); Groningen (209,051); Haarlem (211,124); ΨRotterdam (1,077,818); Tilburg (239,057); Utrecht (549,773), 1996 estimates
CURRENCY – Euro (€) of 100 cents/Gulden (guilder) or florin of 100 cents

NATIONAL ANTHEM – Wilhelmus van Nassouwe (William of Nassau)
NATIONAL FLAG – Three horizontal bands of red, white and blue
LIFE EXPECTANCY (years) – male 75.0; female 81.1
POPULATION GROWTH RATE – 0.6 per cent (1999)
POPULATION DENSITY – 378 per sq. km (1998)
URBAN POPULATION – 89.4 per cent (2000 estimate)

The Kingdom of the Netherlands is a maritime country of western Europe, situated on the North Sea, consisting of 12 provinces (Eastern and Southern Flevoland being amalgamated to form the twelfth province). The land is generally flat and low, intersected by numerous canals and connecting rivers. The principal rivers are the Rhine, Maas, IJssel and Schelde.

## HISTORY AND POLITICS

Following a revolt against Spanish rule under the leadership of William of Orange, the northern provinces were united by the Union of Utrecht (1579) and in 1581 independence was declared. Dutch economic and military power flourished in the 17th and 18th centuries.

The Netherlands were overrun by France in the late 18th century, becoming part of the French Empire until 1814, when the northern and southern Netherlands were united into one kingdom. In 1830 the southern provinces seceded to form Belgium. The Duchy of Luxembourg was made an independent state in 1867.

The Netherlands remained neutral during the First World War but were invaded by Germany during the Second World War and occupied until the war ended. The Netherlands joined the Benelux economic union with Belgium and Luxembourg in 1948 and became a member of NATO in 1949. The Dutch East Indies gained independence as Indonesia in 1949.

In 2001, the Netherlands became the first country in the world to legalise euthanasia and to allow same sex marriages.

The most recent election to the Second Chamber was held on 6 May 1998 and resulted in a centre-left coalition of the Labour Party, People's Party for Freedom and Democracy, and Democrats 66. The state of the parties as at May 1998 was: Labour Party (PvdA) 45; People's Party for Freedom and Democracy (VVD) 38; Christian Democratic Appeal (CDA) 29; Democrats 66 (D66) 14; Green Left 11; others 13.

### POLITICAL SYSTEM

The States-General consists of the *Eerste Kamer* (First Chamber) of 75 members, elected for four years by the Provincial Council; and the *Tweede Kamer* (Second Chamber) of 150 members, elected for four years by voters of 18 years and upwards. Members of the *Tweede Kamer* are paid.

### HEAD OF STATE

*HM The Queen of the Netherlands*, Queen Beatrix Wilhelmina Armgard, KG, GCVO, *born* 31 January 1938; *succeeded* 30 April 1980, upon the abdication of her mother Queen Juliana; *married* 10 March 1966, HRH Prince Claus George Willem Otto Frederik Geert of the Netherlands, Jonkheer van Amsberg; and has *issue*, Prince Willem (*see* below); Prince Johan Friso, *b.* 25 September 1968; Prince Constantijn Christof, *b.* 11 October 1969
*Heir*, HRH Prince Willem Alexander, *b.* 27 April 1967

### CABINET *as at July 2001*

*Prime Minister, General Affairs*, Wim Kok (PvdA)
*Deputy Prime Minister, Economic Affairs*, Annemarie Jorritsma-Lebbink (VVD)
*Deputy PM, Health, Welfare and Sport*, Dr Els Borst-Eilers (D66)
*Agriculture, Nature Management and Fisheries*, Laurens Jan Brinkhorst (D66)
*Defence*, Frank de Grave (VVD)
*Development Co-operation*, Eveline Herfkens (PvdA)
*Education, Cultural Affairs and Science*, Loek Hermans (VVD)
*Finance*, Gerrit Zalm (VVD)
*Foreign Affairs*, Jozias van Aartsen (VVD)
*Housing, Spatial Planning and Environment*, Jan Pronk (PvdA)
*Interior and Kingdom Relations*, Klaas de Vries (PvdA)
*Justice*, Benk Korthals (VVD)
*Major Cities and Integration Policy*, Roger van Boxtel (D66)
*Social Affairs and Employment*, Willem Vermeend (PvdA)
*Transport and Public Works and Water Management*, Tineke Netelenbos (PvdA)

VVD People's Party for Freedom and Democracy; D66 Democrats 66; PvdA Labour Party

### ROYAL NETHERLANDS EMBASSY

38 Hyde Park Gate, London SW7 5DP
Tel: 020-7590 3200
*Ambassador Extraordinary and Plenipotentiary*, HE Baron Willem Oswald Bentinck van Schoonheten, apptd 1999

### BRITISH EMBASSY

Lange Voorhout 10, The Hague, NL-2514 ED
Tel: (00 31) (70) 427 0427
*Ambassador Extraordinary and Plenipotentiary*, HE Colin R. Budd, CMG, apptd 2001

CONSULATE-GENERAL – Amsterdam
CONSULATE – Willemstad (Curaçao); Vice-Consulate – Philipsburg (St Maarten) (both Netherlands Antilles)

BRITISH COUNCIL DIRECTOR, Robert Frost, Keizersgracht 269, NL-1016 ED Amsterdam; e-mail: robert.frost@britcoun.nl

NETHERLANDS-BRITISH CHAMBER OF COMMERCE, The Dutch House, 307–308 High Holborn, London WC1V 7LS

UK OFFICE IN THE HAGUE, Holland Trade House, Bezuidenhoutseweg 181, NL-2594 AH The Hague

## DEFENCE

The Army has 330 main battle tanks, 383 armoured infantry fighting vehicles and 339 armoured personnel carriers. The Navy has four submarines, three destroyers, 12 frigates, 13 combat aircraft and 21 armed helicopters. The Air Force has 157 combat aircraft and 42 armed helicopters.
MILITARY EXPENDITURE – 1.8 per cent of GDP (1999)
MILITARY PERSONNEL – 51,940: Army 23,100, Navy 12,340, Air Force 11,300, Paramilitaries 5,200
CONSCRIPTION DURATION – abolished in August 1996

## ECONOMY

The chief agricultural products are potatoes, wheat, rye, barley, sugar beet, cattle, poultry, pigs, dairy products, vegetables, fruit, flower bulbs, plants and cut flowers and there is an important fishing industry.

Among the principal industries are engineering, electronics, nuclear energy, petrochemicals and plastics, road vehicles, aircraft and defence equipment, shipbuilding repair, steel, textiles of all types, electrical appliances, metal ware, furniture, paper, cigars, sugar, liqueurs, beer, clothing etc.

The majority of the workforce, 71.8 per cent, are engaged in service industries.

GNP – US$397,384 million (1999); US$24,320 per capita (1999)
GDP – US$363,342 million (1997); US$24,906 per capita (1999)
ANNUAL AVERAGE GROWTH OF GDP – 3.4 per cent (2000)
INFLATION RATE – 4.5 per cent (2001)
UNEMPLOYMENT – 2.6 per cent (2001)

### TRADE

The Dutch are traditionally a trading nation. Trade, banking and shipping are of particular importance to the economy. The Netherlands is the sixth largest exporter and third largest agricultural exporter in the world. The geographical position of the Netherlands, at the mouths of the Rhine, Maas and Schelde, brings a large volume of transit trade to and from the interior of Europe to Dutch ports. Principal trading partners are Germany, Belgium/Luxembourg, the UK and France.

In 1999 the Netherlands had a trade surplus of US$16,191 million and a current account surplus of US$22,597 million. Imports totalled US$187,525 million and exports US$200,286 million.

| *Trade with UK* | 1999 | 2000 |
|---|---|---|
| Imports from UK | £12,711,000,000 | £14,188,100,000 |
| Exports to UK | 12,705,400,000 | 14,355,200,000 |

## COMMUNICATIONS

There are 58,133 km of inter-urban roads, of which 2,207 km are motorways. The total extent of navigable rivers including canals is 5,046 km. The total length of the railway system is 2,739 km, of which 1,991 km are electrified. The mercantile marine in 1996 consisted of 379 ships with a total of total 2,795,000 gross registered tons.

There are 64 daily newspapers.

## EDUCATION

Primary and secondary education is given in both denominational and state schools and is compulsory.

The principal universities are at Leiden, Utrecht, Groningen, Amsterdam (two), Nijmegen, Maastricht and Rotterdam, and there are technical universities at Delft, Eindhoven, Enschede and Wageningen (agriculture).

ENROLMENT (percentage of age group) – primary 100 per cent (1996); secondary 91 per cent (1996); tertiary 47.3 per cent (1996)

## OVERSEAS TERRITORIES

### ARUBA

AREA – 75 sq. miles (193 sq. km)
POPULATION – 94,000 (1997)
CAPITAL – ΨOranjestad (population 25,000); and Sint Nicolaas (17,000)
CURRENCY – Aruban florin

The island of Aruba was from 1828 part of the Dutch West Indies and from 1845 part of the Netherlands Antilles. On 1 January 1986 it became a separate territory within the Kingdom of the Netherlands. The 1983 Constitutional Conference agreed that Aruba's separate status would last for ten years from 1986, after which the island would become fully independent. In 1994 this decision was changed and it was decided that Aruba will retain its separate status within the Kingdom of the Netherlands.

*Governor*, Olindo Koolman
*Prime Minister*, Jan Hendrik Eman

| *Trade with UK* | 1999 | 2000 |
|---|---|---|
| Imports from UK | £45,616,000 | £27,709,000 |
| Exports to UK | 13,899,000 | 22,508,000 |

### NETHERLANDS ANTILLES

AREA – 309 sq. miles (800 sq. km)
POPULATION – 215,000 (1997), Curaçao 151,448, Bonaire 14,218, St Maarten 38,567, St Eustatius 1,900, Saba 1,200, 1995
CAPITAL – ΨWillemstad (on Curaçao) (pop. 50,000)
CURRENCY – Netherlands Antilles guilder of 100 cents

The Netherlands Antilles comprise the islands of Curaçao, Bonaire, part of St Maarten, St Eustatius, and Saba in the West Indies. The Netherlands Antilles, which have a 22-member federal parliament, are largely self-governing under the terms of the Realm Statute which took effect in 1954. The part of St Maarten belonging to the Netherlands voted in a non-binding referendum held on 23 June 2000 to secede from the Netherlands Antilles and become an independent state within the Kingdom of the Netherlands. This was rejected by the government of the Netherlands, which did not believe that St Maarten was large enough to be a viable state, but discussions on its future status continue.

*Governor*, Dr Jaime Saleh
*Prime Minister*, Suzy Camelia-Römer

| *Trade with UK* | 1999* | 2000* |
|---|---|---|
| Imports from UK | £40,500,000 | £33,299,000 |
| Exports to UK | 1,603,000 | 8,045,000 |

*Curaçao

## NEW ZEALAND

AREA – 104,454 sq. miles (270,534 sq. km)
POPULATION – 3,823,000 (1999 estimate): 79 per cent European stock, 13 per cent Māori, 5 per cent other Pacific islanders. The main religion is Christianity. In 1991 the principal denominations were Anglican 22.1 per cent, Presbyterian 16.3 per cent, Roman Catholic 15 per cent, Methodist 4.2 per cent, Baptist 2.1 per cent. The official languages are English and Māori

| *Islands* | *Area (sq. miles)* | *Population (census 1996)* |
|---|---|---|
| North Island | 44,281 | 2,749,788 |
| South Island | 58,093 | 930,824 |
| Other islands | 1,362 | 934 |
| Total | 103,736 | 3,681,546 |
| *Territories* | | |
| Tokelau | 5 | 1,487 |
| Niue | 100 | 1,708 (a) |
| Cook Islands | 93 | 18,008 |
| Ross Dependency | 175,000 | — |

(a) 1997 estimate

CAPITAL – ΨWellington (population, 346,700, 1999 estimate)
MAJOR CITIES – ΨAuckland (1,090,400); ΨChristchurch (341,000); ΨDunedin (112,000); Hamilton (169,100); Ψ Napier-Hastings (114,900), 1999 estimates
CURRENCY – New Zealand dollar (NZ$) of 100 cents
NATIONAL ANTHEM – God Save The Queen/God Defend New Zealand
NATIONAL DAY – 6 February (Waitangi Day)
NATIONAL FLAG – Blue ground, with Union Flag in top left quarter, four five-pointed red stars with white borders on the fly
LIFE EXPECTANCY (years) – male 73.9; female 79.3
POPULATION GROWTH RATE – 1.5 per cent (1999)
POPULATION DENSITY – 14 per sq. km (1998)
URBAN POPULATION – 85.8 per cent (2000 estimate)

New Zealand consists of a number of islands in the South Pacific Ocean, and also has administrative responsibility for the Ross Dependency in Antarctica. The two larger islands, North Island and South Island, are separated by a relatively narrow strait. The remaining islands are much smaller and widely dispersed.

Much of the North and South Islands is mountainous. The principal range is the Southern Alps, extending the entire length of the South Island and having its culminating point in Mount Cook/Mount Aoraki (3,754 m/12,349 ft). The North Island mountains include several volcanoes, two of which are active. Of the numerous glaciers in the South Island, the Tasman (18 miles long by 1¼ wide), the Franz Josef and the Fox are the best known. The more important rivers include the Waikato (425 km/270 miles in length), Wanganui (180 miles), and Clutha (210 miles) and lakes include Taupo, 234 sq. miles in area; Wakatipu, 113; and Te Anau, 133.

New Zealand includes, in addition to North and South Islands: Chatham Islands (Chatham, Pitt, South East Islands and some rocky islets, combined area, 965 sq. km (373 sq. miles), largely uninhabited); Stewart Island (area 1,746 sq. km (674 sq. miles), largely uninhabited); the Kermadec Group (Raoul or Sunday, Macaulay, Curtis Islands, L'Esperance, and some islets; population 9–10, all government employees at a meteorological station); Campbell Island, used as a weather station; the Three Kings (discovered by Tasman on the Feast of the Epiphany); Auckland Islands; Antipodes Group; Bounty Islands; Snares Islands and Solander.

New Zealand has a temperate marine climate, but with abundant sunshine. The mean temperature ranges from 15°C in the north to about 9°C in the south. Rainfall in the North Island ranges from 35 to 70 inches and in the South Island from 25 to 45 inches.

## HISTORY AND POLITICS

The discoverers and first colonists of New Zealand were Polynesians, ancestors of the modern-day Māori, who settled the islands between the ninth and 14th centuries. The Dutch navigator, Abel Tasman, sighted the coast in 1642 but did not land, but the British explorer James Cook circumnavigated New Zealand and landed in 1769. Largely as a result of increased British emigration, the country was annexed by the British government in 1840. The British Lieutenant-Governor, William Hobson, proclaimed sovereignty over the North Island by virtue of the Treaty of Waitangi, signed by him and many Māori chiefs, and over the South Island and Stewart Island by right of discovery.

In 1841 New Zealand was created a separate colony distinct from New South Wales. In 1907 the designation was changed to 'The Dominion of New Zealand'.

Following the general election of 27 November 1999, the state of the parties in the House of Representatives was: Labour Party (LP) 49 seats, National Party 39, Alliance Party (AP) 10, Association of Consumers and Tax Payers 9, Green Party 7, New Zealand First 5, United Party 1. The Labour Party and the Alliance Party formed a minority administration with the support of the Green Party.

### POLITICAL SYSTEM

The executive authority is entrusted to a Governor-General appointed by the Crown and aided by an Executive Council, within a unicameral legislature, the House of Representatives. The House of Representatives consists of 120 members elected for three-year terms. In the current parliament, 67 members were elected by the first-past-the-post system, of which six represented Māori electorates, and 53 by proportional representation on a party list basis. A referendum, held simultaneously with the general election in November 1999, approved a reduction in the number of members to 99 in future parliaments.

There is no written constitution.

The judicial system comprises a High Court, a Court of Appeal and district courts having both civil and criminal jurisdiction.

### GOVERNOR-GENERAL

*Governor-General and Commander-in-Chief*, HE Dame Silvia Cartwright , *sworn in* April 2001

### THE EXECUTIVE COUNCIL *as at July 2001*

The Governor-General
*Prime Minister, Arts, Culture and Heritage*, Helen Clark (LP)
*Deputy Prime Minister, Economic Development, Industry, Regional Development*, Jim Anderton (AP)
*Attorney-General, Labour, Treaty of Waitangi Negotiations*, Margaret Wilson (LP)
*Biosecurity*, Jim Sutton
*Commerce, Communications, Information Technology, Assistant Minister of Finance, Revenue and Land Information*, Paul Swain (LP)
*Conservation, Local Government*, Sandra Lee (AP)
*Corrections, Courts, Disarmament and Arms Control, Land Information*, Matt Robson (AP)
*Defence, State-owned Enterprises, Tourism, Veterans' Affairs*, Mark Burton (LP)
*Education, State Services, Sport, Fitness and Leisure*, Trevor Mallard (LP)
*Energy, Fisheries, Forestry, Research, Science and Technology, Crown Research Institutes*, Pete Hodgson (LP)
*Environment, Broadcasting, National Library and Archives New Zealand, Associate Minister of Biosecurity and Education*, Marian Hobbs (LP)
*Foreign Affairs and Trade, Justice*, Phil Goff (LP)
*Health*, Annette King (LP)
*Immigration, Senior Citizens, Accident Insurance*, Lianne Dalziel (LP)
*Māori Affairs*, Parekura Horomia (LP)
*Police, Civil Defence, Internal Affairs, Ethnic Affairs*, George Hawkins (LP)
*Social Services, Employment*, Steve Maharey (LP)
*Transport, Housing, Pacific Island Affairs*, Mark Gosche (LP)
*Treasurer, Finance, Revenue*, Michael Cullen (LP)
*Women's Affairs, Youth Affairs, Statistics*, Laila Harré (AP)

### NEW ZEALAND HIGH COMMISSION

New Zealand House, Haymarket, London SW1Y 4TQ
Tel: 020-7930 8422
*High Commissioner*, HE Paul Clayton East, QC, apptd 1999

### BRITISH HIGH COMMISSION

44 Hill Street (PO Box 1812), Wellington 1
Tel: (00 64) (4) 472 6049
E-mail: bhc.wel@xtra.co.nz
*High Commissioner*, HE Martin Williams, CVO, OBE, apptd 1998

CONSULATE-GENERAL – Auckland
CONSULATE – Christchurch

BRITISH COUNCIL DIRECTOR, Paul Atkins, c/o British High Commission; e-mail: enquiries@britishcouncil.org.nz. Regional office in Auckland

BRITISH CHAMBER OF COMMERCE, PO Box 3029, Level 3, Eagle House, 150-154 Willis Street, Wellington

## DEFENCE

The Army has 77 armoured personnel carriers. The Navy has three frigates, four patrol and coastal vessels and three armed helicopters. The Air Force has 42 combat aircraft.
MILITARY EXPENDITURE – 1.6 per cent of GDP (1999)
MILITARY PERSONNEL – 9,230: Army 4,450, Navy 1,980, Air Force 2,800

## ECONOMY

A far-reaching programme of privatisation was carried out in the 1980s and early 1990s, which resulted in only modest economic growth but increased social inequality, and since December 1999 the government has ruled out further privatisation, increased the powers of trade unions, renationalised accident insurance and raised the top rate of income tax.

Agricultural production is dominated by cattle- and sheep-rearing, for meat, wool, dairy products and other by-products, such as skins, leather, etc. Timber and wood pulp are also important.

Non-metallic minerals such as coal, clay, limestone and dolomite are more important than metallic ones. Coal output in 1997 was 3,664,034 tonnes. Of the metals, the most important are gold and ironsand. Natural gas deposits in the offshore Taranaki Maui field and onshore fields are increasingly being exploited and used for electricity generation and as a premium fuel. Manufacturing is based on food processing, machinery production, motor vehicle assembly, chemicals, electrical and electronic goods, and paper and printing. Tourism is the fastest growing sector of the economy, with 1,539,230 visitors in 1999.

In 1999 New Zealand had a trade deficit of US$421 million and a current account deficit of US$4,334 million.
GNP – US$53,299 million (1999); US$13,780 per capita (1999)
GDP – US$65,291 million (1997); US$14,376 per capita (1999)
ANNUAL AVERAGE GROWTH OF GDP – 4.6 per cent (2000)
INFLATION RATE – 4.0 per cent (2000)
UNEMPLOYMENT – 5.6 per cent (2000)

### TRADE

New Zealand's largest trading partners are Australia, the USA, Japan, and the UK. Main exports include dairy products, meat, timber, fish, fruits and nuts, machinery and aluminium products. Imports include machinery, vehicles, petroleum and petroleum products, textiles, plastics and aircraft. In 1999 imports totalled US$14,301 million and exports US$12,452 million.

| *Trade with UK* | 1999* | 2000* |
|---|---|---|
| Imports from UK | £325,255,000 | £304,054,000 |
| Exports to UK | 591,058,000 | 558,934,000 |

*Includes Niue, Tokelau and Cook Islands

## COMMUNICATIONS

The national railway system is owned and operated by the privately-owned Tranz Rail Ltd. There are 4,439 km of railway track .

In December 1995 there were 2,977 ships registered in New Zealand (gross tonnage 482,180).

There are international airports at Auckland, Christchurch and Wellington. Air New Zealand is the national carrier.

There are 91,864 km of maintained roads.

## EDUCATION

Schools are free and attendance is compulsory between the ages of six and 15. There are 2,226 state and 56 private primary schools and 320 state and 23 private secondary schools. There are seven universities and 25 polytechnics.

## TERRITORIES

### TOKELAU (OR UNION ISLANDS)

Tokelau is a group of atolls, Fakaofo, Nukunonu and Atafu. It was proclaimed part of New Zealand as from 1 January 1949. A Council of Faipule, composed of one elected representative from each atoll, was established in August 1992 to govern Tokelau when the council of elders (General Fono) was not in session. The position of *Ulu-o-Tokelau* (leader) was also established in 1992 and is rotated among the three Faipule members annually. Administrative responsibility for Tokelau lies with the Administrator but in January 1994 his powers were delegated to the General Fono and Council of Faipule. The Tokelau Amendment Act, passed by the New Zealand Parliament in 1996, conferred legislative power on the General Fono. New Zealand provides substantial aid (NZ$8.5 million in year ended 30 June 2001).

*Administrator*, Lindsay Watt
*Ulu-o-Tokelau* (2001), Kuresa Nasau

## THE ROSS DEPENDENCY

The Ross Dependency, placed under the jurisdiction of New Zealand in 1923, is defined as all the Antarctic islands and territories between 160° E. and 150° W. longitude which are situated south of the 60° S. parallel, including Edward VII Land and portions of Victoria Land. Since 1957 a number of research stations have been established in the Dependency.

## ASSOCIATED STATES

### COOK ISLANDS

Included in the realm of New Zealand since June 1901, the Cook Islands group consists of the islands of Rarotonga, Aitutaki, Mangaia, Atiu, Mauke, Mitiaro, Manuae, Takutea, Palmerston, Penrhyn or Tongareva, Manihiki, Rakahanga, Suwarrow, Pukapuka or Danger, and Nassau. The population is mainly Māori; English and Cook Island Māori are the principle languages spoken.

Queen Elizabeth II has a representative on the islands, and there is a New Zealand High Commissioner. Since 1965 the islands have been in free association with New Zealand and enjoyed complete internal self-government, executive power being in the hands of a Cabinet consisting of a prime minister and eight other ministers. There is a 25-member Legislative Assembly. New Zealand has an obligation to assist with foreign affairs and defence if requested. The Cook Islanders are constitutionally guaranteed citizenship both of the Cook Islands and of New Zealand.

Agriculture accounts for 7 per cent of GDP, tourism accounts for 30 per cent and offshore banking and trade are of increasing importance to the economy.

*HM Representative*, Sir Apenera Short, KBE
*Prime Minister*, Terepai Maoate
*New Zealand High Commissioner*, Rob Moore-Jones

### NIUE

A New Zealand High Commissioner is stationed at Niue, which since 1974 has been self-governing in free association with New Zealand. New Zealand is responsible for external affairs and defence, and continues to give financial aid. Executive power is in the hands of a premier and a Cabinet of three drawn from the Assembly of 20 members. The Assembly is the supreme legislative body.

*New Zealand High Commissioner*, Mike Pointer

## NICARAGUA
*República de Nicaragua*

AREA – 50,193 sq. miles (130,000 sq. km). Neighbours: Honduras (north), Costa Rica (south)
POPULATION – 4,919,000 (1997 estimate): three-quarters are of mixed blood, another 15 per cent are white, mostly of pure Spanish descent, and the remaining 10 per cent are West Indians or Indians. The latter group includes the Misquitos, who live on the Atlantic coast. The official language is Spanish and the majority are Roman Catholic, although the English language and the Moravian Church are widespread on the Atlantic coast
CAPITAL – Managua (population, 608,020, 1979 estimate)
MAJOR CITIES – Chinandega (144,291); Granada (72,640); León (158,577); Masaya (78,308)
CURRENCY – Córdoba (C$) of 100 centavos
NATIONAL ANTHEM – Salve A Tí Nicaragua (Hail, Nicaragua)
NATIONAL DAY – 15 September
NATIONAL FLAG – Horizontal stripes of blue, white and blue, with the Nicaraguan coat of arms in the centre of the white stripe
LIFE EXPECTANCY (years) – male 64.8; female 68.8
POPULATION GROWTH RATE – 2.9 per cent (1999)
POPULATION DENSITY – 37 per sq. km (1998)
URBAN POPULATION – 56.1 per cent (2000 estimate)
ILLITERACY RATE – 35.7 per cent (2000)
ENROLMENT (percentage of age group) – primary 77 per cent (1997); secondary 27 per cent (1993); tertiary 12 per cent (1997)

### HISTORY AND POLITICS

Spanish colonisation of Nicaragua began in 1523. Independence was secured in 1838. Guerrillas of the Sandinista National Liberation Front (FSLN) overthrew the government in 1979, but after ten years in power and a civil war against US-backed Contra guerrillas, the Sandinistas lost their parliamentary majority in elections held in February 1990. A coalition of former opposition parties, the Unión Nacional de Opositora (UNO), formed a government. With the defeat of the Sandinistas, the civil war came to an end.

The Liberal Alliance won the legislative election in October 1996 although the Nationalist Liberal Party left the Alliance in May 1997.

#### FOREIGN RELATIONS

Following a long-running dispute between Nicaragua and Honduras concerning their maritime boundaries, the two countries signed a border accord on 7 March 2000, in which they agreed to conduct joint patrols in the Caribbean and the Gulf of Fonseca, and to withdraw all military forces from their mutual frontier. In February 2001 the Nicaraguan government accused Honduras of failing to withdraw its forces from the mutual border. An agreement was reached on 7 June 2001 which permitted observers from the Organisation of American States to monitor the deployment of land and maritime forces on both sides of the frontier.

#### POLITICAL SYSTEM

The head of government is the president, elected for a five-year term, not immediately renewable. The president appoints the Cabinet. There is a unicameral legislature, the National Assembly, with 90 members elected for a six-year term.

A presidential election is due to be held by October 2001.

#### HEAD OF STATE

*President*, Arnoldo Alemán Lacayo, *sworn in* 10 January 1997
*Vice-President*, Leopoldo Navarro

#### CABINET *as at July 2001*

*Agriculture and Livestock*, Augusto Navarro
*Attorney-General*, Julio Centeno Gómez
*Defence*, Ramón Kontorovski
*Development, Industry and Commerce*, Noel Sacasa
*Education, Culture and Sports*, Fernando Robleto
*Environment and Natural Resources*, Roberto Stadthagen
*Family Affairs*, Rosa Argentina López Prado
*Finance*, Estebán Duque-Estrada
*Foreign Co-operation*, Francisco Aguirre Sacasa
*Health*, Mariangeles Arguello
*Interior*, José Marenco Cardenal
*Labour*, Mario Montenegro
*Presidential Adviser*, Emilio Álvarez Montalbán
*Presidential Secretary*, David Castillo
*Tourism*, Lorenzo Guerrero
*Transport and Infrastructure*, David Robleto Lang

#### EMBASSY OF NICARAGUA

Suite 31, Vicarage House, 58-60 Kensington Church Street, London W8 4DP
Tel: 020-7938 2373
*Ambassador Extraordinary and Plenipotentiary*, HE Juan B. Sacasa, apptd 2001

#### BRITISH EMBASSY

PO Box A-169, Plaza Churchill, Reparto 'Los Robles', Managua
Tel: (00 505) (2) 780014/7800887/674050
*Ambassador and Consul-General*, HE Hal Wiles, apptd 2001

### DEFENCE

The Army has 127 main battle tanks and 166 armoured personnel carriers. The Navy has 5 patrol and coastal vessels at three bases. The Air Force has 15 armed helicopters. Full military relations with the USA were restored after 21 years in May 2000.
MILITARY EXPENDITURE – 0.9 per cent of GDP (1999)
MILITARY PERSONNEL – 16,000: Army 14,000, Navy 800, Air Force 1,200
CONSCRIPTION DURATION – 18–36 months

### ECONOMY

The country is mainly agricultural. The major crops are maize, sugar cane, rice, sorghum, beans, bananas and coffee; livestock and timber production are also important. Nicaragua possesses deposits of gold and silver. There were 358,400 tourists in 1997.

In December 2000, the IMF and the World Bank announced a debt relief package worth US$4.5 billion to be made available to Nicaragua during 2001-2; the country's total foreign debt amounted to US$6.5 billion.

In 1999 there was a trade deficit of US$1,133 million and a current account deficit of US$652 million. Imports totalled US$1,846 million and exports US$544 million.
GNP – US$2,012 million (1999); US$430 per capita (1999)
GDP – US$2,018 million (1997); US$442 per capita (1998)
ANNUAL AVERAGE GROWTH OF GDP – 6.4 per cent (1996)
INFLATION RATE – 11.2 per cent (1999)
UNEMPLOYMENT – 13.3 per cent (1998)
TOTAL EXTERNAL DEBT – US$5,968 million (1998)

### Trade

Considerable quantities of foodstuffs are imported as well as cotton goods, jute, iron and steel, machinery and petroleum products. The chief exports are cotton, coffee, beef and sugar.

| *Trade with UK* | 1999 | 2000 |
|---|---|---|
| Imports from UK | £7,178,000 | £6,553,000 |
| Exports to UK | 3,811,000 | 7,180,000 |

## COMMUNICATIONS

The Inter-American Highway runs between the Honduras and the Costa Rican borders; the inter-oceanic highway runs from Corinto on the Pacific coast via Managua to Rama, where there is a natural waterway to Bluefields on the Atlantic; there are 15,478 km of roads. The main airport is at Managua. The chief port is Corinto on the Pacific. There are 252 miles of railway, all on the Pacific side of the country. There are 51 radio stations and five television stations in Managua.

---

# NIGER
*République du Niger*

---

AREA – 489,191 sq. miles (1,267,000 sq. km). Neighbours: Algeria and Libya (north), Chad (east), Nigeria and Benin (south), Mali and Burkina Faso (west). Apart from a small region along the Niger Valley in the south-west near the capital, the country is entirely savannah or desert

POPULATION – 10,493,000 (1997 UN estimate): Hausa (54 per cent) in the south, Songhai and Djerma in the south-west, Fulani, Beriberi–Manga, and nomadic Tuareg in the north. 95 per cent of the population are Muslims, with Christian and Animist minorities. The official language is French. Hausa, Djerma and Fulani are also spoken

CAPITAL – Niamey (population, 392,169, 1988 census)

CURRENCY – Franc CFA of 100 centimes

NATIONAL ANTHEM - Auprès du grand Niger Puissant (By the banks of the mighty great Niger)

NATIONAL DAY – 18 December

NATIONAL FLAG – Three horizontal stripes, orange, white and green with an orange disc in the middle of the white stripe

LIFE EXPECTANCY (years) – male 37.2; female 40.6

POPULATION GROWTH RATE – 3.3 per cent (1999)

POPULATION DENSITY – 8 per sq. km (1998)

URBAN POPULATION – 20.6 per cent (2000 estimate)

MILITARY EXPENDITURE – 1.7 per cent of GDP (1999)

MILITARY PERSONNEL – 5,300: Army 5,200, Air Force 100; Paramilitaries 5,400

CONSCRIPTION DURATION – Two years (selective)

ILLITERACY RATE – 84.3 per cent (2000)

ENROLMENT (percentage of age group) – primary 24 per cent (1996); secondary 6 per cent (1996); tertiary 0.7 per cent (1991)

## HISTORY AND POLITICS

The first French expedition arrived in 1891 and the country was fully occupied by 1914. It decided on 18 December 1958 to remain an autonomous republic within the French Community; full independence outside the Community was proclaimed on 3 August 1960.

The president and government were overthrown in a military coup led by Col. Ibrahim Barre Mainassara on 27 January 1996, who was elected president on 8 July 1996. The pro-Mainassara National Union of Independents for Democratic Renewal won the largest number of seats in legislative elections in November 1996, though these were boycotted by main opposition groups. On 24 November 1997, President Mainassara dismissed the government led by Prime Minister Amadou Boubacar Cissé on grounds of incompetence, and appointed a new government under Ibrahim Hassane Mayaki.

President Mainassara was assassinated on 9 April 1999. On 11 April Major Daouda Mallam Wanke, head of the presidential guard unit responsible for the assassination, was named as the country's new president. In May, President Wanke established a Consultative Council which drafted a new constitution; it was approved by representatives of political groups in June and approved following a national referendum in July. Presidential elections were held in November 1999 and won by Mamadou Tandja of the National Movement for Society in Development (MNSD), who took power on 6 December 1999 and was sworn in as president on 22 December.

### Insurgency

An ethnic Tuareg-based insurgency began in the north of Niger in November 1991; a peace accord was signed with the main group, the Front for the Liberation of Aïr and Azawad (FLAA), in 1995 and two splinter groups agreed to a cease-fire in 1997. All rebel groups had been disarmed by June 1998.

### Head of State

*President*, Mamadou Tandja, *elected* 24 November 1999, *sworn in* 22 December 1999

### Council of Ministers *as at July 2001*

Prime Minister, *Hama Amadou*
*Animal Resources*, Korone Maoude
*Commerce and Industry*, Seini Oumarou
*Communication*, Amadou Elhadj Salifou
*Environment and Desertification*, Issoufou Assoumane
*Equipment and Transport*, Abdou Labo
*Finance*, Ali Badjo Gamatie
*Foreign Affairs, Co-operation and African Integration*, Nassirou Sabo
*Higher Education, Research and Technology*, Amadou Lawal
*Interior and Territorial Administration*, Mahama Manzo
*Justice, Keeper of the Seals, Relations with Parliament*, Ali Sirfi
*Labour and Modernisation of the Administration*, Mireille Ossey
*Mines and Energy*, Yahaya Baare
*National Defence*, Sabiou Dadi Gao
*National Education*, Ari Ibrahim
*Planning*, Baroumi Maliki
*Privatisation and Restructuring of Enterprises*, Alma Oumarou
*Promotion of Small and Medium-sized Enterprises*, Souley Hassane
*Public Health*, Assoumane Amadou
*Rural Development*, Wassalike Boukari
*Social Development, Population, Women's Promotion and Protection of Children*, Aissatou Foumakoye
*Tourism and Cottage Industry*, Rissa ag Boula
*Water Resources, Government Spokesman*, Akoli Daouel
*Youth, Sports and Culture*, Issa Lamine

### Embassy of the Republic of Niger

154 rue de Longchamp, F-75116, Paris
Tel: (00 33) (1) 4504 8060
*Ambassador Extraordinary and Plenipotentiary*, HE Mariama Hima, apptd 1999

BRITISH AMBASSADOR, HE J. François Gordon, CMG, resident at Abidjan, Côte d'Ivoire

## ECONOMY

The cultivation of groundnuts and the production of livestock are the main industries and provide two of the main exports. Other agricultural products include millet, cassava and sugar cane. In 1997, 88.5 per cent of the workforce were engaged in agriculture. There are large uranium deposits at Arlit and Akouta, and this is the main export. Gold deposits exist north-west of Niamey. France and Nigeria are the main trading partners.

In 1995 Niger had a trade deficit of US$18 million and a current account deficit of US$152 million. In 1999 imports totalled US$396 million and exports US$276 million.

GNP – US$1,974 million (1999); US$190 per capita (1999)
GDP – US$1,860 million (1997); US$159 per capita (1998)
ANNUAL AVERAGE GROWTH OF GDP – 3.5 per cent (1996)
INFLATION RATE – 2.3 per cent (1999)
TOTAL EXTERNAL DEBT – US$1,659 million (1998)

| *Trade with UK* | 1999 | 2000 |
|---|---|---|
| Imports from UK | £3,360,000 | £4,196,000 |
| Exports to UK | 2,270,000 | 585,000 |

## NIGERIA
*Federal Republic of Nigeria*

AREA – 356,669 sq. miles (923,768 sq. km). Neighbours: Benin (west), Niger (north), Chad (north-east), Cameroon (east)
POPULATION – 123,897,000 (1997 UN estimate); 88,514,501 (1991 census). The main ethnic groups are Hausa/Fulani, Yoruba and Ibo, and the principal languages are English, Hausa, Yoruba and Ibo. There are some 373 ethnic groups, who speak over 500 different languages. The main religions are Islam (45 per cent, mainly in the north and west) and Christianity (49 per cent), mainly in the south, the remainder being Animists
CAPITAL – Abuja (population, 378,671), declared the federal capital in 1991
MAJOR CITIES – Ibadan (1,295,000); Kaduna (309,600); Kano (699,900); Lagos, the former capital (1,347,000); Ogbomosho (660,600); ΨPort Harcourt (371,000)
CURRENCY – Naira (N) of 100 kobo
NATIONAL ANTHEM – Arise, O Compatriots
NATIONAL DAY – 1 October (Independence Day)
NATIONAL FLAG – Three equal vertical bands, green, white and green
LIFE EXPECTANCY (years) – male 46.8; female 48.2
POPULATION GROWTH RATE – 2.5 per cent (1999)
POPULATION DENSITY – 115 per sq. km (1998)
URBAN POPULATION – 44.0 per cent (2000 estimate)
ILLITERACY RATE – 35.9 per cent
ENROLMENT (percentage of age group) – tertiary 4.1 per cent (1993)

A belt of mangrove swamp forest lies along the entire coastline. North of this there is a zone of tropical rain forest and oil-palms. North of the rain forest, the country rises and the vegetation changes to open woodland and savannah. In the extreme north the country is semi-desert. The Niger and Benue are the main rivers. The climate is tropical. The rainy season is from about April to October. During the dry season the cool *harmattan* wind blows from the desert.

## HISTORY AND POLITICS

The Federation of Nigeria attained independence as a member of the Commonwealth on 1 October 1960 and became a republic in 1963. Originally comprising three regions, the Federation is now divided into 36 states and the Federal Capital Territory.

In 1966 the military took power; in 1979 civil rule was restored after elections at national and state level. The administration was overthrown by the military in December 1983, this regime itself being overthrown in August 1985. An Armed Forces Ruling Council (AFRC) was sworn in and governed until January 1993, when it was replaced by a National Defence and Security Council (NDSC) and a civilian Transitional Council. Full power was handed over to the Transitional Council in August 1993.

Continued instability led Defence Minister Gen. Sanni Abacha to launch a military coup on 17 November 1993 and install himself as head of state. The military regime vowed to hand over power to an elected government in October 1998. In June 1998 Gen. Abacha died of a heart attack and was replaced by Gen. Abdulsalami Abubakar, who promised to continue with the handover to civilian rule and began the release of political prisoners.

A general election was held on 20 February 1999 in which the People's Democratic Party (PDP) won a majority in both houses of parliament; a presidential election was held on 27 February, in which Gen. Olusegun Obasanjo, the PDP candidate, was elected president. President Obasanjo and the civilian administration took office on 29 May 1999.

Several predominantly Muslim northern states introduced the Islamic *Shari'ah* legal system during 2000 (Zamfara, Niger, Kano, Jigawa, Yobe and Borno), which President Obasanjo had declared unconstitutional on 1 November 1999. Bauchi adopted Shari'ah law in June 2001.

### INSURGENCIES

Clashes between Muslim Hausas and Christian Yorubas have occurred in various parts of the country. The debate on Shari'ah law has exacerbated the divisions between Muslims and Christians and there have been sporadic clashes in which hundreds have been killed.

A Yoruba separatist organisation, the Odua People's Congress, was banned on 19 October 2000 following clashes between its members and Hausas in Lagos.

Fighting has also occurred between Ijaw and Ilaje tribesmen in the Niger Delta region and the Isoko and Oleh tribes in Olomoro.

Fighting between Tivs and Hausas in Nassarawa state broke out in June 2001.

### FEDERAL STRUCTURE

| *State* | *Population (1991)* | *Capital* |
|---|---|---|
| Sokoto } | 4,392,391 | Sokoto |
| *Zamfara } | | Gusau |
| Kebbi | 2,062,226 | Birnin-Kebbi |
| Niger | 2,482,367 | Minna |
| Kwara | 1,566,469 | Ilorin |
| Kogi | 2,099,046 | Lokoja |
| Benue | 2,780,398 | Makurdi |
| Plateau } | 3,283,704 | Jos |
| *Nassarawa } | | Lafia |
| Taraba | 1,480,590 | Jalingo |
| Adamawa | 2,124,049 | Yola |
| Borno | 2,596,589 | Maiduguri |
| Yobe | 1,411,481 | Damaturu |
| Bauchi } | 4,294,413 | Bauchi |
| *Gombe } | | Gombe |
| Jigawa | 2,829,929 | Dutse |
| Kano | 5,632,040 | Kano |
| Katsina | 3,878,344 | Katsina |
| Kaduna | 3,969,252 | Kaduna |

| | | |
|---|---|---|
| Federal Capital Territory | 378,671 | Abuja |
| Oyo | 3,488,789 | Ibadan |
| Osun | 2,203,016 | Oshogbo |
| Ogun | 2,338,570 | Abeokuta |
| Lagos | 5,685,781 | Ikeja |
| Ondo } | 3,884,485 | Akure |
| *Ekiti } | | Ado Ekiti |
| Edo | 2,159,848 | Benin City |
| Delta | 2,570,181 | Asaba |
| Rivers } | 3,983,857 | Port-Harcourt |
| *Bayelsa } | | Yenagoa |
| Abia | 2,297,978 | Umuahia |
| Imo } | 2,485,499 | Owerri |
| *Ebonyi } | | Abakaliki |
| Anambra | 2,767,903 | Awka |
| Enugu | 3,161,295 | Enugu |
| Cross River | 1,865,604 | Calabar |
| Akwa Ibom | 2,359,736 | Uyo |

*New state, created on 1 October 1996 by dividing state immediately preceding it in list

### HEAD OF STATE

*President*, Olusegun Obasanjo, elected 27 February 1999, *sworn in* 29 May 1999
*Vice-President*, Abubakar Atiku

### FEDERAL EXECUTIVE COUNCIL *as at August 2001*

*Agriculture and Rural Development*, Mallam Adamu Bello
*Aviation*, Kema Chikwe
*Commerce*, Mustapha Bello
*Communications*, Bello Haliru Mohammed
*Culture and Tourism*, Boma Bromillow-Jack
*Defence*, Gen. Theophilus Yakubu Danjuma
*Education*, Prof. Babalola Aborishade
*Environment*, Alhaji Mohammed Kabir Saidi
*Federal Capital Territory*, Mohammed Abba-Gana
*Finance*, Mallam Adamu Ciroma
*Foreign Affairs*, Alhaji Sule Lamido
*Health*, Prof. Alphonsus Bosa Nwosu
*Industry*, Chief Kolawole Babalola Jamodu
*Information and National Orientation*, Prof. Jerry Gana
*Internal Affairs*, Chief Sunday Afolabi
*Justice, Attorney-General*, Chief Bola Ige
*Labour and Productivity*, Musa Gwadabe
*Ministers in the Presidency*, Chief Bimbola Ogunkelu (*Co-operation and Integration*); Prince Vincent Eze Ogbulafor (*Economic Matters and Special Projects*); Ibrahim Umar Kida (*Government Affairs and NNDC Monitoring*); Yomi Edu (*Special Duties*)
*Police Affairs*, Steven Ibn Akiga
*Power and Steel*, Olusegun Agagu
*Science and Technology*, Prof. Turner Isoun
*Solid Mineral Resources*, Kanu Godwin Agabi
*Sports and Social Development*, Ishaya Mark Aku
*Transport*, Chief Ojo Maduekwe
*Water Resources*, Alhaji Shehu Shagari
*Women and Youth*, Aishatu Ismail
*Works and Housing*, Chief Tony Anenih

### NIGERIA HIGH COMMISSION

9 Northumberland Avenue, London WC2N 5BX
Tel: 020-7839 1244
*High Commissioner*, HE Prince Bola Adesumbo Ajibola, KBE, apptd 1999

### BRITISH HIGH COMMISSION

Shehu Shangari Way (North), Maitama, Abuja
Tel: (00 234) (9) 413 2010/2011/2796/2880
E-mail: consular@abuja.mail.fco.gov.uk
11 Walter Carrington Crescent, Victoria Island, Lagos
Tel: (00 234) (1) 261 9531/9537/9541/9543
*High Commissioner*, HE Philip Thomas, CMG, apptd 2001
*Deputy High Commissioner*, C. Bird
*First Secretary (Political)*, I. Baharie
*Defence Adviser*, Col. J. R. Lemon
LIAISON OFFICES – Ibadan, Kaduna, Kano, Port Harcourt

BRITISH COUNCIL DIRECTOR, Cathy Stephens, c/o British High Commission; e-mail: uju.asoegwu@ng.britishcouncil.org. Branch offices at Enugu, Ibadan, Kaduna, Kano and Lagos

## DEFENCE

The Army has 200 main battle tanks and 380 armoured personnel carriers. The Navy has one frigate, six patrol and coastal vessels and two helicopters at six bases. The Air Force has 91 combat aircraft and 15 armed helicopters.
MILITARY EXPENDITURE – 4.4 per cent of GDP (1999)
MILITARY PERSONNEL – 76,500: Army 62,000, Navy 5,000, Air Force 9,500

## ECONOMY

Nigeria was a predominantly agricultural country until the early 1970s when oil became the principal source of export revenue (over 90 per cent). Recent governments have attempted to stimulate greater self-reliance by encouraging non-oil exports and the use of local rather than imported raw materials.

Much of Nigeria's oil revenue has been squandered on major projects which have failed to generate the predicted returns. Nigeria has also suffered from endemic corruption, especially under Gen. Sani Abacha. Many state and local governments have not published audited accounts for many years. President Obasanjo has attempted to tackle the problem by retiring many army officers suspected of corruption and suspending government contracts signed during the last three months of the previous administration, pending investigations.

Agricultural production has fallen since 1970, largely as a result of a system of marketing boards, which fixed prices for agricultural commodities, often setting prices at levels which were too high or low.

Petrol prices are fixed at a level below market rates. These act as a disincentive to producers to refine their oil, which has resulted in widespread fuel shortages. Three oil refineries are in operation at Port Harcourt, Warri and Kaduna, and steel plants at Warri and Ajaokuta (non-operational). Other projects include natural gas liquefaction, petrochemicals, fertilisers, power stations and irrigation schemes. Tin and calumbite mining on the Jos plateau, textiles and coal mining are also important.

GNP – US$31,600 million (1999); US$310 per capita (1999)
GDP – US$142,920 million (1997); US$724 per capita (1998)
ANNUAL AVERAGE GROWTH OF GDP – 3.3 per cent (1996)
INFLATION RATE – 6.6 per cent (1999)
UNEMPLOYMENT – 4.4 per cent (1998)
TOTAL EXTERNAL DEBT – US$30,315 million (1998)

### TRADE

The principal exports are oil, groundnuts, tin, cocoa, rubber, fish and timber. In 1999 there was a trade surplus of US$4,288 million and a current account surplus of US$506 million. In 1998, imports totalled US$10,002 million and exports US$9,729 million.

| *Trade with UK* | 1999 | 2000 |
|---|---|---|
| Imports from UK | £462,060,000 | £534,725,000 |
| Exports to UK | 129,070,000 | 95,257,000 |

## COMMUNICATIONS

There are 142,837 km of roads. The Nigerian railway system, which is controlled by the Nigerian Railway Corporation, has 3,505 route km of lines. The principal international airlines operate from Lagos, Kano and Port Harcourt. A network of internal air services connects the main centres. The principal seaports are served by a number of shipping lines, including the Nigerian National Line. A nationwide television and radio network is being developed, and ten states have their own television and radio stations.

---

## NORWAY

*Kongeriket Norge*

---

AREA – 125,050 sq. miles (323,877 sq. km) of which Svalbard and Jan Mayen have a combined area of 24,355 sq. miles (63,080 sq. km). Neighbours: Sweden, Finland, Russia (east)
POPULATION – 4,503,000 (2001 estimate). The language is Norwegian and has two forms: Bokmål and Nynorsk. Sami is spoken in the north of the country. The state religion is Evangelical Lutheran
CAPITAL – ΨOslo (population, 499,693, 1998)
MAJOR CITIES – ΨBergen (225,439); ΨKristiansand (70,640); ΨStavanger (106,858); ΨTrondheim (145,778), 1999 estimates
CURRENCY – Krone of 100 øre
NATIONAL ANTHEM – Ja, vi elsker dette landet (Yes, we love this country)
NATIONAL DAY – 17 May (Constitution Day)
NATIONAL FLAG – Red, with white-bordered blue cross
LIFE EXPECTANCY (years) – male 75.1; female 82.1
POPULATION GROWTH RATE – 0.5 per cent (1999)
POPULATION DENSITY – 14 per sq. km (1998)
URBAN POPULATION – 75.5 per cent (2000 estimate)

The coastline is deeply indented with numerous fjords and fringed with rocky islands. The surface is mountainous, consisting of elevated and barren tablelands separated by deep and narrow valleys. At the North Cape the sun does not appear to set from about 14 May to 29 July, causing the phenomenon known as the Midnight Sun; conversely, there is no apparent sunrise from about 18 November to 24 January. During the long winter nights are seen the Northern Lights or Aurora Borealis.

## HISTORY AND POLITICS

Norway was unified under Harald I Fairhair *c.*AD 900 and participated in the Viking expansion from the ninth to the 11th centuries. The accession of Magnus VII (1319) unified the Norwegian and Swedish crowns until his son became King Håkon VI of Norway in 1343. The Norwegian and Danish crowns were united in 1380 and confirmed by the Union of Kalmar (1397) which also brought Sweden under the rule of Queen Margrethe of Denmark. Norway remained a Danish province until transferred to Sweden under the Treaty of Kiel (1814). The union with Sweden was dissolved on 7 June 1905 when Norway regained complete independence.

Norway remained neutral during the First World War and on the outbreak of the Second World War but was invaded by Germany in 1940. Neutrality was abandoned when Norway joined NATO in 1949. Norway became a founder member of EFTA in 1960. The Labour Party governed from 1945 to 1965 when the extensive welfare state system was built. A referendum in 1972 rejected membership of the EC.

The ruling centre-right coalition collapsed in October 1990 over the question of EC membership and was replaced by a minority Labour government. This was returned to power in the general election held on 13 September 1993. A general election was held on 15 September 1997, in which no party won an outright majority. The Labour Party has the largest number of seats (65) but a government was formed by a minority coalition of the Christian Democratic People's Party, the Centre Party and the Liberal Party, led by Kjell Magne Bondevik, which resigned on 9 March 2000 after being defeated in a confidence vote. The Labour Party was invited to form a government the following day and appointed its Cabinet on 17 March. A general election was due to be held on 10 September 2001.

### FOREIGN RELATIONS

The Storting voted in November 1992 to apply to join the European Community. Negotiations with the EU concluded on 1 March 1994 with a proposed accession date of 1 January 1995, subject to parliamentary and national referendum ratifications. However, in a national referendum on 28 November 1994 the electorate voted against joining the EU by 52.4 per cent to 47.6 per cent.

### POLITICAL SYSTEM

Under the 1814 constitution, the 165-member unicameral legislature, the *Storting*, elects one-quarter of its members to constitute the *Lagting* (Upper Chamber), the other three-quarters forming the *Odelsting* (Lower Chamber), dividing when legislative matters are under discussion.

### HEAD OF STATE

*HM The King of Norway*, King Harald V, GCVO, *born* 21 February 1937; *succeeded* 17 January 1991, on the death of his father King Olav V; *married* 29 August 1968, Sonja Haraldsen, and has *issue*, Prince Håkon Magnus (*see below*), and Princess Martha Louise, *born* 22 September 1971
*Heir*;, HRH Crown Prince Håkon Magnus, *born* 20 July 1973

### CABINET *as at July 2001*

*Prime Minister*, Jens Stoltenberg
*Agriculture*, Bjarne Håkon Hanssen
*Children and Family Affairs*, Karita Bekkemellem Orheim
*Co-operation and Development*, Anne Kristin Sydnes
*Cultural Affairs*, Ellen Horn
*Defence*, Bjørn Tore Godal
*Education*, Trond Giske
*Environment*, Siri Bjerke
*Finance*, Karl Eirik Schjøtt-Pedersen
*Fisheries*, Otto Gregussen
*Foreign Affairs*, Thorbjørn Jagland
*Health*, Tore Tønne
*Industry and Trade*, Grete Knudsen
*Justice and Police*, Hanne Harlem
*Labour*, Jørgen Kosmo
*Local Government and Regional Development*, Sylvia Brustad
*Petroleum and Energy*, Olav Akselsen
*Social Affairs*, Guri Ingebrigtsen
*Transport, Communications*, Terje Moe Gustavsen

### ROYAL NORWEGIAN EMBASSY

25 Belgrave Square, London SW1X 8QD
Tel: 020-7591 5500
*Ambassador Extraordinary and Plenipotentiary*, HE Tarald Osnes Brautaset, apptd 2000

### BRITISH EMBASSY

Thomas Heftyesgate 8, N-0244 Oslo
Tel: (00 47) 2313 2700

*Ambassador Extraordinary and Plenipotentiary*, HE Richard Dales, CMG, apptd 1998

BRITISH CONSULAR OFFICES – Oslo; Honorary Consulates at Ålesund, Bergen, Harstad, Kristiansand (South), Kristiansund (North), Stavanger, Tromsø, Trondheim

BRITISH COUNCIL DIRECTOR, Sarah Prosser, Fridtjof Nansens Plass 5, N-0160 Oslo; e-mail: british.council@britishcouncil.no

## DEFENCE

Norway is a member of NATO. The Army has 170 main battle tanks, 157,103 armoured infantry fighting vehicles and 157,225 armoured personnel carriers. The Navy has 1,012 submarines, four frigates and 1,522 patrol and coastal vessels at three bases. The Air Force has 79 combat aircraft.

MILITARY EXPENDITURE – 2.2 per cent of GDP (1999)
MILITARY PERSONNEL – 26,700: Army 14,700, Navy 6,100, Air Force 5,000
CONSCRIPTION DURATION – 12 months

## ECONOMY

The cultivated area is about 10,703 sq. km, 3.5 per cent of the total surface area. Forests cover 23 per cent; the rest consists of highland pastures or uninhabitable mountains. The chief agricultural products are grain, vegetables, milk, furs and timber.

The Gulf Stream causes the sea temperature to be higher than the average for the latitude, which brings shoals of herring and cod into the fishing grounds. In 1997 the catch totalled more than 9 million tonnes. In 1998, dried cod worth €352 million/US$400 million was produced.

The chief industries are oil production and transport, construction, electricity supply, manufactures, agriculture and forestry, fisheries, mining, metal and ferro-alloy production and shipping. Industries providing both manufactured products and services for the development of North Sea energy resources have become increasingly important. In 1998 150,006,000 tonnes of crude oil were produced. Norway produces large amounts of hydro-electric power. GDP was expected to grow by 3.3 per cent in 2000.

GNP – US$149,280 million (1999); US$32,880 per capita (1999)
GDP – US$153,362 million (1997); US$34,277 per capita (1999)
ANNUAL AVERAGE GROWTH OF GDP – 0.9 per cent (2000)
INFLATION RATE – 3.6 per cent (2001)
UNEMPLOYMENT – 3.5 per cent (2000)

### TRADE

The chief imports are motor vehicles, ships and machinery, clothing, foods and textiles. Exports consist chiefly of crude oil and gas, machinery and transport equipment and manufactured goods.

In 1998 Norway had a trade surplus of US$1,566 million and a current account deficit of US$2,161 million. In 1999 imports totalled US$34,041 million and exports US$44,884 million.

| *Trade with UK* | 1999 | 2000 |
|---|---|---|
| Imports from UK | £2,120,383,000 | £2,101,072,000 |
| Exports to UK | 3,762,574,000 | 5,858,714,000 |

## COMMUNICATIONS

The total length of railways open at the end of 1999 was 4,021 km, excluding private lines. There are 90,880 km of public roads in Norway (including urban streets). Scheduled internal air services are operated by Scandinavian Airlines System (SAS) on behalf of Det Norske Luftfartselskap (DNL), by Braathens South American and Far East Airtransport (SAFE), and by Widerøes Flyveselskap AS. There are international airports at Oslo, Bergen and Stavanger. In 1996 there were 64 daily newspapers.

## CULTURE AND EDUCATION

The Norwegian language in both its present forms is closely related to other Scandinavian languages. Independence from Denmark (1814) and resurgent nationalism led to the development of 'new Norwegian' based on dialects, which now has equal official standing with 'bokmål', in which Danish influence is more obvious. Ludvig Holberg (1684–1754) is regarded as the father of Norwegian literature, though the modern period begins with the writings of Henrik Wergeland (1808–45). Some of the famous names are Henrik Ibsen (1828–1906), Bjørnstjerne Bjørnson (1832–1910), Nobel Prizewinner in 1903, and the novelists Jonas Lie (1833–1908), Alexander Kielland (1849–1906), Knut Hamsun (1859–1952) and Sigrid Undset (1882–1949), the latter two also Nobel Prizewinners. Old Norse literature is among the most ancient and richest in Europe.

Education from six to 16 is free and compulsory in the 'basic schools', and free from 16 to 19 years.

ENROLMENT (percentage of age group) – primary 100 per cent (1996); secondary 97 per cent (1996); tertiary 62.0 per cent (1996)

## TERRITORIES

SVALBARD, area 24,295 sq. miles (62,923 sq. km); population 3,700; inhabitants mainly engaged in coal-mining. The Svalbard archipelago consists of the main island, Spitsbergen (15,200 sq. miles), North East Land, the Wiche Islands, Barents and Edge Islands, Prince Charles Foreland, Hope Island, Bear Island and many islands in the neighbourhood of the main group. Glaciers cover 60 per cent of the land area. The sovereignty of Norway over the archipelago was recognised by other nations in 1920 and in 1925 Norway assumed sovereignty

JAN MAYEN ISLAND was joined to Norway by law in 1930

## NORWEGIAN ANTARCTIC TERRITORIES

BOUVET ISLAND was declared a dependency of Norway in 1930

PETER THE FIRST ISLAND was declared a dependency of Norway in 1931

PRINCESS RAGNHILD LAND has been claimed as Norwegian since 1931

QUEEN MAUD LAND was declared Norwegian territory by the Norwegian government in 1939

---

## OMAN
*Saltanat 'Umān*

---

AREA – 82,030 sq. miles (212,457 sq. km). Neighbours: Yemen, Saudi Arabia and the UAE (west)

POPULATION – 2,348,000 (1998 estimate). The official language is Arabic. Islam is the official religion. The majority of the population are Ibadhi Muslims; there is a large Sunni and a small Shia minority. Other religions are tolerated

CAPITAL – ΨMuscat (Masqat) (population, 400,000)

MAJOR CITIES – ΨBarka; Ψ:Mutrah and Ruwi (the commercial centres); ΨSalālah (the main town of Dhofar); ΨSuhār; ΨSūr

CURRENCY – Rial Omani (OR) of 1,000 baisas

NATIONAL ANTHEM - Ya Rabbana elifidh lana jalalat al Saltan (O Lord, protect for us his majesty the Sultan)

NATIONAL DAY – 18 November

NATIONAL FLAG – Red with a white panel in the upper fly and a green one in the lower fly; in the canton the national emblem in white

LIFE EXPECTANCY (years) – male 70.4; female 73.8

POPULATION GROWTH RATE – 3.6 per cent (1999)

POPULATION DENSITY – 7 per sq. km (1998)

URBAN POPULATION – 84.0 per cent (2000 estimate)

Oman lies at the eastern corner of the Arabian peninsula. Sharjah and Fujairah (UAE) separate the main part of Oman from the northernmost part of the state, a peninsula extending into the Strait of Hormuz.

The north and the south of Oman are divided by nearly 400 miles of desert. The Batinah, the coastal plain, is fertile. The Hajjar is a mountain spine running from north-west to south-east and for the most part barren, but valleys penetrate the central massif which are irrigated by wells or a system of underground canals called *falajs* which tap the water table. The two plateaus leading from the western slopes of the mountains descend to the Empty Quarter of the Arabian Desert. Dhofar, the southern province, is the only part of the Arabian peninsula to be touched by the south-west monsoon. Temperatures are more moderate than in the north.

## HISTORY AND POLITICS

Oman became part of the Islamic empire in the seventh century. From the ninth to 16th centuries the area was governed by a succession of religious leaders, or imams of the Ibadhi branch of Islam. The Portuguese established trading posts on the coast in 1507 but were expelled in 1650.

In 1744 Ahmad bin Said Al bu Said established the current ruling dynasty of sultans. The country was divided between the sultan's stronghold in the coastal Muscat-Matrah region and the imam in the interior. The sultan cultivated close relations with Britain and the Sultanate of Muscat and Oman became a British protectorate in 1798. In the late 19th century Dhofar was annexed.

In the 1950s the imam proclaimed an independent state in a revolt which was put down with British assistance. A seven-year-long Marxist uprising was crushed in 1975. The current sultan ousted his father in a palace coup in 1970 and changed the state's name to the Sultanate of Oman. Dhofar is still governed as a separate province and Muscat has special status.

### POLITICAL SYSTEM

A State Consultative Council established in 1981 was replaced by Sultanic decree in 1991 by a *Majlis ash Shoura*, or State Advisory Council. This body, meeting twice a year, consisted of representatives from each of the 59 wilayats, or governorates, of the Sultanate. The Council has the right to review legislation, question ministers and make policy proposals. Effective political power remains with the sultan, who rules by decree and is advised by the Cabinet, which he appoints.

On 16 December 1997 the sultan appointed 41 members to the new *Majlis al-Dawlah* (Council of State). On 15 September 2000 the first direct election to the *Majlis ash-Shoura* (Consultative Council) took place.

### POLITICAL SYSTEM

In November 1996 the sultan decreed Oman to be a hereditary absolute monarchy. The Sultan is advised by the Council of State, whose 41 members are appointed by the Sultan. The 82-member Consultative Council has been directly elected since September 2000. The electorate comprises 175,000 men and women 'of good standing'.

### HEAD OF STATE

*HM The Sultan of Oman*, Sultan HM Qaboos bin Said al-Said, *succeeded* on deposition of Sultan Said bin Taimur, 23 July 1970

### COUNCIL OF MINISTERS *as at July 2001*

*Prime Minister*, The Sultan

*Personal Representative of HM The Sultan*, HH Sayyid Thuwaini bin Shehab al Said

*Deputy Prime Minister for Cabinet Affairs*, HH Sayyid Fahd bin Mamud al-Said

*Agriculture and Fisheries*, Shaikh Salim bin Halil al-Khalili

*Civil Service*, Shaikh Abdel Aziz bin Matar bin Salim al-Azizi

*Commerce, Industry and Minerals*, Maqbul bin Ali bin Sultan

*Defence*, Sayyid Badr bin Saud bin Hareb al-Busaidi

*Diwan of Royal Court*, Sayyid Saif bin Hamad al-Busaidi

*Education and Teaching*, Sayyid Saud bin Ibrahim al-Busaidi

*Foreign Affairs*, Yusuf bin Alawi bin Abdullah

*Health*, Dr Ali bin Mohammed bin Mousa

*Higher Education*, Yahya bin Mahfudh al-Mantheri

*Housing, Electricity and Water*, Shaikh Suhail bin Mustahail bin Salim al-Shamas

*Information*, Hamad bin Muhammad bin Muhsin al-Rashidi

*Interior*, Sayyid Ali bin Hamud al-Busaidi

*Justice*, Shaikh Mohammed bin Abdullah bin Zahir al-Hinai

*Legal Affairs*, Mohammed bin Ali bin Nasir al-Alawi

*Minister of State and Governor of Dhofar*, Shaikh Mohammad bin Ali al-Qatabi
*Minister of State and Governor of Muscat*, Mutasim bin Hamud al-Busaidi
*National Economy and Finance*, Ahmed bin Abdulnabi Makki
*National Heritage and Culture*, HH Sayyid Faisal bin Ali al-Said
*Oil and Gas*, Dr Mohammed bin Hamad bin Saif al-Romhi
*Palace Security*, Gen. Ali bin Majed al-Mamari
*Regional Administrative Areas and Environment*, Dr Khamis bin Mubarak bin Isa al-Alawi
*Religious Property and Affairs*, Shaikh Abdallah bin Mahammed al-Salimi
*Social Affairs, Labour, Training*, Shaikh Amer bin Shuwain al-Hosni
*Special Advisers to the Sultan*, Abd al-Aziz bin Muhammad al-Ruwas (*Cultural Affairs*); Muhammad bin Zubayr (*Economic Planning Affairs*); Shahib ibn Taymur al-Said (*Environment*); Umar bin Abd al-Munim al-Zawawi (*External Liaison*); Salim bin Abdullah al-Ghazali; Mubarak bin Saleh al-Khadouri
*Transport and Telecommunications*, Col. Malik bin Sulaiman al-Ma'amari
*Water Resources*, Lt.-Gen. Hamid bin Said al-Aufi

EMBASSY OF THE SULTANATE OF OMAN
167 Queen's Gate, London SW7 5HE
Tel: 020-7225 0001
*Ambassador Extraordinary and Plenipotentiary*, HE Hussain Ali Abdullatif, apptd 1995

BRITISH EMBASSY
PO Box 300, Muscat, Postal Code 113
Tel: (00 968) 693077
E-mail: becomu@omantel.net.om
*Ambassador Extraordinary and Plenipotentiary*, HE Sir Ivan Callan, KCVO, CMG, apptd 1999

BRITISH COUNCIL DIRECTOR, Colin Hepburn, Road One, Madinat Qaboos West, PO Box 73, Muscat; e-mail: bc.muscat@om.britishcouncil.org. There is also an office in Seeb

## DEFENCE

The Army has 117 main battle tanks and 183 armoured personnel carriers. The Navy has 13 patrol and coastal vessels at five bases. The Air Force has 40 combat aircraft.
MILITARY EXPENDITURE – 10.9 per cent of GDP (1999)
MILITARY PERSONNEL – 43,500: Army 25,000, Navy 4,200, Air Force 4,100, Royal Household 6,500, Paramilitaries 4,400

## ECONOMY

Although there is considerable cultivation in the fertile areas and cattle are raised on the mountains, the backbone of the economy is the oil industry, accounting for about 40 per cent of GDP. Petroleum Development (Oman) (PDO) (owned 60 per cent by the Oman Government) began exporting oil in 1967. Concessions (off and on shore) are held by several major international companies. Oil production in 1998 was 44,788,000 tonnes and natural gas production was 5,200 million cubic metres. The government is actively encouraging the diversification of the economy and private sector development. Tourism is also an expanding area.

In 1998 there was a trade surplus of US$291 million and a current account deficit of US$2,970 million.
GDP – US$15,563 million (1997); US$5,946 per capita (1998)
ANNUAL AVERAGE GROWTH OF GDP – 5.2 per cent (1996)
INFLATION RATE – 0.4 per cent (1999)
TOTAL EXTERNAL DEBT – US$3,629 million (1998)

TRADE

Trade is mainly with the UAE, UK, Japan, South Korea and China. Chief imports are machinery and transport equipment, industrial goods and foodstuffs. Oil accounts for 79 per cent of exports.

In 1998 imports totalled US$5,682 million and exports US$5,508 million.

| *Trade with UK* | 1999 | 2000 |
|---|---|---|
| Imports from UK | £231,359,000 | £278,280,000 |
| Exports to UK | 75,041,000 | 97,445,000 |

## COMMUNICATIONS

Port Qaboos at Mutrah has eight deep-water berths which have been constructed as part of the harbour facilities; a new port is under construction at Suhār. There are some 30,000 km of roads, of which 6,000 km are paved, linking most main population centres of the country with the coast and with the towns of the UAE, though only a trunk road links the north and south of Oman. There are airports at Seeb, Salālah, Sūr, Masirah, Khasab and Diba. Five daily newspapers are published, three in Arabic and two in English.

## SOCIAL WELFARE AND EDUCATION

For many years the Sultanate was a poor country but the advent of oil revenues and the change of regime in 1970 led to the initiation of a wide-ranging development programme, especially concerned with health, education and communications. There are now 47 hospitals and 117 health centres. Mass immunisation programmes have eradicated poliomyelitis and diphtheria; 1,069 schools, with 536,178 pupils, were in operation in 1998. There is one university.
ILLITERACY RATE – 28.1 per cent (2000)
ENROLMENT (percentage of age group) – primary 69 per cent (1996); secondary 56 per cent (1996); tertiary 8 per cent (1997)

---

# PAKISTAN
*Islāmī Jamhūriya-e-Pākistān*

---

AREA – 307,374 sq. miles (796,095 sq. km). Neighbours: Iran (west), Afghanistan (north and north-west), China (north-east), the disputed territory of Kashmir, India (east)
POPULATION – 134,790,000 (1997 UN estimate); 95 per cent Muslim, 3.5 per cent Christian, about 1 per cent Hindu, and 0.5 per cent Buddhist. Urdu is the national language, but is only spoken by a small minority of the population. The most widely used language is Punjabi, followed by Sindi and Pushto. English is used in business, government and higher education
CAPITAL – Islamabad (population, 524,500, 1998 census)
MAJOR CITIES – Faisalabad (1,977,246); ΨKarachi (9,269,265); Lahore (5,063,499); Rawalpindi (1,406,214), 1998 census
CURRENCY – Pakistan rupee of 100 paisa
NATIONAL ANTHEM – Quami Tarana
NATIONAL DAYS – 23 March (Pakistan Day), 14 August (Independence Day)
NATIONAL FLAG – Green with a white crescent and star, and a white vertical strip in the hoist
LIFE EXPECTANCY (years) – male 62.6; female 64.9
POPULATION GROWTH RATE – 2.8 per cent (1999)
POPULATION DENSITY – 165 per sq. km (1998)
URBAN POPULATION – 37.0 per cent (2000 estimate)

Running through Pakistan are five great rivers, the Indus, Jhelum, Chenab, Ravi and Sutlej. The upper reaches of these rivers are in Kashmir, and their sources in the Himalayas.

## HISTORY AND POLITICS

Pakistan was constituted as a Dominion under the Indian Independence Act 1947, becoming a republic on 23 March 1956. Until 1972 Pakistan consisted of two geographical units, West and East Pakistan, separated by about 1,100 miles of Indian territory. East Pakistan's insistence on complete autonomy led to civil war, which broke out on 25 March 1971 and continued until December 1971 when a cease-fire was arranged. The independence of East Pakistan as Bangladesh was proclaimed in April 1972. Under the 1972 Simla Agreement with India, a line of control was established in Kashmir; Pakistan controls an area of 33,653 sq. miles (87,159 sq. km) to the north and west of the line.

Elections held in February 1997 were won by the Pakistan Muslim League with 134 seats. President Farooq Leghari resigned on 2 December 1997 following a dispute with Prime Minster Sharwaz. Muhammad Rafiq Tarar was subsequently elected president.

The government was overthrown by the military under Gen. Pervez Musharraf on 12 October 1999 after the Prime Minister, Nawaz Sharif, had tried to sack him. Gen. Musharraf declared himself chief executive and dissolved the legislature, but left the president in office. Gen. Musharraf established the National Security Council to run the country, comprising the military chiefs of staff and civilian technocrats.

A coalition of 17 of the main political parties, was formed in November 2000 to campaign for the restoration of democracy.

On 20 June 2001, Gen. Musharraf dismissed the elected president, Muhammad Rafiq Tarar and assumed the presidency himself.

Pakistan's membership of the Commonwealth was suspended on 18 October 1999.

### INSURGENCY

Since early 1994 there has been civil disorder in Sind province, especially in Karachi, in two conflicts: armed militants of the Mohajir Qaumi Movement (MQM) Party, which represents Urdu-speaking Indian Muslims who fled from India at partition and their descendants, are fighting for an autonomous Karachi province; and there is an armed conflict between Shia and Sunni fundamentalists.

### POLITICAL SYSTEM

The legislature is bicameral, but was suspended following the coup in October 1999. Under the constitution, the *Majlis as-Shoora* (National Assembly) has a five-year term and comprises 237 members, of whom 207 are directly elected, 10 represent religious minorities and 20 are co-opted women. The Senate has 87 members, with a six-year term; half of the seats are renewed every three years. In January 1997 the interim government set up a Council for Defence and National Security including members of the Cabinet and armed forces to advise on foreign, defence and economic policies. The four provinces each have a provincial assembly and are represented in both legislative chambers.

The National Assembly amended the constitution in April 1997 to remove from the president the power to dismiss the government and dissolve parliament.

### FEDERAL STRUCTURE

| *Province* | *Area (sq. km)* | *Population (1998 census)* | *Capital* |
|---|---|---|---|
| Baluchistan | 347,190 | 6,511,000 | Quetta |
| Federal Capital Territory Islamabad | 906 | 805,000 | — |
| Federally Administered Tribal Areas | 27,220 | 3,138,000 | — |
| North-West Frontier Province | 74,521 | 17,555,000 | Peshawar |
| Punjab | 205,344 | 72,585,000 | Lahore |
| Sind | 140,914 | 29,991,000 | Karachi |

### HEAD OF STATE

*President, Chief Executive, Chief of Army Staff*, Gen. Pervez Musharraf, *sworn in* 20 June 2001

### NATIONAL SECURITY COUNCIL *as at July 2001*

*Chief of Air Staff*, Air Chief Marshal Mushaf Ali Mir
*Chief of Naval Staff*, Adm. Abdul Aziz Mirza
*Commerce, Industry and Production*, Abdul Razzak Daud
*Finance, Revenue, Economic Affairs, Planning, Development and Statistics*, Shaukat Aziz
*Foreign Affairs*, Abdul Sattar
*Interior and Narcotics Control, Capital Administration and Development Divisions*, Lt.-Gen. (retd) Moeenuddin Haider

### FEDERAL MINISTERS *as at July 2001*

*Adviser to the Chief Executive for Food, Agriculture and Livestock*, Shafi Nafiz
*Adviser to the Chief Executive for Foreign Affairs, Law, Justice and Human Rights*, Sharifuddin Pirzada
*Attorney-General*, Aziz A. Munshi
*Chair of the Federal Land Commission*, Imtiaz Ahmad Ghazi
*Communications and Railways*, Lt.-Gen. Javed Asharaf
*Education, Science and Technology*, Zubaida Jalal
*Food and Agriculture*, Khair Mohammad Junejo
*Health*, Abdul Malik Kasi
*Kashmir Affairs, Northern Areas, States and Frontier Regions, Housing and Works*, Abbass Sarfaraz Khan
*Law, Justice, Human Rights and Parliamentary Affairs*, Shahida Jamil
*Local Government and Rural Development, Labour, Environment, Overseas Pakistanis*, Omar Asghar Khan
*Petroleum and Natural Resources*, Usman Aminuddin
*Privatisation*, Altaf M. Saleem
*Religious Affairs*, Mahmood Ahmed Ghazi
*Science and Technology*, Ataur Rahman
*Sports, Culture, Tourism and Minorities Affairs*, S. K. Trassler
*Women's Development, Social Welfare and Special Education, Population Welfare*, Attiya Inayatullah

### HIGH COMMISSION FOR THE ISLAMIC REPUBLIC OF PAKISTAN

35–36 Lowndes Square, London SW1X 9JN
Tel: 020-7664 9200
*High Commissioner*, HE Abdul Kader Jaffer, apptd 2000
*Deputy High Commissioner*, Attiya Mahmood
*Defence and Naval Adviser*, vacant

### BRITISH HIGH COMMISSION

Diplomatic Enclave, Ramna 5, PO Box 1122, Islamabad
Tel: (00 92) (51) 2206071/5
E-mail: bhctrade@isb.comsats.net.pk
*High Commissioner*, HE Hilary Synnott, CMG, apptd 2000
*Deputy High Commissioners*, M. Forbes-Smith *(Islamabad)*; D. D. Pearey *(Karachi)*
First Secretary (Commercial), *M. Pakes*
*Defence and Military Adviser*, Brig. E. Torrens-Spence
DEPUTY HIGH COMMISSION – Karachi
CONSULATE – Lahore

BRITISH COUNCIL DIRECTOR, Peter Ellwood, Block 14, Civic Centre G6, PO Box 1135, Islamabad; e-mail:peter.ellwood@britishcouncil.org.pk. There are offices at Karachi, Lahore and Peshawar

## DEFENCE

On 28 and 30 May 1998, Pakistan carried out six underground nuclear tests, less than a month after India had carried out its own nuclear tests. In doing so, it became the world's seventh declared nuclear power.

The Army has some 2,285 main battle tanks, 1,000 armoured personnel carriers and 20 attack helicopters. The Navy has ten submarines, eight frigates, nine patrol and coastal vessels, five combat aircraft and nine armed helicopters based at Karachi. The Air Force has 353 combat aircraft.

MILITARY EXPENDITURE – 5.7 per cent of GDP (1999)
MILITARY PERSONNEL – 612,000: Army 550,000, Navy 22,000, Air Force 40,000, Paramilitaries 288,000

## ECONOMY

Agriculture employs half the workforce and contributes a quarter of GDP. The principal crops are cotton, rice, wheat and sugar cane. Pakistan has one of the longest irrigation systems in the world, irrigating 42.5 million acres. There are large deposits of rock salt.

Pakistan also produces hides and skins, leather, wool, fertilisers, paints and varnishes, soda ash, paper, cement, fish, carpets, sports goods, surgical appliances and engineering goods, including switchgear, transformers, cables and wires.

In July 2001, the World Bank commended the efforts of the government to stabilise and deregulate the economy and to alleviate poverty.

In 1997 there was a trade deficit of US$2,399 million and a current account deficit of US$1,712 million.

GNP – US$62,915 million (1999); US$470 per capita (1999)
GDP – US$67,122 million (1997); US$458 per capita (1998)
ANNUAL AVERAGE GROWTH OF GDP – 6.0 per cent (1996)
INFLATION RATE – 4.1 per cent (1999)
UNEMPLOYMENT – 5.5 per cent (1998)
TOTAL EXTERNAL DEBT – US$32,229 million (1998)

### TRADE

Principal imports are petroleum products, machinery, fertilisers, transport equipment, edible oils, chemicals and ferrous metals. Principal exports are cotton yarn and cloth, carpets, rice, petroleum products, textiles, leather and fish.

In 1998 imports totalled US$9,800 million and exports US$8,913 million.

| *Trade with UK* | 1999 | 2000 |
|---|---|---|
| Imports from UK | £219,963 | £205,922 |
| Exports to UK | 333,228 | 378,142 |

## COMMUNICATIONS

There are major seaports at Karachi and Port Qasim. The main airports are at Karachi, Islamabad, Lahore, Peshawar and Quetta. Pakistan International Airlines operates air services between the principal cities as well as abroad. There are 86,597 km of roads and 7,344 km of rail track.

## EDUCATION

Education consists of five years of primary education (five to nine years), three years of middle or lower secondary (general or vocational), two years of upper secondary, two years of higher secondary (intermediate) and two to five years of higher education in colleges and universities. Education is free to upper secondary level.

ILLITERACY RATE – 56.7 per cent (2000)
ENROLMENT (percentage of age group) – tertiary 3.0 per cent (1991)

---

# PALAU
*Belu'u era Belau/Republic of Palau*

---

AREA – 177 sq. miles (459 sq. km)
POPULATION – 19,000 (1997 UN estimate); 15,122 (1990 census); 13,900 live on Koror and Babelthaup. The population is Micronesian, and predominantly Roman Catholic with a Protestant minority. Palauan and English are official languages
CAPITAL – Koror (population, 10,493, 1994)
CURRENCY – Currency is that of the USA
NATIONAL FLAG – Light blue with a yellow disc set near the hoist
LIFE EXPECTANCY (years) – male 64.5; female 69.7
POPULATION GROWTH RATE – 2.5 per cent (1999)
POPULATION DENSITY – 40 per sq. km (1998)
URBAN POPULATION – 72.4 per cent (2000 estimate)

The Republic of Palau consists of 340 islands and islets in the western Pacific Ocean, of which eight are inhabited. Part of the Caroline Islands group, the Palau archipelago stretches over 400 miles (644 km) between 2° and 8°N., and 131° and 138°E. Koror island is about 810 miles (1,300 km) south-west of Guam and about 530 miles (852 km) south-east of Manila.

The islands vary in terrain from the highly mountainous to low coral atolls. The climate is tropical with a rainy season lasting from June to October; the average temperature is 27°C (81°F).

## HISTORY AND POLITICS

Spain acquired sovereignty over the Caroline Islands, of which the Palau archipelago is part, in 1886. After defeat in the Spanish-American war of 1898, Spain sold its remaining Pacific possessions, including Palau, to Germany in 1899. On the outbreak of the First World War in 1914, Japan took control of Palau on behalf of the Allied powers, and Japanese administration was confirmed in a League of Nations mandate in 1921. During the Second World War, Allied forces gained control of the archipelago after intense fighting. In 1947 the USA entered into agreement with the UN Security Council to administer the Micronesia area, including Palau, as the UN Trust Territory of the Pacific Islands.

In July 1978, the Palau electorate voted in a referendum not to join the new Federated States of Micronesia and instead became a separate part of the UN Trust Territory. A Compact of Free Association was signed with the USA in 1982 and implemented on 1 October 1994. Under this agreement the USA recognised the Republic of Palau as a fully sovereign and independent state and assumed responsibility for its defence for 50 years.

The last presidential and legislative elections were held on 7 November 2000.

### POLITICAL SYSTEM

Executive power is vested in the president and vice-president, who are elected for four-year terms; the president appoints the Cabinet. There is a bicameral legislature (*Olbiil era Kelulau*) composed of the 16-member House of Delegates (one member elected from each of the 16 constituent states) and the 14-member Senate. There is also a Council of Chiefs to advise the president on matters concerning traditional law and customs. Each of the 16 component states have their own elected governors and legislatures.

HEAD OF STATE

*President*, Tommy Remengesau, *elected* 7 November 2000, *took office* 19 January 2001
*Vice-President, Administration*, Sandra Pierantozzi

CABINET *as at July 2001*

*Commerce and Trade*, George Ngirarsaol
*Community and Cultural Affairs*, Riosang Salvador
*Education*, Billy Kuartei
*Health*, Masao Ueda
*Justice*, Salvador Ingereklii
*Minister of State*, Sabias Anastacio
*Resources and Development*, Marcelino Melairei

BRITISH AMBASSADOR, HE Christopher Haslam, resident at Suva, Fiji

## ECONOMY

The economy remains heavily dependent on US financial support, which the USA is committed to giving under the Compact. Fisheries, tourism, subsistence agriculture and government service are the main areas of employment. Agricultural products include coconuts and copra, and Palau earns significant revenue from the sale of fishing licences to foreign fleets fishing for tuna. The chief exports are fish, mussels, coconuts and copra. Tourism is being developed; there were 75,139 visitors in 1997. There are three airports on Koror, Peleliu and Angaur which have daily flights from Guam operated by Continental Micronesia. There are 61 km of roads, of which 36 km are paved. There is a privately owned television station and a government-operated radio station.

GDP – US$105 million (1997); US$6,448 per capita (1998)
ANNUAL AVERAGE GROWTH OF GDP – 2.6 per cent (1996)

| *Trade with UK* | 1999 | 2000 |
|---|---|---|
| Imports from UK | £65,000 | £78,000 |
| Exports to UK | 1,000 | 1,000 |

## PANAMA
*República de Panamá*

AREA – 29,157 sq. miles (75,517 sq. km). Neighbours: Colombia (east), Costa Rica (west)
POPULATION – 2,815,644 (2000 census): 70 per cent mestizo, 14 per cent mixed Amerindian and black, 10 per cent European, 6 per cent Amerindian. Spanish is the official language
CAPITAL – ΨPanama City (population, 704,117, 2000 census)
CURRENCY – Balboa of 100 centésimos (US notes are also in circulation)
NATIONAL ANTHEM – Alcanzamos Por Fin La Victoria (Victory is ours at last)
NATIONAL DAY – 3 November
NATIONAL FLAG – Four quarters; white with blue star (top, next staff), red (in fly), blue (below, next staff) and white with red star
LIFE EXPECTANCY (years) – male 72.6; female 75.8
POPULATION GROWTH RATE – 1.8 per cent (1999)
POPULATION DENSITY – 37 per sq. km (1998)
URBAN POPULATION – 56.3 per cent (2000 estimate)
MILITARY EXPENDITURE – 1.3 per cent of GDP (1999)
MILITARY PERSONNEL – 11,800 Paramilitaries
ILLITERACY RATE – 8.1 per cent
ENROLMENT (percentage of age group) – primary 91 per cent (1990); secondary 51 per cent (1990); tertiary 31.5 per cent (1996)

## HISTORY AND POLITICS

After a revolt in 1903, Panama declared its independence from Colombia and established a separate government.

On 25 February 1998, President Delvalle was removed by the National Assembly. Presidential elections were held in May 1989 but Gen. Noriega, the Commander of the Defence Forces, annulled the results and on 15 December he assumed power formally as head of state. On 20 December US troops invaded Panama to oust Noriega. Guillermo Endara, believed to have won the May elections, was installed as president. In December 1991 the Legislative Assembly approved a change to the constitution which abolished the armed forces.

The most recent presidential election, on 2 May 1999, was won by Mireya Elisa Moscoso de Gruber of the Union for Panama coalition. Simultaneous legislative elections were won by the New Nation coalition with 46 of the 71 contested seats.

POLITICAL SYSTEM

Legislative power is vested in a unicameral Legislative Assembly of 71 members; executive power is held by the president, assisted by two elected vice-presidents and an appointed Cabinet. Elections are held every five years under a system of universal and compulsory adult suffrage.

HEAD OF STATE

*President*, Mireya Elisa Moscoso de Gruber, *elected* 2 May 1999, *sworn in* 1 September 1999
*First Vice-President*, Arturo Vallarino
*Second Vice-President*, Dominador Kaiser Bazán

CABINET *as at July 2001*

*Agricultural Development*, Pedro Adán Gordón
*Canal Affairs*, Ricardo Martinelli Berrocal
*Commerce and Industry*, Joaquín Jácome Diez
*Education*, Doris Rosas de Mata
*Finance and Economy*, Norberto Delgado
*Foreign Relations*, José Miguel Alemán
*Health*, Fernando Gracia
*Housing*, Miguel Cárdenas
*Interior and Justice*, Winston Spadafora
*Labour and Social Welfare*, Joaquín José Vallarino III
*Presidency*, Ivonne Young Valdez
*Public Works*, Victor Juliao
*Women, Youth and Family*, Alba Ester Tejada de Rolla

EMBASSY OF THE REPUBLIC OF PANAMA
40 Hertford Street, London W1J 7SH
Tel: 020-7493 4646
*Ambassador Extraordinary and Plenipotentiary*, HE Ariadne Singares Robinson, apptd 2000
*Counsellor (Financial and Commercial)*, S. Kheireddine

BRITISH EMBASSY
Torre Swiss Bank, Calle 53 (Apartado 889) Zona 1, Panama City
Tel: (00 507) 269 0866
*Ambassador Extraordinary and Plenipotentiary*, HE Glyn Davies, apptd 1999

## ECONOMY

The soil is moderately fertile, but nearly one-half of the land is uncultivated. The chief crops are bananas, sugar, coconuts, coffee and cereals. Over 13,000 foreign ships are registered in Panama. The shrimping industry plays an important role in the economy. Tourism is the principal foreign currency earner. There are 547 km of railway track and 10,792 km of roads.

GNP – US$8,657 million (1999); US$3,070 per capita (1999)
GDP – US$8,600 million (1997); US$3,287 per capita (1998)
ANNUAL AVERAGE GROWTH OF GDP – 2.5 per cent (1996)
INFLATION RATE – 1.3 per cent (1999)
UNEMPLOYMENT – 13.9 per cent (1998)
TOTAL EXTERNAL DEBT – US$6,689 million (1998)

### TRADE

Imports are mostly manufactured goods, machinery, lubricants, chemicals and foodstuffs. Exports are bananas, petroleum products, shrimps, sugar, meat, coffee and fishmeal.

In 1999 Panama had a trade deficit of US$1,398 million and a current account deficit of US$1,333 million. Imports totalled US$3,516 million and exports US$822 million.

| *Trade with UK*† | 1999 | 2000 |
|---|---|---|
| Imports from UK | £60,689,000 | £48,171,000 |
| Exports to UK | 7,975,000 | 8,153,000 |

†Including Colón Free Zone

## THE PANAMA CANAL ZONE

The Panama Canal Zone was created in 1903 by a contract between Panama and the USA, under which the USA was given the right to build and operate the canal and administer the adjacent territory. With effect from 1 October 1979 the Canal Zone (1,142 sq. km/647 sq. miles) was disestablished, with all areas of land and water within the Zone reverting to Panama. By the 1977 treaty with the USA, the USA was allowed the use of operating bases for the Panama Canal, together with several military bases, but the Republic of Panama was sovereign in all such areas. Control of the Canal reverted to Panama at noon on 31 December 1999.

In the fiscal year 2000, the total number of transits by ocean-going commercial traffic was 12,303; canal net tons totalled 229,459,659; cargo tons totalled 193,714,277.

---

# PAPUA NEW GUINEA

---

AREA – 178,704 sq. miles (462,840 sq. km). Neighbour: Indonesia (west, on New Guinea)
POPULATION – 4,705,000 (1997 UN estimate). English is the official language; Hiri Motu and Neo-Melanesian are widely used
CAPITAL – ΨPort Moresby (population, 173,500, 1990)
MAJOR CITIES – Goroka; Lae; Madang; Mount Hagen; Rabaul; Wewak
CURRENCY – Kina (K) of 100 toea
NATIONAL ANTHEM – Arise All You Sons
NATIONAL DAY – 16 September (Independence Day)
NATIONAL FLAG – Divided diagonally red (fly) and black (hoist); on the red a soaring Bird of Paradise in yellow and on the black five white stars of the Southern Cross
LIFE EXPECTANCY (years) – male 53.4; female 56.6
POPULATION GROWTH RATE – 2.3 per cent (1999)
POPULATION DENSITY – 10 per sq. km (1998)
URBAN POPULATION – 17.4 per cent (2000 estimate)
MILITARY EXPENDITURE – 1.0 per cent of GDP (1999)
MILITARY PERSONNEL – 4,400: Army 3,800, Navy 400, Air Force 200
ILLITERACY RATE – 24.0 per cent (2000)
ENROLMENT (percentage of age group) – tertiary 3.2 per cent (1996)

The country has many island groups, principally the Bismarck Archipelago, a portion of the Solomon Islands, the Trobriands, the D'Entrecasteaux Islands and the Louisade Archipelago. The main islands of the Bismarck Archipelago are New Britain, New Ireland and Manus. Bougainville is the largest of the Solomon Islands within Papua New Guinea.

Papua New Guinea lies within the tropics and has a typically monsoonal climate. Temperature and humidity are uniformly high throughout the year.

## HISTORY AND POLITICS

In 1884 a British protectorate, British New Guinea, was proclaimed over the southern coast of New Guinea (Papua) and the adjacent islands, which were annexed outright in 1888. In 1906 the territory was placed under the authority of Australia. The northern areas were under German administration between 1884 and 1914, when they were occupied by Australian troops and in 1921 became a League of Nations mandate administered by Australia. The territories were occupied by Japan between 1942 and 1945.

From 1970 there was a gradual assumption of powers by the Papua New Guinea government, culminating in formal self-government in December 1973. Papua New Guinea achieved full independence within the Commonwealth on 16 September 1975.

Following elections in June 1997, a coalition government was formed, which was led by the People's Progress Party (PPP).

On 14 March 2001 there was a mutiny by disaffected troops angry at defence cuts and poor equipment and living conditions, who demanded the resignation of the government. The mutineers were granted an amnesty after they peacefully surrendered their weapons on 26 March.

### INSURGENCIES

Following a 1989 insurrection, the Bougainville Revolutionary Army (BRA) declared an independent republic in May 1990. Government forces returned to the island in October 1992, subsequently capturing 90 per cent of rebel-held territory.

A permanent cease-fire came into effect on 30 April 1998, bringing to an end the nine-year civil war. A small group of rebels led by Francis Ona vowed to continue the armed campaign for an independent Bougainville. An interim Bougainville Reconciliation Government was established on 1 January 1999, which renamed itself the Bougainville People's Congress in April. Elections were held in early May. Joseph Kabui, a former rebel leader, was elected president.

Agreement was reached on 26 January 2001 that a referendum on the future of Bougainville should be held within 15 years. The BRA surrendered its weapons during May and a final agreement was reached on 24 June 2001, which granted Bougainville its own system of criminal law, and a separate police force and limited the role of the military.

### POLITICAL SYSTEM

Elections are held every five years. The National Parliament comprises 109 elected members, 20 from regional electorates, the remainder from open electorates. The Governor-General is appointed by parliament for a six-year term. Provincial governments were abolished in August 1995, and replaced with councils combining local and national politicians and headed by an appointed governor.

*Governor-General*, HE Sir Sailas Atopare, GCMG, *appointed* 14 November 1997

NATIONAL EXECUTIVE COUNCIL *as at July 2001*

*Prime Minister, Treasury*, Sir Mekere Morauta, KBE
*Deputy Prime Minister, Forests*, Michael Ogio, CBE
*Agriculture and Livestock*, Muki Taranupi
*Bougainville Affairs*, Moi Avei
*Civil Aviation*, John Tekwie
*Communications and High Technology*, John Kamb
*Correctional Institution Services*, Henry Smith
*Culture and Tourism*, Sir Pita Lus, KBE
*Defence*, Kilroy Genia
*Education*, Prof. John Waiko
*Environment and Conservation*, Herowa Agiwa
*Finance, Planning and Rural Development*, Andrew Kumbakor
*Fisheries*, Ron Ganarafo
*Foreign Affairs*, John Pundari
*Health*, Assik Tomscoll
*Home Affairs*, William Ebenosi
*Housing*, Ludger Mond
*Justice*, Puri Ruing
*Labour and Employment*, Chris Haiveta
*Lands and Physical Planning*, Charlie Benjamin
*Mining*, Peter Ipatas
*Petroleum and Energy*, Roy Yaki
*Police*, Jimson Sauk
*Prime Minister's Office, Multilateral Financial Relationships*, Sir John Kaputin, KBE, CMG
*Privatisation and Corporatisation*, Vincent Auali
*Provincial and Local Government*, Iairo Lasaro
*Public Service*, Philemon Embel, OBE
Iairo Lasaro
*Rural Development*, William Ebenosi
*Trade and Industry*, Tukape Masane
*Transport and Works*, Alfred Pogo

PAPUA NEW GUINEA HIGH COMMISSION
3rd Floor, 14 Waterloo Place, London SW1R 4AR
Tel: 020-7930 0922/7
*High Commissioner*, HE Sir Kina Bona, KBE, apptd 1995

BRITISH HIGH COMMISSION
PO Box 212, Waigani NCD 131, Port Moresby
Tel: (00 675) 325 1643/1645
E-mail: bhcpng@datec.com.pg
*High Commissioner*, HE Simon Mansfield Scadden, apptd 2000

## ECONOMY

A variety of commercial agricultural developments co-exist with the traditional rural economy. In 1995, the government initiated an austerity programme intended to reduce the budget deficit, privatise state assets and eliminate trade tariffs. Following prolonged drought and the financial crisis in south-east Asia, the country is facing its worst financial crisis since independence, with debt servicing amounting to a quarter of government spending.

There are extensive mineral deposits throughout Papua New Guinea, including copper, gold, silver, nickel, bauxite and commercial deposits of oil. The Bougainville copper mine, run by the Anglo-Australian consortium Rio Tinto, closed indefinitely in 1989 because of the unrest on the island. It had provided more than 15 per cent of the country's annual revenue. On 7 September 2000, land-owners on Bougainville filed a damages claim against Rio Tinto, alleging that the company had caused environmental, social and health damage in its running of the mine and that the company had effectively controlled the Papuan military in its operations on Bougainville, which, it was claimed, had resulted in 15,000 civilian deaths.
Industry includes processing of primary products, and brewing, packaging, paint, plywood, and metal manufacturing and the construction industries. A mini-budget was announced in August 1999, which aimed to raise revenue by raising taxes and reducing expenditure.

In 1999 there was a trade surplus of US$856 million and a current account surplus of US$95 million. Imports totalled US$1,188 million and exports US$1,877 million.

GNP – US$3,834 million (1999); US$800 per capita (1999)
GDP – US$4,639 million (1997); US$756 per capita (1998)
ANNUAL AVERAGE GROWTH OF GDP – 3.9 per cent (1999)
INFLATION RATE – 14.9 per cent (1999)
TOTAL EXTERNAL DEBT – US$2,692 million (1998)

| *Trade with UK* | 1999 | 2000 |
|---|---|---|
| Imports from UK | £7,498,000 | £5,374,000 |
| Exports to UK | 47,941,000 | 56,144,000 |

## COMMUNICATIONS

Air Niugini operates regular air services to other countries in the region, as well as internal air services. Several shipping companies operate cargo services to Australia, Europe, the Far East and USA. There are very limited cargo and passenger services between Papua New Guinea main ports, outports, plantations and missions. There are 21,433 km of roads, the most important road being that linking Lae with the populous highlands. Papua New Guinea is linked by international cable to Australia, Guam, Hong Kong, the Far East and the USA.

---

# PARAGUAY
*República del Paraguay*

---

AREA – 157,048 sq. miles (406,752 sq. km). Neighbours: Bolivia (north-west), Brazil (north-east and east), Argentina (south)
POPULATION – 5,359,000 (1997 UN estimate): 95 per cent mestizo. Spanish is the official language of the country but outside the larger towns Guaraní, the language of the largest single group of Amerindian inhabitants, is widely spoken, and is also an official language
CAPITAL – Asunción (population, 718,690)
MAJOR CITIES – Ciudad del Este (133,881); San Lorenzo (133,395)
CURRENCY – Guaraní (Gs) of 100 céntimos
NATIONAL ANTHEM – Paraguayos, República O Muerte (Paraguayans, republic or death)
NATIONAL DAY – 15 May
NATIONAL FLAG – Three horizontal bands, red, white, blue with the National seal on the obverse white band and the Treasury seal on the reverse white band
LIFE EXPECTANCY (years) – male 69.6; female 74.1
POPULATION GROWTH RATE – 2.7 per cent (1999)
POPULATION DENSITY – 13 per sq. km (1998)
URBAN POPULATION – 56.0 per cent (2000 estimate)
MILITARY EXPENDITURE – 1.4 per cent of GDP (1999)
MILITARY PERSONNEL – 20,200: Army 14,900, Navy 3,600, Air Force 1,700; Paramilitaries 14,800
CONSCRIPTION DURATION – One to two years

Paraguay is an inland subtropical state of South America, situated between Argentina, Bolivia and Brazil. It is a country of grassy plains and forested hills. In the angle formed by the Paraná-Paraguay confluence are extensive marshes, one of which, known as Neembucú (or endless) is drained by Lake Ypoa, a large lagoon south-east of the capital. The Chaco, lying between the rivers Paraguay and Pilcomayo and bounded on the north by Bolivia, is a flat plain, rising uniformly towards its western boundary to a height of 1,140 feet; it suffers much from floods and still more from drought, but the building of dams and reservoirs has converted part of it into good pasture for cattle.

## HISTORY AND POLITICS

Paraguay was settled as a Spanish possession in 1537 and became independent in 1811.

Gen. Alfredo Stroessner, dictator from 1954, was overthrown in February 1989 by Gen. Andrés Rodríguez, who was elected president in May 1989. Elections to the parliament were held in December 1991. Amendments to the constitution came into effect in June 1992. The last presidential and legislative elections were held on 10 May 1998. The presidential election was won by Raúl Cubas Grau of the Colorado Party, after its original candidate Gen. Lino Oviedo was banned from standing in elections for his part in a failed coup in 1996. In the legislative election, the distribution of seats in the Senate was: Colorado Party (CP) 24; Democratic Alliance (DA) 20; Blanco Party 1. In the Chamber of Deputies, the CP won 45 seats and the DA 35.

Vice-President Luis María Argaña was assassinated on 23 March 1999, following a power struggle between his supporters and those of President Cubas Grau and Gen. Oviedo. Supporters of Argaña demanded the resignation of the president and an indefinite general strike was called. The Chamber of Deputies voted to initiate impeachment proceedings against President Cubas Grau. He resigned on 28 March and was granted asylum in Brazil. The president of the Senate, Luis González Macchi, was immediately sworn in as the new president. Gen. Oviedo fled to Argentina, where he was granted asylum, but in December fled to Brazil. An attempted coup, thought to be by supporters of Gen. Oviedo, was foiled by government forces on 18 May 2000. Gen. Oviedo was arrested in Brazil on 11 June 2000 pending extradition proceedings.

A vice-presidential election was held on 13 August 2000 and was won by Julio César Franco of the Authentic Radical Liberal Party.

### POLITICAL SYSTEM

The constitution provides for a two-chamber legislature consisting of a 45-member Senate and an 80-member Chamber of Deputies, both elected for five-year terms. Deputies are elected on a regional basis, the number of seats allocated to each regional department being directly proportional to the department's population. Voting is compulsory for all citizens over 18. The president is elected for a five-year term and may not be re-elected. The vice-president may only contest the presidency if he resigns his post six months before the election. The president appoints the Cabinet, which exercises all the functions of government.

### HEAD OF STATE

*President*, Luis González Macchi, *sworn in* 28 March 1999
*Vice-President*, Julio César Franco

### CABINET *as at July 2001*

*Agriculture and Livestock*, Pedro Lino Morel
*Defence*, Adm. Miguel Angel Candia
*Education and Culture*, Dario Zárate Arellano
*Executive Secretary of the Technical Secretariat of Planning and Economic and Social Development of the Republic*, Luis Alberto Meyer
*Finance and Economy*, Francisco Oviedo
*Foreign Affairs*, José Antonio Moreno Ruffinelli
*Industry and Commerce*, Euclides Acevedo
*Interior*, Julio César Fanego
*Justice and Labour*, Silvio Ferreira
*Public Health and Social Welfare*, Martín Chiola
*Public Works, Communications*, Alcides Jiménez
*Secretary for Women's Affairs*, Cristina Muñoz

### EMBASSY OF PARAGUAY

Braemar Lodge, Cornwall Gardens, London SW7 4AQ
Tel: 020-7937 1253/6629
*Ambassador Extraordinary and Plenipotentiary*, Raúl Dos Santos, apptd 1998

### BRITISH EMBASSY

Avda. Boggiani 5848, C/R 16 Boquerón, Asunción
Tel: (00 595) (21) 612611
E-mail: brembasu@rieder.net.py
*Ambassador Extraordinary and Plenipotentiary and Consul-General*, HE Anthony Cantor, apptd 2001

## ECONOMY

President Rodríguez introduced an economic liberalisation programme which has been continued by subsequent governments. In November 2000, Congress approved a privatisation programme. This has reduced foreign debt and attracted foreign investment, notably from Brazil. About half of the population are engaged in agriculture and cattle raising. Cassava, sugar cane, soya, cotton and wheat are the main agricultural products. The forests contain many varieties of timber which find a good market abroad. Paraguay's rivers give it considerable hydroelectric capacity. There is a hydroelectric power station at Acaray which exports surplus power to Argentina and Brazil. Joint projects have been undertaken with Brazil, on a hydroelectric dam at Itaipú (the largest in the world), and with Argentina, at Yacyretá.

GNP – US$8,374 million (1999); US$1,580 per capita (1999)
GDP – US$9,979 million (1997); US$1,629 per capita (1998)
ANNUAL AVERAGE GROWTH OF GDP – 1.3 per cent (1996)
INFLATION RATE – 6.8 per cent (1999)
UNEMPLOYMENT – 8.2 per cent (1996)
TOTAL EXTERNAL DEBT – US$2,304 million (1998)

### TRADE

The chief imports are machinery, fuels and lubricants, vehicles, drinks and tobacco. The chief exports are soya, cotton fibres, meat, timber and coffee. The main trading partners are Brazil, Argentina and the USA.

In 1998 Paraguay had a trade deficit of US$114 million and a current account deficit of US$106 million. In 1997 imports totalled US$3,403 million and exports US$1,089 million.

| *Trade with UK* | 1999 | 2000 |
|---|---|---|
| Imports from UK | £30,460,000 | £24,144,000 |
| Exports to UK | 672,000 | 1,265,000 |

## COMMUNICATIONS

There are direct shipping services from Asunción to Europe and the USA, and river steamer services for internal transport. Eight airlines operate services from Asunción. There are 28,900 km of roads in Paraguay, connecting Asunción with São Paulo via the Bridge of Friendship and Foz de Yguazú, and with Buenos Aires via Puerto Pilcomayo. Many earth roads are liable to be closed or to become impassable in wet weather. There are 441 km of railway track. Rail services, with train ferries, provide internal and international links. Five daily and six weekly newspapers are published in Asunción.

## EDUCATION

Education is free and compulsory. There are 11 universities and one institute of education.
ILLITERACY RATE – 6.7 per cent

ENROLMENT (percentage of age group) – primary 91 per cent (1996); secondary 38 per cent (1996); tertiary 10.3 per cent (1996)

## PERU
*República del Perú*

AREA – 496,225 sq. miles (1,285,216 sq. km). Neighbours: Ecuador and Colombia (north), Brazil and Bolivia (east), Chile (south)
POPULATION – 25,230,000 (1999 estimate): 50 per cent Amerindian, 40 per cent mestizo, 7 per cent European, also Africans, Chinese and Japanese. The official languages are Spanish and Quechua. Aymara is also widely spoken
CAPITAL – Lima (including ΨCallao, population, 7,200,936, 1993 census)
MAJOR CITIES – Arequipa (624,500); Chiclayo (448,400); Chimbote (314,700); Trujillo (521,200)
CURRENCY – New Sol of 100 cénts
NATIONAL ANTHEM – Somos Libres, Seámoslo Siempre (We are free, let us remain so forever)
NATIONAL DAY – 28 July (Anniversary of Independence)
NATIONAL FLAG – Three vertical stripes of red, white, red
LIFE EXPECTANCY (years) – male 65.6; female 69.1
POPULATION GROWTH RATE – 1.6 per cent (1999)
POPULATION DENSITY – 19 per sq. km (1998)
URBAN POPULATION – 72.8 per cent (2000 estimate)
MILITARY EXPENDITURE - 1.6 per cent of GDP (1999)
MILITARY PERSONNEL - 115,000: Army 75,000, Navy 25,000, Air Force 15,000; Paramilitaries 77,000
CONSCRIPTION DURATION - Two years (selective)

The country is traversed throughout its length by the Andes, running parallel to the Pacific coast. There are three main regions, the Costa, west of the Andes, the Sierra or mountain ranges of the Andes, which include the Punas or mountainous wastes below the region of perpetual snow, and the Montaña or Selva, which is the vast area of jungle stretching from the eastern foothills of the Andes to the eastern frontiers of Peru. The coastal area, lying upon and near the Pacific, is not tropical though close to the Equator, being cooled by the Humboldt Current.

### HISTORY AND POLITICS

Peru was conquered in the early 16th century by Francisco Pizarro (1478–1541). He subjugated the Incas (the ruling caste of the Quechua Indians), who had started their rise to power some 500 years earlier, and for nearly three centuries Peru remained under Spanish rule. A revolutionary war of 1821–4 established its independence, declared on 28 July 1821. A military junta ruled Peru from 1968 until 1980 when civilian government was restored.

In April 1992 President Fujimori, faced with increasing terrorist violence, suspended the constitution, dissolved Congress and began to govern by decree. In November 1992 a legislative election was held to an 80-seat Democratic Constituent Congress (CCD) which was installed as an interim legislature and constituent assembly to write a new constitution. Parties supporting Fujimori's suspension of the constitution gained a majority in the CCD. In January 1993, the 1979 constitution was re-established and the CCD declared Fujimori constitutional head of state. The CCD produced a new constitution which was endorsed in a national referendum in October 1993.

Parliamentary and presidential elections were held on 9 April 1995, with President Fujimori winning the first round of the presidential election outright and his Cambio 90-Nueva Mayoría Party winning 67 out of 120 seats in the new *Congreso de la República* (Congress of the Republic).

President Fujimori announced in December 1999 that he would run for a third term of office. Following objections by the opposition, the National Elections Board ruled that Fujimori had been elected president only once since the introduction of the 1993 constitution and was therefore eligible to stand again. President Fujimori was unable to win the first round of the presidential election on 9 April 2000 outright, but polled the most votes. In the simultaneous legislative election, his Peru 2000 alliance won 51 seats, losing its absolute majority. The Peru Possible party won 28 seats and the Moralising Independent Front won nine seats. In the second round of the presidential election on 28 May, President Fujimori was re-elected with 51.2 per cent of the vote after his opponent, Alejandro Toledo of the Peru Possible party refused to campaign, following accusations of widespread ballot rigging in the first round. Although voting was compulsory, Toledo asked his supporters to spoil their ballot papers; he gained 17.7 per cent of the votes and 31.1 per cent of ballot papers were spoiled. The chief of the Organisation of American States observer mission concluded that the entire electoral process had been irregular.

President Fujimori announced on 16 September 2000 that he intended to step down and call a presidential election in which he would not stand. Following his attendance at an APEC summit in Brunei, Fujimori fled to Japan and announced his resignation on 17 November. Congress voted on 21 November to reject Fujimori's resignation and instead dismissed him on the grounds of moral incapacity, and Valentín Paniagua of the Popular Action party was sworn in as interim president the following day.

A general election was held on 8 April 2001 in which the Peru Possible (PP) party won 43 seats and the Peruvian Aprista Party (APRA) won 28 seats. The presidential election was held in two rounds on 8 April and 3 June and was won by the PP candidate, Alejandro Toledo, who was sworn in as president on 28 July, becoming the first Amerindian to hold the position.

#### FOREIGN RELATIONS

A 78-km stretch of the border with Ecuador has been in dispute since 1960. In 1995 an inconclusive border war was fought between the two countries, and in July 1995 a demilitarised zone was established around the disputed area. Four guarantor countries (Argentina, Brazil, Chile and the USA) adjudicated the claims of both countries and produced an agreement which was signed on 26 October 1998 by the presidents of Ecuador and Peru, formally ending the dispute.

#### INSURGENCIES

Since the late 1970s the government has faced violence from drug organisations and insurgencies from two leftist guerrilla movements, the Maoist Sendero Luminoso (Shining Path) and the Movimiento Revolucionario Túpac Amaru (MRTA), with fighting having left 30,000 dead.

Security forces captured the leader of the MRTA in November 1998 and the leader of Shining Path in December 1998.

#### POLITICAL SYSTEM

The constitution, promulgated in December 1993, provides for the president to be able to serve two terms rather than one, as previously; the introduction of the death penalty for treason; and the formation of a new 120-member unicameral Congress. A constitutional panel approved a Bill in August 1996, allowing President Fujimori to stand for a third term in office.

HEAD OF STATE

*President of the Republic*, Alejandro Toledo Manrique, *elected* 3 June 2001, *sworn in* 28 July 2001
*First Vice-President*, vacant
*Second Vice-President*, vacant

CABINET *as at August 2001*

*Prime Minister*, Roberto Dañino
*Agriculture*, Alvaro Enrique Quijanda Salmon
*Defence*, David Waisman
*Economy and Finance*, Pedro Pablo Kuczynski
*Education*, Nicolás Javier Lynch Gamero
*Energy and Mines*, Jaime Quijandria Salmon
*Fisheries*, Javier Edmundo Reategui
*Foreign Affairs*, Diego García Sayan
*Health*, Luis María Solari de la Fuente
*Industry, Tourism, Integration and International Commerce*, Raúl Diez Canseco
*Interior*, Fernando Miguel Rospigliosi
*Justice*, Fernando Olivera Vega
*Labour and Social Promotion*, Fernando Villarán
*Presidency*, Carlos Ricardo Bruce
*Promotion of Women's Affairs and Human Development*, Doris Sánchez
*Transport, Communications, Housing and Construction*, Luis Vicente Chang Reyes

EMBASSY OF PERU
52 Sloane Street, London SW1X 9SP
Tel: 020-7235 1917/2545/3802
*Ambassador Extraordinary and Plenipotentiary*, HE Gilbert Chauny de Porturas Hoyle, apptd 2000

BRITISH EMBASSY
Edificio El Pacifico Washington, Piso 12, Plaza Washington, Avenida Arequipa (PO Box 854), Lima 100
Tel: (00 51) (1) 433 4738/4839
E-mail: britemb@terra.com.pe
*Ambassador Extraordinary and Plenipotentiary*, HE Roger Dudley Hart, CMG, apptd 1999

CONSULAR OFFICE – Lima
HONORARY CONSULATES – Arequipa, Cusco, Iquitos, Piura, Trujillo

BRITISH COUNCIL DIRECTOR, Gail Liesching, Calle Alberto Lynch 110, San Isidro, Lima 27; e-mail: bc.lima@britishcouncil.org.pe
BRITISH-PERUVIAN CHAMBER OF COMMERCE, Parque Francisco Grana 200, Magdalena

## ECONOMY

The chief products of the coastal belt are cotton, sugar and petroleum. There are large tracts of land suitable for cultivation and stock-raising (cattle, sheep, llamas, alpacas and vicuñas) on the eastern slopes of the Andes, and in the mountain valleys maize, potatoes and wheat are grown. The jungle area is a source of timber and petroleum. Other major crops are fruit, vegetables, rice, barley, grapes and coffee. The mountains contain rich mineral deposits and mineral exports include lead, zinc, copper, iron ore and silver. Peru is normally the world's largest exporter of fishmeal.

Since 1990 the government has launched a radical free-market restructuring programme which has rebuilt the foreign exchange reserves, reduced inflation from 7,600 per cent a year in 1990 to four per cent in 1999, cut subsidies and import tariffs, freed interest rates and privatised most state firms. Foreign investment has been encouraged and has grown dramatically. The economic recovery has increased the gap between rich and poor.

Following a slowdown in economic growth, falling output, rising unemployment and a decline in the popularity of the government, further privatisation has been halted.

GNP – US$53,705 million (1999); US$2,390 per capita (1999)
GDP – US$65,169 million (1997); US$2,521 per capita (1998)
ANNUAL AVERAGE GROWTH OF GDP – 2.5 per cent (1996)
INFLATION RATE – 3.5 per cent (1999)
UNEMPLOYMENT – 7.8 per cent (1998)
TOTAL EXTERNAL DEBT – US$32,397 million (1998)

TRADE

The principal imports are machinery, chemicals and pharmaceutical products. The chief exports are minerals and metals, fishmeal, sugar, cotton and coffee.

In 1998 Peru had a trade deficit of US$2,465 million and a current account deficit of US$3,800 million. In 1997 imports totalled US$10,264 million and exports US$6,841 million.

| *Trade with UK* | 1999 | 2000 |
|---|---|---|
| Imports from UK | £48,677,000 | £45,975,000 |
| Exports to UK | 132,403,000 | 142,472,000 |

## COMMUNICATIONS

There are 73,766 km of roads, of which 16,876 km are unsurfaced. The Andean Highway forms a link between the Pacific, the Amazon and the Atlantic. The Pan-American Highway runs along the Peruvian coast connecting it with Ecuador and Chile.

The railway is administered by the government. There are 1,992 km of railway track. There is also steam navigation on the Ucayali and Huallaga, and in the south on Lake Titicaca. Air services are maintained throughout Peru, and there is an international airport at Lima.

## EDUCATION

Education is compulsory and free between seven and 16. There are 51 universities.
ILLITERACY RATE – 10.1 per cent (2000)
ENROLMENT (percentage of age group) – primary 91 per cent (1997); secondary 55 per cent (1997); tertiary 26 per cent (1997)

---

# THE PHILIPPINES
*Repúblika ng Pilipinas*

---

AREA – 115,831 sq. miles (300,000 sq. km)
POPULATION – 76,785,000 (1997 UN estimate). The inhabitants are of Malay stock, with admixtures of Spanish and Chinese blood in many localities. The Chinese minority is estimated at 500,000, with smaller numbers of Spanish, American and Indian. About 90 per cent are Christian, predominantly Roman Catholics. Most of the remainder are Muslims or indigenous animists. The official languages are Filipino and English. Filipino is based on Tagalog, one of the Malay–Polynesian languages. English, the language of government, is spoken by at least 44 per cent of the population. Spanish is now spoken by a very small minority
CAPITAL – ΨManila (population, 8,594,150, 1994)
MAJOR CITIES – Bacolod (402,345); ΨCebu (662,299); ΨDavao (1,008,640); ΨIloilo (334,539); ΨZamboanga (511,139), 1995 UN estimates
CURRENCY – Philippine peso (P) of 100 centavos
NATIONAL ANTHEM – Lupang Hinirang

NATIONAL DAY – 12 June (Independence Day 1898)
NATIONAL FLAG – Equal horizontal bands of blue (above) and red; gold sun with three stars on a white triangle next staff
LIFE EXPECTANCY (years) – male 64.1; female 69.3
POPULATION GROWTH RATE – 2.3 per cent (1999)
POPULATION DENSITY – 251 per sq. km (1998)
URBAN POPULATION – 58.6 per cent (2000 estimate)

There are 11 larger islands and 7,079 other islands. The principal islands (area in sq. km) are: Luzon (104,688); Mindanao (94,630); Samar (13,080); Negros (12,710); Palawan (11,785); Panay (11,515); Mindoro (9,735); Leyte (7,214); Cebu (4,422); Bohol (3,865); Masbate (3,269). Other groups are the Sulu islands (capital, Jolo), Babuyanes and Batanes; the Calamian islands; and Kalayaan Islands.

## HISTORY AND POLITICS

The Philippines were conquered by Spain in 1565 and named Filipinas after Philip II of Spain. Independence was declared on 12 June 1898. In the Spanish–American War of 1898, Manila was captured by American troops and remained under US control until 1946. The Republic of the Philippines came into existence on 4 July 1946.

Ferdinand Marcos was president from 1965 to 1986, when he was forced from power by Corazón Aquino, who took over as president and survived seven coup attempts. Fidel Ramos was elected president in May 1992 and was succeeded by Joseph Estrada, the former Vice-President, in May 1998.

The House of Representatives voted on 13 November 2000 to initiate impeachment proceedings against President Estrada, accusing him of corruption. The trial began on 7 December 2000 in the Senate, but foundered on 16 January 2001 after senators refused to consider evidence which allegedly proved Estrada's guilt, and the trial was indefinitely adjourned on the following day. Up to 500,000 demonstrators, led by Vice-President Gloria Macapagal-Arroyo and supported by former presidents Corazón Aquino and Fidel Ramos, gathered in Manila and called on Estrada to resign. On 19 January, the armed forces announced that they had withdrawn their support from the president and on 20 January the Supreme Court ruled that the presidency was vacant, thus allowing Macapagal-Arroyo to be sworn in. Her legitimacy as president was confirmed by the Supreme Court on 2 March.

Elections were held for the House of Representatives and 13 of the 24 Senate seats on 14 May 2001.

### INSURGENCIES

On 2 September 1996, the government signed an agreement with the Moro National Liberation Front (MNLF) on the creation of an autonomous Muslim region in Mindanao, Palawan, Sulu and Basilan, ending a 24-year rebellion which had left more than 120,000 people dead. The Moro Islamic Liberation Front (MILF), a radical breakaway group, threatened to disrupt the agreement. The Communist New People's Army (NPA) maintains a presence in eastern Mindanao, Negros, Samar, Bicol, the mountains of northern Luzon and Bataan. The NPA signed a cease-fire agreement with the government in December 1993; peace talks were suspended in February 1999. On 23 April 2000, 21 people, including ten foreign tourists, were kidnapped on the Malaysian island of Sipadan and taken to the Philippine island of Jolo by Abu Sayyaf, an Islamic rebel group.

The army captured the MILF military headquarters on 9 July 2000, following which MILF withdrew from peace talks scheduled for August. After military action against MILF was formally ended on 6 February 2001, MILF declared a cease-fire on 3 April and negotiations with the government led to a comprehensive peace deal which came into effect on 22 June.

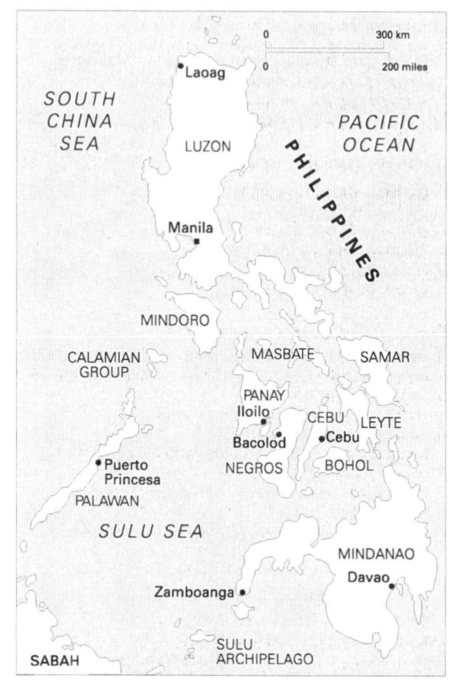


### POLITICAL SYSTEM

A new constitution came into force in July 1987. Legislative authority is vested in a bicameral Congress. The House of Representatives has 250 members, of whom 204 are directly elected and 46 appointed by the President for a three-year term. The Senate has 24 members, of whom 12 are re-elected every three years.

The Autonomous Region of Mindanao consists of four provinces: Sulu, Tawitawi, Lanao del Sur and Maguinadanao. There is a 24-member regional assembly and a governor.

### HEAD OF STATE

*President*, Gloria Macapagal Arroyo, *assumed office* 20 January 2001
*Vice-President, Foreign Affairs*, Teofisto Guingona

### CABINET *as at July 2001*

*Agrarian Reform*, Hernani Braganza
*Agriculture*, Leonardo Montemayor
*Budget and Management*, Emilia Boncodin
*Defence*, Gen. Angelo Reyes
*Education, Culture and Sport*, Raúl Roco
*Energy*, Vicente Perez
*Environment and Natural Resources*, Heherson Álvarez
*Executive Secretary*, Alberto Romulo
*Finance*, José Isidro Camacho
*Health*, Manuel Dayrit
*Housing*, Michael Defensor
*Interior and Local Government*, José Lina
*Justice*, Hernando Perez
*Labour and Employment*, Patricia Santo Tomás
*Presidential Advisor for Special Concerns*, Norberto Gonzales
*Public Works and Highways*, Simeon Datumanong

*Science and Technology*, Estrella Alabastro
*Social Welfare and Development*, Corazón Solimon
*Socio-economic Planning*, Dante Canlas
*Tourism*, Richard Gordon
*Trade and Industry*, Manuel Roxas
*Transportation and Communications*, Pantaleon Álvarez

EMBASSY OF THE PHILIPPINES
9A Palace Green, London W8 4QE
Tel: 020-7937 1600
*Ambassador Extraordinary and Plenipotentiary*, HE César Bautista, apptd 1999
*Defence Attaché*, Capt. F. Angue
*Commercial Attaché*, V. Casim

BRITISH EMBASSY
Floors 15–17 LV Locsin Building, 6752 Ayala Avenue, Corner Makati Avenue, 1226 Makati, Metro Manila (PO Box 2927 MCPO)
Tel: (00 63) (2) 816 7116
E-mail: bremb@skyin.net
*Ambassador Extraordinary and Plenipotentiary*, HE Alan Collins, CMG, apptd 1998

BRITISH COUNCIL DIRECTOR, Rodney Bell, 10th Floor, Taipan Place, Emerald Avenue, Ortigas Centre, Pasig City 1605, Metro Manila; e-mail: britishcouncil@britishcouncil.org.ph

## DEFENCE

The Army has 85 armoured infantry fighting vehicles and 360 armoured personnel carriers. The Navy has one frigate and 60 patrol and coastal vessels at three bases. The Air Force has 47 combat aircraft and 97 armed helicopters.
MILITARY EXPENDITURE – 2.1 per cent of GDP (1999)
MILITARY PERSONNEL – 106,000: Army 66,000, Navy 24,000, Air Force 16,000, Paramilitaries 42,500

## ECONOMY

In 1998, 39.8 per cent of the workforce were engaged in agriculture and in 1997, it accounted for 19.9 per cent of GDP. The chief products are rice, coconuts, sugar cane, bananas, maize and pineapples. There are an increasing number of manufacturing industries and it is the policy of the government to diversify the economy. There are also deposits of copper, coal, gold, silver, chromium, iron and nickel.

The Philippines has been bypassed by the economic growth of most of the rest of south-east Asia since the 1960s, mainly because of the incompetence and corruption of the Marcos regime. Recently, however, an economic reform programme of liberalisation, privatisation and deregulation has been put in place and has led to increased exports, increased foreign investment, and a reduction in inflation. In July 1998, the Bank of the Philippines effectively devalued the peso following attacks from speculators, prompted by the devaluation of the Thai baht. In December 1997, the government unveiled an austerity plan cutting spending by 25 per cent. Prompt and firm measures from the government are credited with limiting the damage caused by the regional economic crisis.

GNP – US$77,967 million (1999); US$1,020 per capita (1999)
GDP – US$82,238 million (1997); US$894 per capita (1998)
ANNUAL AVERAGE GROWTH OF GDP – 5.5 per cent (1996)
INFLATION RATE – 6.7 per cent (1999)
UNEMPLOYMENT – 7.7 per cent (1998)
TOTAL EXTERNAL DEBT – US$47,817 million (1998)

### TRADE

Principal exports are electronic products, machinery and transport equipment, clothing, coconut oil and products, and minerals. Principal imports are fuelstuffs and oils, electronic goods and components, machinery, base metals, transport equipment, textiles and yarns, and cereals. The major trading partners are the USA, Japan, Singapore and Hong Kong.

In 1999 the Philippines had a trade surplus of US$4,962 million and a current account surplus of US$7,912 million. Imports totalled US$31,168 million and exports US$32,188 million.

| *Trade with UK* | 1999 | 2000 |
|---|---|---|
| Imports from UK | £241,165,000 | £274,282,000 |
| Exports to UK | 1,024,775,000 | 1,194,163,000 |

## COMMUNICATIONS

The highway system covers about 187,000 km. The Philippine National Railway operates 429 km of track. There are 415 ports. There are 82 national airports and 137 privately operated airports. Philippine Airlines has regular flights throughout the Far East, to the USA and Europe, in addition to inter-island services.

## EDUCATION

Secondary and higher education is extensive and there are 21 public and 53 private universities recognised by the government, including the Dominican University of Santo Tomás (founded in 1611). There are also 530 other institutions of higher education.
ILLITERACY RATE – 4.6 per cent
ENROLMENT (percentage of age group) – primary 100 per cent (1996); secondary 59 per cent (1996); tertiary 29.0 per cent (1996)

---

# POLAND
*Rzeczpospolita Polska*

---

AREA – 124,808 sq. miles (323,250 sq. km). Neighbours: the Russian Federation (Kaliningrad) (north), Germany (west), the Czech Republic and Slovakia (south), Belarus, Ukraine and Lithuania (east)
POPULATION – 38,695,000 (1997). Roman Catholicism is the religion of 95 per cent of the inhabitants. The language is Polish; there are German, Ukrainian and Belarusian minorities
CAPITAL – Warsaw (population, 1,625,930, 1997 estimate), on the Vistula
MAJOR CITIES – Bydgoszcz (386,551); ΨGdańsk (Danzig) (462,120); Katowice (350,284); Kraków (739,876); Łódź (815,271); Poznań (579,965); ΨSzczecin (Stettin) (418,673); Wrocław (Breslau) (640,509), 1997 estimates
CURRENCY – Złoty of 100 groszy
NATIONAL ANTHEM – Jeszcze Polska Nie Zginęla (Poland has not yet perished)
NATIONAL DAY – 3 May
NATIONAL FLAG – Equal horizontal stripes of white (above) and red
LIFE EXPECTANCY (years) – male 67.9; female 76.6
POPULATION GROWTH RATE – 0.2 per cent (1999)
POPULATION DENSITY – 120 per sq. km (1998)
URBAN POPULATION – 65.6 per cent (2000 estimate)

## HISTORY AND POLITICS

The Polish Commonwealth ceased to exist in 1795 after three successive partitions in 1772, 1793 and 1795 in which Prussia, Russia and Austria shared. The Republic of Poland was proclaimed at Warsaw in November 1918, and its independence guaranteed by the signatories of the Treaty of Versailles.

German forces invaded Poland on 1 September 1939; on 17 September, Russian forces invaded eastern Poland, and on 21 September 1939 Poland was declared by Germany and Russia to have ceased to exist. At the end of the war, its frontiers were redrawn; eastern Poland was ceded to the Soviet Union in return for the German territory east of the rivers Oder and Neisse. A coalition government was formed in which the Polish Workers' Party played a large part. In December 1948, the Polish Workers' Party and the Polish Socialist Party merged to form the Polish United Workers' Party (PUWP). A new constitution modelled on the Soviet constitution was adopted in 1952, and was modified in 1976.

Steep price rises in 1980 prompted strikes which forced the government to allow independent trade unions, including 'Solidarity' led by Lech Wałęsa. The unions agitated for further reforms although their activities were suspended when martial law was in force from December 1981 until July 1983.

A wave of strikes resulted in talks between Wałęsa and the PUWP early in 1989. Multiparty parliamentary elections were held in the summer of 1989, following which the PUWP ceased to be the ruling party. The post-Communist governments have introduced a market economy but economic difficulties and a fragmented parliament have led to a succession of short-lived governments.

Elections held on 21 September 1997 were won by the right-wing Solidarity Electoral Alliance (AWS), a group of 36 parties, which formed a government with the Freedom Union (UW). The AWS won 201 seats in the *Sejm* and 51 in the Senate; the UW won 60 seats in the *Sejm* and 8 in the Senate. On 6 June 2000, the UW withdrew from the government.

President Kwaśniewski was re-elected for a second term in the first round of the presidential election on 8 October 2000, gaining 53.92 per cent of the vote. A general election was due on 23 September 2001.

### Foreign Relations

In July 1997, Poland was invited to join NATO. It has also been approved by the European Commission for membership of the EU, and formal accession talks began in March 1998.

### Political System

A new constitution came into effect on 16 October 1997. The President, directly elected for a maximum of two five-year terms, appoints the Prime Minister and has the right to be consulted over the appointment of the foreign, defence and interior ministers. The National Assembly is the bicameral legislature, comprising a 460-member *Sejm* (Diet) and a Senate of 100 members. Both houses have a four-year term. The Senate is elected on a provincial basis.

### Head of State

*President*, Aleksander Kwaśniewski, *elected* 19 November 1995, *sworn in* 23 December 1995, *re-elected* 8 October 2000

### Council of Ministers *as at July 2001*

*Prime Minister*, Jerzy Buzek (AWS)
*Deputy Prime Minister, Economy, Post and Telecommunications (acting)*, Janusz Steinhoff (AWS)
*Deputy Prime Minister, Labour and Social Policy*, Longin Komołowski (AWS)
*Agriculture and Rural Development*, Artur Balazs (AWS)
*Culture and National Heritage*, Andrzej Zieliński
*Environment*, Antoni Tokarczuk (AWS)
*Finance*, Jarosław Bauc
*Foreign Affairs*, Władysław Bartoszewski
*Health*, Grzegorz Opala
*Internal Affairs and Administration*, Marek Biernacki (AWS)
*Justice*, Stanisław Iwanicki
*National Defence*, Bronisław Komorowski (AWS)
*National Education*, Edmund Wittbrodt (AWS)
*President of the Government Centre of Strategic Studies*, Jerzy Kropiwnicki (AWS)
*Science*, Andrzej Wiszniewski (AWS)
*Transport and Maritime Economy*, Jerzy Widzyk
*Treasury*, Aldona Kamela-Sowińska
*Without Portfolio*, Janusz Pałubicki (AWS) (*Special Services*)

AWS Solidarity Electoral Alliance

### Embassy of the Republic of Poland

47 Portland Place, London W1N 3AG
Tel: 020-7580 4324/9
*Ambassador Extraordinary and Plenipotentiary*, HE Stanisław Komorowski, apptd 1999

### British Embassy

No. 1 Aleje Róz, PL-00-556 Warsaw
Tel: (00 48) (22) 628 1001/5
E-mail: britemb@it.com.pl
*Ambassador Extraordinary and Plenipotentiary*, HE Michael Pakenham, CMG, apptd 2001
Honorary Consulates – Gdańsk, Katowice, Kraków, Poznań, Szczecin, Wrocław (Breslau)

British Council Director, Dr Jeremy Eyres, OBE, Al. Jerozolimskie 59, PL-00–697 Warsaw; e-mail: bc.warsaw@britishcouncil.pl. There is an office in Kraków and libraries in Białystok, Gdańsk, Katowice, Łódź, Lublin, Poznań, Szczecin, Torun and Wrocław
British Chamber of Commerce, Ul. Zimna 2, Mieśkanie 1, PL-00-138 Warsaw

## Defence

The Army has 1,704 main battle tanks, 1,405 armoured infantry fighting vehicles and 33 armoured personnel carriers. The Navy has three submarines, one destroyer, two frigates, 25 patrol and coastal vessels, 28 combat aircraft and 11 armed helicopters at five bases. The Air Force has 267 combat aircraft and ten attack helicopters.
Military Expenditure – 2.1 per cent of GDP (1999)
Military Personnel – 217,290: Army 132,750, Navy 16,860, Air Force 46,200, Paramilitaries 21,500
Conscription Duration – 12 months

## Economy

Poland is well endowed with mineral resources; there are large reserves of brown coal in central and south-western Poland and hard coal in Upper Silesia and the Wałbrzych and Lublin regions; sulphur, copper, zinc, lead, natural gas and salt are also produced.

In 1990, the government embarked upon a series of measures designed to introduce a free-market economy.

The transition to a market economy has been painful, with unemployment doubling between 1990 and 1995 and remaining high. Industrial output has improved and the rate of growth of GDP has increased although inflation remains high.

A programme is underway to modernise the agricultural sector and adapt it to the EU's common agricultural policy.

Poland's major imports are machinery and vehicles, chemical products, leather and textiles, livestock, foodstuffs, luxury goods and metal products. Its major exports are machinery and vehicles, leather and textiles, metal goods, livestock, foodstuffs, luxury goods and chemical products. Germany is Poland's main trading partner.

In 1998 there was a trade deficit of US$12,836 million and a current account deficit of US$6,901 million. In 1999 imports totalled US$45,903 million and exports US$27,397 million.

GNP – US$157,429 million (1999); US$3,960 per capita (1999)

GDP – US$135,623 million (1997); US$4,014 per capita (1999)

Annual Average Growth of GDP – 4.0 per cent (1999)

Inflation Rate – 6.7 per cent (2001)

Unemployment – 15.1 per cent (2001)

Total External Debt – US$47,708 million (1998)

| *Trade with UK* | 1999 | 2000 |
|---|---|---|
| Imports from UK | £1,179,399,000 | £1,307,364,000 |
| Exports to UK | 692,886,000 | 930,677,000 |

## EDUCATION

Elementary education (ages seven to 15) is compulsory and free. Secondary education is optional and free.

Illiteracy Rate – 0.2 per cent (2000)

Enrolment (percentage of age group) – primary 95 per cent (1996); secondary 85 per cent (1996); tertiary 24.7 per cent (1996)

## CULTURE

Polish is a western Slavonic tongue, the Latin alphabet being used.

---

# PORTUGAL
*República Portuguesa*

---

Area – 35,514 sq. miles (91,982 sq. km). Neighbour: Spain (north and east)

Population – 9,990,000 (1995); 9,833,014 (excluding the Azores and Madeira). 94 per cent of the population are Catholic. The language is Portuguese

Capital – ΨLisbon (population, 2,561,225, 1991)

Major Cities – ΨOporto (1,683,000)

Currency – Euro (€) of 100 cents/Escudo (Esc) of 100 centavos

National Anthem – A Portuguesa

National Day – 10 June

National Flag – Divided vertically into unequal parts of green and red with the national emblem over all on the line of division

Life Expectancy (years) – male 72.0; female 79.5

Population Growth Rate –0.0 per cent (1999)

Population Density – 108 per sq. km (1998)

Urban Population – 64.4 per cent (2000 estimate)

## HISTORY AND POLITICS

Portugal was a monarchy from the 12th century until 1910, when an armed rising in Lisbon drove King Manuel II into exile and a republic was set up. A period of political instability ensued until the military stepped in and abolished political parties in 1926. The constitution of 1933 gave formal expression to the corporative 'Estado Novo' (New State) which was personified by Dr Antonio Salazar, Prime Minister 1932–68. Dr Caetano succeeded Salazar as Prime Minister in 1968 but his failure to liberalise the regime or to conclude the wars in the African colonies resulted in his government's overthrow by a military coup on 25 April 1974. There was great political turmoil between April 1974 and July 1976, a period in which most of the colonies gained their independence, but with the failure of an attempted coup by the extreme left in November 1975 the situation stabilised. Full civilian government was restored in 1982.

In the general elections held on 10 October 1999, the Socialist Party was re-elected, winning 115 seats, just one seat short of a majority.

Macao, which had been a Portuguese colony since 1557, was transferred to Chinese sovereignty on 19 December 1999.

In the presidential election held on 14 January 2001, Jorge Sampaio was re-elected, gaining 55.8 per cent of the votes cast.

### Political System

Under the 1976 constitution, amended in 1982 and 1989, the President is elected for a five-year term by universal adult suffrage. The Prime Minister is designated by the largest party in the legislature. Legislative authority is vested in the 230-member Assembly of the Republic, elected by a system of proportional representation every four years. The President retains certain limited powers to dismiss the government, dissolve the Assembly or veto laws.

### Head of State

*President of the Republic*, Jorge Sampaio, *elected* 14 January 1996, *inaugurated* 9 March 1996, *re-elected* 14 January 2001

### Council of Ministers *as at July 2001*

*Prime Minister*, António Guterres
*Deputy Prime Minister, Foreign Affairs*, Jaime Gama
*Agriculture, Rural Development and Fisheries*, Luís Capoulas Santos
*Culture*, Augusto Santos Silva
*Defence*, Rui Pena
*Economy*, Luis Braga da Cruz
*Education*, Julio Pedroso
*Employment and Solidarity*, Paulo Pedroso
*Environment and Territorial Affairs*, José Sócrates Pinto de Sousa
*Finance*, Guilherme d'Oliveira Martins
*Health*, Antonio de Campos
*Infrastructure and Public Works*, Eduardo Ferro Rodrigues
*Interior*, Nuno Teixeira
*Justice*, António da Costa
*Planning*, Elisa Ferreira
*Prime Minister's Office*, António Seguro
*Science and Technology*, José Mariano Gago
*State and Administrative Reforms*, Alberto de Sousa Martins
*Youth and Sport*, José Ribeiro de Almeida

### Portuguese Embassy

11 Belgrave Square, London SW1X 8PP
Tel: 020-7235 5331
*Ambassador Extraordinary and Plenipotentiary*, José Gregório Faria, apptd 1997

### British Embassy

Rua de São Bernardo 33, P-1249-082 Lisbon
Tel: (00 351) (21) 392 4000
E-mail: consular@lisbon.mail.fco.gov.uk
*Ambassador Extraordinary and Plenipotentiary*, HE Sir John Holmes, KBE, CMB, CVO, apptd 1999

Consulate - Oporto

Honorary Consulates – Portimão, Funchal (Madeira), Ribeira Grande (Azores)

British Council Director, Robert Ness, Rua de São Marçal 174, P-1249-062 Lisbon; e-mail: lisbon.enquiries@britcounpt.org. There are also offices at Coimbra, Oporto and Parede

British Portuguese Chamber of Commerce, Rua da Estrela 8, P-1200 Lisbon

## DEFENCE

The Army has 187 main battle tanks and 374 armoured personnel carriers. The Navy has three submarines, six frigates and 30 patrol and coastal vessels at four bases. The Air Force has 51 combat aircraft.

Lisbon is the base of the NATO Iberian Atlantic Command and the USA maintains 980 personnel in mainland Portugal and on the Azores.

Military Expenditure – 2.2 per cent of GDP (1999)
Military Personnel – 44,650; Army 25,650, Navy 11,600, Air Force 7,400; Paramilitaries 45,800
Conscription Duration – Four to 12 months

## ECONOMY

The chief agricultural products are wines, dairy products, potatoes, tomatoes, maize, meat, fruits, olives, wheat, fish, cork and rice. There are extensive forests of pine, cork, eucalyptus and chestnut covering about 38 per cent of the country. Around 13 per cent of the workforce are engaged in agriculture, the highest percentage in the EU. The principal mineral products are limestone, granite, marble, copper, coal, kaolin and wolframite.

The country is moderately industrialised. The principal manufactures are motor vehicle components, clothing and footwear, textiles, machinery, pulp and paper, pharmaceuticals, foodstuffs, chemicals, fertilisers, wood, cork, furniture, cement, glassware and pottery. There are a modern steelworks and large shipbuilding and repair yards at Lisbon and Setúbal, working mainly for foreign shipowners. There are several hydroelectric power stations and two thermal power stations.

Portugal has experienced rapid economic growth since joining the EU in 1986.

Portugal was one of 11 states to adopt the European single currency on 1 January 1999.

GNP – US$110,175 million (1999); US$10,600 per capita (1999)
GDP – US$101,288 million (1997); US$11,438 per capita (1999)
Annual Average Growth of GDP – 3.4 per cent (2000)
Inflation Rate – 4.8 per cent (2001)
Unemployment – 4.5 per cent (2001)

### Trade

The principal imports are machinery, vehicles, textiles, clothing and shoes, agricultural products, chemicals, oil and base metals. The principal exports are textiles, clothing and shoes, machinery, vehicles and automobile parts, wood, pulp, paper and cork, and minerals.

In 1999 Portugal had a trade deficit of US$14,157 million and a current account deficit of US$9,004 million. Imports totalled US$38,461 million and exports US$23,864 million.

| *Trade with UK* | 1999 | 2000 |
|---|---|---|
| Imports from UK | £1,599,300,000 | £1,570,400,000 |
| Exports to UK | 1,732,200,000 | 1,655,400,000 |

## COMMUNICATIONS

There are 3,072 km of railway track , of which 461 km are electrified. There are international airports at Lisbon, Oporto, Faro and Santa Maria and Lages (Azores) and Funchal (Madeira). There are 23 daily newspapers.

## EDUCATION

Education is free and compulsory for nine years from the age of six. Secondary education is mainly conducted in state general unified schools, lyceums, technical and professional schools, but there are also private schools.

## AUTONOMOUS REGIONS

Madeira and The Azores are two administratively autonomous regions of Portugal, having locally elected assemblies and governments.

Madeira is a group of islands in the Atlantic Ocean about 520 miles south-west of Lisbon, and consists of Madeira, Porto, Santo and three uninhabited islands (Desertas). Total area is 300 sq. miles (779 sq. km); population, 257,290 (1995). ΨFunchal in Madeira, the largest island (270 sq. miles), is the capital (population 44,111)

The Azores are a group of nine islands (Flores, Corvo, Terceira, São Jorge, Pico, Faial, Graciosa, São Miguel and Santa Maria) in the Atlantic Ocean; area 895 sq. miles (2,330 sq. km); population, 241,490 (1995). ΨPonta Delgada, on São Miguel, is the capital (population, 137,700). Other ports are ΨAngra, in Terceira (55,900) and ΨHorta (16,300)

---

# QATAR

*Dawlat Qatar*

---

Area – 4,247 sq. miles (11,000 sq. km). Neighbours: United Arab Emirates (south), Saudi Arabia (south-west)
Population – 757,000 (1997 UN estimate). Most of the population is concentrated in the urban district of Doha. Arabic is the official language. Islam is the religion of 95 per cent of the population
Capital – ΨDoha (Ad-Dawhah) (population, 392,384, 1995 estimate)
Major Cities – Ar-Rayyān; Dukhān; ΨMusay'īd; Al-Wakrah
Currency – Qatar riyal of 100 dirhams
National Day – 3 September
National Flag – White and maroon, white portion nearer the mast; vertical indented line comprising 17 angles divides the colours
Life Expectancy (years) – male 71.6; female 74.6
Population Growth Rate – 2.9 per cent (1999)
Population Density – 53 per sq. km (1998)
Urban Population – 92.5 per cent (2000 estimate)
Military Expenditure – 15.4 per cent of GDP (1999)
Military Personnel – 12,330: Army 8,500, Navy 1,730, Air Force 2,100
Illiteracy Rate – 18.7 per cent
Enrolment (percentage of age group) – primary 80 per cent (1993); secondary 69 per cent (1993); tertiary 26.6 per cent (1996)

The state of Qatar covers the peninsula of Qatar in the Gulf from approximately the northern shore of Khor al Odaid to the eastern shore of Khor al Salwa.

## HISTORY AND POLITICS

Qatar was one of nine independent emirates in the Gulf in special treaty relations with the UK until 1971. On 2 April 1970, a provisional constitution for Qatar was proclaimed, providing for the establishment of a Council of Ministers and for the formation of a Consultative Council to assist the Council of Ministers in running the affairs of the state. There are no political parties or legislature; ministers are chosen by the Amir.

The Amir, who had ruled since 22 February 1972, was overthrown on 27 June 1995 by his son and heir, who assumed power as Amir the same day. A coup attempt was thwarted in February 1996.

The Amir announced in November 1998 that a committee of experts would be formed to draft a new constitution and that an elected National Assembly would be established. Municipal elections were held on 8 March 1999, the first in which women were allowed to vote and contest seats.

### FOREIGN RELATIONS

A territorial dispute between Qatar and Bahrain was settled on 16 March 2001 when the International Court of Justice awarded the Hawar islands to Bahrain and the town of Zubarah to Qatar.

### HEAD OF STATE

*HH Amir of Qatar, Minister of Defence and Commander-in-Chief of Armed Forces*, Sheikh Hamad bin Khalifa al-Thani, KCMG, *assumed power* 27 June 1995
*Crown Prince*, HH Sheikh Jassem bin Hamad al-Thani

### COUNCIL OF MINISTERS *as at September 2001*

*Prime Minister, Interior*, HH Shaikh Abdulla bin Khalifa al-Thani
*Deputy Prime Minister*, Shaikh Mohammed bin Khalifa al-Thani
*Awqaf (Religious Endowments) and Islamic Affairs*, Ahmed Abdulla al-Merri
*Civil Service Affairs and Housing*, Shaikh Falah bin Jassim al-Thani
*Communications and Transport*, Shaikh Ahmed bin Nasser al-Thani
*Education, Higher Education and Culture*, Dr Mohammed Abdulrahim Kafoud
*Energy and Industry*, Abdulla bin Hamad al-Attiyah
*Finance, Economy and Trade*, Yousef Hussein Kamal
*Foreign Affairs*, Shaikh Hamad bin Jassem bin Jabr al-Thani
*Internal Affairs*, Shaikh Abdulla bin Khalid al-Thani
*Justice*, Hassan bin Abdulla al-Ghanem
*Municipal Affairs, Agriculture*, Ali Mohammed al-Khater
*Public Health*, Dr Hajr bin Ahmed Hajr

### EMBASSY OF THE STATE OF QATAR

1 South Audley Street, London W1Y 5DQ
Tel: 020-7493 2200
*Ambassador Extraordinary and Plenipotentiary*, HE Nasser bin Hamid M. Al-Khalifa, apptd 2000

### BRITISH EMBASSY

PO Box 3, Doha
Tel: (00 974) 421991
E-mail: bembcomm@qatar.net.qa
*Ambassador Extraordinary and Plenipotentiary*, HE David Wright, OBE, apptd 1997

BRITISH COUNCIL DIRECTOR, Alan Smart, 93 Al Sadd Street, PO Box 2992, Doha; e-mail: alan.smart@qa.britishcouncil.org

## ECONOMY

Although Qatar is a desert country, there are gardens and smallholdings near Doha and to the north, and agriculture is being developed, with self-sufficiency an aim.

The Qatar General Petroleum Corporation is the state-owned company controlling Qatar's interests in oil, gas and petrochemicals. The corporation is responsible for Qatar's oil production onshore and offshore. The large reserves of natural gas in the North Field came into production in September 1991.

Current industries include a steel mill, a fertiliser plant, a cement factory, a petrochemical complex and two natural gas liquids plants. With the exception of the cement works at Umm Bāb, all these industries are at Musay'īd, about 30 miles south of Doha. Qatar is also expanding its infrastructure, including electrical generation and water distillation, roads, houses, and government buildings. The recent drop in demand for crude oil has slowed the economy considerably.

The chief imports are machinery and equipment, manufactures, foodstuffs and livestock, and chemicals.

In 1997 imports totalled US$3,322 million.

GDP – US$9,193 million (1997); US$18,065 per capita (1998)
ANNUAL AVERAGE GROWTH OF GDP – 3.2 per cent (1996)
INFLATION RATE – 2.8 per cent (1997)

| *Trade with UK* | 1999 | 2000 |
|---|---|---|
| Imports from UK | £169,012,000 | £183,994,000 |
| Exports to UK | 24,665,000 | 30,268,000 |

## COMMUNICATIONS

There are 1,210 km of roads, of which 1,089 km are surfaced. Regular air services provided by Gulf Air and Qatar Airways connect Qatar with the other Gulf states, the Middle East, the Indian sub-continent, Africa and Europe. The Qatar Broadcasting Service transmits on medium wave, shortwave and VHF.

---

# ROMANIA
*România*

---

AREA – 92,043 sq. miles (238,391 sq. km). Neighbours: Ukraine (north and east), Moldova (east), Bulgaria (south), Yugoslavia (south-west), Hungary (north-west)
POPULATION – 22,458,000 (1998 estimate); 22,810,035 (1992 census): 89.4 per cent Romanian, 7.1 per cent Hungarian, 1.7 per cent Romany, 0.5 per cent German, 0.3 per cent Ukrainian, 0.04 per cent Jews and others. Religious affiliation: Orthodox 86.8 per cent, Roman Catholic 5 per cent, Reformed 3.5 per cent, Greek Catholic 1 per cent. Romanian is a Romance language with many archaic forms and with admixtures of Slavonic, Turkish, Magyar and French words
CAPITAL – Bucharest (population, 2,027,500, 1997 estimate)
MAJOR CITIES – ΨBraşov (318,000); Constanţa (345,000); Cluj-Napoca (333,000); Craiova (313,000); ΨGalaţi (331,000); Iaşi (348,000); Oradea (222,994); Ploieşti (254,386); Timişoara (334,000), 1997 UN estimates
CURRENCY – Leu (Lei) of 100 bani
NATIONAL ANTHEM – Desteaptăte, române, din somnul cel de moarte (Awake ye, Romanians, from your deadly slumber)
NATIONAL DAY – 1 December
NATIONAL FLAG – Three vertical bands, blue, yellow, red
LIFE EXPECTANCY (years) – male 65.1; female 73.5
POPULATION GROWTH RATE – 0.4 per cent (1999)
POPULATION DENSITY – 94 per sq. km (1998)
URBAN POPULATION – 56.2 per cent (2000 estimate)

## HISTORY AND POLITICS

Romania has its origin in the union of the Danubian principalities of Wallachia and Moldavia in 1859. In 1918 Bessarabia, Bukovina, Transylvania and Banat were united with Romania.

In 1947 Romania became 'The Romanian People's Republic' under the leadership of the Romanian Communist Party. A revolution in December 1989 led to the overthrow of Nicolae Ceauşescu, president since 1965. A provisional government abolished the leading role of the Communist Party and held free elections in May 1990.

In the elections held on 26 November 2000 the Social Democratic Party of Romania (SDPR) gained 155 seats in the Chamber of Deputies and 65 seats in the Senate, becoming the largest party in both houses. The SDPR presidential candidate, Ion Iliescu, obtained 36.35 per cent of the vote in the first round of the presidential election. He won the second round, held on 10 December, obtaining 66.83 per cent of the vote. On 27 December, the SDPR reached an agreement with other centre-right parties to enable it to form a workable minority government.

### Political System

The constitution of 1991 formally makes Romania a multiparty democracy and endorses human rights and a market economy. The parliament comprises the Chamber of Deputies with 345 seats, of which 18 are reserved for ethnic minorities, and the Senate with 140 seats. Both houses are elected for four-year terms.

### Head of State

*President of the Republic*, Ion Iliescu, *elected* 10 December 2000

### Cabinet *as at September 2001*

*Prime Minister*, Adrian Nastase
*Agriculture, Food and Forestry*, Ilie Sârbu
*Communications and Information Technology*, Dan Nica
*Culture and Religious Affairs*, Răzvan Theodorescu
*Defence*, Ioan Mircea Paşcu
*Development and Forecasts*, Cazan Gheorghe Leonard
*Education and Research*, Ecaterina Andronescu
*European Integration*, Hildegard Puwak
*Finance*, Mihai Tănăsescu
*Foreign Affairs*, Mircea Geoană
*Health and Family*, Daniela Bartos
*Industry and Resources*, Ioan Dan Popescu
*Interior*, Ioan Rus
*Justice*, Mihaela Rodica Stanoiu
*Labour, Social Solidarity*, Marian Sarbu
*Minister-Delegate, Ministry for Education and Research*, Serban Constantin Valeca
*Minister-Delegate to the Prime Minister, Chief EU Negotiator*, Vasile Puşcaş
*Parliamentary Relations*, Acsinte Gaspar
*Privatisation*, Ovidiu Muşetescu
*Public Administration*, Octav Cozmâncă
*Public Information*, Vasile Dîncu
*Public Works, Transport and Housing*, Miron Mitrea
*Secretary-General of the Government*, Petru Serban Mihălescu
*Small and Medium Enterprises and Co-operatives*, Silvia Ciornei
*Tourism*, Dan Matei-Agathon
*Water and Environment*, Ilie Aurel Constantin
*Youth and Sports*, Georgiu Gingăraş

### Embassy of Romania

Arundel House, 4 Palace Green, London W8 4QD
Tel: 020-7937 9666
*Ambassador Extraordinary and Plenipotentiary*, HE Radu Onofrei, apptd 1997
*Defence Attaché*, Col. V. Palcău
*Minister-Counsellor*, G. Moloşaga (*Economic*)

### British Embassy

24 Strada Jules Michelet, RO-70154 Bucharest
Tel: (00 40) (1) 312 0303
*Ambassador Extraordinary and Plenipotentiary*, HE Richard Ralph, CVO, CMG, apptd 1999
*Counsellor, Deputy Head of Mission*, A. Pearce
*Defence Attaché*, Col. A. T. Bruce, MBE
*First Secretary (Commercial)*, R. J. Cork

British Council Director, Helen Meixner, Calea Dorobantilor 14, RO-71132 Bucharest; e-mail: bc.romania@britishcouncil.ro. There are libraries in Cluj-Napoca, Constanţa, Iaşi, Sibiu and Timişoara

## DEFENCE

The Army has 1,253 main battle tanks, 1,619 armoured personnel carriers and 177 armoured infantry fighting vehicles. The Navy has one submarine, one destroyer, six frigates, 65 patrol and coastal vessels, seven helicopters and 120 main battle tanks at six bases. The Air Force has 323 combat aircraft and 16 attack helicopters.
Military Expenditure – 1.8 per cent of GDP (1999)
Military Personnel – 207,000: Army 106,000, Navy 20,800, Air Force 43,500, Paramilitaries 75,900
Conscription Duration – 12 months

## ECONOMY

Agriculture employed 37.5 per cent of the workforce in 1997 and contributed 16 per cent of GDP in 1998. The principal crops are cereals, vegetables, flax and hemp. Vines and fruits are also grown. The forests of the mountainous regions are extensive, and the timber industry is important.

There are plentiful supplies of natural gas, together with various mineral deposits including coal, iron ore, bauxite, chromium and uranium in quantities which allow a substantial part of the requirements of industry to be met from local resources. Production of crude oil was 12 million tonnes in 1999.

The economy which was characterised by state-owned and co-operative ownership, excessive centralisation, rigid planning and low efficiency, has been slowly reformed.

Since 1996 the pace of privatisation and restructuring has quickened, subsidies have been reduced and prices liberalised.

An extensive programme of privatisation involving 63 state-owned companies was announced in February 2001.
GNP – US$33,034 million (1999); US$1,520 per capita (1999)
GDP – US$34,843 million (1997); US$1,698 per capita (1998)
Annual Average Growth of GDP – 72.3 per cent (1999)
Inflation Rate – 38.3 per cent (2001)
Unemployment – 6.3 per cent (1998)
Total External Debt – US$9,513 million (1998)

### Trade

The main imports are machines and equipment, minerals, textiles, chemicals and metallurgical products. The main exports are textiles, metallurgical products, machinery components, minerals, chemicals, shoes and transport equipment. Italy, Germany, Russia and France are Romania's most important trading partners.

In 1999 Romania had a trade deficit of US$1,087 million and a current account deficit of US$1,303 million. Imports totalled US$10,392 million and exports US$8,505 million.

| *Trade with UK* | 1999 | 2000 |
|---|---|---|
| Imports from UK | £245,629,000 | £383,053,000 |
| Exports to UK | 260,633,000 | 343,767,000 |

## COMMUNICATIONS

In 1999 there were 11,376 km of railway track, over a third of which was electrified, and 153,358 km of roads, of which 78,213 km are paved and 113 km are motorway. The main national roads largely follow the railway lines and almost all lead to the capital. The principal ports are Constanţa (on the Black Sea), Sulina (on the Danube Estuary), Galaţi, Brăila, Giurgiu and Drobeta-Turnu Severin. The Danube and the Black Sea are linked by a canal completed in 1984.

## EDUCATION

Education is free and primary and secondary education are compulsory. There are state universities in seven cities, 66 private universities, six polytechnics, two commercial academies, and five agricultural colleges.

ILLITERACY RATE – 1.8 per cent

ENROLMENT (percentage of age group) – primary 95 per cent (1996); secondary 73 per cent (1996); tertiary 22.5 per cent (1996)

---

# RUSSIA

*Rossiiskaya Federatsiya – Russian Federation*

---

AREA – 6,592,850 sq. miles (17,075,400 sq. km). Neighbours: Norway, Finland, Estonia, Latvia, Belarus and Ukraine (west), Georgia, Azerbaijan, Kazakhstan, China, Mongolia and North Korea (south). The Kaliningrad enclave borders Lithuania and Poland

POPULATION – 144,900,000 (2001 estimate): 87.5 per cent Russian, 3.5 per cent Tatar, 2.7 per cent Ukrainian, 1.3 per cent ethnic German, 1.1 per cent Chuvash, 0.9 per cent Bashkir, 0.7 per cent Belarusian and 0.7 per cent Mordovian. There are another six minorities with populations of over half a million and more than 130 nationalities in total. The Russian Orthodox Church is the predominant religion, though the Tatars and many in the north Caucasus are Muslims and there are Jewish communities in Moscow and St Petersburg. The language is Russian

CAPITAL – Moscow (population, 8,598,896, 2000 estimate), founded about 1147, became the centre of the rising Moscow principality and in the 15th century the capital of the whole of Russia (Muscovy). In 1325 it became the seat of the Metropolitan of Russia. In 1703 Peter the Great transferred the capital to St Petersburg, but on 14 March 1918 Moscow was again designated as the capital

MAJOR CITIES – ΨSt Petersburg (4,660,800, 2000), from 1914 to 1924 Petrograd and from 1924 to 1991 Leningrad. Other cities: Chelyabinsk (1,111,000); Kazan (1,077,750); Nizhny-Novgorod/Gorky (1,380,100); Novosibirsk/Novonikolayevsk (1,398,350); Omsk (1,785,000); Perm/Molotov (1,050,950); Rostov-on-Don (1,013,635); Samara/Kuibyshev (1,215,050); Ufa (1.098,150); Yekaterinburg/Sverdlovsk (1,275,000), 1997 estimates

CURRENCY – Rouble of 100 kopeks

NATIONAL ANTHEM - Russia, Sacred Our Empire (the former Soviet national anthem, with new lyrics)

NATIONAL DAY – 12 June (Independence Day)

NATIONAL FLAG – Three horizontal stripes of white, blue, red

LIFE EXPECTANCY (years) – male 59.9; female 74.40

POPULATION GROWTH RATE – 0.1 per cent (1999)

POPULATION DENSITY – 9 per sq. km (1998)

URBAN POPULATION – 77.7 per cent (2000 estimate)

ILLITERACY RATE – 0.6 per cent

ENROLMENT (percentage of age group) – primary 93 per cent (1996); tertiary 42.8 per cent (1996)

Russia occupies three-quarters of the land area of the former Soviet Union.

The Russian Federation comprises 89 members: 49 regions (*oblast*) – Amur, Arkhangelsk, Astrakhan, Belgorod, Bryansk, Chelyabinsk, Chita, Irkutsk, Ivanovo, Kaliningrad, Kaluga, Kamchatka, Kemerovo, Kirov, Kostroma, Kurgan, Kursk, Leningrad, Lipetsk, Magadan, Moscow, Murmansk, Nizhny-Novgorod, Novgorod, Novosibirsk, Omsk, Orel, Orenburg, Penza, Perm, Pskov, Rostov, Ryazan, Sakhalin, Samara, Saratov, Smolensk, Sverdlovsk, Tambov, Tomsk, Tula, Tver, Tyumen, Ulyanovsk, Vladimir, Volgograd, Vologda, Voronezh, Yaroslavl; six autonomous territories (*krai*) – Altai, Khabarovsk, Krasnodar, Krasnoyarsk, Primorye, Stavropol; 21 republics – Adygeia, Altai, Bashkortostan, Buryatia, Chechnya, Chuvash, Daghestan, Ingush, Kabardino-Balkar, Kalmykia, Karachai-Cherkessia, Karelia, Khakassia, Komi, Mari-El, Mordovia, North Ossetia (Alania), Sakha, Tatarstan, Tyva, Udmurt; ten autonomous areas – Aga-Buryat, Chuckchi, Evenki, Khanty-Mansi, Komi-Permyak, Koryak, Nenets, Taimyr, Ust-Orda-Buryat, Yamal-Nenets; two cities of federal status – Moscow, St Petersburg; and one autonomous Jewish region, Birobijan.

There are three principal geographic areas: a low-lying flat western area stretching eastwards up to the Yenisei and divided in two by the Ural ridge; the eastern area between the Yenisei and the Pacific, consisting of a number of tablelands and ridges; and a southern mountainous area. Russia has a very long coastline, including the longest Arctic coastline in the world (about 17,000 miles).

The most important rivers are the Volga, the Northern Dvina and the Pechora, the Neva, the Don and the Kuban in the European part, and in the Asiatic part, the Ob, the Irtysh, the Yenisei, the Lena and the Amur, and, further north, Khatanga, Olenek, Yana, Indigirka, Kolyma and Anadyr. Lake Baikal in eastern Siberia is the deepest lake in the world.

## HISTORY AND POLITICS

The Gregorian calendar was not introduced until 14 February 1918. For the events surrounding the 1917 revolutions the dates given here are the Gregorian calendar dates in use in the rest of the world at the time, with the dates in the Julian calendar (OS) in parenthesis.

Russia was formally created from the principality of Muscovy and its territories by Tsar Peter I (The Great) (1682–1725), who initiated its territorial expansion, introduced Western ideas of government and founded St Petersburg. By the end of Peter the Great's reign, the Baltic territories (modern-day Estonia and Latvia) had been annexed from Sweden, and Russia had become the dominant military power of north-eastern Europe. In the 18th century the partitions of Poland and wars with Turkey brought the territories of modern-day Lithuania, Belarus, Ukraine and the Crimea under Russian control, and the colonisation of Siberia east of the Urals began in earnest. Russia overran the Caucasus region (modern-day Armenia, Azerbaijan and Georgia) in the early 19th century, seized Finland from Sweden in 1809 and Bessarabia from Turkey in 1812. Throughout the remainder of the 19th century Russia subdued and annexed the independent Muslim states which later formed the five Central Asian republics.

Discontent caused by autocratic rule, the poor conduct of the military in the First World War and wartime privation led to a revolution which broke out on 12 March (27 February OS) 1917. Tsar Nicholas II abdicated three days later and a provisional government was formed; a republic was proclaimed on 14 September (1 September OS) 1917. A power struggle ensued between the provisional government and the Bolshevik Party which controlled the Soviets (councils) set up by workers, soldiers and peasants. This led to a second revolution on 7 November (25 October OS) 1917 in which the Bolsheviks, led by Lenin, seized power.

Armed resistance to Communist rule developed into an all-out civil war between 'red' Bolshevik forces and 'white' monarchist and anti-Communist forces which lasted until the end of 1922. During the civil war, Russia had been declared a Soviet Republic and other Soviet republics had been formed in Ukraine, Byelorussia and Transcaucasia. These four republics merged to form the Union of Soviet Socialist Republics (USSR) on 30 December 1922.

The Nazi–Soviet pact of August 1939 and the Second World War resulted in further territorial expansion, regaining much of the territory lost in or after 1918, as well as extending Soviet influence to the countries of eastern Europe liberated by Soviet troops. The USSR lost 27 million combatants and civilians in the war.

Joseph Stalin introduced a policy of rapid industrialisation under a series of five-year plans, brought all sectors of industry under government control, abolished private ownership and enforced the collectivisation of agriculture.

Mikhail Gorbachev became Soviet leader in March 1985 and introduced the policies of *perestroika* (complete restructuring) and *glasnost* (openness) in order to revamp the economy, which had stagnated since the 1970s, to root out corruption and inefficiency, and to end the Cold War and its attendant arms race. The retreat from total control by the Communist Party unleashed ethnic and nationalist tensions.

On 19 August 1991 a coup was attempted by hardline elements of the Communist Party, but was defeated by reformist and democratic political groups under the leadership of Russian President Yeltsin. Effective political power was now in the hands of the republican leaders, especially Russian President Yeltsin, and the Soviet Union began to break up as the constituent republics declared their independence. Gorbachev resigned as Soviet President on 25 December 1991 and on 26 December 1991 the USSR formally ceased to exist.

Russia was recognised as an independent state by the EC and USA in January 1992; it took over the Soviet Union's seat at the UN in December 1991.

A new Russian Federal Treaty was signed on 13 March 1992 between the central government and the autonomous republics. Tatarstan and Bashkortostan initially declared themselves independent, but signed the treaty in 1994 after securing considerable legislative and economic autonomy.

President Yeltsin appointed Vladimir Putin as prime minister on 9 August 1999. Yeltsin resigned as President on 31 December 1999 and was replaced in an acting capacity by the Prime Minister, Vladimir Putin, until elections could be held.

The state of the parties in the State *Duma* following the election on 19 December 1999 was: Communist Party 113 seats; Unity 72; Fatherland-All Russia 67; Union of Rightist Forces 29; Yabloko 21; Zhirinovski's Bloc 17; Our Home is Russia 7; DPA 2; Russian All People Unity 2; others 5.

In the presidential election held on 26 March 2000, Vladimir Putin won 52.94 per cent of the vote, in which the turnout was 68.88 per cent, and was formally inaugurated on 7 May 2000.

A new foreign policy doctrine was promulgated in July 2000, which geared foreign policy towards activities which would assist Russia's internal problems.

## Political System

The 1993 constitution enshrines the right to private ownership and the freedoms of press, speech, association, worship and travel, and states that Russia is a multiparty democracy. The President is head of state and of government, head of the Security Council and commander-in-chief of the armed forces. He may chair Cabinet meetings, determine basic government policy, veto legislation, issue decrees and directives, call referendums, and dismiss the government. The President nominates the Prime Minister and deputy Prime Ministers, who must be approved by the State *Duma*.

The President is directly elected for a maximum of two four-year terms. The Prime Minister takes over from the President in the event that he is unable to fulfil his duties.

Legislative power is vested in the Federal Assembly, comprising the Federation Council (upper house) of 178 members, two elected by each of the 89 members of the Russian Federation; the State *Duma* (lower house) of 450 members, of which 225 are elected by constituencies on a first-past-the-post basis and 225 by proportional representation, with a five per cent threshold for representation. The Council is composed of two representatives from each constituent territory of the Federation: the head of the legislative and the head of the executive body. From 2002 the governments and the legislatures of the constituent territories will each elect one representative.

On 1 September 2000, President Putin announced the formation of the State Council of the Russian Federation, a consultative body which consists of the leaders of the 89 republics and regions. The Council has a presidium which is formed on a rotational basis every six months and is chaired by the president of the Russian Federation.

The judicial system consists of a Constitutional Court of 19 members appointed for a 12-year term which protects and interprets the constitution and decides if laws are compatible with it. The Supreme Court adjudicates in criminal and civil laws cases. The Arbitration Court deals with commercial disputes between companies. The new code of civil law came into force in January 1995.

## Insurgencies

The Chechen republic declared its 'independence' in November 1991 after a nationalist coup in the republic. Chechnya refused to sign the Russian Federal Treaty in March 1992. Civil war began in early 1994 between the Chechen government and armed opposition forces of the 'Provisional Chechen Council', tacitly supported by the Russian government. On 9 December 1994 President Yeltsin ordered the Russian military to retake the republic. Chechen forces were finally forced out of Grozny in early February 1995.

The last Russian troops were withdrawn in January 1997 when presidential and legislative elections were also held in Chechnya. A treaty renouncing the use of force to resolve Chechnya's status was signed between Presidents Maskhadov and Yeltsin in May 1997.

On 10 August 1999, Islamic rebels launched an incursion into Dagestan, declaring it to be an independent Islamic state. The Russian government immediately dispatched troops to quell the insurgency; a state of emergency was declared in Chechnya after Russia threatened to attack rebel bases located there.

Russian forces launched airstrikes against Chechnya on 23 September 1999 and on 30 September, Russian ground troops entered the territory. Russian forces captured the Chechen capital, Grozny, on 6 February 2000, forcing the rebels who had defended the city to flee to the southern mountains. Russian troops captured the last Chechen-held town on 29 February, but Chechen guerrilla attacks on Russian targets continued. On 8 June 2000, President Putin imposed temporary direct presidential rule on Chechnya.

## Foreign Relations

A union treaty was signed by the presidents of Russia and Belarus in April 1997. Both countries will retain sovereignty and territorial integrity although citizens of the two countries will also be citizens of the Union. The presidents of the two countries decided in December 1998 to effect a currency union.

A Founding Act was signed by Russia and NATO in May 1997 which lays down the principles of post-Cold War co-operation. A joint permanent council is to be set up.

## HEAD OF STATE

*President*, Vladimir Putin, *elected* 26 March 2000, *inaugurated* 7 May 2000

## GOVERNMENT *as at September 2001*

*Chair*, Mikhail Kasyanov
*Deputy Chairs*, Aleksey Gordeyev (*Agriculture and Food*); Ilya Klebanov; Alexei Kudrin (*Finance*); Viktor Khristenko; Valentina Matviyenko
*Anti-Monopoly and Entrepreneurial Affairs*, Ilya Yuzhanov
*Atomic Energy*, Aleksandr Rumyantsev
*Culture*, Mikhail Shvydkoi
*Defence*, Sergey Ivanov
*Director of the Federal Security Services*, Nikolai Patrushev
*Economic Development and Trade*, German Gref
*Education*, Vladimir Filippov
*Emergencies, Civil Defence, Natural Disasters*, Sergei Shoigu
*Employment and Social Development*, Aleksandr Pochinok
*Energy*, Igor Yusufov
*Federation Affairs, Nationalities and Migration Policy*, Aleksandr Blokhin
*Foreign Affairs*, Igor Ivanov
*Head of Government Administration*, Igor Shuvalov
*Health*, Yuri Shevchenko
*Interior*, Boris Gryzlov
*Justice*, Yuri Chaika
*Natural Resources*, Vitaly Artyukhov
*Press, Broadcasting and Mass Communications*, Mikhail Lesin
*Privatisation*, Farid Gazizullin
*Railways*, Nikolai Aksenenko
*Science, Industry and Technology*, Aleksandr Dondukov
*Secretary of the Security Council*, Vladimir Rushailo
*Social and Economic Development of Chechnya*, Vladimir Yelagin
*Tax and Levy Collection*, Gennady Bukayev
*Telecommunications and Information*, Leonid Reyman
*Transport*, Sergei Frank

## EMBASSY OF THE RUSSIAN FEDERATION

13 Kensington Palace Gardens, London W8 4QX
Tel: 020-7229 2666/3628/6412
*Ambassador Extraordinary and Plenipotentiary*, HE Grigory B. Karasin, apptd 2000
*Minister-Counsellor*, A. Kramarenko
*Defence and Air Attaché*, Maj.-Gen. V. Glagolev
*Counsellor and Consul-General*, A. Lopukhov

## BRITISH EMBASSY

Smolenskaya Naberezhnaya 10, RUS-121099 Moscow
Tel: (00 7) (095) 956 7200
E-mail: britembppas@glas.apc.org
*Ambassador Extraordinary and Plenipotentiary*, HE Sir Roderic Lyne, KBE, CMG, apptd 1999
*Minister and Deputy Head of Mission*, D. Gowan
*Defence and Air Attaché*, Air Cdre J. Jarron
*Counsellor (Economic, Commercial and Science)*, S. Smith
*Consuls-General*: P. McDermott, MVO (Moscow); B. Hay, CMG, MBE (St Petersburg); L. Cross (Ekaterinburg)
CONSULATES-GENERAL - Ekaterinburg, St Petersburg,
HONORARY CONSULATES - Novorossiysk, Vladivostok
BRITISH COUNCIL DIRECTOR, Adrian Greer, Ulitsa Nikoloyamskaya 1, RUS-109189 Moscow; E-mail: bc.moscow@britishcouncil.ru. There are also offices at Ekaterinburg, Nizhni Novgorod, Sochi and St Petersburg

RUSSO-BRITISH CHAMBER OF COMMERCE, Office 6, 6th Floor, Smolenskaya Ploshchad' 3-5, Smolenskiy Passazh, RUS-121099 Moscow; e-mail: mail@rbcc.com

## DEFENCE

Since the demise of the Soviet Union the Russian armed forces have been considerably reduced. In November 2000 it was announced that the armed forces would be reduced to 850,000 personnel by 2005.

A joint CIS air defence system covers Russia, Armenia, Belarus, Kazakhstan, Kyrgyzstan and Uzbekistan.

The Strategic Nuclear Forces have 19 nuclear-powered ballistic missile submarines with 324 missiles, 776 intercontinental ballistic missiles and 100 anti-ballistic missiles.

The Army has about 21,820 main battle tanks, 25,975 armoured personnel carriers and armoured infantry fighting vehicles, and 2,108 helicopters. The Navy has 67 submarines, one aircraft carrier, seven cruisers, 17 destroyers, ten frigates, 108 patrol and coastal vessels, 244 combat aircraft and 107 armed helicopters. The Air Force has 2,733 combat aircraft.

Russia deploys forces in Armenia (3,100), Georgia (5,000), Moldova (2,600) and Tajikistan (8,200). Russia is the world's third largest contributor to peacekeeping operations. An agreement with Ukraine on the division on the Black Sea Fleet was signed in May 1997.

MILITARY EXPENDITURE – 5.1 per cent of GDP (1999)
MILITARY PERSONNEL – 1,004,100: Strategic Nuclear Forces 149,000, Army 348,000, Navy 171,500, Air Force 184,600, Paramilitaries 423,000
CONSCRIPTION DURATION – 18–24 months

## ECONOMY

Under the Soviet regime, an essentially agrarian economy in 1917 was transformed by the early 1960s into the second strongest industrial power in the world. However, by the early 1970s the concentration of resources on the military-industrial complex was causing the civilian economy to stagnate. Free market reforms were introduced by President Gorbachev including the legalisation of small private businesses, the reduction of state control over the economy, and denationalisation and privatisation. The first stage of mass privatisation of state industries began in October 1992 and the central distribution system was abolished with effect from 1 January 1993. By February 1996, 80 per cent of the economy had been privatised.

From 1994 to 1996, the economy began to stabilise with economic reforms judged to have become irreversible. In 1997, for the first time since economic reforms were introduced, Russian GDP grew by 0.4 per cent.

The devaluation of the rouble in 1998 caused the return of growth in the Russian economy in 1999. However, low productivity, overstaffing, and a lack of investment and entrepreneurship remained a problem.

Russia has some of the richest mineral deposits in the world. Coal is mined in the Kuznetsk area, in the Urals, south of Moscow, in the Donets basin and in the Pechora area in the north. Oil is produced in the northern Caucasus, between the Volga and the Urals, and in western Siberia, which also has large deposits of natural gas. A pipeline to bring Caspian oil into Russia via Dagestan and North Ossetia is under construction. Oil production in 2000 was 323.3 million tonnes. Coal and gas deposits in Siberia and the far east (especially Yakutia) are being developed. The Ural mountains contain high-quality iron ore, manganese, copper, aluminium, platinum, precious stones, salt, asbestos, pyrites, coal, oil, etc. Iron ore is also mined near Kursk, Tula, Lipetsk, in several areas in Siberia and in the Kola Peninsula. Non-ferrous metals are found in the Altai, in eastern Siberia, in the northern Caucasus, in the Kuznetsk basin, in the far east

and in the far north. 106 tonnes of gold were produced in 1997.

The vast area and the great variety in climatic conditions are reflected in the structure of agriculture. In the far north reindeer breeding, hunting and fishing are predominant. Further south, timber industry is combined with grain growing. In the southern half of the forest zone and in the adjacent forest-steppe zone, the acreage under grain crops is larger and the structure of agriculture more complex. Between the Volga and the Urals cericulture is predominant (particularly summer wheat), followed by cattle breeding. Beyond the Urals is another important grain-growing and stock-breeding area in the southern part of the western Siberian plain. The southern steppe zone is the main wheat granary of Russia, containing also large acreages under barley, maize and sunflowers. In the extreme south cotton is cultivated. Vine, tobacco and other southern crops are grown on the Black Sea shore of the Caucasus.

Moscow and St Petersburg are still the two largest industrial centres in the country, but new industrial areas have been developed in the Urals, the Kuznetsk basin, in Siberia and the far east.

GNP – US$328,995 million (1999); US$2,270 per capita (1999)

GDP – US$447,103 million (1997); US$1,936 per capita (1998)

Annual Average Growth of GDP – 8.0 per cent (2000)

Inflation Rate – 20.7 per cent (2001)

Unemployment – 13.3 per cent (1998)

Total External Debt – US$183,601 million (1998)

### Trade

Russia's main trading partners are Germany, the USA, Italy, China and the former Soviet states. In 1999 there was a trade surplus of US$35,301 million and a current account surplus of US$24,995 million. Imports totalled US$40,429 million and exports US$74,663 million.

| *Trade with UK* | 1999 | 2000 |
|---|---|---|
| Imports from UK | £537,069,000 | £668,956,000 |
| Exports to UK | 1,360,011,000 | 1,532,019,000 |

## COMMUNICATIONS

The European area of Russia is well served by railways, there are still large areas, notably in the far north and Siberia, with few or no railways.

The most important ports (Taganrog, Rostov and Novorossiisk) lie around the Black Sea and the Sea of Azov. The northern ports are, with the exception of Murmansk, icebound during winter. The far eastern port of Vladivostok, the Pacific naval base of Russia, is kept open by icebreakers all the year round.

The great rivers of European Russia flow outwards from the centre, linking all parts of the plain with the chief ports, an immense system of navigable waterways which carried about 690 million tons of freight in 1988. They are supplemented by a system of canals which provide a through traffic between the White, Baltic, Black and Caspian Seas. The most notable are the White Sea-Baltic Canal, the Moscow-Volga Canal and the Volga-Don Canal linking the Baltic and the White Seas in the north to the Caspian Sea, the Black Sea and the Sea of Azov in the south.

## CULTURE

Russian is a branch of the Slavonic family of languages and is written in the Cyrillic script.

Before the westernisation of Russia under Peter the Great (1682–1725), Russian literature consisted mainly of folk ballads (*byliny*), epic songs, chronicles and works of moral theology. The 18th and 19th centuries saw the development of poetry and fiction. Poetry reached its zenith with Alexander Pushkin (1799–1837), Mikhail Lermontov (1814–41), Alexander Blok (1880–1921), the 1958 Nobel Prize laureate Boris Pasternak (1890–1960), Vladimir Mayakovsky (1893–1930) and Anna Akhmatova (1888–1966). Fiction is associated with the names of Nikolai Gogol (1809–52), Ivan Turgenev (1818–83), Fyodor Dostoevsky (1821–81), Leo Tolstoy (1828–1910), Anton Chekhov (1860–1904), Maxim Gorky (1868–1936), Ivan Bunin (1870–1953), Mikhail Bulgakov (1891–1940), Mikhail Sholokhov (1905–84) and Alexander Solzhenitsyn (*b.* 1918).

Great names in music include Glinka (1804–57), Borodin (1833–87), Mussorgsky (1839–81), Rimsky-Korsakov (1844–1908), Rubinstein (1829–94), Tchaikovsky (1840–93), Rachmaninov (1873–1943), Skriabin (1872–1915), Prokofiev (1891–1953), Stravinsky (1882–1971), Shostakovich (1906–75) and Alfred Schnittke (1934–1998).

## RWANDA
*Repúblika y'u Rwanda*

AREA – 10,169 sq. miles (26,338 sq. km). Neighbours: Burundi (south), Democratic Republic of Congo (west), Uganda (north), Tanzania (east)
POPULATION – 8,310,000 (1997 UN estimate): Hutus 90 per cent, Tutsis 9 per cent, Twa (pygmy) 1 per cent. Kinyarwanda, French and English are the official languages. Swahili is also spoken
CAPITAL – Kigali (population, 116,227)
CURRENCY – Rwanda franc of 100 centimes
NATIONAL ANTHEM - Rwanda rwacu, Rwanda gihugu cyambyage (My Rwanda, Rwanda who gave me birth)
NATIONAL DAY – 1 July
NATIONAL FLAG – Three vertical bands, red, yellow and green with letter R on yellow band
LIFE EXPECTANCY (years) – male 41.2; female 42.3
POPULATION GROWTH RATE – 0.4 per cent (1999)
POPULATION DENSITY – 251 per sq. km (1998)
URBAN POPULATION – 6.2 per cent (2000 estimate)
MILITARY EXPENDITURE – 6.2 per cent of GDP (1999)
MILITARY PERSONNEL – 55,000: Army 49,000, Paramilitaries 6,000
ILLITERACY RATE – 33.0 per cent (2000)
ENROLMENT (percentage of age group) – primary 75 per cent (1991); secondary 8 per cent (1991); tertiary 0.5 per cent (1990)

### HISTORY AND POLITICS

The majority Hutu population rebelled against Tutsi feudal rule (under the Belgian colonial authority) in 1959–61, leading to the massacre of thousands of Tutsis. Large numbers fled into exile in Uganda. Rwanda became an independent republic on 1 July 1962.

Armed Tutsi exiles repeatedly attempted to invade Rwanda in the 1960s and 1970s but were defeated by the predominantly Hutu army. Continued Hutu-Tutsi conflict left thousands dead over a period of 30 years. In October 1990 Rwanda was invaded by the Rwandan Patriotic Front (RPF) of exiled Tutsis and moderate Hutus, who forced the one-party MRND (National Revolutionary Movement for Development) government to introduce a multiparty constitution in 1991. After the government reneged on a 1992 peace agreement, the RPF advanced on Kigali and forced the government to restart negotiations, which led to the August 1993 Arusha peace accord. The accord provided for a transitional period under a broad-based government including the RPF until the 1995 elections, with UN forces in the country throughout the period.

President Habyarimana, who had retained the interim presidency, died on 6 April 1994 in a plane crash widely believed to have been caused by a rocket attack by extremist sections of the Hutu army. The Hutu army and armed militia, the *interahamwe*, then carried out a preplanned act of genocide against the Tutsi minority and moderate Hutus; 800,000 people were massacred in three months. The civil war restarted and the RPF gradually re-established its control over the country, forcing the defeated government forces and two million Hutu refugees into exile. On 18 July 1994 the RPF declared victory and established a broad-based government of national unity in which moderate Hutus were given the presidency and premiership and the RPF took eight of the 22 seats.

The 70-member Transitional National Assembly provided for by the Arusha agreement began operation on 12 December 1994 with the extremist Hutu MRND excluded. Killings by both Hutu militia and government forces continued, and Hutu attacks in central and western Rwanda were frequent in the first half of 1998 and recurred in May and June 2001 in the north west of the country.

At the ICTR in May 1998, former Prime Minister Jean Kambanda pleaded guilty to charges of genocide, the first admission by a senior Hutu official that genocide had taken place. The ICTR announced in December 2000 that it would investigate revenge atrocities committed by the RPF in the wake of the 1994 genocide. The RPF promised its full co-operation. Rwanda has supported a rebellion in the Democratic Republic of Congo led by the Congolese Democratic Rally, a Congolese Tutsi group. Rwandan troops have also been deployed in the Democratic Republic of Congo.

The Transitional National Assembly was extended for four further years on 9 June 1999.

#### POLITICAL SYSTEM

The President is head of state and is elected by the Transitional National Assembly. The President appoints the Council of Ministers.

The Transitional National Assembly was appointed in 1994 for a five-year term, since extended for a further four years. The number of seats in the Assembly was increased from 70 to 74 in September 2000.

#### HEAD OF STATE

*President*, Maj-Gen. Paul Kagame, *appointed* 17 April 2000, *sworn in* 22 April 2000

#### GOVERNMENT *as at September 2001*

The President (FPR)
*Prime Minister*, Bernard Makusa (MDR)
*Agriculture, Livestock, Environment and Rural Development*, Ephraim Kabayija
*Civil Service and Labour*, Sylvie Zainab Kayitesi
*Commerce, Industry and Tourism*, Alexandre Byambabaje
*Defence and National Security*, Col. Emmanuel Habyarimana
*Education, Science and Technology*, Romain Murenzi
*Energy, Water and Natural Resources*, Bonaventure Niyibizi
*Finance and Economic Planning*, Donat Kaberuka
*Foreign Affairs and Regional Co-operation*, André Bumaya
*Gender and Women's Promotion*, Angeline Muganza
*Health*, Ezechias Rwabuhihi
*Internal Affairs*, Jean de Dieu Ntiruhungwa
*Justice and Institutional Relations*, Jean de Dieu Mucyo
*Lands, Resettlement and Environmental Protection*, Laurent Nkusi
*Local Government and Social Affairs*, Désiré Nyandwi
*Public Works, Transport and Communications*, Kalinganire Silas
*Youth, Culture and Sports*, François Ngarambe

FPR Rwandan Patriotic Front; MDR Republican Democratic Movement

#### EMBASSY OF THE REPUBLIC OF RWANDA

Uganda House, 58-59 Trafalgar Square, London WC2N 5DX
Tel: 020-7930 2570
*Ambassador Extraordinary and Plenipotentiary*, HE Rosemary K. Museminali, apptd 2000
*First Secretary*, H. Byamugisha

#### BRITISH EMBASSY

Parcelle No. 1131, Blvd de l'Umuganda, Kacyira-Sud, BP 576 Kigali
Tel: (00 250) 84098/85771/85773
*Ambassador Extraordinary and Plenipotentiary*, HE Graeme Loten, apptd 1998

## ECONOMY

Coffee, tea and sugar are grown. Tin, hides, bark of quinine and extract of pyrethrum flowers are also exported.

In 1998 there was a trade deficit of US$198 million and a current account deficit of US$143 million. In 1999 imports totalled US$253 million and exports US$61 million.

GNP – US$2,041 million (1999); US$250 per capita (1999)
GDP – US$1,016 million (1997); US$225 per capita (1998)
ANNUAL AVERAGE GROWTH OF GDP – 13.3 per cent (1996)
INFLATION RATE – 2.4 per cent (1999)
TOTAL EXTERNAL DEBT – US$1,226 million (1998)

| *Trade with UK* | 1999 | 2000 |
|---|---|---|
| Imports from UK | £1,837,000 | £3,630,000 |
| Exports to UK | 653,000 | 103,000 |

---

# ST CHRISTOPHER AND NEVIS
*The Federation of St Christopher and Nevis*

---

AREA – 101 sq. miles (261 sq. km)
POPULATION – 41,000 (1997 UN estimate). The language is English
CAPITAL – ΨBasseterre (population, 12,200, 1994 estimate)
MAJOR TOWNS – ΨCharlestown (1,700, 1994 estimate), the chief town of Nevis
CURRENCY – East Caribbean dollar (EC$) of 100 cents
NATIONAL ANTHEM – Oh Land of Beauty
NATIONAL DAY – 19 September (Independence Day)
NATIONAL FLAG – Three diagonal bands, green, black and red; each colour separated by a stripe of yellow. Two white stars on the black band
LIFE EXPECTANCY (years) – male 65.0; female 71.2
POPULATION GROWTH RATE – 0.9 per cent (1999)
POPULATION DENSITY – 150 per sq. km (1998)
URBAN POPULATION – 34.1 per cent (2000 estimate)

The state of St Christopher and Nevis is located at the northern end of the eastern Caribbean. It comprises the islands of St Christopher (St Kitts) (68 sq. miles) and Nevis (36 sq. miles). The central area of St Christopher is forest-clad and mountainous, rising to the 3,792 ft Mount Liamuiga. Nevis is separated from the southern tip of St Christopher by a strait two miles wide and is dominated by Nevis Peak, 3,232 ft.

## HISTORY AND POLITICS

St Christopher was the first island in the British West Indies to be colonised (1623). The Territory of St Christopher and Nevis became a State in Association with Britain in 1967. The State of St Christopher and Nevis became an independent nation on 19 September 1983.

On 10 August 1998 a referendum was held in Nevis on the question of independence from St Christopher; although 61.8 per cent voted in favour of secession, it fell short of the two-thirds majority needed for independence.

In the legislative election held on 6 March 2000, the Labour Party won all eight of the seats on St Christopher. On Nevis, the Concerned Citizens' Movement won two seats and the Nevis Reformation Party one seat.

### POLITICAL SYSTEM

Under the constitution, Queen Elizabeth II is Head of State, represented in the islands by the Governor-General. There is a central government with a ministerial system, the head of which is the Prime Minister of St Christopher and Nevis, and a National Assembly located on St Christopher. The National Assembly is composed of the Speaker, three senators (nominated by the Prime Minister and the Leader of the Opposition) and 11 directly elected representatives, who serve a five-year term. On Nevis there is a Nevis Island Administration, the head being styled Premier of Nevis, and a Nevis Island Assembly of five elected and three nominated members.

*Governor-General*, HE Sir Cuthbert Montraville Sebastian, GCMG, OBE, apptd 1996

### CABINET *as at September 2001*

*Prime Minister, Finance, National Security, Planning, Development*, Denzil Douglas
*Deputy Prime Minister, International Trade, Labour, Social Security and Caricom Affairs, Telecommunications and Technology*, Sam Condor
*Agriculture, Fisheries, Co-operatives, Lands and Housing*, Cedric Liburd
*Attorney-General Justice and Legal Affairs*, Delano Bart
*Education, Labour and Social Security*, Timothy Harris
*Foreign Affairs, Education*, Timothy Harris
*Health, Environment*, Earl Asim Martin
*Social Development, Community and Gender Affairs*, Rupert Herbert
*Information, Culture, Youth Affairs and Sports*, Jacinth Henry-Martin
*Public Works, Utilities, Transport and Posts*, Halva Hendrickson
*Tourism, Commerce, Consumer Affairs*, Dwyer Astaphan

### HIGH COMMISSION FOR ST CHRISTOPHER AND NEVIS

2nd Floor, 10 Kensington Court, London W8 5DL
Tel: 020-7460 6500
*High Commissioner for St Christopher and Nevis*, HE James Ernest Williams, apptd 2001

BRITISH HIGH COMMISSIONER, HE John White, resident at Bridgetown, Barbados
*Acting High Commissioner*, S. Murphy

## ECONOMY

The economy of the islands has been based on sugar for over three centuries. Tourism (172,000 visitors in 1996) and light industry, concentrating on distilling, food processing, clothing and electronics, are now being developed. The economy of Nevis centres on small peasant farmers, but a sea-island cotton industry is being developed for export.

The main exports are sugar, lobsters, beverages and electrical equipment. Foodstuffs, energy, machinery and transport equipment are the main imports.

About 70 per cent of homes on St Christopher were damaged by Hurricane Georges in September 1998.

In 1996 imports totalled US$149 million and exports US$22 million.

GNP – US$259 million (1999); US$6,420 per capita (1999)
GDP – US$252 million (1997); US$7,440 per capita (1998)
ANNUAL AVERAGE GROWTH OF GDP – 3.1 per ccent (1996)
INFLATION RATE – 3.9 per cent (1999)
TOTAL EXTERNAL DEBT – US$115 million (1998)

| *Trade with UK* | 1999 | 2000 |
|---|---|---|
| Imports from UK | £6,355,000 | £11,284,000 |
| Exports to UK | 6,409,000 | 7,227,000 |

## COMMUNICATIONS

Basseterre is a port of registry and has deep water harbour facilities. Golden Rock airport, on St Kitts, can take most large jet aircraft; Newcastle airstrip on Nevis can take small aircraft and has night landing facilities. The sea ferry route from Basseterre to Charlestown is 11 miles.

# ST LUCIA

AREA – 240 sq. miles (622 sq. km)
POPULATION – 154,000 (1997 UN estimate). The official language is English. A French creole is spoken by most of the population
CAPITAL – ΨCastries (population, 51,994, 1997 estimate)
CURRENCY – East Caribbean dollar (EC$) of 100 cents
NATIONAL ANTHEM – Sons and Daughters of Saint Lucia
NATIONAL DAY – 22 February (Independence Day)
NATIONAL FLAG – Blue, bearing in centre a device of yellow over black over white triangles having a common base
LIFE EXPECTANCY (years) – male 68.9; female 74.9
POPULATION GROWTH RATE – 1.4 per cent (1999)
POPULATION DENSITY – 244 per sq. km (1998)
URBAN POPULATION – 37.8 per cent (2000 estimate)

St Lucia, the second largest of the Windward group, is 27 miles in length, with an extreme breadth of 14 miles. It is mountainous, its highest point being Mt Gimie (3,145 ft) and for the most part it is covered with forest and tropical vegetation.

## HISTORY AND POLITICS

Possession of St Lucia was fiercely disputed and it constantly changed hands between the British and the French until 1814 when it was ceded to Britain by the Treaty of Paris. It became independent within the Commonwealth on 22 February 1979.

The St Lucia Labour Party defeated the ruling United Workers' Party in a general election on 23 May 1997, winning all but one of the seats in the House of Assembly.

### POLITICAL SYSTEM

The Head of State is Queen Elizabeth II, represented on the island by a St Lucian Governor-General, and there is a bicameral legislature. The Senate has 11 members, six appointed by the ruling party, three by the Opposition and two by the Governor-General. The House of Assembly, which has a life of five years, has 17 elected members and a Speaker, who may be appointed from outside the House.

*Governor-General*, HE Dame Perlette Louisy, apptd 1997

### CABINET *as at September 2001*

*Prime Minister, Finance, Economic Affairs, Information*, Kenny Anthony
*Agriculture, Fisheries*, Cassius Elias
*Commerce, International Financial Services and Consumer Affairs*, Phillip J. Pierre
*Communications, Works, Transport and Public Utilities*, Calixte George
*Community Development, Culture, Local Government and Co-operatives*, Damian Greaves
*Development, Planning, Environment and Housing*, Walter François
*Education, Human Resources Development, Youth and Sport*, Mario Michel
*Foreign Affairs, International Trade*, Julian Hunte
*Health, Human Services, Family Affairs and Women*, Sarah Flood
*Legal Affairs, Labour and Home Affairs*, Velon John
*Tourism, Civil Aviation*, Menissa Rambally

### HIGH COMMISSION FOR ST LUCIA

1 Collingham Gardens, London SW5 0HW
Tel: 020-7370 7123
*High Commissioner for St Lucia*, HE Emmanuel Cotter, MBE, apptd 1998

### OFFICE OF THE BRITISH HIGH COMMISSION

NIS Waterfront Building, 2nd Floor (PO Box 227), Castries
Tel: (00 1 758) 452 2484/5
E-mail: postmaster@castries.mail.fco.gov.uk
*High Commissioner*, HE John White, resident at Bridgetown, Barbados
*Acting High Commissioner*, Douglas Rice

## ECONOMY

The economy is mainly agrarian, with manufacturing based on the processing of agricultural products. Principal crops are bananas, coconuts, cocoa, mangoes, breadfruit, yams and citrus fruit. Attempts are being made to increase industrialisation. The currency is tied to the US dollar at a rate of EC$2.70=US$1.00. There were 414,000 visitors to the island in 1998.

GNP – US$590 million (1999); US$3,770 per capita (1999)
GDP – US$597 million (1997); US$4,081 per capita (1998)
ANNUAL AVERAGE GROWTH OF GDP – 4.1 per cent (1996)
INFLATION RATE – 5.4 per cent (1999)
UNEMPLOYMENT – 20.5 per cent (1997)
TOTAL EXTERNAL DEBT – US$184 million (1998)

### TRADE

The principal exports are bananas, coconut products (copra, edible oils, soap), cardboard boxes, beer, and textile manufactures. The chief imports are flour, meat, machinery, building materials, motor vehicles, manufactured goods, petroleum and fertilisers.

In 1996 St Lucia had a trade deficit of US$184 million and a current account deficit of US$80 million. In 1997 imports totalled US$332 million and exports US$61 million.

| *Trade with UK* | 1999 | 2000 |
|---|---|---|
| Imports from UK | £17,502,000 | £13,771,000 |
| Exports to UK | 34,469,000 | 33,429,000 |

# ST VINCENT AND THE GRENADINES

AREA – 150 sq. miles (388 sq. km)
POPULATION – 114,000 (1997 UN estimate). The language is English
CAPITAL – ΨKingstown (population, 15,466, 1991)
CURRENCY – East Caribbean dollar (EC$) of 100 cents
NATIONAL ANTHEM – St Vincent, Land So Beautiful
NATIONAL DAY – 27 October (Independence Day)
NATIONAL FLAG – Three vertical bands, of blue, yellow and green, with three green diamonds in the shape of a 'V' mounted on the yellow band
LIFE EXPECTANCY (years) – male 71.9; female 75.2
POPULATION GROWTH RATE – 0.8 per cent (1999)
POPULATION DENSITY – 286 per sq. km (1998)
URBAN POPULATION – 54.8 per cent (2000 estimate)

The territory of St Vincent includes certain of the Grenadines, a chain of small islands stretching 40 miles across the Caribbean Sea between Grenada and St Vincent, some of the larger of which are Bequia, Canouan, Mayreau, Mustique, Union Island, Petit St Vincent and Prune Island.

## HISTORY AND POLITICS

St Vincent was discovered by Christopher Columbus in 1498. It was granted by Charles I to the Earl of Carlisle in 1627 and after subsequent grants and a series of occupations alternately by the French and English, it was finally restored to Britain in 1783. St Vincent achieved full independence within the Commonwealth as St Vincent and the Grenadines on 27 October 1979.

The governing New Democratic Party (NDP) won eight seats and the United Labour Party (ULP) seven seats at the election held on 15 June 1998. As a consequence of opposition groups and trade unions pressing for the resignation of the government after the government had approved increased benefits for members of the legislature, the government and opposition agreed that the next general election should be held before 31 March 2001. The election took place on 28 March 2001 and was decisively won by the ULP, who obtained 12 seats. The NDP, who had been in power since 1984, won the remaining three seats.

### POLITICAL SYSTEM

Queen Elizabeth II is Head of State, represented by a Governor-General. The House of Assembly consists of 15 elected members and four Senators appointed by the government and two by the Opposition. It is presided over by a Speaker elected by the House from within or without it.

*Governor-General*, HE Sir Charles James Antrobus, GCMG, OBE, *sworn in* 15 October 1996

### CABINET *as at September 2001*

*Prime Minister, Finance, Planning, Economic Development, Labour, Information, Grenadine Affairs, Legal Affairs*, Ralph Gonsalves
*Deputy Prime Minister, Foreign Affairs, Commerce and Trade*, Louis Straker
*Agriculture, Lands and Fisheries*, Selmon Walters
*Education, Youth Affairs, Sport*, Mike Browne
*Health and the Environment*, Douglas Slater
*Ministers of State*, Montgomery Daniel (*Agriculture, Lands and Fisheries*); Clayton Burgin (*Education, Youth Affairs, Sport*); Conrad Sayers (*Foreign Affairs, Commerce and Trade*)
*National Security, Public Service, Airport Development*, Vincent Beache
*Social Development, Family, Gender Affairs, Ecclesiastical Affairs*, Girlyn Miguel
*Telecommunications, Science, Technology, Industry*, Jerrol Thompson
*Tourism and Culture*, Rene Baptiste
*Transport, Works, Housing*, Julian Francis

### HIGH COMMISSION FOR ST VINCENT AND THE GRENADINES

10 Kensington Court, London W8 5DL
Tel: 020-7565 2874; e-mail: highcommission.svg.uk@cw-com.net
*High Commissioner for St Vincent and the Grenadines*, HE Cenio E. Lewis, apptd 2001

### BRITISH HIGH COMMISSION

Granby Street (PO Box 132), Kingstown
Tel: (00 1 784) 457 1701
*High Commissioner*, HE John White, resident at Bridgetown, Barbados
*Acting High Commissioner*, B. Robertson

## ECONOMY

This is based mainly on agriculture but tourism (216,127 visitors in 1996) and manufacturing industries have been expanding. The main products are bananas, arrowroot, coconuts, cocoa, spices and various kinds of food crops. The main imports are foodstuffs, textiles, lumber, chemicals, motor vehicles and fuel. Bananas account for 40 per cent of exports.

In 1996 St Vincent and the Grenadines had a trade surplus of US$75 million and a current account deficit of US$35 million. In 1999 imports totalled US$201 million and exports US$49 million.

GNP – US$301 million (1999); US$2,700 per capita (1999)
GDP – US$284 million (1997); US$2,815 per capita (1998)
ANNUAL AVERAGE GROWTH OF GDP – 3.6 per cent (1996)
INFLATION RATE – 1.0 per cent (1999)
UNEMPLOYMENT – 19.8 per cent (1991)
TOTAL EXTERNAL DEBT – US$420 million (1998)

| *Trade with UK* | 1999 | 2000 |
|---|---|---|
| Imports from UK | £8,339,000 | £6,151,000 |
| Exports to UK | 20,304,000 | 18,797,000 |

---

# SAMOA

*Ole Malo Tutoatasi o Samoa – Independent State of Samoa*

---

AREA – 1,093 sq. miles (2,831 sq. km)
POPULATION – 170,000 (1997 UN estimate); 162,000 (1989 census), the largest numbers being on Upolu (114,980) and Savai'i (43,150). The Samoans are a Polynesian people, though the population also includes other Pacific Islanders, Euronesians, Chinese and Europeans. The main languages are Samoan and English. The islanders are Christians of different denominations
CAPITAL – ΨApia (population, 36,000, 1989), on Upolu. Robert Louis Stevenson died and was buried at Apia in 1894
CURRENCY – Tala (S$) of 100 sene
NATIONAL ANTHEM – The Banner of Freedom
NATIONAL DAY – 1 June (Independence Day)
NATIONAL FLAG – Red with a blue canton bearing five white stars of the Southern Cross
LIFE EXPECTANCY (years) – male 65.4; female 70.7
POPULATION GROWTH RATE – 1.1 per cent (1999)
POPULATION DENSITY – 59 per sq. km (1998)
URBAN POPULATION – 21.5 per cent (2000 estimate)
ENROLMENT (percentage of age group) –primary 96 per cent (1996); secondary 45 per cent (1995)

Samoa consists of the islands of Savai'i, Upolu, Apolima, Manono, Fanuatapu, Namua, Nuutele, Nuulua and Nuusafee. All the islands are mountainous. Upolu, the most fertile, contains the harbours of Apia and Mulifanua, and Savai'i the harbour of Salelologa.

## HISTORY AND POLITICS

Formerly administered by New Zealand (latterly with internal self-government), Western Samoa became fully independent on 1 January 1962. The state was treated as a member country of the Commonwealth until its formal admission on 28 August 1970. A constitutional amendment came into effect on 4 July 1997 changing the state's name to the Independent State of Samoa.
Suffrage was made universal following a referendum held in 1990.

In the general election held on 4 March 2001, the Human Rights Protection Party won 23 seats, the Samoan National Development Party won 13 seats and 13 seats were won by independents.

POLITICAL SYSTEM

The 1962 constitution provides for a head of state to be elected by the 49-member legislative assembly, the *Fono*, for a five-year term. Initially two of the four Paramount chiefs jointly held the office of head of state for life. When one of the chiefs died in April 1963, Susuga Malietoa Tanumafili II became head of state for life. The Head of State's functions are analogous to those of a constitutional monarch. Executive government is carried out by a Cabinet of Ministers.

HEAD OF STATE

*Head of State for Life*, HH Susuga Malietoa Tanumafili II, GCMG, CBE, *since* 15 April 1963

CABINET *as at September 2001*

*Prime Minister, Foreign Affairs, Attorney-General, Police and Prisons, Immigration, Public Service Commission*, Tuilaepa Sailele Malielegaoi
*Deputy Prime Minister, Finance*, Misa Telefoni Retzlaff
*Agriculture, Forests and Fisheries*, Tuisugaletaua Sofara Aveau
*Customs, Audit, Ombudsman*, Gaiga Tino
*Education*, Fiame Naomi Mata'afa
*Health, Labour*, Mulitalo Siafausa
*Justice*, Seumanu Aita Ah Wa
*Public Works*, Faumuina Liuga
*Tourism, Lands, Survey and Environment*, Tuala Sale Tagaloa
*Trade and Industry*, Hans Joachim Keil
*Transport and Shipping*, Palusalue Faapo II
*Women's Affairs, Internal Affairs, Broadcasting*, Tuala Ainiu Iusi
*Youth, Sports and Culture*, Ulu Vaomalo Ulu Kini

HIGH COMMISSION FOR THE INDEPENDENT STATE OF SAMOA
Franklin D. Rooseveltlaan 123, B-1050 Brussels
Tel: (00 32) (2) 660 8454
*High Commissioner for the Independent State of Samoa*, HE Tau'ili'ili'u'ili Meredith, apptd 1998

BRITISH HIGH COMMISSIONER, HE Martin Williams, CVO, OBE, resident at Wellington, New Zealand
HONORARY CONSULATE – PO Box 2029, Apia

## ECONOMY

Agriculture is the basis of the economy, employing about two-thirds of the labour force and supplying about 40 per cent of GDP and 90 per cent of exports, the principal cash crops (and exports) being coconuts (copra, oil and cream), cocoa and bananas. Efforts are being made to develop fishing on a commercial scale. Manufacturing is very small in scope and concerned largely with processing agricultural products, but is being encouraged by the government. There were over 70,000 visitors in 1996.

Samoa and American Samoa signed a memorandum of understanding on trade, education, health, agriculture and law enforcement in January 2000.

In 1998 Samoa had a trade deficit of US$77 million and a current account surplus of US$20 million. In 1999 imports totalled US$115 million and exports US$20 million.

GNP – US$181 million (1999); US$1,060 per capita (1999)
GDP – US$188 million (1997); US$1,255 per capita (1998)
ANNUAL AVERAGE GROWTH OF GDP – 6.1 per cent (1996)
INFLATION RATE – 2.2 per cent (1998)
TOTAL EXTERNAL DEBT – US$180 million (1998)

| *Trade with UK* | 1999 | 2000 |
|---|---|---|
| Imports from UK | £1,222,000 | £377,000 |
| Exports to UK | 162,000 | 34,000 |

# SAN MARINO
*Repubblica di San Marino*

AREA – 24 sq. miles (61 sq. km). Neighbour: Italy
POPULATION – 26,628 (1997 UN estimate). The official language is Italian and the religion is Roman Catholic
CAPITAL – San Marino (population, 4,357, 1994), on the slope of Monte Titano
CURRENCY – San Marino and Italian currencies are in circulation
NATIONAL DAY – 3 September
NATIONAL FLAG – Two horizontal bands, white, blue (with coat of arms of the republic in centre)
LIFE EXPECTANCY (years) – male 75.3; female 82.0
POPULATION GROWTH RATE – 1.4 per cent (1999)
POPULATION DENSITY – 424 per sq. km (1998)
URBAN POPULATION – 89.4 per cent (2000 estimate)
GDP – US$510 million (1997); US$20,659 per capita (1998)
ANNUAL AVERAGE GROWTH OF GDP – 0.7 per cent (1996)
UNEMPLOYMENT – 4.1 per cent (1998)

## HISTORY AND POLITICS

San Marino is a small republic in the hills near Rimini, on the Adriatic, founded, it is said, by a pious stonecutter of Dalmatia in the fourth century. The republic resisted Papal claims and those of neighbouring dukedoms during the 15th to 18th centuries, and its integrity and sovereignty is recognised and respected by Italy.

The principal products are wine, cereals and fruits, and the main industries are tourism, metals, machinery, textiles and food.

San Marino is in a customs union with the European Union.

Following the general election held on 10 June 2001, the number of seats held in the Grand and General Council was as follows: Christian Democratic Party (PDCS) 25, the Socialist Party (PSS) 15, the Progressive Democratic Party (PPDS) 12, others 8.

POLITICAL SYSTEM

Executive power is vested in the Congress of State composed of ten ministries under the presidency of the two heads of state, who are elected at six-monthly intervals (every April and October). Legislative power is exercised by the 60-member Great and General Council which is elected for a term of five years. A Council of Twelve forms in certain cases a Supreme Court of Justice.

HEADS OF STATE

*Regents*, Two 'Capitani Reggenti'

CONGRESS OF STATE *as at September 2001*

*Education, University, Cultural Institutes*, Pasquale Valentini (PDCS)
*Finance, Budget, Economic Planning, Relations with State Corporations, Transport*, Clelio Galassi (PDCS)
*Foreign and Political Affairs*, Gabriele Gatti (PDCS)
*Health and Social Security*, Sante Canducci (PDCS)
*Industry, Handicrafts, Economic Co-operation*, Maurizio Rattini (PSS)
*Internal Affairs, Post and Telecommunications, Civil Protection, Territory, Environment and Agriculture*, Fiorenzo Stolfi (PSS)

*Justice, Information, Relations with Municipal Authorities*, Pier Marino Menicucci (PDCS)
*Labour and Co-operation*, Pier Marino Mularoni (PDCS)
*Relations with Municipal Authorities, Production, Services*, Cesare Antonio Gasperoni (PDCS)
*Territory, Environment, Agriculture*, Fabio Berardi (PSS)
*Tourism, Commerce and Sport*, Paride Andreoli (PSS)

PDCS Christian Democratic Party; PSS San Marino Socialist Party

BRITISH AMBASSADOR, HE Sir John Shepherd, KCVO, CMG, resident at Rome, Italy

BRITISH CONSULATE-GENERAL FOR SAN MARINO
Lungarno Corsini 2, I-50123 Firenze, Italy.
Tel: (00 39) (55) 284133
*Consul-General*, R. J. Griffiths, OBE

SAN MARINO CONSULATE
Flat 51, 162 Sloane Street, London SW1X 9BS.
Tel: 020-7823 4768
*Consul-General*, M. de Camillo

| *Trade with UK* | 1999 | 2000 |
|---|---|---|
| Imports from UK | £13,009,000 | £8,694,000 |
| Exports to UK | 8,043,000 | 7,595,000 |

## SÃO TOMÉ AND PRÍNCIPE
*República Democrática de São Tomé e Príncipe*

AREA – 372 sq. miles (964 sq. km)
POPULATION – 145,000 (1997 UN estimate). The official language is Portuguese
CAPITAL – ΨSão Tomé (population, 43,420, 1995 estimate)
CURRENCY – Dobra of 100 centavos
NATIONAL ANTHEM - Independência total (Total independence)
NATIONAL DAY – 12 July (Independence Day)
NATIONAL FLAG – Horizontal stripes of green, yellow, green, the yellow of double width and bearing two black stars; and a red triangle in the hoist
LIFE EXPECTANCY (years) – male 62.1; female 64.9
POPULATION GROWTH RATE – 2.2 per cent (1999)
POPULATION DENSITY – 146 per sq. km (1998)
URBAN POPULATION – 46.7 per cent (2000 estimate)

The islands of São Tomé and Príncipe are situated in the Gulf of Guinea, off the west coast of Africa.

### HISTORY AND POLITICS

The islands were first settled by the Portuguese in 1493. In 1951 they became an overseas province of Portugal, and gained full independence on 12 July 1975. A multiparty constitution was approved by referendum in August 1990. The Movement for the Liberation of São Tomé and Príncipe-Social Democratic Party (MLSTP-PSD), which had been the sole legal party since independence, was defeated by the opposition Democratic Convergence Party (PCD) in legislative elections held on 20 January 1991. Miguel Trovoada, an independent, was elected president on 3 March 1991. A government of national unity incorporating opposition party members was appointed on 5 January 1996. President Trovoada was re-elected in July 1996. In September 1996 the government lost a vote of confidence in the National Assembly and a coalition government was installed. Legislative elections were held on 8 November 1998, in which the MLSTP-PSD won 31 of the 55 seats in the National Assembly. Guilherme Posser da Costa was confirmed as Prime Minister by the President on 23 December; the Cabinet was sworn into office on 5 January 1999.

In the presidential election which took place on 29 July 2001, Fradique de Menezes of the Independent Democratic Alliance was elected with 56.31 per cent of the vote.

HEAD OF STATE

*President and Commander-in-Chief of the Armed Forces*, Fradique de Menezes, *elected* 29 July 2001

CABINET *as at September 2001*

*Prime Minister*, Guilherme Posser da Costa
*Deputy Prime Minister, Justice and Parliamentary Affairs, Labour and Public Administration*, Alberto Paulino
*Defence*, Maj. João Quaresma Viegas Bexigas
*Economy, Agriculture, Fisheries, Commerce, Tourism*, Maria das Neves Ceita Batista de Sousa
*Education, Science and Culture, Youth*, Peregrino do Sacramento da Costa
*Foreign Affairs and São Toméan Communities Overseas*, Rafael Branco
*Health, Sports*, Antonio Soares Marques de Lima
*Infrastructure and Natural Resources*, Luis Alberto Carneiro dos Prazeres
*Interior*, Manuel da Cruz Marcal Lima
*Planning, Finance and Co-operation*, Adelino Castelo David
*Secretary of State for Youth, Sport and Professional Training*, Luis Vaz de Sousa Bastos

EMBASSY OF THE DEMOCRATIC REPUBLIC OF SÃO TOMÉ AND PRÍNCIPE
Montgomeryplein, Tervurenlaan 175, B-1150 Brussels
Tel: (00 32) (2) 734 8966
*Chargé d'Affaires*, Antonio de Lima Viegas

BRITISH CONSULATE
Residencial Avenida, Av. Da Independencia CP 257, São Tomé
Tel: (00 239) (12) 21026/7
*British Ambassador*, HE Caroline Elmes, CMG, resident at Luanda, Angola

### ECONOMY

Agriculture accounts for nearly a quarter of GDP and employs nearly 40 per cent of the workforce, with cocoa accounting for 86 per cent of exports in 1997. Drought and mismanagement have led to declining cocoa production, which has resulted in balance of payments deficits.

On 28 April 2000, the IMF approved a three-year credit of US$8.7 million to support the government's 2000-2 economic programme. A further debt reduction package worth about US$200 million was agreed by the IMF and the World Bank on 20 December 2000.

In 1997 imports totalled US$16 million and exports US$5 million.

GNP – US$40 million (1999); US$270 per capita (1999)
GDP – US$44 million (1997); US$210 per capita (1998)
ANNUAL AVERAGE GROWTH OF GDP – 2.2 per cent (1996)
TOTAL EXTERNAL DEBT – US$246 million (1998)

| *Trade with UK* | 1999 | 2000 |
|---|---|---|
| Imports from UK | £3,911,000 | £1,941,000 |
| Exports to UK | 12,000 | 8,000 |

## SAUDI ARABIA
*Al-Mamlaka al-'Arabiyya as-Sa'ūdiyya*

AREA – 830,000 sq. miles (2,149,690 sq. km). Neighbours: UAE and Qatar (east), Jordan, Iraq and Kuwait (north), Yemen and Oman (south)
POPULATION – 21,429,000 (1997 UN estimate); 16,929,294 (1992 census). Islam is the only permitted religion. The language is Arabic

CAPITAL – Riyadh (Ar-Riyād) (population, 3,100,000, 1998 estimate)
MAJOR CITIES – Jiddah (1.5 million); Buraydah; Ad-Dammām; Al-Hofūf; Al-Makkah (Mecca); Al-Madīinah; Tabūk
CURRENCY – Saudi riyal (SR) of 20 qursh or 100 halala
NATIONAL ANTHEM – Long live our beloved King
NATIONAL DAY – 23 September (proclamation and unification of the Kingdom, 1932)
NATIONAL FLAG – Green oblong, white Arabic device in centre: 'There is no God but God and Muhammad is the Prophet of God', and a white scimitar beneath the lettering
LIFE EXPECTANCY (years) – male 71.0; female 72.6
POPULATION GROWTH RATE – 3.0 per cent (1999)
POPULATION DENSITY – 9 per sq. km (1998)
URBAN POPULATION – 85.7 per cent (2000 estimate)

Saudi Arabia comprises most of the Arabian peninsula. The Nejd ('plateau') extends over the centre of the peninsula, including the Nafud and Dahna deserts. The Hejaz ('the boundary') extends along the Red Sea coast to Asir and contains the holy towns of Mecca (Al-Makkah) and Medina (Al-Madīnah). Asir ('inaccessible') is so named for its mountainous terrain, and, with the coastal plain of the Tihama, lies along the southern Red Sea coast from the Hejaz to the border with Yemen. It is the only region to enjoy substantial rainfall. The east and south-east of the country are lower-lying and largely desert.

Mecca (Al-Makkah), about 60 km east of Jeddah, is the birthplace of the Prophet Muhammad, and contains the Great Mosque, within which is the Kaaba (*Ka'abah*) or sacred shrine of the Muslim religion. This is the focus of the annual Hajj ('pilgrimage'). Medina (Al-Madīnah) Al Munawwarah ('The City of Light'), some 300 km north of Al-Makkah, is celebrated as the first city to embrace Islam and as the Prophet Muhammad's burial place.

## HISTORY AND POLITICS

In the 18th century Nejd was an independent state governed from Diriya. It subsequently fell under Turkish rule; in 1913 Abdul Aziz ibn Saud threw off Turkish rule and captured the Turkish province of Al Hasa. In 1920 he captured the Asir and in 1921 the Jebel Shammar territory of the Rashid family. In 1925 he completed the conquest of the Hejaz. Great Britain recognised Abdul Aziz ibn Saud as an independent ruler, King of the Hejaz and of Nejd and its Dependencies, in 1927. The name was changed to the Kingdom of Saudi Arabia in September 1932.

### POLITICAL SYSTEM

Saudi Arabia is a hereditary monarchy, ruled by the sons and grandsons of Abdul Aziz ibn Saud, in accordance with the Islamic Shari'ah law. The line of succession passes from brother to brother according to age, although several sons of ibn Saud renounced their right to the throne. All sons and grandsons of ibn Saud must be consulted before a new king accedes to the throne.

In 1992 King Fahd announced a new Basic Law for the system of government based on Shari'ah law and including rules to protect personal freedoms. The constitution is defined as the Holy Koran (*Qur'an*) and the *Sunnah* (the teachings and sayings of the Prophet Muhammad). The King and the Council of Ministers (established in 1953) retain executive power. A consultative council (*Majlis-ash-Shūra*) of a chairman and 120 members appointed by the King was set up to share power with, and question, the government and to make recommendations to the King. The Majlis-ash-Shūra debates government policy in the areas of the budget, defence, foreign and social affairs. Members of the ruling al-Saud family are excluded from membership of the Council, which has a four-year term and takes decisions by majority vote. Cabinet ministers have terms of four years, with the possibility of a two-year extension.

In 1993 the country was reorganised into 13 provinces: Riyadh; Makkah; Al-Madīnah; Al Qasim; Eastern; Asir; Tabūk; Hā'il; Northern Border; Jīzān; Najrān; Baha; Al-Jawf. Each province has a governor appointed by the King and a council of prominent local citizens to advise the governor on local government, budgetary and planning issues.

### HEAD OF STATE

*Custodian of the Two Holy Mosques and HM The King of Saudi Arabia*, King Fahd ibn Abdul Aziz al-Saud, *born* 1923, *ascended the throne* 1 June 1982
*HRH Crown Prince*, Prince Abdullah ibn Abdul Aziz al-Saud

### COUNCIL OF MINISTERS *as at September 2001*

*Prime Minister*, HM The King
*First Deputy Prime Minister, Commander of the National Guard*, HRH The Crown Prince
*Second Deputy Prime Minister, Defence and Civil Aviation*, HRH Prince Sultan ibn Abdul Aziz al-Saud
*Agriculture and Water Resources*, Abdullah ibn Abdul Aziz ibn Muammar
*Civil Service*, Mohammad ibn Ali al-Fayez
*Commerce*, Osama ibn Jaafar ibn Ibrahim al-Faqih
*Education*, Mohammad ibn Ahmad al-Rashid
*Finance and National Economy*, Ibrahim ibn Abdel Aziz al-Assaf
*Foreign Affairs*, HRH Prince Saud al-Faisal ibn Abdul Aziz al-Saud
*Health*, Osama ibn Abdul-Majid Shabakshi
*Higher Education*, Khalid ibn Muhammad al-Anqari
*Industry and Electricity*, Hashem ibn Abdullah ibn Hashem Yamani
*Information*, Fouad ibn Abdul-Salam Mohammad Farisi
*Interior*, HRH Prince Nayef ibn Abdul Aziz al-Saud
*Islamic Affairs*, Shaikh Salah ibn Abdul-Aziz al-Shaikh
*Justice*, Abdullah ibn Muhammed ibn Ibrahim al-Shaikh
*Labour and Social Affairs*, Ali ibn Ibrahim al-Nemla
*Minister of State*, Ali ibn Talal al-Jehani
*Municipal and Rural Affairs*, Mohammad ibn Ibrahim al-Jarallah
*Oil and Mineral Resources*, Ali Ibrahim al-Naimi
*Pilgrimage Affairs*, Ayad ibn Amin Madani
*Planning, Posts, Telegraphs and Telecommunications*, Khaled ibn Mohammad al-Qussaibi
*Public Works and Housing*, HRH Prince Miteb ibn Abdul Aziz al-Saud
*Transport*, Nasir ibn Muhammad al-Sallum

### ROYAL EMBASSY OF SAUDI ARABIA

30 Charles Street, London W1X 7PM
Tel: 020-7917 3000
*Ambassador Extraordinary and Plenipotentiary*, HE Dr Ghazi Algosaibi, apptd 1992
*Defence Attaché*, Brig.-Gen. A. al-Obaykan
*Cultural Attaché*, A. al-Nasser
*Commercial Attaché*, M. al-Sheddi
*Information Attaché*, Dr F. al-Dakheel

### BRITISH EMBASSY

PO Box 94351, Riyadh 11693
Tel: (00 966) (1) 488 0077
*Ambassador Extraordinary and Plenipotentiary*, HE Sir Derek J. Plumbly, KCMG, apptd 2000

CONSULATE-GENERAL – PO Box 393, Jiddah 21411.
*Consul-General*, A. Henderson
TRADE OFFICE – PO Box 1868, Al-Khobar 31952

BRITISH COUNCIL DIRECTOR, David Burton, OBE, Tower B, 2nd Floor, Al- Mousa Centre, Olaya Street, PO Box 58012, Riyadh 11594; e-mail: enquiry.riyadh@sa.britishcouncil.org. There are also offices in Jiddah and Ad-Dammām

## DEFENCE

The Army has 1,055 main battle tanks, 1,900 armoured personnel carriers, 970 armoured infantry fighting vehicles and 67 helicopters. The Navy has four frigates, 26 patrol and coastal vessels and 21 armed helicopters at eight bases. The Air Force has 417 combat aircraft.

Saudi Arabia is base to the Gulf Co-operational Council Peninsula Shield Force of 7,000 troops. The USA, UK and France station aircraft and support units in the country to patrol the air exclusion zone in southern Iraq.

MILITARY EXPENDITURE – 15.5 per cent of GDP (1999)

MILITARY PERSONNEL – 126,500: Army 75,000, Navy 15,500, Air Force 20,000, Air Defence Force 16,000, National Guard 100,000, Paramilitaries 15,500

## ECONOMY

Saudi Arabia's revenue fell when world oil prices dropped from the mid-1980s onwards, and financial reserves had to be used up to meet budget deficits. However, the sharp rise in world oil prices in 2000 has improved the country's economic prospects.

Agriculture accounted for 6.1 per cent of GDP and engaged 12.2 per cent of the workforce in 1997. The productivity of traditional dryland farming is supplemented by extensive irrigation, desalination and use of aquifers.

The principal industry is oil extraction and processing; 405,200,000 tonnes were produced in 1998. Oil was first found in commercial quantities in 1938. Proven oil reserves of 259 billion barrels account for more than one-quarter of the world's proven reserves. The country is the world's largest oil exporter. Recoverable gas reserves of 204.5 trillion cubic feet, in fields associated with crude oil and those separate from it, are beginning to be exploited; production in 1998 was 46,820 million cubic metres. Mineral exploitation of gold, silver, copper and other minerals is also beginning, with gold production of 5.1 tonnes in 1998.

The government, in a series of five-year development plans begun in 1970, has actively encouraged the establishment of manufacturing industry. Industries have developed in the fields of construction materials, metal fabrication, simple machinery and electrical equipment, food and beverages, textiles, chemicals and plastics.

The seventh development plan, covering 2000–5, was approved in September 2000. It aimed to eliminate the budget and current account deficits, promote economic growth and diversity and introduce legislation to increase the proportion of Saudi Arabian citizens in the workforce.

GNP – US$139,365 million (1999); US$6,910 per capita (1998)

GDP – US$134,825 million (1997); US$7,259 per capita (1998)

ANNUAL AVERAGE GROWTH OF GDP – 0.5 per cent (1996)

INFLATION RATE – 1.4 per cent (1999)

### TRADE

Oil remains the main source of receipts in the balance of payments. The leading suppliers of imports are the USA, the UK, Germany and Japan, and the chief customers for exports are Japan, the USA, South Korea and Singapore. There is a total ban on the importation of alcohol, pork products, firearms, and items regarded as non-Islamic or pornographic.

In 1999 there was a trade surplus of US$22,765 million and a current account deficit of US$1,701 million. In 1998

imports totalled US$30,013 million and exports totalled US$39,775 million.

| *Trade with UK* | 1999 | 2000 |
|---|---|---|
| Imports from UK | £1,528,712,000 | £1,598,179,000 |
| Exports to UK | £874,684,000 | £1,054,304,000 |

## COMMUNICATIONS

There is one railway line from Ad-Dammām to Riyadh, which was opened in 1951 and is operated by the Saudi Government Railway Organisation. The line is being extended to the port of Al-Jubayl on the Gulf. A network of 139,200 km of roads (of which 45,200 km are paved), including an expressway system, connects all the cities and main towns. There are 21 ports, of which the major ones are Ad-Dammām and Al-Jubayl (Gulf) and Jiddah, Yanbu and Jizan (Red Sea). The 15.5 mile-long King Fahd Causeway completed in 1986 connects the Eastern Province to the state of Bahrain and is the world's second longest causeway.

There are international airports at Az-Zahrān (King Fahd), Jiddah (King Abdul Aziz), and Riyadh (King Khalid).

Telecommunications are being rapidly expanded with 1.78 million telephone lines in 1995 and seven earth stations linked to the Intelsat system, allowing direct dialling to 185 countries.

## EDUCATION

With the exception of a few schools for expatriate children, all schools are government-supervised and are segregated for boys and girls. There are universities in Jiddah, Al-Makkah, Riyadh (branches in Abha and Qassim), Ad-Dammām (branch at Al-Hufūf) and Az-Zahrān, and there are Islamic universities in Al-Madīnah and Riyadh together with 83 tertiary colleges. There is great emphasis on vocational training, provided at literacy and artisan skill training centres and more advanced industrial, commercial and agricultural education institutes. Education from kindergarten to university is free, with 22,678 schools in 1998.

ILLITERACY RATE – 18.0 per cent (2000)

ENROLMENT (percentage of age group) – primary 61 per cent (1996); secondary 48 per cent (1996); tertiary 16.3 per cent (1996)

## SENEGAL
*République du Sénégal*

AREA – 75,955 sq. miles (196,722 sq. km). Neighbours: Mauritania (north), Mali (east), Guinea-Bissau and Guinea (south), the Gambia
POPULATION – 9,285,000 (1997 UN estimate), 94 per cent Muslim, 4 per cent Christian, 1 per cent Animist. The official language is French; the principal local language is Wolof. Fulani, Serer, Mandinka, Jola and Sarakole are also spoken
CAPITAL – ΨDakar (population, 1,905,000, 1998 UN estimate)
MAJOR CITIES – Rufisque (150,000); Thiés (248,000); ΨZiguinchor (192,000), 1998 UN estimates
CURRENCY – Franc CFA of 100 centimes
NATIONAL ANTHEM - Pincez tous vos koras, frappez les balafons (All pluck your koras, strike the balafons)
NATIONAL DAY – 4 April
NATIONAL FLAG – Three vertical bands, green, yellow and red; a green star on the yellow band
LIFE EXPECTANCY (years) – male 53.5; female 56.2
POPULATION GROWTH RATE – 2.6 per cent (1999)
POPULATION DENSITY – 46 per sq. km (1998)
URBAN POPULATION – 47.4 per cent (2000 estimate)
MILITARY EXPENDITURE – 1.6 per cent of GDP (1999)
MILITARY PERSONNEL – 9,400: Army 8,000, Navy 600, Air Force 800, Paramilitaries 5,800
CONSCRIPTION DURATION – Two years (selective)
ILLITERACY RATE – 62.7 per cent (2000)
ENROLMENT (percentage of age group) – primary 60 per cent (1997); tertiary 3.4 per cent (1996)

### HISTORY AND POLITICS

Formerly a French colony, Senegal elected in 1958 to remain within the French Community as an autonomous republic. It became independent as part of the Federation of Mali in June 1960 and seceded to form the Republic of Senegal in September 1960.

Abdoulaye Wade, the leader of the Senegalese Democratic Party, was elected in the second round of the presidential election on 19 March 2000 with 58.49 per cent of the vote, thus becoming the first president not to belong to the Socialist Party. The legislative election on 29 April 2001 was won by an alliance of 40 parties, the Sopi (Change) coalition, led by the Senegalese Democratic Party (PDS). Sopi won 89 seats, the Socialist Party (PS), which had been in government, secured only ten seats, and the Alliance of Progress Forces won 11 seats.

#### INSURGENCY

A separatist civil war has been fought in the southern Casamance region for the past 17 years. The government and the Casamance Movement of Democratic Forces (MFDC) agreed a cease-fire on 26 December 1999. A meeting between the two sides in January 2000 agreed to establish a joint body to monitor progress, to withdraw army and rebel forces from occupied villages, and to co-operate on mine clearance and the refugee problem. The government and the MFDC signed a peace agreement on 16 March 2001, but violence in the region increased during the election campaign in April 2001.

#### POLITICAL SYSTEM

A referendum to approve a new constitution took place on 7 January 2001. The constitution, which was approved by 96 per cent of those voting, dissolved the Senate, reduced the number of MPs in the National Assembly from 140 to 120, shortened the presidential term of office to five years, and guaranteed the right to form political parties. A general election for the National Assembly is held every five years.

#### HEAD OF STATE

*President*, Abdoulayé Wade, *elected* 19 March 2000, *sworn in* 1 April 2000

#### COUNCIL OF MINISTERS *as at September 2001*

*Prime Minister*, Mamé Madior Boyé
*Agriculture and Livestock*, Pape Diouf
*Armed Forces*, Youga Sambou
*Civil Service, Labour and Employment*, Yero Deh
*Culture, Tourism and Leisure*, Mamadou Makalou
*Economy and Finance*, Abdoulayé Diop
*Education*, Moustapha Sourang
*Equipment and Transport*, Youssouf Sakho
*Family and Children*, Awa Gueye Kebe
*Fisheries*, Cheikh Saadibou Fall
*Foreign Affairs, African Union and Senegalese Abroad*, Cheikh Tidiane Gadio
*Handicrafts and Industry*, Landing Savane
*Health*, Awa Marie Coll Seck
*Interior*, Maj.-Gen. Mamadou Niang
*Justice and Keeper of the Seals*, Basile Senghor
*Mines, Energy and Water Resources*, Macky Sall
*Ministers-Delegate*, Cheikh Hadjibou Soumare (*Budget*); Thiéwo Cisse Ducoure (*Local Constituencies*)
*Relations with Assemblies*, Mamadou Diop
*Small and Medium Enterprises and Commerce*, Aïcha Agne Pouye
*Social Development and National Solidarity*, Aminata Tall
*Sport*, Joseph Ndong
*Technical and Vocational Training, Basic Education and National Languages*, Bécaye Diop
*Town and Country Planning*, Seydou Sall
*Youth, Environment and Public Hygiene*, Modou Fada Diagne

#### EMBASSY OF THE REPUBLIC OF SENEGAL

39 Marloes Road, London W8 6LA
Tel: 020-7938 4048/7937 7237
*Ambassador Extraordinary and Plenipotentiary*, HE Gabriel Alexandre Sar, apptd 1993

#### BRITISH EMBASSY

20 rue du Docteur Guillet (BP 6025), Dakar
Tel: (00 221) 823 7392/9971
E-mail: britemb@telecomplus.sn
*Ambassador Extraordinary and Plenipotentiary*, HE E. Alan Burner, apptd 1997

BRITISH COUNCIL DIRECTOR, Steve McNulty, 34–36 Blvd de la République, BP 6232, Dakar; e-mail: bc.dakar@enda.sn

### ECONOMY

Around 75 per cent of the workforce are employed in agriculture. Senegal's principal exports are fish, groundnuts (raw and processed) and phosphates. Tourism is also of growing importance as a revenue earner; in 1999 there were some 400,000 overseas visitors. Principal imports are food, machinery, fuel oils and transport equipment. Senegal exports fish, furniture, oilseeds and fruit, rubber, fertilisers and animal fodder to the UK, and imports foodstuffs, cigarettes, chemicals, machinery and transport equipment, vegetable fats and oils, and manufactured goods from the UK.

In 1996 there were 14,576 km of roads, of which 4,271 km were paved. There are 1,225 km of railway track.

In 1997 there was a trade deficit of US$271 million and a current account deficit of US$185 million. In 1999

imports totalled US$1,291 million and exports US$983 million.
GNP – US$4,685 million (1999); US$510 per capita (1999)
GDP – US$4,555 million (1997); US$518 per capita (1998)
Annual Average Growth of GDP – 5.6 per cent (1996)
Inflation Rate – 0.8 per cent (1999)
Total External Debt – US$3,861 million (1998)

| *Trade with UK* | 1999 | 2000 |
|---|---|---|
| Imports from UK | £24,335,000 | £32,253,000 |
| Exports to UK | 10,272,000 | 12,663,000 |

## SEYCHELLES
*The Republic of Seychelles*

Area – 176 sq. miles (455 sq. km)
Population – 80,000 (1998 estimate). The languages are English, French and Créole
Capital – ΨVictoria (population, 24,324, 1987), on Mahé
Currency – Seychelles rupee of 100 cents
National Anthem – Koste Seselwa (Seychellois Unite)
National Day – 18 June
National Flag – Five rays extending from the lower hoist over the whole field, coloured blue, yellow, green, white and red
Life Expectancy (years) – male 64.9; female 70.5
Population Growth Rate – 1.1 per cent (1999)
Population Density – 173 per sq. km (1998)
Urban Population – 63.8 per cent (2000 estimate)
Military Expenditure – 1.8 per cent of GDP (1999)
Military Personnel – 450: Army 200, Paramilitaries 250

Seychelles, in the Indian Ocean, consists of 115 islands spread over 400,000 sq. miles of ocean. There is a relatively compact granitic group, 32 islands in all, with high hills and mountains (highest point about 2,972 ft), of which Mahé is the largest and most populated (90 per cent of the population live on Mahé); and the outlying coralline group, for the most part only a little above sea-level. Although only 4° S. of the Equator, the climate is pleasant though tropical.

### HISTORY AND POLITICS

Proclaimed French territory in 1756, the Mahé group was settled as a dependency of Mauritius from 1770, was captured by a British ship in 1794, and changed hands several times between 1803 and 1814, when it was finally assigned to Great Britain. In 1903 these islands, together with the coralline group, were formed into a separate colony. On 29 June 1976, the islands became an independent republic within the Commonwealth. A coup d'état took place in 1977. Seychelles was a one-party state from 1979 until 1991, when a multiparty democratic system was proposed by President René.

In presidential and legislative elections held in March 1998, President René was re-elected with 67 per cent of the vote, and the Seychelles People's Progressive Front formed a government after winning 30 seats in the National Assembly.

#### Political System

Under the constitution adopted in 1993, multiparty politics was institutionalised, a National Assembly of up to 34 members (23 elected by constituencies, up to 11 by proportional representation) was established and the presidential mandate was set at five years, renewable three times.

#### Head of State

*President, Commander-in-Chief of the Armed Forces, Defence, Interior*, France-Albert René, *assumed office* 5 June 1977; *elected* 1979; *re-elected* 1984, 1989, 1993, 22 March 1998
*Vice-President, Finance, Environment and Transport, Information Technology and Communications*, James Michel

#### Council of Ministers *as at September 2001*

The President
The Vice-President
*Administration*, Noellie Alexander
*Agriculture and Marine Resources*, Dolor Ernesta
*Culture and Information*, Ronald Jumeau
*Education*, Danny Faure
*Employment and Social Affairs*, William Herminie
*Foreign Affairs*, Jérémie Bonnelame
*Health*, Jacquelin Dugasse
*Industry and International Business*, Patrick Pillay
*Land Use and Environment*, Joseph Belmont
*Local Government, Sports and Youth*, Sylvette Pool
*Tourism and Civil Aviation*, Simone de Commarmond

#### Seychelles High Commission

2nd Floor, Eros House, 111 Baker Street, London W1U 6RR
Tel: 020-7224 1660
E-mail:seyhclon@aol.com
*High Commissioner*, HE Bertrand Rassool, apptd 1999

#### British High Commission

Oliaji Trade Centre, PO Box 161 Victoria, Mahé
Tel: (00 248) 225225/225356
E-mail: bhcsey@seychelles.net
*High Commissioner*, HE John Yapp, apptd 1997

### ECONOMY

The economy is based on tourism, fishing, small-scale agriculture and manufacturing, and the re-export of fuel for aircraft and ships. Deep sea tuna fishing by foreign fleets under licence, improved port facilities at Victoria and exports from a tuna canning factory attract growing revenues. The government is attempting to reduce the reliance on tourism, which generates the majority of foreign exchange earnings, by promoting the country as an offshore haven for financial services. There were 128,258 foreign visitors in 1998.
GNP – US$520 million (1999); US$6,540 per capita (1999)
GDP – US$548 million (1997); US$7,378 per capita (1998)
Annual Average Growth of GDP – 3.2 per cent (1996)
Inflation Rate – 2.6 per cent (1998)
Total External Debt – US$187 million (1998)

#### Trade

Principal exports in 1998 were canned tuna, frozen prawns, fish and cinnamon bark. The principal imports were machinery and transport equipment, manufactures, foodstuffs and tobacco, fuel oils and chemicals.

In 1997 there was a trade deficit of US$188 million and a current account deficit of US$63 million. In 1995 imports totalled US$274 million and exports US$100 million.

| *Trade with UK* | 1999 | 2000 |
|---|---|---|
| Imports from UK | £14,215,000 | £14,026,000 |
| Exports to UK | 34,997,000 | 38,647,000 |

## SIERRA LEONE
*The Republic of Sierra Leone*

AREA – 27,699 sq. miles (71,740 sq. km). Neighbours: Guinea (north, north-east), Liberia (south-east)
POPULATION – 4,949,000 (1997 UN estimate). The south is inhabited by peoples whose languages fall into the Mende group; the north by the Temne and smaller groups such as the Limba, Loko, Koranko and Susu
CAPITAL – ΨFreetown (population, 469,776, 1985)
CURRENCY – Leone (Le) of 100 cents
NATIONAL ANTHEM – High We Exalt Thee, Realm of the Free
NATIONAL DAY – 27 April (Independence Day)
NATIONAL FLAG – Three horizontal stripes of leaf green, white and cobalt blue
LIFE EXPECTANCY (years) – male 33.2; female 35.4
POPULATION GROWTH RATE – 1.9 per cent (1999)
POPULATION DENSITY – 64 per sq. km (1998)
URBAN POPULATION – 36.6 per cent (2000 estimate)
MILITARY EXPENDITURE – 1.5 per cent of GDP (1999)
MILITARY PERSONNEL – 3,000: Navy 200 (army disbanded to reform with strength of c.4,000)

## HISTORY AND POLITICS

In the late 18th century a project was begun to settle destitute Africans from England on Freetown peninsula. In 1808 the settlement was declared a Crown colony and became the main base in West Africa for enforcing the 1807 Act outlawing the slave trade. Africans from North America and the West Indies, and Africans rescued from slave ships also settled there. In 1896 a Protectorate was declared over the hinterland.

In 1951 the colony of Freetown and the Protectorate were united and on 27 April 1961 Sierra Leone became a fully independent state within the Commonwealth. In 1971 a republican constitution was adopted and Dr Siaka Stevens became the first executive president. In 1978 Sierra Leone became a one-party state, following approval by Parliament and a referendum.

In September 1991 a new multiparty constitution was adopted and an interim government formed, which was overthrown by a military coup on 29 April 1992. The military government surrendered power to a civilian government on 29 March 1996, following legislative elections on 26–27 February and a run-off election for the presidency on 15 March.

The Sierra Leone People's Party (SLPP) won 27 seats in the 68-member National Assembly and formed a government with the support of the People's Democratic Party and the Democratic Centre Party. The SLPP's candidate, Ahmad Tejan Kabbah, won the presidential contest, attracting 59.4 per cent of the vote.

In May 1997 army officers led by Major Johnny Koroma seized power. President Kabbah fled and a 20-member Armed Forces Revolutionary Council was set up with Koroma as chairman and Revolutionary United Front (RUF) leader Foday Sankoh as Vice-Chairman. In July 1997, a Nigerian-led ECOMOG force was sent to oust Koroma and restore the legitimate government. On 24 October 1997, a peace agreement was reached which provided for Kabbah to return to power within six months and granted immunity from prosecution to Koroma. ECOMOG troops gained control of Freetown on 12 February 1998, and ousted the Koroma regime. President Kabbah returned to Freetown on 10 March 1998.

A general election is due to be held on 14 May 2002.

### INSURGENCY

Since May 1991 government forces have been fighting the RUF whose aim is to force all foreigners out of the country and to nationalise the mining sector. Attacks by the RUF intensified in December 1998 and on 6 January 1999 the RUF attacked Freetown. ECOMOG troops launched a counter-attack on 9–10 January, recapturing the city.

President Kabbah and Foday Sankoh signed a cease-fire agreement on 18 May 1999 and it was agreed in July 1999 that Sankoh would be appointed Vice-President and head the Mineral Resources Commission and that the RUF would be given four cabinet posts. A government of national unity was announced on 2 November 1999. Violence continued, despite the efforts of a UN peacekeeping force, the UN Mission to Sierra Leone (UNAMSIL), which officially took over from ECOMOG on 29 April 2000. The cease-fire agreement collapsed when the RUF abducted 500 UNAMSIL peacekeepers between 30 April–6 May, and on 6 May the RUF used captured UNAMSIL weaponry to launch an advance on Freetown. A temporary British military deployment was despatched to evacuate British, EU and Commonwealth nationals from Freetown. UNAMSIL troops, along with Sierra Leonean Army (SLA) and Nigerian Army troops, went on the offensive and drove the RUF back. RUF leader Foday Sankoh, who had been the Vice-President since November 1999, was arrested on 17 May 2000.

Following the withdrawal of British forces on 14 June 2000, the British government sent an army team to begin a three-year training programme to assist the SLA.

A cease-fire brokered by ECOWAS was signed by the government and the RUF on 11 November 2000, but was never fully implemented. An agreement to end all hostilities was signed by the RUF and the pro-government Civil Defence Forces on 16 May 2001.

### HEAD OF STATE

*President, Defence*, Ahmad Tejan Kabbah, *elected* 15 March 1996
*Vice-President*, Albert Joe Demby

### CABINET *as at September 2001*

The President
The Vice-President
*Agriculture, Forestry and Marine Resources*, Okere Adams
*Attorney-General, Justice*, Solomon Berewa
*Culture and Tourism*, Jumo Jalloh
*Development and Economic Planning*, Kade Sesay
*Education, Youth and Sport*, Alpha Wurie
*Energy and Power*, Chernor Jalloh
*Finance*, Peter Kuyembeh
*Foreign Affairs and International Relations*, Ahmed Ramadan Dumbuya
*Health and Sanitation*, Ibrahim Tejan Jalloh

*Information*, Cecil Blake
*Labour and Industrial Relations*, Alpha Timbo
*Lands, Housing and Country Planning*, Alfred Bobson Sesay
*Mineral Resources*, Alhaji Mohamed Deen
*Political and Parliamentary Affairs*, Abu Aiah Koroma
*Rural Development and Local Government*, James Banda Dauda
*Safety and Security*, Charles Magai
*Social Welfare, Gender, Children's Affairs*, Shirley Gbujama
*Tourism and Culture*, A. B. S. Jumo Jalloh
*Trade and Industry*, Osman Kamara
*Transport and Communications*, Momoh Pujeh
*Works and Maintenance*, S. U. M. Jah

SIERRA LEONE HIGH COMMISSION
Oxford Circus House, 245 Oxford Street, London W1R 1LF
Tel: 020-7287 9884
*High Commissioner*, HE Sulaiman Tejan-Jalloh, apptd 2000

BRITISH HIGH COMMISSION
Spur Road, Freetown
Tel: (00 232) (22) 232563/4/5
E-mail: bhc@sierratel.sl
*High Commissioner*, HE David Alan Jones, apptd 2000

BRITISH COUNCIL DIRECTOR, Rajiv Bendre, PO Box 124, Tower Hill, Freetown; e-mail: bcouncil@sierratel.sl

## ECONOMY

On the Freetown peninsula, farming is largely confined to the production of cassava and crops such as maize and vegetables for local consumption. In the hinterland the principal agricultural product is rice, which is the staple food of the country, and cash crops such as cocoa, coffee, palm kernels and ginger. Cattle production is also important.

The economy depends largely on mineral exports, mainly diamonds, gold and bauxite, although mineral production has been disrupted by the insurgency.

In December 1999, the IMF approved US$21.31 million to assist the government's reconstruction and economic recovery programme.

In 1999 imports totalled US$81 million and exports US$6 million.

GNP – US$653 million (1999); US$130 per capita (1999)
GDP – US$1,151 million (1997); US$154 per capita (1998)
ANNUAL AVERAGE GROWTH OF GDP – 3.6 per cent (1996)
INFLATION RATE – 34.1 per cent (1999)
TOTAL EXTERNAL DEBT – US$1,243 million (1998)

| Trade with UK | 1999 | 2000 |
|---|---|---|
| Imports from UK | £41,308,000 | £77,752,000 |
| Exports to UK | 3,141,000 | 1,676,000 |

## COMMUNICATIONS

Since the phasing out of the railway system in 1974 the road network has been developed considerably; there are now 7,000 miles of roads in the country, 2,000 miles being surfaced. A bridge has been constructed over the Mano River linking Sierra Leone and Liberia.

The Freetown international airport is situated at Lungi. The main port is Freetown, which has one of the largest natural harbours in the world. There are smaller ports at Pepel, Bonthe and Niti.

Radio is operated by the government. Broadcasts are made in several of the indigenous languages, in addition to English and French.

## EDUCATION

Technical education is provided in the two government technical institutes, situated in Freetown and Kenema, in two trade centres and in the technical training establishments of the mining companies. Teacher training is carried out at the University of Sierra Leone, six colleges in the provinces and in the Milton Margai Training College near Freetown.

ILLITERACY RATE – 63.7 per cent (2000)
ENROLMENT (percentage of age group) – tertiary 1.4 per cent (1990)

# SINGAPORE

AREA – 255 sq. miles (660 sq. km)
POPULATION – 4,017,733 (2000 census): Chinese 76.8 per cent, Malays 13.9 per cent, Indians (including those of Pakistani, Bangladeshi and Sri Lankan origin) 7.9 per cent and 1.4 per cent from other ethnic groups. Malay, Mandarin, Tamil and English are the official languages. At least eight Chinese dialects are used. Malay is the national language and English is the language of administration. The religions are Buddhism 42.5 per cent, Islam 14.9 per cent, Christianity 14.6 per cent, Taoism 8.5 per cent, Hinduism 4.0 per cent
CURRENCY – Singapore dollar (S$) of 100 cents
NATIONAL ANTHEM – Majullah Singapura (May Singapore progress)
NATIONAL DAY – 9 August
NATIONAL FLAG – Horizontal bands of red over white; crescent with five five-point stars on red band near staff
LIFE EXPECTANCY (years) – male 75.1; female 80.8
POPULATION GROWTH RATE – 1.7 per cent (1999)
POPULATION DENSITY – 6,255 per sq. km (1998)
URBAN POPULATION – 100.0 per cent (2000 estimate)
MILITARY EXPENDITURE – 5.6 per cent of GDP (1999)
MILITARY PERSONNEL – 60,500: Army 50,000, Navy 4,500, Air Force 6,000; Paramilitaries 108,000
CONSCRIPTION DURATION – 24–30 months
ILLITERACY RATE – 7.6 per cent
ENROLMENT (percentage of age group) – primary 92 per cent (1996); tertiary 38.5 per cent (1996)

Singapore consists of the island of Singapore and 59 islets. Singapore island is 26 miles long and 14 miles in breadth and is situated just north of the Equator off the southern extremity of the Malay peninsula, from which it is separated by the Straits of Johore. A causeway crosses the three-quarters of a mile to the mainland. The climate is hot and humid. Rainfall averages 240 cm a year and temperature ranges from 24° to 32° C (76°–89° F).

## HISTORY AND POLITICS

Singapore, where Sir Stamford Raffles first established a trading post under the East India Company in 1819, was incorporated with Penang and Malacca to form the Straits Settlements in 1826. The Straits Settlements became a Crown colony in 1867. Singapore fell into Japanese hands in 1942 and civil government was not restored until 1946, when it became a separate colony. Internal self-government was introduced in 1959. Singapore became a state of Malaysia in September 1963, but left Malaysia and became an independent sovereign state within the Commonwealth on 9 August 1965. Singapore adopted a republican constitution from that date.

After the general election of 2 January 1997 the People's Action Party (PAP) had 81 seats in Parliament. S. R. Nathan became President of Singapore on 1 September 1999; no election was held as he was the sole candidate.

### POLITICAL SYSTEM

The president is directly elected for a six-year term, and can veto government decisions relating to internal security, the budget, financial reserves and the appointment of senior civil servants. The President appoints the Prime Minister and, on his advice, the members of the Cabinet. There is a Parliament of 83 directly elected members, with up to six further non-constituency members from opposition parties (NCMPs), dependent on their share of the vote, directly elected for a five-year term. Up to nine members can also be nominated by the government for a two-year term (NMPs). In the present parliament, there is one NCMP and nine NMPs.

HEAD OF STATE

*President*, Sellapan Rama Nathan, *took office* 1 September 1999

CABINET *as at September 2001*

*Prime Minister*, Goh Chok Tong
*Senior Minister, Prime Minister's Office*, Lee Kuan Yew
*Deputy Prime Minister, Defence*, Tony Tan Kheng Yam
*Deputy Prime Minister, Prime Minister's Office*, Lee Hsien Loong
*Communications and Information Technology*, Yeo Cheow Tong
*Community Development and Sports, Muslim Affairs*, Abdullah Tarmugi
*Education, Defence*, Rear-Adm. Teo Chee Hean
*Environment (Acting)*, Lim Swee Say
*Finance*, Richard Hu Tsu Tau
*Foreign Affairs and Law*, Shanmugam Jayakumar
*Health, Finance*, Lim Hng Kiang
*Home Affairs*, Wong Kan Seng
*Information and the Arts*, Lee Yock Suan
*Labour*, Lee Boon Yang
*National Development*, Mah Bow Tan
*Trade and Industr*, Brig.-Gen. George Yeo Yong Boon
*Without Portfolio, Prime Minister's Office*, Lim Boon Heng

HIGH COMMISSION FOR THE REPUBLIC OF SINGAPORE

9 Wilton Crescent, London SW1X 8SP
Tel: 020-7235 8315
*High Commissioner*, HE Professor Pang Eng Fong, apptd 1999
*Counsellor*, A. Ismail
*First Secretary*, J. Gopalakrishnan (*Commercial*)

BRITISH HIGH COMMISSION

Tanglin Road, Singapore 247919
Tel: (00 65) 473 9333
E-mail: brit_hc@pacific.net.sg/firecrest
*High Commissioner*, HE Sir Steven Brown, KCVO, apptd 2001

BRITISH COUNCIL DIRECTOR, Les Dangerfield, 30 Napier Road, Singapore 258509; e-mail: britcoun@britishcouncil.org.sg
BRITISH CHAMBER OF COMMERCE, 79 Duxton Road, Singapore 089538

## ECONOMY

Historically Singapore's economy was based on the sale and distribution of raw materials from surrounding countries and on entrepôt trade in finished products. An industrialisation programme launched in 1968 has established a wide range of manufacturing industries, including shipbuilding, iron and steel, micro-electronics, electrical goods, telecommunications equipment, office machinery, scientific instruments, pharmaceuticals, etc. Singapore has also become an important financial services centre with significant insurance and foreign exchange markets, a stock exchange, 149 commercial banks and 79 merchant banks and an oil-refining centre. In February 1998 the government announced substantial liberalising reforms of the financial sector, aimed at allowing the country to compete more competitively with other financial sectors in the region. Singapore has not been as badly affected as its neighbours by the economic crisis in south-east Asia, due in part to currency reserves estimated at US$118 billion; it was praised by the IMF for its adroit response to the crisis, which included wage cuts.

There were 6,958,000 foreign visitors in 1999.

Singapore's major trading partners are the USA, Malaysia, the EU, Hong Kong and Japan.

In 1999 Singapore had a trade surplus of US$11,303 million and a current account surplus of US$21,254 million. Imports totalled US$111,060 million and exports US$114,689 million.

GNP – US$95,429 million (1999); US$29,610 per capita (1999)
GDP – US$96,319 million (1997); US$24,577 per capita (1998)
ANNUAL AVERAGE GROWTH OF GDP – 7.0 per cent (1996)
INFLATION RATE – 0.3 per cent (1998)
UNEMPLOYMENT – 3.2 per cent (1998)

| *Trade with UK* | 1999 | 2000 |
|---|---|---|
| Imports from UK | £1,604,085,000 | £1,627,314,000 |
| Exports to UK | 2,451,004,000 | 2,485,372,000 |

## COMMUNICATIONS

Singapore is one of the largest and busiest seaports in the world, with six terminals, deep water wharves and ship repairing facilities. Ships also anchor in the roads, unloading into lighters. In 2000, the total volume of cargo handled was 325,591,100 tonnes. There were 145,383 ship arrivals in 2000.

The international airport is at Changi, in the east of the island, with 64 airlines operating flights to 50 countries and 24,500,000 passengers using the airport in 1996. There are 25.8 km of railway connected to the Malaysian rail system by the causeway across the Straits of Johore, and 3,027 km of roads.

There are 19 radio and four television channels operated by the Singapore Broadcasting Corporation in the four official languages, and three private broadcasting stations.

Singapore's government has prioritised information technology and telecommunications in its programme to transform the country into a knowledge-based economy by 2010. As at June 2000, there were 59 fixed line telephones, 58.5 mobile phones and 32.9 pagers per cent of population; access to the internet amounted to 54.6 per cent.

---

# SLOVAKIA

*Slovenská Republika – The Republic of Slovakia*

---

AREA – 18,923 sq. miles (49,012 sq. km). Neighbours: Poland (north), Ukraine (east), Hungary (south), Austria (west), the Czech Republic (north-west)
POPULATION – 5,402,547 (2000 estimate): 87.7 per cent are ethnic Slovaks, 10.6 per cent ethnic Hungarians, 1.4 per cent Romany, 1 per cent Czech, with smaller numbers of Ruthenians, Ukrainians and Germans. The population is mainly Christian, some 60 per cent Roman Catholic and 8 per cent Protestant. Slovak is the official language, while Hungarian and Czech are also spoken
CAPITAL – Bratislava (population, 452,278, 1996 estimate), on the Danube
MAJOR CITIES – Košice (241,163), 1996 estimate
CURRENCY – Koruna (Sk) of 100 halierov
NATIONAL ANTHEM – Nad Tatrou sa blýska (Storm over the Tatras)

NATIONAL DAYS – 1 January (Establishment of Slovak Republic); 5 July (Day of the Slav Missionaries); 29 August (Slovak National Uprising); 1 September (Constitution Day)
NATIONAL FLAG – Three horizontal stripes of white, blue, red with the arms all over near the hoist
LIFE EXPECTANCY (years) – male 68.9; female 76.7
POPULATION GROWTH RATE – 0.3 per cent (1999)
POPULATION DENSITY – 110 per sq. km (1998)
URBAN POPULATION – 57.4 per cent (2000 estimate)
ENROLMENT (percentage of age group) – tertiary 22.1 per cent (1996)

The Tatry (Tatras) mountains in the centre and north of Slovakia reach heights of 2,655 m. The major river is the Váh which flows from the Tatry mountains to join the Danube at the Hungarian border. The climate is continental.

## HISTORY AND POLITICS (*see also* Czech Republic, Hungary)

At the end of the 11th century Slovakia became part of the Hungarian state when the Magyars gained control of the area. Following the dissolution of the Austro-Hungarian Empire, Slovakia was amalgamated into Czechoslovakia on 28 October 1918, but became independent in March 1939 as a Nazi puppet state when Germany invaded the Czech lands. Slovakia was liberated by Soviet forces in 1945 and returned to Czechoslovakia. The formation of a federal republic between the Czech lands and Slovakia was the only Prague Spring reform to survive the Soviet invasion of 1968. Following the collapse of Communist rule in 1989, the Czech and Slovak republics began to negotiate the dissolution of the federation into two sovereign states in 1992. Dissolution took effect on 1 January 1993.

A coalition government led by the Movement for a Democratic Slovakia (HZDS) was sworn in on 12 January 1993 but was brought down by a no-confidence vote in March 1994. Legislative elections on 30 September and 1 October 1994 returned the HZDS to power at the head of a three-party coalition which took office on 13 December 1994.

Following the legislative elections on 25–26 September 1998, the HZDS remained the largest party, but a four-party coalition government led by the Slovak Democratic Coalition (SDK) was formed.

The number of seats held by each of the parties in the National Council following the 1998 election was: HZDS 43; SDK 42; Party of the Democratic Left (SDL) 23; Hungarian Coalition Party (SMK) 15; Slovak National Party (SNS) 14; Party of Civic Understanding (SOP) 13. President Kováč's term of office ended on 2 March 1998. The presidential elections were not contested by the ruling HZDS, who were accused by opposition parties of trying to create a constitutional vacuum; since no president was elected by the end of Kováč's term, certain presidential powers were transferred to the prime minister. After the 1998 legislative elections, the National Council voted on 14 January 1999 for direct presidential elections, which were held on 29 May 1999 and won by Rudolf Schuster of the SOP.

On 11 November 2000, a referendum which had been called by the opposition HZDS to demand an early general election failed to obtain the necessary 50 per cent voter turnout; the government had urged voters not to take part.

### POLITICAL SYSTEM

The constitution vests legislative power in the National Council of 150 members directly elected for a four-year term by proportional representation with a five per cent threshold for parliamentary representation. The president is elected for a five-year term, renewable only once, by direct election; executive power is held by the prime minister and Cabinet.

### HEAD OF STATE

*President*, Rudolf Schuster, *elected* 29 May 1999, *sworn in* 15 June 1999

### CABINET *as at September 2001*

*Prime Minister*, Mikuláš Dzurinda (SDK)
*Deputy Prime Ministers*, Ivan Mikloš (SDK) *(Economy)*; Mária Kadlečíkova (SOP) *(European Integration)*; Pál Csáky (SMK) *(Human and Minority Rights and Regional Development)*; Lubomír Fogaš (SDL) *(Legislation)*
*Agriculture*, Pavel Koncoš (SDL)
*Construction and Public Works*, István Harna (SMK)
*Culture*, Milan Knako (SDK)
*Defence*, Jozef Stank (SDL)
*Economy*, Lubomír Harach (SDK)
*Education*, Milan Ftáčnik (SDL)
*Environment*, László Miklós (SMK)
*Finance*, Brigita Schmögnerová (SDL)
*Foreign Affairs*, Eduard Kukan (SDK)
*Health*, Roman Kováč (SDK)
*Interior*, Ivan Šimko (SDK)
*Justice*, Ján Čarnogurský (SDK)
*Labour, Social Affairs and the Family*, Peter Magvaši (SDL)
*Privatisation*, Mária Machová (SOP)
*Transport, Posts and Telecommunications*, Gabriel Palacka (SDK)

### EMBASSY OF THE SLOVAK REPUBLIC

25 Kensington Palace Gardens, London W8 4QY
Tel: 020-7243 0803
*Ambassador Extraordinary and Plenipotentiary*, HE František Dlhopolček, apptd 2000

### BRITISH EMBASSY

Panská 16, SK-811 01 Bratislava
Tel: (00 421) (7) 5441 9632/3
E-mail: bebra@internet.sk
*Ambassador Extraordinary and Plenipotentiary*, HE David Lyscom, apptd 1998

BRITISH COUNCIL DIRECTOR, Jim McGrath, PO Box 68, Panská 17, SK-814 99 Bratislava; e-mail: information.centre@britishcouncil.sk. There are also offices at Banská Bystríca and Košice

BRITISH CHAMBER OF COMMERCE, Cukrova 14, SK-813 39 Bratislava

## DEFENCE

The Army has 275 main battle tanks, 218 armoured personnel carriers and 404 armoured infantry fighting vehicles. The Air Force has 84 combat aircraft and 19 attack helicopters.
MILITARY EXPENDITURE – 1.9 per cent of GDP (1999)
MILITARY PERSONNEL – 38,600; Army 23,800, Air Force 11,500, Paramilitaries 2,600
CONSCRIPTION DURATION – 12 months

## ECONOMY

From independence until mid-1994 Slovakia faced economic difficulties because of the structure of its centrally-planned and inefficiently managed economy, reliant on state-subsidised heavy industries with low productivity, and because of the ambivalent attitude to reform of the HZDS government. In mid-1994 the economic situation stabilised as the Moravčik government implemented a second round of privatisation. The election of an HZDS-led government in October 1994 slowed the pace of reform. Following severe depreciation of the Koruna and the failure of the economy to achieve the anticipated growth targets, the SDK-led government introduced a package of austerity measures on 20 May 1999; the basic rate of VAT was raised, there were increases in energy, water, telecommunications and housing prices, and import taxes were reintroduced.

The EU suspended aid to Slovakia in April 2001 following allegations of the misuse of funds.

Natural resources include brown coal, natural gas, iron ore, antimony, lead, zinc and magnesite.

In 1999 Slovakia had a trade deficit of US$1,109 million and a current account deficit of US$1,155 million. In 1998 imports totalled US$13,604 million and exports US$10,195 million.

GNP – US$20,318 million (1999); US$3,590 per capita (1999)
GDP – US$19,452 million (1997); US$3,653 per capita (1999)
ANNUAL AVERAGE GROWTH OF GDP – 2.9 per cent (2000)
INFLATION RATE – 7.7 per cent (2001)
UNEMPLOYMENT – 18.0 per cent (2000)
TOTAL EXTERNAL DEBT – US$9,893 million (1998)

| *Trade with UK* | 1999 | 2000 |
|---|---|---|
| Imports from UK | £113,518,000 | £157,125,000 |
| Exports to UK | 106,408,000 | 139,797,000 |

## SLOVENIA
*Republika Slovenija*

AREA – 7,821 sq. miles (20,256 sq. km). Neighbours: Austria (north), Hungary (north-east), Croatia (east and south), Italy (west)
POPULATION – 1,967,143 (2001 estimate). The population is mostly Slovenian. There are small Hungarian (0.5 per cent) and Italian (0.1 per cent) minorities, together with a Romany population. The main religion is Roman Catholicism. Slovene is the official language, together with Hungarian and Italian in ethnically mixed regions
CAPITAL – Ljubljana (population, 273,000, 1996 estimate)
MAJOR CITIES – Maribor (100,000), 1996 estimate
CURRENCY – Tolar (SIT) of 100 stotin
NATIONAL ANTHEM – Zdravljica (A Toast)
NATIONAL DAY – 25 June (Statehood Day)
NATIONAL FLAG – Three horizontal stripes of white, blue, red, with the arms in the upper hoist
LIFE EXPECTANCY (years) – male 71.6; female 79.5
POPULATION GROWTH RATE – 0.4 per cent (1999)
POPULATION DENSITY – 98 per sq. km (1998)
URBAN POPULATION – 50.4 per cent (2000)
MILITARY EXPENDITURE – 1.8 per cent of GDP (1999)
MILITARY PERSONNEL – 9,000: Army 9,000; Paramilitaries 4,500
CONSCRIPTION DURATION – Seven months

Slovenia is a small mountainous state which is the most northerly of the former Yugoslav republics. The two major rivers are the Sava and the Drava. There is a short coastline in the south-west 29 miles (46 km) in length on the Adriatic. The climate is a mixture of Mediterranean, continental and alpine.

### HISTORY AND POLITICS

The area that is now Slovenia came under the control of the Habsburg Empire in the 13th and 14th centuries and remained so until the defeat of the Austro-Hungarian Empire in 1918. On 27 October 1918 Slovenia became part of Yugoslavia. In 1941 German forces invaded Yugoslavia and Slovenia was divided between Germany, Italy and Hungary. Slovenia was reformed as a constituent republic of the federal Yugoslav state in May 1945. After a dispute with Italy and nine years of international administration, the Adriatic coast and hinterland were returned to Slovenia in 1954 and Italy retained Trieste.

Slovenian fears of Serbian dominance led the Slovene Assembly in 1989 to amend the republican constitution to lay the basis of a sovereign state. The first democratic elections, held in April 1990, were won by the pro-independence 'Demos' coalition. In a referendum in December 1990, 88 per cent of the electorate voted for independence, which was declared on 25 June 1991. A ten-day war with the Yugoslav National Army followed before the Army called off hostilities and withdrew under the mediation of the EU.

A coalition led by Liberal Democracy of Slovenia (LDS) formed a government following the 1996 legislative election. President Kučan was re-elected on 23 November 1997.

The government lost a vote of confidence on 8 April 2000 and a caretaker government was approved on 8 June 2000.

In the general election which took place on 15 October 2000, the LDS won 34 seats, the Social Democratic Party (SDS) won 14 seats, the United List of Social Democrats (ZLSD) won 11 seats, the Slovene People's Party-Slovene Christian Democrats (SLS-SKD) won 9 seats, New Slovenia won 8 seats, the Democratic Party of Pensioners (DeSUS) won 4 seats and other parties won 10 seats. A coalition government was formed by the LDS, the ZLSD, the SLS-SKD and the DeSUS.

#### FOREIGN RELATIONS

Slovenia signed an association agreement and applied for membership of the EU in June 1996. The EU began formal accession negotiations with Slovenia on 10 November 1998.

#### POLITICAL SYSTEM

The head of state is the president, elected for a five-year term. Executive power is vested in the prime minister and Cabinet of Ministers. The lower house of the legislature, the National Assembly, has 90 members directly elected for a four-year term. The upper house, the 40-member National Council, has an advisory role. The National Assembly is elected on a proportional representation basis, with one seat each reserved for the Italian and Hungarian minorities.

#### HEAD OF STATE

*President*, Milan Kučan, *elected* April 1990, *re-elected* December 1992, 23 November 1997

#### EXECUTIVE COUNCIL *as at September 2001*

*President of the Executive Council (Prime Minister)*, Janez Drnovšek (LDS)
*Agriculture, Forestry and Food*, Franc But (SLS-SKD)
*Culture*, Andreja Rihter (ZLSD)
*Defence*, Anton Grizold (LDS)
*Economic Affairs*, Tea Petrin (LDS)
*Education and Science*, Lucija Čok (LDS)
*Environment and Physical Planning*, Janez Kopač (LDS)
*Finance*, Anton Rop (LDS)
*Foreign Affairs*, Dimitrij Rupel (LDS)
*Health*, Dušan Keber (LDS)
*Information Society*, Pavel Gantar (LDS)
*Internal Affairs*, Rado Bohinc (ZLSD)
*Justice*, Ivo Bizjak (SLS-SKD)
*Labour, Family and Social Affairs*, Vlado Dimovski (ZLSD)
*Transport and Communications*, Jakob Presečnik (SLS-SKD)
*Without Portfolio, European Affairs*, Igor Bavčar (LDS)

LDS Liberal Democracy of Slovenia; SLS-SKD Slovene People's Party-Slovene Christian Democrats; ZLSD United List of Social Democrats

EMBASSY OF THE REPUBLIC OF SLOVENIA
Suite 1, Cavendish Court, 11–15 Wigmore Street, London W1H 9LA
Tel: 020-7495 7775
*Ambassador Extraordinary and Plenipotentiary*, HE Marjan Šetinc, apptd 1998

BRITISH EMBASSY
4th Floor, Trg Republike 3, SI-1000 Ljubljana
Tel: (00 386) (1) 200 3910
E-mail: info@british-embassy.si
*Ambassador Extraordinary and Plenipotentiary*, HE H. Mortimer, LVO, apptd 2000

BRITISH COUNCIL DIRECTOR, Steve Green, Cankarjevo nabrezje 27, SI-1000 Ljubljana; e-mail: info@britishcouncil.si

## ECONOMY

Slovenia's economy has emerged as the most stable of the former Yugoslav economies and the least affected by the end of central planning. Although it has lost its captive export market and cheap supplies of raw materials from other parts of the former Yugoslavia, Slovenia is one of the richest ex-Communist countries. It has successfully re-orientated its exports towards Western markets, its main trading partners being Germany, Italy and France. The privatisation process was completed in 1998.

In 1999 agriculture contributed 4 per cent to the total value of GDP, industry 38.5 per cent and services 59.9 per cent. The main agricultural products are potatoes, wheat, corn, sugar beet and wine. The total land area under cultivation is 517,923 hectares. The major manufacturing sectors are metalworking, electronics, textiles, automotive parts, chemicals, glass products and food-processing. Tourism and transport are major export earners, with 974,300 tourists visiting in 1997.

In 1999 Slovenia had a trade deficit of US$1,157 million and a current account deficit of US$581 million. Imports totalled US$9,952 million and exports US$8,604 million.

GNP – US$19,862 million (1999); US$9,890 per capita (1999)
GDP – US$18,202 million (1997); US$9,798 per capita (1998); estimated to be US$20,294 million and US$10,248 per capita in 1999
ANNUAL AVERAGE GROWTH OF GDP – 5.9 per cent (2000)
INFLATION RATE – 8.5 per cent (2001)
UNEMPLOYMENT – 7.7 per cent (1998)
TOTAL EXTERNAL DEBT – US$4,762 million (1997); US$5,491 million (1999 estimate)

| *Trade with UK* | 1999 | 2000 |
|---|---|---|
| Imports from UK | £143,993,000 | £157,911,000 |
| Exports to UK | 108,685,000 | 126,105,000 |

## COMMUNICATIONS

There are 20,128 km of roads and 1,201 km of rail track, of which 499 km is electrified. Important road and rail communications cross the country from west to east (Milan–Ljubljana–Budapest), and north to south (Munich–Ljubljana–Zagreb–Belgrade–Athens). There are international airports at Ljubljana, Maribor and Portorož (Adriatic Coast). Koper is an important shipment point for goods from Austria, Hungary, the Czech Republic and Slovakia.

## EDUCATION

Education is compulsory and free between the ages of six and 14. There are 816 primary schools (age six–14), 147 secondary or middle schools (age 14–19), 44 colleges and two universities (Ljubljana and Maribor).
ILLITERACY RATE – 0.3 PER CENT (2000)
ENROLMENT (percentage of age group) – primary 95 per cent (1996); tertiary 36.1 per cent (1996)

# SOLOMON ISLANDS

AREA – 11,157 sq. miles (28,896 sq. km)
POPULATION – 408,358 (2000 estimate); 328,723 (1991 census). English is the official language; there are over 80 local languages
CAPITAL – ΨHoniara (population, 40,000, 1991)
CURRENCY – Solomon Islands dollar (SI$) of 100 cents
NATIONAL ANTHEM – God Bless our Solomon Islands
NATIONAL DAY – 7 July (Independence Day)
NATIONAL FLAG – Blue over green divided by a diagonal yellow band, with five white stars in the top left quarter
LIFE EXPECTANCY (years) – male 62.0; female 64.0
POPULATION GROWTH RATE – 3.3 per cent (1999)
POPULATION DENSITY – 14 per sq. km (1998)
URBAN POPULATION – 19.7 per cent (2000 estimate)

Forming a scattered archipelago of mountainous islands and low-lying coral atolls, the Solomon Islands stretches about 900 miles in a south-easterly direction from the Shortland Islands to the Santa Cruz islands. The six biggest islands are Choiseul, New Georgia, Santa Isabel, Guadalcanal, Malaita and Makira. They are characterised by thickly-forested mountain ranges intersected by deep, narrow valleys.

## HISTORY AND POLITICS

The origin of the present Melanesian inhabitants is uncertain. European interest in the islands began in the mid-16th century and continued intermittently for about 300 years, when the inauguration of sugar plantations in Queensland and Fiji (which created a need for labour) and the arrival of missionaries and traders led to increased European interest in the region. Great Britain declared a Protectorate in 1893 over the Southern Solomons, adding the Santa Cruz group in 1898 and 1899. The islands of the Shortland groups were transferred from Germany to Great Britain by treaty in 1900. The Solomon Islands achieved internal self-government in 1976, and became independent in July 1978.

Following legislative elections held on 6 August 1997, the Alliance for Change group, led by the Liberal Party, was the largest party in the National Parliament, winning 21 seats. Bartholomew Ulufa'alu, the Liberal Party leader, was elected prime minister on 27 August 1997. Following his resignation on 13 June 2000, Mannasseh Sogavare was elected prime minister on 30 June and appointed a government of national unity. A general election was due to be held in late 2001, following the failure of a government move to extend the term of the current legislature.

In November 2000, a conference of provincial governmental heads called for the introduction of a federal system of government; some of the islands had earlier threatened secession.

### INSURGENCY

In late 1998 tension between the indigenous inhabitants of Guadalcanal and settlers from other parts of the country, chiefly Malaita, led to violent attacks on the settlers. On 28 June 1999, a peace agreement was signed by representatives of the national and provincial governments and the

Isatabu Freedom Fighters (IFF), a local militant group, following mediation by the Commonwealth special envoy Sitiveni Rabuka.

Following further tension, on 28 February 2000 the government banned the IFF and their rivals the Malaita Eagles Force (MEF), but lifted the ban on 15 May to facilitate peace talks. MEF guerrillas took Prime Minister Ulufa'alu hostage on 5 June 2000 and took over the capital. The prime minister was freed on 10 June and the MEF and the IMF agreed to a two-week truce to allow mediation by a Commonwealth delegation. A peace deal was signed by the IFF and the MEF on 15 October 2000, agreeing to disarm within 30 days. In response, the National Assembly passed a bill granting an amnesty for those involved in the conflict. A peace deal was signed by the IFF and the Marau Eagles Force, a smaller Malaitan militia, on 7 February 2001. Fighting resumed on 18 March on Guadalcanal.

### Political System

The Solomon Islands is a constitutional monarchy. Queen Elizabeth II is represented locally by the Governor-General. Executive authority is exercised by the Cabinet. Legislative power is vested in a unicameral National Parliament of 50 members, elected for a four-year term.

*Governor-General*, HE John Lapli, GCMG, apptd 1999

### Cabinet *as at September 2001*

*Prime Minister*, Manasseh Sogavare
*Deputy Prime Minister, National Unity, Reconciliation and Peace, Police, Justice and Legal Affairs*, William Haomae
*Deputy Prime Minister, Provincial Government and Rural Development*, Nathaniel Waena
*Agriculture and Primary Industries*, Moon Pin Kwan
*Commerce, Employment and Trade*, David Holosivi
*Culture, Tourism and Aviation*, Johnson Koli
*Economic Reform and Structural Adjustment*, Victor Ngele
*Education*, William Gigini
*Finance*, Snyder Rini
*Fisheries and Marine Resources*, George Luilamo
*Foreign Affairs and Trade Relations*, David Sitae
*Forests, Environment and Conservation*, Tommy Chan
*Health and Medical Services*, Allan Paul
*Home and Ecclesiastical Affairs*, Revd Reuben Mesepitu
*Lands and Housing*, Albert Laore
*Mines and Energy*, Walton Naezon
*National Development Planning*, Michael Maina
*Police and Justice*, William Haomae
*Transport, Works and Communication*, Joses Saueha Tahua
*Youth and Women's Affairs*, Hilda Kari

### High Commission of the Solomon Islands

Sint-Michielslaan 28, Box 23, B-1040 Brussels
Tel: (00 32) (2) 2732 7085
*High Commissioner*, HE Robert Sisilo, apptd 1996

### British High Commission

Telekom House, Mendana Avenue (PO Box 676), Honiara
Tel: (00 677) 21705/6
E-mail: bhc@welkam.solomon.com.sb
*High Commissioner*, HE B. Baldwin, apptd 2001

## ECONOMY

The main imports are foodstuffs, consumer goods, machinery and transport materials. Principal exports are timber, fish, palm oil, copra and cocoa.

The economy has suffered gravely since 1998 as a result of the ethnic conflict and the governor of the central bank warned in February 2001 that the economy was close to collapse.

In 1998 there was a trade deficit of US$18 million and a current account surplus of US$8 million. In 1996 imports totalled US$151 million and exports totalled US$162 million.

GNP – US$320 million (1999); US$750 per capita (1999)
GDP – US$341 million (1997); US$712 per capita (1998)
Annual Average Growth of GDP – 6.0 per cent (1996)
Inflation Rate – 8.3 per cent (1999)
Total External Debt – US$152 million (1998)

| *Trade with UK* | 1999 | 2000 |
|---|---|---|
| Imports from UK | £2,534,000 | £481,000 |
| Exports to UK | 9,731,000 | 4,844,000 |

## COMMUNICATIONS

Solomon Airlines operates international services to other Pacific states and Australia. Air Niugini flies from Port Moresby to Honiara. There are about 2,100 km of roads, including those in private plantations, forestry areas and roads built and maintained by councils; only 32 km of roads are paved. Telekom, a company jointly owned by Cable and Wireless and the Solomon Islands government, operates the international and domestic telephone circuits from a ground station in Honiara via the Intelsat Pacific Ocean communication satellite.

---

# SOMALIA

*Jamhuuriyadda Dimoqraadiya Soomaaliya*

---

Area – 246,201 sq. miles (637,657 sq. km). Neighbours: Djibouti, Ethiopia and Kenya (west)
Population – 10,217,000 (1997 UN estimate). Somali and Arabic are the official languages. English and Italian are also spoken
Capital – ΨMogadishu (Muqdisho) (population, 900,000, 1990 estimate)
Major Cities – ΨBerbera (15,000); Boroma (65,000); Burao (15,000); Hargeysa (20,000); ΨKisimaayo (60,000)
Currency – Somali shilling of 100 cents
National Day – under review
National Flag – Five-pointed white star on blue ground
Life Expectancy (years) – male 44.0; female 44.7
Population Growth Rate – 2.5 per cent (1999)
Population Density – 14 per sq. km (1998)
Urban Population – 27.5 per cent (2000 estimate)
Enrolment (percentage of age group) – primary 10 per cent (1985); secondary 3 per cent (1985); tertiary 2.1 per cent (1985)

## HISTORY AND POLITICS

The British protectorate of Somaliland and the Italian trust territory of Somalia were joined and became independent on 1 July 1960. In 1969, the armed forces seized power and established a ruling Revolutionary Council under Siad Barre's leadership.

Siad Barre was overthrown by rebels in January 1991, sparking civil war between rival clan-based movements. The United Somali Congress (USC) seized control in Mogadishu, while the Somali National Movement formed a rival administration in the north. Fighting between the USC and supporters of the Somali National Alliance (SNA) of Gen. Mohammed Aideed devastated Mogadishu and large parts of the south, exacerbating famine conditions. The UN Operation in Somalia proved ineffective in securing aid distribution routes and was replaced on 9 December 1992 by a UN-approved, US-led, United Task Force (UNITAF).

On 4 May 1993, UNITAF handed over to UNOSOM. The UN withdrew its troops in March 1995, enabling

Gen. Aideed's militia to take control of the city's port and airport. On 12 June 1995, Gen. Aideed was ousted as SNA leader by a joint USC-SNA congress which nominated Osman Ali Ato as its leader. Gen. Aideed responded by declaring himself president on 15 June 1995, but was shot dead in July 1996 and was replaced as president by his son, Hussein Aideed.

A peace plan proposed by Djibouti was overwhelmingly supported on 16 November 1999 by representatives of civil society and the armed factions at a forum in Nairobi. A Somali National Reconciliation Conference in Djibouti opened on 2 May 2000, which aimed to lay the foundations of the transitional institutions of the Somali state, but was opposed by the Rahawein Resistance Army, the Somali Patriotic Movement and the leaders of Puntland. The National Reconciliation Conference appointed a transitional national assembly on 13 August, which on 26 August appointed Abdiqassim Salad Hassan as president. President Hassan appointed Ali Khalif Galayadh as prime minister on 3 October 2000. The assembly held an inaugural session in Mogadishu on 2 November 2000 and the prime minister named an interim government composed of members of various clans.

The government attempted to gain control of Mogadishu in March 2001 by ordering armed police onto the streets of Mogadishu to restrict the activities of the militias; the police were withdrawn following heavy fighting but were reintroduced in June.

Fighting between pro- and anti-government militias broke out in the south of the country in July 2001.

### INSURGENCIES

With the downfall of Siad Barre, the SNM took control of the north-west (the former British Somaliland Protectorate) and in May 1991 declared unilateral independence as the 'Somaliland Republic'. A government and legislature was formed which elected Mohammed Ibrahim Egal as president in May 1993; he was re-elected in February 1997. A referendum on a new constitution, which confirmed the independence of Somaliland, was held on 31 May 2001 and was approved by 97.09 per cent of those who voted.

An autonomous administration was proclaimed in north-eastern Somalia on 23 July 1998. Col. Ahmed Abdullahi Yusuf was named as president of the region, calling itself Puntland, and a Cabinet was appointed. On 15 September 1998, a 69-member parliament was inaugurated.

### HEAD OF STATE

*President*, Abdiqassim Salad Hassan, *sworn in* 27 August 2000

### INTERIM CABINET *as at September 2001*

*Prime Minister*, Ali Khalif Galayadh
*Deputy Prime Minister*, Uthman Jama'
*Agriculture*, Yusuf Ma'alin
*Defence*, Abdullahi Boqor Museh
*Education and Training*, Muhammad Meydane Burale
*Environment and Rural Development*, Ali Abdirahman Hirsi
*Finance*, Sayid Ahmed Shaykh Dahir
*Fisheries and Marine Affairs*, Mohamed Qanyare Afrah
*Foreign Affairs*, Ismail Mahmud Hurre Buba
*Health*, Muhammad Nurani Baker
*Higher Education and Guidance*, Muhammad Ali Ahmad
*Industry*, Husayn Mahmud Shaykh Husayn
*Information*, Zakariya Mahmud Haji
*Internal Affairs*, Dahir Sheikh Muhammad Nur
*Justice and Religious Affairs*, Mahmud Umar Farah
*Labour and Sports*, Abdi-al-Aziz Muqtar Ma'alin
*Livestock*, Abd-al-Wahab Ma'alin Mahmud
*National Planning*, Husayn Eelaabe Fahiye

*Ports and Shipping*, Abdiweli Jama' Warsameh
*Posts and Telecommunications*, Ahmad Shaykh Mukhtar
*Public Works*, Si'id Warsameh Abakar
*Reconstruction and Resettlement*, Abdullahi Ga'al Abdi
*Regional Development*, Hasan Farah Hujaleh
*Science and Technology*, Abd-al-Qadir Muhammad Abdulle Madahe
*Trade*, Muhammad Warsameh Ali
*Transport*, Abdi Guled Muhammad
*Water and Minerals*, Hasan Abshir Farah

### SOMALI DIPLOMATIC REPRESENTATION

The Embassy closed in January 1992.

### BRITISH DIPLOMATIC REPRESENTATION

The British Embassy in Mogadishu closed in January 1991.

## ECONOMY

Livestock raising is the main occupation and there is a modest export trade in livestock, skins and hides, which accounted for 38 per cent of exports in 1988. Italy, the Gulf States and Saudi Arabia import the bulk of the banana crop, the biggest export, which accounted for 40 per cent of exports. The principal imports are machinery and transport equipment, industrial goods and foodstuffs.

GDP – US$1,495 million (1997); US$177 per capita (1998)
ANNUAL AVERAGE GROWTH OF GDP – 7.0 per cent (1996)
INFLATION RATE – 81.9 per cent (1988)
TOTAL EXTERNAL DEBT – US$2,635 million (1998)

| *Trade with UK* | 1999 | 2000 |
|---|---|---|
| Imports from UK | £3,079,000 | £11,486,000 |
| Exports to UK | 89,000 | 8,000 |

## SOUTH AFRICA
*Republic of South Africa*

AREA – 470,691 sq. miles (1,219,090 sq. km). Neighbours: Namibia (north-west), Botswana and Zimbabwe (north), Mozambique and Swaziland (north-east), Lesotho, which is completely surrounded by South Africa
POPULATION – 43,054,000 (1999 estimate); 40,583,573 (1996 census): 76.7 per cent African, 10.9 per cent White, 8.9 per cent Coloured, 2.6 per cent Asian. The interim constitution designates 11 official languages: Afrikaans (spoken by 14.4 per cent as a first language); English (8.6 per cent); IsiNdebele (1.5 per cent); IsiXosa (17.9 per cent), IsiZulu (22.9 per cent); Sepedi (9.2 per cent); Sosetho (7.7 per cent); SiSwati (2.5 per cent); Setswana (8.2 per cent); Tshivenda (2.2 per cent); Xitsonga (4.4 per cent). Afrikaans and English are to remain the languages of record although any citizen may correspond official business in his own language. The majority (77 per cent) of the population is Christian. There are also Hindus (1.7 per cent), Muslims (1.1 per cent) and Jews (0.4 per cent)
CAPITAL –The seat of the government is Pretoria (population 1,800,000, 1999 estimate); the seat of the legislature is Cape Town (population, 3,088,028, 1999 estimate); the seat of the judiciary is Bloemfontein (467,400, 1999 estimate)
MAJOR CITIES – ΨDurban (2,589,977); ΨEast London (520,008); Johannesburg (3,800,652); Pietermaritzburg (397,086); ΨPort Elizabeth (1,011,378), 1999 estimates
CURRENCY – Rand (R) of 100 cents
NATIONAL ANTHEMS – Nkosi Sikelel' iAfrika (God Bless Africa); Die Stem Van Suid-Afrika (The Call of South Africa)
NATIONAL DAY – 27 April (Freedom Day)
NATIONAL FLAG – Divided red over blue by a horizontal white-fimbriated green Y; in the hoist a black triangle fimbriated in yellow
LIFE EXPECTANCY (years) – male 47.3; female 49.7
POPULATION GROWTH RATE – 1.8 per cent (1999)
POPULATION DENSITY – 35 per sq. km (1998)
URBAN POPULATION – 50.4 per cent (2000 estimate)

South Africa occupies the southernmost part of the African continent from the courses of the Limpopo, Marico, Molopo, Nosop and Orange Rivers to the Cape of Good Hope, with the exception of Lesotho, Swaziland and the extreme south of Mozambique. To the west, east and south lie the south Atlantic and southern Indian Oceans. Some 1,192 miles (1,920 km) to the south-east of Cape Town lie Prince Edward and Marion Islands, part of South Africa since 1947.

The Orange, with its tributary the Vaal, is the principal river, rising in the Drakensberg and flowing into the Atlantic near the border with Namibia. The Limpopo, or Crocodile River, in the north, rises in North-West Province and flows into the Indian Ocean through Mozambique.

The climate is subtropical, dry and sunny, moderated by the temperate winds from the Atlantic and Indian Oceans. Moist hot air masses from the Indian Ocean are the chief source of rainfall for most of the country.

### HISTORY AND POLITICS

Hunter-gatherers, the San (Bushmen) and Khoikhoi (Hottentots) inhabited southern Africa from *c.*8,000 BC. Their descendants, and those of Bantu-speaking peoples who had migrated south, occupied the area when the Portuguese navigator Bartolomeu Días charted the coast in 1488.

The colony of the Cape of Good Hope was founded by the Dutch at Cape Town in 1652; it was taken by Britain in 1806 and this was confirmed by the London Convention of 1814. The Orange Free State and Transvaal republics were founded by the Boers (the descendants of Dutch settlers), which were recognised by Britain in 1853–4. Natal was annexed to Cape Colony by the British in 1844 and then formed as a separate colony in 1856, to which Zululand was added in 1897 after the British victory in the Zulu wars. Transvaal and the Orange Free State became British colonies after the Boer defeat in the Second Boer War 1899–1902. The self-governing colonies became united in 1910 under the name of the Union of South Africa. Independence within the Commonwealth was gained in 1931 under the Statute of Westminster. South Africa left the Commonwealth and became a republic on 31 May 1961, largely as a result of international condemnation of apartheid and of the Sharpeville massacre.

From 1948, when the Afrikaner National Party came to power, South Africa's social and political structure was based on apartheid, a policy of racial segregation. Opposition protests culminated in the Sharpeville massacre in 1960; the African National Congress (ANC) and other opposition groups were subsequently banned. A new wave of opposition climaxed in 1976 with uprisings in Soweto, in which hundreds were shot dead. In 1984 renewed rioting in the black townships and continuing unrest led to the declaration of a state of emergencywhich was renewed annually until 1990.

As part of its policy of apartheid, the government established a number of black 'homelands'. Six areas (Gazankulu, Lebowa, KwaNdbele, KaNgwane, Qwaqwa and KwaZulu) were designated as self-governing states. A further four (Bophuthatswana, Ciskei, Transkei and Venda) were regarded as independent republics by the South African government but never recognised as such by the UN.

#### MOVES TO DEMOCRACY

The first moves to reform apartheid came into effect in 1984, when a new constitution extended the franchise to the Coloured and Indian populations. However, whites retained effective political power and blacks remained excluded.

In 1989, F. W. de Klerk became president of South Africa and accelerated the process of reform. In 1990, the ban on the ANC and restrictions on other anti-apartheid groups were lifted; Nelson Mandela, the main ANC political detainee, was released. In 1991 the laws implementing apartheid were effectively abolished. In 1992 a referendum amongst the white electorate on continued political reform and a new constitution reached by negotiation was approved by 69 per cent to 31 per cent.

In 1991, the Convention on a Democratic South Africa (CODESA) talks between the government, ANC, Inkatha Freedom Party and other political, business and church groups reached agreement on the establishment of an inter-racial administration and the formation of a five-year coalition government following a multiracial election.

In the country's first multiracial general election held on 26–29 April 1994 the ANC gained 252 seats in the 400-seat National Assembly. In the 90-seat Senate the ANC gained 60 seats.

The parliament has passed two significant pieces of legislation to settle the legacy of the apartheid era. In November 1994 the Restitution of Land Rights Act was passed which established a Commission and a Court to restore the rights of those dispossessed of their land since the 1913 Land Act. In June 1995 the Promotion of National Unity and Reconciliation Act was passed which established a Truth Commission covering the apartheid era, with a remit to assess confessions, grant amnesties for political crimes and set compensation for victims. The first hearing opened on 15 April 1996.

Following legislative and provincial elections held on 2 June 1999, the ANC gained 266 seats in the National Assembly, the Democratic Party (DP) 38 seats, the Inkatha Freedom Party (IFP) 34 seats, the New National Party (NNP) 28 seats, the United Democratic Movement 14 seats, the African Christian Democratic Party 6 seats, and others 14 seats.

On 9 June 1999 the ANC, being one seat short of the two-thirds majority required to amend the constitution, entered into a coalition with the Minority Front, which held just one seat in the National Assembly.

On 14 June 1999 the National Assembly met to select a new president. Thabo Mbeki was elected unopposed and was formally sworn in on 16 June 1999.

### POLITICAL SYSTEM

The final constitution came into effect in 1997. Executive power is vested in a president and Cabinet, with the president elected by the National Assembly. Legislative power is vested in a bicameral parliament, a directly elected 400-member National Assembly elected by proportional representation for a five-year term, and an indirectly elected 90-member National Council of Provinces composed of ten members elected by each of the nine regional legislatures for a five-year term.

The four former provinces (Cape Province, Natal, Orange Free State, Transvaal) have been replaced by nine new regions (Western Cape, Northern Cape, Eastern Cape, Free State, North-West, KwaZulu/Natal, Gauteng, Northern Province, Mpumalanga). Each region has its own premier, a legislature of between 30 and 100 seats elected by proportional representation, and its own constitution.

### HEAD OF STATE

*President, Commander-in-Chief of the Armed Forces*, Thabo Mbeki (ANC), *elected by parliament* 14 June 1999, *sworn in* 16 June 1999
*Executive Deputy President*, Jacob Zuma (ANC)

### CABINET *as at September 2001*

*Agriculture and Land Affairs*, Angela Didiza (ANC)
*Arts, Culture, Science and Technology*, Ben Ngubane (IFP)
*Communications*, Ivy Matsepe-Cassburri (ANC)
*Correctional Services*, Ben Skosana (IFP)
*Defence*, Patrick Lekota (ANC)
*Education*, Kader Asmal (ANC)
*Environmental Affairs and Tourism*, Mohammed Valli Moosa (ANC)
*Finance*, Trevor Manuel (ANC)
*Foreign Affairs*, Nkosazana Dlamini-Zuma (ANC)
*Health*, Mantombazana Tshabala-Msimang (ANC)
*Home Affairs*, Chief Mangosuthu Buthelezi (IFP)
*Housing*, Sankie Mthembi-Mahanyele (ANC)
*Intelligence Service*, Lindiwe Sisulu-Guma (ANC)
*Justice and Constitutional Development*, Penuell Maduna (ANC)
*Labour*, Membathisis Mdladlana (ANC)
*Mineral and Energy Affairs*, Phumzile Mlambo-Necguka (ANC)
*Minister, Office of the President*, Essop Pahad (ANC)
*Provincial and Local Government*, Sidney Mufamadi (ANC)
*Public Enterprises*, Jeffrey Radebe (ANC)
*Public Service and Administration*, Geraldine Fraser-Moleketi (ANC)
*Public Works*, Stella Sigcau (ANC)
*Safety and Security*, Steve Tshwete (ANC)
*Sports and Recreation*, Ngconde Balfour (ANC)
*Trade and Industry*, Alec Erwin (ANC)
*Transport*, Dullah Omar (ANC)
*Water Affairs and Forestry*, Ronnie Kasrils (ANC)
*Welfare and Population Development*, Zola Skweyiya (ANC)

### HIGH COMMISSION FOR THE REPUBLIC OF SOUTH AFRICA

South Africa House, Trafalgar Square, London WC2N 5DP
Tel: 020-7451 7299
*High Commissioner*, HE Cheryl Ann Carolus, apptd 1998
*Deputy High Commissioner*, G. Johannes
*Minister (Economic)*, J. Johnston
Defence Attaché, *Brig.-Gen. S. Sijake*

### BRITISH HIGH COMMISSION

255 Hill Street, Arcadia 0002
Tel: (00 27) (12) 483 1200
E-mail: bhc@icon.co.za
91 Parliament Street, Cape Town 8001
Tel: (00 27) (21) 461 7220
E-mail: britain@icon.co.za
*High Commissioner (Cape Town)*, HE Ann Grant, apptd 2001
*Counsellor, Deputy High Commissioner (Pretoria)*, S. Gass, CMG, CVO
*Counsellor (Political) (Pretoria)*, D. Woods
*Defence and Military Adviser (Pretoria)*, Brig. M. Raworth
*Consul-General and Director of Trade Promotion (Johannesburg)*, N. McInnes

CONSULATES-GENERAL – Cape Town, Johannesburg
CONSULATE – Durban
HONORARY CONSULS – Port Elizabeth, East London

BRITISH COUNCIL DIRECTOR, Clive Gobby, 76 Juta Street, PO Box 30637, Braamfontein 2017, Johannesburg; e-mail: enquiries.johannesburg@britcoun.org.za. There are also offices in Cape Town and Durban

BRITISH CHAMBER OF BUSINESS IN SOUTH AFRICA, PO Box 10329, Johannesburg

## DEFENCE

The new South African National Defence Force (SANDF) was created from the merger of the South African Defence Forces (SADF), the Umkhonto we Sizwe (MK) armed wing of the ANC, the Azanian People's Liberation Army (APLA) of the PAC, and the defence forces of the four former independent homelands.

The Army has 168 main battle tanks, 967 armoured personnel carriers and 1,240 armoured infantry fighting vehicles. The Navy has two submarines and nine patrol and coastal vessels at two bases. The Air Force has 87 combat aircraft and 3 armed helicopters.

MILITARY EXPENDITURE – 1.3 per cent of GDP (1999)
MILITARY PERSONNEL – 63,389: Army 42,490, Navy 5,190, Air Force 9,640

## ECONOMY

Mining is of great importance, employing more than half a million people in 1996. It is the largest source of foreign exchange. The principal minerals produced are gold, coal, diamonds, copper, iron ore, manganese, lime and limestone, uranium, platinum, fluorspar, andalusite, zinc, zirconium, vanadium, titanium and chrome. South Africa is the world's largest producer of gold, platinum, diamonds, manganese, chrome and vanadium, and has the world's largest reserves of chrome ore, manganese, vanadium and andalusite. In 1998 473.8 tonnes of gold were produced.

Agriculture, forestry and fishing accounted for 4.1 per cent of GDP in 1998. Over 70 per cent of land is pasture so livestock farming is widespread and meat and wool important products. There is both highly developed commercial agriculture and subsistence farming. Principal crops are maize, sugar cane, fruits and vegetables, wheat, sorghum, sunflower seeds and groundnuts. Cotton is widely grown, and viticulture is also widespread.

Industries, concentrated most heavily around Johannesburg, Pretoria and the major ports, process foodstuffs, metals and non-metallic mineral products, produce oil from coal, and also produce beverages and tobacco, motor vehicles, chemicals and chemical products, machinery, textiles and clothing, and paper and paper products. Industry contributed 36.6 per cent of GDP in 1998.

Energy production is based upon coal and natural gas and the production of synthetic liquid fuel from coal. One nuclear power station is in operation and others are planned. South Africa exports electricity through its electric grid connections to all states in southern Africa.

Tourism accounts for 4.7 per cent of GDP. In 1997 4.6 million foreign tourists visited South Africa.

The Minister of Public Enterprises announced in December 1999 that the bulk of the state industrial sector was to be sold off or floated on the stock exchange; the areas covered were Telkom, the telecommunications monopoly, Eskom, the state electricity provider, Deskom, the defence company and Transnet, the state transport company.

In 1999 there was a trade surplus of US$3,751 million and a current account deficit of US$464 million. Imports totalled US$26,696 million and exports US$26,707 million.

GNP – US$133,569 million (1999); US$3,160 per capita (1999)
GDP – US$129,094 million (1997); US$3,404 per capita (1998)
ANNUAL AVERAGE GROWTH OF GDP – 3.1 per cent (1996)
INFLATION RATE – 5.2 per cent (1999)
UNEMPLOYMENT – 5.3 per cent (1998)
TOTAL EXTERNAL DEBT – US$24,711 million (1998)

### TRADE

Principal exports are gold, base metals and metal products, coal, diamonds, food (especially fruit) and wool. Principal imports are machinery, chemicals, motor vehicles, metals and metal products, food, inedible raw materials and textiles.

South Africa's main trading partners are Germany, the USA, the UK, Italy and Japan.

| *Trade with UK* | 1999 | 2000 |
|---|---|---|
| Imports from UK | £1,285,218,000 | £1,411,856,000 |
| Exports to UK | 1,707,061,000 | 2,651,501,000 |

## COMMUNICATIONS

There are international airports at Johannesburg, Durban and Cape Town. South African Airways operates international services to Europe, South America, the Far East, Africa, Australia and the USA, and it is the principal operator of domestic flights. Durban is the largest seaport. Other major ports are Cape Town, Port Elizabeth, East London, Saldanha Bay, Mossel Bay and Richards Bay. The national railway system, and most long-distance passenger and freight road transport are run by independent companies. *Spoornet*, the South African rail freight and long-distance passenger carrier, operates 20,319 km of track, 16,946 km of which is electrified.

## CULTURE AND EDUCATION

Seventeen daily newspapers and 15 weekly publications are published, mainly in English. There are three national television channels, a pay-to-view channel and a free-to-air channel. Higher education is provided at 21 universities and 15 other tertiary-level colleges.

ILLITERACY RATE – 14.9 per cent (2000)
ENROLMENT (percentage of age group) – primary 96 per cent (1996); secondary 58 per cent (1996); tertiary 17.2 per cent (1996)

# SPAIN
*España*

AREA – 195,365 sq. miles (505,992 sq. km). Neighbours: Portugal (west), France (north)
POPULATION – 39,410,000 (1996 census): 96 per cent Catholic, 1 per cent Muslim. Castilian Spanish is the official language, although Basque, Catalan, Galician and Valencian, a dialect of Catalan, are spoken and have official status in the autonomous regions where they are spoken
CAPITAL – Madrid (population, 3,084,673, 1996)
MAJOR CITIES – ΨBarcelona (4,748,236); ΨValencia (2,200,319); Málaga (1,224,959); Sevilla (1,719,446); Zaragoza (852,332), 1995
CURRENCY – Euro (€) of 100 cents/Peseta of 100 céntimos
NATIONAL ANTHEM – Marcha Real Española (Spanish royal march)
NATIONAL DAY – 12 October
NATIONAL FLAG – Three horizontal stripes of red, yellow, red, with the yellow of double width
LIFE EXPECTANCY (years) – male 75.3; female 82.1
POPULATION GROWTH RATE – 0.1 per cent (1999)
POPULATION DENSITY – 78 per sq. km (1998)
URBAN POPULATION – 77.6 per cent (2000 estimate)

The interior of the Iberian peninsula consists of an elevated tableland surrounded and traversed by mountain ranges: the Pyrenees, the Cantabrian Mountains, the Sierra de Guadarrama, Sierra Morena, Sierra Nevada, Montes de Toledo, etc. The principal rivers are the Duero, the Tajo, the Guadiana, the Guadalquivir, the Ebro and the Miño.

## HISTORY AND POLITICS

The kingdoms of Castile and Aragón were united in 1479; they captured Granada, the last region of Spain under Moorish rule, in 1492 and conquered Navarra in 1512. In 1492 Columbus reached the Americas on behalf of Spain and began the process of colonisation which led to most of central and south America coming under Spanish rule until their independence in the 19th century. A republic was proclaimed in 1931 and in February 1936 the Popular Front, a left-wing coalition, was elected. In July 1936 a counter-revolution broke out in military garrisons in Spanish Morocco and spread throughout Spain. Civil war ensued until March 1939, when the Popular Front governments in Madrid and Barcelona surrendered to the Nationalists (as Gen. Franco's followers were then named). Gen. Franco became president and ruled the country until his death in 1975, when, according to his wishes, he was succeeded as head of state by Prince Juan Carlos of Bourbon (grandson of Alfonso XIII) and Spain again became a monarchy. The first free election was held on 15 June 1977.

The general election of 12 March 2000 was won by the Popular Party (PP), which won 183 seats in the Congress of Deputies.

### INSURGENCIES

The Basque separatist organisation ETA (*Euzkadi ta Azkatasuna* – Basque Nation and Liberty) has since its formation in 1959 carried out a terrorist campaign of bombings, shootings and kidnappings against the Spanish state and its security forces in an attempt to gain independence for the Basque country. ETA rejected regional autonomy for the Basque country in 1979 as insufficient and continued its campaign, but increased co-operation between French and Spanish security forces had greatly weakened ETA by the early 1990s. On 16 September 1998, ETA announced an indefinite truce, but ended the truce on 28 November 1999. On 23 January

2000, over a million people demonstrated in Madrid against the resumption of ETA terrorist attacks following a car bomb explosion in Madrid on 21 January, in which one person died. The ETA campaign was stepped up in July 2000 and ETA announced in June 2001 that it would continue its terrorist attacks.

### POLITICAL SYSTEM

Under the 1978 constitution there is a bicameral *Cortes Generales* comprising a 350-member Congress of Deputies (*Congreso de los Diputados*) elected for a maximum term of four years, which elects the prime minister; and a Senate (*Senado*) consisting of 208 directly elected representatives and 51 representatives appointed by the assemblies of the autonomous regions.

Since the promulgation of the 1978 constitution, 19 autonomous regions have been established, with their own parliaments and governments. These are Andalucía, Aragón, Asturias, Balearics, the Basque country, Canaries, Cantabria, Castilla-La Mancha, Castilla y León, Cataluña, Ceuta, Extremadura, Galicia, Madrid, Melilla, Murcia, Navarra, La Rioja and Valencia.

### HEAD OF STATE

*HM The King of Spain*, King Juan Carlos I de Borbón, KG, GCVO, *born* 5 January 1938, *acceded to the throne* 22 November 1975, *married* 14 May 1962, Princess Sophie of Greece *and has issue* Príncipe Felipe (*see* below); Infanta Elena Maria Isabel Dominga, *born* 20 December 1963; and Infanta Cristina Federica Victoria Antonia, *born* 13 June 1965

*Heir*, HRH The Prince of the Asturias (Príncipe Felipe Juan Pablo Alfonso y Todos los Santos), *born* 30 January 1968

### CABINET *as at September 2001*

*Prime Minister*, José María Aznar López
*First Deputy Prime Minister, Cabinet Office, Interior*, Mariano Rajoy Brey
*Second Deputy Prime Minister, Economy*, Rodrigo de Rato y Figaredo
*Agriculture, Food and Fisheries*, Miguel Arias Cañete
*Defence*, Federico Trillo-Figueroa y Martínez Conde
*Development*, Francisco Alvárez-Cascos Fernández
*Education, Culture and Sport*, Pilar del Castillo Vera
*Environment*, Jaime Matas Palou
*Foreign Affairs*, Josep Piqué i Camps
*Government Spokesman*, Pío Cabanillas Alonso
*Health and Consumer Affairs*, Celia Villalobos Talero
*Justice*, Angel Acebes Paniagua
*Labour and Social Affairs*, Carlos Aparicio Pérez
*Public Administration*, Jesús Posada Moreno
*Science and Technology*, Anna María Birulés y Bertrán
*Treasury*, Cristóbal Montoro Romero

### SPANISH EMBASSY

39 Chesham Place, London SW1X 8SB
Tel: 020-7235 5555
*Ambassador Extraordinary and Plenipotentiary*, HE The Marqués de Tamarón, apptd 1999
*Minister Counsellor*, José Argüelles
*Defence and Naval Attaché*, Capt. José Carlos Iglesias
*Counsellors*, Manuel Butler (*Commercial and Tourism*); Ignacio Aguirre (*Consular*); Ramón Abaroa (*Cultural*)

### BRITISH EMBASSY

Calle de Fernando el Santo 16, E-28010 Madrid
Tel: (00 34) (91) 700 8200
*Ambassador Extraordinary and Plenipotentiary*, HE Peter Torry, apptd 1998
*Minister, Deputy Head of Mission*, E. Oakden
*Counsellors*, J. Hawkins (*Commercial*); R. Sharpe*Defence and Naval Attaché*, Capt. A. Croke
*Consuls-General*, J. Thomas (*Madrid*); R. Thomson (*Barcelona*); I. Lewis (*Bilbao*)

CONSULATES-GENERAL – Madrid, Barcelona, Bilbao
CONSULATES - Alicante (Alacant), Málaga, Palma de Mallorca, Las Palmas, Seville, Tenerife
VICE-CONSULATES - Ibiza (Eivissa), Menorca
HONORARY CONSULATES – Santander, Vigo

BRITISH COUNCIL DIRECTOR, Peter Sandiford, OBE, Paseo del General Martínez, Campos 31, E-28010 Madrid; e-mail: General.Enquiries@es.britcoun.org. There are offices in Barcelona, Segovia, Seville, Tarrassa and Valencia

BRITISH CHAMBER OF COMMERCE, Passeig de Gràcia 11A, E-08007 Barcelona

## DEFENCE

The Army has 665 main battle tanks, 1,624 armoured personnel carriers and 28 attack helicopters. The Navy has eight submarines, one aircraft carrier, 15 frigates, 33 patrol and coastal vessels, 17 combat aircraft and 27 armed helicopters at seven bases. The Air Force has 211 combat aircraft.

The USA maintains 1,760 naval and 250 air force personnel in Spain.

MILITARY EXPENDITURE – 1.3 per cent of GDP (1999)
MILITARY PERSONNEL – 166,050: Army 100,000, Navy 39,950, Air Force 29,100, Paramilitaries 75,760
CONSCRIPTION DURATION – Nine months

## ECONOMY

The expansion of the economy and accession to the EU have led to reforms in Spanish agriculture, extensive industrial modernisation and widespread privatisation. Agriculture accounted for 3.4 per cent of GDP in 1997 and employed 8.4 per cent of the working population. The country is generally fertile, and olives, oranges, lemons, almonds, pomegranates, bananas, apricots, tomatoes, peppers, cucumbers and grapes are cultivated. Other agricultural products include wheat, barley, oats, rice, hemp and flax. The vine is cultivated widely; in the south-west, around Jerez, sherry and tent wines are produced. Spain has one of Europe's largest fishing industries.

Spain's mineral resources of coal, iron, wolfram, copper, zinc, lead and iron ores are exploited. The principal industrial goods are cars, steel, ships, manufactured goods, textiles, chemical products, footwear and other leather goods. Tourism is a major industry with 58,588,944 tourists in 1999, of whom 26,799,261 were from overseas. Spain successfully met the convergence criteria laid down for EU economic and monetary union and was a participant in the European single currency, the euro, on 1 January 1999.

The centre-right government has withdrawn subsidies from uncompetitive industries, privatised the steel industry and reduced income tax. The economy has been performing well and unemployment has been falling steadily.

In 1999 Spain had a trade deficit of US$29,208 million and a current account deficit of US$12,621 million. Imports totalled US$144,436 million and exports US$109,964 million.

GNP – US$583,082 million (1999); US$14,000 per capita (1999)
GDP – US$531,289 million (1997); US$15,220 per capita (1999)
ANNUAL AVERAGE GROWTH OF GDP – 3.7 per cent (2000)
INFLATION RATE – 1.3 per cent (2000)
UNEMPLOYMENT – 13.7 per cent (2001)

TRADE

The principal imports are manufactures, military hardware, semimanufactures, vehicles, consumer goods, foodstuffs and energy. The principal exports include manufactures, military hardware, vehicles, semimanufactures, foodstuffs, consumer goods and energy.

| *Trade with UK* | 1999 | 2000 |
|---|---|---|
| Imports from UK | £7,021,800,000 | £7,863,700,000 |
| Exports to UK | 5,622,300,000 | 5,757,100,000 |

## EDUCATION

Education is free for those aged six to 18, and compulsory up to the age of 16. Private schools (30 per cent of primary and 60 per cent of secondary schools) have to fulfil certain criteria to receive government maintenance grants. There are 33 public sector universities, the oldest of which, Salamanca, was founded in 1218. Other ancient foundations are Valladolid (1346), Barcelona (1430), Zaragoza (1474), Santiago (1495), Valencia (1500), Seville (1505), Madrid (1508), Granada (1531), Oviedo (1604). Private universities are Deusto in Bilbao, Navarra in Pamplona, Carlos III in Madrid and one in Salamanca.

ILLITERACY RATE – 2.3 per cent (2000)

ENROLMENT (percentage of age group) – primary 100 per cent (1996); secondary 94 per cent (1994); tertiary 51.4 per cent (1996)

## CULTURE

Castilian is the language of more than three-quarters of the population of Spain. Basque, said to have been the original language of Iberia, is spoken in Vizcaya, Guipúzcoa and Álava. Catalan is spoken in Provençal Spain, and Galician, spoken in the north-western provinces, is akin to Portuguese. The governments of these regions actively encourage use of their local languages.

The literature of Spain is one of the oldest and richest in the world, the *Poem of the Cid*, the earliest of the heroic songs of Spain, having been written about 1140. The outstanding writings of its golden age are those of Miguel de Cervantes Saavedra (1547–1616), Lope Felix de Vega Carpio (1562–1635) and Pedro Calderón de la Barca (1600–81). The Nobel Prize for Literature has five times been awarded to Spanish authors: J. Echegaray (1904), J. Benavente (1922), Juan Ramón Jiménez (1956), Vicente Aleixandre (1977) and Camilo José Cela (1989).

## ISLANDS AND ENCLAVES

THE BALEARIC ISLES form an archipelago off the east coast of Spain. There are four large islands (Majorca, Minorca, Ibiza and Formentera), and seven smaller (Aire, Aucanada, Botafoch, Cabrera, Dragonera, Pinto and El Rey). Area 1,935 sq. miles (5,011 sq. km); population 685,088. The archipelago forms a province of Spain, the capital is ΨPalma in Majorca, population 323,138

THE CANARY ISLANDS are an archipelago in the Atlantic, off the African coast, consisting of seven islands and six islets. Area 2,807 sq. miles (7,270 sq. km); population 1,444,626. The Canary Islands form two provinces of Spain: Las Palmas, comprising Gran Canaria, Lanzarote (38,500), Fuerteventura (19,500) and the islets of Alegranza, Roque del Este, Roque del Oeste, Graciosa, Montaña Clara and Lobos, with seat of administration at ΨLas Palmas (373,772) in Gran Canaria; and Santa Cruz de Tenerife, comprising Tenerife, La Palma (76,000), Gomera (31,829), and Hierro (10,000), with seat of administration at ΨSanta Cruz in Tenerife, population estimate 204,948

ISLA DE FAISANES is an uninhabited Franco-Spanish condominium, at the mouth of the Bidassoa in La Higuera bay

ΨCEUTA is a fortified post on the Moroccan coast, opposite Gibraltar. Area 5 sq. miles (13 sq. km); population 70,864

ΨMELILLA is a town on a rocky promontory of the Rif coast, connected with the mainland by a narrow isthmus. Population 58,449. Ceuta and Melilla are autonomous regions of Spain

## OVERSEAS TERRITORIES

The following territories are Spanish settlements on the Moroccan seaboard.

PEÑÓN DE ALHUCEMAS is a bay including six islands; population 366

PEÑÓN DE LA GOMERA (or Peñón de Velez) is a fortified rocky islet; population 450

THE CHAFFARINAS (or Zaffarines) is a group of three islands near the Algerian frontier; population 610

---

# SRI LANKA

*Sri Lanka Prajatantrika Samajawadi Janarajaya*

---

AREA – 25,332 sq. miles (65,610 sq. km)

POPULATION – 18,985,000 (1997 UN estimate): 74 per cent Sinhalese, 12.6 per cent Sri Lankan Tamils, 5.6 per cent Indian Tamils, 7.1 per cent Sri Lankan Moors, 0.7 per cent Burghers, Malays and others. The religion of the majority is Buddhism (69.3 per cent), then Hinduism (15.5 per cent), Islam (7.6 per cent), and Christianity (7.5 per cent). The national languages are Sinhala and Tamil

CAPITAL – ΨColombo (population, 615,000, 1993)

MAJOR CITIES – ΨGalle (971,000); ΨJaffna (879,000); Kandy (1,269,000); ΨTrincomalee (323,000)

CURRENCY – Sri Lankan rupee of 100 cents

NATIONAL ANTHEM – Namo Namo Matha (We all stand together)

NATIONAL DAY – 4 February (Independence Day)

NATIONAL FLAG – On a dark red field, within a golden border, a golden lion passant holding a sword in its right paw, and a representation of a *bo*-leaf, issuing from each corner; and to its right, two vertical stripes of saffron and green also placed within a golden border, to represent the minorities of the country

LIFE EXPECTANCY (years) – male 65.8; female 73.4

POPULATION GROWTH RATE – 1.0 per cent (1999)

POPULATION DENSITY – 286 per sq. km (1998)

URBAN POPULATION – 23.6 per cent (2000 estimate)

ILLITERACY RATE – 8.4 per cent

ENROLMENT (percentage of age group) – tertiary 5.1 per cent (1996)

Sri Lanka (formerly Ceylon) is an island in the Indian Ocean, off the southern tip of India and separated from it by the narrow Palk Strait. Forests, jungle and scrub cover the greater part of the island. In areas over 2,000 ft above sea level grasslands (*patanas* or *talawas*) are found. One of the highest peaks in the central massif is Adam's Peak (7,360 ft), a place of pilgrimage for Buddhists, Hindus and Muslims.

The climate is warm throughout the year, with a high relative humidity. The two main monsoon seasons are mid-May to September (south-west) and November to March (north-east).

## HISTORY AND POLITICS

The Portuguese landed in Ceylon in the early 16th century and founded settlements. The Dutch East India Company controlled the country from 1658 until 1796. The maritime provinces of Ceylon were ceded by the Dutch to the British in 1798, becoming a British Crown Colony in 1802. With the annexation of the Kingdom of Kandy in

1815, all Ceylon came under British rule. Ceylon became a self-governing state and a member of the British Commonwealth on 4 February 1948. A republican constitution was adopted in 1972 and the country was renamed Sri Lanka (meaning 'Resplendent Island').

Eight provincial councils were set up in 1988 under the Indo-Sri Lankan peace accord in an attempt to diffuse ethnic tension. Since then, except for the temporarily merged North-East province, all provinces have had elected provincial councils.

In the presidential election held on 21 December 1999, President Kumaratunga was elected for a second term, gaining 51.37 per cent of the vote. Prime Minister Sirimavo Bandaranaike resigned on 10 August 2000 and was replaced by Ratnasiri Wickremanayake.

In the general election of 10 October 2000 the ruling People's Alliance (PA), a coalition of seven parties led by Chandrika Bandaranaike Kumaratunga, won 107 seats; the United National Party (UNP) 89 seats; and other parties, mainly Muslim and moderate Tamils, 29 seats. The PA formed a government with the support of the Eelam People's Democratic Party (EPDP) and the National Unity Alliance. The government lost its majority on 20 June 2001 when the Sri Lankan Muslim Congress left both the PA and the ruling coalition. The far-left People's Liberation Front agreed on 5 September to support the PA for a period of a year in exchange for economic reforms.

## Insurgencies

The Liberation Tigers of Tamil Eelam (LTTE) guerrilla group has been fighting Sri Lankan forces for control of the Tamil majority areas in the north and east of the country since 1983.

Peace negotiations in 1994, led to a formal cease-fire in January 1995, but fighting resumed in April 1995 after the LTTE had unilaterally broken the cease-fire and negotiations had broken down. A government offensive in April 1996 gained control over almost the entire northern Jaffna peninsula. A second government offensive in May 1997 to take control of a strategic highway on the Jaffna peninsula resulted in losses for the LTTE.

On 22 April 2000, LTTE forces captured the Elephant Pass, the only land link to the Jaffna peninsula. On 3 May 2000, President Kumaratunga imposed a state of war, invoked an ordinance that gave the police wide powers of arrest and confiscation, banned strikes and political rallies and imposed censorship of military, political and economic reporting. All non-essential development projects were suspended and the defence levy sales tax was raised to make more funds available to the military.

The LTTE declared a month-long unilateral cease-fire on 21 December 2000, to facilitate peace talks. The government rejected the cease-fire and troops launched a fresh offensive in the Jaffna peninsula. The LTTE extended the cease-fire in January 2001, and again in February and March, but the government refused to reciprocate, launching a series of attacks on the Jaffna peninsula. The LTTE cease-fire came to an end on 24 April.

## Political System

The 1978 constitution introduced a system of proportional representation. Legislative power is vested in the parliament, whose 225 members are directly elected for a six-year term. Executive power is exercised by the president, elected for six years, and the Cabinet.

## Head of State

*President, Defence, Finance, Planning*, Chandrika Bandaranaike Kumaratunga, *elected* 9 November 1994, *re-elected* 21 December 1999, *sworn in* 22 December 1999

## Cabinet *as at September 2001*

The President
*Prime Minister, Plantation Industries, Buddha Sasana and Religious Affairs*, Ratnasiri Wickremanayake (SLFP)
*Agriculture and Land*, D. M. Jayaratne (SLFP)
*Aviation and Airport Development*, Jeyaraj Fernandopulle (SLFP)
*Constitutional Affairs, Industrial Development*, G. L. Peiris (SLFP)
*Co-operative Development*, H. B. Semasinghe
*Cultural Affairs*, M. C. Gopallawa
*Development and Reconstruction of the East, Rural Housing*, vacant
*Development, Rehabilitation and Reconstruction of the North, Tamil Affairs (North and East)*, Douglas Devananda (EPDP)
*Education*, Susil Premajayantha
*Environment and Forestry*, Mahinda Wijesekera (SLFP)
*Ethnic Affairs and National Integration*, Riginold Cooray
*Fisheries and Aquatic Resources Development*, Mahinda Rajapakse
*Foreign Affairs*, Lakshman Kadirgamar (SLFP)
*Health*, John Senaviratne (SLFP)
*Higher Education and IT Development*, Indika Gunawardena (CPSL)
*Highways*, A. H. M. Fowzie (SLFP)
*Indigenous Medicine*, Tissa Karalliyadda
*Industrial Development*, Maheepala Herath
*Information and Media*, Anura Priyadharshana Yapa
*Internal and External Trade and Commerce, Muslim Religious Affairs, Shipping*, vacant
*Irrigation and Water Resources Management*, Sarath Amunugama
*Justice*, Batty Weerakoon
*Labour*, Alavi Maulana (SLFP)
*Land Development and Minor Export Agriculture*, Salinda Dissanayake
*Livestock Development and Estates Infrastructure*, Arumugam Phondaman (SLWC)
*Mahaweli Development*, Maithripala Sirisena (SLFP)
*Plan Implementation*, Pavithra Wanniarachchi
*Port Development, Development of the South*, Ronnie de Mel
*Post and Telecommunications*, Nimal Siripala De Silva (SLFP)
*Power and Energy*, Gen. Anuruddha Ratwatte (SLFP)
*Provincial Councils and Local Government*, Nandimithra Ekanayake
*Public Administration, Home Affairs, Administrative Reforms*, Richard Pathirana (SLFP)
*Science and Technology*, Leslie Gunawardena
*Social Services, Housing Development for the Fishing Community*, Milroy Fernando
*Tourism, Sports*, Lakshman Kiriella
*Transport*, Dinesh Gunawardena
*Urban Development, Construction and Public Utilities*, Mangala Samaraweera (SLFP)
*Vocational Training*, Amarasiri Dodangoda (SLFP)
*Welfare and Rural Development*, S. B. Dissanayake (SLFP)
*Without Portfolio*, Wijayapala Mendis; Reggie Ranatunga
*Women's Affairs*, Sumedha Jayasena
*Youth Affairs*, Jeewan Kumarathunga

EPDP Eelam People's Democratic Party; SLFP Sri Lanka Freedom Party; CPSL Communist Party of Sri Lanka; SLWC Sri Lanka Workers' Congress

HIGH COMMISSION FOR THE DEMOCRATIC SOCIALIST REPUBLIC OF SRI LANKA
13 Hyde Park Gardens, London W2 2LU
Tel: 020-7262 1841/7
*High Commissioner*, HE Mangala Moonesinghe, apptd 2000
*Deputy High Commissioner*, J. Palipane
*Minister*, N. Magederagamage *(Commerce)*
*Consul*, C. Jayasuriya Arachchi

BRITISH HIGH COMMISSION
190 Galle Road, Kollupitiya, PO Box 1433, Colombo 3
Tel: (00 94) (1) 437336/437343
E-mail: bhc@eureka.lk
*High Commissioner*, HE Linda Duffield, apptd 1999
*Deputy High Commissioner*, M. H. P. Hill
*Defence Adviser*, Lt.-Col. M. Weldon
*First Secretary (Commercial and Economic)*, A. Madeley

BRITISH COUNCIL DIRECTOR, David Hopkinson, 49 Alfred House Gardens, PO Box 753, Colombo 3; e-mail: enquiries@britishcouncil.lk. There is a regional office in Kandy

## DEFENCE

The Army has 25 main battle tanks, 152 armoured personnel carriers and 16 armoured infantry fighting vehicles. The Navy has 39 patrol and coastal vessels at seven bases. The Air Force has 26 combat aircraft and 19 armed helicopters.
MILITARY EXPENDITURE – 5.1 per cent of GDP (1999)
MILITARY PERSONNEL – 115,000: Army 95,000, Navy 10,000, Air Force 10,000, Paramilitaries 88,600

## ECONOMY

The staple products are tea, rubber, copra, spices and gems. There is increasing emphasis on local production of food, especially rice, and plans for the large-scale production of sugar cane, cotton and citrus fruits.

The prinicipal exports are industrial goods, agricultural products (especially tea), and oil derivatives. Principal imports are manufactures, textiles and clothing, capital goods, consumer goods and oil. Tourism is an important industry, with 400,414 foreign visitors in 2000.

In 1998 there was a trade deficit of US$567 million and a current account deficit of US$288 million. In 1999 imports totalled US$5,893 million and exports US$4,599 million.
GNP – US$15,578 million (1999); US$820 per capita (1999)
GDP – US$15,095 million (1997); US$851 per capita (1998)
ANNUAL AVERAGE GROWTH OF GDP – 3.8 per cent (1996)
INFLATION RATE – 4.7 per cent (1999)
UNEMPLOYMENT – 10.6 per cent (1998)
TOTAL EXTERNAL DEBT – US$8,526 million (1998)

| *Trade with UK* | 1999 | 2000 |
|---|---|---|
| Imports from UK | £137,449,000 | £164,308,000 |
| Exports to UK | 343,567,000 | 426,063,000 |

## COMMUNICATIONS

There are 25,952 km of roads in Sri Lanka, of which 11,077 km are surfaced, and a government-run railway system with 1,459 km of lines. A satellite earth station at Padukka provides telecommunication links world-wide. The principal airport is at Katunayake, north of Colombo.

# SUDAN
*Al-Jumhūriyya as-Sūdān*

AREA – 967,500 sq. miles (2,505,813 sq. km). Neighbours: Egypt (north), Eritrea and Ethiopia (east), Kenya, Uganda and the Democratic Republic of Congo (south), Central African Republic, Chad and Libya (west)
POPULATION – 28,993,000 (1997 UN estimate). Arab and Nubian peoples populate the north and centre, Nilotic and Negro peoples the south. Arabic is the official language and Islam the state religion, although the Nilotics of the Bahr el Ghazal and Upper Nile valleys are generally Animists or Christians
CAPITAL – Khartoum (Al-Khartūm) (population, 947,483, 1993 census). The combined population of Khartoum, Khartoum North and Umm Durmān (excluding refugees and displaced people) is estimated at 3,000,000
MAJOR CITIES – Al-Ubayyid (229,425); Nyala (227,183); ΨPort Sudan (Būr Sūdān) (308,195), 1993 census
CURRENCY – Sudanese dinar (SD) of 100 piastres
NATIONAL ANTHEM – Nahnu Djundullah (We are the army of God)
NATIONAL DAY – 1 January (Independence Day)
NATIONAL FLAG – Three horizontal stripes of red, white and black with a green triangle next to the hoist
LIFE EXPECTANCY (years) – male 53.1; female 54.7
POPULATION GROWTH RATE – 2.0 per cent (1999)
POPULATION DENSITY – 11 per sq. km (1998)
URBAN POPULATION – 36.1 per cent (2000 estimate)
MILITARY EXPENDITURE – 4.9 per cent of GDP (1999)
MILITARY PERSONNEL – 104,500: Army 100,000, Navy 1,500, Air Force 3,000; Paramilitaries 15,000
CONSCRIPTION DURATION – Three years

The White Nile, as the Bahr el Jebel, flows through Sudan from Nimule to Wadi Halfa. The Blue Nile flows from Lake Tana on the Ethiopian plateau through Sudan to join the White Nile at Khartoum. The next confluence of importance is at Atbara where the main Nile is joined by the River Atbara. Between Khartoum and Wadi Halfa lie five of the six cataracts.

## HISTORY AND POLITICS

The Anglo-Egyptian Condominium over Sudan was established in 1899 and ended when the Sudan House of Representatives, on 19 December 1955, declared Sudan a fully independent sovereign state. A republic was proclaimed on 1 January 1956, and was recognised by Great Britain and Egypt. Sudan was under military rule from 1958 to 1964, from 1969 to 1986, and from 1989 until presidential and legislative elections were held in March 1996. President al-Bashir was elected with 75.7 per cent of the vote having faced no serious contender. The founding of political parties was legalised on 1 January 1999. In early January 1999, the voting age was lowered to 17 and a new dress code was imposed on women, requiring them to wear headscarves. In December 1999, President al-Bashir suspended the National Assembly and declared a three-month state of emergency, shortly before a vote on constitutional changes, which included the reduction of the powers of the president, was due to be debated. The state of emergency has been extended until the end of 2001.

Presidential and legislative elections were held on 13-23 December 2000, but were boycotted by most opposition parties. President al-Bashir was re-elected, winning 86.5 per cent of votes cast, and the National Congress won 355 of the 360 seats which were up for election. The civil war prevented balloting in three provinces.

### Insurgencies

Nearly 17 years of insurrection in the southern provinces ended in 1972 with the signing of an agreement recognising southern regional autonomy within the Sudanese state. However, insurrection resumed in 1983 and since then there has been civil war in the south of the country between government forces and the Christian and Animist majority in the area, organised into the Sudan People's Liberation Army (SPLA).

The warfare has left an estimated 1.4 million dead, including 300,000 who died in the war-induced famine in 1988 and thousands in a similar situation in 1994. Some three million refugees have fled the fighting, either to the north, to neighbouring states or to the far south near the Ugandan border. The fighting has left large areas of the south desolate and uninhabitable.

### Foreign Relations

In 1995 Sudan's relations with its neighbours, notably Egypt, Eritrea and Uganda, deteriorated as they considered that Sudan was arming Islamic and insurgent groups in their states. On 2 May 1999 a peace agreement was signed with Eritrea. Sudan and the UK agreed to resume full diplomatic representation in June 1999. On 8 December 1999, Sudan and Uganda signed an agreement under which they agreed to cease supporting rebel groups in each other's countries, to disarm and disband such groups and to re-establish full diplomatic links. On 24 December, Sudan and Egypt agreed to normalise their relations and seek a solution to their dispute over the Hala'ib region.

### Head of State

*President, Prime Minister*, Lt.-Gen. Omar Hassan Ahmad al-Bashir, *appointed* 16 October 1993, *elected* 17 March 1996
*First Vice-President*, Maj.-Gen. Ali Osman Mohamad Taha
*Vice-President*, Moses Machar Kashol

### Cabinet *as at September 2001*

The President
*Agriculture and Forestry*, Majdhub al-Khalifah Ahmad
*Animal Resources*, Riek Gai
*Aviation*, Joseph Malwal
*Cabinet Affairs*, Maj.-Gen. al-Hadi Muhammad Awad; Martin Malwal Arop
*Culture and Tourism*, Abd al-Basit Abd al-Majid
*Defence*, Maj.-Gen. Bakri Hassan Salih
*Education*, Ali Tamim Fartak
*Energy and Mining*, Awad Ahmad al-Jaz
*Environment and Construction Development*, Maj.-Gen. al-Tijani Adam al-Tahir
*Finance and National Economy*, Abd al-Rahim Mahmud Hamdi
*Foreign Affairs*, Mustapha Osman Ismail
*Foreign Trade*, Abdel Hamid Mussa Kasha
*Guidance and Awqaf*, Isam Ahmad al-Bashir
*Health*, Ahmad Bilal Uthman
*Higher Education*, Mubarak Muhammad Ali al-Majdhub
*Industry and Investment*, Jalal Yusuf Muhammad al-Dugayr
*Information and Communications*, Mahdi Ibrahim
*Internal Affairs*, Maj.-Gen. Abd al-Rahim Muhammad Husayn
*International Co-operation*, Karam-al-din Abd-al-Mawla
*Irrigation and Water Resources*, Kamal Ali Muhammad
*Justice*, Ali Mohammad Uthman Yassin
*Minister in the Federal Administration Office*, Nafi Ali Nafi
*Presidency*, Lt.-Gen. Salah Muhammad Muhammad Salih
*Presidential Adviser on Authentication*, Ahmad Ali al-Imam
*Presidential Adviser on Legal Affairs and African Industrialisation*, Bedriya Suleiman
*Presidential Adviser on National Security Affairs*, Maj.-Gen. al-Tayyib Ibrahim Muhammad Khayr
*Presidential Adviser on Peace Affairs*, Ghazi Salah al-Din Atabani
*Presidential Adviser on Political Affairs*, Qutbi al-Mahdi
*Relations with the National Assembly*, Abd al-Basit Salih Sabdarat
*Roads and Bridges*, Muhammad Tahir Ila
*Social Development*, Samiyah Ahmad Muhammad
*Science and Technology*, Zubayr Bashir Taha
*Transport*, Lam Akol Ajawin
*Works and Administrative Reform*, Maj.-Gen. Allison Manani Magaya
*Youth and Sport*, Hasan Uthman Rizq

### Embassy of the Republic of the Sudan

3 Cleveland Row, London SW1A 1DD
Tel: 020-7839 8080
*Ambassador Extraordinary and Plenipotentiary*, HE Dr Hasan Abdin, apptd 2000

### British Embassy

PO Box 801, Khartoum East
Tel: (00 249) (11) 777105
E-mail: british@sudanmail.net
*Ambassador Extraordinary and Plenipotentiary*, HE Richard Makepeace, apptd 1999

British Council Director, Don Sloan, 14 Abu Sin Street (PO Box 1253), Khartoum; e-mail: bc.khartoum@bc-khartoum.bcouncil.org

## ECONOMY

Agriculture provides employment for over half the labour force and contributes nearly half of GDP. It is based on large and medium-sized public sector irrigation projects. Mechanised and traditional agriculture is practised in areas of sufficient rainfall. The principal grain crops are *dura* (great millet) and wheat, the staple food of the population. Sesame and groundnuts are other important food crops, which also yield an exportable surplus, and a promising start has been made with castor seed. Sudan still has to achieve self-sufficiency in its production.

In 1999 Sudan had a trade deficit of US$476 million and a current account deficit of US$465 million. In 1998 imports totalled US$1,915 million and exports US$596 million.

GNP – US$9,435 million (1999); US$330 per capita (1999)
GDP – US$1,648 million (1997); US$305 per capita (1998)
Annual Average Growth of GDP – 4.5 per cent (1996)
Inflation Rate – 16.0 per cent (1999)
Total External Debt – US$16,843 million (1998)

### Trade

The principal exports are sesame, cotton and livestock. The chief imports are manufactures, machinery and transport equipment, and raw materials.

| *Trade with UK* | 1999 | 2000 |
|---|---|---|
| Imports from UK | £89,992,000 | £58,198,000 |
| Exports to UK | 6,127,000 | 6,741,000 |

## COMMUNICATIONS

The railway system, adversely affected by the civil war, has a route length of about 5,516 km. There are 11,610 km of roads, of which 4,203 km are paved. Nile river services between Khartoum and Juba have been interrupted by the southern insurrection. Port Sudan is the country's main seaport. Sudan Airways flies services from Khartoum to other parts of Sudan and to other African states, Europe and the Middle East.

## EDUCATION

School education is free for most children but not compulsory, beginning with six years of primary education, followed by three years of secondary education at general secondary schools, the more academic higher secondary schools or vocational schools. The medium of instruction is Arabic. English has not been taught in schools since new Arabisation legislation came into effect in 1991.

In addition to 20 universities there are various technical post-secondary institutes as well as professional and vocational training establishments.

ILLITERACY RATE – 42.9 per cent

ENROLMENT (percentage of age group) – tertiary 3 per cent (1990)

---

# SURINAME

*Republiek Suriname*

---

AREA – 63,037 sq. miles (163,265 sq. km). Neighbours: French Guiana (east), Brazil (south), Guyana (west)

POPULATION – 413,000 (1997 UN estimate): 37 per cent Indians, 31 per cent creoles, 15 per cent Javanese, 10 per cent Africans, small numbers of Amerindians, Chinese and Europeans. The official language is Dutch, the native language is Sranang Tongo, and other widely-used languages are Hindustani and Javanese

CAPITAL – ΨParamaribo (population, 265,000, 1993)

CURRENCY – Suriname guilder of 100 cents

NATIONAL ANTHEM - God zij met ons Suriname (God be with our Suriname)

NATIONAL DAY – 25 November

NATIONAL FLAG – Horizontal stripes of green, white, red, white, green, with a five-pointed yellow star in the centre

LIFE EXPECTANCY (years) – male 68.1; female 73.6

POPULATION GROWTH RATE – 0.4 per cent (1999)

POPULATION DENSITY – 3 per sq. km (1998)

URBAN POPULATION – 74.2 per cent (2000 estimate)

MILITARY EXPENDITURE – 5.5 per cent of GDP (1999)

MILITARY PERSONNEL – 2,040: Army 1,600, Navy 240, Air Force 200

ILLITERACY RATE – 5.8 per cent

## HISTORY AND POLITICS

Formerly known as Dutch Guiana, Suriname remained part of the Netherlands West Indies until 25 November 1975, when it achieved complete independence. The civilian government was ousted in 1980 by the military who appointed a predominantly civilian government in 1982.

The New Front for Democracy, a four-party bloc consisting of the National Party of Suriname (NPS), The Progressive Reform Party, Pertjajah Luhur and the Suriname Labour Party, won 32 of the 51 seats in the elections to the National Assembly on 25 May 2000 and appointed Ronald Venetiaan of the NPS as president on 4 August 2000.

### POLITICAL SYSTEM

The unicameral legislature, the National Assembly, has 51 members, directly elected for a five-year term. The president is elected by a two-thirds majority in the National Assembly, or if the required majority cannot be achieved, by a specially convened United Peoples' Conference, including district and local council representatives, for a five-year term of office.

### HEAD OF STATE

*President*, Ronald Venetiaan, *inaugurated* 4 August 2000
*Vice-President*, Jules Ajodhia

### COUNCIL OF MINISTERS *as at September 2001*

*Agriculture, Animal Husbandry and Fisheries*, Gangaram Panday
*Defence*, Ronald Assen
*Education and Community Development*, Walther Sandriman
*Finance, Natural Resources*, Humphrey Hildenberg
*Foreign Affairs*, Marie Levens
*Health*, Rakieb Khudabux
*Home Affairs, Trade and Industry*, Urmila Joella-Sewnundum
*Justice and Police*, Siegfried Gilds
*Labour and Technological Sciences*, Clifford Marica
*Natural Resources*, Rudi Demon
*Planning and Development Co-operation*, Stanley Raghoebar Singh
*Public Works*, Dewan Balesar
*Regional Development*, Romeo van Russel
*Social Affairs and Housing*, Paul Salam Somohardjo
*Trade and Industry*, John Tjon Tjin Joe
*Transport, Communication and Tourism*, Guno Castelen

### EMBASSY OF THE REPUBLIC OF SURINAME

Alexander Gogelweg 2, NL-2517 JH The Hague, The Netherlands
Tel: (00 31) (70) 365 0844
*Ambassador Extraordinary and Plenipotentiary*, vacant
*Chargé d'Affaires*, N. Stadwijk-Kappel

BRITISH AMBASSADOR, HE Edward Glover, MVO, resident at Georgetown, Guyana

BRITISH CONSULATE, c/o VSH United Buildings, Van 't Hogerhuystraat, PO Box 1860, Paramaribo. *Honorary Consul*, J. J. Healy, MBE

## ECONOMY

Suriname has large timber resources. Rice and sugar cane are the main crops. Bauxite is mined, and is the principal export. Principal trading partners are the Netherlands, the USA and Norway.

In 1998 imports totalled US$552 million and exports US$436 million.

GNP – US$684 million (1998); US$1,660 per capita (1998)

GDP – US$1,538 million (1997); US$2,454 per capita (1998)

ANNUAL AVERAGE GROWTH OF GDP – 3.0 per cent (1996)

INFLATION RATE – 98.9 per cent (1999)

UNEMPLOYMENT – 10.5 per cent (1997)

| *Trade with UK* | 1999 | 2000 |
|---|---|---|
| Imports from UK | £8,299,000 | £10,035,000 |
| Exports to UK | 19,476,000 | 25,917,000 |

---

# SWAZILAND

*Umbuso we Swatini*

---

AREA – 6,704 sq. miles (17,364 sq. km). Neighbours: South Africa (north, west and south), Mozambique (east)

POPULATION – 1,018,000 (1997 UN estimate). The languages are English and Swazi

CAPITAL – Mbabane (population, 38,290, 1986)

MAJOR TOWNS – Manzini (30,000); Hlatikulu; Mhlume; Nhlangano; Pigg's Peak; Siteki

CURRENCY – Lilangeni (E) of 100 cents (South African currency is also in circulation). Swaziland is a member of the Common Monetary Area and its unit of currency *Emalangeni* (singular *Lilangeni*) has a par value with the South African rand
NATIONAL ANTHEM – Ingoma Yesive
NATIONAL DAY – 6 September (Independence Day)
NATIONAL FLAG – Blue with a wide crimson horizontal band bordered in yellow across the centre, bearing a shield and two spears horizontally
LIFE EXPECTANCY (years) – male 45.8; female 46.8
POPULATION GROWTH RATE – 3.0 per cent (1999)
POPULATION DENSITY – 55 per sq. km (1998)
URBAN POPULATION – 26.4 per cent (2000 estimate)
ILLITERACY RATE – 20.2 per cent (2000)
ENROLMENT (percentage of age group) – primary 91 per cent (1996); secondary 38 per cent (1996); tertiary 6 per cent (1996)

The broken mountainous Highveld along the western border, with an average altitude of 4,000 ft, is densely forested, mainly with conifers and eucalyptus; the Middleveld, averaging about 2,000 ft, is a mixed farming area including cotton and pineapples; and the Lowveld in the east was mainly scrubland until the introduction of large sugar-cane plantations. Four rivers, the Komati, Usutu, Mbuluzi and Ngwavuma, flow from west to east.

## HISTORY AND POLITICS

The Kingdom of Swaziland came into being on 25 April 1967 under a self-government constitution and became an independent kingdom, headed by HM Sobhuza II, in membership of the Commonwealth on 6 September 1968.

An illegal general strike was held on 13-14 November 2000 to support a petition demanding the legalisation of political parties, the revocation of restrictive labour laws and the abolition of the right of traditional chiefs to force people to work without pay. The petition had been drawn up by the Swaziland Federation of Trade Unions and a group of illegal political parties. Several trade union and opposition leaders were arrested shortly before the strike took place and during the demonstrations.

### POLITICAL SYSTEM

The King, assisted by his appointed Cabinet, holds considerable executive, legislative and judicial authority. There is a bicameral legislative body comprising a Senate and a House of Assembly. Each of the 55 *Tinkhundla* (administrative districts) directly elects one member to the House of Assembly. The King appoints ten members to the House of Assembly, making 65 in all, who then elect ten members of their own number to the Senate. To these are added 20 senators appointed by the King, bringing the full membership of the Senate to 30. In addition, the King appoints Commissions, who assess public opinion. There are also public gatherings, where any citizen can express an opinion. All political parties are banned.

Legislative elections to the House of Assembly were held on 16–24 October 1998. The members of the Senate were elected and appointed in November 1998.

### HEAD OF STATE

*King of Swaziland*, HM King Mswati III, *inaugurated* 25 April 1986

### CABINET *as at September 2001*

*Prime Minister*, Dr Barnabas Sibusiso Dlamini
*Deputy Prime Minister*, Arthur Khoza
*Agriculture*, Roy Fanourakis
*Economic Planning*, Prince Guduza Dlamini
*Education*, John Carmichael
*Enterprise and Employment*, Lutfo Dlamini
*Finance*, Majozi Sithole
*Foreign Affairs and Trade*, Abednego Ntshangase
*Health and Social Welfare*, Dr Phetsile Dlamini
*Home Affairs*, Prince Sobandla Dlamini
*Housing and Urban Development*, Albert Shabangu
*Justice and Constitutional Development*, Chief Maweni Simelane
*Natural Resources and Energy*, Magwagwa Mdluli
*Public Service and Information*, Mntonzima Dlamini
*Public Works and Transport*, Titus Mlangeni
*Tourism, Environment and Communications*, Stella Lukhele

### KINGDOM OF SWAZILAND HIGH COMMISSION

20 Buckingham Gate, London SW1E 6LB
Tel: 020-7630 6611
*High Commissioner*, HE Revd Percy Mngomezulu, apptd 1994

### BRITISH HIGH COMMISSION

Allister Miller Street, Mbabane
Tel: (00 268) 404 2581/2/3
E-mail: bhc@realnet.co.sz
*High Commissioner*, HE Neil Hook, MVO, apptd 1999

BRITISH COUNCIL DIRECTOR, Paul Feeney, Ground Floor, Lilunga House, Gilfillan Street, Mbabane; e-mail: info@britishcouncil.sz

## ECONOMY

Manufacturing has replaced agriculture as the dominant sector, with timber, textiles and footwear the main products. Agricultural products include sugar cane and fruit. GDP growth rates have declined in the 1990s, partly as a result of lower growth rates in South Africa, on which the Swazi economy is strongly dependent. South Africa accounts for around 60 per cent of exports from Swaziland and about 85 per cent of imports.

In 1998 Swaziland had a trade deficit of US$111 million and a current account surplus of US$17 million. In 1996 imports totalled US$1,174 million and exports US$893 million.

GNP – US$1,379 million (1999); US$1,360 per capita (1999)
GDP – US$1,313 million (1997); US$1,279 per capita (1998)
ANNUAL AVERAGE GROWTH OF GDP – 2.3 per cent (1998)
INFLATION RATE – 6.1 per cent (1999)
TOTAL EXTERNAL DEBT – US$251 million (1998)

| *Trade with UK* | 1999 | 2000 |
|---|---|---|
| Imports from UK | £2,688,000 | £4,932,000 |
| Exports to UK | 30,843,000 | 33,877,000 |

## COMMUNICATIONS

Swaziland's railway is 297 km long and connects with the Mozambique port of Maputo and the South African railway network to Richards Bay. A rail line to the north-west border provides a link to Komatipoort. There are 2,896 km of roads, of which 828 km are paved. Most passenger and goods traffic is carried by privately-owned motor transport services. There is an international airport at Manzini. Royal Swazi National Airways provides scheduled air services to southern and eastern Africa. International telecommunications and television services are provided through a satellite earth station.

## SWEDEN
*Konungariket Sverige*

AREA – 173,732 sq. miles (449,964 sq. km). Neighbours: Norway (west), Finland (east)
POPULATION – 8,894,674 (2001 estimate); 8,745,109 (1993 census). The state religion is Lutheran Protestant, to which over 95 per cent officially adhere. The language is Swedish; in the north there are both Finnish- and Lapp-speaking communities
CAPITAL – ΨStockholm (population, 1,148,953, 1995)
MAJOR CITIES – ΨGothenburg (Göteborg) (454,016); ΨMalmö (248,007); Uppsala (184,507), 1996 estimates
CURRENCY – Swedish krona of 100 öre
NATIONAL ANTHEM – Du Gamla, Du Fria (Thou ancient, thou freeborn)
NATIONAL DAY – 6 June (Day of the Swedish Flag)
NATIONAL FLAG – Yellow cross on a blue ground
LIFE EXPECTANCY (years) – male 77.1; female 81.9
POPULATION GROWTH RATE – 0.4 per cent (1999)
POPULATION DENSITY – 20 per sq. km (1998)
URBAN POPULATION – 83.3 per cent (2000 estimate)

### HISTORY AND POLITICS

Sweden takes its name from the Svear people who inhabited the region during the seventh century AD. The Swedes participated in the Viking expansion during the ninth to 11th centuries and established sovereignty over Finland in the 13th century. The Union of Kalmar (1397) brought Sweden and Norway under Danish rule. Northern Sweden regained its independence following a rebellion by noblemen in 1521 which resulted in the election to the Swedish throne of Gustav I of the house of Vasa.

Sweden's power climaxed in the 17th century under Gustavus II Adolf. The Danes were driven out of southern Sweden, the Baltic coast of Russia was seized and the Swedish army pushed into Germany after vanquishing the Catholic League. Swedish power waned in the 17th and 18th centuries. Finland was lost to Russia in 1809; Norway was ceded to Sweden under the Congress of Vienna (1814–15) but seceded in 1905.

Sweden remained neutral during both World Wars. Post-war party politics was dominated by Social Democrat-led coalitions which established a mixed economy and a generous welfare state. Right-wing and centrist parties held power from 1976–82 and 1991–4. Sweden applied for EU membership in July 1991 and acceded to the EU on 1 January 1995.

In the general election held on 20 September 1998 the Social Democrats remained the largest party in the legislature with 131 seats and formed a minority government.

#### POLITICAL SYSTEM

Sweden is a constitutional monarchy, with the monarch retaining purely ceremonial functions as head of state. Under the Act of Succession 1810 (with amendments) the throne is hereditary in the House of Bernadotte. The constitution is based upon the Instrument of Government 1974, which amended the 1810 Act and removed from the monarch the roles of appointing the prime minister and signing parliamentary bills into law. A 1979 amendment vested the succession in the monarch's eldest child irrespective of sex.

Executive power is vested in the prime minister and Council of Ministers. There is a unicameral legislature (*Riksdag*) of 349 members elected by universal suffrage on a proportional representation basis (with a 4 per cent threshold for representation) for four years. The Council of Ministers (*Statsråd*) is responsible to the *Riksdag*.

Sweden is divided into 24 counties (*län*) and 288 municipalities (*kommun*).

#### HEAD OF STATE

*HM The King of Sweden*, Carl XVI Gustaf, KG, *born* 30 April 1946, *succeeded* 15 September 1973, *married* 19 June 1976 Fräulein Silvia Renate Sommerlath and has *issue*, Crown Princess Victoria (*see* below); Prince Carl Philip Edmund Bertil, Duke of Värmland, *born* 13 May 1979; Princess Madeleine Thérèse Amelie Josephine, Duchess of Hälsingland and Gästrikland, *born* 10 June 1982
*Heir*, HRH Crown Princess Victoria Ingrid Alice Désirée, Duchess of Västergötland, *born* 14 July 1977

#### CABINET *as at September 2001*

*Prime Minister*, Göran Persson
*Deputy Prime Minister*, Lena Hjelm-Wallén
*Agriculture, Food and Fisheries, Gender Equality Affairs*, Margareta Winberg
*Culture*, Marita Ulvskog
*Defence*, Björn von Sydow
*Education and Science*, Thomas Östros
*Environment*, Kjell Larsson
*Finance*, Bosse Ringholm
*Foreign Affairs*, Anna Lindh
*Health and Social Affairs*, Lars Engqvist
*Industry, Employment and Communications*, Björn Rosengren
*Justice*, Thomas Bodström

#### EMBASSY OF SWEDEN
11 Montagu Place, London W1H 2AL
Tel: 020-7917 6400
*Ambassador Extraordinary and Plenipotentiary*, HE Mats Bergquist, CMG, apptd 1997
*Defence Attaché*, Col. M. Engman
*Consul-General*, G. Dannerljung
*Counsellor (Economic Affairs)*, P. Wallén

#### BRITISH EMBASSY
Skarpögatan 6–8, Box 27819, S-115 93 Stockholm
Tel: (00 46) (8) 671 3000
*Ambassador Extraordinary and Plenipotentiary*, HE John Grant, CMG, apptd 1999
*Counsellor, Consul-General and Deputy Head of Mission*, vacant
*Counsellor (Economic and Commercial)*, P. Mathers, LVO
*Military Attaché*, Wg Cdr. P. Leadbetter, MVO

CONSULAR OFFICES – Stockholm, Gothenburg
HONORARY CONSULATES – Malmö, Sundsvall

BRITISH COUNCIL DIRECTOR , Jim Potts, PO Box 27819, S-115 93 Stockholm; e-mail: info@britishcouncil.se
BRITISH-SWEDISH CHAMBER OF COMMERCE, PO Box 16050, Jakob Torg, 4th floor, S-10321 Stockholm

### DEFENCE

The Army has 537 main battle tanks, 646 armoured personnel carriers and 1,210 armoured infantry fighting vehicles. The Navy has nine submarines and 45 patrol and coastal vessels at four bases. The Air Force has 250 combat aircraft.

Sweden has a policy of non-alignment in peace and neutrality in war, and it maintains a 'total defence' which includes peacetime organisations for civil, economic and psychological defence.

It was announced in March 1999 that the size of the armed forces was to be reduced by about 50 per cent in line with budget cuts and the perceived diminished threat to Sweden's security.

MILITARY EXPENDITURE – 2.3 per cent of GDP (1999)
MILITARY PERSONNEL – 52,700: Army 35,100, Navy 9,200, Air Force 8,400, Paramilitaries 600
CONSCRIPTION DURATION – Seven to 15 months

## ECONOMY

Less than 10 per cent of the land area is farmland and less than 3 per cent of the labour force is employed in farming, although Sweden is more than 80 per cent self-sufficient in food.

Industrial prosperity is based on natural resources: forests, mineral deposits and water power. The forests cover about half the total land surface and sustain timber, finished wood products, pulp and paper milling industries. The mineral resources include iron ore, lead, zinc, sulphur, granite, marble, precious and heavy metals (the latter not exploited) and extensive deposits of low-grade uranium ore. Industries based on mining are important but it is the general engineering industry that provides 80 per cent of Sweden's exports, especially specialised machinery and systems, motor vehicles, aircraft, electrical and electronic equipment, pharmaceuticals, plastics and chemical industries.

Hydroelectricity supplies 15 per cent of energy needs. Sweden has no significant indigenous resources of conventional hydrocarbon fuels and relies for 50 per cent of its energy needs upon imported oil and coal.

Sweden experienced a deep recession between 1992 and 1994. The centre-right government, elected in 1991, introduced austerity measures and free market economic reforms. In October 1997 Sweden decided not to join European economic and monetary union (EMU) at the first stage; however, a referendum on EMU membership is to be held after the general election due in September 2002.

Unemployment has been falling steadily since 1997.

In 1998 there was a trade surplus of US$17,632 million and a current account surplus of US$4,639 million. In 1999 imports totalled US$68,453 million and exports US$84,812 million.

GNP – US$236,940 million (1999); US$25,040 per capita (1999)
GDP – US$227,757 million (1997); US$27,256 per capita (1999)
ANNUAL AVERAGE GROWTH OF GDP – 2.3 per cent (2000)
INFLATION RATE – 1.5 per cent (2001)
UNEMPLOYMENT – 5.3 per cent (2001)

### TRADE

About 45 per cent of industrial output is exported, mainly in the form of cars, trucks, machinery, and electrical and communications equipment. Sweden conducts 70 per cent of its trade with EFTA and the rest of the EU.

| *Trade with UK* | 1999 | 2000 |
|---|---|---|
| Imports from UK | £3,769,000,000 | £3,987,700,000 |
| Exports to UK | 4,397,700,000 | 4,740,800,000 |

## COMMUNICATIONS

The total length of railroads is 10,939 km. The road network is about 210,000 km in length. The mercantile marine amounted in 1996 to 2,950,000 gross tonnage. Regular domestic air traffic is maintained by the Scandinavian Airlines System and by Malmö Aviation. Regular European and intercontinental air traffic is maintained by the Scandinavian Airlines System.

## EDUCATION

The state system provides nine years' free and compulsory schooling from the age of seven to 16 in the comprehensive elementary schools. 95 per cent continue into further education of two to four years' duration in the upper secondary schools and a unified higher education system administered in six regional areas containing one of the universities: Uppsala (founded 1477); Lund (1668); Stockholm (1878); Gothenburg (1887); Umeå (1963) and Linköping (1967). There are 40 institutions of higher education including three technical universities in Stockholm, Gothenburg and Luleå.

ENROLMENT (percentage of age group) – primary 100 per cent (1996); secondary 99 per cent (1996); tertiary 50.3 per cent (1996)

## CULTURE

Swedish belongs, with Danish and Norwegian, to the North Germanic language group. Swedish literature dates back to King Magnus Eriksson, who codified the old Swedish provincial laws in 1350. With his translation of the Bible, Olaus Petri (1493–1552) formed the basis for the modern Swedish language. Literature flourished during the reign of Gustavus III, who founded the Swedish Academy in 1786. Notable Swedish writers include Almquist (1795–1866), Strindberg (1849–1912) and Lagerlöf (1858–1940), Nobel Prizewinner in 1909. Contemporary authors include Lagerquist (1891–1974), Nobel Laureate in 1951, Martinson (1904–78) and Johnson (1900–76), Nobel Laureates jointly in 1974. The Swedish scientist Alfred Nobel (1833–96) founded the Nobel Prizes for literature, science and peace.

---

# SWITZERLAND

*Schweizerische Eidgenossenschaft – Confédération Suisse – Confederazione Svizzera - Confederaziun Svizra*

---

AREA – 15,940 sq. miles (41,284 sq. km). Neighbours: France (west and north-west), Germany (north), Austria and Liechtenstein (east), Italy (south)
POPULATION – 7,120,000 (1998 estimate): 46.1 per cent Roman Catholic, 40 per cent Protestant, 5 per cent other religions and 8.9 per cent without religion. The official languages are German (the first language of 63.7 per cent), French (19.2 per cent), Italian (7.6 per cent) and Romansch (0.6 per cent). German is the dominant language in 19 of the 26 cantons; French in Fribourg, Jura, Geneva, Neuchâtel, Valais and Vaud; Italian in Ticino; and Romansch in parts of Graubünden
CAPITAL – Bern (population, 319,292, 1996 estimate)
MAJOR CITIES – Basel (404,418); Geneva (446,217); Lausanne (284,707); Lucerne (181,015); Winterthur (117,328); Zürich (929,070), 1996 estimates
CURRENCY – Swiss franc of 100 rappen (or centimes)
NATIONAL ANTHEM – Trittst im Morgenrot Daher (Radiant in the morning sky)
NATIONAL DAY – 1 August
NATIONAL FLAG – Square and red, bearing a couped white cross
LIFE EXPECTANCY (years) – male 75.6; female 83.0
POPULATION GROWTH RATE – 0.8 per cent (1999)
POPULATION DENSITY – 172 per sq. km (1998)
URBAN POPULATION – 67.7 per cent (2000 estimate)

Switzerland is the most mountainous country in Europe. The Alps, from 1,700 to 4,634 m (5,000 to 15,217 ft) in height, occupy its southern and eastern frontiers and the chief part of its interior; the Jura mountains rise in the north-west. The Alps occupy 61 per cent, and the Jura mountains 12 per cent of the country. The highest peak, Mont Blanc, Pennine Alps (4,807 m/15,782 ft) is partly in France and partly in Italy; Monte Rosa (4,634 m/15,217 ft) and Matterhorn (4,478 m/14,780 ft) are partly in Switzerland and partly in Italy. The highest wholly Swiss peaks are Finsteraarhorn (4,274 m/14,026 ft), Aletschhorn (4,195/

13,711), Jungfrau (4,158/13,671), Mönch (4,099/13,456), Eiger (3,970/13,040), Schreckhorn (4,078/13,385), and Wetterhorn (3,701/12,150) in the Bernese Alps, and Dom (4,545/14,918), Weisshorn (4,506/14,803) and Breithorn (4,165/13,685). The Swiss lakes include Lakes Maggiore, Zürich, Lucerne, Neuchâtel, Geneva, Constance, Thun, Zug, Lugano, Brienz and the Walensee.

## HISTORY AND POLITICS

The Romans invaded the area populated by Helvetii tribes in the first century BC and named the region Helvetia. The Roman Empire was overrun in the fifth century AD by Germanic tribes who are the ancestors of the modern Swiss.

The Swiss confederation was formed as an alliance of three cantons in 1291 and achieved full independence under the Peace of Westphalia (1648), having been a province of the Holy Roman Empire since 1033. French Revolutionary forces seized Switzerland in 1789 and named it the Helvetic Republic. Independence was not restored until the Congress of Vienna (1815), which also joined Geneva and Valais to the confederation and instituted perpetual neutrality in foreign affairs. In 1847 a war broke out between the Protestant and Roman Catholic cantons, the latter being defeated. A new constitution was adopted in 1848 which enhanced the powers of the central government.

Proportional representation was introduced in 1919 and has ensured coalition governments throughout the 20th century. Women were given the vote in 1971.

On 24 October 1999, the ruling coalition, comprising the Social Democrats, the Swiss People's Party, the Radical Democratic Party and the Christian Democrats, in power since 1959, was re-elected with 173 of the 200 seats in the National Council.

### Foreign Relations

The Federal Council voted in 1992 to apply for European Community membership. The European Economic Area (EEA) Treaty between the EC and EFTA, which extends the provisions of the EC single internal market to EFTA states, was rejected in a national referendum on 6 December 1992. Switzerland is consequently the only EFTA state outside the EEA. Switzerland has observer status at the UN. On 21 May 2000, a referendum on seven bilateral agreements with the EU, which would progressively reduce trade barriers and allow the free movement of people between Switzerland and the EU, was passed, with 67.2 per cent of voters in favour.

The government plans to hold a referendum on UN membership in 2002 or 2003.

### Political System

The federal government consists of the Federal Assembly of two chambers, a National Council (*Nationalrat*) of 200 members, and a States Council (*Ständerat*) of 46 members (two from each canton and one from each demi-canton). Members of the National Council are elected for four years, elections taking place in October. The executive power is in the hands of a Federal Council (*Bundesrat*) of seven members, elected for four years by the Federal Assembly and presided over by the president of the Confederation. Each year the Federal Assembly elects from the Federal Council the president and the vice-president. Not more than one person from the same canton may be elected a member of the Federal Council; however, there is a tradition that Italian- and French-speaking areas should between them be represented on the Federal Council by at least two members.

### Confederal Structure

There are 23 cantons, three of which are subdivided, making 26 in all. Each canton has its own government. The main language in 19 of the cantons is German; in the others it is French (*) or Italian (†).

| *Canton* | *Area (sq. km)* | *Population (1999)* |
|---|---|---|
| Aargau | 1,404 | 540,600 |
| Appenzell-Ausserrhoden | 243 | 53,700 |
| Appenzell-Innerrhoden | 173 | 14,900 |
| Basel-Country (Basel-Landschaft) | 517 | 258,600 |
| Basel-Town (Basel-Stadt) | 37 | 188,500 |
| Bern | 5,961 | 943,400 |
| *Fribourg | 1,671 | 234,300 |
| *Geneva | 282 | 403,100 |
| Glarus | 685 | 38,700 |
| Graubünden/Grischun | 7,105 | 186,000 |
| *Jura | 837 | 68,800 |
| Lucerne (Luzern) | 1,493 | 345,400 |
| *Neuchâtel | 803 | 165,600 |
| Nidwalden | 276 | 37,700 |
| Obwalden | 491 | 32,200 |
| St Gallen | 2,026 | 447,600 |
| Schaffhausen | 299 | 73,600 |
| Schwyz | 909 | 128,200 |
| Solothurn | 791 | 243,900 |
| Thurgau | 991 | 227,300 |
| †Ticino | 2,812 | 308,500 |
| Uri | 1,077 | 35,500 |
| *Valais | 5,225 | 275,600 |
| *Vaud | 3,212 | 616,300 |
| Zürich | 1,729 | 1,198,600 |
| Zug | 239 | 97,800 |

### Federal Council *as at September 2001*

*President of the Swiss Confederation* (2001), *Transport, Communications, Energy*, Moritz Leuenberger (SPS)
*Vice-President* (2001), Finance,, Kaspar Villiger (FDP)
*Federal Chancellor*, Annemarie Huber-Hotz
*Defence, Civil Protection and Sport*, Samuel Schmid (SVP)
*Economic Affairs*, Pascal Couchepin (FDP)
*Finance*, Kaspar Villiger (FDP)
*Foreign Affairs*, Joseph Deiss (CVP)
*Interior*, Ruth Dreifuss (SPS)
*Justice and Police*, Ruth Metzler-Arnold (CVP)

CVP Christian Democratic People's Party; SPS Social Democratic Party; FDP Radical Democratic Party; SVP Swiss People's Party

### Embassy of Switzerland

16–18 Montagu Place, London W1H 2BQ
Tel: 020-7616 6000
*Ambassador Extraordinary and Plenipotentiary*, HE Bruno Max Spinner, apptd 2000
*Minister*, R. Reich
*Defence Attaché*, Col. W. Knüsli
*Consul-General*, U. Hunn
*Counsellor*, D. Furgler (*Economic and Financial*)

### British Embassy

Thunstrasse 50, CH-3005 Bern
Tel: (00 41) (31) 359 7700
*Ambassador Extraordinary and Plenipotentiary*, HE Basil Eastwood, CMG, apptd 2001
*Counsellor, Deputy Head of Mission and Director of Trade Promotion, Consul-General for Liechtenstein*, D. Roberts
*Commercial Attachés*, B. Haessig, S. Valdettaro, H. Küpfer
*Defence Attaché*, Lt.-Col. E. J. Gould

Consulate-General – Geneva

CONSULAR OFFICES - Basel, Bern (at Embassy), Lugano, Montreux, Valais, Zürich

BRITISH COUNCIL DIRECTOR , Caroline Morrissey, Sennweg 2, PO Box 532, CH-3000 Bern 9; e-mail: britishcouncil@britishcouncil.ch

BRITISH-SWISS CHAMBER OF COMMERCE, Freiestrasse 155, CH-8032 Zürich

## DEFENCE

The Army has 556 main battle tanks, 1,103 armoured personnel carriers, 435 armoured infantry fighting vehicles and 60 helicopters. The Air Force has 154 combat aircraft.

A referendum proposing the reduction of military expenditure over a ten-year period was held on 26 November 2000; the proposal was rejected by 62.3 per cent of those voting.

MILITARY EXPENDITURE – 1.3 per cent of GDP (1999)
MILITARY PERSONNEL – 3,470 active (351,200 to be mobilised: Army 321,000, Air Force 30,200)
CONSCRIPTION DURATION – 15 weeks, then ten refresher courses

## ECONOMY

Agriculture is followed chiefly in the valleys and the central plateau, where cereals, flax, hemp, wine and tobacco are produced, and fruits and vegetables are grown. Dairying and stock-raising are the principal industries; there are 308,924 hectares of open arable land, 111,133 ha of cultivated grassland and 628,976 ha of natural grassland and pasture. The forests cover about 28 per cent of the whole surface.

The chief manufacturing industries comprise engineering and electrical engineering, metalworking, chemicals and pharmaceuticals, textiles, watchmaking, woodworking, foodstuffs, publishing and footwear. Banking, insurance and tourism are major industries. In 1997, 4.6 per cent of the workforce was employed in agriculture, 26.8 per cent in industry and 68.6 per cent in services.

GNP – US$273,856 million (1999); US$38,350 per capita (1999)
GDP – US$254,994 million (1997); US$36,247 per capita (1999)
ANNUAL AVERAGE GROWTH OF GDP – 2.6 per cent (2000)
INFLATION RATE – 1.0 per cent (2001)
UNEMPLOYMENT – 1.7 per cent (2001)

### TRADE

The principal imports are machinery, chemicals, vehicles, metals, textiles, precision instruments, watches and jewellery. The principal exports are machinery, chemicals, precision instruments, watches and jewellery, and metals.

In 1998 Switzerland had a trade surplus of US$988 million and a current account surplus of US$24,547 million. In 1999 imports totalled US$75,438 million and exports US$76,122 million.

| *Trade with UK* | 1999 | 2000 |
|---|---|---|
| Imports from UK | £2,827,403,000 | £3,155,615,000 |
| Exports to UK | 5,629,363,000 | 5,745,145,000 |

## COMMUNICATIONS

There were in 1995, 5,041 km of railway tracks and 70,975 km of roads, of which 1,540 km were national highways. The merchant marine consisted in 1995 of 174 vessels with a total gross tonnage of 4.36 million tonnes. Goods handled at Basel Rhine ports amounted to 13 million tonnes. Swissair, the national airline, flies to and from the airports at Zürich, Geneva and Basel.

## EDUCATION

Education is controlled by cantonal and communal authorities. Primary education is free and compulsory. School age varies, generally seven to 14, with secondary education from age 12 to 15. Special schools make a feature of commercial and technical instruction. Universities are Basel (founded 1460), Bern (1834), Fribourg (1889), Geneva (1873), Lausanne (1890), Zürich (1832), and Neuchâtel (1909), the technical universities of Lausanne and Zürich and the economics university of St Gall.

ENROLMENT (percentage of age group) – primary 100 per cent (1993); secondary 79 per cent (1990); tertiary 32.6 per cent (1996)

## CULTURE

Famous painters include Arnold Böcklin (1827-1901) and Paul Klee (1879-1940). The Dada movement began in Zürich. Le Corbusier (Charles-Édouard Jeanneret) (1887-1966) was one of the most influential 20th century architects. Modern authors who have achieved international fame include Karl Spitteler (1845–1924) and Hermann Hesse (1877–1962), awarded the Nobel Prize for Literature in 1919 and 1946 respectively.

In 1993 there were 96 daily newspapers published (76 German, 16 French, four Italian).

---

# SYRIA
*Al-Jumhūriyya Al-'Arabiyya as-Sūriyya*

---

AREA – 71,498 sq. miles (185,180 sq. km). Neighbours: Lebanon (west), Israel and Jordan (south-west), Iraq (east), Turkey (north)
POPULATION – 15,653,000 (1997 UN estimate): mostly Muslim. Arabic is the principal language, but Kurdish, Turkish and Armenian are spoken among significant minorities and a few villages still speak Aramaic, the language spoken by Christ and the Apostles. English has taken over from French as the main foreign language
CAPITAL – Damascus (Dimashq) (population, 1,549,000, 1994)
MAJOR CITIES – Halab (Aleppo) (1,542,000); Hamāh (273,000); Hims (558,000); ΨAl-Lādhiqīyah, the principal port (303,000), 1994 estimates
CURRENCY – Syrian pound (S$) of 100 piastres
NATIONAL ANTHEM - Humata al Diyari alaykum salaam (Defenders of the Realm on you be peace)
NATIONAL DAY – 17 April
NATIONAL FLAG – Red over white over black horizontal bands, with two green stars on central white band
LIFE EXPECTANCY (years) – male 64.6; female 67.1
POPULATION GROWTH RATE – 2.7 per cent (1999)
POPULATION DENSITY – 84 per sq. km (1998)
URBAN POPULATION – 54.5 per cent (2000 estimate)

The Orontes flows northwards from the Lebanon range across the northern boundary to Antakya (Antioch, Turkey). The Euphrates crosses the northern boundary near Jerablus and flows through north-eastern Syria to the boundary of Iraq.

The region is rich in historical remains. Damascus (Dimishq ash-Sham) is said to be the oldest continuously inhabited city in the world (although Halab disputes this claim), having existed as a city for over 4,000 years. The city contains the Omayed Mosque, the Tomb of Saladin, and the 'street which is called Straight' (Acts 9:11), while to the north-east is the Roman outpost of Dmeir and further east is Palmyra. On the Mediterranean coast at Amrit are ruins of the Phoenician town of Marath, and of Crusaders' fortresses at Markab, Sahyoun, and Krak des Chevaliers. One of the oldest alphabets in the world has been discovered at Ugarit (Ras Shamra), a Phoenician village near Al-Lādhiqīyah. Hittite cities dating from 2000 to 1500 BC, have been explored on the west bank of the Euphrates at Jerablus and Kadesh.

## HISTORY AND POLITICS

Once part of the Ottoman Empire, Syria came under French mandate after the First World War. Syria became an independent republic during the Second World War; the first independently elected parliament met in August 1943, but foreign troops were in occupation until April 1946. Syria remained an independent republic until 1958, when it became part, with Egypt, of the United Arab Republic. It seceded from the United Arab Republic in September 1961.

Elections to the 250-seat People's Council in November 1998 resulted in the National Progressive Front retaining all of its 167 seats unchallenged. This seven-party bloc is dominated by the Ba'ath Party, its allies being the Arab Socialist Union, Socialist Unionist Party, Arab Socialist Movement, Syrian Communist Party and Socialist Unionist Democratic Party. Independents, who are predominantly businessmen, won 83 seats. Mahmoud Zubi, who had been prime minister since 1987, resigned on 7 March 2000 and was replaced by Mustafa Mohamad Miro on 13 March. Zubi committed suicide on 21 May following his expulsion from the Ba'ath Party amid allegations of corruption.

President Hafez al-Assad, who had seized power in a military coup in 1970 and been elected president in 1971 and re-elected in 1978, 1985, 1992 and 1999, died on 10 June 2000. On 18 June, his son, Bashar al-Assad, was unanimously elected as leader by the Ba'ath Party, on 27 June the legislature nominated him for the presidency, and on 10 July he was elected president, gaining 97.29 per cent of the votes cast.

### POLITICAL SYSTEM

The constitution promulgated in 1973 declares that Syria is a democratic, popular socialist state, and that the Arab Socialist Renaissance (Ba'ath) Party, which has been the ruling party since 1963, is the leading party in the state and society. The president is head of state and is elected by parliament for a seven-year term. The legislature, the *Majlis al-Chaab* (People's Council) has 250 members directly elected for a four-year term.

### HEAD OF STATE

*President*, Bashar al-Assad, *elected by parliament* 27 June 2000, *approved by referendum* 10 July 2000
*Vice-Presidents*, Abdel Halim Khaddam, Zuheir Masharqa

### CABINET *as at September 2001*

*Prime Minister*, Mohamad Mustafa Miro
*Deputy Prime Minister, Defence*, First Lt.-Gen. Mustafa Tlass
*Deputy Prime Minister, Economic Affairs*, Khaled Raad
*Deputy Prime Minister, Service Affairs*, Mohamad Naji Otri
*Agriculture and Agrarian Reform*, Assa'ad Mustafa
*Awqaf (Religious Endowments)*, Mohamad Abd ar-Ra'uf Ziyadah
*Communications*, Radwan Martini
*Construction and Building*, Nihad Mushantat
*Culture*, Maha Qannut
*Economy and Foreign Trade*, Mohamad al-Imadi
*Education*, Mahmood al-Sayed
*Electricity*, Munib bin Assa'ad Saem al-Daher
*Finance*, Khaled al-Mahayni
*Foreign Affairs*, Farouk al-Shara'
*Health*, Mohamad Iyad al-Shatti
*Higher Education*, Hassan Risheh
*Housing and Utilities*, Husam al-Safadi
*Industry*, Ahmad Hamo
*Information*, Adnan Omran
*Interior*, Mohamad Harba
*Irrigation*, Taha al-Atrash
*Justice*, Nabil al-Khatib
*Labour and Social Affairs*, Baria al-Qodsi
*Local Administration*, Salam al-Yaseen
*Petroleum and Mineral Resources*, Mohamad Maher bin Hosni Jamal
*Presidential Affairs*, Haitham Duahi
*Supply and Internal Trade*, Usama Ma'a al-Bared
*Tourism*, Qassem Maqdad
*Transport*, Makram Obeid

### EMBASSY OF THE SYRIAN ARAB REPUBLIC

8 Belgrave Square, London SW1X 8PH
Tel: 020-7245 9012
*Ambassador Extraordinary and Plenipotentiary*, HE Dr Sami Glaiel, apptd 2001

### BRITISH EMBASSY

Kotob Building, 11 Mohammad Kurd Ali Street, Malki, Damascus (PO Box 37)
Tel: (00 963) (11) 373 9241/2/3/7
*Ambassador Extraordinary and Plenipotentiary*, HE H. Hogger, apptd 2000

CONSULATE – Halab

BRITISH COUNCIL DIRECTOR, David Baldwin, OBE, Maysaloun Street, Shalaan, PO Box 33105, Damascus; e-mail: britcoun@bc-damascus.bcouncil.org. There is also an office in Halab

## DEFENCE

The Army has 4,850 main battle tanks, 1,500 armoured personnel carriers and 2,250 armoured infantry fighting vehicles. The Navy has two frigates, 18 patrol and coastal vessels and 24 armed helicopters at three bases. The Air Force has 589 combat aircraft and 87 armed helicopters.

Syria maintains a force of some 22,000 men in Lebanon; 1,035 UN troops are deployed on the Golan Heights.

MILITARY EXPENDITURE – 5.6 per cent of GDP (1999)
MILITARY PERSONNEL – 316,000: Army 215,000, Navy 6,000, Air Force 40,000, Air Defence Command 55,000, Paramilitaries 108,000
CONSCRIPTION DURATION – 30 months

## ECONOMY

Agriculture accounted for 25.9 per cent of GDP in 1997; fruit, vegetables, wheat and barley are the main crops, but the cotton crop is the highest in value. Large areas are coming under cultivation in the north-east of the country as a result of irrigation from the Thawra dam. Industry accounted for 27.2 per cent of GDP in 1997. There are an increasing number of light assembly plants as Syria's industrialisation programme develops. Leather goods, wool and silk, textiles, vegetable oil, soap, sugar, plastics and metal utensils are produced. Oil production is proceeding in the region of Deir ez Zor. A pipeline has been built to the Mediterranean port of Banias, via Hims. Two oil refineries are in production at Hims and Banias. Oil production in 1998 was 29,300,000 tonnes. Syria also has gas reserves, deposits of phosphate and rock salt, and produces asphalt.

On 2 December 2000, President al-Assad authorised the establishment of private banks and a stock market and the flotation of the Syrian pound.

A free trade agreement was signed with Iraq in February 2001.

GNP – US$15,172 million (1999); US$970 per capita (1999)

GDP – US$64,926 million (1997); US$2,509 per capita (1998)
ANNUAL AVERAGE GROWTH OF GDP – 5.9 per cent (1996)
INFLATION RATE – 0.5 per cent (1998)
UNEMPLOYMENT – 6.8 per cent (1991)
TOTAL EXTERNAL DEBT – US$22,435 million (1998)

### TRADE

The principal imports are manufactures, metals and metal goods, machinery, foodstuffs and transport equipment. Principal exports include oil and oil derivatives, agricultural products (chiefly fruit and vegetables, cotton and wheat) and textiles.

In 1998 Syria had a trade deficit of US$172 million and a current account surplus of US$59 million. In 1999 imports totalled US$3,832 million and exports US$3,464 million.

| *Trade with UK* | 1999 | 2000 |
|---|---|---|
| Imports from UK | 81,499,000 | £71,410,000 |
| Exports to UK | 83,664,000 | 56,794,000 |

## COMMUNICATIONS

Although railway lines run from Damascus to both Beirut and 'Ammān, train services go only to 'Ammān as much of the Lebanese line has been dismantled. A track has been opened connecting Hims with Damascus. A track links Hims, Hamāh, Halab, Deir ez Zor and Qamishliye to the Iraqi frontier. There are 2,750 km of rail track. All the principal towns in the country are connected by roads which vary from modern dual carriageways to narrow country lanes. There are 39,377 km of roads, of which 10,078 km are unpaved. An internal air service operates between all major towns. The main international airport is at Damascus and there are also flights from Halab, Al-Kamishli, Al-Lādhiqīyah and Deir Ez-Zor.

There are eight national daily newspapers.

## EDUCATION

Education is under state control and although a few of the schools are privately owned, they all follow a common syllabus. Elementary education is free at state schools and is compulsory from the age of seven. Secondary education is not compulsory and is free only at the state schools. There are universities at Damascus, Halab, Tishrin, Al-Lādhiqīyah and the Ba'ath University, Hims.
ILLITERACY RATE – 25.6 per cent (2000)
ENROLMENT (percentage of age group) – primary 91 per cent (1996); secondary 38 per cent (1996); tertiary 15.7 per cent (1996)

---

# TAIWAN

*Chung-hua Min-kuo – Republic of China*

---

AREA – 13,800 sq. miles (35,742 sq. km)
POPULATION – 22,277,000 (2000 estimate). Mandarin Chinese has been the official language since 1949. Now Taiwanese, spoken by 85 per cent of the population, is growing in importance
CAPITAL – Taipei (population, 2,646,000, 2000 estimate)
MAJOR CITIES – ΨKaohsiung (1,461,996); ΨKeelung (381,695), Taichung (916,279); Tainan (721,264), 1998
CURRENCY – New Taiwan dollar (NT$) of 100 cents
NATIONAL ANTHEM - San min chu I (Our Aim Shall Be to Found a Free Land)
NATIONAL DAY – 10 October
NATIONAL FLAG – Red, with blue quarter at top next staff, bearing a 12-point white sun

An island in the China Sea, Taiwan, formerly Formosa, lies 90 miles east of the Chinese mainland. The eastern part of the main island is mountainous and forested. Mt Morrison (Yu Shan) (13,035 ft) and Mt Sylvia (Tz'u-kaoshan) (12,972 ft) are the highest peaks. The western plains are watered by many rivers.

Territories include the Pescadores Islands (50 sq. miles), some 35 miles west of Taiwan, as well as Kinmen (Quemoy) (68 sq. miles) and Matsu (11 sq. miles) which are only a few miles from mainland China.

## HISTORY AND POLITICS

Settled for centuries by the Chinese, the island was ceded by China to Japan in 1895 and remained part of the Japanese empire until Japan's defeat in 1945. Nationalist Kuomintang (KMT) leader Gen. Chiang Kai-shek withdrew to Taiwan in 1949, towards the end of the war against the Communist regime in mainland China, after which the territory continued under his presidency until his death in 1975. He was succeeded as president by his son Gen. Chiang Ching-kuo who ruled until his death in 1988, when Vice-President Lee Teng-hui was appointed president. Martial law was lifted in 1987 after 38 years.

In 1991, President Lee announced that the 'period of Communist rebellion' on the Chinese mainland was over, recognising *de facto* the People's Republic of China. The announcement also ended emergency measures which had frozen political life on Taiwan since 1949. In 1991–2 power shifted away from mainlanders to native Taiwanese with the forcible retirement of the 'Senior Parliamentarians' who had retained their seats since being elected on the mainland in 1948. The new parliament, the Legislative Yuan, gained control of the budget, of law-making and of the appointment of the prime minister. A general election to the Legislative Yuan on 5 December 1998 was won by the KMT with 123 of the 225 seats; the pro-independence Democratic Progressive Party (DPP) won 70 seats; the pro-reunification New Party won 11 seats; independents and minor parties won 21 seats.

President Chen Shui-bian won the presidential election on 18 March 2000 with 39 per cent of the vote, ahead of two KMT candidates, and took office on 20 May.

A general election was due to be held on 1 December 2001.

### FOREIGN RELATIONS

Taiwan (Nationalist China) held China's seat on the UN Security Council until 25 October 1971 when it was replaced by the People's Republic of China. The Republic of China is recognised by less than 30 states.

Direct tourism, trade and communications links between mainland China and the Taiwanese islands of Kinmen and Matsu were inaugurated on 2 January 2001, the first direct links between Taiwan and the People's Republic of China since 1949.

### POLITICAL SYSTEM

The legislature is bicameral. The Legislative Yuan has 225 members, 176 elected and 49 appointed proportionately by party, and serves a three-year term. Constitutional reforms passed by the Legislative Yuan in 1994 provide for the president and vice-president to be directly elected for four-year terms (previously the president was elected by parliament). The National Assembly, which had previously been an elected upper chamber, voted on 24 April 2000 to transform itself into a largely ceremonial body, to be convened when necessary to consider constitutional amendments, the impeachment of a president, or territorial changes. Members will be appointed proportionally by the parties in the Legislative Yuan.

HEAD OF STATE

*President*, Chen Shui-bian, *elected* 18 March 2000, *sworn in* 20 May 2000
*Vice-President*, Annette Lu

EXECUTIVE YUAN *as at September 2001*

*Prime Minister*, Chang Chun-hsiung
*Deputy Prime Minister*, Lai In-jaw
*Administrator, Environmental Protection Administration*, Hao Lung-pin
*Chairs of Commissions*, Youharni Yisicacafute (*Aboriginal Affairs*); Hu Ching-piao (*Atomic Energy Commission*); Hsu Cheng-kuang (*Mongolian and Tibetan Affairs*); Lin Feng-mei (*National Youth Commission*); Chang Fu-mei (*Overseas Chinese Affairs, State Minister*); Hsu Hsin-yi (*Physical Education*); Lin Chia-cheng (*Research, Development and Evaluation*); Yang Teh-chih (*Veterans' Affairs*)
*Chairs of Councils*, Chen Hsi-huang (*Agriculture*); Huang Hsih-cheng (*Central Election Commission*); Chen Yu-hsiu (*Cultural Affairs*); Chen Po-chih (*Economic Planning and Development*); Chen Chu (*Labour Affairs*); Tsai Ying-wen (*Mainland Affairs*); Wei Che-ho (*National Science Council*)
*Directors*, Wang Chun (*Coast Guard Administration*); Tu Cheng-sheng (*National Palace Museum*)
*Directors-General*, Lin Chuan (*Budget, Accounting and Statistics*); Chu Wu-hsien (*Central Personnel Administration*); Lee Ming-liang (*Department of Health*); Su Cheng-ping (*Government Information Office, Government Spokesman*)
*Economic Affairs*, Lin Hsin-yi
*Education*, Tseng Chih-lang
*Finance*, Yen Ching-chang
*Foreign Affairs*, Tien Hung-mao
*Interior and State Minister*, Chang Po-ya
*Justice*, Chen Ding-nan
*National Defence*, Wu Hsih-wen
*Secretary-General of the Executive Yuan*, Chiou I-jen
*Transport and Communications*, Yeh Chu-lan
*Without Portfolio*, Lin Neng-pai (*Chair of Public Construction Commission*); Chen Ching-huang; Chung Ching; Hu Sheng-cheng; Tsai Ching-yen

TAIPEI REPRESENTATIVE OFFICE, 50 Grosvenor Gardens, London, SW1W 0EB

BRITISH COUNCIL DIRECTOR, Geoff Evans, 7-F-1, British Trade and Cultural Office, 99 Jen Ai Road, Section 2, Taipei 10625; e-mail: inquiries@britishcouncil.org.tw. There is a regional office in Kaohsiung
BRITISH TRADE AND CULTURAL OFFICE, 8-10th Floor, Fu Key Building, 99 Jen Ai Road, Section 2, Taipei 100; e-mail: inquiries@britishcouncil.org.tw

## DEFENCE

The Army has 739 main battle tanks, 950 armoured personnel carriers, 225 armoured infantry fighting vehicles and 20 aircraft. The Navy has four submarines, 12 destroyers, 21 frigates, 59 patrol and coastal vessels, 31 combat aircraft and 21 armed helicopters at four bases. The Air Force has 570 combat aircraft.

The USA announced in April 2001 that it was to sell four destroyers and 12 submarine hunter aircraft to Taiwan.
MILITARY EXPENDITURE – 5.2 per cent of GDP (1999)
MILITARY PERSONNEL – 370,000: Army 240,000, Navy 62,000, Air Force 68,000; Paramilitaries 26,650
CONSCRIPTION DURATION – Two years

## ECONOMY

Taiwan has transformed itself from a mainly agricultural country to a highly developed industrial economy. The industrial base has expanded to include steel, shipbuilding, chemicals, cement, machinery, electrical equipment and textiles. In 1997 agriculture contributed 3.5 per cent of GDP, manufacturing 36.3 per cent and services 60.2 per cent. Continued trade surpluses have led to one of the largest foreign exchange reserves of any country in the world. Direct shipping between Taiwan and China, which had been suspended in 1949, resumed in April 1997.

The soil is very fertile, producing sugar, rice, sweet potatoes, tea, fruit and tobacco. Livestock provided a third of the value of Taiwan's agricultural produce in 1996. Mineral resources are meagre. Taiwan produces one-tenth of its coal needs and some natural gas. There are important fisheries. The principal seaports are Keelung and Kaohsiung situated in the north and south of the island respectively.
UNEMPLOYMENT – 2.8 per cent (1998)

TRADE

The principal exports are electronic goods, machinery, metal goods, textiles, plastic products, and toys and games. The main imports are oil, chemicals, machinery and natural resources. The main trading partners are the USA, Japan, Hong Kong, Germany, and the Republic of Korea.

In 1999 imports totalled US$110,957 million and exports US$121,496 million.

| *Trade with UK* | 1999 | 2000 |
|---|---|---|
| Imports from UK | £867,643,000 | £1,014,207,000 |
| Exports to UK | 2,737,748,000 | 3,691,710,000 |

## TAJIKISTAN
*Respublika i Tojikiston*

AREA – 55,251 sq. miles (143,100 sq. km). Neighbours: Uzbekistan (north-west), Kyrgyzstan (north-east), China (east), Afghanistan (south)
POPULATION – 6,218,000 (2000): 62 per cent Tajik, 23 per cent Uzbek and 8 per cent Russian, with smaller numbers of Tatars, Kyrgyz, Germans and Ukrainians. The people are predominantly Sunni Muslim. The main languages are Tajik, Uzbek and Russian. Tajik is close to the Farsi spoken in Iran
CAPITAL – Dushanbe (population, 528,600, 1993 estimate)
CURRENCY – Somoni of 100 dirams
NATIONAL DAY – 9 September (Independence Day)
NATIONAL FLAG – Three horizontal stripes of red, white and green with the white of double width and charged with a crown and seven stars, all in gold
LIFE EXPECTANCY (years) – male 65.1; female 70.1
POPULATION GROWTH RATE – 1.6 per cent (1999)
POPULATION DENSITY – 42 per sq. km (1998)
URBAN POPULATION – 27.5 per cent (2000 estimate)
MILITARY EXPENDITURE – 7.6 per cent of GDP (1999)
MILITARY PERSONNEL – 6,000: Army 6,000; Paramilitaries 1,200
CONSCRIPTION DURATION – Two years
ILLITERACY RATE – 0.8 per cent
ENROLMENT (percentage of age group) – tertiary 20.4 per cent (1996)

The republic includes the Gorno-Badakhstan Autonomous Province and the Kulyab, Kurgan-Tyubinsk and Khodzhent Provinces. The country is mountainous with the Pamir highlands in the east and the high ridges of the Pamir-Altai system in the centre. Plains are formed by wide stretches of the Syr-Darya valley in the north and of the Amu-Darya in the south. The country has areas prone to earthquakes, and a continental climate.

## HISTORY AND POLITICS

The area that is now Tajikistan was conquered by Alexander the Great in the fourth century BC and remained under Greek and Greco-Persian rule for 200 years, until the Kingdom of Kusha was established, based on Bacharia (Bukhara). Tajikistan was invaded by both the Arabs and the Samanid Persians between the seventh and ninth centuries AD. The cities of Bukhara and Samarkand were two of the most important cultural and educational centres in the Islamic world.

The Tajiks lived under the control of various feudal emirates until the area was subsumed within the Russian Empire in 1868. At the time of the Russian revolution in 1917 the central Asian emirates attempted to re-establish their independence. Soviet power was re-established in northern Tajikistan by 1 April 1918, when the Turkestan Soviet Socialist Republic was formed, and the Bukhara emirate was overthrown by Soviet forces in 1920. In 1924 the Tajikistan Autonomous Soviet Socialist Republic was formed as part of the Uzbek Republic before Tajikistan was given full republican status within the Soviet Union in 1929. Stalin deprived the Tajiks of Bukhara and Samarkand, which remained in Uzbekistan, and during Soviet rule 1,000,000 Uzbeks and 800,000 Russians were settled in Tajikistan.

Tajikistan declared independence from the Soviet Union on 9 September 1991. The Islamic-Democratic alliance formed a government in September 1992 but civil war broke out as forces loyal to the former Communist regime rebelled against the new government. By early November, pro-Communist forces controlled virtually all the country and the Supreme Soviet installed Emomaly Rakhmonov as its Speaker and head of state.

A cease-fire in October 1994 allowed presidential and parliamentary elections to be held, which were won by Emomaly Rakhmonov and the ruling (former Communist) People's Democratic Party of Tajikistan (HDKT), although the elections were boycotted by most opposition groups. Fighting restarted in early 1995. A peace agreement was signed in December 1996 which provided for the formation of a National Reconciliation Commission (NRC), a general amnesty and an exchange of prisoners. The agreement has held, although there have been sporadic outbreaks of violence since it was signed. A referendum was held on constitutional amendments demanded by the opposition on 26 September 1999 and was approved by the electorate. It amended the 1994 constitution to create a bicameral legislature, extended the president's term of office from five to seven years and allowed the formation of religious political parties. Legislation to allow the formation of a bicameral legislature was passed in December 1999.

Presidential elections which took place on 6 November 1999 resulted in a landslide victory for the incumbent President Rakhmonov, who gained over 96 per cent of the vote in a poll which the Organisation for Security and Co-operation in Europe had refused to monitor due to restrictions imposed on candidates and political parties. Oqil Oqilov was named as prime minister on 20 December when President Rakhmonov announced a new government. Following an election to the Assembly of Representatives on 27 February and 12 March 2000, the HDKT won 30 of the 63 seats, gaining 64.5 per cent of the vote; the Communist Party won 13 seats, the Islamic Renaissance Party won 2 and independent candidates won 15 seats, with three seats remaining vacant. An election to the National Assembly was held on 23 March.

### POLITICAL SYSTEM

Under the new constitutional arrangements, the president serves a single seven-year term. The new bicameral legislature consists of a 63-seat *Majlisi Mamoyandogan* (Assembly of Representatives), which is directly elected and serves a five-year term, and the *Majlisi Milli* (National Assembly), which has 33 members, 25 of which are elected for a five-year term by five regional assemblies and eight are appointed by the president. Administratively Tajikistan is divided into two regions and one autonomous region.

### HEAD OF STATE

*President*, Emomaly Sharipovich Rakhmonov, *elected by Supreme Soviet* 19 November 1992, *elected* 6 November 1994, *re-elected* 6 November 1999

### COUNCIL OF MINISTERS *as at September 2001*

*Prime Minister*, Oqil Oqilov
*First Deputy Prime Minister, Relations with CIS States*, Haji Akbar Turajonzoda
*Deputy Prime Ministers*, Kozidavlat Koimdodov; Nigina Sharapova; Zokir Vazirov; Maj.-Gen. Saidamir Zuhurov
*Agriculture*, Tursun Rahmatov
*Chairs of State Committees*, Matlubkhon Davlatov (*Administration of Affairs of State*); Ismat Eshmirzoyev (*Construction and Architecture*); Ayub Aliyev (*Industry and Mining*); Khayrulloyev Sadullo (*Land Resources and Reclamation*); Salomsho Muhabbatov (*Oil and Gas*); Muhammadjon Davlatov (*Precious Metals*); Rahimov Sayfullo (*Radio and Television*)
*Culture*, Abdurahim Rahimov
*Defence*, Lt.-Gen. Sherali Khayrulloyev
*Economics and Trade*, Hakim Soliyev
*Education*, Safarali Radzhabov
*Emergency Situations and Civil Defence*, Maj.-Gen. Mirzo Ahmadovoch Zieyev
*Energy*, Abdullo Yorov
*Environmental Protection and Water Resources*, Ismail Davlatov
*Finance*, Anvarsho Muzaffurov
*Foreign Affairs*, Talbak Nazarov
*Grain*, Bekmurod Urokov
*Health*, Alamkhon Ahmedov
*Interior*, Lt.-Gen. Homiddin Sharipov
*Justice*, Halifabobo Hamidov
*Labour, Employment and Social Welfare*, Rafiqa Ghaniyevna Musoyeva
*Security*, Khayruddin Abdurahimov
*Transport and Roads*, Abdujalol Salimov

### HONORARY CONSULATE

33 Ovington Square, London SW3 1LJ
*Honorary Consul*, Benjamin Brahms

BRITISH AMBASSADOR, HE Christopher Ingham, apptd 1998, resident at Tashkent, Uzbekistan

## ECONOMY

In January 1994 Tajikistan entered into a monetary union with Russia, effectively handing over monetary control to Russia in exchange for a US$100 million loan needed to prevent an economic collapse following the civil war. The Tajik rouble replaced the Russian rouble in May 1995. The economy is being reformed and privatisation undertaken in order to attract foreign investment. In 1997 GDP grew by 1.7 per cent and industry grew by 9 per cent.

Agriculture is the major sector of the economy, concentrating on cotton-growing and cattle-breeding. Tajikistan also has rich mineral deposits of mercury, lead, zinc, oil, gold and uranium. Industry specialises in the production of clothing and textiles.

A new currency, the somoni, was introduced on 30 October 2000, replacing the Tajik rouble at a value of one somoni to 1,000 Tajik roubles.

GNP – US$1,749 million (1999); US$290 per capita (1999)
GDP – US$1,056 million (1997); US$219 per capita (1998)
ANNUAL AVERAGE GROWTH OF GDP – 8.3 per cent (2000)
UNEMPLOYMENT – 2.7 per cent (1997)
TOTAL EXTERNAL DEBT – US$1,070 million (1998)

| *Trade with UK* | 1999 | 2000 |
|---|---|---|
| Imports from UK | £3,038,000 | £1,035,000 |
| Exports to UK | 2,696,000 | 2,602,000 |

## TANZANIA

*Jamhuri ya Muungano wa Tanzania – United Republic of Tanzania*

AREA – 341,216 sq. miles (883,749 sq. km). Neighbours: Kenya and Uganda (north), Mozambique (south), Malawi and Zambia (south-west), Rwanda, Burundi and the Democratic Republic of Congo (west)
POPULATION – 32,923,000 (1997 UN estimate). Africans form a large majority, with European, Asian, and other non-African minorities. The African population consists mostly of tribes of mixed Bantu race. The official languages are Swahili and English
CAPITAL – Dodoma (population, 85,000, 1988)
MAJOR CITIES – ΨDar es Salaam (1,096,000), the economic and administrative centre; Mbeya (194,000); Mwanza (252,000); ΨTanga (172,000), 1985 estimates
CURRENCY – Tanzanian shilling of 100 cents
NATIONAL ANTHEM – Mungu Ibariki Afrika (God Bless Africa)
NATIONAL DAY – 26 April (Union Day)
NATIONAL FLAG – Green (above) and blue; divided by diagonal black stripe bordered by gold, running from bottom (next staff) to top (in fly)
LIFE EXPECTANCY (years) – male 44.4; female 45.6
POPULATION GROWTH RATE – 2.8 per cent (1999)
POPULATION DENSITY – 36 per sq. km (1998)
URBAN POPULATION – 32.9 per cent (2000 estimate)
MILITARY EXPENDITURE – 1.7 per cent of GDP (1999)
MILITARY PERSONNEL – 34,000: Army 30,000, Navy 1,000, Air Force 3,000; Paramilitaries 1,400
CONSCRIPTION DURATION – Two years

Tanzania comprises Tanganyika, on the mainland of east Africa, and the island of Zanzibar. The greater part of the country is occupied by the central African plateau from which rise, among others, Mt Kilimanjaro (19,340 ft), the highest point on the continent of Africa, and Mt Meru (14,974 ft). The Serengeti National Park covers an area of 6,000 sq. miles in the Arusha, Mwanza and Mara Regions.

### HISTORY AND POLITICS

Tanganyika became an independent state and a member of the British Commonwealth on 9 December 1961, and a republic within the Commonwealth on 9 December 1962. Zanzibar, comprising the islands of Zanzibar, Pemba and Mafia, was formerly ruled by the Sultan of Zanzibar and was a British Protectorate until 10 December 1963 when it became an independent state within the Commonwealth. On 26 April 1964 Tanganyika united with Zanzibar to form the United Republic of Tanzania.

The sole legal political party from 1977 to 1992 was the Chama Cha Mapinduzi – the Revolutionary Party of Tanzania (CCM). The constitution was amended in 1992 to allow multiparty politics, with the stipulation that all parties must be active in both the mainland and in Zanzibar and that parties must not be formed on regional, religious, tribal or racial grounds.

The first multiparty presidential and parliamentary elections were held in October and November 1995 and were won by the CCM.

Presidential and general elections were held on 29 October 2000. President Mkapa was re-elected, winning 71.7 per cent of the vote, and the CCM won an overwhelming majority in the National Assembly. In Zanzibar, Amani Abeid Karume, the CCM candidate, was elected president and the CCM won a majority, but the results were disputed following violent protests and the annulment of the results in 16 of the 50 constituencies by the National Electoral Commission because of irregularities. A rerun was held in the 16 constituencies on 5 November, but it was boycotted by six opposition parties, who claimed that the irregularities had not been confined to those constituencies and demanded that there should be a rerun for all constituencies in Zanzibar. All 16 seats were won by the CCM. A series of demonstrations in protest at the conduct of the elections was organised by the main opposition party, the Civic United Front, in January 2001.

### POLITICAL SYSTEM

The president is directly elected and may serve two terms. The National Assembly contains up to 296 members, of whom 280 are directly elected, five are chosen by the Zanzibar House of Representatives, up to ten members are appointed by the president and one seat is reserved for the Attorney-General. Constituency members are elected at a general election held at a maximum of five-yearly intervals.

Although Zanzibar has its own president, government and 60-member House of Representatives, Tanganyika is governed by the government of the Union. The president of Zanzibar is also a member of the Union Cabinet.

### HEAD OF STATE

*President of the United Republic*, Benjamin Mkapa, *elected* 29 October 1995, *re-elected* 5 November 2000
*Vice-President*, Ali Mohamed Sheni
*President of Zanzibar*, Amani Abeid Karume

### CABINET *as at September 2001*

The President
The Vice-President
*Prime Minister*, Frederick Sumaye
*Agriculture and Food*, Charles Keenja
*Attorney-General*, Andrew Cheng
*Communications and Transport*, Mark Mwandosya
*Community Development, Women's Affairs and Children*, Asha-Rose Migiro
*Co-operatives and Marketing*, George Kahama
*Defence*, Philemon Sarungi
*Education*, James Mungai
*Energy and Mineral Resources*, Edgar Maokola-Majogo
*Finance*, Basil Mramba
*Foreign Affairs and International Co-operation*, Jakaya Kikwete
*Health*, Anna Abdallah
*Home Affairs*, Mohammed Seif Khatib
*Justice and Constitutional Affairs*, Harith Bakari Mwapachu
*Labour, Youth Development and Sport*, Juma Athumani Kapuya
*Land, Housing and Urban Development*, Gideon Cheyo
*Ministers of State in the President's Office*, Mary Nagu *(Civil Service)*; Abdallah Kigoda *(Planning and Privatisation)*; Brig.-Gen. Hassan Ngwiliza (*Regional Administration and Local Government*); Wilson Masilingi *(Security)*
*Ministers of State in the Prime Minister's Office*, William Lukuvi (*Information and Policy*); Ramadhani Mapuri
*Ministers of State in the Vice-President's Office*, Daniel Yona Ndhiwa; Arcado Ntagwiza
*Natural Resources, Tourism and Environment*, Zakia Meghji
*Science, Technology and Higher Education*, Pius Ng'wandu

*Trade and Industry*, Iddi Simba
*Water and Livestock Development*, Edward Lowassa
*Works*, John Magufuli

HIGH COMMISSION FOR THE UNITED REPUBLIC OF TANZANIA
43 Hertford Street, London W1Y 8DB
Tel: 020-7499 8951/4
*Acting High Commissioner*, Mawazo Paul Kaducha

BRITISH HIGH COMMISSION
Social Security House, Samora Avenue (PO Box 9200), Dar es Salaam
Tel: (00 255) (22) 2117659/64
E-mail: bhc.dar@dar.mail.fco.gov.uk
*High Commissioner*, HE R. Clarke, apptd 2001

BRITISH COUNCIL DIRECTOR, Tom Cowin, Samora Avenue/Ohio Street, PO Box 9100, Dar es Salaam; e-mail: info@britishcouncil.or.tz

## ECONOMY

In 1997, 81.7 per cent of the workforce were employed in agriculture and agricultural produce accounted for 52 per cent of GDP in 1996. The islands of Zanzibar and Pemba produce a large part of the world's supply of cloves and clove oil; coconuts, coconut oil and copra are also produced. Tanzania's chief exports are coffee, cotton and cashew nuts. The chief imports are capital equipment, oil and oil derivatives, and consumer goods. Industry, which accounts for 14 per cent of GDP, is largely concerned with the processing of raw material for export or local consumption; secondary manufacturing industries include factories for the manufacture of leather and rubber footwear, knitwear, razor blades, cigarettes and textiles, and a wheat flour mill.

In 1998 Tanzania had a trade deficit of US$776 million and a current account deficit of US$956 million. In 1999, imports totalled US$1,636 million and exports US$541 million.

GNP – US$8,515 million (1999); US$240 per capita (1999)
GDP – US$7,684 million (1997); US$213 per capita (1998)
ANNUAL AVERAGE GROWTH OF GDP – 4.2 per cent (1996)
INFLATION RATE – 7.9 per cent (1999)
TOTAL EXTERNAL DEBT – US$7,603 million (1998)

| *Trade with UK* | 1999 | 2000 |
|---|---|---|
| Imports from UK | £63,431,000 | £56,664,000 |
| Exports to UK | 18,397,000 | 30,223,000 |

## COMMUNICATIONS

The main ports are Dar es Salaam, Tanga, Mtwara, Zanzibar, Mkoani and Wete, in addition to Mwanza, Musoma and Bukoba on Lake Victoria and Kigoma on Lake Tanganyika. Coastal shipping services connect the mainland to Zanzibar, and lake services are operated on Lake Tanganyika and Lake Malaŵi with neighbouring countries. The principal international airports are Dar es Salaam, Kilimanjaro and Zanzibar. There are two railway systems; one connecting Dar es Salaam to Zambia, and the second having two main lines running from Dar es Salaam, one to northern Tanzania and Kenya and the other to Lakes Tanganyika and Victoria. There are more than 3,000 km of railtrack.

## EDUCATION

The school system is administered in Swahili but the government is making efforts to improve English standards for the purposes of secondary and higher education. All Tanzanian secondary schools are expected to include practical subjects in the basic course. There are three institutes of higher education: the University of Dar es Salaam, Sokoine University of Agriculture in Morogoro and an open university.

ILLITERACY RATE – 24.8 per cent
ENROLMENT (percentage of age group) – primary 48 per cent (1997); tertiary 0.6 per cent (1997)

---

# THAILAND
*Prathes Thai – Kingdom of Thailand*

---

AREA – 198,115 sq. miles (513,115 sq. km). Neighbours: Malaysia (south), Myanmar (west), Laos and Cambodia (east)
POPULATION – 61,691,000 (1997 census). The principal language is Thai, a monosyllabic, tonal language of the Indo-Chinese linguistic family, with a vocabulary strongly influenced by Sanskrit and Pali. It is written in an alphabetic script derived from ancient Indian scripts. Significant minorities speak Chinese (in urban areas), Lao (in the north-east), Khmer (in the east) and Malay (in the far south). The principal religion is Buddhism (94.37 per cent), with Muslim and Christian minorities
CAPITAL – ΨBangkok (population, 7,358,300, 1998 estimate)
MAJOR CITIES – Chiang Mai (159,000); Chon Buri (229,400); Nakhon Ratchasima (260,500); Nanthanburi (476,300); Songkhla (288,000), 1998 estimates
CURRENCY – Baht of 100 satang
NATIONAL ANTHEM – Pleng Chart
NATIONAL DAY – 5 December (The King's Birthday)
NATIONAL FLAG – Five horizontal bands, red, white, dark blue, white, red (the blue band twice the width of the others)
LIFE EXPECTANCY (years) – male 66.0; female 70.4
POPULATION GROWTH RATE – 1.0 per cent (1999)
POPULATION DENSITY – 119 per sq. km (1998)
URBAN POPULATION – 21.6 per cent (2000 estimate)

Thailand, formerly known as Siam, is divided geographically into four: the centre is a plain; to the north-east there is a plateau area and to the north-west mountains. The south of Thailand consists of a narrow mountainous peninsula. The principal rivers are the Chao Phraya in the central plains, and the Mekong on the northern and north-eastern borders.

## HISTORY AND POLITICS

The Thai nation was founded in the 13th century. Although occupied by Burma in the 18th century, Thailand is the only country in the region not to have been colonised by a European power.

Following a revolution in 1932, Thailand became a constitutional monarchy. After a military coup in February 1991, a new constitution was approved under which the military would have significant political power. Parties aligned with the military won the general election in March 1992, but mass demonstrations held in Bangkok, with the help of the King, forced the government from power. Military power was curbed, the 1978 constitution was restored and the interim government sacked military chiefs.

Parliamentary elections in September 1992 resulted in a majority for those parties not allied with the military. The first election to the Senate was held on 4 March 2000. A rerun was held in 78 seats on 29 April following evidence of fraud. Further reruns were necessary for some seats.

A general election took place on 6 January 2001. The Thai Rak Thai (TRT) party won 248 seats and formed a coaltion with the Chart Thai party and the New Aspiration party.

### Foreign Relations

Laos occupied two Thai islands in the Mekong river on 19 August 2000 and evicted the inhabitants, claiming that it had jurisdiction over all the islands in the Mekong under a 1926 treaty.

On 9–11 February 2001, fighting occurred between the Thai army and Myanmarese troops who had crossed the border in pursuit of rebels in Chiang Rai province; several Myanmarese soldiers were killed in the incident. The two countries agreed on 19-20 June to resolve the border tension and co-operate on fighting drug production and smuggling.

### Political System

The constitution provides for a National Assembly consisting of a 200-member Senate, directly elected on a non-party basis for a six-year term, and a 500-member House of Representatives elected by universal adult suffrage, 400 elected in single-member constituencies and 100 from party lists, for a term of four years.

### Head of State

*HM The King of Thailand*, King Bhumibol Adulyadej, *born* 5 December 1927; *succeeded his brother* 9 June 1946; *married* 28 April 1950 Mom Rajawongse Sirikit Kitiyakara; *crowned* 5 May 1950; and has *issue*, Princess Ubol Ratana, *born* 6 April 1951; Crown Prince Maha Vajiralongkorn (*see* below); Princess Maha Chakri Sirindhorn, *born* 2 April 1955; Princess Chulabhorn, *born* 4 July 1957

*Heir*, HRH Crown Prince Maha Vajiralongkorn, *born* 28 July 1952; *married* 3 January 1977 Soamsawali Kitiyakra

### Cabinet *as at September 2001*

*Prime Minister, Education*, Thaksin Shinawatra (TRT)
*Deputy Prime Ministers*, Gen. Chawalit Yongchaiyudh (TRT) (*Defence*); Daj Boonlong (TRT) (*Labour and Social Welfare*); Pongpol Adireksan (TRT); Pitak Intravitayanant (TRT); Suwit Khunkitti (TRT)
*Ministers to the Prime Minister's Office*, Jaturon Chaisan (TRT); Krasae Chanawong (TRT); Gen. Thammarak Isarakuan na Ayuthaya (TRT); Somsak Thepsutin (TRT)
*Agriculture and Co-operatives*, Chuchief Harnsawad (TRT)
*Commerce*, Adisai Bodharamik (TRT)
*Finance*, Somkit Chatusipitak (TRT)
*Foreign Affairs*, Surakiet Sathirathai (TRT)
*Industry*, Suriya Rungruangkit (TRT)
*Interior*, Purachai Piumsombun (TRT)
*Justice*, Pongthep Thepkanchana (CT)
*Public Health*, Sudarat Keyuraphan (TRT)
*Science, Technology and Environment*, Sontaya Kunplome (CT)
*Transport and Communications*, Wanmuhadnoor Matha (NAP)
*University Affairs*, Suthum Sangpathom (TRT)

CT Chart Thai; NAP New Aspiration Party; TRT Thai Rak Thai

### Royal Thai Embassy

29–30 Queen's Gate, London SW7 5JB
Tel: 020-7589 2944
*Ambassador Extraordinary and Plenipotentiary*, HE Sir Vidhya Rayananonda, KCVO, apptd 1994
*Minister and Deputy Head of Mission*, A. Manasvanich
*Defence and Naval Attaché*, Capt. J. Poocharoenyos
*Minister*, S. Sarayudh *(Commercial)*

### British Embassy

Wireless Road, Bangkok 10330
Tel: (00 66) (2) 2530 1919
*Ambassador Extraordinary and Plenipotentiary*, HE Lloyd Barnaby Smith, apptd 2000
*Deputy Head of Mission and Counsellor*, P. West
*Defence Attaché*, Col. A. Singer
*Counsellor (Commercial)*, D. Wyatt
*Consul*, D. Fisher

Consulate – Chiang Mai

British Council Director, Bhaskar Chakravarti, 254 Chulalongkorn Soi 64, Siam Square, Phayathai Road, Pathumwan, Bangkok 10330; e-mail: bc.bangkok@britcoun.or.th. There is also an office in Chiang Mai

British Chamber of Commerce, BP Building 18th Floor, Unit 1810, 54 Asoke Road (Sukhumvit 21), Bangkok 10110

## DEFENCE

The Army has 282 main battle tanks, 970 armoured personnel carriers and four attack helicopters. The Navy has one aircraft carrier, 14 frigates, 88 patrol and coastal vessels, 67 combat aircraft and five armed helicopters at five bases. The Air Force has 153 combat aircraft.
Military Expenditure – 1.9 per cent of GDP (1999)
Military Personnel – 301,000: Army 190,000, Navy 68,000, Air Force 43,000, Paramilitaries 115,600

## ECONOMY

Thailand was one of the countries worst affected by the economic crisis in south-east Asia. Many Thai banks had borrowed heavily to finance the booming property market, and suffered when the market collapsed. In May 1997 the stock market fell to an eight-year low. In July 1997 the government allowed the currency to float freely, resulting in a *de facto* devaluation of 20 per cent and triggering a currency crisis throughout south-east Asia. On 5 August 1997, an IMF loan of US$16.7 billion was announced, in return for emergency financial reforms. However, these reforms were only implemented after a delay and were seen by the markets as inadequate, further damaging economic confidence. The government resigned on 3 November 1997, and was replaced by an eight-party coalition. The Thai economy contracted by about 8 per cent in 1998. In March 1999, the government announced a package of tax cuts and increased spending designed to stimulate the economy.

The banking system remains in crisis with nearly half of all loans non-performing, as many businesses had became heavily indebted during the financial crisis and are now unable to repay their loans.

The agricultural sector employs around half of the labour force. In 1997 it contributed 11 per cent of GDP. Rice remains the most important crop; other main crops are sugar, maize, sorghum, cassava, rubber, tobacco, kenaf and jute. In recent years fishing and livestock production have gained importance. There are reserves of oil, natural gas and lignite; mineral resources include tin, tungsten, lead and iron.

Important industrial sectors include textiles, transportation vehicles and equipment, construction materials, brewing, petroleum refining, electrical appliances, plastics, computers and parts, and integrated circuits. In 1997, industry contributed 39.8 per cent of GDP. Since 1982 tourism has been the main foreign exchange earner. In 1998, there were 7.8 million foreign visitors.
GNP – US$121,051 million (1999); US$1,960 per capita (1999)
GDP – US$153,909 million (1997); US$1,890 per capita (1998)
Annual Average Growth of GDP – 6.0 per cent (1996)
Inflation Rate – 0.3 per cent (1999)

UNEMPLOYMENT – 4.5 per cent (1998)
TOTAL EXTERNAL DEBT – US$86,172 million (1998)

## TRADE

Thailand's main exports are computers and parts, cars, integrated circuit boards, precious stones, rice, maize, canned sea food, fabrics, sugar and tin. Main imports are crude oil, chemicals, electrical goods, industrial machinery, iron, steel and transport equipment.

In 1999 Thailand had a trade surplus of US$13,477 million and a current account surplus of US$11,050 million. Imports totalled US$41,526 million and exports US$58,392 million.

| *Trade with UK* | 1999 | 2000 |
|---|---|---|
| Imports from UK | £465,796,000 | £580,796,000 |
| Exports to UK | 1,346,599,000 | 1,661,419,000 |

## COMMUNICATIONS

The road network totalled 64,600 km in 1996, of which 62,985 km were paved. Navigable waterways have a length of about 1,100 km in the dry season and 1,600 km in the wet season. There are 3,940 km of railways. Bangkok is the international airport, though airports at Chiang Mai, Phuket and Hat Yai also receive international flights. Most major provincial towns have airports. There are two important ports in the country. Bangkok, which is a river port, can serve vessels up to 27 ft draught. The deep-sea port at Sattahip caters for larger vessels. Phuket and Songkhla deep-water ports have already been completed and are the first to be managed privately under a ten-year concession. There are 3,999 km of principal waterways.

In September 1999, the government approved a plan to build a 350-km gas pipeline from the Gulf of Thailand to Songkhla province, where it would link with the Malaysian network.

## EDUCATION

Primary education is compulsory and free, and secondary education in government schools is free. Private universities and colleges are playing an increasing role in higher education. Out of 43 universities and other similar higher institutes of learning, 21 are private.
ILLITERACY RATE – 4.4 per cent
ENROLMENT (percentage of age group) – tertiary 22.1 per cent (1996)

---

# TOGO
*République Togolaise*

---

AREA – 21,925 sq. miles (56,785 sq. km). Neighbours: Ghana (west), Burkina Faso (north), Benin (east)
POPULATION – 4,567,000 (1997 UN estimate). The official language is French; Ewe, Watchi and Kabiyé are the main indigenous languages
CAPITAL – ΨLomé (population, 366,476, 1983)
CURRENCY – Franc CFA of 100 centimes
NATIONAL ANTHEM - Écartons tous mauvais esprit qui gêne l'unité nationale (Let us discard all ill feelings which harm national unity)
NATIONAL DAY - 27 April
NATIONAL FLAG – Five alternating green and yellow horizontal stripes; a quarter in red at top next staff bearing a white star
LIFE EXPECTANCY (years) – male 48.9; female 50.8
POPULATION GROWTH RATE – 2.8 per cent (1999)
POPULATION DENSITY – 77 per sq. km (1998)
URBAN POPULATION – 33.3 per cent (2000 estimate)
MILITARY EXPENDITURE – 2.3 per cent of GDP (1999)
MILITARY PERSONNEL – 6,950: Army 6,500 Navy 200, Air Force 250; Paramilitaries 750
CONSCRIPTION DURATION – Two years (selective)
ILLITERACY RATE – 42.9 per cent (1997)
ENROLMENT (percentage of age group) – primary 81 per cent (1996); secondary 18 per cent (1990); tertiary 3.6 per cent (1996)

## HISTORY AND POLITICS

The first president of Togo, Sylvanus Olympio, was assassinated in 1963. In 1967, there was an army coup d'état and the army commander Lt.-Col. (later Gen.) Eyadéma named himself president. In April 1990, following increasing popular pressure, the government was forced to concede a political amnesty, the introduction of a multiparty constitution and a national conference. In August 1991 the national conference stripped President Eyadéma of all powers, banned the *Rassemblement du peuple togolais* (RPT), which had been the sole legal party, and elected Kokou Koffigoh as prime minister of an interim government.

Troops loyal to President Eyadéma three times attempted to overthrow Koffigoh (in October, November and December 1991) but were frustrated by pro-democracy supporters. A new multiparty constitution was approved by referendum in September 1992. In November, Eyadéma, who had regained the position of head of state in August 1992, ordered the Army to crush civil unrest and a general strike against his rule. In February 1993, as violence continued, Koffigoh and Eyadéma agreed on the formation of a crisis government, which the national conference and the Collective Democratic Opposition-2 (COD-2) declared illegal.

The presidential election of 21 June 1998 was won by Gen. Eyadéma. Opposition politicians and EU observers expressed serious doubts over the conduct of the election.

Legislative elections to the 81-seat National Assembly were held on 21 March 1999. Opposition parties, who had refused to accept the results of the presidential election in 1998, boycotted the election, with the result that the ruling RPT gained 79 seats, the remaining two seats being won by independents. Eugene Koffi Adoboli was appointed prime minister on 22 May 1999 and a new Cabinet was appointed on 18 June. The government and opposition parties reached an agreement in July 1999 that a fresh election would be held in March 2000 and President Eyadéma agreed not to run in the 2003 presidential elections. The legislative election was postponed and was due to be held on 14 and 28 October 2001.

### HEAD OF STATE

*President*, Gen. Gnassingbé Eyadéma, *assumed office* 14 April 1967 *re-elected* 1986, 1993, 21 June 1998

### GOVERNMENT *as at September 2001*

*Prime Minister*, Agbeyomé Kodjo
*Agriculture, Livestock and Fisheries*, Komikpime Bamenante
*Civil Service, Labour and Employment*, Kokou Tozoun
*Commerce, Industry, Transport and Development of the Free Zone*, Dama Dramani
*Communication and Civic Education*, Bawa Semedo
*Culture, Youth and Sport*, Komi Klassou
*Defence*, Brig.-Gen. Assani Tidjani
*Economic Affairs, Finance and Privatisation*, Tankpadja Lalle
*Environment and Forest Resources*, Koffi Adade
*Equipment, Mines, Energy, Post and Telecommunications*, Andjo Tchamdja
*Interior, Security and Decentralisation*, Col. Sising Akawilou Walla
*Justice and Keeper of the Seals*, Brig.-Gen. Séyi Méméne
*Minister-Delegate at the Prime Minister's Office, in charge of the Private Sector*, Angèle Aguigah

*Minister of State, Foreign Affairs and Co-operation*, Kofi Panou
*National Education and Research*, Koffi Sama
*Planning and Urban and Rural Development*, Simféïtchéou Pré
*Public Health*, Charles Kondi Agba
*Regional Integration, Parliamentary Relations*, Joseph Kokoh Koffigoh
*Social Affairs, Promotion of Women and Child Protection*, Irène Ashir Aissah
*Technical Education and Professional Training*, Edo Kodjo Maurille Agbobli
*Tourism, Handicrafts and Leisure*, Kossi Assimaidou

EMBASSY OF THE REPUBLIC OF TOGO
8 rue Alfred-Roll, F-75017 Paris, France
Tel: (00 33) (1) 4380 1213
*Ambassador Extraordinary and Plenipotentiary*, vacant

BRITISH AMBASSADOR, HE Rod Pullen, resident at Accra, Ghana
There is a Consulate (BP 20050) and a Commercial Office (BP 9224) in Lomé.

## ECONOMY

Although the economy remains largely agricultural, exports of phosphates have superseded agricultural products as the main source of export earnings. Other exports include palm kernels, copra and manioc.

In December 1998 the EU announced that it would not resume developmental aid to Togo following irregularities in the country's election process.

In 1998 Togo had a trade deficit of US$133 million and a current account deficit of US$140 million. Imports totalled US$631 million and exports US$411 million.
GNP – US$1,398 million (1999); US$320 per capita (1999)
GDP – US$1,400 million (1997); US$344 per capita (1998)
ANNUAL AVERAGE GROWTH OF GDP – 6.0 per cent (1996)
INFLATION RATE – 0.1 per cent (1999)
TOTAL EXTERNAL DEBT – US$1,448 million (1998)

| *Trade with UK* | 1999 | 2000 |
|---|---|---|
| Imports from UK | £19,556,000 | £20,515,000 |
| Exports to UK | 1,361,000 | 1,504,000 |

---

# TONGA
*Pule'anga Tonga/Kingdom of Tonga*

---

AREA – 288 sq. miles (747 sq. km)
POPULATION – 100,000 (1997 UN estimate). The languages are Tongan and English
CAPITAL – ΨNuku'alofa (population, 29,018, 1986), on Tongatapu
CURRENCY – Pa'anga (T$) of 100 seniti
NATIONAL ANTHEM – E, 'Otua Mafimafi (Oh, Almighty God Above)
NATIONAL DAY – 4 June (Emancipation Day)
NATIONAL FLAG – Red with a white canton containing a couped red cross
LIFE EXPECTANCY (years) – male 68.3; female 72.8
POPULATION GROWTH RATE – 0.3 per cent (1999)
POPULATION DENSITY – 151 per sq. km (1998)
URBAN POPULATION – 38.0 per cent (2000 estimate)
ILLITERACY RATE – 42.9 per cent (2000)

Tonga, or the Friendly Islands, comprises a group of islands situated in the southern Pacific some 450 miles east-south-east of Fiji. The largest island, Tongatapu, was discovered by Tasman in 1643. Most of the islands are of coral formation, but some are volcanic (Tofua, Kao and Niuafoou or 'Tin Can' Island).

## HISTORY AND POLITICS

The Kingdom of Tonga is an independent constitutional monarchy within the Commonwealth. Prior to 4 June 1970 it had been a British-protected state for 70 years. The constitution provides for a government consisting of the Sovereign, an appointed privy council which functions as a Cabinet, a legislative assembly and a judiciary. The 30-member legislative assembly comprises the King, the 11-member privy council, nine hereditary nobles elected by their peers, and nine popularly elected representatives who hold office for three years. The most recent election took place on 12 March 1999.

### HEAD OF STATE

*King of Tonga*, HM King Taufa'ahau Tupou IV, GCMG, GCVO, KBE, *born* 4 July 1918, *acceded* 16 December 1965
*Heir*, HRH Crown Prince Tupouto'a

### CABINET *as at September 2001*

*Prime Minister, Agriculture and Fisheries, Civil Aviation and Communications, Foreign Affairs and Defence*, HRH Prince 'Ulukalala Lavaka Ata
*Deputy Prime Minister, Justice and Attorney-General*, Tevita Tupou
*Education*, Tūtoatasi Fakafanua
*Finance*, Siosiua Utoikamanu
*Governor of Ha'apai*, Malupo
*Governor of Vava'u*, Capt. S. M. Tuita
*Health*, Viliami Tangi
*Labour, Commerce and Industries, Tourism*, Masaso Paunga
*Lands, Survey, and Natural Resources*, Fielakepa
*Police, Prisons and Fire Services, Immigration*, Clive Edwards
*Works, Marines and Ports, Environment*, Cecil Cocker

TONGA HIGH COMMISSION
36 Molyneux Street, London W1H 6AB
Tel: 020-7724 5828
*High Commissioner*, HE Col. Fetu'utolu Tupou, apptd 2000

BRITISH HIGH COMMISSION
PO Box 56, Nuku'alofa
Tel: (00 676) 24285/24395
E-mail: britcomt@kalianet.to
*High Commissioner*, HE Brian Connelly, apptd 1998

## ECONOMY

The economy is primarily agricultural; the main crops are coconuts, vanilla, yams, taro, cassava, groundnuts, squash pumpkins and other fruits. Fish is an important staple food, though recent shortfalls have led to canned fish being imported. Industry is based on the processing of agricultural produce, and the manufacture of foodstuffs, clothing and sports equipment.
GNP – US$172 million (1999); US$1,720 per capita (1999)
GDP – US$175 million (1997); US$1,614 per capita (1998)
ANNUAL AVERAGE GROWTH OF GDP – 1.6 per cent (1996)
INFLATION RATE – 4.5 per cent (1999)
TOTAL EXTERNAL DEBT – US$65 million (1998)

### TRADE

The principal exports are fish and vanilla. The principal imports are manufactures, foodstuffs, machinery and transport equipment and combustible fuels.

In 1996 imports totalled US$75 million and exports US$9 million.

| *Trade with UK* | 1999 | 2000 |
|---|---|---|
| Imports from UK | £1,467,000 | £1,883,000 |
| Exports to UK | 260,000 | 470,000 |

## TRINIDAD AND TOBAGO
*The Republic of Trinidad and Tobago*

AREA – 1,981 sq. miles (5,130 sq. km)
POPULATION – 1,293,000 (1997 UN estimate). The language is English. The main religions are Roman Catholicism (29.4 per cent of the population), Hinduism (23.8 per cent); Anglicanism (10.9 per cent); Islam (5.8 per cent) and Presbyterianism (3.4 per cent)
CAPITAL – ΨPort of Spain (population, 43,396, 1994)
MAJOR CITIES – San Fernando (55,784); ΨScarborough, the main town of Tobago
CURRENCY – Trinidad and Tobago dollar (TT$) of 100 cents
NATIONAL ANTHEM - Forged from the love of liberty
NATIONAL DAY – 31 August (Independence Day)
NATIONAL FLAG – Black diagonal stripe bordered with white stripes, running from top by staff, all on a red field
LIFE EXPECTANCY (years) – male 68.7; female 73.4
POPULATION GROWTH RATE – 0.7 per cent (1999)
POPULATION DENSITY – 250 per sq. km (1998)
URBAN POPULATION – 74.1 per cent (2000 estimate)
MILITARY EXPENDITURE – 0.9 per cent of GDP (1999)
MILITARY PERSONNEL – 2,700: Army 2,000, Coast Guard 700

Trinidad, the most southerly of the West Indian islands, lies seven miles off the north coast of Venezuela. The island is about 50 miles in length by 37 miles in width. Two mountain systems, the Northern and Southern Ranges, stretch across almost its entire width and a third, the Central Range, lies diagonally across its middle portion; otherwise the island is mostly flat.

Tobago lies 19 miles north-east of Trinidad. The island is 32 miles long at its widest point, and 11 miles wide.

Corozal Point and Icacos Point, the north-west and south-west extremities of Trinidad, enclose the Gulf of Paria. West of Corozal Point lie several islands, of which Chacachacare, Huevos, Monos and Gaspar Grande are the most important.

The climate is tropical. There is a dry season from December to May, and a wet season from June to November broken by a short dry season (the *Petit Carême*) in September and October.

## HISTORY AND POLITICS

Trinidad was discovered by Columbus in 1498, was colonised in 1532 by the Spaniards, capitulated to the British in 1797, and was ceded to Britain under the Treaty of Amiens (1802). Tobago was discovered by Columbus in 1498. Dutch colonists arrived in 1632; Tobago subsequently changed hands numerous times until it was ceded to Britain by France in 1814 and amalgamated with Trinidad in 1888. The Territory of Trinidad and Tobago became an independent state and a member of the British Commonwealth on 31 August 1962, and a republic in 1976.

The most recent general election on 11 December 2000 produced 19 seats for the ruling United National Congress (UNC), 16 seats for the People's National Movement (PNM) and one seat for the National Alliance for Reconstruction.

### POLITICAL SYSTEM

The president is elected for five years by all members of the Senate and the House of Representatives. The House of Representatives has 36 members, directly elected for a five-year term, and the Senate has 31, of whom 16 are appointed on the advice of the prime minister, six on the advice of the Leader of the Opposition and nine at the discretion of the president. Legislation was passed in September 1980 which afforded Tobago a degree of self-administration through the 15-member Tobago House of Assembly, of whom 12 are directly elected and three chosen by the House for a four-year term.

### HEAD OF STATE

*President*, HE Arthur N. Robinson, *elected* 14 February 1997

### CABINET *as at September 2001*

*Prime Minister*, Basdeo Panday
*Attorney-General, Legal Affairs*, Ramesh Lawrence Maharaj
*Communications and Information Technology*, Ralph Maraj
*Community Empowerment, Sport, Consumer Affairs*, Manohar Ramsaran
*Education*, Kamla Persad-Bissessar
*Energy and Energy Industries*, Lindsay Gillette
*Enterprise Development, Foreign Affairs, Tourism*, Mervyn Assam
*Environment*, Adesh Nanan
*Finance, Planning and Development*, Gerard Yetming
*Food Production and Marine Resources*, Trevor Sudama
*Health*, Hamza Rafeeq
*Housing and Settlements*, Sadiq Baksh
*Human Development, Youth and Culture*, Ganga Singh
*Infrastructure Development, Local Government*, Carlos John
*Integrated Planning and Development*, John Humphrey
*Labour, Manpower Development and Industrial Relations*, Harry Partrap
*Transport*, Jearlean John

### HIGH COMMISSION OF THE REPUBLIC OF TRINIDAD AND TOBAGO

42 Belgrave Square, London SW1X 8NT
Tel: 020-7245 9351
*High Commissioner*, vacant
*Deputy High Commissioner*, Sandra McIntyre-Trotman

### BRITISH HIGH COMMISSION

19 St Clair Ave, St Clair, Port of Spain
Tel: (00 1 868) 622 2748/8960. E-mail: csbhc@opus.co.tt
*High Commissioner*, HE P. G. Harborne, apptd 1999
BRITISH COUNCIL, c/o British High Commission; e-mail: bctt@opus.co.tt

## ECONOMY

Trinidad and Tobago's main source of revenue is from oil. Production of domestic crude was 6.3 million tonnes in 1998. Trinidad has large reserves of natural gas, and in March 2000, an agreement was signed to expand significantly the production of liquefied natural gas. In May, it was announced that an additional natural gas deposit of some 56,600 million cubic metres had been discovered and the discovery of a further deposit of some three trillion cubic feet was announced in September. An integrated steel plant, two anhydrous ammonia plants, four methanol plants, one urea plant and one iron carbide plant have been constructed at Point Lisas. An industrial complex, including an iron and steel production plant, is developing around San Fernando.

Fertilisers, tyres, clothing, soap, furniture and foodstuffs are manufactured locally while motor vehicles, radios, TV sets, and electro-domestic equipment are assembled from parts, mainly from Japan. The main agricultural products are sugar, cocoa, coffee, horticultural products and teak. There were 265,900 tourists in 1996.

In 1998 Trinidad and Tobago had a trade surplus of US$741 million and a current account surplus of US$644 million. Imports totalled US$2,999 million and exports US$2,258 million.

GNP – US$6,142 million (1999); US$4,390 per capita (1999)

GDP – US$5,614 million (1997); US$4,622 per capita (1998)

ANNUAL AVERAGE GROWTH OF GDP – 3.1 per cent (1996)

INFLATION RATE – 3.6 per cent (1999)

UNEMPLOYMENT – 14.2 per cent (1998)

TOTAL EXTERNAL DEBT – US$2,193 million (1998)

| *Trade with UK* | 1999 | 2000 |
|---|---|---|
| Imports from UK | £143,339,000 | £76,031,000 |
| Exports to UK | 53,433,000 | 49,710,000 |

## COMMUNICATIONS

There are some 9,586 km of roads in Trinidad and Tobago. The three main ports are Scarborough (Tobago), Port of Spain and Point Lisas where new industries powered by local natural gas are located. The national airline is BWIA West Indies Airways Ltd, and the international airport, Piarco, is at Port of Spain.

## EDUCATION

Education is free at all state-owned and government-assisted denominational schools and certain faculties at the University of the West Indies. Attendance is compulsory for children aged six to 12 years, after which attendance at free secondary schools is determined by success in the secondary school entrance examination at 11 years. There are three technical institutes, two teachers' training colleges, and one of the three branches of the University of the West Indies is located in Trinidad. A medical teaching complex at Mt Hope operates in collaboration with the University of the West Indies.

ILLITERACY RATE – 1.8 per cent

ENROLMENT (percentage of age group) – primary 88 per cent (1996); secondary 65 per cent (1992); tertiary 8.2 per cent (1996)

# TUNISIA

*Al-Jumhūriyya at-Tūnisiyya*

AREA – 63,170 sq. miles (163,610 sq. km). Neighbours: Algeria (west), Libya (south)

POPULATION – 9,457,000 (1997). Arabic is the official language

CAPITAL – ΨTunis (population, 1,830,634, 1997)

MAJOR CITIES – ΨBizerte (484,250); ΨSfax (732,865); ΨSousse (435,075), 1996

CURRENCY – Tunisian dinar of 1,000 millimes

NATIONAL ANTHEM – Himat Al Hima (Defenders of the homeland)

NATIONAL DAY – 20 March

NATIONAL FLAG – Red with a white disc containing a red crescent and star

LIFE EXPECTANCY (years) – male 67.0; female 67.9

POPULATION GROWTH RATE – 1.7 per cent (1999)

POPULATION DENSITY – 57 per sq. km (1998)

URBAN POPULATION – 65.5 per cent (2000 estimate)

MILITARY EXPENDITURE – 1.7 per cent of GDP (1999)

MILITARY PERSONNEL – 35,000: Army 27,000, Navy 4,500, Air Force 3,500; Paramilitaries 12,000

CONSCRIPTION DURATION – 12 months (selective)

## HISTORY AND POLITICS

A French Protectorate from 1881 to 1956, Tunisia became an independent sovereign state on 20 March 1956. In 1957 the Constituent Assembly abolished the monarchy and elected M. Bourguiba president of the Republic. In March 1975 the National Assembly proclaimed M. Bourguiba as president for life. He was deposed on 7 November 1987 and succeeded by President Zine el-Abidine Ben Ali, who was subsequently elected in 1989 and re-elected in 1994. President Ben Ali was elected for a third term of office on 24 October 1999, gaining 99.4 per cent of the vote; there were two other candidates. A parallel legislative election was won by the Democratic Constitutional Rally (RCD), who gained 91.6 per cent of the vote, winning 148 of the 182 seats in the National Assembly *(Majlis al-Nuwaab)*. The Movement of Social Democrats (MDS) won 13 seats, the Unionist Democratic Union (UDU) and the Party of People's Unity (PUP) won 7 seats each, the Movement for Renewal (MR) won 5 seats and the Social-Liberal Party won 2 seats.

The country is divided into 23 regions (*gouvernorats*) each administered by a governor.

### HEAD OF STATE

*President*, Gen. Zine el-Abidine Ben Ali, *took office* 7 November 1987, *elected* 2 April 1989, *re-elected* 20 March 1994, 24 October 1999

### CABINET *as at September 2001*

*Prime Minister*, Mohammed Ghannouchi
*Agriculture*, Sadok Rabah
*Communications Technologies*, Ahmed Friaâ
*Culture*, Abdelbaki Hermassi
*Economic Development*, Abdellatif Saddam
*Education*, Moncer Rouissi
*Environment and Land Development*, Mohamed Nabli
*Finance*, Taoufik Baccar
*Foreign Affairs*, Habib Ben Yahia
*Higher Education*, Sadok Chaâbane
*Industry*, Moncef Ben Abdallah
*Interior*, Abdallah Kaäbi
*International Co-operation and Foreign Investment*, Fethi Merdassi
*Justice*, Bechir Takali
*Minister-Delegate to the Prime Minister in charge of Human Rights, Communications and Relations with the National Assembly*, Afif Hendaoui
*Minister of State, Special Adviser to the President*, Abdelaziz Ben Dhia
*National Defence*, Dali Jazi
*Public Health*, Abdelkrim Zbidi
*Public Works and Housing*, Slaheddine Belaid
*Religious Affairs*, Jelloul Jribi
*Secretary-General to the Government*, Mohamed Rachid Kechiche
*Secretary-General to the Presidential Office*, Ahmed Eyadh Ouederni
*Social Affairs*, Hedi M'henni
*State Property, Real Estate Affairs*, Ridha Grira
*Tourism, Leisure and Handicrafts*, Mondher Zenaidi
*Trade*, Taher Sioud
*Transport*, Hassine Chouk
*Vocational Training and Employment*, Faiza Kefi
*Women and the Family*, Neziha Zarrouk
*Youth, Childhood and Sport*, Abderrahim Zouari

### TUNISIAN EMBASSY

29 Prince's Gate, London SW7 1QG
Tel: 020-7584 8117
*Ambassador Extraordinary and Plenipotentiary*, HE Khemaies Jhinaoui, apptd 1999

### BRITISH EMBASSY

5 Place de la Victoire, Tunis 1000 RP
Tel: (00 216) (1) 341444

E-mail: british.emb@planet.tn
*Ambassador Extraordinary and Plenipotentiary*, HE Ivor Rawlinson, OBE, apptd 1998
*Consul*, J. Hancock (*Deputy Head of Mission*)
HONORARY CONSULATE – Sfax

BRITISH COUNCIL DIRECTOR, John Whitehead (*Cultural Attaché*), c/o British Embassy; e-mail: general.enquiries@bc-tunis.bcouncil.org

## ECONOMY

Agriculture employed 25.7 per cent of the workforce in 1997 and in 1998 accounted for 12 per cent of GDP. The valleys of the northern region support large flocks and herds and contain rich agricultural areas in which cereal crops, citrus fruits, dates, melons, potatoes, peppers and tomatoes are grown. Vines and olives are extensively cultivated. Crude oil production in 1998 was 3.9 million tonnes. Gas has also been discovered off the east coast but is only exploited in small quantities. Tourism is the main foreign exchange earner and there were 4.7 million visitors in 1998.

In 1999 Tunisia had a trade deficit of US$2,141 million and a current account deficit of US$503 million. Imports totalled US$8,466 million and exports US$5,872 million.

GNP – US$19,757 million (1999); US$2,100 per capita (1999)
GDP – US$19,004 million (1997); US$2,138 per capita (1998)
ANNUAL AVERAGE GROWTH OF GDP – 6.9 per cent (1996)
INFLATION RATE – 2.7 per cent (1999)
UNEMPLOYMENT – 16.2 per cent (1989)
TOTAL EXTERNAL DEBT – US$11,078 million (1998)

### TRADE

The chief exports are manufactures, textiles and leather goods, phosphates, mechanical and electronic products, agricultural products and energy. The chief imports are manufactures, raw materials and semi-manufactures, consumer goods, capital goods, and foodstuffs. France remains the main trading partner.

Tunisia became an associate of the EC in 1969. In July 1995 a new EU-Tunisian partnership agreement was signed which aims to modernise Tunisia's economy and improve its competitiveness with a view to creating a free trade zone with the EU by 2008.

| *Trade with UK* | 1999 | 2000 |
|---|---|---|
| Imports from UK | £107,398,000 | £133,290,000 |
| Exports to UK | 83,873,000 | 109,727,000 |

## EDUCATION

There are 90 centres of higher education, of which six are universities (four in Tunis, one each in Sousse and Sfax). There are plans to establish two new universities in Jendouba and Gafsa..

ILLITERACY RATE – 29.2 per cent
ENROLMENT (percentage of age group) – primary 98 per cent (1996); secondary 43 per cent (1991); tertiary 13.7 per cent (1996)

---

## TURKEY
*Türkiye Çumhuriyeti*

---

AREA – 314,508 sq. miles (814,578 sq. km). Neighbours: Greece (west), Bulgaria (north), Georgia, Armenia, Nakhichevan (Azerbaijan) and Iran (east), Syria and Iraq (south)
POPULATION – 66,620,120 (2000 estimate); 62,865,574 (1997 census). Islam ceased to be the state religion in 1928 but 98.99 per cent of the population are Muslim. The main religious minorities, which are concentrated in Istanbul and on the Syrian frontier, are Greek Orthodox, Armenian, Syrian Christian, and Jewish. The language is Turkish; Kurdish is widely spoken in the south-east of the country
CAPITAL – Ankara (Angora), in Asia (population, 3,294,220, 1997 estimate). Ankara (or Ancyra) was the capital of the Roman Province of *Galatia Prima*, and a marble temple (now in ruins), dedicated to Augustus, contains the *Monumentum* (*Marmor*) *Ancyranum*, inscribed with a record of the reign of Augustus Caesar
MAJOR CITIES – Adana (1,272,892); Bursa (1,484,838); Gaziantep (866,567); ΨIstanbul (8,506,026); ΨIzmir (2,554,363); Konya (1,140,016), 1997 estimates. Istanbul, in Europe, is the former capital. The Roman city of Byzantium, it was selected by Constantine the Great as the capital of the Roman Empire about AD 328 and renamed Constantinople. Istanbul contains the celebrated church of St Sophia, which, after becoming a mosque, was made a museum in 1934. It also contains Topkapi, former palace of the Ottoman Sultans, which is also a museum
CURRENCY – Turkish lira (TL)
NATIONAL ANTHEM – Istiklal Marsi (The Independence March)
NATIONAL DAY – 29 October (Republic Day)
NATIONAL FLAG – Red, with white crescent and star
LIFE EXPECTANCY (years) – male 69.7; female 69.9
POPULATION GROWTH RATE – 1.7 per cent (1999)
POPULATION DENSITY – 83 per sq. km (1999)
URBAN POPULATION – 75.3 per cent (2000 estimate)

Turkey in Europe consists of Eastern Thrace, including the cities of Istanbul and Edirne, and is separated from Asia by the Bosporus at Istanbul and by the Dardanelles (about 40 miles in length with a width varying from one to four miles). Turkey in Asia comprises the whole of Asia Minor or Anatolia.

## HISTORY AND POLITICS

On 29 October 1923 the National Assembly declared Turkey a republic and elected Gazi Mustafa Kemal (later known as Kemal Atatürk) president. In 1945 a multiparty system was introduced but in 1960 the government was overthrown by the armed forces. A new constitution was adopted in 1961 and a civilian government took office. Civilian governments remained in power until September 1980 when mounting problems with the economy and terrorism led to a military takeover.

Following the general election in November 1983 the military leadership handed over power to a civilian government.

Following elections on 18 April 1999, the Democratic Left Party (DSP) won the most seats and formed a coalition with the Nationalist Action Party (MHP) and the Motherland Party (ANAP). Hadep, the pro-Kurdish People's Democracy Party, won control of several towns in south-eastern Turkey in simultaneous local elections.

### INSURGENCIES

Since 1984 Turkey has been fighting armed guerrillas of the Marxist Kurdistan Workers' Party (PKK) in the south-east of the country where Kurds are the majority population. The leader of the PKK. Abdullah Öcalan was captured by Turkish authorities in February 1999 in Kenya and returned to Turkey to stand trial, where he was found guilty of treason on 31 May and sentenced to death on 29 June 1999. The Turkish government announced on 12 January 2000 that it would suspend the execution, pending an appeal. The PKK announced on 8 February

2000 that it had renounced violence and removed the word 'Kurdistan', which is illegal in Turkey, from its title.

## Political System

A new constitution, extending the powers of the president, was approved in 1982. It provided for the separation of powers between the legislature, executive and judiciary, and the holding of free elections to the unicameral Grand National Assembly, which now has 550 members elected every five years.

Turkey is divided for administrative purposes into 81 *il* with subdivisions into *ilçe* and *nahiye*. Each *il* has a governor (*vali*) and elective council.

## Head of State

*President*, Ahmet Necdet Sezer, *elected by parliament for a seven-year term* 5 May 2000, *took office* 16 May 2000

## Cabinet *as at September 2001*

*Prime Minister*, Bülent Ecevit (DSP)
*Deputy Prime Minister, EU Relations*, Mesut Yilmaz (ANAP)
*Deputy Prime Ministers, Ministers of State*, Devlet Bahçeli (MHP); Hasan Hüsamettin Özkan (DSP)
*Ministers of State*, Mustafa Yılmaz (DSP); Şükrü Sina Gürel (DSP); Fikret Ünlü (DSP); Hasan Gemici (DSP); Mehmet Keçeciler (ANAP); Yılmaz Karakoyunlu (ANAP); Nejat Arseven (ANAP); Tunca Toskay (MHP); Faruk Bal (MHP); Ramazan Mirzaoğlu (MHP); Edip Safter Gaydalı (ANAP); Şuayip Üşenmez (MHP); Abdulhaluk Çay (MHP); Recep Önal (DSP); Kemal Derviş *(Economy)*
*Agriculture and Village Affairs*, Hüsnü Yusuf Gökalp (MHP)
*Culture*, Mustafa İstemihan Talay (DSP)
*Energy and Natural Resources*, Zeki Çakan (ANAP)
*Environment*, Fevzi Aytekin (DSP)
*Finance*, Sümer Oral (ANAP)
*Foreign Affairs*, İsmail Cem (DSP)
*Forestry*, İbrahim Nami Çağan (DSP)
*Health*, Osman Durmuş (MHP)
*Interior*, Rüştü Kazım Yücelen (ANAP)
*Justice*, Hikmet Sami Türk (DSP)
*Labour and Social Security*, Yaşar Okuyan (ANAP)
*National Defence*, Sabahattin Çakmakoğlu (MHP)
*National Education*, Metin Bostancıoğlu (DSP)
*Public Works and Housing*, vacant
*Tourism*, Mustafa Taşar (ANAP)
*Trade and Industry*, *Transport* (*acting*), Ahmet Kenan Tanrıkulu (MHP)

ANAP Motherland Party; DSP Democratic Left Party; MHP Nationalist Action Party

## Turkish Embassy

43 Belgrave Square, London SW1X 8PA
Tel: 020-7393 0202
*Ambassador Extraordinary and Plenipotentiary*, HE Korkmaz Haktanır, apptd 2000
*Minister Counsellor*, Irfan Acar

## British Embassy

Şehit Ersan Caddesi 46/A, Çankaya, Ankara
Tel: (00 90) (312) 455 3344
E-mail: britembank@fco.gov.uk

*Ambassador Extraordinary and Plenipotentiary*, HE David Logan, KCMG, apptd 1997
*Counsellor, Deputy Head of Mission*, D. Fitton
*Counsellor (Commercial)*, C. Innes-Hopkins
*Defence and Military Attaché*, Brig. K. Winfield
*Consul-General (Istanbul)*, R. Short, CMG

Consulate-General – Istanbul
Consulate – Izmir
Honorary Consulates – Antalya, Bodrum, Marmaris, Mersin

British Council Director, Ray Thomas, Esat Caddesi No: 41, Kucukesat, TR-06660 Ankara; e-mail: bc.ankara@britishcouncil.org.tr. Regional offices in Istanbul and Izmir

British Chamber of Commerce of Turkey Inc., Mesrutiyet Caddessi No. 18, Ashhan Kat. 6, Tepebasi/ Beyoglu, TR-80050 Istanbul

## DEFENCE

The Army has 4,205 main battle tanks, 3,643 armoured personnel carriers, 650 armoured infantry fighting vehicles and 37 attack helicopters. The Navy has 14 submarines, 22 frigates, 49 patrol and coastal vessels and 16 armed helicopters at eight bases. The Air Force has 505 combat aircraft.

Between 150,000 and 200,000 troops are stationed in the south-east of the country to prevent Kurdish insurgency.

Since its invasion of Cyprus in 1974, Turkey has maintained forces in the north of the island and at present has about 36,000 men stationed there.

As a member of NATO, Turkey is host to the Headquarters Allied Land Forces South-Eastern Europe and the Sixth Allied Tactical Air Force Headquarters. US (2,040 personnel) and UK (160 personnel) air force detachments are based at Incirlik air base in southern Turkey to patrol the air exclusion zone over northern Iraq.
Military Expenditure – 5.5 per cent of GDP (1999)
Military Personnel – 609,700: Army 495,000, Navy 54,600, Air Force 60,100; Paramilitaries 220,200
Conscription Duration – 18 months

## ECONOMY

Agricultural production accounted for 14.4 per cent of GDP in 2000. About 40 per cent of the working population is employed in agriculture. The principal crops are wheat, barley, rice, tobacco, sugar beet, tea, olives, grapes, figs and hazelnuts. Most of the crops are grown on the fertile littoral. Tobacco, sultana and fig cultivation is centred around Izmir, where substantial quantities of cotton are also grown. The main cotton area is in the Cukurova plain around Adana.

The main export minerals are chromite and boron. Tourism is a major industry, with over 7.5 million visitors in 1999.

The bulk of the country's requirements in sugar, cotton, woollen and silk textiles, and cement, is produced locally. Other industries include vehicle assembly, paper, glass and glassware, iron and steel, leather and leather goods, sulphur refining, canning and rubber goods, soaps and cosmetics, pharmaceutical products, and prepared food-stuffs.

A customs union with the EU came into force on 1 January 1996 which was expected to boost the economy, although Greece has managed to suspend EU aid packages. A gas deal worth £14,800 million was signed with Iran in August 1996 which provided for a 20-year supply of Iranian gas.

Turkey was accepted as a candidate for EU membership in December 1999.

Following a banking crisis in December 2000 in which ten banks had to be taken into state ownership, the IMF authorised US$7,500 million in new loans to Turkey in 2001, in addition to the US$2,900 million already agreed.

A public row between the president and the prime minister concerning allegations of corruption within the Cabinet led to a financial crisis on 22-23 February 2001, in which interest rates rose and the lira fell by 36 per cent against the US dollar. An economic recovery plan was unveiled in March 2001, which envisaged restructuring the country's banking system and privatising indebted state industries, beginning with Türk Telekom and Turkish Airlines. In May, the IMF authorised US$15,700 million of loans to Turkey.

GNP – US$201,188 million (2000); US$2,986 per capita (2000)
GDP – US$183,314 million (1999); US$2,807 per capita (1999)
ANNUAL AVERAGE GROWTH OF GDP – 7.2 per cent (2000)
INFLATION RATE – 37.5 per cent (2001)
UNEMPLOYMENT – 6.3 per cent (2000)
TOTAL EXTERNAL DEBT – US$114,324 million (2000)

### TRADE

The main imports are machinery, crude oil and petroleum products, iron and steel, vehicles, medicines, chemicals and electrical appliances. Agricultural commodities (cotton, tobacco, fruits, nuts, livestock) represented 13.9 per cent of total exports in 2000. Other exports are minerals, textiles, glass and cement. Germany, the USA and Italy are the main trading partners.

In 2000 Turkey had a trade deficit of US$26,728 million and a current account deficit of US$9,819 million. Imports totalled US$54,503 million and exports US$27,775 million.

| *Trade with UK* | 1999 | 2000 |
|---|---|---|
| Imports from UK | £1,253,992,000 | £1,858,018,000 |
| Exports to UK | 1,279,905,000 | 1,519,103,000 |

### COMMUNICATIONS

The rail network is run by the State Railways Administration. There are about 10,933 km of railway track and 62,672 km of state highways, including 1,749 km of motorways. There are 156 ports. The Bosporus is spanned by two bridges; plans are being drawn up for a third fixed link between the two continents. The state airline (THY) operates all internal services.

### EDUCATION

Education is free and secular, and since August 1997, compulsory from the ages of six to 14. There are elementary, secondary and vocational schools. There are 69 universities in Turkey.

ILLITERACY RATE – 14.8 per cent (2000)
ENROLMENT (percentage of age group) – primary 91 per cent (1998); secondary 50 per cent (1998); tertiary 21 per cent (1998)

### CULTURE

Turkish is a Ural-Altaic language. Turkish was written in Arabic script until 1928 when a version of the Roman alphabet reflecting Turkish phonetics was adopted.

---

## TURKMENISTAN
*Turkmenostan Respublikasy*

---

AREA – 188,456 sq. miles (488,100 sq. km). Neighbours: Iran and Afghanistan (south), Uzbekistan (east and north), Kazakhstan (north-west)
POPULATION – 3,808,900 (2000 estimate); 4,483,000 (1996 census): 77 per cent Turkmen, 9.2 per cent Uzbek, 6.7 per cent Russian, together with smaller numbers of Kazakhs, Tatars, Ukrainians and Armenians. Most of the population are Sunni Muslims. The main languages are Turkmen (72 per cent), Russian (9 per cent), Uzbek (9 per cent). Turkmen is one of the Turkic languages
CAPITAL Ashgabat (population, 407,000, 1990)
MAJOR CITIES – Chardzhou (164,000); Tashauz (114,000), 1990
CURRENCY – Manat of 100 tenge
NATIONAL DAY – 27–28 October (Independence Day)
NATIONAL FLAG – Green with a vertical carpet pattern near the hoist in black, white and wine-red; and in the lower part of the carpet design two laurel branches; in the upper hoist a crescent and five stars, all in white
LIFE EXPECTANCY (years) – male 61.0; female 65.3
POPULATION GROWTH RATE – 2.0 per cent (1999)
POPULATION DENSITY – 10 per sq. km (1998)
URBAN POPULATION – 44.8 per cent (2000 estimate)
MILITARY EXPENDITURE – 3.3 per cent of GDP (1999)
MILITARY PERSONNEL – 17,500: Army 14,500, Air Force 3,000
CONSCRIPTION DURATION – 24 months
ILLITERACY RATE – 2.3 per cent
ENROLMENT (percentage of age group) – tertiary 21.7 per cent (1990)

The republic comprises five regions: Ashgabat; Chardzhou; Krasnovodsk; Mary; and Tashauz. The country is a low-lying plain fringed by hills in the south. Ninety per cent of the plain is taken up by the Obe Kara-Kum (Black Sands) desert. The climate is hot and dry.

### HISTORY AND POLITICS

Situated at the crossroads of Central Asia, the area that is now Turkmenistan has been invaded and occupied by many empires: Persian; Greek under Alexander the Great; Parthian; Mongol. From the early 19th century until 1886 Turkmenistan was gradually incorporated into the Russian Empire. Soviet control over Turkmenistan was established on 30 April 1918 when it became an Autonomous Soviet Socialist Republic. Turkmenistan became a full republic of the Soviet Union in February 1925.

Turkmenistan declared its independence from the Soviet Union on 27 October 1991 and gained UN membership on 2 March 1992.

The autocratic government of President Niyazov has prevented any effective political opposition or free press through harassment and the continuation of authoritarianism. The political leadership has rejected political pluralism and instead a cult of personality has developed around President Niyazov. The Supreme Soviet voted on 30 December 1993 to extend the term of President

Niyazov to 2002 and this was confirmed by a 99.99 per cent vote in a referendum on 15 January 1994. On 28 December 1999, the legislature removed the limit on his term of office, effectively making him life president. The Communist Party, renamed the Democratic Party (DP), remains in power. Legislative elections to the *Khalk Maslakhaty* held on 5 April 1998 were won by the Democratic Party. General elections were held on 12 December 1999, in which all 50 seats in the *Majlis* were won by candidates of the DP, the sole legal party.

### FOREIGN RELATIONS

In 1992 joint Turkmen–Russian armed forces of 34,000 army and air force personnel were established and remain in operation. In late 1993 Turkmen–Russian agreements were signed allowing Russian troops to protect the borders with Iran and Afghanistan, Russian citizens to undergo military training in Turkmenistan, Turkmen officers to train in Russia, and Turkmenistan to bear the cost of Russian forces in the country. Agreement on dual citizenship for ethnic Russians in Turkmenistan was also reached. In December 1993 Turkmenistan signed the CIS charter to become a full CIS member and in January 1994 became a member of the CIS economic union.

### POLITICAL SYSTEM

The 1992 constitution declares the president head of state and government. The legislature is the 50-member *Majlis* (formerly the Supreme Soviet). The *Khalk Maslakhaty* (People's Council) is a supervisory body with no legislative powers. The *Majlis* approved an amendment to the constitution on 28 December 1999, allowing President Niyazov to remain in power indefinitely.

### HEAD OF STATE

*President*, Saparmurad Niyazov, *elected* 27 October 1990, *re-elected* 21 June 1992, *appointed head of government* 18 May 1992, *elected by referendum for an eight-year term* 15 January 1994, *term extended indefinitely* 28 December 1999

### COUNCIL OF MINISTERS *as at September 2001*

*Prime Minister*, The President
*Deputy Prime Ministers*, Rejep Saparov (*Agriculture*); Berdymurad Rezhdepov (*Communications and Transport*); Muhammetnazar Hudaygulyyev (*Construction and Construction Materials Industry*); Gurbanberdy Begendzhov (*Defence*); vacant (*Economy and Finance*); Amangeldi Atayev (*Energy and Industry*); Gurbanguli Berdymuhamedov (*Health and the Pharmaceutical Industry*); Yolly Gurbanmuradov; Seitbay Gandimov (*Interbank Council*); Djamal Geklenova (*Textile Industry*)
*Chairmen*, Muhamed Nazarov (*Committee for National Security*); Nepesov Arslan Sakoyevich (*Committee for Tourism and Sports*); Tirkish Tyrmyev (*State Border Service*); Seyitguly Chareyev (*State Committee for Land Use and Land Reform*); Ilyas Mahtumovich Chariyev (*State Commodity and Raw Materials Exchange*); Ovezgeldy Atayev (*Supreme Court*)
*Culture*, Orazgeldi Aydogdiyev
*Education*, Annagurban Ashirov
*Foreign Affairs*, Rashid Meredov
*General Public Prosecutor*, Kurbanbibi Atadjanova
*Interior*, Maj.-Gen. Poran Berdiev
*Justice*, Gen. Gurbanmuhamed Kasimov
*Natural Resources and Environmental Protection*, Matkarim Rajapov
*Oil and Gas Industry and Mineral Resources*, Gurban Nazarov
*Social Security*, Enebay Ataeva
*Trade and Foreign Economic Relations*, Dortguly Aidogdyev
*Water Resources*, Gurbangeldi Velmyradov

### EMBASSY OF TURKMENISTAN

2nd Floor South, St George's House, 14/17 Wells Street, London W1P 3FP
Tel: 020-7255 1071
*Ambassador Extraordinary and Plenipotentiary*, HE Chary Babaev, apptd 1999

### BRITISH EMBASSY

3rd Floor, Office Building, Four Points Ak Altin Hotel, Ashgabat
Tel: (00 993) (12) 510616/510861/510862
E-mail: beasb@online.tm
*Ambassador Extraordinary and Plenipotentiary*, HE Fraser Wilson, MBE, apptd 1998

## ECONOMY

The large reserves of natural gas and the foreign revenue that they earn make the country economically viable and have enabled the government to maintain low stable prices for basic commodities and utilities.

The principal industries are cotton cultivation, stock-raising and mineral extraction, together with natural gas production and the long-established silk industry. Some fisheries exist along the Caspian Sea coast. Arable land is irrigated by the Niyazov canal, which cuts through the Kara Kum desert. There are estimated reserves of some 700 million tonnes of oil and 8,000,000 million cubic metres of natural gas. Natural gas is exported by pipeline to Ukraine and western Europe. A pipeline through Iran and Turkey was opened in 1997, and a pipeline to Pakistan is under construction. Agreement on building a further pipeline under the Caspian Sea, through Azerbaijan and Georgia, to supply gas to Turkey was reached in November 1999. In 1997 there was a trade deficit of US$231 million and a current account deficit of US$580 million.

GNP – US$3,205 million (1999); US$660 per capita (1999)
GDP – US$796 million (1997); US$582 per capita (1998)
ANNUAL AVERAGE GROWTH OF GDP – 3.0 per cent (1996)
TOTAL EXTERNAL DEBT – US$2,266 million (1998)

| Trade with UK | 1999 | 2000 |
|---|---|---|
| Imports from UK | £16,139,000 | £9,335,000 |
| Exports to UK | 2,763,000 | 2,807,000 |

## TUVALU

AREA – 10 sq. miles (26 sq. km)
POPULATION – 10,000 (1997 UN estimate). About 1,500 Tuvaluans work overseas, mostly in Nauru, or as seamen. The people are almost entirely Polynesian. The principal languages are Tuvaluan and English. A large majority of the population is Christian, predominantly Protestant
CAPITAL – ΨFongafale (population, 2,856)
CURRENCY – The Australian dollar ($A) of 100 cents is legal tender. In addition there are Tuvalu dollar and cent coins in circulation
NATIONAL ANTHEM – Tuvalu Mo Te Atua (Tuvalu for the Almighty)
NATIONAL DAY – 1 October (Independence Day)
NATIONAL FLAG – Light blue ground with Union flag in top left quarter and nine five-pointed gold stars in the fly
LIFE EXPECTANCY (years) – male 63.9; female 65.5
POPULATION GROWTH RATE – 2.8 per cent (1999)
POPULATION DENSITY – 428 per sq. km (1998)
URBAN POPULATION – 52.2 per cent (2000 estimate)

Tuvalu comprises nine coral atolls situated in the south-west Pacific around the point at which the International Date Line cuts the Equator. Few of the atolls are more than 12 ft above sea level or more than half a mile in width. The vegetation consists mainly of coconut palms.

## HISTORY AND POLITICS

Tuvalu, formerly the Ellice Islands, formed part of the Gilbert and Ellice Islands Colony until 1 October 1975, when separate constitutions came into force. Separation from the Gilbert Islands was implemented on 1 January 1976. On 1 October 1978 Tuvalu became a fully independent state within the Commonwealth.

In April 1998, Prime Minister Bikenibeu Paeniu was sworn in for a second term of office; he was forced to resign following his defeat in a motion of no confidence on 15 April 1999 and on 27 April was succeeded by Ionatana Ionatana.

Following the death of Ionatana Ionatana on 8 December 2000, Faimalaga Luka was chosen to replace him as prime minister on 23 February 2001.

Tuvalu became a full member of the UN on 17 February 2000.

### POLITICAL SYSTEM

The constitution provides for a prime minister and four other ministers, who must be members of the 13-member parliament, 12 of whom are directly elected. The prime minister presides at meetings of the Cabinet, which consists of the five Ministers and is attended by the Attorney-General. Local government services are provided by elected Island Councils.

*Governor-General*, Sir Tomasi Puapua

### CABINET *as at September 2001*

*Prime Minister, Home Affairs and Rural Development, Natural Resources and Environment*, Faimalaga Luka
*Attorney-General*, Teleti Teo
*Education, Sports and Culture, Health, Women's and Community Affairs*, Teagai Esekia
*Foreign Affairs, Tourism, Trade, Commerce, Finance and Economic Planning*, Lagitupu Tuilimu
*Works, Energy and Communications*, Samuelu Penitala Teo

### HONORARY CONSULATE OF TUVALU

Tuvalu House, 230 Worple Road, London SW20 8RH
Tel: 020-8879 0985
*Honorary Consul*, Iftikhar Ayaz

BRITISH HIGH COMMISSIONER, HE Michael Price, LVO, resident at Suva, Fiji

## ECONOMY

Most people still practise a subsistence economy, the main staples of the diet being coconuts and fish. The main imports are foodstuffs, semi-manufactures, machinery and transport equipment and fuels. The main exports are copra and fish, though philatelic sales provide a major source of revenue and handicraft sales are increasing. However, Tuvalu is almost entirely dependent on foreign aid. In August 1998, Tuvalu signed a deal worth about US$50 million over ten years with a US media company, granting rights to use the country's internet suffix of '.tv'.

Funafuti has an airfield from which a service operates regularly to Fiji and Kiribati, and is also the only port.

GDP – US$14 million (1997); US$1,215 per capita (1998)
ANNUAL AVERAGE GROWTH OF GDP – 2.6 per cent (1996)

| *Trade with UK* | 1999 | 2000 |
|---|---|---|
| Imports from UK | £51,000 | £328,000 |
| Exports to UK | 33,000 | 4,000 |

## SOCIAL WELFARE

All islands are served by a dispensary and a primary school. A maritime training school caters for 60 boys a year. There is a 30-bed hospital at Funafuti.

---

## UGANDA
*Republic of Uganda*

---

AREA – 93,065 sq. miles (241,038 sq. km). Neighbours: Democratic Republic of Congo (west), Sudan (north), Kenya (east), Tanzania and Rwanda (south)
POPULATION – 21,479,000 (1997 UN estimate): 17 per cent Baganda, 12 per cent Karamojong; many other ethnic groups including Basogo, Iteso, Langi, Rwanda, Bagisu, Acholi, Lugbara, Bunyoro and Batobo. The official language is English. The main local vernaculars are of Bantu, Nilotic and Hamitic origins. Ki-Swahili is generally understood
CAPITAL – Kampala (population, 750,000, 1990)
MAJOR CITIES – Jinja (45,000); Masaka (29,000); Mbale (28,000)
CURRENCY – Uganda shilling of 100 cents
NATIONAL ANTHEM – Oh Uganda
NATIONAL DAY – 9 October (Independence Day)
NATIONAL FLAG – Six horizontal stripes of black, yellow, red, with a white disc in the centre containing the badge of a crested crane
LIFE EXPECTANCY (years) – male 41.9; female 42.4
POPULATION GROWTH RATE – 2.8 per cent (1999)
POPULATION DENSITY – 87 per sq. km (1998)
URBAN POPULATION – 14.2 per cent (2000 estimate)
MILITARY EXPENDITURE – 2.5 per cent of GDP (1999)
MILITARY PERSONNEL – 50,000: Ugandan People's Defence Force 50,000, Paramilitaries 1,800

Large parts of Lakes Victoria, Edward and Albert (Mobuto) are within Uganda's boundaries, as are Lakes Kyoga, Kwania, George and Bisina (formerly Salisbury) and the course of the River Nile from its outlet from Lake Victoria to the Sudan border at Nimule.

Despite its tropical location, the climate is tempered by its situation some 3,000 ft above sea level, and well over that altitude in the highlands of the Western and Eastern Regions. Uganda has three National Parks and a fourth (Lake Mburo) has been designated.

## HISTORY AND POLITICS

Uganda became an independent state within the Commonwealth on 9 October 1962, after some 70 years of British rule. A republic was instituted in 1967.

In 1971 an army coup took place and Maj.-Gen. Idi Amin, the army commander, proclaimed himself head of state. In 1979, following uprisings and military intervention by Tanzania, President Amin was overthrown. Dr Milton Obote became president in 1980 but was ousted by a military coup in 1985. A military council was installed but the National Resistance Movement led by Yoweri Museveni captured Kampala in January 1986, securing control of the rest of the country in the following few months. Yoweri Museveni was sworn in as president in January 1986.

President Museveni won the first direct presidential election on 9 May 1996. Supporters of the president won a majority of seats in legislative elections on 27 June. The ban on political party activity introduced by President Museveni in 1986, was endorsed in a referendum held on 29 June 2000, in which 90.7 per cent of those voting backed the continuation of the no party 'Movement' system, in which political parties were allowed to exist, but not to contest elections.

President Museveni was re-elected on 12 March 2001, winning 69.3 per cent of the vote. Nemgroup, the country's non-governmental election monitoring group, found various irregularities, but ruled that these had not been of sufficient magnitude to affect the outcome. A general election was held on 26 June in which most seats were won by supporters of the no party 'Movement' system.

### Political System

A Constituent Assembly was elected in March 1994 to draft a new constitution. The constitution, promulgated on 8 October 1995, endorsed the existing non-party political system. The president, who is head of government, is directly elected for a five-year term. The legislature, the 276-seat National Assembly, is also directly elected for a five-year term; 214 members are elected by constituencies and 62 are elected indirectly to represent particular groups.

### Head of State

*President*, Yoweri Museveni, *sworn in* 29 January 1986, *elected* 9 May 1996, *re-elected* 12 March 2001
*Vice-President*, Specioza Wandira Kazibwe

### Cabinet *as at September 2001*

The President
The Vice-President
*Prime Minister*, Apollo Nsibambi
*First Deputy Prime Minister, Internal Affairs*, Eriya Kategaya
*Second Deputy Prime Minister, Disaster Preparedness*, Brig. Moses Ali
*Third Deputy Prime Minister, Foreign Affairs*, James Wambogo Wapakhabulo
*Minister in the Office of the Prime Minister*, George Mondo Kagonyera
*Ministers in the Office of the President*, Kweronda Ruhemba (*Economic Monitoring*); Miria Matembe (*Ethics and Integrity*); Basoga Nsadhu (*Information*); Elizabeth Okwir (*Office of the Vice-President*); Ruhakana Rugunda (*Presidency*)
*Agriculture, Animal Industry and Fisheries*, Kisamba Mugwera
*Attorney-General*, Francis Ayume
*Defence*, Amama Mbabazi
*Disaster Preparedness and Refugees*, Maj. Tom Butiime
*Education and Sports*, Kiddu Makubuya
*Energy and Minerals*, Syda Bbumba
*Finance, Planning and Economic Development*, Gerald Sendawula
*Gender*, Zoe Bakoko-Bakoru
*Health*, Jim Katugogu Muhwezi
*Justice and Constitutional Affairs*, Janet Mukwaya
*Local Government*, Jaberi Bidandi-Ssalli
*Parliamentary Affairs*, Rebecca Kadaga
*Presidency*, Gilbert Balibaseka Bokenya
*Public Service*, Henry Muganwa Kajura
*Tourism, Trade and Industry*, Edward Rugumayo
*Water, Lands and Environment*, Ruhakana Rugunda
*Works, Housing and Communications*, John Nassasira

### Uganda High Commission

Uganda House, 58–59 Trafalgar Square, London WC2N 5DX
Tel: 020-7839 5783
*High Commissioner*, HE Prof. George Kirya, apptd 1990
*Counsellor*, D. Nyakairu
*First Secretary*, A. Kafeero
Financial Attaché, *A. Bamweyana*

### British High Commission

10–12 Parliament Avenue, PO Box 7070, Kampala
Tel: (00 256) (41) 257054/9
E-mail: bhcinfo@starcom.co.ug
*High Commissioner*, HE Tom Phillips, CMG, apptd 2000
*Deputy High Commissioner*, C. Skilton
*Defence Adviser*, Lt.-Col. C. Thom, OBE

British Council Director, Sue Beaumont *(First Secretary)*, IPS Building, Parliament Avenue, PO Box 7070, Kampala;
e-mail: bc.kampala@britishcouncil.or.ug

## ECONOMY

Since 1988 the government has been successfully implementing an IMF recovery programme. In December 1998, the IMF pledged US$2.2 billion in economic assistance over a three-year period. On 8 February 2000, the IMF pledged a further US$139 million in debt relief, and the International Development Association (IDA) announced that it would give assistance of US$629 million over 20 years. In March, donor countries pledged at least US$2,000 million over three years to support economic development.

The principal export earners are coffee, tobacco, cotton and tea. Hydroelectricity is produced from the Owen Falls power station, some of which is exported to Kenya, Tanzania and Rwanda. The principal food crops are plantains, sugar cane, cassava, maize and sorghum; livestock raising and inshore fishing are also important.

In 1997 Uganda had a trade deficit of US$467 million and a current account deficit of US$388 million. In 1999 imports totalled US$1,341 million and exports US$517 million.

GNP – US$6,794 million (1999); US$320 per capita (1999)
GDP – US$6,258 million (1997); US$347 per capita (1998)
Annual Average Growth of GDP – 5.9 per cent (1996)
Inflation Rate – 6.4 per cent (1999)
Total External Debt – US$3,935 million (1998)

| *Trade with UK* | 1999 | 2000 |
|---|---|---|
| Imports from UK | £37,192,000 | £37,761,000 |
| Exports to UK | 10,706,000 | 9,190,000 |

## COMMUNICATIONS

There is an international airport at Entebbe, and eight other airfields around the country. Having no sea coast, Uganda is dependent upon rail and road links to Mombasa and Dar es Salaam for its trade. There are 1,241 km of railways and 27,000 km of roads, of which only 1,800 km are paved.

## EDUCATION

Education is a joint undertaking by the government, local authorities and voluntary agencies. In 1995 Uganda had an estimated 7,905 primary schools, 774 secondary schools, and various technical training institutions and universities. In 1996, the Universal Primary Programme was launched, under which four children per family are entitled to receive free primary education.

Illiteracy Rate – 32.7 per cent (2000)
Enrolment (percentage of age group) – tertiary 1.9 per cent (1996)

## UKRAINE
*Ukraïna*

AREA – 233,090 sq. miles (603,700 sq. km). Neighbours: Belarus (north), Russia (north and east), Romania and Moldova (south-west), Hungary, Slovakia and Poland (west)
POPULATION – 49,908,000 (2000 estimate); 51,471,000 (1989 census): 73 per cent Ukrainian, 22 per cent Russian, with smaller numbers of Jews, Belarusians, Moldovans, Tatars, Poles, Hungarians and Greeks. The majority religion is Orthodox Christianity. There are also large numbers of Uniates and Reformed Protestants in the Transcarpathian region and a sizeable Jewish community in Kiev. The official language is Ukrainian. Russian is the language of 22 per cent of the population
CAPITAL – Kiev (Kyiv) (population, 2,620,900, 1998 estimate)
MAJOR CITIES – Dnipropetrovsk (1,122,400); Donetsk (1,065,400); Kharkiv (1,521,400); Lviv (793,700), ΨOdesa (1,027,400), Zaporizhzhya (863,100), 1998 estimates
CURRENCY – Hryvna of 100 kopiykas
NATIONAL ANTHEM - Shche ne vmerla, Ukraïna (Thou hast not perished, Ukraine)
NATIONAL DAY – 24 August (Independence Day)
NATIONAL FLAG – Two horizontal stripes of blue over yellow
LIFE EXPECTANCY (years) – male 64.4; female 74.4
POPULATION GROWTH RATE – 0.3 per cent (1999)
POPULATION DENSITY – 84 per sq. km (1998)
URBAN POPULATION – 68.0 per cent (2000 estimate)
ILLITERACY RATE – 1.2 per cent
ENROLMENT (percentage of age group) – tertiary 41.7 per cent (1996)

Ukraine consists of 24 regions (Cherkasy, Chernihiv, Chernivtsi, Dnipropetrovsk, Donetsk, Ivano-Frankivsk, Kharkiv, Kherson, Khmelnytsky, Kyiv, Kirovohrad, Luhansk, Lviv, Mykolaïv, Odesa, Poltava, Rivne, Sumy, Ternopil, Transcarpathia, Vinnitsa, Volyn, Zaporizhya and Zhytomyr) and the Autonomous Republic of Crimea.

Most of Ukraine forms a plain with small elevations. The Carpathian mountains lie in the south-western part of the republic. The main rivers are the Dnieper with its tributaries, the Southern Bug and the Northern Donets (a tributary of the Don). The climate is temperate continental with a Mediterranean climate in the south of the Crimean Peninsula.

## HISTORY AND POLITICS

The earliest Slavic state was formed in the middle reaches of the Dnieper River with its capital at Kyiv in the ninth century AD. The state lasted until Kyiv fell to the Tatar-Mongols in 1240. For the next four centuries Ukraine was invaded and ruled by Poles and Lithuanians. Kyiv was liberated from the Poles in 1648 and in 1654 Ukraine became a protectorate of Russia.

Ukraine declared its independence in 1918, but was invaded by Poland in 1919 before becoming a constituent republic of the USSR on 30 December 1922.

Ukraine declared itself independent of the Soviet Union on 24 August 1991. Independence was confirmed by a referendum held on 1 December 1991 and Leonid Kravchuk was elected to the presidency.

In the June 1994 presidential election Leonid Kuchma defeated President Kravchuk.

In legislative elections held in March 1998, the Communist Party of Ukraine won 119 seats, well short of an overall majority, but making it the largest party in the legislature. The Popular Democratic Party won 84 seats, and the People's Movement of Ukraine 46. OSCE observers voiced concerns at serious shortcomings in the electoral process.

President Kuchma won a second term of office in a presidential election on 14 November 1999, receiving 56.25 per cent of the vote.

In January 2000, the Supreme Council split into two factions following a failed attempt by the pro-government faction to remove the Speaker, Oleksandr Tkachenko, from office. The minority left-wing faction remained in control of the Supreme Council building until the pro-government majority faction forcibly took control of the Supreme Council building on 8 February 2000.

### INSURGENCIES

A pro-Russian majority in the Crimean parliament voted to make Crimea an autonomous republic in September 1991, which was accepted by Ukraine, but then voted for independence, which was not accepted, and the declaration of independence was rescinded in May 1992. Elections to the Crimean parliament in August 1995 saw a dramatic drop in support for pro-Russian parties. Arkady Demydenko was appointed Prime Minister of Crimea on 26 February 1996. A new constitution, which gave Crimea property and budget rights, came into effect in January 1999.

A referendum in June 1994 in the Donbass region of eastern Ukraine in favour of closer economic ties with Russia and making Russian an official language was overwhelmingly passed, as was one in the Crimea in favour of dual Russian–Ukrainian citizenship.

### FOREIGN RELATIONS

Since the demise of the Soviet Union, Russia and Ukraine have clashed over defence issues.

Under a January 1994 USA–Russia–Ukraine Treaty, Ukraine agreed to transfer its nuclear arsenal to Russia for dismantling, which was completed in May 1996. In return Ukraine received a territorial guarantee from Russia, a cancellation of a large part of its debt to Russia, and nuclear security guarantees from Russia and the USA.

In May 1997, a treaty of friendship and co-operation was signed with Russia. Agreement was also reached over the division of the former Soviet Black Sea Fleet.

In February 1998, a treaty on economic co-operation was signed between Ukraine and Russia which aimed to strengthen industrial and commercial links and move towards the introduction of the free movement of goods, services, capital and labour.

Ukraine signed a partnership and co-operation agreement with the EU in June 1994 and in July 1997 signed the NATO-Ukraine Charter to enhance co-operation on peacekeeping.

### POLITICAL SYSTEM

The unicameral Supreme Council has 450 members, who serve a four-year term. Half of the seats in the Supreme Council are elected from single-seat constituencies by a simple majority, and the other 225 are to be filled by proportional representation from party lists, with a 4 per cent threshold for representation. A member may only be elected if the turnout in the electoral district is above 50 per cent.

### HEAD OF STATE

*President*, Leonid Kuchma, *elected* 10 July 1994, *sworn in* 19 July 1994, *re-elected* 14 November 1999

### CABINET *as at September 2001*

*Prime Minister*, Anatoliy Kinakh
*First Deputy Prime Minister*, Oleh Dubyna

*First Deputy Prime Minister for Economic Issues*, Vasyl Rohovyy
*Deputy Prime Ministers*, Leonid Kozachenko; Volodymyr Semynozhenko
*Agriculture*, Ivan Kyrylenko
*Culture and Art*, Yuriy Bohutskiy
*Defence*, Gen. Oleksandr Kuzmuk
*Economy*, Oleksandr Shlapak
*Education and Science*, Vasyl Kremen
*Emergency Situations and Protection of the Population from the aftermath of Chernobyl*, Vasyl Durdanynets
*Energy and Fuel*, Stanislav Stashevskiy
*Environment and Natural Resources*, Serhiy Kurykin
*Finance*, Ihor Mityukov
*Foreign Affairs*, Anatoliy Zlenko
*Government Secretary*, Volodymyr Yatsuba
*Health Protection*, Vitaliy Moskalenko
*Industrial Policy*, Vasyl Hureyev
*Interior*, Yuriy Smirnov
*Justice*, Syuzanna Stanik
*Labour and Social Policy*, Ivan Sakhan
*Transport*, Valeriy Pustovoytenko

There are also 11 heads of state committees.

UKRAINIAN EMBASSY
60 Holland Park, London W11 3SJ
Tel: 020-7727 6312
E-mail: emb_gb@mfa.gov.ua
*Ambassador Extraordinary and Plenipotentiary*, HE Volodymyr Vassylenko, apptd 1998
*Minister Plenipotentiary*, I. Prokopchuk*Defence Attaché*, Col. O. Chornohuz

BRITISH EMBASSY
UA-01018 Kyiv Desyatinna 9
Tel: (00 380) (44) 462 0011/2/4
E-mail: ukembinf@sovam.com
*Ambassador Extraordinary and Plenipotentiary*, HE Roland Smith, CMG, apptd 1999
*Consul-General and Deputy Head of Mission*, D. Maclaren
*Defence Attaché*, Capt. R. Drewett, MBE
*First Secretary (Commercial)*, R. Cook

BRITISH COUNCIL DIRECTOR - Liliana Biglou, 4/12 Vul. Hryhoriya Skovorody, UA-04070 Kyiv; e-mail: enquiry@britishcouncil.org.ua. There are regional offices in Donetsk, Kharkiv, Lviv and Odesa

## DEFENCE

The Constitution bans the stationing of foreign troops on Ukrainian soil, but permits Russia to retain naval bases.

The Army has 3,895 main battle tanks, 1,770 armoured personnel carriers, 3,048 armoured infantry fighting vehicles and 247 attack helicopters. The Navy has one submarine, four principal surface combat vessels and ten patrol and coastal vessels at six bases. The Air Force has 911 combat aircraft.

MILITARY EXPENDITURE – 2.9 per cent of GDP (1999)
MILITARY PERSONNEL – 303,800: Army 151,200, Navy 13,000, Air Force 96,000, Paramilitaries 116,600
CONSCRIPTION DURATION – 18 months to two years

## ECONOMY

The Communist-led government of 1991–4 was characterised by economic mismanagement and opposition to economic reforms. Successive governments were unable to gain consensus for a reform programme, which delayed economic restructuring. Ukraine joined the CIS economic union as an associate member in 1993.

Since his election in 1999, President Kuchma has introduced a wide-ranging economic reform programme. Continuing economic difficulties led to the devaluation of the hryvna in February 1999. In March 2000, the IMF issued an interim statement about the alleged misuse of foreign currency reserves, saying that Ukraine had received IMF funds in 1997–8 that it would not have received had the true state of the country's reserves been known. The IMF has suspended its loan programme to Ukraine until investigations are completed.

Metal processing, the manufacture of machinery, and the chemical and petrochemical industries are major contributors to Ukraine's GDP; mining and metallurgy account for more than 40 per cent of exports. The southern part of the country contains a coal-mining and iron and steel industrial area. Ukraine also contains engineering and chemical industries and ship building yards on the Black Sea coast. Ukrainian agricultural production is good with large areas under cultivation with wheat, cotton, flax and sugar beet; stock-raising is very important. There are large deposits of coal and salt in the Donets Basin, of iron ore in Kryvyi Rih and near Kerch in the Crimea, of manganese in Nikopol, and of quicksilver in Nikitovka.

The major ports are Odesa, Mykolaïv, Kerch and Sevastopol.

Russia is the main trading partner, accounting for 24 per cent of exports and 41.7 per cent of imports in 2000. Turkey, Germany, the USA and Turkmenistan are also major trading partners.

In 1999 there was a trade deficit of US$482 million and a current account surplus of US$834 million. Imports totalled US$11,846 million and exports US$11,582 million.

GNP – US$41,991 million (1999); US$750 per capita (1999)
GDP – US$49,677 million (1997); US$823 per capita (1998)
ANNUAL AVERAGE GROWTH OF GDP – 50.5 per cent (2000)
INFLATION RATE – 18.9 per cent (2001)
UNEMPLOYMENT – 11.3 per cent (1998)
TOTAL EXTERNAL DEBT – US$12,718 million (1998)

| *Trade with UK* | 1999 | 2000 |
|---|---|---|
| Imports from UK | £145,449,000 | £154,670,000 |
| Exports to UK | 48,494,000 | 65,465,000 |

## UNITED ARAB EMIRATES
*Dawlat Al-Amārat Al-'Arabiyya Al-Muttahida*

AREA – 32,278 sq. miles (83,600 sq. km) approximately. Neighbours: Oman (north-east and east), Saudi Arabia (south and west), Qatar (north-west)
POPULATION – 2,815,000 (1999 estimate), of which 75 per cent are expatriates. The official language is Arabic, and English is widely spoken. The established religion is Islam
CAPITAL – Abu Dhabi (Abū Żaby) (population, 450,000)
CURRENCY – UAE dirham (Dh) of 100 fils
NATIONAL DAY – 2 December
NATIONAL FLAG – Horizontal stripes of green over white over black with vertical red stripe in the hoist
LIFE EXPECTANCY (years) – male 72.2; female 75.6
POPULATION GROWTH RATE – 2.5 per cent (1999)
POPULATION DENSITY – 33 per sq. km (1998)
URBAN POPULATION – 85.9 per cent (2000 estimate)

The United Arab Emirates is situated in the south-east of the Arabian peninsula. Six of the emirates lie on the shore of the Gulf between the Musandam peninsula in the east and the Qatar peninsula in the west while the seventh, Fujairah, lies on the Gulf of Oman. The climate varies between hot and humid in May to September and mild with erratic rainfall in October to April.

## HISTORY AND POLITICS

The United Arab Emirates (formerly the Trucial States) is composed of seven emirates (Abu Dhabi, Ajman, Dubai, Fujairah, Ras al-Khaimah, Sharjah and Umm al-Qaiwain) which came together as an independent state on 2 December 1971 when they ended their individual special treaty relationships with the British government (Ras al-Khaimah joined the other six on 10 February 1972). On independence, the Union Government assumed full responsibility for all internal and external affairs apart from some internal matters that remained the prerogative of the individual emirates.

### FOREIGN RELATIONS

Relations with Iran remain strained over Iran's illegal occupation of three UAE islands in the Gulf (Abu Musa and the Two Tunbs).

### POLITICAL SYSTEM

Overall authority lies with the Supreme Council of the seven emirate rulers, each of whom also governs in his own territory. The president and vice-president are elected every five years by the Supreme Council from among its members. The Supreme Council appoints the Council of Ministers. A 40-member Federal National Council, comprising eight members each from Abu Dhabi and Dubai, six each from Sharjah and Ras al-Khaimah and four each for Fujairah, Umm al-Qaiwain and Ajman, appointed by the rulers of each emirate, studies draft laws referred to it by the Council of Ministers.

The legal system consists of both secular and religious courts guided by the Islamic philosophy of justice. Individual emirates retain their own penal codes and courts alongside a federal court system and penal code.

### FEDERAL STRUCTURE

Each emirate has its separate government, with Abu Dhabi having an executive council chaired by the Crown Prince.

| *Emirate* | *Area (sq. km)* | *Population (1997)* |
|---|---|---|
| Abu Dhabi (Abū Żaby) | 67,340 | 1,017,000 |
| Ajman ('Ujman) | 259 | 137,000 |
| Dubai (Dubayy) | 3,885 | 757,000 |
| Fujairah (Al-Fujayrah) | 1,165 | 83,000 |
| Ras al-Khaimah (Ra's al-Khaymah) | 1,700 | 152,000 |
| Sharjah (Ash-Shariqah) | 2,590 | 439,000 |
| Umm al-Qaiwain (Umm al-Qaywayn) | 777 | 39,000 |

### HEAD OF STATE

*President*, HH Sheikh Zayed bin Sultan al-Nahyan (*Abu Dhabi*), *elected* 1971, *re-elected* 1976, 1981, 1986, 1991, 1996, April 2001 *Vice-President, Prime Minister*, HH Sheikh Maktoum bin Rashid al-Maktoum (*Dubai*)

### SUPREME COUNCIL

The President
The Vice-President
HH Sheikh Sultan bin Mohammed al-Qassimi (*Sharjah*)
HH Sheikh Saqr bin Mohammed al-Qassimi (*Ras Al-Khaimah*)
HH Sheikh Hamad bin Mohammed al-Sharqi (*Fujairah*)
HH Sheikh Humaid bin Rashid al-Nuaimi (*Ajman*)
HH Sheikh Rashid bin Ahmad al-Mualla (*Umm al-Qaiwain*)

### COUNCIL OF MINISTERS *as at September 2001*

The Vice-President
*Deputy Prime Minister*, Sheikh Sultan bin Zayed al-Nahyan
*Agriculture and Fisheries*, Saeed Mohammed al-Raqabani
*Communications*, Ahmed Humaid al-Tayir
*Defence*, HH Gen. Sheikh Mohammed bin Rashid al-Maktoum
*Economy and Commerce*, HH Sheikh Fahim bin Sultan al-Qassimi
*Education and Youth*, Ali Abd al-Aziz al-Sharhan
*Electricity and Water*, Humaid bin Nasir al-Uways
*Finance and Industry*, HH Sheikh Hamdan bin Rashid al-Maktoum
*Foreign Affairs*, Rashid Abdullah al-Nuaimi
*Health*, Hamad Abdul Rahman al-Madfa
*Higher Education and Scientific Research*, HH Sheikh Nahyan bin Mubarak al-Nahyan
*Information and Culture*, HH Sheikh Abdullah bin Zayed al-Nahyan
*Interior*, Lt.-Gen. Mohammed Saeed al-Badi
*Justice, Islamic Affairs and Awqaf (Religious Endowments)*, Mohammed Nakhira al-Dhahiri
*Labour and Social Affairs*, Matar Humaid al-Tayir
*Petroleum and Mineral Resources*, Ubayd bin Sayf al-Nasiri
*Planning*, HH Sheikh Humaid bin Ahmed al-Mualla
*Public Works and Housing*, Rakadh bin Salem al-Rakadh

### EMBASSY OF THE UNITED ARAB EMIRATES

30 Princes Gate, London SW7 1PT
Tel 020-7581 1281
*Ambassador Extraordinary and Plenipotentiary*, HE Easa Saleh al-Gurg, CBE, apptd 1991
*Military Attaché*, Col. M. al-Hamadi
*Cultural Attaché*, A. al-Marri

### BRITISH EMBASSIES

PO Box 248, Abu Dhabi
Tel: (00 971) (2) 632 6600
*Ambassador Extraordinary and Plenipotentiary*, HE Patrick Nixon, CMG, OBE, apptd 1998
*Counsellor and Deputy Head of Mission*, A. McKenzie, MBE
*Defence and Military Attaché*, Col. A. Malkin

PO Box 65, Dubai
Tel: (00 971) (4) 397 1070
*Counsellor and Consul-General*, S. Collis
*Deputy Head of Mission*, N. E. Cole, OBE

BRITISH COUNCIL DIRECTOR, Robert Sykes, Villa no. 7, Al-Nasr Street, Khalidiya, PO Box 46523, Abu Dhabi; e-mail: information@britishcouncil.org.ae. There is also an office in Dubai

## DEFENCE

The Army has 331 main battle tanks, 620 armoured personnel carriers and 433 armoured infantry fighting vehicles. The Navy has 16 patrol and coastal vessels. The Air Force has 101 combat aircraft and 49 armed helicopters.
MILITARY EXPENDITURE – 6.2 per cent of GDP (1999)
MILITARY PERSONNEL – 65,000: Army 59,000, Navy 2,000, Air Force 4,000

## ECONOMY

The UAE is the Gulf's third largest oil producer after Saudi Arabia and Iran, with oil reserves of 98,200 million barrels and gas reserves of 5,800 million cubic metres. Oil production in 1999 accounted for 25.6 per cent of GDP. Other important sectors of the economy are manufacturing (aluminium, cement, chemicals, fertilisers, pharmaceuticals, ship repair), government services, construction, transport, communications and financial services. Tourism is growing in importance, with 1,919,000 visitors in 1994. Agricultural production (vegetables, dates, fruit, eggs, flowers, olives, animal husbandry) has increased due to large-scale water desalination and irrigation projects, with 2,359,479 hectares of agricultural land in 1999. There is no personal or corporate taxation apart from on oil companies and foreign banks. There are several free zones, where overseas companies can trade tax-free.

There are 15 major ports, of which nine are modern container terminals. Six international airports (Dubai, Abu Dhabi, Sharjah, Ras al-Khaimah, Fujairah, Al Ain) are in operation.

Oil revenues over the past 30 years have enabled the government to invest heavily in education, health and social services, housing, transport and communications infrastructure, and agriculture, and enabled the UAE's citizens to have one of the highest GDPs per capita in the world.

GNP – US$48,673 million (1998); US$17,870 per capita (1998)

GDP – US$46,614 million (1997); US$19,506 per capita (1998)

ANNUAL AVERAGE GROWTH OF GDP – 9.9 per cent (1996)

| *Trade with UK* | 1999 | 2000 |
|---|---|---|
| Imports from UK | £1,402,947,000 | £1,598,022,000 |
| Exports to UK | 666,536,000 | 648,758,000 |

## EDUCATION AND SOCIAL WELFARE

In 1999 there were 687 government schools, where education is free; and 398 private schools. There are five universities. There were 31 federal hospitals in 2000, and 17 more are due to be completed by 2005.

ILLITERACY RATE – 23.5 per cent (2000)

ENROLMENT (percentage of age group) – primary 78 per cent (1996); secondary 71 per cent (1996); tertiary 11.9 per cent (1996)

# UNITED KINGDOM

*United Kingdom of Great Britain and Northern Ireland*

AREA –. 93,784 sq. miles (242,900 sq. km), of which England 50,351 sq. miles (130,410 sq. km), Wales 8,015 sq. miles (20,758 sq. km), Scotland 30,420 sq. miles (78,789 sq. km), Northern Ireland 5,467 sq. miles (14,160 sq. km). Neighbour: Republic of Ireland (south and west)

POPULATION – 59,110,000 (1997 UN estimate); England 48,903,000, Wales 2,917,000, Scotland 5,137,000, Northern Ireland 1,649,000 (1996 UN estimates). The language is English, of West Germanic origin, with a vocabulary heavily influenced by French, Latin and Greek. Welsh is spoken by 18.7 per cent of the population of Wales, Scots is spoken by 30 per cent of the population of Scotland; there are also small numbers of Scottish and Irish Gaelic speakers. There are 39.4 million Christians (of which 26.1 million Anglicans, 5.7 million Roman Catholics and 2.6 million Presbyterians), nearly 2 million Muslims, 400,000 Sikhs, 380,000 Hindus, 285,000 Jews, 25,000 Buddhists and 25,000 Jains

CAPITAL – ΨLondon, (population, 7,074,265, 1996 estimate) (capital of the UK and England)

MAJOR CITIES – Belfast (297,300) (capital of Northern Ireland); Birmingham, (population 861,041); Bradford (457,344); Bristol (399,600); Cardiff/Caerdydd (315,040) (capital of Wales); Dudley (304,615); Edinburgh (452,806) (capital of Scotland); Glasgow (611,440); Leeds (680,722); Liverpool (452,450); Manchester (404,861); Sheffield (501,202); Wakefield (310,915); Wigan (306,521), 1996 estimates

CURRENCY – Pound sterling (£) of 100 pence

NATIONAL ANTHEM – God save the Queen

NATIONAL DAY – St David's Day (Wales only) 1 March, St Patrick's Day (N. Ireland only) 17 March, St George's Day (England only) 23 April, St Andrew's Day (Scotland only) 30 November

NATIONAL FLAG – A red cross and a red diagonal cross on a white cross and a white diagonal cross on a blue ground (*see* The National Flag)

LIFE EXPECTANCY (years) – male 74.7; female 79.7

POPULATION GROWTH RATE – 0.2 per cent (1997)

POPULATION DENSITY – 241 per sq. km (1998)

URBAN POPULATION – 89.5 per cent (2000 estimate)

The United Kingdom consists of Great Britain (formed of Scotland in the north, Wales in the west of the central portion of the island, and England, which occupies the rest of the island), the north-eastern part of the island of Ireland, and the Hebrides, Orkney and Shetland Islands, the Isle of Wight, Anglesey and the Isles of Scilly. The United Kingdom is bounded on the south by the English Channel, on the east by the Straits of Dover and the North Sea, and on the north and west by the Atlantic Ocean. The North Channel and the Irish Sea separate Northern Ireland from Great Britain.

## HISTORY AND POLITICS

The United Kingdom is formed of four constituent nations: England, Wales, Scotland and Northern Ireland (*see* Ireland *and* Local Government – England, Wales, Scotland for early history of individual countries).

The Normans, who had invaded England in 1066, established control over Wales by 1300; Wales was politically assimilated to England under the Act of Union of 1535.

Following the death of Queen Elizabeth I, James VI of Scotland succeeded to the English throne as James I of England in 1603; an Act of Union was proclaimed in 1707, under which the seat of Scottish Government was transferred to London.

The Norman English had established control over most of Ireland in the 12th century, but their influence waned. King Henry VIII re-established English control over Ireland and was declared king of Ireland by a parliament summoned in Dublin in 1541. The United Kingdom of Great Britain and Ireland was established by the Act of Union in 1801.

By the early twentieth century, the United Kingdom had acquired a substantial empire, which included Australia, Canada, the Indian subcontinent, Malaysia, New Zealand, and extensive territories in Africa, the West Indies and the Pacific.

Ireland was partitioned in 1921 and the Irish Free State became a republic in 1949. Northern Ireland remained part of the United Kingdom, governed by a Northern Ireland parliament.

Beginning with the independence of India and Pakistan in 1947, a process of decolonisation began.

The Labour government elected in 1945 nationalised iron and steel, transport and the utilities. Prime Minister Margaret Thatcher, who was in power from 1979 to 1989, broke the post-war consensus. Her Conservative government privatised state-owned industries and reduced the influence of the trade unions.

The Labour Party won the general election held on 1 May 1997 and retained power in the general election held on 7 June 2001 winning 413 seats; the Conservative Party won 166 seats, the Liberal Democrats 52 seats, the Ulster Unionist Party six seats, the Scottish Nationalist Party and the Democratic Unionist Party five seats each, Plaid Cymru and Sinn Féin four seats each, the Social and Democratic Labour Party three seats, and the Kidderminster Hospital and Health Concern won one seat and one seat was held by the Speaker.

Referendums held in Scotland and Wales in September 1997 produced majorities in favour of devolution. The first elections to the Scottish Parliament and the Welsh National Assembly took place in May 1999.

### Northern Ireland

Following the partition of Ireland in 1921, the Protestant Unionists held a permanent majority in the government and administration of Northern Ireland. A Roman Catholic civil rights campaign in the late 1960s led to rioting, sectarian violence and terrorist activity conducted by the Irish Republican Army (IRA), an Irish nationalist paramilitary organisation, and several Protestant paramilitary organisations. Following the resignation in 1972 of the Northern Ireland government, the Northern Ireland parliament was abolished and replaced with direct rule from London.

Several attempts were made by successive governments to restore power to a devolved government which was acceptable to both the Catholic and Protestant communities.

In November 1985 the governments of the UK and the Republic of Ireland signed the Anglo-Irish Agreement, under which both parties agreed to improve cross-border co-operation and that Northern Ireland should remain part of the UK for as long as the majority of the population wished it to remain so.

The 'Good Friday Agreement', which proposed the establishment of a Northern Ireland Assembly, along with a cross-border ministerial council and a consultative body of ministers from the UK, the Republic of Ireland and the Northern Irish, Scottish and Welsh assemblies, was put to a referendum in May 1998 and was endorsed by the electorate. At the same time, a referendum was held in the Republic of Ireland to repeal its constitutional claim to Northern Ireland; this was also endorsed by voters. The first election for the Northern Ireland Assembly was held in June 1998.

Power was devolved to the Northern Ireland Assembly in December 1999. The Assembly was suspended in February 2000 owing to the lack of progress made in talks with the IRA on decommissioning its weaponry, but it was reinstated in May 2000 following further negotiations.

### Political System

Parliament consists of the House of Commons and the House of Lords. The House of Commons has 659 directly-elected members, whose term of office is a maximum of five years. The House of Lords is appointed and consists of 92 hereditary peers, over 500 life peers, certain senior judges, and 26 bishops of the Church of England.

England is divided into 34 county councils (subdivided into 238 district councils), 46 unitary authorities, 36 metropolitan borough councils, 32 London borough councils and the Corporation of London. Wales has 22 unitary authorities, Scotland has 32 unitary authorities and Northern Ireland has 26 single-tier district councils.

### Head of State

*HM by the Grace of God, of the United Kingdom of Great Britain and Northern Ireland and of her other Realms and Territories Queen, Head of the Commonwealth, Defender of the Faith*, Queen Elizabeth II, *born* 21 April 1926; *succeeded* 6 February 1952; *crowned* 2 June 1953; *married* 20 November 1947, HRH The Prince Philip, Duke of Edinburgh, KG, KT, OM, GBE, AC, QSO, PC (Prince Philip of Denmark and Greece), and has *issue* HRH The Prince of Wales (*see* below); HRH The Princess Royal (Princess Anne Elizabeth Alice Louise), KG, GCVO, *b.* 15 August 1950; HRH The Duke of York (Prince Andrew Albert Christian Edward), CVO, ADC(P), *b.* 10 March 1964; HRH The Earl of Wessex (Prince Edward Antony Richard Louis), CVO, *b.* 10 March 1964

*Heir*, HRH The Prince of Wales (Prince Charles Philip Arthur George), KG, KT, GCB and Great Master of the Order of the Bath, AK, QSO, PC, ADC(P), *born* 14 November 1948, *married* Lady Diana Frances Spencer (Diana, Princess of Wales); and has *issue* HRH Prince William of Wales (Prince William Arthur Philip Louis), *b.* 21 June 1982; HRH Prince Henry of Wales (Prince Henry Charles Albert David), *b.* 15 September 1984

### Cabinet *as at September 2001*

*Prime Minister, First Lord of the Treasury, Civil Service*, Tony Blair
*Deputy Prime Minister, First Secretary of State*, John Prescott
*Chancellor of the Exchequer*, Gordon Brown
*Chief Secretary to the Treasury*, Andrew Smith
*Culture, Media and Sport*, Tessa Jowell
*Defence*, Geoff Hoon
*Education and Skills*, Estelle Morris
*Environment, Food and Rural Affairs*, Margaret Beckett
*Foreign and Commonwealth Affairs*, Jack Straw
*Health*, Alan Milburn
*Home Office*, David Blunkett
*International Development*, Clare Short
*Lord Chancellor*, Lord Irvine of Lairg
*Lord Privy Seal, Leader of the House of Lords*, Lord Williams of Mostyn
*Northern Ireland*, John Reid
*Parliamentary Secretary, Treasury, Chief Whip*, Hilary Armstrong
*President of the Council and Leader of the House of Commons*, Robin Cook
*Scotland*, Helen Liddell
*Trade and Industry*, Patricia Hewitt
*Transport, Local Government and the Regions*, Stephen Byers
*Wales*, Paul Murphy
*Without Portfolio, Labour Party Chair*, Charles Clarke
*Work and Pensions*, Alistair Darling

## DEFENCE

The Army has 616 main battle tanks, 3,278 armoured personnel carriers and 737 armoured infantry fighting vehicles. The Navy has 16 submarines, 3 carriers, 11 destroyers, 20 frigates, 23 patrol and coastal combatants, 34 combat aircraft, and 120 armed helicopters at five bases. The Air Force has 429 combat aircraft

Military Expenditure – 2.6 per cent of GDP (1999)
Military Personnel – 212,450: Strategic Forces 1,900, Army 113,950, Navy 43,770, Air Force 54,730

## ECONOMY

Service industries accounted for 69.1 per cent of GDP and 74.8 per cent of employment in 1998. The UK is a major international financial centre, with particular expertise in the fields of banking, currency trading, insurance and shipping. The London Stock Exchange and commodity markets are among the largest in the world.

Manufacturing contributed 29.5 per cent of GDP and employing 23.4 per cent of the workforce in 1997. There is a wide range of manufacturing industry, covering areas such as chemicals, textiles and clothing, furniture, engineering, foodstuffs, metals and minerals, printing and publishing.

Agriculture employs less than 2 per cent of the workforce. The most important crops grown are barley, forestry products, oats, potatoes, oilseed rape, sugar beets and wheat. There is extensive livestock farming and fishing is an important, though declining, industry.

The UK has extensive reserves of natural gas, oil and coal. In 1998 the UK produced 124,222,000 tonnes of crude oil; proven reserves are estimated at 770 million tonnes. Gas production totalled 95,614 million cubic metres; reserves are estimated at 590,000 million cubic metres. Coal production amounted to 41,428,000 tonnes in 1998. Other minerals mined include limestone, sandstone, clay, chalk and gravel. Metals mined include aluminium, copper, lead and zinc.

The United Kingdom was at the forefront of the Industrial Revolution in the 18th and 19th centuries, but by the 1950s, its manufacturing industry had declined relative to other developed nations.

The economy has revived since 1980 following a period of extensive privatisation and the closure of many unproductive companies.

GNP – US$1,403,844 million (1999) US$22,640 per capita (1999)
GDP – US$1,283,335 million (1997) US$24,228 per capita (1999)
ANNUAL AVERAGE GROWTH OF GDP – 2.6 per cent (2000)
INFLATION RATE – 2.7 per cent (2001)
UNEMPLOYMENT – 5.2 per cent (2000)

### TRADE

The principal imports are machinery and transport equipment, manufactured goods, semi-manufactures, chemicals, foodstuffs and livestock, and raw materials. The principal exports are machinery and transport equipment, chemical products, semi-manufactures, manufactured goods, chemical products, mineral fuels, and foodstuffs and livestock.

The majority of trade is with other member states of the EU. The USA and Japan are important trading partners and the UK also trades extensively with other Commonwealth nations.

In 1999 there was a trade deficit of US$43,069 million and a current account surplus of US$20,639 million. Imports totalled US$317,968 million and exports US$268,211 million.

## COMMUNICATIONS

There were 371,900 km (231,100 miles) of roads in 1999, of which 3,316 km (2,060 miles) were motorways. There are about 32,000 km (20,000 miles) of railway track. The Channel Tunnel links the UK railway system to those of mainland Europe. About 5,200 km (3,200 miles) of waterways are navigable and there are many commercial ports, the most important of which are London, Grimsby and Immingham, Tees and Hartlepool, and Forth. The total tonnage handled by British ports amounted to some 566 million tonnes in 1999. There are over 150 commercial airports, of which London Heathrow (the world's busiest international airport), London Gatwick, and Manchester are the most important.

## EDUCATION

Full-time education is compulsory between the ages of five and 16 in Great Britain and four and 16 in Northern Ireland. Education between the ages of 16 and 18 is voluntary, although most pupils remain in education until 18. There are 87 universities and 64 other tertiary level colleges. In addition, the Open University offers distance higher education. (*see* Education)

ENROLMENT primary 99 per cent (1996); secondary 91 per cent (1996); tertiary 52.3 per cent (1996)

## CULTURE

Old English was a highly inflected language. Middle English developed following the Norman invasion, when the language became grammatically simpler and acquired a large number of Norman loan words. The dialect of the East Midlands, as spoken in London, became the basis for standard Modern English.

Modern English has spread from the United Kingdom with differences in spelling, usage and grammar to North America, Australasia and many other parts of the world.

Great names in English literature include Geoffrey Chaucer (*c*.1343–1400), William Shakespeare (1564–1616), probably the greatest writer in the English language, and the novelists Jane Austen (1775–1817), Charlotte Brontë (1816–1855), Emily Brontë (1818–1848), George Eliot (1819–1880), Charles Dickens (1812–1870), Thomas Hardy (1840–1928), Rudyard Kipling (1865–1936) and Graham Greene (1904–1991)

NB Statistics used in this entry are obtained from international sources for ease of comparison with other countries, rather than from the UK government sources used elsewhere in *Whitaker's Almanack*, and may therefore differ.

---

## UNITED STATES OF AMERICA

---

AREA – 3,536,382 sq. miles (9,156,119 sq. km). Neighbours: Canada (north), Mexico (south)
POPULATION – 276,059,000 (2000 estimate). The language is English. There is a significant Spanish-speaking minority
CAPITAL – Washington DC (population, 7,285,206, 1998 estimate). The area of the District of Columbia (with which the City of Washington is considered co-extensive) is 61 sq. miles, with a resident population (1998 estimate) of 523,124. The District of Columbia is governed by an elected mayor and City Council
MAJOR CITIES – ΨChicago (2,802,079); Dallas (1,075,894); ΨDetroit (970,196); ΨHouston (1,786,691); ΨLos Angeles (3,597,556); ΨNew York (7,420,166); ΨPhiladelphia (1,436,287); Phoenix (1,198,064); San Antonio (1,114,130); ΨSan Diego (1,220,666), 1998 estimates
CURRENCY – US dollar (US$) of 100 cents
NATIONAL ANTHEM – The Star-Spangled Banner
NATIONAL DAY – 4 July (Independence Day)
NATIONAL FLAG – Thirteen horizontal stripes, alternately red and white, with blue canton in the hoist showing 50 white stars in nine horizontal rows of six and five alternately (known as the Star-Spangled Banner)
LIFE EXPECTANCY (years) – male 73.8; female 79.7
POPULATION GROWTH RATE – 0.9 per cent (1999)
POPULATION DENSITY – 29 per sq. km (1998)
URBAN POPULATION – 77.2 per cent (2000 estimate)

The coastline has a length of about 2,069 miles on the Atlantic, 7,623 miles on the Pacific, 1,060 miles on the Arctic, and 1,631 miles on the Gulf of Mexico.

The principal river is the Mississippi-Missouri-Red (3,710 miles long), traversing the whole country to its mouth in the Gulf of Mexico. The chain of the Rocky Mountains separates the western portion of the country from the remainder. West of these, bordering the Pacific coast, the Cascade Mountains and Sierra Nevada form the outer edge of a high tableland, consisting in part of stony and sandy desert and partly of grazing land and forested mountains, and including the Great Salt Lake, which extends to the Rocky Mountains. In the eastern states large forests still exist, the remnants of the forests which formerly extended over all the Atlantic slope. The highest point is Mount McKinley (20,320 ft) in Alaska, and the lowest point of dry land is in Death Valley (Inyo, California), 282 ft below sea level.

## Area and Population

| | Total land area 1990 (sq. km) | Population census 1990 |
|---|---|---|
| The United States (a) | 9,159,116 | 248,709,873 |
| Outlying areas under US jurisdiction | 10,929 | 3,862,431 |
| *Territories* | 10,888 | 3,862,238 |
| Puerto Rico | 8,875 | 3,522,037 |
| Guam | 544 | 133,152 |
| US Virgin Islands | 346 | 101,809 |
| American Samoa | 200 | 46,773 |
| Northern Mariana Is. | 464 | 43,345 |
| *Other US possessions* | 41 | 193 |
| Population abroad (b) | – | 925,845 |
| Total | 9,170,045 | 253,498,149 |

(a) the 50 states and the Federal District of Columbia
(b) excludes US citizens temporarily abroad on business

## Resident Population by Race 2000 Estimate *(Thousands)*

| | |
|---|---|
| White | 226,861 |
| Black | 35,470 |
| *American Indian | 2,448 |
| Asian and Pacific Islanders | 11,279 |
| †Hispanic origin | 32,832 |
| Total | 276,059 |

*Includes Eskimo and Aleut
†Persons of Hispanic origin may be of any race

## Immigration

From 1820 to 1998, 64,599,082 immigrants were admitted to the United States. Total number of immigrants in 1998 was 660,477, of which 298,390 came from North and South America (131,575 from Mexico), 219,696 from Asia and 90,793 from Europe.

# HISTORY AND POLITICS

The area which is now the USA was first inhabited by nomadic hunters who probably arrived from Asia *c.*30,000 BC. The first (failed) European colony was founded by Sir Walter Raleigh in 1585. By 1733 there were 13 British colonies, composed largely of religious non-conformists who had left Britain to escape persecution; the French and Spanish had also founded colonies.

The War of Independence broke out in 1775 largely because of the colonists' objection to being taxed by, but having no representation in, the British Parliament. The forces of the British government were defeated with French, Spanish and Dutch assistance. The Declaration of Independence which inaugurated the United States of America was signed on 4 July 1776; Britain recognised American sovereignty in 1783. The first federal constitution was drawn up in 1787; ten amendments, termed the Bill of Rights, were added in 1791. The 13 original states of the Union ratified the constitution between 1787 and 1790. Vermont, Kentucky and Tennessee were admitted in the 1790s but most of the states acceded in the 19th century as the opening up of the centre and west led to the creation of new states and European or neighbouring countries ceded or sold their territories to the USA.

The Civil War (1861–5) was fought over the issue of slavery, which was integral to the economy of the southern states but was opposed by the northern states. The northern states defeated the Confederacy of southern states (South Carolina, Georgia, Alabama, Florida, Mississippi, Louisiana).

The USA emerged as a world economic and military superpower in the 20th century and played a decisive role in the two world wars, in which it was engaged between 1917 and 1918, and between 1941 and 1945. Its economic and military (including nuclear) supremacy gave the USA a key role in shaping the post-war world.

## Political System

By the constitution of 17 September 1787 (to which amendments were added in 1791, 1798, 1804, 1865, 1868, 1870, 1913, 1920, 1933, 1951, 1961, 1964, 1967, 1971 and 1992), the government of the United States is entrusted to three separate authorities: the executive (the president and Cabinet), the legislature (Congress) and the judicature.

The president is indirectly elected by an electoral college every four years. There is also a vice-president, who, should the president die, becomes president for the remainder of the term. The tenure of the presidency is limited to two terms.

The president, with the consent of the Senate, appoints the Cabinet officers and all the chief officials. He makes recommendations of a general nature to Congress, and when laws are passed by Congress he may return them to Congress with a veto. But if a measure so vetoed is again passed by both Houses of Congress by two-thirds majority in each House, it becomes law, notwithstanding the objection of the president. The president must be at least 35 years of age and a native citizen of the United States.

### *Presidential elections*

Each state elects (on the first Tuesday after the first Monday in November of the year preceding the year in which the presidential term expires) a number of electors (members of the electoral college), equal to the whole number of Senators and Representatives to which the state may be entitled in the Congress. The electors for each state meet in their respective states on the first Monday after the second Wednesday in December following, and vote for a president by ballot. The ballots are then sent to Washington, and opened on 6 January by the President of the Senate in the presence of Congress. The candidate who has received a majority of the whole number of electoral votes cast is declared president for the ensuing term. If no one has a majority, then from the highest on the list (not exceeding three) the House of Representatives elects a president, the votes being taken by states, the representation from each state having one vote. A presidential term begins at noon on 20 January.

## Head of State

*President of the United States*, George Walker Bush, *born* 6 July 1946, *elected* 7 November 2000, *sworn in* 20 January 2001. Republican
*Vice-President*, Richard B. Cheney, *born* 30 January 1941

## The Cabinet *as at September 2001*

*Agriculture*, Ann Veneman
*Attorney-General*, John Ashcroft
*Commerce*, Don Evans
*Defence*, Donald Rumsfeld
*Education*, Rod Paige
*Energy*, Spencer Abraham
*Health and Human Services*, Tommy Thompson
*Housing and Urban Development*, Mel Martinez
*Interior*, Gale Norton
*Labour*, Elaine Chao
*Secretary of State*, Colin Powell
*Transportation*, Norman Mineta
*Treasury*, Paul O'Neill
*Veterans' Affairs*, Anthony Prinicipi
Other senior positions:

*Permanent Representative to the UN (acting)*, James Cunningham
*Chair, Council of Economic Advisers*, R. Glenn Hubbard
*White House Chief of Staff*, Andrew Card
*National Security Adviser*, Condoleezza Rice
*Environmental Protection Agency*, Christine Todd Whitman
*Federal Emergency Management Agency*, Joseph Allbaugh
*Director, National Drug Control Policy*, John Walters
*Director, National Economic Council*, Lawrence Lindsey
*Director, Office of Management and Budget*, Mitch Daniels
*Director, Small Business Administration*, Hector Barreto
*President's Counsellor*, Karen Hughes
*Trade Representative*, Robert Zoellick
*White House Counsel*, Alberto Gonzales
*Director of CIA*, George Tenet
*Director of FBI*, Robert Mueller III
*Chairman, Federal Reserve Board of Governors*, Alan Greenspan

### UNITED STATES EMBASSY

24 Grosvenor Square, London W1A 1AE
Tel: 020-7499 9000
*Ambassador Extraordinary and Plenipotentiary*, HE William S. Farish, apptd 2001
*Deputy Chief of Mission*, G. Davies
*Defence and Naval Attaché*, Capt. S. Barnett
*Minister-Counsellors*, L. A. Lohman (*Administrative*); D. Katz (*Commercial*); W. G. Griffith (*Consular*); M. Dworken (*Political*)

### BRITISH EMBASSY

3100 Massachusetts Avenue NW, Washington DC 20008
Tel: (00 1) (202) 588 6500
*Ambassador Extraordinary and Plenipotentiary*, HE Sir Christopher Meyer, KCMG, apptd 1997
*Ministers*, A. Brenton, CMG; S. J. Pickford (*Economic*); S. French (*Defence Material*)
*Head of British Defence Staff and Defence Attaché*, Air Vice-Marshal J. Thompson, CB
*Counsellor*, W. Townend (*Management and Consul-General*)
*Consul-General (New York) and Director-General of Trade and Investment*, T. Harris, CMG

BRITISH CONSULATES-GENERAL – Atlanta, Boston, Chicago, Houston, Los Angeles, New York and San Francisco

BRITISH VICE-CONSULATE – Orlando

BRITISH CONSULATES – Anchorage, Charlotte, Dallas, Denver, Kansas City, Miami, Minneapolis, Nashville, New Orleans, Philadelphia, Phoenix, Pittsburgh, Portland, St Louis, Salt Lake City, San Diego, San Jose, Seattle and Puerto Rico

BRITISH COUNCIL DIRECTOR, David Blagbrough (*Cultural Attaché*), c/o British Embassy; e-mail: enquiries@britishcouncil-usa.org

BRITISH-AMERICAN CHAMBER OF COMMERCE, 20th floor, 52 Vanderbilt Avenue, New York NY 10017; UK OFFICE, 8 Staple Inn, Holborn, London WC1V 7QH

## THE CONGRESS

Legislative power is vested in two houses, the Senate and the House of Representatives. The Senate has 100 members, two Senators from each state, elected for the term of six years, and each Senator has one vote.

The House of Representatives consists of 435 Representatives, directly elected in each state for a two-year term, a resident commissioner from Puerto Rico and a delegate each from American Samoa, the District of Columbia, Guam and the Virgin Islands.

Members of the 107th Congress were elected on 7 November 2000. The 107th Congress is constituted as follows:

*Senate* – Republicans 49; Democrats 50; Independent 1; total 100
*House of Representatives* – Republicans 219; Democrats 210; Independent 2; vacant 4; total 435
*President of the Senate*, The Vice-President
*Senate Majority Leader*, Tom Daschle (*D*), *South Dakota*
*Speaker of the House of Representatives*, J. Dennis Hastert (*R*), *Illinois*
*Secretary of the Senate*, Gary Sisco
*Clerk of the House of Representatives*, Jeff Trandahl

## THE JUDICATURE

The federal judiciary consists of three sets of federal courts: the Supreme Court at Washington DC, consisting of a Chief Justice and eight Associate Justices, with original jurisdiction in cases where a state is a party to the suit, and with appellate jurisdiction from inferior federal courts and from the judgments of the highest courts of the states; the United States Courts of Appeals, dealing with appeals from district courts and from certain federal administrative agencies, and consisting of 168 circuit judges within 13 circuits; the 94 United States district courts served by 575 district court judges.

### THE SUPREME COURT

US Supreme Court Building, Washington DC 20543

*Chief Justice*, William H. Rehnquist, *Arizona*, apptd 1986

*Associate Justices*
John Paul Stevens, *Illinois*, apptd 1975
Sandra Day O'Connor, *Arizona*, apptd 1981
Antonin Scalia, *Virginia*, apptd 1986
Anthony M. Kennedy, *California*, apptd 1988
David H. Souter, *New Hampshire*, apptd 1990
Clarence Thomas, *Georgia*, apptd 1991
Ruth Bader Ginsburg, *New York*, apptd 1993
Stephen Breyer, *Massachusetts*, apptd 1994

*Clerk of the Supreme Court*, William K. Suter

In 1999 there were 11,635,090 recorded offences: murder and non-negligent manslaughter 15,530; forcible rape 89,110; robbery 409,670; aggravated assault 916,380; burglary 2,099,700; larceny-theft 6,957,400; motor vehicle theft 1,147,300.

## DEFENCE

Each military department is separately organised and functions under the direction, authority and control of the Secretary of Defence. The Air Force has primary responsibility for the Department of Defence space development programmes and projects.

Under strategic command the USA has 432 submarine-launched ballistic missiles, 550 inter-continental ballistic missiles, 208 heavy nuclear-capable bombers and 60 strategic defence interceptor aircraft together with multiple intelligence satellites, radars and early warning systems throughout the world.

The Army has 7,900 main battle tanks, 6,710 armoured infantry fighting vehicles, 15,200 armoured personnel carriers, 292 aircraft and 1,502 armed helicopters.

The Navy has 18 strategic submarines, 55 tactical submarines, 12 aircraft carriers, 27 cruisers, 52 destroyers, 35 frigates, 21 patrol and coastal vessels, 243 amphibious and support ships, 1,456 combat aircraft and 222 armed helicopters.

The Marine Corps has 403 main battle tanks and 1,321 amphibious armoured vehicles. The Air Force has 208 long-range strike aircraft, 2,529 tactical combat aircraft and 216 helicopters.

The major deployments of US personnel overseas are: Germany (57,580); South Korea (36,630); Japan (39,750); Italy (10,500); UK (11,340); Turkey (2,040).

MILITARY EXPENDITURE – 3.1 per cent of GDP (1999)

MILITARY PERSONNEL – 1,365,800: Army 471,700, Navy 370,700, Marine Corps 169,800, Coast Guard 42,140, Air Force 353,600

## ECONOMY AND FINANCE

In 2000 central government budget receipts totalled US$2,025.0 billion and outlays US$1,788.1 billion. The largest items of expenditure were: defence US$293.9 billion, social security US$409.4 billion, income security US$247.4 billion, debt interest US$223.2 billion. In the year to the end of September 2000, US$58,364 million was spent on education, US$154,215 million on health, US$197,115 million on Medicare, US$247,380 million on income security, US$409,437 million on social security and US$47,084 million on veterans' benefits and services.

At the end of the 1999 financial year the total gross federal debt stood at US$5,606,087 million; it was estimated to be US$5,768,957 million at the end of the 2001 financial year.

GNP – US$8,879,500 million (1999); US$30,600 per capita (1999)

GDP – US$7,824,008 million (1997); US$33,836 per capita (1999)

ANNUAL AVERAGE GROWTH OF GDP – 3.4 per cent (2000)

INFLATION RATE – 3.4 per cent (2001)

UNEMPLOYMENT – 4.2 per cent (2001)

### GROSS DOMESTIC PRODUCT BY INDUSTRY 1999

| | US$ billions |
|---|---|
| *Private industries* | 8,140.8 |
| Agriculture, forestry, fisheries | 125.4 |
| Mining | 111.8 |
| Construction | 416.4 |
| Manufacturing | 1,500.8 |
| Transportation and public utilities | 779.6 |
| Wholesale trade | 643.3 |
| Retail trade | 856.4 |
| Finance, insurance, and real estate | 1,792.1 |
| Services | 1,986.9 |
| *Government and government enterprises* | 1,158.4 |
| Statistical discrepancy | –71.9 |
| TOTAL | 9,227.3 |

### AGRICULTURE

The total number of farms in 1999 was 2,194,070 with a total area of land in farms of 947,340,000 acres, and an average acreage per farm of 432 acres. Principal crops are maize for grain, soybeans, wheat, hay, cotton, tobacco, grain sorghums, potatoes, oranges and barley. Gross income from farming in 1998 was US$223 billion. Cash receipts from all crops in 1998 was US$102 billion and from livestock and livestock products US$95 billion.

### MINERALS

The value of non-fuel raw mineral production in 1997 totalled an estimated US$39 billion. Mineral exports in 1997 were valued at US$37 billion, and imports at US$58 billion. In 1998 the following quantities of minerals were produced: iron ore 62,931,000 tonnes; marketable phosphate rock 44,200,000 tonnes; copper 1,858,900 tonnes; zinc 755,000 tonnes; lead 415,000 tonnes.

### ENERGY

Production in 1999 was 72.45 quadrillion BTU, principally coal, natural gas and crude oil. Petroleum accounted for almost half of energy exports of 3.82 quadrillion BTU. Net imports were 23.73 quadrillion BTU, of which crude oil was 18.69 quadrillion BTU, to meet consumption of 97.16 quadrillion BTU (quadrillion=$10^{15}$).

### TRADE

In 1999 the USA had a trade deficit of US$344,822 million and a current account deficit of US$338,916 million. Imports totalled US$1,059,435 million and exports US$702,098 million.

| *Trade with UK* | 1999 | 2000 |
|---|---|---|
| Imports from UK | £24,373,101,000 | £29,417,790,000 |
| Exports to UK | 25,212,005,000 | 29,332,236,00000 |

## COMMUNICATIONS

In 1999 there were 3.91 million miles of public roads and streets. Surfaced roads and streets account for 61.3 per cent of the total. The ocean-going merchant marine on 1 January 1999 consisted of 29,827 vessels with a capacity of 73.7 million tonnes. According to preliminary figures, US domestic and international scheduled airlines in 2000 carried 665,042,491 passengers over 692,008,214,000 revenue passenger miles.

## EDUCATION

All the states and the District of Columbia have compulsory school attendance laws. In general, children are obliged to attend school from seven to 16 years of age.

Most of the revenue for public elementary and secondary school purposes comes from federal, state, and local governments. Less than three per cent comes from gifts and from tuition and transportation fees.

Among the better-known universities are: Harvard, founded at Cambridge, Mass. in 1636, and named after John Harvard of Emmanuel College, Cambridge, England, who bequeathed to it his library and a sum of money in 1638; Yale, founded at New Haven, Connecticut, in 1701; Princeton, NJ, founded 1746.

ILLITERACY RATE – 0.5 per cent

ENROLMENT (percentage of age group) – primary 95 per cent (1996); secondary 90 per cent (1996); tertiary 80.9 per cent (1996)

---

## US TERRITORIES, ETC

---

Responsibility within the federal government for the United States insular areas other than Puerto Rico and Kingman Reef lies with the United States Department of the Interior, either the Office of Insular Affairs (for American Samoa, Guam, the Northern Mariana Islands, the United States Virgin Islands, Navassa Island (3 sq. miles), Palmyra Atoll (1.56 sq. miles) and Wake Atoll (2.5 sq. miles) (shared with the United States Army Space and Missile Defense Command)) or the United States Fish and Wildlife Service (for Baker Island (0.59 sq. miles), Howland Island (1 sq. mile) and Jarvis Island (1.66 sq. miles), Midway Atoll (2 sq. miles) and Johnston Atoll (0.98 sq. miles) (shared with the Defense Special Weapons Agency)). Four of the eight populated insular areas are represented in the United States House of Representatives, Puerto Rico by a resident commissioner and American Samoa, Guam and the United States Virgin Islands each by a delegate. Although represented in the United States House of Representatives by a delegate, the

District of Columbia was an incorporated territory for only three years, from 21 February 1871 to 20 June 1874.

## THE COMMONWEALTH OF PUERTO RICO

AREA – 3,427 sq. miles (8,875 sq. km)
POPULATION – 3,860,091 (1998 estimate); 3,522,037 (1990 census). The majority of the inhabitants are of Spanish descent, and Spanish and English are the official languages
CAPITAL – ΨSan Juan, population of the municipality (1998 estimate), 439,427. Other major towns are: Bayamón (233,797); Carolina (190,469); ΨPonce (191,469)

Puerto Rico (Rich Port) is an island of the Greater Antilles group in the West Indies.

Puerto Rico was discovered in 1493 by Columbus. It was a Spanish possession until 1898, when the USA took formal possession as a result of the Spanish-American War.

The 1952 constitution establishes the Commonwealth of Puerto Rico with full powers of local government. The Legislative Assembly consists of two elected houses: the Senate of 27 members and the House of Representatives of 51 members. The term of the Legislative Assembly is four years. The Governor is popularly elected for a term of four years. Residents of Puerto Rico are US citizens. Puerto Rico is represented in Congress by a resident commissioner, elected for a term of four years, who has a seat in the House of Representatives but not a vote, although he has a right to vote on those committees of which he is a member.

Principal agricultural products are milk, poultry, coffee, plantains, meat, ornamental plants, eggs, fish and seafood, and fruits and vegetables. Most valuable areas of manufacturing are chemicals and allied products, metal products and machinery, and food processing.

*Governor*, Sila María Calderón

| TRADE WITH UK | 1999 | 2000 |
|---|---|---|
| Imports from UK | £437,008,000 | £272,549,000 |
| Exports to UK | 262,520,000 | 435,486,000 |

## GUAM

AREA – 212 sq. miles (549 sq. km)
POPULATION – 156,000 (1997 estimate): 43 per cent Chamorro stock mingled with Filipino and Spanish blood. The Chamorro language belongs to the Malayo-Polynesian family, but with considerable admixture of Spanish. Chamorro and English are the official languages; most Chamorro residents are bilingual
CAPITAL – Hagatna. Port of entry, ΨApra

Guam is the largest of the Mariana Islands, in the north Pacific Ocean.

Guam was occupied by the Japanese in December 1941 but was recaptured by US forces in 1944. Under the Organic Act of Guam 1950, Guam has statutory powers of self-government, and any person born in Guam is a US citizen. A 21-member unicameral legislature is elected biennially. The Governor and Lieutenant-Governor are popularly elected. There is also a District Court of Guam, with original jurisdiction in cases under federal law.

Guam's two main sources of revenue are tourism and US military spending.

*Governor*, Carl Gutierrez

## AMERICAN SAMOA

AREA – 77 sq. miles (199 sq. km)
POPULATION – 63,000 (1997 estimate)
CAPITAL – ΨPago Pago (population, 3,519)

American Samoa consists of the islands of Tutuila, Aunu'u, Ofu, Olesega, Ta'u, Rose and Swains Islands. Tutuila, the largest of the group, has an area of 52 sq. miles and a magnificent harbour at Pago Pago. The remaining islands have an area of about 24 sq. miles. Tuna and copra are the chief exports.

Those born in American Samoa are US non-citizen nationals, but some have acquired citizenship through service in the United States armed forces or other naturalisation procedure. The 1960 constitution grants American Samoa a measure of self-government, with certain powers reserved to the US Secretary of the Interior. There is a bicameral legislature with popularly

## THE STATES OF THE UNION

The United States of America is a federal republic consisting of 50 states and the federal District of Columbia and of organised territories. Of the present 50 states, 13 are original states, seven were admitted without previous organisation as territories, and 30 were admitted after such organisation.

| STATE (with date and *order* of admission) | LAND AREA sq. km | POPULATION (1999 estimate) | CAPITAL | GOVERNOR (end of term in office) | |
|---|---|---|---|---|---|
| Alabama (AL) (1819) (*22*) | 131,443 | 4,369,862 | Montgomery | Don Siegelman (*D*) | (2002) |
| Alaska (AK) (1959) (*49*) | 1,477,268 | 619,500 | Juneau | Tony Knowles (*D*) | (2002) |
| Arizona (AZ) (1912) (*48*) | 294,333 | 4,778,332 | Phoenix | Jane Dee Hull (*R*) | (2002) |
| Arkansas (AR) (1836) (*25*) | 134,875 | 2,551,373 | Little Rock | Mike Huckabee (*R*) | (2002) |
| California (CA) (1850) (*31*) | 403,971 | 33,145,121 | Sacramento | Gray Davis (*D*) | (2002) |
| Colorado (CO) (1876) (*38*) | 268,658 | 4,056,133 | Denver | Bill Owens (*R*) | (2002) |
| Connecticut (CT) § (1788) (*5*) | 12,550 | 3,282,031 | Hartford | John Rowland (*R*) | (2002) |
| Delaware (DE) § (1787) (*1*) | 5,063 | 753,538 | Dover | Ruth Ann Minner (*D*) | (2004) |
| Florida (FL) (1845) (*27*) | 139,853 | 15,111,244 | Tallahassee | Jeb Bush (*R*) | (2002) |
| Georgia (GA) § (1788) (*4*) | 150,010 | 7,788,240 | Atlanta | Roy Barnes (*D*) | (2002) |
| Hawaii (HI) (1959) (*50*) | 16,637 | 1,185,497 | Honolulu | Ben Cayetano (*D*) | (2002) |
| Idaho (ID) (1890) (*43*) | 214,325 | 1,251,700 | Boise | Dirk Kempthorne (*R*) | (2002) |
| Illinois (IL) (1818) (*21*) | 143,987 | 12,128,370 | Springfield | George Ryan (*R*) | (2002) |
| Indiana (IN) (1816) (*19*) | 92,904 | 5,942,901 | Indianapolis | Frank O'Bannon (*D*) | (2004) |
| Iowa (IA) (1846) (*29*) | 144,716 | 2,869,413 | Des Moines | Tom Vilsack (*D*) | (2002) |
| Kansas (KS) (1861) (*34*) | 211,922 | 2,654,052 | Topeka | Bill Graves (*R*) | (2002) |
| Kentucky (KY) (1792) (*15*) | 102,907 | 3,960,825 | Frankfort | Paul Patton (*D*) | (2003) |
| Louisiana (LA) (1812) (*18*) | 112,836 | 4,372,035 | Baton Rouge | M. J. Mike Foster (*R*) | (2004) |
| Maine (ME) (1820) (*23*) | 79,939 | 1,253,040 | Augusta | Angus King (*I*) | (2002) |
| Maryland (MD) § (1788) (*7*) | 25,316 | 5,171,634 | Annapolis | Parris Glendening (*D*) | (2002) |
| Massachusetts (MA) § (1788) (*6*) | 20,300 | 6,175,169 | Boston | Argeo Paul Cellucci (*R*) | (2002) |
| Michigan (MI) (1837) (*26*) | 147,136 | 9,863,775 | Lansing | John Engler (*R*) | (2002) |
| Minnesota (MN) (1858) (*32*) | 206,207 | 4,775,508 | St Paul | Jesse Ventura (*Reform*) | (2002) |
| Mississippi (MS) (1817) (*20*) | 121,506 | 2,768,619 | Jackson | David Ronald Musgrove (*D*) | (2004) |
| Missouri (MO) (1821) (*24*) | 178,446 | 5,468,338 | Jefferson City | Bob Holden (*D*) | (2004) |
| Montana (MT) (1889) (*41*) | 376,991 | 882,779 | Helena | Judy Martz (*R*) | (2004) |
| Nebraska (NE) (1867) (*37*) | 199,113 | 1,660,028 | Lincoln | Mike Johanns (*R*) | (2002) |
| Nevada (NV) (1864) (*36*) | 284,396 | 1,809,253 | Carson City | Kenny Guinn (*R*) | (2002) |
| New Hampshire (NH) § (1788) (*9*) | 23,231 | 1,201,134 | Concord | Jeanne Shaheen (*D*) | (2002) |
| New Jersey (NJ) § (1787) (*3*) | 19,215 | 8,143,412 | Trenton | Christine Whitman (*R*) | (2002) |
| New Mexico (NM) (1912) (*47*) | 314,334 | 1,739,844 | Santa Fé | Gary Johnson (*R*) | (2002) |
| New York (NY) § (1788) (*11*) | 122,310 | 18,196,601 | Albany | George Pataki (*R*) | (2002) |
| North Carolina (NC) § (1789) (*12*) | 126,180 | 7,650,789 | Raleigh | Mike Easley (*D*) | (2004) |
| North Dakota (ND) (1889) (*39*) | 178,695 | 633,666 | Bismarck | John Hoeven (*R*) | (2004) |
| Ohio (OH) (1803) (*17*) | 106,067 | 11,256,654 | Columbus | Bob Taft (*R*) | (2002) |
| Oklahoma (OK) (1907) (*46*) | 177,877 | 3,358,044 | Oklahoma City | Frank Keating (*R*) | (2002) |
| Oregon (OR) (1859) (*33*) | 248,646 | 3,316,154 | Salem | John Kitzhaber (*D*) | (2002) |
| Pennsylvania (PA) § (1787) (*2*) | 116,083 | 11,994,016 | Harrisburg | Tom Ridge (*R*) | (2002) |
| Rhode Island (RI) § (1790) (*13*) | 2,707 | 990,819 | Providence | Lincoln Almond (*R*) | (2002) |
| South Carolina (SC) § (1788) (*8*) | 77,988 | 3,885,736 | Columbia | Jim Hodges (*D*) | (2002) |
| South Dakota (SD) (1889) (*40*) | 196,571 | 733,133 | Pierre | William Janklow (*R*) | (2002) |
| Tennessee (TN) (1796) (*16*) | 106,759 | 5,483,535 | Nashville | Don Sundquist (*R*) | (2002) |
| Texas (TX) (1845) (*28*) | 678,358 | 20,044,141 | Austin | George W. Bush (*R*) | (2002) |
| Utah (UT) (1896) (*45*) | 212,816 | 2,129,836 | Salt Lake City | Mike Leavitt (*R*) | (2004) |
| Vermont (VT) (1791) (*14*) | 23,956 | 593,740 | Montpelier | Howard Dean (*D*) | (2002) |
| Virginia (VA) § (1788) (*10*) | 102,558 | 6,872,912 | Richmond | James Gilmore (*R*) | (2002) |
| Washington (WA) (1889) (*42*) | 172,445 | 5,756,361 | Olympia | Gary Locke (*D*) | (2004) |
| West Virginia (WV) (1863) (*35*) | 62,384 | 1,806,928 | Charleston | Bob Wise (*D*) | (2004) |
| Wisconsin (WI) (1848) (*30*) | 140,672 | 5,250,446 | Madison | Tommy Thompson (*R*) | (2002) |
| Wyoming (WY) (1890) (*44*) | 251,501 | 479,602 | Cheyenne | Jim Geringer (*R*) | (2002) |
| Dist. of Columbia (DC) (1791) | 159 | 519,000 | — | Anthony Williams (*D*) (*Mayor*) | |
| **OUTLYING TERRITORIES AND POSSESSIONS** | | | | | |
| American Samoa | 200 | 62,093* | Pago Pago | Tauese Pita Sunia (*D*) | (2004) |
| Guam | 544 | 149,101* | Hagatna | Carl Gutierrez (*D*) | (2002) |
| Northern Mariana Islands | 464 | 66,611* | Saipan | Pedro P. Tenorio (*R*) | (2002) |
| Puerto Rico | 8,875 | 3,860,091* | San Juan | Sila María Calderón (*D*) | (2004) |
| US Virgin Islands | 346 | 118,382* | Charlotte Amalie | Charles Wesley Turnbull (*D*) | (2002) |

§The 13 original states
*D* Democratic Party; *I* Independent; *R* Republican Party
* 1998 estimates

elected representatives and traditionally elected senators, and a popularly elected Governor.

*Governor*, Tauese Pita Sunia

## THE UNITED STATES VIRGIN ISLANDS

AREA – 134 sq. miles (347 sq. km)
POPULATION – 114,483 (1997 estimate)
CAPITAL – ΨCharlotte Amalie (population, 12,331, 1990), on St Thomas

The US Virgin Islands were purchased from Denmark and came under US sovereignty in 1917. There are three main islands, St Thomas (28 sq. miles), St Croix (84 sq. miles), St John (20 sq. miles) and about 50 small islets or cays, mostly uninhabited.

Under the provisions of the Revised Organic Act of the Virgin Islands 1954, legislative power is vested in the Legislature, a unicameral body composed of 15 senators popularly elected for two-year terms. The Governor is popularly elected. Those born in the US Virgin Islands are US citizen nationals. A referendum is to take place at a future date to determine the future political status of the islands.

*Governor*, Charles Wesley Turnbull

| *Trade with UK* | 1999 | 2000 |
|---|---|---|
| Imports from UK | £5,881,000 | £4,083,000 |
| Exports to UK | 591,000 | 4,963,000 |

## NORTHERN MARIANA ISLANDS

AREA – 179 sq. miles (464 sq. km)
POPULATION – 63,763 (1997 estimate)
SEAT OF GOVERNMENT – Saipan (population, 52,706, 1995 census)

The USA administered the Northern Mariana Islands as part of a UN Trusteeship until the trusteeship agreement was terminated in 1986, bringing fully into effect a 1976 congressional law establishing the Northern Mariana Islands as a Commonwealth under US sovereignty. Most of the then residents became US citizens. Those born subsequently in the Northern Mariana Islands are US citizen nationals. There is a popularly elected bicameral legislature and a popularly elected Governor.

*Governor*, Pedro P. Tenorio

---

# URUGUAY
*República Oriental del Uruguay*

---

AREA – 67,574 sq. miles (175,016 sq. km). Neighbours: Argentina (west), Brazil (north and east)
POPULATION – 3,312,000 (1997 UN estimate): predominantly of Spanish and Italian descent. Spanish is the official language. Many Uruguayans are Roman Catholics. There is no established church
CAPITAL – ΨMontevideo (population, 1,303,182, 1996)
MAJOR CITIES – Melo; Mercedes; Minas; ΨPaysandú; Punta del Este; Rivera; Salto
CURRENCY – Uruguayan peso of 100 centésimos
NATIONAL ANTHEM – Orientales, La Patria O La Tumba (Uruguayans, the fatherland or death)
NATIONAL DAY – 25 August (Declaration of Independence, 1825)
NATIONAL FLAG – Four blue and five white horizontal stripes surcharged with sun on a white ground in the top corner, next flagstaff
LIFE EXPECTANCY (years) – male 70.5; female 77.8
POPULATION GROWTH RATE – 0.7 per cent (1999)
POPULATION DENSITY – 19 per sq. km (1998)
URBAN POPULATION – 91.3 per cent (2000 estimate)
MILITARY EXPENDITURE – 2.3 per cent of GDP (1999)
MILITARY PERSONNEL – 23,700: Army 15,200, Navy 5,500, Air Force 3,000, Paramilitaries 920

The country consists mainly of undulating grassy plains. The principal river is the Rio Negro (with its tributary the Yi), flowing from north-east to south-west into the Rio Uruguay. The climate is temperate.

## HISTORY AND POLITICS

Uruguay (or the *Banda Oriental*, as the territory lying on the eastern bank of the Uruguay River was then called) formed part of Spanish South America from 1726 to 1814, when it was annexed by the Argentine Confederation and then Portugal, becoming a province of Brazil. In 1825, the country threw off Brazilian rule. Uruguay was declared an independent state in 1828 and was inaugurated as a republic in 1830.

General elections held in 1984 marked the return to civilian rule after 11 years of presidential rule with military support. The first fully free presidential and legislative elections since 1971 were held in 1989, and were won by the National (Blanco) Party (NP).

The presidential election on 31 October and 28 November 1999 was won by Jorge Batlle Ibáñez of the Colorado Party (CP), who gained 51.5 per cent of the vote in the second round of the election. The legislative elections for both houses of the General Assembly, which were held simultaneously with the first round of the presidential election, resulted in the Progressive Encounter-Broad Front (EP-FA) winning 40 seats, the CP 33 seats, the NP 22 seats and the New Space party (NE) four seats in the House of Representatives, with the EP-FA winning 12 seats, the CP ten seats, the NP seven seats and the NE one seat in the Senate. A coalition government of the CP and the NP was formed.

### POLITICAL SYSTEM

Under the constitution the president (who may serve only a single term of five years) appoints a council of ministers and a Secretary (Planning and Budget Office), and the vice-president presides over Congress. The Congress consists of a Chamber of 99 deputies and a Senate of 30 members (plus the vice-president), elected for five years by proportional representation.

The republic is divided into 19 Departments, each with an elected governor and legislature.

### HEAD OF STATE

*President*, Jorge Batlle Ibáñez, *elected* 28 November 1999, *took office* 1 March 2000
*Vice-President*, Luis Hierro López

### COUNCIL OF MINISTERS *as at September 2001*

The President
*Economy and Finance*, Alberto Bensión (CP)
*Education and Culture*, Antonio Mercador (NP)
*Foreign Relations*, Didier Opertti (CP)
*Health*, Horacio Fernández Ameglio (CP)
*Housing, Territorial Regulation and Environment*, Carlos Cat (NP)
*Industry, Energy and Mines*, Sergio Abreu (NP)
*Interior*, Guillermo Sterling (CP)
*Labour and Social Security*, Álvaro Alonso (NP)
*Livestock, Agriculture and Fisheries*, Gonzalo González (NP)
*National Defence*, Luis Brezzo (CP)
*Planning and Budget*, Ariel Davrieux (NP)
*Tourism*, Alfonso Varela (CP)
*Transport and Public Works*, Lucio Cáceres (CP)
CP Colorado Party; NP National (Blanco) Party;

EMBASSY OF THE ORIENTAL REPUBLIC OF URUGUAY
2nd Floor, 140 Brompton Road, London SW3 1HY
Tel: 020-7589 8835
*Ambassador Extraordinary and Plenipotentiary*, HE Dr Miguel Jorge Berthet, apptd 2001

BRITISH EMBASSY
Calle Marco Bruto 1073, 11300 Montevideo (PO Box 16024)
Tel: (00 598) (2) 622 3650/3630
*Ambassador Extraordinary and Plenipotentiary*, HE John Everard, apptd 2001

BRITISH-URUGUAYAN CHAMBER OF COMMERCE, Avenida Libertador Brig. Gen., Lavalleja 1641, P2, Of 202, Montevideo

## ECONOMY

Agriculture accounted for 8.2 per cent of GDP in 1998 and employed 13.1 per cent of the workforce in 1997. Beef, mutton and wool are produced and rice, wheat, barley, linseed and sunflower seed are cultivated. Other foodstuffs (citrus, wine, beer), fishing and textile industries are also of importance.

Industry accounted for 26.5 per cent of GDP in 1998. Textiles, tyres, sheet-glass, three-ply wood, cement, leather-curing, beet-sugar, plastics, household consumer goods and edible oils are produced. Exploited minerals include clinker, dolomite, marble and granite.

Much of the economy is in the hands of state monopolies and there has been only limited market liberalisation. In October 2000, the House of Representatives approved a plan to privatise 40 per cent of the state telecommunications company Ancel.

GNP – US$20,604 million (1999); US$5,900 per capita (1999)
GDP – US$19,677 million (1997); US$6,333 per capita (1998)
ANNUAL AVERAGE GROWTH OF GDP – 4.8 per cent (1996)
INFLATION RATE – 5.7 per cent (1999)
UNEMPLOYMENT – 10.1 per cent (1998)
TOTAL EXTERNAL DEBT – US$7,600 million (1998)

### TRADE

The major exports are meat, meat by-products and livestock, agricultural products and textiles. The principal imports are machinery and transport equipment and chemical products. Principal trading partners are Brazil, Argentina, the USA and Germany.

In 1999 Uruguay had a trade surplus of US$868 million and a current account surplus of US$605 million. Imports totalled US$3,357 million and exports US$2,232 million.

| *Trade with UK* | 1999 | 2000 |
|---|---|---|
| Imports from UK | £66,430,000 | £58,555,000 |
| Exports to UK | 41,566,000 | 35,596,000 |

## COMMUNICATIONS

There are over 50,000 km of roads, including 12,000 km of national highways, and over 2,000 km of standard gauge railway in use. A state-owned airline, PLUNA, provides international services, and internal passenger and limited freight services are provided by TAMU, a branch of the Uruguayan Air Force. The international airport of Carrasco lies 12 miles outside Montevideo. The River Uruguay is navigable from its estuary to Salto, 200 miles north, and the Negro is also navigable as far as Mercedes. In December 1998, the Senate approved the construction of a 45-km bridge across the River Plate, linking Uruguay and Argentina.

## EDUCATION

Primary and secondary education is compulsory and free, and technical and trade schools and evening courses for adult education are state controlled. The university at Montevideo (founded in 1849) has ten faculties and a new university has been built at Salto.
ILLITERACY RATE – 2.2 per cent
ENROLMENT (percentage of age group) – primary 93 per cent (1996); tertiary 29.5 per cent (1996)

---

# UZBEKISTAN
*O'zbekiston Respublikasy*

---

AREA – 172,742 sq. miles (447,400 sq. km). Neighbours: Kazakhstan (north and west), Kyrgyzstan and Tajikistan (east), Afghanistan and Turkmenistan (south)
POPULATION – 24,600,000 (2000 estimate): 72 per cent Uzbek, 8 per cent Russian, 5 per cent Tajik and 4 per cent Kazakh, with smaller numbers of Tatars, Kara-Kalpaks, Koreans, Ukrainians and Kyrgyz. The predominant religion is Sunni Muslim. Islam is tolerated within strict bounds; it is allowed to play no part in politics. The official language is Uzbek (72 per cent). Russian (8 per cent), Tajik (5 per cent) and Kazakh (4 per cent) are also spoken. Uzbek is one of the Turkic group of languages. In 1994 the government approved a six-year programme for the transfer of the Uzbek language to a Latin script
CAPITAL – Tashkent (population, 2,200,000, 1998 estimate)
MAJOR CITIES – Samarkand (361,800), which contains the Gur-Emir (Tamerlane's Mausoleum); Bukhara (237,100), which contains the Samanid Mausoleum and the Ulughbek Madrassah
CURRENCY – Soum of 100 tiyin
NATIONAL DAY – 1 September (Independence Day)
NATIONAL FLAG – Three horizontal stripes of blue, white, green, with the white fimbriated in red; on the blue near the hoist a crescent and twelve stars, all in white
LIFE EXPECTANCY (years) – male 65.8; female 71.2
POPULATION GROWTH RATE – 1.7 per cent (1999)
POPULATION DENSITY – 54 per sq. km (1998)
URBAN POPULATION – 36.9 per cent (2000 estimate)
MILITARY EXPENDITURE – 3.9 per cent of GDP (1999)
MILITARY PERSONNEL – 59,100: Army 50,000, Air Force 9,100, Paramilitaries 20,000
CONSCRIPTION DURATION – 18 months
ILLITERACY RATE – 2.8 per cent
ENROLMENT (percentage of age group) – tertiary 32.9 per cent (1992)

Uzbekistan occupies the south-central part of former Soviet Central Asia, lying between the high Tienshan Mountains and the Pamir highlands in the east and south-east and sandy lowlands in the west and north-west, in the basin of the Amudarya and Syrdarya rivers. Uzbekistan consists of the Republic of Karakalpakstan and 12 regions: Andijan, Bukhara, Jizak, Fergana, Kashka-Darya, Khorezm, Namanghan, Navoi, Samarkand, Surhan-Darya, Syr-Darya and Tashkent. Most of the country is a plain with huge waterless deserts, and several large oases which form the main centres of population and economic life. The climate is hot, continental and dry.

## HISTORY AND POLITICS

In the 13th century the area that is now Uzbekistan became the centre of a great Muslim empire under Amir Timur (Tamerlane), with its capital at Samarkand. By the beginning of the 19th century three independent Khanates, Khiva, Kokand and Bukhara, existed in what is now Uzbekistan. These were annexed to the Russian Empire in the second half of the 19th century. In November 1917 a Communist revolution broke out in Tashkent and by 1921, all of Uzbekistan had been absorbed into the Soviet Union.

Uzbekistan declared its independence from the Soviet Union on 1 September 1991. Its independence was confirmed in a referendum on 29 December and recognised internationally. Elections to the new *Oliy Majlis* were held on 25 December 1994 and won by the ruling People's Democratic Party (PDP) and its allies.

The government of President Karimov is formed by the People's Democratic Party. Despite the constitutionally guaranteed freedom of religion and thought, and respect for human rights and multiparty democracy, censorship is still widely used and little political opposition is tolerated. The main opposition parties, Erk (Freedom) and Birlik (Unity) nationalist parties, have been continually banned since the introduction of the multiparty constitution in December 1992, but five political parties are legally registered. In March 1995 President Karimov's term of office was extended to 2000 by a national referendum and he won a further five-year term in a presidential election held on 9 January 2000, gaining 91.9 per cent of the vote. The election result attracted criticism from the Organisation for Security and Co-operation in Europe, who claimed no real opposition candidate had been allowed to stand. Legislative elections were held on 5 and 19 December 1999; the People's Democratic Party and its allies won 123 seats. The remaining seats were won by independent candidates and citizens' groups.

### Insurgencies

The Islamic Movement of Uzbekistan (IMU), which seeks to overthrow the government and establish an Islamic state, was founded in 1996. Many IMU members have trained in camps in Afghanistan and the organisation is thought to be financed by the Taliban. Whilst they have carried out car bombings in Tashkent, their activities have centred on the Fergana valley and they have clashed with Kyrgyz armed forces.

### Foreign Relations

Uzbekistan has actively supported international efforts to resolve the conflict in Afghanistan. It was announced in February 1999 that Uzbekistan was to withdraw from the collective security treaty of the Commonwealth of Independent States. Uzbekistan is a member of the UN, OSCE, UNESCO, WHO and many other international organisations.

### Political System

Under the constitution of December 1992, the president and government hold executive power. The president may serve a maximum of two five-year terms and has the power to dissolve the 250-member unicameral Supreme Assembly (*Oliy Majlis*), which may not remove or impeach the president.

### Head of State

*President*, Islam Karimov, *elected* 29 December 1991, *elected by referendum for a five-year term* 26 March 1995, *re-elected* 9 January 2000

### Cabinet *as at September 2001*

*Chairman of the Cabinet*, The President
*Prime Minister*, Utkur Sultanov
*First Deputy Prime Minister, Macroeconomics and Statistics*, Rustam Azimov
*Deputy Prime Ministers*, Turop Kholtaev *(Agriculture and Water Resources)*; Valery Ataev *(Power and Electrification)*; Bakhtiyor Alimjanov; Dilbar Ghulomova; Rustam Junusov; Mirabror Usmanov
*Chairman, National Parliament*, Erkin Khalilov
*Communications*, Abduwahid Djurabaev
*Cultural Affairs*, Khairulla Djuraev
*Defence*, Kodir Gulomov
*Education*, R. Djuraev
*Finance*, Mamarizo Normurodov
*Foreign Affairs*, Abdulaziz Kamilov
*Foreign Economic Relations*, Elyor Majidovich Ganiev
*Health*, Feruz Nazirov
*Higher and Secondary Specialised Education*, Saidahror Gulamov
*Interior*, Zakir Almatov
*Justice*, Abdusamad Polvonzoda
*Labour and Social Security*, Okiljon Abidov
*Macroeconomics and Statistics*, Rustam Shoabdurakhmanov
*Municipal Economy*, Gafurjan Mukhamedov

### Embassy of the Republic of Uzbekistan

41 Holland Park, London W11 2RP
Tel: 020-7229 7679
*Ambassador Extraordinary and Plenipotentiary*, HE Alisher Faizullaev, apptd 1999

### British Embassy

Ul. Gulyamova 67, UZ-700000 Tashkent
Tel: (00 99871) 1206451/1206288
*Ambassador Extraordinary and Plenipotentiary*, HE Christopher Ingham, apptd 1998
British Council Director, Michael Moore, MBE, 11 D. Kounoev Street, Tashkent; e-mail: bc.tashkent@bc-tashkent.sprint.com

## ECONOMY

Uzbekistan's economy is based on intensive agricultural production, which accounted for 29.1 per cent of GDP in 1997 and engaged 46 per cent of the workforce in 1995. Cotton production is approximately 4 million tonnes per year, made possible by extensive irrigation schemes. Textile manufacture, silk production and leather goods are also important. Wheat, potatoes and rice are widely grown. In addition there are some agricultural and textile machinery plants and several chemical combines. Uzbekistan possesses extensive mineral deposits. Copper, uranium, oil, gold and many other metals are extracted. In 1998 oil output was 8.0 million tonnes, and gas production was 55 billion cubic metres. The Muruntao mine is the largest open-cast gold mine in the world; in 1998, 81 tonnes of gold were produced. Total gold reserves are estimated at more than 5,000 tonnes.

Foreign direct investment exceeds US$9 billion. South Korea, the USA, Japan, Turkey and the UK are the main investors. Uzbekistan is a member of the CIS economic union.

GNP – US$17,613 million (1999); US$720 per capita (1999)
GDP – US$9,892 million (1997); US$470 per capita (1998)
Annual Average Growth of GDP – 4.8 per cent (1999)
Unemployment – 4.4 per cent (2000)
Total External Debt – US$3,162 million (1998)

| *Trade with UK* | 1999 | 2000 |
|---|---|---|
| Imports from UK | £30,555,000 | £16,107,000 |
| Exports to UK | 23,678,000 | 14,629,000 |

## VANUATU

*Ripablik Blong Vanuatu*

AREA – 4,706 sq. miles (12,189 sq. km)
POPULATION – 189,618 (2000 UN estimate). About 95 per cent are Melanesian, the rest being mostly Micronesian, Polynesian and European. The national language is Bislama, but English and French are also official languages
CAPITAL – ΨPort Vila (population, 26,100, 1993), on Efate
MAJOR TOWN – Luganville (8,800, 1993), on Espiritu Santo
CURRENCY – Vatu of 100 centimes
NATIONAL ANTHEM – Nasonal sing sing blong Vanuatu
NATIONAL DAY – 30 July (Independence Day)
NATIONAL FLAG – Red over green with a black triangle in the hoist, the three parts being divided by fimbriations of black and yellow, and in the centre of the black triangle a boar's tusk overlaid by two crossed fern leaves
LIFE EXPECTANCY (years) – male 58.7; female 63.0
POPULATION GROWTH RATE – 2.5 per cent (1999)
POPULATION DENSITY – 15 per sq. km (1998)
URBAN POPULATION – 20.0 per cent (2000 estimate)
ENROLMENT (percentage of age group) – primary 74 per cent (1989); secondary 17 per cent (1991)

Vanuatu is situated in the South Pacific Ocean. It includes 13 large and some 70 small islands, of coral and volcanic origin, including the Banks and Torres Islands in the north. The principal islands are Vanua Lava, Espiritu Santo, Maewo, Pentecost, Ambae, Malekula, Ambrym, Epi, Efate, Erromango, Tanna and Aneityum. Most islands are mountainous and there are active volcanoes on several. The climate is oceanic tropical, moderated by the south-east trade winds which blow between May and October. At other times winds are variable and cyclones may occur.

### HISTORY AND POLITICS

Vanuatu, the former Anglo-French Condominium of the New Hebrides, became an independent republic within the Commonwealth on 30 July 1980. Parliament consists of 52 members, directly elected for a term of four years. A Council of Chiefs advises on matters of custom. Executive power is held by the prime minister (elected from and by parliament) and a Council of Ministers who are responsible to parliament. The president is elected for a five-year term by the presidents of the six provincial governments and the members of parliament. The most recent legislative election took place on 6 March 1998, following which a multiparty coalition government was formed under Prime Minister Barak Sope. The most recent presidential election took place on 24 March 1999 and was won by Fr John Bani.

Following a no-confidence motion against Prime Minister Sope, Eduard Napatei of the Vanu'aku Pati (VP) became prime minister on 13 April 2001 and appointed a Cabinet consisting of VP and Union of Moderate Parties (UMP) members.

#### HEAD OF STATE

*President*, HE Fr John Bani, *elected* 24 March 1999

#### COUNCIL OF MINISTERS *as at September 2001*

*Prime Minister*, Edward Natapei (VP)
*Deputy Prime Minister*, Serge Vohor (UMP)
*Agriculture, Forestry and Fisheries*, Willy Posen (UMP)
*Comprehensive Reform Programme*, Willie Ollie (VP)
*Education*, Jacques Sese (UMP)
*Finance*, Joe Carlo Bomal (VP)
*Foreign Affairs*, Alain Mahé (UMP)
*Health*, Clement Leo (VP)
*Infrastructure, Public Utilities*, Jacklyn Rueben Titek (VP)
*Internal Affairs*, Joe Natuman (VP)
*Lands and Mineral Resources*, Sela Molisa (VP)
*Ni-Vanuatu Business Development*, Daniel Bangtor (VP)
*Youth and Sports*, Henri Taga (UMP)

HIGH COMMISSIONER TO GREAT BRITAIN, vacant, resident at Port Vila, Vanuatu

#### BRITISH HIGH COMMISSION

KPMG House, Rue Pasteur, PO Box 567, Port Vila
Tel: (00 678) 23100
E-mail: bhcvila@vanuatu.com.vu
*High Commissioner*, HE Michael Hill, OBE, apptd 2000

### ECONOMY

Most of the population is employed on plantations or in subsistence agriculture. Subsistence crops include yams, taro, manioc, sweet potato and breadfruit; principal cash crops are copra, cocoa and coffee. Cattle are kept on the plantations and beef is the second largest export. There is a small light industrial sector. Principal exports are copra, meat (frozen, tinned and chilled), timber and cocoa. The main trading partner is Japan.

There were about 50,000 tourists in 1997. The absence of direct taxation has led to growth in the finance and associated industries.

In 1998 Vanuatu had a trade deficit of US$42 million and a current account surplus of US$5 million. Imports totalled US$88 million and exports totalled US$34 million.

GNP – US$227 million (1999); US$1,170 per capita (1999)
GDP – US$252 million (1997); US$1,276 per capita (1998)
ANNUAL AVERAGE GROWTH OF GDP – 3.0 per cent (1996)
INFLATION RATE – 3.3 per cent (1998)
TOTAL EXTERNAL DEBT – US$63 million (1998)

| *Trade with UK* | 1999 | 2000 |
|---|---|---|
| Imports from UK | £153,000 | £115,000 |
| Exports to UK | 307,000 | 26,000 |

## VATICAN CITY STATE

*Status Civitatis Vaticanae/Stato della Città del Vaticano*

AREA – 0.2 sq. miles (0.44 sq. km). Neighbour: Italy
POPULATION – 1,000 (1994 UN estimate). The languages are Latin and Italian
CAPITAL – Vatican City (population, 766, 1988)
CURRENCY – Italian currency is legal tender
NATIONAL DAY – 22 October (Inauguration of present Pontiff)
NATIONAL FLAG – Square flag; equal vertical bands of yellow (next staff), and white; crossed keys and triple crown device on white band
POPULATION GROWTH RATE – 0.0 per cent (1997)
POPULATION DENSITY – 2,273 per sq. km (1997)
URBAN POPULATION – 100.0 per cent (2000 estimate)
GDP – US$9 million (1997); US$19,962 per capita (1997)
ANNUAL AVERAGE GROWTH OF GDP – 0.7 per cent (1996)

The office of the ecclesiastical head of the Roman Catholic Church (Holy See) is vested in the Pope, the Sovereign Pontiff. For many centuries the Sovereign Pontiff exercised temporal power but by 1870 the Papal States had become part of unified Italy. The temporal power of the Pope was in suspense until the treaty of 1929 which recognised the full and independent sovereignty of the Holy See in the City of the Vatican.

*Sovereign Pontiff*, His Holiness Pope John Paul II (Karol Wojtyła), *born* at Wadowice (Kraków, Poland), 18 May 1920, *elected* Pope in succession to Pope John Paul I, 16 October 1978

SECRETARIAT OF STATE *as at September 2001*

*Secretary of State*, Cardinal Angelo Sodano, *apptd* December 1990
*Assistant Secretary of State*, Archbishop Leonardo Sandri
*Secretary for Relations with States*, Archbishop Jean-Louis Tauran

APOSTOLIC NUNCIATURE
54 Parkside, London SW19 5NE
Tel: 020-8946 1410/7971
*Apostolic Nuncio*, HE Archbishop Pablo Puente, apptd 1997

BRITISH EMBASSY TO THE HOLY SEE
91 Via dei Condotti, I–00187 Rome
Tel: (00 39) (6) 6992 3561
*Ambassador Extraordinary and Plenipotentiary*, HE Mark Pellew, CVO, LVO, apptd 1997

| *Trade with UK* | 1999 | 2000 |
|---|---|---|
| Imports from UK | £847,000 | £714,000 |
| Exports to UK | — | 78,000 |

## VENEZUELA
*República Bolivariana de Venezuela*

AREA – 352,145 sq. miles (912,050 sq. km). Neighbours: Colombia (west), Guyana (east), Brazil (south)POPULATION – 24,169,744 (2000 estimate): 67 per cent mestizo, 21 per cent white, 10 per cent black and 2 per cent Amerindian. The language is Spanish. 96 per cent of the population is Roman Catholic
CAPITAL – Caracas (population, 3,672,779, 1996 estimate)
MAJOR CITIES – Barquisimeto (793,565); ΨMaracaibo (1,660,233); Maracay (449,180); Valencia (1,225,342), 1997 estimates
CURRENCY – Bolívar (Bs) of 100 céntimos
NATIONAL ANTHEM – Gloria Al Bravo Pueblo (Glory to the brave people)
NATIONAL DAY – 5 July
NATIONAL FLAG – Three horizontal stripes of yellow, blue, red with an arc of seven white stars on the blue stripe
LIFE EXPECTANCY (years) – male 70.9; female 76.2
POPULATION GROWTH RATE – 2.2 per cent (1999)
POPULATION DENSITY – 25 per sq. km (1998)
URBAN POPULATION – 86.9 per cent (2000 estimate)
ILLITERACY RATE – 7.0 per cent
ENROLMENT (percentage of age group) – primary 84 per cent (1996); secondary 22 per cent (1996); tertiary 28.5 per cent (1991)

Included in the area of the South American republic of Venezuela are 72 islands off the coast, with a total area of about 14,650 sq. miles, the largest being Margarita (area, about 400 sq. miles).

The mountains are the Eastern Andes and Maritime Andes, running south-west to north-east. The main range is known as the Sierra Nevada de Mérida, and contains Pico Bolivar (16,411 ft) and Picacho de la Sierra (15,420 ft). The principal river is the Orinoco, with innumerable affluents, the main river exceeding 1,600 miles in length. The upper waters of the Orinoco are united with those of the Rio Negro (a Brazilian tributary of the Amazon) by a natural river or canal, known as the Casiquiare. The coastal regions contain many lagoons and lakes, of which Maracaibo (area 8,296 sq. miles) is the largest lake in South America.

The climate is tropical, except where modified by altitude or tempered by sea breezes.

### HISTORY AND POLITICS

The first Spanish settlement was established at Cumaná in 1520. During the 18th century there were a number of uprisings against Spanish rule, and troops led by Simón Bolívar finally defeated the Spanish in 1823. Venezuela became an independent republic in 1830.

On 25 April 1999, a referendum on convening a constituent assembly to rewrite the constitution was passed and an election to decide the members of the constituent assembly was held on 25 July 1999. The new constitution was approved in a referendum held on 15 December and was proclaimed on 20 December.

The National Congress was dissolved on 4 January 2000 pending elections to the new National Assembly, which were due to be held on 28 May, but were postponed. In the presidential election held on 30 July 2000, President Chávez was re-elected, winning 59 per cent of the vote. In the simultaneous election for the National Assembly, the Fifth Republic Movement (MVR) won 76 seats, Democratic Action 29 seats, Movement towards Socialism 21 seats, and other parties 39 seats.

The National Assembly granted President Chávez Frías the power to rule by decree in industrial and economic policy and matters concerning the civil service for a period of one year on 7 November 2000.

POLITICAL SYSTEM

Under the 1999 constitution, the country was renamed the Bolivarian Republic of Venezuela, a unicameral legislature, the National Assembly, was created, and the post of vice-president instituted. The president, who is directly elected, serves a six-year term, which is renewable once only. The vice-president is appointed by the president. Legislative power is exercised by the 165-member *Asamblea Nacional* (National Assembly), which is directly elected for a five-year term.

FEDERAL STRUCTURE

Venezuela is divided into 22 states and two federal districts.

| *State* | *Area (sq. km)* | *Population (2000 estimate)* | *Capital* |
|---|---|---|---|
| Amazonas | 175,750 | 100,325 | Puerto Ayacucho |
| Anzoátegui | 43,300 | 1,140,369 | Barcelona |
| Apure | 76,500 | 466,931 | San Fernando |
| Aragua | 7,014 | 1,481,453 | Maracay |
| Barinas | 35,200 | 583,521 | Barinas |
| Bolívar | 238,000 | 1,306,651 | Ciudad Bolívar |
| Carabobo | 4,650 | 2,106,264 | Valencia |
| Cojedes | 14,800 | 262,154 | San Carlos |
| Delta Amacuro | 40,200 | 137,939 | Tucupita |
| Falcón | 24,800 | 747,672 | Coro |
| Federal District | 1,930 | 2,284,924* | Caracas |
| Federal Dependencies | 120 | —— | |
| Guárico | 64,986 | 638,638 | San Juan |
| Lara | 19,800 | 1,581,121 | Barquisimeto |
| Mérida | 11,300 | 744,986 | Mérida |
| Miranda | 7,950 | 2,607,163 | Los Teques |
| Monagas | 28,900 | 599,764 | Maturín |
| Nueva Esparta | 1,150 | 377,701 | La Asunción |
| Portuguesa | 15,200 | 830,441 | Guanare |

| | | | |
|---|---|---|---|
| Sucre | 11,800 | 824,764 | Cumaná |
| Táchira | 11,100 | 1,031,158 | San Cristóbal |
| Trujillo | 7,400 | 587,280 | Trujillo |
| Yaracuy | 7,100 | 518,902 | San Felipe |
| Zulia | 63,100 | 3,209,626 | Maracaibo |

* Includes Federal Dependencies

## HEAD OF STATE

*President*, Hugo Chávez Frías, *elected* 6 December 1998, *sworn in* 2 February 1999, re-elected 30 July 2000
*Vice-President*, Adina Bastidas

## COUNCIL OF MINISTERS *as at September 2001*

*Attorney-General*, Isaias Rodriguez
*Defence*, José Vicente Rangel
*Education*, Héctor Navarro Diaz
*Energy and Mines*, Álvaro Silva Calderón
*Environment and Renewable Natural Resources*, Ana Elisa Osorio
*Finance*, Nelson Merentes
*Foreign Relations*, Col. Luís Alfonso Davila
*Health*, María Lourdes Urbaneja
*Industry and Commerce*, Luisa Romero Bermudez
*Infrastructure*, Gen. Eliecer Hurtado Soucre
*Interior and Justice*, Luís Miquilena
*Labour*, Blancanieves Portocarrero
*Planning and Development*, Jorge Giordani
*Science and Technology*, Carlos Genatios

## VENEZUELAN EMBASSY

1 Cromwell Road, London SW7 2HR
Tel: 020-7584 4206/7
*Ambassador Extraordinary and Plenipotentiary*, HE Alfredo Toro-Hardy, apptd 2001
*Defence Attaché*, Capt. C. Briceño-Corales

## BRITISH EMBASSY

Edificio Torre Las Mercedes (Piso 3), Avenida La Estancia, Chuao (Apartado 1246), Caracas 1061
Tel: (00 58) (21) 2993 4111/4224
E-mail: britishembassy@internet.ve
*Ambassador Extraordinary and Plenipotentiary*, HE Dr John Hughes, apptd 2000
*Deputy Head of Mission*, S. J. le Jeune d'Allegeershecque
*Defence Attaché*, Capt. E. Searle
*First Secretary (Commercial)*, S. Seaman, MBE

CONSULAR OFFICES – Maracaibo, Margarita, Mérida, San Cristobal, Valencia

BRITISH COUNCIL DIRECTOR, Jonathan Greenwood, Piso 3, Torre Credit card, Av. Principal El Bosque, El Bosque, Caracas; e-mail: bc-venezuela@britishcouncil.org.ve

BRITISH-VENEZUELAN CHAMBER OF COMMERCE, Torre Británica, Piso 11, Altamira Sur, Caracas 1062A

## DEFENCE

The Army has 81 main battle tanks, 290 armoured personnel carriers and five attack helicopters. The Navy has two submarines, six frigates, six patrol and coastal vessels, seven combat aircraft and eight armed helicopters at nine bases. The Air Force has 124 combat aircraft and 31 armed helicopters.
MILITARY EXPENDITURE – 1.5 per cent of GDP (1999)
MILITARY PERSONNEL – 79,000: Army 34,000, Navy 15,000, Air Force 7,000, National Guard 23,000
CONSCRIPTION DURATION – 30 months (selective)

## ECONOMY

President Hugo Chávez Frías pledged in December 1998 that his government would cut public spending and tackle tax evasion and corruption.

Agriculture comprises large-scale commercial farms together with subsistence farming. Land distribution is very uneven, with 1 per cent of farms occupying 46 per cent of arable land and 250,000 smallholdings occupying less that 2 per cent of arable land.

Products of the tropical forest region include orchids, wild rubber, timber, mangrove bark, balata gum and tonka beans. Agricultural products include corn, bananas, cocoa beans, coffee, cotton, rice, maize, sugar, sesame, groundnuts, potatoes, tomatoes, other vegetables, sisal and tobacco. There is an extensive beef and dairy farming industry.

The principal industry is petroleum and gas, which together account for 78 per cent of exports. There are eight refineries. The Orinoco heavy oil belt is being developed; estimates put recoverable resources at 73,000 million barrels in 1996.

Aluminium is abundant. Rich iron ore deposits in eastern Venezuela have been developed. Other industry includes a wide variety of manufacturing and component assembly, principally petrochemicals, gold, diamonds and foodstuffs.

On 2 February 2000, President Chávez announced reductions in the rate of value-added tax, a reduction in personal taxes, the abolition of bank debit tax, and tax exemptions in certain key areas of the economy.
GNP – US$87,313 million (1999); US$3,670 per capita (1999)
GDP – US$83,774 million (1997); US$4,107 per capita (1998)
ANNUAL AVERAGE GROWTH OF GDP – 1.6 per cent (1996)
INFLATION RATE – 23.6 per cent (1999)
UNEMPLOYMENT – 10.1 per cent (1998)
TOTAL EXTERNAL DEBT – US$37,003 million (1998)

## TRADE

Apart from oil, the main exports are bauxite, iron ore, agricultural products and basic manufactures. The main imports are machinery and transport equipment, chemicals and foodstuffs. The USA and Colombia are the major trading partners.

In 1998 Venezuela had a trade surplus of US$2,748 million and a current account surplus of US$2,562 million. In 1999 imports totalled US$14,789 million and exports US$19,852 million.

| *Trade with UK* | 1999 | 2000 |
|---|---|---|
| Imports from UK | £203,201,000 | £221,382,000 |
| Exports to UK | 149,992,000 | 215,126,000 |

## COMMUNICATIONS

There are about 62,000 km of roads, some 24,000 km of them paved. Road and river communications have made railways of negligible importance in Venezuela except for carrying iron ore in the south-east, though the government is expanding the network, and there are now some 336 km of railway lines.

The Orinoco is navigable for ocean-going ships (up to 40 ft draught) for 150 miles upstream, by large steamers for 700 miles, and by smaller vessels some 900 miles upstream. There are seven Venezuelan airlines which between them have a comprehensive network of internal and international flights. There is an international airport at Caracas.

## VIETNAM
*Công Hòa Xã Hôi Chu Nghĩa Viêt Nam*

AREA – 128,066 sq. miles (331,689 sq. km). Neighbours: China (north), Laos and Cambodia (west)
POPULATION – 77,515,000 (1997 UN estimate). The language is Vietnamese. French, English and Khmer are also spoken
CAPITAL – Hanoi (population, 1,073,760, 1992 estimate)
MAJOR CITIES – Hai Phong (1,447,523); Ho Chi Minh City (3,924,435)
CURRENCY – Dông of 10 hào or 100 xu
NATIONAL ANTHEM – Tien Quan Ca (The troops are advancing)
NATIONAL DAY – 2 September
NATIONAL FLAG – Red, with yellow five-point star in centre
LIFE EXPECTANCY (years) – male 64.7; female 68.8
POPULATION GROWTH RATE – 1.9 per cent (1999)
POPULATION DENSITY – 234 per sq. km (1998)
URBAN POPULATION – 19.7 per cent (2000 estimate)
ILLITERACY RATE – 6.7 per cent (2000)
ENROLMENT (percentage of age group) – primary 95 per cent (1980); tertiary 6.9 per cent (1996)

### HISTORY AND POLITICS

Vietnam became a unified state at the end of the 18th century, with the assistance of France, whose influence on the region grew. In 1899 the Indo-Chinese Union was proclaimed, uniting Vietnam with Cambodia and Laos under French rule. Vietnam was under Japanese occupation from 1940-1945; insurrection by Communist, Nationalist and Revolutionary forces led to a French withdrawal in 1954 and the division of the country into Communist North Vietnam and non-communist South Vietnam. War broke out between the two countries in 1961, which lasted until 1975. North and South Vietnam were reunified in 1976 under the name of the Socialist Republic of Vietnam. The national flag, anthem and capital of North Vietnam were adopted, and Saigon was renamed Ho Chi Minh City.

#### INSURGENCY

There was unrest among the Montagnard ethnic minority in the central highlands in February 2001, which was thought to have been caused by resentment towards northern migrants who were settling in the region due to the expansion of coffee farming.

#### POLITICAL SYSTEM

Effective power lies with the Vietnamese Communist Party (VCP), its highest executive body being the Central Committee, elected by a Party Congress on a national basis. The Politburo and the Secretariat of the Central Committee exercise the real power.

The constitution of 1992 reaffirmed Communist Party rule but also formalised free market economic reforms.

A new National Assembly (*Quoc-Hoi*) was elected on 20 July 1997; the VCP holds 384 of the 450 seats. The president is elected for a five-year term by the members of the National Assembly .

#### HEAD OF STATE

*President*, Tran Duc Luong, *elected* 25 September 1997
*Vice-President*, Nguyen Thi Binh

#### POLITBURO

*Secretary-General of the VCP*, Nong Duc Manh
Politburo Standing Board, *Le Hong Anh; Le Minh Huong; Nguyen Khoa Diem; Nguyen Minh Triet; Nguyen Phu Trong; Nguyen Tan Dzung; Nong Duc Manh; Phan Van Khai; Nguyen Van An; Pham Van Tra; Phan Dien; Tran Dinh Hoan; Truong Quang Duoc; Truong Tan Sang; Tran Duc Luong*

#### COUNCIL OF MINISTERS *as at September 2001*

*Prime Minister*, Phan Van Khai
*Deputy Prime Ministers*, Nguyen Tan Dzung *(Co-ordinator for Deputy Prime Ministers, Economy, Industry, Combating Smuggling and Trade Fraud, Renovation of Enterprise Management)*; Nguyen Manh Cam *(Foreign Affairs, Foreign Trade)*; Nguyen Cong Tan *(Agriculture, Food Production, Forestry, Aquaculture, Capital Construction, Rural Development, Poverty Alleviation and Agricultural Industrialisation)*; Pham Gia Khiem *(Science, Technology, Environment, Hydro-meteorology, Posts, Education, Training, Culture, Arts, Press and Information, Public Health and Sports)*
*Agriculture and Rural Development*, Le Huy Ngo
*Aquatic Resources*, Ta Quang Ngoc
*Child Protection and Care*, Tran Thi Thanh Thanh
*Construction*, Nguyen Manh Kiem
*Culture and Information*, Pham Quang Nghi
*Education and Training*, Nguyen Minh Hien
*Ethnic Minorities and Mountain Regions*, Hoang Duc Nghi
*Finance*, Nguyen Sinh Hung
*Foreign Affairs*, Nguyen Dy Nien
*Government Personnel and Organisation*, Do Quang Trung
*Government Secretariat*, Lai Van Cu
*Governor, State Bank*, Le Duc Thuy
*Industry*, Dang Vu Chu
*Interior and Public Security*, Lt.-Gen. Le Minh Huong
*Justice*, Nguyen Dinh Loc
*Labour, War Invalids and Social Affairs*, Tran Dinh Hoan
*National Defence*, Gen. Pham Van Tra
*Physical Training and Sports*, Nguyen Danh Thai
*Planning and Investment*, Tran Xuan Gia
*Population Activities and Family Planning*, Tran Thi Trung Chien
*Public Health*, Do Nguyen Phuong
*Science, Technology and Environment*, Chu Tuan Nha
*State Inspectorate*, Ta Huu Thanh
*Trade*, Vu Khoan
*Transport*, Le Ngoc Hoan

#### EMBASSY OF THE SOCIALIST REPUBLIC OF VIETNAM

12–14 Victoria Road, London W8 5RD
Tel: 020-7937 1912
*Ambassador Extraordinary and Plenipotentiary*, HE Vuong Thua Phong, apptd 1998
*Minister–Counsellor*, Nguyen Trung Thanh
*Commercial Counsellor*, Dinh Van Hoi

#### BRITISH EMBASSY

Central Building, 31 Hai Ba Trung, Hanoi
Tel: (00 84) (4) 825 2510/826 7560/5
E-mail: behanoi@fpt.vn
*Ambassador Extraordinary and Plenipotentiary*, HE Warwick Morris, apptd 2001
*Deputy Head of Mission, Consul*, M. McLachlan
*Second Secretary (Commercial)*, R. Lally

CONSULATE-GENERAL – Ho Chi Minh City

BRITISH COUNCIL DIRECTOR, David Cordingley *(Cultural Attaché)*, 40 Cat Linh Street, Dong Da, Hanoi; e-mail: bchanoi@britishcouncil.org.vn. There is a regional office in Ho Chi Minh City

## DEFENCE

The Army has 1,315 main battle tanks, 1,180 armoured personnel carriers and 300 armoured infantry fighting vehicles. The Navy has two submarines, six frigates and 42 patrol and coastal vessels at seven principal bases. The Air Force has 189 combat aircraft and 26 armed helicopters.

MILITARY EXPENDITURE – 3.1 per cent of GDP (1999)
MILITARY PERSONNEL – 484,000: Army 412,000, Navy 42,000, People's Air Force 30,000; Paramilitaries 40,000
CONSCRIPTION DURATION – Two to three years

## ECONOMY

Vietnam experienced economic difficulties following the imposition of socialist reforms in the south after 1975. However, economic reforms, known as 'Doi Moi' liberalisation, were instituted in 1986 and have had significant success. The state's share of control has been greatly reduced in most sectors, leading to significant improvement in agricultural production, with Vietnam becoming a major rice exporter. Industry has grown and now contributes 30 per cent of GDP. Building materials, chemicals, machinery and foodstuffs are the main products.

Foreign investment has been actively encouraged and was further boosted by Vietnam's accession to ASEAN in August 1995, but the level of foreign investment has begun to fall in response to the lack of economic reform and the difficult local business environment. A stock exchange was opened in July 2000. Oil production has increased and large natural gas reserves have been found offshore, though these are also claimed by China.

A bilateral trade agreement between Vietnam and the USA was signed in July 2000.

In June 2001, the World Bank granted Vietnam a US$250 million poverty reduction loan and the EU announced that it would commit €2.6 billion in aid.

In 1997 imports totalled US$11,271 million and exports US$8,900 million.

GNP – US$28,733 million (1999); US$370 per capita (1999)
GDP – US$25,225 million (1997); US$336 per capita (1998)
ANNUAL AVERAGE GROWTH OF GDP – 9.3 per cent (1996)
TOTAL EXTERNAL DEBT – US$22,359 million (1998)

| *Trade with UK* | 1999 | 2000 |
|---|---|---|
| Imports from UK | £79,245,000 | £93,182,000 |
| Exports to UK | 305,508,000 | 385,449,000 |

---

## YEMEN
*Al-Jumhūriyya Al-Yamaniyya*

---

AREA – 203,850 sq. miles (527,968 sq. km). Neighbours: Saudi Arabia (north), Oman (east)
POPULATION – 17,048,000 (1995 census). The language is Arabic
CAPITAL – Sana'ā (population, 926,595, 1995)
MAJOR CITIES – ΨAden ('Adan) (400,783), the former capital of South Yemen; Al-Hudaydah (246,068); Ta'izz (290,107), 1993 estimates
CURRENCY – Riyal of 100 fils
NATIONAL ANTHEM – Raddidi Ayyatuha ad Dunya nashidi (Repeat, O World, my song)
NATIONAL DAY – 22 May
NATIONAL FLAG – Horizontal bands of red, white and black
LIFE EXPECTANCY (years) – male 57.3; female 58.0
POPULATION GROWTH RATE – 4.7 per cent (1999)
POPULATION DENSITY – 32 per sq. km (1998)
URBAN POPULATION – 24.7 per cent (2000 estimate)
ILLITERACY RATE – 53.8 per cent (2000)
ENROLMENT (percentage of age group) – tertiary 4.2 per cent (1996)

Included in the state of Yemen are the offshore islands of Perim and Kamarān in the Red Sea, and Suqutrā in the Gulf of Aden. The border with Saudi Arabia, except for the north-west corner, is unclear and is being delineated following an agreement between the two countries signed on 12 June 2000. The highlands and central plateau, and the highest portions of the maritime range in the south, form the most fertile part of Arabia, with abundant but irregular rainfall. The north is largely composed of mountains and desert, and rainfall is generally scarce.

## HISTORY AND POLITICS

Turkish occupation of North Yemen (1872–1918) was followed by the rule of the Hamid al-Din dynasty until a revolution in 1962 overthrew the monarchy and the Yemen Arab Republic was declared. The People's Republic of South Yemen was set up in 1967 when the British government ceded power to the National Liberation Front, bringing to an end 129 years of British rule in Aden and some years of protectorate status in the hinterland. Negotiations towards merging the two states began in 1979 and unification was proclaimed on 22 May 1990. The constitution was approved by referendum in May 1991.

A power struggle between the former Northern and Southern Yemen élites in mid-1993 led to civil war on 5 May 1994 between the unmerged Northern and Southern forces. Aden was captured by victorious Northern forces on 7 July, ending the civil war.

After the war a coalition government of the General People's Congress and the Islamic Islah was formed and the constitution amended. Gen. Saleh was elected president by the House of Representatives for a five-year term. Multiparty democracy, a free market economy and Sharia law are enshrined in the constitution.

A general election in April 1997 was won by the ruling General People's Congress. President Ali Abdullah Saleh was re-elected in the first direct presidential election held on 23 September 1999, winning 96.3 per cent of the vote.

### POLITICAL SYSTEM

The 1991 constitution was amended following a referendum on 20 February 2001. The president is directly elected and serves a seven-year term which may be renewed once only. The unicameral legislature, the House of Representatives (*Majlis an-Nowab*), has 301 directly-elected members, who serve a six-year term. In addition, there is an advisory Shura Council, which is appointed by the president and has 111 members.

### HEAD OF STATE

*President*, Field Marshal Ali Abdullah Saleh, *took office* 22 May 1990, *elected* 1 October 1994, *re-elected* 23 September 1999
*Vice-President*, Maj.-Gen. Abd Rabbah Mansur Hadi

### COUNCIL OF MINISTERS *as at September 2001*

*Prime Minister*, Abd al-Qadir Abd al-Rahman Bajammal
*Deputy Prime Minister, Finances*, Alawi Salih al-Salami
*Agriculture and Irrigation*, Ahmad Salim al-Jabali
*Awqaf (Religious Endowments) and Religious Guidance*, Qasim al-A'jam
*Civil Service and Social Security*, Abd-al-Wahhab Rawih
*Communications*, Abd-al-Malik al-Mu'allimi
*Construction, Housing and Urban Planning*, Abdullah Husayn al-Daf'i
*Culture*, Abd-al-Wahhab al-Rawhani
*Defence*, Maj.-Gen. Abdallah Ali Ulaywah

*Education*, Fadl Abu-Ghanim
*Electricity and Water*, Yahyah al-Abyad
*Expatriate Affairs*, Abduh Ali Qudati
*Fisheries*, Ali Hasan al-Ahmadi
*Foreign Affairs*, Abu-Bakr Abdallah al-Qirdi
*Higher Education and Scientific Research*, Yahya Muhammad Abdullah al-Shu'aybi
*Industry and Trade*, Abd al-Rahman Muhammad Ali Uthman
*Information*, Husayn Dayfallah al-Awadi
*Interior*, Rashad al-Alimi
*Justice*, Al-Qadi Ahmad Aqabat
*Legal and Parliamentary Affairs*, Abdullah Ahmad Ghanim
*Local Administration*, Sadiq Amin Abu Ra's
*Ministers of State*, Wahibah Fari (*Human Rights*); Alawi Hasan al-Attas (*Parliamentary and Council of Ministers' Affairs*); Maj.-Gen. Abdallah Husayn al-Bashiri (*Secretary-General of the Presidency*); Khalid al-Sharif; Muhammad Ali Yasir; Muhsin al-Yusufi
*Oil and Mineral Resources*, Rashid Ba-Rabba
*Planning and Development*, Ahmad Muhammad Sufan
*Public Health and Population*, Abd-al-Nasir Manibari
*Social Affairs and Labour*, Abd-al-Karim al-Arhabi
*Technical Education and Vocational Training*, Muhammad Abdallah al-Batani
*Tourism and Environment*, Abd-al-Malik Abd-al-Rahman al-Iryani
*Transport and Marine Affairs*, Capt. Sa'id Yafi'i
*Youth and Sport*, Abd al-Rahman Muhammad al-Akwa

EMBASSY OF THE REPUBLIC OF YEMEN
57 Cromwell Road, London SW7 2ED
Tel: 020-7584 6607
*Ambassador Extraordinary and Plenipotentiary*, HE Dr Hussein Abdullah al-Amri, apptd 1995

BRITISH EMBASSY
129 Haddah Road, PO Box 1287, Sana'ā'
Tel: (00 967) (1) 264 081/2/3/4
*Ambassador Extraordinary and Plenipotentiary*, HE Frances Guy, apptd 2001
*Deputy Head of Mission and Consul*, M. Lamport

BRITISH COUNCIL DIRECTOR, Adrian Chadwick, 3rd Floor, Administrative Tower, Sana'ā' Trade Centre, Algiers Street, PO Box 2157, Sana'ā'; e-mail: britishcouncil@britishcouncil.org.ye

## DEFENCE

The Army has 990 main battle tanks, 440 armoured personnel carriers and 200 armoured infantry fighting vehicles. The Navy has 12 patrol and coastal vessels at two bases. The Air Force has 49 combat aircraft and eight attack helicopters.
MILITARY EXPENDITURE – 6.7 per cent of GDP (1999)
MILITARY PERSONNEL – 66,300: Army 61,000, Navy 1,800, Air Force 3,500; Paramilitaries 70,000

## ECONOMY

The economy has been seriously damaged by the civil war. However, the war had little effect on oil production, which amounted to 18.3 million tonnes in 1998 and accounted for 94 per cent of exports in 1995. An agreement was signed with the French oil company Total in September 1995 for the exploitation of liquefied natural gas over a 25-year period and the construction of a gas liquefication plant by 2000. Despite the production of oil Yemen remains one of the poorest states in the world. Tourism has been hampered by the prevalence of kidnapping. The principal imports are machinery and transport equipment, raw materials, and foodstuffs and livestock.

Agriculture is the main occupation of the inhabitants, accounting for 54 per cent of the workforce in 1997 and 18 per cent of GDP in 1998. This is largely of a subsistence nature, sorghum, sesame, millet, wheat and barley being the chief crops. Exports include cotton, coffee, fruit, vegetables and hides. Imports include food and animals

In 1998 Yemen had a trade deficit of US$701 million and current account deficit of US$228 million. Imports totalled US$2,167 million and exports US$1,497 million.
GNP – US$6,088 million (1999); US$350 per capita (1999)
GDP – US$5,185 million (1997); US$354 per capita (1998)
ANNUAL AVERAGE GROWTH OF GDP – 4.4 per cent (1996)
TOTAL EXTERNAL DEBT – US$4,138 million (1998)

| *Trade with UK* | 1999 | 2000 |
|---|---|---|
| Imports from UK | £64,815,000 | £52,480,000 |
| Exports to UK | 3,575,000 | 6,248,000 |

# YUGOSLAVIA

*Savezna Republika Jugoslavija – Federal Republic of Yugoslavia*

AREA – 39,449 sq. miles (102,173 sq. km). Neighbours: Hungary (north), Romania and Bulgaria (east), the Former Yugoslav Republic of Macedonia and Albania (south), Bosnia-Hercegovina and Croatia (west)
POPULATION – 10,616,000 (1997 UN estimate): 67.6 per cent Serb and Montenegrin, 16.5 per cent Albanian, 3.2 per cent Muslim Slavs, 3.3 per cent Hungarian, with smaller numbers of Romanies, Croats, Slovaks and Bulgarians. The majority religion is Serbian Orthodox, with significant Muslim and small Roman Catholic minorities. The main language is Serbian (74 per cent), with Albanian and Hungarian minorities. Serbian is a South Slav language written in the Cyrillic script
CAPITAL – Belgrade (population, 1,597,599, 1997 estimate)
MAJOR CITIES – Kragujevac (181,061); Niš (250,104); Novi Sad (178,896); Podgorica (162,172), the capital of Montenegro; Priština (241,565); Subotica (146,075), 1997 estimates
CURRENCY – New dinar of 100 paras
NATIONAL ANTHEM – Hej, Sloveni, Jošte Živi Reč Naših Dedova (Oh! Slavs, our ancestors' words still live)
NATIONAL DAY – 27 April
NATIONAL FLAG – Three horizontal stripes of blue, white, red
LIFE EXPECTANCY (years) – male 71.8; female 76.4
POPULATION GROWTH RATE – 0.5 per cent (1999)
POPULATION DENSITY – 104 per sq. km (1998)
URBAN POPULATION – 52.2 per cent (2000 estimate)
MILITARY EXPENDITURE – 12.4 per cent of GDP (1999)
MILITARY PERSONNEL – 97,700: Army 74,000, Navy 7,000, Air Force 16,700
CONSCRIPTION DURATION – 12–15 months
ILLITERACY RATE – 6.7 per cent
ENROLMENT (percentage of age group) – primary 69 per cent (1990); secondary 62 per cent (1990); tertiary 21.9 per cent (1996)

The climate is continental. Montenegro and southern Serbia are extremely mountainous, while the north is dominated by the low-lying plains of the Danube. The major rivers are: the Danube, which flows through the north of Serbia to Romania and Bulgaria; the Sava, which flows eastwards from Bosnia to join the Danube at Belgrade; the Drina, which flows along most of the Serbian–Bosnian border to join the Sava; and the Morava, which flows from the extreme south to join the Danube in the north.

## HISTORY AND POLITICS

Serbia emerged from the rule of the Byzantine Empire in the 13th century to form a large and prosperous state in the Balkans. Defeat by the Turks in 1389 led to almost 500 years of Turkish rule. After gaining autonomy within the Ottoman Empire in 1815, Serbia became fully independent in 1878 and a kingdom in 1881. Montenegro was part of the Serbian state before it was conquered by the Turks in the fifteenth century; it became independent in 1878. At the end of the First World War Serbia and Montenegro joined with the former Austro-Hungarian provinces of Slovenia, Croatia and Bosnia-Hercegovina to form the 'Kingdom of Serbs, Croats and Slovenes' which was renamed Yugoslavia in 1929. Yugoslavia was occupied by Axis forces in 1941 and reformed as a Communist federal republic under the presidency of partisan leader Josip Tito in 1945.

Tito died in 1980 and was succeeded by a rotating federal presidency which was unable to contain the growing nationalist movements. Efforts by the six republican presidents to negotiate a new federal or confederal structure for the country failed in 1991. On 25 June 1991 Slovenia and Croatia declared their independence from Yugoslavia.

In Croatia the ethnic Serb minority refused to accept Croatia's independence and fighting began in July 1991 between Croat Defence Forces and Serbian guerrillas backed by the Yugoslav National Army (JNA). By September 1991 this had escalated into war between Croatia and Yugoslavia. The war in Croatia continued until January 1992 when the EU and the UN were able to bring about a cease-fire (*see* Croatia).

Macedonia declared its independence on 18 September 1991.

Bosnia-Hercegovina declared its independence on 1 March 1992. Independence was supported by the Bosniacs (Muslims) and Croats but rejected by the ethnic Serbs and fighting between Bosniacs and Serbs broke out in March 1992. The JNA intervened against the Bosniacs but in May 1992 withdrew to Serbia and Montenegro (*see* Bosnia-Hercegovina).

On 27 April 1992 the two remaining republics of the former Socialist Federal Republic of Yugoslavia, Serbia and Montenegro, announced the formation of a new Yugoslav federation, which they invited Serbs in Croatia and Bosnia-Hercegovina to join.

Legislative elections were held in Montenegro in May 1998 and were won by reformists led by President Djukanović.

Kosovo has been under UN administration since June 1999.

Presidential and legislative elections were held on 24 September 2000, but were largely boycotted in Montenegro after its government had urged the population not to vote. The Democratic Opposition of Serbia (DOS) became the largest party in both chambers of parliament. In the presidential election, the Federal Election Commission announced that President Slobodan Milošević of the Socialist Party of Serbia (SPS), had obtained 40.23 per cent of votes and his rival, Vojislav Koštunica of the DPS, had won 48.22 per cent, just short of the 50 per cent necessary to win without a second round, although an independent monitoring organisation had given Koštunica a clear majority. Koštunica denounced the official result as fraudulent and refused to participate in the second round, scheduled for 8 October. Tension grew and on 28 September, the Serb Orthodox Church declared that Koštunica was the elected president and the Yugoslav Army guaranteed that it would not involve itself in politics. The next day, the Serbian Radical Party (SRP), one of the coalition partners in the Milošević regime, declared its support for Koštunica. A general strike began on 2 October. On 5 October, opposition supporters stormed the parliament building and took over the television station and the state news agency and by evening the media organisations were declaring Koštunica to be the elected president. Milošević accepted his defeat on 6 October and Koštunica was sworn in the following day. Following a period of uncertainty, the DOS and the SPS agreed to dissolve parliament and form a transitional government until a fresh election could be held for the Serbian Parliament. In the federal parliament, the DOS, who had won 138 seats, formed a coalition government with the Socialist People's Party of Montenegro (SPP), who had 28 seats.

An election to the Serbian Parliament was held on 23 December 2000, in which the DOS won an overwhelming victory, obtaining 176 of the 250 seats. The SPS won 37, the SRP won 23 and the Party of Serbian Unity won 14.

In Montenegro, which had steadily removed itself from the influence of Serbia, the government coalition collapsed on 29 December 2000. A legislative election was held on 22 April 2001, in which the pro-independence Victory Belongs to Montenegro (VBM) alliance, led by the Democratic Party of Socialists (DPS), won 36 of the 77 seats. The pro-Yugoslav Together for Yugoslavia alliance, led by the SPP, won 33 seats. The VBM alliance formed a coalition government with the pro-independence Liberal League, which had six seats.

Former President Slobodan Milošević was arrested on 1 April 2001 and on 28 June, he was handed over to the UN International Criminal Tribunal for the Former Yugoslavia, which in May 1999 had indicted him on charges of crimes against humanity.

### INSURGENCIES

The province of Kosovo in the south of Serbia is more than 90 per cent ethnically Albanian. In 1989, Slobodan Milošević, then leader of the League of Communists of Serbia, revoked Kosovo's autonomous status, resulting in the progressive exclusion of the Albanian majority from public life. Following clashes between ethnic Albanians and Serbian police in February and March 1998, the Serbian military attacked civilians in the province on the pretext of eliminating support for the Kosovo Liberation Army (KLA), an ethnic Albanian organisation fighting for independence for the province. The international community condemned the brutality of the Serbian forces and a UN arms embargo was imposed on Yugoslavia, but the situation deteriorated with clashes between the KLA and security forces becoming commonplace. International organisations detailed widespread human rights abuses by the security forces; NATO and Russia ordered both sides to attend a peace conference in Paris on 6 February 1999, which was unsuccessful. Tens of thousands of Kosovar Albanians fled when Yugoslav forces began to attack Kosovar villages. Following warnings to the Yugoslav authorities, NATO commenced air strikes against military targets in Yugoslavia on 24 March 1999. Over eight hundred thousand people fled or were forced to leave their homes and sought refuge in Albania, Macedonia or Montenegro, which, although part of the Yugoslav Federation, had refused to become involved in the fighting; more than five hundred thousand people were displaced within Kosovo. NATO intensified its bombing campaign, now targeting industrial, communications and power links.

On 27 May 1999, the UN War Crimes Tribunal indicted President Milošević of Yugoslavia, President Milutinović of Serbia, and other senior Yugoslav officials for crimes against humanity.

On 3 June President Milošević accepted a peace plan agreed by NATO and Russia and on 10 June Yugoslav forces began to withdraw; NATO air operations were immediately suspended and NATO and Russian forces entered Kosovo the following day. By 20 June all Yugoslav forces had been withdrawn from Kosovo and the Kosovar refugees had begun to return. Since the Yugoslav withdrawal, Kosovo has been under the administration of the UN's Interim Administration Mission in Kosovo (UNMIK), who have established the Kosovo Transitional Council composed of four UN and four Kosovar representatives. The NATO-led Kosovo Force (KFOR) has established five command sectors, administered by UK, US, French, German and Italian troops respectively. In addition, parts of the French, German and US sectors are patrolled by Russian troops. KFOR has facilitated the disarming of the KLA and the return of over 850,000 Kosovar Albanian refugees, but at least 200,000 Kosovar Serbs have fled, fearing reprisal attacks, which have frequently occurred.

In May 2001, the UN Interim Administration Mission in Kosovo (UNMIK), announced that elections to a legislative assembly would be held on 17 November 2001. The assembly would have powers over health, education and the environment, but UNMIK would retain final authority.

Armed fighters belonging to the ethnic Albanian Liberation Army of Preševo, Medvedja and Bujanovac (UCPMB) launched attacks on Serbs in Albanian populated areas of southern Serbia in November 2000. The rebels wanted to annex these areas into Kosovo. A cease-fire was negotiated by KFOR on 27 November, but it collapsed on 1 December. A further cease-fire was signed on 12 March 2001 after NATO agreed to permit Yugoslav forces to enter the demilitarised buffer zone which had been established on the Serbian side of the border with Kosovo in 1999.

## POLITICAL SYSTEM

The Federal Republic has a bicameral parliament with a 138-seat (108 Serbian, 30 Montenegrin) lower house, the Chamber of Citizens, and a 40-seat (20 Serbian, 20 Montenegrin) upper house, the Chamber of Republics. Both houses are directly elected and serve four-year terms. Executive power is vested in a federal president and government.

## HEAD OF STATE

*Federal President*, Vojislav Koštunica, *elected* 24 September 2000

## FEDERAL GOVERNMENT *as at September 2001*

*Prime Minister*, Dragiša Pešić (SNP)
*Deputy Prime Minister, Foreign Trade Relations*, Miroljub Labus (DOS)
*Agriculture*, Sasa Vitosević (DOS)
*Defence*, Slobodan Krapović (SNP)
*Development and Science*, Vuko Domazetović
*Economy and Internal Trade*, Petar Trojanović
*Finance*, Jovan Ranković
*Foreign Affairs*, Goran Svilanović (DOS)
*Information*, Slobodan Orlić
*Interior*, Zoran Živković (DOS)
*Justice*, Savo Marković
*Labour, Health and Social Policy*, Miodrag Kovač (SNP)
*Law*, Mirko Petrović
*National and Ethnic Communities*, Rasim Ljajić (DOS)
*Religions*, Bogoljub Sijaković (SNP)
*Sports and Youth*, Vojislav Andrić (DOS)
*Transportation and Telecommunications*, Božidar Milović
*Without Portfolio*, Velimir Radojević (SNP)
DOS Democratic Opposition of Serbia; SNP Montenegrin Socialist National Party

## MONTENEGRO

AREA – 5,331 sq. miles (13,812 sq. km)

POPULATION – 615,000: 62 per cent Montenegrin, 14.5 per cent Bosniac, 6.5 per cent Albanian and 3 per cent Serb
CAPITAL – Podgorica (population, 117,875, 1991)

The Montenegrin Social Democrat Party (former Communists) won multiparty elections in November 1996 for the 85-seat republican assembly and formed a government. The most recent presidential election was won by Milo Djukanović, a reformist candidate favouring greater independence for the province.

*President*, Milo Djukanović, *elected* 19 October 1997
*Prime Minister*, Filip Vujanović
BRITISH COUNCIL, British Council Information Centre, Brace Zlaticanina 10, 81000 Podgorica; e-mail: eadbic@cg.yu

## SERBIA

AREA – 34,175 sq. miles (88,538 sq. km)
POPULATION – 9,300,000, of whom 66 per cent are Serbs
CAPITAL – Belgrade (population, 1,597,599, 1991)

Serbia includes the provinces of Kosovo (population 1.6 million), of great historic importance to Serbs, and Vojvodina (population 2 million); the autonomy of both was ended in September 1990. Vojvodina, with its capital at Novi Sad, has a large Hungarian minority (21 per cent). Kosovo, with its capital at Priština, is predominantly Albanian (90 per cent). Following the conflict in Kosovo, more than 200,000 people have been left homeless and entire villages have been destroyed.

The Socialist Party of Serbia (SPS) (formerly the Communists) emerged as the largest party in multiparty elections for the 250-seat National Assembly, held in November 1996, although the results of the election were disputed.

*President*, Milan Milutinović
*Prime Minister*, Zoran Djindjić

## EMBASSY OF THE FEDERAL REPUBLIC OF YUGOSLAVIA

5 Lexham Gardens, London W8 5JJ.
Tel: 020-7370 6105
*Ambassador Extraordinary and Plenipotentiary*, HE Dr Vladeta Janković, apptd 2001

## BRITISH EMBASSY

Resavska 46, YU-11000 Belgrade
Tel: (00) (381) (11) 645055
*Ambassador Extraordinary and Plenipotentiary*, HE C. Crawford, CMG, apptd 2000

BRITISH COUNCIL DIRECTOR, Muriel Kirton, Generala Zdanova 34, YU-11000 Belgrade; e-mail;bcyu@britcoun.org.yu

## ECONOMY

Since 1991 the economy has been devastated by the wars in Croatia and Bosnia-Hercegovina, by the UN economic sanctions and trade embargo, and because of the lack of free-market reforms. Only the country's agricultural self-sufficiency has kept it afloat. In 1997, agriculture accounted for 21.3 per cent of GDP and employed 22.6 per cent of the workforce.

Industrial production remains extremely low and there is high unemployment, estimated to be around 40 per cent in 1997.

Economic sanctions and NATO bombing in 1999 further damaged the already fragile economy. GDP in 2000 was roughly 40 per cent of 1989 levels and more than a quarter of the workforce is without employment.

GDP – US$17,000 million (1997); US$1,124 per capita (1998)
ANNUAL AVERAGE GROWTH OF GDP – 4.3 per cent (1996)
INFLATION RATE – 117.4 per cent (1991)
TOTAL EXTERNAL DEBT – US$13,742 million (1998)

| *Trade with UK* | 1999 | 2000 |
|---|---|---|
| Imports from UK | £27,038,000 | £32,524,000 |
| Exports to UK | 15,573,000 | 14,821,000 |

# ZAMBIA

*Republic of Zambia*

AREA – 290,587 sq. miles (752,618 sq. km). Neighbours: Democratic Republic of Congo and Tanzania (north), Malawi (east), Mozambique, Zimbabwe and Namibia (south), Angola (west)
POPULATION – 9,881,000 (1997 UN estimate). English is the official language; other languages spoken include Bemba, Kaonda, Lozi, Lunda, Luvale, Nyanja and Tonga
CAPITAL – Lusaka (population, 982,362, 1990)
MAJOR CITIES – Chingola (186,769); Kabwe (348,571166,519); Kitwe (348,571); Luanshya (147,747); Mufulira (175,025); Ndola (376,311)
CURRENCY – Kwacha (K) of 100 ngwee
NATIONAL ANTHEM – Stand and Sing of Zambia, Proud and Free
NATIONAL DAY – 24 October (Independence Day)
NATIONAL FLAG – Green with three small vertical stripes, red, black and orange (next fly); eagle device on green above stripes
LIFE EXPECTANCY (years) – male 38.0; female 39.0
POPULATION GROWTH RATE – 2.4 per cent (1999)
POPULATION DENSITY – 12 per sq. km (1998)
URBAN POPULATION – 39.6 per cent (2000 estimate)
MILITARY EXPENDITURE – 2.5 per cent of GDP (1999)
MILITARY PERSONNEL – 21,600: Army 20,000, Air Force 1,600, Paramilitaries 1,400
ILLITERACY RATE – 22.0 per cent (2000)
ENROLMENT (percentage of age group) – primary 75 per cent (1996); secondary 16 per cent (1994); tertiary 2.5 per cent (1996)

Zambia lies on the plateau of Central Africa. With the exception of the valleys of the Zambezi, the Luapula, the Kafue and the Luangwa rivers, and the Luano valley, elevations vary from 3,000 to 5,000 feet above sea level, but in the north-east the plateau rises to occasional altitudes of over 6,000 feet. Although Zambia lies within the tropics, and fairly centrally in the African land mass, its elevation relieves it from extremely high temperatures and humidity.

## HISTORY AND POLITICS

Northern Rhodesia came under British rule in 1889. It achieved internal self-government when the Federation of Rhodesia and Nyasaland was dissolved in 1963 and became an independent republic within the Commonwealth on 24 October 1964 under the name of Zambia.

Zambia was a one-party state (the United National Independence Party) from 1973 until 1990, when pressure from opposition groups led to a new constitution (August 1991) and multiparty legislative and presidential elections in October 1991. The Movement for Multiparty Democracy (MMD) won 125 of the 150 seats in parliament, and the MMD candidate Frederick Chiluba defeated Kenneth Kaunda, who had ruled since independence, in the presidential election; Kaunda was later stripped of his Zambian citizenship. President Chiluba and the MMD were re-elected in November 1996.

Presidential and legislative elections were due to be held by November 2001.

### HEAD OF STATE

*President*, Frederick J. Chiluba, *elected* October 1991, *re-elected* 18 November 1996
*Vice-President*, Enoch Kavindele

### CABINET *as at September 2001*

*Agriculture, Food and Fisheries*, Misheck Shiinda
*Commerce, Trade and Industry*, Yusuf Badat
*Communications and Transport*, Augustine Mwape
*Community Development and Social Services*, Jane Chikwata
*Defence*, Joshua Simunyandi
*Education*, Rueben Musakabantu
*Energy and Water Development*, David Saviye
*Environment and Natural Resources*, Bothwell Nyangu
*Finance and Economic Development*, Katele Kalumba
*Foreign Affairs*, Keli Walubita
*Health*, Levison Mumba
*Home Affairs*, vacant
*Information and Broadcasting*, Vernon Johnson Mwaanga
*Labour and Social Security*, Newstead Zimba
*Lands*, Abel Chambeshi
*Local Government and Housing*, Bates Namuyamba
*Mines and Mineral Development*, Chitalu Sampa
*Presidential Affairs, Legal Affairs*, Eric Silwamba
*Science, Technology and Vocational Training*, Valentine Kayope
*Tourism*, Michael Mabenga
*Without Portfolio*, Michael Sata
*Works and Supply*, vacant
*Youth, Sport and Child Development*, Peter Chintala

### HIGH COMMISSION FOR THE REPUBLIC OF ZAMBIA

2 Palace Gate, London W8 5NG
Tel: 020-7589 6655
*High Commissioner*, HE Silumelume Mubukwanu, apptd 2001
*Deputy High Commissioner*, G. Alikipo
*Defence Adviser*, Brig.-Gen. M. Lisita

### BRITISH HIGH COMMISSION

5210 Independence Avenue (PO Box 50050), 15101 Ridgeway, Lusaka
Tel: (00 260) (1) 251133
E-mail: brithc@zamnet.zm
*High Commissioner*, HE Thomas Young, apptd 1997
*Deputy High Commissioner*, P. Nessling

BRITISH COUNCIL DIRECTOR, Brendan McSharry, Heroes Place, Cairo Road (PO Box 34571), Lusaka; e-mail: info@britishcouncil.org.zm

## ECONOMY

In 1991, the MMD government began the transition from a state-controlled economy to a free market system. Privatisation has been encouraged, foreign exchange controls have been removed and the Kwacha has been floated. Price subsidies and tariffs have been lowered or abolished, but increased imports have affected manufacturing. In 1997, 71.1 per cent of the workforce were engaged in agriculture, which accounted for 17 per cent of GDP in 1998. Principal agricultural products are maize, sugar, groundnuts, cotton, livestock, vegetables and tobacco. The principal exports are copper and cobalt. The principal imports are industrial goods, machinery and transport equipment, fuel and foodstuffs.

In 1997 imports totalled US$819 million and exports US$915 million.

GNP – US$3,222 million (1999); US$320 per capita (1999)
GDP – US$3,865 million (1997); US$413 per capita (1998)
ANNUAL AVERAGE GROWTH OF GDP – 6.5 per cent (1996)
INFLATION RATE – 24.8 per cent (1997)
TOTAL EXTERNAL DEBT – US$6,865 million (1998)

| *Trade with UK* | 1999 | 2000 |
|---|---|---|
| Imports from UK | £24,024,000 | £28,353,000 |
| Exports to UK | 15,184,000 | 12,649,000 |

## ZIMBABWE
*Republic of Zimbabwe*

AREA – 150,872 sq. miles (390,757 sq. km). Neighbours: Zambia (north), Mozambique (east), South Africa (south), Botswana and Namibia (west)
POPULATION – 11,904,000 (1997 UN estimate); 10,400,000 (1992 census): 77 per cent Shona, 17 per cent Ndebele, 1.4 per cent Europeans. The official language is English, with Shona the largest indigenous language group
CAPITAL – Harare (population, 1,189,103, 1992)
MAJOR CITIES – Bulawayo (621,742), the largest town in Matabeleland; Chitungwiza (274,912)
CURRENCY – Zimbabwe dollar (Z$) of 100 cents
NATIONAL ANTHEM – Ngaikomberarwe Nyika Ye Zimbabwe (Blessed be the country of Zimbabwe)
NATIONAL DAY – 18 April (Independence Day)
NATIONAL FLAG – Seven horizontal stripes of green, yellow, red, black, red, yellow, green; a white, black-bordered, triangle based on the hoist containing the national emblem
LIFE EXPECTANCY (years) – male 40.9; female 40.0
POPULATION GROWTH RATE – 1.7 per cent (1999)
POPULATION DENSITY – 32 per sq. km (1998)
URBAN POPULATION – 35.3 per cent (2000 estimate)
MILITARY EXPENDITURE – 6.1 per cent of GDP (1999)
MILITARY PERSONNEL – 40,000: Army 35,000, Air Force 5,000; Paramilitaries 21,800

## HISTORY AND POLITICS

European colonisation of Zimbabwe began in 1890 when settlers forcibly acquired Shona lands, followed by the seizure of Ndebele lands in 1893. It became a self-governing colony under the name of Southern Rhodesia in 1923. A unilateral declaration of independence on 11 November 1965, which resulted in UN sanctions against the country, was finally terminated on 12 December 1979. Following elections in February 1980 the country became independent on 18 April 1980 as the Republic of Zimbabwe, a member of the British Commonwealth.

The independence constitution was amended in 1987, making the presidency an executive post. The president is popularly elected for a six-year term, appoints the Cabinet and can veto parliamentary bills. The unicameral legislature, the House of Assembly, has 150 members: 120 elected, ten traditional chiefs and 20 others appointed by the president.

President Mugabe was re-elected for a six-year term in March 1996, following the withdrawal of the other two contenders. The most recent general election was held on 24—25 June 2000. The Zimbabwe African National Union – Patriotic Front (ZANU-PF) won 62 of the 120 elective seats and the Movement for Democratic Change (MDC), a new opposition grouping formed by various civic groups and the Zimbabwe Congress of Trade Unions, won 57 seats. There was widespread intimidation and violence against the opposition during the election campaign.

In April 2001, a campaign of intimidation was carried out by 'war veterans' and ZANU-PF activists on businesses and industries which were thought to support the MDC.

The country is divided into eight provinces: Manicaland, Masvingo, Matabeleland North, Matabeleland South, Midlands, Mashonaland West, Mashonaland Central and Mashonaland East.

## LAND REFORM

Following independence, about 30 per cent of agricultural land remained in the possession of around 4,000 white farmers. They employed nearly 300,000 workers and accounted for about 70 per cent of the country's agricultural production and about a third of foreign currency earnings. A further 37 per cent of agricultural land was in the possession of 1.2 million black peasant farmers, mainly engaged in subsistence farming. Most of this land was located in less fertile, drought-prone regions. Land reform was designed to achieve a more equitable distribution of land.

By 1997 the state had acquired 3.4 million hectares of land, but either left it fallow or distributed it to members of the government. The 1990 amendments to the 1980 constitution had made provision for the compulsory acquisition of farms, with compensation to be paid to the owners.

The occupation of white-owned farms by protestors, led by former veterans of the war against the white minority regime, began in February 2000. On 17 March 2000 the Supreme Court ordered the police to evict the black war veterans who had occupied around 600 white-owned farms. The police ignored the judgement with the support of President Mugabe. On 6 April, the House of Assembly approved the Land Acquisition Act, which amended the constitution to enable the government to take over white-owned farms without compensation and redistribute them to landless blacks. A meeting of representatives of the British and Zimbabwean governments on 27 April 2000 failed to resolve the crisis and on 3 May the UK imposed an embargo on weapons sales to Zimbabwe, making financial support for land reform dependent on an end to the farm occupations.

The Supreme Court ruled on 10 November 2000 that the compulsory land seizures were illegal and ordered the removal of squatters. The government rejected the ruling and accelerated the land acquisition programme. On 21 December, the Supreme Court directed the President to produce a land distribution programme within six months and to protect white farmers whose land had been occupied by squatters.

Following a Commonwealth meeting on 6 September 2001, Zimbabwe agreed to end the illegal land occupations and restore the rule of law in return for international assistance.

HEAD OF STATE

*Executive President, C.-in-C. of the Defence Forces*, Robert Gabriel Mugabe, *elected* 30 December 1987, *re-elected* March 1990, March 1996
*Vice-Presidents*, Simon Vengesai Muzenda; Joseph Msika

CABINET *as at September 2001*

The President
*Defence*, Sidney Tigere Sekeramayi
*Education, Sport and Culture*, Aeneas Chigwedere
*Environment and Tourism*, Francis Nhema
*Finance and Economic Development*, Simba Makoni
*Foreign Affairs*, Stanislaus Mudenge
*Health and Child Welfare*, Timothy Stamps
*Higher Education and Technology*, Samuel Mubengegwi
*Home Affairs*, John Nkomo
*Industry and International Trade*, Herbert Murerwa
*Information and Publicity*, Jonathan Moyo
*Justice, Legal and Parliamentary Affairs*, Patrick Chinamas
*Lands, Agriculture and Resettlement*, Joseph Made
*Local Government, Public Works and National Housing*, Ignatius Chombo
*Mines and Energy*, Edward Chindori Chininga
*National Security*, Nicholas Goche
*Public Service, Labour and Social Welfare*, July Moyo
*Rural Resources and Water Development*, Joyce Mujuru
*Transport and Communications*, Swithen Mombeshora
*Youth Development, Gender, Employment Creation*, Elliot Manyika

HIGH COMMISSION OF THE REPUBLIC OF ZIMBABWE
Zimbabwe House, 429 Strand, London WC2R 0QE
Tel: 020-7836 7755
*High Commissioner*, HE Simbarashe Simbanenduku Mumbengegwi, apptd 1999
*Deputy High Commissioner*, Pavelyn Tendai Musaka
*Minister-Counsellor*, M. Manhuna
*Defence Adviser*, Col. J. Murozvi
*Senior Commercial Attaché*, J. Foroma

BRITISH HIGH COMMISSION
Corner House, Samora Machel Avenue/Leopold Takawira Street (PO Box 4490), Harare
Tel: (00 263) (4) 772990/774700
*High Commissioner*, HE Brian Donnelly, CMG, apptd 2001
*Deputy High Commissioner*, D. Corner
*Defence Adviser*, Col. J. Field, CBE
*First Secretary (Commercial)*, D. Seddon

BRITISH COUNCIL DIRECTOR, Marcus Milton, 23 Jason Moyo Avenue, PO Box 664, Harare; e-mail: general.enquiries@britishcouncil.org.zw. There is a regional office in Bulawayo

## ECONOMY

A programme of free-market economic reforms was introduced in 1990, but has only been partially implemented. The economy remains highly regulated and weak, inflation and unemployment remain high and rises in the prices of basic commodities and fuel have resulted in widespread strike action and protests. Agriculture accounted for 28 per cent of GDP in 1998 and two-thirds of the workforce are engaged in agriculture, but the activities of squatters and the government land acquisition campaign have had a dramatic effect on productivity at commercial farms, preventing the planting of many crops. Tobacco remains the most important crop in terms of export (Zimbabwe is the largest exporter in the world), and maize the most important for domestic consumption. Other crops include wheat, cotton, sugar, horticultural products, fruit and vegetables.

The manufacturing sector is very dependent on the agricultural sector for raw materials and on imports e.g. fuel oil, steel products and chemicals, as well as heavy machinery and items of transport. The mining sector, although contributing a relatively small portion to GDP, is important to the economy as a foreign exchange earner. Almost all mineral production is exported. Gold is the most important product; others are asbestos, diamonds, silver, nickel, copper, platinum, chrome ore, tin, iron ore and cobalt. There is a successful ferro-chrome industry and a substantial steel works which has been heavily subsidised by government.

The budget for 2001 aimed to reduce the budget deficit though drastic cuts in defence, education and health spending, but increased spending on land resettlement. Fuel prices were raised in November 2000 by 14.6 per cent.

The principal exports are agricultural products (especially tobacco), manufactured goods and unprocessed minerals. The principal imports are machinery and transport equipment, manufactures, chemical products, oil and oil products, and foodstuffs. The main trading partners are South Africa and the UK.

In 1996 imports totalled US$2,803 million and exports US$2,406 million.

GNP – US$6,302 million (1999); US$520 per capita (1999)
GDP – US$8,990 million (1997); US$548 per capita (1998)
ANNUAL AVERAGE GROWTH OF GDP – 6.0 per cent (1996)
INFLATION RATE – 31.8 per cent (1998)
TOTAL EXTERNAL DEBT – US$4,716 million (1998)

| *Trade with UK* | 1999 | 2000 |
| --- | --- | --- |
| Imports from UK | £73,689,000 | £42,782,000 |
| Exports to UK | 122,696,000 | 99,873,000 |

## EDUCATION

Education is compulsory, and the language of instruction is English. Over 80 per cent of schools are government-aided. There are four universities; the University of Zimbabwe was founded in 1955.

ILLITERACY RATE – 7.3 per cent
ENROLMENT (percentage of age group) – tertiary 6.6 per cent (1996)

# UK Overseas Territories

## ANGUILLA

AREA – 37 sq. miles (96 sq. km)
POPULATION – 12,394 (1998 estimate)
CAPITAL – The Valley (population, 2,400, 1994)
CURRENCY – East Caribbean dollar (EC$) of 100 cents
FLAG – British blue ensign with the coat of arms and three dolphins in the fly
POPULATION GROWTH RATE – 8.6 per cent (1998)
POPULATION DENSITY – 84 per sq. km (1998)
GDP – US$88 million (1997)

Anguilla is a flat coralline island in the Caribbean, about 16 miles in length, three and a half miles in breadth at its widest point and its area is about 37 sq. miles (96 sq. km). The island is covered with low scrub and fringed with white coral-sand beaches. The climate is pleasant, with temperatures in the range of 24-30°C throughout the year.

### HISTORY AND POLITICS

Anguilla has been a British colony since 1650. For much of its history it was linked administratively with St Christopher, but three months after the Associated State of Saint Christopher (St Kitts)-Nevis-Anguilla came into being in 1967, the Anguillans repudiated government from St Kitts. A Commissioner was installed in 1969 and in 1976 Anguilla was given a new status and separate constitution. Final separation from St Kitts and Nevis was effected on 19 December 1980 and Anguilla reverted to a British dependency. A new constitution was introduced in 1982, providing for a Governor, an Executive Council comprising four elected Ministers and two ex-officio members (the Attorney-General and Deputy Governor), and a 12-member legislative House of Assembly, consisting of seven elected members, two nominated members, two ex-officio members (the Attorney-General and Deputy Governor) and presided over by a Speaker. The most recent general election was held in March 2000.

*Governor*, HE Peter Johnson, *apptd* 2000
*Deputy Governor*, Roger Cousins, OBE, *apptd* 1997

EXECUTIVE COUNCIL *as at June 2001*

*Chairman*, The Governor
*Chief Minister*, Osbourne Fleming
*Attorney-General*, Ronald Scipio
*Communications, Public Utilities and Works*, Kenneth Harrigan
*Finance*, Victor Banks
*Social Services*, Eric Reid
*Member*, The Deputy Governor

### ECONOMY

Low rainfall limits agricultural output and export earnings are mainly from sales of fish and lobsters. Tourism has developed rapidly in recent years and accounts for most of the island's economic activity. In 1998 there were 43,874 tourists and a further 69,922 day visitors.

| TRADE WITH UK | 1999 | 2000 |
|---|---|---|
| Imports from UK | £2,058,000 | £2,984,000 |
| Exports to UK | 27,000 | 17,000 |

## ASCENSION
– *see* St Helena

## BERMUDA

AREA – 20 sq. miles (53 sq. km)
POPULATION – 64,000 (1994 UN estimate)
CAPITAL – ΨHamilton (population, 2,277, 1994)
CURRENCY – Bermuda dollar of 100 cents
FLAG – British red ensign with the shield of arms in the fly
LIFE EXPECTANCY (years) – male 71.1; female 77.8
POPULATION GROWTH RATE – 0.1 per cent (1997)
POPULATION DENSITY – 1,199 per sq. km (1998)
GDP – US$2,311 million (1997); US$38,652 per capita (1998)

The Bermudas, or Somers Islands, are a cluster of about 100 small islands (about 20 of which are inhabited) situated in the west of the Atlantic Ocean, the nearest point of the mainland being Cape Hatteras in North Carolina, about 570 miles distant.

### HISTORY AND POLITICS

The colony derives its name from Juan Bermudez, a Spaniard, who sighted it before 1515. No settlement was made until 1609 when Sir George Somers, who was shipwrecked there on his way to Virginia, colonised the islands.

Internal self-government was introduced in 1968. There is a Senate of 11 members and an elected House of Assembly of 40 members. The Governor retains responsibility for external affairs, defence, internal security and the police, although administrative matters for the police service have been delegated to the Minister of Labour, Home Affairs and Public Safety. Independence from the UK was rejected in a referendum in August 1995.

The last general election was held on 9 November 1998. The Progressive Labour Party won 26 of the 40 seats.

*Governor and Commander-in-Chief*, HE Thorold Masefield, CMG, *apptd* 1997
*Deputy Governor*, Tim Gurney

CABINET *as at June 2001*

*Premier*, Jennifer Smith
*Deputy Premier, Minister of Finance*, C. Eugene Cox
*Attorney-General*, Dame Lois Brown-Evans
*Education*, L. Milton Scott
*Environment, Development, Opportunity and Government Services*, Terry E. Lister
*Health and Family Services*, Nelson Bascome, Jr
*Labour, Home Affairs and Public Safety*, Paula A. Cox
*Telecommunications and E-Commerce*, M. D. Renee Webb
*Tourism*, David H. Allen
*Transport*, Ewart Brown
*Works and Engineering*, W. Alex Scott
*Youth, Sport and Recreation*, Dennis P. Lister

### ECONOMY

The islands' economic structure is based on tourism and international company business, attracted by the low level of taxation and sophisticated telecommunications system.

In 1998 a total of 557,868 visitors arrived by air and cruise ship.

Locally manufactured concentrates, perfumes, cut flowers and pharmaceuticals are the islands' leading exports. Little food is produced except vegetables and fish, other foodstuffs being imported.

In November 1995, the US, UK and Canadian governments handed over 1,500 acres of land (roughly 10 per cent of the colony), to the government. The land, which had been used for military bases, included an airport on St David's Island.

| TRADE WITH UK | 1999 | 2000 |
|---|---|---|
| Imports from UK | £183,655,000 | £325,861,000 |
| Exports to UK | 29,092,000 | 1,766,000 |

## COMMUNICATIONS

One daily and two weekly newspapers are published in Bermuda. Three commercial companies operate radio and television services, including a cable-television system. The Bermuda Telephone Company, TeleBermuda, and Cable and Wireless provide telecommunications links to more than 140 countries.

## EDUCATION

Free elementary education was introduced in 1949. Free secondary education was introduced in 1965 for those children in the aided and maintained schools who were below the upper limit of the statutory school age of 18.

## THE BRITISH ANTARCTIC TERRITORY

AREA – 660,000 sq. miles (1,709,340 sq. km.)
POPULATION – No permanent population
FLAG – British white ensign, without the cross of St George, with the coat of arms of the Territory in the fly

The British Antarctic Territory was designated in 1962 and consists of the areas south of 60°S. latitude and bounded by longitudes 20°W. and 80°W. The territory includes the South Orkney Islands, the South Shetland Islands, the mountainous Antarctic Peninsula (highest point Mount Jackson, 10,443 ft above sea level) and all adjacent islands, and the land mass extending to the South Pole. The territory has no indigenous inhabitants and the British population consists of the scientists and technicians at the British Antarctic Survey stations. These numbered 37 during the 1999-2000 winter, but this number increases considerably in the southern hemisphere's summer months with the arrival of field scientists. Argentina, Brazil, Bulgaria, Chile, China, Korea (South), Poland, Russia, Spain, Ukraine, Uruguay and the USA also have scientific stations in the territory.

The territory is administered by a Commissioner, resident in London.

*Commissioner* (non-resident), Alan Edden Huckle, *apptd* 2001

## THE BRITISH INDIAN OCEAN TERRITORY

AREA – 23 sq. miles (59 sq. km.)
POPULATION – No permanent population
FLAG – Divided horizontally into blue and white wavy stripes, with the Union Flag in the canton and a crowned palm-tree over all in the fly

The British Indian Ocean Territory was established by an Order in Council in 1965 and included islands formerly administered from Mauritius and the Seychelles. The islands of Farquhar, Desroches and Aldabra became part of the Seychelles when it became independent in 1976; since then the Territory has consisted of the Chagos Archipelago only. The Chagos Archipelago consists of six main groups of islands situated on the Great Chagos Bank and covering some 21,000 sq. miles (54,389 sq. km). The largest and most southerly of the Chagos Islands is Diego Garcia, a sand cay with a land area of about 17 sq. miles approximately 1,100 miles east of Mahé, used as a joint naval support facility by Britain and the USA.

The other main island groups of the archipelago, Peros Banhos (29 islands with a total land area of 4 sq. miles) and Salamon (11 islands with a total land area of 2 sq. miles) are uninhabited. The islands have a tropical maritime climate, with average temperatures between 25°C and 29°C in Diego Garcia, and rainfall in the whole archipelago of 90–100 inches a year.

The islands' former inhabitants (the Ilois) were expelled between 1967 and 1973 to allow for the construction of the naval base, most being resettled in Mauritius. Following legal action by representatives of the Ilois, on 3 November 2000 the High Court overturned the ordinance that had required the Ilois to seek permission to visit the territory, effectively granting them the right of return.

*Commissioner*, Alan Edden Huckle, *apptd* 2001
*Administrator*, Louise Savill, *apptd* 1996

| TRADE WITH UK | 1999 | 2000 |
|---|---|---|
| Imports from UK | £1,406,000 | £976,000 |
| Exports to UK | 863,000 | 145,000 |

## BRITISH VIRGIN ISLANDS

AREA – 58 sq. miles (151 sq. km)
POPULATION – 20,254 (2001 estimate; by island: Tortola 16,630; Virgin Gorda 3,063; Anegada 204; Jost Van Dyke 176; other islands 181)
CAPITAL – ΨRoad Town (population, 6,667, 2001 estimate)
CURRENCY – US dollar (US$) (£ sterling and EC$ also circulate)
FLAG – British blue ensign with the shield of arms in the fly
POPULATION GROWTH RATE – 2.0 per cent (2000)
POPULATION DENSITY – 132 per sq. km (2000)
URBAN POPULATION – 61.1 per cent (2000 estimate)
GDP – US$528 million (1997); US$26,787 per capita (1997)
ANNUAL AVERAGE GROWTH OF GDP – 4.7 per cent (2000)

The Virgin Islands, divided between the UK and the USA, are situated at the eastern extremity of the Greater Antilles. Those of the group which are British number 46, of which 11 are inhabited, and have a total area of about 58 sq. miles (151 sq. km). The principal islands are Tortola, the largest (area, 21 sq. miles), Virgin Gorda (8 sq. miles), Anegada (15 sq. miles) and Jost Van Dyke (3½ sq. miles).

Apart from Anegada, which is a flat coral island, the British Virgin Islands are hilly, being an extension of the Puerto Rico and the US Virgin Islands archipelago. The highest point is Sage Mountain on Tortola which rises to a height of 1,780 feet.

The islands lie within the trade winds belt and possess a sub-tropical climate. The average temperature varies from 22°–28° C in winter to 26°–31° C in summer. Average annual rainfall is 53 inches.

## HISTORY AND POLITICS

Under the 1977 constitution the Governor, appointed by the Crown, remains responsible for defence and internal security, external affairs and the civil service but in other matters acts in accordance with the advice of the Executive Council. The Executive Council consists of the Governor as Chairman, one ex-officio member (the Attorney-General), the Chief Minister and three other ministers. The Legislative Council consists of a Speaker chosen from outside the Council, one ex-officio member (the Attorney-General), and 13 elected members returned from ten electoral districts.

*Governor*, HE Frank Savage, CMG, OBE, LVO, *apptd* 1998
*Deputy Governor*, Elton Georges, OBE

EXECUTIVE COUNCIL *as at May 2001*

*Chairman*, The Governor
*Chief Minister and Minister of Finance*, Ralph O'Neal, OBE
*Deputy Chief Minister*, Alvin Christopher
*Attorney-General*, Cherno Jallow
*Communications and Works*, Alvin Christopher
*Education and Culture*, Andrew Fahie
*Health and Welfare*, Ethlyn Smith
*Natural Resources and Labour*, Julian Frazer

## ECONOMY

Tourism is the main industry but the financial centre is growing steadily in importance. Other industries include a rum distillery, three stone-crushing plants and factories manufacturing concrete blocks and paint. The major export items are fresh fish, gravel, sand, fruit and vegetables; exports are largely confined to the US Virgin Islands. Chief imports are building materials, machinery, cars and beverages.

| TRADE WITH UK | 1999 | 2000 |
|---|---|---|
| Imports from UK | £5,371,000 | £14,171,000 |
| Exports to UK | 2,499,000 | 4,524,000 |

## COMMUNICATIONS

The principal airport is on Beef Island, linked by bridge to Tortola, and an extended runway of 3,600 ft enables larger aircraft to call. There is a second airfield on Virgin Gorda and a third on Anegada. There are direct shipping services to the UK and the USA and fast passenger services connect the main islands by ferry.

# CAYMAN ISLANDS

AREA – 102 sq. miles (264 sq. km)
POPULATION – 40,786 (1999 census)
CAPITAL – ΨGeorge Town (population, 20,626, 1999 census)
CURRENCY – Cayman Islands dollar (CI$) of 100 cents
FLAG – British blue ensign with the arms on a white disc in the fly
POPULATION GROWTH RATE – 5.0 per cent (1999)
POPULATION DENSITY – 154 per sq. km (1999)
URBAN POPULATION – 100.0 per cent (2000 estimate)
GDP – US$928 million (1997); US$23,382 per capita (1996)
ANNUAL AVERAGE GROWTH OF GDP – 4.0 per cent (1996)

The Cayman Islands consist of three islands, Grand Cayman, Cayman Brac, and Little Cayman. About 150 miles south of Cuba, the islands are divided from Jamaica, 180 miles to the south-east, by the Cayman Trench, the deepest part of the Caribbean. The nearest point on the US mainland is Miami in Florida, 450 miles to the north. Cooled by trade winds, the annual average temperature and rainfall are 28.5°C and 50.7 inches respectively.

## HISTORY AND POLITICS

The colony derives its name from the Carib word for the crocodile, 'caymanas', which appeared in the log of the first English visitor to the islands, Sir Francis Drake. Although tradition has it that the first settlers arrived in 1658, the first recorded settlers arrived in 1666–71. The first recorded permanent settlers followed the first land grant by Britain in 1734. The islands were placed under direct control of Jamaica in 1863. When Jamaica became independent in 1962, the islands opted to remain under the British Crown.

The constitution provides for a Governor, a Legislative Assembly and an Executive Council, and effectively allows a large measure of self-government. Unless there are exceptional reasons, the Governor accepts the advice of the Executive Council, which comprises three official members and five ministers elected from the 15 elected members of the Assembly. The official members also sit in the Assembly. The Governor has responsibility for the police, civil service, defence and external affairs. The Governor handed over the presidency of the Legislative Assembly to the Speaker in 1991. The normal life of the Assembly is four years; the most recent general election was held on 8 November 2000.

*Governor*, HE Peter Smith, CBE, *apptd* 1999

EXECUTIVE COUNCIL *as at November 2000*

*President*, The Governor
*Chief Secretary*, James Ryan, MBE
*Attorney-General*, David Ballantyne
*Education, Human Resources and Culture*, Roy Bodden
*Financial Secretary*, George McCarthy, OBE
*Health and Information Technology*, Linford Pierson
*Planning, Communication and Works*, Kurt Tibbetts
*Tourism, Environment and Transport*, McKeeva Bush
*Speaker of Legislative Assembly*, Capt. Mabry Kirkconnell, MBE

CAYMAN ISLANDS GOVERNMENT OFFICE, 6 Arlington Street, London SW1A 1RE. Tel: 020-7491 7772. *Government Representative*, Jennifer Dilbert

## ECONOMY

With a complete absence of direct taxation, the Cayman Islands has become successful over the past 30 years as an offshore financial centre. With representation from 69 countries, there were, at the end of 2000, 449 banks and trust companies, of which local offices were maintained by 117. In addition, there were 668 licensed insurance companies and 59,922 registered companies. The Cayman Islands stock exchange opened in January 1997. Tourism, with an emphasis on scuba diving, has also been developed successfully. There were 406,620 visitors by air and 1,030,857 cruise ship callers in 2000.

The two industries support a heavy imbalance in trade resulting from the need to import most of what is consumed and used on the islands, and have created a thriving local economy. Import duty and fees from financial centre operations have provided revenue enabling the government to undertake heavy investment in education (which is provided free to all four to 16-year olds), health and other social programmes.

| TRADE WITH UK | 1999 | 2000 |
|---|---|---|
| Imports from UK | £10,561,000 | £25,013,000 |
| Exports to UK | 1,023,000 | 18,234,000 |

## FALKLAND ISLANDS

AREA – 4,700 sq. miles (12,173 sq. km)
POPULATION – 2,221 (1996 census)
CAPITAL – ΨStanley (population, 1,636, 1996 census)
CURRENCY – Falkland pound of 100 pence
FLAG – British blue ensign with the arms on a white disc in the fly
POPULATION GROWTH RATE – 0.0 per cent (1997)
URBAN POPULATION – 89.7 per cent (2000 estimate)

The Falkland Islands, the only considerable group in the South Atlantic, lie about 300 miles east of the Straits of Magellan. They consist of East Falkland (area 2,610 sq. miles; 6,759 sq. km), West Falkland (2,090 sq. miles; 5,413 sq. km) and over 700 small islands. Mount Usborne (E. Falkland), the loftiest peak, rises 2,312 feet above sea level. The islands are chiefly moorland.

The climate is cool. At Stanley the mean monthly temperature varies between 24° C in January and –5° C in July.

### HISTORY AND POLITICS

The Falklands were sighted first by Davis in 1592, and then by Hawkins in 1594; the first known landing was by Strong in 1690. A settlement was made by France in 1764; this was subsequently sold to Spain, but the latter country recognised Great Britain's title to a part at least of the group in 1771. The first British settlement was established in 1765. After Argentina declared independence from Spain, the Argentine government in 1820 proclaimed its sovereignty over the Falklands and a settlement was founded in 1826. The settlement was destroyed by the Americans in 1831. In 1833 occupation was resumed by the British for the protection of the seal-fisheries, and the islands were permanently colonised. Argentina continued to claim sovereignty over the islands (known to them as *las Islas Malvinas*), and in pursuance of this claim invaded the islands on 2 April 1982 and also occupied South Georgia. A naval and military force dispatched from Great Britain recaptured South Georgia on 25 April and after landing at San Carlos on 21 May, recaptured the islands from the Argentines, who surrendered on 14 June 1982. A British naval and military garrison of 1,700 personnel remains in the area. Under the 1985 constitution, the Governor is advised by an Executive Council consisting of three elected members of the Legislative Council and two ex-officio members, the Chief Executive and the Financial Secretary. The Legislative Council consists of eight elected members and the same two ex-officio members.

*Governor and Chairman of the Executive Council*, HE Donald Lamont, *apptd* 1999
*Chief Executive*, Dr Michael D. Blanch
*Attorney-General*, David G. Lang, CBE, QC
*Commander, British Forces, Falkland Islands*, Air Cdre John A. Cliffe
*Financial Secretary*, Derek F. Howatt

FALKLAND ISLANDS GOVERNMENT OFFICE, Falkland House, 14 Broadway, London SW1H 0BH. Tel: 020-7222 2542. *Government Representative*, Miss S. Cameron

### ECONOMY

The economy was formerly based solely on agriculture, principally sheep farming with a little dairy farming for domestic requirements and crops for winter fodder. Since the establishment of an interim conservation and management fishing zone around the islands in 1987 and the consequent introduction of a licensing regime for vessels fishing within the 200-mile zone, the economy has diversified. Income from the associated fishing activities, mainly for illex squid, is now the largest source of revenue. The increase in government revenue from fishing licences has led to the establishment of a substantial health, education and welfare system. The islands are now self-financing except for defence. Chief imports are provisions, alcoholic beverages, timber, clothing and hardware. Tourism is a small but expanding industry. At 30 June 2000 the government had a budget surplus of £11.9 million.

In 1996, the Falkland Islands government awarded licences to five consortia to search for offshore hydrocarbons to the north of the islands. By the end of 1998, no commercially viable accumulations of oil had been found, but the exploration revealed the presence of organic-rich source rock, indicating the presence of considerable quantities of oil in the North Falkland basin. Further exploratory searches are planned.

An EU-standard abattoir was due to open in 2001, enabling the Falkland Islands to export meat to the European Union.

| TRADE WITH UK | 1999 | 2000 |
|---|---|---|
| Imports from UK | £16,228,000 | £22,064,000 |
| Exports to UK | 24,946,000 | 6,704,000 |

## GIBRALTAR

AREA – 2.3 sq. miles (6.0 sq. km)
POPULATION – 28,000 (2000 estimate)
CAPITAL – ΨGibraltar
CURRENCY – Gibraltar pound of 100 pence
FLAG – White with a red stripe along the lower edge; over all a red castle with a key hanging from its gateway
POPULATION GROWTH RATE – 1.4 per cent (1997)
POPULATION DENSITY – 4,239 per sq. km (1998)
URBAN POPULATION – 100.0 per cent (2000 estimate)

Gibraltar is a rocky promontory which juts southwards from the south-east coast of Spain, with which it is connected by a low isthmus. It is about 20 miles (32 km) from the opposite coast of Africa. The town stands at the foot of the promontory on the west side.

### HISTORY AND POLITICS

Gibraltar was captured in 1704, during the War of the Spanish Succession, by a combined Dutch and English force, and was ceded to Great Britain by the Treaty of Utrecht (1713). Several attempts have been made to retake it, the most celebrated being the great siege of 1779 to 1783, when General Eliott held it for three years and seven months against a combined French and Spanish force. The Treaty of Utrecht stipulates that if Britain ever relinquishes its colonial rights over Gibraltar the colony would return to Spain. In a 1967 referendum on the colony's status, 12,138 people voted to remain a British Dependent Territory and 44 voted to join Spain. Spain closed the border with Gibraltar from 1969 to 1985 and refused to engage in any trade.

The House of Assembly consists of an independent Speaker, 15 elected members, the Attorney-General and the Financial and Development Secretary.

The Gibraltar government has recently been pressing

for more local autonomy especially in its relations with the EU, and this has led to tension with the UK and Spanish governments. Gibraltar is part of the EU (with the UK government responsible for enforcing EU directives affecting Gibraltar) but is not a fully-fledged member and is exempt from the Common Customs Tariff and the Common Agricultural Policy. Value added tax is not applied. The Gibraltar Social Democrats won the last election in February 2000.

*Governor and Commander-in-Chief*, HE the Rt. Hon. David Durie, CMG
*Commander British Forces, HM Naval Base, Gibraltar*, Cdre A. N. Willmett
*Deputy Governor*, P. A. Speller
*Attorney-General*, R. Rhoda
*Chief Justice*, Derek Schofield
*Chief Minister*, Peter Caruana
*Deputy Chief Minister, Trade, Industry and Telecommunication*, Keith Azopardi
*Education, Training, Culture and Health*, Dr Bernard Linares
*Employment and Consumer* Affairs, Hubert Corby
*Housing*, Jaime Netto
*Public Services, Environment, Sport and Youth*, Ernest Britto
*Social Affairs*, Yvette Del Agua
*Speaker*, John Alcantara , CBE
*Tourism and Transport*, Joe Holliday

## ECONOMY

Gibraltar has an extensive shipping trade and is a popular shopping centre and tourist resort. The chief sources of revenue are the port dues, the rent of the Crown estate in the town, and duties on consumer items. The free port tradition of Gibraltar is still reflected in the low rates of import duty. A financial services industry is expanding, based on Gibraltar's status as an offshore financial centre. However, many jobs have been lost as a result of reductions in the British naval and military presence.

A total of 6,303 merchant ships (133.97 million gross registered tons aggregate) entered the port during 2000. There are 53 km of roads.

| Trade with UK | 1999 | 2000 |
|---|---|---|
| Imports from UK | £93,355,000 | £121,599,000 |
| Exports to UK | 12,791,000 | 11,547,000 |

## EDUCATION

Education is compulsory and free for children between the ages of five and 15 whose parents are ordinarily resident in Gibraltar. Scholarships are available for higher education in Britain. The total enrolment in government schools was 4,980 in September 2000.

# MONTSERRAT

Population – 5,200 (2001 estimate)
Capital – ΨPlymouth (destroyed by volcanic activity)
Currency – East Caribbean dollar (EC$) of 100 cents
Flag – British blue ensign with the shield of arms in the fly
Population Growth Rate – 0.0 per cent (1997)
Population Density – 105 per sq. km (1998)
Urban Population – 18.4 per cent (2000 estimate)
GDP – US$25 million (1999); US$5,600 per capita (1999)

Montserrat is about 11 miles long and seven miles wide. It is volcanic with several hot springs. About two-thirds of the island is mountainous, the rest capable of cultivation but volcanic activity has caused the evacuation of two-thirds of the island.

## HISTORY AND POLITICS

Discovered by Columbus in 1493, Montserrat became a British colony in 1632. The first settlers were predominantly Irish indentured servants from St Christopher. Montserrat was captured by the French in 1664, 1667 and 1782 but the island reverted to Britain within a few years on each occasion and was finally assigned to Great Britain in 1783.

A ministerial system was introduced in Montserrat in 1960. The Executive Council is presided over by the Governor and is composed of four elected members (the Chief and three other Ministers) and two ex-officio members (the Attorney-General and the Financial Secretary). The four Ministers are appointed from the members of the political party or coalition holding the majority in the Legislative Council. The Legislative Council consists of the Speaker, two ex-officio members (the Attorney-General and the Financial Secretary), two nominated members and nine elected members. Following elections in April 2001 the elected element of the legislature comprised the following parties: New People's Liberation Movement 7; National Progressive Party 2.

*Governor*, HE Anthony Longrigg, CMG, *apptd* 2001

Executive Council *as at May 2001*

*President*, The Governor
*Chief Minister and Minister of Finance and Economic Development*, Dr John Osborne
*Agriculture, Lands, Housing and the Environment*, Margaret Dyer-Howe
*Attorney-General*, Brian Cottle
*Communications and Works*, Dr Lowell Lewis
*Education, Health and Community Services*, Idabelle Meade
*Financial Secretary*, John Skerritt

## ECONOMY

The economy, which consists of tourism, related construction activities, offshore business services and agriculture, has been seriously affected by relocation to the north of the island due to volcanic activity.

| Trade with UK | 1999 | 2000 |
|---|---|---|
| Imports from UK | £1,414,000 | £1,104,000 |
| Exports to UK | 71,000 | 120,000 |

# PITCAIRN ISLANDS

Area – 2 sq. miles (5 sq. km)
Population – 54 (1999). Since 1887 the islanders have generally been adherents of the Seventh-day Adventist Church
Currency – Currency is that of New Zealand
Flag – British blue ensign with the arms in the fly.

Pitcairn is the chief of a group of islands situated about midway between New Zealand and Panama in the South Pacific Ocean. The island rises in cliffs to a height of 1,100 feet and access from the sea is possible only at Bounty Bay, a small rocky cove, and then only by surf boats. The other three islands of the group (Henderson, lying 105 miles east-north-east of Pitcairn, Oeno, lying 75 miles north-west, and Ducie, lying 293 miles east) are all uninhabited.

Mean monthly temperatures vary between 66°F (19°C) in August and 75°F (24°C) in February and the average annual rainfall is 80 inches. With an equable climate, the island is very fertile and produces both tropical and subtropical trees and crops.

### HISTORY AND POLITICS

First settled in 1790 by the Bounty mutineers and their Tahitian companions, Pitcairn was left uninhabited in 1856 when the entire population was resettled on Norfolk Island. The present community are descendants of two parties who, not wishing to remain on Norfolk, returned to Pitcairn in 1859 and 1864 respectively.

Pitcairn became a British settlement under the British Settlement Act 1887, and was administered by the Governor of Fiji from 1952 until 1970, when the administration was transferred to the British High Commission in New Zealand and the British High Commissioner was appointed Governor. The local Government Ordinance of 1964 provides for a Council of ten members of whom six are elected.

*Governor of Pitcairn, Henderson, Ducie and Oeno Islands*, HE Martin J. Williams, CVO, OBE (*British High Commissioner to New Zealand*)
*Island Mayor*, Steve Christian

### ECONOMY

The islanders live by subsistence gardening and fishing. Wood carvings and other handicrafts are sold to passing ships and to a few overseas customers. Other than small fees charged for gun and driving licences there are no taxes and government revenue is derived almost solely from the sale of postage stamps and income from investments. Communication with the outside world is maintained by cargo vessels travelling between New Zealand and Panama which call at irregular intervals, and by means of a satellite service providing telephone, telex and fax facilities.

| TRADE WITH UK | 1999 | 2000 |
|---|---|---|
| Imports from UK | £333,000 | £245,000 |
| Exports to UK | 12,000 | 1,000 |

### EDUCATION

Education is compulsory between the ages of five and 15. Secondary education in New Zealand is encouraged by the administration, which provides scholarships and bursaries. Medical care is provided by a registered nurse when a doctor is not present.

## ST HELENA

AREA – 47 sq. miles (122 sq. km)
POPULATION – 6,000 (1994 UN estimate)
CAPITAL – ΨJamestown (population, 884, 1998)
CURRENCY – St Helena pound (£) of 100 pence
FLAG – British blue ensign with the shield of arms in the fly
POPULATION GROWTH RATE – 0.8 per cent (1998)
POPULATION DENSITY – 49 per sq. km (1997)
URBAN POPULATION – 39.2 per cent (1998)
ILLITERACY RATE – 3.6 per cent (1998)

St Helena is situated in the South Atlantic Ocean, 955 miles south of the Equator, 702 miles south-east of Ascension, 1,140 miles from the nearest point of the African continent, 1,800 miles from the coast of South America and 1,694 miles from Cape Town. It is 10.5 miles long and 6.5 broad.

St Helena is of volcanic origin, and consists of numerous rugged mountains, the highest rising to 2,700 feet (820 m), interspersed with picturesque ravines. Although within the tropics, the south-east trade winds keep the temperature mild and equable.

### HISTORY AND POLITICS

St Helena was probably discovered by the Portuguese navigator, João da Nova in 1502. It was used as a port of call for vessels of all nations trading to the East until it was annexed by the Dutch in 1633. It was never occupied by them, however, and the English East India Company seized it in 1659. From 1815 to 1821 the island was lent to the British government as a place of exile for the Emperor Napoleon Bonaparte who died in St Helena on 5 May 1821, and in 1834 it was annexed to the British Crown.

The island was settled by the East India Company in the 17th and 18th centuries with planters and company soldiers from England and slaves from the Indian subcontinent and Madagascar.

The government of St Helena is administered by a Governor, with the aid of a Legislative Council, consisting of a Speaker, three ex-officio members (Chief Secretary, Financial Secretary and Attorney-General) and 12 elected members. Five committees of the Legislative Council are responsible for the overseeing of the activities of the five biggest government departments and have in addition a wide range of statutory and administrative functions. The Governor is also assisted by an Executive Council of the three ex-officio members and the chairmen of the Council committees.

*Governor*, HE David Hollamby, *apptd* 1999
*Attorney-General*, Kurt de Freitas, OBE
*Chief Administrative Health Officer*, Robert Essex
*Chief Agriculture and Natural Resources Officer*, Roderick J. Steele
*Chief Auditor*, Rupert Bladon
*Chief Development Officer*, Mrs Corinda S. S. Essex
*Chief Education Officer*, John Price
*Chief Employment and Social Services Officer*, John MacDonald
*Chief Engineer*, vacant
*Chief Finance Officer*, Desmond H. Wade
*Chief Justice*, Geoffrey W. Martin, OBE
*Chief Personnel Officer*, Mrs Sylvia I. Ellick
*Chief Secretary*, Michael J. Clancy
*Chief of Police*, G. G. Yon
*Deputy Secretary*, Ms Ethel C. Yon
*Financial Secretary*, Matthew J. Young
*Postmistress*, Mrs Iva I. Henry

### ECONOMY

St Helena was intended as a maritime base, with an economy dedicated to the provision of supplies for shipping and the local garrison, rather than as a self-sufficient colony. St Helena still receives an annual grant from the UK which amounted to £3.184 million in 1999. The only significant export is canned and frozen fish. The other exports are a small amount of high quality coffee and cottage industry products (including lace, decorative woodwork and beadwork). James's Bay, on the north-west of the island, possesses a good anchorage. There is as yet no airport or airstrip. Shortages of staple goods arose following panic buying when the sole supply ship broke down in November 1999, highlighting St Helena's isolation.

| TRADE WITH UK | 1999 | 1998 |
|---|---|---|
| Imports from UK | £8,781,000 | £10,043,000 |
| Exports to UK | 1,111,000 | 297,000 |

## ASCENSION ISLAND

AREA – 34 sq. miles (88 sq. km)
POPULATION – 980 (2001 census)
CAPITAL – ΨGeorgetown
CURRENCY – Currency is that of St Helena or the UK

The small island of Ascension lies in the South Atlantic some 750 miles north-west of the island of St Helena. It is a rocky peak of purely volcanic origin. The highest point (Green Mountain), some 2,817 ft, is covered with lush vegetation. The island is a breeding area for green turtles and for the sooty tern, or wideawake. Other wildlife includes feral donkeys and sheep, nine varieties of sea birds, including the indigenous Ascension frigate bird, and five of land birds.

Ascension Island's residents consist of the employees and families of the British organisations, of the contractors of the US Air Force and RAF and of the Ascension Island government.

British forces returned to the island in April 1982 in support of operations in the Falkland Islands. At present there are about 25 RAF personnel on the island together with some 200 civilian workers supporting the air link to the Falklands.

### HISTORY AND POLITICS

Ascension is said to have been discovered by João da Nova in 1501 and two years later was visited on Ascension Day by Alphonse d'Albuquerque, who gave the island its present name. It was uninhabited until the arrival of Napoleon in St Helena in 1815 when a small British naval garrison was stationed on the island. As HMS *Ascension* it remained under the supervision of the Board of Admiralty until 1922, when it was made a dependency of St Helena.

The British Foreign Secretary appoints the Administrator who is responsible to the Governor resident in St Helena. There is a small police force, bank and post office. The Ascension Island government is responsible for health and education. The Ascension Island Works and Services Agency operates the port and provides other public services such as road and building maintenance.

*Administrator*, Geoffrey Fairhurst, *apptd* 1999

### COMMUNICATIONS

Cable and Wireless PLC operates the international telephone and cable services and maintains an internal telephone service. The BBC opened its Atlantic relay station broadcasting to Africa and South America in 1967. There is a monthly shipping service and two flights a week by RAF Tristars which transit Ascension en route to the Falkland Islands. US aircraft and ships service the American base.

## TRISTAN DA CUNHA

AREA – 38 sq. miles (98 sq. km)
POPULATION – 288 (1994 UN estimate)
CAPITAL – ΨEdinburgh of the Seven Seas
CURRENCY – Currency is that of the UK

Tristan da Cunha is the chief island of a group of islands in the South Atlantic which lies some 1,260 nautical miles (2,333 km) south-south-west of St Helena.

All the islands are volcanic and steep-sided with cliffs or narrow beaches. Tristan itself has a single volcanic cone rising to 6,760 feet (2,060 m)

The islands have a warm-temperate oceanic climate which is damp and windy. Rainfall averages 66 inches a year on the coast of Tristan da Cunha.

Population is centred in the settlement of Edinburgh on Tristan da Cunha. In addition, there is a meteorological station maintained on Gough Island by the South African government. Inaccessible Island and the Nightingale Islands are uninhabited.

### HISTORY AND POLITICS

Tristan da Cunha was discovered in 1506 by a Portuguese admiral (Tristão da Cunha) after whom it was named. In 1760 a British naval officer visited the islands and gave his name to Nightingale Island. In 1816 the group was annexed to the British Crown and a garrison was placed on Tristan da Cunha, but this force was withdrawn in 1817. Corporal William Glass remained at his own request with his wife and two children. This party, with two others, formed a settlement. In 1827 five women from St Helena, and afterwards others from Cape Colony, joined the party.

Due to its position on a main sailing route the colony thrived, with an economy based on trading with whalers, sealers and other passing ships. However, the replacement of sail by steam and the opening of the Suez Canal in the late 19th century led to decline.

In October 1961 a volcano, believed to have been extinct for thousands of years, erupted and the danger of further volcanic activity led to the evacuation of inhabitants to the UK. An advance party returned to Tristan da Cunha in 1963 and subsequently the main body of the islanders returned to the island.

### GOVERNMENT

In 1938 Tristan da Cunha and the neighbouring islands of Inaccessible, Nightingale and Gough were made dependencies of St Helena. They are administered by the Governor of St Helena through a resident Administrator, with headquarters at Edinburgh. Under a constitution introduced in 1985, the Administrator is advised by an Island Council of eight elected members, of whom one must be a woman, and three appointed members. There is universal suffrage at 18. Elections are held every three years.

*Administrator*, Brian Baldwin, *apptd* 1998

### ECONOMY

The island is almost financially self-sufficient; UK government aid finances training scholarships and a resident medical officer at the hospital. The main industries are crayfish fishing, fish-processing and agriculture, with the shore-based fishing industry having been developed with the construction of the boat harbour in 1967 and the re-establishment of the lobster factory in 1966. There are no taxes, income being derived from the royalties from the rock lobster fishery around the islands, interest from the reserve fund, and the sales of stamps and handicrafts, as well as vegetables, to passing ships. Tourism is increasing, the island being on the itinerary of several environmental tours. Apart from the fishing industry, the other main employer is the administration itself. There is a school catering for children up to age 15. Healthcare and education are free for the islanders.

### COMMUNICATIONS

Scheduled visits to the island are restricted to about six calls a year by fishing vessels from Cape Town and annual calls of the RMS *St Helena* and the *SA Agulhas*, also from Cape Town. A wireless station on the island is in daily contact with Cape Town and a radio-telephone service was established in 1969, the same year that electricity was introduced to all the islanders' homes. A marine satellite system providing direct dialling telephone, telex and fax facilities was installed in 1992. Since 1998 the island has had internet and e-mail facilities, as well as a public telephone. Cable television was introduced in 2001.

## SOUTH GEORGIA AND THE SOUTH SANDWICH ISLANDS

AREA – 1,580 sq. miles (4,092 sq. km)
POPULATION – No permanent population

South Georgia is an island 800 miles east-south-east of the Falkland group. The population comprises a small military garrison (which is due to be withdrawn in 2001 and replaced by a scientific research station operated by the British Antarctic Survey) and the curator of the museum at King Edward Point, and staff of the British Antarctic Survey at Bird Island, to the north-west of South Georgia.

The South Sandwich Islands lie some 470 miles south-east of South Georgia. The group is a chain of uninhabited, actively volcanic islands about 150 miles long, with a wholly Antarctic climate.

The present constitution came into effect in 1985. It provides for a Commissioner who, for the time being, is the officer administering the government of the Falkland Islands.

In 1993 the UK government decreed an extension of Crown sovereignty and jurisdiction from 12 miles around South Georgia and the South Sandwich Islands to 200 miles around each in order to preserve marine stocks.

*Commissioner for South Georgia and the South Sandwich Islands*, Donald Lamont, *apptd* 1999

## TURKS AND CAICOS ISLANDS

AREA – 166 sq. miles (430 sq. km)
POPULATION – 23,000 (1999 estimate)
CAPITAL – ΨGrand Turk (population, 3,691, 1994)
CURRENCY – US dollar (US$)
FLAG – British blue ensign with the shield of arms in the fly
POPULATION GROWTH RATE – 3.2 per cent (1997)
POPULATION DENSITY – 36 per sq. km (1998)
URBAN POPULATION – 45.2 per cent (2000 estimate)

The Turks and Caicos Islands are about 50 miles south-east of the Bahamas of which they are geographically an extension. There are over 30 islands, of which eight are inhabited, covering an estimated area of 166 sq. miles (430 sq. km). The principal island and seat of government is Grand Turk.

The islands lie in the trade wind belt. The average temperature varies from 24°–27° C in the winter to 29°–32° C in the summer and humidity is generally low. Average rainfall is 21 inches a year.

### HISTORY AND POLITICS

A constitution was introduced in 1988, and amended in 1993, which provides for an Executive Council and a Legislative Council. The Executive Council is presided over by the Governor and comprises the Chief Minister and five elected Ministers, together with the ex-officio Chief Secretary and Attorney-General.

At the general election of 4 March 1999, the People's Democratic Movement won nine seats and the Progressive National Party four seats in the Legislative Council.

*Governor*, HE Mervyn T. Jones, *apptd* 2000

EXECUTIVE COUNCIL *as at June 2001*

*President*, The Governor
*Attorney-General*, David Jeremiah
*Chief Minister*, Derek H. Taylor
*Chief Secretary*, Cynthia Astwood, MBE
*Ministers*, Hilly Ewing (*Deputy Chief Minister*); Larry Coalbrooke; Noel Skippings; Oswald Skippings; Clarence Selver

### ECONOMY

The most important industries are fishing, tourism and offshore finance. The islands were visited by 151,000 tourists in 2000.

| TRADE WITH UK | 1999 | 2000 |
|---|---|---|
| Imports from UK | £1,284,000 | £864,000 |
| Exports to UK | 67,000 | 251,000 |

### COMMUNICATIONS

The principal airports are on the islands of Grand Turk and Providenciales. Air services link Providenciales with London, Miami, Fort Lauderdale, Atlanta, Jamaica, the Bahamas, Haiti and the Dominican Republic. An internal air service provides a regular service between the principal islands. There are direct shipping services to the USA (Miami). A comprehensive telephone and telex service is provided by Cable and Wireless (WI) Ltd.

# Events of the Year

## 1 September 2000 to 31 August 2001

### BRITISH AFFAIRS

#### SEPTEMBER 2000

**4.** Cabinet Office Minister (Mo Mowlam) announced that she would be standing down as an MP at the next general election. **5.** 150 British paratroopers were flown into Sierra Leone, on standby to rescue the six British soldiers being held hostage by a rebel faction. **6.** The Government came under increasing pressure to reduce the VAT on fuel as petrol prices were expected to reach almost 87 pence a litre, due to the rising price of crude oil. **8.** Protesters in France set up road blocks at refineries and fuel depots to highlight the high cost of fuel. **9.** The fuel shortages continued as people began panic buying after Shell warned that the majority of their pumps would be dry by the end of the week. **10.** A British paratrooper was killed when airborne forces freed six captured soldiers in a raid deep in the Sierra Leone jungle. **11.** Following reports showing that over a quarter of all British petrol stations were dry, the Prime Minister (Tony Blair) declared that he would not cave in to the protestors. **12.** A limited number of tankers were released from blockades around the country in order to meet the needs of the emergency services and other essential industries. 90% of petrol stations remained closed. **13.** Troops were put on standby to intervene in the fuel crisis as the health service went on emergency alert. Schools and businesses closed and supermarkets introduced rationing. **14.** Protesters lifted the blockades at oil refineries around the country but threatened that the blockades would return if taxes on fuel were not cut within 60 days. **19.** The Tories called for the resignation of the Chancellor of the Exchequer (Gordon Brown) over allegations that he lied about a £1 million donation to the Labour Party by the head of Formula One motor racing Bernie Ecclestone.

#### OCTOBER 2000

**4.** The Conservative spokesperson for Home Affairs (Anne Widdecombe) was criticised by her own party for proposing that individuals caught in possession of cannabis should receive an automatic minimum fine of £100 and a criminal record. **11.** Scotland's First Minister (Donald Dewar) died of a brain haemorrhage following a fall outside his Edinburgh residence. Thousands attended the funeral of former East End gangster Reggie Kray. **14.** Former Paymaster General, Geoffrey Robinson, accused Peter Mandelson of initiating discussions about a home loan in the scandal that forced them both to resign. Figures showed that the size of secondary school classes had grown to a ten year high due to a shortage of teachers. **19.** Hundreds of thousands of doses of a polio vaccine were recalled by the Department of Health after it was discovered that it had been produced with material from British cows, in breach of European guidelines in force since 1999. **23.** It was announced that Railtrack was to receive a five-year grant of £4.7 billion from the rail industry regulator to 'deliver a modern safe railway with greater public accountability'. The Labour MP for Glasgow Springburn (Michael Martin) was elected Speaker of the House of Commons. **24.** Sir Edward Heath announced he was to retire from Parliament at the next election. French-owned rail company Connex became the first train operating company to lose its franchise since privatisation. Railtrack announced the immediate closure of the Scottish west coast mainline for urgent maintenance, causing major disruptions in Scotland. **26.** The official BSE inquiry found that Ministers and Whitehall were guilty of repeatedly misleading the public about the threat to human health posed by mad cow disease, but did not deliberately lie or protect farming interests at the cost of consumers. The House of Lords voted to delay part-privatisation of air traffic control until after the general election.

#### NOVEMBER 2000

**4.** Samples collected by researchers from the *Sunday Times* found traces of cocaine on surfaces in lavatories in the House of Commons. John Prescott, announced that an extra £51 million would be spent on improving flood defences around the British Isles over the next four years in response to the extreme flooding taking place around the country. **6.** Surgeons at St Mary's Hospital, Manchester, undertook the operation to separate Siamese twins Jodie and Mary following a ruling by the Court of Appeal. As surgeons suspected, the weaker twin Mary later died. Alan Milburn signed an agreement to recruit up to 5,000 nurses from Spain in order to address the shortfall within the NHS. **8.** In response to growing fears of public protest the Chancellor (Gordon Brown) in his pre-budget speech announced that duty on fuel would be frozen at current levels until April 2002. **10.** Fuel protesters began their convoy from Newcastle to London. **13.** For the third time in two years, the House of Lords rejected Government proposals to lower the age of consent from 18 to 16 for homosexuals. **15.** A report compiled by the Better Regulation Taskforce claimed that farmers in Britain were being driven to bankruptcy due to EU 'red tape'. A rebellion by 37 Labour MPs over plans to privatise the national air traffic control service was beaten by a Government majority of 93. **20.** The Agriculture Minister (Nick Brown) warned Tony Blair that BSE infected beef of French origin could be entering the UK due to legal loopholes in the importing mechanism and insufficient checking. Members of the European Union including the United Kingdom declared their commitment to a military European Rapid Reaction Force in a meeting in Brussels. **23.** By-elections took place for the seats of West Bromwich West (winner John Robertson (Lab) with a majority of 6,337), Preston (winner Mark Hendrick (Lab/Co-op) with a majority of 4,426) and Glasgow Anniesland (winner Adrian Bailey (Lab/Co-op) with a majority of 3,232). **27.** The Prime Minister met with the head of Railtrack and other train operating companies, emphasising that the rail network should be restored to its normal timetable by Christmas.

#### DECEMBER 2000

**3.** The Metropolitan Police Commissioner said that inner-city policing was in crisis due to difficulties in recruiting and retaining sufficient police officers and called on Government to provide resources to make up the shortfall of 3,000. **6.** The Queen's speech marked the official re-opening of Parliament. **18.** Brighton and Hove, Wolverhampton and Inverness were awarded city status. In an attempt to alleviate pressure on the National Health Service, the Government announced that the majority of nurses would receive a 3.7% pay increase and GPs a 3.9% increase. Senior nurses and nurses working in Inner London would get a larger increase of up to 9%. **19.** Camelot won the right to continue to run the National Lottery for another seven years, beating the rival bid from Richard Branson's People's Lottery. **20.** Following the second reading of the Hunting Bill, the Home Secretary (Jack Straw) stated in the House of Commons that he was in favour of the regulation of hunting with dogs rather than its abolition. **27.** John Prescott ordered an inquiry into why 1,000 Christmas travellers were stranded at Stansted airport after all train links to London were cancelled.

### January 2001

**2.** Speculation about the identity of a £2 million donor to the Labour Party's election fund ended when the publisher Lord Hamlyn announced that it came from him. Following calls for an inquiry by war veterans, the Ministry of Defence admitted that it was aware of the health risks of using depleted uranium ammunition during the Gulf War and the Balkan conflicts. In a reversal of Government policy, the Defence Minister (John Spellar) announced that a voluntary screening programme would be introduced for all personnel and civilians deployed to the Balkans with concerns about their health. **3.** A series of checks undertaken by inspection teams revealed that more than one in three hospitals did not meet basic hygiene standards. **10.** Head Teachers of Schools, Chief Examiners and Trade Unions warned the Government that the examining boards were facing a serious shortage of qualified A-level markers which could lead to the collapse of the delivery of exam results in the summer. **15.** Railtrack announced that it needed an advance of £1 billion from the Government in funding if it was to avoid scrapping new schemes such as the Channel tunnel Rail Link. **16.** Figures released by the Metropolitan Police in September 2000 which showed that 281 officers from ethnic minorities had joined the service, were reported to be inaccurate: 214 of the officers came from Irish and other Caucasian backgrounds. A British couple was widely criticised for paying £8,200 to adopt twin baby girls over the Internet. **17.** MPs voted by a majority of more than 200 for an outright ban on hunting with dogs. **23.** The Northern Ireland Secretary (Peter Mandelson) admitted that he had personally intervened in the passport application of the wealthy Indian businessmen Srichand Hinduja, who later contributed £1 million to the Millennium Dome project. Mr Mandelson denied that he had given any preferential treatment to Mr Hinduja's family but resigned the following day. The Rt. Hon. John Reid was immediately appointed to be the new Northern Ireland Secretary, and in turn, Helen Liddell was appointed Secretary of State for Scotland to replace him. **25.** Figures released by the Home Office showed that Britain had become the most popular destination for asylum-seekers, with over 10,000 arriving in the year 2000. **26.** The Alder Hey Hospital in Liverpool and the Birmingham Children's Hospital admitted they had routinely removed the thymus glands from children undergoing heart surgery and sold them to a French drug company, without prior knowledge or consent of the children's parents. **29.** Peers voted 177 to 95 against a motion in the House of Lords, proposed by Baroness Young, to prevent the sale of the morning-after pill over the counter in pharmacies.

### February 2001

**7.** Tony Blair stated during Prime Minister's questions that a re-elected Labour Government would set a two-year deadline for deciding whether the conditions for entry into the single European currency have been met. **15.** The Strategic Rail Authority announced that it was to strip Railtrack of its responsibility for expanding the rail network after deciding that the company could not stop costs spiralling out of control. **18.** John Prescott ordered a complete reorganisation of the rules governing the sale of the Millennium Dome. **21.** The first case of foot-and-mouth disease for 20 years was discovered at an abattoir in Essex. The European Commission immediately imposed a world-wide ban on shipments of all cattle and meat until March 1. The Pope appointed the Archbishop of Westminster, The Most Reverend Cormack Murphy-O'Connor, as a Cardinal. **22.** The third case of foot-and-mouth disease was confirmed and 600 farms around Britain were under emergency restrictions. **23.** The Government banned livestock movements throughout the country for seven days as the number of confirmed outbreaks of foot-and-mouth-disease rose to six. **24.** Mass culls of pigs and cattle got underway in an attempt to prevent further spread of foot-and-mouth-disease. **25.** Fears were raised that Britain might have exported the disease to France through exports from a farm in Devon, which was later found to be infected. The number of British outbreaks grew to 8. **27.** As a result of the outbreak horse racing was suspended for a week, a £5,000 fine was introduced for walking on closed footpaths, and the ban on movement of animals was extended by a further two weeks. Tony Blair and Gordon Brown approved £167 million in compensation for beef, sheep and dairy farmers.

### March 2001

**1.** Cases of foot-and-mouth were confirmed in Scotland and Northern Ireland for the first time since the start of the outbreak. **2.** The House of Commons passed a Bill to allow priests and clergymen to sit as MPs. **6.** The European Commission suspended all livestock markets in the EU for two weeks in an unprecedented emergency measure aimed at preventing the spread of foot-and-mouth. **7.** The Chancellor (Gordon Brown) presented the Budget to the House of Commons. **8.** Bluebird, the jet-powered boat in which Donald Campbell died while attempting to break the world water speed record in 1967, was recovered from the waters of Coniston. **14.** The Prince of Wales donated £500,000 to farmers who were dealing with the outbreak of the disease. **27.** Control of Britain's air traffic control was awarded to the Airline Group – including British Airways, Virgin Atlantic and British Midland, who had promised to spend £1 billion on improving the system. **29.** Princess Margaret suffered a third stroke. **31.** Tony Blair confirmed that the General Election and all English local elections would be postponed due to the foot-and-mouth crisis.

### April 2001

**7.** The Countess of Wessex was forced to resign from her PR company R-JH, after a reporter, claiming to be a potential client, recorded her making unsuitable remarks about the Government, the monarchy and British affairs. **8.** The Scottish Executive announced that it was to post a senior civil servant in the USA in a bid to boost tourism and inward investment links. **11.** Scotland's premier farming event, The Royal Highland Show, was cancelled due to the foot-and-mouth outbreak. **22.** The Department of Health launched an investigation into the effects of the inhalation of smoke and pollution from pyres used to burn foot-and-mouth diseased animals. The Queen appointed the Most Reverend Peter Hollingworth, Archbishop of Brisbane, as

Australia's new Governor-General. **23.** David Hart, The General Secretary of the National Association of Head Teachers, asked for a Government enquiry into pay and conditions in schools. **26.** The Government created the first of 15 'people's peers'. The Master of Dominicans, Fr. Timothy Radcliffe stated that the Roman Catholic Church was in a state of institutional crisis and needed reform. **27.** British Roman Catholic bishops agreed to create a national child protection unit to vet potential child abuse by clergy, lay staff or volunteers. **28.** A Californian businessman, Dennis Tito, paid £14 million to the Russian space agency to go on an eight-day excursion orbiting the earth on the Soyuz spacecraft. **29.** The Army admitted to supplying untreated waste food to the pig farm where the foot-and-mouth broke out.

## May 2001

**1.** May Day demonstrators held anti-capitalist protests in London, 6,000 police officers were drafted in to keep the peace. Stephen Byers announced that new mothers would have the right to 52 weeks unpaid maternity leave, but would have to give employers additional notice. The Association of British Insurers agreed to reduce the use of genetic test results for insurance policies worth £300,000 or more following recommendations by the Human Genetics Commission. **2.** The NHS admitted that one in three women with cervical cancer had been wrongly given the all-clear. Statistics from the United Kingdom Central Council showed a 70% rise in the number of foreign nurses registering to work in the UK. **3.** Mike Tomlinson, the Chief Inspector of OFSTED, said that basic school inspections would continue every six years, but the amount of information that schools had to provide would be 'streamlined'. **4.** Oxford University announced the creation of a £15 million institute to study the Internet. **6.** A survey by The Institute of Education in London found that more than 5,000 maths teachers were needed in Britain to reduce the chronic shortfall of qualified teachers. **7.** It was announced that schools in Southwark, where Damilola Taylor was stabbed to death in a gang attack, were to be given their own full-time police officers to tackle crime. **8.** An official industrial investigation found that Railtrack was aware that the line at Hatfield was cracked two years before the derailment, which caused four deaths. **11.** Fuel protesters demonstrated at refineries and petrol stations prior to the general election in a bid to force the Prime Minister to cut fuel tax. **12.** A study commissioned by the Police Federation found that Britain had the lowest number of officers per capita among comparable countries. **18.** It was announced that train companies had recovered all their lost passenger business resulting from the Hatfield train disaster. Figures released from the Child Support Agency showed that the number of absent mothers targeted by the CSA had increased from 23,300 in 1996 to 61,000. **20.** Doug McAvoy, General Secretary of the National Union of Teachers, said that regulation should be introduced to protect children from advertisers marketing products by sending text messages to their mobile phones. **21.** The European Commission labelled Windermere unfit for bathing in an annual survey of seaside and freshwater holiday resorts. A report showed that women smokers were twice as likely to suffer from chest cancer as men who smoke the same number of cigarettes. **25.** Cancer-causing chemicals from foot-and-mouth funeral pyres may have contaminated milk on nearby farms, said the Food Standard Agency. The Ministry of Agriculture Fisheries and Food (MAFF) said the total number of foot-and-mouth cases was likely to be 3,000 – almost double the official total of 1,640. **26.** Rioting occurred in Oldham, as fighting broke out between whites and Asians.

## June 2001

**4.** A report by the National Audit Office found that some hospital trusts 'massaged' waiting lists to reduce the numbers. British Airways agreed to compensate more than 500 stewardesses who were transferred to lower paid ground duties after they became pregnant. **6.** A report by the Royal Society for The Prevention of Accidents found that nearly three million people were injured at home every year, of whom 4,000 died. Timothy McVeigh, in prison for the Oklahoma City bombing, which killed 168 people, withdrew his appeal against receiving the death sentence. **7.** Tony Blair became the first Labour leader to secure a second full term in office after another landslide general election victory. The election had the lowest turnout since 1918. For full details of the new cabinet *see* p. 289. **8.** William Hague resigned as Leader of the Conservative Party following his party's defeat at the General Election. **10.** Around a million people in Britain could be suffering from undiagnosed diabetes, which could result in life-threatening complications according to a report issued by Diabetes UK. **11.** Following a ruling by the European Commission, employers must consult their employees before taking any decisions on redundancies and closures. The new legislation will take effect in three years time. **11.** Janardan Dhasmana, a surgeon involved in the Bristol heart babies scandal, operated on 38 children of whom 20 died according to the General Medical Council. **12.** Philanthropist Sir Paul Getty made a £5 million donation to the Conservative Party to boost the party leadership contest. The Education and Skills Secretary (Estelle Morris) ordered an emergency review of the new sixth-form curriculum. **13.** The Family Planning Association won the right to a judicial review over abortion rights in Northern Ireland. **15.** The surviving Siamese twin Gracie Attard (alias Jodie) went home to Gozo after being released from St Mary's Hospital, Manchester. **17.** The first of two parole hearings took place to decide whether the two boys convicted of the murder of Jamie Bulger would be released from detention. **18.** Liberal Democrat Leader (Charles Kennedy) completed a reshuffle of his front bench team: Norman Baker became the junior spokesperson on Home Affairs; Colin Breed became junior agricultural spokesman; David Heath became spokesman on work, family and pensions; and Sarah Gidley – deputy spokeswoman on health and women's issues. The Serious Fraud Office began an investigation into the collapse of Independent Insurance, whose liquidation affected more than 40,000 British firms. **20.** Cancer-causing chemical 3-MCPD was found in a number of imported soy sauces. **26.** Shahid Malik, a member of the Government's National Executive Committee and the Commission for Racial Equality, was hit by a police riot shield and beaten by officers whilst intervening during disturbances in Burnley. **29.** British tourists were stranded at airports in the Balearic Islands, after bus drivers went on strike over pay. **30.** The Prince of Wales told an inquiry into the future of the monarchy, that the Earl and Countess of Wessex must give up their business careers entirely if they were to continue to receive royal privileges and participate in official duties. British Members of the European Parliament (MEPs) were given a 36% pay rise to £61,488 per year.

## July 2001

**2.** The Government set new academic targets for 14-year-olds to increase literacy and numeracy levels by 2004, 75% of 14-year-olds will be expected to achieve level 5 in national curriculum tests in English, maths and information technology. Liverpool Airport was renamed Liverpool John Lennon Airport. **3.** Bumi Shagaya, an eleven-year old schoolgirl from Brixton, London, went missing whilst on a school trip in Dieppe, France. *The Sun* newspaper was cleared by the Press Complaints Committee for breaking its code of conduct after paying for Ronnie Biggs, his son and Bruce Reynolds, a fellow Great Train Robber, to fly back to Britain. Under new Government welfare reform plans individuals claiming invalidity benefit will have to have to prove every three years that they are still unwell. **5.** Bumi Shagaya's, dead body was found floating in the Lac de Caniel near Dieppe. MPs voted in favour of an increase to their pay, pensions, expenses and allowances worth £24,000 per year. Kenneth Clarke, Michael Portillo, David Davis, Iain Duncan Smith and Michael Ancram were nominated for leadership of the Conservative Party. **7.** Lord Jenkins and Lord Baker, both former Home Secretaries, called for the possession of cannabis to be decriminalised. Around 120 police officers were injured and two people were stabbed during a riot in Bradford, following disturbances between far right gangs and Asian youths. **8.** The Church of England's General Synod announced that it would end its secret selection of bishops. Members of the Royal family would maintain the right to pursue business careers in new guidelines drawn up by senior officials and approved by the Queen. **10.** London Mayor (Ken Livingstone) announced plans to cut traffic congestion in the capital by introducing a £5 charge for traffic entering central London, the scheme is likely to be implemented in 2003. Jean Corston, MP for Bristol East, became the first woman to be elected chairman of the Parliamentary Labour Party. The Royal Navy announced plans to replace warships designed in the 1960s with six new generation Type 45 destroyers costing £4.5 billion which would create 3,000 new jobs. John Prescott was appointed head of a new Cabinet committee responsible for drawing up policy and reform. Labour MPs called for the banning of far right organisations following the race riots in Bradford. **11.** The Government abandoned most of its A-level education reforms by scrapping its key skills tests for A/S-level exams. **14.** SMA Nutrition baby milk was withdrawn from sale amid fears that it might have been responsible for a recent case of infant botulism. **17.** The Government fired Bob Kiley as the Chairman of London Transport, two months after his appointment to oversee reforms of the Government's Public Private Partnership. **19.** US President George Bush began a state visit to Britain and met the Queen at Buckingham Palace. **20.** Three police officers were injured when 120 youths rioted following a peaceful protest over the death of Derek Bennett, who was shot dead by a police marksman. **25.** The Home Office announced that the backlog for asylum applications had risen to 47,000. The Food Standards Agency announced fines up to £500 on restaurants, pubs, food manufacturers or supermarkets that misled the members of the public about food descriptions. Forty-seven British tourists returned to Heathrow airport after fleeing a Tamil Tiger attack at Colombo airport in Sri Lanka. **26.** James Archer, 27, the son of Lord Jeffrey Archer of Western-Super-Mare, was banned from working in the city by the Securities and Futures Authority over a 'blatant attempt to swindle the stock market'. **29.** Ministers ordered an investigation into allegations that farmers were deliberately spreading foot-and-mouth to gain compensation. Channel 4 apologised to victims of sex abuse following the screening of a spoof about media treatment of paedophilia; the programme *Brass Eye* was condemned by Government ministers and some 500 complaints were received from the general public. MPs called for an investigation into allegations of teachers' cheating following the results of national tests. **30.** Ken Livingstone lost his High Court attempt to block the Government's part-privatisation plans for the London Underground. A report by the Day Care Trust, entitled The Price Parents Pay, found that one in eight parents could not afford to send their children to nursery or a childminder. **31.** Louis Farrakhan, the leader of the Nation of Islam, was given leave to enter Britain after a High Court Judge overruled a ban by the Home Office. The Prime Minister (Tony Blair) made a historic visit to Argentina to meet both President de la Rua of Argentina and President Cardoso of Brazil.

### August 2001

**2.** A car bomb exploded at Ealing tube station; several people were injured and a nearby pub was damaged in the explosion. 2,000 teachers were to be given Government help to buy their homes. Queen Elizabeth the Queen Mother received a blood transfusion for anaemia at King Edward VII Hospital in London. British tourists on a cruise of the Spice Islands were attacked by machete-wielding robbers on the island of Shungu Mbili. **4.** The Queen Mother celebrated her 101st birthday. The Church of England's General Synod appointed a review group to look at ways of modernising the practice of reading marriage banns. The European Commission announced that the Department of Health could face legal action if it refused to allow British NHS patients to obtain surgical treatment abroad. The Government launched a national register to match children with families wishing to adopt, in an attempt to reduce the numbers of young people in care. It was announced by the Roman Catholic and Church of England that clergymen previously jailed for paedophile offences were to be treated in safe houses financed by church parishes. **5.** Leader of the Liberal Democrats (Charles Kennedy) announced that he was likely to end his party's links with Labour by ending the Joint Cabinet Committee (JCC) established four years ago by Tony Blair and Paddy Ashdown. Hundreds of asylum-seekers marched in Glasgow in protest over the death of a 22-year-old Turkish man who police believe was killed in a racist attack. **7.** Three Welsh teenagers in Pill, Newport South Wales, contracted typhoid fever, the first outbreak in Britain for nine years. **9.** A report by The Howard League for Penal Reform stated that conditions in young offenders institutes failed to meet standards set by the United Nations. **20.** The British Medical Association issued a warning to general practitioners to combat female genital mutilation, a cultural practice carried out amongst some refugee communities in the UK. Baroness Thatcher, the former Conservative Prime Minister, gave her support to Ian Duncan Smith's candidacy as the next Conservative Party leader. British paratroopers went on standby to fly to Macedonia to begin collecting arms from Albanian National Liberation Army rebels. **23.** Britain supplied a further 1,000 troops to 'Operational Essential Harvest' as part of the NATO peace keeping force in Macedonia. **24.** It was revealed that Edgar Griffin, a Conservative official who has been campaigning for Ian Duncan Smith, is the father of Nick Griffin, the leader of the far-right British National Party (BNP). Ken Livingstone won a legal case to force the Government to publish a report on its £13 billion plan to part-privatise the tube. **25.** Alan Milburn announced that the Government would change the law so that British NHS patients could obtain medical treatment in other EU member states. Tony Blair ordered a review of student tuition fees and loans following fears that it might deter school-leavers in lower income groups from going to university. **26.** 6 new cases of foot-and-mouth were confirmed in three days in Hexham, Northumberland. **28.** It was announced that the top civil servants were to receive a 50% pay rise, plus bonus payments to bring their salaries in line with the private sector. Street crime rose by 20% between January and July 2001 according to figures published by Scotland Yard. **30.** Government officials announced that health ministers were preparing guidelines for the primary care trusts to enable patients to receive treatment in other EU member states.

## NORTHERN IRELAND AFFAIRS

### SEPTEMBER 2000

**20.** A missile was fired at the M16 building in Vauxhall, London causing at least one explosion but minimal damage. It was thought to be the responsibility of the Real IRA although no group claimed responsibility. **21.** Police found part of a rocket-propelled grenade launcher in a park 300 yards from the MI6 building. **25.** Forty school children escaped injury when a gunman opened fire on their school bus in Miegh, South Armagh. **28.** The last inmates of Maze Prison were released. **29.** The Government announced that convicted IRA terrorists on the run in the Irish Republic and America will be allowed to return home to Northern Ireland and would qualify for immediate freedom under the Good Friday Agreement.

### OCTOBER 2000

**3.** Ulster Unionist Party leader (David Trimble) came under increasing pressure to resign from the Northern Ireland power sharing Executive if the IRA did not relinquish their arms by Christmas. **9.** The BBC current affairs programme Panorama was granted the right to name the suspects in the Omagh bombing by the High Court. Relatives of some of the victims objected, fearing that the programme could prejudice any subsequent trial. **17.** Three men were arrested in connection with the Omagh bombing.

### NOVEMBER 2000

**5.** Intelligence from the Royal Ulster Constabulary and Ireland's Garda Siochana showed that there were two Real IRA units operating in Britain, which initiated a tightening of security in the run-up to Christmas. **7.** The Government announced plans to provide £11 million of compensation to widows of RUC officers killed by the IRA. **11.** Security services intercepted a horsebox packed with explosives, thought to be heading for London. **12.** Police seized a bomb, believed to be the work of the Real IRA, being driven in a van eight miles from Enniskillen.

### DECEMBER 2000

**12.** US President Bill Clinton began a visit to Northern Ireland with the objective of ending the political deadlocks, which developed within the power-sharing executive over issues including the decommissioning of weapons and policing reforms.

### JANUARY 2001

**1.** The Fermanagh and South Tyrone MP Ken Maginnis announced that he would not be standing at the next election. **28.** David Trimble, the First Minster of the Northern Ireland Assembly, raised hopes in a television interview that the IRA were on the verge of decommissioning their weapons. **29.** The Belfast High Court ruled that David Trimble's ban on Sinn Féin ministers attending North-South ministerial councils was illegal as it was designed to put pressure on the IRA to decommission weapons. Mr Trimble lodged an appeal against the decision and insisted that the ban would remain in place.

### FEBRUARY 2001

**7.** Unionist and Republican politicians voiced their concerns about the future of the peace process. Unionists stated that the process could not continue without the immediate decommissioning of IRA weapons, of which it saw no sign, while the leader of Sinn Féin, stated that the escalation of Loyalist violence was causing a collapse in confidence in the Good Friday agreement.

### MARCH 2001

**4.** A taxi bomb exploded outside the BBC's London headquarters, injuring one man; the attack was believed to have been carried out by the Real IRA. **7.** The IRA issued a statement saying that it had entered into discussions with the decommissioning body, and that British Government 'must deliver on it obligations'. **30.** Michael McKevitt, the brother-in-law of IRA hunger striker Bobby Sands was charged in the Irish Republic with directing terrorism.

### APRIL 2001

**1.** Sinn Féin Education Minister (Martin McGuinness) accused the Northern Ireland Secretary (John Reid) of dishonesty and putting the Good Friday Agreement in jeopardy after demanding an IRA surrender. **4.** The Cabinet Office Minister (Mo Mowlam) retracted an earlier comment to newspaper executives that Martin McGuinness was 'a murderer and a terrorist'.

### MAY 2001

**2.** Martin McGuinness admitted to being second-in-command in Londonderry on Bloody Sunday. **4.** The European Court of Human Rights ordered the Government to pay compensation to the families of the IRA men killed by the SAS and the Royal Ulster Constabulary in the 1980s and 1990s. **7.** David Trimble told the UUP that he would resign as First Minister of the Northern Ireland Assembly on 1 July 2001 if there has been no progress from the IRA on decommissioning their weapons. **9.** An inquiry into the death of 14 civilians killed during the Bloody Sunday uprising in 1972 found that an MI5 agent, who claimed that the Northern Ireland Education Minister fired the first shot, which sparked the events, was a 'reliable operator'. **15.** The US Government declared the Real IRA a foreign terrorist organisation and moved to freeze the assets of any individual or group linked to the paramilitaries in the US.

### JUNE 2001

**4.** The Ministry of Defence informed the second Bloody Sunday inquiry that 200 British soldiers would be at risk from dissident IRA squads if they were required to give evidence in Londonderry. **6.** During the general election the UUP won 5 seats remaining the largest party one seat ahead of Sinn Féin and 2 seats ahead of the SDLP. Sinn Féin became the largest single party on Belfast City Council. **18.** Riot police were mobilised to protect Catholic children going to school in north Belfast after clashes between rival gangs. **20.** Plastic bullets were fired and petrol bombs were thrown, injuring members of the RUC during sectarian rioting in North Belfast. **30.** David Trimble resigned his post as Northern Ireland First Minister. Reg Empey was nominated as caretaker, triggering a six-week period in which to resolve the decommissioning issue.

### JULY 2001

**1.** The Northern Ireland Parades Commission banned the Orange Order's Drumcree March at Portadown for the third successive year. **8.** Party political talks attended by Tony Blair and Bertie Ahern (Irish Prime Minister) at Weston Park, Staffordshire failed to find a breakthrough over decommissioning. **10.** The Ulster Freedom Fighters withdrew their support from the Good Friday agreement. **11.** Around 55 officers were injured during rioting in Belfast, following celebrations by Orangemen to commemorate the 311th anniversary of the Battle of the Boyne. **13-14.** Political talks reconvened at Weston Park. The meeting ended without agreement. **22-27.** The British and Irish Governments spent a week preparing a final make or break non-negotiable deal to offer pro-agreement parties.

### August 2001

**1.** The funeral of an 18 year-old Protestant boy killed by the Ulster Defence Association took place, his father, a paramedic, had been unable to revive him at the scene. **2.** Lord Saville, tribunal chairman of the 'Bloody Sunday' inquiry, upheld his request, that the soldiers who shot dead 13 Roman Catholic men and youths in a civil rights demonstration in 1972, must return to Londonderry to give evidence. **9.** John Reid suspended the devolved institutions for 24 hours. **11.** Devolution was restored, giving the parties a six-week deadline to agree a new deal. **13.** Three suspected Provisional IRA men were detained in Bogotá, on suspicion of training Colombian FARC guerrillas. **14.** The Provisional IRA withdrew its proposal on decommissioning their weapons six days after making the offer. **20.** The SDLP gave its support to the British Government's attempt to encourage Roman Catholics to join the proposed police service in Northern Ireland. **31.** The Northern Ireland Secretary ordered the Northern Ireland Police to review the Ulster Defence Association's cease-fire.

## ACCIDENTS AND DISASTERS

### September 2000

**4.** 3 people were taken to hospital, one of them unconscious, when a Central line London Underground train broke down in a tunnel for two hours between Bank and Liverpool Street. **8.** 41 people, including 20 British holidaymakers, were injured in the USA when their tour bus crashed in Nevada. **15.** The Environment agency issued flood warnings to five English counties as an average month's rainfall fell in one day. The Meteorological Office reported that London had experienced 40 mm of rain between 5 a.m. and 5 p.m. **27.** More than 70 people were killed when a Greek ferry struck rocks in seas off the Aegean Island of Paros.

### October 2000

**10.** Serious flooding hit Kent and Sussex causing millions of pounds worth of damage and leaving many people homeless. **17.** 4 people died and 33 were injured when an express train travelling to Leeds derailed at Hatfield shortly after leaving Kings Cross station. **18.** Railtrack admitted that they knew about the faulty track, thought to have caused the Hatfield train crash, but had decided its repair was not a priority. Gerald Corbett, Chief Executive of Railtrack, later resigned. **26.** Two people were treated for shock after a train derailed at Virginia Water, Surrey; leaves on the line were thought to have caused the accident. **27.** A Royal Navy Merlin helicopter crashed into the sea off the coast of Raasay, near Skye, all five crewmembers were rescued. **28.** A tornado swept through Bognor Regis, West Sussex causing £5 million worth of damage. **29.** 5 people were killed when torrential rain and 90 mph winds caused flooding and massive disruption throughout the south of England and Wales. Continued bad weather caused flood waters to rise in the following days with Yorkshire, Shropshire and the West Country particularly badly effected. **31.** A Singapore Airlines jumbo jet bound for Los Angeles crashed on take-off from Taipei Airport in high winds, killing 95 passengers on board. It was later thought that it had taken off from the wrong runway and may have hit earthmoving equipment. The Italian registered tanker Ievoli Sun sank 11 miles off the coast of Alderney in the English Channel, prompting fears that her leaking cargo of highly toxic styrene posed a serious environmental threat.

### November 2000

**6.** 27 people were airlifted to safety after three yachts were caught in storms off the Bay of Biscay. The death toll for the spate of storms and flooding which hit the British Isles reached 12, following an accident in Tunbridge Wells in which a tree fell on top of a car, killing the two occupants. **10.** Figures released showed a 140% increase in accidents involving police cars between 1998 and 1999. **11.** More than 150 people were killed, including one Briton, when a ski train caught fire in a tunnel in the Austrian Alps. **26.** The front three carriages of a Virgin train travelling from London Euston to Glasgow became derailed at Mossend South Junction, near Motherwell, causing minor injuries to a number of passengers. **30.** At least 60 people burned to death when a leaking oil pipeline caught fire engulfing the village of Ebute-Oko in Lagos.

### December 2000

**2.** A holiday jet flying from Birmingham to Paphos, Cyprus, came within 100ft of colliding with a US Airforce F15 jet over Northamptonshire. **3.** Typhoon Rumbia killed at least 24 people and injured many more when it struck the southern and central regions of the Philippines. **17.** The US State of Alabama suffered widespread devastation when it was hit by a band of tornadoes causing the deaths of 12 people in the town of Tuscaloosa and injuring many others throughout the state. **25.** 309 people died in a fire in an illegal discotheque in Luoyang, China.

### January 2001

**3.** The prompt actions of a signalman prevented two trains from crashing with more than 400 passengers on board, when a signal failure allowed them to leave London's Victoria Station simultaneously. **13.** An earthquake measuring 7.6 on the Richter scale hit Central America causing widespread devastation throughout the region. 260 houses in Las Colinas near San Salvador, the capital of El Salvador, were buried under a mudslide, killing at least 349 people. **22.** The wildlife and marine animals in the Galapagos Islands region were put in serious danger after the oil tanker Jessica ran aground near the island of San Cristóbal, leaking 144,000 gallons of fuel oil. **26.** An earthquake measuring between 6.0 and 7.9 on the Richter scale hit the western India state of Gujarat and southern Pakistan causing widespread devastation. India's Defence Minister stated that it was anticipated that the death toll would rise to around 20,000.

### February 2001

**6.** More than 50 people were injured and 32 needed hospital treatment when hydrochloric acid leaked into the ventilation systems of two factories in Staffordshire. **11.** The submarine USS Greenville collided with and sank a Japanese fisheries training ship off the coast of Hawaii. The US coastguard rescued 26 people on board the ship while 9 remained missing. **28.** 10 people were killed and 33 seriously injured when a Land Rover careered off the M62 in Yorkshire down a railway embankment and into the path of an approaching express train in Selby, North Yorkshire. The express train was derailed but remained upright and continued to move forward, colliding with an oncoming coal train.

MARCH 2001

**7.** The inquiry into the Selby train crash has concluded that the rail industry could not have reasonably prevented the collisions. **12.** 9 people were injured when two rush-hour trains clipped each other at Hither Green, south east London when both tried to join the same track.

APRIL 2001

**2.** 27 British holiday makers died when their coach fell into a South African ravine after their driver pressed the wrong pedal.

MAY 2001

**10.** Around 100 people were killed during a stampede at a football match between two top African teams in Ghana. **22.** A South Atlantic storm hit the UK Overseas Territory Tristan da Cunha, wiping out its power supply and wrecking buildings. **25.** 23 people were killed, and around 300 injured at a wedding in Jerusalem when the third floor of a banqueting hall collapsed.

JUNE 2001

**9.** A 37 year-old man with a history of schizophrenia stabbed and killed 8 children at a Japanese primary school. **23.** Around 40 people died during an earthquake in Arequipa, Peru. 59 people were killed in Southern India when part of a bridge collapsed as three train carriages passed over it, and fell in to the river Kadalundi.

JULY 2001

**22.** A Briton was injured and 6 other people were held during a police raid on the Genoa Social Forum in Italy. The organisation had organised an anti-capitalist march during the G8 summit. **29.** 3 children were killed when their mother's boyfriend lost control of the car he was driving and plunged into a lake at the Blue Lagoon, a Bedfordshire picnic area.

AUGUST 2001

**7.** Two workmen were killed and others were injured during an explosion at a power station in Teeside. **20.** Amelia Ward, the 16 year-old daughter of a senior judge, died in a climbing accident during a school trip to South Africa. **26.** British school pupils were rescued from a Himalayan mountain after their group leader, an RAF officer, used a satellite positioning device to raise a distress signal, received by a military base 100 miles from their school.

---

## ARTS AND THE MEDIA

---

SEPTEMBER 2000

**5.** The Millennium Dome received a further emergency payment from the Government of £47 million to avoid bankruptcy. **12.** The Japanese bid for the Millennium Dome, worth £105 million, was withdrawn, once again putting the future of the Dome in doubt. **14.** The BBC announced that Lorraine Heggessey was to take over as controller of BBC 1. Craig Phillips, from Liverpool, won the popular Channel Four game show *Big Brother*, following a television vote of 7.5 million people.

OCTOBER 2000

**3.** The BBC announced that it would be changing the *Nine O'Clock News* bulletin to a new 10 p.m. slot and moving its *Panorama* programme from Monday to Sunday despite misgivings by BBC news journalists and the Culture Secretary Chris Smith. **10.** A Michelangelo drawing of a woman in mourning, valued at £8 million, was discovered in the library of Castle Howard. **11.** An anonymous donor, who claimed to be on her deathbed, donated two rare miniature portraits to the Dulwich Art Gallery.

NOVEMBER 2000

**16.** English Heritage accused the trustees of the British Museum of 'dereliction of duty' when it was discovered that the new portico, constructed as a £100 million lottery-aided development of the Great Court, had been built using French limestone instead of Portland stone from Dorset. **19.** The Culture Secretary (Chris Smith) warned the governor of the BBC that action should be taken if viewing figures or programme quality were affected by the showing of nightly news bulletins on both BBC and ITV at ten o'clock. **20.** The Press Complaints Commission ruled that photos taken of Prince William whilst hiking in the South American jungle, which appeared in *OK!* magazine, were obtained as a result of 'persistent pursuit' and the publication was therefore guilty of 'harassment and breach of privacy'. The ratings war between the BBC and ITV was exacerbated when the final episode of the BBC's long running sitcom 'One Foot in the Grave' was beaten in the ratings by ITV's 'Who wants to be a Millionaire', when Judith Keppel won the million pound prize for the first time. **22.** Richard Desmond, the founder of Northern and Shell Media, bought Express Newspapers. **28.** The German photographer Wolfgang Tillmans won the Turner prize.

DECEMBER 2000

**4.** A record £2.9 million was paid by an anonymous bidder for the painting *My Naked Wife Watching Her Own Body* by the surrealist artist Salvador Dali at an auction at Sotheby's, London. **12.** It was announced in the Government's Communications White Paper that the Independent Television Commission, the Broadcasting Standards Commission and a number of other organisations would be merged into a new television and radio regulatory body called the Office of Communications (Ofcom). **14.** A newly discovered handwritten draft manuscript of the Circe episode of *Ulysses* by James Joyce, fetched over £1 million at Christie's in New York. **18.** An advertising poster for the Yves Saint Laurent perfume *Opium* featuring a naked image of the model Sophie Dahl, was banned by the Advertising Standards Authority for causing offence. **21.** Pierre-Yves Gerbeau, the Chief Executive of the Millennium Dome, annouced that the final lottery grant of £47 million awarded to the Dome in September was hoped to be returned as it had not been spent. **22.** Three masked men forced their way into Sweden's National Museum and stole two paintings by Renoir titled *Young Parisienne* and *Conversation* and a Rembrandt self portrait, valued in total at around £20 million. They later held the paintings to ransom.

JANUARY 2001

**8.** A Ph.D. student discovered documentation which revealed that Stonehenge had undergone considerable restoration to straighten and re-erect some of its stones between 1901 and 1964. **9.** Archaeologists excavating the site of a 2nd century villa in the City of London discovered a cache of 43 Roman gold coins (Aureii) which had been hidden beneath its floorboards. **10.** It was announced that

ITV would move its main nightly news bulletin back to the ten o'clock slot for three nights of the week, following a compromise deal with the Independent Television Commission. **11.** Tony Hall, the head of BBC News, was announced as the next executive director of the Royal Opera House, London. **13.** Six diary notebooks written by Rudyard Kipling were discovered in a desk at the Macmillan publishing house after lying undiscovered for nearly 75 years. **23.** The Whitbread Prize for book of the year went to Matthew Kneale for his historical novel *English Passengers*. **28.** A review of the Royal Shakespeare Company by its main funding body, the Arts Council, concluded that the company should concentrate on 'more and better' works of Shakespeare, which it said accounted for only half of the company's repertoire at that time.

### February 2001

**4.** Greg Dyke the director-general of the BBC announced that 750 employees would be made redundant in the coming year. **6.** The magazine *Mad About Boys*, which was heavily criticised by the children's charity *Kidscape* for pushing children into grown up behaviour, was banned by Woolworths and placed under review by WH Smith. **12.** Liz Forgan was appointed chairman of the National Heritage Memorial Fund, the body which buys art and collections of historic importance for Britain. **15.** Figures published by the Public Lending Right showed that Catherine Cookson was the most popular author amongst library users for the 15th year.

### March 2001

**3.** Disney bought the rights to Winnie-the-Pooh books for £240 million in the most lucrative deal in British literary history. **8.** Dame Ninette de Valois, the founder of British ballet, died at the age of 102. **9.** Part of a panel from the Temple of Apollo at Bassae, a 400 BC Greek freeze on show in the British Museum, was stolen from the display. **16.** The television fundraiser Comic Relief raised more than £23 million on the night of its broadcast.

### April 2001

**5.** A lifesize bronze Roman arm, believed to be from a statue of the emperor Nero, was unearthed in the City of London. **6.** The skeleton of a Parisi tribal queen thought to be the predecessor of Boadicea was discovered in a Middle Iron Age burial ground in the village of Wetwang, near Driffield West Yorkshire. **23.** Michael Longley, the Northern Irish poet, was awarded The Queen's gold medal for poetry. **29.** Nelson Mandela, the former South African president, hosted a concert in Trafalgar Square in celebration of the freedom of South Africa.

### May 2001

**11.** Tate Modern was voted the most popular art museum in the world, having received 5.2 million visitors in its first year. **24.** Adrian Noble, artistic director at The Royal Shakespeare Company, established a one-year postgraduate course, due to his concern that drama schools were failing to train actors in classical theatre in favour of television.

### June 2001

**5.** Kate Grenville won the Orange prize for Fiction for *The Idea of Perfection*. **6.** Mark Wallinger, the official British entrant at the Venice Biennale exhibition, caused controversy by flying the Union Jack flag in the colours of the Irish tricolour over his exhibition. A photograph album containing pictures of Alice Liddell, the inspiration for Lewis Carroll's children's book *Alice in Wonderland*, sold for £465,500 at auction. **25.** Marc Quinn, 37, won the £25,000 Charles Wollaston prize for a marble sculpture of a one-armed woman. **26.** Monet's painting *Haystacks, Last Rays of the Sun* sold for £10 million at Sotheby's. Paintings by Gainsborough, including *The Belotto*, worth more than £2 million, were stolen from Russborough House, Co. Wicklow. The *Sherborne Missal*, an illuminated prayer book from the Middle Ages, worth £15 million was donated to the British Library.

### July 2001

**3.** The City of London Sinfonia gained a £1 million sponsorship deal with Marsh & McLennan Companies. **4.** Prehistoric engravings dating 30,000 years ago were discovered in underground caves in the Dordogne, south-western France. **10** The drawing *The Horse and Rider* by Leonardo da Vinci sold for £8.14 million at Christie's in London. **11.** A drawing by Michelangelo left undiscovered in a scrapbook in a library at Castle Howard, fetched £5.94 million at auction to a London dealer. **16.** The Culture Secretary (Tessa Jowell) approved the Arts Council of England plans to restructure the organisation despite objections from the Regional Arts Boards. **29.** Fans celebrated the centenary of the publication of the first episode of Conan Doyle's book, *The Hound of the Baskervilles*. Central Government gave a grant of £250 million to 13 national galleries and museums, most in London. The other regional areas received funds via local authorities at around £250 million divided between 2,000 museums.

### August 2001

**2.** A sculpture, made of crushed animal bones, entitled *The Naked Christ*, on display in Shrewsbury Abbey, was criticised for being unsuitable for children. **5.** An old cornet, that Louis Armstrong learnt to play whilst at the Colored Waifs Home for Boys in New Orleans, was sold at auction on the Internet by Sotheby's. The mother of murdered toddler James Bulger and children's campaigners protested against a stage play *The Age of Consent* at the Edinburgh Festival Fringe about a child who was abducted and killed. **19.** Officials at the Department for Culture, Media and Sport confirmed that the Greek government had written to the Culture Secretary (Tessa Jowell) asking for the return of the 2,300 year old Elgin Marbles removed from the Acropolis by Lord Elgin in 1779. **22.** A 600 year old glass depiction of the face of Lady Godiva went on display in Coventry, West Midlands.

## CRIMES AND LEGAL AFFAIRS

### September 2000

**1.** The head teacher of a school in Cardiff who was convicted of slapping a pupil won her appeal, but remained suspended from her post whilst new allegations that she mistreated pupils were investigated. **4.** Judges in the case of Siamese twins Jodie and Mary ruled that the twins should be separated against their parents' wishes. **12.** The British owner of the Thai guesthouse, where the Welsh backpacker Kirsty Jones was murdered, was arrested in connection with her death. **21.** Alan Milburn, the Health Secretary, confirmed that there would be a full public enquiry into the Harold Shipman murders. Serial rapist Nicholas Edwards was jailed for life after an unprecedented legal ruling that women he had already been cleared of raping could give evidence against him. Derek Hooper, a former special constable, was jailed for 18 years after being convicted of 40 child sex charges. The High Court ruled that Camelot were to be given a further chance to bid for the National Lottery license, stating that the decision to block them from the bidding process was unlawful and unfair. **22.** The Court of Appeal rejected attempts to prevent the separation of the Siamese twins known as Mary and Jodie. **25.** The Duchess of York's former aid, Jane Andrews, was remanded in custody after appearing before magistrates charged with the murder of her boyfriend, Tim Cressman. Police shot dead a former British mercenary, Kirk Davies, after he threatened a number of people around the town of Selby, North Yorkshire, with an air rifle. **26.** Lord Archer of Western-Super-Mare was charged with perjury and conspiracy to pervert the course of justice over allegations surrounding his libel case against the Daily Star. **29.** Police Constable Alan Paull was jailed for five years for raping a drunken colleague at a work party.

### October 2000

**5.** Police investigating the disappearance of a mother and her four children discovered three bodies in the shed behind their home in Cornwall and two buried in a field four miles away. All were strangled. **8.** Jennifer Cormack won damages of £345,000 after being wrongly diagnosed with cancer, which had resulted in her having to undergo 14 operations that included having both breasts removed, and a hysterectomy. Dame Elizabeth Butler-Sloss, head of the High Court's family division, ruled that doctors were allowed to withdraw artificial feeding from two patients who were in a state of 'living death', saying that the move would not infringe on their right to life. **14.** Police began an investigation into the deaths of more than 50 patients in the care of Ann David, a senior hospital intensive care specialist at Basildon hospital in Essex. Alan Milburn ordered an urgent enquiry into the abnormally high death rate amongst heart transplant patients at St George's Hospital, Tooting. **17.** The Enigma machine, stolen from Bletchley Park in June, was returned anonymously to the office of Jeremy Paxman. The Court of Appeal ruled that the body of James Hanratty, who was hanged in 1962 for the notorious A6 murder, should be exhumed in the interests of justice. **22.** Iain Hay Gordon began proceedings in the Court of Appeal in an attempt to get his 1953 conviction for murdering Patricia Curran quashed. **26.** Lord Woolfe, the Lord Chief Justice, ruled that Robert Thompson and Jon Venables, the killers of Jamie Bulger, should serve a minimum of eight years in detention. The ruling meant that the boys would be eligible for parole in February 2001.

### November 2000

**6.** The Equal Opportunities Commission announced that it would back Jane Coker and Martha Osamor, who brought a case against the Lord Chancellor for appointing a friend, Garry Hart as his special adviser without first advertising the post. **7.** Robbers attempted to steal the 203-carat diamond, the *Millennium Star* from the Millennium Dome by smashing into the site on a JCB bulldozer. **9.** Robert Deadman, an ordained Roman Catholic priest known as Father James, was convicted of indecently assaulting four of his female parishioners. **11.** Following a challenge from three media groups, the Home Secretary, the Attorney General and the Official Solicitor backed the High Court in a move to preserve the ban on publicity in the media about the killers of Jamie Bulger. **13.** The High Court ruled that the killers of Jamie Bulger were to be given new identities upon their release to protect them from revenge attacks. **15.** The former butler to Princess Diana, Harold Brown, was arrested in connection with the alleged theft of a £500,000 wedding present to the Princess. Michael Abram, the man who broke into the home of George Harrison and repeatedly stabbed him, was ordered to be held indefinitely in a secure hospital by Oxford Crown Court. Lord Jeffrey Archer of Western-Super-Mare appeared at Bow Street Magistrates' Court and was ordered to stand trial at the Central Criminal Court on 12 December 2000 accused of perverting the course of justice. **17.** A man from Derby was arrested in connection with the theft of the Enigma Machine, which was stolen from the Bletchley Park centre in April 2000. **24.** The record producer and recording artist Jonathan King was charged with the sexual assault of a number of boys in the late 1970s and early 1980s. **28.** Damilola Taylor, a ten-year-old Nigerian boy bled to death when he was attacked and stabbed in the leg on his way home from school in Peckham, London. The Netherlands became the first country to legalise euthanasia, by the passing of a bill that guaranteed doctors immunity from prosecution for mercy killings under a number of strict conditions.

### December 2000

**4.** The Crown Prosecution Service announced that two police marksmen who shot and killed a man they believed to be carrying a shot gun but who was in fact carrying a table leg, would not face criminal charges. **5.** Charges of child abuse against the former manager of Southampton Football Club, David Jones, were dropped when one of the four alleged victims refused to testify. **11.** Police renewed their search for the body of the Suzy Lamplugh, the estate agent from Fulham who went missing in 1986, looking specifically in the area around the former Norton Army Barracks in Worcestershire. **15.** The serial killer Harold Shipman refused to assist in police investigations into the deaths of a further 200 people. **21.** Dr Robert Ayling, a GP working in Kent, was found guilty of the indecent assault of 13 female patients and was sentenced to four years in prison. The Government ordered an inquiry into how Dr Ayling was allowed to continue to practice for two years after he was charged. Kurdish demonstrators took over two pods of the London Eye and threatened to set fire to themselves in protest against alleged human rights abuse in Turkish jails. **25.** Six Indian soldiers and three Kashmiri students were killed when a British Muslim suicide bomber blew up his car outside an Indian Army barracks in Srinagar, Kashmir. **29.** The cabin crew of a British Airways jumbo jet with 389 passengers on board, was attacked by a man during a flight from Gatwick to Nairobi. The man managed to disengage the auto-pilot causing the plane to nosedive before the crew and passengers overpowered him and the plane was landed safely.

### January 2001

**1.** An Algerian man was stabbed and later died in what was thought to be a racially motivated attack outside a restaurant in Soho, London. **5.** The Government passed a dossier to the police and the Crown Prosecution Service which gave the names of 250 people who died in suspicious circumstances whilst under the medical care of the serial killer, Dr Harold Shipman. **8.** The High Court judge, Dame Elizabeth Butler Sloss, granted the killers of James Bulger, Jon Venables and Robert Thompson the right to lifelong anonymity via a ban on publicity concerning the new identities they would be given on release from prison. The ban applied to the media throughout England and Wales raising suspicions that their identities would eventually be revealed by foreign media. **15.** In a landmark case Steven Thoburn, a market trader, appeared in court accused of refusing to sell fruit in kilos and grams, as legally required by the amended Weights and Measures Act of 1985, introduced to bring Britain in line with the rest of the European Community. **16.** Home Office statistics revealed that violent crime increased in 2000 even though crime overall had fallen by 0.2%. **18.** The music publisher Boosey and Hawkes won its legal battle against Disney after claiming that Disney's payment for the rights to use Igor Stravinsky's *The Rite of Spring* in its animated film *Fantasia* did not extend to the film's release on video 52 years later. **31.** A Libyan intelligence service agent, Abdul Baset Ali al-Megrahi was sentenced to life imprisonment by a Scottish Court in the Netherlands for the Lockerbie bombing which killed 270 people. His alleged accomplice Al-Amin Khalifa Fhimah was acquitted.

### February 2001

**2.** David Mulcahy was sentenced to life imprisonment for the murder of three women and the rape of 12 others after his accomplice John Duffy, who was convicted and imprisoned in 1998, gave evidence against him at the trial. **6.** Michael Stone, who was convicted for the murders of Lin and Megan Russell and the attempted murder of Josie Russell, won his case in the Court of Appeal which ruled that a key trial witness, Barry Thompson, had been a police informant and therefore his testimony was unreliable. The following day the court ruled that he should be re-tried. Roy Whitting, a 42-year-old mechanic, was charged with the murder of eight-year-old Sarah Payne, who went missing in July 2000 whilst playing with her brothers and sister in a field Kingston Gore, West Sussex. Her body was found 16 days later partially buried off the A29 near Pulborough. A gunman, identified as Robert Pickett from Indiana, USA, opened fire outside the White House whilst President George Bush Jnr was inside the building. He was eventually shot in the leg and overpowered by Secret Service agents. **13.** Judge Kenneth MacRae was criticised by children's charities after jailing members of the world's largest internet paedophile ring for a maximum of 30 months. **15.** Six Liverpool supporters were stabbed in clashes with rival fans before the UEFA Cup match against AS Roma. **16.** An appeal by the father of murdered toddler, Jamie Bulger, to block the early release of Jamie's killers was rejected by the High Court. **26.** Barry George, the man accused of murdering TV presenter Jill Dando, appeared at the Central Criminal Court for his opening hearing.

### March 2001

**2.** A second severed torso was pulled from a London waterway in less than two months, prompting fears that a serial killer might be at large. **3.** A car bomb exploded outside the BBC Television Centre in West London, injuring a London Underground worker. The bomb was thought to be the work of the dissident Irish terrorist group the Real IRA. **6.** Judith and Alan Kilshaw, the British couple who adopted American twin girls through an Internet agency, had their adoption annulled by an American court. **7.** Peter Noble was sentenced to 15 years in jail for killing six people in a car accident after drinking 13 pints of lager and two Bacardi Breezers. **13.** The Princess Royal was fined £400 for driving her Bentley at 93mph when she was late for an official engagement in August. **15.** A nurse at Wrexham Park Hospital in Slough was arrested after the deaths of four children on a paediatric ward. **21.** The remains of James Hanratty were exhumed in an effort to prove that he was not guilty of the murder of Michael Gregston on the A6 in 1961. He was hanged in April 1962.

### April 2001

**3.** DNA taken from the exhumed body of James Hanratty, the man hanged for the A6 murder in 1961, matched pieces of evidence from the crime scene. Perry Wacker, the Dutch driver in whose lorry 58 illegal Chinese immigrants suffocated as they entered Dover, was jailed for 14 years. **9.** The trial of Leeds players Lee Bowyer and Jonathon Woodgate, accused of assaulting an Asian student, was halted following a prejudicial report in a tabloid newspaper. A date for retrial was later set. **14.** A bomb thought to be the work of the Real IRA exploded on the doorstep of a Royal Mail sorting office in Hendon, north-west London, no one was hurt in the blast. **23.** A 15-year-old schoolboy, who terrorised a community in Manchester with threats of murder and fire-bombings, was banned by Manchester Magistrates' from coming within a one-mile radius of the area for ten years. Anton Malloth, an 89 year old former nazi guard at Theresienstadt concentration camp, went on trial for the murder of hundreds of prisoners in Czechoslovakia. **26.** The preliminary hearing of David Shayler, former MI5 officer charged under the Official Secrets Act for passing information to *The Mail on Sunday* began at the High Court.

### May 2001

**2.** The former chairman of Sotheby's and Christie's was charged with criminal collusion over commissions paid by clients during the 1990's in New York. **3.** Ronnie Biggs, the Great Train Robber, e-mailed Detective Chief Superintendent John Coles, head of the Flying Squad, to obtain documentation to allow him to return to the UK. **7.** Ronnie Biggs returned to Britain and was taken to Belmarsh prison under a warrant issued for his arrest for being unlawfully at large since his escape from Wandsworth Prison in 1965. **11.** The deaths of 466 patients of the serial killer Harold Shipman were to be investigated by an official public inquiry. **12.** The driver of the Land Rover involved in the Selby rail disaster was charged with causing the death of ten people by reckless driving. **15.** It was announced that supermarkets would be allowed to reduce the prices of medicines and vitamins after the Community Pharmacy Action Group, representing small pharmacies, withdrew its opposition to a High Court action brought by the Office of Fair Trading to end price fixing. **19.** Women police officers won the right in a legal test to refuse to walk the beat if it clashed with their childcare arrangements. **20.** Lord Philips of Worth Matravers, Master of the Rolls, called for a state no-fault compensation scheme for medical accidents to cut the cost of going to court. **23.** The family of Timothy Evans, who was wrongly hanged for the 10 Rillington Place murders in 1950, began a claim for compensation. **29.** Lord Archer of Western-Super-Mare, former Conservative Vice-Chairman, appeared at the Central Criminal Court, accused of forging his diary to provide a false alibi during a libel trial in 1987. **31.** A Shari'ah court in Saudi Arabia sentenced four British men to up to 500 lashes and up to two-and-a-half years each in jail for defying the Saudi prohibition laws.

### June 2001

**4.** Lord Archer's former secretary told an inquiry that she had faked a diary that gave the peer a false alibi for the evening when he allegedly consorted with a prostitute, the Peer later used it as evidence during a libel action against the *Daily Star* newspaper. **5.** Ian Brady, the Moors murderer, was denied the right to starve himself to death by a High Court Judge. **6.** The entertainer Michael Barrymore was arrested over suspected drug offences following the drowning of a guest in his swimming pool during an all-night party in March. A Belgian jury found two Catholic nuns guilty of war crimes for their part in the murder of 7,000 ethnic Tutsis in Rwanda. Richard Boeken was awarded £2.17 billion by a US court. Mr Boeken suffered from lung and brain cancer and previously smoked up to two packets of cigarettes per day. **10.** Timothy Mc Veigh, the Oklahoma City bomber, was executed in Indiana, USA. **11.** A blackmailer who failed in an attempt to extort £5 million from Tesco via a parcel bomb campaign was sentenced to 16 years imprisonment at Dorchester Crown Court. **18.** Two of the photographers who pursued Diana, Princess of Wales, on the night of her death in 1997 were charged under French privacy laws in connection with the accident. **20.** Mohammed Al-Fayed lost his High Court attempt to recover £500,000 legal costs from the backers who provided a fund for Neil Hamilton's unsuccessful 'cash for questions' libel trial. **22.** Robert Thompson and Jon Venables, both 18, were granted parole on life licence after serving eight years for the murder of toddler Jamie Bulger. **26.** Four teenagers were charged with the murder of Damilola Taylor, and remanded into local authority secure accommodation after appearing before West London Youth Court. **28.** Slobodan Milosevic, the former president of the Federal Republic of Yugoslavia was flown to the Hague to stand trial for 'crimes against humanity,' including mass murder and the deportation of Kosovo Albanians. Microsoft had the decision to break up the software company overruled by the US Court of Appeal.

JULY 2001

**2.** Barry George was sentenced to life imprisonment at the Central Criminal Court for the murder of TV presenter Jill Dando. **10.** The High Court ruled that internet service providers would not automatically face criminal sanction if they publish details about the new identities of the Jamie Bulger killers Jon Venables and Robert Thompson. **13.** Two British tourists, Joanne Lees and boyfriend Peter Falconio, were abducted by a man at gun-point. Joanne Lees escaped but her boyfriend was not found. **15.** A man brandishing a fake gun was shot dead by police in South London. **16.** A 14 year old boy became the first persistent offender to be tagged under a new Home Office funded computer system. **18.** A terminally ill man, who was suffering from multiple sclerosis and pneumonia began a legal action under the Human Rights Act to win the right to die at home. The Law Society announced plans to monitor incompetent solicitors whose performance repeatedly failed to meet a high professional standard. It was revealed that Derek Bennett, who was shot dead by police in South London, was a psychiatric patient at the Maudsley Hospital. **19.** Lord Archer of Western-Super-Mare began a four-year sentence for perjury at Belmarsh prison. **25.** Scotland Yard's Serious Fraud Office began an investigation into allegations that millions of pounds went missing from a fundraising campaign organised by Lord Archer to help Kurdish refugees. **26.** The Criminal Cases Review commission sent the case of a man hanged 74 years ago for the murder of his mother to the Court of Appeal, following a two-year investigation. It is the oldest case that the commission has referred since its formation in 1977.

AUGUST 2001

**2.** Police forces around the world were searching DNA databases to find a match to DNA samples believed to belong to the gunman who ambushed a British couple in the Australian outback. An international arrest warrant was issued to capture Alberto Fujimori, the former president of Peru, on charges of dereliction of duty. **10.** Neil Hamilton, the former Government minister, and his wife were arrested over an alleged rape. The couple was later released on bail. **13.** Neil and Christine Hamilton provided the police with an alibi for their whereabouts during the alleged rape claim. **14.** Nadine Milroy-Sloan, the woman who claimed that she was sexually assaulted by Neil and Christine Hamilton, waived her rights to anonymity and discussed the case in a tabloid newspaper. **16.** Paul Burrell, 43, the former butler of Diana Princess of Wales, appeared in court accused of stealing thousands of personal possessions of the princess. **19.** A 26-year-old man was arrested in connection with the murder of a Kurdish refugee who was stabbed to death near Sighthill, Glasgow. He and an accomplice had been charged in the same day with the assault and robbery of a German tourist. **20.** Masked raiders stole computer hardware from the Express Newspapers halting production of later editions of the *Daily Express* and *Daily Star*. **24.** Ken Livingstone won the second round of his High Court case against the Government over its part-privatisation plans for the tube. **27.** The police dropped the case against Neil and Christine Hamilton who were accused of a serious sexual assault.

## ECONOMIC AND BUSINESS AFFAIRS

SEPTEMBER 2000

**1.** The DIY retailer Wickes agreed to a £289 million hostile take-over bid by Focus Do-It-All. The market value of Manchester United Football Club fell by £25 million due to rows over the proposed abolition of transfer fees. **15.** The Chief Executive of the London Stock Exchange, Gavin Casey announced his resignation after its shareholders called on him to stand down. Ford announced that it would not pursue its £5 billion bid to take-over the South Korean car manufacturer Daewoo. **19.** Cadbury Schweppes expanded its drinks business when they acquired the Snapple Beverage Group for £1.03 billion. **19.** Official figures revealed that the number of pensioners living in households with incomes below half of the national average had risen by almost 100,000 since the last election. **26.** Car manufacturers Reliant announced that it would cease production of the Robin in December 2000.

OCTOBER 2000

**3.** A report by the United Nations Conference on Trade and Developments showed that Britain was the single most popular destination for inward investment into Europe and the biggest global investor last year. **31.** Honda suspended plans to build its new Super Mini in Great Britain blaming the weakness of the Euro against the pound and uncertainty over the pricing of cars, relocating the manufacture to Japan. Alliance and Leicester announced it would cut 1,500 jobs in a drive to reduce costs by £100 million by 2003.

NOVEMBER 2000

**3.** Welsh Water was sold to a consortium of businesses and local authorities for £2.4 billion under a plan for it to become a not-for-profit utility. **5.** The Director-General of the CBI, Digby Jones, criticised the Government's employment legislation, claiming that it had cost businesses more that £12.3 billion in red tape. **6** The European Commission announced that it would sue the American tobacco firms Philip Morris and R. J. Reynolds for their involvement in smuggling untaxed cigarettes into the EU. **20.** The Treasury raised £38 million pounds by selling broadband fixed-wireless access licences, which would allow Telecom companies to beam high-speed Internet data directly to homes using satellite technology. **21.** Nationwide Building Society pre-empted a suspected cut in base rates by reducing its variable mortgage rate by 0.2%. **27.** Casenove, the 177-year-old stock-broking partnership, announced that it would float with an estimated value of £1.5 billion. **30.** Royal Scottish Assurance, the mortgage endowment arm of the Royal Bank of Scotland, was fined a record £2 million because of failings in its mortgage endowment products.

DECEMBER 2000

**6.** The high street electrical retailer Dixons accepted a £1.62 billion take-over bid by Freeserve, the UK Internet service provider. **7.** Virgin Atlantic announced plans to create 1,700 jobs through expansion of staff at London's Gatwick Airport. Abbey National rejected an informal take-over bid by Lloyds TSB prompting suspicion that Lloyds would launch a hostile bid. **11.** The Competition Commission cut the powers of Ofgem, the electricity regulator, by stating a new 'good behaviour' licence condition imposed on the electricity market was unnecessary to protect the public interest. **12.** The car manufacturer Vauxhall announced that it would cease production at its Luton plant early in 2002 resulting in the loss of 6,500 jobs. **19.** Airbus Industrie announced the launch of its superjumbo, the A380, which is expected to bring 22,000 new jobs to the UK. **28.** A report in *The Times*, which stated that a group of brain tumour victims in the United States were planning to sue mobile phone companies such as Vodaphone and BT, caused their value to drop by £5 billion on the stock market. **29.** The Internet company Letsbuyit.com asked that dealing in its shares be suspended until it could restructure its finances.

JANUARY 2001

**3.** The US Federal Reserve cut interest rates by half a point to 6% in response to a risk of economic weakness. **8.** It was announced that Orange, the mobile phone company, would be floated on the stock market in London and Paris with an estimated value of £45 billion. **9.** The Post Office announced that it would be changing its name to Consignia and introducing a new logo at a cost of £2 million. **16.** Inflation was at the lowest levels since current records began in 1976 averaging 2.1% for the year 2000. **23.** Clara Furse was appointed as the new chief executive of the London Stock Exchange. **24.** GNER announced that if it won a 20 year contract to operate the South West Trains franchise, it would move Clapham Junction train station 500 yards to the east of its existing site in order to increase the number of lines to Waterloo and Victoria stations. **30.** Amazon.com, the internet retailer announced that it was to cut 1,300 jobs and close distribution centres in a major strategy rethink. **31.** Lloyds TSB offered an £18.7 billion conditional take-over bid for the Abbey National pre-empting the decision of the Office of Fair Trading as to whether such a merger would be a threat to customer choice.

FEBRUARY 2001

**1.** Britain's biggest steel manufacturer Corus announced 6,000 redundancies at its five main sites across the country and warned that further job cuts might be necessary. **6.** The International Monetary Fund suggested Britain and Europe were not ready to converge in the form of a single currency due their divergent economic cycles. It was stated that Britain's business cycle was more in line with that of the USA and that early adoption of the Euro would lead to higher inflation in Britain.

MARCH 2001

**2.** The Conservative Party treasurer (Lord Ashcroft) announced that he planned to raise £42 million (US$61 million) by selling shares on Wall Street. Lord Ashcroft gave more than £1 million to the Conservative Party last year. Boeing, the American aircraft manufacturer joined forces with Britain's leading airlines in a bid to take over air traffic control. The FTSE 100 index dropped 50 points to its lowest level since February 1999, following a number of US profit warnings. **13.** Telecom giants Motorola and Cable and Wireless announced that they were to cut a total of 11,000 jobs across the world, including up to 2,700 in Britain. **29.** Marks and Spencer announced that they were cutting 4,400 jobs and planned to pull out of Europe and America in an attempt to boost the ailing profits.

APRIL 2001

**10.** Tesco announced that they were to create approximately 900 jobs in Scotland in the following six months. **23.** BPB, the UK building materials company, and four other construction firms were accused of price fixing by the European Commission. **26.** The International Monetary Fund (IMF) warned policymakers around the world to respond 'rapidly and decisively to a weakening global economy' if they wanted to prevent recession. It was announced that Nasdaq, the US stock market, would become a public company in its own right with an estimated value of $2.5 billion. **27.** It was revealed that Matalan, the discount clothes chain, lost £350 million from its market capitalisation.

MAY 2001

**3.** The Royal & Sun Alliance made a £93 million loss on the sale of its Swinton chain of high street insurance brokers to MMA, the French mutual insurer. **4.** The Halifax building society and the Bank of Scotland agreed a £28 billion merger. **7.** The London Stock Exchange launched an inquiry into the share price of Shire Pharmaceuticals prior to the merger with BioChem Pharma. HSBC and Merill Lynch launched a US$1 billion joint banking venture. **21.** Competition watchdogs in Britain and in the USA are set to investigate the US$4.95 billion acquisition of Clairol by Proctor and Gamble. **23.** The Westbourne Group, a Canadian plumbing business, acquired Woseley, the UK building products group, for £250 million. **29.** Vodafone, the mobile phone company, announced a £8.1 billion pre-tax loss. **31.** Guinness made 140 people redundant in Dundalk, Ireland; as part of their redundancy package they will each receive free alcohol for the next 10 years.

JUNE 2001

**6.** Carlton and Granada, the owners of ITV, signed a £50 million deal with Coca-Cola to sponsor their coverage of Premier League soccer. Safeway announced plans to create 12,000 new jobs in the UK. **9.** Virgin and Sprint, a leading US telecom group, have formed a joint mobile phone venture. **12.** Nokia, the mobile phone company, lost £22.5 billion of its market value after issuing a profit warning.

JULY 2001

**2.** Emap, the magazine and radio group, sold Primedia, its American Magazine business, for £366 million. It originally paid £950 million for the company in 1999. **4.** Marconi announced plans to cut 4,000 jobs worldwide, jobs in its eleven UK sites would also be affected. **10.** Hutchinson 3G became Britain's fifth mobile phones network operator after signing a £500 million deal with Motorola. The Trade and Industry Secretary (Patricia Hewitt) blocked the merger between Abbey National and Lloyds TSB as it would have reduced competition on the high street. **18.** JP Morgan Chase, the second largest US bank, announced a 61% reduction in profits, after writing off US$1 billion (£700 million) of investment in telecom companies. **25.** A survey for *Management Today* found that UK chief executives' pay had risen by 29% over the past two years. **26.** Dolphin Telecom, the provider of radio communications to British taxi firms and emergency services, filed for bankruptcy protection. **30.** The Department of Trade and Industry warned women against joining a bogus investment scheme operating in the UK, 'Women Empowering Women'.

AUGUST 2001

**14.** It was announced that thirteen of the UK's top 100 companies faced a shortfall in their pension schemes due to falling interest rates and lower return on equities. **19.** The publishing group Pearson launched 200 book titles on line via its new ePenguin venture. **20.** Fujitsu, the Japanese personal computer company, announced plans to make several hundred British workers redundant over the next 12 months. Cammell Laird shipyard announced the sacking of 117 workers at its Birkenhead and Tyneside yards. **21.** Stelios Haji-Ioannou, the founder of Easyjet airlines announced plans to diversify in to banking. **25.** Britannia, the in-house airline of Thompson Travel, announced plans to reduce its 3,500 British workforce by 500. **28.** CityReach, the computer data centre company, was placed in administration after its backers failed to find a trade buyer or additional finance. **30.** The European Central Bank cut interest rates by a quarter-point to 4.25%. A public inquiry into Equitable Life, which cut the value of almost a million pension funds by 16%, was announced.

## ENVIRONMENT AND SCIENCE

SEPTEMBER 2000

**8.** Scientists from Nasa reported that the largest ever hole in the ozone layer has opened up over Antarctica and the southern tip of Latin America. The hole covered an area of 11 million square miles. **14.** A report funded by the Department of Health found that BSE could be spread by blood transfusions. **18.** British scientists unveiled plans to create an early warning system which would detect asteroids on a collision course with Earth. **19.** A report by the Government revealed that traces of pesticide were found in nearly half the fruit and vegetables sampled by Government inspectors in 1999. Scientists at Imperial College and Hammersmith Hospital discovered a natural protein involved in prostate cancer, which could be suppressed by the same family of drugs as the common pain-killer. **23.** It was revealed that up to 8 cows had contracted BSE since measures were introduced in 1996 to eradicate the disease. **24.** A report by the Cancer Research Campaign showed that lung cancer had overtaken breast cancer as the main cause of cancer deaths among women. **27.** Dozens of new species of plants, birds, reptiles and insects were discovered by a British-led expedition to a formerly closed part of Cambodia. **28.** Sir Robert May, the Government's Chief Scientific Adviser, reported that the level of plants and animals at risk of extinction was becoming critical, with one in four mammals and one in eight birds deemed seriously endangered.

OCTOBER 2000

**5.** The South African Medical Research Council announced that they would be conducting the first trials of an AIDS vaccine on humans in South Africa and America. **7.** Britain's first major refuge for red squirrels was opened at Thirlmere, in the Lake District, in a bid to save them from extinction. The red-bearded anotrichium, one of the world's rarest types of seaweed, was recorded in British Waters for the first time in over 100 years. The discovery came during a project to map marine life off the north-west coast of Wales. **22.** Scientists discovered a method of screening embryos for fatal chromosomal defects that could slash the rate of failed pregnancies.

NOVEMBER 2000

**5.** Scientists from the International Council for the Exploration of the Sea met in Copenhagen to discuss the possibility of closing the North Sea to cod fishermen due to the dwindling numbers of remaining stock. **6.** A consortium of organisations including the British Trust for Ornithology and the RSPB are to conduct a Government backed research project into the dwindling numbers of certain British native birds, such as the house sparrow and starling. **8.** BNFL were fined £15,000 for discharging 5,000 gallons of bleach into the Irish Sea from its Wylfa Nuclear power station. **10.** The International Council for the Exploration of the Sea warned that the North Sea had been fished almost to exhaustion and immediate measures were needed to control the situation. **17.** The Government predicted that Britain would achieve the 23% reduction of the emission of gasses linked with global warming required by the Kyoto protocol. **20.** John Prescott revealed plans to reward people financially for buying or converting their cars to run on green fuels, such as liquid petroleum or natural gas.

DECEMBER 2000

**4.** The fossilised remains of the earliest known human ancestor, Millennium Man, were discovered in Kenya predating previous discoveries by 1.5 million years. **19.** 40,000 people had to be evacuated from their homes when the volcano *Popocateptl* situated on the edge of Mexico City erupted twice. **26.** Following a period of panic when contact was lost for a period of 24 hours with the 15-year-old Mir space station, a British expert claimed that the station could crash into Earth with some pieces surviving re-entry if Russian mission control lost permanent radio contact with it. **27.** A ten-day-old baby white rhino born at Whipsnade Wild Animal Park made its first appearance in public. **29.** A red kite bird was spotted for the first time in 120 years in the centre of London.

JANUARY 2001

**2.** Health officials revealed that the UK's vaccination programme had virtually wiped out the brain disease Meningitis C. **3.** Scientists reported the results of investigations commissioned by the EU and the Swiss Government which showed that global warming had increased temperatures in the rocks and mud of the Alps by 1-2°C causing permafrost to melt and increasing the risk of mudslides and rockfalls throughout the Europe's alpine regions. **8.** The Ministry of Agriculture launched a scheme to halt the decline of the song thrush whose population had declined by 55% since 1970. **9.** A total lunar eclipse during which the moon appeared to turn dark red was clearly visible in most regions of the British Isles. **10.** Scientists in America announced they had created the world's first genetically modified monkey, which had received an extra gene from a jellyfish. They suggested that the baby rhesus monkey, which was named ANDi, could help to hasten the development of treatments for a range of diseases. Archaeologists and the Egyptian government called for urgent measures to be taken to prevent the Nile from eroding away hieroglyphics on the walls of some of Egypt's best know temples, including the temple at Karnak. **26.** Scientists from two biotechnology companies announced that they had mapped the complete genetic code of rice which they claim would allow its nutritional qualities and pest resistance to be enhanced.

FEBRUARY 2001

**3.** Researchers at University College London and the British Antarctic Survey announced that over the past eight years the Pine Island glacier, which covers 10% of the western Antarctic ice-sheet, had thinned by 33 feet and retreated inland by three miles. **11.** One of the world's rarest birds, the small blue macaw, was reported to have vanished from the wild after the last known specimen disappeared from Bahia in north eastern Brazil.

MARCH 2001

**1.** Scientists said that the freezing cold weather conditions had contributed to the spread of foot-and-mouth disease. Half of Britain's butterfly species have declined over the past 200 years, with nearly a third of the species suffering a 50% fall in numbers according to a survey by the Butterfly Conservation charity and the Centre for Hydrology. **3.** Research commissioned by the National Radiological Protection Board (NRPB), the Government radiation watchdog, officially established a link between high voltage power cables and cancer for the first time. **5.** Tony Blair announced a £100 million investment in wind, solar and wave power. **23.** The Met Office announced that official figures showed the last 12 months to have been the wettest since records began in 1766. **31.** The Government reported spending £2.6 million on research to create Genetically Modified fast-growing fish for human consumption.

APRIL 2001

**4.** It was announced that there had been 24 confirmed cases of tuberculosis centred around a Leicester secondary school. A screening programme for local children was immediately adopted. British scientists announced the discovery of a cluster of 'orphan' planets without a central star to orbit. Some astronomers disputed the suggestion that the new objects could be planets. **8.** Conservation groups asked the Government to add the willow tit, starling, lesser spotted woodpecker, marsh tit, yellowhammer and lapwing to its list of birds in danger. **9.** It was announced that the Bronze Age timber circle knows as 'Seahenge' was to be reburied after heritage experts failed to find it a fixed address. Astronomers claimed that the earth needs more greenhouse gas emissions to prevent atmospheric cooling that could lead to the start of a new Ice Age. **22.** Scientists in the USA threatened to boycott all scientific journals that refused to back the creation of a free online public library of science.

MAY 2001

**5.** A draft report prepared for the Asian Development Bank found that a Chinese project to build up to nine dams along the Mekong River in Indo-China might pose a threat to people, wild life and water systems. **8.** A previously unknown species of predatory dinosaur, a cousin of Tyrannosaurus Rex was discovered on the Isle of Wight. **18.** The first test tube foals, Eezee and Quickzee, were born in Britain using an in-vitro fertilisation. **23.** A fruit tree in Worcester was discovered to grow both apples and pears. **26.** Doctor's devised a new heart bypass operation that could be carried out without opening up the patient's chest. Scientists created the first test tube eaglet via artificial insemination. **31.** Scientists discovered remains of a Paralititan Stromeri in Egypt, one of the biggest dinosaurs to have lived on earth.

JUNE 2001

**2.** Site engineers revealed that the ground underneath the Millennium Dome contained contaminated waste. **12.** The Port of London Health Authority issued a ban on collecting mussels, oysters, clams and cockles from the Essex side of the Thames estuary after dangerous toxins were found in them. **13.** A report by *Which* magazine found that improvements to the quality of British beaches had encouraged more UK holidaymakers to holiday in Britain. Officials in Brussels called for a reduction in North Sea cod and hake fishing in order to prevent further depletion of fish stocks.

JULY 2001

**11.** British Airways and other international Airlines agreed not to transport whale meat and blubber on their planes as part of a campaign to stop Norway resuming exports after a 15 year ban. **16.** An international team of workers, including 16 Britons, began a rescue operation to raise the Kursk submarine. Environmentalists feared that the salvage operation could cause the nuclear reactors on board to leak. **17.** The Government introduced strict rules to prevent developers from building on land that might be at risk from flood damage. **21.** The Department of Health was considering banning the re-use of surgical equipment for fear that it may spread CJD. **23.** Ministers from 180 countries agreed to a deal that will ratify the Kyoto treaty on climate change next year, the US did not take part. **30.** The UK water regulator the Office of Water Services (Ofwat) called for an improvement in service standards after it emerged that water companies had spent £700 million less on vital infrastructure work than they had agreed following a review in the year 2000.

AUGUST 2001

**2.** A report by the Food Standard agency claimed that BSE might have been present in sheep a decade ago. Red Kite birds nested in West Yorkshire and raised around eight chicks according to the Royal Society for the Protection of Birds. A red panda at a British wildlife park became the first in the world to give birth in captivity. **4.** Eight British women volunteered to be impregnated with cloned embryos as part of an attempt to produce the first human clone in a clinic in Rome. **13.** A 20 year-old British woman made a remarkable recovery after receiving a revolutionary drug treatment for CJD, the human form of BSE. **15.** Japanese scientists created a miniature 'microbull' sculpture that is seven thousandths of a millimetre high and the size of a single blood cell. Scientists hoped that that the technique could be adapted to make small machines to deliver drugs inside the human body. **19.** British and Colombian students have discovered a new bird species, the Chestnut-capped piha that lives in the Andes tropical rainforest.

---

## SPORT

---

SEPTEMBER 2000

**4.** England defeated the West Indies to win the Wisden Trophy for the first time in 31 years. **12.** Gianluca Vialli was sacked as coach of Chelsea Football Club after alleged disagreements with players and management. **13.** Surrey became County Cricket Champions. **15.** The Games of the XXVII Olympiad were opened in Sydney with a spectacular four hour ceremony. Gary Thornhill was stripped of his British featherweight boxing title and banned for six months after testing positive for drugs. **16.** Britain's Jason Queally won Britain's first Olympic gold medal in the 1km cycling time trial. Claudio Ranieri was appointed as Chelsea's new manager. **21.** Four times world champion motorbike rider Carl Fogarty announced his retirement . **23.** Steve Redgrave set an Olympic record by winning his fifth consecutive gold medal at the games as part of the coxless fours. A total of 12 world records were broken in Sydney as the world's top swimmers put on an unprecedented aquatic display of speed and agility. **25.** Mark Loram became the first Briton since 1992 to become the Speedway world champion.

OCTOBER 2000

**1.**The closing ceremony of the Sydney Olympics took place. Britain celebrated their best performance in the Olympics for 80 years with 28 medals. **7.** Kevin Keegan announced his resignation as manager of the national team after its defeat against Germany. **8.** Michael Schumacher led Ferrari to its first Formula 1 title in 21 years. **15.** In golf, Spain defeated South Africa to take the Dunhill Cup at St Andrews. **22.** Peter Taylor, the Leicester County manager, was appointed temporary manager of the England football team. **23.** Jaguar Racing's driver Johnny Herbert retired from Formula 1 after 12 years and 159 races. **31.** Sven-Göran Eriksson was appointed as the new manager of the England Football team amongst considerable controversy that the job should not have gone to a foreigner. An official report into cricket match-fixing by India's Central Bureau of Investigation alleged former England captain Alex Stewart accepted £5,000 for information on pitches and match conditions. He later denied the allegations.

NOVEMBER 2000

**2.** Garry Kasparov lost his title as the world's chess champion for the first time in 15 years to Vladimir Kramnik. **6.** Chris Hutchings was dismissed from his role as manager of Bradford City football club after only a dozen league matches. **12.** Lennox Lewis successfully defended his World Heavyweight Champion of the World title by defeating challenger David Tua of New Zealand over twelve rounds by a large points advantage. **18.** A last minute try by Dan Luger gave England the victory against world champions Australia in a Rugby Union match to win the Cook Cup. **21.** A number of players in the England Rugby Union squad went on strike in a pay dispute with the Rugby Football Union. **24.** The Spanish Paralympic team for the Sydney 2000 games were found to have cheated in a number of events, most markedly in basketball after a journalist posing as one of the athletes disclosed that the team consisted of 15 members who did not have mental or physical handicaps.

DECEMBER 2000

**10.** The five times Olympic gold medallist in rowing, Steve Redgrave, won the BBC Sports Personality of the Year award. The second prize went to the heptathlete Denise Lewis and third prize to paralympian Tanni Grey-Thompson. During trials for a round-the-world race the yachtsman Pete Goss and his team were forced to abandon their £4.5 million *Team Philips* catamaran due to high winds, 850 miles off the coast of Ireland. In tennis, Pat Cash ended John McEnroe's three-year reign as the Honda Challenge seniors champion with a victory at the Albert Hall, London. **11.** In cricket, England beat Pakistan in Karachi to win its first test match against them for 38 years. Murray Walker, the Formula One racing commentator announced that he would retire at the end of next season bringing his 52 year career to a close. **16.** An inquiry was launched when the featherweight boxer Paul Ingle collapsed at the end of a championship fight against Mbulelo Botile and had to undergo emergency surgery to remove a blood clot from his brain. **18.** Silverstone Circuit secured a deal with the British Racing Drivers' Club to continue to host the British Grand Prix until 2015. **29.** Gayl King became the first woman to compete on equal terms with men in the World Darts Championships.

JANUARY 2001

**9.** Sven-Göran Eriksson, who was appointed in October 2000 to become the England Football team's new coach, left his job as the coach of the Italian football team Lazio. **15.** Michael Johnson, the only man to have won the 200 and 400 metre Olympic titles, announced that he would be retiring from athletics at the end of the season. **18.** Bruce Grobbelaar, the former Liverpool goalkeeper, faced a legal bill of £1.5 million when a Court of Appeal jury overturned his libel action victory against *The Sun*, following allegations of match fixing. **27.** Andrew Magee scored a hole-in-one on a par-four hole at a tournament in Scottsdale, Arizona in the United States. This had never been achieved since the formation of the US PGA tour and has only happened once during a European tournament. **27.** Jennifer Capriati, the teenage phenomenon who recently spent a number of years out of professional tennis competition, beat Martina Hingis to win the Australian Open, her first Grand Slam title.

FEBRUARY 2001

**11.** Ellen MacArthur became the fastest woman and the fastest Briton to circumnavigate the globe single-handedly when she arrived in Sables d'Olonne in her yacht *Kingfisher* at the end of the Vendée Globe yacht race.

MARCH 2001

**1.** Alan Street, the British figure skating champion, finished sixth at the World Junior Figure Skating Championships in Sofia, Bulgaria. It was the highest place achieved by a British skater at an international skating Union championship since 1998. Josh Hall finished ninth place in the Vendée Globe race and became the third British skipper to complete the race. **5.** International football players' salaries could match the top American baseball players under terms agreed by the European Commission and the international football authorities. The main beneficiaries would be leading players who now earned £50,000 a week in Premiership League football. **6.** Racing resumed at Lingfield race course after a seven-day suspension due to the foot-and-mouth disease outbreak. **9.** The Badminton Horse Trials was cancelled due to foot-and-mouth disease restrictions. **16.** Tottenham Hotspur sacked its manager George Graham. **24.** England defeated Finland 2–1 in their World Cup Qualifier at Anfield. **30.** British rower Jim Shekhdar completed his 8,000-mile voyage to become the first man to cross the Pacific Ocean non-stop and unaided.

APRIL 2001

**7.** Red Marauder, ridden by Richard Guest, won the Grand National after only two horses managed to finish the race. **22.** Lennox Lewis lost his heavyweight title after being knocked out in the fifth round by Hasim Rahman during their fight in South Africa. Edgar Davids, the Juventus Holland midfield player, tested positive for nandrolone, a banned steroid. Russian school boy Alexey Korobkin's cricketing performance at Dover College earned him an entry in Wisden, the cricketers' Almanack. **23.** Manchester United FC paid £19 million for Ruud van Nistelrooy, making him the most expensive player in British football. **25.** Michele Alboreto, the formula one racing driver, was killed whilst testing an Audi sports car in

Lausitzring, near Dresden. **30.** Teddy Sheringham won The Player of the Year award, and Steven Gerrard won The Young Player of the Year award at the Professional Footballers' Association (PFA) awards ceremony.

MAY 2001

**5.** Coventry City was relegated from the Premiership after 34 years in the First Division. **22.** Kathy Freeman, the Olympic 400 metres gold winner, won the Sports Woman of the Year Award at the Laureus World Sports Awards held in Monte Carlo. Sir Steve Redgrave, five times olympic gold medal winner, was awarded a lifetime achievement award. **24.** Lee Westwood was awarded the Vardon Trophy as the winner of the Order of Merit and as Europe's leading golfer. **26.** Lord Condon's report into match fixing in cricket was published. **6.** The English football team beat Greece to qualify for the world cup.

JUNE 2001

**9.** Galileo won the Vodafone Epsom Derby recording the second fastest time in the event's history. Jennifer Capriati won the French Open after winning the longest third set in the championship's history.

JULY 2001

**2.** Pete Sampras was beaten by a former junior Wimbledon champion Roger Federer, a 19-year-old from Switzerland. **4.** Tim Henman won a place in the semi-finals at Wimbledon. **5.** Helen Tew, 89, completed a double Atlantic crossing in a 26ft gaff-rigged cutter. **8.** Tim Henman was knocked out of Wimbledon men's semi-final by Goran Ivanisević. Venus Williams won her second singles title at Wimbledon. **9.** Goran Ivanisević, unseeded, won the men's Wimbledon final. Real Madrid FC broke the world record transfer fee by signing Zinedine Zidane from Juventus FC for £48 million. **26.** British swimmer Joanna Fargus won the bronze medal in the 200 metres backstroke at the World Swimming Championships in Fukuoka, Japan, bringing the British medal total to four. **29.** Michael Schumacher, the Formula 1 champion, escaped a serious injury when his Ferrari was rammed from behind by the Prost of Luciano Burti at more than 100 mph at the start of the German Grand Prix.

AUGUST 2001

**9.** Premier rugby player Julian White lost his court case to break his contract with Bristol and move to a different rugby club. **19.** Michael Schumacher won the Hungarian Grand Prix matching Alain Prost's record of 51 grand prix wins and four driver's world championships. **22.** Sir Geoff Hurst, the hat-trick hero of England's 1966 World Cup win over West Germany agreed to sell his commemorative medal to his former football club West Ham for £150,000. **25.** Mathew Pinsett and James Cracknell became the first sportsmen to win gold medals for both the coxless and coxed pairs at Lucerne, Switzerland. **31.** The England football team beat Germany 5–1 during World Cup qualifier. Footballer Michael Owen scored a hat-trick.

---

## AFRICA

---

SEPTEMBER 2000

**6.** In Zimbabwe, an official forecast predicted that the 2001 tobacco crop would be at least 30 per cent below the 2000 harvest if the planned seizure of 3,270 farms went ahead. **9.** Maria Stevens, the widow of a white Zimbabwean farmer who was beaten and murdered by a gang of veterans, filed a US$400 million case against Robert Mugabe in New York. **10.** A British paratrooper was killed in Sierra Leone when airborne forces freed six captured British soldiers who had been taken hostage by the West Side Boys militia near Forodugu; 12 others were wounded in the attack, in which 25 members of the West Side Boys were killed. **11.** In the general election in Mauritius, the ruling coalition was defeated by the Mauritian Socialist Movement and the Mauritian Militant Movement, who won 54 of the 62 contested seats. **14.** In South Africa, the health committee of the ANC urged President Mbeki to acknowledge that HIV was the cause of AIDS; the Confederation of South African Trade Unions (COSATU) had previously urged him to do so. **17.** In Egypt, the flogging of prisoners was outlawed. **18.** In Côte d'Ivoire, President Gen. Robert Guëi survived an assassination attempt after rebels fought their way into the presidential palace. **20.** India announced it was to withdraw its troops from the UN Mission to Sierra Leone following demands from other countries for the Indian head of the peacekeeping force, Maj.-Gen. Vijay Jetley, to be replaced. In Zimbabwe, 2,500 squatters were evicted by police from nine white-owned farms. **26.** In Zimbabwe, almost 2,000 white farmers and black farm workers went on a law and order march in Karoi after a white farmer was brutally assaulted by a mob of squatters near the town.

OCTOBER 2000

**1.** The World Bank announced that Zimbabwe was to be listed among the world's poorest countries, following its failure to maintain its debt repayments. **3.** In Algeria, Islamic extremists killed 14 members of the same family in the village of Ouled Amrane.. **8.** In Côte d'Ivoire, the Supreme Court barred Alassane Ouattara, the leader of the main opposition party, and 14 other prospective candidates from standing in the presidential election on 22 October. **14-17.** In Nigeria, more than 100 people were killed in three days of ethnic violence in Lagos. **16–19.** In Zimbabwe, rioters fought with police in some of Harare's poorest townships after the price of bread rose 34 per cent and bus fares rose 20 per cent; troops were sent in to quell the riots. **17.** In South Africa, President Mbeki handed over responsibility for government policy on AIDS to a newly established committee following severe criticism of his views. **20–22.** An emergency Arab League summit was held in Cairo, Egypt, to discuss the security situation in Israel; £625 million in aid was pledged to the Palestinians. **24.** In Côte d'Ivoire, the government dissolved the electoral commission and declared that President Robert Guëi had been re-elected in the presidential election held on 22 October. **25.** In Zimbabwe, President Mugabe said that the national reconciliation policy that his government had officially followed since coming to power in 1980 was at an end, and that all whites who had fought in the former Rhodesian armed forces would be put on trial for genocide; however, parliamentary approval would be required to repeal the amnesty. **26.** Laurent Gbagbo was sworn in as president of Côte d'Ivoire after the National Electoral Commission declared that he had won the election with 59.36 per cent of the vote. It was estimated that about 155 people were killed in fighting as Christians, who had backed Laurent Gbagbo, fought Muslims, who had supported Alassane Ouattara, who had not been allowed to stand. **26.** In Zimbabwe, the MDC presented a parliamentary motion calling for the removal of the President, accusing him of gross misconduct and wilful violation of the constitution. **29.** In the Tanzanian general election, polling was cancelled in 16 out of 50 constituencies in Zanzibar; the opposition boycotted a rerun in the 16 constituencies on 6 December

NOVEMBER 2000

**1.** In Malawi, President Miluzi ordered the sale of 39 Mercedes-Benz limousines worth £1.72 million that had been bought for government ministers; the proceeds were to be put towards poverty reduction. **6.** In Ethiopia, Emperor Haile Selassie, the country's last emperor who was deposed in 1974 and died the following year, was reburied in Addis Ababa's Holy Trinity Cathedral. **9.** In Tanzania, the government of Zanzibar released 18 opposition supporters who had been held for three years on treason charges. **10.** In Sierra Leone, talks between the government and Revolutionary United Front (RUF) rebels began. On 14 November, the government and the rebels signed a 30-day cease-fire; the Royal Marines had carried out an amphibious landing near Freetown as part of an operation to deter the RUF from launching a new campaign. **10.** Zimbabwe's Supreme Court declared the government's land seizures illegal. **14.** In Swaziland, a two-day illegal national strike was held to demand democratic reforms. **15.** In Egypt, the legislative election was won by the ruling National Democratic Party, who won 388 of the 454 seats. **15.** President Taylor of Liberia accused the UK of fomenting the civil war in Sierra Leone and said that the flooding in the UK was God's punishment. **20.** In Guinea-Bissau, the former head of the military junta, Gen. Ansumane Mane, challenged President Kumba Yalla by declaring himself head of the army; troops loyal to the government drove him out of his military base on 23 November and shot him dead on 30 November. **27.** In Zimbabwe, the ruling Zanu-PF won a by-election in Marondera West; the MDC had abandoned its campaign after violent attacks by Zanu-PF supporters resulted in the death of one person and dozens injured. **30.** In Zimbabwe, the Supreme Court threw out a government decree withdrawing citizenship from those with British passports.

DECEMBER 2000

**4-5.** In Côte d'Ivoire, at least nine people were killed in violence between protestors and security forces in Abidjan. **7.** In the presidential election in Ghana, John Kufuor of the New Patriotic Party won 57.4 per cent of the vote; Vice President John Atta Mills of the ruling National Democratic Congress won 42.6 per cent. In Guinea, about 360 people were killed, more than 1,000 injured and thousands more fled their homes during fierce fighting in the town of Guékedou between rebels and government forces; on 11 December, government troops killed at least 150 rebels in Kissidougou. **10.** In Zimbabwe, where the High Court had been due to hear a case brought by the opposition Movement for Democratic Change contesting the legitimacy of the election of 38 Zanu-PF MPs during the general election in June 2000, President Mugabe issued a decree that allowed Zanu-PF MPs to retain their seats even if found guilty of electoral fraud. **12.** Ethiopia and Eritrea signed a peace treaty ending their two-year border dispute; it was agreed that an independent international commission would delineate the frontier. **13-23.** In Sudan, presidential and parliamentary elections were held over a ten-day period; President Omar Bashir was re-elected with 86 per cent of the vote. There was no voting in rebel-held areas of the south and the main opposition parties did not take part. **20.** In Zimbabwe, President Mugabe announced that the government had now completed its listing of white-owned land for compulsory acquisition; 2,540 white-owned farms had been listed, about 80 per cent of the land owned by white farmers.

JANUARY 2001

**7.** In Côte d'Ivoire, at least eight people died during a failed coup d'état. **10.** In Nigeria, Muslims burned down about 40 hotels and bars in Maiduguri in reaction to the lunar eclipse, which they blamed on sinners. **15.** The presidents of Kenya, Tanzania and Uganda announced the launch of a revived East African Community; the previous one collapsed 23 years ago. **16.** In the Democratic Republic of Congo, President Laurent Kabila was shot dead by one of his bodyguards; the government only admitted his death on 18 January after his son, Maj.-Gen. Joseph Kabila, had been proclaimed head of state. **25.** In Nigeria, President Olusegun Obasanjo dissolved the Cabinet on 24 January. **26.** Maj.-Gen. Joseph Kabila was sworn in as president of the Democratic Republic of Congo. **27.** In Tanzania, up to 32 people were killed and one police officer decapitated in the port and capital of Zanzibar when police opened fire on demonstrators from the main opposition party who were calling for a re-run of elections.

FEBRUARY 2001

**1.** In Tanzania, up to 100 people were feared dead after a police helicopter fired on civilians in two boats fleeing the violence on Zanzibar. **7.** In the Democratic Republic of Congo, President Joseph Kabila called for negotiations to end the civil war. **9.** In South Africa, an ANC MP, Andrew Feinstein, called on the government to answer allegations that senior officials had siphoned off millions of pounds in a 1999 arms deal. **16.** In Zimbabwe, Morgan Tsvangirai, the leader of the MDC, was charged with inciting the violent overthrow of the government. **24.** In the Democratic Republic of Congo, UN observers moved into position to monitor a withdrawal by Rwandan Armed Forces. **25.** In Cape Verde, Pedro Pires, the African Party for the Independence of Cape Verde (PAICV) candidate, won the second round of the presidential election by a margin of just 17 votes.

MARCH 2001

**2.** Former President Nelson Mandela accused the ANC of being as intolerant and corrupt as South Africa's white leaders during the apartheid years, saying that the party's reputation had been tarnished by a series of financial scandals and abuses of power. **7.** The UN Security Council voted unanimously to ban diamond exports from Liberia in punishment for its support of the rebel Revolutionary United Front in Sierra Leone; it also imposed an arms embargo. **12.** In Uganda, at least 12 civilians were killed and scores injured in pre-election clashes between members of the presidential protection unit and supporters of opposition candidates. **14.** In Uganda, President Yoweri Museveni was declared the winner of the Ugandan presidential election, gaining 69.3 per cent of the vote, but his main rival, Kizza Besigye, who got 27.8 per cent, said the vote had been rigged and demanded a new poll. **20.** The Foreign Affairs Minister, Stan Mudenge, rejected a decision by Commonwealth ministers to send an urgent mission to Harare to express concern at intimidation of the country's journalists and judiciary, saying the UK had irregularly sponsored it. **21.** In Zimbabwe, the Commercial Farmers' Union rejected a proposal to accept President Mugabe's land seizure plan, but reaffirmed its absolute commitment to land reform and a negotiated settlement with the government. **25.** In Burundi, more than 200 bodies were discovered in mass graves in a suburb of Bujumbura, the result of recent fighting between Hutu rebels and government troops. In Zimbabwe, the government announced that it had begun compensating white farmers whose land had been seized for improvements such as roads or buildings. **27.** In Somalia at least seven people were reported killed as gun battles erupted throughout the city between the forces of the transitional government and a rebel militia. **28.** In Kenya, President Moi dismissed three senior civil servants who had been appointed to fight corruption. **29.** UN troops began deploying in Congo to guard the 500 unarmed UN observers monitoring a cease-fire and a buffer zone between pro-government forces and rebels in the east of the country.

APRIL 2001

**3.** In Zimbabwe, parliament passed a series of measures to ban foreign funding of any political party and to tighten the regulations on the establishment of private radio and television stations. **6.** In Zambia, Tilenji Kaunda, the son of former president Kenneth Kaunda, was appointed leader of the opposition United National Independence Party. **11.** In Rwanda, the government ordered the arrest of former Prime Minister Pierre Céléstin Rwigema, who was accused of participating in the 1994 genocide. **17.** In Zimbabwe, President Mugabe insisted that he would stand for re-election. **18.** In Burundi, an attempted coup by junior army officers was put down by the army. **25.** In South Africa, Safety and Security Minister Steve Tshwete accused three senior members of the ruling ANC of plotting to kill President Mbeki. **25.** In Zimbabwe, pro-government mobs stormed at least 20 organisations linked to Harare's white community. **26.** In Zimbabwe, Morgan Tsvangirai, the leader of the opposition MDC, won an appeal that overturned his defeat in last year's parliamentary election. Lawyers for the winning candidate, Kenneth Manyonda of the ruling Zanu-PF, said that they would appeal. **27.** In the Democratic Republic of Congo, Ugandan troops found the bodies of six Red Cross workers near Bunia. **29.** President Yoweri Museveni of Uganda announced that the country would immediately withdraw its armed forces from the Democratic Republic of Congo.

MAY 2001

**2.** In Algeria, thousands of Berbers demonstrated in Algiers in protest at police repression and arabisation in the Kabyle region; around 80 people had been killed during several days of rioting preceding the march. **3.** In Zambia, more than 30 MPs signed a motion to impeach President Chiluba for abuse of power; the following day the president announced that he would not seek to amend the constitutional limit on a president serving more than two terms. **6.** In Zimbabwe, the trial began of MDC leader Morgan Tsvangirai on charges of treason. **7.** UN sanctions against Liberia came into force; the sanctions had been approved on 7 March, but the government had been given two months to end its support for RUF rebels in Sierra Leone. **10.** The British Council closed its offices in Zimbabwe after repeated threats of invasion by war veterans. **12.** In Somalia, 80 people died in fighting between government troops and militias battling for control of the port in Mogadishu. **15.** In Sierra Leone, government troops and rebels agreed to suspend hostilities and prepare to disarm; a cease-fire had been agreed in November 2000, but clashes had continued. **18.** In Zimbabwe, President Mugabe authorised arrests among the mobs that have invaded hundreds of white-owned businesses. **23.** In Tristan da Cunha, winds of up to 120 mph destroyed a community centre and the island's only pub; there were no casualties. **24.** In Zimbabwe, the Commercial Farmers' Union offered almost 2.5 million acres of land to poor blacks, together with free technical advice and £800,000 for seed and fertiliser. **28.** In the Central African Republic, rebel soldiers attacked the home of President Ange-Félix Patasse in a failed coup attempt in which about 12 people were killed. **31.** More than a million voters in the former British protectorate of Somaliland voted in a referendum on independence from the rest of Somalia. In South Africa, the Truth and Reconciliation Commission, which attempted to settle grievances from the apartheid era, closed its investigations after five years of work.

JUNE 2001

**4.** In Zimbabwe, Chenjerai Hitler Hunzvi, the leader of the War Veterans' Association, died in Harare. He was given a state funeral on 8 June. **12.** In Zimbabwe, a black commercial farmer who had been an MDC candidate in the 2000 general election was ordered off his farm. **13.** The price of petrol rose by 74 per cent in Zimbabwe. The Zimbabwe Congress of Trade Unions threatened to call a general strike if the government refused to reverse the fuel price rise. **14.** In Algeria, up to half a million pro-democracy demonstrators marched on the presidential compound. **17.** In Algeria, Islamist guerrillas killed twenty soldiers in an ambush in the Chelf region. **20.** President Mugabe of Zimbabwe agreed to support a Commonwealth ministerial mission to investigate ways in which relations with the UK government could be repaired. **26.** In Swaziland, King Mswati III signed a decree that made any criticism of the king a criminal offence. **29.** The Zimbabwean government listed another 2,030 white-owned farms for seizure.

JULY 2001

**3.** In the Democratic Republic of Congo, nearly 300 people were killed in a witch-hunt around Aru near the Ugandan border; more than 80 suspects were arrested by the Ugandan armed forces. **4-5.** A general strike was held in Zimbabwe; more than half of the workforce stayed at home in defiance of the government. **5.** Zimbabwean Finance Minister Simba Makoni launched an international appeal for aid to prevent a famine. **12.** Kenyan President arap Moi urged his people to abstain from sex for two years to curb the spread of AIDS. **23.** In Burundi, an attempted coup was mounted in an effort to derail a peace deal intended to end eight years of civil war.

AUGUST 2001

**2.** In Zimbabwe, Agriculture Minister Joseph Made told delegates to the congress of the Commercial Farmers' Union that the government now intended to seize 21 million acres, rather than the 12.5 million acres it had previously claimed for resettlement**6.** In Zimbabwe, 22 white farmers were arrested on charges of public violence and assault after they responded to an appeal for help by a white landowner; they were granted bail on August 20. **9.** In the Comoros, the civilian administration was ousted in a military coup. **9-10.** In Zimbabwe, mobs of squatters attacked and looted 29 white-owned farms near Chinhoyi. **10.** In Swaziland, King Mswati III announced an extension of his powers after an opinion gathering exercise revealed that the majority of the population wanted an absolute monarchy. **11.** In Zimbabwe, about 300 white Zimbabwean women and children were evacuated from Doma after armed squatters ransacked farms in the district. **13.** In Algeria, 17 people were killed in an ambush by suspected Islamist rebels near Sidi M'hamed Benaouda. **18.** The Zimbabwean government refused to grant permission to the International Committee of the Red Cross to set up refugee camps for black farm labourers forced off the white-owned farms where they had worked. **23.** Gambia expelled the British Deputy High Commissioner, Bharat

Joshi, who had attended an opposition party meeting. **26.** The Zimbabwe Council of Churches issued a pastoral letter criticising the government for the breakdown of law and order. **29.** In Zimbabwe, thousands of acres of white-owned farmland were set ablaze by government supporters. **30.** Govan Mbeki, a veteran leader of the anti-apartheid struggle in South Africa and father of President, Thabo Mbeki, died aged 91.

## THE AMERICAS

### SEPTEMBER 2000

**17.** In Peru, President Alberto Fujimori announced that there would be a new presidential election in march 2001, at which he would not stand, after a secret video showed his most senior adviser, Vladimiro Montesinos, head of the National Intelligence Service (SIN) allegedly bribing an opposition politician. **18.** In the USA, an airline passenger was beaten and kicked to death by other passengers when he tried to break into the flight deck and attack the crew on a flight from Phoenix to Salt Lake City. **25.** In Chile, the trial of former President Gen. Pinochet was delayed to allow medical tests to be carried out to establish his mental health. **29.** In Bolivia, at least nine people died and up to 95 were injured in protests by farmers against plans to restrict the growth of coca, the raw material for cocaine.

### OCTOBER 2000

**18.** The US Senate passed legislation easing its trade embargo on Cuba, by allowing the sale of American food and medicine to Cuba. **22.** In Canada, Prime Minister Jean Chrétien announced that there would be a general election on 27 November 2000. **27.** Argentina formally requested the extradition of Augusto Pinochet in connection with the 1974 assassination of a Chilean general in Buenos Aires. **27.** In the USA, the Microsoft Corporation called in the FBI to investigate hackers who were reported to have copied the source code blueprints of the latest version of Windows and Office products.

### NOVEMBER 2000

**7.** In the USA, presidential and legislative elections took place. The outcome depended on Florida, whose 25 electoral college results would decide who became president, where the Republican candidate, George W. Bush, led by 1,784 votes from a total of almost six million cast in the state. As the winning margin was less than 0.5 per cent, Florida law demanded an automatic recount, which began the following day. Al Gore, the Democratic candidate, who had already conceded defeat, retracted his concession when the recount was announced. **9.** In the Florida recount, George W. Bush's lead fell from 1,784 votes to 225 after the results of the recounts in 65 of Florida's 67 counties had been declared; the Democrats indicated that they would not accept the results of the recount, citing several irregularities, among which was the rejection of 19,120 ballots in Palm Beach County because voters had selected more than one candidate on a ballot slip whose design was widely criticised. **11.** Republican presidential candidate George W. Bush initiated legal action to try to prevent a manual recount of votes in Florida's Volusia, Palm Beach, Broward and Miami-Dade counties. **14.** In Colombia, Revolutionary Armed Forces of Colombia (FARC) guerrillas suspended peace talks with the government, claiming that the authorities had not taken sufficient action against right-wing paramilitaries. **16.** President Clinton became the first US president to visit Vietnam since the victory of the Communist North over the US-backed South in 1975. **18.** In the US presidential election, the count of absentee postal ballots added to the recounted results left George W. Bush with a 930-vote lead over Al Gore in Florida. **20.** President Alberto Fujimori of Peru submitted his resignation; the next day, the leader of Congress, Valentin Paniagua, was named to lead a caretaker government until elections scheduled for 8 April 2001. **22.** In Peru, Valentin Paniagua was sworn in and appointed Javier Pérez de Cuéllar, the former secretary-general of the UN, as prime minister; the Peruvian Congress rejected President Fujimori's resignation and dismissed him instead. Florida's Supreme Court ruled that the revised results of manual recounts which were being conducted in Volusia, Palm Beach, Broward and Miami-Dade counties would only be accepted if they were returned by 26 November. Miami-Dade county, the most populous in Florida, suspended its hand count, saying it could not complete it in time. Dick Cheney, the Republican vice-presidential candidate, suffered a minor heart attack. **23.** The last result was declared for the US Senate leaving the Democrats and Republicans with 50 seats each. The Florida Supreme Court denied Al Gore's request to order officials in Miami-Dade to reverse their decision to abandon their recount. **26.** In Haiti, Jean-Bertrand Aristide was elected president, securing 91.7% of the vote. George W. Bush was certified as the winner of the presidential election in Florida by a majority of 537 votes, giving him enough Electoral College votes to claim the presidency; the Democratic Party immediately challenged the certification. **28.** In Canada, the Liberal Party retained power in the legislative election, winning 173 seats; the main opposition party, the Canadian Alliance, won 66 seats.

### DECEMBER 2000

**1.** Vicente Fox was inaugurated as President of Mexico. In Chile, Gen. Augusto Pinochet was place under house arrest after being charged by Judge Juan Guzmán with involvement in 55 murders and 18 kidnappings in the months after the coup against the socialist government of Salvador Allende in 1973. On 11 December, the Appeal Court ruled that the correct procedures had not been followed and ordered the release of Gen. Pinochet; on 20 December, the Supreme Court rejected an appeal by Judge Guzmán to overturn the Appeal Court's order. **4.** The US Supreme Court set aside the earlier decision of the Florida Supreme Court to extend a deadline for hand recounts at the request of the Democrats. On 8 December, the Florida Supreme Court upheld the Democrats' challenge and ordered a manual recount in Miami-Dade county. On 14 December, the US Supreme Court ruled that that there was no longer enough time to complete a recount in accordance with constitutional standards within the time available. **6.** In Florida, Democrat lawyers brought cases in Seminole and Martin counties, alleging that Republicans had illegally corrected about 25,000 absentee ballot applications. On 8 December, Circuit Court judges decided the corrections were in clear breach of electoral law, but ruled that discarding the votes was unacceptable. **11.** In the general election in Trinidad and Tobago, the ruling United National Congress won 19 of the 36 seats; the opposition People's National Movement won 16 seats. **13.** Governor George W. Bush became president-elect of the United States after Vice-President Al Gore conceded defeat. **15.** The Governor of Florida, Jeb Bush, established a bipartisan body to reform the Florida electoral system. **18.** In the USA, the 43rd Collegium of Electors met in 50 state capitals, giving George W. Bush 271 votes of the total of 538, one more than he needed to claim the presidency. **29.** In Colombia, Diego Turbay, the head of the congressional peace commission, was shot dead in an ambush in the province of Caqueta. Rebels from the Revolutionary Armed Forces of Colombia (FARC) were thought to be to blame for the attack

JANUARY 2001

**15.** A recount of disputed ballots in Miami-Dade county showed that George W. Bush would have gained an additional 251 votes and Al Gore 245; it had been thought that the county would have won Al Gore the presidency had the recount not been stopped. **18.** In Chile, doctors who examined Gen. Augusto Pinochet declared that he was suffering from mild vascular dementia, but might still be able to stand trial; he was served with an arrest order on murder and kidnapping charges on 31 January. **19.** The USA paid China US$28 million compensation for the damage done to the Chinese embassy in Belgrade embassy during the 1999 bombing campaign against Yugoslavia. **20.** George W. Bush was sworn in as the 43rd president of the USA in Washington DC. **22.** President Bush banned international agencies from using US funds to fund abortions abroad. **29.** President Bush announced the formation of the White House Office of Faith-Based and Community Initiatives, which would dispense billions of dollars of government funds to religious organisations for social welfare.

FEBRUARY 2001

**3.** In Ecuador, a state of emergency was imposed following a dispute with indigenous Indians over economic austerity measures imposed by the government that involved increases in fuel prices; it was lifted on 10 February. **7.** Jean-Bertrand Aristide was sworn in as president of Haiti. **9.** In Colombia, the Revolutionary Armed Forces guerrilla movement agreed to resume formal peace talks to try to end the 37-year civil war with the government at a meeting with President Pastrana. **14.** Ten Caribbean countries, nine of them former British colonies, signed an agreement to create a regional Supreme Court that would replace the Privy Chamber. **16.** The Supreme Court of Canada refused to extradite two Canadian citizens accused of murder to the USA, because Washington State, where the murders were committed, had the death penalty.

MARCH 2001

**8.** In the USA, the House of Representatives voted by 230 to 198 in favour of President Bush's proposed tax cuts. The Chilean Appeal Court voted by 2-1 to drop 57 counts of murder and 18 kidnapping charges against Gen. Augusto Pinochet, but ruled that he should still face trial for covering up the crimes after they took place; he was released on bail on 14 March. **12.** In Mexico, the leaders of the Zapatista movement met with President Fox to commence negotiations aimed at ending the seven-year revolt. **13.** The USA and Canada banned the import of all EU meat and livestock following the first case of foot and mouth disease in France. **19.** In Guyana, the ruling People's Progressive Party/Civil Alliance won the general election. **20.** The Florida Secretary of State, Katherine Harris, announced that punch card ballots would be replaced by an optical scanning system in future elections. **29.** President Bush announced that the USA would not ratify the 1997 Kyōto protocol, which aimed to reduce harmful emissions by 2010; world leaders condemned the decision.

APRIL 2001

**5.** The US Senate voted down President Bush's tax cutting proposals by 53 votes to 47. **12–16.** In the USA, there was rioting in Cincinnati and a curfew was imposed after an unarmed black man was shot dead by police.

MAY 2001

**16.** The US State Department designated the Real IRA and the 32-County Sovereignty Movement as terrorist organisations. **18.** Canadian Foreign Minister John Manley called for his country to replace the Queen as its head of state. **24.** In the US Senate, Senator Jim Jeffords defected from the Republican party and became an independent; the Senate had been evenly divided between Republicans and Democrats, which had given the Republican Vice President Dick Cheney the casting vote. **29.** Four Islamic terrorists were convicted in New York of the bombing of two US embassies in Kenya and Tanzania in 1998 in which 224 people were killed.

JUNE 2001

**4.** In the Peruvian presidential election, Alejandro Toledo obtained 52 per cent of the vote, becoming the first Amerindian to be elected president. **7.** In Argentina, former President Carlos Menem was arrested and charged with involvement in illegal arms sales to Ecuador and Croatia while both countries were subject to international embargoes. **12.** In the USA, Mohamed Rashed Daoud al-Owhali, a Saudi Arabian, was jailed for life for the1998 bombing of the US embassy in Kenya. **19.** In Canada, Prime Minister Jean Chrétien was accused of embarrassing his country after voicing his disapproval of knighthoods bestowed upon two British-Canadians who possessed dual citizenship; Canadian citizens were not permitted to receive honours.

JULY 2001

**7-11.** In Jamaica, 28 people died in violence that spread out from Kingston across the country; the entire army was mobilised to restore order. **9.** In Chile, the Court of Appeal suspended legal action against the former dictator Gen. Pinochet because of his deteriorating health. **30.** In Canada, the government approved the use of marijuana for medical purposes and announced the establishment of a government-run centre for cultivating the drug.

AUGUST 2001

**1.** The US House of Representatives voted by 265 – 162 to ban therapeutic cloning, which involved creating embryos to treat diseases. **6.** The president of Bolivia, Gen. Hugo Banzer, resigned after he was diagnosed as having cancer; vice-president Jorge Quiroga was sworn in as president the following day. **17.** The Cuban government announced that Niall Connolly, an IRA suspect accused by the Colombian army of training the FARC Marxist rebels, was Sinn Féin's Latin American representative; he had been arrested on 11 August together with two other suspected IRA members.

---

## ASIA

---

SEPTEMBER 2000

**3.** Sri Lankan government forces launched an attack on Tamil Tiger rebels on the Jaffna peninsular. Government forces captured Chavakachcheri, the second largest town on the peninsular, on 18 September. **6.** In Afghanistan, the Taliban militia captured Taloqan, the political headquarters of the opposition Northern Alliance. In Indonesia, three UN workers were murdered by militiamen in Atambua, West Timor, when the offices of the UNHCR and International Organisation for Migration (IOM) were attacked. The following day, the UN and other aid agencies withdrew their staff to East Timor. **9.** In China, an explosion in the Xinjiang region which killed 60 people and injured more than 300 was believed to have been caused by Uygur separatists. **10.** In the Hong Kong legislative election, the Democratic Party remained the largest in the Legislative Council, but the pro-China Democratic Alliance for the betterment of Hong Kong gained seats. **14.** In Myanmar, Aung San Suu Kyi was freed after 12 days of house arrest. On 21 September, she was escorted home from Yangon's main railway station after attempting to leave the capital by train. **18.** President Kim Dae-jung of South Korea inaugurated the commencement of work on restoring road and railway links to North Korea. **21.** North Korea invited nine European countries, including the UK, to open full embassies in Pyongyang. **23.** In Indonesia, former President Suharto was examined by an independent medical team to determine his fitness to stand trial for corruption. **25.** The North and South Korean defence ministers met for the first time since the Korean War. In Nepal, at least 15 police officers were killed and more than 20 seriously injured when nearly 2,000 Maoist guerrillas attacked the district police station in Dolpa district; the rebels later broke into a local jail, releasing the prisoners, and attacked a local bank, stealing more than £300,000 in cash. **28.** In Indonesia, a court threw out a corruption case against former President Gen. Suharto after doctors had pronounced him unfit to stand trail. The following day, President Wahid called for the case against the former President to be reopened and accused judges of accepting bribes to dismiss the case. **29.** In India former Prime Minister P. V. Narasimha Rao was convicted of bribing MPs to support his Congress government during a confidence motion in 1993. On 12 November, he was sentenced to three years in jail, but was granted bail pending an appeal.

OCTOBER 2000

**1.** In China, several hundred protesters from the banned Falun gong sect forced the closure of Tiananmen Square on China's national day; on 10 November, the government described the Falun gong sect as an enemy of the nation, whose aim was to overthrow the socialist system. **2.** In Sri Lanka, a parliamentary candidate and 18 other people were killed when a bomb exploded during a meeting of the Sri Lanka Muslim Congress in Muttur. **3.** In Taiwan, Prime Minister Gen. Tang Fei resigned. **4.** India announced that it had agreed to purchase arms worth several billion pounds from Russia during a visit by President Putin. **7.** In Indonesia, at least 30 people died in clashes between security forces and independence activists in Irian Jaya province.

**10.** In the Sri Lankan general election, the People's Alliance won 107 seats and the United National Party won 89 of the 225 seats. In Pakistan, Gen. Pervez Musharraf promised that provincial and general elections would be held by 2002. **11.** In the Philippines, Cardinal Sin, the Roman Catholic primate, demanded the resignation of President Joseph Estrada, who had been accused of receiving more than £5.3 million in payoffs from an illegal lottery; Vice-President Gloria Macapagal Arroyo resigned the following day. **13.** Ratnasiri Wickremanayake was sworn in as Prime Minister of Sri Lanka. **16.** In China, Abduhelil Abdulmejit, a Muslim separatist leader responsible for uprisings in Xinjiang province, was tortured to death by prison guards. **22.** In North Korea, a US delegation led by Madeleine Albright visited to assess if the country were serious about ending its isolation, during which President Kim Jong-il promised to halt the country's long-range missile programme. **23.** In Sri Lanka, the Trincomalee naval base was attacked by Tamil Tigers; six service personnel and 18 Tamil Tigers were killed and a transport ship was sunk. **28.** In Pakistan, 17 political parties formed a coalition, the Grand Democratic Alliance, with the aim of restoring democracy. **29.** In Afghanistan, Taliban leaders announced a ban on the cultivation of opium. **31.** In Taiwan, parliament tabled a motion to dismiss the government.

NOVEMBER 2000

**3.** The UK High Court ruled that hundreds of former inhabitants of the British Indian Ocean Territory who had been evicted by the British Government in the late 1960's to make way for a US airbase had been evicted illegally; the UK government announced that it would draft legislation to allow them to return. **6.** In the Philippines, a congressional committee passed a motion to commence impeachment proceedings against President Estrada. **19.** India ordered its security forces in Jammu and Kashmir state to suspend all operations against pro-independence guerrillas during the Muslim holy month of Ramadan; the cease-fire, which began on 27 November, was ignored by the United Jihad Council, a collection of 14 groups fighting Indian rule in Kashmir. **20.** In Japan, Prime Minister Yoshiro Mori survived a no-confidence motion when rebels in his party abandoned a plan to join the opposition and vote against him. **24.** In Cambodia, about 80 armed men attempted to stage a coup, which failed when eight of them were killed and 30 arrested. **30.** In Nepal, more than 150 Maoist terrorists blew up a police post in Kumal, killing 11 policemen and injuring six others.

DECEMBER 2000

**7.** In the Philippines, the trial of President Estrada opened; he faced charges of bribery, corruption, betrayal of public trust and culpable violation of the Constitution. **10.** The Pakistani army announced that the imprisoned former Prime Minister Nawaz Sharif was to be released to go into exile in Saudi Arabia. **12.** The UK and North Korea agreed to establish diplomatic relations. **20.** In Afghanistan, the ruling Taliban announced that it was closing the UN mission to the country in response to a UN Security Council arms embargo imposed the previous day in an attempt to force the surrender of the wanted Saudi terrorist Osama bin Laden. **21.** In Sri Lanka, Tamil Tiger rebels declared that a month-long cease-fire would begin on 25 December. The following day, government forces launched an attack that left at least 76 people from both sides died. **24.** In Indonesia, a series of bomb explosions in Christian churches killed 15 people; two men were arrested on 26 December in connection with the bombings. **25.** In India, a man from Birmingham, Mohammed Bilal, launched a suicide bomb attack at an army base in Srinagar, Kashmir, in which at least seven people were killed. **26—28.** In Nepal, four people died in clashes between protestors and police after rumours spread that a popular Indian actor, Hrithik Roshan, had made derogatory remarks about Nepal in a television interview. **30.** In the Philippines, a suspected Islamic extremist was arrested after at least 14 people died and almost 100 were wounded in a series of bomb blasts in Manila.

JANUARY 2001

**2.** In Cambodia, the National Assembly approved a law allowing the prosecution by a mixed UN-Cambodian court of Khmer Rouge leaders responsible for the deaths of an estimated 1.7 million people in slave labour camps and torture centres between 1975-9; the law was approved by the Senate on 15 January. **2.** Two Taiwanese ships made the first legal direct trip to Mainland China since 1949, when a ban on travel, post and communications was imposed. **3.** Indian troops launched an offensive against Muslim separatists in northern Kashmir, after the Hizbul Mujahidin ended the cease-fire that it had unilaterally declared 11 days before. **5.** An emergency meeting of the leaders of Kazakhstan, Uzbekistan, Kyrgyzstan and Tajikistan was held to co-ordinate efforts to counter Islamic terrorism in Central Asia sponsored by the Taliban regime in Afghanistan. **6.** In the general election in Thailand, the Thai Rak Thai party won the greatest number of seats in the Lower House; following re-runs in 62 constituencies on 29 January after evidence of malpractice was found in the original ballots, the Thai Rak Thai had won 248 seats. **8.** In India, The Maha Kumbh Mela (Great Pitcher Festival), a 12-yearly Hindu festival, began in Allahabad, Uttar Pradesh; on 24 January, the most auspicious day of the 42-day festival, more than 30 million Hindus bathed in the Ganges. In Pakistan, the military government announced that from 1 July 2001 all financial transactions would be conducted in accordance with Shari'ah law. **10.** In Myanmar, a UN special envoy announced that the pro-democracy leader Aung Suu Kyi had met members of the military junta to discuss national reconciliation. **11.** In Indonesia, six men suspected of murdering three UN aid workers in West Timor in September 2000 went on trial. **19.** In the Philippines, Vice President Gloria Macapagal Arroyo took over as president after Joseph Estrada was forced from office after the armed forces and police withdrew their support and most of the cabinet resigned. In Afghanistan, the Taliban government ordered three days of prayer for rain and snow to end a drought. **24.** In Singapore, Prime Minister Goh Chok Tong announced that he intended to hand over power in 2007 to Deputy Prime Minister Lee Hsien Loong. **27.** In Iran, a military court sentenced three Iranian intelligence agents to death and imposed life sentences on five others for the murders of dissidents in 1998. **29.** In Indonesia, about 10,000 protestors tried to storm parliament, demanding the resignation of President Wahid over corruption scandals; the following day, a parliamentary commission investigating two corruption scandals linked to the president concluded that he gave false testimony in one and probably had a role in the other.

### February 2001

**1.** The Indonesian parliament formally censured President Abdurrahman Wahid over his alleged involvement in two financial corruption scandals; thousands of women marched to the presidential palace to call for the president's resignation. **4.** In Indonesia's Maluku province, more than 1,000 Christians from the islands of Kesui and Teor islands in Maluku province were forcibly converted to Islam and circumcised. **8.** Vietnam closed the Central Highlands region to foreigners and deployed troops to suppress protests by members of ethnic minority groups over the relocation to their region of lowland Vietnamese. **14.** In Afghanistan, the anti-Taliban United Front captured the town of Bamiyan in the Hazarajat region on 13 February. **20.** In the Philippines, President Gloria Arroyo announced that military operations against the Moro Islamic Liberation Front, the main Islamic separatist group, were to be suspended. **21.** In India, the Maha Kumbh Mela came to an end; more than 100 million Hindus were thought to have attended. **23.** In the Indonesian province of Central Kalimantan, around 200 people were killed following six days of violence by native Dayaks against migrants from the island of Madura; thousands of Maduran settlers fled the island. **24.** In Pakistan, police arrested more than 1,000 members of the Islamic group Sipah-i-Sahaba before the planned execution on 28 February of one of its members for the murder of an Iranian diplomat. **26.** In Afghanistan, the Taliban ordered the destruction of all statues, claiming that they were classified as idols under Islamic law.

### March 2001

**1.** In Afghanistan, the Taliban militia said that they had begun to destroy all idols, including the two largest standing Buddhas in the world, despite appeals from the UN and several governments to save the statues. **11.** In Malaysia, five people died in ethnic fighting between Malays and ethnic Indians in Kuala Lumpur. **12–13.** In Indonesia, thousands of students besieged the presidential palace demanding the resignation of President Abdurrahman Wahid. **13.** In East Timor, two people died in violence in Viquequeto following the arrest of three men at a political rally on 8 March. **14.** In India, the president of the ruling Bharatiya Janata Party, Bangaru Laxman, resigned after he was secretly filmed accepting a bribe from journalists posing as arms dealers. The following day, the Minister of Defence, George Fernandes, resigned but denied any role in the arms bribery scandal. **18.** In Iran, the revolutionary court banned all activities by the Iran Freedom Movement, the main opposition party. **19.** Japan reduced its interest rate to zero per cent in a move to stave off recession. **27.** In the Philippines, the Moro Islamic Liberation Front agreed to a cease-fire and peace talks with the government. **28.** In China, preliminary census results showed that the population had risen to 1,270 million. **29.** In East Timor, the independence leader José Xanana Gusmão resigned from the National Council, the interim legislature, and said that he would not contest the planned presidential election.

### April 2001

**1.** A Chinese pilot was killed in a collision with a US EP-3 spy plane in international airspace 65 miles off the island of Hainan; the US Navy aircraft was forced to make an emergency landing on Hainan. The 24 crewmembers were held until 11 April when Adm. Joseph Prueher, the US ambassador to China, formally apologised for the incident. **2.** In Nepal, Maoist rebels killed 42 policemen in two attacks in Rukumkot and Maina Pokhari. **7.** In Nepal, at least 47 people including 29 policemen were killed when Maoist rebels bombed a police post in Dailekh district. **8.** In Iran, about 40 members of the liberal opposition were arrested and charged with plotting to overthrow the Islamic system. **12.** In China, at least 89 convicted people were executed in one day under the 'strike hard' campaign against organised crime. **17-19.** Clashes between border troops on the Bangladesh-India border led to the deaths of 18 soldiers. **19.** South Korean Foreign Minister Han Seung-soo warned that President Bush's hard-line policy towards North Korea was undermining efforts to forge closer ties between the two Koreas. In Pakistan, the Supreme Court ruled that the trial of former Prime Minister Benazir Bhutto on corruption charges had been rigged. **25.** In Cambodia, Prime Minister Hun Sen announced that there would be a referendum on whether to keep or cremate the remains of the Khmer Rouge. **26.** In Japan, Junichiro Koizumi was inaugurated as prime minister. In Pakistan, more than 500 people were arrested to prevent a pro-democracy rally in Karachi. **29.** In Singapore, an anti-government rally took place, the first since independence 35 years ago. **30.** In Indonesia, the House of Representatives voted by 363 to 52 to censure President Wahid over two corruption scandals.

### May 2001

**1.** In the Philippines four people died and more than 30 were injured after an attempt was made to storm the presidential palace in Manila. In Indonesia, the House of Representatives censured President Abdurrahman Wahid for a second time.
**4.** In Afghanistan, a mob attacked the Iranian consulate office in Herat after a bomb explosion inside a mosque killed at least eight worshippers, including an exiled Iranian Sunni Muslim dissident cleric; the consulate was closed the following day. **17.** In Iran, the transport minister and several junior ministers and members of parliament were killed in a plane crash. **18.** China rejected an offer by President Chen Shui-bian of Taiwan to hold discussions on bilateral relations during the APEC summit in October. **22.** In Afghanistan, the Taliban authorities announced that the Hindu minority would be compelled to wear an identity label on their clothing. **23.** India ended its unilateral six-month cease-fire in Kashmir, blaming continuing terrorist activity. **28.** The Indonesian Parliament voted to proceed with impeachment hearings against President Wahid despite an attempt by his supporters to storm the building. **29.** The Pakistani leader Gen. Pervez Musharraf accepted an invitation from Indian Prime Minister Atal Behari Vajpayee to discuss the Kashmir dispute in New Delhi.

### June 2001

**1.** In Nepal, King Birendra and Queen Aishwarya were killed by their son, Crown Prince Dipendra, when he opened fire with an automatic rifle in the Narayanhiti royal palace in Kathmandu; he killed 14 people before shooting himself. **2.** The funeral of the murdered Nepalese King and Queen took place. Crown Prince Dipendra, who was in a coma, was declared king. **3.** In Bangladesh, at least 10 people were killed and 20 injured when a bomb exploding during Mass in a church in Gopanlganj district. **4.** In Nepal, Prince Gyanendra was crowned as king following the death of King Dipendra. Riots broke out in Kathmandu as protestors blamed the new king and his son for the killings. In Afghanistan, the Taliban announced that foreign aid workers and journalists were to come under the jurisdiction of Islamic law and the religious police.
**8.** In Iran, President Mohammed Khatami was re-elected with over 76 per cent of the vote. **12.** In Afghanistan, Taliban troops attacked the town of Yakowlang in the Hazarajat region of central Afghanistan, burning down every building, after recapturing it from United Front forces the previous day. **16.** In Afghanistan, the UN World Food Programme closed 130 bakeries after the Taliban banned women from working in them. **18.** In Thailand, Prime Minister Thaksin Shinawatra appeared in court and admitted having failed to declare more than £170 million. **20.** In Pakistan, the leader of the military government, Gen. Pervaiz Musharraf, assumed the presidency and formally dissolved parliament, which had been suspended since the 1999 coup.

### July 2001

**3.** China returned the US spy plane that had been forced to land on 1 April following a collision with a Chinese warplane. **11.** In Sri Lanka, President Kumaratunga suspended parliament when her governing alliance lost its majority. **14–16.** In India, Prime Minister Atal Bihari Vajpayee met with the Pakistani Chief Executive Gen. Pervez Musharraf at a summit in Agra, but failed to agree a joint declaration. **19.** In Nepal, Prime Minister Girija Prasad Koirala resigned after demands for his removal by Maoist guerrillas who had been holding 71 policemen hostage since 12 July. **21.** Thirty-one people were killed and 15 wounded in Kashmir when suspected guerrillas attacked a route along which thousands of Hindu pilgrims were trekking to a mountain shrine. The following day, at least 15 Hindus were massacred the village of Peddar. A decree issued by President Saparmurad Niyazov of Turkmenistan ordered that non-Turkmens would have to pay a dowry of US$50,000 to the state if they wished to marry a local woman. **23.** In Indonesia, the House of Representatives voted to oust President Abdurrahman Wahid and replace him with Vice-President Megawati Sukarnoputri; Wahid initially refused to accept his dismissal, locking himself inside the presidential palace, but fled the country on 26 July. **23.** In Nepal, the government and Maoist rebels announced a cease-fire and agreed to hold talks to end the five-year insurgency in which at least 1,600 people have died. **29.** In Japan, the Liberal Democrat-led ruling coalition won 72 of the 121 seats that were up for election the Upper House. **31.** The first British embassy was opened in North Korea.

### August 2001

**7.** In the Philippines, the Moro Islamic Liberation Front signed a formal cease-fire with the government and agreed to begin negotiating a peace settlement. **9.** The Japanese Foreign Minister, Makiko Tanaka, announced that she would dock her own salary to atone for scandals in the foreign ministry prior to her taking office. **10.** In Indonesia, at least 30 civilians were found massacred in Aceh province; the Free Aceh Movement claimed that the military had committed the atrocity in revenge for an attack on a military post. **14.** In Pakistan, President Musharraf announced that legislative and provincial elections would take place between 1 and 11 October 2002. **17.** In Nepal, the Hindu practice of untouchability was outlawed. **21.** In Sri Lanka, Tamil Tiger rebels attacked a police camp in Ampara district, killing 17 police officers and wounding 18. **30.** East Timor held its first free general election; Fretilin, the independence movement, was expected to win a convincing victory. In Nepal, a government delegation met with Maoist rebels to attempt to begin a dialogue aimed at ending the Maoist insurgency.

## AUSTRALASIA AND THE PACIFIC

### September 2000

**11.** At least eight people, including five policemen, were injured in Melbourne as about 2,000 anti-globalisation protesters blockaded the opening of the World Economic Forum.

### October 2000

**15.** In the Solomon Islands, the two militia groups, the Malaita Eagle Force and the Isatabu Freedom Movement, signed a peace deal intended to end a two-year ethnic war that had claimed 70 lives.

### November 2000

**2.** In Fiji, rebel soldiers from the Counter Revolutionary Warfare Unit mutinied in Suva; the army put down the insurrection. **15.** In Fiji, interim Prime Minister Laisenia Qarase rejected a High Court ruling which had declared the interim government illegal and ordered the reinstatement of the previous Prime Minister, Mahendra Chaudhry.

### March 2001

**1.** In Fiji, the interim government was declared illegal and the president was ordered to step down in a court ruling by five international appeal judges, which found that the multi-racial 1997 constitution was still the supreme law of Fiji; the ruling stated that President Ratu Josefa Iloilo should reassemble MPs from the previous parliament, then relinquish power by 15 March. **14.** In Fiji, the president appointed Ratu Tevita Momoedonu to head a caretaker government to lead the country until fresh elections could be held and formally dismissed former Prime Minister Mahendra Chaudhry. **26.** Rebel soldiers in Papua New Guinea, who mutinied after the government announced plans to halve the size of the army, ended their 13-day rebellion after the government dropped the plans and offered an amnesty.

### May 2001

**8.** In New Zealand, Prime Minister Helen Clark announced that the air force was to scrap all its combat and trainer aircraft and that the navy's only frigate would not be replaced.

### July 2001

**11.** In Fiji, George Speight and 12 of his accomplices were ordered to stand trial for treason. **16.** George Speight was allowed to register as a candidate in the forthcoming general election.

### August 2001

**28.** In Australia, 438 Afghan refugees who were rescued from a sinking raft by a Norwegian vessel demanded to be taken to the Australian territory of Christmas Island; they were refused permission to disembark, which caused a flurry of international protests.

## EUROPE

### September 2000

**8.** The final report of the panel of three 'wise men' appointed by the EU to investigate Austria's human rights record urged the EU to end sanctions, as it had found no evidence that the Austrian government had breached the European Convention on Human Rights, and stated that Austria's treatment of ethnic minorities was better than many EU member states; the sanctions were lifted on 12 September. **11.** In Slovakia, an opposition-sponsored referendum which demanded an early legislative election failed when only about one-fifth of those eligible voted; the participation of at least 50 per cent of the electorate was required by the constitution to carry the demand. **13.** Spanish police arrested 19 suspected members of ETA, the armed Basque separatist group, and searched the offices of Herri Batasuna, ETA's legal political ally, in Bilbao and Pamplona. **15.** In France, the leader of the Basque terrorist organisation ETA, Ignacio Gracia Arregui, was arrested in Bidart. **20.** Yugoslav President Slobodan Milosević addressed Serb nationalists in the northern town of Berane during his first visit to Montenegro in four years, and accused the Montenegrin President Djukanović of selling out to the West. In Yugoslavia, an opposition rally in Belgrade was attended by more than 150,000 people. The Spanish government announced tougher measures against terrorism and street violence in the Basque country. **23.** In the Czech Republic, about 1,000 protestors demonstrated against the annual meeting of the IMF and World Bank and brought the centre of Prague to a standstill; on 26 September, around 10,000 anti-capitalist protestors attacked banks, department stores and fast-food outlets; 64 policeman and 20 demonstrators were injured. In Spain, almost 100,000 people demonstrated against the ETA killings in Donostia/San Sebastián. **24.** In France, a referendum to reduce the length of the presidential term of office from seven years to five was passed with 73.2 per cent of those voting approving the plan; only 30.2 per cent of the electorate voted. In a referendum in Switzerland, 63.7 per cent of voters rejected a proposal to cut the number of foreigners living in the country from 20 per cent to 18 per cent. **25.** In Yugoslavia, at least 40,000 people gathered in Belgrade's central square to celebrate the defeat of President Milošević in the presidential election before the official results had been announced. **26.** In the first round of the Yugoslav presidential election, the official results gave Vojislav Koštunica 48.22 per cent and President Slobodan Milošević 40.23 per cent of the vote; candidates were required to gain over 50 per cent of the vote to win without a second round being required. Opposition parties, independent monitors and even one party in the ruling coalition had proclaimed Mr Koštunica the outright winner with 54 per cent of the vote; a second round was scheduled for 8 October. In the concurrent legislative election, the coalition of the Socialists, the United Yugoslav Left and the pro-Serb Socialist People's Party in Montenegro won 72 out of 138 seats in the lower house and 26 of 40 seats in the upper house. The elections were boycotted by more than 75 per cent of voters in Montenegro and 90 per cent in Kosovo. **27.** In France, President Chirac was put under pressure by his own party to reveal his role in an illegal party funding scandal, which concerned a videotape purporting to show a bribe being given in 1986 in Chirac's presence while he was mayor of Paris. **28.** In the Danish referendum on the adoption of the European single currency, 53.1 per cent of those who voted rejected the adoption of the Euro; the turnout was 88 per cent. Serbia's opposition threatened to bring the country to a halt by calling a general strike; amid controversy over who had won the presidential election. **29.** In Spain, riot police cleared blockades at the country's largest biggest fuel distribution centre after more than three weeks of protests over fuel prices.

### October 2000

**2.** In Serbia, a general strike began in protest at the official results of the Yugoslav presidential election. The Pope canonised 120 Chinese martyrs and apologised for errors committed by missionaries in China. **3.** In Switzerland, Finance Minister Kaspar Villiger revealed that the country had frozen £57 million from about 100 secret bank accounts linked to Slobodan Milošević. **4.** The Yugoslav presidential election result was annulled by the country's Supreme Court, citing irregularities in the conduct of the election; it recommended that fresh elections should be held in July 2001. In France, the Senate rejected a government attempt to bring the country into line with European laws on sexual equality by allowing women to work at night in manual and industrial employment. **5.** In Yugoslavia, President Milošević went into hiding after an estimated one million people took to the streets of Belgrade and stormed parliament and other government buildings; on the following day, he announced his resignation, saying that he had received official information that Vojislav Koštunica had won the election. **7.** Vojislav Koštunica was sworn in as president of Yugoslavia. In Luxembourg, Crown Prince Henri became Grand Duke after the formal abdication of his father, Jean. **8.** In Poland, Aleksander Kwaśniewski won a second term of office in the presidential election, winning 53.9 per cent of the vote. In Lithuania, the result of the general election was inconclusive, but on 12 October, a grouping of four centrist parties, the New Union, Lithuanian Liberal Union, Modern Christian Democrats and the Centre Union, announced that they were to form a coalition government. In Belgium, the far-right Vlaams Blok made significant advances in local elections, winning 20 seats in Antwerp's 55-member city council. **9.** In Spain, the chief prosecutor of the Supreme Court of Andalucia, Luís Portero, was murdered in Granada by the ETA. **10.** The Presidents of Russia, Belarus, Kazakhstan, Kyrgyzstan and Tajikistan signed a treaty establishing the Eurasian Economic Community. **12.** In France, the Defence Minister, Alain Richard, ordered the French Foreign Legion to accept female recruits. **13.** The Bosnian Muslim leader, Alija Izetbegović, resigned from the country's three-member presidency due to ill health; Halid Genjac replaced him as the representative of the Muslim community. **15.** In Slovenia, the centre-left Liberal Democrats won 34 of the 90 seats in the general election, becoming the largest party in the legislature. In Belarus, opposition parties boycotted the legislative election; only 54 of the 565 candidates were not supporters of President Lukashenko and the OSCE declared that the conduct of the election had not met normal democratic standards. **16.** In Yugoslavia, an agreement was reached between reformers and allies of ex-President Milošević to share power until a legislative election on 23 December. **24.** President Koštunica said that Slobodan Milošević would stand trial and acknowledged that the Yugoslav security forces had committed atrocities in Kosovo. The UN was to be allowed to reopen its office in Belgrade to prosecute those responsible for war crimes committed in the former Yugoslavia. The Italian parliament voted to abolish national service. **25.** At an informal Balkans summit in Skopje, President Rexhep Mejdani of Albania demanded that President Koštunica should denounce his predecessor, Slobodan Milošević, and hand him over to an international court, he also demanded that all Yugoslav officials involved in the oppression of Kosovo Albanians should be sacked and brought to trial. **29.** The pacifist leader Ibrahim Rugova claimed a landslide victory for his Democratic League of Kosovo over former Kosovo Liberation Army guerrillas in the province's first democratic elections. **30.** In Kosovo, the Democratic League of Kosovo won civic elections in 21 of 27 municipalities. The turnout was nearly 80 per cent. A car bomb in Madrid planted by ETA killed José Francisco Querol, a Supreme Court judge.

### November 2000

**2.** In Serbia, democratic and human rights groups demanded the resignation of secret police chief Rade Marković, after a leaked document implicated the security agency in the assassination of journalist Slavko Curuvija in April 1999. **5.** In Azerbaijan, the incumbent New Azerbaijan party won the legislative election, securing about 70 per cent of the votes cast; foreign observers denounced the poll as unfair. **7.** The Roman Catholic Church in Germany announced that it would issue payments of about £1,500 per person in compensation to Second World War slave labourers. In France, following disclosures of an outbreak of bovine spongiform encephalopathy, (BSE), President Jacques Chirac called for an immediate ban on feed containing animal remains. **9.** In Germany, more than 200,000 people marched through Berlin to protest against neo-Nazi anti-Semitic and racist attacks. **11.** In the legislative election in Bosnia-Hercegovina, the multi-ethnic Social Democratic Party and the Muslim Party for Democratic Action emerged as the largest parties in the Muslim-Croat Federation; Serb nationalists remained in control of Republika Srpska. **16.** Yugoslavia announced the re-establishment of diplomatic relations with the USA, the UK, France and Germany. Russia announced that it would resume arms supplies to Iran. **19.** In Azerbaijan, up to 15,000 people marched through Baku demanding a fresh election and the annulment of the legislative election on 5 November; demonstrations also took place in other towns. **20.** In Russia, President Putin announced that 2,600 soldiers had been killed in Chechnya since the fighting began in 1999; he criticised military standards, training and goals. **21.** In Spain, ETA terrorists assassinated Ernest Lluch, the former health minister, in Barcelona. On 23 November, nearly a million people demonstrated against ETA in Barcelona; Prime Minister José Maria Aznar was among the marchers. **23.** The European Court of Human Rights ruled that the Greek government had violated the human rights of former King Constantine when it seized his property after he was deposed; the Court ordered the Greek government to devise a compensation offer within six months. **23.** In Kosovo, British peacekeepers announced that they had arrested 10 suspected Kosovar Albanian guerrillas and seized a lorry packed with weapons. Xhemajl Mustafa, a senior political adviser to the political leader Ibrahim Rugova, was shot dead in Priština. **26.** In Romania, the primary round of the presidential election resulted in the Communist candidate, Ion Iliescu, winning 37 per cent of the vote and Corneliu Vadim Tudor, a nationalist, winning 28 per cent; the other four candidates were eliminated.

### December 2000

**5.** The trial in the Netherlands of the two Libyans suspected of the Lockerbie bombing was adjourned until January 2001 to await documents from Syria, which the defence believed were crucial to its case. **6.** In Serbia, the Serbian Socialist Party selected former President Slobodan Milošević to head its list of candidates contesting the general election on 23 December. In France, about 60,000 people from throughout Europe demonstrated in Nice against globalisation and for of workers' rights. **7.** In Austria, an anti-EU umbrella organisation composed mainly of environmental organisations announced that it had collected almost double the 100,000 signatures needed to force a parliamentary debate and vote on membership of the EU. **8.** In Germany, the last remaining watchtower from the Berlin wall was demolished. **12.** At a UN conference on organised crime in Palermo, Italy, 142 nations signed the first legally binding UN convention on fighting organised crime. **15.** In Ukraine, the last functioning reactor at the Chernobyl nuclear plant was closed. **18.** In Kosovo, rebel Albanian separatists fired at US and Russian KFOR troops from within the five-kilometre buffer zone between Kosovo and Serbia. The KFOR troops had been destroying a road near Gornje Karačevo used by rebels to smuggle arms from Kosovo into the security zone. **19.** In Yugoslavia, President Vojislav Koštunica called on NATO to allow paramilitary forces to enter the border buffer zone to end a campaign by ethnic Albanian guerrillas in the Preševo valley. He asked for the buffer zone to be reduced by at least half. In the Netherlands, parliament passed legislation to permit homosexual couples to marry and adopt children. **19–22.** Turkish security forces stormed 20 jails in an attempt to end a two-month hunger strike by more than 1,100 prisoners, twenty-one prisoners were killed in the operation and many more wounded. **20.** In France, members of the National Assembly voted to postpone the legislative election that had been planned for March 2001 until after the presidential election due to be held in May 2001. **21.** Austria became the first EU country to impose a ban on German beef, a move that was approved by the European Commission. **24.** In Yugoslavia, the 18-party Democratic Opposition of Serbia (DOS) won 176 of the 250 seats in the general election; the Socialist Party of Serbia came second with 37 seats. **26.** The president of Moldova, Petru Lucinschi, announced the dissolution of parliament following its failure to elect his successor. In Russia, the old Soviet national anthem was officially restored, but was to remain wordless until new lyrics are agreed. **28.** In Romania, a left-wing minority government was appointed by parliament. **29.** In Montenegro, the government collapsed after the National Party withdrew from the ruling coalition.

### January 2001

**1.** Greece formally adopted the Euro, becoming the 12th EU member state to do so. **2.** In Germany, women were given the right to join frontline units of the armed forces. **9.** Biljana Plavsić, a former president of the Republika Srpska, the Bosnian Serb entity in Bosnia-Hercegovina, surrendered herself to the UN War Crimes Commission in The Hague; on 11 January she pleaded not guilty to nine counts of genocide and crimes against humanity. **14.** In Portugal, Jorge Sampãio was re-elected president with 55.8 per cent of the vote. **18.** The Belgian government announced the decriminalisation of the use and possession of cannabis for personal consumption. Turkey recalled its ambassador from Paris in protest at a vote by the French parliament recognising massacres of Armenians by the Ottoman Empire in 1915 as genocide. **24.** In Russia, the Duma voted to impose limits on the immunity granted to all post-Soviet Russian presidents after leaving office and the Defence Ministry announced that it would reduce troop numbers in Chechnya in February. **26.** In Russia, President Putin warned that US plans for a missile defence shield and NATO proposals to expand eastward could seriously damage Russia's relationship with the West. **29.** In Germany, Defence Minister Rudolf Scharping announced that 59 military bases would be closed as part of a cost-cutting programme. Riots broke out in Zürich, Switzerland, in protest at the annual meeting of the World Economic Forum in Davos. **31.** In the Lockerbie trial at Camp Zeist, the Netherlands, Abdelbaset Ali Mohmed Al Megrahi was found guilty of the murder of 270 people and was told that he must serve at least 20 years in a Scottish prison. The other suspect, Al Amin Khalifa Fhimah, was found not guilty. In Turkey, a Kurdish True Path Party MP, Fevzi Sihanlioglu, died after being involved in a fight in the parliamentary chamber with fellow MPs. On 1 February, two MPs from the Nationalist Action Party who were charged with involuntary manslaughter said that they would give up their parliamentary immunity to face trial.

### February 2001

**1.** The Vatican replaced its first 1929 constitution with a new basic law, incorporating amendments made since then and dropping all reference to the death penalty, which was abolished in 1969. **5.** Albanian separatists in the Preševo valley in southern Serbia launched a sustained attack against Yugoslav security forces. **6.** The Danish Cabinet announced that it would end its large subsidies to the Færoe Isles in four years' time if the inhabitants backed the plan of their Prime Minister, Anfinn Kallsberg, to seek full independence by 2012 in a referendum on the issue planned for 26 May. **8.** In Ukraine, the prosecutor general's office announced that President Leonid Kuchma had been questioned over allegations that he ordered the death of a journalist, George Gongadze, who had exposed government corruption. In Germany, former Chancellor Helmut Kohl agreed to pay a fine of about £100,000 in return for not facing further criminal investigation of breach of trust allegations. **12.** Ukraine and Russia agreed to reconnect the power grids of the two countries, create a joint aerospace consortium and build a bridge connecting Russia to the Crimean peninsula. **16.** In Kosovo, a bus carrying Serb civilians was attacked, leaving seven people dead and 21 more injured near the town of Podujevo. **19.** In Russia, at least 20 Russian soldiers were killed and 20 wounded near Grozny, Chechnya. **22.** The Turkish government abandoned its currency control policy, causing the lira to fall by almost 30 per cent against the US dollar. **24.** In Yugoslavia, the former head of the secret police, Rade Marković, was arrested over the attempted assassination of a political opponent, Vuk Drasković, in October 1999. **25.** In the Moldovan general election, the Communist Party won 50.2 per cent of the vote.

### March 2001

**4.** In Switzerland, a referendum proposing the immediate commencement of negotiations to join the EU was rejected by 76.7 per cent of those who voted. Macedonia closed all border crossings with Kosovo after three soldiers were killed near a border village occupied by ethnic Albanian guerrillas. **5.** In Portugal, the Infrastructure Minister, Jorge Coelho, resigned, saying he accepted responsibility for the collapse of a road bridge over the river Douro near Entre-os-Rios in which at least 70 people died. **7.** In Bosnia-Hercegovina, Ante Jelavić, the Bosnian Croat member of the three-man collective presidency and other senior Bosnian Croat officials were sacked by Wolfgang Petritsch, the senior international administrator, after their party announced plans to break the alliance with the country's Muslims.

**8.** NATO acted to halt an insurrection by ethnic Albanians rebels on the Macedonian side of the border with Kosovo, capturing the main rebel headquarters in the Macedonian village of Tanusevci and allowing Yugoslav forces back into a border zone they had been forbidden to enter for two years. In France, the Basque separatist organisation ETA stole 1.5 tonnes of explosives from a warehouse near Grenoble. **12–30.** In Macedonia, the armed forces launched an offensive to drive out ethnic Albanian forces, who had occupied five villages near the Kosovan border. **22.** In Poland, President Aleksander Kwaśniewski vetoed a £7,000 million compensation payment to hundreds of thousands of people whose property had been seized by the Communists, saying that the economy could not afford it. **25.** Yugoslav forces re-entered much of the buffer zone bordering Kosovo with the agreement of NATO in an attempt to halt the activities of ethnic Albanian rebels in border regions of southern Serbia. **26–27.** In Germany, anti-nuclear protesters occupied sections of railway line to try to prevent a train full of nuclear waste from travelling to Dannenberg to be buried in a salt mine. **30.** In Spain, the Basque terrorist group ETA warned tourists to stay away from Spanish tourist resorts.

### April 2001

**2.** In Yugoslavia, former President Slobodan Milošević admitted that the Yugoslav government had secretly paid the cost of arming rebel Serbs in Croatia and Bosnia during the break-up of the former Yugoslavia. **4.** The Moldovan Parliament elected the Communist Party leader Vladimir Voronin as president. **5.** In Yugoslavia, Justice Minister Vladan Batić, declined to accept the arrest warrants for Slobodan Milošević brought from the International Tribunal for the Former Yugoslavia. **10.** In the Netherlands, the States General, the country's upper house, passed legislation by 46 to 28 to legalise euthanasia. **11.** In Turkey, hundreds of thousands of people protested in cities across the country to demand the resignation of Prime Minister Bülent Ecevit over his failure to control the country's economic crisis. **19.** The

Italian government approved plans to construct a bridge linking Sicily to the mainland. **22.** In Montenegro, the Democratic Party of Socialists and other pro-independence parties won 44 of the 77 seats in the general election. **24.** In France, Employment Minister Elisabeth Guigou announced a package of measures to bolster the rights of workers facing redundancy and to penalise companies suspected of laying them off to boost profits. **24.** The Yugoslav army charged 183 of its members with war crimes in the Kosovo conflict. **26.** In Ukraine, Prime Minister Viktor Yushchenko was dismissed by parliament. **29.** In Macedonia, eight members of the security forces were killed in an ambush by members of the ethnic Albanian National Liberation Army (NLA).

MAY 2001

**3.** In Macedonia, government forces attacked an ethnic Albanian village, ending their two-month cease-fire following the killing of 10 soldiers and police by the outlawed NLA. In Serbia, Slobodan Milošević was served with an arrest warrant issued by the International War Crimes Tribunal for the Former Yugoslavia. **6.** In Bosnia-Hercegovina, thousands of Bosnian Serb nationalists attacked Muslims and international officials, forcing the cancellation of a ceremony to mark the rebuilding of a mosque in Banja Luka. **8.** In Macedonia, it was announced that a coalition government of national unity was to be formed to avert the threat of civil war. **14.** In the Italian general election, the Centre-Right House of Liberty alliance won 368 seats in the 630-seat Chamber of Deputies and 177 seats of the 315 seats in the Senate. **16.** More than 7,000 Bosnian Croat soldiers who mutinied in support of separatists trying to carve out an ethnic Croat state returned to barracks following an agreement between nationalist generals and the central government. **21.** In Serbia, ethnic Albanian rebels agreed to disband, announcing that their aims would now be better served through political debate. **24.** The coalition government of Northern Cyprus collapsed amid disagreement over its stance on the future of the divided island. In Macedonia, the army and police launched an offensive against more than 10 rebel-held villages near Kumanovo. **28.** In the general election in Cyprus, the Communist Akel party won 34.7 per cent of the vote, making it the largest party.

JUNE 2001

**5.** Serbian Interior Minister Dušan Mihailović admitted the existence of three mass graves within Serbia containing the remains of Albanian Kosovars who were killed during the war in 1999. **8.** The Irish electorate voted against the ratification of the Treaty of Nice; only about 35 per cent of the electorate voted. **14.** President Boris Trajkovski made an official request for NATO help in disarming the NLA; the NLA had earlier made NATO involvement a pre-requisite for disarmament. **15.** Macedonian political leaders held talks on concessions to ethnic Albanians in an attempt to halt an all-out war. **15-16.** In Sweden, 25,000 protestors demonstrated in Gothenburg against the EU summit that was taking place in the city; there was widespread violence and over 500 people were arrested. **17.** In the general election in Bulgaria, the National Movement for Simeon II won 43.4 per cent of the vote, obtaining 120 seats of the 240 seats. **22.** In Turkey, Virtue, the main opposition party, was ruled illegal by the country's highest court, which judged it to be a focal point for pro-Islamic and anti-secular activity. **22-24.** Macedonian forces ended a tenuous 11-day cease-fire and launched a three-day campaign against NLA positions in the village of Aracinovo until the NLA agreed to withdraw its forces. **25.** In the Macedonian capital Skopje, Slav nationalists stormed parliament in protest against the government allowing NATO forces to escort NLA fighters from Aracinovo to safety. **28.** Yugoslavia extradited Slobodan Milošević to the UN tribunal in The Hague where he faced four charges of crimes against humanity and violations of the laws or customs of war for his responsibility for the conduct of the Kosovo campaign; further crimes committed in the Bosnian and Croatian wars were likely to be added. **30.** In Yugoslavia, Prime Minister Zoran Zizić and other ministers resigned in protest at the extradition of Milošević.

JULY 2001

**1.** In Austria, protestors attacked police and smashed cars and shop windows in a demonstration against a meeting of the World Economic Forum in Salzburg. **3.** In Cyprus, following the arrest of Marios Matsakis, an MP who had protested at the construction of a communications aerial in the RAF base at Akrotiri, more than 1,000 Greek Cypriots stormed the base and released him; 40 policemen and soldiers were injured in the attack. Former Yugoslav President Slobodan Milošević made his first appearance at his UN war crimes trial and refused to enter a plea on charges against humanity, saying that he did not recognise the authority of the court. **4.** In Bosnia-Hercegovina, the Prime Minister of the Republika Srpska, Mladen Ivanić, declared that the state was preparing to hand over the war crimes suspects Radovan Karadzić and Ratko Mladić to the UN War Crimes Tribunal for the Former Yugoslavia. **5.** In Macedonia, ethnic Albanian rebels and the Macedonian army signed separate cease-fire deals with NATO. **8.** In Croatia, four Cabinet ministers resigned in protest at the government's decision to hand over two generals accused of war crimes against Serb civilians in the mid-1990s. **9.** The Russian-appointed head of the Chechen administration, Mufti Akhmad Kadyrov, accused the Russian military of tormenting, humiliated and robbing people. **16.** The Russian President, Vladimir Putin, signed a friendship treaty with President Jiang Zemin of China. **17.** In Bulgaria the National Movement of the former King Simeon II of Bulgaria agreed to form a coalition government with the ethnic-Turkish Movement for Rights and Freedom. **24.** Macedonia closed its border with Kosovo after accusing peace envoys of siding with the country's ethnic Albanian minority in negotiations between the two sides. Demonstrators attacked the British and German embassies and UN offices in Skopje. A commission of Catholic and Jewish historians announced that it had suspended its study of the Church's role in the Holocaust because the Vatican had refused to release material from its archives. **25.** In Bulgaria, Simeon Saxe-Coburgotski, the former King Simeon II was appointed Prime Minister.

AUGUST 2001

**6.** In Macedonia, talks to end the conflict between the government and the NLA broke down after Macedonian hard-liners added new demands. **12.** Macedonian security forces shot dead five unarmed ethnic Albanian villagers and burnt at least a dozen houses in Ljuboten; the Interior Ministry claimed that the five killed were terrorists. **13.** In Macedonia, leaders of the Slav and Albanian parties signed an agreement aimed at tending the fighting and clearing the way for NATO troops to take up their positions within two weeks; the agreement accorded equal status to Christianity and Islam and made Albanian an official language. **15.** NATO authorised the deployment to Macedonia of troops for the Essential Harvest task force. **30.** In Macedonia, demonstrators tried to prevent deputies from entering the parliament building to debate the ratification of the peace agreement.

## THE MIDDLE EAST

### SEPTEMBER 2000

**4.** The first round of the Lebanese general election took place. Selim al-Hoss, the incumbent prime minister, conceded defeat when it became obvious that Rafik al-Hariri had won a large majority. **10.** The Palestinian Central Council decided to delay its declaration of Palestinian statehood, which it had promised for 13 September, for at least two months. **12.** Israeli Prime Minister Ehud Barak set out proposals, known as a civil revolution, which were designed to reduce the influence of religious leaders on daily life; the proposed changes included the introduction of civil marriage, allowing buses and El Al flights on the Sabbath and closing the religious affairs ministry. **18.** In Jordan, a military court sentenced six Islamic militants to death for plotting a bombing campaign against Jews and Christians during the Millennium celebrations at the start of the year. **23.** The US ambassador to Israel, Martin Indyk, was suspended pending an investigation into alleged security violations. **27.** In Israel, the Attorney General announced that there was insufficient evidence to prosecute former Prime Minister Binyamin Netanyahu on corruption charges. **28.** Violent unrest occurred in Jerusalem following a visit to the Temple Mount by Ariel Sharon, the opposition leader.

### OCTOBER 2000

**1.** Palestinians protested throughout the West Bank and Gaza Strip; three Israeli soldiers and at least 28 Palestinians were killed and 700 people were reported wounded. There was also fighting between Jews and Arabs in major towns in Israel. **2.** Seven Israeli Arabs were killed in clashes inside Israel, the first to die in political clashes since 1976. **5.** An agreement aimed at ending the violence on the West Bank and Gaza was reached by the Israeli Prime Minister, Ehud Barak, and the leader of the Palestinian National Authority, Yasser Arafat, in talks hosted by Madeleine Albright in Paris. **7.** The Israeli air force bombed targets in Lebanon after Lebanese Hezbollah guerrillas captured three soldiers in a border raid. **8.** In the West Bank, Jewish settlers blocked roads and stoned Palestinian cars; in Tiberias, a crowd set fire to a mosque; the following day, thousands of Israeli Arabs demonstrated in Nazareth. **10.** In Yemen, a suicide bomb attack in Aden killed 17 US sailors dead and injured 35 others. **11.** Israeli helicopters launched rocket attacks on Yasser Arafat's compound in Gaza, a police station at Ramallah and a police academy in Jericho in revenge for the lynching of three Israeli soldiers in a police station in Ramallah. On 18 October, an Israeli undercover unit seized eight suspected members of the Palestinian mob that had lynched the Israeli soldiers; another two suspects were arrested on 25 June 2001. **12.** Oman cut diplomatic ties with Israel. **14.** A Saudi Arabian Airlines Boeing 777-200 carrying 90 passengers, of whom 40 were British, was seized by four terrorists on a flight from Jiddah to Heathrow and ordered to fly to Baghdād; the hostages were freed on the following day and flown back to Jiddah. The Iraqi authorities announced on 6 November that the hijackers had been granted political asylum. **16–17.** A crisis summit was hosted by the USA in Sharm el-Sheik, Egypt; an agreement was reached between the Israeli and Palestinian delegations in which both sides agreed to issue statements calling for an end to violence. **21.** Israel announced that it intended to suspend diplomatic contact with the Palestinian Authority because it had failed to keep to the agreed cease-fire. **23.** In Lebanon, President Gen. Lahoud appointed Rafiq al-Hariri as Prime Minister designate. **31.** On a state visit to Israel, Federal Chancellor Gerhard Schröder of Germany accidentally extinguished the eternal flame at the Yad Vashem Holocaust memorial in Jerusalem.

### NOVEMBER 2000

**5.** In Iraq, the national airline, Iraqi Airways resumed domestic flights through the Western-imposed no-fly zones in defiance of the UN. **9.** A leading member of al-Fatah, the mainstream wing of the Palestine Liberation Organisation, Hussein Abayad, was killed in a helicopter rocket attack launched by Israel. The following day al-Fatah announced that it was at war with Israel. In Kuwait, four people were arrested on charges of planning terrorist attacks on US targets in the Gulf. **13.** Palestinian-ruled towns in the West Bank were cordoned off by the Israeli army following the killing of four Jewish settlers. **20.** Israeli helicopters attacked Palestinian targets in the Gaza Strip in retaliation for the bombing of a school bus, in which two teachers were killed. **21.** The Palestinian National Authority authorised its policemen to open fire in self-defence against Israeli forces in those areas that were under full Palestinian sovereignty. Egypt recalled its ambassador to Tel Aviv in protest at Israel's handling of the security situation. **22.** In Israel, two people were killed and about 55 were injured when a bus was bombed near Tel Aviv. **26.** At least four members of al-Fatah were killed in an ambush by an Israeli commando unit near the West Bank village of Habla. **26.** An Israeli soldier was killed and several were injured by a bomb planted by Hezbollah guerrillas near the Lebanese border; Israel responded with a bombing raid on three suspected Hezbollah positions in Lebanon. **30.** The PLO rejected an Israeli offer to negotiate a partial peace deal, in which Israel would hand over a further 10 per cent of the West Bank to connect the patches of autonomous territory and recognise Palestinian statehood, annexing some Jewish settlements in return, leaving the final status of Jerusalem and the return of Palestinian refugees to be decided within three years.

### DECEMBER 2000

**3.** Israeli Prime Minister Ehud Barak warned President Bashar al-Assad of Syria that continued support for Hezbollah guerrillas would result in Israeli military strikes against Syrian targets. **4.** Israeli helicopters opened fire on buildings in Bethlehem to defend Rachel's Tomb, a Jewish shrine, against a Palestinian assault. **9.** In Israel, Prime Minister Ehud Barak resigned and was immediately adopted as the Labour Party's candidate for the forthcoming election. **19.** In Bahrain, a committee appointed by the Emir recommended the introduction of a bicameral parliament and suffrage for women. **23.** Israeli and Palestinian negotiators met President Clinton for peace talks in Washington. **28.** In Israel, two soldiers were killed when a bomb exploded at the Sufa border crossing to the Gaza Strip. Thirteen people were injured when two pipe bombs exploded on a bus in Tel Aviv.

### JANUARY 2001

**1.** In Netanya, Israel, over 40 people were injured in a car bomb explosion. **8.** In Jerusalem, thousands demonstrated in protest at Prime Minister Barak's proposal to divide the Old City between Israel and the Palestinians. **16.** Palestinian police announced that six people suspected

of collaborating with Israeli security forces had been executed and that a further 40 were under arrest. **17.** Gunmen in Gaza City shot the head of Palestinian television, Hisham Mekki, dead; the Al-Aqsa Martyrs' Brigade, a dissident faction of the al-Fatah party, claimed responsibility.
**21—27.** Peace talks between Israel and the Palestinians opened in Taba, Egypt, but ended without a peace deal.

FEBRUARY 2001

**6.** In Israel, Ariel Sharon was elected prime minister winning 62.3 per cent of the vote. **7.** Prime Minister-elect Ariel Sharon declared Jerusalem to be the centre of the eternal and indivisible capital of the Jewish people. **14.** In Israel, a Palestinian bus driver drove into a bus queue of soldiers and commuters in Tel Aviv, killing eight people and injuring 20. **15.** In Bahrain, a referendum to approve a package of liberal reforms to create a partially elected parliament, an independent judiciary and to limit the powers of the Emir was approved by 98.4 per cent of voters; women were allowed to vote for the first time. **16.** In Iraq, the UK and the USA launched the biggest air raid on targets around Baghdad since operation Desert Fox in December 1998, damaging six new command-and-control facilities and involving at least 80 aircraft. An Israeli soldier was killed and three wounded in a cross-border rocket attack by Lebanese Hezbollah militants. **19.** Israeli and US soldiers began tests on the Patriot air-defence system.

MARCH 2001

**4.** In Israel, a suicide bomber blew himself up in Netanya, killing three people and wounding about 60. **5.** In Saudi Arabia, 35 people were crushed to death and a number of others injured at the annual Muslim pilgrimage, the Hajj, during the ritual stoning of pillars symbolising the devil near the holy city of Mecca (Al-Makkah). **8.** In Israel, Prime Minister Ariel Sharon announced an eight-party coalition government that was backed by 72 of the 120 MPs. **12.** In Kuwait, service personnel were killed and seven injured when a US Navy Hornet jet dropped a 500lb bomb on a group of military observers during a training mission. **27.** Two bombs exploded in Jerusalem; a suicide bomber was killed and 42 people were wounded in the attacks. **28.** The Israeli army bombed six bases of Force 17, Yasser Arafat's presidential guard, in response to three bombings, the third of which killed two teenagers. **31.** Israel jailed 600 reserve soldiers in an attempt to halt a growing rebellion against military service in the West Bank and Gaza Strip.

APRIL 2001

**1.** Israeli Special Forces seized six members of Yasser Arafat's Force 17 guard in Jilijiheh, a town in Palestinian-controlled territory. **7.** In Lebanon, a military court sentenced 12 former members of the South Lebanon Army to death for collaboration with Israel during its occupation of Lebanon. **4.** Israeli Foreign Minister Shimon Peres held formal talks with Palestinian negotiators in Athens. **15.** Israeli warplanes killed three soldiers and wounded six in a raid on a Syrian radar station in Lebanon; the attack was in retaliation for the earlier killing of an Israeli soldier by Hezbollah guerrillas. **16.** Israeli ships and helicopters fired missiles at bases of the Force 17 security unit in central Gaza, after Palestinian mortar bombs fell on the Israeli town of Sderot. **29.** In Yemen, President Ali Abdullah Saleh offered to exchange five Britons who had been convicted of terrorist offences in Yemen for the London-based Islamic cleric, Abu Hamza al-Masri, whom the Yemeni authorities believed had ordered the attacks.

MAY 2001

**6.** Pope John Paul II became the first leader of the Roman Catholic Church to set foot inside a mosque when he entered the Great Ummayyid Mosque in Damascus together with the Mufti, Sheikh Ahmed Kuftaro. **18.** In Israel, five Israelis were killed in a Hamas suicide bomb attack in Netanya; Israel bombed a security headquarters in Nablus and fired rockets at targets in Ramallah, Gaza and Tulkarem in retaliation. **21.** Gen. Colin Powell, the US Secretary of State, urged the Israelis to use non-lethal responses to unarmed demonstrators and the Palestinians to prevent gunmen from firing on Israeli positions from Palestinian-controlled areas. **26.** The 56 member states of the Organisation of the Islamic Conference agreed to halt all political contact with Israel. **29.** Israeli and Palestinians security officials resumed talks in Ramallah.

JUNE 2001

**1.** In Israel, a Palestinian suicide bomber blew himself up in a crowd of teenagers outside a Tel Aviv disco killing 18 people and injuring more than 75; Yasser Arafat, the leader of the Palestinian National Authority, agreed to an immediate and unconditional cease-fire the following day. **4.** Iraq halted its official crude oil exports in an attempt to raise world oil prices. **5.** The family of a Palestinian man who was shot dead by Jews donated his organs to be transplanted to three Israelis. **11.** In Yemen, the USA closed its embassy in Aden, citing terrorist threats. **12.** Yasser Arafat accepted terms for a cease-fire with Israel after talks with the CIA director, George Tenet. **14.** In Lebanon, Syrian troops began to withdraw from strategic positions in Beirut.

JULY 2001

**11.** In Iraq, the Supreme Council for the Islamic Revolution in Iraq (SCIRI), a Shi'a Muslim dissident group backed by Iran, launched a rocket attack against government targets in Baghdad. **16.** In Israel, a suicide bomber blew himself up at a railway station in Binyamina, killing two people and injuring 11. Islamic Jihad claimed responsibility. **17.** Israeli helicopter gunships killed two senior Hamas members in Bethlehem. **20.** Israel launched artillery attacks on Hebron and two Christian districts of Bethlehem were shelled. **22.** In Yemen, four men were jailed for terms of between four and 15 years for a grenade attack on the British embassy in Sana'ā' in October 2000. **27.** Israeli tanks shelled Palestinian security posts on the West Bank in retaliation for the shooting hours earlier of an Israeli teenager by Palestinian guerrillas. **30.** Two senior Hamas members were killed in an Israeli missile attack.

AUGUST 2001

**5.** A Palestinian opened fire on soldiers outside the largest army base in Tel Aviv, wounding 10 people. **7.** US combat aircraft bombed an Iraqi air defence site after being tracked by Iraqi artillery. **9.** In Jerusalem, a Palestinian suicide bomber blew himself up in a pizza restaurant in Jerusalem killing at least 15 people and injuring more than 100. Israeli fighter jets attacked the police station in the Palestinian-controlled West Bank city of Ramallah. **10.** British and US aircraft launched four raids on Iraqi air defence sites. Israeli troops and police seized key offices and buildings used by the PLO in Jerusalem. **14.** Israeli troops conducted a four-hour raid on the Palestinian-run West Bank town of Jenin, levelling the main police station with armoured bulldozers. US F16 jets bombed a mobile

Iraqi radar battery which had tracked NATO aircraft. **26.** Three Israeli soldiers were killed by Palestinian commandos in the Gaza Strip. The military responded with a wide-scale air and land assault, destroying Palestinian security headquarters in four towns. **28-30.** Israeli tanks occupied Beit Jala, a Palestinian Christian town near Bethlehem to silence gunfire directed at Jerusalem.

## EUROPEAN UNION

### September 2000

**5.** The European Parliament approved plans to create an EU Foreign Service, with its own embassies and training academy, and co-ordinated representation in international organisation. **22.** Central banks of the Group of Seven industrialised nations bought billions of euros on foreign exchanges as fears grew that the currency's performance was jeopardising economic growth.

### October 2000

**6.** The Council of Ministers agreed to extend the powers of Europol, the European Police Office, to enable it to investigate money-laundering stemming from all forms of crime. **9.** The European Council agreed to the unconditional lifting of all sanctions against Yugoslavia. **13.** At the European Council summit in Biarritz, agreement was reached in principle to allow groups of member states that wished to proceed to closer union to do so independently of others. **17.** The Council of Ministers approved a directive that will make illegal discrimination in the workplace on the grounds of age, disability, religion or sexual orientation and called for penalties against countries that had high levels of money laundering. **26.** Yugoslavia was admitted to the EU's Stability Pact for south eastern Europe.

### November 2000

**7.** The European Commission announced that it was launching legal action against Philip Morris, R. J. Reynolds, Japan Tobacco and Nabisco Group for their alleged involvement in smuggling cigarettes into the EU. **8.** The annual Enlargement Strategy Paper praised all the applicant countries except Turkey for meeting the political requirements of EU membership. **15.** The Court of Auditors refused to certify the 1999 EU budget. It criticised the European Commission and the member states for mismanagement of funds. The mistakes amounted to between 5.5 and 7 per cent of the £60,000 million budget, but the majority were accumulated small errors and incorrect expenditure, rather than fraud. **16.** A German general, Lt.-Gen. Klaus Schuwirth, was appointed the EU's Director of Military Staff, with the task of creating a rapid reaction force of 60,000 by 2003. **24.** Leaders of the EU and Albania, Bosnia-Hercegovina, Croatia, Macedonia and Yugoslavia met at the EU-Balkans summit in Zagreb; the EU offered £2.4 billion in economic aid, duty-free access to EU markets and eventual membership of the EU to the five Balkan states.

### December 2000

**7-11.** At the EU summit in Nice, a new EU treaty was finalised which was intended to reform the EU prior to the accession of new member states; the treaty would increase qualified majority voting, limit the size of the Commission and strengthen the powers of the Commission President. **15.** The EU ordered drastic cuts in North Sea fishing quotas. The UK's share of the cod quota was cut by 45 per cent.

### January 2001

**24.** The Economic and Monetary Affairs Commissioner, Pedro Solbes, formally reprimanded Ireland for tax cuts which were overheating the economy and causing higher inflation. The EU and Norway agreed to ban cod fishing in the North Sea for a two-and-a-half-month period from mid-February until the end of April. **26.** The European Court of Justice suspended the European Parliament's decision to bar the French far-right leader Jean-Marie Le Pen.

### February 2001

**12.** The government of the Republic of Ireland was reprimanded by the Commission for its lack of action in controlling inflation; the UK was rebuked for allowing the British economy to move into deficit.

### March 2001

**2.** The EU granted 48 of the poorest countries quota- and tariff-free access to the EU market. **6.** The European Commission suspended all livestock markets in the EU for two weeks aimed at preventing the foot and mouth epidemic in the UK from spreading. **30.** Gen. Gustav Hägglund, the chief of the Finnish army, was chosen to head the Military Committee. **31.** The EU declared that it would ratify the Kyōto treaty regardless of the USA.

### April 2001

**5.** The Council of Ministers agreed to develop a European satellite navigation system; the first satellites were due to be launched by 2005. **26.** The EU suspended aid to Slovakia after allegations of large-scale theft of EU funds by the head of the Department of Foreign Assistance, Roland Tóth, who was under investigation for fraud.

### June 2001

**13.** Agriculture and Fisheries Commissioner Franz Fischler warned that further drastic cuts would need to be made during 2001 to preserve fish stocks.

### July 2001

**18.** Internal Market Commissioner Frits Bolkestein declared that the UK would be brought before the European Court of Justice if British customs staff did not relax their rigid interpretation of EU guidelines on the amount of alcohol and cigarettes which could be brought into the UK.

### August 2001

**6.** The European Commission launched a fraud enquiry into compensation payments to British farmers following a highly critical report by EU veterinary inspectors on the government's handling of the foot and mouth epidemic.

## INTERNATIONAL RELATIONS

### September 2000

**5.** The UN Millennium Summit opened in New York; more than 150 presidents, prime ministers and rulers, the largest gathering of world leaders in history, gathered for the three-day meeting. **27.** The UN compensation commission agreed that Iraq should pay £11 billion in compensation to the Kuwaiti Petroleum Company for the oil-well fires started by retreating Iraqi troops in the Gulf War.

### October 2000

**10.** Ireland, Norway, Colombia, Singapore and Mauritius won two-year terms on the UN Security Council. **25.** The

UN Secretary-General announced that Ruud Lubbers would be the next UN High Commissioner for Refugees.

NOVEMBER 2000

**1.** The UN General Assembly accepted Yugoslavia as a member; it had been suspended in 1992. **25.** The World Climate Change Conference ended in acrimony after a 12 day attempt to persuade world leaders to agree to legally binding reductions in greenhouse gases; Deputy Prime Minister John Prescott walked out after a British attempt to reach a compromise between the EU and the US positions was rejected. **30.** The IMF approved loans of nearly £425 million to Pakistan. The loan, for a period of ten months, was to prevent Pakistan from defaulting on its £26 billion debt in January.

DECEMBER 2000

**9.** Hans Hækkerup, the Danish Defence Minister, was named as the new head of the United Nations mission in Kosovo; he was to assume his new role in January 2000.

JANUARY 2001

**14.** The UN War Crimes Tribunal announced that Slobodan Milošević and four other former Serbian leaders should be arrested and surrendered to the tribunal to stand trial for human rights abuses against ethnic Albanians in Kosovo. **23.** A report issued by the International Labour Office declared that a third of the world's work force were unemployed or under-employed. **24.** The Chief Prosecutor of the UN War Crimes Tribunal, Carla Del Ponte, broke off talks with President Koštunica of Yugoslavia on 23 January after they failed to agree on the extradition of war criminals.

FEBRUARY 2001

**22.** The UN War Crimes Tribunal sentenced three Bosnian Serbs to between 12 and 28 years in prison for using rape and sexual slavery as a weapon of war during the 1992-1995 conflict. **26.** The UN War Crimes Tribunal jailed the former Vice-President of the Croatian Republic of Herceg-Bosna, the former self-declared Croat state within Bosnia-Herzegovina, Dario Kordić, for 25 years after finding him guilty of ordering the massacre of hundreds of Muslims in the Lasva Valley between 1991-1994. **27.** The annual UN human rights report stated that a million North Koreans had died of starvation and related diseases since 1995; North Korea was named as one of the three worst human rights abusers along with Cuba and Myanmar. UNICEF announced that it had airlifted more than 2,800 demobilised child soldiers away from the front lines in southern Sudan.

MARCH 2001

**2.** At a summit of the Organisation of African Unity in Libya, the heads of state and government of some 40 countries proclaimed the birth of the African Union, designed to unite Africa politically and economically; the formal birth of the union would effectively take place only when it had been ratified by at least 36 of the 53 member states. **20.** The Commonwealth Ministerial Action Group decided that the foreign ministers of Barbados, Australia and Nigeria should be sent to have talks with the Zimbabwean government. Zimbabwe said that it would not co-operate. **21.** NATO's decision-making North Atlantic Council unanimously called for the KFOR peacekeeping mission in Kosovo to be reinforced with additional troops.

APRIL 2001

**22.** At the Summit of the Americas in Québec, leaders of 34 countries signed plans to establish a free trade zone by 2005; the summit had been delayed by anti-globalisation protests.

MAY 2001

**3.** The USA was voted off the UN Human Rights Commission for the first time since 1947.

JUNE 2001

**15.** Uzbekistan became a member of the Shanghai Co-operation Organisation and together with the five original members, China, Russia, Kazakhstan, Kyrgyzstan and Tajikistan, signed the Shanghai pact, which aimed to combat ethnic and religious militancy, while promoting trade and investments. **29.** In a ruling upholding Turkey's decision in 1998 to dissolve the pro-Islamic Welfare Party, the European Court of Human Rights ruled that Islamic parties could be banned if they posed a threat to civil order and secular democracy. It justified its ruling on the basis that the Welfare Party had planned to institute Shari'ah law, which would have conflicted with the values embodied in the European convention on Human Rights.

JULY 2001

**9.** The OAU held its final summit before it was renamed the African Union; the summit was addressed by UN Secretary-General Kofi Annan, who told delegates to emulate the EU. **20.** A G8 summit was held in Genoa, Italy, which was accompanied by violent protests in which one demonstrator was shot dead and 184 people were injured; the summit agreed to a campaign to raise US$1 billion to combat AIDS and other diseases was begun. **23.** The UN climate treaty talks in Bonn agreed a compromise deal on the Kyōto Treaty, which was signed by all the participants except the USA. **25.** The USA rejected a proposed protocol strengthen the 1972 Biological Weapons Convention. All of the other 53 participating states had supported it.

AUGUST 2001

**2.** At the International War Crimes Tribunal for the Former Yugoslavia, Gen. Radislav Krstić, a senior Bosnian Serb officer, was convicted of genocide for the murder of more than 7,000 Muslims at Srebrenica and sentenced to 46 years imprisonment. **12-14.** At the South African Development Community summit in Blantyre, Malawi, a final communiqué was issued expressing concern at the situation in Zimbabwe. **22.** The NATO North Atlantic Council issued orders for troops to go to Macedonia to collect weapons handed over by the ethnic Albanian NLA.

# Obituaries

1 SEPTEMBER 2000 TO 31 AUGUST 2001

Adams, Douglas, author, aged 49 – *d.* 11 May 2001, *b.* 11 March 1952

Aldington, Lord, KCMG, CBE, DSO, TD, PC, soldier, businessman and politician, aged 86 – *d.* 7 December 2000, *b.* 25 May 1914

Alexander, Sir Kenneth, principal of Stirling University 1981–86; and Chairman of the Highlands and Islands Development Board 1976–80, aged 79 – *d.* 27 March 2001, *b.* 14 March 1922

Amichai, Yehuda, poet, aged 76 – *d.* 22 September 2000, *b.* 1924

Andrew, Professor Raymond, FRS, physicist, aged 79 – *d.* 27 May 2001, *b.* 27 June 1921

Ardbrecknish, Lord Mackay of, deputy leader of the Opposition in the House of Lords 1998–01, aged 62 – *d.* 21 February 2001, *b.* 15 November 1938

Astor, The Hon. Sir John, MBE, Conservative MP Sutton Division 1951–59 and farmer, aged 82 – *d.* 10 September 2000, *b.* 29 August 1918

Aylmer, Dr Gerald, FBA, historian and former Master of St Peter's College, Oxford 1978–91, aged 74 – *d.* 17 December 2000, *b.* 30 April 1926

Baker, The Very Revd Thomas, former Dean of Worcester 1975–86, aged 79 – *d.* 25 September 2000, *b.* 22 December 1920

Baker, Tom, GC, coalminer and soldier, aged 88 – *d.* 7 December 2000, *b.* 14 April 1912

Balthus, James Aldridge, painter, aged 92 – *d.* 18 February 2001, *b.* 29 February 1908

Bamford, Joseph Cyril, CBE, created the JCB digger, aged 84 – *d.* 1 March 2001, *b.* 21st June 1916

Bandaranaike, Sirimavo, Prime Minister of Sri Lanka 1960–65; 1970–77; 1994–00, aged 84 – *d.* 10 October 2000, *b.* 17 April 1916

Baroness Denton of Wakefield, Jean, CBE, Northern Ireland Minister 1994–97 and champion racing car driver, aged 65 – *d.* 5 February 2001, *b.* 29 December 1935

Beattie, Sir David, GCVO, QSO, QC, Governor General of New Zealand 1980–85, aged 76 – *d.* 4 February 2001, *b.* 29 February 1924

Beddington, Rosa, FRS, biologist, aged 45 – *d.* 23 March 1956, *b.* 18 May 2001

Bedford, Eric, CVO, chief architect to the Ministry of Works 1950–70, aged 91 – *d.* 28 July 2001, *b.* 23 August 1909

Beeley, Sir Harold, KCMG, CBE, former British Ambassador to Cairo 1961–64; 1967–70, aged 92 – *d.* 27 July 2001, *b.* 15 February 1909

Beith, Sir John, KCMG, ambassador to Israel 1963–65, ambassador to Belgium 1969–74, aged 86 – *d.* 4 September 2000, *b.* 4 April 1914

Bellwin, Lord Irwin Norman, Conservative Under-Secretary of State at the Department of Environment 1979–83 and Minister of State 1983–84, aged 78 – *d.* 11 February 2001, *b.* 7 February 1923

Bevins, Anthony, political correspondent and journalist, aged 58 – *d.* 23 March 2001, *b.* 16 August 1942

Bodmer, Lady Julia, FAMS, FRCP, scientist, aged 66 – *d.* 29 January 2001, *b.* 31 July 1934

Borge, Victor, 91, comic pianist, aged 91 – *d.* 23 December 2000, *b.* 3 January 1909

Bradbury, Sir Malcolm, CBE, critic and novelist, aged 68 – *d.* 27 November 2000, *b.* 7 September 1932

Bradman, Sir Donald, Australian cricket captain, aged 92 – *d.* 25 February 2001, *b.* 27 August 1908

Brooks, Gwendolyn, poet, aged 83 – *d.* 3 December 2000, *b.* 7 June 1917

Brower, David, founder of Friends of the Earth, aged 88 – *d.* 5 November 2000, *b.* 1 July 1912

Burns, Robert, president of the World War I Veterans' Association, aged 104 – *d.* 29 October 2000, *b.* 12 November 1895

Cawley, Sir Charles, CBE, chief scientist, Ministry of Power 1959–67, aged 93 – *d.* 8 November 2000, *b.* 17 May 1907

Chaban-Delmas, Jacques, Prime Minister of France 1969–72; Mayor of Bordeaux 1947–97, aged 85 – *d.* 10 November 2000, *b.* 7 March 1915

Christian, Professor Jack, FRS, metallurgist, aged 74 – *d.* 27 February 2001, *b.* 9 April 1926

Cole, Sir Colin, KCB, KCVO, Garter Principal King of Arms 1978–82, aged 87 – *d.* 19 February 2001, *b.* 29 September 2001

Como, Perry, American Singer, aged 87 – *d.* 12 May 2001, *b.* 18 May 1912

Compston, Vice-Admiral Sir Peter, KCB, Supreme Allied Commander Atlantic 1968–79, *d.* 20 August 2000, *b.* 12 September 1915

Conway, Russ, DSM, pianist, aged 75 – *d.* 16 November 2000, *b.* 2 September 1925

Countess of Ranfurly, Hermione, OBE, diarist, aged 87 – *d.* 11 February 2001, *b.* 13 November 1913

Cram, Donald, American chemist and joint winner of the Nobel Prize for Chemistry in 1987, aged 82 – *d.* 17 June 2001, *b.* 22 August 1919

Critchley, Sir Julian, author and Conservative MP for Rochester and Chatham 1959–64 and for Aldershot 1970–97, aged 69 – *d.* 9 September 2000, *b.* 8 December 1930

de Valois, Dame Ninette, OM, CH, DBE, founder-director of the Royal Ballet, aged 102 – *d.* 8 March 2001, *b.* 5 June 1898

Dearnley, Christopher, LVO, organist and director of music at St. Paul's Cathedral 1968–90, aged 70 – *d.* 15 December 2000, *b.* 11 February 1930

Denmark, Queen Ingrid of, Danish Queen Mother, aged 90 – *d.* 7 November 2000, *b.* 28 March 1910

Devi, Phoolan, Indian politician, aged 37 – *d.* Shot dead on 25 July 2001, *b.* 10 August 1963

Dewar, Donald, PC, First Minister of the Scottish Executive, Scottish Parliament 1999–00, aged 63 – *d.* 11 October 2000, *b.* 21 August 1937

Diamond, John, journalist and broadcaster, aged 47 – *d.* 2 March 2001, *b.* 10 May 1953

Duke of Sutherland (6th), John, TD, landowner and art collector, aged 85 – *d.* 21 September 2000, *b.* 10 May 1915

Dunham, Professor Sir Kingsley, FRS, geologist, aged 91 – *d.* 5 April 2001, *b.* 2nd January 1910

Edwards, Leslie, OBE, ballet dancer, aged 84 – *d.* 8 February 2001, *b.* 6 August 1916

Estenssoro, Victor Paz, President of Bolivia 1950s, 1960's and 1985, aged 93 – *d.* 7 June 2001, *b.* 2nd October 1907

Fletcher-Cooke, Sir Charles, Conservative MP for Darwen 1951–83; MEP 1977–79, aged 86 – *d.* 24 February 2001, *b.* 5 May 1914
Fock, Jeno, Prime Minister of Hungary 1967–75, aged 85 – *d.* 23 May 2001, *b.* 17 May 1916
Foster, Sir Richard, director of the National Museums and Galleries on Merseyside 1986–01, aged 59 – *d.* 8 March 2001, *b.* 3 October 1941
Francis, Mary, researcher and author, aged 76 – *d.* 30 September 2000, *b.* 17 June 1924
Fryd, Judy, CBE, founder of Mencap, aged 90 – *d.* 20 October 2000, *b.* 31 October 1909
Giedroyc, Jerzy, Polish publisher and editor, aged 94 – *d.* 14 September 2000, *b.* 27 July 1906
Gilmour, Dr Alan, CVO, CBE, director of the NSPCC 1979–89, aged 72 – *d.* 18 July 2001, *b.* 30 August 1928
Glasspole, Sir Florizel, GCMG, GCVO, Governor-General of Jamaica 1973–90, aged 91 – *d.* 25 November 2000, *b.* 25 September 1909
Gooding, Air Vice-Marshall Keith, CB, CBE, RAF Officer, aged 87 – *d.* 4 March 2001, *b.* 2 September 1913
Graham, Alastair, FRS, professor of Zoology, aged 94 – *d.* 12 December 2000, *b.* 6 November 1906
Green, The Revd Fred Pratt, MBE, Methodist minister, hymn writer and poet, aged 97 – *d.* 22 October 2000, *b.* 2 September 1903
Greenhill of Harrow, Lord, GCMG, OBE, Under Secretary of State, Foreign and Commonwealth Office and Head of the Diplomatic Service, 1969–73, aged 87 – *d.* 8 November 2000, *b.* 7 November 1913
Gross, Al, pioneer of mobile telecommunications, aged 82 – *d.* 21 December 2000, *b.* 22 February 1918
Grylls, Sir Michael, MP for Chertsey 1970–74; North West Surrey 1974–97 and free-marketer, aged 66 – *d.* 7 February 1934, *b.* 21 February 1934
Guiness, Lady, children's writer and artist, aged 86 – *d.* 18 October 2000, *b.* 16 October 1914
Hamilton, Liam, chief Justice of Ireland 1994–00, aged 81 – *d.* 29 November 2000, *b.* 30 December 1928
Hanley, Sir Michael, Director-General of M15 1972–78, aged 82 – *d.* 1 January 2001, *b.* 24 February 1918
Hanna, William, American animator, aged 90 – *d.* 22 March 2001, *b.* 14 July 1910
Harmar-Nicholls, Lord, Conservative MP for Peterborough 1950–74; Member of the European Parliament 1979–84, aged 87 – *d.* 15 September 2000, *b.* 1 November 1912
Harris of Greenwich, Lord (John Henry), Labour Home Office minister, aged 71 – *d.* 1 April 2001, *b.* 5 April 1930
Hartwell, Lord, MBE, TD, proprietor of The Daily Telegraph 1954–85, aged 89 – *d.* 2 April 2001, *b.* 18 May 1911
Hastings, Professor Adrian, FBA, theologian and historian, aged 71 – *d.* 30 May 2001, *b.* 23 June 1929
Hattersley, Enid, Lord Mayor of Sheffield 1981–82, aged 96 – *d.* 17 May 2001, *b.* 19 September 2001
Hayr, Air Marshal Sir Kenneth, CBE, CB, KCB, KBE, New Zealand born holder of the Kuwait Liberation Order (1st Grade), aged 66 – *d.* (accidentally) 3 June 2001, *b.* 13 April 1935
Hearst, Randolph A., newspaper mogul, aged 85 – *d.* 18 December 2000, *b.* 2 December 1915
Helou, Charles, President of Lebanon 1964–70, aged 88 – *d.* 7 January 2001, *b.* 25 December 1912
Hewlett, William, co-founder of Hewlett-Packard, aged 87 – *d.* 12 January 2001, *b.* 20 May 1913
Hickman, John, CMG, ambassador to Chile 1982–87 and author, aged 73 – *d.* 23rd February 2001, *b.* 3rd July 1927
Hinds, Harvey, Labour Party Chief Whip in the Greater London Council 1967–86, aged 80 – *d.* 1 September 2000, *b.* 29 August 1920
Hinton, Milt, jazz double bassist, aged 90 – *d.* 19 December 2000, *b.* 23 June 1910
Hoddinott, Sir John, CBE, police chief constable of Hampshire 1988–99, aged 56 – *d.* 13 August 2001, *b.* 21 September 1944
Holder, Sir Paul, DFC, DSO, CB, FRS, pilot, aged 89 – *d.* 22 April 2001, *b.* 2 September 1912
Hollan-Martin, Lady, DBE, DL, Chairman of NSPCC 1969–87, aged 86 – *d.* 18 June 2001, *b.* 26 June 1914
Hooker, John Lee, American blues guitarist, aged 83 – *d.* 21 June 2001, *b.* 22 August 1920
Hoyle, Sir Fred, FRS, astronomer and writer, aged 86 – *d.* 20 August 2001, *b.* 24 June 1915
Hughes, The Right Revd John, CBE, Suffragan Bishop of Croydon 1956–77, *d.* 21 July 2001, *b.* 12 April 1908
Ingstad, Helge, Scandinavian writer and explorer, aged 101 – *d.* 29 March 2001, *b.* 30 December 1899
Jacob, Sir Jack, QC, senior Master of the Supreme Court, Queen's Bench Division 1975–80, aged 92 – *d.* 26 December 2000, *b.* 5 June 1908
Jamieson, Major David, VC, Officer who gained the VC for defending the bridgehead over the River Orne whilst wounded, aged 80 – *d.* 5 May 2001, *b.* 1 October 1920
Jeffrey, Betty, OAM, Australian nursing sister and war hero, aged 92 – *d.* 13 September 2000, *b.* 14 May 1908
Jennens, David, oarsman, aged 71 – *d.* 27 September 2000, *b.* 4 April 1929
John Howe, The Right Revd, Bishop of St Andrews, Dunkeld and Dunblane1955; 1969–82 and Secretary General of the Anglican Consultative Council, aged 80 – *d.* 26 April 2001, *b.* 14 July 1920
Johnson, Air Vice-Marshal Johnnie, CB, CBE, DSO and two bars, DFC, fighter pilot, aged 85 – *d.* 30 January 2001, *b.* 9 March 1915
José, Queen Marie, Queen of Italy for 27 days in May 1946, aged 94 – *d.* 27 January 2001, *b.* 4 August 1906
Ju-Yung, Chung, founder of Hyundai, aged 85 – *d.* 21March 2001, *b.* 25 November 1915
Kabila, Laurent, President of the Democratic Republic of Congo 1997–01, aged 61 – *d.* (shot dead) 16 January 2001, *b.* 27 November 1939
Kaujau, Konrad, forger of the 'Hitler Diaries', aged 62 – *d.* 12 September 2000, *b.* 27 June 1938
Kenneally, John, VC, Lance Corporal Irish Guard, aged 79 – *d.* 27 September 2000, *b.* 15 March 1921
Kenward, Betty, KBE, society columnist, aged 94 – *d.* 24 January 2001, *b.* 14 July 1906
Kilburn, Prof Tom, CBE, FRS, pioneer of the computer, aged 79 – *d.* 17 January 2001, *b.* 11 August 1921
King Birendra of Nepal, Bir Bikram Shah, Himalayan Monarch 1972–01, aged 55 – *d.* (Shot dead) 1 June 2001, *b.* 28 December 1945
King Dipendra of Nepal, Bir Bikram Shah Dev, Himalyan Monarch for 2 days in June 2001, aged 29 – *d.* (gunshot wounds) 4 June 2001, *b.* 27 June 1971
Knapp, Jimmy, general secretary, National Union of Railwaymen 1983–90, aged 60 – *d.* 13 August 2001, *b.* 29 September 1940
Kohl, Hannelore, wife of former German Chancellor, aged 68 – *d.* (suicide) 5 July 2001, *b.* 7 March 1933
Korda, Alberto, Cuban photographer, aged 72 – *d.* 25 May 2001, *b.* 14 September 1928
Kramer, Stanley, American film producer and director, aged 87 – *d.* 19 February 2001, *b.* 29 September 1913
Lang, Lieutenant-General Sir Derek, KCB, DSO, MC, GOC-IN-C, Scottish Infantry man, aged 87 – *d.* 7 April 2001, *b.* 7 October 1913

Lasdun, Sir Denys, CH, CBE, architect, aged 86 – *d.* 11 January 2001, *b.* 8 September 1914
Lawton, Sir Frederick, Lord Justice of Appeal 1972–76, aged 89 – *d.* 3 February 2001, *b.* 21 December 1911
Lees-Spalding, Rear-Admiral Tim, naval engineer, aged 81 – *d.* 20 July 2001, *b.* 16 June 1920
Lemmon, Jack, American actor, aged 76 – *d.* 27 June 2001, *b.* 8 February 1925
Lincoln, Frances, publisher, aged 55 – *d.* 26 February 2001, *b.* 20 March 1945
Longlord, Lord, Lord Privy Seal and Leader of the House of Lords 1964–68 and campaigner, aged 95 – *d.* 3 August 2001, *b.* 5 December 1905
Lord Cledwyn of Penrhos, Hughes, Labour Leader in the House of Lords 1982–92, aged 84 – *d.* 22 February 2001, *b.* 14 September 1916
Lord Cocks of Hartcliffe, Michael, Labour Chief Whip 1976–85, aged 71 – *d.* 26 March 2001, *b.* 19 August 1929
Lord Mackay of Ardbrecknish, Deputy Leader of the Opposition in the Lords 1998–01; Under Secretary at the Scottish Office 1982–87, aged 62 – *d.* 21 February 2001, *b.* 15 November 1938
Lord Onslow of Woking, Cranley Gordon Douglas, KCMG, Chairman of The 1922 Committee 1984–92 and former MP for Woking 1961–64, aged 74 – *d.* 13 March 2001, *b.* 8 June 1926
Ludlum, Robert, author, aged 73 – *d.* 12 March 2001, *b.* 25 May 1927
Macdonald, Vice-Admiral Sir Roderick, KBE, Nato Chief of Staff 1976–79, and artist, aged 79 – *d.* 19 January 2001, *b.* 25 February 1921
Mackworth-Young, Sir Robin, GCVO, librarian of Windsor Castle 1958–85, aged 80 – *d.* 5 December 2000, *b.* 12 February 1920
MacNeish, Richard, archaeologist, aged 82 – *d.* 16 January 2001, *b.* 29 April 1918
Madden, Adm. Sir Charles, GCB, Commander-in-Chief Home Fleet 1963–65, aged 38 – *d.* 12 April 2001, *b.* 10 August 1962
McTaggart, David, Chairman of Greenpeace 1979–91, aged 68 – *d.* 23 March 2001, *b.* 24 June 1932
Melville, Sir Ronald, KCB, Permanent Secretary to the Ministry of Aviation 1963–66, aged 89 – *d.* 4 June 2001, *b.* 9 March 1912
Mendoza, Maurice, CVO, MSM, conservationist, aged 79 – *d.* 11 October 2000, *b.* 1 May 1921
Miller, Canon Paul, Canon of Derby 1966–81 and Chaplin to the Queen 1981–83, aged 82 – *d.* 18 October 2000, *b.* 8 October 1918
Ming, General Duong Van, President of South Vietnam in 1995 for three days, aged 85 – *d.* 6 August 2001, *b.* 16 February 1916
Molloy, Lord William John, Labour MP for Ealing North, aged 82 – *d.* 26 May 2001, *b.* 26 October 1918
Morley, Eric, impresario, aged 82 – *d.* 9 November 2000, *b.* 26 September 1918
Morpurgo, Professor Jack, professor of American Literature, University of Leeds 1969–83, and author, aged 82 – *d.* 2 October 2000, *b.* 26 April 1918
Morrison, John, CBE, FBA, classicist, first President of Wolfson College , Cambridge 1966–80, aged 87 – *d.* 25 October 2000, *b.* 15 June 1913
Narayan, R. K., FRSL, Indian Novelist, aged 94 – *d.* 13 May 2001, *b.* 10 October 1906
Nunburnholme, Lord, 5th Baron Nunburnholme, aged 65 – *d.* 20 November 2000, *b.* 27 May 1935
O'Connor, Air Vice-Marshall Patrick, OBE, CB, RAF medical officer, *d.* 3 May 2001, *b.* 21 August 1914
O'Connor, Sir Patrick, Lord Justice of Appeal 1980–89, aged 86 – *d.* 3 May 2001, *b.* 29 December 1914
Olsen, Gary, actor, aged 42 – *d.* 13 September 2000, *b.* 3 November 1957
Pahlavi, Princess Leila, daughter of the Late Shah of Iran, aged 31 – *d.* (Drug overdose) 10 June 2001, *b.* Born around 1970
Palmer, Charles, OBE, Chairman of the British Olympic Association 1983–88, aged 71 – *d.* 17 August 2001, *b.* 15 April 1930
Pamphilj, Princess Orietta Doria, British custodian of European art, aged 78 – *d.* 19 November 2000, *b.* 22 April 1922
Peyrefitte, Roger, French author, aged 93 – *d.* 6 November 2000, *b.* 17 August 1907
Phipps, The Right Revd Simon, MC, Bishop of Lincoln 1974–86, aged 79 – *d.* 29 January 2001, *b.* 6 July 1921
Plowden, Lady Bridget, DBE, chair of the Central Advisory Council for Education (England); chair of the IBA 1975–80, aged 90 – *d.* 29 September 2000, *b.* 5 May 1910
Plowden, Lord, GBE, KCB, economic adviser 1947–53, aged 94 – *d.* 15 February 2001, *b.* 6 January 1907
Pontin, Sir Frederick William, KT, founder of Pontin's Holiday Camps, aged 93 – *d.* 2 October 2000, *b.* 24 October 1906
Porteous, Colonel Patrick, VC, war hero of the Dieppe raid, aged 82 – *d.* 9 October 2000, *b.* 1 January 1918
Prebble, John, OBE, writer and historian, aged 85 – *d.* 30 January 2001, *b.* 23 June 1915
Professor Christain, Jack, FRS, International Metallurgist, aged 74 – *d.* 27 February 2001, *b.* 9 April 1926
Queen Aiswarya of Nepal, Himalayan monarch, aged 51 – *d.* (shot dead) 1 June 2001, *b.* 7 November 1949
Quinn, Anthony, hollywood actor, aged 86 – *d.* 3 June 2001, *b.* 21 April 1915
Rabin, Leah, peace campaigner, wife of the assassinated former Israeli Prime Minister Yitzhak Rabin, aged 72 – *d.* 12 November 2000, *b.* 8 April 1928
Railton, Dame Ruth, OBE, DBE, founder and artistic director of the National Youth Orchestra 1948–65, aged 85 – *d.* 23 February 2001, *b.* 14 December 1915
Rajya Laxmi Devi Rana, Queen Aiswarya of Nepal, Himalayan Monarch, aged 51 – *d.* (shot dead) 1 June 2001, *b.* 7 November 1949
Rapaport, Rosemary, founder of the Purcell School and violinist, aged 83 – *d.* 8 June 2001, *b.* 29 March 1918
Raphael, Sarah, painter, aged 40 – *d.* 10 January 2001, *b.* 10 August 1960
Rawson, Michael, athlete, aged 66 – *d.* 25 October 2000, *b.* 26 May 1934
Read, General Sir Anthony, GCB, CBE, DSO, MC, quartermaster-General of the Army 1969–72, aged 87 – *d.* 22 September 2000, *b.* 10 September 1913
Reilly, Tommy, MBE, harmonica player, aged 81 – *d.* 25 September 2000, *b.* 21 August 1919
Ridley, Sir Harold, FRS, ophthalmic surgeon, aged 94 – *d.* 25 May 2001, *b.* 10 July 1906
Robards, Jason, actor, aged 78 – *d.* 26 December 2000, *b.* 26 July 1922
Roberts, The Rt Revd Edward, Bishop of Ely 1964–77, aged 93 – *d.* 29 June 2001, *b.* 18 April 1908
Rogers, William, United States Secretary of State 1968–73, aged 87 – *d.* 2 January 2001, *b.* 23 June 1913
Ross, Alan, OBE, editor of the London Magazine 1975–2001, aged 78 – *d.* 14 February 2001, *b.* 6 May 1922
Rotherham, Professor Leonard, CBS, FRS, Rotherham, aged 87 – *d.* 23 March 2001, *b.* 31 August 1913
Runciman, Sir Steven, CH, FBA, historian, aged 97 – *d.* 1 November 2000, *b.* 7 July 1903
Sage, Lorna, literary critic and scholar, aged 57 – *d.* 11 January 2001, *b.* 13 January 1943

Sampson, Nicos, Cypriot Newspaper publisher and President of Cyprus for eight days in July 1974, aged 66 – *d.* 9 May 2001, *b.* 16 December 1934
Sanger, Ruth, FRS, scientist, aged 82 – *d.* 4 June 2001, *b.* 6 June 1918
Sann, Son, Prime Minister of Cambodia 1967–68, aged 89 – *d.* 19 December 2000, *b.* 15 October 1911
Scatchard, Vice-Admiral Jack, CB, DSC and two bars, Naval officer Second-in-command Far East Fleet 1962–64, aged 90 – *d.* 22 June 2001, *b.* 5 September 1910
Schindler, Rabbi Alexander, leader of the America's Jewish Reform movement for 22 years, aged 75 – *d.* 15 November 2000, *b.* 4 October 1925
Sealy, Thodore, OJ, CBE, Jamaican born Editor of the 'Gleaner' newspaper, aged 91 – *d.* 18 June 2001, *b.* 6 November 1909
Secombe, Sir Harry, comedian and singer, aged 79 – *d.* 11 April 2001, *b.* 8 September 1921
Shackleton, Len, Sunderland and England footballer, aged 78 – *d.* 28 November 2000, *b.* 22 May 1922
Shepard, Mary, artist and illustrator, aged 90 – *d.* 4 September 2000, *b.* 25 December 1909
Shepherd, Lord, PC and Former Leader of The House of Lords 1974–76, aged 82 – *d.* 5 April 2001, *b.* 27 September 1918
Sieff of Brimpton, Lord Marcus Joseph, OBE, Chairman of Marks & Spencer 1972–84, aged 87 – *d.* 23 February 2001, *b.* 2 July 1913
Simmons, Jack, OBE, historian, aged 85 – *d.* 3 September 2000, *b.* 30 August 1915
Sims, Joan, actress, aged 71 – *d.* 28 June 2001, *b.* 9 May 1930
Sithole, The Revd Ndabaningi, African nationalist leader 1963–78, aged 80 – *d.* 12 December 2000, *b.* 31 July 1920
Southern, Sir Richard, FBA, historian, aged 88 – *d.* 6 February 2001, *b.* 8 February 1912
Speeding, Sir David, KCMG, CVO, OBE, M16 Chief 1994–99, aged 58 – *d.* 13 June 2001, *b.* 7 March 1943
Stakis, Sir Reo, Greek -born founder of Stakis Hotel, aged 88 – *d.* 28 August 2001, *b.* 13 March 1913
Stern, William T., CBE, botanical authority, aged 90 – *d.* 16 April 1911, *b.* 9 May 2001
Storr, Anthony, psychiatrist, aged 80 – *d.* 17 March 2001, *b.* 18 May 1920
Synnot, Admiral Sir Anthony, Commander of Defence Force Staff 1979–82, aged 79 – *d.* 4 July 2001, *b.* 5 January 1922
Talbot, Godfrey, LVO, OBE, broadcaster, aged 91 – *d.* 3 September 2000, *b.* 8 October 1908
Taylor, The Right Revd John, Bishop of Winchester 1975–85, aged 86 – *d.* 30 January 2001, *b.* 11 September 1914
Terrington, Lord, OBE, DSO, Conservative MP for Oxford 1959–66 and 1970–74; Parliamentary Secretary in the Ministry of Aviation 1961–62; Joint Under-Secretary of State at the Home Office 1962–64, aged 83 – *d.* 13 February 2001, *b.* 11 May 1917
Temple, The Rt Revd Frederick, Suffragan Bishop of Malmesbury 1973–83, aged 84 – *d.* 26 November 2000, *b.* 24 November 1916
Therond (with an accent over 'e'), Roger, Editor of Paris - Match 1976–99, aged 76 – *d.* 23 June 2001, *b.* 24 October 1924
Titov, Gherman, cosmonaut, aged 65 – *d.* 20 September 2000, *b.* 11 September 1935
Tjupurrula, Johnny Warrangkula, Aboriginal Artist, aged (around) 76 – *d.* 11 February 2001, *b.* born around 1925
Tonbridge, Lord Cowdrey of, cricketer, aged 67 – *d.* 4 December 2000, *b.* 24 December 1932
Trewby, Vice-Admiral Sir Allan, naval engineer, aged 84 – *d.* 23 July 2001, *b.* 8 July 1917
Trudeau, Pierre, Prime Minister of Canada 1968–79 and 1980–84, aged 80 – *d.* 28 September 2000, *b.* 18 October 1919
Tuke, Sir Anthony, Chairman of Barclays Bank 1973–81, aged 80 – *d.* 6 March 2001, *b.* 22 August 1920
Tyson, Alan, CBE, FBA, musicologist and psychoanalyst, aged 74 – *d.* 10 November 2000, *b.* 27 October 1926
Vanden Boeynants, Paul, Prime Minister of Belgium 1966–68; 1978–79, aged 81 – *d.* 9 January 2001, *b.* 22 May 1919
Venables, Bernard, MBE, angler and writer, aged 94 – *d.* 21 April 2001, *b.* 14 February 1907
Wakefield, Rev Gordon, Methodist minister and scholar, aged 79 – *d.* 11 September 2000, *b.* 15 January 1921
Walker, David, astronaut who made four shuttle flights including the 'Atlantis', aged 56 – *d.* 23 April 2001, *b.* 20 May 1944
Walker, General Sir Walter, KCB, CBE, DSO and two bars, fighting General, aged 89 – *d.* 12 August 2001, *b.* 11 November 1911
Warsaw, Baroness Ryder of, CMG; OBE, social worker, aged 77 – *d.* 2 November 2000, *b.* 3 July 1923
Watson, Colin, obituaries Editor of The Times 1956–82, aged 81 – *d.* 6 January 2001, *b.* 15 May 1919
Waugh, Auberon, journalist, aged 61 – *d.* 16 January 2001, *b.* 17 November 1939
Weir, Jack, General Secretary of the Presbyterian Church in Ireland 1964–85, aged 81 – *d.* 18 September 2000, *b.* 24 March 1919
Welch, David, CBE, former Chief Executive of the Royal Parks, aged 66 – *d.* 18 September 2000, *b.* 13 December 1933
Wilcox, Desmond, broadcaster, aged 69 – *d.* 6 September 2000, *b.* 21 May 1931
Williams, Michael, actor, aged 65 – *d.* 11 January 2001, *b.* 9 July 1935
Willimer, Professor Neil, FRS, biologist and author, aged 98 – *d.* 8 April 2001, *b.* 15 August 1902
Winning, Cardinal Thomas, Catholic Archbishop of Glasgow 1974–2001, aged 76 – *d.* 17 June 2001, *b.* 3 June 1925
Winstone, Howard, MBE, boxer, aged 61 – *d.* 30 September 2000, *b.* 15 April 1939
Wise, Audrey, MP, labour MP for Coventry South West 1974–79; Preston 1987–2000, aged 65 – *d.* 2 September 2000, *b.* 4 January 1935
Woodfield, Sir Philip, KCB, CBE, permanent Secretary to the Northern Ireland Office 1981–83, aged 77 – *d.* 17 September 2000, *b.* 30 August 1923
Woods, Donald, CBE, South African Editor and author, aged 67 – *d.* 19 August 2001, *b.* 15 December
Wright, Fred, FRSA, amateur archaeologist, aged 83 – *d.* 18 May 2001, *b.* 21 June 1918
Yates, Paula, television presenter, aged 40 – *d.* 17 September 2000, *b.* 24 April 1960
Young, Gavin, foreign correspondent and author, aged 72 – *d.* 18 January 2001, *b.* 24 April 1928
Ystradfellte, Baroness Brooke of, DBE, joint vice-chairman of the Conservative Party 1954–64; chairman of the Godolphin and Latymer School 1960–78, aged 92 – *d.* 1 September 2000, *b.* 14 January 1908

# Archaeology

## Stonehenge

Stonehenge, perhaps the most easily visualised of all British prehistoric sites, is rarely out of the news. One of the first scheduled Ancient Monuments in the 19th century and an early designation as a World Heritage Site in the 20th, Stonehenge continues to attract attention, although not so much recently for any excavation work undertaken at the site but rather for the considerable public interest in improving its interpretation. The term 'national disgrace' has been applied to the setting of the stones on more than one occasion over the last half-century and to do something about this state of affairs was the challenge facing English Heritage when it was set up in 1984. Various schemes had been proposed, but in 1998 English Heritage, the National Trust and the Highways Agency, with the support of the relevant local authorities, published a master plan. Reviewing recent progress Giles Worsley writes in *The Daily Telegraph* for Saturday 14 July 2001 'within the last three years key steps have been taken. The Highways Agency has announced that it wishes to sink the A303 in a tunnel as it passed Stonehenge and to close the other road, the A344. English Heritage has bought a 70-acre site outside the World Heritage Site at Countess East on the edge of Amesbury, two miles to the east of the stones, where it plans to build a new visitor centre. And agreement has been reached in principle about the way the stones should be presented, no longer as a quick half-hour stop for bus parties, but as a half day in a remarkable Stone Age landscape, littered with nearby barrows and other historic remains as well as Stonehenge'.

Further, it was reported in the media in April 2001 that architects had been appointed to design a new visitor centre which would be some two miles from the stones themselves. The firm chosen is Denton Corker Marshall of Melbourne, Australia, which is known for its office towers in Sydney as well as the Melbourne Museum. This Australian architectural practice with a strong background in planning has already been short-listed for a number of other commissions in the UK. No plans are yet available but Barrie Marshall, one of the three partners, is quoted as saying that: 'The building will be subtle, low key, more about earth and sky than a building which stands up and says 'look at me, aren't I clever', it's incredibly important to us that the building doesn't even with a hint take away anything of the impact of Stonehenge'. Giles Worsley's final comment is instructive: 'It is easy to be cynical about Stonehenge. The English ability to sort out the monument seems to be on a par with their ability to win Wimbledon. There are still real issues to be resolved. The question of how visitors will get from the new building to the stones remains controversial and everything depends on persuading the Heritage Lottery Fund to underwrite the work. But English Heritage has made an interesting choice in Denton Corker Marshall who might, just might, pull it off this time'.

## The Hyena Den

A very good example of how the unexpected still surprises archaeologists is the excavation carried out at the village of Glaston, some two miles east of Uppingham in Rutland. Farmland, which was to be sold for re-development, was investigated because an adjacent sand quarry had already revealed Bronze Age cremations as well as the remains of a large Anglo-Saxon cemetery. The surprise, however, was the discovery of Palaeolithic remains which indicated a major open-air site of that period, some 40,000 years ago. The report in *Current Archaeology* (April 2001) is enlightening, but two aspects of the site may be noted in particular. The first was the discovery of a flint blade identified as a 'leaf-point', a type better known from continental sites. As the report in *Current Archaeology* continues: 'Of course, the presence of the leaf-point need not indicate the presence of people it may have arrived in the soft tissue of an animal. We do however have further evidence that people made use of the site, perhaps only for a few hours, but they were certainly there. Fairly near to the spot where the leaf-point was discovered lay a flint core. This piece had by no means reached the end of its productive life and was of sufficient size to have been capable of producing more blade blanks. Indeed it appears that one of the last episodes of working on the core was the careful preparation of the core platform as a precursor to further removals. For some unknown reason however, this work was never completed. Excavation in the immediate area of the core (between several large rafts) revealed a concentration of large waste flakes one of which could quite conceivably have been a 'blank' for another leaf-point and a dense scatter of tiny flint chips and spalls. So in one small, well located area of the site we have the remains of almost every stage in the flint reduction process clear evidence of the presence of people'.

The second aspect of the site of general interest was the discovery of a spotted hyena den, the first in Britain to be clearly an open-air site. 'The remains of hyena feasting littered the area and gnawed bones chiefly of woolly rhinoceros but also woolly mammoth, reindeer, wolverine and arctic hare were recovered. This den was 'centred on a cluster of large limestone rocks. Around and within the nooks and crannies created by the rocks, a mass of woolly rhinoceros bones was discovered, many with distinctive pitmarks indicating gnawing. Some had apparently been deliberately pushed beneath the lip of one of the rocks, perhaps stored for a later meal. Several fossilised hyena droppings were also found amongst the bones. Analysis of them may shed light on the contemporary environment should they contain traces of pollen'.

## Re-dated Boats

The three boats found at Ferriby in East Yorkshire by Ted Wright in 1937, 1940 and 1963 are all justifiably famous. An exhibition at Hull and East Riding Museum mounted for National Science Week in March 2001 and associated media coverage drew attention to the fact that refinements in archaeological dating techniques have suggested that the 1963 plank boat could claim to be the oldest in Western Europe. One of the justifications for retaining objects in museums is that they are available for further study, long after their date of discovery, as scientific techniques improve. It is reported that the boat discovered in 1963 dates to about 2030BC–1780BC with the most likely date being 1900BC, with the other boats being several hundred years later. The facts that the 52 foot long boat was made from oak planks sewn together with yew branches, had room for 18 oarsmen and perhaps a mast suggested that it could possibly have sailed to and from the Continent allowing it to be dubbed, perhaps inevitably, 'Britain's oldest cross-Channel ferry'.

## Silbury Hill

Silbury Hill, a 130-foot-high earthen mound built between 2080 and 2000 BC for an unknown, but perhaps ritual purpose, is one of the most distinctive monuments in the prehistoric complex at Avebury in Wiltshire.

Classed in the 20th century as a World Heritage Site, because of its prominence, Silbury Hill attracted investigators over recent centuries and in particular shafts were dug into the colossal mound in 1849, 1867, 1886 and 1968. But an earlier mine shaft dug by the Duke of Northumberland in 1776 led to the partial collapse of the top of Silbury Hill prompting investigations by English Heritage, using a seismic scan so it was reported in May 2001, to discover the extent of the instability of the Hill caused by all these previous probes. Not only is the purpose of Silbury Hill unknown, but also there has been a long-standing debate as to whether there are tunnels or burial chambers within the mound; the seismic survey by English Heritage could perhaps resolve some of these problems as well as giving vital information to secure the future well-being of this most prominent of ancient monuments.

## Iron Age Gold

Media interest was aroused in March 2001 by an inquest under the 1996 Treasure Act into the discovery of two Iron Age solid gold torcs or necklaces which had been found and declared under the Portable Antiquities Scheme by Kevin Halls, a metal detectorist, in the vicinity of Winchester. A report in *Minerva* (May/June 2001) reports that: 'The two torcs (neckrings), four brooches, and two bracelets recovered by a metal detectorist are the most important group of finds of their kind to come to light in over a decade. Both sets of jewellery, weighing a total of one kilogram of gold, were deposited between 60 and 20BC, which was a time of profound upheaval in Britain, coinciding with Julius Caesar's invasion in 55 and 54BC and the country's transformation from an Iron Age to a Roman culture. The torcs have attracted particular interest because they are stylistically unique, combining Roman and Greek metalworking techniques (inter-linked gold wire) with British artistic concepts. They undoubtedly belonged to two aristocratic Iron Age individuals and were highly prestigious status symbols'. The find spot was recorded and excavated but, it is reported by Sean Kingsley in *Minerva* that: 'since no archaeological structure, burial, or even any other artefacts were uncovered, J. D. Hill of the British Museum, an expert on Iron Age Britain, has concluded that the Winchester Hoard was probably a lavish religious 'gift to the gods' offered by two important Britons, perhaps even a king and queen'.

Celtic gold continued to attract attention in the media with the sale in London on 25 April 2001 of a six inch long gold clasp dating from the 3rd century BC. This fibula depicted a young warrior surrounded by fierce animals and usage suggests that it had been worn regularly by its presumably aristocratic owner. The recent history of the piece can be traced from a titled family in Europe in the 19th century, to America in the years after 1945 and thence to the British Museum where it has been on display since 1993. This exquisite piece sold at auction for £1,103,750 in London on 25 April 2001 and was acquired by the British Museum.

## A Carnyx

A Carnyx was a vertical trumpet much used in the ancient world, not least by the Celtic people when defying the Romans as when Claudius invaded Britain in 43AD. From the remains of the Deskford Carnyx found in North Eastern Scotland in about 1816, and from five other surviving fragments plus depictions in Roman sculpture and on coins, Fraser Hunter, an archaeologist of the National Museum of Scotland, was, with colleagues, able to reconstruct the instrument for a demonstration to the British Association in September 2000. The Carnyx was designed to look like a wild boar with its snout upturned and the skin-folds and ears reflected in the metal. John Kenny, who was described as the only person knowing how to play the Carnyx, described it as a 'primordial brass instrument'.

## Chariot Burials

The inhumation of presumed aristocrats with their chariots in the middle Iron Age is a burial rite in Britain substantially restricted to East Yorkshire, although there are strong links with the Celts in Gaul, especially the Parisi who gave their name to Paris, where chariot burials are also found.

The latest discovery is at the well-known site of Wetwang in East Yorkshire during excavations sponsored by English Heritage, in the course of which an Iron Age woman was found buried alongside her chariot; the latter was sufficiently highly decorated as to include coral from the Mediterranean area. David Miles, the chief archaeologist for English Heritage, is reported as saying that: 'It may be the earliest chariot burial so far and could help us solve the mystery of who these people were and why they buried their dead in a way that was different from other Iron Age Britons'. The buried woman was clearly a person of some significance, an aristocrat or probably a queen, as women in Iron Age societies are known to have exercised power in their own right.

Archaeology is full of surprises and, given that chariot burials tend to be restricted to Yorkshire with continental parallels, an Iron Age chariot found buried in Edinburgh was quite unexpected. The discovery is reported in *Minerva* (July/August 2001) by Geoffrey Borwick; the note states that: 'An Iron Age chariot found during industrial development in Edinburgh is unique in Scotland and rare by any standards. Only a few metres away is evidence of several burial mounds, completely truncated, although their surrounding ring ditches remain. They indicate the remains of a Neolithic, Bronze Age, or perhaps Iron Age cemetery of which the chariot grave was probably a part. In a very fragile condition with only the metal part surviving the remains were removed complete with the original soil for what will be a detailed and time-consuming examination in the conservation laboratory. Provisionally a 3rd century BC date has been ascribed to the chariot'.

## Gladiator

The popular success in the cinema of the film *Gladiator* and the Special Exhibition at the British Museum entitled *Gladiators and Caesars: The Power of Spectacle in Ancient Rome* signalled a revival of interest in Roman popular entertainment, not least the bloody spectacles in the Colosseum in Rome and other amphitheatres throughout the Empire including that in London. From artistic depictions it has been known that women as well as men fought in the arena, although it is less clear whether these were serious contests or a form of light entertainment. A television programme gave prominence to archaeological discoveries in London which suggested that the remains of a female gladiator may have been excavated; if that is the correct deduction from the burial group, then it is a rare discovery indeed.

The excavation itself has been written up and published by the Museum of London Archaeology Service as *A Romano-British Cemetery on Watling Street: Excavations at 165 Great Dover Street, Southwark, London* by Anthony Mackinder in the Molas Archaeology Studies Series 4 published in 2000. The report relates to excavations carried out in 1996 and 1997 in Southwark which 'uncovered important new evidence of burials and structures associated with a Roman roadside cemetery to the south-east of the settlement'. Of the 25 inhumation and five cremation burials from the site, one cremation burial in particular caught the imagination of the wider public. This consisted of 'the cremated remains of a female with at least nine pottery tazze, eight pottery lamps and an exceptional array of plant remains, many imported from the Mediterranean, including stone pine, white almond and the first occurrence in London of date fruit. Images on the lamps included Anubis and a gladiator'. As Angela Wardle writes in the report: 'The cremated remains are those of a woman and one should consider the possibility that she was a gladiator, a practice which may have been more common than is generally realised. Clearly an interpretation of the cremation burial as that of a female gladiator can only be speculative and may indeed be too simplistic, but it is certainly possible. An alternative, and perhaps more acceptable interpretation, is that the lamp symbolises funeral games, the origin of gladiatorial combat in Republic times'.

## A Roman POW Camp

Near Hexham in Northumberland are the remains of the Roman fort of Vindolanda which lies about a mile to the south of Hadrian's Wall, pre-dating the latter by about 20-30 years. Occupied throughout the entire period of Roman domination the fort has yielded many important discoveries and the media reported on the excavation of some 13 stone huts with a diameter of about six feet and arranged back-to-back in rows of five, with the suggestion that there could have been some 300 of these huts within the walls of the fort. Patricia Birley, the Deputy Director of the Vindolanda Trust is reported as stating that while unlikely to have been used by Roman soldiers, 'It is possible that they were for hostages, although they could have been used for people who were friendly to the occupation, but who were under threat and so might have had temporary shelter'. It is further suggested that the huts could be related to the uprising near Edinburgh which took place between 209 and 211AD when hostages were taken.

## Roman Gold Coins

In the course of an archaeological excavation in 2000 at Plantation Place near Fenchurch Street by the Museum of London Archaeology Service, a hoard of gold coins was found; this is the first from Roman London with only four other Roman gold coin hoards of comparable date being known from Britain. Jenny Hall, Roman Curator at the Museum of London, describes the hoard in *Minerva* (March/April 2001) noting that: 'The coins were discovered by an archaeologist from the Museum of London Archaeology Service within an area where the remains of a large Roman stone building had been recorded. Large amounts of richly decorated wall plaster, mosaic *tesserae*, and fragments of tessellated floor indicated that the building was of high status and may have been residential. The coins were found adjacent to the remains of one of the walls. The close distribution of the coins implies that they were probably held together in some kind of a textile purse or bag; some staining in the soil also suggested that they had been held in a wooden container. This had been placed in the corner of a stone-lined area, possibly a deposit box, underneath the floor of one of the rooms. The 43 gold coins span a period of 109 years. The earliest were issued under the Emperor Nero in AD65-66 and the latest, an *aureus* of the Emperor Marcus Aurelius, dates to AD174. The hoard consists solely of gold coins, which were not intended for everyday circulation but would have been used as bullion by administrators, bankers, or rich merchants'. This very important coin hoard has now passed into the collections of the Museum of London.

## The Stanchester Hoard

In *Minerva* (May/June 2001) Paul Robinson, Curator of the Wiltshire Heritage Museum in Devizes, describes the Stanchester Hoard found by a 14-year old schoolboy from Marlborough. 'The hoard comprises altogether 1196 gold, silver, and copper coins, with a fragmentary base-metal fingering. It was concealed in a dull grey-ware pot manufactured at the Alice Holt kiln factory near Farnham in Surrey a pottery kiln which provided much of the common domestic pottery in use in southern Britain in the later years of the Roman period in Britain'. After describing the coins Dr Robinson notes that 'The latest coins present were imported into Britain either in, or after 406, making this the latest dated hoard to have been discovered so far in Wiltshire. None of the *siliquae* have been clipped; that pernicious late Roman practice which can infuriate present-day collectors. Clipping was often carried out in order to make the coins conform in weight with later coins struck at a lower weight. This suggests that such clipping in Britain took place after 406'.

The association of the hoard with the nearby Roman villa at Stanchester is seen to be of particular significance, not least because 'chester', derived from the Latin *castra* meaning military camp was given by the Saxons to former Roman sites to which they accorded a particular significance. 'Dr Margaret Gelling, who is the leading place-name specialist in England, has suggested that the Saxons may have done this when a villa also had a regional administrative role either at the end of the Roman period, or in the obscure years that followed the departure of the Romans until all Britain finally became subject to the Saxons. Stanchester lies a short distance south of the earthwork known today as Wansdyke (Woden's Ditch). Was the villa perhaps the base from which this 12-mile-long defence system was administered and policed in the Dark Ages? The new hoard helps to confirm the villa's importance at this time for its late date suggests it may have been concealed after Britain ceased to be part of the Roman empire'.

## Floral Street Brooch

In the *London Archaeologist* (Spring 2001) is a note that the excavation of 'the first Saxon cemetery in central London, at Floral Street next to the Royal Opera House, led to the discovery of a rare 7th-century Saxon brooch, the first of its kind to be found in London. It is intricately worked with panels of gold, and set with garnets forming a geometric pattern around a central boss, indicating its owner was of great wealth and importance'. John Clark, Curator of

Medieval Collections at the Museum of London, is reported in the press as suggesting that it belonged to a noblewoman or a princess adding 'The style was very fashionable among aristocratic ladies in Kent in the seventh century'. Not only is this brooch the first of its kind to be found in London but also one of only 18 in Britain as a whole.

### SYPHILIS

A recurrent debate amongst historians of disease is whether or not Christopher Columbus returned to Europe from the New World bringing syphilis with him. Evidence suggesting that he did not and that the disease existed in Europe already is reported from research carried out at English Heritage's Ancient Monuments Laboratory on a girl's skeleton from Rivenhall churchyard in Essex dating to between 1295 and 1445. Pitting of the bones, which is a sign of syphilis, is present on these remains which pre-date Columbus's voyage of 1492. In press reports Dr Simon Mays, who led the research team, is quoted as saying: 'It seems that syphilis or a related disease was present in Europe before Columbus returned from America'.

### LIMEHOUSE

Excavations during 2000 at the site of 43-53 Narrow Street, Limehouse in London's East End are reported by Gary Brown in *Minerva* (May/June 2001). After dealing with the evidence for the earliest occupation of the site attention is drawn to the post-medieval period. 'The earliest buildings at the site date to the late 16th century, and there were continual modifications throughout the succeeding century; indeed, property boundaries established in the 16th century appear to have been retained virtually intact until commercial redevelopment of the area in the 19th century. In the 17th century the buildings increased in number and quality and almost certainly represent merchant and seafarers' housing, workshops, and stores. To the rear of the properties were the usual lined and unlined cess and rubbish pits, and it is from these that an exceptional range of artefacts were recovered'. The explanation given relates to the political situation of the time with Protestant England engaging in trade and conflict across the world. 'Some of Narrow Street's inhabitants are known to have been sailors and privateers. For example, Christopher Newport was the Master's 'mate' on the *Drake* in 1587 and lost an arm in an attempt to capture two Mexican ships off Cuba in 1590. Other privateers or pirates who are known to have lived in the area include William Bushell, Michael Geare, and Captain Paramour. It is significant that much of the more unusual ceramics recovered from the excavations originated from countries, and by extension their colonies, that England was at war with (or in regular conflict with) at the time. The imported part of the assemblage is composed for the most part of material from Spain and North Italy, but of types made for the domestic rather than the export market and rarely found outside Spain or its colonies. Other *exotica* included Mexican coins, and ceramics from the Far East, Turkey, and Persia. The significance of the latter lies in the fact that at this time Turkey was a waning power in the Mediterranean and that Morocco, Algiers, Tunis, and Tripoli became established havens for pirates. The relative wealth of the inhabitants was also demonstrated by material collected from parts of Europe that the English were not in conflict with, such as Portugal and Germany, as well as from various locations in England'.

### 18TH CENTURY DISSECTIONS

The act of 1752 which permitted surgeons to dissect publicly the corpses of murderers was the background behind an unusual excavation in Oxford. It was reported in the media that in the grounds of the Museum of the History of Science in Oxford more than 2,000 bones were discovered during excavations by Thames Valley Archaeological Services. Graham Hull, the Director of the excavation, is reported as remarking that many of the bones had been sawed and there was also evidence of chemical experiments from the large number of chemical vessels recovered. From University records it was clear that the pit in which the bones were found was excavated when the University Anatomy Department moved in 1767. The fact that the excavation recovered remains of children as well suggests that body-snatchers could have been another source as well as executed criminals.

### THE SILVER TROWEL AWARD

As in many other areas of modern life, so in archaeology there are awards for excellence. The biennial British Archaeological Awards were founded in 1976 and now, in the words of *Current Archaeology* (April 2001) 'have grown till they encompass 12 awards covering every aspect of British archaeology. The aim of the Awards is to reward good practice in British archaeology, to acknowledge the help received from non-archaeologists and to raise the profile of archaeology'. Of particular interest in the 2000 awards was the fact that the highest prize, the Silver Trowel, sponsored by Spear & Jackson, was awarded to the Portable Antiquities Scheme, which had already won the Virgin Holidays Award for presenting projects to the public. To quote from the *Current Archaeology* report: 'The winner was the Portable Antiquities Scheme, established to promote the voluntary recording of archaeological finds by members of the public. This had its origins in the Treasure Act 1996, and is funded by the Department for Culture, Media & Sport, the British Museum, the Heritage Lottery Fund and many local partners. After the initial pilot, the scheme was expanded to cover over half of England and the whole of Wales. The results of the first 2 years of the scheme are impressive: 13,500 archaeological objects recorded in its first year and over 20,000 in its second year demonstrating that a voluntary approach can be successful. Direct and personal contact with the general public has been undertaken by the Finds Liaison Officers. They talked to metal detecting clubs and local archaeological societies, hold finds identification days, organise museum displays of recent finds made by members of the public, as well as day schools and other events. National and regional newsletters attractively highlight successful practice through case studies. There is also a popular website at www.finds.org.uk'.

Useful background information to the Portable Antiquities Scheme is to be found in an article by Dr Richard Hobbs in *mda information* (July 2001). Dr Hobbs explains why 'The Portable Antiquities Scheme was introduced at the end of 1997 as a complement to the Treasure Act which became law in 1996'. The latter greatly improved the old law of Treasure Trove in that it allowed objects associated with treasure to be included in the group under consideration and also removed the necessity of trying to decide at a coroner's inquest as to what had been the intention of the person burying the items in the first place. However, as Dr Hobbs explains, 'the Act does not apply to the vast majority of archaeological objects found in England and Wales which are not composed of gold and silver, for instance Bronze Age axes, and, for this reason, the government initiated a series of pilot schemes to record these finds. The underlying motivation however to this initiative was to address the large scale and highly politicised issue of metal detecting'. While metal detector enthusiasts were finding items of potential archaeological interest 'prior to the scheme it did not fall within anyone's remit to actually provide a means by which this material could be assessed. The voluntary scheme provides a means by which this material can be recorded, without relying on the goodwill of over-stretched museum staff and other individuals working within the heritage sector'.

## The Valetta Convention

In March 2001 the British Government signed the Valetta Convention of 1992 which was an update of the European Convention on the Protection of the Archaeological Heritage (the London Convention) of 1969. While many welcome the action of the British Government as a further step in protecting the archaeological heritage and support is offered by bodies such as English Heritage and the Institute of Field Archaeologists, others have expressed a note of caution. *Current Archaeology* (June 2001) sets out the issues and sounds a warning note under the heading of 'Government to Outlaw the Amateurs?' The problem is seen to lie in Article 3 of the Convention which 'requires states party to the revised Convention to establish a system regulating the conduct of archaeological activities, whether on public or private land. World-wide it is common for states to require a person intending to engage in such activities to obtain a permit' The explanatory notes continue that Article 3 'requires destructive techniques to be carried out only by qualified, specially authorised persons. This does not mean to say that members of the general public cannot be engaged on excavation, but it means they must be under the control of a qualified person who is responsible for the excavation'. It is reported that the Council for Independent Archaeology has launched a campaign to stop Article 3 and in this it is fully supported by the editors of *Current Archaeology* who write 'Article 3 of the Valetta Convention will stifle the independent. You cannot claim to back the amateur and at the same time call for bans on 'unauthorised' work. You have to choose one or the other: freedom or control'. The amateur tradition in British archaeology is a long and honourable one and many would regret its demise, if that were to be the effect of the Valetta Convention when interpreted into British law.

# Architecture

NEW PARLIAMENTARY BUILDING
Westminster, London
*Architect*: Michael Hopkins & Partners

There can be few development sites in the world of such sensitivity as that upon which Portcullis House, the new parliamentary building for 210 Members of Parliament and their staff, has recently been completed. Overlooking the embankment of the Thames between the brick and stone Arts and Crafts architecture of Norman Shaw's New Scotland Yard and the towering gothic icon of Big Ben, this stretch of London's riverside is one of the most familiar set pieces in western architecture and a daunting challenge for any designer. It is no surprise then that the new building has not been completed without causing a degree of controversy in a number of camps, for it is a robust and challenging essay in contemporary design whose appearance is in many ways determined by the logistics of the brief and the context and the environmental regime adopted in its implementation.

The building fills a complete rectangular city block, and a consistent architectural vocabulary has been developed for all four external elevations as well as the substantial inner courtyard, derived directly from structural and servicing systems. This is manifested most evidently in the dark, stubby and brooding chimneys which punctuate the roofline and gather to their bases the spreading finger-like ducts articulating the panelled bronze roof structure. The chimneys provide an overarching rhythm to the otherwise repetitive composition, simplifying the building's mass into a simply understood 4 bays by 5 bays rectangle.

The plan is simplicity itself - a courtyard format with surrounding wings of cellular offices, inner and outer, with a central circulation spine and vertical circulation, lifts and stairs, at the four corners. The offices, each MP has an individually allocated room, are typically arranged in pairs with a shared staff room in between, all three spaces accessible from the central corridor. The MPs' offices each have a projecting bay window incorporating a bench seat, a feature which allows the occupants to enjoy their superlative views over the neighbouring streets and buildings, and which lends a characteristic articulation to the facades, alternating with the plain glazed openings of the staff accommodation. The MPs' offices are arranged on four principal floors, while some lucky members occupy occasional suites, squeezed in between the roof plant rooms in an attic storey, with views both to the inner courtyard and out over Westminster and the river, accessed by their own private stairways off the central corridor. The first floor accommodates the major meeting rooms for conferences, functions, select committee meetings and similar activities, while at the principal 'ground' level the main entrance and security control gives access to the central courtyard and surrounding it, a library, a restaurant, a self-service café and central kitchen.

The simplicity of the plan, however, belies the complexity of the structural and services framework of the building. The structural system derives its form from influences that emanate from far under ground, where the complexities of the multi-level underground station and the crisscrossing Circle, District and Jubilee lines, (Westminster - *see* Almanack 2000), constrain the internal points of support to just six massive columns, set within the perimeter box of retaining walls. The weight of the entire building is therefore resolved into the inner and outer walls. The loads on the outer perimeter walls are taken down via stone columns expressed on the elevation, the blocks of Derbyshire gritstone increasing in width with each progressive storey to express the accumulating load pattern. The external columns form a sheltered arcade at ground floor on the Bridge Street and Embankment facades and their loads are then transferred directly to the perimeter box beneath. The internal columns are organised in a similar fashion at the upper levels, but within the first floor storey height are gathered onto six enormous prefabricated arches that transmit the loads onto the six columns rising from below. Spanning some 23 metres, these arches form the dominant elements of the enclosed internal courtyard which rises through three storeys and is covered by a dramatic glass roof. Internal and external columns support a series of wave-form prefabricated white concrete floor slabs giving a clear span of 13.2 metres across the building, the curving soffits expressed within the individual offices and highlighted by concealed uplighting.

The severe structural constraints generated other ingenious solutions. For example four enormous steel transfer structures located at the external corners provide the means of support for much of the roof and for the vertical circulation cores. At each corner a pair of lifts and an enveloping staircase is suspended from the high level transfer beams by means of high tensile steel rods running the height of the building.

The stone piers of the external elevations define the cellular module of the internal office planning, and enclose aluminium bronze framed windows and spandrel panels, with the alternating projecting oriel windows also framed in aluminium bronze and capped by projecting fixed horizontal prismatic louvres. These shade the windows from the sun and also reflect light up onto the curved soffits of the precast concrete vaults to the offices. Each stone column is also embraced by a pair of aluminium bronze air handling ducts rising on each side to the eaves/cornice line and connecting directly to the angled roof ducts which meet in the air handling chimneys at ridge level. Each pair of ducts delivers a fresh air supply to the raised floor plenums and exhausts stale air taken at high level over the oriel windows of the offices. Groups of ducts are gathered together and connected to a complex arrangement of mechanical plant in the roof level plant rooms which filter and condition the fresh air intake and dispell stale exhaust gases after passing them through a heat exchange mechanism. The faceted louvred bases to the flues provide a point of fresh air intake while the chimneys themselves exhaust stale air through the open cowls at the top.

The entire roofscape including the chimneys features the same dark bronze cladding material used for the window panels and there is the strong influence of industrial aesthetics evident in what is a muscular, authoritative and almost sinister composition. There is no doubt that the new building more than stands its ground in the face of its illustrious neighbours, and it is to be hoped that the very evident attention to quality of materials and detailing and the originality and integrity of the design will endear it to the citizenry as time passes and overcome the initial controversy about its unconventional appearance. MPs can surely have few causes for complaint about the standard of accommodation, putting aside matters of cost, and can quietly enjoy one of the most stunning interior spaces in the capital as they arrive through the entrance foyer facing Embankment or emerge from the tunnel underneath Bridge Street linking directly with the Houses of Parliament.

At the heart of the building is the great courtyard, a formal landscaped space with groves of fig trees emerging from formal planted beds either side of a central water feature in the form of low stone rimmed 'tables' of shimmering water, the whole composition capped by a stunning clear glazed roof that gives superb views up into the space defined by the walls of the office wings and their dominating chimneys. The roof structure is an arching lattice of flitched American oak beams connected by stainless steel node castings, from which stainless steel tension rods emanate to form a secondary opposing lattice supporting the panels of clear glass on patch fittings at their corners. Around the perimeter of the vault the lines of force are resolved into tapering angled struts which fan out from the sculpted capitals which form the springing point for the six arches supporting the internal building structure atop the massive columns projecting from below.

The entire architecture of this superb building is predicated on the exploitation of the potential of structure and services as the driving force behind the aesthetic realisation and the design benefits greatly from the resulting sense of purpose and seeming inevitability. Designed to last 200 years, quality oozes from every surface and the building certainly has the grand air of dignified calm befitting a major public building. As time passes it will no doubt be viewed as money well spent and will be held up as an exemplar for buildings of its type.

## THE EDEN PROJECT

St Austell, Cornwall
*Architect:* Nicholas Grimshaw & Partners

The Eden Project is one of the most remarkable and memorable products of the Millennium Commission's sponsorship of building projects. Within months of its full opening in March 2001 it has imprinted itself on the public consciousness like few other buildings of the recent past. Its initial success, despite Cornwall's isolation from much of mainland Britain, stems from the combination of a broad educational and research agenda, exploring global biodiversity and humanity's close relationship with and dependence on plants, and a spectacular setting, which provides a rewarding experience for the general public.

Set in what was originally the almost lunar-like landscape of a worked out china clay pit near St Austell, its two primary elements quite literally bubble up from the floor of the quarry, hugging the rugged contours and steep sides of the former workings, which are now being softened by new terracing and planting. Like giant accretions of monster soap bubbles, the two climate controlled greenhouses, or 'biomes', each provide differing internal environments, one recreating the rainforest of the humid tropics, the other the warm temperate climate of the Mediterranean region.

Each of the biomes is constructed in four segments, each segment comprising part of the surface of a sphere whose radial point coincides with the notional circumference of the adjacent sphere. Each segment differs in radius from the next, creating larger and smaller 'bubbles'. The structure of the biomes is generated by a three dimensional space frame in which an outer layer, an icosahedral geodesic skin of hexagonal frames like a curving honeycomb pattern is braced by an inner layer of slender tubular sections forming a pattern of hexagons, pentagons and triangles. The geometry of inner and outer skins is directly related and the skins are separated and linked by circular hollow sections located at the nodes of the hexagons and pentagons. The hexagonal panes of the outer skin are infilled with inflated 'pillows' of translucent ETFE (ethyltetrafluoroethylene) foil, a very lightweight material which is highly transparent to a broad spectrum of natural daylight, particularly ultraviolet light, thus rendering it ideal for a conservatory application where lightness and transparency of structure as well as cladding is most important. The foil is triple layered within each hexagonal frame and thus acts to retain much of the heat generated by solar energy. The panes vary considerably in size, the largest being nearly 11 metres across with a surface area of 75 square metres, and the largest dome has a radius of 65 metres, thus enclosing an enormous volume. The larger of the biomes is 240 metres long, 55 metres high and 110 metres wide covering an area of approximately 1.5 hectares. Despite their large size, the panes are incredibly light, (the material itself has 1 per cent of the weight of glass), and this has permitted considerable savings in the overall weight of the structure compared with a glass based solution.

The location of the biomes within the quarry was largely determined by the desire to embrace the quarry walls and terraces within the internal landscapes and by computer modelling of potential building forms against site topography and sun path criteria. Thus the tropics biome was placed against the north face of the pit to maximise sunlight and solar heat gain, the temperate biome curving away to the south east. As the pit was still being worked during the early design stages this presented the engineers with a difficult design problem, as the structure was being defined in advance of a final survey of the worked out quarry. However one of the major advantages of the modular geodesic structure is that it can relatively easily adapt to differing perimeter conditions without generating major design changes, simply by adding or eliminating a number of hexagonal panes.

The two biomes are joined together by a link structure containing a large double height café space, in front of raised walkways leading from the central approach out to the two biomes. Behind the walkways are placed various support facilities for the public and the horticulturists. The link building is a complete contrast to the glistening bubbles of the biomes. The roof over the café space is formed from sloping steel trusses supported on raking columns and braced to the rear two storey support facilities for stability. The trusses have their curved face uppermost and are set out at different angles along the building's length to generate a warped roof plane. This is covered with metal decking supporting a green roof system that is allowed to sweep down to ground level at the connection point to each of the biomes. This device adds support to the visual image of the transparent domes emerging from the green floor of the quarry and successfully integrates a substantial amount of building structure into the landscape. Access to the link and thereby to the biomes is made by way of a path that winds down the opposite slope from the Visitor Centre which controls public access to the site.

The Visitor Centre, also designed by Grimshaw, follows the contours of the site with a dramatically curved plan form in which two single storey buildings define a long curving courtyard or street, partially covered by a tensile fabric roof. The smaller of the buildings is cut into the hillside, with a 'green' roof helping to absorb the considerable bulk of the staff rooms, plant and public lavatories which it houses into the landscape setting. The main building is banana-shaped in plan, its north facade bulging outwards towards the quarry and offering a panoramic view of the biomes below. Its three main spaces accommodate an exhibition/interpretation hall, cafeteria and shop and a conference facility. The materials used in the construction reflect the underlying ethos of the Eden project and involve traditional techniques and low embodied energy. The sheltered internal street elevation features the use of rammed earth walling, a Cornish tradition, made with material salvaged from the site. The centre also incorporates gabion walls, utilising rocks obtained from blasting operations during the construction of the biome foundations. On the outer face, areas of glazed walling contrast with the use of Western Red Cedar as cladding shingles and horizontal boarding. Oversailing the central 'street', the long tensioned fabric canopy swoops up and down over a series of raking timber posts and oversails the adjacent structures, providing shelter from sun and rain.

This is a project firmly based on the principles of ecology and celebrating the variety and importance of the natural world, and it is entirely fitting that it explores the principles of sustainability and energy conservation in both its construction and continuing operation. It has been an ambitious project, but its enormous popular success in such a short period of time demonstrates that the substantial £86 million overall cost (£57 million for the biomes) has been well spent. Further developments are planned, including a third biome to explore 'arid' climates, a separate education centre and a possible hotel. In the meantime the regeneration of Cornwall is being substantially aided by the influx of visitors and the creation of new jobs. The initiators and designers alike deserve great credit for turning such a potentially bleak natural asset into a place where excitement, entertainment, education and beauty can be found in equal measure.

## RESTORATION OF THE GREAT COURT, BRITISH MUSEUM

London

*Architect*: Foster & Partners

Robert Smirke's original design for the British Museum, built in neo-Greek style between 1823 and 1852, laid out the gallery accommodation behind the famous colonnaded front and portico of the south wing with ranges of rooms enclosing a huge open courtyard, with classical porticoed entrances placed in the centre of each wing. The museum quickly developed and grew however, and the overwhelming demand for space led to the construction in the 1850s within this courtyard of the famous central reading room by Robert's brother, Sydney Smirke, and the subsequent infilling of the remaining spaces with rooms for book storage. The magnificent reading room, thus engulfed, became an almost entirely internal space, with no significant external presence or elevations, a strange fate for a building possessing a dome larger than St Paul's Cathedral.

This remained the situation until the relocation of the British Library to its new building alongside St Pancras Station (*see* Almanack 1999) presented the opportunity to recreate the courtyard as a major public space and at the same time resolve a number of problems with the access and circulation through the museum and the by now inadequate arrival and reception facilities. The conceptual idea for the project was essentially very simple; remove the book storage accretions around the Reading Room, restore the resulting space into a noble public forum providing easy access to all parts of the museum, and ensure all year round use and accessibility by enclosing the entire courtyard space with a glass roof.

Like many simple ideas however it required high levels of skill in the application of engineering and structural techniques to make the end result look as effortless as it does. The new glazed roof is the key element in the design, assuring the year round viability of the spaces and presenting the most obvious, and clearly contemporary visual addition. It is continuously supported around its perimeter by the massive brick walls of the surrounding building and spans without visible or intermediate means of support onto a ring beam supported by new composite steel and concrete columns placed around the original cast-iron structure of the reading room. These have been completely concealed within a new French Cabra limestone skin cladding. The reading room therefore now has a proper formal external elevation worthy of its interior. The structure of the roof is a self supporting steel lattice vaulting the space between central drum and surrounding quadrangle, the height of the vault reflecting the uneven spans front to back and side to side. The variable geometry is complex, having to resolve a clear span from a rectangular perimeter to a circular centre, which added to the fact that the centre of the reading room drum is some 5 metres north of the courtyard centre point, meant that every glazed panel, there are 3,312 of them, had to be individually sized. The modular dimensions of the lattice grid were dictated by the optimum size for the triangular glazed panels, which are double glazed with low emissivity glass and have been given a 55 per cent dot matrix to reduce the effects of solar gain and glare and create a softer character of lighting.

In order to provide additional space for retail areas, café and restaurant spaces and associated back up facilities, a new structure has been inserted, elliptical in plan, but pushed towards the north wrapping round the newly cased central Reading Room. Approaching from the south through the main entrance the visitor is confronted by monumental stone staircases sweeping up within a stone balustrade around the drum form to the first of two newly inserted floor levels in the swelling of the plan form between the drum and the north face of the courtyard. This houses a new temporary exhibition and gallery space and is capped by an upper terrace accessed by further curving stairs, which functions as a semi-open restaurant space, partially enclosed with its own tensile fabric roof but otherwise open to the upper expanses of the Great Court space and offering unexpected close-up views of the intricate classical stone detailing of the north portico. From here, a narrow stainless steel and glass bridge link provides a visually tenuous but important circulation link into the second floor gallery spaces of the original building. It is a featherlight touch and point of release at the apex of the enveloping stoneclad balustrade's inexorable climb from courtyard to cornice level as it embraces the Reading Room.

The decision to clear the courtyard space of the bookstore buildings has enabled a substantial area of new accommodation to be carved out by excavating the resulting free courtyard area down to a depth of as much as nine metres. This space is allocated to the new Clore Education Centre, which contains two auditoria and a range of seminar rooms accessed from a large foyer area, as well as the new Sainsbury African Galleries located under the northern part of the courtyard. The foyer to the Education Centre is accessed by two staircases which open up the southern side of the courtyard either side of the newly reconstructed south portico.

Restoration and reconstruction of the original 19th Century fabric has been as important a part of the overall project as the purely new build elements. The facades of the courtyard had to be extensively refurbished, including patching with new stone and rebuilding in some areas. The entrance hall, expanded in 1878 by a third bay during extensions to the south wing, has been restored to its original size and now gives immediate access to the new Court through the south portico. Following painstaking investigation of surviving paint finishes the original 1846 colour scheme has been reinstated in the entrance hall.

The south portico, demolished for the 1878 extensions, has been completely rebuilt in a matching ionic order, the opportunity being taken to include two new lifts embedded into the solid outer corners of the projecting structure. A considerable public furore developed over the selection of the particular form of limestone used for the portico but it was surely the correct decision not to tear it down and insist on Portland stone. The stone used is French Anstrude Roche Clair Limestone, an almost identical material with a long history of use in the country (eg at Canterbury Cathedral). Having not been exposed to 150 years of London's grimy atmosphere the new work was always bound to look newer then the other courtyard facades, and the precision of its cutting bears witness to its late 20th Century origins, and thus expresses an honesty that attempts at disguise would have subverted.

The crowning glory and focal point of the Great Court remains the magisterial volume of the Reading Room, one of the great library spaces of the world, and one resonant with the memories of important historical figures, both literary and political. This has now been made freely accessible to the public and houses a collection of books related to the Museum's collections. The original radiating layout of desks has been retained, so members of the public can study selected volumes at the very positions formerly used by Marx, Gandhi and Kipling. The room has been immaculately restored to its 1850s' colour scheme of ivory white, gold and turquoise, a warm, rich but light combination of colours that emphasises the soaring volume and thus adds to the sense of surprise experienced upon entering the space through the small simple entrance opening cut into the new stone skin opposite the main entrance and flanked by the winding staircases. This deliberately underplayed point of transition is to be marked by a new polished stainless steel sculpture by the artist Anish Kapoor.

The enduring achievement of this project is not only the creation of this wonderful new space, and its much needed associated facilities but also the way in which it liberates the other areas of the museum with a much more user-friendly pattern of circulation, enabling the visitor to cross freely between selected areas of interest among the very extensive collections without endlessly tramping through labyrinthine corridors and other galleries.

On a much wider scale it has at last created a public pedestrian route through a substantial slice of Bloomsbury, from Great Russell Street and the newly laid out forecourt to the south, through the Portico to the Great Court and on to the North Library and out again into Montague Place. It is now firmly enmeshed with the urban map and provides an enjoyable and enlightening experience for passing visitor and keen student alike.

The project has cost in the region of £100 million, of which £30 million was provided by the Millennium Commission, and £15.75 million from the Heritage Lottery Fund, together with a gift of £20 million from the Weston family and contributions from a wide range of private sources. Once the furore over the south portico stone has subsided it will be clearly seen that the architect has achieved a radical, sensitive and lasting improvement to a world famous institution which has made its once hidden heart a major public forum capable of realising the intentions behind the quotation from Tennyson which is set into the new stonework of the courtyard floor - " .. and let thy feet ....... millenniums hence ....... be set in midst of knowledge".

## GLASGOW SCIENCE CENTRE

Govan, Glasgow, Scotland

*Architect (Science Mall and Imax):* Building Design Partnership

*Tower Concept Architect:* Richard Horden Associates

The newly completed Glasgow Science Centre is a complex of three futuristically styled buildings set on a narrow promontory site adjacent to the River Clyde in Govan, a relic from the decay of Glasgow's industrial past, where the former docks of Princes Quay have been filled in and which formed the site of the 1988 Glasgow Garden Festival. The three buildings, linked together and approached through a separate fabric roofed entrance pavilion, comprise an Imax cinema, a Science Mall containing several exhibition levels, and a dramatic wind-orientated tower, giving distant views over the Glasgow region and the mountains to the north.

The Science Centre tower is the tallest building in Scotland at 120 metres above river level, and was originally a 1992 competition winning design by Richard Horden for a new landmark building for a completely different site in the city centre, later transferred to the Science Centre project. Although continually orientated in response to the prevailing wind direction and boasting sleek and slender aerofoil modelling, changes of direction are effected mechanically by rotating the base upon which the tower is constructed rather than by wind applied forces. The steel structure of the tower utilises structural principles involved in the design of aeroplane wings. The main shaft is solid and teardrop shaped on plan, and comprises a triangular and braced framework of tubular columns surrounding a spiral escape staircase supported by a central tubular steel column. The shaft is clad with curved silver anodised aluminium panels, and is flanked on each side by an aerofoil-shaped steel outrigger that curves and tapers as it rises towards the viewing cabin at the top. Every 12 metres in height, the outriggers are braced by 250mm square hollow section curved steel ribs both to the main shaft and to a tail section, which is again a square hollow section clad in silver anodised aluminium panels to form a slim aerofoil section.

Two panoramic lift cars rise up within the wing-like framework, either side of a steel lattice guide tower braced to the rear of the main shaft, conveying passengers from the concourse level to the viewing cabin, which is constructed from glass reinforced gypsum and looks very much like the body of a large helicopter. Its tail links with the mast tail, which resolves vertically into a 24 metre high carbon fibre mast. At the base of the tower is a circular motor driven horizontal disc supported by 24 roller bearings set in a concrete ring beam which is supported by a series of raking steel columns. The weight of the tower is resolved into a tapering framework that terminates in a massive solid steel casting set into a thrust bearing in the middle of a dramatic pit at the centre of the concourse.

A tunnel connects the tower concourse to the principal building of the three, the Science Mall. This is a long, sleek, ground-hugging form like an upturned silver boat hull on one side, contrasting with a cut away facade on the other, infilled by a sloping glazed wall. The geometry of the hull-shaped form is that of a section of a torus, tilted at an angle, and its structural frame is formed from a two-way spanning diagrid of tubular steel members. This underlying diagonal pattern is expressed on the metallic exterior which is clad with titanium panels. The pattern of diamond shaped panels is subtly highlighted by plain narrow strips defining groups of 4 panelled 'tiles' about 4.5 metres square. The titanium cladding, manufactured in the USA and finished in Japan, has a textured finish rather than a pure high polish and this gives the material not only a more consistent finish but a more subtle diffused reflectivity.

The gallery exhibition areas occupy the ground and three upper levels, the internal structure being visually independent of the enclosing envelope, with fair face finish concrete columns, walls and floor slabs contrasting with the metallic outer structure and skin. The central bay of this internal structure supports pairs of angled struts in an inverted V-format providing points of support for the curving roof's diagrid frame. For much of the curving length of the plan form the hull profile is cut away to the height of the ground storey to reveal an inward sloping glazed wall, and as the diagrid structural frame is also curtailed at the head of the glazing, support is taken down on further V-shaped pairs of tapering metal struts set inside the line of glazing. These are braced back to the leading edge of the first floor slab.

The third building, which houses an Imax cinema auditorium, is a much more compact form, curving on all sides, its glistening shape suggestive of a huge bubble of mercury perched on the quayside, its pneumatic form cut away along one side to reveal a curving and sloping glazed screen lighting the foyer areas. The bubble form curves in on itself where the skin touches the ground, in contrast to the spreading form of the Science Mall, and has therefore resulted in the adoption of a completely different structural solution. This involves the use of a wraparound steel space frame, its complex geometry calculated by computer, assembled on site from a kit of parts. Steel purlins attached to the space frame support steel liner trays containing insulation which act as a base for the water-proof membrane beneath the cladding. In view of the geometry of the envelope, the titanium cladding has been applied as a series of strips, alternate wide strips made up of horizontal panels contrasting with vertical narrow continuous rib-like strips which help to define the three dimensional form and reflect the underlying structure. The building is partially surrounded by shallow water pools, partly to protect the titanium finish from the effects of human contact, but these serve also to heighten the effects of the titanium's silver finish, picking up the moving reflections from the surface of the water.

This is an important project playing its full part in the wider programme of regeneration of run down areas of Glasgow. It offers the general public an absorbing and educational experience that not only acknowledges Glasgow's past but in its manner of presentation and in the style of the buildings is very firmly focussed on the future. It deals with all things scientific in a modern and accessible way and shows the work of talented exhibition designers to good effect. The £32 million cost of the overall project will prove of lasting value if the young of today and future generations have their understanding of, and interest in, the principles of science heightened by the wide ranging displays and hands on experiments which are made available in this fascinating and futuristic set of buildings.

## NEW LIBRARY BUILDING

Coventry University

*Architect:* Short & Associates

The new Lanchester Library at Coventry University is one of a growing number of buildings whose distinctive visual appearance reflects an overriding preoccupation with the principles of low energy consumption and sustainability, linked to a philosophy of natural ventilation wherever feasible. The University's brief was for a flexible deep-plan building naturally ventilated. Principles of natural ventilation effected from perimeter windows typically produce narrow floor plates rather than deep plan formats, and opening external windows would also have proved counterproductive in controlling noise and air pollution from surrounding roads. Accordingly the designers decided to turn the building in on itself and apply the natural ventilation approach through a series of internal light and air shafts.

The resulting building provides approximately 11,000 sq metres of library space on four floors, the bulk of the accommodation housed within a block 46 metres square. The square plan form is divided into four quarters around a central atrium whose base occurs at first floor level, and whose glazed walls cant outwards to create a larger void at the upper levels. In the centre of each quarter there is a further lightwell that also functions as an air shaft, the combined pattern of voids set out like the five on a dice.

The four outer voids are used as supply air shafts, fed by 1.5 metre high plenums set immediately below the ground floor slab and connected to fresh air inlets at low level. The ventilation system is driven by the stack effect of the heat gain from occupants and other sources such as computers, which is sufficient to draw fresh air in via these four supply shafts to replace warm stale air which rises and exhausts via the central atrium and additional triangular stacks located around the building perimeter. These additional stacks number a total of twenty, four triangular ones on each face and one square one in each corner, and being expressed as tall tower like features rising high above the parapet level are the major determinants of the external architectural form and appearance.

The flow of air through the building is finely controlled by a building energy management system (BEMS) which determines flow rates through inlet and outlet openings based on external temperature and $CO_2$ and temperature readings in each quarter of the building. Fresh air can be preheated if required at the base of each of the supply air-wells, and additional heating can be provided by radiators around the perimeter. Air is supplied to each floor through grilles placed near floor level around the glazed enclosures. Rising warm air is then extracted through high level grilles placed just below the soffit of the exposed precast concrete floor slabs, within the depth of the castellated steel beams that support the floor. The holes within the castellated beams permit air to flow horizontally across the exposed concrete surfaces towards the extract shafts, and the stack movement is assisted by a generous storey height that gives a 4.4 metre high internal space.

The BEMS works on a 24 hour basis, and is able to increase ventilation at night to dissipate heat that may be built up during the day, thus making use of the thermal mass of the building's structure to warm or cool the building during the day as appropriate. Energy use is predicted to be about 20 per cent of that for a typical air-conditioned building and about 25 per cent of that for a typical open plan naturally ventilated building, even though none of the intake air is recirculated.

At the fourth floor level, the square plan form of the main building is cut away symetrically at each corner to reveal two sides of the emerging supply air lightwells, and provide an L-shaped roof terrace. While this helps with the amount of natural daylight available through the glazed sides of the shafts at lower floor levels, it renders the shaft itself liable to solar gain, and is therefore protected from this by a secondary glazed screen. Additional extract towers are provided serving just the fourth floor level as computer modelling highlighted potential over-heating problems if this top level was connected to the central atrium because of possible re-entry of exhausted air from below.

Despite being a steelframed superstructure, and the expressed external ducts being steel framed and suspended from the main frame, the external architectural expression is one of massive brick walls, with heavily recessed and modelled bands of window openings set into large areas of plain buff coloured brickwork, accentuated by the substantial floor to floor height, dominated by the soaring profiles of the brick clad ventilation ducts or chimneys and their intricately detailed 'pots'. To maintain the loadbearing illusion the projecting triangular ducts are visually supported from circular columns at the lowest level, and on the south west and south east elevations also support projecting vertical sunshades.

The ventilation chimney stacks are terminated by large cowls, with oversailing panels of wind baffles constructed of double rows of half tubular metal sections set vertically around all four sides and displaced one to the other by half a module, like ranks of sliced organ pipes. The chimneys are topped by canted flat roof sections sloping in to the centre. The design of the wind baffles was subjected to extensive wind tunnel tests to ensure that prevailing winds would not drive air back into the exhaust shafts.

The monumental expression and high degree of articulation of the main block is further enhanced by rectangular stair towers, separated from the main floor plan and expressed as free standing elements placed at seemingly arbitrary angles to the main facade, one on each elevation. Three of these contain simple auxiliary/escape staircases, the fourth is larger, and incorporates a grander public staircase and lavatory facilities.

The entire square floorplan of the main building is thus devoted exclusively to library related functions and permits a high degree of flexibility in future arrangements of facilities. The presence of the interior lightwells produces areas of greater and lesser daylight value throughout the floor plan, the more internal spaces being generally devoted to bookstack areas, while user seating areas are placed around the lightwells and the perimeter to take advantage of stronger light levels.

Even the main entrance and its associated facilities are separated from the library 'box' in order to maintain flexibility. A long entrance corridor runs along one side, with adjoining café and bookshop as separate angular structures. The glazed entry concourse gathers approach and circulation routes from a number of directions and resolves them into a last minute 90° turn into the entrance control point at the centre of the south east elevation.

Since its opening, library usage has exceeded expectations and there can be little doubt that such a distinctive landmark has firmly imprinted itself on the minds of the students. At a cost of £17.5 million the building has been produced within tight budgeting constraints, and these are reflected in the robust no-nonsense handling of details and materials. In terms of the wider agenda of energy conscious design it serves as a useful exemplar of the application of natural ventilation techniques to deep plan buildings and will therefore help in the diversification of low energy sustainable development in the future. To date it appears that the intended parameters for the internal environment and user comfort have been satisfactorily achieved without the need for mechanical intervention.

# Broadcasting

## TELEVISION

Greg Dyke's first full year as director general of the BBC made the year in television a particularly bruising period for the two main terrestrial networks, ITV and BBC1. Dyke's decision to shift the 9 O'Clock News to 10pm - giving rivals ten days' notice – unleashed an intense ratings battle that had a knock-on effect on all the main channels. The move, originally planned for autumn 2001, exposed weaknesses in the BBC's own schedules because executives had not been given enough time to prepare and stockpile viewer-friendly drama and entertainment capable of performing strongly at 9pm.

As competition for ratings reached new levels of ferocity, there was greater pressure than ever for peak time shows to deliver big numbers and more emphasis on 'event' programming. This might be a soap special, a big feature film, or football match – or a short, two or three-part drama featuring a high celebrity quotient. These 'events' could then be promoted aggressively in the hope of luring viewers, increasingly fickle and with more channels to choose from. The continued proliferation of channels was reflected in ITV re-branding itself in the summer as ITV1.

Against this background the satellite and cable stations, led by BSkyB digital service, Sky Digital, continued their slow but inexorable march into the territory of the terrestrial war horses.

### ITV and BBC1 Go Head to Head

Sometimes, as the year progressed, it became more difficult than ever to distinguish any real differences between the offerings of ITV and BBC1, more populist than ever with shows like *Celebrity Sleepover*. They fought for the same on screen talent, (ex-EastEnders actor Ross Kemp appeared in an ITV version of *A Christmas Carol* while *The Frank Skinner Show* transferred straight from BBC1 to ITV). Meanwhile the BBC finally hit the jackpot with a successful game show of their own to rival *Who Wants To Be A Millionaire?*, but lacking its huge appeal.

*The Weakest Link*, a knockout contest in which contestants competed against one another to answer general knowledge questions, had begun as a daytime programme on BBC2, helping to boost the channel's overall popularity. The show gave a huge lift to the career of its 'sadistic' presenter Anne Robinson.

This general drift towards a more populist agenda led viewers and critics to complain that the BBC was abandoning public service. There was also concern that ITV, granted extra advertising airtime by the Independent Television Commission in return for agreeing to reinstate *News At Ten*, was ruining the viewing experience by interrupting their favourite shows with too many commercial breaks. The additional advertising minutes, however, were a mixed blessing because they came at precisely the time that difficulties in the American economy and the crash in internet and telecom companies were forcing advertisers to reduce their spend, particularly on ITV. By the end of the year, the cost of buying an advertising slot in Coronation Street had reportedly fallen from £90,000 to £70,000. Channel 4 too was caught up in the frenzy for ratings. Nowhere was this more apparent than when the station successfully poached Richard and Judy of *This Morning* fame from ITV in the spring.

### Panorama Marginalised

There was all-round condemnation following the BBC's decision to marginalise its once proud flagship current affairs show, *Panorama*, shifted from Monday evenings to a post-10pm position on Sundays, where fewer people were likely to tune in. Ironically, *Panorama's* final Monday night offering, *Who Bombed Omagh?*, was one of the most successful and powerful editions of the programme in recent memory leading to several awards for its intrepid reporter, John Ware, and an audience of 4.2 million. There was speculation that *Who Bombed Omagh?*, which revealed the identities of the terrorists who committed the Omagh outrage, was responsible for a terrorist attack when a car bomb was detonated by police outside BBC Television Centre in February. Fortunately, there were no casualties although the bomb caused extensive damage to the building's reception area.

*Panorama* was not the only well-known BBC programme to be given a back seat in the schedules as BBC1 devoted itself more to drama, entertainment and sport, particularly soccer and, amazingly, boxing. The Evening Standard's TV critic, Victor Lewis Smith, summed up the feeling of many when he wrote: 'I'm appalled that *Omnibus* is no longer on BBC1, because the raison d'etre of a public service broadcaster, surely, is a willingness to transmit challenging material to a mass audience.'

### Reality Mania

Dyke and the BBC played little part in what represented the biggest small screen phenomenon of 2000-2001. This was the rise of the so-called reality show, propelled by Channel 4's iconic *Big Brother*, but also in evidence on ITV, Channel 5, and Sky One with series such as *Popstars*, *Survivor*, *The Mole* and *Temptation Island*. What these programmes – part game show, part docusoap – had in common was putting members of the public - preferably young and good looking - at the centre of a voyeuristic contest that offered the possibility of overnight celebrity and riches.

*Big Brother* featured a group of strangers who had to survive and form relationships with each other surrounded by cameras and cut off from the outside world. Each week one of the group would be evicted by audience vote until only one remained. *Big Brother* was, according to the newspapers, TV's biggest talking point of the year. Most of the press (tabloid and broadsheet alike) gave saturation coverage to the goings on inside the *Big Brother* house.

In the summer, Helen, the runner-up to Brian, received the kind of media attention normally reserved for show business stars, footballers and members of the royal family. Significantly, although a special celebrity version of the show - shown in the spring as part of the fund raising venture, *Comic Relief* - generated widespread interest, this was nothing compared with the response to the original show. Sceptics, however, wondered if the whole thing was exploitative and uncomfortably voyeuristic - more TV trivia aimed squarely at a consumer and celebrity obsessed generation. How long would it be, asked the critics, before the next *Big Brother* resorted to showing live sex in peak time to keep audiences coming back for more? Commenting about television per se, Jonathan Miller, once a small screen regular but now devoting his energies to the stage, remarked that these days the medium was like 'taking a warm bath in dirty water'. For some, the remark perfectly summed up *Big Brother* and its ilk.

### Interactive TV

Undeniably, *Big Brother* offered an insight into how TV might be viewed in the future. As well as the daily updates on Channel 4 from the *Big Brother* house in London's East End, there was continuous coverage via the internet, and on Channel 4's new digital station, E4, launched in January. The latter proved so successful that in homes with digital TV, during the series in the summer, E4 was more popular than Sky One, traditionally the most watched of the non-terrestrial services. Votes for eviction could be made either via conventional phone lines or direct from people's remote controls in households with digital TV. Incidentally, digital interactive TV also enabled the BBC to provide coverage from Wimbledon allowing viewers to select the match of their choice, rather than the one chosen for them by the broadcaster.

While in sheer numbers the ratings generated by the spate of reality shows fell well below those for the big league soaps (audiences for *Big Brother* were around five million compared with 12 million for *Coronation Street* or *EastEnders*) or drama perennials like ITV's *Heartbeat*, they were particularly popular with viewers in their teens and 20s. Earlier in the year ITV struck gold with a different sort of reality format, *Popstars*. The idea was that aspiring chart toppers were auditioned by a panel of entertainment industry experts. The winners were then put together to form a pop group. The power of prime-time Saturday night TV and the hype surrounding the show ensured that the winners, Hear'Say, had a number one record.

But reality TV was not failure proof, as ITV discovered in May when *Survivor*, set on a remote Malaysian island, flopped badly. *Survivor*, unlike the majority of reality shows, was actually a British invention, created by Charlie Parsons, mastermind of Channel 4's *The Big Breakfast*. It had taken American audiences by storm, but critics suggested that British viewers resented the melodramatic production, more like a traditional game show than the laid back approach of *Big Brother*.

### Soap Wars

The intense competition between channels acted as a further brake on the mainstream networks' innate tendency to play safe and avoid taking any real creative risks. This explains why the hours devoted to soap operas on ITV and BBC1 reached a new peak. ITV led the way by adding a fifth weekly episode of *Emmerdale* in the autumn and re-introducing the much ridiculed *Crossroads*. The BBC finally announced plans to introduce a fourth weekly installment of *EastEnders*, launched in August. The decision to screen an extra *EastEnders* was another sign of Dyke's populism; for years John Birt, Dyke's predecessor, had vetoed plans to increase the number of soaps on the BBC. Not to be outdone Channel 5, which throughout the year struggled to live down its image as a second-class station, poached the rights from ITV to Antipodean teen soap, *Home and Away*.

In an attempt to stop audiences grabbing the remote control and changing channels, more attention than ever was paid to beefing up the storylines of the leading soaps. *Coronation Street*, which celebrated its 40th birthday with a live episode on December 8, featured a highly controversial rape, while *EastEnders* ensured front-page coverage in the tabloids by introducing a storyline involving incest.

The shooting of Phil Mitchell in *EastEnders* was a reminder that although audiences continued to fragment, the right programme could still draw a massive following. The anticipation surrounding the episode in which the identity of Phil's attacker was revealed - his ex-girlfriend Lisa - was so keen that the kick off for Liverpool's crunch UEFA Cup semi final in Spain was delayed by 15 minutes. Nearly 18 million viewers tuned in. Not since the Who shot JR? storyline in Dallas back in 1980 had a TV soap generated such enormous interest.

### Drama

It was not a vintage year for fresh, groundbreaking TV drama. In such a competitive atmosphere, ITV and BBC 1 attempted to outgun each other by screening a succession of two or three part mini series that could be easily publicised in advance; ITV offered programmes like *Tough Love*, starring Ray Winstone, and *My Fragile Heart*, featuring Sarah Lancashire. BBC1 responded with a series of Crime Doubles; one of the best was *Second Sight*, written by Paula Milne, and with Clive Owen playing optically challenged detective Ross Tanner.

As ever, the main channels continued to invest heavily in tried-and-tested drama series. Veteran ITV programme, *London's Burning*, returned for a 13th run; *Cold Feet* reappeared for the third time, and customs and excise yarn, *The Knock* was back after a long absence for a celebrity-studded four part run. There was praise for Ken Stott, playing the central character in ITV's crime drama, *The Vice*. ITV's prison saga, *Bad Girls*, drew big audiences but critics did not see the point of some of its more violent scenes. One old timer axed after failing to perform was Irish caper, *Ballykissangel*, principally because its stars Stephen Tompkinson and Dervla Kirwin had left and show, while another of its leading actors, Tony Doyle, had died.

ITV's one new autumn hit drams series, *Fat Friends*, stood out from the usual mix of crime and medical stories. Written by Kay Mellor and starring daughter Gaynor Faye plus Alison Steadman, Meera Syal and Josie Lawrence, this six-parter about a group of weight watchers was an instant success. Meanwhile John Thaw, later revealed to be suffering from cancer, bowed out as *Inspector Morse*, when the last ever Morse story, The Remorseful Day, was shown by ITV in the autumn, the 33rd film since the programme made its debut in 1987.

BBC1 continued to struggle with fiction, accumulating several high profile flops in the autumn and winter seasons. The much-hyped *Sins*, starring Pete Postlethwaite, failed to win a big audience, while an eagerly anticipated two-part dramatisation of Nancy Mitford's *Love In A Cold Climate* was felt by critics to be too condensed - despite a cast boasting Alan Bates, Sheila Gish and Celia Imrie. Even Paul Abbott, writer of *Clocking Off*, *Reckless* and *Cracker*, was, said critics, not at his best in the three-part eternal triangle saga, *Best of Both Worlds*, also on BBC1. But there was acclaim for Kieran Prendiville's harrowing one-off BBC1 drama, *Care*, examining child abuse and starring Steven Mackintosh.

Overall, period drama was less in evidence than in previous years. BBC1's attempt to add a new twist to literary adaptation by filming a serial based on a 20th century book, rather than a classic from an earlier era, Kingsley's Amis's post-war novel, *Take A Girl Like You*, was only a partial success. Arguably the year's most ambitious drama was BBC2's *Land Of Plenty*, adapted from Tim Pears' story of a successful small town industrialist and his family set over four decades starting in the 1950s.

Commented the Radio Times' Alison Graham: 'In this very strange world of ours, where you feel that if anyone could get away with it they would wallpaper the schedules with soaps, *Heartbeat* and *Who Wants To Be A Millionaire?* there's something intensely noble about a commitment to ten weeks of arty, frequently pretentious drama'. Also on BBC2, Tony Garnett's latest TV drama, *Attachments*, set in the world of dot-com start-ups, drew attention, but failed to repeat the success of his earlier series, *This Life*. More remarkable was Stephen Poliakoff's *Perfect Strangers*, starring Michael Gambon, Lindsay Duncan, Claire Skinner, Toby Stephens and Matthew MacFadyen.

On Channel 4, a new legal series, *North Square*, was acknowledged by critics to be one of the station's more successful attempts at contemporary drama since the ground-breaking *Queer As Folk*. But unfortunately *North Square* failed to prove popular enough for Channel 4 to commission another series. Another work place saga, *Teachers*, that portrayed members of the profession in a far from flattering light provoking complains from education authorities, is, however, set to return.

### Comedy Makes an Impression

In entertainment, Channel 4 had a generally successful year but did cause controversy with an edition of *Brass Eye* satirising media hysteria to paedophiles, winning praise for the hidden camera series, *Trigger Happy TV*, and *Rory Bremner's* merciless send ups of politicians; over on BBC1, another impressionist, *Alistair McGowan*, also kept audiences smirking. It was after all an election year but public apathy towards the polls and the continued down grading of current affairs on TV muted the impact of the small screen's election coverage. Graham Norton went from strength to strength and the station even secured a modest hit with *Black Books*, its most successful sitcom since *Father Ted*. Written by Dylan Moran and Graham Linehan, the action revolved around an alcoholic Basil-Fawlty-like bookshop owner.

Generally, given TV's historic difficulty in developing successful new sitcom, the year contained several unexpected highlights in this field. On BBC1 *My Family* starring Robert Lindsay and Zoe Wanamaker got off to a promising start. Two gems, *The Office*, featuring Ricky Gervais, and *Life As We Know It*, arrived late in the year: both from the BBC, the latter was created by *Waiting For God* writer Michael Aitkens and was well performed by a cast led by Stephanie Cole and Richard Wilson; in the autumn Wilson had made his final appearance as Victor Meldrew in the last ever series of *One Foot In The Grave*. Another success was Paul Whitehouse's black comedy, *Happiness*, a fresh insight into midlife crisis.

Granada's *The Royle family* continued to reach the comic heights. So too did Victoria Wood in one of the genuine triumphs of the Christmas schedules, *Victoria Wood With All The Trimmings*. Brian Hunt writing in the Daily Telegraph singled out the show for praise saying: 'In television terms, this millennial Christmas was determinedly secular to the point where it felt like nothing more than an indulgent bank holiday - one of the few highlights was *Victoria Wood With All the Trimmings* – frequently funny in just a liberatingly daft way, but held together by a backbone of stiff satire.' In one acutely observed sketch, Wood satirised the BBC's new found enthusiasm for digital niche channels complaining that the Corporation was devoting all its energies to services like BBC Upmarket and BBC Knitwear.

She had a point. In the autumn the BBC had announced plans to re-launch digital channels, BBC Choice and BBC Knowledge as BBC3 and 4, catering, respectively for the under-25s and more up-market viewers; in addition the BBC said it wanted to invest in two dedicated children's services (one for the pre-school audience and one for older children). In order to proceed with these plans, the BBC needed approval from the government. By the summer of 2001, permission had still not been granted, but it was widely expected that it would eventually be forthcoming.

### Simon Schama Brings History Alive

In documentary, one of the year's undoubted highlights was *Simon Schama's History of Britain*, screened in two installments, beginning in the autumn and continuing in the spring. The final five-parts will be shown in autumn 2001. This ambitious, highly personal programme, commentators agreed, represented a perfect match of presenter and the medium of TV to recreate some of the most important stories from Britain's past. Admirers, of whom there was no shortage, praised the way Schama provided an accessible and enthusiastic guide to the nation's history covering such subjects as The English Civil War, the reign of Oliver Cromwell, and the beginnings of the British empire.

While Schama was sure-footed, there was a feeling that perhaps Sir David Attenborough was not at his very best in his latest series, *State Of The Planet*, shown by BBC1 in the autumn. However, the programme evinced an unusually polemical edge tackling head on the problems of global warming and other environmental concerns.

On BBC2, the winter provided two stand-out documentaries, *The Rise and Sprawl of the Middle Classes* and *Walk On By*, an especially intelligent look at the history of the popular song. At the other end of the spectrum, Louis Theroux supplied BBC2 with a string of irreverent documentaries.

Channel 4 followed up the successful *The 1900 House* with its wartime equivalent, *The 1940s House*, and won approval for its coverage of the Kumbh Meia festival in India, normally ignored by British TV. Less impressive was the station's axing of the *Tour de France*, one of the highlights of its summer line-up since the station's early days almost 20 years earlier. The decision was yet another example of how even a public service broadcaster like Channel 4 could no longer afford to take as many risks by backing programmes of minority appeal.

## RADIO

Radio had much to celebrate during the year 2000-2001. When the latest listening figures were published in August, it emerged that audiences were now spending more time tuned to the radio than watching TV - an average of 3.48 hours a day compared with 3.46 sitting in front of the box. At the BBC, Radio 2 went from strength to strength, adding nearly a million new listeners in the second quarter of 2001. Listening levels for Radios 3 and 4 were slightly down, while Radio 5 Live recorded a slight increase. After suffering from a dip in popularity earlier in the year Radio 1's new look, introduced in March, appeared to be reaping benefits as its share of listening grew by 0.5 per cent. In the commercial sector, audience sizes were generally static, but with a challenging economic background and greater choice, this part of the market looked surprisingly stable.

There were some worries within the industry that the new Communications Bill, published in December, would do radio few favours. Of particular concern was that the proposed, new, all-encompassing communications regulator, Ofcom, would neglect radio and spend too much energy on television and telecommunications.

However, the one real note of caution was struck by the continued failure of digital radio to make an impact. In September, the BBC revealed plans for five new digital stations involving an investment of £20m. The services included two stations for ethnic minorities (Asian and black), an enhanced Radio Five Live, a drama and comedy network and another aimed at the 'post Beatles generation'. The hope was that these would be up and running by the beginning of the New Year, but, in common with the BBC's plans for digital TV, by August there was still no sign of the government granting the necessary permission for these digital stations to get underway.

### Digital Doldrums

In any case, digital radio sets remained in short supply. In April it was reported that only 0.1 per cent of the population had digital radio. This was despite predictions that by the end of 2001, there would be more than 300 digital radio stations on air in the UK.

In fact, unknown to most listeners, Britain now boasted 178 different digital services. 'Around 80 per cent of the population are already able to receive digital quality radio,' claimed Ralph Bernard, head of GWR (owners of Classic FM).

With receivers costing upwards of £300, they were still regarded as too expensive to become established as a mass consumer item. However, following predictions that the price would fall to about £100 by mid-2002, the age of digital radio may finally be about to dawn.

The slow progress of digital notwithstanding, the mood in the radio industry remained upbeat. Writing in the annual report of industry regulator, the Radio Authority, chair Richard Hooper said: 'We have few fears for the future of what is sometimes referred to as 'traditional' terrestrially delivered radio. It is already clear that the development of Internet Radio, and other services delivered over telecommunications networks, serve to enhance and reinvigorate the appeal of radio to the public at large. The remarkable growth in patronage of radio, at a time when other broadcast media seem to be in relative decline, once again illustrates the ability of the radio medium, born a century ago, to renew itself in the face of technological and market challenges.'

Veteran radio writer Gillian Reynolds expressed a similar sentiment, albeit in a more light hearted way, when she wrote an article in the Daily Telegraph in April in which she discussed the highly rewarding relationship celebrities had with radio. Reynolds revealed that Mick Jagger owned 20 radios, and while he was addicted to BBC Radio's *Test Match Special*, he despised phone-ins and commercials. Britain's highest paid radio presenter Chris Tarrant, who renewed his contract (reputed to be worth £1 million a year) with London's Capital Radio in July, emerged as a fan of Radio 4 drama. Paul McCartney, meanwhile, summed up radio's appeal by rejoicing in how it sets the imagination free and stimulates parts not normally reached by other media.

The ex-Beatle, presumably, was referring to Radio 4. During the year the network's desire to reach a younger audience was evident in two major departures. The first involved clearing the FM schedules on Boxing Day to make way for a marathon, uninterrupted reading of J. K. Rowling's *Harry Potter and the Philosopher's Stone*. The narrator was Stephen Fry and the broadcast lasted eight hours. Radio 4 controller Helen Boaden hailed the programme as a 'landmark in family memory'. At its peak 3.4 million listeners tuned in, with almost 400,000 staying with Harry Potter throughout the entire broadcast. But not everyone was happy. Some listeners complained when they had to switch over to long wave in order to avoid the children's hero and hear network favourites like *Desert Island Discs*, *The Archers* and *Front Row*.

### Radio 4 Goes For It

For Radio 4, the year's other turning point was the launch on Easter Sunday of a dedicated children's programme - seen as long overdue by many parents worried that their offspring would never fall into the habit of listening to speech radio. In fact, it was three years since Radio 4 last made room in its schedules for a regular children's show. 'I have always believed that the BBC has a responsibility to offer children a chance to hear quality speech programmes aimed at them,' explained Boaden. 'I want *Go For It* to capture the interests and passions of the modern child; stories, jokes, music, computer games, films, sport, TV and so on. It's a big challenge but I know that like any Radio 4 listeners our young audience will tell us what they think very quickly.'

But *Go For It* disappointed critics. They suggested that the mix of popular culture seemed more like children's TV than children's radio, and audience figures were small. Fortunately, Radio 4's traditional audience seemed generally pleased with what they were offered during the year and remarkably loyal; research by market analysts Claritas showed that 64.6 per cent of Radio 4's audience listen every day, by far the highest figure for any British station. In January, *The Archers* celebrated its 50th anniversary; there was even a party attended by Prince Charles, a long-standing fan of the rural soap. Throughout the year, drama remained strong. Highlights included a five-part adaptation of Dickens' *Little Dorrit* narrated by Iain McKellen and starring Margaret Tyzack as Mrs Clennam; Kevin Wong's *Green Fingers* starring Roy Hudd; *Funeral Catering in the 21st Century* by Iain Heggie and Robin Brooks' *The Man Who Knew Everything*. Another peak was the single-voice play, *The Duvet Lady* written by Peter Tinniswood - starring and inspired by Billie Whitelaw, and a serialisation of Vikram Seth's epic love story, *A Suitable Boy*, adapted and directed by John Dryden.

In entertainment, the second series of media satire, *The Sunday Format*, won widespread acclaim. One critic described it as 'a perfect comedy format.' On Friday evenings, *Dead Ringers* continued to delight taking pot shots at celebrities, politicians, and Radio 4 as it revealed the dark side of presenters Brian Perkins and Michael Buerk. As ever, controversy was never far away from *Today*. There was a row over the use of author Frederick Forsyth as a right wing polemicist on the Saturday edition of the show when a listener contacted *Feedback* to say he didn't expect to hear such viewers on the BBC. The Spectator retorted: 'I suspect the listener was just shocked at hearing politician incorrectness, we so rarely do.'

The BBC also faced criticism over its decision to switch off shortwave broadcasts of the *World Service* in the United States, Australia and New Zealand. Protestors said that more than one million listeners would be left without access to the BBC. But the Corporation said that the money saved would enable it to invest in reaching people in the developing world hitherto deprived of its broadcasts. Meanwhile, added the BBC, those in the affected areas could switch to FM, satellite or the internet to listen to the World Service. 'But the internet is not radio,' said protester Ralph Brandi. 'It does not serve as a suitable replacement.' Undeterred, the signal was turned off on July 1.

### Battle for Breakfast Listeners

The battle for the breakfast radio audience drew one high-profile casualty when in June, Virgin Radio sacked its former star DJ and one-time owner, Chris Evans. He claimed he was off work ill but he was photographed drinking in his local pub. Evans' departure was a relief for the station because ratings for his show had gone into a steep decline. Chris Tarrant told the Evening Standard that any talent that Evans had once had was now 'a long way down the bottom of a pint glass.'

Radio 1's breakfast presenter Sara Cox may not have been to everyone's liking (Terry Wogan launched an attack on her in the Sunday Telegraph for 'dumbing down' the BBC), but her audience grew throughout the year reaching 7.8 million - beating Wogan's Radio 2 following by almost one million. On a somber note, one of the original architects of Radio 1, producer turned presenter, John Walters, died suddenly in July, aged 63.

Radio 2's new golden boy was Jonathan Ross, saluted by the Radio Times with a cover story, thanks to the success of his Saturday morning show. Even John Peel declared himself a fan. Ross had made it possible for a generation who grew up with Radio 1 to come out of the closet and admit they now listen to Radio 2, commented the Radio Times.

Overall nearly 11 million listeners were tuning in every week to Radio 2, voted station of the year at the Sony Radio Awards in May. This was almost 700,000 more than Radio 1. In July it was announced that in an attempt to strengthen further its popularity with listeners in their 30s and 40s, Radio 2 would launch an album chart in the autumn of 2001 fronted by Simon Mayo. 'Our audience buys albums and many of the great artists develop some of their best work within the context of albums - performers like Van Morrison, Paul Weller and Bruce Springsteen,' explained Radio 2 controller Jim Moir.

Radio 3 tended to keep a low profile throughout the year. But there was a general recognition that despite failing to significantly increase audience size, the network was developing into a more wide-ranging cultural station by devoting greater space to jazz and world music, in addition to its time-honoured commitment to the classical canon. Classic FM, Radio 3's commercial rival, confirmed in August that its audience was more than three times the size of Radio 3's with over seven million regular listeners.

# Conservation and Heritage

## THE NATURAL ENVIRONMENT

### ACCESS TO COUNTRYSIDE

The Countryside and Rights of Way Act came into force on 30 January 2001. Dubbed the 'Right to Roam' Act by the press, it also gave a measure of increased protection for Sites of Special Scientific Interest (SSSIs), for example by making it an offence for anyone to damage an SSSI deliberately and obliging all public bodies and privatised utilities to help conserve them. The Act applies to England and Wales only; separate legislation will be needed in Scotland.

The Act promises rather less than a general right to roam. It does however open up commons, moorland, mountain and heath, although any area can be closed off for up to 28 days a year for safety reasons, for routine management like heather burning, or to protect wildlife. In addition people with dogs can be excluded from grouse moors or fields during lambing. The process of consulting landowners and defining open-access land on maps is expected to take until 2005.

Increased public access is not likely to become a serious threat to wildlife. Most of the Wildlife Trust's 2,000 or so nature reserves are already open to the public. The vast majority of walkers stick to paths and rights of way, and cause little or no disturbance. There have been problems with vandals and loose dogs, but the Trust believes that, on balance, it is better to give people access to wild places, since this helps promote nature conservation.

### FOOT-AND-MOUTH CRISIS

The foot-and-mouth outbreak in 2000 resulted in the slaughter of more than three and a half million cattle, sheep and pigs and cost more than the entire year's agricultural production. It highlighted the complex trade in livestock, which brings animals from one part of the country to another and so helped spread the disease. It also underlined the fact that in some areas the rural economy depends on tourism at least as much as farming.

After the outbreak, the then Ministry of Agriculture briefly considered a plan to slaughter deer and any other wild animals that might conceivably carry the foot-and-mouth virus before abandoning it as unworkable. The long-term environmental consequences of the mass slaughter of farm animals depends on whether the current subsidised over-production in hill areas is tackled. An immediate consequence was the effective suspension of conservation work, including the common bird census, over much of the country. It probably also contributed to the closure of the old, environment-unfriendly Ministry of Agriculture, and its new incarnation within a holistic-sounding Department for the Environment, Food and Rural Affairs (DEFRA). The nature conservation world is clear about what *should* happen: a massive shift of agricultural subsidies in support of sustainable, environment-friendly farming and an end to headage payments for sheep which have so severely damaged the ecology of upland areas. Others would scrap the whole subsidy-based system, force farmers to carry their own costs, and turn back the clock on animal breeding and GM crops. Much will depend on what system the British people decide they want.

### COUNTRYSIDE SURVEY

The results of the government's latest Countryside Survey, which were published in November 2000, is one of mixed fortunes for the natural environment and wildlife. On one hand, the diversity of arable field margins has increased, and hedgerow loss has been halted (except in Northern Ireland). There were small increases in broad-leaved woodland (up 5 per cent since 1990) and lowland ponds (6 per cent), but decreases in acid and calcareous grassland by 10 and 18 per cent respectively. Northern Ireland lost nearly a third of its 'neutral' meadow grassland sites since 1990. Water quality in rivers has improved and we are planting more native trees. On the other hand, the survey reveals falling diversity in unimproved grassland and streamside vegetation. Road verges showed signs of increasing nutrient levels and decreasing plant diversity, with a growing tendency towards domination by tall-growing plants like Cow Parsley, Hogweed and Stinging Nettle. A related survey by Plantlife showed that many counties are slowly losing plant diversity at the rate of roughly one species per year. It seems that the underlying reason is the contamination of the environment by chemicals, especially nitrogen from emissions and farm fertiliser, and phosphorus from intensive livestock farming. In effect, soil is becoming more fertile and water more eutrophic. Both encourage competition from a relatively few species and the result is decreasing diversity.

### BIODIVERSITY

The Biodiversity Challenge group of voluntary wildlife bodies produced a report on the progress of Biodiversity Action Plan, *Biodiversity Counts*. Echoing the government's pronouncement that biodiversity contributes to the quality of human life, it analysed threats and reported on the successes and failures of the plan so far. Some 450 species plans have been prepared, covering most forms of life except microscopic species. However, none of the 450 rare or declining species are yet out of danger, and some, like the marsh fritillary butterfly or the capercaillie, continue to decline. The main constraints on improving their lot are considered to be the Common Agricultural Policy and the lack of commitment in some quarters to 'delivering BAP targets'. Agri-environment schemes were criticised as being of limited benefit to wildlife, and water management was considered poor. The report admitted that another obstacle to success was inadequate knowledge. Much biodiversity planning is based on guesswork. 'Significant progress' included the establishment of a National Biodiversity Network providing access to biodiversity information, and the production of red data books. Challenges we face over the next five years include changing the CAP by switching support from production to sustainable development, reducing carbon emissions by 20 per cent and implementing EU directives on habitat protection and water management. In effect biodiversity is becoming another word for nature conservation, although one supplying a more 'holistic' remit.

### GLOBAL WARMING

Climate research from Scotland, Norway and the Faröe Islands shows that global warming has begun to interfere with ocean circulation. Paradoxically this could result in colder weather if the Gulf Stream, which keeps Britain 5°C warmer than expected at our latitudes, is diverted away from our coasts. Scientists measuring the force of the cold, relatively dense water that drives the Gulf Stream found that it had decreased by 20 per cent in the past fifty years. The government also saw the unusually wet autumn of 2000 as a 'wake-up call' on climate change. Scientists are now predicting more frequent extreme weather.

The natural habitats most at risk from climate change and rising sea levels are salt-marsh, chalk streams, bogs, and mountain habitats that depend on snow. If the English Channel rises by 65 cm over the next 50 years as predicted, much of the present tidal mud flats and marshes on the south and east coast will be lost. The RSPB calculates that some 40 square miles of tidal flats will go by 2013. Another prediction is the spread of invasive foreign species, especially water plants like the swamp stonecrop (*Crassula helmsii*), a native of Australia widely used as an oxygenator in garden ponds. Some native species are slowly expanding their range northwards, probably in response to climate change, among them butterflies like the orange-tip, gatekeeper and large skipper. However, Britain's island isolation will make it difficult for non-migratory species to move in from the continent to take advantage of warming conditions. Hence the predicted results of global warming on British wildlife are nearly all bad.

### Lottery Funding

The Heritage Lottery Fund is a principal source of funds for nature conservation. Land and Countryside accounted for 22 per cent of Heritage Lottery handouts, which in the past year totalled £326 million. Among the major projects is Tomorrow's Heathland Heritage, launched in 1997 to help conserve and restore the UK's lowland heathland, one of our most endangered habitats. The work involves enclosing sites and introducing grazing animals, and also a programme of scrub-cutting to restore open heather or grass. Local authorities, environment agencies and voluntary bodies contribute to the project, which is co-ordinated by English Nature.

The Lottery also funds land purchase for nature conservation purposes. Grants made in 2000-2001 helped conservation bodies to extend nature reserves at Aston Rowant, Oxon and Queendown Warren, Kent, and a community trust to acquire the 1,173 ha estate at Middle Inver in the Assynt district of north-west Scotland. It pledged £3.7 million to the Scottish Wildlife Trust for a five-year programme of works on 96 nature reserves throughout Scotland. It helped the Gwent Wildlife Trust acquire grassland of special interest at Springdale Farm and restore ancient woodland in the Wye Valley. The visitor centre at Achnasheen on the Beinn Eighe National Nature Reserve was remodelled, and a new woodland trail built, with help from the Heritage Lottery Fund.

### Hastings Bypass

Road building was back in the news with a pair of bypass proposed for Hastings costing £130 million. They threatened to damage two nature reserves, seven Sites of Special Scientific Interest, a designated wetland and an ancient wood. The government's commissioned report failed to identify all the wildlife sites on its route. At issue was not only habitat loss and fragmentation but the loss of beauty and tranquillity in the attractive well-wooded countryside surrounding the city. The scheme was approved by the South East England Regional Assembly (a newly devolved development body), but turned down by the Secretary of State, largely on environmental grounds.

A timely report, *Roads to Ruin*, by Friends of the Earth examined the environmental cost of the Labour government's road-building programme, destined to expand again after the fuel protests of 2000. Not surprisingly, they lamented the government's apparent abandonment of its much-vaunted integrated transport strategy, and predicted a new generation of Swampies taking to the trees and building tunnels as they did in the mid-1990s.

### Special Areas of Conservation

The number of Special Areas of Conservation (SACs) in Britain is to be increased at the behest of the European Union, which found its initial list inadequate to preserve important wildlife habitats. The number in England is to be raised from 147 to 228, and will include the North York Moors, Ashdown Forest, the Severn Estuary and Thorne Moors. The latter site has long been a bone of contention between the peat-digging industry and conservationists, and the implication of the new ruling is that industrial digging will have to stop. If so, the peat industry will demand compensation. This brings the number of SACs in Britain to 576 sites covering 360,000 hectares. The EU Habitats Directive which set them up requires that SACs are maintained to the highest standards, and managed in such a way that biodiversity is not lost. They include inshore marine areas, and have also been extended into the open sea to provide protection for dolphins and basking shark. SACs are the responsibility of the government's wildlife agencies, but are funded by the European Union. Together they form a network of European sites designated on similar criteria and are, in effect, a 'Common Conservation Policy' for Europe.

### Beavers and Boars

Another step in the long drawn-out plan to reintroduce beavers to Britain was made in 2001. Scottish Natural Heritages' proposal to release beavers in a fenced enclosure in Knapdale Forest was approved by local residents. So long as the Scottish Parliament approves the plan, 12 European beavers will be released there for a 5-year trial period, to see whether they adapt successfully to Scottish conditions. Beavers were hunted to extinction in the Middle Ages, but research suggests that Scotland could support up to 1,000 animals. Enthusiasts are promoting the beaver as a natural 'waterways engineer', helping to purify river water by its dam-building. It is claimed they will also help to control flooding and preserve natural wetlands. Britain is one of the last suitable European countries to reintroduce beavers. Reintroduction attempts have been generally successful in restoring the animal's natural range across Europe from the Netherlands to Poland.

The wild boar has returned to Britain by a different route by escaping from farms. Free-living boars are now established in at least two well-wooded areas in southern England. A study in 1998 estimated that about 100 animals lived on the borders of Kent and East Sussex and 12 to 20 in Dorset. Normal breeding would produce about 500 wild boars by 2008, even if no more manage to escape. Not all of these animals are pure-bred wild boars, since farms cross them with domestic breeds to increase their productivity. Wild boar are mainly nocturnal, and are rarely seen. Their presence can be detected by field signs, such as muddy wallows and disturbed ground where the animals have been rooting, and also by their droppings and tracks. Although they are not dangerous unless cornered, wild boars can attack livestock like newborn lambs, eat flower bulbs, like bluebells, orchids and wild daffodils, and have the potential to spread disease to pig units. Whether or not they are here to stay will depend on our willingness to tolerate them.

### Otters and Water Voles

The well-loved water vole has become Britain's most

endangered wild mammal, having declined by 88 per cent since 1989. Current numbers are estimated at 875,000 compared with around seven million in the 1980s. They seem close to extinction in south-west England. The main reason is predation by the American mink, against which the vole seems to be helpless. Contributory reasons include pollution, the loss of bankside vegetation and insensitive river engineering. It is thought that the voles stand a better chance of escaping the mink where the bankside vegetation is at least 10 metres broad. Conservationists are concentrating efforts on 'key sites' which still have reasonably healthy numbers of water voles. The Environment Agency has asked the government to invest £4 million in a programme of mink trapping, similar to that which controlled and eventually eliminated the coypu in the 1970s and 1980s. There is little chance, however, of eliminating the mink. There is a ray of hope in the slow recovery, helped by reintroductions, of the otter. In the south-west, mink numbers are falling as otters increase, and it is possible that the re-establishment of the otter on river systems will oust the smaller mink and give the water vole some respite – time will tell. Unfortunately the problem is not confined to Britain. Thanks to escapes from fur-farms, the mink is on the rampage across western Europe, from the Netherlands to Italy.

### Fish Crisis

WWF published a report, *Fish of the Day*, which highlights the lack of sustainability in our fishery policies. Improved technology, including deep-sea trawling, has reduced the stocks of some commercial fish to dangerously low levels, and trawl nets are also damaging life on the sea bed. The EU responded by placing nearly a quarter of the North Sea off-limits to cod, whiting and haddock fishing, but some scientists believe that even deeper cuts may be needed to restore the fisheries. Modern techniques can reduce target species very quickly, especially those which reproduce slowly. A deep sea fish, the orange roughy, which was scarcely fished for before the 1980s, has declined by 76 per cent since 1991 and 1998 because of over-fishing. The once common skate, a bycatch of trawler nets, has been all but wiped out from the Irish Sea, and is now listed as an endangered species.

The survival of the Atlantic salmon is also precarious, according to WWF. Its loss from 309 river systems in North America and Europe is probably due to a combination of falling water quality, acid rain and fish farm escapes, which spread sea-lice and disease, and may reduce genetic resistance. The solution, say WWF, is not to stop eating fish but to broaden our tastes to include species currently off the menu, like pollack or saithe. Hitherto, short-term concern for the fishing industry has always over-ridden the long-term survival of fish stocks, with all too predictable results.

### Not a Species

Analysis of DNA is changing previous ideas about how species are related. It also, on occasion, shows that a plant or animal is not what it seems. Biodiversity planners are interested in a small, annual plant of chalk downs called the Early or English Gentian (*Gentianella anglica*), which is found nowhere else in the world, not even on similar chalk downs on the opposite side of the English Channel. For this reason it has received special protection as an endemic species. However, DNA fingerprinting at Cambridge University Botanic Garden made a surprise revelation. The DNA of Early Gentian is identical to the commoner Autumn Gentian (*G. amarella*) – which means it is not a species at all, only a dwarf, early flowering variety of Autumn Gentian. It probably 'evolved' in the past 150 years since despite its distinctiveness, no one noticed the Early Gentian until 1883. Conservationists now have to decide whether it should continue to be a 'target species'. On the other hand, DNA analysis is also producing new species – for example, there is no longer one species of Fragrant Orchid in Britain but three, and there are also said to be many genetically distinct forms of Chiffchaff and Crossbill.

### National Parks for Scotland

In July 2000 the Scottish Parliament passed a Bill to establish National Parks in Scotland. The stated aim is 'to conserve and enhance the natural and cultural heritage' and also to promote sustainable use and development. The first Scottish National Park is likely to be Loch Lomond and the Trossachs, followed by The Cairngorms, which received official approval for National Park status in December 2000. Scotland's first two National Parks will benefit from previous experience and from the fact that much of the land within them is already in public ownership. However, achieving a satisfactory balance between conservation and human needs has been difficult. Cairngorm now has a funicular railway and speedboats race on the waters of Loch Lomond. The record of National Parks in England and Wales has been disappointing in wildlife terms, since National Park status had little influence on how an owner farmed his land. In Scotland, the emphasis is likely to be on tourist development, but there is potential for beneficial land management too.

## THE BUILT ENVIRONMENT

### The Heritage Review

The Heritage Review, which was overarching activity at the time of last year's overview, finally emerged in November 2000 although under the much catchier title of 'The Power of Place'. Although articulated by English Heritage and published by it, the findings and recommendations were the result of the most extensive democratic exercise that the Government has ever launched in the field of Heritage. A broad consultation process, a MORI Opinion Poll, working parties on specific matters and an Executive Steering Group on which English Heritage nominees were in a small minority, has resulted in an unprecedented statement of collective wisdom on the Historic Built Environment. And democratic it certainly hoped to be – the MORI poll, a research study on Attitudes towards the Heritage, showed that only 2% said they had no interest in Heritage whatsoever and 77% disagreed that 'We preserve too much of this country's heritage'. Exactly the same percentage felt that their lives were enriched by historic buildings and sites and a further 76% disagreed with the statement that anything after 1950 does not count as Heritage. The majority felt that public funds should be used to preserve historic buildings and 51% of the population visited an historic attraction in the year before compared with just 50% attending the cinema and 17%, a football match. The recommendations to Government from the Review included:

Equalisation of VAT charged on repairs to listed buildings at 5%, thus going beyond the stated Government objective in the November Pre-Budget Statement of 2000 that the reduction should be extended to churches only (a move not yet implemented or endorsed by the EU at the time of writing); a requirement that every planning authority should produce an empty property strategy; the setting by Government of funding targets for English Heritage and local authorities to clear the backlog of repairs to buildings, monuments, parks and gardens at risk within 10 years; the commissioning of a full review of the management and maintenance of public parks; the promotion of good quality new design in historic contexts (an initiative already started and involving the newly founded Commission for Architecture and the Built Environment); the introduction of a statutory duty of care on the owners of listed buildings, scheduled monuments and registered parks and gardens, supported by appropriate financial assistance; the establishment of a national conservation training forum; placing the historic environment at the heart of education and using it as part of the National Curriculum; establishing more local Architecture Centres; increasing control over damaging change within conservation areas; the commissioning of regular reports to monitor the condition of the historic environment; the transformation of the current Sites and Monuments Records held by county councils into IT-friendly and properly curated Historic Environment Record Centres at each principal local centre and the extension of responsibilities of 'Green Ministers' to encompass the historic environment.

The Government promised a considered response to the Review by March but this had not emerged at the time of writing. The delay was to some extent explained by the complete clear-out of Ministers within the Department for Culture, Media and Sport as a result of the post-Election reshuffle, the new Secretary of State being Tessa Jowell and the new Arts Minister (with responsibility for the Built Environment), Baroness Blackstone. The departure of Chris Smith and Alan Howarth was generally regretted within the sector.

## Urban and Rural White Papers

The Autumn of 2000 and the Winter of 2000 saw a positive paper storm, for alongside 'The Power of Place' came the long awaited Urban and Rural White Papers issued by the then Department of the Environment, Transport and the Regions. Although both clearly examined, and made promises on, areas much broader than the historic environment, the importance of the latter was acknowledged. The Paper on Cities lifted the heart with its reference to the country's 'priceless architectural heritage' stating 'We have historic towns and cities that are famous the world over'. 'We have fine squares, elegant terraces and a legacy of great civic buildings'. The Paper pledged: the establishment of up to 12 more Urban Regeneration Companies; a comprehensive programme to improve the quality of parks (many of them historic); a major Urban Summit with a stocktaking agenda to be held in 2002; the commissioning of guides for property owners and developers on residential conversion; a requirement on Government Departments and other public sector landlords to report annually on their performance in bringing empty properties back into use; an increase in the budgets for the Regional Development Agencies from £1.2 billion as at present to £1.7 billion in 2003/2004; the creation of 6,000 on-line centres funded by Government based in 'community centres, schools, churches or even converted buses'; further assistance to help people repair their own homes; the preparation by the English Tourism Council of a national strategy for revitalising England's seaside resorts (all of which are historic sites of the 18th, 19th or early 20th centuries); and the establishment of a new Cabinet Committee on Urban Affairs and within the then DETR, of an Urban Policy Unit. The Paper also drew renewed attention to the Chancellor's Pre-Budget Statement in November which included a reduced rate of VAT on the cost of converting residential properties into a different number of dwellings, immediate tax relief to property owners for the cost of converting redundant space over shops and other commercial premises into flats for letting and an adjustment to the zero rate of VAT to provide relief for the sale of renovated houses that had been empty for 10 years or more.

The Rural White Paper offered, among other things, 50% mandatory rate relief for village shops, pubs and garages, the introduction of a presumption against the closure of rural schools (the majority of which are listed), a new £37 million scheme to regenerate market towns, and the continuation of the Redundant Building Grant Scheme which assists farmers to convert agricultural buildings into benign non-agricultural use generating employment and saving the often historic buildings concerned from decay and demolition.

## Heritage Lottery Fund

The Heritage Lottery Fund (HLF) towers over all other sources of money for the historic environment with some 38% of its expenditure of more than £300 million going towards historic buildings and sites between 1999 and 2001. The year 2001 saw delegation by HLF on decisions on most applications for up to £1 million to nine new Committees for the English Regions, including London.

Among the decisions announced in the year under review, (with the grant amount given in parenthesis) were: the old Royal Naval College, Greenwich (£8,721,000) to secure the future of three of the outstanding buildings by Wren and Webb surrounding the Grand Square for the use of both the University of Greenwich and Trinity College of Music; the Water Hall, Birmingham (£516,000) to allow a Grade II* listed building to be transformed into a gallery of modern art; Ancoats, Manchester (£4,830,000) to conserve one of the greatest concentrations of early industrial buildings in the country described plausibly as 'the world's first factory suburb', visited and recorded by Frederick Engels; Birkenhead Park, Wirral (£6,578,000) to restore what is considered to be Britain's most important historic urban park, opened in 1847, designed by Joseph Paxton and the model for New York's Central Park; The Royal Military Canal, Hythe, Kent (£2,512,000) constructed between 1804 and 1806 as part of the land defences against the possible invasion by Napoleon, to allow both conservation and improved access; Birmingham Town Hall (£9,800,000) to meet the escalating repair needs of one of the great Classical monuments of the Midlands, of 1832 by Charles Hansom currently closed to the public in view of its condition; Kirkstall Abbey, Leeds (£3,396,000) to restore the fabric and landscape of one of the best preserved of all Cistercian abbeys, set in a wooded valley north-west of Leeds; The Victoria County Histories (£179,500) to pay for a pilot study of the single most important agency engaged in the production of local history (with a strong architectural content); St. Margaret's Church, Toxteth, Liverpool (£343,000) to bring back from the brink a Grade II* listed church of 1869 by G. E. Street which would otherwise face certain closure; The British Hinduism Oral History Project (£86,200) to create an oral history archive recording all aspects of the history and culture of the Hindu community of Britain; the Lawrence Olivier Archive (£500,000) to facilitate the conservation and cataloguing at the British Library of the papers of the country's greatest 20th century actor; The Esplanade Heritage Centre, Rochdale, Lancashire (£1,100,000) to conserve one of the town's more important 19th century civic buildings; the former Oxford Station (£1,225,000) to permit the re-erection at Quainton, Buckinghamshire of the former LNWR station of 1851, an important pioneer in the use of prefabrication; the Nenthead Mines Heritage Centre at Alston, Cumbria (£599,500) for further conservation work at a dramatic mining landscape manifesting lead and zinc working and smelting from the 18th century; creating a new Centre for Buckinghamshire Studies at Aylesbury (£463,500); Hardwick Hall, Derbyshire (£2.5 million) to allow the National Trust to continue its programme of repairs and improvements; Gloucester Blackfriars (£2,930,000) to enable the City Council to rehouse the Town Museum in a new annexe to be built adjacent to the Gloucester Blackfriars, the 13th century Dominican priory in the middle of the city; Heaton Park, Manchester (£4,973,000) for the second phase of the conservation campaign, bringing the total grant aid to more than £9 million, the largest grant ever given by the HLF to a park restoration project as part of a regime which should see £250 million going to Urban Parks; and the Old Town Hall, Crediton, Devon (£478,500) to buy and convert this listed building into a community centre.

Grants offered are increasingly being translated into projects completed and open to the public. These included: The Millennium Galleries at Sheffield opened in April 2001 with a rehoused Ruskin Gallery; Bede's World, Jarrow (HLF contribution: £3.08 million) opened by the Queen in December 2000; Stanley Mills, Perthshire where 30 flats have been created in Scotland's most dramatic complex of mills which had previously faced demolition; The Museum of the History of Science, Oxford which opened in May (HLF grant: £1.195 million); and St. Andrew's in the Square, Glasgow where this spectacular church of 1739 has been reopened as an artistic and conference centre.

### Other New Attractions

The HLF is not of course the only funder of new attractions and amenities. Other historic buildings opened or reopened after programmes of repair and conversion in the last 12 months including: Beckford's Tower in Bath, partly occupied by the Landmark Trust which has itself launched a £10 million appeal to raise money to take similar buildings into care; the New Armouries Building in the Tower of London of 1663 which reopened in February; The Wellington Arch at London's Hyde Park Corner, open to the public for the first time after English Heritage had completed a £1.5 million programme of repairs; Somerset House in the Strand where the public is able to wander through the great courtyard with the sound of playing fountains and move through onto the terrace facing the river; the Museum of Domestic Design and Architecture in the London Borough of Barnet; Nunhead Cemetery, Southwark which reopened to the public in March 2001 after completion of Phase I of a comprehensive conservation campaign; The National War Museum of Scotland, now resited in the north-west corner of Edinburgh Castle; the new Visitor Centre at Painshill Park, Cobham in Surrey interpreting one of the most famous of all 18th century planned landscapes which opened in the Spring of 2001; John Keats' home at Hampstead which reopened after a comprehensive programme of repairs; the Royal Gunpowder Mills at Waltham Abbey on the Essex/Hertfordshire border which opened to the public for the first time on 6 April 2001 offering views of a site where gunpowder production was continuous from the mid-1660s to 1991; and, finally, the Museum of British Pewter which opened in the Summer of 2001 at Harvard House, Stratford-on-Avon, Warwickshire.

In 2000 and 2001 hundreds of historic buildings were open to the public for a number of given weekends as part of the increasingly ambitious and successful Heritage Open Days programme, organised by the Civic Trusts for England, Wales and Scotland.

### England

The 'lead body' for the historic environment in England is English Heritage. Its latest Annual Report, that for 1999-2000 published in November 2000, highlights achievements despite an actual reduction in the baseline grant aid from the Department for Culture, Media and Sport by some £1.7 million in real terms. Pledges for the future promise only stasis as the organisation would be no better off than at present despite a promised extra £7 million in 2002-2003 and £9 million in the year thereafter. It was some small compensation that it was able to increase its own earned income to £26.2 million, largely by welcoming almost 12 million people to its 409 historic properties.

EH's principal impact on the outside world is through its grant programme and through education. On the former, a major announcement was made in the course of the year on the Ditherington Flax Mill at Shrewsbury built in 1797 and claimed to be 'the first iron framed building in the world'. EH's total offer to the Mill itself and to the surrounding mill housing was £750,000 (a further £2.8 million has been offered by Advantage West Midlands, the new less formal name for the Regional Development Agency). The total grant aid offered in 1999-2000 was £35.1 million, thus allowing 108 of the 1,428 entries on the 1999 Buildings at Risk Register to be removed (even if this was offset by 141 new entries for the lists for 2000). The Summer of 2001 saw EH's announcement of the third round of Heritage Economic Regeneration Schemes (HERS) which gave £9 million to 59 areas, the highest grant being £150,000 to Burnley Town Centre and Padiham in Lancashire. More conventional heritage benefited in January 2001 with the offer of £2.5 million for the year 2001-2002 to England's cathedrals, bringing the total offer over 10 years to £34.5 million. The 27 beneficiaries in 2001-2002 included Salisbury, with three offers amounting to £407,000, although comparative youth was no impediment – Guildford built in the 1930s picked up a modest £8,000, Liverpool's Roman Catholic Cathedral by Frederick Gibberd got £90,000 for repairs to the 'pyramids' built over the great spiral staircase to Lutyens' crypt, while Truro, J. L. Pearson's magnum opus of the mid-19th century, received £127,000.

EH's educational role expanded enormously as a result of its absorption in 1999 of the former Royal Commission on the Historical Monuments for England. The year 2000-2001 saw the publication of major studies on thatching, construction in cob and earth, a Directory of Building Sands and Aggregates, a guide to Post War Listing, the historic architecture of prisons and, perhaps most intriguingly of all, an assessment of Britain's programme of bombing decoys of World War II, including an attempted replica of the entire city of Bristol.

### Listing

EH's other major impact on the lives of the general public is through its role as principal adviser to the Secretary of State at the Department for Culture, Media and Sport on statutory listing. The EH Annual Report 1999-2000 states that 2,349 buildings were recommended for spot listing to Government and only 1% were turned down. There were 349 additions to the schedule of ancient monuments, bringing the total to 18,351. By May 2000 there were 1,368 entries on the Register of Historic Parks and Gardens with, perhaps surprisingly, the greatest concentration of 128 in London. The number of conservation areas at the end of 2000 was just short of 9,000, whilst the grand total of listed buildings as last announced was 373,484 as at December 1999.

Individual listings announced in the 12 months up to the middle of 2001 included: the megastructure of Brunswick Square in Bloomsbury of 1963 by Patrick Hodgkinson; the Rotunda in Birmingham of 1960, the only survivor from the loathed Bull Ring; the History Faculty Building at Cambridge of 1964-68 by James Stirling; the monuments to Captain George Vancouver who gave his name to the Canadian city of 1798 at Petersham in Surrey; Mary Sumner House, Tufton Street, Westminster, the purpose-built headquarters of the Mothers' Union of 1925; the remaining buildings of the Royal Naval Cordite Factory at Holton Heath, near Wareham, Dorset of 1916; the railway stations at Ramsgate and Margate by Maxwell Fry who went on to so loudly embrace the International Modern style; the Grand Hotel, Clacton-on-Sea, Essex of 1892, the earliest building 'with a complete and coherent structural steel system'; a purpose-built veterinary surgery at Swindon; the Cistercian Trappist monastery at Woodleigh, Devon of 1902, abandoned as early as 1921; the D-Day embarcation slipways at Torquay, Devon of 1943; Broadmoor Hospital at Crowthorne, Berkshire of 1863 built as the State Asylum for Criminal Lunatics; a cricket pavilion of 1904 at Uttoxeter, Staffordshire; 'possibly the earliest surviving football grandstand in England' at Great Yarmouth, Norfolk of 1890; the Roman Catholic Cathedral at Clifton, Bristol of 1969-73; a rare 19th century manure sump at Ruyton, Shropshire; and 173 High Street, Berkhamsted, Hertfordshire, previously passed by but now found after some opening up to be a late 13th century shop.

### Wales

The latest available report of Cadw, the Welsh equivalent of English Heritage, covering the period up to 31 March 2000 states that 1,263 extra buildings had been listed in the preceding 12 months, bringing the total to 23,751. Fifty-two of the new listings were chapels, themselves the subject of a special thematic survey. The total of scheduled ancient monuments rose to 3,267, an increase over the year of 121. The principal new attraction was Haverfordwest Priory which opened in October 1999 and boasts what is claimed to be 'the only restored medieval abbey garden in Britain'. Grant aid to outsiders in the year totalled £1,280,443 in grants to outstanding secular buildings, £506,398 to buildings in use for worship and £449,349 for schemes in Conservation Areas. Cadw also issued a very useful guide on medieval church archaeology, whilst the National Museums and Galleries of Wales offered 'The Medieval Tiles of Wales', a major study in that area. 'Gwent/Monmouthshire' became the latest 'Buildings of Wales' volume.

### Scotland

In 1999-2000 Historic Scotland offered 110 grants for repairs worth over £10 million, including £540,000 to the Wynd Centre, the former church of St. John at Paisley. Like EH south of the Border, it is also the principal adviser to Government on listing and two of the more unusual recommendations in the year were the Tote Tower at Lanark Racecourse, the first 'robot bookie in Scotland' and the sheep dyke on North Ronaldsay, Orkney which was built to keep the sheep on the rocky shore whilst they grazed on the seaweed. HS also continued a distinguished publishing programme with major works on fire risk management in heritage buildings, the conservation of historic graveyards, historic Scottish roofing, and the carved stones of Scotland. The Royal Commission on the Ancient and Historical Monuments of Scotland, which is a strictly separate organisation, included among its acquisitions in the year a pocketbook and manual owned by Thomas Stevenson, son of Robert and father of Robert Louis who, with his brothers, carried out experiments into lighthouse illumination. Properties surveyed included the home of the writer Naomi Mitchison on Argyll where she lived between 1937 and her death in 1999.

### Threats Mounted and Averted

Major conservation campaigns of the 12 months up to July 2001 embraced: Hurstwood Great Barn, Burnley, Lancashire, listed Grade II* where the application to demolish was swiftly refused; St. Mary's, Buckden in Cambridgeshire where an audacious new extension was planned; Llawhaden House, Pembrokeshire, threatened with demolition after a devastating fire; Pallant House, Chichester, West Sussex, the subject of a controversial proposal for a Modernist extension to a Grade I listed Georgian townhouse; the 'Eye of York', near Cliffords Tower, the subject of a scheme for a major retail redevelopment; the Roman Catholic Cathedral of 1872 at Middlesbrough, Cleveland, consumed in an arsonist blaze after years of dereliction; and the Free Trade Hall, Manchester, where the interior of the Grade II* listed building was to be obliterated so that the shell could be skewered to the ground by a huge new multi-storey hotel. Other buildings have been reprieved, most notably Glentworth Hall, Lincolnshire, derelict for years, Manningham Mills, Bradford in Yorkshire, one of the greatest monuments of the Industrial Revolution in the North, now purchased for conversion by the developers Urban Splash, and St. Matthias Church, Poplar in the East End of London, now to be taken over by a Pentecostal Church following repair by a trust which in turn rescued the building from disuse and vandalism.

Organisations established to save church buildings have also seen a year of consolidation and expansion. The Churches Conservation Trust, which owns 330 redundant Anglican churches too important to be demolished or converted, has taken into care the granite church of 1814 at Princetown in Devon which served the warders of Dartmoor Prison. The Historic Chapels Trust, the equivalent body for nonconformist chapels in England, has completed its programme of repairs at Cote Baptist Chapel in Oxfordshire and has just won a substantial HLF grant for the conservation of the German Lutheran church in Alie Street, Tower Hamlets. The Friends of Friendless Churches accepted three new vestings in Wales in 2001: Derwen in Clwyd, Ynyscynhaearn in Gwynedd and Llandeloy in Pembrokeshire.

### Miscellanea

The Charity Commission published an important document on its attitude towards 'Preservation and Conservation' which recognised quite expressly for the first time that 'Conservation of the environment' is a charitable purpose.

The Plowden Medal, introduced in memory of the wall painting conservator Anna Plowden who died in 1997 and is given to a distinguished member of the 'conservation profession' went in 2001 to Donald Insall, CBE, the conservation architect.

A Centre for Historic Buildings Collections and Sites was opened at University College London in March 2001.

The same month also saw the launch of the United Kingdom and Ireland Blue Shield organisation (UKIRB), a 'non-governmental body which aims to raise awareness of the risks, both manmade and natural, to cultural heritage'.

# Dance

This was a year that saw many of Britain's leading dance companies at a crossroads looking backwards with affection and pride, and forwards with both confidence and trepidation. The Royal Ballet lost its founder Dame Ninette de Valois, who died in March 2001, and its director Sir Anthony Dowell, who retired at the end of the season. The new director, Ross Stretton, comes from the Australian Ballet and therefore represents an unprecedented break from the company's past. English National Ballet's director, Derek Deane, also left during the season, in which the company celebrated its 50th anniversary. Northern Ballet Theatre passed the season without a director after Stefano Giannetti's resignation in April 2000; the new director, David Nixon, took over in August 2001. Rambert Dance Company celebrated its 75th anniversary during the year and appointed a new chairman and a new executive director. Siobhan Davies Dance Company, still looking for a permanent rehearsal base, closed down temporarily at the end of 2000. The dance world in Britain will look very, and possibly fundamentally, different in the coming year.

Dame Ninette de Valois was born Edris Stannus in Co. Wicklow, Ireland on 6 June 1898 and died on 8 March 2001 at the age of 102. She was an accomplished dancer, and performed with the Massine-Lopokova company and then, from 1923, with Diaghilev's Ballets Russes in Monte Carlo. She opened her first school, the London Academy of Choreographic Art, in 1926. Her collaboration with the Old Vic's manager, Lilian Baylis, led to the foundation of the Vic-Wells Ballet when the new Sadler's Wells Theatre opened in 1931. The company grew and developed and, particularly during the war, nurtured a growing audience for ballet in Britain. It was renamed the Sadler's Wells Ballet, and was invited to re-open the Royal Opera House in 1946. International success followed, and in 1956 the company was granted a royal charter and became the Royal Ballet. Throughout the period of this growth, de Valois had been the company's artistic director and guiding force, encouraging the talents of the company's first ballerina, Alicia Markova, its founding choreographer, Frederick Ashton, its music director, Constant Lambert, and in due course its greatest star, Margot Fonteyn.

De Valois was herself a notable choreographer, creating *The Rake's Progress* in 1935 and *Checkmate* in 1937 amongst other works, but subsequently concentrated largely on running the company. She resigned in 1963 and became director of the Royal Ballet School, a position she held until 1971. She remained until her death a figure of enormous influence at the Royal Ballet, both company and school. De Valois was largely (although not, as she often said, solely) responsible for the growth and success of the Royal Ballet, and indeed for the development of ballet in Britain; she shaped the careers of generations of dancers, choreographers and teachers, and always had the vision to seize opportunities others may not even have seen.

Lack of vision was the criticism most regularly thrown at the Royal's retiring director, Sir Anthony Dowell. He took over the company in 1986, and although he undeniably presided over a huge improvement in the technical standards of the dancers, this was never combined with an artistic or stylistic vision or a clear sense of direction. His problems were exacerbated in recent years by the closure of the Royal Opera House and the financial and administrative nightmares that accompanied it, and he must be congratulated for holding the company together through these lean and difficult years. Although his choice of repertoire was generally uninspired and his productions of *Swan Lake* and *The Sleeping Beauty* were controversial, he did bring forward a number of highly talented dancers (including Darcey Bussell, Viviana Durante, Jonathan Cope and Sarah Wildor) and imported the international stars Sylvie Guillem and Irek Mukhamedov. But it is as a dancer that Dowell will be best remembered; he danced his first leading roles under de Valois' directorship, and went on to create major roles for both Frederick Ashton (most notably Oberon in *The Dream* in 1964, which initiated his great partnership with Antoinette Sibley) and Kenneth MacMillan (including Des Grieux in *Manon* in 1974). He combined a pure and elegant technique with sensitivity, intense musicality and a great sense of theatre, and he epitomised the English style of classical ballet.

The biggest challenge for Ross Stretton, who took over as director in September 2001, may be to preserve this distinctive English style in the face of the increasing 'globalisation' of the ballet world. He will not be helped in this task by his unfamiliarity with the company. But his pedigree as a director is sound, and he inherits a troupe of extremely talented dancers and the richest repertoire in the world.

Dowell's last season as director was, ironically, his most successful. It saw a repertoire including many of the most notable works associated with his own dancing career, and it also saw two major new talents bursting forth in splendour. Excellent performances of *Ondine*, *Shadowplay*, *The Song of the Earth*, *Les Noces*, *Symphonic Variations*, *Lilac Garden*, *Gloria*, *Triad*, and *The Firebird* were among the pleasures of the season. A partly redesigned version of MacMillan's *Romeo and Juliet* was less successful, and the year sadly saw the deaths of the ballet's designer, Nicholas Georgiadis, who collaborated with MacMillan on many important works, and of its first Escalus, Leslie Edwards, who joined the Vic-Wells Ballet in 1933 and was an outstanding dancer-actor and director of the Royal Ballet Choreographic Group; he retired from the company in 1993.

*Romeo and Juliet* did, however, give great opportunities to two outstanding new dancers in the company. Tamara Rojo was already known as a talented dramatic dancer from her years with English National Ballet; she joined the Royal Ballet at the beginning of the season and now has a repertoire worthy of her talents. Her affinity with MacMillan works in particular is evident, and her performances as Juliet and in *The Song of the Earth* were revelatory. She also applies her intelligence, her dramatic skills and her formidable technique to the classics, showing us in her performances why these works have survived. Alina Cojocaru, a 19-year-old Romanian who joined the company in November 1999, was known before this year only to a handful of insiders. In February 2000 she took over at short notice the lead role in *Symphonic Variations*, regarded by many as the Royal Ballet's signature work, and danced this difficult work as if she had known it all her life. This season she danced Clara in *The Nutcracker*, Juliet and Giselle in quick succession, and was promoted to principal dancer status in a blaze of publicity. She is a fragile-looking dancer who nevertheless has great technical strength, and she dances with rare musicality and an apparently effortless poetry.

The Royal Ballet's two new works of the season met with mixed success: Michael Corder's *Dance Variations* was an attractive, lyrical work, but Ashley Page's *This House Will Burn* was a long, self-indulgent and badly over-designed piece from a choreographer who seems to have lost his way. More encouraging new work was staged as part of the Artists' Development Initiative (ADI) run by principal dancer Deborah Bull in the studio theatres at the Royal Opera House. This saw the continuation of an interesting collaboration between Royal Ballet dancers and the contemporary choreographer Wayne McGregor. Last year McGregor created *Symbiont(s)* for Royal Ballet dancers as part of the same initiative; in spring 2001 he returned and re-staged the work, while dancers from his own company, Random Dance Company, performed *Aeon III*. The last element of the triple bill, *brainstate*, brought together dancers from both companies in an intriguing fusion of styles. The success of the ADI led to the appointment of Deborah Bull as artistic director of the Linbury Studio Theatre and the Clore Studio Upstairs from January 2002; she therefore retired as a dancer at the end of the 2000-2001 season. The Royal Ballet's music director, Andrea Quinn, left during the year to take up her new appointment at New York City Ballet, and Tony Hall, formerly head of news at the BBC, was appointed chief executive of the Royal Opera House.

English National Ballet (ENB) celebrated its 50th anniversary on 16 January 2001 with a gala at the London Coliseum that also honoured the 90th birthday of its co-founder, Dame Alicia Markova. It was a happy evening that stood out in a distinctly turbulent season. Derek Deane announced in October 2000 that he would resign as artistic director at the end of the season after eight years in charge; he was known to be unhappy about the cancellation of some planned new works for the company. In the event he left before the end of the season, and he will be replaced by the former ENB dancer Matz Skoog, a Swede who has been artistic director of the Royal New Zealand Ballet since 1996. Deane leaves behind a company in good technical shape and he has maintained a reasonable repertoire given the inevitable financial constraints; his tenure, however, may be remembered largely for the introduction of large-scale arena productions that garnered much publicity for the company but did little for its artistic stature. His most recent production of *Swan Lake*, premiered in October 2000, was described as a re-staging of the arena production mounted in 1997; in fact it was a beautiful, straightforward version incorporating Ashton's superb waltz and *pas de quatre* and with excellent new designs by Peter Farmer. This is a parting gift to be treasured. Skoog would appear to be a good choice to lead the company as he is familiar with its strengths and its problems and he seems to be level-headed but not unambitious about ENB's future. He aims to clear the company's deficit by the end of the 2001-2 season, and should have more room to manoeuvre in 2002-3, when ENB's Arts Council grant increases from £4.48 million to £5.08 million. He will be assisted by the company's new executive director, Christopher Nourse, and by Anthony Twiner, who was appointed music director in February 2001.

Rambert Dance Company's 75th anniversary was celebrated in a more relaxed fashion in June 2001. The company's first work was *A Tragedy of Fashion*, which marked the beginning of Frederick Ashton's choreographic career in 1926. The landmark was celebrated by an anniversary season at Sadler's Wells Theatre in London, an exhibition at the Theatre Museum and a film season at the National Film Theatre. This is a company secure in its past and confident about its future. It appointed a new chairman, Prudence Skene (a former executive director of the then Ballet Rambert from 1975 to 1986) and a new executive director, Sue Wyatt (formerly general manager of The Cholmondeleys and The Featherstonehaughs dance companies). The company undertook a large-scale tour of Australia, New Zealand and Singapore in spring 2001, and mounted a range of good-quality new productions as well as excellent pieces from the existing repertoire. It also performed for the first time at the Linbury Studio Theatre at the Royal Opera House.

Birmingham Royal Ballet (BRB) had a comparatively quiet season compared to the other leading dance companies. It was unable to use its home theatre, the Birmingham Hippodrome, which is being redeveloped, and so took advantage of the new Lowry centre in Salford. The big new work of the season was part 2 of the epic *Arthur*, choreographed by the company's director, David Bintley. Unfortunately *Arthur Part 2* was as turgid and uninspired as last season's part 1. Bintley is however maintaining the Ashton repertoire with a care that the Royal Ballet itself would do well to emulate, and won the award for Outstanding Contribution to Dance given for the first time by the dance section of the Critics' Circle in January 2001. Bintley, who sadly chose not to apply for the directorship of the Royal Ballet, was awarded a CBE in the Queen's Birthday Honours in June 2001. The company toured the USA in the autumn of 2000, and appointed former BRB dancer Kevin O'Hare as company manager.

Northern Ballet Theatre's lack of an artistic director during the year may be a defence for its dire new production, *Jekyll and Hyde*, that was premiered in February 2001. The choreography was by Massimo Moricone with designs by Alessandro Ciammarughi and a commissioned score by Philip Wilby; the whole amounted to a gimmicky and worthless production with little dance interest and no sense of drama. When this became evident, Mark Skipper, the company's executive director, had the courage to pull the production and replace it with the same choreographer's vastly superior *Romeo and Juliet*. The season was also improved by a revival of Michael Pink's excellent *Dracula*, that was presented in a horror double bill by the company at Sadler's Wells Theatre. The company took its production of *A Christmas Carol* to China in December 2000. Northern Ballet Theatre's premises in Leeds were badly damaged by fire in March 2001, but the company has now been given by Leeds City Council the site it needs for its new premises, and is close to raising the funds required to proceed with the project. Its Arts Council funding is also to be increased by about 25 per cent in the next two years. The new director, David Nixon, came to the company from BalletMet, Columbus, USA, in August 2001, thus ending the long interregnum.

Scottish Ballet mounted a disappointing new full-length production, its first for seven years. *Aladdin*, with choreography by Robert Cohan, a commissioned score by Carl Davis and designs by Lez Brotherston, brought no credit to its distinguished creators. The company does not seem to have successfully resolved questions over its identity and direction that have been raised for the last few years. It has, however, gained greater administrative stability, and now shares a board with Scottish Opera.

Richard Alston Dance Company suffers from no crisis of artistic identity. Alston continues to create fluent works for his company, and was awarded a CBE in the New Year's Honours. His new works this season were *Tremor*, to Shostakovich, and *Fever*, to Monteverdi. Siobhan Davies Dance Company, founded by Davies in 1988, has reached an *impasse* both financially and, to some extent, artistically. Her new work in autumn 2000, *Of Oil and*

*Water*, was set to music by Orlando Gough and had designs by David Buckland; the combination of talents was less persuasive than usual. At the end of 2000 Davies announced that the company would close down for 18 months while a permanent rehearsal base was sought. The Laban Institute plans to move from New Cross to purpose-built premises in Deptford in August 2002, and The Place in London is due to reopen shortly after its £7 million redevelopment. The absence of The Place left several contemporary dance festivals without a venue this year. Resolution! moved to the Bloomsbury Theatre for a slightly shorter season than usual, but Spring Loaded did not take place. Dance Umbrella used a range of venues and mounted performances by Merce Cunningham Dance Company, DV8 Physical Theatre (with Lloyd Newson's intriguing new work, *Can We Afford This*), Random Dance Company (which subsequently gained revenue funding from the Arts Council and has attracted major sponsorship from Ericsson), Trisha Brown Dance Company and the Siobhan Davies work mentioned above. It also presented Akram Khan, who is gaining a growing reputation for his work that fuses Kathak dance with contemporary dance; he is a charismatic dancer and choreographer, and won the award from the dance section of the Critics' Circle for Most Promising Newcomer in January 2001.

Other notable new works in the year under review included Kim Brandstrup's *The Art of Storytelling* for his Arc Dance Company, which celebrated its 15th anniversary in 2000, and Matthew Bourne's *The Car Man* for Adventures in Motion Pictures (AMP); this was set to Rodion Shchedrin's *Carmen* suite and was (very) loosely based on Bizet's opera, with designs by Lez Brotherston. Bourne, who was awarded an OBE in the New Year's Honours, has plenty of ideas and a well developed commercial and theatrical sense, but from a dance perspective his work is fairly limited. AMP takes up residency at the Old Vic in 2002.

Leading visitors to the UK included the Béjart Ballet and the Paul Taylor Dance Company, which both performed at Sadler's Wells Theatre in autumn 2000. Houston Ballet opened their first London season for 18 years at the same theatre in April 2001 with Ben Stevenson's production of *Cleopatra*, which was deemed to be entirely unsuccessful. Dutch National Ballet gave a short and very successful season at Sadler's Wells in May 2001, and the Cullberg Ballet performed at the Barbican Theatre in June 2001. The Bolshoi sent some of its dancers to give a season at Drury Lane at short notice in April-May 2001, and the full strength of the Kirov returned to the Royal Opera House for a lavish season in June-July 2001. La Scala Ballet brought Sylvie Guillem's production of *Giselle* to the Royal Opera House in August 2001, followed immediately by the triumphant return of Helgi Tomasson's San Francisco Ballet.

An auction was held at Christie's in London in December 2000 of costumes, letters and other items belonging to Dame Margot Fonteyn, who died in 1991. Although the Royal Opera House, the Royal Ballet School and the Theatre Museum did acquire some important items, many others went overseas and to private collectors. This was a sad outcome for a historic collection.

Ballet's biggest publicity boost for years came in the shape of major feature film, *Billy Elliot*, dealing with the balletic aspirations of a young boy from a northern mining town during the Miners' Strike of the mid 1980s. The film was more than a sentimental tear-jerker; it, and particularly its young star, Jamie Bell, did manage to convey the excitement and exhiliration of ballet, as well as the hard work and dedication required to become a dancer. The Royal Ballet School, foremost guardian of our future dancers, is planning to move to new premises alongside the Royal Ballet in Covent Garden, and an extra £1 million of government funding for this project was announced in June 2001. A dance school in the north will also be added to the three schools in the south currently providing government-funded places for talented dancers, presumably in the hope that real-life 'Billy Elliots' will be encouraged to take up this inspiring and supremely demanding art form.

## PRODUCTIONS

### Royal Ballet

Founded 1931 as the Vic-Wells Ballet

Royal Opera House, Covent Garden, London WC2E 9DD

World premières:

*Dance Variations* (Michael Corder), 28 October 2000. A one-act ballet. Music, Richard Rodney Bennett; design, Anthony Ward. Cast led by Darcey Bussell and Jonathan Cope

*This House Will Burn* (Ashley Page), 7 March 2001. A one-act ballet. Music, Orlando Gough; sets, Stephen Chambers; costumes, Jon Morrell. Dancers, Laura Morera, Mara Galeazzi, Zenaida Yanowsky, Alina Cojocaru, Johan Kobborg, Inaki Urlezaga, Ricardo Cervera, Edward Watson, Joshua Tuifua

Full-length ballets from the repertoire: *Swan Lake* (Petipa/Ivanov, prod. Dowell 1987), *Ondine* (Ashton, 1958), *The Nutcracker* (Ivanov, prod. Wright 1984 with revisions 1999), *La file mal gardée* (Ashton, 1960), *Romeo and Juliet* (MacMillan, 1965), *Giselle* (Coralli/Perrot, prod. Wright 1985), *Coppélia* (de Valois after Ivanov and Cecchetti, 1954).

One-act ballets and *pas de deux* from the repertoire: *Shadowplay* (Tudor, 1967), *Marguerite and Armand* (Ashton, 1963), *La Valse* (Ashton, 1958), *Symphonic Variations* (Ashton, 1946), *Lilac Garden* (Tudor, 1936), *Gloria* (MacMillan, 1980), *Triad* (MacMillan, 1972), *The Concert* (Robbins, 1956), *The Firebird* (Fokine, 1910), *Agon* (Balanchine, 1957), *Les Noces* (Nijinska, 1923), *The Dream* (Ashton, 1964), *Song of the Earth* (MacMillan, 1965), *The Sleeping Beauty pas de deux* (Petipa, prod. Dowell 1994), *Monotones II* (Ashton, 1966), *Manon pas de deux* (MacMillan, 1974), *Don Quixote pas de deux* (Petipa, 1869), *A Month in the Country* (Ashton, 1976).

On 23 May 2001 at the Royal Opera House the company staged a gala, *A Knight at the Ballet*, that paid tribute to the career of its director, Sir Anthony Dowell, who retired at the end of the season.

Dancers from the company participated in various works in the Clore Studio Upstairs at the Royal Opera House, working with choreographers including Wayne McGregor, Cathy Marston and Tom Sapsford as part of the Artists' Development Initiative. Dancers also took part in a programme on 12 November 2000 in the Linbury Studio Theatre at the Royal Opera House celebrating the 150th anniversary of the birth of Enrico Cecchetti and highlighting his influence on the work of Sir Frederick Ashton.

The company toured to the USA in June 2001, performing *Les Rendezvous* (Ashton, 1933), *Thais pas de deux* (Ashton, 1971), *Symphonic Variations*, *Marguerite and Armand* and *La fille mal gardée* in Washington DC, and *Swan Lake* in Boston.

### Birmingham Royal Ballet

Founded 1946 as the Sadler's Wells Opera Ballet

Birmingham Hippodrome, Thorp Street, Birmingham B5 4AU

World première:
*Arthur, Part 2* (David Bintley), 9 May 2001. A full-length ballet. Music, John McCabe; sets, Peter J. Davison; costumes, Jasper Conran. Cast led by Wolfgang Stollwitzer, Leticia Muller, Monica Zamora, Andrew Murphy, Robert Parker and Joseph Cipolla
Full length ballets from the repertoire: *The Two Pigeons* (Ashton, 1961), *The Nutcracker* (Ivanov, prod. Wright, additional choreography by Redmon, 1990), *La fille mal gardée* (Ashton, 1960), *Arthur, Part 1* (Bintley, 2000).
One-act ballets from the repertoire: *Scènes de Ballet* (Ashton, 1948), *Dante Sonata* (Ashton, 1940), *Enigma Variations* (Ashton, 1968), *Five Brahms Waltzes in the Manner of Isadora Duncan* (Ashton, 1975), *Walk to the Paradise Garden* (Ashton, 1972), *Tweedledum and Tweedledee* (Ashton, 1977), *Voices of Spring* (Ashton, 1977), *Concerto Barocco* (Balanchine, 1941), *Powder* (Welch, 1998), *In the Upper Room* (Tharp, 1986).
In addition to a season at the Alexandra Theatre in Birmingham, the company toured to Plymouth (three seasons), Sunderland, Bradford and Manchester (two seasons each) and London (Sadler's Wells Theatre).
The company also toured to the USA (New York and Chicago) in September-October 2000 with a repertoire of *Edward II* (Bintley, 1995), *Slaughter on Tenth Avenue* (Balanchine, 1936), *The Shakespeare Suite* (Bintley, 1999) and *The Nutcracker Sweeties* (Bintley, 1996).

ENGLISH NATIONAL BALLET
Founded 1950 as London Festival Ballet
Markova House, 39 Jay Mews, London SW7 2ES

World première:
*Swan Lake* (Petipa/Ivanov, prod. Deane), 16 October 2000. Music, Tchaikovsky; design, Peter Farmer. Cast led by Monica Perego and Patrick Armand
Full-length ballets from the repertoire: *The Nutcracker* (Deane, 1997), *Giselle* (Coralli/Perrot, prod. Deane 1994), *Romeo and Juliet* (Deane, 1998).
One-act ballets from the repertoire: *Les Sylphides* (Fokine, 1909), *Voluntaries* (Tetley, 1973), *Etudes* (Lander, 1948), *Le Corsaire pas de deux* (Petipa), *Swan Lake Act II pas de deux*, *Impromptu* (Deane, 1982), *Don Quixote pas de deux* (after Petipa).
The full company toured to Southampton (three seasons), Bristol, Liverpool, Manchester (two seasons), Oxford, London (the Coliseum and the Royal Albert Hall) and Bristol.
In March-April 2001 the company split into two groups and went on two small-scale tours (called *Tour de Force*). One group toured *Apollo* (Balanchine, 1928), *Perpetuum Mobile* (Hampson, 1997) and *Grand Pas* from *Paquita* (Petipa/Deane) to Swindon, Poole, Blackpool, Woking, Truro and Malvern. The other group toured *Square Dance* (Balanchine, 1957), *Don Quixote pas de deux*, *Flower Festival in Genzano pas de deux* (Bournonville, 1858), *The Sleeping Beauty pas de deux* and *Who Cares?* (Balanchine, 1970) to Tunbridge Wells, Cambridge, Scunthorpe and Barnstaple.
In April 2001 the company toured *Swan Lake* to Japan (Tokyo, Osaka and Nagoya) and in July-August 2001 it took *Romeo and Juliet* to Australia (Sydney, Brisbane, Melbourne, Adelaide and Perth).
On 16 January 2001 the company staged a gala at the London Coliseum to mark its 50th anniversary.

RAMBERT DANCE COMPANY
Founded 1926 as the Marie Rambert Dancers
94 Chiswick High Road, London W4 1SH

World premières:
*7DS (Seven Deadly Sins)* (Didy Veldman), 20 September 2000. Score, Luca Mainardi; design, Miriam Buether. Dancers, Antonia Grove, Miranda Lind, Ana Luján Sanchez, Rachel Poirier, Angela Towler and Deirdre Chapman
*The Celebrated Soubrette* (Javier de Frutos), 1 November 2000. Score, Michael Daugherty; design, Jackie Galloway
*Twin Suite 2* (Kinson Productions/Glenn Wilkinson), 2 May 2001. Music, Aphex Twin; design, Dody Nash
*At Any Time* (Rafael Bonachela), 2 May 2001. Music, Bach; design, Angela de la Cruz. Cast led by Elizabeth Old
*Unrest* (Richard Alston), 20 June 2001. Music, Arvo Pärt; design, Jeanne Spaziani
*detritus* (Wayne McGregor), 20 June 2001. Music, Scanner; sets, Vicki Mortimer; costumes, Ben Maher

Company premières:
*She Was Black* (Mats Ek, 1995), 4 October 2000. Music, Gorecki and a traditional throat song, *Kongerei*; design, Peder Freiij
*Hurricane* (Christopher Bruce, 2000), 2 May 2001. A solo. Music, Bob Dylan. Dancer, David Hughes
*Cheese* (Jeremy James, 2000), 12 June 2001. Music, Peter Morris; design, Fiona Chillcot. Dancers, Antonia Grove, Ana Luján Sanchez, Samantha Smith, Rafael Bonachela, Conor O'Brien
*Symphony of Psalms* (Jirí Kylián, 1978), 12 June 2001. Music, Stravinsky; sets, William Katz; costumes, Joop Stokvis

Works from the repertoire: *Embrace Tiger and Return to Mountain* (Tetley, 1968), *Ghost Dances* (Bruce, 1981), *Sergeant Early's Dream* (Bruce, 1984), *Moonshine* (Bruce, 1993), *Swansong* (Bruce, 1987), *Beach Birds* (Cunningham, 1991), *Rooster* (Bruce, 1991), *Sounding* (Davies, 1989), *Pierrot Lunaire* (Tetley, 1962).
The company performed in Manchester, High Wycombe, Edinburgh, London (two seasons at Sadler's Wells Theatre and one at the Linbury Studio Theatre at the Royal Opera House), Plymouth, Sheffield, and Aberdeen. It also toured to Australia (Perth, Adelaide and Melbourne), New Zealand (Wellington and Auckland) and Singapore in March-April 2001, performing *Rooster*, *Ghost Dances*, *Meeting Point* (Bruce, 1996), and *Gaps, Laps and Relapse* (James, 1998). It then performed *Beach Birds*, *Swansong* and *Meeting Point* in Cologne, Germany, in April 2001.

RICHARD ALSTON DANCE COMPANY
Founded 1994
Cecil Sharp House, 2 Regent's Park Road, London NW1 7AY
All works danced by the company are choreographed by Richard Alston.

World premières:
*Tremor*, 13 October 2000. Music, Shostakovich; costumes, Elizabeth Baker
*Fever*, 27 February 2001. Music, Monteverdi; costumes, Elizabeth Baker
Works from the repertoire: *Waltzes in Disorder* (1998), *Roughcut* (1999), *The Signal of a Shake* (2000), *Slow Airs (Almost All)* (1999), *Red Run* (1998), *A Sudden Exit* (1999).
The company performed in Cambridge (two seasons), Horsham, High Wycombe, Manchester, Brecon, Malvern, Edinburgh, Nottingham, Norwich, Brighton, Stevenage, Canterbury, Oxford, London (Queen Elizabeth Hall), Sheffield, Blackpool and Woking.

Scottish Ballet
Founded 1956 as the Western Theatre Ballet
261 West Princes Street, Glasgow G4 9EE

World première:
*Aladdin* (Robert Cohan), 20 December 2000. A full-length work. Score, Carl Davis; sets, Lez Brotherston (realized by Colin Falconer); costumes, Colin Falconer. Cast led by Jésus Pastor, Linda Packer and Michele di Molfetta

Company première:
*Carmen* (Robert North, 1997), 4 May 2001. Score, Christopher Benstead; design, Luisa Spinatelli. Cast led by Mar Moreno and Jésus Pastor
Full-length ballet from the repertoire: *Romeo and Juliet* (North, 1990).
The company performed in Aberdeen (three seasons), Edinburgh (three seasons), Inverness (three seasons) and Glasgow (two seasons).
It also gave three performances of *Carmen* at the Sintra Festival, Portugal, in August 2001.

# Film

Truth 24 frames a second, Jean-Luc Godard's famous definition of cinema may soon become an anachronism. The movies' relationship to 'truth' has always been debatable and fraught with contradiction, but it's quite possible that the frame itself won't last much longer. Already more and more films are being shot on digital video technology (this year the most notable were the Dogme brethren's *The King Is Alive* and *Julian Donkey-boy*, Lars von Trier's non-Dogme musical *Dancer in the Dark*, and Spike Lee's *Bamboozled*), and now the industry is eyeing up digital distribution networks. 'Truth bytes' may have to be the cineaste's new catchphrase.

While first-time and independent film-makers are turning to digital cameras to cut down on film stock and crewing costs, the most obvious signs of change are in high-end Hollywood productions, where computer generated imagery (CGI) is coming to dominate the look and feel of the movies. In the summer of 2001 the big studio blockbusters were *AI: Artificial Intelligence* (Spielberg's film based on the late Stanley Kubrick's sci-fi project), *Evolution* (a sci-fi comedy with CGI aliens on Earth), *Cats & Dogs* (a children's movie about CGI dogs battling it out with CGI cats), *Lara Croft: Tomb Raider* (with Angelina Jolie as the computer game action heroine), *Dr Dolittle 2* (Eddie Murphy and CGI animals), *Jurassic Park III* (Téa Leoni and CGI dinosaurs), *Shrek* (a CGI animated fairytale) and *Final Fantasy: The Spirits Within* – this last another computer game spin-off, but notable for electing to tell its adult sci-fi story with 'realistic' CGI creations rather than through live actors. If it's questionable whether computer programmers can match the humanity of a great actor, there's little doubt they can achieve uncanny verisimilitude (and industry Bible 'Variety' opined that the performances in *Final Fantasy* were no worse than in most sci-fi movies). When Oliver Reed died before completing his role in *Gladiator*, director Ridley Scott was able to resurrect him for crucial shots by way of CGI. No-one could spot the difference. The sad truth is that very few Hollywood movies ask actors to go beyond a few basic, pre-programmed emotional registers as it is; watching the part-live action *Cats & Dogs*, you sometimes have to pinch yourself to remember that Jeff Goldblum and Elizabeth Perkins are 'human-generated'.

That's the downside to the way Hollywood still panders to a perceived teenage taste for spectacle and shock, elements which guarantee multiplex exposure across the globe. *Gladiator* – on the face of it a less obvious CGI movie – is actually a good case in point, for this old fashioned historical epic would not have been deemed commercially viable ten or fifteen years ago (the 'sword and sandal' genre died out at the end of the 1960s), but eschewed the costs of building huge sets and filling them with thousands of hungry extras by recreating them digitally. In this way we can see that CGI technology is setting the agenda just as surely as CinemaScope transformed pictures in the 1950s. Of course it would be absurd to suggest that actors are facing imminent redundancy (and anyway they've never been in higher demand as 'voice artists'), but it's not surprising that so many movie stars turn to the stage for artistic fulfilment (Jessica Lange trod London's boards this year in *A Long Day's Journey Into Night*, so did many others) or take to directing their own, more personal movies: Steve Buscemi with *Animal Factory* (starring Willem Dafoe and Edward Furlong) and Sean Penn with *The Pledge* (starring Jack Nicholson) for example. Sadly – typically – both these fine, character-based films struggled to gain more than token distribution.

Average production costs continue to rise ($55 million with half that again in marketing costs). So do ticket prices and (in the UK) the number of cinema screens (in the US that statistic dropped in 2000 for the first time in more than a decade). Yet in the US nearly ten cinema chains filed for bankruptcy this year and profit margins are shrinking. Jerry Bruckheimer's production *Pearl Harbor* became the most expensively budgeted movie ever approved by a studio (as opposed to the likes of *Titanic*, which went massively over-budget) at a widely-reported $135 million. Buena Vista spent another $5 million on a lavish premiere on a US aircraft carrier docked in *Pearl Harbor*, where the stars greeted the world's press. Yet Bruckheimer and his director Michael Bay deferred their usual fees, as did cast members Ben Affleck, Kate Beckinsale, Josh Hartnett and Cuba Gooding Jr. It was estimated the film would have to make in the region of $500 million to turn a profit. Such is the juggernaut of Hollywood distribution across the world it will probably do it, eventually – despite scathing reviews which quite rightly pointed out how the film shirked historical responsibility for tepid adolescent romance and heavy-handed myth-mongering. Again, this was a film put into production to capitalise on CGI; the Japanese raid on the US fleet constitutes no less than 43 minutes of screen time. Yet for all the ultimately numbing carnage, Bay is careful to ensure that nothing is too horrific: at this kind of budget, a PG certificate is a pre-requisite.

For six months this year – longer in some quarters – the industry was entirely over-shadowed by the looming prospect of the strikes threatened by the Writers Guild of America (scheduled for June 2001) and the Screen Actors Guild (due to kick in a month later). The issue for both unions was the crucial question of residual payments for ancillary markets – the markets where the studios really make their profits: sales to television companies, video rentals and DVD retail (with Internet distribution still the big, elusive prize). Had they gone ahead, the strikes could have paralysed the industry – so the studios rushed dozens of movies into production in the first half of 2001, with casts and crews working double-time to get them in the can. (By June, Warners apparently had 35 films in the bag, more than enough to see them through a two-year strike). Looking on the bright side, these movies may turn out to be closer to the writers' original intentions than those which go through the usual script factory doctoring, that is to say quirkier, and possibly more subversive, but the fear has to be they'll look like just what they are: rush jobs.

In the event, negotiations went up to the wire but compromises left honours more or less even – though not before the studios had rid themselves of most of their costly 'house-keeping deals', whereby they pay the overheads on a star or director's development company in return for first-refusal on their projects.

The strike threat seems to have concentrated some minds at least. It's by no means unusual for a director to take three years between getting projects on the screen; such is the lumbering pace and uncertainty of Hollywood. Yet this year Robert Zemeckis shot the first half of *Cast Away*, then went straight into the suspense film *What Lies Beneath* as Tom Hanks grew his beard and lost weight for the second half. Steven Spielberg edited *AI* by night and shot *Minority Report* by day.

Meanwhile his Dreamworks SKG studio went from strength to strength, scoring critical and commercial hits with *Chicken Run* and *Shrek*, and winning the Best Picture Oscar for *Gladiator*. Director Ridley Scott was still taking his bow for that dubious triumph when he released *Hannibal*, an inert, style-conscious sequel to *The Silence of the Lambs* – and went straight into production on *Black Hawk Down*, about the ill-fated US intervention in Somalia.

Scott was matched by Steven Soderbergh, who became the first director in 60 years to pick up two Oscar nominations as Best Director in the same year. Julia Roberts was named Best Actress for her performance as working class legal crusader *Erin Brockovich*, and Soderbergh also won, this time for *Traffic*, an ambitious dissection of American drug culture(s), inspired by the British TV series 'Traffik'. Evidently not one to rest on his laurels, Soderbergh has since shot his remake of the old Ratpack vehicle *Oceans 11* with an all-star cast.

Perhaps the most enthusiastically received American film of the year was in Cantonese, Ang Lee's *Crouching Tiger, Hidden Dragon*. Produced by Columbia, a division of the Japanese conglomerate Sony, this romantic action movie in the Chinese 'wuxia' chivalric story tradition was conceived as a mainstream movie for Asian territories with art-house credentials for the West. As it turned out, the film's graceful, gravity-defying acrobatics and charismatic stars (Chow Yun-Fat, Michelle Yeoh and Zhang Ziyi) proved equally popular with young audiences in the US and across Europe as they did across Asia. Ironically this was one 'Hollywood' film which dispensed with CGI entirely and staged all its remarkable stunts physically, with wire tricks developed in the Hong Kong film industry. The most successful subtitled film ever made, this was either a one-off, or an exciting portent of how a truly global cinema might work, depending on your point of view.

No-one could pretend it was a vintage year for American movies. Among the Independents, bright spots were few and far between. Sundance 2000 winners *Girlfight* and *You Can Count on Me* couldn't turn good reviews into good box-office. Artisan faced the same problem with the nihilistic addiction drama *Requiem for a Dream*, and fell flat on their face with the disastrous *Blair Witch 2*, a flop which jeopardised the future of the company. The Shooting Gallery was also reported to be in financial trouble. Miramax has long since given up its indie credentials, if not its pretensions. Harvey Weinstein decided to make his annual Oscar push with the thoroughly bland and whimsical *Chocolat*, a de-politicised take on Joanne Harris's best-seller. In common with his rivals, Weinstein passed on Christopher Nolan's *Memento*, easily the most ingenious thriller of the year (with Guy Peirce as a man with no short-term memory, the film builds into a nightmare of uncertainty), forcing the film-makers to form their own distribution company – and reap the rewards themselves.

It was not a great year for British cinema either (though patriots can stake a claim to both *Gladiator* and *Memento* if they choose to), but as always two or three films beat the odds to show what can be done. The lottery franchisees produced little or nothing to enhance their battered reputations, and it was a matter of national shame that not one British film made the official selection at Cannes 2001. Admittedly, Cannes 2000 rejected Terence Davies' sublime Edith Wharton adaptation, *House of Mirth*, as did Venice, but the general point stands: British cinema is inhospitable ground for artists at the moment. And as the luckless franchisees have shown, commercial orientation is no guarantee of success.

At least *Billy Elliott* was a genuine home-grown hit, a feel-good movie set against the backdrop of the miners' strike, it featured a winning performance from young Jamie Bell as a northern lad encouraged to make the most of his natural gift for ballet by teacher Julie Walters. A bit rose-tinted and 'grim up North', but still a notable first film from acclaimed stage director Stephen Daldry to put beside Sam Mendes' *American Beauty* triumph last year.

To everyone's surprise, it seemed, Jonathan Glazer finally made a British gangster film worth seeing. *Sexy Beast* had a novel, dreamy robbery sequence for its climax, but essentially this was a Pinteresque two-hander pitting Ben Kingsley's East End bulldog Don Logan against Ray Winstone's adamantly retired Costa del Sol ex-pat, Gal. Don wants him to come back for one last job, and won't take 'no' for an answer. Something has to give, but when it does it comes as a totally believable shock. Splendidly acted (with Kingsley laying Gandhi's ghost to rest once and for all) this was enthralling stuff.

Britain's most consistent production outfit, Working Title, delivered the goods again with *Bridget Jones's Diary*. Directed by author Helen Fielding's friend Sharon Maguire, the film retained the book's sarky wit but toned down Bridget's neurotic self-consciousness. Texan Renee Zellweger hit the right note (and the right size) as a normal, unhealthy-looking woman about town, and Hugh Grant excelled as her posh publisher, Daniel. (Colin Firth was wittily cast as D'Arcy). This is the kind of mid-level, self-deprecating comedy the British do well. In its own way, Aardman Animation's *Chicken Run* fits the same bill. What Working Title and the rest are hoping is that the industry can step up a level and beat Hollywood for higher stakes – but that still looks a tall order.

Budgeted at $40 million, Working Title's *Captain Corelli's Mandolin* (co-produced with Miramax) illustrated some of the pitfalls. A WWII romance, it skirted the novel's controversial politics but its opportunist casting of Nicolas Cage as an Italian, John Hurt and Penelope Cruz as Greeks failed to bring diverse ethnic stereotypes to life, leaving the audience with little more than a sumptuous but misleading tourist brochure of a movie. Another WWII movie, *Enemy at the Gates* fell at the same gate. This was a European production – the most expensive ever at $95 million – directed by a French man, Jean-Jacques Annaud, shot in Berlin and set during the siege of Stalingrad, but in English, starring Jude Law, Joseph Fiennes and Rachel Weisz. Muddy and bloody, you wouldn't call it 'touristic', but audiences just weren't interested.

Interestingly, European film-makers did make real impact on the box-office this year, but only on home ground. In the first six months of 2001, seven of the top ten money-makers in France were French films – an extraordinary success. They were led by Jean-Pierre Jeunet's charming comic fable *Amélie Poulain de Montmartre*, an innocuous modern day fairytale which somehow became embroiled in a political debate about the true (multi-ethnic) face of modern France. Comedies like *Le Gout des Autres* and stylish action movies like *Brotherhood of the Wolf* were popular locally, but couldn't hope to make serious inroads internationally.

Similarly, German films scored well in Germany, Spanish films in Spain. It would be rash to suggest that Hollywood's long hegemony is under threat, but it's interesting that audiences do seem to be looking for alternative perspectives and films which connect, however fleetingly, with their own cultures.

Of course national cultures are in perpetual flux, and never more so than in the era of globalisation. As politicians and protesters everywhere fought to get some sort of grip on the New World Order, film-makers reflected a general frustration with rampant capitalism, social division and powerlessness in many of the outstanding movies of the year: from Britain, Pawel Pawelikowski's asylum-seekers' love story *Last Resort*; from France, Michael Haneke's fractured study of urban alienation Code: *Unknown; from Mexico*; Alejandro Gonzalez Inarritu's savage *Amores Perros*; and from Sweden, Roy Andersson's black comic allegory *Songs from the Second Floor*.

The most profound and moving film of the year also reflected these anxieties: Edward Yang's *A One and A Two* ('*YiYi*') is a simple but enormously sympathetic portrait of a family coping – with some difficulty – with the depersonalising pressures of modern life in Taipei. An old lady goes into a coma, and the doctor advises her relatives to go in and speak to her each day. This rite inspires tearful confessionals from some, gossipy chit-chat from others, but allows Yang to put each of them under the microscope: there is NJ, the old lady's son-in-law, a partner in a financially shaky computer firm who is thrown when he bumps into an ex-girlfriend at his brother-in-law's wedding; NJ's wife Min-Min, who comes to realise the emptiness of her own life as she deals with her mother's mortality; their teenage daughter Ting-Ting, on the cusp of discovering love for the first time; and their eight-year-old boy Yang-Yang, intent on his own photographic pursuits, including a project photographing the back of people's heads ('Very avant-garde' sniffs his teacher).

Like a good number of recent Hollywood heroes and anti-heroes – Lester Burnham in *American Beauty* might be their figurehead – NJ is beginning to wonder whether he has wasted his prime. He suspects that, like his brother-in-law, he didn't marry the love of his life. Furthermore he's no longer confident of his vocation. A man of integrity, he is disgusted by his partners' fast and loose business ethics, their rampant opportunism and cynicism. 'Where is our dignity?' he wants to know. Only an encounter with a gnomic Japanese games designer, Mr Ota, restores his morale. Delegated to look after this VIP, NJ takes him to a karaoke club where the two men communicate in their one common language, English, about their love for another: music. It's a beautiful, tender, ineffably touching scene, in a film that is full of such heart-rending recognitions. *A One and a Two* is long and slow, sentimental, old fashioned in a way, shot in a patient, discreet, rational style antithetical to prevailing trends in Western cinema – but it's a movie that speaks to the spiritual void in our times with essential good faith in humanity.

## FILM AWARD WINNERS

### Academy Awards 2000

Best picture - *Gladiator*
Best director - Steven Soderbergh, *Traffic*
Best actor - Russell Crowe, *Gladiator*
Best actress - Julia Roberts, *Erin Brockovich*
Best supporting actor - Benicio Del Toro, *Traffic*
Best supporting actress - Marcia Gay Harden, *Pollock*
Best original screenplay - Cameron Crowe, *Almost Famous*
Best adapted screenplay - Stephen Gaghan, *Traffic*
Best foreign language film - *Crouching Tiger Hidden, Dragon*
Best original score - *Crouching Tiger, Hidden Dragon*
Best original song - *Things Have Changed*
Best cinematography - *Crouching Tiger, Hidden Dragon*
Best art direction - *Crouching Tiger, Hidden Dragon*
Best film editing – *Traffic*
Best costume design - *Gladiator*
Best sound – *Gladiator*
Best sound effects editing – *U-571*
Best visual effects - *Gladiator*
Best make-up - *Dr. Seuss' in: How the Grinch Stole Christmas*
Best animated short - *Father and Daughter*
Best documentary feature - *Into the Arms of Strangers: Stories of Kindertransport*
Best short documentary - *Big Mama*
Best short film - *Quiero Ser*

### BAFTA Awards 2000

Best film - *Gladiator*
David Lean award (best achievement in direction) - Ang Lee, *Crouching Tiger, Hidden Dragon*
Best actor - Jamie Bell, *Billy Elliot*
Best actress - Julia Roberts, *Erin Brockovich*
Best supporting actor -Benicio Del Toro, *Traffic*
Best supporting actress - Julie Walters, *Billy Elliot*
Alexander Korda award (British film of the year) - *Billy Elliot*
Best foreign language film – *Crouching Tiger, Hidden Dragon*
Best original screenplay -Cameron Crowe, *Almost Famous*
Best adapted screenplay - Stephen Gaghan, *Traffic*
Academy Fellowships -Albert Finney
Michael Balcon Award for contribution to British cinema: Mary Selway

### Golden Globe Awards 2001

Best picture - *Gladiator*
Best actress in drama - Julia Roberts, *Erin Brockovich*
Best actor in drama - Tom Hanks, *Cast Away*
Best actress in musical or comedy - Renee Zellweger, *Nurse Betty*
Best actor in musical or comedy - George Clooney, *O Brother, Where Art Thou*
Best supporting actress - Kate Hudson, *Almost Famous*
Best supporting actor - Benicio Del Toro, *Traffic*
Best director - Ang Lee, *Crouching Tiger, Hidden Dragon*
Best screenplay - Stephen Gaghan, *Traffic*
Best original song - Wonder Boys, *Things Have Changed*

# Literature

Despite the fact that book five of the Harry Potter series was not published in 2001, J. K. Rowling continued to dominate the bestseller lists. All four previous books regularly occupied the top slots, and the paperback of *Harry Potter and the Goblet of Fire*, out in July, sold more than 100,000 copies in its first official week of publication alone (though booksellers squabbled because a publication embargo was broken, and several chains sold the paperback early). The fifth book, *Harry Potter and the Order of the Phoenix*, had always been scheduled for 2002, contrary to press reports that the author had writer's block. In fact in March Rowling produced, in aid of Comic Relief Red Nose Day, two short books which are mentioned in the novels: *Quidditch Through the Ages by Kenilworthy Whisp*, published by '*Whizz Hard Books*' (Ron Weasley's favourite book) and *Fantastic Beasts and Where to Find Them by Newt Scamander, from 'Obscurus Books*'. They cost £2.50 each, were published around the world by Bloomsbury and by Scholastic in the US, sold more than 400,000 copies each and, thanks to the generosity of booksellers, printers, typesetters and paper suppliers, between them raised some £1.5m to tackle poverty and promote social justice. Bestselling authors Helen Fielding and Delia Smith also wrote special books to raise money for Comic Relief. *Delia's Chocolate Selection* (New Crane) sold at a rate of 50,000 copies a week to begin with, and *Bridget Jones's Guide to Life* (Picador) at a rate of some 30,000 copies.

Comic Relief was not Harry's only contribution to charity. J. K. Rowling signed up a reported $150m deal for global marketing rights in the first film of the Harry Potter books. The deal included, at the author's insistence, a commitment to fund community-based reading schemes.

Harry Potter was also the subject of a groundbreaking media initiative. On Boxing Day Radio Four broadcast a reading by Stephen Fry of Harry Potter and the Philosopher's Stone in its entirety, which occupied an unprecedented eight hours of airtime. Fry's unabridged audiotape of the fourth book, 16 tapes long, also helped to perpetuate Harry fervour when it came out in the summer. Merchandise, especially stationery, T-shirts and games, was ubiquitous, and tantalising trailers, released months early, stoked excitement about the release of the Warner Brothers film of the first book in November 2001. Harry's publishers, Bloomsbury, found its stock soared: two directors made £150,000 in one day buying and selling shares (bought at a low price set by a longstanding contractual agreement), and the publisher was named Publisher of the Year in the British Book Awards. The Queen, who devoted a day (22 March) to the book trade by visiting Pimlico Library and Waterstone's flagship bookshop in Piccadilly, and inviting luminaries of the industry to Buckingham Palace, also paid a visit to Bloomsbury's Soho offices, and heard the story of Harry's success from those who helped it happen.

Although there was hardly a week of the year when a book by J. K. Rowling did not appear in the top five bestsellers, there were books that managed to nudge Harry aside. Some were romances and thrillers by predictably bestselling authors, such as Danielle Steel, with *Irresistible Forces*, *The House on Hope Street* and *Leap of Faith* (Transworld), Dick Francis with *Second Wind* (Pan), Catherine Cookson with yet more posthumous books coming out of the cupboard: *A House Divided*, *Kate Hannigan's Girl* and *Silent Lady* (Transworld), Patricia Cornwell with *Last Precinct* (Little, Brown), Stephen King with *Dreamcatcher* (Hodder), Wilbur Smith with *Warlock* (Macmillan) and John Grisham with *The Brethren* and *A Painted House* (Century/Arrow). Some were old favourites producing sequels to past successes, such as Sue Townsend with *Adrian Mole: The Cappuccino Years* (Penguin), Terry Pratchett with *The Fifth Elephant*, *The Truth and Thief of Time* (Transworld), Frank McCourt, still going strong with his second volume of his memoirs, *'Tis* (Flamingo), and Andy McNab with more SAS adventure in *Crisis Four* (Corgi). Among celebrity autobiographies, actress Martine McCutcheon's *Who Does She Think She Is?* (Century/Arrow), Carry On star Barbara Windsor's *All of Me* (Headline), and footballer David Beckham's *My World*, were big sellers. This doubtless inspired the payment of a seven-figure advance to Beckham's wife Victoria for a book based on two years of her diaries, for publication by Michael Joseph in September 2001. (Also commanding huge sums were Hillary Clinton, rumoured to have been paid £850,000 by Headline for UK & Commonwealth rights in her memoir of eight years in the White House, and also pop star Robbie Williams. Ebury is believed to have paid £800,000 for an illustrated tour diary authored by Mark McCrum, for publication in September 2001).

The craze for text messaging made *Wan2Tlk* (Michael O'Mara) and its spin-offs bestsellers that came out of left field. Dave Pelzer told the story of the most unimaginably awful childhood abuse in *A Child Called 'It'* and its sequels *The Lost Boy* and *A Man Called Dave* (Orion), which were runaway bestsellers. Also more successful than expected were Tony Parsons' comic novel of single fatherhood, *Man and Boy* (HarperCollins), which sold nearly 600,000 copies, and his subsequent *One for My Baby*, which also climbed the bestseller lists. Films gave a fillip to Helen Fielding, bringing Bridget Jones back up the bestseller lists, with the original Diary and its sequel *The Edge of Reason* (Picador), after Hugh Grant and Colin Firth got involved, and to Joanne Harris, whose novel *Chocolat* came round for second helpings after the screen adaptation, along with her later novels *Blackberry Wine* and *Five Quarters of the Orange* (Transworld). Television gave a lot of books a leg up into the bestseller lists, not all of them lowbrow. David Starkey's tie-in biography of the Virgin Queen, *Elizabeth*, and Simon Schama's *History of Britain* were among them. Meanwhile TV cooks Jamie Oliver (*Return of the Naked Chef*) and Nigella Lawson (*Nigella Bites*) continued to be flavour of the month, or dishes of the day, for months on end.

A television connection was not necessarily, however, a guarantee of success. The most publicised flop of the year was the autobiography of television presenter Anthea Turner, entitled, many thought aptly, *Fools Rush In*. The public mood turned against Turner, stoked by the tabloid newspapers, who were engaged in their own internecine war of exclusives and spoilers. Turner, a divorcee, let *Hello* magazine photograph her second wedding, and free chocolate bars, distributed to guests at one a. m. as a promotional gimmick, sealed her unpopularity. She was reviled as someone who would do anything for publicity, and after that no kind of promotion could encourage sales. The publisher was left with a large pile of returns, an unearned advance, a new understanding that not all publicity is good publicity, and a sobering awareness of the vagaries of celebrity.

The Booker Prize underwent something of a revamp, with a redesigned website, bookshops displayed new promotional material, and carried a CD of readings from the shortlisted books. The BBC took over coverage from Channel 4, promising to support the broadcasting of the awards ceremony with a schedule of related coverage and to appeal to younger viewers, to show that writers were 'no longer just old codgers in tweeds'. Channel 4's last Booker programme, in autumn 2000, did not broadcast the ceremony live, which meant that the suspense of the news that Margaret Atwood had won with *The Blind Assassin* (published by Bloomsbury) was undermined by the fact that the winner appeared on Booker's website half an hour before the announcement was screened. But this did not diminish a general delight, given that Atwood had been nominated for the Booker three times in the past. Simon Jenkins, chair of the judges, said that *The Blind Assassin* demonstrated Atwood's 'immense emotional range, as well as her poet's eye for both telling detail and psychological truth.' Atwood said she planned to use the £21,000 prize money to make donations to environmental charities.

One of the books shortlisted in 2000, *The Deposition of Father McGreevy* (Arcadia Books), by Irish-born but US-based writer Brian O'Doherty prompted a county councillor in the Irish Republic to call for a 'fatwa' against the author. The book concerned a small Irish community that descended into pagan and bestial acts. The councillor, Michael Healy-Rae of Kerry County Council, announced that he had changed his mind after meeting the author for a radio debate in Dublin.

In 2001 the newsworthy Booker development was that the judges published their longlist for the first time, and that not only were there, as in most years, surprise omissions, but the list also included several unlikely books. The obvious exclusion from the longlist was *Fury* by previous laureate Salman Rushdie, whose *Midnight's Children* had even won the 'Booker of Bookers' on the prize's 21st anniversary. But the inclusions were still more remarkable. Among them, unprecedentedly, was a children's book, Philip Pullman's *The Amber Spyglass* (Scholastic), the third volume of his *His Dark Materials* trilogy, and already a persistent bestseller. Also on the longlist were Nick Hornby and Melvyn Bragg, whom many in the past had deemed too 'middlebrow' to be Booker contenders. Hornby's *How to be Good*, a tale of moral dilemmas in the professional classes, was already a bestseller, and Bragg's *Son of War*, sequel to his W. H. Smith-award winning Soldier's Return had garnered high critical praise. Also on the longlist was a very little known author, published by a small press, Zvi Jagendorf, with *Wolfy* and the *Strudelbakers* (Dewi Lewis Press).

The £30,000 Orange Prize, for women writers only, once again aroused controversy by enlisting a 'jury of men' to select their own shortlist from the Orange Prize longlist. (One commentator speculated that the next Orange prize - in its pursuit of newsworthiness - would be 'judged underwater'). The votes of the shadow judges would not count in the final decision, but their opinions would fuel the debate about whether men's tastes differ from women's, and provide a backdrop for research Orange had initiated into how gender affects reading habits. The male jury, comprising of journalist John Walsh, novelist Paul Bailey and bookseller Paul Henderson, obliged by being disparaging about the quality of the books on the longlist, which had been chosen by journalist Rosie Boycott (former editor of the Daily Express), singer/songwriter Suzanne Vega, novelist Emily Perkins, Kate Adie, chief news correspondent of the BBC, and Rachel Holmes, managing editor of online bookseller Amazon. The shortlists both panels went on to select overlapped by only one book - but, just to confound everyone, that overlapping book was the one both juries chose as the overall winner, Kate Grenville's beautifully crafted story of romance between two unlikely people who had given up on love, *The Idea of Perfection*. The real jury (but not the men) had also shortlisted the 2000 Booker prizewinner, Margaret Atwood's *The Blind Assassin*, which also went to prove that literary prize judging is not rocket science for either sex.

The book that was felt to have 'got away' from the 2000 Booker shortlist was Zadie Smith's acclaimed debut novel of multi-cultural Britain *White Teeth* (Hamish Hamilton), which was also shortlisted for the 2000 Orange Prize but did not win. But it went on to win the Whitbread first novel prize and the Guardian First Fiction award (for which Smith was the only British author shortlisted), the $10,000 Frankfurt e-book award for a work of fiction converted into an e-book, the Commonwealth Writer's Prize 2001 in the best first book category (worth £3,000) and the W. H. Smith new talent award (worth £5,000).

Another success story of the year, in the swings and roundabouts of literary prizes, was Matthew Kneale's tale of war, shipwreck, evolution and race on a nineteenth-century ship sailing to Tasmania, *English Passengers* (published, like *White Teeth*, by Hamish Hamilton), which had been beaten by Atwood to the Booker Prize but went on to be voted the surprise winner of the Whitbread Book of the Year. Meanwhile, W. H. Smith changed its awards system to let the public vote for its choices between January and March 2001. Five books were shortlisted in each of eight categories ranging from new talent to business writing. The ninth prize, the W. H. Smith Literary Award, was not voted for by the public. The winners, taking a total prize money of £45,000, included (apart from Zadie Smith) J. K. Rowling, Maeve Binchy, David Starkey and Jamie Oliver. Philip Roth won the literary award for *The Human Stain* (Vintage). Peter Carey won the overall £10,000 Commonwealth Writer's Prize for his novel *The True History of the Kelly Gang* (Faber). And the $100,000 main Frankfurt e-book award for the best book originally published as an e-book was shared between David Maraniss, for his work of non-fiction *When Pride Still Mattered* (Simon & Schuster) and E. M. Schorb for a novel, *Paradise Square* (Denliger's Publishers Ltd). The organisers were criticised, however, for being too heavily influenced by their main sponsor, Microsoft, and for failing to come up with a clear definition of an e-book.

E-books did take a step forward when Random House UK became the first British trade publisher to enter the e-book market, with a list of more than 100 fiction and non-fiction books drawn from Random House and Transworld's backlists. It then offered authors a half share in revenue from e-books, on the principle that royalties should be higher than for printed books because they are easier to produce.

BBC Worldwide became the first large trade publisher to publish an e-book in the UK, when in November 2000 it released a tie-in, Rupert Smith's *On the Edge*, in digital form, but there were technical glitches at first, which did not inspire confidence in the medium. Author Stephen King also suspended his online serial novel, *The Plant*, for which readers had paid in instalments, on the grounds that he needed to concentrate on other work. This angered fans, and upset e-book advocates since King was perceived as one of the pioneers of the digital revolution. King argued that his story had not ended, just gone into 'hibernation'.

Electronic publishing also lost one of its most enthusiastic advocates in 2001, when Douglas Adams, best known as the author of *The Hitchhiker's Guide to the Galaxy*, died suddenly at the age of 49. Journalist and author John Diamond also died, losing his long battle against throat cancer, which was chronicled in his newspaper columns and his bestselling book *C: Cowards Get Cancer Too*. His death inspired a huge amount of media coverage, and his unfinished book, *Snake Oil*, an attack on the charlatanism of alternative medicine, was edited by his brother-in-law Dominic Lawson and published posthumously in July (Vintage).

Book-related controversies of the year included the announcement by the British Library that it wanted to collect printed works 'more selectively', revealed in proposals for its strategy for the next five years. Storage space was 'expected to run out by 2006'. Many felt that selectivity was an erosion of what the British Library was known for. The Library has its job cut out, though, because the news was also revealed this year that book output, which had slowed slightly in the 1990s, had started to accelerate again. The number of books published in the UK in 2000 rose by 5.7% to a new record of 116,415 books a year.

Also making news headlines was the publication of the controversial memoirs of sacked MI5 agent Richard Tomlinson, *The Big Breach, From Top Secret to Maximum Security* (Mainstream). The author was alleged to have waived his copyright four years before publication, so that copyright was held by the Crown. The book went ahead despite government opposition, and further claims followed that Tomlinson was 'merely a pawn of Russian Intelligence' which wanted the book published 'to gain revenge for *The Mitrokhin Archive*' - according to the author of *The Mitrkhin Archive*, Christopher Andrew.

Another book that raised the question of what was ethical for publishers to print or booksellers to sell was a book on the psychology of serial killers by Moors murderer Ian Brady, *The Gates of Janus: Serial Killing and Its Analysis*, with an introduction by Colin Wilson. The US and UK publisher was Feral House, based in California, though the book had a UK distributor, Turnaround. Arguments ensued about the right to free speech, the sensibilities of victims' families, and who should be entitled to profit.

And a children's book fuelled an argument that books for youngsters should be marked with warning stickers if they contain adult material. Former Carnegie Medal winner Melvin Burgess's new novel, *Lady: My Life as a Bitch* (Andersen Press) is the story of a promiscuous teenager who turns into a dog, and comes to enjoy a life untrammelled by human responsibilities. It was argued that those who thought the book advocated promiscuity missed its irony, and its playfulness.

Also controversial was HarperCollins alleged decision to 'downplay' the overtly Christian sentiments in C. S. Lewis's *The Chronicles of Narnia*. An overwhelming tide of opinion insisted that the books should be left as the author wrote them. Besides, disentangling the Christian imagery from the books would seem to be an impossible task - since Aslan the lion is a Christlike figure who couldn't be edited out.

The winner of the Carnegie Medal, Beverley Naidoo, courted controversy by accusing the government of 'paying lip service' to countering racism in schools. Her winning book, *The Other Side of Truth* (Penguin), told the story of Nigerian refugee children in Britain, and stimulated debate around asylum issues in the UK.

Also conscious of the climate of the times was children's author Michael Morpurgo, who surprised his publisher Macmillan by sending a completely different book from the one he had been commissioned to write. *Out of the Ashes* was inspired by passion and born of the author's experience of farming communities during the foot and mouth crisis. It was the narrative of a 13-year-old girl whose family farm is quarantined and its animals slaughtered. A donation from each copy sold went to the Supporting Farmers in Crisis Fund.

And there were several other conspicuous successes among the children's books of 2001. Harry Potter's popularity changed the climate in which children's books were published, creating a feeling that the potential for children to be readers should never be underestimated (a view shared by the newly appointed Children's laureate, Anne Fine). Meanwhile J. K. Rowling's decision not to allow Harry Potter to be submitted for the Smarties Prize cleared the way for a win for scriptwriter William Nicholson's fantasy *The Wind Singer* (Mammoth). Penguin did its utmost to promote Eoin Colfer's spoof cop drama *Artemis Fowl*, described by the author as 'Die Hard with fairies', into Harry Potteresque sales; it did well but not that well. It was outsold, despite the marketing, by Philip Pullman's complex (Booker long-listed) *The Amber Spyglass*, which was a triumph of literary sophistication over hype.

## LITERARY PRIZEWINNERS

Nobel Laureate in Literature 2000 - Gao Xingjian
Commonwealth Writers Prize 2001 - Peter Carey, *True History of the Kelly Gang*
Best first book - Zadie Smith, White Teeth
Prix Goncourt 1999 - Jean-Marie Laclavetine - *Premiere Ligne*
Booker Prize 2000 - Margaret Atwood, *The Blind Assassin*
Whitbread Prize 2000: overall winner - Matthew Kneale, *English Passengers*
First novel - Zadie Smith, *White Teeth*
Biography - Lorna Sage, *Bad Blood*
Poetry - John Burnside, *The Asylum Dance*
Children's novel - Jamila Gavin, *Coram Boy*
Smarties Prize 2000 (children's books):
Age 0–5 - Bob Graham, *Max*
Age 6–8 - Jacqueline Wilson, *Lizzie Zipmouth*
Age 9–11 - William Nicholson, *The Wind Singer*
Crime Writers Association 2000:
Gold Dagger (fiction) - Jonathan Lethem, *Motherless Brooklyn*
Gold Dagger (non-fiction) - Edward Bunker, *Mr Blue*
Silver Dagger (fiction) - Donna Leon, *Friends in High Places*
Short Story Dagger - Denise Mina, *Helena and the Babies*
British Book Awards 2000:
Author - Nigella Lawson, *How to be a Domestic Goddess; Baking and the Art of Comfort Cooking*
Book of the Year - Tony Parsons, *Man and Boy*
Newcomer - Zadie Smith, *White Teeth*
Children's - Philip Pullman – *The Amber Spyglass*
Lifetime achievement - Ernest Hecht
Encore Award 2001 (second novel) Anne Enright, *What Are You Like?*
Orange Award 2001 (women writers) - Kate Grenville, *The Idea of Perfection*
Somerset Maugham Awards 2001 - Edward Platt, *Leadville;* Ben Rice, *Pobby and Dingan*
Betty Trask Prize 2001 (first novel by an author under 35) - Zadie Smith, *White Teeth*
McKitterick Prize 2001 (first novel by a writer over 40) - Giles Waterford, *The Long Afternoon*
W H Smith Prize 2001 (voted for by the public):
Literary Award - Philip Roth, *The Human Stain*
Fiction - Maeve Binchy, *Scarlet Fever*
New Talent, Zadie Smith, *White Teeth*
Biography and Autobiography - David Starkey, *Elizabeth*
General Knowledge - Simon Schama, *A History of Britain*
Business - Cynthia Crossen, *The Rich and How They Got That Way*
Travel: Bill Bryson, *Down Under*
Home and Leisure, Jamie Oliver, *The Return of the Naked Chef*
Children's - J. K. Rowling, *Harry Potter and the Goblet of Fire*
Cholmondeley Awards 2001 (poetry) - Ian Duhig, *Mersey Goldfish*; Paul Durcan, *Greetings to Our Friends in Brazil*; Kathleen Jamie, *Autonomous Regions*; Grace Nichols, *Asana and the Animals*
Sunday Times Young Writer of the Year Award 2001 - Zadie Smith, *White Teeth*
T. S. Eliot Prize 2000 (poetry) - Michael Longley, *The Weather in Japan*
Parker Romantic Novel of the Year - Cathy Kelly, *Someone Like You*
Carnegie Prize 2000 (children's) Beverley Naidoo, *The Other Side of Truth*
Kate Greenaway 1999 (children's illustrated) – Helen Oxenbury, *Alice's Adventures in Wonderland*
David Cohen British Literature Prize 2001 (lifetime achievement, biennial) – Doris Lessing
Samuel Johnson Prize 2001 (for Non-Fiction) - Michael Burleigh, *The Third Reich: A New History*

# Opera

The centenary of the death of Verdi, which occurred in Milan on 21 January 1901, affected nearly every opera house in the world during this season. Most companies had at least one or two, if not several, Verdi operas in their repertory, and those that could not manage a new production, for whatever reason, brought out old ones. The Royal Opera, which had had to abandon its ambitious project of staging all Verdi's operas by 2001, revived three of its productions, *La traviata, Otello* and *Falstaff.* 2001 is also the bicentenary of the birth of Vincenzo Bellini, and the Royal Opera revived *I Capuleti e i Montecchi* in his honour. Although the length of the season at Covent Garden was almost back to normal, there were only four new productions. The most interesting of these was Hans Werner Henze's *Boulevard Solitude*, mounted in celebration of the composer's 75th birthday. This version of the story of Manon Lescaut, set in Paris in the 1940s, is now nearly forty years old, but Henze's music still sounds fresh and urgent, while a magnificent production by Nikolaus Lehnhoff, which fully used the new technical facilities of the theatre, was very well received by the audience. The loudest cheers, however, were reserved for Henze himself, who attended the first performance.

Götz Friedrich, the controversial German director, who staged two cycles of Wagner's *Ring* at Covent Garden, died in December 2000 at the age of 70. His first cycle, completed in 1975, was highly praised for its insight into 'the labyrinthine motives of the drama', and in 1976 Friedrich became chief director of the Royal Opera. Subsequent productions included Weber's *Der Freischutz*, Mozart's *Idomeneo* and in 1991 the British premiere of the three-act version of Berg's *Lulu*, with his wife Karan Armstrong in the title role, which was enormously successful. His second *Ring* cycle at Covent Garden, in 1984-85, was a modification of a Berlin production which did not really fit the stage. Friedrich also directed *Tristan und Isolde* for English National Opera in 1985.

The Linbury Studio at the Royal Opera House played host to several enterprising companies during the year, in particular to Music Theatre Wales, which gave the London premiere of Michael Berkeley's chamber opera *Jane Eyre*, which had received its premiere at the 2000 Cheltenham Festival. One of the two Laurence Olivier Awards for Opera in 2000, the Best New Production, was awarded to the Royal Opera for Martinu's *The Greek Passion*. The Award for Outstanding Achievement in Opera went to Mark-Anthony Turnage and Amanda Holden, composer and librettist respectively of *The Silver Tassie*, premiered by English National Opera. ENO's commission for 2001, David Sawer's *From Morning to Midnight*, also scored a great success; based on a play by Georg Kaiser, the German Expressionist, the opera was developed (as had been *The Silver Tassie*) in ENO's studio over a two year period, and consequently did not suffer from the usual teething troubles of new, untried operas. A second commission, Martin Butler's short opera *A Better Place*, received its premiere at the end of the season.

ENO embarked on a four-year project to return their much loved home, the London Coliseum, to its original glory by 2004, the centenary of the theatre. Designed by the incomparable theatre architect Frank Matcham, the Coliseum urgently needs restoration, both inside and out. Having learnt a lesson from the Royal Opera's difficulties while absent from Covent Garden and homeless, ENO intend to keep the periods of closure to a minimum, extending the summer recesses and doing nearly all the work with the theatre open. The restoration of the exterior has already begun. The project will cost more than £30 million; of this, £12 million has been allocated from the Arts Council Lottery Fund, with a possible 6.50 million extra from the Heritage Lottery Fund. ENO will provide the rest, and have already found £3 million.

The new cycle of Wagner's *Ring* (in English) starting with concert performances of *The Rhinegold* in January 2001, will develop into a complete, staged cycle in the restored theatre in 2005. Meanwhile the recording of ENO's previous *Ring*, completed in 1973 and conducted by Reginald Goodall, was re-released. The Brunnhilde of that performance, English soprano Rita Hunter, died in April 2001, aged 68. A member of ENO for many years, she also sang Santuzza in *Cavalleria rusticana*, Senta in *The Flying Dutchman*, Donna Anna in *Don Giovanni*, Leonora in *Il trovatore*, Elisabeth in *Don Carlos* and Amelia in *A Masked Ball*, but Brunnhilde remained her finest role, which she also sang at the Metropolitan Opera, New York, Munich, Barcelona, Chicago, Seattle and Sydney.

ENO's celebration of the Millennium and its contribution to the Verdi centenary was a three-month season consisting of eight new productions of Italian operas from *Monteverdi* to *Dallapiccola*, including *Nabucco* and the Verdi *Requiem*. These productions, though staged by various directors, all had sets designed by Stefanos Lazaridis, whose 'theme' was the scaffolding erected round the auditorium (the scaffolding, though suggested by the renovation, was nothing to do with it). Obviously this suited some of the operas better than others, but for those with large choruses, like Puccini's *Manon Lescaut*, Leoncavallo's *La Bohème* and the two Verdi items, the scaffolding proved ideal. Later ENO staged another Verdi opera, *Il trovatore*, jointly directed by Nicholas Payne, the General Manager, and Paul Daniel, the Music Director. Both are extremely good at their own jobs, but they should leave direction to the experts. This was underlined by the revival of David Pountney's superb staging of Shostakovich's *Lady Macbeth of Mtsensk*.

This was altogether a good year for Shostakovich, whose three completed stage works could be seen in London during a three-week period in May 2001. As well as *Lady Macbeth* at the Coliseum, *The Nose*, his comic opera based on a story by Gogol, was on view at the Lyric Hammersmith, in an exhilarating performance by a touring company, The Opera Group, while Opera North brought a new production of the musical comedy, *Cheryomushki* or *Paradise Moscow*, to Sadler's Wells Theatre. This light-hearted piece, dating from 1959, about some apartments that become available in a newly built tower block in a Moscow suburb, was immensely enjoyable in Pountneys's imaginative staging and witty translation. The score is a brilliant confection of Viennese operetta, American musical and the composer's own inimitable style. Otherwise, Opera North chose the theme of German Romanticism, with Schuman's *Genoveva*, premiered at the 2000 Edinburgh Festival brought into the repertory, while a 'dramatised concert version' of *Tristan und Isolde* was performed in the newly-furbished Leeds Town Hall.

Scottish Opera paid lip service to Verdi with a revival of *Il trovatore*, but the company's main efforts were directed towards the *Ring* cycle, staged by Tim Albery, being built up, season by season. With *Das Rheingold* firmly in the repertory, *Die Walkure* was introduced as part of the 2001 Edinburgh Festival. An education project undertaken by Scottish Opera for All will also focus on *Die Walkure*. Other operas at the Festival were *Die Zauberflote* from the Aix-en-Provence Festival, and a number of concert performances, including Berlioz' *Les Troyens* given in two parts by the BBC Scottish Symphony Orchestra, Rameau's *Zoroastre* performed by Les Arts Florissants, and Messiaen's *Saint François d'Assise* by the Netherlands Philharmonic Radio Orchestra.

Carlo Rizzi, Musical Director of Welsh National Opera for the last nine years, gave up the position at the end of July 2001. He has been hugely successful during his years in Cardiff, conducting a very wide repertory. To end his tenure he conducted a much-admired new production of Janáček's *Kát'a Kabanová*; the final performance, at the Apollo Theatre in Oxford, which has notoriously tricky acoustics, was orchestrally superb, as well as perfectly balanced between stage and 'pit' (a facility lacking in the Apollo). Rizzi returns to WNO as a guest in the 2001-2002 season. Another highly successful WNO production was Tchaikovsky's *Queen of Spades*, directed by Richard Jones, which won the 2000 Royal Philharmonic Society Award for Outstanding Achievement in Opera - the third year running that WNO had won this award. The *Queen of Spades* was authentically conducted by Vladimir Jurowski, the young Russian musician who was appointed Music Director of Glyndebourne Festival Opera in January 2001. He will make his conducting debut at Glyndebourne in 2002.

Meanwhile Glyndebourne's General Director, Nicholas Snowman, resigned in November 2000 after two years in the position. His successor was announced in March 2001 as David Pickard, for the last eight years Chief Executive of the Orchestra of the Age of Enlightenment, which frequently plays at Glyndebourne, and indeed played on the opening night of the 2001 season, conducted by Sir Simon Rattle, in a new production of *Fidelio*. It was extremely interesting to hear Beethoven's opera played on period instruments, although the staging was not greatly liked. Sir Peter Hall, returning to Glyndebourne after an absence of several years, directed a successful production of Verdi's *Otello* (its first production at Glyndebourne), designed by John Gunter, and set in a colonial outpost of the Venetian republic in the 18th century. Even more successful was a revival of Hall's staging of Britten's *A Midsummer Night's Dream*, originally produced in 1981 at the old theatre. The magical settings were designed by John Bury, who adapted them to the new, larger stage before his untimely death in 2000.

Garsington Opera, continuing its search for Rossini and Strauss rarities, gave the British premiere of *La gazzetta*, first performed in Naples in 1816. Though not one of Rossini's comic masterpieces, it has a good libretto based on a play by Goldoni, *Marriage by Competition*. Strauss's domestic drama *Intermezzo*, which was produced at Glyndebourne in the 1980s, is perfect summer evening entertainment for Country House Opera. The Aldeburgh Festival featured Britten's *The Rape of Lucretia*, staged by the young Scottish director David MacVicar, a joint production with ENO, where the opera scored a success later in the season. Aldeburgh also presented the British premiere of *Kantan and Damask Drum*, Alexander Goehr's triptych of short operas based on Japanese Noh plays, which were later staged by Almeida Opera at its temporary home in King's Cross.

As usual, Almeida Opera also staged a world premiere, in this case *God's Liar* by John Casken, based on a story by Tolstoy, *Father Sergius*. A co-production with Théâtre de la Monnaie in Brussels, it opened in King's Cross before going on to Brussels. Aidan Lang, Artistic Director of the Buxton Festival, presented a significantly expanded programme, whose chief attraction was a special festival production of *Un giorno di regno*, Verdi's second opera (and first comedy). The Early Opera Company offered Handel's comic opera *Partenope*; Music Theatre Wales staged Peter Maxwell Davies' *To the Lighthouse*, while The Opera Group brought their touring production of *The Nose*, already mentioned. Operas performed at the 2001 Promenade Concerts at the Royal Albert Hall included the Glyndebourne *Fidelio*; *Royal Palace* by Kurt Weill, Bartok's *Duke Bluebeard's Castle* together with *Le Visage nuptial*, a work for two female soloists and chorus by Pierre Boulez, who conducted both works, and the Verdi *Requiem*.

The deaths were announced of three baritones who specialised in Verdi operas. Canadian baritone Louis Quilico, who died aged 75, sang frequently at Covent Garden during the late 1950s and 1960s. His Verdi roles included Amonasro in *Aida*, Germont in *La traviata*, Rigoletto, Posa in *Don Carlos*, Miller in *Luisa Miller*, Iago in *Otello*, and Falstaff, which he sang with his son Gino, also a baritone, as Ford. Keith Latham, the English baritone who died in January 2001 aged only 46, was a member of Opera North, where he sang Don Carlo in *Ernani*, Luna in *Il trovatore*, Amonasro, Germont, Macbeth, Count of Toulouse in *Jérusalem* and Giacomo in *Giovanna d'Arco*. For ENO he sang Ford, Paolo in *Simon Boccanegra* and Rigoletto. Delme Bryn-Jones, the Welsh baritone who died in May 2001 aged 66, was a member of the Royal Opera during the 1960s, when his roles included Ford, Paolo, Rigoletto and Renato in *Un ballo in maschera*. He also appeared frequently for WNO, singing Macbeth, Germont, Rigoletto, Ford and Nabucco.

Jess Walters, an American baritone who died in October 2001 aged 91, joined the Covent Garden Opera Company - later the Royal Opera - in 1947. During the 12 seasons he sang in London, he gave 680 performances of twenty roles, that included Wozzeck, Marcello in *La Bohème*, Jupiter in *The Olympians* by Arthur Bliss, the Count in *The Marriage of Figaro*, Choroebus in *The Trojans* and Wolfram in *Tannhäuser*. Victor Braun, the Canadian baritone who died in January 2001 aged 65, specialised in works by Berg, Bartok, Henze and Berio. He made his Covent Garden debut in 1969 singing the title role in the British premiere of Humphrey Searle's *Hamlet*. Other roles that he sang in London included Eugene Onegin, Posa in *Don Carlos*, Golaud in *Pelléas et Mélisande* and Balstrode in *Peter Grimes*. He also sang Baron Prus in Janacek's *The Makropulos Case* in 1995.

## PRODUCTIONS

In the summaries of company activities shown below, the dates in brackets indicate the year that the current productions entered the company's repertory.

### ROYAL OPERA

Founded 1946
Royal Opera House, Covent Garden, London WC2E 9DD
Productions from the repertory: *Tosca* (1964), *Billy Budd* (1995), *Les Contes d'Hoffmann* (1980), *Kátă Kabanová* (1994), *La traviata* (1994), *Falstaff* (1999), *Palestrina* (1997), *Turandot* (1984), *I Capuleti e i Montecchi* (1984), *Otello* (1987), *Die Entfuhrung aus dem Serail* (1987)

New productions:
*Tristan und Isolde* (Wagner), 14 October 2000. Conductor, Bernard Haitink; director/designer, Herbert Wernicke. Jon Frederic West (Tristan), Gabriele Schnaut (Isolde), Petra Lang (Brangäne), Alan Titus (Kurwenal), Peter Rose (King Marke), Christopher Booth-Jones (Melot).

*La Cenerentola* (Rossini), 16 December 2000. Conductor, Mark Elder; directors, Patrick Caurier and Moshe Leise; set designer, Christian Fenouillat; costume designer, Augustino Cavalca. Sonia Ganassi (Cenerentola), Juan Diego Florez (Don Ramiro), Nicole Tibbels (Clorinda), Leah-Marian Jones (Tisbe), Marcin Bronikowski (Dandini), Simone Alaimo (Don Magnifico), Michele Pertusi (Alidoro).

*Boulevard Solitude* (Henze), 20 March 2001. Conductor, Bernhard Kontarsky; director, Nikolaus Lehnhoff; designer, Tobias Hoheisel. Pär Lindskog (Armand), Alexandra von der Weth (Manon), Chris Merritt (Lilaque père), Wolfgang Rauch (Lescaut), Graeme Broadbent (Lilaque fils).

*The Queen of Spades* (Tchaikovsky), Conductor, Bernard Haitink; director, Francesca Zambello; set designer Peter J. Davison; costume designer, Nicky Gillibrand. Vladimir Galouzine (Ghermann), Nikolai Putilin (Count Tomsky), Dmitri Hvorostovsky (Prince Yeletsky), Josephine Barstow (Countess), Karita Mattila (Lisa), Viktoria Vizin (Paulina), Jenny Grahn (Prilepa).

### English National Opera

Founded 1931
London Coliseum, St Martin's Lane, London WC2N 4BS
Productions from the repertory: *The Cunning Little Vixen* (1988), *Carmen* (1995), *Il trittico* (1998), *The Barber of Seville* (1987), *Falstaff* (1997), *Lady Macbeth of Mtsensk* (1987).

New productions:
*Manon Lescaut* (Puccini), 18 September 2000. Conductor, Paul Daniel; director, Keith Warner; designer, Stefanos Lazaridis. Nina Stemme (Manon), Martin Thompson (Des Grieux), David Kempster (Lescaut), Mark Richardson (Geronte), John Graham-Hall (Edmondo/Dancing Master/Lamplighter).

*The Coronation of Poppea* (Monteverdi), 19 September 2000. Conductor, Harry Christophers; director, Steven Pimlott; set designer, Stefanos Lazaridis; costume designer, Ingeborg Bernerth. Alice Coote (Poppea), David Walker (Nero), Eric Owens (Seneca), Michael Chance (Otho), Sarah Connolly (Octavia), Anne-Marie Owens (Arnalta), Susan Gritton (Drusilla).

*La Gioconda* (Ponchielli), 23 September 2000. Concert performance. Conductor, Paul Daniel; Jane Eaglen (Gioconda), Dennis O'Neill (Enzo), Anne-Marie Owens (Laura), Alastair Miles (Alvise), Catherine Wyn-Rogers (La Cieca).

*The Turk in Italy* (Rossini), 11 October 2000. Conductor, Michael Lloyd; director, David Fielding; set designer, Stefanos Lazaridis; costume designer, Nicky Gillibrand. Judith Howarth (Fiorilla), Jeremy White (Selim), Donald Maxwell (Geronio), Thomas Allen (Prosdocimo), Toby Spence (Narciso), Nerys Jones (Zaida), Ryland Davies (Albazar).

*La Bohème* (Leoncavallo), 2 November 2000. Conductor, Mark Shanahan; director, Tim Albery; set designer, Stefanos Lazaridis; costume designer, Jon Morrell. Christine Rice (Musetta), Rhys Meirion (Marcello), Sandra Ford (Mimi), Riccardo Simonetti (Rodolfo), Paul Whelan (Schaunard), Leslie John Flanagan (Colline).

*The Prisoner* (Dallapiccola), 17 November 2000. Conductor, Richard Hickox; director, Neil Armfeld; set designer, Stefanos Lazaridis; costume designer, Tess Schofield. Peter Coleman-Wright (Prisoner), Susan Bullock (The Mother), Peter Bronder (Gaoler/Grand Inquisitor)

*Nabucco* (Verdi), 30 November 2000. Conductor, Mikko Franck; director, David Pountney; set designer, Stefanos Lazaridis; costume designer, Marie-Jeanne Lecca. Bruno Caproni (Nabucco), Lauren Flanigan (Abigaille), John Daszak (Ismaele), Alastair Miles (Zaccaria).

*Requiem* (Verdi), 9 December 2000. Conductor, Paul Daniel; director, Phyllida Lloyd; designer, Stefanos Lazaridis. Claire Weston (soprano), Susan Parry (mezzo), Rafael Rojas (tenor), David Pittsinger (bass).

*The Rhinegold* (Wagner), 26 January 2001. Semi-staged. Conductor, Paul Daniel; Matthew Best (Wotan), Susan Parry (Fricka), John Graham-Hall (Loge), Peter Sidhom (Alberich), Richard Roberts (Mime), Stephen Richardson (Fasolt), Patricia Bardon (Erda).

*Il trovatore* (Verdi), 9 April 2001. Conductor, Paul Daniel; directors, Nicholas Payne/Paul Daniel; set designer, Conor Murphy; costume designer Leon E. Wiebers. Sandra Ford (Leonora), Julian Gavin (Manrico), Sally Burgess (Azucena), David Kempster (Count di Luna), Clive Bayley (Ferrando).

*From Morning to Midnight* (David Sawer), 27 April 2001, world premiere. Conductor, Martyn Brabbins; director, Richard Jones; designer, Steward Laing. John Daszak (Cashier), Kathryn Harries (The Lady), Susan Bickley (Wife/Hostess/Salvation Army Officer), Linda Kitchen (Daughter/Hostess/Prostitute), Robert Poulton (Bank Manager/Steward/Pimp/Family Man), Menai Davies (Mother), Gail Pearson (Salvation Army Girl).

*Don Giovanni* (Mozart), 31 May 2001. Conductor, Joseph Swensen; director, Calixto Bieito; set designer, Alfonso Flores; costume designer, Merce Paloma. Garry Magee (Don Giovanni), Nathan Berg (Leporello), Claire Rutter (Donna Anna), Claire Weston (Donna Elvira), Paul Nilon (Don Ottavio), Linda Richardson (Zerlina), Leslie John Flanagan (Masetto), Philip Ems (Commendatore).

*The Rape of Lucretia* (Britten), 21 June 2001. Conductor, Paul Daniel; director, David MacVicar; designer, Yannis Thavoris. Sarah Connolly (Lucretia), Orla Boylan (Female Chorus), John Mark Ainsley (Male Chorus), Christopher Maltman (Tarquinius), Clive Bayley (Collatinus), Leigh Melrose (Junius), Catherine Wyn-Rogers (Bianca), Mary Nelson (Lucia).

*A Better Place* (Martin Butler), 4 July 2001, world premiere. Conductor, Paul Daniel; director, Lenka Udovici; designer, Soutra Gilmour. Rebecca de Pont Davies (Suzanne), Mark le Brocq (Siward), Gail Pearson (Karen), Roderick Williams (Michel).

### Opera North

Founded 1978
Grand Theatre, 40 New Briggate, Leeds LS1 6NU
Productions from the repertory: *The Marriage of Figaro* (1996), *La rondine* (1994), *Pelléas et Mélisande* (1995), *Eugene Onegin* (1998)

New productions:
*Genoveva* (Schumann), 5 September 2000. Conductor, Steven Sloane; director, David Pountney; set designer, Ralph Koltai; costume designer, Sue Wilmington. Patricia Schuman (Genoveva), Sally Burgess (Margaretha), Paul Nilon (Golo), Christopher Purves (Siegfried).

*Elixir of Love* (Donizetti), 21 December 2000. Conductor, David Parry; director, Daniel Slater; designer, Robert Innes Hopkins. Mary Hegarty (Adina), Paul Nilon

(Nemorino), Richard Whitehouse (Belcore), Christopher Purves (Dr Dulcamara).

*Tristan und Isolde* (Wagner), 27 January 2001, Leeds Town Hall. Conductor, Steven Sloane; director/designer, Keith Warner. Susan Bullock (Isolde), Mark Lundberg (Tristan), Anne-Marie Owens (Brangäne), John Wegner (Kurwenal), Donald McIntyre (King Marke).

*Paradise Moscow* (Shostakovich), 3 May 2001. Conductor, Gerald McBurney; director, David Pountney; designer, Robert Innes Hopkins. Rachel Taylor (Lusyr), Alan Oke (Sergei), Loren Geeting (Boris), Richard Angas (Drebednyov), Campbell Morrison (Barabashkin), Janie Dee (Lidochka), Steven Beard (Barburov), Daniel Broad (Sasha), Gillian Kirkpatrick (Masha), Margaret Preece (Vava).

Performances were given at the Grand Theatre, Leeds, and on tour at Newcastle, Salford Quays, Nottingham, Hull, Norwick, Sheffield, and London (Sadler's Wells)

### Scottish Opera

Founded 1962
39 Elmbank Crescent, Glasgow G2 4PT
Productions from the repertory: *Das Rheingold* (2000), *L'elisir d'amore* (1994), *Don Giovanni* (1995), *Il trovatore* (1992), *Inez de Castro* (1996).

New productions:
*Madama Butterfly* (Puccini), 5 December 2000. Conductor, Guido Ajmone-Marsan; director, David MacVicar; designer Yannis Thavorin. Natalia Dercho (Butterfly), Jane Irwin (Suzuki), Ian Storey (Pinkerton), Jason Howard (Sharpless), Peter Van Hulle (Goro), Heather Ross (Kate Pinkerton).

*Die Walkure* (Wagner), 26 August 2001, as part of Edinburgh Festival. Conductor, Richard Armstrong; director, Tim Albery; designers, Hildegard Bechtler and Ana Jebsen. Ursula Furi-Bernhard (Sieglinde), Elizabeth Byrne (Brunnhilde), Anne Mason (Fricka), Jan Kyhle (Siegmund), Matthew Best (Wotan), Carsten Stabell (Hunding). Performances were given at the Theatre Royal, Glasgow, and on tour in Edinburgh, Aberdeen, Inverness.

### Welsh National Opera

Founded 1946
John Street, Cardiff CF1 4SP
Productions from the repertory: *Carmen* (1997), *La traviata* (1988), *Beatrice and Benedict* (1994), *Tosca* (1994), *The Magic Flute* (1979).

New productions:
*The Queen of Spades* (Tchaikovsky), 16 September 2000. Conductor, Vladimir Jurowski; director, Richard Jones; designer, John Macfarlane. Vitali Taraschenko (Gherman), Robert Hayward (Count Tomsky), Garry Magee (Prince Yeletsky), Susan Gorton (The Countess), Susan Chilcott (Lisa), Emma Selwyn (Paulina).

*Orphée et Eurydice* (Gluck), 2 October 2000. Conductor, Paul McCreesh; directors, Patrice Caurier and Moshe Leiser; designers, Christian Fenouilhat and Agostino Cavalca. Katarina Karnéus (Orphee), Natalie Christie (Eurydice), Jeni Bern (L'Amour).

*Le nozze di Figaro* (Mozart), 10 February 2001. Conductor, Rinaldo Alessandrini; director, Neil Armfield; designer, Dale Ferguson. Nicola Ulivieri (Figaro), Nuccia Focile (Susanna), Gidon Saks (Count Almaviva), Geraldine McGreevy (Countess Almaviva), Imelda Drumm (Cherubino), Donald de Stefano (Doctor Bartolo), Robert Tear (Don Basilio), Anne Mason (Marcellina).

*Kát'a Kabanová* (Janáček), 19 May 2001. Conductor, Carlo Rizzi; director Katie Mitchell; designer Vickie Mortimer. Nuccia Focile (Katya), Suzanne Murphy (Kabanicha), Claire Bradshaw (Varvara), Ian Storey (Boris), Nicholas Sears (Kudrjas), Peter Hoare (Tichon), Alan Fairs (Dikoj).

Performances were given at the New Theatre, Cardiff and on tour in Oxford, Southampton, Liverpool, Birmingham, Belfast, Bristol, Swansea and Llandudno.

### Glyndebourne Festival Opera

Founded 1934
Glyndebourne, Lewes, East Sussex BN8 5UU
The Festival ran from 17 May to 26 August 2001. *A Midsummer Night's Dream* (1981), *Le nozze di Figaro* (2000), *The Makropulos Case* (1995), *The Last Supper* (2000, GTO) were revived.

New productions:
*Fidelio* (Beethoven), 17 May 2001. Conductor, Sir Simon Rattle; director, Deborah Warner; set designer, Jean Kalman; costume designer, John Bright. Charlotte Margiono (Leonore), Lisa Milne (Marzelline), Kim Begley (Florestan), Timothy Robinson (Jaquino), Reinhard Hagen (Rocco), Steven Page (Don Pizarro), Alan Opie (Don Fernando).

*Otello* (Verdi), 21 July 2001. Conductor, Richard Farnes; director, Sir Peter Hall; designer John Gunter. David Rendall (Otello), Susan Chilcott (Desdemona), Anthony Michaels-Moore (Iago), Peter Auty (Roderigo), Kurt Streit (Cassio), Jean Rigby (Emilia).

### Glyndebourne Touring Opera

*Le nozze di Figaro* (2000), *Fidelio* (2001) and *Rodelinda* (1998) were performed at Glyndebourne, Woking, Norwich, Milton Keynes, Plymouth, Oxford and Stoke-on-Trent.

### Garsington Opera

Founded 1989
Garsington Manor, Garsington, Oxford OX44 9DH
The season ran from 9 June to 8 July 2001.

New productions:
*Die Zauberflöte* (Mozart), 9 June 2001. Conductor, Steuart Bedford; director, James Macdonald; designer Rae Smithe. Alan Ewing (Sarastro), Rufus Miller (Tamino), Felicity Hammond (Pamina), Jennifer Rhys-Davis (Queen of the Night), Riccardo Novaro (Papageno), Bibi Heal (Papagena).

*La gazzetta* (Rossini), 12 June 2001, British premiere. Conductor, Corrado Rovaris; director, Marco Gandini; set designer, Edoardo Sanchi; costume designer, Carlo Poggioli. Carla Huhtanen (Lisette), Mark Milhofer (Alberto), Robert Poulton (Filippo), Donald Maxwell (Don Pomponio), Kate Flowers (Madame La Rosa).

*Intermezzo* (Strauss), 26 June 2001. Conductor, Elgar Howarth; director/designer, David Fielding. Yvonne Kenny (Christine), Tom Erik Lie (Robert), Lynda Russell (Anna), Jeffrey Lloyd-Roberts (Baron Lummer).

### English Touring Opera

Founded 1980 as Opera 80.
*The Rake's Progress* (Stravinsky) and *The Magic Flute* (Mozart) were toured to Richmond, Canterbury, Weston-super-Mare, Bath, Wolverhampton, High Wycombe, York and Buxton, between 18 October and 2 December 2000.

*Manon* (Massenet) and *The Magic Flute* were toured to Cambridge, Reading, Brighton, Poole, Jersey, Leicester, Truro, Exeter, Lincoln, Crawley, Yeovil, Cheltenham, Preston, Ulverston, Darlington, Perth and Wimbledon, between 24 April to 2 June 2001.

# Parliament

In an attempt to ensure that the Government's legislative programme would be completed by the end of the 1999–2000 session, the House of Lords returned from the Summer Recess nearly a whole month earlier than the House of Commons on 27 September 2000.

The Committee stage of the Countryside and Rights of Way Bill began on 27 September (first of six days in Committee) and some 480 amendments had been tabled with no fewer than 163 from the Government. The second day of Committee on 3 October saw the Lords complete a marathon session of more than 17 hours – rising at 7.58 a.m., its first overnight sitting since 1988. Although the Government suffered no defeats on votes in Committee they offered several concessions in an attempt to ensure the smooth passage of the Bill at Report Stage on 1 November. The Government offered amendments on making the feeding of animals an offence, the extension of exclusion for abuse of access rights to 72 hours, new amendments concerning dogs on access land and occupiers' liability. On the second day of Report Stage (7 November) the Lords had to sit until 1.36 am. Although not defeated again, the Third Reading sitting on 23 November was unusually long and went on until 12.14 p.m. Under a guillotine motion, MPs completed consideration of Lords amendments on 29 November and the Bill received Royal Assent on 30 November.

The reintroduced Criminal Justice (Mode of Trial) (No 2) Bill (the first having been rejected by the Lords on 20 January 2000), limiting the number of cases that would come before a jury trial was due to receive a Second Reading in the House of Lords on 28 September. The bill was passed by 184 votes to 88, a majority against the Government of 96 and so the Bill was withdrawn.

Lord Mackay of Ardbrecknish, Conservative Deputy Leader in the Lords opened the Committee stage on the Freedom of Information Bill on 17 October. No defeats were inflicted on the Government in the passage through the Lords and the Bill received Royal Assent on 30 November.

On the first day of Report Stage on the Transport Bill on 26 October the Lords defeated the Government over its plans to privatise the National Air Traffic Services (NATS) when an amendment moved by Conservative Transport spokesman Lord Brabazon of Tara to Clause 43 was passed by 112 votes to 90, a majority against the Government of 22 and a New Clause on Pension Entitlements for NATS Employees moved by Lord Brett (Labour) was passed by 78 votes to 77, a majority against the Government of 1. These defeats were overturned in the Commons on 15 November but some 37 Labour backbenchers voted against the Government. Although Ministers pledged to protect workers' pension rights in a bid to reassure rebel Labour peers, the Lords insisted on their amendments on 27 November by 132 votes to 125, a majority against the Government of 7. With time in the session running out a compromise was agreed in the Commons on 28 November when MPs voted by 302 votes to 205 to agree to delay the planned sell-off until February, giving the Government time to reassure those concerned about the safety of the proposals although among the Labour rebels former Transport Minister Gavin Strang said it would be a 'huge mistake' for the Government to put the entire Bill in jeopardy and Gwyneth Dunwoody, Chair of the Commons Transport Select Committee warned the Government that 'the partial privatisation of NATS is a mistake.' The Lords agreed this compromise on 29 November and the amended Bill received Royal Assent the next day.

At Report Stage on the Criminal Justice and Court Services Bill on 31 October the Government suffered a number of defeats on the setting up of a new national probation service for England and Wales. A Conservative amendment moved by Education spokesman Baroness Blatch to Clause 2 to make criminals aware of the effect of their crimes was passed by 131 voted to 112, a majority against the Government of 19; a second defeat on a Baroness Blatch amendment to Clause 4 also insisting that new local boards should be named 'local probation boards', which was passed by 147 votes to 114, a majority against the Government of 33; a third defeat came over the issue of who should appoint local chief probation officers (CPOs) when a Baroness Blatch amendment to Schedule 1 insisting that CPOs should be appointed by the local probation boards was passed by 185 votes to 121, a majority against the Government of 64; a fourth defeat also on Schedule 1 came on a Baroness Blatch amendment over the arrangements for holding and managing land or property, which was passed by 178 votes to 133, a majority against the Government of 45; a fifth on Clause 5 when a Baroness Blatch amendment concerning supervision of offenders was passed by 180 votes to 126, a majority against the Government of 54. Another defeat was inflicted on Clause 7 when an amendment moved by Lord Windlesham (Conservative) to ensure that the functions of the Chief Inspector of Probation and Her Majesty's Chief Inspector of Prisons remained totally separate was passed by 188 votes to 120, a majority against the Government of 60. On a guillotine motion many of these defeats were overturned on 14 November in the Commons. Although the Lords tried to insist on their amendments to Schedule 1 on 28 November by rejecting the Commons reasons by 139 votes to 116, a majority against the Government of 33, this too was overturned by the Commons on 30 November, when the Bill received Royal Assent.

In the final week of the session, Government Ministers moved to 'guillotine' debate on a total of five key pieces of legislation. MPs were only given three hours to debate 666 amendments to the Political Parties, Elections and Referendums Bill that overhauled the way political parties are funded; discussion on the Disqualifications Bill, allowing members of the Irish parliament to sit in the House of Commons and Northern Ireland assembly and the Police (Northern Ireland) Bill was curtailed. And in an attempt to complete its legislative programme, the Government used the Parliament Act to override opposition in the Lords and ensure that the Sexual Offences (Amendment) Bill to lower the age of homosexual consent to 16 got onto the statute books (defeated twice by Peers in Committee on 13 November on amendments moved by Baroness Young (Conservative) – the first an amendment on Reduction of Age of Consent passed by 205 votes to 144, a majority against the Government of 61 and the second on Abuse of Position of Trust passed by 139 votes to 124 a majority against the Government of 15). This it duly did on 30 November.

On their return on 23 October, the first business of the House of Commons was to elect a new Speaker following the surprise retirement of Betty Boothroyd. Twelve MPs put their names forward for consideration. The eventual victor was Michael Martin, Labour MP for Glasgow Springburn who secured 370 votes in favour with only 8 against. This despite the fact that conventionally the successful candidate would have been from the Conservative Party in the 'buggins turn' principle. Following this a promise was made that the new Modernisation Committee would look into the election of future Speakers and come up with an improved system. These new proposals were debated in the Commons on 22 March 2001.

Business in the Commons in the spill-over period consisted mainly of waiting for the Lords to send back Bills that had already been scrutinised by MPs. Having made an announcement to the Press over the previous weekend the Minister for the Armed Forces John Spellar was forced to come to the House on 24 October to make a statement on the withdrawal of the Royal Navy's nuclear-powered, hunter-killer submarines from active service.

On 31 October Deputy Prime Minster John Prescott made a statement on Government aid following the violent storms that had swept across the country – 'we have measures in place to deal with the immediate effects of this storm. We need to take a longer term look at how we can as a country be better placed to deal with the extreme weather events which we expect to be more frequent in future.'

The fuel protests of the summer led to Home Secretary Jack Straw reporting to MPs on 2 November about the new contingency arrangements being put in place in the event of further blockades of fuel or other essential supplies, following the national disruptions in September.

On 7 November Junior Defence Minister Lewis Moonie announced that the Government had decided in recognition of the unique circumstances of their captivity, to make a single ex-gratia payment of £10,000 to each of the surviving members of the British groups who were held prisoner by the Japanese during the Second World War.

On 8 November Chancellor of the Exchequer Gordon Brown made his annual pre-budget statement which included an across the board duty freeze on all fuels until April 2002 and reform of vehicle excise duty for hauliers. As usual the Secretary of State for Social Security Alistair Darling made the annual benefits uprating statement the following day.

On 14 November the Secretary of State for Health Alan Milburn made a statement on the resources available to the National Health Service and the Government's priorities for reform of the NHS.

On 20 November the House approved the recommendations of the Modernisation Committee for continuing the experiment with changes to Parliamentary procedure by 283 votes to 18, a majority of 265. On 22 November Geoff Hoon made a statement about recent developments in European Defence collaboration with the formation of the Rapid Defence Force, reiterating that 'A British Prime Minister, answerable to this House, will always have the final say over the use and deployment of British armed forces.'

On 27 November John Prescott reported back to the House on the outcome of the climate change talks in the Hague 'a real disappointment for all those concerned.' On 28 November he announced the publication of the Rural White Paper – 'our aim is a living, working countryside, with better access, for all people to enjoy.' On 29 November Alistair Darling announced the decision on putting right the confusion on Inherited SERPS, with proposals to give full protection to every pensioner; to give younger people adequate notice of the change to SERPs rules and to provide transitional arrangements for those approaching retirement age.

The 1999–2000 Session of Parliament ended when Parliament was prorogued on 30 November, much later than normal. Some eleven Bills received Royal Assent.

The 2000–01 Session of Parliament was opened by the Queen's Speech on 6 December outlining the fourth legislative programme of the Government and containing proposals for fifteen Bills for what was likely to be a shortened session with the prospect of a General Election being called in the Spring. Four Bills that were to be introduced in draft were also mentioned. The Bills continued to build on manifesto commitments and concentrate on two key public concerns – cutting crime and improving public services. Perhaps confirming that this was indeed to be a shortened session, Tony Blair's speech was reserved for an attack upon the Opposition. After six days of debate the Speech was approved by 317 votes to 183, a Government majority of 134 on 13 December. The ensuing session was dominated by the impression that this was indeed to be a shortened session, with a General Election to be called in the Spring and although the Government had much less trouble from the House of Lords the session was marked by various backbench MPs objecting to the way business was handled with programming motions and deferred divisions on outstanding matters being held en bloc every Wednesday and therefore forcing extra divisions as a matter of course in protest and objecting on principle to agreeing to any matters, however small, without debate, adding to the impression that the Government were 'control freaks'.

On 11 December Tony Blair reported back to the House of Commons on the outcome of the Nice European Council when he said, 'It is possible in our judgement to fight Britain's corner, get the best out of Europe for Britain and exercise real authority and influence in Europe. That is as it should be. Britain is a world power. To stand aside from the key alliance – the European Union – right on our doorstep, is not advancing Britain's interests; it is betraying Britain's interests.' On 12 December Culture Secretary Chris Smith published a Communications White Paper with plans set up 'modern regulation for a modern world.' On 13 December Trade and Industry Secretary Stephen Byers made an announcement on the decision by General Motors to end car production at its Vauxhall plant in Luton and the steps the Government would take to assist the community.

The Vehicles (Crime) Bill to make it harder for criminals to dispose of stolen vehicles by introducing powers to regulate the motor salvage industry and require operators to register with local authorities, keep records and for the police to have right of entry to registered premises without warrant had an unopposed Second Reading in the House of Commons on 18 December. As a protest at the tight programming of all Government legislation the Opposition parties voted against the programming motion but it was still passed by 305 votes to 147, a Government majority of 158. The Bill was not amended in Committee, received its Third Reading on 30 January. Its passage through the House of Lords, once the Junior Transport Minister Lord Whitty had reassured peers at Second Reading on 15 February that 'there is no intention to make [a compulsory EU sign with stars on number plates] mandatory' was smooth and the Bill received Royal Assent on 10 April. The Private Security Industry Bill (Lords), to establish a new Security Industry Authority to eliminate criminality from the industry and raise professional standards was given a Second Reading in the House of Lords. This uncontroversial measure completed its passage through the Lords with Third Reading on 15 March before moving to the House of Commons for Second Reading on 28 March. The Bill received Royal Assent on 11 May. On 19 December, during a free vote the House of Commons approved the draft Human Fertilisation and Embryology (Research Purposes) Regulations to allow stem cell research by 366 votes to 174, a majority of 192. There was a row over why this issue was being dealt with by secondary rather than primary legislation, therefore in the words of opponents of the measure making it easier to pass and stifling debate. When the measure was debated in the House of Lords on 22 January, an amendment moved by Lord Walton of Detchant (Cross Bencher) to set up a Select Committee to look into the matter was agreed. In the House of Lords the Special Educational Needs and Disability Bill (Lords), to strengthen the right of children with Special Educational Needs (SEN) to be educated in mainstream schools and to introduce disability discrimination rights in the provision of education, was given a Second Reading on 19 December. Minister of State at the Department for Education and Employment Baroness Blackstone thought the Bill proved the Government's commitment to 'a fairer, more tolerant society where every individual is valued and appreciated for what he or she can do, not labeled for what he or she cannot do.' Baroness Blatch welcomed the Bill. It completed its Lords stages with three Grand Committee sessions in the Moses Room and Third Reading on 1 March and moved to the Commons for Second Reading on 20 March. The Bill received Royal Assent on 11 May.

One of the Government's most contentious pieces of legislation in the session, the Hunting Bill, a short bill with three options to provide for an almost total ban on hunting with dogs; a compulsory regulatory system which would require all those who wanted to hunt to obtain a licence; or a voluntary system of self-regulation, had its Second Reading in the House of Commons on 20 December by 373 votes to 158, a majority of 215. With feelings running high, votes were also forced on both the Programming Motion and the Money Resolution for the Bill and MPs refused to let through other secondary business that night. The Bill was taken in Committee of the Whole House on 17 January when MPs had a chance for a free vote on which of the three options they favoured. 1 – voluntary self-regulation was defeated by 399 votes to 155, a majority of 244; 2 – licencing (the so called Middle Way) was defeated by 382 votes to 182 (both Jack Straw and William Hague voted for this option – Tony Blair did not vote), a majority of 200; and 3 – outright ban was approved by 387 votes to 174, a majority of 213. This was the Clause that was debated in Standing Committee, and was approved at Third Reading on 27 February by 319 votes to 140, a majority of 179. Second Reading in the House of Lords on 12 March was passed without division during a debate that continued until 1.51 am. Agreement was reached the next day, by 189 votes to 129, to allow the Lords to make their choice of the three options proposed and in Committee on 26 March they voted as follows: 1 – voluntary self-regulation was approved by 249 votes to 108, a majority of 141; 2 – licencing was defeated by 202 votes to 122, a majority of 80; and 3 – outright ban was defeated by 317 votes to 68, a majority of 249. This is the option that would have been discussed in detail in Committee but in the event no further progress was made and the Bill fell with the calling of the General Election.

On 20 December the Secretary of State for Health Alan Milburn announced the publication of a White Paper on Adoption outlining reforms that 'will transform the life chances of hundreds hopefully thousands of children.' On 21 December the House of Lords gave a Second Reading to the Regulatory Reform Bill (Lords), to reduce the burden of existing regulation and to ensure that proposed legislation imposes as few burdens as possible. Conservative Trade and Industry spokesman Baroness Buscombe did not oppose the Bill in principle but was keen to debate the detail. The Bill completed its passage through the Lords with Third Reading on 26 February and had its Second Reading in the Commons on 19 March by 284 votes to 151, a Government majority of 133. The Bill received Royal Assent on 10 April.

The wholly uncontroversial Criminal Defence Service (Advice and Assistance) Bill (Lords) also received a Second Reading that day, going on to obtain Royal Assent on 10 April.

Returning after the Christmas Recess the House of Commons debated the Second Reading of the Homes Bill, to make home buying and selling in England and Wales faster, more transparent and consumer friendly by introducing a sellers pack of standard, essential information for prospective buyers, on 8 January. After Committee the Bill received an unopposed Third Reading on 7 February and was sent to the House of Lords on 28 March. The Bill fell due to the calling of the General Election. On 9 January the Minister for the Armed Forces John Spellar made a statement on the possible exposure of United Kingdom forces to depleted uranium in the Balkans. On 10 January the Health and Social Care Bill, to enable the setting up of a National Health Performance Fund from which the Secretary of State could make payments direct to NHS Trusts and Primary Care Trusts in addition to the conventional funding route through health authorities (which would also give the Secretary of State the power to replace the management team of NHS bodies in cases of persistent or catastrophic failure) was given a Second Reading by 324 votes to 118, a Government majority of 206. After completing Committee the Bill was given a Third Reading on 14 February by 310 votes to 168, a Government majority of 142 and moved to the House of Lords for Second Reading on 26 February, when Conservative Health spokesman Earl Howe expressed particular concern about the proposed abolition of Community Health Councils and about Clause 67 on the restriction on the collection of anonymised patient data. At Report Stage on 24 April the Government were defeated when a New Clause on the Reform of Community Health Councils (CHCs) moved by Earl Howe, which would ensure that the proposed new patient advocacy and liaison service councils would retain the independent function performed by the CHCs, was passed by 162 votes to 121, a majority against the Government of 41. The Bill therefore received Royal Assent on 11 May.

On 15 January after a statement from Junior International Development Minister George Foulkes on the Government's response to the earthquake in El Salvador, the Minister for Local Government and the Regions Hilary Armstrong made a statement about the national strategy for neighbourhood renewal action plan. The Capital Allowances Bill, the first Bill to be produced by the Inland Revenue tax law rewrite project, to modernise direct tax legislation and make it clearer and easier to use received its Second Reading. This uncontroversial Bill cleared both Houses without amendment and received Royal Assent on 23 March. The House of Lords on 15 January gave a Second Reading to the International Criminal Court Bill (Lords), to enable the UK to ratify the statute of the International Criminal Court (ICC) and become a founding member of the Court. This Bill also cleared both Houses without amendment and received Royal Assent on 11 May. On 16 January Alan Milburn made a statement announcing an inquiry into the alleged storage of corpses at Bedford Hospital. The Childrens' Commissioner for Wales Bill, to extend the powers of the Commissioner to include schools and hospitals, with extra powers to examine the cases of individual children and power to review the operations of the Welsh Assembly affecting children was given a Second Reading. The Bill was not amended in Committee and received an unopposed Third Reading on 8 February before moving to the House of Lords for Second Reading on 19 February. It received Royal Assent on 11 May. In the House of Lords on 16 January the Social Security Fraud Bill (Lords), enacting the recommendations of Lord Grabiner's report *The Informal Economy* by giving powers to tackle persistent offenders, was given a Second Reading. The Bill completed its Lords stages with Third Reading on 8 March and moved to the Commons for Second Reading on 27 March. The Bill received Royal Assent on 11 May.

The Culture and Recreation Bill (Lords), simplifying and clarifying the way in which cultural and sporting quangos operate and reducing their number was given a Second Reading in the House of Lords on 18 January. The Bill was not discussed any further and fell with the calling of the General Election.

The Tobacco Advertising and Promotion Bill, to ban the advertising and promotion of tobacco products in the United Kingdom received a Second Reading by 316 votes to 11, a Government majority of 305 in the House of Commons on 22 January. The Bill completed its Committee stage and had a Third Reading by 327 votes to 5, a Government majority of 322 on 13 February before moving to the House of Lords for Second Reading on 28 March. The Bill was lost due to the calling of the General Election.

On 23 January the Social Security Contributions (Share Options) Bill addressing concerns about the effects of aligning the income tax and national insurance treatment of employee share options had its Second Reading. The Opposition did not vote against the Bill. It received an unopposed Third Reading on 8 February and moved to the Lords for Second Reading on 2 April. The Bill received Royal Assent on 11 May.

On 29 January the Secretary of State for International Development Clare Short made a statement on the Government's response to the earthquake in India. The Criminal Justice and Police Bill had an unopposed Second Reading. Jack Straw said, 'the Bill has a simple aim: it is to aid the police and the courts in further reducing crime and the fear of crime.' Unopposed Third Reading on 14 March was followed by Second Reading in the Lords on 2 April. The Bill received Royal Assent on 11 May. In the House of Lords on 29 January the Commonhold and Leasehold Reform Bill (Lords), to reform the purchase of freeholds by leaseholders and to create commonhold, a new form of tenure for flat owners was given a Second Reading. The Bill had five sessions in Grand Committee in the Moses Room and returned to the Lords to begin its Report Stage but the Bill was lost when the General Election was called.

On 30 January Alan Milburn published the report of the Redfern inquiry into the Royal Liverpool Children's NHS Trust (Alder Hey Hospital) and announced that the law would be changed to enshrine the concept of informed consent. On 31 January the Foreign Secretary Robin Cook made a statement on the result of the Lockerbie bombing trial in the Hague, 'at last the relatives know that a fair trial in an open court has seen justice done.' On 1 February Stephen Byers made a statement on the Government's reaction to the announcement by Corus PLC of major redundancies in the steel industry. The Chairman of Corus, Sir Brian Moffat was called before both the Trade and Industry Select Committee (on 14 February) and the Welsh Affairs Select Committee (on 2 May) to explain the company's actions.

On 6 February the House of Commons (Removal of Clergy Disqualification) Bill, to allow serving and former ministers of religion to become MPs was given a Second Reading by 278 votes to 57, a Government majority of 221 in the House of Commons. Opposition MPs were concerned that this legislation was in fact being introduced to benefit one individual, David Cairns, a Minister who wished to stand as the Labour candidate in Greenock and Inverclyde in the General Election, and therefore objected on principle. Committee of the Whole House and Third Reading (passed by 196 to 15) were concluded on 1 March and the Bill moved to the House of Lords for Second Reading on 27 March. The Bill received Royal Assent on 11 May.

On 9 February Liberal Democrat MP Norman Baker having asked several questions about the affair, raised the matter of the Hinduja Brothers and their application for a British passport in an adjournment debate, a case that had major implications for the Secretary of State for Northern Ireland Peter Mandelson, who had resigned over his role in it on 24 January and the Minister for Europe Keith Vaz.

On 12 February the Secretary of State for Education and Employment David Blunkett announced the publication of a Green Paper on Schools 'to create a schools system appropriate to the 21st century.'

The House of Commons returned from the short February half-term recess on 26 February to three statements. Jack Straw announced the publication of a White Paper on Criminal Justice. Following Junior Agriculture Minister Baroness Hayman's statement in the House of Lords on 21 February on the outbreak of Foot-and-Mouth disease in Essex, Agriculture Minister Nick Brown used this first opportunity to update MPs on the outbreak of the disease in the United Kingdom for the first time in 20 years – 11 cases having been confirmed by then. Finally Geoff Hoon made a statement about coalition operations to enforce the no-fly zones over Iraq.

On 5 March Stephen Byers made a statement in the House of Commons publishing the Bain report on the National Minimum Wage and accepting the recommendation that it be increased to £4.10 per hour from October. On 6 March the International Development Bill, to establish in legislation the reduction of poverty as the aim of the United Kingdom's development assistance was given an unopposed Second Reading. Although the Bill completed its Commons stages it fell when the General Election was called.

Gordon Brown delivered his fifth Budget statement on 7 March, generally seen as a something for everyone, pre-election budget with modest tax cuts and pledges to help working families and defend public services.

Foot-and-Mouth dominated the next few weeks of Parliament. Gradually any concensus on the issue between the Government and the Opposition broke down. Nick Brown updated MPs on developments on 8 March but was criticised by Tim Yeo for failing to give more details about compensation schemes. Culture Secretary Chris Smith reported on the consequences for rural tourism of the outbreak on 14 March. Nick Brown again updated MPs on developments on 15 March, when the number of confirmed cases had risen to 240 and had concluded that 'the disease has spread mainly through movement of sheep and subsequent mixing of animals at a small number of livestock markets.' On 20 March Environment Minister Michael Meacher reported back on the work of the rural taskforce to date whose 'first priority remains to eradicate the disease as soon as possible . . . and is working urgently to develop measures to alleviate the impact' Conservative Environment spokesman Archie Norman thought the measures announced would be 'widely welcomed as far as they go . . . but it is clear that the extent of the crisis has been widely underestimated. The countryside is now risking meltdown and permanent loss of business.' The Conservatives initiated debates on the outbreak on 21 March.

On 23 March Deputy Prime Minister John Prescott announced the publication of the independent Clarke Inquiry report into the sinking of the Marchioness in 1989 – 'responsibility has at long last been attributed and laid at the door of the skippers, the owners and the managers of both vessels.'

On 26 March Tony Blair reported back on the outcome of the European Council in Stockholm over the weekend and outlined the agenda for enlargement and economic reform in Europe. The Adoption and Children Bill, to amend existing outdated adoption legislation was given a Second Reading in the Commons.

On 27 March Nick Brown updated MPs on developments in the foot-and-mouth outbreak. 668 cases had been confirmed. There was a backlog of 264,000 animals awaiting slaughter. The cause of the outbreak seemed to be from imported meat that was then used as pigswill. The Ministry of Agriculture, Fisheries and Food had now called on the army for assistance and were bringing more vets into the front line.

On 29 March Ulster Unionist MP Roy Beggs made a personal statement in the House concerning his breach of rules concerning the registering of an interest.

On 2 April Jack Straw made the long expected announcement that due to the foot-and-mouth outbreak the local elections scheduled to be held on 3 May in England and 26 May in Northern Ireland would now be postponed until 7 June (and, by implication the General Election as well). A short bill would be introduced to allow candidates and local authorities who had already incurred costs to be compensated. What was actually two bills (The Elections Bill and the Elections Publications Bill) were rushed through all their stages and received Royal Assent on 10 April.

On 9 April Nick Brown updated MPs on foot-and-mouth, with 1,144 confirmed cases and 478,000 animals awaiting slaughter. Tim Yeo criticised him for failing to learn the lessons of the 1967 outbreak, the delay in calling in the army and the slowness in consulting epidemiologists about the likely spread of the disease. The Finance Bill, implementing the proposals from the Budget was given a Second Reading by 319 votes to 175, a Government majority of 144. Committee of the Whole House was held on 23 and 24 April and despite the calling of the General Election the Bill got through without any amendments and received Royal Assent on 11 May.

Returning from the Easter Recess MPs were updated on the work of the Rural Taskforce by Michael Meacher on 23 April, 'a total package for immediate practical help to the rural economy of more than £200 million.'

On 25 April Stephen Byers made an announcement on the Government's response to the closure of the Motorola factory in Bathgate. This was followed by a Liberal Democrat debate on the Rural Economy. On 26 April Nick Brown made his ninth statement to MPs on the foot-and-mouth outbreak. 1,141 cases had been confirmed, 152,000 animals were awaiting slaughter and some 218,000 carcasses were awaiting disposal. Restrictions had been lifted on certain areas where there had been no new cases for 30 days.

On 30 April the Rating (Former Agricultural Premises and Rural Shops) Bill, a measure to give rate relief to certain premises, had its Second Reading in the House of Commons.

Despite being introduced so late in the session the Bill received Royal Assent on 11 May.

On 2 May Chris Smith reported to the Commons on the collapse of the Football Association's plans for the Wembley National Stadium project. He had asked the existing ministerial group to look at alternative solutions. A group of Labour backbench MPs continued to block any progress on the City of London (Ward Elections) Bill, a Private Bill which they felt it denied justice and representation to many in its reform of the Corporation of London. Nick Brown updated MPs on the foot-and-mouth outbreak with 1,537 confirmed cases with no backlog of animals waiting for disposal. Restrictions had also been lifted in 10 different areas, where there had been no new cases for thirty days.

On 8 May Tony Blair announced the date of the General Election as 7 June. Business managers then agreed a rushed timetable to get through as much of the outstanding legislation as could be agreed. On 9 May Edward Heath, who was standing down after 51 years as an MP was allowed to make a personal statement to the House.

Parliament was dissolved on 11 May. On the same day some thirteen Government Bills received Royal Assent and in the 2000/01 session some 21 Government Bills were passed, with no Private Members' Bills making progress.

Following another landslide victory for the Labour Party, winning a Commons majority of 167, the new Parliament met for the State Opening and Queen's Speech on 20 June which set out the first legislative programme of the second term of the New Labour Government. It contained proposals for twenty Bills for the session, which will last until October 2002, and mentioned four Bills that would be introduced in draft and one further Bill that was being prepared. The Bills were designed to build on manifesto commitments and concentrate on reforming and transforming public services (particularly education, health and crime) and on boosting business and enterprise. William Hague who had announced that he would be standing down as Leader felt that the Queen's Speech ignored more than it included. He was particularly keen, in the light of the poor turn out at the General Election, for more to be done on the reform of Parliament. The Queen's Speech was debated for six days and on 27 June was passed by 334 votes to 207, a Government majority of 127.

On 21 June the Secretary of State for Environment, Food and Rural Affairs Margaret Beckett updated the House of Commons on developments in the foot-and-mouth outbreak since Parliament had been dissolved. Some 1,771 cases had been confirmed in the United Kingdom (including four in Northern Ireland) but the number of daily cases had fallen to one.

On 25 June the Minister for Police, Courts and Drugs John Denham replied to a Private Notice Question from Peter Pike (Labour) in the House of Commons on riots in Burnley over the previous weekend. On 28 June the House approved a motion proposed by the Modernisation Committee agreeing to the programming of all Bills at all stages by 268 votes to 130, a Government majority of 138.

On 2 July the Secretary of State for Northern Ireland John Reid made a statement in the House of Commons on the situation in Northern Ireland following the resignation of the First Minister David Trimble.

In the few weeks before the Summer Recess the Government concentrated on re-introducing Bills that had been lost in the previous Parliament due to the calling of the election and on bills to enable the United Kingdom to carry out international treaty obligations. All the legislation was again subject to strict timetabling.

The International Development Bill (Lords) was reintroduced in identical form, designed to establish the reduction of poverty as the central aim of the United Kingdom's international development effort. It had its Second Reading in the House of Lords on 2 July. Committee stage was completed on 16 July with only minor Government amendments. Earlier in the day the Lords had approved a controversial new Code of Conduct for Peers despite the reservation of certain Peers such as Lord Kingsland (Conservative).

The Land Registration Bill (Lords) intended to reform the system of land registration to promote greater electronic conveyancing had its Second Reading in the House of Lords on 3 July and completed its Committee stage on 17, 19 and 23 July.

The European Communities (Finance) Bill, to allow the adoption of the amended system for financing the annual EC budget as agreed at the 1999 Berlin European Council had its Second Reading in the House of Commons on 3 July. Introducing the debate Chief Secretary to the Treasury Andrew Smith called it 'a good deal for the United Kingdom and an important step for the EU. The Bill completed Committee of the Whole House on 19 July without amendment.

The European Communities (Amendment) Bill to enable the United Kingdom to ratify the Treaty of Nice had its Second Reading in the House of Commons on 4 July. Second reading was passed by 385 votes to 148, a Government majority of 237. The Bill completed Committee of the Whole House on 11, 17 and 19 July without amendment.

In the House of Commons on 5 July MPs voted to increase their salaries, pensions and allowances well above the rate of inflation as recommended by the Senior Salaries Review Body by 276 votes to 42, a majority of 234.

The Commonhold and Leasehold Reform Bill (Lords), a measure to reform the purchase of freeholds by leaseholders and to create commonhold, a new form of tenure for flat owners, was reintroduced and had its Second Reading in the House of Lords on 5 July. The Lord Chancellor Lord Irvine of Lairg suggested that the Government had listened to the criticisms of the previous Bill and had introduced important new clauses to Part II of the Bill.

Two new Bills were introduced in the House of Commons before the Summer recess. The Homelessness Bill, a measure not outlined in the Queen's Speech. The Bill completed its Committee Stage without amendment.

The Export Control Bill, to improve the controls by setting out the purposes for which export controls may be imposed, and by providing new controls on the trafficking and brokering of weapons and related equipment, had an unopposed Second Reading in the House of Commons on 9 July. There was an objection from all Opposition parties to the continued tight programming of this and all Government legislation and so the Programme Motion was opposed, although comfortably passed by 318 votes to 62, a Government majority of 256.

In the House of Lords on 9 July the Travel Concessions (Eligibility) Bill (Lords) to make age entitlement for concessionary travel fares the same for men and women at the age of sixty had its Second Reading. It completed its Committee stage on 24 July without amendment.

On 10 July the Home Secretary David Blunkett made a statement on the disturbances in Bradford over the previous weekend. This was followed by a statement by the Secretary of State for Defence Geoff Hoon on the procurement strategy for the Type 45 Destroyer based on a proposal by BAe Systems. In the House of Lords the British Overseas Territories Bill (Lords) had its Second Reading on 10 July. The Bill, not outlined in the Queen's Speech will grant British citizenship, with the right of abode in the United Kingdom, to British Dependent Territories citizens in qualifying overseas territories. It completed its Committee stage on 24 July without amendment.

In the final week before the Summer Recess the Government were accused of trying to exercise too much control over Parliament when the nominations for the membership of the powerful Commons Select Committees were announced and it appeared that the much respected and long-serving Labour Chairs of two Committees (Gwyneth Dunwoody [Transport] and Donald Anderson [Foreign Affairs]) had been dropped, for what seemed to be taking too critical a line of the Government in their reports. The Government suffered two defeats on the votes for the Foreign Affairs Committee (by 301 votes to 232, a majority against the Government of 69) and the Transport, Local Government and the Regions Committee (by 308 votes to 221, a majority against the Government of 87). New motions which replaced the two Members on the Committees were approved on 19 July and the two were duly re-elected as Chairs by their respective Committees.

William Hague made his last appearance in the House as Leader of the Opposition at Prime Minister's Question Time on 18 July. Later that day the Alan Milburn announced the publication of the Kennedy inquiry into the care and management of children treated at the Bristol Royal Infirmary.

The following day (19 July) saw the final appearance of defeated Conservative Leadership challenger Michael Portillo (who had announced that he was retiring from front-line politics following his failure to secure the nomination of his fellow Conservative MPs) at the Dispatch Box during Treasury Questions.

The House of Commons rose for the Summer Recess on 20 July. The House of Lords continued to sit until and on 23 July they were informed of the imprisonment of one of their number, Lord Archer of Weston-super-Mare and, in response to a PNQ from Lord Luke (Conservative), the Leader of the Lords Lord Carter made a statement on the Government's decision to review arrangements for disinfecting farms contaminated by foot-and-mouth disease. On 24 July the Minister of State at the Department for Transport, Local Government and the Regions Lord Falconer of Thoroton made a statement in response to a PNQ from Lord Peyton of Yeovil (Conservative) justifying the dismissal of London Transport Commissioner Bob Kiley as Chairman of London Underground. The Lords rose for the Summer Recess after business on 24 July.

## PUBLIC ACTS OF PARLIAMENT 2000-2001

This list of Public Acts commences with eleven Public Acts which received the Royal Assent before September 1, 2000. Those Public Acts which follow received the Royal Assent after August 31 2000. The date stated after each Act is the date on which it came into effect.

*Finance Act 2000*, c. 17 (various dates) grants certain duties, alters others, and amends the law relating to the National Debt and the Public Revenue; makes further provision for charitable donations; employee share ownership and pension schemes; enterprise incentives, research and development; and incentives to use electronic communications.

*Sea Fishing Grants (Charges) Act 2000*, c. 18 (July 28, 2000) makes provision to ensure the validity of charges made in the administration of certain grant schemes relating to sea fishing.

*Child Support, Pensions and Social Security Act 2000*, c. 19 (various dates, some to be appointed) amends the law relating to child support, occupational and personal pensions, war pensions, social security benefits, social security administration and national insurance contributions; amends the Family Law Reform Act 1969 and the Family Law Act 1986.

*Government Resources and Accounts Act 2000*, c. 20 (various dates, some to be appointed) makes provision about government resources and accounts; provides for financial assistance for a body established to participate in public-private partnerships; and for connected purposes.

*Learning and Skills Act 2000*, c. 21 (various dates, some to be appointed) establishes the Learning and Skills Council for England and the National Council for Education and Training for Wales; and makes other provision for education and training.

*Local Government Act 2000*, c. 22 (various dates, some to be appointed) makes provision with respect to the functions and procedures of local authorities, local authority elections, and grants and housing benefit in respect of certain welfare services; amends the Children Act 1989; and for connected purposes.

*Regulation of Investigatory Powers Act 2000*, c. 23 (various dates, some to be appointed) makes provision in relation to the interception of communications, the acquisition and disclosure of data relating to communications, the carrying out of surveillance, the use of covert human intelligence sources and the acquisition of the means by which electronic data protected by encryption or passwords may be decrypted or accessed; and for many connected purposes.

*Census (Amendment) Act 2000*, c. 24 (July 28, 2000) amends the 1920 Act to enable particulars to be required in respect of religion.

*Football (Disorder) Act 2000*, c. 25 (July 28, 2000 except s.1 on a day to be appointed) provides for the prevention of violence or disorder at or in connection with association football matches.

*Postal Services Act 2000*, c. 26 (various dates, some to be appointed) establishes the Postal Services Commission and the Consumer Council for Postal Services; provides for the licensing of certain postal services and for a universal service; the vesting of the property, rights and liabilities of the Post Office in a company nominated by the Secretary of State; and for the subsequent dissolution of the Post Office; and for connected purposes.

*Utilities Act 2000*, c. 27 (various dates, some to be appointed) provides for the establishment and functions of the Gas and Electricity Markets Authority and the Gas and Electricity Consumer Council and amends the legislation regulating the gas and electricity industries; and for connected purposes.

*Health Services Commissioners (Amendment) Act 2000*, c. 28 (February 23, 2001) amends the 1993 Act.

*Trustee Act 2000*, c. 29 (various dates, some to be appointed) amends the law relating to trustees and persons having the investment powers of trustees.

*Licensing (Young Persons) Act 2000*, c. 30 (January 23, 2001) makes provision in connection with the sale and consumption of intoxicating liquor in cases involving persons under eighteen; and for connected purposes.

*Warm Homes and Energy Conservation Act 2000*, c. 31 (November 23, 2000 except in Wales s. 2 on a day to be appointed) requires the Secretary of State to publish and implement a strategy for reducing fuel poverty and to require the setting of targets for the implementation of that strategy; and for connected purposes.

*Police (Northern Ireland) Act 2000*, c. 32 (various dates, some to be appointed) makes provision in relation to policing in Northern Ireland.

*Fur Farming (Prohibition) Act 2000*, c. 33 ( s. 5 on January 23, 2001, ss 1–4 on a day to be appointed but not before January 1, 2003) prohibits the keeping of animals solely or primarily for slaughter for the value of their fur and provides for the making of payments in respect of the related closure of certain businesses.

*Race Relations (Amendment) Act 2000*, c. 34 (various dates, some to be appointed) extends further the application of the 1976 Act to the police and other public authorities and amends the exemption under that Act for acts carried out for the purpose of safeguarding national security; and for connected purposes.

*Children (Leaving Care) Act 2000*, c. 35 (various dates, some to be appointed) makes provision about children and young persons who are being, or have been, looked after by a local authority; replaces section 24 of the Children Act 1989; and for connected purposes.

*Freedom of Information Act 2000*, c. 36 (November 30, 2000) makes provision for the disclosure of information held by public authorities or by persons providing services for them; amends the Data Protection Act 1998 and the Public Records Act 1958; and for connected purposes.

*Countryside and Rights of Way Act 2000*, c. 37 (various dates, some to be appointed) makes new provision for public access to the countryside; amends the law relating to public rights of way; enables traffic regulation orders to be made for the purpose of conserving an area's natural beauty; makes provision with respect to the driving of mechanically propelled vehicles elsewhere than on roads; amends the law relating to nature conservation and the protection of wildlife; makes further provision with respect to areas of outstanding natural beauty; and for connected purposes.

*Transport Act 2000*, c. 38 (various dates, some to be appointed) makes provision about transport.

*Insolvency Act 2000*, c. 39 (various dates, some to be appointed) amends the law about insolvency and the

Company Directors Disqualification Act 1986; and for connected purposes.

*Protection of Animals (Amendment) Act 2000*, c. 40 (January 30, 2001) enables provision to be made for the care, disposal or slaughter of animals to which proceedings under the Protection of Animals Act 1911, s. 1 relate.

*Political Parties, Elections and Referendums Act 2000*, c. 41 (various dates, some to be appointed) establishes an Electoral Commission; makes provision for the registration and finances of political parties; donations and expenditure for political purposes; election and referendum campaigns and the conduct of referendums; election petitions and other legal proceedings in connection with elections; reduces the qualifying periods set out in the Representation of the People Act 1985; makes pre-consolidation amendments relating to European Parliamentary Elections; and for connected purposes.

*Disqualification Act 2000*, c. 42 (November 30, 2000) removes the disqualification for membership of the House of Commons and the Northern Ireland Assembly of persons who are members of the legislature of Ireland (the Oireachtas); disqualifies for certain offices which may be held by members of the Northern Ireland Assembly persons who are or will become ministers of the Government of Ireland or chairmen or deputy chairmen of committees of the Dail Eireann or the Seanad Eireann or of joint committees of the Oireachtas; makes provision with respect to who may be chairman or deputy chairman of a statutory committee of the Assembly or a member of the Northern Ireland Assembly Commission.

*Criminal Justice and Court Services Act 2000*, c. 43 (various dates, some to be appointed) establishes a National Probation Service for England and Wales and a Children and Family Court Advisory and Support Service; makes further provision for the protection of children and about dealing with persons suspected of, charged with or convicted of offences; and amends the law relating to access to information held under the Road Traffic Act 1988, Pt III; and for connected purposes.

*Sexual Offences (Amendment) Act 2000*, c. 44 (various dates, some to be appointed) reduces the age at which, makes provision with respect to the circumstances in which, certain sexual acts are lawful; makes it an offence for a person aged 18 or over to engage in sexual activity with or directed towards a person under that age if he is in a position of trust in relation to that person; and for connected purposes.

*Consolidated Fund (No. 2) Act 2000*, c. 45 (December 21, 2000) applies certain sums out of the Consolidated Fund to the service of the year ending on March 31, 2001.

*Consolidated Fund Act 2001*, c. 1 (March 22, 2001) authorises the use of resources for the service of the year ending on March 31, 2002 and applies certain sums out of the Consolidated Fund to the service of the years ending on March 31, 2000, 2001 and 2002.

*Capital Allowances Act 2001*, c. 2 (various dates) restates, with minor changes, certain enactments relating to capital allowances.

*Vehicles (Crime) Act 2001*, c. 3 (various dates, some to be appointed) regulates motor salvage operators and registration plate suppliers; makes further provision for preventing or detecting vehicle crime; enables the Secretary of State to make payments in respect of certain expenditure relating to vehicle crime; and for connected purposes.

*Criminal Defence Service (Advice and Assistance) Act 2001*, c. 4 (April 10, 2001) clarifies the extent of the duties of the Legal Services Commission under the Access to Justice Act 1999.

*Election Publications Act 2001*, c. 5 (April 10, 2001) makes provision for postponing the operation of certain enactments relating to election publications; and for connected purposes.

*Regulatory Reform Act 2001*, c. 6 (April 10, 2001) enables provision to be made for the purpose of reforming legislation which has the effect of imposing burdens affecting persons in the carrying on of any activity and enables codes of practice to be made with respect to the enforcement of restrictions, requirements and conditions; and for connected purposes.

*Elections Act 2001*, c. 7 (April 10, 2001) postpones local elections in England and Wales and Northern Ireland, requires polls for different elections in Northern Ireland to be taken together if they are to be taken on the same day; and consequential provisions.

*Appropriation Act 2001*, c. 8 (May 11, 2001) appropriates the supplies authorised in this Session of Parliament.

*Finance Act 2001*, c. 9 (May 11, 2001) grants certain duties, alters others, and amends the law relating to the national debt and the public revenue; makes further provision in connection with finance.

*Special Education Needs and Disability Act 2001*, c. 10 (various dates, some to be appointed) amends Education Act 1996 Pt 4; makes further provision against discrimination on the grounds of disability, in schools and other educational establishments; and for connected purposes.

*Social Security Fraud Act 2001*, c. 11 (various dates, some to be appointed) makes provision for the purposes of the law relating to social security, about the obtaining and disclosure of information; makes provision for restricting the payment of social security benefits and war pensions in the case of persons convicted of offences relating to such benefits or pensions and about the institution of proceedings for such offences.

*Private Security Industry Act 2001*, c. 12 (various dates, some to be appointed) makes provision for the regulation of the private security industry.

*House of Commons (Removal of Clergy Disqualification) Act 2001*, c. 13 (May 11, 2001) removes any disqualification from membership of the House of Commons that arises by reason of a person having been ordained or being a minister of a religious denomination and continues the disqualification of Lords Spiritual from such membership.

*Rating (Former Agricultural Premises and Rural Shops) Act 2001*, c. 14 (various dates, some to be appointed) makes provision about non-domestic rating in respect of hereditaments including land or buildings which were formerly agricultural and in respect of food stores in rural settlements.

*Health and Social Care Act 2001*, c. 15 (various dates, some to be appointed) amends the law relating to the NHS; provides for the exercise of functions by Care Trusts under partnership arrangements under the Health Act 1999 and makes further provision in relation to such arrangements; makes further provision in relation to social care services and the supply or other processing of patient information; extends the categories of appropriate practitioners in relation to prescription-only medicinal products; and for connected purposes.

*Criminal Justice and Police Act 2001*, c. 16 (various dates, some to be appointed) makes provision for combating crime and disorder; about the disclosure of information relating to criminal matters and about powers of search and seizure; and for connected purposes.

*International Criminal Court Act 2001*, c. 17 (day or days to be appointed) gives effect to the Statute of the International Criminal Court and provides for offences under the law of England and Wales and Northern Ireland corresponding to offences within the jurisdiction of that Court; and for connected purposes.

*Children's Commissioner for Wales Act 2001*, c. 18 (various dates, some to be appointed) makes further provision about the Children's Commissioner for Wales.

*Armed Forces Act 2001*, c. 19 (various dates, some to be appointed) continues the Army Act 1955, the Air Force Act 1955 and the Naval Discipline Act 1957; makes further provision in relation to the armed forces and the Ministry of Defence Police; and for connected purposes.

*Social Security Contributions (Share Options) Act 2001*, c. 20 (May 11, 2001) makes provision about the payment of NICs in respect of share options and similar rights obtained by persons as directors or employees during the period beginning April 6, 1999 and ending May 19, 2000.

WHITE PAPERS, REPORTS ETC

International Development White Paper on '*Eliminating World Poverty: Making Globalisation Work for the Poor*' was presented to Parliament by the Secretary of State for International Development on 11 December 2000. The white paper sets out the following proposals to meet the Government's commitment to eliminate world poverty.

- Work with other government departments and agencies, to manage globalisation, so that poverty is reduced and the international Development targets are achieved.
- Encourage economic growth that is 'equitable and environmentally sustainable.'
- Assist developing countries to reform their 'economic management' and build effective government structures.
- Work to decrease corruption, increase human rights and provide a public forum for poor peoples opinions.
- Work with other agencies to reduce violent conflict, including more restrictions on arms trading.
- Encourage better education for the poor, especially in new technologies, and to share skills and knowledge with other countries.
- Focused UK global research on the needs of the poor and extending 'intellectual property regimes' for the poor.
- Assisting developing countries to gain private finance.
- To strengthen the global financial system to assist developing countries in opening their capital accounts.
- To encourage international involvement and investment, competition and tax to promote and protect the interests of developing nations.
- Create interest from national and trans-national companies to invest in developing companies.
- Work to encourage an open rules-based international trading system, and promote equitable trade rules.
- Help to reduce trade barriers both in developed and developing countries to encourage new trade opportunities.
- Decrease the contribution made by developing countries to global environmental degradation.
- Work with developing countries to ensure that their poverty reduction policies do not adversely affect the management of their environmental resources.
- Provide a platform for developing countries to take part in international negotiations.
- Increase the percentage of global development assistance spent in poor countries to support their poverty reduction policies.
- Introduce a new Development bill to replace the Overseas Development and Co-Operation Act (1980).
- Generate faster provision of debt relief for poorer countries that are attempting to reduce poverty.
- Strengthening the system of international accountability, so that developing countries are part of the decision making process.

*Reforming the Mental Health Act* was presented to Parliament by the Secretary of State for Health and the Home Secretary on 20 December 2000. The report concerns parts I and II of the Mental Health Act. Part I 'The New Legal Framework' looks at the Government's plans for new mental health legislation, and explains how the legislation will affect patients. Part II 'High Risk Patients' details the Government's arrangements for high risk patients who represent a threat to public safety.
The new mental health legislation will:

- Become part of the new arrangements for improving the 'quality and consistency' of health and social care services for people who suffer from mental health problems.
- Provides a new structure for the use of 'compulsory powers' to detain members of society who pose a 'serious threat' to others due to their mental illness.
- The legislation will create a single framework for the use of compulsory powers for care and treatment, this will include the following; common criteria, a common pathway for assessment, the approval of a plan of care treatment by the Mental Health Tribunal and better safeguards for patients.

*Department of Trade and Industry* white paper '*Opportunity for All in a World of Change*' was presented to Parliament by the Secretary of Trade and Industry and the Secretary of State for Education and Employment on 13 February 2001. The paper is concerned with what Government, businesses and individuals should do to provide economic success in the next decade. It included the following main proposals:

- Improvement of living standards and opportunities for all across the UK by launching a £75 million incubator fund, managed by the Small Business Service to provide support and advice to new buisinesss.
- The Government has established an Enterprise Scholarship Scheme for exceptional young graduates from abroad, particularly in 'hi-tech'subjects to develop their careers or start a business in the UK.
- Strengthening ties with businesses abroad and working towards global economic integration, by launching a global partnership programme to help UK firms collaborate with domestic and overseas companies.
- Increasing literacy and numeracy investment by spending an extra £150 on literacy training.
- Working to train individuals and the workforce with vocational, technical, information and communication technology skills and qualifications.
- The Government plans to establish university centres and new technology institutes in the regions.
- Ensuring investment, competition and innovation in businesses, such as e-science, research on genomics, broadband technology and digital TV.

Home Office white paper '*Criminal Justice: The Way Ahead*' presented by the Secretary of State for the Home Department on 26 February 2001. As part of an evidence-based programme to reduce crime and it's causes. This included programmes funding by the *Department for Education and Employment, Department of Health and †Department of the Environment, Transport and the Regions, continuing with initiatives like Sure Start for pre-school children and the Neighbourhood Renewal Strategy to help deprived areas. Also, the white paper develops the policies set out under the 2000 Spending Review .The main proposals of the white paper were:

- The radical overhaul and reform of the current Criminal Justice System (CJS), especially the Criminal Prosecution Service (CPS) and the Youth Justice System.
- Catching and convicting more offenders and increasing the percentage of criminals brought to justice in proportion to crimes reported to the police.
- Increasing resources to combat drug related crimes.
- Ensuring that punishments fit the crime to help break re-offending patterns.

- Focusing on the needs of the victims of crimes.
- Combating international and organised crime.
- Increasing staff numbers in the CJS.
- Improving the information and communication technology of the CJS, through providing a £1.4 billion investment in 2001 to 2002, rising to £2.7 billion in 2003 to 2004.
- Incorporating new procedures making it easier for courts to deliver justice including; simplified rules of evidence for magistrates and juries; improved access by jurors and witnesses to written statements and interview transcripts.
- Assisting the police with reducing crime via a 21 per cent increase in police funding between 2001 to 2004, including £500 million to fund Airwave a new national secure digital radio system, and increased funding to recruit an additional 9,000 recruits between 2000 to 2003.

*Department of Health White Paper 'Valuing People: A New Strategy for Learning Disability for the 21st Century'* was presented to Parliament by the Secretary of State for Health on 20 March 2001. It explains the Government's plans to increase the life opportunities for people with learning difficulties and their families by bettering their education, care, health and leisure opportunities. The four main principles are:

- *Rights*, by incorporating legislation that gives equal rights to all citizens, including the Human Rights Act 1998, Race Relations Act 1976, the Sex Discrimination Act 1975 and the Disability Discrimination Act 1995. As well as providing guidance to electoral administrators on helping disabled people, including those with learning disabilities with registering to vote and voting to enforce their civil rights.
- *Independence*, creating a non-dependent individual by encouraging their use of public services.
- *Choice*, in areas of housing, work and the provision of care by of those with learning disabilities thus providing them with opportunities to direct their daily lives.
- *Inclusion*, so that people with learning difficulties can do every day leisure and sporting activities such as going swimming or to the cinema. The Government has created a new Learning Disability Development Fund of up to £50 million per annum from April 2001, consisting of £20 million capital and £30 revenue.

Spending Review for 2001:
The Cabinet Office Department Expenditure Limits for 2001 to 2002 was £147,347,000. The gross Administrative cost limit was £124,293,000. The Cabinet also provided grants above £250,000 to the following organisations; £845,000 to the Civil Service Benevolent Fund; £1,322,000 to the Civil Service Sports Council and £265,000 to the Civil Service Retirement Fellowship. The spending review was presented to Parliament by the Minister for the Civil Service and Chief Secretary to the Treasury on 30 March 2001.

- The Chancellor of Exchequer's Departments Expenditure Limits for 1999 to 2000 was £2 billion above the Budget 2000 estimate of £1 billion. Instead of carrying forward the full amount the Government decided that £½ a billion of the additional 'underspend' should be used to repay debt, with the remaining £1½ billion spread equally between 2001 to 2002. The Budget 2000 provided an additional £2 billion for the NHS in 2000 to 2001, while the November 2000 pre-budget report provided an additional £200 million for school buildings across the UK in 2000 to 2001. Under the spending review targets for 2001 to 2004 the Department plans to raise the 'trend rate' of growth from the current estimate of 2.5 per cent by 2004, and to fix inflation at 2.5 per cent as specified by the Bank of England's remit. The spending review was presented to Parliament by the Chancellor of the Exchequer and Chief Secretary to the Treasury on 2 April 2001.
- The Home Office spending resources from a base line of £8.2 billion in 2000 to 2001 will increase to £9.6 billion in 2001 to 2002, £10.3 billion in 2002 to 2003 and £10.6 billion in 2003 to 2004. The spending review provided for increased spending on law and order and asylum totalling £2.6 billion for 2001 to 2003. The spending review was presented to Parliament by the Secretary of State for the Home Department and the Chief Secretary to the Treasury Department on 30 March 2001.
- The Department for International Development's total Department Expenditure Limits for 2003 to 2004 will be £399 million. The spending review was presented to Parliament by the Secretary of State for International Development and the Chief Secretary to the Treasury Department on 26 March 2001.
- ‡The Ministry of Agriculture, Fisheries and Food, and the Intervention Board and the Forestry Commission Department Expenditure Limits spending plans for 2003 to 2004 will be £1,103 million, the total Annual Managed Expenditure will be £2,244. The spending review was presented to Parliament by the Secretary of State for the Ministry of Agriculture, Fisheries and Food and the Chief Secretary to the Treasury Department on 30 March 2001.
- British Trade International cash requirement for 2002 to 2003 will be £391 million and 2003 to 2004 will be £399 million. The spending review was presented to Parliament by the Secretary of State for Trade and Industry the Secretary of State for Foreign and Commonwealth Affairs and the Chief Secretary to the Treasury Department on 30 March 2001.
- The Food Standards Agency Departmental spending plans for 20001 to 2002 was £114,746 million, 2002 to 2003 will be £122,045 and £2003 to 2004 will be £121,951. The spending review was presented to Parliament by the Secretary of State for Health and the Chief Secretary to the Treasury Department on 30 March 2001.
- The Department for Culture, Media and Sport received an increase in departmental funding from £1,015 million in 2000 to 2001 to £1,240 million in 2003 to 2004. This includes an increase settlement for sport and the arts by £100 million, including £10.5 million support for the 2002 Commonwealth Games in Manchester. The spending review was presented to Parliament by the Secretary of State for Culture, Media and Sport and the Chief Secretary to the Treasury on 10 April 2001.
- The Education and Employment Department spending review announced a growth in spending on education and training in England between 2000 to 2001 and 2003 to 2004 will be 5.7 per cent a year, and between and between 2003 to 2004 at 6.7 per cent a year. Capital expenditure on education and training will rise by an average of 18 per cent a year in real terms between 2000 to 2001 and 2003 to 2004. By 2003 to 2004 the Departments spending on education and training in England will be over £10.5 billion more than in 2000 to 2001. The spending review was presented to Parliament by the Secretary of State for Education and Employment and the Chief Secretary to the Treasury Department on 28 March 2001.

- The Inland Revenue's net cash requirement for the year ending 2002 will be £2,398,476,000 million. This sum will be to fund payments such as; providing tax relief to certain bodies and making rate payments to Local Authorities on behalf of certain bodies. The spending review was presented to Parliament by the Paymaster General and the Chief Secretary to the Treasury Department on 28 March 2001.
- The Department for Health expenditure for 2003 to 2004 will be £57.0 billion for England and £69.5 billion for the UK. The spending review was presented to Parliament by the Secretary of State for Health and the Chief Secretary to the Treasury Department on 2 May 2001.
- The Wales Office (Office of the Secretary of State for Wales) Departmental Expenditure Limits will be £9,499.466 million in 2003 to 2004 and Annual Managed Expenditure for the same period will be £1,265.937 million. The spending review was presented to Parliament by the Secretary of State for Wales and the Chief Secretary to the Treasury Department on 30 March 2001.
- The Ministry of Defence expenditure plans for 2003 to 2004 will be £31,973 million and for the same period the capital budget will be £6,184 million. The Department anticipates sales of assets and surplus land between April 2001 to March 2004 will raise £600 million. The spending review was presented to Parliament by the Secretary of State for Defence and the Chief Secretary to the Treasury Department on 2 April 2001.
- The Northern Ireland Office total budget for 2000 to 2001 was £8.7 billion with £7.6 billion set aside for the reinstatement and operation of the devolved institutions, and just under £1.1 billion for the Northern Ireland Office. The spending review was presented to Parliament by the Secretary of State for Northern Ireland the Chief Secretary to the Treasury Department on 3 March 2001.
- ≠The Department of Social Security total Departmental Expenditure Limits for 2002 to 2003 will be £4,264 million and the Annual Managed Expenditure for the same period will be £105,011. The total resource budget for the same period is £4,156 million. During 2003 to 2004 the Departmental Expenditure Limits will be £109,735 million. The spending review was presented to Parliament by the Secretary of State for Social Security and the Chief Secretary to the Treasury Department on 30 March 2001.
- Lord Chancellor's Departmental Expenditure Limits for 2002 to 2003 will be £2,836 million and £2,744 million for the Annual Managed Expenditure during the same period. During 2003 to 2004 the Departmental Expenditure Limits will be £2,845 million and £2,756 million for the Annual Managed Expenditure for the same period. The Departments spending plans include the HM Land Registry, Public Records Office and the Northern Ireland Court Sérvice. The spending review was presented to Parliament by the Lord Chancellor and the Chief Secretary to the Treasury Department on 30 March 2001.
- The Foreign and Commonwealth Office total Departmental Expenditure Limits will be £1,260 million during 2002 to 2003. During 2003 to 2004 the Departmental Expenditure Limits will be £207 million and the total Annual Managed Expenditure during the same period will be £1,146 million. The spending review was presented to Parliament by the Secretary of State for Foreign *the Chief Secretary to the Treasury Department on 2 April 2001.*
- The Scotland Office's investment in public expenditure is expected to increase by £3.4 billion over the previous provision during 2000 to 2001. The Department will also gain an extra £200 million for devolved services in Scotland over the next three years. The spending review was presented to Parliament by the Secretary of State for Scotland and the Chief Secretary to the Treasury Department on 30 March 2001.
- The Law Officer's Departmental Expenditure Limit for the Serious Fraud Office was £21,350,000 for 2001 to 2002. This provision was £7.4 per cent higher than the final net provision for 2000 to 2001. The spending review was presented to Parliament by the Attorney General and the Chief Secretary to the Treasury Department on 30 March 2001.
- †The Department of the Environment, Transport and the Regions Departmental Expenditure Limit for 2002 to 2003 will be £53,297 million and the total Annual Managed Expenditure during the same period will be £7,627 million. The Departmental Expenditure Limit for 2003 to 2004 will be £58,380 million and the total Annual Managed Expenditure during the same period will be £7,548 million. The spending review was presented to Parliament by the Deputy Prime Minister, the Secretary of State for Environment, Transport and the Regions and the Chief Secretary to the Treasury Department on 30 March 2001.

*Regulatory Impact Assessments: 1 July to 31 December 2000* was presented to Parliament by the Minister of the Cabinet Office and the Chancellor of the Duchy of Lancaster on 3 April 2001. It included the following review of the '*Good Policy Making: A Guide to Regulatory Impact Assessment*' published in August 2000:

The guidance proposed that new regulations should not be introduced without a full appraisal of the alternatives available to the Government. They also recommended that the Government should not under take any new regulations until a comprehensive analysis of the risks, costs and benefits had taken place. Ministers should be satisfied that the benefits of any new regulation justify the costs prior to the Government deciding on a new policy strategy.

Following the General Election and a Cabinet reshuffle in June 2001 the Government departments below have changed responsibilities and or titles:

* The Former Department for Education and Employment has now become the Department for Education and Skills.

† The Former Department of Environment, Transport and the Regions has now become The Department of Transport, Local Government and the Regions.

‡ The Former Ministry of Agriculture, Fisheries and Food, has now become the Department of Environment, Food and Rural Affairs.

≠The former Department of Social Security has now become the Department for Work and Pensions.

# The Queen's Awards for Enterprise

The Queen's Award for Export Achievement and The Queen's Award for Technological Achievement were instituted by royal warrant in 1975. The two separate awards took the place of The Queen's Award to Industry, which had been instituted in 1965. In 1992 the scheme was extended with the launch of a third award, The Queen's Award for Environmental Achievement. In December 1998 it was announced that a review committee, chaired by the Prince of Wales, would examine all aspects of the awards and recommend any changes it felt necessary The three awards are now: The Queen's Award for International Trade, The Queen's Award for Innovation and The Queen's Award for Environmental Achievement.

The awards differ from a personal royal honour in that they are given to a unit as a whole, management and employees working as a team. They may be applied for by any organisation within the United Kingdom, the Channel Islands or the Isle of Man which meet the criteria for the awards.

Awards are held for five years and holders are entitled to fly the appropriate award flag and to display the emblem on the packaging of goods produced in this country, on the goods themselves, on the unit's stationery, in advertising and on certain articles used by employees. Units may also display the emblem of any previous current awards during the five years.

Awards are announced on 21 April (the birthday of The Queen) and published formally in a special supplement to the London Gazette.

AWARDS OFFICE

All enquiries about the scheme and requests for application forms should be made to: The Secretary, The Queen's Awards Office, 151 Buckingham Palace Road, London SW1W 9SS. Tel: 020-7222 2277. Alternatively, a variety of information about the awards can be found at www.queensawards.org.uk.

## INTERNATIONAL TRADE

The criteria for an award for international trade are "outstanding achievement in international trade, resulting in substantial growth in overseas earnings and in commercial success, sustained over not less than three years, to levels which are outstanding for the goods and services concerned and for the size of the applicant's operations" or "continuous achievement in international trade, resulting in substantial overseas earnings with growth and commercial success, sustained over not less than six years, to levels which are outstanding for the goods or services concerned and for the size of the applicant's operations".

In 2001, The Queen's Award for International Trade was conferred on the following concerns:

AVX Limited, MLC Division, Londonderry - multi-layer ceramic capacitors

Abercombie and Kent Europe Ltd, Burford, Oxfordshire - De-luxe travel services

Adder Technology Ltd, Bar Hill, Cambridge - Computer peripheral equipment

Aircom International, Redhill, Surrey - Enterprise integrated software solution, consultancy and product support

Aircontrol Technologies Ltd, Staines, Middlesex - Environmental life support systems

Aortech Technologies Ltd, Bellsill, Lanarkshire - Replacement heart valves

Asset Security Managers Ltd, London - Specialist broking/advice on kidnap and ransom, product extortion and wrongful detention insurance

The Association of Chartered Certified Accountants, London - Professional examinations and membership

Julius Baer Investments Ltd, London - Investment advice

Bibby Line Limited, London - Offshore and marine vessel oprations

Nigel Burgess Ltd, London - Luxury yacht brockerage, charter and management

Celador, London - Television programmes

Chemence, Corby - Engineering adhesives and sealants for industrial, consumer and medical markets

C and J Clark Ltd, Street, Somerset - Footwear

Colefax and Fowler Limited, London - Soft furnishings

Cooke Optics Limited, Thurmaston, Leicester - A range of prime 35mm lenses

Coombe Castle International Limited, Corhsam, Wiltsire - Cheese and dairy products

G. Costa and Co Ltd, Aylesford, Kent - Pan-oriental foods, including Chinese, Thai and Japanese ingredients, authentic sauces, dips, noodles and rice

Delaware International Advisers Limited, London - Investment management

Digital Vision Limited, London - Production and distribution of royalty free digital photography and film footage

Domino Printing Sciences Plc, Bar Hill Cambridge - Ink jet and laser coding and marking equipment

Fibercore Limited, Southampton - Optical fibres

Gaffney, Cline and Associates Limited, Alton, Hampshire - Consultancy services to the energy industry

Glassbond (N.W.) Ltd, St Helens, Merseyside - Specialist cements and moulding powders

Glotel Plc, London - Telecommunications and networking consultancy

Group 4 Technology Limited, Tewkesbury, Gloucestershire - Access control equipment

Henrion, Ludlow and Schmidt Ltd, London - Corporate identity consultancy services

ISG Thermal Systems Ltd, Basildon, Essex - Thermal imaging cameras

The Independent Fragrance Company, Northampton - Specialised fragrances

Ivory and Ledoux Limited, London - Fruit juice concentrates and purees, frozen and canned fruit, vegetables and fish

J and H Sales (International Ltd), London - Waste paper (secondary fibres) for recycling

Junior Hagen Ltd, London - Exclusive fashion trimmings and accessories

KW International t/a KWI, London - Computer software offering a completely integrated trading, risk management and settlement platform for energy markets
Labtech Limited, Presteigne, Powys - Microwave printed circuits
Land Rover, Solihull, West Midlands - Four wheel drive vehicles
Less Common Metals Ltd, Birkenhead, Merseyside - Reactive metal alloys
Eli Lilly and Company Limited, Basingstoke - Pharmaceuticals and animal health products
London Business School, London - Business education and post graduate business degree programmes
M.O.S. (Miko Oilfield Supplies Ltd), Shipley, West Yorkshire - Oilfield cranes and lifting appliances
Malmic Lace Ltd, Ruddington, Nottingham - Lace, trimmings, elastic and rigid braids
Martin-Baker Aircraft Company Ltd, Uxbridge, Middlesex - Aircraft ejection seats
Mecatherm International Ltd, Kinswinford, West Midlands - Industrial furnaces and ovens
Media Audits Ltd, London - Media consultancy and evaluation services
Milton keynes Pressings Ltd, Bletchley, Milton Keynes - Metal pressings and welded assemblies
JPMorgan Investor Services EMEA, London - Investor services
NGF Europe Limited, St Helens, Merseyside - Rubber impregnated glass fibre cords
Nutrition Trading (International) Ltd, Studley, Warwickshire - Speciality animal feeds
Oceanair Marine Ltd, Chichester, West Sussex - Blinds and flyscreens for windows and hatches for boats and vehicles
Oxford Instruments Plasma Technology Ltd, Yatton, Bristol - Plasma processing and ion beam etching and deposition equipment
Oyster Marine Limited, Ipswich - Deck saloon cruising yachts
PAV Data Systems Ltd, Windermere, Cumbria - Wireless optical data transmission systems using infra-red lasers
Paradise Datacom Limited, Tiptree, Essex - Satellite communications equipment
Phase 1 Clinical Trials Unit Limited, Derriford, Plymouth - Clinical research on compounds for the pharmaceutical industry
Pinacl Cables, Ryhl, Denbighshire - Fibre optic cables
Quasar Microwave Technology Ltd, Newton Abbot, Devon - microwave frequency waveguide components
Randox Laboratories Ltd, Crumlin, County Antrim - diagnostic kits for medical, veterinary and environmental monitoring
Renishaw plc, Wotton-under-Edge, Gloucestershire - Metrology products enabling measurement to international standards
Rochford Thompson Equipment Ltd, Newbury, Berkshire - Passport reading equipment
Scottish Biomedical, Glasgow - Biomedical consultancy services
Shadbolt and Co, Reigate, Surrey - Commercial legal services
Shipley Europe Limited, Coventry - Speciality chemicals
David S Smith Worldwide Dispensers, London - Precision engineered plastic taps, dispensers and valves
Software 2000 Limited, Oxford - Driver software technologies for printers and copiers
Special Commissions Department, Spink and Son Ltd, London - Decorations, medals and presentation gifts
Stoneridge-Pollak Limited, Cheltenham, Gloucestershire - Electro-mechanical switches for the automotive industry
Targus Europe Ltd, Hounslow, Middlesex - Accessories for mobile computers
Thermomax Limited, Bangor, County Down - Vacuum tube solar collectors for water heating and also refrigeration controllers
M and A Thomson Litho Ltd, East Kilbride, Glasgow - Printing material and software
Throne International Boiler Services Limited, Bilston, Wolverhampton - Refurbishment and repair of industrial boilers
The University of Nottingham, Nottingham - Higher educational and research facilities
Vicon Motion Systems Limited, Oxford - Systems capturing the dimensional movement of objects, particularly the human body
Vision in Business Ltd, London - Business information services
Wagtech International Ltd, Thatcham, Berkshire - Laboratory, water and environmental testing equipment
John Wood Group Plc, Aberdeen - New generation contracting, solutions and services to the global energy industries
Wykes, A division of Peel Street and Co Ltd, Leicester - Covered plastic yarns
Zenith Print and Packaging Ltd, Treforest, Pontypridd - Printed giftset packaging

## INNOVATION

The criteria for an award for innovation are "outstanding innovation, resulting in substantial improvement in business performance and commercial success, sustained over not less than two years, to levels which are outstanding for the goods or services concerned and for the size of the applicant's operations" or "continuous innovation and development, resulting in substantial improvement in business performance and commercial success, sustained over not less than five years, to levels which are outstanding for the goods or services concerned and for the size of the applicant's operations." Achievement may be assessed in any of the following fields: invention, design, production, performance, marketing, distribution, after sales support.

In 2001, The Queen's Award for Innovation was conferred on the following concerns:

ACCO Technologies Plc, Shefford, Bedfordshire - ACO KerbDrain - a combined kerbstone and drainage channel
Aircom International, Redhill, Surrey - Enterprise integrated software solution designed farradio network engineering
Aireshelta Ltd, Huddersfield, West Yorkshire - Aireshower portable decontamination unit
Andel Limited, Huddersfield, West Yorkshire - Floodline 128 leak detection system
BBC Research and Development, Tadworth, Surrey - Digital terrestrial television receiver demodulator chip

Biomet Merck Ltd, Bridgend, Wales - Oxford Unicompartmental Knee, Phase 3
Biosurgical Research Unit, Surgical Materials Testing Laboratory, Princess of Wales Hospital, Bridgend, Wales – sterile maggots of Lucilia sericata
Bromcom Computers Plc, London - Wireless registration systems for schools and colleges
Cooke Optics Limited, Thurmaston, Leicester - 35mm lenses for the film industry
Debenhams Plc - The wedding Services, London - Multi-channel wedding services, offering gift lists and planning services instore, on-line or by telephone
EME (Electro Medical Equipment) Ltd, Brighton, East Sussex - The provision of neonatal respiratory support
Easysoft Limited, Wetherby - *Easysofy Data Access*
Feralco (UK) Ltd, Widnes, Cheshire - *Production of new teatment additive for wastewater and paper processing*
Fish Guidance Systems Ltd, Fawley, Hampshire - *Fish guidance system for prevention of fish kill at power stations*
Forticrete Roofing Products, Leighton Buzzard, Bedfordshire - *Gemini concrete roof tile*
Geneva Technology Ltd, Cambourne, Cambridge - *Genva customer billing software for telecommunications*
Hanovia Ltd, Slough, Berkshire - *SuperTOC Lamp*
Joseph Heler Limited, Nantwich Cheshire
Innovation Research and Technology plc, Wokingham, Berkshire - DatalabelTM - innovation and low cost RF tag technology
Jobserve Ltd, Tiptree, Essex - Job vacancy advertising by e-mail and website
LSI Logic (Europe) Ltd, Brachnell, Berkshire - Digital terrestrial television receiver demodulator chip
Land Rover - Gaydon product Development Centre, Graydon Warwickshire - Hill descent control system for 4 x 4 vehicles
Magiglo Ltd, Broadstairs, Kent - Design of gas fires
Melles Griot Limited, Ely Cambridgeshire - Design and manufacture of nanometric positioning equipment
PAV Data Systems Ltd, Windermere, Cumbria - Wirelss optical data transmission equipment
Pfizer Limited, Sandwich, Kent - Sildenafil (Viagra) for the treatment of erectile dysfunction
Polymer Reprocessors Limited, Knowsley, Wales - Mechanical compact disc recycling processes
Process Systems Enterprise Systems, London - advanced process modelling simulation software and optimisation and services
QAS Systems Ltd, London - QuickAddress range of address management software
Rotork Controls Ltd, Bath - Rotork IQ electric valve actuator
Segnet Ltd, Wickford, Essex - RPM-S RF upstream cross-connect segmentation router for broadband multmedia systems management
Silberline Ltd, Leven, Fife - Silvet metal pigment in novel granular form
Solvent Resource Management Limited, Morecambe, Lanarkshire - Processing and reclamation of containers of waste chemicals
Sortex Limited, London - Niagara: a machine for simultaneous colour and shape sorting of fruit and vegetables
Titan Airways Ltd, Stanstead, Essex - Provision of immediate and short notice aircraft availability
Tritech International Limited, Westhill, Aberdeenshire - SeaKing range of networked subsea tools and sensor
UPU Industries Ltd, Dromore, County Down - Bale crop conservation technologies
Unitec Cermaics Ltd, Stafford - An yttria stabilised zirconia powder for automotive oxygen sensors
Urbis Lighting Ltd, Basingstoke, Hampshire - The Sealsafe sealed beam street lighting optic
VG Systems Ltd t/a Thermo VG Semicon, East Grinstead, West Sussex - Equipment for the manufacture of advanced semiconductor devices
Vicon Motion Systems Limited, Oxford - Systems capturing the 3-dimensional movement of objects, particularly the human body
Waterside Manufacturing Limited t/a Englands Safety Equipment, Harbourne, Birmingham - Multi-purpose life saving equipment

## ENVIRONMENTAL ACHIEVEMENT

The criteria for an award for Environmental Achievement includes "an outstanding advance in environmental performance resulting in a substantial improvement in business performance and commercial success."

In 2001, The Queen's Award for Environmental Achievement was conferred on the following concerns:

B&Q plc, Eastleigh, Hampshire - QUEST (Quality, Ethics, Safety) programme
Bettys and Taylors Group Ltd, Harrogate, North Yorkshire - Holistic management of resources
Bovince Limited, London - Sustainability development programme
Buro Happold Limited, Bath - Engineering sustainable buildings, with research and innovation reducing impact upon the built environment
Cooks' Delight Ltd, Berkhampsted, Hertfordshire - organic food
The Cotwold Water Park Society Limited, Cirencester, Gloucestershire - sustainable recreation and conservation
Greenbanks Country Hotel and Restaurant, Wendling, Norfolk - Exceptional facilities for the disabled and able bodied to share
Kodak Limited, Hemel Hempstead, Hertfordshire - Consistent improvement of environmental management systems and procedures
Leeds Environmental Design Associated, Leeds - Sustainability in building design
The North of England Zoological Society, Chester - Chester Zoo revitalisation
Safeway plc - Supply Division, Hayes, Middlesex - Rail freight strategy
Scottish Power plc, Generation Division, Glasgow - Gas reburn, cost effective Nox reduction technology
Southampton Geothermal Heating Company Ltd, Crawley, West Sussex - District energy network using combined heat and power and geothermal energy
Woking Borough Council, Energy Services, Woking, Surrey - Community energy systems
The Yeo Valley Organic Company Ltd, Cannington, Somerset - Organic dairy supply chain

# Science and Discovery

## Jupiter's Auroral Outburst

The Hubble Space Station has hit the headlines by photographing an enormous auroral flare near to Jupiter's north pole. On the night of 21 September 1999, Hunter Waite and a colleague at the University of Michigan monitored the two-hour burst with a special filter on the Hubble Space Spectrograph (STIS). It was ten times more powerful than the most energetic outburst previously recorded. The flare extended over a range of several thousand kilometres and during the burst it brightened and faded by a factor of 30 within one minute.

The intensity of aurora on the planet is roughly 1,000 times greater than that experienced on Earth. The mechanism is not yet fully understood although the outburst on 21 September is squarely attributed to sudden changes in the intensity of the solar wind, the cause of terrestrial displays.

A knowledge of the exact location of the big outburst has enabled Waite to pinpoint the centre of the burst to about 50 Jovian radii from the planet. Data from an Explorer satellite has also shown that the outburst coincided with a dip in the intensity of the solar wind.

Data from the Cassini spaceprobe flyby of Jupiter in December 2000 and the Galileo spacecraft have yet to be analysed so interest now awaits to see if more details can be deduced about this spectacular event.

## X-Rays from Deep Space

Building on the results from ROSAT, the first of the deep space x-ray satellites, NASA's Chandra X-Ray Observatory (CXO) was launched in July 1999. With a resolving power ten times that of the earlier probe it has made tremendous strides in the study of the universe at x-ray wavelengths. In addition to seeing further into space it has made an interesting discovery. An object seen in the constellation Fornax has been found to be a new type of quasar.

By pointing CXO at two small areas of sky for the equivalent of two days, it has revealed much interesting information. The exposures are known as the Chandra Deep Fields. Deep Field North is the smaller of the two and covers an area with sides measuring about 2.5 arcminutes. This is less than one tenth of the apparent size of the Moon in the sky. It lies in the constellation of Ursa Major and the total exposure time was just over 5.8 days, collected from observations spread over 15 months. The Deep Field South, lying in the constellation of Fornax and exposed for 10.8 days penetrated much farther into space and covered an area about a quarter the angular size of the Moon. Almost every point of light within this region is a distinct active galaxy or quasar, billions of light years distant and each powered by a black hole. However one of these objects has caused much interest and is thought to be a new type of astronomical object and given the title Type-2 Quasar.

This new type is thought to be an earlier manifestation of the more usual Type-1 quasar. Type-2 quasars are surrounded by vast clouds of gas and dust which makes them invisible at optical wavelengths but not at x-ray wavelengths. They are thought to be much older than the normal quasars with ages about nine to 12 billion light years.

## Mars' Giant Volcano not so Large

The discovery by Mariner 9 in 1972 of the giant shield volcano known now as Olympus Mons put the volcano as the tallest mountain in the Solar System with a height of between 26 and 27 km above the Martian equivalent of sea level. Subsequent data from the Mars Global Surveyor (MGS) has shown that it is not quite so tall and has a height of 21.3 km.

The latest value is the result of a more accurate knowledge of the shape of the planet. Earlier values for altitude were based on a hypothetical surface by an atmospheric pressure of 6.1 millibars – the pressure of the triple point when water can exist simultaneously as a gas, liquid or solid. It was always understood that this was not accurate but it provided a reference point.

Now, from the results of MGS's hundreds of millions of altitude soundings it has been found that the planet's mean radius is 2 km larger than the previously accepted figure. Using the laser-altimeter measurements this reduces the height of Olympus Mons. There are complications in deriving the new value because standing water would behave oddly in the vicinity of the volcano. The mountain has not sunk into the martian crust to achieve the iceberg-style equilibrium with gravity as it can with terrestrial mountains but it sits like an Arizona sized bump on top of the planet's thick rigid exterior. This distorts any water table beneath it, drawing liquid up by more than 1 km, providing a height of 22.7 km for the volcano. However, the MGS scientists strongly favour the use of the sea level areoid to be the standard reference level.

## Coelacanths

The sensational discovery in 1938, when fishermen caught the first coelacanth off the coast of South Africa, produced many theories of why this so-called relic of the past still existed. But since then many such creatures have been discovered over quite a range of the Indian Ocean lying between the African mainland and Madagascar.

Most of the specimens have been found near to the Comoros Islands but in the last few months of the year 2000, divers saw and filmed the first off Sodwana Bay on the north-east coast of South Africa. It is thought that there must be a viable population in that region.

Phillip Heemstra of the JLB Smith Institute of Ichthyology in Grahamstown, fully described the discovery in a recent issue of the South African Journal of Science. He has also said that the divers filmed a juvenile as well as two adults. It is thought unlikely that they had strayed from the Comoros area because coelacanths have an unusually low metabolism and move very slowly. Studies carried out over the last 10 years by Hans Fricke of the Max Plank Institute in Germany have shown that the coelacanths tend to remain in one area and not move about very much.

Heemstra is of the opinion that coelacanths are more widespread than originally thought and live in undersea caverns too deep to be caught by fishermen's nets or seen by divers. He plans to raise an expedition to tag the Sodwana coelacanths and compare their DNA with the first one caught from further north.

## Mass Extinctions in Earth' s History

It is now generally accepted that the huge impact structure located in the Yucatan Peninsula in Mexico was responsible for the wiping out of the dinosaurs some 65 million years ago. Recently there has been much thought into what happened to cause other mass extinctions, known to have punctuated the Earth's geological past. New evidence has come to light to indicate that the most devastating extinction known to have occurred on the Earth was caused indirectly by an impact that took place some 250 million years ago. This destroyed about 90% of life on Earth involving almost all marine species and up to 70% of land vertebrates. No direct evidence for the location of the crater caused by the impact has been found. American geologists have found tell-tale evidence from rocks in Japan, China and Hungary. This evidence involves complex carbon molecules called buckminsterfullerenes (usually called buckyballs) that contain unusual isotopes of helium and argon. The team leader, Luann Becker, of the University of Washington has said that these isotopes form in carbon stars where the extreme temperatures and pressures existing in stars are the only conditions known in the natural world which would permit noble gases to be forced into the fullerene.

Although the gas-laden fullerenes were formed outside the solar system, they must have reached the Earth via a comet or an asteroid. It has been estimated that the object which hit the Earth was about 6-12 km in diameter, comparable to the size of the object which hit Mexico. It is believed that the impact was not responsible for the overwhelming loss of life as there is evidence that the event coincided with widespread volcanic activity in Siberia and other severe climatic changes.

## Behaviour of the Earth's Magnetic Field

The Earth's magnetic field can be illustrated in its simplest form as that formed by a bar magnet situated deep in the Earth's interior but unfortunately for a long time now this picture has been shown to be unsatisfactory in many ways. For example the temperatures existing in the core of the Earth are well in excess of what is called the Curie Point, a temperature which differs for different substances and above which the mineral loses all magnetic properties. Magnetite, the most important magnetic mineral has a Curie Point at about 578 degrees centigrade and no mineral is known to have a Curie Point above 800 degrees.

As a mineral cools at or near to the surface and falls below the critical point it will become magnetised parallel to the local magnetic field existing at that time. Subsequent studies of minerals provide data on the direction of the magnetic field existing at that time. Studies of a large number of rocks in various parts of the world have provided information on the way the Earth's magnetic field has varied over the years.

Studies have shown that in addition to long periods when the magnetic field has been generally the same as that existing today, there have been long periods of time when the magnetic field has been reversed. The current epoch, known as the Brunhes epoch, extends backwards in time for about 700,000 years, when the field was reversed for nearly two million years, except for two very brief periods when the field was normal again. However much of the data deduced from rock studies falls off rapidly as we go back in time. The picture is fairly well documented up to about 50,000 years ago but for earlier periods only relative intensities have been available.

Recent work, carried out by American geologists on sea floor measurements of the magnetic field over the Eastern Pacific Rise has produced much more precise data of the geomagnetic intensity during the past 780,000 years, covering the Brunhes into the beginning of the Matuyama periods, the results of which are in general agreement with those obtained from earlier studies. The technique employed in this new survey for collecting data from the geomagnetic intensity in the ocean crust will no doubt be extended further into the past and hence provide more reliable information on the early days of the Earth's magnetic field.

## New Theory for Human Origins

Scientists in Australia have analysed the DNA from a skeleton of a man who died about 60,000 years ago and found that it differed from anything seen before. It is the oldest DNA ever recovered from human remains.

The analysis showed that whilst the man was completely anatomically modern, he belong to a genetic lineage that is now extinct. This challenges the belief that all modern humans have descended from a group that migrated from Africa about 100,000 years ago.

Mungo Man, as it is now called because it was found on the shores of Lake Mungo in southeast Australia in 1974, was thought to be from radio carbon dating about 30,000 years old but recent work using three different techniques found the skeleton to be twice that age. Simon Easteal, an evolutionary geneticist at the Australian National University in Canberra analysed the sequence of a single gene from Mungo man's mitochondria, the powerhouse of cells whose small genome is passed down the female line and compared it with sequences of the same gene from nine other early Australians of ages ranging from 8,000 to 15,000 years as well as 3,000 contemporary people around the world and chimpanzees, pygmy chimps and two European Neanderthals. His analysis showed that chimps were the first to break off the evolutionary path leading modern man. Next were the Neanderthals followed by Mungo Man and finally the line that has led to the most recent common ancestor of contemporary people, including the ancient Australians but not Mungo Man. The research has showed that modern people arrived in Australia before the new lineage arrived. This conflicts sharply with the 'out of Africa' theory for human origins. This new find suggests that Mungo Man's ancestors evolved in Asia and some migrated to Australia where the line vanished. It is possible that the clan could have been wiped out by newcomers, but much more research is needed before a clear picture of man's origins is obtained.

## A Jurassic Shrew

A fossil skull of a shrew-like creature has been found in the Yunnan Province in China and is thought to be from the smallest mammal discovered from the age of the dinosaurs some 195 million years ago. The 13 mm long skull weighs 2 grams. It has been named Hadrocodium and lived on small insects and worms.

Studies of the skull showed it to be between half and a third as long as the skull of other relatives of the mammals living at the same time and had a larger brain than its contemporaries. This suggests that it was most closely related to the common ancestors of all mammals. Fossils of mammals are distinguished from those of reptiles by their skull and jaw bones. Three bones which form part of the reptile's jaw became part of the middle ear in mammals and in this case the bones must have migrated into the skull. The investigators claim that it is easier for jaws and teeth to evolve smaller than it is for similar evolution of the brain, eye and ear. It is thought that this could have been the critical stage in evolving the sharp hearing that primarily nocturnal mammals needed to survive in the age of the dinosaurs.

### Jupiter's Moon Europa

The Galileo spacecraft has for some time now been observing the four main satellites of Jupiter in great detail as well as the planet itself. All four satellites have provided sensational discoveries but Europa, the second of the four main ones from the planet and only slightly smaller than our own Moon, has provided much interesting information which could lead to even greater sensations.

An earlier low-level pass by Galileo provided a detailed record of the magnetic field surrounding the satellite and this data has now been used to make a strong case for a global ocean lying not too far below the icy exterior of the moon. The strong perturbations to Jupiter's magnetic field has been put down to two possible causes. Either Europa has its own magnetic field as does its neighbour Gannymede, or the overall Jovian field induces a weaker counterpart in the electrically conducting layer such as an ocean beneath the surface. Surveys carried out by Galileo during periods when the Jovian magnetic field was orientated in different directions indicated that the European field changed in step with the planet's variations. This indicates that the satellite's field was induced.

Margaret G. Kivelson of the University of California in Los Angeles claims that the induction model requires a shell that has closed paths for currents to flow from the equator to the poles over most of the body. She claims that this layer is more likely to be a true liquid than a slush. Although there is strong evidence for the existence of a liquid layer below the visible surface, it will require sending another spacecraft to Europa and to orbit it for an extended period. Plans are being made to launch this in 2006.

### Age of the Universe

One of the biggest problems in astronomy is the determination of the age of the Universe. Many different techniques have been used, most depending on a determination of the rate of expansion based on the velocity of distant galaxies, or the luminosity of the very faint white dwarf stars. But the methods depend on assumptions about the nature of the objects being observed. The resulting values for the age of the universe have been scattered over a large range of values from nine to 16 Gyr.

Recently methods involving entirely new techniques based on radioactive isotopes have contributed greatly to arriving at a reliable age. A method based on the abundance of radioactive thorium in stars showed the possibility of this new approach. The half life for 235 Th is 14.1 Gyr which is rather too long for this particular problem. Thorium has been detected in several metal-poor stars but in smaller amounts than that seen in relatively near stars, implying that the metal poor stars are much older. The estimates of the errors in the ages are very large, so thorium is of limited use.

Much more favourable is uranium with a half life of 238 U of 4.5 Gyr. For a high mass star born early in the life of a galaxy, it would end its life as a supernova explosion, resulting in radioactive thorium and uranium being thrown into the interstellar medium. The next generation of stars would capture some of this material and its presence would be detected by spectroscopic studies.

Such material has been found in stars in the outer regions of the galaxy in the galactic hole. The presence of thorium and uranium has provided a very reliable tool for age determination. The differing decay rates allow quite accurate estimates of the age of the stars and from this the investigators have suggested that the age of the universe is about 12.5 Gyr with an uncertainty of 3.5 Gyr. Further work in this field will obviously improve the accuracy of the value, especially with the new generation of large telescopes coming into operation.

### The Milky Way's Black Hole

Evidence has gradually been gathered to support the belief that a large black hole exists in the centre of our own galaxy, the Milky Way. Over the last few years, astronomers have made accurate measurements of the motions of more than 100 luminous giant stars very close to the centre of the galaxy, by means of large telescopes, infrared detectors and high resolution imaging techniques. All the objects under surveillance lie within arcseconds of the radio source known as Sagittarius A*, which many astronomers believe is powered by a super massive black hole. The stars in question have been found to have proper motions corresponding to speeds up to 1,400 km per second. This motion indicates that Sgr A* contains two to three million times the mass of the Sun.

Andrea M. Ghez of the University of California at Los Angeles and colleagues have attempted, using the 10 metre Keck 1 telescope in Hawaii to measure not only the velocity of the stars but also their acceleration. By comparing observations made over the last four years of high resolution near infrared images, they found three stars within 0.4 arcseconds of SGr A* where their trajectories curved by measurable amounts. This data indicated that they are behaving as if they are being attracted by a mass equivalent to 2.6 million solar masses lying within 0.006 light years of the radio source. The results indicate an increase in the mass of the object at the centre of the Milky Way by a factor of 10. Very few astronomers doubt that an object so massive and small could be anything else but a black hole. It has however been suggested that a massive pool of neutrons could be a possibility. Work still goes on and the team is now trying to measure the star's line of sight velocities in an attempt to determine their motions in three dimensions.

### Mars Lander Found

One of NASA's experimental space probes sent to explore Mars involved making a soft landing in the south polar region of the planet. The lander arrived in the region of the south pole in December 1999, but during the descent the mission control lost contact. Investigations into what went wrong revealed that a software error switched off the thrusters too early sending the probe crashing to the surface.

Subsequently, a military organisation, the National Imagery and Mapping Agency (NIMA), which specialises in collecting information from surveillance photographs, offered to help by studying photographs taken by the Mars Global Surveyor. The results of studying 40 such photos has revealed that NIMA believes it has found the spacecraft sitting upright on the Martian surface.

However, NASA's Space Science chief, Ed Weiler, says he is not convinced because the data is based on a single photograph. He feels that evidence should be based also on the other images of the area taken by Mars Global Surveyor. He also says that the photograph of the crashed lander covers just two or three pixels of the million pixel image and to really understand what happened to the lander you would need a resolution about 10 times better than that currently available.

NIMA is at present discussing the find with NASA but no definite results have been made public.

### Rendezvous with Asteroid Eros

After one or two problems had been sorted out during the journey of the first spacecraft designed specifically to study the asteroid 433 Eros, the Near Earth Asteroid Rendezvous (NEAR) satellite, named Shoemaker after the death of the planetary geologist Eugene Shoemaker, arrived in the vicinity of the minor planet in February 2000. As it orbited Eros, a relatively small body measuring only 33 km by 13 km, it photographed its surface in detail and revealed many geological oddities. Many thousands of close range images were recorded. Most of the small features on the surface were probably caused by continual bombardment from meteoroids rather than internal processes. However, it has been difficult to explain the scarcity of large boulders and small craters. Preliminary analysis showed a very large number of small boulders, a saturation of large craters but far fewer small craters than would be expected. In addition, the photographs revealed features attributed to unknown erosion processes. Flat surfaces inside the larger craters, called ponds, have been found to be horizontal and very smooth, suggesting fluid-like motion.

On 12 February 2001, the spacecraft was taken out of its 35 km radius orbit and it landed gently on the surface of Eros at a speed of 1.8 metres per second (brisk walking speed) without any airbags or other protective devices. It survived the landing and started transmitting from the surface. The data, whilst in orbit and after landing, has enabled scientists to confirm that Eros was never completely molten and that it is a primitive mix of metal and silicate materials largely unaltered since the formation of the Solar System.

### The Edge of the Solar System

It was less than ten years ago when the first transneptunian asteroid (1992 QB1) was discovered and since then the region beyond the orbit of Neptune has been the target of intense research. By the beginning of the year 2001, more than 340 objects had been found in this region, now called the Kuiper Belt and it is thought that the region contains millions of small icy bodies.

As more and more objects were discovered, astronomers began to draw a remarkable conclusion. It appears that the Solar System may end abruptly. American scientists found that the number of bodies larger than 160 km appears to drop off dramatically beyond a distance of about 55 astronomical units (au) from the Sun. 1 au is the distance of the Earth from the Sun. Neptune lies about 30 au from the Sun. Pluto has a rather eccentric orbit and it is about 55 au from the Sun when it is farthest away. It is thought that many objects lie farther out, but the increasing number of objects discovered did not support the theory for the large bodies. It was thought that the equipment available should have detected objects larger than 160 km out to distances of 65 au but none have been found at distances in excess of 55 au. This result was obtained from the Cerro Tololo Inter-American Observatory in Chile. An independent survey, using the Canada-France-Hawaii Telescope, found 86 new objects but none more than 50 to 55 au distant.

There are several possible explanations. Perhaps there is much less material than expected beyond 55 au or perhaps the larger objects are replaced by numerous small objects as yet undetected.

Of the larger bodies, one roughly a quarter the size of Pluto was discovered in the last year and was found to be moving in a Pluto-like 2-3 resonance with Neptune. But the highlight of the year was the discovery of an object with a diameter of 900 km and at a distance of 45 au. If the size is found to be correct it certainly challenges Ceres as the largest known minor planet. Another surprise was the discovery of a binary system, two objects roughly 200 and 150 km across, orbiting some 40,000 km apart. To give this some scale, Pluto and Charon, 2,300 and 1,200 km respectively, are separated by 19,000 km.

### A Different Type of Dinosaur

The general picture of dinosaurs built up in the minds of the general public is the bone crushing jaws of such creatures as Tyrannosaurus rex. However some dinosaurs attacked their prey not by biting it but by slashing its flesh like a medieval knight wielding a mace. A new type of dinosaur, Allosaurus, slammed its upper jaw into its victim, ripping off flesh with its sharp teeth, in a similar manner to that of the Komono Dragon.

Although Allosaurus lived in the late Jurassic, some 85 million years earlier than T. rex, it has left more fossils but strangely it has not been studied in detail.

In her studies of dinosaurs Emily Rayfield of the University of Cambridge, examined Allosaurus's jaw muscles and found that its bite was by no means pathetic but no where near as big as that of a lion. Its bite was about a quarter of that of T. rex or of a modern crocodile. Rayfield constructed a complete model of the skull from a specimen found in Wyoming and calculated the force needed by its jaws to break the skull of a living animal and found it was many times stronger than that necessary to withstand a biting force. A combination of a strong light skull and a weak bite indicated to Rayfield that Allosaurus had a different feeding habit, perhaps by opening its jaws wide and slamming its upper jaw into its prey.

The technique used by T. rex was atypical, says Tom Holtz, a dinosaur palaeontologist at the University of Maryland in College Park. Most other dinosaurs were more lightly built and adapted methods according to their build.

### Ticks on Dinosaurs

A 90 million year old fossil tick has been found in a block of amber on a building site in New Jersey. Being the oldest tick ever found, it suggests that ticks existed 50 million years earlier than previously thought. So claims Hans Klompen, an entomologist at Ohio State University. Mites, the parent group of ticks, are thought to be the first land animals, some 400 million years ago, but it was thought that ticks did not evolve until much later, about 42 million years ago. The oldest ticks known previously had been found in South America.

This new discovery is a soft tick about half a millimetre long. Earlier studies indicated that soft ticks evolved in South America, long before it was geologically joined to North America. Klompen says that this new find does not fit in with a South American origin. He is of the opinion that the tick was brought to New Jersey by a migratory seabird. This idea is based on the fact that the 40 kg block of amber also contains a small piece of feather that possibly came from the bird. To support this he says that some of the modern relatives of the ticks prey on seabirds.

Because modern ticks feed also on reptiles as well as birds and mammals, Klompen thinks that contemporary relatives of the New Jersey object also fed on the blood of dinosaurs as well as birds.

### Jupiter's Family of Moons

It is quite certain that the number of moons circling the planet Jupiter is now 28, all of the recent discoveries having orbits well outside the orbits of the four major satellites that have hit the headlines over the last few years.

In 1975 Charles Kowal recorded a faint object moving near to Jupiter in photographs taken with the 48-inch Schmidt telescope on Mount Palomar. It was observed again a few weeks later from Kitt Peak and then lost. On 20 November 2000, Scott Sheppard and colleagues at the University of Hawaii's Institute for Astronomy, using the 2.2 metre reflector at Mauna Kea recorded a faint moving object and tracked its position over the next few days. Data was sent to the IAU Minor Planet Center in Cambridge, Massachusetts where calculations carried out by Gareth Williams and Brian Marsden showed that this new object was the same as that observed by Kowal. The object is thought to be about 15 km in diameter and orbits the planet in 129 days at a distance of about 7.4 million kilometres. During the same period of observation, Scott Sheppard located a dozen new objects and these observations were also sent to the Minor Planet Center. Marsden confirmed that 10 of them were in fact new moons of the planet, bringing the total number up to 28. All these new objects are fairly small with diameters in the range of 3 to 8 km. Nine of these new objects have retrograde orbits about 22 km from Jupiter whilst the tenth has a prograde orbit 12 million km from the planet. It is thought that all these new objects had a common parent body.

### Biodiversity Theories in Turmoil

Until recently it has been generally accepted that biodiversity mushroomed after the mass extinction some 250 million years ago, with new species developing at an ever increasing rate. However, this basic assumption has now been challenged and it is thought that the levels of biodiversity have stayed largely unchanged since that time.

John Altoy of the University of California at Santa Barbara claims that if recent investigations are shown to be correct, then biodiversity and hence evolution must be regulated more by predation and competition between species than by ecological factors such as climate.

The explosion theory was based on work carried out by Jack Sepkoski in the 1970s but because of the lack of computer power the necessary simplification in the modelling led to a substantial bias which has subsequently shown to be false. Altoy and Charles Marshal at Harvard University re-examined the data base by compiling data on thousands of fossilised clams, molluscs and other marine invertebrates. They divided the prehistoric record into slots with time widths of 10 million years and statistically examined the results. They found that the biodiversity stayed constant or even decreased during the Palaeozoic period whereas the earlier studies suggested a rapid expansion. The new work revealed only a small rise in biodiversity over the period 164 to 24 million years ago.

Although the data base used covers only marine fossils from the northern hemisphere, work is now being carried out to fill in the gaps in the record. It is also planned to re-examine the previously accepted Cambrian explosion.

### Origin of Man

It has been generally accepted that modern humans descended via the earliest known hominid species, Australopithecus afarensis, dated from between three to four million years ago, and known popularly as fossil Lucy. However this theory has been put in doubt by the discovery of a skull and additional pieces of jaw and teeth unearthed in a gully in Kenya. The fossils have been classified as part of a previously unknown hominid species dubbed "flat-faced human from Kenya" - Kenyanthropus platyops. This new fossil also dates from a similar age to Lucy.

It has several features which distinguish it from Lucy. It has a less protruding jaw and more pronounced cheek-bones, giving it an appearance more like hominids 1.5 million years younger. It has very small teeth. It is thought that the two species had different diets and lifestyles.

Obviously there will be much debate about whether this new find is really a new species, but Bill Kimbal, an expert at the Institute of Human Origins at Arizona State University at Tempe has examined the skull and is of no doubt that it represents a new lineage. Maeve Leakey, palaeontologist at the National Museum of Kenya in Nairobi, says that at the present time it is not possible to decide whether modern man is related to Lucy or to K platyops. The search goes on for more evidence.

### Spinning Black Holes

Tod Strohmayer of NASA's Goddard Space Flight Center in Greenbelt, Maryland, has provided data obtained from the Rossi X-ray Explorer satellite to show that a black hole with a mass of about 7 times that of the Sun and at a distance of 10,000 light years from the Earth is actually rotating exceedingly fast. He noticed that the x-rays from the object waxed and waned roughly 450 times per second. Strohmeyer is of the opinion that the radiation is coming from a blob of hot matter travelling in the smallest stable orbit around the black hole. The oscillation is so fast that this material must be in an orbit smaller than Einstein's theory allows if the black hole is not rotating. If the black hole is spinning, however, it distorts space in a way that permits closer orbits of material and hence more rapidly oscillating x-rays. Astrophysicists have said that there is no way around the speed limit for a non-rotating black hole and so it is thought that this new explanation is correct.

The discovery may provide solution for the explanation of gamma ray bursts recorded from deep space. One theory says that the bursts occur when very big stars collapse to form a black hole but the crucial condition is the spin of the star. If it spins too fast then the x-rays just fizzle out but if it spins too slowly the black hole absorbs all the energy needed to produce the gamma rays.

The solution to the problem lies in future work by measuring the spin of a large number of black holes.

### Fermi Pressure

Strange things happen as material is cooled down to temperatures near to absolute zero, about -273 degrees centigrade, but the information gathered provides much useful data on the structure of dead stars such as white dwarfs and neutron stars.

Recently a cloud of lithium atoms were cooled to the lowest temperature ever reached, about a quarter of a millionth of a degree above absolute zero and the gas was seen to develop "Fermi Pressure", a strange quantum effect which stops superdense stars collapsing completely. Fermi pressure will only occur in a gas of fermions, subatomic particles which include electrons and neutrons. Fermions obey a quantum rule which does not permit them from occupying the same energy states. Consequently, at enormous pressures or very low temperatures, the particles fill all lowest energy states available, forming a degenerate Fermi gas. The particles are therefore prevented from getting any closer to each other, creating the Fermi pressure. This prevents gravity from crushing dense stars into black holes and produces stabilised dead stars such as white dwarfs and neutron stars.

Randall Hulet of Rice University in Houston, Texas cooled down a cloud of lithium-6 atoms, which are fermions, and just close to absolute zero the cloud became degenerate and resisted any further shrinking as the temperature dropped. Earlier experiments had produced a partially degenerate potassium cloud at 0.3 millionths of a degree kelvin but on this occasion the scientists were able to photograph the size of the cloud, thus demonstrating the existence of the Fermi pressure.

### The Dark Side of the Universe

Much research has been carried out over many years to try and identify and quantify the dark matter which exists in the universe. Recent work in the United States has revealed the existence of a cluster of invisible galaxies. The cluster was found by an analysis of the effect it had on light coming from more distant galaxies.

Last year European astronomers located a single dark galaxy as it distorted the light from more distant galaxies but the discovery was not confirmed independently. Recently however, Tony Tyson, David Wittman and colleagues at the Lucent Technologies' Bell Laboratory in New Jersey, have made a similar discovery which they later confirmed by picking up very faint light from the cluster. Using the Blanco 4-metre telescope at the Cerro Tololo Inter-American Observatory in Chile, they examined 31,000 distant galaxies within a patch of sky half a degree across. They then used a computer to combine their shapes to give an average shape. They thought that as most galaxies are elliptical, because of a random orientation, the average shape should be circular. But it turned out that the resultant shape was elliptical, indicating that dark matter lying between them and the Earth was distorting the images. The computer study revealed the existence of 26 dark galaxies in the intervening space. By examining the red-shifts of the distant galaxies with the amount the intervening galaxies distorted their light, it was possible to estimate the distances to the dark clusters.

There is no doubt that the results are only the forerunner of many discoveries about the hitherto unknown dark galaxies.

### Stellar Orbits for three Bodies

Newton developed equations of motion which can describe exactly how two bodies orbit each other. The universe is full of cases of binary systems which can be explained mathematically, but cases involving three bodies have presented huge problems and it is impossible to calculate all the possible periodic orbits directly.

In the 16th and 17th centuries mathematicians derived some simple solutions. Leonhard Euler showed mathematically that three planets with equal masses and equally spaced along a straight line would have a stable orbit if the two outer members orbited the central one. Joseph Lagrange showed that three celestial bodies at the corners of an equilateral triangle would rotate about its centre. Another arrangement of three can exist when two bodies orbit each other and these orbit about the third, very similar to the Moon orbiting the Earth and they in turn orbit the Sun.

Recently a computer solution has revealed that three objects of equal mass can have a stable orbit by following each other round a figure of 8. This is the simplest orbit to be confirmed in more than a century. So far no such cases have been found in space and it is thought that only a few will exist. Douglas Heggie of Edinburgh University feels that if one is found it is strong evidence for the existence of extraterrestrial intelligence.

In practice orbital analysis is complicated by the fact that it is rarely the case and possibly virtually non-existent when three bodies have the same mass. In many cases, bodies orbiting another have virtually a negligible mass compared with the dominant gravitational pull of the primary. Such is the case for artificial satellites orbiting the Earth.

### The Oldest Meteorite

Many meteorites are located each year but most fall into well defined classes. If they are seen to fall and are recovered fairly quickly they provide useful data by not being spoiled by terrestrial contamination. Now and again, a fireball is seen to cross the sky and the resulting meteorite is quickly recovered. Such was the case when in the dawn twilight of 18 January 2000, several fireballs were observed crossing the sky from Tagish Lake, Yukon, Canada. Within a few days about a dozen pieces of meteorite had been recovered and chemical analysis showed them to be of a relatively rare type. In fact, the analysis showed them to be the most primitive rock ever found.

The meteorite was found to be a CI carbonaceous chondrite, a type found in less than 1% of all meteorite finds. Peter G. Brown and colleagues from the University of Western Ontario subjected the meteorite to exhaustive tests and found its overall composition to be very similar to that of the Sun, indicating that it was very old. Because such primitive material is rich in volatile substances, it is rare that they survive the entry through the atmosphere. In this case it was possible to deduce the track through the atmosphere and just prior to the entry into the atmosphere, the object's size and its orbit prior to Earth encounter could be determined. It is considered that it resembles a group known as the Apollo asteroids, which orbit the Sun in the middle of the Minor Planet belt lying between the orbits of Mars and Jupiter.

Research in the event is still in progress and it is possible that even more sensational results may emerge with time.

### Studies in BSE and Scrapie

Outbreaks in BSE and Scrapie in cattle and sheep and their possible association with vCJD, the human form of BSE, have rarely been out of the news for the last few years. One line of thought being investigated by scientists in Britain is that sheep may have caught BSE after being fed food originating from infected cattle and that people subsequently eating the lamb may then risk catching vCJD. The big problem with the investigation is that it takes a very long time to detect the difference between BSE and Scrapie. The technique currently employed involves injecting brain tissues from a dead sheep into mice that are susceptible to both BSE and Scrapie. The time it takes for the mice to die provides the necessary data but the process takes nearly two years. The results so far are not definite enough to give a positive answer.

Research workers at the government's Veterinary Laboratory Agency in Weybridge, Surrey have now found a new test which can speed up the process. Martin Jeffrey and colleagues have found that BSE and Scrapie can be identified separately by staining sheep brain tissue with a cocktail of prion antibodies. As these antibodies stick to the abnormal proteins they provide easily identified specific patterns which immediately enable BSE and Scrapie to be individually recognised.

There are still many unanswered questions before a satisfactory solution can be achieved for this nasty problem affecting mankind.

### Planet-Star Division no longer Valid

Until recently the separation of planets from stars was quite logical. Planets were objects orbiting a star and shone only by reflected starlight whereas a star shone by its own nuclear processes. But this distinction has been gradually eroded and now it appears that in many cases there is no way of separating them. Modern telescopes have enabled astronomers to find abundant evidence for objects ranging in size from that of Jupiter to that of a normal star and which could fall into either category. Of particular interest are the results using the Japanese Subaru 8.3 metre telescope in Hawaii, of the deep infrared images of the star forming region S106 in our own Galaxy, lying in the constellation of Cygnus at a distance of roughly 2000 light years.

S106 appears to contain hundreds of faint objects with masses less than that of an ordinary star. In particular many are less than 0.08 times the mass of the Sun and therefore too small to sustain the nuclear fusion of hydrogen, the basic mechanism for stars to shine. It is thought that they may be brown dwarfs.

Some of the objects have masses of only a few times that of Jupiter and are classed as floating small objects. At the centre of S106 lies a young massive star (IRS4- infrared source 4). It is about 100,000 years old and has a mass of 20 times that of the Sun.

Material appears to be flowing away from IRS4. The huge disc of gas and dust surrounding the star blots out light from the central region of S106. The ultraviolet light from IRS4 ionises the surrounding hydrogen creating a blue emission region, but towards the edge of the cloud is a red reflection nebula, the dust particles reflecting the light from IRS4.

### An Ancient Supernova

When a star explodes to produce a supernova, an exceptionally bright object in the sky for a few days, a small remnant is left behind. This is known as a pulsar. They are relatively rare events in any one galaxy and the only one well documented in our own Milky Way Galaxy has been the well observed supernova recorded in 1054 AD, the remnant of which can now be seen as the Crab nebula, the centre of which is a pulsar.

NASA's Chandra X-ray Observatory has now provided evidence that a pulsar, spinning at 14 times per second, and discovered in 1997, is located at the exact centre of a supernova remnant known as G11.2-0.3. The observation implies that the pulsar was formed during the supernova explosion of 386AD, an event recorded in Chinese records of that time. The Chinese recorded the existence of a new star between mid-April and mid-May of 386 AD.

Like all new discoveries the facts do not agree fully with the theories previously put forward to explain such events and questions have been raised about the behaviour of pulsars especially during their infancies. Earlier work, deduced from data obtained from a Japanese satellite designed to study cosmology and astrophysics, had led astronomers to think the age of the pulsar was roughly 24,000 years. New research carried out by the Chandra team suggests that the pulsar may have had the same spin rate as it has at the present time. This could mean that pulsars generally spin more slowly than previously thought.

### Our Receding Glaciers

In spite of the intense arguments that are taking place regarding the glaciation the Earth experienced some 700 million years ago, when it is thought by some scientists that glaciation reached the equator whilst others prefer what they call the slushball model in which the tropics did not freeze completely, it is felt that a satisfactory explanation for this event will be a long time in coming. Whether this explanation will solve the situation existing at the moment is open to debate.

A study of the current conditions indicates that glaciers all over the world are shrinking. There has been much evidence to indicate that over the last few years individual glaciers such as those on Mt Kilimanjaro and in Montana's Glacier National Park have been receding but infrared and visual photographs taken by the Japanese instrument ASTER on board NASA's Terra space vehicle show that glaciers all over the world are receding.

Rick Wessels of the US Geological Survey in Flagstaff, Arizona, compared images taken by ASTER with aerial photographs taken as long ago as 20 years and found that all glaciers in the Himalayas, Alps and Pyrenees have shrunk by hundreds of metres and some by even kilometres. Studies have also showed that lakes formed at the end of glaciers have grown considerably and that the water contains a much higher concentration of sediment than was present even 10 years ago.

The equipment used by ASTER consists of three telescopes taking photographs at three specific wavelengths, two in the infrared and one in the visual range. This enabled the investigators to distinguish between snow, ice and debris covered ice as well as determining the temperature to within 0.5 degree.

### Toxic Chemical Spill in Spain

The chemical spill from the Aznalcóllar pyrite mine near Seville, Spain, on 24 April 1998 became headlines in the national press for a few days. The mine is near to the Doñana National Park, declared a World Heritage Site in 1994 and the park is an important stopover for over six million migrating birds. The spillage took place when two million tonnes of tailings broke through a dam together with 5.5 million cubic metres of acidic water laced with heavy metals into the Agrio and Guadiamar rivers and into the Entramuros Marshes on the edge of the National Park.

A huge effort has taken place to clean up the water and remove the poisonous sludge but many poisons have entered the food chain. Just after the flood, scientists at the Doñana Biological Station found that birds living in the area had potentially lethal levels of heavy metals in their blood and after three years the scientists have found that the white storks living in the area are suffering from continual genetic damage. Felipe Cortés of the University of Seville tested blood taken from white stork chicks 14 months after the spill and found that they had levels of genetic damage between 10 and 20 times greater than those living further away. DNA damage in eggs and sperm could be inherited by future generations and cause birth defects. It is also reported that kites in the park have also been badly affected.

Although every effort has been made to clean up the area it is accepted that the very heavy metal pollution will cause long term damage to the animals in the park and is exceptionally dangerous to the birds in general.

## An Alternative to Pesticides

One of the biggest problems met by farmers all over the world is the fighting of pests which eat or destroy crops. In the richer countries emphasis has been placed on pesticides etc, but in the poorer areas of the third world this is far too expensive. In the last few years, however, the problem has been tackled from an entirely new angle, with results that seem to provide the answer without the involvement of huge costs.

Ziadin Khan, who works at the Mbita Point Research Station on the shores of Lake Victoria in Kenya claims that crop yields have increased by as much as 60 to 70% and in some cases over 100% by a host of low-tech innovations.

East Africa is an area where there are two major pests affecting the production of maize, the staple diet of the area. One of these is the insect called the stem borer. Its larvae eat though as much as one third of the crop. Khan discovered that the borer is attracted much more to a local weed, napier grass. The technique is to plant napier grass along the side of the maize and the larvae of the stem borer are attracted to the grass which produces a sticky substance that traps and kills the larvae.

The other major pest is Striga a parasite plant which wrecks many billions of pounds worth of maize each year. Weeding Striga is one of the most time consuming activity of African women farmers. Khan has found that planting another weed called Desmodium with the maize produces a chemical that Striga does not like and therefore does not grow.

These new techniques are spreading rapidly over much of East Africa with great success. Khan is now investigating other techniques to kill common pests.

## Feathered Dinosaurs

Over the last few years there have been many sensational discoveries about dinosaurs but the recent discovery of two species that are feathered like birds is possibly the most bizarre. One of these creatures is incredibly related to giant meat-eating dinosaur Tyrannosaurus rex. The fossils of these newly discovered dinosaurs were found in the desert of New Mexico which geologists say was a swampy forest some 90 million years ago. Both creatures possessed features similar to present day birds, suggesting that they may have been covered with feathers.

The first of these new creatures is a member of the carnivorous theropod group of dinosaurs but it appears to have evolved to live on a diet of vegetation. Named Nothronychus, it was sloth-like in appearance and weighed about a tonne. It was 4.6 to 6 metres long and stood between 3 and 3.6 metres high. In general appearance it was very similar to T. rex. It walked upright on two stout hind legs and had a relatively short tail, a long neck and long arms. Its dextrous hands had 4-inch curved claws on its fingers. It had a small head and was equipped with leaf-shaped teeth designed for shredding vegetation. It had a very large stomach allowing it to digest plant food.

The second discovery was a small carnivore from the coelurosaur family and was just over 2 metres long and about a metre high. It fed probably on small animals such as lizards and mammals, but it is thought that it may have scavenged from much larger corpses. It has been described as "the coyote of the Cretaceous period". It has yet to be given a name.

## The Missing Solar Neutrinos

A fundamental problem has been puzzling solar physicists for some 30 years. Scientists have been continually arguing whether or not the Solar Model was correct or whether the equipment available was not giving the correct results. The Solar Model showed that the Sun was emitting vast numbers of neutrinos but the detectors were only able to identify a small percentage of those thought to be emitted.

There are three types of neutrinos, the electron neutrino, the muon neutrino and the tau neutrino. The basic solar theory states that the nuclear reactions on the Sun produce only electron neutrinos and much effort has been made to construct equipment to pick up these neutrinos. One such observatory, the Sudbury Neutrino Observatory (SNO) is a detector buried 2 km underground in a nickel mine in Ontario. The detector consists of 1,000 tonnes of heavy water surrounded by 10,000 photomultipliers. More than a thousand billion electron neutrinos pass through the SNO every second but only a handful are detected. The rate of detection was compared with data collected from Super-Kamiokande particle detector (Super-K) in Mozumi, Japan. The Super-K was also able to detect muon and tau neutrinos but not as efficiently as it detected electron neutrinos. The SNO results were found to be much lower than the Super-K inclusive rate and it was found that electron neutrinos were being converted into muon and tau neutrinos. In fact about 60% of the electron neutrinos were being converted on route to the earth.

It has been found that the three forms of neutrinos can change from one form to another and it is now accepted that the flux of neutrinos starting from the Sun is in complete agreement with the Standard Solar model.

The latest results also confirm that neutrinos have mass, first reported by the Super-K in 1998. This contradicts the prevailing theory of particle physics. So much more research is required before this problem is sorted out.

# Theatre

Theatregoers became increasingly irritated by the failure of big stars to turn up to work. Sometimes even the understudies were ill. At the curtain call of one performance of *My Fair Lady* at the National Theatre, Jonathan Pryce playing Henry Higgins stepped forward and wryly announced 'This will be your first Eliza but it is my second of the day – and my third of this week. Any member of the audience interested in playing Eliza can find applications at the door'. The casting of soap star Martine McCutcheon as the cockney flower girl created huge interest especially in the tabloids, which usually pay little attention to the National Theatre. McCutcheon, unlike her predecessors such as Julie Andrews and Audrey Hepburn, has more in common with Eliza's background at the beginning of the musical than with her transformation into a lady. In spite of problems with her voice, she struggled through the first night and won glowing reviews. From then on she was plagued with illness and instructed not to perform by her doctors. Fortunately, most nights she had an excellent understudy in Alexandra Jay.

Musicals do make huge demands vocally and it has become customary for the leads not to play every performance although audiences aren't always informed of this when they book their tickets. Fans, however, became frustrated by the increasing number of no-shows. A particular offender was Dannii Minogue in *Notre Dame de Paris*. She rarely appeared on a Monday night although those who booked for Mondays weren't always aware of this until they arrived in the Dominion foyer; this, in spite of the fact that the show is marketed on her name. It wasn't only the musicals that had problems. The Almeida Theatre cast Anna Friel as Lulu, a hugely demanding role for an actress as she is hardly ever offstage in a long play. Friel injured herself before the show opened and then again during the run. There was no understudy in this case and performances had to be cancelled altogether.

There were other complaints about the West End in a difficult year hit by the aftermath of Hatfield on the railways as well as a shortage of American tourists put off by the foot and mouth crisis. Andrew Lloyd Webber and Cameron Mackintosh (who announced this year that he was giving up producing new musicals) banded together to complain about the grimy state of the streets surrounding their theatres. They felt that the inadequacies of the tube, the problems of parking, crime, drugs and general filth all contributed to deterring people from making a visit to the West End. Sir Richard Eyre, ex-director of the National Theatre, was much quoted for saying that theatre can be 'ball-breakingly, bowel-churningly bad'. His comments on a three-day conference on the state of theatre also covered tickets prices, the price of drinks and programmes. Director Deborah Warner whose radical production of *Medea* was staged in the West End persuaded her producers to drop ticket prices from £35 to £10 for those under 25 in the belief that excessively high ticket prices were deterring younger audiences. The scheme attracted a warm response.

## West End

The most bizarre event of the year was Jeffrey Archer's decision to appear in his own play *The Accused* as a heart surgeon charged with murdering his wife, knowing full well that the run was likely to coincide with his own trial for perjury and perverting the course of justice. In the event he was charged just nine hours before the play opened in the Theatre Royal, Windsor prior to the West End. Archer has written plays before but it was the first time he appeared himself, sitting in silence for the first two acts and then taking the stand at the end. One critic stated that 'to describe his acting as wooden would be to insult even the humblest piece of furniture'. A novelty feature was the chance for the audience to decide whether or not he was guilty by pressing handsets in front of their seats. The play had no more to recommend it than his previous efforts but the timing and his own appearance onstage guaranteed him plenty of publicity.

Fortunately, the West End had more to offer. There was the usual smattering of stars. Jessica Lange came over from the United States to give a heartbreaking performance as the morphine-addicted Mary Tyrone in Eugene O'Neill's *Long Day's Journey into Night*'. A less happy star import was Daryl Hannah who sank without trace in *The Seven Year Itch*. Macaulay Culkin made an unlikely debut on the London stage in Richard Nelson's *Madame Melville*, the story of a young American pupil in Paris who is seduced on the rebound by his glamorous thirtysomething schoolteacher (Irène Jacob). Culkin's efforts to escape his past, as a child actor and star of *Home Alone*, weren't entirely convincing. Whether he can play anything apart from a gawky, shy teenager remains to be seen. In complete contrast, Alistair Beaton's *Feelgood* made a timely opening at Hampstead Theatre prior to the election and then moved into the West End. A satire on New Labour, spin, and the party's obsessive preoccupation with keeping power at any cost, it was enhanced by Henry Goodman's performance as a manic combination of Alastair Campbell and Peter Mandelson.

Harold Pinter's 70th birthday was marked with a cracking production of *The Caretaker* in which Michael Gambon gave an award-winning performance as the whining tramp who rats on Aston, the gentle, younger man who gives him shelter in his junk-filled attic, played brilliantly by Douglas Hodge. Gambon was ingratiating, racist and treacherous in the riveting revival directed by playwright Patrick Marber. His disgusting long johns and distressed vest made his boastful claims to have eaten with the best quite risible. Other events to mark Pinter's birthday included a production of his adaptation of Proust's *Remembrance of Things Past* at the National. In 2001, a new pairing of his two short political plays *Mountain Language* and *Ashes to Ashes* opened at the Royal Court.

'The Mousetrap' celebrated its 20,000 performance. Elsewhere there were calls to bring Agatha Christie's whodunits into the 21st century, but *The Mousetrap* succeeds because it has never been updated and provides a nostalgic look at a world that has all but vanished. There's a reassuring board in the foyer that clocks up the number of performances. In 1952, the year that *The Mousetrap* opened, there would have been no possibility of *Puppetry of the Penis* reaching the West End stage. Apart from public taste, the Lord Chancellor would have banned it, as Nicholas de Jongh makes clear in his award-winning account of theatrical censorship in the 20th century called *Politics, Prudery and Perversions*. *Puppetry of the Penis* first pitched up at the Edinburgh Festival before coming down to the West End. The two Australian performers describe themselves as 'Grandmasters of the ancient art of genital origami'. In contrast, Eve Ensler brought her one-woman show *The Vagina Monologues* into the West End in which she draws on her many interviews with women. The show has a serious purpose as well as being an entertainment and Ensler has performed it in countries where religious fundamentalism denies women the chance to feel free to talk about their bodies. As in the USA, a number of celebrities joined her onstage including Maureen Lipman, Mariella Frostrup, Meera Syal and Jerry Hall.

An unusual hit was *Shockheaded Peter* originally seen in 1988 at the Lyric Hammersmith. On the strength of rave reviews in New York, it came into the West End. The combined talents of Martyn Jacques and the Tiger Lillies plus Phelim McDermott and Julian Crouch produced a deliciously evil show based on *Struwwelpeter*, the 19th century cautionary tales by Heinrich Hoffman. To his own accordion accompaniment, a white-faced Jaques warbled in his falsetto voice of the terrible things that happen to children who misbehave. Julian Bleach played a sinister master of ceremonies, and designer Crouch paid tribute to the Victorian theatre with a set that consisted of painted flats, traps, huge puppets and ornate wigs.

### Musicals

Andrew Lloyd Webber surprised everybody by announcing that he was collaborating with comedian and writer Ben Elton on a new, musical. The result was *The Beautiful Game* which, in a 'Romeo and Juliet' story, followed the fortunes of a team of talented teenage footballers in Northern Ireland. In a break from such scenically spectacular pieces as *Phantom of the Opera* and *Sunset Boulevard*, *The Beautiful Game* was simply staged with no special effects and, unusually, included dialogue as well as lyrics by Elton. Lloyd Webber's music was both romantically melodic and plangent in such songs as *God's Own Country* and *Our Kind Love*, and drew on Irish jigs and ballads. Although *The Beautiful Game* received much better reviews than Lloyd Webber has become accustomed to in recent years, it still closed after a fairly short run.

The French musical *Napoleon* was an old-fashioned romantic account of Napoleon's life that placed the responsibility for his political downfall on the break-up of his relationship with Josephine. It quickly met its own Waterloo. The RSC attempted to replicate the success, many years ago, of *Les Miserables* with its musical version of the children's classic *The Secret Garden*. It was hugely popular in Stratford but in London it failed to attract enough families while adults assumed it was for children. Very different was *Closer to Heaven* the long awaited collaboration between the Pet Shop Boys and Jonathan Harvey. Harvey's sardonic slow moving storyline was immersed in the doings of gay club land and an immoral pop music scene. The Evening Standard's Best Musical Event was awarded to Adventures in Motion Pictures, *The Car Man* (subtitled 'an auto-erotic thriller') located in a garage in small town America circa 1960 and performed to a jazzed-up version of Bizet's 'Carmen'. One of the oddest musical events was *Road to Heaven* presented by LIFT at the Lyric Hammersmith and performed by a company aged between 70 and 90 giving rousing versions of pop songs such as *Stairway to Heaven* and *Staying Alive*. The Donmar salvaged the reputation of Stephen Sondheim's *Merrily we Roll Along* which originally only lasted 16 performances on Broadway in 1981. Travelling backwards in time, its examination of how talent can go sour perhaps proved too cynical initially for Broadway audiences but Michael Grandage's production made the story work as well as the always popular songs.

### National Theatre

The National's year was very much dominated by the publicity surrounding *My Fair Lady*. Artistic director Trevor Nunn took advantage of a co-production with Cameron Mackintosh to create a sure-fire banker for his own theatre before it moved into the Drury Lane in the West End. Few questioned the quality of his production but there were complaints about his choice of a musical that is already regularly revived and also about the abandonment of the repertoire system in the Lyttelton throughout its run. Once again there was controversy over Trevor Nunn's leadership. Supporters claim that he is the great director of classics and that the National is lucky to have him. Critics complain about his poor leadership, his refusal to create a team of associates, his bad choice of new plays, and his taste for the old-fashioned and traditional. After the remarkably high standard of last year's ensemble, a successor was formed, this time headed by Tim Supple and Irish director Conall Morrison. The rumour mill began to turn with the news that Trevor Nunn had to step in to help out on Supple's production of *Romeo and Juliet* in the Olivier with Chiwetel Ejiofor and Charlotte Randle as the blighted lovers. A postponed opening meant that Supple's prior commitments to the RSC took him away before the press night. Reviews when it finally opened were cool. Then Conall Morrison's production of *Peer Gynt* also ran into trouble and Trevor Nunn had to intervene again. Morrison was eventually retired home to Ireland on doctor's orders. The ensemble was abandoned and the actors had their contracts terminated early. Nunn's judgment was criticised in choosing two relatively inexperienced directors although he defended himself stoutly. He had stalwart backing from his board, but in April announced that he would not be seeking a second term when his contract expired in 2002 although he would stay on until a successor was found. The list of names likely to be approached was remarkably similar to those when Nunn himself was appointed. Most people's favourite, Stephen Daldry, is now heavily involved in a film career after the success of *Billy Elliot*. But those who want the National to have a radical edge look to him to provide it. Both Jude Kelly and Nicholas Hytner are said to be interested in the job but at the time of writing no announcement had been made.

In spite of fielding flak, the National did have its triumphs and won most of the year's awards. Simon Russell Beale was a heartbreakingly moving *Hamlet* in a production by John Caird that stripped the play of its politics. Zinnie Harris' new play *Further than the Furthest Thing* about the fate of the inhabitants of Tristan da Cunha after a volcano erupted, provided a mammoth role for Paola Dionisotti as the doughty leader in exile determined that she and her fellow islanders should be allowed to return home. Four revivals gave much pleasure: Trevor Nunn's own production of *The Cherry Orchard* with real life siblings Corin and Vanessa Redgrave playing Madame Ranevskaya and her brother Gaev; Howard Davies' production of Arthur Miller's *All My Sons* with Julie Walters; Nicholas Hytner's production of *The Winter's Tale* with Alex Jennings as the tortured Leontes; and Jeremy Sams' revival of Michael Frayn's spoof of old-fashioned touring theatre, *Noises Off*. By far the most fascinating show at the National, however, was *The Far Side of the Moon* written, directed and performed by Robert Lepage. The one man show mingled the story of the space race between the Americans and Russians with the relationship of two brothers, one a romantic struggling to finish his thesis on the effects of space travel on popular culture and the other a sleek, successful TV weatherman only interested in making money. A huge mirror that filled the width of the stage and reflected the audience was a reminder of the once-held belief that the moon reflected the earth and it culminated with the sight of Lepage apparently floating in space. A brilliant mix of the cosmic and domestic, the production was a visitor to the National, as was Complicite's *Mnemonic*, both giving an indication of the direction the National should take to stay in touch with modern audiences.

The RSC announced changes too but to its organisation rather than its personnel. For years the company has been struggling with the reluctance of the best actors to commit themselves to a long term contract: they prefer to keep their options open in case a high-earning film or television job comes along. A few years ago, contracts were reduced from two years to eighteen months without having the desired effect. The company's directors are also aware that many of the most exciting Shakespearean productions in recent years have taken place in unusual, specifically chosen venues. In contrast, the RSC directors are confined to working in the company's own spaces. In May, Artistic Director Adrian Noble announced radical changes including the scrapping of the permanent company of actors and abandoning its London home at the Barbican. Instead, the company will look to a wide variety of London venues including West End theatres, the Roundhouse and the Young Vic to stage its productions in London. Shorter seasons with actors employed for specific plays may attract big names back to the company. It was announced that Ralph Fiennes and Kenneth Branagh had already signed up to appear in productions next year. Praised by everybody was Noble's intention to set up a Shakespearean academy which in the summer of 2002 will be led by director Declan Donnellan in an attempt to give young actors just out of drama school the classical training they lack. The main concern is whether the company will be able to preserve its identity in London where it will have no regular base. The big losers are the company's permanent backstage staff, especially in London, as technical teams, like the actors, will be employed on a one-off basis. These changes will be further exacerbated when the company hears whether or not it has won its lottery bid to re-design the Memorial Theatre in Stratford.

When Noble last announced that the RSC was reducing its season at the Barbican, there was consternation that it would be difficult to find productions to fill he main stage. The Barbican's summer season of international visitors, however, has now become so well established that there are no such fears. *Tantalus* was a joint venture between the RSC, the Barbican and Denver College in Colorado, the last picking up most of the Bill. It was a project which Sir Peter Hall had been discussing with John Barton for over twenty years. John Barton's 10 hour epic re-telling of the Trojan Wars often introducing unfamiliar material was rehearsed for 26 weeks in Colorado where director and author fell out over cuts introduced by Hall. The result, which opened in Britain at the new Lowry Centre in Salford, was admired for its design, its ambition and for Greg Hicks' doubling as Priam and Agamemnon.

Although the RSC's future plans divided commentators and naturally caused distress among those who were losing their jobs, the company was generally seen to have had a good year, particularly with its millennium staging of Shakespeare's History plays from *Richard II* to *Richard III* employing four different directors and a number of different styles. Michael Boyd, in particular, created clarity out of the *Henry VI* trilogy of power struggles, reversals, and civil wars. The biggest criticism was that there were too few possibilities to see the cycle in its entirety.

In a year of 'Hamlets', a controversial production by Steven Pimlott saw Samuel West playing a modern day Prince sharing a joint with Rosencrantz and Guildenstern and with Kerry Condon as a punkish Ophelia. New plays proliferated in Stratford, the most notable being *The Lieutenant of Inishmore* a monstrous satire on the IRA by Martin McDonagh depicting IRA members as sentimental – more concerned about their pet cat than human beings – ignorant of history, as well as psychotically violent. Peter Whelan's *A Russian in the Woods* was a subtle rites-of-passage play about a young idealistic soldier finding himself in a divided Berlin after the war, answerable to people with very different beliefs from his own. Peter Barnes' *Jubilee* debunked the idealisation of Shakespeare and the Shakespearean industry in a chaotic fashion.

At the Royal Court, the home of new plays, Gary Mitchell's examination of the RUC, *The Force of Change*, was moved to the Downstairs theatre from the Theatre Upstairs. Mitchell won the Evening Standard's award for most promising playwright, which for the first time included a cheque for £30,000. David Hare's *My Zinc Bed* was an intense study of addiction with Tom Wilkinson, Julia Ormond and Steven Mackintosh farming an emotional triangle in which it was unclear who was the outsider. The Theatre Upstairs had the most interesting season with David Eldridge's examination of teachers, sex and friendship in *Under the Blue Sky;* Rebecca Gilman's look at political correctness and racism in a liberal institution in *Spinning into Butter* and Caryl Churchill's powerful *Far Away*, an apocalyptic, surreal vision of a world at war. Downstairs Kevin Elyot's disturbing *Mouth to Mouth* with Lindsay Duncan was hugely popular at the Royal Court although it fared less well in the West End. Much of the year, however, was taken up with staging almost all the works of Sarah Kane, the young playwright who committed suicide in 1999. Most critics revised their first damaging opinions of her devastating play *Blasted*.

Many theatres benefited from the Government's announcement of an additional £25m to go into theatre across the country. Between 2001 and 2003, the newly built Theatre by the Lake in Cumbria will receive an increase in grant of 233%, the Contact Theatre in Manchester 91%, the Soho theatre in London 130% and the Oxford Playhouse 405%. Announcing these increases the previous Culture Secretary, Chris Smith, said: 'This extra investment will have many wide-ranging benefits: to audiences, allowing ticket prices to remain affordable and quality to remain high; to artists, to allow experimentation and ensure a reasonable standard of living; and to organisations so that they can invest in training and support new writing.

The Almeida, another theatre to benefit, moved temporarily to a converted coach station in an insalubrious part of King's Cross while its Islington home base is renovated with lottery money. Typically it went out in a spectacular fashion. Jonathan Kent's production of *The Tempest* included Aidan Gillen as Ariel swimming in a huge tank beneath the stage. When not swimming, he was talking to Ian McDiarmid's bitter Prospero swinging upside down on a rope. The new temporary space provides two flexible spaces, a wonderful spacious bar and has grass growing on its roof. Nicholas Wright's excellent adaptation of the Lulu plays opened the season but Anna Friel's Lulu failed to make the necessary impact. Far more exciting was Neil La Bute's tense, provocative new play *The Shape of Things* which explored the nature of art. Rachel Weisz as the ruthless artist smartens up a fellow student, changes his relationship with his friends, gets his teeth fixed, and even persuades him to have plastic surgery.

All the time, he believes he is in a relationship rather than being shaped up as her future exhibit. David Lan made his mark as the new artistic director of the Young Vic. He quickly laid out his policy of turning his theatre into a place for the training of young directors many of who find it difficult to make the jump from studio to main theatres. His own evocative production of the American classic *A Raisin in the Sun* drew attention to a play that has rarely been seen over here. In collaboration with LIFT, the theatre also brought over Peter Brook's production of *Le Costume*, a heartbreaking tale of a South African couple in which the husband discovers his wife has been unfaithful and forces her to treat the lover's discarded suit as a guest. Brook's simple style perfectly suited the subject matter. The veteran director revealed once again that theatre is about the rapport between actor and audience rather than spectacular scenic effects.

PRODUCTIONS
September 2000 to August 2001

## LONDON PRODUCTIONS

ADELPHI, WC2. *Chicago*, since November 1997

ALBERY, WC2. (11 October 2000) *The Guardsman* (Ferenc Molnar, adapt. Frank Marcus) with Greta Scacchi Michael Pennington, Nickolas Grace and Georgina Hale; director, Janet Suzman. (18 January) *Far Away* (Caryl Churchill) with Linda Bassett, Kevin McKidd, Annabelle Seymour-Julien; director, Stephen Daltry. (22 March) *A Midsummer Night's Dream* (Shakespeare) with Dawn French, Jemma Redgrave, Will Keen, Tilly Blackwood; director, Matthew Francis. (18 July) *A Servant to Two Masters* (Carlo Goldoni, adapt. Lee Hall from a literal translation Gwenda Pandolfi) with Jason Watkins; director, Tim Supple.

ALDWYCH, WC2. *Whistle Down the Wind*, since July 1998. (27 February 2001) *The Secret Garden* (lyrics Marsha Norman, music Lucy Simon, based on the novel by Frances Hodgon Burnett) with Philip Quast, Peter Polycarpou, Linzi Hateleye, Meredith Braun; director, Adrian Noble.

APOLLO, W1. (17 October 2000) *Fallen Angels* (Noel Coward) with Felicity Kendal, Frances de la Tour, Eric Carte and James Woolley; director, Michael Rudman. (17 April) *The Female Odd Couple* (Neil Simon) with Jenny Seasgrove, Paul Wilcox.

APOLLO VICTORIA, SW1. *Starlight Express*, since March 1984

ARTS THEATRE, WC1E. (27 September 2000) *Another Country* (Julian Mitchell) with Alex Avery, James De Courcy, Martin Hutson and Neil Jones; director, Stephen Henry. (22 January) *Entertaining Mrs Sloane* (Orton) with Alison Steadman, Clive Francis, Neil Stuke; director, Terry Johnson. (31 May) *Closer to Heaven* (Book John Harvey, music and lyrics Neil Tennant and Chris Lowe - The Pet Shop Boys) director, Gemma Bodinetz.

BARBICAN, EC2. (3 November 2000) *The Duchess of Malfi* (John Webster) with Aisling O'Sullivan, Ken Bones, Colin Tierney and Neil Dudgeon; director, Gale Edwards. (29 November) *The Comedy of Errors* (William Shakespeare) with Jacqueline Defferary, Paul Greenwood, Anthony Howell and Ian Hughes; director, Lynne Parker. (18 December) *The Rivals* (Richard Brinsley Sheridan) with Jack Chissick, Wendy Craig, Jacqueline Defferary and Robert Goodale; director, Lindsay Posner. (17 January) *Romeo and Juliet* (William Shakespeare) with Alexandra Gilbreath, Adrian Schiller, David Tennant and Alfred Burke; director, Michael Boyd. (21 February) *Henry IV: Part I* and *Part II* (William Shakespeare) with Desmond Barrit, Nancy Carroll, Clifford Rose and David Troughton; director, Michael Attenborough. (22 March) *Henry V* (Shakespeare) with David Acton, Richard Bremmer, Sam Cox and Alexis Daniel; director, Edward Hall. (2 May) *Tantalus* (John Barton, adapt. Peter Hall) with Greg Hicks, Ann Mitchell and David Ryall; director, Peter Hall and Edward Hall.

THE PIT. (27 September 2000) *Secret Fall of Constance Wilde* (Thomas Kilroy) director, Patrick Mason. (1 November) *The Tempest* (Shakespeare) with Zubin Varla, Nikki Amuka-Bird, Nicholas Day and Oliver Dimsdale; director, James Macdonald. (21 December) *Richard II* (Shakespeare) with David Killick, David Troughton, Samuel West and Alfred Burke; director, Steven Pimlott. (2 January) *As You Like It* (Shakespeare) with Nancy Carrol, Alexandra Gibreath, Adrian Schiller and Declan Conlon; director, Gregory Doran. (21 December) *Richard II* (Shakespeare) with David Killick, David Troughton, Samuel West and Alfred Burke; director, Steven Pimlott. (16 January) *La Lupa* (Giovanni Verga, new version David Lan) with Brid Brennan, Karen Bryson, Declan Conlon and Mali Harries; director, Simona Gonella. (20 February) *Back to Methuselah* (George Bernard Shaw) with Karen Bryson, Nina Conti, Julian Curry and Don Gallagher; director, David Fielding. (7 March) *Loveplay* (Moira Buffini) with Simon Coates, Ian Dunn, Niamh Linehan; director, Anthony Clark. (27 March) *Luminosity* (Nick Stafford) with Susan Engel, Karen Bryson, Simon Coates; director, Gemma Bodinetz.

BUSH, W12. (24 October 2000) *Howie the Rookie* (Mark Rowe) with Aidan Kelly and Karl Shiels, director, Mike Bradwell. (15 November) *Hijra* (Ask Kotak) with Sharon Maharaj, Charubala Chokshi, Leena Dhingra; director, Ian Brown. (13 December) *The Messiah* (Patrick Barlow with additional material Jude Kelly, Julian Hough and John Ramm) with Patrick Barlow and John Ramm.

CAMBRIDGE, WC2. (5 September 2000) *The Beautiful Game* (Andrew Lloyd Webber and Ben Elton) with Ben Goddard, Jamie Golding, Frank Grimes and Dale Meeks; director, Robert Carsen.

COMEDY, SW1. (23 October 2000) *The Mystery of Charles Dickens* (Peter Ackroyd) with Simon Callow; director, Patrick Garland. (15 November) *The Caretaker* (Harold Pinter) with Michael Gambon, Rupert Graves and Douglas Hodge; director, Rob Howell. (22 February) *Under the Doctor* (Peter Tilbury) with Peter Davison, Anton Rogers, Polly Maberley, Emma Pike; director, Fiona Laird. (2 April) *Ghosts* (Henrik Ibsen, adapt. Richard Harris) with Francesca Annis, Anthony Andrews, Martin Hutson, Robin Soans; director, Robin Phillips. (23 July) *Nixon's Nixon* (Russell Lees) with Tim Donohue, Keith Jochim; director, Charles Towers.

CRITERION, W1. *The Complete Works of William Shakespeare (Abridged)* and *The Complete History of America (Abridged)*, since 1996

DOMINION, W1. *Notre-Dame de Paris*, since May 2000

DONMAR WAREHOUSE, WC2. (25 September 2000) *To the Green Fields Beyond* (Nick Whitby) with Ray Winstone, Dougray Scott, Hugh Dancy and Finbar Lynch; director, Sam Mendes. (11 December) *Merrily We Roll Along* (Stephen Sondheim and George Furth) with Daniel Evans, Julian Ovenden and Samantha Spiro; director, Michael Grandage. (15 March) *Boston Marriage* (David Mamet) with Zoe Wanamaker, Anna Chancello, Lyndsey Marshall. (1 May) *Tales from Hollywood* (Christopher Hampton); director, John Crowley. (4 July) *A Lie of the Mind* (Sam Shepard) with

Sinead Cusack, Keith Bartlett, Anna Calder-Marshall, Catherine McCormack; director, Wilson Milam.

DRURY LANE THEATRE ROYAL, WC2. *Witches of Eastwick*, since July 2000. (13 March 2001) *The League of Gentlemen* (Jeremy Dyson, Mark Gatiss, Steve Pemberton and Reece Shearsmith) performed and directed by the authors.

DUCHESS, WC2. *Copenhagen*, since February 1999. (30 April 2001) *Blue/Orange* (Joe Penhall) with Chiwetel Ejiofor, Andrew Lincoln, Bill Nighy.

DUKE OF YORK, WC2. since *Stones in his Pockets* (Mary Jones) August 2000 with Sean Campion and Conleth Hill; director, Ian McElhinney, transferred from the New Ambassadors

FORTUNE, WC2. *The Woman in Black*, since June 1989

GARRICK, WC2. *An Inspector Calls*, the 1992 National Theatre production, since 1995. (26 April 2001) *Feelgood* (Alistair Beaton) with Henry Goodman, Nigel Planer, Sian Thomas, Amita Dhiri; director, Max Stafford-Clark.

GIELGUD, W1. *The Graduate*, since April 2000

GLOBE, SE1. (18 April 2001) *Umabatha: The Zulu Macbeth* (Shakespeare, trans. Msomi) with a cast of 40 Zulu warriors. (12 May) *King Lear* (Shakespeare) with Julian Glover; director, Barry Kyle. (27 May) *Macbeth* (Shakespeare) with Jasper Britton; director, Tim Carroll. (30 June) *Cymbeline* (Shakespeare) with Mark Rylance; director, Mike Alfreds. (18 July) *Comedy of Errors* (Shakespeare) with Mansai Nomura.

HAYMARKET THEATRE ROYAL, SW1. (2 October 2000) *The Blue Room* (David Hare, adapt. from Arthur Schnitzier's *La Ronde*) with Michael Higgs and Camilla Power; director, Loveday Ingram. (5 December) *The Accused* (Jeffrey Archer) with Jeffrey Archer, Edward Petherbridge, Tony Britton and Edward de Souza; director, Val May. (7 February) *Japes* (Simon Gray) with Toby Stephens, Jasper Britton and Clare Swinburne; director, Peter Hall. (24 May) *The Beau* (Ron Hunchinson) with Peter Bowles, Richard McCabe; director, Caroline Hunt.

HER MAJESTY' S, SW1. *Phantom of the Opera*, since October 1986

LONDON PALLADIUM, W1. *The King and I*, since May 2000. (5-17 February 2001) *The Nutcracker* (Tchaikovsky) performed the Chisnau National Ballet; director, Yuri Grigorovich.

LYCEUM, WC2. *The Lion King*, since 1999

LYRIC, W1. (11 September 2000) *Brief Encounter* (Noel Coward, adapt. Andrew Taylor) with Jenny Seagrove, Christopher Cazenove, Brian Deacon and Elizabeth Power; director, Roger Redfarn. (21 November) *Long Day's Journey into Night* (Eugene O'Neill) with Jessica Lange and Charles Dance; director, Robin Phillips. (14 March) *Semi-Monde* (Noel Coward) with Nichola McAuliffe, John Carlise, Sophie Ward and Ben Bates; director, Philip Prowse. (August 2001) *Mostly Sondheim: Barbara Cook* with Barbar Cook, accompanied Willie Harper.

NEW AMBASSADORS, WC2. (4 September 2000) *In Flame* (Charlotte Jones) with Kerry Fox, Marcia Warren, Jason Hughes and Rosie Cavaliero; director, Anna Mackmin. (2 November) *A Doll's House* (Henrik Ibsen, trans. Michael Mayer) with Anne-Marie Duff, Paterson Joseph, Pip Donagh and Jude Akuwudike; director, Polly Teale. (17 December) *Servant of Two Masters* (Carlo Goldoni, adapt. Lee Hall from a translation Gwenda Pandolfi) with Jason Watkins; director, Tim Supple. (5 February) *Berkoff's Women* (Steven Berkoff) with Linda Marlowe. (19 February) *Port Authority* (Conor McPherson) with Jim Norton, Steven Brennan and Eanna MacLiam; director, Conor McPherson. (3 April) *Mill on the Floss* (George Elliot, adapt. Helen Edmundson), directors Nancy Meckler and Polly Teale. (10 May) *The Vagina Monologues* (Eve Ensler) with Eve Ensler, Maureen Lipman, Sophie Okonedo, Edie Falco; director, Eve Ensler. (3 July) *One for the Road* (Harold Pinter) with Harold Pinter.

NEW END, NW3. (14 November 2000) *Shylock* (Gareth Armstrong) with Gareth Armstrong; director, Frank Barrie. (14 November) *Achtung Kabarett!* (Ron Hart) with Alexandra Valavelska; director, Kate Flatt. (13 December) *Alice through the Looking Glass* (Carroll, adapt. and composed Stephen Daltry, co-written and commissioned Pamela Barlow).

NEW LONDON, WC2. *Cats*, since May 1981

OLD VIC, SE1. (13 September 2000) *The Car Man 'An Auto-Erotic Thriller'* (Terry Davies and Rodion Shchedrin, adapt. Georges Bizet) with Alan Vincent, Ewan Wardrop, Will Kemp and Ben Hartley; director, Matthew Bourne. (12 February) *Life x3* (Yasmina Reza, trans. Christopher Hampton) with Mark Rylance, Imelda Staunton, Harriet Walter and Oliver Cotton. (1 March) *Lulu* (Frank Wedekind, new version Nicholas Wright) with Anna Friel; director, Jonathan Kent.

OPEN AIR, REGENT'S PARK (11 June 2001) *A Midsummer Night's Dream* (Shakespeare) director, Alan Strachan. (15 June) *Love's Labours Lost* (Shakespeare) director, Rachel Kavanaugh. (26 July) *Where's Charley?* (Music and lyrics Frank Loesser, book George Abbott, based on Brandon Thomas' *Charley Aunt*) director, Ian Talbot. (5 August) *Voices from Ambridge in Come Rain Come Shine* (devised Gareth Armstrong and Malcolm McKee) directors, Gareth Armstrong and Malcolm McKee. (10 August) *Desires of Frankenstein* (James Martin Charlton) director, Simon Green. (27 August) *Pirates of Penzance* (Gilbert and Sullivan) director, Ian Talbot.

PALACE, WC2. *Les Miserables*, since December 1985

PHOENIX, WC1. *Blood Brothers*, since November 1991

PICCADILLY, W1. *La Cava The Musical*, since August 2000. (19 February 2001) *Shockheaded Peter* (adapt. from Heinrich Hoffman's *Struwwelpeter*, music Martin Jacques) directors Julian Crouch and Phelim McDermott. (3 May) *Noises Off* (Michael Frayn) with Lyn Redgrave, director, Jeremy Sams.

PLAYHOUSE, WC2. (8 September 2000) *Hedwig and the Angry Inch* (John Cameron Mitchell and Stephen Trask) with Michael Cerveris; director, Peter Askin. (29 November) *Thunderbirds F.A.B.* (Andrew Dawson and Gavin Robertson) with Andrew Dawson and Gavin Robertson. (17 April) *Pub Landlord: My Gaff Rules* with Al Murray and Jason Freeman.

PRINCE EDWARD, W1. *Mamma Mia*, since April 1999

PRINCE OF WALES, W1. *Fosse*, since February 2000. (23 March 2001) *The Witches of Eastwick* (book and lyrics John Dempsey, music Dana Rowe) transfer from Drury Lane.

QUEENS, W1. (9 October 2000) *The Seven Year Itch* (George Axelrod) with Daryl Hannah, Rolf Saxon, Myriam Acharki and William Hope; director, Michael Radford. (13 December) *The Hobbit* (J R R Tolkien, adapt. Glynne Robbins) with Toby Gafney, James Adair, Clive Kneller and Michael Geary; director, Roy Marsden. (30 January) *Medea* (Euripides, trans. Kenneth McLeish and Frederic Raphael) with Fiona Shaw, Jonathan Clarke, Siobhan McCarthy and Jonathan Slinger; director, Deborah Warner. (21 May) *All You Need is Love* with Linda John-Pierre, Jon Boydon, Jacqui Dubois, Peter Elridge.

ROYAL COURT DOWNSTAIRS SW1. (14 September 2000) *My Zinc Bed* (David Hare) with Steven Mackintosh, Julia Ormond and Tom Wilkinson; director, David Hare. (8 November) *The Force of Change* (Gary Mitchell) with Sean Caffrey, Stuart Graham, Gerard Jordan and Stephen Kennedy; director, Robert Delamere. (4 December) I Just Stopped to *See* the Man (Stephen Jeffreys) with Sophie Okenedo; director, Richard Wilson. (6 February) *Mouth to Mouth* (Kevin Elyot) with Lindsay Duncan, Michael Maloney, Barnaby Kay and Andrew McKay; director, Ian Rickson. (3 April) *Blasted* (Sarah Kane) with Neil Dudgeon, Tom Jordan Murphy, Kelly Reilly; director, James Macdonald. (10 May 2001) *4.48 Psychosis* (Sarah Kane) director, James Macdonald. (10 May) *Crave* (Sarah Kane) director, James Macdonald. (26 June) *Mountain Language/Ashes to Ashes* (Harold Pinter) with Gabrielle Hamilton, Anastasia Hille; director, Katie Mitchell. (28-30 June) *Alive from Palestine* (Al Kasaba).

ROYAL COURT UPSTAIRS, SW1. (19 September 2000) *Under the Blue Sky* (David Eldridge) with Jonathan Cullen, Samantha Edmonds, Sheila Hancock and Lisa Palfrey; director, Rufus Norris. (18 October) *Good-bye Roy* (Holly Baxter Baine), director, Annabelle Comyn; *Made of Stone* (Leo Butler) director, Deborah Bruce; *Drag-on* (Holly Baxter Baine) director, Emmanuel De Nasciemento; *Local* (written and directed Arzhang Pezhman). (30 November) *Far Away* (Caryl Churchill) with Linda Bassett; director, Stephen Daldry. (9 January) *Spinning into Butter* (Rebecca Gilman) with Emma Fielding, Jordan Frieda, Mido Hamada and David Horovitch; director, Dominic Cooke. (13 February) *Credible Witness* (Timberlake Wertenbaker) with Anthony Barclay, Olympia Dukakis and Vincent Ebrahim; director, Sacha Wares. (15 March) *Spirit* (Improbable Theatre production) with Guy Dartnell, Phelim McDermott and Lee Simpson; directors, Julian Crouch and Arlene Audergon. (23 April) *Presence* (David Harrower) director, James Kerr. (22 May) *Herons* (Simon Stephens) director, Simon Usher. (19 June) *Clubland* (Roy Williams) director, Indhu Rubasingham.

ROYAL NATIONAL THEATRE, SE1, COTTESLOE. (6 July) *All My Sons* (Arthur Miller) with Ben Daniels, James Hazeldine, Catherine McCormack, Julie Walters; director, Howard Davies. (21 September) *The Cherry Orchard* (Anton Chekhov, new version David Lan) with Vanessa Redgrave, Corin Redgrave, Eve Best and Michael Bryant; director, Trevor Nunn. (10 October) *Further than the Furthest Thing* (Zinnie Harris) with Arlene Cockburn, Paolo Dionisotti, Darell D'Silva and Gary McInnes; director, Irina Brown. (7 November) *In Extremis/De Profundis* (Neil Bartlett/Oscar Wilde, ed. Merlin Holland) with Corine Redgrave and Sheila Hancock. (23 November) *Remembrance of Things Past* (Marcel Proust, adapt. Harold Pinter and Di Trevis) with John Bett, John Burgess, Branwell Donaghey and Janine Duvitski; director, Di Trevis; transferred to Olivier 23 February. (20 February) *Playboy of the Western World* (J. M. Synge) with Derbhle Crotty, Sorcha Cusack, James Ellis; Annie Farr; director, Fiona Buffini. (8 March) *The Walls* (Colin Teevan) director, Mick Gordon. (20 March) *Good Woman of Setzuan* (Bertolt Brecht, new version Tanika Gupta) with Deborah Asante, Matthew Ashford, David Baker, Agron, Tim Crouch; director, Colin Peters. (8 May) *Finding the Sun/Marriage Play* (Edward Albee) with Sheila Burrell, Sheila Gish, Bill Paterson; director, Anthony Page. (13 June) *Howard Katz* (Patrick Marber) with Ron Cook, Ashley Jensen, Cherry Morris, Trevor Peacock; director, Patrick Marber. (9 August) *Humble Boy* (Charlotte Jones) with Diana Rigg, Simon Russell Beale, Denis Quilley, Cathryn Bradshaw; director, John Caird.

LYTTELTON. (5 September 2000) *Hamlet* (Shakespeare) with Simon Russell Beale, Cathryn Bradshaw, Sara Kestelman and Peter McEnery; director, John Caird. (5 October) *Noises Off* (Michael Frayn) with Susie Blake, Patricia Hodge, Christopher Benjamin and Peter Egan; director, Jeremy Sams. (7 December) *Life x 3* (Yasmina Reza, trans. Christopher Hampton) with Mark Rylance and Imelda Staunton; director, Matthew Warchus. (2 February) *Mnemonic* (Simon McBurney) with Katrin Cartlidge, Richard Catz, Simon McBurney and Tim McMullan; director, Simon McBurney. (15 March) *My Fair Lady* (music Frederick Loewe, book and lyrics Alan Jan Lerner) with Martine McCutcheon, Jonathan Price, Nicholas Le Prevost; director, Trevor Nunn. (10 July) *The Far Side of the Moon* (Robert Lepage and Ex Machina) with Robert Lepage; director, Robert Lepage. (7 August 2001) *All My Sons* (Arthur Miller) with Ben Daniels, Laurie Metcalfe, Nigel Cooke, Charles Edwards; director, Howard Davies.

OLIVIER. (3 October 2000) *Romeo and Juliet* (Shakespeare) with Chiwetel Ejiofor, Charlotte Randle, John Burgess and Jeff Diamond; director, Tim Supple. (13 November) *Peer Gynt* (Henrik Ibsen, new version Frank McGuinness) with Sorcha Cusack, Jeff Diamond, Annie Farr and Olwen Fouere; director, Conall Morrison. (18 December) *Singin' in the Rain* (story and screenplay Betty Comden and Adolph Freed, music Nacio Herb Brown, lyrics Arthur Freed) with Mark Shannon, Zoe Hart, Paul Robinson and Sarah Cortez; director, Jude Kelly. (3 February) *The Cherry Orchard* (Anton Chekhov, new version David Lan) transferred from Cottesloe with Vanessa Redgrave, Corin Redgrave, Eve Best, Michael Bryant; director, Trevor Nunn. (23 February) *Remembrance of Things Past* (Marcel Proust, adapt. Harold Pinter and Di Trevis) transferred from Cottesloe with John Bett, John Burgess, Branwell Donaghey; director, Di Trevis. (11 April) *The Ramayana* (in a new version Peter Oswald) with Charlotte Bicknell, Vincent Ebrahim, George Eggay, Andrew French; director, Indhu Rubasingham. (23 May) *The Winter's Tale* (Shakespeare) with Alex Jennings; director, Nicholas Hytner. (11 June) *Hamlet* (Shakespeare) with Simon Russell-Beale, Denis Quilley, Sara Kestelman; director, John Caird. (20 July) *The Relapse (or Virtue in Danger)* (John Vanbrugh) with Brian Blessed, Paul Bradley, Alex Jennings; director, Trevor Nunn.

ST MARTINS, WC2. *The Mousetrap*, since March 1974

SAVOY, WC2. (15 September 2000) *The Mikado* (Gilbert and Sullivan) with The D'Oyly Carte Opera Company; director, Ian Judge. (17 January) *The Importance of Being Earnest* (Wilde) with Patricia Routledge, Alistair Petrie, Theo Fraser Steele and Jonathan Elsom; director, Christopher Morahan. (20 April) *The Pirates of Penzance* (Gilbert and Sullivan) with Royce Mills, James Cleverton, Gareth Jones, Charlotte Page; director, Stuart Maunder. (2 July) *Naughty Baby* with Ute Lemper.

SHAFTESBURY THEATRE, WC2. (30 September 2000) *Napoleon* (Andrew Sabiston and Timothy Williams) with Paul Baker; Anastasia Barzee; director, Francesca Zambello. (17 April) *Baddiel and Skinner Unplanned* with David Baddiel and Frank Skinner. (20 August) *Peggy Sue Got Married* (music Bob Gaudio, lyrics and book Arlene Sarner and Jerry Leichtling) with Ruthie Henshall, Andrew Kennedy.

STRAND, WC2. *Buddy*, since October 1995

UPSTAIRS AT THE GATEHOUSE, N6. (4 October 2000) *Counterpoint* (Shirlie Roden) with Catherine Debenham-Taylor, Fiona Mack, Glen McCready, Jon Emmanuel.

VAUDEVILLE, WC2. (18 October 2000) *Madame Melville* (Richard Nelson) with Macaulay Culkin, Irene Jacob and Madeleine Potter; director, Richard Nelson. (15 March 2001) *God Only Knows* with Derek Jacobi, Francesca Hunt, Margot Leicester; director, Antony Page.

WHITEHALL, SW1. (20 September 2000) *Puppetry of the Penis* with Simon Morley and David Friend. (31 January) *Bouncers* (John Godber) with Andrew Dennis, Andrew Dunn, Zach Lee, John Godber. (2 May) *Official Tribute to the Blues Brothers* with Brad Henshaw, Simon Foster, Antonio Fargas; director, David Leland.

WYNDHAM'S, WC2. *Art*, since October 1996

YOUNG VIC, SE1. (15 September 2000) *Julius Caesar* (Shakespeare) with Dorian Healy, Lloyd Owen, Robert Cavanagh and Marcus D'Amico; director, David Lan. (6 December) *The Three Musketeers* (Alexandre Dumas) director, Julian Webber. (24 January) *Le Costume* (Can Themba, adapt. Barney Simon) director, Peter Brook. (15 February) *Six Characters in Search of an Author* (Luigi Pirandello, new translation David Harrower) director, Richard Jones. (24 April) *Henry VI: Part 1: The War Against France* and *Henry VI: Part 2: England's Fall* (Shakespeare) with Richard Cordsey, Geff Frances, Aidan McArdle and Jake Nightingale; director, Michael Boyd. (25 April) *Henry VI: Part 3: The Chaos* (Shakespeare) with Richard Cordery, Geff Francis, Aidan McArdle and Jake Nightingale; director, Michael Boyd. (11 April) *Richard III* (Shakespeare) with Richard Cordery, Fiona Bell, Tom Beard and Aidan McArdle; director, Michael Boyd. (1 June) *A Raisin in the Sun* (Lorraine Hansbury) with Daniel Anthony, William Chubb, Adrian Fergus Fuller, Lennie James; director, David Lan. (12 June) *Streetcar to Tennessee* (Tennessee Williams) director, Timothy Sheader. (25 July) *Action* (Sam Shepard) director, Arlette Kim George. (22 August) *The Tragedy of Hamlet* (Shakespeare) director, Peter Brook.

## OUTSIDE LONDON

CHICHESTER: FESTIVAL *Pal Joey* (music Richard Rogers, lyrics Lorenz Hart, book John O'Hara) director, Loveday Ingram. (13 November) *Jeffrey Bernard is Unwell* (Keith Waterhouse). (12 December) *Godspell* (music and lyrics Stephen Schwartz, book Michael Tebelak). (5 March) *An Ideal Husband* (Oscar Wilde) with Barbara Murray, Patrick Ryecart, Richard Todd. (23 May) *On the Razzle* (adapt. from comedy by Johann Nestroy) director, Peter Wood. (6 June) *The Winslow Boy* (Terence Rattigan) director, Christopher Morahan. (19 July) *My One and Only* (lyrics George and Ira Gershwin, book Peter Stone and Timothy S. Mayer) director, Loveday Ingram. (22 August) *Three Sisters* (Anton Chekhov) director, Loveday Ingram.

MINERVA (28 October 2000) *Hysteria* (Terry Johnson) director, Loveday Ingram. (15 March) *The Silver Sword* (adapt. Stuart Henson, book Ian Serrailier) director, Dale Rooks. (29 May) *Song of Singapore* director, Roger Redfarn. (11 July) *In Celebration* (David Storey) director, Sean Holmes. (8 August) *The Secret Rapture* (David Hare) director, Indhu Rubasingham.

EDINBURGH: ROYAL LYCEUM (24 October 2000) *Romeo and Juliet* (Shakespeare) with Garry Collins and Kanunu Kirimi. (16 January) *A Listening to Heaven* (Torben Betts) director, Muriel Romanes. (13 February) *A View from the Bridge* (Arthur Miller). (27 March) *Guys and Dolls* (based on a story by Damon Runyon, music and lyrics Frank Loesser) with Elaine C. Smith; director, Kenny Ireland. (1 May) *Woyzeck* (George Buchner, new version David Harrower).

LEEDS: COURTYARD AND QUARRY THEATRES: (4 May) *Broken Glass* (Arthur Miller) with Clare Burt, Michael Elwyn, Kevin McMonagle; director, Ian Brown. (13 June) *2001: A Ramayan Oddysey* director, Jatinder Verma. (22 June) *Shylock: Shakespear's Alien* with Patrick Stewart. (19 July) *Wanted Man* (Toby Jones) with Toby Jones and Edward Woodall; director, Edward Kemp. (28 August) *Johnson over Jordan* (J B Priestley) with Patrick Stewart; director, Jude Kelly.

LEICESTER: HAYMARKET: (7 September 2000) *When We are Married* (J. B. Priestly) director, Paul Kerryson. (3 October) *A Doll's House* (Henrick Ibsen., trans. Michael Meyer) directors Polly Tweale and Yvonne McDevitt. (5 October) *Picture Me* (Noel Greig) director, Wendy Harris. (13 October) *The Crucible* (Arthur Miller) director, Paul Kerryson. (25 October) *Two Old Ladies* (Gurpeet Bhatti and Harvey Virdi) director, Nona Shepphard. (1 November) *Crazy Lady*, written and directed Nona Shepphard. (28 November) *Pyar - Love* (inspired Lorca's *Blood Wedding*) director, Mark Powell. (9 February) *Rent* (Jonathan Larson) director, Paul Kerryson. (24 March) *East is East* (Ayub Khan-Din) director, Nona Shepphard. (5 April) *The Winter's Tale* (Shakespeare) director, Gary Brown and Sarah Chiswell. (20 April) *A Little Night Music* (music and lyrics Stephen Sondheim, book Hugh Wheeler) director, Paul Kerryson. (8 June) *2001: A Ramayan Oddysey* (Jatinder Verma).

MANCHESTER: ROYAL EXCHANGE: (6 September 2000) *Ghosts* (Henrik Ibsen) with Frances Tomelty, David Horovitch, Paul Hilton; director, Gregory Hersov. (10 October) *The Critic and Dispute* (Richard Brinsley Sheridan and Pierre Marivaux) director, Matthew Lloyd. (15 November) *Snake in Fridge* (Brad Fraser) with Adam Sims, Adam James, Christopher Colquhoun; director, Braham Murray. (13 December) *The Magistrate* (Arthur Wing Pinero) with Richard O'Callaghan, Russell Dixon, Gordon Langford-Rowe; director, Gregory Hersov. (31 January) *A Moon for the Bisbegotten* (Eugene O'Neill) with Helen Schlesinger, Gerard Murphy, Jnr. Finbar Lynch; director, Matthew Lloyd. (28 February) *The Taming of the Shrew* (Shakespeare) with Joseph Alessi, John Branwell, Nick Cavaliere; director, Helena Kaut-Howson. (18 April) *Les Blancs* (Lorraine Hansberry). (27 June) *The Fall Guy* (George Feydeau, trans. Braham Murray and Robert Cogo-Fawcett) with Rachel Pickup, David Fielder, Chook Sibtain; director, Matthew Lloyd.

LIBRARY THEATRE: (5 September 2000) *Resident Alien* (Tim Fountain). (22 September) *The Beauty Queen of Leenane* (Martin McDonagh) director, Roger Haines. (27 October) *Closer* (Patrick Marber) director, Chris Honer. (23 January) *Rita, Sue and Bob Too* (Andrea Dunbar). (2 February) *Death of a Salesman* (Arthur Miller) director, Chris Honer. (20 March) *Feelgood* (Alistair Beaton). (27 March) Moll Flanders (dramatis. Les Smith). (25 May) *The Importance of Being Earnest* (Oscar Wilde).

SCARBOROUGH: STEPHEN JOSEPH (24 May 2001) *GamePlan* (written and directed by Alan Ayckbourn). (28 June) *FlatSpin* (written and directed by Alan Ayckbourn). (2 August) *Whispers Along the Patio* (David Cregan) director, Sam Walters. (30 August) *RolePlay* (written and directed by Alan Ayckbourn).

SHEFFIELD: CRUCIBLE (8 December 2001) *Guys and Dolls* (based on a story and characters of Damon Runyon, music and lyrics by Frank Loesser, book by Jo Swerling and Abe Burrows) director, Rachel Kavanaugh. (1 February) *The Man Who Had All The Luck* (Arthur Miller) director, David Hunt. (8 March) *Edward II* (Christopher Marlowe) with Joseph Fiennes; director, Michael Grandage. (31 May) *The Arbor* (Andrea Dunbar) director, Anna Mackmin.

SOUTHAMPTON: NUFFIELD (1 February 2001) *Spike* (Simon Day) with Richard Briers, Ann Davies and Lucy Briers; director, Dominic Hills. (26 April) *The Shagaround* (Maggie Neville) director, John Doyle.

STRATFORD: ROYAL SHAKESPEARE THEATRE (28 November 2000) *The Secret Garden* (lyrics Marsha Norman, music Lucy Simon, based on the novel Frances Hodgon Burnett) director, Adrian Noble. (6 February) *The Duchess of Malfi* (John Webster) director, Gale Edwards. (2 May) *Hamlet* (Shakespeare) director, Steven Pimlott. (10 May) *Twelfth Night* (Shakespeare) director, Lindsay Posner. (26 July) *Julius Caesar* (Shakespeare) director, Edward Hall.

SWAN (13 December 2000) *Henry VI: Parts 1, 2 and 3* (Shakespeare) director, Michael Boyd. (14 February) *Richard III* (Shakespeare) director, Michael Boyd. (28 March) *King John* (Shakespeare) director, Gregory Doran. (19 April) *Love in a Wood* (William Wycherley) director, Tim Supple. (19 July) *Jubilee* (Peter Barnes) director, Gregory Doran.

THE OTHER PLACE (30 November 2000) *The Tempest* (Shakespeare) director, James Macdonald. (29 March) *A Russian in the Woods* (Peter Whelan) director, Robert Delamere. (18 April) *The Lieutenant of Inishmore* (Martin McDonagh) director, Wilson Milam. (18 July) *The Prisoner's Dilemma* (David Edgar) director, Michael Attenborough.

# Weather

JULY 2000

Statistically, this was the dullest July since 1992 and the wettest since 1993. It was mostly cool and often cloudy, especially in the east. It was sunnier and warmer in the west. Thunderstorms caused local flooding in Surrey and Sussex during the first week but it was sunny and very warm during the third week. July was more unsettled with some thunder during the last week. The 1st–8th saw a slack low pressure area persisted for most of the time, with associated fronts migrating slowly southwards, bringing showery conditions to many places. Temperatures were near normal at first but it became cooler later. The 1st to the 5th were particularly wet with widespread outbreaks of rain and thundery showers. Overnight on the 4th–5th many southern counties of England were affected by an area of heavy thundery rain resulting in falls between three and four inches over parts of Surrey and Sussex. Local flooding was reported from the Redhill and Reigate area. After the clearance of a thundery rain belt from the south coast early on the 7th things became relatively drier and brighter for a time as a weak ridge of high pressure extended from the Azores high. During the 9th–11th the cloudy cool theme continued as low pressure moved south-east to the south North Sea. Winds became northerly with widespread outbreaks of rain and thundery showers. The 12th–16th saw low pressure centred to the east. North west and north winds brought mainly cloudy cool weather especially to eastern parts of England. Apart from some heavy rain early on the 13th around London it was mostly dry with western areas enjoying some good sunny periods. Over the 17th–24th high pressure was in control much of the time resulting in mostly dry warm or very warm weather, Wolverhampton reached 28°C on the 21st. There were long sunny periods and light winds particularly over central and western areas. Mostly clear nights allowed early morning mist and fog patches to form in places. East coast counties were cloudier and cooler. As the high pressure centre moved north a more organised area of cloud and occasional light rain or drizzle affected some east coast counties from the 22nd. The 25th–31st was more unsettled conditions returned with fairly wide-spread thundery showers on the 27th, 28th and 29th some were accompanied by hail. There were local patches of early morning mist and fog. Heavy rain affected north Wales and northern England on the 31st.

AUGUST 2000

August was changeable and mostly warm seeing thundery outbreaks alternated with warm dry sunny spells. It was hot at times in the south and some funnel clouds were observed in places. The 1st–3rd saw a low centred to the west transferred to the North Sea, filling as it did so. There were outbreaks of thundery rain on the 2nd–3rd especially over south-east England and East Anglia, with over two inch falls reported from parts of Sussex during the 3rd. During the 4th–11th, high pressure allowed mostly very warm weather with good sunny periods particularly in eastern and south-east England. It was mainly dry but showers, some thundery, broke out in places on the 7th, with more storms affecting Kent, Sussex and parts of Essex on the 8th. Wales and north-west England had less sunshine though staying warm. Northern England had heavy rain on the 9th while north-west areas were cloudy with rain and drizzle on the 10th. Over the 12th–17th an unsettled period generally with fairly frequent rain and thundery outbreaks affecting Wales, northern England and the Midlands later. South-east England and East Anglia were mostly dry, though hot at first on the 12th and 13th, temperatures returned to near normal by the 16th and 17th. Eastern and south-east England continued to benefit the most with good sunny periods. From the 18th–21st more thundery rain affected the Midlands, Wales and East Anglia, especially on the 18th. It was mainly rather cool with sunny periods. South-east England had most sunshine and was mainly dry. During the 21st heavy hail and thunderstorms were active over North Wales, the Pennines/Yorkshire and Humberside, with pronounced funnel clouds in attendance. Hail drifted to six inches in places, while 54 mm of rain fell in an hour at Bowland in the Pennines. Over the 22nd–24th high pressure to the north-east and mainly dry sunny weather prevailed, apart from some thundery rain in the extreme south-west of England. It became hot in the south later. The 25th–28th saw more thundery outbreaks especially in the south and east, where it was very warm or hot at first with Jersey Airport reaching 31°C and Southampton 30°C both on the 25th. One-inch hail smashed car windscreens at Lands End later the same day. The 29th–31st was mostly dry and sunny at first with some early morning mist and fog in places but rain, occasionally heavy, spread from the north-west during the 31st reaching London by evening.

SEPTEMBER 2000

Statistically this was the dullest September since 1994 and the wettest since 1981. It was very unsettled with frequent outbreaks of rain, heavy and thundery at times. A short hot sunny spell arrived on the second week but there was also local flooding in places. The 1st–9th saw mostly unsettled conditions as a series of lows passed close by. Some places had thundery rain at first, while the 3rd and 4th were mainly dry and sunny under a transient ridge of high pressure, but rain affected north-west areas later. Further rain broke out in most parts, with thunder reported in south-east England on the 5th. Over north Wales the rain was heavy at times, however England stayed mainly dry on the 7th. It became quite windy in places on the 6th and 7th with a deep depression south of Iceland. Temperatures were generally near normal with sunny periods between the wet spells. The 10th–13th was a mainly dry quiet period with some sunny and very warm or hot weather over much of the region. Hawarden near Chester touched 29°C on the 11th. Northern England was cloudier and cooler with outbreaks of rain, the lower temperatures moving south by the 13th. During the 14th–19th, apart from a mainly dry day on the 16th, a very wet period ensued with frequent outbreaks of rain, heavy and thundery in many places. Yorkshire, Cornwall and the Channel coast counties were particularly affected. Walderton in West Sussex collected 84 mm during the 15th, while many locations in south-east England experienced local flooding from thunderstorms. The 20th–23rd was rather cool with sunny periods and some thundery rain, heavy at times in the north, was followed by drier weather on the 22nd. The 23rd became very warm and sunny. The 24th–27th saw another very wet spell with frequent outbreaks of rain, heavy and thundery at times, as frontal systems crossed the region from the south-west. The 27th became windy especially over western parts as a vigorous

Atlantic low became centred off south-west Ireland. The 28th–30th saw more sunny periods and showers (some thundery) as the low over southern Ireland drifted slowly south-east to south-west England and filled. Some showers on the 30th were quite heavy in places, notably over north-west London around midday, moving into the Midlands later. A waterspout was spotted near Brighton, with a funnel cloud reported from Lincolnshire. Some parts were affected by mist and fog patches early in the morning and later in the evening.

### October 2000

Statistically, this was the wettest October since 1987 and the dullest since 1991. Generally, it was a very wet unsettled month. There was severe local flooding in Sussex and parts of Kent during the second week and a very stormy last week caused widespread flooding. Over the 1st–8th passing depressions and their associated frontal troughs provided a chilly mixed bag of weather. Most places had spells of rain or showers, sometimes heavy, with a gust of 71 kts recorded at Capel Curig/Gwynedd on the 3rd. There were sunny periods at times, with mainly dry weather on the 2nd and 3rd. Some showers turned thundery on the 5th especially in the south, while a transient ridge gave mainly dry conditions during the 6th. A cold wet day on the 7th gave way to scattered showers on the 8th. The 9th–12th was a very wet period as a complex low lingered over northern parts bringing much rain and wind on the 9th–10th. The situation was compounded later on the 11th–12th by a slow moving area of heavy rain and showers affecting Sussex and adjacent areas of Kent. Torrential downpours gave between four and six inches of rain overnight in many places causing severe local flooding, Plumpton in East Sussex received 144 mm of rain in 24 hours. The 13th–22nd saw more changeable weather as low pressure to the north-west drove belts of rain and showers across the region. Some days had good sunny periods and temperatures near normal. The 14th was cloudy with rain and drizzle while the 17th and 20th were wet in most places. The south-east and East Anglia were rather cold, cloudy and wet at times during the 21st and 22nd. The 23rd–26th was more unsettled as Atlantic depressions passed close by. Brisk westerly winds carried scattered showers to many places, most frequent and heaviest in western areas. The 27th–31st saw another very wet spell commenced, culminating in a severe storm and heavy rain during the 29th–30th as a deep depression crossed northern parts. Gusts between 70 and 80 kts were common around coasts with a gust of 84 kts recorded at Mumbles/Swansea. Flooding was widespread especially in the south as another two inches of rain fell, with some places in East Sussex collecting near 360 mm (over 14 inches) for the month. Bognor/West Sussex suffered damage from a tornado, while snow fell over higher parts of the Midlands and northern England. Some places in south-east England had their wettest month on record.

### November 2000

Statistically, this was the wettest November since 1970. It was very wet and unsettled, with widespread flooding at first. It was stormy at times especially in the west. Temperatures were mostly near normal with some overnight frost mid-month and it was very mild at the end of the month. The 1st–4th saw a very wet start as low pressure to the west moved northwards. Bands of rain and showers affected many places, especially western areas. Thunder was reported from Sussex on the 3rd, however England was mostly sunny on the 4th. During the 5th–8th a deep low moved from South West approaches to the English Channel then to the North Sea bringing copious amounts of rain and strong winds to many areas. Some of the showers became thundery on the 6th and 7th, but were mainly scattered by the 8th. Over the 9th–14th, low pressure moved from Iceland to Ireland, then to Scotland and the North Sea. Rain and showers affected many parts, in particular a slow moving cold front on the 11th–12th brought much wind and rain. Sunny intervals and clear skies later allowed some overnight frost. During the 15th–20th, after a chilly start (Redhill in Surrey recorded minus 6°C early on the 15th) a deep low off Iceland migrated to Scotland by 19th and 20th bringing yet more spells of rain and showers. Later some showers turned thundery, with sleet and snow reported over northern hills. The 21st–27th saw a very wet and disturbed period as a series of Atlantic depressions passed close by. Wind and rain were the dominant themes, especially on the 21st, 25th and 27th. Thunder accompanied some of the showers later during the 25th and 26th. A gust of 80 kts was recorded at Mumbles/Swansea on the 25th. After a rather cold start it became milder later. On the 27th another depression brought rain, hill and coastal fog and very mild air from the south. The 28th and 29th were mostly very mild and cloudy. Some heavy rain affected northern England on the 28th, while more showery conditions prevailed during the 29th particularly around western coasts. As the month ended further rain spread across from the south-west. Some places in Gwynedd/north Wales received more than 460 mm or 18 inches of rain.

### December 2000

Statistically, this was the mildest December since 1994. December was very mild and very wet during its first half with frequent gales and squally showers. There was some fog and frost during the third week and it was much colder with snow last week. The 1st–6th was wet and unsettled but very mild as complex low pressure to the west brought bands of rain and showers across the region. The rain was heavy at times especially in the west, however showers on the 2nd and 6th were mainly scattered. Eastern counties of England as usual were the most favoured for sunny periods. The 7th–13th saw some more deep depressions passed the region, in particular on the 7th–8th, and 12th–13th. It continued very mild and very wet especially during the 7th–8th and 12th. There were frequent squally thundery showers notably on the 8th, 9th, 10th and 13th, and a funnel cloud was seen at Scunthorpe. Coastal gales were frequent with a gust of 81 kts at Mumbles on the 13th. During the 14th–18th, after some showers there was a chilly spell with some fog and night frost. Where fog persisted it was cold or very cold. On the 18th milder weather and rain spread from the south. The 19th–22nd was mild and mostly wet at first with some hill and coastal fog, thereafter mainly overcast with temperatures not far from normal, although the south east became rather cold. The 23rd–27th saw pressure high over Greenland and low to the east and south colder weather edged slowly southwards. Wintry showers fell over northern England during Christmas day but there was rain further south. By the 26th and 27th it was cold or very cold everywhere though mainly dry, later on the 27th a band of rain and snow moved into western districts. Snow fell widely during the 28th, heavy in places in Wales and the north but only a few centimetres deep over southern counties. Snow showers in Wales, the north and north-east of England on the 29th contained the odd clap of thunder, earlier in the day minus 14.4°C was recorded at Credenhill/Hereford. Snow depths were about 10 cm in the Midlands and north Wales to between 8 and 15 cm in north-east England. Day temperatures stayed below freezing in places on the 29th and 30th especially in fog. After a mainly cold, dry, sunny day on the 30th, mild, wet and windy weather returned with a gust of 87 kts reported from the Lizard lighthouse.

### January 2001

Statistically this was the sunniest January since 1959. It was a very sunny month with temperatures and rainfall near average. It began with a wet and mild start, mainly dry for a fortnight, then colder with a little snow. The fourth week began mild wet and windy but frost and fog returned at month's end. Outbreaks of rain and showers were heavy at times particularly in the west. The 5th–11th saw a complex low-pressure area over the region migrated to southern Scandinavia by the 9th. There were scattered showers, some wintry, especially in northern and western areas, however south-east parts were often dry and mainly sunny. High pressure near Iceland then moved to central Scotland by 10th and 11th producing strong and cold easterly or north-easterly winds over southern England. From the 12th–20th, high-pressure slowly receded east to St Petersburg by 18th. The weather was mostly dry and sunny at first under the high pressure, but much colder from the 16th onwards with frost and fog at night. The fog was slow to clear at times in the morning. During the 18th to the 20th weak low pressure systems affected the region with snow falling in places. Some snow flurries were experienced in southern counties during the 18th, while a few centimetres of snow carpeted East Anglia on the 19th and also in places in north east England. Redesdale/Northumberland and Redhill/Surrey recorded minus 8.0°C early on the 19th and 20th. From the 21st–25th there was low pressure to the west and north west and a very mild, wet and windy period ensued, preceded by some snow in central and northern areas. Sunny periods alternated with bands of rain and showers, some of which were heavy and accompanied by thunder especially in the west and north. A gust of 63 kts was recorded at Llanbedr/Gwynedd on the 23rd. The period of the 26th–31st began with a wet start with outbreaks of rain, sleet and snow but the 27th, 28th and 29th were mainly sunny and dry with some fog and frost at night. An occluded front became stalled over England and Wales during the last two days. Although mild in the south west most places were rather cold with overnight frost, patchy fog and outbreaks of light rain and drizzle.

### February 2001

Statistically it was the coldest February since 1996, and the wettest since 1995. It was sunny and wet overall, very wet in south-east England and East Anglia, wet and unsettled during the first fortnight, then dry with fog and frost at night. The last week was colder with some snow later in the north. The 1st–8th saw a complex low pressure centred over the UK during this period, with bands of rain and showers affecting the region, sometimes heavy and accompanied by thunder. After a cold start with a little snow in the north it became mostly mild or very mild, especially in the south. A gust of 73 kts was recorded at Mumbles [south Wales] on the 6th, thundery rain broke out over southern counties of England on the 7th. A ridge of high pressure on the 9th gave way to more wind and rain on the 10th and 11th, north-west areas were particularly wet. A small active depression over south-east England on the 12th gave copious amounts of rain in many places before migrating to the extreme south-east by evening. High pressure dominated from the 13th–20th allowing much dry weather with frost and fog at night, and sunny periods by day, although the fog was slow to clear in places. Temperatures stayed chilly in areas where fog lingered. South-east England and East Anglia were more cloudy at times. The anticyclone receded westwards from the 21st–25th and low pressure over Scandinavia and north-westerly winds brought increasingly colder air southwards from the arctic. Though cloudy at first it became generally sunny later but with some severe frosts at night inland. Counties bordering the North Sea had wintry showers from time to time leaving a dusting of snow in places. Sennybridge in Powys recorded minus 8.8°C on the morning of the 25th. From the 26th–28th a depression off south-west Scotland moved south to Brittany, its associated fronts giving significant falls of snow in northern England and north Wales overnight the 27th and 28th, especially over high ground. Boltshope Park/Durham had 33 cm of snow on the morning of the 28th. Further south there were outbreaks of rain, sleet and snow.

### March 2001

Statistically, this was the wettest March since 1988. It was mostly cold with some snow at times especially in the north and over high ground. Relatively sunny and dry in the north and northwest. Dull and wet in the south and south-east of England and East Anglia. From the 1st–5th it was mostly dry but with generally slack winds and snow cover in many places especially in the north, some very low temperatures were recorded. Boltshope Park in Durham which had 30 cm of snow on the 1st, fell to minus 17.1°C overnight the 2nd–3rd. There was some wintry showers over eastern and south-east counties of England; otherwise most places had sunny periods, prolonged in the north and north-west. Light southerly winds and sunshine on the 5th gave a mild day. With a complex low pressure centred to the west and north-west from the 6th–12th a wet but very mild period ensued. Bands of rain and showers (some heavy with thunder) affected a number of areas more especially in the south and south-east and East Anglia. The 6th in particular was very wet, with more heavy rain on the 11th and 12th, the south-east and East Anglia again bearing the brunt. North-western areas saw the most sun. As the low pressure moved away to Scandinavia from the 13th–19th a new centre became established to the south-west, with fronts becoming slow moving over southern areas of England and Wales. It was generally dry at first except in the south and south-west where some heavy thundery rain broke out. During the 16th and 17th a rain band made some progress northwards with sleet and snow on its northern flank. A low near the English Channel on the 18th brought some rain, sleet and snow to many areas before moving to the continent. A ridge of high pressure on the 19th gave a mainly sunny day. Mild in the south at first, colder later. Weather fronts from the 20th–23rd made erratic progress northwards again bringing rain to many areas, preceded by sleet and snow especially over high ground and in the north. Wales had significant falls, and snowploughs were used on Exmoor where 5–8 cm of snow fell. It became very mild for a time in the south later. The 24th–26th saw easterly winds bring mainly cold, cloudy conditions with patchy rain and drizzle to most places. During the 27th–29th rain and showers, some heavy with hail and thunder affected many southern areas as an Atlantic depression moved across the region. A funnel cloud was reported from Guildford in Surrey and Newmarket. The 30th–31st was much warmer but with patchy rain and drizzle, Guernsey reached 17.5°C on the 31st.

### April 2001

Statistically, this was the coolest April since 1989. It was changeable and very wet overall. The month began with a wet start with some thundery rain at times, followed by a short dry sunny spell folowed by a cold third week with northerly winds and wintry showers. Frequent outbreaks of rain, thundery showers and hail featured for the remainder of the month. The 1st–10th was a wet unsettled period as a series of depressions passed to the north of Scotland or traversed eastwards across northern England. Although warm or very warm and dry at first (London reached 21.5°C on the 2nd), periods of rain and showers, some thundery and heavy affected many places soon after. Capel Curig/Gwynedd recorded a gust of 57 kts on the 5th. Some places in North Wales received from two to three inches of rain during the 5th and 6th. It became chilly later with some overnight frost in the north. There was some hill and coastal fog in the west at first on the 9th. The 11th–13th was mainly dry and sunny but rather cold under transient high pressure, allowing some overnight frost. Patchy rain and drizzle affected Wales and south-west England during the 12th and 13th. The 14th–20th saw cold northerly or north-westerly winds prevailing as pressure rose to the west and depressions tracked south-east from the Iceland area to Denmark. There were showers, some thundery, from time to time, these showers became distinctly wintry during the 18th to the 20th with hail, sleet, and snow mixed in. North Wales and counties adjacent to the North Sea were especially affected. There was widespread overnight frost, Sennybridge/Powys fell to minus 4.4°C early on the 19th. The 21st–28th was rather cold wet and unsettled as a complex area of low pressure encroached upon and established itself over the region from the North Atlantic. Bands of rain and showers often heavy with thunder and hail mixed in, were the prevailing feature of the weather, however most places had some sunny periods. The 22nd was very cold and wet as fronts became slow moving over western areas, Cynwyd/Denbighshire only just rose above 4°C. Bristol reported a heavy thunderstorm on the 24th and there was some damaging hail in Norfolk on the 25th. A funnel cloud was observed off the Norfolk coast on the 26th. The remaining days to the 28th saw more thundery showers in many areas. The 29th–30th saw a drier finish to the month as rain and some scattered thundery showers over southern England slowly petered out. There were good sunny spells in remaining areas of England and Wales.

### May 2001

Statistically it was the sunniest May since 1997. It was very warm with some thunder after a chilly start. There was a cool wet spell with thunderstorms mid month. It was mostly dry very warm and sunny thereafter, more changeable towards end of month. The 1st–3rd was rather unsettled and mostly cold with some thundery rain especially in south-east England and East Anglia. Drier and brighter in the north-west. The 4th–12th saw high pressure firmly established off Scotland the weather was mainly dry and sunny especially in the north. There was patchy fog at times especially around coasts. Many places had overnight frost at first, Shapfell/Cumbria fell to minus 3.9°C early on the 7th. Some thundery rain with hail and spectacular lightning broke out overnight the 9th–10th mainly over south-east England, East Anglia and south-west England. Thunderstorms also occurred over the south-east Midlands on the 11th. By the 11th and 12th it had become very warm or hot in many areas with prolonged sunshine, Southampton peaked at 27.3°C on the 12th. During the 13th–17th, low pressure centres traversing the region brought frequent outbreaks of heavy thundery rain to many areas, especially in the south, south-east and Midlands, with some localities experiencing torrential downpours. It was very warm at first but became colder later, the 17th being especially cold, wet and windy. From the 18th–25th, after some scattered showers and thundery outbreaks petered out on the 18th, high pressure migrated quickly from the south-west to cover the region. Although somewhat cloudy at first in north-western areas long sunny periods soon prevailed everywhere. Dry, warm or very warm conditions were established, especially in Wales and western areas. Counties nearer the relatively cool North Sea had their temperatures moderated to some extent by the onshore breezes. As the high pressure moved south over the 26th–27th, more changeable (though still warm) weather began to affect the region. As weak fronts crossed England and Wales, patchy rain and drizzle with hill and coastal fog affected many western and north western areas, with the rain being heavy over north Wales on the 27th. From the 28th–31st the warm or very warm theme continued with most places having long sunny periods, although there were areas of patchy rain in the west at first. During the 30th heavy rain affected northern England, and thunder was reported from Norfolk later. The 31st was cooler with showers down the east coast of England.

### June 2001

Statistically, This was the driest June since 1996. It was a dry sunny month especially in the south. Wet in north-east England and East Anglia. A cool first half with some thunderstorms followed by a wet thundery spell mid month. A heatwave during the last week ended with an outbreak of scattered thunderstorms. After some outbreaks of rain or showers on the 1st and 2nd a dry two days followed with good sunny periods, although it was often on the cool side. The 5th–10th saw low pressure close by to the north or north-east a rather unsettled rather wet period ensued. On the 5th heavy thunderstorms in the West Country gave two inches of rain at Newquay/Cornwall. After some scattered showers on the 6th, heavy thundery rain affected a number of places particularly in the north and east coast counties down to the Wash. Temperatures were in the cool category, though with good sunny periods especially in the south. A funnel cloud was seen off the Cornish coast and near Shoreham/West Sussex on the 8th. Redhill/Surrey recorded minus 1.8°C early on the 9th a near record for the south-east region. The 11th–13th was rather cool, mostly cloudy few days and generally dry, apart from some isolated light showers. During the 14th–16th a mainly cool, very wet spell occurred as a depression in the south-west approaches took up residence over southern England. Rain and showers often heavy and thundery broke out in many places. From the 17th–20th, after showers cleared from the east coast, a drier regime prevailed, but with some patchy rain in the north. The south became very warm with good sunny periods and Herne Bay reached 27°C on the 20th. The 21st–26th was virtually dry as high pressure sat close by giving long sunny periods in most parts. During the 24th to the 26th it became hot in many areas especially the south. Thundery rain affected north Wales early on the 26th and north-east England later that day, as falling pressure heralded an end to the heat-wave. Some thunderstorms also touched East Sussex and Kent in the evening. At Barbourne near Worcester a high of 32.6°C was reached that day, the highest for the UK so far this year. During the 27th–30th, after some thunderstorms moved away from east coast counties and East Anglia early on the 27th, a relatively cooler, fresher and more changeable weather pattern became established. Sunny spells alternated with occasional outbreaks of rain or showers, some of these were thundery over the Midlands and Eastern England later on the 29th.

## AVERAGE AND GENERAL VALUES 1999–2001 (JUNE)

| | *Rainfall (mm)* Average 1961–90 | 1999 | 2000 | 2001 | *Temperature (°C)* Average 1961–90 | 1999 | 2000 | 2001 | *Bright Sunshine (hrs per day)* Average 1961–90 | 1999 | 2000 | 2001 |
|---|---|---|---|---|---|---|---|---|---|---|---|---|
| ENGLAND AND WALES | | | | | | | | | | | | |
| January | 77 | 120 | 195 | 70 | 3.8 | 7.7 | 4.7 | 3.4 | 1.6 | 2.1 | 3.3 | 2.5 |
| February | 55 | 47 | 190 | 90 | 3.8 | 5.1 | 6.0 | 4.4 | 2.4 | 3.0 | 3.9 | 3.2 |
| March | 63 | 64 | 112 | 86 | 5.6 | 7.2 | 7.2 | 5.1 | 3.5 | 3.8 | 4.8 | 3.0 |
| April | 53 | 72 | 101 | 93 | 7.7 | 9.2 | 7.6 | 7.5 | 4.9 | 5.6 | 6.4 | 4.8 |
| May | 56 | 53 | 61 | 42 | 10.9 | 12.6 | 11.7 | 12.1 | 6.2 | 5.7 | 5.9 | 7.5 |
| June | 58 | 78 | 75 | 39 | 13.9 | 13.6 | 14.5 | 13.8 | 6.4 | 7.0 | 6.9 | – |
| July | 56 | 88 | 62 | – | 15.7 | 17.1 | 15.0 | – | 6.0 | 7.6 | 5.2 | – |
| August | 68 | 66 | 66 | – | 15.6 | 16.0 | 16.3 | – | 6.0 | 5.1 | 6.3 | – |
| September | 70 | 173 | 121 | – | 13.6 | 15.3 | 14.5 | – | 4.5 | 5.3 | 3.9 | – |
| October | 77 | 110 | 177 | – | 10.7 | 10.6 | 10.3 | – | 3.2 | 4.0 | 3.1 | – |
| November | 81 | 184 | 169 | – | 6.6 | 7.6 | 6.8 | – | 2.2 | 2.5 | 2.1 | – |
| December | 82 | 261 | 124 | – | 4.7 | 4.7 | 5.6 | – | 1.5 | 2.0 | 1.5 | – |
| YEAR | 796 | 1316 | 1453 | – | 9.4 | 10.5 | 10.0 | – | 4.0 | 4.5 | 3.9 | – |
| SCOTLAND | | | | | | | | | | | | |
| January | 117 | 138 | 185 | 86 | 3.1 | 3.7 | 4.1 | 1.9 | 1.3 | 1.4 | 1.5 | 1.8 |
| February | 78 | 88 | 190 | 91 | 3.1 | 3.4 | 4.0 | 2.4 | 2.4 | 2.9 | 2.3 | 2.7 |
| March | 94 | 79 | 112 | 74 | 4.6 | 5.3 | 5.8 | 2.8 | 3.2 | 3.8 | 2.7 | 4.1 |
| April | 60 | 74 | 101 | 70 | 6.5 | 7.4 | 5.6 | 5.7 | 4.8 | 4.9 | 4.6 | 4.8 |
| May | 67 | 81 | 61 | 41 | 9.3 | 9.8 | 9.5 | 10.4 | 5.6 | 5.9 | 7.9 | 7.1 |
| June | 67 | 87 | 75 | 87 | 12.1 | 11.1 | 11.1 | 11.0 | 5.6 | 5.1 | 5.4 | 4.8 |
| July | 74 | 88 | 51 | – | 13.6 | 14.0 | 12.9 | – | 4.9 | 5.4 | 5.2 | – |
| August | 92 | 66 | 110 | – | 13.5 | 13.2 | 13.6 | – | 4.9 | 5.1 | 4.7 | – |
| September | 111 | 173 | 151 | – | 11.5 | 12.8 | 12.1 | – | 3.5 | 3.5 | 3.4 | – |
| October | 120 | 110 | 221 | – | 9.1 | 9.1 | 8.6 | – | 2.6 | 2.2 | 2.8 | – |
| November | 118 | 184 | 164 | – | 5.3 | 6.2 | 5.0 | – | 1.7 | 1.5 | 1.8 | – |
| December | 115 | 261 | 170 | – | 3.9 | 2.4 | 3.8 | – | 1.0 | 1.2 | 1.1 | – |
| YEAR | 1113 | 1429 | 1591 | – | 7.9 | 8.2 | 8.0 | – | 3.5 | 3.6 | 3.6 | – |

*Source:* Data provided by the Met Office

## WEATHER RECORDS

WORLD RECORDS

| | |
|---|---|
| Maximum air temperature<br>San Louis, Mexico, 11 August 1933 | 57.8°C/136°F |
| Minimum air temperature<br>Vostok, Antarctica, 21 July 1983 | –89.2°C/–128.56°F |
| Greatest rainfall in one day<br>Cilaos, Isle de Réunion, 16 March 1952 | 1870 mm/73.62 in |
| Greatest rainfall in one calendar month<br>Cherrapunji, Assam, July 1861 | 9300 mm/366.14 in |
| Greatest annual rainfall total<br>Cherrapunji, Assam, 1861 | 22,990 mm/905.12 in |
| Fastest gust of wind<br>Mt Washington Observatory, USA, 12 April 1934 | 201 knots/231 mph |

UNITED KINGDOM RECORDS

| | |
|---|---|
| Maximum air temperature<br>Cheltenham, Glos, 3 August 1990 | 37.1°C/98.8°F |
| Minimum air temperature<br>Braemar, Grampian, 11 February 1895 and 10 January 1982 | –27.2°C/–17°F |
| Greatest rainfall in one day<br>Martinstown, Dorset, 18 July 1955 | 280 mm/11 in |
| Greatest annual rainfall total<br>Sprinkling Tarn, Cumbria, 1954 | 6528 mm/257 in |
| Fastest gust of wind<br>Cairngorm, Highland, 20 March 1986 | 150 knots/173 mph |
| Fastest low-level gust*<br>Fraserburgh, Grampian, 13 February 1989 | 123 knots/141.7 mph |
| Highest mean hourly speed<br>Great Dun Fell, Cumbria, December 1974 | 92 knots/106 mph |
| Highest low-level mean hourly speed*<br>Shoreham-by-Sea, Sussex, 16 October 1987 | 72 knots/83 mph |

* below 200 m/656 ft

## WIND FORCE MEASURES

The *Beaufort Scale* of wind force has been accepted internationally and is used in communicating weather conditions. Devised originally by Admiral Sir Francis Beaufort in 1805, it now consists of the numbers 0–17, each representing a certain strength or velocity of wind at 10 m (33 ft) above ground in the open.

| *Scale no.* | *Wind Force* | *mph* | *knots* |
|---|---|---|---|
| 0 | Calm | 1 | 1 |
| 1 | Light air | 1–3 | 1–3 |
| 2 | Slight breeze | 4–7 | 4–6 |
| 3 | Gentle breeze | 8–12 | 7–10 |
| 4 | Moderate breeze | 13–18 | 11–16 |
| 5 | Fresh breeze | 19–24 | 17–21 |
| 6 | Strong breeze | 25–31 | 22–27 |
| 7 | High wind | 32–38 | 28–33 |
| 8 | Gale | 39–46 | 34–40 |
| 9 | Strong gale | 47–54 | 41–47 |
| 10 | Whole gale | 55–63 | 48–55 |
| 11 | Storm | 64–72 | 56–63 |
| 12 | Hurricane | 73–82 | 64–71 |
| 13 | – | 83–92 | 72–80 |
| 14 | – | 93–103 | 81–89 |
| 15 | – | 104–114 | 90–99 |
| 16 | – | 115–125 | 100–108 |
| 17 | – | 126–136 | 109–118 |

## TEMPERATURE, RAINFALL AND SUNSHINE

At selected climatological reporting stations, July 2000–June 2001 and calendar year 2000

Ht height (in metres) of station above mean sea level
°C mean air temperature
Rain total monthly rainfall
Sun monthy total (hours)

*Source:* Data provided by the Met Office

| | | *July 2000* | | | *August 2000* | | | *September 2000* | | | *October 2000* | | |
|---|---|---|---|---|---|---|---|---|---|---|---|---|---|
| | Ht m | °C | Rain mm | Sun hrs | °C | Rain mm | Sun hrs | °C | Rain mm | Sun hrs | °C | Rain mm | Sun hrs |
| Lerwick | 82 | 11.1 | 28.2 | 87.9 | 11.9 | 87.5 | 109.2 | 11.2 | 145.6 | 91.7 | 9.3 | 144.9 | 1.9 |
| Stornoway | 15 | 12.8 | 22.7 | 141.5 | 13.8 | 74.7 | 146.6 | 12.7 | 97.3 | 133.2 | 9.8 | 190.3 | 96.2 |
| Dyce | 65 | 12.9 | 15.0 | 122.3 | 14.2 | 81.6 | 148.0 | 12.4 | 102.4 | 109.9 | 9.0 | 120.2 | 3.1 |
| Eskdalemuir | 242 | 13.2 | 76.1 | 173.2 | 13.3 | 158.9 | 127.1 | 12.0 | 188.3 | 79.4 | 7.7 | 251.3 | 69.9 |
| Aldergrove | 68 | 15.1 | 14.2 | 156.4 | 15.5 | 133.5 | 182.2 | 13.9 | 134.2 | 115.7 | 9.3 | 147.2 | 103.8 |
| Leeds | 64 | 15.5 | 47.0 | 134.2 | 17.3 | 41.2 | 193.4 | 14.8 | 131.4 | 116.4 | 10.6 | 121.7 | 105.5 |
| Valley | 10 | 15.4 | 74.0 | 230.8 | 16.0 | 59.0 | 211.4 | 14.9 | 137.6 | 122.2 | 11.3 | 209.0 | 102.6 |
| Coleshill | 98 | 15.4 | 24.9 | n/a | 16.9 | 62.0 | n/a | 14.8 | 126.1 | n/a | 10.5 | 120.2 | n/a |
| Skegness | 6 | 14.5 | 34.5 | 129.6 | 17.3 | 43.8 | 217.3 | 15.5 | 90.8 | 115.0 | 10.8 | 84.0 | 1115.1 |
| Bristol | 42 | 17.3 | 54.1 | 199.8 | 18.2 | 103.4 | 212.6 | 16.0 | 141.8 | 121.0 | 11.6 | 194.4 | 102.6 |
| St Mawgan | 103 | 15.8 | 58.0 | 222.6 | 16.6 | 80.8 | 178.2 | 15.1 | 166.6 | 146.9 | 11.2 | 181.8 | 105.1 |
| Hastings | 45 | 15.8 | 43.0 | n/a | 17.8 | 48.1 | 249.8 | 16.4 | 122.0 | 143.8 | 12.2 | 200.9 | 99.4 |

| | *November 2000* | | | *December 2000* | | | *The Year 2000* | | | *January 2001* | | | *February 2001* | | |
|---|---|---|---|---|---|---|---|---|---|---|---|---|---|---|---|
| | °C | Rain mm | Sun hrs | °C | Rain mm | Sun hrs | °C | Rain mm | Sun hrs | °C | Rain mm | Sun hrs | °C | Rain mm | Sun hrs |
| Lerwick | 6.6 | 182.4 | 59.2 | 4.7 | 140.4 | 16.3 | 7.5 | 117.0 | 95.0 | 4.4 | 79.7 | 40.9 | 1.9 | 140.3 | 84.9 |
| Stornoway | 6.2 | 110.8 | 52.3 | 5.5 | 148.1 | 23.1 | 9.0 | 115.0 | 112.0 | 4.0 | 60.5 | 78.7 | 3.7 | 64.8 | 65.5 |
| Dyce | 5.5 | 138.4 | 92.9 | 4.4 | 119.7 | 42.5 | 8.4 | 72.0 | 125.0 | 2.9 | 63.0 | 72.3 | 2.6 | 83.0 | 82.6 |
| Eskdalemuir | 4.5 | 218.1 | 36.8 | 3.2 | 234.9 | 43.5 | 7.9 | 160.4 | 99.2 | 1.7 | 91.6 | 50.3 | 1.6 | 138.8 | 72.3 |
| Aldergrove | 5.9 | 111.0 | 40.4 | 4.9 | 117.0 | 33.1 | 10.0 | 82.0 | 120.2 | 3.4 | 39.6 | 76.4 | 3.9 | 55.3 | 94.3 |
| Leeds | 7.0 | 125.1 | 57.8 | 5.7 | 68.8 | 53.5 | 10.6 | 72.0 | 124.0 | 3.7 | 28.3 | 82.1 | 4.5 | 60.8 | 108.9 |
| Valley | 8.4 | 220.0 | 40.3 | 6.7 | 127.0 | 40.3 | 10.7 | 98.5 | 141.3 | 4.9 | 51.6 | 93.6 | 5.1 | 92.0 | 83.4 |
| Coleshill | 6.9 | 121.4 | n/a | 5.2 | 124.1 | n/a | 10.3 | 73.3 | n/a | 3.0 | 51.8 | n/a | 4.4 | 83.6 | n/a |
| Skegness | 7.2 | 111.4 | 81.8 | 5.7 | 53.8 | 62.9 | 10.7 | 61.2 | 137.3 | 3.8 | 32.9 | 101.2 | 4.5 | 61.7 | 81.7 |
| Bristol | 8.3 | 146.0 | 66.9 | 7.4 | 111.2 | 57.5 | 11.7 | 97.8 | 131.3 | 5.1 | 58.8 | 79.2 | 6.1 | 64.0 | 103.5 |
| St Mawgan | 8.4 | 187.0 | 68.0 | 7.8 | 170.6 | 64.9 | 11.0 | 105.0 | 138.0 | 5.7 | 123.6 | 70.9 | 6.7 | 71.2 | 114.3 |
| Hastings | 8.5 | 178.7 | 78.8 | 7.3 | 110.4 | 54.8 | 11.3 | 88.7 | 84.8 | 5.1 | 135.9 | 105.2 | 5.9 | 105.2 | 84.8 |

| | *March 2001* | | | *April 2001* | | | *May 2001* | | | *June 2001* | | |
|---|---|---|---|---|---|---|---|---|---|---|---|---|
| | °C | Rain mm | Sun hrs | °C | Rain mm | Sun hrs | °C | Rain mm | Sun hrs | °C | Rain mm | Sun hrs |
| Lerwick | 3.0 | 95.3 | 121.1 | 5.3 | 65.2 | 158.7 | 8.5 | 29.7 | 186.2 | 9.4 | 54.0 | 138.6 |
| Stornoway | 4.5 | 54.0 | 155.6 | 6.4 | 56.9 | 165.5 | 10.4 | 32.7 | 205.1 | 10.8 | 55.3 | 164.9 |
| Dyce | 3.2 | 108.8 | 114.5 | 6.6 | 45.8 | 170.2 | 10.9 | 21.4 | 255.8 | 11.9 | 44.2 | 154.7 |
| Eskdalemuir | 1.8 | 73.4 | 107.1 | 5.3 | 99.0 | 114.6 | 10.5 | 37.6 | 236.8 | 11.0 | 94.2 | 104.8 |
| Aldergrove | 4.5 | 47.8 | 127.7 | 7.1 | 58.2 | 142.6 | 12.2 | 44.2 | 224.5 | 12.9 | 57.2 | 128.4 |
| Leeds | 5.2 | 41.0 | 122.4 | 8.0 | 67.3 | 133.5 | 13.1 | 26.8 | 230.4 | 14.5 | 18.0 | 173.4 |
| Valley | 5.8 | 45.4 | 159.6 | 7.8 | 81.8 | 173.8 | 12.4 | 44.4 | 255.1 | 13.5 | 30.7 | 212.8 |
| Coleshill | 5.0 | 85.4 | n/a | 7.7 | 110.7 | n/a | 12.3 | 53.6 | n/a | 14.0 | 50.4 | n/a |
| Skegness | 5.4 | 46.3 | 99.9 | 7.6 | 70.5 | 140.3 | 11.4 | 24.7 | n/a | 13.9 | 26.2 | n/a |
| Bristol | 6.7 | 96.2 | 81.3 | 9.1 | 79.0 | 168.3 | 13.9 | 38.8 | n/a | 15.9 | 32.2 | n/a |
| St Mawgan | 7.4 | 117.0 | 92.7 | 8.6 | 92.8 | 160.0 | 12.7 | 21.4 | 289.3 | 14.3 | 78.0 | 256.6 |
| Hastings | 6.4 | 143.1 | 70.5 | 8.7 | 72.1 | 165.5 | 13.3 | 24.1 | 275.1 | 15.0 | 14.0 | 289.3 |

## METEOROLOGICAL OBSERVATIONS London (Heathrow)

Temperature maxima and minima cover the 24-hour period 9 - 9 h; mean wind speed is 10 m above ground; rainfall is for the 24 hours starting on 9 h on the day of entry; sunshine is for the 24 hours. *Source:* Data provided by the Met Office

### JULY 2000

| *Day* | Temperature Max C° | Temperature Min C° | Wind knots | Sun hrs | Rain mm |
|---|---|---|---|---|---|
| 1 | 20.9 | 14.4 | 4.0 | 3.0 | 0.2 |
| 2 | 22.3 | 13.0 | 2.8 | 3.0 | 0.2 |
| 3 | 23.3 | 14.2 | 3.7 | 5.8 | Trace |
| 4 | 18.3 | 15.4 | 4.4 | 0.0 | 17.0 |
| 5 | 17.1 | 13.7 | 2.9 | 0.0 | Trace |
| 6 | 22.7 | 12.6 | 3.6 | 3.7 | 0.4 |
| 7 | 17.9 | 13.5 | 6.8 | 4.0 | 0.0 |
| 8 | 17.9 | 11.5 | 6.0 | 1.4 | 0.6 |
| 9 | 19.1 | 13.8 | 8.1 | 1.1 | 9.0 |
| 10 | 16.1 | 11.8 | 8.5 | 1.3 | 10.4 |
| 11 | 16.3 | 9.6 | 5.8 | 5.0 | Trace |
| 12 | 18.7 | 7.5 | 6.0 | 3.0 | 4.2 |
| 13 | 20.9 | 13.6 | 6.0 | 2.7 | 4.8 |
| 14 | 16.9 | 12.9 | 8.0 | 0.7 | Trace |
| 15 | 18.1 | 9.1 | 7.1 | 7.4 | Trace |
| 16 | 18.2 | 9.8 | 4.5 | 7.6 | 0.0 |
| 17 | 22.6 | 9.8 | 1.9 | 11.7 | 0.0 |
| 18 | 24.7 | 10.9 | 3.4 | 10.7 | 0.0 |
| 19 | 25.2 | 13.0 | 3.9 | 14.6 | 0.0 |
| 20 | 25.3 | 14.9 | 3.7 | 11.7 | 0.0 |
| 21 | 25.9 | 14.4 | 5.9 | 14.4 | 0.0 |
| 22 | 21.6 | 12.9 | 9.2 | 9.5 | Trace |
| 23 | 19.0 | 12.8 | 8.8 | 0.8 | Trace |
| 24 | 17.2 | 12.9 | 6.6 | 0.1 | Trace |
| 25 | 19.0 | 12.8 | 1.4 | 0.7 | 0.0 |
| 26 | 23.4 | 13.9 | 3.4 | 8.6 | 0.0 |
| 27 | 25.0 | 15.1 | 3.8 | 7.5 | Trace |
| 28 | 20.9 | 14.5 | 3.9 | 4.5 | 5.8 |
| 29 | 24.9 | 13.4 | 4.6 | 9.0 | 0.2 |
| 30 | 24.8 | 13.7 | 3.8 | 9.5 | 0.0 |
| 31 | 25.3 | 16.1 | 5.8 | 11.7 | 0.0 |

### AUGUST 2000

| *Day* | Temperature Max C° | Temperature Min C° | Wind knots | Sun hrs | Rain mm |
|---|---|---|---|---|---|
| 1 | 24.5 | 14.8 | 5.7 | 8.8 | 0.0 |
| 2 | 23.5 | 13.0 | 9.1 | 7.8 | 4.2 |
| 3 | 19.7 | 15.0 | 5.0 | 3.1 | 5.8 |
| 4 | 22.4 | 14.6 | 4.2 | 8.0 | 0.0 |
| 5 | 24.2 | 12.2 | 3.0 | 8.5 | Trace |
| 6 | 24.7 | 16.0 | 4.8 | 4.1 | Trace |
| 7 | 23.0 | 17.4 | 4.0 | 2.0 | 0.0 |
| 8 | 22.6 | 16.2 | 3.1 | 2.8 | 5.6 |
| 9 | 23.9 | 14.5 | 6.7 | 3.9 | 0.0 |
| 10 | 25.4 | 16.5 | 6.3 | 6.1 | Trace |
| 11 | 24.9 | 15.3 | 2.9 | 7.4 | 0.0 |
| 12 | 27.4 | 13.4 | 5.1 | 12.8 | Trace |
| 13 | 23.6 | 15.1 | 6.0 | 0.9 | 1.0 |
| 14 | 23.7 | 17.9 | 9.6 | 1.4 | Trace |
| 15 | 24.4 | 14.3 | 8.0 | 8.2 | Trace |
| 16 | 23.1 | 14.7 | 8.8 | 7.9 | 0.1 |
| 17 | 23.1 | 14.7 | 7.8 | 8.1 | 2.4 |
| 18 | 19.9 | 13.2 | 5.3 | 0.1 | 0.6 |
| 19 | 23.2 | 14.2 | 6.0 | 10.7 | 0.0 |
| 20 | 21.7 | 12.4 | 3.4 | 6.4 | 0.0 |
| 21 | 22.2 | 10.3 | 5.0 | 11.6 | 0.0 |
| 22 | 22.7 | 10.6 | 5.3 | 8.0 | 0.0 |
| 23 | 23.9 | 13.3 | 8.4 | 13.1 | 0.0 |
| 24 | 27.0 | 12.8 | 5.6 | 12.4 | 0.0 |
| 25 | 26.2 | 14.7 | 11.8 | 10.9 | 2.2 |
| 26 | 19.7 | 18.3 | 5.1 | 0.0 | 3.8 |
| 27 | 21.8 | 13.2 | 4.2 | 4.5 | 3.8 |
| 28 | 20.1 | 11.6 | 3.0 | 7.7 | 1.2 |
| 29 | 21.8 | 10.3 | 2.2 | 8.4 | 0.0 |
| 30 | 22.2 | 13.0 | 5.5 | 9.5 | 0.0 |
| 31 | 22.6 | 10.5 | 6.2 | 6.3 | 1.6 |

### SEPTEMBER 2000

| *Day* | Temperature Max C° | Temperature Min C° | Wind knots | Sun hrs | Rain mm |
|---|---|---|---|---|---|
| 1 | 18.9 | 13.0 | 5.8 | 2.7 | 4.6 |
| 2 | 19.9 | 11.7 | 5.8 | 4.2 | 0.8 |
| 3 | 18.6 | 9.4 | 4.8 | 9.8 | 0.0 |
| 4 | 20.5 | 6.9 | 2.5 | 11.0 | 0.0 |
| 5 | 20.4 | 10.9 | 6.3 | 1.6 | 0.4 |
| 6 | 20.7 | 14.1 | 8.3 | 4.8 | 0.8 |
| 7 | 20.3 | 8.6 | 7.0 | 0.7 | Trace |
| 8 | 20.2 | 15.0 | 4.9 | 0.0 | 4.4 |
| 9 | 22.3 | 15.6 | 2.8 | 2.2 | 0.2 |
| 10 | 25.6 | 14.8 | 2.4 | 11.0 | 0.0 |
| 11 | 27.5 | 15.6 | 5.0 | 9.7 | 0.0 |
| 12 | 24.0 | 16.0 | 6.7 | 6.7 | 0.0 |
| 13 | 21.0 | 13.9 | 3.8 | 2.9 | 0.0 |
| 14 | 21.6 | 12.4 | 6.5 | 3.0 | 11.0 |
| 15 | 18.5 | 16.0 | 6.0 | 1.3 | 19.6 |
| 16 | 18.2 | 13.4 | 7.6 | 0.9 | 0.0 |
| 17 | 20.6 | 11.7 | 5.3 | 0.9 | 0.0 |
| 18 | 16.8 | 13.6 | 6.6 | 0.0 | 13.8 |
| 19 | 15.6 | 11.9 | 4.8 | 0.0 | 16.4 |
| 20 | 16.9 | 10.4 | 6.6 | 3.5 | 0.4 |
| 21 | 18.6 | 7.2 | 6.6 | 2.9 | 1.0 |
| 22 | 21.5 | 14.3 | 6.8 | 8.5 | Trace |
| 23 | 24.8 | 14.1 | 9.9 | 10.6 | 0.0 |
| 24 | 16.8 | 13.6 | 5.5 | 1.3 | 11.0 |
| 25 | 18.5 | 10.7 | 6.8 | 4.7 | 6.8 |
| 26 | 20.7 | 12.1 | 8.5 | 4.3 | 0.4 |
| 27 | 18.2 | 11.7 | 12.1 | 3.3 | 5.4 |
| 28 | 18.4 | 13.2 | 7.5 | 5.8 | 3.4 |
| 29 | 18.9 | 11.5 | 8.5 | 7.1 | Trace |
| 30 | 17.9 | 12.3 | 2.4 | 6.7 | 5.4 |

### OCTOBER 2000

| *Day* | Temperature Max C° | Temperature Min C° | Wind knots | Sun hrs | Rain mm |
|---|---|---|---|---|---|
| 1 | 18.6 | 7.7 | 4.6 | 6.7 | 10.0 |
| 2 | 15.3 | 9.9 | 7.1 | 0.3 | 0.2 |
| 3 | 16.4 | 8.5 | 8.4 | 0.0 | 0.8 |
| 4 | 16.3 | 12.7 | 6.6 | 4.0 | 0.2 |
| 5 | 15.7 | 11.1 | 6.5 | 7.3 | 0.8 |
| 6 | 15.1 | 5.4 | 4.0 | 8.6 | 5.0 |
| 7 | 13.2 | 9.1 | 3.7 | 0.0 | 8.6 |
| 8 | 15.6 | 9.5 | 4.0 | 6.1 | 0.0 |
| 9 | 12.4 | 5.6 | 6.1 | 0.5 | 24.0 |
| 10 | 13.3 | 6.3 | 9.6 | 3.5 | 8.8 |
| 11 | 14.3 | 6.7 | 8.5 | 5.1 | 3.8 |
| 12 | 13.5 | 8.0 | 2.0 | 1.1 | 4.2 |
| 13 | 16.0 | 6.4 | 1.0 | 4.2 | Trace |
| 14 | 13.9 | 8.2 | 4.2 | 0.0 | Trace |
| 15 | 15.6 | 7.8 | 1.5 | 4.7 | 2.8 |
| 16 | 13.9 | 10.8 | 4.0 | 0.1 | 1.6 |
| 17 | 14.9 | 5.1 | 5.0 | 7.2 | 5.0 |
| 18 | 16.3 | 9.4 | 6.5 | 0.1 | 1.0 |
| 19 | 15.2 | 7.6 | 4.0 | 9.2 | 0.0 |
| 20 | 14.1 | 7.0 | 5.0 | 0.1 | 20.2 |
| 21 | 11.5 | 10.4 | 3.1 | 0.0 | 0.2 |
| 22 | 14.3 | 9.6 | 3.7 | 0.3 | Trace |
| 23 | 16.0 | 9.4 | 10.0 | 4.0 | 0.2 |
| 24 | 14.2 | 9.7 | 8.9 | 0.0 | 0.2 |
| 25 | 15.3 | 11.0 | 12.6 | 2.2 | Trace |
| 26 | 14.5 | 7.1 | 7.9 | 6.3 | 3.0 |
| 27 | 15.4 | 9.5 | 9.3 | 0.0 | 9.0 |
| 28 | 16.0 | 11.8 | 12.2 | 0.0 | 7.2 |
| 29 | 13.4 | 7.8 | 15.9 | 5.4 | 36.6 |
| 30 | 11.3 | 8.6 | 17.8 | 4.4 | 1.6 |
| 31 | 13.3 | 6.3 | 10.5 | 6.6 | 0.4 |

## NOVEMBER 2000

| | Temperature Max C° | Min C° | Wind knots | Sun hrs | Rain mm |
|---|---|---|---|---|---|
| *Day* 1 | 11.6 | 7.0 | 9.9 | 6.9 | 6.0 |
| 2 | 10.9 | 3.6 | 9.2 | 3.2 | 5.2 |
| 3 | 11.4 | 5.7 | 4.6 | 6.2 | Trace |
| 4 | 11.4 | 2.9 | 3.3 | 6.8 | Trace |
| 5 | 10.9 | 2.5 | 9.5 | 1.0 | 24.8 |
| 6 | 11.0 | 7.0 | 6.6 | 0.2 | 5.4 |
| 7 | 10.7 | 7.7 | 5.5 | 1.0 | 1.0 |
| 8 | 9.2 | 6.4 | 6.1 | 0.1 | Trace |
| 9 | 10.2 | 6.1 | 7.7 | 0.2 | Trace |
| 10 | 12.1 | 3.7 | 6.0 | 5.9 | 0.8 |
| 11 | 12.8 | 5.3 | 12.7 | 0.0 | 8.8 |
| 12 | 11.1 | 8.3 | 6.3 | 5.0 | 0.2 |
| 13 | 10.8 | 2.4 | 2.5 | 7.6 | 0.2 |
| 14 | 8.7 | 1.2 | 0.8 | 5.4 | 0.4 |
| 15 | 10.2 | -1.2 | 2.8 | 0.5 | 5.6 |
| 16 | 10.4 | 1.0 | 6.7 | 4.5 | 0.1 |
| 17 | 9.4 | 0.4 | 4.5 | 2.5 | Trace |
| 18 | 11.9 | 2.2 | 6.1 | 1.0 | 3.2 |
| 19 | 10.9 | 7.2 | 6.7 | 1.1 | 0.8 |
| 20 | 7.0 | 2.0 | 2.7 | 2.5 | 0.2 |
| 21 | 10.1 | 3.8 | 6.8 | 0.4 | 4.6 |
| 22 | 10.9 | 4.0 | 12.3 | 3.4 | 0.2 |
| 23 | 8.4 | 3.3 | 3.3 | 0.0 | 5.4 |
| 24 | 11.0 | 2.7 | 5.4 | 3.3 | 1.4 |
| 25 | 11.6 | 5.0 | 10.3 | 0.0 | 6.8 |
| 26 | 10.5 | 7.3 | 12.7 | 4.9 | Trace |
| 27 | 14.0 | 3.7 | 7.0 | 0.0 | 9.0 |
| 28 | 15.6 | 7.4 | 11.0 | 0.0 | 1.2 |
| 29 | 14.2 | 10.0 | 9.1 | 0.2 | 0.8 |
| 30 | 12.2 | 6.3 | 8.7 | 1.1 | 7.4 |

## DECEMBER 2000

| | Temperature Max C° | Min C° | Wind knots | Sun hrs | Rain mm |
|---|---|---|---|---|---|
| *Day* 1 | 13.7 | 8.9 | 11.4 | 0.0 | 1.6 |
| 2 | 12.9 | 9.6 | 7.6 | 3.8 | 0.2 |
| 3 | 11.3 | 3.7 | 6.8 | 5.2 | 7.2 |
| 4 | 13.8 | 6.7 | 13.9 | 0.8 | 4.6 |
| 5 | 13.4 | 11.3 | 12.9 | 0.0 | 3.0 |
| 6 | 12.7 | 11.1 | 10.9 | 0.0 | 0.4 |
| 7 | 14.3 | 7.1 | 9.5 | 0.0 | 13.6 |
| 8 | 12.4 | 8.4 | 15.8 | 3.7 | 2.2 |
| 9 | 11.5 | 7.6 | 10.6 | 2.9 | 2.4 |
| 10 | 13.4 | 9.0 | 12.8 | 0.9 | 6.0 |
| 11 | 14.2 | 9.3 | 14.3 | 0.0 | 2.4 |
| 12 | 13.7 | 12.7 | 15.6 | 0.0 | 10.0 |
| 13 | 12.2 | 9.4 | 17.1 | 3.3 | Trace |
| 14 | 9.5 | 5.3 | 7.0 | 5.0 | 0.6 |
| 15 | 7.1 | 2.2 | 4.6 | 7.0 | 0.0 |
| 16 | 4.4 | -1.1 | 1.5 | 0.3 | 0.2 |
| 17 | 6.3 | 1.0 | 1.7 | 0.1 | 0.4 |
| 18 | 8.2 | 3.1 | 5.8 | 0.0 | 2.8 |
| 19 | 10.0 | 5.8 | 6.5 | 0.0 | Trace |
| 20 | 9.8 | 7.0 | 8.9 | 0.0 | Trace |
| 21 | 6.7 | 6.2 | 7.8 | 0.0 | Trace |
| 22 | 5.9 | 3.1 | 5.6 | 0.0 | 0.0 |
| 23 | 6.6 | 2.8 | 6.9 | 0.0 | 2.0 |
| 24 | 6.5 | 4.0 | 7.5 | 0.0 | 6.2 |
| 25 | 4.3 | 3.9 | 13.2 | 0.0 | Trace |
| 26 | 2.5 | 1.0 | 9.3 | 0.0 | 0.0 |
| 27 | 3.0 | 1.5 | 5.7 | 0.1 | 1.8 |
| 28 | 2.9 | -3.5 | 3.0 | 4.1 | 0.0 |
| 29 | 1.2 | -5.5 | 2.1 | 5.6 | Trace |
| 30 | 3.1 | -5.3 | 5.0 | 7.2 | 0.0 |
| 31 | 10.1 | -4.6 | 10.2 | 0.0 | 6.3 |

## JANUARY 2001

| | Temperature Max C° | Min C° | Wind knots | Sun hrs | Rain mm |
|---|---|---|---|---|---|
| *Day* 1 | 11.1 | -0.5 | 11.7 | 2.0 | 3.2 |
| 2 | 10.8 | 9.0 | 12.8 | 0.3 | 3.4 |
| 3 | 10.5 | 3.5 | 9.3 | 2.9 | 8.0 |
| 4 | 9.4 | 3.7 | 7.8 | 0.1 | 4.6 |
| 5 | 7.6 | 6.7 | 4.4 | 0.0 | Trace |
| 6 | 8.5 | 3.1 | 5.4 | 4.5 | 0.4 |
| 7 | 7.4 | 2.3 | 5.2 | 7.4 | 0.0 |
| 8 | 7.8 | 1.7 | 4.0 | 3.3 | 0.6 |
| 9 | 5.6 | 0.0 | 3.2 | 2.6 | 0.0 |
| 10 | 6.4 | 1.3 | 12.5 | 0.0 | Trace |
| 11 | 5.5 | 4.3 | 15.7 | 0.0 | 0.0 |
| 12 | 7.4 | 4.2 | 14.9 | 3.7 | 0.0 |
| 13 | 7.6 | 1.5 | 7.8 | 7.4 | 0.0 |
| 14 | 7.5 | 1.5 | 8.3 | 7.6 | 0.0 |
| 15 | 4.9 | 2.2 | 8.7 | 5.1 | 0.0 |
| 16 | 3.5 | -2.2 | 4.0 | 4.3 | 0.0 |
| 17 | 4.8 | -2.9 | 1.3 | 4.8 | 0.0 |
| 18 | 3.3 | -2.5 | 0.1 | 2.0 | 0.0 |
| 19 | 2.1 | -3.9 | 0.8 | 0.0 | Trace |
| 20 | 2.4 | -2.6 | 1.7 | 0.9 | 3.4 |
| 21 | 7.9 | -2.6 | 5.5 | 0.0 | 4.4 |
| 22 | 9.9 | 1.9 | 8.0 | 0.0 | 4.2 |
| 23 | 12.3 | 5.4 | 13.0 | 0.0 | 18.0 |
| 24 | 10.0 | 6.8 | 11.8 | 7.4 | 2.2 |
| 25 | 8.8 | 4.8 | 7.4 | 3.9 | 1.2 |
| 26 | 8.6 | 3.8 | 6.9 | 3.6 | 17.8 |
| 27 | 7.2 | 0.9 | 6.3 | 6.7 | 0.0 |
| 28 | 6.6 | -1.1 | 1.9 | 5.8 | 0.0 |
| 29 | 4.4 | -0.2 | 2.2 | 0.7 | 1.2 |
| 30 | 5.2 | 0.4 | 4.8 | 0.0 | 1.6 |
| 31 | 5.6 | 3.8 | 2.3 | 0.0 | 1.0 |

## FEBRUARY 2001

| | Temperature Max C° | Min C° | Wind knots | Sun hrs | Rain mm |
|---|---|---|---|---|---|
| *Day* 1 | 6.1 | -1.1 | 2.3 | 0.1 | 5.5 |
| 2 | 8.8 | -0.1 | 4.3 | 0.0 | 3.6 |
| 3 | 11.0 | 5.3 | 6.4 | 3.2 | 6.0 |
| 4 | 11.0 | 4.2 | 7.9 | 0.0 | 10.4 |
| 5 | 11.7 | 7.2 | 10.3 | 0.1 | 4.4 |
| 6 | 12.5 | 8.1 | 17.3 | 2.6 | 1.8 |
| 7 | 12.2 | 7.9 | 9.6 | 3.1 | 15.8 |
| 8 | 5.5 | 5.5 | 9.7 | 0.0 | 2.4 |
| 9 | 7.5 | 1.2 | 2.9 | 5.8 | 0.0 |
| 10 | 12.1 | 1.2 | 9.6 | 0.0 | 1.0 |
| 11 | 13.7 | 6.3 | 16.6 | 0.0 | 0.6 |
| 12 | 11.6 | 11.5 | 12.0 | 0.0 | 8.8 |
| 13 | 10.6 | 2.9 | 4.1 | 9.0 | 0.0 |
| 14 | 10.7 | 1.2 | 3.1 | 9.0 | 0.0 |
| 15 | 9.0 | 2.4 | 1.5 | 5.8 | 0.2 |
| 16 | 10.1 | 0.0 | 3.3 | 3.2 | 0.0 |
| 17 | 9.1 | 0.2 | 2.1 | 7.8 | 0.0 |
| 18 | 8.1 | 1.0 | 0.8 | 3.6 | 0.0 |
| 19 | 7.6 | -0.6 | 2.1 | 2.4 | 0.0 |
| 20 | 8.5 | -0.5 | 1.4 | 5.1 | Trace |
| 21 | 12.1 | 1.5 | 4.2 | 0.5 | Trace |
| 22 | 10.6 | 4.9 | 5.0 | 3.2 | 0.4 |
| 23 | 7.4 | 4.7 | 6.0 | 5.6 | 0.4 |
| 24 | 5.3 | 1.6 | 5.2 | 8.1 | 0.3 |
| 25 | 5.5 | -1.7 | 4.1 | 9.7 | Trace |
| 26 | 7.5 | 0.2 | 7.0 | 2.5 | 4.8 |
| 27 | 6.6 | 1.2 | 4.0 | 1.9 | 0.2 |
| 28 | 4.7 | 2.2 | 6.6 | 0.0 | 3.0 |

## MARCH 2001

| Day | Temperature Max C° | Temperature Min C° | Wind knots | Sun hrs | Rain mm |
|---|---|---|---|---|---|
| 1 | 4.3 | 1.0 | 6.1 | 0.7 | Trace |
| 2 | 3.5 | -2.6 | 3.4 | 2.2 | 0.2 |
| 3 | 3.8 | -0.5 | 7.7 | 3.6 | Trace |
| 4 | 5.0 | 0.7 | 4.0 | 0.1 | Trace |
| 5 | 8.1 | -4.3 | 3.7 | 8.4 | 0.0 |
| 6 | 13.1 | 0.6 | 9.6 | 7.1 | 6.2 |
| 7 | 15.1 | 4.4 | 5.8 | 3.7 | 0.3 |
| 8 | 10.5 | 7.0 | 3.0 | 0.0 | 7.0 |
| 9 | 13.3 | 6.3 | 5.2 | 1.6 | 0.8 |
| 10 | 14.9 | 9.3 | 5.9 | 1.9 | 0.4 |
| 11 | 13.8 | 9.8 | 4.7 | 0.3 | 7.4 |
| 12 | 11.4 | 3.9 | 5.3 | 5.6 | 4.2 |
| 13 | 10.0 | 4.7 | 4.9 | 2.7 | 0.6 |
| 14 | 11.4 | 1.3 | 2.6 | 5.0 | 0.4 |
| 15 | 9.8 | 5.2 | 1.0 | 2.9 | 1.0 |
| 16 | 9.1 | 6.9 | 7.1 | 0.0 | 11.0 |
| 17 | 4.1 | 3.7 | 7.0 | 0.0 | 9.6 |
| 18 | 6.5 | 1.6 | 6.0 | 0.7 | 0.6 |
| 19 | 6.8 | 1.5 | 4.6 | 6.3 | 0.0 |
| 20 | 4.3 | 2.6 | 14.0 | 0.0 | 11.2 |
| 21 | 6.8 | 2.3 | 7.3 | 0.0 | 2.6 |
| 22 | 14.1 | 3.5 | 2.9 | 1.6 | 6.8 |
| 23 | 10.8 | 6.6 | 2.8 | 0.0 | 4.4 |
| 24 | 9.6 | 7.5 | 4.5 | 0.1 | Trace |
| 25 | 6.6 | 4.9 | 6.1 | 0.3 | Trace |
| 26 | 7.0 | 3.7 | 5.3 | 0.0 | Trace |
| 27 | 9.3 | 3.5 | 8.2 | 0.2 | 12.8 |
| 28 | 10.8 | 6.8 | 5.0 | 1.9 | 6.8 |
| 29 | 11.6 | 4.3 | 3.1 | 7.3 | 0.6 |
| 30 | 13.1 | 2.8 | 4.8 | 10.8 | 0.4 |
| 31 | 15.5 | 7.4 | 9.5 | 3.2 | Trace |

## APRIL 2001

| Day | Temperature Max C° | Temperature Min C° | Wind knots | Sun hrs | Rain mm |
|---|---|---|---|---|---|
| 1 | 15.3 | 9.7 | 3.8 | 2.1 | 0.0 |
| 2 | 19.5 | 7.8 | 6.1 | 6.5 | 2.0 |
| 3 | 14.4 | 6.2 | 8.3 | 6.9 | 6.2 |
| 4 | 11.5 | 6.9 | 10.1 | 5.2 | 1.8 |
| 5 | 12.2 | 4.3 | 9.1 | 0.7 | 5.8 |
| 6 | 14.0 | 7.4 | 9.2 | 0.5 | 0.4 |
| 7 | 12.1 | 4.9 | 7.3 | 5.7 | 1.2 |
| 8 | 12.7 | 4.2 | 6.2 | 6.9 | 10.2 |
| 9 | 17.5 | 6.5 | 4.8 | 5.8 | 0.2 |
| 10 | 12.9 | 8.4 | 7.6 | 3.5 | 0.5 |
| 11 | 11.7 | 6.2 | 5.0 | 1.8 | 0.0 |
| 12 | 13.5 | 6.3 | 2.9 | 3.5 | Trace |
| 13 | 10.8 | 5.0 | 4.0 | 8.3 | Trace |
| 14 | 11.3 | 2.8 | 4.7 | 0.0 | 3.0 |
| 15 | 12.8 | 6.4 | 6.8 | 3.6 | 0.6 |
| 16 | 9.6 | 5.2 | 4.6 | 1.6 | Trace |
| 17 | 11.2 | 0.9 | 4.4 | 7.2 | 1.2 |
| 18 | 9.0 | 3.5 | 6.3 | 7.4 | 0.2 |
| 19 | 10.1 | 0.6 | 5.1 | 10.2 | 1.4 |
| 20 | 9.1 | 2.2 | 6.6 | 3.5 | 0.2 |
| 21 | 10.9 | 2.6 | 3.1 | 7.3 | 0.0 |
| 22 | 11.7 | 4.3 | 7.5 | 4.2 | 7.6 |
| 23 | 14.0 | 6.6 | 3.8 | 5.3 | 1.2 |
| 24 | 12.7 | 5.0 | 6.5 | 3.1 | 4.0 |
| 25 | 12.9 | 5.5 | 5.2 | 4.3 | 2.4 |
| 26 | 15.2 | 5.0 | 5.7 | 6.0 | Trace |
| 27 | 15.0 | 6.4 | 2.7 | 3.2 | 3.6 |
| 28 | 14.3 | 8.1 | 7.0 | 8.5 | 10.8 |
| 29 | 12.5 | 6.1 | 4.1 | 3.5 | 2.0 |
| 30 | 13.5 | 5.8 | 3.7 | 2.2 | Trace |

## MAY 2001

| Day | Max C° | Min C° | Wind knots | Sun hrs | Rain mm |
|---|---|---|---|---|---|
| 1 | 10.8 | 6.8 | 8.5 | 0.0 | 3.2 |
| 2 | 15.0 | 6.8 | 3.8 | 3.2 | 6.2 |
| 3 | 17.2 | 6.5 | 5.0 | 4.3 | Trace |
| 4 | 13.4 | 5.7 | 6.3 | 10.6 | 0.0 |
| 5 | 13.4 | 3.5 | 5.9 | 9.9 | 0.0 |
| 6 | 12.8 | 4.1 | 6.8 | 3.4 | 0.0 |
| 7 | 15.4 | 5.2 | 5.6 | 5.7 | 0.0 |
| 8 | 17.3 | 4.8 | 4.1 | 13.8 | 0.0 |
| 9 | 17.6 | 5.4 | 4.1 | 1.3 | 0.2 |
| 10 | 23.0 | 9.1 | 4.2 | 8.0 | 0.0 |
| 11 | 26.1 | 12.8 | 5.0 | 12.2 | 0.0 |
| 12 | 24.9 | 11.1 | 5.5 | 14.5 | 0.0 |
| 13 | 24.9 | 11.8 | 4.3 | 6.7 | 0.2 |
| 14 | 15.1 | 11.6 | 3.2 | 0.0 | Trace |
| 15 | 19.0 | 10.0 | 3.0 | 5.6 | 5.8 |
| 16 | 15.7 | 10.9 | 6.2 | 4.7 | 4.8 |
| 17 | 11.3 | 7.4 | 10.8 | 0.2 | 5.6 |
| 18 | 16.5 | 7.0 | 4.8 | 4.4 | 0.0 |
| 19 | 16.1 | 7.1 | 1.3 | 0.2 | 0.0 |
| 20 | 18.2 | 11.0 | 3.0 | 2.1 | 0.0 |
| 21 | 18.1 | 8.3 | 5.3 | 14.7 | 0.0 |
| 22 | 19.3 | 8.4 | 7.2 | 13.1 | 0.0 |
| 23 | 22.6 | 8.7 | 4.9 | 13.5 | 0.0 |
| 24 | 23.3 | 10.5 | 5.2 | 13.4 | 0.0 |
| 25 | 20.7 | 10.4 | 4.7 | 7.4 | 0.0 |
| 26 | 23.2 | 12.2 | 3.5 | 9.5 | Trace |
| 27 | 21.2 | 13.9 | 6.6 | 1.3 | Trace |
| 28 | 24.6 | 15.5 | 7.9 | 7.8 | 0.0 |
| 29 | 22.5 | 11.2 | 4.9 | 14.0 | 0.0 |
| 30 | 23.2 | 11.6 | 4.6 | 14.6 | 0.0 |
| 31 | 19.1 | 11.5 | 5.3 | 7.9 | 0.0 |

## JUNE 2001

| Day | Max C° | Min C° | Wind knots | Sun hrs | Rain mm |
|---|---|---|---|---|---|
| 1 | 19.1 | 9.2 | 7.6 | 1.7 | Trace |
| 2 | 16.6 | 12.5 | 10.0 | 4.7 | 0.6 |
| 3 | 16.8 | 6.4 | 5.8 | 15.2 | 0.0 |
| 4 | 20.3 | 7.6 | 4.5 | 7.3 | 0.0 |
| 5 | 20.6 | 9.3 | 4.1 | 6.5 | 0.2 |
| 6 | 19.4 | 11.1 | 8.5 | 1.9 | 1.4 |
| 7 | 18.0 | 8.3 | 7.7 | 12.4 | 0.0 |
| 8 | 16.8 | 7.0 | 4.5 | 12.4 | 0.0 |
| 9 | 17.7 | 5.6 | 3.3 | 8.4 | 5.4 |
| 10 | 15.1 | 9.1 | 6.1 | 6.4 | 0.6 |
| 11 | 18.0 | 5.9 | 4.5 | 8.5 | 0.0 |
| 12 | 18.5 | 11.9 | 2.9 | 1.9 | 0.0 |
| 13 | 21.6 | 11.7 | 4.4 | 7.6 | 0.0 |
| 14 | 21.5 | 10.1 | 6.1 | 9.6 | 1.2 |
| 15 | 20.5 | 12.8 | 7.5 | 6.2 | 15.9 |
| 16 | 16.5 | 13.2 | 5.9 | 0.2 | 12.8 |
| 17 | 15.6 | 12.3 | 6.7 | 0.5 | Trace |
| 18 | 17.9 | 9.2 | 3.4 | 6.7 | 0.0 |
| 19 | 21.8 | 11.5 | 5.8 | 12.4 | 0.0 |
| 20 | 24.6 | 11.9 | 6.2 | 12.5 | 0.0 |
| 21 | 21.5 | 12.3 | 4.9 | 15.1 | 0.0 |
| 22 | 22.4 | 10.5 | 6.0 | 14.1 | 0.0 |
| 23 | 23.7 | 11.2 | 7.8 | 11.0 | 0.0 |
| 24 | 27.4 | 13.2 | 3.3 | 13.1 | 0.0 |
| 25 | 29.1 | 15.9 | 7.7 | 14.0 | 0.0 |
| 26 | 31.9 | 17.3 | 10.4 | 12.1 | Trace |
| 27 | 25.1 | 16.8 | 8.8 | 7.2 | 0.0 |
| 28 | 22.7 | 14.8 | 10.8 | 5.6 | 1.0 |
| 29 | 21.3 | 16.2 | 11.3 | 1.9 | Trace |
| 30 | 23.3 | 15.5 | 9.5 | 10.9 | Trace |

# Sports Results

For 2002 sports fixtures, *see* pages 12–13

## ALPINE SKIING

### World Championships 2001 St Anton/Arlberg, Austria

Men

*Super Giant Slalom*: Daron Rahlves (USA) 1:21.46
*Combined*: Kjetil Andre Aamodt (Norway) 2:58.25
*Slalom Combined*: Kjetil Andre Aamodt (Norway) 1:31.81
*Downhill Combined*: Paul Accola (Switzerland) 1:25.55
*Downhill*: Hannes Trinkl (Austria) 1:38.74
*Giant Slalom*: Michael von Gruenigen (Switzerland) 2:23.80
*Slalom*: Mario Matt (Austria) 1:39.66

Women

*Super Giant Slalom*: Regine Cavagnoud (France) 1:23.44
*Combined*: Martina Ertl (Germany) 2:55.65
*Downhill Combined*: Kirsten L. Clark (USA) 1:25.85
*Slalom Combined*: Martina Ertl (Germany) 1:28.29
*Downhill*: Michaela Dorfmeister (Austria) 1:36.20
*Giant Slalom*: Sonja Nef (Switzerland) 2:19.01
*Slalom*: Anja Paerson (Sweden) 1:32.95

### World Cup 2000–1

Men

*Combined*: Lasse Kjus (Norway), 100 points
*Downhill*: Hermann Maier (Austria), 576 points
*Slalom*: Benjamin Raich (Austria), 625 points
*Giant Slalom*: Hermann Maier (Austria), 622 points
*Super Giant Slalom*: Hermann Maier (Austria), 420 points
*Overall*: Hermann Maier (Austria), 1,618 points

Women

*Combined*: Janica Kostelic (Croatia), 100 points
*Downhill*: Isolde Kostner (Italy), 596 points
*Slalom*: Janica Kostelic (Croatia), 824 points
*Giant Slalom*: Sonja Nef (Switzerland), 676 points
*Super Giant Slalom*: Régine Cavagnoud (France), 577 points
*Overall*: Janica Kostelic (Croatia), 1,256 points

## AMERICAN FOOTBALL

*AFC Championship 2001*: Baltimore Ravens beat Tennessee Titans 22–20
*NFC Championship 2001*: New York Giants beat Minnesota Vikings 41–0
*XXXV American Superbowl 2001*: (Tampa Bay, 28 January): Baltimore Ravens beat New York Giants 34–7

## ANGLING

### National Coarse Championships 2001

*Division*: 2 – *see Stop Press*
*Venue*: Grand Union Canal, 22 September *no. of teams*: 62
*Individual winner*: D. Brookes Jnr.
*Team winner*: Passies N.B.C.

*Division*: 3
*Venue*: Stanforth, Keadby and New Junction Canal *no. of teams*: 55
*Individual winner*: B. Smith
*Team winners*: Handsworth Angling

*Division*: 4
*Venue*: Basingstoke Canal; *no. of teams*: 48
*Individual winner*: John Clarke
*Team winners*: Fosters Tipton VDE

*Division*: 5
*Venue*: River Trent; *no. of teams*: 35
*Individual winner*: P. Harrop
*Team winners*: Team Peninsula Marazion

*Ladies' Championship*
*Venue*: Stainforth and Keadby Canal
*Winner*: Linda Cooke

## ASSOCIATION FOOTBALL

### LEAGUE COMPETITIONS 2000–1

England and Wales

*Premiership*
1. Manchester United, 80 points
2. Arsenal, 70 points

*Relegated*: Manchester City, 34 points; Coventry City, 34 points; Bradford City, 26 points

*Division 1*
1. Fulham, 101 points
2. Blackburn Rovers, 91 points

*Third promotion place*: Bolton Wanderers
*Relegated*: Huddersfield, Queens Park Rovers, Tranmere Rovers

*Division 2*
1. Millwall, 93 points
2. Rotherham United, 91 points

*Third promotion place*: Walsall
*Relegated*: Bristol Rovers, Luton Town, Swansea City, Oxford United

*Division 3*
1. Brighton and Hove Albion, 92 points
2. Chesterfield, 89 points
3. Cardiff City, 82 points

*Fourth promotion place*: Blackpool
*Relegated*: Barnet

*Football Conference*
*Champions*: Rushden and Diamonds, 86 points

*League of Wales*: Barry Town, 77 points

Scotland

*Premier Division*
1. Celtic, 97 points
2. Rangers, 82 points

*Division 1*
1. Livingston, 76 points
2. Ayr United, 69 points

*Relegated*: Morton, 35 points; Alloa Athletic, 32 points

*Division 2*
1. Partick Thistle, 75 points
2. Arbroath, 58 points

*Relegated*: Queen's Park, 40 points; Stirling Albion, 32 points

*Division 3*
1. Hamilton Academicals, 76 points
2. Cowdenbeath, 76 points

*Bottom*: Elgin City, 22 points

NORTHERN IRELAND

*Irish League Championship*: Linfield, 75 points

FRANCE

*French League Champions*: Nantes, 68 points

GERMANY

*German League Champions*: Bayern Munich, 63 points

ITALY

*Italian League Champions*: Roma, 75 points

HOLLAND

*Dutch League Champions*: PSV Eindhoven, 83 points

SPAIN

*Spanish League Champions*: Real Madrid, 80 points

## CUP COMPETITIONS

ENGLAND

*FA Cup final 2001*: Liverpool beat Arsenal 2–1
*Worthington (League) Cup final 2001:* Liverpool beat Birmingham 1–1 (5-4 on penalties)
*LDV Vans Trophy final 2001:* Port Vale beat Brentford 2–1
*FA Vase final 2001:* Taunton beat Birkhampstead 2–1
*FA Trophy final 2001:* Canvey Island beat Forest Green Rovers 1–0
*Charity Shield 2001*: Liverpool beat Manchester United 2–1
*Women's FA Cup final 2001*: Arsenal beat Fulham 1–0
*Women's League 2001*: Arsenal, 52 points

WALES

*Welsh Cup final 2001*: Barry Town beat TNS 2–0
*League of Wales Cup final 2001*: Caersws beat Barry Town 2–0

SCOTLAND

*Scottish Cup final 2001* (Hampden Park, 26 May): Celtic beat Hibernian 3–0
*League Cup final 2001* (Hampden Park, 18 March) : Celtic beat Kilomarnock 3–0

NORTHERN IRELAND

*Irish Cup final*: Glentoran beat Linfield 1–0

EUROPE

*European Champions' Cup final 2001* (Paris): Bayern Munich beat Valencia 1–1 (won on penalties)
*UEFA Cup final*: Liverpool beat Alaves 5–4
*European Super Cup final 2001*: Galatasaray beat Real Madrid 2–1
*InterToto Cup final 2000*: Aston Villa (England); Paris St-Germain, (France); Troyes Aube Champagne (France) qualified for the UEFA Cup

## INTERNATIONALS

AFRICA

*African Nationals Cup 2001*: Cameroon beat Nigeria 2–2 (4–3 on penalties)

## FOOTBALLER OF THE YEAR

2000 – Zinedine Zidane (France)
1999 - Rivaldo (Brazil)
1998 - Zinedine Zidane (France)
1997 - Ronaldo (Brazil)
1996 - Ronaldo (Brazil)
1995 - George Weah (Liberia)
1994 - Romario (Brazil)
1993 - Roberto Baggio (Italy)
1992 - Marco van Basten (Netherlands)

# ATHLETICS

## WORLD HALF MARATHON CHAMPIONSHIPS

Cancun, Mexico, 12 November 2000

MEN

*Individual*: Paul Tergat (Kenya) 1 hr. 03 min. 47 sec.
*Team result*: Kenya, 3 hr. 11 min 38 sec.

WOMEN

*Individual*: Paula Radcliffe (GBR) 1 hr. 09 min. 07 sec.
*Team result*: Romania 3 hr. 34 min. 22 sec.

## EUROPEAN CROSS-COUNTRY CHAMPIONSHIPS

Malmo, Sweden, 10 December 2000

SENIOR MEN (9705m)

*Individual*: Paulo Guerra (Portugal) 29 min. 29 sec.
*Team*: France 23 points

SENIOR WOMEN (4945m)

*Individual*: Katalin Szentgyörgyi (Hungary) 16 min. 34 sec.
*Team*: Portugal 18 points

JUNIOR MEN (6135m)

*Individual*: Wolfram Müller (Germany) 18 min. 58 sec.
*Team*: Portugal 21 points

JUNIOR WOMEN (4950 m)

*Individual*: Jessica Augusto (Portugal) 12 mins. 55 sec.
*Team*: Great Britain 21 points

## AAA INDOOR CHAMPIONSHIPS

Birmingham, 27–28 January 2001

MEN

| | min. | sec. |
|---|---|---|
| 60 *metres*: John Skeete (Horrow) | | 6.59 |
| 200 *metres*: Allyn Condon (Sale) | | 20.66 |
| 400 *metres*: Daniel Caines (Birchfield) | | 45.75 |
| 800 *metres*: Eddie King (Sale) | 1 | 49.98 |
| 1,500 *metres*: Angus Maclean (Team Solent) | 3 | 48.02 |
| 3,000 *metres*: Mark Miles (Belgrave) | 8 | 19.89 |
| 60 *metres hurdles*: Domanic Bradley (Birchfield) | 7 | 84 |
| 3,000 *metres walk*: Robert Hefferan (Ireland) | 11 | 19.27 |

| | metres |
|---|---|
| *High jump*: Samson Oni (Belgrave) | 2.20 |
| *Pole vault*: Tine Thomas (Cardiff) | 5.35 |
| *Long jump*: Christopher Tomlinson (Mandate) | 7.41 |
| *Triple jump*: Julian Golley (TVH) | 16.22 |
| *Shot*: Emeka Udechuku (Loughborough) | 18.19 |
| *Heptathlon*: John Heanley (Windsor) | 5148 points |

WOMEN

| | min. | sec. |
|---|---|---|
| 60 *metres*: Marcia Richardson (Windsor) | | 7.28 |
| 200 *metres*: Catherine Murphy (Shaftesbury) | | 23.35 |
| 400 *metres*: Catherine Murphy (Shaftesbury) | | 62.31 |
| 800 *metres*: Kelly Holmes (Ealing) | 2 | 05.26 |
| 1,500 *metres*: Freda Davoren (Ireland) | 4 | 19.85 |

| | min. | sec. |
|---|---|---|
| 3,000 *metres*: Maria Lynch (Ireland) | 9 | 35.92 |
| 60 *metres hurdles*: Melanie Wilkins (Windsor) | | 8.20 |
| 3,000 *metres walk*: Gillian O'Sullivan (Ireland) | 12 | 23.45 |

| | metres |
|---|---|
| *High jump*: Susan Jones (Trafford) | 1.85 |
| *Pole vault*: Janine Whitlock (Trafford) | 4.05 |
| *Long jump*: Ann Danson (Sale) | 5.97 |
| *Triple jump*: Michelle Griffiths (Windsor) | 13.25 |
| *Shot*: Lieja Koeman (Netherlands) | 17.26 |
| *Pentathlon*: Kelly Sotherton (Birchfield) | 4116 points |

### World Championships

Edmonton, Alberta, Canada, 3–12 August 2001

#### Men

| | hr. | min. | sec. |
|---|---|---|---|
| 100 *metres*: Maurice Greene (USA) | | | 9.82 |
| 200 *metres*: Konstandinos Kedéris (Greece) | | | 20.04 |
| 400 *metres*: Avard Moncur (Bahamas) | | | 44.64 |
| 800 *metres*: André Bucher (Switzerland) | | 1 | 43.70 |
| 1,500 *metres*: Hichman El Guerrouj (Morrocco) | | 3 | 30.68 |
| 5,000 *metres*: Richard Limo (Kenya) | | 13 | 00.77 |
| 10,000 *metres*: Charles Kamathi (Ethiopia) | | 27 | 53.25 |
| *Marathon*: Gezahegne Abera (Ethiopia) | 2 | 12 | 42 |
| 3,000 *metres steeplechase*: Reuben Kosgei (Kenya) | | 8 | 16 |
| 110 *metres hurdles*: Allen Johnson (USA) | | | 13.04 |
| 400 *metres hurdles*: Felix Sánchez (Dominican Republic) | | | 47.49 |
| 4 × 100 *metres relay*: USA | | | 37.96 |
| 4 × 400 *metres relay*: USA | | 2 | 57.54 |
| 20 *km walk*: Roman Rasskazov (Russia) | 1 | 20 | 31 |
| 50 *km walk*: Robert Kiorzeniowski (Poland) | 3 | 42 | 8 |

| | metres |
|---|---|
| *High jump*: Martin Buss (Germany) | 2.36 |
| *Pole vault*: Dmitri Markov (Australia) | 6.05* |
| *Long jump*: Iván Pedroso (Cuba) | 8.40 |
| *Triple jump*: Jonathan Edwards (GB) | 17.92 |
| *Shot*: John Godina (USA) | 21.87 |
| *Discus*: Lars Riedel (Germany) | 69.72* |
| *Javalin*: Jan Zelezney (Czech Republic) | 92.80* |
| *Decathlon*: Tomas Dvorak (Czech Republic) | 8,902 points |

#### Women

| | hr. | min. | sec. |
|---|---|---|---|
| 100 *metres*: Zhana Pintusevich-Block (Ukraine) | | | 10.82 |
| 200 *metres*: Marion Jones (USA) | | | 22.39 |
| 400 *metres*: Amy Mbacke Thiam (Senegal) | | | 49.86 |
| 800 *metres*: Maria Mutola (Mozambique) | | 1 | 57.17 |
| 1,500 *metres*: Gabriela Szabo (Romania) | | 4 | 00.57 |
| 5,000 *metres*: Olga Yegorova (Russia) | | 15 | 3.39 |
| 10,000 *metres*: Tulu Deratu (Ethiopia) | | 34 | 48.81 |
| *Marathon*: Lidia Simon (Romania) | 2 | 26 | 1 |
| 100 *metres hurdles*: Anjanette Kirkland (USA) | | | 12.42 |
| 400 *metres hurdles*: Nezha Biduane (Morocco) | | | 53.34 |
| 4 × 100 *metres relay*: USA | | | 41.71 |
| 4 × 400 *metres relay*: Jamaica | | 3 | 20.65 |
| 20 *km walk*: Oliumpiada Ivanova (Russia) | 1 | 27 | 48 |

| | metres |
|---|---|
| *High jump*: Hestrie Cloete (South Africa) | 2.0 |
| *Pole vault*: Stacy Draglia (USA) | 4.75 |
| *Long jump*: Fiona May (Italy) | 7.02 |
| *Triple jump*: Tatyana Lebedeva (Russia) | 15.25 |
| *Shot*: Yanina Korolchik (Bulgaria) | 20.61 |
| *Discus*: Natalya Sadova (Russia) | 68.57 |
| *Hammer*: Yipsi Moreno (Cuba) | 70.65 |
| *Javelin*: Osleidys Menendez (Cuba) | 69.53* |
| *Heptathlon*: Yelena Prokhorova (Russia) | 6,694 points |

*Championship record

### World Indoor Championships

Lisbon, Portugal, March 2001

#### Men

| | min. | sec. |
|---|---|---|
| 60 *metres*: Tim Harden (USA) | | 6.44 |
| 200 *metres*: Shawn Crawford (USA) | | 20.63 |
| 400 *metres*: Daniel Caines (GB) | | 46.40 |
| 800 *metres*: Yuri Borzakovski (Russia) | 1 | 44.49 |
| 1,500 *metres*: Rui Silva (Portugal) | 3 | 51.06 |
| 3,000 *metres*: Hichman El Guerrouj (Morocco) | 7 | 37.74 |
| 60 *metres hurdles*: Terrence Trammell (USA) | | 7.51 |
| 4 × 400 *metres relay*: Poland | 3 | 4.47 |

| | metres |
|---|---|
| *High jump*: Stefan Holm (Sweden) | 2.32 |
| *Pole vault*: Lawrence Johnson (USA) | 5.95 |
| *Long jump*: Iván Pedroso (Cuba) | 8.43 |
| *Triple jump*: Paolo Camossi (Italy) | 17.32 |
| *Shot*: John Godina (USA) | 20.82 |
| *Decathlon*: Roman Šebrle (Czech Republic) | 6,420 points |

WOMEN

| | min. | sec. |
|---|---|---|
| 60 *metres*: Chandra Sturrup (Bahamas) | | 7.05 |
| 200 *metres*: Juliet Campbell (Jamaica) | | 22.64 |
| 400 *metres*: Sandie Richards (Jamaica) | | 51.04 |
| 800 *metres*: Maria Mutola (Mozambique) | 1 | 59.74 |
| 1,500 *metres*: Hasna Benhassi (Morocco) | 4 | 10.83 |
| 3,000 *metres*: Olga Yergorova (Russia) | 8 | 37.48 |
| 60 *metres hurdles*: Anjanette Kirkland (USA) | | 7.85 |
| 4 × 400 *metres relay*: Russia | 3 | 30 |

| | metres |
|---|---|
| *High jump*: Kajsa Bergqvist (Sweden) | 2.00 |
| *Pole vault*: Pavla Hamácková (Czech Republic) | 4.56 |
| *Long jump*: Dawn Burrell (USA) | 7.03 |
| *Triple jump*: Tereza Marinova (Bulgaria) | 14.91 |
| *Shot*: Larisa Peleshenko (Russia) | 19.84 |
| *Pentathlon*: Natalya Sazanovich (Belarus) | 4,850 points |

NATIONAL CROSS-COUNTRY CHAMPIONSHIPS

Stowe, 26 February 2001

MEN

*Individual*: Mike Openshaw (Birchfield) 36 min. 52 sec.
*Team*: Bingley, 162 points

WOMEN

*Individual*: Liz Yelling (Bedford) 28 min. 8 sec.
*Team*: Sale, 61 points

WORLD CROSS-COUNTRY CHAMPIONSHIPS

Dublin, Ireland, March 2001

SENIOR MEN (12.3 KM)
*Individual*: Mohammed Mourhit (Belgium), 39min. 53sec
*Team*: Kenya, 33 points

SENIOR MEN (4,100 M)
*Individual*: Enock Koech (Kenya), 12min. 40sec
*Team*: Kenya, 13 points

SENIOR WOMEN (7,700 M)
*Individual*: Paula Radcliffe (GB), 27min. 49sec.
*Team*: Kenya, 18 points

SENIOR WOMEN (4,100 M)
*Individual*: Gete Wami (Ethiopia), 14min. 46sec.
*Team*: Ethiopia, 26 points

LONDON MARATHON

15 April 2001

*Men*: Abdelkader El Mouaziz (Morocco), 2hr 7min. 11sec.
*Women*: Deratu Tulu (Ethiopia), 2hr 23min. 56sec.

EUROPEAN CUP SUPER LEAGUE

Bremen, Germany, 23–24 June 2001

MEN

| | min. | sec. |
|---|---|---|
| 100 *metres*: Mark Lewis-Francis (GBR), | | 10.13 |
| 200 *metres*: Konstadinos Kenderis (Greece) | | 20.31 |
| 400 *metres*: Marc Raquil (France) | | 44.95 |
| 800 *metres*: Pawel Czapiewski (Poland) | 1 | 48.28 |
| 1,500 *metres*: Jose Redolat (Spain) | 3 | 45.81 |
| 3,000 *metres*: Driss Maazouzi (France) | 7 | 52.26 |
| 5,000 *metres*: Ismail Sehir (France), | 13 | 50.47 |
| 3,000 *metres steeplechase*: Boubdallah Tahri (France) | 8 | 38.02 |
| 110 *metres hurdles*: Yevgeni Pechonkin (Russia) | | 13.38 |
| 400 *metres hurdles*: Fabrizio Mori (Italy) | | 48.39 |
| 4 × 100 *metres relay*: Italy | | 38.89 |
| 4 × 400 *metres relay*: Poland | 3 | 79 |

| | metres |
|---|---|
| *High jump*: Yaroslav Rybakov (Russia) | 2.28 |
| *Pole vault*: Michael Stolle (Germany) | 5.75 |
| *Long jump*: Danila Burkenya (Russia) | 7.89 |
| *Triple jump*: Jonathan Edwards (GBR) | 17.26 |
| *Shot*: Manuel Martinez, (Spain) | 21.03 |
| *Discus*: Lars Riedel (Germany) | 66.63 |
| *Hammer*: Szymon Ziolkowski (Poland) | 88.87 |
| *Javelin*: Kostadinos Gatsiovdis, (Greece) | 88.33 |
| Decathlon, Alexander Yurkon (Ukraine) | 8380 points |
| *Team points*: Poland 107 points; France | 97 points; |

WOMEN

| | min. | sec. |
|---|---|---|
| 100 *metres*: Marina Kislova (Russia) | | 11.23 |
| 200 *metres*: Natalya Safrannikova, (Belarus) | | 22.18 |
| 400 *metres*: Grit Breuer (Germany) | | 50.49 |
| 800 *metres*: Inna Mistyukevich (Russia) | 1 | 59.09 |
| 1,500 *metres*: Violeta Szekely (Romania), | 4 | 06.43 |
| 3,000 *metres*: Kathy Butler (GBR) | 9 | 03.71 |
| 5,000 *metres*: Yelena Zadorozanaya (Russia) | 14 | 40.47 |
| 100 *metres hurdles*: Irina Korotya (Russia) | | 13.06 |
| 400 *metres hurdles*: Yuliya Nosova (Russia) | | |
| 4 × 100 *metres relay*: Germany | | 43.02 |
| 4 × 400 *metres relay*: Germany | 3 | 23.81 |

| | metres |
|---|---|
| *High jump*: Susan Jones (GBR) | 1.95 |
| *Pole vault*: Svetlana Feofanova (Russia) | 4.60 |
| *Long jump*: Heike Drechsler (Germany) | 6.79 |
| *Triple jump*: Tatyana Lebedyeva (Russia) | 14.89 |

| | min. | sec. |
|---|---|---|
| *Shot*: Nadine Kleinert-Schmitt (Germany) | | 19.30 |
| *Discus*: Franka Dietzsch (Germany) | | 64.04 |
| *Hammer*: Olga Tsander (Belarus) | | 68.40 |
| *Javelin*: Nikola Tomeckova (Czech Republic) | | 64.77 |
| *Heptathlon*: Svetlana Sokolova (Russia) | | 6270 points |

*Team points*: Russia 126.6 points; Germany 117 points; France 86 points; Great Britain 82 points; Romania 78 points; Italy 72.5 points; Belarus 70 points; Czech Republic 47 points

## AAA Championships

Birmingham, 13–15 July 2001

### Men

| | min. | sec. |
|---|---|---|
| 100 *metres*: Dwain Chambers (Belgrave) | | 10.01 |
| 200 *metres*: Marlon Devonish (Coventry) | | 20.52 |
| 400 *metres*: Mark Richardson (WSE Hounslow) | | 45.79 |
| 800 *metres*: Neil Speaight (Belgrave) | 1 | 49.63 |
| 1,500 *metres*: John Mayock (Barnsley) | 3 | 44.05 |
| 5,000 *metres*: Jon Wild (Sale) | 13 | 52.72 |
| 10,000 *metres*: Llyn Tromans (Coventry) | 28 | 31.33 |
| 3,000 *metres steeplechase*: Benedict Whitby (WSE Hounslow) | 8 | 32.68 |
| 110 *metres hurdles*: Tony Jarrett (Enfield and Haringey) | | 13.66 |
| 400 *metres hurdles*: Chris Rawlinson (Belgrave) | | 48.68 |
| 5,000 *metres walk*: Lloyd Finch (Leicester) | 20 | 47.23 |

| | metres |
|---|---|
| *High jump*: Ben Challenger (Belgrave) | 2.17 |
| *Pole vault*: Paul Williamson (TVH) | 5.30 |
| *Long jump*: Nathan Morgan (Birchfield) | 7.80 |
| *Triple jump*: Jonathan Edwards (Gateshead) | 17.59 |
| *Shot*: Mark Proctor (Newham, EB) | 18.38 |
| *Discus*: Glen Smith (Birchfield) | 59.99 |
| *Hammer*: Mick Jones (Belgrave) | 74.40 |
| *Javelin*: Mark Roberson (Newham EB) | 80.80 |
| *Decathlon*: John Heanley (WSE Hounslow) | 712 points |

### Women

| | min. | sec. |
|---|---|---|
| 100 *metres*: Sarah Wilhemy (Southend) | | 11.41 |
| 200 *metres*: Sarah Reilly (Birchfield/Ireland) | | 23.42 |
| 400 *metres*: Lesley Owusu (WSE Hounslow) | | 52.27 |
| 800 *metres*: Kelly Holmes (Ealing) | 2 | 02.61 |
| 1,500 *metres*: Helen Pattinson (Preston) | 4 | 14.49 |
| 5,000 *metres*: Jo Pavey (Bristol) | 15 | 15.98 |
| 10,000 *metres*: Penny Thackery (Wakefield) | | |
| 100 *metres hurdles*: Diane Allahgreen (Liverpool) | | 13.11 |
| 400 *metres hurdles*: Sinead Dudgeon (Edinburgh) | | 56.37 |
| 5,000 *metres walk*: Niobe Menendez (Steyning) | 23 | 46.30 |

| | metres |
|---|---|
| *High jump*: Susan Jones (Trafford) | 1.91 |
| *Pole vault*: Janine Whitlock (Trafford) | 4.40 |
| *Long jump*: Ann Danson (Sale) | 6.15 |
| *Triple jump*: Ashia Hansen (Shatesbury-Barnet) | 14.09 |
| *Shot*: Joanne Duncan (Woodford Green) | 16.84 |
| *Discus*: Shelly Drew (Belgrave) | 67.22 |
| *Hammer*: Lorraine Shaw, | 66.97 |
| *Javelin*: Karen Martin (Derby) | 54.82 |
| *Heptathlon*: Laura Redmond (Edinburgh) | 5,068 points |

## IAFF Grand Prix Final

Doha, Qatar, 5 October 2000

### Men

| | min. | sec. |
|---|---|---|
| 100 *metres*: Darren Campbell (GBR) | | 10.25 |
| 400 *metres*: Mark Richardson (GBR) | | 45.20 |
| 1,500 *metres*: Noah Ngeny (Kenya) | 3 | 36.62 |
| 3,000 *metres*: Luke Kipkosgei (Kenya) | 7 | 46.21 |
| 400 *metres hurdles*: Angelo Taylor (USA) | | 48.14 |

| | metres |
|---|---|
| *High jump*: Vyacheslav Voronin (Russia) | 2.32 |
| *Pole vault*: Tim Lobinger (Germany) | 5.70 |
| *Triple jump*: Jonathan Edwards (GBR) | 17.12 |
| *Shot*: Andy Bloom (USA) | 21.81 |
| *Hammer*: Andrey Skvaruk (Ukraine) | 81.43 |

### Women

| | min. | sec. |
|---|---|---|
| 100 *metres*: Marion Jones (USA) | | 11.00 |
| 400 *metres*: Lorraine Graham (Jamaica) | | 50.21 |
| 1,500 *metres*: Violete Beclea-Szekely (Romania) | 4 | 15.63 |
| 3,000 *metres*: Sonia O'Sullivan (Ireland) | 8 | 52.01 |
| 100 *metres hurdles*: Gail Devers (USA) | | 12.85 |

| | min. | sec. |
|---|---|---|
| | | metres |
| *Long jump*: Heike Daute-Drechsler (Germany) | | 7.07 |
| *Discus*: Franka Dietzsch (Germany) | | 65.41 |
| *Javelin*: Sonia Bisset (Cuba) | | 65.87 |

IAFF GRAND PRIX FINAL

Melbourne, Australia,9 September 2001

MEN

| | min. | sec. |
|---|---|---|
| *200 metres*: Shawn Crawford (USA) | | 20.37 |
| 800 *metres*: André Bucher (Switzerland) | 1 | 46.91 |
| 1,500 *metres*: Hicham El Guerrous (Morocco) | 3 | 31.25 |
| 3,000 *metres*: Paul Bitok (Kenya) | 7 | 53.85 |
| 3,000 *metres steeplechase*: Brahim Boulami (Morocco) | 8 | 16.14 |
| | | metres |
| *Long jump*: Younes Moudnik (Morocco) | | 8.23 |
| *Discus*: Virgilius Alekna (Lithuania) | | 64.42 |
| *Javelin*: Jan Zelezny (Czech Republic) | | 64.42 |

WOMEN

| | min. | sec. |
|---|---|---|
| 200 *metres*: Leonie Mani (Cameroon) | | 22.93 |
| 800 *metres*: Maria Mutola (Mozambique) | 1 | 59.78 |
| 1,500 *metres*: Violeta Szekely (Romania) | 4 | 03.46 |
| 3,000 *metres*: Tatyana Tomashova (Russia) | 9 | 30.93 |
| 400 *metres hurdles*: Tonya Buford-Bailey (USA) | | 54.58 |
| | | metres |
| *High jump*: Hestrie Cloete (South Africa) | | 1.98 |
| *Pole vault*: Stacy Dragila (USA) | | 4.50 |
| *Triple jump*: Tereza Marinova (Bulgaria) | | 14.77 |
| *Shot*: Astrid Rumbernuss (Germany) | | 18.94 |
| *Hammer*: Kamila Skolimowska (Poland) | | 71.71 |
| *Men's overall winner*: André Bucher (Switzerland) | | 102 points |
| *Women's overall winner*: Violeta Szekely (Romania) | | 116 points |

GB v. USA v. RUSSIA

Scotstoun, Glasgow, 1 July 2001

MEN

| | min. | sec. |
|---|---|---|
| 100 *metres*: John Drummond (USA) | | 10.10 |
| 200 *metres*: Kevin Little (USA) | | 20.31 |
| 400 *metres*: Mark Richardson (GBR) | | 46.20 |
| 800 *metres*: Yuri Borzakovsky (Russia) | 1 | 48.50 |
| 1500 *metres*: Seneca Lassiter (USA) | 3 | 50.78 |
| 110 *metres hurdles*: Allen Johnson (USA) | | 13.31 |
| 400 *metres hurdles*: Angelo Taylor (USA) | | 49.01 |
| 4 × 100 *metres relay*: Great Britain | | 38.69 |
| | | metres |
| *High jump*: Charles Austin (USA) | | 2.25 |
| *Triple jump*: Jonathan Edwards (GBR) | | 17.66 |
| *Discus*: John Godina (USA) | | 65.54 |
| *Javelin*: Breaux Greer (USA) | | 85.74 |

WOMEN

| | min. | sec. |
|---|---|---|
| 100 *metres*: Chryste Gaines (USA) | | 11.19 |
| 400 *metres*: Katherine Merry (GBR) | | 51.03 |
| 1,500 *metres*: Olga Yegorova (Russia) | 4 | 02.76 |
| 100 *metres hurdles*: Svetlana Laukhova (Russia) | | 12.76 |
| 3,000 *metres steeplechase*: Elizabeth Jackson (USA) | 9 | 48.72 |
| 4 × 100 *metres relay*: Russia | | 43.84 |
| | | metres |
| *Long jump*: Olga Rublyova (Russia) | | 6.80 |

*Overall Team Points*: USA 135 points; Great Britain 131 points; Russia 111 points

GOODWILL GAMES 2001

ATHLETICS

MEN

| | hr | min. | sec. |
|---|---|---|---|
| 100 *metres*: Dwain Chambers (GB) | | | 10.11 |
| 200 *metres*: Shawn Crawford (USA) | | | 20.17 |
| 400 *metres*: Gregory Haughton (Jamaica) | | | 45.02 |
| 800 *metres*: William Yiampoy (Kenya) | | 1 | 46.49 |
| 1,500 *metres (mile)*: Noah Ngeny (Kenya) | | 3 | 56.64 |
| 5,000 *metres*: Paul Bitok (Keyna) | | 15 | 26.10 |
| 10,000 *metres*: Assefa Mezgebu (Ethiopia) | | 28 | 06.48 |
| 3,000 *metres steeplechase*: Brahim Boulami (Morocco) | | 8 | 17.73 |
| 110 *metres hurdles*: Allen Johnson (USA) | | | 13.16 |
| 400 *metres hurdles*: Felix Sanchez (Dominican Republic) | | | 48.47 |
| 4 × 100 *metres relay*: Great Britain | | | 38.71 |

| | hr | min. | sec. |
|---|---|---|---|
| 4 × 400 *metres relay*: United States of America | | 3 | 00.52 |
| 20 *km walk*: Nathan Deakes (Australia) | 1 | 19 | 48.10* |

| | metres |
|---|---|
| *High jump*: Stefan Holm (Sweden) | 2.33 |
| *Pole vault*: Tim Mack (USA) | 5.80 |
| *Long jump*: I van Pedroso (Cuba) | 8.16 |
| *Triple jump*: Jonathan Edwards (GB) | 17.26 |
| *Shot*: Adam Nelson (USA) | 20.91 |
| *Discus*: Frantz Kruger (South Africa) | 67.84* |
| *Hammer*: Koji Murofushi (Japan) | 82.94 |
| *Javelin*: Jan Zelezny (Czech Republic) | 87.52* |
| *Decathlon*: T. Dvorak (Czech Republic) | 8,514 points |

WOMEN

| | hr. | min. | sec. |
|---|---|---|---|
| 100 *metres*: Marion Jones (USA) | | | 10.84* |
| 200 *metres*: Debbie Ferguson (Bahamas) | | | 22.80 |
| 400 *metres*: Ana Guevara (Mexico) | | | 50.32 |
| 800 *metres*: Maria Mutola (Mozambique) | | 1 | 58.76 |
| 1,500 *metres (mile)*: Violeta Szekely (Romania) | | 4 | 38.03 |
| 5,000 *metres*: Olga Yegorova (Russia) | | 15 | 12.22 |
| 10,000 *metres*: Derartu Tulu (Ethiopia) | | 31 | 48.19* |
| 3,000 *metres steeplechase*: Melissa Rollison (Australia) | | 9 | 30.70* |
| 100 *metres hurdles*: Gail Devers (USA) | | | 12.61 |
| 400 *metres hurdles*: Tatyana Tereshchuk-Antipova (Ukraine) | | | 54.47 |
| 4 × 100 *metres relay*: World Team | | | 42.95 |
| 4 × 400 *metres relay*: United States of America | | 3 | 24.63 |
| 20 *km walk*: Olimpiada Ivanova (Russia) | 1 | 26 | 52.30** |

| | metres |
|---|---|
| *High jump*: Hestrie Cloete (South Africa) | 2.0 |
| *Pole vault*: Stacy Dragila (USA) | 4.55* |
| *Long jump*: Maurren Higa Maggi (Brazil) | 6.94 |
| *Triple jump*: Tatyana Lebedeva (Russia) | 14.58 |
| *Shot*: Larisa Peleshenko (Russia) | 18.65 |
| *Discus*: Ellina Zvereva (Bulgaria) | 66.36 |
| *Javelin*: Osleidys Menendez (Cuba) | 66.14 |
| *Hammer*: Kamilia Skolimowska (Poland) | 70.31 |
| *Heptathlon*: N. Roshchupkina (Russia) | 6,373 points |

BASKETBALL

MEN – United States of America

BEACH VOLLEYBALL

MEN – Brazil
WOMEN – Brazil

BOXING

48*kg*: Ronald Siler (USA)
54*kg*: Guillermo Rigondeaux (Cuba)
60*kg*: Mario Kindelan (Cuba)
67*kg*: Yudel Jhonson (Cuba)
75*kg*: Gaidarbek Gaidaibekov (Russia)
91*kg*: Odlaniel Solis (Cuba)

CYCLING

MEN

10 *km scratch race*: Mark Renshaw (Australia)
20 *km points race*: Greg Henderson (New Zealand) 25 points
30 *km Madison*: Greg Henderson and Hayden Godfrey (New Zealand) 28 points
*Elimination race*: Brett Aitken (Australia)
*Keirin*: Rene Wolff (Germany)
*Sprint*: Sean Eadie (Australia)

WOMEN

10 *km scratch race*: Susan Panzer (Germany)
15 *km points race*: Erin Mirabella (USA) 23 points
*Elimination race*: Katrin Meinke (Germany)
*Sprint*: Katrin Meinke (Germany)

DIVING

MEN

1 *metre springboard*: Wang Tianling (China) 466.98 points
3 *metre springboard*: Dmitri Sautin (Russia) 487.71 points
10 *metre platform*: Tian Liang (China) 535.17 points
3 *metre synchronised springboard*: Peng Bo and Wang Kenan (China) 353.52 points
10 *metre synchronised platform*: Hu Jia and Tian Liang (China) 360.93 points

WOMEN

1 *metre springboard*: Guo Jingjing (China) 301.86 points
3 *metre springboard*: Guo Jingjing (China) 344.94 points
10 *metre platform*: Duan Qing (China) 391.59 points
3 *metre synchronised springboard*: Guo Jingjing and Wu Minxia (China) 331.08 points
10 *metre synchronised platform*: Li Rao and Li Ting (China) 315.36 points

FIGURE SKATING

*Ladies*: Irina Slutskaya (Russia)
*Mens*: Evgeni Plushenko (Russia)
*Ice dance*: Irina Lobacheva and Ilia Averbukh (Russia)
*Pairs*: Elena Berezhnaya and Anton Sikharulidze (Russia)

GYMNASTICS

MEN

*Overall*: Marian Dragulescu (Romania) 56.048 points
*Individual Apparatus Champions*
*Floor*: Jordan Jovtchev (Bulgaria) 9.375 points
*Pommel Horse*: Marius Urzica (Romania) 9.762 points
*Rings*: Szilveszter Csollany (Hungary) 9.775 points
*Vault*: Lu Bin (China) 9.556 points
*Parallel Bars*: Huang Xu (China) 9.675 points
*High Bar*: Philippe Rizzo (Australia) 9.737 points

WOMEN

*Overall*: Sabina Cojocar (Romania) 36.854 points

*Individual Apparatus Champions*

*Floor*: Elena Zamolodchikova (Russia) 8.950 points

*Beam*: Sun Xiaojiau (China) 9.662 points

*Vault*: Elena Zamolodchikova (Russia) 9.393 points

*Assymetric Bars*: Svetlana Khorkina (Russia) 9.712 points

RHYTHMIC GYMNASTICS

*Overall*: Irina Chashchina (Russia) 113.550 points

*Individual Apparatus Champions*

*Rope*: Alina Kabaeva (Russia) 28.875 points

*Hoop*: Irina Chaschchina (Russia) 28.525 points

*Ball*: Alina Kabaeva (Russia) 28.725 points

*Clubs*: Alina Kabaeva (Russia) 29.200 points

SURF LIFESAVING

*Overall team*: Australia 535 points

SWIMMING

MEN

50 *metres freestyle*: Bartosz Kizierowski (Poland) 22.36sec.
100 *metres freestyle*: Michael Klim (Australia) 48.81sec.
200 *metres freestyle*: Grant Hackett (Australia) 1min 47.95sec.
400 *metres freestyle*: Ian Thorpe (Australia) 3min. 45.40sec.
1,500 *metres freestyle*: Grant Hackett (Australia) 15min. 01.25sec.*
50 *metres backstroke*: Bartosz Kizierowski (Poland) 25.63sec.
100 *metres backstroke*: Matthew Welsh (Australia) 54.87sec.
200 *metres backstroke*: Ray Hass (Australia) 1min. 59.95sec.
50 *metres breaststroke*: Jarrod Marrs (USA) 28.50sec.
100 *metres breaststroke*: Kosuke Kitajima (Japan) 1min. 01.76sec.
200 *metres breaststroke*: Terence Parkin (South Africa) 2min. 13.21sec.
50 *metres butterfly*: Geoff Huegill (Australia) 23.63sec.*
100 *metres butterfly*: Michael Klim (Australia) 52.51sec.*
200 *metres butterfly*: Tom Malchow (USA) 1min. 55.27sec.*
200 *metres individual medley*: Thomas Wilkens (USA) 2min. 02.05sec.
400 *metres individual medley*: Thomas Wilkens (USA) 4min. 17.93sec.
4 × 100 *metres freestyle relay*: Australia 3min. 16.32sec.
4 × 100 *metres medley relay*: Australia 3min. 38.26sec.

WOMEN

50 *metres freestyle*: Inge de Bruijn (Netherlands) 25.00sec.*
100 *metres freestyle*: Sarah Ryan (Australia) 55.38sec.*
200 *metres freestyle*: Lindsay Benko (USA) 1min. 59.71sec.
400 *metres freestyle*: Jingwen Tang (China) 4min. 11.40sec.
800 *metres freestyle*: Yana Klochkova (Ukraine) 8min. 38.51sec.
50 *metres backstroke*: Haley Cope (USA) 28.89sec.*
100 *metres backstroke*: Mai Nakamura (Japan) 1min. 01.46sec.
200 *metres backstroke*: Clementine Stoney (Australia) 2min. 13.54sec.
50 *metres breaststroke*: Brooke Hanson (Australia) 31.91sec.
100 *metres breaststroke*: Brooke Hanson (Australia) 1min. 09.25sec.
200 *metres breaststroke*: Beatrice Caslaru (Romania) 2min. 28.61sec.
50 *metres butterfly*: Inge de Bruijn (Netherlands) 26.48sec.*
100 *metres butterfly*: Martina Maravcova (Slovakia) 52.28sec*
200 *metres butterfly*: Maki Mita (Japan) 2min. 09.15sec.
200 *metres individual medley*: Beatrice Caslaru (Romania) 2min. 14.91sec.
400 *metres Individual medley*: Yana Klochkova (Ukraine) 4min. 41.12sec.
4 × 100 *freestyle relay*: Europe 3min. 42.40sec.
4 × 100 *medley relay*: Australia 4min. 03.96sec.

TRAMPOLINE

MEN – Aleksandr Moskalenko (Russia) 71.50 points
WOMEN – Anna Dogonadze-Lilkendey (Germany) 68.00 points

TRIATHLON

MEN – Chris Meeormack (Australia) 1hr 47min. 26.43sec.
WOMEN – Loretta Harrop (Australia) 1hr 59min. 44.59sec.

WEIGHT-LIFTING

MEN

85 *kg snatch*: Sergo Chakhoyan (Australia) 181.50 kg**
105+ *kg snatch*: Victor Scerbatihs (Latvia) 195.0 kg

WOMEN

65 *kg snatch*: Valentina Popova (Russia) 113.50 kg**

*denotes Games Record
**denotes World Record

---

## BADMINTON

---

ENGLISH NATIONAL CHAMPIONSHIPS 2001

Burgess Hill, Bournemouth, February

*Men's Singles*: Colin Haughton beat Mark Constable 2–1
*Ladies Singles*: Julia Mann beat Tracey Hallam 2–0
*Men's Doubles*: Simon Archer and Nathan Robertson beat Chris Hunt and Julian Robertson 2–0
*Ladies Doubles*: Gail Emms and Jo Wright beat Ella Miles and Sara Sankey 2–1
*Mixed Doubles*: Simon Archer and Gail Emms beat Graham Hurrell and Sarah Hardaker 2–0

SCOTTISH NATIONAL CHAMPIONSHIPS 2001

Edinburgh, February

*Men's Singles*: B. Flockhart beat R. Blair 2–0
*Ladies' Singles*: S. Hughes beat F. Sneddon 2–1
*Men's Doubles*: A. Gatt and C. Robertson beat R. Blair and R. Hogg 2–0
*Ladies Doubles*: R. Pickering and S. Watt beat K. McEwan and C. Tedman 2–0
*Mixed Doubles*: R. Hogg and K. McEwan beat C. Robertson and R. Pickering 2–1

ALL-ENGLAND CHAMPIONSHIPS 2001

Birmingham, March

*Men's Singles*: Pulella Gopichand (India) beat Chen Hong (China) 2–0
*Ladies Singles*: Gong Zhichao (China) beat Zhou Mi (China) 2–0
*Men's Doubles*: Tony Gunawan and Halim Heryanto (Indonesia) beat Sigit Budiarto and Candra Wijaya (Indonesia) 2–1
*Ladies Doubles*: Gao Ling and Sui Huang (China) beat Wei Yili and Zhang Jiewen (China) 2–1
*Mixed Doubles*: Zhang Jun and Gao Ling (China) beat Michael Sogaard and Rikke Olsen (Denmark) 2–1

## BASEBALL

*American League Championship Series 2000*: New York Yankees beat Seattle Mariners 4–2
*National League Championship Series 2000*: New York Mets beat St Louis Cardinals 4–1
*World Series 2000*: New York Yankees beat New York Mets 4–1

## BASKETBALL

### MEN

*National Cup final 2001*: Leicester beat Sheffield 84–75

### NORTH AMERICA

*National Basketball League (NBA)*
*Eastern Conference final 2001*: Philadelphia 76ers beat Milwaukee Bucks 4–3 (best of 7 series)
*Western Conference final 2001*: Los Angeles Lakers beat San Antonio Spurs 4–0 (best of 7 series)
*NBA final 2001*: Los Angeles Lakers beat Philadelphia 76ers 4–1 (best of 7 series)

## BOWLS – OUTDOOR

### MEN

NATIONAL CHAMPIONSHIPS 2001
Worthing, August

*Singles*: Gordon Charlton (Kent 'B') beat Mark Clarke (Warwickshire 'A') 21–18
*Pairs*: Maurice Miller and Tony Merrell (Cambridgeshire 'A') beat Ray Ottley and Mark Overington (Surrey 'A') 18–17
*Triples*: Nottinghamshire 'A' beat Kent 'A' 21–11
*Fours*: Derbyshire 'A' beat Durham 'A' 17–16
*Middleton Cup (Inter-County Championship) final 2001*: Cumbria beat Kent 113-110

## BOWLS – INDOOR

### THE 66TH OPEN

### MEN

*Singles*: M. Brown beat J. Riddington 21–11
*Pairs*: J. Cooke and A. Sprake beat I. Mackenzie and G. Starks 24–12
*Triples*: R. Puddephatt, G. Gough and P. Lawrence beat D. Fairall, S. Fielder and R. Cheater 20–10

### WOMEN

*Singles*: L. Watkins beat J. Westmore 21–18
*Pairs*: B. Crane and H. Marke beat A. Hathaway and M. Goodwin 31–7
*Triples*: J. Westmore, V. Bramble and L. May beat J. Currek, S. Gard and D. Oliver 20–13

## BOXING

### PROFESSIONAL BOXING

as at 1 September 2001

### WORLD BOXING COUNCIL (WBC) CHAMPIONS

*Heavy*: Hasim Rahman (USA)
*Cruiser*: Juan Carlos Gomez (Cuba)
*Light-heavy*: Roy Jones Jnr (USA)
*Super-middle*: Eric Lucas (Canada)
*Middle*: Bernard Hopkins (USA)
*Light-middle*: Oscar de la Hoya (USA)
*Welter*: Shane Moseley (USA)
*Light-welter*: Kostya Tszyu (Australia)
*Light*: Jose Luis Castillo (Mexico)
*Super-Feather*: Floyd Mayweather (USA)
*Feather*: Erik Morales (Mexico)
*Super-bantam*: Willie Jorrin (USA)
*Bantam*: Veeraphol Sahaprom (Thailand)
*Light-bantam*: Masamori Tokuyama (Japan)
*Fly*: Pongsaklek Wonjongkam (Thailand)
*Light-fly*: Yosam Choi (Korea)
*Straw*: Jose Antonio Aguirre (Mexico)

### WORLD BOXING ASSOCIATION (WBA) CHAMPIONS

*Heavy*: John Ruiz (USA)
*Cruiser*: Virgil Hill (USA)
*Light-heavy*: Roy Jones Jnr (USA)
*Super-middle*: Byron Mitchell (USA)
*Middle*: Felix Trinidad (Puerto Rico)
*Light-middle*: vacant
*Welter*: Andrew Lewis (Guyana)
*Light-welter*: Kostya Tszyu (Australia)
*Light*: Julien Lorcy (France)
*Super-feather*: Joel Casamayor (Cuba)
*Feather*: Derrick Gainer (USA)
*Super-bantam*: vacant
*Bantam*: vacant
*Light-bantam*: Celes Kobayashi (Japan)
*Fly*: Eric Morel (USA)
*Light-fly*: Rosendo Alverez (Nicaragua)
*Straw*: Yutaka Niida (Japan)

### WORLD BOXING ORGANISATION (WBO) CHAMPIONS

*Heavy*: Wladimir Klitschko (Ukraine)
*Cruiser*: Johnny Nelson (England)
*Light-heavy*: Daruisz Michalczewski (Germany)
*Super-middle*: Joe Calzaghe (Wales)
*Middle*: vacant
*Light-middle*: vacant
*Welter*: Daniel Santos (Puerto Rico)
*Light-welter*: DeMarcus Corley (USA)
*Light*: Artur Grigorian (Uzbekistan)
*Super-feather*: Acelino Frietas (Brazil)
*Feather*: Julio Pablo Chacon (Argentina)
*Super-bantam*: Agapito Sanchez (Dominican Republic)
*Bantam*: Mauricio Martinez (Panama)
*Light-bantam*: Pedro Alcazar (Panama)
*Fly*: Fernando Montiel (Mexico)
*Light-fly*: Nelson Dieppa (Puerto Rico)
*Straw*: Kermin Guardia (Colombia)

### INTERNATIONAL BOXING FEDERATION (IBF) CHAMPIONS

*Heavy*: Hasim Rahman (USA)
*Cruiser*: Vassily Jirov (Kazakhstan)
*Light-heavy*: Roy Jones Jnr (USA)
*Super-middle*: Sven Ottke (Germany)
*Middle*: Bernard Hopkins (USA)
*Light-middle*: vacant
*Welter*: Vernon Forrest (USA)
*Light-welter*: Zab Judah (USA)
*Light*: Paul Spadafora (USA)
*Super-feather*: Steve Forbes (USA)
*Feather*: Frankie Toledo (USA)
*Super-bantam*: Manny Pacquiao (Philippines)
*Bantam*: Tim Austin (USA)
*Super-fly*: Felix Machado (Venezuela)

*Fly*: Irene Pacheco (Colombia)
*Light-fly*: Ricardo Lopez (Mexico)
*Straw*: Robert Leyva (Mexico)

BRITISH CHAMPIONS
*Heavy*: Danny Williams
*Cruiser*: Scott Bruce
*Light-heavy*: Neil Simpson
*Super-middle*: David Starie
*Middle*: Howard Eastman
*Light-middle*: Wayne Alexander
*Welter*: Harry Dhami
*Light-welter*: vacant
*Light*: Bobby Vanzie
*Super-feather*: Michael Gomez
*Feather*: Scott Harrison
*Super-bantam*: Patrick Mullings
*Bantam*: Nicky Booth
*Fly*: Jason Booth

## CHESS

*British Championships 2001*: Joseph Gallagher

## CRICKET

### TEST SERIES

ENGLAND V. SRI LANKA
*Galle* (22–26 February 2001): Sri Lanka beat England by an innings and 28 runs. Sri Lanka 470–5; England 256 and 189.
*Kandy* (7–11 March 2001): England beat Sri Lanka by 3 wickets. Sri Lanka 297 and 250. England 387 and 161–7
*Colombo* (15–19 March 2001): England beat Sri Lanka by 4 wickets. Sri Lanka 241 and 81. England 249 and 74–6

ENGLAND V. PAKISTAN
*Lahore* (15–19 November 2000): Match drawn. England 480–8 dec. and 77-4; Pakistan 401
*Faisalabad* (29 November–3 December 2000): Match drawn. Pakistan 316 and 269–3; England 342 and 125–5
*Karachi* (7–11 December 2000): England beat Pakistan by 6 wickets. Pakistan 405 and 158; England 388 and 176–4

ENGLAND V. PAKISTAN
*Lord's* (17–20 May 2001): England beat Pakistan by and innings and 9 runs. England 391; Pakistan 203–5 and 179
*Old Trafford* (31 May–4 June 2001): Pakistan beat England by 108 runs. Pakistan 403 and 323; England 357 and 261

ENGLAND V. AUSTRALIA
*Edgbaston* (5–8 July): Australia beat England by an innings and 118 runs. England 294; Australia 576
*Lord's* (19–22 July): Australia beat England by 8 wickets. England 187 and 227; Australia 401
*Trent Bridge* (2–4 August): Australia beat England by 7 wickets. England 185 and 162; Australia 190 and 158–3
*Headingley* (16–20 August): England beat Australia by 6 wickets. Australia 447 and 176-4 dec.; England 309 and 315–4
*Oval* (23–27 August): Australia beat England by an innings and 25 runs. Australia 641-4 dec.; England 432 and 184

### ONE-DAY INTERNATIONALS

ICC KNOCK-OUT 2000
*Nairobi* (3 October): India beat Kenya by 8 wickets. India 209–2; Kenya 208–9
*Nairobi* (4 October): Sri Lanka beat West Indies by 108 runs. Sri Lanka 287–6; West Indies 179
*Nairobi* (5 October): England beat Bangladesh by 8 wickets. England 236–2; Bangladesh 232–8
*Nairobi* (7 October): India beat Australia by 20 runs. India 265–9; Australia 245
*Nairobi* (8 October): Pakistan beat Sri Lanka by 9 wickets. Pakistan 195–1; Sri Lanka 194
*Nairobi* (9 October): New Zealand beat Zimbabwe by 64 runs. New Zealand 265–7; Zimbabwe 201
*Nairobi* (10 October): South Africa beat England by 8 wickets. South Africa 184–2; England 182
*Nairobi* (11 October): New Zealand beat Pakistan by 4 wickets. New Zealand 255–6; Pakistan 252
*Nairobi* (13 October): India beat South Africa by 95 runs. India 295–6; South Africa 200
*Nairobi* (15 October): New Zealand beat India by 4 wickets. New Zealand 265–6; India 264–6

ENGLAND V. PAKISTAN
*Karachi* (24 October 2000): England beat Pakistan by 5 wickets. England 306–5; Pakistan 304–9
*Lahore* (27 October 2000): Pakistan beat England by 8 wickets. Pakistan 214–2; England 211–9
*Rawalpindi* (30 October 2000): Pakistan beat England by 6 wickets. Pakistan 161–4; England 158

TRIANGULAR TOURNAMENT 2000
20 October: Sri Lanka beat India by 5 wickets. Sri Lanka 225–5; India 224–8
21 October: Sri Lanka beat Zimbabwe by 7 wickets. Sri Lanka 229–3; Zimbabwe 225–4
22 October: India beat Zimbabwe by 13 runs. India 265–8; Zimbabwe 252-6
25 October: Sri Lanka beat Zimbabwe by 123 runs. Sri Lanka 276–9; Zimbabwe 153
26 October: India beat Zimbabwe by 3 wickets. India 219–7; Zimbabwe 218–9
27 October: Sri Lanka beat India by 68 runs. Sri Lanka 294–5; India 226
29 October: Sri Lanka beat India by 245 runs. Sri Lanka 299–5; India 54

### NATWEST SERIES 2001

*Birmingham* (7 June): Pakistan beat England by 108 runs. Pakistan 273–6; England 165
*Cardiff* (9 June): Australia beat Pakistan by 7 wickets. Pakistan 257; Australia 258–3
*Bristol* (10 June): Australia beat England by 5 wickets. England 264–4; Australia 272–5
*London* (12 June): Pakistan beat England by 2 runs. Pakistan 242-8; England 240
*Manchester* (14 June): Australia beat Pakistan by 125 runs. Australia 208–7; Pakistan 86
*Chester-le-Street* (16 June): match abandoned
*Leeds* (17 June): Pakistan beat England (conceded match). England 156; Pakistan 153–4
*Nottingham* (19 June): Pakistan beat Australia by 36 runs. Pakistan 290–9; Australia 254
*London* (21 June): Australia beat England by 8 wickets. England 176; Australia 177–2
*Final, London* (23 June): Australia beat Pakistan by 9 wickets to win the series. Pakistan 152; Australia 156–1

### OTHER INTERNATIONAL DOMESTIC CHAMPIONSHIPS

*Australia*: ACB Cup 2000–1: Western Australia, 36.4 points
*India*: Deodhar Trophy: Match drawn. Central Zone 298–8; South Zone 298; Irani Trophy 2000–1: Rest of India beat Mumbai by 10 wickets. Mumbai 260 and 184; Rest of India 389 and 58–0; Ranji Trophy 2000–1:

Baroda beat Railways by 21 runs. Baroda 243 and 373; Railways 394 and 201

*New Zealand*: Shell Super Max 2000–1: Wellington beat Auckland by 8 wickets. Auckland 99–2 and 63–6; Wellington 111–6 and 53–2; Shell Cup 2000–1: Canterbury 12 points; Shell Trophy 2000–1: Wellington, 34 points

*Pakistan*: One Day Tournament (Associations), 2000–1: Karachi Cricket Association beat Sheikpura Cricket Association by 79 runs. Karachi 278–5; Shiekpura 199; One Day Tournament (Departments) 2000–1:Habib Bank Limited beat National Bank of Pakistan by 8 wickets. National Bank of Pakistan 192; Habib Bank 196-2; Patrons Trophy 2000–1: Pakistan Customs beat National Bank of Pakistan by 4 wickets. National Bank of Pakistan 365 and 110; Pakistan Customs 321 and 155; Quaid-e-Azam Trophy 2000-1: Lahore Cricket Association Blues beat Karachi Cricket Association by 1 wicket. Karachi 297 and 104; Lahore 218 and 185

*South Africa*: Standard Bank Cup 2000–1: KwaZulu Natal beat Northerns by 3 wickets. Northerns 214–4; KwaZulu Natal 217–7; SuperSport Series 2000–1: Western Province beat Border by an innings and 26 runs. Borders 252 and 191; Western Province 469

*West Indies*: Busta Cup 2000–1: Jamaica beat Guyana on 1st innings score. Jamaica 375 and 161-4; Guyana 290

*Zimbabwe*: Logan Cup 2000–1: Matabeleland beat CFX Academy by an innings and 62 runs. CFX Academy 320 and 126; Matabeleland 508-8 dec.

### OTHER RESULTS 2001

*Benson and Hedges Cup final*: Surrey beat Gloucestershire by 47 runs. Surrey 244; Gloucestershire 197

*C & G Trophy final:* Somerset beat Leicester by 41 runs. Somerset 271–5; Leicestershire 230

*County Championship Cricket 2001*: *Division 1*, Yorkshire 219 points; *Relegated*, Northamptonshire 148 points; Glamorgan, 133 points; Essex ,166 points

*Division 2*, *Promoted*, Sussex, 208 points; Hampshire, 192 points; Warwickshire, 185 points

*Norwich Union League*, *Division 1*, Kent Spitfires 50; *Relegated*, Gloucestershire Gladiators, 26 points; Surrey Lions, 24 points; Northamptonshire Steelbacks, 14 points

*Division 2*, *Promoted*, Durham Dynamos, 42 points; Worcestershire Royals, 40 points

*Varsity Match* (*one-day*)*:* Oxford beat Cambridge by 8 wickets. Cambridge 177–8; Oxford 178–2

*Varsity Match* (*three-day*): Oxford beat Cambridge by 3 wickets. Cambridge 296 and 233; Oxford 325 and 207–7

## CURLING

### EUROPEAN CHAMPIONSHIPS 2000
Oberstdorf, Germany

MEN

Finland beat Denmark 8–7

WOMEN

Sweden beat Norway 9–4

### WORLD CHAMPIONSHIPS 2001
Lausanne, Switzerland

MEN

Sweden beat Switzerland 6–3

WOMEN

Canada beat Sweden 5–2

## CYCLING

### WORLD ROAD CYCLING CHAMPIONSHIPS 2001

MEN

*Time trial:* Serhiy Honchar (Ukraine) 56:21.75
*Road race:* Romans Vainsteins (Latvia) 6hr 15:28

WOMEN

*Time trial:* Mari Holden (USA) 33:14.62
*Road race:* Zinaida Stahurskaia (Belarus) 3hr 17:39

*Tour of Italy 2001*: Gilberto Simoni (Italy), Lampre
*Tour de France 2001*: Lance Armstrong (USA), US Postal Service
*Tour of Spain 2001*: Jose Maria Jamenez (Spain)

### WORLD CUP STANDINGS 2001

1. Erik Dekker (Netherlands); 2. Erik Zabel (Germany); 3. Romans Vainsteins (Latvia)

### UCI STANDINGS 2001

1. Lance Armstrong (USA); 2. Davide Rebellin (Italy); 3. Erik Zabel (Germany)

### WORLD TRACK CHAMPIONSHIPS 2000

MEN

*1km time trial*: Arnaud Tournant (France) 1:01.619
*Individual pursuit*: Jens Lehmann (Germany) 4:21.836
*Keiren*: Frederic Magne (France) 10.695
*Madison*: Germany (Stefan Steinweg, Erik Weispfennig) 28pts
*Olympic sprint*: France (Laurent Gane, Florian Rousseau, Arnaud Tournant) 44.627
*Points race*: Rosello Joan Llaneras (Spain) 19pts
*Sprint*: Jan van Eijden (Germany) Run 1–11.229; Run 2–10.680
*Team pursuit*: Germany (Sebastian Siedler, Daniel Becke, Guido Fulst, Jens Lehmann) 4:01.322

WOMEN

*500m time trial*: Natalia Markovnichenko (Belarus) 34.838
*Individual pursuit*: Yvonne McGregor (GB) 3:35.274
*Points race*: Marion Clignet (France) 15pts
*Sprint*: Natalia Markovnichenko (Belarus) Run 1–11.703; Run 3–11.885

## DARTS

*Embassy World Championship 2001*: John Walton (England) beat Ted Hankey (England) 6–2

## EQUESTRIANISM

*Badminton Horse Trials 2001*: cancelled due to foot and mouth disease
*British Open Horse Trials 2001* (Gatcombe Park): cancelled due to foot and mouth disease
*Burghley Horse Trials 2001*: Blyth Tait (New Zealand) on Ready Teddy

## ETON FIVES

*Amateur Championship (Kinnaird Cup) 2001*: Ed Wass and Jamie Halstead beat James Toop and Matthew Wiseman 3–1
*Alan Barber Cup final 2001*: Old Cholmeleians beat Old Olavians 2–1
*County Championship final 2001*: Kent beat Warwickshire 2–1
*League Championship (Douglas Keeble Cup) 2001*: Old Cholmeleians beat Old Olavian I 2–1

*Holmwoods Schools' Championship 2001*: Highgate I (A. S. Varma and H. Young) beat Highgate II (O. D. Rodwell and G. A. Eleftheriou) 3–0

*Holmwoods Preparatory Schools' Tournament 2001*: Highgate I (A. O'Callaghan and M. Little) beat Ludgrove I (A. Cornwallis and J. Rowland Clark) 2–0

## FENCING

### MEN

#### BRITISH CHAMPIONS 2001

*Foil*: Richard Kruse (Salle Paul)
*Epée*: Greg Allen (Haverstock)
*Sabre*: Chris Jamieson (Edinburgh)
*Corble Cup 2001* (International Sabre World Cup Series): Wiradech Kothny (Germany)
*Glasgow Cup 2001* (International Epée World Cup Series): Fabrice Jeannet (France)

### WOMEN

#### BRITISH CHAMPIONS 2001

*Foil*: Linda Strachan (Salle Boston)
*Epée*: Georgina Usher (LTFC)
*Sabre*: Louise Bond-Williams (Shakespeare Swords)
*Ipswich Cup 2001* (international epée world cup series): Tatiana Logounova (Russia)

## GOLF (MEN)

### THE MAJOR CHAMPIONSHIPS 2001

*US Masters* (Augusta, Georgia, 5–8 April): Tiger Woods (USA), 272
**US Open* (Tulsa, Oklahoma, 14–17 June): Retief Goosen (South Africa), 276
*The Open* (Royal Lytham and St Annes, 19–22 July): David Duvall (USA), 274
*US PGA Championship* (Atlanta, Georgia, 16–19 August): David Toms (USA), 265
* Woods becomes the first player in history to consecutively win the four majors

### MAJOR TEAM EVENTS 2000

*Alfred Dunhill Cup final* (St Andrews, 12–15 October): Spain beat South Africa 2–1
*Presidents Cup* (Lake Manassas, Virginia, 19–22 October): United States beat Internationals 21 ½ to 10 ½

### WORLD RANKINGS (as at 2 September 2001)

1. Tiger Woods (USA); 2. Phil Mickelson (USA); 3. David Duval (USA); 4.Ernie Els (South Africa); 5. Vijay Singh (Fiji)

### EUROPEAN TOUR ORDER OF MERIT 2001

1. Retief Goosen (South Africa); 2. Darren Clarke (Northern Ireland); 3. Thomas Björn (Denmark); 4. Padraig Harrington (Ireland); 5. Colin Montgomerie (Scotland)

### PGA EUROPEAN TOUR 2000–1

*Volvo Masters* (Jerez, Spain): Pierre Fulke (Sweden), 272
*WGC-American Express Championship* (Valderrama, Spain): Mike Weir (Canada), 277
*Johnnie Walker Classic* (Bangkok, Thailand): Tiger Woods (USA), 263
*WGC-Andersen Consulting Match Play* (Victoria, Australia): Steve Stricker (USA)
*Alfred Dunhill Championship* (Johannesburg, South Africa): Adam Scott (Australia), 267
*Mercedes-Benz South African Open* (East London, South Africa): Mark McNulty (Zimbabwe), 280
*Heineken Classic* (Perth, Australia): Mark Campbell (New Zealand), 270
*Greg Norman Holden International* (Sydney, Australia): Aaron Baddeley (Australia), 271
*Carlsberg Malaysian Open* (Malaysia): Vijay Singh (Fiji), 274
*Caltex Singapore Masters* (Singapore): Vijay Singh (Fiji), 263
*Dubai Desert Classic* (Dubai): Thomas Björn (Denmark), 266
*Qatar Masters* (Doha, Qatar): Tony Johnstone (Zimbabwe), 274
*Madeira Island Open* (Santo da Serra, Portugal): Des Smyth (Ireland), 270
*Sao Paulo Brazil Open* (Sao Paulo): Darren Fichardt (South Africa), 195
*Open de Argentina* (Buenos Aires): Angel Cabrera (Argentina), 268
*Moroccan Open* (Rabat, Morocco): Ian Poulter (England), 277
*Open de España* (Girona, Spain): Robert Karlsson (Sweden), 277
*Algarve Portuguese Open* (Quinta do Lago Algarve, Portugal): Phillip Price (Wales), 273
*Novotel Perrier Open de France* (Villette d'Anthon, France): José Maria Olazabal (Spain), 268
*Benson and Hedges International Open* (Belfry): Henrik Stenson (Sweden), 275
*Deutsche Bank - SAP Open TPC of Europe* (Heidelberg, Germany): Tiger Woods (USA), 266
*Volvo PGA Championship* (Wentworth): Andrew Oldcorn (GB), 272
*Victor Chandler British Masters* (Milton Keynes): Thomas Levet (France), 274**
*The Compass Group English Open* (Forest of Arden): Peter O'Malley (Australia), 275
*The Great North Open* (Northumberland): Andrew Coltart (GB), 277
*Murphy's Irish Open* (Cork, Ireland): Colin Montgomerie (GB), 266
*Smurfit European Open* (Dublin, Ireland): Darren Clark (GB), 273
*Scottish Open* (Loch Lomond): Reteif Goosen (South Africa), 268
*TNT Dutch Open* (Noordwijk, Netherlands): Bernhard Langer (Germany), 269
*Volvo Scandinavian Masters* (Barsebäck, Sweden): Colin Montgomerie (GB), 274
*The Celtic Manor Resort Wales Open* (Newport): Paul McGinley (Ireland), 138
*West of Ireland Open* (Ireland): Tobias Dier (Germany), 271
*WGC-NEC Invitational* (Akron, Ohio): Tiger Woods (USA), 268**
*Scottish PGA Championship* (Gleneagles): Paul Casey (England), 274
*BMW International Open* (Munich, Germany): John Daly (USA), 261
*Omega European Masters* (Crans-sur-Sierre, Switzerland): Ricardo Gonzalez (Argentina), 268
*WGC-American Express Championship* (St Louis, Missouri): *cancelled*

### TROPHÉE LANCÔME (PARIS, FRANCE)

Sergio Garcia (Spain) 266

### MAJOR TEAM EVENTS

*Ryder Cup* (Belfry): postponed until September 2002 due to the World Trade Centre bombings in New York on 11 September 2001

AMATEUR CHAMPIONSHIPS
*British Amateur Championship 2001* (Prestwick and Kilmarnock): Michael Hoey (Ireland) by 1 hole
*English Amateur Championship 2001* (Saunton): Scott Godfrey
*Welsh Amateur Championship 2001* (Royal Porthcawl Golf Club): Craig Williams
*Scottish Amateur Championship 2001* (Downfield): Barry Hume
*Brabazon Trophy (English Open Strokeplay) 2001* (Royal Birkdale): Richard Walker (England), 280
*Welsh Open Strokeplay 2001* (Llandudno, Maesdu Golf Club): Jonathan Lupton, 266
*Scottish Open Strokeplay 2001* (Nairn and Nairn Dunbar): John Sutherland (Australia), 279
*Lytham Trophy 2001* (Royal Lytham Golf Club): Richard McEvoy (England), 276
*Berkshire Trophy 2001* (The Berkshire): Greg Evans (England), 283
*Home International Championship 2001* (Carnoustie): *see Stop Press*
*After a play-off

## GOLF (WOMEN)

EUROPEAN TOUR ORDER OF MERIT 2000:
1. Raquel Carriedo (Spain); 2. Elisabeth Esterl (Germany); 3. Sophie Gustafson (Sweden); 4. Samantha Head (England); 5. Anna Berg (Sweden)

EUROPEAN LPGA TOUR 2000–1
*Ladies World Cup of Golf* (Limerick, Ireland): Sweden, 425
*Mexx Sport Open* (Zandvoort, Netherlands): Tina Fischer (Germany), 211
*Solheim Cup* (Loch Lomond): Europe beat USA
*Marrakech Palmeraie Open* (Marrakech, Morocco): Alison Munt (Australia), 207
*ANZ Ladies Masters* (Goldcoast, Australia): Karrie Webb (Australia), 271
*AAMI Womens Australian Open* (Melbourne, Australia): Sophie Gustafson (Sweden), 276
*Taiwan Ladies Open* (Taiwan): Raquel Carriedo (Spain), 212
*Nedbank Mastercard South African Masters* (Johannesburg): Samantha Head (GB), 210
*Le Perla Italian Open* (Poggio dei Medici), Paula Marti (Spain), 283
*Ladies French Open* (St Aubin): Suzann Pettersen (Norway), 280
*Evian Masters* (Evian les Bains): Rachel Teske (Australia), 273
*Kellogg's All-Bran Ladies British Masters* (Mottram Hall, Cheshire): Paula Marti (Spain), 209
*WPGA Championship of Europe* (Royal Porthcaw, nr Bridgend): Helen Alfredson (Sweden), 276
*Weetabix Women's British Open* (Sunningdale, Surrey): Se Ri Pak (Korea), 277
*Compaq Open* (Österäkers, Sweden): Raquel Carriedo (Spain), 284
*Ladies German Open* (Berlin): Karine Icher (France), 210
*Mexx Sport Open* (Zandvoort, Netherlands): Karine Icher (France), 212
*Ladies Irish Open* (Faithlegg, Waterford): Racquel Carriedo (Spain), 200
*Samsung World Championship 2000* (Vallejo, California): Julie Inkster (USA), 274
*US Women's Open 2001* (Merit Club, Libertyville, Illinois): Karrie Webb (Australia), 273

AMATEUR CHAMPIONSHIPS
*British Open Championship 2001* (Ladybank Golf Club, Scotland): Marta Prieto (Spain), won by 4/3 in final
*English Amateur Championship 2001* (West Sussex Golf Club): Rebecca Hudson, won on 20th hole in final
*English Strokeplay 2001* (Stoneham Golf Club): Caroline Marron, 291
*European Amateur Team Championship 2001* (Golf de Meis, Spain): Sweden

## GREYHOUND RACING

2000
*Cesarewitch* (Catford): Lady Jean
*East Anglian Derby* (Yarmouth): Courts Legal
*Gold Collar* (Catford): Castlelyons Dani
*Laurels* (Belle Vue): Courts Legal
*The Derby* (Milton Keynes): Glowing Wave
*Oaks* (Wimbledon): Ragga Juju
*St Leger* (Wimbledon): Palace Issue
*Television Trophy* (Wimbledon): Sexy Delight

2001
*Grand National* (Wimbledon): Kish Jaguar
*Grand Prix* (Walthamstow): Palace Issue
*William Hill Derby* (Wimbledon): Rapid Ranger
*Bass Brewers Greyhound Derby* (Peterborough): Kinda Magic
*Kent Derby* (Sittingbourne): Pinewood Blue
*Ladbroke Golden Jacket* (Crayford): Blues Best Tayla
*The Masters* (Reading): Marshalls June
*Pall Mall* (Oxford): Kinda Majic
*The Regency* (Brighton): Solid Magic
*Scurry Gold Cup* (Catford): Kalooki Jet
*Select Stakes* (Nottingham): Sonic Flight
*Summer Cup* (Milton Keynes): Santas Supreme

## GYMNASTICS

BRITISH MEN'S CHAMPIONSHIPS 2001
Stoke-on-Trent, July

*British Champion*: David Eaton (Hinckley)
*Individual Apparatus Champions*
*Floor*: Darren Gerrard (Stoke-on-Trent)
*Pommel Horse*: Ross Brewer (Sutton S of G)
*Rings*: Scott Mirceta (Stoke-on-Trent)
*Vault*: Darren Gerrard (Stoke-on-Trent)
*Parallel Bars*: Ross Brewer (Sutton S of G)
*High Bar*: David Eaton (Hinckley)

BRITISH WOMEN'S CHAMPIONSHIPS 2001
Guildford, July

*British Champion*: Elizabeth Tweddle (City of Liverpool)
*Individual Apparatus Champions*
*Floor*: Nicola Willis (South Essex)
*Beam*: Holly Murdock (Salto)
*Vault*: Holly Murdock (Salto)
*Assymetric Bars*: Elizabeth Tweddle (City of Liverpool)

## HOCKEY

MEN
*English Hockey League Premier Division 2001*: Reading
*English Hockey League Premiership final 2001*: Surbiton beat Guildford 1–0
*National Indoor Club Championship final 2001*: Guildford beat Old Loughtonians 7–6

*County Championship final 2001*: Warwickshire beat Cheshire 5–3 (APS)

WOMEN

*English Hockey League Premier Division 2001*: Fyffes Leicester

*English Hockey League Premiership final 2000:* Slough beat Ipswich 3–1

*English Hockey Indoor League Premier Division 2001*: Slough beat Chelmsford 5–2

## HORSE-RACING

### RESULTS

CAMBRIDGESHIRE HANDICAP
(1839) Newmarket, 1 mile

1997 Pasternak (4y), (9st 1lb), G. Duffield
1998 Lear Spear (3y), (8st 4lb), N. Pollard
1999 She's Our Mare (6y), (7st 12lb), F. Norton
2000 Katy Nowaitee (4y), (8st, 8lb), J. Reid

PRIX DE L'ARC DE TRIOMPHE
(1920) Longchamp, 1½ miles

1997 Peintre Célèbre (3y), (8st 11lb), O. Peslier
1998 Sagamix (3y), (8st 11lb), O. Peslier
1999 Montjeu (3y), (8st 11lb), M. Kinane
2000 Sinndar (3y), (8st, 11lb), J. P. Murtagh

CESAREWITCH
(1839) Newmarket, 2 miles and about 2 f

1997 Turnpole (6y), (7st 10lb), L. Charnock
1998 Spirit of Love (3y), (8st 8lb), O. Peslier
1999 Top Cees (9y), (8st 10lb), K. Fallon
2000 Heros Fatal (6y), (8st), G. Carter

CHAMPION STAKES
(1877) Newmarket, 1 mile, 2 f

1997 Pilsudski (5y), (9st 2lb), M. Kinane
1998 Alborada (3y), (8st 8lb), G. Duffield
1999 Alborada (4y), (8st 13lb), G. Duffield
2000 Kalanisi (5y), (9st 2lb), J. Murtagh

*HENNESSY GOLD CUP
(1957) Newbury, 3 miles and about 2½ f

1997 Suny Bay (8y), (11st 8lb), G. Bradley
1998 Teeton Mill (9y), (10st 5lb), N. Williamson
1999 Ever Bless (6y), (10st), T. J. Murphy
2000 Kings Road (8y), (10st), J. Goldstein

*KING GEORGE VI CHASE
(1937) Kempton, about 3 miles

1997 See More Business (7y), (11st), A. Thornton
1998 Teeton Mill (9y), (11st), N. Williamson
1999 See More Business (9y), (11st), M. A. Fitzgerald
2000 First Gold (8y), T. Dounan

*DUBAI WORLD CUP
(1957) Dubai, 1 mile and 2 f

2000 Dubai Millennium (4y), (10st 8lb), L. Dettori
2001 Captain Steve (4y), J. D. Bailey

*CHAMPION HURDLE
(1927) Cheltenham, 2 miles and about ½ f

1998 Istabraq (6y), (12st), C. Swan
1999 Istabraq (7y), (12st), C. Swan
2000 Istabraq (8y), (12st), C. Swan
2001 cancelled due to foot and mouth crisis

*QUEEN MOTHER CHAMPION CHASE
(1959) Cheltenham, about 2 miles

1998 One Man (10y), (12st), B. Harding
1999 Call Equiname (9y), (12st), M. Fitzgerald
2000 Edredon Bleu (8y), (12st), A. P. McCoy
2001 cancelled due to foot and mouth crisis

*CHELTENHAM GOLD CUP
(1924) 3 miles and about 2½ f

1998 Cool Dawn (10y), (12st), A. Thornton
1999 See More Business (9y), (12st), M. Fitzgerald
2000 Looks Like Trouble (8y), (12st), R. Johnson
2001 cancelled due to foot and mouth crisis

LINCOLN HANDICAP
(1965) Doncaster, 1 mile

1998 Hunters Of Brora (8y), (9st), J. Weaver
1999 Right Wing (5y), (9st 5lb), T. Quinn
2000 John Ferneley (5y), (8st, 10lb), F. Fortune
2001 Nimello (5y), (8st 9lb), J. Fortune

*GRAND NATIONAL
(1837) Liverpool, 4 miles and about 4 f

1998 Earth Summit (10y), (10st 5lb), C. Llewellyn
1999 Bobbyjo (9y), (10st), P. Carberry
2000 Papillon (9y), (10st 12lb), R. Walsh
2001 Red Marauder (11y), (10st 5lb), R. Guest

Record times: 8 minutes 47.8 seconds by Mr Frisk in 1990; 9 minutes 1.9 seconds by Red Rum in 1973

*WHITBREAD GOLD CUP
(1957) Sandown, 3 miles and about 5 f

1998 Call It A Day (8y), (10st 10lb), A. Maguire
1999 Eulogy (9y), (10st), B. Fenton
2000 Beau (7yr), (10st 9lb), C. Llewellyn
2001 Ad hoc (7y), (10st 4lb), R. Walsh

JOCKEY CLUB STAKES
(1894) Newmarket, 2 miles, 24 yds

1997 Time Allowed (4y), (8st 6lb), J. Reid
1998 Romanov (4y), (8st 9lb), J. Reid
1999 Rainbow High (4y), (9st), M. Hills
2000 Millenary (4y), (9st), P. Eddery

PRIX DU JOCKEY CLUB
(1836) Chantilly, 1½ miles

1998 Dream Well (9st 2lb), C. Asmussen
1999 Montjeu (9st 2lb), C. Asmussen
2000 Volvoreta (9st), T. Thulliez
2001 Anabaa Blue (3y), C. Soumillion

ASCOT GOLD CUP
(1807) Ascot, 2 miles and about 4 f

1998 Kayf Tara (4y), (9st), L. Dettori
1999 Enzeili (4y), (9st), J. Murtagh
2000 Kayf Tara (6y), (9st 2lb), M. J. Kinane
2001 Royal Rebel (5y), (9st 2lb), J. P. Murtagh

IRISH DERBY
(1866) Curragh, 1½ miles, for three-year-olds

1998 Dream Well (9st), C. Asmussen
1999 Montjeu (9st), C. Asmussen
2000 Sinndar (9st), J. P. Murtagh
2001 Galileo (3y), (9st), M. Kinane

ECLIPSE STAKES
(1886) Sandown, 1 mile and about 2 f

1998 Daylami (4y), (9st 7lb), F. Dettori
1999 Compton Admiral (3y), (8st 10lb), D. Holland
2000 Giant's Causeway (3y), (8st 10lb), G. Duffield
2001 Medicean (9st 4lb), K. Fallon

## THE CLASSICS
### ONE THOUSAND GUINEAS

(1814) Rowley Mile, Newmarket, for three-year-old fillies

| *Year* | *Winner* | *Betting* | *Owner* | *Jockey* | *Trainer* | *No. of Runners* |
|---|---|---|---|---|---|---|
| 1998 | Cape Verdi | 100–30 | Godolphin | F. Dettori | Saeed bin Suroor | 16 |
| 1999 | Wince | 4–1 | Prince K. Abdulla | K. Fallon | H. Cecil | 22 |
| 2000 | Lahan | 14–1 | Hamdan Al Maktoum | R. Hills | J. Gosden | 18 |
| 2001 | Ameerat | | Sheikh Ahmed Al Maktoum | P. Robinson | M. A. Jarvis | 15 |

Record time: 1 minute 36.71 seconds by Las Meninas in 1994

### TWO THOUSAND GUINEAS

(1809) Rowley Mile, Newmarket, for three-year-olds

| *Year* | *Winner* | *Betting* | *Owner* | *Jockey* | *Trainer* | *No. of Runners* |
|---|---|---|---|---|---|---|
| 1998 | King of Kings | 7–2 | Mrs J. Magnier/M. Tabor | M. Kinane | A. O'Brien | 18 |
| 1999 | Island Sands | 10–1 | Godolphin | F. Dettori | Saeed bin Suroor | 16 |
| 2000 | King's Best | 13–2 | Saeed Suhail | K. Fallon | Sir Michael Stoute | 27 |
| 2001 | Golan | | Lord Weinstock | K. Fallon | Sir Michael Stoute | 18 |

Record time: 1 minute 35.08 seconds by Mister Baileys in 1994

### THE DERBY

(1780) Epsom, 1 mile and about 4 f, for three-year-olds

The first winner was Sir Charles Bunbury's Diomed in 1780. The owners with the record number of winners are Lord Egremont, who won in 1782, 1804, 1805, 1807, 1826 (also won five Oaks); and the late Aga Khan, who won in 1930, 1935, 1936, 1948, 1952. Other winning owners are: Duke of Grafton (1802, 1809, 1810, 1815); Mr J. Bowes (1835, 1843, 1852, 1853); Sir J. Hawley (1851, 1858, 1859, 1868); the 1st Duke of Westminster (1880, 1882, 1886, 1899); and Sir Victor Sassoon (1953, 1957, 1958, 1960).

Record times are: 2 min. 32.31 sec. by Lammtarra in 1995; 2 min. 33.80 sec. by Mahmoud in 1936; 2 min. 33.84 sec. by Kahyasi in 1988; 2 min. 33.88 by High-Rise in 1998; 2 min. 33.9 sec. by Reference Point in 1987.

The Derby was run at Newmarket in 1915–18 and 1940–5.

| *Year* | *Winner* | *Betting* | *Owner* | *Jockey* | *Trainer* | *No. of Runners* |
|---|---|---|---|---|---|---|
| 1998 | High Rise | 20–1 | Sheikh Mohammed Obaidh Al Maktoum | O. Peslier | L. Cumani | 15 |
| 1999 | Oath | 13–2 | Prince Ahmed Salman | K. Fallon | H. Cecil | 16 |
| 2000 | Sinndar | 7–1 | Aga Khan | J. Murtahg | J. Oxx | 8 |
| 2001 | Galileo | | Mrs John Magnier | M. Kinane | A. O'Brien | 12 |

### THE OAKS

(1779) Epsom, 1 mile and about 4 f, for three-year-old fillies

| *Year* | *Winner* | *Betting* | *Owner* | *Jockey* | *Trainer* | *No. of Runners* |
|---|---|---|---|---|---|---|
| 1997 | Reams of Verse | 5–6 | Prince K. Abdulla | K. Fallon | H. Cecil | 12 |
| 1998 | Shahtoush | 12–1 | Mrs D. Nagle/Mrs J. Magnier | M. Kinane | A. O'Brien | 8 |
| 1999 | Ramruma | 3–1 | Prince Fahd Salman | K. Fallon | H. Cecil | 10 |
| 2000 | Love Divine | 9–4 | Lordship Stud | T. Quinn | H. Cecil | 18 |
| 2001 | Imagine | | Mrs John Magnier | M. Kinane | A. O'Brien | 14 |

Record time: 2 minutes 34.19 seconds by Intrepidity in 1993

### ST LEGER

(1776) Doncaster, 1 mile and about 6 f, for three-year-olds

| *Year* | *Winner* | *Betting* | *Owner* | *Jockey* | *Trainer* | *No. of Runners* |
|---|---|---|---|---|---|---|
| 1997 | Silver Patriarch | 5–4 | P. Winfield | P. Eddery | J. Dunlop | 10 |
| 1998 | Nedawi | 5–2 | Godolphin | J. Reid | Saeed bin Suroor | 9 |
| 1999 | Mutafaweq | 11–2 | Godolphin | R. Hills | Saeed bin Suroor | 9 |
| 2000 | Goggles | 14–1 | Mrs J. Powell | C. Rutter | H. Candy | 22 |
| 2001 | Millenany | | L. Neil Jones | T. Quinn | J. L. Dunlop | 11 |

Record time: 3 minutes 1.60 seconds by Coronach in 1926 and Windsor Lad in 1934

King George VI and Queen Elizabeth Diamond Stakes
(1952) Ascot, 1 mile and about 4 f

1998 Swain (6y), (9st 7lb), L. Dettori
1999 Daylami (5y), (9st 7lb), L. Dettori
2000 Montjeu (4y), (9st 7lb), M. J. Kinane
2001 Galileo (3y), (8st 9lb), M. Kinane

Goodwood Cup
(1812) Goodwood, about 2 miles

1998 Double Trigger (7y), (9st 5lb), D. Holland
1999 Kayf Tara (5y), (9st 7lb), L. Dettori
2000 Royal Rebel (4y), (9st 2lb), M. J. Kinane
2001 Persian Punch (8y), T. Quinn
*National Hunt
†Run on 6 January 1996 because of bad weather

## Statistics

Winning Flat Owners 2000

| | |
|---|---|
| H. H. Aga Khan | £1,651,752 |
| Hamdan Al-Maktoum | 1,409,963 |
| K. Abdulla | 1,311,115 |
| Godolphin | 1,209,630 |
| Mrs J. Magnier and M. Tabor | 1,002,356 |
| M. Tabor | 679,337 |
| Maktoum Al Maktoum | 559,208 |
| Cheveley Park Stud | 525,274 |
| M. Tabor and Mrs J. Magnier | 454,008 |
| S. Suhail | 336,655 |

Winning Flat Trainers 2000

| | |
|---|---|
| Sir Michael Stoute | £2,803,216 |
| J. L. Dunlop | 1,602,101 |
| M. Johnston | 1,583,281 |
| R. Hannon | 1,542,333 |
| A. P. O'Brien (Ireland) | 1,520,674 |
| J. H. M. Gosden | 1,499,406 |
| Saeed bin Suroor | 1,209,630 |
| M. R. Channon | 1,046,226 |
| H. R. A. Cecil | 1,036,870 |
| B. W. Hills | 814,541 |

Winning Flat Sires 2000

| | *Races won* | *Stakes* |
|---|---|---|
| Sadler's Wells by Northern Dancer | 45 | £1,652,281 |
| Storm Cat by Storm Bird | 9 | 1,082,746 |
| Grand Lodge by Chief's Crown | 31 | 894,773 |
| Danehill by Danzig | 31 | 671,640 |
| Unfuwain by Northern Dancer | 30 | 641,009 |
| Rainbow Quest by Blushing Groom | 37 | 636,587 |
| Indian Ridge by Ahonoora | 58 | 604,459 |
| Doyoun by Mill Reef | 6 | 542,225 |
| Diesis by Sharpen Up | 22 | 527,262 |
| Machiavellian by Mr Prospector | 36 | 516,723 |

Winning Flat Jockeys 2000

| | *1st* | *2nd* | *3rd* | *Unpl.* | *Total mts* |
|---|---|---|---|---|---|
| K. Darley | 155 | 141 | 113 | 588 | 997 |
| T. Quinn | 140 | 120 | 91 | 432 | 783 |
| P. Eddery | 127 | 91 | 79 | 520 | 817 |
| R. Hughes | 102 | 98 | 81 | 507 | 788 |
| J. Fortune | 93 | 81 | 66; | 457 | 697 |
| A. Culhane | 92 | 111 | 90 | 658 | 951 |
| L. Newman | 87 | 62 | 63 | 520 | 732 |
| N. Callan | 80 | 80 | 79 | 511 | 750 |
| R. Hills | 81 | 49 | 56 | 273 | 459 |
| S. Sanders | 80 | 76 | 79 | 499 | 734 |

Winning National Hunt Trainers 2000–1

| | |
|---|---|
| M. C. Pipe | £1,289,693 |
| P. F. Nicholls | 1,091,125 |
| N. J. Henderson | 822,842 |
| P. J. Hobbs | 712,229 |
| Miss V. Williams | 667,832 |
| N. B. Mason | 537,993 |
| N. A. Twiston-Davies | 528,052 |
| Mrs M. Reveley | 475,721 |
| J. J. O'Neill | 395,164 |
| Miss H. C. Knight | 382,712 |

Winning National Hunt Jockeys 2000–1

| | *1st* | *2nd* | *3rd* | *Unpl.* | *Total mts* |
|---|---|---|---|---|---|
| A. P. McCoy | 191 | 131 | 82 | 371 | 775 |
| R. Johnson | 161 | 156 | 139 | 437 | 893 |
| A. Dobbin | 84 | 54 | 33 | 252 | 423 |
| A. Maguire | 79 | 72 | 50 | 265 | 466 |
| M. A. Fitzgerald | 78 | 64 | 55 | 197 | 394 |
| N. Williamson | 76 | 56 | 62 | 243 | 437 |
| A. Thornton | 54 | 62 | 61 | 310 | 487 |
| C. Llewellyn | 54 | 50 | 52 | 328 | 484 |
| T. J. Murphy | 54 | 42 | 50 | 266 | 412 |
| J. Tizzard | 50 | 39 | 48 | 179 | 316 |

The above statistics have been provided by *Timeform*, publishers of the *Racehorses* and *Chasers and Hurdlers* annuals

## ICE HOCKEY

Men

*World Championships 2001*: Czech Republic beat Finland 3-2 in overtime

Women

*World Championships 2001*: Canada beat USA 3–2

National Hockey League

*Eastern Conference final 2001*: New Jersey Devils beat Pittsburgh Penguins 4–1 (best of 7 series)
*Western Conference final 2001*: Colorado Avalanche beat St Louis Blues 4–1 (best of 7 series)
*Stanley Cup final 2001*: Colorado Avalanche beat New Jersey Devils 4–3 (best of 7 series)
*Super League Champions 2001*: Sheffield Steelers

## ICE SKATING

British Championships 2000
Ayr, Scotland, November

*Men*: Alan Street
*Women*: Zoe Jones
*Pairs*: Marika Humphreys and Vitaly Baranov
*Ice Dance*: Tiffany Sifkas and Andrew Seabrook

European Championships 2001
Bratislava, Slovakia, January

*Men*: Evgeni Plushenko (Russia)
*Women*: Irina Slutskaya (Russia)
*Pairs*: Elena Berezhnaya and Anton Sikharulidze (Russia)
*Ice Dance*: Barbara Fusar Poli and Maurizio Margaglio (Italy)

World Championships 2001
Vancouver, British Columbia, Canada March

*Men*: Evgeni Plushenko (Russia)
*Women*: Michelle Kwan (USA)
*Pairs*: Jamie Salé and David Pelletier (Canada)
*Ice Dance*: Barbara Fusar Poli and Maurizio Margaglio (Italy)

## JUDO

British National Championships 2000
Wolverhampton, December

Men

*Heavyweight* (over 100 kg): Daniel Sargent (Dartford)
*Light-heavyweight* (100 kg): Keith Davis (Wandsworth Lightning)
*Middleweight* (90 kg): Winston Gordon (Wandsworth Lightning)
*Welter* (81 kg): Luke Preston (Camberley)
*Lightweight* (73 kg): Darren Warner (Neil Adams)
*Junior lightweight* (66 kg): James Warren (Budokwai)
*Bantamweight* (60 kg): Jamie Johnson (Ryecroft)

Women

*Heavyweight* (over 78 kg): Simone Callender (Takei)
*Light-heavyweight* (78 kg): Michelle Rogers (SKK)
*Middleweight* (70 kg): Rachel Wilding (Camberley)
*Welter* (63 kg): Sarah Clark (Kodokwai)
*Lightweight* (57 kg): Natalie Barry (Bacup)
*Junior lightweight* (52 kg): Georgina Singleton (Pinewood)
*Bantamweight* (48 kg): Donna Robertson (SJC Alba)

## MOTOR CYCLING

500 cc Grand Prix 2000

*Brazilian* (Rio): Valentino Rossi (Italy), Honda
*Japanese* (Motegi): Kenny Roberts (USA), Suzuki
*Australian* (Phillip Island): Max Biaggi (Italy), Yamaha
*Riders' Championship 2001:* 1. Kenny Roberts (USA), Suzuki; 2. Valentino Rossi (Italy), Honda; 3. Max Biaggi (Italy), Yamaha

500 cc Grand Prix 2001

*Japan* (Suzuka): Valentino Rossi (Italy), Honda
*South Africa* (Welkom): Valentino Rossi (Italy), Honda
*Spanish* (Jerez): Valentino Rossi (Italy), Honda
*French* (Le Mans): Max Biaggi (Italy), Yamaha
*Italian* (Mugello): Alex Barros (Brazil), Honda
*Catalunya* (Barcelona): Valentino Rossi (Italy), Honda
*Dutch* (Assen): Max Biaggi (Italy), Yamaha
*British* (Donington Park): Valentino Rossi (Italy), Honda
*German* (Sachsenring): Max Biaggi (Italy), Yamaha
*Czech* (Brno): Valentino Rossi (Italy), Honda
*Portugal* (Estoril): Valentino Rossi (Italy), Honda
*Valencia*: Sete Gibernau (Spain), Suzuki

250 cc Grand Prix 2000

*Brazilian* (Rio): Daijiro Katoh (Japan), Honda
*Japanese* (Motegi): Daijiro Katoh (Japan), Honda
*Australian* (Phillip Island): Olivier Jacque (France), Yamaha
*Riders' Championship 2000:* 1. Olivier Jacque (France), Yamaha; 2. Shinya Nakano (Japan), Yamaha; 3. Daijiro Katoh (Japan), Honda

250 cc Grand Prix 2001

*Japan* (Suzuka): Daijiro Katoh (Japan), Honda
*South Africa* (Welkom): Daijiro Katoh (Japan), Honda
*Spanish* (Jerez): Daijiro Katoh (Japan), Honda
*French* (Le Mans): Daijiro Katoh (Japan), Honda
*Italian* (Mugello): Tetsuya Harada (Japan), Aprillia
*Catalunya* (Barcelona): Daijiro Katoh (Japan), Honda
*Dutch* (Assen): Jeremy McWilliams (GB), Aprillia
*British* (Donington Park): Daijiro Katoh (Japan), Honda
*German* (Sachsenring): Marco Melandri (Italy), Aprillia
*Czech* (Brno): Tetsuya Harada (Japan), Aprillia
*Portugal* (Estoril): Daijiro Katoh (Japan), Honda
*Valencia*: Daijiro Katoh (Japan), Honda

125 cc Grand Prix 2000

*Brazilian* (Rio): Simone Sanna (Italy), Honda
*Japanese* (Motegi): Roberto Locatelli (Italy), Aprillia
*Australian* (Phillip Island): Masao Azuma (Japan), Honda
*Riders' Championship 2000:* 1. Roberto Locatelli (Italy), Aprillia; 2. Youichi Ui (Japan), Derbi; 3. Emilio Alzamora (Spain), Honda

125 cc Grand Prix 2001

*Japan* (Suzuka): Masao Azuma (Japan), Honda
*South Africa* (Welkom): Youichi Ui (Japan), Derbi
*Spanish* (Jerez): Masao Azuma (Japan), Honda
*French* (Le Mans): Manuel Poggiali (Italy), Gilera Racing
*Italian* (Mugello): Noboru Ueda (Japan), Technical Sports Racing
*Catalunya* (Barcelona): Lucio Cecchinello (Italy), MS Aprillia LCR
*Dutch* (Assen): Antonio Elias (Spain), Telefonica Movistar Jnr Team
*British* (Donington Park): Youichi Ui (Japan), Derbi Racing
*German* (Sachsenring): Simone Sanna (Italy), Safilo Oxydo Racing
*Czech* (Brno): Antonio Elias (Spain), Telefonica Movistar Jnr Team
*Portugal* (Estoril): Manuel Poggiali (Italy), Gilera Racing
*Valencia*: Manuel Poggiali (Italy), Gilera Racing

*Senior TT 2001, Isle of Man*: cancelled due to foot and mouth disease
*Junior TT 2001, Isle of Man*: cancelled due to foot and mouth disease

World Superbikes 2000

*Great Britain* (Brands Hatch): Race 1–J. Reynolds (GB), Ducati; Race 2–Colin Edwards (USA), Honda
*World Superbike Champion 2000*: Colin Edwards (USA), Honda 400 points

2001

*Spain* (Valencia): Race 1–Troy Corser (Australia), Aprilia; Race 2–Troy Corser (Australia), Aprilia
*South Africa* (Kyalami): Race 1–Colin Edwards (USA), Honda; Race 2–Ben Bostrom (USA), Ducati
*Australia* (Philip Island): Race 1–Colin Edwards (USA), Honda; Race 2–Cancelled due to rain
*Japan* (Sugo): Race 1–Makoto Tomada (Japan), Honda; Race 2–Makoto Tomada (Japan), Honda
*Italy* (Monza): Race 1–Troy Bayliss (Australia), Ducati; Race 2–Troy Bayliss (Australia), Ducati
*Great Britain* (Donington): Race 1–Neil Hodgson (GB), Ducati; Race 2–Pierfrancesco Chili (Italy), Suzuki
*Germany* (Hockenheim): Race 1–Colin Edwards (USA), Honda; Race 2–Troy Bayliss (Australia), Ducati
*San Marino* (Misano): Race 1–Troy Bayliss (Australia), Ducati; Race 2-Ben Bostrom (USA), Ducati
*United States* (Laguna Seca): Race 1–Ben Bostrom (USA), Ducati; Race 2–Ben Bostrom (USA), Ducati
*Great Britain* (Brands Hatch): Race 1–Ben Bostrom (USA), Ducati; Race 2–Ben Bostrom (USA), Ducati
*Germany* (Oschersleben): Race 1-Colin Edwards (USA), Honda; Race 2-Ruben Xaux (Spain), Ducati
*Netherlands* (Assen): Race 1-Troy Bayliss (Australia), Ducati; Race 2– Troy Bayliss (Australia), Ducati
*Italy* (Italy): *see Stop Press*

## MOTOR RACING

FORMULA ONE GRAND PRIX 2000
*Japanese* (Suzaka): Michael Schumacher (Germany), Ferrari
*Malaysian* (Kuala Lumpa): Michael Schumacher (Germany), Ferrari
*Drivers' World Championship 2000:* 1. Michael Schumacher (Germany), Ferrari, 108 points; 2. Mika Hakkinen (Finland), McLaren-Mercedes, 89 points; 3. David Coulthard (GB) McLaren-Mercedes, 73 points
*Constructors' World Championship 2000:* 1. Ferrari, 170 points; 2. McLaren-Mercedes, 152 points; 3. Williams-BMW, 36 points

FORMULA ONE GRAND PRIX 2001
*Australian* (Melbourne): (4 March) Michael Schumacher (Germany), Ferrari
*Malaysian Grand Prix* (Kuala Lumpur): (18 March) Michael Schumacher (Germany), Ferrari
*Brazilian Grand Prix* (São Paulo): (1 April) David Coulthard (GB), McLaren-Mercedes
*San Marino Grand Prix* (Imola): (15 April) Ralf Schumacher (Germany), Williams-BMW
*Spanish Grand Prix* (Barcelona): (29 April) Michael Schumacher (Germany), Ferrari
*Austrian Grand Prix* (Spielberg): (13May) David Coulthard (GB), McLaren-Mercedes
*Monaco Grand Prix* (Monaco): (27 May) Michael Schumacher (Germany), Ferrari
*Canadian Grand Prix* (Montreal): (10 June) Ralf Schumacher (Germany), Williams-BMW
*European Grand Prix* (Nurburgring): (24 June) Michael Schumacher (Germany), Ferrari
*French Grand Prix* (Magny-Cours): (1 July) Michael Schumacher (Germany), Ferrari
*British Grand Prix* (Silverstone): (15 July) Mika Hakkinen (Finland), McLaren-Mercedes
*German Grand Prix* (Hockenheim): (29 July) Ralf Schumacher (Germany), Williams-BMW
*Hungarian Grand Prix* (Hungaroring): (19 August) Michael Schumacher (Germany), Ferrari*
*Belgian Grand Prix* (Spa-Francorchamps): (2 September) Michael Schumacher (Germany), Ferrari**
*Italian Grand Prix* (Monza): (16 September) Juan Pablo Montoya (Colombia), Williams-BMW
*United States Grand Prix* (Indianapolis): (30 September) *see Stop Press*
*Michael Schumacher becomes 2001 World Champion and Ferrari claim the Constructors' Championship
**Michael Schumacher becomes the winning driver in F1 by winning his 52nd Grand Prix
*Indianapolis 500 2001*: Helio Castroneves (Brazil), Team Penske
*Le Mans 24-hour Race 2001*: Emanuele Pirro (Italy), Frank Biela (Germany) and Tom Kristensen (Denmark), Audi
*Paris-Dakar-Cairo Rally*: Cars – Jutta Kleinschmidt (Germany), Mitsubishi; Motorcycles – Fabrizio Meoni (Italy) KTM; Trucks – Karel Loprais (Czech Republic), Tatra

## MOTOR RALLYING

2000
*Corsica Rally*: Gilles Panizzi (France), Peugeot
*San Remo Rally*: Gilles Panizzi (France), Peugeot
*Rally Australia*: Marcus Gronholm (Finland), Peugeot
*Network Q Rally of Great Britain*: Richard Burns (GB), Subaru
*Drivers' World Championship 2000*: Marcus Gronholm (Finland), 65 points
*Manufacturers' World Championship 2000*: Peugeot, 111 points

2001
*Monte Carlo Rally*: Carlos Sainz (Spain), Ford
*Swedish Rally*: Harri Rovanpera (Finland), Peugeot
*Rally of Portugal*: Tommi Makinen (Finland), Mitsubishi
*Catalunya Rally*: Didier Auriol (France), Peugeot
*Argentine Rally*: Colin McRae (GB), Ford
*Cyprus Rally*: Colin McRae (GB), Ford
*Acropolis Rally*: Colin McRae (GB), Ford
*Safari Rally*: Tommi Makinen (Finland), Mitsubishi
*Rally Finland*: Marcus Gronholm (Finland), Peugeot

*Rally of Wales 2001*: cancelled due to foot-and-mouth disease
*Scottish Rally 2001*: Justin Dale (GB), Peugeot
*Pirelli Rally 2001*: cancelled due to foot-and-mouth disease
*MSA Rally 2001*: cancelled due to foot-and-mouth disease

## NETBALL

*Inter-County Championship final 2001*: not held due to foot and mouth disease
*National Clubs Championship 2001*: Wealden beat Queens 72–34
*English Counties League Championship 2001*: Division 1 – Essex Met
*National Clubs League Championship 2001*: Oakwood Netball Club

## NORDIC EVENTS

BIATHLON WORLD CHAMPIONSHIPS 2001
Pokljuka, Slovenia

MEN
*10km sprint*: Pavel Rostovtsev (Russia) 24min. 40.30sec.
*12.5km pursuit*: Pavel Rostovtsev (Russia) 34min. 21.30sec.
*15km mass start*: Raphael Poiree (France) 39min. 28.20sec.
*20km individual*: Paavo Puurunen (Finland) 55min. 05.60sec.
4 × *7.5km relay*: France 1hr 12min. 56.70sec.

WOMEN
*7.5km sprint*: Kati Wilhelm (Germany) 21min. 56.20sec.
*10km pursuit*: Liv Grete Skjelbreid-Poiree (Norway) 32min. 13.50sec.
*12.5km mass start*: Magdalena Forsberg (Sweden) 38min. 38.60sec.
*15km individual*: Magdalena Forsberg (Sweden) 45min. 13.00sec.
4 × *7.5km relay*: Russia 1hr 29min. 02.80sec.

BIATHLON OVERALL CHAMPIONS 2001

MEN
1. Raphael Poiree (France), 921 points; 2. Ole Einar Bjoerndalen (Norway), 911 points; 3. Frode Andresen (Norway), 712 points

WOMEN
1. Magdalena Forsberg (Sweden), 1,021 points; 2. Liv Grete Skjelbreid-Poiree (Norway), 804 points; 3. Olena Zubrilova (Ukraine), 774 points

### CROSS-COUNTRY WORLD CHAMPIONSHIPS 2001

Lahti, Finland

MEN

*Sprint*: Tor Arne Hetland (Norway) 8min. 02.20sec.
*10km classic*: Per Elofsson (Sweden) 47min. 15.50sec.
*15km classic*: Per Elofsson (Sweden) 39min. 26.00sec.
*30km classic*: Andrus Veerpalu (Estonia) 1hr 14min. 7.00sec.
*50km freestyle*: Johann Muehlegg (Spain) 2hr 5min. 27sec.
4 × *10km*: Finland 1hr 36min. 15sec.

WOMEN

*Sprint*: Sabina Valbursa (Italy) 9min. 45.80sec.
*5km classic*: Virpi Kuitunen (Finland) 13min. 12.10sec.
*10km classic*: Bente Skari (Norway) 26min. 55.50sec.
*15km classic*: Bente Skari (Norway) 43min. 54.80sec.

CROSS-COUNTRY OVERALL CHAMPIONS 2001

MEN

1. Per Elofsson (Sweden), 765 points; 2. Johann Muehlegg (Spain), 710 points; 3. Odd-Björn Hjelmeset (Norway), 504 points

WOMEN

1. Julija Tchepalova (Russia), 1,074 points; 2. Larissa Lazutina (Russia), 903 points; 3. Stefania Belmondo (Italy), 809 points

### NORDIC-COMBINED 2001 WORLD CHAMPIONSHIPS

Lahti, Finland

*7.5km*: 1. Marco Baacke (Germany); 2. Samppa Lajunen (Finland); 3. Ronny Ackermann (Germany)
*15km*: 1. Bjarte Engen Vik (Norway); 2. Samppa Lajunen (Finland); 3. Felix Gottwald (Austria)

OVERALL CHAMPIONS 2001

1. Felix Gottwald (Austria) 1,785 points; 2. Ronny Ackermann (Germany), 1,342 points; 3. Marco Baacke (Germany), 1,209 points

### SKI-JUMPING WORLD CHAMPIONSHIPS 2001

Lahti, Finland

*90m*: 1. Adam Malysz (Poland); 2. Martin Schmitt (Germany); 3. Martin Hoellwarth (Austria)
*116m*: 1. Martin Schmitt (Germany); 2. Adam Malysz (Poland); 3. Janne Ahonen (Finland)

OVERALL CHAMPIONS 2001

1. Adam Malysz (Poland), 1,051 points; 2. Martin Schmitt (Germany), 772 points; 3. Janne Ahonen (Finland), 646 points

## POLO

*Prince of Wales Trophy final 2001*: Royal Pahang beat Woodchester 13–11
*Queen's Cup final 2001*: Geebung beat Les Lions 13–8
*Gold Cup (British Open) final 2001*: Geebung beat Black Bears
*Coronation Cup 2001*: Argentina beat England 10–9 in the 7th Chukha
*Prince Philip Trophy 2001*: Black Bears beat England 'A' 12–10
*Arena Gold Cup 2001*: cancelled
*Varsity Match 2001*: Oxford beat Cambridge 6–0

## RACKETS

*Professional Singles Championship final 2001*: Neil Smith beat Toby Sawrey-Cookson 3–1
*British Open Singles Championship final 2001*: James Male beat Mark Hubbard 4–0
*British Open Doubles Championship final 2001*: James Male and Mark Hue Williams beat A. Smith-Bingham and G. Smith-Bingham 4–2
*H.K. Foster Cup final 2001* (public schools' single championship): Jamie Stout (Cheltenham) beat Alex Coldicott (Cheltenham) 3–1
*Varsity Match 2001*: Cambridge beat Oxford 3–1

## REAL TENNIS

*Professional Singles Championship final 2001*: Robert Fahey beat Tim Chisholm 6–2, 5–6, 6–2, 6–1
*Professional Doubles Championship final 2001*: Chris Bray and Nick Wood beat Frank Filippelli and Mike Gooding 6–3, 2–6, 6–4, 6–2
*British Open Singles Championship final 2001*: Robert Fahey beat Chris Bray 6–4, 6–0, 6–3
*British Open Doubles Championship final 2000*: Chris Bray and Nick Wood beat Tim Chisholm and Julian Snow 6–3, 2–6, 3–6, 6–2, 6–1
*Amateur Singles Championship final 2001*: Julian Snow beat M. Howard 6–0, 6–1, 6–0
*Amateur Doubles Championship final 2001*: James Willcocks and Alexis Hombrecher beat Julian Snow and James Acheson Gray 5–6, 6–4, 6–3, 6–3
*Henry Leaf Cup final 2001* (public schools' old boys' doubles championship): Stowe (Peter Jarvis and Richaard Elmitt) beat Canford (Matthew Ronaldson and Simon de Halpert) 6–4, 6–1
*Women's World Singles Championship final 2001*: Penny Lumley beat Sally Jones 6–1, 6–3
*Women's British Open Singles Championship final 2001*: Penny Lumley beat Sally Jones 6–1, 6–3
*Women's British Open Doubles Championship final 2001*: Penny Lumley and Jo Iddles beat Charlotte Cornwallis and Alex Garside 1–6, 6–3, 6–2

## ROAD WALKING

RWA MEN'S NATIONAL 20 KM WALK
Sheffield, 7 July 2001
*Individual*: Andy Penn (Nuneaton), 1hr. 31 min. 09 sec.
*Team*: Road Hoggs, 273 points

RWA WOMEN'S NATIONAL 20 KM WALK
Sheffield, 7 July 2001
*Individual*: Sheila Bull (Midland Vets), 2 hr. 18 min. 53 sec.
*Team*: no team finished

RWA MEN'S NATIONAL 50 KM WALK
Victoria Park, 25 March 2001
*Individual*: Mike Smith (Coventry), 4 hr. 33 min. 17 sec.
*Team*: Surrey WC, 185 points

RWA WOMEN'S NATIONAL 5 KM WALK
Victoria Park, 25 March 2001
*Individual*: Sharon Tonks, 24 min. 51 sec.
*Team*: Dartford, 281 points

RWA MEN'S NATIONAL 35 KM WALK
Birmingham, 5 May 2001
*Individual*: Mark Easton (Surrey WC), 2 hr. 55 min. 20 sec.
*Team*: Coventry Godiva, 281 points

RWA WOMEN'S NATIONAL 10 KM WALK
Birmingham, 5 May 2001
*Individual*: Olive Loughnane (Ireland), 46 min. 35 sec.
*Team*: Steyning 285 points

EUROPEAN CUP, RACE WALKING
Dudince, Slovakia, 19 May 2001
MEN (20km)
*Individual*: Viktor Burayav (Belarus), 1 hr. 19 min. 30sec.
*Team*: Russia, 13 points
MEN (50km)
*Individual*: Jesús Angel Garlia (Spain), 3 hr. 44 min. 26 sec.
*Team*: Russia, 11 points
WOMEN (20km)
*Individual*: Olimpiada Ivanova (Russia), 1 hr. 26 min. 48 sec.
*Team*: Russia, 8 points

## ROWING

### NATIONAL CHAMPIONSHIPS 2001
Nottingham, July

MEN
*Coxed pairs*: no race this year
*Coxless pairs*: Robert Gordons University/Aberdeen Boat Club 7:27.96
*Coxed fours*: Nottinghamshire County Rowing Association 7:03.92
*Coxless fours*: Oxford University Boat Club
*Single sculls*: M. Langridge (Nautilus Rowing Club) 7:44.81
*Double sculls*: Nottinghamshire County Rowing Association 7:09.98
*Quad sculls*: Tideway Scullers School 6:57.04
*Eights*: Oxford University Boat Club/Isis Boat Club 6:06.74

WOMEN
*Coxless pairs*: Thames Tradesman's Rowing Club 8:30.25
*Coxed fours*: Thames Rowing Club 7:36.72
*Coxless fours*: Kingston Rowing Club 7:50.59
*Single sculls*: E. Butler-Stoney (Wallingford Rowing Club) 9:10.61
*Double sculls*: Hereford Rowing Club 8:13.54
*Quad sculls*: Nautilus Rowing Club 7:27.65
*Eights*: Thames Rowing Club 7:09.51

### THE 147th UNIVERSITY BOAT RACE
Putney–Mortlake, 4 miles 1 f, 180 yd, 24 March 2001

Oxford beat Cambridge by 3 lengths; 18 min. 4 sec. Cambridge have won 76 times, Oxford 69 and there has been one dead heat. The record time is 16 min. 19 sec., rowed by Cambridge in 1998

### HENLEY ROYAL REGATTA 2001
*Grand Challenge Cup*: H.A.V.K. Mladost and V.K. (Croatia) beat Sydney Rowing Club and University of Technology (Australia) by 4 ¾ lengths
*Ladies' Challenge Plate*: Dartmouth Rowing Club (USA) beat Princeton University (USA) by a canvas
*Thames Challenge Cup*: Koninklijike Roeivereniginjg Club (Belgium) beat Thames Rowing Club 'A' by 2½ lengths
*Temple Challenge Cup*: Harvard University 'A' (USA) beat Oxford Brookes University 'A' by 1 length
*Princess Elizabeth Challenge Cup*: The King's School (Australia) beat Radley College by 1¾ lengths
*Stewards' Challenge Cup*: Leander Club and Queen's Tower beat Gorge Rowing Centre (Canada) by 4 lengths
*Prince Philip Challenge Cup*: Leander Club and Oxford Brooks University beat Moseley Boat Club and Oxford University easily
*Queen Mother Challenge Cup*: Leander Club beat London Rowing Club by 2¾ lengths
*Visitors' Challenge Cup*: Oxford Brookes University and Taurus Boat Club beat Moseley Boat Club by 1½ lengths
*Wyfold Challenge Cup*: Leander Club beat Nottinghamshire County Rowing Association 'A' by a canvas
*Britannia Challenge Cup*: Nottinghamshire County Rowing Association beat Durham University 'A' by 3 lengths
*Fawley Challenge Cup*: Southport School and St Joseph's College (Australia) beat Maidenhead Rowing Club and Marlow Rowing Club by 1¾ lengths
*Silver Goblets and Nickalls' Challenge Cup*: J. E. Cracknell and M. C. Pinsent beat P. M. Haining and N. J. Strange easily
*Double Sculls Challenge Cup*: T. Kucharski and R. Sycz (Poland) beat P. P. Gardner and I. J. Lawson by 4 lengths
*Diamond Challenge Sculls*: D. S. Free (Australia) D. T. Hallett (Canada) by 4 lengths
*Princess Royal Challenge Cup*: E. Karsten (Belarus) beat K. Rutschow-Stomporowski (Germany) by 4½ lenghts
*Men's Quadruple Sculls*: University of Technology (Australia) and Nottinghamshire County Rowing Club beat Leander Club by 2½ lengths
*Women's Quadruple Sculls*: Potsdamer Ruder-Gesellschaft E.V. 'A' (Germany) beat Nautilus Rowing Club easily
*Henley Prize*: Australian Institute of Sport (Australia) beat Nautilus Rowing Club by 2¾ lengths

### OTHER ROWING EVENTS
*Oxford Torpids 2001*: *Men*, Oriel; *Women*, St Catherine's
*Oxford Summer Eights 2001*: *Men*, Oriel; *Women*, Pembroke
*Head of the River 2001*: *Men*,Queens Tower I; *Women*: Thames Rowing Club 'A'
*Scullers Head of the River 2001*: G. Pooley (Crabtree Boat Club)
*Doggett's Coat and Badge 2001*: Nicholas Beasley (Poplar and Blackwall Rowing Club)
*Thames World Sculling Challenge 2000*: *Men*,Iztok Cop; *Women*,Katrin Rutchow

## RUGBY FIVES

*National Singles Championship final 2000*: Neil Roberts beat Hamish Buchanan 15–8, 15–1
*National Doubles Championship final 2001*: John Beswick and Neil Roberts beat Hamish Buchanan and Robin Perry 15–3, 15–13
*National Club Championship final 2001*: Alleyn Old Boys beat Manchester YMCA 110–70
*National Schools' Singles Championship final 2001*: A. Lee (St Paul's) beat J. Bristow (Winchester) 6–11, 11–8, 11-3
*National School' Doubles Championship final 2001*: St Paul's I beat St Paul's II 7–11, 11–8,11–5
*Varsity Match 2001*: Oxford beat Cambridge 246–215

## RUGBY LEAGUE

### Competitions

*Super League Grand Final 2000* (Old Trafford, 14 October): St Helens beat Wigan Warriors 29–16
*Challenge Cup final 2001* (Twickenham, 28 April): St Helens beat Bradford 13–6
*Northern Ford Premiership Grand Final 2001* (Rochdale, 28 July): Widnes Vikings beat Oldham 24–14
*Varsity Match 2001* (Richmond, 9 March): Oxford beat Cambridge 22–16

## RUGBY UNION

### Six Nations' Championship 2001

| | | |
|---|---|---|
| 3 February | Rome | Ireland 41, Italy 22 |
| | Cardiff | England 44, Wales 15 |
| 4 February | Paris | France 16, Scotland 6 |
| 17 February | Dublin | Ireland 22, France 15 |
| | London | England 80, Italy 23 |
| | Edinburgh | Scotland 28, Wales 28 |
| 3 March | Rome | France 30, Italy 19 |
| | London | England 43, Scotland 3 |
| | Cardiff | Wales v. Ireland postponed |
| 17 March | Paris | Wales 43, France 35 |
| | Edinburgh | Scotland 23, Italy 19 |
| 24 March | Dublin | England v. Ireland postponed |
| | London | England 48, France 19 |
| 8 April | Rome | Wales 33, Italy 23 |
| 22 September | Edinburgh | Scotland 32, Ireland 10 |

*The Championship has been subject to serious delay and will not be completed until the Autumn of 2001*

### Heineken European Cup 2000–1

*European Cup final 2001* (Twickenham, 19 May): Leicester Tigers beat Stade Francais 34–30
*European Shield final 2001* (Toulouse, 20 May): Harlequins beat Narbonne 42–33
*Super 12 final 2001* (26 May): Brumbies (Australia) beat Sharks (South Africa) 36–6
*Women's (Inaugural) Five Nations' Championship 2000*: England

### Domestic Competitions

*Zurich Premiership*: *Division 1*, Leicester Tigers, points 82; *Division 2*, London Wasps, points 72
*National League*: *Division 1*, *Promoted*, Leeds, *Relegated*, Orrell and Waterloo; *Division 2*, *Promoted*, Bracknell, Rugby Lions
*County Championship final 2001*: Yorkshire beat Devon 16–9
*Tetley's Bitter Cup final 2001*: Newcastle Fallons beat NEC Harlequins 30–27
*Scottish Premiership*: *Division 1*, Hawick, 74 points; *Division 2*, Stirling County, 64 points; *Division 3*, Murrayfield Wanderers, 69 points
*Scottish Cup final 2001*: Boroughmuir beat Melrose 39–15
*Welsh National League*: *Premier Division*, Swansea, 54 points; *Division 1*, Aberavon, 79 points; *Division 2*, Bedwas, 81 points
*Welsh Challenge Cup final 2001*: Newport beat Neath 13–8
*Irish League*: *Division 1*, Munster
*Services Championship 2000*: Navy beat Army 31–20
*Varsity Match 2000*: Oxford beat Cambridge 19–16
*Middlesex Sevens final 2001*: The British Army beat the Newcastle Fallons 45–21

## SHOOTING

### 132nd National Rifle Association Imperial Meeting

Bisley, July 2001

*Queen's Prize*: D. J. Pickering, 150.27 v-bulls
*Grand Aggregate*: P. M. Patel, 699.104 v-bulls
*Prince of Wales Prize*: P. R. Bain, 75.13 v-bulls
*St George's Vase*: D. J. Pickering, 150.22 v-bulls
*Allcomers' Aggregate*: P. M. Jory, 375.50 v-bulls
*National Trophy*: England, 2058.240 v-bulls
*Kolapore Cup*: Great Britain, 1189.160 v-bulls
*Chancellor's Trophy*: Cambridge University RA, 114.108 v-bulls
*Musketeers Cup*: Edinburgh A Team, 591.182 v-bulls
*Vizianagram Trophy*: House of Commons, 548.28 v-bulls
*County Long-Range Championship*: Surrey, 298.34 v-bulls
*Mackinnon Challenge Cup*: England, 1154.120 v-bulls
*The Ashburton*: Uppingham 476 (Cadet GP rifle used, so therefore no v-bulls)
*The Elcho*: Scotland, 1541.83 v-bulls
*The Albert*: N. M. Bartlett 210.16 v-bulls
*Hopton Challenge Cup*: J. S. Collings 973.98 v-bulls

## SHORT-TRACK SPEED SKATING

### European Championships 2001

The Hague, Netherlands

#### Men

500 *metres*: Maurizio Carnino (Italy) 43:170sec.
1,000 *metres*: Bruno Loscos (France) 1min. 30.842sec.
1,500 *metres*: Bruno Loscos (France) 2min. 19.296sec.
3,000 *metres*: Cees Juffermans (Netherlands) 5min. 07.689sec.
5,000 *metres relay*: Italy 7min. 15.968sec.
*Overall*: Bruno Loscos (France)

#### Women

500 *metres*: Evgennia Radanova (Bulgaria) 45.360sec.
1,000 *metres*: Evegenia Radanova (Bulgaria) 1min. 36.665sec.
1,500 *metres*: Evgenia Radanova (Bulgaria) 2min. 35.542sec.
3,000 *metres*: Evegenia Radanova (Bulgaria) 5min. 51.694sec.
3,000 *metres relay*: Bulgaria 4 min. 28.970sec.
*Overall*: Evgenia Radanova (Bulgaria)

### World Championships 2001

Jeonju City, Korea

#### Men

500 *metres*: JiaJun Li (China) 43.433sec.
1,000 *metres*: JiaJun Li (China) 1min. 32.034sec.
1,500 *metres*: Marc Gagnon (Canada) 2min. 20.325sec.
3,000 *metres*: Apolo Anton Ohno (USA) 5min. 36.664sec.
3,000 *metres relay*: United States 7min. 15.885sec.

#### Women

500 *metres*: Chunlu Wang (China) 45.779sec.
1,000 *metres*: Yang Yang A (China) 1min. 45.664sec.
1,500 *metres*: Yang Yang A (China) 2min. 40.448sec.
3,000 *metres*: Yang Yang A (China) 5min. 43.454sec.
3,000 *metres relay*: China 4min. 25.927sec.

## SPEED SKATING

European Championships 2001 Baselga di Pine, Italy

MEN

500 *metres*: Ids Postma (Netherlands) 36.95sec.
1,500 *metres*: Dmitry Shepel (Russia) 1min. 49.42sec.
5,000 *metres*: Bart Veldkamp (Belgium) 6min. 33.65sec.
10,000 *metres*: Bart Veldkamp (Belgium) 13min. 38.72sec.
*Overall*: 1. Dmitry Shepel (Russia) 156.167 points; 2. Bart Veldkamp (Belgium) 156.224 points; 3. Ids Postma (Netherlands) 156.410

WOMEN

500 *metres*: Claudia Pechstein (Germany) 39.88sec.
1,500 *metres*: Renate Groenewold (Netherlands) 2min. 00.26sec.
3,000 *metres*: Gunda Niemann-Stirnemann (Germany) 4min. 08.54sec.
5,000 *metres*: Gunda Niemann-Stirnemann (Germany) 7min. 05.67sec.
*Overall*: 1.Gunda Niemann-Stirnemann (Germany) 166.136 points; 2. Claudia Pechstein (Germany) 167.026 points; 3. Wieteke Cramer (Netherlands) 169.525 points

WORLD CHAMPIONSHIPS 2001

Budapest, Hungary

MEN

500 *metres*: Christian Breuer (Germany) 37.55sec.
1,500 metres: Ids Postma (Netherlands) 1min. 54.12sec.
5,000 metres: Bart Veldkamp (Belgium) 6min. 43.69sec.
10,000 metres: Bart Veldkamp (Belgium) 13min. 44.19sec.

WOMEN

500 metres: Anni Friesinger (Germany) 39.99sec.
1,500 metres: Anni Friesinger (Germany) 2min. 03.38sec.
3,000 metres: Renate Groenewold (Netherlands) 4min. 16.57sec.
5,000 metres: Claudia Pechstein (Germany) 7min. 21.68sec.

SPRINT WORLD CHAMPIONSHIPS 2001

Inzell, Germany

OVERALL

Men: 1. Michael Ireland (Canada); 2. Hiroyasu Shimizu (Japan); 3. Jeremy Wotherspoon (Canada)
Women: 1. Monique Garbrecht-Enfeldt (Germany); 2. Eriko Sanmiya (Japan); 3. Catriona Lemay Doan (Canada)

## SNOOKER

2000–1

*Champions Cup*: (Croydon) Ronnie O'Sullivan (England) beat Mark J. Williams (Wales) 7–5
*British Open*: (Plymouth) Peter Ebdon (England) beat Jimmy White (England) 9–6
*Grand Prix*: (Telford) Mark J. Williams (Wales) beat Ronnie O'Sullivan (England) 9–5
*Regal Scottish Masters*: (Motherwell) Ronnie O'Sullivan (England) beat Stephen Hendry (Scotland) 9–6
*Benson & Hedges Championship*: (Malvern) Shaun Murphy beat Stuart Bingham 9–7
*Liverpool Victoria UK Championship*: (Bournemouth) John Higgins (Scotland) beat Mark J. Williams (Wales) 10–4
*China International*: (Shenzhen) Ronnie O'Sullivan (England) beat Mark J. Williams (Wales) 9–3
*Nations Cup*: (Reading) Scotland beat Republic of Ireland 6–2
*Regal Welsh Open*: (Cardiff) Ken Doherty (Ireland) beat Paul Hunter (England) 9–2
*Benson & Hedges Masters*: (Wembley) Paul Hunter (England) beat Fergal O'Brien (Ireland) 10–9
*Malta Grand Prix*: (Valetta) Stephen Hendry (Scotland) beat Mark J. Williams (Wales) 7–1
*Thailand Masters*: (Bangkok) Ken Doherty (Ireland) beat Stephen Hendry (Scotland) 9–3
*Benson & Hedges Irish Masters*: (Kildare) Ronnie O'Sullivan (England) beat Stephen Hendry (Scotland) 9–8
*Regal Scottish Masters*: (Aberdeen) Peter Ebdon (England) beat Ken Doherty (Ireland) 9–7
*Embassy World Championship*: (Sheffield) Ronnie O'Sullivan (England) beat John Higgins (Scotland) 18–14

## SQUASH RACKETS

MEN

*World Junior Championships 2000*: Kareem Darwich (Egypt) beat Gregory Gaultier (France) 9–1, 9–3, 9–7
*World Junior Team Championships 2000*: England beat Egypt 2–1
*European Team Championship final 2001*: England beat France 4–0
*National Championship final 2001*: Lee Beachill (Yorks) beat Nick Taylor (Lancs) 15–13, 15–5, 15–8
*Tournament of Champions 2001*: Peter Nicol (Scotland) beat Jonathon Power (Canada) 15–9, 15–12, 13–15, 13–15, 15–11

WOMEN

*World Open Championship final 2000*: Carol Owens (Australia) beat Leilani Joyce (New Zealand) 7–9, 3–9, 10–8, 9–6, 9–1
*World Team Championship final 2000*: England beat Australia 2–1
*World Grand Prix Final 2001*: Sarah Fitz-Gerald (Australia) beat Leilani Joyce (New Zealand) 9–6, 9–5, 9–1
*European Team Championship final 2001:* England beat Denmark 3–0
*National Championship final 2001*: Sue Wright (Kent) beat Fiona Geaves (Glos) 10–9, 9–2, 3–9, 10–8

## SWIMMING

WORLD CHAMPIONSHIPS 2001
Fukuoka, Japan, July

MEN

50 *metres freestyle*: Anthony Ervin (USA) 22.09
100 *metres freestyle*: Anthony Ervin (USA) 48.33*
200 *metres freestyle*: Ian Thorpe (Australia) 1:44.06**
400 *metres freestyle*: Ian Thorpe (Australia) 3:40.17**
800 *metres freestyle*: Ian Thorpe (Australia) 7:39.16**
1,500 *metres freestyle*: Grant Hackett (Australia) 14:34.56**
50 *metres backstroke*: Randall Bal (USA) 25.34
100 *metres backstroke*: Matt Welsh (Australia) 54.31
200 *metres backstroke*: Aaron Peirsol (USA) 1:15.13*
50 *metres breaststroke*: Oleg Lisogor (Ukraine) 27.52
100 *metres breaststroke*: Roman Sloudnov (Russia) 1:00.16
200 *metres breaststroke*: Brendan Hansen (USA) 2:10.69
50 *metres butterfly*: Geoff Huegill (Australia) 23.50
100 *metres butterfly*: Lars Frolander (Sweden) 52.10
200 *metres butterfly*: Michael Phelps (USA) 1:54.58**
200 *metres medley*: Massimiliano Rosolino (Italy) 1:59.71
400 *metres medley*: Alessio Boggiatto (Italy) 4:13.15
4 × 100 *metres freestyle relay*: Australia 3:14.10
4 × 200 *metres freestyle relay*: Australia 7:04.66**
4 × 100 *metres medley relay*: Australia 3:35.35*

WOMEN

50 *metres freestyle*: Inge de Bruijn (Netherlands) 24.47
100 *metres freestyle*: Inge de Bruijn (Netherlands) 54.18
200 *metres freestyle*: Giaan Rooney (Australia) 1:58.57
400 *metres freestyle*: Yana Klochkova (Ukraine) 4:07.30
800 *metres freestyle*: Hannah Stockbauer (Germany) 8:24.66
1,500 *metres freestyle*: Hannah Stockbauer (Germany) 16:01.02
50 *metres backstroke*: Haley Cope (USA) 28.51
100 *metres backstroke*: Natalie Coughlin (USA) 1:00.37
200 *metres backstroke*: Diana Iuliana Mocanu (Romania) 2:09.94
50 *metres breaststroke*: Luo Xuejuan (China) 30.84
100 *metres breaststroke*: Luo Xuejuan (China) 1:07.18*
200 *metres breaststroke*: Agnes Kovacs (Hungary) 2:24.90*
50 *metres butterfly*: Inge de Bruijn (Netherlands) 25.90
100 *metres butterfly*: Petria Thomas (Australia) 58.27*
200 *metres butterfly*: Petria Thomas (Australia) 2:06.73*
200 *metres medley*: Martha Bowen (USA) 2:11.93
400 *metres medley*: Yana Klochkova (Ukraine) 4:36.98
4 × 100 *metres freestyle relay*: Germany 3:39.58
4 × 200 *metres freestyle relay*: Great Britain 7:58.69
4 × 100 *metres medley relay*: Australia 4:01.50*
* denotes Championship Record
** denotes World Record

BRITISH CHAMPIONSHIPS 2001
Manchester - April

MEN

50 *metres backstroke*: Neil Willey (University of Bath) 25.06
100 *metres backstroke*: Adam Ruckwood (City of Birmingham) 56.40
200 *metres backstroke*: Simon Militis (Portsmouth Northsea) 2:02.73
50 *metres breaststroke*: James Gibson (LCLM/WITS) 27.79
100 *metres breaststroke*: Darren Mew (University of Bath) 1:01.52
200 *metres breaststroke*: Ian Edmond (City of Edinburgh) 2:15.50
50 *metres butterfly*: Mark Foster (University of Bath) 24.12
100 *metres butterfly*: James Hickman (City of Leeds) 53.53
200 *metres butterfly*: Stephen Parry (Stockport Metro) 1:58.42
50 *metres freestyle*: Mark Foster (University of Bath) 22.62
100 *metres freestyle*: Paul Palmer (University of Bath) 24.74
200 *metres freestyle*: Paul Palmer (University of Bath) 1:48.85
400 *metres freestyle*: Paul Palmer (University of Bath) 3:51.82
800 *metres freestyle*: Adam Faulkner (Nova Centurion) 8:01.77
1,500 *metres freestyle*: Graeme Smith (Stockport Metro) 15:27.02
200 *metres medley*: Adrian Turner (City of Salford) 2:04.19
400 *metres medley*: Simon Militis (Portsmouth Northsea) 4:19.90

WOMEN

50 *metres backstroke*: Sarah Price (Barnet Copthall) 29.57
100 *metres backstroke*: Sarah Price (Barnet Copthall) 1:01.32
200 *metres backstroke*: Joanna Fargus (University of Bath) 2:11.81
50 *metres breaststroke*: Zoe Baker (City of Sheffield) 31.99
100 *metres breaststroke*: Jaime King (Univesity of Bath) 1:09.64
200 *metres breaststroke*: Jaime King (University of Bath) 2:28.10
50 *metres butterfly*: Rosalind Brett (Loughborough University) 27.53
100 *metres butterfly*: Georgina Lee (Camphill Edwardians) 1:00.137
200 *metres butterfly*: Georgina Lee (Camphill Edwardians) 2:10.21
50 *metres freestyle*: Alison Sheppard (Milngavie and Bearsden) 25.07
100 *metres freestyle*: Rosalind Brett (Loughborough University) 55.78
200 *metres freestyle*: Karen Legg (Ferndown) 2:01.12
400 *metres freestyle*: Rebecca Cooke (Reading) 4:13.73
800 *metres freestyle*: Rebecca Cooke (Reading) 8:34.91
1,500 *metres freestyle*: Rebecca Cooke (Reading) 16:21.75
200 *metres medley*: Kathryn Evans (Nova Centurion) 2:18.13
400 *metres medley*: Holly Fox (Reading) 4:49.09

NATIONAL CHAMPIONSHIPS 2001
Sheffield, July

MEN

50 *metres freestyle*: Matthew Kidd (Leatherhead) 23.46
100 *metres freestyle*: Matthew Kidd (Leatherhead) 50.98
200 *metres freestyle*: Franck Southon (France) 1:52.87
400 *metres freestyle*: Stuart Trees (City of Leeds) 3:57.61
800 *metres freestyle*: Nathan Hayes (Portsmouth Northsea) 8:25.93
1,500 *metres freestyle*: Ross Hughes (Eess/Bres) 16:02.09
50 *metres backstroke*: Simon Burnett (Wycombe District) 27.21
100 *metres backstroke*: Franck Southon (France) 57.88
200 *metres backstroke*: Franck Southon (France) 2:03.55
50 *metres breaststroke*: Adam Whitehead (City of Coventry) 28.79
100 *metres breaststroke*: Chris Cook (City of Newcastle) 1:03.57
200 *metres breaststroke*: Chris Cook (City of Newcastle) 2:18.13
50 *metres butterfly*: David Bennett (Beks/Pors) 24.99
100 *metres butterfly*: James Hickman (City of Leeds) 53.98
200 *metres butterfly*: James Hickman (City of Leeds) 1:58.94
200 *metres medley*: James Hickman (City of Leeds) 2:04.18
400 *metres medley*: Robin Frances (University of Bath) 4:27.39
4 × 100 *metres freestyle relay*: France 3:51.31
4 × 200 *metres freestyle relay*: University of Bath 7:42.01

WOMEN

50 *metres freestyle*: Jennifer Lyes (T5LS/EALS) 26.39
100 *metres freestyle*: Janine Pietsch (Germany) 56.62
200 *metres freestyle*: Karen Nisbet (City of Leeds) 2:02.70
400 *metres freestyle*: Holly Fox (Reading) 4:16.80
800 *metres freestyle*: Marion Perrotin (France) 8:45.94
1,500 *metres freestyle*: Marion Perrotin (France) 16:41.79
50 *metres backstroke*: Janine Pietsch (Germany) 4:19.36
100 *metres backstroke*: Zoe Cray (Ipswich) 1:03.44
200 *metres backstroke*: Charlotte Evans (Dartmouth D) 2:35.95
50 *metres breaststroke*: Joanne Mullins (Orpington OJ) 33.62
100 *metres breaststroke*: Charlotte Evans (Bournemouth D) 1:12.29
200 *metres breaststroke*: Charlotte Evans (Bournemouth D) 2:35.95
50 *metres butterfly*: Malia Metella (France) 28.07
100 *metres butterfly*: Malia Metella (France) 1:01.76

*200 metres butterfly*: Margaretha Pedder (Portsmouth Northsea) 2:11.64
*200 metres medley*: Sarah Whewell (City of Newcastle) 2:18.94
*400 metres medley*: Holly Fox (Reading) 4:50.51
*4 × 100 metres freestyle relay*: Nova Centurion 4:19.36
*4 × 200 metres freestyle relay*: France 8:28.04

## TABLE TENNIS

### WORLD CHAMPIONSHIPS 2001
Osaka, Japan, April–May

*Men's Singles*: Wang Liqin (China) beat Kong Linghui (China) 3–2
*Women's Singles*: Wang Nan (China) beat Lin Ling (China) 3–1
*Men's Doubles*: Wang Liqin and Yan Sen (China) beat Kong Linghui and Lui Gouliang (China) 3–0
*Women's Doubles*: Li Ju and Wang Nan (China) beat Yang Ying and Sun Jin (China) 3–0
*Mixed Doubles*: Yang Ying and Qin Zhijian (China) beat Oh Sang Eun and Kim Moo Kyo (Korea) 3–0

### ENGLISH NATIONAL CHAMPIONSHIPS 2001
Sheffield, March

*Men's Singles*: Matthew Syed (Surrey) beat Alex Perry (Devon) 2–0
*Women's Singles*: Nicola Deaton (Derbys) beat Kubrat Owolabi (Middx) 2–1
*Men's Doubles*: Alan Cooke (Derbys) and Bradley Billington (Derbys) beat Andrew Baggaley (Bucks) and Terry Young (Berks) 2–0
*Women's Doubles*: Nicola Deaton (Derbys) and Helen Lower (Staffs) beat Linda Radford (Essex) and Kubrat Owolabi (Middx) 2–1
*Mixed Doubles*: Alan Cooke (Derbys) and Nicola Deaton (Derbys) beat Alex Perry (Devon) and Helen Lower (Staffs) 2-0
*Men's Under 21 Singles*: Andrew Rushton (Lancs) beat Michael Isherwood (Derbys) 2–1
*Women's Under 21 Singles*: Louise Durrant (Notts) beat Georgina Walker (Notts) 2–1

## TENNIS

### AUSTRALIAN OPEN CHAMPIONSHIPS 2001
Melbourne, 15–28 January

*Men's Singles*: Andre Agassi (USA) beat Arnaud Clement (France) 6–4, 6–2, 6–2
*Women's Singles*: Jennifer Capriati (USA) beat Martina Hingis (Switzerland) 6–4, 6–3
*Men's Doubles*: Jonas Björkman (Sweden) and Todd Woodbridge (Australia) beat Wayne Black (Zimbabwe) and David Prinosil (Germany) 6–1, 5–7, 6–4, 6–4
*Women's Doubles*: Venus Williams (USA) and Serena Williams (USA) beat Lindsay Davenport (USA) and Corina Morariu (USA) 6–2, 4–6, 6–4
*Mixed Doubles*: Ellis Ferreira (South Africa) and Corina Morariu (USA) beat Joshua Eagle (Australia) and Barbara Schett (Austria) 6–1, 6–3

### FRENCH OPEN CHAMPIONSHIPS 2001
Paris, 28 May–10 June

*Men's Singles*: Gustavo Kuerten (Brazil) beat Alex Corretja (Spain) 6–7, 7–5, 6–2, 6–0
*Women's Singles*: Jennifer Capriati (USA) beat Kim Clijsters (Belgium) 1–6, 6–4, 12–10
*Men's Doubles*: Mahesh Bhupathi (India) and Leander Paes (India) beat Petr Pala (Czech Republic) and Pavel Vizner (Czech Republic) 7–6, 6–3
*Women's Doubles*: Paola Suarez (Argentina) and Virginia Ruano Pascual (Spain) beat Conchita Martinez (Spain) and Jelena Dokic (Yugoslavia) 6–2, 6–1
*Mixed Doubles*: Virginia Ruano Pascual (Spain) and Tomas Carbonell (Spain) beat Paola Suarez (Argentina) and Jaime Oncins (Brazil) 7–5, 6–3

### ALL-ENGLAND CHAMPIONSHIPS 2001
Wimbledon, 20 June–7 July

*Men's Singles*: Goran Ivanisevic (Croatia) beat Patrick Rafter (Australia) 6–3, 3–6, 6–3, 2–6, 9–7
*Women's Singles*: Venus Williams (USA) beat Justine Henin (Belgium) 6–1, 3–6, 6–0
*Men's Doubles*: Jared Palmer (USA) and Don Johnson (USA) beat Jiri Novak (Czech Republic) and David Rikl (Czech Republic) 6–4, 4–6, 6–3, 7–6
*Women's Doubles*: Lisa Raymond (USA) and Rennae Stubbs (Australia) beat Kim Clijsters (Belgium) and Ai Sugiyama (Japan) 6–4, 6–3
*Mixed Doubles*: Leos Friedl (Czech Republic) and Daniela Hantuchova (Slovakia) and Mike Bryan (USA) and Liezel Huber (South Africa) 4–6, 6–3, 6–2

### US OPEN CHAMPIONSHIPS 2001
New York, 29 August–9 September

*Men's Singles*: Lleyton Hewitt (Australia) beat Pete Sampras (USA) 7–6, 6–1, 6–1
*Women's Singles*: Venus Williams (USA) beat Serena Williams (USA) 6–2, 6–4
*Men's Doubles*: Wayne Black (Zimbabwe) and Kevin Ullyet (Zimbabwe) beat Jared Palmer (USA) and Don Johnson (USA) 7–6, 2–6, 6–3
*Women's Doubles*: Lisa Raymond (USA) and Rennae Stubbs (Australia) beat Cara Black Zimbabwe and Elena Likhovtseva (Russia) 6–3, 6–4
*Mixed Doubles*: Rennae Stubbs (Australia) and Todd Woodbridge (USA) beat Lisa Raymond (USA) and Leander Paes (India) 6–4, 5–7, 11–9

### TEAM CHAMPIONSHIPS

*Davis Cup final 2000*: Spain beat Australia 3–1
*Fed Cup final 2000*: USA beat Spain 5–0

## VOLLEYBALL

### MEN
*World League 2001*: Brazil beat Italy 3–0

### WOMEN
*Grand Prix final 2001*: USA beat China 3–1

### BEACH VOLLEYBALL

### MEN
*World Championships 2001*: Argentina

### WOMEN
*World Championships 2001*: Brazil

# Sports Records

## ATHLETICS WORLD RECORDS
AS AT 18 SEPTEMBER 2001

All the world records given below have been accepted by the International Amateur Athletic Federation except those marked with an asterisk* which are awaiting homologation. Fully automatic timing to 1/100th second is mandatory up to and including 400 metres. For distances up to and including 10,000 metres, records will be accepted to 1/100th second if timed automatically, and to 1/10th if hand timing is used.

### MEN'S EVENTS

| TRACK EVENTS | hr. | min. | sec. |
|---|---|---|---|
| 100 metres | | | 9.79 |
| Maurice Greene, USA, 1999 | | | |
| 200 metres | | | 19.32 |
| Michael Johnson, USA, 1996 | | | |
| 400 metres | | | 43.18 |
| Michael Johnson, USA, 1999 | | | |
| 800 metres | | 1 | 41.11 |
| Wilson Kipketer, Denmark, 1997 | | | |
| 1,000 metres | | 2 | 11.96 |
| Noah Ngeny, Kenya, 1999 | | | |
| 1,500 metres | | 3 | 26.00 |
| Hicham El Guerrouj, Morocco, 1998 | | | |
| 1 mile | | 3 | 43.13 |
| Hicham El Guerrouj, Morocco, 1999 | | | |
| 2,000 metres | | 4 | 44.79 |
| Hicham El Guerrouj, Morocco, 1999 | | | |
| 3,000 metres | | 7 | 20.67 |
| Daniel Komen, Kenya, 1996 | | | |
| 5,000 metres | | 12 | 39.36 |
| Haile Gebrselassie, Ethiopia, 1998 | | | |
| 10,000 metres | | 26 | 22.75 |
| Haile Gebrselassie, Ethiopia, 1998 | | | |
| 20,000 metres | | 56 | 55.6 |
| Arturo Barrios, Mexico, 1991 | | | |
| 21,101 metres (13 miles 196 yards 1 foot) | 1 | 00 | 00.0 |
| Arturo Barrios, Mexico, 1991 | | | |
| 25,000 metres | 1 | 13 | 55.8 |
| Toshihiko Seko, Japan, 1981 | | | |
| 30,000 metres | 1 | 29 | 18.8 |
| Toshihiko Seko, Japan, 1981 | | | |
| Marathon | 2 | 05 | 42 |
| Khalid Khannouchi, Morocco, 1999 | | | |
| 110 metres hurdles (3 ft 6 in) | | | 12.91 |
| Colin Jackson, GB, 1993 | | | |
| 400 metres hurdles (3 ft 0 in) | | | 46.78 |
| Kevin Young, USA, 1992 | | | |
| 3,000 metres steeplechase | | 7 | 55.28* |
| Brahim Boulami, Morocco 2001 | | | |

| RELAYS | min. | sec. |
|---|---|---|
| 4×100 metres | | 37.40 |
| USA, 1992, 1993 | | |
| 4×200 metres | 1 | 19.11 |
| Santa Monica TC, 1992 | | |
| 4×400 metres | 2 | 54.20 |
| USA, 1998 | | |
| 4×800 metres | 7 | 03.89 |
| GB, 1982 | | |
| 4×1,500 metres | 14 | 38.8 |
| Federal Republic of Germany, 1977 | | |

| FIELD EVENTS | metres | ft | in |
|---|---|---|---|
| High jump | 2.45 | 8 | 0½ |
| Javier Sotomayor, Cuba, 1993 | | | |
| Pole vault | 6.14 | 20 | 1¾ |
| Sergei Bubka, Ukraine, 1994 | | | |
| Long jump | 8.95 | 29 | 4½ |
| Mike Powell, USA, 1991 | | | |
| Triple jump | 18.29 | 60 | 0¼ |
| Jonathan Edwards, GB, 1995 | | | |
| Shot | 23.12 | 75 | 10¼ |
| Randy Barnes, USA, 1990 | | | |
| Discus | 74.08 | 243 | 0 |
| Jürgen Schult, GDR, 1986 | | | |
| Hammer | 86.74 | 284 | 7 |
| Yuriy Sedykh, USSR, 1986 | | | |
| Javelin | 98.48 | 323 | 1 |
| Jan Zelezny, Czech Rep., 1996 | | | |
| Decathlon† | 9,026* points | | |
| Roman Sebrle, Czech Rep., 2001 | | | |

† Ten events comprising 100 m, long jump, shot, high jump, 400 m, 110 m hurdles, discus, pole vault, javelin, 1500 m

| WALKING (TRACK) | hr. | min. | sec. |
|---|---|---|---|
| 20,000 metres | 1 | 17 | 25.6 |
| Bernard Segura, Mexico, 1994 | | | |
| 29,572 metres (18 miles 660 yards) | 2 | 00 | 00.0 |
| Maurizio Damilano, Italy, 1992 | | | |
| 30,000 metres | 2 | 01 | 44.1 |
| Maurizio Damilano, Italy, 1992 | | | |
| 50,000 metres | 3 | 40 | 57.9 |
| Thierry Toutain, France, 1996 | | | |

### WOMEN'S EVENTS

| TRACK EVENTS | | min. | sec. |
|---|---|---|---|
| 100 metres | | | 10.49 |
| Florence Griffith-Joyner, USA, 1988 | | | |
| 200 metres | | | 21.34 |
| Florence Griffith-Joyner, USA, 1988 | | | |
| 400 metres | | | 47.60 |
| Marita Koch, GDR, 1985 | | | |
| 800 metres | | 1 | 53.28 |
| Jarmila Kratochvilova, Czechoslovakia, 1983 | | | |
| 1,500 metres | | 3 | 50.46 |
| Qu Yunxia, China, 1993 | | | |
| 1 mile | | 4 | 12.56 |
| Svetlana Masterkova, Russia, 1996 | | | |
| 3,000 metres | | 8 | 06.11 |
| Wang Junxia, China, 1993 | | | |
| 5,000 metres | | 14 | 28.09 |
| Jiang Bo, China, 1997 | | | |
| 10,000 metres | | 29 | 31.78 |
| Wang Junxia, China, 1993 | | | |
| Marathon | 2 | 20 | 43 |
| Tegla Loroupe, Kenya, 1999 | | | |
| 100 metres hurdles (2 ft 9 in) | | | 12.21 |
| Yordanka Donkova, Bulgaria, 1988 | | | |
| 400 metres hurdles (2 ft 6 in) | | | 52.61 |
| Kim Batten, USA, 1995 | | | |

| Relays | min. | sec. |
|---|---|---|
| 4×100 metres<br>GDR, 1985 | | 41.37 |
| 4×200 metres<br>USA, 2000 | 1 | 27.46* |
| 4×400 metres<br>USSR, 1988 | 3 | 15.17 |
| 4×800 metres<br>USSR, 1984 | 7 | 50.17 |

| Field Events | metres | ft | in |
|---|---|---|---|
| High jump<br>Stefka Kostadinova, Bulgaria, 1987 | 2.09 | 6 | 10¼ |
| Pole vault<br>Stacy Dragila, USA, 2000 | 4.81* | 15 | 7 |
| Long jump<br>Galina Chistiakova, USSR, 1988 | 7.52 | 24 | 8¼ |
| Triple jump<br>Inessa Kravets, Ukraine, 1995 | 15.50 | 50 | 10¼ |
| Shot<br>Natalya Lisovskaya, USSR, 1987 | 22.63 | 74 | 3 |
| Discus<br>Gabriele Reinsch, GDR, 1988 | 76.80 | 252 | 0 |
| Hammer<br>Mihaela Melinte, Romania, 1999 | 75.97 | 249 | 2 |
| Javelin (new implement in 1999)<br>Osleidys Menendez, Cuba, 2001 | 71.54m* | *234 | 7 |
| Heptathlon†<br>Jackie Joyner-Kersee, USA, 1988 | 7,291 points | | |

†Seven events comprising 100 m hurdles, shot, high jump, 200 m, long jump, javelin, 800 m

## ATHLETICS NATIONAL (UK) RECORDS
AS AT 9 SEPTEMBER 2000

Records set anywhere by athletes eligible to represent Great Britain and Northern Ireland

### MEN

| Track Events | hr. | min. | sec. |
|---|---|---|---|
| 100 metres<br>Linford Christie, 1993 | | | 9.87 |
| 200 metres<br>John Regis, 1994 | | | 19.87 |
| 400 metres<br>Iwan Thomas, 1997 | | | 44.36 |
| 800 metres<br>Sebastian Coe, 1981 | | 1 | 41.73 |
| 1,000 metres<br>Sebastian Coe, 1981 | | 2 | 12.18 |
| 1,500 metres<br>Sebastian Coe, 1985 | | 3 | 29.67 |
| 1 mile<br>Steve Cram, 1985 | | 3 | 46.32 |
| 2,000 metres<br>Steve Cram, 1985 | | 4 | 51.39 |
| 3,000 metres<br>David Moorcroft, 1982 | | 7 | 32.79 |
| 5,000 metres<br>David Moorcroft, 1982 | | 13 | 00.41 |
| 10,000 metres<br>Jon Brown, 1998 | | 27 | 18.14 |
| 20,000 metres<br>Carl Thackery, 1990 | | 57 | 28.7 |
| 20,855 metres<br>Carl Thackery, 1990 | 1 | 00 | 00.0 |
| 25,000 metres<br>Ron Hill, 1965 | 1 | 15 | 22.6 |
| 30,000 metres<br>Jim Alder, 1970 | 1 | 31 | 30.4 |
| 3,000 metres steeplechase<br>Mark Rowland, 1988 | | 8 | 07.96 |
| 110 metres hurdles<br>Colin Jackson, 1993 | | | 12.91 |
| 400 metres hurdles<br>Kriss Akabusi, 1992 | | | 47.82 |

| Relays | min. | sec. |
|---|---|---|
| 4×100 metres<br>GB team, 1999 | | 37.73 |
| 4×200 metres<br>GB team, 1989 | 1 | 21.29 |
| 4×400 metres<br>GB team, 1996 | 2 | 56.60 |
| 4×800 metres<br>GB team, 1982 | 7 | 03.89 |

| Field Events | metres | ft | in |
|---|---|---|---|
| High jump<br>Steve Smith, 1992, 1993 | 2.37 | 7 | 9¼ |
| Pole vault<br>Nick Buckfield, 1998 | 5.80 | 19 | 0¼ |
| Long jump<br>Lynn Davies, 1968 | 8.23 | 27 | 0 |
| Triple jump<br>Jonathan Edwards, 1995 | 18.29 | 60 | 0¼ |
| Shot<br>Geoff Capes, 1980 | 21.68 | 71 | 1½ |
| Discus<br>Perris Wilkins, 1998 | 66.64 | 218 | 8 |
| Hammer<br>Martin Girvan, 1984 | 77.54 | 254 | 5 |
| Javelin<br>Steve Backley, 1992 | 91.46 | 300 | 1 |
| Decathlon<br>Daley Thompson, 1984 | | 8,847 points | |

| Walking (Track) | hr. | min. | sec. |
|---|---|---|---|
| 20,000 metres<br>Ian McCombie, 1990 | 1 | 23 | 26.5 |
| 30,000 metres<br>Christopher Maddocks, 1984 | 2 | 19 | 18 |
| 50,000 metres<br>Paul Blagg, 1990 | 4 | 05 | 44.6 |
| 26,037 metres (16 miles 315 yards)<br>Ron Wallwork, 1971 | 2 | 00 | 00.0 |

### WOMEN

| Track Events | min. | sec. |
|---|---|---|
| 100 metres<br>Kathy Cook, 1981 | | 11.10 |
| 200 metres<br>Kathy Cook, 1984 | | 22.10 |
| 400 metres<br>Kathy Cook, 1984 | | 49.43 |
| 800 metres<br>Kelly Holmes, 1995 | 1 | 56.21 |
| 1,500 metres<br>Kelly Holmes, 1997 | 3 | 58.07 |
| 1 mile<br>Zola Budd, 1985 | 4 | 17.57 |
| 3,000 metres<br>Paula Radcliffe, 2001 | 8 | 26.97** |
| 5,000 metres<br>Paula Radcliffe, 2001 | 14 | 32.44* |

| | | | |
|---|---|---|---|
| 10,000 metres<br>Paula Radcliffe, 1999 | | 30 | 27.13* |
| 100 metres hurdles<br>Angela Thorp, 1996 | | | 12.80 |
| 400 metres hurdles<br>Sally Gunnell, 1993 | | | 52.74 |

| Relays | min. | sec. |
|---|---|---|
| 4×100 metres<br>GB team, 1980 | | 42.43 |
| 4×200 metres<br>GB team, 1977 | 1 | 31.57 |
| 4×400 metres<br>GB team, 1991 | 3 | 22.01 |
| 4×800 metres<br>GB team, 1971 | 8 | 23.8 |

| Field Events | metres | ft | in |
|---|---|---|---|
| High jump<br>Diana Elliott, 1982<br>Susan Jones, 2001* | 1.95 | 6 | $4\frac{3}{4}$ |
| Pole vault<br>Janine Whitlock, 2001 | 4.40* | 14 | 4 |
| Long jump<br>Beverley Kinch, 1983 | 6.90 | 22 | $7\frac{3}{4}$ |
| Triple jump<br>Ashia Hansen, 1997 | 15.15 | 49 | $8\frac{1}{2}$ |
| Shot<br>Judy Oakes, 1988 | 19.36 | 63 | $6\frac{1}{4}$ |
| Discus<br>Margaret Ritchie, 1981 | 67.48 | 221 | 5 |
| Hammer<br>Lorraine Shaw, 2001 | 68.15* | 223 | 5 |
| Javelin<br>Fatima Whitbread, 1986 | 77.44 | 254 | 1 |
| Heptathlon<br>Denise Lewis, 2000 | | 6,831* points | |

*Awaiting ratification

## SWIMMING WORLD RECORDS
AS AT 9 SEPTEMBER 2000

| Men | min. | sec. |
|---|---|---|
| 50 metres freestyle<br>Alexander Popov, Russia | | 21.64 |
| 100 metres freestyle<br>Pieter van den Hoogenband, Netherlands | | 47.84 |
| 200 metres freestyle<br>Ian Thorpe, Australia | 1 | 44.06 |
| 400 metres freestyle<br>Ian Thorpe, Australia | 3 | 40.17 |
| 800 metres freestyle<br>Ian Thorpe, , Australia | 7 | 39.16 |
| 1,500 metres freestyle<br>Grant Hackett, Australia | 14 | 34.56 |
| 100 metres breaststroke<br>Roman Sloudnov, Russia | | 59.94 |
| 50 metres breaststoke<br>Ed Moses, USA | | 27.39 |
| 200 metres breaststroke<br>Mike Barrowman, USA | 2 | 10.16 |
| 50 metres butterfly<br>Geoff Heugill, Australia | | 23.44 |
| 100 metres butterfly<br>Michael Klim, Australia | | 51.81 |
| 200 metres butterfly<br>Michael Phelps, USA | 1 | 54.58 |
| 50 metres backstroke<br>Lenny Krayzelburg, USA | | 24.99 |
| 100 metres backstroke<br>Lenny Krayzelburg, USA | | 53.60 |
| 200 metres backstroke<br>Lenny Krayzelburg, USA | 1 | 55.87 |
| 200 metres medley<br>Jani Sievinen, Finland | 1 | 58.16 |
| 400 metres medley<br>Tom Dolan, USA | 4 | 11.76 |
| 4×100 metres freestyle relay<br>Australia | 3 | 13.67 |
| 4×200 metres freestyle relay<br>Australia | 7 | 04.66 |
| 4×100 metres medley relay<br>USA | 3 | 33.73 |

| Women | min. | sec. |
|---|---|---|
| 50 metres freestyle<br>Inge de Bruin, Netherlands | | 24.13 |
| 100 metres freestyle<br>Inge de Bruin, Netherlands | | 53.77 |
| 200 metres freestyle<br>Franziska van Almsick, Germany | 1 | 56.78 |
| 400 metres freestyle<br>Janet Evans, USA | 4 | 03.85 |
| 800 metres freestyle<br>Janet Evans, USA | 8 | 16.22 |
| 1,500 metres freestyle<br>Janet Evans, USA | 15 | 52.10 |
| 50 metres breaststroke<br>Penny Heyns, South Africa | | 30.83 |
| 100 metres breaststroke<br>Penny Heyns, South Africa | 1 | 06.52 |
| 200 metres breaststroke<br>Qi Hui (China) | 2 | 22.99 |
| 50 metres butterfly<br>Inge de Bruin, Netherlands | | 25.64 |
| 100 metres butterfly<br>Inge de Bruin, Netherlands | | 56.61 |
| 200 metres butterfly<br>Susan O'Neill, Australia | 2 | 05.81 |
| 50 metres backstroke<br>Sandra Volker, Germany | | 28.25 |
| 100 metres backstroke<br>Cihong He, China | 1 | 00.16 |
| 200 metres backstroke<br>Krisztina Egerszegi, Hungary | 2 | 06.62 |
| 200 metres medley<br>Wu Yanyan, China | 2 | 09.72 |
| 400 metres medley<br>Yana Klochkova, Ukraine | 4 | 33.59 |
| 4×100 metres freestyle relay<br>USA | 3 | 36.61 |
| 4×200 metres freestyle relay<br>GDR | 7 | 55.47 |
| 4×100 metres medley relay<br>USA | 3 | 58.30 |

# Weights and Measures

## SI UNITS

The Système International d'Unités (SI) is an international and coherent system of units devised to meet all known needs for measurement in science and technology. The system was adopted by the eleventh Conférence Générale des Poids et Mesures (CGPM) in 1960. A comprehensive description of the system is given in *SI The International System of Units* (HMSO). The British Standards describing the essential features of the International System of Units are *Specifications for SI units and recommendations for the use of their multiples and certain other units* (BS 5555:1993) and *Conversion Factors and Tables* (BS 350, Part 1:1974).

The system consists of seven base units and the derived units formed as products or quotients of various powers of the base units. Together the base units and the derived units make up the coherent system of units. In the UK the SI base units, and almost all important derived units, are realised at the National Physical Laboratory and disseminated through the National Measurement System.

### Base Units

metre (m)=unit of length
kilogram (kg)=unit of mass
second (s)=unit of time
ampere (A)=unit of electric current
kelvin (K)=unit of thermodynamic temperature
mole (mol)=unit of amount of substance
candela (cd)=unit of luminous intensity

### Derived Units

For some of the derived SI units, special names and symbols exist; those approved by the CGPM are as follows:

hertz (Hz)=unit of frequency
newton (N)=unit of force
pascal (Pa)=unit of pressure, stress
joule (J)=unit of energy, work, quantity of heat
watt (W)=unit of power, radiant flux
coulomb (C)=unit of electric charge, quantity of electricity
volt (V)=unit of electric potential, potential difference, electromotive force
farad (F)=unit of electric capacitance
ohm (Ω)=unit of electric resistance
siemens (S)=unit of electric conductance
weber (Wb)=unit of magnetic flux
tesla (T)=unit of magnetic flux density
henry (H)=unit of inductance
degree Celsius (°C)=unit of Celsius temperature
lumen (lm)=unit of luminous flux
lux (lx)=unit of illuminance
becquerel (Bq)=unit of activity (of a radionuclide)
gray (Gy)=unit of absorbed dose, specific energy imparted, kerma, absorbed dose index
sievert (Sv)=unit of dose equivalent, dose equivalent index
radian (rad)=unit of plane angle
steradian (sr)=unit of solid angle

Other derived units are expressed in terms of base units. Some of the more commonly used derived units are the following:

Unit of area=square metre ($m^2$)
Unit of volume=cubic metre ($m^3$)
Unit of velocity=metre per second ($m\ s^{-1}$)
Unit of acceleration=metre per second squared ($m\ s^{-2}$)
Unit of density=kilogram per cubic metre ($kg\ m^{-3}$)
Unit of momentum=kilogram metre per second ($kg\ m\ s^{-1}$)
Unit of magnetic field strength=ampere per metre ($A\ m^{-1}$)
Unit of surface tension=newton per metre ($N\ m^{-1}$)
Unit of dynamic viscosity=pascal second (Pa s)
Unit of heat capacity=joule per kelvin ($J\ K^{-1}$)
Unit of specific heat capacity=joule per kilogram kelvin ($J\ kg^{-1}\ K^{-1}$)
Unit of heat flux density, irradiance=watt per square metre ($W\ m^{-2}$)
Unit of thermal conductivity=watt per metre kelvin ($W\ m^{-1}\ K^{-1}$)
Unit of electric field strength=volt per metre ($V\ m^{-1}$)
Unit of luminance=candela per square metre ($cd\ m^{-2}$)

### SI Prefixes

Decimal multiples and submultiples of the SI units are indicated by SI prefixes. These are as follows:

| *multiples* | *submultiples* |
|---|---|
| yotta (Y)$\times 10^{24}$ | deci (d)$\times 10^{-1}$ |
| zetta (Z)$\times 10^{21}$ | centi (c)$\times 10^{-2}$ |
| exa (E)$\times 10^{18}$ | milli (m)$\times 10^{-3}$ |
| peta (P)$\times 10^{15}$ | micro (μ)$\times 10^{-6}$ |
| tera (T)$\times 10^{12}$ | nano (n)$\times 10^{-9}$ |
| giga (G)$\times 10^{9}$ | pico (p)$\times 10^{-12}$ |
| mega (M)$\times 10^{6}$ | femto (f)$\times 10^{-15}$ |
| kilo (k)$\times 10^{3}$ | atto (a)$\times 10^{-18}$ |
| hecto (h)$\times 10^{2}$ | zepto (z)$\times 10^{-21}$ |
| deca (da)$\times 10$ | yocto (y)$\times 10^{-24}$ |

## METRIC UNITS

The metric primary standards are the metre as the unit of measurement of length, and the kilogram as the unit of measurement of mass. Other units of measurement are defined by reference to the primary standards.

### Measurement of Length

Kilometre (km)=1000 metres
Metre (m) is the length of the path travelled by light in vacuum during a time interval of 1/299 792 458 of a second
Decimetre (dm)=1/10 metre
Centimetre (cm)=1/100 metre
Millimetre (mm)=1/1000 metre

### Measurement of Area

Hectare (ha)=100 ares
Decare=10 ares
Are (a)=100 square metres
Square metre=a superficial area equal to that of a square each side of which measures one metre
Square decimetre=1/100 square metre

Square centimetre=1/100 square decimetre
Square millimetre=1/100 square centimetre

MEASUREMENT OF VOLUME

Cubic metre ($m^3$)=a volume equal to that of a cube each edge of which measures one metre
Cubic decimetre=1/1000 cubic metre
Cubic centimetre (cc)=1/1000 cubic decimetre
Hectolitre=100 litres
Litre=a cubic decimetre
Decilitre=1/10 litre
Centilitre=1/100 litre
Millilitre=1/1000 litre

MEASUREMENT OF CAPACITY

Hectolitre (hl)=100 litres
Litre (l or L)=a cubic decimetre
Decilitre (dl)=1/10 litre
Centilitre (cl)=1/100 litre
Millilitre (ml)=1/1000 litre

MEASUREMENT OF MASS OR WEIGHT

Tonne (t)=1000 kilograms
Kilogram (kg) is equal to the mass of the international prototype of the kilogram
Hectogram (hg)=1/10 kilogram
Gram (g)=1/1000 kilogram
*Carat (metric)=1/5 gram
Milligram (mg)=1/1000 gram

*Used only for transactions in precious stones or pearls

METRICATION IN THE UK

The European Council Directive 80/181/EEC, as amended by Council Directive 89/617/EEC, relates to the use of units of measurement for economic, public health, public safety or administrative purposes in the member states of the European Union. The provisions of the directives were incorporated into British law by the Weights and Measures Act 1985 (Metrication) (Amendment) Order 1994 and the Units of Measurement Regulations 1994; these instruments amended the Weights and Measures Act 1985. Parallel statutory rules amending Northern Ireland weights and measures legislation were made in May 1995.

The general effect of the 1994 and 1995 legislation is to end the use of imperial units of measurement for trade, replacing them with metric units – *see* below for timetable for UK metrication. Imperial units can, however, be used in addition to metric units, as supplementary indications.

## IMPERIAL UNITS

The imperial primary standards are the yard as the unit of measurement of length and the pound as the unit of measurement of mass. Other units of measurement are defined by reference to the primary standards. Most of these units are no longer authorized for use in trade in the UK – *see* below.

MEASUREMENT OF LENGTH

Mile=1760 yards
Furlong=220 yards
Chain=22 yards
Yard (yd)=0.9144 metre
Foot (ft)=1/3 yard
Inch (in)=1/36 yard

MEASUREMENT OF AREA

Square mile=640 acres
Acre=4840 square yards
Rood=1210 square yards
Square yard (sq. yd)=a superficial area equal to that of a square each side of which measures one yard
Square foot (sq. ft)=1/9 square yard
Square inch (sq. in)=1/144 square foot

MEASUREMENT OF VOLUME

Cubic yard=a volume equal to that of a cube each edge of which measures one yard
Cubic foot=1/27 cubic yard
Cubic inch=1/1728 cubic foot

MEASUREMENT OF CAPACITY

Bushel=8 gallons
Peck=2 gallons
Gallon (gal)=4.54609 cubic decimetres
Quart (qt)=1/4 gallon
*Pint (pt)=1/2 quart
Gill=1/4 pint
*Fluid ounce (fl oz)=1/20 pint
Fluid drachm=1/8 fluid ounce
Minim (min)=1/60 fluid drachm

MEASUREMENT OF MASS OR WEIGHT

Ton=2240 pounds
Hundredweight (cwt)=112 pounds
Cental=100 pounds
Quarter=28 pounds
Stone=14 pounds
*Pound (lb)=0.453 592 37 kilogram
*Ounce (oz)=1/16 pound
*†Ounce troy (oz tr)=12/175 pound
Dram (dr)=1/16 ounce
Grain (gr)=1/7000 pound
Pennyweight (dwt)=24 grains
Ounce apothecaries=480 grains
Drachm (1)=1/8 ounce apothecaries
Scruple (1)=1/3 drachm

*Units of measurement still authorised for use for trade in the UK
†Used only for transactions in gold, silver or other precious metals, and articles made therefrom

PHASING-OUT OF IMPERIAL UNITS IN THE UK

Since 1965 the United Kingdom has been adopting metric weights and measures in response to the adoption of metric units as the international system of measurement.

Goods sold loose by weight (mainly fresh foods) from January 1 2000 are required to be sold in grams and kilograms. Retailers can continue to display the price per imperial unit alongside the price per metric unit. Consumers can continue to express in ounces and pounds the quantity they wish to buy. Retailers will weigh out the equivalent quantity in grams and kilograms.

The Weights and Measures Units of Measurement Regulations 1995 (Statutory Instrument 1995 No. 1804) require that metric units should be used for all economic, public health, public safety and administrative purposes.

Units of measurement authorised for use in specialised fields are:

| *Unit* | *Field of application* |
|---|---|
| fathom | Marine navigation |
| fluid ounce, pint | Beer, cider, water, lemonade, fruit juice in returnable containers |
| ounce, pound | Goods for sale loose from bulk |
| therm | Gas supply |

Units of measurement authorized for use in specialized fields from 1 October 1995, without time limit

| *Unit* | *Field of application* |
|---|---|
| inch<br>foot<br>yard<br>mile | Road traffic signs, distance and speed measurement |
| pint | Dispense of draught beer or cider<br>Milk in returnable containers |
| acre | Land registration |
| troy ounce | Transactions in precious metals |

## MEASUREMENT OF ELECTRICITY

Units of measurement of electricity are defined by the Weights and Measures Act 1985 as follows:

ampere (A)=that constant current which, if maintained in two straight parallel conductors of infinite length, of negligible circular cross-section and placed 1 metre apart in vacuum, would produce between these conductors a force equal to $2\times10^{-7}$ newton per metre of length
ohm (Ω)=the electric resistance between two points of a conductor when a constant potential difference of 1 volt, applied between the two points, produces in the conductor a current of 1 ampere, the conductor not being the seat of any electromotive force
volt (V)=the difference of electric potential between two points of a conducting wire carrying a constant current of 1 ampere when the power dissipated between these points is equal to 1 watt
watt (W)=the power which in one second gives rise to energy of 1 joule
kilowatt (kW)=1000 watts
megawatt (MW)=one million watts

## WATER AND LIQUOR MEASURES

1 cubic foot=62.32 lb
1 gallon=10 lb
1 cubic cm=1 gram
1000 cubic cm=1 litre; 1 kilogram
1 cubic metre=1000 litres; 1000 kg; 1 tonne
An inch of rain on the surface of an acre (43560 sq. ft)=3630 cubic ft=100.992 tons
*Cisterns:* A cistern $4\times2\frac{1}{2}$ feet and 3 feet deep will hold brimful 186.963 gallons, weighing 1869.63 lb in addition to its own weight

### Water for Ships

Kilderkin=18 gallons
Barrel=36 gallons
Puncheon=72 gallons
Butt=110 gallons
Tun=210 gallons

### Bottles of Wine

Traditional equivalents in standard champagne bottles:
Magnum=2 bottles
Jeroboam=4 bottles
Rehoboam=6 bottles
Methuselah=8 bottles
Salmanazar=12 bottles
Balthazar=16 bottles
Nebuchadnezzar=20 bottles

A quarter of a bottle is known as a *nip*
An eighth of a bottle is known as a *baby*

## ANGULAR AND CIRCULAR MEASURES

60 seconds (″)=1 minute (′)
60 minutes=1 degree (°)
90 degrees=1 right angle or quadrant
Diameter of circle×3.1416=circumference
Diameter squared×0.7854=area of circle
Diameter squared×3.1416=surface of sphere
Diameter cubed×0.523=solidity of sphere
One degree of circumference×57.3=radius*
Diameter of cylinder×3.1416; product by length or height, gives the surface
Diameter squared×0.7854; product by length or height, gives solid content

*Or, one radian (the angle subtended at the centre of a circle by an arc of the circumference equal in length to the radius)=57.3 degrees

## MILLION, BILLION, ETC.

| *Value in the UK* | | |
|---|---|---|
| Million | thousand×thousand | $10^6$ |
| *Billion | million×million | $10^{12}$ |
| Trillion | million×billion | $10^{18}$ |
| Quadrillion | million×trillion | $10^{24}$ |
| *Value in USA* | | |
| Million | thousand×thousand | $10^6$ |
| *Billion | thousand×million | $10^9$ |
| Trillion | million×million | $10^{12}$ |
| Quadrillion | million×billion US | $10^{15}$ |

*The American usage of billion (i.e. $10^9$) is increasingly common, and is now universally used by statisticians

## NAUTICAL MEASURES

### Distance

Distance at sea is measured in nautical miles. The British standard nautical mile was 6080 feet but this measure has been obsolete since 1970 when the international nautical mile of 1852 metres was adopted by the Hydrographic Department of the Ministry of Defence. The cable (600 feet or 100 fathoms) was a measure approximately one-tenth of a nautical mile. Such distances are now expressed in decimal parts of a sea mile or in metres.

Soundings at sea were recorded in fathoms (6 feet). Depths are now expressed in metres on Admiralty charts.

### Speed

Speed is measured in nautical miles per hour, called knots. A ship moving at the rate of 30 nautical miles per hour is said to be doing 30 knots.

| *knots* | *m.p.h.* | *knots* | *m.p.h.* |
|---|---|---|---|
| 1 | 1.1515 | 9 | 10.3636 |
| 2 | 2.3030 | 10 | 11.5151 |
| 3 | 3.4545 | 15 | 17.2727 |
| 4 | 4.6060 | 20 | 23.0303 |
| 5 | 5.7575 | 25 | 28.7878 |
| 6 | 6.9090 | 30 | 34.5454 |
| 7 | 8.0606 | 35 | 40.3030 |
| 8 | 9.2121 | 40 | 46.0606 |

### Tonnage

Under the Merchant Shipping Act 1854, the tonnage of UK-registered vessels was measured in tons of 100 cubic feet. The need for a universal method of measurement led to the adoption of the International Convention on Tonnage Measurements of Ships 1969, which measures, in cubic metres, all the internal spaces of a vessel for the gross tonnage and those of the cargo compartments for the net tonnage. The convention has applied since July 1982 to new ships, ships which needed to be remeasured because of substantial alterations, and ships whose owners requested remeasurement. On 18 July 1994 the convention became mandatory and all vessels should have been remeasured by that date; however, there is a backlog and some vessels have not yet been remeasured.

## DISTANCE OF THE HORIZON

The limit of distance to which one can see varies with the height of the spectator. The greatest distance at which an object on the surface of the sea, or of a level plain, can be seen by a person whose eyes are at a height of five feet from the same level is nearly three miles. At a height of 20 feet the range is increased to nearly six miles, and an approximate rule for finding the range of vision for small heights is to increase the square root of the number of feet that the eye is above the level surface by a third of itself. The result is the distance of the horizon in miles, but is slightly in excess of that in the table below, which is computed by a more precise formula. The table may be used conversely to show the distance of an object of given height that is just visible from a point on the surface of the earth or sea. Refraction is taken into account both in the approximate rule and in the table.

| *Height in feet* | *range in miles* |
|---|---|
| 5 | 2.9 |
| 20 | 5.9 |
| 50 | 9.3 |
| 100 | 13.2 |
| 500 | 29.5 |
| 1,000 | 41.6 |
| 2,000 | 58.9 |
| 3,000 | 72.1 |
| 4,000 | 83.3 |
| 5,000 | 93.1 |
| 20,000 | 186.2 |

## TEMPERATURE SCALES

The SI (International System) unit of temperature is the kelvin, which is defined as the fraction 1/273.16 of the temperature of the triple point of water (i.e. where ice, water and water vapour are in equilibrium). The zero of the Kelvin scale is the absolute zero of temperature. The freezing point of water is 273.15 K and the boiling point (as adopted in the International Temperature Scale of 1990) is 373.124 K.

The Celsius scale (formerly centigrade) is defined by subtracting 273.15 from the Kelvin temperature. The Fahrenheit scale is related to the Celsius scale by the relationships:

temperature °F=(temperature °C×1.8)+32
temperature °C=(temperature °F–32)÷1.8

It follows from these definitions that the freezing point of water is 0°C and 32°F. The boiling point is 99.974°C and 211.953°F.

The temperature of the human body varies from person to person and in the same person can be affected by a variety of factors. In most people body temperature varies between 36.5°C and 37.2°C (97.7–98.9°F).

*Conversion between scales*

| °C | °F | °C | °F | °C | °F |
|---|---|---|---|---|---|
| 100 | 212 | 60 | 140 | 20 | 68 |
| 99 | 210.2 | 59 | 138.2 | 19 | 66.2 |
| 98 | 208.4 | 58 | 136.4 | 18 | 64.4 |
| 97 | 206.6 | 57 | 134.6 | 17 | 62.6 |
| 96 | 204.8 | 56 | 132.8 | 16 | 60.8 |
| 95 | 203 | 55 | 131 | 15 | 59 |
| 94 | 201.2 | 54 | 129.2 | 14 | 57.2 |
| 93 | 199.4 | 53 | 127.4 | 13 | 55.4 |
| 92 | 197.6 | 52 | 125.6 | 12 | 53.6 |
| 91 | 195.8 | 51 | 123.8 | 11 | 51.8 |
| 90 | 194 | 50 | 122 | 10 | 50 |
| 89 | 192.2 | 49 | 120.2 | 9 | 48.2 |
| 88 | 190.4 | 48 | 118.4 | 8 | 46.4 |
| 87 | 188.6 | 47 | 116.6 | 7 | 44.6 |
| 86 | 186.8 | 46 | 114.8 | 6 | 42.8 |
| 85 | 185 | 45 | 113 | 5 | 41 |
| 84 | 183.2 | 44 | 111.2 | 4 | 39.2 |
| 83 | 181.4 | 43 | 109.4 | 3 | 37.4 |
| 82 | 179.6 | 42 | 107.6 | 2 | 35.6 |
| 81 | 177.8 | 41 | 105.8 | 1 | 33.8 |
| 80 | 176 | 40 | 104 | *zero* | 32 |
| 79 | 174.2 | 39 | 102.2 | – 1 | 30.2 |
| 78 | 172.4 | 38 | 100.4 | – 2 | 28.4 |
| 77 | 170.6 | 37 | 98.6 | – 3 | 26.6 |
| 76 | 168.8 | 36 | 96.8 | – 4 | 24.8 |
| 75 | 167 | 35 | 95 | – 5 | 23 |
| 74 | 165.2 | 34 | 93.2 | – 6 | 21.2 |
| 73 | 163.4 | 33 | 91.4 | – 7 | 19.4 |
| 72 | 161.6 | 32 | 89.6 | – 8 | 17.6 |
| 71 | 159.8 | 31 | 87.8 | – 9 | 15.8 |
| 70 | 158 | 30 | 86 | –10 | 14 |
| 69 | 156.2 | 29 | 84.2 | –11 | 12.2 |
| 68 | 154.4 | 28 | 82.4 | –12 | 10.4 |
| 67 | 152.6 | 27 | 80.6 | –13 | 8.6 |
| 66 | 150.8 | 26 | 78.8 | –14 | 6.8 |
| 65 | 149 | 25 | 77 | –15 | 5 |
| 64 | 147.2 | 24 | 75.2 | –16 | 3.2 |
| 63 | 145.4 | 23 | 73.4 | –17 | 1.4 |
| 62 | 143.6 | 22 | 71.6 | –18 | 0.4 |
| 61 | 141.8 | 21 | 69.8 | –19 | –2.2 |

## PAPER MEASURES

*Printing Paper*
516 sheets=1 ream
2 reams=1 bundle
5 bundles=1 bale

*Writing Paper*
480 sheets=1 ream
20 quires=1 ream
24 sheets=1 quire

### BROWN PAPERS

| | *inches* | | *inches* |
|---|---|---|---|
| Casing | 46×36 | Imperial Cap | 29×22 |
| Double Imperial | 45×29 | Haven Cap | 26×21 |
| Elephant | 34×24 | Bag Cap | 24×19½ |
| Double Four Pound | 31×21 | Kent Cap | 21×18 |

### PRINTING PAPERS

| | *inches* | | *inches* |
|---|---|---|---|
| Foolscap | 17×13½ | Double Large Post | 33×21 |
| Double Foolscap | 27×17 | Demy | 22½×17½ |
| Quad Foolscap | 34×27 | Double Demy | 35×22½ |
| Crown | 20×15 | Quad Demy | 45×35 |
| Double Crown | 30×20 | Music Demy | 20×15½ |
| Quad Crown | 40×30 | | |

| | | | |
|---|---|---|---|
| Double Quad Crown | 60×40 | Medium | 23×18 |
| Post | 19×15½ | Royal | 25×20 |
| Double Post | 31½×19½ | Super Royal | 27½×20½ |
| | | Elephant | 28×23 |
| | | Imperial | 30×22 |

WRITING AND DRAWING PAPERS

| | *inches* | | *inches* |
|---|---|---|---|
| Emperor | 72×48 | Copy or Draft | 20×16 |
| Antiquarian | 53×31 | Demy | 20×15½ |
| Double Elephant | 40×27 | Post | 19×15 |
| Grand Eagle | 42×28 | Pinched Post | 18½×14 |
| Atlas | 34×26 | Foolscap | 17×13½ |
| Colombier | 34½×23½ | Double Foolscap | 26½×16½ |
| Imperial | 30×22 | Double Post | 30½×19 |
| Elephant | 28×23 | Double Large Post | 33×21 |
| Cartridge | 26×21 | Double Demy | 31×20 |
| Super Royal | 27×19 | Brief | 16½×13 |
| Royal | 24×19 | Pott | 15×12½ |
| Medium | 22×17½ | | |
| Large Post | 21×16½ | | |

## INTERNATIONAL PAPER SIZES

The basis of the international series of paper sizes is a rectangle having an area of one square metre, the sides of which are in the proportion of 1:2. The proportions 1:2 have a geometrical relationship, the side and diagonal of any square being in this proportion. The effect of this arrangement is that if the area of the sheet of paper is doubled or halved, the shorter side and the longer side of the new sheet are still in the same proportion 1:2. This feature is useful where photographic enlargement or reduction is used, as the proportions remain the same.

Description of the A series is by capital A followed by a figure. The basic size has the description A0 and the higher the figure following the letter, the greater is the number of sub-divisions and therefore the smaller the sheet. Half A0 is A1 and half A1 is A2. Where larger dimensions are required the A is preceded by a figure. Thus 2A means twice the size A0; 4A is four times the size of A0.

### SUBSIDIARY SERIES

B sizes are sizes intermediate between any two adjacent sizes of the A series. There is a series of C sizes which is used much less. A is for magazines and books, B for posters, wall charts and other large items, C for envelopes particularly where it is necessary for an envelope (in C series) to fit into another envelope. The size recommended for business correspondence is A4.

Long sizes (DL) are obtainable by dividing any appropriate sizes from the two series above into three, four or eight equal parts parallel with the shorter side in such a manner that the proportion of 1:2 is not maintained, the ratio between the longer and the shorter sides being greater than 2:1. In practice long sizes should be produced from the A series only.

It is an essential feature of these series that the dimensions are of the trimmed or finished size.

A SERIES

| | *mm* | | *mm* |
|---|---|---|---|
| A0 | 841×1189 | A6 | 105×148 |
| A1 | 594×841 | A7 | 74×105 |
| A2 | 420×594 | A8 | 52×74 |
| A3 | 297×420 | A9 | 37×52 |
| A4 | 210×297 | A10 | 26×37 |
| A5 | 148×210 | | |

B SERIES

| | *mm* | | *mm* |
|---|---|---|---|
| B0 | 1000×1414 | B6 | 125×176 |
| B1 | 707×1000 | B7 | 88×125 |
| B2 | 500×707 | B8 | 62×88 |
| B3 | 353×500 | B9 | 44×62 |
| B4 | 250×353 | B10 | 31×44 |
| B5 | 176×250 | | |

| C SERIES | | DL | |
|---|---|---|---|
| | *mm* | | *mm* |
| C4 | 324×229 | DL | 110×220 |
| C5 | 229×162 | | |
| C6 | 114×162 | | |

## BOUND BOOKS

The book sizes most commonly used are listed below. Approximate centimetre equivalents are also shown. International sizes are converted to their nearest imperial size, e.g. A4=D4; A5=D8.

| | | *inches* | *cm* |
|---|---|---|---|
| Crown 32mo | C32 | 2½×3 | 6×9 |
| Crown 16mo | C16 | 3×5 | 9×13 |
| Foolscap 8vo | F8 | 4×6 | 11×17 |
| Demy 16mo | D16 | 4×5 | 11×14 |
| Crown 8vo | C8 | 5×7½ | 13×19 |
| Demy 8vo | D8 | 5×8 | 14×22 |
| Medium 8vo | M8 | 5×9 | 15×23 |
| Royal 8vo | R8 | 6×10 | 16×25 |
| Super Royal 8vo | suR8 | 6×10 | 17×25 |
| Foolscap 4to | F4 | 6×8½ | 17×22 |
| Crown 4to | C4 | 7½×10 | 19×25 |
| Imperial 8vo | Imp8 | 7½×11 | 19×28 |
| Demy 4to | D4 | 8×11 | 22×29 |
| Royal 4to | R4 | 10×12½ | 25×31 |
| Super Royal 4to | suR4 | 10½×13½ | 25×34 |
| Crown Folio | Cfol | 10½×15 | 25×38 |
| Imperial Folio | Impfol | 11½×15 | 28×38 |

Folio=a sheet folded in half

Quarto (4to)=a sheet folded into four
Octavo (8vo)=a sheet folded into eight
Books are usually bound up in sheets of 16, 32 or 64 pages. Octavo books are generally printed 64 pages at a time, 32 pages on each side of a sheet of quad.

## CONVERSION TABLES FOR WEIGHTS AND MEASURES

Bold figures equal units of either of the columns beside them; thus: 1 cm=0.394 inches and 1 inch=2.540 cmrhtext>conversion tables for weights and measures

| LENGTH | | | AREA | | | VOLUME | | | WEIGHT (MASS) | | |
|---|---|---|---|---|---|---|---|---|---|---|---|
| *Centimetres* | | *Inches* | *Square cm* | | *Square in* | *Cubic cm* | | *Cubic in* | *Kilograms* | | *Pounds* |
| 2.540 | **1** | 0.394 | 6.452 | **1** | 0.155 | 16.387 | **1** | 0.061 | 0.454 | **1** | 2.205 |
| 5.080 | **2** | 0.787 | 12.903 | **2** | 0.310 | 32.774 | **2** | 0.122 | 0.907 | **2** | 4.409 |
| 7.620 | **3** | 1.181 | 19.355 | **3** | 0.465 | 49.161 | **3** | 0.183 | 1.361 | **3** | 6.614 |
| 10.160 | **4** | 1.575 | 25.806 | **4** | 0.620 | 65.548 | **4** | 0.244 | 1.814 | **4** | 8.819 |
| 12.700 | **5** | 1.969 | 32.258 | **5** | 0.775 | 81.936 | **5** | 0.305 | 2.268 | **5** | 11.023 |
| 15.240 | **6** | 2.362 | 38.710 | **6** | 0.930 | 98.323 | **6** | 0.366 | 2.722 | **6** | 13.228 |
| 17.780 | **7** | 2.756 | 45.161 | **7** | 1.085 | 114.710 | **7** | 0.427 | 3.175 | **7** | 15.432 |
| 20.320 | **8** | 3.150 | 51.613 | **8** | 1.240 | 131.097 | **8** | 0.488 | 3.629 | **8** | 17.637 |
| 22.860 | **9** | 3.543 | 58.064 | **9** | 1.395 | 147.484 | **9** | 0.549 | 4.082 | **9** | 19.842 |
| 25.400 | **10** | 3.937 | 64.516 | **10** | 1.550 | 163.871 | **10** | 0.610 | 4.536 | **10** | 22.046 |
| 50.800 | **20** | 7.874 | 129.032 | **20** | 3.100 | 327.742 | **20** | 1.220 | 9.072 | **20** | 44.092 |
| 76.200 | **30** | 11.811 | 193.548 | **30** | 4.650 | 491.613 | **30** | 1.831 | 13.608 | **30** | 66.139 |
| 101.600 | **40** | 15.748 | 258.064 | **40** | 6.200 | 655.484 | **40** | 2.441 | 18.144 | **40** | 88.185 |
| 127.000 | **50** | 19.685 | 322.580 | **50** | 7.750 | 819.355 | **50** | 3.051 | 22.680 | **50** | 110.231 |
| 152.400 | **60** | 23.622 | 387.096 | **60** | 9.300 | 983.226 | **60** | 3.661 | 27.216 | **60** | 132.277 |
| 177.800 | **70** | 27.559 | 451.612 | **70** | 10.850 | 1147.097 | **70** | 4.272 | 31.752 | **70** | 154.324 |
| 203.200 | **80** | 31.496 | 516.128 | **80** | 12.400 | 1310.968 | **80** | 4.882 | 36.287 | **80** | 176.370 |
| 228.600 | **90** | 35.433 | 580.644 | **90** | 13.950 | 1474.839 | **90** | 5.492 | 40.823 | **90** | 198.416 |
| 254.000 | **100** | 39.370 | 645.160 | **100** | 15.500 | 1638.710 | **100** | 6.102 | 45.359 | **100** | 220.464 |

| *Metres* | | *Yards* | *Square m* | | *Square yd* | *Cubic m* | | *Cubic yd* | *Metric tonnes* | | *Tons (UK)* |
|---|---|---|---|---|---|---|---|---|---|---|---|
| 0.914 | **1** | 1.094 | 0.836 | **1** | 1.196 | 0.765 | **1** | 1.308 | 1.016 | **1** | 0.984 |
| 1.829 | **2** | 2.187 | 1.672 | **2** | 2.392 | 1.529 | **2** | 2.616 | 2.032 | **2** | 1.968 |
| 2.743 | **3** | 3.281 | 2.508 | **3** | 3.588 | 2.294 | **3** | 3.924 | 3.048 | **3** | 2.953 |
| 3.658 | **4** | 4.374 | 3.345 | **4** | 4.784 | 3.058 | **4** | 5.232 | 4.064 | **4** | 3.937 |
| 4.572 | **5** | 5.468 | 4.181 | **5** | 5.980 | 3.823 | **5** | 6.540 | 5.080 | **5** | 4.921 |
| 5.486 | **6** | 6.562 | 5.017 | **6** | 7.176 | 4.587 | **6** | 7.848 | 6.096 | **6** | 5.905 |
| 6.401 | **7** | 7.655 | 5.853 | **7** | 8.372 | 5.352 | **7** | 9.156 | 7.112 | **7** | 6.889 |
| 7.315 | **8** | 8.749 | 6.689 | **8** | 9.568 | 6.116 | **8** | 10.464 | 8.128 | **8** | 7.874 |
| 8.230 | **9** | 9.843 | 7.525 | **9** | 10.764 | 6.881 | **9** | 11.772 | 9.144 | **9** | 8.858 |
| 9.144 | **10** | 10.936 | 8.361 | **10** | 11.960 | 7.646 | **10** | 13.080 | 10.161 | **10** | 9.842 |
| 18.288 | **20** | 21.872 | 16.723 | **20** | 23.920 | 15.291 | **20** | 26.159 | 20.321 | **20** | 19.684 |
| 27.432 | **30** | 32.808 | 25.084 | **30** | 35.880 | 22.937 | **30** | 39.239 | 30.481 | **30** | 29.526 |
| 36.576 | **40** | 43.745 | 33.445 | **40** | 47.840 | 30.582 | **40** | 52.318 | 40.642 | **40** | 39.368 |
| 45.720 | **50** | 54.681 | 41.806 | **50** | 59.799 | 38.228 | **50** | 65.398 | 50.802 | **50** | 49.210 |
| 54.864 | **60** | 65.617 | 50.168 | **60** | 71.759 | 45.873 | **60** | 78.477 | 60.963 | **60** | 59.052 |
| 64.008 | **70** | 76.553 | 58.529 | **70** | 83.719 | 53.519 | **70** | 91.557 | 71.123 | **70** | 68.894 |
| 73.152 | **80** | 87.489 | 66.890 | **80** | 95.679 | 61.164 | **80** | 104.636 | 81.284 | **80** | 78.737 |
| 82.296 | **90** | 98.425 | 75.251 | **90** | 107.639 | 68.810 | **90** | 117.716 | 91.444 | **90** | 88.579 |
| 91.440 | **100** | 109.361 | 83.613 | **100** | 119.599 | 76.455 | **100** | 130.795 | 101.605 | **100** | 98.421 |

| *Kilometres* | | *Miles* | *Hectares* | | *Acres* | *Litres* | | *Gallons* | *Metric tonnes* | | *Tons (US)* |
|---|---|---|---|---|---|---|---|---|---|---|---|
| 1.609 | **1** | 0.621 | 0.405 | **1** | 2.471 | 4.546 | **1** | 0.220 | 0.907 | **1** | 1.102 |
| 3.219 | **2** | 1.243 | 0.809 | **2** | 4.942 | 9.092 | **2** | 0.440 | 1.814 | **2** | 2.205 |
| 4.828 | **3** | 1.864 | 1.214 | **3** | 7.413 | 13.638 | **3** | 0.660 | 2.722 | **3** | 3.305 |
| 6.437 | **4** | 2.485 | 1.619 | **4** | 9.844 | 18.184 | **4** | 0.880 | 3.629 | **4** | 4.409 |
| 8.047 | **5** | 3.107 | 2.023 | **5** | 12.355 | 22.730 | **5** | 1.100 | 4.536 | **5** | 5.521 |
| 9.656 | **6** | 3.728 | 2.428 | **6** | 14.826 | 27.276 | **6** | 1.320 | 5.443 | **6** | 6.614 |
| 11.265 | **7** | 4.350 | 2.833 | **7** | 17.297 | 31.822 | **7** | 1.540 | 6.350 | **7** | 7.716 |
| 12.875 | **8** | 4.971 | 3.327 | **8** | 19.769 | 36.368 | **8** | 1.760 | 7.257 | **7** | 8.818 |
| 14.484 | **9** | 5.592 | 3.642 | **9** | 22.240 | 40.914 | **9** | 1.980 | 8.165 | **9** | 9.921 |
| 16.093 | **10** | 6.214 | 4.047 | **10** | 24.711 | 45.460 | **10** | 2.200 | 9.072 | **10** | 11.023 |
| 32.187 | **20** | 12.427 | 8.094 | **20** | 49.421 | 90.919 | **20** | 4.400 | 18.144 | **20** | 22.046 |
| 48.280 | **30** | 18.641 | 12.140 | **30** | 74.132 | 136.379 | **30** | 6.599 | 27.216 | **30** | 33.069 |
| 64.374 | **40** | 24.855 | 16.187 | **40** | 98.842 | 181.839 | **40** | 8.799 | 36.287 | **40** | 44.092 |
| 80.467 | **50** | 31.069 | 20.234 | **50** | 123.555 | 227.298 | **50** | 10.999 | 45.359 | **50** | 55.116 |
| 96.561 | **60** | 37.282 | 24.281 | **60** | 148.263 | 272.758 | **60** | 13.199 | 54.431 | **60** | 66.139 |
| 112.654 | **70** | 43.496 | 28.328 | **70** | 172.974 | 318.217 | **70** | 15.398 | 63.503 | **70** | 77.162 |
| 128.748 | **80** | 49.710 | 32.375 | **80** | 197.684 | 363.677 | **80** | 17.598 | 72.575 | **80** | 88.185 |
| 144.841 | **90** | 55.923 | 36.422 | **90** | 222.395 | 409.137 | **90** | 19.798 | 81.647 | **90** | 99.208 |
| 160.934 | **100** | 62.137 | 40.469 | **100** | 247.105 | 454.596 | **100** | 21.998 | 90.719 | **100** | 110.231 |

# Abbreviations

| | |
|---|---|
| A | Associate of |
| AA | Alcoholics Anonymous |
| | Automobile Association |
| AAA | Amateur Athletic Association |
| AB | Able-bodied seaman |
| ABA | Amateur Boxing Association |
| abbr(ev) | abbreviation |
| ABM | Anti-ballistic missile |
| abr | abridged |
| ac | alternating current |
| a/c | account |
| AC | Aircraftman |
| | (*Ante Christum*) Before Christ |
| | Companion, Order of Australia |
| ACAS | Advisory, Conciliation and Arbitration Service |
| ACT | Australian Capital Territory |
| AD | (*Anno Domini*) In the year of our Lord |
| ADC | Aide-de-Camp |
| ADC (P) | Personal ADC to The Queen |
| adj | adjective |
| Adj | Adjutant |
| ad lib | (*ad libitum*) at pleasure |
| Adm | Admiral |
| | Admission |
| adv | adverb |
| AE | Air Efficiency Award |
| AEEU | Amalgamated Engineering and Electrical Union |
| AEM | Air Efficiency Medal |
| AFC | Air Force Cross |
| AFM | Air Force Medal |
| AG | Adjutant-General |
| | Attorney-General |
| AGM | air-to-ground missile |
| | annual general meeting |
| AH | (*Anno Hegirae*) In the year of the Hegira |
| AI | Artificial intelligence |
| AIDS | Acquired immune deficiency syndrome |
| AIM | Alternative Investment Market |
| alt | altitude |
| am | (*ante meridiem*) before noon |
| AM | (*Anno mundi*) In the year of the world |
| | amplitude modulation |
| amp | ampere |
| | amplifier |
| ANC | African National Congress |
| anon | anonymous |
| ANZAC | Australian and New Zealand Army Corps |
| AO | Air Officer |
| | Officer, Order of Australia |
| AOC | Air Officer Commanding |
| AONB | Area of Outstanding Natural Beauty |
| AS | Anglo-Saxon |
| ASA | Advertising Standards Authority |
| | Amateur Swimming Association |
| asap | as soon as possible |
| ASB | Alternative Service Book |
| ASEAN | Association of South East Asian Nations |
| ASH | Action on Smoking and Health |
| ASLEF | Associated Society of Locomotive Engineers and Firemen |
| ASLIB | Association for Information Management |
| ATC | Air Training Corps |
| AUC | (*ab urbe condita*) In the year from the foundation of Rome |
| | (*anno urbis conditae*) In the year of the founding of the city |
| AUT | Association of University Teachers |
| AV | Audio-visual |
| | Authorized Version (*of Bible*) |
| AVR | Army Volunteer Reserve |
| AWOL | Absent without leave |
| b | born |
| | bowled |
| BA | Bachelor of Arts |
| BAA | British Airports Authority |
| | British Astronomical Association |
| BAF | British Athletics Federation |
| BAFTA | British Academy of Film and Television Arts |
| Bart | Baronet |
| BAS | Bachelor in Agricultural Science |
| | British Antarctic Survey |
| BBC | British Broadcasting Corporation |
| BBSRC | Biotechnology and Biological Sciences Research Council |
| BC | Before Christ |
| | British Columbia |
| B Ch (D) | Bachelor of (Dental) Surgery |
| BCL | Bachelor of Civil Law |
| B Com | Bachelor of Commerce |
| BD | Bachelor of Divinity |
| BDA | British Dental Association |
| BDS | Bachelor of Dental Surgery |
| B Ed | Bachelor of Education |
| BEM | British Empire Medal |
| B Eng | Bachelor of Engineering |
| BFI | British Film Institute |
| BFPO | British Forces Post Office |
| BL | British Library |
| B Litt | Bachelor of Letters *or* of Literature |
| BM | Bachelor of Medicine |
| | British Museum |
| BMA | British Medical Association |
| B Mus | Bachelor of Music |
| BOTB | British Overseas Trade Board |
| Bp | Bishop |
| B Pharm | Bachelor of Pharmacy |
| B Phil | Bachelor of Philosophy |
| Br(it) | Britain |
| | British |
| BR | British Rail |
| Brig | Brigadier |
| BSc | Bachelor of Science |
| BSE | Bovine spongiform encephalopathy |
| BSI | British Standards Institution |
| BST | British Summer Time |
| Bt | Baronet |
| BTEC | Business and Technology Education Council |
| B Th | Bachelor of Theology |
| Btu | British thermal unit |
| BVM | (*Beata Virgo Maria*) Blessed Virgin Mary |
| BVMS | Bachelor of Veterinary Medicine and Surgery |
| c | (*circa*) about |
| C | Celsius |
| | Centigrade |
| | Conservative |
| CA | Chartered Accountant (*Scotland*) |
| CAA | Civil Aviation Authority |
| CAB | Citizens' Advice Bureau |
| Cantab | (of) Cambridge |
| Cantuar: | of Canterbury (*Archbishop*) |
| CAP | Common Agricultural Policy |
| Capt | Captain |
| Caricom | Caribbean Community and Common Market |
| Carliol: | of Carlisle (*Bishop*) |
| CB | Companion, Order of the Bath |
| CBE | Commander, Order of the British Empire |
| CBI | Confederation of British Industry |
| CC | Chamber of Commerce |
| | Companion, Order of Canada |
| | City Council |
| | County Council |
| | County Court |
| CCC | County Cricket Club |
| CCF | Combined Cadet Force |
| C Chem | Chartered Chemist |
| CD | Civil Defence |
| | compact disc |
| | Corps Diplomatique |
| Cdr | Commander |
| Cdre | Commodore |
| CDS | Chief of the Defence Staff |
| CE | Christian Era |
| | Civil Engineer |
| C Eng | Chartered Engineer |
| Cestr: | of Chester (*Bishop*) |
| CET | Central European Time |
| | Common External Tariff |
| cf | (*confer*) compare |
| CF | Chaplain to the Forces |
| CFC | Chlorofluorocarbon |
| CFS | Chronic Fatigue Syndrome |
| CGC | Conspicuous Gallantry Cross |
| Cgeol | Chartered Geologist |
| CGM | Conspicuous Gallantry Medal |
| CGS | Centimetre-gramme-second (*system*) |
| | Chief of General Staff |
| CH | Companion of Honour |
| ChB/M | Bachelor/Master of Surgery |
| CI | Channel Islands |
| | The Imperial Order of the Crown of India |
| CIA | Central Intelligence Agency |
| Cicestr: | of Chichester (*Bishop*) |
| CID | Criminal Investigation Department |
| CIE | Companion, Order of the Indian Empire |
| cif | cost, insurance and freight |
| C-in-C | Commander-in-Chief |
| CIPFA | Chartered Institute of Public Finance and Accountancy |
| CIS | Commonwealth of Independent States |
| CJD | Creutzfeld-Jakob disease |

| | |
|---|---|
| C Lit | Companion of Literature |
| CLJ | Commander, Order of St Lazarus of Jerusalem |
| CM | (*Chirurgiae Magister*) Master of Surgery |
| CMG | Companion, Order of St Michael and St George |
| CND | Campaign for Nuclear Disarmament |
| c/o | care of |
| CO | Commanding Officer |
| | conscientious objector |
| COD | Cash on delivery |
| C of E | Church of England |
| COI | Central Office of Information |
| Col | Colonel |
| Con | Conservative |
| *cons* | consecrated |
| Cpl | Corporal |
| CPM | Colonial Police Medal |
| CPRE | Council for the Protection of Rural England |
| CPS | Crown Prosecution Service |
| CPVE | Certificate of Pre-Vocational Education |
| CRE | Commission for Racial Equality |
| CSA | Child Support Agency |
| CSE | Certificate of Secondary Education |
| CSI | Companion, Order of the Star of India |
| CVO | Commander, Royal Victorian Order |
| d | (*denarius*) penny |
| DA | District Attorney (*USA*) |
| DBE | Dame Commander, Order of the British Empire |
| dc | direct current |
| DC | District Council |
| | District of Columbia |
| DCB | Dame Commander, Order of the Bath |
| D Ch | (*Doctor Chirurgiae*) Doctor of Surgery |
| DCL | Doctor of Civil Law |
| DCM | Distinguished Conduct Medal |
| DCMG | Dame Commander, Order of St Michael and St George |
| DCMS | Department for Culture, Media and Sport |
| DCVO | Dame Commander, Royal Victorian Order |
| DD | Doctor of Divinity |
| DDS | Doctor of Dental Surgery |
| DDT | dichlorodiphenyl-trichloroethane |
| del | (*delineavit*) he/she drew it |
| DEFRA | Department for Environment, Food and Rural Affairs |
| DFC | Distinguished Flying Cross |
| DfES | Department for Education and Skills |
| DFID | Department for International Development |
| DFM | Distinguished Flying Medal |
| DG | (*Dei gratia*) By the grace of God |
| DH | Department of Health |
| DHA | District Health Authority |
| Dip Ed | Diploma in Education |
| Dip HE | Diploma in Higher Education |
| Dip Tech | Diploma in Technology |
| DJ | Disc jockey |
| DL | Deputy Lieutenant |
| D Litt | Doctor of Letters *or* of Literature |
| DM | Deutsche Mark |
| D Mus | Doctor of Music |
| DNA | deoxyribonucleic acid |
| DNB | *Dictionary of National Biography* |
| do | (*ditto*) the same |
| DoE | Department of the Environment |
| DOS | Disk operating system (*computer*) |
| DP | Data processing |
| D Ph or D Phil | Doctor of Philosophy |
| DPP | Director of Public Prosecutions |
| Dr | Doctor |
| D Sc | Doctor of Science |
| DSC | Distinguished Service Cross |
| DSM | Distinguished Service Medal |
| DSO | Companion, Distinguished Service Order |
| DTI | Department of Trade and Industry |
| DTLR | Department of Transport, Local Government and the Regions |
| DTP | Desk-top publishing |
| Dunelm: | of Durham (*Bishop*) |
| DV | (*Deo volente*) God willing |
| DWP | Department for Work and Pensions |
| E | East |
| Ebor: | of York (*Archbishop*) |
| EBRD | European Bank for Reconstruction and Development |
| EC | European Community |
| ECG | Electrocardiogram |
| ECGD | Export Credits Guarantee Department |
| ECSC | European Coal and Steel Community |
| ECU | European Currency Unit |
| ED | Efficiency Decoration |
| EEC | European Economic Community |
| EEG | Electroencephalogram |
| EFA | European Fighter Aircraft |
| EFTA | European Free Trade Association |
| eg | (*exempli gratia*) for the sake of example |
| EIB | European Investment Bank |
| EMS | European Monetary System |
| EMU | European Monetary Union |
| EOC | Equal Opportunities Commission |
| EPSRC | Engineering and Physical Sciences Research Council |
| ER | (*Elizabetha Regina*) Queen Elizabeth |
| ERD | Emergency Reserve Decoration |
| ERM | Exchange Rate Mechanism |
| ERNIE | Electronic random number indicator equipment |
| ESA | European Space Agency |
| ESP | Extra-sensory perception |
| ESRC | Economic and Social Research Council |
| ETA | *Euzkadi ta Askatasuna* (Basque separatist organization) |
| et al | (*et alibi*) and elsewhere |
| | (*et alii*) and others |
| etc | (*et cetera*) and the other things/and so forth |
| et seq | (*et sequentia*) and the following |
| EU | European Union |
| Euratom | European Atomic Energy Commission |
| Exon: | of Exeter (*Bishop*) |
| *f* | (*forte*) loud |
| F | Fahrenheit |
| | Fellow of |
| FA | Football Association |
| FANY | First Aid Nursing Yeomanry |
| FAO | Food and Agriculture Organization (*UN*) |
| FBA | Fellow, British Academy |
| FBAA | Fellow, British Association of Accountants and Auditors |
| FBI | Federal Bureau of Investigation |
| FIMgt | Fellow, Institute of Management |
| FBS | Fellow, Botanical Society |
| FC | Football Club |
| FCA | Fellow, Institute of Chartered Accountants in England and Wales |
| FCCA | Fellow, Chartered Association of Certified Accountants |
| FCGI | Fellow, City and Guilds of London Institute |
| FCIA | Fellow, Corporation of Insurance Agents |
| FCIArb | Fellow, Chartered Institute of Arbitrators |
| FCIB | Fellow, Chartered Institute of Bankers |
| | Fellow, Corporation of Insurance Brokers |
| FCIBSE | Fellow, Chartered Institution of Building Services Engineers |
| FCII | Fellow, Chartered Insurance Institute |
| FCIPS | Fellow, Chartered Institute of Purchasing and Supply |
| FCIS | Fellow, Institute of Chartered Secretaries and Administrators |
| FCIT | Fellow, Chartered Institute of Transport |
| FCMA | Fellow, Chartered Institute of Management Accountants |
| FCO | Foreign and Commonwealth Office |
| FCP | Fellow, College of Preceptors |
| FD | (*Fidei Defensor*) Defender of the Faith |
| FE | Further Education |
| fec | (*fecit*) made this |
| ff | (*fecerunt*) made this (*pl*) |
| | folios following |
| *ff* | (*fortissimo*) very loud |
| FFA | Fellow, Faculty of Actuaries (*Scotland*) |
| | Fellow, Institute of Financial Accountants |
| FFAS | Fellow, Faculty of Architects and Surveyors |
| FFCM | Fellow, Faculty of Community Medicine |
| FFPHM | Fellow, Faculty of Public Health Medicine |
| FGS | Fellow, Geological Society |
| FHS | Fellow, Heraldry Society |
| FHSM | Fellow, Institute of Health Service Management |
| FIA | Fellow, Institute of Actuaries |
| FIBiol | Fellow, Institute of Biology |
| FICE | Fellow, Institution of Civil Engineers |
| FICS | Fellow, Institution of Chartered Shipbrokers |
| FIEE | Fellow, Institution of Electrical Engineers |
| FIERE | Fellow, Institution of Electronic and Radio Engineers |
| FIFA | International Association Football Federation |
| FIM | Fellow, Institute of Metals |

|  |  |
|---|---|
| FIMM | Fellow, Institution of Mining and Metallurgy |
| FInstF | Fellow, Institute of Fuel |
| FInstP | Fellow, Institute of Physics |
| FIQS | Fellow, Institute of Quantity Surveyors |
| FIS | Fellow, Institute of Statisticians |
| FJI | Fellow, Institute of Journalists |
| fl | (*floruit*) flourished |
| FLA | Fellow, Library Association |
| FLS | Fellow, Linnaean Society |
| FM | Field Marshal |
| | frequency modulation |
| fo | folio |
| FO | Flying Officer |
| fob | free on board |
| FPhS | Fellow, Philosophical Society |
| FRAD | Fellow, Royal Academy of Dancing |
| FRAeS | Fellow, Royal Aeronautical Society |
| FRAI | Fellow, Royal Anthropological Institute |
| FRAM | Fellow, Royal Academy of Music |
| FRAS | Fellow, Royal Asiatic Society |
| | Fellow, Royal Astronomical Society |
| FRBS | Fellow, Royal Botanic Society |
| | Fellow, Royal Society of British Sculptors |
| FRCA | Fellow, Royal College of Anaesthetists |
| FRCGP | Fellow, Royal College of General Practitioners |
| FRCM | Fellow, Royal College of Music |
| FRCO | Fellow, Royal College of Organists |
| FRCOG | Fellow, Royal College of Obstetricians and Gynaecologists |
| FRCP | Fellow, Royal College of Physicians, London |
| FRCPath | Fellow, Royal College of Pathologists |
| FRCPE *or* FRCPEd | Fellow, Royal College of Physicians, Edinburgh |
| FRCPI | Fellow, Royal College of Physicians, Ireland |
| FRCPsych | Fellow, Royal College of Psychiatrists |
| FRCR | Fellow, Royal College of Radiologists |
| FRCS | Fellow, Royal College of Surgeons of England |
| FRCSE *or* FRCSEd | Fellow, Royal College of Surgeons of Edinburgh |
| FRCSGlas | Fellow, Royal College of Physicians and Surgeons of Glasgow |
| FRCSI | Fellow, Royal College of Surgeons in Ireland |
| FRCVS | Fellow, Royal College of Veterinary Surgeons |
| FREconS | Fellow, Royal Economic Society |
| FREng | Fellow, Royal Academy of Engineering |
| FRGS | Fellow, Royal Geographical Society |
| FRHistS | Fellow, Royal Historical Society |
| FRHS | Fellow, Royal Horticultural Society |
| FRIBA | Fellow, Royal Institute of British Architects |
| FRICS | Fellow, Royal Institution of Chartered Surveyors |
| FRMetS | Fellow, Royal Meteorological Society |
| FRMS | Fellow, Royal Microscopical Society |
| FRNS | Fellow, Royal Numismatic Society |
| FRPharmS | Fellow, Royal Pharmaceutical Society |
| FRPS | Fellow, Royal Photographic Society |
| FRS | Fellow, Royal Society |
| FRSA | Fellow, Royal Society of Arts |
| FRSC | Fellow, Royal Society of Chemistry |
| FRSE | Fellow, Royal Society of Edinburgh |
| FRSH | Fellow, Royal Society of Health |
| FRSL | Fellow, Royal Society of Literature |
| FRTPI | Fellow, Royal Town Planning Institute |
| FSA | Fellow, Society of Antiquaries |
| FSS | Fellow, Royal Statistical Society |
| FSVA | Fellow, Incorporated Society of Valuers and Auctioneers |
| FT | *Financial Times* |
| FTI | Fellow, Textile Institute |
| FTII | Fellow, Chartered Institute of Taxation |
| FZS | Fellow, Zoological Society |
| G7 | Group of Seven (Canada, France, Germany, Italy, Japan, UK, USA) |
| GATT | General Agreement on Tariffs and Trade |
| GBE | Dame/Knight Grand Cross, Order of the British Empire |
| GC | George Cross |
| GCB | Dame/Knight Grand Cross, Order of the Bath |
| GCE | General Certificate of Education |
| GCHQ | Government Communications Headquarters |
| GCIE | Knight Grand Commander, Order of the Indian Empire |
| GCLJ | Knight Grand Cross, Order of St Lazarus of Jerusalem |
| GCMG | Dame/Knight Grand Cross, Order of St Michael and St George |
| GCSE | General Certificate of Secondary Education |
| GCSI | Knight Grand Commander, Order of the Star of India |
| GCVO | Dame/Knight Grand Cross, Royal Victorian Order |
| GDP | Gross domestic product |
| Gen | General |
| GHQ | General Headquarters |
| GM | George Medal |
| GMB | General, Municipal, Boilermakers and Allied Trades Union |
| GMT | Greenwich Mean Time |
| GNP | Gross national product |
| GNVQ | General National Vocational Qualification |
| GOC | General Officer Commanding |
| GP | General Practitioner |
| Gp Capt | Group Captain |
| GSA | Girls' Schools Association |
| HAC | Honourable Artillery Company |
| HB | His Beatitude |
| HBM | Her/His Britannic Majesty('s) |
| HCF | Highest common factor |
| | Honorary Chaplain to the Forces |
| HE | Her/His Excellency |
| | Higher Education |
| | His Eminence |
| HGV | Heavy Goods Vehicle |
| HH | Her/His Highness |
| | Her/His Honour |
| | His Holiness |
| HIM | Her/His Imperial Majesty |
| HIV | Human immunodeficiency virus |
| HJS | (*hic jacet sepultus*) here lies buried |
| HM | Her/His Majesty('s) |
| HMAS | Her/His Majesty's Australian Ship |
| HMC | Headmasters' Conference |
| HMI | Her/His Majesty's Inspector |
| HML | Her/His Majesty's Lieutenant |
| HMS | Her/His Majesty's Ship |
| HMSO | Her/His Majesty's Stationery Office |
| HNC | Higher National Certificate |
| HND | Higher National Diploma |
| HOLMES | Home Office Large Major Enquiry System |
| Hon | Honorary |
| | Honourable |
| hp | horse power |
| HP | Hire purchase |
| HQ | Headquarters |
| HR | Human resources |
| HRH | Her/His Royal Highness |
| HSE | Health and Safety Executive |
| | (*hic sepultus est*) here lies buried |
| HSH | Her/His Serene Highness |
| HWM | High water mark |
| I | Island |
| IAAS | Incorporated Association of Architects and Surveyors |
| IAEA | International Atomic Energy Agency |
| IATA | International Air Transport Association |
| ibid | (*ibidem*) in the same place |
| IBRD | International Bank for Reconstruction and Development |
| ICAO | International Civil Aviation Organization |
| ICBM | Inter-continental ballistic missile |
| ICFTU | International Confederation of Free Trade Unions |
| ICJ | International Court of Justice |
| ICRC | International Committee of the Red Cross |
| id | (*idem*) the same |
| IDA | International Development Association |
| IDD | International direct dialling |
| ie | (*id est*) that is |
| IEA | International Energy Agency |
| IFAD | International Fund for Agricultural Development |
| IFC | International Finance Corporation |
| IHS | (*Iesus Hominum Salvator*) Jesus the Saviour of Mankind |
| ILO | International Labour Office/ Organization |
| ILR | Independent local radio |
| IMF | International Monetary Fund |
| IMO | International Maritime Organization |
| Inc | Incorporated |
| incog | (*incognito*) unknown, unrecognized |
| INLA | Irish National Liberation Army |
| in loc | (*in loco*) in its place |

| | |
|---|---|
| Inmarsat | International Maritime Satellite Organization |
| INRI | (*Iesus Nazarenus Rex Iudaeorum*) Jesus of Nazareth, King of the Jews |
| inst | (*instant*) current month |
| Intelsat | International Telecommunications Satellite Organization |
| Interpol | International Criminal Police Commission |
| IOC | International Olympic Committee |
| IOM | Isle of Man |
| IOU | I owe you |
| IOW | Isle of Wight |
| IQ | Intelligence quotient |
| IRA | Irish Republican Army |
| IRC | International Red Cross |
| Is | Islands |
| ISBN | International Standard Book Number |
| ISO | Imperial Service Order |
| | International Standards Organization |
| ISSN | International Standard Serial Number |
| ITC | Independent Television Commission |
| ITN | Independent Television News |
| ITU | International Telecommunication Union |
| ITV | Independent Television |
| JP | Justice of the Peace |
| K | Köchel numeration (*of Mozart's works*) |
| KBE | Knight Commander, Order of the British Empire |
| KCB | Knight Commander, Order of the Bath |
| KCIE | Knight Commander, Order of the Indian Empire |
| KCLJ | Knight Commander, Order of St Lazarus of Jerusalem |
| KCMG | Knight Commander, Order of St Michael and St George |
| KCSI | Knight Commander, Order of the Star of India |
| KCVO | Knight Commander, Royal Victorian Order |
| KG | Knight of the Garter |
| KGB | (*Komitet Gosudarstvennoi Besopasnosti*) Committee of State Security (*USSR*) |
| kHz | kiloHertz |
| KKK | Ku Klux Klan |
| KLJ | Knight, Order of St Lazarus of Jerusalem |
| ko | knock out (*boxing*) |
| KP | Knight, Order of St Patrick |
| KStJ | Knight, Order of St John of Jerusalem |
| Kt | Knight |
| KT | Knight of the Thistle |
| kV | Kilovolt |
| kW | Kilowatt |
| kWh | Kilowatt hour |
| L | Liberal |
| Lab | Labour |
| Lat | Latitude |
| lbw | leg before wicket |
| lc | lower case (*printing*) |
| LCJ | Lord Chief Justice |

| | |
|---|---|
| LCM | Least/lowest common multiple |
| LD | Liberal Democrat |
| LDS | Licentiate in Dental Surgery |
| LEA | Local Education Authority |
| LHD | (*Literarum Humaniorum Doctor*) Doctor of Humane Letters/Literature |
| Lib | Liberal |
| Lic | (*Licenciado*) lawyer (*Spanish*) |
| Lic Med | Licentiate in Medicine |
| Lit | Literary |
| Lit Hum | (*Literae Humaniores*) Faculty of classics and philosophy, Oxford |
| Litt D | Doctor of Letters |
| LJ | Lord Justice |
| LLB | Bachelor of Laws |
| LLD | Doctor of Laws |
| LLM | Master of Laws |
| LM | Licentiate in Midwifery |
| LMS | Local management in schools |
| LMSSA | Licentiate in Medicine and Surgery, Society of Apothecaries |
| loc cit | (*loco citato*) in the place cited |
| log | logarithm |
| Londin: | of London (*Bishop*) |
| Long | Longitude |
| LS | (*loco sigilli*) place of the seal |
| LSA | Licentiate of Society of Apothecaries |
| Lsd | (*Librae, solidi, denarii*) £, shillings and pence |
| LSE | London School of Economics and Political Science |
| Lt | Lieutenant |
| LTA | Lawn Tennis Association |
| Ltd | Limited (liability) |
| LTh *or* L Theol | Licentiate in Theology |
| LVO | Lieutenant, Royal Victorian Order |
| LW | long wave |
| LWM | Low water mark |
| M | Member of |
| | Monsieur |
| MA | Master of Arts |
| Maj | Major |
| max | maximum |
| MB | Bachelor of Medicine |
| MBA | Master of Business Administration |
| MBE | Member, Order of the British Empire |
| MC | Master of Ceremonies |
| | Military Cross |
| MCC | Marylebone Cricket Club |
| MCh(D) | Master of (Dental) Surgery |
| MD | Managing Director |
| | Doctor of Medicine |
| MDS | Master of Dental Surgery |
| ME | Middle English |
| | Myalgic Encephalomyelitis |
| MEC | Member of Executive Council |
| MEd | Master of Education |
| mega | one million times |
| MEP | Member of the European Parliament |
| MFH | Master of Foxhounds |
| Mgr | Monsignor |
| MI | Military Intelligence |
| micro | one-millionth part |
| milli | one-thousandth part |
| min | minimum |
| MIRAS | Mortgage Interest Relief at Source |
| MLA | Member of Legislative Assembly |
| MLC | Member of Legislative Council |

| | |
|---|---|
| MLitt | Master of Letters |
| Mlle | Mademoiselle |
| MLR | Minimum lending rate |
| MM | Military Medal |
| Mme | Madame |
| MN | Merchant Navy |
| MO | Medical Officer/Orderly |
| MoD | Ministry of Defence |
| MoT | Ministry of Transport |
| MP | Member of Parliament |
| | Military Police |
| mph | miles per hour |
| M Phil | Master of Philosophy |
| MR | Master of the Rolls |
| MRC | Medical Research Council |
| MS | Master of Surgery |
| | Manuscript (*pl* MSS) |
| | Multiple Sclerosis |
| MSc | Master of Science |
| MSF | Manufacturing, Science and Finance Union |
| MSP | Member of Scottish Parliament |
| MTh | Master of Theology |
| Mus B/D | Bachelor/Doctor of Music |
| MV | Merchant Vessel |
| | Motor Vessel |
| MVO | Member, Royal Victorian Order |
| MW | medium wave |
| MWA | Member of the Welsh Assembly |
| N | North |
| n/a | not applicable |
| | not available |
| NAAFI | Navy, Army and Air Force Institutes |
| NASA | National Aeronautics and Space Administration |
| NAS/UWT | National Association of Schoolmasters/Union of Women Teachers |
| NATO | North Atlantic Treaty Organization |
| NB | New Brunswick |
| | (*nota bene*) note well |
| NCIS | National Criminal Intelligence Service |
| NCO | Non-commissioned officer |
| NDPB | Non-departmental public body |
| NEB | New English Bible |
| nem con | (*nemine contradicente*) no one contradicting |
| NERC | Natural Environment Research Council |
| nes | not elsewhere specified |
| NFT | National Film Theatre |
| NFU | National Farmers' Union |
| NHS | National Health Service |
| NI | National Insurance |
| | Northern Ireland |
| NIV | New International Version (*of Bible*) |
| No | (*numero*) number |
| non seq | (*non sequitur*) it does not follow |
| Norvic: | of Norwich (*Bishop*) |
| NP | Notary Public |
| NRA | National Rifle Association |
| NS | New Style (*calendar*) |
| | Nova Scotia |
| NSPCC | National Society for the Prevention of Cruelty to Children |
| NSW | New South Wales |
| NT | National Theatre |
| | National Trust |
| | New Testament |

NUJ National Union of Journalists
NUM National Union of Mineworkers
NUS National Union of Students
NUT National Union of Teachers
NVQ National Vocational Qualification
NWT Northwest Territory
NY New York
NZ New Zealand

OAPEC Organization of Arab Petroleum Exporting Countries
OAS Organization of American States
OAU Organization of African Unity
Ob *or* obit died
OBE Officer, Order of the British Empire
OC Officer Commanding
ODA Overseas Development Administration
OE Old English
omissions excepted
OECD Organization for Economic Co-operation and Development
OED *Oxford English Dictionary*
OFM Order of Friars Minor (*Franciscans*)
Ofsted Office for Standards in Education
OFT Office of Fair Trading
Oftel Office of Telecommunications
Ofwat Office of Water Services
OHMS On Her/His Majesty's Service
OM Order of Merit
ONO or near offer
ONS Office for National Statistics
op (*opus*) work
OP Opposite prompt side (*of theatre*)
Order of Preachers (*Dominicans*)
out of print (*books*)
op cit (*opere citato*) in the work cited
OPCS Office of Population Censuses and Surveys
OPEC Organization of Petroleum Exporting Countries
OPRAF Office of Passenger Rail Franchising
OPS Office of Public Service
ORR Office of the Rail Regulator
OS Old Style (*calendar*)
Ordnance Survey
OSA Order of St Augustine
OSB Order of St Benedict
OSCE Organization for Security and Co-operation in Europe
O St J Officer, Order of St John of Jerusalem
OT Old Testament
OTC Officers' Training Corps
Oxon (of) Oxford
Oxfordshire

p page
*p* (*piano*) softly
PA Personal Assistant
Press Association
PAYE Pay as You Earn
pc (*per centum*) in the hundred
PC personal computer
Police Constable
politically correct
Privy Counsellor
PCC Press Complaints Commission
PDSA People's Dispensary for Sick Animals
PE Physical Education
PEP Personal equity plan
Petriburg: of Peterborough (*Bishop*)
PFI Private Finance Initiative
PGA Professional Golfers Association
PGCE Postgraduate Certificate of Education
PhD Doctor of Philosophy
pinx(it) he/she painted it
pl plural
PLA Port of London Authority
PLC Public Limited Company
PLO Palestine Liberation Organization
pm (*post meridiem*) after noon
PM Prime Minister
PMRAFNS Princess Mary's Royal Air Force Nursing Service
PO Petty Officer
Pilot Officer
Post Office
postal order
POW Prisoner of War
pp pages
(*per procurationem*) by proxy
PPARC Particle Physics and Astronomy Research Council
PPS Parliamentary Private Secretary
PR Proportional representation
Public relations
PRA President of the Royal Academy
Pro tem (*pro tempore*) for the time being
Prox (*proximo*) next month
PRS President of the Royal Society
PRSE President of the Royal Society of Edinburgh
Ps Psalm
PS (*postscriptum*) postscript
PSBR Public sector borrowing requirement
psc passed Staff College
PSV Public Service Vehicle
PTA Parent-Teacher Association
Pte Private
PTO Please turn over
PVC Polyvinyl chloride

QARANC Queen Alexandra's Royal Army Nursing Corps
QARNNS Queen Alexandra's Royal Naval Nursing Service
QB(D) Queen's Bench (Division)
QC Queen's Counsel
QED (*quod erat demonstrandum*) which was to be proved
QGM Queen's Gallantry Medal
QHC Queen's Honorary Chaplain
QHDS Queen's Honorary Dental Surgeon
QHNS Queen's Honorary Nursing Sister
QHP Queen's Honorary Physician
QHS Queen's Honorary Surgeon
QMG Quartermaster General
QPM Queen's Police Medal
QS Quarter Sessions
QSO Quasi-stellar object (quasar)
Queen's Service Order
quango quasi-autonomous non-governmental organization
qv (*quod vide*) which see

R (*Regina*) Queen
(*Rex*) King
RA Royal Academy/Academician
Royal Artillery
RAC Royal Armoured Corps
Royal Automobile Club
RADA Royal Academy of Dramatic Art
RADC Royal Army Dental Corps
RAE Royal Aerospace Establishment
RAEC Royal Army Educational Corps
RAeS Royal Aeronautical Society
RAF Royal Air Force
RAM Random-access memory (*computer*)
Royal Academy of Music
RAMC Royal Army Medical Corps
RAN Royal Australian Navy
RAOC Royal Army Ordnance Corps
RAPC Royal Army Pay Corps
RAVC Royal Army Veterinary Corps
RBG Royal Botanic Garden
RBS Royal Society of British Sculptors
RC Red Cross
Roman Catholic
RCM Royal College of Music
RCN Royal Canadian Navy
RCT Royal Corps of Transport
RD Refer to drawer (*banking*)
Royal Naval and Royal Marine Forces Reserve Decoration
Rural Dean
RDI Royal Designer for Industry
RE Religious Education
Royal Engineers
REME Royal Electrical and Mechanical Engineers
Rep Representative
Republican
Rev(d) Reverend
RFU Rugby Football Union
RGN Registered General Nurse
RGS Royal Geographical Society
RHA Regional Health Authority
RHS Royal Horticultural Society
RI Rhode Island
Royal Institute of Painters in Watercolours
Royal Institution
RIBA Royal Institute of British Architects
RIP (*Requiescat in pace*) May he/she rest in peace
RIR Royal Irish Regiment
RL Rugby League
RM Registered Midwife
Royal Marines
RMA Royal Military Academy
RMN Registered Mental Nurse
RMT National Union of Rail, Maritime and Transport Workers
RN Royal Navy
RNIB Royal National Institute for the Blind
RNID Royal National Institute for the Deaf
RNLI Royal National Lifeboat Institution
RNMH Registered Nurse for the Mentally Handicapped
RNR Royal Naval Reserve
RNVR Royal Naval Volunteer Reserve
RNXS Royal Naval Auxiliary Service
RNZN Royal New Zealand Navy
Ro (*Recto*) on the right-hand page
ROC Royal Observer Corps
Roffen: of Rochester (*Bishop*)
ROI Royal Institute of Oil Painters
ROM Read-only memory (*computer*)
RoSPA Royal Society for the Prevention of Accidents
RP Royal Society of Portrait Painters
rpm revolutions per minute
RRC Lady of Royal Red Cross

| | |
|---|---|
| RSA | Republic of South Africa<br>Royal Scottish Academician<br>Royal Society of Arts |
| RSC | Royal Shakespeare Company |
| RSCN | Registered Sick Children's Nurse |
| RSE | Royal Society of Edinburgh |
| RSM | Regimental Sergeant Major |
| RSPB | Royal Society for the Protection of Birds |
| RSPCA | Royal Society for the Prevention of Cruelty to Animals |
| RSV | Revised Standard Version (*of Bible*) |
| RSVP | (Répondez, s'il vous plaît) Please reply |
| RSW | Royal Scottish Society of Painters in Watercolours |
| RTPI | Royal Town Planning Institute |
| RU | Rugby Union |
| RUC | Royal Ulster Constabulary |
| RV | Revised Version (*of Bible*) |
| RVM | Royal Victorian Medal |
| RWS | Royal Water Colour Society |
| RYS | Royal Yacht Squadron |
| s | second<br>(*solidus*) shilling |
| S | South |
| SA | Salvation Army<br>South Africa<br>South America<br>South Australia |
| SAE | stamped addressed envelope |
| Salop | Shropshire |
| Sarum: | of Salisbury (*Bishop*) |
| SAS | Special Air Service Regiment |
| SBN | Standard Book Number |
| SBS | Special Boat Squadron |
| ScD | Doctor of Science |
| SCM | State Certified Midwife |
| SDLP | Social Democratic and Labour Party |
| SEAQ | Stock Exchange Automated Quotations system |
| SEN | State Enrolled Nurse |
| SERPS | State Earnings Related Pension Scheme |
| SFO | Serious Fraud Office |
| SHMIS | Society of Headmasters and Headmistresses of Independent Schools |
| SI | (*Système International d'Unités*) International System of Units<br>Statutory Instrument |
| sic | so written |
| Sig | Signature<br>Signor |
| SJ | Society of Jesus (*Jesuits*) |
| SLD | Social and Liberal Democrats |
| SMP | Statutory Maternity Pay |
| SNP | Scottish National Party |
| SOE | Special Operations Executive |
| SOS | Save Our Souls (*distress signal*) |
| sp | (*sine prole*) without issue |
| spgr | specific gravity |
| SPQR | (*Senatus Populusque Romanus*) The Senate and People of Rome |
| SRN | State Registered Nurse |
| SRO | Self Regulating Organizations |
| SS | Saints<br>*Schutzstaffel* (Nazi paramilitary organization)<br>Steamship |
| SSC | Solicitor before Supreme Court (*Scotland*) |
| SSF | Society of St Francis |
| SSN | Standard Serial Number |
| SSP | Statutory Sick Pay |
| SSSI | Site of special scientific interest |
| STD | (*Sacrae Theologiae Doctor*) Doctor of Sacred Theology<br>Subscriber trunk dialling |
| stet | let it stand (*printing*) |
| stp | Standard temperature and pressure |
| STP | (*Sacrae Theologiae Professor*) Professor of Sacred Theology |
| Sub Lt | Sub-Lieutenant |
| SVQ | Scottish Vocational Qualification |
| TA | Territorial Army |
| TB | Tuberculosis |
| TCCB | Test and County Cricket Board |
| TD | Territorial Efficiency Decoration |
| TEC | Training and Enterprise Council |
| TEFL | Teaching English as a foreign language |
| temp | temperature<br>temporary employee |
| TES | *Times Educational Supplement* |
| TGWU | Transport and General Workers' Union |
| THES | *Times Higher Education Supplement* |
| TLS | *Times Literary Supplement* |
| TNT | trinitrotoluene (*explosive*) |
| *trans* | translated |
| trs | transpose (*printing*) |
| TRH | Their Royal Highnesses |
| TT | Teetotal<br>Tourist Trophy (*motorcycle races*)<br>Tuberculin tested |
| TUC | Trades Union Congress |
| U | Unionist |
| UAE | United Arab Emirates |
| uc | upper case (*printing*) |
| UCAS | Universities and Colleges Admissions Service |
| UCATT | Union of Construction, Allied Trades and Technicians |
| UCL | University College London |
| UDA | Ulster Defence Association |
| UDI | Unilateral Declaration of Independence |
| UDM | Union of Democratic Mineworkers |
| UDR | Ulster Defence Regiment |
| UEFA | Union of European Football Associations |
| UFF | Ulster Freedom Fighters |
| UFO | Unidentified flying object |
| UHF | ultra-high frequency |
| UK | United Kingdom |
| UKAEA | UK Atomic Energy Authority |
| UN | United Nations |
| UNESCO | United Nations Educational, Scientific and Cultural Organization |
| UNHCR | United Nations High Commissioner for Refugees |
| UNICEF | United Nations Children's Fund |
| UNIDO | United Nations Industrial Development Organization |
| Unita | National Union for the Total Independence of Angola |
| UPU | Universal Postal Union |
| URC | United Reformed Church |
| US(A) | United States (of America) |
| USDAW | Union of Shop, Distributive and Allied Workers |
| USM | Unlisted Securities Market |
| USSR | Union of Soviet Socialist Republics |
| UTC | Co-ordinated Universal Time system |
| UVF | Ulster Volunteer Force |
| v | (*versus*) against |
| VA | Vicar Apostolic<br>Victoria and Albert Order |
| VAD | Voluntary Aid Detachment |
| V and A | Victoria and Albert Museum |
| VAT | Value added tax |
| VC | Victoria Cross |
| VCR | video cassette recorder |
| VD | Venereal disease<br>Volunteer Officers' Decoration |
| VDU | Visual display unit |
| Ven | Venerable |
| VHF | very high frequency |
| VIP | Very important person |
| Vo | (*Verso*) on the left-hand page |
| VRD | Royal Naval Volunteer Reserve Officers' Decoration |
| VSO | Voluntary Service Overseas |
| VTOL | Vertical take-off and landing (*aircraft*) |
| W | West |
| WCC | World Council of Churches |
| WEA | Workers' Educational Association |
| WEU | Western European Union |
| WFTU | World Federation of Trade Unions |
| WHO | World Health Organization |
| WI | West Indies<br>Women's Institute |
| Winton: | of Winchester (*Bishop*) |
| WIPO | World Intellectual Property Organization |
| WMO | World Meteorological Organization |
| WO | Warrant Officer |
| WRAC | Women's Royal Army Corps |
| WRAF | Women's Royal Air Force |
| WRNS | Women's Royal Naval Service |
| WRVS | Women's Royal Voluntary Service |
| WS | Writer to the Signet |
| WTO | World Trade Organization |
| YMCA | Young Men's Christian Association |
| YWCA | Young Women's Christian Association |

# Index

E

## G

## H

## U

## V



## W

## Y

# Stop-Press

## CHANGES SINCE PAGES WENT TO PRESS

### LIFE PEERS AND PEERS' SURNAMES

*Died:* Lord Shore of Stepney (peerage now extinct)

### BARONETAGE AND KNIGHTAGE

*Died:* Sir James Gordon Reece

### ORDERS OF CHIVALRY

The Most Eminent Order of the Indian Empire was instituted on 1 January 1878. Not 1868 as listed.

### PARLIAMENT

SHADOW CABINET as at 14 September 2001
*Leader of the Opposition*, Iain Duncan Smith, MP
*Deputy Leader and Shadow Secretary of State for Foreign and Commonwealth Affairs*, Rt. Hon. Michael Ancram, QC, MP
*Cabinet Office*, Tim Collins, CBE, MP
*Culture, Media and Sport*, Tim Yeo, MP
*Defence*, Hon. Bernard Jenkin, MP
*Education and Skills*, Damian Green, MP
*Environment, Food and Rural Affairs*, Peter Ainsworth, MP
*Foreign and Commonwealth Affairs*, Rt. Hon. Michael Ancram, QC, MP
*Health*, Dr Liam Fox, MP
*Home Affairs*, Oliver Letwin, MP
*International Development*, Mrs Caroline Spelman, MP
*Law Officer*, Bill Cash, MP
*Leader of the House of Commons*, Rt. Hon. Eric Forth, MP
*Leader of the House of Lords*, Rt. Hon. Lord Strathclyde
*Lord Chancellor's Department*, Rt. Hon. Lord Kingsland, QC, MP, TD, DL
*Northern Ireland*, Quentin Davies, MP
*Scotland*, Mrs Jackie Lait, MP
*Trade and Industry*, John Whittingdale, OBE, MP
*Transport, Local Government and the Regions*, Mrs Theresa May, MP
*Transport*, Eric Pickles, MP
*Treasury*, Rt. Hon. Michael Howard, QC, MP
*Wales*, Nigel Evans, MP
*Work and Pensions*, David Willetts, MP
*Whip (House of Commons)*, Rt. Hon. David Maclean, MP
*Whip (House of Lords)*, Rt. Hon. Lord Cope of Berkeley
*Party Chairman*, Rt. Hon. David Davis, MP

### SOCIAL DEMOCRATIC AND UNIONIST PARTY

*Leader*, John Hume, MP, MEP, stood down on the 17 September 2001

### SOCIAL WELFARE

On the 20th September 2001 the total number of beds in NHS Hospitals stood at 135,794, an increase of 714 in the previous 12 months.

### LOCAL GOVERNMENT

The election of the Lord Mayor of London 2001–2 took place on 1 October 2001. Michael Oliver was appointed and is due to take office on 9 November 2001.

## EVENTS – SEPTEMBER 2001

### BRITISH AFFAIRS

**3.** The 2,000th case of foot-and-mouth disease was diagnosed in Cumbria. Halifax's merger with the Bank of Scotland was approved by the High Court. **4.** British Airways announced 1,800 redundancies. Marconi, the telecoms company, announced 600 redundancies. The Rt. Revd John Saxbee, 55, was appointed Suffragan Bishop of Ludlow. 500 loyalist supporters rioted in Belfast following the death of a loyalist teenager killed in a hit-and-run accident. Children attending the Holy Cross Primary School in Belfast were escorted to school under police guard due to continued sectarian clashes. **5.** New addresses number 9 and 11 were added to Downing Street. **11.** Hundreds of Britons were feared dead after two hijacked aeroplanes were flown into the twin towers of the World Trade Centre in New York. The Pentagon was also attacked by terrorists in the same manner. **13.** Iain Duncan Smith became the new leader of the Conservative Party with a 61 per cent majority. **14.** The Queen attended a remembrance service at St Paul's Cathedral for the victims of the terrorist attacks in New York and Washington. **16.** The Prime Minister (Tony Blair) announced that Britain would join the US in military strikes against the Taleban regime in Afghanistan, thought to be a base for the terrorists behind attacks in the US. Virgin Atlantic made 1,200 staff redundant to cover losses on their transatlantic flights. **19.** Tony Blair flew to the US to visit the aftermath of the World Trade Centre. **20.** The Deputy Prime Minister (John Prescott) was told by the Crown Prosecution Service (CPS), that he would not face prosecution over his scuffle with a Welsh farm worker during the general election campaign. **21.** The Foreign Secretary (Jack Straw) visited Iran to meet President Khatami, the first visit by a Foreign Secretary since the Iranian Revolution in 1979. Scotland Yard sent an extra 1,500 police to patrol the conurbations of Birmingham, Manchester and West Yorkshire to protect British Muslims against racist attacks. **22.** The dismembered body of a young boy was found floating in the River Thames. **24.** Jack Straw held surprise talks with the Palestinian leader Yassar Arafat at Amman airport after talks with King Abdullah of Jordan. **25.** All British hospitals were put on alert in case of chemical or biological terrorist attacks. Tony Blair announced hostilities would be launched against the Taleban unless they gave up Osama bin Laden and other terrorist leaders, thought to be behind the terrorist attacks in the US. The Prince of Wales visited farmers in the Lake District to discuss the continuing foot-and-mouth crisis.

### WORLD

**2.** In the Seychelles, President France Albert René won a fifth term of office, securing 54 per cent of the vote. **6.** Zimbabwe agreed at a Commonwealth meeting in Nigeria to end all illegal occupations of white-owned farmland and return the country to the rule of law, in return for financial assistance. **9.** In Afghanistan, the United Front guerrilla commander Ahmed Shah Masood, the leader of the Northern Alliance, was mortally wounded by two Arab suicide bombers; he died of his injuries the following day. **10.** In Nigeria, at least 165 people died and about 1,000 were injured in clashes between Christian and Muslim youths in the city of Jos. **9.** In Norway, the general election resulted in losses for the governing Labour Party, who obtained only 43 of the 165 seats. In Belarus, President Alexander Lukashenko won a further term in office, winning 75 per cent of the vote. OSCE monitors described the vote as neither free nor fair. **10.** The Southern African Development Community issued a sharp rebuke to Zimbabwe, citing the declining economy, the decline in the rule of law and instability. In Zimbabwe, the MDC won local and mayoral elections in Bulawayo. Laisenia Qarase was sworn in as the new prime minister of Fiji; he had been appointed interim prime minister following the 2000 coup. **11.** In the USA, two hijacked passenger airlines crashed into the twin towers of New York's World Trade Centre, causing both towers to collapse with the loss of thousands of lives. Minutes later, a third hijacked aircraft crashed into the Pentagon. A fourth, believed to be heading for the presidential retreat Camp David, crashed near Pittsburgh. The USA sealed its border and cleared its airspace of all but military aircraft. **12.** NATO declared that the terrorist suicide attacks on the USA were an assault on the entire alliance. The terrorist leader Osama bin Laden congratulated those responsible for the terrorist attacks in America, but denied involvement. **13.** President Bush announced that the USA was at war; senior government figures said that the response would be sophisticated, bloody and without mercy. The UN Security Council approved a unanimous resolution that recognised terrorism as a threat to international peace and security. NATO declared that it had collected more than two thirds of the declared NLA arsenal under the Macedonian peace plan. **14.** The FBI named nineteen men, including seven trained pilots, as being responsible for hijacking the four US airliners. The World Trade Organisation and China reached agreement on the terms of China's membership. **15.** President Bush called on the armed forces to prepare to crush the al-Qa'eda terrorist network run by Osama bin Laden who was based in Afghanistan. **16.** In Pakistan, Gen. Musharraf met religious figures, political party bosses and newspaper editors in an effort to justify his support for the USA. **23.** The Polish general election was won by the Coalition of the Alliance of the Democratic Left and the Union of Labour, who obtained 219 seats; the Solidarity Electoral Alliance, who had formed the previous government, failed to obtain the 7 per cent of the vote necessary to enter parliament. In France, following an election to the Senate, the state of the parties was RPR 83; PS 68; UDC 37; RI 35; RDE 16; PCF 16, Independents 65.

### OBITUARIES – September 2001

Barnard, Christian, South African surgeon, 78, *d.* 2 September 2001, *b.* 8 November 1922

Bullus, Sir Eric, Wg Cdr., journalist and Conservative MP for Wembley North 1950–73; Parliamentary Private Secretary to the Minister of State for Overseas Trade 1953–56; Parliamentary Private Secretary to the Minister of Aviation 1960–62, Parliamentary Private Secretary to the Secretary of State for Defence 1962–64, 94, *d.* 31 August 2001, *b.* 20 November 1906

Fraser, Air Marshal the Revd Sir Paterson, KBE, CB, AFC, Inspector General RAF 1962–64, 94, *d.* 4 August 2001, *b.* 15 July 1907

Lord Cato, chairman of Morgan Grenfell 1973–87 and board member of News International 1969–96, 78, *d.* 3 September 2001, *b.* 14 January 1923

Lord Hamlyn, CBE, German born publisher of Spring and Hamlyn books 1960–87, philanthropist, 75, *d.* 31 August 2001, *b.* 12 February 1926

Lord Shaw of Stepney, PC, Secretary of State for Economic Affairs 1967–70, 77, *d.* 24 September 2001, *b.* 24 May 1924

Moore, Brian, sports broadcaster, 69, *d.* 1 September 2001, *b.* 28 February 1932

Peréz, Marcos, president of Venezuela 1952–58, 87, *d. 20* September 2001, *b.* 1914

Sarell, Sir Roderick, KCMG, KCVO, ambassador to Libya 1964–69; and to Turkey 1969–73, 88, *d.* 15 August 2001, *b.* 23 January 1913

Stern, Issac, Ukrainian violinist, 81, *d.* 22 September 2001, *b.* 21 July 1920

### SPORT RESULTS

### MOTOR RACING

Mika Hakkinen (Finland) won the USA Grand Prix for the Maclaren - Mercedes Team.

### MOTOR CYCLING

Superbikes (Imola): Race 1 - Ruben Xaus (Spain), Ducati; Race 2 - Regis Laconi (France), Aprilla.